# 1992 FLAT ANNUAL

## The Jockey Club's Official Form Book

Complete record of all Turf and
All-Weather Flat Racing in Great Britain
from November 12th, 1991 to
November 9th, 1992

Published by Raceform Ltd
Compton, Newbury, Berkshire, RG16 0NL
Tel: 0635 578080

Registered as a newspaper at the Post Office.

Printed by Woolnough Bookbinding Ltd.,
Irthlingborough, Northants

© Raceform Ltd 1992

### ISBN 0-900611-19-7

● Cover Photo: Alan Johnson

THE WESTERN MEETING CLUB, AYR RACECOURSE,
2 WHITLETTS ROAD, AYR. KA8 0JE
TELEPHONE (0292) 264179
TELEX 777459   FAX (0292) 610140

## SCOTLAND'S PREMIER RACECOURSE
### 1993 Fixtures

### JANUARY

Saturday, 2nd (N.H.)
Thursday, 21st (N.H.)
Saturday, 30th (N.H.)

### FEBRUARY

Friday, 12th (N.H.)
Saturday, 13th (N.H.)

### MARCH

Friday, 12th (N.H.)
Saturday, 13th (N.H.)

### APRIL

**(Scottish National Meeting)**
Friday, 16th (N.H.)
Saturday, 17th (N.H.)

### MAY

Saturday, 22nd
Monday, 24th

### JUNE

Friday, 18th
Saturday, 19th

### JULY

Saturday, 17th
Monday, 19th
Friday (eve), 23rd
Saturday, 24th

### AUGUST

Saturday 7th
Thursday 19th

### SEPTEMBER

**(Western Meeting)**
Thursday, 16th
Friday, 17th
Saturday, 18th

### OCTOBER

Saturday, 9th (N.H.)

### NOVEMBER

Friday, 12th (N.H.)
Saturday, 13th (N.H.)

### DECEMBER

Tuesday, 28th (N.H.)

FULL FACILITIES FOR OWNERS, TRAINERS AND
JOCKEYS. HELICOPTER LANDING FACILITIES IN
CENTRE OF COURSE

## "WELCOME TO AYR"

# *The Professional*

# CONTENTS

# INDEX TO ADVERTISERS

# HOW TO READ RACEFORM

**THE OFFICIAL GOING,** shown after the date of each meeting, is recorded in the following stages:-

Hard;   Firm;   Good to firm;   Good;   Good to soft;
Soft;   Heavy
Going for All-Weather meetings is recorded in the stages - Slow; Standard; Fast

**GOING ALLOWANCE,** assessed in seconds per furlong, is an estimation of the ground, taking into account the race times compared with the Raceform Standard Times, the wind and other elements.

**GOING ASSESSED ON TIME** is shown in parentheses after the going allowance: Hard (H); Firm (F); Good (G); Yielding (Y); Soft (S); Heavy (Hvy) and for All-Weather meetings: Fast (Fs); Standard (Std); Slow (Sl).

**WIND** is included for every Turf meeting in the U.K. Apart from 'nil', 'almost nil' and squally, wind conditions are shown in degrees of 'against', 'across' and 'behind'.

**VISIBILITY** is Good unless stated.

**STARTING STALLS** are shown in the form 'Stalls high' or 'Stalls low', indicating that (looking from the Stands) the stalls are POSITIONED on the high (left) or low (right) side of the course. All races are started by stalls unless otherwise stated.

**RACE NUMBERS** are the same as those in Raceform Note-Book. All French and Irish Group races are covered, plus **all** races abroad in which a British trained horse has taken part. However, usually they are not received in time to insert in strict **date** order. All race numbers for Foreign and Irish meetings carry the suffix 'a'.

**PRIZE MONEY** — penalty values down to sixth place (when applicable)

**DISTANCE OF RACE** on courses that have two tracks of the same distance (st) indicates straight course and (rnd) indicates round.

**(AWT)** immediately after the distance denotes a race run on an all-weather (Equitrack or Fibresand) surface.

**THE FIGURES** on the left of each horse's name represent the number of the race in which it last ran. An asterisk indicates a win and a small figure ($^2$, $^3$, $^4$, $^5$, $^6$) positions down to sixth. A figure in italics indicates a previous performance from an all-weather track.

**ADJUSTED OFFICIAL RATING -** The figure in **bold type** and in brackets immediately following the horse's name indicates the Official Jockey Club rating, at entry, after the following additions have been made:
(i) Overweight carried by rider.
(ii) The number of pounds out of the handicap (if applicable)
(iii) Penalties incurred after the publication of the weights.
However, please note that **no** adjustments have been made for:
(i) Weight-for-age.
(ii) Riders' claims.

**BLINKERS** shown after runner's name thus (bl).
Hood thus (h)
Visor thus (v)
Hood and blinkers are shown (h & b)
Hood and visor are shown (h & v)

**EYESHIELD** details are shown in the comments-on-running.

**TRAINER** is shown in italics for every runner.

**AGE,** shown immediately before the weight carried, does not appear in those races confined to one age group.

**WEIGHTS** shown are actual weight carried. Small figures in parentheses against weight denotes overweight carried in lbs.

(7x) = including 7lb. extra for win after publication of weights.

‡$^3$, ‡$^5$, ‡$^7$ = apprentice allowance deducted

**LONG HANDICAP WEIGHTS** runners allotted a lower-than-minimum weight at entry (**handicaps only**) are shown directly under the commentary of the last horse in each race.

## APPRENTICE ALLOWANCES

The holders of apprentice jockeys' licences under the provisions of Rule 60(iii) are permitted to claim the following allowances in Flat races:

7lb until they have won 15 Flat races run under the Rules of any recognised Turf Authority; thereafter 5lb until they have won 50 such Flat races; thereafter 3lb until they have won 85 such Flat races.

These allowances can be claimed in the Flat races set out below, with the exception of races confined to apprentice jockeys:

(a) All handicap and all selling races

(b) All other races with guaranteed prize money of not more than £8000

**THE DRAW** for places at the start is shown after each jockey's name.

**THE OFFICIAL DISTANCES** between the first six horses are shown on the right-hand side immediately preceding their position at the finish.

Distances beyond sixth place may be shown after inspection of race-finish photographs. Unknown positions are shown in saddle-cloth number order.

**WITHDRAWN** horses, that fail to come under orders after entering the parade ring, are included in the Index to Past Racing (with W after the race number); side reference, odds and reason for withdrawal (if known) are shown in italics below the bottom horse of the race.

**4(C) Tattersall's Committee Rules on Betting States -**

In the case of bets made at a price on the day of the race before it has been officially notified that a horse has been withdrawn before coming under Starter's Orders, the liability of a layer against any horse remaining in the race, win or place, will be reduced in accordance with the following scale depending on the odds current against the withdrawn horse at the time of such official notification.

(a) if the current odds are 30/100 or longer odds on by 75p. in the £.

(b) if shorter odds on than 30/100 up to and including 2/5 by 70p. in the £.

(c) if shorter odds on than 2/5 up to and including 8/15 by 65p. in the £.

(d) if shorter odds on than 8/15 up to and including 8/13 by 60p. in the £.

(e) if shorter odds on than 8/13 up to and including 4/5 by 55p. in the £.

(f) if shorter odds on than 4/5 up to and including 20/21 by 50p. in the £.

(g) if shorter odds on than 20/21 up to and including 6/5 by 45p. in the £.

(h) if over 6/5 up to and including 6/4 by 40p. in the £.

(i) if over 6/4 up and including 7/4 by 35p. in the £.

(j) if over 7/4 up and including 9/4 by 30p. in the £.

(k) if over 9/4 up and including 3/1 by 25p. in the £.

(l) if over 3/1 up to and including 4/1 by 20p. in the £.

(m) if over 4/1 up and including 11/2 by 15p. in the £.

(n) if over 11/2 up to and including 9/1 by 10p. in the £.

(o) if over 9/1 up to and including 14/1 by 5p. in the £.

(p) if over 14/1 the liability would be unchanged.

(q) in the case of two or more horses being withdrawn the total deduction shall not exceed 75p. in the £.

Ante-post bets are not affected and S.P. bets are also not affected, except in cases where insufficient time arises for a fresh market to be formed, when the above named scale of reductions will apply.

**STEWARDS' ENQUIRY,** except in special circumstances, is included only if it concerns a prize winner(s).

**TOTE** prices include £1 stake. Dual Forecast dividends are shown in parentheses.

**OWNER** of the winner is shown immediately after the Tote, then the winning **trainer's location**, the **breeder** of the winner, the number of runners, result of seller and details regarding any claimed horse. Friendly claims are not detailed.

**RACE-TIMES** in Great Britain (except **official times** which are electrically recorded and shown to **100th of a second**) are clocked by Raceform's own watch-holders. Figures in parentheses following the time show the number of seconds slower than standard for the course distance. Raceform Standard Times' were compiled originally from times recorded on Good or Firm going after adjustments had been made for weight carried either above or below a norm of 9st. Times equal to and faster than standard are shown as (equals standard) and (U1.8). Record times are shown either refering to the 2-y-o record (1 under 2y best) or the overall record (1 under best).

**SPEED FIGURES** The numbers at the end of each race indicate the Speed Figures of the first six (in post-the-post order) after each horse has been brought to 9st. and calculations made for going, wind and distances behind winner.

Example: SF — 100/96/94/80/77/74.

To find Speed Figures for future races add 1 point for each 1lb. weighted below 9st. and deduct 1 point for each 1lb. above 9st. Highest resultant figure is best.

**INDEX TO FLAT RACING -** Please note that names of horses are indexed strictly as spelt and include country codes, e.g. Elect (USA) comes **after** Electro.

# Abbreviations

**Most of the contents explain themselves but to save space the following abbreviations are frequently used:**

**THE PARADE RING - Classification of horses on looks:**

| | | |
|---|---|---|
| **v nice c** = very nice colt: outstanding in looks | **h.d.w** = has done well: improved in looks | **lw** = looked very fit |
| **nice c** = nice colt: very good sort | **scope** = scope for development | **bkwd** = backward in condition |
| **gd sort** = well made: above average on looks | **cmpt** = compact | **str** = strong |
| | **lt-f** = light-framed | **swtg** = sweating excessively |
| **wl grwn** = well grown | **unf** = unfurnished: not furnished to frame | **t** = tubed |
| **w'like** = workmanlike | **nt grwn** = not grown | **b** = bandaged fore |
| | | **b.hind** = bandaged hind |

**THE RUNNING**

| | | |
|---|---|---|
| **a** = always | **bnd** = bend | **disp** = disputed |
| **abt** = about | **btn** = beaten | **disq** = disqualified |
| **a.p** = always prominent | **bttr** = better | **dismntd** = dismounted |
| **appr** = approaching | **c** = came | **dist** = distance (240y from finish) |
| **awrdd** = awarded | **ch** = chance | **div** = division |
| **b.b.v** = broke blood vessel | **chal** = challenge(d) | **drvn** = driven |
| **b.d** = brought down | **chsd** = chased | **dwlt** = dwelt |
| **bdly** = badly | **circ** = circuit | **edgd** = edged |
| **bef** = before | **cl** = close | **effrt** = effort |
| **bel** = below | **clr** = clear | **ent** = entering |
| **bhd** = behind | **comf** = comfortably | **ev ch** = every chance |
| **bk** = back | **cpld** = coupled | **ex** = extra |
| **blkd** = baulked | **crse** = course | **f** = furlong |
| **bmpd** = bumped | **ct** = caught | **fdd** = faded |

| | | |
|---|---|---|
| **fin** = finish(ed) | **no imp** = no impression | **rt** = right |
| **fnd** = found | **nr** = near | **s** = start |
| **fnl** = final | **nrr** = nearer | **sddle** = saddle |
| **fr** = from | **nrst fin** = nearest at finish | **s.h.** = short head |
| **gd** = good | **nt** = not | **shkn** = shaken |
| **gng** = going | **nvr** = never | **s.i.s.** = slowly into stride |
| **grad** = gradually | **one pce** = one paced | **slt** = slight |
| **grnd** = ground | **out** = from finish | **sme** = some |
| **½-wy** = half-way | **outpcd** = outpaced | **sn** = soon |
| **hd** = head | **pce** = pace | **spd** = speed |
| **hdd** = headed | **pl** = place | **s.s** = started slowly |
| **hdwy** = headway | **plcd** = placed | **st** = straight |
| **hld** = held | **plld** = pulled | **stdy** = steady |
| **hmpd** = hampered | **press** = pressure | **str** = strong |
| **hrd rdn** = hard ridden | **prog** = progress | **styd** = stayed |
| **imp** = impression | **prom** = prominent | **swtchd** = switched |
| **ins** = inside | **p.u** = pulled up | **swvd** = swerved |
| **jnd** = joined | **qckn** = quicken | **tch** = touch |
| **jst** = just | **qckly** = quickly | **thro** = through |
| **kpt** = kept | **r** = race | **thrght** = throughout |
| **l** = length | **racd** = raced | **t.o** = tailed off |
| **ld** = lead | **rch** = reach | **trckd** = tracked |
| **ldr** = leader | **rcvr** = recover | **u.p** = under pressure |
| **lft** = left | **rdn** = ridden | **w** = with |
| **m** = mile | **rdr** = rider | **wd** = wide |
| **mde** = made | **reard** = reared | **whn** = when |
| **mid div** = mid division | **ref** = refused | **wknd** = weakened |
| **m.n.s** = made no show | **rn** = ran | **wl** = well |
| **n.d** = no danger | **rnd** = round | **wnr** = winner |
| **n.g.t** = not go through | **r.o.** = ran on | **wnt** = went |
| **nk** = neck | **rr** = rear | **w.r.s** = whipped round start |
| **n.m.r** = not much room | **rn wl** = ran well | |
| **no ex** = no extra pace | **rspnse** = response | |

The utmost care is taken to ensure accuracy but the Proprietors accept no responsibility for error.

# KEY TO RACE-READERS INITIALS

| | | | |
|---|---|---|---|
| (AA) | –Alan Amies | (KH) | –Keith Hewitt |
| (AK) | –Anthony Kemp | (LMc) | –Lee McKenzie |
| (CR) | –Colin Roberts | (Mk) | –Iain Mackenzie |
| (Dk) | –David Dickinson | (NR) | –Neville Ring |
| (DS) | –Desmond Stoneham | (O'R) | –Tom O'Ryan |
| (GB) | –Gordon Brown | (P) | –John Penney |
| (Hn) | –John Hanmer | (RC) | –Robert Carter |
| (IM) | –Ivor Markham | (SM) | –Stephen Mellish |
| (J) | –Mike Jones | (T) | –Mary Trueman |
| | (WG) | –Walter Glynn | |

# HOW TO READ RACEFORM

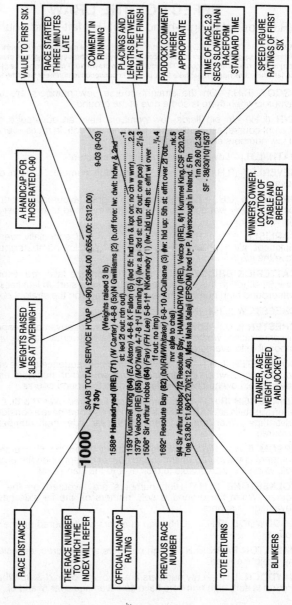

**RACE DISTANCE**

**THE RACE NUMBER TO WHICH THE INDEX WILL REFER**

**OFFICIAL HANDICAP RATING**

**PREVIOUS RACE NUMBER**

**TOTE RETURNS**

**BLINKERS**

**VALUE TO FIRST SIX**

**RACE STARTED THREE MINUTES LATE**

**COMMENT IN RUNNING**

**PLACINGS AND LENGTHS BETWEEN THEM AT THE FINISH**

**PADDOCK COMMENT WHERE APPROPRIATE**

**TIME OF RACE 2.3 SECS SLOWER THAN RACEFORM STANDARD TIME**

**SPEED FIGURE RATINGS OF FIRST SIX**

**WEIGHTS RAISED 3LBS AT OVERNIGHT**

**A HANDICAP FOR THOSE RATED 0-90**

**WINNER'S OWNER, LOCATION OF STABLE AND BREEDER**

**TRAINER, AGE, WEIGHT CARRIED AND JOCKEY**

**1000**
7f 30y

SAAB TOTAL SERVICE H'CAP (0-90) £2364.00 £664.00: £312.00      9-03 (9-03)
(Weights raised 3 lb)

1588⁴ **Hamadryad (IRE)** (71) (W Carter) 4-8-8 (5x)N Gwilliams (2) (b.off fore: lw: dwlt: hdwy & 2nd
st: led 2f out: rdn out)...........................................................................1

1193⁵ Kummel King (64) (EJ Alston) 4-8-6 K Fallon (5) (led 5f: hld rdn & kpt on: no ch w wnr).....2.2
1379¹ Veloce (IRE) (55) (MO'Neill) 4-7-8 +³J Fanning (4) (lw: a.p 3rd st: rdn 2f out: one pce)......2½.3
1508⁴ Sir Arthur Hobbs (64) (Fav) (FH Lee) 5-8-11* NKennedy ( ) (lw: hld up: 4th st: effrt wl over
1f out: no imp)........................................................................................¼.4

1692⁴ Resolute Bay (82) (bl)(RMWhitaker) 6-9-10 ACulhane (3) (lw: hld up: 5th st: effrt over 2f out:
nvr able to chal)......................................................................nk.5

9/4 Sir Arthur Hobbs, 7/2 Resolute Bay, HAMMADRYAD (IRE), Veloce (IRE), 6/1 Kummel King.CSF £20.20,
Tote £3.80: £1.60 £2.70 (£12.40). Miss Maha Kalaji (EPSOM) bred by P. Myerscough in Ireland. 5 Rn
1m 29.60 (2.30)
SF - 38/30/10/15/37

ix

# EFFECT OF THE DRAW

## (R.H.) denotes right-hand and (L.H.) left-hand courses.

**RULES OF RACING No. 28 (v):** The Starter shall call over the names of the runners and, for Flat races, assign the horses to the places drawn by lot, all horses taking their place at the Start in the order drawn for them. The rider who has drawn No. 1 must always be placed on the left and other riders must take their places in consecutive numbers from the left.

**ASCOT** (R.H.)—On the straight course, low numbers are slightly favoured when there is some give in the ground.

**AYR** (L.H.)—In big fields, low numbers have an advantage on the straight course, especially when the ground is soft. In races over 7f and 8f low numbers are favoured.

**BATH** (L.H.)—Low numbers are slightly favoured.

**BEVERLEY** (R.H.)—In 5f.—8f. races high numbers have a distinct advantage.

**BRIGHTON** (L.H.)—Low numbers are slightly favoured in sprint races except in very wet conditions, when jockeys tend to tack over to the stands' side.

**CARLISLE** (R.H.)—High numbers are favoured, especially over sprint distances, although when the ground rides soft, low numbers appear to have the edge.

**CATTERICK BRIDGE** (L.H.)—Low numbers are favoured, especially over 6f, although this can be negated by a slow start. In late season on soft ground high numbers have the advantage on the straight course.

**CHEPSTOW** (L.H.)—No significant effect.

**CHESTER** (L.H.)—Low numbers have a distinct advantage, especially in sprint races, where a slow start and a high draw can be virtually impossible to overcome.

**DONCASTER** (L.H.)—The draw is of little consequence on the straight course except when the ground is soft, when high numbers have an advantage. Low numbers are favoured on the round course.

**EDINBURGH** (R.H.)—High numbers are favoured over 7f & 8f. Over 5f when the stalls are on the stands' side, low numbers have a considerable advantage. When the stalls are on the far side, high numbers are favoured.

**EPSOM** (L.H.)—High numbers are favoured on the 5f course. Low numbers are favoured on the round course except when the ground is soft, when it is fashionable to tack over to the stands' rail.

**FOLKESTONE** (R.H.)—High numbers are favoured on the round course. When the ground is soft, runners on the far side have the advantage in sprints.

**GOODWOOD** (R.H.)—(L.H) High numbers are favoured on the round course.

**HAMILTON PARK** (R.H.)—High numbers are favoured, especially on the straight course.

**HAYDOCK** (L.H.)—Low numbers are favoured over 7f & 8f. When the ground is soft, high numbers have an advantage over 5f and 6f.

**KEMPTON** (R.H.)—Over 5f & 6f, when the stalls are on the stands' side and the ground is soft, a low draw is a great advantage. When the stalls are placed on the far side (high), a high number is essential.

**LEICESTER** (R.H.)—Low numbers have an advantage, especially when the ground is soft.

**LEOPARDSTOWN** (L.H.)—Low numbers are at a disadvantage on the sprint course.

**LINGFIELD** (L.H.)—**Turf:** High numbers are generally favoured in races on the straight course, though this may be negated by heavy ground. **AWT:** Low numbers are favoured, an advantage which can be accentuated by a fast break.

**LONGCHAMP** (R.H.)—A low draw is important on the straight course (remembering that the French invariably number from the rail outwards).

**NEWBURY** (L.H.)—High numbers have a slight advantage on the straight course, especially on soft ground.

**NEWCASTLE** (L.H.)—No significant effect, except on soft & heavy ground when low numbers have a marked advantage.

**NEWMARKET** (R.H.)—Rowley Mile Course: No significant effect. July Course: No significant effect.

**NOTTINGHAM** (L.H.)—On the straight course the position of stalls gives the best indication which side is favoured, especially in big fields. Low numbers are slightly favoured on the round course.

**PONTEFRACT** (L.H.)—Low numbers are favoured.

**REDCAR** (L.H.)—High numbers are favoured on the straight course.

**RIPON** (R.H.)—Low numbers are favoured on the straight course, high numbers on the round course.

**SALISBURY** (R.H.)—Low numbers are favoured in sprints when the ground is soft.

**SANDOWN** (R.H.)—High numbers enjoy a considerable advantage in 5f races when the ground is soft.

**SOUTHWELL** (L.H.)—Low numbers are favoured, an advantage which can be accentuated by a fast break.

**THIRSK** (L.H.)—High numbers are favoured on the straight course, except when the ground is soft. In 7f and 8f races with big fields low numbers have an advantage.

**WARWICK** (L.H.)—Low numbers are favoured.

**WINDSOR** (R.H.)—It is generally considered that high numbers have the advantage in sprints but the advantage is not great.

**WOLVERHAMPTON** (L.H.)—High numbers are slightly favoured in 5f races, except when the ground is soft.

**YARMOUTH** (L.H.)—High numbers have a slight advantage on the straight course.

**YORK** (L.H.)—Low numbers have an advantage on the straight course, especially when the ground is testing.

# JOCKEY CLUB SCALE OF WEIGHT FOR AGE

Expressed as the number of pounds that is deemed the average horse in each group falls short of maturity at different dates and distances.

| Distance Furlongs | Age | JAN 1/15 | JAN 16/31 | FEB 1/14 | FEB 15/28 | MARCH 1/15 | MARCH 16/31 | APRIL 1/15 | APRIL 16/30 | MAY 1/15 | MAY 16/31 | JUNE 1/15 | JUNE 16/30 | JULY 1/15 | JULY 16/31 | AUGUST 1/15 | AUGUST 16/31 | SEPT 1/15 | SEPT 16/30 | OCT 1/15 | OCT 16/31 | NOV 1/15 | NOV 16/31 | DEC 1/15 | DEC 16/31 |
|---|---|---|---|---|---|---|---|---|---|---|---|---|---|---|---|---|---|---|---|---|---|---|---|---|---|
| 5 | 2 | – | 15 | – | 15 | – | 47 | 44 | 41 | 38 | 36 | 34 | 32 | 30 | 28 | 26 | 24 | 22 | 20 | 19 | 18 | 17 | 17 | 16 | 16 |
|   | 3 | 15 | – | 15 | – | 14 | 13 | 12 | 11 | 10 | 9 | 8 | 7 | 6 | 5 | 4 | 3 | 2 | 2 | 1 | 1 | 1 | – | 1 | – |
| 6 | 2 | – | 16 | – | 16 | – | 14 | – | 13 | 44 | 41 | 38 | 36 | 33 | 31 | 28 | 26 | 24 | 22 | 21 | 20 | 19 | 18 | 17 | 17 |
|   | 3 | 16 | – | 16 | – | 15 | – | 13 | 12 | 11 | 10 | 9 | 8 | 7 | 6 | 5 | 4 | 3 | 3 | 2 | 2 | 1 | 1 | 1 | – |
| 7 | 2 | – | 18 | – | 18 | – | 17 | – | 15 | – | 14 | – | 10 | 44 | 41 | 38 | 35 | 31 | 29 | 27 | 25 | 23 | 21 | 20 | 19 |
|   | 3 | 18 | – | 18 | – | 17 | – | 16 | 15 | 12 | 11 | 10 | 9 | 8 | 6 | 5 | 4 | 3 | 3 | 2 | 2 | 1 | 1 | 1 | – |
| 8 | 2 | – | 20 | – | 18 | – | 19 | – | 16 | – | 15 | – | 11 | – | 8 | 37 | 30 | 25 | 22 | 19 | 17 | 16 | 15 | 19 | 19 |
|   | 3 | 20 | 1 | 18 | – | 18 | 17 | 16 | 14 | 13 | 12 | 11 | 10 | 9 | 8 | 7 | 6 | 6 | 4 | 4 | 3 | 2 | 2 | 1 | 1 |
| 9 | 2 | 20 | 1 | 19 | 1 | 20 | 19 | 18 | 17 | 15 | 14 | 13 | 12 | – | 9 | 37 | 34 | 31 | 28 | 26 | 24 | 23 | 22 | 21 | 21 |
|   | 3 | 22 | 2 | 21 | – | 22 | 2 | 18 | – | 15 | 13 | 11 | 10 | 10 | 9 | 7 | – | 5 | 4 | 4 | 3 | 3 | 2 | 2 | 1 |
| 10 | 3 | 23 | 3 | 22 | 2 | 23 | 3 | 21 | 20 | 19 | 18 | 16 | 15 | 13 | 12 | 10 | 9 | 7 | 6 | 5 | 5 | 4 | 4 | 3 | 1 |
| 11 | 3 | 4 | – | 3 | – | 22 | 1 | 21 | 1 | 19 | – | 16 | 15 | 13 | 12 | 10 | 9 | 8 | 7 | 6 | 6 | 5 | 5 | 4 | 4 |
| 12 | 3 | 4 | – | 4 | – | 23 | 2 | 22 | 2 | 20 | – | 17 | 16 | 14 | 13 | 11 | 10 | 9 | 8 | 7 | 7 | 6 | 6 | 5 | 5 |
| 13 | 3 | 5 | – | 4 | – | 24 | 2 | 23 | 2 | 21 | 1 | 18 | 17 | 15 | 14 | 12 | 11 | 10 | 9 | 8 | 8 | 7 | 7 | 6 | 6 |
| 14 | 3 | 5 | – | 5 | – | 25 | 3 | 24 | 3 | 23 | 2 | 19 | 18 | 16 | 15 | 13 | 12 | 11 | 10 | 9 | 9 | 8 | 8 | 7 | 7 |
| 15 | 3 | 6 | – | 5 | – | 26 | 4 | 26 | 3 | 26 | 4 | 20 | 1 | 17 | 16 | 14 | 13 | 12 | 11 | 10 | 10 | 9 | 9 | 8 | 8 |
| 16 | 3 | 6 | – | 6 | – | 28 | 4 | 27 | 3 | 28 | 5 | 20 | 1 | 18 | 17 | 15 | 14 | 13 | 12 | 11 | 11 | 10 | 10 | 9 | 9 |
| 18 | 3 | 7 | – | 7 | – | 31 | 6 | 29 | 5 | 26 | 4 | 22 | 2 | 19 | 18 | 17 | 16 | 15 | 14 | 13 | 13 | 12 | 11 | 10 | 10 |
| 20 | 3 | 8 | – | 8 | – | 33 | 7 | 31 | 6 | 28 | 5 | 24 | 3 | 20 | 19 | 18 | 17 | 16 | 15 | 14 | 14 | 13 | 12 | 11 | 9 |

# *Raceform*

## ALL-WEATHER
## FLAT RACING 1991

Complete record of
All-Weather Flat Racing
from November 12th to December 28th,
1991

3371—**SOUTHWELL (L-H)** Fibresand
**Tuesday, November 12th [Standard]**
Going Allowance: minus 0.30 sec per fur (FS)

Wind: fresh across

Stalls: 1st, 3rd & 5th high, remainder low

**4004** HENRY BOOT (NORTHERN) CLAIMING STKS (I) £2285.20 (£632.20: £301.60)
1½m (AWT) 12-15 (12-16)

**Admiral's Mistress (IRE)** *(PJMakin)* 3–8-3 TSprake (7) (lt-f: bit bkwd: hld up: hdwy & 5th st: rdn 2f out: c wde: led wl ins fnl f) ............................—1

3950 Tristiorum **(62)** (bl) *(JEtherington)* 4–8-2(4) ‡7JWeaver (5) (dwlt: sn rcvrd: 2nd st: led over 2f out wl ins fnl f) ............................ 1½.2

3889* Irish Native (IRE) **(70)** (bl) *(CASmith)* 3–8-11 AProud (4) (hld up: 4th st: ev ch & n.m.r over 1f out: nt rcvr) ............................ 2½.3

3777² Jeethgaya (USA) **(50)** (Fav) *(AHide)* 3–8-5(3) WRyan (9) (stdy hdwy fr ½-wy: 3rd st: rdn & ev ch whn hung lft appr fnl f: nt qckn) ............................ s.h.4

3262⁶ Abigail's Dream *(DBurchell)* 4–8-4 LCharnock (11) (led 7f tl over 2f out: wknd fnl f) ............................ 3½.5

3478 Royal Acclaim **(53)** (v) *(JMBradley)* 6–8-7(2) JWilliams (10) (hld up & 6th st: one pce fnl 2f) ............................ 3½.6

Swagman (USA) **(45)** *(CRBeever)* 4–8-9 DMcKeown (1) (led 5f: wknd over 3f out) hd.7

1503 Gin and Orange **(43)** (v) *(JRJenkins)* 5–8-6 TQuinn (2) (chsd ldrs: 7th & btn st) ...... 3½.8

3135 Sharp Issue (USA) **(28)** (bl) *(MCChapman)* 3–7-12 GBardwell (8) (w ldr: rdn 5f out: sn wknd: t.o) ............................ 9

3830 Al Manhal (IRE) **(45)** *(RHollinshead)* 3–8-7(5) ‡7CorrineCripps (3) (a bhd: t.o fr ½-wy) ............................ 10

3885 Cahelia (IRE) *(JIHarris)* 3–8-2(5) ‡7GForster (6) (lw: a in rr: t.o fnl 3f) ............................ 11

2/1 Jeethgaya (USA), 5/2 Irish Native (IRE)(6/4—3/1), 7/2 Abigail's Dream, 8/1 Swagman (USA), 12/1 Tristiorum(op 8/1), ADMIRAL'S MISTRESS (IRE)(8/1—14/1), 14/1 Royal Acclaim, 20/1 Gin and Orange, 33/1 Ors. CSF £140.85, Tote £19.60: £2.80 £2.40 £1.30 (£112.50). Mr Lynn Wilson (MARLBOROUGH) bred by Edward M. Daly in Ireland. 11 Rn; Abigail's Dream clmd D Spencer £8,178
2m 39.9 (4.9)
SF—4/–/4/–/–/–

**4005** EAST MIDLANDS ELECTRICITY CLAIMING STKS (I) £2488.20 (£690.20: £330.60)
6f (AWT) 12-45 (12-50)

3791 **Hansom Lad (60)** *(WWHaigh)* 8–8-8 DMcKeown (4) (chsd ldrs: effrt on ins over 1f out: rdn to ld last stride) ............................—1

3966² Cronk's Courage **(57)** (bl) (Fav) *(GLewis)* 5–8-5 MHills (15) (lw: led tl ct cl home) hd.2

3946² Wellsy Lad (USA) **(66)** *(DWChapman)* 4–8-7 SWood (16) (a.p: hrd rdn over 2f out: r.o wl ins fnl f) ............................ 1.3

3517⁵ Drummer's Dream (IRE) **(36)** *(MrsNMacauley)* 3–8-1 AMcGlone (7) (prom: hrd rdn over 1f out: sn btn) ............................ 4.4

3717 Super Heights **(53)** *(MissAJWhitfield)* 3–8-10 DaleGibson (12) (hdwy 2f out: r.o wl ins fnl f) ............................ nk.5

2504 Rambo Express **(65)** (v) *(ICampbell)* 4–8-4 ‡5DBiggs (10) (a.p: swtchd r over 1f out: wknd fnl f) ............................ 2.6

3876 Harlequin Girl **(39)** *(KTIvory)* 3–8-0 GBardwell (2) (nvr plcd to chal) ............................ 1½.7

3900⁶ The Shanahan Bay **(65)** (bl) *(EEldin)* 6–8-9 BRaymond (13) (s.i.s: hdwy ½-wy: rdn over 1f out: sn btn) ............................ 2.8

3044 Petropower (IRE) **(50)** *(MO'Neill)* 3–8-4 JFortune (8) (prom: rdn over 2f out: sn wknd) ............................ ¾.9

3625 Long Lane Lady **(43)** *(JMackie)* 5–8-0 AProud (6) (nvr nr ldrs) ............................ 1½.10

3863 Cross Mags **(47)** *(DBurchell)* 4–8-2 LCharnock (1) (prom: hmpd & lost pl after 1f: n.d after) ............................ 3.11

3804 Green's Stubbs **(37)** *(ABarrow)* 4–8-7 NAdams (14) (outpcd) ............................ 2½.12

3699 Heartburn **(35)** (bl) *(JDBethell)* 3–7-13 TyroneWilliams (9) (swtg: prom over 3f) ........ 13

Sporting Heritage (IRE) (bl) *(DJGMurray-Smith)* 3–8-10 CRutter (3) (w'like: bkwd: s.s: outpcd) ............................ 14

3133 Hot Tootsie **(31)** *(JBalding)* 4–8-6 AClark (5) (s.s: a bhd) ............................ 15

3427 Oratel Flyer **(42)** (v) *(RThompson)* 4–8-6(2) JCarroll (11) (outpcd) ............................ 16

7/2 Cronk's Courage, 4/1 Wellsy Lad (USA), The Shanahan Bay, 11/1 HANSOM LAD(7/1—12/1), Long Lane Lady, 12/1 Rambo Express(op 6/1), 14/1 Super Heights, Drummer's Dream (IRE), Cross Mags, 20/1 Sporting Heritage (IRE), 25/1 Oratel Flyer, Petropower (IRE), Harlequin Girl, Green's Stubbs, 33/1 Hot Tootsie. CSF £49.82, Tote £29.30: £5.30 £1.90 £2.30 (£47.30). Mrs V. Haigh (MALTON) bred by S. I. G. Hunt. 16 Rn; Cronk's Courage clmd M P Russell £4,447
1m 16.2 (2.2)
SF—14/10/8/–/–/–

**4006** COOPERS LYBRAND DELOITTE H'CAP (0-100) £2407.00 (£667.00: £319.00)
5f (AWT)
1-15 (1-18)

(Weights raised 2 lb)

3873 **Abom Swift (80)** (bl) (AHide) 3–9-10 WRyan (1) (swvd lft s: racd alone far side: hdwy over 1f out: r.o to ld ins fnl f) ..................... —1

3961 **Very Bold (53)** (PDEvans) 3–7-11 DaleGibson (11) (a.p stands' side: rdn & r.o ins fnl f) ..................... 1.2

3961 **Sully's Choice (USA) (55)** (bl) (DWChapman) 10–7-13 SWood (14) (lw: a.p stands' side: ev ch fnl f: r.o) ..................... ½.3

3996² **Joe Sugden (62)** (bl) (Fav) (PHowling) 7–8-6 NCarlisle (3) (hdwy ½-wy: ev ch ins fnl f: unable qckn) ..................... s.h.4

3768⁵ **Beckingham Ben (53)** (bl) (JPLeigh) 7–7-11 TyroneWilliams (9) (a.p: rdn & kpt on ins fnl f) ..................... hd.5

2974 **Lady of the Fen (69)** (MrsNMacauley) 3–8-8 ‡5DBiggs (5) (lw: led: edgd lft & hdd ins fnl f) ..................... nk.6

3821⁵ **Greetland Rock (70)** (bl) (JBerry) 3–9-0 JCarroll (12) (disp ld stands' side: rdn & wknd fnl f) ..................... 1½.7

3996 **Ballasecret (75)** (RDickin) 3–8-12 ‡7DMeredith (13) (chsd ldrs stands' side 4f) ..................... nk.8

3301 **Brisas (65)** (bl) (TFairhurst) 4–8-6 ‡3JFanning (6) (spd over 3f) ..................... 2½.9

3946³ **Mimining (51)** (bl) (GMMoore) 5–7-9⁽¹⁾ JQuinn (4) (nvr nr to chal) ..................... nk.10

3961³ **Lincstone Boy (IRE) (50)** (bl) (ASmith) 3–7-8⁽¹⁾ NAdams (7) (spd 3f) ..................... 1½.11

2046⁵ **Lucy Dancer (IRE) (64)** (MMcCormack) 3–8-8 AClark (10) (outpcd) ..................... 4.12

2763 **More Larks (IRE) (54)** (bl) (MBJames) 3–7-12⁽¹⁾ AProud (2) (outpcd) ..................... 1½.13

3947 **Glencroft (78)** (bl) (DWChapman) 7–9-1 ‡7SDWilliams (8) (t: outpcd) ..................... 2.14

LONG HANDICAP: Lincstone Boy (IRE) 7-3.

2/1 Joe Sugden, 15/2 Mimining, 17/2 Lady of the Fen(12/1—8/1), 10/1 Greetland Rock, ABOM SWIFT, 12/1 Glencroft, Ballasecret(op 7/1), Brisas(op 8/1), 14/1 Lucy Dancer (IRE), Sully's Choice (USA), Beckingham Ben, Very Bold, Lincstone Boy (IRE), 33/1 More Larks (IRE). CSF £137.60, CT £1,809.45. Tote £13.60: £2.00 £3.70 £5.30 (£169.40). Mr Victor Sujanani (NEWMARKET) bred by Dunchurch Lodge Stud. 14Rn
60.4 sec (1.4)
SF—52/21/21/27/17/27

**4007** HENRY BOOT (NORTHERN) CLAIMING STKS (II) £2264.90 (£626.40: £298.70)
1½m (AWT)
1-45 (1-45)

3564⁶ **Intricacy (56)** (LadyHerries) 3–8-4 NDay (1) (lw: hdwy ½-wy: wnt 4th st: led over 1f out: sn clr) ..................... —1

2265⁴ **Qualitair Blazer (40)** (JRJenkins) 4–8-1 TyroneWilliams (10) (a.p: 2nd & rdn st: ev ch over 1f out: one pce) ..................... 8.2

3374 **Tempering (80)** (DWChapman) 5–9-2 SWood (6) (led: sn clr: hdd over 1f out: sn btn) ..................... hd.3

1464 **Chronological (62)** (MHTompkins) 5–8-6 ‡5CHodgson (7) (bkwd: bhd: hdwy & 7th st: nt rch ldrs) ..................... 3½.4

3589⁶ **Suluk (USA) (57)** (RHollinshead) 6–8-5 TQuinn (8) (bhd: effrt over 2f out: nt pce to chal) ..................... 7.5

3825⁶ **Have a Care (58)** (RCharlton) 3–8-0 SRaymont (5) (chsd ldrs: 5th st: wknd 2f out) ..................... 1.6

3808 **John Shaw (USA) (78)** (Fav) (WJHaggas) 3–9-0 MHills (9) (lw: chsd ldrs tl 3rd & wkng st) ..................... 1.7

3822 **Ihsaas (MPNaughton)** 4–8-2 ‡3JFanning (4) (bkwd: chsd ldrs: 6th st: wknd 2f out) ..................... 1.8

3955⁵ **Edward Seymour (USA) (62)** (PCalver) 4–8-11 NCarlisle (11) (a in rr) ..................... 9

1675³ **Kevinsline (IRE) (35)** (bl) (ICampbell) 3–7-9⁽²⁾ ‡5DBiggs (3) (chsd ldr 4f: wknd 5f out: t.o) ..................... 10

3885 **Kennington Samara** (RTJuckes) 3–7-10 NAdams (2) (still bkwd: a bhd: t.o) ..................... 11

Evens John Shaw (USA), 11/2 INTRICACY, Tempering(3/1—6/1), 8/1 Chronological, 10/1 Have a Care, 16/1 Suluk (USA), 20/1 Qualitair Blazer, 25/1 Edward Seymour (USA), 33/1 Ors. CSF £95.99, Tote £5.40: £1.70 £3.20 £3.30 (£31.20). Lavinia Duchess of Norfolk (LITTLEHAMPTON) bred by Lavinia Duchess of Norfolk. 11 Rn
2m 37.7 (2.7)
SF—27/8/22/5/—/—

**4008** ROYAL BANK OF SCOTLAND H'CAP (0-70) £2569.40 (£713.40: £342.20)
1m (AWT)
2-15 (2-18)

3902⁵ **Kristis Girl (57)** (DHaydnJones) 4–9-1 TyroneWilliams (13) (3rd st: led over 1f out: all out) ..................... —1

3791² **Sir Arthur Hobbs (57)** (FHLee) 4–9-1 RLappin (17) (w ldrs: led over 4f out tl over 1f out: r.o wl) ..................... nk.2

3915 **Mac's Princess (USA) (63)** (WAO'Gorman) 3–9-4 DMcKeown (5) (bhd: gd hdwy 2f out: r.o ins fnl f) ..................... ¾.3

3771³ Mca Below the Line **(66)** (bl) *(WJPearce)* 3–9-2 ‡⁵GHusband (15) (6th st: one pce fnl 2f) ........................................................................ 2.4
3915* Bescaby Boy **(63)** *(JWharton)* 5–9-7 JWilliams (8) (nrst fin) ..................... 1.5
3915⁴ Habeta (USA) **(65)** (Fav) *(JWWatts)* 5–9-2 ‡⁷JWeaver (2) (nvr nrr) ............... 3.6
3886 Cartel **(61)** *(JLHarris)* 4–9-5 BRaymond (3) (dwlt: gd hdwy & 5th st: wknd over 1f out) ................................................................................................ 1.7
  *1928* Evening Star **(59)** *(AHide)* 5–8-12 ‡⁵DBiggs (9) (bit bkwd: n.d) .............. s.h.8
3796 Lock Keeper (USA) **(60)** *(JMackie)* 5–9-4 AProud (6) (lw: prom 5f) ........... 1.9
3988 Doulab's Image **(70)** *(JAGlover)* 4–9-7 ‡⁷SDWilliams (14) (n.d) ............. 1½.10
3131⁵ Crofter's Cline **(68)** (v) *(MO'Neill)* 7–9-10 DNicholls (1) (4th st: wknd 2f out) ..... 1.11
3051 Come Home Alone **(60)** *(RHannon)* 3–9-1 AMcGlone (16) (2nd st: wknd 2f out) ..... 2.12
3988 Dodgy **(59)** (bl) *(WJHaggas)* 4–9-3 NDay (10) (b: n.d) .......................... 1½.13
3915 Miss Sarajane **(55)** *(RHollinshead)* 7–8-13 WRyan (12) (prom 4f) ............. 5.14
3148⁶ Stairway to Heaven (IRE) **(63)** (bl) *(CRBeever)* 3–8-13 ‡⁵CHodgson (4) (n.d) ..... 2½.15
  Gushy **(55)** *(CRBeever)* 5–8-13 TQuinn (11) (b: bkwd: t.o) .............................. 16
1851 Nuclear Express **(62)** (bl) *(DJWintle)* 4–9-6 NAdams (7) (rdn along: led over 3f: wknd qckly: t.o) ........................................................................................ 17

**4/1** Habeta (USA), **7/1** Crofter's Cline, **8/1** Bescaby Boy(op 5/1), Sir Arthur Hobbs, **10/1** Mca Below the Line, Doulab's Image, Stairway to Heaven (IRE)(12/1—8/1), **12/1** Cartel, Dodgy(op 8/1), **14/1** KRISTIS GIRL, Lock Keeper (USA), **16/1** Mac's Princess (USA), Come Home Alone, Miss Sarajane, **20/1** Evening Star, Nuclear Express, **25/1** Gushy. CSF £126.29, CT £1,702.22. Tote £16.30: £3.50 £2.30 £4.70 £3.30 (£59.20). Mrs S. T. Mantle (PONTYPRIDD) bred by Benham Stud. 17 Rn     1m 43.9 (5.9)

---

**4009**     EAST MIDLANDS ELECTRICITY CLAIMING STKS (II)    £2467.90 (£684.40: £327.70)
        6f (AWT)                                                    2-45 (2-48)

3996 **Everset (FR) (76)** *(WJMusson)* 3–8-10 AMackay (14) (lw: hdwy 4f out: led over 1f out. jst hld on) ........................................................................................ —1
3791 In a Whirl (USA) **(42)** (bl) *(NACallaghan)* 3–7-11 NCarlisle (5) (hdwy 3f out: ev ch fnl f: r.o) ............................................................................................... s.h.2
3984⁶ Euroblake **(72)** *(TDBarron)* 4–8-9 AlexGreaves (8) (swtg: hdwy on ins over 1f out: str run fnl f: fin fast) ........................................................................ s.h.3
3873⁴ Zanoni **(83)** (Fav) *(MAJarvis)* 4–9-2 BRaymond (4) (lw: led 3f: wknd over 1f out) ..... 3.4
3911 Sally's Son **(69)** (bl) *(WAO'Gorman)* 5–8-2 ‡⁵EmmaO'Gorman (13) (hdwy 3f out: one pce fnl 2f) ........................................................................................... 1½.5
3961 Sir Tasker **(52)** *(JLHarris)* 3–8-6 TQuinn (11) (lw: prom: led over 2f out tl over 1f out: wknd fnl f) ................................................................................... 3½.6
3409 Able Princess **(50)** (bl) *(MrsNMacauley)* 3–7-10 ‡⁵DBiggs (7) (prom 4f) ........... 4.7
3741 Dawn Success **(80)** *(DWChapman)* 5–8-9 SWood (9) (nvr trbld ldrs) ............. ½.8
3946 Dorking Lad **(58)** *(MHTompkins)* 9–8-4 ‡⁵CHodgson (12) (n.d) .................. 1.9
3724 Supreme Optimist **(29)** (bl) *(REPeacock)* 7–8-4 ‡³JFanning (2) (b: spd over 3f) ..... 1½.10
3634 Gina's Delight **(30)** *(JWharton)* 3–7-13 JQuinn (16) (n.d) ............................ ½.11
3771 Quinzii Martin **(48)** *(DHaydnJones)* 3–8-10 TyroneWilliams (6) (prom 4f) ...... 2.12
3372 Yeoman Force **(77)** (v) *(JMBradley)* 5–7-10 ‡⁷MichaelBradley (3) (n.d) ........ 1½.13
  Secret Contract **(28)** *(REBarr)* 6–8-4 SWebster (1) (prom 4f) ........................ ¾.14
3850 Jolly Fisherman (IRE) **(39)** (bl) *(MCChapman)* 3–8-8 GBardwell (15) (a bhd) ..... nk.15
  Godsall **(44)** *(MrsNMacauley)* 4–8-2 NAdams (10) (bkwd: w ldrs: led over 3f out tl wknd over 2f out) ...................................................................................... 1½.16

**10/11** Zanoni, **7/1** Euroblake, **8/1** Dawn Success(op 4/1), **11/1** EVERSET (FR)(7/1—12/1), **12/1** Sally's Son(op 8/1), **14/1** Dorking Lad, **16/1** Yeoman Force, **20/1** In a Whirl (USA), Able Princess, **25/1** Sir Tasker, Quinzii Martin, **33/1** Jolly Fisherman (IRE), Secret Contract, Godsall, **50/1** Ors. CSF £201.42, Tote £16.80: £4.70 £4.30 £2.00 (£149.30). Broughton Thermal Insulation (NEWMARKET) bred by Societe Aland in France. 16 Rn     1m 15.3 (1.3)
                                         SF—34/20/31/26/6/-

---

**4010**     GAY KELLEWAY 'THE SPORT RACELINE' STKS (Mdn 2-Y.O) £2731.80 (£759.80: £365.40)                                                     1m (AWT)                     3-15 (3-18)

  **Lord Vivienne (IRE)** (Fav) *(PFICole)* 9-0 TQuinn (9) (bit bkwd: 5th st: led 2f out: edgd lft: r.o wl) ............................................................................................ —1
3487 Aegaen Lady **(50)** *(JEtherington)* 8-2 ‡⁷JWeaver (14) (led over 3f: ev ch 2f out: one pce) ................................................................................................... 3.2
3704 Brotherlyaffection *(RHollinshead)* 9-0 WRyan (15) (7th st: r.o one pce fnl 2f) ....... 3.3
  Cold Shower (IRE) *(JAGlover)* 8-7 ‡⁷SWilliams (2) (w'like: hld up: hdwy on ins & n.m.r over 1f out: bttr for r) ..................................................................... 6.4
3844 Our John **(51)** *(RonaldThompson)* 9-0 DNicholls (5) (led over 4f out: hdd 2f out: wknd fnl f) ................................................................................................. s.h.5
3949 Absent Lyric (IRE) **(64)** (bl) *(TDBarron)* 8-9 AlexGreaves (3) (hdwy on ins & 4th st: hrd rdn & wknd over 1f out) .................................................................. s.h.6

3882 Shirl *(WJHaggas)* 8-9 JFortune (12) (3rd st: wknd 2f out) ............................ ½.7
3648⁶ Free Transfer (IRE) *(PFTulk)* 9-0 BRaymond (11) (w ldrs: 2nd st: wknd 2f out) ...... 1½.8
Pip's Optimist *(PJFeilden)* 8-7 ‡7StephenDavies (7) (leggy: unf: bkwd: 6th st: wknd 2f out) ................................................................................................ 10.9
3869 Shayna Maidel *(WJHaggas)* 8-9 NDay (6) (nvr nr ldrs) ...................................... 1.10
2940 Elite Reg *(PFICole)* 9-0 CRutter (8) (a bhd) ...................................................... 2.11
3106 Majestic Maybe (IRE) **(51)** *(THCaldwell)* 8-2 ‡7MHumphries (1) (a bhd: t.o) ...... 12
3881 Element Ofsurprise *(CaptJWilson)* 8-9 MWood (17) (swtg: t.o) ............................ 13
Spectrum Star *(ACStewart)* 8-9 MHills (16) (w lke: leggy: lw: bhd fnl 3f: t.o) ...... 14
3616 Hall Porter **(50)** *(RMWhitaker)* 9-0 ACulhane (10) (prom: hrd rdn 6f out: sn wknd: t.o) ...................................................................................................................... 15
3881 Caherea School *(JPLeigh)* 8-9 DMcKeown (4) (bkwd: t.o) .................................. 16

**2/1** LORD VIVIENNE (IRE)(op 4/5), **4/1** Spectrum Star, **6/1** Free Transfer (IRE), **8/1** Shirl, Our John(op 20/1), **12/1** Absent Lyric (IRE), Shayna Maidel, **16/1** Pip's Optimist, **18/1** Cold Shower (IRE), **20/1** Majestic Maybe (IRE), Aegaen Lady, **25/1** Elite Reg, **33/1** Caherea School, Element Ofsurprise, **50/1** Ors. CSF £45.26, TOTE £2.50: £2.70 £3.80 £6.60 (£152.20). Mrs Jane Lewis (WHATCOMBE) bred by Binfield Manor Farms Ltd in Ireland. 16 Rn                                                                                     1m 43.2 (5.2)

---

**4011**      AUTUMN NURSERY (0-75) £2508.50 (£696.00: £333.50)  **7f (AWT)**      3-45 (3-48)

3880 **Ferdia (IRE) (58)** *(RHollinshead)* 8-7 WRyan (2) (hld up: gd hdwy 2f out: r.o to ld ins fnl f: r.o) ........................................................................................................... —1
3922 Empeeka (USA) **(64)** *(WAO'Gorman)* 8-8 ‡5EmmaO'Gorman (11) (hld up: gd hdwy 2f out: ev ch whn hung lft ins fnl f: r.o) .............................................................. 1.2
3310 Debsy Do (USA) **(55)** *(SGNorton)* 8-8 JFortune (16) (a.p: led 3f tl ins fnl f: r.o) ...... hd.3
3383 Sie Amato (IRE) **(59)** *(CaptJWilson)* 8-8 GBardwell (1) (lw: led 4f: 2nd st: one pce fnl 2f) ................................................................................................................. 3½.4
3880 Runnel **(61)** (bl) *(DWChapman)* 8-10 SWood (7) (lw: 3rd st: wknd 1f out) ............ 5.5
3548³ Everso Irish **(55)** *(MHTompkins)* 8-4 TyroneWilliams (8) (lw: nvr nr to chal) ............ 4.6
3844⁴ Up the Punjab **(72)** *(SDow)* 9-7 TQuinn (15) (b.nr hind: hdwy on ins & 5th st: wknd over 1f out) ....................................................................................................... nk.7
3583 Risk Zone **(55)** (Fav) *(RHannon)* 8-4 MHills (14) (n.d) ...................................... 1½.8
3862 Chris Hughton (IRE) **(70)** *(JAkehurst)* 9-5 SWhitworth (3) (prom 4f) .................. 1½.9
3849⁵ Capital Idea (IRE) **(62)** *(RonaldThompson)* 8-11 RPElliott (13) (n.d) .................. 3.10
3316 Phil-Man **(52)** *(TFairhurst)* 7-12 ‡3JFanning (9) (n.d) ........................................ nk.11
3880⁵ Coastal Express **(70)** *(EWeymes)* 9-5 DaleGibson (6) (4th st: wknd qckly 2f out) .. ½.12
3474 Just-Go-Again **(52)** *(JMJefferson)* 8-1 LCharnock (10) (6th st: wknd 2f out) .......... 2.13
3767 Daily Sport August **(69)** *(MCChapman)* 8-11 ‡7SWilliams (5) (t.o) ...................... 14
*3964* Kingchip Boy **(53)** *(MJRyan)* 7-11 ‡5DBiggs (4) (sddle slipped: t.o) ...................... 15

**9/2** Risk Zone, **6/1** Empeeka (USA)(op 4/1), Everso Irish, **7/1** Chris Hughton (IRE), **8/1** Sie Amato (IRE)(op 5/1), **9/1** Up the Punjab(op 5/1), **10/1** Coastal Express, Runnel, Capital Idea (IRE), **14/1** Debsy Do (USA), FERDIA (IRE), **16/1** Phil-Man, Kingchip Boy, **20/1** Daily Sport August, **25/1** Just-Go-Again. CSF £101.37, CT £1,142.12. Tote £14.00: £2.20 £3.20 £5.70 (£105.20). Mr Noel Sweeney (UPPER LONGDON) bred by Noel Sweeney in Ireland. 15 Rn                                                                        1m 30.5 (3.3)
                                                                                                      SF—12/9/4/—/—/—

T/Plpt: Not won; £2,005.25 to Newbury 13/11/91.                                                              IM/KH

---

3962—**LINGFIELD (L-H)** Equitrack
**Thursday, November 14th [Standard]**
Going Allowance: minus 0.60 sec per fur (FS)                        *Racing delayed half hour - power failure*

---

**4015**      LEVIATHAN CLAIMING STKS (I) (2-Y.O) £2186.80 (£604.80: £288.40)
            **1m (AWT)**                                                                      12-40 (1-12)

3728 **Lady Linnet (69)** (Jt-Fav) *(PFICole)* 8-1 CRutter (7) (hdwy over 3f out: led ins fnl f: drvn out) ........................................................................................................ —1
3820 Stylish Gentleman **(63)** (Jt-Fav) *(CTinkler)* 8-4 MBirch (5) (eyeshield: led over 4f out tl ins fnl f: r.o) ................................................................................................... 1½.2
3680⁶ Honey Vision **(49)** (bl) *(GHEden)* 8-1⁽³⁾ GCarter (10) (a.p: ev ch ins fnl f: r.o) ...... s.h.3
3820 A Nymph Too Far (IRE) **(66)** *(DrJDScargill)* 7-12 JQuinn (3) (a.p: hrd rdn over 1f out: unable qckn) ................................................................................................ 2.4
3903 Shakinski **(50)** *(MJRyan)* 7-12 GBardwell (8) (hdwy fnl 2f: nvr nrr) ...................... 2.5
3880² Super-Sub **(62)** *(MJFetherston-Godley)* 8-3⁽¹⁾ TQuinn (11) (hdwy over 2f out: one pce) ............................................................................................................... ¾.6
3949 Perforate **(70)** *(SirMarkPrescott)* 8-7 CNutter (4) (lw: nvr nr to chal) ..................... 3½.7
3628 Rustic Wedding **(54)** *(GBBalding)* 7-12 NCarlisle (1) (prom 4f) ............................ s.h.8

```
3922  High Post (46) (DMarks) 8-9  AClark (12) (hdwy over 3f out: wknd over 2f out) ......... hd.9
3881  Bright Fantastic (IRE) (47) (bl) (RFJohnsonHoughton) 8-6  AMunro (6) (lw: a
                                                                              bhd) ...................................... 7.10
3963⁴  Tyrone Flyer (67) (TJNaughton) 8-11  MHills (2) (b.hind: led over 3f) ...................... 7.11
3278  Lock Lane (IRE) (40) (PFTulk) 8-5  AMcGlone (9) (a bhd) ................................... 6.12
```

**11/4** LADY LINNET, Stylish Gentleman(2/1—7/2), **4/1** Super-Sub, **5/1** Perforate, **10/1** Honey Vision, Rustic Wedding, **14/1** Tyrone Flyer, Shakinski, **16/1** A Nymph Too Far (IRE), **33/1** Ors. CSF £11.98, Tote No win or place dividends declared. Mr N. C. Kersey (WHATCOMBE) bred by Bridge End Bloodstock. 12 Rn; Stylish Gentleman clmd J Daniels £3,550                                          1m 38.8 (hand) (0.8)
                                                                              SF—3/1/—/—/—/—

---

## 4016
E.B.F. ALBION STKS (Mdn 2-Y.O) £2402.40 (£666.40: £319.20)
**7f (AWT)**                                                                1-10 (1-41)

```
3727³  Liability Order (73) (RBoss) 9-0  BRaymond (7) (a.p: led over 1f out: r.o wl) ............ —1
3898²  Constructivist (IRE) (Fav) (BWHills) 9-0  MHills (9) (hdwy over 2f out: rdn over 1f
                                                             out: unable qckn) ............................. 2½.2
        Fengari (PTWalwyn) 9-0  TQuinn (2) (unf: scope: bit bkwd: a.p: r.o one pce fnl 2f)  1½.3
3982  In the Game (IRE) (48) (MissAJWhitfield) 8-9  RFox (3) (led over 5f: one pce) ......... hd.4
3962⁵  Amazon Express (CEBrittain) 9-0  AMunro (8) (no hdwy fnl 2f) ......................... 3.5
3982  Thor Power (IRE) (DTThom) 9-0  JWilliams (6) (nvr nr to chal) ........................... 1.6
3624  Tronchetto (IRE) (SirMarkPrescott) 9-0  CNutter (4) (prom 4f) ........................ 1½.7
        Storm Drum (PJMakin) 9-0  WNewnes (10) (leggy: bit bkwd: nvr nrr) ............... hd.8
        Child Star (FR) (DMarks) 8-9  AClark (12) (lt-f: dwlt: a bhd) ......................... hd.9
        Bold Boris (RWArmstrong) 9-0  BCrossley (1) (neat: bkwd: a bhd) ................. nk.10
3872  Our Eddie (BGubby) 9-0  JQuinn (13) (a bhd) ................................................ ½.11
3963³  Lindeman (SDow) 9-0  GCarter (5) (prom 5f) ................................................ 4.12
```

**5/6** Constructivist (IRE)(1/2—Evens), **4/1** Tronchetto (IRE), **6/1** Lindeman, **8/1** LIABILITY ORDER, **11/1** Amazon Express, **14/1** Fengari(10/1—16/1), **16/1** Storm Drum(12/1—20/1), **20/1** Bold Boris(op 10/1), **33/1** Ors. CSF £16.43, Tote No win or place dividends declared. Madagans Plc (NEWMARKET) bred by N. J. Dent. 12 Rn                                                                      1m 25.9 (hand) (0.9)
                                                                              SF—24/16/11/5/1/—

---

## 4017
LEVIATHAN CLAIMING STKS (II) (2-Y.O) £2186.80 (£604.80: £288.40)
**1m (AWT)**                                                                1-40 (2-07)

```
4011  Kingchip Boy (53) (MJRyan) 7-12 ‡⁵DBiggs (10) (a.p: hrd rdn over 3f out: led last
                                                             stride) ............................................ —1
3964⁴  Clare Kerry Lass (72) (Fav) (TJNaughton) 8-9 ‡⁵CHodgson (2) (b: hdwy over 2f
                                              out: led wl over 1f out: hrd rdn fnl f: hdd last stride) ................... hd.2
3964  Easy Does it (60) (v) (CCElsey) 8-0  JQuinn (8) (led over 4f out tl wl over 1f out:
                                                             unable qckn) ..................................... 2½.3
3692⁶  Grog (IRE) (52) (MRChannon) 8-9  BRouse (4) (hdwy over 2f out: ev ch over 1f
                                                             out: one pce) .................................... 1.4
4001  Great Hall (54) (WGRWightman) 8-8⁽¹⁾ JWilliams (9) (b.hind: hdwy fnl 2f: nvr nrr) ..... 3.5
3964  Play Risky (IRE) (bl) (PAKelleway) 8-3  AMunro (1) (led over 3f: wknd over 3f out) ... 6.6
3616  Victor Romeo (66) (WJPearce) 8-9  DNicholls (7) (a mid div) .......................... ¾.7
3844  Green's Exhibit (60) (RAkehurst) 8-3  TyroneWilliams (6) (prom over 3f) ............... 3.8
3701  Meadow Game (IRE) (WGMTurner) 7-12  GBardwell (5) (s.s: a wl bhd) ................. 2.9
3872  Dangina (ASReid) 8-3  CRutter (11) (b: b.hind: a bhd) .................................... 1½.10
3548  Bay Chieftain (bl) (MrsLStubbs) 8-5  MBirch (3) (a wl bhd) .............................. 8.11
        Sun Glory (IRE) (WJarvis) 8-5⁽¹⁾ WRyan (12) (unf: bhd fnl 4f) .......................... 2.12
```

**7/4** Clare Kerry Lass, **4/1** Victor Romeo, **11/2** Green's Exhibit(op 7/2), **13/2** Grog (IRE), **10/1** Sun Glory (IRE)(op 5/1), **14/1** Easy Does it(8/1—16/1), Play Risky (IRE), **20/1** KINGCHIP BOY, Great Hall(op 12/1), **25/1** Meadow Game (IRE), **33/1** Ors. CSF £55.34, Tote No win or place dividends declared. Four Jays Racing Partnership (NEWMARKET) bred by R. M. Scott. 12 Rn                                          1m 39.4 (hand) (1.4)

---

## 4018
EAGLE H'CAP (0-90) £2877.60 (£798.60: £382.80)  **1½m (AWT)**              2-10 (2-34)

```
3968*  Mr Wishing Well (57) (RJRWilliams) 5—7-9 (5x) JQuinn (8) (gd hdwy over 4f out:
                                                             led over 1f out: drvn out) ..................... —1
3852⁴  Mysterious Maid (USA) (70) (JPearce) 4—8-8  TQuinn (12) (hdwy over 3f out: hrd
                                                             rdn over 1f out: no wl ins fnl f) .............. s.h.2
3852  Venturist (USA) (84) (JHMGosden) 4—9-8  AMcGlone (16) (b.nr fore: a.p: led
                                                             over 2f out tl over 1f out: r.o) ............... 1.3
3992  Age of Miracles (76) (CACyzer) 4—9-0  DMcKeown (4) (rdn 7f out: hdwy over 1f
                                                             out: r.o wl ins fnl f) .......................... nk.4
3919³  Quick Ransom (66) (Fav) (MJohnston) 3—7-11  NCarlisle (5) (rdn thrght: hdwy 3f
                                                             out: r.o ins fnl f) ............................ 1½.5
```

3874⁵ Briery Fille **(59)** *(AHide)* 6–7–4⁽⁴⁾ ‡⁷PTurner (9) (hdwy fnl 2f: r.o) .......................... 1½.6
3302⁶ Kiska (USA) **(76)** *(BWHills)* 3–8–0⁽²⁾ ‡⁷JWeaver (11) (a.p: led over 3f out tl over 2f
out: wknd over 1f out) .............................................. ½.7
3965³ Art Form (USA) **(74)** *(CACyzer)* 4–8–5 ‡⁷TMcLaughlin (15) (nvr nrr) ...................... s.h.8
652 Caspian Beluga **(62)** *(MrsAKnight)* 3–7–2 ‡⁵BDoyle (3) (a mid div) ..................... ¾.9
3967³ Rapporteur (USA) **(90)** *(CCElsey)* 5–10–0 WNewnes (6) (b: lw: led over 8f) .......... 2.10
3857 Northern Flyer **(74)** *(PTWalwyn)* 3–8–5 AMunro (2) (prom 9f) ............................ nk.11
3564 Scotoni **(63)** *(RJO'Sullivan)* 5–7–10⁽²⁾ ‡⁵DBiggs (14) (s.s: a bhd) ..................... 15.12
3867 Ryewater Dream **(62)** *(DRCElsworth)* 3–7–7 NAdams (13) (prom over 7f) ............. 2.13
1776³ Applianceofscience **(60)** (bl) *(ASReid)* 4–7–12 CRutter (7) (bhd fnl 4f) ............. 5.14
1113² Master Line **(55)** *(HCandy)* 10–7–7 GBardwell (10) (b: a bhd) ........................ 2.15
3915 Sarabah (IRE) **(78)** *(GHarwood)* 3–8–9 AClark (1) (lw: hdwy on ins over 6f out:
wknd over 4f out) ............................................. 1½.16

LONG HANDICAP: Briery Fille 7-0, Caspian Beluga 7-6, Ryewater Dream 7-5.

**100/30** Quick Ransom, **4/1** MR WISHING WELL, **15/2** Rapporteur, Venturist (USA), **8/1** Kiska (USA),
**10/1** Mysterious Maid (USA), **12/1** Art Form (USA), **14/1** Age of Miracles, Sarabah (IRE), Briery Fille, **16/1**
Master Line, **20/1** Northern Flyer, Scotoni, Ryewater Dream, **33/1** Ors. CSF £46.71, CT £283.15. Tote No win
or place dividends declared. Mr Steven Astaire (NEWMARKET) bred by Mrs John Trotter. 16 Rn
2m 31.49 (0.49)
SF—4/16/28/19/–/–

**4019** CENTAUR H'CAP (0-70) £2461.20 (£683.20: £327.60) **1¼m (AWT)** 2-40 (3-02)

3874² **Queen of India (USA) (66)** (Fav) *(JHMGosden)* 3–9–10 WRyan (11) (rdn &
hdwy over 6f out: led over 1f out: r.o wl) ............................. —1
3688² Chloes Diamond (IRE) **(58)** *(JLSpearing)* 3–9–2 TQuinn (6) (a.p: led over 3f out tl
over 1f out: unable qckn) ............................................. 1½.2
3515⁴ Samurai Gold (USA) **(50)** (v) *(PTWalwyn)* 3–8–8 BRouse (8) (lw: a.p: ev ch wl
over 1f out: one pce) ................................................. ½.3
3915 Adjacent (IRE) **(58)** *(BWHills)* 3–8–9 ‡⁷JWeaver (13) (hdwy over 2f out: r.o one
pce) ..................................................................... 2½.4
1514 Pleasure Ahead **(48)** *(MRChannon)* 4–8–11 LornaVincent (4) (hdwy 3f out: r.o
ins fnl f) ................................................................. 1½.5
3984 Toshiba Comet Too (IRE) **(57)** *(WJPearce)* 3–9–1 DNicholls (1) (no hdwy fnl 2f) ... 1½.6
3999* On Y Va (USA) **(58)** *(RJRWilliams)* 4–9–7 (5x) MHills (12) (b.off hind: a.p: ev ch 2f
out: wknd over 1f out) .............................................. 3.7
3967⁴ Double Echo (IRE) **(58)** (bl) *(JDBethell)* 3–9–2 AMunro (2) (lw: led over 6f) ............. 4.8
3847 Crown Reserve **(66)** *(MJRyan)* 3–9–10 GCarter (5) (a bhd) ................................ 1½.9
3905 Overpower **(56)** *(MHTompkins)* 7–9–0 ‡⁵CHodgson (14) (a bhd) ................. nk.10
92³ Gipsy King **(66)** *(PAKelleway)* 3–9–3 ‡⁷ABates (10) (eyeshield: bhd fnl 6f) ........... 10.11
1652 El Volador (USA) **(RJO'Sullivan)* 4–8–12 ‡⁵DBiggs (9) (a bhd) ........................... 8.12
4008 Gushy **(55)** (bl) *(CRBeever)* 5–9–4 DMcKeown (3) (b: bhd fnl 4f) ..................... 10.13
3968⁴ Dr Maccarter (USA) **(65)** (bl) *(CCElsey)* 4–9–9 ‡⁵EmmaO'Gorman (7) (virtually
ref to: a t.o) ......................................................... dist.14

**5/2** QUEEN OF INDIA (USA), **7/2** El Volador, **11/2** Adjacent (IRE), **15/2** Double Echo (IRE)(12/1—7/1), **8/1** Dr
Maccarter (USA), **12/1** Chloes Diamond (IRE), On Y Va (USA), **14/1** Samurai Gold (USA), **16/1** Gushy, **25/1**
Gipsy King, Crown Reserve, Toshiba Comet Too (IRE), Pleasure Ahead, **33/1** Overpower. CSF £34.55, CT
£354.05. Tote £3.70: £1.60 £2.80 £4.70 (£18.40). Mrs Roger Waters (NEWMARKET) bred by Robert
Courtney and Mr Congleton in USA. 14 Rn
2m 7.12 (2.12)
SF—29/18/9/5/4/5

**4020** BULWARK H'CAP (0-90) £2739.00 (£759.00: £363.00) **7f (AWT)** 3-10 (3-29)

3381⁴ **Helawe (80)** (bl) *(SirMarkPrescott)* 8–9–7 BRaymond (11) (mde all: hrd rdn fnl f:
r.o wl) ................................................................. —1
3372³ African Chimes **(70)** *(WAO'Gorman)* 4–8–6 ‡⁵EmmaO'Gorman (1) (a.p: nt clr run
& snatched up ins fnl f: swtchd rt: r.o wl) .......................... hd.2
3617 Bold Habit **(87)** *(WJPearce)* 6–9–9 ‡⁵GHusband (9) (gd hdwy over 1f out: r.o wl
ins fnl f) ............................................................... s.h.3
3911* Pytchley Night **(82)** *(DMorris)* 4–9–2 ‡⁷StephenDavies (4) (lw: rdn & hdwy over 1f
out: r.o ins fnl f) ..................................................... 1½.4
3645 Domicksky **(82)** *(MJRyan)* 3–9–7 MTebbutt (3) (a.p: ev ch 2f out: one pce) .......... 2½.5
3914 Grey Starling **(60)** *(RCharlton)* 3–7–13 SRaymont (5) (lw: a.p: hrd rdn wl over 1f out:
one pce) .............................................................. s.h.6
3813⁶ Cape Pigeon (USA) **(72)** *(LGCottrell)* 6–8–13 AMunro (15) (lw: nvr nr to chal) ....... 1½.7
3645 Graf (USA) **(84)** *(MrsLPiggott)* 4–9–11 LPiggott (13) (eyeshield: nvr nrr) ............. hd.8
3873⁵ Able Jet (USA) **(77)** (bl) *(MrsNMacauley)* 3–9–2 DMcKeown (10) (lw: prom over
4f) ...................................................................... hd.9
3847⁶ Gabbiadini **(77)** (v) *(MHTompkins)* 4–9–4 TyroneWilliams (16) (prom 5f) ............. s.h.10

3966[4] Nigel's Lucky Girl **(66)** (Jt-Fav) *(RGuest)* 3–8-5[(1)] NDay (6) (bhd fnl 2f) .............. s.h.**11**
3902 Cash a Million (FR) **(56)** *(PDCundell)* 3–7-9 JQuinn (3) (a bhd) ..................... 1½.**12**
3801* La Belle Vie **(65)** *(JHBaker)* 5–8-6 GCarter (2) (a bhd) ........................... ¾.**13**
1866 Predictable **(70)** *(MrsAKnight)* 5–8-11 AlexGreaves (7) (bhd fnl 3f) ............... 3½.**14**
3897 Pims Classic **(78)** *(WJHaggas)* 3–9-3 MHills (14) (lw: a bhd) ..................... nk.**15**
3873[2] Assignment **(80)** (Jt-Fav) *(JFfitch-Heyes)* 5–9-7 TQuinn (8) (a bhd) ........... 1½.**16**
*Stewards Enquiry: Obj. to Helawe by O'Gorman overruled.*

**13/2** Assignment, Nigel's Lucky Girl(tchd 4/1), **8/1** Grey Starling, HELAWE, **9/1** Gabbiadini, Cape Pigeon (USA), **10/1** Pytchley Night, La Belle Vie, **12/1** Graf (USA), African Chimes, Domicksky, Bold Habit, **14/1** Pims Classic, **16/1** Cash a Million (FR), **20/1** Ors. CSF £102.92, CT £1,074.55. Tote £12.60: £3.20 £2.90 £2.00 £4.00 (£20.50). Mr A. R. C. Finn (NEWMARKET) bred by Miss Ann C. Leighton Hardman. 16Rn
1m 24.21 (U.79)
SF—56/40/56/44/41/18

## 4021    ARK ROYAL H'CAP (0-70) £2186.80 (£604.80: £288.40)    5f (AWT)    3-40 (3-58)

3804 **Pendor Dancer (48)** (bl) *(BForsey)* 8–8-7[(3)] JWilliams (1) (hld up: led ins fnl f: r.o wl) ......................... —**1**
3000 Imco Double (IRE) **(49)** *(EEldin)* 3–8-8 LPiggott (8) (a.p: hrd rdn fnl f: r.o wl) ........... hd.**2**
2879 Inswinger **(43)** *(WGRWightman)* 5–8-2 TyroneWilliams (2) (outpcd: hdwy over 1f out: r.o wl ins fnl f) ........................... hd.**3**
3721[2] Barbara's Cutie **(44)** *(MBlanshard)* 3–8-3 NAdams (5) (led over 3f out tl ins fnl f: r.o) ......................... ¾.**4**
3966 Tachyon Park **(50)** (v) *(PHowling)* 9–8-9 BCrossley (4) (outpcd: hdwy over 1f out: nvr nrr) ........................... nk.**5**
3966* Rushanes **(67)** *(TCasey)* 4–9-5 (7x) ‡7SWilliams (10) (nvr nr to chal) ......... 2½.**6**
3900 Ski Captain **(60)** *(PHowling)* 7–9-5 WNewnes (9) (outpcd) ..................... 2½.**7**
4006[6] Lady of the Fen **(69)** *(MrsNMacauley)* 3–10-0 SKeightley (6) (spd over 3f) ......... nk **8**
3966 Village Pet **(53)** *(HABennett)* 3–8-1½ JCurant (7) (bhd fnl 3f) ................. 3½.**9**
2361 Ever so Artistic **(56)** (bl) (Fav) *(PHowling)* 4–9-1 CRutter (3) (led over 1f: wknd over 1f out) ......................... 1.**10**

**7/2** Ever so Artistic, **4/1** Rushanes, Barbara's Cutie, **6/1** Ski Captain, **7/1** Lady of the Fen, **12/1** PENDOR DANCER, Tachyon Park, Imco Double (IRE), **14/1** Inswinger, **25/1** Village Pet. CSF £131.88, CT £1,850.68. Tote £10.30: £1.50 £2.40 £3.60 (£283.60). Mr D. A. Bay (TAUNTON) bred by Mrs P. A. Brown. 10Rn
59.51 sec (U.49)
SF—43/43/36/34/39/39
T/Plpt: £49.50 (24.1 Tckts).    AK

## 4004—SOUTHWELL (L-H) Fibresand
### Tuesday, November 19th [Standard]
Going Allowance: minus 0.25 sec per fur (FS)    Wind: str across

## 4022    RIVER IDLE STKS (I) (Mdn 2-Y-O) £2346.10 (£649.60: £310.30)
**7f (AWT)**    12-20 (12-24)

**Macs Bid (CAN)** *(WAO'Gorman)* 8-9 ‡5EmmaO'Gorman (9) (lengthy: bit bkwd: a gng wl: 4th st: led over 1f out: sn clr) ......................... —**1**
3619 Ballyranter *(HJCollingridge)* 9-0 VSmith (11) (bhd: hdwy over 1f out: r.o) ........... 6.**2**
3964 Watersong *(DRLaing)* 8-9 TyroneWilliams (4) (3rd st: ev ch over 1f out: one pce) hd.**3**
Our Man in Havana (Fav) *(PFICole)* 9-0 TQuinn (1) (unf: scope: 2nd st: ev ch over 1f out: one pce) ......................... 2½.**4**
3773 Another Nut **(46)** *(PDEvans)* 8-9 NAdams (6) (led tl hdd over 1f out: sn btn) ...... 2½.**5**
3959 Roger Rabbit (FR) *(RBoss)* 9-0 BRaymond (12) (hmpd 4f out: c wd & 6th st: sn rdn: wknd wl over 1f out) ......................... 3.**6**
2645 Medbourne (IRE) **(54)** *(JLHarris)* 8-9 DMcKeown (8) (s.i.s: nvr trbld ldrs) ..... hd.**7**
3989 Tales of Wisdom *(SirMarkPrescott)* 8-9 GDuffield (5) (outpcd) ..................... hd.**8**
Blackwater Panther (IRE) *(CNAllen)* 8-9 ‡5DBiggs (2) (leggy: unf: chsd ldrs 4f) ....... ¾.**9**
3945 Bold Mood *(JBerry)* 9-0 JCarroll (7) (5th st: wknd 2f out) ......................... 7.**10**
3917 Noble Vienna (USA) *(RHollinshead)* 9-0 WRyan (3) (a bhd) ....................... 1½.**11**
3896 Saruk (IRE) *(DRCElsworth)* 8-9 JWilliams (13) (a in rr) ......................... ½.**12**
3916 Scarborough Hill (IRE) *(MHTompkins)* 8-9 ‡5CHodgson (10) (chsd ldrs 2f) ........ 2.**13**

**5/2** Our Man in Havana, **4/1** Roger Rabbit (FR)(10/1—7/2), **9/1** MACS BID (CAN)(op 4/1), Bold Mood(op 4/1), Tales of Wisdom(op 6/1), **14/1** Saruk (IRE)(op 8/1), **16/1** Scarborough Hill (IRE), **20/1** Blackwater Panther (IRE), Noble Vienna (USA), **25/1** Medbourne (IRE), Watersong, **33/1** Ors. CSF £208.97, Tote £9.20: £2.50 £3.00 £5.90 (£3.50). Mr M. McDonnell (NEWMARKET) bred by Anderson Farms in Canada. 13Rn
1m 30.1 (2.9)
SF—25/12/6/3/–/–

**4023** HUMBER CLAIMING STKS (I) £2346.10 (£649.60: £310.30)
1¾m (AWT)                                                    12-50 (12-53)

4007* **Intricacy (56)** (Fav) (LadyHerries) 3–8-8 NDay (1) (chsd ldrs: 3rd st: led 2f out: sn clr) .................................................................................... —1
4007³ Tempering **(80)** (DWChapman) 5–9-7 SWood (9) (led 12f out: one pce appr fnl f) .......... 4.2
4004³ Irish Native (IRE) **(70)** (bl) (CASmith) 3–9-0 AProud (5) (bhd: hdwy & 5th st: styd on: nt rch ldrs) ............................................................................ 3.3
4007² Qualitair Blazer **(40)** (JRJenkins) 4–8-7 TyroneWilliams (10) (a.p: 2nd st: wknd 2f out) ........................................................................................... 6.4
3920⁵ Noted Strain (IRE) **(57)** (PJMakin) 3–8-7 TSprake (11) (hdwy 7f out: 4th st: one pce fnl 2f) .............................................................................. ½.5
4007⁴ Chronological **(62)** (MHTompkins) 5–8-9 ‡⁵CHodgson (2) (hdwy 8f out: 6th & wkng st) ..................................................................................... 12.6
Hostess Quickly (MRChannon) 4–8-7 JWilliams (3) (b.hind: 7th & wkng st) ............ 10.7
4007 Ihsaas (MPNaughton) 4–8-9 DMcKeown (7) (t.o fr ½-wy) .......................................... 6.8
4003⁵ Hellespont (IRE) **(68)** (CAAustin) 3–8-1 ‡⁵BDoyle (13) (effrt 7f out: wknd over 4f out: t.o) ................................................................................... 15.9
3867 Brora Rose (IRE) **(40)** (bl) (JDBethell) 3–7-13 DaleGibson (4) (prom 4f: t.o) ........... 8.10
Daunting Prospect (MCChapman) 7–8-4 ‡⁷SWilliams (6) (chsd ldr 8f: t.o) .............. 15.11
Woodstock Lodge (USA) **(41)** (DRFranks) 3–8-7 RFox (8) (a bhd: t.o) ....................... 12.12
Al Billal (JDCzerpak) 3–8-9 NAdams (12) (unf: s.i.s: prom ½-wy: t.o) ...................... 10.13

**4/5 INTRICACY, 9/2 Chronological, 8/1 Tempering**(op 5/1), **17/2 Irish Native (IRE), 12/1 Noted Strain** (IRE)(op 7/1), **14/1 Qualitair Blazer, 16/1 Hellespont** (IRE)(12/1—20/1), **Brora Rose (IRE), 20/1 Hostess** Quickly, **25/1 Woodstock Lodge (USA), Al Billal, 33/1 Ors. CSF £10.22, Tote £2.00: £1.20 £2.30 £2.80** (£5.10). Lavinia Duchess of Norfolk (LITTLEHAMPTON) bred by Lavinia Duchess of Norfolk. 13 Rn; Intricacy clmd C C Elsey £16,270                                              3m 8.5 (6.5)

**4024** TRENT NAVIGATION NURSERY (0-75) £2386.70 (£661.20: £316.10)
6f (AWT)                                                    1-20 (1-22)

(Weights raised 1 lb)
3917 **Dublin Indemnity (USA) (52)** (bl) (NACallaghan) 8-0 NAdams (11) (hdwy over 2f out: led wl ins fnl f: r.o wl) ............................................................ —1
3985 Baileys by Name **(67)** (MJohnston) 9-1 DMcKeown (10) (led over 3f out tl wl ins fnl f) ............................................................................................ 1.2
3855 Peace Formula (IRE) **(62)** (RHollinshead) 8-10 WRyan (4) (bhd: hdwy wl over 1f out: r.o ins fnl f) ...................................................................... hd.3
3728 Doesyoudoes **(61)** (DTThom) 8-9 TyroneWilliams (14) (chsd ldrs: 3rd st: one pce fnl f) ............................................................................... 1½.4
3962 Flim Flam Aly (USA) **(59)** (bl) (MrsNMacauley) 8-7 AlexGreaves (9) (hdwy over 1f out: nrst fin) ................................................................ ½.5
1515⁴ Mighty Lady (IRE) **(73)** (MRChannon) 9-7 JWilliams (16) (nvr rchd ldrs) ............... 3½.6
4011⁵ Runnel **(58)** (bl) (DWChapman) 8-6 SWood (3) (hmpd s: bhd tl styd on fnl 2f: nt rch ldrs) ............................................................................... hd.7
3616 Sizzling Rose **(54)** (WCarter) 8-2 GCarter (7) (6th st: wknd 2f out) .......................... ¾.8
3945 Bee Dee Ell (USA) **(55)** (MissLAPerratt) 8-0 ‡³JFanning (5) (5th st: wknd 2f out) ...... ¾.9
3959³ Stoproveritate **(68)** (Jt-Fav) (SGNorton) 9-2 NCarlisle (6) (a in rr) ............................ 2.10
3964³ Certain Lady **(58)** (Jt-Fav) (GBlum) 7-13 ‡⁷CHawksley (15) (a in rr) ........................ 1½.11
3949 Jiggerak **(67)** (SGNorton) 8-8 ‡⁷OPears (1) (led over 2f: 4th st: wknd over 2f out) 1½.12
3764 Merls Pearl **(52)** (bl) (JAGlover) 8-0 GBardwell (13) (a bhd) ...................................... 4.13
3945 Froinech **(51)** (TDBarron) 7-13 DaleGibson (12) (dwlt: a bhd) ..................................... ½.14
4011 Daily Sport August **(60)** (MCChapman) 8-3 ‡⁵BDoyle (2) (w ldrs: 2nd st: wknd qckly) ........................................................................................... 10.15

**11/2 Certain Lady, Stoproveritate, 6/1 Jiggerak, 8/1 Runnel**(op 5/1), **Flim Flam Aly (USA)**(op 5/1), **11/1** Baileys by Name(8/1—12/1), **Peace Formula (IRE), 12/1 Mighty Lady (IRE), 14/1 Doesyoudoes, Froinech**(op 8/1), **DUBLIN INDEMNITY (USA), Daily Sport August, 16/1 Merls Pearl, 25/1 Ors. CSF £154.12, CT** £1,611.63. Tote £19.60: £11.50 £2.30 £3.60 (Wnr or 2nd w any £2.70). Mr R. K. Carvill (NEWMARKET) bred by Katalpa Farm in USA. 15 Rn                                 1m 16.6 (2.6)
                                                            SF—4/15/9/2/–/–

**4025** HUMBER CLAIMING STKS (II) £2325.80 (£643.80: £307.40)
1¾m (AWT)                                                    1-50 (1-52)

4007⁵ **Suluk (USA) (57)** (RHollinshead) 6–8-10 WRyan (2) (hdwy & 4th st: styd on u.p to ld cl home) ............................................................................... —1
3965⁵ Glenstal Priory **(40)** (Fav) (PFICole) 4–8-4 TQuinn (12) (a.p: 2nd st: led 2f out tl ct nr fin) ..................................................................................... 1.2
1534 Mississippi Beat (USA) **(39)** (v) (MPNaughton) 4–8-10 DMcKeown (9) (a.p: 3rd st: one pce fnl f) .......................................................................... 2½.3

*4004* Swagman (USA) **(45)** *(CRBeever)* 4–9-0 TyroneWilliams (8) (led tl hdd 2f out: wknd 1f out) ..................................................................................................... 12.4
3960 Grey Commander **(42)** *(MBrittain)* 3–8-0 ‡⁵SMaloney (10) (chsd ldrs: 5th & wkng st) ................................................................................................................. 8.5
*4004* Sharp Issue (USA) **(28)** *(MCChapman)* 3–7-11 ‡⁵DBiggs (7) (bhd: hdwy & poor 6th st: n.d) .......................................................................................... 1½.6
3379 Allez-Oops **(35)** *(ASmith)* 4–8-5 SWebster (3) (a bhd) .............................................. 12.7
*2759* Aughton Ridge (IRE) **(29)** *(MCChapman)* 3–7-7 ‡³JFanning (5) (chsd ldr 6f) ........... 1.8
*4004* Gin and Orange **(43)** (v) *(JRJenkins)* 5–8-12 WNewnes (6) (hld up: effrt 6f out: eased whn btn 3f out) ........................................................................... 8.9
1213 Dandoon **(65)** *(JDCzerpak)* 4–9-0 ‡⁷DMiddleton (11) (s.i.s: sn rcvrd: prom over 8f) ........................................................................................................ 6.10
3883⁴ Blazing Pearl **(35)** *(JLHarris)* 3–7-12 GBardwell (1) (sn bhd: t.o) .......................... 30.11
Fit for Life (IRE) (bl) *(MrsLStubbs)* 3–8-7 MBirch (4) (unf: a t.o) ............................. 30.12

**7/2** Glenstal Priory, **9/2** SULUK (USA), **5/1** Swagman (USA), **7/1** Dandoon, Blazing Pearl, **17/2** Grey Commander, **11/1** Fit for Life (IRE), **12/1** Mississippi Beat (USA), **20/1** Gin and Orange, Allez-Oops, **25/1** Ors. CSF £20.60, Tote £5.80: £1.80 £1.60 £1.80 (£5.70). Mr Anthony White (UPPER LONGDON) bred by Dolphin B'stock & B'stock Investments, Ltd. in USA. 12 Rn     3m 12.2 (10.2)

---

**4026**    EAST MIDLANDS ELECTRICITY H'CAP (0–70) £2569.40 (£713.40: £342.20)
       1½m (AWT)                                      2-20 (2-22)

3997 **Duggan (58)** *(RJRWilliams)* 4–9-2 NDay (12) (lw: hdwy 6f out: 5th st: r.o fnl f: led post) ....................................................................................... —1
3809 Magic Secret **(67)** *(PCHaslam)* 3–9-2 ‡³JFanning (7) (4th st: led 2f out tl hdd post) s.h.2
*4008⁵* Bescaby Boy **(63)** *(JWharton)* 5–8-7 JWilliams (4) (hld up & bhd: hdwy over 3f out: r.o fnl f) .................................................................................. 1½.3
3992 Golden Torque **(70)** *(RBastiman)* 4–9-7 ‡⁷HBastiman (8) (hld up & bhd: hdwy 6f out: 7th st: hrd rdn & one pce fnl 2f) ............................................. 2.4
3992 Western Dynasty **(66)** *(MJRyan)* 5–9-5 ‡⁵DBiggs (1) (no hdwy fnl 2f) ................... 4.5
3991³ Breckenbrough Lad **(57)** *(TDBarron)* 4–9-1 AlexGreaves (10) (hdwy 5f out: 6th st: wknd over 1f out) ....................................................................... 2½.6
3950 Tanoda **(50)** *(MBrittain)* 5–8-3 ‡⁵SMaloney (11) (hrd rdn & 2nd st: wknd 2f out) .... 6.7
3960⁴ Carlingford (USA) **(56)** *(HATWhiting)* 5–9-0 SWebster (17) (w ldr: led over 3f out tl wknd 2f out) ..................................................................... 1½.8
3709 War Beat **(58)** *(PJBevan)* 3–8-10 DMcKeown (13) (prom over 8f) ........................... 5.9
3269 Smartie Lee **(58)** *(PFICole)* 4–9-2 TQuinn (16) (n.d) .............................................. 1½.10
3950 Sunflower Seed **(46)** *(PJMakin)* 4–8-4 WNewnes (5) (led over 8f) ........................... 1½.11
3874 Bairn Free **(46)** *(DWPArbuthnot)* 3–7-7⁽¹⁾ ‡⁵BDoyle (3) (b.hind: s.i.s: a bhd) .......... ½.12
1843 Lord Advocate **(48)** *(MPNaughton)* 3–8-0 DaleGibson (9) (bit bkwd: a bhd) ........... ½.13
3776⁵ Singing Reply (USA) **(64)** *(JHMGosden)* 3–9-2 WRyan (14) (b: b.hind: t.o) ............. 15.14
King Trevisio **(43)** *(JLHarris)* 5–8-1 NCarlisle (6) (bkwd: bhd fnl 4f: t.o) ................. 1½.15
3494 In Truth **(51)** *(DWChapman)* 3–8-3 SWood (15) (prom 8f: t.o) ................................. 6.16
3469⁵ Buzzards Crest **(41)** *(BobJones)* 6–7-13 GBardwell (2) (eyeshield: bit bkwd: a bhd: t.o) ..................................................................................... 2.17
2410³ Bedouin Prince (USA) **(48)** *(CRBeever)* 4–8-6 TyroneWilliams (18) (bit bkwd: t.o) 10.18

**7/2** Western Dynasty, **6/1** Bescaby Boy, Golden Torque(op 4/1), **8/1** Breckenbrough Lad(6/1—10/1), Magic Secret(10/1—12/1), **9/1** Singing Reply (USA)(op 6/1), **10/1** Carlingford (USA), Buzzards Crest, **14/1** Bedouin Prince (USA), **16/1** Tanoda, Smartie Lee, **16/1** Tanoda, Sunflower Seed, **20/1** DUGGAN, **25/1** Bairn Free, War Beat, **33/1** Ors. CSF £182.75, CT £1,015.35. Tote £56.30: £12.80 £1.90 £2.00 £1.90 (Wnr or 2nd w any £5.00). Mr F. Hornett (NEWMARKET) bred by M. Sinclair and J. Fisher. 18 Rn     2m 41 (6)
                                           SF—12/11/13/9/–/–

---

**4027**    NATIONAL PLANT & TRANSPORT H'CAP (0–70) £2508.50 (£696.00: £333.50)
       7f (AWT)                                          2-50 (2-59)

*4020²* **African Chimes (70)** (Fav) *(WAO'Gorman)* 4–9-9 ‡⁵EmmaO'Gorman (14) (hld up: stdy hdwy & 7th st: edgd lft over 1f out: led ins fnl f: comf) .....—1
3988 Kinlacey **(55)** *(BAMcMahon)* 4–8-13 WRyan (10) (4th st: led ins fnl f: sn hdd: nt qckn) ............................................................................................ 1½.2
3999 Silks Princess **(52)** *(MJRyan)* 5–8-10 JMcLaughlin (11) (2nd st: led over 2f out tl hdd & no ex ins fnl f) ................................................................. 2½.3
*4008\** Kristis Girl *(DHaydnJones)* 4–9-6 (5x) TyroneWilliams (5) (led over 1f: 3rd st: hrd rdn over 1f out: nt qckn) ...................................................... ½.4
4005⁵ Super Heights **(53)** *(MissAJWhitfield)* 3–8-9 DaleGibson (15) (gd hdwy 3f out: one pce fnl 2f) .......................................................................... 6.5
2991 Precious Air (IRE) **(60)** *(DenysSmith)* 3–9-2 BCrossley (7) (dwlt: nvr nr to chal) .... 1½.6

*400*>3 Wellsy Lad (USA) **(66)** *(DWChapman)* 4–9–10 SWood (12) (6th st: no hdwy fnl 2f) ........................................................................... ½.7
3771 Wsom (IRE) **(58)** (v) *(MO'Neill)* 3–9–0 GCarter (13) (nvr trbld ldrs) ......... nk.8
3958 Silly's Brother **(52)** *(NBycroft)* 3–8–10 SWebster (16) (5th st: wknd 2f out) .... 3.9
*4008* Stairway to Heaven (IRE) **(63)** (bl) *(CRBeever)* 3–8–12 ‡7JWeaver (3) (n.d) ...... 2½.10
3625 Swingaway Lady **(67)** *(GRichards)* 3–9–9 MBirch (1) (n.d) .................... 3½.11
3801² Bill Moon **(52)** *(PJFeilden)* 5–8–3 ‡7StephenDavies (8) (bhd fnl 3f) ....... 1½.12
*4008* Cartel **(61)** *(JLHarris)* 4–9–5 BRaymond (4) (s.i.s: sn rcvrd: led over 5f out tl over 2f out: wknd qckly) ............................... ¾.13
*70*4 Jumby Bay **(64)** *(MJohnston)* 5–9–8 RPElliott (6) (prom tl hrd rdn & wknd 4f out) ..... 2.14
*3966*3 Count Me Out **(51)** *(JPearce)* 6–8–9 TQuinn (9) (a bhd) ........................ nk.15
*3150*3 Inseyab (8/1) Withdrawn (uns rdr & bolted bef s) : not under orders

**4/1 AFRICAN CHIMES, 11/2 Bill Moon, 15/2 Cartel, 8/1 Silks Princess, 10/1 Kinlacey, 11/1 Wellsy Lad (USA), Kristis Girl, 12/1 Count Me Out, 14/1 Swingaway Lady, Wsom (IRE), 16/1 Jumby Bay, Super Heights, 20/1 Stairway to Heaven (IRE), 25/1 Ors. CSF £42.98, CT £287.21. Tote £5.30: £2.00 £2.50 £4.20 (£67.50). Mr D. G. Wheatley (NEWMARKET) bred by Noel Cogan. 15 Rn**
1m 29.1 (1.9)
SF—54/39/28/36/7/9

**4028** MERSEY CANAL H'CAP (0-90) £2407.00 (£667.00: £319.00) **6f (AWT)** 3-20 (3-29)

3674 Plain Fact **(73)** *(SirMarkPrescott)* 6–9–1 GDuffield (14) (hld up: stdy hdwy & 5th st: led ins fnl f: r.o wl) ........................................ —1
3958* Languedoc **(71)** *(HATWhiting)* 4–8–13 SWebster (13) (hdwy 2f out: r.o ins fnl f) ........ 3.2
3996 Pretonic **(69)** *(MJohnston)* 3–8–10 RPElliott (10) (3rd st: led over 1f out tl ins fnl f) 1½.3
*4005*² Cronk's Courage **(59)** (v) *(EJAlston)* 5–8–1 BCrossley (2) (4th st: one pce fnl 2f) ...... nk.4
3988 Brown Fairy (USA) **(72)** *(MrsNMacauley)* 3–8–8 ‡5DBiggs (11) (7th st: no hdwy fnl 2f) ........................................... 3.5
*4009*3 Euroblake **(72)** (Fav) *(TDBarron)* 4–9–0 AlexGreaves (7) (bhd tl hdwy fnl f: nrst fin) ........................................... s.h.6
*4009*5 Sally's Son **(69)** *(WAO'Gorman)* 5–8–6 ‡5EmmaO'Gorman (12) (hdwy over 2f out: nvr nr to chal) ........................... s.h.7
3996 Arc Lamp **(55)** *(JAGlover)* 5–7–11 DaleGibson (6) (led 2f: 2nd st: wknd over 1f out) ....................................... 3.8
*4020*5 Domicksky **(82)** *(MJRyan)* 3–9–9 MTebbutt (1) (led 4f out: hdd over 1f out: wknd fnl f) ....................................... nk.9
3318 Rancho Mirage **(75)** *(MrsNMacauley)* 4–9–3 DMcKeown (9) (dwlt: n.d) .............. ¾.10
3771 Pesidanamich (IRE) **(80)** *(TDBarron)* 3–9–0 ‡7VHalliday (8) (n.d) ............ 2½.11
3993 Whippet **(86)** *(CAAustin)* 7–9–9 ‡5BDoyle (15) (n.d) ................... 1.12
1866⁴ Sno Serenade **(83)** *(MDods)* 5–9–11 GBaxter (4) (bit bkwd: n.d) ............ s.h.13
3873 Lyndon's Linnet **(65)** *(KRBurke)* 3–8–6 GCarter (16) (s.i.s: hdwy & 6th st: wknd 2f out) ....................................... s.h.14
3961* Tauber **(76)** *(PatMitchell)* 7–9–1 ‡3SO'Gorman (3) (sn outpcd: t.o) ........ 7.15
3996 Breezy Day **(78)** *(BAMcMahon)* 5–9–6 TQuinn (5) (sn t.o: p.u 4f out) ................ 0

**4/1 Euroblake(7/1—8/1), 6/1 Tauber(op 4/1), 8/1 Domicksky, Cronk's Courage, Pretonic, Languedoc(op 5/1), 9/1 PLAIN FACT(op 6/1), 14/1 Sally's Son(10/1—16/1), Pesidanamich (IRE), 16/1 Rancho Mirage, 20/1 Breezy Day(op 7/1), Arc Lamp, Brown Fairy (USA)(op 8/1), 25/1 Ors. CSF £78.94, CT £557.17. Tote £10.80: £4.20 £2.60 £2.50 £2.60 (£50.60). Mr G. Moore (NEWMARKET) bred by Clanville Lodge Stud. 16 Rn**
1m 14.3 (0.3)
SF—65/51/42/32/27/32

**4029** RIVER IDLE STKS (II) (Mdn 2-Y.O) £2346.10 (£649.60: £310.30) **7f (AWT)** 3-50 (3-57)

3799² **Spanish Miner (USA)** (Fav) *(AAScott)* 9-0 BRaymond (7) (b: b.hind: chsd ldr: 2nd st: led over 2f out: sn clr) ........................... —1
3957 Big Easy (IRE) *(MrsJCecil)* 9-0 BCrossley (12) (eyeshield: 3rd & rdn st: chsd wnr fnl 2f: no imp) ............................... 5.2
Jade Green *(PJMakin)* 8-9 TSprake (2) (b: leggy: bit bkwd: dwlt: hdwy 2f out: nt rch ldrs) ............................... 6.3
*4010*² Aegaen Lady **(50)** *(JEtherington)* 8-2 ‡7JWeaver (1) (led over 4f: wknd over 1f out) ............................... 10.4
3990⁶ Santana Lady (IRE) *(MJHeaton-Ellis)* 8-9 GCarter (8) (4th st: wknd over 2f out) .. 2½.5
Nothing Compares *(JWHills)* 8-9 MHills (11) (unf: s.i.s: rdn along: 5th st: wknd over 2f out) ........................... 2.6
*3963* Pie Hatch (IRE) *(SirMarkPrescott)* 8-9 GDuffield (4) (outpcd) ............ 5.7
3893 Blushing Opal **(40)** *(BEllison)* 8-9 GBaxter (10) (poor 6th st: sn bhd) ......... 1½.8
3945 Red Springs (IRE) *(JGFitzGerald)* 8-7 ‡7MHunt (5) (outpcd) ............ hd.9
3375 Honey Day *(SRBowring)* 8-9 SWebster (3) (bhd fnl 4f) ............ 3.10
2179 Dot's Jester *(EJAlston)* 9-0 DMcKeown (9) (bit bkwd: a bhd: t.o) ............ 7.11

**5/4** SPANISH MINER (USA)(6/4—Evens), **9/4** Santana Lady (IRE)(6/4—5/2), **6/1** Big Easy (IRE)(5/1—8/1), **12/1** Jade Green(op 5/1), Aegaen Lady(op 5/1), Nothing Compares(op 6/1), **50/1** Ors. CSF £9.29, Tote £3.20: £1.10 £3.00 £1.80 (£13.70). Sir Anthony Page-Wood (NEWMARKET) bred by Courtney & Richardson in USA. 11 Rn

1m 29.4 (2.2)
SF—41/26/3/–/–/–

T/Plpt: £793.90 (0.5 Tckts); £536.43 to Kempton 20/11/91.

CR/KH

---

4015—**LINGFIELD (L-H)** Equitrack

## Thursday, November 28th [Standard]

Going Allowance: minus 0.30 sec per fur (FS)

**4030**     VITTORIA CLAIMING STKS (I) (3 & 4-Y.O) £2226.00 (£616.00: £294.00)
           1½m (AWT)                                        11-55 (11-58)

4019⁴ **Adjacent (IRE) (58)** *(Fav) (BWHills)* 3–8-1 RHills (7) (a.p: led over 3f out: rdn over 1f out: r.o wl) ...................... —1

3998³ Absolutely Right **(44)** *(RAkehurst)* 3–8-5 TQuinn (10) (lw: hdwy 4f out: ev ch over 1f out: r.o) ...................... 2½.2

3905⁵ Sharp Top **(41)** *(MJRyan)* 3–7-8 ‡⁵DBiggs (8) (a.p: one pce fnl 3f) ...................... 6.3

4019⁵ Pleasure Ahead **(46)** *(MRChannon)* 4–8-10 LornaVincent (1) (a.p: one pce fnl 3f) ...... 1.4

2915⁴ Shar Emblem *(SDow)* 3–7-10⁽²⁾ ‡⁷MJermy (4) (lost pl after 3f: late hdwy: r.o) .........3½.5

2015 Line Drummer (USA) *(PAKelleway)* 3–8-8⁽¹⁾ ‡⁷ABates (9) (b: eyeshield: nvr nr to chal) ...................... 1½.6

3404 Billy Lomond (IRE) **(53)** *(CACyzer)* 3–8-8 DMcKeown (11) (bhd fnl 4f) ...................... 8.7

3386 Nailem **(33)** *(RPCHoad)* 4–8-10 SWhitworth (5) (chsd ldr tl wknd over 3f out) ...................... 7.8

3430⁴ Brunswick Blue (IRE) **(43)** (bl) *(JSutcliffe)* 3–8-8 MHills (3) (led tl wknd over 3f out) ...................... 1½.9

4019⁶ Toshiba Comet Too (IRE) **(53)** *(WJPearce)* 3–8-5 GDuffield (2) (rdn 8f out: sn bhd) ...................... 10.10

3565 North-West One (IRE) *(HJCollingridge)* 3–8-10 JQuinn (12) (s.s: hdwy over 4f out: wknd 3f out) ...................... 2½.11

**11/8** ADJACENT (IRE)(Evens—6/4), **4/1** Absolutely Right, **11/2** Brunswick Blue (IRE)(op 7/2), **9/1** Pleasure Ahead(8/1—12/1), Toshiba Comet Too (IRE)(op 5/1), **12/1** Billy Lomond (IRE), **14/1** Sharp Top(10/1—16/1), **16/1** Shar Emblem(op 10/1), **20/1** North-West One (IRE), Line Drummer (USA), **33/1** Nailem. CSF £8.21, Tote £3.00: £1.10 £1.40 £2.60 (£3.90). Mrs J. M. Corbett (LAMBOURN) bred by Brownstown Stud Farm in Ireland. 11 Rn; Adjacent (IRE) clmd J Daniels £6,250 2m 32.16 (2.76)

SF—23/22/–/13/–/1

**4031**     BUSACO RIDGE STKS (I) (Mdn 2-Y.O) £2088.80 (£576.80: £274.40)
           5f (AWT)                                          12-25 (12-28)

4000⁶ **Inherent Magic (IRE)** *(MMcCormack)* 8-9 WNewnes (3) (lw: a.p: hrd rdn over 1f out: r.o wl to ld last strides) ...................... —1

3364 Myasha (USA) **(78)** *(Fav) (MrsLPiggott)* 9-0 AMunro (6) (eyeshield: led tl last strides) ...................... nk.2

4024⁴ Doesyoudoes **(61)** *(DTThom)* 8-9 TyroneWilliams (8) (a.p: ev ch 1f out: r.o) ......... 1½.3

3723 Wilco **(56)** *(AndrewTurnell)* 9-0 RHills (1) (w ldr tl wknd over 1f out) ...................... 2½.4

3964 Man of the Season (USA) **(58)** *(MrsNMacauley)* 9-0 DMcKeown (5) (lw: no hdwy fnl 2f) ...................... hd.5

4024⁶ Mighty Lady (IRE) **(73)** *(MRChannon)* 8-9 JWilliams (4) (outpcd: nrst fin) ...................... 1½.6

4000 Spectacle Jim *(JO'Donoghue)* 9-0 NAdams (7) (prom 3f) ...................... 3½.7

1528 Shakiri *(JAkehurst)* 8-9 SWhitworth (2) (s.s: a wl bhd) ...................... 8.8

**2/1** Myasha (USA), **11/4** INHERENT MAGIC (IRE), **4/1** Mighty Lady (IRE), **6/1** Doesyoudoes(7/2—7/1), **10/1** Man of the Season (USA)(op 6/1), **11/1** Wilco(7/1—12/1), **20/1** Shakiri(op 12/1), **33/1** Spectacle Jim. CSF £8.71, Tote £3.50: £1.60 £1.30 £3.20 (£5.80). Orchid Racing & Bloodstock Limited (WANTAGE) bred by Mrs M. McStay in Ireland. 8 Rn 59.73 sec (1.53)

SF—35/39/28/23/22/11

**4032**     VITTORIA CLAIMING STKS (II) (3 & 4-Y.O) £2206.40 (£610.40: £291.20)
           1½m (AWT)                                        12-55 (12-57)

3783 **Storm Orphan (35)** *(MissBSanders)* 4–8-7 DaleGibson (6) (hdwy 4f out: led over 1f out: r.o wl) ...................... —1

3078 Plectrum *(BWHills)* 3–8-5 MHills (11) (b.hind: sn prom: led 3f out tl over 1f out: r.o) ...................... 1½.2

4026 Lord Advocate **(48)** (v) *(MPNaughton)* 3–8-8 DMcKeown (12) (led 5f out to 3f out: one pce) ...................... 7.3

*4019* Crown Reserve (60) *(MJRyan)* 3–8-7 GCarter (8) (a.p: one pce fnl 3f) ............ 2½.4
3955² Blackdown (70) *(Fav)* *(CWeedon)* 4–9-2 MBirch (3) (hdwy 5f out: rdn over 2f out: one pce) .................................................................................... 1.5
*3920* Dazzle the Crowd (IRE) (50) *(CACyzer)* 3–8-8 AMorris (5) (hdwy & hrd rdn 5f out: wknd 2f out) ..................................................................... 1½.6
3591 Hubbers Favourite (42) *(MJHeaton-Ellis)* 3–8-0 AMackay (1) (nvr nr to chal) ........ 1½.7
*4023* Hostess Quickly *(MRChannon)* 4–8-8(1) JWilliams (7) (b.hnd: a bhd) .................. nk.8
3998⁶ Mister Major (35) *(LJHolt)* 3–8-3 NAdams (2) (led 1f: wknd 5f out) .................. 2.9
4025⁴ Swagman (USA) (45) (bl) *(CRBeever)* 4–8-13 TyroneWilliams (4) (led after 1f: rdn & hdd 5f out: wknd qckly) ......................................... 10.10
3801 Verro (USA) (40) (bl) *(JABennett)* 4–9-2 JQuinn (10) (prom 6f: t.o) ............ 12.11
Red Bomber *(KOCunningham-Brown)* 3–8-10 TQuinn (9) (b: w'like: lw: s.s: a wl bhd: t.o) ............................................................ nk.12

**6/4** Blackdown, **3/1** Plectrum(op 7/4), **8/1** Swagman (USA)(6/1—10/1), **10/1** Hostess Quickly(op 6/1), Crown Reserve(op 6/1), **12/1** Lord Advocate, **16/1** Dazzle the Crowd (IRE), Hubbers Favourite, **20/1** Mister Major, Red Bomber(op 10/1), STORM ORPHAN, **33/1** Verro (USA). CSF £81.27, Tote £64.20: £6.90 £1.70 £4.00 (£246.70). Mr T. Scully (EPSOM) bred by T. Scully. 12 Rn
                                              2m 33 (3.60)
                                            SF—21/16/5/–/6/–

---

## 4033

SALAMANCA APP'CE H'CAP (0-70) £2500.40 (£694.40: £333.20)
1¼m (AWT)                             1-25 (1-27)

3997 **Princess Roxanne** (49) (bl) *(Fav)* *(ABailey)* 4–8-4 ‡⁷PBowe (5) (hld up: led wl over 1f out: r.o wl) ......................................... —1
3416* Tara's Delight (62) *(MJRyan)* 4–9-10 DBiggs (10) (a.p: led over 3f out tl wl over 1f out) ...................................................... 5.2
3997⁶ Miss Mirror (59) *(WJHaggas)* 3–9-3 FNorton (7) (lw: led over 4f out tl over 3f out: one pce) ............................................ 2½.3
*3968* Smith's Peak (46) *(RJO'Sullivan)* 7–8-5 ‡³CMunday (9) (hdwy 3f out: one pce fnl 2f) ...................................................... nk.4
4019³ Samurai Gold (USA) (52) (v) *(PTWalwyn)* 3–8-7 ‡³JWeaver (3) (a.p: no hdwy fnl 2f) ...................................................... nk.5
3968⁵ Carpet Slippers (51) (bl) *(JDBethell)* 5–8-13 SO'Gorman (1) (prom tl wknd over 2f out) ...................................................... 4.6
2931⁴ Misty Goddess (IRE) (55) *(MAJarvis)* 3–8-13 KRutter (2) (nvr nr to chal) .......... 4.7
3576 Northern Conqueror (IRE) (68) *(TJNaughton)* 3–9-12 CHodgson (6) (eyeshield: b: nvr nrr) ..................................................... 2.8
3897 El Dominio (60) *(KOCunningham-Brown)* 3–9-1 ‡³MarkDenaro (11) (b: a bhd) ..... 2½.9
543 Go Forum (46) *(JSutcliffe)* 6–8-5 ‡³JTate (8) (b: bit bkwd: a bhd) ............. 4.10
578 Blazing Fen (52) *(MrsNMacauley)* 3–8-10 AlexGreaves (13) (b: lw: a bhd) ...... ½.11
4019² Chloes Diamond (61) *(JLSpearing)* 3–9-5 GHusband (4) (led tl wknd over 4f out) ..................................................... 7.12
3426 Just One (IRE) (50) (bl) *(MMcCormack)* 3–8-5 ‡³StephenDavies (12) (hrd rdn 6f out: sn bhd) ................................................. 3.13
3915⁵ Ballerina Bay (50) *(DTThom)* 3–8-8 EmmaO'Gorman (14) (reard up & s.s: a wl bhd: t.o) .................................................. 20.14

*Stewards Enquiry: Weaver suspended 7-10/12/91 (careless riding).*

**11/2** PRINCESS ROXANNE, **6/1** Ballerina Bay, **13/2** Miss Mirror, Chloes Diamond (IRE), **7/1** Tara's Delight, **8/1** Samurai Gold (USA), **10/1** Smith's Peak(7/1—14/1), **12/1** Misty Goddess (IRE), **14/1** Carpet Slippers, Go Forum, Northern Conqueror (IRE), **25/1** El Dominio, Just One (IRE), **33/1** Blazing Fen. CSF £42.71, CT £240.76. Tote £6.70: £3.20 £3.20 £2.80 (£20.10). Mrs M. O'Donnell (NEWMARKET) bred by Mrs C. Van C. Anthony. 14 Rn
                                             2m 6.04 (3.04)
                                     SF—30/40/28/15/16/14

---

## 4034

CORUNNA H'CAP (0-80) £2490.00 (£690.00: £330.00)
           1m (AWT)                          1-55 (1-57)

4028² **Languedoc** (71) *(Jt-Fav)* *(HATWhiting)* 4–9-7 AMunro (10) (swtg: a gng wl: qcknd to ld ins fnl f) ................................... —1
*4020* Gabbiadini (74) (v) *(MHTompkins)* 4–9-10 TyroneWilliams (12) (hdwy led over 2f out tl ins fnl f) .......................................... 3½.2
3823 Dance on Sixpence (68) (v) *(HJCollingridge)* 3–9-2 JQuinn (5) (a.p: r.o ins fnl f) ... s.h.3
3519 Ain'tlifelikethat (54) (bl) *(TJNaughton)* 4–8-4 GCarter (9) (b: dwlt: hdwy 4f out: ev ch 2f out: nt qckn) ............................. 4.4
*4018* Scotoni (58) *(RJO'Sullivan)* 5–8-3 ‡⁵DBiggs (4) (lw: w ldr: led over 4f out tl over 2f out) ................................... 2.5
3473* Angelo's Double (IRE) (75) *(Jt-Fav)* *(JHMGosden)* 3–9-9 WRyan (6) (b: b.hind: a.p: ev ch 2f out: sn wknd) ........................ 2½.6
3620 Martini Executive (72) *(WJPearce)* 3–9-6 SKeightley (11) (nrst fin) ............ hd.7
2834 Will He Or Wont He (IRE) (65) (v) *(CNAllen)* 4–8-13 WWharton (2) (a bhd) ........ ½.8
*4020* Pims Classic (73) *(WJHaggas)* 3–9-7 MHills (1) (prom 4f) ........................ 1½.9
I'Ll Soon Know (58) *(BPalling)* 4–8-8(3) JWilliams (8) (bhd fnl 4f) ................ ¾.10

3531 Clipper One **(68)** *(KOCunningham-Brown)* 3–9-2 TQuinn (3) (b: lw: led over 3f:
　　sn wknd) ............................................................................................................... 10.**11**
　　　Polyroll **(78)** *(MRChannon)* 5–10-0 LornaVincent (7) (bit bkwd: prom 4f) ........... ¾.**12**

**3/1** LANGUEDOC(op 2/1), Angelo's Double (IRE)(op 6/4), **6/1** Gabbiadini, **8/1** Dance on Sixpence, **12/1** Ain'tlifelikethat, Pims Classic, **14/1** Clipper One, **20/1** Martini Executive, Will He Or Wont He (IRE), Scotoni, **25/1** I'Ll Soon Know, **33/1** Polyroll. CSF £19.96, CT £119.59. Tote £3.50: £1.70 £2.00 £3.00 (£16.20).
Langdale Racing Stables (MELSONBY) bred by Danton Stud Farm Co Ltd. 12 Rn　　　　1m 38.29 (1.59)
　　　　　　　　　　　　　　　　　　　　　　　　　　　　　　　　　　　SF—47/39/30/6/–/11

---

**4035**　　　BADAJOZ H'CAP (0-90) £2669.70 (£739.20: £353.10)　**7f (AWT)**　　　2-25 (2-30)

4020[4] **Pytchley Night (82)** *(DMorris)* 4–8-13 ‡[7]StephenDavies (6) (a:p: led over 1f out:
　　r.o wl) ...................................................................................................................... —**1**
4020[3] **Bold Habit (90)** *(WJPearce)* 6–9-9 ‡[5]GHusband (7) (hdwy 2f out: ev ch fnl f:
　　r.o) ....................................................................................................................... nk.**2**
4005 **The Shanahan Bay (61)** (v) *(MrsNMacauley)* 6–7-13[(1)] AMunro (3) (hdwy 2f out:
　　r.o ins fnl f) ........................................................................................................... 4.**3**
3909 **Spring High (56)** (bl) *(KTIvory)* 4–7-8[(1)] NAdams (8) (a:p: led over 3f out tl over 1f
　　out) ........................................................................................................................ 2.**4**
4020* **Helawe (84)** (bl) *(SirMarkPrescott)* 8–9-8 GDuffield (10) (lw: rdn along: nvr nr to
　　chal) ................................................................................................................... 3½.**5**
3863[4] **Cee-En-Cee (61)** (v) *(MMcCourt)* 7–7-13 CRutter (11) (outpcd: nrst fin) ............... 3½.**6**
3864 **Grand Guignol (70)** *(GWragg)* 3–8-1 ‡[5]FNorton (4) (w ldrs tl wknd over 2f out) ......... 4.**7**
4019 **On Y Va (USA) (56)** (Fav) *(RJRWilliams)* 4–7-5[(1)] ‡[3]JFanning (1) (b.off hind: led
　　over 3f: wknd over 1f out) ................................................................................... s.h.**8**
3057[3] **State Governor (72)** *(NACallaghan)* 3–8-1 ‡[7]JTate (2) (b: w ldrs tl wknd over 2f
　　out) ...................................................................................................................... 2½.**9**
4006 **Lucy Dancer (IRE) (59)** *(MMcCormack)* 3–7-9 GBardwell (9) (a bhd) ............... hd.**10**
3864 **Pusey Street Boy (55)** *(JRBosley)* 4–7-7 RFox (5) (lw: a bhd) .................................. 1.**11**
　　　　　　LONG HANDICAP: Spring High 6-11, On Y Va (USA) 7-5, Pusey Street Boy 6-11.

**3/1** On Y Va (USA), **9/2** Grand Guignol, **5/1** Bold Habit, **11/2** Helawe, PYTCHLEY NIGHT, **10/1** State Governor, Cee-En-Cee, **14/1** The Shanahan Bay, **20/1** Lucy Dancer (IRE), **25/1** Pusey Street Boy, **33/1** Spring High. CSF £33.27, CT £345.38. Tote £10.20: £2.40 £2.10 £3.80 (£15.80). Mr J. J. Higgins (NEWMARKET) bred by G. W. Robinson. 11 Rn　　　　　　　　　　　　　　　　　　　　　　　　　　　　　　1m 24.41 (0.41)
　　　　　　　　　　　　　　　　　　　　　　　　　　　　　　　　SF—61/70/34/23/40/6

---

**4036**　　　BUSACO RIDGE STKS (II) (Mdn 2-Y.O) £2069.20 (£571.20: £271.60)
　　　　　**5f (AWT)**　　　　　　　　　　　　　　　　　　　　　　　　　2-55 (2-56)

3668 **Appealing Times (USA) (71)** *(WAO'Gorman)* 8-9 ‡[5]EmmaO'Gorman (5) (a:p:
　　rdn over 1f out: r.o to ld last strides) ................................................................... —**1**
4000[2] **Battle Colours (IRE)** (Fav) *(SirMarkPrescott)* 9-0 GDuffield (4) (led: rdn ins fnl f:
　　hdd last strides) ................................................................................................. s.h.**2**
3340 **Jaromic** *(PFTulk)* 9-0 WRyan (6) (b: w ldr tl wknd over 1f out) ........................... 5.**3**
　　　**Walkonthemoon** *(MMcCormack)* 8-9 WNewnes (1) (neat: s.s: a wl bhd) ............... 6.**4**

**10/11** Battle Colours (IRE), **11/8** APPEALING TIMES (USA), **7/1** Walkonthemoon(op 7/2), **20/1** Jaromic(op 10/1). CSF £2.98, Tote £2.60 (£1.40). Times of Wigan (NEWMARKET) bred by Harry T. Mangurian Jnr in USA. 4 Rn　　　　　　　　　　　　　　　　　　　　　　　　　　　　　　59.66 sec (1.46)
　　　　　　　　　　　　　　　　　　　　　　　　　　　　　　　　SF—36/40/20/–

---

**4037**　　　ALMARAZ NURSERY (0-85) £2511.00 (£696.00: £333.00)　**1m (AWT)**　　3-25 (3-27)

4010* **Lord Vivienne (IRE) (73)** (Fav) *(PFICole)* 9-3 TQuinn (12) (a gng wl: hung lft
　　over 1f out: led ins fnl f: r.o) ............................................................................... —**1**
3962[2] **Paper Clip (63)** *(JDBethell)* 8-7 TyroneWilliams (1) (led over 3f out: edgd rt 1f out:
　　hdd ins fnl f) ..................................................................................................... 1½.**2**
4017[2] **Clare Kerry Lass (72)** *(TJNaughton)* 8-11 ‡[5]CHodgson (9) (eyeshield: b: a:p: ev
　　ch whn squeezed 1f out: nt qckn) ..................................................................... 2½.**3**
3963* **Sybaritic Sam (IRE) (74)** *(NACallaghan)* 9-4 WNewnes (4) (lw: a:p: one pce fnl
　　2f) ......................................................................................................................... 2.**4**
4016* **Liability Order (73)** *(RBoss)* 9-3 DMcKeown (6) (a:p: one pce fnl 2f) ...................... hd.**5**
3945[4] **Kay Beeyou (IRE) (64)** *(TThomsonJones)* 8-8 SWhitworth (3) (prom over 5f) ......... ¾.**6**
4016 **Lindeman (65)** *(SDow)* 8-9 JWilliams (10) (s.s: nrst fin) .......................................... 4.**7**
3957[3] **Lady St Lawrence (USA) (69)** *(SirMarkPrescott)* 8-13 GDuffield (8) (lw: a bhd) ....... hd.**8**
3680 **Dragon Spirit (77)** *(AHide)* 9-7 WRyan (7) (nvr nr to chal) ...................................... 10.**9**
3949 **Mystery Lad (IRE) (62)** *(NACallaghan)* 7-13 ‡[7]JTate (5) (lw: a bhd) ...................... nk.**10**
3903[6] **Charmonix (64)** *(GWragg)* 8-3 ‡[5]FNorton (11) (a bhd) ....................................... 3½.**11**
2489 **Jubal Early (IRE) (72)** (bl) *(CNAllen)* 9-2 GBardwell (2) (led over 4f: wknd qckly:
　　t.o) ....................................................................................................................... 15.**12**

**5/2** LORD VIVIENNE (IRE)(7/4—3/1), **11/4** Liability Order(4/1—5/1), **9/2** Sybaritic Sam (IRE)(4/1—6/1), **8/1** Paper Clip, **10/1** Clare Kerry Lass(8/1—12/1), Lady St Lawrence (USA), **12/1** Charmonix(op 8/1), **14/1** Kay Beeyou (IRE), **16/1** Mystery Lad (IRE), **20/1** Ors. CSF £25.30, CT £166.75. Tote £2.90: £1.50 £1.60 £4.20 (£14.20). Mrs Jane Lewis (WHATCOMBE) bred by Binfield Manor Farms Ltd in Ireland. 12 Rn

1m 39.43 (2.73)
SF—26/11/7/8/6/–

T/Plpt: £81.40 (11.2 Tckts). Hn

---

4022—**SOUTHWELL (L-H)** Fibresand

## Friday, November 29th [Standard]

Going Allowance: minus 0.20 sec per fur (FS)                      Wind: slt across

Stalls: 1st, 3rd & 4th high, remainder low

**4038**   DAISY CLAIMING STKS (I)   £2386.70 (£661.20: £316.10)
           **1m 3f (AWT)**                                          12-00 (12-02)

| | | |
|---|---|---|
| 3905³ | **Hand Painted** (41) (JPearce)  7–8–6  GCarter (4) (b: lw: a:p: 2nd st: shkn up to ld wl ins fnl f: r.o) | —1 |
| 4023³ | Irish Native (IRE) (70) (bl) (Jt-Fav) (CASimpson)  3–9–5  AProud (1) (led tl hdd wl ins fnl f) | ½.2 |
| 3885⁵ | All the King's Men (IRE) (65) (Jt-Fav) (PFICole)  3–8–12  TQuinn (6) (hdwy 6f out: 3rd st: rdn over 2f out: styd on one pce) | 8.3 |
| 4023⁵ | Noted Strain (IRE) (57) (PJMakin)  3–8–7  WNewnes (5) (hdwy & 6th st: styd on fnl 2f) | hd.4 |
| 3967 | Vanroy (80) (v) (Jt-Fav) (JRJenkins)  7–9–7  JWilliams (2) (b.hind: hld up: effrt 4f out: n.d) | 8.5 |
| 3998 | Friendlypersuasion (IRE) (45) (RHollinshead)  3–8–10  WRyan (11) (chsd ldrs: 5th st: wknd wl over 1f out) | ¾.6 |
| 3792 | Corporate Type (IRE) (DWChapman)  3–8–3  SWood (9) (prom: 4th st: wknd over 2f out) | 8.7 |
| 3902 | Logarithm (40) (PJMakin)  3–8–4  TSprake (7) (prom 5f) | 1½.8 |
| | Norma Jean (MHTompkins)  5–8–4(1) ‡5CHodgson (12) (prom tl wknd over 4f out) | s.h.9 |
| 3065³ | Lady Baraka (IRE) (46) (ICampbell)  3–8–3 ‡5DBiggs (8) (chsd ldrs 5f) | hd.10 |
| | Persian Dipper (RBastiman)  3–8–5(1) DMcKeown (3) (w'like: leggy: s.s: a bhd) | 11 |
| 3135 | Un Souverain (27) (MCChapman)  3–8–5  SWebster (10) (stumbled s: a bhd) | 12 |
| 3920³ | Drinks Party (IRE) (40) (JWharton)  3–8–1 ‡3JFanning (13) (bhd fr ½-wy) | 13 |

**5/1** Vanroy, Irish Native (IRE), All the King's Men (IRE)(op 3/1), **6/1** Drinks Party (IRE), HAND PAINTED(op 10/1), Norma Jean, **8/1** Noted Strain (IRE), **12/1** Friendlypersuasion (IRE), Logarithm, **14/1** Lady Baraka (IRE), **20/1** Corporate Type (IRE), **25/1** Persian Dipper, **33/1** Un Souverain. CSF £38.66, Tote £9.00: £1.70 £2.90 £3.50 (£19.40). Mrs Margaret Baxter (NEWMARKET) bred by Mrs R. M. Vella. 13 Rn   2m 25.3 (3.8)
SF—32/44/21/15/13/–

**4039**   IRIS STKS (I) (Mdn F & M) £2386.70 (£661.20: £316.10)  **1m (AWT)**   12-25 (12-29)

| | | |
|---|---|---|
| 3994⁶ | **Super Sally** (Fav) (MJRyan)  4–8–9 ‡5DBiggs (10) (2nd st: led over 2f out: clr fnl f) | —1 |
| 4008³ | Mac's Princess (USA) (65) (WAO'Gorman)  3–8–12  DMcKeown (7) (hdwy over 2f out: styd on: nrst fin) | 4.2 |
| 1110 | Supadupa (27) (MrsBarbaraWaring)  4–9–0  NHowe (6) (outpcd & bhd: hdwy over 1f out: nt rch ldrs) | 4.3 |
| 3414⁶ | Singing Nelly (BWHills)  3–8–12  MHills (13) (s.i.s: hdwy & 5th st: wknd over 1f out) | 2½.4 |
| 3011³ | Swinging Lady (58) (WWHaigh)  3–8–12  ACulhane (4) (hdwy 5f out: 6th st: no imp) | 2.5 |
| | Dulzura (29) (APJarvis)  3–8–12  NAdams (3) (led tl hdd over 2f out: sn wknd) | 2½.6 |
| 3948 | Harry's Lady (IRE) (50) (TTThomsonJones)  3–8–12  SWhitworth (14) (hdwy u.p over 2f out: wknd fnl f) | s.h.7 |
| | Kay's Dilemma (IRE) (MichaelCunningham, Ireland)  3–8–12  JWilliams (5) (4th st: wknd 2f out) | 3.8 |
| 3876⁴ | Goodbye Maggie (IRE) (37) (bl) (MJFetherston-Godley)  3–8–12  TQuinn (9) (a in rr) | 3.9 |
| 4009 | Godsall (39) (MrsNMacauley)  4–8–7 ‡7MadeleineSmith (12) (lw: racd wd: 3rd st: sn wknd) | s.h.10 |
| 4005 | Heartburn (32) (bl) (JDBethell)  3–8–12  RHills (1) (swtg: prom 3f) | 11 |
| 45 | Pleasant Company (PABlockley)  4–8–7 ‡7GParkin (2) (outpcd) | 12 |
| | Another Warning (IRE) (LordHuntingdon)  3–8–12  AMcGlone (8) (w'like: bit bkwd: s.i.s: a bhd: t:o) | 13 |
| | Collina Del Fonte (JBalding)  3–8–12  JFortune (11) (cmpt: scope: bit bkwd: prom to ½-wy) | 14 |

**2/1** SUPER SALLY, **5/2** Mac's Princess (USA)(3/1—4/1), **4/1** Singing Nelly(2/1—9/2), **8/1** Another Warning (IRE)(op 4/1), **12/1** Kay's Dilemma (IRE)(op 8/1), Harry's Lady (IRE), **14/1** Goodbye Maggie (IRE), Swinging Lady, **16/1** Supadupa, **20/1** Heartburn, **33/1** Dulzura, Pleasant Company, **50/1** Collina Del Fonte. CSF £8.76, Tote £3.10: £1.60 £1.20 £3.40 (£4.10). Mr Leonard Seale (NEWMARKET) bred by R. Duggan.
14 Rn          1m 42.9 (3.6)
SF—17/8/–/–/–/–

---

**4040**      DAFFODIL H'CAP (0-90) £2467.90 (£684.40: £327.70)    1¾m (AWT)    12-50 (12-55)

4018   **Art Form (USA) (72)** (CACyzer) 4–9-9 WRyan (9) (bhd: hdwy 5f out: led over 2f out: styd on wl) ............................................. —1

4023*   Intricacy (61) (Fav) (CCElsey) 3–8-5 (5x) NDay (13) (bhd: hdwy 6f out: 4th & nt clr run st: styd on fnl f) ............................................. 1½.2

4018⁵   Quick Ransom (64) (MJohnston) 3–8-8 DMcKeown (7) (w ldr: led 3f out: sn hdd: no ex) ............................................. 6.3

3992   Discord (63) (v) (LordHuntingdon) 5–9-0 DaleGibson (4) (hld up: hdwy & 3rd st: wknd 2f out) ............................................. 7.4

4026⁵   Western Dynasty (66) (MJRyan) 5–9-3 GCarter (14) (lw: bhd: hdwy 6f out: 6th st: wknd over 1f out) ............................................. 8.5

4018²   Mysterious Maid (USA) (72) (JPearce) 4–9-9 JWilliams (1) (nvr rchd ldrs) ......... hd.6

4025³   Mississippi Beat (USA) (47) (v) (MPNaughton) 4–7-7(5) ‡⁵FNorton (12) (bhd: effrt 5f out: n.d) ............................................. 10.7

3987⁶   Castoret (72) (JWHills) 5–9-9 MHills (11) (hdwy 6f out: 5th st: eased whn btn fnl 2f) ............................................. 1.8

3987   Native Magic (70) (RWArmstrong) 5–9-7 RHills (2) (prom: hmpd appr st: sn lost pl) ............................................. 1.9

3776⁴   Robins Find (IRE) (66) (JGFitzGerald) 3–8-10 MWood (5) (chsd ldrs 10f) ......... 12.10

3965*   Qualitair Aviator (73) (JFBottomley) 5–9-10 GBardwell (3) (led tl hdd 3f out: wknd qckly) ............................................. 7.11

1103²   Blushing Belle (72) (PFICole) 3–9-2 TQuinn (6) (bhd fr ½-wy: t.o) ............... 15.12

3830⁴   Daleside (63) (TFairhurst) 3–8-4 ‡³JFanning (10) (prom tl wknd over 4f out) ....... 1½.13

4002⁵   Marine Society (72) (PTWalwyn) 3–9-2 MBirch (8) (lw: prom 7f) ............... 10.14

LONG HANDICAP: Mississippi Beat (USA) 7-4.

**9/4** Intricacy, **7/1** Discord(5/1—8/1), **15/2** Qualitair Aviator, **8/1** Castoret, ART FORM (USA)(10/1—14/1), **9/1** Mysterious Maid (USA)(6/1—10/1), Blushing Belle, Quick Ransom(op 5/1), **11/1** Western Dynasty, **16/1** Marine Society, **20/1** Ors. CSF £28.12, CT £160.32. Tote £12.90: £4.10 £1.80 £2.00 (£25.20). Mr R. M. Cyzer (HORSHAM) bred by Morgan's Ford Farm and Elizabeth Thomas in USA. 14 Rn    3m 3.3 (4)
SF—41/20/11/3/–/–

---

**4041**      DAISY CLAIMING STKS (II) £2386.70 (£661.20: £316.10)   1m 3f (AWT)   1-20 (1-22)

4023²   **Tempering (75)** (Fav) (DWChapman) 5–9-10 SWood (3) (mde all: clr over 3f out: eased over 1f out) ............................................. —1

4019   Gipsy King (61) (bl) (PAKelleway) 3–8-11 WNewnes (5) (hdwy 6f out: 3rd st: rdn over 1f out: styd on: no ch w wnr) ............................................. 3.2

4023⁴   Qualitair Blazer (45) (JRJenkins) 4–8-11 SWhitworth (13) (a.p: 2nd st: one pce fnl 2f) ............................................. 2½.3

2840³   Spring Tern (USA) (56) (bl) (RO'Leary) 3–8-13 MBirch (2) (prom: lost pl 8f out: hdwy & 4th st: one pce fnl 2f) ............................................. 5.4

2448   What a Card (25) (DenysSmith) 3–7-10 JQuinn (9) (hdwy 5f out: 5th st: sn wknd)   3½.5

3920⁶   Temple Island (IRE) (PJMakin) 3–8-6 TSprake (8) (bhd: hdwy over 3f out: n.d) ........ 3.6

  Qualitair Sweetie (JFBottomley) 4–9-5 GBardwell (4) (lw: bhd: effrt 5f out: 7th & no hdwy st) ............................................. 5.7

4019   Gushy (48) (CRBeever) 5–9-0 JWilliams (12) (b: a bhd) ............................................. 5.8

3495⁵   Ivan the Terrible (IRE) (67) (MissSJWilton) 3–8-5 ‡⁵FNorton (10) (prom 6f) ............ ¾.9

402   Dorsey (42) (PJFeilden) 4–8-1 ‡⁷StephenDavies (7) (6th & wkng st) ............... 7.10

3018   Nafplion (16) (bl) (REPeacock) 6–7-13 ‡³JFanning (11) (b: prom 6f) ............... 2½.11

3884⁵   Lanceval (FR) (CAAustin) 5–9-7 DMcKeown (1) (a bhd: t.o) ............................................. 12

**8/13** TEMPERING, **6/1** Temple Island (IRE)(op 4/1), **7/1** Qualitair Blazer, **9/1** Spring Tern (USA)(op 6/1), **10/1** Ivan the Terrible (IRE), **14/1** Gipsy King, **16/1** Qualitair Sweetie, **20/1** What a Card, **33/1** Lanceval (FR), Gushy, Dorsey, **40/1** Nafplion. CSF £13.22, Tote £1.80: £1.30 £2.10 £2.30 (£6.50). Mr Michael Hill (YORK) bred by Lord Howard de Walden. 12 Rn    2m 26.2 (4.7)
SF—41/22/17/9/–/–

---

**4042**      EAST MIDLANDS ELECTRICITY H'CAP (0-70) £2407.00 (£667.00: £319.00) 6f (AWT)                 1-50 (1-58)

4028⁴   **Cronk's Courage (59)** (v) (Jt-Fav) (EJAlston) 5–9-9 MHills (14) (led after 2f: hld on wl fnl f) ............................................. —1

*3966* Precentor **(57)** (bl) *(JDBethell)* 5–9-7 RHills (6) (hdwy over 2f out: hung lft ins fnl f: r.o towards fin) .................................................. hd.2
*4027* Count Me Out **(51)** *(JPearce)* 6–9-1 GBardwell (8) (bhd: hdwy over 2f out: r.o wl) 2½.3
*4021⁶* Rushanes **(64)** *(TCasey)* 4–9-9 ‡⁵FNorton (3) (a chsng ldrs: rdn & one pce fnl 2f) ..... ½.4
*4028* Arc Lamp **(55)** *(JAGlover)* 5–9-5 DaleGibson (12) (a in tch: styd on one pce fnl 2f) ½.5
*3947\** Meeson Times **(52)** *(BEllison)* 3–9-1 WRyan (13) (a.p: kpt on one pce fnl 2f) ...... nk.6
*4027³* Silks Princess **(52)** (Jt-Fav) *(MJRyan)* 5–9-2 JMcLaughlin (10) (nvr trbld ldrs) ...... 1½.7
*3051* Pretty Poppy **(54)** *(PMitchell)* 3–9-3 JWilliams (2) (s.i.s: hdwy ½-wy: nvr rchd ldrs) 1.8
*4006³* Sully's Choice **(55)** (bl) (Jt-Fav) *(DWChapman)* 10–9-5 SWood (4) (cl up early: outpcd appr st: n.d after) ................. 2.9
*4006²* Very Bold **(54)** *(PDEvans)* 3–8-12 ‡⁵LNewton (9) (b: led 2f: cl up tl wknd over 2f out) .................................................. 1.10
*4027⁶* Precious Air (IRE) **(60)** *(DenysSmith)* 3–9-9 DNicholls (15) (s.i.s: hdwy after 2f: no imp) .......................................... nk.11
*3966* Erik Odin **(51)** *(MrsLPiggott)* 4–8-8 ‡⁷WAldwinckle (11) (eyeshield: b.hind: outpcd fr ½-wy) ................................ 1½.12
*3984* Stoneleigh Abbey (IRE) **(57)** (bl) *(RDEWoodhouse)* 3–9-6 SWhitworth (1) (bhd fr ½-wy) .................................................. 3.13
*4006⁵* Beckingham Ben **(53)** *(JPLeigh)* 7–9-3 ACulhane (5) (cl up 4f: eased whn btn) ..... ½.14
*580* Ensharp (USA) **(60)** *(JPLeigh)* 5–9-10 DMcKeown (7) (bkwd: chsd ldrs over 3f: wknd qckly) ........................................... 1.15

**6/1** CRONK'S COURAGE, Silks Princess, Sully's Choice (USA), 7/1 Precentor, 8/1 Rushanes, 11/1 Very Bold, 12/1 Arc Lamp, Meeson Times(op 8/1) Erik Odin, 14/1 Beckingham Ben(op 8/1), 16/1 Count Me Out, 20/1 Ensharp (USA), 25/1 Ors. CSF £46.12, CT £584.23. Tote £8.20: £2.20 £2.20 £5.80 (£28.70). Mr M. P. Russell (PRESTON) bred by M. Andree. 15 Rn 1m 16 (2.6)
SF—33/30/14/20/14/9

**4043** COOPERS LYBRAND DELOITTE NURSERY £2467.90 (£684.40: £327.70)
**7f (AWT)** (Weights raised 4 lb) 2-20 (2-25)
*4011³* **Debsy Do (USA) (60)** *(SGNorton)* 8-12 JFortune (5) (lw: led 2f: w ldrs: led over 2f out: rdn & r.o) ......................................... —1
*3949⁶* Talented Ting (IRE) **(69)** *(PCHaslam)* 9-7 DMcKeown (2) (led after 2f tl over 2f out: r.o) ................................................ 1.2
*4015⁶* Super-Sub **(58)** *(MJFetherston-Godley)* 8-10 TQuinn (6) (a chsng ldrs: kpt on same pce fnl 2f) .......................... 2.3
*4024\** Dublin Indemnity (USA) **(59)** (bl) (Fav) *(NACallaghan)* 8-11 (7x) NAdams (13) (lw: pushed along & bhd: hdwy 2f out: r.o) .. 1½.4
*4024³* Peace Formula (IRE) **(62)** *(RHollinshead)* 9-0 WRyan (1) (lw: hdwy u.p 4f out: styd on: no imp) ............................ nk.5
*4015²* Stylish Gentleman **(65)** *(CTinkler)* 9-3 MBirch (3) (outpcd & bhd: hdwy 2f out: nrst fin) ...................................... nk.6
*3592* Invigilate **(52)** *(HATWhiting)* 8-4 SWebster (14) (s.i.s: hdwy over 2f out: r.o wl) ...... ½.7
*4017³* Easy Does it **(53)** (v) *(CCElsey)* 8-5 JQuinn (15) (in tch tl outpcd fnl 2f) ......... 5.8
*4024⁵* Flim Flam Aly (USA) **(59)** (bl) *(MrsNMacauley)* 8-11 AlexGreaves (11) (sn outpcd: hdwy 2f out: nvr trbld ldrs) ......... hd.9
*3408* Penny Drops **(52)** *(LordHuntingdon)* 8-4 DaleGibson (12) (prom over 4f) ............ 3.10
*4000* Affa **(58)** *(TThomsonJones)* 8-10 SWhitworth (16) (b: chsd ldrs over 4f) ............ nk.11
*4011⁴* Sie Amato (IRE) **(59)** *(CaptJWilson)* 8-11 GBardwell (9) (cl up tl wknd over 2f out)2½.12
*3890* Profit Stream **(62)** *(MWEasterby)* 8-7 ‡⁷JWeaver (4) (dwlt: n.d) .................... 1½.13
*3945* Sunrays (IRE) **(57)** *(CWCElsey)* 8-9 WNewnes (7) (chsd ldrs 4f) .................... 3½.14
*1372* Mary's Special **(51)** *(CNAllen)* 8-0 ‡³DBiggs (8) (lost tch fnl 3f) ................ nk.15
*3963* Wheeler's Wonder (IRE) **(59)** *(CEBrittain)* 8-11 GCarter (10) (s.s: n.d) .......... 1½.16

**3/1** Dublin Indemnity (USA)(9/2—5/2), 6/1 Peace Formula (IRE), 7/1 Affa, 17/2 Stylish Gentleman, 10/1 DEBSY DO (USA), Invigilate(op 16/1), 12/1 Sie Amato (IRE), Talented Ting (IRE)(op 8/1), Super-Sub, Flim Flam Aly (USA), Penny Drops(op 7/1), 14/1 Profit Stream, 16/1 Easy Does it, Wheeler's Wonder (IRE), 20/1 Mary's Special, 25/1 Sunrays (IRE). CSF £131.82, CT £1,375.66. Tote £10.20: £2.10 £3.20 £5.40 £1.60 (£140.30). Mr S. G. Norton (BARNSLEY) bred by Cambus Kenneth Farm in USA. 16 Rn 1m 29.2 (2.6)
SF—38/44/27/23/25/27

**4044** ROSE STKS (Mdn 2-Y.O) £2691.20 (£748.20: £359.60) **7f (AWT)** 2-50 (2-52)
*4011²* **Empeeka (USA) (70)** (h) (Jt-Fav) *(WAO'Gorman)* 8-9 ‡⁵EmmaO'Gorman (10) (hdwy ent st: led over 1f out: r.o wl) —1
*4029²* Big Easy (IRE) (Jt-Fav) *(MrsJCecil)* 9-0 TQuinn (14) (eyeshield: lw: a.p: led over 2f out tl over 1f out: kpt on) 1½.2
Stylus *(MRStoute)* 9-0 PD'Arcy (6) (unf: scope: bit bkwd: a cl up: chal 2f out: kpt on) 1.3
Flamingo Rose (IRE) *(HRACecil)* 8-9 WRyan (7) (w'like: scope: bhd: hdwy 2f out: styd on) 10.4

xxx

40296 Nothing Compares *(JWHills)* 8-9 RHills (12) (in tch: effrt appr st: nvr able to chal) ........ s.h.5
Red Archer *(PJMakin)* 9-0 WNewnes (2) (unf: bkwd: nvr nr to chal) ...................... nk.6
39835 Don't Drop Bombs (USA) *(AAScott)* 9-0 JFortune (8) (cl up: led 3f out: sn hdd & wknd) ........................................................................................................................ 3.7
40166 Thor Power (IRE) *(DTThom)* 9-0 JWilliams (9) (bhd tl sme late hdwy) ................... d.h.7
General John (IRE) *(PCHaslam)* 9-0 DMcKeown (16) (w'like: bkwd: s.i.s: nvr plcd to chal) ........................................................................................................ nk.9
3700 Lord Leitrim *(NACallaghan)* 9-0 GCarter (15) (bhd: gd hdwy ½-wy: sn prom: wknd 2f out) ........................................................................................... 1.10
3728 Lizzie Drippin (CAN) *(MDIUsher)* 8-9 CRutter (13) (nvr wnt pce) ...................... ½.11
4022 Blackwater Panther (IRE) *(CNAllen)* 9-0 WWharton (5) (s.i.s: a bhd) ................. 2½.12
39632 Esprit Fort (USA) (70) *(BWHills)* 8-9 MHills (1) (led tl hdd 3f out: btn whn hmpd 2f out) ........................................................................................................................ s.h.13
3340 Don't Move (IRE) *(MHTompkins)* 8-4 ‡5CHodgson (4) (bit bkwd: sn outpcd) ........ s.h.14
3056 Ace Girl (67) *(SRBowring)* 8-2 ‡7KiriBeeching (11) (chsd ldrs to st) ................... s.h.15
4017 Sun Glory (IRE) *(WJarvis)* 8-9 NDay (3) (cl up tl wknd 3f out) ........................... ¾.16

3/1 EMPEEKA (USA)(op 10/1), Big Easy (IRE)(5/1—5/2), **4/1** Don't Drop Bombs (USA), 9/2 Flamingo Rose (IRE)(2/1—5/2), **6/1** Esprit Fort (USA)(op 4/1), **10/1** Stylus(op 7/2), **14/1** Red Archer, 20/1 Ace Girl, 25/1 General John (IRE), 33/1 Blackwater Panther (IRE), Thor Power (IRE), Don't Move (IRE), Nothing Compares, 50/1 Ors. CSF £14.12, Tote £5.60: £2.10 £1.50 £4.50 (£9.20). Maclaine Racing (NEWMARKET) bred by John Fernung & Carrel Eakle in USA. 16 Rn
1m 28.7 (2.1)
SF—44/42/39/4/3/7

## 4045

IRIS STKS (Mdn F & M) £2366.40 (£655.40: £313.20)  1m (AWT)  3-20 (3-21)

3778 Litmore Dancer (55) *(JDBethell)* 3–8-12 RHills (6) (mde all: edgd rt fnl 2f: r.o) ........ —1
Shaurni Girl *(RVKing)* 3–8-12 VSmith (2) (leggy: unf: a chsng ldrs: styd on fnl 2f: nt poo to chal) ...................................................................................................... 2½.2
3796 Macquarie Ridge (USA) (39) *(BHanbury)* 3–8-12 MHills (13) (cl up tl outpcd fnl 2f) ..................................................................................................................... 2½.3
3946 Quiet Victory (47) *(MissLCSiddall)* 4–9-0 MBirch (10) (a chsng ldrs: rdn & no imp fnl 3f) ................................................................................................................... 6.4
3706 Hepburn (IRE) (42) *(MJFetherston-Godley)* 3–8-12 TQuinn (7) (sn outpcd & bhd: styd on fnl 3f: n.d) .................................................................................... 2½.5
3984 Ballater Lass (IRE) (46) *(JWharton)* 3–8-12 JWilliams (9) (lw: outpcd & bhd: hdwy appr st: no imp) ...................................................................................... 3.6
4005 Harlequin Girl (39) *(KTIvory)* 3–8-12 GBardwell (3) (outpcd fr ½-wy) ................ hd.7
3766 Bingo Bongo (38) *(DBurchell)* 4–9-0 DMcKeown (8) (in tch to st) ...................... nk.8
First Sapphire *(WJarvis)* 4–9-0 NDay (4) (unf: scope: s.s: nvr nr to chal) .............. 1½.9
39115 Barachois Princess (USA) (38) *(RHollinshead)* 4–9-0 WRyan (1) (n.d) ................ 10
1575 Restless Niece (Fav) *(TDBarron)* 3–8-12 AlexGreaves (14) (bit bkwd: gd spd over 4f) ......................................................................................................... 11
1743 Maria Medici (54) *(MrsLPiggott)* 3–8-12 GCarter (12) (eyeshield: b: b.hind: bit bkwd: outpcd after 3f) ............................................................................. 12
2534 Green's Bonheur (46) *(MPNaughton)* 3–8-12 JakiHouston (11) (bhd fr ½-wy) ......... 13
Absent Minded (25) *(JDooler)* 5–8-11 ‡3JFanning (5) (bkwd: sn outpcd: wl t.o) ...... 14

9/2 Restless Niece (Fav), 6/1 Maria Medici, LITMORE DANCER, 13/2 Green's Bonheur, 7/1 First Sapphire(op 2/1), Barachois Princess (USA), 8/1 Ballater Lass (IRE), 10/1 Macquarie Ridge (USA)(14/1—8/1), 10/1 Quiet Victory, Hepburn (IRE), 12/1 Harlequin Girl, 14/1 Bingo Bongo, 20/1 Ors. CSF £125.40, Tote £10.10: £2.80 £6.00 £6.30 (Wnr or 2nd w any £2.30). Mrs David Shirley (DIDCOT) bred by David and Mrs Shirley. 14Rn
1m 42 (2.7)
SF—33/25/17/1/–/–

T/Plpt: £25.00 (45.9 Tckts).

CR/AA

## 4038—**SOUTHWELL (L-H)** Fibresand
### Wednesday, December 4th [Standard]
Going Allowance: minus 0.25 sec per fur (FS)

## 4046

MACBETH STKS (I) (Mdn 2-Y.O) £2407.00 (£667.00: £319.00)
**1m (AWT)**  11-55 (11-58)

Citiqueen (IRE) (Jt-Fav) *(HRACecil)* 8-2 ‡7StephenDavies (13) (cmpt: scope: chsd ldrs: rdn over 3f out: led over 1f out: r.o) ............................. —1
Sir Pageant (Jt-Fav) *(PFICole)* 9-0 TQuinn (4) (w'like: bit bkwd: outpcd: hdwy 2f out: r.o ins fnl f) ...................................................................................... 2.2
39624 Quiet Miss *(DRCElsworth)* 8-9 JWilliams (1) (eyeshield: lost pl after 3f: hdwy over 1f out: styd on fnl f) ......................................................................... 3.3

4010³ Brotherlyaffection (56) (RHollinshead) 9-0 WRyan (6) (led 1f: led 3f out tl over 1f out: sn btn) ...................................................................... ½.4

4022² Ballyranter (56) (HJCollingridge) 9-0 JQuinn (9) (chsd ldrs: styd on one pce fnl 2f) ...................................................................... 1.5

4044 Blackwater Panther (IRE) (CNAllen) 8-7 ‡⁷MichaelDenaro (12) (bhd: hdwy over 2f out: nt rch ldrs) ...................................................................... 2.6

3995 Slight Risk (65) (PAKelleway) 8-9 GBardwell (11) (eyecover: led after 1f: hdd 3f out: wknd 2f out) ...................................................................... ½.7

4044 Thor Power (IRE) (60) (DTThom) 9-0 BRaymond (3) (no hdwy fnl 2f) .............. 3.8

Cellito (IRE) (WAO'Gorman) 8-9 ‡5EmmaO'Gorman (2) (cmpt: bkwd: prom tl wknd over 1f out) ...................................................................... nk.9

4022 Medbourne (IRE) (44) (JLHarris) 8-4 ‡5FNorton (5) (s.i.s: a in rr) .............. ¾.10

Lady Dundee (USA) (MrsJCecil) 8-9 GDuffield (7) (neat: unf: bit bkwd: s.i.s: drvn along: a in rr) ...................................................................... 6.11

2728 Spanish Rhapsody (48) (MDIUsher) 8-9 NAdams (8) (bit bkwd: sn bhd) ............ 12

968⁴ Briginski (JWPayne) 8-9 ASkingle (10) (a in rr: t.o) ...................................................................... 13

4/1 Sir Pageant, CITIQUEEN (IRE)(op Evens), 5/1 Ballyranter (56)(op 10/1), 6/1 Quiet Miss, 13/2 Lady Dundee (USA)(op 3/1), 8/1 Cellito (IRE)(op 4/1), 10/1 Brotherlyaffection, 14/1 Briginski, 16/1 Slight Risk, 20/1 Medbourne (IRE), 25/1 Ors. CSF £21.51. Tote £4.70: £3.30 £1.40 £1.60 (£4.80). Mr Ivan Allan (NEWMARKET) bred by Ivan W. Allan in Ireland. 13 Rn
1m 42.9 (3.6)
SF—4/10/–/–/–/–

---

**4047**    JULIUS CAESAR CLAIMING STKS (I)  £2325.80 (£643.80: £307.40)
6f (AWT)                                    12-25 (12-28)

4028* Plain Fact (82) (Fav) (SirMarkPrescott) 6-8-7 GDuffield (1) (chsd ldrs: led over 1f out: pushed out) ...................................................................... —1

1061 Friendly Claim (IRE) (77) (TDBarron) 3–8-5 AlexGreaves (6) (hdwy 2f out: r.o: nt rch wnr) ...................................................................... 2.2

3946⁴ Miss Aragon (40) (MissLCSiddall) 3–8-6 TQuinn (2) (chsd ldrs: outpcd over 2f out: hdwy over 1f out: styd on ins fnl f) ...................................................................... 6.3

4042⁴ Rushanes (64) (TCasey) 4–8-2 ‡5FNorton (7) (led 1f: led over 2f out: hdd over 1f out: wknd ins fnl f) ...................................................................... ¾.4

4005⁶ Rambo Express (60) (v) (ICampbell) 4–7-12 ‡3DBiggs (5) (led after 1f: hdd over 2f out: ev ch over 1f out: sn wknd) ...................................................................... 1.5

3946 Kabera (33) (DWChapman) 3–8-1 SWood (8) (a bhd) ...................................................................... 2.6

4009 Dawn Success (73) (DWChapman) 5–8-0 ‡7WMaher (9) (s.i.s: outpcd) ............ hd.7

Cleo Modena (IRE) (MO'Neill) 3–8-6 JFortune (3) (w'like: s.i.s: a bhd) ............ 2½.8

3308 Where's Carol (MBrittain) 3–7-11⁽⁶⁾ ‡5SMaloney (4) (bhd fr ½-wy: t.o) ............ 15.9

8/15 PLAIN FACT, 6/1 Rushanes(5/1—8/1), 7/1 Friendly Claim, 10/1 Rambo Express, 11/1 Dawn Success(5/1—12/1), 16/1 Where's Carol, Miss Aragon, 33/1 Cleo Modena (IRE), 50/1 Kabera. CSF £5.95. Tote £1.70: £1.10 £1.90 £2.80 (£3.80). Mr G. Moore (NEWMARKET) bred by Clanville Lodge Stud. 9Rn
1m 14.9 (1.5)
SF—33/23/–/–/–/–

---

**4048**    HAMLET NURSERY  £2549.10 (£707.60: £339.30)    7f (AWT)    12-55 (12-59)

4043⁶ Stylish Gentleman (65) (CTinkler) 8-4 MBirch (7) (eyeshield: led after 1f: hdd over 1f out: hrd rdn to ld wl ins fnl f: all out) ...................................................................... —1

4044* Empeeka (USA) (77) (h) (WAO'Gorman) 8-11 (7x) ‡5EmmaO'Gorman (4) (hld up: hdwy over 2f out: nt clr run over 1f out: swtchd rt & r.o in s fnl f) ...................................................................... hd.2

4029* Spanish Miner (USA) (82) (Fav) (AAScott) 9-7 BRaymond (11) (b: b.hind: lw: chsd ldrs: led over 1f out tl wl ins fnl f: unable qckn) ...................................................................... hd.3

4043 Invigilate (58) (HATWhiting) 7-6⁽⁴⁾ ‡5FNorton (1) (a.p: ev ch over 1f out: styd on fnl f) ...................................................................... hd.4

4011* Ferdia (IRE) (66) (RHollinshead) 8-5 WRyan (9) (hld up: hdwy over 2f out: styd on: nt rch ldrs) ...................................................................... 3½.5

3957⁴ Little Nod (68) (MJCamacho) 8-2 ‡5SMaloney (16) (chsd ldrs: styd on one pce fnl 2f) ...................................................................... nk.6

3407⁶ Rosa Why (IRE) (66) (WJarvis) 8-5 MHills (3) (chsd ldrs: no hdwy fnl 2f) ............ nk.7

1980 Gone Bust (IRE) (74) (RFJohnsonHoughton) 8-13 TQuinn (13) (prom tl wknd wl over 1f out) ...................................................................... 6.8

4043 Sie Amato (IRE) (59) (CaptJWilson) 7-12 GBardwell (8) (led 1f: wknd 3f out) .......... hd.9

4043² Talented Ting (69) (PCHaslam) 8-5 ‡3JFanning (10) (lw: effrt over 3f out: nvr nr ldrs) ...................................................................... nk.10

3844 Heart Flutter (62) (bl) (JHetherton) 8-1 DaleGibson (2) (lw: a bhd) .................. 2½.11

3956⁵ Feeling Foolish (IRE) (63) (SGNorton) 7-13 ‡3DBiggs (14) (s.i.s: a in rr) .......... 3.12

3764 And Me (56) (DTThom) 7-9 JQuinn (5) (a bhd) .......................................... nk.13
3619 Evening Dress (54) (TThomsonJones) 7-7 SWood (6) (bhd fr ½-wy) ................. nk.14
3106 Lady of Letters (56) (TThomsonJones) 7-9(2) NAdams (15) (n.d) ...................... 2½.15
    LONG HANDICAP: Invigilate 7-5, Evening Dress 7-1, Lady of Letters 7-3.
    Stewards Enquiry: Birch suspended 13-14/12/91 (excessive use of whip).

**13/8** Spanish Miner (USA), **4/1** Empeeka (USA)(7/2—11/2), **11/2** Talented Ting (IRE), **7/1** Rosa Why (IRE)(6/1—10/1), **8/1** Ferdia (IRE), **14/1** STYLISH GENTLEMAN, Feeling Foolish (IRE), **16/1** Gone Bust (IRE), Invigilate, **20/1** Sie Amato (IRE)(op 10/1), Little Nod, **25/1** Heart Flutter, **33/1** Ors. CSF £75.73, CT £136.11. Tote £15.90: £2.30 £2.10 £1.70 (£45.90). Mr Tony S. K. Wong (MALTON) bred by J. L. Acklam.
15 Rn                                                     1m 28.8 (2.2)
                                               SF—31/37/46/15/15/11

---

**4049**      JULIUS CAESAR CLAIMING STKS (II)   £2325.80 (£643.80: £307.40)
             **6f (AWT)**                                          1-25 (1-30)

4027 **Wellsy Lad (USA) (64)** (DWChapman) 4–8-3 SWood (5) (prom: led 2f out: rdn out) .......................................................................................................... —1
4027* African Chimes (78) (Fav) (WAO'Gorman) 4–8-6 ‡⁵EmmaO'Gorman (4) (hld up: hdwy 3f out: ev ch 1f out: styd on one pce) .............................. ½.2
    Swingaway Lady (62) (bl) (GRichards) 4–7-12 JQuinn (6) (eyeshield: bhd: hdwy over 1f out: nrst fin) .......................................................................... 5.3
    Awesome Power (MichaelCunningham,Ireland) 5–8-8(5) JWilliams (1) (effrt ½-wy: styd on fnl 2f) ................................................................................ nk.4
4028 Rancho Mirage (72) (MrsNMacauley) 4–8-5 GDuffield (3) (b: chsd ldrs: rdn over 1f out: sn btn) ....................................................................................... nk.5
4009 Supreme Optimist (29) (bl) (REPeacock) 7–7-10 ‡⁵FNorton (8) (b: led 4f: wknd fnl f) ................................................................................................................ 1.6
3500 Answersnotproblomo (IRE) (bl) (AWDenson) 3–7-10 NAdams (2) (rdn over 2f out: no imp) ................................................................................................. 5.7
1642⁵ Cossack Noir (35) (MPNaughton) 3–8-1 JakiHouston (7) (chsd ldrs to ½-wy) ...... 2½.8
    Daniel Challenger (JPSmith) 3–8-5 TSprake (9) (dwlt: a bhd) ............................ 9

**8/11** African Chimes, **9/2** WELLSY LAD, **6/1** Rancho Mirage(op 4/1), **9/1** Awesome Power(op 9/2), **12/1** Swingaway Lady, **33/1** Answersnotproblems (IRE), Supreme Optimist, **50/1** Ors. CSF £7.94, Tote £5.30: £1.30 £1.10 £4.00 (£2.00). Mr J. M. Chapman (YORK) bred by Mrs. Helen K. Groves in USA. 9Rn
                                               1m 15.4 (2)
                                             SF—19/20/–/–/–/–

---

**4050**      LILLEY DEVELOPMENTS H'CAP (0-70)   £2407.00 (£667.00: £319.00)
             **2m (AWT)**                                          1-55 (1-57)

3987 **Moving Out (69)** (Fav) (SirMarkPrescott) 3–10-0 GDuffield (6) (mde all: styd on wl fnl 3f: comf) ........................................................................................... —1
3960² Bridge Player (43) (DMoffatt) 4–8-3 ‡⁷DarrenMoffatt (8) (a chsng ldrs: kpt on u.p fnl 3f: no imp) ........................................................................................... 4.2
3775⁴ Racing Raskal (31) (CaptJWilson) 4–7-9 ‡³DBiggs (7) (a.p: effrt over 4f out: one pce) ................................................................................................................ 5.3
2126 Jawani (IRE) (47) (DrJDScargill) 3–8-6 GBardwell (3) (bit bkwd: chsd ldrs after 6f tl outpcd fnl 3f) .................................................................................... 1½.4
    Mississippi Beat (USA) (42) (v) (MHTompkins) 4–8-9(2) JWilliams (4) (lw: bhd: hdwy 5f out: sn rdn & no imp) ............................................................... 4.5
4023⁶ Chronological (53) (v) (MHTompkins) 5–9-1 ‡⁵CHodgson (12) (effrt & hdwy 7f out: rdn & btn 3f out) ........................................................................... 10.6
3797⁴ Caroles Clown (30) (MJHaynes) 5–7-4 ‡⁷DToole (9) (prom tl lost pl 8f out: hdwy over 2f out: styd on) ..................................................................................... 2½.7
4002 Carly-B (IRE) (39) (bl) (PHowling) 3–7-7(3) ‡⁵FNorton (14) (cl up: rdn 5f out: wknd over 3f out) ...................................................................................................... 3.8
4032 Mister Major (36) (LJHolt) 3–7-9(1) NAdams (13) (cl up tl rdn & wknd 4f out) ........... 12.9
3765⁵ Dancing Days (46) (bl) (JParkes) 5–8-13 DaleGibson (1) (bhd: effrt ½-wy: n.d) ...... 8.10
4025* Suluk (USA) (48) (RHollinshead) 6–9-1 WRyan (11) (lw: sn pushed along: a rr div: eased whn btn fnl 3f) ............................................................................. 4.11
4025⁶ Sharp Issue (USA) (36) (bl) (MCChapman) 3–7-6(2) ‡³JFanning (2) (a bhd) ........ 1½.12
4023 Ihsaas (40) (MPNaughton) 4–8-7 JakiHouston (5) (bhd most of wy) .................... 5.13
4023 Daunting Prospect (35) (MCChapman) 7–7-11(6) ‡⁵SMaloney (15) (bhd fr ½-wy) 1½.14
    LONG HANDICAP: Sharp Issue (USA) 7-1.

**7/2** MOVING OUT, **5/1** Suluk (USA), **6/1** Bridge Player, Chronological(op 4/1), Caroles Clown, **8/1** Carly-B (IRE), **10/1** Mississippi Beat (USA)(7/1—11/1), **12/1** Racing Raskal, **14/1** Dancing Days, **16/1** Mister Major, **25/1** Ihsaas, Jawani (IRE), **33/1** Sharp Issue (USA), **50/1** Daunting Prospect. CSF £26.23, CT £224.16. Tote £7.00: £2.40 £2.10 £2.90 (£13.00). Mr Fahd Salman (NEWMARKET) bred by Newgate Stud Ltd. 14Rn
                                                   3m 37.9 (11.9)

**4051**    KING LEAR CLAIMING STKS (2-Y.O) £2467.90 (£684.40: £327.70)
         **6f (AWT)**                                      2-25 (2-29)

*4024* **Runnel (58)** *(DWChapman)* 8-0 SWood (1) (mde all: clr appr fnl f & eased) ............ —1
*4036\** Appealing Times (USA) **(71)** *(Fav) (WAO'Gorman)* 8-6 ‡⁵EmmaO'Gorman (13)
                            (lw: a.p: styd on fnl 2f: no ch w nnr) ............................................. 3.2
3995 Patrician Magician **(83)** *(RJRWilliams)* 8-8 RonHillis (11) (chsd ldrs: styd on fnl
                            2f: nvr able to chal) ....................................................................... s.h.3
*3959\** Little Saboteur **(58)** (bl) *(PJMakin)* 8-1 TSprake (16) (chsd ldrs tl outpcd fnl 2f) ......... 4.4
3166 Ready to Draw (IRE) **(61)** *(RonaldThompson)* 8-1 AProud (3) (stdy hdwy 2f out:
                            r.o) ..................................................................................................... 3.5
      Swale Side *(MrsGRReveley)* 8-6 MHills (9) (w'like: bkwd: dwlt: bhd tl r.o fnl 2f) .... ¾.4.6
3471 Miss Narnia **(51)** *(APJarvis)* 7-9⁽¹⁾ NAdams (8) (chsd ldrs tl rdn & btn over 2f out) .. 1.7
*4022* Scarborough Hill (IRE) *(MHTompkins)* 7-13 DaleGibson (4) (nvr nrr) ........................ 1.8
4001⁵ Queen of Pendona **(47)** *(HATWhiting)* 7-6⁽²⁾ ‡⁵FNorton (5) (n.d) ........................... 1½.9
*4043* Mary's Special **(51)** *(CNAllen)* 7-8 GBardwell (6) (w ldrs to st) ................................. 1.10
      Bold Melody *(PCHaslam)* 7-11 ‡³JFanning (12) (leggy: unf: nvr wnt pce) ............. hd.11
3890 Grubby *(RHollinshead)* 7-5⁽²⁾ ‡⁷MHumphries (15) (n.d) ..................................... 1.12
*4024* Daily Sport August **(54)** *(MCChapman)* 7-1 JakiHouston (10) (nvr wnt pce) .......... 1.13
4022⁵ Another Nut **(47)** *(PDEvans)* 7-10⁽³⁾ ‡⁵SMaloney (14) (spd over 3f) ........................ nk.14
*4031⁶* Mighty Lady (IRE) **(69)** *(MRChannon)* 7-11 JQuinn (3) (prom over 3f) ................. 2½.15
643 Lady Dooley (IRE) **(48)** *(JWharton)* 7-9⁽²⁾ ‡³DBiggs (7) (bit bkwd: sn bhd) ......... 15.16

**6/4** Appealing Times (USA), **4/1** Patrician Magician(2/1—9/2), **5/1** Little Saboteur(op 3/1), **8/1** Mighty Lady
(IRE), **11/1** RUNNEL(8/1—12/1), **12/1** Ready to Draw (IRE)(16/1—10/1), **14/1** Swale Side, **16/1** Bold
Melody, **20/1** Miss Narnia, Mary's Special, **25/1** Another Nut, **33/1** Ors. CSF £30.13, Tote £10.80: £2.10
£1.60 £2.50 (£17.20). Mr E. Stockdale (YORK) bred by Ruckmans Farm. 16 Rn
                                                    1m 15.3 (1.9)
                                                   SF—18/12/13/–/–/–

**4052**    KING HENRY VI H'CAP (0-80) £2589.70 (£719.20: £345.10)
         **1m (AWT)**                                        2-55 (2-57)

*4028⁶* **Euroblake (72)** *(TDBarron)* 4-9-13 AlexGreaves (8) (bhd: hdwy ½-wy: rdn to ld
                            ins fnl f) ............................................................................................. —1
*4039\** Super Sally **(78)** *(MJRyan)* 4-10-2 (5x) ‡³DBiggs (16) (chsd ldrs: led wl over 1f
                            out tl ins fnl f) ................................................................................... 2.2
*4008* Evening Star **(58)** *(AHide)* 5-8-13 JWilliams (11) (bhd tl hdwy 2f out: r.o towards
                            fin) ....................................................................................................... 1.3
*4034\** Languedoc **(78)** *(Fav) (HATWhiting)* 4–10-0 (5x) ‡⁵FNorton (5) (lw: chsd ldrs: led
                            over 2f out tl wl over 1f out: no ex) ............................................... 2½.4
3850³ Golden Chip (IRE) **(62)** *(APStringer)* 3–9-1 SWebster (1) (a chsng ldrs: rdn ent
                            st: r.o one pce) ................................................................................. 1½.5
*4041\** Tempering **(75)** *(DWChapman)* 5–10-2 (5x) SWood (4) (lw: sn chsng ldrs: effrt
                            ent st: nt qckn fnl 2f) ...................................................................... ½.6
3925 Croft Valley **(70)** *(RMWhitaker)* 4–9-11 ACulhane (15) (styd on fnl 2f: nvr nrr) .......... 4.7
*4008* Doulab's Image **(66)** *(JAGlover)* 4–9-0 ‡⁷SWilliams (17) (bhd: hdwy over 2f out:
                            n.d) ..................................................................................................... ½.8
3948 Tulfarris **(55)** (v) *(DMoffatt)* 4-8-5 ‡⁵CHodgson (4) (nvr bttr than mid div) ............. 2½.9
4035³ The Shanahan Bay **(60)** (bl) *(MrsNMacauley)* 6–9-1 GDuffield (7) (led tl hdd &
                            wknd over 2f out) ............................................................................. hd.10
3823\* Diamond Inthe Dark (USA) **(65)** *(CTinkler)* 3–9-4 MBirch (14) (hmpd sn after s: nt
                            rcvr) ..................................................................................................... 1.11
3809 Falcons Dawn **(57)** (v) *(MO'Neill)* 4-8-12 JFortune (13) (cl up to st) ..................... hd.12
3915 Barkston Singer **(66)** *(MrsNMacauley)* 4–9-1 CDwyer (2) (s.i.s: a rr div) ............... 1½.13
3958 Huso **(70)** *(PCHaslam)* 3–9-9 BRaymond (10) (hdwy u.p appr st: sn btn) ............... hd.14
*4034* Will He Or Wont He (IRE) **(65)** (v) *(CNAllen)* 3–8-11 ‡⁷MichaelDenaro (3) (s.s: a
                            bhd) ..................................................................................................... 1½.15
3958 Good Time Boy **(58)** *(MBrittain)* 3–8-6 ‡⁵SMaloney (9) (in tch to st: sn wknd) ....... 1½.16
*4008* Crofter's Cline **(64)** (v) *(MO'Neill)* 7–9-5 DNicholls (6) (chsd ldrs to ½-wy: wknd
                            qckly) ................................................................................................... 17

**7/2** Languedoc, **9/2** EUROBLAKE(6/1—4/1), **5/1** Tempering, **7/1** Golden Chip (IRE)(op 16/1), **9/1** Super
Sally, Diamond Inthe Dark (USA), Huso(op 11/2), **10/1** Doulab's Image, **12/1** Croft Valley, **14/1** Barkston
Singer, Crofter's Cline, **16/1** The Shanahan Bay, Evening Star, **20/1** Falcons Dawn, **25/1** Tulfarris, Will He Or
Wont He (IRE), **33/1** Good Time Boy. CSF £53.02, CT £607.75. Tote £6.10: £2.30 £4.50 £6.20 £1.60
(£24.20). Mr W. G. Swiers (THIRSK) bred by Viscount Leverhulme. 17 Rn
                                                    1m 42.3 (3.6)
                                              SF—38/35/15/22/4/17

**4053**    MACBETH STKS (II) (Mdn 2-Y.O) £2386.70 (£661.20: £316.10)
         **1m (AWT)**                                        3-25 (3-27)

*4017⁴* **Grog (IRE) (60)** *(MRChannon)* 9-0 LornaVincent (2) (mde all: comf) ..................... —1

Receptionist (Fav) *(HRACecil)* 8-9 WRyan (6) (w'like: bit bkwd: a chsng ldrs: rdn
along over 3f out: styd on towards fin) ...................... 2.2
Alternation (FR) *(PFICole)* 8-9 TQuinn (4) (lt-f: a in tch: hdwy u.p ent st: no imp) ...... 2.3
3908[6] Noble Singer *(HThomsonJones)* 8-9 RHills (8) (a chsng ldrs: styd on u.p fnl 2f) ...... nk.4
French Revolution (FR) *(MichaelCunningham,Ireland)* 8-10[(1)] JWilliams (9) (lt-f:
unf: s.i.s: sn rcvrd: styd on fnl 2f: nvr able to chal) ......... 1.5
4010 Free Transfer (IRE) *(PFTulk)* 9-0 MBirch (5) (lw: chsd ldrs tl outpcd fnl 2f) ............ 4.6
3701 Granite Boy **(63)** *(PJFeilden)* 9-0 CDwyer (3) (gd spd over 5f) ...................... 1.7
3982 Aide Memoire (IRE) *(CBBBooth)* 8-9 ACulhane (12) (outpcd & bhd: sme hdwy 2f
out: n.d) ................................................ hd.8
3945 Cindy's Baby *(JJO'Neill)* 8-4 ‡[5]CHodgson (11) (s.i.s: hdwy after 3f: n.d) ........ 1½.9
4016 Storm Drum *(PJMakin)* 9-0 BRaymond (1) (nvr wnt pce) ...................... ¾.10
3963[5] Winter Lightning *(PTWalwyn)* 8-9 NHowe (13) (a bhd) ........................ 2.11
3881 Expansionist (bl) *(AHide)* 9-0 MHills (7) (sn outpcd & bhd) .................... 2½.12
3780 Petty Cash *(DrJDScargill)* 8-9 GBardwell (10) (spd over 4f: wknd qckly) ........ ¾.13

**11/8** Receptionist(6/4—8/11), **5/1** Alternation (FR)(op 2/1), **6/1** GROG (IRE)(tchd 14/1), Granite Boy(op
20/1), **8/1** Noble Singer, French Revolution (FR)(op 4/1), **10/1** Expansionist(8/1—16/1), **16/1** Storm Drum,
**20/1** Winter Lightning, **25/1** Ors. CSF £16.57, Tote £10.70: £2.40 £1.10 £4.00 (£12.60). Mrs D. Hanson
(UPPER LAMBOURN) bred by Michael P. Keane in Ireland. 13 Rn　　　　1m 43.8 (4.5)
SF—3/–/–/–/–/–/–

T/Plpt: £14.90 (46.9 Tckts).　　　　　　　　　　　　　　　　　　　　　　　　CR/AA

---

4030—**LINGFIELD** (L-H) Equitrack
## Thursday, December 5th [Standard]
Going Allowance: minus 0.25 sec per fur (FS)

Stalls: 1st, 3rd & 5th high, remainder low

### 4054
DANCING FLOOR CLAIMING STKS (I)　£2324.00 (£644.00: £308.00)
**1m (AWT)**　　　　　　　　　　　　　　　　　　　　　11-40 (11-50)

4038[5] **Vanroy (80)** (v) (Fav) *(JRJenkins)* 7-9-2 JWilliams (11) (b.hind: hld up on
outside: hdwy tl led over 1f out: r.o) .......................... —1
3176 Wileys Folly **(44)** *(SDow)* 5–8-5[(4)] TQuinn (4) (a.p: ev ch over 1f out: unable
qckn) ................................................. 3.2
3909 Kirby Opportunity **(43)** *(JPearce)* 3–7-11 GBardwell (8) (outpcd & hrd rdn 4f out:
hdwy over 1f out: fin wl) .................................... nk.3
4035 State Governor **(72)** *(NACallaghan)* 3–7-11 ‡[7]JTate (3) (b: b.off hind: led over 6f) ... hd.4
4009 Quinzii Martin **(48)** *(DHaydnJones)* 3–8-8 WRyan (9) (rdn over 3f out: hdwy over
1f out: n.d) ............................................... nk.5
3885[6] Kevinsbelle **(42)** *(ICampbell)* 3–7-10 ‡[3]DBiggs (12) (prom tl wknd 2f out) ........... 3½.6
3902 Sergeant Meryll **(39)** (v) *(PHowling)* 7–8-0 ‡[5]FNorton (7) (a mid div) .............. nk.7
2819 Petivara **(43)** *(SDow)* 4–8-1 JQuinn (6) (nvr nrr) ............................... 2.8
4028 Whippet **(80)** (bl) *(CAAustin)* 7–8-11 NDay (1) (lw: gd spd 6f: wknd qckly) ...... 7.9
3885 Daisy Grey **(34)** (bl) *(ASReid)* 3–7-13[(2)] NAdams (2) (bhd fnl 3f) ................. ½.10
4038 Norma Jean *(MHTompkins)* 5–8-1 DaleGibson (10) (a bhd) ................. hd.11
4005 Sporting Heritage (IRE) (bl) *(DJGMurray-Smith)* 3–8-7 CRutter (5) (bhd fnl 5f:
t.o) ................................................ dist.12

**9/4** VANROY(3/1—2/1), **11/4** State Governor, **6/1** Kirby Opportunity(tchd 14/1), **8/1** Whippet(4/1—14/1),
**11/1** Norma Jean(7/1—12/1), **12/1** Sergeant Meryll, Wileys Folly(6/1—14/1), **16/1**
Kevinsbelle(12/1—20/1), Petivara(10/1—201/1), **33/1** Quinzii Martin, Sporting Heritage (IRE), **40/1** Daisy
Grey. CSF £29.31, Tote £3.60: £1.70 £2.10 £1.90 (£18.90). Mr Derek Garrad (ROYSTON) bred by S.
Taberner. 12 Rn　　　　　　　　　　　　　　　　　　　　1m 38.22 (1.52)
SF—49/29/20/19/29/6

### 4055
THREE HOSTAGES STKS (I)　£2108.40 (£582.40: £277.20)
**6f (AWT)**　　　　　　　　　　　　　　　　　　　　12-10 (12-17)

4036[2] **Battle Colours (IRE) (75)** (Fav) *(SirMarkPrescott)* 9-0 GDuffield (8) (lw: a.p: led
over 1f out: r.o wl) ........................................ —1
4031[4] Wilco **(56)** *(AndrewTurnell)* 9-0 RHills (6) (led 3f out tl hdd over 1f out: unable
qckn) .................................................. 3½.2
4031[3] Doesyoudoes **(65)** (v) *(DTThom)* 8-9 TQuinn (1) (plld hrd: chsd ldrs 4f: one pce) 4.3
4031 Spectacle Jim *(JO'Donoghue)* 9-0 NAdams (7) (s.s: hdwy over 1f out: r.o one
pce) ................................................... ¾.4
3964 Savalaro **(60)** *(JFfitch-Heyes)* 8-4 ‡[5]FNorton (5) (led 3f) ........................ nk.5
3872 Classic Exhibit *(AHide)* 9-0 WRyan (2) (bhd fnl 2f) ......................... 1½.6

*3963* Shapely Deb *(DRLaing)* 8-9 SWhitworth (4) (eyeshield: outpcd & hrd rdn 4f out: sn wknd) ................................................................................ 6.7
4000 Googly **(51)** *(WGRWightman)* 8-9 JWilliams (3) (a bhd) ............................................ 7.8

**8/11** BATTLE COLOURS (IRE), **9/2** Classic Exhibit, **5/1** Doesyoudoes, **14/1** Wilco, **20/1** Savalaro(op 12/1), **33/1** Googly, **50/1** Ors. CSF £10.43, Tote £1.80: £1.10 £1.80 £1.60 (£6.30). Mr Garth Insoll (NEWMARKET) bred by Stackallan Stud in Ireland. 8 Rn
1m 13.27 (2.67)
SF—16/2/–/–/–/–

---

## 4056

DANCING FLOOR CLAIMING STKS (II)  £2324.00 (£644.00: £308.00)
**1m (AWT)**
12-40 (12-44)

*3175⁶* **Crosby (75)** *(PAKelleway)* 5-8-5 TQuinn (8) (eyeshield: swtg: hdwy over 3f out: led wl over 1f out: drvn out) ............................................................. —1
*3911⁶* Say You Will **(42)** (v) *(MPNaughton)* 7-8-7 NCarlisle (9) (hdwy over 2f out: r.o wl fnl f) .......................................................................................... ½.2
3984 Les Amis **(47)** *(MJRyan)* 4—7-11 ‡³DBriggs (6) (hdwy over 2f out: r.o fnl f) ............... 2.3
*4035⁴* Spring High **(45)** (bl) *(KTIvory)* 4—7-13 NAdams (2) (led over 6f: one pce) ............... ¾.4
3897² Something Quick (IRE) **(74)** (Fav) *(RHannon)* 3—8-9 AMcGlone (5) (bhd tl hdwy over 2f out: one pce) ................................................................ 6.5
3515 Video Wall **(52)** *(SDow)* 3—7-11 ‡⁷MJermy (11) (a.p: ev ch 2f out: sn wknd) ............ hd.6
*4049⁴* Awesome Power *(MichaelCunningham,Ireland)* 5—8-7 JWilliams (4) (a mid div) ...... 4.7
2957 Old Speckled Hen **(55)** *(MJFetherston-Godley)* 3—7-6 ‡⁵FNorton (1) (prom 6f) ......... 1.8
3801 Please Please Me (IRE) **(36)** *(KOCunningham-Brown)* 3—7-11 JQuinn (7) (b: a bhd) ...................................................................................... 1½.9
*4021³* Inswinger **(45)** *(WGRWightman)* 5—8-8⁽¹⁾ SWhitworth (3) (hdwy over 4f) ............... 5.10
3832 Woodlands Grey **(28)** *(PAPritchard)* 5—8-6 GBardwell (10) (dwlt: a bhd) ............... 2.11
Melfa **(32)** (bl) *(AJDenson)* 6—8-2 RHills (12) (prom over 3f) ................................ 6.12

**11/8** Something Quick (IRE), **3/1** CROSBY, **10/1** Old Speckled Hen, Les Amis, Inswinger(6/1—11/1), **12/1** Spring High, **14/1** Awesome Power, Say You Will, **20/1** Video Wall, **33/1** Ors. CSF £43.86, Tote £5.00: £1.50 £4.40 £4.60 (£54.60). Mr R. B. Belderson (NEWMARKET) bred by Hesmonds Stud Ltd. 12 Rn
1m 39.09 (2.39)
SF—25/25/9/9/1/–

---

## 4057

RICHARD HANNAY H'CAP (0-70) £2441.60 (£677.60: £324.80)  **7f (AWT)** 1-10 (1-13)

*3966⁵* **Kissavos (49)** (v) *(CCElsey)* 5-8-4 ‡⁵FNorton (12) (hdwy over 2f out: led ins fnl f: r.o wl) ............................................................................ —1
*4035⁶* Cee-En-Cee **(61)** (bl) *(MMcCourt)* 7—9-7 TQuinn (11) (b.hind: a.p: led over 3f out tl ins fnl f: unable qckn) ..................................................... 1½.2
*4027⁵* Super Heights **(52)** (bl) *(MissAJWhitfield)* 3—8-11 DaleGibson (15) (a.p: ev ch 2f out: one pce) .......................................................... hd.3
2364³ Sarum **(48)** *(CPWildman)* 5—8-8 CRutter (4) (a.p: one pce fnl 2f) ........................... s.h.4
*4042³* Count Me Out **(50)** *(JPearce)* 6—8-10 GBardwell (3) (lw: hdwy 2f out: one pce fnl f) ....................................................................................... 2½.5
*4034⁴* Ain'tlifelikethat **(54)** (bl) *(TJNaughton)* 4—9-0 MHills (5) (b: a.p: one pce fnl 2f) ...... s.h.6
*4042* Silks Princess **(51)** *(MJRyan)* 5—8-11 GDuffield (1) (led over 1f: one pce fnl 2f) ... 1.7
3600 Vuchterbacher **(51)** *(PFTulk)* 5—8-4 ‡⁷TWilson (8) (b: a mid div) ........................... 1.8
*4039²* Mac's Princess (USA) **(64)** *(WAO'Gorman)* 3—9-4 ‡⁵EmmaO'Gorman (2) (wl bhd over 4f: hdwy over 1f out: nvr nrr) .......................... s.h.9
*4033* Ballerina Bay **(50)** (v) *(DTThom)* 3—8-6 JWilliams (14) (a bhd) .............................. 2.10
3825 Idir Linn (IRE) **(47)** *(DJGMurray-Smith)* 3—8-6 RWernham (16) (a bhd) ................. nk.11
*3966* Penando **(51)** *(EAWheeler)* 3—8-3 ‡⁷BThomas (9) (eyeshield: a bhd) ..................... ½.12
451⁶ Danzig Lad (USA) **(50)** *(MPNaughton)* 3—8-9 NCarlisle (7) (bit bkwd: bhd fnl 3f) ... 3.13
Catalani **(68)** *(TJNaughton)* 6—9-9 ‡⁵CHodgson (6) (b: b.nr hind: bit bkwd: prom over 3f) ............................................................ 1½.14
3796 Winter Pearl **(47)** *(RHannon)* 3—8-6 AMcGlone (10) (led over 5f out tl over 3f out: sn wknd) .......................................................................... nk.15
*3966* Scots Law **(52)** *(RJO'Sullivan)* 4—8-9 ‡³DBiggs (13) (a bhd) ................................. 2½.16

**11/2** KISSAVOS(6/1—10/1), **6/1** Silks Princess, **7/1** Mac's Princess (USA), Vuchterbacher, **15/2** Ballerina Bay, **8/1** Cee-En-Cee, **10/1** Count Me Out(op 5/1), Sarum, **12/1** Ain'tlifelikethat, **14/1** Super Heights(op 8/1), **16/1** Scots Law(op 10/1), Winter Pearl, **25/1** Danzig Lad (USA), **33/1** Ors. CSF £49.77, CT £550.48. Tote £9.80: £1.10 £3.60 £3.80 £2.20 (£18.60). Mr C. Arnold (LAMBOURN) bred by Falconet Inc. 16 Rn
1m 25.94 (1.94)
SF—39/46/35/31/25/28

---

## 4058

FLEURETS H'CAP (0-80) £2343.00 (£648.00: £309.00)  **5f (AWT)**   1-40 (1-42)

*4009⁶* **Sir Tasker (51)** *(JLHarris)* 3—8-5 TQuinn (5) (mde all: clr over 1f out: comf) ............. —1

4021* Pendor Dancer (54) (bl) (Fav) (BForsey) 8–8–8(3) JWilliams (8) (a.p: rdn over 1f out: unable qckn) .................................................... 3½.2

3829 Slip-a-Snip (71) (GBBalding) 4–9–11 AMcGlone (9) (a.p: hrd rdn over 1f out: one pce) ............................................................ 1½.3

4028 Tauber (72) (PatMitchell) 7–9–9 ‡3SO'Gorman (4) (hdwy wl over 1f out: one pce fnl f) ...................................................... 1.4

2253 Murmuring (52) (SDow) 5–8–3 ‡3DBiggs (7) (prom over 3f) ..................... 3.5

3768 Pigalle Wonder (48) (WHolden) 3–8–2 SDawson (6) (prom 3f) ............... 2½.6

4021⁵ Tachyon Park (48) (v) (PHowling) 9–8–2 NCarlisle (10) (outpcd) ............ 1½.7

3996 Maid Welcome (74) (bl) (MrsNMacauley) 4–10–0 SWhitworth (1) (bhd fnl 3f) ....... 2½.8

4042 Beckingham Ben (53) (bl) (JPLeigh) 7–8–7 ACulhane (2) (rdn thrght: bhd fnl 2f) ..... nk.9⁹

4021 Ever so Artistic (54) (bl) (PHowling) 4–8–3 ‡5FNorton (3) (lw: hmpd over 4f out: a bhd) ........................................................... ½.10

**100/30** Pendor Dancer, **4/1** Tauber, **7/1** Slip-a-Snip, **8/1** Maid Welcome(tchd 12/1), **10/1** Beckingham Ben, **11/1** Murmuring, **12/1** SIR TASKER & Ors. CSF £47.66, CT £276.78. Tote £11.30: £2.10 £1.10 £3.40 (£38.70). Mr C. Conway (MELTON MOWBRAY) bred by W. H. Joyce. 10 Rn 59.47 sec (1.27) SF–41/30/41/35/3/–

---

**4059** GREENMANTLE H'CAP (0–70) £2304.40 (£638.40: £305.20)
**1m 5f (AWT)** 2-10 (2-11)

4034⁵ **Scotoni (58)** (Fav) (RJO'Sullivan) 5–9–7 ‡3DBiggs (5) (a.p: chsd ldr over 3f out: hrd rdn fnl 2f: led last stride) ........................ —1

3413⁶ Sailor Boy (61) (RAkehurst) 5–9–13 TQuinn (2) (lw: led 3f: led 5f out: hrd rdn over 2f out: hdd last stride) ............................... s.h.2

3968³ Windsor Park (USA) (47) (KSBridgwater) 5–8–13 JWilliams (13) (hdwy over 3f out: r o one pce fnl 2f) ...................................... 7.3

3968 Bronze Runner (40) (EAWheeler) 7–7–13 ‡7BThomas (4) (eyeshield: hdwy 4f out: one pce fnl 2f) ............................................. 1½.4

4026* Duggan (62) (RJRWilliams) 4–10–0 NDay (3) (hdwy over 3f out: one pce fnl 2f) ...... nk.5

4032* Storm Orphan (40) (MissBSanders) 4–8–6 (5x) DaleGibson (9) (hdwy 6f out: one pce fnl 2f) ................................................ nk.6

4030⁵ Shar Emblem (48) (SDow) 3–8–1 ‡7MJermy (14) (hdwy fnl 2f: nvr nrr) ..................... 10.7

3212 Daddy's Darling (46) (JTGifford) 6–8–12 RHills (15) (lw: nvr nr to chal) ........................ 3½.8

3967 Al Shareef (42) (DBurchell) 6–8–8 GBardwell (16) (prom 10f) ............. 5.9

4003⁶ Coolness (USA) (55) (JHMGosden) 3–9–1 MHills (6) (prom over 9f) ..... 4.10

4032³ Lord Advocate (42) (v) (PMNaughton) 3–8–2 NCarlisle (1) (lw: prom 9f) ............... hd.11

3968 Paint the Lily (49) (DCJermy) 3–8–9 TSprake (12) (bhd fnl 4f) .................. hd.12

3950 Malenoir (USA) (56) (WJPearce) 3–9–2 MBirch (8) (b.hind: bhd fnl 4f) .................. 3.13

3864 Gibbot (36) (bl) (PHowling) 6–7–11 ‡5FNorton (11) (led 10f out to 5f out: wknd over 3f out) ................................................ 2.14

3783 Spirit Level (50) (CRBarwell) 3–8–10 NAdams (10) (bhd fnl 6f: t.o) ................ dist.15

**11/4** SCOTONI, **9/2** Storm Orphan(op 9/4), **13/2** Duggan(5/1—8/1), **15/2** Sailor Boy, **11/1** Windsor Park (USA)(8/1—12/1), Lord Advocate, **12/1** Daddy's Darling, **14/1** Spirit Level, Bronze Runner, **16/1** Shar Emblem(op 10/1—20/1), Coolness (USA)(op 10/1), **20/1** Malenoir (USA), Al Shareef, **25/1** Gibbot, **33/1** Paint the Lily. CSF £25.29, CT £198.08. Tote £4.80: £3.10 £3.50 £2.70 (£18.00). Mr R. J. O'Sullivan (BOGNOR REGIS) bred by M. J. Simmonds. 15 Rn 2m 46.88 (3.38) SF–41/46/18/1/29/6

---

**4060** THIRTY NINE STEPS H'CAP (0–90) £2646.60 (£732.60: £349.80)
**1¼m (AWT)** 2-40 (2-41)

3967* **Crossillion (81)** (GWragg) 3–9–3 ‡5FNorton (7) (gd hdwy over 2f out: led ins fnl f: r.o wl) ................................................. —1

4018 Rapporteur (USA) (83) (CCElsey) 5–10–0 JWilliams (6) (b: hdwy 4f out: hrd rdn over 3f out: ev ch ins fnl f: unable qckn) ...................... 1½.2

4033* Princess Roxanne (50) (bl) (Fav) (ABailey) 4–7–9(1) JQuinn (8) (a.p: led 2f out tl ins fnl f: one pce) ................................... 2.3

3632³ Premier Dance (53) (DHaydnJones) 4–7–12 DaleGibson (1) (hdwy 3f out: one pce fnl 2f) ...................................................... ¾.4

3991 Bengal Tiger (IRE) (53) (JAkehurst) 3–7–5(1) ‡3JFanning (10) (b.nr fore: a.p: hrd rdn over 3f out: wknd over 1f out) ......................... 2.5

4018 Northern Flyer (68) (PTWalwyn) 3–8–9 MBirch (4) (prom 6f) ....................... 1½.6

3967² Belmoredean (73) (RJO'Sullivan) 6–9–1 ‡3DBiggs (2) (led 8f) ................... 2½.7

3925* Scales of Justice (82) (JWHills) 3–9–13 RHills (9) (hdwy 5f out: wknd 2f out) .......... s.h.8

1065³ Sianema (70) (DRLaing) 3–8–11 SWhitworth (3) (b: a bhd) ...................... 10.9

4026 Sunflower Seed (48) (PJMakin) 4–7–7 GBardwell (5) (prom 5f: t.o) ............... 25.10

LONG HANDICAP: Bengal Tiger (IRE) 7-5, Sunflower Seed 6-13.

**7/4** Princess Roxanne, **100/30** Scales of Justice, **6/1** CROSSILLION(4/1—7/1), Belmoredean, **7/1** Rapporteur (USA), **10/1** Bengal Tiger (IRE)(tchd 20/1), **20/1** Premier Dance, **50/1** Ors. CSF £44.55, CT £93.56. Tote £7.00: £2.60 £1.50 £1.80 (£19.20). Mr G. Wragg (NEWMARKET) bred by Hascombe and Valiant Studs. 10 Rn    2m 6.03 (3.03)
SF—48/56/19/20/9/24

## 4061
THREE HOSTAGES STKS (II) (Mdn 2-Y.O) £2108.40 (£582.40: £277.20)
**6f (AWT)**    3-10 (3-11)

| | | | |
|---|---|---|---|
| 3945³ | **Burning Point (IRE) (73)** (Fav) (SirMarkPrescott) 9-0 GDuffield (2) (lw: mde all: hrd rdn over 1f out: r.o wl) | —1 |
| 4036³ | Jaromic **(60)** (PFTulk) 9-0 MBirch (6) (b: a.p: chsd wnr over 3f out: r.o) | 2.2 |
| 3497 | Anna Manana **(63)** (WJPearce) 8-9 DaleGibson (7) (outpcd: nvr nr to chal) | 10.3 |
| 3340 | Flat Rate **(50)** (JWhite) 8-4 ‡⁵FNorton (1) (spd over 3f) | ½.4 |
| | Minoan Light (IRE) (RHannon) 9-0 AMcGlone (5) (w'like: bit bkwd: s.s: t.o 4f: nvr nrr) | nk.5 |
| 3562 | Wild Persian (IRE) (PatMitchell) 8-9 ASkingle (4) (a bhd) | 4.6 |
| 4022³ | Watersong (DRLaing) 8-9 SWhitworth (3) (p.u 5f out: broke leg: dead) | 0 |

**10/11** BURNING POINT (IRE), **7/2** Watersong(op 8/1), **5/1** Anna Manana, **7/1** Minoan Light (IRE)(op 3/1), **12/1** Jaromic, **16/1** Flat Rate(op 10/1), **40/1** Wild Persian (IRE). CSF £12.22, Tote £1.80: £1.40 £2.30 (£4.50). Mrs David Thompson (NEWMARKET) bred by Chippenham Lodge Stud. 7 Rn    1m 14.35 (3.75)
T/Plpt: £123.70 (6.4 Tckts).    SM/AK

---

4046—**SOUTHWELL (L-H)** Fibresand
## Thursday, December 12th [Standard]
Going Allowance: 5f: minus 0.15 sec; Rest: 0.05 sec per fur (FS)    Wind: nil   Vis: poor

Stalls: high

## 4062
MANSFIELD CIVIC THEATRE CLAIMING STKS (I)    £2407.00 (£667.00: £319.00)
**1½m (AWT)**    12-00 (12-02)

| | | | |
|---|---|---|---|
| 4026² | **Magic Secret (70)** (Fav) (PCHaslam) 3-8-7 ‡³JFanning (12) (lw: a.p: led over 3f out: pushed out) | —1 |
| 4025⁵ | Grey Commander **(39)** (MBrittain) 3-7-12(3) ‡⁵SMaloney (1) (rdn & gd hdwy 5f out: 5th st: r.o ins fnl f) | 2.2 |
| 3136 | Qualitair Flyer **(26)** (JFBottomley) 9-8-7 GBardwell (10) (gd hdwy 5f out: 2nd st: one pce fnl 2f) | 6.3 |
| 4032 | Swagman (USA) **(41)** (CRBeever) 4-8-4(1) ‡⁵CHodgson (4) (bhd: sn rdn along: hdwy 4f out: 4th st: wknd over 1f out) | hd.4 |
| 4038 | Corporate Type (IRE) **(35)** (DWChapman) 3-7-13 SWood (7) (mde most over 8f: 3rd st: wknd 2f out) | 5.5 |
| | Star Oats (GRichards) 5-8-7 JQuinn (2) (prom 8f) | s.h.6 |
| 3494³ | Free Minx **(52)** (MrsVAAconley) 5-8-4 ‡⁷GParkin (6) (rdn 6f out: n.d) | 8.7 |
| 4030* | Adjacent (IRE) **(58)** (MDixon) 3-8-0 RFox (8) (disp ld 7f: wknd over 3f out) | 1.8 |
| 4045² | Shaurni Girl (RVKing) 3-8-10 VSmith (13) (chsd ldrs 8f) | 3½.9 |
| 3618 | Mara Askari **(69)** (JLHarris) 3-8-5 TQuinn (11) (prom tl 6th & wkng st) | ½.10 |
| 4045⁶ | Ballater Lass (IRE) **(40)** (JWharton) 3-7-12 DaleGibson (3) (a bhd: t.o) | 12.11 |
| 4041⁶ | Temple Island (IRE) **(58)** (PJMakin) 3-8-3(1) TSprake (5) (hrd rdn 5f out: bhd fnl 4f: t.o) | ½.12 |
| | Rodmarton (APJarvis) 4-8-4 NAdams (9) (bhd fnl 4f: t.o) | 1½.13 |

**6/4** MAGIC SECRET, **5/2** Adjacent (IRE), **6/1** Mara Askari, **10/1** Shaurni Girl, **16/1** Free Minx, Rodmarton, **20/1** Temple Island (IRE), Grey Commander, Swagman (USA), **25/1** Star Oats, **33/1** Ors. CSF £32.87, Tote £3.00: £1.60 £9.50 £7.50 (£48.00). Hambleton Thoroughbreds Plc (MIDDLEHAM) bred by Gainsborough Stud Management Ltd. 13 Rn    2m 43.8 (9.6)
SF—3/-/-/-/-/-

## 4063
ALADDIN H'CAP (0-70) £2447.60 (£678.60: £324.80)    **5f (AWT)**    12-30 (12-35)

| | | | |
|---|---|---|---|
| 4021² | **Imco Double (IRE) (51)** (CNAllen) 3-8-10 JMcLaughlin (17) (a.p: led wl over 1f out: comf) | —1 |
| 4026⁶ | Meeson Times **(49)** (BEllison) 3-8-8 DMcKeown (15) (a.p: r.o fnl f: nt trble wnr) | 2½.2 |
| 4005⁴ | Drummer's Dream (IRE) **(43)** (MrsNMacauley) 3-7-13 ‡³DBiggs (11) (hdwy over 1f out: r.o) | 1½.3 |
| 4021⁴ | Barbara's Cutie **(43)** (MBlanshard) 3-8-2 JQuinn (18) (led over 3f) | s.h.4 |
| 4058⁸² | Pendor Dancer **(51)** (bl) (Fav) (BForsey) 8-8-10 JWilliams (13) (no hdwy fnl 2f) | nk.5 |
| 3947² | Shedad (USA) **(55)** (TDBarron) 3-9-0 AlexGreaves (8) (nvr nr to chal) | 1½.6 |

*4021* Lady of the Fen **(66)** *(MrsNMacauley)* 3-9-4 ‡[7]SWilliams (2) (led far side: wknd fnl f) ................................................. ½.7
3876 Strip Cartoon (IRE) **(35)** (bl) *(SRBowring)* 3-7-8[(1)] NAdams (7) (prom 3f) ................ 1.8
*4009* Able Princess **(45)** (bl) *(MrsNMacauley)* 3-7-11 ‡[7]JMarshall (10) (n.d) .................. ½.9
*4058*\* Sir Tasker **(58)** *(JLHarris)* 3-9-3 (7x) TQuinn (3) (prom over 3f) ......................... ½.10
4057 Penando **(51)** (bl) *(EAWheeler)* 3-8-10 TSprake (16) (n.d) ............................ hd.11
*4042*\* Cronk's Courage **(64)** (v) *(EJAlston)* 5-9-9 MHills (5) (unruly s: n.d) ................ nk.12
4042 Very Bold **(53)** *(PDEvans)* 3-8-12 DaleGibson (4) (prom 3f) ........................ s.h.13
*2758*3 Sobering Thoughts **(43)** (bl) *(DWChapman)* 5-8-2 SWood (4) (bit bkwd: chsd ldrs 3f) ................................................. ½.14
*3966*6 Goldvein (SWE) **(64)** (bl) *(WAO'Gorman)* 3-9-9 DNicholls (6) (lw: prom 3f) ......... ¾.15
*4005* Oratel Flyer **(34)** (bl) *(RThompson)* 4-7-7 RFox (12) (n.d) ............................ 1.16
3946 Johanna Thyme **(52)** *(RBastiman)* 4-8-4[(8)] ‡[7]HBastiman (9) (lw: sn wl bhd) ....... 2.17
*4045* Green's Bonheur **(43)** *(MPNaughton)* 3-7-13 ‡[3]JFanning (14) (sn wl bhd: t.o) ...... **18**

**5/1** Pendor Dancer(tchd 8/1) **6/1** Sobering Thoughts, Sir Tasker, **9/1** Shedad (USA), **10/1** Barbara's Cutie, Lady of the Fen, Cronk's Courage, **12/1** Meeson Times, IMCO DOUBLE (IRE)(op 8/1), **14/1** Goldvein (SWE), **16/1** Very Bold(10/1—20/1), Johanna Thyme, Green's Bonheur, **20/1** Strip Cartoon (IRE), Drummer's Dream (IRE), Able Princess, **33/1** Ors. CSF £151.74, CT £2,637.97. Tote £56.90: £7.30 £3.20 £7.00 £3.20 (£155.80). Mrs L. Ahmet (NEWMARKET) bred by Ardoon Stud in Ireland. 18 Rn  59.9 sec (1.9)
SF—43/31/16/18/25/23

---

**4064**　MANSFIELD CIVIC THEATRE CLAIMING STKS (II)　£2407.00 (£667.00: £319.00)
**1½m (AWT)**　1-00 (1-01)

*4054*3 **Kirby Opportunity (43)** *(JPearce)* 3-7-7 GBardwell (2) (a.p: wnt 2nd st: r.o u.p to ld nr fin) ......................................... —1
*4038*2 Irish Native (IRE) **(66)** (bl) *(CASmith)* 3-8-5 ‡[5]CHodgson (3) (led: hrd rdn over 1f out: hdd nr fin) ................................ nk.2
3822 Flash Bulb **(42)** *(JHetherton)* 4-8-4 LCharnock (6) (lw: hdwy 6f out: 4th st: one pce fnl 2f) ......................................... 10.3
*4052*6 Tempering **(83)** (Fav) *(DWChapman)* 5-9-5 SWood (10) (lw: prom: 3rd st: wknd 2f out) ................................................. 4.4
4041 Qualitair Sweetie **(42)** *(JFBottomley)* 4-8-7 JQuinn (9) (hdwy 6f out: poor 5th & wkng st) ................................................. 15.5
*3889*6 Brantfell **(44)** *(TFairhurst)* 3-7-9 ‡[3]JFanning (7) (prom 9f) ....................... hd.6
　La Reine Rouge (IRE) *(PJMakin)* 3-8-5 TSprake (11) (lengthy: hdwy 6f out: poor 6th st: t.o) ................................................. 8.7
2334 Top Spinner *(DHaydnJones)* 3-7-9 RFox (8) (a bhd: t.o) ........................ 2½.8
*4030*6 Line Drummer (USA) *(PAKelleway)* 3-8-5 TQuinn (4) (eyeshield: b: prom 9f: t.o) ...... 5.9
*4004*2 Tristiorum **(58)** (bl) *(WClay)* 4-8-7 ACulhane (12) (bhd fnl 6f: t.o) .............. ½.10
462 Moon Reef **(45)** *(CDBroad)* 5-7-13 NAdams (5) (b: a in rr: t.o) ................. 8.11
*Stewards Enquiry: Hodgson suspended 27/12/91-11/1/92 (excessive use of whip)*

**5/6** Tempering, **7/2** Irish Native (IRE), **7/1** KIRBY OPPORTUNITY(op 3/1), **8/1** Tristiorum(op 5/1), **16/1** Line Drummer (USA), **25/1** La Reine Rouge (IRE), Flash Bulb, Moon Reef, **33/1** Ors. CSF £31.95, Tote £6.20: £2.40 £1.30 £4.00 (£7.40). Mr Peter Bradley (NEWMARKET) bred by Highfield Stud Ltd. 11 Rn
2m 40.9 (6.7)
SF—18/29/8/15/–/–

---

**4065**　PACEMAKER UPDATE INTERNATIONAL H'CAP (0-100)　£2305.50 (£638.00: £304.50)
**7f (AWT)**　1-30 (1-31)

3891 **Super Benz (78)** *(TFairhurst)* 5-8-10 ‡[3]JFanning (8) (mde all: clr 3f out: unchal) ...... —1
1977 Dorset Duke **(85)** *(GWragg)* 4-9-6 MHills (4) (b: 4th st: rdn & r.o on pce fnl 2f) ......... 4.2
*4028*5 Brown Fairy (USA) **(70)** *(MrsNMacauley)* 3-8-1 ‡[3]DBiggs (7) (lw: 5th st: r.o one pce fnl 2f) ......................................... 2½.3
3925 Mac's Fighter **(93)** (bl) *(WAO'Gorman)* 6-10-0 DMcKeown (2) (6th st: no hdwy fnl 2f) ................................................. 7.4
3925 Mystic Crystal (IRE) **(82)** (bl) *(WAO'Gorman)* 3-8-11 ‡[5]EmmaO'Gorman (9) (chsd wnr: 2nd st: wknd 2f out) ................ hd.5
*4052*\* Euroblake **(79)** (Fav) *(TDBarron)* 4-9-0 (7x) AlexGreaves (3) (lw: hld up & bhd: nvr nr ldrs) ................................... 2.6
*4006* Mimining **(60)** *(GMMoore)* 5-7-9[(2)] JQuinn (6) (lw: 3rd st: wknd 2f out) ............... 5.7
*2725*\* Spanish Love **(59)** *(MMcCormack)* 5-7-8[(1)] GBardwell (1) (sn wl bhd) ............. 1½.8
3724 Sobriety **(58)** (bl) *(MBJames)* 6-7-7 SWood (5) (dwlt: t.o) ........................ 12.9
LONG HANDICAP: Mimining 6-11, Spanish Love 5-10, Sobriety 5-10.

**7/2** Euroblake, **4/1** SUPER BENZ, Brown Fairy, **5/1** Dorset Duke, **6/1** Mac's Fighter(4/1—13/2), **15/2** Mystic Crystal (IRE)(op 5/1), **20/1** Mimining, **33/1** Ors. CSF £22.51, CT £74.87. Tote £4.10: £2.20 £2.90 £1.90 (£10.10). Mr David F. Bramley (MIDDLEHAM) bred by Scarteen Stud. 9 Rn
1m 30.9 (4.3)
SF—42/40/11/17/–/–

**4066**　　WISHY WASHY STKS (Mdn 2-Y.O) £2447.60 (£678.60: £324.80)
　　　　　**7f (AWT)**　　　　　　　　　　　　　　　　　　2-00 (2-05)

| | |
|---|---|
| 496² | **Donegal Dandy (IRE)** (Jt-Fav) *(JARToller)* 9-0　DaleGibson (8) (stumbled s: 4th st: led 1f out: r.o) .................................................. —1 |
| 4046 | Cellito (IRE) *(WAO'Gorman)* 9-0　JWilliams (7) (hdwy & 5th st: r.o ins fnl f) ............... 1.2 |
| 4010⁴ | Cold Shower (IRE) (Jt-Fav) *(JAGlover)* 8-7 ‡⁷SWilliams (2) (w ldr: 2nd st: ev ch over 1f out: nt qckn) .................................. 3½.3 |
| 4051 | Another Nut (44) *(PDEvans)* 8-9　NAdams (1) (led over 5f: sn wknd) ...................... 1.4 |
| | Golden Sickle (USA) (Jt-Fav) *(WAO'Gorman)* 8-9 ‡⁵EmmaO'Gorman (10) (w'like: bit bkwd: 3rd st: led over 1f out: sn hdd & wknd) ................ 3.5 |
| 4053 | Cindy's Baby *(JJO'Neill)* 8-4 ‡⁵CHodgson (13) (nvr nr to chal) ............................... 1.6 |
| | For All Time *(LordHuntingdon)* 8-9　DMcKeown (6) (w'like: scope: bit bkwd: nvr trbld ldrs) ................................ s.h.7 |
| 3630⁶ | Tazamisha *(RHollinshead)* 8-9　MHills (3) (n.d) .................................... hd.8 |
| | Heavyweight (IRE) *(SirMarkPrescott)* 9-0　GDuffield (12) (wl grwn: bkwd: 6th st: wknd 2f out) .................................. 1½.9 |
| | Ergon *(PJFeilden)* 8-9　CDwyer (4) (lengthy: unf: n.d) ................................ 6.10 |
| 3805⁵ | Gay Ming *(RHollinshead)* 8-2 ‡⁷AGarth (5) (n.d) .................................... 1½.11 |
| | Barryben *(WMBrisbourne)* 9-0　AProud (11) (bkwd: t.o) ............................... 12 |
| | Counter Blast *(WHolden)* 8-2 ‡⁷BRussell (9) (lengthy: bkwd: t.o) ..................... 13 |

**9/2** Golden Sickle (USA)(7/1—4/1), DONEGAL DANDY (IRE)(14/1—4/1), Cold Shower (IRE), **5/1** Heavyweight (IRE)(op 5/2), **7/1** For All Time(op 7/4), **8/1** Cellito (IRE)(6/1—10/1), **11/1** Tazamisha, **20/1** Gay Ming, Counter Blast, **33/1** Ors. CSF £38.04. Tote £5.30: £1.90 £3.00 £1.70 (£48.20). Mr S. R. Bullard (NEWMARKET) bred by Deepwood Farm Stud in Ireland. 13 Rn　　　　　　　1m 33.7 (7.1)
　　　　　　　　　　　　　　　　　　　　　　　　　　　　　　SF—4/1/–/–/–/–

**4067**　　LARRY GRAYSON NURSERY　£2366.40 (£655.40: £313.20)　6f (AWT)　2-30 (2-30)
　　　　　　　　　　　　(Weights raised 2 lb)

| | |
|---|---|
| 38205 | **Meltonby (58)** *(JHetherton)* 7-5(1) ‡³JFanning (8) (lw: 3rd st: led over 1f out: drvn out) .................................. —1 |
| 4051* | Runnel (65) (Jt-Fav) *(DWChapman)* 8-11 (7x)　SWood (7) (5th & rdn st: hung lft 1f out: nt qckn) ........................... 1½.2 |
| 4031* | Inherent Magic (IRE) (68) (Jt-Fav) *(MMcCormack)* 8-4　AClark (2) (lw: 2nd st: led over 2f out tl over 1f out: nt qckn) ................. 2.3 |
| 4051 | Miss Narnia (57) *(APJarvis)* 7-0 ‡⁷SHawkes (3) (4th st: one pce fnl 2f) ...................... 1.4 |
| 4043 | Profit Stream (58) *(MWEasterby)* 7-8(1)　LCharnock (6) (6th st: hdwy 2f out: nt rch ldrs) ................................ 1.5 |
| 3985 | Dublin Rainbow (59) *(MBrittain)* 7-9(2)　JQuinn (1) (led over 3f: sn wknd: t.o) ............. 15.6 |
| 4010 | Element Ofsurprise (61) *(CaptJWilson)* 7-6(4) ‡⁵DHarrison (5) (outpcd: t.o) ................. 8.7 |
| | LONG HANDICAP: Meltonby 7-4, Miss Narnia 7-0, Profit Stream 7-6, Dublin Rainbow 6-12, Element Ofsurprise 6-9. |

**2/1** Inherent Magic (IRE), Runnel, **100/30** MELTONBY, **8/1** Profit Stream(op 12/1), **16/1** Miss Narnia, **33/1** Dublin Rainbow, **50/1** Element Ofsurprise. CSF £9.78, CT £13.64. Tote £3.90: £1.70 £1.70 (£5.80). Mr J. Hetherton (MALTON) bred by Woodd{t}ton Stud Ltd. 7 Rn　　　　　　　1m 18.2 (4.8)

**4068**　　WIDOW TWANKY H'CAP (0-70) £2508.50 (£696.00: £333.50)　1m (AWT)　3-00 (3-03)

| | |
|---|---|
| 4052⁵ | **Golden Chip (IRE) (62)** *(APStringer)* 3-9-11　SWebster (5) (4th st: r.o u.p to ld last strides) ........................... —1 |
| 4057 | Silks Princess (50) *(MJRyan)* 5-9-1　JMcLaughlin (10) (lw: led 6f out tl hdd last strides) ................................ nk.2 |
| 4057 | Mac's Princess (USA) (64) *(WAO'Gorman)* 3-9-8 ‡⁵EmmaO'Gorman (3) (b.nr hind: hdwy over 1f out: r.o ins fnl f) ............... 2½.3 |
| 4027⁴ | Kristis Girl (61) *(DHaydnJones)* 4–9-12　AClark (8) (2nd st: one pce fnl 2f) ................. 2.4 |
| 4035 | On Y Va (USA) (52) *(RJRWilliams)* 4-8-12 ‡⁵CHodgson (13) (b.nr hind: 3rd st: wknd over 1f out) ........................ ¾.5 |
| 3832² | Sandmoor Denim (49) *(SRBowring)* 4–9-0　AProud (4) (lw: hdwy & 6th st: nvr nr to chal) ................................ 3½.6 |
| 4027² | Kinlacey (59) *(BAMcMahon)* 4–9-3 ‡⁷SSanders (14) (5th st: wknd over 1f out) ...... 1½.7 |
| 4052³ | Evening Star (58) (Fav) *(AHide)* 5–9-9　JWilliams (11) (lw: hdwy & 8th st: nt rch ldrs) ................................ 2.8 |
| 4042 | Stoneleigh Abbey (IRE) (50) (bl) *(RDEWoodhouse)* 3-8-13　SWhitworth (7) (bhd tl sme late hdwy) .......................... 3.9 |
| 4052 | Diamond Inthe Dark (USA) (65) *(CTinkler)* 3–10-0　MBirch (17) (chsd ldrs: 7th & rdn st: sn wknd) ......................... 2.10 |
| 4049³ | Swingaway Lady (62) (bl) *(GRichards)* 3-9-11　DMcKeown (15) (eyeshield: n.d) .... hd.11 |
| 4034 | I'Ll Soon Know (52) *(BPalling)* 4–9-3　JQuinn (1) (n.d) ............................ 1½.12 |
| 4033³ | Miss Mirror (58) *(WJHaggas)* 3–9-7　MHills (12) (led 2f: rdn & wknd over 3f out) ...... 2.13 |

3984 Miss Broughton **(52)** *(WJMusson)* 3–9-1 JHBrown (6) (a bhd) ................................ 3.14
3771 Warrior Prince **(52)** *(RMWhitaker)* 3–9-1 ACulhane (16) (chsd ldrs 3f) ................ 1½.15
    4027 Stairway to Heaven (IRE) (20/1) Withdrawn (ref to ent stalls) : not under orders

**3/1** Evening Star(op 6/1), **7/1** Miss Mirror, **8/1** Sandmoor Denim, Silks Princess, Kristis Girl, **10/1** Kinlacey(op 6/1), On Y Va (USA), Mac's Princess (USA), **12/1** GOLDEN CHIP (IRE), **16/1** Swingaway Lady, Diamond Inthe Dark (USA), **20/1** Miss Broughton, **25/1** I'Ll Soon Know, **33/1** Ors. CSF £103.20, CT £925.81. Tote £20.20: £5.60 £4.50 £2.70 (£37.40). Mr A. H. Jackson (THIRSK) bred by C. and J. Sandys and Barbara McCourt in Ireland. 15 Rn
        1m 44.2 (4.9)
        SF—44/33/32/30/14/5

T/Plpt: £297.10 (5.3 Tckts).        KH

---

4054—**LINGFIELD (L-H)** Equitrack

## Saturday, December 14th [Standard]

Going Allowance: minus 0.40 sec per fur (FS)        Vis: mod races 1-7, poor race 8

**4069**    NORTHERN RACING SERVICES CLAIMING STKS (I) (Mdn) £2324.00 (£644.00: £308.00)
        1¼m (AWT)        12-00 (12-01)

*4059* Lord Advocate (42) (v) *(MPNaughton)* 3–8-1 ‡³JFanning (3) (a.p: led over 3f out: drvn out) ................................................. —1
*4045⁵* Hepburn (IRE) **(42)** *(MJFetherston-Godley)* 3–7-8 ‡⁵DHarrison (1) (led over 6f: hrd rdn & rallied over 1f out: edgd rt: r.o) ................................. 1½.2
    Athclare (IRE) (bl) (Jt-Fav) *(JAkehurst)* 3–8-7 DMcKeown (9) (a.p: r.o one pce fnl 3f) ................................. nk.3
*4030⁴* Pleasure Ahead **(46)** *(MRChannon)* 4–8-7 LornaVincent (14) (dwlt: bhd tl gd hdwy over 1f out: fin wl) ................................. hd.4
*4038⁴* Noted Strain (IRE) **(52)** *(PJMakin)* 3–8-3 TSprake (13) (hdwy over 5f out: one pce fnl 3f) ................................. ½.5
*4041²* Gipsy King **(61)** (bl) *(PAKelleway)* 3–8-10 TQuinn (10) (mid div tl styd on fnl 2f) ........ 2.6
33595 Kir (IRE) **(62)** (Jt-Fav) *(MMcCormack)* 3–8-7 AClark (12) (hrd rdn & hdwy 7f out: wknd over 3f out) ................................. 8.7
3997 Don't Cry **(53)** *(JDBethell)* 3–8-2 DaleGibson (5) (rdn thrght: nvr nr) ................................. 1½.8
*4054* Quiet Victory **(44)** *(MissLCSiddall)* 4–8-1 ‡³SO'Gorman (2) (lw: prom 5f) ................. s.h.9
3706 Hold Fast (IRE) **(45)** *(HCandy)* 3–8-3 CRutter (7) (prom 5f) ................................. 4.10
2806⁴ Ma Petite Chou **(35)** *(PHayward)* 4–7-9 ‡⁵FNorton (11) (bhd fnl 4f) ................................. 4.11
3053 Zaxis **(37)** (v) *(ASReid)* 3–7-9⁽¹⁾ JQuinn (6) (rdn 5f out: sn wknd) ................................. ¾.12
    Wise Friend (USA) *(CPWildman)* 3–8-3 NAdams (4) (rdn thrght: a bhd) ................................. 2.13
2351 Prince Bollinger **(36)** (bl) *(CLPopham)* 4–8-3 RFox (8) (a bhd: t.o fnl 7f) ................ dist.14

**100/30** Kir (IRE)(2/1—7/2), Athclare (IRE), **9/2** Gipsy King(4/1—6/1), **8/1** Pleasure Ahead(tchd 12/1), Noted Strain (IRE), **12/1** Quiet Victory, **16/1** Hepburn (IRE)(12/1—20/1), **20/1** LORD ADVOCATE, **25/1** Zaxis, Ma Petite Chou, Hold Fast (IRE), **33/1** Ors. CSF £274.86, Tote £29.20: £4.70 £3.90 £3.20 (Wnr or 2nd w any £7.40). Mr W. J. Kelly (RICHMOND) bred by London Thoroughbred Services Ltd. 14 Rn    2m 7.74 (4.74)

**4070**    LYDIA STKS (I) (Mdn 2-Y-O) £2206.40 (£610.40: £291.20)  **7f (AWT)**  12-30 (12-32)

3990 **Parlemo (IRE)** *(JDBethell)* 9-0 DMcKeown (5) (lw: hdwy 3f out: str run fnl f: led nr fin) ................................. —1
*4015³* Honey Vision **(62)** (bl) *(GHEden)* 8-9 JWilliams (8) (s.i.s: gd hdwy to ld over 5f out: clr over 2f out: ct nr fin) ................................. 1½.2
*4053* Granite Boy **(63)** *(PJFeilden)* 9-0 CDwyer (2) (prom tl lost pl 5f out: gd hdwy over 1f out: r.o) ................................. 2½.3
3872³ Courtenay Bee (Fav) *(WJarvis)* 9-0 NDay (6) (a.p: one pce fnl 3f) ................................. hd.4
    Mediator *(PFICole)* 9-0 TQuinn (4) (w'like: scope: rdn thrght: nvr nr to chal) ............. 2.5
*4036⁴* Walkonthemoon *(MMcCormack)* 8-9 AClark (1) (led over 1f: rdn & wknd 3f out) ....... 3.6
3092⁵ Atyaaf (USA) *(MJHeaton-Ellis)* 8-9 DaleGibson (7) (lw: a mid div) ................................. 1.7
*4061⁴* Flat Rate **(50)** *(JWhite)* 8-4 ‡⁵FNorton (10) (lw: prom to ½-wy) ................................. 3½.8
*4046* Briginski *(JWPayne)* 8-9 ASkingle (3) (a bhd: t.o) ................................. 20.9
    Plan More Action (IRE) *(JAkehurst)* 9-0 JCurant (9) (leggy: lw: dwlt: a wl bhd: t.o) ....... 4.10

**11/8** Courtenay Bee(10/11—6/4), **9/2** Granite Boy(10/1—4/1), **6/1** Mediator(op 9/4), **8/1** Honey Vision(tchd 12/1), **10/1** Atyaaf (USA)(8/1—14/1), **16/1** Walkonthemoon, **20/1** PARLEMO (IRE), Plan More Action (IRE)(op 12/1), **33/1** Flat Rate, **50/1** Briginski. CSF £149.81, Tote £13.20: £4.50 £2.30 £3.10 (£89.30). Mr P. T. Yu (DIDCOT) bred by John O'Connor in Ireland. 10 Rn    1m 26.16 (2.16)
        SF—25/15/12/11/5/–

**4071**    ATROPOS H'CAP (0-100) £2914.60 (£805.60: £383.80)  **6f (AWT)**  1-00 (1-01)
        (Weights raised 6 lb)

*4049²* **African Chimes (78)** (bl) *(WAO'Gorman)* 4–9-0 ‡⁵EmmaO'Gorman (3) (hld up: eased out wl over 1f out: led 1f out: comf) ................................. —1

3900⁵ Respectable Jones **(83)** *(GBBalding)* 5–9-10 JWilliams (7) (bhd tl hdwy over 1f out: r.o) ........................................................................................... 3½.2

4020 Assignment **(78)** *(JFfitch-Heyes)* 5–9-5 TQuinn (1) (b.hind: led 1f: led 3f out: hdd 1f out: one pce) ......................................................................... hd.3

4028³ Pretonic **(69)** (Jt-Fav) *(MJohnston)* 3–8-10 RPElliott (4) (lw: no hdwy fnl 2f) ......... 2½.4

3807 Toshiba Comet **(82)** (bl) *(WJPearce)* 4–9-9 DMcKeown (5) (a.p: rdn 3f out: wknd over 1f out) .................................................................................. ½.5

4058⁴ Tauber **(69)** (Jt-Fav) *(PatMitchell)* 7–8-7 ‡³SO'Gorman (2) (led 5f out: hdd 3f out: wknd over 1f out) ............................................................. ½.6

4042 Erik Odin **(56)** *(MrsLPiggott)* 4–7-6⁽⁴⁾ ‡⁵FNorton (6) (eyeshield: b.hind: outpcd) ......... 7.7

110 Domino Trick **(53)** *(AMoore)* 3–7-8⁽¹⁾ GBardwell (8) (a bhd) ............................... 15.8

LONG HANDICAP: Erik Odin 7-2.

**7/2** Tauber(op 9/4), Pretonic, **4/1** Assignment, **11/2** Toshiba Comet, **6/1** AFRICAN CHIMES(7/2—7/1), **8/1** Respectable Jones, **16/1** Erik Odin, **50/1** Domino Trick. CSF £45.91, CT £191.91. Tote £6.90: £1.60 £2.40 £1.40 (£32.00). Mr D. G. Wheatley (NEWMARKET) bred by Noel Cogan. 8 Rn      1m 11.97 (1.37)
SF—25/34/15/–/7/–

---

**4072** HOTSPUR H'CAP (0-85) £2385.00 (£660.00: £315.00) **2m (AWT)**    1-30 (1-33)

4059 **Shar Emblem (48)** *(SDow)* 3–7-9⁽¹⁾ JQuinn (2) (hdwy 7f out: led over 1f out: rdn out) ............................................................................................................... —1

4040² Intricacy **(66)** (Jt-Fav) *(CCElsey)* 3–8-13 NDay (7) (hld up: hdwy 6f out: led over 2f out: hdd over 1f out: unable qckn) ........................................ 2.2

4026 Smartie Lee **(54)** (bl) *(PFlCole)* 4–8-9 TQuinn (8) (a.p: rdn 5f out: one pce fnl 3f)   2½.3

4059 Daddy's Darling **(42)** *(JTGifford)* 6–7-11 DaleGibson (9) (hdwy over 3f out: one pce fnl 2f) ..................................................................................... 5.4

4050 Caroles Clown **(38)** *(M.IHaynes)* 5–7-0 ‡⁷DToole (1) (nvr nrr) ......................... 2.5

4050⁵ Mississippi Beat (USA) **(39)** (bl) *(MPNaughton)* 4–7-5 ‡³JFanning (4) (led 8f out tl over 2f out: sn wknd) .................................................... 7.6

4059² Sailor Boy **(67)** (Jt-Fav) *(RAkehurst)* 5–9-8 MHills (5) (led 8f: wknd 5f out: eased whn btn 3f out) ................................................................ 15.7

4040 Qualitair Aviator **(73)** *(JFBottomley)* 5–10-0 GBardwell (6) (prom 9f) ................. 3.8

3818 Tsar Alexis (USA) **(39)** *(CLPopham)* 3–9-2 TSprake (3) (prom 7f: t.o fnl 4f) ............ 25.9

LONG HANDICAP: Caroles Clown 6-11.

**5/2** Sailor Boy, Intricacy, **6/1** Smartie Lee, **7/1** Qualitair Aviator, **11/1** Daddy's Darling(8/1—12/1), **12/1** Mississippi Beat (USA)(op 8/1), **16/1** SHAR EMBLEM, **20/1** Caroles Clown(12/1—20/1), **33/1** Tsar Alexis (USA). CSF £51.73, CT £247.35. Tote £14.10: £2.90 £1.10 £1.70 (£45.30). Mr T. R. Pearson (EPSOM) bred by Brickfield Bloodstock Agency Ltd. 9 Rn      3m 23.4 (0.4)
SF—12/29/22/5/–/–

---

**4073** WITCH OF ENDOR H'CAP (0-70) £2402.00 (£666.40: £319.20)
1½m (AWT)      2-00 (2-04)

4033⁶ **Carpet Slippers (48)** *(JDBethell)* 5–8-11 DMcKeown (15) (rdn & hdwy 3f out: qcknd to ld nr fin) ........................................................... —1

4002² Fiala (IRE) **(69)** *(JHMGosden)* 3–9-12 MHills (11) (a.p: led 2f out: rdn fnl f: hdd nr fin) ....................................................................................... ½.2

4050⁴ Jawani (IRE) **(46)** *(DrJDScargill)* 3–8-3 JQuinn (7) (a.p: rdn 6f out: ev ch 1f out: r.o) ..................................................................................... nk.3

4059⁴ Bronze Runner **(39)** *(EAWheeler)* 7–7-9 ‡⁷BThomas (3) (eyeshield: s.s: hdwy over 2f out: r.o wl ins fnl f) ............................................ 1½.4

4018* Mr Wishing Well **(60)** (Jt-Fav) *(RJRWilliams)* 5–9-2 ‡⁷SWilliams (8) (lw: hdwy 4f out: hrd rdn over 2f out: ev ch over 1f out: one pce) ........... nk.5

4060⁵ Bengal Tiger (IRE) **(50)** (bl) *(JAkehurst)* 3–8-4 ‡³SO'Gorman (5) (led 7f out to 2f out: sn wknd) ................................................ 10.6

4059⁶ Storm Orphan **(46)** *(MissBSanders)* 4–8-9 DaleGibson (14) (nvr nr to chal) ........... 4.7

4059* Scotoni **(65)** *(RJO'Sullivan)* 5–9-7 ‡⁷CMunday (4) (lw: led 5f: hrd rdn & wknd over 4f out) .................................................................... hd.8

4018⁶ Briery Fille **(52)** (Jt-Fav) *(AHide)* 6–9-1 NDay (12) (a mid div) ........................... 5.9

244 Bursana **(40)** *(JLSpearing)* 5–8-3 GBardwell (1) (lw: rdn thrght: a bhd) ............... 1.10

2337⁶ Erevnon **(63)** *(JLHarris)* 4–9-12 JWilliams (16) (rdn & hdwy 6f out: wknd over 3f out) ....................................................................... 4.11

3998* Priceless Fantasy **(45)** *(PatMitchell)* 4–8-3 ‡⁵KRutter (13) (rdn: a bhd) ............... 4.12

3089 Talish **(55)** *(TDBarron)* 3–8-12 TQuinn (10) (prom 8f: eased whn btn 3f out) ......... 4.13

4032⁴ Crown Reserve **(54)** *(MJRyan)* 3–8-8 ‡³DBiggs (9) (bhd fnl 4f) ......................... ½.14

3550 Frescobaldo (USA) **(62)** *(MPNaughton)* 5–9-8 ‡³JFanning (2) (prom 4f: bhd fnl 6f) .................................................................... ½.15

2622 Vinton Va **(50)** *(RABennett)* 6–8-13 JCurant (6) (wl bhd fnl 5f: t.o) ................. 16

**6/1** Briery Fille(op 12/1), Mr Wishing Well, **8/1** Talish, **9/1** Fiala (IRE)(6/1—10/1), Frescobaldo (USA), Bengal Tiger (IRE), **10/1** Priceless Fantasy, **11/1** Scotoni, **14/1** Storm Orphan, Bursana, Bronze Runner, **16/1** Crown Reserve, **25/1** CARPET SLIPPERS, Erevnon, Jawani (IRE), **33/1** Vinton Va. CSF £219.62, CT £5,096.04. Tote £24.50: £3.90 £2.50 £9.90 £3.30 (£59.50). Mrs G. Fane (DIDCOT) bred by Mrs G. Fane. 16Rn

2m 31.60 (2.2)
SF—27/41/17/6/26/–

---

**4074**    NORTHERN RACING SERVICES CLAIMING STKS (II) (Mdn) £2340.40 (£638.40: £305.20)  **1¼m (AWT)**    2-30 (2-34)

| | | |
|---|---|---|
| 4019 | **Double Echo (IRE) (55)** *(JDBethell)* 3–8–13 DMcKeown (10) (hld up: nt clr run 3f out: str run fnl f: led nr fin) | —1 |
| | Ibsen *(PJMakin)* 3–8–11 TSprake (8) (unf: bit bkwd: hld up: stdy hdwy on bit over 2f out: shkn up & r.o wl ins fnl f) | 1.2 |
| 4030² | **Absolutely Right (59)** (Fav) *(RAkehurst)* 3–8–4(1) TQuinn (4) (a.p: led over 2f out: clr 1f out: ct nr fin) | s.h.3 |
| 4032² | **Plectrum (50)** (Fav) *(BWHills)* 3–7–8 GBardwell (13) (rdn thrght: hdwy fnl 2f: nvr nrr) | 7.4 |
| 3920 | **Buddy's Friend (IRE) (51)** *(RJRWilliams)* 3–8–7 MHills (14) (a.p: ev ch over 2f out: one pce) | ½.5 |
| 7593 | **Great Impostor** *(PTWalwyn)* 3–8–5 GDuffield (1) (outpcd: gd hdwy 3f out: hrd rdn 2f out: one pce) | 2.6 |
| 3576⁵ | **Lady Poly (43)** *(MissBSanders)* 3–8–2 DaleGibson (9) (hrd rdn & no hdwy fnl 3f) | 10.7 |
| 4057 | **Danzig Lad (USA) (46)** (v) *(MPNaughton)* 3–7–11 ‡3JFanning (6) (a.p: led over 3f out tl over 2f out: wknd qckly) | 7.8 |
| | **Rushey Sands** *(JTGifford)* 3–7–8 RFox (11) (w'like: nvr nr to chal) | s.h.9 |
| 4039 | **Kay's Dilemma (IRE)** *(PAKelleway)* 3–8–8(2) JWilliams (5) (eyeshield: bhd fnl 4f) | ¾.10 |
| 1499 | **Shining Wood (50)** (bl) *(ASReid)* 3–8–0 CRutter (3) (lod over 6f) | 0½.11 |
| 4033 | **Just One (IRE) (47)** (bl) *(MMcCormack)* 3–8–0 AClark (12) (a bhd) | 2.12 |
| 4041 | **Dorsey (41)** (v) *(PJFeilden)* 4–8–10(1) CDwyer (7) (prom 6f) | ½.13 |
| 3885⁴ | **Replicate (52)** *(MJCharles)* 3–7–10(2) JQuinn (2) (prom 6f) | 8.14 |

**15/8** Plectrum(11/10—2/1), **3/1** Absolutely Right(tchd 9/2), **9/2** Shining Wood(14/1—4/1), **9/1** Replicate(9/2—9/1), **12/1** DOUBLE ECHO (IRE)(8/1—14/1), Great Impostor(8/1—14/1), **14/1** Rushey Sands, **16/1** Ibsen(10/1—20/1), **33/1** Lady Poly, **50/1** Ors. CSF £171.94, Tote £13.70: £3.60 £8.90 £1.60 (£297.40). Mrs John Lee (DIDCOT) bred by A. Tarry in Ireland. 14 Rn; Plectrum clmd C J Welch£4,253

2m 5.99 (2.99)
SF—29/27/19/–/–/–

---

**4075**    LA REVE H'CAP (0-95) £2822.00 (£782.00: £374.00)  **1m (AWT)**    3-00 (3-05)

| | | |
|---|---|---|
| 4052² | **Super Sally (80)** *(MJRyan)* 4–8–12 ‡3DBiggs (8) (hld up: led over 1f out: pushed out) | —1 |
| 4056* | **Crosby (72)** *(PAKelleway)* 5–8–7 TQuinn (10) (eyeshield: hdwy 3f out: r.o ins fnl f) | ½.2 |
| 3967⁶ | **Super Morning (60)** *(GBBalding)* 5–7–9 DaleGibson (6) (lw: hdwy fnl 3f: r.o) | nk.3 |
| 4065⁴ | **Mac's Fighter (93)** (bl) *(WAO'Gorman)* 6–9–9 ‡5EmmaO'Gorman (4) (hld up: hdwy fnl 2f: nvr nrr) | 4.4 |
| 4057 | **Scots Law (58)** *(RJO'Sullivan)* 4–7–7 GBardwell (11) (lw: led over 6f: one pce) | nk.5 |
| 4056² | **Say You Will (59)** (v) *(MPNaughton)* 7–7–5(1) ‡3JFanning (12) (prom 6f) | 3½.6 |
| 4035* | **Pytchley Night (87)** *(DMorris)* 4–9–1 ‡7StephenDavies (3) (lw: prom 6f) | 1½.7 |
| 4043³ | **Dance on Sixpence (70)** (v) *(HJCollingridge)* 3–8–3 JQuinn (7) (hdwy over 2f out: wknd over 1f out) | ½.8 |
| 3747 | **Kaths Choice (63)** *(HJCollingridge)* 3–7–3(3) ‡7CHawksley (5) (s.s: a bhd) | 3½.9 |
| 4054* | **Vanroy (73)** (v) (Fav) *(JRJenkins)* 7–8–8(1) JWilliams (2) (b: b.hind: sme hdwy 3f out: wknd 2f out) | nk.10 |
| 3051 | **Blues Balidar (60)** *(JLSpearing)* 3–7–7 RFox (9) (a bhd) | 8.11 |
| 4035⁵ | **Helawe (84)** (bl) *(SirMarkPrescott)* 8–9–5 GDuffield (1) (w ldr 5f: wkng whn bdly hmpd on ins 2f out) | 1.12 |

LONG HANDICAP: Scots Law 6-11, Say You Will 6-10, Kaths Choice 6-6, Blues Balidar 7-2.

**7/2** Vanroy(5/1—3/1), **9/2** Pytchley Night(6/1—4/1), **6/1** Helawe(op 10/1), **13/2** SUPER SALLY, **8/1** Dance on Sixpence, **9/1** Mac's Fighter, Super Morning, **11/1** Crosby(8/1—12/1), **12/1** Say You Will, **50/1** Blues Balidar, Scots Law, **66/1** Kaths Choice. CSF £68.54, CT £589.22. Tote £8.40: £3.10 £2.60 £2.60 (£41.70). Mr Leonard Seale (NEWMARKET) bred by R. Duggan. 12 Rn

1m 36.71 (0.01)
SF—50/43/30/46/15/2

---

**4076**    LYDIA STKS (II) (Mdn 2-Y-O) £2206.40 (£610.40: £291.20)  **7f (AWT)**    3-30 (3-34)

| | | |
|---|---|---|
| 4046³ | **Quiet Miss** *(DRCElsworth)* 8–9 JWilliams (10) (eyeshield: a.p: led over 1f out: pushed out) | —1 |

3668 Amadeus Aes **(84)** (v) *(Fav)* *(DMorris)* 8-7 ‡⁷StephenDavies (1) (led over 5f: unable qckn) ............................................................................ 3.2

4061³ Anna Manana **(57)** (bl) *(WJPearce)* 8-9 GDuffield (6) (a.p: ev ch over 1f out: one pce) ................................................................................ 1½.3

4044 Esprit Fort (USA) **(66)** *(BWHills)* 8-9 MHills (2) (a.p: one pce fnl 2f) ................... 2½.4

4017⁵ Great Hall **(55)** (bl) *(WGRWightman)* 9-0 TQuinn (3) (b.hind: spd over 4f) ............ 1½.5

4016 Child Star (FR) *(DMarks)* 8-9 AClark (9) (outpcd: nvr nrr) ................................ 12.6

Albany Spark *(GHEden)* 9-0 DaleGibson (A) (unf: bkwd: s.s: a.t.o) ............ 15.7

4031 Shakiri *(JAkehurst)* 8-9 SWhitworth (8) (a bhd: t.o) ...................................... 4.8

4051 Mighty Lady (IRE) **(61)** *(MRChannon)* 8-9 LornaVincent (5) (bhd fnl 3f: t.o) ......... 12.9

3613 Sharling *(JHMGosden)* 8-9 DMcKeown (4) (hld up: 4th & ev ch whn fell 2f out) ......... 0

2/1 Amadeus Aes, **11/4** Sharling(5/1—5/2), **100/30** Esprit Fort (USA)(op 7/1), **4/1** QUIET MISS, **12/1** Anna Manana(tchd 20/1), **16/1** Child Star (FR), **25/1** Mighty Lady (IRE), **50/1** Ors. CSF £12.87, Tote £5.90: £1.30 £1.30 £2.20 (£8.50). Mr G. M. Gee (WHITSBURY) bred by D. R. C. Elsworth. 10 Rn        1m 26.25 (2.25)
SF—20/9/6/–/–/–

T/Plpt: £2,521.80 (0.25 Tckts). £2,555.96 to Newton Abbot 16/12/91.                     SM/LMc

4062—**SOUTHWELL (L-H)** Fibresand
### Tuesday, December 17th [Standard]
Going Allowance: 5f: minus 0.35 sec; Rest: nil sec per fur (FS)                    Wind: slt across

Stalls: 2nd, 3rd & 7th high, remainder low

**4077**     LITTONDALE CLAIMING STKS (I)   £2285.20 (£632.20: £301.60)
              **6f (AWT)**                                   12-00 (12-02)

4047² **Friendly Claim (IRE) (74)** *(TDBarron)* 3–8-4 ‡⁷VHalliday (1) (cl up: led wl over 1f out: styd on u.p) .......................................................... —1

4047* **Plain Fact (82)** *(Fav)* *(SirMarkPrescott)* 6–9-3 GDuffield (9) (lw: chsd ldrs: effrt & swtchd wl over 1f out: nt qckn towards fin) ............................ 2½.2

4058 Maid Welcome **(70)** (bl) *(MrsNMacauley)* 4–8-1 ‡⁵EmmaO'Gorman (7) (led tl hdd wl over 1f out: sn outpcd) ................................................... 6.3

3370 Beatle Song **(68)** *(CJHill)* 3–8-4 NAdams (2) (lw: bhd tl styd on fnl 2f: n.d) ........... 3.4

4056⁶ Video Wall **(50)** (v) *(SDow)* 3–8-0 ‡⁷MJermy (6) (chsd ldrs over 3f: sn wknd) ....... 3½.5

Our Amber *(DWChapman)* 4–8-4 SWood (5) (s.i.s: n.d) .................................. 2.6

3911 Sally Fay (IRE) **(62)** *(TKersey)* 3–8-5⁽¹⁾ SWebster (3) (lw: lost pl after 2f: n.d after) ..................................................................... ½.7

3958⁴ Henry Will **(45)** *(TFairhurst)* 7–8-6 ‡³JPanning (8) (a outpcd & wl bhd) ............... 6.8

4039 Collina Del Fonte *(JBalding)* 3–8-6 LCharnock (4) (bit bkwd: lost tch fr ½-wy) ....... 5.9

**1/2** Plain Fact, **9/2** FRIENDLY CLAIM (IRE), **9/1** Maid Welcome, **10/1** Beatle Song, **25/1** Video Wall, Henry Will, Sally Fay (IRE), **33/1** Ors. CSF £7.16, Tote £6.10: £1.20 £1.30 £1.30 (£2.70). Mr Stephen Woodall (THIRSK) bred by Mrs K. Twomey in Ireland. 9 Rn        1m 16.6 (3.2)
SF—26/29/–/–/–/–

**4078**     GARSDALE H'CAP (0-70) £2407.00 (£667.00: £319.00)   **5f (AWT)**     12-30 (12-31)

4063² **Meeson Times (49)** *(BEllison)* 3–8-11 MHills (8) (lw: chsd ldrs: sn drvn along: styd on to ld wl ins fnl f) ................................................... —1

4063 Lady of the Fen **(66)** *(MrsNMacauley)* 3–10-0 SKeightley (9) (lw: led tl hdd & no ex wl ins fnl f) ..................................................................... ¾.2

4063³ Drummer's Dream (IRE) **(43)** *(MrsNMacauley)* 3–8-2 ‡³DBiggs (4) (lw: a chsng ldrs: kpt on fnl f) ......................................................... nk.3

4009² In a Whirl (USA) **(58)** *(DWChapman)* 3–9-6 TQuinn (7) (lw: s.i.s: hdwy over 1f out: styd on nr fin) .................................................... nk.4

4063* Imco Double (IRE) **(58)** *(Fav)* *(CNAllen)* 3–9-6 (7x) JMcLaughlin (5) (lw: chsd ldrs: rdn 2f out: nt qckn fnl f) .............................. ¾.5

4063⁶ Shedad (USA) **(55)** (bl) *(TDBarron)* 3–9-3 AlexGreaves (6) (chsd ldrs tl wknd appr fnl f) ............................................................... ¾.6

4063 Strip Cartoon (IRE) **(34)** (bl) *(SRBowring)* 3–7-10 NAdams (2) (cl up over 3f) ......... 1.7

3717 Lazy Hill **(31)** *(DWChapman)* 4–7-7 SWood (3) (spd 3f: sn wknd) ...................... 1½.8

244 Bursar **(40)** *(WHolden)* 4–7-9⁽⁹⁾ ‡⁷BRussell (1) (s.i.s: a bhd) ........................ 2.9

LONG HANDICAP: Lazy Hill 7-2, Bursar 7-6.

**6/4** Imco Double (IRE), **6/1** Drummer's Dream (IRE), **13/2** MEESON TIMES, In a Whirl (USA)(op 4/1), **8/1** Shedad (USA), Lady of the Fen, **10/1** Strip Cartoon (IRE), **33/1** Ors. CSF £52.19, CT £295.88. Tote £5.40: £1.70 £2.60 £2.10 (£23.70). Mr Charles Castle (MALTON) bred by Mrs M. Chubb. 9 Rn        60.7 sec (2.7)
SF—8/22/–/12/9/–

## 4079

WHARFDALE NURSERY (0-75) £2305.50 (£638.00: £304.50)   **5f (AWT)**   1-00 (1-02)

3769⁵ **Creche (61)** (bl) *(MrsNMacauley)* 8-7 NDay (4) (lw: mde all: clr over 1f out: pushed out) .............................................................. —1
4051² Appealing Times (USA) **(75)** (Fav) *(WAO'Gorman)* 9-2 ‡5EmmaO'Gorman (9) (lw: in tch: hdwy 2f out: styd on: no imp) ........................ 5.2
4031² Myasha (USA) **(72)** *(MrsLPiggott)* 8-11 ‡7MichaelDenaro (1) (eyeshield: chsd wnr: rdn ½-wy: no imp) ........................................... 5.3
3964 Fort Hope (58) (bl) *(TJNaughton)* 8-4 TQuinn (12) (b: drvn along thrght: hdwy ½-wy: no imp) ................................................ ¾.4
4044 Ace Girl (60) (bl) *(SRBowring)* 8-6 AProud (5) (sn drvn along: no imp) ............ 3.5
4055³ Doesyoudoes (60) (v) *(DTThom)* 8-1 ‡5KRutter (8) (effrt ½-wy: nvr rchd ldrs) .......... ½.6
4031⁵ Man of the Season (USA) **(62)** (bl) *(MrsNMacauley)* 8-8 AlexGreaves (11) (nvr trbld ldrs) .................................................... 2½.7
4051 Mary's Special **(47)** *(CNAllen)* 7-7 GBardwell (2) (nvr nr to chal) ................... 2½.8
4051 Daily Sport August **(48)** *(MCChapman)* 7-5 ‡3JFanning (10) (wnt lft s: spd to ½-wy: sn lost pl) ........................................ 10.9
3085 Uraragskal **(50)** *(JAkehurst)* 7-10⁽²⁾ NAdams (3) (sn bhd) ...................... 1½.10
2593⁴ Mykindofmusic **(59)** *(MJHaynes)* 8-5 RFox (7) (dwlt: n.d) .......................... nk.11
2140 Roaring Trade **(48)** *(JBalding)* 7-8 LCharnock (13) (bit bkwd: a bhd) ............ ½.12
4061² Jaromic **(65)** *(PFTulk)* 8-11 MBirch (6) (b: sn bhd) ................................ 1.13
LONG HANDICAP: Mary's Special 7-4.

**11/4** Appealing Times (USA), **3/1** Myasha (USA), **7/1** Jaromic, **8/1** Man of the Season (USA), Fort Hope, **10/1** Doesyoudoes, **12/1** CRECHE, **16/1** Mykindofmusic, **20/1** Ace Girl, **25/1** Mary's Special, **33/1** Ors. CSF £44.44, CT £117.45. Tote £10.20: £2.60 £1.50 £2.00 (£14.20). Mrs N. Macauley (MELTON MOWBRAY) bred by Bacton Stud. 13 Rn                                         58.7 sec (0.7)
                                                                      SF—44/33/8/–/–/–

## 4080

LITTONDALE CLAIMING STKS (II)   £2264.90 (£626.40: £298.70)
**6f (AWT)**                                                    1-30 (1-32)

4049* **Wellsy Lad (USA) (67)** (Fav) *(DWChapman)* 4–8-11 SWood (3) (lw: mde most: comf) ............................................................ —1
4028 Pesidanamich (IRE) **(76)** (bl) *(TDBarron)* 3–8-13 AlexGreaves (7) (chsd ldrs: ev ch over 2f out: rdn & r.o one pce) .............................. 1½.2
3634⁵ Qualitair Rhythm (IRE) **(40)** *(JHetherton)* 3–8-1 ‡3DBiggs (4) (dwlt: wl bhd tl r.o wl fnl 2f) .................................................... hd.3
4049⁶ Supreme Optimist **(35)** (bl) *(REPeacock)* 7–8-7 TQuinn (9) (b: disp ld to ½-wy: btn whn hung bdly lft 1f out) .................................... 4.4
4047⁶ Kabera (33) *(DWChapman)* 3–8-5 DaleGibson (8) (prom tl outpcd fr ½-wy) ....... 2½.5
437 Ping Pong **(50)** *(TFairhurst)* 3–7-11 ‡3JFanning (5) (bit bkwd: chsd ldrs to st: sn wknd) ......................................................... 3½.6
4049⁵ Rancho Mirage **(66)** *(MrsNMacauley)* 4–8-9 NDay (1) (b: reluctant to r: a wl bhd) 2.7
Clefti's Slipper *(CJHill)* 3–8-0 NAdams (6) (unf: bit bkwd: outpcd & lost tch after 2f) .......................................................... 10.8
2827 Impetulence **(33)** *(WStorey)* 5–7-12 JQuinn (2) (dwlt: a wl bhd) ................. 1.9

**4/7** WELLSY LAD (USA) (tchd 6/4), **5/1** Rancho Mirage, Pesidanamich (IRE)(op 7/4), **10/1** Ping Pong(8/1—12/1), **20/1** Qualitair Rhythm (IRE), Supreme Optimist, **33/1** Clefti's Slipper, Impetulence, **50/1** Kabera. CSF £4.58, Tote £1.70: £1.10 £1.80 £3.50 (£2.90). Mr J. M. Chapman (YORK) bred by Mrs. Helen K. Groves in USA. 9 Rn                                                       1m 18.9 (5.5)

## 4081

SOUTHWELL H'CAP (Amateurs) (0-80) £2650.60 (£736.60: £353.80)
**1m (AWT)**                                                    2-00 (2-02)

4063 **Cronk's Courage (64)** (v) *(EJAlston)* 5–11-0 ‡5MrRWilkinson (9) (lw: mde all: clr 2f out: kpt on) ..................................................... —1
4057 Ballerina Bay **(47)** (v) *(DTThom)* 3–10-1 MissIDWJones (15) (a chsng ldrs: styd on fnl 2f: nvr able to chal) ....................................... 2½.2
3984⁵ Night Transaction **(47)** (Fav) *(AHide)* 4–10-2 MrsLPearce (13) (a.p: hdwy over 1f out: nt qckn ins fnl f) ........................................... ½.3
4033² Tara's Delight **(65)** *(MJRyan)* 4–11-1⁽¹⁾ ‡5MrWDixon (4) (a chsng ldrs: one pce fnl 2f) ................................................................... 1½.4
2827 East Barns (IRE) **(42)** (bl) *(TDBarron)* 3–9-10 MrsAFarrell (2) (s.i.s: sn in tch: outpcd over 2f out: styd on nr fin) ..................................... ¾.5
4032 Verro (USA) **(46)** (bl) *(JABennett)* 4–9-10⁽⁷⁾ ‡5MissAPurdy (8) (a chsng ldrs: one pce fnl 3f) ................................................................ 3.6
2697⁴ Krisfield **(51)** *(TPMcGovern)* 6–10-1 ‡5MissLHarwood (12) (lw: styd on fnl 2f: nvr rchd ldrs) .................................................... 2½.7

3606 The Minder (FR) **(40)** *(DAWilson)* 4–9-9 MissEBronson (5) (effrt appr st: nvr nr ldrs) .................................................................................................. 1½.8
4064² Irish Native (IRE) **(66)** (bl) *(CASmith)* 3–11-1 ‡5MrAPhillips (16) (b: dwlt: bhd tl r.o fnl f) ......................................................................................... nk.9
4047 Dawn Success **(68)** *(DWChapman)* 5–11-4 ‡5MrJWeymes (3) (dwlt: n.d) .............. 6.10
3389 Tapestry Dancer **(46)** *(MJHaynes)* 3–10-0 MissYHaynes (1) (outpcd after 3f: n.d after) ........................................................................................................ 3½.11
2281⁴ Srivijaya **(74)** *(MrsJJordan)* 4–11-10(1) ‡5MrKHolder (6) (lw: spd to ½-wy) ....... 1½.12
4042 Ensharp (USA) **(58)** *(JPLeigh)* 5–10-8(2) ‡5MrSGollings (7) (in tch to ½-wy) ...... 10.13
Racecall Gold Card **(62)** *(TKersey)* 4–10-12(24) ‡5MrPWinks (17) (bhd fr ½-wy) ... 1½.14
3385 Spirit Sam **(38)** *(RVKing)* 6–9-2 ‡5MrSRees (11) (bhd fr ½-wy) ......................... 7.15
4035 Lucy Dancer (IRE) **(52)** *(MMcCormack)* 3–10-1 ‡5MissSFarrant (10) (chsd ldrs to st: wknd qckly) .................................................................................... 5.16
Bold Answer **(38)** *(MCChapman)* 8–9-2 ‡5MrPClose (14) (bit bkwd: dwlt: a wl bhd) ........................................................................................................... 17

LONG HANDICAP: Racecall Gold Card 9-5, Spirit Sam 8-7, Bold Answer 8-2.

**5/1** Night Transaction, **11/2** Ballerina Bay, Tara's Delight, **7/1** East Barns (IRE), **8/1** Irish Native (IRE), **9/1** Krisfield, **10/1** CRONK'S COURAGE(8/1—12/1), Dawn Success, **12/1** Srivijaya, **14/1** Tapestry Dancer, **16/1** Verro (USA), **20/1** The Minder (FR), Lucy Dancer (IRE), **33/1** Ensharp (USA), Racecall Gold Card, **50/1** Ors. CSF £66.37, CT £295.51. Tote £17.50: £3.40 £3.00 £1.10 £1.70 (£48.90). Mr M. P. Russell (PRESTON) bred by M. Andree. 17 Rn                                                                    1m 48.1 (8.8)

---

**4082**  COVERDALE CLAIMING STKS (2-Y.O) £2549.10 (£707.60: £339.30)
7f **(AWT)**                                                                                          2-30 (2-34)

4067² Runnel **(74)** *(DWChapman)* 8-1 SWood (10) (lw: mde all: easily) ........................... —1
4067* Meltonby **(54)** (Fav) *(JHetherton)* 7-6 ‡3JFanning (7) (lw: a chsng ldrs: effrt ent st: no imp) .................................................................................................. 5.2
4051³ Patrician Magician **(77)** *(RJRWilliams)* 8-3 ‡3DBiggs (4) (a chsng ldrs: kpt on one pce fnl 2f) ............................................................................................ 1½.3
3995⁴ Silver Samurai **(66)** *(RHollinshead)* 8-4 TQuinn (11) (lw: hdwy to chase ldrs ½-wy: styd on: no imp) .......................................................................... 1½.4
4029⁴ Aegaen Lady **(54)** *(JEtherington)* 7-11 LCharnock (15) (chsd ldrs tl wknd ins fnl f) 6.5
4053* Grog (IRE) **(74)** *(MRChannon)* 8-6 LornaVincent (12) (lw: in tch: no imp fnl 3f) ...... 6.6
4051⁶ Swale Side *(MrsGRReveley)* 8-5 MHills (13) (outpcd & bhd tl sme late hdwy) ............ 8.7
1611 Swing O'The Kilt **(44)** *(PCalver)* 7-9 DaleGibson (8) (sn outpcd & bhd: styd on fnl f) ...................................................................................................... 5.8
3524 Toll Booth *(WStorey)* 7-9(2) JQuinn (9) (nvr trbld ldrs) ......................................... 1½.9
3865 Orchard Bay **(46)** *(DRTucker)* 7-7 GBardwell (2) (outpcd fr ½-wy) ......................... 1.10
Full Flight *(RBastiman)* 7-9(2) NCarlisle (3) (small: lt-f: s.s: a bhd) ......................... 10.11
4051 Queen of Pendona **(41)** (v) *(HATWhiting)* 7-8(1) RFox (1) (outpcd & bhd fr ½-wy) 1½.12
3985 Grand Time **(74)** *(CJHill)* 7-12 NAdams (6) (bhd fr ½-wy) ..................................... 1.13
4066 Counter Blast *(WHolden)* 7-11 ‡7BRussell (5) (bkwd: s.s: a wl bhd) ..................... hd.14
4066 Barryben *(WMBrisbourne)* 8-4 AProud (14) (bit bkwd: dwlt: a outpcd & wl bhd) ..... 15.15

**3/1** Meltonby, **9/2** RUNNEL, **5/1** Silver Samurai, **6/1** Patrician Magician(op 4/1), **7/1** Grog (IRE), Swale Side, **12/1** Grand Time, **16/1** Aegaen Lady, **25/1** Full Flight, Orchard Bay, **33/1** Ors. CSF £18.85, Tote £5.70: £1.60 £1.90 £2.20 (£7.80). Mr E. Stockdale (YORK) bred by Ruckmans Farm. 15 Rn                           1m 30.7 (4.1)
SF—26/2/8/6/–/–

---

**4083**  WINDERMERE H'CAP (0-70) £2528.80 (£701.80: £336.40)  1¾m **(AWT)**  3-00 (3-03)

4050⁶ **Chronological (50)** (v) *(MHTompkins)* 5–8-8 ‡5CHodgson (1) (dwlt: hdwy 9f out: led wl over 1f out: styd on) .............................................................. —1
4041³ Qualitair Blazer **(48)** *(JRJenkins)* 4–8-11 SWhitworth (12) (led tl hdd wl over 1f out: one pce) ................................................................................. 3½.2
4059³ Windsor Park (USA) **(47)** *(KSBridgwater)* 5–8-10 JWilliams (5) (lw: mid div tl hdwy 2f out: r.o nr fin) ......................................................................... 3.3
4062 Free Minx **(52)** *(MrsVAAconley)* 5–8-8 ‡7GParkin (15) (hdwy u.p over 2f out: styd on wl) ...................................................................................................... 2½.4
660⁴ Peak District **(40)** *(KSBridgwater)* 5–8-3 RFox (13) (lw: w ldr tl wknd ent st) ......... ¾.5
3987 Dalby Dancer **(58)** *(BAMcMahon)* 7–9-0 ‡7SSanders (16) (bit bkwd: a chsng ldrs: effrt appr st: wknd over 2f out) ................................................. hd.6
3994 Negatory (USA) **(65)** *(MCChapman)* 4–9-7 ‡7SWilliams (18) (outpcd & lost tch after 6f: r.o fnl 2f) .............................................................................. 5.7
3779⁶ Welcoming Arms **(45)** *(PCalver)* 4–8-8 DaleGibson (8) (lw: outpcd & bhd 8f out: sme late hdwy) .......................................................................... 3.8
4040 Daleside **(57)** *(TFairhurst)* 3–8-11 ‡3JFanning (2) (cl up tl wknd over 4f out) ......... 2.9
3379⁶ Demokos (FR) **(41)** *(APStringer)* 6–8-4(1) SWebster (6) (lw: sn outpcd & bhd: sme hdwy ent st: n.d) ................................................................. 10.10
963 Obeliski **(54)** *(PCHaslam)* 5–8-10 ‡7MichaelDenaro (4) (lw: nvr trbld ldrs) .......... 1½.11

3374 Mubaaris **(57)** *(BRichmond)* 8–9-6 MHills (10) (b: sn outpcd & bhd) .................... s.h.**12**
4064[5] Qualitair Sweetie **(42)** *(JFBottomley)* 4–8-5 GBardwell (3) (chsd ldrs tl wknd appr
st) ........................................................................................................................ 8.**13**
3834[3] Dodger Dickins **(36)** (Fav) *(RHollinshead)* 4–7-13 NCarlisle (7) (lw: sn outpcd &
bhd) ...................................................................................................................... 3.**14**
3718 First Bid **(44)** (v) *(RMWhitaker)* 4–8-7 ACulhane (14) (chsd ldrs tl wknd qckly
over 2f out) ............................................................................................................ 8.**15**
4062 Mara Askari **(69)** *(JLHarris)* 3–9-12 TQuinn (9) (sn outpcd & bhd) ................... s.h.**16**
4018 Master Line **(47)** *(HCandy)* 10–8-10 CRutter (11) (b.hind: bhd fnl 5f) ............... 6.**17**
633[5] Tharsis **(40)** (Fav) *(RJWeaver)* 6–8-3 SWood (17) (sn outpcd & bhd) ............... ¾.**18**

**3/1** Dodger Dickins(5/1—5/2), **7/1** Obeliski, Dalby Dancer(5/1—8/1), **8/1** Negatory (USA)(op 12/1), **10/1** Windsor Park (USA), Qualitair Blazer, CHRONOLOGICAL(op 8/1), Welcoming Arms, Demokos (FR)(op 8/1), Peak District, **14/1** First Bid, **16/1** Master Line, Daleside, Mara Askari, Free Minx, **20/1** Tharsis, **33/1** Ors. CSF £137.84, CT £1,180.34. Tote £8.00: £3.20 £1.90 £3.30 £6.20 (£36.70). Hirst Kidd & Rennie Ltd - Oldham Chron (NEWMARKET) bred by Mrs S. M. Rogers. 18 Rn                               3m 13.1 (13.8)

T/Plpt: £9.80 (148.25 Tckts).                                                                                            AA

4069—**LINGFIELD (L-H)** Equitrack

## Wednesday, December 18th [Standard]

Going Allowance: minus 0.30 sec per fur (FS)

**4084**       SELMA STKS (I) (Mdn 2-Y.O) £2186.80 (£632.80: £288.40)   **1m (AWT)** 12-15 (12-16)

3901[5] **Judge and Jury (70)** (bl) (Fav) *(MJFetherston-Godley)* 9-0 JWilliams (6) (a.p:
rdn over 4f out: led over 3f out: drvn out) ................................................ —**1**
4053[4] Noble Singer *(HThomsonJones)* 8-9 RHills (9) (lw: a.p: chsd wnr fnl 3f: r.o ins fnl
f) ............................................................................................................................ ¾.**2**
4044 Lord Leitrim (IRE) *(NACallaghan)* 9-0 WNewnes (7) (hdwy 4f out: one pce fnl 3f) 5.**3**
4070[5] Mediator *(PFICole)* 9-0 TQuinn (4) (lw: rdn along: no hdwy fnl 3f) ..................... 5.**4**
4044[5] Nothing Compares *(JWHills)* 8-9 MHills (1) (led over 4f) .................................. 1.**5**
3819 Litho Bold Flasher *(WJPearce)* 9-0 AClark (8) (w ldr 4f: sn wknd) .................... 4.**6**
4048 And Me **(50)** *(DTThom)* 8-9 JQuinn (3) (a bhd) ................................................ ½.**7**
4000 True Mood *(JDBethell)* 8-9 SDawson (2) (a wl bhd) ..................................... 8.**8**
4061[5] Minoan Light (IRE) *(RHannon)* 9-0 AMcGlone (5) (a wl bhd: t.o) ...................... 3½.**9**

**2/1** JUDGE AND JURY, **3/1** Mediator(op 7/4), **4/1** Noble Singer(op 9/4), **6/1** Nothing Compares(14/1—5/1), **14/1** Minoan Light (IRE)(op 7/1), Litho Bold Flasher, Lord Leitrim (IRE), **20/1** True Mood(op 12/1), **50/1** And Me. CSF £10.37, Tote £2.80: £1.10 £1.60 £8.20 (£7.70). Mr M. E. Cole (EAST ILSLEY). 9 Rn       1m 40.25 (3.55)
                                                                                                            SF—10/3/–/–/–/–

**4085**       SELMA STKS (II) (Mdn 2-Y.O) £2167.20 (£599.20: £285.60)
              **1m (AWT)**                                                                        12-45 (12-47)

4037[2] **Paper Clip (68)** (Fav) *(JDBethell)* 8-9 GDuffield (9) (a.p: hrd rdn fnl 3f: r.o to ld wl
ins fnl f) ............................................................................................................... —**1**
4037 Mystery Lad (IRE) **(56)** (bl) *(NACallaghan)* 9-0 WNewnes (2) (led: clr 3f out: hdd
wl ins fnl f) ........................................................................................................... ¾.**2**
2112[5] Level Up *(RGuest)* 8-9 NDay (6) (hdwy over 3f out: rn wd over 1f out: r.o one pce) ¾.**3**
Good as Gold (IRE) *(JLSpearing)* 8-9 GBardwell (3) (w'like: nvr nrr) ............... 4.**4**
Hawkish (USA) *(PMitchell)* 9-0 AClark (4) (w'like: bkwd: s.s: nrst fin) ............ 7.**5**
4053[6] Free Transfer (IRE) *(PFTulk)* 9-0 MBirch (5) (bhd fnl 5f) ................................. 5.**6**
Mississippi Queen *(RJRWilliams)* 8-9 MHills (7) (unf: hdwy 4f out: wknd over 2f
out) ........................................................................................................................ 1.**7**
4053[3] Alternation (FR) *(PFICole)* 8-9 TQuinn (1) (chsd ldr over 4f: wknd qckly) ............... ¾.**8**
3548 Spy in the Sky (BAR) **(50)** *(RHannon)* 9-0 AMcGlone (8) (prom 4f) ..................... 6.**9**

**11/8** PAPER CLIP(4/5—13/8), **5/2** Alternation (FR), **7/1** Level Up(op 3/1), **12/1** Mystery Lad (IRE)(20/1—8/1), Free Transfer (IRE), **14/1** Mississippi Queen(op 8/1), **16/1** Spy in the Sky (BAR)(op 8/1), **20/1** Ors. CSF £17.85, Tote £2.30: £1.40 £1.30 £2.80 (£11.10). Mr D. B. Ziff (DIDCOT) bred by Highfield Stud Ltd. 9 Rn                                                                                        1m 39.31 (2.61)
                                                                                                            SF—20/23/16/4/–/–

**4086**       TOINHA CLAIMING STKS   £2245.60 (£621.60: £296.80)   **5f (AWT)**    1-15 (1-16)

3863 **Sports Post Lady (IRE) (65)** *(CJHill)* 3–7-10 NAdams (5) (led 2f: led over 1f out:
r.o wl) .................................................................................................................... —**1**
4063 Sir Tasker **(62)** *(JLHarris)* 3–8-6 TQuinn (2) (led after 2f tl over 1f out: r.o) ................. 5.**2**
4058[3] Slip-a-Snip **(70)** (Fav) *(GBBalding)* 4–7-12 CRutter (6) (a.p: ev ch over 1f out: nt
qckn) ...................................................................................................................... 1½.**3**

4058 Ever so Artistic **(51)** (bl) *(PHowling)* 4–8-11 JWilliams (9) (b.hind: lw: a same pl) .... 2½.4
4063 Oratel Flyer **(34)** *(RThompson)* 4–7-13 RFox (8) (lw: nvr nr to chal) ....................... 1½.5
4057 Catalani **(63)** *(TJNaughton)* 6–7-12 DaleGibson (3) (b.nr hind: no hdwy fnl 3f) ......... 1.6
4063 Able Princess **(45)** *(MrsNMacauley)* 3–7-9 ‡3DBiggs (1) (lw: nvr trbld ldrs) ............ nk.7
4021 Village Pet **(48)** *(RABennett)* 3–8-2(1) JCurant (7) (b: a bhd) ............................ 3½.8
4071 Domino Trick **(52)** *(AMoore)* 3–7-10 GBardwell (4) (a bhd) ............................. 4.9

**11/10** Slip-a-Snip, **4/1** SPORTS POST 'LADY (IRE), **9/2** Sir Tasker, **9/1** Catalani(6/1—10/1), **20/1** Able Princess(op 12/1), Ever so Artistic(op 12/1), **33/1** Domino Trick, **50/1** Ors. CSF £20.12, Tote £4.80: £1.50 £1.50 £1.20 (£17.50). Mr C. John Hill (BARNSTAPLE) bred by J. Mamakos in Ireland. 9Rn

58.50 sec (0.30)
SF—46/36/24/27/9/4

## 4087
S.K. FINANCE & LEASING STKS (Mdn 3-Y.O) £2167.20 (£599.20: £285.60)
1½m (AWT)
1-45 (1-47)

4023 **Brora Rose (IRE) (34)** *(JDBethell)* 8-9 RHills (10) (hdwy 5f out: led wl over 1f out: r.o) ........ —1
40692 Hepburn (IRE) **(42)** (Fav) *(MJFetherston-Godley)* 8-9 TQuinn (11) (hdwy after 4f: ev ch 1f out: nt qckn) .................................................. 1.2
4074 Shining Wood **(50)** *(ASReid)* 8-4 ‡5KRutter (9) (late hdwy: nrst fin) .................. ¾.3
2235 Grey Dancer **(47)** *(JWhite)* 9-0 JWilliams (4) (bhd tl gd hdwy 3f out: one pce fnl 2f) ... 6.4
4062 Shaurni Girl *(RVKing)* 8-4 ‡5LNewton (12) (led 4f out tl wl over 1f out) ............. 2½.5
3390 Valued Friend (USA) *(JJBridger)* 8-7 ‡7RachelBridger (1) (lw: wl bhd tl sme late hdwy) ................................................................. 3½.6
4059 Malenoir (USA) **(53)** (bl) *(WJPearce)* 9-0 LCharnock (7) (led 5f out to 4f out: sn btn) ........ 5.7
4050 Carly-B (IRE) **(34)** (bl) *(PHowling)* 8-9 JMcLaughlin (5) (a bhd) ...................... 5.8
4069 Wise Friend (USA) *(CPWildman)* 9-0 CRutter (6) (a bhd: t.o) ....................... 25.9
4033 Blazing Fen **(47)** *(MrsNMacauley)* 9-0 AlexGreaves (2) (b: led tl wknd qckly 5f out: t.o) .......... ¾.10
Budget *(AJChamberlain)* 9-0 LornaVincent (3) (b: chsd ldr tl wknd qckly over 5f out: t.o) ........ nk.11
2880 Lisbon Lass *(PHowling)* 8-9 NAdams (8) (t.o fnl 5f) ..................... dist.12

**9/4** Hepburn (IRE), **9/2** Shining Wood(6/1—4/1), **6/1** Shaurni Girl(op 7/2), **7/1** Malenoir (USA)(op 9/2), **8/1** Blazing Fen, **11/1** BRORA ROSE (IRE)(op 6/1), **14/1** Grey Dancer(op 8/1), **16/1** Wise Friend (USA), **33/1** Ors. CSF £33.64, Tote £7.40: £2.50 £1.20 £2.10 (£8.60). Mrs S. M. Burley (DIDCOT) bred by Mrs M. Beaumont in Ireland. 12 Rn

2m 35.35 (5.95)

## 4088
DANNY DENT H'CAP (0-80) £2637.00 (£732.00: £351.00)  **7f (AWT)**    2-15 (2-24)
(Weights raised 8 lb)

4019 El Volador **(47)** *(RJO'Sullivan)* 4–8-0 ‡3DBiggs (7) (hdwy over 1f out: str run to ld cl home) ........ —1
4057* Kissavos **(54)** (v) *(CCElsey)* 5–8-10 TQuinn (15) (lw: a.p: rdn fnl 4f: r.o ins fnl f) ..... 1½.2
4057 Vuchterbacher **(49)** *(PFTulk)* 5–7-12 ‡7TWilson (16) (b: a.p: led 2f out tl ins fnl f: led wl ins fnl f tl nr fin) ....... nk.3
37475 Unanimous (IRE) **(67)** *(NACallaghan)* 3–9-8 WNewnes (5) (gd late hdwy: nrst fin) .. ¾.4
40574 Sarum **(48)** *(CPWildman)* 5–8-4 CRutter (10) (a.p: rdn fnl 3f: styd on) ............ ½.5
40422 Precentor **(61)** (bl) (Fav) *(JDBethell)* 5–9-3 RHills (4) (gd hdwy 2f out: led ins fnl f: sn hdd) ....... ¾.6
40573 Super Heights **(52)** (bl) *(MissAJWhitfield)* 3–8-7 DaleGibson (11) (led 5f: r.o one pce) ....... 2½.7
Gun Rule **(63)** *(DRLaing)* 7–9-5 GDuffield (8) (prom tl wknd 2f out) .............. 1½.8
40714 Pretonic **(69)** *(MJohnston)* 3–9-10 RPElliott (2) (prom over 4f) .................. ½.9
2746 Pure Bliss **(45)** *(RJHodges)* 4–8-1 JQuinn (6) (prom over 4f) ..................... ¾.10
40572 Cee-En-Cee **(62)** *(MMcCourt)* 7–9-4 RWernham (9) (a bhd) ...................... hd.11
Tylers Wood **(56)** *(SDow)* 6–8-12 NDay (13) (bit bkwd: n.d) .......................... 1½.12
3984 Mai Pen Rai **(52)** *(CJHill)* 3–8-7 NAdams (12) (a bhd) ............................. 3.13
4075 Blues Balidar **(55)** (bl) *(JLSpearing)* 3–8-10 RFox (14) (n.d) ..................... 4.14
3902 Absent Forever (20/1) Withdrawn (bolted bef s) : not under orders

**4/1** Precentor(op 13/2), **9/2** Kissavos(6/1—7/2), **6/1** Sarum(9/2—7/1), **9/1** Unanimous (IRE)(7/1—12/1), **10/1** Gun Rule, Cee-En-Cee(op 5/1), Vuchterbacher, **12/1** Pretonic(8/1—14/1), **14/1** Super Heights, **16/1** EL VOLADOR(op 10/1), **20/1** Mai Pen Rai(op 12/1), **50/1** Ors. CSF £79.99, CT £695.49. Tote £39.10: £8.90 £2.50 £3.90 (£112.70). Mr I. A. Baker (BOGNOR REGIS) bred by L. and Mrs Hutch. 14 Rn 1m 25.32 (1.32)

SF—35/40/27/49/29/40

## 4089
EUROPEAN GOLF PATRONS H'CAP (0-100) £2914.60 (£805.60: £383.80)
1¼m (AWT)
2-45 (2-50)

4075* **Super Sally (85)** *(MJRyan)* 4–9-10 (5x) ‡3DBiggs (7) (a.p: led over 2f out: all out) .....—1

4060² Rapporteur (USA) **(86)** (Fav) *(CCElsey)* 5–10-0 WNewnes (4) (b: lw: hdwy 3f
out: ev ch fnl f: r.o) ............................................................................. s.h.**1**
4060 Belmoredean **(73)** *(RJO'Sullivan)* 6–9-1 GDuffield (3) (a.p: ev ch fnl f: r.o) ...... s.h.**3**
4052 Will He Or Wont He (IRE) **(61)** (bl) *(CNAllen)* 3–8-0 GBardwell (5) (chsd ldr: led 5f
out tl over 2f out) ................................................................................... 12.**4**
4035 Pusey Street Boy **(51)** *(JRBosley)* 4–7-7 RFox (1) (lw: led 5f) ............................ 3.**5**
3227 Marjons Boy **(53)** (v) *(CDBroad)* 4–7-9⁽²⁾ NAdams (2) (lw: a bhd) ................ ¾.**6**
4052 Barkston Singer **(56)** *(MrsNMacauley)* 4–7-12 DaleGibson (6) (a bhd) .............. nk.**7**
3565 Liu Liu San (IRE) **(58)** *(PButler)* 3–7-6⁽⁴⁾ ‡5DHarrison (9) (a bhd) .................... 6.**8**
3511 Turbo-R **(54)** *(AJChamberlain)* 3–7-0 ‡7KimMcDonnell (8) (prom 5f) ............... ¾.**9**
LONG HANDICAP: Pusey Street Boy 7-1, Marjons Boy 6-12, Liu Liu San (IRE) 6-9, Turbo-R 6-4.

**5/4** Rapporteur (USA)(op 7/1), **11/4** SUPER SALLY(2/1—3/1), **100/30** Belmoredean, **7/1** Barkston Singer,
**20/1** Will He Or Wont He (IRE), **25/1** Pusey Street Boy, **33/1** Marjons Boy, **66/1** Ors. CSF £6.64, CT £10.39.
Tote £3.30: £1.80 £1.30 £1.10 (£3.10). Mr Leonard Seale (NEWMARKET) bred by R. Duggan. 9Rn
2m 7.37 (4.37)
SF—36/39/25/–/–/–

---

**4090**    CHRISTINA H'CAP (0-70) £2324.00 (£644.00: £308.00)  **6f (AWT)**   3-15 (3-28)
(Weights raised 2 lb)

4058⁵ **Murmuring** **(49)** *(SDow)* 5–8-10 TQuinn (10) (w ldrs: led over 3f out: r.o wl) ........... —**1**
4052 The Shanahan Bay **(59)** (v) *(MrsNMacauley)* 6–9-6 NDay (4) (a.p: hrd rdn 2f out:
ev ch 1f out: r.o) .................................................................................. 3.**2**
3876 Proud Brigadier (IRE) **(55)** *(WCarter)* 3–8-11 ‡5NGwilliams (7) (s.s: hdwy fnl 2f:
nvr nrr) ................................................................................................ 1.**3**
4047⁴ Rushanes **(63)** (Fav) *(TCasey)* 4–9-3 ‡7SWilliams (9) (w ldrs: ev ch 2f out: nt
qckn) .................................................................................................. 1.**4**
4058 Tachyon Park **(45)** (bl) *(PHowling)* 9–8-6 NCarlisle (3) (a.p: no hdwy fnl 2f) ............. 4.**5**
4042 Pretty Poppy **(50)** *(PMitchell)* 3–8-11 JWilliams (5) (a abt oamo pl) .................... 1½.**6**
967 Jovial Kate (USA) **(56)** *(MDIUsher)* 4–9-3 CRutter (2) (bit bkwd: nvr nr chal) ........ 1½.**7**
4056 Inswinger **(44)** *(WGRWightman)* 5–8-5 SDawson (1) (a bhd) .............................. 4.**8**
4039⁶ Dulzura **(43)** *(APJarvis)* 3–8-4 NAdams (11) (led over 2f: wknd over 2f out) ............ ½.**9**
3801 Grey Tudor **(46)** (v) *(CNAllen)* 4–8-7 GBardwell (6) (a bhd) ................................ ½.**10**
One Heart **(34)** *(RJHodges)* 6–7-9⁽²⁾ JQuinn (3) (a wl bhd: t.o) ........................ 12.**11**
LONG HANDICAP: One Heart 7-0.

**7/2** Rushanes, **9/2** Inswinger, **5/1** The Shanahan Bay, **6/1** MURMURING(op 4/1), **8/1** Proud Brigadier (IRE),
Pretty Poppy, **12/1** Tachyon Park(op 8/1), Dulzura(op 6/1), **16/1** Grey Tudor, **33/1** Jovial Kate (USA), **100/1**
One Heart. CSF £33.73, CT £221.08. Tote £4.00: £2.70 £2.50 £1.60 (£13.30). Mr J. A. Redmond (EPSOM)
bred by J. A. Redmond. 11 Rn
1m 12.23 (1.63)
SF—27/25/12/14/–/–

T/Plpt: £21.60 (69.05 Tckts).                                              Hn

---

# LINGFIELD (L-H) Equitrack
## Friday, December 27th [Standard]
Going Allowance: minus 0.25 sec per fur (FS)

**4091**    LIGHT BRIGADE CLAIMING STKS (I)  £2167.20 (£599.20: £285.60)
       **6f (AWT)**                               12-25 (12-26)

4071² **Respectable Jones** **(83)** (Fav) *(GBBalding)* 5–8-11 JWilliams (6) (led over 3f
out: rdn out) ....................................................................................... —**1**
4090* Murmuring **(49)** *(SDow)* 5–8-5 TQuinn (7) (chsd wnr fnl 3f: no imp) .................. 4.**2**
4071⁵ Toshiba Comet **(80)** (bl) *(WJPearce)* 4–8-4 ‡7GParkin (3) (swtg: rdn 4f out: nvr nr
to chal) ............................................................................................. 3.**3**
4090 Jovial Kate (USA) **(56)** *(MDIUsher)* 4–8-2 CRutter (5) (swtg: led over 2f: wknd
over 2f out) ........................................................................................ ½.**4**
4086⁶ Catalani **(63)** *(TJNaughton)* 6–8-1 DaleGibson (4) (prom 3f) ............................ 3.**5**
4086 Domino Trick **(47)** (bl) *(AMoore)* 3–7-13 GBardwell (8) (rdn thrght: bhd fnl 3f) ...... 15.**6**
1502 Cotton Bank (IRE) **(40)** *(PButler)* 3–8-7 SWhitworth (1) (lw: a bhd) .................... 5.**7**
3386 Katy's Pet **(40)** *(RPCHoad)* 3–7-13 NAdams (2) (lft at s: virtually t.n.p: wl t.o) ........ dist.**8**

**5/6** RESPECTABLE JONES, **7/2** Murmuring, **4/1** Toshiba Comet, **16/1** Catalani, **25/1** Jovial Kate (USA), **50/1**
Ors. CSF £4.00, Tote £2.00: £1.10 £1.20 £1.20 (£2.50). Mrs Ernest Weinstein (DORCHESTER) bred by E.
and Mrs Weinstein. 8 Rn
1m 12.49 (1.89)
SF—29/7/–/–/–/–

---

**4092**    THIN RED LINE STKS (Mdn 2-Y.O) £2265.20 (£627.20: £299.60)
       **1m (AWT)**                               12-55 (12-58)

4070⁴ **Courtenay Bee** *(WJarvis)* 9-0 TQuinn (3) (led over 3f out: all out) ........................ —**1**

4084² Noble Singer *(HThomsonJones)* 8-9 JWilliams (1) (a.p: ev ch fnl f: r.o wl) .............. ½.**2**
4070³ Granite Boy **(62)** *(PJFeilden)* 9-0 CDwyer (9) (hdwy 4f out: ev ch fnl f: r.o wl) ....... s.h.**3**
4085³ Level Up (Fav) *(RGuest)* 8-9 NDay (4) (lw: a.p: ev ch over 2f out: hrd rdn & wknd
      over 1f out) ..................................................................................... 6.**4**
4084⁶ Litho Bold Flasher *(WJPearce)* 9-0 LCharnock (8) (outpcd: nvr nr to chal) ............... 8.**5**
3508 Simon Ellis (IRE) **(50)** *(DRLaing)* 9-0 TyroneWilliams (2) (led over 4f: wknd over
      2f out) ........................................................................................... 6.**6**
4084 True Mood *(JDBethell)* 8-9 SDawson (6) (bhd fnl 4f) ........................................... 7.**7**
Jolly Jester *(TJNaughton)* 9-0 DaleGibson (10) (lt-f: dwlt: a bhd) ........................ 2½.**8**
Reach Me Not (IRE) *(CHolmes)* 8-4 ‡⁵KRutter (5) (unf: s.s: a wl bhd) ................... 25.**9**

**7/4** Level Up, **100/30** Noble Singer, **7/2** COURTENAY BEE, **9/2** Granite Boy, **20/1** Jolly Jester, **33/1** Litho Bold
Flasher, True Mood, **50/1** Ors. CSF £14.52, Tote £3.50: £1.70 £1.20 £2.40 (£4.70). Mrs Guen Boyle
(NEWMARKET) bred by J. L. Woolford. 9 Rn       1m 39.29 (2.59)
                                           SF—31/24/28/5/–/–

## 4093       SEBASTOPOL H'CAP (0-80) £2259.00 (£624.00: £297.00)    **1m 5f (AWT)**    1-25 (1-32)

4073² Fiala (IRE) **(72)** (Jt-Fav) *(JHMGosden)* 3–10-0 MHills (7) (lw: hld up: led over 3f
      out: rdn clr 2f out: easily) ................................................................. —**1**
4083² Qualitair Blazer **(48)** *(JRJenkins)* 4–9-9 SWhitworth (5) (b.hind: swtg: a.p: r.o
      one pce fnl 3f) ................................................................................ 8.**2**
4072 Sailor Boy **(64)** *(RAkehurst)* 5–9-11 TQuinn (6) (led 11f out tl over 3f out: one
      pce) ............................................................................................. 2½.**3**
4073* Carpet Slippers **(52)** (Jt-Fav) *(JDBethell)* 5–8-13 RHills (8) (lw: rdn 5f out: hdwy
      4f out: one pce fnl 3f) ...................................................................... nk.**4**
4072* Shar Emblem **(52)** *(SDow)* 3–8-8 JQuinn (4) (rdn 7f out: no hdwy fnl 3f) ............ 4.**5**
3899³ With Gusto **(38)** *(KOCunningham-Brown)* 4–7-13 SDawson (3) (b: b.hind: led 2f:
      wknd 3f out: eased whn btn over 2f out) .............................................. 20.**6**
4089 Liu Liu San (IRE) **(42)** *(PButler)* 3–7-12 GBardwell (2) (rdn 9f out: a bhd: t.o fnl 4f)   25.**7**
4087³ Shining Wood (13/2) Withdrawn : not under orders

**11/4** Carpet Slippers, FIALA (IRE), **4/1** Shar Emblem, **9/2** Qualitair Blazer, Sailor Boy, **10/1** With Gusto, **50/1**
Liu Liu San (IRE). CSF £15.42, CT £49.99. Tote £4.30: £2.30 £2.70 (£14.00). Mr C. A. B. St. George
(NEWMARKET) bred by M. L. Page in Ireland. 7 Rn       2m 46.14 (2.64)
                                           SF—55/20/31/18/5/–

## 4094       CRIMEA H'CAP (0-80) £2490.00 (£690.00: £330.00)    **1¼m (AWT)**      1-55 (1-59)

4074* **Double Echo (IRE) (62)** *(JDBethell)* 3–9-4 RHills (9) (hdwy 4f out: led wl over 1f
      out: drvn out) ................................................................................. —**1**
4081⁴ Tara's Delight **(64)** *(MJRyan)* 4–9-6 ‡³DBiggs (3) (a.p: bmpd after 1f: hrd rdn over
      1f out: r.o wl fnl f) ........................................................................... 1½.**2**
4075³ Super Morning **(61)** (Fav) *(GBBalding)* 5–9-6 JWilliams (1) (rapid hdwy 5f out:
      led over 3f out tl wl over 1f out: unable qckn) ..................................... 3½.**3**
4054² Wileys Folly **(49)** *(SDow)* 5–8-1 ‡⁷MJermy (8) (hdwy 5f out: one pce fnl 2f) ........... hd.**4**
4060³ Princess Roxanne **(56)** (bl) *(ABailey)* 4–8-8 ‡⁷PBowe (12) (a.p: one pce fnl 2f) ...... 2½.**5**
2240 Race to Time (IRE) **(60)** *(RAkehurst)* 3–9-2 TQuinn (14) (rdn 7f out: hdwy over 2f
      out: nvr nrr) .................................................................................... nk.**6**
4088⁴ Unanimous (IRE) **(67)** *(NACallaghan)* 3–9-2 ‡⁷JTate (7) (rdn 6f out: hdwy 3f out:
      nvr nr to chal) ................................................................................ nk.**7**
3699³ Gallant Effort (IRE) **(48)** *(SDow)* 3–8-4 JQuinn (2) (outpcd) ................................ 12.**8**
4060⁴ Premier Dance **(52)** *(DHaydnJones)* 4–8-11 DaleGibson (15) (outpcd: nvr nrr) ...... ½.**9**
3785³ Internal Affair **(44)** *(JPearce)* 3–7-7 ‡⁷ALiggins (5) (prom 5f) ................................ ½.**10**
3122 Helios **(64)** *(RSimpson)* 3–9-6 GDuffield (11) (b: led over 5f) ................................ 2½.**11**
4034 Martini Executive **(68)** *(WJPearce)* 3–9-10 LCharnock (10) (s.s: a bhd) ................ s.h.**12**
4089⁶ Marjons Boy **(42)** (v) *(CDBroad)* 4–8-1 NAdams (13) (rdn 6f out: a bhd) ................ ½.**13**
4089⁴ Will He Or Wont He (IRE) **(61)** (v) *(CNAllen)* 3–8-10 ‡⁷MichaelDenaro (4) (bmpd
      after 1f: led over 4f out tl over 3f out: sn wknd) .................................... ½.**14**
3803 Modesto (USA) **(60)** *(KOCunningham-Brown)* 3–9-2 MHills (6) (b: prom 5f) ......... nk.**15**
4060 Sianema **(24)** *(DRLaing)* 3–9-6 TyroneWilliams (16) (b: s.s: a bhd) ..................... ¾.**16**

**7/2** Super Morning, **4/1** Princess Roxanne, **7/1** Tara's Delight, Unanimous (IRE), **8/1** DOUBLE ECHO (IRE),
**9/1** Premier Dance, **11/1** Wileys Folly(12/1—8/1), **12/1** Race to Time (IRE), **14/1** Will He Or Wont He (IRE),
**16/1** Gallant Effort (IRE), Helios, **25/1** Marjons Boy, Martini Executive, Internal Affair, **33/1** Ors. CSF £66.25,
CT £221.65. Tote £6.80: £1.40 £1.50 £1.50 £4.10 (£32.50). Mrs John Lee (DIDCOT) bred by A. Tarry in
Ireland. 16 Rn       2m 6.06 (3.06)
                                           SF—48/47/40/20/22/29

## 4095       ALMA H'CAP (0-90) £2715.90 (£752.40: £359.70)    **7f (AWT)**      2-25 (2-28)

4075 **Pytchley Night (86)** *(DMorris)* 4–9-7 ‡⁷StephenDavies (6) (lw: hdwy over 2f out:
      led over 1f out: all out) ...................................................................... —**1**

I

4045* Litmore Dancer **(55)** *(JDBethell)* 3–7–5 ‡5DHarrison (7) (dwlt: gd hdwy 2f out: hrd rdn over 1f out: r.o wl fnl f) ................................................ ½.2

4065⁵ Mystic Crystal (IRE) **(78)** (bl) *(WAO'Gorman)* 3–9–0 ‡5EmmaO'Gorman (5) (wl bhd 5f: gd hdwy over 1f out: fin wl) ................................................ 1.3

4090³ Proud Brigadier (IRE) **(60)** *(WCarter)* 3–7–10⁽⁵⁾ ‡5NGwilliams (4) (a.p: ev ch 2f out: one pce) ................................................ 1½.4

4088 Gun Rule **(63)** *(DRLaing)* 7–8–5 MHills (11) (prom over 5f) ................................................ 2.5

4075 Helawe **(82)** (bl) *(SirMarkPrescott)* 8–9–10 GDuffield (3) (led over 5f) ................................................ s.h.6

4075² Crosby **(74)** *(PAKelleway)* 5–9–2 TQuinn (2) (eyeshield: hmpd over 3f out: no hdwy fnl 2f) ................................................ 1.7

3911 Dumbreck **(54)** *(ABailey)* 4–7–10 JQuinn (8) (prom over 4f) ................................................ ¾.8

4065² Dorset Duke **(85)** (Fav) *(GWragg)* 4–9–8 ‡5FNorton (1) (b: hrd rdn 3f out: nvr nrr) ................................................ ¾.9

4027 Jumby Bay **(59)** *(MJohnston)* 5–8–1 RPElliott (12) (lw: hdwy over 5f out: ev ch 2f out: sn wknd) ................................................ ½.10

4088 Tylers Wood **(56)** *(SDow)* 6–7–12 DaleGibson (9) (lw: bhd fnl 2f) ................................................ 4.11

4088 Absent Forever **(58)** (bl) *(WRMuir)* 3–7–13 CRutter (10) (prom 4f) ................................................ 2½.12

**5/2** Dorset Duke, **4/1** Crosby, **5/1** PYTCHLEY HUNT(tchd 8/1), **7/1** Litmore Dancer, **17/2** Helawe, **10/1** Absent Forever(tchd 16/1), Gun Rule, **12/1** Proud Brigadier (IRE), **16/1** Dumbreck, Mystic Crystal (IRE), **50/1** Ors. CSF £40.29, CT £491.74. Tote £6.30: £3.10 £2.30 £5.50 (£39.30). Mr J. J. Higgins (NEWMARKET) bred by G. W. Robinson. 12 Rn
1m 24.88 (.88)
SF—67/35/55/32/35/53

---

**4096**　　LIGHT BRIGADE CLAIMING STKS (II) £2147.60 (£593.60: £282.80)
6f **(AWT)**　　　　　　　　　2-55 (2-58)

4075⁴ Mac's Fighter **(90)** (v) (Fav) *(WAO'Gorman)* 6–9–2 ‡5EmmaO'Gorman (1) (wl bhd 3f: gd hdwy over 2f out: led wl ins fnl f: pushed out) .............—1

3807 Gorinsky (IRE) **(84)** *(JBerry)* 3–8–13 JCarroll (4) (b) (led: hrd rdn & hdd wl ins fnl f: r.o wl) ................................................ nk.2

4071³ Assignment **(78)** *(JFfitch-Heyes)* 5–9–0 TQuinn (5) (b.hind: chsd ldr: hrd rdn & ev ch ins fnl f: r.o) ................................................ 1½.3

4088 Cee-En-Cee **(62)** *(MMcCourt)* 7–8–9 RWernham (7) (lost pl 3f out: styd on fnl f) ....... 6.4

4090 Inswinger **(44)** *(WGRWightman)* 5–8–7 JWilliams (3) (outpcd: rdn & hdwy 3f out: one pce fnl 2f) ................................................ 1½.5

4086⁵ Oratel Flyer **(29)** *(RThompson)* 4–8–4 RFox (6) (spd 4f) ................................................ ½.6

Anne's Bank (IRE) *(AMoore)* 3–8–2 NAdams (2) (lw: bhd fnl 2f) ................................................ 12.7

**6/4** MAC'S FIGHTER, **9/4** Gorinsky (IRE), **11/4** Assignment, **10/1** Cee-En-Cee, **20/1** Inswinger(tchd 12/1), **33/1** Anne's Bank (IRE), **40/1** Oratel Flyer. CSF £5.31, Tote £2.70: £1.50 £1.70 (£3.80). Mr M. McDonnell (NEWMARKET) bred by R. M. West. 7 Rn
1m 12.26 (1.66)
SF—39/35/30/1/–/–

---

**4097**　　INKERMAN NURSERY (0-75) £2069.20 (£571.20: £271.60)　**7f (AWT)**　3-25 (3-27)

4076* Quiet Miss **(72)** *(DRCElsworth)* 9-4 JWilliams (3) (rdn & lost pl 5f out: rallied over 1f out: str run fnl f: led nr fin) ................................................—1

4043⁴ Dublin Indemnity (USA) **(60)** (bl) *(NACallaghan)* 8-6 GDuffield (4) (hdwy 4f out: hrd rdn & led ins fnl f: hdd nr fin) ................................................ ½.2

3945* Jefferson Davis (IRE) **(75)** *(WJPearce)* 9-0 ‡7GParkin (5) (plld hrd: led after 1f tl ins fnl f: unable qckn) ................................................ 3.3

4070* Parlemo (IRE) **(70)** (Fav) *(JDBethell)* 9-2 RHills (2) (jnd ldr over 3f out: wknd over 1f out) ................................................ 2.4

2072 Thursley **(63)** *(HJCollingridge)* 8-9 JQuinn (1) (lw: led 1f: rdn & no hdwy fnl 3f) ....... s.h.5

4037 Jubal Early **(66)** (bl) *(CNAllen)* 8-5 ‡7MichaelDenaro (6) (a bhd) ................................................ 15.6

**9/4** Parlemo (IRE), **11/4** QUIET MISS, **7/2** Jefferson Davis (IRE)(op 7/1), Dublin Indemnity (USA), **14/1** Thursley, **25/1** Jubal Early (IRE). CSF £11.88, Tote £2.90: £1.30 £2.70 (£6.60). Mr G. M. Gee (WHITSBURY) bred by D. R. C. Elsworth. 6 Rn
1m 26.58 (2.58)
SF—39/25/24/20/12/–

T/Plpt: £133.30 (8.85 Tckts).
LMc

---

4077—**SOUTHWELL (L-H)** Fibresand
## Saturday, December 28th [Standard]
Going Allowance: 0.10 sec per fur (SL)
　　　　　　　　　　　　　　　　　　　Wind: slt bhd

Stalls: high 1, 3 & 4, rest low

**4098**　　TURKEY CLAIMING STKS (I)　£2407.00 (£667.00: £319.00)
1½m **(AWT)**　　　　　　　　　12-25 (12-25)

3950⁵ Lara's Baby (IRE) **(64)** (Fav) *(RAkehurst)* 3–8–0 ‡5FNorton (8) (a.p: led on bit wl over 2f out: rdn out fnl f) ................................................—1

4064* **Kirby Opportunity (49)** *(JPearce)* 3–7-13 GBardwell (2) (chsd ldrs: 5th st: rdn 2f out: no imp fnl f) ............................................................ 3.2

4069⁴ **Pleasure Ahead (46)** *(MRChannon)* 4–8-7 LornaVincent (14) (hdwy & 4th st: rdn over 2f out: sn btn) ................................................ 12.3

4069⁶ **Gipsy King (58)** (bl) *(PAKelleway)* 3–8-8 GDuffield (13) (sn rdn along: hdwy 8f out: 3rd st: wknd 2f out) .................................... 1½.4

Orpen (IRE) *(WAO'Gorman)* 3–8-5 ‡⁵EmmaO'Gorman (15) (bit bkwd: led after 3f tl wl over 2f out: sn btn) ........................................ 4.5

4064³ **Flash Bulb (42)** *(JHetherton)* 4–8-3 LCharnock (7) (sn outpcd & bhd: nvr rchd ldrs) ........................................................ 1½.6

4083⁵ **Peak District (40)** (bl) *(KSBridgwater)* 5–8-9 RFox (6) (led 2f: 6th st: eased whn btn appr fnl f) ........................................ nk.7

**Tristan's Comet (35)** *(JLHarris)* 4–8-9 JQuinn (4) (bit bkwd: nvr nr to chal) ............ 2.8

4069 **Kir (IRE) (55)** (bl) *(MMcCormack)* 3–8-8 AClark (9) (8th st: no hdwy) ................. 1½.9

3955 **Design Wise (30)** *(DMoffatt)* 7–7-12 ‡⁷DarrenMoffatt (5) (n.d) ............................ 3.10

4062² **Grey Commander (36)** *(MBrittain)* 3–8-3 ‡⁵SMaloney (10) (a bhd) ..................... 4.11

4083 **Daleside (57)** *(TFairhurst)* 3–8-5 ‡³JFanning (1) (led after 2f: sn hdd: 7th & wkng st) ........................................................ 4.12

4073 **Talish (53)** *(TDBarron)* 3–8-11 TQuinn (11) (a bhd) ...................................... ½.13

4062⁵ **Corporate Type (IRE) (33)** *(DWChapman)* 3–7-12 SWood (12) (bhd fr ½-wy) ...... ¾.14

**Smart Performer (80)** *(NTinkler)* 6–9-7 KimTinkler (3) (bkwd: hmpd & lost tch after 2f: t.o after) ........................................ 15

**100/30** LARA'S BABY (IRE)(op 6/4), **7/2** Kirby Opportunity, **7/1** Talish, **10/1** Gipsy King, Grey Commander, Orpen (IRE), **11/1** Peak District, Kir (IRE)(op 7/1), **14/1** Pleasure Ahead, Flash Bulb(op 12/1), Smart Performer, **25/1** Ors. CSF £16.48, Tote £4.60: £2.10 £1.90 £3.10 (£12.70). Larabuild Contractors (EPSOM) bred by Killarkin Stud in Ireland. 15 Rn                    2m 41 (6.8)
SF—30/23/7/5/–/–

**4099**      MISTLETOE H'CAP (0-60) £2589.70 (£719.20: £345.10)      **7f (AWT)**      12-55 (12-55)

4088³ **Vuchterbacher (49)** *(PFTulk)* 5–8-10 ‡⁷TWilson (15) (b: hdwy & 4th st: c wd & led over 1f out: rdn out) .......................... —1

4068⁵ **On Y Va (USA) (50)** *(RJRWilliams)* 4–9-4 NDay (6) (hdwy 3f out: ev ch 1f out: r.o) ... 1.2

4078⁴ **In a Whirl (USA) (58)** *(DWChapman)* 3–9-11 TQuinn (10) (chsd ldrs: 5th st: led wl over 1f out: sn hdd: kpt on u.p) .................. ¾.3

4078⁶ **Shedad (USA) (55)** *(TDBarron)* 3–9-8 AlexGreaves (1) (led over 5f: one pce) ...... 3½.4

4081³ **Night Transaction (47)** *(AHide)* 4–9-1 DaleGibson (5) (lw: bhd tl r.o fnl 2f) ............ nk.5

4056 **Awesome Power (60)** *(CRNelson)* 5–9-9 ‡⁵FNorton (16) (r.o fnl 2f: nrst fin) ............ nk.6

4068 **Kinlacey (59)** *(BAMcMahon)* 4–9-13 GDuffield (12) (nvr nrr) ............................ 4.7

4039⁴ **Singing Nelly (59)** *(BWHills)* 3–9-4 MHills (2) (chsd ldrs: 7th st: sn btn) ........ 2½.8

4039⁵ **Swinging Lady (55)** *(WWHaigh)* 3–9-5 ‡³JFanning (4) (8th st: sn no imp) .... s.h.9

4081 **Krisfield (51)** *(TPMcGovern)* 6–9-5 JQuinn (14) (s.i.s: nvr rchd ldrs) ............ 2½.10

4057⁵ **Count Me Out (48)** *(JPearce)* 6–9-2 RPrice (13) (prom: 3rd st: sn wknd) ............ 2.11

4075⁵ **Scots Law (50)** *(RJO'Sullivan)* 4–9-4 GBardwell (8) (chsd ldr: 2nd st: sn wknd) .... ½.12

**Northern Rocket (53)** *(JPLeigh)* 4–9-0 ‡⁷SWilliams (9) (bkwd: hdwy & 6th st: sn wknd) .................................. 4.13

2164⁵ **Damaaz (IRE) (58)** (v) *(JSWainwright)* 3–9-4 ‡⁷GParkin (11) (bit bkwd: a bhd) .... 1½.14

4081 **Ensharp (USA) (56)** (bl) *(JPLeigh)* 5–9-10 ACulhane (3) (prom 3f) ..................... 15.15

**9/4** Singing Nelly(op 8/1), **6/1** VUCHTERBACHER(9/2—7/1), **7/1** Awesome Power, **15/2** Night Transaction(op 5/1), **8/1** Scots Law(op 12/1), **9/1** On Y Va (USA)(op 6/1), Count Me Out(op 8/1), **10/1** Shedad (USA), In a Whirl (USA), **12/1** Kinlacey, Krisfield, **16/1** Swinging Lady, **20/1** Ors. CSF £68.55, CT £518.03. Tote £6.80: £2.10 £3.00 £2.40 (£11.20). Mrs D. Carvalho (NEWMARKET) bred by Mrs D. Z. Carvalho. 15 Rn                    1m 30.8 (4.2)
SF—43/48/53/39/31/38

**4100**      TURKEY CLAIMING STKS (II) £2386.70 (£661.20: £316.10)
**1½m (AWT)**                                                     1-25 (1-26)

4038* **Hand Painted (50)** (Fav) *(JPearce)* 7–8-3 GDuffield (13) (hld up: hdwy 6f out: 3rd st: chal on bit appr fnl f: shkn up & led ins fnl f) ......... —1

4062⁴ **Swagman (USA) (37)** *(CRBeever)* 4–8-6 ‡⁵FNorton (10) (a.p: 2nd st: led over 1f out: hdd ins fnl f: no ch w wnr) .................. 3.2

3699 **Barichste (47)** *(BAMcMahon)* 3–7-11 ‡⁷SSanders (5) (chsd ldrs: 5th st: one pce fnl 2f) ........................................ 3½.3

4073 **Frescobaldo (USA) (58)** *(MPNaughton)* 5–9-4 ‡³JFanning (4) (led 6f out tl over 1f out: rdn & no ex) ............................ 1½.4

4060[6] Northern Flyer **(65)** *(MCChapman)* 3–8-9 ‡[7]SWilliams (11) (hdwy 4f out: nvr rchd ldrs) .................................................................................................. 12.5

4039[3] Supadupa **(43)** *(MrsBarbaraWaring)* 4–8-10 NHowe (7) (hdwy & 8th st: rdn 2f out: no imp) ............................................................................................... s.h.6

1243[6] Two Badges (IRE) **(60)** *(MrsAKnight)* 3–7-11 ‡[3]DBiggs (6) (bkwd: prom tl 4th & wkng st) ................................................................................................. 1½.7

Top Prize *(MBrittain)* 3–8-3 ‡[5]SMaloney (1) (unf: bkwd: dwlt: nvr trbld ldrs) .............. 8.8

2501[4] Elegant Approach **(45)** *(WWHaigh)* 3–8-1 JQuinn (12) (hdwy 5f out: 6th st: sn btn) .................................................................................................. 12.9

Vinstan *(CASmith)* 5–9-7 AProud (15) (b: bkwd: a bhd) ........................................ ½.10

4004 Al Manhal (IRE) **(34)** *(RHollinshead)* 3–8-13[4] ‡[7]CorrineCripps (9) (a bhd) ......... 1½.11

4038 Persian Dipper *(RBastiman)* 3–8-4[1] ‡[7]HBastiman (8) (bit bkwd: chsd ldrs tl 6th & wkng st) ................................................................................................. 2½.12

4056 Melfa **(34)** (bl) *(AWDenson)* 3–8-5[2] MHills (2) (b.hind: led 4f: sn wknd) ............ hd.13

4077[6] Our Amber *(DWChapman)* 4–8-4 SWood (3) (prom 6f) ........................................ 14

**Evens** HAND PAINTED(op 6/4), **9/1** Frescobaldo (USA), **10/1** Supadupa, Elegant Approach(op 6/1), Northern Flyer(op 6/1), **11/1** Two Badges (IRE)(8/1—12/1), Vinstan, **12/1** Swagman (USA), **20/1** Melfa, **25/1** Top Prize, Barichste, Persian Dipper, **33/1** Ors. CSF £15.85, Tote £2.30: £1.20 £3.00 £12.60 (£6.60). Mrs Margaret Baxter (NEWMARKET) bred by Mrs R. M. Vella. 14 Rn; Hand Painted clmd Mrs L Payne£3,020

2m 41.2 (7)
SF—31/28/12/30/–/–

**4101**      NATIONAL PLANT & TRANSPORT H'CAP (0-80) £2325.80 (£643.80: £307.40)
1¾m (AWT)      1-55 (1-56)

4050[2] **Bridge Player (45)** *(DMoffatt)* 4–8-5 ‡[7]DarrenMoffatt (5) (hdwy 8f out: 5th st: led ins fnl f: pushed out) ................................................................................ —1

4083* Chronological **(57)** (v) *(MHTompkins)* 5–9-10 (7x) TQuinn (1) (hld up: hdwy 5f out: 4th st: led over 2f out: hdd ins fnl f: no ex) ............... 1½.2

4072[2] Intricaty **(67)** *(CCElsey)* 3–9-9 ‡[5]FNorton (11) (bhd: hdwy over 2f out: rdn & r.o fnl f) ............................................................................................ 1½.3

4083[6] Dalby Dancer **(58)** *(BAMcMahon)* 7–9-11 GDuffield (9) (chsd ldr: 2nd st: one pce fnl 2f) ................................................................................................. 3½.4

4081 Irish Native (IRE) **(65)** (bl) *(CASmith)* 3–9-12 AProud (6) (led tl hdd over 2f out: wknd fnl f) .............................................................................................. 2.5

4050[3] Racing Raskal **(30)** *(CaptJWilson)* 4–7-8 ‡[3]DBiggs (7) (chsd ldrs tl wknd over 4f out) ................................................................................................. 5.6

3632 Queens Tour **(39)** *(MBrittain)* 6–8-1 ‡[5]SMaloney (3) (chsd ldrs: 6th & wkng st) ......... 6.7

3589[5] Anderson Rose **(34)** *(CaptJWilson)* 3–7-6[2] ‡[3]JFanning (10) (prom: 7th & wkng st) .. nk.8

4073[4] Bronze Runner **(40)** *(EAWheeler)* 7–8-0 ‡[7]BThomas (4) (eyeshield: hld up: hdwy 7f out: 3rd st: sn wknd) ............................................................................ ¾.9

3069 Never Cry Wolf **(43)** *(LJCodd)* 3–7-11[11] ‡[7]RMitchell (2) (a bhd: t.o fnl 8f) ................. 10

3021 Spring Forward **(33)** (bl) *(REPeacock)* 7–8–0 JQuinn (8) (bkwd: t.o fnl 6f) ................. 11

LONG HANDICAP: Anderson Rose 7-3, Never Cry Wolf 7-0.

**7/4** Chronological(op 3/1), **7/2** Intricaty, **11/2** BRIDGE PLAYER, **7/1** Bronze Runner, **8/1** Dalby Dancer, **9/1** Irish Native (IRE)(op 6/1), **10/1** Racing Raskal, **20/1** Spring Forward, Queens Tour, **25/1** Ors. CSF £16.84, CT £38.42. Tote £6.70: £1.40 £1.40 £1.70 (£6.80). D. A. & M. Lambert and Partners (CARTMEL) bred by Swettenham Stud. 11 Rn

3m 9.8 (10.5)

**4102**      CHRISTMAS CLAIMING STKS (2-Y.O) £2346.10 (£649.60: £310.30)
1m (AWT)      2-25 (2-25)

4048 **Feeling Foolish (IRE) (58)** (v) *(SGNorton)* 7-13[1] ‡[7]OPears (5) (bhd: hdwy over 3f out: hrd rdn to ld ins fnl f) ................................................. —1

4082* Runnel **(65)** *(DWChapman)* 9-1 SWood (10) (led tl hdd & no ex ins fnl f) ............ 2½.2

3293[6] Bassio (BEL) **(75)** *(CNAllen)* 8-7 ‡[7]MichaelDenaro (4) (bhd: hdwy over 1f out: kpt on) ................................................................................................. 3½.3

4048[6] Little Nod **(65)** *(MJCamacho)* 8-3 ‡[5]SMaloney (3) (chsd ldrs: 3rd st: one pce) ...... 2.4

4051 Bold Melody *(PCHaslam)* 8-0 ‡JFanning (1) (chsd ldrs: 5th st: sn rdn & no imp) ....... 1.5

4082[4] Silver Samurai **(66)** *(RHollinshead)* 8-7 ACulhane (6) (chsd ldr: 2nd st: rdn & wknd 2f out) .......................................................................................... 2½.6

4015* Lady Linnet **(65)** (Fav) *(PFICole)* 8-3 TQuinn (8) (chsd ldrs: effrt & 4th st: sn btn) ..... s.h.7

4085 Mississippi Queen *(RJRWilliams)* 8-0 DaleGibson (9) (chsd ldrs tl 6th & btn st) ........ 7.8

2976 Resa Girl *(JSWainwright)* 7-11 JQuinn (2) (bit bkwd: dwlt: a bhd) ........................... 12.9

4066[2] Cellito (IRE) *(WAO'Gorman)* 8-6 ‡[5]EmmaO'Gorman (7) (lw: nvr plcd to chal) ......... 2.10

7/4 Lady Linnet(op 3/1), 7/2 Runnel, 4/1 Cellito (IRE), 8/1 Silver Samurai, Bassio (BEL)(op 5/1), 9/1 Little Nod(op 6/1), 10/1 FEELING FOOLISH (IRE), 20/1 Bold Melody, 25/1 Ors. CSF £47.47, Tote £9.80: £2.80 £1.70 £2.60 (£51.80). Mr M. Turner (BARNSLEY) bred by Mrs J. O'Halloran in Ireland. 10 Rn; Feeling Foolish (IRE) clmd A Hoyle £6,025

1m 44.8 (5.5)
SF—14/22/3/–/–/–

**4103**  CHRISTMAS PUDDING H'CAP (0-80) £2325.80 (£425.60 each)
**6f (AWT)**  2-55 (3-00)

| | | |
|---|---|---|
| 4088 | **Super Heights (52)** (bl) (MissAJWhitfield) 3–8-2 DaleGibson (12) (t.o 3f: c wd ent st: rapid hdwy over 1f out: led nr fin) | —1 |
| 4077* | Friendly Claim (IRE) (81) (TDBarron) 3–9-10 (7x) ‡7VHalliday (8) (chsd ldrs: 7th st: led 1f out tl ct nr fin) | 1½.2 |
| 3521 | Tudorgateway (63) (v) (MHTompkins) 3–8-6 ‡7SMulvey (13) (t.o 3f: c wd ent st: r.o fnl 2f: fin wl) | d.h.2 |
| 3437 | Flying Promise (57) (RABennett) 3–8-2 ‡5FNorton (10) (gd hdwy 2f out: ev ch ins fnl f: no ex nr fin) | nk.4 |
| 4027 | Silly's Brother (47) (NBycroft) 5–7-11 LCharnock (3) (led 1f: outpcd & 8th st: swtchd lft & r.o appr fnl f) | nk.5 |
| 4080* | Wellsy Lad (USA) (74) (DWChapman) 4–9-10 (7x) TQuinn (9) (lw: a.p: 3rd st: ev ch over 1f out: one pce) | hd.6 |
| 4090² | The Shanahan Bay (59) (v) (MrsNMacauley) 6–8-9 NDay (2) (in tch: effrt 3f out: n.m.r over 1f out: sn btn) | 1.7 |
| 4063 | Sobering Thoughts (43) (bl) (DWChapman) 5–7-7 SWood (7) (chsd ldrs: 5th st: ev ch over 1f out: wknd fnl f) | 2.8 |
| 4090⁵ | Tachyon Park (46) (bl) (PHowling) 9–7-10(1) NCarlisle (5) (w ldr: 2nd st: wknd over 1f out) | 1.9 |
| 4028 | Breezy Day (78) (BAMcMahon) 5–9-7 ‡7JBramhill (1) (led 5f out to 1f out: wknd qckly) | 2½.10 |
| 4080⁶ | Ping Pong (50) (TFairhurst) 3–7-11 ‡3JFanning (4) (chsd ldrs: 6th st: sn btn) | hd.11 |
| 3710 | Castle Cary (46) (TCraig) 5–7-10(3) JQuinn (6) (b.hind: a bhd) | 3½.12 |
| 4081* | Cronk's Courage (71) (v) (EJAlston) 5–9-7 (7x) MHills (11) (chsd ldr: 4th st: wknd 2f out) | 1½.13 |

LONG HANDICAP: Sobering Thoughts 7-6, Castle Cary 6-10.

7/4 The Shanahan Bay(op 7/2), 6/1 Cronk's Courage(op 7/2), 7/1 Sobering Thoughts(10/1—12/1), Wellsy Lad (USA)(op 4/1), 8/1 Friendly Claim (IRE)(op 5/1), 10/1 Tachyon Park, 12/1 Silly's Brother, 14/1 Tudorgateway, Breezy Day, 16/1 Ping Pong, SUPER HEIGHTS, 20/1 Castle Cary, 25/1 Flying Promise. CSF w FC £70.82, w T £108.77, CT w FC & T £856.73, w T & FC £888.04. Tote £32.50: £6.40 £3.00 FC, £4.90 T (w FC £89.60, w T £179.20). Mr B. Pagliaroli (LAMBOURN) bred by Aston Park Stud. 13 Rn 1m 17.3 (3.9)
SF—22/38/20/15/9/35

**4104**  IVY NURSERY (0-75) £2346.10 (£649.60: £310.30) **1m (AWT)**  3-30 (3-32)
(Weights raised 8 lb)

| | | |
|---|---|---|
| 4082² | **Meltonby (65)** (JHetherton) 9-0 ‡7SWilliams (9) (led after 1f: hld on wl fnl f) | —1 |
| 3293² | Sure to Win (IRE) (62) (Fav) (ABailey) 8-11 ‡7StephenDavies (4) (in tch: hdwy & 5th st: swtchd & r.o fnl f) | ½.2 |
| 4046⁵ | Ballyranter (59) (HJCollingridge) 9-1 JQuinn (3) (lw: hld up: hdwy & 7th st: ev ch over 1f out: one pce) | ¾.3 |
| 4082⁵ | Aegaen Lady (54) (JEtherington) 8-10 LCharnock (5) (hdwy over 3f out: c wd: one pce appr fnl f) | ¾.4 |
| 4043³ | Super-Sub (59) (MJFetherston-Godley) 9-1 TQuinn (11) (lw: a.p: 3rd st: ev ch over 1f out: btn fnl f) | s.h.5 |
| 4044 | Lizzie Drippin (CAN) (48) (MDIUsher) 8-4 CRutter (2) (r.o fnl 2f: nvr able to chal) | 10.6 |
| 4066 | Tazamisha (53) (RHollinshead) 8-2 ‡7AGarth (1) (nvr nrr) | 2.7 |
| 3145⁶ | Dark Midnight (IRE) (63) (PCHaslam) 9-5 AlexGreaves (10) (sn chsng wnr: 2nd st: wknd 2f out) | 2½.8 |
| 4046 | Medbourne (IRE) (44) (JLHarris) 7-9 ‡5FNorton (6) (hmpd 4f out: n.d after) | 3.9 |
| 3288⁵ | Do the Business (IRE) (55) (CNAllen) 8-4 ‡7MichaelDenaro (12) (chsd ldrs tl 6th & wkng st) | 1.10 |
| 2542 | Whirlygig (53) (JSWainwright) 8-9(1) CDwyer (7) (led 1f: wknd 4f out) | s.h.11 |
| 4044 | Don't Move (IRE) (57) (MHTompkins) 8-13 DaleGibson (13) (sn bhd) | 2½.12 |
| 3017 | Phargold (IRE) (49) (PCHaslam) 8-2 ‡3JFanning (8) (b.nr hind: prom: 4th st: wknd qckly) | 1½.13 |

11/4 Sure to Win (IRE)(4/1—2/1), 9/2 Super-Sub(4/1—6/1), 5/1 Ballyranter, 13/2 MELTONBY(4/1—7/1), 10/1 Aegaen Lady, Phargold (IRE), 11/1 Medbourne (IRE), 12/1 Dark Midnight (IRE), 16/1 Whirlygig, 20/1 Don't Move (IRE)(op 12/1), Tazamisha, 25/1 Ors. CSF £25.63, CT £93.63. Tote £8.30: £2.10 £1.80 £2.20 (£13.10). Mr J. Hetherton (MALTON) bred by Woodditton Stud Ltd. 13 Rn 1m 44.9 (5.6)
SF—28/23/25/18/22/–

T/Plpt: £109.00 (14.15 Tckts). Dk

# *Raceform*

## TURF AND ALL-WEATHER FLAT RACING 1992

Complete record of
Turf and All-Weather Flat Racing
from January 1st to November 9th, 1992

## EVRY (R-H)
### Wednesday, November 13th [Soft]
Going Allowance: 1.10 sec per fur (S)

**1a**  PRIX BELLE DE NUIT (listed race) (3 & 4-Y.O.F) £12220.00  **1½m**

**Gloria Mundi (FR)** *(France)* 4–8–11 DBoeuf .................. —1
Sheriyna (FR) *(France)* 3–8–9 WMongil .................. 4.2
SPECIFICITY (USA) *(JHMGosden)* 3–8–9 WRyan .................. hd.3
BLUE BIRDS FLY *(RCharlton)* 3–8–9 ABadel (btn more than 16l by wnr) .................. 12
Tote 6.00f: 2.20f 2.60f 4.30f (23.80f). Mrs M. Levesque (F.Doumen,FRANCE) bred by Jean Saucede in France. 12 Rn                                               2m 45.4 (14.81)
SF—82/71/70

## LEOPARDSTOWN (L-H)
### Sunday, November 17th [Good to soft]
Going Allowance: 0.90 sec per fur (S)

**2a**  MONARCH PROPERTIES KNOCKAIRE STKS (listed race)  IR£8625.00  **7f**

**Regal Crest (USA)** *(Ireland)* 3–8–13 SCraine .................. —1
Blue Daisy (USA) *(Ireland)* 3–8–12 JPMurtagh .................. 1.2
Gogarty (IRE) (bl) *(Ireland)* 3–8–8 WJSupple .................. 3.3
TROJAN CROWN (IRE) (bl) *(GWragg)* 3–8–10 WJO'Connor .................. 1.4
THE AUCTION BIDDER *(RHollinshead)* 4–8–10 WRyan (btn further 7l) .................. 8
Tote £10.50: £2.40 £1.50 £2.80 (£14.40). Mr R. Leah (A.J.Maxwell,IRELAND) bred by Joseph Arriola in USA. 10 Rn                                               1m 35.2 (9.2)
SF  55/51/38/37/34

## CAPANNELLE (R-H)
### Sunday, November 17th [Heavy]

**3a**  PREMIO GUIDO BERARDELLI (Gp 2) (2-Y.O) £32154.00  **1¼m**

**JAPE (USA)** *(PFICole)* 2–8–11 AMunro .................. —1
JAIRZINHO (USA) *(RHannon)* 2–8–11 WCarson .................. 1½.2
Brace Blu (USA) *(Italy)* 2–8–11 GDettori .................. ¾.3
ALLARME SOCIALE (USA) *(BHanbury)* 2–8–11 JCaro (btn further 3l) .................. 6
GOVERNOR'S IMP (USA) *(MBell)* 2–8–11 LPiggott (btn 57l by wnr) .................. 18
Tote 87L: 71L 51L 31L (881L). Mr Fahd Salman (WHATCOMBE) bred by Kinderhill Select Bloodstock in USA.
18 Rn                                               2m 10.9

**4a**  PREMIO UMBRIA (Gp 3)  £27561.00  **6f**

**Arranvanna** *(Italy)* 3–9–3 VMezzatesta .................. —1
Dream Talk *(France)* 4–9–6 CAsmussen .................. 1.2
Glen Jordan *(Italy)* 5–9–6 GDettori .................. 2.3
NICHOLAS (USA) *(MrsLPiggott)* 5–9–6 LPiggott (btn further 7l) .................. 6
SECRET THING (USA) *(CEBrittain)* 2–8–4 JCaro (btn 17l by wnr) .................. 10
Tote 77L: 24L 30L 23L (163L). A.J.B.Stable (A.Renzoni,ITALY) bred by Highclere Stud. 16 Rn    1m 12.9

## HOLLYWOOD PARK (L-H)
### Sunday, November 17th [Firm]

**5a**  HOLLYWOOD DERBY (I) (Grade 1) (3-Y.O) £56995.00  **1m 1f (turf)**

**Eternity Star (USA)** *(America)* 3–8–10 EDelahoussaye .................. —1
Native Boundary (USA) *(America)* 3–8–10 CMcCarron .................. 1¾.2
Perfectly Proud (USA) *(America)* 3–8–10 KDesormeaux .................. hd.3
SATIN FLOWER (USA) *(JHMGosden)* 3–8–10 PValenzuela (btn further 1¾l) .................. 6
Tote 6.20 (1-2) 4.00 9.00 (1-2-3) 3.20 6.60 9.60 (SF: 70.20). Mr P. Wall (R. Frankel,AMERICA) bred by Lucy Young Ruspoli Trust in USA. 11 Rn                                               1m 47.2

**6a**  HOLLYWOOD DERBY (II) (Grade 1) (3-Y.O) £56995.00  **1m 1f (turf)**

**Olympio (USA)** *(America)* 3–8–10 EDelahoussaye .................. —1
Bistro Garden (USA) *(France)* 3–8–10 CMcCarron .................. ½.2
River Traffic (USA) *(America)* 3–8–10 ASolis .................. 1½.3
CLARET (IRE) *(MajorWRHern)* 3–8–10 GStevens (btn further 5½l) .................. 9
Tote 6.80 (1-2) 3.80 4.40 (1-2-3) 3.40 3.40 5.60 (SF: 30.80). Verne H.Winchell Jnr. (R.McAnally,AMERICA) bred by Verne H. Winchell Jnr. in USA. 10 Rn                                               1m 47

## 1a—EVRY (R-H)

### Wednesday, November 20th [Heavy]
Going Allowance: 1.05 sec per fur (S)

**7a**    PRIX DES CHENES (Gp 3) (2-Y.O.C & F) £20367.00  **1m**

**Litron (GER)** *(Germany)* 2–8-9  DIlic ...................................... —**1**
Greek Air (IRE) *(France)* 2–8-6  DBoeuf ................................ 2½.**2**
Saintry (USA) *(France)* 2–8-11  GGuignard ............................ 3.**3**
MOUGINS (IRE) *(DRCElsworth)* 2–8-9  CAsmussen ............... nk.**4**
Tote 7.10f: 2.90f 1.80f (SF: 33.20f). Mrs S. Wewering (T.Grieper,GERMANY) bred by Mrs S.Hager in Germany. 7 Rn                                                  1m 47.7 (10.3)
                                                                   SF—66/58/51/48

## MARSEILLE (R-H)

### Saturday, November 23rd [Good]

**8a**    GRAND PRIX DE MARSEILLE (listed race) £30550.00  **1¼m**

**KNIFEBOX (USA)** *(JHMGosden)* 3–8-11  WCarson ................ —**1**
Muroto *(France)* 5–9-3  ESaint-Martin ................................ 3½.**2**
Michel Georges *(France)* 3–8-11  CLeScrill ....................... s.h.**3**
Tote 9.00f: 2.70f 1.80f 1.70f (18.90f). Sheikh Mohammed (NEWMARKET) bred by Barbara Hunter in USA.
12 Rn                                                                2m 2.1

## BORDEAUX (R-H) Le Bouscat

### Sunday, November 24th [Heavy]

**9a**    GRAND PRIX DE BORDEAUX (listed race)  £20367.00  **1½m**

1a* **Gloria Mundi (FR)** *(France)* 4–8-11  DBoeuf .................. —**1**
Last King (FR) *(France)* 3–9-0  CLeScrill ......................... 3½.**2**
Windsider (USA) *(France)* 3–8-11  J-RDubosc ..................... ½.**3**
SHARP IMPOSTER (USA) *(HRACecil)* 3–9-0  WRyan (btn further 2l) ...... **5**
Tote 5.00f: 2.00f 5.90f 2.70f (93.70f). Mrs M-J Levesque (F.Doumen,FRANCE) bred by Jean Saucede in France. 13 Rn                                                No time taken

## TOKYO (L-H)

### Sunday, November 24th [Firm]

**10a**    JAPAN CUP (Grade 1)  £621762.00  **1½m**

**Golden Pheasant (USA)** *(America)* 5–8-13  GStevens ........... —**1**
Magic Night (FR) *(France)* 3–8-5  ABadel ......................... 1½.**2**
Shaftesbury Avenue (AUS) *(Austrailia)* 5–8-13  DGauci ......... 1½.**3**
Mejiro McQueen (JPN) *(Japan)* 4–8-13  YTake ..................... 1½.**4**
Rough Habit (NZ) *(NewZealand)* 5–8-13  JCassidy ............... ½.**5**
Wajd (USA) *(France)* 4–8-9  TJarnet ................................. 1¼.**6**
ROCK HOPPER *(MRStoute)* 4–8-13  PatEddery .................... nose.**7**
Fujiyama Kenzan (JPN) *(Japan)* 3–8-9  SKojima ................. 1¾.**8**
Main Caster (JPN) *(Japan)* 5–8-9  KMinai ......................... ½.**9**
Carib Song (JPN) *(Japan)* 5–8-13  MShibata ..................... ½.**10**
DRUM TAPS (USA) *(LordHuntingdon)* 5–8-13  LDettori .......... nk.**11**
TERIMON *(CEBrittain)* 5–8-13  MRoberts .......................... 1½.**12**
Splash of Colour *(France)* 4–8-13  FHead ......................... nk.**13**
Mejiro Ardan (JPN) *(Japan)* 6–8-13  MTamura ................... 6.**14**
George Monarch (JPN) *(Japan)* 6–8-13  SHayata ................ 2½.**15**

9/10 Mejiro McQueen (JPN), 5/1 Magic Night (FR), 86/10 Drum Taps (USA), 99/10 Rock Hopper, 126/10 Terimon, 141/10 Shaftesbury Avenue (AUS), 172/10 GOLDEN PHEASANT (USA), 24/1 Rough Habit (NZ), 25/1 Carib Song (JPN), 35/1 Wajd (USA), 42/1 Fujiyama Kenzan (JPN), 46/1 Mejiro Ardan (JPN), 55/1 Splash of Colour, 97/1 George Monarch (JPN), 126/1 Main Caster (JPN). Tote 18.20Y: 5.70Y 2.50Y 5.50Y (667.00Y). Mr W.Gretzky and Summer Stable (C.Whittingham,AMERICA) bred by Carelaine Farm & Vintage Meadow Farm in USA. 15 Rn                                                   2m 24.7

## 3a—CAPANNELLE (R-H)

### Sunday, November 24th [Heavy]

**11a**    PREMIO UNIRE CONSIGLIO EUROPEO ROMA VECCHIA (Gp 3)  £91870.00  **1¾m**

**SNURGE** *(PFICole)* 4–9-3  TQuinn .................................. —**1**

HIEROGLYPHIC (IRE) *(JHMGosden)* 3–8-8 WCarson .......................................... 2.2
Turgeon (USA) *(France)* 5–9-3 CAsmussen ...................................................... 4.3
SOUGHT OUT (IRE) *(MRStoute)* 3–8-5 BRaymond (btn further 10¾l) ............... 5
GOLDLINE SEEKER (bl) *(MAJarvis)* 3–8-8 BJovine (btn 22¼l by wnr) ............... 6
SHAMBO *(CEBrittain)* 4–8-13 JReid (btn 25l by wnr) ...................................... 7
Tote 57L: 17L 32L 13L (454L). Mr M. Arbib (WHATCOMBE) bred by Kilcarn Stud. 13 Rn           3m 15.6

## SAINT-CLOUD  (L-H)

### Tuesday, November 26th [Heavy]

Going Allowance: 1.30 sec per fur (Hvy)

**12a**    PRIX FILLE DE L'AIR (Gp 3) (F & M) £20367.00  1¼m 110y

**Fabulous Hostess (USA)** *(France)* 3–8-13 GGuignard ...................................... —1
On Credit (FR) *(France)* 3–8-9 ELegrix .......................................................... 1½.2
La Tirana (FR) *(France)* 4–8-11 WMongil ........................................................ 1½.3
FILIA ARDROSS (bl) *(ACStewart)* 5–9-4 RHills (btn further 5¾l) ....................... 8
DARTREY (IRE) *(MRStoute)* 3–8-9 LPiggott (btn 10¾l by wnr) .......................... 9
Tote 4.00f: 1.80f 2.70f 1.70f (29.50f). Mr J. Wertheimer (Mrs C. Head, FRANCE) bred by Wertheimer & Frere
in USA. 12 Rn                                                                      2m 26.2 (14.9)
SF—87/79/79

### 7a—EVRY  (R-H)

### Wednesday, November 27th [Heavy]

Going Allowance: 1.00 sec per fur (S)

**13a**    PRIX CONTESSINA (listed race)  £12220.00  6f 110y

**Zanadiyka (FR)** *(France)* 3–9-6 WMongil ...................................................... —1
PUNCH N'RUN (bl) *(RHannon)* 3–9-6 LPiggott ............................................... 1½.2
Idefix (USA) *(France)* 5–9-6 FHead ............................................................... hd.3
Tote 3.20f: 1.50f 3.90f 2.40f (30.00f). H. H. Aga Khan (A. de Royer-Dupre, FRANCE) bred by H.H. Aga Khan in
France. 11 Rn                                                                       1m 23.27 (7.57)
SF—81/75/74

### 5a—HOLLYWOOD PARK  (R-H)

### Friday, November 29th [Firm]

**14a**    HOLLYWOOD TURF EXPRESS H'CAP (I)  £32060.00  5f 110y

**Gundaghia (USA)** *(America)* 4–8-2 CNakatani ................................................ —1
Club Champ (USA) *(America)* 3–8-4 EDelahoussaye ...................................... ½.2
Sun Brandy (USA) *(America)* 4–8-3 CMcCarron ............................................. 1½.3
HAKY (FR) *(WAO'Gorman)* 3–8-2 KDesormeaux (btn further 4¾l) ................... 8
FURAJET (USA) *(AAScott)* 2–7-12 WCarson (btn further nk) ........................... 9
Tote 9.80 (1-2) 5.20 6.00 (1-2-3) 3.60 4.60 3.00. J.K.Goodman & R.Kieckhefer (Bob Baffert, AMERICA)
bred by John K. Goodman & Robert Kieckhefer in USA. 9 Rn                                61.4 sec

## HOLLYWOOD PARK  (L-H)

### Saturday, November 30th [Firm]

**15a**    CITATION H'CAP (I) (Grade 2)  £53161.00  1m 1f (turf)

**Notorious Pleasure (USA)** *(America)* 5–8-6 LPincay ...................................... —1
Somethingdifferent (USA) *(America)* 4–8-2 DFlores ....................................... 1¼.2
Classic Fame (USA) *(America)* 3–8-6 EDelahoussaye .................................... ¾.3
NUCLEUS (USA) *(JHMGosden)* 3–8-6 WCarson (btn further 6l) ...................... 7
Tote 9.00 (1-2) 4.60 10.20 (1-2-3) 3.40 5.80 3.80 (SF: 98.60). Robert, Karen, Marc, Michael and Richard
Levey (D. Vienna, AMERICA) bred by A. R. Bucci & J. R. Bramble in USA. 8 Rn                 1m 45.8

**16a**    MIESQUE STKS (I) (2-Y.O.F) £32060.00  1m (turf)

**More Than Willing (USA)** *(America)* 2–8-6 EDelahoussaye .............................. —1
Stormagain (USA) *(France)* 2–8-3 CMcCarron ............................................... nk.2
Looie Capote (USA) *(America)* 2–8-6 KDesormeaux ....................................... 2¼.3
SNOW FOREST (USA) *(JHMGosden)* 2–8-2 WCarson (btn further 5l) ............... 8
Tote 7.00 (1-2) 3.00 3.20 (1-2-3) 2.60 2.60 4.40 (SF: 19.00). Mr R.E. Hibbert (R. Reash, AMERICA) bred by
Robert E. Hibbert in USA. 8 Rn                                                      1m 35.4

**17a**    CITATION H'CAP (II) (Grade 2)  £53161.00  1m 1f

**Fly Till Dawn (USA)** *(America)* 5–8-7 LPincay .............................................. —1

Best Pal (USA) *(America)* 3–8-7 KDesormeaux ...................................... 1¾.2
Wolf (CHI) *(America)* 4–8-7 EDelahoussaye ...................................... nk.3
LORD CHARMER (USA) *(JHMGosden)* 4–8-1 WCarson (btn further 1¾l) ............ 5
Tote 21.00 (1-2) 8.40 7.00 (1-2-3) 4.00 3.80 2.60 (SF: 101.60). Mrs T.L.Gleis (D. Vienna,AMERICA) bred by Mrs Josephine Gleis in USA. 8 Rn
1m 45.8

# HOLLYWOOD PARK (L-H)

## Sunday, December 1st [Firm]

### 18a
HOIST THE FLAG STKS (I) (2-Y.O) £38743.00 **1m (turf)**

**Silver Ray (USA)** *(America)* 2–8-2 MPedroza ...................................... —1
Thinkernot (USA) *(America)* 2–8-3 CMcCarron ...................................... 1¼.2
African Colony (USA) *(America)* 2–8-2 LPincay ...................................... hd.3
GOLD DESERT (IRE) *(RCharlton)* 2–8-2 DFlores ...................................... nk.4
VYING VICTOR (USA) *(CFWall)* 2–8-2 KDesormeaux (btn further 7¾l) ............ 8
Tote 11.20 (1-2) 6.60 6.80 (1-2-3) 4.60 4.00 6.40 (SF: 87.80). Mr & Mrs J. S. Moss (B. Mayberry, AMERICA) bred by P.B.Walden in USA. 9 Rn
1m 35

### 19a
HOIST THE FLAG STKS (II) (2-Y.O) £37189.00 **1m (turf)**

**Contested Bid (USA)** *(France)* 2–8-2 CNakatani ...................................... —1
Turbulent Kris (USA) *(America)* 2–8-2 KDesormeaux ...................................... 1¾.2
Sevengreenpairs (USA) *(America)* 2–8-2 FMartinez ...................................... 4.3
FAIR CRACK (IRE) *(RHannon)* 2–8-9 BRaymond (btn further 11¼l) ............ 8
Tote 7.60 (1-2) 5.00 8.60 (1-2-3) 4.00 5.60 7.80 (SF: 55.20). Juddmonte Farms (M. Zilber, FRANCE) bred by Juddmonte Farms Inc. in USA. 9 Rn
1m 34.4

### 20a
THE MATRIARCH (Grade 1) (F & M) £56995.00 **1m 1f (turf)**

**Flawlessly (USA)** *(America)* 3–8-8 CMcCarron ...................................... —1
Fire the Groom (USA) *(America)* 4–8-11 GStevens ...................................... 1¾.2
Free At Last *(America)* 4–8-11 EDelahoussaye ...................................... ½.3
SUSURRATION (USA) *(BWHills)* 4–8-11 WCarson (btn further 20l) ............ 13
Tote 14.60 (1-2) 6.00 4.60 (1-2-3) 4.60 3.40 6.60 (SF: 63.20). Harbor View Farm (C.Whittingham.AMERICA) bred by Harbor View Farm in USA. 14 Rn
1m 46.6

# HOLLYWOOD PARK (L-H)

## Saturday, December 7th [Firm]

### 21a
ALLEZ FRANCE H'CAP (listed race) (3-Y.O.F) £25311.00 **1m 110y (turf)**

**Exchange (CAN)** *(America)* 3–8-5[1] LPincay ...................................... —1
Gold Fleece (USA) *(America)* 3–8-4 ASolis ...................................... 1¼.2
5a[6] SATIN FLOWER (USA) *(JHMGosden)* 3–8-10 CMcCarron ...................................... nk.3
Tote 12.20 (1-2) 6.60 9.80 (1-2-3) 4.00 5.00 3.00 (SF: 104.20). Mr Sidney H.Craig (B.Spawr, AMERICA) bred by Kinghaven Farms Ltd. in Canada. 9 Rn
1m 40.8

## 12a—SAINT-CLOUD (L-H)

## Saturday, December 7th [Heavy]
Going Allowance: 1.40 sec per fur (Hvy)

### 22a
PRIX LE FABULEUX (listed race) £12220.00 **1¼m 110y**

12a[3] **La Tirana (FR)** *(France)* 4–8-5[1] WMongil ...................................... —1
Fleur Du Manoir (FR) *(France)* 5–8-4 DBoeuf ...................................... ½.2
After the Sun (USA) *(France)* 3–8-4 ESaint-Martin ...................................... s.nk.3
8a* KNIFEBOX (USA) *(JHMGosden)* 3–8-11 WCarson (btn further 1¾l) ............ 5
Tote 3.80f: 1.50f 1.70 2.30f (8.60f). Marquesa de Moratalla (A de Royer-Dupre, FRANCE) bred by Horse Breeding Corp. & Olivier Nicol in France. 11 Rn
2m 26.5 (16.2)
SF—76/74/73

## SHA TIN (L-H) Hong Kong

## Sunday, December 15th [Good to firm]

### 23a
HONG KONG INVITATION BOWL £82562.00 **7f**

**Additional Risk (IRE)** *(Ireland)* 3–8-13 MJKinane ...................................... —1
Mastermind (FR) *(HongKong)* 4–9-0 GMosse ...................................... 1¾.2
Concert King (AUS) *(HongKong)* 4–9-0 BThomson ...................................... 1¼.3
SHALFORD (IRE) *(RHannon)* 3–8-13 BRaymond ...................................... hd.4

Tote HK341.60: HK65.80 HK34.20 HK21.70 (HK1,960.30). Moyglare Stud Farm Ltd. (D.K.Weld,IRELAND) bred by Moyglare Stud Farm Ltd. in Ireland. 14 Rn　　　　　　　　　　　　　　　　　1m 21.9

**24a**　　　HONG KONG INVITATION CUP　£123843.00　**1m 1f**

    **River Verdon** (HongKong) 4–9-0 GMosse .................................................. —**1**
    Prudent Manner (Ireland) 4–9-0 MJKinane ................................................. 1.**2**
    Majestic Boy (NZ) 5–9-0 SDye .............................................................. 1½.**3**
    KARINGA BAY (DenysSmith) 4–9-0 BRouse (btn further 1¾l) ................... **14**
Tote HK26.40: HK13.60 HK32.30 HK39.90 (HK174.70). Sir O.Cheung and R.Arculli (D.Hill,HONG KONG) bred by R.Arculli. 14 Rn　　　　　　　　　　　　　　　　　　　　1m 49.8

## SOUTHWELL (L-H) Fibresand

## Wednesday, January 1st [Standard]
Going Allowance: nil sec per fur (FS)

**25**　　　LEAP YEAR CLAIMING STKS (I)　£2206.40 (£610.40: £291.20)
    **1m 3f (AWT)**　　　　　　　　　　　　　　　　　12-35 (12-36)

    **Give Me Hope (IRE) (47)** (RGBrazington) 4–7-11 JQuinn (6) (a.p: 2nd st: led wl
        over 1f out: comf) .............................................................. —**1**
    Frescobaldo (USA) **(58)** (MPNaughton) 6–8-13 ‡⁵BDoyle (1) (lw: led tl hdd & no
        ex wl over 1f out) ............................................................... 3.**2**
    Magic Secret **(70)** (Fav) (PCHaslam) 4–8-13 ‡³JFanning (5) (lw: w ldr tl rdn & 3rd
        st: one pce) ....................................................................... 5.**3**
    Little Red Hen (OO'Neill) 7–8-4⁽²⁾ AMcGlone (7) (bit bkwd: prom: 4th st: sn rdn &
        no imp) .............................................................................. 6.**4**
    Athclare (IRE) (bl) (JAkehurst) 4–8-5 DaleGibson (4) (chsd ldrs tl 5th & btn st) .... 7.**5**
    Blue Disc **(36)** (CRBeever) 7–8-9 ‡⁷MichaelDenaro (3) (bit bkwd: bhd fr ½-wy) ....... 10.**6**
    Rodmarton (APJarvis) 5–8-8⁽¹⁾ SWhitworth (9) (hdwy u.p 6f out: 6th & btn st) ......... 3.**7**
    Bold Answer **(20)** (MCChapman) 9–8-5⁽¹⁾ ‡⁷SWilliams (2) (s.i.s: a bhd: t.o) ........... dist.**8**

4/6 Magic Secret, 7/2 Athclare (IRE)(op 9/4), **13/2** Frescobaldo (USA), **8/1** GIVE ME HOPE (IRE), **20/1** Little Red Hen(op 12/1), **25/1** Blue Disc, **33/1** Ors. CSF £55.26, Tote £9.70: £1.30 £1.10 £1.10 £1.00. R.J.B. Owen (REDMARLEY) bred by K. Hsu and A. R. G. Cherry-Downes in Ireland. 8 Rn　　2m 28.3 (6.8)
                                          SF—12/25/15/–/–/–

**26**　　　NEW YEAR H'CAP (0-70) £2226.00 (£616.00: £294.00)　**1¾m (AWT)**　　1-05 (1-06)

    **Brora Rose (IRE) (43)** (Fav) (JDBethell) 4–7-10 ‡⁷DHarrison (7) (sn outpcd &
        pushed along: rdn & 5th st: styd on to ld wl ins fnl f) ...................... —**1**
    Obeliski **(50)** (PCHaslam) 6–8-13 ‡³JFanning (1) (led 10f out tl hdd & no ex wl ins
        fnl f) ................................................................................. ½.**2**
    Enfant du Paradis (IRE) **(45)** (PDEvans) 4–8-0 ‡⁵SMaloney (5) (lw: hld up: hdwy
        7f out: 3rd st: ev ch 2f out: one pce fnl f) ................................ 1½.**3**
    Mississippi Beat (USA) **(37)** (v) (MPNaughton) 5–7-12 ‡⁵BDoyle (3) (hdwy & 4th
        st: kpt on fnl f) .................................................................. 1.**4**
    Jawani (IRE) **(47)** (v) (DrJDScargill) 4–8-7 JQuinn (4) (lw: hdwy 7f out: 2nd st:
        wknd over 2f out) ............................................................... 5.**5**
    Searcy **(48)** (h) (DBurchell) 4–8-8 LCharnock (2) (prom 8f: wknd & poor 6th st:
        t.o) .................................................................................. dist.**6**
    Corporate Type (IRE) **(33)** (DWChapman) 4–7-7 SWood (8) (led 4f: wknd 6f out:
        t.o) .................................................................................. 10.**7**
    Randama **(62)** (DJWintle) 5–10-0 JWilliams (6) (t.o fnl 6f) ......................... dist.**8**

2/1 BRORA ROSE (IRE), **5/2** Jawani (IRE), **6/1** Obeliski, **7/1** Mississippi Beat (USA), **8/1** Enfant du Paradis (IRE), **12/1** Searcy, **20/1** Randama, **25/1** Corporate Type (IRE). CSF £13.68, CT £71.51. Tote £3.10: £1.20 £2.70 £1.90 (£15.90). Mrs S. M. Burley (DIDCOT) bred by Mrs M. Beaumont in Ireland. 8 Rn
                                    3m 9.8 (10.5)

**27**　　　LEAP YEAR CLAIMING STKS (II)　£2206.40 (£610.40: £291.20)　**1m 3f (AWT)** 1-35 (1-35)

    **Hand Painted (50)** (Fav) (JPearce) 8–8-6 ‡⁵RPrice (3) (hld up: hdwy 5f out: 6th
        st: led on bit 1f out: sn clr: easily) ........................................ —**1**
    Quinzii Martin **(49)** (DHaydnJones) 4–8-9 JWilliams (5) (hdwy 5f out: led ent st tl
        hdd 1f out: no ch w wnr) ..................................................... 8.**2**
    Noushy (KSBridgwater) 4–8-2⁽¹⁾ AProud (8) (plld hrd: led tl hdd ent st: one pce) ....... 2.**3**
    Rajaya (USA) **(57)** (bl) (RO'Leary) 4–8-7 LCharnock (6) (bit bkwd: hld up: r.o fnl
        2f: nrst fin) ....................................................................... 3.**4**
    Sweet 'n' Low **(42)** (PJFeilden) 5–8-4 ‡⁷MichaelDenaro (9) (bit bkwd: prom: 4th
        st: sn btn) ........................................................................ ¾.**5**

Talish (53) (bl) *(TDBarron)* 4–8–13  AlexGreaves (4) (s.i.s: hdwy after 3f: 3rd st: rdn & wknd 2f out) ......................................................... nk.6
Al Shareef (40) (h) *(DBurchell)* 7–8–11  SWhitworth (1) (n.d) ........................... 4.7
Charming Gift (51) (bl) *(RJRWilliams)* 5–8–10  MHills (2) (prom: 5th st: sn wknd) ....... 3.8
Jimmy Pip (35) *(BAMcMahon)* 5–8–3 ‡⁷SSanders (7) (chsd ldrs 7f) ...................... 10.9

**11/8** HAND PAINTED, **5/2** Charming Gift, **6/1** Noushy(op 10/1), **8/1** Al Shareef, **10/1** Talish, **12/1** Quinzii Martin, **14/1** Rajaya (USA), **20/1** Sweet 'n' Low, **50/1** Jimmy Pip. CSF £18.93, Tote £2.10: £1.50 £1.90 £2.10 (£8.30). Mrs Margaret Baxter (NEWMARKET) bred by Mrs R. M. Vella. 9 Rn; Hand Painted clmd H Ramsden £6,659                                                                            2m 31.4 (9.9)

**28**   NEW YEAR RESOLUTION H'CAP (0-90) £2265.20 (£627.20: £299.60)
        **1m (AWT)**                                                          2-05 (2-05)

**Super Sally (86)** *(MJRyan)* 5–9-11 ‡³DBiggs (5) (hdwy & 4th st: hrd rdn to ld nr fin) ................................................................................ —1
Euroblake (77) (Fav) *(TDBarron)* 5–9-5  AlexGreaves (2) (hdwy & 2nd st: led over 1f out: hdd & unable qckn nr fin) .............................. hd.2
Cee-Jay-Ay (63) *(JBerry)* 5–8-5  JCarroll (1) (dwlt: r.o appr fnl f: nrst fin) ......... 4.3
Mac's Princess (USA) (65) *(WAO'Gorman)* 4–8-1 ‡⁵EmmaO'Gorman (3) (lw: hld up: hdwy & 6th st: unable qckn fnl f) .......................... ½.4
Fair Dare (55) *(CBBBooth)* 4–7-7⁽³⁾ ‡³JFanning (6) (led tl hdd over 1f out: sn btn) 2.5
Kristis Girl (60) *(DHaydnJones)* 5–8-2  DaleGibson (8) (plld hrd: w ldr tl 3rd & rdn st: wknd fnl f) ................................................ 1½.6
Carrolls Marc (IRE) (72) *(PJFeilden)* 4–8-6 ‡⁷MichaelDenaro (4) (bkwd: prom tl 5th & btn st) .................................................... 8.7
Dawn Success (64) *(DWChapman)* 6–8-6  SWood (7) (w ldrs tl wknd qckly 4f out) ¾.8
LONG HANDICAP: Fair Dare 7-2.

**7/4** Euroblake, **3/1** Mac's Princess (USA)(op 5/1), **4/1 SUPER SALLY**, **11/2** Cee-Jay-Ay, **6/1** Kristis Girl, **12/1** Dawn Success, **14/1** Carrolls Marc (IRE), **20/1** Fair Dare. CSF £12.57, CT £38.59. Tote £4.60: £1.70 £1.60 £1.60 (£3.30). Exors of the late Mr Leonard Seale (NEWMARKET) bred by R. Duggan. 8 Rn     1m 43.4 (4.1)
                                                                          SF—48/41/15/9/–/–

**29**   NEW ERA CLAIMING STKS (3-Y.O) £2147.60 (£593.60: £282.80)   6f (AWT)   2-35 (2-35)

**Pop to Stans (80)** *(TDBarron)* 8-2  AlexGreaves (3) (hld up: mod 5th st: rapid hdwy to ld over 1f out: sn clr) ............................ —1
Golden Sickle (USA) (Fav) *(WAO'Gorman)* 8-2 ‡⁵EmmaO'Gorman (1) (led wl over 4f: no ch w wnr) ...................................... 8.2
Palacegate Racing (77) *(JBerry)* 8-6  JCarroll (5) (lw: chsd ldrs: 2nd st: ev ch 2f out: one pce) .................................................. 3½.3
Runnel (79) *(DWChapman)* 8-10  SWood (4) (hmpd after 1f: 3rd st: no imp) ......... 1½.4
Miss Narnia (52) *(APJarvis)* 7-7⁽²⁾ ‡³JFanning (2) (chsd ldrs: 4th st: sn btn) ........ 3½.5

**2/1** Golden Sickle (USA)(tchd 5/1), **9/4** Palacegate Racing, **5/2** Runnel, **9/2 POP TO STANS**(3/1—5/1), **16/1** Miss Narnia. CSF £13.73, Tote £6.40: £2.20 £1.60 (£14.20). Mr W. G. Spink (THIRSK) bred by Lincoln Collins. 5 Rn                                                                          1m 16.8 (3.4)
                                                                          SF—20/–/–/–/–

**30**   'HAIR OF THE DOG' H'CAP (3-Y.O) (0-90) £2030.00 (£560.00: £266.00)
        **6f (AWT)**                                                          3-05 (3-05)

**Palacegate King (53)** *(JBerry)* 7-8⁽¹⁾  LCharnock (2) (mde all: hld on wl fnl f) ........... —1
Patrician Magician (71) *(RJRWilliams)* 8-5 ‡⁷MichaelDenaro (3) (lw: hld up: hdwy & 4th st: ev ch ins fnl f: no ex nr fin) .............. 1.2
Appealing Times (USA) (75) *(WAO'Gorman)* 8-11 ‡⁵EmmaO'Gorman (4) (chsd ldr tl 3rd st: no imp appr fnl f) .......................... 1½.3
Try Leguard (IRE) (80) (Fav) *(WCarter)* 9-7  JWilliams (1) (chsd ldrs tl 5th st: n.d after) ...................................................... 5.4
Meltonby (72) *(JHetherton)* 8-10 (7x) ‡³JFanning (5) (dwlt: hdwy & 2nd st: ev ch 2f out: sn btn) ...................................... nk.5

**7/4** Try Leguard (IRE), **3/1** Appealing Times (USA), **7/2** Meltonby, Patrician Magician, **8/1 PALACEGATE KING**(op 5/1). CSF £32.83, Tote £6.30: £2.20 £2.70 (£17.80). Palacegate Corporation Ltd (COCKERHAM) bred by Miss E. Streatfeild. 5 Rn                                                              1m 16.9 (3.5)
                                                                          SF—10/17/17/7/–

**31**   HOGMANAY H'CAP (0-70) £2402.40 (£666.40: £319.20)   7f (AWT)   3-35 (3-36)

**Doulab's Image (63)** (bl) (Fav) *(JAGlover)* 5–9-2 ‡⁷SWilliams (16) (hdwy & 9th st: led over 1f out: sn pushed clr: comf) .................... —1

State Governor **(65)** *(DWChapman)* 4–9-11 SWood (8) (led after 1f: hdd over 1f out: no ch w wnr) ............................................................................ 4.2
Les Amis **(47)** *(MJRyan)* 5–8-4 ‡³DBiggs (12) (r.o wl appr fnl f: nrst fin) ................ 2½.3
Sandmoor Denim **(46)** *(SRBowring)* 5–8-6 AProud (3) (prom: 4th st: rdn & one pce appr fnl f) ................................................................................ nk.4
Pims Classic **(68)** (bl) *(WJHaggas)* 4–10-0 MHills (4) (prom: 2nd st: rdn & wknd wl over 1f out) ............................................................ 3½.5
Saladan Knight **(60)** (bl) *(JGFitzGerald)* 7–8-13 ‡⁷MHunt (13) (eyeshield: bit bkwd: hld up: r.o fnl 2f: nvr able to chal) ................................ hd.6
Pilar **(47)** *(MrsNMacauley)* 4–8-7 DaleGibson (10) (prom: 3rd st: wknd over 2f out) ................................................................................ 2.7
Miss Knight **(49)** *(RBastiman)* 5–8-2(3) ‡⁷HBastiman (7) (nvr trbld ldrs) ............ s.h.8
My Alibi (IRE) **(40)** (bl) *(WCarter)* 4–7-9 ‡⁵NGwilliams (11) (lost pl 4f out: n.d after) 1½.9
Daley Brioche **(47)** *(PCHaslam)* 4–8-4 ‡³JFanning (15) (b: lw: chsd ldrs: 6th st: sn btn) ................................................................................ 1½.10
Say You Will **(44)** (v) *(MPNaughton)* 8–8-7 AMcGlone (14) (n.d) .................... 1.11
Foursingh **(64)** (bl) *(CBBBooth)* 4–9-10 ACulhane (2) (bit bkwd: hmpd after 3f: bhd after) ................................................................................ 3.12
Hinari Hi Fi **(43)** *(PDEvans)* 7–7-12 ‡⁵SMaloney (6) (prom: 7th st: sn wknd) ...... 2½.13
Summer Sands **(46)** *(JLHarris)* 4–8-6 JWilliams (5) (b.off hind: chsd ldrs tl 8th & btn st) ................................................................................ 3.14
Godsall **(40)** (bl) *(MrsNMacauley)* 5–8-0 JQuinn (1) (led 1f: 5th & wkng st) .......... 4.15
Shedad (USA) **(52)** *(TDBarron)* 4–8-5 ‡⁷VHalliday (9) (reard stalls: s.v.s: a t.o) ... dist.16

**11/4** DOULAB'S IMAGE, **4/1** Sandmoor Denim(op 6/1), **13/2** Say You Will, **7/1** Shedad (USA), **10/1** Daley Brioche(12/1—8/1), **11/1** Les Amis(op 7/1), **12/1** Saladan Knight, Pims Classic, State Governor(9/1—14/1), **14/1** Hinari Hi Fi(op 8/1), **20/1** Miss Knight(op 10/1), **25/1** Summer Sands, **33/1** Ors. CSF £38.11, CT £309.19. Tote £4.70: £1.70 £3.40 £1.80 £1.50 (£21.10). Claremont Management Services (WORKSOP) brod by Hadi Al Tajir. 16 Rn
1m 30.3 (3.7)
**3F**—47/44/15/10/27/10

T/Plpt: £161.90 (5.6 Tckts). Dk

## SOUTHWELL (L-H) Fibresand
### Friday, January 3rd [Standard]
Going Allowance: 5f: minus 0.20 sec (FS); Rest: nil sec per fur (F)

**32**     OSBERTON CLAIMING STKS (I) (Mdn 4-Y.O) £2206.40 (£610.40: £291.20)
       **7f (AWT)**                                      12-10 (12-11)

**Ringland (USA)** *(PCHaslam)* 9-4 ‡³JFanning (7) (lw: a.gng wl: 3rd st: led over 2f out: sn wl clr: easily) ........................................................ —1
Qualitair Rhythm (IRE) **(47)** **(Fav)** *(JHetherton)* 7-9 ‡³DBiggs (1) (sn rdn & bhd: r.o fnl 2f: no ch w wnr) ............................................ 10.2
Dashing April **(63)** *(DTThom)* 8-7(1) JWilliams (4) (bit bkwd: hdwy & poor 5th st: r.o one pce fnl 2f) ............................................ 2½.3
Strip Cartoon (IRE) **(30)** (bl) *(SRBowring)* 7-13 NAdams (2) (led over 4f: no ch w wnr: wknd fnl f) ............................................ 2½.4
Cleo Modena (IRE) *(MO'Neill)* 8-0 JQuinn (11) (chsd ldr: 2nd st: wknd over 2f out) ................................................................ 4.5
Kabera **(33)** *(DWChapman)* 7-13 SWood (8) (no hdwy fnl 3f) .................... 4.6
Miss Aragon **(48)** *(MissLCSiddall)* 7-6 ‡⁵FNorton (10) (lw: prom: 4th st: rdn & wknd 2f out) ............................................ 1.7
Restless Niece **(40)** *(TDBarron)* 8-6 AlexGreaves (6) (a bhd) ...................... 1.8
Green's Bonheur **(40)** *(MPNaughton)* 7-8(3) ‡⁵BDoyle (9) (a bhd) .......... 3½.9
Pick and Choose **(48)** *(JPLeigh)* 7-12 LCharnock (12) (bkwd: prom: poor 6th & wkng st: t.o) ............................................ 2½.10
Hannah Brown (IRE) **(34)** *(BAMcMahon)* 7-7(2) ‡⁷JBramhill (3) (bit bkwd: t.o) ........ nk.11
Company Cash *(RBastiman)* 9-0 ‡⁷HBastiman (5) (bkwd: a bhd: t.o) ................ 1½.12

**5/2** Qualitair Rhythm (IRE)(3/1—11/8), **11/4** Miss Aragon(op 5/1), **100/30** RINGLAND (USA)(2/1—9/2), **12/1** Dashing April(op 6/1), Restless Niece(7/1—14/1), **20/1** Green's Bonheur, Strip Cartoon (IRE), **33/1** Kabera, **40/1** Ors. CSF £10.97, Tote £5.80: £1.20 £1.10 £2.70 (£6.00). Mr S. A. B. Dinsmore (MIDDLEHAM) bred by Robinson Farm in USA. 12 Rn
1m 29.9 (3.3)
**SF**—54/1/5/–/–/–

**33**     CHATSWORTH H'CAP (0-70) £2245.60 (£621.60: £296.80)    **5f (AWT)**     12-40 (12-42)

**Sir Tasker (61)** *(JLHarris)* 4–9-8 JWilliams (9) (mde all: rdn over 1f out: r.o wl) ........ —1
In a Whirl (USA) **(58)** *(DWChapman)* 4–9-2 ‡³JFanning (12) (a.p: rdn over 1f out: r.o ins fnl f) ............................................ ½.2

Meeson Times **(52)** (Fav) (BEllison) 4—8-13 MHills (4) (a.p: ev ch over 1f out: r.o) .......... hd.3
Drummer's Dream (IRE) **(43)** (MrsNMacauley) 4—8-1 ‡3DBiggs (8) (a chsng ldrs: r.o fnl f) .......... hd.4
Lazy Hill **(32)** (DWChapman) 5—7-7 SWood (11) (prom: lost pl 2f out: r.o ins fnl f) .......... 1½.5
Rushanes **(63)** (TCasey) 5—9-3 ‡7SWilliams (10) (lw: prom over 3f) .......... 1½.6
Hinari Video **(64)** (MJohnston) 7—9-11 RPElliott (7) (lw: hdwy & edgd lft over 2f out: ev ch over 1f out: wknd ins fnl f) .......... nk.7
Beaumont's Keep **(34)** (TDBarron) 6—7-9 LCharnock (6) (hdwy & carried lft over 2f out: ev ch over 1f out: wknd fnl f) .......... ½.8
Barbara's Cutie **(43)** (MBlanshard) 4—7-13 ‡5FNorton (3) (spd 3f) .......... ¾.9
Lady of the Fen **(67)** (MrsNMacauley) 4—10-0 SKeightley (2) (spd 3f: t.o) .......... 6.10
Rancho Mirage **(62)** (MrsNMacauley) 5—9-9 NDay (1) (b: outpcd: t.o) .......... 5.11

LONG HANDICAP: Lazy Hill 7-1.

**5/1** Meeson Times, **6/1** In a Whirl (USA)(op 4/1), Barbara's Cutie, Rushanes(8/1—5/1), Lady of the Fen, **8/1** Rancho Mirage, Drummer's Dream (IRE), **10/1** SIR TASKER(op 11/2), Beaumont's Keep, **12/1** Hinari Video, **33/1** Lazy Hill. CSF £66.69, CT £312.87. Tote £13.10: £3.00 £1.60 £2.30 (£44.80). Mr C. Conway (MELTON MOWBRAY) bred by W. H. Joyce. 11 Rn
60.2 sec (2.2)
SF—44/36/32/19/5/23

---

**34**     BRAMHAM CLAIMING STKS (3-Y.O) £2147.60 (£593.60: £282.80)    **7f (AWT)**    1-10 (1-11)

29⁴ Runnel **(79)** (Fav) (DWChapman) 9-4 SWood (1) (mde all: easily) .......... —1
30² Patrician Magician **(71)** (RJRWilliams) 8-7 ‡7MichaelDenaro (2) (b.hind: wnt 2nd & rdn st: no imp) .......... 6.2
Whirlygig **(52)** (bl) (JSWainwright) 8-2 JQuinn (4) (rdn over 3f out: poor 4th st: n.d) .......... 6.3
29⁵ Miss Narnia **(50)** (bl) (APJarvis) 8-2 NAdams (5) (chsd wnr tl 3rd & rdn st: sn wknd) .......... 5.4
Bold Melody (PCHaslam) 8-3 ‡3JFanning (3) (5th st: a last) .......... 1½.5

**5/4** RUNNEL, **11/8** Patrician Magician, **9/1** Miss Narnia(10/1—14/1), **10/1** Bold Melody, **25/1** Whirlygig. CSF £3.18, Tote £1.60: £1.40 £1.10 (£2.10). Mr E. Stockdale (YORK) bred by Ruckmans Farm. 5 Rn
1m 31.9 (5.3)
SF—24/-/-/-/-

---

**35**     BURGHLEY H'CAP (0-70) £2265.20 (£627.20: £299.60)    **1m 3f (AWT)**    1-40 (1-41)

Qualitair Flyer **(31)** (JFBottomley) 10-7-7 GBardwell (11) (lw: a.p: 2nd st: led over 2f out: hrd rdn: r.o wl) .......... —1
Mr Wishing Well **(60)** (RJRWilliams) 6—9-8 MBirch (4) (b.hind: 3rd st: ev ch over 2f out: one pce) .......... 3½.2
In Truth **(45)** (DWChapman) 4—8-3 SWood (2) (led over 8f: r.o one pce) .......... s.h.3
Cheerful Times **(56)** (Fav) (BAMcMahon) 9—8-11 ‡7SSanders (6) (hld up: hdwy & 6th st: one pce fnl 2f) .......... 1½.4
Barkston Singer **(51)** (MrsNMacauley) 5—8-10 ‡3DBiggs (7) (s.i.s: hdwy 5f out: 4th st: wknd over 1f out) .......... 4.5
Evening Star **(58)** (AHide) 6—9-6 JWilliams (3) (hmpd & lost pl after 1f: hdwy 5f out: 5th st: wknd 2f out) .......... 5.6
Pleasure Ahead **(46)** (MRChannon) 5—8-8 LornaVincent (8) (prom 6f) .......... 2½.7
Indivisible **(37)** (RHollinshead) 6—7-6⁽⁶⁾ ‡7MHumphries (9) (a bhd) .......... 1½.8
Va Utu **(49)** (RDEWoodhouse) 4—8-0 ‡7GParkin (10) (rdn 6f out: sn bhd) .......... hd.9
East Barns (IRE) **(43)** (TDBarron) 4—8-1⁽¹⁾ AlexGreaves (1) (a in rr) .......... 1½.10
Balaat (USA) **(69)** (MCChapman) 4—9-6 ‡7SWilliams (5) (bit bkwd: w ldr tl hrd rdn & wknd 4f out: t.o) .......... 11

LONG HANDICAP: Qualitair Flyer 7-4, Indivisible 7-0.

**9/4** Cheerful Times(5/2—7/2), **11/4** Mr Wishing Well(7/2—9/4), **7/1** Evening Star, East Barns (IRE)(op 4/1), **12/1** Pleasure Ahead, **14/1** In Truth, Barkston Singer, QUALITAIR FLYER, **16/1** Va Utu, **20/1** Balaat (USA), **33/1** Indivisible. CSF £51.59, CT £523.60. Tote £10.20: £2.10 £1.70 £2.80 (£24.20). Qualitair Holdings Limited (MALTON) bred by Red House Stud. 11 Rn
2m 29.1 (7.6)
SF—3/25/5/10/1/1

---

**36**     OSBERTON CLAIMING STKS (II) (Mdn 4-Y.O) £2206.40 (£610.40: £291.20)    **7f (AWT)**    2-10 (2-13)

31 Shedad (USA) **(52)** (Fav) (TDBarron) 8-2 AlexGreaves (3) (mde all: rdn out) .......... —1
Swinging Lady **(55)** (WWHaigh) 7-13 ‡5FNorton (1) (chsd wnr: 2nd st: hrd rdn over 1f out: r.o) .......... 1½.2
Buddy's Friend (IRE) **(51)** (RJRWilliams) 8-7 MHills (11) (hdwy & 4th st: r.o ins fnl f) .......... 2.3
Danzig Lad (USA) **(44)** (v) (MPNaughton) 7-10 ‡5BDoyle (5) (3rd st: one pce fnl 2f) .......... 5.4

Heartburn (36) *(JDBethell)* 7-5(4) ‡7DHarrison (6) (7th st: no hdwy fnl 2f) .......... 6.5
Pigalle Wonder (45) *(WHolden)* 8-4 AMcGlone (2) (b: prom over 3f) .......... nk.6
Able Princess (40) *(MrsNMacauley)* 7-10 JQuinn (12) (lw: prom over 3f) .......... 1½.7
Scravels Saran (IRE) (40) (bl) *(DrJDScargill)* 7-8 GBardwell (10) (n.d) .......... hd.8
Goldvein (SWE) (63) (bl) *(WAO'Gorman)* 8-10(1) DNicholls (9) (dwlt: hdwy & poor 6th st: wknd 2f out) .......... 2½.9
Carnfield *(JAGlover)* 7-12 DaleGibson (4) (bkwd: prom: 5th & wkng st: t.o) .......... 10
Uppance *(DWChapman)* 7-8 SWood (8) (bkwd: s.s: a in rr: t.o) .......... 11
Daniel Challenger *(JPSmith)* 8-1 NAdams (7) (outpcd: t.o) .......... 12

2/1 SHEDAD (USA)(5/2—7/2), 100/30 Goldvein (SWE)(op 2/1), 7/1 Pigalle Wonder, 8/1 Swinging Lady, 9/1 Buddy's Friend (IRE), 12/1 Scravels Saran (IRE), 14/1 Heartburn, Danzig Lad (USA), 16/1 Able Princess, 25/1 Carnfield, Uppance, 33/1 Daniel Challenger. CSF £19.05, Tote £3.80: £1.80 £1.50 £2.10 (£7.70). Mr T. D. Barron (THIRSK) bred by Indian Creek, Ashram Enterprises et al. in USA. 12 Rn        1m 30.1 (3.5)
SF—35/27/29/3/–/–

**37**    WINDSOR STKS (Mdn 3-Y.O) £2167.20 (£599.20: £285.60)    **1m (AWT)**    2-40 (2-41)

**General John (IRE)** *(PCHaslam)* 8-11 ‡3JFanning (1) (mde all: rdn 2f out: r.o wl) .......... —1
Hand on Heart (IRE) *(WJHaggas)* 8-9 NDay (7) (b.off hind: leggy: hld up: wnt 2nd 4f out: rdn over 1f out: one pce) .......... 2½.2
Rosa Why (63) (Fav) *(WJarvis)* 8-9 MHills (6) (swtg: 4th & rdn st: r.o one pce fnl 2f) .......... 8.3
Optical (IRE) *(HATWhiting)* 9-0 NAdams (5) (lt-f: bit bkwd: prom: rdn 4f out: 3rd st: wknd 2f out) .......... 3½.4
Serious Action *(SirMarkPrescott)* 9-0 CNutter (9) (w'like: prom 3f: poor 6th st) .......... 1½.5
Bold Boris *(RWArmstrong)* 9-0 JWilliams (2) (outpcd) .......... 3.6
High Success *(WAO'Gorman)* 8-9 ‡5EmmaO'Gorman (8) (wl grwn: bkwd: outpcd) .......... 3.7
Peace Formula (IRE) *(RHollinshead)* 9-0 ACulhane (3) (poor 5th st: sn bhd) .......... nk.8
Bilberry *(JHetherton)* 8-9 LCharnock (4) (w'like: leggy: s.s: a in rr) .......... s.h.9

3/1 Rosa Why (IRE)(op 7/4), 4/1 GENERAL JOHN (IRE)(op 12/1), 9/2 Peace Formula (IRE), 5/1 High Success, 6/1 Serious Action, Hand on Heart (IRE)(op 3/1), 10/1 Bold Boris, 14/1 Bilberry, 33/1 Optical (IRE). CSF £28.59, Tote £4.30: £1.70 £2.10 £1.40 (£48.20). Lord Scarsdale (MIDDLEHAM) bred by R. M. Fox in Ireland. 9 Rn        1m 45.8 (6.5)

**38**    BADMINTON APP'CE H'CAP (3-Y.O) (0-60) £2324.00 (£644.00: £308.00)    **1m (AWT)**    3-10 (3-11)

**Buddy (IRE) (58)** *(MBell)* 9-0 ‡5EBentley (11) (w ldr: led 5f out: clr over 1f out: easily) .......... —1
Lizzie Drippin (CAN) (48) *(MDIUsher)* 8-9 DHarrison (7) (hdwy & 4th st: r.o fnl f: no ch w wnr) .......... 3½.2
Brotherlyaffection (61) *(RHollinshead)* 9-3 ‡5GParkin (6) (3rd st: one pce fnl 2f) .......... 1½.3
Invigilate (60) (Fav) *(HATWhiting)* 9-7 OPears (2) (wnt 2nd 4f out: ev ch over 2f out: wknd fnl f) .......... 3.4
Energic (IRE) (48) *(CNAllen)* 8-9 MichaelDenaro (5) (5th st: no hdwy fnl 2f) .......... hd.5
Swing O'The Kilt (40) *(PCalver)* 7-10 ‡5CHawksley (4) (s.s: nvr nr ldrs) .......... 10.6
Shirl (45) *(WJHaggas)* 7-13 ‡7SallyRadfordHowes (8) (bit bkwd: bhd fnl 4f) .......... 1½.7
Queen of Pendona (40) *(HATWhiting)* 7-10 ‡5DarrenMoffatt (1) (t.o fnl 6f) .......... 2½.8
Daily Sport August (45) *(MCChapman)* 8-6 SWilliams (9) (sn t.o) .......... 2½.9
Kalar (46) *(DWChapman)* 8-2 ‡5VHalliday (10) (bkwd: led 3f: wknd 4f out: poor 6th st: t.o) .......... 10
Medbourne (IRE) (44) (bl) *(JLHarris)* 8-5 CMunday (3) (lw: reluctant to r: a t.o) .......... 11

9/4 Invigilate(op 4/1), 3/1 Energic (IRE)(6/1—5/2), 11/2 BUDDY (IRE)(op 5/2), 6/1 Brotherlyaffection, 10/1 Medbourne (IRE), 11/1 Shirl, 16/1 Daily Sport August, Lizzie Drippin (CAN), 25/1 Kalar, Queen of Pendona, 33/1 Swing O'The Kilt. CSF £81.68, CT £505.70. Tote £6.00: £2.00 £3.10 £2.00 (£27.80). E. and B. Productions (Theatre) Ltd (NEWMARKET) bred by Limestone Stud in Ireland. 11 Rn        1m 46.6 (7.3)
T/Plpt: £11.00 (81.3 Tckts).        KH

# LINGFIELD (L-H) Equitrack
## Saturday, January 4th [Standard]
Going Allowance: minus 0.25 sec per fur (FS)

**39**    SAN SEBASTIAN STKS (Mdn) £2245.60 (£621.60: £296.80)    **6f (AWT)**    12-55 (12-59)

**Myasha (USA) (71)** (Fav) *(MrsLPiggott)* 3-8-7(2) JWilliams (4) (eyeshield: b.hind: hld up: rdn over 1f out: led wl ins fnl f: r.o wl) .......... —1

Shocking Times *(RSimpson)* 3-8-5[5] SWhitworth (5) (hld up: led over 1f out tl wl ins fnl f: r.o wl) .................... nk.2

Easy Match *(CJHill)* 6-9-2 NAdams (8) (rdn thrght: hdwy 4f out: hrd rdn 2f out: one pce) .................... 10.3

Lonesome Dove (IRE) *(JWhite)* 4-8-11 ‡[5]FNorton (11) (str: scope: outpcd: nvr nr to chal) .................... 1½.4

Savinien (IRE) *(PJFeilden)* 3-8-5 DaleGibson (3) (neat: lw: b.nr hind: led over 4f) 1½.5

Reach Me Not (IRE) *(CHolmes)* 3-8-0 RFox (6) (bit bkwd: swtg: bhd fnl 3f) .................... ½.6

Camino a Ronda *(PatMitchell)* 3-7-7 ‡[7]CHawksley (10) (small: lt-f: b.hind: hdwy 4f out: wknd 2f out) .................... 2½.7

Plan More Action (IRE) *(JAkehurst)* 3-8-0 ‡[5]RPrice (2) (lw: lost pl over 4f out: nt rcvr) .................... 5.8

5/4 MYASHA (USA), 5/2 Shocking Times(2/1—3/1), 4/1 Easy Match(7/2—6/1), 7/1 Lonesome Dove (IRE)(4/1—8/1), 10/1 Savinien (IRE)(op 5/1), 33/1 Ors. CSF £5.19, Tote £2.10: £1.10 £1.40 £2.30 (£2.20). Mr J. D. Ashenheim (NEWMARKET) bred by B. C. Jones, Cook & McMillan in USA. 8 Rn    1m 14.57 (3.97)

**40**    VIGO CLAIMING STKS  £2402.40 (£666.40: £319.20)  1½m (AWT)    1-25 (1-29)

**Kirby Opportunity (52)** *(Fav)* *(JPearce)* 4-7-6 ‡[7]CHawksley (11) (rdn 7f out: hdwy over 4f out: led over 2f out: comf) .................... —1

Adjacent (IRE) (56) *(MDixon)* 4-7-12 ‡[5]NGwilliams (9) (hdwy 5f out: hrd rdn over 1f out: styd on fnl f) .................... 4.2

Line Drummer (USA) *(PAKelleway)* 4-8-8 JWilliams (16) (eyeshield: b: s.i.s: gd hdwy 7f out: led 5f out tl over 2f out: one pce) .................... 4.3

Glenstal Priory (40) *(PFICole)* 5-8-2 CRutter (13) (hdwy 6f out: one pce fnl 3f) .................... nk.4

Don't Cry (43) *(JDBethell)* 4-7-11 DaleGibson (10) (hdwy 4f out: nvr nr to chal) .................... 12.5

Fact Or Fiction (59) (v) *(MissBSanders)* 6-8-12 ‡[5]FNorton (12) (led after 3f to 5f out: hrd rdn & wknd over 3f out) .................... ¾.6

Abigail's Dream *(JRJenkins)* 5-9-2 SWhitworth (5) (prom 7f) .................... 8.7

Lifetimes Ambition (48) *(TCasey)* 4-7-10[1] ‡[3]DBiggs (7) (b: lw: prom 8f) .................... s.h.8

Hepburn (IRE) (44) *(MJFetherston-Godley)* 4-7-4[2] ‡[7]DHarrison (4) (led 3f: wknd 5f out) .................... 2.9

Adjaristan (52) *(RSimpson)* 5-8-2 ‡[5]RPrice (2) (a bhd) .................... hd.10

Camomile *(DMorley)* 4-7-11 JQuinn (14) (s.i.s: a bhd) .................... ¾.11

Carlowitz (USA) *(AMoore)* 4-8-2 NAdams (8) (leggy: bit bkwd: a bhd) .................... 2½.12

Sailor Boy (63) *(RAkehurst)* 6-8-9 MHills (6) (bhd fnl 5f) .................... ½.13

Shy Maiden (IRE) (bl) *(CWeedon)* 4-7-13 RFox (15) (prom 6f) .................... 1½.14

Tender Reach (36) *(RVoorspuy)* 4-7-7 JakiHouston (1) (swtg: bhd fnl 5f) .................... 2.15

Chloes Diamond (IRE) (59) *(JLSpearing)* 4-7-13 GBardwell (3) (rdn 8f out: prom 9f: eased whn btn 2f out) .................... s.h.16

4/1 KIRBY OPPORTUNITY, 5/1 Chloes Diamond (IRE)(op 7/2), 13/2 Glenstal Priory(10/1—16/1), 9/1 Line Drummer (USA), 11/1 Lifetimes Ambition, 14/1 Sailor Boy, Hepburn (IRE)(4/1—7/1), 14/1 Adjaristan(op 8/1), Adjacent (IRE)(8/1—16/1), 16/1 Fact Or Fiction, Don't Cry, 20/1 Shy Maiden (IRE)(op 12/1), 25/1 Carlowitz (USA), 33/1 Ors. CSF £61.50, Tote £5.10: £1.90 £2.70 £3.40 (£22.10). Mr Peter Bradley (NEWMARKET) bred by Highfield Stud Ltd. 16 Rn    2m 31.95 (2.55)

SF—23/21/23/16/–/–

**41**    SANTIAGO H'CAP (0-80) £2206.40 (£610.40: £291.20)  1¼m (AWT)    2-00 (2-05)

**El Dominio (54)** *(KOCunningham-Brown)* 4-8-11 GBardwell (2) (b: rdn 5f out: hdwy 3f out: led 1f out: r.o wl) .................... —1

Double Echo (IRE) (68) *(Jt-Fav)* *(JDBethell)* 4-9-4 ‡[7]DHarrison (14) (stdd s: wl bhd 6f: rdn & gd hdwy over 1f out: fin wl) .................... 1½.2

Tara's Delight (68) *(MJRyan)* 5-9-11 ‡[3]DBiggs (10) (hdwy 6f out: ev ch 1f out: unable qckn) .................... 6.3

Modesto (USA) (54) *(KOCunningham-Brown)* 4-8-11 SWhitworth (12) (b: led 9f: wkng whn n.m.r ins fnl f) .................... 2.4

Dance on Sixpence (68) (v) *(HJCollingridge)* 4-9-11 JQuinn (11) (hdwy 5f out: one pce fnl 3f) .................... 4.5

31[5] Pims Classic (68) (bl) *(WJHaggas)* 4-9-11 MHills (8) (prom 8f) .................... 2½.6

Wileys Folly (48) *(SDow)* 6-8-8 JWilliams (3) (b.hind: lw: hrd rdn over 3f out: nvr nr to chal) .................... 4.7

Shamshom Al Arab (IRE) (45) *(WCarter)* 4-7-11 ‡[5]NGwilliams (13) (hdwy 7f out: rdn 5f out: wknd over 3f out) .................... 1½.8

Pure Bliss (41) *(RJHodges)* 5-8-1 DaleGibson (6) (no hdwy fnl 3f) .................... ¾.9

Ballerina Bay (47) *(Jt-Fav)* *(DTThom)* 4-8-4 NAdams (1) (lost pl over 5f out: bhd whn hmpd over 4f out) .................... ½.10

Shaurni Girl (50) *(RVKing)* 4-8-2 ‡[5]LNewton (7) (prom over 7f) .................... ½.11

Tapestry Dancer (40) (v) *(MJHaynes)* 4-7-11 RFox (5) (prom 6f) .................... 2.12

Ardent Groom (IRE) **(49)** *(TMJones)* 4–8–1[1] ‡5RPrice (9) (lost pl over 4f out: nt
rcvr) .................................................................................................................. 12.13
*Tanegrus (16/1) Withdrawn (bolted circuit bef s) : not under orders*

**3/1** Double Echo (IRE), Ballerina Bay, **9/2** Tara's Delight, **13/2** Wileys Folly, **12/1** Shaurni Girl, **14/1** Dance on
Sixpence, **16/1** Shamsham Al Arab (IRE), Pims Classic, **25/1** Tapestry Dancer, **33/1** EL DOMINIO & Ors. CSF
£122.89, CT £494.81. Tote £35.80: £5.80 £1.10 £2.30 (£47.00). Mr M. D. Brunton (STOCKBRIDGE) bred
by Mrs I. A. Balding. 13 Rn　　　　　　　　　　　　　　　　　　　　　　　　　　　2m 5.93 (2.93)
　　　　　　　　　　　　　　　　　　　　　　　　　　　　　　　　　　　　SF—43/47/42/24/30/25

**42**　　　BILBAO H'CAP (0-70) £2422.00 (£672.00: £322.00)　**7f (AWT)**　　　2-30 (2-37)

**El Volador (51)** (Jt-Fav) *(RJO'Sullivan)* 5–8–6 ‡3DBiggs (4) (rdn & hdwy 3f out:
led ins fnl f: rdn out) .................................................................................. —1
Sarum **(47)** *(CPWildman)* 6–8–5 CRutter (2) (lw: hdwy 2f out: ev ch ins fnl f: r.o) 2.2
Sally's Son **(66)** *(WAO'Gorman)* 6–9–5 ‡5EmmaO'Gorman (13) (hld up: led wl
over 1f out tl ins fnl f: r.o) ......................................................................... nk.3
Beatle Song **(66)** *(CJHill)* 4–9–3 ‡7DHarrison (12) (hdwy 4f out: ev ch over 1f out:
one pce) ..................................................................................................... 2½.4
Kreischim (IRE) **(48)** *(MMadgwick)* 4–8–1[2] ‡5RPrice (3) (hdwy over 2f out: nvr
nrr) ............................................................................................................. 2½.5
Kissavos **(55)** (v) *(CCElsey)* 6–8–13 TRogers (10) (lw: a.p: led over 2f out tl wl
over 1f out: sn wknd) ................................................................................... s.h.6
Windsor Highness **(48)** *(MPMuggeridge)* 5–8–6 DaleGibson (9) (lw: outpcd:
hdwy fnl 3f: r.o) ........................................................................................... 1½.7
Cee-En-Cee **(59)** (bl) (Jt-Fav) *(MMcCourt)* 8–9–3 RWernham (7) (w ldrs: led over
3f out tl wknd over 2f out: wknd over 1f out) ............................................... ½.8
Tylers Wood **(50)** *(SDow)* 7–8–8 JWilliams (11) (b.hind: s.s: hdwy over 4f out:
one pce fnl 3f) ............................................................................................. hd.9
Phil-Blake **(40)** *(SMellor)* 5–7–12 RFox (1) (b: swtg: hld up: lost pl 4f out: styd on
fnl 2f) .......................................................................................................... ½.10
Helios **(61)** *(RSimpson)* 4–9–5 SWhitworth (16) (led after 1f tl wknd over 3f out) ..... ¾.11
Orba Gold (USA) **(66)** *(RJManning)* 4–9–3 ‡7ABates (15) (b: wknd 1f: wknd over 3f
out) .............................................................................................................. 1.12
Sergeant Meryll **(40)** (v) *(PHowling)* 8–7–7[1] ‡5FNorton (8) (s.s: sme hdwy 5f out:
wknd over 3f out) ......................................................................................... 2½.13
Verro (USA) **(39)** (bl) *(JABennett)* 5–7–11 JQuinn (6) (wl bhd fnl 4f) ........................ 1½.14
Precious Air (IRE) **(54)** *(AMoore)* 4–8–12 NAdams (14) (prom 4f) ............................ ½.15
Answersnotproblems (IRE) **(39)** (bl) *(AWDenson)* 4–7–11 GBardwell (5) (lw: a
bhd) ............................................................................................................. 4.16

**3/1** EL VOLADOR, Cee-En-Cee(op 5/1), **4/1** Kissavos, **9/2** Sarum(6/1—4/1), **13/2** Beatle Song, **11/1** Windsor
Highness(op 20/1), **12/1** Sally's Son, **16/1** Helios, Phil-Blake, **20/1** Sergeant Meryll, **25/1** Precious Air (IRE),
**33/1** Ors. CSF £20.05, CT £146.70. Tote £3.90: £1.80 £2.10 £3.10 £2.20 (£20.30). Mr I. A. Baker (BOGNOR
REGIS) bred by L. and Mrs Hutch. 16 Rn　　　　　　　　　　　　　　　　　1m 25.13 (1.13)
　　　　　　　　　　　　　　　　　　　　　　　　　　　　　　　　　　　SF—48/41/54/44/20/31

**43**　　　LIMA H'CAP (0-80) £2186.80 (£604.80: £288.40)　**6f (AWT)**　　　3-00 (3-08)

**Super Heights (58)** (bl) *(MissAJWhitfield)* 4–8–6 DaleGibson (5) (outpcd: gd
hdwy over 1f out: str run fnl f: led nr fin) ..................................................... —1
Murmuring **(60)** *(SDow)* 6–8–8 JWilliams (4) (rdn & gd hdwy over 1f out: r.o wl ins
fnl f) ............................................................................................................ 1½.2
Assignment **(78)** *(JFfitch-Heyes)* 6–9–7 ‡5FNorton (10) (lw: a.p: led 2f out: hrd rdn
fnl f: hdd nr fin) ............................................................................................ nk.3
Inswinger **(49)** *(WGRWightman)* 6–7–4[4] ‡7DHarrison (11) (hdwy over 2f out: ev
ch ins fnl f: r.o) ............................................................................................ s.h.4
336 Rushanes **(63)** *(TCasey)* 5–8–11 WNewnes (9) (hdwy over 1f out: ev ch ins fnl f:
r.o) .............................................................................................................. s.h.5
Jovial Kate (USA) **(52)** *(MDIUsher)* 5–8–0 CRutter (6) (a.p: one pce fnl 2f) ............... 4.6
Everset (FR) **(73)** *(WJMusson)* 4–9–0 ‡7PBowe (3) (outpcd: nvr nrr) ........................ ½.7
Sports Post Lady (IRE) **(65)** (Fav) *(CJHill)* 4–8–13 NAdams (2) (lw: led 4f: wknd
over 1f out) .................................................................................................. 2½.8
Lucky Blue **(64)** *(JCFox)* 5–8–12 SWhitworth (7) (bit bkwd: gd spd 4f) ...................... ½.9
Tauber **(67)** *(PatMitchell)* 8–8–12 ‡3SO'Gorman (1) (lost pl 4f out: rallied wl over 1f
out: sn wknd) ............................................................................................... 4.10
LONG HANDICAP: Inswinger 7-4.

**1/2** Murmuring, **2/1** Sports Post Lady (IRE)(11/4—7/4), **5/1** Assignment, **7/1** Everset (FR)(9/2—8/1), **8/1**
Tauber(op 5/1), SUPER HEIGHTS, **12/1** Rushanes(op 8/1), **14/1** Inswinger(12/1—20/1), **20/1** Jovial Kate
(USA)(op 10/1), **33/1** Lucky Blue. CSF £49.48, CT £224.67. Tote £10.00: £3.60 £1.80 £1.60 (£14.30). Mr
B. Pagliaroli (LAMBOURN) bred by Aston Park Stud. 10 Rn　　　　　　　　1m 12.63 (2.03)
　　　　　　　　　　　　　　　　　　　　　　　　　　　　　　　　　　　SF—22/18/30/–/18/–

**44**     SANTANDER H'CAP (3-Y.O) (0-60) £2049.60 (£565.60: £268.80)    **5f (AWT)**    3-30 (3-37)

**Doesyoudoes (60)** (v) *(DTThom)* 9-7 JWilliams (2) (chsd ldr: led over 2f out: drvn out) ............................................ —1
Mykindofmusic **(59)** *(MJHaynes)* 9-6 RFox (1) (swtg: rdn thrght: hdwy over 1f out: fin wl) ............................................ 3.2
Ossie **(50)** *(BPalling)* 8-4 ‡⁷StephenDavies (6) (outpcd: hdwy over 1f out: r.o wl ins fnl f) ............................................ s.h.3
Fort Hope **(55)** (bl) (Fav) *(TJNaughton)* 9-2 MHills (4) (b: led over 3f out: unable qckn fnl f) ............................................ ¾.4
Do the Business (IRE) **(50)** *(CNAllen)* 8-4 ‡⁷MichaelDenaro (5) (outpcd: gd hdwy fnl f: fin wl) ............................................ ½.5
Flat Rate **(45)** *(JWhite)* 8-1 ‡⁵FNorton (3) (s.s: outpcd: nvr nrr) ............................................ 3.6

**2/1** Fort Hope, **9/4** DOESYOUDOES, **7/2** Mykindofmusic, **11/2** Do the Business (IRE)(10/1—5/1), **6/1** Flat Rate, **14/1** Ossie. CSF £10.93, Tote £3.00: £1.40 £2.20 (£5.50). Mr Stanley C. Bass (NEWMARKET) bred by J. S. Bell. 6 Rn
60.53 sec (2.33)
SF—35/22/5/14/–/–

T/Plpt: £34.10 (39.4 Tckts).
LMc

**25—SOUTHWELL (L-H)** Fibresand

**Friday, January 10th [Standard]**

Going Allowance: 0.05 per fur (SL)                    Wind: slt half bhd

Stalls: low

**45**     LEICESTERSHIRE CLAIMING STKS (I)    £2265.20 (£627.20: £299.60)
**7f (AWT)**                                                                12-25 (12-29)

**African Chimes (87)** *(WAO'Gorman)* 5–8–9 ‡⁵EmmaO'Gorman (6) (5th st: shkn up to ld 1f out: comf) ............................................ —1
Wellsy Lad (USA) **(73)** *(DWChapman)* 5–8–8 SWood (10) (2nd st: led over 2f out tl over 1f out: r.o one pce) ............................................ 4.2
28² Euroblake **(77)** (Fav) *(TDBarron)* 5–8–11 AlexGreaves (1) (4th st: ev ch 1f out: one pce) ............................................ 1½.3
Inseyab **(65)** *(PCHaslam)* 4–8–0 ‡⁷NicolaHowarth (9) (3rd st: led over 1f out: sn hdd: wknd fnl f) ............................................ 2½.4
Catundra (IRE) **(78)** *(MrsAKnight)* 4–8–3 JQuinn (12) (lw: 7th st: wknd 2f out) ...... 8.5
Beechwood Cottage **(49)** (bl) *(ABailey)* 9–8–3 ‡⁵ATucker (14) (bkwd: 8th st: wknd 2f out) ............................................ ¾.6
King Ferdinand **(69)** *(DRTucker)* 5–8–2 ‡⁷TanyaMayne (3) (bkwd: s.i.s: nvr trbld ldrs) ............................................ hd.7
Count Me Out **(44)** (bl) *(JPearce)* 7–8–1 ‡⁵RPrice (2) (led over 4f) ............................................ 4.8
Persian Satan (IRE) *(CJHill)* 4–8–3 NAdams (8) (bit bkwd: sn rdn along & outpcd) 3½.9
Call for Rooney **(54)** *(ASmith)* 4–8–6⁽¹⁾ SWebster (7) (bkwd: outpcd) ............................................ nk.10
36 Uppance *(DWChapman)* 4–7–11 ‡³JFanning (5) (prom: 6th & wkng st) ............................................ nk.11
Little Miss Polly *(CJHill)* 4–7–10 ‡⁷DHarrison (4) (bkwd: s.s: t.o) ............................................ 15.12
Bracken Bay *(TKersey)* 5–7–13 DaleGibson (13) (b: bkwd: t.o) ............................................ 12.13

**15/8** Euroblake, **2/1** AFRICAN CHIMES, **6/1** Inseyab, **13/2** Wellsy Lad (USA)(op 4/1), **14/1** King Ferdinand, **16/1** Catundra (IRE), **20/1** Count Me Out, **25/1** Beechwood Cottage, Call for Rooney, **50/1** Little Miss Polly, Persian Satan (IRE), Uppance, **66/1** Bracken Bay. CSF £16.03, Tote £2.10: £2.50 £2.80 £1.10 (£7.10). Mr D. G. Wheatley (NEWMARKET) bred by Noel Cogan. 13 Rn
1m 30.3 (3.7)
SF—45/32/30/11/–/–

**46**     EAST MIDLANDS H'CAP (Amateurs) (0-70) £2265.20 (£627.20: £299.60)
**1¾m (AWT)**                                                               12-55 (12-57)

27* **Hand Painted (59)** (Fav) *(CRBeever)* 8–11–6 (7x) MrsLPearce (6) (b: bhd tl hdwy 6f out: 4th st: styd on to ld ins fnl f) ............................................ —1
Carlingford (USA) **(51)** *(HATWhiting)* 6–10–7 ‡⁵MrGreen (9) (bkwd: hdwy after 4f: slt ld 7f out: hdd ins fnl f) ............................................ 2.2
Kovalevskia **(40)** *(DAWilson)* 7–10–1 MissEBronson (3) (hdwy & 5th st: styd on fnl 2f) ............................................ 2½.3
Aberfoyle (IRE) **(55)** *(ICampbell)* 4–10–5 ‡⁵MissSKelleway (5) (eyeshield: led after 4f tl 7f out: 2nd st: one pce fnl 2f) ............................................ 3.4
Chronological **(60)** (v) *(MHTompkins)* 6–11–2 ‡⁵MrMJenkins (8) (prom 9f) ............................................ 12.5
26² Obeliski **(50)** *(PCHaslam)* 6–10–11 MissJFeilden (10) (prom: lost pl 5f out: poor 6th st) ............................................ 7.6
Malenoir (USA) **(50)** (bl) *(WJPearce)* 4–10–0⁽³⁾ ‡⁵MrDDurrant (13) (a bhd) ............................................ ½.7
26³ Enfant du Paradis (IRE) **(45)** *(PDEvans)* 4–9–9 ‡⁵MrWMcLoughlin (12) (prom 8f) ..... ½.8

*35*[2] Mr Wishing Well **(61)** *(RJRWilliams)* 6–11-3[(1)] ‡[5]MrSAstaire (4) (b.hind: hdwy 7f out: 3rd st: wknd 2f out) ........................ 2½.9

Harpley **(43)** *(SEKettlewell)* 5–9-13 ‡[5]MrsDKettlewell (7) (bit bkwd: led 4f: wknd qckly 8f out: t.o) ........................ 12.**10**

*27*[4] Rajaya (USA) **(57)** (bl) *(RO'Leary)* 4–10-7 ‡[5]MrKDavies (11) (prom 8f: t.o) ........... 12.**11**

Vinstan **(57)** *(CASmith)* 6–10-13 ‡[5]MrAPhillips (1) (b: bit bkwd: t.o) ........................ 6.**12**

Cold Marble (USA) **(59)** (v) *(DRTucker)* 7–11-1 ‡[5]MissSRowe (2) (prom 7f: t.o) ........ **13**

**3/1** HAND PAINTED, **9/2** Obeliski, **5/1** Chronological, **6/1** Mr Wishing Well(op 7/2), **8/1** Enfant du Paradis (IRE), **10/1** Kovalevskia, **11/1** Carlingford (USA), **12/1** Rajaya (USA)(tchd 20/1), **14/1** Aberfoyle (IRE), Harpley, **20/1** Malenoir (USA), **33/1** Ors. CSF £37.61, CT £286.77. Tote £4.30: £2.50 £4.20 £2.40 (£36.20). Mrs B. Ramsden (GRANTHAM) bred by Mrs R. M. Vella. 13 Rn     3m 12.9 (13.6)
                                   SF—19/2/–/–/–/–

## 47   YORKSHIRE CLAIMING STKS (3-Y.O) £2245.60 (£621.60: £296.80)
**1m (AWT)**     1-25 (1-26)

**Silver Samurai (66)** *(RHollinshead)* 8-2 ‡[7]EHusband (6) (led 4f out: clr 2f out: easily) ........................ —1

Mr Snuggs (IRE) **(MHTompkins)** 8-9[(2)] RCochrane (3) (neat: bit bkwd: dwlt: 3rd st: hrd rdn fnl 2f: no ch w wnr) ........................ 12.2

*34** Runnel **(79)** *(DWChapman)* 9-7 SWood (1) (led 4f out: 2nd st: wknd 2f out) ........... 4.3

Quiet Miss **(75)** (Fav) *(DRCElsworth)* 8-12 JWilliams (2) (eyeshield: lw: prom: 5th & wkng st) ........................ 2½.4

So Great *(WWHaigh)* 8-11 ACulhane (5) (b: w'like: bit bkwd: dwlt: 4th st: wknd over 2f out) ........................ 1½.5

*38* Medbourne (IRE) **(40)** (bl) *(JLHarris)* 7-10[(1)] ‡[5]SMaloney (4) (reluctant to r: last st: at o) ........................ 30.6

**4/6** Quiet Miss(tchd 5/4), **15/8** Runnel, **11/1** ‡[5]SILVER SAMURAI, **14/1** Mr Snuggs (IRE)(op 6/1), **20/1** So Great(op 8/1), **50/1** Medbourne (IRE). CSF £108.01, Tote £17.90: £2.90 £2.40 (£13.40). Mrs B. Facchino (UPPER LONGDON) bred by Elisha Holdings. 6 Rn     1m 44.7 (5.4)
                                     SF—13/–/–/–/–/–

## 48   DERBYSHIRE H'CAP (0-70) £2304.40 (£638.40: £305.20)   **1½m (AWT)**   1-55 (1-55)

(Weights raised 1 lb)

**Alle-Roy (61)** *(MHTompkins)* 4–9-10 RCochrane (6) (lw: 6th st: hdwy & swtchd ins 2f out: str run to ld last strides) ........................ —1

*26*[4] Mississippi Beat (USA) **(37)** (v) *(MPNaughton)* 5–8-0 ‡[5]BDoyle (8) (hdwy 8f out: 2nd st: led wl over 1f out: edgd lft & ct last strides) ........................ nk.2

Swagman (USA) **(45)** *(CRBeever)* 5–8-13 ACulhane (5) (led 6f out tl wl over 1f out: wknd fnl f) ........................ 5.3

*35** Qualitair Flyer **(35)** *(JFBottomley)* 10–8-3 (7x) GBardwell (3) (hdwy 5f out: sn hrd rdn: 3rd st: wknd over 1f out) ........................ 8.4

Fusion **(40)** *(REarnshaw)* 8–8-8 JWilliams (7) (b: bkwd: hld up: 4th st: wknd 2f out) ........................ 10.5

*25** Give Me Hope (IRE) **(54)** (Fav) *(RGBrazington)* 4–9-3 (7x) JQuinn (1) (5th st: wknd 2f out) ........................ 3.6

Polyplate **(45)** *(MJRyan)* 4–8-5 ‡[3]DBiggs (4) (bkwd: a bhd: t.o) ........................ 8.7

*35*[3] In Truth **(45)** *(DWChapman)* 4–8-8 SWood (9) (lw: led 6f: sn wknd: t.o) ........................ 6.8

Vanda's Girl **(45)** *(ABailey)* 4–8-3 ‡[5]ATucker (2) (bit bkwd: w ldr 7f: wknd qckly: t.o) ........................ 25.9

**3/1** Give Me Hope (IRE), **4/1** Qualitair Flyer, **9/2** Fusion(op 8/1), **5/1** In Truth(op 5/2), **7/1** Swagman (USA), **10/1** Mississippi Beat (USA), ALLE-ROY, **25/1** Ors. CSF £92.84, CT £672.36. Tote £7.00: £2.70 £1.80 £2.10 (£40.60). Mr M. H. Tompkins (NEWMARKET) bred by Mrs M. S. Thomas. 9 Rn     2m 42.3 (8.1)
                                     SF—35/10/13/–/–/–

## 49   LEICESTERSHIRE CLAIMING STKS (II)   £2265.20 (£627.20: £299.60)
**7f (AWT)**     2-25 (2-32)

**Bold Habit (94)** (Fav) *(WJPearce)* 7–9-0 ‡[5]GHusband (3) (hdwy & 5th st: led wl ins fnl f: r.o) ........................ —1

Shabanaz **(85)** *(THCaldwell)* 7–8-4 ‡[7]StephenDavies (11) (bit bkwd: s.s: gd hdwy fnl 2f: fin wl) ........................ 1½.2

Pesidanamich (IRE) **(72)** (bl) *(TDBarron)* 4–8-9 AlexGreaves (12) (led: sn clr: c wd st: hdd wl ins fnl f) ........................ s.h.3

Luzum **(67)** (bl) *(JAGlover)* 8–8-6[(2)] ‡[7]SWilliams (2) (bkwd: hdwy & 6th st: one pce fnl 2f) ........................ 2½.4

Tudorgateway **(65)** (v) *(MHTompkins)* 4–8-11 RCochrane (9) (wnt 2nd st: wknd 2f out) ........................ 5.5

Orpen (IRE) (bl) *(WAO'Gorman)* 4–8–4[1] ‡[5]EmmaO'Gorman (7) (rdn 2f out: nvr nr to chal) ........................................................................ s.h.**6**
Mushy Boff **(49)** *(CJHill)* 4–8–3 NAdams (1) (prom over 3f) ........................ ¾.**7**
Courting Newmarket **(46)** *(MrsAKnight)* 4–8–5 ‡[3]DBiggs (10) (bit bkwd: 3rd st: wknd 2f out) ................................................................... 1½.**8**
Stone Flake (USA) **(70)** *(PJHobbs)* 6–8–7 JWilliams (4) (bit bkwd: n.d) ............... 5.**9**
River Way **(38)** *(CJHill)* 4–8–0[2] ‡[5]RPrice (5) (a bhd) ........................ ½.**10**
Cossack Noir **(35)** *(MPNaughton)* 4–8–3 JakiHouston (13) (4th st: wknd over 2f out) ........................................................................... 2.**11**
Our Amber *(DWChapman)* 5–8–2 SWood (8) (prom 3f: t.o) ........................ 12.**12**
Lady Khadija **(35)** *(GPKelly)* 6–7–10 ‡[7]JMarshall (6) (bkwd: t.o) ............... 2.**13**

**4/5** BOLD HABIT, **9/2** Pesidanamich (IRE), **9/1** Tudorgateway, **11/1** Orpen (IRE)(8/1—12/1), **16/1** Luzum(op 8/1), **20/1** Shabanaz, **25/1** Stone Flake (USA), Mushy Boff, **33/1** Courting Newmarket, **50/1** Cossack Noir, Our Amber, River Way (IRE), **66/1** Lady Khadija. CSF £17.71. Tote £1.90: £1.50 £6.70 £1.10 (£77.90). Mr Roger Sterry (HAMBLETON) bred by R. Butters. 13 Rn                1m 30.4 (3.8)
                                                            SF—49/34/38/27/17/9

**50**          NOTTINGHAMSHIRE H'CAP (0-80) £2324.00 (£644.00: £308.00)    **1m (AWT)**  2-55 (2-59)
                                    (Weights raised 3 lb)
*31\** **Doulab's Image (70)** (bl) *(JAGlover)* 5–9–3 (7x) ‡[7]SWilliams (6) (lw: hld up: hdwy & 8th st: led ins fnl f: r.o wl) .................................................. —**1**
*28[4]* Mac's Princess (USA) **(65)** *(WAO'Gorman)* 4–8–13 ‡[5]EmmaO'Gorman (16) (hdwy over 2f out: r.o ins fnl f) .......................................... 1½.**2**
*35* East Barns (IRE) **(42)** (bl) *(TDBarron)* 4–7–6 ‡[3]JFanning (1) (5th st: r.o one pce fnl 2f) ........................................................................... 1½.**3**
Model Nurse **(44)** *(MrsAKnight)* 5–7–5[5] ‡[7]DHarrison (14) (lw: hdwy 4f out: 4th st: led over 1f out tl ins fnl f) .............................................. 1½.**4**
Golden Ancona **(55)** *(MBrittain)* 9–8–4 ‡[5]SMaloney (4) (bkwd: hdwy over 2f out: nvr nr to chal) ....................................................................... 1.**5**
Predictable **(67)** *(MrsAKnight)* 6–9-7 JWilliams (13) (hdwy & 6th st: one pce fnl 2f) ........................................................................... hd.**6**
Golden Chip (IRE) **(68)** *(APStringer)* 4–9-7 SWebster (10) (hdwy & 7th st: rdn over 1f out: one pce) ................................................. s.h.**7**
*31[2]* State Governor **(65)** *(DWChapman)* 4–9-4 SWood (12) (lw: led 4f out tl wknd over 1f out) ........................................................... 6.**8**
*31* Foursingh **(64)** (bl) *(CBBBooth)* 4–9-3 ACulhane (11) (n.d) .................. 1½.**9**
*35* Balaat (USA) **(69)** *(MCChapman)* 4–9-1 ‡[7]MichaelDenaro (15) (n.d) ............ 2.**10**
*28[5]* Fair Dare **(47)** *(CBBBooth)* 4–8-0 DaleGibson (8) (n.d) ...................... 5.**11**
Tyrian Purple (IRE) **(52)** *(RHollinshead)* 4–7-12 ‡[7]MHumphries (5) (3rd st: wknd over 2f out) ............................................................... s.h.**12**
Pusey Street Boy **(43)** *(JRBosley)* 5–7-11 NAdams (2) (led 4f: 2nd st: wknd 2f out) ........................................................................... s.h.**13**
*42* Orba Gold (USA) **(66)** *(RJManning)* 4–8-12 ‡[7]ABates (9) (bhd fnl 4f) .......... 3½.**14**
Damaaz (IRE) **(52)** (v) *(JSWainwright)* 4–8-5 LCharnock (7) (bhd fnl 4f: t.o) ......... 4.**15**
Polyroll **(70)** *(MRChannon)* 6–9-10 JQuinn (3) (bhd fnl 4f: t.o) .................. 2.**16**
                    LONG HANDICAP: Model Nurse 7-5.

**2/1** DOULAB'S IMAGE, **13/2** Mac's Princess (USA), **9/1** Predictable, Golden Chip (IRE)(op 6/1), East Barns (IRE), **10/1** State Governor, **14/1** Polyroll, **16/1** Orba Gold (USA), Fair Dare, Tyrian Purple (IRE), Golden Ancona, **20/1** Pusey Street Boy, Model Nurse, **25/1** Damaaz (IRE), **33/1** Ors. CSF £16.71. CT £97.98. Tote £3.00: £2.10 £1.50 £2.40 £4.00 (£8.70). Claremont Management Services (WORKSOP) bred by Hadi Al Tajir. 16 Rn                                                 1m 43.7 (4.4)
                                                            SF—43/34/8/2/12/28

**51**          LINCOLNSHIRE H'CAP (3-Y.O) (0-70) £2186.80 (£604.80: £288.40)    **7f (AWT)**  3-25 (3-26)
*30\** **Palacegate King (59)** *(JBerry)* 8-10 (7x) RCochrane (1) (lw: led 5f out: hrd rdn over 1f out: all out) ................................................... —**1**
Ready to Draw (IRE) **(60)** *(RonaldThompson)* 8-6 ‡[5]SMaloney (10) (lw: 3rd st: ev ch ins fnl f: r.o) ..................................................... ½.**2**
*38\** Buddy (IRE) **(59)** (Fav) *(MBell)* 8-3[1] ‡[7]EBentley (8) (led 2f: 2nd st: r.o one pce fnl 2f) ........................................................................... 2½.**3**
Profit Stream **(56)** *(MWEasterby)* 8-7 LCharnock (2) (4th st: no hdwy fnl 2f) ......... 3½.**4**
Granite Boy **(70)** *(PJFeilden)* 9-0 ‡[7]MichaelDenaro (7) (nvr nr to chal) ............... ½.**5**
Sure to Win (IRE) **(66)** *(ABailey)* 8-10 ‡[7]StephenDavies (4) (5th st: wknd 2f out) .... 6.**6**
*38* Kalar **(46)** *(DWChapman)* 7-11 SWood (6) (a bhd) .......................... 1½.**7**
*38[4]* Invigilate **(60)** *(HATWhiting)* 8-11 NAdams (5) (6th st: wknd 2f out) ............ ½.**8**
Rythmic Style **(64)** *(TDBarron)* 9-1 AlexGreaves (3) (bit bkwd: a bhd) ............... ¾.**9**
Cellito (IRE) **(63)** (h) *(WAO'Gorman)* 8-9 ‡[5]EmmaO'Gorman (9) (bit bkwd: a bhd) 1½.**10**

**6/4** Buddy (IRE), **11/4** Sure to Win (IRE)(4/1—5/2), **11/2** PALACEGATE KING(4/1—6/1), **10/1** Invigilate, **11/1** Rythmic Style, Profit Stream, **12/1** Ready to Draw (IRE), **14/1** Granite Boy, Cellito (IRE), **33/1** Kalar. CSF £67.89, CT £138.45. Tote £4.80: £1.80 £1.10 £1.80 (£58.00). Palacegate Corporation Ltd (COCKERHAM) bred by Miss E. Streatfeild. 10 Rn
1m 30.7 (4.1)
SF—39/33/22/15/20/–

T/Plpt: £536.30 (1.7 Tckts).
KH

## 39—LINGFIELD (L-H) Equitrack
## Saturday, January 11th [Standard]
Going Allowance: minus 0.40 sec per fur (FS)

### 52    COWSLIP STKS (Mdn 3-Y.O) £2186.80 (£604.80: £288.40)    1¼m (AWT)    1-20 (1-23)

| | | |
|---|---|---|
| **Noble Singer (65)** (Fav) (HThomsonJones) 8-9 RHills (6) (led over 3f out: rdn out) | —1 | |
| Alternation (FR) (PFICole) 8-9 CRutter (3) hdwy 4f out: r.o one pce fnl 2f) | 2½.2 | |
| 38² Lizzie Drippin (CAN) (50) (MDIUsher) 8-9 JWilliams (1) (swtg: gd hdwy 4f out: ev ch over 2f out: c wd bnd wl over 1f out: unable qckn) | 1½.3 | |
| Good as Gold (IRE) (JLSpearing) 8-9 GBardwell (4) (hmpd on ins & swtchd 5f out: hdwy 4f out: one pce fnl 2f) | 1.4 | |
| Colouring Book (IRE) (MJHaynes) 8-2‡7DToole (8) (no hdwy fnl 3f) | 6.5 | |
| 37⁶ Bold Boris (RWArmstrong) 9-0 BCrossley (7) (prom 7f) | 1.6 | |
| Sun Glory (IRE) (WJarvis) 8-9 NDay (9) (outpcd) | 1½.7 | |
| True Mood (JDBethell) 8-9 MHills (2) (led 5f: wknd qckly: t.o) | 20.8 | |
| Mississippi Queen (RJRWilliams) 8-9 RCochrane (5) (plld hrd: chsd ldr: led 5f out tl over 3f out: wknd qckly: t.o) | 1½.9 | |

**11/10** NOBLE SINGER, **3/1** Good as Gold (IRE)(tchd 9/2), **11/2** Alternation (FR)(3/1—6/1), **13/2** Lizzie Drippin (CAN), **16/1** Sun Glory (IRE), **20/1** Colouring Book (IRE)(op 6/1), **25/1** Bold Boris, **33/1** Ors. CSF £8.06, Tote £2.30: £1.00 £2.30 £1.20 (£8.30). Mr W. J. Gredley (NEWMARKET) bred by Stetchworth Park Stud Ltd. 9 Rn
2m 8.66 (5.66)

### 53    DAFFODIL H'CAP (0-90) £2646.60 (£732.60: £349.80)    1m (AWT)    1-50 (1-52)

| | | |
|---|---|---|
| **Dorset Duke (84)** (GWragg) 5–9-8 MHills (10) (b: dwlt: gd hdwy 6f out: hrd drvn fnl f: led last strides) | —1 | |
| 32* Ringland (USA) (82) (Fav) (PCHaslam) 4–9-2 ‡3JFanning (8) (a.p: led over 3f out: hrd rdn fnl f: hdd last strides) | hd.2 | |
| 28* Super Sally (89) (MJRyan) 5–9-10 ‡3DBiggs (5) (hdwy 4f out: prom whn stumbled over 2f out: unable qckn) | 4.3 | |
| Mac's Fighter (90) (v) (WAO'Gorman) 7–9-9 ‡5EmmaO'Gorman (1) (lw: rdn over 3f out: hdwy fnl 2f: nvr nrr) | 3½.4 | |
| Crosby (73) (PAKelleway) 6–8-11 WNewnes (6) (eyeshield: rdn & no hdwy fnl 3f) | 2.5 | |
| 43³ Assignment (78) (JFfitch-Heyes) 6–8-11 ‡5BDoyle (4) (b.hind: lost pl over 6f out: styd on fnl 2f) | 1½.6 | |
| Litmore Dancer (60) (JDBethell) 4–7-4(3) ‡7DHarrison (3) (chsd ldr over 4f: wknd 2f out) | 3½.7 | |
| 43 Everset (FR) (71) (WJMusson) 4–8-8 RCochrane (7) (bhd fnl 3f) | 3½.8 | |
| 41 Tanegrus (69) (DRCElsworth) 4–8-6 JWilliams (9) (eyeshield: lw: led over 4f) | 2½.9 | |
| Neroli (70) (APJones) 4–8-7 NAdams (2) (bhd fnl 4f: t.o) | 15.10 | |

**3/1** Ringland (USA), **9/2** Super Sally, **11/2** Litmore Dancer, **13/2** DORSET DUKE(op 9/2), Mac's Fighter, **10/1** Assignment, Crosby, Everset (FR), **16/1** Tanegrus, **25/1** Neroli. CSF £25.93, CT £90.78. Tote £6.90: £1.70 £1.70 £2.30 (£16.40). Mr G. Wragg (NEWMARKET) bred by Sir Robin McAlpine. 10 Rn    1m 36.77 (0.07)
SF—58/51/47/35/17/12

### 54    BLUEBELL CLAIMING STKS (3-Y.O) £2167.20 (£599.20: £285.60)    5f (AWT)    2-20 (2-22)

| | | |
|---|---|---|
| **Creche (71)** (bl) (Fav) (MrsNMacauley) 8-7 NDay (2) (mde all: clr 2f out: easily) | —1 | |
| 30³ Appealing Times (USA) (74) (WAO'Gorman) 8-10 ‡5EmmaO'Gorman (5) (lw: chsd wnr fnl 2f: r.o one pce) | 2.2 | |
| 44² Mykindofmusic (59) (bl) (MJHaynes) 7-10 RFox (6) (s.s: hrd rdn 3f out: hdwy wl over 1f out: r.o ins fnl f) | 1.3 | |
| 39² Shocking Times (66) (RSimpson) 8-6 SWhitworth (4) (lw: chsd wnr: rdn 3f out: wknd 2f out) | 5.4 | |
| 44* Doesyoudoes (70) (v) (DTThom) 8-6(2) JWilliams (1) (s.i.s: outpcd) | 3.5 | |
| 39⁵ Savinien (IRE) (PJFeilden) 8-5 DaleGibson (3) (lw: bhd fnl 3f) | 15.6 | |

**13/8** CRECHE, **5/2** Shocking Times(3/1—9/2), **4/1** Appealing Times (USA), **6/1** Doesyoudoes, **8/1** Mykindofmusic, **25/1** Savinien (IRE). CSF £8.38, Tote £2.50: £1.50 £3.20 (£5.80). Mrs N. Macauley (MELTON MOWBRAY) bred by Bacton Stud. 6 Rn
60.46 sec (2.26)
SF—8/3/–/–/–/–

**55** VIOLET H'CAP (0-80) £2238.00 (£618.00: £294.00) **1m 5f (AWT)** 2-50 (2-51)

41* **El Dominio (60)** *(KOCunningham-Brown)* 4–8-8 GBardwell (2) (b: rdn & hdwy 4f out: led over 1f out: drvn out) .................. —1
Fiala (IRE) **(80)** (Fav) *(JHMGosden)* 4–10-0 MHills (7) (chsd ldr: led 4f out tl over 1f out: unable qckn) ............... 4.2
26⁵ Jawani (IRE) **(47)** (v) *(DrJDScargill)* 4–7-9⁽²⁾ JQuinn (3) (hld up: rdn & ev ch 2f out: one pce) ............... 1.3
26* Brora Rose (IRE) **(49)** *(JDBethell)* 4–7-4⁽²⁾ ‡⁷DHarrison (1) (rdn along fnl 6f: nvr nrr) ......... 7.4
40² Adjacent (IRE) **(56)** *(MDixon)* 4–7-13 ‡⁵NGwilliams (4) (prom 10f) ............... 2½.5
40 Lifetimes Ambition **(50)** *(TCasey)* 4–7-9⁽⁵⁾ ‡³DBiggs (5) (b: bhd fnl 3f) ............... 2½.6
Norwick Star **(48)** *(TMJones)* 4–7-10⁽³⁾ NAdams (6) (led 9f: hrd rdn: wknd qckly: eased fnl 2f) .......... 25.7
LONG HANDICAP: Norwick Star 6-6.

**11/10** Fiala (IRE), **4/1** Brora Rose (IRE)(3/1—9/2), **7/1** EL DOMINIO(op 4/1), **17/2** Adjacent (IRE), **9/1** Jawani (IRE)(5/1—10/1), **10/1** Lifetimes Ambition, **50/1** Norwick Star. CSF £14.38, Tote £9.20: £3.40 £1.10 (£4.70). Mr M. D. Brunton (STOCKBRIDGE) bred by Mrs I. A. Balding. 7 Rn
2m 47.40 (3.90)
SF—3/15/–/–/–/–

**56** PRIMROSE H'CAP (0-60) £2343.60 (£649.60: £310.80) **1¼m (AWT)** 3-20 (3-24)

41⁴ **Modesto (USA) (50)** (Fav) *(KOCunningham-Brown)* 4–9-5 SWhitworth (13) (b: lw: mde all: rdn 3f out: r.o wl) .................. —1
Samurai Gold (USA) **(51)** (v) *(PTWalwyn)* 4–9-6 RCochrane (5) (a.p: rdn 4f out: r.o ins fnl f) ......... 2.2
27² Quinzii Martin **(47)** *(DHaydnJones)* 4–9-2 JWilliams (8) (hdwy over 3f out: chsd wnr 2f out tl ins fnl f: one pce) ............ 4.3
31³ Les Amis **(46)** *(MJRyan)* 5–9-1 ‡³DBiggs (12) (hld up: hrd rdn & hdwy over 1f out: r.o wl ins fnl f) ............ 1½.4
Miss Broughton **(47)** *(WJMusson)* 4–8-9 ‡⁷PBowe (14) (hdwy 2f out: nvr nr to chal) ............ 3.5
42 Windsor Highness **(44)** *(MPMuggeridge)* 5–9-2 JMcLaughlin (2) (outpcd: nvr nrr) nk.6
Night Transaction **(46)** *(AHide)* 5–9-4 DaleGibson (10) (lw: no hdwy fnl 3f) ............ 2.7
27 Charming Gift **(48)** (bl) *(RJRWilliams)* 5–9-6 NDay (9) (b: outpcd: nvr nr to chal) ............ 2.8
40³ Line Drummer (USA) **(56)** (bl) *(PAKelleway)* 4–9-4 ‡⁷ABates (3) (b: lw: prom 7f) ......... 4.9
Lord Advocate **(49)** (v) *(MPNaughton)* 4–9-1 ‡³JFanning (11) (chsd wnr 6f: wknd over 2f out) ............ dht.9
Misty Goddess (IRE) **(51)** *(MAJarvis)* 4–9-6 MHills (1) (bhd fnl 4f) ............ 10.11
Foreign Assignment (IRE) **(52)** *(JWhite)* 4–9-2 ‡⁵RPrice (4) (rdn 8f out: a bhd) ............ ½.12
31 Summer Sands **(46)** *(JLHarris)* 4–8-8 ‡⁷CMunday (6) (b.off hind: prom 6f) ............ ½.13
Krisfield **(48)** (bl) *(TPMcGovern)* 7–9-6 JQuinn (7) (bhd fnl 4f) ............ 1½.14

**15/2** MODESTO (USA)(14/1—7/1), **8/1** Krisfield, Windsor Highness(op 5/1), Quinzii Martin, Les Amis(op 5/1), Night Transaction(op 5/1), **17/2** Lord Advocate, **9/1** Line Drummer (USA), **10/1** Misty Goddess (IRE), Samurai Gold (USA)(8/1—12/1), **14/1** Charming Gift, **20/1** Foreign Assignment (IRE), **33/1** Ors. CSF £74.41, CT £563.41. Tote £7.80: £2.80 £3.70 £1.80 (£13.70). Mr D. Bass (STOCKBRIDGE) bred by Rhydian Morgan-Jones in USA. 14 Rn
2m 6.62 (3.62)
SF—29/26/14/10/–/4

**57** POPPY APP'CE H'CAP (0-70) £2265.20 (£627.20: £299.60) **6f (AWT)** 3-50 (3-56)

42³ **Sally's Son (66)** *(WAO'Gorman)* 6–9-13 EmmaO'Gorman (9) (hdwy 2f out: led wl ins fnl f: r.o wl) .................. —1
Furiella **(49)** *(PCHaslam)* 4–8-10 JFanning (12) (gd hdwy 3f out: led over 1f out tl wl ins fnl f: hrd rdn: r.o) ............ ¾.2
31 Say You Will **(44)** (v) *(MPNaughton)* 4–8-5 BDoyle (7) (hdwy fnl 2f: r.o) ............ 2.3
33² In a Whirl (USA) **(58)** (Fav) *(DWChapman)* 4–9-5 GHusband (3) (bdly hmpd & lost pl 5f out: rallied over 1f out: r.o) ............ nk.4
Proud Brigadier (IRE) **(55)** *(WCarter)* 4–9-2 NGwilliams (13) (hdwy 3f out: chsd wnr over 2f out tl over 1f out: one pce) ............ 2.5
36* Shedad (USA) **(51)** *(TDBarron)* 4–8-12 SMaloney (5) (led after 1f: lw: clr over 2f out: hdd & wknd over 1f out) ............ 1.6
Sunwind **(37)** *(RJHodges)* 6–7-9 ‡³CHawksley (10) (hrd rdn & no hdwy fnl 3f) ........ 1½.7
43⁶ Jovial Kate (USA) **(48)** *(MDIUsher)* 5–8-9 DHarrison (11) (a mid div) ............ nk.8

The Shanahan Bay **(60)** (v) *(MrsNMacaulay)* 7–9–7  DBiggs (2) (prom whn hmpd
5f out: nt rcvr) ........................................................................... 1.9
43⁵ Rushanes **(63)** *(TCasey)* 5–9–10  RPerham (1) (led 1f: wknd 2f out) .................... s.h.10
Across the Bay **(60)** *(SDow)* 5–9–4 ‡³MJermy (4) (outpcd) .................... 3½.11
43 Lucky Blue **(59)** *(JCFox)* 5–9–6  ATucker (6) (prom over 3f) ................ 1½.12
Stockair **(41)** *(RJHodges)* 6–7–13⁽⁷⁾ ‡³SDrowne (8) (dwlt: a bhd) ......... 2.13
Notanotherone (IRE) **(54)** (bl) *(JELong)* 4–9–1  RPrice (14) (a bhd) ......... 4.14

**4/1** In a Whirl (USA), **5/1** SALLY'S SON, **6/1** The Shanahan Bay(op 4/1), **8/1** Rushanes, Shedad (USA),
Furiella, **10/1** Proud Brigadier (IRE), **12/1** Say You Will, **20/1** Jovial Kate (USA), Across the Bay, **25/1** Lucky
Blue, **33/1** Notanotherone (IRE), **50/1** Ors. CSF £41.38, CT £416.24. Tote £4.20: £1.80 £3.00 £5.40
(£23.20). Mr W. A. O'Gorman (NEWMARKET) bred by R. Duggan. 14 Rn     1m 13.19 (2.59)
T/Plpt: £39.70 (45.2 Tckts).                                         LMc

## 45—SOUTHWELL (L-H) Fibresand
### Wednesday, January 15th [Standard]
Going Allowance: 5f: minus 0.35 sec; Rest: minus 0.05 sec (FS)

**58**     SNOW WHITE H'CAP (0-90) £2226.00 (£616.00: £294.00)    5f **(AWT)**    1-20 (1-20)

33³ **Meeson Times (52)** *(BEllison)* 4–7–11  NCarlisle (14) (gd hdwy 2f out: led ins fnl
f: r o u.p) ................................................................................ —1
On the Edge **(80)** *(TDBarron)* 4–9–11  AlexGreaves (2) (lw: stdd s: bhd: hdwy
over 1f out: r.o wl u.p) ........................................................... hd.2
33 Hinari Video **(62)** *(MJohnston)* 7–8–7  RPElliott (7) (hdwy ½-wy: styd on wl fnl f) .....1½.3
Very Dicey **(78)** *(SDow)* 4–9–9  RCochrane (5) (w ldrs: led 2f out tl ins fnl f: sn
wknd) ................................................................................... ½.4
Gorinsky (IRE) **(81)** *(JBerry)* 4–9–12  JCarroll (3) (chsd ldrs: nt qckn fnl 2f) ............ 1.5
Sully's Choice (USA) **(54)** (bl) *(DWChapman)* 11–7–13  SWood (13) (nvr rchd ldrs) .. hd.6
Breezy Day **(75)** *(BAMcMahon)* 6–8–13 ‡⁷JBramhill (12) (lw: chsd ldrs: rdn ½-wy:
wknd over 1f out) ................................................................... s.h.7
Maid Welcome **(68)** (bl) *(MrsNMacaulay)* 5–8–8 ‡⁵EmmaO'Gorman (9) (lw: s.i.s:
bhd: sme hdwy ½-wy: n.d) ...................................................... nk.8
57² Furiella **(49)** (Fav) *(PCHaslam)* 4–7–5 ‡³JFanning (10) (sn drvn along: effrt ½-wy:
sn btn) ................................................................................... 1½.9
Tachyon Park **(48)** (bl) *(PHowling)* 10–7–7  GBardwell (8) (nvr wnt pce) ................. ½.10
Misdemeanours Girl (IRE) **(54)** *(MRChannon)* 4–7–13  JQuinn (11) (a in rr) ......... s.h.11
33* Sir Tasker **(64)** *(JLHarris)* 4–8–9  MHills (1) (chsd ldrs 3f: sn lost pl) ................. 1.12
33 Lady of the Fen **(64)** *(MrsNMacaulay)* 4–8–9  JMcLaughlin (4) (lw: led 3f: sn
wknd) ................................................................................... 1.13
Glencroft **(73)** (bl) *(DWChapman)* 8–8–11 ‡⁷SWilliams (6) (bit bkwd: outpcd
½-wy: effrt over 1f out: sn wknd) ........................................... 1½.14
LONG HANDICAP: Tachyon Park 7-0.

**4/1** Furiella, **9/2** MEESON TIMES, **8/1** Sir Tasker(op 5/1), **9/1** Very Dicey, **10/1** Gorinsky (IRE), Maid
Welcome, **12/1** Lady of the Fen, Hinari Video, **14/1** Sully's Choice (USA), Breezy Day, **16/1**
Misdemeanours Girl (IRE), On the Edge(op 10/1), **20/1** Tachyon Park, **25/1** Glencroft. CSF £69.63, CT
£755.66. Tote £5.40: £1.90 £2.70 £4.20 (£37.90). Mr Charles Castle (MALTON) bred by Mrs M. Chubb. 14
Rn                                               58.8 sec (0.8)
                                           SF—32/59/35/49/48/20/33

**59**     JACK AND THE BEANSTALK CLAIMING STKS   £2382.80 (£660.80: £316.40)
    1½m **(AWT)**                                          1-50 (1-51)

**Lara's Baby (IRE) (64)** (Fav) *(RAkehurst)* 4–8–8  RCochrane (9) (b.nr fore: trckd
ldrs: led over 4f out: pushed clr over 1f out: eased nr fin) ................... —1
40* Kirby Opportunity **(56)** *(JPearce)* 4–7–13 ‡⁵RPrice (10) (lw: chsd ldrs: jnd wnr 4f
out: kpt on wl u.p fnl 2f) ......................................................... 1½.2
Le Temeraire *(NTinkler)* 6–9–9  KimTinkler (6) (w ldrs: led 7f out tl over 4f out: one
pce) ...................................................................................... 8.3
Shadowland (IRE) **(56)** *(GAPritchard-Gordon)* 4–8–7  WRyan (8) (hld up & bhd:
gd hdwy over 4f out: sn rdn & no imp) ...................................... 4.4
Top Prize *(MBrittain)* 4–8–5  SWebster (3) (led 5f: hrd rdn & lost pl over 3f out) ......... nk.5
First Sapphire *(WJarvis)* 5–8–9  NDay (5) (effrt ½-wy: sn drvn along & no imp) ......... 8.6
Brantfell **(39)** *(TFairhurst)* 4–7–13 ‡³JFanning (2) (lw: plld hrd: hld up & a bhd) ........ 1½.7
Bell Turret **(26)** *(AWPotts)* 5–8–10 ‡³DBiggs (1) (plld hrd: bhd fnl 5f) ................. 3½.8
Toshiba Comet Too (IRE) **(51)** (bl) *(WJPearce)* 4–8–13  DNicholls (7) (plld hrd:
wnt prom ½-wy: hrd rdn & wknd 5f out) .................................... 2.9
Flirting **(24)** *(JMulhall)* 8–8–5  SMorris (11) (in tch tl wknd 5f out) ....................... 5.10
Canonised *(RGBrazington)* 8–8–12  JQuinn (4) (t.o) ........................................... 11

**8/11** LARA'S BABY (IRE), **9/4** Kirby Opportunity, **14/1** Shadowland (IRE)(op 7/1), **16/1** First Sapphire, **20/1** Toshiba Comet Too (IRE), Le Temeraire(op 12/1), **33/1** Canonised, Brantfell, **50/1** Ors. CSF £2.92. Tote £2.00: £1.10 £1.10 £9.90 (£2.00). Larabuild Contractors (EPSOM) bred by Killarkin Stud in Ireland. 11 Rn
2m 39.4 (5.2)
SF—36/24/32/8/5/–

---

**60**  D J JONES PAPER BEDDING H'CAP (0-90) £2069.20 (£571.20: £271.60)
**1¾m (AWT)**
2-20 (2-20)

552 **Fiala (IRE) (80)** (Jt-Fav) *(JHMGosden)* 4–9-0 MHills (1) (mde all: pushed along: styd on strly fnl 2f: comf) ..................................................................... —1
Dalby Dancer **(55)** *(BAMcMahon)* 8–7-9 NCarlisle (4) (chsd ldrs: kpt on fnl 2f: no imp) .............................................................................. 2½.2
46* **Hand Painted (62)** (Jt-Fav) *(CRBeever)* 8–7-9 (5x) ‡7DHarrison (2) (b: lw: hld up: effrt over 2f out: sn drvn along & kpt on same pce) .................. 2½.3
465 Chronological **(65)** (v) *(MHTompkins)* 6–7-12(5) ‡7SMulvey (6) (bhd: effrt u.p 4f out: kpt on: nrst fin) ................................................. 3½.4
48 In Truth **(59)** *(DWChapman)* 4–7-7 SWood (3) (in tch tl rdn & outpcd 5f out) ............. 8.5
King High **(88)** *(ASReid)* 5–9-7 ‡7KRutter (7) (b: chsd ldrs: drvn along 8f out: lost pl over 4f out) ............................................................... 10.6
466 Obeliski **(53)** *(PCHaslam)* 6–7-4 ‡3JFanning (5) (chsd wnr tl rdn & wknd over 3f out) ....................................................................... 1½.7
LONG HANDICAP: In Truth 6-7.

**6/4** Hand Painted, FIALA (IRE), **7/1** Chronological, **12/1** Dalby Dancer(op 7/1), **14/1** Obeliski(op 8/1), **40/1** In Truth, **50/1** King High. CSF £16.72, Tote £2.00: £1.40 £4.00 (£18.40). Mr C. A. B. St. George (NEWMARKET) bred by M. L. Page in Ireland. 7 Rn
3m 4.6 (3.4)
SF—40/16/11/7/–/–

---

**61**  ALADDIN CLAIMING STKS (3-Y-O) £2167.20 (£599.20: £285.60)  **6f (AWT)**
2-50 (2-50)

293 **Palacegate Racing (77)** *(JBerry)* 9-2 JCarroll (3) (lw: chsd ldrs: rdn to ld 2f out: jst hld on) ....................................................................... —1
29* **Pop to Stans (85)** (Fav) *(TDBarron)* 9-2 AlexGreaves (4) (trckd ldrs: effrt 2f out: r.o wl u.p ins fnl f) .............................................. hd.2
Dark Midnight (IRE) **(60)** *(PCHaslam)* 8-9(2) RCochrane (8) (chsd ldrs: styd on u.p fnl 2f: nvr able to chal) ................................. 4.3
Life's a Breeze *(MRChannon)* 8-9 LornaVincent (1) (cmpt: sn outpcd: hdwy over 1f out: r.o nr fin) ......................................................... nk.4
473 Runnel **(85)** *(DWChapman)* 9-4 SWood (6) (led tl hdd & wknd 2f out) ................ 1½.5
Indigo Blue (IRE) *(NACallaghan)* 8-7 WNewnes (7) (b.hind: s.i.s: hdwy ½-wy: sn wl outpcd) .................................................................. 10.6
Rumbled Again (IRE) *(TDBarron)* 8-4 LCharnock (5) (t: s.s: sn w ldr: rdn & wknd qckly over 2f out) ........................................ 3.7
Dogma *(DWChapman)* 7-11 ‡3JFanning (2) (small: neat: bit bkwd: s.s: a wl bhd) 15.8

**4/5** Pop to Stans, **4/1** Runnel, PALACEGATE RACING, **12/1** Dark Midnight (IRE)(op 8/1), **14/1** Indigo Blue (IRE)(op 8/1), **25/1** Life's a Breeze, **33/1** Rumbled Again (IRE), **50/1** Dogma. CSF £7.58, Tote £4.20: £1.50 £1.20 £2.90 (£3.10). Palacegate Corporation Ltd (COCKERHAM) bred by D. Rabey. 8 Rn
1m 16.2 (2.8)
SF—40/39/16/15/18/–

---

**62**  SLEEPING BEAUTY H'CAP (3-Y-O) (0-80) £2088.80 (£576.80: £274.40)
**1m (AWT)**
3-20 (3-20)
(Weights raised 1 lb)

**Dublin Indemnity (USA) (62)** (bl) (Fav) *(NACallaghan)* 8-11 WNewnes (3) (trckd ldrs: led over 1f out: r.o strly) ........................... —1
Ferdia (IRE) **(66)** *(RHollinshead)* 9-1 WRyan (7) (lw: hld up: effrt over 3f out: r.o u.p fnl 2f: nt rch wnr) .............................. 2½.2
Up the Punjab **(72)** *(SDow)* 9-7 RCochrane (2) (effrt over 3f out: r.o one pce fnl 2f) ................................................................ ½.3
Lady of Letters **(50)** *(TThomsonJones)* 7-13 NAdams (6) (led after 1f tl hdd & wknd over 1f out) ...................................... 4.4
Super-Sub **(61)** *(MJFetherston-Godley)* 8-3 ‡7DHarrison (1) (sn bhd: effrt on outside over 2f out: n.d) .............................. 1½.5
343 Whirlygig **(47)** (bl) *(JSWainwright)* 7-7 ‡3JFanning (4) (chsd ldrs tl rdn & lost pl over 3f out) ...................................... 10.6
Thursley **(58)** *(HJCollingridge)* 8-7 JQuinn (5) (lw: led 1f: chsd ldrs tl wknd over 2f out) ................................................. nk.7

**9/4** DUBLIN INDEMNITY (USA), **5/2** Ferdia (IRE), **5/1** Up the Punjab, **11/2** Super-Sub(4/1—6/1), **6/1** Thursley(op 7/2), **20/1** Ors. CSF £8.09, Tote £3.90: £1.80 £1.60 (£3.70). Mr R. K. Carvill (NEWMARKET) bred by Katalpa Farm in USA. 7 Rn
1m 42.3 (3)
SF—46/42/46/11/10/–

**63**      SWAN LAKE H'CAP (0-80) £2343.60 (£649.60: £310.80)    **1m (AWT)**     3-50 (3-51)

(Weights raised 9 lb)

42[6] **Kissavos (53)** (CCElsey) 6–8-12 TRogers (1) (b.hind: trckd ldrs: r.o u.p fnl f: led last stride) .................................................................... —1

50[2] Mac's Princess (USA) **(62)** (Fav) (WAO'Gorman) 4–9-1 ‡[5]EmmaO'Gorman (11) (hld up & bhd: rapid hdwy 4f out: led 2f out: edgd lft: jst ct) ... s.h.2

Question of Degree **(36)** (NTinkler) 6–7-9 KimTinkler (9) (lw: sn pushed along & outpcd: hdwy over 1f out: r.o nr fin) .................................... 1½.3

50[5] Golden Ancona **(55)** (MBrittain) 9–9-0 RCochrane (4) (sn bhd: styd on fnl 2f: nt rch ldrs) ......................................................................... ¾.4

Hawaii Storm (FR) **(36)** (MissAJWhitfield) 4–7-8 NAdams (7) (b.nr hind: led tl hdd f2f out: wknd nr fin) ............................................. s.h.5

56[4] Les Amis **(46)** (MJRyan) 5–8-2 ‡[3]DBiggs (5) (chsd ldrs tl wknd over 1f out) ...... 2½.6

49[4] Luzum **(65)** (bl) (JAGlover) 8–9-3 ‡[7]SWilliams (3) (lw: trckd ldrs: effrt & n.m.r over 1f out: fnd nil fnl f) ............................................................. nk.7

35[6] Evening Star **(56)** (AHide) 6–8-8 ‡[7]KRutter (2) (sn bhd: sme hdwy over 2f out: sn wknd) ................................................................................... 5.8

50 State Governor **(66)** (DWChapman) 4–9-10 SWood (8) (chsd ldrs tl wknd 2f out)   1½.9

Henry Will **(45)** (TFairhurst) 8–8-1 ‡[3]JFanning (6) (sn rr div & drvn along) ........... 2½.10

Gibbot **(36)** (bl) (PHowling) 7–7-9 GBardwell (12) (in tch: sn pushed along: wknd over 3f out) .................................................................... 4.11

32[3] Dashing April **(54)** (DTThom) 4–8-5 ‡[7]DHarrison (10) (chsd ldrs: sn drvn along: lost pl 3f out) .............................................................. hd.12

49[5] Tudorgateway **(65)** (v) (MHTompkins) 4–9-2 ‡[7]SMulvey (13) (reluctant to r: a wl bhd) ........................................................................... 1.13

*Stewards Enquiry: Rogers suspended 24-25/1/92 (excessive use of whip).*

**9/4** Mac's Princess (USA), **7/1** Evening Star, Golden Ancona(9/1—6/1), **8/1** KISSAVOS(op 5/1), **9/1** Les Amis, **10/1** Luzum, **12/1** State Governor, Tudorgateway, Question of Degree, **14/1** Henry Will, Dashing April, **25/1** Gibbot, **33/1** Hawaii Storm (FR). CSF £26.65, CT £211.17. Tote £8.50: £2.10 £1.20 £5.90 (£9.30). Red Nose Racing (LAMBOURN) bred by Falconet Inc. 13 Rn    1m 43 (3.7)

SF—35/37/12/29/8/8

T/Plpt: £17.70 (81.45 Tckts).        WG

## SOUTHWELL (L-H) Fibresand
### Friday, January 17th [Standard]
Going Allowance: minus 0.20 sec per fur (FS)           Wind: slt half bhd   Vis: misty

Stalls: Races 2 & 4 high, Rest low

**64**      TIMOTHY CLAIMING STKS (I)   £2226.00 (£616.00: £294.00)   **1m (AWT)**    12-51 (12-59)

41[3] **Tara's Delight (66)** (MJRyan) 5–8-4 ‡[3]DBiggs (10) (a.p: wnt 2nd st: led 2f out: hld on gamely) ............................................................ —1

45[3] Euroblake **(78)** (Fav) (TDBarron) 5–8-12 AlexGreaves (5) (hld up: hdwy over 3f out: 5th st: unable qckn nr fin) ....................................... s.h.2

Petropower (IRE) **(45)** (MO'Neill) 4–8-6 JFortune (1) (led 6f: kpt on same pce fr over 1f out) ................................................................. 3.3

49[2] Shabanaz **(85)** (THCaldwell) 7–8-12 ‡[7]StephenDavies (7) (hld up: hdwy & 4th st: kpt on one pce fnl 2f) ................................................... 4.4

28 Carrolls Marc (IRE) **(69)** (PJFeilden) 4–8-9[(1)] RCochrane (2) (chsd ldr: 3rd st: wknd wl over 1f out) ........................................... 6.5

Porick **(23)** (v) (DMoffatt) 4–7-9 ‡[7]DarrenMoffatt (4) (bit bkwd: dwlt: hdwy after 1f: 6th & btn st) .................................................... 6.6

King Trevisio **(43)** (bl) (JLHarris) 6–8-5[(1)] MHills (8) (s.s: effrt ½-wy: no imp: t.o) ....... 7.7

32 Green's Bonheur **(30)** (MPNaughton) 4–7-7 ‡[5]BDoyle (9) (b.off fore: a bhd: t.o) ....... 4.8

Great Music **(39)** (JSWainwright) 4–8-3 JQuinn (3) (chsd ldrs 4f: sn lost pl: t.o) ......... 4.9

Rockalong (MJCharles) 7–7-13[(4)] ‡[7]SSanders (6) (bkwd: a bhd: t.o) .................... 10.10

**5/4** Euroblake, **7/4** Shabanaz, **100/30** TARA'S DELIGHT, **25/1** Carrolls Marc (IRE), **33/1** Green's Bonheur, Great Music, **40/1** Petropower (IRE), **50/1** King Trevisio, **66/1** Ors. CSF £7.81, Tote £5.30: £1.10 £1.10 £7.70 (£4.30). Mr W. G. Dixon (NEWMARKET) bred by Burton Agnes Stud Co Ltd. 10 Rn   1m 41.7 (2.4)

SF—30/37/22/16/–/–

**65**      COWSLIP H'CAP (3-Y.O) (0-70) £2030.00 (£560.00: £266.00)   **5f (AWT)**    1-25 (1-27)

51 **Kalar (39)** (DWChapman) 7-9 SWood (4) (chsd ldr: rdn 2f out: led over 1f out: r.o wl) ...................................................................... —1

44[5] Do the Business (IRE) **(49)** (CNAllen) 8-2 ‡[3]DBiggs (1) (s.s: bhd: rdn over 1f out: r.o wl nr fin) ........................................................ 1½.2

It's Only Money **(65)** (Fav) *(THCaldwell)* 9-0 ‡⁷StephenDavies (2) (bit bkwd: led tl over 1f out: sn rdn: one pce) .............................................. ¾.3

44⁴ Fort Hope **(54)** (bl) *(TJNaughton)* 8-10 MHills (3) (b: chsd ldrs: rdn wl over 1f out: wknd ins fnl f) .............................................. 2½.4

Kick on Majestic (IRE) **(56)** *(NBycroft)* 8-7 ‡⁵EmmaO'Gorman (5) (bkwd: s.s: rdn ½-wy: a bhd) .............................................. 3½.5

**7/4** It's Only Money, **2/1** Fort Hope, **7/2** Do the Business (IRE), **6/1** Kick on Majestic (IRE), **16/1** KALAR. CSF £61.72, Tote £15.80: £5.10 £1.40 (£15.00). Mr C. C. Pryor (YORK) bred by C. C. and Mrs Pryor. 5Rn
61.3 sec (3.3)

**66**   TIMOTHY CLAIMING STKS (II)   £2226.00 (£616.00: £294.00)   **1m (AWT)**   1-55 (2-00)

32⁵ **Cleo Modena (IRE)** *(MO'Neill)* 4—7-11 ‡⁵SMaloney (1) (mde all: rdn out) .............. —1

Awesome Power **(59)** (Fav) *(CRNelson)* 6—8-11 RCochrane (7) (hdwy 5f out: 3rd st: styd on u.p fnl f) .............................................. 1½.2

36³ Buddy's Friend (IRE) **(51)** *(RJRWilliams)* 4—8-8 MHills (6) (chsd ldr: 2nd st: rdn & no ex ins fnl f) .............................................. 2.3

36 Carnfield *(JAGlover)* 4—8-1 NCarlisle (5) (hdwy & 6th st: styd on one pce appr fnl f) .............................................. 2.4

50 Foursingh **(58)** *(CBBBooth)* 4—8-8 ACulhane (3) (hdwy over 2f out: nvr nr to chal) 3½.5

36⁴ Danzig Lad (USA) **(42)** (v) *(MPNaughton)* 4—7-13 ‡⁵BDoyle (9) (dwlt: sn rcvrd: 4th st: wknd 2f out: t.o) .............................................. 10.6

33 Rancho Mirage **(56)** *(MrsNMacauley)* 4—8-8⁽¹⁾ NDay (2) (b: bit bkwd: prom: 5th st: wknd 2f out: t.o) .............................................. 2½.7

45 Uppance *(DWChapman)* 4—7-12 SWood (4) (a bhd: rn wd ent st: t.o) ............ ½.8

My Three Girls (IRE) **(39)** *(HJCollingridge)* 4—8-1 JQuinn (8) (bit bkwd: chsd ldrs to ½-wy: sn wknd: t.o) .............................................. 20.9

Absaloui **(38)** *(WGMTurner)* 4—8-3 GBardwell (10) (bolted bef s: a bhd: wl t.o) .... dist.10

**10/11** Awesome Power, **11/4** Buddy's Friend (IRE), **8/1** Foursingh(op 4/1), **Rancho Mirage**(op 5/1), **16/1** Danzig Lad (USA)(op 8/1), **20/1** CLEO MODENA (IRE), **33/1** Carnfield, **40/1** Absaloui, **50/1** Uppance, **66/1** My Three Girls (IRE). CSF £38.17, Tote £14.40: £2.80 £1.30 £1.10 (£15.80). Mrs Jan Heaven (LYDIATE) bred by R. Goodwin in Ireland. 10 Rn
1m 43.2 (3.9)
SF—1/10/1/–/–/–

**67**   BROWN JACOBSON H'CAP (0-100) £2108.40 (£582.40: £277.20)   **1½m (AWT)**   2-25 (2-26)

(Weights raised 12 lb)

**Qualitair Blazer (49)** *(JRJenkins)* 5—8-9 SWhitworth (1) (b: chsd ldrs: 3rd st: shkn up to ld over 1f out: r.o) .............................................. —1

25³ Magic Secret **(68)** *(PCHaslam)* 4—9-7 ‡³JFanning (3) (b.off hind: led: rdn ent st: hdd over 1f out: rallied gamely fnl f) .............................................. nk.2

25² Frescobaldo (USA) **(62)** *(MPNaughton)* 6—9-3 ‡⁵BDoyle (5) (chsd ldr: 2nd st: ev ch over 1f out: one pce) .............................................. 1½.3

Duggan **(61)** (Fav) *(RJRWilliams)* 5—9-7 RCochrane (4) (hld up: 4th st: effrt & ev ch over 1f out: wknd fnl f) .............................................. 2.4

50 Balaat (USA) **(59)** *(MCChapman)* 4—8-8 ‡⁷SWilliams (2) (hld up & bhd: 5th st: rdn over 1f out: no imp) .............................................. ½.5

**7/4** Duggan, **3/1** Frescobaldo (USA), **100/30** Magic Secret(op 2/1), **4/1** QUALITAIR BLAZER, **12/1** Balaat (USA)(16/1—20/1). CSF £15.96, Tote £4.80: £2.40 £1.90 (£6.20). Brooke (Enfield Wash) Ltd (ROYSTON) bred by Neriad (UK) Ltd. 5 Rn
2m 40.1 (5.9)
SF—12/23/16/16/2

**68**   YORKSHIRE FOG CLAIMING STKS (3-Y.O) £2167.20 (£599.20: £128.80 each)   **7f (AWT)**   2-55 (2-55)

51* **Palacegate King (58)** *(JBerry)* 9-2 JCarroll (4) (lw: mde all: rdn over 1f out: hld on gamely) .............................................. —1

61² Pop to Stans **(85)** (Fav) *(TDBarron)* 9-2 AlexGreaves (3) (prom: 2nd st: sustained chal fnl f: r.o) .............................................. nk.2

30⁵ Meltonby **(70)** *(JHetherton)* 8-8 WNewnes (7) (chsd wnr 4f: outpcd & 5th st: swtchd rt 2f out: styd on) .............................................. 4.3

38³ Brotherlyaffection **(62)** *(RHollinshead)* 8-7 WRyan (5) (a.p: 3rd st: one pce fnl 2f) d.h.3

51² Ready to Draw (IRE) **(60)** *(RonaldThompson)* 8-7 ‡⁵SMaloney (1) (s.i.s: hdwy 4f out: 4th st: wknd 2f out) .............................................. 6.5

34² Patrician Magician **(73)** *(RJRWilliams)* 8-9 ‡⁵CHodgson (2) (b.hind: chsd ldrs: lost pl & 6th st: sn btn) .............................................. 1½.6

Simon Ellis (IRE) **(50)** *(DRLaing)* 8-5 MHills (8) (a outpcd: t.o) .............................................. 10.7

51 Rythmic Style **(64)** *(TDBarron)* 8-4 LCharnock (6) (hdwy fr ½-wy: t.o) .............................................. 5.8

*Stewards Enquiry: Carroll suspended 26-27/1/92 (excessive use of whip).*

**Evens** Pop to Stans(tchd 6/4), **5/1** Meltonby, PALACEGATE KING, **8/1** Patrician Magician(op 5/1), **9/1** Ready to Draw (IRE)(op 6/1), **12/1** Brotherlyaffection, **25/1** Rythmic Style, **33/1** Simon Ellis (IRE). CSF £10.41, Tote £4.90: £1.50 £1.20 M £0.60 B £0.90 (£3.90). Palacegate Corporation Ltd (COCKERHAM) bred by Miss E. Streatfeild. 8 Rn
1m 28.9 (2.3)
SF—46/45/25/24/6/3

**69**      FOXGLOVE STKS (Mdn 3-Y.O) £2108.40 (£582.40: £277.20)    **1m (AWT)**     3-25 (3-25)

37² **Hand on Heart (IRE)** *(Fav) (WJHaggas)* 8-9 NDay (1) (b.off hind: led after 4f: clr
     ent st: eased cl home) ..................................................................... —1
     Fengari *(PTWalwyn)* 9-0 RCochrane (2) (bit bkwd: led 4f: lost pl & 4th st: swtchd
     rt 1f out: styd on ins fnl f) ................................................................ 2.2
     Calcutta Queen *(MrsJCecil)* 8-9 BCrossley (3) (bkwd: prom: styd on fnl f)   hd.3
     Buzzards Bellbuoy *(HJCollingridge)* 9-0 JQuinn (4) (w'like: bkwd: s.i.s: hdwy &
     3rd st: wknd 1f out) ........................................................................ nk.4
37 High Success *(WAO'Gorman)* 8-9 ‡⁵EmmaO'Gorman (5) (bit bkwd: chsd ldrs:
     5th st: wknd 2f out) ........................................................................ 2.5
47⁵ So Great *(WWHaigh)* 9-0 ACulhane (6) (b: dwlt: a bhd: 6th st: t.o) ........... 15.6

**5/4** HAND ON HEART (IRE)(Evens—6/4), **7/4** Fengari, **7/1** Calcutta Queen(op 5/2), **17/2** Buzzards Bellbuoy, **11/1** High Success(8/1—12/1), **25/1** So Great. CSF £3.90, Tote £2.90: £1.40 £1.60 (£3.10). Mrs M. M. Haggas (NEWMARKET) bred by Kellsboro House Stud in Ireland. 6 Rn
1m 43.9 (4.6)
SF—2/1/–/–/–/–

**70**      RYEGRASS H'CAP (0-80) £2304.40 (£638.40: £305.20)    **7f (AWT)**     3-55 (4-00)
           (Weights raised 4 lb)

On Y Va (USA) **(52)** *(RJRWilliams)* 5–8-4 JQuinn (15) (b.hind: hld up: 6th st: led
     ins fnl f: r.o strly) .......................................................................... —1
31⁶ Saladan Knight **(59)** *(JGFitzGerald)* 7–8-4 ‡⁷MHunt (7) (chsd ldrs: 3rd st: led 2f
     out tl ins fnl f) .............................................................................. 3½.2
28 Dawn Success **(60)** *(DWChapman)* 6–8-12 GBaxter (4) (hld up: hdwy over 1f
     out: fin wl) .................................................................................. nk.3
49 Cossack Noir **(44)** *(MPNaughton)* 4–8-7⁽³⁾ ‡⁵BDoyle (8) (hdwy fnl 2f: nt rch ldrs) ... nk.4
49³ Pesidanamich (IRE) **(72)** (bl) *(TDBarron)* 4–9-3 ‡⁷VHalliday (10) (led after
     2f to 2f out: sn rdn & btn) ............................................................... ¾.5
     Silly's Brother **(47)** *(NBycroft)* 6–7-13 GBardwell (11) (chsd ldrs: 4th st: wknd
     over 1f out) ................................................................................. 3½.6
     Brown Fairy (USA) **(68)** *(MrsNMacauley)* 4–9-3 ‡³DBiggs (1) (chsd ldrs: no hdwy
     fnl 2f) ....................................................................................... 1.7
     Minizen Music (IRE) **(45)** *(MBrittain)* 4–7-4⁽⁴⁾ ‡⁷DWright (9) (bit bkwd: 2f: 2nd
     st: hrd rdn & wknd over 1f out) ......................................................... nk.8
     Warrior Prince **(50)** *(RMWhitaker)* 4–7-11⁽⁴⁾ ‡⁵SMaloney (2) (nvr plcd to chal) ...... 1½.9
45⁴ Inseyab **(65)** *(PCHaslam)* 4–9-0 ‡³JFanning (16) (s.i.s: effrt & 7th st: sn wknd) ...... 3.10
36² Swinging Lady **(50)** *(WWHaigh)* 4–8-2 LCharnock (3) (spd over 4f) ..................... ½.11
     Gun Rule **(60)** *(DRLaing)* 8–8-12 MHills (13) (b: s.i.s: hdwy & 5th st: wknd 2f out)   2.12
32⁶ Kabera **(41)** *(DWChapman)* 4–7-7 SWood (6) (a in rr) ...................................... hd.13
     Morpick **(55)** *(JPLeigh)* 5–8-7 ACulhane (5) (bkwd: sn outpcd) ........................ 1½.14
42 Verro (USA) **(43)** *(JABennett)* 5–7-9⁽²⁾ NCarlisle (14) (eyeshield: chsd ldrs tl
     wknd 2f out: t.o) .......................................................................... 5.15

LONG HANDICAP: Cossack Noir 7-1, Kabera 6-10, Verro (USA) 7-1.

**5/2** Pesidanamich (IRE)(7/2—9/2), **6/1** ON Y VA (USA)(op 7/2), **7/1** Silly's Brother, **15/2** Brown Fairy (USA), **8/1** Inseyab, **10/1** Swinging Lady, **12/1** Saladan Knight(op 8/1), **14/1** Morpick, **20/1** Dawn Success, Verro (USA), **33/1** Cossack Noir, Warrior Prince, Minizen Music (IRE), **50/1** Kabera. CSF £73.34, CT £1,261.89. Tote £5.50: £2.40 £3.20 £3.40 (£65.40). Mr T. F. Hornett (NEWMARKET) bred by Pillar Stud, Inc. in USA. 15 Rn
1m 28.9 (2.3)
SF—34/23/30/8/32/3

T/Plpt: £19.90 (50.55 Tckts).                                               IM

## 52—**LINGFIELD (L-H)** Equitrack
## Saturday, January 18th [Standard]
Going Allowance: minus 0.10 sec per fur (FS)

**71**      DOWN H'CAP (0-70) £2324.00 (£644.00: £308.00)    **1½m (AWT)**     12-55 (12-57)

**Strat's Legacy (41)** *(DWPArbuthnot)* 5–8-0⁽¹⁾ ‡⁵RPrice (3) (b.hind: a.p: led over
     2f out: clr over 1f out: eased nr fin) .................................................... —1
     Plectrum **(50)** *(JLSpearing)* 4–8-10 GBardwell (7) (a.p: led over 4f out tl over 2f
     out: unable qckn) ......................................................................... 3½.2
     Sharp Top **(42)** *(MJRyan)* 4–7-13 ‡³DBiggs (1) (a.p: one pce fnl 2f) ................. nk.3
     Carpet Slippers **(52)** (Fav) *(JDBethell)* 6–9-2 WRyan (10) (rdn & no hdwy fnl 3f) ..... 12.4

Aude la Belle (FR) **(59)** *(MrsAKnight)* 4–8-12 ‡7DHarrison (2) (w ldr: led 5f out tl
over 4f out: sn wknd) ........................................................ 3½.5
Saville Way **(33)** *(WJMusson)* 5–7-6(3) ‡5BDoyle (9) (eyeshield: nvr nr to chal) ......... 4.6
Luthior (FR) **(64)** *(RSimpson)* 6–10-0 SWhitworth (6) (a bhd) ............................... 1½.7
Kaths Choice **(45)** *(HJCollingridge)* 4–8-5 JQuinn (4) (swtg: plld hrd: bhd fnl 5f) ...... 10.8
Glowing Mantle (IRE) **(43)** *(REPeacock)* 4–8-0 ‡3JFanning (5) (led 7f) ................... nk.9
45 Persian Satan (IRE) **(46)** *(CJHill)* 4–8-6 NAdams (8) (bhd fnl 8f) ........................ 12.10

**9/4** Carpet Slippers, **5/1** Saville Way, Sharp Top, STRAT'S LEGACY, **11/2** Plectrum, **14/1** Luthior (FR), Aude
la Belle (FR), **16/1** Kaths Choice(12/1—20/1), **25/1** Persian Satan (IRE), **33/1** Glowing Mantle (IRE). CSF
£31.59, CT £134.08. Tote £4.20: £2.10 £1.60 £2.00 (£30.50). Mr Jack Blumenow (COMPTON) bred by
Exors of the late A. Stratton Smith. 10 Rn                                   2m 35.71 (6.31)
                                                                            SF—11/14/2/–/–/–

**72**          TYRONE STKS (Mdn 3-Y.O) £2167.20 (£599.20: £285.60)      **7f (AWT)**     1-25 (1-28)

**Sand Table** (Fav) *(LordHuntingdon)* 9-0 WRyan (4) (w'like: bit bkwd: a.p: led
over 1f out: easily) ......................................................... —1
Easy Does it **(48)** (v) *(CCElsey)* 8–9 WNewnes (8) (w ldr: led over 3f out tl one over 1f
out: unable qckn) .......................................................... 7.2
62⁵ Super-Sub **(61)** *(MJFetherston-Godley)* 8-9 CRutter (5) (led over 3f: one pce) 3½.3
54⁴ Shocking Times **(65)** *(RSimpson)* 8-9 SWhitworth (2) (unruly stalls: hdwy over
2f out: one pce) ........................................................... 2½.4
29² Golden Sickle (USA) *(WAO'Gorman)* 8-9 ‡5EmmaO'Gorman (3) (prom over 4f) . 3.5
Smudgemupum *(MissBSanders)* 9-0 BCrossley (6) (unf: bit bkwd: s.i.s: a bhd) ¾.6
Albany Spark *(GHEden)* 9-0 RCochrane (7) (a bhd) ............................... hd.7
Floating Rate **(54)** *(JWhite)* 8-4 ‡5RPrice (1) (a bhd) ........................ 2½.8

**11/8** SAND TABLE, **5/2** Golden Sickle (USA), **4/1** Shocking Times(3/1—11/2), **13/2** Super-Sub, **20/1** Floating
Rate(op 12/1), Easy Does it(op 12/1), **33/1** Albany Spark, **40/1** Smudgemupum. CSF £25.21, Tote £2.80: £1.10
£1.90 £3.10 (£35.70). Lord Derby (WEST ILSLEY) bred by Stanley Estate and Stud Co. 8 Rn      1m 26.58 (2.58)
                                                                            SF—50/24/13/5/–/–

**73**          ARMAGH H'CAP (3-Y.O) (0-80) £2280.00 (£630.00: £300.00)     **7f (AWT)**     1-55 (1-55)
                  (Weights raised 3 lb)
**Jefferson Davis (IRE) (71)** (Jt-Fav) *(WJPearce)* 9-3 DNicholls (4) (lw: plld hrd:
led over 1f out: r.o wl) ..................................................... —1
30⁴ Try Leguard (IRE) **(75)** *(WCarter)* 9-2 ‡5NGwilliams (3) (lw: hld up: hrd rdn over 2f
out: r.o ins fnl f) ......................................................... 1.2
62³ Up the Punjab **(72)** *(SDow)* 8-11 ‡7MJermy (5) (b.hind: lw: led 4f out to 3f
out: led wl over 1f out: sn hdd: unable qckn) ............................... 1.3
68⁶ Patrician Magician **(73)** *(RJRWilliams)* 9-0 ‡5CHodgson (2) (b.hind: led 3f: wknd
wl over 1f out) ............................................................ 5.4
39* Myasha (USA) **(69)** (Jt-Fav) *(MrsLPiggott)* 9-1 RCochrane (1) (eyeshield:
b.hind: a.p: led 3f out tl wl over 1f out: sn wknd) ......................... 4.5

**5/2** Up the Punjab(4/1—7/1), JEFFERSON DAVIS (IRE), Myasha (USA), **4/1** Try Leguard (IRE), **8/1** Patrician
Magician(op 5/1). CSF £12.10, Tote £2.80: £1.90 £3.00 (£39.10). The Confederacy (HAMBLETON) bred by
Rose O'Reilly in Ireland. 5 Rn                                               1m 26.95 (2.95)
                                                                            SF—48/44/36/24/13

**74**          FERMANAGH H'CAP (0-100) £2369.40 (£653.40: £310.20)      **1¼m (AWT)**     2-25 (2-26)

**Rapporteur (USA) (86)** (Fav) *(CCElsey)* 6–9-13 WNewnes (2) (b: lw: mde all:
qcknd wl over 1f out: hrd rdn: r.o wl) ...................................... —1
46 Mr Wishing Well **(60)** *(RJRWilliams)* 6–8-1 JQuinn (1) (lw: hld up: r.o one pce fnl
2f) ...................................................................... 1.2
53³ Super Sally **(87)** *(MJRyan)* 5–9-11 ‡3DBiggs (4) (chsd wnr: ev ch over 2f out: one
pce) ..................................................................... 1.3
Sianema **(58)** *(DRLaing)* 4–7-10 GBardwell (3) (b: s.s: rdn over 4f out: ev ch over
2f out: wknd over 1f out) .................................................. 5.4

**5/6** RAPPORTEUR (USA), **7/4** Super Sally, **6/1** Mr Wishing Well, **20/1** Sianema. CSF £5.38, Tote £1.80
(£2.80). Mr Richard Berenson (LAMBOURN) bred by Thomas P. Whitney in USA. 4 Rn      2m 7.02 (4.02)
                                                                            SF—63/35/57/18

**75**          ANTRIM CLAIMING STKS  £2402.40 (£666.40: £319.20)      **6f (AWT)**     2-55 (2-56)

45* **African Chimes (89)** (Fav) *(WAO'Gorman)* 5–8-10 ‡5EmmaO'Gorman (1)
(hdwy over 3f out: led wl over 1f out: rdn out) ............................. —1
49* Bold Habit **(94)** *(WJPearce)* 7–9-0 ‡5GHusband (12) (s.s: hdwy wl over 1f out: r.o
ins fnl f) ................................................................. 4.2
Respectable Jones **(83)** *(GBBalding)* 6–8-12 WNewnes (9) (lw: a.p: led over 2f
out tl wl over 1f out: unable qckn) ........................................ 2.3

43² Murmuring (60) *(SDow)* 6–8–6 JQuinn (3) (b.hind: a.p: one pce fnl 2f) ...................... 5.4
53⁶ Assignment (77) *(JFfitch-Heyes)* 6–8–11 RCochrane (7) (b.hind: hrd rdn over 2f
    out: nvr nr to chal) ............................................................................................. 1½.5
49 Courting Newmarket (46) *(MrsAKnight)* 4–8–4 ‡³DBiggs (4) (led over 3f) .................. 1.6
39⁴ Lonesome Dove (IRE) *(JWhite)* 4–8–0(1) ‡⁵RPrice (6) (outpcd) ............................... 4.7
43 Sports Post Lady (IRE) (62) *(CJHill)* 4–8–6 NAdams (5) (spd 3f) .............................. 1.8
57 Lucky Blue (52) *(JCFox)* 5–8–7 BCrossley (10) (lw: outpcd) ................................... hd.9
Supreme Optimist (39) (bl) *(REPeacock)* 8–8–3 ‡³JFanning (8) (b: spd 3f) ............. 3.10
Scottish Tina *(AMoore)* 4–8–0 SDawson (2) (s.i.s: a bhd) ..................................... 2.11

**2/1** AFRICAN CHIMES, **11/1** Bold Habit(op 6/4), **4/1** Respectable Jones, **6/1** Assignment, **8/1**
Murmuring(tchd 12/1), **16/1** Sports Post Lady (IRE)(op 10/1), **33/1** Lucky Blue, **50/1** Ors. CSF £7.89, Tote
£2.80: £1.20 £1.50 £1.60 (£3.50). Mr D. G. Wheatley (NEWMARKET) bred by Noel Cogan. 11 Rn
1m 11.79 (1.19)
SF—60/48/38/12/11/–

**76**    LONDONDERRY H'CAP (0-60) £2402.40 (£666.40: £319.20)  **2m (AWT)**  3-25 (3-27)

55³ **Jawani (IRE) (46)** (v) (Jt-Fav) *(DrJDScargill)* 4–8–9 JQuinn (9) (hdwy 7f out: led
    over 3f out: clr over 2f out: eased nr fin) ............................................................. —1
46 Malenoir (USA) (45) (v) *(WJPearce)* 4–8–8 DNicholls (8) (a.p: chsd wnr fnl 2f: no
    imp) ................................................................................................................... 3.2
Take Issue (40) *(JSutcliffe)* 7–8–10 WRyan (13) (lw: hdwy over 4f out: one pce fnl
    2f) ..................................................................................................................... 4.3
55⁶ Lifetimes Ambition (45) *(TCasey)* 4–8–5 ‡DBiggs (6) (hdwy over 3f out: one pce
    fnl 2f) ................................................................................................................ nk.4
Shar Emblem (52) (Jt-Fav) *(SDow)* 4–9–1 RCochrane (2) (b.hind: no hdwy fnl 3f) .... 5.5
46³ Kovalevskia (40) *(DAWilson)* 7–8–10(1) WNewnes (4) (hdwy over 2f out: nvr nrr) .... hd.6
Touching Times (55) *(GAPritchard-Gordon)* 4–8–13 ‡⁵SMaloney (14) (nvr nrr) ........ 2.7
25⁶ Blue Disc (36) (bl) *(CRBeever)* 7–7–13 ‡⁷DIlarrison (5) (prom over 12f) ................ 1½.8
Free Minx (49) *(MrsVAAconley)* 4–8–12 ‡⁷GParkin (7) (prom over 11f) ................... 4.9
Bursana (38) *(JLSpearing)* 6–8–8 GBardwell (3) (led 7f out tl over 3f out: sn
    wknd) ................................................................................................................ ½.10
40 Adjaristan (52) *(RSimpson)* 5–9–3 ‡⁵ATucker (11) (prom 12f) ............................. 4.11
Jarrwah (46) *(JLSpearing)* 4–8–9 CRutter (1) (led 9f: wknd over 3f out) ................. 6.12
First Stage (58) *(JGMO'Shea)* 5–9–9 ‡⁵BDoyle (10) (hdwy 8f out: wknd over 4f
    out) ................................................................................................................. 12.13
Sand Castle (45) *(PHowling)* 11–9–1 JMcLaughlin (12) (hdwy bhd: bhd fnl 5f) ...... 10.14

**9/2** Shar Emblem, JAWANI (IRE)(tchd 8/1), **5/1** Take Issue, **6/1** Touching Times, **7/1** Kovalevskia, **8/1**
Bursana(tchd 16/1), **10/1** Free Minx, **11/1** Blue Disc(op 5/1), **20/1** First Stage, Malenoir (USA)(op 12/1),
Lifetimes Ambition, **33/1** Ors. CSF £86.66, CT £435.04. Tote £7.00: £3.30 £11.80 £2.70 (£75.50). Mrs
Susan Scargill (NEWMARKET) bred by Barronstown Bloodstock Ltd in Ireland. 14 Rn   3m 27.96 (4.96)
SF—29/25/23/17/22/15

T/Plpt: £313.10 (3.15 Tckts).                                   AK

## 71—LINGFIELD (L–H) Equitrack
### Tuesday, January 21st [Standard]
Going Allowance: minus 0.05 sec per fur (FS)

**77**    COWES CLAIMING STKS (I) £2167.20 (£599.20: £285.60)  **1m (AWT)**  1-10 (1-11)

45⁶ **Beechwood Cottage (49)** *(ABailey)* 9–8–2 ‡⁵BDoyle (8) (outpcd: gd hdwy over
    1f out: led ins fnl f: rdn out) ............................................................................. —1
53⁵ Crosby (72) (Fav) *(PAKelleway)* 4–8–9 WNewnes (5) (eyeshield: lw: hdwy 3f out:
    hrd rdn over 1f out: ev ch ins fnl f: unable qckn) ................................................. 2.2
Beau Dada (IRE) (61) *(JWhite)* 4–7–13(1) ‡⁵ATucker (2) (hdwy 2f out: r.o one pce) .. nk.3
57 Across the Bay (55) *(SDow)* 5–8–2 ‡⁷MJermy (6) (b.hind: hdwy over 1f out: one
    pce) ................................................................................................................ 1½.4
Sooty Tern (45) *(JMBradley)* 5–8–4 ‡³JFanning (9) (a.p: hrd rdn over 1f out: ev ch
    ins fnl f: one pce) ............................................................................................ 1½.5
66³ Buddy's Friend (IRE) (51) *(RJRWilliams)* 4–8–12 MHills (4) (led over 4f out tl ins
    fnl f: eased whn btn) ......................................................................................... 5.6
63⁶ Les Amis (43) *(MJRyan)* 5–7–13 ‡³DBiggs (1) (led over 3f: wknd 3f out) ................. ½.7
Red Dollar (h) *(BGubby)* 7–8–5 JQuinn (10) (bit bkwd: a bhd) ............................... 2.8
42⁵ Kreischim (IRE) (46) *(MMadgwick)* 4–8–2(1) ‡⁵RPrice (3) (prom over 4f) ............... 4.9

**6/4** Crosby, **4/1** Beau Dada (IRE), **5/1** Les Amis, **8/1** Buddy's Friend (IRE)(op 5/1), **12/1** BEECHWOOD
COTTAGE, **14/1** Kreischim (IRE)(op 8/1), Across the Bay(op 8/1), **16/1** Sooty Tern(op 10/1), **33/1** Red Dollar.
CSF £29.45, Tote £22.30: £3.00 £1.20 £1.10 (£13.50). Mrs A. Madgwick (NEWMARKET) bred by W. J.
O'Regan. 9 Rn                                        1m 39.81 (3.11)
SF—35/36/25/23/20/13

**78**  VENTNOR STKS (Mdn 3-Y.O) £2128.00 (£588.00: £280.00)  1¼m (AWT)  1-40 (1-42)

52² **Alternation (FR)** (Fav) *(PFICole)* 8-9 CRutter (4) (lw: hdwy 5f out: led over 3f out: easily) ............................................................ —1
Child Star (FR) *(DMarks)* 8-9 GBaxter (4) (a.p: led 4f out tl over 3f out: no imp) .... 6.2
52⁵ Colouring Book (IRE) *(MJHaynes)* 8-2 ‡7DToole (2) (nvr nr to chal) ...................... 4.3
Eau D'Espoir (48) *(JLSpearing)* 8-9 RCochrane (1) (hdwy over 4f out: wknd over 2f out) .......................................................... 8.4
37 Bilberry *(JHetherton)* 8-9 WNewnes (3) (prom over 5f) .................................... 15.5
Elgin (52) *(ABailey)* 9-0 GCarter (5) (lw: led 6f) ............................................ 20.6

4/7 ALTERNATION (FR), 11/2 Elgin(6/1—4/1), 15/2 Eau D'Espoir(op 5/1), 12/1 Colouring Book (IRE)(op 8/1), Child Star (FR)(op 6/1), 20/1 Bilberry(op 10/1). CSF £7.35, Tote £1.10: £1.10 £3.30 (£4.80). Mr Ray Taylor (WHATCOMBE) bred by Ahmad Fustok in France. 6 Rn
2m 10.07 (7.07)
SF—19/7/–/–/–/–

**79**  COWES CLAIMING STKS (II)  £2147.60 (£593.60: £282.80)  1m (AWT)  2-10 (2-11)

64* **Tara's Delight (66)** (Fav) *(MJRyan)* 5—8-4 ‡3DBiggs (5) (a.p: led over 3f out: comf) .......................................................... —1
Merseyside Man (55) (v) *(DrJDScargill)* 6—8-3 JQuinn (3) (lw: a.p: hrd rdn over 1f out: unable qckn) .................................... 2½.2
Marzocco (55) *(JFfitch-Heyes)* 4—8-8 SWhitworth (9) (b.nr hind: a.p: one pce fnl 2f) ................................................ 2.3
70 Inseyab (65) *(PCHaslam)* 4—8-0 ‡7NicolaHowarth (6) (hdwy 2f out: one pce) ....... 1½.4
Royal Acclaim (47) (v) *(JMBradley)* 7—7-10 ‡7MichaelBradley (7) (wl bhd 6f: hdwy fnl f: r.o) .......................................... 2½.5
45⁵ Catundra (IRE) (60) *(MrsAKnight)* 4—7-10 ‡7DHarrison (2) (led over 4f: wknd over 1f out) ................................................ nk.6
43⁴ Inswinger (42) *(WGRWightman)* 6—8-5 GCarter (4) (a bhd) ................................ 1½.7
Anne's Bank (IRE) *(AMoore)* 4—7-13 NAdams (8) (prom 6f) .......................... 2.8
Replicate (46) *(MJCharles)* 4—7-13 GBardwell (1) (prom over 4f) ................... 10.9

4/5 TARA'S DELIGHT, 5/1 Inswinger(tchd 10/1), 11/2 Inseyab, 10/1 Catundra (IRE)(7/1—12/1), 14/1 Merseyside Man, 16/1 Royal Acclaim, 20/1 Replicate, 25/1 Marzocco, 33/1 Anne's Bank (IRE). CSF £13.06, Tote £1.30: £1.00 £6.90 £13.20 (£23.00). Mr W. G. Dixon (NEWMARKET) bred by Burton Agnes Stud Co Ltd. 9 Rn
1m 39.88 (3.18)
SF—36/27/26/13/1/–

**80**  SHANKLIN H'CAP (0-90) £2554.20 (£706.20: £336.60)  6f (AWT)  2-40 (2-42)

57* **Sally's Son (73)** *(WAO'Gorman)* 6—8-8 ‡5EmmaO'Gorman (2) (lw: hld up: led ins fnl f: r.o wl) .......................................... —1
58⁴ Very Dicey (78) *(SDow)* 4-9-4 WRyan (8) (b.hind: led over 4f out tl ins fnl f: r.o) ... hd.2
58³ Hinari Video (62) *(MJohnston)* 7—7-13 ‡3JFanning (5) (hdwy 2f out: r.o one pce) ....... 4.3
57 Jovial Kate (USA) (53) *(MDIUsher)* 5—7-0 ‡7KimMcDonnell (6) (led over 1f: one pce fnl 2f) ........................................ ¾.4
43* Super Heights (63) (bl) *(MissAJWhitfield)* 4—8-3 DaleGibson (4) (no hdwy fnl 2f) .... 1½.5
53² Ringland (USA) (84) (Fav) *(PCHaslam)* 4—9-10 RCochrane (1) (lw: outpcd) ........... ½.6
Gabibti (IRE) (63) *(BGubby)* 4—8-3 JQuinn (3) (prom over 3f) ....................... 2½.7
LONG HANDICAP: Jovial Kate (USA) 6-12.

9/4 Ringland (USA), 11/4 SALLY'S SON, 4/1 Super Heights, 11/2 Hinari Video, 6/1 Very Dicey, 16/1 Gabibti (IRE), 33/1 Jovial Kate (USA). CSF £18.13, CT £76.45. Tote £3.30: £3.70 £2.10 (£16.80). Mr W. A. O'Gorman (NEWMARKET) bred by R. Duggan. 7 Rn
1m 13.81 (3.21)
SF—24/33/–/–/–/–

**81**  NEWPORT H'CAP (0-70) £2324.00 (£644.00: £308.00)  1¼m (AWT)  3-10 (3-12)

**Princess Roxanne (54)** (bl) *(ABailey)* 5—8-11 ‡7PBowe (2) (a.p: led over 1f out: comf) .......................................... —1
Littledale (USA) (52) *(DJGMurray-Smith)* 6—9-2 RCochrane (5) (a.p: ev ch over 1f out: unable qckn) ............................ 6.2
56* Modesto (USA) (56) (Fav) *(KOCunningham-Brown)* 4—9-3 SWhitworth (6) (b: led over 8f: one pce) ................................ ¾.3
Smith's Peak (45) (bl) *(RJO'Sullivan)* 8—8-6 ‡3DBiggs (11) (a.p: hrd rdn over 4f out: r.o one pce fnl 2f) ........................ 2.4
32 Restless Niece (35) *(TDBarron)* 4—7-7 ‡3JFanning (14) (hdwy over 2f out: one pce)2½.5
48⁴ Qualitair Flyer (32) *(JFBottomley)* 10—7-10 GBardwell (4) (nvr nr to chal) .......... 1.6
Searching Star (51) *(PAKelleway)* 4—8-12 WNewnes (10) (eyeshield: nvr nrr) ......... 5.7
56⁵ Miss Broughton (43) *(WJMusson)* 4—8-4 GCarter (1) (no hdwy fnl 3f) .............. s.h.8
63 Gibbot (37) *(PHowling)* 7—7-10⁽¹⁾ ‡5NGwilliams (13) (a bhd) ..................... 1.9

Queen of Dreams **(45)** *(DrJDScargill)* 4–8–6 JQuinn (8) (prom over 7f) .................. 6.**10**
*48*6 Give Me Hope (IRE) **(50)** *(RGBrazington)* 4–8–4 ‡7SWilliams (12) (bhd fnl 3f) ........ ½.**11**
Evening Affair **(45)** *(WHolden)* 6–8–9 SDawson (9) (b.nr fore: b.hind: a bhd) .... d.h.**11**
Tenayestelign **(64)** *(DMarks)* 4–9–11 GBaxter (3) (bit bkwd: chsd ldr over 5f) ...... 1½.**13**
*36* Scravels Saran (IRE) **(33)** *(DrJDScargill)* 4–7–8(1) DaleGibson (7) (a bhd) .......... 10.**14**

**100/30** Modesto (USA)(op 7/4), **4/1** Littledale (USA)(tchd 8/1), **11/2** Smith's Peak, **6/1** PRINCESS ROXANNE(op 4/1), **8/1** Miss Broughton(op 5/1), **9/1** Qualitair Flyer, **12/1** Give Me Hope (IRE)(op 8/1), **14/1** Searching Star, **16/1** Restless Niece(op 10/1), **20/1** Tenayestelign, **25/1** Queen of Dreams, **33/1** Ors. CSF £30.79, CT £87.94. Tote £10.90: £2.20 £1.60 £2.00 (£22.00). Mrs M. O'Donnell (NEWMARKET) bred by Mrs C. Van C. Anthony. 14 Rn    2m 7.06 (4.06)
SF—51/44/43/28/10/11

**82**    YARMOUTH H'CAP (3-Y.O) (0-60) £2186.80 (£604.80: £288.40)   **7f (AWT)**    3-40 (3-40)

**Level Up (56)** *(RGuest)* 9-3 NDay (4) (hdwy over 2f out: nt clr run over 1f out: swtchd & led wl ins fnl f: drvn out) ................................................ —**1**
Kipini **(46)** *(WJMusson)* 8-0 ‡7PBowe (9) (hdwy 2f out: ev ch ins fnl f: r.o) ................ nk.**2**
*51* Invigilate **(55)** *(HATWhiting)* 9-2 NAdams (2) (led: hrd rdn over 1f out: hdd wl ins fnl f: unable qckn) .................................................. 1½.**3**
*65*2 Do the Business (IRE) **(49)** *(CNAllen)* 8-7 ‡3DBiggs (8) (a.p: hrd rdn over 1f out: one pce) ............................................................ 1½.**4**
*61*3 Dark Midnight (IRE) **(58)** *(Fav)* *(PCHaslam)* 9-5 RCochrane (7) (lw: ap: one pce fnl 2f) ........................................................ ½.**5**
*52* Mississippi Queen **(47)** *(RJRWilliams)* 8-7 JQuinn (3) (prom over 4f) ...................... 7.**6**
Papa Westray **(60)** *(TDBarron)* 9-7 AlexGreaves (1) (spd over 3f) ...................... 1½.**7**
*44*3 Ossie **(50)** *(BPalling)* 8-11 WRyan (5) (a bhd) ........................................ s.h.**8**
Great Hall **(55)** *(WGRWightman)* 9-2 MHills (6) (b.hind: a bhd) .......................... ¾.**9**

**3/1** Dark Midnight (IRE), **4/1** Do the Business (IRE), **9/2** Ossie, LEVEL UP(op 3/1), **8/1** Invigilate, Papa Westray, Kipini, **20/1** Great Hall, **25/1** Mississippi Queen. CSF £38.49, CT £260.31. Tote £5.20: £2.10 £4.70 £3.20 (£47.40). Mr Christopher P. J. Brown (NEWMARKET) bred by J. F. Watson. 9 Rn    1m 27.88 (3.88)
SF—40/22/33/19/29/–

**83**    RYDE H'CAP (0-70) £2206.40 (£610.40: £291.20)   **1m 5f (AWT)**    4-10 (4-10)

*67*2 **Magic Secret (68)** *(PCHaslam)* 4–10-0 RCochrane (8) (lw: a.p: rdn over 4f out: led ins fnl f: r.o wl) ................................................ —**1**
*46*2 Carlingford (USA) **(53)** *(HATWhiting)* 6–9-3 JCarroll (7) (hld up: led over 2f out tl ins fnl f: r.o) ........................................... ¾.**2**
*76** Jawani (IRE) **(51)** (v) *(DrJDScargill)* 4–8-11 (5x) JQuinn (9) (chsd ldr: led 5f out tl over 2f out: unable qckn) ................................ 3.**3**
*55*5 Adjacent (IRE) **(52)** *(MDixon)* 4–8-7 ‡5NGwilliams (1) (b.off hind: hdwy wl over 1f out: one pce) ........................................... 8.**4**
*55** El Dominio **(64)** *(Fav)* *(KOCunningham-Brown)* 4–9-10 GBardwell (5) (b: nvr nr to chal) .......................................... 1½.**5**
Nocturnal Reverie (USA) **(33)** (bl) *(TJNaughton)* 5–7-4(3) ‡7DHarrison (4) (b: b.hind: a bhd) ...................................... 1½.**6**
*56*6 Windsor Highness **(40)** (bl) *(MPMuggeridge)* 5–8-4 DaleGibson (6) (hdwy over 4f out: wknd over 2f out) ................................... hd.**7**
Wise Friend (USA) **(38)** *(CPWildman)* 4–7-12 CRutter (2) (led 8f) .......................... 12.**8**
Top it All **(39)** *(MJRyan)* 4–7-10(1) ‡3DBiggs (3) (prom 7f) .......................... 5.**9**

**7/4** El Dominio, **9/4** Jawani (IRE), **6/1** MAGIC SECRET(op 4/1), **7/1** Carlingford (USA), **12/1** Adjacent (IRE), Windsor Highness, **20/1** Nocturnal Reverie (USA)(op 12/1), Top it All, **50/1** Wise Friend (USA). CSF £44.66, CT £112.35. Tote £5.60: £2.70 £1.20 £1.40 (£14.40). Hambleton Thoroughbreds Plc (MIDDLEHAM) bred by Gainsborough Stud Management Ltd. 9 Rn    2m 49.86 (6.36)
SF—44/31/19/–/13/–

T/Plpt: £34.40 (36.05 Tckts).    AK

## 58—**SOUTHWELL (L-H)** Fibresand
## **Friday, January 24th [Standard]**
Going Allowance: 0.45 sec per fur (SL)

**84**    OCTOPUS H'CAP (0-80) £2226.00 (£616.00: £294.00)   **1¾m (AWT)**    1-25 (1-26)

**Qualitair Aviator (71)** *(JFBottomley)* 6–10-0 GBardwell (4) (a cl up: led 5f out: styd on u.p: fin lame) .............................................. —**1**
*60*2 Dalby Dancer **(55)** *(Fav)* *(BAMcMahon)* 8–8-12 RCochrane (2) (b: lw: a chsng ldrs: kpt on fnl 2f: nt pce to chal) ............................... 5.**2**

67* Qualitair Blazer **(56)** *(JRJenkins)* 5–8–13 (7x) SWhitworth (8) (b: lw: a chsng ldrs: one pce fnl 3f) .................................................................. 3.3

67⁵ Balaat (USA) **(59)** *(MCChapman)* 4–8–4 ‡⁷SWilliams (3) (hld up: stdy hdwy 4f out: effrt over 2f out: no rspnse) .................................................. 2½.4

49 Stone Flake (USA) **(60)** *(PAKelleway)* 6–9–3 MHills (1) (eyeshield: led tl hdd 5f out: grad wknd fnl 3f) .................................................................. 4.5

56 Lord Advocate **(44)** (v) *(MPNaughton)* 4–7–7 ‡³JFanning (10) (nvr bttr than mid div) ........................................................................................ ¾.6

Intricacy **(68)** *(CCElsey)* 4–9–6 WNewnes (9) (lw: bhd: hdwy ½-wy: rdn appr st: n.d) .................................................................................... nk.7

76 Blue Disc **(38)** (bl) *(CRBeever)* 7–7–9(2) LCharnock (7) (b: chsd ldrs: outpcd 7f out: sn bhd) .......................................................................... 10.8

Robins Find (IRE) **(61)** *(JGFitzGerald)* 4–8–13 WRyan (6) (b: b.hind: bit bkwd: a outpcd & bhd) ................................................................ nk.9

Pondered Bid **(44)** *(PatMitchell)* 8–7–8 ‡⁷CHawksley (2) (eyeshield: a bhd) ............ 10

Final Ace **(50)** *(MissSJWilton)* 5–8–7 JFortune (11) (lw: t.o fr ½-wy: virtually p.u) ...... 11

**2/1** Dalby Dancer **(4/1** Intricacy, **11/2** Qualitair Blazer, **10/1** QUALITAIR AVIATOR, **11/1** Balaat (USA), **14/1** Pondered Bid, **16/1** Final Ace, Lord Advocate, Robins Find (IRE), **20/1** Blue Disc, **33/1** Stone Flake (USA). CSF £28.67, CT £114.17. Tote £8.50: £2.50 £1.10 £2.60 (£19.90). Qualitair Holdings Limited (MALTON) bred by Qualitair Engineering. 11 Rn                                                                       3m 16.7 (17.4)

**85**  HALIBUT CLAIMING STKS (3-Y.O) £2167.20 (£599.20: £285.60)  **1m (AWT)**  1-55 (1-57)

68³ **Meltonby (70)** (Fav) *(JHetherton)* 8-12 WNewnes (6) (mde all: easily) .................. —1

Little Nod **(65)** *(MJCamacho)* 8-11 LCharnock (7) (bit bkwd: a chsng wnr: drvn along & no imp fnl 3f) ................................................................... 8.2

47* Silver Samurai **(80)** *(RHollinshead)* 8-11 ‡⁷EHusband (4) (lw: a chsng ldrs: rdn appr st: no imp) ........................................................................ 6.3

Malcesine (IRE) *(CaptJWilson)* 8-8 JFortune (5) (lt-f: bit bkwd: in tch tl outpcd 4f out: sme late hdwy: n.d) ................................................................ hd.4

Don't Move (IRE) **(50)** (v) *(MHTompkins)* 7-12 ‡⁷SMulvey (9) (sn outpcd & bhd) ... 10.5

54⁵ Doesyoudoes **(66)** *(DTThom)* 8-11 RCochrane (2) (hld up: hdwy & prom 4f out: rdn ent st: sn btn) ...................................................................... hd.6

True Touch *(TDBarron)* 8-12 AlexGreaves (1) (neat: scope: bit bkwd: bhd fr ½-wy) ...................................................................................... 4.7

Kashgar *(DWChapman)* 8-7 SWood (3) (str: w'like: bkwd: s.s: a bhd) ................... nk.8

**7/4** MELTONBY, **11/4** Silver Samurai, **5/1** Little Nod, **7/1** Doesyoudoes, **12/1** True Touch, **20/1** Malcesine (IRE), **33/1** Ors. CSF £9.89, Tote £2.70: £1.10 £1.80 £1.10 (£6.70). Mr J. Hetherton (MALTON) bred by Woodditton Stud Ltd. 8 Rn                                                                       1m 47.3 (8)
SF–32/7/–/–/–/–

**86**  SHARK H'CAP (0-90) £2245.60 (£621.60: £296.80)  **1m (AWT)**  2-25 (2-26)

74³ **Super Sally (87)** *(MJRyan)* 5–9-10 ‡³DBiggs (10) (lw: trckd ldrs gng wl: led over 1f out: pushed along & sn clr) .................................................. —1

Mystic Crystal (IRE) **(78)** (bl) *(WAO'Gorman)* 4–8-12 ‡⁵EmmaO'Gorman (11) (chsd ldrs: led over 2f out tl over 1f out: one pce) ............................. 6.2

53* Dorset Duke **(88)** *(GWragg)* 5–10-0 MHills (4) (b: lw: cl up: chal 3f out: sn rdn: r.o one pce) ....................................................................... ½.3

70³ Dawn Success **(60)** *(DWChapman)* 6–8-0 SWood (6) (lw: prom tl outpcd & lost pl ½-wy: hdwy 2f out: styd on) ............................................. ¾.4

Usa Dollar **(65)** (h) *(BGubby)* 5–8-5 JQuinn (7) (effrt ent st: no imp) .................. 2½.5

50⁶ Predictable **(64)** *(MrsAKnight)* 6–7-11 ‡⁷DHarrison (9) (hld up: gd hdwy & prom appr st: sn rdn: no ex) ..................................................... hd.6

50* Doulab's Image **(73)** (bl) (Fav) *(JAGlover)* 5–8-6 ‡⁷SWilliams (2) (lw: in tch after 3f: effrt ent st: sn btn) ................................................... 3.7

53 Everset (FR) **(70)** *(WJMusson)* 4–8-9 RCochrane (8) (chsd ldrs: outpcd appr st: no imp after) ............................................................. 2.8

Quinta Royale **(55)** (bl) *(JRJenkins)* 5–7-9 LCharnock (3) (chsd ldrs: hrd drvn appr st: sn btn) .................................................................. 1½.9

Gulmarg **(80)** *(MHTompkins)* 5–9-1 ‡⁵CHodgson (1) (led tl hdd & wknd over 2f out) .......................................................................... 1½.10

Sno Serenade **(78)** *(MDods)* 6–9-4 GBaxter (5) (hmpd after 1f: sn wl bhd) ........... 12.11

**7/2** Doulab's Image, **11/2** SUPER SALLY, **6/1** Dorset Duke(op 4/1), **7/1** Predictable, **8/1** Mystic Crystal (IRE), **9/1** Usa Dollar, **10/1** Dawn Success(op 6/1), **16/1** Everset (FR), Gulmarg(op 7/1), **20/1** Quinta Royale, **25/1** Sno Serenade. CSF £43.47, CT £245.41. Tote £5.80: £1.50 £3.50 £2.40 (£16.90). Exors of the late Mr Leonard Seale (NEWMARKET) bred by R. Duggan. 11 Rn                                                         1m 47.3 (8)
SF–44/14/28/–/–/–

**87**     OYSTER CLAIMING STKS   £2441.60 (£677.60: £324.80)    **6f (AWT)**     2-55 (2-59)

32⁴ **Strip Cartoon (IRE) (30)** (bl) *(SRBowring)* 4–8-3 NAdams (4) (lw: mde all: clr ent st: all out) ............................................................................. —1

Miss Calculate **(55)** *(CaptJWilson)* 4–8-9 JFortune (6) (a chsng ldrs: styd on fnl f: nrst fin) ..................................................................................... ½.2

70² Saladan Knight **(59)** (bl) *(JGFitzGerald)* 7–8-9 ‡7MHunt (10) (eyeshield: hdwy on outside ent st: rdn & nt qckn fnl f) ................................................ 1½.3

Friendly Claim (IRE) **(83)** *(TDBarron)* 4–9-6 AlexGreaves (2) (in tch: effrt over 2f out: styd on) ...................................................................................... 1½.4

63 Tudorgateway **(65)** *(MHTompkins)* 4–7-12 ‡7SMulvey (15) (dwlt: hdwy on outside ent st: styd on one pce fnl 2f) ........................................................ 1.5

Toshiba Comet **(77)** (v) *(WJPearce)* 5–9-4 DNicholls (11) (lw: a chsng ldrs: no hdwy fnl 2f) .................................................................................. ¾.6

Flying Promise **(57)** *(RABennett)* 4–8-5 WRyan (3) (lw: effrt ent st: styd on: no imp) ........................................................................................ 1.7

Harry's Joy **(32)** *(CJHill)* 4–7-5 ‡7DHarrison (14) (c wd & rdn st: no imp after) ............ ¾.8

Beckingham Ben **(50)** *(JPLeigh)* 8–8-10 GCarter (12) (chsd ldrs 4f: grad wknd) ... 1½.9

75⁶ Courting Newmarket **(46)** *(MrsAKnight)* 4–8-6 ‡3DBiggs (7) (nvr trbld ldrs) .......... 1½.10

70 Morpick **(55)** *(JPLeigh)* 5–8-8 ACulhane (13) (lw: nvr plcd to chal) ...................... 1½.11

Mitsubishi Video (IRE) **(APStringer)** 4–8-3 JQuinn (1) (bit bkwd: chsd ldrs to st) ... nk.12

Tigani **(99)** *(DWChapman)* 6–9-3 ‡7SWilliams (8) (bit bkwd: n.d) ........................... 4.13

45² Wellsy Lad (USA) **(75)** (Fav) *(DWChapman)* 5–8-10 SWood (5) (lw: sn bhd) ............ 1.14

45 Bracken Bay *(TKersey)* 5–7-12 GBardwell (9) (b: squeezed out after 1f: sn wl bhd) ................................................................................................. 15

**9/4** Wellsy Lad (USA), **11/4** Friendly Claim (IRE)(7/2–(2), **8/1** Toshiba Comet(op 5/1), **10/1** Saladan Knight, Tigani(op 5/1), **14/1** Morpick(op 8/1), **16/1** Flying Promise, Tudorgateway, **20/1** Mitsubishi Video (IRE), **25/1** Courting Newmarket, **33/1** Miss Calculate, Beckingham Ben, **40/1** Harry's Joy, **50/1** STRIP CARTOON (IRE), **100/1** Bracken Bay. CSF £960.17, Tote £28.70: £5.40 £5.30 £3.90 (£404.70). Mrs Irene Pryce (EDWINSTOWE) bred by John Kelly in Ireland. 15 Rn    1m 2m (6.6)
SF—11/15/9/14/–/5

**88**     CRAB H'CAP (0-90) £2226.00 (£616.00: £294.00)    **1m 3f (AWT)**     3-25 (3-31)

67³ **Frescobaldo (USA) (62)** *(MPNaughton)* 6–7-13 ‡5BDoyle (2) (mde all: styd on wl fnl 3f) ................................................................................................ —1

59* Lara's Baby (IRE) **(71)** *(RAkehurst)* 4–8-9 (7x) RCochrane (6) (b. nr fore: lw: trckd ldrs: chal on bit 3f out: rdn 2f out: no ex) ......................... 4.2

Westfield Moves (IRE) **(59)** *(HJCollingridge)* 4–7-4(1) ‡7CHawksley (5) (chsd ldrs: outpcd appr st: no imp after) ................................................ 2.3

60³ Hand Painted **(65)** *(CRBeever)* 8–8-2 ‡5RPrice (4) (lw: rr div: drvn along appr st: styd on fnl 2f: nrst fin) ........................................................ 2½.4

35⁴ Cheerful Times **(58)** *(BAMcMahon)* 9–7-9(2) ‡5SMaloney (9) (chsd ldrs: effrt appr st: one pce) ........................................................................ s.h.5

Crossillion **(87)** (Fav) *(GWragg)* 4–9-11 MHills (1) (cl up tl wknd ent st) .................. 2½.6

74² Mr Wishing Well **(60)** *(RJRWilliams)* 6–7-13 ‡3DBiggs (8) (b. nr hind: effrt over 4f out: sn drvn along: n.d) ........................................................ 10.7

Mai Pen Rai **(59)** *(CJHill)* 4–7-4(4) ‡7DHarrison (7) (a bhd) .................................... 2.8

63⁴ Golden Ancona **(54)** *(MBrittain)* 9–7-3(2) ‡7DWright (11) (outpcd & bhd) ................ 1½.9

Priceless Fantasy **(52)** *(PatMitchell)* 5–7-5(1) ‡3JFanning (3) (eyeshield: a bhd) ... 1½.10

Qualitair Sweetie **(51)** *(JFBottomley)* 5–7-7 GBardwell (10) (b.nr fore: chsd wnr tl wknd qckly appr st) .................................................................. hd.11

LONG HANDICAP: Mai Pen Rai 7-2, Priceless Fantasy 6-11, Qualitair Sweetie 6-9.

**3/1** Crossillion, **4/1** Lara's Baby (IRE), **5/1** Mr Wishing Well, **7/1** FRESCOBALDO (USA), **8/1** Cheerful Times(op 5/1), **10/1** Hand Painted(op 5/1), **14/1** Westfield Moves (IRE), Golden Ancona, **16/1** Priceless Fantasy, **33/1** Ors. CSF £33.22, CT £347.10. Tote £8.50: £1.80 £1.60 £3.70 (£23.80). Mr M. P. Naughton (RICHMOND) bred by Mr N. B. Hunt in USA. 11 Rn    2m 30.7 (9.2)
SF—43/45/22/29/21/46

**89**     LOBSTER H'CAP (0-70) £2284.80 (£632.80: £302.40)    **7f (AWT)**     3-55 (3-59)

**Foolish Touch (60)** *(WJMusson)* 10–9-1 ‡7PBowe (6) (b: bhd: gd hdwy to ld ins fnl f: r.o) ....................................................................................... —1

Grand Guignol **(66)** *(GWragg)* 4–10-0 RCochrane (13) (bhd: hdwy over 1f out: r.o wl) ..................................................................................... 1.2

57⁶ Shedad (USA) **(50)** *(TDBarron)* 4–8-12 AlexGreaves (11) (cl up: led over 4f out: c wd st: sn rdn: hdd ins fnl f: kpt on) ........................................ 1½.3

49 Mushy Boff **(49)** *(CJHill)* 4–8-4 ‡7DHarrison (9) (hdwy ent st: kpt on one pce fnl f) ... hd.4

63 State Governor **(65)** *(DWChapman)* 4–9-13 SWood (12) (chsd ldrs: chal 2f out: nt qckn ins fnl f) ............................................................ ½.5

 70* On Y Va (USA) (59) (Fav) (RJRWilliams) 5–9-2 (7x) ‡5CHodgson (10) (lw: a chsng ldrs: one pce fnl 2f) ............ 5.6
66⁴ Carnfield (37) (JAGlover) 4–7-13 NCarlisle (5) (stdd s: hdwy 3f out: nvr trbld ldrs) 2.7
70⁴ Cossack Noir (36) (MPNaughton) 4–7-7(1) ‡5BDoyle (7) (sme hdwy over 2f out: nvr trbld ldrs) ............ 4.8
63⁵ Hawaii Storm (FR) (36) (MissAJWhitfield) 4–7-12 NAdams (4) (led tl hdd over 4f out: wknd 2f out) ............ 1½.9
31⁴ Sandmoor Denim (45) (bl) (SRBowring) 5–8-7 AProud (1) (chsd ldrs: hmpd after 1f: wknd over 2f out) ............ 3.10
 63 Luzum (65) (bl) (JAGlover) 8–9-6 ‡7SWilliams (8) (lw: effrt ent st: sn btn) 2.11
Blazing Fen (40) (MrsNMacauley) 4–7-13 ‡3DBiggs (2) (b: w ldrs tl wknd qckly ent st) ............ 3.12
63³ Question of Degree (36) (NTinkler) 6–7-12 KimTinkler (14) (lw: in tch to st) ............ 13
Good Time Boy (53) (MBrittain) 4–9-1 GCarter (15) (n.d) ............ 14
Kevinsbelle (41) (ICampbell) 4–7-10 ‡7MGriffiths (3) (prom to st) ............ 15

3/1 On Y Va (USA), 15/2 Sandmoor Denim, 8/1 Cossack Noir, 10/1 Shedad (USA), Question of Degree, Hawaii Storm (FR), Grand Guignol(op 6/1), 11/1 Mushy Boff, 12/1 Carnfield(op 20/1), 14/1 Luzum, FOOLISH TOUCH, 20/1 State Governor, Blazing Fen, 25/1 Ors. CSF £141.76, CT £1,345.30. Tote £19.10: £5.20 £4.70 £8.90 (£68.10). Broughton Thermal Insulation (NEWMARKET) bred by R. Lycett-Green. 15 Rn

1m 33.9 (7.3)
SF—38/48/27/18/39/13

T/Plpt: £485.40 (7.65 Tckts). 

AA

## 77—LINGFIELD (L-H) Equitrack
### Saturday, January 25th [Standard]
Going Allowance: minus 0.10 sec per fur (FS)

Vis: misty

**90**     WESTMINSTER STKS (Mdn) £2363.20 (£655.20: £313.60)   1½m (AWT)   1-20 (1-21)

 48² **Mississippi Beat (USA) (38)** (v) (MPNaughton) 5–8-13 ‡5BDoyle (13) (lw: hdwy 5f out: led over 1f out: rdn out) ............ —1
 40 Carlowitz (USA) (AMoore) 4–9-0 CandyMorris (12) (a.p: led over 3f out tl over 1f out: unable qckn) ............ 2½.2
71⁵ Aude la Belle (FR) (56) (MrsAKnight) 4–8-2 ‡7DHarrison (14) (hdwy 5f out: hrd rdn 2f out: one pce) ............ 5.3
40⁵ Don't Cry (43) (JDBethell) 4–8-9 WRyan (5) (hdwy over 2f out: one pce) ............ ½.4
Soda Popinski (USA) (ICampbell) 4–8-11 ‡3DBiggs (1) (lw: a.p: one pce fnl 2f) ............ s.h.5
 63 Dashing April (49) (DTThom) 4–8-9 MHills (4) (nvr nr to chal) ............ 3.6
81² Littledale (USA) (52) (Fav) (DJGMurray-Smith) 6–9-4 RCochrane (7) (led 11f out tl over 3f out: wknd wl over 1f out) ............ 3½.7
Valued Friend (USA) (40) (JJBridger) 4–8-8(1) ‡7RachelBridger (11) (dwlt: hdwy 9f out: wknd 4f out) ............ 3.8
27⁵ Sweet 'n' Low (42) (bl) (PJFeilden) 5–8-11 ‡7MichaelDenaro (6) (lw: a bhd) ............ 2½.9
Gipsy King (55) (PAKelleway) 4–9-0 WNewnes (2) (eyeshield: hdwy 6f out: wknd over 4f out) ............ ½.10
59⁶ First Sapphire (WJarvis) 5–8-13 NDay (8) (lw: prom over 8f) ............ hd.11
Striking Distance (JFfitch-Heyes) 5–9-4 GBaxter (12) (b: b. drfd: a bhd) ............ 4.12
Dashwood (USA) (DCJermy) 5–9-4 GBardwell (9) (bkwd: s.s: a bhd) ............ 7.13
Soughaan's Pride (IRE) (33) (RABennett) 4–8-4 ‡5RPrice (3) (led 1f: wknd 9f out: t.o) ............ 25.14

6/4 Littledale (USA)(op Evens), 9/2 Soda Popinski (USA)(op 8/1), 7/1 Gipsy King(op 4/1), 8/1 Aude la Belle (FR), 10/1 Mississippi Beat (USA)(op 6/1), 12/1 Striking Distance(op 7/1), 16/1 First Sapphire, Dashing April(op 10/1), Don't Cry(op 6/1), 20/1 Soughaan's Pride (IRE), Dashwood (USA), Sweet 'n' Low, 33/1 Ors. CSF £266.74, Tote £8.10: £2.40 £14.50 £2.10 (£345.70). Mr Michael O'Grady (RICHMOND) bred by Offutt-Cole Farm in USA. 14 Rn

2m 37.21 (7.81)
SF—9/5/–/–/–/–

**91**     HUNGERFORD CLAIMING STKS (3-Y.O) £2147.60 (£593.60: £282.80)   1¼m (AWT)   1-50 (1-50)

 **Slight Risk (55)** (PAKelleway) 7-10 GBardwell (8) (eyecover: lw: a.p: led over 5f out: hrd rdn over 1f out: r.o wl) ............ —1
73⁴ Patrician Magician (69) (RJRWilliams) 8-0 ‡3DBiggs (3) (a.p: hrd rdn over 2f out: unable qckn) ............ 5.2
Feeling Foolish (IRE) (75) (v) (Fav) (TFairhurst) 8-8 ‡3JFanning (4) (lw: plld hrd: a.p: rdn over 4f out: one pce) ............ 1.3
 52 Sun Glory (IRE) (WJarvis) 7-3 ‡7DHarrison (7) (no hdwy fnl 3f: sddle slipped) ............ 2½.4
A Nymph Too Far (IRE) (63) (DrJDScargill) 7-10 JQuinn (1) (prom 8f) ............ 4.5
Court Room (45) (AMoore) 8-3 CandyMorris (2) (led over 4f) ............ 10.6

Red for Danger **(60)** *(MDixon)* 8-2 ‡⁵NGwilliams (6) (bit bkwd: a bhd) ...................... 15.7
Uraragskal **(45)** *(JAkehurst)* 7-10 DaleGibson (5) (a bhd) ........................................ 6.8

**6/5** Feeling Foolish (IRE), **3/1** Patrician Magician, **9/2** A Nymph Too Far (IRE)(op 3/1), **8/1** SLIGHT
RISK(6/1—9/1), **12/1** Red for Danger, **20/1** Sun Glory (IRE), **25/1** Uraragskal, **33/1** Court Room. CSF
£31.35, Tote £13.20: £2.70 £1.20 £1.10 (£8.50). Mrs G. E. Kelleway (NEWMARKET) bred by Mrs G. E.
Kelleway. 8 Rn                                                                                       2m 10.40 (7.40)

## 92

VAUXHALL H'CAP (0-90) £2577.30 (£712.80: £339.90)   **7f (AWT)**   2-20 (2-21)

75³ **Respectable Jones (82)** *(GBBalding)* 6—9-8 WNewnes (2) (b.nr fore: hld up: led
1f out: rdn out) ............................................................................... —1
53⁴ Mac's Fighter **(88)** (v) *(WAO'Gorman)* 7—9-9 ‡⁵EmmaO'Gorman (7) (hdwy
over 2f out: ev ch ins fnl f: r.o) ................................................... ½.2
70⁵ Pesidanamich (IRE) **(71)** (bl) *(TDBarron)* 4—8-11 AlexGreaves (4) (a.p: led wl
over 1f out: sn hdd: unable qckn) ................................................ 4.3
Vuchterbacher **(59)** *(PFTulk)* 6—7-6⁽⁴⁾ ‡⁷TWilson (3) (b: a.p: led 2f out tl wl over 1f
out: sn wknd) ............................................................................... 2½.4
Second Adventure **(62)** (bl) *(DJGMurray-Smith)* 4—8-2 CRutter (1) (bhd fnl 3f) .......... 4.5
Super Benz **(87)** *(TFairhurst)* 6—9-10 ‡³JFanning (6) (led 5f) ................................. 2½.6
80⁵ Super Heights **(63)** (bl) *(MissAJWhitfield)* 4—8-3 DaleGibson (5) (bhd fnl 3f) .......... 3.7

**100/30** Mac's Fighter, **4/1** Super Benz, **9/2** RESPECTABLE JONES, Vuchterbacher, **6/1** Pesidanamich
(IRE)(op 4/1), **9/1** Super Heights, **12/1** Second Adventure. CSF £18.17, Tote £4.70: £2.70 £1.90 (£6.50).
Mrs Ernest Weinstein (DORCHESTER) bred by E. and Mrs Weinstein. 7 Rn        1m 25.96 (1.96)
                                                                           SF—67/66/42/15/13/27

## 93

ALBERT H'CAP (0-70) £2343.60 (£649.60: £310.80)   **1m (AWT)**   2-50 (2-51)

**Martini Executive (65)** (bl) *(WJPearce)* 4—10-0 DNicholls (9) (lw: rdn & hdwy
over 2f out: led 1f out: r.o wl) ..................................................... —1
42* El Volador **(56)** (Fav) *(RJO'Sullivan)* 5—9-3 ‡³DBiggs (12) (hdwy over 3f out: ev ch
over 1f out: unable qckn) ............................................................. 5.2
42² Sarum **(48)** *(CPWildman)* 6—8-12 CRutter (8) (hdwy over 4f out: ev ch over 1f
out: one pce) .............................................................................. 2.3
28⁶ Kristis Girl **(57)** *(DHaydnJones)* 5—9-7 RCochrane (3) (a.p: led over 3f out to 1f
out: one pce) .............................................................................. nk.4
32² Qualitair Rhythm (IRE) **(47)** *(JHetherton)* 4—8-10 JQuinn (5) (lw: hdwy over 1f
out: r.o ins fnl f) ......................................................................... 1½.5
Lady Baraka (IRE) **(43)** *(ICampbell)* 4—7-13 ‡⁷MGriffiths (7) (hdwy over 1f out: nvr
nrr) .......................................................................................... ½.6
53 Litmore Dancer **(55)** *(JDBethell)* 4—9-4 RHills (6) (a.p: ev ch over 1f out: wknd fnl
f) ............................................................................................. s.h.7
77⁴ Across the Bay **(55)** *(SDow)* 5—8-12 ‡⁷MJermy (10) (b.hind: prom 6f) ....................... ¾.8
79³ Marzocco **(55)** *(JFfitch-Heyes)* 4—9-4 SWhitworth (11) (b.nr hind: bhd fnl 3f) ............ 3.9
50⁴ Model Nurse **(55)** *(MrsAKnight)* 5—8-0 ‡⁷DHarrison (1) (prom over 5f) ................. hd.10
Sunley Sparkle **(54)** *(DRGandolfo)* 4—8-12 ‡⁵RPerham (2) (led over 4f) ............... 1½.11

**7/4** El Volador, **9/2** Sarum(8/1—4/1), **7/1** MARTINI EXECUTIVE(tchd 12/1), **10/1** Qualitair Rhythm (IRE),
Litmore Dancer, **11/1** Across the Bay, **12/1** Marzocco, Model Nurse(op 7/1), **20/1** Ors.
CSF £19.93, CT £58.36. Tote £10.10: £2.20 £1.60 £1.60 (£12.80). Mr Roger Jelley (HAMBLETON) bred by
T. F. M. Corrie. 11 Rn                                                       1m 39.48 (2.78)
                                                                           SF—60/34/23/31/15/2

## 94

TOWER STKS (Mdn 3-Y.O) £2069.20 (£571.20: £271.60)   **1m (AWT)**   3-20 (3-23)

37³ **Rosa Why (IRE) (64)** *(WJarvis)* 8-5⁽¹⁾ ‡⁵EmmaO'Gorman (3) (hld up: qcknd to ld
2f out: clr over 1f out: easily) ...................................................... —1
Well Bought (IRE) **(NAGraham)** 8-9 JQuinn (1) (b.hind: unf: a.p: ev ch 2f out: no
imp) ........................................................................................ 10.2
69³ Calcutta Queen (Fav) *(MrsJCecil)* 8-9 BCrossley (6) (lw: led 6f out to 2f out: one
pce) ........................................................................................ 2½.3
French Revolution (FR) *(PAKelleway)* 8-9 WNewnes (2) (eyeshield: prom over
3f) .......................................................................................... 4.4
39⁶ Reach Me Not (IRE) *(CHolmes)* 8-9 RFox (5) (bit bkwd: swtg: led 2f: wknd over 4f
out) ......................................................................................... 20.5
Midyanzie *(CHolmes)* 8-9 WRyan (4) (leggy: unf: bit bkwd: dwlt: bhd fnl 5f: t.o) ... dist.6

**5/4** Calcutta Queen(tchd 4/5), **7/2** French Revolution (FR)(5/2—4/1), Well Bought (IRE), **9/2** ROSA WHY
(IRE)(4/1—6/1), **25/1** Midyanzie, **33/1** Reach Me Not (IRE). CSF £19.11, Tote £6.20: £1.70 £2.40 (£9.10).
Mr Jerry Sung (NEWMARKET) bred by Jerry Sung in Ireland. 6 Rn               1m 40.49 (3.79)
                                                                           SF—22/–/–/–/–/–

**95**  CHELSEA H'CAP (0-70) £2206.40 (£610.40: £291.20)  **5f (AWT)**  3-50 (3-51)

58 **Sir Tasker (64)** (JLHarris) 4–9-11 RCochrane (8) (lw: a.p: led 1f out: all out) ............ —1
804 Jovial Kate (USA) **(44)** (Fav) (MDIUsher) 5–8-5 CRutter (1) (lost pl over 2f out:
  rallied fnl f: fin wl) ............................................................... s.h.2
58* Meeson Times **(56)** (BEllison) 4–9-3 MHills (7) (lw: rdn over 2f out: str run fnl f: fin
  wl) ............................................................................................... s.h.3
Slip-a-Snip **(67)** (GBBalding) 5–9-9 ‡5RPrice (10) (b: lw: led 4f: r.o) ...................... 1.4
Pendor Dancer **(54)** (bl) (BForsey) 9–9-1 SWhitworth (6) (a.p: ev ch 2f out:
  unable qckn) ............................................................................. 2.5
573 Say You Will **(44)** (v) (MPNaughton) 8–8-0 ‡5BDoyle (2) (lw: no hdwy fnl 2f) ............ 1.6
Greetland Rock **(67)** (bl) (PHowling) 4–10-0 JMcLaughlin (9) (no hdwy fnl 2f) ...... 1½.7
Goodbye Maggie (IRE) **(37)** (MJFetherston-Godley) 4–7-5 ‡7DHarrison (5) (a bhd) 1.8
The Noble Oak (IRE) **(50)** (MMcCormack) 4–8-11 WNewnes (3) (a bhd) ................. ½.9
Fontaine Lady **(40)** (TThomsonJones) 5–8-1 DaleGibson (4) (a bhd) .................. 2½.10

**4/1** Jovial Kate (USA), **9/2** Meeson Times(op 3/1), **11/2** Fontaine Lady, **6/1** SIR TASKER, **7/1** Pendor Dancer,
**8/1** Say You Will, Slip-a-Snip, **12/1** Goodbye Maggie (IRE), **14/1** Greetland Rock, **20/1** The Noble Oak (IRE).
CSF £29.43, CT £109.79. Tote £5.20: £2.10 £1.50 £1.60 (£19.10). Mr C. Conway (MELTON MOWBRAY)
bred by W. H. Joyce. 10 Rn                                                         60.74 sec (2.54)
                                                                                  SF—50/29/40/42/26/7

T/Plpt: £48.60 (67.1 Tckts).

                                                                                  AK

**84—SOUTHWELL (L-H)** Fibresand

## Wednesday, January 29th [Standard]

Going Allowance: 5f: minus 0.10 sec; Rest: nil sec per fur (FS)                    Vis:mod

Stalls: 5f high

**96**  FISKERTON CLAIMING STKS (3-Y.O) £2265.20 (£627.20: £299.60)  **5f (AWT)**  1-40 (1-43)

54* **Creche (76)** (bl) (Fav) (MrsNMacauley) 9-5 NDay (10) (mde all: clr over 1f out:
  v.easily) ....................................................................................... —1
Grubby **(49)** (RHollinshead) 7-8 ‡7AGarth (5) (chsd ldrs tl outpcd ½-wy: styd on
  wl ins fnl f) ................................................................................. 8.2
Ever so Lonely **(68)** (bl) (ABailey) 7-13 ‡5BDoyle (8) (chsd ldrs: rdn ½-wy: kpt on
  fnl f) ................................................................................................. hd.3
61* Palacegate Racing **(80)** (JBerry) 9-0 JCarroll (1) (chsd ldrs: rdn 2f out: sn btn) ...... 2.4
653 It's Only Money **(68)** (bl) (THCaldwell) 9-0 MWood (9) (chsd wnr tl wknd over 1f
  out) ................................................................................................ hd.5
First Gold (JWharton) 8-13 JWilliams (6) (sn wl outpcd: styd on appr fnl f) ........ 1½.6
39 Camino a Ronda (PatMitchell) 7-13 ‡7CHawksley (7) (b.hind: sn wl bhd: kpt on nr
  fin) ................................................................................................ 1½.7
Swale Side (MrsGRReveley) 8-9 MHills (3) (s.i.s: outpcd ½-wy: sn bhd) ................. 5.8
Counter Blast 8-8(4) (WHolden) 8-8(4) ‡7MichaelDenaro (4) (bit bkwd: s.i.s: a wl bhd: t.o) ... 9
Laggard's Quest (CDBroad) 8-11 NAdams (2) (s.i.s: sn wl bhd: t.o) ................... 10

**11/10** CRECHE, **3/1** Palacegate Racing, **9/2** Ever so Lonely, **10/1** It's Only Money, **16/1** First Gold, **20/1** Swale
Side, **33/1** Ors. CSF £36.07, Tote £1.80: £1.10 £21.20 £2.00 (£41.80). Mrs N. Macauley (MELTON
MOWBRAY) bred by Bacton Stud. 10 Rn                                                60.2 sec (2.2)
                                                                                  SF—41/-/-/-/-/

**97**  OLLERTON H'CAP (0-70) £2382.80 (£660.80: £316.40)  **1½m (AWT)**  2-10 (2-12)

846 **Lord Advocate (44)** (v) (MPNaughton) 4–7-8 ‡5BDoyle (6) (trckd ldrs: led over 2f
  out: styd on wl fnl f) ....................................................................... —1
Uninvited **(40)** (JAGlover) 5–7-13 NCarlisle (1) (trckd ldrs: kpt on u.p fnl 2f) ........... 3½.2
593 Le Temeraire **(69)** (NTinkler) 6–10-0 KimTinkler (2) (led tl over 2f out: one pce) ....3½.3
Shining Wood **(43)** (Fav) (ASReid) 4–7-12 RFox (14) (effrt appr st: styd on fnl 2f:
  nt rch ldrs) .................................................................................. ½.4
713 Sharp Top **(43)** (MJRyan) 4–7-9(1) ‡3DBiggs (8) (effrt over 3f out: kpt on: nvr nr to
  chal) ............................................................................................ 3½.5
485 Fusion **(39)** (REarnshaw) 8–7-12(2) PBurke (4) (b: chsd ldrs: one pce fnl 2f) .......... nk.6
I'M Special (IRE) **(41)** (v) (AHarrison) 4–7-10 LCharnock (16) (chsd ldrs: drvn
  along 6f out: wknd 2f out) ............................................................. 2½.7
605 In Truth **(43)** (DWChapman) 4–7-12 SWood (5) (chsd ldrs tl outpcd 3f out: kpt on
  fnl f) ............................................................................................... nk.8
884 Hand Painted **(65)** (CRBeever) 8–9-3 ‡7MichaelDenaro (13) (b: lw: bhd tl styd on
  appr fnl f) ..................................................................................... 2½.9
81 Give Me Hope (IRE) **(50)** (RGBrazington) 4–8-5 JQuinn (15) (nvr nr ldrs) ........... 1½.10

     Bedouin Prince (USA) **(45)** *(CRBeever)* 5–8-4  MHills (7) (hld up: hdwy fnl 2f: nvr
         plcd to chal) ................................................ ½.11
     Erevnon **(59)** *(JLHarris)* 5–9-4  RCochrane (10) (trckd ldrs tl rdn & lost pl ent st) ...... 1.12
     Spanish Whisper **(37)** *(JRBostock)* 5–7-10[2]  NAdams (11) (prom 5f: bhd fnl 4f) ... 12.13
81[5] Restless Niece **(39)** *(TDBarron)* 4–7-5[1] ‡[3]JFanning (12) (lw: bhd: effrt appr st:
         sn wknd) ..................................................... 12.14
     Camden Knight **(37)** *(NBycroft)* 7–7-10  GBardwell (17) (a bhd) ........................... 2.15
79[6] Catundra (IRE) **(60)** *(MrsAKnight)* 4–8-8 ‡[7]DHarrison (9) (stdd s: hld up & a bhd)   nk.16
   81 Searching Star **(52)** *(PAKelleway)* 4–8-7[1]  WNewnes (4) (eyeshield: wl t.o fnl 4f) ..... 17
         LONG HANDICAP: Restless Niece 7-4.

**6/1** Shining Wood, **15/2** Sharp Top, Hand Painted, **9/1** Restless Niece(op 6/1), **10/1** Erevnon, Le Temeraire,
**12/1** I'M Special (IRE), In Truth, LORD ADVOCATE, Give Me Hope (IRE), **14/1** Fusion, Spanish Whisper, **16/1**
Bedouin Prince (USA), Camden Knight, Searching Star, **20/1** Uninvited, **25/1** Catundra (IRE). CSF £220.79,
CT £2,283.55. Tote £18.70: £4.30 £2.30 £3.20 £1.40 (wnr or 2nd with any £3.90). Mr W. J. Kelly
(RICHMOND) bred by London Thoroughbred Services Ltd. 17 Rn               41.3 (7.1)
                                                              SF—9/7/29/–/–/

## 98    STAYTHORPE CLAIMING STKS (3-Y.O) £2088.80 (£576.80: £274.40)
      **7f (AWT)**                                                       2-40 (2-42)

68[2] Pop to Stans **(80)** (Fav) *(TDBarron)* 9-7  AlexGreaves (3) (chsd ldrs: c wd ent st:
         led 2f out: clr 1f out: drvn out) .......................... —1
61[4] Life's a Breeze *(MRChannon)* 9-2  LornaVincent (5) (w ldr: kpt on u.p fnl 2f: no ch
         w wnr) ....................................................... 12.2
68* Palacegate King **(81)** *(JBerry)* 9-9  JCarroll (2) (lw: led to 2f out: wknd fnl f) ............ 2.3
  51 Cellito (IRE) **(56)** *(WAO'Gorman)* 9-0 ‡[5]EmmaO'Gorman (4) (lw: sn chsng ldrs:
         drvn along appr st: sn wknd) ............................. 12.4
     Forza Azzurri (IRE) **(48)** *(MrsNMacauley)* 9-0  NDay (1) (unruly s: lost pl ½-wy:
         sn bhd) ..................................................... 2.5

**11/10** POP TO STANS(Evens—6/4), **7/4** Palacegate King, **4/1** Life's a Breeze, **16/1** Cellito (IRE)(op 10/1),
**66/1** Forza Azzurri (IRE). CSF £5.59. Tote £2.10: £1.10 £2.40 (£5.60). Mr W. G. Spink (THIRSK) bred by
Lincoln Collins. 5 Rn                                                          1m 30.7 (4.1)
                                                         SF—44/3/4/–/–

## 99    AVERHAM H'CAP (3-Y.O) (0-90) £2049.60 (£565.60: £268.80)   **1m (AWT)**    3-10 (3-10)
                               (Weights raised 1 lb)

62[2] **Ferdia (IRE) (66)** (Jt-Fav) *(RHollinshead)* 8-12  WRyan (4) (effrt appr st: sn rdn &
         hung lft: led jst ins fnl f: sn clr) ......................... —1
62[4] Lady of Letters **(49)** *(TThomsonJones)* 7-9[2]  NAdams (5) (led tl hdd just ins fnl f:
         sn wknd) ..................................................... 4.2
69* Hand on Heart (IRE) **(69)** (Jt-Fav) *(WJHaggas)* 9-1  NDay (3) (b. off hind: chsd
         ldrs: hrd drvn appr st: wknd over 1f out) .............. 2½.3
65[5] Kick on Majestic (IRE) **(53)** *(NBycroft)* 7-13  SWood (1) (s.s: nvr rchd ldrs) ............... 3.4
47[4] Quiet Miss **(75)** *(DRCElsworth)* 9-7  JWilliams (2) (chsd ldrs tl lost pl appr st: sn
         bhd) ........................................................ hd.5
         LONG HANDICAP: Lady of Letters 7-4.

**2/1** Hand on Heart (IRE), FERDIA (IRE)(op 3/1), **4/1** Quiet Miss(op 5/2), **11/2** Kick on Majestic (IRE), **20/1**
Lady of Letters. CSF £23.44. Tote £2.90: £1.10 £4.10 (£16.70). Mr Noel Sweeney (UPPER LONGDON) bred
by Noel Sweeney in Ireland. 5 Rn                                             1m 45 (5.7)
                                                         SF—13/–/–/–/

## 100    MANSFIELD H'CAP (0-80) £2226.00 (£616.00: £294.00)   **1m (AWT)**    3-40 (3-41)
                               (Weights raised 1 lb)

93* **Martini Executive (72)** (bl) (Fav) *(WJPearce)* 4–9-8 (7x)  DNicholls (9) (lw: hld
         up gng wl: smooth hdwy over 2f out: led over 1f out: pushed out) —1
  41 Ballerina Bay **(45)** (v) *(DTThom)* 4–7-9  JQuinn (4) (effrt appr st: styd on appr fnl f:
         no ch w wnr) ................................................ 2.2
  93 Model Nurse **(48)** *(MrsAKnight)* 5–7-5[5] ‡[7]DHarrison (5) (led 1f: led over 3f out tl
         over 1f out: one pce) ..................................... 3½.3
86[4] Dawn Success **(60)** *(DWChapman)* 6–8-11  SWood (7) (bhd tl styd on fnl 2f) .......... 2.4
     Master Ofthe House **(48)** *(MDHammond)* 6–7-10 ‡[3]JFanning (3) (trckd ldrs: effrt
         over 2f out: btn whn hmpd over 1f out) ................. 3½.5
  86 Doulab's Image **(73)** (bl) *(JAGlover)* 5–9-3 ‡[7]SWilliams (6) (trckd ldrs tl lost pl 2f
         out) ......................................................... 2.6
  63 Evening Star **(59)** (v) *(AHide)* 6–8-3[7] ‡[7]KRutter (8) (effrt appr st: sn lost pl) ............ 3.7
50[3] East Barns (IRE) **(43)** (bl) *(TDBarron)* 4–7-7  LCharnock (1) (lw: prom tl lost pl
         appr st: n.d after) ...................................... s.h.8
     Sharp to Oblige **(46)** (v) *(RMWhitaker)* 5–7-6[2] ‡[5]BDoyle (2) (led after 1f tl over 3f
         out: sn wknd & wl bhd) ................................. 15.9
         LONG HANDICAP: East Barns (IRE) 7-4.

**Evens** MARTINI EXECUTIVE(tchd 6/4), **7/1** Dawn Success(op 4/1), Doulab's Image(op 7/2), **17/2** Evening Star, **9/1** Ballerina Bay(op 5/1), **10/1** East Barns (IRE), **14/1** Model Nurse, Master Ofthe House, **20/1** Sharp to Oblige. CSF £11.18, CT £81.74. Tote £1.90: £1.10 £2.90 £3.20 (£7.20). Mr Roger Jelley (HAMBLETON) bred by T. F. M. Corrie. 9 Rn
1m 43.5 (4.2)
SF—45/12/–/11/–/–

**101** MORTON H'CAP (0-70) £2128.00 (£588.00: £280.00) **7f (AWT)** 4-10 (4-11)

89 **Question of Degree (36)** (bl) *(NTinkler)* 6–8–0 KimTinkler (1) (s.i.s: gd hdwy on outside 2f out: edgd lft: styd on wl u.p to ld wl ins fnl f) ...............—1
89 Sandmoor Denim **(45)** *(SRBowring)* 5–8–9 SWebster (3) (sn chsng ldrs: drvn along appr st: led over 1f out: wknd nr fin) ................ 3.2
Mca Below the Line **(64)** (bl) *(WJPearce)* 4–10–0 DNicholls (7) (hld up: gd hdwy on outside 2f out: kpt on: nvr nr to chal) ................ 2½.3
89³ Shedad (USA) **(50)** *(TDBarron)* 4–9–0 AlexGreaves (6) (lw: led tl hdd & wknd over 1f out) ................ 2.4
92⁴ Vuchterbacher **(55)** (Fav) *(PFTulk)* 6–8–12 ‡⁷TWilson (8) (b: sn chsng ldrs: rdn & no imp 2f out) ................ hd.5
89 Cossack Noir **(40)** *(MPNaughton)* 4–7–13 ‡⁵BDoyle (5) (effrt & chsd ldrs appr st: lost pl 2f out) ................ 5.6
Station Express (IRE) **(35)** *(RHollinshead)* 4–7–6⁽³⁾ ‡⁷MHumphries (2) (s.i.s: a in rr) ................ 3.7
89⁵ State Governor **(62)** *(DWChapman)* 4–9–12 SWood (4) (chsd ldrs tl lost pl appr st) s.h.8
89 Luzum **(61)** (bl) *(JAGlover)* 8–9–4 ‡⁷SWilliams (9) (lw: chsd ldr tl wknd over 2f out) nk.9
89 Carnfield **(42)** *(JAGlover)* 4–8–6 NCarlisle (10) (nvr nr ldrs) ................ ¾.10

**11/4** Vuchterbacher, **4/1** Shedad (USA), **7/1** State Governor, Mca Below the Line, **8/1** Sandmoor Denim, Carnfield, **10/1** Cossack Noir, **12/1** QUESTION OF DEGREE, Luzum, **16/1** Station Express (IRE). CSF £98.50, CT £668.34. Tote £25.10: £4.40 £2.10 £3.10 (£34.70). Mr Philip J. Grundy (MALTON) bred by J. Hanson and R. Ogden. 10 Rn
1m 29.9 (3.3)
SF—36/36/47/27/24/–

T/Plpt: £1,655.20 (1.1 Tckts).
WG

## SOUTHWELL (L-H) Fibresand
### Friday, January 31st [Standard]
Going Allowance: 0.05 sec per fur (SL) Wind: almost nil Vis: v.poor
*Racing delayed due to fog*

Stalls: high 1st & 2nd, remainder low

**102** DANETHORPE STKS (Mdn) £2049.60 (£565.60: £268.80) **5f (AWT)** 1-40 (2-10)

**Lets Go Sabo** *(DWChapman)* 4–9–0 SWood (6) (bit bkwd: mde all: rdn & hld on gamely) ................—1
33⁴ Drummer's Dream (IRE) **(43)** (Fav) *(MrsNMacauley)* 4–8–6 ‡³DBiggs (2) (w ldrs: rdn ½-wy: r.o wl nr fin) ................ s.h.2
Galaxy Express **(42)** *(GHEden)* 4–9–0 GCarter (4) (bit bkwd: prom: rdn over 1f out: one pce) ................ 2.3
32 Company Cash (bl) *(RBastiman)* 4–8–7 ‡⁷HBastiman (5) (chsd ldrs: rdn 2f out: no imp) ................ ¾.4
66⁶ Danzig Lad (USA) **(42)** (v) *(MPNaughton)* 4–8–9 ‡⁵BDoyle (1) (outpcd tl styd on ins fnl f) ................ hd.5
Petank (IRE) *(PatMitchell)* 4–9–0 ASkingle (3) (bit bkwd: outpcd: t.o) ................ 6.6

**2/7** Drummer's Dream (IRE), **8/1** Galaxy Express(op 4/1), Danzig Lad (USA)(op 4/1), **20/1** LETS GO SABO(op 10/1), **25/1** Company Cash, **40/1** Petank (IRE). CSF £25.92, Tote £16.40: £3.50 £1.10 (£8.20). Mr Bill Waddington (YORK) bred by B. C. Taylor. 6 Rn
61.6 sec (3.6)
SF—38/29/31/21/22/3

**103** BALDERTON H'CAP (0-70) £2304.40 (£638.40: £305.20) **1¾m (AWT)** 2-10 (2-36)
(Weights raised 3 lb)
**Bridge Player (50)** (Jt-Fav) *(DMoffatt)* 5–8–5 ‡⁷DarrenMoffatt (11) (hld up: hdwy ½-wy: led 2f out: jst hld on) ................—1
76² Malenoir (USA) **(46)** (v) *(WJPearce)* 4–8–3 LCharnock (12) (hld up: hdwy over 3f out: styd on strly fnl f) ................ hd.2
84² Dalby Dancer **(57)** (Jt-Fav) *(BAMcMahon)* 8–9–5 RCochrane (1) (a.p: led over 3f out: rdn & hdd 2f out: sn btn) ................ 10.3
What a Card **(36)** *(DenysSmith)* 4–7–0 ‡⁷CTeague (10) (chsd ldrs: styd on one pce fnl 3f) ................ 10.4

Gilbert's Girl (35) (*CJHill*) 5–7–6(4) ‡5BDoyle (9) (bhd: styd on fnl 2f: nvr nrr) .............. 3.5
84 Pondered Bid (44) (*PatMitchell*) 8–7–13 ‡7CHawksley (3) (s.i.s: sn chsng ldrs: no
  ch fnl 3f) ..................................................................... 2.6
Flitcham (42) (*JRBostock*) 5–7–13(4) ‡5RPrice (8) (bit bkwd: nvr nr ldrs) ................ 1½.7
84⁵ Stone Flake (USA) (60) (bl) (*PAKelleway*) 6–9–8 WNewnes (2) (led early: bhd fnl
  4f) ..................................................................... ¾.8
46 Enfant du Paradis (IRE) (45) (*PDEvans*) 4–8–2 JQuinn (5) (t.o) ........................ 10.9
Showaca (36) (*RFMarvin*) 4–7–7 RFox (4) (chsd ldrs early: no ch fnl 3f: t.o) ......... ¾.10
Negatory (USA) (62) (*MCChapman*) 5–9–10 SWebster (6) (a bhd: t.o) .............. 2½.11
Unassuming (40) (v) (*JSWainwright*) 4–7–11(1) NCarlisle (13) (b.nr hind: hrd rdn
  3f out: sn bhd: t.o) ..................................................................... 2½.12
46 Cold Marble (USA) (50) (*DRTucker*) 7–8–7 ‡5RPerham (7) (w ldr early: t.o fnl 3f)  30.13
  LONG HANDICAP: What a Card 6-10, Gilbert's Girl 7-1, Showaca 7-6.

**5/2** BRIDGE PLAYER, Dalby Dancer, **8/1** Malenoir (USA), **9/1** Negatory (USA), **11/1** Stone Flake (USA), **12/1** Pondered Bid(op 8/1), **14/1** Enfant du Paradis (IRE), Flitcham, Unassuming, **20/1** Showaca, Gilbert's Girl, **33/1** Ors. CSF £23.56, CT £52.78. Tote £3.10: £2.80 £1.50 £1.40 (£13.60). D. A. & M. Lambert and Partners (CARTMEL) bred by Swettenham Stud. 13 Rn                                  3m 11.9 (12.6)

**104**  EAKRING CLAIMING STKS (3-Y.O) £2167.20 (£599.20: £285.60)  **1m (AWT)** 2-40 (3-01)

**Early Star** (*TDBarron*) 9-5 AlexGreaves (3) (bit bkwd: chsd ldrs: led fnl f: r.o wl) —1
85* Meltonby (69) (Fav) (*JHetherton*) 9-3 WNewnes (1) (lw: led ½-wy: hdd & no ex
  fnl f) ..................................................................... 2.2
Cold Shower (IRE) (*JAGlover*) 8-10 ‡7SWilliams (6) (hdwy 3f out: styd on wl ins
  fnl f) ..................................................................... 1½.3
85³ Silver Samurai (80) (*RHollinshead*) 8-12 ‡7EHusband (4) (a.p: ev ch 2f out: one
  pce) ..................................................................... 4.4
Walkonthemoon (*MMcCormack*) 8-12 JFortune (2) (led early: ev ch 2f out: wknd
  fnl f) ..................................................................... nk.5
69⁵ High Success (WAO'Gorman) 9-2 ‡5EmmaO'Gorman (5) (lw: chsd ldrs tl wknd
  fnl 3f) ..................................................................... 6.6
Tamasha (69) (*CJHill*) 8-12 NAdams (8) (a bhd: t.o) ........................ 12.7
85 Kashgar (*DWChapman*) 8-10 SWood (7) (bit bkwd: a bhd: t.o) ................ 10.8

**1/2** Meltonby, **15/2** EARLY STAR(4/1—8/1), **10/1** Silver Samurai, **12/1** Cold Shower (IRE), Tamasha(op 6/1), **14/1** High Success, **20/1** Walkonthemoon, **66/1** Kashgar. CSF £11.39, Tote £8.80: £2.20 £1.50 £3.40 (£3.60). Mr E. Buck (THIRSK) bred by Somerhall Bloodstock Ltd. 8 Rn                                  1m 45.3 (6)
SF—21/13/–/–/–/–/

**105**  ANNESLEY H'CAP (3-Y.O) (0-90) £2069.20 (£571.20: £271.60)  **6f (AWT)**  3-10 (3-25)

51³ **Buddy (IRE) (62)** (*MBell*) 8-0 ‡3DBiggs (6) (led after 1f: hrd rdn fnl f: all out) ..............—1
Inherent Magic (IRE) (68) (*MMcCormack*) 8-9 WNewnes (1) (led early: effrt 2f
  out: hrd rdn & ev ch fnl f: r.o) ..................................................................... s.h.2
73* Jefferson Davis (IRE) (75) (Fav) (*WJPearce*) 9-2 DNicholls (3) (chsd ldrs: hrd
  rdn 2f out: kpt on one pce) ........................................ 2.3
54² Appealing Times (USA) (74) (*WAO'Gorman*) 8-10 ‡5EmmaO'Gorman (5) (bhd tl
  r.o ins fnl f) ..................................................................... 6.4
Fighter Squadron (59) (*JAGlover*) 8-0 NCarlisle (4) (bit bkwd: chsd ldrs 4f: sn
  outpcd) ..................................................................... 5.5
96⁴ Palacegate Racing (80) (*JBerry*) 9-7 JCarroll (4) (hdwy ½-wy: rdn to chal 2f out:
  wknd qckly appr fnl f) ..................................................................... 1½.6
65* Kalar (52) (*DWChapman*) 7-7 SWood (7) (spd over 3f: sn lost tch: t.o) ........ 8.7
  LONG HANDICAP: Kalar 7-0.

**9/4** Jefferson Davis (IRE), **11/4** Appealing Times (USA), **5/1** BUDDY (IRE), **7/1** Inherent Magic (IRE)(op 4/1), Palacegate Racing, **16/1** Kalar, **33/1** Fighter Squadron. CSF £32.93, Tote £4.00: £4.20 £3.20 (£25.20). E. and B. Productions (Theatre) Ltd (NEWMARKET) bred by Limestone Stud in Ireland. 7 Rn      1m 16.7 (3.3)
SF—26/34/33/3/–/–

**106**  FACKLEY CLAIMING STKS £2441.60 (£677.60: £324.80)  **1m (AWT)**  3-40 (3-50)

64² **Euroblake (75)** (Fav) (*TDBarron*) 5–9–4 AlexGreaves (1) (hld up: led 2f out: sn
  clr: unchal) ..................................................................... —1
66² Awesome Power (59) (*CRNelson*) 6–9–3 RCochrane (11) (a.p: ev ch 2f out: one
  pce) ..................................................................... 7.2
Simply Candy (IRE) (*APStringer*) 4–8–6 JQuinn (6) (chsd ldrs: rdn over 2f out:
  one pce) ..................................................................... 1½.3
31 Pilar (45) (*MrsNMacauley*) 4–8–3 ‡7MadeleineSmith (10) (racd wd: prom tl
  outpcd fnl 2f) ..................................................................... ¾.4

87 Flying Promise **(57)** *(RABennett)* 4–8-10 WRyan (9) (b.nr hind: sme hdwy u.p fnl 2f: nvr nrr) .................................................................................. 3.5
45 King Ferdinand **(69)** *(DRTucker)* 5–8-11 ‡⁵RPerham (4) (led 6f: sn rdn & wknd) ...... nk.6
25⁴ Little Red Hen *(OO'Neill)* 7–8-4 RFox (12) (a in rr) ...................................... 2½.7
Sassy Lassy (IRE) **(63)** *(DBurchell)* 4–8-13 LCharnock (7) (chsd ldrs 5f) ............... nk.8
Mummy's Emerald **(70)** *(NTinkler)* 4–8-11 KimTinkler (3) (a in rr) ...................... ½.9
Armaiti **(73)** *(DRTucker)* 4–9-0 GBaxter (5) (bit bkwd: t.o) .............................. 6.10
45 Little Miss Polly *(CJHill)* 4–8-7 NAdams (2) (bkwd: prom to ½-wy: sn wknd: t.o) .... 30.11
Top One **(58)** *(CJHill)* 7–9-2 GCarter (8) (bit bkwd: w ldrs 5f: sn wknd: t.o) ............ hd.12

**4/5** EUROBLAKE(tchd 6/4), **5/1** Mummy's Emerald(tchd 8/1), **7/1** Awesome Power(op 9/2), **10/1** Armaiti(op 6/1), King Ferdinand(op 6/1), **12/1** Sassy Lassy (IRE)(op 8/1), **16/1** Flying Promise, Pilar, **20/1** Simply Candy (IRE)(op 10/1), Top One(op 9/2), **33/1** Little Red Hen, **50/1** Little Miss Polly. CSF £8.91, Tote £2.20: £1.30 £1.90 £2.50 (£6.30). Mr W. G. Swiers (THIRSK) bred by Viscount Leverhulme. 12 Rn
1m 44.5 (5.2)
SF—32/10/–/–/–/–

**107** CARLTON-ON-TRENT H'CAP (3-Y.O) (0-80) £2128.00 (£588.00: £280.00)
**7f (AWT)**
4-10 (4-15)

38⁵ **Energic (IRE) (52)** *(CNAllen)* 7-4⁽⁴⁾ ‡⁷DHarrison (4) (mde all: rdn along ½-wy: drew clr fnl f) ........................................................ —1
68⁵ Ready to Draw (IRE) **(62)** *(Jt-Fav)* *(RonaldThompson)* 8-2 ‡⁵SMaloney (5) (a.p: ev ch 2f out: r.o one pce) ............................................... 3.2
73² Try Leguard (IRE) **(76)** *(WCarter)* 9-2 ‡⁵NGwilliams (1) (chsd ldrs: effrt & ev ch 2f out: one pce) ................................................ nk.3
82 Papa Westray **(60)** *(TDBarron)* 8-5 AlexGreaves (3) (wl bhd & outpcd tl r.o ins fnl f) ...................................................................... 4.4
68³ Brotherlyaffection **(62)** *(RHollinshead)* 8-7 WRyan (6) (hld up: effrt 3f out: no imp) ...................................................................... 5.5
82² Kipini **(49)** *(Jt-Fav)* *(WJMusson)* 7-8⁽¹⁾ JQuinn (2) (chsd ldrs: rdn over 2f out: sn btn) ............................................................... 1½.6
LONG HANDICAP: Energic (IRE) 7-3, Kipini 7-5.

**5/2** Kipini, Ready to Draw, **4/1** Try Leguard (IRE)(op 5/2), **5/1** Brotherlyaffection(4/1—6/1), **12/1** ENERGIC (IRE)(op 7/1) & Ors. CSF £38.16, Tote £14.60: £5.00 £2.20 (£33.80). Mr P. J. McBride (NEWMARKET) bred by Damastown Stud in Ireland. 6 Rn
1m 30.7 (4.1)
SF—20/23/36/13/–/–

T/Plpt: £99.80 (21.35 Tckts).
IM

90—**LINGFIELD (L-H)** Equitrack
## Saturday, February 1st [Standard]
Going Allowance: minus 0.20 sec per fur (F)
Vis: bad

**108** CHURCHILL STKS (Mdn 3-Y.O) £2186.80 (£604.80: £288.40) **6f (AWT)** 1-50 (1-51)

**Summer Express** *(JLSpearing)* 9-0 DNicholls (1) (leggy: lt-f: lw: chsd ldr 4f out: shkn up 1f out: led ins fnl f: r.o wl) ..................................... —1
Honey Vision **(70)** (bl) *(Fav)* *(GHEden)* 8-9 JWilliams (3) (led: hrd rdn over 1f out: hdd ins fnl f: r.o) ..................................................... 2.2
Telegraphic *(MBell)* 9-0 MHills (5) (neat: bit bkwd: s.s: hdwy 3f out: one pce fnl 2f) . 12.3
Charmonix **(58)** *(GBlum)* 8-9 GBardwell (4) (lost pl 4f out: nt rcvr) ..................... 1.4
94⁶ Midyanzie *(CHolmes)* 8-9 RFox (2) (plld hrd: shkn up 3f out: nvr nr to chal) ............... 5.5
54⁶ Savinien (IRE) *(PJFeilden)* 9-0 RCochrane (7) (b.nr hind: bhd fnl 2f) ................. 5.6

**8/13** Honey Vision(Evens—4/7), **2/1** Telegraphic(6/4—9/4), **10/1** SUMMER EXPRESS(op 6/1), Savinien (IRE), **25/1** Midyanzie, **33/1** Charmonix. CSF £17.51, Tote £8.30: £2.60 £1.10 (£4.40). Mr Graham Treglown (ALCESTER) bred by Aramstone Stud Co. 6 Rn
1m 15.14 (4.54)

**109** CRUSADER CLAIMING STKS £2382.80 (£660.80: £316.40) **7f (AWT)** 2-20 (2-20)

75* **African Chimes (94)** *(Fav)* *(WAO'Gorman)* 5–9-2 ‡⁵EmmaO'Gorman (3) (hld up: led wl ins fnl f: pushed out) ............................. —1
75² Bold Habit **(92)** *(WJPearce)* 7–9-0 ‡⁵GHusband (9) (lw: hdwy 3f out: led over 1f out tl wl ins fnl f: r.o wl) ..................................... 1½.2
80⁶ Ringland (USA) **(83)** *(PCHaslam)* 4–9-7 RCochrane (4) (chsd ldr: led wl over 1f out: sn hdd: unable qckn) ................................. 3½.3
87⁶ Toshiba Comet **(76)** (bl) *(WJPearce)* 5–8-9 DNicholls (8) (hdwy 3f out: ev ch 2f out: wknd fnl f) ................................................. 2.4
93⁴ Kristis Girl **(56)** *(DHaydnJones)* 5–8-5 ‡³JFanning (1) (plld hrd: nt clr run 2f out: swtchd & rdn over 1f out: one pce) ..................... 2½.5

Clipper One **(63)** *(KOCunningham-Brown)* 4–8-0 ‡³DBiggs (2) (b: s.i.s: rdn 3f out: hdwy 2f out: wknd over 1f out) ................................................ ¾.6
*79* Anne's Bank (IRE) **(AMoore)** 4–7-13 NAdams (5) (led over 5f) ................................ 10.7
Nazare Blue **(43)** *(MrsBarbaraWaring)* 5–8-11 NHowe (6) (b: prom 3f) ................... ¾.8
Bay Mountain **(34)** *(MDixon)* 6–8-7 GBardwell (7) (a bhd) ................................ 2½.9

**11/8** AFRICAN CHIMES, **2/1** Bold Habit, **9/2** Ringland (USA), **10/1** Toshiba Comet, **14/1** Kristis Girl, **20/1** Nazare Blue, Clipper One, **50/1** Ors. CSF £4.76, Tote £2.20: £1.10 £1.20 £2.30 (£2.70). Mr D. G. Wheatley (NEWMARKET) bred by Noel Cogan. 9 Rn
1m 25.39 (1.39)
SF—60/53/49/31/19/12

**110**    CHALLENGER H'CAP (0-90) £2438.70 (£673.20: £320.10)  1½m (AWT)    2-50 (2-51)

*74\** **Rapporteur (USA) (88)** (Fav) *(CCElsey)* 6–10-0 WNewnes (2) (b: mde all: qcknd 5f out: rdn out) ................................................ —1
*83⁵* El Dominio **(64)** *(KOCunningham-Brown)* 4–8-0 GBardwell (3) (b: lw: chsd wnr 6f out: rdn 2f out: r.o wl ins fnl f) ................................ ¾.2
Belmoredean **(73)** *(RJO'Sullivan)* 7–8-13 RCochrane (1) (no hdwy fnl 3f) ............. 20.3
Winoski **(72)** *(DLWilliams)* 4–8-8 WRyan (4) (bit bkwd: rdn 6f out: bhd fnl 2f) ...... 15.4

**11/10** RAPPORTEUR (USA), **7/4** Belmoredean, **3/1** El Dominio, **10/1** Winoski. CSF £4.88, Tote £2.40 (£2.00). Mr Richard Berenson (LAMBOURN) bred by Thomas P. Whitney in USA. 4 Rn    2m 36.12 (6.72)
SF—23/–/–/–

**111**    CHIEFTAIN APP'CE H'CAP (0-70) £2324.00 (£644.00: £308.00)
1¼m (AWT)    3-20 (3-23)

**Premier Dance (51)** *(DHaydnJones)* 5–9-1 JFanning (5) (hdwy 4f out: hrd rdn fnl f: led last strides) ................................ —1
*81³* Modesto (USA) **(56)** *(KOCunningham-Brown)* 4–8-13 ‡⁵SWilliams (12) (b: lw: led 7f out: rdn 2f out: hdd last strides) ................................ nk.2
*81^* Princess Roxanne **(03)** (Ul) (Fav) *(ADailey)* 5–9-0 ‡⁴Dowe (Ω) (lw: a.p: ev ch ins fnl f: r.o wl) ................................ nk.3
*56* Charming Gift **(44)** *(RJRWilliams)* 5–8-0 ‡⁸GMitchell (7) (a.p: rdn & r.o wl ins fnl f) 1½.4
*93⁶* Lady Baraka (IRE) **(41)** *(ICampbell)* 4–7-9 ‡⁸MGriffiths (3) (nvr nr to chal) ............ 12.5
Our Topsie **(42)** *(FJO'Mahony)* 5–8-6 NWilliams (8) (b.nr fore: s.s: nvr nrr) ............. ½.6
*71\** Strat's Legacy **(45)** *(DWPArbuthnot)* 5–8-9 RPrice (9) (b.hind: a bhd) ................... 5.7
*79⁵* Royal Acclaim **(47)** (v) *(JMBradley)* 9–8-7 ‡⁸MichaelBradley (4) (bhd fnl 4f) .......... 1.8
*88* Mai Pen Rai **(50)** *(CJHill)* 4–8-12 ATucker (10) (s.i.s: a wl bhd) ........................... 12.9
Scots Law **(46)** *(RJO'Sullivan)* 5–8-10 DBiggs (6) (lw: led 3f: wknd over 4f out) ....... 4.10
Enterprise Lady (FR) **(43)** *(RJHodges)* 5–8-2 ‡⁵CHawksley (11) (swtg: s.i.s & stumbled s: a bhd) ................................ ½.11
*79⁴* Inseyab **(54)** *(PCHaslam)* 4–8-8 ‡⁸NicolaHowarth (1) (lw: rdn along: prom over 5f: t.o) ................................ 8.12

**2/1** Princess Roxanne, **3/1** Strat's Legacy, **5/1** Modesto (USA)(op 3/1), **13/2** PREMIER DANCE, **15/2** Lady Baraka (IRE), **10/1** Inseyab(8/1—12/1), **12/1** Charming Gift, **14/1** Scots Law, **16/1** Mai Pen Rai, **20/1** Royal Acclaim, Enterprise Lady (FR), **33/1** Our Topsie. CSF £43.34, CT £86.78. Tote £7.20: £2.40 £2.20 £1.20 (£11.90). Mrs Carol Sheppard (PONTYPRIDD) bred by Brick Kiln Stud Farm. 12 Rn    2m 7.62 (4.62)
SF—35/32/40/15/–/–

**112**    CENTURION H'CAP (0-60) £2382.80 (£660.80: £316.40)  **1m (AWT)**    3-50 (3-54)

*56³* **Quinzii Martin (46)** (v) *(DHaydnJones)* 4–9-0 JWilliams (7) (led 5f out: clr 2f out: rdn out) ................................ —1
*93²* El Volador **(56)** (Fav) *(RJO'Sullivan)* 5–9-7 ‡³DBiggs (3) (lw: a.p: hrd rdn over 1f out: r.o wl ins fnl f) ................................ 1½.2
*93³* Sarum **(47)** *(CPWildman)* 6–9-1 CRutter (2) (hdwy 4f out: chsd wnr 3f out: hrd rdn over 1f out) ................................ hd.3
*93⁵* Qualitair Rhythm (IRE) **(45)** *(WWHaigh)* 4–8-13 JQuinn (12) (hdwy 2f out: hrd rdn & r.o ins fnl f) ................................ 2½.4
Petticoat Power **(56)** *(MrsBarbaraWaring)* 6–9-10 NHowe (10) (b: no hdwy fnl 3f) 3½.5
*63\** Kissavos **(57)** *(CCElsey)* 6–9-11 TRogers (6) (lw: a abt same pl) ......................... hd.6
*77\** Beechwood Cottage **(64)** *(ABailey)* 9–9-11 ‡⁷PBowe (11) (nvr nrr) ....................... 4.7
*93* Across the Bay **(52)** *(SDow)* 5–9-6 WNewnes (1) (b.hind: led 3f: wknd 3f out) ........ 3.8
Jumby Bay **(53)** *(MJohnston)* 6–9-7 RPElliott (8) (w ldrs over 4f: wknd 2f out) ........ 1½.9
Parisian Express (FR) **(46)** *(KOCunningham-Brown)* 4–8-7 ‡⁷SWilliams (9) (b: s.i.s: a wl bhd) ................................ 10.10
*39³* Easy Match **(56)** *(CJHill)* 6–9-4 RCochrane (4) (a bhd) ................................ 2½.11
Wave Master **(57)** *(RJHodges)* 5–9-11 MHills (5) (wl bhd fnl 5f) ......................... 5.12

**2/1** El Volador, **7/2** Qualitair Rhythm (IRE)(op 12/1), **7/1** Kissavos, Sarum, Beechwood Cottage(8/1—12/1), **10/1** Across the Bay(8/1—12/1), **11/1** Petticoat Power, QUINZII MARTIN, **16/1** Jumby Bay(op 10/1), Easy Match(op 10/1), **25/1** Ors. CSF £33.59, CT £152.41. Tote £15.90: £2.20 £2.00 £3.00 (£11.40). Monolithic Refractories Ltd (PONTYPRIDD) bred by Lord Fairhaven. 12 Rn    1m 39.11 (2.41)
SF—40/42/35/25/25/25

## 113      COMET H'CAP (0-70) £2382.80 (£660.80: £316.40)    6f (AWT)      4-20 (4-22)

| | | | |
|---|---|---|---|
| 95³ | **Meeson Times (59)** (Fav) (BEllison) 4–9-6 MHills (12) (lw: hdwy 3f out: led ins fnl f: rdn out) | —1 | |
| 33 | Beaumont's Keep (32) (TDBarron) 6–7-7 LCharnock (3) (dwlt: hdwy on ins 2f out: r.o ins fnl f) | 2½.2 | |
| 80³ | Hinari Video (61) (MJohnston) 7–9-8 RPElliott (8) (led 4f out tl ins fnl f: unable qckn) | 1½.3 | |
| | Yeoman Force (57) (v) (JMBradley) 6–8-11 ‡⁷MichaelBradley (2) (bit bkwd: hdwy fnl 2f: r.o) | 2½.4 | |
| 42 | Cee-En-Cee (56) (v) (MMcCourt) 8–8-12 ‡⁵ATucker (9) (nvr nr to chal) | 2.5 | |
| | Grand Time (60) (CJHill) 3–8-5 WRyan (7) (lw: led 2f: wknd over 2f out) | 1.6 | |
| 75⁴ | Murmuring (61) (SDow) 6–9-8 JWilliams (1) (b.hind: no hdwy fnl 2f) | hd.7 | |
| | Sareen Express (IRE) (34) (bl) (MrsJCDawe) 4–7-6⁽²⁾ ‡³JFanning (14) (s.s: wl bhd 4f: nvr nrr) | ¾.8 | |
| 58 | Misdemeanours Girl (IRE) (50) (MRChannon) 4–8-11 JQuinn (4) (prom over 3f) | ¾.9 | |
| 95 | Greetland Rock (65) (bl) (PHowling) 4–9-12 JMcLaughlin (10) (gd spd 4f) | 1.10 | |
| | Oratel Flyer (34) (v) (RThompson) 5–7-9 RFox (5) (outpcd) | 1½.11 | |
| | Miss Bell Ringer (47) (CJHill) 4–8-8 NAdams (6) (bit bkwd: dwlt: a bhd) | 1.12 | |
| 53 | Neroli (65) (v) (APJones) 4–9-12 RCochrane (13) (a bhd: t.o) | 13 | |
| | Easy Delta (48) (CHolmes) 3–7-7 GBardwell (11) (b.nr hind: a bhd: t.o) | 14 | |

LONG HANDICAP: Beaumont's Keep 7-6, Sareen Express (IRE) 7-5, Easy Delta 7-3.

**3/1** MEESON TIMES, **9/2** Hinari Video, Murmuring, **11/2** Beaumont's Keep(12/1—5/1), **15/2** Misdemeanours Girl (IRE), **8/1** Cee-En-Cee, **14/1** Miss Bell Ringer, **20/1** Grand Time, Oratel Flyer, Greetland Rock, **25/1** Neroli, **33/1** Ors. CSF £20.95, CT £70.62. Tote £4.50: £1.90 £2.50 £1.10 (£13.50). Mr Charles Castle (MALTON) bred by Mrs M. Chubb. 14 Rn
         1m 13.75 (3.15)
         SF—19/–/4/–/–/–

T/Plpt: £6.40 (223.45 Tckts).                        LMc

## 108— LINGFIELD (L-H) Equitrack
### Tuesday, February 4th [Standard]
Going Allowance: minus 0.20 sec per fur (FS)

## 114      HANSOM CLAIMING STKS   £2245.60 (£621.60: £296.80)    1m 5f (AWT)    1-40 (1-41)

| | | | |
|---|---|---|---|
| 59² | **Kirby Opportunity (58)** (Fav) (JPearce) 4–7-11⁽²⁾ ‡⁵RPrice (12) (lw: a.gng wl: led 4f out: sn clr: eased fnl f) | —1 | |
| 90³ | Aude la Belle (FR) (48) (MrsAKnight) 4–7-10⁽¹⁾ ‡³DBiggs (8) (hdwy over 2f out: r.o wl ins fnl f) | ¾.2 | |
| 84³ | Qualitair Blazer (54) (JRJenkins) 5–8-8 SWhitworth (10) (b: a.p: rdn 4f out: r.o one pce) | 7.3 | |
| | Vaniski (45) (v) (MrsBarbaraWaring) 5–8-13 NHowe (3) (b: rdn along: nvr nrr) | 4.4 | |
| 97⁴ | Shining Wood (43) (ASReid) 4–8-0 ‡⁷KRutter (13) (led 5f out to 4f out: wknd fnl f) | 2½.5 | |
| 84 | Intricacy (66) (CCElsey) 4–8-12 WNewnes (11) (b: lw: nrst fin) | 6.6 | |
| 90 | Dashwood (USA) (DCJermy) 5–8-0 ‡⁷MJermy (1) (a bhd) | 12.7 | |
| 76⁴ | Lifetimes Ambition (43) (TCasey) 4–7-13 JQuinn (5) (bhd fnl 4f) | 15.8 | |
| 90⁶ | Dashing April (47) (DTThom) 4–8-8 MHills (9) (a bhd) | 7.9 | |
| 71 | Glowing Mantle (IRE) (40) (REPeacock) 4–7-9 ‡³JFanning (4) (lw: bhd fnl 5f) | 2.10 | |
| | Northern Conqueror (IRE) (63) (bl) (TJNaughton) 4–8-10 ‡⁵RPerham (2) (b: prom 8f) | 1.11 | |
| | Romola Nijinsky (PDEvans) 4–8-8 WRyan (7) (b: led 8f: wknd qckly) | 12.12 | |

**2/1** KIRBY OPPORTUNITY, **5/1** Romola Nijinsky, **6/1** Intricacy, **7/1** Qualitair Blazer, **10/1** Shining Wood(8/1—16/1), **14/1** Northern Conqueror (IRE), **16/1** Lifetimes Ambition, **20/1** Aude la Belle (FR)(op 12/1), Vaniski(op 12/1), Dashing April(op 12/1), **33/1** Ors. CSF £37.24, Tote £3.00: £1.10 £1.90 £2.50 (£23.30). Mr Peter Bradley (NEWMARKET) bred by Highfield Stud Ltd. 12 Rn
         2m 47.50 (4)
         SF—17/14/12/9/–/–

## 115      BROUGHAM H'CAP (0-60) £2343.60 (£649.60: £310.80)    1¼m (AWT)    2-10 (2-12)
### (Weights raised 1 lb)

| | | | |
|---|---|---|---|
| 111² | **Modesto (USA) (56)** (Fav) (KOCunningham-Brown) 4–9-9 SWhitworth (12) (b: chsd ldr: led over 3f out: r.o wl) | —1 | |
| 56² | Samurai Gold (USA) (54) (v) (PTWalwyn) 4–9-7 RCochrane (14) (led tl over 3f out: nt qckn) | 2.2 | |
| 66⁵ | Foursingh (52) (bl) (CBBBooth) 4–9-5 ACulhane (3) (a.p: r.o one pce fnl 2f) | 2.3 | |
| | Riviera Rainbow (57) (DRCElsworth) 4–9-10 JWilliams (6) (eyeshield: lw: hdwy 4f out: r.o ins fnl f) | 2.4 | |
| | Little Big (40) (BJCurley) 5–8-9 JQuinn (13) (lw: hdwy over 4f out: styd on: nt rch ldrs) | nk.5 | |

*83* Windsor Highness **(37)** (bl) *(MPMuggeridge)* 5–8–6[1] MHills (11) (lw: s.s: hdwy
7f out: wknd 3f out) ........................................... 1½.6
   Crown Reserve **(49)** (bl) *(MJRyan)* 4–8-13 ‡³DBiggs (7) (s.s: hdwy over 4f out:
wknd over 2f out) ........................................... 2.7
   Lady Poly **(39)** (bl) *(MissBSanders)* 4–8–6 BCrossley (2) (wl bhd fnl 4f) .............. 4.8
*90* Gipsy King **(52)** (bl) *(PAKelleway)* 4–9-5 GBardwell (9) (prom 5f) .............. 1½.9
   Internal Affair **(42)** *(JPearce)* 4–8–4 ‡⁵RPrice (5) (a bhd) .............. 1½.10
*77* Kreischim (IRE) **(42)** *(MMadgwick)* 4–8–9 GBaxter (1) (wl bhd fnl 5f) .............. 1½.11
   Always Alex **(40)** *(PDEvans)* 5–8–9 WRyan (8) (b: a wl bhd: t:o) .............. 30.12
*100³* Model Nurse **(40)** *(MrsAKnight)* 5–8-4 ‡⁵BDoyle (10) (bhd fnl 4f: t:o) .............. 6.13

**4/1 MODESTO (USA), 5/1** Samurai Gold (USA), **11/2** Riviera Rainbow(4/1—6/1), **6/1** Always Alex, **8/1** Crown
Reserve, **10/1** Model Nurse, **12/1** Little Big(op 5/1), **14/1** Lady Poly, Windsor Highness, **16/1** Internal Affair,
**20/1** Gipsy King, **25/1** Ors. CSF £24.01, CT £409.88. Tote £4.80: £1.30 £1.80 £16.80 (£4.20). Mr D. Bass
(STOCKBRIDGE) bred by Rhydian Morgan-Jones in USA. 13 Rn
2m 7.24 (4.24)
SF—47/41/35/36/23/17

**116**    LANDAU H'CAP (3-Y.O) (0-80) £2343.00 (£648.00: £309.00)   **1¼m (AWT)**   2-40 (2-41)

*91\** **Slight Risk (67)** *(PAKelleway)* 9-1 GBardwell (2) (eyecover: mde all: all out) ......... —1
*52\** Noble Singer **(65)** (Jt-Fav) *(HThomsonJones)* 8-13 RHills (6) (lw: a.p: ev ch 1f
out: r.o) ........................................... 1½.2
*51⁶* Sure to Win (IRE) **(62)** (Jt-Fav) *(ABailey)* 8-10 GCarter (4) (dropped rr 5f out:
hdwy 3f out: hrd rdn over 1f out: r.o) ........................................... s.h.3
   Bassio (BEL) **(73)** *(CNAllen)* 9-0 ‡⁷MichaelDenaro (9) (hld up: hdwy 4f out: ev ch
1f out: nt qckn) ........................................... nk.4
*78\** Alternation (FR) **(64)** *(PFICole)* 8-12 CRutter (8) (rdn 4f out: styd on: nt rch ldrs) ...... 2.5
*78⁴* Eau D'Espoir **(50)** *(JLSpearing)* 7-12[2] AMackay (7) (nvr nr to chal) ............ 15.6
*91¹* Cun Glory (IRE) **(50)** *(WJarvis)* 0 C NDay (1) (prom 6f) ............ ¾.7
   And Me **(50)** *(DTThom)* 7-12 JQuinn (5) (prom 5f) ............ 6.8
*72³* Super-Sub **(60)** *(MJFetherston-Godley)* 8-8 JWilliams (3) (a bhd) ............ 1½.9

**5/2** Sure to Win (IRE), Noble Singer, **4/1** Alternation (FR), **8/1** Super-Sub, **9/1** Bassio (BEL), SLIGHT
RISK(6/1—10/1), **20/1** Eau D'Espoir, Sun Glory (IRE), **33/1** And Me. CSF £31.28, CT £68.79. Tote £14.50:
£4.60 £1.30 £1.50 (£11.40). Mrs G. E. Kelleway (NEWMARKET) bred by Mrs G. E. Kelleway. 9 Rn
2m 8.15 (5.15)
SF—30/25/21/24/18/–

**117**    PHAETON APP'CE H'CAP (0-70) £2245.60 (£621.60: £296.80)   **1m (AWT)**   3-10 (3-12)

*112³* **Sarum (47)** *(CPWildman)* 6–8-10 DBiggs (1) (mde virtually all: all out) ......... —1
   Sunset Street (IRE) **(60)** *(SDow)* 4–9-9 MJermy (3) (b.hind: w wnr: ev ch fnl 2f:
r.o) ........................................... ¾.2
*100* East Barns (IRE) **(40)** (bl) *(TDBarron)* 4–8-3 JFanning (8) (a.p: r.o one pce fnl 2f) ...... ¾.3
*79²* Merseyside Man **(55)** (v) *(DrJDScargill)* 6–9-4 KRutter (7) (gd hdwy over 1f out:
one pce ins fnl f) ........................................... 3.4
*112* Beechwood Cottage **(64)** *(ABailey)* 9–9-13 PBowe (4) (nvr nrr) ............ nk.5
*63²* Mac's Princess (USA) **(65)** (Fav) *(WAO'Gorman)* 4–10-0 EmmaO'Gorman (11)
(dwlt: hdwy over 3f out: nvr nr to chal) ........................................... 1½.6
   Grown At Rowan **(61)** *(MMadgwick)* 5–9-10 ATucker (9) (swtg: prom tl rdn &
wknd over 2f out) ........................................... 1½.7
   Curtain Up (FR) **(41)** *(BForsey)* 5–8-4 RPrice (5) (bhd fnl 4f) ............ 12.8
*109* Bay Mountain **(34)** *(MDixon)* 6–7-11 NGwilliams (6) (b.nr hind: a wl bhd) ...... ¾.9
   Please Please Me (IRE) **(36)** *(KOCunningham-Brown)* 4–7-13 BDoyle (2) (b: w
ldrs tl wknd over 4f out) ........................................... 3.10
   Royal Course **(30)** (v) *(BEllison)* 7–7-7 CHawksley (10) (b: t.o fnl 4f) ............ 25.11
LONG HANDICAP: Royal Course 7-2.

**9/4** Mac's Princess (USA), **3/1** SARUM, **5/1** Merseyside Man, **10/1** Sunset Street (IRE), Grown At Rowan(op
6/1), East Barns (IRE), **12/1** Please Please Me (IRE), **14/1** Beechwood Cottage, **25/1** Curtain Up (FR), **33/1**
Bay Mountain, **50/1** Royal Course. CSF £31.61, CT £250.35. Tote £5.30: £1.60 £1.40 £3.10 (£43.10). Mr
W. Wildman (SALISBURY) bred by Miss Suzannah Armstrong. 11 Rn
1m 39.76 (3.06)
SF—27/38/16/22/30/26

**118**    VICTORIA STKS (Mdn) £2108.40 (£582.40: £277.20)   **7f (AWT)**   3-40 (3-41)

   **Sauvignon (IRE) (59)** (Fav) *(RGuest)* 4–8-9 NDay (2) (in rr tl hdwy 3f out: str run
to ld ins fnl f) ........................................... —1
*81* Queen of Dreams **(40)** *(DrJDScargill)* 4–8-9 JQuinn (8) (a.p: led over 3f out tl ins
fnl f) ........................................... 2.2
*113* Sareen Express (IRE) **(30)** (bl) *(MrsJCDawe)* 4–8-11 ‡³JFanning (4) (lost pl over
3f out: gd hdwy fnl f) ........................................... 2.3

102[5] Danzig Lad (USA) **(42)** (v) *(MPNaughton)* 4—8-9 ‡[5]BDoyle (7) (dwlt: hdwy 4f out: one pce fnl 2f) ..................... 2½.4

95 Goodbye Maggie (IRE) **(34)** (bl) *(MJFetherston-Godley)* 4—8-9 WNewnes (5) (led over 4f out tl over 3f out: wknd 2f out) ..................... hd.5

Skip Tracer **(38)** *(KTIvory)* 4—9-0 JWilliams (6) (bhd fnl 4f) ..................... 5.6

Jeethgaya (USA) **(56)** *(BSmart)* 4—8-9 WRyan (3) (lw: led over 2f: wknd qckly: t.o) ..................... 15.7

36 Goldvein (SWE) **(58)** (bl) *(WAO'Gorman)* 4—9-0 RCochrane (1) (ref to r: t.n.p) ..................... 0

**7/4** SAUVIGNON (IRE)(tchd 4/5), **5/2** Jeethgaya (USA), Goldvein (SWE)(op 4/1), **10/1** Danzig Lad (USA), **20/1** Goodbye Maggie (IRE)(op 12/1), Skip Tracer, Queen of Dreams(op 12/1), **25/1** Sareen Express (IRE). CSF £31.22, Tote £2.50: £1.10 £1.50 £3.10 (£15.20). Mr Christopher P. J. Brown (NEWMARKET) bred by Mrs P. Grubb in Ireland. 8 Rn ..................... 1m 26.63 (2.63)
SF—35/29/25/15/14/4

**119**     DOG CART H'CAP (Amateurs) (0-70) £2206.40 (£610.40: £291.20)
**6f (AWT)**     4-10 (4-13)

87 **Courting Newmarket (50)** *(MrsAKnight)* 4—10-13 ‡[5]MrDSalter (7) (a.p: led wl ins fnl f: r.o) ..................... —1

57 Rushanes **(60)** *(TCasey)* 5—11-9 ‡[5]MissEFolkes (11) (a.p: led ins fnl f: sn hdd: r.o) ..................... 2.2

45 Count Me Out **(43)** (bl) *(JPearce)* 7—10-11 MrsLPearce (1) (lw: gd hdwy fnl f: fin wl) ..................... s.h.3

70 Verro (USA) **(33)** (bl) *(JABennett)* 5—9-10[(1)] ‡[5]MissAPurdy (8) (b.nr fore: nrst fin) ..................... 3½.4

42 Precious Air (IRE) **(47)** *(AMoore)* 4—10-10 ‡[5]MrKGoble (3) (nvr nrr) ..................... 2½.5

95 The Noble Oak (IRE) **(48)** (bl) *(MMcCormack)* 4—10-11 ‡[5]MissSFarrant (4) (led after 1f: sn wknd qckly & hdd ins fnl f) ..................... ¾.6

79 Inswinger **(42)** *(WGRWightman)* 6—10-5 ‡[5]MrGKille (10) (no hdwy fnl 2f) ..................... ½.7

95[2] Jovial Kate (USA) **(47)** (Fav) *(BEllison)* 5—11-1 MrSLyons (6) (prom 3f) ..................... nk.8

113[2] Beaumont's Keep **(31)** *(TDBarron)* 6—9-13 MissEBronson (12) (b.hind: outpcd) ..................... ¾.9

95 Fontaine Lady **(38)** *(TThomsonJones)* 5—10-6 MissABillot (2) (led 1f: wknd qckly over 1f out) ..................... ½.10

31 Hinari Hi Fi **(43)** *(PDEvans)* 7—10-6 ‡[5]MrWMcLaughlin (9) (b.off hind: prom 3f) ..................... nk.11

Barbezieux **(37)** (bl) *(TJNaughton)* 5—10-0 ‡[5]MrsJNaughton (5) (b: bit bkwd: a wl bhd) ..................... 5.12

**9/4** Jovial Kate (USA), **11/4** Beaumont's Keep, **6/1** The Noble Oak (IRE), **7/1** Fontaine Lady(5/1—8/1), **8/1** Inswinger, Count Me Out, **11/1** Rushanes(op 10/1), **20/1** Barbezieux, **50/1** COURTING NEWMARKET & Ors. CSF £625.79, CT £6,244.76. Tote £56.10: £8.10 £3.00 £3.40 (£423.50). Mr Geo Taylor (CULLOMPTON) bred by R. H. Cowell and Mrs B. R. Abel Smith. 12 Rn ..................... 1m 14.64 (4.04)
SF—10/12/–/–/–/–

T/Plpt: £195.30 (8.4 Tckts).     Hn

96—**SOUTHWELL (L-H)** Fibresand
**Friday, February 7th [Standard]**
Going Allowance: 0.20 sec per fur (SL)     Wind: fresh half bhd

**120**     NEW BALDERTON CLAIMING STKS £2382.80 (£660.80: £316.40)
**1m 3f (AWT)**     1-55 (1-57)

97[3] **Le Temeraire (69)** *(NTinkler)* 6—9-2 KimTinkler (7) (led after 2f: hrd rdn fnl f: r.o) ..................... —1

106[3] Simply Candy (IRE) *(APStringer)* 4—7-10 JQuinn (13) (hdwy 5f out: 2nd st: ev ch 2f out: unable qckn ins fnl f) ..................... ¾.2

48* Alle-Roy **(63)** (Fav) *(MHTompkins)* 4—8-11 RCochrane (4) (in rr: hdwy over 1f out: hrd rdn & r.o ins fnl f) ..................... 1½.3

64[6] Porick **(23)** (v) *(DMoffatt)* 4—7-5 ‡[7]DarrenMoffatt (11) (prom: 5th st: one pce fnl f) ..................... hd.4

106 Little Red Hen *(OO'Neill)* 7—7-10 NAdams (5) (hdwy & 4th st: rdn over 1f out: one pce) ..................... 3½.5

Fit for Life (IRE) *(MrsNMacauley)* 4—8-0 NCarlisle (12) (led 2f: 6th & wkng st) ..................... 10.6

101[6] Cossack Noir **(33)** *(MPNaughton)* 4—7-7 ‡[5]BDoyle (9) (bhd: hdwy & 3rd st: sn btn) ..................... 2.7

56 Misty Goddess (IRE) **(44)** *(MAJarvis)* 4—7-9 ‡[3]DBiggs (3) (a in rr) ..................... 1½.8

86 Quinta Royale **(49)** *(JRJenkins)* 5—8-7 GBardwell (2) (prom: rdn 5f out: wknd over 3f out) ..................... 12.9

Belarius **(54)** *(REBarr)* 4—8-0 LCharnock (8) (sn pushed along: hdwy 6f out: wknd over 3f out: t.o) ..................... dist.10

Northern Flyer **(62)** *(MCChapman)* 4—8-10 SWebster (6) (chsd ldrs tl wknd qckly 5f out: p.u & dismntd over 3f out: lame) ..................... 0

**2/1** Alle-Roy, **4/1** LE TEMERAIRE, **11/2** Simply Candy (IRE)(op 3/1), **8/1** Misty Goddess (IRE), **10/1** Northern Flyer, **11/1** Quinta Royale(op 7/1), **12/1** Cossack Noir(op 8/1), **16/1** Belarius, **20/1** Porick, Little Red Hen, **25/1** Fit for Life (IRE). CSF £25.90, Tote £5.40: £1.50 £1.50 £1.90 (£19.10). Mr Dave Douglas (MALTON) bred by Petra Bloodstock Agency Ltd. 11 Rn
2m 31.7 (10.2)
SF—22/–/12/–/–/–

**121**    LANGFORD APP'CE H'CAP (0-60) £2461.20 (£683.20: £327.60)    **6f (AWT)**    2-25 (2-29)

87³  **Saladan Knight (60)** (bl) *(JGFitzGerald)* 7–9-7 ‡⁷MHunt (10) (eyeshield: hld up: hdwy over 1f out: swtchd rt & r.o to ld nr fin) ................................ —1
87²  Miss Calculate **(56)** *(CaptJWilson)* 4–9-7 ‡³GParkin (15) (4th st: led over 1f out tl hdd nr fin) ................................ ¾.2
101⁴  Shedad (USA) **(50)** *(TDBarron)* 4–9-1 ‡³VHalliday (7) (led over 3f out: hdd over 2f out: ev ch ins fnl f: nt qckn) ................................ 1½.3
102²  Drummer's Dream (IRE) **(43)** (Fav) *(MrsNMacauley)* 4–8-11 DBiggs (4) (led over 4f out: sn hdd: 2nd st: ev ch fnl f: unable qckn nr fin) .......... hd.4
58  Furiella **(51)** *(PCHaslam)* 4–8-12 ‡⁷NicolaHowarth (9) (chsd ldrs: rdn over 1f out: styd on same pce) ................................ 1½.5
58⁶  Sully's Choice (USA) **(52)** (bl) *(DWChapman)* 11–9-3 ‡³SWilliams (6) (3rd st: led over 2f out tl over 1f out: wknd ins fnl f) ................................ 2½.6
98⁴  Cellito (IRE) **(56)** *(WAO'Gorman)* 3–8-8  EmmaO'Gorman (1) (nvr rchd ldrs) .......... ½.7
87*  Strip Cartoon (IRE) **(51)** (bl) *(SRBowring)* 4–8-12 ‡⁷MHarris (11) (hdwy & 6th st: wknd over 1f out) ................................ 1½.8
87  Morpick **(54)** *(JPLeigh)* 5–9-5 ‡³HBastiman (3) (led after 1f: sn hdd: hmpd & 5th st: sn btn) ................................ ½.9
Ping Pong **(45)** *(TFairhurst)* 4–8-13  JFanning (14) (a in rr) ................................ 3.10
50  Damaaz (IRE) **(45)** (v) *(JSWainwright)* 4–8-13  SMaloney (5) (bhd fr ½-wy) .......... ½.11
113  Miss Bell Ringer **(47)** *(CJIll)* 4–9-1  ATucker (0) (n.d) ................................ nk.12
95⁶  Say You Will **(42)** (v) *(MPNaughton)* 8–8-10  BDoyle (16) (n.d) ................................ 1½.13
106⁵  Flying Promise **(57)** *(RABennett)* 4–9-11  KRutter (12) (bhd fr ½-wy) .......... ¾.14
Catalani **(49)** *(TJNaughton)* 7–9-3  RPerham (2) (b: b.nr hind: chsd ldrs: bdly hmpd wl over 3f out: nt rcvr: t.o) ................................ 12.15

**6/1** Drummer's Dream (IRE), **8/1** Furiella, Morpick(12/1—7/1), **17/2** Sully's Choice (USA)(6/1—9/1), **9/1** SALADAN KNIGHT(op 6/1), **10/1** Miss Calculate(op 6/1), Shedad (USA)(op 6/1), Say You Will(op 5/1), **12/1** Strip Cartoon (IRE)(op 7/1), **14/1** Catalani, Miss Bell Ringer, **16/1** Cellito (IRE), **20/1** Ors. CSF £89.65, CT £827.94. Tote £11.50: £3.10 £2.10 £2.50 (£26.30). Mrs A. F. Budge (MALTON) bred by Woodditton Stud Ltd. 15 Rn
1m 19.2 (5.8)
SF—15/15/3/–/–/–

**122**    GAMSTON H'CAP (0-90) £2206.40 (£610.40: £291.20)    **2m (AWT)**    2-55 (2-57)

103²  **Malenoir (USA) (51)** (v) *(WJPearce)* 4–7-7  LCharnock (5) (lw: mde all: clr over 2f out: unchal) ................................ —1
Clifton Hampden **(71)** *(LadyHerries)* 4–8-13  WRyan (1) (lw: bhd: outpcd 8f out: poor 5th st: hdwy over 2f out: styd on) ................................ 12.2
Unpaid Member **(47)** *(JWharton)* 8–7-6 ‡³JFanning (3) (hdwy & 2nd st: wknd 2f out) ................................ 1½.3
103³  Dalby Dancer **(57)** *(BAMcMahon)* 8–8-5  NCarlisle (4) (chsd ldrs: pushed along 8f out: wknd over 4f out: poor 4th st: t.o) ................................ 15.4
60*  Fiala (IRE) **(86)** (Fav) *(JHMGosden)* 4–10-0  MHills (2) (chsd wnr over 12f: 3rd & wkng st: t.o) ................................ 6.5
Paulinus **(51)** *(DenysSmith)* 4–7-0 ‡⁷CTeague (6) (a bhd: t.o & 6th st) ................................ 15.6
LONG HANDICAP: Malenoir (USA) 7-2, Paulinus 7-1.

**4/5** Fiala (IRE), **7/2** MALENOIR (USA), **13/2** Dalby Dancer(5/1—3/1), **7/1** Clifton Hampden(7/2—8/1), **12/1** Unpaid Member(10/1—16/1), **33/1** Paulinus. CSF £24.14, Tote £5.80: £1.80 £2.50 (£12.90). Mr John Purcell (HAMBLETON) bred by King Ranch Inc. in USA. 6 Rn
3m 49 (23)

**123**    OLD CLIPSTONE CLAIMING STKS (3-Y.O) £2245.60 (£621.60: £296.80)
**1m (AWT)**    3-25 (3-27)

116⁴  **Bassio (BEL) (73)** *(CNAllen)* 8-2 ‡⁷MichaelDenaro (6) (a.p: 2nd st: led wl over 2f out: rdn out) ................................ —1
104*  Early Star (Fav) *(TDBarron)* 8-10  AlexGreaves (1) (chsd ldrs: 4th st: rdn over 1f out: styd on same pce) ................................ 1½.2
Firefighter *(RHollinshead)* 8-5⁽¹⁾ WRyan (2) (lw: prom: lost pl & 6th st: swtchd rt over 1f out: styd on) ................................ 2½.3
91²  Patrician Magician **(69)** *(RJRWilliams)* 8-1 ‡³DBiggs (7) (5th st: styd on same pce fnl 2f) ................................ 8.4

91³ Feeling Foolish (IRE) (75) (v) (TFairhurst) 8-3 ‡³JFanning (3) (n.d) ............... 2.5
37⁴ Optical (IRE) (HATWhiting) 8-4 LCharnock (9) (led over 5f: sn wknd) ................. ½.6
99³ Hand on Heart (IRE) (70) (WJHaggas) 8-4 ‡⁵EmmaO'Gorman (5) (dwlt: hdwy &
                3rd st: wknd over 2f out) ................................................... 4.7
108⁴ Charmonix (58) (GBlum) 7-11 GBardwell (8) (sn bhd) .................................. 3.8
Turning Heads (CaptJWilson) 7-12⁽³⁾ AMackay (4) (small: unf: s.i.s: hdwy 5f out:
                wknd 3f out) ............................................................ ½.9

**5/6** Early Star(11/10—4/5), **4/1** BASSIO (BEL), **7/1** Feeling Foolish (IRE)(op 7/2), **10/1** Hand on Heart (IRE),
Patrician Magician, **20/1** Turning Heads, Optical (IRE), Firefighter, **33/1** Charmonix. CSF £7.85, Tote £4.50:
£1.50 £1.10 £4.00 (£3.30). Mrs Shirley Darby (NEWMARKET) bred by P. Madelein in Belgium. 9Rn
                                                                          1m 47 (7.7)

**124**        HALAM H'CAP (0-70) £2304.40 (£638.40: £305.20)        7f (AWT)        3-55 (3-59)

89⁴ **Mushy Boff (49)** (CJHill) 4–8-6 ‡³DBiggs (8) (hdwy & 6th st: led wl ins fnl f: r.o wl)     —1
89² Grand Guignol (68) (Fav) (GWragg) 4–10-0 WRSwinburn (9) (prom: led 4f out:
                rdn over 1f out: hdd wl ins fnl f: no ex) ................................. 1½.2
117⁶ Mac's Princess (USA) (65) (bl) (WAO'Gorman) 4–9-6 ‡⁵EmmaO'Gorman (5)
                (s.i.s: bhd: hdwy over 2f out: rdn over 1f out: styd on) ...............2½.3
101² Sandmoor Denim (41) (SRBowring) 5–8-1 NAdams (2) (led 5f out to 4f out: 2nd
                st: wknd 1f out) ......................................................... 3½.4
41⁶ Pims Classic (62) (WJHaggas) 4–9-8 MHills (1) (led 2f: 3rd st: wknd 2f out) ......... 2.5
Obsidian Grey (67) (BAMcMahon) 5–9-13 RCochrane (12) (chsd ldrs: 7th st:
                one pce fnl 2f) ........................................................... 3.6
D'Altagnan (48) (SMellor) 6–8-8  DanaMellor (4) (nvr trbld ldrs) ...................... 1.7
106⁴ Pilar (45) (MrsNMacauley) 4–7-12 ‡⁷MadeleineSmith (11) (4th st: wknd over 2f
                out) ...................................................................... nk.8
Sobering Thoughts (41) (DWChapman) 6–8-1 SWood (3) (chsd ldrs: 5th st:
                wknd over 2f out) ........................................................ 1½.9
87⁵ Tudorgateway (63) (v) (MHTompkins) 4–9-2 ‡⁷MGodsafe (10) (dwlt: a bhd) ......... ¾.10
Yonge Tender (56) (bl) (JWharton) 5–9-2 JWilliams (7) (bit bkwd: chsd ldrs over
                3f) ....................................................................... ½.11
Hamilton Lady (IRE) (40) (DMoffatt) 4–7-7 ‡⁷DarrenMoffatt (6) (bkwd: dwlt: a
                bhd) .................................................................... s.h.12
87 Harry's Joy (35) (CJHill) 4–7-9⁽¹⁾ JQuinn (13) (bhd fr ½-wy: t.o) ...................10.13

**2/1** Grand Guignol, **4/1** Sandmoor Denim, **6/1** Mac's Princess (USA), **7/1** MUSHY BOFF, **12/1** Obsidian Grey,
**14/1** Pims Classic, **16/1** Tudorgateway(op 10/1), Yonge Tender(op 10/1), **20/1** Pilar, Sobering
Thoughts(10/1—25/1), **25/1** Harry's Joy, **33/1** Ors. CSF £21.03, CT £84.97. Tote £7.90: £2.50 £1.70 £1.90
(£14.50). Mr C. John Hill (BARNSTAPLE) bred by Newschoice Ltd. 13 Rn
                                                                          1m 31.9 (5.3)
                                                                   SF—33/50/34/4/19/15

**125**        MANSFIELD H'CAP (0-60) £2578.80 (£716.80: £344.40)        1½m (AWT)        4-25 (4-26)

**Heir of Excitement (30)** (APStringer) 7–7-12 JQuinn (4) (a.p: 4th st: led over 1f
                out: sn rdn & r.o wl) ..................................................... —1
Qualitair Sound (IRE) (57) (JFBottomley) 4–9-7 GBardwell (6) (chsd ldr: 2nd st:
                led over 2f out tl over 1l over 1f out: r.o) ................................ hd.2
83² Carlingford (USA) (53) (Fav) (HATWhiting) 6–9-7 JCarroll (1) (led over 9f: ev ch
                fnl f: nt qckn) ........................................................... 2½.3
97 Spanish Whisper (35) (JRBostock) 5–7-12 ‡⁵RPrice (12) (prom: rdn 5f out: 5th st:
                styd on fnl 2f) .......................................................... 3½.4
Watch Tower Bay (IRE) (39) (RBoss) 4–8-3 GCarter (17) (chsd ldrs: poor 6th st:
                one pce fnl 3f) ........................................................... 5.5
97 Bedouin Prince (USA) (45) (CRBeever) 5–8-13 MHills (2) (sn pushed along: lost
                pl 4f out: n.d after) ..................................................... 5.6
88 Mr Wishing Well (56) (RJRWilliams) 6–9-3 ‡⁷SWilliams (16) (b.nr hind: hld up:
                hdwy 7f out: 3rd st: wknd over 1f out) .................................... 7.7
97⁶ Fusion (37) (REarnshaw) 8–8-5 PBurke (10) (b: pushed along 7f out: no ch fnl 3f)     5.8
Milly Black (IRE) (48) (JLHarris) 4–9-1⁸ RCochrane (7) (b.off fore: nvr trbld ldrs)   1½.9
97² Uninvited (40) (JAGlover) 5–8-8 NCarlisle (13) (rdn 6f out: bhd fnl 3f) ........... 2.10
Carefree Times (50) (JNorton) 5–9-4 ACulhane (13) (bhd fnl 3f) ...................... ½.11
103⁶ Pondered Bid (41) (PatMitchell) 8–8-2 ‡⁷CHawksley (5) (dwlt: a bhd) ............. ½.12
100⁴ Dawn Success (59) (DWChapman) 6–9-13 SWood (8) (a bhd) ....................... 6.13
Spring Tern (USA) (56) (bl) (RO'Leary) 4–9-6 LCharnock (3) (chsd ldrs 6f) .......... 5.14
Opening Overture (USA) (55) (CNAllen) 6–9-2‡⁷MichaelDenaro (14) (bit bkwd: a
                bhd) ...................................................................... 6.15
71⁶ Saville Way (29) (bl) (WJMusson) 5–7-11 AMackay (9) (b.hind: bhd fr ½-wy: t.o) 12.16

**9/4** Carlingford (USA), **7/1** Dawn Success, Mr Wishing Well, **8/1** Uninvited, **9/1** Watch Tower Bay (IRE), Qualitair Sound (IRE)(op 6/1), **10/1** Saville Way, **14/1** Pondered Bid, Milly Black (IRE), **16/1** Bedouin Prince (USA)(op 8/1), Fusion(8/1—20/1), **20/1** Spring Tern (USA), Carefree Times, **25/1** HEIR OF EXCITEMENT & Ors. CSF £241.19, CT £660.47. Tote £28.10: £2.30 £3.00 £1.20 £7.80 (Wnr or 2nd w any £9.10). Mr D. M. Hetherington (THIRSK) bred by Mrs N. B. Parr. 16 Rn　　　　　2m 43.6 (9.4)

SF—14/36/31/1/–/–

T/Plpt: £59.90 (25.75 Tckts).　　　　　　　　　　　　　　　　　　　　　　CR

## 114—LINGFIELD (L-H) Equitrack
## Saturday, February 8th [Standard]
Going Allowance: minus 0.20 sec per fur (FS)

| 126 | NECTARINE STKS (Mdn) £2147.60 (£593.60: £282.80) | 1¼m (AWT) | 1-30 (1-33) |
|---|---|---|---|

*35* **Pleasure Ahead (43)** (MRChannon) 5–8–7 ‡[7]PTurner (4) (hld up: rdn over 3f out: led over 2f out: r.o wl) ........................................................................ —1
*90[2]* Carlowitz (USA) (Fav) (AMoore) 4–8–12 CandyMorris (3) (lw: gd hdwy over 1f out: hrd rdn: r.o wl) ........................................................................ 3½.2
*111[6]* Our Topsie (35) (FJO'Mahony) 5–8–4 ‡[5]NGwilliams (10) (b: a.p: hrd rdn over 1f out: unable qckn) ........................................................................ 1.3
*57* Sunwind (35) (RJHodges) 6–9–0 RCochrane (1) (hdwy over 4f out: one pce fnl 2f) ¾.4
*117* Bay Mountain (34) (bl) (MDixon) 6–9–0 SWhitworth (9) (b.nr hind: led over 7f) ... 2.5
Grey Dancer (42) (JWhite) 4–8–12 JWilliams (2) (nvr nr to chal) ........................ 4.6
Clear Idea (IRE) (45) (CRNelson) 4–8–12 MHills (1) (b: a bhd) ........................ 6.7
Red Bomber (KOCunningham-Brown) 4–8–12 WNewnes (6) (b: prom over 6f) ....... 2.8
*40* Hepburn (IRE) (42) (MJFetherston-Godley) 4–8–7 WRyan (8) (lw: chsd ldr 6f) ...... s.h.9
*64* Green's Bonheur (30) (v) (MPNaughton) 4–8–2 ‡[5]BDoyle (7) (a bhd) ................. 6.10

**9/4** Carlowitz (USA), **9/2** Hepburn (IRE)(op 3/1), **5/1** PLEASURE AHEAD, **6/1** Our Topsie(op 10/1), **10/1** Clear Idea (IRE)(op 4/1), **12/1** Grey Dancer, Green's Bonheur, **20/1** Red Bomber(op 8/1), Sunwind, **40/1** Bay Mountain. CSF £15.68, Tote £6.20: £1.50 £1.40 £2.30 (£9.80). Mighty Quinn Racing (II) Limited (UPPER LAMBOURN) bred by Joseph O'Brien. 10 Rn　　　　　　　　　　2m 10.02 (7.02)

SF—3/1/–/–/–/–

| 127 | DAMSON CLAIMING STKS £2324.00 (£644.00: £308.00) | 1m (AWT) | 2-00 (2-06) |
|---|---|---|---|

*77[5]* **Sooty Tern (45)** (JMBradley) 5–8–1 NAdams (6) (lw: led over 2f: led over 4f out: qcknd over 2f out: drvn out) ........................................................ —1
*79\** Tara's Delight (68) (Jt-Fav) (MJRyan) 5–8–0 ‡[3]DBiggs (8) (a.p: chsd wnr over 2f out: hrd rdn over 1f out: r.o) ........................................................ ¾.2
*92[2]* Mac's Fighter (90) (bl) (Jt-Fav) (WAO'Gorman) 7–9–2 ‡[5]EmmaO'Gorman (9) (lw: hdwy over 2f out: rdn over 1f out: unable qckn) ........................ 1.3
*77[6]* Buddy's Friend (IRE) (50) (RJRWilliams) 4–8–3 MHills (1) (hdwy over 1f out: one pce) ........................................................................ 2½.4
*77[3]* Beau Dada (IRE) (54) (JWhite) 4–8–2 GCarter (7) (a.p: one pce fnl 2f) ................. 2½.5
Cone Lane (37) (BGubby) 6–7–13 JQuinn (3) (prom 6f) ........................ 1.6
Harry's Going (40) (RJHodges) 4–7–6 ‡[7]CHawksley (4) (prom over 5f) ............ 8.7
*109* Nazare Blue (43) (MrsBarbaraWaring) 5–8–9 NHowe (2) (b: bhd fnl 3f) ............ 3.8
Saysana (36) (AMoore) 5–8–6 CandyMorris (5) (lw: led over 5f out tl over 4f out: sn wknd) ........................................................................ 1½.9
Chaff (34) (DMorris) 5–8–2 BCrossley (10) (a bhd) ........................ ½.10

**11/8** Tara's Delight, Mac's Fighter, **9/1** Beau Dada (IRE), **16/1** SOOTY TERN, Buddy's Friend (IRE), **50/1** Ors. CSF £36.23, Tote £15.00: £3.20 £1.10 £1.10 £1.10 £2.20 (£24.20). Mr J. M. Bradley (CHEPSTOW) bred by Sheikh Mohammed bin Rashid al Maktoum. 10 Rn; Tara's Delight clmd M McDonnell £9,162　　1m 39.79 (3.09)

SF—16/13/26/5/–/–

| 128 | GREENGAGE H'CAP (0-100) £2531.10 (£699.60: £333.30) | 1m (AWT) | 2-30 (2-32) |
|---|---|---|---|

*86[3]* **Dorset Duke (87)** (GWragg) 5–9–8 WRSwinburn (2) (mde all: all out) ........... —1
*86\** Super Sally (93) (Fav) (MJRyan) 5–9–11 ‡[3]DBiggs (4) (lw: a.p: ev ch fnl 2f: hrd rdn: r.o wl) ........................................................................ s.h.2
*86[5]* Usa Dollar (64) (bl) (BGubby) 5–7–13 JQuinn (3) (a.p: hrd rdn over 1f out: ev ch ins fnl f: r.o wl) ........................................................ hd.3
*86[2]* Mystic Crystal (IRE) (78) (v) (WAO'Gorman) 4–8–8 ‡[5]EmmaO'Gorman (5) (hld up: rdn & ev ch over 2f out: wknd over 1f out) ........................ 12.4
*86* Gulmarg (75) (MHTompkins) 5–8–5[1] ‡[5]CHodgson (1) (plld hrd: a bhd: t.o) ........... 25.5

**6/4** Super Sally, **5/2** DORSET DUKE, **9/2** Mystic Crystal (IRE)(tchd 7/2), **7/1** Usa Dollar, **16/1** Gulmarg(op 8/1). CSF £6.00, Tote £3.60: £2.10 £1.90 (£2.90). Mr G. Wragg (NEWMARKET) bred by Sir Robin McAlpine. 5 Rn　　　　　　　　　　　　　　　　　1m 38.59 (1.89)

SF—56/58/31/4/–

**129** CHERRY H'CAP (3-Y.O) (0-90) £2280.00 (£630.00: £300.00) **7f (AWT)** 3-00 (3-01)

107³ **Try Leguard (IRE) (76)** *(WCarter)* 9-2 GCarter (6) (a.p: led over 1f out: rdn out) —1
105* **Buddy (IRE) (66)** *(MBell)* 7-13 ‡⁷PTurner (8) (lw: a.p: led wl over 1f out: sn hdd: r.o) ³/₄.2
82* **Level Up (61)** *(RGuest)* 7-12 ‡³DBiggs (1) (hdwy wl over 1f out: r.o one pce) 3.3
107* **Energic (IRE) (54)** (Fav) *(CNAllen)* 7-8 GBardwell (7) (led 6f out tl wl over 1f out: sn wknd) 2¹/₄.4
72² **Easy Does it (61)** (v) *(CCElsey)* 8-1 JQuinn (5) (lw: hdwy over 3f out: wknd over 1f out) 2.5
73³ **Up the Punjab (71)** *(SDow)* 8-4 ‡⁷MJermy (3) (led 1f: wknd over 4f out) 1¹/₂.6
104⁶ **High Success (59)** *(WAO'Gorman)* 7-8 ‡⁵BDoyle (4) (a bhd) 2¹/₂.7
**Dancing Beau (IRE) (81)** *(MrsLPiggott)* 9-7 RCochrane (2) (eyeshield: bit bkwd: a bhd) ¹/₂.8

**3/1** Energic (IRE), **4/1** Level Up, **5/1** Buddy (IRE), TRY LEGUARD (IRE), **7/1** Up the Punjab, **8/1** Dancing Beau (IRE), **11/1** Easy Does it, **14/1** High Success. CSF £28.20, CT £99.28. Tote £7.30: £2.10 £1.10 £1.60 (£17.20). Mr J. P. Devaney (EPSOM) bred by D. P. McConnell in Ireland. 8 Rn 1m 26.38 (2.38)
SF—45/26/16/4/5/3

**130** PEACH H'CAP (0-90) £2259.00 (£624.00: £297.00) **5f (AWT)** 3-30 (3-31)
(Weights raised 5 lb)

95* **Sir Tasker (67)** *(JLHarris)* 4–8-10 RCochrane (2) (lw: a.p: led over 2f out: rdn out) —1
80* **Sally's Son (77)** *(WAO'Gorman)* 6–9-1 ‡⁵EmmaO'Gorman (5) (lw: lost pl over 2f out: rallied over 1f out: r.o) 3.2
80² **Very Dicey (81)** (Fav) *(SDow)* 4–9-10 JWilliams (4) (led over 3f out tl over 2f out: unable qckn) ¹/₂.3
113³ **Hinari Video (60)** *(MJohnston)* 7–8-3 RPElliott (6) (lw: lost pl over 2f out: rallied fnl f: r.o) 1.4
95⁴ **Slip-a-Snip (67)** *(GBBalding)* 5–8-5 ‡⁵RPrice (1) (b: led over 1f: wknd over 2f out) 5.5
113 **Greetland Rock (62)** (bl) *(PHowling)* 4–8-5 GCarter (3) (a wl bhd) 5.6

**5/2** Very Dicey, **7/2** Hinari Video, SIR TASKER, **4/1** Sally's Son(3/1—5/1), **5/1** Slip-a-Snip, **14/1** Greetland Rock. CSF £16.87, Tote £4.20: £1.80 £1.30 (£7.70). Mr C. Conway (MELTON MOWBRAY) bred by W. H. Joyce. 6 Rn 59.25 sec (1.05)
SF—55/48/55/30/12/–

**131** PLUM H'CAP (0-70) £2186.80 (£604.80: £288.40) **1¹/₂m (AWT)** 4-00 (4-02)

**Present Times (30)** *(AMoore)* 6–7-11 NAdams (8) (hld up: led 2f out: comf) —1
71² **Plectrum (50)** *(JLSpearing)* 4–8-13 DNicholls (3) (plld hrd: a.p: ev ch 2f out: unable qckn) 1¹/₂.2
77 **Red Dollar (47)** *(BGubby)* 7–9-0 JQuinn (4) (a.p: hrd rdn over 2f out: one pce) 2.3
81 **Tenayestelign (54)** *(DMarks)* 4–9-3 GBaxter (2) (led 10f: one pce) 2¹/₂.4
83⁴ **Adjacent (IRE) (50)** *(MDixon)* 4–8-8 ‡⁵NGwilliams (5) (b.off hind: lw: hdwy fnl 2f: r.o: nvr nrr) s.h.5
97⁵ **Sharp Top (41)** *(MJRyan)* 4–8-1 ‡³DBiggs (11) (a.p: hrd rdn over 2f out: one pce)' 1¹/₂.6
81 **Evening Affair (38)** *(WHolden)* 6–8-5 AMcGlone (9) (b.nr fore: a bhd) 2.7
90* **Mississippi Beat (USA) (45)** (v) *(MPNaughton)* 5–8-7 ‡⁵BDoyle (6) (bhd fnl 9f) hd.8
**Merchant of Venice (65)** *(MHTompkins)* 4–9-7 ‡⁷DavidWilliams (10) (bit bkwd: a bhd) 7.9
110² **El Dominio (64)** (Fav) *(KOCunningham-Brown)* 4–9-13 SWhitworth (1) (b: lw: rdn 5f out: bhd fnl 4f) 3.10
**Burracoppin (45)** *(MrsBarbaraWaring)* 5–8-12 NHowe (7) (b: hdwy 7f out: wknd over 4f out) 4.11

**2/1** El Dominio, **3/1** Mississippi Beat (USA), **11/2** Plectrum(4/1—6/1), **6/1** Sharp Top, **10/1** Adjacent (IRE)(op 6/1), Tenayestelign, PRESENT TIMES, **12/1** Merchant of Venice, **33/1** Red Dollar, Evening Affair, **40/1** Burracoppin. CSF £65.45, CT £1,641.08. Tote £13.70: £3.30 £2.60 £12.10 (£23.00). Mrs S. M. Green (BRIGHTON) bred by Mrs M. Upsdell. 11 Rn 2m 35.38 (5.98)
T/Plpt: £32.50 (48.45 Tckts). AK

120—**SOUTHWELL (L-H)** Fibresand
## Wednesday, February 12th [Standard]
Going Allowance: 5f: 0.25 sec; Rest: 0.35 sec per fur (SL)

**132** DARLTON CLAIMING STKS £2245.60 (£621.60: £296.80) **5f (AWT)** 1-50 (1-52)

58 **Maid Welcome (66)** (bl) *(MrsNMacauley)* 5–8-2 ‡⁷MadeleineSmith (11) (lw: mde all: r.o fnl 2f) —1

58⁵ Gorinsky (IRE) **(79)** *(JBerry)* 4–9–0 JCarroll (10) (a chsng wnr: kpt on one pce fnl f) ........................................................................ 1½.2

58² On the Edge **(83)** (Fav) *(TDBarron)* 4–9–2 AlexGreaves (5) (dwlt: outpcd & bhd tl r.o wl fnl f) ............................................................ 6.3

87 Tigani **(90)** (bl) *(DWChapman)* 6–8–10 ‡⁷SWilliams (7) (a chsng ldrs: one pce fnl 2f) .................................................................... hd.4

Brisas **(60)** (v) *(TFairhurst)* 5–8–11 ‡³JFanning (2) (a chsng ldrs: sn drvn along: no imp fr ½-wy) ..................................................... 1½.5

Lonely Lass **(45)** *(LJBarratt)* 6–7–13 LCharnock (8) (sn drvn along: edgd rt fnl 2f: no imp) ........................................................ nk.6

Hitchin a Ride (v) *(MPMuggeridge)* 5–9–0 RMuggeridge (6) (chsd ldrs: outpcd ½-wy: n.d after) ................................................. 1½.7

87 Wellsy Lad (USA) **(75)** *(DWChapman)* 5–8–12 SWood (12) (lw: broke wl: sn outpcd & bhd: no ch whn hmpd ins fnl f) ................. ½.8

119⁶ The Noble Oak (IRE) **(48)** (bl) *(MMcCormack)* 4–8–9 WNewnes (3) (lw: outpcd after 2f) ................................................................. 1.9

58 Lady of the Fen **(61)** *(MrsNMacauley)* 4–8–2 ‡³DBiggs (1) (lw: racd wd: spd to ½-wy) ........................................................ 4.10

87 Beckingham Ben **(50)** (bl) *(JPLeigh)* 8–8–10 ACulhane (9) (dwlt: a bhd) ................. 1.11

Factuelle **(55)** *(DRTucker)* 5–8–5 NAdams (4) (s.i.s: a bhd) ......................... 3.12

**11/8** On the Edge(2/1—5/4), **5/2** Gorinsky (IRE), **8/1** Hitchin a Ride(op 20/1), **10/1** MAID WELCOME, **11/1** Wellsy Lad (USA), Tigani(op 6/1), **16/1** Brisas, Lady of the Fen(op 10/1), **20/1** Factuelle, Beckingham Ben, Lonely Lass, **25/1** The Noble Oak (IRE). CSF £38.25, Tote £13.50: £2.40 £2.00 £1.40 (£22.80). Mr Stephen Roots (MELTON MOWBRAY) bred by Doublet Ltd. 12 Rn
61.6 sec (3.6)
SF—41/47/25/18/13/–

**133** ASKHAM H'CAP (3-Y-O) (0-80) £2167.20 (£599.20: £285.60) **5f (AWT)** 2-20 (2-22)

113⁶ **Grand Time (57)** *(OJHill)* 7 0 ‡⁷DDiggs (2) (chsd ldrs: led jst ins fnl f: r.o) ................. 1

96* Creche **(88)** (bl) *(MrsNMacauley)* 10-1 NDay (4) (lw: a cl up: led ovr 1f out tl ins fnl f: r.o) ................................................. ½.2

105² Inherent Magic (IRE) **(71)** *(MMcCormack)* 8-12 WNewnes (6) (lw: s.i.s: nt clr run & swtchd after 1f: r.o wl fnl f) ............ 2.3

96² Grubby **(56)** *(RHollinshead)* 7-4(2) ‡⁷AGarth (7) (lw: a chsng ldrs: sn drvn along: kpt on same pce fnl 2f) ................ 1½.4

96³ Ever so Lonely **(62)** (bl) *(ABailey)* 8-3 GCarter (3) (squeezed out s: chsd ldrs: chal 2f out: wknd 1f out) ................. s.h.5

96⁵ It's Only Money **(64)** (bl) *(THCaldwell)* 8-2 ‡³JFanning (8) (led tl hdd & wknd over 1f out) ............................... ½.6

129² Buddy (IRE) **(66)** *(MBell)* 8-0 ‡⁷PTurner (9) (lw: sn outpcd & bhd: hung lft fr ½-wy) 2½.7

105⁵ Fighter Squadron **(55)** (v) *(JAGlover)* 7-10 JQuinn (1) (wnt lft s: a bhd) ................. 1.8

105 Kalar **(52)** *(DWChapman)* 7-7 SWood (5) (sn outpcd & bhd) ......................... hd.9

LONG HANDICAP: Kalar 7-0.

**Evens** Creche(tchd 6/4), **4/1** Buddy (IRE)(9/2—3/1), **13/2** Inherent Magic (IRE), **11/1** It's Only Money, Ever so Lonely, GRAND TIME(8/1—12/1), **12/1** Grubby, **20/1** Kalar, **33/1** Fighter Squadron. CSF £23.01, CT £79.84. Tote £15.10: £2.90 £1.40 £1.80 (£24.90). Mr C. John Hill (BARNSTAPLE) bred by D. Gill. 9Rn
62.6 sec (4.6)
SF—14/46/21/–/–/5/2

**134** BARNBY H'CAP (0-80) £2226.00 (£616.00: £294.00) **1½m (AWT)** 2-50 (2-51)

(Weights raised 5 lb)

88³ **Westfield Moves (IRE) (59)** *(HJCollingridge)* 4–8–13 ‡⁷CHawksley (4) (lw: chsd ldrs: qcknd to ld over 3f out: sn drvn clr) ................ —1

97* Lord Advocate **(49)** (v) (Fav) *(MPNaughton)* 4–8-5 ‡⁵BDoyle (8) (in tch: outpcd appr st: r.o wl fnl 2f) ................................ 3½.2

Irish Native (IRE) **(63)** (bl) *(CASmith)* 4–9–10 AProud (2) (bhd tl hdwy over 2f out: styd on wl) ....................................... 8.3

97 In Truth **(41)** *(DWChapman)* 4–8–2 SWood (1) (lw: mde most tl hdd over 3f out: sn outpcd) ...................................... 1.4

Margs Girl **(56)** *(TFairhurst)* 5–9–4 ‡³JFanning (7) (lw: w ldr tl outpcd 4f out: grad wknd) ............................................ 1.5

114 Dashing April **(47)** *(DTThom)* 4–8–8 JQuinn (3) (chsd ldrs tl wknd over 3f out) .......... 8.6

111 Mai Pen Rai **(45)** *(CJHill)* 4–8–6 NAdams (6) (effrt 5f out: n.d) ..................... 5.7

122⁶ Paulinus **(45)** *(DenysSmith)* 4–8–6 LCharnock (5) (chsd ldrs: sn drvn along: wknd over 4f out) ................................... 2.8

Elhudhud **(51)** (bl) *(DRTucker)* 5–8-9 ‡⁷TanyaMayne (9) (a bhd: t.o) ..................... 9

**5/2** Lord Advocate, **7/2** WESTFIELD MOVES (IRE), **4/1** Margs Girl, **5/1** Irish Native (IRE), **12/1** In Truth, Mai Pen Rai, **14/1** Dashing April, **20/1** Elhudhud, **33/1** Paulinus. CSF £12.21, CT £39.05. Tote £5.20: £1.10 £1.20 £3.10 (£4.00). Mr A. G. Wakley (NEWMARKET) bred by Eugene Matthews in Ireland. 9Rn
2m 46.7 (12.5)
SF—16/1/4/–/–/–/

**135**　　EAST MARKHAM CLAIMING STKS (3-Y.O) £2167.20 (£599.20: £285.60)
　　　　　**7f (AWT)**　　　　　　　　　　　　　　　　　　　　　3-20 (3-22)

98* **Pop to Stans (85)** (Fav) *(TDBarron)* 9-3 AlexGreaves (1) (lw: hld up: c wd & effrt
　　　　ent st: led wl over 1f out: r.o wl) ............................................. —1
85² Little Nod (63) *(MJCamacho)* 7-13 LCharnock (4) (mde most tl hdd wl over 1f out:
　　　　kpt on same pce) ............................................. 8.2
104⁵ Walkonthemoon *(MMcCormack)* 7-11 JQuinn (6) (chsd ldrs: rdn appr st: styd on
　　　　one pce) ............................................. 3½.3
98³ Palacegate King (72) *(JBerry)* 8-9 JCarroll (7) (w ldr tl wknd 2f out) ............ 2½.4
　　　Lord Naskra (USA) *(WAO'Gorman)* 8-5 ‡⁵EmmaO'Gorman (2) (b: lengthy: bit
　　　　bkwd: s.i.s: a bhd) ............................................. 12.5
　　　Injaka Boy (bl) *(KWhite)* 8-2 NAdams (5) (chsd ldrs to st: wknd qckly) ......... 20.6
104 Kashgar *(DWChapman)* 7-7 SWood (3) (bit bkwd: dwlt: a outpcd & bhd) ....... 8.7

**4/5** POP TO STANS, **9/4** Palacegate King, **7/1** Little Nod(op 9/2), **11/1** Lord Naskra (USA)(8/1—12/1), **16/1**
Walkonthemoon, **40/1** Injaka Boy, **100/1** Kashgar. CSF £7.04, Tote £2.40: £1.10 £4.20 (£4.20). Mr W. G.
Spink (THIRSK) bred by Lincoln Collins. 7 Rn　　　　　　　　　　　　　　　　1m 32.4 (5.8)
　　　　　　　　　　　　　　　　　　　　　　　　　　　　　　　　SF—52/10/–/–/–/–

**136**　　FARNDON STKS (Mdn 3-Y.O) £2206.40 (£610.40: £291.20)　**1m (AWT)**　3-50 (3-51)

**Admirals Secret (USA)** *(CFWall)* 9-0 NDay (9) (lw: chsd ldrs: led 2f out: hung lft:
　　　　r.o u.p fnl f) ............................................. —1
123³ Firefighter *(RHollinshead)* 9-0 WRyan (8) (prom tl outpcd 4f out: hdwy 2f out: kpt
　　　　on) ............................................. 2.2
　　　Raaya *(WAO'Gorman)* 8-4 ‡⁵EmmaO'Gorman (4) (leggy: s.i.s: bhd tl hdwy ent st:
　　　　nt qckn fnl f) ............................................. 5.3
91⁶ Court Room (45) (bl) *(AMoore)* 9-0 NAdams (10) (hdwy appr st: sn chsng ldrs:
　　　　one pce fnl 2f) ............................................. 5.4
　　　Trump *(SirMarkPrescott)* 9-0 GDuffield (1) (lengthy: unf: bit bkwd: s.s: sn chsng
　　　　ldrs: outpcd & lost tch 4f out: n.d after) ............................................. 3½.5
78⁶ Elgin (47) (bl) *(ABailey)* 9-0 DNicholls (7) (trckd ldrs: led over 3f out tl hdd 2f out:
　　　　sn wknd) ............................................. 1.6
　　　Boogie Bopper (IRE) (71) (Fav) *(MBell)* 9-0 MHills (3) (lw: disp ld tl hdd over 3f
　　　　out: sn wknd) ............................................. 6.7
94² Well Bought (IRE) *(NAGraham)* 8-9 JQuinn (5) (b.hind: chsd ldrs tl outpcd 4f out:
　　　　sn wknd) ............................................. 1½.8
　　　Loose Zeus (USA) *(CFWall)* 8-7 ‡⁷TWilson (2) (disp ld tl hdd & wknd over 3f out) ½.9

**6/4** Boogie Bopper (IRE), **3/1** Firefighter, **8/1** Well Bought (IRE)(op 4/1), Raaya(op 4/1), Trump(op 4/1), **10/1**
Elgin(op 20/1), **11/1** ADMIRALS SECRET (USA)(op 20/1), **25/1** Loose Zeus (USA), **33/1** Court Room. CSF
£43.66, Tote £14.90: £10.90 £1.60 £1.50 (£72.50). Mr Walter Grubmuller (NEWMARKET) bred by Haras
Santa Maria de Araras & Peter Brant in USA. 9 Rn　　　　　　　　　　　　1m 49.7 (10.4)

**137**　　SOUTHWELL H'CAP (0-70) (Amateurs) £2402.40 (£666.40: £319.20)
　　　　　**1m (AWT)**　　　　　　　　　　　　　　　　　　　　　4-20 (4-24)
　　　　　　　　　　　　　(Weights raised 1 lb)
100² **Ballerina Bay (47)** (v) (Fav) *(DTThom)* 4–11-0 MissIDWJones (13) (in tch: hdwy
　　　　ent st: led over 2f out: sn clr) ............................................. —1
117³ East Barns (IRE) (35) (bl) *(TDBarron)* 4–10-2 MrsAFarrell (11) (effrt appr st: styd
　　　　on u.p) ............................................. 5.2
　　　Buzzards Crest (36) *(BobJones)* 7–9-12 ‡⁵MissDJJones (3) (sn outpcd & wl bhd:
　　　　r.o wl fnl 3f) ............................................. 2½.3
119³ Count Me Out (43) (bl) *(JPearce)* 7–10-10 MrsLPearce (2) (trckd ldrs: effrt ent st:
　　　　swtchd over 1f out: no imp) ............................................. 3½.4
88 Priceless Fantasy (41) *(PatMitchell)* 5–10-3 ‡⁵MissLGlayzer (17) (bhd tl styd on
　　　　wl fnl 3f: nrst fin) ............................................. 1½.5
　　　Great Impostor (50) *(PTWalwyn)* 4–11-3 MrJDurkan (12) (nvr nrr) ............ 4.6
119⁵ Precious Air (IRE) (47) *(AMoore)* 4–10-9 ‡⁵MrKGoble (15) (effrt ent st: nvr trbld
　　　　ldrs) ............................................. 1½.7
86⁶ Predictable (61) (v) *(MrsAKnight)* 6–11-9 ‡⁵MrDSalter (16) (chsd ldrs tl wknd
　　　　over 2f out) ............................................. nk.8
115³ Model Nurse (41) *(MrsAKnight)* 5–10-3 ‡⁵MissEFolkes (4) (chsd ldrs to st) ......... s.h.9
59 Toshiba Comet Too (IRE) (45) (bl) *(WJPearce)* 4–10-7 ‡⁵MrDDurrant (9) (chsd
　　　　ldrs tl wknd 3f out) ............................................. s.h.10
　　　North-West One (IRE) (39) *(HJCollingridge)* 4–10-1 ‡⁵MrPClose (10) (n.d) ......... s.h.11
50 Tyrian Purple (IRE) (48) *(RHollinshead)* 4–11-1 MrsGRees (5) (lw: disp ld tl hdd
　　　　& wknd over 2f out) ............................................. 3.12
117⁵ Beechwood Cottage (59) *(ABailey)* 9–11-7 ‡⁵MrAMcPherson (1) (dwlt: a bhd) ...... ¾.13

Salman (USA) **(50)** *(SGNorton)* 6–11-3　MrSLyons (6) (in tch to st) ...................... ¾.**14**
106⁶ King Ferdinand **(54)** *(DRTucker)* 5–11-2 ‡⁵MissSRowe (7) (n.d) ......................... 2½.**15**
Blake's Treasure **(40)** (v) *(TThomsonJones)* 5–10-7　MissABillot (14) (lw: disp ld
tl hdd & wknd over 2f out) ............................ 1½.**16**
Sidney Smith (IRE) **(51)** *(EHOwenjun)* 4–10-13 ‡⁵MrTMarlow (8) (sn bhd: t.o) ........... **17**

**11/2** BALLERINA BAY, **7/1** Salman (USA), Count Me Out(5/1—8/1), **15/2** Model Nurse, **17/2** East Barns
(IRE)(op 5/1), **10/1** Blake's Treasure, Predictable, **12/1** Great Impostor, **14/1** Beechwood
Cottage(10/1—16/1), Buzzards Crest, **16/1** Tyrian Purple (IRE), Priceless Fantasy, **20/1** Toshiba Comet Too
(IRE), King Ferdinand, Sidney Smith (IRE), Precious Air (IRE), **33/1** North-West One (IRE). CSF £52.45, CT
£595.84. Tote £6.20: £1.20 £3.40 £2.20 £1.50 (£10.80). Mrs Carol Whitwood (NEWMARKET) bred by Mrs
C. Whitwood and N. E. C Sherwood. 17 Rn　　　　　　　　　　　　　　1m 48.8 (9.5)
　　　　　　　　　　　　　　　　　　　　　　　　　　　　　　SF—28/1/–/–/–/–

T/Plpt: £8.50 (185.1 Tckts).　　　　　　　　　　　　　　　　　　　　　　　AA

# SOUTHWELL (L-H) Fibresand
## Friday, February 14th [Standard]
Going Allowance: 0.35 sec per fur (SLW)　　　　　　　　Wind: mod half against

**138**　　SEALED WITH A LOVING KISS H'CAP (0-60) £2402.40 (£666.40: £319.20)
　　　　**1¾m (AWT)**　　　　　　　　　　　　　　　　　　　1-50 (1-52)

114² **Aude la Belle (FR) (47)** *(MrsAKnight)* 4–8-8 ‡³DBiggs (12) (hld up: hdwy 5f out:
2nd st: led over 1f out: r.o wl) ..............................—**1**
122³ Unpaid Member **(47)** *(JWharton)* 8–8-13 ‡³JFanning (11) (prom: led 5f out tl over
1f out: nt qckn) ...............................................2.**2**
114⁵ Shining Wood **(43)** *(ASReid)* 4–8-0⁽¹⁾ ‡⁷KRutter (14) (hdwy 6f out: 3rd st: r.o one
pce tnl 2f) ....................................................1½.**0**
131 Mississippi Beat (USA) **(45)** (v) *(MPNaughton)* 5–8-9 ‡⁵BDoyle (8) (bhd tl gd
hdwy & 5th st: out pce fnl 2f) .............................hd.**4**
103* Bridge Player **(55)** (Fav) *(DMoffatt)* 5–9-3 ‡⁷DarrenMoffatt (5) (lw: a chsng ldrs:
4th st: one pce fnl 2f) ......................................½.**5**
60⁴ Chronological **(59)** (v) *(MHTompkins)* 6–9-7 ‡⁷SMulvey (4) (lw: hld up: rdn 6f out:
nvr nr to chal) ...............................................12.**6**
Norfolk Lass **(40)** *(MCPipe)* 4–8-4　LCharnock (13) (nvr trbld ldrs) ...........................nk.**7**
122* Malenoir (USA) **(55)** (v) *(WJPearce)* 4–9-5 (5x)　DNicholls (6) (bhd fnl 4f) ..........10.**8**
Ballerina Rose **(28)** *(OO'Neill)* 5–7-11　NAdams (9) (bit bkwd: hld up: hdwy 7f out:
wknd 4f out) .................................................2½.**9**
Atlantic Way **(30)** *(CJHill)* 4–7-8　GBardwell (10) (a bhd) .....................................s.h.**10**
Grey Commander **(38)** *(MBrittain)* 4–8-2⁽²⁾　GCarter (1) (bhd fnl 7f) ........................1.**11**
Dale Park **(45)** *(NTinkler)* 6–9-0　KimTinkler (3) (bit bkwd: w ldr tl wknd 6f out) ......nk.**12**
Beaumood **(46)** (bl) *(CTinkler)* 6–9-1　MBirch (15) (eyeshield: lw: prom: rdn 6f
out: 6th & wkng st) .........................................nk.**13**
103 Flitcham **(38)** *(JRBostock)* 5–8-2 ‡⁵RPrice (2) (led 9f: sn hrd rdn & wknd: t.o) .........15.**14**
90⁴ Don't Cry **(45)** *(JDBethell)* 4–8-9　WRyan (7) (t.o) ..........................................8.**15**

**4/1** Bridge Player, **11/2** Malenoir (USA), **7/1** Flitcham, **8/1** Beaumood, Chronological(op 5/1), **12/1** AUDE LA
BELLE (FR), Norfolk Lass, **14/1** Dale Park, Mississippi Beat (USA), **16/1** Don't Cry, Ballerina Rose, Unpaid
Member, **20/1** Shining Wood, Grey Commander, **25/1** Atlantic Way. CSF £177.37, CT £3,443.57. Tote
£6.00: £2.20 £4.60 £4.40 (£69.20). Mrs Val Rapkins (CULLOMPTON) bred by J. P. de Gaste in France. 15
Rn　　　　　　　　　　　　　　　　　　　　　　　　　　　　　3m 13.6 (16)

**139**　　CUPID CLAIMING STKS £2382.80 (£660.80: £316.40)　**1½m (AWT)**　　2-20 (2-23)

88² **Lara's Baby (IRE) (73)** (Fav) *(RAkehurst)* 4–8-10　RCochrane (5) (lw: b.nr fore:
a.p: led 3f out: drvn out) .................................—**1**
120* Le Temeraire **(69)** *(NTinkler)* 6–9-8　KimTinkler (9) (lw: prom: outpcd 4f out: 4th
st: styd on fnl 2f) ...........................................3½.**2**
114* Kirby Opportunity **(56)** *(JPearce)* 4–8-1 ‡⁵RPrice (1) (lw: led 9f: r.o one pce) .............2.**3**
114³ Qualitair Blazer **(54)** *(JRJenkins)* 5–8-10　SWhitworth (2) (b: a.p: 3rd & hrd rdn st:
wknd 2f out) .................................................8.**4**
124 Hamilton Lady (IRE) **(40)** *(DMoffatt)* 4–7-5 ‡⁷DarrenMoffatt (7) (bhd tl some hdwy
fnl 2f: n.d) ...................................................12.**5**
Aldington Noble *(CCTrietline)* 5–8-3 ‡⁵BDoyle (12) (dwlt: some hdwy & poor 6th
st: n.d) .......................................................2½.**6**
120⁵ Little Red Hen *(OO'Neill)* 7–8-1　NAdams (4) (prom tl wknd 6f out: poor 5th st) ..........6.**7**
Northern Vision *(PABlockley)* 5–8-11 ‡⁷JDennis (8) (sme hdwy 7f out: nvr nr ldrs) .....3.**8**
Un Souverain **(27)** *(MCChapman)* 4–8-7 ‡⁷SWilliams (10) (dwlt: a in rr) ...................2½.**9**
Elissa *(GPKelly)* 6–8-7⁽³⁾　DNicholls (6) (bit bkwd: a in rr) ....................................hd.**10**
32 Hannah Brown (IRE) **(25)** *(BAMcMahon)* 4–7-10　LCharnock (11) (bhd fnl 6f: t.o) .....7.**11**

**4/5** LARA'S BABY (IRE), **9/4** Kirby Opportunity(7/4—11/4), **10/1** Qualitair Blazer, Le Temeraire, **33/1** Northern Vision, Little Red Hen, **50/1** Un Souverain, **66/1** Hannah Brown (IRE), **100/1** Ors. CSF £9.31, Tote £1.60: £1.20 £1.90 £1.20 (£6.40). Normandy Developments (London) (EPSOM) bred by Killarkin Stud in Ireland. 11 Rn
         2m 45.7 (11.5)
SF—23/28/3/—/—/—

**140**    LOVE CHANGES EVERYTHING H'CAP (0-90) £2147.60 (£593.60: £282.80)
      6f (AWT)                                  2-50 (2-52)

109⁴ **Toshiba Comet (70)** (bl) *(WJPearce)* 5–9-1 DNicholls (7) (hdwy & 4th st: hrd rdn over 1f out: led last strides) ............................................................. —1

87⁴ Friendly Claim (IRE) **(83)** *(TDBarron)* 4–9-7 ‡⁷VHalliday (4) (lw: 3rd st: led over 1f out tl hdd last strides) ..................................................................... hd.2

Mossy Rose **(56)** *(LordHuntingdon)* 6–7-12 ‡³DBiggs (5) (hdwy & nt clr run 2f out: r.o wl ins fnl f) ................................................................ hd.3

121* Saladan Knight **(60)** (bl) (Fav) *(JGFitzGerald)* 7–7-12 ‡⁷MHunt (1) (eyeshield: lw: hld up: gd hdwy & 5th st: rdn 2f out: r.o one pce) ........................ 2½.4

70 Swinging Lady **(54)** *(WWHaigh)* 4–7-8⁽⁶⁾ ‡⁵FNorton (3) (no hdwy fnl 3f) ........... 3.5

101 State Governor **(60)** *(DWChapman)* 4–8-5 SWood (6) (lw: w ldr: led over 2f out tl over 1f out: wknd fnl f) .......................................................... ½.6

Corn Futures **(71)** *(JPLeigh)* 4–9-2 ACulhane (4) (bit bkwd: hld up: 6th st: wknd over 1f out) ................................................................................ 1½.7

70 Minizen Music (IRE) **(52)** *(MBrittain)* 4–7-4⁽⁴⁾ ‡⁷DWright (2) (led over 3f: 2nd st: sn wknd) ..................................................................... 2.8

Goody Four Shoes **(62)** *(DRTucker)* 4–8-2 ‡⁵RPrice (8) (a bhd: t.o) ................... 7.9

LONG HANDICAP: Swinging Lady 7-4, Minizen Music (IRE) 6-13.

**5/4** Saladan Knight, **11/2** TOSHIBA COMET, **9/1** State Governor, **10/1** Mossy Rose(6/1—11/1), Friendly Claim (IRE), Corn Futures, **14/1** Swinging Lady, **20/1** Minizen Music (IRE), **33/1** Goody Four Shoes. CSF £49.93, CT £468.52. Tote £7.20: £1.90 £1.70 £2.30 (£14.80). Mike Clynes Associates Ltd (HAMBLETON) bred by Mrs Nikki A. Collins. 9 Rn
         1m 18 (4.6)
SF—51/56/32/22/6/15

**141**    SWEET NOTHINGS CLAIMING STKS (3-Y.O) £2049.60 (£565.60: £268.40)
      1m (AWT)                                 3-25 (3-28)

**Mad Militant (IRE) (85)** *(RHollinshead)* 9-2 WRyan (5) (lw: hld up: wnt 2nd st: led 2f out: sn clr) ............................................................. —1

104² Meltonby **(72)** *(CWCElsey)* 8-9 WNewnes (2) (lw: led 6f: rdn & r.o one pce) ...... 4.2

123² Early Star (Fav) *(TDBarron)* 9-2 AlexGreaves (1) (lw: hld up: 3rd st: rdn & wknd over 2f out) ..................................................................... 12.3

123* Bassio (BEL) **(73)** *(CNAllen)* 8-11 ‡⁷MichaelDenaro (4) (lw: chsd ldr tl 4th & wkng st) ...................................................................... 8.4

104 Tamasha **(60)** *(CJHill)* 8-2 NAdams (3) (lost tch 5f out: poor 5th st: t.o) .......... 15.5

**2/1** Early Star, **85/40** Bassio (BEL), **3/1** Meltonby, **5/1** MAD MILITANT (IRE), **20/1** Tamasha. CSF £18.41, Tote £6.10: £2.40 £2.10 (£8.60). Mrs B. Facchino (UPPER LONGDON) bred by Cloghran Stud Farm Co in Ireland. 5 Rn
         1m 45.7 (6.4)
SF—48/29/—/—/—

**142**    PILLOW TALK STKS (Mdn) £2186.80 (£604.80: £288.40)    **1m (AWT)**      3-55 (3-56)

127⁴ **Buddy's Friend (IRE) (50)** *(RJRWilliams)* 4–8-11 MHills (2) (lw: chsd ldrs: wnt 2nd st: led 2f out: drvn out) ....................................................... —1

115⁴ Riviera Rainbow **(57)** *(DRCElsworth)* 4–8-11 WNewnes (3) (lw: bhd tl gd hdwy & 5th st: rdn & edgd lft over 1f out: r.o ins fnl f) ........................ 1½.2

Amphigory (v) (Fav) *(LordHuntingdon)* 4–8-11 WRSwinburn (6) (lw: led 6f: r.o one pce) ....................................................................... nk.3

118³ Sareen Express (IRE) **(30)** (bl) *(MrsJCDawe)* 4–8-8 ‡³JFanning (8) (hld up: hdwy 4th st: wknd 2f out) ................................................. 8.4

Daisy Grey **(32)** (bl) *(ASReid)* 4–7-13 ‡⁷PBowe (7) (prom tl 7th & wkng st) .......... 4.5

120⁴ Porick **(23)** (v) *(DMoffatt)* 4–8-4 ‡⁷DarrenMoffatt (5) (lw: hld up & plld hrd: a bhd) .. 2½.6

79 Replicate **(41)** *(MJCharles)* 4–8-8⁽²⁾ RCochrane (4) (hld up: gd hdwy on ins 4f out: 3rd st: plld out: sn wknd) .................................... 2½.7

Orchanda **(42)** *(MrsAKnight)* 4–8-3 ‡³DBiggs (1) (a bhd) ............................. 5.8

Martini's Courier **(35)** *(REBarr)* 5–8-11 SWebster (10) (b: prom tl 6th & wkng st) .... 1½.9

64 Rockalong **(27)** *(MJCharles)* 7–7-13 ‡⁷SSanders (9) (bhd fnl 4f: t.o) .............. 12.10

**11/10** Amphigory, **7/2** BUDDY'S FRIEND (IRE), **6/1** Riviera Rainbow(op 5/2), **16/1** Sareen Express (IRE), Porick(12/1—20/1), **20/1** Daisy Grey, Orchanda, **33/1** Replicate, Martini's Courier, **50/1** Rockalong. CSF £22.21, Tote £5.40: £1.30 £1.60 £1.20 (£4.90). Mr Colin G. R. Booth (NEWMARKET) bred by John and Mrs McNamara in Ireland. 10 Rn
         1m 46.9 (7.6)
SF—25/20/19/—/—/—

## 143

SAY IT WITH ROSES H'CAP (0-70) £2324.00 (£644.00: £308.00)  **7f (AWT)**  4-25 (4-26)

| | | |
|---|---|---|
| 112[6] | **Kissavos (56)** (v) (CCElsey) 6–9-0 TRogers (10) (b.hind: 4th & carried wd st: hrd rdn 2f out: led cl home) | —1 |
| 92[3] | Pesidanamich (IRE) **(70)** (bl) (TDBarron) 4–10-0 AlexGreaves (9) (a.p: c wd & 2nd st: ev ch over 1f out: rallied ins fnl f) | ¾.2 |
| 112* | Quinzii Martin **(51)** (v) (DHaydnJones) 4–8-9 WNewnes (7) (lw: led tl hdd cl home) | 1.3 |
| 119[4] | Verro (USA) **(35)** (bl) (JABennett) 5–7-7 GBardwell (12) (b: hdwy 3f out: r.o ins fnl f) | nk.4 |
| 101* | Question of Degree **(43)** (bl) (NTinkler) 6–8-1 KimTinkler (4) (hdwy 2f out: r.o ins fnl f) | ½.5 |
| 118[2] | Queen of Dreams **(40)** (DrJDScargill) 4–7-9 ‡3DBiggs (8) (chsd ldr: 2nd st: ev ch 2f out: kpt on fnl f) | ½.6 |
| | Chaplins Club (USA) **(48)** (bl) (DWChapman) 12–8-6 KDarley (11) (bit bkwd: s.i.s: hdwy 3f out: c wd st: r.o fnl f) | ½.7 |
| | Carousella **(56)** (CEBrittain) 4–8-9 ‡5BDoyle (14) (s.i.s: nvr nr to chal) | 1.8 |
| 89* | Foolish Touch **(64)** (Fav) (WJMusson) 10–9-1 ‡7PBowe (1) (b: lw: sn wl bhd: nrst fin) | 1½.9 |
| | Spanish Realm **(45)** (MBrittain) 5–8-3 GCarter (13) (bit bkwd: 6th st: wknd over 2f out) | 1½.10 |
| 121 | Morpick **(54)** (JPLeigh) 5–8-12 ACulhane (6) (lw: prom: sn rdn along: 5th & wknd st) | ½.11 |
| 124 | Sobering Thoughts **(41)** (bl) (DWChapman) 6–7-13 SWood (2) (hmpd after s: hdwy over 3f out: wknd 2f out) | ¾.12 |
| | Thatchenne **(47)** (bl) (PRHedger) 7–8-0 ‡5ATucker (3) (a bhd) | 3½.13 |
| 101 | Carnfield **(41)** (JAGlover) 4–7-8[(6)] ‡5FNorton (5) (7th st: wknd 2f out) | 5.14 |

LONG HANDICAP: Verro (USA) 7-4, Carnfield 7-6.

**4/1** Foolish Touch, **5/1** Question of Degree, **6/1** Quinzii Martin, **8/1** Queen of Dreams(op 12/1), KISSAVOS, Pesidanamich (IRE), **14/1** Carnfield, Verro (USA), Thatchenne, **16/1** Spanish Realm, **20/1** Carousella(op 12/1), Morpick, Chaplins Club (USA)(op 12/1), **25/1** Sobering Thoughts. CSF £68.52, CT £384.62. Tote £10.60: £2.20 £2.20 £2.70 (£21.90). Red Nose Racing bred by Falconet Inc. 14 Rn

1m 33 (6.4)
SF—41/53/31/14/20/12

T/Plpt: £77.20 (20.55 Tckts). KH

---

## Saturday, February 15th [Standard]
Going Allowance: 5f: minus 0.45 sec; Rest: minus 0.20 sec (FS)

## 144

LOVELY MAUREEN TAYLOR CLAIMING STKS  £2304.40 (£638.40: £305.20)
1¼m (AWT)  1-20 (1-24)

| | | |
|---|---|---|
| 126* | **Pleasure Ahead (43)** (MRChannon) 5–7-10 ‡7PTurner (8) (hdwy over 2f out: led ins fnl f: rdn out) | —1 |
| 106[2] | Awesome Power **(60)** (CRNelson) 6–8-8[(1)] RCochrane (1) (hdwy 5f out: led over 1f out tl ins fnl f: unable qckn) | 1½.2 |
| | Paper Craft (MJohnston) 5–8-3 RPElliott (10) (bit bkwd: a.p: led over 3f out tl over 1f out: one pce) | 1½.3 |
| 111[4] | Charming Gift **(42)** (Fav) (RJRWilliams) 5–7-9 ‡7GMitchell (4) (a.p: r.o one pce fnl 2f) | 3½.4 |
| 109 | Anne's Bank (IRE) (AMoore) 4–7-11 ‡3DBiggs (2) (nvr nr to chal) | ½.5 |
| | Absolutely Right **(55)** (RAkehurst) 4–8-5 SDawson (9) (b.nr hind: prom over 7f) | hd.6 |
| 41 | Wileys Folly **(42)** (SDow) 6–8-2 GCarter (6) (lw: prom 8f) | hd.7 |
| 120[2] | Simply Candy (IRE) **(40)** 4–7-9 ‡5FNorton (13) (no hdwy fnl 3f) | 3.8 |
| | Invocation **(35)** (AMoore) 5–8-7 NAdams (5) (lw: led over 6f: wknd over 1f out) | 1½.9 |
| | Applianceofscience **(53)** (bl) (ASReid) 5–8-9 MHills (7) (mid div 8f) | 2.10 |
| | Ergana **(28)** (WHolden) 5–7-12 GBardwell (11) (a bhd) | 15.11 |
| 126 | Red Bomber (KOCunningham-Brown) 4–8-13 WNewnes (3) (b: lw: a bhd) | 2½.12 |
| | Dons-Best-Boy **(44)** (JPearce) 4–7-12 ‡5RPrice (12) (prom over 4f) | 3.13 |

**7/2** Charming Gift, **4/1** Awesome Power(op 9/4), **9/2** PLEASURE AHEAD, **5/1** Absolutely Right, Simply Candy (IRE)(7/2—6/1), **10/1** Wileys Folly, **12/1** Paper Craft, **20/1** Ergana, Applianceofscience, **25/1** Ors. CSF £23.96, Tote £7.10: £1.30 £1.10 £4.00 (£4.70). Mighty Quinn Racing (II) Limited (UPPER LAMBOURN) bred by Joseph O'Brien. 13 Rn; Pleasure Ahead clmd J Daniels £4,250

2m 6.94 (3.94)
SF—23/32/24/9/10/17

**145**

T.I.M. DARLING DIANA STKS (Mdn 3-Y.O) £2284.80 (£632.80: £302.40)
**6f (AWT)**                                                    1-50 (1-53)

> **In the Game (IRE) (57)** *(MissAJWhitfield)* 8-9 NAdams (9) (mde virtually all: rdn out) ............................................................. —1
121 Cellito (IRE) **(53)** (Fav) *(WAO'Gorman)* 8-9 ‡5EmmaO'Gorman (8) (a.p: ev ch over 1f out: unable qckn) ......................................... 3½.2
Oeightnineeight (USA) *(DRCElsworth)* 8-9 RCochrane (2) (eyeshield: unf: bit bkwd: outpcd: hdwy over 2f out: r.o ins fnl f) ................... ½.3
108² Honey Vision **(68)** (bl) *(GHEden)* 8-9 GCarter (3) (a.p: rdn over 3f out: ev ch 2f out: one pce) ................................................... 1.4
82 Ossie **(49)** *(BPalling)* 8-7 ‡7StephenDavies (6) (prom over 2f) ............. 6.5
Ferry Girl (USA) *(DRCElsworth)* 8-9 WNewnes (5) (eyeshield: lt-f: s.s: a bhd) ......... 5.6
96 Camino a Ronda *(PatMitchell)* 8-2 ‡7CHawksley (4) (a bhd) ........... 11½.7
Saruk (IRE) *(JJBridger)* 8-6 ‡3DBiggs (1) (bit bkwd: a bhd) ........... 20.8
113 Easy Delta **(40)** *(CHolmes)* 8-9 SDawson (7) (prom over 2f) ............ 2½.9

7/4 Cellito (IRE)(op 3/1), 9/4 Honey Vision(6/4—5/2), 5/1 Oeightnineeight (USA)(op 5/2), 15/2 IN THE GAME (IRE)(5/1—8/1), 10/1 Ferry Girl (USA)(op 5/1), 16/1 Ossie(12/1—20/1), 20/1 Camino a Ronda, 33/1 Ors. CSF £20.97, Tote £13.70: £5.20 £1.10 £1.30 (£19.00). Mr Andreas Sofroniou (LAMBOURN) bred by Miss Honora Corridan in Ireland. 9 Rn        1m 13.09 (2.49)
SF—21/7/5/1/–/–

**146**

JANET BODEN H'CAP (0-95) £2369.40 (£653.40: £310.20) **1¼m (AWT)**    2-20 (2-21)

115* **Modesto (USA) (62)** *(KOCunningham-Brown)* 4—7-10 ‡3DBiggs (3) (b: lw: mde all: qcknd over 2f out: hrd rdn over 1f out: r.o wl) .......... —1
117⁴ Merseyside Man **(55)** (v) *(DrJDScargill)* 6—7-5(1) ‡3JFanning (4) (hld up: rdn over 2f out: r.o ins fnl f) ....................................... 11½.2
110* Rapporteur (USA) **(89)** (Fav) *(CCElsey)* 6-10-0 WNewnes (1) (b: lw: chsd wnr: rdn over 2f out: unable qckn) ................................. s.h.3
Army of Stars **(81)** *(CEBrittain)* 7—9-1 ‡5BDoyle (2) (lw: hld up: rdn over 3f out: wknd wl over 1f out) .................................... 6.4

LONG HANDICAP: Merseyside Man 7-4.

11/8 Rapporteur (USA), 9/4 MODESTO (USA), 3/1 Army of Stars(tchd 5/1), 8/1 Merseyside Man. CSF £13.86, Tote £2.90 (£14.70). Mr D. Bass (STOCKBRIDGE) bred by Rhydian Morgan-Jones in USA. 4 Rn    2m 7.16 (4.16)
SF—21/13/49/24

**147**

DEBBIE AND LAUREN RUSSELL H'CAP (0-80) £2280.00 (£630.00: £300.00) **1m (AWT)**    2-50 (2-52)

94* **Rosa Why (IRE) (61)** *(WJarvis)* 7-11 ‡5FNorton (4) (outpcd: rdn over 4f out: hdwy over 3f out: led ins fnl f: drvn out) ..................... —1
116³ Sure to Win (IRE) **(63)** (bl) *(ABailey)* 7-11 ‡7PBowe (5) (a.p: led 2f out: rn wd bnd wl over 1f out: sn hdd: r.o ins fnl f) ............... nk.2
Tadora (IRE) **(62)** *(CJBenstead)* 8-3(1) MHills (2) (hld up: rdn over 2f out: swtchd lft over 1f out: r.o one pce) ........................... 11½.3
129* Try Leguard (IRE) **(81)** *(WCarter)* 9-8 GCarter (1) (led 1f: led over 3f out to 2f out: led over 1f out tl ins fnl f: unable qckn) ......... 1.4
62* Dublin Indemnity (USA) **(67)** (bl) (Fav) *(NACallaghan)* 8-1 ‡7JTate (7) (b: b.nr hind: led 7f out tl over 3f out: sn wknd) ................. 8.5
Basilica **(75)** *(CEBrittain)* 8-11 ‡5BDoyle (6) (eyeshield: a wl bhd) ........... 15.6
99² Lady of Letters **(53)** *(TThomsonJones)* 7-8(1) NAdams (3) (prom over 3f) ........... 7.7

LONG HANDICAP: Lady of Letters 7-5.

11/4 Dublin Indemnity (USA), 3/1 Sure to Win (IRE)(op 5/1), Try Leguard (IRE), 4/1 ROSA WHY (IRE)(op 2/1), 9/1 Lady of Letters, 14/1 Basilica, 25/1 Tadora (IRE). CSF £15.96, Tote £4.60: £2.40 £4.20 (£8.70). Mr Jerry Sung (NEWMARKET) bred by Jerry Sung in Ireland. 7 Rn    1m 38.37 (1.67)
SF—33/32/33/49/4/–

**148**

CAROLINE COPEMAN CLAIMING STKS (3-Y.O) £2108.40 (£582.40: £277.20) **1m (AWT)**    3-20 (3-21)

129⁶ **Up the Punjab (68)** (Fav) *(SDow)* 7-7 ‡5FNorton (5) (a.p: led over 2f out: drvn out) —1
54³ Mykindofmusic **(58)** (bl) *(MJHaynes)* 7-10 RFox (8) (s.s: hdwy 4f out: ev ch over 1f out: unable qckn) .......................... 1½.2
91⁵ A Nymph Too Far (IRE) **(55)** *(DrJDScargill)* 7-5 ‡3JFanning (1) (lost pl over 5f out: rallied over 1f out: r.o) ........................... 5.3
123⁴ Patrician Magician **(69)** *(RJRWilliams)* 7-10 ‡3DBiggs (4) (led over 5f) ........... s.h.4

Pace E Salute *(SDow)* 7-13⁽²⁾ ‡⁷MJermy (3) (lw: s.s: nvr nr to chal) .........................3½.5
72⁶ Smudgemupum *(MissBSanders)* 8-7 BCrossley (7) (prom over 4f) ......................... 5.6
Sizzling Rose **(50)** *(WCarter)* 7-12 ‡⁵NGwilliams (2) (hld up: rdn over 2f out: sn
wknd) .................................................................. nk.7
108⁵ Midyanzie *(CHolmes)* 7-12⁽⁴⁾ SDawson (6) (s.s: a bhd: t.o) .................................. dist.8

**5/4** UP THE PUNJAB, **7/2** Patrician Magician, **4/1** Mykindofmusic, **12/1** A Nymph Too Far (IRE), **16/1**
Sizzling Rose, **20/1** Smudgemupum, Pace E Salute, **33/1** Midyanzie. CSF £6.34, Tote £2.30: £1.30 £1.40
£2.10 (£3.10). Mr Ray Hawthorn (EPSOM) bred by Giles W. Pritchard-Gordon. 8 Rn       1m 39.98 (3.28)
SF—5/3/–/–/–/–/

**149**　　　　JACK AND GILL COLE H'CAP (0-80) £2196.00 (£606.00: £288.00)　**5f (AWT)** 3-50 (3-51)

130* **Sir Tasker (76)** (Fav) *(JLHarris)* 4–10-0 RCochrane (5) (lw: chsd ldr: led 2f out:
qcknd over 1f out: drvn out) ........................................ —1
75 Sports Post Lady (IRE) **(60)** *(CJHill)* 4–8-9 ‡³DBiggs (6) (lw: lost pl over 2f out:
rallied fnl f: r.o) ....................................................... 1.2
Ski Captain **(57)** *(PHowling)* 8–8-9 WNewnes (4) (led 3f: unable qckn) ..................... 1.3
119² Rushanes **(61)** *(TCasey)* 5–8-13 GCarter (3) (outpcd: hdwy fnl f: r.o) .............. nk.4
113* Meeson Times **(68)** *(BEllison)* 4–9-6 MHills (2) (outpcd: rdn over 3f out: nvr nr to
chal) ....................................................................... 1½.5
119* Courting Newmarket **(56)** *(MrsAKnight)* 4–8-8 AlexGreaves (1) (outpcd) ................ 2.6

**2/1** SIR TASKER, **5/2** Sports Post Lady (IRE)(op 4/1), **7/2** Meeson Times(op 9/4), **11/2** Rushanes, **10/1**
Courting Newmarket(6/1—12/1), **14/1** Ski Captain(op 8/1). CSF £7.33, Tote £3.00: £1.20 £2.60 (£4.60). Mr
C. Conway (MELTON MOWBRAY) bred by W. H. Joyce. 6 Rn                              58.66 sec (0.46)
SF—60/37/33/36/37/17

T/Plpt: £17.45 (12.65 Tckts).　　　　　　　　　　　　　　　　　　　　　　　　　　　AK

## 144—**LINGFIELD (L-H)** Equitrack
### Tuesday, February 18th [Standard]
Going Allowance: minus 0.20 sec per fur (FS)

**150**　　　　DOROTHY L. SAYERS STKS (Mdn) £2030.00 (£560.00: £266.00)　**5f (AWT)** 1-50 (1-51)

102³ **Galaxy Express (43)** *(GHEden)* 4–9-0 ‡⁷PTurner (3) (mde all: r.o) ................. —1
61⁶ Indigo Blue (IRE) **(53)** (Fav) *(NACallaghan)* 3–8-1 GCarter (4) (b.hind: w wnr: ev
ch over 1f out: wknd) ................................................. 2.2
49 Our Amber **(38)** *(DWChapman)* 5–9-2 SWood (2) (a same pl: one pce fnl 2f) ............ 5.3
Caerulia **(32)** (bl) *(WJPearce)* 4–8-11 ‡⁵BDoyle (1) (s.s: a last) ................................. 2.4

**4/6** Indigo Blue, (IRE), **6/4** GALAXY EXPRESS, **10/1** Our Amber, **25/1** Caerulia. CSF £2.90, Tote £2.70
(£1.40). Mr M. F. Eden (NEWMARKET) bred by D. Lowe. 4 Rn                          60.68 sec (2.48)
SF—30/9/4/–

**151**　　　　HELEN McINNES CLAIMING STKS (3-Y.O) £2088.80 (£576.80: £274.40)
　　　　　　　**6f (AWT)**　　　　　　　　　　　　　　　　　　　　　　　　　　2-20 (2-22)

108* **Summer Express** *(JLSpearing)* 8-13 DNicholls (3) (a.p: led over 2f out: all out) ...... —1
133* Grand Time **(57)** (Jt-Fav) *(CJHill)* 8-5 ‡³DBiggs (4) (hld up: ev ch fnl f: no ex) ....... hd.2
105⁴ Appealing Times (USA) **(72)** (Jt-Fav) *(WAO'Gorman)* 8-8 ‡⁵EmmaO'Gorman (5)
(outpcd: hdwy over 1f out: nrst fin) ............................... 1½.3
82⁴ Do the Business (IRE) **(51)** *(CNAllen)* 7-12⁽¹⁾ ‡⁷GForster (3) (one pce fnl 2f) ........... hd.4
72⁴ Shocking Times **(65)** *(RSimpson)* 7-13⁽¹⁾ ‡⁵ATucker (2) (led over 3f: ev ch ins fnl f:
wknd nr fin) ............................................................ 1½.5
Rocky Bay **(44)** *(DHaydnJones)* 8-2 AMackay (1) (w ldr over 2f: sn wknd) ............. 10.6

**9/4** Grand Time, Appealing Times (USA), **100/30** SUMMER EXPRESS, **5/1** Shocking Times, **16/1** Do the
Business (IRE)(10/1—20/1), **25/1** Rocky Bay. CSF £10.55, Tote £3.50: £6.50 £1.40 (£1.90). Mr Graham
Treglown (ALCESTER) bred by Aramstone Stud Co. 6 Rn                               1m 14.57 (3.97)

**152**　　　　EVELYN ANTHONY H'CAP (0-90) £2531.10 (£699.60: £333.30)　**7f (AWT)**　2-50 (2-51)

**Pytchley Night (89)** *(DMorris)* 5–9-7 ‡⁷StephenDavies (3) (lw: hld up: led over 2f
out: hld on wl) ....................................................... —1
130² Sally's Son **(83)** (Fav) *(WAO'Gorman)* 6–8-12 (5x) ‡⁵EmmaO'Gorman (4) (lw:
a.p: hmpd wl over 1f out: r.o wl ins fnl f) ..................... ½.2
121 Say You Will **(58)** (v) *(MPNaughton)* 8–7-6⁽⁴⁾ ‡⁵BDoyle (6) (hdwy 3f out: hrd rdn:
r.o one pce) ........................................................... 3.3

113 Murmuring **(60)** (SDow) 6–7–10 ‡3DBiggs (1) (prom over 4f) ............................. 2.4
41 Tapestry Dancer **(54)** (MJHaynes) 4–7-7 RFox (5) (a bhd) ........................... 2¹/₂.5
92⁵ Second Adventure **(59)** (bl) (DJGMurray-Smith) 4–7-12 CRutter (2) (led over 4f) 6.6
LONG HANDICAP: Say You Will 6-7, Tapestry Dancer 5-13.
*Stewards Enquiry: Obj. to Pytchley Night by Emma O'Gorman overruled.*

5/4 Sally's Son(4/5—11/8), 9/4 PYTCHLEY NIGHT, 7/1 Murmuring, Say You Will, 10/1 Second Adventure, 50/1
Tapestry Dancer. CSF £5.22, Tote £4.20: £3.50 £2.20 (£2.40). Mr J. J. Higgins (NEWMARKET) bred by G. W.
Robinson. 6 Rn
1m 25.66 (1.66)
SF—61/50/21/19/8/–

**153**
MARGERY ALLINGHAM H'CAP (0-70) £2343.60 (£649.60: £310.80)
**1m (AWT)**
3-20 (3-23)

117* Sarum **(49)** (CPWildman) 6–9-1 CRutter (7) (a.p: led wl over 1f out: drvn out) ........ —1
101³ Mca Below the Line **(62)** (bl) (WJPearce) 4–10-0 DNicholls (4) (a.p: swtchd
outside over 1f out: r.o wl ins fnl f) ............................... 2.2
142⁴ Sareen Express (IRE) **(40)** (bl) (MrsJCDawe) 4–8-1 ‡⁵ATucker (6) (swtg: w ldrs:
ev ch 2f out: r.o one pce) ............................... nk.3
126⁴ Sunwind **(35)** (RJHodges) 6–7-8 ‡7CHawksley (8) (lw: a.p: rdn over 2f out: r.o one
pce) ............................... 2.4
117² Sunset Street (IRE) **(60)** (Fav) (SDow) 4–9-12 TQuinn (1) (led over 4f out tl wl
over 1f out) ............................... 2¹/₂.5
143⁶ Queen of Dreams **(40)** (DrJDScargill) 4–8-3 ‡3DBiggs (3) (lw: mid div whn bdly
hmpd over 4f out: nt rcvr) ............................... ¾.6
121 Damaaz (IRE) **(40)** (v) (JSWainwright) 4–8-1 ‡⁵SMaloney (2) (lw: a bhd) ........ 2¹/₂.7
Dutch Czarina **(47)** (MissBSanders) 4–8-13 WNewnes (11) (a bhd) ............... 12.8
118* Sauvignon (IRE) **(59)** (RGuest) 4–9-11 NDay (9) (a bhd) ............................. 2¹/₂.9
Deepwood Nanusket **(34)** (MMadgwick) 6–8-0 SDawson (5) (led over 3f) ........... hd.10
Mazin **(33)** (CJBenstead) 4–7-8⁽¹⁾ ‡⁵FNorton (10) (b: a bhd: t.o fnl 3f) ............... 10.11

5/2 Sunset Street (IRE), 4/1 Sauvignon (IRE), SARUM, 5/1 Mca Below the Line, 10/1 Queen of
Dreams(8/1—12/1), 11/1 Sunwind, 14/1 Dutch Czarina(10/1—16/1), Sareen Express (IRE), 33/1 Ors. CSF
£24.18, CT £232.81. Tote £5.10: £1.40 £3.10 £5.60 (£25.40). Mr W. Wildman (SALISBURY) bred by Miss
Suzannah Armstrong. 11 Rn
1m 40.28 (3.58)
SF—23/30/2/–/13/–

**154**
AGATHA CHRISTIE H'CAP (0-70) £2284.80 (£632.80: £302.40)
**1¼m (AWT)**
3-50 (3-54)
(Weights raised 3 lb)

146² **Merseyside Man (51)** (v) (DrJDScargill) 6–9-1 ‡7KRutter (3) (a.p: led 3f out: r.o
wl) ............................... —1
115³ Foursingh **(52)** (bl) (CBBBooth) 4–9-7 ACulhane (4) (a.p: ev ch over 1f out: nt
qckn) ............................... 2¹/₂.2
131 Evening Affair **(34)** (bl) (WHolden) 6–8-5 TQuinn (5) (a.p: ev ch 2f out: one pce) ... ¹/₂.3
144* Pleasure Ahead **(48)** (Fav) (MDixon) 5–9-0 (5x) ‡⁵NGwilliams (8) (s.s: rdn over 3f
out: nrst fin) ............................... 2¹/₂.4
126 Clear Idea (IRE) **(35)** (CRNelson) 4–7-13 ‡⁵FNorton (12) (b: lw: a.p: led over 4f
out to 3f out) ............................... 2¹/₂.5
124 D'Altagnan **(35)** (SMellor) 6–9-1 DanaMellor (1) (lw: nvr nr to chal) ............ 2¹/₂.6
115 Crown Reserve **(44)** (MJRyan) 4–8-13 JMcLaughlin (10) (prom 6f) ............... 1.7
Rarfy's Dream **(50)** (JEBanks) 4–8-12 ‡7JSwinnerton (9) (lw: s.s: a bhd) ........ 4.8
118⁶ Skip Tracer **(35)** (KTIvory) 4–8-4 NAdams (11) (led over 5f: t.o) ............... 15.9
Luks Akura **(44)** (MJohnston) 4–8-6 ‡7MBaird (2) (bit bkwd: a bhd: t.o) ......... 2.10
Red Sparky **(35)** (WJPearce) 4–8-4 SWebster (6) (bhd fnl 5f: t.o) ............... 25.11
90 Littledale (USA) (9/2) Withdrawn (kicked at s) : not under orders

9/4 Pleasure Ahead, 5/2 MERSEYSIDE MAN, 6/1 Foursingh, Crown Reserve, 8/1 Evening Affair, Rarfy's
Dream, 16/1 Luks Akura, Clear Idea (IRE), 20/1 D'Altagnan, 33/1 Ors. CSF £19.39, CT £103.50. Tote £3.00:
£1.10 £1.20 £4.50 (£16.80). Mrs Susan Scargill (NEWMARKET) bred by A. G. Martin. 11 Rn
2m 6.54 (3.54)
SF—46/47/30/34/14/25

**155**
GEORGETTE HEYER H'CAP (0-60) £2324.00 (£644.00: £308.00)
**1½m (AWT)**
4-20 (4-23)

103⁵ Gilbert's Girl **(33)** (CJHill) 5–8-4 TQuinn (4) (a.p: hrd rdn over 1f out: r.o to ld last
strides) ............................... —1
131⁴ Tenayestelign **(51)** (DMarks) 4–9-5 GBaxter (12) (a.p: led over 3f out tl last
strides) ............................... s.h.2
131* Present Times **(34)** (Fav) (AMoore) 6–8-5 NAdams (5) (hld up: ev ch over 1f out:
nt qckn) ............................... 2¹/₂.3

125* Heir of Excitement **(34)** *(APStringer)* 7–8–0 ‡⁵FNorton (9) (lw: prom tl outpcd over 2f out: r.o fnl f) ............ 1.4

125 Mr Wishing Well **(53)** *(RJRWilliams)* 6–9–5 ‡⁵CHodgson (14) (hdwy over 3f out: one pce fnl 2f) ............ ¾.5

126³ Our Topsie **(31)** *(FJO'Mahony)* 5–7–11 ‡⁵NGwilliams (10) (b.nr fore: nvr nr to chal) ............ 2.6

115⁵ Little Big **(35)** (bl) *(BJCurley)* 5–8–6 WRyan (2) (lw: led tl wknd over 3f out) ............ 1½.7

134² Lord Advocate **(49)** (v) *(MPNaughton)* 4–8–12 ‡⁵BDoyle (13) (bhd & rdn along: nrst fin) ............ 1.8

Broughton Blues (IRE) **(49)** *(WJMusson)* 4–9–3 MWigham (8) (a bhd) ............ 2.9

83 Wise Friend (USA) **(32)** *(CPWildman)* 4–8–0 CRutter (1) (a wl bhd) ............ 3½.10

131² Plectrum **(51)** *(JLSpearing)* 4–9–5 DNicholls (6) (chsd ldr tl wknd qckly over 3f out) ............ nk.11

131³ Red Dollar **(46)** *(BGubby)* 7–9–0 ‡³DBiggs (3) (b.hind: lw: bhd fnl 4f) ............ 3.12

115 Kreischim (IRE) **(36)** *(MMadgwick)* 4–7–13⁽¹⁾ ‡⁵ATucker (7) (a bhd) ............ 13

**11/4** Present Times, **7/2** Plectrum(7/1—8/1), **6/1** Little Big(3/1—9/1), Heir of Excitement, **7/1** Mr Wishing Well, **15/2** Lord Advocate(5/1—8/1), **8/1** Tenayestelign, **14/1** Red Dollar, Broughton Blues (IRE), Our Topsie, **20/1** GILBERT'S GIRL, **33/1** Kreischim (IRE), **50/1** Wise Friend (USA). CSF £180.66, CT £546.22. Tote £19.50: £9.10 £2.80 £3.80 (£124.20). Mr A. G. Newcombe (BARNSTAPLE) bred by T. Newcombe. 13 Rn
2m 33.87 (4.47)
SF—21/35/16/9/26/–

T/Plpt: £71.20 (19 Tckts).                                                                      Hn

# CAGNES-SUR-MER (L-H)
## Wednesday, February 12th [Firm]

**156a**    PRIX DU LOGIS DU PIN (Mdn 3-Y.O) F5160.00  **1m**

**Social Revolution (USA)** *(France)* 3–8–8 AJunk ............ —1
Clever Chap (USA) (bl) *(France)* 3–8–11 RLaplanche ............ nk.2
Sweet N'Bubbly (USA) *(France)* 3–8–4 ‡⁵TMajorcryk ............ 1.3
FLIGHT LIEUTENANT (USA) *(PMitchell)* 3–8–11 BRaymond (btn further nk) ............ 5
Tote 7.60f: 2.00f 2.00f 1.90f (16.00f). Mr C. Bauer (C. Bauer, FRANCE) bred by High Line Management Ltd. in USA. 14 Rn                                                                      1m 42.8

# 132—SOUTHWELL (L-H) Fibresand
## Friday, February 21st [Standard]
Going Allowance: 0.30 sec per fur (SL)

**157**    NEW HOUGHTON STKS (Mdn 3-Y.O) £2226.00 (£616.00: £294.00)
**7f (AWT)**                                                              2-10 (2-14)

**Native Idol (USA)** *(JRFanshawe)* 9–0 WRSwinburn (12) (small: sn trckng ldrs: led over 2f out: sn clr) ............ —1
Qualitair Idol *(JFBottomley)* 8–9 GBardwell (1) (w'like: sn bhd: hdwy over 2f out: r.o ins fnl f) ............ 7.2
37 Peace Formula (IRE) **(60)** *(RHollinshead)* 9–0 WRyan (3) (mid-div tl styd on fnl f) ............ 2.3
98⁵ Forza Azzurri (IRE) **(48)** *(MrsNMacauley)* 9–0 NDay (7) (led tl over 4f out: one pce fnl 2f) ............ s.h.4
Keen Wit (Jt-Fav) *(LordHuntingdon)* 8–9 LDettori (2) (unf: scope: bit bkwd: hld up: effrt over 2f out: kpt on fnl f) ............ 1½.5
96⁶ First Gold *(JWharton)* 8–11 ‡³JFanning (4) (stdy hdwy over 2f out: hmpd 1f out: nvr plcd to chal) ............ 1½.6
136³ Raaya (Jt-Fav) *(WAO'Gorman)* 8–4 ‡⁵EmmaO'Gorman (11) (chsd ldr: led over 4f out tl over 2f out: sn wknd) ............ ¾.7
Swynford Flyer *(JFBottomley)* 8–9 GCarter (9) (leggy: s.i.s: sn chsng ldrs: lost pl 3f out) ............ 1½.8
108³ Telegraphic *(MBell)* 9–0 MHills (5) (bit bkwd: hmpd & lost pl after 2f: n.d after) ............ 2.9
Efharisto *(CEBrittain)* 8–9 ‡⁵BDoyle (10) (bit bkwd: nvr nr ldrs) ............ 4.10
145⁵ Ossie **(49)** *(BPalling)* 8–7 ‡⁷StephenDavies (8) (chsd ldrs tl wknd qckly 3f out: sn bhd) ............ 20.11
Bitmac Boy *(MrsPABarker)* 9–0 SWebster (6) (chsd ldrs 3f: sn bhd) ............ 1.12

**7/2** Keen Wit, Raaya(op 7/1), **4/1** NATIVE IDOL (USA)(op 5/4), **11/2** Efharisto(5/2—6/1), **9/1** Telegraphic(4/1—10/1), **12/1** Peace Formula (IRE), **20/1** First Gold, **25/1** Ossie, Qualitair Idol, **33/1** Ors. CSF £82.89, Tote £4.40: £2.70 £8.00 £2.60 (£155.10). Mr David Thompson (NEWMARKET) bred by Cheveley Park Stud in USA. 12 Rn                                                          1m 34.5 (7.9)
SF—13/–/–/–/–/–

**158**    MAPLEBECK CLAIMING STKS  £2284.80 (£632.80: £302.40)   1m (AWT)  2-40 (2-43)

    Battle Standard (CAN) (CTinkler) 5–8-8 MBirch (12) (trckd ldrs: led over 2f out:
        r.o u.p fnl f) ................................................................ —1
106* Euroblake (75) (Fav) (TDBarron) 5–8-6 AlexGreaves (7) (lw: hdwy over 3f out:
        rdn to chal 2f out: nt qckn fnl f) ................................ 2.2
    Merchant House (IRE) (WHolden) 4–7-13 NAdams (5) (led after 2f tl wknd over 2f
        out) ................................................................................ 8.3
  40 Chloes Diamond (IRE) (57) (JLSpearing) 4–7-10 ‡³JFanning (8) (effrt over 3f out:
        styd on same pce fnl 2f) .......................................... ¾.4
    Green's Seago (USA) (67) (JLHarris) 4–7-13 ‡⁵FNorton (11) (lw: a chsng ldrs: no
        imp fnl 3f) ........................................................................ ½.5
137⁶ Great Impostor (50) (PTWalwyn) 4–7-10 ‡³DBiggs (1) (chsd ldrs tl grad wknd fnl
        2f) ................................................................................ ¾.6
    Tipperary Azul (IRE) (MHTompkins) 4–8-9 RCochrane (4) (bit bkwd: s.s: bhd tl
        kpt on u.p fnl 2f) ...................................................... hd.7
    Mofador (GER) (74) (FHLee) 8–8-8 RLappin (6) (bkwd: led after 1f to 6f out:
        wknd over 2f out) ........................................................ 2.8
  124 Pilar (40) (MrsNMacauley) 4–7-9 ‡⁷MadeleineSmith (9) (chsd ldrs tl wknd over 2f
        out) ............................................................................ 1½.9
106 Armaiti (66) (DRTucker) 4–8-0 GBardwell (2) (nvr nr ldrs) ................................ 2½.10
    Gemdoubleyou (FJordan) 4–7-5 ‡⁷CHawksley (3) (s.s: a bhd) ................................ 5.11
    Escape Talk (20) (JDooler) 5–7-11 RFox (10) (sn wl bhd) ................................ 2½.12
  59 Bell Turret (26) (AWPotts) 5–8-2 AProud (14) (a in rr) ................................ 2.13
    Red and Gold (NZ) (MrsSOliver) 9–8-2 AMackay (13) (in tch 3f: sn wl bhd: t.o) ......... 14

**5/6** Euroblake(Evens—4/6), **6/1** Mofador (GER), **8/1** Great Impostor(12/1—14/1), **12/1** BATTLE STANDARD
(CAN)(op 5/1), **14/1** Green's Seago (USA), Tipperary Azul (IRE)(op 6/1), **16/1** Armaiti, **20/1** Chloes Diamond
(IRE), Pilar, **33/1** Merchant House (IRE), **50/1** Gemdoubleyou, Escape Talk, Bell Turret, **100/1** Red and Gold
(NZ). CSF £21.94, Tote £14.70: £2.80 1.40 £19.80 (£14.90). Mr Steven Astaire (MALTON) bred by
Brushwood Stable in Canada. 14 Rn              1m 47.2 (7.9)
                                        SF—12/4/–/–/–/–

**159**    LAXTON H'CAP I (0-70)  £2128.00 (£588.00: £280.00)   6f (AWT)   3-10 (3-12)

132⁵ Brisas (60) (bl) (TFairhurst) 5–9-1 ‡³JFanning (3) (mde most: clr 1f out: unchal) ...... —1
143² Pesidanamich (IRE) (70) (bl) (Fav) (TDBarron) 4–10-0 AlexGreaves (5) (chsd
        ldrs: brought v.wd ent st: sn rdn: wknd fnl f) ................................ 6.2
121² Miss Calculate (59) (CaptJWilson) 4–9-3 JFortune (4) (chsd ldrs: one pce fnl 2f) ...... 4.3
134⁶ Dashing April (45) (v) (DTThom) 4–8-0 ‡³DBiggs (1) (sn wl bhd a drvn along) ............ 2.4
121 Strip Cartoon (IRE) (52) (bl) (SRBowring) 4–8-3⁽¹⁾ ‡⁷MHarris (6) (disp ld after 1f tl
        over 3f out: wknd 2f out) ........................................ 1.5
121 Miss Bell Ringer (42) (CJHill) 4–8-0 NAdams (2) (lw: s.s: a bhd) ...................... 2½.6

**7/4** Pesidanamich (IRE)(5/4—2/1), **11/4** Miss Calculate, **11/2** BRISAS, **7/1** Miss Bell Ringer(op 4/1), **15/2**
Strip Cartoon (IRE)(5/1—8/1), **16/1** Dashing April. CSF £14.34, Tote £7.30: £2.70 £1.70 (£5.70). Mr Brian
Cann (MIDDLEHAM) bred by Mrs J. E. Young. 6 Rn             1m 18.3 (4.9)
                                     SF—39/28/1/–/–/–

**160**    HARDWICK H'CAP (3-Y.O)(0-90) £2049.60 (£565.60: £268.80)   7f (AWT)   3-40 (3-40)

107⁵ Brotherlyaffection (63) (RHollinshead) 7-6⁽⁶⁾ ‡⁷MHumphries (1) (lw: trckd ldr:
        kpt on fnl f: led nr fin) ............................................ —1
129⁴ Energic (IRE) (61) (CNAllen) 7-6⁽⁴⁾ ‡⁵BDoyle (3) (b.off hind: led: rdn a edgd rt 2f
        out: jst ct) ................................................................ hd.2
    By Hand (80) (Jt-Fav) (WJHaggas) 9-2 MHills (2) (trckd ldrs: effrt over 2f out:
        wknd 1f out) ............................................................ 4.3
135* Pop to Stans (92) (Jt-Fav) (TDBarron) 10-0 (7x) AlexGreaves (4) (chsd ldrs:
        brought wd ent st: sn rdn: btn wl over 1f out) ................ 2½.4
        LONG HANDICAP: Brotherlyaffection 7-6, Energic (IRE) 7-3.

**2/1** Pop to Stans(op 4/5), By Hand, **3/1** Energic (IRE)(4/1—5/1), **9/2** BROTHERLYAFFECTION. CSF £15.48,
Tote £5.40 (£3.20). Mrs R. Hollinshead (UPPER LONGDON) bred by W. H. A. Dodds. 4 Rn  1m 33.3 (6.7)
                                       SF—9/8/20/24

**161**    KIRKBY-IN-ASHFIELD APP'CE H'CAP (0-90) £2128.00 (£588.00: £280.00)
    1½m (AWT)                                  4-10 (4-11)

    Horizon (IRE) (67) (bl) (TThomsonJones) 4–8-11 DBiggs (5) (lw: mde all: clr 2f
        out: eased towards fin) ............................................ —1
146⁴ Army of Stars (81) (CEBrittain) 7–10-0 BDoyle (6) (a chsng wnr: kpt on u.p fnl 2f:
        no imp) ...................................................................... 3.2

124[5] Pims Classic **(57)** *(WJHaggas)* 4–7–10 ‡[5]SallyRadford-Howes (3) (effrt 5f out: kpt on same pce fnl 2f) ....................................................................................... 4.3

134* Westfield Moves (IRE) **(66)** (Fav) *(HJCollingridge)* 4–8–7 (7x) ‡[3]CHawksley (1) (lw: effrt 5f out: sn drvn along & no imp) ........................................................ 4.4

134[5] Margs Girl **(56)** *(TFairhurst)* 5–8–3 JFanning (2) (effrt 5f out: rdn & wknd over 2f out) ..................................................................................................... 2½.5

Admiral's Mistress (IRE) **(60)** *(PJMakin)* 4–8–4 TSprake (8) (bit bkwd: gd hdwy 5f out: wknd over 2f out: fin tired) ..................................................................... 8.6

Thrill **(50)** *(KGWingrove)* 4–7–8[(1)] FNorton (4) (b: bit bkwd: chsd ldrs tl wknd 6f out: sn wl bhd) .................................................................................... 12.7

Count Barachois (USA) **(69)** *(DMorris)* 4–8–13 StephenDavies (7) (drvn along & lost pl 7f out: sn bhd) .................................................................................... 7.8

LONG HANDICAP: Thrill 6-12.

**13/8** Westfield Moves (IRE)(5/2—6/4), **5/1** HORIZON (IRE), **6/1** Margs Girl, **13/2** Admiral's Mistress (IRE)(op 4/1), **7/1** Army of Stars, **16/1** Count Barachois (USA), Pims Classic, **50/1** Thrill. CSF £33.60, CT £413.92. Tote £5.60: £1.60 £1.30 £3.00 (£16.20). Mrs Solna Thomson Jones (UPPER LAMBOURN) bred by Mrs Nuala Clarke in Ireland. 8 Rn    2m 43.8 (9.6)
SF—37/48/8/11/2/–

**162**    LAXTON H'CAP (II) (0-70)  £2108.40 (£582.40: £277.20)    **6f (AWT)**    4-40 (4-41)

Orient Air **(60)** (bl) *(TDBarron)* 4–10–0 AlexGreaves (5) (mde all: clr over 1f out: rdn out) ....................................................................................................... —1

140[5] Swinging Lady **(45)** *(WWHaigh)* 4–8–8 ‡[5]FNorton (2) (a chsng wnr: rdn 2f out: kpt on) ................................................................................................................. 4.2

137[4] Count Me Out **(44)** (Fav) *(JPearce)* 7–8–7 ‡[5]RPrice (6) (s.i.s: bhd tl styd on u.p fnl 2f: nvr nr to chal) ..................................................................................... 2.3

Sir Arthur Hobbs **(60)** *(FHLee)* 5–10–0 RLappin (4) (bit bkwd: chsd ldrs tl rdn & wknd over 1f out) ................................................................................................ 4.4

142 Rockalong **(27)** *(MJCharles)* 7–7–9 NAdams (7) (chsd ldrs tl wknd over 2f out: sn bhd) ........................................................................................................ 20.5

132 Factuelle **(56)** *(DRTucker)* 5–9–10 GBardwell (1) (sn outpcd & bhd) .................. 4.6

The Huyton Lady **(32)** (bl) *(MBJames)* 4–8–0 AMackay (3) (bit bkwd: chsd ldrs tl rdn & wknd over 3f out: sn wl bhd) ........................................................... 15.7

**85/40** Count Me Out(7/2—2/1), **7/2** Swinging Lady, **5/1** ORIENT AIR(3/1—6/1), Sir Arthur Hobbs(op 6/4), **7/1** Factuelle, **25/1** The Huyton Lady, **33/1** Rockalong. CSF £19.90, Tote £6.80: £3.40 £2.10 (£15.70). Mrs I. M. Raine (THIRSK) bred by Mrs I. M. Raine. 7 Rn    1m 18.7 (5.3)
SF—44/12/3/8/–/–

T/Plpt: £1,469.30 (0.85 Tckts); £297.84 to Kempton 22/2/92.    WG

150—**LINGFIELD (L-H)** Equitrack

## Saturday, February 22nd [Standard]
Going Allowance: minus 0.20 sec per fur (FS)

**163**    NEEDLES H'CAP (0-70) £2304.40 (£638.40: £305.20)    **5f (AWT)**    2-10 (2-11)

149[4] **Rushanes (61)** *(TCasey)* 5–9–9 ‡[5]FNorton (4) (led 1f: led ins fnl f: all out) ................ —1

145[2] Cellito (IRE) **(54)** (bl) *(WAO'Gorman)* 3–8–1 ‡[5]EmmaO'Gorman (9) (hld up: hdwy over 1f out: str run fnl f: fin wl) ............................................................. s.h.2

85[6] Doesyoudoes **(65)** (v) *(DTThom)* 3–8–9 RCochrane (2) (hrd rdn & hdwy over 1f out: ev ch fnl f: r.o wl) ...................................................................................... hd.3

95[5] Pendor Dancer **(52)** (bl) *(BForsey)* 3–8–0 SWhitworth (7) (swtg: chsd ldr over 3f out: ev ch ins fnl f: r.o wl) ...................................................................................... hd.4

130[4] Hinari Video **(58)** (Jt-Fav) *(MJohnston)* 7–9–11 RPElliott (3) (lost pl 3f out: rallied ins fnl f: fin wl) ................................................................................................... 1½.5

133[6] It's Only Money **(61)** (bl) *(THCaldwell)* 3–8–6 ‡[7]StephenDavies (8) (lw: led 4f out tl ins fnl f: unable qckn) ................................................................................. ½.6

149[3] Ski Captain **(57)** (Jt-Fav) *(PHowling)* 8–9–10 WNewnes (6) (a.p: rdn over 2f out: one pce) ......................................................................................................... ½.7

119 Barbezieux **(32)** (bl) *(TJNaughton)* 5–7–10 ‡[3]JFanning (3) (b: dwlt: wl bhd over 3f: gd hdwy over 1f out: nvr nrr) ....................................................................... 1.8

113 Misdemeanours Girl (IRE) **(47)** *(MRChannon)* 4–8–7 ‡[7]PTurner (5) (outpcd: hdwy over 1f out: nvr nr to chal) ................................................................... 1.9

**3/1** Hinari Video(9/2—5/1), Ski Captain, **5/1** RUSHANES, **13/2** Pendor Dancer, **7/1** Cellito (IRE)(op 7/2), **9/1** Doesyoudoes(op 6/1), **12/1** It's Only Money(op 7/1), **16/1** Misdemeanours Girl (IRE)(op 10/1), **25/1** Barbezieux. CSF £37.32, CT £281.14. Tote £6.60: £1.80 £2.10 £2.10 (£7.40). Mr M. Mac Carthy (UPPER LAMBOURN) bred by M. MacCarthy. 9 Rn    60.10 sec (1.90)
SF—51/29/43/44/44/23

**164**    HURST POINT CLAIMING STKS (3-Y.O) £2186.80 (£604.80: £288.40)
        **1m (AWT)**                                 2-40 (2-42)

*148*3  **A Nymph Too Far (IRE) (55)** *(DrJDScargill)* 7-9 ‡³JFanning (2) (led 3f out: rdn out) .................................................................................................... —1
*148*2  **Mykindofmusic (62)** (bl) *(Jt-Fav)* *(MJHaynes)* 8-0 RFox (5) (rdn & hdwy 3f out: plld out over 1f out: r.o wl nr fin) ......................................... nk.2
*141*4  **Bassio (BEL) (73)** *(Jt-Fav)* *(CNAllen)* 8-12 ‡7MichaelDenaro (7) (hdwy 4f out: ev ch ins fnl f: r.o) ........................................................... nk.3
*129*5  **Easy Does it (57)** (v) *(CCElsey)* 7-9 ‡5FNorton (3) (led 4f out to 3f out: hrd rdn wl over 1f out: unable qckn) ........................................ 4.4
      **Lindeman (63)** *(SDow)* 9-1 TQuinn (6) (s.s: hdwy 3f out: one pce fnl 2f) ...... 1½.5
      **Cue Directors (IRE) (50)** *(WJPearce)* 8-0 LCharnock (4) (lost pl over 4f out: rdn & no hdwy 3f) ............................................................ 8.6
      **Rhythmic Echo (55)** *(PHowling)* 8-8(1) WNewnes (1) (bit bkwd: led after 1f to 4f out: sn wknd) ........................................................ 5.7
*148*6  **Smudgemupum** *(MissBSanders)* 8-9 BCrossley (9) (bhd fnl 3f) .................. nk.8
*148*5  **Pace E Salute** *(SDow)* 8-2 GCarter (8) (dwlt: a bhd) ........................ ¾.9
*145*  **Saruk (IRE)** *(JJBridger)* 7-12 NAdams (10) (prom 4f) ...................... 6.10

**9/4** Mykindofmusic(op 6/4), Bassio (BEL), **6/1** Easy Does it(op 4/1), **8/1** A NYMPH TOO FAR (IRE), **11/1** Pace E Salute(6/1—12/1), **14/1** Lindeman(10/1—16/1), **20/1** Rhythmic Echo, **25/1** Smudgemupum, **33/1** Cue Directors (IRE), **50/1** Saruk (IRE). CSF £6.70, CT £24.58. Tote £7.90: £2.80 £1.40 (£1.10). Mr M. Gill-Anderson (NEWMARKET) bred by Loughbrown Stud in Ireland. 10 Rn       1m 41 (4.30)

**165**    EDDYSTONE H'CAP (0-100) £2861.40 (£790.40: £376.20)  **1m (AWT)**   3-10 (3-11)

*128*2  **Super Sally (93)** *(MJRyan)* 5-9-11 ‡3DBiggs (1) (hld up: shkn up over 1f out: led ins fnl f: r.o wl) .................................................... —1
*128*3  **Usa Dollar (64)** (bl) *(Fav)* *(BGubby)* 5-7-13 NAdams (4) (lw: rdn & hdwy 6f out: led over 2f out tl ins fnl f: unable qckn) ............... 1.2
*128*\*  **Dorset Duke (88)** *(GWragg)* 5-9-9 WRSwinburn (6) (lost pl 6f out: rdn along fnl 5f: rallied over 1f out: r.o) .......................... 2½.3
*146*\*  **Modesto (USA) (63)** *(KOCunningham-Brown)* 4-7-12 GBardwell (2) (b: lw: led: rdn 5f out: hdd 4f out: r.o one pce) .......................... ¾.4
      **Go Executive (89)** *(CEBrittain)* 4-9-5 ‡5BDoyle (3) (lw: chsd ldr: led 4f out tl over 2f out: wknd fnl f) .................................... nk.5
*64*4  **Shabanaz (77)** *(THCaldwell)* 7-8-5 ‡7StephenDavies (5) (bhd fnl 5f) .......... 12.6

**2/1** Usa Dollar(op 7/2), **11/4** Dorset Duke, **7/2** SUPER SALLY(op 2/1), **4/1** Modesto, **10/1** Go Executive, **20/1** Shabanaz. CSF £10.81, Tote £3.40: £2.00 £1.60 (£8.50). Mrs L. Seale (NEWMARKET) bred by R. Duggan. 6 Rn        1m 38.15 (1.45)
                                                         SF—66/37/53/26/46/–

**166**    BISHOP'S ROCK APP'CE H'CAP (0-70) £2304.40 (£638.40: £305.20)
        **2m (AWT)**                                       3-45 (3-46)

*138*\*  **Aude la Belle (FR) (51)** *(MrsAKnight)* 4-8-10 DBiggs (10) (rdn & hdwy 6f out: n.m.r over 1f out: qcknd & led ins fnl f: r.o wl) ......... —1
*83*3  **Jawani (IRE) (51)** (v) *(DrJDScargill)* 4-8-10 KRutter (8) (hdwy 10f out: chsd ldr 6f out: rdn 4f out: ev ch 1f out: unable qckn) ...... 3.2
*155*2  **Tenayestelign (51)** *(DMarks)* 4-8-10 EmmaO'Gorman (9) (a.p: led 6f out tl ins fnl f: one pce) ........................................ 1½.3
      **Caroles Clown (29)** *(MJHaynes)* 6-7-3 ‡5DToole (3) (b.hind: led 10f: one pce) ...... 5.4
*76*  **Sand Castle (38)** *(PHowling)* 11-8-3 DebbieBiggs (2) (wl bhd 14f: gd hdwy over 1f out: r.o) ........................................ hd.5
*144*  **Applianceofscience (46)** (bl) *(ASReid)* 8-8-11 PTurner (5) (prom 10f) ....... 15.6
*114*  **Lifetimes Ambition (43)** *(TCasey)* 4-8-2 FNorton (4) (prom 10f) ............. 12.7
*155*  **Wise Friend (USA) (34)** *(CPWildman)* 4-8-7 CHawksley (6) (prom 8f) ......... 3.8
      **Ta Wardle (28)** *(MJBolton)* 8-7-7 JFanning (1) (lw: bhd fnl 7f) .............. 1.9
      **Megan's Flight (63)** *(THCaldwell)* 7-10-0 StephenDavies (4) (t.o fnl 7f: virtually p.u fnl 2f) ............................................ dist.10

               LONG HANDICAP: Wise Friend (USA) 7-5, Ta Wardle 7-3.

**9/4** Jawani (IRE), **5/2** AUDE LA BELLE (FR), **9/2** Tenayestelign, **13/2** Caroles Clown(op 4/1), **9/1** Lifetimes Ambition, **20/1** Applianceofscience, Megan's Flight(op 12/1), **25/1** Sand Castle, Ta Wardle, **33/1** Wise Friend (USA). CSF £8.50, CT £21.92. Tote £3.70: £1.40 £1.50 £1.50 (£4.00). Mrs Val Rapkins (CULLOMPTON) bred by J. P. de Gaste in France. 10 Rn       3m 27.57 (4.57)
                                                          SF—18/15/13/–/–/–

**167**　DURLSTON HEAD STKS (Mdn 3-Y.O) £2363.20 (£655.20: £315.60)
1¼m (AWT)　　　　　　　　　　　　　　　　　　　4-20 (4-23)

**Khrisma** (Fav) *(MrsJCecil)* 8-9 BCrossley (5) (w'like: a:p: chsd ldr over 2f out: hrd rdn 1f out: qcknd to ld wl ins fnl f) ............... —1

69² Fengari *(PTWalwyn)* 9-0 RCochrane (8) (hdwy to ld 4f out: rdn clr 2f out: ct wl ins fnl f) ............... ½.2

Copy Lane (IRE) (57) *(MRChannon)* 9-0 WNewnes (3) (rdn over 4f out: hdwy fnl 2f: r.o) ............... 7.3

51⁵ Granite Boy (67) *(PJFeilden)* 9-0 AShoults (2) (b.off hind: a:p: hrd rdn 3f out: one pce fnl 2f) ............... ¾.4

Major Risk *(PAKelleway)* 9-0 GBardwell (4) (lw: led 6f) ............... 2.5

52⁴ Good as Gold (IRE) *(JLSpearing)* 8-9 DNicholls (7) (rdn & hdwy 3f out: wknd wl over 1f out) ............... 2.6

147⁶ Basilica (68) *(CEBrittain)* 8-9 ‡5BDoyle (9) (eyeshield: chsd ldr 6f: wknd 2f out) ............... 2½.7

78² Child Star (FR) *(DMarks)* 8-9 GBaxter (1) (nvr nr to chal) ............... nk.8

147³ Tadora (IRE) (62) *(CJBenstead)* 9-0 MHills (10) (prom 8f) ............... 1½.9

Dream Sweet Dreams (USA) *(BHanbury)* 8-2 ‡7VBray (6) (neat: s.i.s: a bhd: t.o) ............... 25.10

**6/4** KHRISMA, **3/1** Tadora (IRE), **9/2** Fengari(op 9/4), **7/1** Granite Boy(5/1—8/1), **11/1** Good as Gold (IRE)(8/1—12/1), **12/1** Basilica, **14/1** Child Star (FR), **Dream Sweet Dreams (USA)(op 8/1), **25/1** Ors. CSF £10.03, Tote £2.70: £1.40 £1.40 £12.00 (£4.90). Lord Howard de Walden (NEWMARKET) bred by Lord Howard de Walden. 10 Rn
　　　　　　　　　　　　　　　　　　　　　　　　2m 8.45 (5.45)
　　　　　　　　　　　　　　　　　　　　SF—21/25/11/9/5/–

**168**　DUNGENESS POINT H'CAP (3-Y.O) (0-80) £2364.00 (£654.00: £312.00)
1¼m (AWT)　　　　　　　　　　　　　　　　　　　4-50 (4-51)

(Weights raised 2 lh)

147* **Rosa Why (IRE) (64)** *(WJarvis)* 8-9 ‡5EmmaO'Gorman (1) (chsd ldr: led 3f out: clr over 1f out: comf) ............... —1

116* **Slight Risk (71)** (Fav) *(PAKelleway)* 9-7 GBardwell (5) (eyecover: led 7f: rdn: no imp) ............... 7.2

Beam Me Up Scotty (IRE) (65) *(PMitchell)* 9-1 TQuinn (2) (a.p: rdn 5f out: one pce fnl 4f) ............... 8.3

62 Thursley (53) *(HJCollingridge)* 7-10 ‡7CHawksley (4) (rdn & no hdwy fnl 4f) ............... 10.4

Victor Romeo (62) *(WJPearce)* 8-12 DNicholls (3) (bit bkwd: bhd fnl 5f) ............... 3.5

Akura (IRE) (50) *(MJohnston)* 7-7 ‡7MBaird (6) (bit bkwd: rn wd bnds after 1f & 6f out: t.o fnl 4f) ............... 7.6

116⁶ Eau D'Espoir (45) *(JLSpearing)* 7-6 ‡3JFanning (7) (s.s: rdn along: a bhd: t.o fnl 4f) ............... 5.7

**6/4** Slight Risk, **13/8** ROSA WHY (IRE)(Evens—7/4), **9/1** Victor Romeo, **10/1** Beam Me Up Scotty (IRE), **14/1** Eau D'Espoir, Thursley, **33/1** Akura (IRE). CSF £4.29, Tote £2.40: £1.40 £1.70 (£1.70). Mr Jerry Sung (NEWMARKET) bred by Jerry Sung in Ireland. 7 Rn
　　　　　　　　　　　　　　　　　　　　　　　　2m 7.03 (4.03)
　　　　　　　　　　　　　　　　　　　　SF—35/33/11/–/–/–

T/Plpt: £10.20 (185.6 Tckts).　　　　　　　　　　　　　　　　　　LMc

## 157—**SOUTHWELL (L-H)** Fibresand
### Wednesday, February 26th [Standard]
Going Allowance: 0.35 sec per fur (SL)

**169**　EDINGLEY CLAIMING STKS　£2422.00 (£672.00: £322.00)　1½m (AWT) 2-10 (2-12)

**Tempering (80)** *(DWChapman)* 6-9-5 SWood (14) (bit bkwd: mde all: rdn & hld on wl appr fnl f) ............... —1

139* Lara's Baby (IRE) (72) (Fav) *(RAkehurst)* 4-8-6 RCochrane (3) (b.nr fore: b.off hind: a:p: ev ch 3f out: rdn & nt qckn appr fnl f) ............... 2½.2

139² Le Temeraire (70) *(NTinkler)* 6-9-2 KimTinkler (10) (lw: hdwy 5f out: kpt on one pce fnl 2f) ............... 1½.3

138⁴ Mississippi Beat (USA) (45) (v) *(MPNaughton)* 5-8-3 ‡5BDoyle (15) (hdwy 5f out: nvr able to chal) ............... 8.4

Ramble (USA) *(JABOld)* 5-8-9 RFox (6) (prom tl wknd 3f out) ............... 7.5

Guest Player (56) (bl) *(TJNaughton)* 5-8-4 GCarter (2) (b: bhd tl sme hdwy fnl 2f) ............... 10.6

125 Fusion (33) (bl) *(REarnshaw)* 8-8-10 JCarroll (4) (b: bit bkwd: trckd ldrs tl rdn & wknd 3f out) ............... hd.7

Trendy Auctioneer (IRE) (44) *(MCPipe)* 4-8-9⁽²⁾ JWilliams (7) (sn wl bhd: nvr rchd ldrs) ............... 1½.8

138 Norfolk Lass (37) (bl) *(MCPipe)* 4-7-11 ‡3DBiggs (11) (nvr trbld ldrs) ............... 1½.9

Conjuring (USA) (bl) *(GThorner)* 4–9-2  RWernham (12) (prom 8f) .............. 12.**10**
139 Elissa *(GPKelly)* 6–7-10 ‡7JMarshall (5) (a bhd) .................................... 1¹/₂.**11**
97 Give Me Hope (IRE) **(46)** *(GHYardley)* 4–8-3 ‡⁵FNorton (1) (lw: chsd wnr 6f) .. nk.**12**
142⁶ Porick **(42)** (v) *(DMoffatt)* 4–7-10 ‡7DarrenMoffatt (8) (a bhd) ..................... 3¹/₂.**13**
Noble Fellow *(PMMcEntee)* 5–8-2 ‡7CHawksley (13) (bhd fnl 4f: t.o) .................... **14**
Petony (IRE) **(38)** *(CWCElsey)* 4–8-0  LCharnock (9) (plld hrd: prom 4f: t.o) ........ **15**

**4/6** Lara's Baby (IRE), **15/2** Le Temeraire(6/1—10/1), **10/1** Give Me Hope (IRE)(20/1—8/1), **11/1** TEMPERING(op 7/1), **14/1** Ramble (USA)(op 7/1), Mississippi Beat (USA)(op 7/1), **20/1** Trendy Auctioneer (IRE)(op 10/1), Guest Player(op 10/1), Norfolk Lass, **25/1** Fusion, Conjuring (USA), **33/1** Noble Fellow, Porick, Petony (IRE), **100/1** Elissa. CSF £19.32, Tote £17.90: £4.60 £1.60 £1.00 (£7.70). Mr Michael Hill (YORK) bred by Lord Howard de Walden. 15 Rn                                    2m 45.2 (11)
                                                                                SF–37/19/26/–/–/–

**170**    FENTON STKS (Mdn 3-Y.O) £2088.80 (£576.80: £274.40)    **1m (AWT)**    2-40 (2-42)

168⁶ **Akura (IRE) (50)** *(MJohnston)* 8-9  RPElliott (5) (mde all: rdn & styd on fnl 2f) ... –**1**
136² Firefighter **(64)** (Fav) *(RHollinshead)* 9-0  WRyan (2) (lw: a.p: effrt over 2f out:
                                                    unable qckn appr fnl f) ...................... 2¹/₂.**2**
136⁵ Trump *(SirMarkPrescott)* 9-0  GDuffield (6) (lw: a.p: one pce fnl 2f) ................ 1¹/₂.**3**
69⁴ Buzzards Bellbuoy *(HJCollingridge)* 8-7 ‡7CHawksley (4) (bit bkwd: chsd ldrs:
                                                    rdn 2f out: sn btn) .......................... 10.**4**
Set the Fashion (v) *(LordHuntingdon)* 9-0  WRSwinburn (3) (bit bkwd: cmpt: sn
                                                    rdn & bhd: effrt 3f out: no imp) .............. 12.**5**
Amber Glow (IRE) *(LJCodd)* 9-0  VSmith (1) (leggy: unf: bit bkwd: s.i.s: sn rcvrd:
                                                    bhd fnl 4f) .................................. 6.**6**

**6/4** Firefighter, **4/1** Set the Fashion(op 7/4), **9/2** Buzzards Bellbuoy(op 5/2), **11/2** Trump, Amber Glow (IRE)(op 20/1), **16/1** AKURA (IRE)(12/1—20/1). CSF £39.47, Tote £59.90: £13.00 £1.30 (£44.70). Mark Johnston Racing Ltd (MIDDLEHAM) bred by J. Mamakos in Ireland. 6 Rn                    1m 48.9 (9.6)

**171**    BECKINGHAM H'CAP (3-Y.O) (0-90) £2147.60 (£593.60: £282.80)
           **1m (AWT)**                                                              3-10 (3-11)

107⁴ **Papa Westray (55)** *(TDBarron)* 7-7 ‡³JFanning (4) (lw: trckd ldrs: rdn to ld wl
                                                    over 1f out: sn drew clr) .................... –**1**
129 High Success **(54)** (bl) *(WAO'Gorman)* 7-4 ‡⁵BDoyle (1) (a.p: rdn & kpt on appr
                                                    fnl f) ........................................ 3.**2**
Elsharh (IRE) **(54)** *(JAGlover)* 7-2⁽²⁾ ‡7CHawksley (7) (bhd: rdn 3f out: styd on
                                                    appr fnl f) .................................. 2.**3**
99* Ferdia (IRE) **(73)** (Jt-Fav) *(RHollinshead)* 9-0  WRyan (5) (in tch: rdn 2f out: kpt
                                                    on one pce) ................................. 3¹/₂.**4**
Clare Kerry Lass **(72)** *(TJNaughton)* 8-8 ‡⁵CHodgson (9) (bit bkwd: swtg: in tch:
                                                    styd on one pce u.p fnl 2f) .................. 3.**5**
160² Energic (IRE) **(53)** (Jt-Fav) *(CNAllen)* 7-8  GBardwell (6) (b.off hind: prom: led
                                                    over 2f out tl wl over 1f out: sn wknd) ....... 6.**6**
Dance Scene (IRE) **(80)** *(DRCElsworth)* 9-7  JWilliams (8) (eyeshield: effrt 4f
                                                    out: no ch fnl 2f) ........................... 2¹/₂.**7**
99⁴ Kick on Majestic (IRE) **(52)** *(NBycroft)* 7-7  SWood (2) (lost pl 4f out: no ch after)   4.**8**
147 Lady of Letters **(54)** *(TThomsonJones)* 7-9⁽²⁾  NAdams (3) (sn rdn along: led tl
                                                    hdd & wknd over 2f out) .................... ¹/₂.**9**
LONG HANDICAP: Kick on Majestic (IRE) 7-5, Lady of Letters 7-4.

**7/2** Energic (IRE), Ferdia (IRE), **9/2** PAPA WESTRAY(6/1—7/1), **5/1** Dance Scene (IRE), **10/1** Clare Kerry Lass, **11/1** Lady of Letters(8/1—12/1), **12/1** Kick on Majestic (IRE)(8/1—14/1), **16/1** Ors. CSF £61.15, CT £952.35. Tote £5.30: £1.50 £5.40 £5.10 (£99.10). Miss N. J. Barron (THIRSK) bred by T. Anthony. 9 Rn  1m 47.6 (8.3)

**172**    CLAYPOLE H'CAP (0-70) £2324.00 (£644.00: £308.00)    **7f (AWT)**    3-40 (3-43)

137² **East Barns (IRE) (39)** (bl) *(TDBarron)* 4–7-7 ‡⁵BDoyle (3) (dwlt: hdwy after 2f:
                                                    plld out over 1f out: r.o u.p to ld nr fin) ..... –**1**
124² Grand Guignol **(69)** (Fav) *(GWragg)* 4–9-9 ‡⁵FNorton (5) (a.p: led wl over 1f out:
                                                    hdd & unable qckn nr fin) ................... 1.**2**
Sciacca **(37)** *(SMellor)* 5–7-10  DanaMellor (9) (lw: prom: led over 2f out: hdd wl
                                                    over 1f out: one pce) ....................... 7.**3**
124* Mushy Boff **(53)** *(CJHill)* 4–8-9 ‡³DBiggs (2) (lw: chsd ldrs: one pce fnl 2f) ..... 5.**4**
Ruth's Gamble **(66)** *(DWChapman)* 4–9-11  SWood (11) (bit bkwd: chsd ldrs:
                                                    no hdwy fnl 2f) ............................. hd.**5**
Cool Enough **(42)** *(MrsJRRamsden)* 11–8-1  AMackay (4) (lw: nvr plcd to chal) 1¹/₂.**6**
121 Ping Pong **(39)** (bl) *(TFairhurst)* 4–7-9 ‡³JFanning (12) (led tl hdd & wknd over 2f
                                                    out) ......................................... nk.**7**
124 Yonge Tender **(52)** (bl) *(JWharton)* 5–8-11  JWilliams (8) (bhd fnl 4f) ............ 1.**8**

153[4] Sunwind **(35)** *(RJHodges)* 6–7–8 GBardwell (1) (prom tl outpcd after 3f: n.d after) 1.9
143 Morpick **(50)** *(JPLeigh)* 5–8–9 DNicholls (7) (prom over 5f: sn wknd) ............... 2.10
153 Damaaz (IRE) **(43)** (bl) *(JSWainwright)* 4–7–11[3] ‡5SMaloney (10) (chsd ldrs 4f) . 11
143 Chaplins Club (USA) **(48)** (bl) *(DWChapman)* 12–8–7 KDarley (6) (dwlt: brought
      wd ent st: a bhd) ...................................................................................... 12

**7/4** Grand Guignol, **4/1** Mushy Boff(3/1—9/2), **7/1** EAST BARNS (IRE), **10/1** Cool Enough(op 5/1), Sunwind, **14/1** Chaplins Club (USA), **16/1** Yonge Tender, **20/1** Ruth's Gamble, Damaaz (IRE), Sciacca, **25/1** Ors. CSF £18.92, CT £217.22. Tote £6.50: £1.90 £1.10 £2.90 (£7.80). Mrs M. Baggott (THIRSK) bred by P. J. Mulhall in Ireland. 12 Rn                                                    1m 32.8 (6.2)
SF–23/50/2/–/15/–

**173**    DUNHAM-ON-TRENT H'CAP (0-80) £2265.20 (£627.20: £299.60)
          **6f (AWT)**                                                      4-10 (4-11)

140★ **Toshiba Comet (73)** (bl) *(WJPearce)* 5–10–0 DNicholls (8) (hdwy 3f out: rdn to
      ld ins fnl f) ............................................................................................. —1
140[4] Saladan Knight **(65)** (bl) *(JGFitzGerald)* 7–8–13 ‡7MHunt (3) (eyecover: bhd: gd
      hdwy over 1f out: nt rch wnr) ................................................................ 1.2
162★ Orient Air **(67)** (bl) (Fav) *(TDBarron)* 4–9–8 (7x) AlexGreaves (1) (led after 1f tl
      over 3f out: sn led again: clr over 1f out: hdd & no ex nr fin) 2.3
  57 The Shanahan Bay **(60)** (v) *(MrsNMacauley)* 7–9–1 NDay (2) (b: led 1f: wknd 2f
      out) ...................................................................................................... 10.4
      Princess Jestina (IRE) **(51)** *(GHYardley)* 4–8–1 ‡5FNorton (6) (nvr trbld ldrs) ....... 1.5
132 Lady of the Fen **(60)** *(MrsNMacauley)* 4–8–8 ‡7SWilliams (9) (lw: prom: led over
      3f out: c wd & hdd st: wknd over 1f out) .................................... 1¹⁄₂6
140 Goody Four Shoes **(59)** *(DRTucker)* 4–8–9 ‡5RPrice (7) (bhd fnl 3f) ................ 1¹⁄₂7
150[3] Our Amber **(38)** *(DWChapman)* 5–7–7 SWood (4) (chsd ldrs over 3f) ............. 1¹⁄₂8
102★ Lets Go Sabo **(52)** *(DWChapman)* 4–8–4 ‡3JFanning (5) (sn bhd) .................. 1¹⁄₂9

**5/2** Orient Air(op 6/4), **4/1** TOSHIBA COMET, **11/2** Saladan Knight, **6/1** The Shanahan Bay, **10/1** Lets Go Sabo, **12/1** Lady of the Fen, **14/1** Princess Jestina (IRE), **25/1** Ors. CSF £22.79, CT £32.71. Tote £4.10: £1.80 £2.50 £1.70 (£15.60). Mike Clynes Associates Ltd (HAMBLETON) bred by Mrs Nikki A. Collins. 9 Rn   1m 19.5 (6.1)
SF–34/15/16/–/–/–

**174**    CLAPWELL STKS (Mdn) £2265.20 (£627.20: £299.60)      **6f (AWT)**      4-40 (4-44)

      **Daros** *(MrsJRRamsden)* 3–8–5 MHills (10) (w'like: leggy: bit bkwd: trckd ldrs:
      led wl over 1f out: sn clr: easily) ........................................................ —1
      Eastleigh **(70)** (Fav) *(RHollinshead)* 3–8–5 WRyan (6) (chsd ldrs: rdn & r.o appr
      fnl f: no ch w wnr) .............................................................................. 2.2
135[5] Lord Naskra (USA) *(WAO'Gorman)* 3–8–2[2] ‡5EmmaO'Gorman (11) (dwlt:
      hdwy 3f out: kpt on fnl f) ..................................................................... 2.3
121[4] Drummer's Dream (IRE) **(43)** *(MrsNMacauley)* 4–8–13 ‡3DBiggs (5) (chsd ldrs:
      one pce fnl 2f) ................................................................................... s.h.4
      Colour Solutions *(TDBarron)* 3–8–1[1] AlexGreaves (3) (unf: scope: dwlt: hdwy
      over 3f out: wknd over 1f out) ............................................................. ¹⁄₂5
      Petaurista *(MJohnston)* 3–7–11 ‡3JFanning (8) (s.i.s: rdn & hdwy 3f out: nvr rchd
      ldrs) ................................................................................................... 7.6
151[4] Do the Business (IRE) **(50)** (v) *(CNAllen)* 3–7–12 ‡7GForster (7) (prom: led 3f out
      tl wl over 1f out: sn wknd) ................................................................... 7.7
      Comiskey Park (IRE) *(DWChapman)* 3–8–5 SWood (2) (str: bkwd: chsd ldrs
      over 3f) ............................................................................................. 1¹⁄₂8
157[4] Forza Azzurri (IRE) **(48)** *(MrsNMacauley)* 3–8–5 NDay (4) (lw: w ldrs 4f) ............. 2.9
      Clefti's Slipper *(CJHill)* 4–9–2 NAdams (1) (bit bkwd: led 3f: sn wknd) ........... 1¹⁄₂10
135[6] Injaka Boy (bl) *(KWhite)* 3–7–12 ‡7AGarth (9) (sn bhd) ..................................... 11

**7/4** Eastleigh(6/4—9/4), **4/1** Do the Business (IRE)(5/1—6/1), **6/1** Drummer's Dream (IRE)(4/1—7/1), **10/1** Lord Naskra (USA)(7/1—12/1), **11/1** Colour Solutions(op 6/1), Forza Azzurri (IRE)(16/1—10/1), **12/1** Petaurista(op 6/1), **14/1** Comiskey Park (IRE), **16/1** DAROS(op 5/1), **33/1** Ors. CSF £43.46, Tote £10.90: £4.80 £1.80 £2.20 (£9.30). Mr K. E. Wheldon (THIRSK) bred by Juddmonte Farms. 11 Rn     1m 19.1 (5.7)
SF–19/11/–/10/–/–

T/Plpt: £67.30 (18.15 Tckts).                                                      Dk

**156a—CAGNES-SUR-MER  (L-H)**
**Sunday, February 23rd [Good]**

**175a**    PRIX POLICEMAN (3-Y.O) £11352.00    1¼m

      **Wedding Ring (IRE)** *(France)* 3–9–0 MBoutin ................................................ —1
      Holly Counsel (FR) *(France)* 3–8–6 GElorriaga-Santos ................................... ¹⁄₂2

Hundred Hours (IRE) *(France)* 3-8-6 GBianchi ................................................ 6.3
156a⁵ FLIGHT LIEUTENANT (USA) *(PMitchell)* 3-8-7 BRaymond (btn further 1l) ............. 6
Tote 2.30f: 1.50f 2.10f 2.10f (10.40f). Mr R.C.Strauss (R. Collet,FRANCE) bred by R.M.Aubert & R.C.Strauss in
Ireland. 8 Rn
2m 5.2

169— **SOUTHWELL (L-H)** Fibresand

## Friday, February 28th [Standard]

Going Allowance: 0.25 sec per fur (SL)
Wind: slt across

Stalls: 1st high, remainder low

**176** SKEDBY H'CAP (0-90) £2088.80 (£576.80: £274.40) **1³⁄₄m (AWT)** 2-10 (2-14)

138² **Unpaid Member (48)** (Fav) *(JWharton)* 8-8-2 ‡³JFanning (5) (lw: led after 1f: clr
appr fnl f) ...................................................... —1
155 Lord Advocate (50) (v) *(MPNaughton)* 4-7-12 ‡⁵BDoyle (4) (prom: 3rd st: chsd
wnr fnl 2f: no imp) ................................................ 5.2
Steppey Lane (69) *(WWHaigh)* 7-9-12 RCochrane (1) (led 1f: chsd wnr tl wknd
fnl 2f) ............................................................... 3¹⁄₂.3
120³ Alle-Roy (63) *(MHTompkins)* 4-8-11 ‡⁵CHodgson (3) (lw: hld up: outpcd 5f out:
4th st: rdn over 1f out: styd on same pce) ........................... 1.4
Shooting Lodge (IRE) (13/2) Withdrawn : not under orders — Rule 4 applies

5/2 UNPAID MEMBER, 3/1 Alle-Roy(op 6/4), 4/1 Steppey Lane, 9/2 Lord Advocate. CSF £8.80, Tote £3.10:
£1.80 (£10.90). Mr W. Fletcher (MELTON MOWBRAY) bred by Sledmere Stud Co Ltd. 4 Rn 3m 18 (18.7)

**177** WELLOW CLAIMING STKS (3-Y.O) £2167.20 (£599.20: £285.60)
**1m (AWT)** 2-40 (2-43)

141★ **Mad Militant (IRE) (85)** (Fav) *(RHollinshead)* 8-6 WRyan (7) (lw: sn chsng ldrs:
4th st: led 2f out: sn clr) ........................................... —1
141² Meltonby (72) *(NTinkler)* 7-11 KimTinkler (6) (lw: chsd ldr: led 3f out: hdd 2f out:
styd on same pce) .................................................. 7.2
148⁴ Patrician Magician (66) *(RJRWilliams)* 7-13 JQuinn (3) (prom: 3rd st: no hdwy
fnl 2f) .............................................................. 3.3
123⁵ Feeling Foolish (IRE) (69) (bl) *(TFairhurst)* 7-13 ‡³JFanning (5) (chsd ldrs: 5th
st: wknd 2f out) .................................................... 3¹⁄₂.4
72 Albany Spark *(GHEden)* 7-11⁽²⁾ ‡⁷PTurner (4) (poor 6th st: n.d) .............. 2¹⁄₂.5
Sunrays (IRE) (51) *(CWCElsey)* 7-8 LCharnock (1) (bhd fnl 2f) ............... 3.6
85⁴ Malcesine (IRE) *(CaptJWilson)* 7-9⁽¹⁾ ‡³DBiggs (2) (dwlt: bhd fr ¹⁄₂-wy) ........ hd.7
123 Turning Heads *(CaptJWilson)* 7-2⁽¹⁾ ‡⁷CHawksley (8) (a bhd) .............. 8.8
Evening Session (IRE) *(JNorton)* 7-12⁽⁶⁾ ‡⁷OPears (9) (bhd fnl 3f) ............ 1¹⁄₂.9

8/11 MAD MILITANT (IRE), 7/1 Meltonby(op 7/2), 8/1 Patrician Magician, 9/1 Feeling Foolish (IRE)(op 6/1),
12/1 Malcesine (IRE), 25/1 Sunrays (IRE), Turning Heads, 50/1 Ors. CSF £5.89, Tote £1.70: £1.10 £1.60 £1.60
(£2.70). Mrs B. Facchino (UPPER LONGDON) bred by Cloghran Stud Farm Co in Ireland. 9 Rn 1m 45.7 (6.4)
SF—26/-/-/-/-/-

**178** THURGATON H'CAP (0-80) £2245.60 (£621.60: £296.80) **1m (AWT)** 3-10 (3-11)

127★ **Sooty Tern (58)** *(JMBradley)* 5-8-7 NAdams (1) (led over 5f: clr appr fnl f) ........ —1
100★ Martini Executive (79) (bl) (Fav) *(WJPearce)* 4-10-0 DNicholls (2) (lw: hld up:
5th st: ev ch 2f out: hrd rdn 1f out: styd on same pce) ....... 2¹⁄₂.2
137 Tyrian Purple (IRE) (50) *(RHollinshead)* 4-7-6⁽⁶⁾ ‡⁷MHumphries (9) (lw: led over
2f: 2nd st: wknd over 1f out) ...................................... 4.3
158² Euroblake (75) *(TDBarron)* 5-9-5 ‡⁵BDoyle (8) (dwlt: hdwy over 2f out: nvr rchd
ldrs) ................................................................. ³⁄₄.4
127² Tara's Delight (59) *(WAO'Gorman)* 5-8-3 ‡⁵EmmaO'Gorman (7) (3rd st: ev ch
over 2f out: wknd wl over 1f out) ................................... ¹⁄₂.5
Loudest Whisper (63) *(KSBridgwater)* 4-8-12 JWilliams (4) (nvr trbld ldrs) ..... 5.6
124⁶ Obsidian Grey (64) *(BAMcMahon)* 5-8-13 RCochrane (3) (chsd ldrs: 4th st:
wknd 2f out) ....................................................... 3.7
137★ Ballerina Bay (57) (v) *(DTThom)* 4-8-6 JQuinn (6) (effrt 3f out: c wd st: wknd st) nk.8
Lombard Ships (59) *(MO'Neill)* 5-8-8 JFortune (5) (prom: 6th & wkng st) ....... 3¹⁄₂.9
Shannon Express (71) *(MDHammond)* 5-9-6 SDawson (10) (bhd fr ¹⁄₂-wy) ..... 8.10
LONG HANDICAP: Tyrian Purple (IRE) 7-6.

100/30 Martini Executive(9/4—4/1), 7/2 Tara's Delight, 11/2 Obsidian Grey, 13/2 Euroblake, 7/1 Ballerina
Bay(op 9/2), 10/1 SOOTY TERN, 14/1 Shannon Express(tchd 25/1), 16/1 Tyrian Purple (IRE), 20/1 Lombard
Ships, 25/1 Loudest Whisper. CSF £40.52, CT £486.21. Tote £12.40: £3.60 £1.10 £4.10 (£24.00). Mr J. M.
Bradley (CHEPSTOW) bred by Sheikh Mohammed bin Rashid al Maktoum. 10 Rn 1m 45.4 (6.1)
SF—31/44/-/21/3/-

**179**    CLAYPOLE STKS (Mdn)(F & M) £2206.40 (£610.40: £291.20)    **1m (AWT)**  3-40 (3-42)

**Money Spinner (USA)** (*LordHuntingdon*) 3-8-5 WRyan (3) (led over 6f out: pushed clr appr fnl f) ............................................. —1
97  Restless Niece (31) (*TDBarron*) 4-9-10 AlexGreaves (6) (bhd: hdwy & 4th st: styd on fnl 2f: nrst fin) ........................... 12.2
157  Raaya (bl) (Fav) (*WAO'Gorman*) 3-8-2(2) ‡5EmmaO'Gorman (7) (lw: chsd ldr: 2nd st: wknd over 1f out) ........................ 1.3
Kay's Dilemma (IRE) (*PAKelleway*) 4-9-3 ‡7ABates (2) (bit bkwd: 3rd st: wknd 2f out) ......................................... 1¹/₂.4
Starlight Wonder (43) (*REBarr*) 6-9-10 DNicholls (5) (s.i.s: effrt & 5th st: n.d) 3¹/₂.5
154  Red Sparky (35) (*WJPearce*) 4-9-10 SWebster (4) (poor 6th st: a bhd) ........... hd.6
Jodie Bobs (*RDEWoodhouse*) 3-8-5 PBurke (1) (led over 1f: t.o fnl 3f) .......... dist.7

9/4 Raaya, 3/1 MONEY SPINNER (USA)(op 5/4), 9/2 Restless Niece, 6/1 Starlight Wonder, 12/1 Kay's Dilemma (IRE), 14/1 Red Sparky(tchd 25/1), 40/1 Jodie Bobs. CSF £14.28, Tote £3.60: £1.80 £2.90 (£6.00). The Queen (WEST ILSLEY) bred by The Queen in USA. 7 Rn        1m 47 (7.7)
SF—5/–/–/–/–/–

**180**    RAVENSHEAD H'CAP (0-90) £2167.20 (£599.20: £285.60)    **6f (AWT)**  4-10 (4-12)
(Weights raised 4 lb)
119  **Jovial Kate (USA) (52)** (*BEllison*) 5-7-9(2) NCarlisle (1) (led 1f: 3rd st: led 1f out: rdn out) ........................................... —1
Empeeka (USA) (84) (h) (*WAO'Gorman*) 3-8-6 ‡5EmmaO'Gorman (6) (lw: hdwy & 5th st: ev ch fnl f: nt qckn cl home) ..................... 1¹/₂.2
159*  Brisas (67) (bl) (*TFairhurst*) 5-8-7 (7x) ‡3JFanning (4) (lw: 2nd st: led 2f out: hdd 1f out: kpt on same pce) ....................... 3.3
132²  Gorinsky (IRE) (79) (*JBerry*) 4-9-8 JCarroll (7) (led 5f out: hdd 2f out: wknd appr fnl f) ........................................... 1¹/₂.4
132³  On the Edge (81) (Fav) (*TDBarron*) 4-9-10 AlexGreaves (3) (bhd: styd on fnl 2f: nrst fin) ........................................... 1.5
58  Glencroft (69) (bl) (*DWChapman*) 8-8-5 ‡7OPears (5) (t: prom: 4th st: wknd 2f out) ........................................... 7.6
132  Wellsy Lad (USA) (73) (*DWChapman*) 5-9-2 SWood (2) (prom over 2f: poor 6th st) ........................................... ³/₄.7
LONG HANDICAP: Jovial Kate (USA) 7-4.

11/4 On the Edge, 3/1 Brisas, 4/1 Gorinsky (IRE), 7/1 Empeeka (USA), 8/1 Wellsy Lad (USA), 9/1 JOVIAL KATE (USA), 25/1 Glencroft. CSF £58.32, Tote £12.10: £2.40 £2.70 (£36.10). Mr Philip Serbert (MALTON) bred by Northwest Farms in USA. 7 Rn        1m 18.3 (4.9)
SF—13/18/7/16/14/–

**181**    BEESTHORPE STKS (Mdn) £2128.00 (£588.00: £280.00)    **7f (AWT)**  4-40 (4-41)

102⁴  **Company Cash** (bl) (*RBastiman*) 4-8-7 ‡7HBastiman (2) (mde all: clr 2f out: easily) ........................................... —1
124³  Mac's Princess (USA) (64) (bl) (Fav) (*WAO'Gorman*) 4-8-4 ‡5EmmaO'Gorman (3) (hld up: hdwy & c wd st: styd on appr fnl f: nrst fin) ....... 5.2
118⁴  Danzig Lad (USA) (40) (v) (*MPNaughton*) 4-9-0 GCarter (6) (chsd wnr: 2nd st: wknd 2f out) ........................................... 6.3
159⁴  Dashing April (41) (v) (*DTThom*) 4-8-9 JWilliams (4) (a in rr) ........................ 2.4
118⁵  Goodbye Maggie (IRE) (34) (bl) (*MJFetherston-Godley*) 4-8-9 WNewnes (8) (prom: 4th st: wknd over 2f out) ........................... 2¹/₂.5
150⁴  Caerulia (32) (bl) (*WJPearce*) 4-8-9 DNicholls (5) (chsd ldrs: 3rd st: wkng st: t.o) 30.6
Stewards Enquiry: Carter suspended 8-11/3/92 (excessive use of whip).

1/3 Mac's Princess (USA), 7/1 COMPANY CASH, 10/1 Dashing April, Danzig Lad (USA), 20/1 Goodbye Maggie (IRE), 25/1 Caerulia. CSF £9.80, Tote £9.10: £2.40 £1.10 (£6.10). Mrs P. Churm (WETHERBY) bred by Cheveley Park Stud Ltd. 6 Rn        1m 31.4 (4.8)
SF—47/29/21/10/2/–

T/Plpt: £378.50 (3.85 Tckts).        CR

163—**LINGFIELD (L-H)** Equitrack
## Saturday, February 29th [Standard]
Going Allowance: minus 0.30 sec per fur (FS)

**182**    BUZZARD STKS (Mdn 3-Y.O) £2108.40 (£582.40: £277.20)    **7f (AWT)**  2-10 (2-12)

135³  **Walkonthemoon** (*MMcCormack*) 8-9 WNewnes (3) (mde all: clr over 2f out: unchal) ........................................... —1

Miss Orient (Fav) *(WAO'Gorman)* 8-4 ‡⁵EmmaO'Gorman (4) (unf: a.p: chsd wnr
over 2f out: no imp: fnl lame) ............................................ 10.2
157 Telegraphic *(MBell)* 9-0 MHills (7) (hdwy 2f out: nvr nr to chal) ....... 2½.3
Amazon Express *(CEBrittain)* 8-9 ‡⁵BDoyle (2) (rdn thrght: lost pl 4f out: styd on
fnl f) ............................................................ hd.4
136 Well Bought (IRE) *(NAGraham)* 8-4 ‡⁵FNorton (1) (b.hind: no hdwy fnl 3f) .... 2.5
Dilkush *(LJHolt)* 8-7 ‡⁷CAvery (5) (wl grwn: bkwd: s.s: t.o over 5f: nvr nrr) ....... 8.6
Jaromic (65) *(PFTulk)* 9-0 WRyan (8) (bit bkwd: chsd wnr over 4f) ............ hd.7
Spectacle Jim *(JO'Donoghue)* 9-0 NAdams (6) (lw: bhd fnl 2f) ................... 2.8
136⁴ Court Room (43) (v) *(AMoore)* 9-0 CandyMorris (9) (a bhd) ................ 5.9

11/4 Miss Orient, 100/30 Amazon Express, 9/2 Telegraphic(6/1—8/1), 11/2 Jaromic(op 11/4), 15/2
WALKONTHEMOON, 8/1 Well Bought (IRE), 16/1 Spectacle Jim(op 10/1), 20/1 Dilkush(op 8/1), 33/1 Court
Room. CSF £27.72, Tote £6.40: £1.20 (£25.70). Mr Brian North (WANTAGE) bred by Catridge Farm Stud Ltd. 9
Rn                                                                            1m 26.44 (2.44)
                                                                              SF—27/–/–/–/–/–

**183**          HARRIER CLAIMING STKS     £2206.40 (£610.40: £291.20)    **7f (AWT)**    2-40 (2-41)

144 **Invocation** *(AMoore)* 5-8-5 NAdams (5) (chsd ldr: led over 3f out to 1f out: led
ins fnl f: all out) ................................................... —1
109★ African Chimes (95) (Fav) *(WAO'Gorman)* 5-9-2 ‡⁵EmmaO'Gorman (4) (hdwy
3f out: led 1f out tl ins fnl f: r.o wl) ............................... s.h.2
Dazzle the Crowd (IRE) (47) *(CACyzer)* 4-8-10 GCarter (1) (outpcd: hdwy fnl
2f: nvr nrr) ......................................................... 3½.3
River Chase (IRE) (75) *(KCBailey)* 4-8-8 MHills (2) (b.hind: lw: led over 3f: one
pce fnl 2f) .......................................................... 3½.4
132 Hitchin a Ride *(MPMuggeridge)* 5-9-2 JWilliams (3) (prom 4f) ............. 1½.5
102⁶ Petank (IRE) *(PatMitchell)* 4–7-11 ‡⁷RTurner (6) (eyeshield: wl bhd fnl 3f) ...... 25.6

1/4 African Chimes, 9/2 River Chase (IRE), 20/1 Hitchin a Ride(op 10/1), 33/1 Dazzle the Crowd (IRE), 40/1
INVOCATION, 50/1 Petank (IRE). CSF £49.30, Tote £27.30: £4.20 £1.10 (£7.30). Mr R. Kiernan (BRIGHTON)
bred by Juddmonte Farms. 6 Rn                                                 1m 25.86 (1.86)
                                                                              SF—31/41/24/11/–/–

**184**          WILLIAM HILL H'CAP (Amateurs) (0-70) £2363.20 (£655.20: £313.60)
                 1¼m (AWT)                                                    3-10 (3-11)
                                   (Weights raised 5 lb)

144² **Awesome Power (57)** (Fav) *(CRNelson)* 6–11-12 MissJWinter (4) (a.p: led ins
fnl f: rdn out) ...................................................... —1
Thundering (26) *(AWJones)* 7–9-9⁽²⁾ MissIDWJones (12) (chsd ldr: led 6f out tl
ins fnl f: r.o) ....................................................... ¾.2
Mardior (30) *(WGRWightman)* 4–9-6 ‡⁵MrGKille (5) (led 4f: ev ch over 1f out:
unable qckn) ........................................................ 3.3
137 North-West One (IRE) (34) *(HJCollingridge)* 4–9-10 ‡⁵MrPClose (9) (hdwy 3f
out: rdn & r.o ins fnl f) ............................................. 2½.4
154⁵ Clear Idea (IRE) (33) *(CRNelson)* 4-10-0 MissABillott (13) (a.p: ev ch 2f out: hrd
rdn over 1f out: wknd fnl f) ......................................... hd.5
115 Internal Affair (35) *(JPearce)* 4-10-2 MrsLPearce (1) (no hdwy fnl 3f) ......... 12.6
Green's Cassatt (USA) (50) *(WMBrisbourne)* 4-11-3 MissYHaynes (8) (lost pl
5f out: nvr nr to chal) .............................................. 2½.7
155⁶ Our Topsie (28) (bl) *(FJO'Mahony)* 5–9-6 ‡⁵MissDianaJones (6) (b.nr fore:
prom 5f) ............................................................. 1½.8
Castleacre (43) *(CASmith)* 6-10-7 ‡⁵MrAPhillips (3) (b.off hind: a bhd) ....... 2½.9
137⁵ Priceless Fantasy (39) *(PatMitchell)* 5–10-3 ‡⁵MissLGlayzer (10) (lw: a bhd) .... ¾.10
Hills of Hoy (57) *(KCBailey)* 6–11-7 ‡⁵MrsTBailey (2) (a bhd) .............. nk.11
143⁴ Verro (USA) (35) (bl) *(JABennett)* 5–9-13 ‡⁵MissAPurdy (7) (b: mid div over 6f) .. 1.12
                 LONG HANDICAP: Thundering 9-3.

3/1 AWESOME POWER, 9/2 Our Topsie, 7/1 Clear Idea (IRE), Hills of Hoy, Priceless Fantasy, 8/1 Internal Affair,
9/1 Green's Cassatt (USA)(6/1—11/1), 10/1 Verro (USA), 12/1 Castleacre(op 8/1), 33/1 Ors. CSF £84.29, CT
£2,544.92. Tote £3.90: £1.60 £11.00 £31.10 (£123.10). Mr Garrett J. Freyne (UPPER LAMBOURN) bred by G.
J. Freyne. 12 Rn                                                             2m 9.33 (6.33)
                                                                              SF—47/14/5/4/7/–

**185**          SPARROWHAWK H'CAP (0-100) £2888.00 (£798.00: £380.00)    **7f (AWT)**    3-40 (3-42)
                                   (Weights raised 2 lb)

137 **Predictable (63)** *(MrsAKnight)* 6–7-9⁽⁴⁾ ‡³DBiggs (3) (mde all: rdn out) ...... —1
101⁵ Vuchterbacher (63) *(PFTulk)* 6–7-5⁽⁵⁾ ‡⁷TWilson (5) (b: chsd wnr: ev ch 2f out:
rdn & r.o) ........................................................... 2.2

165⁵ Go Executive **(89)** (Jt-Fav) *(CEBrittain)* 4-9-5 ‡⁵BDoyle (2) (lost pl over 5f out: rallied over 1f out: r.o wl ins fnl f) ........................... 3¹/₂.3
152² Sally's Son **(78)** (Jt-Fav) *(WAO'Gorman)* 6-8-8 ‡⁵EmmaO'Gorman (1) (lw: a.p: rdn over 3f out: one pce fnl 2f) ........................... ¹/₂.4
Gorytus Star **(60)** *(DHaydnJones)* 6-7-2 ‡⁷SianWilliams (4) (bit bkwd: n.d) ..... 10.5
Lucky Noire **(68)** *(GHarwood)* 4-8-3 RHills (6) (b: b.hind: a bhd) ........................ 8.6
LONG HANDICAP: Vuchterbacher 7-2.

**7/4** Sally's Son, Go Executive, **6/1** Lucky Noire, **8/1** Vuchterbacher(op 5/1), **9/1** PREDICTABLE(6/1—10/1), **33/1** Gorytus Star. CSF £62.15, Tote £12.00: £4.30 1.50 (£11.50). Mr L. J. Hawkings (CULLOMPTON) bred by Newsells Park Stud. 6 Rn
1m 24.97 (0.97)
SF−31/25/42/29/–/–

## 186  MERLIN H'CAP (0-70) £2324.00 (£644.00: £308.00)    6f **(AWT)**    4-10 (4-11)

152⁴ **Murmuring (58)** *(SDow)* 6-9-3 JWilliams (3) (hld up: led wl ins fnl f: pushed out) −1
145* In the Game (IRE) **(59)** (Fav) *(MissAJWhitfield)* 3-8-2 NAdams (4) (led over 4f out tl wl over 1f out: led ins fnl f: sn hdd: r.o) ................. 1¹/₂.2
162³ Count Me Out **(43)** (bl) *(JPearce)* 7-7-11 ‡⁵RPrice (8) (rdn along: hdwy over 1f out: r.o wl ins fnl f) ........................... nk.3
119 Inswinger **(39)** *(WGRWightman)* 6-7-12 TyroneWilliams (10) (a.p: ev ch 2f out: unable qckn) ........................... 1¹/₂.4
163* Rushanes **(64)** *(TCasey)* 5-9-4 ‡⁵FNorton (2) (led over 1f: led wl over 1f out tl wknd ins fnl f) ........................... nk.5
149⁶ Courting Newmarket **(56)** *(MrsAKnight)* 4-8-12 ‡³DBiggs (7) (a.p: rdn over 2f out: one pce) ........................... hd.6
132 The Noble Oak (IRE) **(46)** *(MMcCormack)* 4-8-5 JQuinn (11) (lw: a.p: ev ch 2f out: wknd over 1f out) ........................... 3.7
174 Do the Business (IRE) **(41)** *(CNAllen)* 3-7-12 GBardwell (1) (outpcd: nvr nrr) .. 1.8
163 Misdemeanours Girl (IRE) **(44)** *(MRChannon)* 4-7-12 ‡⁵BDoyle (6) (s.i.s: outpcd: nvr nr to chal) ........................... hd.9
86 Everset (FR) **(68)** *(WJMusson)* 4-9-6 ‡⁷PBowe (5) (eyeshield: bhd fnl 4f) .. 1.10
Judgement Call **(67)** *(PHowling)* 5-9-12 WNewnes (9) (a bhd) ........................ 1.11

**100/30** In the Game (IRE), **6/1** Misdemeanours Girl (IRE)(tchd 9/1), Rushanes(op 4/1), **7/1** Count Me Out, **5/2** MURMURING, **12/1** Courting Newmarket, The Noble Oak (IRE), Inswinger(op 8/1), **14/1** Do the Business (IRE), **25/1** Ors. CSF £29.41, CT £163.41. Tote £6.60: £2.00 1.50 1.80 (£15.90). Mr J. A. Redmond (EPSOM) bred by J. A. Redmond. 11 Rn
1m 13.22 (2.62)
SF−15/–/–/–/–/–

## 187  BARN OWL H'CAP (0-80) £2553.00 (£708.00: £339.00)    1¹/₂m **(AWT)**    4-40 (4-41)

165⁴ **Modesto (USA) (63)** *(KOCunningham-Brown)* 4-9-0 SWhitworth (13) (b: mde all: rdn out) ........................... −1
Caspian Beluga **(55)** *(MrsAKnight)* 4-8-1 ‡⁵FNorton (7) (a.p: chsd wnr fnl 3f: r.o) 2.2
144⁶ Absolutely Right **(52)** *(RAkehurst)* 4-8-3 SDawson (10) (rdn & hdwy 5f out: r.o wl ins fnl f) ........................... nk.3
Munday Dean **(65)** *(DWPArbuthnot)* 4-9-2 MHills (6) (b.hind: chsd ldr 9f: r.o one pce) ........................... hd.4
139³ Kirby Opportunity **(59)** (Fav) *(JPearce)* 4-8-5 ‡⁵RPrice (1) (a.p: r.o one pce fnl 2f) ........................... 2.5
126² Carlowitz (USA) **(44)** *(AMoore)* 4-7-9⁽²⁾ NAdams (8) (rdn & hdwy 4f out: nvr nr to chal) ........................... s.h.6
97 Searching Star **(43)** *(PAKelleway)* 4-7-2 GBardwell (5) (no hdwy fnl 2f) ........ 1.7
Windsor Park (USA) **(45)** *(KSBridgwater)* 6-7-13 DaleGibson (12) (hdwy fnl 2f: nvr nrr) ........................... 2.8
155 Broughton Blues (IRE) **(46)** *(WJMusson)* 4-7-11 AMackay (14) (eyeshield: a mid div) ........................... 3.9
154² Foursingh **(53)** (bl) *(CBBBooth)* 4-8-4 ACulhane (2) (prom 10f) ........................ 3.10
134³ Irish Native (IRE) **(62)** (bl) *(CASmith)* 4-8-13 AProud (9) (a.t.o) ........................ 25.11
143 Carousella **(55)** *(CEBrittain)* 4-8-1 ‡⁵BDoyle (11) (bhd fnl 5f: t.o) ........................ 1¹/₂.12
131 El Dominio **(62)** *(KOCunningham-Brown)* 4-8-10 ‡³DBiggs (4) (b: lw: a bhd: t.o) 2¹/₂.13
Julfaar (USA) **(74)** *(JPearce)* 5-10-0 WNewnes (3) (bit bkwd: bhd fnl 4f: t.o) 3¹/₂.14

**9/2** Kirby Opportunity, **5/1** MODESTO (USA), **6/1** Carousella, **13/2** Munday Dean(14/1—6/1), **8/1** Absolutely Right, Foursingh, **10/1** Carlowitz (USA), Irish Native (IRE)(op 6/1), El Dominio(8/1—12/1), **14/1** Windsor Park (USA), **20/1** Broughton Blues (IRE), **25/1** Searching Star, Caspian Beluga, **33/1** Julfaar (USA). CSF £115.72, CT £932.15. Tote £3.40: £1.90 5.80 2.70 (Wnr or 2nd w any £1.90). Mr D. Bass (STOCKBRIDGE) bred by Rhydian Morgan-Jones in USA. 14 Rn
2m 32.42 (3.02)
SF−34/17/18/30/15/4

T/Plpt: £553.80 (3.5 Tckts).

LMc

182—**LINGFIELD (L-H)** Equitrack
**Tuesday, March 3rd [Standard]**
Going Allowance: minus 0.40 sec per fur (FS)

### 188

COLUMBUS H'CAP (0-60) £2128.00 (£588.00: £280.00)  **5f (AWT)**  2-10 (2-11)

163⁵ **Hinari Video (57)** (Fav) (MJohnston) 7–9–12 DMcKeown (8) (a.p: r.o to ld wl ins
fnl f: drvn out) .................................................................. —1
132 Beckingham Ben (47) (JPLeigh) 8–9–2 DNicholls (1) (lw: led: hrd rdn over 1f
out: hdd wl ins fnl f: r.o) ........................................................ nk.2
186⁴ Inswinger (39) (WGRWightman) 6–8–8 TyroneWilliams (4) (a.p: rdn along: r.o
one pce fnl 2f) .................................................................. 2.3
33 Barbara's Cutie (41) (MBlanshard) 4–8–10 RCochrane (9) (a.p: one pce fnl 2f) .. 2.4
Ever so Artistic (52) (v) (PHowling) 5–9–2 ‡5FNorton (3) (lw: w ldr tl wknd over 1f
out) ......................................................................... 3¹/₂.5
150★ Galaxy Express (48) (GHEden) 4–8–10 ‡7PTurner (5) (outpcd) ............... ¹/₂.6
130⁶ Greetland Rock (59) (bl) (PHowling) 4–9–7 ‡7DebbieBiggs (2) (outpcd) ........... 1.7
163⁴ Pendor Dancer (52) (bl) (BForsey) 9–9–7 JWilliams (7) (swtg: dwlt: a bhd) ...... s.h.8
183⁶ Petank (IRE) (34) (PatMitchell) 4–7–10 ‡7RTurner (6) (a wl bhd) ................ 4.9

3/1 HINARI VIDEO, 7/2 Pendor Dancer, 9/2 Ever so Artistic, 5/1 Inswinger, 13/2 Galaxy Express, 10/1 Barbara's
Cutie, 12/1 Greetland Rock, 20/1 Beckingham Ben, 33/1 Petank (IRE). CSF £51.23, CT £269.59. Tote £5.10:
£2.20 £5.70 £2.00 (£38.00). Mark Johnston Racing Ltd (MIDDLEHAM) bred by Confey Stud Farm Ltd. 9 Rn
59.50 sec (1.30)
SF—46/35/19/13/5/–

### 189

COOK CLAIMING STKS (3-Y.O) £2088.80 (£576.80: £274.40)  **7f (AWT)**  2-40 (2-41)

151³ **Appealing Times (USA) (69)** (WAO'Gorman) 8-8 ‡5EmmaO'Gorman (3) (mde
all: clr 2f out: r.o) .............................................................. —1
135² Little Nod (63) (MJCamacho) 7-13 LCharnock (2) (w wnr over 4f: r.o one pce) 3¹/₂.2
164⁴ Easy Does it (56) (v) (CCElsey) 7-8(1) ‡5FNorton (6) (a.p: one pce fnl 2f) ......... 10.3
151★ Summer Express (70) (JLSpearing) 8-11 DNicholls (1) (rdn over 3f out: nvr nr
to chal) ..................................................................... 1¹/₂.4
164★ A Nymph Too Far (IRE) (56) (Fav) (DrJDScargill) 7-5 ‡3JFanning (7) (bhd fnl 3f) nk.5
164 Rhythmic Echo (52) (PHowling) 7-13 NCarlisle (4) (bhd fnl 4f) ................... 6.6
150² Indigo Blue (IRE) (46) (NACallaghan) 7-10 JQuinn (5) (prom 4f) ............... 3¹/₂.7

7/4 A Nymph Too Far (IRE), 4/1 Little Nod, APPEALING TIMES (USA), Summer Express(3/1—9/2), 10/1 Easy
Does it, 16/1 Indigo Blue (IRE), 20/1 Rhythmic Echo. CSF £19.26, Tote £4.10: £2.50 £2.50 (£14.50). Times of
Wigan (NEWMARKET) bred by Harry T. Mangurian Jnr in USA. 7 Rn; Little Nod clmd A Spargo £4,125
1m 25.32 (1.32)
SF—32/12/–/–/–/–

### 190

WITTENBORG UK LTD H'CAP (0-90) £2631.60 (£727.60: £346.80)
**1¹/₄m (AWT)**  3-10 (3-11)

187★ **Modesto (USA) (68)** (Fav) (KOCunningham-Brown) 4–9–6 (5x) ‡3DBiggs (4) (b:
lw: led tl over 2f out: hrd rdn & led wl over 1f out: r.o) —1
110³ Belmoredean (72) (RJO'Sullivan) 7–10–0 GDuffield (2) (a.p: r.o ins fnl f) ......... 1¹/₂.2
178⁵ Tara's Delight (59) (WAO'Gorman) 3–8–10 ‡5EmmaO'Gorman (3) (a.p: led over
2f out tl wl over 1f out) ......................................................... hd.3
154★ Merseyside Man (56) (v) (DrJDScargill) 6–8–5 ‡7KRutter (1) (jnd ldrs over 2f out:
rn wd wl over 1f out: nt rcvr) ................................................. 2¹/₄.4
142★ Buddy's Friend (IRE) (54) (RJRWilliams) 4–8–9 MHills (5) (lw: prom tl rdn & nt
qckn wl over 1f out) ........................................................... ¹/₂.5
Will He Or Wont He (IRE) (55) (CNAllen) 4–8–3 ‡7GForster (6) (wl bhd fnl 5f) .... 12.6

9/4 MODESTO (USA), 3/1 Merseyside Man, 4/1 Buddy's Friend (IRE), Tara's Delight, 11/2 Belmoredean(4/
1—6/1), 25/1 Will He Or Wont He (IRE). CSF £13.82, Tote £2.30: £1.70 £2.90 (£8.00). Mr D. Bass
(STOCKBRIDGE) bred by Rhydian Morgan-Jones in USA. 6 Rn
2m 7.77 (4.77)
SF—18/23/4/–/–/–

### 191

VASCO DA GAMA STKS (Mdn 3-Y.O) £2186.80 (£604.80: £288.40)
**1¹/₄m (AWT)**  3-40 (3-42)

167² **Fengari** (Fav) (PTWalwyn) 9-0 RCochrane (11) (hdwy 6f out: hrd rdn & led 1f
out: r.o wl) .................................................................. —1
167⁴ Granite Boy (60) (PJFeilden) 9-0 AShoults (2) (b.off hind: led 1f: led 5f out to 1f
out: r.o) ..................................................................... 2¹/₂.2
168³ Beam Me Up Scotty (IRE) (61) (PMitchell) 9-0 JWilliams (6) (a.p: rdn over 3f
out: r.o one pce) ............................................................. 1.3

170⁵ Set the Fashion (v) *(LordHuntingdon)* 9-0 DMcKeown (7) (hdwy 6f out: r.o one
pce fnl 3f) ...................................................................................... ¾.4
167³ Copy Lane (IRE) **(57)** *(MRChannon)* 9-0 WNewnes (5) (led 7f out to 5f out: sn
btn) ...................................................................................... 5.5
167 Child Star (FR) *(DMarks)* 8-9 GBaxter (4) (led after 1f to 7f out: wknd qckly 5f
out) ...................................................................................... 10.6
157² Qualitair Idol *(JFBottomley)* 8-9 GBardwell (4) (plld hrd: bhd fnl 4f) ............ 1½.7
68 Simon Ellis (IRE) **(47)** *(DRLaing)* 9-0 TyroneWilliams (8) (bhd fnl 4f) ............ 1½.8
164⁵ Lindeman **(63)** *(SDow)* 9-0 TQuinn (10) (b.hind: s.s: bhd most of wy) ........ 12.9
167⁵ Major Risk *(PAKelleway)* 8-11 ‡³DBiggs (9) (a wl bhd) ................................ 2.10
145 Easy Delta **(35)** *(CHolmes)* 8-9 SDawson (3) (prom 4f: t.o fnl 4f) ................ 30.11

**Evens** FENGARI(4/6—11/10), **6/1** Copy Lane (IRE)(8/1—5/1), **7/1** Lindeman, Qualitair Idol(op 4/1), **10/1** Beam
Me Up Scotty (IRE), **12/1** Granite Boy, **14/1** Child Star (FR), Set the Fashion, **20/1** Major Risk, **25/1** Simon Ellis
(IRE), **50/1** Easy Delta. CSF £15.37, Tote £1.70: £1.50 £3.00 £4.20 (£10.10). Fairly Stable (LAMBOURN) bred
by Hesmonds Stud Ltd. 11 Rn
2m 7.75 (4.75)
SF—13/8/6/4/1/—

**192** MARCO POLO H'CAP (0-80) £2301.00 (£636.00: £303.00)   **1m (AWT)**   4-10 (4-11)
(Weights raised 11 lb)

153★ **Sarum (55)** (Fav) *(CPWildman)* 4-9-10 CRutter (1) (a.p: led over 1f out: r.o) ..... —1
127⁵ Beau Dada (IRE) **(52)** *(JWhite)* 4-9-7 GCarter (6) (gd hdwy over 1f out: fin wl) nk.2
153⁶ Queen of Dreams **(39)** *(DrJDScargill)* 4-8-5 ‡³JFanning (8) (a.p: led over 2f out
tl over 1f out: hrd rdn: one pce) ...................................................... 2½.3
144 Wileys Folly **(42)** *(SDow)* 6-8-11 TQuinn (5) (b.hind: hdwy 4f out: rdn over 2f
out: one pce) ...................................................................................... ¾.4
154 Luks Akura **(40)** *(MJohnston)* 4-8-9 DMcKeown (4) (w ldr: led 4f out tl over 2f
out: sn wknd) ...................................................................................... 3.5
153 Dutch Czarina **(43)** (v) *(MissBSanders)* 4-8-12 WNewnes (2) (nvr nr to chal) ..... 0.6
111 Scots Law **(41)** *(RJO'Sullivan)* 5-8-7 ‡³DBiggs (2) (led 4f: t.o) ................ 20.7

**7/4** SARUM, **5/2** Wileys Folly, **4/1** Queen of Dreams, **11/2** Beau Dada (IRE), **8/1** Scots Law(op 12/1), **12/1** Dutch
Czarina, **16/1** Luks Akura(10/1—20/1). CSF £12.41, CT £33.42. Tote £1.90: £1.60 £2.30 (£4.60). Mr W.
Wildman (SALISBURY) bred by Miss Suzannah Armstrong. 7 Rn
1m 39.35 (2.65)
SF—23/19/—/—/—/

**193** CABOT H'CAP (Amateurs) (0-70) £2324.00 (£644.00: £308.00)
**1m 5f (AWT)**   4-40 (4-41)
(Weights raised 7 lb)

**Classic Account (58)** (Fav) *(JAkehurst)* 4-11-4 ‡⁵MrEReitel (2) (lw: mde
virtually all: r.o wl) ...................................................................................... —1
76⁶ Kovalevskia **(36)** *(DAWilson)* 7-10-4 MissEBronson (10) (hdwy 4f out: ev ch ins
fnl f: r.o) ...................................................................................... ½.2
Crosby Place **(45)** (bl) *(MJHaynes)* 6-10-13 MissYHaynes (5) (bit bkwd: hdwy
6f out: ev ch 2f out: r.o one pce) ...................................................... 3.3
184 Priceless Fantasy **(39)** *(PatMitchell)* 5-10-2 ‡⁵MissLGlayzer (7) (hdwy 5f out:
one pce fnl 3f) ...................................................................................... 8.4
88 Qualitair Sweetie **(39)** *(JFBottomley)* 5-10-2 ‡⁵MissAPurdy (3) (nvr nrr) ............ ½.5
184³ Mardior **(39)** *(WGRWightman)* 4-9-9 ‡⁵MrGKille (1) (w wnr tl wknd qckly 2f out) . 2.6
125 Pondered Bid **(38)** *(PatMitchell)* 8-10-6 MissIDWJones (11) (swtg: a bhd) ........ 12.7
76 Bursana **(35)** *(JLSpearing)* 6-9-12 ‡⁵MissTSpearing (4) (a bhd) ...................... ½.8
Against You **(60)** *(RAkehurst)* 5-11-9 ‡⁵MrRByrne (12) (prom 6f) ...................... 5.9
Emperor Chang (USA) **(48)** *(PABlockley)* 5-10-11 ‡⁵MrKGreen (9) (bit bkwd:
bhd fnl 7f) ...................................................................................... 3½.10
142 Orchanda **(35)** *(MrsAKnight)* 4-10-0 MissABillot (6) (prom 8f: t.o) ................ 12.11
LONG HANDICAP: Mardior 9-9, Orchanda 9-12.

**2/1** CLASSIC ACCOUNT(tchd 3/1), **7/2** Kovalevskia, **9/2** Bursana, **11/2** Crosby Place(op 7/2), **11/1** Against You,
**14/1** Mardior(op 8/1), **16/1** Emperor Chang (USA), **20/1** Ors. CSF £9.81, CT £28.91. Tote £2.90: £2.00 £1.90
£1.60 (£7.40). Mr E. Reitel (UPPER LAMBOURN) bred by Home Stud Ltd. 11 Rn
2m 49.41 (5.91)
SF—21/2/5/—/—/—

T/Plpt: £49.30 (28 Tckts).
Hn

169—**SOUTHWELL (L-H)** Fibresand

**Friday, March 6th [Standard]**
Going Allowance: 12f: 0.20 sec; Rest: 0.40 sec per fur (SL)
Stalls: 4th high, remainder low

**194** RUFFORD APP'CE STKS (Mdn) £2343.60 (£649.60: £310.80)   **6f (AWT)**   2-30 (2-33)

162² Swinging Lady **(46)** *(WWHaigh)* 4-9-2 FNorton (2) (mde all: rdn clr over 2f out:
eased nr fin) ...................................................................................... —1

163² Cellito (IRE) **(57)** (bl) (Fav) *(WAO'Gorman)* 3-8-6　EmmaO'Gorman (11) (lw: stdy hdwy ½-wy: rdn & no imp fnl 2f) ................................ 3½.2

143 Carnfield **(34)** (v) *(JAGlover)* 4-9-2　SWilliams (7) (chsd ldrs: effrt over 2f out: nt pce to chal) ..................................................... 1½.3

133⁴ Grubby **(53)** *(RHollinshead)* 3-7-12 ‡³AGarth (5) (prom tl wknd wl over 1f out) . nk.4

Miss Moody **(36)** *(JMBradley)* 6-8-11 ‡⁵MichaelBradley (10) (styd on u.p fnl 2f: nvr nrr) ..................................................... 1½.5

North Flyer **(53)** *(BAMcMahon)* 3-8-3 ‡³SSanders (9) (prom over 3f) ................. ¾.6

Native Lass (IRE) **(36)** *(JBalding)* 3-7-12 ‡³ClaireBalding (1) (chsd wnr 3f: rdn & wknd ent st) ..................................................... 4.7

Educated Pet **(46)** *(MJohnston)* 3-8-1 ‡⁵MBaird (4) (bit bkwd: s.s: a bhd) ......... 3.8

Friendly Song **(48)** (bl) *(TFairhurst)* 4-9-2　JFanning (8) (hdwy 3f out: sn rdn & wknd) ..................................................... ½.9

174 Comiskey Park (IRE) *(DWChapman)* 3-8-6　OPears (6) (bit bkwd: chsd ldrs to ½-wy: sn lost pl) ..................................................... ¾.10

Ingenuity *(LordHuntingdon)* 3-8-1 DHarrison (3) (small: bit bkwd: sn rdn along: a bhd: t.o) ..................................................... 8.11

**5/2** Cellito (IRE)(7/4—11/4), **4/1** Ingenuity, **5/1** Grubby, SWINGING LADY, **12/1** Educated Pet, **14/1** Friendly Song, **16/1** Carnfield, **20/1** North Flyer, Comiskey Park (IRE), **33/1** Ors. CSF £16.82, Tote £4.80: £1.60 £1.50 £2.80 (£5.10). Mrs P. A. Valentine (MALTON) bred by Brian Mills. 11 Rn
1m 20.6 (7.2)
SF–6/–/–/–/–/–

**195**　　SKEGBY CLAIMING STKS (3-Y.O) £2186.80 (£604.80: £288.40)　　**6f (AWT)** 3-00 (3-02)

174³ Lord Naskra (USA) *(WAO'Gorman)* 8-4 ‡⁵EmmaO'Gorman (6) (s.i.s: hdwy ½-wy: hung lft appr fnl f: r.o to ld cl home) ..................... —1

177³ Patrician Magician **(66)** (bl) *(RJRWilliams)* 7-12 ‡³DBiggs (8) (chsd ldr: rdn to ld 2f out: hdd nr fin) ..................................................... s.h.2

160⁴ Pop to Stans **(89)** (Fav) *(TDBarron)* 9-7　AlexGreaves (4) (chsd ldrs: hmpd over 1f out: swtch rt & r.o strly fnl f) ..................................................... ¾.3

Monti Beppo **(56)** *(LJBarratt)* 7-7⁽²⁾ ‡⁵FNorton (1) (led 4f : kpt on ins fnl f) ......... ½.4

174² Eastleigh **(70)** *(RHollinshead)* 9-3　WRyan (5) (lw: prom: rdn & unable qckn fnl f) sh.5

157 Bitmac Boy *(MrsPABarker)* 7-13 ‡³JFanning (3) (prom 3f: wknd qckly: t.o) ......... 25.6

Aldington Peach *(BAMcMahon)* 7-13 ‡⁵SMaloney (2) (unf: s.i.s: a bhd: t.o) ......... 6.7

Moniaive *(WClay)* 8-4 ‡⁷KRutter (3) (lt-f: bkwd: dwlt: a outpcd & bhd: t.o) ......... 20.8

**6/5** Pop to Stans, **7/2** Patrician Magician(op 11/2), **9/2** Eastleigh, **11/2** LORD NASKRA (USA), **25/1** Monti Beppo, **33/1** Aldington Peach, **50/1** Ors. CSF £22.83, Tote £6.00: £1.10 £1.30 £1.10 (£11.70). Curley O'Gorman (NEWMARKET) bred by Barbara Hunter in USA. 8 Rn
1m 19.6 (6.2)
SF–14/7/28/–/21/–

**196**　　EAST MIDLANDS ELECTRICITY H'CAP (0-90) £2069.20 (£571.20: £271.60)
**6f (AWT)**　　　　　　　　　　　　　　　　　　　　　　　3-30 (3-32)

92⁶ Super Benz **(84)** (Fav) *(TFairhurst)* 6-9-11 ‡³JFanning (2) (mde all: rdn 2f out: clr fnl f: v.easily) ..................................................... —1

92 Super Heights **(61)** (bl) *(MissAJWhitfield)* 4-8-5　DaleGibson (1) (bhd: hdwy u.p appr fnl f: nvr nrr) ..................................................... 4.2

149⁵ Meeson Times **(68)** *(BEllison)* 4-8-12　MHills (4) (b: lw: hld up in tch: effrt 2f out: rdn & no ex fnl f) ..................................................... 3.3

162⁶ Factuelle **(50)** *(DRTucker)* 5-7-8　GBardwell (5) (spd over 4f) ..................... 4.4

Asterix **(79)** (v) *(JMBradley)* 4-9-9　JWilliams (6) (bkwd: hdwy ½-wy: wknd 2f out) ..................................................... 3½.5

132⁴ Tigani **(81)** (bl) *(DWChapman)* 6-9-11　SWood (3) (chsd wnr 4f: sn rdn & btn) .. ¾.6

**15/8** SUPER BENZ, **5/2** Meeson Times, **5/1** Super Heights, **11/2** Tigani, **12/1** Asterix, **25/1** Factuelle. CSF £10.06, Tote £2.40: £1.50 £2.50 (£5.10). Mr David F. Bramley (MIDDLEHAM) bred by Scarteen Stud. 6 Rn
1m 19.6 (6.2)
SF–35/–/–/–/–/–

**197**　　MILTON H'CAP (0-90) £2226.00 (£616.00: £294.00)　　**1½m (AWT)**　　4-00 (4-00)

161★ Horizon (IRE) **(72)** (bl) (Fav) *(TThomsonJones)* 4-9-0 ‡³DBiggs (1) (led after 3f: rdn & styd on strly fnl 2f) ..................................................... —1

Broom Isle **(54)** *(MrsAKnight)* 4-7-8⁽⁶⁾ ‡⁵FNorton (2) (bkwd: a.p: 2nd st: jnd wnr u.p 2f out: one pce fnl f) ..................................................... 3½.2

161² Army of Stars **(79)** *(CEBrittain)* 7-9-8 ‡⁵BDoyle (3) (lw: chsd ldrs: 4th & rdn st: styd on ins fnl f) ..................................................... 3½.3

161³ Pims Classic **(56)** *(WJHaggas)* 7-9-0 ‡⁷SallyRadford-Howes (7) (b.nr fore: led 3f: 3rd st: one pce fnl 2f) ..................................................... ¾.4

176★ Unpaid Member **(53)** *(JWharton)* 8-7-12 (5x) ‡³JFanning (4) (chsd ldr: 5th & btn st) ..................................................... 15.5

169³ Le Temeraire (70) (NTinkler) 6-9-4 KimTinkler (5) (stdd s: hdwy ½-wy: 6th st: nvr nr ldrs) ............................................................................................................... 3.6

169⁴ Mississippi Beat (USA) (45) (v) (MPNaughton) 5-7-0 ‡7CHawksley (6) (sn pushed along: a bhd: 7th st) ....................................................................................... 2.7

**Evens** HORIZON (IRE), **5/1** Army of Stars, **13/2** Unpaid Member, **15/2** Le Temeraire(5/1—8/1), **10/1** Mississippi Beat (USA), **14/1** Pims Classic, **40/1** Broom Isle. CSF £26.39, Tote £1.70: £1.10: £3.90 (£14.10). Mrs Solna Thomson Jones (UPPER LAMBOURN) bred by Mrs Nuala Clarke in Ireland. 7 Rn                    2m 42.2 (8)
SF—44/17/38/16/–/–

## 198 TUXFORD STKS (Mdn) £2206.40 (£610.40: £291.20) 1m (AWT) 4-30 (4-36)

112⁴ **Qualitair Rhythm (IRE) (45)** (bl) (Fav) (ICampbell) 4-8-9 BRaymond (4) (hld up: stdy hdwy & 3rd st: led on bit over 2f out: sn clr: canter) —1

179⁴ Kay's Dilemma (IRE) (PAKelleway) 4-8-6 ‡3DBiggs (7) (led 3f: 2nd st: chsd wnr fnl 2f: no imp) ........................................................................................................ 15.2

Persuasius (IRE) (59) (WJPearce) 4-9-0 DNicholls (2) (prom: 4th st: no hdwy fnl 2f) ............................................................................................................................... 8.3

181³ Danzig Lad (USA) (40) (v) (MPNaughton) 4-9-0 GCarter (10) (chsd ldrs: 5th st: sn rdn & btn) ........................................................................................................... 2.4

Hanjessdan (DHaydnJones) 4-9-0 JWilliams (8) (bkwd: bhd: hdwy ½-wy: 6th st: styd on one pce) ..................................................................................................... 1½.5

First Home (PatMitchell) 4-8-7 ‡7RTurner (3) (bkwd: chsd ldrs 5f: sn lost tch) .. s.h.6

179² Restless Niece (31) (TDBarron) 4-8-9 AlexGreaves (1) (led after 3f tl over 2f out: sn rdn & btn) ..................................................................................................... 5.7

Rustic Hunter (IRE) (CJHill) 4-9-0 NAdams (5) (bit bkwd: s.s: a bhd) ..................... 5.8

Oka Flow (55) (bl) (PABlockley) 4-8-7 ‡7GParkin (9) (prom: rdn along ½-wy: wknd) .............................................................................................................................. 8.9

142 Replicate (36) (MJCharles) 4-8-9 RCochrane (6) (s.s: a bhd: t.o) .................. ½.10

**11/8** QUALITAIR RHYTHM (IRE), **7/2** Persuasius (IRE), **11/2** Restless Niece, **10/1** Danzig Lad (USA), **12/1** Kay's Dilemma (IRE)(op 8/1), **14/1** Replicate, Hanjessdan, Oka Flow, **25/1** First Home, **33/1** Rustic Hunter (IRE). CSF £18.48, Tote £2.40: £1.30: £2.40 £1.10 (£12.70). Mr M. J. Spore (NEWMARKET) bred by Brendan Powell in Ireland. 10 Rn                                                                                    1m 46.6 (7.3)
SF—32/–/–/–/–/–

## 199 NORMANTON H'CAP (0-70) £2343.60 (£649.60: £310.80) 7f (AWT) 5-00 (5-04)

89 **Hawaii Storm (FR) (36)** (MissAJWhitfield) 4-7-8(1) NAdams (11) (b.nr hind: a.p: led 3f out: sn clr: eased nr fin) ..................................................................... —1

100⁶ Doulab's Image (70) (JAGlover) 5-9-7 ‡7SWilliams (9) (hld up & bhd: hdwy 2f out: nrst fin) ....................................................................................................... 3.2

111 Royal Acclaim (45) (v) (JMBradley) 7-7-10(3) ‡7MichaelBradley (6) (bhd: hdwy over 1f out: fin wl) ................................................................................................ 1.3

143³ Quinzii Martin (52) (v) (Fav) (DHaydnJones) 4-8-10 JWilliams (5) (hdwy 4f out: 3rd st: chsd wnr fnl 2f: wknd ins fnl f) ........................................................... nk.4

159⁵ Strip Cartoon (IRE) (49) (bl) (GBlum) 4-8-7 SWebster (7) (led 4f: 2nd st: rdn & wknd appr fnl f) ............................................................................................. 4.5

31 Miss Knight (46) (RBastiman) 5-8-4 DMcKeown (1) (prom tl hmpd & lost pl after 2f: 6th st: rdn & no hdwy fnl 2f) .................................................................... nk.6

172⁶ Cool Enough (42) (MrsJRRamsden) 11-7-11 ‡3DBiggs (2) (mid div: effrt 2f out: nt trble ldrs) ................................................................................................... 4.7

143 Foolish Touch (64) (WJMusson) 10-9-8 AMackay (10) (eyeshield: b: s.i.s: a in rr) ............................................................................................................................. hd.8

132⁶ Lonely Lass (45) (LJBarratt) 6-8-3 LCharnock (4) (chsd ldrs tl 5th & wkng st) ... 2.9

172 Ping Pong (39) (bl) (TFairhurst) 4-7-8 ‡3JFanning (8) (prom: 4th st: sn wknd) nk.10

158 Armaiti (61) (DRTucker) 4-9-5 GBardwell (3) (uns rdr & bolted bef s: a bhd: t.o) 8.11

LONG HANDICAP: Hawaii Storm (FR) 7-6.

**100/30** Quinzii Martin, **9/2** Cool Enough, **11/2** Foolish Touch, **6/1** Doulab's Image(op 4/1), **7/1** Miss Knight, **10/1** Strip Cartoon (IRE), **12/1** Ping Pong, **16/1** Armaiti, Lonely Lass, Royal Acclaim, **20/1** HAWAII STORM (FR). CSF £127.22, CT £1,808.04. Tote £18.60: £4.10 £2.30 £4.80 (£146.70). Mr Andreas Sofroniou (LAMBOURN) bred by Horse France in France. 11 Rn                                                                        1m 32.7 (6.1)
SF—20/38/10/23/8/4

T/Plpt: £37.40 (38.2 Tckts).                                                                                                IM

## 188—LINGFIELD (L-H) Equitrack

### Saturday, March 7th [Standard]

Going Allowance: minus 0.60 sec per fur (FS)

## 200 PISCES STKS (Mdn 3-Y-O) £2108.40 (£582.40: £277.20) 1m (AWT) 1-55 (1-58)

191² **Granite Boy (60)** (Fav) (PJFeilden) 9-0 AShoults (4) (led 2f: led 4f out: qcknd 2f out: easily) ...................................................................................................... —1

170³ Trump *(SirMarkPrescott)* 9-0 GDuffield (3) (led 6f out to 4f out: rdn over 2f out: no imp) ............................................................ 6.2
Witches Coven *(MBell)* 8-9 MHills (7) (rdn & hdwy over 4f out: one pce fnl 3f) ... 2.3
Prove It's Gold *(TMJones)* 8-9 JWilliams (2) (neat: dwlt: rdn along: nvr nr to chal) ............................................................ 5.4
157⁵ Keen Wit *(LordHuntingdon)* 8-9 DMcKeown (1) (w ldrs 4f) ........................... 3.5
Dominant Serenade (68) *(PWHarris)* 9-0 WNewnes (5) (rdn along: bhd fnl 5f) ... 8.6
182 Court Room (43) (bl) *(AMoore)* 9-0 BRouse (6) (a bhd) ..................................... 5.7

**15/8** GRANITE BOY, **3/1** Witches Coven(op 2/1), **9/2** Trump(op 3/1), **11/2** Keen Wit(op 3/1), **9/1** Dominant Serenade(8/1—12/1), **33/1** Ors. CSF £9.63, Tote £3.10: £1.20 £2.10 (£8.90). Mr C. V. Lines (NEWMARKET) bred by Grange Stud (UK). 7 Rn                                1m 40.97 (4.27)

---

## 201    ACE PRIVATE AMBULANCE CARE CLAIMING STKS    £2226.00 (£616.00: £294.00)
**7f (AWT)**                                                                2-25 (2-28)

183★ **Invocation (48)** *(AMoore)* 5-8-7 NAdams (7) (lw: mde all: clr over 1f out: drvn out) ............................................................ —1
173★ Toshiba Comet (78) (bl) *(Jt-Fav)* *(WJPearce)* 5-8-8 DNicholls (5) (chsd wnr 4f out: hrd rdn over 1f out: r.o ins fnl f) ........................................ 1¹⁄₂.2
127³ Mac's Fighter (89) (bl) *(Jt-Fav)* *(WAO'Gorman)* 7-9-2 ‡5EmmaO'Gorman (2) (rdn along: hdwy 3f out: r.o ins fnl f) ............................ 2.3
180 Wellsy Lad (USA) (70) *(DWChapman)* 5-8-3 SWood (4) (no hdwy fnl 3f) ...... 7.4
186⁶ Courting Newmarket (54) *(MrsAKnight)* 4-8-2 ‡3DBiggs (1) (nvr nr to chal) ...... nk.5
The Square Centre (USA) *(PBurgoyne)* 4-8-5 TQuinn (3) (bit bkwd: rdn & lost pl 5f out: rallied 3f out: wknd 2f out) ............................ nk.6
183⁵ Hitchin a Ride *(MPMuggeridge)* 5-9-7 JWilliams (8) (a bhd) ........................... 10.7
153 Deepwood Nanusket (31) *(MMadgwick)* 6-7-11⁽¹⁾ SDawson (9) (prom 4f) ......... 5.8
126⁵ Bay Mountain (32) (bl) *(MDixon)* 6-8-3 GBardwell (6) (b.hind: s.i.s: a bhd) ...... 1¹⁄₂.9

**13/8** Mac's Fighter, Toshiba Comet, **8/1** INVOCATION, Wellsy Lad (USA), **16/1** Courting Newmarket(op 10/1), **33/1** The Square Centre (USA), Bay Mountain, **50/1** Ors. CSF £20.08, Tote £8.10: £1.70 £1.40 £1.10 (£5.30). Mr R. Kiernan (BRIGHTON) bred by Juddmonte Farms. 9 Rn; Invocation clmd W O'Gorman £8,210
                                                                1m 24.71 (0.71)
                                                                SF—19/17/19/–/–/–

---

## 202    RAPPORTEUR STKS    £4113.00 (£1224.00: £582.00: £261.00)
**1¹⁄₄m (AWT)**                                                             2-55 (2-57)

**Tanfith (CAN)** *(JEBanks)* 5-8-9 ‡3DBiggs (1) (swtg: hld up: led over 2f out: clr over 1f out: comf) ............................................ —1
146³ Rapporteur (USA) (89) *(Fav)* *(CCElsey)* 6-9-5 WNewnes (2) (b: rdn along: hdwy 4f out: ev ch 3f out: unable qckn) ............................ 7.2
Rising Tempo (IRE) (63) *(CACyzer)* 4-8-11 GCarter (3) (rdn & hdwy 4f out: ev ch 3f out: one pce) ............................................ 2.3
169★ Tempering (80) *(DWChapman)* 6-9-5 SWood (5) (led 5f out tl over 2f out: sn wknd) ............................................................ 2¹⁄₂.4
187⁶ Carlowitz (USA) (41) *(AMoore)* 4-8-11 BRouse (6) (b: lw: led 3f: rdn, hmpd & stumbled over 3f out: wknd qckly) ............................ 20.5
Wingfield (USA) *(DRCElsworth)* 4-9-4 JWilliams (4) (eyeshield: lw: led 7f out to 5f out: sn wknd) ............................................ 15.6

**8/11** Rapporteur (USA), **5/2** TANFITH (CAN)(op 5/1), **5/1** Tempering, **11/1** Wingfield (USA)(op 9/2), **33/1** Carlowitz (USA), **50/1** Rising Tempo (IRE). CSF £4.76, Tote £4.60: £1.80 £1.10 (£3.80). Miss Karen Barton (NEWMARKET) bred by Roger Laurin in Canada. 6 Rn                        2m 4.83 (1.83)
                                                                SF—17/13/1/4/–/–

---

## 203    CONQUEST CUP (H'cap) (0-110) £10770.00 (£3210.00: £1530.00: £690.00)
**1m (AWT)**                                                                3-25 (3-28)

152★ **Pytchley Night (90)** *(Fav)* *(DMorris)* 5-8-13 ‡7StephenDavies (5) (lw: hdwy 4f out: hrd rdn over 1f out: led wl ins fnl f: all out) .................. —1
165★ Super Sally (98) *(MJRyan)* 5-9-11 ‡3DBiggs (7) (hdwy over 2f out: led ins fnl f: sn hdd: r.o wl) ........................................ hd.2
178² Martini Executive (81) (bl) *(WJPearce)* 4-8-11 DNicholls (10) (gd hdwy over 3f out: led over 1f out tl ins fnl f: r.o) .................... 1.3
178⁴ Euroblake (75) *(TDBarron)* 5-8-5 AlexGreaves (4) (rdn 3f out: hdwy fnl 2f: r.o) 1¹⁄₂.4
165² Usa Dollar (66) (bl) *(BGubby)* 5-7-10 JQuinn (11) (hdwy 3f out: ev ch ins fnl f: unable qckn) ...................................... ³⁄₄.5
143★ Kissavos (68) (v) *(CCElsey)* 6-7-7⁽⁵⁾ ‡5FNorton (1) (b.hind: a.p: one pce fnl 2f) 1¹⁄₂.6
183² African Chimes (95) (bl) *(WAO'Gorman)* 5-9-6 ‡5EmmaO'Gorman (3) (led 5f out tl over 1f out: wknd fnl f) ................................ 3¹⁄₂.7

185[2] Vuchterbacher **(67)** *(PFTulk)* 6–7–4[(4)] ‡7TWilson (8) (b: a.p: ev ch over 2f out: wknd wl over 1f out) ..... 1½.**8**
Shake Town (USA) **(79)** *(MHTompkins)* 4–8–4 ‡5CHodgson (6) (bhd fnl 5f) ..... 2½.**9**
153 Sauvignon (IRE) **(63)** *(RGuest)* 4–7–0 ‡7CHawksley (9) (s.s: a bhd) ................. ¾.**10**
Conjurer **(74)** *(RSimpson)* 5–8–4[(4)] WRyan (2) (led 3f: t.o) ................. 20.**11**
LONG HANDICAP: Kissavos 7-5, Vuchterbacher 7-5, Sauvignon (IRE) 7-0.

**4/1** PYTCHLEY NIGHT, **9/2** Martini Executive, Super Sally(3/1—5/1), **13/2** African Chimes, Usa Dollar(9/2—7/1), **10/1** Shake Town (USA)(7/1—11/1), **12/1** Kissavos, **14/1** Euroblake, **16/1** Vuchterbacher, **33/1** Sauvignon (IRE), **40/1** Conjurer. CSF £20.90, CT £76.34. Tote £6.80: £1.90 £1.50 £1.80 (£7.50). Mr J. J. Higgins (NEWMARKET) bred by G. W. Robinson. 11 Rn
1m 37.54 (0.84)
SF—22/26/9/–/–/–

## 204

LIBRA H'CAP (0-90) £3687.50 (£1100.00: £525.00: £237.50)    **7f (AWT)**    3-55 (3-56)
(Weights raised 7 lb)

189★ **Appealing Times (USA) (78)** *(WAO'Gorman)* 3–8–2[(2)] (7x) ‡5EmmaO'Gorman (5) (chsd ldr: led over 1f out: rdn out) ................. —**1**
Domicksky **(78)** *(MJRyan)* 4–9–10 NDay (3) (lw: a.p: hrd rdn over 1f out: r.o wl ins fnl f) ................. nk.**2**
185★ Predictable **(66)** *(MrsAKnight)* 6–8–9 ‡3DBiggs (1) (lw: led over 5f: rdn & r.o) hd.**3**
140[3] Mossy Rose **(58)** *(LordHuntingdon)* 6–7–11 ‡7DHarrison (6) (outpcd: hdwy over 2f out: hrd rdn over 1f out: str run fnl f: fin wl) ................. nk.**4**
147 Try Leguard (IRE) **(81)** *(WCarter)* 3–8–10 GCarter (4) (outpcd) ................. 12.**5**
Languedoc **(78)** *(MPNaughton)* 5–9–10 LCharnock (2) (hrd rdn 4f out: bhd fnl 3f) 5.**6**
186★ Murmuring **(65)** *(SDow)* 6–8–11 TQuinn (7) (rdn along fnl 5f: wknd 3f out) ...... 1½.**7**
173[4] The Shanahan Bay **(58)** (v) *(MrsNMacauley)* 7–8–4 DMcKeown (4) (b: bhd fnl 4f) 3.**8**

**3/1** Predictable, **7/2** Mossy Rose, **5/1** APPEALING TIMES (USA), **11/2** Try Leguard (IRE), **8/1** Domicksky(op 5/1), **10/1** Languedoc, **11/1** Murmuring(op 7/1), **14/1** The Shanahan Bay. CSF £39.09, CT £125.74. Tote £4.40: £1.70 £3.60 £1.40 (£32.40). Times of Wigan (NEWMARKET) bred by Harry T. Mangurian Jnr in USA. 8 Rn
1m 23.74 (U.26)
SF—29/50/34/21/10/9

## 205

REPQUIP-TERRA-VAC H'CAP (0-80) £2950.00 (£880.00: £420.00: £190.00) **2m (AWT)**    4-25 (4-27)

125[3] Carlingford (USA) **(54)** *(MPNaughton)* 6–8–3 LCharnock (2) (lw: led 3f: led 2f out: rdn out) ................. —**1**
Postage Stamp **(67)** *(JPearce)* 5–9–2 JMcLaughlin (12) (led after 3f to 4f out: rallied ins fnl f: r.o wl) ................. ½.**2**
166★ Aude la Belle (FR) **(56)** *(MrsAKnight)* 4–7–11 ‡3DBiggs (3) (hdwy 3f out: r.o ins fnl f) ................. 1½.**3**
76[5] Shar Emblem **(51)** *(SDow)* 4–7–9[(2)] JQuinn (9) (stdy hdwy 7f out: r.o one pce fnl 2f) ................. 5.**4**
115 Gipsy King **(49)** *(PAKelleway)* 4–7–7 GBardwell (6) (a.p: led 4f out to 2f out: snatched up wl over 1f out: sn wknd) ................. ¾.**5**
187 El Dominio **(63)** *(KOCunningham-Brown)* 4–8–7[(2)] WNewnes (10) (b: lw: prom over 13f) ................. 1½.**6**
Coleridge **(72)** *(DShaw)* 4–9–2 GCarter (5) (bit bkwd: rdn over 6f out: wknd over 3f out) ................. 7.**7**
166[5] Sand Castle **(49)** *(PHowling)* 11–7–7[(5)] ‡5FNorton (11) (rdn 9f out: bhd fnl 4f) ...... 1.**8**
Honey Dancer **(66)** *(MissAJWhitfield)* 8–9–1 GBaxter (1) (bhd fnl 6f) ................. 10.**9**
Sir Dancelot (USA) **(53)** *(RSimpson)* 4–7–11 SDawson (8) (b: wl bhd fnl 8f) .... ½.**10**
Art Form (USA) **(79)** *(CACyzer)* 5–9–7 ‡7TMcLaughlin (7) (a bhd: t.o fnl 8f) .... dist.**11**
LONG HANDICAP: Gipsy King 7-3, Sand Castle 6-12.
*Stewards Enquiry: Obj. by McLaughlin to Carlingford overruled.*

**2/1** Postage Stamp, **9/4** Aude la Belle (FR), **6/1** Shar Emblem(op 4/1), **9/1** CARLINGFORD (USA)(op 5/1), **10/1** El Dominio, Art Form (USA)(6/1—12/1), **14/1** Sir Dancelot (USA)(op 7/1), **20/1** Coleridge(op 12/1), **25/1** Honey Dancer, **33/1** Ors. CSF £28.00, CT £52.68. Tote £5.30: £1.10 £1.60 £1.80 (£17.30). Mrs H. H. Wane (RICHMOND) bred by Hugh G. King, III in USA. 11 Rn
3m 23 (equals standard)
T/Plpt: £7.80 (214 Tckts).
LMc

## 200—**LINGFIELD (L-H)** Equitrack

## Tuesday, March 10th [Standard]

Going Allowance: minus 0.40 sec per fur (F)

## 206

WATERINGBURY APP'CE STKS (I) (Mdn) £2128.00 (£588.00: £280.00) **1¼m (AWT)**    1-55 (1-56)

142[2] **Riviera Rainbow (52)** *(Jt-Fav)* *(DRCElsworth)* 4–8–11 ‡3JHunter (5) (eyeshield: chsd ldr over 6f out: led over 2f out: clr over 1f out: r.o wl) .. —**1**

Smiling Chief (IRE) **(60)** *(CACyzer)* 4–8–11 ‡3AMorris (8) (bit bkwd: a.p: rdn over
　　6f out: one pce fnl 3f) ...................................................................... 10.2
*178*6 Loudest Whisper **(58)** (Jt-Fav) *(KSBridgwater)* 4–9–0 BDoyle (2) (led over 7f:
　　wknd wl over 1f out) ....................................................................... 1.3
Carol's Pet (IRE) *(JEBanks)* 4–8–9 DBiggs (3) (bit bkwd: s.s: rdn & hdwy over 4f
　　out: wknd over 1f out) ...................................................................... 4.4
High Kabour *(WGMTurner)* 6–8–7 ‡3TWilson (1) (nvr nr to chal) ................... 1/2.5
*138* Ballerina Rose **(24)** *(OO'Neill)* 5–8–7 ‡3EHusband (7) (bhd fnl 5f) ............ s.h.6
Lunagraphe (USA) *(BobJones)* 4–8–6 ‡3CHawksley (4) (swtg: hdwy over 4f out:
　　wknd 3f out) ..................................................................................... 3.7
Manaolana **(42)** *(AMoore)* 4–8–4 ‡5RMoogan (6) (b: chsd ldr over 3f: t.o) ......... 25.8

**7/4** Loudest Whisper, RIVIERA RAINBOW, **5/1** Carol's Pet (IRE)(7/1—9/2), **9/1** Smiling Chief (IRE)(op 4/1), **10/1**
Lunagraphe (USA)(tchd 16/1), **14/1** Manaolana, **25/1** Ballerina Rose, **33/1** High Kabour. CSF £17.59, Tote
£1.90: £1.10 £3.20 £1.20 (£33.70). Sir Clement Freud (WHITSBURY) bred by J. L. C. Pearce. 8 Rn
　　　　　　　　　　　　　　　　　　　　　　　　　　　　　　　　　　　2m 6.4 (3.4)
　　　　　　　　　　　　　　　　　　　　　　　　　　　　　　　　　　SF–24/1/2/–/–/–

**207**　　　TONBRIDGE CLAIMING STKS　　£2284.80 (£632.80: £302.40)　　**6f (AWT)**　2-25 (2-26)

*130*3 **Very Dicey (81)** (Fav) *(SDow)* 4–9–0 TQuinn (7) (b.hind: mde all: clr over 2f out:
　　unchal) .................................................................................................. —1
*201*3 Mac's Fighter **(89)** (v) *(WAO'Gorman)* 7–9–5 ‡5EmmaO'Gorman (10) (hdwy
　　over 1f out: r.o) ................................................................................... 5.2
*186*3 Count Me Out **(44)** (bl) *(JPearce)* 7–8–8 ‡5RPrice (5) (lw: a.p: one pce fnl 3f) ... 11/2.3
*201*2 Toshiba Comet **(78)** (bl) *(WJPearce)* 5–9–2 DNicholls (9) (hdwy over 4f out: rdn
　　over 3f out: one pce) ............................................................................ 2.4
*137* Precious Air (IRE) **(43)** *(AMoore)* 4–8–10 BRouse (3) (nvr nr to chal) ............ s.h.5
Erris Express **(76)** *(KTIvory)* 7–9–0 MWigham (6) (eyeshield: b: nvr nrr) ............. 3/4.6
*82* Great Hall **(47)** *(WGRWightman)* 3–7–13 GBardwell (1) (b.hind: rdn thrght: nvr
　　nrr) ..................................................................................................... 11/2.7
*75* Lonesome Dove (IRE) *(JWhite)* 4–8–12 SWhitworth (2) (a bhd) ................... 10.8
*164* Saruk (IRE) *(JJBridger)* 3–7–9(2) NAdams (8) (chsd wnr 4f) ...................... 3/4.9
*201*5 Courting Newmarket **(54)** *(MrsAKnight)* 4–8–13 ‡3DBiggs (4) (bhd fnl 3f) ..... 21/2.10
Milan Fair *(DLWilliams)* 8–8–13 VSmith (11) (bit bkwd: outpcd) .................. 31/2.11

**6/4** VERY DICEY, **5/2** Toshiba Comet, **3/1** Mac's Fighter, **12/1** Erris Express(op 8/1), **16/1** Courting Newmarket,
**20/1** Count Me Out, **25/1** Lonesome Dove (IRE), **33/1** Ors. CSF £6.82, Tote £3.60: £1.00 £1.70 £7.50 (£8.10).
Mrs G. R. Smith (EPSOM) bred by G. R. Smith (Thriplow) Ltd and Lord Edwin McAlpine. 11 Rn; Very Dicey clmd S
Whitworth £6,599　　　　　　　　　　　　　　　　　　　　　　　　　　1m 11.95 (1.35)
　　　　　　　　　　　　　　　　　　　　　　　　　　　　　　　　　SF–25/10/–/–/–/–

**208**　　　GOODWINS H'CAP (0-80) £2385.00 (£660.00: £315.00)　　**7f (AWT)**　2-55 (2-56)

*204*★ **Appealing Times (USA) (76)** (Fav) *(WAO'Gorman)* 3–8–12 (7x) ‡5 Emma
　　O'Gorman (3) (mde virtually all: rdn out) .............................................. —1
*192*★ Sarum **(62)** *(CPWildman)* 6–9–6 (7x) CRutter (2) (lw: hld up: hrd rdn over 1f out:
　　r.o) ...................................................................................................... 11/2.2
Zinbaq **(42)** *(CJBenstead)* 6–8–0 JQuinn (2) (a.p: rdn over 1f out: unable qckn) 3/4.3
*199*★ Hawaii Storm (FR) **(41)** *(MissAJWhitfield)* 4–7–13 (7x) NAdams (8) (b.nr hind:
　　a.p: hrd rdn over 2f out: one pce) ......................................................... 11/2.4
*152*3 Say You Will **(46)** (v) *(MPNaughton)* 8–8–4 DMcKeown (6) (prom 4f) ........... 3.5
*192* Scots Law **(41)** (bl) *(RJO'Sullivan)* 5–7–6 ‡7CHawksley (4) (rdn thrght: a bhd) . 11/2.6
*204*3 Predictable **(66)** *(MrsAKnight)* 6–9–5 ‡5FNorton (5) (lw: w wnr over 4f: eased
　　whn btn ins fnl f) ................................................................................. nk.7
*172*4 Mushy Boff **(53)** *(CJHill)* 4–8–8 ‡3DBiggs (1) (a bhd) .............................. s.h.8

**3/1** APPEALING TIMES (USA), **7/2** Predictable, **4/1** Sarum, **5/1** Hawaii Storm (FR), **6/1** Say You Will, **12/1** Mushy
Boff, **20/1** Ors. CSF £14.58, CT £175.54. Tote £3.20: £1.10 £1.10 £4.90 (£2.60). Times of Wigan
(NEWMARKET) bred by Harry T. Mangurian Jnr in USA. 8 Rn　　　　　　　1m 25.99 (1.99)
　　　　　　　　　　　　　　　　　　　　　　　　　　　　　　　　　SF–26/29/7/1/–/–

**209**　　　SPRING H'CAP (0-100) £2710.80 (£748.80: £356.40)　　**6f (AWT)**　3-25 (3-26)

*186* **Misdemeanours Girl (IRE) (47)** *(MRChannon)* 4–7–6(4) ‡5BDoyle (7) (mde
　　virtually all: rdn out) ............................................................................ —1
*185*4 Sally's Son **(78)** (Fav) *(WAO'Gorman)* 6–9–9 ‡5EmmaO'Gorman (2) (a.p: hrd
　　rdn over 1f out: r.o wl ins fnl f) ............................................................. hd.2
*186*5 Rushanes **(64)** *(TCasey)* 5–8–9 ‡5FNorton (3) (w wnr: ev ch 1f out: unable qckn) 11/2.3
Joe Sugden **(62)** (bl) *(PHowling)* 5–8–9 NCarlisle (6) (a.p: one pce fnl 2f) ...... 4.4
*204* Murmuring **(65)** *(SDow)* 6–9–1 JWilliams (1) (b.hind: outpcd: hdwy over 1f out:
　　r.o) ...................................................................................................... s.h.5

*196*² Super Heights **(61)** (bl) *(MissAJWhitfield)* 4-8-11 DaleGibson (4) (prom 4f) .... 1¹/₂.**6**
*173* Goody Four Shoes **(55)** *(DRTucker)* 4-8-0⁽¹⁾ ‡⁵RPrice (5) (lw: a bhd) ................ 10.**7**
　　　　LONG HANDICAP: Misdemeanours Girl (IRE) 7-4.

**5/2** Sally's Son, **7/2** Super Heights, Rushanes, **5/1** Joe Sugden, **8/1** Murmuring, MISDEMEANOURS GIRL (IRE), **25/1** Goody Four Shoes. CSF £27.18, Tote £14.50: £3.90 £1.80 (£26.10). Mr M. G. Michaels (UPPER LAMBOURN) bred by A. F. O'Callaghan in Ireland. 7 Rn　　　　1m 12.07 (1.47)
　　　　　　　　　　　　　　　　　　　　　　　　　　　SF—1/31/11/–/–/–

**210**　　TUNBRIDGE WELLS H'CAP (0-60) £2520.00 (£700.00: £336.00)
　　　　　1¹/₄m (AWT)　　　　　　　　　　　　　　　　　3-55 (3-58)

*183*³ **Dazzle the Crowd (IRE) (47)** *(CACyzer)* 4-9-0 GDuffield (2) (hdwy over 3f out:
　　　　hrd rdn over 1f out: led ins fnl f: r.o wl) ...................................... —**1**
*184*\* Awesome Power **(60)** (Fav) *(CRNelson)* 6-10-0 JReid (7) (a.p: led wl over 1f
　　　　out tl ins fnl f: r.o) ...................................................... 1.**2**
*166*⁶ Applianceofscience **(42)** (bl) *(ASReid)* 5-8-10 BCrossley (9) (b: a.p: led over 4f
　　　　out tl wl over 1f out: sn wknd) ........................................... 8.**3**
*192*⁴ Wileys Folly **(42)** *(SDow)* 6-8-10 TQuinn (10) (b.hind: hdwy over 3f out: one
　　　　pce fnl 2f) ................................................................ 2¹/₂.**4**
*134* Mai Pen Rai **(42)** (v) *(CJHill)* 4-8-6 ‡³DBiggs (4) (led 1f: wknd over 2f out) ......... 4.**5**
*192*⁵ Luks Akura **(40)** *(MJohnston)* 4-8-7 DMcKeown (8) (led 9f out to 7f out: wknd 5f
　　　　out) ..................................................................... 3¹/₂.**6**
　　　　Pickles **(52)** *(PCHaslam)* 4-9-2 ‡JFanning (14) (dwlt: hdwy 8f out: hrd rdn over
　　　　3f out: sn wknd) ......................................................... 2¹/₂.**7**
*172*³ Sciacca **(34)** *(SMellor)* 5-8-2 DanaMellor (13) (led 7f out tl over 4f out: sn wknd) 2¹/₂.**8**
*190*⁵ Buddy's Friend (IRE) **(54)** *(RJRWilliams)* 4-9-7 MHills (6) (lw: prom 7f) ........... 3¹/₂.**9**
*193*⁴ Priceless Fantasy **(37)** *(PatMitchell)* 5-8-2 ‡³SO'Gorman (12) (a wl bhd) .......... 8.**10**
　　　　Yeoman Bound **(40)** *(KTIvory)* 4-8-7 MWigham (1) (a bhd) ........................... 1¹/₂.**11**
*154* Littledale (USA) **(53)** *(DJGMurray-Smith)* 6-9-7 RCochrane (5) (reluctant to r:
　　　　p.u 9f out) ................................................................ 0
*190*⁶ Will He Or Wont He (IRE) **(55)** (v) *(CNAllen)* 4-9-1 ‡⁷GForster (3) (ref to r: t.n.p) .... 0

**7/2** Awesome Power, **4/1** DAZZLE THE CROWD (IRE), **5/1** Buddy's Friend (IRE), **11/2** Littledale (USA), **8/1** Applianceofscience, Wileys Folly, **9/1** Pickles(op 6/1), **10/1** Mai Pen Rai, Luks Akura, **16/1** Priceless Fantasy, Sciacca, **25/1** Will He Or Wont He (IRE), **33/1** Yeoman Bound. CSF £21.04, CT £110.52. Tote £9.20: £3.00 £2.20 £3.00 (£12.70). Mr R. M. Cyzer (HORSHAM) bred by J. B. Clarke in Ireland. 13 Rn　　2m 5.29 (2.29)
　　　　　　　　　　　　　　　　　　　　　　　　　　　SF—36/48/14/9/–/–

**211**　　PANTILES H'CAP (0-70) £2226.00 (£616.00: £294.00)　　1¹/₂m (AWT)　　4-25 (4-27)
　　　　　　　　　　　　　　　　　(Weights raised 5 lb)

*187*² **Caspian Beluga (58)** *(MrsAKnight)* 4-9-8 ‡⁵FNorton (7) (hdwy 5f out: hrd rdn
　　　　over 3f out: led ins fnl f: all out) ........................................ —**1**
*115*² Samurai Gold (USA) **(57)** (v) (Fav) *(PTWalwyn)* 4-9-6 RCochrane (10) (lw: a.p:
　　　　led 6f out tl over 3f out: ev ch ins fnl f: r.o wl) ......................... hd.**2**
*111* Strat's Legacy **(44)** *(DWPArbuthnot)* 5-8-5 ‡⁵RPrice (8) (b.hind: a.p: led over 3f
　　　　out tl ins fnl f: unable qckn) ............................................ 2¹/₂.**3**
*184*⁴ North-West One (IRE) **(33)** *(HJCollingridge)* 4-7-10 JQuinn (9) (hdwy 5f out:
　　　　hrd rdn over 2f out: one pce) ............................................. 7.**4**
*81*⁴ Smith's Peak **(43)** (bl) *(RJO'Sullivan)* 8-8-6 ‡³DBiggs (11) (a.p: one pce fnl 2f) .. 1.**5**
*154*³ Evening Affair **(34)** (bl) *(WHolden)* 6-8-0 NAdams (4) (b.nr fore: hrd rdn over 3f
　　　　out: nvr nr to chal) ...................................................... 1¹/₂.**6**
*176*² Lord Advocate **(47)** (v) *(MPNaughton)* 4-8-10 GHind (6) (hdwy over 4f out:
　　　　wknd 3f out) ............................................................. 2.**7**
　　　　Saint Bene't (IRE) **(55)** *(PCHaslam)* 4-9-4 DMcKeown (5) (rdn over 8f out: a
　　　　mid div) .................................................................. 1¹/₂.**8**
*144*⁴ Charming Gift **(44)** *(RJRWilliams)* 5-8-3 ‡⁷GMitchell (3) (bhd fnl 5f) ............. 1¹/₂.**9**
*205*⁶ El Dominio **(61)** *(KOCunningham-Brown)* 4-9-10 WNewnes (12) (b: lw: bhd fnl
　　　　5f) ...................................................................... 8.**10**
　　　　Merry Marigold **(52)** *(JDRoberts)* 6-9-4 JWilliams (1) (b: a wl bhd) ............... hd.**11**
　　　　Billy Lomond (IRE) **(47)** (bl) *(CACyzer)* 4-8-10 GDuffield (2) (led 6f) ............ ³/₄.**12**

**7/2** Samurai Gold (USA), **5/1** CASPIAN BELUGA, Lord Advocate, Strat's Legacy, **15/2** Charming Gift, **8/1** Smith's Peak, El Dominio, **9/1** North-West One (IRE), Saint Bene't (IRE), **10/1** Evening Affair, **14/1** Ors. CSF £27.17, CT £95.53. Tote £17.00: £2.20 £1.80 £1.20 (£14.10). Mr L. J. Hawkings (CULLOMPTON) bred by Wretham Stud. 12 Rn　　　　2m 31.73 (2.33)
　　　　　　　　　　　　　　　　　　　　　　　　　　　SF—31/34/14/–/–/–

**212**　　WATERINGBURY APP'CE STKS (II) (Mdn) £2108.40 (£582.40: £277.20)
　　　　　1¹/₄m (AWT)　　　　　　　　　　　　　　　　　4-55 (4-56)

　　　　**With Gusto (32)** *(KOCunningham-Brown)* 5-9-1 StephenDavies (6) (a.p: led
　　　　over 2f out: rdn out) ..................................................... —**1**

La Reine Rouge (IRE) *(PJMakin)* 4-8-9 TSprake (8) (a.p: ev ch wl over 1f out: r.o) ............................................................................................ 1.2

1423 Amphigory (Fav) *(LordHuntingdon)* 4-9-0 DHarrison (4) (hdwy over 3f out: ev ch over 2f out: unable qckn) ........................................ 4.3

1533 Sareen Express (IRE) **(40)** (bl) *(MrsJCDawe)* 4-9-0 DBiggs (5) (led over 7f: one pce) ............................................................................. s.h.4

184 Our Topsie **(26)** *(FJO'Mahony)* 5-8-10 NGwilliams (2) (nvr nr to chal) ............ 5.5

1266 Grey Dancer **(35)** *(JWhite)* 4-9-0 RPrice (1) (rdn thrght: a bhd) ................ 1.6

158 Tipperary Azul (IRE) *(MHTompkins)* 4-9-0 CHodgson (3) (prom over 5f) ..... 20.7
Champenoise *(MBell)* 4-8-9 PTurner (7) (a bhd) ................................. 15.8

**6/4** Amphigory, **5/2** Tipperary Azul (IRE), Champenoise, **8/1** Sareen Express (IRE), **14/1** Grey Dancer, La Reine Rouge (IRE), **16/1** WITH GUSTO(12/1—20/1), **20/1** Our Topsie. CSF £191.81, Tote £14.80: £2.70 £3.50 £1.20 (£115.50). Mr M. D. Brunton (STOCKBRIDGE) bred by Lt-Comdr P. S. Emmet and Partner. 8 Rn
2m 5.87 (2.87)
SF—32/24/21/20/6/8

T/Plpt: £7.80 (144.55 Tckts).                                                    AK

## 194—SOUTHWELL (L-H) Fibresand
### Saturday, March 14th [Standard]
Going Allowance: 5f: minus 0.10 sec (FS); Rest: 0.10 sec (SL)          Wind: fresh bhd

Stalls: 2nd & 5th high, remainder low

**213**    IN THE FRAME CLAIMING STKS    £2905.00 (£805.00: £385.00)
       **7f (AWT)**                                                  2-25 (2-28)

203 **African Chimes (93)** (Fav) *(WAO'Gorman)* 5-9-2 ‡5EmmaO'Gorman (3) (lw: hld up: hdwy & 5th st: led wl over 1f out: sn clr) ................. —1

1425 Daisy Grey **(32)** (bl) *(ASReid)* 4-7-6 ‡7PMcCabe (6) (b: prom: 3rd st: styd on same pce fnl 2f) ................................................................ 4.2

Gabbiadini **(76)** *(MHTompkins)* 4-9-0 ‡5CHodgson (1) (lost pl after 2f: hdwy over 2f out: kpt on) ................................................................... 2½.3

172 Morpick **(47)** (bl) *(JPLeigh)* 5-8-7 DNicholls (7) (led tl hdd wl over 1f out: rdn & no ex) .................................................................................. 1½.4

Breezed Well **(80)** *(CNAllen)* 6-8-4 ‡7GForster (11) (bit bkwd: hdwy & 7th st: styd on fnl f: nvr able to chal) ................................................. 2.5

139 Northern Vision (bl) *(PABlockley)* 5-8-11 KFallon (5) (chsd ldrs: 6th st: one pce fnl 2f) ...................................................................................... ½.6

184 Green's Cassatt (USA) **(47)** *(WMBrisbourne)* 4-8-2 AProud (2) (styd on fnl 2f: n.d) ................................................................................................ hd.7

Faynaz **(56)** *(WRMuir)* 6-8-8 SWhitworth (10) (bkwd: 2nd st: wknd 2f out) ......... 8.8

1583 Merchant House (IRE) **(59)** *(WHolden)* 4-8-6 NAdams (8) (b.nr hind: prom tl 4th & wkng st) ........................................................................ 1½.9

2016 The Square Centre (USA) *(PBurgoyne)* 4-8-9 TQuinn (4) (a bhd) ............... s.h.10
Bolton Flyer *(OO'Neill)* 6-8-4 JLowe (9) (bit bkwd: bhd fr ½-wy) ............ 4.11

**8/11** AFRICAN CHIMES, **6/1** Gabbiadini(op 3/1), **10/1** Breezed Well(op 9/2), **12/1** Merchant House (IRE), Faynaz, **16/1** Green's Cassatt (USA), **20/1** The Square Centre (USA), **25/1** Ors. CSF £22.01, Tote £1.80: £1.10 £8.90 £1.80 (£29.10). Mr D. G. Wheatley (NEWMARKET) bred by Noel Cogan. 11 Rn
1m 31.4 (4.8)
SF—40/8/19/10/1/6

**214**    DEAD CERT H'CAP (0-95) £2733.50 (£756.00: £360.50)    1½m (AWT)    2-55 (2-55)

**Lord Hastie (USA) (72)** *(SGNorton)* 4-9-0 ‡7OPears (8) (lw: chsd ldr: 2nd st: led over 2f out: hung lft fnl f: r.o) ........................................ —1

1443 Paper Craft **(53)** (bl) *(MJohnston)* 5-8-5 DMcKeown (5) (led over 9f: hmpd 1f out: styd on same pce) ................................................... 2.2

1972 Broom Isle **(55)** *(MrsAKnight)* 4-7-13 ‡5FNorton (7) (lw: hdwy 7f out: 4th st: styd on fnl f) .............................................................................. 2.3

Shaffaaf (USA) **(59)** *(PDEvans)* 4-8-8 JQuinn (10) (bit bkwd: hld up: hdwy 6f out: 3rd st: rdn over 2f out: no imp) ....................................... 3½.4

Majed (IRE) **(75)** *(NACallaghan)* 4-9-3 ‡7JTate (6) (chsd ldrs: 5th st: no hdwy fnl 3f) ............................................................................................. hd.5

169 Conjuring (USA) **(64)** (bl) *(GThorner)* 4-8-13 RWernham (2) (in tch: pushed along 7f out tl wknd 3f out) ....................................................... 12.6

197★ Horizon (IRE) **(79)** (bl) (Fav) *(TThomsonJones)* 4-9-11 ‡3DBiggs (3) (sn pushed along & bhd: styd on fnl 3f: n.d) ................................... 2½.7

187 Irish Native (IRE) **(60)** (bl) *(CASmith)* 4-8-9 AProud (9) (prom over 7f) ........... s.h.8

125 Dawn Success **(57)** *(DWChapman)* 6–8-9 SWood (4) (lw: prom to ½-wy) ...... 1¹/2.**9**
81⁶ Qualitair Flyer **(41)** *(JFBottomley)* 10–7-7 GBardwell (1) (lw: hdwy & 6th st: wknd over 2f out) ............................................................................. 3.**10**
LONG HANDICAP: Qualitair Flyer 6-11.

**11/4** Horizon (IRE)(op 11/8), **3/1** LORD HASTIE (USA), **9/2** Broom Isle(op 3/1), **7/1** Majed (IRE), **10/1** Paper Craft, **11/1** Dawn Success, **12/1** Shaffaaf (USA)(op 20/1), Irish Native (IRE), Qualitair Flyer, **20/1** Conjuring (USA). CSF £32.88, CT £128.28. Tote £4.40: £1.80 £2.40 £2.20 (£15.50). Mrs Joy Bendall (BARNSLEY) bred by Upland Farm Park Series 6 in USA. 10 Rn                     2m 41.2 (7)
SF—42/29/19/21/29/1

## 215
SMOKESCREEN H'CAP (3-Y.O) (0-110) £10820.00 (£3260.00: £1580.00: £740.00)
**7f (AWT)**                                            3-25 (3-30)

141³ **Early Star (74)** *(TDBarron)* 8-7 KDarley (3) (lw: led over 1f: 3rd st: led over 1f out: hld on wl) ............................................................ —**1**
174* **Daros (84)** *(MrsJRRamsden)* 8-10 ‡7JWeaver (14) (lw: prom: 5th st: ev ch fnl f: unable qckn nr fin) ........................................................ nk.**2**
72* **Sand Table (82)** *(LordHuntingdon)* 9-1 BRaymond (10) (lw: hld up: hdwy & nt clr run 2f out: swtchd lft appr fnl f: r.o wl) ...................... hd.**3**
133 **Buddy (IRE) (68)** *(MBell)* 7-8 ‡7PTurner (12) (lw: chsd ldrs: led 3f out: hdd over 1f out: styd on one pce fnl f) .................................. 1¹/2.**4**
180² **Empeeka (USA) (86)** (h) (Fav) *(WAO'Gorman)* 9-0 ‡5EmmaO'Gorman (7) (hld up: hdwy over 2f out: rdn over 1f out: no imp) .................. nk.**5**
157* **Native Idol (USA) (85)** *(JRFanshawe)* 9-4 WRSwinburn (2) (lw: chsd ldrs: 6th st: no hdwy fnl 2f) ............................................. 4.**6**
195³ **Pop to Stans (88)** *(TDBarron)* 9-7 AlexGreaves (6) (effrt ½-wy: nvr nr ldrs) ........ 6.**7**
**Debsy Do (USA) (67)** *(SGNorton)* 7-9 ‡5FNorton (4) (bit bkwd: chsd ldrs: 4th st: sn wknd) ...................................................... 1¹/2.**8**
164³ **Bassio (BEL) (74)** (v) *(CNAllen)* 8-7 NOochrane (1) (a in rr) ...................... ¹/2.£.**0**
**Master Planner (87)** *(CACyzer)* 9-6 GCarter (5) (led over 5f out: hdd 3f out: 2nd st: sn wknd) ......................................................... ³/4.**10**
160* **Brotherlyaffection (65)** *(RHollinshead)* 7-5⁽¹⁾ ‡7MHumphries (9) (prom: nt clr run ent st: sn btn) ..................................... 4.**11**
**Parlemo (IRE) (76)** *(JDBethell)* 8-9 RHills (15) (bit bkwd: a bhd) ................ 2¹/2.**12**
**Wild Honour (IRE) (88)** *(WRMuir)* 9-7 SWhitworth (8) (bit bkwd: n.d) ............. ³/4.**13**
129³ **Level Up (61)** *(RGuest)* 7-8⁽¹⁾ JQuinn (11) (s.i.s: a bhd) ...................... 2.**14**

**4/1** Empeeka (USA)(8/1—5/2), **9/2** Native Idol (USA)(5/2—5/1), **11/2** Daros(7/2—6/1), Sand Table(op 3/1), **10/1** EARLY STAR, Debsy Do (USA), Bassio (BEL)(op 8/1), **14/1** Buddy (IRE), Pop to Stans(op 8/1), **16/1** Brotherlyaffection, Level Up, **25/1** Ors. CSF £78.10, CT £381.83. Tote £26.00: £4.10 £4.30 £1.90 (£69.60). Mr E. Buck (THIRSK) bred by Somerhall Bloodstock Ltd. 14 Rn          1m 31.3 (4.7)
SF—33/35/39/13/32/24

## 216
BANKER CLAIMING STKS (3-Y.O) £2856.00 (£791.00: £378.00)
**1m (AWT)**                                            3-55 (3-57)

177* **Mad Militant (IRE) (87)** (Fav) *(RHollinshead)* 9-0 WRyan (2) (lw: hld up: smooth hdwy & 4th st: led over 2f out: pushed out) ............ —**1**
**Grog (IRE) (74)** *(MRChannon)* 8-0 ‡5BDoyle (6) (led over 5f: rdn appr fnl f: no ch w wnr) ................................................................ 2¹/2.**2**
174 **Forza Azzurri (IRE) (55)** *(MrsNMacauley)* 8-5⁽¹⁾ NDay (3) (chsd ldrs: 5th st: styd on u.p fnl 2f) ......................................... 10.**3**
177 **Malcesine (IRE) (55)** *(CaptJWilson)* 8-3⁽¹⁾ GCarter (7) (chsd ldr tl 3rd st: wknd 2f out) 3.**4**
47² **Mr Snuggs (IRE) (55)** *(BJMcMath)* 8-4 JQuinn (4) (prom: 2nd st: rdn & wknd over 2f out) ..................................................... 5.**5**
191 **Qualitair Idol (55)** *(JFBottomley)* 8-0 GBardwell (8) (lw: in tch: 6th st: sn rdn & wknd) 10.**6**
177 **Turning Heads (55)** *(CaptJWilson)* 7-13 JLowe (1) (dwlt: a bhd) .................. 2¹/2.**7**
**Stratford Lady (55)** *(JAGlover)* 7-13 NCarlisle (5) (bit bkwd: a bhd) .......... nk.**8**

**1/2** MAD MILITANT (IRE), **7/1** Qualitair Idol(5/1—8/1), Grog (IRE), **14/1** Forza Azzurri (IRE)(op 7/1), Mr Snuggs (IRE), **20/1** Malcesine (IRE)(op 10/1), Stratford Lady, **33/1** Turning Heads. CSF £4.96, Tote £1.50: £1.10 £1.90 £2.90 (£3.10). Mrs B. Facchino (UPPER LONGDON) bred by Cloghran Stud Farm Co. in Ireland. 8 Rn          1m 45.9 (6.6)
SF—13/-/-/-/-/-

## 217
HOT MONEY H'CAP (0-100) £6108.00 (£1824.00: £872.00: £396.00)
**5f (AWT)**                                            4-25 (4-27)

(Weights raised 6 lb)
173⁶ **Lady of the Fen (57)** *(MrsNMacauley)* 4–7-7 ‡5FNorton (4) (lw: led 3f out: drvn out) ................................................................ —**1**

Roseate Lodge **(80)** *(RWArmstrong)* 6–9-7 BCrossley (1) (bit bkwd: bhd: rdn ½-wy: r.o wl fnl f) .................................................................. 1½.2
*121⁶* Sully's Choice (USA) **(52)** (bl) *(DWChapman)* 11–7-7 SWood (5) (sn drvn along: prom: kpt on one pce fnl f) .................................. s.h.3
*133²* Creche **(90)** (bl) (Fav) *(MrsNMacauley)* 3–9-3 NDay (2) (led 2f: unable qckn ins fnl f) ...................................................................... s.h.4
*132★* Maid Welcome **(77)** (bl) *(MrsNMacauley)* 5–8-11 ‡⁷MadeleineSmith (16) (lw: chsd ldrs: kpt on same pce fnl f) ................................. nk.5
*58* Breezy Day **(73)** *(BAMcMahon)* 6–9-0 TQuinn (15) (chsd ldrs: no hdwy appr fnl f) 1.6
*188★* Hinari Video **(62)** *(MJohnston)* 7–8-3 DMcKeown (3) (lw: spd over 3f) .............. nk.7
*180★* Jovial Kate (USA) **(58)** *(BEllison)* 5–7-13 NCarlisle (13) (lw: sn drvn along: nvr able to chal) ................................................................ nk.8
*149★* Sir Tasker **(83)** *(JLHarris)* 4–9-10 RCochrane (6) (chsd ldrs: no hdwy fnl 2f) ...... 1.9
*173³* Orient Air **(66)** (bl) *(TDBarron)* 4–8-7 KDarley (12) (n.d) .............................. nk.10
*57⁴* In a Whirl (USA) **(58)** *(DWChapman)* 4–7-13 JQuinn (7) (r.o fnl 2f: nvr rchd ldrs) 2.11
*149²* Sports Post Lady (IRE) **(62)** *(CJHill)* 4–8-0 ‡³DBiggs (9) (unruly stalls: n.d) ....... 2.12
*209★* Misdemeanours Girl (IRE) **(56)** *(MRChannon)* 4–7-6⁽⁴⁾ (7x) ‡⁵BDoyle (8) (bhd fr ½-wy) ..................................................................... 1½.13
*180⁵* On the Edge **(78)** *(TDBarron)* 4–9-5 AlexGreaves (14) (dwlt: a bhd) ............... hd.14
Crail Harbour **(61)** *(PCHaslam)* 6–7-13 ‡³JFanning (11) (bit bkwd: bhd fr ½-wy) s.h.15
*196⁶* Tigani **(75)** (bl) *(DWChapman)* 6–8-9 ‡⁷SWilliams (10) (rdn along ½-wy: sn bhd) nk.16
LONG HANDICAP: Sully's Choice (USA) 7-5, Misdemeanours Girl (IRE) 7-2.

**9/2** Creche, **5/1** Sir Tasker, **7/1** Sports Post Lady (IRE), **17/2** Orient Air(6/1—9/1), **9/1** Maid Welcome, On the Edge(op 6/1), **10/1** Jovial Kate (USA), Hinari Video, **14/1** Crail Harbour, Misdemeanours Girl (IRE), Breezy Day, In a Whirl (USA), **20/1** LADY OF THE FEN, Tigani, **25/1** Sully's Choice (USA), **33/1** Roseate Lodge. CSF £501.58, CT £13,756.43. Tote £30.60: £5.00 £6.80 £8.40 £1.90 (£143.90). Mr P. Mingay (MELTON MOWBRAY) bred by R. A. G. Robinson. 16 Rn      59.7 sec (1.7)

SF—35/47/18/41/34/33

**218**     ODDS AGAINST STKS (Mdn 3-Y.O) £2385.00 (£660.00: £315.00)
        **6f (AWT)**                         4-55 (4-57)

*195⁵* Eastleigh **(72)** *(RHollinshead)* 9-0 WRyan (4) (lw: chsd ldrs: led over 1f out: pushed out) ........................................................................... —1
Blake End (USA) (Fav) *(WAO'Gorman)* 9-0 RCochrane (3) (prom: led over 2f out: hdd over 1f out: styd on same pce fnl f) ....................... 5.2
*98²* Life's a Breeze *(MRChannon)* 9-0 WRSwinburn (8) (lw: prom: outpcd over 2f out: styd on fnl f) .............................................................. 1½.3
*174⁵* Colour Solutions *(TDBarron)* 8-9 AlexGreaves (5) (in tch: styd on fnl 2f) .......... 2½.4
*194* Educated Pet **(43)** *(MJohnston)* 9-0 DMcKeown (12) (hdwy over 2f out: styd on) ¾.5
*194* Ingenuity *(LordHuntingdon)* 8-9 BRaymond (10) (chsd ldrs tl wknd appr fnl f) s.h.6
Phil-Man **(55)** *(TFairhurst)* 8-11 ‡³JFanning (1) (bit bkwd: nrst fin) .................... 2.7
*194⁶* North Flyer **(50)** *(BAMcMahon)* 9-0 TQuinn (7) (n.d) ................................. 5.8
Miss Kingfisher (USA) **(62)** *(SGNorton)* 8-2 ‡⁷OPears (6) (bit bkwd: bhd fr ½-wy) 2.9
Weekend Girl **(36)** *(WMBrisbourne)* 8-9 AProud (13) (a bhd) ......................... 1½.10
*182* Jaromic **(61)** (bl) *(PFTulk)* 9-0 MBirch (9) (led over 3f) ................................. 7.11
*44⁶* Flat Rate **(41)** (v) *(WJPearce)* 8-9 LCharnock (11) (sn rdn along: a in rr) .......... 8.12
Shadaylou (IRE) **(63)** (bl) *(MrsJJordan)* 8-9 GCarter (2) (prom to ½-wy) ............ 8.13

**15/8** Blake End (USA)(4/7—2/1), **4/1** EASTLEIGH(3/1—6/1), Life's a Breeze(6/1—7/2), **6/1** Colour Solutions, **12/1** Flat Rate, Ingenuity(op 8/1), **14/1** Jaromic, North Flyer, **16/1** Phil-Man, Miss Kingfisher (USA), Shadaylou (IRE), **33/1** Ors. CSF £13.46, Tote £8.60: £2.20 £1.50 £1.40 (£5.30). Mr J. E. Bigg (UPPER LONGDON) bred by Hever Castle Stud. 13 Rn      1m 17.8 (4.4)

SF—22/2/–/–/–/–

T/Plpt: £35.70 (51.3 Tckts).                                    CR

## 213— SOUTHWELL (L-H) Fibresand

### Wednesday, March 18th [Standard]

Going Allowance: 0.20 sec per fur (SL)                  Wind: slt half bhd

Stalls: 1st, 2nd & 4th low, remainder high

**219**     BLUE TIT H'CAP (0-90) £2245.60 (£621.60: £296.80)    **5f (AWT)**    2-10 (2-14)
                        (Weights raised 1 lb)
*217⁴* **Creche (90)** (bl) (Jt-Fav) *(MrsNMacauley)* 3–9-2 ‡⁷SWilliams (2) (lw: prom: led 3f out: rdn & edgd lft fnl f) ........................................... —1
*217³* Sully's Choice (USA) **(50)** (bl) *(DWChapman)* 11–7-10 SWood (4) (in tch: rdn over 2f: r.o fnl f) ......................................................... ¾.2

188² Beckingham Ben (51) *(JPLeigh)* 8–7–11 JQuinn (3) (lw: prom: ev ch 2f out: one pce) ................................................................. 1½.3
194³ Carnfield (49) (v) *(JAGlover)* 4–7–2⁽²⁾ ‡7CHawksley (6) (prom: ev ch 2f out: sn wknd) .......................................................... 1½.4
217 Hinari Video (62) (Jt-Fav) *(MJohnston)* 7–8–8 DMcKeown (7) (lw: chsd ldrs: one pce appr fnl f) ........................................ hd.5
Slades Hill (56) *(TDBarron)* 5–8–2⁽²⁾ AlexGreaves (8) (bit bkwd: led 2f: wknd wl over 1f out) .................................................... 4.6
Barrys Gamble (78) (bl) *(TFairhurst)* 6–9–7 ‡3JFanning (5) (bit bkwd: s.s: nvr nr ldrs) .......................................................... 2.7
173 Lets Go Sabo (50) *(DWChapman)* 4–7–10 JLowe (1) (outpcd) .......................... 3.8
LONG HANDICAP: Carnfield 7-4.

**7/2** CRECHE, Hinari Video, **9/2** Sully's Choice (USA), **6/1** Beckingham Ben, **7/1** Barrys Gamble(5/1—8/1), **10/1** Slades Hill, **16/1** Carnfield(20/1—25/1), **20/1** Lets Go Sabo(op 10/1). CSF £17.26, CT £72.37. Tote £3.90: £1.40 £1.50 £1.70 (£8.00). Mr Brian Pollins (MELTON MOWBRAY) bred by Bacton Stud. 8 Rn   61.5 sec (3.5)
SF—52/39/24/9/28/8

## 220    THRUSH H'CAP (0–80)   £2108.40 (£582.40: £277.20)   1³⁄₄m (AWT)    2-40 (2-42)

176³ **Steppey Lane (67)** *(WWHaigh)* 7–9–1 DMcKeown (8) (lw: hdwy 8f out: led 3f out: eased ins fnl f) ............................................. —1
Suluk (USA) (51) *(RHollinshead)* 7–7–6⁽³⁾ ‡7MHumphries (1) (lw: in tch: hdwy over 3f out: kpt on) ............................................... 2½.2
202⁴ Tempering (80) *(DWChapman)* 6–10–0 SWood (2) (lw: led 11f: one pce appr fnl f) .................................................................................. 3½.3
205³ Aude la Belle (FR) (56) (Fav) *(MrsAKnight)* 4–7–12 ‡3DBiggs (3) (in tch: no imp fnl 3f) ......................................................................... 8.4
Springs Welcome (71) *(CACyzer)* 6–8–12 ‡7TMcLaughlin (9) (bit bkwd: wl bhd tl mod late hdwy) ................................................. 10.5
97 Erevnon (55) *(JLHarris)* 5–7–12 ‡5BDoyle (7) (lw: chsd ldrs 9f: sn wknd) .......... 3.6
Singular Run (66) (bl) *(MrsJCDawe)* 6–9–0 JWilliams (5) (chsd ldr 10f: wknd qckly) ........................................................................................ 1.7
193 Pondered Bid (51) *(PatMitchell)* 8–7–6⁽⁶⁾ ‡7RTurner (4) (sn rdn & bhd) ............ 2.8
Shikari Kid (48) *(PABlockley)* 5–7–3⁽³⁾ ‡7AGarth (6) (bhd fnl 8f) ..................... 3½.9
LONG HANDICAP: Pondered Bid 6-10, Shikari Kid 6-10.

**2/1** Aude la Belle (FR), **9/2** Suluk (USA)(op 9/4), **5/1** STEPPEY LANE, **13/2** Tempering, **17/2** Springs Welcome, Erevnon(12/1—8/1), **16/1** Shikari Kid, **25/1** Pondered Bid, **33/1** Singular Run. CSF £25.64, CT £132.85. Tote £5.10: £1.20 £2.00 £2.30 (£11.10). Dr C. I. Emmerson (MALTON) bred by Southdown Stud. 9 Rn
3m 12.1 (12.8)

## 221    ROBIN CLAIMING STKS   £2226.00 (£616.00: £294.00)   6f (AWT)    3-10 (3-16)

213★ **African Chimes (93)** (Fav) *(WAO'Gorman)* 5–9–2 ‡5EmmaO'Gorman (8) (lw: hld up: hdwy over 2f out: n.m.r 1f out: qcknd to ld nr fin) .... —1
180⁴ Gorinsky (IRE) (76) (bl) *(JBerry)* 4–8–10 JCarroll (5) (lw: prom: led over 2f out: rdn 1f out: ct nr fin) ............................................ ½.2
213⁴ Morpick (47) (bl) *(JPLeigh)* 5–8–10 DNicholls (3) (led 3f: ev ch 1f out: kpt on) ... 1.3
201⁴ Wellsy Lad (USA) (65) *(DWChapman)* 5–8–10 SWood (7) (lw: chsd ldrs: rdn 2f out: one pce ins fnl f) ..................................................... 3.4
Prime Mover (69) *(DBurchell)* 4–8–10 DMcKeown (12) (bit bkwd: dwlt: sn rcvd: rdn & edgd rt 2f out: no imp) ................................... 3.5
207⁶ Erris Express (76) (bl) *(KTIvory)* 7–8–9 MWigham (6) (eyeshield: b: n.d) .......... nk.6
199 Lonely Lass (41) (bl) *(LJBarratt)* 6–7–12 LCharnock (1) (chsd ldrs: led 3f out: sn hdd & wknd) ............................................................... 5.7
213⁶ Northern Vision (bl) *(PABlockley)* 5–8–7 ‡7JDennis (10) (nvr nr to chal) .......... hd.8
Regal Tiger *(MrsJCDawe)* 7–8–8 JWilliams (4) (sn outpcd) ........................... 1½.9
Twilight Falls (34) *(MJCamacho)* 7–9–4 NConnorton (2) (bkwd: a bhd) .......... hd.10
Last Straw (33) *(AWJones)* 4–8–5 GDuffield (4) (chsd ldrs 3f) ....................... 3.11
173⁵ Princess Jestina (IRE) (47) *(GHYardley)* 4–8–0 ‡5FNorton (9) (hmpd s: a bhd) 1½.12

**6/4** AFRICAN CHIMES(op 8/11), **4/1** Gorinsky (IRE)(tchd 6/1), Prime Mover(5/1—3/1), **8/1** Morpick(6/1—10/1), **11/1** Erris Express, **14/1** Wellsy Lad (USA), Lonely Lass(12/1—20/1), **20/1** Twilight Falls, Princess Jestina (IRE)(14/1—25/1), **25/1** Northern Vision, **100/1** Ors. CSF £8.48, Tote £2.40: £1.10 £2.00 £2.30 (£2.80). Mr D. G. Wheatley (NEWMARKET) bred by Noel Cogan. 12 Rn
1m 17.7 (4.3)
SF—40/32/28/16/4/2

## 222    WOODPECKER STKS (Mdn)   £2304.40 (£638.40: £305.20)   1½m (AWT)    3-40 (3-46)

**Maamur (USA)** (Fav) *(DBurchell)* 4–9–5 RCochrane (8) (bit bkwd: trckd ldrs: led 3f out: rdn clr appr fnl f: easily) ..................................... —1
206³ Loudest Whisper (58) *(KSBridgwater)* 4–9–0 ‡5BDoyle (5) (a.p: rdn & styd on appr fnl f) ................................................................... 10.2

212² La Reine Rouge (IRE) *(PJMakin)* 4-8-9 ‡⁵TSprake (7) (hdwy 5f out: rdn over 2f out: sn btn) ....................................................... ¹/₂.3

212 Tipperary Azul (IRE) *(MHTompkins)* 4-8-12 ‡⁷SMulvey (4) (r.o fnl 4f: nvr able to chal) .................................................................... 4.4

Illogical (36) *(JWharton)* 5-8-13 ‡³JFanning (11) (lw: led 9f: wknd wl over 1f out) 2.5

169⁵ Ramble (USA) *(JABOld)* 5-9-2 RFox (14) (in tch: no imp fnl 3f) ............... 12.6

Jadidh (bl) *(MrsJCDawe)* 4-9-0 JWilliams (3) (lw: bhd: rdn & hdwy over 3f out: sn no imp) ...................................................................... 6.7

179⁶ Red Sparky (29) *(WJPearce)* 4-9-0 DNichols (13) (nvr nr to chal) ............. 4.8

Statia (IRE) (50) *(DonEnricoIncisa)* 4-9-0 KimTinkler (1) (chsd ldr tl wknd 4f out) .................................................................................. 2¹/₂.9

Ullswater *(ASReid)* 6-9-0 ‡⁷PMcCabe (9) (b: a bhd) ................................ 7.10

139⁶ Aldington Noble *(CCTrietline)* 5-9-7 JLowe (2) (a bhd: t.o) ................... 15.11

198 Oka Flow (45) (bl) *(PABlockley)* 4-8-12 ‡⁷JDennis (10) (bhd fnl 6f: t.o) ......... 6.12

59 Canonised *(RGBrazington)* 8-9-7 JQuinn (6) (a bhd: t.o fnl 6f) ................ 13

Torkabar (USA) *(GAHam)* 7-9-7 JCarroll (12) (b: ref to r: t.n.p) ................ 0

**5/4** MAAMUR (USA), **4/1** La Reine Rouge (IRE)(3/1—5/1), **7/1** Jadidh(op 7/2), **8/1** Ramble (USA), Loudest Whisper, **12/1** Tipperary Azul (IRE), Torkabar (USA)(8/1—14/1), **14/1** Oka Flow (IRE), **16/1** Statia (IRE), **33/1** Ors. CSF £13.97, Tote £3.10: £1.10 £3.20 £1.60 (£15.90). Park Industrial Supplies (Wales) Ltd bred by Maverick Productions Ltd in USA. 14 Rn                     2m 42.9 (8.7)
SF—40/15/9/4/1/–

**223**      STARLING H'CAP (0-80) (3-Y.O) £2128.00 (£588.00: £280.00)      **1m (AWT)** 4-10 (4-19)
(Weights raised 4 lb)

**Eriny (USA) (54)** *(SGNorton)* 8-4 KDarley (9) (chsd ldr: led over 2f out: clr over 1f out: pushed out) ........................................................ —1

104⁴ Silver Samurai (67) *(RHollinshead)* 8-10 ‡⁷EHusband (2) (lw: hld up: hdwy 3f out: chsd wnr fnl 2f: no imp) ...................................... 10.2

148* Up the Punjab (68) *(SDow)* 9-4 JWilliams (4) (lw: chsd ldrs: one pce fnl 2f) ... ¹/₂.3

Libra Legend (USA) (67) *(CEBrittain)* 9-0 ‡³RonHillis (6) (bit bkwd: in tch: kpt on fnl 2f: nvr able to r) ............................................. 2¹/₂.4

177² Meltonby (71) *(NTinkler)* 9-7 KimTinkler (5) (bhd: effrt 3f out: sn no imp) ....... 8.5

170* Akura (IRE) (59) (Fav) *(MJohnston)* 8-9 DMcKeown (7) (lw: led over 5f: sn wknd) ................................................................................. 2.6

135 Kashgar (43) *(DWChapman)* 7-7 SWood (1) (prom 4f: wknd qckly: t.o) ............... 7
LONG HANDICAP: Kashgar 7-4.

200² Trump (5/1) Withdrawn (broke out of stalls) : not under orders

**11/4** Akura (IRE), **3/1** Up the Punjab, **9/2** Meltonby, **5/1** ERINY (USA), **6/1** Silver Samurai, **8/1** Libra Legend (USA), **20/1** Kashgar. CSF £31.80, CT £95.19. Tote £7.30: £2.20 £4.00 (£40.70). Mr R. W. Cousins (BARNSLEY) bred by Arthur I. Appleton in USA. 7 Rn                     1m 44.6 (5.3)
SF—35/11/17/5/–/–

**224**      BLACKBIRD STKS (Mdn) £2324.00 (£644.00: £308.00)      **1m (AWT)**      4-40 (4-46)

198² **Kay's Dilemma (IRE)** *(PAKelleway)* 4-8-13 ‡³DBiggs (4) (lw: led 3f: led over 2f out: rdn & edgd lft nr fin) ........................................ —1

170² Firefighter (63) *(RHollinshead)* 3-8-4 WRyan (5) (lw: chsd ldrs: rdn over 3f out: styng on whn nt clr run over 1f out & ins fnl f) ................. ³/₄.2

Mill Burn *(ICampbell)* 3-8-4 GDuffield (11) (hdwy 4f out: ev ch over 1f out: one pce) ................................................................................ hd.3

Heniu (USA) (Fav) *(LordHuntingdon)* 3-8-4 DMcKeown (7) (w'like: scope: bit bkwd: s.i.s: sn pushed along: gd hdwy appr fnl f: fin wl) ... s.h.4

212⁴ Sareen Express (IRE) (40) (bl) *(MrsJCDawe)* 4-9-7 JWilliams (8) (chsd ldr: led 5f out tl over 2f out: wknd ins fnl f) ......................... hd.5

194 Comiskey Park (IRE) *(DWChapman)* 3-8-4 SWood (10) (hdwy 3f out: no imp fnl 2f) .................................................................................. 1¹/₂.6

Escadaro (USA) *(SGNorton)* 3-7-11 ‡⁷OPears (6) (dwlt: n.d) ....................... 7.7

126 Hepburn (IRE) (35) *(RGBrazington)* 4-9-2 JQuinn (2) (nvr nr to chal) ............. 2.8

Weapon Exhibition (v) *(GAHam)* 5-9-2 RCochrane (3) (nvr trbld ldrs) ............. hd.9

Persian Anthem (IRE) *(GWragg)* 3-7-8 ‡⁵FNorton (9) (unf: chsd ldrs 4f) ........... 4.10

198⁶ First Home *(PatMitchell)* 5-9-0 ‡⁷RTurner (1) (bhd fnl 5f) ...................... 6.11

Yours Or Mine (IRE) *(DWChapman)* 4-8-9 ‡⁷SWilliams (10) (bkwd: prom 5f) ....... 12

**5/4** Heniu (USA), **3/1** Persian Anthem (IRE)(7/2—6/1), **11/2** Firefighter(3/1—6/1), **11/1** KAY'S DILEMMA (IRE), **12/1** Sareen Express (IRE), **14/1** Escadaro (USA), **16/1** Yours Or Mine (IRE), Hepburn (IRE), Weapon Exhibition, **25/1** Ors. CSF £74.17, Tote £11.90 £2.20 £1.50 £14.20 (£9.80). Mr Alexander Pereira (NEWMARKET) bred by Michael F. Fogarty in Ireland. 12 Rn                     1m 47.5 (8.2)

T/Plpt: £104.50 (15 Tckts).                                                                    Dk

# DONCASTER (L-H)
## Thursday, March 19th [Good]
Going Allowance: St: 0.30 sec per fur; Rnd: nil sec per fur (G)　　　Wind: fresh half against

Stalls: high

**225**　　RACEFORM APP'CE H'CAP (0-80) £2826.00 (£786.00: £378.00)
　　　　　1¹/₄m 60y
　　　　　　　　　　　　　　　　　　　　　　　　　　　　　　　　2-00 (2-13)

**Mr Confusion (IRE)** (65) *(SGNorton)* 4-8-12 ‡⁷OPears (21) (lw: chsd ldrs: led
　　　wl over 2f out: r.o) ............................................................................ —1
165⁶ Shabanaz (70) (bl) *(THCaldwell)* 7-9-4 ‡⁷StephenDavies (11) (hdwy 4f out:
　　　chsd wnr fnl 2f: kpt on) ....................................................... 1¹/₂.2
　　Tanoda (50) *(MBrittain)* 6-7-12 ‡⁷DWright (17) (styd on wl fnl 3f: nrst fin) .... 2¹/₂.3
　　Rive-Jumelle (IRE) (68) *(MBell)* 4-9-1 ‡⁷PTurner (2) (bit bkwd: mid div: hdwy 3f
　　　out: wknd appr fnl f) .............................................................. nk.4
　　Supertop (47) *(PWHarris)* 4-7-10 ‡⁵ATucker (18) (bit bkwd: mde most tl hdd wl
　　　over 2f out: grad wknd) ........................................................ 2¹/₂.5
　　Glastondale (38) *(TDBarron)* 6-7-0 ‡⁷DarrenMoffatt (25) (mid div: effrt & wnt lft
　　　over 2f out: styd on) ............................................................. ¹/₂.6
161⁴ Westfield Moves (IRE) (58) *(HJCollingridge)* 4-8-5 ‡⁷CHawksley (3) (lw: in tch:
　　　effrt 4f out: one pce) ............................................................ hd.7
88⁵ Cheerful Times (53) *(BAMcMahon)* 9-8-3 ‡⁵SMaloney (16) (lw: hdwy 4f out:
　　　chsg ldrs 2f out: wknd 1f out) ............................................. 1¹/₂.8
184 Hills of Hoy (57) *(KCBailey)* 6-8-5 ‡⁷CMunday (20) (lw: bhd: hdwy 3f out: nvr
　　　rchd ldrs) ................................................................................ 1.9
　　Mardessa (70) *(FHLee)* 4-9-5 ‡⁵NKennedy (19) (bit bkwd: s.i.s: effrt appr st:
　　　styd on fnl 2f) ...................................................................... 5.10
　　Nakora Bistraya (USA) (70) *(GAPritchard-Gordon)* 5-9-6 ‡⁵DHarrison (12) (sn
　　　wl bhd: styd on fnl 3f) ......................................................... 1¹/₂.11
　　Pant Llin (60) *(FJordan)* 6-8-10 ‡⁵RPrice (6) (n.d) ................................. s.h.12
　　Rose Glen (62) (bl) *(ABailey)* 6-8-10 ‡⁷PBowe (15) (hdwy 8f out: wknd over 3f
　　　out) ..................................................................................... 2¹/₂.13
　　Abingdon Flyer (IRE) (61) *(RHannon)* 4-8-9 ‡⁵RPerham (23) (swtg: n.d) ..... s.h.14
　　Mingus (USA) (71) *(MrsJRRamsden)* 5-9-5 ‡⁷JWeaver (14) (nvr nr to chal) ..... 3.15
　　Ikteshaf (74) *(BHanbury)* 4-9-7 ‡⁷VBray (22) (b.off hind: prom to st) ........... ³/₄.16
190² Belmoredean (71) *(RJO'Sullivan)* 7-9-9 ‡³DBiggs (1) (chsd ldrs tl wknd 4f out) nk.17
103 Unassuming (46) (bl) *(JSWainwright)* 4-7-7⁽⁷⁾ ‡⁷AGarth (7) (n.d) ................ 1.18
　　Golden Torque (69) *(RBastiman)* 5-9-3 ‡⁷HBastiman (5) (bkwd: n.d) ........... hd.19
　　Chatham Island (72) *(CEBrittain)* 4-9-7 ‡⁸BDoyle (4) (lw: chsd ldrs to st) ............ 20
　　Colonel Fairfax (46) *(JWWatts)* 4-7-9 ‡⁵FNorton (8) (bit bkwd: hdwy appr st:
　　　wknd 4f out) ............................................................................... 21
178★ Sooty Tern (51) (Fav) *(JMBradley)* 5-8-3 ‡³JFanning (24) (lw: swtg: w ldr tl wknd
　　　4f out) ......................................................................................... 22
　　Valatch (63) (v) *(DenysSmith)* 4-8-10 ‡⁷GForster (13) (chsd ldrs to st) ................. 23
　　　　　LONG HANDICAP: Glastondale 7-5.
　　197⁴ Pims Classic (20/1) Withdrawn (bolted gng to s) : not under orders
　　Diving (USA) (66/1) Withdrawn (rdr uns & inj on wy to s) : not under orders

**7/1** Sooty Tern, **17/2** Rive-Jumelle (IRE), **11/1** Cheerful Times, Westfield Moves (IRE), Colonel Fairfax,
Belmoredean, Chatham Island, **14/1** Mingus (USA), Supertop, Abingdon Flyer (IRE), MR CONFUSION (IRE), **16/1**
Golden Torque, Hills of Hoy, Mardessa, **20/1** Nakora Bistraya (USA), Glastondale, Rose Glen, **25/1** Ikteshaf, **33/1**
Ors. CSF £391.70, CT £12,593.92. Tote £13.20: £2.80 £10.70 £8.10 £1.60 (£301.50). Mr R. Fenwick-Gibson
(BARNSLEY) bred by D. P. O'Brien in Ireland. 23 Rn　　　　　　　　　　2m 12.88 (5.88)
　　　　　　　　　　　　　　　　　　　　　　　　　　　　　　　SF—39/42/17/33/9/–

**226**　　PHILIP CORNES BROCKLESBY STKS (2-Y.O. C & G) £3687.50 (£1100.00: £525.00:
　　　　　£237.50)　　**5f**
　　　　　　　　　　　　　　　　　　　　　　　　　　　　　　　　2-35 (2-36)

**Touch Silver** *(BWHills)* 8-11 DHolland (3) (neat: chsd ldrs: led 1f out: r.o wl) .... —1
　　Nominator *(RHollinshead)* 8-11 WCarson (7) (str: cmpt: s.i.s: sn chsng ldrs:
　　　chal over 1f out: nt qckn) ................................................. 1¹/₂.2
　　Sabre Rattler (Fav) *(JBerry)* 8-11 JCarroll (10) (w'like: scope: lw: mde most tl
　　　hdd 1f out: no ex) ............................................................. hd.3
　　Second Chance (IRE) *(PMitchell)* 8-11 JWilliams (5) (w'like: scope: s.i.s: rn
　　　green & bhd tl r.o fnl 2f) .................................................... 5.4
　　Duke of Dreams *(MrsGRReveley)* 8-11 KDarley (1) (rangy: scope: s.i.s: hdwy 2f
　　　out: styd on) ..................................................................... 3.5
　　Sharro *(PAKelleway)* 8-11 AMunro (9) (leggy: unf: bit bkwd: w ldrs 3f: grad
　　　wknd) ............................................................................... hd.6

Plum First *(NBycroft)* 8-11 SWebster (8) (w'like: str: bit bkwd: spd over 3f) ..... 1¹/₂.**7**
Gone Prospecting (USA) *(RHannon)* 8-11 BRaymond (4) (unf: scope: lw: gd
spd 3f) ....................................................................................................................... hd.**8**
Cracker Jack *(TFairhurst)* 8-8 ‡³JFanning (6) (wl grwn: scope: bit bkwd: s.i.s:
n.d) ........................................................................................................................... 2.**9**
Gorodenka Boy *(MrsJJordan)* 8-11 ACulhane (2) (lt-f: unf: cl up to ¹/₂-wy: sn
wknd) ......................................................................................................................... 7.**10**

**8/13** Sabre Rattler(op 6/4), **5/1** Gone Prospecting (USA)(3/1—6/1), **7/1** Nominator(4/1—8/1), **9/1** TOUCH
SILVER(5/1—10/1), Sharro(6/1—10/1), **12/1** Second Chance (IRE)(op 5/1), **20/1** Duke of Dreams, **25/1**
Cracker Jack, **33/1** Ors. CSF £72.20, Tote £9.90: £2.30 £1.60 £1.20 (£38.10). Mr John Leat (LAMBOURN) bred
by J. J. Leat. 10 Rn                                                                       63.38 sec (4.68)
                                                                                            SF—33/27/26/6/–/–

**227**    RACEFORM UPDATE H'CAP (3-Y.O) (0-100) £3557.50 (£1060.00: £505.00: £227.50)
           **5f**                                                                3-05 (3-14)

(Weights raised 2 lb)
**Cindora (IRE) (86)** *(MHTompkins)* 8-8 ‡⁵CHodgson (7) (bhd: effrt 2f out:
swtchd & r.o wl ins fnl f) ............................................................................ —**1**
Echo-Logical **(94)** (Fav) *(JBerry)* 9-7 JCarroll (1) (h.d.w: stdd s: sn cl up: led wl
over 1f out: r.o: jst ct) ................................................................................. hd.**2**
*133³* Inherent Magic (IRE) **(71)** *(MMcCormack)* 7-12 WCarson (2) (lw: cl up: led
¹/₂-wy tl wl over 1f out: kpt on same pce) .............................................. 1¹/₂.**3**
Trove **(90)** *(MrsNMacauley)* 9-3 LDettori (3) (h.d.w: lw: chsd ldrs: rdn chal 1f
out: kpt on) ................................................................................................... hd.**4**
Angels Answer (IRE) **(71)** *(MrsJJordan)* 7-12 SWood (4) (spd 3f) .................... 7.**5**
Boulabas (IRE) **(71)** *(MO'Neill)* 7-12 JLowe (5) (bit bkwd: outpcd fr ¹/₂-wy) .... 1.**6**
*163³* Doesyoudoes **(67)** (v) *(DTThom)* 7-8⁽¹⁾ JQuinn (6) (led to ¹/₂-wy: sn wknd) ... 1.**7**

**3/1** Echo-Logical, **100/30** Inherent Magic (IRE), **7/2** Trove, **11/2** CINDORA (IRE), **8/1** Doesyoudoes(op 5/1),
**12/1** Boulabas (IRE), **14/1** Angels Answer (IRE). CSF £20.47, Tote £6.60: £2.60 £2.10 (£13.20). Mark
Tompkins Racing (NEWMARKET) bred by P. Myerscough in Ireland. 7 Rn          62.21 sec (3.51)
                                                                            SF—54/66/37/55/8/4

**228**    DONCASTER SHIELD (Stks)    £7180.00 (£2140.00: £1020.00: £460.00)
           **1¹/₂m**                                                            3-40 (3-41)

**Luchiroverte (IRE) (111)** (Fav) *(CEBrittain)* 4-8-13 MRoberts (7) (lw: trckd
ldrs: chal 4f out: led over 2f out: r.o) ....................................................... —**1**
Gulf Palace (USA) **(87)** *(RAkehurst)* 7-8-12 LDettori (1) (a.p: effrt over 3f out:
r.o) ............................................................................................................... 1¹/₂.**2**
Lift and Load (USA) **(94)** *(RHannon)* 5-8-12 JReid (3) (a chsng ldrs: rdn over 2f
out: r.o) ....................................................................................................... nk.**3**
Arcadian Heights **(103)** *(GWragg)* 4-8-13 WRSwinburn (2) (led tl hdd over 2f
out: btn whn bit wnr appr fnl f) ................................................................ 1¹/₂.**4**
Spinning **(105)** *(IABalding)* 5-8-12 RCochrane (5) (hld up: hdwy appr st: effrt 3f
out: hung lft & nvr able to chal) ............................................................... 2¹/₂.**5**
Per Quod (USA) **(111)** *(BHanbury)* 7-9-4 BRaymond (8) (hdwy appr st: outpcd
4f out: r.o nr fin) ........................................................................................ 1.**6**
Uluru (IRE) **(93)** *(MrsJRRamsden)* 4-8-10 AMunro (6) (effrt ent st: nvr able to
chal) .............................................................................................................. 5.**7**
Sarwan (IRE) *(APStringer)* 4-8-10 JFortune (4) (a bhd: lost tch fnl 5f) ........... 30.**8**

**13/8** LUCHIROVERTE (IRE), **7/2** Arcadian Heights, **9/2** Spinning(op 3/1), **7/1** Lift and Load (USA), **8/1** Per Quod
(USA), **12/1** Uluru (IRE), **33/1** Gulf Palace (USA), **66/1** Sarwan (IRE). CSF £38.60, Tote £2.70: £1.20 £2.70
£2.30 (£22.50). The Dowager Lady Beaverbrook (NEWMARKET) bred by Stonethorn Stud Farms Ltd in Ireland. 8
Rn                                                                          2m 34.84 (4.24)
                                                                           SF—57/53/52/50/44/48/30

**229**    'BACK A WINNER BY TRAIN' H'CAP (0-80) £3418.00 (£1024.00: £492.00: £226.00)
           **1¹/₂m**                                                            4-10 (4-13)

**Whitechapel (USA) (66)** *(LordHuntingdon)* 4-9-4 WRSwinburn (2) (trckd ldrs
gng wl: led on bit over 2f out: shkn up & sn clr) .................................... —**1**
Welshman **(54)** *(MBlanshard)* 6-8-8 RCochrane (1) (lw: hrd rdn to ld after 1f:
hdd over 2f out: kpt on) ............................................................................ 1¹/₂.**2**
Saffaah (USA) **(60)** *(WRMuir)* 5-9-0 SWhitworth (7) (a chsng ldrs: chal 3f out:
one pce fnl 2f) ........................................................................................... ¹/₂.**3**
Eire Leath-Sceal **(64)** *(MBrittain)* 5-9-4 KDarley (3) (a.p: effrt 4f out: styd on one
pce) ............................................................................................................... 8.**4**
Paper Dance **(62)** *(RJHolder)* 4-9-0 JWilliams (15) (stdd s: hld up & bhd: r.o wl
fnl 2f) .......................................................................................................... ³/₄.**5**

187 Searching Star **(48)** *(PAKelleway)* 4–8-0 GBardwell (10) (effrt ent st: hdwy 4f
out: no imp) ............................................................................. nk.6
Grey Power **(70)** *(MrsGRReveley)* 5–9-10 BRaymond (11) (bit bkwd: in tch: effrt
over 4f out: one pce) ............................................................. ¾.7
214* Lord Hastie (USA) **(77)** **(Fav)** *(SGNorton)* 4–9-8 (5x) ‡⁷OPears (12) (lw: hld up:
smooth hdwy 4f out: effrt 3f out: wknd 2f out) .................... hd.8
West With the Wind **(59)** *(GMMoore)* 5–8-13 KFallon (4) (sn pushed along:
hdwy 4f out: no imp) .............................................................. 3.9
Mysterious Maid (USA) **(70)** *(JPearce)* 5–9-5 ‡⁵RPrice (8) (bit bkwd: bhd: effrt 4f
out: n.d) ................................................................................ 1½.10
Run High **(63)** *(PMitchell)* 9–9-0 ‡³SO'Gorman (14) (swtg: bit bkwd: bhd tl sme
late hdwy) ............................................................................. hd.11
Vallance **(75)** *(PWHarris)* 4–9-13　PaulEddery (9) (bit bkwd: chsd ldrs tl wknd 3f
out) ....................................................................................... 7.12
187 Carousella **(55)** *(CEBrittain)* 4–8-7 MRoberts (5) (a rr div) ........................ nk.13
Clear Light **(64)** *(CASmith)* 4–9-4 MWigham (6) (led 1f: cl up tl wknd 4f out) ....... 14
187 Julfaar (USA) **(74)** *(JPearce)* 5–10-0 WNewnes (13) (swtg: n.d) ................... 15
Gallant Effort (IRE) **(48)** *(SDow)* 4–8-0 GCarter (16) (in tch to st: eased whn btn) 16

**4/1** Lord Hastie (USA)(3/1—9/2), **9/2** Saffaah (USA)(7/2—11/2), **7/1** WHITECHAPEL (USA), **15/2** Eire
Leath-Sceal, **10/1** Welshman, **11/1** Grey Power, **12/1** West With the Wind, **14/1** Mysterious Maid (USA), **16/1**
Paper Dance, Carousella, **20/1** Gallant Effort (IRE), Vallance, **25/1** Clear Light, **33/1** Ors. CSF £71.72, CT
£321.57. Tote £6.50: £1.70 £1.40 £2.10 £2.20 (£28.70). The Queen (WEST ILSLEY) bred by The Queen in USA.
16 Rn　　　　　　　　　　　　　　　　　　　　　　　　　　　　　　　　　　　　　2m 35.88 (5.28)
　　　　　　　　　　　　　　　　　　　　　　　　　　　　　　　　　SF—51/38/43/31/25/10

**230**　　HALL GATE STKS (Mdn 3-Y.O) £2427.00 (£672.00: £321.00)　　1¼m 60y　4-40 (4-43)

Touch Paper (USA) **(Fav)** *(BWHills)* 9-0 SCauthen (7) (lw: hld up: smooth
hdwy ent st: shkn up to ld 1f out: r.o) .................................. —1
In the Money (IRE) *(RHollinshead)* 9-0 SPerks (8) (a cl up: led over 2f out: hdd
1f out: kpt on) ...................................................................... 1½.2
Fassfern (USA) *(MrsJCecil)* 9-0 PaulEddery (11) (lw: led tl hdd over 2f out: one
pce) ...................................................................................... 5.3
Illuminating *(MrsJRRamsden)* 8-3(1) ‡⁷JWeaver (5) (a cl up: kpt on one pce fnl
2f) ......................................................................................... 4.4
Northern Kingdom (USA) *(SGNorton)* 9-0 DNicholls (3) (wl grwn: scope: bit
bkwd: in tch: drvn along appr st: styd on: no imp) ................. 2.5
Tree Frog (IRE) *(LordHuntingdon)* 8-9 DMcKeown (2) (bhd & rdn along ½-wy:
nvr trbld ldrs) ....................................................................... 7.6
Nigelschinapalace *(MissSJWilton)* 8-9 ‡⁵FNorton (4) (unf: in tch: hdwy appr st:
wknd 3f out) ......................................................................... nk.7
Tees Gazette Girl *(MrsGRReveley)* 8-9 JLowe (6) (a outpcd & bhd) ................... 10.8
The Titan Ghost *(BAMcMahon)* 9-0 WRyan (10) (swtg: bit bkwd: chsd ldrs tl
wknd 3f out) ......................................................................... 1½.9
Kut-El-Amara *(CWCElsey)* 9-0 JCarroll (9) (w'like: scope: bit bkwd: s.s: a bhd) 12.10

**11/8** TOUCH PAPER (USA), **2/1** Fassfern (USA), **5/1** Illuminating(6/1—9/1), **9/1** Tree Frog (IRE), **14/1** Northern
Kingdom (USA), **25/1** In the Money (IRE), Kut-El-Amara, **33/1** The Titan Ghost, **50/1** Ors. CSF £32.94, Tote
£2.30: £1.10 £2.80 £1.60 (£16.70). Sheikh Mohammed (LAMBOURN) bred by Wooden Horse Investments in
USA. 10 Rn　　　　　　　　　　　　　　　　　　　　　　　　　　　　　　　　　2m 13.55 (6.55)
　　　　　　　　　　　　　　　　　　　　　　　　　　　　　　　　　SF—35/32/22/3/10/–

T/Trio: Race 5: £53.90 (14.5 Tckts). T/Plpt: £66.50 (82.65 Tckts).　　　　　　　　　　　　AA

# DONCASTER (L-H)
## Friday, March 20th [Good]
Going Allowance: St: 0.30 sec per fur; Rnd: nil sec per fur (G)　　　Wind: fresh half against

Stalls: high

**231**　　SOUTH YORKSHIRE (S) STKS (Mdn 2-Y.O) £2070.00 (£570.00: £270.00)
　　　　　5f
　　　　　　　　　　　　　　　　　　　　　　　　　　　　　　　　1-40 (1-43)

Classic Storm *(JBerry)* 8-9 JCarroll (4) (blind nr eye: w'like: scope: lw: cl up:
led over 2f out: sn drvn clr) .................................................. —1
Shadow Jury *(MrsGRReveley)* 9-0 KDarley (10) (cmpt: hdwy ½-wy: shkn up
over 1f out: r.o) .................................................................... 3.2
Egg *(TDBarron)* 9-0 AlexGreaves (11) (leggy: scope: in tch: hdwy & hung lft
over 2f out: kpt on same pce u.p fnl f) ................................. ¾.3

Luckifosome *(PDEvans)* 8-9  JQuinn (3) (unf: hdwy 2f out: nt qckn fnl f) ............ ¾.**4**
Nellie's Gamble *(APStringer)* 8-9  JFortune (9) (unf: scope: bhd & outpcd early:
hdwy wl over 1f out: kpt on) ...................................... 3½.**5**
Mantlepiece (IRE) *(TDBarron)* 8-4 ‡⁵SMaloney (12) (small: neat: led: hdd over 2f
out: sn btn) ...................................... 1½.**6**
Costa Verde *(KWHogg)* 8-9  WRyan (1) (w'like: bkwd: s.s. hdwy over 2f out: nvr
plcd to chal) ...................................... nk.**7**
Ukam's Lady (Fav) *(RHannon)* 8-9  PatEddery (8) (neat: scope: in tch: drvn
along ½-wy: sn btn) ...................................... 1½.**8**
Cheltenham Windows *(MWEasterby)* 9-0  TLucas (6) (leggy: b.hind: nvr nr ldrs) 1½.**9**
Purbeck Centenary *(MRChannon)* 9-0  TQuinn (5) (cmpt: scope: bit bkwd:
prom tl rdn & wknd wl over 1f out) ...................................... 1.**10**
Genesis Four *(JRJenkins)* 9-0  SWhitworth (2) (neat: unf: lw: sn outpcd) ......... 2.**11**
Spotland Lass *(WGMTurner)* 8-4 ‡⁵TSprake (7) (leggy: a in rr) ...................... 1½.**12**
What Bliss *(DWChapman)* 8-9  SWood (13) (unf: scope: bkwd: s.s. a bhd) .... 3½.**13**
Badenoch Burner *(NTinkler)* 9-0  KimTinkler (14) (w'like: lw: hung lft thrght: gd
spd tl wknd u.p wl over 1f out) ...................................... 2½.**14**

**15/8** Ukam's Lady(5/4—9/4), **5/1** Badenoch Burner(op 8/1), CLASSIC STORM(op 5/2), **11/2** Purbeck
Centenary(op 7/2), **6/1** Shadow Jury, **12/1** Egg, Luckifosome, **14/1** Nellie's Gamble(op 8/1), **16/1** Cheltenham
Windows, Spotland Lass, **20/1** Ors. CSF £40.00, Tote £4.10: £1.90 £2.80 £4.90 (£21.40). Mr D. J. Ayres
(COCKERHAM) bred by Concorde Breeding and Racing International P'Ship. 14 Rn; No bid   63.47 sec (4.77)
SF—29/22/19/11/–/–

**232**     FORTE H'CAP (Ladies) (0-70) £2070.00 (£570.00: £270.00)     **1¼m 60y**   2-10 (2-19)
(Weights raised 1 lb)

     **I Perceive (54)** *(FHLee)* 5-10-6  MrsSGRees (13) (lw: a wl plcd: hdwy on bit 3f
out: led 2f out: sn clr) ...................................... —**1**
  42 Phil-Blake (38) *(SMellor)* 5-9-4  MrsEMellor (20) (swtg: a.p: led over 2f out: sn
hdd & no ch w wnr) ...................................... 7.**2**
 111³ Princess Roxanne (56) (bl) (Fav) *(ABailey)* 5-9-3 ‡⁵MissCRadband (11) (hdwy
u.p 3f out: kpt on one pce fnl 2f) ...................................... 3½.**3**
     Panico (36) (v) *(MissSEHall)* 5-9-2  MissEBronson (5) (mid div: hdwy over 2f
out: styd on same pce) ...................................... 2½.**4**
     Lots of Luck (51) *(JPearce)* 9-10-3  MrsLPearce (6) (lw: stdy hdwy on ins whn
hmpd 3f out: styd on wl fnl f) ...................................... 2½.**5**
 178 Ballerina Bay (61) (v) *(DTThom)* 4-10-12  MissIDWJones (14) (in tch: effrt 3f
out: no imp fnl 2f) ...................................... s.h.**6**
 137³ Buzzards Crest (40) *(BobJones)* 7-9-1 ‡⁵MissDianaJones (17) (effrt over 4f out:
nvr able to chal) ...................................... 1½.**7**
     Glenscar (39) *(JLSpearing)* 6-9-0 ‡⁵MissTSpearing (21) (hdwy over 2f out: nvr
nrr) ...................................... ¾.**8**
 193³ Crosby Place (49) (bl) *(MJHaynes)* 6-10-1  MissYHaynes (16) (lw: mid div: effrt
over 3f out: n.d) ...................................... 3.**9**
 210 Priceless Fantasy (46) *(PatMitchell)* 5-9-7 ‡⁵MissLGlayzer (3) (n.d) .......... 2½.**10**
     Northern Lion (43) *(RThompson)* 9-9-4 ‡⁵MissHCarrington (9) (chsd ldrs tl rdn
& wknd 3f out) ...................................... 1.**11**
     Rag Time Belle (44) *(MWEckley)* 6-9-5⁽¹⁰⁾ ‡⁵MissJRussell (22) (swtg: chsd ldr:
led wl over 3f out tl hdd & wknd over 2f out) ...................................... s.h.**12**
     Golden Beau (34) *(AHarrison)* 10-8-9 ‡⁵MrsGHarrison (15) (swtg: bhd: sme
hdwy on outside over 3f out: n.d) ...................................... ½.**13**
     Roses Have Thorns (48) *(DMorris)* 5-9-9 ‡⁵MrsLCrofts (4) (stdd s: sn wl bhd:
sme late hdwy) ...................................... nk.**14**
  64⁵ Carrolls Marc (IRE) (52) (v) *(PJFeilden)* 4-10-3  MissJFeilden (10) (n.d) ......... ¾.**15**
     Brown Carpet (41) *(CAHorgan)* 5-9-2⁽⁷⁾ ‡⁵MissDPomeroy (12) (n.d) .......... 1.**16**
     Latin Quartet (62) (bl) *(LJCodd)* 4-10-8 ‡⁵MissCBurgess (19) (sn drvn along:
chsd ldrs to st) ...................................... 1.**17**
     Raawi (48) *(JNorton)* 4-9-13  MissLEaton (18) (in tch tl wknd over 3f out) ....... ¾.**18**
     Okaz (USA) (35) *(JSMoore)* 7-8-10 ‡⁵MrsSMoore (2) (b: a bhd) ...................... 2.**19**
 169 Give Me Hope (IRE) (46) (bl) *(GHYardley)* 4-9-6 ‡⁵MissAYardley (8) (swtg: led tl
hdd & wknd wl over 3f out) ...................................... 2½.**20**
     Scotoni (54) *(RJO'Sullivan)* 6-10-6  MissABillot (1) (n.d) ...................... 21
 137 King Ferdinand (69) (v) *(DRTucker)* 5-11-2 ‡⁵MissSRowe (23) (n.d) .......... 22
LONG HANDICAP: Rag Time Belle 8-10, Golden Beau 8-10, Brown Carpet 8-10.
*139 Un Souverain (100/1) Withdrawn (bolted bef s) : not under orders*

**6/1** Princess Roxanne, **8/1** Buzzards Crest, Crosby Place, **9/1** Scotoni, **10/1** Ballerina Bay, Lots of Luck, **12/1** I
PERCEIVE, Panico(op 8/1), **14/1** Raawi, Roses Have Thorns, **16/1** Carrolls Marc (IRE), Latin Quartet(12/1—20/
1), **20/1** Phil-Blake, **25/1** Priceless Fantasy, Give Me Hope (IRE), Golden Beau, Glenscar, **40/1** Brown Carpet,
**50/1** Ors. CSF £216.88, CT £1,450.44. Tote £12.20: £2.70 £7.60 £2.00 £3.70 (£231.50). Mr F. H. Lee
(WILMSLOW) bred by R. Hodgins. 22 Rn                                                   2m 13.63 (6.63)
SF—54/24/30/10/20/28

**233**  HOLROYD CONSTRUCTION GROUP H'CAP (0-90) £3200.00 (£950.00: £450.00: £200.00)
1m (rnd)                                                                      2-40 (2-47)

**King of Chance (IRE) (68)** *(MrsJRRamsden)* 4–8-3 ‡⁷JWeaver (11) (in tch: gd
hdwy over 2f out: disp ld fnl f: r.o wl) ..................................... —1

State Dancer (USA) **(86)** *(MMoubarak)* 5–10-0 LDettori (12) (chsd ldr: led over
2f out: disp ld 1f out: r.o) ........................................................... s.h.2

Abso **(67)** *(RHannon)* 4–8-9 JReid (9) (hdwy over 2f out: edgd lft & kpt on wl fnl
f) ...................................................................................................... 1¹⁄₂.3

Rousitto **(70)** *(RHollinshead)* 4–8-12 RCochrane (2) (s.s: hdwy 2f out: styd on
strly ins fnl f) ................................................................................. 2¹⁄₂.4

Nordic Brave **(67)** *(MBrittain)* 6–8-9 PatEddery (5) (prom: rdn wl over 2f out: no
ex appr fnl f) ................................................................................... 2¹⁄₂.5

Mango Manila **(79)** *(CAHorgan)* 7–9-7 SCauthen (3) (a wl in tch: grad lost pl fnl
2f) ...................................................................................................... ¹⁄₂.6

Bengal Tiger (IRE) **(56)** (bl) *(JAkehurst)* 4–7-7⁽⁵⁾ ‡⁵FNorton (7) (nvr nr ldrs) ..... 1¹⁄₂.7

Lord Oberon (IRE) **(77)** *(RJO'Sullivan)* 4–9-2 ‡³DBiggs (15) (effrt over 2f out: nt
rch ldrs) ............................................................................................ nk.8

En Attendant (FR) **(77)** *(BHanbury)* 4–9-5 BRaymond (6) (hld up: hdwy on ins
whn nt clr run fnl 3f: nt rcvr) .......................................................... 1¹⁄₂.9

Just a Step **(82)** *(MMcCormack)* 6–9-10 WNewnes (19) (nvr plcd to chal) ...... ¹⁄₂.10

Capital Bond (IRE) **(68)** *(RJHolder)* 4–8-10 JWilliams (14) (in tch to st) ......... 1¹⁄₂.11

203★ Pytchley Night **(78)** (Fav) *(DMorris)* 5–8-13 ‡⁷StephenDavies (10) (gd hdwy
over 2f out: sn rdn: wknd fnl f) ...................................................... nk.12

Srivijaya **(70)** (bl) *(MrsJJordan)* 5–8-12 ACulhane (1) (hld up in tch: effrt on ins
& n.m.r 3f out: sn wknd) ................................................................. nk.13

Wild Prospect **(70)** *(CTinkler)* 4–8-12 MBirch (8) (led tl hdd over 2f out: sn
wknd) .............................................................................................. ³⁄₄.14

Northern Printer **(72)** *(MO'Neill)* 7–9-0 JFortune (18) (in tch to st: sn lost pl) ... ¹⁄₂.15

Too Eager **(61)** (bl) *(MWEasterby)* 6–8-9 KDarley (4) (prom to st: sn wknd) ... hd.16

Vague Dancer **(71)** *(MrsJRRamsden)* 6–8-13 AMunro (16) (effrt on outside
over 3f out: sn btn) .......................................................................... 2¹⁄₂.17

199 Foolish Touch **(62)** *(WJMusson)* 10–7-11 ‡⁷PBowe (17) (sn bhd) .................. ¹⁄₂.18

Stylish Gent **(70)** *(NTinkler)* 5–8-12 KimTinkler (13) (prom to ¹⁄₂-wy: sn btn) ... ³⁄₄.19

LONG HANDICAP: Bengal Tiger (IRE) 7-6.

**11/2** Pytchley Night, **13/2** KING OF CHANCE (IRE), **7/1** Vague Dancer, **12/1** Mango Manila, Nordic Brave, **14/1**
Abso, State Dancer (USA), Capital Bond (IRE), Rousitto, **16/1** Foolish Touch, En Attendant (FR), Lord Oberon
(IRE), Stylish Gent, **25/1** Too Eager, Just a Step, **33/1** Bengal Tiger (IRE), Srivijaya, Wild Prospect, **50/1** Northern
Printer. CSF £85.60, CT £1,133.37. Tote £9.00: £1.90 £2.60 £3.40 £2.40 (£131.90). Mr David Thompson
(THIRSK) bred by Ardenode Stud Ltd. in Ireland. 19 Rn                          1m 42.71 (6.41)

**234**  CYSTIC FIBROSIS RESEARCH CUP (H'cap) (0-110) £6400.00 (£1900.00: £900.00:
£400.00)  2¹⁄₄m                                                              3-10 (3-14)
(Weights raised 24 lb)

205 **Coleridge (72)** (v) *(DShaw)* 4–8-10 GCarter (18) (stdy hdwy 8f out: led over 3f
out: r.o wl) ...................................................................................... —1

Bardolph (USA) **(71)** *(PFICole)* 5–9-1 TQuinn (14) (b.off hind: lw: a.p: rdn & ev ch
over 2f out: one pce appr fnl f) ...................................................... ¹⁄₂.2

Tamarpour (USA) **(73)** (v) (Jt-Fav) *(MCPipe)* 5–9-3 MRoberts (2) (b: bhd:
pushed along 10f out: styd on fnl 2f: nrst fin) ............................... 3.3

Dom Wac **(78)** *(MBell)* 4–9-2 MHills (16) (lw: in tch: hdwy on bit to chal 3f out:
wknd over 1f out) ............................................................................ 3¹⁄₂.4

Castle Secret **(80)** (h) *(DBurchell)* 6–9-10 DMcKeown (4) (mid div: effrt 4f out:
one pce fnl 2f) ................................................................................. 1¹⁄₂.5

Taroudant **(67)** *(RJHolder)* 5–8-11 JWilliams (5) (wnt in tch ¹⁄₂-wy: effrt 4f out:
wknd fnl 2f) ..................................................................................... s.h.6

Jinxy Jack **(79)** *(GRichards)* 8–9-9 DNicholls (9) (trckd ldrs: drvn along 5f out:
btn & eased over 1f out) ................................................................ 1¹⁄₂.7

Farsi **(78)** *(RHollinshead)* 4–9-2 SPerks (11) (effrt & hdwy 5f out: btn whn hmpd
2f out: n.d after) .............................................................................. 1¹⁄₂.8

205★ Carlingford (USA) **(56)** *(MPNaughton)* 6–8-0 LCharnock (7) (chsd ldrs tl rdn &
wknd 3f out) ..................................................................................... 7.9

Fight to Win (USA) **(63)** *(IABalding)* 4–7-12 ‡³SO'Gorman (17) (lw: cl up: led 5f
out tl hdd & wknd over 3f out) ....................................................... 2¹⁄₂.10

Maggies Lad **(56)** *(LJCodd)* 4–7-8⁽¹⁾ LJLowe (14) (led tl hdd 5f out: sn bhd) ..... 8.11

205 Honey Dancer **(66)** *(MissAJWhitfield)* 8–8-10 NAdams (6) (a.p: rdn & ev ch
over 3f out: sn btn) .......................................................................... ¹⁄₂.12

Wings of Freedom (IRE) **(56)** (bl) *(APJenkins)* 4–7-8⁽¹⁾ NCarlisle (10) (effrt &
hdwy to chase ldrs 5f out: wknd over 3f out) ............................... 1.13

Patroclus **(52)** *(RVoorspuy)* 7–7-10⁽³⁾ SDawson (15) (nvr nr ldrs: no ch fnl 5f) . 6.14

Prince Sobur **(56)** *(MBlanshard)* 6–8-0(1) DHolland (8) (bhd fnl 4f) .............. 2½.**15**
Cabochon **(75)** *(DMorley)* 5–9-5 MBirch (3) (t.o fnl 5f) ........................... 10.**16**
46[4] Aberfoyle (IRE) **(55)** *(PAKelleway)* 4–7-7 GBardwell (12) (swtg: prom early: sn
lost pl: t.o) ............... s.h.**17**
Kayfaat (USA) **(69)** *(Jt-Fav)* *(MCPipe)* 4–8-7 PatEddery (13) (lw: a bhd: lost tch
9f out: t.o fnl 5f) ............................. **18**
LONG HANDICAP: Maggies Lad 7-4, Patroclus 6-12.

**13/2** Kayfaat (USA), Tamarpour (USA), **7/1** Cabochon, **8/1** Bardolph (USA), **9/1** Farsi, **10/1** Fight to Win (USA),
**12/1** Carlingford (USA), Dom Wac, Taroudant, **14/1** Jinxy Jack, **16/1** Maggies Lad, Castle Secret, **20/1** Prince
Sobur, **25/1** Wings of Freedom (IRE), **33/1** Aberfoyle (IRE), **50/1** Honey Dancer, COLERIDGE, **100/1** Patroclus.
CSF £379.00, CT £2,696.01. Tote £84.30: £16.30 £2.10 £2.20 £2.40 (£558.50). Mr P. J. Sheehan
(ASHINGTON) bred by W. and R. Barnett Ltd. 18 Rn                                    4m 3.82 (11.12)

---

**235** CYSTIC FIBROSIS STKS (Mdn 3-Y.O) £2070.00 (£570.00: £270.00)
1m (st)                                                                    3-40 (3-48)

Mizaaya *(MRStoute)* 9-0 PatEddery (4) (lw: hld up: stdy hdwy on outside
½-wy: rdn to ld 1f out: edgd rt & r.o) ..................... —**1**
Glasgow (Fav) *(BWHills)* 9-0 SCauthen (10) (hld up: effrt & swtchd over 1f out:
r.o strly nr fin) .......................................... 2.**2**
Sudanor (IRE) *(MJHeaton-Ellis)* 9-0 JReid (1) (chsd ldrs: effrt over 2f out: led
over 1f out: sn hdd & nt ackn) ............................ nk.**3**
170[4] Buzzards Bellbuoy *(HJCollingridge)* 9-0 JQuinn (5) (lw: mid div: hdwy over 1f
out: r.o wl nr fin) ........................................ 2.**4**
Mathal (USA) *(MRStoute)* 9-0 WRSwinburn (11) (in tch: shkn up over 2f out: nt
pce of ldrs) ............................................. s.h.**5**
Sky Hunter (USA) **(87)** *(RHannon)* 9-0 BRaymond (15) (lw: plld hrd: hld up in
tch: gd hdwy & ev ch over 1f out: wknd nr fin) ........... s.h.**6**
Houlston's Will *(MrsJRRamsden)* 8-9 AMunro (9) (hld up: hdwy whn bdly
hmpd over 1f out: nt rcvr) ................................ 1½.**7**
Desert Force (IRE) *(MMoubarak)* 9-0 LDettori (3) (w ldrs tl rdn & wknd wl over 1f
out) .................................................... 1.**8**
4a Secret Thing (USA) **(102)** *(CEBrittain)* 9-0 MRoberts (13) (mde most tl hdd &
wknd over 1f out) ........................................ 2½.**9**
Landowner (IRE) *(JHMGosden)* 9-0 GHind (12) (chsd ldrs tl rdn & grad wknd
fnl 2f) ................................................. 1½.**10**
Tahitian *(MrsJRRamsden)* 9-0 TLucas (2) (nvr nr to chal) ................... hd.**11**
Regal Lover *(MBell)* 9-0 MHills (17) (in tch tl outpcd fnl 3f) ............... 1½.**12**
Northern Blade (IRE) *(RHollinshead)* 9-0 WRyan (6) (bhd: sme hdwy 2f out:
n.d) ................................................... 1½.**13**
High Mind (FR) *(MissLCSiddall)* 9-0 RCochrane (7) (w'like: s.s: a in rr) ......... 2½.**14**
The Old Chapel *(BAMcMahon)* 9-0 TQuinn (8) (w ldrs 5f) ................... 2½.**15**
Linpac Express *(CWCElsey)* 9-0 KFallon (16) (w'like: s.s: a bhd) ........... 6.**16**
170[6] Amber Glow (IRE) *(LJCodd)* 9-0 VSmith (14) (t.o) .......................... 20.**17**

**5/2** Glasgow(2/1—3/1), **7/2** Secret Thing (IRE), **5/1** Desert Force (IRE), **8/1** Sky Hunter (USA), **10/1** MIZAAYA,
**12/1** Regal Lover (IRE), Landowner (IRE)(op 8/1), **14/1** Houlston's Will(op 8/1), Sudanor (IRE), **16/1** Mathal
(USA)(op 10/1), **33/1** Northern Blade (IRE), Tahitian, **50/1** Ors. CSF £36.43, Tote £14.20: £3.40 £2.00 £4.80
(£17.70). Maktoum Al Maktoum (NEWMARKET) bred by Cheveley Park Stud Ltd. 17 Rn    1m 43.71 (7.21)
SF—28/22/21/15/14/13

---

**236** C.F. JUBILEE H'CAP (0-100) £3840.00 (£1140.00: £540.00: £240.00)    5f  4-10 (4-15)

Amron **(67)** *(JBerry)* 5–7-10 NCarlisle (8) (a.p: led 1f out: styd on strly nr fin) .... —**1**
Panikin **(90)** *(JWharton)* 4–9-5 JWilliams (12) (hdwy wl over 1f out: r.o wl fnl f: nt
rch wnr) ............................................... 3.**2**
Never so Sure **(78)** *(MrsJRRamsden)* 4–8-0 ‡7JWeaver (15) (bdly hmpd &
dropped rr 2f out: swtchd lft & styd on wl fnl f) ........... 1½.**3**
Gondo **(71)** (v) *(EJAlston)* 5–7-9 ‡5NKennedy (6) (mde most tl hdd 1f out: no ex) hd.**4**
Tbab (IRE) **(95)** *(CEBrittain)* 4–9-10 MRoberts (1) (w ldr: rdn 2f out: nt ackn fnl f) 1½.**5**
Terrhars (IRE) **(99)** *(RHannon)* 4–9-9 ‡5RPerham (9) (chsd ldrs tl rdn & one pce
appr fnl f) ............................................. hd.**6**
217[6] Breezy Day **(78)** *(BAMcMahon)* 6–8-7 TQuinn (5) (effrt 2f out: nt rch ldrs) ......... ¾.**7**
Paddy Chalk **(79)** *(LJHolt)* 6–8-8 JReid (7) (b: n.d) ........................ ¾.**8**
163 Ski Captain **(64)** *(PHowling)* 8–7-4 ‡3JFanning (11) (w ldrs: drvn along ½-wy:
wknd over 1f out) ...................................... ¾.**9**
217 Tigani **(90)** (bl) *(DWChapman)* 6–9-5 SWood (13) (rdn along ½-wy: nvr able to
chal) .................................................. 1½.**10**
Eager Deva **(93)** *(RHollinshead)* 5–9-8 SPerks (10) (lw: chsd ldrs: n.m.r & wknd
wl over 1f out) ........................................ hd.**11**

217 Sir Tasker (76) *(JLHarris)* 4–8–5 RCochrane (3) (in tch: effrt ½-wy: wknd appr fnl f) ....................................................................... ¾.12
209⁴ Joe Sugden (64) (v) *(PHowling)* 8–7-7 NAdams (14) (spd to ½-wy) .............. hd.13
217⁵ Maid Welcome (69) (bl) (Fav) *(MrsNMacauley)* 5–7-7⁽¹⁾ ‡⁵FNorton (4) (lw: w ldrs over 3f) ................................................................................ 1.14
Miami Banker (83) (bl) *(WRMuir)* 6–8-12 SWhitworth (2) (a in rr) ...................... 1.15
LONG HANDICAP: Ski Captain 7-3.

**6/1** Maid Welcome, **7/1** AMRON, **15/2** Never so Sure, **8/1** Terrhars (IRE), **9/1** Sir Tasker, Tbab (IRE), Eager Deva, **10/1** Joe Sugden, **14/1** Gondo, **16/1** Breezy Day, Paddy Chalk, **20/1** Miami Banker, **25/1** Ski Captain, Panikin, **50/1** Tigani. CSF £144.96, CT £1,227.84. Tote £6.90: £2.60 £5.70 £3.20 (£161.40). Mr Roy Peebles (COCKERHAM) bred by Llety Stud. 15 Rn            61.13 sec (2.43)
SF—63/74/49/43/66/64

T/Trio: Race 3: Any 2 from first 3 w any £10.60 (62.1 Tckts), Race 4: Any 2 from first 3 w any £12.90 (54.1 Tckts). T/Plpt: £817.30 (6.4 Tckts).            O'R

# DONCASTER (L-H)
## Saturday, March 21st [Good]
Going Allowance: 0.55 sec per fur (Y)            Wind: str against

Stalls: high

**237**            E.B.F. GREY FRIARS STKS (Mdn 2-Y.O) £2831.50 (£784.00: £374.50)    **5f**  2-00 (2-04)

**Other One** *(NCWright)* 8-9 GDuffield (7) (lt-f: scope: hdwy 2f out: led ins fnl f: r.o) ............................................................................... —1
Totally Unique (USA) *(MBell)* 9-0 MHills (5) (neat: str: s.i.s: hdwy 2f out: r.o nr fin) ......................................................................................... 1½.2
Greenwich Chalenge *(WCarter)* 8-9 ‡³NGwilliams (6) (unf. scope: b.hind: cl up: led ½-wy: wandered: hdd & no ex ins fnl f) ........................ nk.3
Night Melody (IRE) *(RHannon)* 9-0 KDarley (2) (str: cmpt: sn cl up: chal 2f out: rn green: wknd ins fnl f) ........................................................ 2.4
Moscatop (IRE) *(RHollinshead)* 9-0 WRyan (9) (w'like: s.i.s: bhd tl r.o wl fnl f) . 1½.5
Chummy's Friend (IRE) (Fav) *(BWHills)* 8-9 PatEddery (1) (neat: scope: cl up: outpcd ½-wy: no imp) ........................................................ 1½.6
Two Moves in Front (IRE) *(JBerry)* 9-0 JCarroll (3) (w'like: scope: bit bkwd: led to ½-wy: grad wknd) ............................................. 1½.7
Magic Pearl *(EJAlston)* 8-9 KFallon (10) (leggy: unf: bit bkwd: gd spd over 3f) nk.8
The Wend *(DTThom)* 8-9 JQuinn (4) (small: neat: sn outpcd & bhd) ................. 2.9
Gold Desire *(MBrittain)* 9-0 AMunro (8) (leggy: unf: bit bkwd: sn outpcd & bhd) 6.10

**2/1** Chummy's Friend (IRE), **9/4** Two Moves in Front (IRE), **11/2** Totally Unique (USA), **7/1** Night Melody (IRE)(op 9/2), **11/1** Gold Desire, **14/1** Moscatop (IRE), **20/1** Magic Pearl, **25/1** OTHER ONE & Ors. CSF £149.20, Tote £31.40: £4.10 £1.60 £6.00 (£87.90). Mr W. J. Gredley (NEWMARKET) bred by Stetchworth Park Stud Ltd. 10 Rn            64.41 sec (5.71)
SF—36/35/24/26/20/9

**238**            DONCASTER EXHIBITION CENTRE STKS (Mdn 3-Y.O) £2427.00 (£672.00: £321.00)
**7f**            2-30 (2-32)

**Forest Tiger (USA)** (Fav) *(MMoubarak)* 9-0 LDettori (4) (rangy: scope: trckd ldrs gng wl: led over 2f out: impressive) ................................ —1
Rebel Call *(RHannon)* 9-0 BRaymond (9) (rangy: scope: bit bkwd: s.i.s: sn pushed along: hdwy ½-wy: r.o: no ch w wnr) ................. 3½.2
Klingon (IRE) *(RHollinshead)* 9-0 SPerks (3) (wl grwn: bit bkwd: s.s: hdwy over 2f out: r.o wl) ................................................................. 1½.3
Open Agenda (IRE) *(BWHills)* 9-0 PatEddery (6) (w'like: scope: a in tch: hdwy over 2f out: nt qckn appr fnl f) ...................................... ½.4
Mashakel (USA) *(BHanbury)* 9-0 WRSwinburn (8) (lengthy: prom: effrt over 2f out: no imp) .......................................................... 1½.5
Canon Kyle (IRE) *(MHEasterby)* 9-0 MBirch (12) (wl grwn: scope: bit bkwd: chsd ldrs: edgd lft over 2f out: grad wknd) ..................... 4.6
Hi-Tech Honda (IRE) *(CEBrittain)* 9-0 MRoberts (2) (str: cmpt: bkwd: effrt 3f out: nvr trbld ldrs) ............................................................. ¾.7
Fangio *(WGMTurner)* 8-9 ‡⁵TSprake (1) (w'like: bit bkwd: led tl hdd & wknd over 2f out) .................................................................... 1½.8
Boursin (IRE) *(PCalver)* 9-0 DMcKeown (11) (lengthy: scope: cl up: hung lft fr ½-wy: grad wknd) ........................................................ ½.9
Cellist *(RThompson)* 9-0 AProud (10) (unf: bit bkwd: spd over 4f) ................. ¾.10
Treasure Beach *(MBrittain)* 9-0 KDarley (7) (unf: in tch 4f) ...................... ¾.11
Our Eileen *(ASReid)* 8-9 RCochrane (5) (unf: s.s: a bhd) ................................ 12

**6/5** FOREST TIGER (USA)(4/6—11/8), **4/1** Open Agenda (IRE)(3/1—5/1), **6/1** Rebel Call, **9/1** Mashakel (USA), **10/1** Hi-Tech Honda (IRE), **12/1** Canon Kyle (IRE), **25/1** Boursin (IRE), Klingon (IRE), **33/1** Ors. CSF £9.31, Tote £2.10: £1.10 £2.00 £6.10 (£5.00). Ecurie Fustok (NEWMARKET) bred by Buckram Oak Farm in USA. 12 Rn
1m 31.30 (7.90)
SF—37/26/21/19/14/2

**239**    TETLEY BITTER DONCASTER MILE (Stks) (listed race) £14490.00 (£4320.00: £2060.00: £930.00)    1m (st)    3-00 (3-01)

215² Daros *(MrsJRRamsden)* 3–8–0 AMunro (2) (lw: hld up & bhd: hdwy ½-wy: r.o u.p fnl f to ld cl home) .................................................... —1
202* Tanfith (CAN) *(JEBanks)* 5–9–3 BRaymond (4) (lw: chsd ldrs: led wl over 1f out: hrd rdn & r.o: jst ct) ............................................ hd.2
My Memoirs **(100)** *(RHannon)* 3–8–0 AMcGlone (3) (chsd ldrs: outpcd over 2f out: styng on whn nt clr run fr over 1f out) ...................... 1½.3
Soleil Dancer (IRE) **(100)** *(MMcCormack)* 4–9–3 JReid (5) (swtg: led over 6f: grad wknd) ................................................ 4.4
Man From Eldorado (USA) **(Fav)** *(GHarwood)* 4–9–6 RCochrane (1) (in tch: effrt 3f out: sn rdn & no imp) ........................................ 1½.5
Shot Stopper **(59)** *(MJHeaton-Ellis)* 4–8–12 LDettori (6) (bhd: drvn along & n.m.r over 2f out: n.d) ..................................... 1½.6
Marcham (IRE) *(BWHills)* 4–9–3 SCauthen (7) (hld up & bhd: effrt ½-wy: n.d) .. nk.7
Ernestan **(100)** *(MHEasterby)* 3–8–3 MBirch (8) (outpcd whn hmpd wl over 2f out: sn wl bhd) ................................................ 8

**5/2** Man From Eldorado (USA), **5/1** Tanfith (CAN), **11/2** Marcham (IRE), **6/1** Soleil Dancer (IRE), Ernestan(op 4/1), **7/1** My Memoirs, **9/1** DAROS(14/1—8/1), **66/1** Shot Stopper. CSF £48.00, Tote £9.60: £1.80 £1.70 £1.90 (£30.40). Mr K. E. Wheldon (THIRSK) bred by Juddmonte Farms. 8 Rn
1m 43.17 (6.67)
SF—51/67/45/50/48/35/39

**240**    WILLIAM HILL LINCOLN H'CAP    £45552.50 (£13670.00: £6585.00: £3042.50)
1m (st)    3-40 (3-47)

(Weights raised 4 lb)
High Low (USA) **(75)** *(WJHaggas)* 4–8–0 JQuinn (17) (mde all stands' side: qcknd clr 3f out: r.o wl) ............................... —1
Mudaffar (IRE) **(83)** *(RWArmstrong)* 4–8–8 LPiggott (5) (lw: hdwy far side 3f out: r.o u.p fnl f: nrst fin) ............................. 1½.2
Democratic (USA) **(89)** *(MBell)* 4–9–0 AMunro (6) (b: lw: a cl up: led far side over 2f out: nt qckn fnl f) ......................... 1½.3
Ashdren **(83)** *(AHarrison)* 5–8–8 KFallon (22) (racd stands' side: hdwy 2f out: r.o: nrst fin) ................................ 2½.4
Linpac West **(96)** *(CWCElsey)* 6–9–7 LDettori (1) (lw: a chsng ldrs far side: kpt on one pce fnl 3f) ...................... ½.5
213³ Gabbiadini **(77)** *(MHTompkins)* 5–8–2 AMackay (19) (racd stands' side: effrt ½-wy: styd on: no imp) .................. ½.6
204² Domicksky **(82)** *(MJRyan)* 4–8–7 NDay (10) (hdwy far side ½-wy: styd on: nvr able to chal) ........................ nk.7
204⁶ Languedoc **(77)** *(MPNaughton)* 5–8–2 LCharnock (23) (lw: a chsng ldrs stands' side: rdn 3f out: no hdwy) ............... ½.8
Maggie Siddons **(86)** *(CJHill)* 4–8–11 PatEddery (14) (stdd s: racd far side: swtchd lft & hdwy ½-wy: rdn 2f out: sn btn) ........ 1½.9
185³ Go Executive **(89)** *(CEBrittain)* 4–9–0 MRoberts (16) (swtg: prom stands' side tl outpcd fnl 3f) ............... nk.10
217² Roseate Lodge **(80)** (Jt-Fav) *(RWArmstrong)* 6–8–5 WCarson (9) (racd far side: hdwy ½-wy: rdn & btn appr fnl f) ......... ¾.11
Two Left Feet **(96)** *(SirMarkPrescott)* 5–9–7 GDuffield (7) (racd far side: in tch: effrt 3f out: wknd wl over 1f out) ......... ½.12
203² Super Sally **(86)** *(MJRyan)* 5–8–8 ‡3DBiggs (2) (lw: in tch far side tl outpcd fnl 2f) ½.13
Sharpalto **(77)** *(MrsGRReveley)* 4–8–2 GHind (11) (bit bkwd: racd far side: bhd: gd hdwy over 3f out: wknd over 1f out) ......... 1.14
Barford Lad **(74)** *(JRFanshawe)* 5–7–13 GCarter (21) (chsd ldrs stands' side over 5f) .............................. 2½.15
Karazan **(85)** *(JGFitzGerald)* 5–8–3 ‡7MHunt (24) (prom stands' side 5f) ......... ½.16
Montpelier Boy **(86)** (Jt-Fav) *(LordHuntingdon)* 4–8–11 WRSwinburn (20) (lw: cl up stands' side tl wknd over 2f out) ............. ¾.17
Gaelic Myth (USA) **(99)** *(TStack,Ireland)* 5–9–10 SCraine (8) (swtg: lw: in tch far side 5f) ........................... nk.18
Pelorus **(83)** *(DRCElsworth)* 7–8–1 ‡7JHunter (18) (lw: spd stands' side 5f) ..... 1.19
Rise Up Singing **(86)** (bl) *(RHannon)* 4–8–6 ‡5RPerham (13) (led far side after 2f tl over 2f out: wknd) ..................... 1½.20

Jimlil **(84)** *(BPalling)* 4–8-9 WRyan (3) (led far side 2f: chsd ldrs tl wknd 3f out) 2½.**21**
Take Two **(80)** *(JWhite)* 4–8-5 SWhitworth (12) (racd far side: prom 5f) ........ 1½.**22**
203 Shake Town (USA) **(79)** *(MHTompkins)* 4–8-4 RHills (4) (chsd ldrs far side 5f:
sn wknd) ............................................................................................ 4.**23**
Glassblower **(75)** *(RAkehurst)* 5–7-9 ‡5FNorton (15) (lw: racd far side: wl bhd fnl
3f) ................................................................................................. 12.**24**

**6/1** Montpelier Boy(op 14/1), Roseate Lodge(op 9/1), **9/1** Super Sally, **12/1** Domicksky, Maggie Siddons, **14/1**
Barford Lad, **16/1** Pelorus, Mudaffar (IRE), HIGH LOW (USA), Gaelic Myth (USA), **20/1** Go Executive, Democratic
(USA), Linpac West, Rise Up Singing, **22/1** Gabbiadini, Take Two, **33/1** Shake Town (USA), Ashdren, **40/1** Two
Left Feet, **50/1** Ors. CSF £224.63, CT £4,572.39. Tote £14.10: £4.10 £3.70 £6.20 £11.20 (£175.10). Mr B.
Haggas (NEWMARKET) bred by Emory Alexander in USA. 24 Rn          1m 42.74 (6.24)
SF—58/61/62/48/59/38/42

**241**      CAMMIDGE TROPHY (Stks) (listed race) £9218.75 (£2750.00: £1312.50: £593.75)
           **6f**                                                         4-15 (4-16)

**Fylde Flyer (91)** *(JBerry)* 3–8-2 JCarroll (1) (lw: disp ld: led 1f out: edgd rt: r.o) —1
Notley **(111)** *(Jt-Fav)* *(RHannon)* 5–9-7 BRaymond (9) (lw: hdwy 2f out: n.m.r:
r.o wl nr fin) ...................................................................................... s.h.**2**
Letsbeonestaboutit **(89)** (bl) *(MrsNMacauley)* 6–9-2 DMcKeown (3) (disp ld 4f:
sn outpcd: hdwy over 1f out: r.o) ................................................... ½.**3**
Stack Rock **(87)** *(EJAlston)* 5–8-11 KFallon (7) (bit bkwd: disp ld tl led 2f out:
hdd 1f out: no ex) ............................................................................ hd.**4**
Duplicity (IRE) **(100)** *(LJHolt)* 4–9-2 WCarson (2) (effrt ½-wy: n.m.r: styd on fnl
f: no imp) ......................................................................................... 1½.**5**
Montendre **(110)** *(Jt-Fav)* *(MMcCormack)* 5–9-7 JReid (10) (in tch: effrt 2f out:
hmpd over 1f out: n.d) ..................................................................... ¾.**6**
Reshift **(06)** *(MBell)* 4 8 11 MHillo (6) (outpcd ½e wy: n.d after) ...................... 2½.**7**
2275 Angels Answer (IRE) **(71)** *(MrsJJordan)* 3–7-11 SWood (4) (n.m.r & outpcd
½-wy: n.d after) ............................................................................... 4.**8**
2a The Auction Bidder **(94)** *(RHollinshead)* 5–9-2 SPerks (8) (lw: prom 3f: sn lost pl) 1.**9**
*Stewards Enquiry: Obj. to Fylde Flyer by Raymond overruled.*

**11/4** Montendre, Notley, **6/1** Duplicity (IRE), **8/1** FYLDE FLYER, Stack Rock, Reshift, **16/1** The Auction Bidder,
**50/1** Letsbeonestaboutit, **100/1** Angels Answer (IRE). CSF £27.01, Tote £6.60: £1.80 £1.70 £2.90 (£11.10).
Blackpool Gazette & Herald Ltd (COCKERHAM) bred by W. L. Caley. 9 Rn          1m 17.11 (6.11)
SF—32/50/43/37/37/39

**242**      INSUREX EXPO-SURE GROUP H'CAP (3-Y.O) (0-90) £4662.50 (£1400.00: £675.00:
           £312.50)   **7f**                                              4-45 (4-50)

**Big Leap (IRE) (80)** *(MMoubarak)* 8-11 LDettori (3) (lw: a gng wl: effrt over 1f
out: qcknd to ld ins fnl f) ............................................................... —1
218★ Eastleigh **(70)** *(RHollinshead)* 8-1 AMunro (4) (lw: racd stands' side: in tch: r.o
wl nr fin) ........................................................................................... 2½.**2**
Double Feature (IRE) **(62)** *(MrsJRRamsden)* 7-7 JLowe (20) (racd stands' side:
cl up: led over 1f out tl ins fnl f: nt qckn) ..................................... s.h.**3**
215★ Early Star **(79)** *(TDBarron)* 8-10 AlexGreaves (6) (lw: hdwy 2f out: r.o nr fin) ... 2½.**4**
Crept Out **(68)** *(MissSEHall)* 7-8 ‡5FNorton (11) (bit bkwd: hdwy over 1f
out: r.o) ............................................................................................ 3½.**5**
Sovereign Rock (IRE) **(69)** *(RHannon)* 8-0 WCarson (5) (disp ld 5f: eased ins fnl
f) ....................................................................................................... nk.**6**
Pageboy **(86)** *(PCHaslam)* 9-3 DaleGibson (8) (bit bkwd: in tch: kpt on same
pce fnl 2f) ........................................................................................ ¾.**7**
Misunderstanding (IRE) **(88)** *(MrsJRRamsden)* 8-12 ‡7JWeaver (14) (bit bkwd:
chsd ldrs tl grad wknd fnl 2f) ......................................................... 1½.**8**
Reel of Tulloch (IRE) **(82)** *(PCHaslam)* 8-13 DMcKeown (13) (bit bkwd: bhd tl
stdy late hdwy) ............................................................................... nk.**9**
Amthaal (USA) **(74)** *(MRStoute)* 8-5 PatEddery (7) (trckd ldrs: led 2f out:
sn hdd & wknd) .............................................................................. hd.**10**
Stoproveritate **(64)** *(SGNorton)* 7-9 LCharnock (12) (s.s: nrst fin) ..................... hd.**11**
1576 First Gold **(62)** *(JWharton)* 7-4 ‡3JFanning (4) (nvr trbld ldrs) ..................... s.h.**12**
Major's Law (IRE) **(86)** *(CEBrittain)* 9-3 MRoberts (21) (bit bkwd: led stands'
side to ½-wy: sn wknd) ................................................................... 2.**13**
Stag Night **(68)** *(CTinkler)* 7-8(6) ‡5SMaloney (1) (bit bkwd: chsd ldrs 5f) ......... ½.**14**
2154 Buddy (IRE) **(69)** *(MBell)* 7-7 ‡7PTurner (9) (lw: disp ld 5f: sn wknd) ............ nk.**15**
Lifetime Fame **(74)** (bl) *(JWPayne)* 8-5 RCochrane (15) (n.d) .......................... ½.**16**
2045 Try Leguard (IRE) **(80)** *(WCarter)* 8-11 JReid (2) (spd over 4f) ...................... nk.**17**
Sylvan (IRE) **(90)** *(CFWall)* 9-7 NDay (10) (prom over 4f) ............................... ¾.**18**
Freephone (CAN) **(63)** *(JWHills)* 7-8 NCarlisle (16) (lw: unruly stalls: n.d) ...... 2½.**19**

Lombard Ocean **(72)** *(MO'Neill)* 8-3 JFortune (19) (racd stands' side: outpcd fr ¹/₂-wy) .......................................................... 1¹/₂.**20**
Spot the Earlybird (USA) **(63)** *(NTinkler)* 7-8 SWood (17) (racd stands' side: outpcd fr ¹/₂-wy) ............................................. 10.**21**
LONG HANDICAP: First Gold 7-5, Stag Night 7-2.

**9/4** Amthaal (USA), **17/2** Early Star, **9/1** Sovereign Rock (IRE), BIG LEAP (IRE)(op 6/1), **10/1** Eastleigh, Double Feature (IRE), **12/1** Misunderstanding (IRE), Reel of Tulloch (IRE), **14/1** Major's Law (IRE), **16/1** Buddy (IRE), Try Leguard (IRE), **20/1** Crept Out (IRE), Pageboy, **25/1** Sylvan (IRE), First Gold, Lifetime Fame, **33/1** Ors. CSF £100.22, CT £864.73. Tote £10.60: £2.30 £2.10 £2.30 £1.80 (£53.60). Ecurie Fustok (NEWMARKET) bred by The Mount Coote Partnership in Ireland. 21 Rn                     1m 30.91 (7.51)
SF—41/23/14/23/–/–

**243**     MARCH STKS (Mdn) £2511.00 (£696.00: £333.00)     **1³/₄m 132y**     5-15 (5-17)

Star Quest **(77)** *(JRJenkins)* 5-9-0 PatEddery (10) (trckd ldrs: led over 4f out: hld on wl fnl f) ................................................ —**1**
56 Line Drummer (USA) *(PAKelleway)* 4-8-11 MRoberts (14) (b: a:p: effrt 2f out: chal ins fnl f: no ex nr fin) ..................................... hd.**2**
Equity Card (IRE) *(GAPritchard-Gordon)* 4-8-11 WRSwinburn (1) (lw: hdwy 4f out: ev ch over 1f out: nt qckn) ...................................... 2¹/₂.**3**
Signor Sassie (USA) **(74)** *(NTinkler)* 4-8-11 RCochran (12) (lw: a:p: chal 4f out: outpcd fnl 2f) ................................................. 10.**4**
Albertito (FR) *(RHollinshead)* 5-9-0 SPerks (6) (hdwy appr st: ch over 2f out: one pce) ........................................................ ³/₄.**5**
214⁶ Conjuring (USA) (bl) *(GThorner)* 4-8-11 RWernham (13) (chsd ldrs fr ¹/₂-wy: chal ent st: wknd 3f out) ....................................... 3¹/₂.**6**
138³ Shining Wood **(46)** *(JSWainwright)* 4-8-6 MBirch (7) (lw: led tl hdd & wknd over 4f out) ............................................................ 5.**7**
120⁰ Fit for Life (IRE) (bl) *(MrsNMacauley)* 4-8-11 LDettori (5) (lw: prom tl wknd over 4f out) ............................................................ 7.**8**
131 Burracoppin **(45)** *(MrsBarbaraWaring)* 5-9-0 NHowe (3) (chsd ldrs tl wknd appr st) .......................................................... 3.**9**
Cardea Castle (IRE) **(38)** *(BEllison)* 4-8-11 NCarlisle (9) (a rr div) ........ 12.**10**
Tumbling (USA) *(RAllan)* 4-8-11 BRaymond (2) (bit bkwd: bhd: effrt appr st: n.d) ................................................................ hd.**11**
Shrewd Girl (USA) (Fav) *(BWHills)* 4-8-6 DHolland (4) (plld hrd early: stdd & bhd after 3f: hdwy & prom appr st: rdn & wknd 3f out) ... 1¹/₂.**12**
Bosambo (USA) **(70)** *(CLPopham)* 4-8-6 ‡⁵RPerham (11) (cl up to ¹/₂-wy: wknd) **13**

**11/8** Shrewd Girl (USA), **7/2** STAR QUEST, **5/1** Equity Card (IRE), **9/1** Albertito (FR)(op 16/1), **10/1** Signor Sassie (USA), Line Drummer (USA), **14/1** Tumbling (USA), **20/1** Shining Wood, **33/1** Fit for Life (IRE), Burracoppin, Bosambo (USA), Conjuring (USA), **50/1** Cardea Castle (IRE). CSF £39.96, Tote £4.50: £1.90 £3.50 £1.90 (£49.70). Mr A. Escudero (ROYSTON) bred by Juddmonte Farms. 13 Rn                3m 18.22 (14.62)
SF—34/30/25/–/–/–

T/Trio: Race 4: £1864.20 (2 Tckts), Race 6: £181.70 (7.2 Tckts). T/Plpt: £2,998.00 (3.55 Tckts).     AA

## 206—LINGFIELD (L-H) Equitrack

### Saturday, March 21st [Standard]

Going Allowance: minus 0.20 sec per fur (FS)

**244**     FRESH & FROZEN CLAIMING STKS     £903.60 (£249.60: £118.80)
1m 5f (AWT)                                                  2-20 (2-20)

187⁵ **Kirby Opportunity (58)** (Fav) *(JPearce)* 4-7-12 ‡⁵RPrice (3) (lw: a:p: led over 3f out: clr over 2f out r.o wl) ........................... —**1**
40 Sailor Boy **(61)** *(RAkehurst)* 6-8-7 TQuinn (2) (lw: rdn thrght: chsd ldr 5f: r.o one pce fnl 3f) ........................................... 6.**2**
John Shaw (USA) **(70)** *(WJHaggas)* 4-9-0 WNewnes (7) (led over 9f: one pce) 2.**3**
197⁶ Le Temeraire **(69)** *(NTinkler)* 6-9-7 KimTinkler (6) (a:p: hrd rdn over 3f out: one pce) ........................................................ ³/₄.**4**
205 Sand Castle **(37)** *(PHowling)* 11-8-3⁽²⁾ ‡⁷DebbieBiggs (1) (nvr nr to chal) ......... 12.**5**
Pims Gunner (IRE) **(66)** *(DBurchell)* 4-8-11 JWilliams (5) (a bhd) ..................... 8.**6**
211 Billy Lomond (IRE) **(42)** *(CACyzer)* 4-7-11 ‡⁷TMcLaughlin (4) (lw: bhd fnl 5f) .. 2¹/₂.**7**
110⁴ Winoski **(66)** *(DLWilliams)* 4-8-9 NAdams (8) (bhd fnl 4f) ................................ 2.**8**

**15/8** KIRBY OPPORTUNITY(op 9/2), **4/1** John Shaw (USA)(op 2/1), **5/1** Winoski(4/1—6/1), **11/2** Le Temeraire, **6/1** Pims Gunner (IRE), **8/1** Sailor Boy(op 5/1), **25/1** Billy Lomond (IRE), **33/1** Sand Castle. CSF £16.58, Tote £3.10: £1.30 £1.60 £2.00 (£14.70). Mr Peter Bradley (NEWMARKET) bred by Highfield Stud Ltd. 8 Rn; Sailor Boy clmd A S Reid £5,000                               2m 45.81 (2.31)
SF—35/32/35/40/–/–

## 245
**BANKERS & BOOZERS H'CAP** (0-70) £979.20 (£271.20: £129.60)
**6f (AWT)**                                                    2-50 (2-51)
(Weights raised 2 lb)

| | |
|---|---|
| 218[5] **Educated Pet (47)** *(MJohnston)* 3-7-7 NAdams (3) (lw: mde all: drvn out) ........ | —1 |
| 188[3] Inswinger **(38)** (Fav) *(WGRWightman)* 6-7-12 GBardwell (6) (w wnr: ev ch ins fnl f: r.o) .................................................. | 1/2.2 |
| 209[3] Rushanes **(63)** *(TCasey)* 5-9-9 WNewnes (7) (a.p: hrd rdn & ev ch over 1f out: r.o) .................................................. | 1/2.3 |
| 213[2] Daisy Grey **(45)** (bl) *(ASReid)* 4-7-12 ‡7PMcCabe (4) (b: a.p: one pce fnl 2f) ...... | 1.4 |
| Erik Odin **(47)** *(MrsLPiggott)* 5-8-0 ‡7GMilligan (5) (eyeshield: b.hind: bit bkwd: nvr nr to chal) .................................................. | 1.5 |
| 185[5] Gorytus Star **(56)** *(DHaydnJones)* 6-8-11 ‡5RPrice (2) (a bhd) ........................ | 11/2.6 |
| 209[5] Murmuring **(64)** *(SDow)* 6-9-10 JWilliams (8) (b.hind: a bhd) .................... | 31/2.7 |
| 188[5] Ever so Artistic **(50)** (v) *(PHowling)* 5-8-10 JMurray (1) (lw: prom 3f) ............ | 31/2.8 |

LONG HANDICAP: Educated Pet 7-6.

**3/1** Inswinger, **100/30** Rushanes, **9/2** Daisy Grey, **11/2** Murmuring, **8/1** EDUCATED PET(op 5/1), **10/1** Erik Odin(op 6/1), **12/1** Ever so Artistic(7/1—14/1), **25/1** Gorytus Star. CSF £29.88, CF £86.29. Tote £7.70: £1.80 £1.40 £1.40 (£12.30). Mr Billy Morgan (MIDDLEHAM) bred by Highfield Stud Ltd. 8 Rn   1m 12.79 (2.19)
SF—11/14/37/8/6/11

## 246
**ABBEY LIFE H'CAP** (0-70) £1576.00 (£436.00: £208.00)   **1½m (AWT)**   3-20 (3-20)

| | |
|---|---|
| 187[4] **Munday Dean (65)** *(DWPArbuthnot)* 4-9-4 ‡5RPrice (2) (chsd ldr: led over 4f out: clr over 1f out: comf) .................................................. | —1 |
| 211* Caspian Beluga **(61)** *(MrsAKnight)* 4-8-12 ‡7OPears (1) (a.p: hrd rdn over 3f out: r.o one pce) .................................................. | 5.2 |
| 190* Modesto (USA) **(70)** (Fav) *(KOCunningham-Brown)* 4-9-7 ‡7StephenDavies (7) (b: led over 7f: then one pce fnl 2f) .................................................. | 3/4.3 |
| 202[3] Rising Tempo (IRE) **(68)** *(CACvzer)* 4-9-12 WNewnes (6) (lw: a.p: hrd rdn over 3f out: one pce) .................................................. | 31/2.4 |
| 211[6] Evening Affair **(33)** (bl) *(WHolden)* 6-7-7 NAdams (5) (bhd fnl 5f) .................... | 10.5 |
| 187 Broughton Blues (IRE) **(43)** *(WJMusson)* 4-8-1 JHBrown (4) (eyeshield: lw: bhd fnl 5f) .................................................. | 1/2.6 |
| Race to Time (IRE) **(58)** *(RAkehurst)* 4-9-2 TQuinn (3) (lw: bhd fnl 7f: t.o whn p.u wl over 1f out: dismntd) .................................................. | 0 |

LONG HANDICAP: Evening Affair 7-6.

**5/2** Modesto (USA), **7/2** MUNDAY DEAN, **4/1** Caspian Beluga, **5/1** Rising Tempo (IRE)(tchd 9/1), **6/1** Race to Time (IRE)(5/1—8/1), **12/1** Broughton Blues (IRE)(tchd 25/1), **14/1** Evening Affair(10/1—16/1). CSF £16.99, Tote £5.30: £2.10 £1.70 (£8.10). Mr N. A. Woodcock (COMPTON) bred by Mrs Anne Sutton. 7 Rn
2m 34.23 (4.83)
SF—32/16/23/21/-/-

## 247
**FREDK. ROE CLAIMING STKS** (3-Y.O) £895.20 (£247.20: £117.60)
**5f (AWT)**                                                    3-50 (3-52)

| | |
|---|---|
| 194[2] **Cellito (IRE) (54)** (v) *(WAO'Gorman)* 8-6 ‡5EmmaO'Gorman (4) (a.p: lft in ld wl over 1f out: edgd lft ins fnl f: rdn out) .................................... | —1 |
| Ipsilante *(NACallaghan)* 7-13 BCrossley (2) (w'like: outpcd: hdwy on ins over 1f out: snatched up ins fnl f: r.o) .................................................. | 3/4.2 |
| 163[6] It's Only Money **(59)** *(THCaldwell)* 8-1 ‡7StephenDavies (5) (hld up: bmpd over 2f out: r.o ins fnl f) .................................................. | 1/2.3 |
| Corley Flower **(51)** *(PDCundell)* 8-0 EJohnson (1) (w ldr: one pce fnl 2f) .......... | 3.4 |
| Cranfield Comet **(74)** (bl) (Fav) *(JBerry)* 8-11 TQuinn (3) (qcknd & led over 2f out: rn v.wd bnd & hdd wl over 1f out: nt rcvr) .................................... | 3.5 |
| 207 Saruk (IRE) *(JJBridger)* 8-1 NAdams (6) (led over 2f: wknd over 1f out) .......... | s.h.6 |

Stewards Enquiry: Obj. to Cellito (IRE) by Crossley overruled.

**40/85** Cranfield Comet, **100/30** CELLITO (IRE), **7/1** It's Only Money(4/1—8/1), **9/1** Ipsilante(op 4/1), **33/1** Corley Flower, **50/1** Saruk (IRE). CSF £28.17, Tote £3.40: £2.00 £3.20 (£8.50). Mr R. A. Meadows (NEWMARKET) bred by Ballykisteen Stud Ltd in Ireland. 6 Rn; Ipsilante clmd A S Reid £5,308   60.41 sec (2.21)
SF—28/18/18/5/4/–

## 248
**LANCASTER STKS** (Mdn 3-Y.O) £878.40 (£242.40: £115.20)   **6f (AWT)**   4-20 (4-29)

| | |
|---|---|
| 207 **Great Hall (45)** *(WGRWightman)* 9-0 JWilliams (3) (hdwy wl over 1f out: led wl ins fnl f: rdn out) .................................................. | —1 |
| 189[3] Easy Does it **(55)** (v) *(CCElsey)* 8-9 WNewnes (1) (led 1f: led wl over 1f out tl wl ins fnl f: r.o: originally plcd 3rd, s.h) .................................... | 3/4.2 |
| 171[2] High Success **(56)** (bl) *(WAO'Gorman)* 8-9 ‡5EmmaO'Gorman (2) (wl bhd over 3f: gd hdwy wl over 1f out: r.o ins fnl f: originally plcd 2nd, 3/4l) .................................................. | s.h.3 |

218  Jaromic **(57)** (bl) *(PFTulk)* 9-0  AShoults (4) (led 5f out tl rn wd bnd & hdd wl over
1f out: wknd ins fnl f) ................................................................ 8.4

*Stewards Enquiry: Original placings revised under Rule 26 (ii). All bets settled on original result.*

**11/10** Easy Does it, **2/1** High Success, **5/1** Jaromic, **9/1** GREAT HALL(6/1—10/1). CSF £23.83, Tote £5.30
(£4.60). Mrs J. M. Joyce (UPHAM) bred by Dorothea Viscountess Kelburn. 4 Rn    1m 14.17 (3.57)
SF—5/–/–/–

**249**    BEAUFORT H'CAP (0-70) £1260.80 (£348.80: £166.40)    **1¼m (AWT)**    4-50 (4-53)

210★ **Dazzle the Crowd (IRE) (57)** *(Fav)* *(CACyzer)* 4-9-1 TQuinn (8) (lw: rdn 5f out:
hdwy over 3f out: led over 1f out: r.o wl) .............................. —1
210²  Awesome Power **(68)** *(CRNelson)* 6-9-6 ‡⁷DRThompson (2) (hld up: nt clr run
2f out: r.o wl ins fnl f) ............................................... ¾.2
192²  Beau Dada (IRE) **(56)** *(JWhite)* 4-9-0 JWilliams (3) (a.p: led over 2f out tl over 1f
out: unable qckn) ....................................................... 3½.3
212★  With Gusto **(53)** *(KOCunningham-Brown)* 5-8-5 ‡⁷StephenDavies (7) (b:
b.hind: a.p: led over 3f out tl over 2f out: one pce) ................... 2½.4
      Texan Clamour (FR) **(60)** *(JSMoore)* 4-8-13 ‡⁵RPrice (1) (b.off hind: a.p: led 5f
out tl over 3f out: sn wknd) ........................................... 10.5
193⁶  Mardior **(40)** *(WGRWightman)* 4-7-5⁽⁵⁾ ‡⁷DHarrison (9) (prom over 6f) ............ s.h.6
190⁴  Merseyside Man **(54)** (v) *(DrJDScargill)* 6-8-6 ‡⁷KRutter (5) (hdwy 5f out: wknd
4f out) ................................................................. 10.7
207   Milan Fair **(36)** *(DLWilliams)* 8-7-9 NAdams (4) (led 5f: wknd over 3f out) ......... 1.8
210⁶  Luks Akura **(35)** *(MJohnston)* 4-7-7 GBardwell (6) (a bhd) .......................... 1.9
                                    LONG HANDICAP: Mardior 7-0, Luks Akura 7-5.

**2/1** DAZZLE THE CROWD (IRE)(3/1—7/2), **4/1** With Gusto, **9/2** Merseyside Man, **5/1** Beau Dada
(IRE)(4/1—6/1), **6/1** Awesome Power, **9/1** Texan Clamour (FR)(6/1—10/1), **14/1** Luks Akura, **33/1** Mardior,
**40/1** Milan Fair. CSF £14.89, CT £51.27. Tote £3.80: £1.60 £2.10 £2.40 (£4.20). Mr R. M. Cyzer (HORSHAM)
bred by J. B. Clarke in Ireland. 9 Rn    2m 7.33 (4.33)
SF—38/41/28/14/2/–

T/Plpt: £789.50 (1.55 Tckts).    AK

# FOLKESTONE  (R-H)
## Monday, March 23rd [St course Heavy, Rnd Soft]
Going Allowance: 1.00 sec per fur (S)

**250**    ALKHAM CLAIMING STKS    £2284.80 (£632.80: £302.40)    **1m 1f 149y**    1-45 (1-47)

214⁵  **Majed (IRE) (69)** *(Fav)* *(NACallaghan)* 4-9-5 PatEddery (1) (hld up in rr: gd
hdwy on ins 3f out: 3rd st: led over 1f out: r.o) .................. —1
158⁶  Great Impostor *(PTWalwyn)* 4-8-10 JReid (7) (hdwy & 4th st: chsd wnr fnl f: no
imp) .................................................................... 2½.2
      Metternich *(MHTompkins)* 7-8-13 CHodgson (12) (bit bkwd: led over 1f: led
3f out tl wl over 1f out) ............................................... 5.3
      Molly Splash **(42)** *(CACyzer)* 5-8-4 ‡⁷AMorris (14) (bit bkwd: hdwy & 6th st: one
pce fnl 2f) ............................................................. nk.4
213⁵  Breezed Well *(CNAllen)* 6-9-1 ‡⁷GForster (2) (nvr nr to chal) ........................ 2.5
      Jaeger (USA) **(63)** *(JRJenkins)* 5-9-2 SWhitworth (13) (lw: led 8f out: rdn & hdd
3rd st: wknd over 1f out) ............................................... 2½.6
      Run Free *(PatMitchell)* 7-9-3 AMunro (8) (nvr nrr) .................................... 8.7
115⁵  Lady Baraka (IRE) **(41)** *(ICampbell)* 4-8-10 AMackay (3) (a bhd) .................... hd.8
      Rushluan *(RJHodges)* 4-8-9² MRoberts (5) (bit bkwd: prom 6f) ......................... 1½.9
42    Sergeant Meryll **(37)** *(PHowling)* 8-8-10 ‡⁵FNorton (11) (5th st: wknd 2f out) .. ½.10
      Viceroy Gem (IRE) **(41)** *(RJHolder)* 4-8-13 JWilliams (6) (bhd most of wy) ...... 1.11
      Stormy Praise (USA) **(44)** *(WGMTurner)* 8-8-10 ‡⁵TSprake (9) (prom 7f) ........ ¾.12
      Monte Bre *(RAkehurst)* 6-9-4 RCochrane (10) (prom 7f: t.o) ........................... 10.13
213   The Square Centre (USA) *(PBurgoyne)* 4-9-0 TQuinn (4) (a bhd: t.o) ................. 1½.14

**11/10** MAJED (IRE), **11/2** Breezed Well(3/1—6/1), **13/2** Jaeger (USA), **10/1** Monte Bre(6/1—12/1), Viceroy
Gem (IRE)(6/1—8/1), **14/1** Rushluan(10/1—16/1), Lady Baraka (IRE)(8/1—16/1), **20/1** Run Free, Sergeant
Meryll, **33/1** Ors. CSF £44.26, Tote £2.40: £1.50 £3.40 £5.40 (£25.80). Mr N. A. Callaghan (NEWMARKET) bred
by Rowlane Investments in Ireland. 14 Rn; Majed (IRE) clmd N Callaghan £9,100    2m 17.2 (19.5)
SF—5/–/–/–/–/–

**251**    SHORNCLIFFE STKS (Mdn 3-Y.O) £1932.00 (£532.00: £252.00)
**1m 1f 149y**    2-15 (2-16)

**In the Picture (IRE) (70)** *(RHannon)* 9-0 AMcGlone (10) (lw: 2nd st: led wl over
1f out: r.o) ............................................................. —1

Mujid (IRE) *(HThomsonJones)* 9-0 RHills (8) (a.p: led over 2f out tl wl over 1f
out) ............................................................................................................... 6.2

Hawkish (USA) *(PMitchell)* 9-0 TQuinn (4) (bit bkwd: hdwy & 4th st: one pce fnl
2f) ................................................................................................................... 8.3

Bernie Silvers *(GLewis)* 9-0 PaulEddery (5) (led tl over 2f out: 3rd st: one pce) 1½.4

American Boogie (FR) *(CEBrittain)* 9-0 MRoberts (1) (w'like: bit bkwd: rdn 7f
out: nvr nr to chal) ....................................................................................... 8.5

Anar (IRE) **(58)** *(WCarter)* 9-0 JReid (2) (a bhd) .......................................... nk.6

Baher (USA) **(Fav)** *(NACallaghan)* 9-0 PatEddery (3) (w'like: bit bkwd: bhd &
rdn along: hdwy 5f out: 5th & btn st) ......................................................... 5.7

Sun Eclipse (IRE) *(MMcCormack)* 8-9 WNewnes (6) (lw: bhd fnl 6f) ............... 1½.8

Lord Belmonte (IRE) *(CACyzer)* 9-0 GCarter (9) (chsd ldr 5f: 6th & btn st: t.o) . 12.9

Midnight Galaxy *(ANLee)* 9-0 JQuinn (7) (bit bkwd: a bhd: t.o) ..................... 25.10

**9/4** Baher (USA), **4/1** IN THE PICTURE (IRE), **5/1** Bernie Silvers(op 3/1), Mujid (IRE), **8/1** American Boogie (FR), **10/1** Anar (IRE)(op 6/1), **12/1** Hawkish (USA), **20/1** Sun Eclipse (IRE), **50/1** Ors. CSF £23.47, Tote £6.40: £1.90 £1.20 £2.60 (£13.60). Mrs Diana Attwood (MARLBOROUGH) bred by Barronstown Stud in Ireland. 10 Rn
2m 19.1 (21.4)

**252**     LEVY BOARD STKS (Mdn 3-Y.O) £2226.00 (£616.00: £294.00)    **6f 189y**    2-45 (2-47)

**Thinking Twice (USA)** *(PWHarris)* 9-0 GDuffield (3) (gd hdwy 2f out: led over 1f
out: r.o) ........................................................................................................... —1

Precious Wonder *(PButler)* 9-0 GBaxter (11) (5th st: styd on fnl 2f) ............... 4.2

Everybodys Talking (Jt-Fav) *(CEBrittain)* 9-0 MRoberts (12) (str: lw: 6th st: ev
ch over 1f out: nt qckn) ................................................................................ 3½.3

Sartigila *(JWPayne)* 8-9 RCochrane (7) (bit bkwd: 4th st: led wl over 1f out: sn
hdd) .................................................................................................................. 1½.4

Hugging **(70)** *(MMcCormack)* 8-9 WNewnes (8) (nvr nrr) .............................. 1½.5

Grey Cphas *(MMcCormack)* 9-0 JReid (10) (w'like: bit bkwd: nrst fin) ............. hd.6

Bold Mood *(JBerry)* 9-0 GCarter (2) (2nd st: wknd over 1f out) ..................... 5.7

Dare to Dream (IRE) *(GLewis)* 9-0 PaulEddery (4) (bit bkwd: nvr nr to chal) .... 1½.8

Formal Invitation (IRE) *(GLewis)* 9-0 BRouse (9) (a bhd) ................................ 1½.9

191 Lindeman *(SDow)* 9-0 JWilliams (5) (3rd st: wknd 2f out) ........................ ½.10

218³ Life's a Breeze *(MRChannon)* 9-0 TQuinn (1) (led after 1f tl wknd wl over 1f
out) .................................................................................................................. 2½.11

Yatoo (IRE) **(72)** (Jt-Fav) *(RHannon)* 9-0 PatEddery (13) (lw: led 1f: nt clr run 2f
out: eased whn btn) ....................................................................................... 3.12

182⁶ Dilkush *(LJHolt)* 9-0 AMcGlone (6) (bit bkwd: a bhd: t.o) ..................... 25.13

**7/2** Everybodys Talking, Yatoo (IRE)(op 7/4), **4/1** Life's a Breeze(5/1—6/1), **8/1** Sartigila(12/1—7/1), **10/1** THINKING TWICE (USA)(8/1—12/1), Hugging, Precious Wonder(12/1—16/1), **14/1** Bold Mood(op 6/1), **20/1** Grey Cphas, **25/1** Formal Invitation (IRE), **50/1** Ors. CSF £98.59, Tote £20.40: £4.40 £1.40 £2.10 (£280.80). Mrs P. W. Harris (BERKHAMSTED) bred by Pendley Farm in USA. 13 Rn
1m 35.2 (13.6)
SF–1/–/–/–/–/–

**253**     ALDINGTON H'CAP (0-70) £2363.20 (£655.20: £313.60)    **6f**     3-15 (3-18)

112 **Across the Bay (58)** (v) *(SDow)* 5-9-5 TQuinn (4) (b.nr fore: a.p: led over 1f
out: r.o wl) ...................................................................................................... —1

Risk Zone **(56)** *(RHannon)* 3-8-3[1] PaulEddery (8) (a.p: ev ch 1f out: nt qckn) .. 2.2

Malunar **(67)** *(MHTompkins)* 7-9-9 ‡5CHodgson (1) (a.p: ev ch over 1f out: nt
qckn) ................................................................................................................ 3.3

208³ Zinbaq **(42)** (Fav) *(CJBenstead)* 6-8-3 JQuinn (6) (lw: rdn over 2f out: styd on:
nt rch ldrs) ....................................................................................................... 3½.4

Domiana **(40)** *(MBlanshard)* 4—7-10 ‡5FNorton (16) (bit bkwd: chsd ldr: ev ch
over 1f out: one pce) ..................................................................................... 2.5

Swing Lucky **(42)** *(KTIvory)* 4—9-10 LPiggott (17) (b: prom over 4f:
eased whn btn) ............................................................................................... 2½.7

Liffey River (USA) **(63)** *(MrsLPiggott)* 4-9-10 RCochrane (2) (b.hind: nrst fin) ... 1½.8

Dawn's Delight **(47)** *(KTIvory)* 14-8-8 RCochrane (2) (b.hind: nrst fin) ........... 1½.8

Barlogan **(63)** *(CFWall)* 4-9-10 NDay (12) (nvr nr to chal) ............................ s.h.9

A Little Precious **(64)** *(JRBostock)* 6-9-11 GDuffield (14) (n.d) ...................... s.h.10

186 The Noble Oak (IRE) **(50)** (bl) *(MMcCormack)* 4-8-11 JReid (13) (lw: led tl wknd
qckly over 1f out) .......................................................................................... ½.11

203⁶ Kissavos **(57)** (v) *(CCElsey)* 6-9-4 TRogers (9) (lw: prom 3f) ................ 2.12

Red Verona **(53)** *(EAWheeler)* 3—7-7[2] ‡7BThomas (10) (n.d) ................... 2.13

Teanarco (IRE) **(62)** *(RJHolder)* 4-9-9 GCarter (5) (prom 3f) ....................... ½.14

Cotton Bank (IRE) **(38)** (v) *(PButler)* 4-7-13 AProud (11) (n.d) .................... 5.15

36⁶ Pigalle Wonder **(48)** (bl) *(WHolden)* 4-8-9 AMunro (7) (spd 3f) ............. 2½.16

Grey Illusions (25/1) Withdrawn (spread plate at s) : not under orders

11/4 Zinbaq, **7/1** Kissavos(5/1—8/1), Malunar, **10/1** A Little Precious(op 6/1), Liffey River (USA)(tchd 16/1), **12/1** Risk Zone(op 8/1), Domiana, **14/1** Teanarco (IRE)(10/1—16/1), **16/1** Barlogan(op 10/1), Pigalle Wonder, **20/1** Dawn's Delight(op 12/1), **33/1** Swing Lucky, ACROSS THE BAY, The Noble Oak (IRE), Red Verona, **50/1** Cotton Bank (IRE). CSF £342.33, CT £2,791.87. Tote £28.60: £3.70 £3.90 £1.50 £1.30 (£379.10). Mr J. A. Redmond (EPSOM) bred by Patrick McGrath and Liam Slattery. 16 Rn 1m 20 (9.3)

SF—39/15/23/–/–/–

### 254
ROCHESTER GRADUATION STKS  £2259.00 (£624.00: £297.00)  **5f**  3-45 (3-47)

**Arctic Appeal (IRE) (86)** (Fav) (JBerry) 3–8–6 GCarter (6) (mde virtually all: r.o wl) .................................................. —1
Allthruthenight (IRE) **(82)** (LJHolt) 3–8–11 JReid (1) (lw: a.p: r.o ins fnl f) .... 5.2
Freddie Lloyd (USA) **(88)** (Jt-Fav) (NACallaghan) 3–8–11 PatEddery (2) (w ldrs: rdn over 1f out: nt qckn) ............................ nk.3
Isdar (USA) **(92)** (Jt-Fav) (HThomsonJones) 3–8–11 RHills (5) (spd over 3f) .... 2¹/₂.4
Ednego Bay (IRE) **(73)** (MMcCormack) 4–9–0 WNewnes (4) (outpcd) ............... 7.5

**15/8** Freddie Lloyd (USA), Isdar (USA), **11/4** ARCTIC APPEAL (IRE), **7/1** Allthruthenight (IRE)(6/1—10/1), **20/1** Ednego Bay (IRE)(10/1—25/1). CSF £18.11, Tote £4.10: £1.70 £2.40 (£6.70). Mr Yahya Nasib (COCKERHAM) bred by Hamilton Bloodstock (UK) Ltd in Ireland. 5 Rn 66.4 sec (7.6)

SF—40/25/24/14/–/–

### 255
HEADCORN STKS (Mdn 2-Y-O)  £1932.00 (£532.00: £252.00)  **5f**  4-15 (4-16)

**George Roper** (MRChannon) 9-0 BRouse (3) (w'like: a.p: rdn over 1f out: led ins fnl f: r.o) .......................................... —1
Always Risky (PAKelleway) 8-9 MRoberts (6) (leggy: led over 2f: led over 1f out tl ins fnl f) ........................................ 1¹/₂.2
Petite Lass (WCarter) 8-4 ‡⁵NGwilliams (8) (neat: w ldr: led over 2f out tl over 1f out) ................................................ 5.3
Polity Prince (LJHolt) 9-0 JReid (4) (w'like: no hdwy fnl 2f) ...................... 3.4
Critical Mass (Fav) (JBerry) 9-0 GCarter (2) (cmpt: bit bkwd: prom 3f) ........... 3.5
Jazitina (MJHaynes) 8-2 ‡⁷DToole (7) (lt-f: nvr nr to chal) ...................... hd.6
Huesca (JRJenkins) 8-9 JWilliams (4) (leggy: lt-f: a bhd) ........................ 4.7

**15/8** Critical Mass(Evens—2/1), **9/4** Always Risky(tchd 4/1), **9/2** GEORGE ROPER(op 3/1), **5/1** Polity Prince(5/2—6/1), **9/1** Jazitina(6/1—10/1), Petite Lass(5/1—10/1), **14/1** Huesca(op 8/1). CSF £16.12, Tote £6.00: £3.50 £1.80 (£12.10). Mr K. Higson (UPPER LAMBOURN) bred by Mrs R. D. Peacock. 7 Rn 67.4 sec (8.6)

SF—28/17/–/–/–/–

### 256
KINGSNORTH H'CAP (3-Y-O) (0-70) £2304.40 (£638.40: £305.20)  **1¹/₂m**  4-45 (4-47)
(Weights raised 3 lb)

**Jack Button (IRE) (67)** (v) (BobJones) 9-7 NDay (9) (mde virtually all: clr over 2f out: r.o wl) .......................................... —1
Lady St Lawrence (USA) **(59)** (Jt-Fav) (SirMarkPrescott) 8-13 GDuffield (7) (lw: 2nd st: hrd rdn: r.o one pce) ............................ 5.2
Thor Power (IRE) **(49)** (DTThom) 8-3 JQuinn (12) (4th st: r.o one pce fnl 2f) .. ¹/₂.3
1824 Amazon Express **(62)** (CEBrittain) 9-2 MRoberts (3) (hdwy & 6th st: one pce fnl 2f) .............................................. 8.4
Oco Royal **(67)** (bl) (JFfitch-Heyes) 9-7 AMackay (4) (nvr nr to chal) ......... 2¹/₂.5
1165 Alternation (FR) **(62)** (PFICole) 9-2 TQuinn (6) (rdn along: hdwy 2f out: nt rch ldrs) ................................................ 8.6
Miss Pin Up **(48)** (bl) (PatMitchell) 8-2 AMunro (8) (5th st: wknd 2f out) ...... 1¹/₂.7
A a Bamba **(63)** (Jt-Fav) (NACallaghan) 9-3 PatEddery (10) (lw: w wnr 9f: 3rd & btn st) ........................................... 2.8
1682 Slight Risk **(67)** (PAKelleway) 9-7 GBardwell (11) (eyecover: prom 9f) ........ 4.9
1915 Copy Lane (IRE) **(57)** (MRChannon) 8-11 BRouse (5) (prom 7f) ................ nk.10
168 Eau D'Espoir **(47)** (JLSpearing) 8-1 RFox (1) (a wl bhd) ..................... 5.11
783 Colouring Book (IRE) **(52)** (MJHaynes) 8-6 AMcGlone (2) (lw: t.o fnl 6f) ..... 12

**11/4** Lady St Lawrence (USA), A a Bamba(5/2—4/1), **7/1** Alternation (FR)(5/1—8/1), **10/1** Slight Risk(op 6/1), **11/1** Amazon Express(op 7/1), **12/1** Miss Pin Up, **14/1** Oco Royal(op 6/1), JACK BUTTON (IRE)(20/1—33/1), **20/1** Colouring Book (IRE)(op 12/1), **33/1** Ors. CSF £49.45, CT £713.98. Tote £10.40: £3.60 £1.20 £10.00 (£29.90). A. and B. Racing (NEWMARKET) bred by Empress Syndicate in Ireland. 12 Rn 3m 1.3 (27.8)

T/Plpt: £2,220 (0.25 Tckts); £2,060.77 to Sandown 24/3/92.

Hn

## LEICESTER (R-H) Tuesday, March 24th

257  **Abandoned**—Waterlogged

# CATTERICK (L-H)
**Wednesday, March 25th [Good]**
Going Allowance: 0.50 sec per fur (Y)                    Wind: fresh across

Stalls: low

**263**    E.B.F. ORAN STKS (Mdn 2-Y.O) £2301.00 (£636.00: £303.00)    5f    2-15 (2-16)

**Bright Gem** *(TFairhurst)* 8-6 ‡³JFanning (5) (cmpt: unf: mde all: hld on wl fnl f) . —1
Annie Rose *(TDBarron)* 8-9 AlexGreaves (3) (cmpt: scope: trckd ldrs: rn
v.green early: hdwy ½-wy: chal over 1f out: kpt on) .......... nk.2
Two Times Twelve (IRE) *(Fav) (JBerry)* 9-0 JCarroll (7) (leggy: bit bkwd: dwlt:
hdwy ½-wy: edgd lft: r.o) .......................... 2½.3
Pinkerton's Silver *(MHEasterby)* 9-0 MBirch (6) (neat: unf: cl up tl rdn & btn
appr fnl f) ............................ 1½.4
Never in Touch *(MBrittain)* 8-9 KDarley (1) (unf: s.i.s: hdwy ½-wy & edgd rt:
carried lft over 1f out: btn whn hmpd ins fnl f) ............ ¾.5
Glow of Hope *(EJAlston)* 8-9 KFallon (4) (cmpt: bit bkwd: s.i.s: sn chsng ldrs:
wknd 1f out) ............................ ¾.6
Canazei *(DonEnricoIncisa)* 8-9 KimTinkler (2) (neat: sn outpcd & bhd) ............ 6.7

**11/8** Two Times Twelve (IRE), **9/4** BRIGHT GEM, **7/2** Annie Rose, **12/1** Glow of Hope, **16/1** Pinkerton's Silver(op
8/1), **20/1** Never in Touch, **50/1** Canazei. CSF £10.19, Tote £4.30: £2.40 £2.10 (£4.30). Mr J. A. Turney
(MIDDLEHAM) bred by J. and S. Evans. 7 Rn                    63.7 sec (6.2)
SF—18/20/15/9/1/—

**264**    FORCETT PARK (S) STKS (3 & 4-Y.O) £2402.40 (£666.40: £319.20)    7f    2-45 (2-47)

**Emerald Earo** *(63) (EWeymes)* 3 9 1⁽¹⁾ GHind (2) (chsd ldrs: led ins fnl f: r.o) —1
153²  Mca Below the Line *(65)* (bl) *(Fav) (WJPearce)* 4-9-11 DNicholls (9) (a chsng
ldrs: led over 1f out: sn hdd: styd on nr fin) ...................... nk.2
Miss Parkes *(JBerry)* 3-8-0 GCarter (20) (bit bkwd: in tch: effrt ent st: styd on wl
fnl f) ............................ 2½.3
101  Station Express (IRE) *(32)* *(BEllison)* 4-9-4 ‡7JWeaver (6) (hdwy over 2f out: r.o) hd.4
159²  Pesidanamich (IRE) *(65)* (bl) *(TDBarron)* 4-9-11 AlexGreaves (1) (led tl hdd
over 1f out: grad wknd) ...................... 1½.5
Chance Report *(42)* *(FHLee)* 4-9-2 RLappin (18) (b.hind: swtg: prom: kpt on
same pce fnl 2f) ...................... 1½.6
51⁴  Profit Stream *(MWEasterby)* 3-8-5 KDarley (17) (lw: bhd: hdwy on outside appr
st: r.o) ............................ 1½.7
Super Marco *(57)* *(WWHaigh)* 3-8-5 DMcKeown (8) (lw: hmpd & lost pl after 1f:
hdwy over 1f out) ...................... 1.8
123⁶  Optical (IRE) *(MPNaughton)* 3-8-5 LCharnock (11) (hld up & bhd: hmpd appr
st: nvr plcd to chal) ...................... 3.9
Foxes Diamond *(BEllison)* 4-9-2 NCarlisle (16) (n.d) ................... ½.10
Rowandene (IRE) *(MHEasterby)* 3-8-5 MBirch (12) (bhd tl sme late hdwy) ..... ½.11
224  Yours Or Mine (IRE) *(DWChapman)* 4-9-2 SWood (13) (bit bkwd: s.s: hmpd & c
wd st: n.d) ............................ ½.12
Scu's Lady (IRE) *(29)* *(ASmith)* 4-9-2 SWebster (14) (s.i.s: n.d) ............ ½.13
Stoneleigh Abbey (IRE) *(45)* (v) *(DMoffatt)* 4-9-7 AMunro (3) (chsd ldrs 5f) .. 2½.14
Who's That Lady *(MHEasterby)* 3-7-9 ‡5SMaloney (7) (prom tl sltly hmpd & lost
pl appr st) ............................ nk.15
Chiparopai (IRE) *(WStorey)* 4-8-9 MichaelDenaro (19) (b: n.d) ............ ½.16
106  Mummy's Emerald *(NTinkler)* 4-9-2 KimTinkler (5) (s.i.s: a bhd) ............ nk.17
172  Damaaz (IRE) (v) *(JSWainwright)* 4-9-7 KFallon (4) (w ldrs to st: wknd qckly) .. 18
Jiggerak *(64)* (v) *(SGNorton)* 3-7-11 ‡7OPears (10) (b: prom tl hmpd & uns rdr
appr st) ............................ 0

**100/30** Mca Below the Line, **9/2** Pesidanamich (IRE), **13/2** Jiggerak, **7/1** Mummy's Emerald, **10/1** EMERALD
EARS, **12/1** Miss Parkes, Rowandene (IRE), **14/1** Profit Stream, **16/1** Chiparopai (IRE), **20/1** Super Marco,
Who's That Lady, **25/1** Optical (IRE), Chance Report, **33/1** Foxes Diamond, **50/1** Scu's Lady (IRE), Damaaz
(IRE), Stoneleigh Abbey (IRE), **100/1** Ors. CSF £42.22, Tote £12.50: £3.10 £2.10 £2.70 (£38.50). Mr F. Town
(LEYBURN) bred by Mrs N. Napier. 19 Rn; No bid                    1m 31 (7.8)
SF—22/42/9/26/28/14

**265**    GODS SOLUTION H'CAP (0-80) £2856.00 (£791.00: £378.00)    5f 212y    3-15 (3-17)

121⁵  **Furiella** *(54)* *(PCHaslam)* 4-8-5 DMcKeown (8) (lw: chsd ldrs & c wd st: hung lft
u.p: styd on to ld wl ins fnl f) ...................... —1
Cronk's Courage *(62)* (v) *(EJAlston)* 6-8-13 MHills (11) (led: edgd rt fnl 2f: hdd
& btn whn sltly hmpd cl home) ...................... 1.2

Plain Fact **(75)** *(SirMarkPrescott)* 7–9-12 GDuffield (6) (lw: trckd ldrs: effrt 2f out: kpt on one pce fnl f) .................................................. 1¹/₂.**3**

217 In a Whirl (USA) **(49)** *(DWChapman)* 4–8-0 SWood (4) (bhd & effrt over 2f out: styd on wl) ...................................................................... ³/₄.**4**

217 Orient Air **(65)** (bl) (Fav) *(TDBarron)* 4–8-9 ‡⁷JWeaver (2) (effrt appr st: sn rdn: nvr rchd ldrs) ................................................................. 3¹/₂.**5**

207⁴ Toshiba Comet **(77)** (bl) *(WJPearce)* 5–10-0 DNicholls (12) (hdwy on outside appr st: c wd: sn rdn & no imp) ............................................. 3.**6**

Drum Sergeant **(53)** *(JParkes)* 5–8-4 NCarlisle (1) (s.s: bhd tl styd on fnl 2f) ... 1¹/₂.**7**

Hob Green **(62)** *(MrsJRRamsden)* 3–7-13 AMunro (3) (nvr plcd to chal) ....... hd.**8**

180³ Brisas **(60)** (bl) *(TFairhurst)* 5–8-8 ‡³JFanning (13) (chsd ldrs: c wd st & grad wknd) ................................................................................ 2¹/₂.**9**

Oyston's Life **(57)** *(JBerry)* 3–7-8 NAdams (9) (effrt appr st: n.d) ................. ³/₄.**10**

143 Spanish Realm **(49)** *(MBrittain)* 5–8-0 JLowe (1) (sn bhd) ........................ ¹/₂.**11**

241 Angels Answer (IRE) **(71)** *(MrsJJordan)* 3–8-8 ACulhane (10) (chsd ldrs: edgd lft & wknd fnl 3f) ..................................................................... 1¹/₂.**12**

173² Saladan Knight **(62)** (bl) *(JGFitzGerald)* 7–8-13 MBirch (5) (lw: prom: c wd st: sn wknd) ............................................................................. 7.**13**

**9/2** Orient Air, **5/1** Plain Fact, **6/1** Saladan Knight, **8/1** In a Whirl (USA), **10/1** Hob Green, Cronk's Courage, Brisas, Toshiba Comet, **14/1** Drum Sergeant, Oyston's Life, **16/1** Angels Answer (IRE), FURIELLA, **25/1** Spanish Realm. CSF £155.73, CT £843.97. Tote £15.90: £3.40 £3.90 £2.50 (£119.20). Mr W. J. Hall (MIDDLEHAM) bred by Langham Hall Bloodstock. 13 Rn
1m 16.2 (5.7)
SF—37/41/48/19/14/21

**266**  TOYTOP STKS (2-Y.O) £2387.20 (£659.20: £313.60)  **5f**  3-45 (3-46)

**Lucky Parkes** (Fav) *(JBerry)* 8-6 JCarroll (7) (neat: cl up: led after 2f: clr appr fnl f: r.o) ......................................................................................... —**1**

Isotonic *(GMMoore)* 8-6 KFallon (6) (cmpt: bit bkwd: s.i.s: hdwy ¹/₂-wy: r.o: no ch w wnr) ............................................................................. 3.**2**

Principal Player (USA) *(WBentley)* 8-11 JLowe (2) (leggy: scope: a chsng ldrs: kpt on one pce fnl 2f) .......................................................... 1¹/₂.**3**

Sison (IRE) *(RMWhitaker)* 8-11 ACulhane (4) (cmpt: bkwd: chsd ldrs: effrt ¹/₂-wy: no hdwy) ................................................................. 2.**4**

226 Gorodenka Boy *(MrsJJordan)* 8-11 MHills (1) (sn drvn along: no imp fr ¹/₂-wy) . 2.**5**

Exodus (IRE) *(MHEasterby)* 8-11 KDarley (5) (cmpt: unf: dwlt: nvr trbld ldrs) .. 1¹/₂.**6**

231 What Bliss (bl) *(DWChapman)* 8-6 SWood (3) (led 2f: hung lft & sn wknd) ........ 8.**7**

**4/5** LUCKY PARKES, **3/1** Sison (IRE), **7/1** Isotonic, **9/1** Principal Player (USA), **14/1** Exodus (IRE)(op 6/1), **25/1** Gorodenka Boy, **33/1** What Bliss. CSF £7.04, Tote £2.00: £1.60 £2.50 (£5.30). Mr Joseph Heler (COCKERHAM) bred by Joseph Heler. 7 Rn
63.6 sec (6.1)
SF—20/8/9/1/–/–

**267**  YARM H'CAP (0-70) £2406.00 (£666.00: £318.00)  **1m 5f 175y**  4-15 (4-17)

225⁶ **Glastondale (36)** (Jt-Fav) *(TDBarron)* 6–7-7 ‡³JFanning (1) (lw: mde virtually all: hld on wl fnl 2f) ............................................................... —**1**

Bollin Magdalene **(44)** (bl) *(MHEasterby)* 4–7-10 ‡⁵SMaloney (4) (cl up: chal 7f out: outpcd over 2f out: styd on wl fnl f) ................................... s.h.**2**

220* Steppey Lane **(72)** (Jt-Fav) *(WWHaigh)* 7–10-4 (4x) DMcKeown (9) (lw: in tch: pushed along 6f out: hdwy 2f out: styd on: nvr able to chal) 2¹/₂.**3**

138⁵ Bridge Player **(43)** *(DMoffatt)* 5–7-10 ‡⁷DarrenMoffatt (11) (lw: bhd: reminders 7f out: hdwy 6f out: no imp over 2f out) ....................................... 10.**4**

Demokos (FR) **(42)** *(APStringer)* 7–8-2 JFortune (3) (chsd ldrs: outpcd 5f out: no imp after) .......................................................................... 5.**5**

Not Yet **(41)** *(EWeymes)* 8–8-1⁽¹⁾ GHind (5) (bit bkwd: bhd: sme hdwy ent st: nvr rchd ldrs) ............................................................................. 1.**6**

243 Shining Wood **(47)** *(JSWainwright)* 4–8-4⁽¹⁾ MBirch (7) (prom to st) ............. 1.**7**

Smoke **(48)** *(JParkes)* 6–8-8 NCarlisle (8) (b: bit bkwd: nvr nr ldrs) .................. ¹/₂.**8**

Angelica Park **(53)** *(JWharton)* 6–8-13 JWilliams (10) (swtg: hdwy 8f out: lost pl 5f out) ................................................................................. 6.**9**

Bonny's Game **(36)** (bl) *(CWCElsey)* 4–7-7 JLowe (2) (chsd ldrs tl outpcd 6f out: sn wknd) ........................................................................ 7.**10**

225 Diving (USA) **(48)** *(MrsVAAconley)* 4–8-5 PBurke (12) (a bhd) ....................... 3.**11**

55⁴ Brora Rose (IRE) **(43)** *(JDBethell)* 4–8-0 RHills (6) (bhd fnl 6f) .................... 2.**12**

LONG HANDICAP: Bonny's Game 7-3.

**4/1** GLASTONDALE, Steppey Lane, **9/2** Bridge Player(op 3/1), **7/1** Brora Rose (IRE), **12/1** Smoke(op 8/1), **14/1** Angelica Park, Demokos (FR), **16/1** Bollin Magdalene(op 10/1), **20/1** Shining Wood, Not Yet, **25/1** Diving (USA), **33/1** Bonny's Game. CSF £55.89, CT £243.46. Tote £4.90: £2.10 £3.50 £2.00 (£168.80). Mr J. Baggott (THIRSK) bred by Lord Harrington. 12 Rn
3m 11 (15.8)
SF—/–/24/–/–/–

**268**     WHORLTON STKS (Mdn 3-Y.O) £2226.00 (£616.00: £294.00)     1¹/₂m 44y   4-45 (4-47)

**Romansh** (Fav) *(GWragg)* 9-0 WRSwinburn (4) (lw: trckd ldr: led wl over 1f out: shkn up & r.o: comf) ................................................................ —1

Salu *(JEtherington)* 8-9 KDarley (5) (bit bkwd: trckd ldrs: effrt ent st: r.o: nt pce of wnr) .................................................................................. 3¹/₂.2

Natral Exchange (IRE) **(85)** *(JWHills)* 9-0 RHills (3) (led tl hdd wl over 1f out: kpt on same pce) ............................................................................. 1.3

Drummer Hicks **(62)** *(EWeymes)* 9-0 DMcKeown (2) (trckd ldrs: effrt appr st: sn rdn & one pce) .......................................................................... 2.4

38   Queen of Pendona **(34)** *(DMoffatt)* 8-9 GHind (1) (outpcd & lost tch 7f out: n.d after) ........................................................................................... 25.5

**6/4** ROMANSH, **15/8** Natral Exchange (IRE), **4/1** Drummer Hicks(tchd 6/1), **8/1** Salu(op 5/1), **100/1** Queen of Pendona. CSF £10.93, Tote £2.00: £1.10 £2.30 (£4.70). Sheikh Mohammed (NEWMARKET) bred by White Lodge Stud Ltd. 5 Rn                                                                 2m 55.6 (21.6)

**269**     SPRINGTIME H'CAP STKS (0-70) £2595.00 (£720.00: £345.00)     7f     5-15 (5-17)

203⁴  **Euroblake (48)** *(TDBarron)* 5-8-6 AlexGreaves (10) (lw: gd hdwy 2f out: r.o u.p fnl f to ld cl home) ........................................................................ —1

Nordan Raider **(35)** *(MJCamacho)* 4-7-7 LCharnock (8) (lw: trckd ldrs: led & qcknd over 2f out: edgd rt & no ex nr fin) ......................................... 1.2

The Devil's Music **(42)** *(MrsJRRamsden)* 8-8-0 AMunro (3) (lw: a chsng ldrs: rdn 2f out: nvr able to chal) .................................................................. 5.3

135⁴  Palacegate King **(63)** *(JBerry)* 3-8-5 JCarroll (6) (lw: led after 1f tl wnr 2f out: grad wknd) ................................................................................... 7.4

Par de Luxe **(40)** (bl) *(BWMurray)* 5-7-9 ‡³JFanning (12) (cl up tl wknd 2f out) .... 1.5

Spanish Verdict **(54)** *(DenysSmith)* 5-8-5 ‡⁷CTeague (11) (a chsng ldrs: no imp over 2f out) ........................................................................................... ³/₄.6

199   Cool Enough **(42)** *(MrsJRRamsden)* 11-8-0 RHills (7) (lw: trckd ldrs: effrt ent st: no imp) .......................................................................................... 1¹/₂.7

Kawwas **(35)** *(WHolden)* 7-7-7 JLowe (5) (s.i.s: hdwy 2f out: n.d) ................... 1.8

233   Srivijaya **(70)** *(MrsJJordan)* 5-10-0 ACulhane (14) (s.i.s: n.d) ...................... 2¹/₂.9

Miss Brightside **(38)** *(ASmith)* 4-7-10 AMackay (9) (w ldrs to st: sn wknd) .. hd.10

233   Too Eager **(67)** (bl) (Fav) *(MWEasterby)* 6-9-11 KDarley (1) (b: outpcd & lost tch after 2f: n.d after) ........................................................................... nk.11

Tequila Gold **(38)** *(JJO'Neill)* 4-7-10 NCarlisle (13) (n.d) ............................. ³/₄.12

233   Wild Prospect **(70)** *(CTinkler)* 5-10-0 MBirch (2) (led 1f: lost pl appr st) ......... 3.13

171   Lady of Letters **(51)** *(TThomsonJones)* 3-7-7 NAdams (5) (sn outpcd & bhd) . 2.14

LONG HANDICAP: Nordan Raider 7-4, Kawwas 7-5, Lady of Letters 7-3.

**4/1** Too Eager, **5/1** EUROBLAKE, **13/2** Palacegate King, **7/1** The Devil's Music, **8/1** Cool Enough, Wild Prospect(op 5/1), **10/1** Tequila Gold, **16/1** Miss Brightside, Kawwas, **20/1** Srivijaya, **25/1** Ors. CSF £111.91, CT £784.15. Tote £3.80: £1.40 £5.40 £2.30 (£74.30). Mr W. G. Swiers (THIRSK) bred by Viscount Leverhulme. 14 Rn                                                                          1m 29.8 (6.6)
                                                                                 SF—46/30/22/6/–/–

T/Plpt: £350.10 (6.95 Tckts).                                                             AA

# BRIGHTON (L-H)

## Thursday, March 26th [Good]

Going Allowance: 0.15 sec per fur (G)                                 Wind: fresh half bhd

Stalls: low

**270**     CHURCHILL SQUARE STKS (Mdn 3-Y.O) £1932.00 (£532.00: £252.00)
            **5f 213y**                                                     2-00 (2-01)

218²  **Blake End (USA)** (Fav) *(WAO'Gorman)* 9-0 RCochrane (4) (lw: mde all: rdn out) —1

Prince Rodney **(66)** *(RHannon)* 9-0 WCarson (1) (3rd st: chsd wnr fnl 2f: r.o) ... ³/₄.2

Tulapet *(SDow)* 8-9 TQuinn (5) (bit bkwd: chsd wnr 4f: sn wknd) ..................... 10.3

Savalaro **(58)** *(JFfitch-Heyes)* 8-9 AMackay (3) (4th st: no hdwy fnl 3f) ............ 3¹/₂.4

Placid Lady (IRE) *(WCarter)* 8-9 BRaymond (2) (dwlt: 5th st: a wl bhd) .......... 12.5

**2/5** BLAKE END (USA), **4/1** Prince Rodney, **12/1** Tulapet(op 8/1), **14/1** Placid Lady (IRE)(op 8/1), **33/1** Savalaro. CSF £2.35, Tote £1.40: £1.10 £1.70 (£1.60). Tamdown Ltd (NEWMARKET) bred by Harry T. Mangurian Jnr in USA. 5 Rn                                                                     1m 12.3 (3.9)
                                                                                 SF—40/37/–/–/–

**271**  SHEEPCOTE VALLEY H'CAP (0-80) £2259.00 (£624.00: £297.00)
1m 3f 196y                                                2-30 (2-33)

**Sparkler Gebe (47)** *(RJO'Sullivan)* 6-7-9 JQuinn (3) (led over 4f out: all out) .... —1
Kaher (USA) **(80)** (Fav) *(NACallaghan)* 5-10-0 PatEddery (1) (3rd st: rdn over 3f
      out: r.o ins fnl f) ............................................................ nk.2
Polistatic **(46)** *(CAHorgan)* 5-7-8[1] DaleGibson (4) (s.s: hdwy 5f out: 2nd st:
      hrd rdn over 2f out: r.o one pce) ............................ 1½.3
212[3] Amphigory **(57)** *(LordHuntingdon)* 4-8-3 AMunro (6) (6th st: hrd rdn over 1f
      out: r.o one pce) .............................................. 1.4
 225 Pims Classic **(60)** *(WJHaggas)* 4-8-6 NDay (5) (b.nr fore: 5th st: hrd rdn over 2f
      out: one pce) ................................................. 1½.5
Hear a Nightingale **(56)** *(RJHodges)* 5-8-4 WCarson (8) (chsd ldr over 7f: 4th
      st: wknd over 3f out) ........................................ 20.6
Predestine **(59)** *(MMadgwick)* 7-8-2[5] ‡5RPerham (7) (b: bhd fnl 3f) ................ 10.7
Do the Right Thing **(70)** *(JABOld)* 4-9-2 BRaymond (2) (led over 7f) ................ 15.8
      *Stewards Enquiry: Quinn suspended 4-7/4/92 (excessive use of whip).*

**11/8** Kaher (USA)(11/10—13/8), **5/1** Amphigory, **6/1** Do the Right Thing, **7/1** Polistatic(op 9/2), **8/1**
Predestine(tchd 12/1), Pims Classic, **14/1** Hear a Nightingale(op 8/1), **50/1** SPARKLER GEBE. CSF £114.60, CT
£531.89. Tote £80.50: £8.50 £1.20 £2.30 (£183.30). Sparkler Filters (Great Britain) Ltd (BOGNOR REGIS) bred
by P. Nelson. 8 Rn                                                2m 40.5 (flag) (13.5)

**272**  ELM GROVE CLAIMING STKS  £2324.00 (£644.00: £308.00)
1m 3f 196y                                                3-00 (3-02)

187[3] **Absolutely Right (45)** *(RAkehurst)* 4-8-12 TQuinn (9) (b.nr hind: hdwy over 5f
      out: 4th st: led over 2f out: clr over 1f out: comf) .............. —1
244* Kirby Opportunity **(45)** (Fav) *(JPearce)* 4-8-3 ‡5RPrice (2) (led 4f out tl over 2f
      out: unable qckn) ............................................. 8.2
226[6] Ramble (USA) *(JABOld)* 5-8-12 RFox (3) (3rd st: one pce fnl 3f) ...................... 3.3
 225 Abingdon Flyer (IRE) **(61)** *(RHannon)* 4-8-9 ‡5RPerham (6) (led over 6f out to 4f
      out: 2nd st: wknd 3f out) ..................................... 4.4
Silver Ancona (bl) *(JO'Donoghue)* 8-8-5 ‡7TMcLaughlin (8) (nvr nr to chal) ..... 2½.5
Singing Reply (USA) **(61)** *(DMarks)* 4-8-5 ‡7AntoinetteArmes (7) (nvr nrr) ........... 7.6
206[5] High Kabour *(WGMTurner)* 6-8-4 ‡5TSprake (11) (5th st: wknd over 3f out) ........ 8.7
244[3] John Shaw (USA) **(73)** *(WJHaggas)* 4-9-4 NDay (4) (lw: led over 5f) ............... nk.8
155[3] Present Times **(30)** *(AMoore)* 6-9-1 BRouse (1) (6th st: wknd over 3f out) ........ ½.9
131[5] Adjacent (IRE) **(58)** *(MDixon)* 4-8-6 DaleGibson (10) (b: bhd fnl 6f) .............. 12.10

**11/8** Kirby Opportunity, **3/1** John Shaw (USA), **5/1** ABSOLUTELY RIGHT(op 8/1), **13/2** Abingdon Flyer (IRE),
**10/1** Adjacent (IRE), **20/1** Present Times, **25/1** High Kabour, **33/1** Ors. CSF £12.41, Tote £4.80: £1.10 £1.80
£14.90 (£6.30). Automarque (Bournemouth) Ltd (EPSOM) bred by R. S. Cockerill (Farms) Ltd. 10 Rn
                                                                 2m 40.3 (flag) (13.3)

**273**  HOLLINGBURY H'CAP (0-70) £2363.20 (£655.20: £313.60)    1m 1f 209y    3-30 (3-34)

 41[2] **Double Echo (IRE) (65)** *(JDBethell)* 4-9-10 AMunro (1) (lw: 2nd st: led 3f out:
      pushed out) ................................................... —1
Tiger Claw (USA) **(54)** (Fav) *(RJHodges)* 6-9-0 WCarson (12) (3rd st: ev ch
      over 2f out: unable qckn) ..................................... 7.2
Joli's Great **(52)** *(MJRyan)* 4-8-8 ‡3DBiggs (15) (6th st: hrd rdn over 2f out: one
      pce) .......................................................... 2½.3
Noted Strain (IRE) **(55)** *(PJMakin)* 4-9-0 BRaymond (4) (hdwy 5f out: r.o one
      pce fnl 2f) .................................................... nk.4
  93 Marzocco **(55)** *(JFfitch-Heyes)* 4-9-0 AMackay (13) (rdn & hdwy over 1f out:
      nvr nrr) ...................................................... 7.5
Castle Galah **(33)** *(SWoodman)* 5-7-7 JQuinn (2) (no hdwy fnl 3f) .................... 4.6
Solid Steel (IRE) **(50)** *(AMoore)* 4-8-9 CandyMorris (9) (prom 5f) .................... 6.7
 154 Rarfy's Dream **(45)** *(JEBanks)* 4-7-13 ‡5LNewton (7) (a mid div) .................... nk.8
166[3] Tenayestelign **(52)** *(DMarks)* 4-8-11 AMcGlone (14) (hdwy 5f out: wknd 4f out) 5.9
210[4] Wileys Folly **(47)** *(SDow)* 6-8-7 TQuinn (11) (4th st: eased whn btn fnl 2f) ...... 6.10
144[5] Anne's Bank (IRE) **(48)** *(AMoore)* 4-8-7 BRouse (6) (lw: 5th st: wknd 3f out) 3½.11
Silver Cannon (USA) **(34)** *(RVoorspuy)* 10-7-8[1] NCarlisle (10) (b: a bhd) ....... 1.12
 113 Neroli **(69)** *(APJones)* 4-9-7 ‡7JWeaver (5) (led 7f) ............................... 2.13
115[6] Windsor Highness **(44)** *(MPMuggeridge)* 5-8-4 DaleGibson (3) (a bhd) ....... 1½.14
 201 Deepwood Nanusket **(35)** *(MMadgwick)* 6-7-9[2] SDawson (8) (prom 6f) ......... 7.15
      LONG HANDICAP: Castle Galah 7-4, Silver Cannon (USA) 7-4, Deepwood Nanusket 7-4.

5/2 Tiger Claw (USA), **3/1 DOUBLE ECHO (IRE)**, **4/1** Joli's Great, **15/2** Tenayestelign, **10/1** Wileys Folly, **12/1** Anne's Bank (IRE)(op 7/1), Rarfy's Dream, **14/1** Noted Strain (IRE), **16/1** Marzocco, **20/1** Windsor Highness, **25/1** Solid Steel (IRE), **33/1** Neroli, **50/1** Silver Cannon (USA), Deepwood Nanusket, **100/1** Castle Galah. CSF £11.97, CT £31.72. Tote £3.50: £1.20 £1.50 £1.90 (£4.90). Mrs John Lee (DIDCOT) bred by A. Tarry in Ireland.
15 Rn                                                                                                      2m 8.4 (10.4)
                                                                                                           SF—21/–/–/–/–/–

**274**      FALMER STKS (Mdn 3-Y-O) £1932.00 (£532.00: £252.00)      7f 214y      4-00 (4-03)

2356 **Sky Hunter (USA) (87)** (Fav) *(RHannon)* 9-0 BRaymond (1) (lw: 2nd st: led 3f
       out: rdn out) ......................................................................................... —1
     Dune River *(SirMarkPrescott)* 9-0 GDuffield (5) (bit bkwd: 3rd st: rdn 3f out:
       unable qckn) ......................................................................................... 4.2
     Dexter Chief *(IABalding)* 9-0 RCochrane (4) (leggy: 5th st: hdwy over 1f out: r.o)  nk.3
     Silica (USA) *(JHMGosden)* 8-9 PatEddery (2) (nt grwn: led 4f out to 3f out: one
       pce) ....................................................................................................... 1½.4
     Alkarif (USA) (72) *(AAScott)* 9-0 WCarson (3) (led 4f: 4th st: eased whn btn over
       2f out) .................................................................................................... 20.5
     Bella Run *(RJHodges)* 8-4 ‡5TSprake (6) (bit bkwd: bhd fnl 6f) .......................... ½.6

**6/4** SKY HUNTER (USA), **2/1** Dune River, **13/2** Silica (op 2/1), **7/1** Alkarif (USA)(op 4/1), **12/1** Dexter Chief(op 4/1), **66/1** Bella Run. CSF £4.50, Tote £2.50: £1.30 £1.70 (£2.70). A. F. Budge (Equine) Limited (MARLBOROUGH) bred by Mrs Lucy G. Bassett in USA. 6 Rn                         1m 40.1 (7.9)
                                                                                                           SF—3/–/–/–/–/–

**275**      ROEDEAN H'CAP (3-Y-O) (0-80) £2280.00 (£630.00: £300.00)      5f 213y      4-30 (4-31)

     **Ponsardin (80)** (Fav) *(SirMarkPrescott)* 9-7 GDuffield (2) (lw: 3rd st: led over 2f
       out: rdn out) .......................................................................................... 1
     Golden Proposal (52) *(MBell)* 7-7 JQuinn (4) (2nd st: ev ch over 2f out: unable
       qckn) ...................................................................................................... 5.2
     Duty Sergeant (IRE) (67) *(MPMuggeridge)* 8-8 AMunro (5) (b.hind: 5th st:
       hdwy over 1f out: one pce) ...................................................................... 1½.3
208* Appealing Times (USA) (78) *(WAO'Gorman)* 9-0 ‡5EmmaO'Gorman (1) (led 2f:
       4th & styd far side st: wknd over 2f out) .................................................. 20.4
     Truthful Image (72) (bl) *(MJRyan)* 8-13 RCochrane (3) (led 4f out tl over 2f out:
       sn wknd) ................................................................................................. 6.5
                         LONG HANDICAP: Golden Proposal 7-5.

**7/4** PONSARDIN, **2/1** Truthful Image(6/4—9/4), **7/2** Appealing Times (USA), **6/1** Duty Sergeant (IRE), **14/1** Golden Proposal(op 8/1). CSF £18.31, Tote £2.70: £1.60 £1.50 (£9.40). Mr W. E. Sturt (NEWMARKET) bred by D. A. and Mrs Hicks. 5 Rn                                                         1m 12.6 (4.2)
                                                                                                           SF—41/–/2/–/–

T/Plpt: £22.80 (96.95 Tckts).                                                                              AK

# WOLVERHAMPTON (L-H)
## Thursday, March 26th [Heavy]
Going Allowance: 5f: 0.90 sec per fur; Rest: 1.10 sec per fur (S)                Wind: slt half bhd

Stalls: high

**276**      CYCLAMEN STKS (Mdn 3-Y-O) £2206.40 (£610.00: £291.20)      5f      2-10 (2-12)

     **Uccello (69)** *(LJHolt)* 9-0 JReid (8) (lw: hdwy over 2f out: led ins fnl f: r.o wl) .... —1
     Nigals Friend (73) (Fav) *(DHaydnJones)* 9-0 JWilliams (10) (a.p: led 2f out tl ins
       fnl f: unable qckn) ................................................................................. 3.2
     We're All Game (57) *(BCMorgan)* 8-9 JLowe (1) (led 3f: r.o one pce fnl f) ......... 2½.3
     Murray's Mazda (IRE) (51) *(JBerry)* 9-0 JCarroll (7) (prom: rdn wl over 1f out: sn
       btn) ........................................................................................................ ½.4
     Preamble *(MrsJRRamsden)* 8-9 TLucas (4) (bhd: hdwy fnl 2f: nvr nrr) ............. 1½.5
174  Injaka Boy (v) *(KWhite)* 9-0 NAdams (3) (chsd ldrs: rdn 2f out: no imp) ......... 1½.6
     Speed Oil *(RBastiman)* 8-7 ‡7HBastiman (5) (outpcd: a bhd) ........................ 1½.7
     Rivet *(MBlanshard)* 9-0 MRoberts (6) (bit bkwd: spd to ½-wy: sn lost tch) ........ ½.8
1944 Grubby (49) *(RHollinshead)* 8-9 WRyan (9) (a in rr) .................................... nk.9
     Millefiori *(KSBridgwater)* 8-9 AProud (2) (neat: unf: s.s: swvd lft s: a outpcd: t.o) 10.10
       *Stewards Enquiry: Lucas fined £290 under Rule 151 (ii) (failure to ensure best possible placing).*

**2/1** Nigals Friend, **3/1** UCCELLO, **7/2** Preamble(op 7/4), **13/2** Murray's Mazda (IRE), **10/1** We're All Game, **11/1** Grubby(8/1—12/1), **14/1** Speed Oil, **16/1** Rivet, Millefiori, **50/1** Injaka Boy. CSF £10.32, Tote £5.50: £1.80 £1.80 £1.30 (£14.70). Mr K. F. Khan (BASINGSTOKE) bred by D. A. and Mrs Hicks. 10 Rn     65.5 sec (8.2)
                                                                                                           SF—26/14/–/2/–/–

**277**          LILAC H'CAP (0-70) £2735.60 (£761.60: £366.80)    **1m**          2-40 (2-48)

    **Solid (IRE) (50)** *(JRJenkins)* 4–8-8 SWhitworth (13) (hld up: hdwy over 2f out:
    r.o strly to ld nr fin) ................................................................................. —1
199³ Royal Acclaim **(47)** (v) *(JMBradley)* 7–7-12 ‡⁷MBradley (8) (hdwy 3f out: ev ch
    ins fnl f: r.o) ......................................................................................... nk.2
896 On Y Va (USA) **(69)** *(RJRWilliams)* 5–9-13 DHolland (2) (hld up: hdwy 3f out: led
    1f out tl ct cl home) ............................................................................. nk.3
    Friendlypersuasion (IRE) **(46)** *(RHollinshead)* 4–8-4⁽¹⁾ WRyan (5) (hdwy ½-wy:
    rdn & unable qckn fnl f) ........................................................................ 2.4
1992 Doulab's Image **(70)** (bl) *(JAGlover)* 5–9-7 ‡⁷SWilliams (18) (chsd ldrs: led over
    2f out to 1f out: one pce) ..................................................................... 2.5
    Sunset Reins Free **(48)** (v) *(EJAlston)* 7–8-6⁽²⁾ KFallon (15) (lw: bhd & sn
    pushed along: hdwy 2f out: nrst fin) ...................................................... nk.6
124⁴ Sandmoor Denim **(54)** *(SRBowring)* 5–8-5 ‡⁷MHarris (16) (bit bkwd: s.s: styd on
    fnl 2f: nvr nrr) ..................................................................................... ¾.7
    Quietly Impressive (IRE) **(60)** (Fav) *(MBell)* 4–9-4 MHills (20) (5th st: ev ch 2f
    out: sn rdn & wknd) ............................................................................. ¾.8
    Execution Only (IRE) **(58)** (v) *(JWWatts)* 4–9-2 WRSwinburn (14) (prom: 4th st:
    wknd 2f out) ......................................................................................... 1¹/₂.9
    Jolizal **(44)** *(DMorris)* 4–8-2 BCrossley (19) (bit bkwd: bhd tl sme late hdwy) ... 6.10
214 Dawn Success **(60)** *(DWChapman)* 6–9-4 SWood (6) (lw: nvr nr to chal) ...... 3¹/₂.11
    Tender Moment (IRE) **(65)** *(CEBrittain)* 4–9-9 MRoberts (17) (prom: 6th st:
    eased whn btn appr fnl f) ..................................................................... 2.12
88 Golden Ancona **(52)** *(MBrittain)* 9–8-10 KDarley (3) (n.d) ................................ 5.13
178 Obsidian Grey **(67)** *(BAMcMahon)* 5–9-11 LDettori (7) (lw: n.d) .................. 3¹/₂.14
181★ Company Cash **(62)** (bl) *(RBastiman)* 4–8-13 ‡⁷HBastiman (11) (led 2f: 3rd st:
    wknd 3f out) ......................................................................................... nk.15
253⁶ Swing Lucky **(42)** (bl) *(KTIvory)* 7–7-9 ‡⁵FNorton (10) (b: prom: 2nd st: led over
    4f out tl over 2f out: wknd qckly: t.o) .................................................... 10.16
154 Crown Reserve **(47)** *(MJRyan)* 4–8-5 PaulEddery (9) (spd 5f: sn lost tch: t.o) ..... 17
64³ Petropower (IRE) **(44)** *(MO'Neill)* 4–8-2⁽²⁾ JFortune (4) (b.off hind: led after 2f:
    hdd over 4f out: grad wknd: t.o) ............................................................ 18
    Travel Token **(53)** *(LJHolt)* 4–8-11 NAdams (1) (bhd fr ¹/₂-wy: t.o) .................. 19
    Royal Dartmouth **(48)** *(BRMillman)* 7–8-6 GBaxter (12) (bhd fr ¹/₂-wy:
    virtually p.u ins fnl f: t.o) ....................................................................... 20

**9/2** Quietly Impressive (IRE), **7/1** On Y Va (USA)(8/1—4/1), **10/1** Swing Lucky(op 6/1), Sunset Reins Free, Royal
Dartmouth (USA), **11/1** Doulab's Image, **12/1** SOLID (IRE), **16/1** Dawn Success, Execution Only (IRE), Company
Cash, **20/1** Petropower (IRE), Sandmoor Denim, Golden Ancona, Crown Reserve, Royal Acclaim,
Friendlypersuasion (IRE), **33/1** Ors. CSF £211.09, CT £1,641.60. Tote £25.80: £4.80 £12.10 £2.30 £7.80 (Wnr
or 2nd w any £6.70). Mr J. McBarron (ROYSTON) bred by Barronstown Stud in Ireland. 20 Rn  1m 50.4 (13.1)
                                        SF–29/18/46/17/28/12


**278**          FORGET-ME-NOT (S) STKS (3 & 4-Y.O) £2676.80 (£744.80: £358.40)    **1m** 3-10 (3-19)

151⁶ **Rocky Bay (42)** *(DHaydnJones)* 3–8-1 DHolland (16) (led to ¹/₂-wy: led 2f out:
    r.o wl) ................................................................................................. —1
    Taunting (IRE) *(MBlanshard)* 4–9-9 JReid (8) (lw: hdwy 3f out: chsd wnr appr fnl
    f: r.o) ................................................................................................... 2¹/₂.2
230 Nigelschinapalace (bl) *(MissSJWilton)* 3–8-1 ‡⁵FNorton (15) (plld hrd: 3rd st:
    led 4f out to 2f out: sn rdn & btn) ......................................................... 6.3
273 Noushy *(KSBridgwater)* 4–8-11 ‡⁷MichaelDenaro (17) (hdwy 3f out: nt rch ldrs) . 4.4
242 Stag Night **(57)** (Fav) *(CTinkler)* 3–8-6 KDarley (11) (prom: 6th st: kpt on one
    pce fnl 3f) ............................................................................................ 2.5
198⁵ Hanjessdan *(DHaydnJones)* 4–9-9 JWilliams (6) (nvr plcd to chal) ................... 10.6
    Nicholas Star *(REPeacock)* 3–8-1 ‡⁵ATucker (4) (leggy: lt-f: s.s: styd on fnl 2f:
    nvr nrr) ................................................................................................ s.h.7
221 Princess Jestina (IRE) *(GHYardley)* 4–8-13 ‡⁵NKennedy (5) (chsd ldrs: 7th st:
    no imp fnl 3f) ....................................................................................... 2¹/₂.8
189⁶ Rhythmic Echo **(50)** *(PHowling)* 3–8-7⁽¹⁾ WNewnes (13) (prom: 5th st: sn lost
    tch) ..................................................................................................... ¹/₂.9
    Tsar Alexis (USA) **(59)** (bl) *(CLPopham)* 4–9-9 PaulEddery (14) (a bhd) ........ 3¹/₂.10
    Between Two Fires **(57)** *(JBerry)* 3–8-6 JCarroll (3) (prom: 2nd st: wknd over 2f
    out) ..................................................................................................... s.h.11
    Dots Dee *(JMBradley)* 3–7-8 ‡⁷MBradley (7) (bkwd: a bhd) ......................... hd.12
164 Pace E Salute **(41)** *(SDow)* 3–8-3⁽²⁾ MRoberts (10) (prom: 4th st: sn rdn & wknd) 6.13
218 Weekend Girl **(36)** *(WMBrisbourne)* 3–8-1 AProud (2) (lw: n.d) .................... hd.14
    My Moody Girl (IRE) **(43)** *(CRBarwell)* 3–8-1 NAdams (1) (s.s: a bhd: t.o) ...... 2¹/₂.15
    Flying Petal *(CJHill)* 4–9-4 GHind (12) (bkwd: s.s: t.o fnl 4f) ......................... 16

**7/4** Stag Night(6/4—9/4), **13/2** Between Two Fires(op 4/1), Noushy(op 4/1), **7/1** Nigelschinapalace, **11/1** Taunting (IRE), **12/1** Rhythmic Echo, **14/1** Tsar Alexis (USA), **16/1** Pace E Salute, **20/1** Weekend Girl, ROCKY BAY, Nicholas Star, Princess Jestina (IRE), **25/1** Hanjessdan, **33/1** My Moody Girl (IRE), **50/1** Ors. CSF £217.59, Tote £24.90: £4.00 £4.40 £7.10 (£104.60). Miss Karen Harris (PONTYPRIDD) bred by Mrs M. L. Parry and P. M. Steele-Mortimer. 16 Rn; No bid
1m 51.4 (14.1)
SF—7/21/–/–/–/–

### 279    PRIMROSE H'CAP (0-70) £2480.80 (£688.80: £330.40)    5f    3-40 (3-50)

| | | | |
|---|---|---|---|
| | **Penny Hasset (42)** *(MWEasterby)* 4-8-4 MBirch (7) (a.p stands' side: rdn to ld 2f out: r.o wl) | | —1 |
| 1995 | Strip Cartoon (IRE) **(49)** (bl) *(SRBowring)* 4-8-4(2) ‡#7MHarris (5) (lw: racd centre: led 3f: rdn & no ex fnl f) | | 2½.2 |
| | Peggy Mainwaring **(56)** *(RJHolder)* 3-8-5 PaulEddery (4) (chsd ldrs: kpt on one pce fnl f) | | 3½.3 |
| 140 | Minizen Music (IRE) **(43)** *(MBrittain)* 4-8-5 KDarley (14) (r.o u.p fnl f: nvr nrr) | nk.4 |
| | Chateau Nord **(60)** *(JBerry)* 3-8-9 JCarroll (16) (w ldrs stands' side: ev ch 2f out: wknd over 1f out) | nk.5 |
| | No Quarter Given **(66)** *(PSFelgate)* 7-10-0 MRoberts (11) (bit bkwd: s.s: sn chsng ldrs: eased whn btn fnl f) | 2.6 |
| 66 | Uppance **(36)** *(DWChapman)* 4-7-12 SWood (15) (chsd ldrs stands' side over 3f) | 1½.7 |
| 133 | Fighter Squadron **(53)** (bl) *(JAGlover)* 3-8-2 GHind (8) (dwlt: hdwy ½-wy: nvr able to chal) | nk.8 |
| | Ballad Dancer **(58)** *(Fav)* *(EJAlston)* 7-9-6 JWilliams (1) (racd far side: spd 3f) | 2½.9 |
| | R a Express **(46)** *(BAMcMahon)* 7-8-8 LDettori (3) (spd centre 3f) | 2½.10 |
| | Queen's Tickle **(59)** *(APJarvis)* 3-8-8 SWhitworth (12) (outpcd) | ½.11 |
| 1884 | Barbara's Cutie **(45)** *(MBlanshard)* 4-8-7(1) JReid (2) (racd far side: spd 3f) | 1½.12 |
| 219⁴ | Carnfield **(30)** (v) *(JAGlover)* 4 7 6 ‡#7CHawksley (9) (spd 3f) | 1½.13 |
| 196⁴ | Factuelle **(54)** *(DRTucker)* 5-9-2 GBardwell (10) (outpcd) | 2½.14 |
| 169 | Petony (IRE) **(38)** *(CWCElsey)* 4-8-0 JLowe (13) (lw: outpcd: t.o) | 4.15 |

**9/2** Ballad Dancer, **7/1** Chateau Nord, **9/1** Queen's Tickle, R a Express, **10/1** PENNY HASSET, Peggy Mainwaring, Carnfield, Factuelle(op 16/1), **12/1** Barbara's Cutie, No Quarter Given, **20/1** Minizen Music (IRE), **25/1** Fighter Squadron, Petony (IRE), Strip Cartoon (IRE), **33/1** Uppance. CSF £201.06, CT £2,311.33. Tote £19.10: £3.70 £3.50 £5.40 (£462.20). Mrs Anne Henson (SHERIFF HUTTON) bred by Mrs Anne Henson. 15 Rn
64.1 sec (6.8)
SF—44/34/22/21/24/35

### 280    NARCISSUS STKS (Mdn 3-Y.O) £2088.80 (£576.80: £274.40)    1½m 70y    4-10 (4-13)

| | | | |
|---|---|---|---|
| | **Goldsmiths' Hall** *(Fav)* *(GWragg)* 9-0 SCauthen (4) (lw: mde all: sn clr: canter) | | —1 |
| | For Mog (USA) *(CEBrittain)* 9-0 MRoberts (2) (dwlt: wnt 2nd 8f out: rdn ent st: no imp) | | 10.2 |
| | Line of Kings *(DMorley)* 8-7 ‡#7EBentley (1) (lengthy: scope: bit bkwd: s.s: 3rd st: wknd over 3f out) | | 20.3 |
| | My Grain *(RHollinshead)* 8-9 SPerks (3) (bkwd: chsd wnr over 4f: 4th & btn st) | 10.4 |

**1/5** GOLDSMITHS' HALL, **5/1** For Mog (USA), **15/2** Line of Kings(5/1—8/1), **33/1** My Grain. CSF £2.03, Tote £1.20 (£1.70). Sheikh Mohammed (NEWMARKET) bred by White Lodge Stud Ltd. 4 Rn    3m 3.3 (31.6)

### 281    TULIP APP'CE H'CAP (3-Y.O) (0-70) £2343.60 (£649.60: £310.80)

1m 200y    4-40 (4-45)

| | | | |
|---|---|---|---|
| 223★ | **Eriny (USA) (59)** *(Fav)* *(SGNorton)* 8-10 (5x) OPears (10) (a.p: 4th st: led 4f out: sn clr: unchal) | | —1 |
| 224² | Firefighter **(57)** *(RHollinshead)* 8-3 ‡#5JFordham (7) (lw: hld up: hdwy 3f out: rdn & no imp fnl 2f) | | 10.2 |
| | Galley Gossip **(62)** *(MrsJRRamsden)* 8-13 PBowe (8) (bit bkwd: s.i.s: hdwy 3f out: nvr nr to chal) | | ½.3 |
| 171 | Kick on Majestic (IRE) **(51)** *(NBycroft)* 8-2 JMarshall (9) (prom: 5th st: effrt 4f out: wknd over 1f out) | 7.4 |
| 218 | North Flyer **(48)** *(BAMcMahon)* 7-13 SSanders (4) (led over 4f: wknd 3f out) | 1½.5 |
| 104³ | Cold Shower (IRE) **(60)** *(JAGlover)* 8-11 CHawksley (5) (bhd: rdn along 4f out: nt rch ldrs) | 1½.6 |
| | Master Shikari **(54)** *(JEBanks)* 8-0 ‡#5JSwinnerton (3) (prom: 2nd st: wknd 3f out) | 6.7 |
| 223³ | Up the Punjab **(68)** *(SDow)* 9-5 MJermy (6) (lw: hmpd after 1f: 3rd st: rdn & wknd 3f out) | 5.8 |
| | Tronchetto (IRE) **(59)** *(SirMarkPrescott)* 8-10 EBentley (1) (lw: sn pushed along: 6th & btn st: t.o) | 5.9 |
| | Bartolomeo (USA) **(70)** *(MrsJRRamsden)* 9-7 JTate (2) (bkwd: a bhd: t.o fnl 3f) dist.10 |

**5/2** ERINY (USA), **7/2** Cold Shower (IRE), **8/1** Firefighter(op 5/1), **9/1** Up the Punjab(6/1—10/1), Tronchetto (IRE), **10/1** Bartolomeo (USA)(op 5/1), **12/1** Galley Gossip(op 8/1), **20/1** North Flyer(op 12/1), **25/1** Ors. CSF £19.90, CT £171.93. Tote £3.70: £1.10 £1.30 £4.60 (£10.40). Mr R. W. Cousins (BARNSLEY) bred by Arthur I. Appleton in USA. 10 Rn                                                                    2m 4.7 (16.2)

T/Plpt: £1,837.20 (1.15 Tckts).                                                                                           IM

## 2a—LEOPARDSTOWN  (L-H)
### Tuesday, March 17th [Good to soft]
Going Allowance: 0.20 sec per fur (G)

**282a**     CASTROL SYNTRON X E.B.F. STKS (Mdn 2-Y.O) IR£5520.00     **5f**

        SOBER LAD (IRE) *(JBerry)* 2–9–0 JCarroll ................................................ —**1**
        Galaxy Star (IRE) *(Ireland)* 2-9-0 WJO'Connor ..................................... nk.**2**
        Irish Wedding (IRE) *(Ireland)* 2-8-11 RHughes ................................... 4$^{1}/_{2}$.**3**
Tote £1.50: £1.20 £3.30 £2.80 (£22.20). Mr F.Viner (COCKERHAM) bred by John Kent in Ireland. 9 Rn
                                       62.9 sec (3.9)
                                   SF–42/41/20

## 22a—SAINT-CLOUD  (L-H)
### Tuesday, March 17th [Heavy]
Going Allowance: 0.60 sec per fur (Y)

**283a**     PRIX EXBURY (Gp 3)     £20640.00     **1$^{1}/_{4}$m**

        **Fortune's Wheel (IRE)** *(France)* 4-8-11 MBoutin ................................. —**1**
8a³ Michel Georges *(France)* 4-8-9 CLeScrill ..................................... $^{3}/_{4}$.**2**
        Glity (USA) *(France)* 4-9-4 ELegrix ................................................. 1$^{1}/_{2}$.**3**
Tote 2.50f: 1.40f 1.60f 3.00f (7.50f). Mr R.C.Strauss (R.Collet,FRANCE) bred by Kilfrush Stud Farm in Ireland. 14 Rn                                                                   2m 13.7 (9.7)
                                       SF–61/56/63

## MAISONS-LAFFITTE  (L-H)
### Thursday, March 19th [Soft]

**284a**     PRIX COR DE CHASSE (listed race)     £12384.00     **6f**

        **Rayon Bleu (FR)** *(France)* 5-9-4 MBoutin ...................................... —**1**
        Botanic (USA) *(France)* 3-8-7 TJarnet ............................................. hd.**2**
        MEDAILLE D'OR (bl) *(JWPayne)* 4-9-4 GGuignard ......................... 2$^{1}/_{2}$.**3**
        Ganges (USA) *(France)* 4-9-8 FHead ............................................. $^{1}/_{2}$.**4**
Tote 7.50f: 1.90f 2.20f 4.60f (25.00f). Ecurie A.B.U. (Alain Bates,FRANCE) bred by Wertheimer et Frere in France. 8 Rn                                                                   1m 12.4

## BEVERLEY  (R-H)
### Friday, March 27th [Good]
Going Allowance: 0.40 sec per fur (G)                          Wind: fresh half against

Stalls: high

**285**     WITHERNSEA H'CAP (0-80) £2880.50 (£798.00: £381.50)     **7f 100y**     2-30 (2-32)

        **Colossus (64)** *(CEBrittain)* 4-9-1 MRoberts (13) (lw: mde all: clr over 1f out: drvn out) ................................................................................. —**1**
        Laurel Queen (IRE) **(58)** *(JBerry)* 4-8-9 JCarroll (10) (bit bkwd: s.i.s: gd hdwy 2f out: n.m.r: styd on wl u.p ins fnl f) ....................................... 1$^{1}/_{2}$.**2**
269* Euroblake **(53)** (Fav) *(TDBarron)* 5-8-4 (5x) AlexGreaves (7) (hld up: smooth hdwy 2f out: effrt over 1f out: unable qckn) ................................ 1$^{1}/_{2}$.**3**
        Norfolkiev (FR) **(59)** *(MMoubarak)* 6-8-10 GBaxter (9) (trckd ldrs: effrt over 2f out: edgd rt & kpt on same pce) ..................................... 2$^{1}/_{2}$.**4**
208⁴ Hawaii Storm (FR) **(42)** *(MissAJWhitfield)* 4-7-7 NAdams (4) (a chsng ldrs: squeezed 1f out: one pce) ................................................. s.h.**5**
203³ Martini Executive **(72)** (bl) *(WJPearce)* 4-9-9 DNicholls (2) (lw: hld up & bhd: effrt 3f out: nvr rchd ldrs) ....................................... 1$^{1}/_{2}$.**6**
203⁵ Usa Dollar **(65)** (bl) *(BGubby)* 5-9-2 JQuinn (1) (hdwy over 2f out: nvr nr to chal) 1$^{1}/_{2}$.**7**
        Sleepline Fantasy **(67)** *(MRChannon)* 7-9-4 TQuinn (8) (trckd ldrs: effrt 2f out: btn whn n.m.r ins fnl f) .......................................... $^{1}/_{2}$.**8**

162⁴ Sir Arthur Hobbs *(57) (FHLee)* 5–8-8 RLappin (11) (bhd: styd on appr fnl f: n.d) hd.9
217 Jovial Kate (USA) *(47) (BEllison)* 5–7-12 NCarlisle (6) (chsd wnr tl wknd 2f out) 2.10
140 Corn Futures *(71) (JPLeigh)* 4–9-8 DMcKeown (5) (a in rr) .............................. 2.11
Duckington *(77) (MHEasterby)* 8–10-0 MBirch (12) (bit bkwd: rn wl 5f: eased
whn btn) ........................................ ³⁄₄.12
Pimsboy *(56)* (bl) *(PABlockley)* 5–8-7 GHind (3) (prom tl lost pl 2f out: sn bhd) 8.13
Arabian King *(74) (MBrittain)* 4–9-11 KDarley (14) (s.i.s: a bhd) ................... 3.14
LONG HANDICAP: Hawaii Storm (FR) 7-6.

**7/2** Euroblake, **9/2** Norfolkiev (FR), **6/1** Sleepline Fantasy, **13/2** Martini Executive, **7/1** COLOSSUS, **10/1** Usa Dollar, Duckington, Laurel Queen (IRE), **12/1** Sir Arthur Hobbs, Jovial Kate (USA), **14/1** Arabian King, **16/1** Hawaii Storm (FR), **25/1** Ors. CSF £79.80, CT £273.02. Tote £8.00: £2.40 £2.80 £2.00 (£33.40). Capt. M. Lemos (NEWMARKET) bred by Flinders Enterprises S A. 14 Rn
1m 36.1 (5.9)
SF—57/46/36/34/16/41

**286** SCARBOROUGH SPA (S) STKS (2-Y.O) £2284.80 (£632.80: £302.40)  **5f**  3-00 (3-09)

231² **Shadow Jury** (Fav) *(MrsGRReveley)* 8-11 KDarley (16) (lw: mde all: clr over 1f
out: easily) .......................................... —1
231 Costa Verde *(KWHogg)* 8-6 WRyan (14) (s.s: gd hdwy 2f out: r.o wl ins fnl f) ..... 2.2
Ruby Cooper *(JWharton)* 8-6 JWilliams (2) (neat: scope: sn outpcd: hdwy over
1f out: r.o nr fin) ...................................... 3¹⁄₂.3
237 The Wend *(DTThom)* 8-6 JQuinn (12) (w wnr tl wknd over 1f out) .................... 1.4
Yeveed (IRE) *(MHEasterby)* 8-6 MBirch (11) (neat: unf: chsd ldrs to ¹⁄₂-wy: grad
wknd) ................................................. hd.5
Laxey Flyer *(JBerry)* 8-6 JCarroll (15) (neat: bit bkwd: in tch to ¹⁄₂-wy) .......... s.h.6
Take Your Partner (IRE) *(MJohnston)* 8-6 DMcKeown (3) (neat: a chsng ldrs:
kpt on fnl 2f) ......................................... hd.7
Craigie Boy *(JPLeigh)* 8-11 DNicholls (7) (leggy: unf: sn bhd: stdy hdwy over 1f
out: r.o) ............................................... ³⁄₄.8
231³ Egg *(TDBarron)* 8-11 AlexGreaves (4) (sn outpcd) ..................................... 1¹⁄₂.9
Red Ronnie *(JBerry)* 8-6 GCarter (10) (lt-f: unf: chsd ldrs tl wknd ¹⁄₂-wy) ........ ³⁄₄.10
231⁵ Nellie's Gamble *(APStringer)* 8-6 JFortune (5) (sn bhd) ............................... 4.11
Hazy Dazy *(WGMTurner)* 8-1 ‡⁵TSprake (9) (neat: nvr nr ldrs) ....................... nk.12
Brave Bidder *(BGubby)* 8-6 RFox (6) (b.off hind: neat: unf: a outpcd) ............. 1.13
Get Daily Sport *(PAKelleway)* 8-6 PaulEddery (13) (small: neat: gd spd 3f:
wknd) .................................................. nk.14
Dardanelle *(TFairhurst)* 8-3 ‡³JFanning (1) (cmpt: unf: sn drvn along: lost tch
¹⁄₂-wy) ................................................. 15
Farabout *(JPLeigh)* 8-6 KFallon (8) (lt-f: unf: uns rdr gng to s: sn wl bhd) ........ 16

**Evens** SHADOW JURY(op 6/4), **4/1** Costa Verde, **10/1** Get Daily Sport, **12/1** Laxey Flyer(op 7/1), Egg(op 8/1), **14/1** Red Ronnie(op 8/1), Yeveed (IRE)(op 5/1), **16/1** Nellie's Gamble(op 10/1), **20/1** Take Your Partner (IRE), The Wend, Farabout, Hazy Dazy, Brave Bidder(op 10/1), **25/1** Ors. CSF £7.30, Tote £2.20: £1.30 £1.70 £10.20 (£4.00). Mr P. D. Savill (SALTBURN) bred by J. S. Bell. 16 Rn; Bt in 8,200 gns
67.2 sec (5.7)
SF—23/10/–/–/–/–

**287** HUTTON CRANSWICK AUCTION STKS (Mdn 2-Y.O) £2382.80 (£660.80: £316.40)
**5f**
3-30 (3-39)

**Calisar** *(WGMTurner)* 7-13 ‡⁵TSprake (10) (unf: chsd ldrs: styd on u.p to ld ins
fnl f) .................................................. —1
Stardust Express *(MJohnston)* 8-7 DMcKeown (3) (leggy: disp ld tl led ¹⁄₂-wy:
wknd ins fnl f) ......................................... 1¹⁄₂.2
Royal Folly (IRE) *(CWCElsey)* 7-13 JLowe (9) (scope: sn wl bhd: gd hdwy over
1f out: fin strly) ....................................... nk.3
Master Sinclair (IRE) *(RHollinshead)* 8-4 WCarson (4) (cmpt: scope: sn chsng
ldrs: rn green & drvn along: kpt on fnl 2f) ............ ³⁄₄.4
Colfax Starlight *(BSRothwell)* 7-13 RFox (13) (small: neat: sn wl bhd: stdy hdwy
2f out: r.o nr fin) ...................................... 7.5
Wrightmill (IRE) *(CTinkler)* 8-7 MBirch (12) (lt-f: neat: chsd ldrs tl wknd ¹⁄₂-wy) 1¹⁄₂.6
Be Polite (IRE) *(MBell)* 7-12 ‡⁷PTurner (2) (small: lt-f: rn green & sn outpcd) .... 2¹⁄₂.7
Common Gain (IRE) (Fav) *(JBerry)* 8-4 JCarroll (7) (cmpt: scope: disp ld to
¹⁄₂-wy: wknd over 1f out) ............................. 3¹⁄₂.8
Miramichi Bay *(MrsVAAconley)* 8-4 PBurke (11) (leggy: sn outpcd) ................. ¹⁄₂.9
Great Mashhor *(JSWainwright)* 8-5⁽¹⁾ WNewnes (8) (unf: uns rdr gng to s: dwlt:
a bhd) ................................................. 1.10
226 Cracker Jack *(TFairhurst)* 8-10 ‡³JFanning (5) (chsd ldrs tl lost pl ¹⁄₂-wy) ....... 11
Arkendale Diamond (USA) *(WJPearce)* 8-10 DNicholls (1) (leggy: scope: swvd
lft s: a bhd) .......................................... 12
Fortune Inn *(JSWainwright)* 7-13 LCharnock (6) (lt-f: unf: s.s: a t.o) ................ 13

**11/4** Common Gain (IRE), **3/1** Master Sinclair (IRE)(tchd 2/1), **6/1** Wrightmill (IRE)(op 7/2), **13/2** Be Polite (IRE), **9/1** Stardust Express, **10/1** Arkendale Diamond (USA)(op 5/1), Miramichi Bay, Royal Folly (IRE), **14/1** Great Mashhor, Cracker Jack, **16/1** CALISAR, **20/1** Colfax Starlight, **33/1** Fortune Inn. CSF £161.32, Tote £50.00: £6.20 £3.90 £4.30 (£531.70). Mr A. Poole (SHERBORNE) bred by W. M. Comerford. 13 Rn    68.5 sec (7)

**288**   BRIDLINGTON BAY STKS (Mdn) £2265.20 (£627.20: £299.60)    2m 35y    4-00 (4-05)

      **Peak District** *(KSBridgwater)* 6-9-0 ‡5ATucker (10) (a chsng ldrs: kpt on wl u.p fnl 2f to tl post) ...................................................... —1

*176*  Shooting Lodge (IRE) **(75)** (Fav) *(JRJenkins)* 4-9-0 WCarson (8) (lw: chsd ldrs: drvn along 5f out: slt ld ins fnl f: jst ct) ........................ s.h.2

      Pink Gin *(MissSEHall)* 5-9-5 MBirch (11) (lw: hld up: gd hdwy u.p & c wd ent st: slt ld over 1f out: hdd ins fnl f: no ex) ............................ 1.3

*243⁴*  Signor Sassie (USA) **(74)** *(NTinkler)* 4-9-0 KimTinkler (5) (hld up: hdwy 6f out: prom 2f out: one pce) ................................................ 2¹/₂.4

      See the Light (bl) *(MrsVAAconley)* 5-9-0 PBurke (1) (a chsng ldrs: kpt on one pce fnl 2f) ........................................................ 5.5

*205⁵*  Gipsy King *(PAKelleway)* 4-9-0 BRaymond (12) (b.off fore: chsd ldrs tl wknd over 2f out) ....................................................... 15.6

      Peatswood *(MRChannon)* 4-9-0 LornaVincent (3) (prom: led 6f out tl over 2f out: sn wknd) ....................................................... 10.7

      Arctic Oats *(WWHaigh)* 7-9-0 DMcKeown (9) (bhd & drvn along 6f out) ............ 4.8

      Bold Resolution (IRE) **(46)** *(CACyzer)* 4-9-0 GCarter (7) (jnd ldr 6f out: led over 2f out tl hdd & wknd qckly over 1f out) ........................... ³/₄.9

      Khojohn **(43)** *(RDEWoodhouse)* 4-8-7 ‡7GParkin (4) (prom tl drvn along & lost pl ¹/₂-wy) .......................................................... 8.10

      Cometti Star *(JWharton)* 8-9-5 JWilliams (6) (led & sn clr: wknd & hdd 6f out: sn bhd) ................................................................ 20.11

      Nishara *(NBycroft)* 4-8-9 SWebster (2) (wl bhd fr ¹/₂-wy) ...................... 25.12

        Stewards Enquiry: Tinkler suspended 5-8/4/92 (improper use of whip).

**Evens** Shooting Lodge (IRE), **4/1** Pink Gin, **6/1** Signor Sassie (USA)(op 4/1), Peatswood(op 4/1), **20/1** PEAK DISTRICT, Gipsy King, **25/1** Arctic Oats, **33/1** Ors. CSF £40.23, Tote £32.90: £7.00 £1.30 £1.60 (£33.50). Mr Bill Neale (LAPWORTH) bred by The Banstead Manor Stud. 12 Rn    3m 51.3 (20.6)

**289**   LECONFIELD STKS (Mdn 3-Y-O) £1932.00 (£532.00: £252.00)    7f 100y    4-30 (4-34)

      **Brightness** *(MMoubarak)* 8-9 TQuinn (6) (neat: scope: lw: mde all: clr over 1f out: r.o strly) ................................................... —1

      Pridian (IRE) (Fav) *(GWragg)* 9-0 WRSwinburn (1) (lw: a chsng wnr: effrt 2f out: sn rdn & no imp) ................................................ 3¹/₂.2

      Arctic Splendour (USA) *(PWChapple-Hyam)* 8-9 LDettori (2) (chsd ldrs: rdn & prom over 2f out: sn wknd) ...................................... 12.3

      Scottish Park **(71)** *(JPLeigh)* 8-9 KFallon (8) (bhd: sme hdwy 2f out: n.d) .......... 4.4

      Canaan Lane *(AHarrison)* 8-11 ‡3JFanning (7) (w'like: leggy: s.i.s: hdwy on outside ent st: rdn & lost pl 2f out) ................................... nk.5

      Sea Lord *(KWHogg)* 9-0 WRyan (5) (chsd ldrs tl lost pl appr st) ................... 8.6

*238*  Treasure Beach *(MBrittain)* 9-0 KDarley (3) (a in rr) ............................ 4.7

      Lord Lambson *(RMWhitaker)* 9-0 AGilhane (4) (w'like: abd fnl 3f) ................. 4.8

**8/11** Pridian (IRE), **3/1** BRIGHTNESS, **6/1** Arctic Splendour (USA), **14/1** Scottish Park, **16/1** Treasure Beach, **25/1** Canaan Lane, Lord Lambson, **50/1** Sea Lord. CSF £5.58, Tote £4.00: £1.30 £1.10 £1.40 (£2.40). Ecurie Fustok (NEWMARKET) bred by Lord Haddington. 8 Rn    1m 36.5 (6.3)
                                                     SF—45/39/–/–/–/–

**290**   HORNSEA MERE H'CAP (3-Y-O) (0-100) £3114.00 (£927.00: £441.00: £198.00)    1m 1f 207y    5-00 (5-03)

*216²*  **Grog (IRE) (67)** *(MRChannon)* 7-7⁽²⁾ ‡5BDoyle (5) (trckd ldr: led over 2f out: clr over 1f out: comf) ........................................ —1

      Holiday Island **(72)** *(CEBrittain)* 8-3 MRoberts (1) (bhd: effrt 4f out: sn drvn along: styd on same pce fnl 2f: no ch w wnr) ........................... 10.2

      Majal (IRE) **(90)** *(BHanbury)* 9-7 BRaymond (4) (led & sn clr: hdd over 2f out: wknd over 1f out) .................................................... ³/₄.3

*171⁴*  Ferdia (IRE) **(72)** *(RHollinshead)* 8-3 WCarson (3) (lw: hld up: effrt 4f out: n.d) .. 8.4

      Wild Fire **(84)** (Fav) *(GWragg)* 9-1 WRSwinburn (6) (chsd ldrs tl lost pl 4f out: sn wl bhd & eased) .................................................. 25.5

      Simply George **(77)** *(RBoss)* 8-8 LDettori (2) (chsd ldrs: drvn along 4f out: sn lost pl & wl bhd) ................................................... 12.6

**9/4** Wild Fire, **7/2** Majal (IRE), Simply George, **11/2** Holiday Island, **9/1** Ferdia (IRE), **10/1** GROG (IRE). CSF £53.38, Tote £9.70: £2.50 £2.00 (£13.20). Mrs D. Hanson (UPPER LAMBOURN) bred by Michael P. Keane in Ireland. 6 Rn    2m 10.9 (8.9)
                                                     SF—30/20/36/2/–/–

T/Plpt: £3,268.90 (0.6 Tckts); £1,767.00 to Beverley 28/3/92.
                                                       WG

## BEVERLEY (R-H)
**Saturday, March 28th [Good]**
Going Allowance: 0.40 sec per fur (G)　　　　　　　　Wind: slt half against

Stalls: high

**291**　　　STEVE MASSAM (S) STKS　£2500.40 (£694.40: £333.20)　**2m 35y**　2-30 (2-31)

**Dari Sound (IRE) (43)** *(JGFitzGerald)* 4-8-10 TLucas (17) (hld up: hmpd over
　　　　5f out: hdwy over 2f out: styd on to ld wl ins fnl f) ................ —1
　97　Hand Painted (57) **(Fav)** *(CRBeever)* 8-8-13 ‡⁷JWeaver (16) (b: hld up: smooth
　　　　hdwy appr st: led 2f out: hung rt: hdd & no ex nr fin) ......... ¾.2
　243　Fit for Life (IRE) (42) (bl) *(MrsNMacauley)* 4-8-10 BRaymond (15) (hld up:
　　　　hdwy appr st: hung bdly rt 2f out: styd on) ........................ 3.3
　138　Don't Cry (45) *(JDBethell)* 4-8-6(1) DHolland (12) (in tch: hdwy appr st: rdn 2f out:
　　　　hung rt ins fnl f: no imp) ............................... 4.4
　48　Polyplate (MJRyan) 4-8-6(1) RCochrane (5) (lw: a.p: led wl over 2f out: hdd 2f
　　　　out: grad wknd) .......................................... 2½.5
　　　Racing Raskal (30) *(Capt.JWilson)* 5-9-1 JFortune (8) (a.p: effrt appr st: one
　　　　pce) ........................................................ 1½.6
　125　Milly Black (IRE) (48) *(JLHarris)* 4-8-5 JQuinn (4) (hdwy 6f out: sn prom: one
　　　　pce fnl 2f) ................................................. nk.7
　　　One for the Chief *(RMWhitaker)* 4-8-10 ACulhane (10) (bhd & pushed along:
　　　　hdwy 6f out: no imp) ....................................... 2.8
　211　Saint Bene't (IRE) (55) *(PCHaslam)* 4-8-10 DMcKeown (1) (chsd ldrs: hrd drvn
　　　　7f out: wknd ent st) ....................................... 8.9
　　　My Turn Next (32) *(KWHogg)* 4-8-5 GCarter (9) (trckd ldrs gng wl tl rdn & wknd
　　　　over 2f out) ................................................ ½.10
　　　Spoof (44) *(MDHammond)* 5-8-10 KDarley (11) (cl up: led 5f out tl wl over 2f
　　　　out: sn btn) ............................................... hd.11
　　　Herberto (USA) *(NTinkler)* 5-9-1 KimTinkler (6) (wl bhd tl sme late hdwy) ..... 1½.12
　　　Kandiysha (IRE) *(JParkes)* 4-8-5 NCarlisle (2) (hld up & bhd: hdwy 6f out: wknd
　　　　3f out) .................................................... 12.13
　125　Spring Tern (USA) (56) (bl) *(RO'Leary)* 4-9-1 MBirch (7) (led: rdn 6f out: hdd 5f
　　　　out: wknd 3f out) .......................................... 14
　169　Elissa *(GPKelly)* 6-8-10 KFallon (14) (b.nr fore: chsd ldrs: pushed along after
　　　　5f: sn wknd) ............................................... 15
　　　No Credibility *(BRichmond)* 10-9-1 ‡⁵ATucker (3) (b: cl up to ½-way: sn bhd) ...... 16
　　　Mothers Day Magic *(JDooler)* 6-8-10 NConnorton (13) (wl bhd fnl 7f) ........... 17

11/2 Hand Painted, 6/1 Saint Bene't (IRE), 13/2 DARI SOUND (IRE), Milly Black (IRE), 7/1 Herberto (USA),
Spring Tern (USA), 9/1 Spoof, 10/1 Don't Cry, 16/1 One for the Chief, 20/1 Fit for Life (IRE), Racing Raskal,
Kandiysha (IRE), Polyplate, 33/1 My Turn Next, 50/1 Ors. CSF £42.45, Tote £11.20: £4.30 £1.90 £3.40
(£35.70). Mrs K. D. Leckenby (MALTON) bred by Ash Hill Stud in Ireland. 17 Rn; No bid　　3m 46.6 (15.9)

**292**　　　MARTIN PLENDERLEITH STKS (2-Y.O) £2635.50 (£728.00: £346.50)　**5f**　3-00 (3-02)

**Toocando (IRE)** *(CNAllen)* 7-13 ‡⁷GForster (5) (small: cmpt: hld up: smooth
　　　　hdwy to ld over 1f out: shkn up & r.o) .................... —1
　　　So so *(TDBarron)* 8-6 AlexGreaves (3) (leggy: unf: chsd ldrs: chal 2f out: kpt on
　　　　one pce fnl f) ............................................. 5.2
　237²　Totally Unique (USA) **(Fav)** *(MBell)* 8-11 MHills (1) (cl up: chal ½-wy: rdn & nt
　　　　qckn appr fnl f) ........................................... 1½.3
　　　Field of Vision (IRE) *(MJohnston)* 8-11 DMcKeown (4) (small: cmpt: bit bkwd:
　　　　s.i.s: sn disp ld: wknd over 1f out) ...................... 3.4
　　　Fanfan (IRE) *(MHEasterby)* 8-6 KDarley (2) (cmpt: bit bkwd: a chsng ldrs: no
　　　　imp fnl 2f) ................................................ ½.5
　　　Price Rumpus (IRE) *(JBerry)* 8-11 GCarter (6) (leggy: led tl hdd & wknd over 1f
　　　　out) ....................................................... 2½.6

4/5 Totally Unique (USA), 4/1 Field of Vision (IRE)(op 5/2), 9/2 Price Rumpus (IRE)(op 3/1), 10/1 TOOCANDO
(IRE)(op 20/1), 14/1 So so, 20/1 Fanfan (IRE)(op 10/1). CSF £97.69, Tote £13.60: £2.90 £3.70 (£75.10).
Shadowfax Racing (NEWMARKET) bred by Tim Corridan in Ireland. 6 Rn　　　　　65.9 sec (4.4)
　　　　　　　　　　　　　　　　　　　　　　　　　　　　SF—37/24/23/11/4/–

**293**　　　YORKSHIRE TELEVISION H'CAP (0-90) £3106.00 (£928.00: £444.00: £202.00)
　　　　　**1m 100y**　　　　　　　　　　　　　　　　　　　　　3-30 (3-33)

**Habeta (USA) (62)** *(JWWatts)* 6-8-2 GDuffield (4) (lw: in tch: effrt over 1f out:
　　　　r.o u.p to ld nr fin) ...................................... —1

Langtry Lady **(84)** *(MJRyan)* 6-9-10 RCochrane (11) (hld up: swtchd & effrt 2f
out: ev ch ins fnl f: r.o) ............................................................................ hd.2

50 Golden Chip (IRE) **(64)** *(APStringer)* 4-8-4 JFortune (1) (cl up: led 3f out &
qcknd clr: hrd rdn fnl f: nt qckn & hdd nr fin) ................................ s.h.3

Fox Chapel **(69)** *(JGFitzGerald)* 5-8-9 TLucas (5) (broke wl: stdd: effrt 2f out:
no imp) ............................................................................................................ 3.4

Surrey Dancer **(63)** *(BHanbury)* 4-8-0 ↑⁵BDoyle (8) (hld up & bhd: hdwy on ins
over 2f out: n.m.r & nvr able to chal) .................................................... 2.5

Elegant Touch **(77)** (Fav) *(MMoubarak)* 3-8-0⁽²⁾ GCarter (12) (hld up: effrt over
2f out: one pce) ........................................................................................ hd.6

Sally Fay (IRE) **(60)** *(TKersey)* 4-8-0 JQuinn (7) (chsd ldrs tl outpcd fnl 2f) ...... hd.7

Choral Sundown **(54)** *(BWMurray)* 6-7-5 ‡³JFanning (6) (b: bit bkwd: led 1f:
chsd ldrs tl wknd 2f out) ...................................................................... d.h.7

70 Brown Fairy (USA) **(68)** *(MrsNMacauley)* 4-8-8 NCarlisle (3) (swtg: trckd ldrs tl
wknd wl over 1f out) ................................................................................ 1.9

Matts Boy **(72)** *(MissSEHall)* 4-8-12 MBirch (10) (outpcd appr st: n.d) .......... 1.10

Cashtal Dazzler **(70)** *(NTinkler)* 5-8-10 KimTinkler (2) (bit bkwd: led after 1f to 3f
out: sn lost pl) .......................................................................................... 11

*Tusky (12/1) Withdrawn (reard & lame at s) : not under orders — Rule 4 applies*

**5/2** Elegant Touch, **6/1** Matts Boy, **7/1** Brown Fairy (USA), **8/1** HABETA (USA)(op 5/1), **9/1** Langtry Lady, **11/1**
Fox Chapel, **12/1** Choral Sundown, **14/1** Surrey Dancer, **16/1** Cashtal Dazzler, **20/1** Golden Chip (IRE), **50/1** Sally
Fay (IRE). CSF £63.42, CT £1,073.38. Tote £9.60: £2.40 £1.90 £4.30 (£19.10). Mr R. D. Bickenson
(RICHMOND) bred by Spendthrift Farm, Inc. in USA. 11 Rn                            1m 49.9 (7.2)
SF—31/52/31/27/15/9

---

**294**   BBC RADIO HUMBERSIDE H'CAP (0-90) £2782.50 (£770.00: £367.50)   **5f** 4-00 (4-02)

217 **Misdemeanours Girl (IRE) (58)** *(MRChannon)* 4-8-2 ‡⁵BDoyle (5) (a chsng
ldrs: styd on to ld wl ins fnl f) .......................................................... —1

265 Drum Sergeant **(53)** (v) *(JParkes)* 5-8-2 NCarlisle (3) (s.i.s: hdwy after 2f: led 1f
out: hdd & nt qckn wl ins fnl f) ............................................................ 1.2

217 Crail Harbour **(61)** *(PCHaslam)* 6-8-10 DMcKeown (7) (sn chsng ldrs: effrt 2f
out: kpt on u.p fnl f) ................................................................................ hd.3

Dokkha Oyston (IRE) **(79)** *(JBerry)* 4-9-7 ‡⁷SHaworth (1) (bit bkwd: in tch: hdwy
2f out: nvr able to chal) ...................................................................... 1½.4

219² Sully's Choice (USA) **(54)** (bl) *(DWChapman)* 11-8-3 SWood (9) (lw: led 4f:
grad wknd) ............................................................................................ 1.5

Fourwalk **(65)** *(MrsNMacauley)* 8-9-0 BRaymond (2) (lw: bhd: hdwy 2f out: no
imp) .................................................................................................... 2½.6

186 Everset (FR) **(73)** *(WJMusson)* 4-9-8 RCochrane (8) (lw: bhd: effrt & n.m.r 2f
out: no imp) ............................................................................................ hd.7

219⁵ Hinari Video **(52)** (Fav) *(MJohnston)* 7-8-1 RPElliott (4) (lw: racd wd: prom over
3f) ...................................................................................................... 3½.8

219 Barrys Gamble **(78)** (bl) *(TFairhurst)* 6-9-10 ‡³JFanning (6) (chsd ldrs over 3f) 3½.9

87 Bracken Bay **(45)** *(TKersey)* 5-7-8⁽¹⁾ JQuinn (10) (b: w ldr to ½-wy: sn wknd) 1½.10

LONG HANDICAP: Bracken Bay 6-7.

**9/2** Hinari Video, **5/1** Sully's Choice (USA), **11/2** Crail Harbour, **13/2** Barrys Gamble, MISDEMEANOURS GIRL
(IRE), **8/1** Drum Sergeant, Dokkha Oyston (IRE), Fourwalk, **12/1** Everset (FR), **100/1** Bracken Bay. CSF £52.75,
CT £278.19. Tote £8.60: £1.80 £2.40 £1.60 (£18.30). Mr M. G. Michaels (UPPER LAMBOURN) bred by A. F.
O'Callaghan in Ireland. 10 Rn                                                                   66.2 sec (4.7)
SF—34/30/37/42/20/21

---

**295**   PETER ADAMSON H'CAP (3-Y.O)(0-90) £2532.00 (£702.00: £336.00)
**7f 100y**                                                                4-30 (4-35)

**Doyce (63)** *(JEtherington)* 9-0 NConnorton (1) (bit bkwd: hld up: hdwy 3f out:
led over 1f out: hdwy & jst hld on) .................................................... —1

Nicely Thanks (USA) **(70)** *(TDBarron)* 9-7 AlexGreaves (12) (h.d.w: bit bkwd:
hld up & bhd: hdwy 2f out: r.o wl nr fin) ............................................ hd.2

216⁴ Malcesine (IRE) **(50)** *(CaptJWilson)* 8-1 JFortune (8) (lw: plld hrd: in tch: hdwy
& ev ch 1f out: kpt on) ............................................................................ 1.3

168⁴ Thursley **(58)** *(HJCollingridge)* 8-9 JQuinn (9) (trckd ldrs: disp ld 2f out tl over 1f
out: grad wknd) .................................................................................... 3½.4

218 Miss Kingfisher (USA) **(62)** *(SGNorton)* 8-6 ‡⁷OPears (3) (effrt & c wd st: styd on:
nt pce o) ................................................................................................ 2.5

218 Phil-Man **(55)** *(TFairhurst)* 8-3 ‡JFanning (6) (chsd ldrs: ev ch 2f out: wknd 1f
out) ...................................................................................................... nk.6

Daaris (USA) **(68)** *(DMorley)* 9-5 BRaymond (10) (nt grwn: cl up: disp ld 2f out tl
wknd over 1f out) ................................................................................ 2.7

224⁶ Comiskey Park (IRE) **(49)** *(DWChapman)* 8-0 SWood (2) (bhd tl sme late hdwy) 2½.8

224³ Mill Burn (52) (Fav) (ICampbell) 8-3 GDuffield (11) (lw: chsd ldrs: rdn appr st: sn wknd) .......................................................................................... hd.9
Broughton's Tango (IRE) (50) (WJMusson) 8-1 JHBrown (4) (b: bhd: sme hdwy 2f out: n.d) ............................................................................... ¾.10
Syke Lane (47) (RMWhitaker) 7-12 PBurke (5) (nt grwn: hld up: effrt over 2f out: n.d) ....................................................................................... 3½.11
182* Walkonthemoon (61) (v) (MMcCormack) 8-12 WNewnes (13) (led tl hdd wl over 1f out: sn wknd) ........................................................... 12
Parisienne King (USA) (60) (FHLee) 8-11 DMcKeown (7) (cl up tl wknd 2f out) ... 13

4/1 Mill Burn(op 6/1), 5/1 Daaris (USA), 11/2 Walkonthemoon, 13/2 Nicely Thanks (USA), 10/1 DOYCE, Thursley, 12/1 Phil-Man, Syke Lane, Broughton's Tango (IRE)(op 8/1), 14/1 Miss Kingfisher (USA), 20/1 Comiskey Park (IRE), Parisienne King (USA), 25/1 Malcesine (IRE). CSF £71.31, CT £1,462.72. Tote £11.10: £2.70 £2.50 £12.70 (£17.60). Lord Matthews (MALTON) bred by Lord Victor Matthews. 13 Rn  1m 37.3 (7.1)
SF—38/44/21/18/9/5

**296**    JUDI MURDEN STKS (Mdn 3-Y.O) £2284.80 (£632.80: £302.40)
           1m 1f 207y                                                      5-00 (5-04)

Daru (USA) (v) (JHMGosden) 9-0 GHind (4) (w'like: s.i.s: sn in tch: swvd lft over 1f out: r.o wl to ld wl ins fnl f) ............................................................ —1
West Stow (MRStoute) 9-0 RCochrane (10) (small: lengthy: in tch: effrt ent st: styd on to ld ins fnl f: sn hdd & no ex) ............................................ 1.2
Legendary (IRE) (PWChapple-Hyam) 9-0 DHolland (7) (chsd ldrs: pushed along appr st: led over 1f out: hdd & nt qckn ins fnl f) ...... 1½.3
Rock Hard (WJarvis) 9-0 MTebbutt (11) (trckd ldrs: stdy hdwy ent st: chal over 1f out: hrd rdn & nt qckn) ...................................................... hd.4
Chipper (RBoss) 9-0 DMcKeown (2) (outpcd & lost pl appr st: styd on wl fnl 2f) 2½.5
Glowing Devil (IDBarron) 9-0 AlexGreaves (3) (trckd ldrs: ehln up 2f out: one pce) .................................................................................. 4.6
Owner's Dream (USA) (88) (Jt-Fav) (BHanbury) 9-0 BRaymond (6) (led tl hdd over 1f out: eased whn btn) .............................................. 5.7
Amalfi (JPearce) 8-4 ‡5RPrice (1) (outpcd & bhd appr st: n.d after) ................. nk.8
235 Tahitian (66) (MrsJRRamsden) 9-0 TLucas (12) (prom tl lost pl appr st) ............ 5.9
Lady Reem (USA) (Jt-Fav) (MMoubarak) 8-9 GCarter (5) (leggy: lt-f: unf: w ldrs tl wknd over 2f out) ................................................................ hd.10
224 Escadaro (USA) (SGNorton) 8-7 ‡7OPears (9) (sn pushed along & a bhd) ......... 11
Nishiki (USA) (RMWhitaker) 8-9 ACulhane (8) (lt-f: unf: a bhd) ....................... 12

11/4 Owner's Dream (USA), Lady Reem (USA), 5/1 West Stow, Legendary (IRE), 10/1 Rock Hard(op 6/1), DARU (USA), 11/1 Chipper, 14/1 Tahitian, 25/1 Nishiki (USA), 33/1 Ors. CSF £61.07, Tote £9.60: £3.10 £1.90 £2.20 (£8.50). Sheikh Mohammed (NEWMARKET) bred by Albert G. Clay & Charlotte Clay Buxton in USA. 12 Rn
2m 11.9 (9.9)
SF—41/39/36/35/30/22

T/Plpt: £4,618.90 (1.15 Tckts).                                                          AA

# WARWICK (L-H)
## Saturday, March 28th [Soft, Heavy patches]
Going Allowance: 5f - 6f: 0.80 sec; Rest: 1.20 sec per fur (S)                   Wind: nil

Stalls: Races 1 & 4 low, rest flag start

**297**    OLD MILVERTON STKS (Mdn 2-Y.O) £1932.00 (£532.00: £252.00)    5f    2-15 (2-17)

Palacegate Episode (IRE) (JBerry) 8-9 JCarroll (5) (unf: led after 2f: sn clr: eased nr fin) ......................................................................... —1
Stormy Heights (JRJenkins) 8-9 SWhitworth (2) (lt-f: chsd ldrs: wnt 2nd 2f out: no imp) ..................................................................................... 7.2
Not so Generous (IRE) (WGMTurner) 8-4 ‡5TSprake (6) (leggy: lt-f: unf: chsd ldrs: rdn 2f out: no imp) ................................................... 8.3
237³ Greenwich Chalenge (Fav) (WCarter) 8-9 ‡5NGwilliams (4) (b.hind: bhd: rdn along ½-wy: styd on ins fnl f) ............................................... 2½.4
Duchess Dianne (IRE) (RJHolder) 8-9 JWilliams (7) (neat: bkwd: nvr nr ldrs) .. 1½.5
226 Gone Prospecting (USA) (RHannon) 8-9 ‡5RPerham (3) (lw: led 2f: rdn & wknd 2f out) ............................................................................... 4.6
Bella's Boy (BPalling) 8-7 ‡7StephenDavies (1) (w'like: lengthy: bit bkwd: s.s: a bhd) ............................................................................. 2½.7
Lochore (RIngram) 9-0 CDwyer (8) (small: unf: bkwd: s.s: a bhd: t.o) .............. 6.8
Gaynor Goodman (IRE) (JSMoore) 8-9 BRouse (9) (scope: bkwd: outpcd: bhd fr ½-wy: t.o) ................................................................ 15.9

**9/4** Greenwich Chalenge, **7/2** Gone Prospecting (USA), **4/1** PALACEGATE EPISODE (IRE)(op 5/2), **8/1** Lochore(tchd 33/1), Not so Generous (IRE)(op 4/1), **12/1** Stormy Heights, **25/1** Bella's Boy, **33/1** Ors. CSF £42.96, Tote £3.00: £1.90 £3.70 £2.10 (£12.60). Palacegate Corporation Ltd (COCKERHAM) bred by Brendan and Sheila Powell in Ireland. 9 Rn
65.1 sec (7.1)
SF—33/5/–/–/–/–/

## 298

WELLESBOURNE H'CAP (3-Y.O) (0-80) £3422.80 (£1023.40: £490.20: £223.60)
6f
2-45 (2-48)

242⁶ **Sovereign Rock (IRE) (69)** (Fav) (RHannon) 8-10 WCarson (2) (chsd ldr: 2nd st: hrd rdn to ld cl home) .................................................. —1
Sonderise (66) (NTinkler) 8-7 LDettori (5) (3rd st: led over 1f out: hrd rdn & ct cl home) .................................................................... hd.2
227³ Inherent Magic (IRE) (71) (MMcCormack) 8-12 JReid (10) (hdwy & 5th st: kpt on one pce u.p fnl f) .................................................. 5.3
Hawa Layaam (IRE) (74) (AAScott) 9-1 WRSwinburn (4) (a.p: 4th st: rdn over 1f out: one pce) ............................................................... hd.4
Stormswept (USA) (69) (PWChapple-Hyam) 8-3 ‡7BThomas (3) (bit bkwd: hld up: effrt 2f out: nrst fin) .................................................. 4.5
189⁴ Summer Express (70) (JLSpearing) 8-11 DNicholls (1) (led tl over 1f out: rdn & wknd fnl f) .......................................................... 1¹/₂.6
248★ Great Hall (57) (WGRWightman) 7-7⁽²⁾ ‡5FNorton (8) (b.hind: nvr nr to chal) ... 1¹/₂.7
Abigails Boy (HOL) (56) (DrJDScargill) 7-11 GBardwell (9) (bkwd: chsd ldrs: 6th st: sn wknd) ............................................................ 1¹/₂.8
Palacegate Gold (IRE) (66) (RJHodges) 8-2 ‡5TSprake (6) (bkwd: a bhd: t.o) .. 10.9
Mustahil (IRE) (77) (RJHodges) 9-4 TQuinn (11) (bkwd: a bhd: t.o) .................. 4.10
Sea Crusader (60) (MBlanshard) 8-1 CRutter (12) (bkwd: prom tl 7th & wkng st: t.o) ....................................................................................... 12.11
Elanmatina (IRE) (80) (CFWall) 9-7 NDay (7) (bkwd: a bhd: t.o) ...................... 4.12

**11/8** SOVEREIGN ROCK (IRE), **6/1** Hawa Layaam (IRE)(op 4/1), **7/1** Inherent Magic (IRE)(tchd 11/1), Sonderise, **10/1** Great Hall, Stormswept (USA), **12/1** Summer Express, **14/1** Elanmatina (IRE), **16/1** Mustahil (IRE), **33/1** Ors. CSF £12.48, CT £49.89. Tote £2.00: £1.10 £2.00 £2.50 (£5.40). Mr P. A. Howell (MARLBOROUGH) bred by K. Molloy in Ireland. 12 Rn
1m 19.1 (7.1)
SF—50/46/31/33/5/7

## 299

DUNSMORE H'CAP (0-80) £3478.70 (£1040.60: £498.80: £227.90)
1¹/₄m 169y
3-20 (3-21)

**Myfontaine (53)** (KTIvory) 5-8-4 GBardwell (5) (hld up: gd hdwy to ld 3f out: sn wl clr: unchal) ............................................................. —1
Eastern Magic (70) (JAkehurst) 4-9-1 ‡5RPerham (1) (hdwy ¹/₂-wy: 4th st: r.o one pce fnl 2f) .................................................................. 8.2
Famous Beauty (49) (RHollinshead) 5-7-7 ‡7AGarth (2) (bit bkwd: prom: 5th st: kpt on same pce fnl 2f) ................................................ hd.3
Muddy Lane (48) (BRMillman) 4-7-7⁽⁵⁾ ‡5FNorton (4) (bhd: hdwy 4f out: kpt on fnl f) ..................................................................................... 4.4
Lookingforarainbow (IRE) (56) (BobJones) 4-8-6 VSmith (19) (prom: 2nd st: rdn & wknd ins fnl f) ..................................................... ¹/₂.5
Latour (77) (CEBrittain) 4-9-13 MRoberts (15) (bit bkwd: chsd ldrs 6f: sn wknd) 8.6
Weekday Cross (IRE) (55) (JRJenkins) 4-9-8 GBaxter (17) (chsd ldrs: no hdwy fnl 2f) ..................................................................................... hd.7
Admiralty Way (63) (MO'Neill) 6-9-0 AMackay (7) (bhd: sme hdwy fnl 3f: nvr nrr) hd.8
214 Horizon (IRE) (72) (bl) (TThomsonJones) 4-9-5 ‡3DBiggs (10) (led to 3f out: 3rd st: sn wknd: t.o) .................................................. 12.9
213 Bolton Flyer (43) (OO'Neill) 6-7-8⁽¹⁾ NAdams (6) (t.o) ................................... 12.10
Hello My Darling (IRE) (73) (WRMuir) 4-9-9 SWhitworth (3) (bit bkwd: prom tl rdn & wknd 4f out: t.o) ........................................... 2¹/₂.11
Dosseri (54) (RJO'Sullivan) 4-8-4 WRyan (8) (bkwd: disp ld over 6f: 6th & wkng st: t.o) ............................................................................. 1¹/₂.12
Our Slimbridge (48) (CNWilliams) 4-7-12 JLowe (11) (a bhd: t.o) .................... 1¹/₂.13
225³ Tanoda (50) (Fav) (MBrittain) 6-8-1 WCarson (14) (s.i.s: sn rdn along: a bhd: t.o) ...................................................................................... 1.14
232 Glenscar (43) (JLSpearing) 6-7-8⁽¹⁾ RFox (9) (t.o) ...................................... 1¹/₂.15
111★ Premier Dance (46) (DHaydnJones) 5-7-11 DaleGibson (18) (t.o) ............... 3.16
Dyd (65) (FJordan) 4-9-1 JWilliams (12) (b: bhd fr ¹/₂-wy: t.o) ........................ 17
Ante Up (IRE) (73) (JAkehurst) 4-9-9 LDettori (16) (lw: s.v.s: ref to r after 1f) ...... 0
Devil's Soul (62) (RAkehurst) 4-8-12 AMunro (13) (s.v.s: wl bhd tl p.u over 1f out) ......................................................................................... 0

LONG HANDICAP: Bolton Flyer 7-5, Glenscar 6-13.

**4/1** Tanoda, **13/2** Hello My Darling (IRE), **9/1** Latour, **10/1** Premier Dance, Devil's Soul, Admiralty Way, **12/1** Dosseri, **14/1** Lookingforarainbow (IRE), Horizon (IRE), **16/1** Ante Up (IRE), **20/1** Famous Beauty, Eastern Magic, Weekday Cross (IRE), **25/1** Our Slimbridge, Muddy Lane, MYFONTAINE, Dyd, **33/1** Ors. CSF £418.44, CT £8,817.07. Tote £22.40: £3.90 £2.90 £8.90 £4.10 (£426.00). Mr K. T. Ivory (RADLETT) bred by Farmleigh Partners. 19 Rn
2m 31.9 (18.4)
SF—38/33/10/2/14/19

---

### 300
BINTON CLAIMING STKS   £2520.00 (£700.00: £336.00)   **5f**   3-50 (3-52)

245³ **Rushanes (51)** *(TCasey)* 5–8–11 ‡5FNorton (9) (chsd ldrs: shkn up over 1f out: led ins fnl f: sn clr) ...... —1

Hotfoot Hannah (IRE) *(PSFelgate)* 4–8–12 WRyan (4) (bit bkwd: b: s.s: hdwy fnl 2f: no ch w wnr) ...... 4.2

238 Fangio *(WGMTurner)* 3–7–13 ‡5TSprake (5) (b.off hind: w ldrs: led over 1f out tl ins fnl f) ...... 2.3

221 Regal Tiger *(MrsJCDawe)* 7–8–12 JWilliams (11) (sme hdwy fnl 2f: nvr nrr) ...... 4.4

Blazing Sensation *(DWPArbuthnot)* 4–8–8 SWhitworth (2) (bit bkwd: nvr nr to chal) ...... 1.5

Certain Lady (63) *(GBlum)* 3–7–3 ‡7CHawksley (8) (bkwd: nvr nrr) ...... 1.6

Johnston's Express (IRE) *(EJAlston)* 4–9–3 ‡7SKnott (12) (nvr gng pce of ldrs) ...... 5.7

236 Eager Deva (92) (Fav) *(RHollinshead)* 5–9–5 WCarson (6) (disp ld over 3f: wknd qckly) ...... 1½.8

Unveiled *(RJHodges)* 4–9–0 TQuinn (13) (chsd ldrs 3f) ...... 1½.9

Three Lucky (IRE) *(MDIUsher)* 4–9–5 CRutter (7) (swtg: bkwd: outpcd fr ½-wy) 1½.10

St Piran's Lass *(RJHolder)* 3–7–11 NAdams (3) (unf: outpcd) ...... hd.11

I Broke the Rules (IRE) (41) *(AJChamberlain)* 3–7–3(1) ‡7GMilligan (10) (outpcd) 2½.12

Super Rocky (80) *(JBerry)* 3–8–7 JCarroll (1) (led tl over 1f out: wkng whn stumbled & fell ins fnl f) ...... 0

**7/4** Eager Deva(Evens—15/8), **9/4** Super Rocky, **7/1** RUSHANES(tchd 16/1), **9/1** Fangio, **10/1** Unveiled, **15/2** Certain Lady, **33/1** St Piran's Lass, **50/1** Johnston's Express (IRE), Three Lucky (IRE), Blazing Sensation, Hotfoot Hannah (IRE), Regal Tiger, **66/1** I Broke the Rules (IRE). CSF £228.36, Tote £6.40: £1.40 £10.40 £1.80 (£104.10). Mr M. Mac Carthy (UPPER LAMBOURN) bred by M. MacCarthy. 13 Rn
65.5 sec (7.5)
SF—27/12/–/–/–/–

---

### 301
COVENTRY CUP (H'cap) (0-100) £3785.00 (£1130.00: £540.00: £245.00)   **1¾m 194y**   4-25 (4-26)

197³ **Army of Stars (81)** *(CEBrittain)* 7–9–1 MRoberts (7) (lw: led 6f: 2nd st: led 2f out: clr fnl f) ...... —1

228² Gulf Palace (USA) (90) *(RAkehurst)* 7–9–10 TQuinn (9) (lw: a.p: 3rd st: ev ch 2f out: one pce) ...... 7.2

229³ Saffaah (USA) (63) *(WRMuir)* 5–7–11 WCarson (4) (lw: plld hrd: led after 6f to 2f out: sn rdn & btn) ...... 2.3

Shoofe (USA) (79) *(DMorley)* 4–8–10 NDay (10) (hld up & bhd: hdwy 4f out: 5th st: nt rch ldrs) ...... 6.4

Jackson Flint (94) *(HThomsonJones)* 4–9–11 RHills (6) (bkwd: hld up: hdwy 6f out: 4th & rdn st: sn btn) ...... 10.5

Sir Crusty (60) *(OO'Neill)* 10–7–8(1) NAdams (11) (bkwd: wl bhd tl styd on fnl 2f) s.h.6

229⁴ Eire Leath-Sceal (65) *(MBrittain)* 5–7–13(1) AMunro (3) (lw: hdwy ½-wy: rdn 5f out: sn wknd: 6th st) ...... ½.7

Al Mutahm (USA) (80) (Fav) *(JABOld)* 4–8–11 LDettori (5) (lw: lost pl ½-wy: t.o: bridle broke) ...... 8.8

Ocean Lad (63) *(AJChamberlain)* 9–7–4(4) ‡7GMilligan (8) (b: bkwd: lost pl ½-wy: sn t.o) ...... 30.9

LONG HANDICAP: Sir Crusty 6-7, Ocean Lad 5-13.

**5/2** Al Mutahm (USA), **4/1** Saffaah (USA)(op 5/2), Gulf Palace (USA)(3/1—9/2), **5/1** Shoofe (USA)(tchd 8/1), **6/1** ARMY OF STARS, **7/1** Jackson Flint(tchd 14/1), **11/1** Eire Leath-Sceal, **250/1** Ors. CSF £29.48, CT £99.40. Tote £6.20: £2.10 £1.50 £1.80 (£13.40). The Army of Stars Partnership (NEWMARKET) bred by Stetchworth Park Stud Ltd. 9 Rn
3m 35.7 (26.7)
SF—14/16/–/–/–/–

---

### 302
KNOWLE STKS (Mdn 3-Y.O.F) £1932.00 (£532.00: £252.00)   **1m**   4-55 (4-56)

**Waterfowl Creek (IRE)** (Fav) *(GWragg)* 8–11 WRSwinburn (5) (lt-f: lw: hld up: 5th st: led 1f out: r.o wl) ...... —1

Juniper Berry (IRE) *(PWChapple-Hyam)* 8–11 LDettori (4) (a.p: 2nd st: led over 2f out to 1f out: unable qckn fnl f) ...... 3.2

Edge of Darkness *(JWHills)* 8–11 RHills (9) (leggy: lt-f: prom: 4th & rdn st: ev ch over 1f out: sn wknd) ...... 8.3

Humour (IRE) *(CFWall)* 8-11  NDay (2) (bit bkwd: hld up: 7th st: styd on u.p fnl:
nvr nrr) ........................................................................ 1¹/₂.4
Chatino *(CEBrittain)* 8-11  SCauthen (3) (still unf: bit bkwd: chsd ldr: 3rd st:
wknd wl over 1f out) ...................................................... 2¹/₂.2
Tajigrey *(BWLunness)* 8-11  JLowe (8) (bkwd: led tl hdd & wknd over 2f out: t.o) 15.6
Tiffany Gem (IRE) *(LordHuntingdon)* 8-11  DaleGibson (1) (unf: a in rr: t.o fnl 3f) 2.7
Fine as Fivepence **(41)** *(MrsAKnight)* 8-6 ‡⁵FNorton (4) (bit bkwd: a bhd: t.o) .... 4.8
Gallery Note (IRE) *(BWHills)* 8-4 ‡⁷SBusfield (7) (plld hrd: prom tl 6th & wkng st:
t.o) ............................................................................. ³/₄.9
Barjonal *(JJBridger)* 8-11  NAdams (6) (bkwd: a bhd: t.o) ................................. 15.10

**2/1** WATERFOWL CREEK (IRE), **11/4** Juniper Berry (IRE)(7/4—3/1), **100/30** Chatino, **5/1** Edge of Darkness(op
20/1), **10/1** Tiffany Gem (IRE)(op 5/1), **14/1** Humour (IRE), **25/1** Gallery Note (IRE), **33/1** Fine as Fivepence,
**50/1** Tajigrey, **100/1** Barjonal. CSF £8.31, Tote £3.40: £1.30 £1.50 £1.10 (£4.70). Sir Philip Oppenheimer
(NEWMARKET) bred by Hascombe and Valiant Studs in Ireland. 10 Rn                      1m 51.2 (14.2)
SF—28/19/–/–/–/

T/Plpt: £2,916.10 (0.65 Tckts); £1,379.28 to Newcastle 30/3/92.                                    IM

## 250—FOLKESTONE (R-H)  Monday, March 30th

303  **Abandoned**—Waterlogged

# NEWCASTLE (L-H)
## Monday, March 30th [Soft]
Going Allowance: 0.60 sec per fur (Y)                                      Wind: slt half bhd

Stalls: high

### 310
'MONKEY BUSINESS' STKS (Mdn 3-Y.O) £2072.00 (£572.00: £272.00)   **6f** 2-30 (2-31)

**Taufan Blu (IRE)** *(Fav)* *(MJohnston)* 8-9  DMcKeown (1) (w ldr: led 1f out: edgd
rt: r.o) ........................................................................ —1
Saddlehome (USA) **(83)** *(RMWhitaker)* 9-0  SCauthen (4) (led: edgd lft most of
wy: hdd 1f out: no ex) .................................................. 2¹/₂.2
Vive le Roi (IRE) *(MrsJRRamsden)* 9-0  TLucas (2) (lengthy: unf: trckd ldrs: effrt
3f out: sn rdn & btn) .................................................... 10.3
Sally Tadpole *(NTinkler)* 8-9  KimTinkler (3) (bit bkwd: prom tl outpcd over 2f
out) ........................................................................... 3.4

**4/5** TAUFAN BLU (IRE), **2/1** Saddlehome (USA), **6/1** Vive le Roi (IRE)(op 4/1), **14/1** Sally Tadpole(op 8/1). CSF
£2.69, Tote £1.70 (£1.20). Hambleton Lodge Equine Premix Ltd (MIDDLEHAM) bred by Mrs S. O'Riordan in
Ireland. 4 Rn                                                                     1m 18.21 (6.71)
SF—33/28/–/–

### 311
'GO WEST' SPRINT H'CAP (0-90) £2820.00 (£840.00: £400.00: £180.00)
**5f**                                                                   3-00 (3-01)

236* **Amron (77)** *(JBerry)* 5-9-1  NCarlisle (3) (a.p: hdwy to ld over 1f out: shkn up &
sn qcknd clr) ............................................................... —1
236³ Never so Sure **(79)** *(Fav)* *(MrsJRRamsden)* 4-8-10 ‡⁷JWeaver (6) (hld up: effrt
2f out: sn rdn & nt pce to chal) .................................... 6.2
Macrobian **(90)** *(MHEasterby)* 8-10-0  MBirch (2) (bit bkwd: a chsng ldrs: kpt
on one pce fnl 2f) ........................................................ nk.3
Sigama (USA) **(80)** *(FHLee)* 6-8-13 ‡⁵NKennedy (1) (bit bkwd: led tl hdd over 1f
out: no ex) .................................................................. 2.4
Real Stunner **(73)** *(MPNaughton)* 5-8-11  GHind (5) (chsd ldrs: kpt on one pce
fnl 2f) ....................................................................... ¹/₂.5

**6/4** Never so Sure, **13/8** AMRON, **6/1** Sigama (USA), **9/1** Real Stunner(op 5/1), **12/1** Macrobian. CSF £4.26,
Tote £2.10: £1.80 £1.10 (£1.80). Mr Roy Peebles (COCKERHAM) bred by Llety Stud. 5 Rn  62.87 sec (4.47)
SF—72/43/60/37/33

### 312
'AT THE CIRCUS' H'CAP (0-70) £2469.00 (£684.00: £327.00)   **2m 19y**  3-30 (3-32)

**Needwood Muppet (48)** *(BCMorgan)* 5-8-13  SCauthen (12) (lw: trckd ldrs
gng wl: led over 1f out: shkn up & sn clr) ....................... —1
267² Bollin Magdalene **(44)** (bl) *(MHEasterby)* 4-7-13 ‡⁵SMaloney (14) (a cl up: led
over 2f out tl over 1f out: kpt on one pce) ....................... 3¹/₂.2
Broctune Grey **(60)** *(MrsGRReveley)* 8-9-11  KDarley (1) (lw: hld up & bhd:
pushed along & hdwy 6f out: styd on: no imp) ................. 6.3
K-Brigade **(49)** *(CWCElsey)* 7-9-0  BRaymond (4) (lw: led 2f: led ¹/₂-wy tl hdd
over 2f out: sn btn) ...................................................... nk.4

Northants **(49)** (Fav) *(WStorey)* 6–9–0 SWebster (5) (b: sn pushed along: a in
tch: hdwy appr st: no imp) .................................................................. 15.5
Deb's Ball **(62)** *(DMoffatt)* 6–9–8 ‡⁵CHodgson (7) (hld up & bhd: effrt ½-wy: nvr
trbld ldrs) ........................................................................................ 20.6
Buckingham Band (USA) **(54)** *(FHLee)* 4–9–0 RLappin (6) (bit bkwd: prom tl
outpcd ½-wy: n.d after) .................................................................... 8.7
229 West With the Wind **(56)** *(GMMoore)* 5–9–7 KFallon (3) (chsd ldrs: drvn along
appr st: sn btn) ................................................................................ 1½.8
Cosmic Dancer **(49)** *(AHide)* 5–8–7 ‡⁷JWeaver (8) (hld up: effrt appr st: n.d) .... nk.9
Moment of Truth **(39)** *(PMonteith)* 8–8–1 ‡³JFanning (11) (sn cl up: rdn & wknd
appr st) .......................................................................................... 8.10
220² Suluk (USA) **(45)** *(RHollinshead)* 7–8–10 WRyan (2) (lw: led after 2f tl hdd ½-wy:
wknd appr st) .................................................................................. 11
Mystery Band (USA) **(41)** *(MrsSJSmith)* 6–8–6 NConnorton (13) (blind nr eye:
prom to ½-wy: sn wknd) .................................................................. 12
Brusque (USA) **(35)** *(DonEnricoIncisa)* 8–8–0 KimTinkler (9) (bit bkwd: a bhd:
virtually p.u ins fnl f) ...................................................................... 13

**7/2** Northants, **9/2** Bollin Magdalene, **5/1** NEEDWOOD MUPPET, **8/1** Deb's Ball, **10/1** K-Brigade, **12/1** Suluk
(USA), West With the Wind, **14/1** Broctune Grey, **16/1** Buckingham Band (USA), Cosmic Dancer, **20/1** Moment
of Truth, **25/1** Brusque (USA), **33/1** Mystery Band (USA). CSF £275.23, Tote £5.10: £2.20 £1.40 £10.40 £18.00
(£26.54). Mr D. G. Blagden (BURTON-ON-TRENT) bred by Needwood Stud. 13 Rn    3m 44.51 (19.01)
SF–3/–/5/–/–/–

---

**313**  'HORSE FEATHERS' CLAIMING STKS (3-Y.O) £2586.50 (£714.00: £339.50)
**1m 1f 9y**
4-00 (4-01)

Philgun **(52)** *(CWCElsey)* 7-7 ‡⁵SMaloney (3) (chsd ldrs: effrt ent st: led wl over
1f out: r.o) ...................................................................................... —1
223² Silver Samurai **(67)** (Jt-Fav) *(RHollinshead)* 8-6 WRyan (6) (lw: hld up: stdy
hdwy 3f out: effrt over 1f out: nt pce of wnr) .................................... 3.2
223⁶ Akura (IRE) **(54)** *(MJohnston)* 8-0 RPElliott (5) (led early: cl up: led over 2f out tl
wl over 1f out: one pce) .................................................................. 7.3
147² Sure to Win (IRE) **(65)** (bl) *(DMorris)* 8-3 ‡⁷StephenDavies (2) (hld up:
hdwy on bit ent st: swtchd & effrt 2f out: nt r.o) .............................. 5.4
177⁴ Feeling Foolish (IRE) **(62)** (bl) *(TFairhurst)* 8-2 ‡³JFanning (1) (sn bhd: hdd over
2f out: wknd qckly) ........................................................................ 2.5
Bantel Brigadier **(45)** *(RAllan)* 8-0 JLowe (4) (bkwd: wl bhd fnl 3f) .................... 20.6

**11/4** Silver Samurai, Sure to Win (IRE), **3/1** Feeling Foolish (IRE)(op 6/4), **5/1** PHILGUN, **11/2** Akura (IRE), **33/1**
Bantel Brigadier. CSF £17.99, Tote £5.20: £1.90 £1.20 (£5.30). Mr C. D. Barber-Lomax (MALTON) bred by Mrs
M. Morley. 6 Rn    2m 4.21 (11.91)

---

**314**  'ANIMAL CRACKERS' STKS (Mdn 3-Y.O) £2072.00 (£572.00: £272.00)
**1¼m 32y**
4-30 (4-32)

Viardot (IRE) (Fav) *(MRStoute)* 9-0 SCauthen (1) (lw: trckd ldrs: led over 2f out:
shkn up & qcknd: easily) ................................................................ —1
White Willow *(BHanbury)* 9-0 BRaymond (7) (w'like: bit bkwd: hld up & bhd:
hdwy 3f out: styd on: no ch w wnr) .................................................. 2.2
235 Linpac Express *(CWCElsey)* 9-0 KDarley (3) (cl up: led over 5f out tl over 2f out:
one pce) ........................................................................................ 1½.3
238³ Klingon (IRE) *(RHollinshead)* 9-0 MBirch (6) (a.p: effrt & ev ch over 2f out: one
pce) .............................................................................................. 1½.4
Massiba (IRE) *(BHanbury)* 8-9 WRyan (6) (lengthy: bit bkwd: hld up & bhd: stdy
hdwy 3f out: no ex appr fnl f) .......................................................... 1.5
Tidal River *(DenysSmith)* 8-2 ‡⁷CTeague (2) (bit bkwd: led tl hdd over 5f out:
wknd ent st) .................................................................................. 15.6

**1/3** VIARDOT (IRE), **6/1** Klingon (IRE), **9/1** Massiba (IRE)(op 5/1), **10/1** White Willow, **25/1** Linpac Express, **33/1**
Tidal River. CSF £4.75, Tote £1.30: £1.10 £2.60 (£2.90). Sheikh Mohammed (NEWMARKET) bred by
Barronstown Stud in Ireland. 6 Rn    2m 21.92 (15.22)
SF–8/4/1/–/–/–

---

**315**  'DUCK SOUP' H'CAP (0-70) £2784.00 (£774.00: £372.00)  **1¼m 32y**
5-00 (5-03)

El Nido **(50)** *(MJCamacho)* 4-8-7 NConnorton (5) (hld up: effrt 2f out: r.o wl to
ld cl home) .................................................................................... —1
131⁶ Sharp Top **(41)** *(MJRyan)* 4-7-12 GBardwell (4) (lw: trckd ldrs: led over 3f out:
qcknd clr: no ex nr fin) .................................................................. ½.2
Miss Hyde (USA) **(62)** *(JAGlover)* 3-8-0 DHolland (2) (a.p: effrt over 2f out: kpt
on one pce) .................................................................................. 8.3

249 Luks Akura **(44)** (bl) *(MJohnston)* 4–8-1 RPElliott (10) (led 6f out tl over 3f out: one pce) ......... 4.4

225 Colonel Fairfax **(41)** *(JWWatts)* 4–7-12 JLowe (8) (hld up: effrt appr st: rdn & no imp) ......... 8.5

Puffy **(52)** *(GMMoore)* 5–8-10 KFallon (14) (bkwd: effrt ent st: kpt on: n.d) ...... 1¹/₂.6

Be the Best **(54)** *(MPNaughton)* 4–8-11 LCharnock (9) (bhd: sme hdwy over 2f out: nvr nr to chal) ......... 8.7

Errema **(47)** *(CTinkler)* 7–8-5 MBirch (6) (bit bkwd: led 4f: cl up tl grad wknd fnl 3f) ......... 1¹/₂.8

Rawaan (FR) **(39)** *(NTinkler)* 5–7-11 KimTinkler (7) (s.i.s: n.d) ......... 1¹/₂.9

Barney O'Neill **(61)** *(JJO'Neill)* 6–9-5 BRaymond (1) (bkwd: in tch to st) ......... 5.10

232* I Perceive **(64)** *(Fav)* *(FHLee)* 5–9-8 RLappin (13) (lw: hld up & bhd: c wd & effrt st: rdn & n.d) ......... s.h.11

Aussie Aisle (IRE) **(53)** *(DMoffatt)* 4–8-5 ‡⁵CHodgson (12) (prom to st) ......... 2.12

161 Count Barachois (USA) **(69)** *(DMorris)* 4–9-12 MTebbutt (11) (chsd ldrs to st: sn wknd & eased) ......... 5.13

Kind Style (IRE) **(42)** *(RHollinshead)* 4–7-6 ‡⁷AGarth (3) (bit bkwd: chsd ldrs to st) ......... 4.14

**6/4** I Perceive, **6/1** Colonel Fairfax, **7/1** Miss Hyde (USA), **10/1** EL NIDO, Puffy, **12/1** Sharp Top, **14/1** Be the Best, **16/1** Rawaan (FR), **20/1** Luks Akura, Aussie Aisle (IRE), Count Barachois (USA), Barney O'Neill, **25/1** Kind Style (IRE), **33/1** Errema. CSF £119.93, CT £831.53. Tote £9.80: £2.50 £3.20 £2.30 (£42.60). Mr H. Roberts (MALTON) bred by M. J. Camacho. 14 Rn ........ 2m 18.56 (11.86)

SF—34/24/10/3/–/–

T/Plpt: £165.50 (35.45 Tckts).

AA

257—**LEICESTER (R-H) Tuesday, March 31st**

316 **Abandoned**—Waterlogged

## HAMILTON (R-H)
### Wednesday, April 1st [Heavy]

Going Allowance: 0.85 sec per fur (S)          Wind: mod half against     *Flag start: All races*

**323**          E.B.F. CAMPSIE STKS (Mdn 2-Y.O) £2477.80 (£685.80: £327.40)       **5f 4y**   2-15 (2-18)

**Key to My Heart (IRE)** *(DMoffatt)* 9-0 JFortune (8) (leggy: trckd ldrs: effrt 2f out: styd on wl to ld cl home) ......... —1

226³ Sabre Rattler **(Fav)** *(JBerry)* 9-0 TQuinn (6) (lw: s.i.s: hdwy ¹/₂-wy: led over 1f out: no ex nr fin) ......... ¹/₂.2

Boldville Bash (IRE) *(TDBarron)* 9-0 KDarley (3) (w'like: leggy: bit bkwd: a chsng ldrs: rdn 2f out: kpt on fnl f) ......... 3.3

266³ Principal Player (USA) *(WBentley)* 9-0 JLowe (4) (chsd ldrs: outpcd 2f out: no imp after) ......... 3¹/₂.4

286² Costa Verde *(KWHogg)* 8-9 LCharnock (5) (bale: wandered u.p 2f out: hdd & wknd appr fnl f) ......... 1¹/₂.5

226 Plum First *(NBycroft)* 9-0 SWebster (2) (s.s: nt rcvr) ......... nk.6

231 Spotland Lass *(WGMTurner)* 8-4 ‡⁵TSprake (9) (lw: spd 3f) ......... 8.7

Sensabo *(MissLAPerratt)* 8-6 ‡³JFanning (7) (cmpt: bkwd: sn outpcd & wl bhd) ......... 25.8

**Evens** Sabre Rattler(1/2—5/4), **5/1** Costa Verde, Boldville Bash (IRE), **10/1** Principal Player (USA)(op 6/1), **12/1** KEY TO MY HEART (IRE)(op 9/2), **16/1** Sensabo, **25/1** Plum First, **33/1** Spotland Lass. CSF £23.18, Tote £9.10: £1.40 £1.10 £3.30 (£11.80). Mrs Maureen Pickering (CARTMEL) bred by Miss Fiona Meehan in Ireland. 8 Rn ........ 66.1 sec (7.8)

SF—29/27/15/1/–/–

**324**          HAMILTON ENTERPRISE DEVELOPMENT CO. MEDIAN AUCTION STKS (Mdn 3-Y.O) £1932.00 (£532.00: £252.00)       **5f 4y**       2-45 (2-46)

**Double Blue** *(MJohnston)* 8-10 DMcKeown (3) (unf: hdwy ¹/₂-wy: led ins fnl f: styd on wl) ......... —1

Music Dancer *(JBerry)* 9-0 TQuinn (5) (a.p: rdn ¹/₂-wy: hdwy appr fnl f: nt qckn nr fin) ......... 1¹/₂.2

264 Optical (IRE) *(MPNaughton)* 9-0 LCharnock (6) (a chsng ldrs: rdn ¹/₂-wy: ev ch 1f out: no ex) ......... nk.3

Cocos Island (USA) **(Fav)** *(PWChapple-Hyam)* 9-0 KFallon (1) (chsd ldrs: outpcd ¹/₂-wy: no imp after) ......... 5.4

Don't Run Me Over **(46)** *(BCMorgan)* 9-0 KDarley (7) (led & sn clr: wknd & hdd ins fnl f) ......... 1¹/₂.5

Crimson Consort (IRE) **(40)** *(DonEnricoIncisa)* 9-0 KimTinkler (2) (outpcd & bhd after 2f) ................ 12.6
Ebony Isle *(PMonteith)* 8-2 ‡³JFanning (4) (neat: bit bkwd: dwlt: a wl bhd) ........ 4.7

**6/4** Cocos Island (USA)(op Evens), **2/1** Music Dancer(op Evens), **3/1** DOUBLE BLUE(op 8/1), **8/1** Optical (IRE), **20/1** Don't Run Me Over, **33/1** Ebony Isle, **50/1** Crimson Consort (IRE). CSF £9.54, Tote £4.00: £2.00 £1.90 (£7.10). Mr R. W. Huggins (MIDDLEHAM) bred by The Queen. 7 Rn
65.5 sec (7.2)
SF—37/35/34/14/8/–/

**325**    'HOME IN ON HAMILTON' H'CAP (0-80) £3019.20 (£836.20: £399.60)
          **6f 5y**                                                    3-15 (3-16)

265² **Cronk's Courage (62)** (v) *(EJAlston)* 6–8-13 KFallon (4) (lw: mde all: rdn 2f out: styd on wl) ............................ —1
265⁶ Toshiba Comet **(77)** (bl) *(WJPearce)* 5–10-0 DNicholls (6) (sn pushed along: hdwy 2f out: swtchd over 1f out: nrst fin) ............... 4.2
221⁴ Wellsy Lad (USA) **(54)** *(DWChapman)* 5–8-5 TQuinn (2) (a.p: effrt ½-wy: no ch whn bmpd ins fnl f) ............ 2¹/2.3
Sea Devil **(76)** (Fav) *(MJCamacho)* 6–9-13 NConnorton (11) (a chsng ldrs: hdwy u.p 2f out: sn btn) ............ ¹/2.4
279⁴ Minizen Music (IRE) **(43)** *(MBrittain)* 4–7-8 JLowe (5) (b. off fore: a chsng ldrs: rdn ½-wy: no hdwy) ............ 2¹/2.5
Pretonic **(67)** *(MJohnston)* 4–9-4 DMcKeown (9) (outpcd: styd on fnl 2f: n.d) .. nk.6
172 Chaplins Club (USA) **(48)** (bl) *(DWChapman)* 12–7-13 SWood (7) (s.i.s: n.d) . 2¹/2.7
She's Special **(79)** (v) *(MissLAPerratt)* 3–9-0 ‡³JFanning (8) (chsd ldrs 4f) ........ hd.8
Castle Cary **(42)** *(TCraig)* 6–7-7 AMackay (1) (bit bkwd: chsd wnr over 3f) ...... 1¹/2.9
294³ Crail Harbour **(61)** *(PCHaslam)* 6–8-12 KDarley (10) (dwlt: a bhd) ............ 3¹/2.10
265 Spanish Realm **(49)** *(MBrittain)* 5-7-7 ‡7DWright (3) (s.s: a wl bhd) ................ 8.11
LONG HANDICAP: Castle Cary 7-5

**9/4** Sea Devil(3/1—2/1), **9/2** CRONK'S COURAGE(op 3/1), Crail Harbour, **8/1** Minizen Music (IRE), **10/1** Wellsy Lad (USA), **11/2** Chaplins Club (USA), Pretonic, Toshiba Comet, **20/1** She's Special, **33/1** Ors. CSF £52.43, CT £466.69. Tote £9.50: £2.10 £4.30 £3.00 (£37.60). Mr M. P. Russell (PRESTON) bred by M. Andree. 11 Rn
1m 18.4 (8.4)
SF—33/32/–/19/–/–/

**326**    BOTHWELL ROAD (S) H'CAP (0-60) £2500.40 (£694.40: £333.20)
          **1m 65y**                                                  3-45 (3-47)
          (Weights raised 1 lb)

**Tynron Doon (58)** *(JBerry)* 3–8-11 LCharnock (8) (disp ld tl led 4f out: styd on wl u.p) ............................ —1
253 Dawn's Delight **(47)** *(KTIvory)* 14–9-2 MWigham (17) (b.hind: a chsng ldrs: kpt on fnl f) ............ 1¹/2.2
199⁶ Miss Knight **(47)** *(RBastiman)* 5–9-2 NConnorton (3) (in tch: hdwy over 2f out: ev ch 1f out: nt qckn) ............ nk.3
250 Stormy Praise (USA) **(44)** (bl) *(WGMTurner)* 8–8-8 ‡5TSprake (16) (lw: a chsng ldrs: effrt over 3f out: one pce appr fnl f) ........ 2.4
267 Diving (USA) **(48)** *(MrsVAAconley)* 4–9-3 PBurke (9) (disp ld tl hdd 4f out: ev ch tl wknd 1f out) ............ 1¹/2.5
277 Golden Ancona **(52)** *(MBrittain)* 9–9-7 KDarley (6) (a.p: one pce fnl 3f) ........ 1¹/2.6
Great Service **(48)** *(GMMoore)* 5–9-3 KFallon (18) (lw: pushed along & bhd: sme hdwy 3f out) ............ 3¹/2.7
291 My Turn Next **(32)** *(KWHogg)* 4–7-8 ‡7DarrenMoffatt (10) (outpcd & bhd tl styd on fnl 2f) ............ d.h.7
Valley of Time (FR) **(39)** *(PMonteith)* 4–8-5 ‡³JFanning (2) (in tch tl wknd over 2f out) ............ 6.9
Master Plan (FR) **(33)** *(MissLAPerratt)* 6–8-2 SWood (7) (chsd ldrs 6f) .......... 2¹/2.10
Brown as a Berry (IRE) **(40)** *(WStorey)* 4–8-9 SWebster (11) (bhd most of wy) .... 11
Lucky Barnes **(52)** (bl) *(PABlockley)* 5–9-7 DNicholls (1) (chsd ldrs tl wknd 3f out) ............ 12
Lazy Rhythm (USA) **(42)** (Fav) *(RAkehurst)* 6–8-11 TQuinn (14) (bdly hmpd appr st: nt rcvr) ............ 13
264 Scu's Lady (IRE) **(29)** *(ASmith)* 4–7-12 JLowe (13) (bhd most of wy) ................ 14
Fen Princess (IRE) **(55)** *(PCHaslam)* 4–9-10 DMcKeown (12) (bit bkwd: mid div whn hmpd & fell over 6f out) ............ 0
Go Tally-Ho **(48)** (v) *(JJO'Neill)* 4–9-3 JFortune (15) (b: rr div whn hmpd & uns rdr over 6f out) ............ 0

**2/1** Lazy Rhythm (USA), **6/1** Great Service(op 4/1), **8/1** Valley of Time (FR)(5/1—9/1), **9/1** Stormy Praise (USA), **10/1** Dawn's Delight, **14/1** Miss Knight, **16/1** TYNRON DOON, Master Plan (FR), Go Tally-Ho, Golden Ancona, Fen Princess (IRE), **25/1** My Turn Next, **33/1** Lucky Barnes, Diving (USA), **50/1** Ors. CSF £156.69, CT £2,093.75. Tote £15.50: £3.00 £1.30 £1.70 £2.20 (£121.90). Mr D. G. Rogers (COCKERHAM) bred by Mrs C. A. Dickson. 16 Rn; No bid
2m 0.6 (17.3)

**327**     CHATELHERAULT CLAIMING STKS (Mdn) £1932.00 (£532.00: £252.00)
1m 1f 36y                                   4-15 (4-18)

291   **Saint Bene't (IRE) (55)** (PCHaslam) 4-9-2 KDarley (15) (pushed along appr st: hdwy 4f out: led 2f out: sn rdn clr) ............................. —1

Grey Record **(51)** (MrsGRReveley) 4-9-0 ‡⁷DarrenMoffatt (9) (chsd ldrs: nt clr run 3f out: swtchd lft: styd on: no ch w wnr) ............... 8.2

Acquisition (SGPayne) 5-9-4 SWebster (5) (in tch: hdwy on outside 2f out: styd on) ................................................................. 3.3

144   Simply Candy (IRE) (v) **(Fav)** (APStringer) 4-9-0 PBurke (10) (a.p: effrt 3f out: r.o one pce) ....................................................... 1¹/₂.4

264   Chiparopai (IRE) (WStorey) 4-8-5 ‡⁷MichaelDenaro (1) (b: bhd tl styd on wl fnl 3f: nrst fin) ......................................................... 3¹/₂.5

264   Yours Or Mine (IRE) (DWChapman) 4-9-0 SWood (11) (chsd ldrs: led 3f out to 2f out: sn btn) ...................................................... 2¹/₂.6

267   Shining Wood **(46)** (JSWainwright) 4-8-9 ‡⁵SMaloney (8) (led tl hdd 3f out: sn btn) ................................................................ 1¹/₂.7

300   Johnston's Express (IRE) (EJAlston) 4-9-11 KFallon (4) (w ldrs tl wknd over 2f out) .................................................................... 5.8

Sparkling Vision (MrsGRReveley) 3-7-10 JLowe (6) (bit bkwd: in tch & rdn appr st: n.d after) ...................................................... ¹/₂.9

177⁶   Sunrays (IRE) **(49)** (CWCElsey) 3-7-4 ‡³JFanning (12) (prom tl wknd 3f out) 1¹/₂.10

Misty Night **(25)** (PMonteith) 4-8-6 ‡⁷SWilliams (7) (a bhd) ...................... 1¹/₂.11

289⁶   Sea Lord (KWHogg) 3-8-3 AMackay (2) (a bhd) .................................... 3¹/₂.12

222   Statia (IRE) **(50)** (DonEnricoIncisa) 4-9-1 KimTinkler (13) (a bhd) ............. hd.13

Remember the Alamo (JJO'Neill) 6-9-2 ‡⁷MHunt (14) (a bhd) .............. 5.14

242   Spot the Earlybird (USA) **(58)** (bl) (NTinkler) 3-7-12 LCharnock (3) (chsd ldrs tl rdn & wknd over 3f out) ...................................... 3.15

**7/2** Simply Candy (IRE), **5/1** Sparkling Vision, **8/1** SAINT BENE'T (IRE), **9/1** Grey Record(7/1—12/1), **10/1** Statia (IRE), Shining Wood, Sunrays (IRE), **12/1** Remember the Alamo, **14/1** Johnston's Express (IRE), **16/1** Spot the Earlybird (USA), **25/1** Ors. CSF £70.81, Tote £11.20: £3.90 £2.50 £5.20 (£8.90). Hambleton Thoroughbreds Plc (MIDDLEHAM) bred by Kilfrush Stud Ltd in Ireland. 15 Rn       2m 12.1 (17.8)

**328**     STRATHCLYDE PARK APP'CE H'CAP (0-70) £2382.80 (£660.80: £316.40)
1m 3f 16y                                   4-45 (4-47)

**Sillars Stalker (IRE) (35)** (Fav) (MrsJRRamsden) 4-7-13 RHavlin (3) (in tch: effrt over 2f out: led ins fnl f: r.o) ............................. —1

Santaray **(51)** (JMackie) 6-9-2 SWilliams (10) (lw: hld up: smooth hdwy to ld over 3f out: sn clr: hdd & no ex ins fnl f) ........................ 2.2

Needwood Poppy **(29)** (BCMorgan) 4-7-7 DarrenMoffatt (7) (bhd: hdwy 5f out: styd on u.p: nrst fin) .......................................... 1¹/₂.3

138   Grey Commander **(42)** (MBrittain) 4-8-6 DWright (5) (led early: cl up: led 5f out tl over 3f out: one pce) .......................................... 2¹/₂.4

Long Furlong **(60)** (RAkehurst) 4-9-10 OPears (11) (chsd ldrs tl wknd over 3f out) .............................................................. 25.5

60   Obeliski **(53)** (PCHaslam) 6-9-4 MichaelDenaro (2) (nvr nr ldrs) ............... ¹/₂.6

Arrow Dancer **(45)** (JJO'Neill) 6-8-7 ‡³JFordham (9) (lw: cl up tl rdn & wknd 4f out) ....................................................................... hd.7

Bobby on the Bank **(28)** (SGPayne) 6-7-4 ‡³PRoberts (1) (chsd ldrs tl wknd 4f out) .............................................................. 12.8

269   Tequila Gold **(38)** (JJO'Neill) 4-8-2 MHunt (8) (n.d) .............................. 15.9

222   Oka Flow **(40)** (bl) (PABlockley) 4-8-1 ‡³JDennis (4) (sn led: hdd 5f out: sn lost pl: wl t.o) ......................................................... 10

LONG HANDICAP: Bobby on the Bank 7-6.

**9/4** SILLARS STALKER (IRE)(op 5/4), **3/1** Long Furlong(op 5/1), **4/1** Santaray(3/1—9/2), **13/2** Obeliski, **14/1** Grey Commander, Tequila Gold, **16/1** Bobby on the Bank, **33/1** Ors. CSF £11.16, CT £197.04. Tote £2.90: £1.10 £1.80 £4.00 (£6.70). Sillars Civil Engineering (THIRSK) bred by Martyn J. McEnery in Ireland. 10 Rn     2m 39.5 (20.5)

T/Plpt: £87.90 (38.3 Tckts).                                              AA

## 270— BRIGHTON (L-H)

### Thursday, April 2nd [Good to soft]

Going Allowance: 0.20 sec per fur (G)                          Wind: almost nil

Stalls: low

**329**     SEVEN DIALS STKS (2-Y.O) £2385.00 (£660.00: £315.00)    **5f 59y**    2-15 (2-16)

**Moodiesburn (IRE)** (Fav) (ABailey) 8-6 AMackay (8) (unf: 4th st: led 2f out: rdn out) ................................................................. —1

255* George Roper *(MRChannon)* 9-4 BRouse (5) (led over 3f: unable qckn) ......... 2½.2
　　Awesome Risk *(GLewis)* 8-6 PaulEddery (2) (unf: 3rd st: rdn over 2f out: one
　　　　pce) ............................................................................................................... 3½.3
　　Christian Spirit *(RHannon)* 8-6 ‡⁵RPerham (7) (leggy: bit bkwd: 6th st: one pce
　　　　fnl 2f) ........................................................................................................... 3.4
255³ Petite Lass *(WCarter)* 8-1 ‡⁵NGwilliams (9) (2nd st: wknd over 2f out) ............... 3½.5
255 Huesca *(JRJenkins)* 8-1 ‡⁵RPrice (6) (bhd fnl 3f) ........................................... hd.6
　　Selectable *(MDIUsher)* 8-6 CRutter (4) (neat: 5th st: wknd 3f out) ................... 2½.7
　　Bird Hunter *(NACallaghan)* 8-11 PatEddery (10) (leggy: bit bkwd: s.s: a bhd) .. hd.8
　　Arogant Fool *(DAWilson)* 8-11 GCarter (4) (cmpt: dwlt: a bhd) ......................... 6.9

**5/4** MOODIESBURN (IRE)(op 2/1), **9/4** George Roper(2/1—9/2), **6/1** Christian Spirit(4/1—13/2), **8/1** Bird
Hunter(op 3/1), **14/1** Awesome Risk(op 5/1), **16/1** Petite Lass, **33/1** Ors. CSF £4.68, Tote £2.30: £1.10 £1.30
£4.40 (£4.00). Mr D. W. Rolt (TARPORLEY) bred by Lodge Park Stud in Ireland. 9 Rn　　64.1 sec (3.8)
　　　　　　　　　　　　　　　　　　　　　　　　　　　　　　　　　　　　　　　SF—36/38/12/–/–/–

**330**　　LEVY BOARD STKS (Mdn 3-Y.O) £2363.20 (£655.20: £313.60)
　　　　　1m 1f 209y　　　　　　　　　　　　　　　　　　　　2-50 (2-52)

　　**Desert Zone (USA)** *(PFICole)* 9-0 AMunro (4) (w'like: scope: lw: 6th st: rdn
　　　　over 2f out: led over 1f out: comf) ................................................................. —1
　　Boloardo *(CEBrittain)* 9-0 MRoberts (7) (unf: scope: 5th st: ev ch over 1f out:
　　　　unable qckn) ............................................................................................... 8.2
　　Esbooain (FR) *(LMCumani)* 9-0 SCauthen (10) (bit bkwd: 3rd st: led 3f out tl
　　　　over 1f out: one pce) .................................................................................. 5.3
266⁵ Oco Royal **(67)** (bl) *(JFfitch-Heyes)* 9-0 GBaxter (3) (4th st: wknd over 2f out) .... 5.4
235 Landowner (IRE) *(JHMGosden)* 9-0 GHind (5) (bit bkwd: s.s: nvr nr to chal) .. 1.5
　　Storm Drum *(PJMakin)* 9-0 JReid (9) (nvr nr) .............................................. hd.6
　　Timurid (FR) *(JLDunlop)* 9-0 WCarson (8) (bit bkwd: nvr nrr) ..................... s h 7
200⁶ Dominant Serenade **(68)** *(PWHarris)* 9-0 PaulEddery (4) (led 7f) ................... 6.8
235⁵ Mathal (USA) *(Fav)* *(MRStoute)* 9-0 PatEddery (11) (lw: 2nd st: wknd over 2f
　　　　out) ............................................................................................................. 8.9
116 And Me **(50)** *(DTThom)* 8-9 JQuinn (8) (a bhd) ............................................. 4.10
251 Sun Eclipse (IRE) **(50)** (bl) *(MMcCormack)* 8-9 WNewnes (2) (prom 6f) ......... 20.11

**15/8** Mathal (USA), **2/1** DESERT ZONE (USA)(4/1—7/4), **4/1** Esbooain (FR)(3/1—5/1), **9/1** Boloardo(5/1—12/
1), **14/1** Timurid (FR)(op 8/1), **20/1** Landowner (IRE)(op 10/1), **50/1** Dominant Serenade, Oco Royal, **66/1** Ors.
CSF £19.13, Tote £3.10: £1.10 £4.20 £1.30 (£26.80). Mr Fahd Salman (WHATCOMBE) bred by Michael D.
Baudhuin in USA. 11 Rn　　　　　　　　　　　　　　　　　　　　　　　　　　2m 6.8 (8.8)
　　　　　　　　　　　　　　　　　　　　　　　　　　　　　　　　　　　SF—32/16/16/–/–/–

**331**　　OVINGDEAN H'CAP (0-70) £2539.60 (£705.60: £338.80)　　1m 3f 196y　　3-25 (3-28)

315² **Sharp Top (41)** *(MJRyan)* 4-7-11 WCarson (8) (a.p: led 4f out: r.o wl) ............... —1
272* Absolutely Right **(49)** *(Fav)* *(RAkehurst)* 4-8-5 (4x) TQuinn (1) (b.nr hind: lw:
　　　　hdwy 5f out: 6th st: ev ch 2f out: unable qckn) ..................................... 5.2
273⁴ Noted Strain (IRE) **(55)** *(PJMakin)* 4-8-11 BRaymond (5) (hdwy 4f out: one pce
　　　　fnl 2f) ......................................................................................................... 4.3
184⁵ Clear Idea (IRE) **(44)** *(CRNelson)* 4-7-11 ‡³DBiggs (10) (b: 5th st: rdn over 2f
　　　　out: wknd fnl f) .......................................................................................... 2½.4
271* Sparkler Gebe **(51)** *(RJO'Sullivan)* 6-8-9 (4x) JQuinn (6) (hdwy 4f out: wknd
　　　　over 1f out) ................................................................................................. 1½.5
　　Greenwich Bambi **(59)** *(WCarter)* 4-9-1 RCochrane (2) (nvr nr to chal) .......... 1½.6
243² Line Drummer (USA) **(72)** *(PAKelleway)* 4-10-0 MRoberts (19) (b: lw: 2nd st:
　　　　wknd over 2f out) ....................................................................................... 2.7
115 Lady Poly **(43)** *(MissBSanders)* 4-7-13 BCrossley (14) (4th st: wknd over 2f
　　　　out) ............................................................................................................. 3½.8
　　Romanian **(55)** *(ARDavison)* 4-8-11 JReid (7) (a mid div) ............................ 3½.9
　　Midday Show (USA) **(70)** *(JRJenkins)* 4-8-11 SWhitworth (17) (nvr nrr) ......... hd.10
169⁶ Guest Player **(50)** (bl) *(TJNaughton)* 5-8-1 ‡7JWeaver (15) (b: led 8f: 3rd st:
　　　　wknd over 3f out) ....................................................................................... nk.11
229 Mysterious Maid (USA) **(67)** *(JPearce)* 5-9-6 ‡⁵RPrice (18) (a mid div) .......... 1½.12
225 Pant Llin **(55)** *(FJordan)* 6-8-13 WNewnes (16) (prom 8f) ........................... ½.13
206 Manaolana **(42)** *(AMoore)* 4-7-12 CRutter (4) (a bhd) ................................. 3.14
244² Sailor Boy **(45)** *(ASReid)* 9-9-5 WRyan (12) (a bhd) .................................... 8.15
　　Paint the Lily **(47)** *(DCJermy)* 4-8-3 GBardwell (13) (prom 8f) .................... 1½.16
　　Albury Grey **(44)** *(RCurtis)* 5-8-2 GCarter (11) (a bhd) .............................. 6.17
　　Willow Blue **(49)** *(TPMcGovern)* 5-8-5 NAdams (20) (a bhd: t.o) ................... 20.18
272⁵ Silver Ancona **(43)** (bl) *(JO'Donoghue)* 8-8-1 DHolland (3) (reluctant to r: a t.o) .. hd.19
　　Di Stefano **(60)** (bl) *(GHarwood)* 4-9-2 AClark (9) (prom 8f: virtually p.u over 2f
　　　　out: t.o) ...................................................................................................... dist.20

**5/2** Absolutely Right, **7/2** SHARP TOP, **5/1** Greenwich Bambi(op 8/1), **12/1** Line Drummer (USA), Sparkler Gebe(op 7/1), **14/1** Noted Strain (IRE), **20/1** Guest Player, Di Stefano, Mysterious Maid (USA), **25/1** Sailor Boy, **33/1** Romanian (IRE), Clear Idea (IRE), Lady Poly. **50/1** Ors. CSF £11.97, CT £98.61. Tote £4.60: £1.20 £1.50 £2.90 £6.50 (£4.60). Malpass Bros Ltd (NEWMARKET) bred by Limestone Stud. 20 Rn      2m 38 (flag) (11)

**332**     BRIGHTON FESTIVAL H'CAP (3-Y.O) (0-80) £2616.00 (£726.00: £348.00)
           **6f 209y**                                                          4-00 (4-02)

| | | |
|---|---|---|
| **Magnificent (69)** *(MAJarvis)* 8-3 ‡⁷KRutter (4) (hdwy over 2f out: led 1f out: drvn out) | | —**1** |
| Bold Setko (IRE) **(61)** *(JMPEustace)* 8-2 DHolland (5) (3rd st: led 2f out to 1f out: r.o wl) | | hd.**2** |
| *215* Parlemo (IRE) **(70)** *(JDBethell)* 8-11 AMunro (2) (s.s: gd hdwy over 1f out: r.o wl) | | 3¹⁄₂.**3** |
| *223⁴* Libra Legend (USA) **(67)** *(CEBrittain)* 8-8 MRoberts (9) (2nd st: ev ch 2f out: unable qckn) | | ³⁄₄.**4** |
| Battle Colours (IRE) **(74)** *(SirMarkPrescott)* 9-1 GDuffield (12) (bit bkwd: hdwy & n.m.r 3f out: r.o ins fnl f) | | 1.**5** |
| Another Vintage **(55)** *(PDCundell)* 7-10 EJohnson (8) (led 6f out to 2f out: one pce) | | nk.**6** |
| Rock Song (IRE) **(57)** *(PFICole)* 7-12 CRutter (13) (lw: 5th st: one pce fnl 3f) .. | | 1¹⁄₂.**7** |
| Christian Warrior **(80)** *(RHannon)* 9-2 ‡⁵RPerham (15) (nvr nr to chal) | | 2.**8** |
| Lonesome Train (USA) **(65)** *(JHMGosden)* 8-6 GHind (10) (lw: nvr nrr) | | s.h.**9** |
| Googly **(52)** *(WGRWightman)* 7-7 GBardwell (1) (hdwy over 3f out: wknd over 1f out) | | 1¹⁄₂.**10** |
| *167* Tadora (IRE) **(58)** *(CJBenstead)* 7-13 JQuinn (7) (4th st: nt clr run over 2f out: sn wknd) | | nk.**11** |
| 269 Lady of Letters **(52)** *(TThomsonJones)* 7-7 AMackay (3) (a bhd) | | 6.**12** |
| Confound (IRE) **(52)** *(JAkehurst)* 7-7 NAdams (6) (bit bkwd: bhd fnl 3f) | | 6.**13** |
| Cheshire Annie (IRE) **(64)** *(WCarter)* 8-5 GCarter (14) (lw: 6th st: wknd over 2f out) | | 2¹⁄₂.**14** |
| Roly Wallace **(66)** *(KTIvory)* 8-4 ‡³DBiggs (16) (led 1f: wknd 4f out) | | 1¹⁄₂.**15** |
| 253² Risk Zone **(55)** (Fav) *(RHannon)* 7-10 WCarson (11) (bhd fnl 3f) | | 1¹⁄₂.**16** |
| LONG HANDICAP: Googly 7-0, Lady of Letters 7-2, Confound (IRE) 7-5. | | |

**7/4** Risk Zone(op 11/4), **9/2** Battle Colours (IRE), **11/2** MAGNIFICENT, **10/1** Cheshire Annie (IRE)(12/1—8/1), **12/1** Rock Song (IRE)(tchd 20/1), **14/1** Parlemo (IRE), Libra Legend (IRE), **20/1** Roly Wallace, Bold Setko (IRE), Tadora (IRE), **25/1** Christian Warrior, Lonesome Train (USA), **33/1** Another Vintage, Confound (IRE), Lady of Letters, **50/1** Googly. CSF £105.50, CT £1,370.97. Tote £7.60: £1.90 £11.00 £2.90 £2.00 (£234.70). Mrs P. L. Yong (NEWMARKET) bred by Nasrullah Holdings. 16 Rn
1m 25.4 (5.4)
SF—27/25/23/18/22/2

**333**     HURSTPIERPOINT (S) H'CAP (0-60) £2520.00 (£700.00: £336.00)
           **6f 209y**                                                          4-35 (4-36)

| | | |
|---|---|---|
| *245⁴* **Daisy Grey (45)** (bl) *(ASReid)* 4-8-11 ‡⁷PMcCabe (8) (b: led over 4f out: rdn out) | | —**1** |
| 250 Sergeant Meryll **(37)** *(PHowling)* 8-8-5 ‡⁵FNorton (18) (4th st: ev ch over 1f out: unable qckn) | | 1¹⁄₂.**2** |
| *137* Beechwood Cottage **(43)** (bl) *(ABailey)* 9-8-9 ‡⁷PBowe (12) (hdwy over 2f out: r.o ins fnl f) | | 1.**3** |
| *152⁵* Tapestry Dancer **(46)** *(MJHaynes)* 4-9-5 WCarson (15) (5th st: one pce fnl 2f) | | 3¹⁄₂.**4** |
| *184⁶* Internal Affair **(44)** (Fav) *(JPearce)* 4-8-12 ‡⁵RPrice (5) (hdwy 3f out: ev ch over 1f out: wknd fnl f) | | ³⁄₄.**5** |
| Foo Foo (IRE) **(36)** *(DMarks)* 4-8-9 AClark (11) (bit bkwd: prom 5f) | | 4.**6** |
| Tina's Angel **(34)** *(JCFox)* 5-8-7 NAdams (14) (nvr nr to chal) | | hd.**7** |
| *181⁴* Dashing April **(48)** *(DTThom)* 4-9-7 MRoberts (13) (dwlt: nvr nrr) | | ¹⁄₂.**8** |
| Miss Precocious **(38)** *(DShaw)* 4-8-11 GCarter (17) (bit bkwd: nvr nrr) | | 1¹⁄₂.**9** |
| *154* Skip Tracer **(38)** (bl) *(KTIvory)* 4-8-8 ‡³DBiggs (7) (2nd st: wknd over 2f out) | | 1¹⁄₂.**10** |
| 253 Cotton Bank (IRE) **(38)** *(PButler)* 4-8-11 AProud (3) (b: a bhd) | | 1.**11** |
| Swift Stream **(51)** *(ABarrow)* 4-9-10 JReid (1) (bhd fnl 3f) | | 2.**12** |
| *158* Gemdoubleyou **(47)** *(FJordan)* 4-9-6 WNewnes (10) (a bhd) | | ¹⁄₂.**13** |
| Monscoma (IRE) **(48)** *(ARDavison)* 4-9-7 JWilliams (16) (a bhd) | | 3.**14** |
| Cheeky Chaplin **(38)** *(DRGandolfo)* 6-8-6 ‡⁵RPerham (9) (led over 2f: 3rd st: wknd over 3f out) | | 12.**15** |
| Sockem **(41)** (bl) *(CNWilliams)* 5-9-0 BRaymond (9) (6th st: wknd over 2f out) | | hd.**16** |

**11/2** Internal Affair, **6/1** DAISY GREY (op 4/1), Sockem(op 5/1), **7/1** Sergeant Meryll, Tapestry Dancer, **8/1** Miss Precocious(op 14/1), **10/1** Foo Foo (IRE)(tchd 16/1), Dashing April, **12/1** Beechwood Cottage(op 8/1), **14/1** Swift Stream, **20/1** Monscoma (IRE), Gemdoubleyou, **33/1** Ors. CSF £47.55, CT £455.03. Tote £6.90: £2.50 £2.50 £1.70 £1.80 (£34.40). Mr A. S. Reid (THURLEIGH) bred by Cheveley Park Stud Ltd. 16 Rn; No bid
1m 26.9 (6.9)
SF—14/5/6/5/—/—

**334**     SOUTHWICK STKS (Mdn 3-Y-O) £1932.00 (£532.00: £252.00)     6f 209y   5-05 (5-06)

235 **Secret Thing (USA) (100)** (Fav) *(CEBrittain)* 9-0 MRoberts (7) (2nd st: led over
3f out: comf) ............................................................................................ —1
        Baluga *(GHarwood)* 9-0 AClark (5) (bit bkwd: led over 3f: rdn & ev ch over 1f
out: r.o) ................................................................................................... 1.2
252² Precious Wonder *(PButler)* 9-0 RCochrane (3) (3rd st: ev ch over 1f out: unable
qckn) ................................................................................................... 3½.3
        Sunley Silks *(MRChannon)* 8-9 CRutter (8) (w'like: lw: 5th st: r.o one pce fnl 2f) 2½.4
        Chinaman **(61)** *(WGRWightman)* 9-0 JWilliams (4) (bit bkwd: nvr nr to chal) ... 2½.5
        Rio Trusky *(MDIUsher)* 9-0 TQuinn (6) (4th st: wknd over 2f out) ...................... 2.6
        Odoen (USA) *(MRChannon)* 9-0 LornaVincent (1) (bit bkwd: dwlt: 6th st: a bhd) hd.7
252 Dare to Dream (IRE) *(GLewis)* 9-0 PaulEddery (9) (dwlt: a bhd) .................... hd.8

**10/11** SECRET THING (USA), **3/1** Sunley Silks(tchd 9/2), **9/2** Precious Wonder, **9/1** Baluga(op 9/4), **33/1**
Chinaman, **66/1** Ors. CSF £9.07, Tote £2.00: £1.10 £1.10 £1.40 (£3.80). Mr Luciano Gaucci (NEWMARKET)
bred by Sandra M. Fourbush & Calumet Farm in USA. 8 Rn                          1m 25.5 (5.5)
                                                                                SF—37/34/23/10/7/1

**335**     PYECOMBE APP'CE STKS   £2382.80 (£660.80: £316.40)     1m 1f 209y   5-35 (5-36)

240 **Two Left Feet (93)** (Fav) *(SirMarkPrescott)* 5-9-5 KRutter (5) (3rd st: led over 2f
out: easily) ............................................................................................ —1
        Sea Goddess *(WJarvis)* 4-7-9 ‡5GMilligan (2) (lw: led 4f out tl over 2f out: unable
qckn) ................................................................................................... 3.2
278² Taunting (IRE) *(MBlanshard)* 4-8-12 DHarrison (12) (6th st: hrd rdn over 2f out:
r.o ins fnl f) ............................................................................................ 1.3
250³ Metternich *(MHTompkins)* 7-8-7 ‡5DavidWilliams (3) (s.s: hdwy over 2f out: r.o) 2½.4
        Secretary of State *(PFICole)* 6 8 12 JDCmith (6) (b: blcwd: lcd 0f: 2nd st: wknd
over 2f out) .......................................................................................... 1½.5
        Knights (NZ) *(MrsSOliver)* 6-8-12 TWilson (10) (hdwy fnl 2f: r.o) ...................... 6.6
        Prince Lyphard *(RAkehurst)* 6-8-7 ‡5LCarter (4) (hdwy fnl 2f: nvr nrr) .............. ¾.7
250⁴ Molly Splash **(42)** *(CACyzer)* 5-8-0 AMorris (11) (4th st: wknd over 2f out) ....... ¾.8
        Empire Blue *(PFICole)* 9-9-5 PTurner (14) (b: bit bkwd: dwlt: bhd fnl 3f) ......... 2½.9
239 Marcham (IRE) **(97)** *(BWHills)* 4-9-5 CMunday (7) (lw: 5th st: wknd over 1f out) 1.10
        Al Skeet (USA) **(37)** *(AMoore)* 6-8-12 PBowe (8) (dwlt: a bhd) ...................... 7.11
224 Weapon Exhibition (bl) *(GAHam)* 5-8-6⁽⁶⁾ MichaelDenaro (13) (a bhd) ............ 3.12
        Singing Detective **(25)** *(RCurtis)* 5-8-5 NGWilliams (1) (a bhd) ...................... 2.13
        Marjons Boy **(42)** (bl) *(CDBroad)* 5-9-5 EHusband (9) (a bhd) ...................... 8.14

**6/4** TWO LEFT FEET(tchd 9/4), **3/1** Marcham (IRE)(tchd 2/1), **5/1** Sea Goddess, **13/2** Secretary of State, **11/1**
Empire Blue, **14/1** Taunting (IRE), **20/1** Prince Lyphard, **25/1** Singing Detective, Metternich, **33/1** Knights (NZ),
Marjons Boy, Molly Splash, Weapon Exhibition, **50/1** Al Skeet (USA). CSF £10.83, Tote £2.80: £1.90 £1.90
£2.90 (£18.30). Mr P. W. W. Molins (NEWMARKET) bred by Stud-On-The-Chart. 14 Rn     2m 8.1 (10.1)
                                                                                SF—24/–/9/–/1/–

T/Plpt: £72.60 (30.55 Tckts).                                                    AK

# KEMPTON (R-H)
## Friday, April 3rd [Good to soft]
Going Allowance: 0.55 sec per fur (Y)                                Wind: almost nil

Stalls: centre

**339**     POLYANTHUS AUCTION STKS (Mdn 2-Y-O) £2539.60 (£705.60: £338.80)
            **5f**                                                          1-40 (1-46)

        **Tuscan Dawn** *(JBerry)* 8-9 PatEddery (3) (unf: racd stands' side: hdwy over 2f
out: led over 1f out: all out) ................................................................ —1
        Auntie Ginger *(PButler)* 8-0 AProud (4) (leggy: lt-f: racd stands' side: rdn &
hdwy over 1f out: r.o wl ins fnl f) ...................................................... s.h.2
297 Gaynor Goodman (IRE) *(JSMoore)* 7-10⁽¹⁾ ‡5ATucker (2) (racd stands' side:
a.p: led 2f out tl over 1f out: unable qckn) ...................................... 2.3
        Hung Parliament *(BWHills)* 8-2 DHolland (13) (unf: scope: rdn & hdwy over 1f
out: r.o ins fnl f) ................................................................................ 1.4
        Glowing Dancer *(JRJenkins)* 8-11 MRoberts (1) (leggy: bit bkwd: racd stands'
side: led 3f: eased whn btn ins fnl f) ................................................ ½.5
        Tigerspike (IRE) *(MMcCormack)* 8-7 JReid (5) (unf: bit bkwd: racd stands' side:
dwlt: nvr nr to chal) ........................................................................ 5.6
        Moonstruck Bard *(AHide)* 8-5 BRouse (7) (unf: bit bkwd: racd stands' side:
prom over 3f) ................................................................................... hd.7

226⁴ Second Chance (IRE) *(PMitchell)* 8-7 JWilliams (12) (spd 3f) .............................. 1.8
Chinnery (IRE) *(JMPEustace)* 8-9 RCochrane (14) (w'like: bit bkwd: prom over
2f) ....................................................................................................... ³/₄.9
Heber Spring (IRE) *(RHannon)* 8-7 BRaymond (16) (leggy: bit bkwd: prom over
3f: eased whn btn fnl f) ................................................................. s.h.10
Aberdeen Heather *(DRCElsworth)* 8-13 SCauthen (17) (str: lw: spd over 3f) . 3.11
Waterlord (IRE) *(CGCox)* 8-7 AClark (8) (neat: prom 3f) .......................... 1¹/₂.12
Toff Sundae *(GLewis)* 8-7 PaulEddery (11) (w'like: hdwy over 2f out: wknd over
1f out) ........................................................................................... hd.13
Runnett Dancer (IRE) *(MRStoute)* 8-13 WRSwinburn (9) (w'like: bit bkwd: a bhd) 2.14
Lady Relko *(RVoorspuy)* 8-0 SDawson (6) (lt-f: racd stands' side: bhd fnl 2f) s.h.15
Surprise Offer (Fav) *(RHannon)* 8-6 ‡5RPerham (10) (und: bkwd: gd spd 3f) .... ¹/₂.16
Threeofus *(KTIvory)* 8-11 MWigham (20) (unf: bkwd: s.s: a wl bhd) ............. 1¹/₂.17
Madame Cresson *(GAPritchard-Gordon)* 8-4 AMcGlone (19) (leggy: lt-f: bit
bkwd: gd spd over 3f) ..................................................................... 5.18
Persian Gusher (IRE) *(SDow)* 8-7 TQuinn (18) (leggy: lt-f: a bhd) ............... 2.19

**9/2** Surprise Offer, **6/1** Aberdeen Heather(tchd 9/1), **7/1** Runnett Dancer (IRE)(op 3/1), **8/1** Second Chance
(IRE), Hung Parliament, TUSCAN DAWN(6/1—12/1), **12/1** Moonstruck Bard, Persian Gusher (IRE), **14/1** Toff
Sundae, Heber Spring (IRE)(op 7/1), Threeofus, **16/1** Glowing Dancer, **20/1** Chinnery (IRE), Madame Cresson,
**25/1** Waterlord (IRE), Tigerspike (IRE), **33/1** Gaynor Goodman (IRE), **40/1** Auntie Ginger, **50/1** Lady Relko. CSF
£275.39, Tote £6.60: £3.60 £23.70 £17.60 (£156.00). Miss Antonia Taverner (COCKERHAM) bred by F. Hines.
19 Rn
                                                              65.69 sec (6.69)
                                                              SF—16/6/–/–/–/–

**340**      FLORENCE NAGLE GIRL APP'CE H'CAP (0-70) £2700.00 (£750.00: £360.00)
             **1m 1f**                                                     2-10 (2-16)

233 **Bengal Tiger (IRE) (50)** (bl) *(JAkehurst)* 4-8-10 KimMcDonnell (9) (led over 7f
              out tl over 1f out: rdn: led last stride) ...................................... —1
         Always Ready (39) *(RLee)* 6-7-13 MadeleineSmith (10) (b: 2nd st: led over 1f
              out tl hdd last stride) ....................................................... s.h.2
232³ Princess Roxanne (56) (bl) (Fav) *(ABailey)* 5-8-11 ‡5WendyMcLaughlin (14)
              (dwlt: 3rd st: edgd rt ins fnl f: unable qckn) .............................. 2.3
232⁶ Ballerina Bay (58) (v) *(DTThom)* 4-8-13 ‡5BeverleyBrett (13) (hdwy over 3f out:
              r.o ins fnl f) ................................................................... 1¹/₂.4
         Salbyng (57) *(JWHills)* 4-9-3 EmmaO'Gorman (8) (bit bkwd: 4th st: one pce fnl
              2f) ................................................................................. hd.5
246⁶ Broughton Blues (IRE) (43) *(WJMusson)* 4-7-12 ‡5SallyRadford-Howes (15)
              (5th st: one pce fnl 2f) .................................................... 1¹/₂.6
249⁴ With Gusto (49) *(KOCunningham-Brown)* 5-8-9 DebbieBiggs (4) (b.hind: led
              over 1f: one pce fnl 2f) ................................................... ³/₄.7
         Lady Lacey (53) (v) *(GBBalding)* 5-8-13 TraceyPurseglove (6) (bit bkwd: hdwy
              4f out: one pce fnl 2f) ..................................................... 2.8
         Acqua Noir (34) *(AWJones)* 5-7-3⁽¹⁾ ‡5ClaireBalding (2) (nvr nr to chal) ...... ¹/₂.9
244⁵ Sand Castle (36) *(PHowling)* 11-7-5⁽¹⁾ ‡5KateMason (11) (a mid div) ......... 5.10
220⁵ Springs Welcome (63) *(CACyzer)* 6-9-4 ‡5SamanthaBenney (16) (s.s: nvr nrr) 1.11
203 Sauvignon (IRE) (59) *(RGuest)* 4-9-5 AntoinetteArmes (17) (a mid div) ....... ³/₄.12
         Peter Pumpkin (35) (bl) *(RVoorspuy)* 4-7-7 JakiHouston (1) (b: a bhd) ...... 2.13
220 Singular Run (61) *(MrsJCDawe)* 6-9-2 ‡5MariePlowright (5) (a bhd) .......... 3.14
         Scossa (USA) (49) *(JLSpearing)* 4-8-9 DonnaHayman (18) (6th st: wknd over
              2f out) ........................................................................... 1¹/₂.15
185⁶ Lucky Noire (68) *(GHarwood)* 4-10-0 GayeHarwood (7) (bhd fnl 3f) ........... s.h.16
         Easter Term (45) *(RJHolder)* 4-8-0 ‡5RobynFullelove (12) (bit bkwd: bhd fnl 6f) . 17
         Tendresse (IRE) (57) *(DRTucker)* 4-8-12 ‡5SianWilliams (19) (s.i.s: a bhd) ..... 18
                                   LONG HANDICAP: Acqua Noir 7-6.

**6/1** Princess Roxanne, **13/2** BENGAL TIGER (IRE), **7/1** Salbyng, **9/1** Ballerina Bay, **10/1** Sauvignon (IRE), Always
Ready(tchd 16/1), Lady Lacey, **12/1** Lucky Noire, **14/1** Tendresse (IRE), Springs Welcome, With Gusto, **16/1**
Broughton Blues (IRE), **20/1** Acqua Noir, **25/1** Scossa (USA), **33/1** Ors. CSF £66.80, CT £377.73. Tote £7.40:
£1.90 £2.30 £1.10 £3.90 (£104.60). Mr A. P. Johnston (UPPER LAMBOURN) bred by Barronstown Bloodstock
Ltd in Ireland. 18 Rn
                                                              1m 58.72 (8.72)
                                                              SF—40/28/34/31/34/10

**341**      LABURNUM GRADUATION STKS (3-Y.O) £3574.00 (£1072.00: £516.00: £238.00)
             **1m (J.C)**                                                   2-45 (2-48)

         **Pollen Count (USA)** (Fav) *(JHMGosden)* 8-11 SCauthen (1) (lw: 4th st: led
              over 1f out: rdn out) ....................................................... —1
         Free Flyer (IRE) *(MMoubarak)* 9-3 LDettori (12) (3rd st: led over 2f out tl over 1f
              out: unable qckn) ........................................................... 2.2

Jeune **(101)** *(GWragg)* 9-3 WRSwinburn (3) (led over 4f: 2nd st: ev ch over 2f out: one pce) .......................... 1½.3

Bobzao (IRE) **(105)** *(WCarter)* 9-3 JReid (7) (lw: 5th st: one pce fnl 2f) .......... 4.4

Spartan Shareef (IRE) *(CEBrittain)* 8-11 MRoberts (2) (lw: 6th st: one pce fnl 3f) 1½.5

Haroldon (IRE) *(BPalling)* 8-11 RCochrane (10) (a.p: led over 3f out tl over 2f out: sn wknd) .......................... s.h.6

Hierarch (USA) *(LordHuntingdon)* 8-11 AMunro (14) (unf: scope: rdn & hdwy over 1f out: r.o) .......................... 2½.7

252★ Thinking Twice *(PWHarris)* 9-3 WNewnes (5) (nvr nr to chal) .................. 6.8

Alsaarm (USA) **(102)** *(JLDunlop)* 9-3 WCarson (4) (h.d.w: bit bkwd: a mid div) 3½.9

Vivitz (IRE) **(63)** *(GBBalding)* 8-11 JWilliams (11) (a bhd) .......................... 2.10

235★ Mizaaya **(86)** *(MRStoute)* 9-3 PatEddery (9) (lw: hdwy over 2f out: eased whn btn over 1f out) .......................... ½.11

Baharlilys *(NCWright)* 8-6 GDuffield (8) (plld hrd: rdn over 4f out: a bhd) ...... 3½.12

Nocatchim *(BWHills)* 8-11 DHolland (15) (s.s: a bhd) .......................... 1½.13

Probation *(BRMillman)* 8-11 GBaxter (6) (bit bkwd: a bhd) .......................... 12.14

Brooks Express (FR) *(RAkehurst)* 8-11 TQuinn (13) (leggy: bit bkwd: a bhd) .... 5.15

**2/1** POLLEN COUNT (USA), **3/1** Free Flyer (IRE)(5/2—5/1), **13/2** Mizaaya, **10/1** Jeune, Bobzao (IRE), Hierarch (USA), **11/1** Alsaarm (USA)(8/1—12/1), **12/1** Haroldon (IRE), Spartan Shareef (IRE), **14/1** Brooks Express (FR), **20/1** Nocatchim, **25/1** Baharlilys, Thinking Twice, **50/1** Probation, **66/1** Vivitz (IRE). CSF £10.04, Tote £3.40: £1.70 £2.10 £2.30 (£5.40). Sheikh Mohammed (NEWMARKET) bred by Muckler Stables Incorporated in USA. 15 Rn
1m 43.35 (6.75)
SF—61/61/56/44/35/32

**342** JONNIE MULLINGS MEMORIAL H'CAP (0-80) £3496.00 (£1048.00: £504.00: £232.00)
1½m
3-20 (3-22)

**Western Dynasty (66)** *(MJRyan)* 6-9-5 LDettori (3) (3rd st: led over 1f out: hrd rdn: r.o wl) .......................... —1

Rare Detail (IRE) **(72)** *(MrsLPiggott)* 4-9-9 LPiggott (4) (hdwy over 2f out: hrd rdn over 1f out: r.o wl) .......................... 1.2

214³ Broom Isle **(48)** *(MrsAKnight)* 4-7-8 ‡5FNorton (16) (2nd st: ev ch over 2f out: unable qckn) .......................... 6.3

301 Eire Leath-Sceal **(64)** *(MBrittain)* 5-9-3 KDarley (21) (4th st: one pce fnl 3f) ..... hd.4

Rosgill **(69)** (Jt-Fav) *(PMitchell)* 6-9-8 MRoberts (20) (edgd rt & hdwy 2f out: r.o) ¾.5

Crabby Bill **(47)** (bl) *(MissBSanders)* 5-8-0 BCrossley (19) (hdwy over 1f out: r.o) .......................... hd.6

Mahrajan **(65)** *(CJBenstead)* 8-9-4 RCochrane (11) (gd hdwy over 1f out: r.o) ... s.h.7

Mubin (IRE) **(73)** *(CCElsey)* 4-9-10 WNewnes (18) (w ldr: led over 5f out tl over 1f out: sn wknd) .......................... 3.8

211² Samurai Gold (USA) **(50)** (Jt-Fav) *(PTWalwyn)* 4-8-1 AMunro (8) (5th st: wknd over 2f out) .......................... 1½.9

Full Quiver **(63)** (v) *(MrsBarbaraWaring)* 7-9-2 NHowe (15) (b.off fore: hdwy over 3f out: 6th st: wknd over 1f out) .......................... 1½.10

Green's Van Goyen (IRE) **(68)** *(RAkehurst)* 4-9-5 TQuinn (1) (hdwy 4f out: wknd over 2f out) .......................... 3½.11

Indian Slave (IRE) **(55)** *(RGuest)* 4-8-6 GBaxter (12) (a mid div) .......................... 2.12

249★ Dazzle the Crowd (IRE) **(52)** *(CACyzer)* 4-8-3 GCarter (17) (a mid div) ........... 3.13

River Island (USA) **(75)** *(JABOld)* 4-9-12 BRaymond (13) (nvr nrr) .............. s.h.14

Lark Rise (USA) **(67)** *(CWeedon)* 4-9-4 JReid (10) (a mid div) .......................... hd.15

Rousillon to Be **(46)** *(MissBSanders)* 5-7-13 DanaMellor (9) (led over 6f) ........ 4.16

Sedgy Mead **(47)** *(PJJones)* 4-7-12[1] AMcGlone (22) (bhd fnl 6f) .......................... hd.17

Moot Point (USA) **(67)** *(JRJenkins)* 4-9-4 PatEddery (14) (bit bkwd: a bhd) ... hd.18

232 Buzzards Crest **(40)** *(BobJones)* 7-7-7 JQuinn (6) (hdwy 4f out: wknd 3f out) ... 19

246³ Modesto (USA) **(65)** *(KOCunningham-Brown)* 4-8-13 ‡3DBiggs (7) (b: rdn thrght: prom over 6f) .......................... 20

Sweet Request **(67)** *(JRBostock)* 4-9-4 SWhitworth (5) (a bhd) .......................... 21

246★ Munday Dean **(68)** *(DWPArbuthnot)* 4-9-0 ‡5RPrice (2) (prom over 6f) .......................... 22

LONG HANDICAP: Buzzards Crest 7-3.

**7/1** Rosgill, Samurai Gold (USA)(tchd 11/1), **10/1** WESTERN DYNASTY, **11/1** Dazzle the Crowd (IRE), **12/1** Munday Dean(op 8/1), Rare Detail (IRE), **14/1** Green's Van Goyen (IRE), Moot Point (USA), Broom Isle, Eire Leath-Sceal, Modesto (USA), **16/1** Full Quiver, Mubin (IRE), **20/1** Crabby Bill, Rousillon to Be, Buzzards Crest, **25/1** Indian Slave (IRE), River Island (USA), Lark Rise (USA), Mahrajan, **33/1** Sweet Request, **66/1** Sedgy Mead. CSF £121.08, CT £1,566.00. Tote £16.00: £3.30 £3.20 £6.80 £3.90 (£332.20). Mr M. F. Kentish (NEWMARKET) bred by M. F. Kentish. 22 Rn
2m 42.18 (11.98)
SF—51/53/12/34/37/14/31

**343** MAGNOLIA STKS (listed race) £9000.00 (£2700.00: £1300.00: £600.00)
1¼m
3-55 (3-59)

**Red Bishop (USA) (101)** (Fav) *(JHMGosden)* 4-8-11 SCauthen (2) (rdn & hdwy over 2f out: led over 1f out: comf) .......................... —1

Crystal Path (FR) *(MMoubarak)* 4-8-6 LDettori (3) (5th st: hrd rdn over 1f out:
unable qckn) ............................................................................ 3¹/₂.**2**
Ile de Chypre *(GHarwood)* 7-9-6 AClark (5) (led over 8f: one pce) ..................... 2.**3**
Busted Rock **(85)** *(MrsLPiggott)* 7-8-11 LPiggott (1) (hdwy over 1f out: r.o) .... 1¹/₂.**4**
Hateel **(109)** *(PTWalwyn)* 6-9-6 WCarson (10) (bit bkwd: hld up: 3rd st: ev ch
over 1f out: wknd fnl f) ............................................................ 3.**5**
Fire Top **(91)** *(RAkehurst)* 7-8-11 RCochrane (11) (6th st: wknd over 1f out) .. 3¹/₂.**6**
Green's Ferneley (IRE) **(100)** *(RCharlton)* 4-8-11 PatEddery (7) (nvr nr to chal) 2.**7**
Heart of Darkness **(105)** *(IABalding)* 4-8-11 JReid (9) (lw: no hdwy fnl 3f) .......... 1.**8**
Cooley's Valve (IRE) **(91)** *(BWHills)* 4-8-11 DHolland (8) (2nd st: wknd 2f out) hd.**9**
Percy's Girl (IRE) *(GWragg)* 4-8-7⁽¹⁾ WRSwinburn (12) (4th st: wknd over 2f
out) ................................................................................ ³/₄.**10**
Prince Russanor *(JLDunlop)* 4-8-11 MRoberts (4) (a bhd) .............................. s.h.**11**
Meqdaam (USA) *(RAkehurst)* 5-8-11 TQuinn (6) (bit bkwd: bhd fnl 5f) .......... nk.**12**

**7/2** RED BISHOP (USA), **9/2** Crystal Path (FR), **5/1** Percy's Girl (IRE), **6/1** Hateel(tchd 9/1), Heart of Darkness,
**8/1** Prince Russanor, **10/1** Ile de Chypre, **11/1** Cooley's Valve (IRE), **12/1** Green's Ferneley (IRE), **20/1** Busted
Rock, Fire Top, **33/1** Meqdaam (USA). CSF £21.17, Tote £4.20: £1.60 £2.70 £2.80 (£5.80). Mr Ali Saeed
(NEWMARKET) bred by Pillar Stud Inc in USA. 12 Rn                                    2m 11.15 (9.15)
SF—62/50/60/48/51/35/31

**344**     SYRINGA H'CAP (0-90) £3392.00 (£1016.00: £488.00: £224.00)     **6f**     4-30 (4-37)

233⁵ **Nordic Brave (67)** *(MBrittain)* 6-8-5 KDarley (23) (racd far side: mde virtually
all: drvn out) ............................................................................... —**1**
253★ Across the Bay **(66)** (v) *(SDow)* 5-8-4⁽¹⁾ (7x) TQuinn (24) (racd far side: w wnr:
ev ch fnl f: r.o wl) ........................................................ ¹/₂.**2**
236 Paddy Chalk **(76)** *(LJHolt)* 6-9-0 JReid (8) (b: a.p: rdn over 1f out: r.o) ........... 1¹/₂.**3**
Baysham (USA) **(80)** *(BRMillman)* 6-9-4 GBaxter (22) (racd far side: a.p:
rdn over 1f out: unable qckn) .......................................... 1.**4**
Pharoah's Dancer **(60)** *(EAWheeler)* 5-7-7⁽⁵⁾ ‡⁵FNorton (20) (racd far side: a.p:
one pce fnl f) ............................................................... hd.**5**
Darakah **(65)** *(CJHill)* 5-7-12 ‡³DBiggs (1) (hdwy over 1f out: r.o ins fnl f) ........... hd.**6**
Merryhill Maid (IRE) **(65)** *(JLHarris)* 4-8-3 DHolland (13) (gd spd over 4f) ....... 1¹/₂.**7**
How's Yer Father **(71)** *(RJHodges)* 6-8-9 RCochrane (21) (hld
up: hrd rdn over 1f out: one pce) ................................. 2.**8**
Luna Bid **(65)** *(MBlanshard)* 9-8-3 CRutter (16) (racd far side: nvr nr to chal) .. hd.**9**
285⁴ Norfolkiev (FR) **(59)** *(MMoubarak)* 6-7-4 ‡⁷DonnaHayman (2) (prom 3f) .......... hd.**10**
Piquant **(79)** (Fav) *(LordHuntingdon)* 5-9-3 WRSwinburn (4) (bit bkwd: sme
hdwy over 2f out: wknd over 1f out) ......................... nk.**11**
Lord High Admiral (CAN) **(69)** *(RHannon)* 4-8-2 ‡⁵RPerham (11) (lw: gd spd
over 4f) ................................................................ 1¹/₂.**12**
Saafend **(67)** *(JSutcliffe)* 4-8-5 BRouse (3) (bit bkwd: outpcd) ..................... ³/₄.**13**
Olifantsfontein **(71)** *(RSimpson)* 4-8-9 GDuffield (5) (s.s: nvr nrr) .................. 3¹/₂.**14**
253 Grey Illusions **(56)** *(LJHolt)* 4-7-8 NAdams (9) (outpcd) ........................ ¹/₂.**15**
253³ Malunar **(67)** *(MHTompkins)* 7-8-5 RHills (15) (racd far side: outpcd) ............. hd.**16**
Candle King (IRE) **(64)** *(MJFetherston-Godley)* 4-8-2 AMunro (10) (a bhd) ... nk.**17**
233 Foolish Touch **(60)** *(WJMusson)* 10-7-12 AMackay (6) (a bhd) .................. ¹/₂.**18**
Nawwar **(57)** *(CJBenstead)* 8-7-9 JQuinn (7) (outpcd) .................................. 1.**19**
240 Go Executive **(87)** *(CEBrittain)* 4-9-11 MRoberts (17) (racd far side: outpcd) ...... 20
Highland Magic (IRE) **(65)** *(MJFetherston-Godley)* 4-7-10 ‡⁷DHarrison (18)
(racd far side: outpcd) .............................................. 21
199 Armaiti **(73)** *(DRTucker)* 4-8-11 GBardwell (25) (racd far side: outpcd) ............. 22
92★ Respectable Jones **(73)** *(GBBalding)* 6-8-11 JWilliams (19) (racd far side: bhd
fnl 2f) ................................................................... 23
42⁴ Beatle Song **(72)** *(RJHodges)* 4-8-10 WCarson (12) (lw: outpcd) ..................... 24
Fivesevenfiveo **(66)** *(RJHodges)* 4-7-13 ‡⁵TSprake (14) (outpcd) .................. 25
LONG HANDICAP: Pharoah's Dancer 7-2.

**6/1** Piquant(op 16/1), **7/1** NORDIC BRAVE(6/1—11/1), **10/1** Lord High Admiral (CAN), **11/1** Malunar,
Respectable Jones(8/1—12/1), Candle King (IRE), **12/1** Across the Bay(op 7/1), Paddy Chalk, **14/1**
Saafend(20/1—12/1), Go Executive, Baysham (USA), Highland Magic (IRE), Norfolkiev (FR), **16/1** Beatle Song,
How's Yer Father, Darakah, **20/1** Luna Bid, **25/1** Pharoah's Dancer, Armaiti, Foolish Touch, Fivesevenfiveo,
Merryhill Maid (IRE), **33/1** Ors. CSF £98.73, CT £965.12. Tote £9.00: £2.80 £4.60 £3.40 £9.20 (£22.40). Mr Mel
Brittain (WARTHILL) bred by Tsarina Stud. 25 Rn                                    1m 16.74 (5.44)
SF—48/45/49/49/23/27

T/Trio: Race 4: £682.20 (1.1 Tckts). T/Plpt: £376.20 (5.9 Tckts).                              AK

244—**LINGFIELD (L-H)**
**Saturday, April 4th [Turf Soft, AWT Standard]**
Going Allowance: Turf: 0.80 sec (S); AWT: minus 0.45 sec (FS)     Wind: almost nil
Stalls: high     *Flag start: 4th Race*

**345**     HOLIDAY CLUB PONTINS STKS (Mdn 2-Y.O) £2382.80 (£660.80: £316.40)
5f     1-40 (1-48)

2554 **Polity Prince** *(LJHolt)* 9-0 JReid (2) (a.p: hrd rdn over 2f out: led nr fin) ............ —1
Defenceless *(RHannon)* 8-9 BRouse (6) (neat: bit bkwd: led: hrd rdn over 1f
    out: hdd nr fin) ................................................................................ ½.2
Iron Merchant (IRE) *(RAkehurst)* 9-0 TQuinn (5) (w'like: a.p: hrd rdn over 2f out:
    r.o ins fnl f) ................................................................................... nk.3
Zuno Warrior *(GLewis)* 9-0 PaulEddery (8) (w'like: bit bkwd: outpcd: hdwy over
    1f out: r.o ins fnl f) .......................................................................... 2.4
Pilgrim Bay (IRE) *(Fav)* *(JBerry)* 9-0 PatEddery (3) (leggy: scope: lw: w ldr: ev
    ch 2f out: hrd rdn over 1f out: eased whn btn nr fin) ........... 2.5
Ballaindy *(WGMTurner)* 8-4 ‡5TSprake (7) (lt-f: s.s: nvr nr to chal) ...................... 2.6
Chatworth Grey *(PHowling)* 8-9 JMurray (4) (unf: bkwd: dwlt: a bhd) .............. 12.7
Buck the Tiger *(RHannon)* 9-0 AMcGlone (1) (unf: a bhd) ................................... 2.8
Sheila's Secret (IRE) *(WCarter)* 8-4 ‡5NGwilliams (9) (neat: bkwd: bhd fnl 3f) ...... 1.9

7/4 Pilgrim Bay (IRE)(5/4—2/1), 9/2 Zuno Warrior, Iron Merchant (IRE)(tchd 8/1), 7/1 Sheila's Secret (IRE)(op
4/1), 9/1 Defenceless(op 4/1), 14/1 POLITY PRINCE(op 4/1), 25/1 Ors. CSF £114.12, Tote £13.70: £2.40 £3.60
£2.30 (£56.20). Mrs S. Khan (BASINGSTOKE) bred by H. Khan. 9 Rn     65.09 sec (8.09)
     SF—28/26/25/17/9/–

**346**     CHAIR CLAIMING STKS (3-Y.O) £2128.00 (£588.00: £280.00)
1½m (AWT)     2-10 (2-11)

**Perforate (60)** *(SirMarkPrescott)* 8-3 GDuffield (4) (b.hind: led over 8f: led over
    2f out: r.o wl) ................................................................................... —1
2566 Alternation (FR) (62) *(Fav)* *(PFICole)* 8-4 TQuinn (1) (a.p: led over 3f out tl over
    2f out: unable qckn) ........................................................................ 3.2
1913 Beam Me Up Scotty (IRE) (61) *(PMitchell)* 8-5 JWilliams (5) (a.p: ev ch over 2f
    out: one pce) ................................................................................... 7.3
302 Fine as Fivepence (45) *(MrsAKnight)* 7-7(4) ‡5FNorton (2) (t.o fnl 6f: sddle
    slipped) ........................................................................................... 30.4
256 Colouring Book (IRE) (47) *(MJHaynes)* 7-1 ‡7DToole (3) (t.o fnl 6f) ............ 2½.5

13/8 Alternation (FR), 15/8 Beam Me Up Scotty (IRE), 5/2 PERFORATE, 14/1 Colouring Book (IRE), 33/1 Fine as
Fivepence. CSF £6.69, Tote £3.00: £1.70 £1.10 (£3.20). Sir Mark Prescott (NEWMARKET) bred by Hesmonds
Stud Ltd. 5 Rn     2m 32.92 (3.52)

**347**     KENTUCKY DERBY TRIAL STKS (3-Y.O) £4308.00 (£1284.00: £612.00: £276.00)
1¼m (AWT)     2-40 (2-43)

**Thyer (USA)** *(JSBolger,Ireland)* 9-7 CRoche (3) (leggy: scope: lw: hld up: led
    wl over 1f out: r.o wl) ....................................................................... —1
Rokeby (105) *(IABalding)* 9-7 JReid (1) (b.off hind: lw: led tl rn wd bnd & hdd wl
    over 1f out: unable qckn) ................................................................. 2½.2
Hero's Light (USA) (90) *(PFICole)* 9-4 AMunro (4) (chsd ldr tl carried wd bnd wl
    over 1f out: one pce) ........................................................................ 1.3
Balla Jidaal (USA) (105) *(Fav)* *(MRStoute)* 9-7 PatEddery (2) (lw: plld hrd: hld
    up: carried wd bnd wl over 1f out: one pce) ..................................... 2.4
Freni (41) *(MDIUsher)* 8-9 JWilliams (5) (bhd fnl 4f: t.o) ................................... 30.5

Evens Balla Jidaal (USA), 2/1 THYER (USA)(6/4—9/4), 11/2 Rokeby(op 3/1), 8/1 Hero's Light (USA)(6/1—9/
1), 100/1 Freni. CSF £11.49, Tote £2.50: £1.20 £1.90 (£6.20). Maktoum Al Maktoum (IRELAND) bred by Cherry
Valley Farm Inc. & E. A. Cox Jnr in USA. 5 Rn     2m 5.43 (2.43)
     SF—38/33/28/27/–

**348**     BRITVIC SOFT DRINKS MEDIAN AUCTION GRADUATION STKS (3-Y.O) £2520.00 (£700.00:
£336.00)    7f     3-15 (3-17)

**Irek** *(LordHuntingdon)* 9-0 JReid (3) (unf: lw: a.p: led over 1f out: rdn out) ........ —1
Sebosan (80) *(AHide)* 9-7 WRyan (6) (a.p: hrd rdn over 1f out: r.o) .................... 5.2

Grand Fellow (IRE) *(JDBethell)* 9-0 AMunro (8) (hdwy over 2f out: hrd rdn over 1f out: r.o) ................................................................. nk.3
Allmosa *(TJNaughton)* 8-9 GCarter (4) (leggy: hdwy over 2f out: r.o one pce) .. ¾.4
Efra *(RHannon)* 9-0 PatEddery (11) (led over 5f: eased whn btn wl ins fnl f) ...... 1½.5
Will Soon *(HCandy)* 9-0 CRutter (7) (lw: hld up: shkn up over 1f out: r.o wl) ... s.h.6
First Century (IRE) **(98)** (Fav) *(PFICole)* 9-7 TQuinn (2) (bit bkwd: prom 5f) ...... 5.7
Coniston Lake (IRE) *(GLewis)* 9-0 BRouse (13) (hld up: nvr nr to chal) ............ 2½.8
Elton Ledger (IRE) **(83)** *(AAScott)* 9-7 BRaymond (10) (lw: prom 5f) ................ nk.9
Mastamist *(RVoorspuy)* 9-0 JWilliams (11) (w'like: bit bkwd: a bhd) ............... 6.11
Rostands Hero (IRE) **(50)** *(HJCollingridge)* 9-0 NHowe (14) (bit bkwd: bhd fnl 3f) 6.11
Spanish Glory *(IABalding)* 8-9 RCochrane (9) (a bhd) .................................. nk.12
Peerage Prince **(79)** *(PatMitchell)* 9-4 ‡³SO'Gorman (12) (a bhd) .................... 10.13
Mansber (IRE) **(56)** *(PatMitchell)* 9-0 GDuffield (5) (plld hrd: a bhd) ............... 10.14

**11/10** First Century (IRE), **100/30** IREK(7/4—7/2), **13/2** Elton Ledger (IRE), **9/1** Will Soon, **16/1** Peerage Prince, Sebosan(12/1—20/1), **20/1** Spanish Glory(op 12/1), **33/1** Grand Fellow (IRE), Coniston Lake (IRE), Efra, **66/1** Ors. CSF £51.85, Tote £3.30: £1.90 £3.10 £5.80 (£23.80). Sheikh Mohammed (WEST ILSLEY) bred by Somerhall Bloodstock Ltd. 14 Rn
1m 32.9 (hand) (11.6)
SF—10/2/–/–/–/–

**349** BRIAN LIVESEY DECORATORS H'CAP (0-80) £2633.60 (£729.60: £348.80)
5f
3-45 (3-49)

Coppermill Lad **(48)** *(LJHolt)* 9-7-11 NAdams (2) (rdn over 3f out: hdwy over 1f out: r.o ins fnl f: fin 2nd, 2l: awrdd r) ........................... —1
265³ Plain Fact **(75)** (Fav) *(SirMarkPrescott)* 7-9-10 GDuffield (7) (lw: dwlt: hdwy 2f out: r.o ins fnl f: fin 3rd, s.h: plcd 2nd) ...................... 2
163 Barbezieux **(44)** (bl) *(TJNaughton)* 5-7-4 ‡³JFanning (10) (a.p: hrd rdn over 1f out: wknd ins fnl f: fin 4th, 5l: plcd 3rd) ...................... 3
43 Tauber **(63)** *(PatMitchell)* 8-8-9 ‡SO'Gorman (9) (chsd wnr 4f: fin 5th, 3½l: plcd 4th) ........................................................................... 4
87 Mitsubishi Video (IRE) **(79)** *(DrJDScargill)* 4-10-0 JWilliams (3) (nvr nr to chal) ¾.6
Restore **(58)** (bl) *(RVoorspuy)* 9-8-7 PaulEddery (8) (prom over 3f) ............. nk.7
294 Everset (FR) **(70)** *(WJMusson)* 4-9-5 RCochrane (6) (bhd fnl 2f) ............. 2½.8
Frimley Parkson **(44)** *(PHowling)* 8-7-7 JLowe (1) (bhd fnl 2f) ................... 2.9
Spitzabit **(50)** *(PatMitchell)* 8-7-6⁽⁶⁾ ‡⁷RTurner (5) (bhd fnl 2f) ............... 1½.10
Wanda **(65)** *(KRBurke)* 5-9-0 DHolland (4) (mde all: rdn out: fin 1st: disq: plcd last) ................................................................................... 0

LONG HANDICAP: Barbezieux 7-1, Frimley Parkson 7-6, Spitzabit 7-3.
*Stewards Enquiry: Wanda disq. (prohibited substance (procaine) in urine).*

**7/4** Plain Fact(op 7/2), **11/2** Wanda(9/2—7/1), **7/1** Tauber(5/1—8/1), **8/1** COPPERMILL LAD(op 5/1), **10/1** Barbezieux(8/1—12/1), **14/1** Frimley Parkson, Restore, Everset (FR), **25/1** Mitsubishi Video (IRE), **33/1** Spitzabit. CSF £42.09, CT £93.09. Tote £5.70: £1.60 £1.80 £1.40 (£21.50). Mr L. J. Holt (BASINGSTOKE) bred by Miss J. Samuel. 10 Rn
63.25 sec (6.25)
SF—35/30/56/2/7/23

**350** BOVRIL H'CAP (3-Y.O) (0-90) £2607.80 (£720.80: £343.40) 1¼m (AWT) 4-20 (4-21)

290★ Grog (IRE) **(80)** *(MRChannon)* 8-13 ‡⁵BDoyle (3) (lw: chsd ldr: rdn over 2f out: led nr fin) ............................................................... —1
256 Slight Risk **(71)** *(PAKelleway)* 8-9 GBardwell (5) (eyecover: b: led: hrd rdn fnl f: hdd nr fin) ........................................................................ hd.2
Elizabethan Air **(55)** *(ANLee)* 7-0 ‡⁷CHawksley (2) (hld up: one pce fnl 3f) ...... 10.3
281★ Eriny (USA) **(73)** (Fav) *(SGNorton)* 8-4 ‡⁷OPears (4) (hld up: hrd rdn over 3f out: one pce) ........................................................................ 1.4
Mr Ziegfeld (USA) **(83)** *(SirMarkPrescott)* 9-7 GDuffield (1) (lw: bhd fnl 5f) ....... 10.5
LONG HANDICAP: Elizabethan Air 6-13.

**5/4** Eriny (USA), **3/1** GROG (IRE)(op 2/1), **7/2** Mr Ziegfeld (USA), **11/2** Slight Risk, **40/1** Elizabethan Air. CSF £16.33, Tote £2.80: £1.80 £2.80 (£9.60). Mrs D. Hanson (UPPER LAMBOURN) bred by Michael P. Keane in Ireland. 5 Rn
2m 6.25 (3.25)
SF—21/16/–/–/–/–

**351** LEISURE PROJECTS H'CAP (0-80) £2422.00 (£672.00: £322.00)
7f (AWT)
4-50 (4-53)

Ain'tlifelikethat **(51)** (bl) *(TJNaughton)* 5-7-10 ‡³JFanning (1) (b: dwlt: gd hdwy over 1f out: led nr fin) ................................................. —1
209² Sally's Son **(80)** *(WAO'Gorman)* 6-9-9 ‡⁵EmmaO'Gorman (10) (hdwy over 2f out: ev ch wl ins fnl f: r.o wl) ................................................ hd.2
208² Sarum **(63)** (Jt-Fav) *(CPWildman)* 6-8-11 CRutter (4) (hdwy over 1f out: ev ch wl ins fnl f: r.o wl) ................................................................. hd.3

201* Invocation **(76)** (AMoore) 5-9-10 NAdams (11) (lw: led: hrd rdn over 1f out: hdd
nr fin) ............................................................... ¹/₂.4

245⁶ Gorytus Star **(54)** (Jt-Fav) (DHaydnJones) 6-7-11 ‡⁵RPrice (14) (chsd ldr: ev ch
ins fnl f: r.o) .................................................... nk.5

224⁵ Sareen Express (IRE) **(45)** (MrsJCDawe) 4-7-0 ‡⁷CHawksley (3) (nvr nr to chal)  3.6

Helawe **(80)** (bl) (SirMarkPrescott) 9-10-0 GDuffield (9) (bit bkwd: hdwy over 3f
out: one pce) ................................................... ¹/₂.7

253⁴ Zinbaq **(45)** (CJBenstead) 6-7-7 JLowe (13) (a.p: one pce fnl 2f) ............ 2.8

Concert Pitch **(50)** (BPalling) 13-7-7⁽⁵⁾ ‡⁵BDoyle (6) (bit bkwd: nvr nrr) ............ ¹/₂.9

208 Predictable **(66)** (MrsAKnight) 6-8-11 ‡³DBiggs (15) (lw: prom 5f) .......... 2.10

Anatroccolo **(46)** (v) (CAHorgan) 5-7-8⁽¹⁾ DaleGibson (2) (b: b.hind: prom over
3f) .......................................................... 3¹/₂.11

224* Kay's Dilemma (IRE) **(48)** (PAKelleway) 4-7-5 ‡⁵FNorton (5) (bhd fnl 3f) ......... 1.12

184 Verro (USA) **(45)** (bl) (JABennett) 5-7-7 GBardwell (8) (dwlt: a bhd) ............ 13

300⁴ Regal Tiger **(45)** (MrsJCDawe) 7-7-7 RFox (12) (a bhd) ................. 14

LONG HANDICAP: Zinbaq 7-4, Concert Pitch 7-4, Verro (USA) 6-8, Regal Tiger 6-11.

**4/1** Sarum(tchd 6/1), Gorytus Star(op 20/1), **9/2** Invocation, **7/1** Sally's Son(op 4/1), **8/1** Predictable, **9/1** Helawe(6/1—10/1), Kay's Dilemma (IRE)(12/1—8/1), **11/1** Zinbaq(6/1—12/1), **14/1** Sareen Express (IRE)(10/1—16/1), **20/1** AIN'TLIFELIKETHAT, **40/1** Ors. CSF £149.88, CT £623.88. Tote £14.80: £3.40 £3.00 £2.10 (£108.90). Mrs Marilyn Lipman (EPSOM) bred by Miss B. Galway-Greer. 14 Rn     1m 24.51 (0.51)
SF—27/53/40/51/23/3/44

T/Plpt: £194.20 (7.75 Tckts).                                                                    AK

## 276—WOLVERHAMPTON (L-H)

### Monday, April 6th [Soft becoming Heavy]

Going Allowance: Races 1 & 2. 0.70 sec; Rest. 1.00 ooo per fur (S)          Wind· almost nil

Stalls: high

**352**     TRILLIUM STKS (Mdn 2-Y.O) £2363.20 (£655.20: £313.60)     **5f**     2-30 (2-34)

231⁴ Luckifosome (PDEvans) 8-9 LDettori (1) (a.p: led appr fnl f: drvn out) .............. —1

231 Ukam's Lady (RHannon) 8-4 ‡⁵RPerham (6) (hmpd s: sn chsng ldrs: shkn up
over 1f out: r.o) .......................................... ³/₄.2

Heathyards Gem (RHollinshead) 8-9 WRyan (11) (lt-f: a.p: ev ch wl over 1f out:
unable qckn) ............................................... 1¹/₂.3

Silly Sally (WGMTurner) 8-4 ‡⁵TSprake (10) (neat: prom: rdn & no ex appr fnl f) . 1.4

Trentesimo (IRE) (Fav) (JBerry) 9-0 PatEddery (4) (neat: cmpt: bkwd: led tl hdd
& wknd appr fnl f) ........................................ ¹/₂.5

Finmental (IRE) (ABailey) 9-0 AMackay (2) (lt-f: bkwd: v.slowly away: styd on
appr fnl f: nvr nrr) ....................................... 4.6

Stay Great (WCarter) 9-0 AMunro (9) (lt-f: outpcd) ....................... hd.7

The Cut (MJohnston) 8-9 GDuffield (7) (small: bkwd: swvd lft s: sn prom: wknd
over 1f out) .............................................. 2.8

Burishki (GAPritchard-Gordon) 8-9 NCarlisle (5) (small: cmpt: bkwd: outpcd) ... 4.9

Easy Touch (MDIUsher) 8-9 CRutter (3) (lt: unf: s.s: swvd rt s: a bhd) ......... 1¹/₂.10

The Rover's (RonaldThompson) 9-0 RPElliott (8) (lengthy: outpcd: t.o) ......... 12.11

**2/1** Trentesimo (IRE)(5/4—5/2), **6/1** LUCKIFOSOME(op 3/1), **13/2** Ukam's Lady, **8/1** The Cut(op 5/1), Burishki(12/1—7/1), **11/1** Finmental (IRE)(5/1—12/1), **12/1** Heathyards Gem(25/1—10/1), **14/1** Stay Great, **25/1** Silly Sally, **33/1** Ors. CSF £40.28, Tote £4.90: £2.30 £2.40 £1.70 (£36.60). Mr P. D. Evans (WELSHPOOL) bred by Roy Ashford. 11 Rn                                                    65.5 sec (8.2)
SF—1/-/-/-/-/-/-

**353**     WALLFLOWER (S) STKS (3-Y.O) £2324.00 (£644.00: £308.00)     **7f**     3-00 (3-07)

Karamoja (NAGraham) 9-0 RCochrane (17) (w'like: lw: s.i.s: hdwy 3f out: rdn
to ld ins fnl f: r.o) ....................................... —1

Man of the Season (USA) **(59)** (Fav) (JAkehurst) 9-0 PatEddery (15) (bit bkwd:
hld up: hdwy to ld appr fnl f: hdd & no ex ins fnl f) .............. 3.2

189² Little Nod **(65)** (JWhite) 9-0 MRoberts (12) (a.p: 2nd st: led 4f out tl appr fnl f: sn
wknd) ..................................................... 12.3

276 Speed Oil **(55)** (RBastiman) 8-7 ‡⁷HBastiman (14) (b: a.p: 6th st: jnd ldrs 2f out:
sn rdn & wknd) ........................................... 1¹/₂.4

191 Simon Ellis (IRE) **(47)** (v) (DRLaing) 9-0 SWhitworth (9) (rdn along thrght: styd
on fnl f: nvr nrr) ......................................... 5.5

Spareathought (CNAllen) 8-2 ‡⁷GForster (3) (leggy: chsd ldrs over 4f) ......... 5.6

264 Profit Stream **(54)** (MWEasterby) 9-0 KDarley (4) (rdn ¹/₂-wy: no imp) ......... 6.7

278 My Moody Girl (IRE) **(31)** *(CRBarwell)* 8-9 JWilliams (7) (nvr nr to chal) ............ 2.8
Another Nut **(44)** *(PDEvans)* 8-9 LDettori (5) (prom: 3rd st: wknd 3f out) ......... s.h.9
Nun the Wiser (IRE) **(48)** *(BAMcMahon)* 8-9 MHills (16) (a bhd) ...................... ¹/₂.10
Gunmaker *(RJHolder)* 9-0 ADicks (13) (w'like: bkwd: s.i.s: a bhd) .................. ³/₄.11
Our John **(50)** *(RonaldThompson)* 9-0 DNicholls (2) (chsd ldrs: 5th st: wknd
    over 2f out) ................................................................. hd.12
Orchard Bay **(46)** *(DRTucker)* 9-1 NAdams (8) (m.n.s) .................................... hd.13
Morjinski Dancer *(RSimpson)* 8-4 ‡5ATucker (10) (w'like: lw: s.s: a bhd) ...... ³/₄.14
298 Palacegate Gold (IRE) **(63)** *(RJHodges)* 9-1 ‡5TSprake (11) (lw: prom: 4th st:
    rdn & wknd over 2f out) ................................................... s.h.15
123 Charmonix **(47)** *(GBlum)* 8-9 GDuffield (1) (a in rr: t.o) ............................ 7.16
276 Millefiori *(KSBridgwater)* 8-9 AProud (6) (led 3f: wknd qckly: t.o) ................ 7.17

**3/1** Man of the Season (USA), **7/2** Little Nod(2/1—4/1), **5/1** Speed Oil(op 10/1), **10/1** Profit Stream(7/1—12/1), KARAMOJA(8/1—12/1), **12/1** Spareathought(8/1—14/1), **16/1** Palacegate Gold (IRE)(op 8/1), **20/1** Our John, **25/1** Simon Ellis (IRE), Another Nut, Charmonix, Gunmaker, **33/1** Ors. CSF £38.46, Tote £5.40: £4.20 £2.80 £2.10 (£28.80). Mr Paul G. Jacobs (NEWMARKET) bred by Mrs M. H. Hunter. 17 Rn; Bt in 7,000 gns
                                                                          1m 33.6 (9.3)
                                                                          SF—34/25/–/–/–/–

**354**    HYACINTH H'CAP (0-90) £2500.40 (£694.40: £333.20)    1¹/₂m 70y    3-30 (3-35)
                    (Weights raised 2 lb)

301 **Al Mutahm (USA) (80)** (Jt-Fav) *(JABOld)* 4–9-4 LDettori (11) (lw: hld up: hdwy
    4f out: led on bit over 2f out: sn clr: eased fnl f) ..................... —1
    Belafonte **(65)** *(RJHolder)* 5–8-0 ‡5ATucker (8) (hdwy ent st: ev ch appr fnl f: no
    ch w wnr) ................................................................ 2¹/₂.2
222★ Maamur (USA) **(71)** (Jt-Fav) *(DBurchell)* 4–8-9 RCochrane (2) (prom: 2nd st:
    one pce fnl 2f) ........................................................... 1¹/₂.3
299³ Famous Beauty **(57)** *(RHollinshead)* 5–7-8⁽⁴⁾ ‡7AGarth (13) (hdwy & 3rd st: led
    over 2f out: sn hdd: one pce) ............................................ 1.4
    Saint Ciel (USA) **(75)** *(FJordan)* 4–8-13 WNewnes (1) (lw: hdwy fnl 2f: nrst fin) .. 8.5
    Franciscan **(55)** *(BPreece)* 5–7-9⁽²⁾ JLowe (10) (lw: chsd ldrs: 7th st: wknd over
    2f out) .................................................................. s.h.6
    Hillzah (USA) **(86)** *(RBastiman)* 4–9-3 ‡7HBastiman (9) (s.i.s: nvr nr to chal) ..... nk.7
    One for the Pot **(66)** *(MPNaughton)* 7–8-6 AMunro (4) (a bhd) ..................... 1¹/₂.8
240 Jimlil **(80)** *(BPalling)* 4–9-4 RHills (5) (led 6f out tl over 2f out: sn wknd) ......... 6.9
155 Plectrum **(60)** *(JLSpearing)* 4–7-12 RFox (12) (prom tl 6th & wkng st) ........... 2¹/₂.10
229 Vallance **(70)** *(PWHarris)* 4–8-8 PaulEddery (7) (a bhd) ............................ 1¹/₂.11
214⁴ Shaffaaf (USA) **(61)** *(PDEvans)* 4–7-8⁽²⁾ ‡5FNorton (3) (prom: 5th st: wknd over
    2f out) .................................................................. ¹/₂.12
    Auvillar (USA) **(55)** (v) *(OO'Neill)* 4–7-7 LCharnock (14) (lw: led over 6f: sn lost
    tch: t.o) ................................................................. dist.13
    Almoojid **(64)** *(RJBaker)* 6–8-4 AMcGlone (6) (a bhd: t.o fr ¹/₂-wy) ............... dist.14
    LONG HANDICAP: Famous Beauty 7-3, Franciscan 7-5, Auvillar (USA) 6-13.

**11/4** Maamur (USA), AL MUTAHM (USA), **5/1** One for the Pot, **12/1** Auvillar (USA)(op 20/1), **16/1** Jimlil(op 10/1), Saint Ciel (USA)(op 10/1), Famous Beauty, Shaffaaf (USA), Vallance(op 10/1), Belafonte, **25/1** Hillzah (USA), **33/1** Plectrum, **50/1** Franciscan, **66/1** Almoojid. CSF £43.15, CT £124.01. Tote £3.50: £1.90 £4.10 £1.90 (£21.30). Mr W. E. Sturt (WROUGHTON) bred by John Valentine and Mary Bradley in USA. 14 Rn
                                                                          2m 55.5 (23.8)

**355**    CROCUS CLAIMING STKS (3-Y.O) £2480.80 (£688.80: £330.40)    1m 200y    4-00 (4-05)

281² **Firefighter (57)** *(RHollinshead)* 8-12 WRyan (12) (hdwy & 4th st: led over 2f
    out: all out) ............................................................. —1
107² Ready to Draw (IRE) **(63)** *(RonaldThompson)* 8-6 RPElliott (11) (prom: 5th st:
    jnd wnr over 2f out: hrd rdn & nt qckn wl ins fnl f) .................... 1.2
    High Post **(49)** *(DMarks)* 7-13 JLowe (9) (hdwy over 2f out: nvr nrr) ............. 8.3
    Holy Wanderer (USA) **(59)** *(DWPArbuthnot)* 7-13⁽⁵⁾ ‡5RPrice (2) (hdwy 3f out:
    styd on ins fnl f) ........................................................ ³/₄.4
264 Jiggerak **(63)** (v) *(SGNorton)* 7-10 ‡5SMaloney (10) (2nd st: led over 3f out tl
    over 2f out: sn wknd) .................................................... 4.5
    Leigh Crofter **(75)** *(RJHolder)* 8-10 NAdams (7) (hdwy & 6th st: rdn 3f out: sn
    btn) ..................................................................... 8.6
    Sabzy *(PDEvans)* 7-9 RFox (15) (w'like: nvr nrr) ...................................... 10.7
    Elsa **(43)** *(RJHolder)* 7-12 ‡7SDrowne (14) (nvr plcd to chal) ..................... hd.8
278★ Rocky Bay **(53)** (Fav) *(DHaydnJones)* 8-1 DHolland (4) (led tl hdd over 3f out:
    sn wknd) ................................................................. 1.9
    Fly for Gold (IRE) *(DWPArbuthnot)* 8-4 MRoberts (13) (b.hind: a in rr) ........... 5.10
    Expansionist *(AHide)* 8-6 PaulEddery (6) (a bhd) ................................... 6.11

256 Miss Pin Up **(46)** (bl) *(PatMitchell)* 8-0⁽²⁾ AMunro (1) (bhd fr ½-wy: t.o) .......... nk.**12**
    Have a Nightcap **(63)** *(MAJarvis)* 8-13 BRaymond (3) (prom tl 7th & wkng st) 1½.**13**
278³ Nigelschinapalace (bl) *(MissSJWilton)* 7-9⁽¹⁾ ‡5FNorton (5) (sn prom: 3rd st:
                     wknd over 3f out: t.o) .............................................. 2½.**14**
    Tender Look (IRE) *(ANLee)* 7-6 ‡3JFanning (16) (b: prom 4f: sn wknd: t.o) ..... 20.**15**
    Magnetic Prince **(40)** *(GBlum)* 7-6 ‡7CHawksley (8) (bit bkwd: a bhd: t.o) ........ 1.**16**
           *Stewards Enquiry: Elliott suspended 15-18/4/92 (excessive use of whip).*

**7/2** Rocky Bay, **11/2** FIREFIGHTER(7/2—6/1), **13/2** Have a Nightcap, **7/1** Leigh Crofter, **10/1** Jiggerak, Ready to Draw (IRE)(op 6/1), Miss Pin Up(op 6/1), Nigelschinapalace, **20/1** Holy Wanderer (USA), **25/1** Fly for Gold (IRE), Expansionist, **33/1** Sabzy, Tender Look (IRE), High Post, **50/1** Ors. CSF £55.64, Tote £6.40: £2.50 £2.80 £15.30 (£8.60). Mrs B. Facchino (UPPER LONGDON) bred by Sir Stephen Hastings. 16 Rn     2m 4.6 (16.1)

---

**356**      BLUEBELL STKS (3-Y.O.F) £2206.40 (£610.40: £291.20)    **1m**      4-30 (4-32)

    **Rockawhile (IRE)** **(Fav)** *(HRACecil)* 8-11 PatEddery (9) (rangy: scope: a.p: led
           ent st: clr over 1f out: v.easily) .................................................... —**1**
    Flourishing (IRE) **(94)** *(GWragg)* 8-13 ‡5FNorton (8) (hdwy & 3rd st: chsd wnr fnl
           2f: no imp) .................................................................................... 5.**2**
    Hymn Book (IRE) *(MRStoute)* 8-11 WRSwinburn (5) (effrt over 2f out: nvr plcd
           to chal) ................................................................................... 3½.**3**
302⁴ Humour (IRE) *(CFWall)* 8-11 NDay (10) (4th st: wknd over 2f out) ............... 2.**4**
    Eleckydo *(RJHodges)* 8-6 ‡TSprake (7) (swtg: bkwd: chsd ldrs 5f: sn outpcd) . 4.**5**
    Flute (USA) *(CEBrittain)* 8-11 MRoberts (3) (lw: dwlt: nvr nr to chal) .......... 20.**6**
    Briginski **(33)** *(KRBurke)* 8-11 DHolland (6) (led tl rn wd & hdd ent st: rdn 3f out:
           sn wknd) ................................................................................. ½.**7**
    Princess Dechtra (IRE) *(RHollinshead)* 8-11 LDettori (4) (6th st: wknd over 3f
           out) .......................................................................................... ½.**8**
    Hot Sound *(BWLunness)* 8-11 JLowe (1) (scope: s.s. a bhd: t.o) ...................... 26.**9**
    Alizarin *(BCMorgan)* 8-11 GDuffield (2) (w'like: bkwd: prom: 5th st: sn lost pl:
           t.o) ........................................................................................ dist.**10**

**1/2** ROCKAWHILE (IRE)(tchd 4/5), **9/2** Hymn Book (IRE)(6/1—4/1), **6/1** Flourishing (IRE)(op 7/2), **8/1** Flute (USA), **14/1** Princess Dechtra (IRE), **16/1** Humour (IRE), **100/1** Briginski, **200/1** Eleckydo, **400/1** Ors. CSF £4.87, Tote £1.40: £1.10 £2.70 £1.20 (£2.40). Mr L. Marinopoulos (NEWMARKET) bred by Swettenham Stud in Ireland. 10 Rn     1m 54.6 (17.3)

---

**357**      DAFFODIL H'CAP (0-70) £2343.60 (£649.60: £310.80)    **5f**      5-00 (5-02)
                                (Weights raised 2 lb)
279⁶ **No Quarter Given (64)** *(PSFelgate)* 7-9-10 MRoberts (15) (chsd ldrs: rdn 2f
           out: kpt on to ld wl ins fnl f) ....................................................... —**1**
279⋆ Penny Hasset **(51)** **(Fav)** *(MWEasterby)* 4-8-11 TLucas (7) (a.p: rdn to ld ins fnl
           f: sn hdd & nt qckn) ................................................................. 1.**2**
   351 Verro (USA) **(39)** (bl) *(JABennett)* 5-7-13 DHolland (12) (hdwy over 1f out: fin
           wl) ........................................................................................ 1½.**3**
300⋆ Rushanes **(60)** *(TCasey)* 5-9-1 ‡5FNorton (5) (lw: a.p: rdn over 2f out: ev ch
           appr fnl f: unable qckn) ................................................................ 1.**4**
245⋆ Educated Pet **(46)** *(MJohnston)* 3-7-8 NAdams (6) (lw: w ldrs: led ½-wy tl ins
           fnl f) ...................................................................................... 1½.**5**
    Iron King **(62)** *(JLSpearing)* 6-9-8 LDettori (8) (bit bkwd: hdwy over 1f out: nt
           pce to chal) .............................................................................. ½.**6**
276⁶ Injaka Boy **(50)** (v) *(KWhite)* 3-7-5 ‡7AGarth (4) (lw: effrt appr fnl f: nvr nrr) ...... 1½.**7**
247³ It's Only Money **(64)** *(THCaldwell)* 3-8-5 ‡7JWeaver (1) (chsd ldrs: no hdwy fnl f) 1.**8**
    Lucy Dancer (IRE) **(57)** *(CGCox)* 4-9-3 AClark (5) (spd over 3f) ........................ s.h.**9**
    Stocktina **(44)** *(RJHodges)* 5-7-13 ‡5TSprake (9) (swtg: led to ½-wy: wknd wl
           over 1f out) .............................................................................. nk.**10**
    Fay Eden (IRE) **(60)** *(RJHodges)* 4-8-13 ‡7SDrowne (11) (bit bkwd: bhd fnl 2f) 3.**11**
    Tina Meena Lisa **(47)** *(EHOwenjun)* 3-7-9⁽²⁾ JLowe (2) (n.d) .......................... 1.**12**
279 Factuelle **(51)** *(DRTucker)* 5-8-11 GBardwell (16) (spd to ½-wy: sn lost pl) ..... 7.**13**
279 R a Express **(44)** *(BAMcMahon)* 7-8-4 NCarlisle (14) (n.d) ......................... hd.**14**
13¹⁵ Ever so Lonely **(70)** *(ABailey)* 3-9-4 GCarter (13) (chsd ldrs 3f: sn lost pl) ..... hd.**15**
   351 Regal Tiger **(35)** (bl) *(MrsJCDawe)* 7-7-9 RFox (10) (outpcd) ...................... nk.**16**
           LONG HANDICAP: Tina Meena Lisa 7-5.

**7/2** Penny Hasset, **9/2** NO QUARTER GIVEN, Rushanes, **7/1** Educated Pet, **10/1** Stocktina, **12/1** R a Express, **14/1** It's Only Money, Iron King, **20/1** Fay Eden (IRE), Ever so Lonely, Factuelle, **33/1** Verro (USA), Injaka Boy, Regal Tiger, **50/1** Lucy Dancer (IRE), **100/1** Tina Meena Lisa. CSF £20.02, CT £442.14. Tote £5.50: £1.90 £1.50 £2.30 £1.70 (19.50). Mr P. S. Felgate (MELTON MOWBRAY) bred by Sean Madigan. 16 Rn   64.6 sec (7.3)
                                                SF—64/47/29/41/14/40

T/Plpt: £9.30 (292.3 Tckts).                                               IM

## PONTEFRACT (L-H)
### Tuesday, April 7th [Good to soft, Soft patches]
Going Allowance: 5f-8f: 0.90 sec (S); rest: 0.60 sec per fur (Y)　　　　　Wind: almost nil

Stalls: low

**358**　　　BARBICAN H'CAP (0-70) £2931.00 (£816.00: £393.00)　　**1¼m 6y**　　2-45 (2-47)

　　　**Katy's Lad (57)** (BAMcMahon) 5-9-1 TQuinn (1) (lw: mde all: qcknd clr ent st: eased nr fin) .......................................................................................................... —1
225⁵ Supertop (46) (PWHarris) 4-8-4 PaulEddery (17) (lw: a.p: chsd wnr over 2f out: no imp) ........................................................................................................ 2½.2
　　　Taylors Prince (56) (HJCollingridge) 5-8-7 ‡7CHawksley (5) (in tch: hdwy 3f out: sn rdn & one pce) ........................................................................................ 7.3
277² Royal Acclaim (49) (v) (JMBradley) 7-8-0 ‡7MichaelBradley (12) (bhd: hdwy ½-wy: styd on fnl 3f: nvr nrr) ................................................................. 5.4
331* Sharp Top (46) (Fav) (MJRyan) 4-8-4 (5x) WCarson (15) (lw: in tch: effrt 4f out: no imp) ................................................................................................... 1½.5
　　　Floating Line (60) (PWigham) 4-9-4 MWigham (16) (bit bkwd: chsd ldrs tl wknd appr st) ..................................................................................................... 1½.6
　41 Shamshom Al Arab (IRE) (45) (WCarter) 4-8-3 AMunro (10) (lw: hdwy 4f out: rdn & no imp) .................................................................................. 1.7
　　　Boogy Lady (IRE) (46) (ICampbell) 4-8-4 AMackay (8) (styd on fnl 3f: nvr nr to chal) ......................................................................................................... hd.8
250² Great Impostor (51) (RJHodges) 4-8-9 MRoberts (4) (drvn along 4f out: nvr trbld ldrs) ............................................................................................. 2½.9
277⁶ Sunset Reins Free (47) (v) (EJAlston) 7-8-5⁽¹⁾ KFallon (14) (lw: hdwy on outside ½-wy: rdn & btn 2f out) ....................................................... 1½.10
　　　Bustino Bay (43) (DShaw) 4-8-1⁽³⁾ GCarter (3) (bit bkwd: chsd ldrs tl grad wknd fnl 3f) ....................................................................................................... 4.11
　　　Enchanted Flyer (41) (TWDonnelly) 5-7-8⁽²⁾ ‡5FNorton (13) (bkwd: bhd & drvn along 4f out: n.d) ................................................................... 3.12
206* Riviera Rainbow (57) (DRCElsworth) 4-9-1 JWilliams (19) (lw: a bhd) .......... 2.13
　　　Sally Forth (60) (JRBostock) 6-8-13 ‡5RPrice (2) (bit bkwd: in tch tl wknd over 3f out) ................................................................................................................ 1.14
　　　Ackers Wood (57) (KRBurke) 4-9-1 AShoults (4) (prom 6f) ....................................... nk.15
　　　Hypnotist (58) (WBentley) 5-8-13 ‡3JFanning (6) (chsd wnr tl wknd 3f out) ..... ½.16
225 Mingus (USA) (69) (MrsJRRamsden) 5-9-13 TLucas (11) (n.d) ...................... 1½.17
137 Salman (USA) (49) (SGNorton) 6-8-0 ‡7OPears (9) (lw: bhd: hdwy on outside 4f out: wknd over 2f out) ..................................................................................... 18
315⁴ Luks Akura (44) (v) (MJohnston) 4-8-2 RPElliott (18) (racd wd: prom 6f) ........ 19

2/1 Sharp Top, 7/1 Riviera Rainbow, KATY'S LAD, 15/2 Supertop, 10/1 Sunset Reins Free, Great Impostor, 12/1 Shamshom Al Arab (IRE), 14/1 Royal Acclaim, Salman (USA), 20/1 Mingus (USA)(op 12/1), 25/1 Taylors Prince, Luks Akura, Boogy Lady (IRE), Hypnotist, 33/1 Ackers Wood, Bustino Bay, 50/1 Ors. CSF £60.94, CT £1,182.18. Tote £8.80: £1.60 £3.40 £5.30 £3.00 (£64.00). Mr J. W. Butler (TAMWORTH) bred by Peter Doyle.
19 Rn　　　　　　　　　　　　　　　　　　　　　　　　　　　　2m 19.9 (11.6)
　　　　　　　　　　　　　　　　　　　　　　　　　　　　SF—45/29/11/–/–/–

**359**　　　BENTLEY MEMORIAL (S) H'CAP (0-60) £2559.20 (£711.20: £341.60)　　**6f**　　3-15 (3-19)

　221 **Twilight Falls (41)** (Fav) (MJCamacho) 7-8-11 NConnorton (7) (chsd ldrs: led wl over 1f out: rdn & r.o wl) .................................................................. —1
　325 Chaplins Club (USA) (48) (bl) (DWChapman) 12-9-4 KDarley (5) (bhd: hdwy ½-wy: r.o: no ch w wnr) ......................................................................... 3.2
207³ Count Me Out (43) (bl) (JPearce) 7-8-8 ‡5RPrice (6) (hdwy over 2f out: styd on wl: nrst fin) .............................................................................................. 1.3
325⁵ Minizen Music (IRE) (42) (MBrittain) 4-8-12 JLowe (11) (lw: cl up: led over 2f out tl wl over 1f out: sn btn) ....................................................................... 2½.4
326³ Miss Knight (47) (RBastiman) 5-9-3 WCarson (14) (lw: hdwy 2f out: styd on wl) hd.5
264⁴ Station Express (IRE) (38) (BEllison) 4-7-13⁽¹⁾ ‡7JWeaver (1) (lw: broke wl: sn outpcd: hdwy u.p 2f out: nvr able to chal) ........................................... s.h.6
　　　Mystic Panther (49) (bl) (RJHolder) 4-9-5 ADicks (3) (hdwy ½-wy: swtchd & chsd ldrs appr fnl f: nt qckn) ........................................................... 1.7
279 Ballad Dancer (56) (EJAlston) 7-9-12 KFallon (12) (chsd ldrs over 4f) ............. 1½.8
275² Golden Proposal (53) (MBell) 3-8-10 MHills (17) (hdwy 4f out) ........................ 4.9
　　　Super Ted (37) (WJMusson) 5-8-7 JHBrown (15) (b: bhd tl sme late hdwy) .. nk.10
　　　Blazing Pearl (35) (JLHarris) 4-8-5 PaulEddery (2) (sn outpcd & bhd: sme late hdwy) ......................................................................................................... 2.11

221[6] Erris Express (58) *(KTIvory)* 7-10-0 MWigham (10) (b: hmpd after s: nvr nr to chal) ............................................................. 1½.**12**
264 Foxes Diamond (40) *(BEllison)* 4-8-5 ‡5ATucker (13) (outpcd fr ½-wy) ... 2.**13**
Cashtal Queen (56) *(JBerry)* 3-8-13 LPiggott (9) (b: lw: led tl hdd over 2f out: sn wknd) ............................................................. 1½.**14**
277 Petropower (IRE) (40) *(MO'Neill)* 4-8-10 AMackay (18) (spd over 3f: wknd qckly) **15**
56 Summer Sands (43) *(JLHarris)* 4-8-13 DHolland (8) (b: lost tch fr ½-wy) ........... **16**
Miss Pinocchio (41) *(RRLamb)* 5-8-6 ‡5SMaloney (16) (lw: a bhd) .................. **17**
The Right Time (53) (bl) *(JParkes)* 7-8-9 NCarlisle (4) (bit bkwd: in tch: hdwy ½-wy: wknd wl over 1f out) ............................................. **18**

**5/2** TWILIGHT FALLS(op 5/1), **6/1** Station Express (IRE), **7/1** Miss Knight, **17/2** Chaplins Club (USA)(14/1—7/1), **9/1** Cashtal Queen, **10/1** Ballad Dancer(8/1—12/1), **11/1** Count Me Out, Golden Proposal(op 7/1), **12/1** Minizen Music (IRE), The Right Time, **14/1** Erris Express, **20/1** Mystic Panther, Petropower (IRE), Summer Sands, **25/1** Blazing Pearl, **33/1** Ors. CSF £28.46, CT £210.14. Tote £4.50: £1.40 £3.30 £3.80 £2.90 (£40.50).
Mr Clifford Smith (MALTON) bred by Ballinacurra Stud. 18 Rn; Bt in 4,800 gns
1m 22.9 (8.9)
SF—27/22/8/2/6/–

**360** HEY GROUP TROPHY (Stks) £3557.50 (£1060.00: £505.00: £227.50)
1¼m 6y
3-45 (3-46)

Torchon (109) *(Fav) (GWragg)* 4-9-0 WRSwinburn (3) (lw: a:p: effrt 3f out: hrd rdn to ld ins fnl f: sn hdd: lft in ld nr fin) ................................. —**1**
Starlight Flyer *(MMoubarak)* 5-8-8 TQuinn (2) (cl up tl outpcd 3f out: hdwy u.p to ld ins fnl f: veered rt & hdd nr fin) ................................. 1.**2**
Kansk (94) *(JHMGosden)* 4-8-11 RCochrane (1) (led tl hdd & no ex ins fnl f) . 1½.**3**
Swift Sword (97) *(MrsGRReveley)* 4-8-8 KDarley (5) (in tch tl outpcd over 3f out: hdwy over 1f out: nvr able to chal) ............................ 1½.**4**

**5/6** TORCHON, **4/1** Kansk(op 5/2), Starlight Flyer, **6/1** Swift Sword. CSF £4.14, Tote £1.90 (£3.10). Oir Robin McAlpine (NEWMARKET) bred by Sir Robin McAlpine. 4 Rn
2m 21.5 (13.2)
SF—28/20/20/14

**361** BEAST FAIR STKS (Mdn 2-Y.O) £2427.00 (£672.00: £321.00) **5f** 4-15 (4-16)

266[2] **Isotonic** *(GMMoore)* 8-9 KFallon (4) (lw: cl up: led ½-wy: edgd rt fnl 2f: r.o wl) . —**1**
226[2] Nominator *(Fav) (RHollinshead)* 9-0 WCarson (10) (lw: a cl up: disp ld over 1f out: btn whn sltly hmpd ins fnl f) ............................... 3½.**2**
Reasons for Love (IRE) *(JJO'Neill)* 8-9 AMunro (5) (lt-f: cl up tl outpcd & lost pl ½-wy: hdwy ins fnl f: fin wl) ........................... 3.**3**
Irish Roots (IRE) *(CTinkler)* 9-0 MBirch (3) (lt-f: a chsng ldrs: nt qckn ins fnl f) ... ½.**4**
226[5] Duke of Dreams *(MrsGRReveley)* 9-0 KDarley (2) (lw: sn pushed along: hdwy ½-wy: nt qckn appr fnl f) ........................... s.h.**5**
Peak Fitness *(JAGlover)* 9-0 DNicholls (1) (unf: s.i.s: nvr nr ldrs) .................. 10.**6**
Surprise Partner *(MJohnston)* 9-0 TQuinn (9) (leggy: scope: prom: sn pushed along: wknd 2f out) ........................... hd.**7**
Mrs Dawson *(DrJDScargill)* 8-9 RCochrane (11) (lt-f: unf: s.s: nt rcvr) ............... hd.**8**
Border Dream *(WGMTurner)* 8-9 ‡5TSprake (6) (wl grwn: lengthy: scope: nvr wnt pce) ........................... ¾.**9**
Latin Leader *(MrsJRRamsden)* 9-0 TLucas (7) (w'like: scope: bit bkwd: prom early: lost tch fr ½-wy) ........................... 2½.**10**
Tom Piper *(JBerry)* 9-0 LPiggott (8) (lt-f: led to ½-wy: sn wknd: eased fnl f) ... 1.**11**

**5/2** Nominator(op 5/4), **4/1** Tom Piper, **5/1** Latin Leader, **7/1** Duke of Dreams, Surprise Partner(14/1—16/1), ISOTONIC, **8/1** Reasons for Love (IRE), **14/1** Mrs Dawson, **20/1** Irish Roots (IRE), Peak Fitness, **50/1** Border Dream. CSF £25.93, Tote £6.80: £1.60 £1.60 £2.30 (£6.20). Mr J. Burgess (MIDDLEHAM) bred by Mrs S. M. Sands and M. Yiapatos. 11 Rn
69.2 sec (7.7)
SF—31/22/5/8/7/–

**362** LEVY BOARD H'CAP (0-75) £3321.50 (£924.00: £444.50) **2m 1f 22y** 4-45 (4-46)

Dodger Dickins (39) *(RHollinshead)* 5-7-7 NCarlisle (2) (bhd: hdwy 3f out: r.o wl to ld wl ins fnl f) ........................... —**1**
125 Carefree Times (50) *(JNorton)* 5-7-13 ‡5FNorton (4) (a.p: effrt 4f out: ev ch over 2f out: wknd fnl f) ........................... nk.**2**
Tactical Mission (IRE) (68) *(JAkehurst)* 4-9-4 TQuinn (5) (cl up: led ½-wy tl over 1f out: one pce) ........................... 3.**3**
Yorkshire Holly (58) *(MAvison)* 9-8-12 MBirch (11) (a cl up: chal over 4f out: outpcd fnl 2f) ........................... 2½.**4**
Mandalay Prince (40) *(TKersey)* 8-7-8[(1)] DaleGibson (10) (drvn along 4f out: styd on: no imp) ........................... 2½.**5**

Topcliffe **(43)** (v) *(MrsVAAconley)* 5–7-11[(1)] PBurke (6) (a in tch: hdwy 4f out: one pce fnl 2f) ............................................. hd.6

291★ Dari Sound (IRE) **(52)** *(JGFitzGerald)* 4–8-2 GDuffield (1) (in tch: effrt 4f out: ev ch over 2f out: sn rdn & btn) ............................. ¹⁄₂.7

Marlin Dancer **(39)** *(MissBSanders)* 7–7-7 GBardwell (14) (effrt on outside 6f out: sn rdn & btn) ............................................ 25.8

131 Merchant of Venice **(52)** *(MHTompkins)* 4–8-2 AMackay (9) (in tch: drvn along over 4f out: sn btn) ........................... 1¹⁄₂.9

Bonanza **(39)** *(MrsGRReveley)* 5–7-7 JLowe (16) (drvn along ¹⁄₂-wy: sn lost tch) 7.10

331 Sailor Boy **(61)** *(ASReid)* 6–9-1 BCrossley (15) (bhd & rdn after 6f: n.d) ....... 7.11

234 Cabochon **(74)** (Fav) *(DMorley)* 5–10-0 WCarson (13) (prom tl wknd over 4f out) 12

Take One **(55)** *(RRLamb)* 6–8-4 ‡⁵SMaloney (12) (lost tch fnl 6f) ..................... 13

Daleside **(60)** (bl) *(TFairhurst)* 4–8-7 ‡³JFanning (17) (n.d) ...................... 14

244 Winoski **(69)** *(DLWilliams)* 4–9-5 WRyan (18) (a outpcd & bhd) ................. 15

271⁶ Hear a Nightingale **(52)** *(RJHodges)* 5–8-6 MRoberts (20) (a bhd: t:o) .......... 16

288★ Peak District **(65)** *(KSBridgwater)* 6–9-0 ‡⁵ATucker (8) (prom to ¹⁄₂-wy: sn wknd: t:o) ....................................................... 17

Knight of Honour **(60)** (v) *(MDods)* 4–8-10 KFallon (7) (t:o) ...................... nk.9 ... 18

Military Honour **(55)** (bl) *(MWEasterby)* 7–8-9 TLucas (12) (t.o fnl 4f) ......... 19

Ragtime **(43)** *(ASReid)* 5–7-4[(4)] ‡⁷PMcCabe (3) (sddle slipped: led to ¹⁄₂-wy: p.u 3f out) ...................................................... 0

LONG HANDICAP: Dodger Dickins 7-4, Mandalay Prince 7-6, Marlin Dancer 7-6, Bonanza 7-6, Ragtime 7-6.

**11/2** Cabochon, **13/2** Marlin Dancer, **8/1** Dari Sound (IRE), Merchant of Venice, **10/1** DODGER DICKINS, Bonanza, Peak District, **11/1** Tactical Mission (IRE), **14/1** Topcliffe, **16/1** Hear a Nightingale, Yorkshire Holly, **20/1** Military Honour, Ragtime, **25/1** Carefree Times, Sailor Boy, Winoski, **33/1** Ors. CSF £222.01, CF £2,543.80. Tote £7.60: £1.50 £6.10 £5.20 £2.70 (£213.90). Dickins Ltd (UPPER LONGDON) bred by J. F. O'Malley. 20 Rn                                                                       4m 6 (26)

---

**363**    SPRING STKS (Mdn 3-Y.O) £2658.00 (£738.00: £354.00)    **6f**    5-15 (5-18)

235 **The Old Chapel (59)** *(BAMcMahon)* 9-0 TQuinn (8) (w ldr: led 2f out: sn qcknd clr: all out) ................................................ —1

Scarlatine (IRE) (Fav) *(JHMGosden)* 8-9 RCochrane (6) (lw: a chsng ldrs: rdn 2f out: styd on strly nr fin) ........................... ³⁄₄.2

Rural Lad *(MrsJRRamsden)* 9-0 TLucas (16) (scope: bhd: stdy hdwy ent st: r.o strly) ....................................................... 4.3

252⁴ Sartigila *(JWPayne)* 8-9 AMunro (18) (a chsng ldrs: nt qckn fnl 2f) .............. 5.4

Dandy Desire *(BCMorgan)* 9-0 JLowe (7) (bhd tl hdwy over 1f out: r.o) ............. 2.5

Sammy Slew (USA) *(SGNorton)* 9-0 DNicholls (11) (chsd ldrs: hmpd appr st: styd on one pce) ................................................ 2.6

Yazaly (USA) *(AAScott)* 9-0 WRSwinburn (14) (bit bkwd: a chsng ldrs: rdn 2f out: no hdwy) ................................................. ³⁄₄.7

Tagetes *(JPearce)* 8-4 ‡⁵RPrice (1) (led 4f: sn wknd) ...................... 2.8

Don't Worry (IRE) **(57)** *(MHTompkins)* 9-0 DaleGibson (5) (bhd tl styd on fnl 2f) nk.9

Hester Stanhope *(PWHarris)* 8-9 WNewnes (4) (nvr bttr than mid div) ........ 1¹⁄₂.10

247² Ipsilante (ASReid) 8-9 BCrossley (3) (chsd ldrs 4f: sn wknd) .................. 2.11

Al-Dahlawia (IRE) *(GAPritchard-Gordon)* 8-9 GCarter (9) (nvr trbld ldrs) ....... 3¹⁄₂.12

289² Pridian (IRE) *(GWragg)* 9-0 MRoberts (12) (lw: lost tch fr ¹⁄₂-wy) ............ 7.13

Nest *(LordHuntingdon)* 8-9 LDettori (17) (bit bkwd: bhd fr ¹⁄₂-wy) ........... 1¹⁄₂.14

Mash the Tea (IRE) *(HJCollingridge)* 9-0 VSmith (10) (str: cmpt: bit bkwd: s.i.s: a bhd) ....................................................... 1¹⁄₂.15

Bright Paragon (IRE) *(BRichmond)* 8-7 ‡⁷SWilliams (13) (rangy: scope: bit bkwd: in tch over 3f: sn wknd) ....................... 8.16

Dancing Gem *(JMBradley)* 8-9 ‡⁵ATucker (15) (leggy: bkwd: s.i.s: a bhd) ...... 6.17

**5/4** Scarlatine (IRE), **9/2** Pridian (IRE), **11/2** Yazaly (USA)(4/1—6/1), **10/1** Nest, **12/1** THE OLD CHAPEL(op 33/1), Sammy Slew (USA), **14/1** Ipsilante, **16/1** Hester Stanhope, **20/1** Sartigila, Tagetes, **25/1** Don't Worry (IRE), **33/1** Rural Lad, **50/1** Ors. CSF £29.07, Tote £19.10: £2.50 £1.60 £18.50 (£42.10). R. A. Holdings Ltd (TAMWORTH) bred by Roldvale Ltd. 17 Rn                                           1m 25.5 (11.5)

---

**364**    HARDWICK H'CAP (0-70) £2973.00 (£828.00: £399.00)    **1m 4y**    5-45 (5-49)

204⁴ **Mossy Rose (56)** *(LordHuntingdon)* 6–9-0 JReid (8) (chsd ldrs: led over 2f out: all out) .................................................. —1

315 Errema **(47)** *(CTinkler)* 7–8-5 KDarley (16) (a.p: effrt 2f out: r.o u.p: jst failed) .. hd.2

277⁵ Doulab's Image **(68)** (bl) *(JAGlover)* 5–9-5 ‡⁷SWilliams (6) (trckd ldrs: effrt 2f out: styd on: nt pce to chal) ..................... 1¹⁄₂.3

Veloce (IRE) **(56)** *(MO'Neill)* 4–9-0 LDettori (15) (in tch: hdwy 3f out: styd on wl) ³⁄₄.4

277 Execution Only (IRE) **(53)** (v) *(JWWatts)* 4–8-11 WRSwinburn (3) (mid div & rdn ¹⁄₂-wy: hdwy 2f out: styd on wl) ......................... s.h.5

293³ Golden Chip (IRE) **(66)** *(APStringer)* 4–9-10 JFortune (17) (hld up & bhd tl hdwy over 2f out: r.o) ........................................................ 1¹/₂.6
277⁴ Friendlypersuasion (IRE) **(46)** *(RHollinshead)* 4–8-4⁽¹⁾ WRyan (1) (mid div: nt clr run appr st: r.o appr fnl f) ................... 1¹/₂.7
293 Sally Fay (IRE) **(58)** *(TKersey)* 4–9-2 DNichols (9) (lw: effrt 3f out: styd on: no imp) ................................ 1.8
269³ The Devil's Music **(42)** *(MrsJRRamsden)* 8–8-0 AMunro (19) (lw: a.p: effrt over 2f out: rdn & no imp) .................... 5.9
225 Sooty Tern **(46)** (Fav) *(JMBradley)* 5–7-11 ‡⁷MichaelBradley (2) (lw: w ldrs 5f: one pce) ............................. ³/₄.10
Zeppeki (IRE) **(68)** *(MDHammond)* 4–9-9 ‡³JFanning (5) (nvr trbld ldrs) ........ 2¹/₂.11
No Decision **(55)** *(MWEasterby)* 5–8-13 TLucas (11) (bhd tl sme late hdwy) . s.h.12
Little Rousillon **(64)** *(ACStewart)* 4–9-8 MRoberts (18) (lw: chsd ldrs over 5f) 3¹/₂.13
Spring to the Top **(64)** *(JWPayne)* 5–9-8 RCochrane (21) (n.d) .................... ¹/₂.14
I'M Electric **(46)** *(RCurtis)* 6–8-4⁽¹⁾ NDay (14) (bit bkwd: a bhd) .................... nk.15
326 Great Service **(48)** *(GMMoore)* 5–7-13 ‡⁷JWeaver (12) (hld up & bhd: n.d) ... 1¹/₂.16
326 Go Tally-Ho **(48)** (v) *(JJO'Neill)* 4–8-6 DHolland (22) (lw: chsd ldrs tl rdn & wknd 2f out) ............................ 4.17
Wsom (IRE) **(59)** *(JMCarr)* 4–9-3 SMorris (20) (bit bkwd: chsd ldrs 5f) ........ 3¹/₂.18
100⁵ Master Ofthe House **(48)** *(MDHammond)* 6–8-6 MBirch (7) (led tl hdd over 2f out: wknd qckly) ........................ hd.19
253 A Little Precious **(62)** *(JRBostock)* 6–9-6 GDuffield (13) (bhd: sme hdwy ¹/₂-wy: sn wknd) ................................ 1.20
Deputy Tim **(56)** *(RBastiman)* 9–8-7 ‡⁷HBastiman (10) (bkwd: n.d) ........... nk.21

7/1 Sooty Tern, 8/1 MOSSY ROSE, Little Rousillon, 9/1 Spring to the Top, Friendlypersuasion (IRE), Doulab's Image(12/1—8/1), 10/1 Execution Only (IRE), Golden Chip (IRE), 12/1 Go Tally-Ho, 14/1 The Devil's Music, Deputy Tim, A Little Precious, 16/1 Veloce (IRE), Great Service, 20/1 Master Ofthe House, 25/1 No Decision, Zoppeki (IRE), 33/1 Wsom (IRE), Errema 40/1 Sally Fay (IRE), 50/1 I'M Electric. CSF £240.30, CT £2,261.88. Tote £8.90: £1.90 £11.80 £2.20 £6.70 (£310.20). Mr Stanley J. Sharp (WEST ILSLEY) bred by C. L. Loyd. 2 f Run
1m 53.2 (11.6)
SF—34/24/33/26/22/30

T/Plpt: £617.30 (6.55 Tckts).　　　　　　　　　　　　　　　　　　　　　　　　　　AA

# RIPON (R-H)

## Wednesday, April 8th [Soft]

Going Allowance: 0.55 sec per fur (Y)　　　　　　　　　　　　　　　Wind: almost nil

Stalls: low

**365**　　E.B.F. FOUNTAINS STKS (Mdn 2-Y.0) £2406.00 (£666.00: £318.00)　5f　2-25 (2-27)

297⁴ **Greenwich Chalenge** *(WCarter)* 9-0 JReid (8) (b.hind: mde all: r.o wl u.p fnl f) . —1
237 Magic Pearl *(EJAlston)* 8-9 KFallon (3) (hdwy ¹/₂-wy: styd on wl fnl f) .............. 1¹/₂.2
Puenta Aguila *(MHEasterby)* 9-0 MBirch (6) (lt-f: unf: a chsng ldrs: nt qckn fnl 2f) ...................... 1¹/₂.3
263³ Two Times Twelve (IRE) (Fav) *(JBerry)* 9-0 PatEddery (11) (chsd wnr: rdn over 1f out: hung lft & wknd ins fnl f) ........ ³/₄.4
292⁴ Field of Vision (IRE) *(MJohnston)* 9-0 TQuinn (2) (chsd ldrs: rdn 2f out: sn btn) . 5.5
Blue Radiance *(TFairhurst)* 8-6 ‡³JFanning (10) (lt-f: unf: s.i.s: kpt on fnl 2f: nvr nr to chal) .......................... nk.6
Nicky Mygirl *(MBrittain)* 8-9 KDarley (1) (lt-f: lw: prom: hmpd ¹/₂-wy: no d after) .. ¹/₂.7
Perdition (IRE) *(WJPearce)* 8-9 LCharnock (4) (neat: scope: nvr nr ldrs) ........ 1¹/₂.8
Riston Lady (IRE) *(BSRothwell)* 8-9 RFox (5) (small: unf: sn outpcd: sme hdwy u.p ¹/₂-wy: n.d) ................... 1¹/₂.9
Hawaymyson (IRE) *(APStringer)* 9-0 JFortune (7) (cmpt: scope: bit bkwd: s.i.s: rn green & a in rr) ............. 1¹/₂.10
Bold Philip *(WJPearce)* 9-0 DNicholls (9) (w'like: str: bit bkwd: s.s: a wl bhd) .. 8.11
Dunnington *(MWEasterby)* 8-9 TLucas (12) (lt-f: unf: swvd bdly rt s: a wl bhd) nk.12

7/4 Two Times Twelve (IRE), 11/4 Field of Vision (IRE), 7/1 GREENWICH CHALENGE, 11/1 Puenta Aguila, 12/1 Bold Philip(op 8/1), Dunnington, 14/1 Magic Pearl, 16/1 Blue Radiance, Riston Lady (IRE), 20/1 Perdition (IRE), 25/1 Ors. CSF £96.14, Tote £6.50: £1.80 £4.60 £3.10 (£100.90). Mr J. A. Bird (EPSOM) bred by T. G. Mills Ltd.
12 Rn　　　　　　　　　　　　　　　　　　　　　　　　　　　　　64.8 sec (6.2)
SF—31/20/19/16/–/–

**366**　　DANBY (S) H'CAP (0-60) (3-Y.0) £2441.60 (£677.60: £324.80)　1m　3-00 (3-02)

**Futures Gift (IRE) (54)** *(AWPotts)* 9-2 AProud (17) (stdy hdwy over 2f out: led over 1f out: rdn & hld on nr fin) ................................... —1

313³ Akura (IRE) **(54)** (Jt-Fav) *(MJohnston)* 9-2 TQuinn (8) (effrt appr st: styd on u.p fnl 2f: ev ch ins fnl f: nt qckn nr fin) ............................................. ¹/₂.2

Eurotwist **(50)** *(TDBarron)* 8-12 AlexGreaves (5) (hdwy 3f out: styd on same pce appr fnl f) ........................................................................ 2.3

216 Stratford Lady **(50)** *(JAGlover)* 8-12 DNicholls (15) (s.i.s: hdwy u.p 3f out: nvr rchd ldrs) ........................................................................ 1.4

Lyn's Return (IRE) **(56)** *(RSimpson)* 8-13 ‡5ATucker (6) (lw: chsd ldrs: led over 2f out tl over 1f out: sn wknd) .......................................... 2¹/₂.5

107⁶ Kipini **(47)** *(WJMusson)* 8-2 ‡7PBowe (3) (kpt on fnl 3f: nvr plcd to chal) ............. 3.6

Reach for Glory **(58)** *(RMWhitaker)* 9-6 ACulhane (16) (bit bkwd: hdwy over 2f out: nvr rchd ldrs) .......................................................... 1.7

215 Brotherlyaffection **(59)** *(RHollinshead)* 9-0 ‡7MHumphries (19) (lw: bhd: effrt & hung bdly rt over 3f out: hung bdly lft over 1f out: n.d) ... 1¹/₂.8

281⁴ Kick on Majestic (IRE) **(47)** *(NBycroft)* 8-9 MBirch (7) (lw: chsd ldrs tl wknd 2f out) ................................................................................ ³/₄.9

Classic Exhibit **(56)** *(AHide)* 9-4 WRyan (11) (lw: s.i.s: bhd: hdwy over 2f out: nvr plcd to chal) .......................................................... 5.10

Mummys Rocket **(47)** *(MO'Neill)* 8-9 AMackay (20) (sn bhd) ...................... 1¹/₂.11

Lady Randolph **(53)** *(ICampbell)* 8-8 ‡7JWeaver (4) (bit bkwd: nvr nr ldrs) ...... s.h.12

Hot Punch **(54)** *(PCalver)* 9-2 SPerks (12) (chsd ldrs: ev ch 3f out: sn wknd) ... 2.13

278⁵ Stag Night **(55)** (v) *(CTinkler)* 9-3 KDarley (9) (chsd ldrs: rdn over 3f out: wknd over 2f out) .......................................................... 2¹/₂.14

295⁶ Phil-Man **(51)** *(TFairhurst)* 8-10 ‡3JFanning (10) (chsd ldrs to st: sn lost pl) ... s.h.15

324³ Optical (IRE) **(50)** (Jt-Fav) *(MPNaughton)* 8-12 LCharnock (14) (chsd ldrs: rdn over 3f out: sn wknd) .......................................... 5.16

Lift Boy (USA) **(52)** *(DenysSmith)* 9-0 BRouse (1) (n.d) .................................. 2¹/₂.17

148 Sizzling Rose **(50)** *(WCarter)* 8-7 ‡5NGwilliams (18) (led: edgd lft over 4f out: hdd & wknd over 2f out) ................................................ ¹/₂.18

252 Bold Mood **(59)** *(JBerry)* 9-7 PatEddery (13) (lw: chsd ldrs tl lost pl 3f out: sn bhd) ............................................................................. 8.19

Chester Belle **(50)** *(PCHaslam)* 8-12 BRaymond (2) (wl bhd fnl 3f) .............. 12.20

13/2 Akura (IRE), Optical (IRE), 8/1 Lady Randolph(op 12/1), Stag Night, 9/1 Bold Mood, 10/1 FUTURES GIFT (IRE), 11/1 Kipini, 12/1 Brotherlyaffection, Classic Exhibit(op 8/1), Chester Belle, Phil-Man, 14/1 Eurotwist, Lyn's Return (IRE), Reach for Glory, Kick on Majestic (IRE), 20/1 Ors. CSF £80.35, CT £867.57. Tote £35.20: £6.50 £2.00 £6.20 £9.30 (£136.40). Mr T. Marshall (BARTON-ON-HUMBER) bred by Miss H. Dean in Ireland. 20 Rn; Bt in 7,400 gns ............................................................ 1m 50.1 (12.4)

**367** ROECLIFFE STKS (2-Y-O) £2488.80 (£686.80: £326.40) **5f** 3-30 (3-32)

297★ **Palacegate Episode (IRE)** (Fav) *(JBerry)* 8-13 PatEddery (2) (mde all: pushed wl clr over 1f out) .......................................... —1

Local Heroine *(JBerry)* 8-6 TQuinn (1) (cmpt: str: bit bkwd: sn drvn along: wnt poor 2nd 2f out: no ch w wnr) .................. 12.2

329² George Roper *(MRChannon)* 9-4 BRouse (3) (chsd wnr: rdn ¹/₂-wy: sn wknd) 3¹/₂.3

30/100 PALACEGATE EPISODE (IRE), 3/1 George Roper(op 5/1), 10/1 Local Heroine. CSF £3.11, Tote £1.30 (£2.20). Palacegate Corporation Ltd (COCKERHAM) bred by Brendan and Sheila Powell in Ireland. 3 Rn 64.8 sec (6.2)
SF—30/–/–

**368** GREWELTHORPE H'CAP (0-95) £4537.20 (£1356.60: £649.80: £296.40) **1¹/₄m** 4-00 (4-05)

Revif (FR) **(74)** *(ACStewart)* 4–8-7 MRoberts (15) (trckd ldrs gng wl: led on bit over 2f out: impressive) ................................ —1

Mesleh **(89)** (Fav) *(JHMGosden)* 5–9-8 SCauthen (7) (bit bkwd: chsd ldrs: effrt over 3f out: kpt on wl: no ch w wnr) .......................... 2.2

233⁴ Rousitto **(71)** *(RHollinshead)* 4–8-4⁽¹⁾ RCochrane (1) (s.i.s: bhd: gd hdwy on outside over 2f out: r.o wl nr fin) .......................... nk.3

293⁵ Surrey Dancer **(62)** *(BHanbury)* 4–7-9 RFox (9) (hdwy 4f out: kpt on same pce fnl 2f) ........................................................ 2.4

88⁶ Crossillion **(84)** *(GWragg)* 4–8-12 ‡5PRobinson (17) (chsd ldrs tl wknd 2f out) ...... 5.5

225 Mardessa **(69)** *(FHLee)* 4–8-2 PaulEddery (2) (s.i.s: bhd: hdwy 3f out: nvr nr ldrs) ¹/₂.6

Admirals Seat **(60)** *(MrsJRRamsden)* 4–7-7 NCarlisle (4) (hld up & bhd: stdy hdwy 2f out: nvr plcd to chal) ................................ hd.7

233 Vague Dancer **(70)** *(MrsJRRamsden)* 6–8-3 AMunro (14) (lw: mid div: sme hdwy over 2f out: nvr nr ldrs) .......................... 2.8

225² Shabanaz **(74)** (v) *(THCaldwell)* 7–8-7⁽¹⁾ LDettori (10) (lw: chsd ldrs: drvn along appr st: lost pl over 2f out) ...................... nk.9

293⁴ Fox Chapel **(70)** *(JGFitzGerald)* 5–7-10⁽¹⁾ ‡7MHunt (13) (lw: nvr trbld ldrs) ........ 5.10

Touch Above (60) *(TDBarron)* 6–7-4 ‡³JFanning (1) (bit bkwd: a in rr) .......... 1½.11
No Submission (USA) (83) *(CRNelson)* 6–9-2 JReid (3) (lw: chsd ldrs tl n.m.r & lost pl 3f out) ............... ½.12
Azureus (IRE) (69) *(MrsGRReveley)* 4–8-2 JLowe (16) (sn bhd & drvn along) 2½.13
Jalmusique (95) *(MHEasterby)* 6–10-0 MBirch (8) (bit bkwd: led over 6f out tl over 2f out: eased whn btn) ............... 4.14
299 Admiralty Way (61) *(MO'Neill)* 6–7-8[1] AMackay (6) (a in rr) ............... 3.15
Latosky (62) *(JNorton)* 4–7-9[2] JQuinn (5) (in tch: sn drvn along: lost pl over 3f out) ............... 7.16
Green Medina (IRE) (81) *(MBell)* 4–9-0 MHills (12) (led tl over 6f out: wknd qckly 3f out) ............... 10.17
LONG HANDICAP: Admirals Seat 7-6, Admiralty Way 7-5, Latosky 6-12.

**6/4** Mesleh, **7/2** REVIF (FR)(3/1—5/1), **10/1** Rousitto, Surrey Dancer, **12/1** Crossillion, No Submission (USA), Admirals Seat, **16/1** Green Medina (IRE), Shabanaz, Vague Dancer, Fox Chapel, **20/1** Touch Above, Admiralty Way, Jalmusique, **25/1** Mardessa, Azureus (IRE), **40/1** Latosky. CSF £10.70, CT £55.97. Tote £6.40: £2.00 £1.30 £1.70 £2.70 (£5.00). S. Corman Ltd (NEWMARKET) bred by Petra Bloodstock Ltd in France. 17 Rn
2m 14.5 (11)
SF–38/49/30/17/18/7

**369** STUDLEY ROYAL H'CAP (3-Y.O) (0-80) £3096.90 (£858.40: £410.70)
1½m 60y                                                    4-30 (4-38)

230³ **Fassfern (USA) (70)** *(Jt-Fav)* *(MrsJCecil)* 9-2 PaulEddery (14) (chsd ldrs: led over 6f out: swvd lft over 4f out: hrd rdn & r.o wl u.p fnl 2f) .. —1
Eleganza (IRE) (67) *(NTinkler)* 8-13 MBirch (15) (lw: hld up: stdy hdwy 3f out: chal & rdn over 1f out: no ex nr fin) ............... nk.2
268* Romansh (75) *(Jt-Fav)* *(GWragg)* 9-7 SCauthen (7) (lw: trckd ldrs: chal & rdn over 1f out: unable qckn) ............... 1.3
256* Jack Button (IRE) (73) (v) *(BobJones)* 9-5 NDay (10) (otyd on u.p fnl 2f: hung rt & nt rch ldrs) ............... 5.4
Mr News (IRE) (62) *(WJPearce)* 8-8 DNicholls (16) (a chsng ldrs: effrt over 2f out: styd on one pce) ............... 3.5
256³ Thor Power (IRE) (52) *(DTThom)* 7-7[3] ‡⁵FNorton (9) (chsd ldrs: bmpd over 4f out: sn disp ld: wknd over 2f out) ............... 2½.6
Mayo Man (IRE) (47) *(MrsGRReveley)* 7-7 JLowe (4) (bkwd: s.i.s: sn bhd & drvn along: hdwy & wandered u.p over 2f out: nvr rchd ldrs) 1.7
251⁶ Anar (IRE) (53) *(WCarter)* 7-13 AMunro (12) (sn bhd: sme hdwy over 2f out: n.d) ............... 2.8
171⁹ Elsharh (IRE) (54) *(JAGlover)* 8-0 GCarter (13) (sn bhd: n.d) ............... 6.9
Sioux Perfick (50) *(CWThornton)* 7-3‡⁷KSked (2) (lw: in tch tl outpcd ent st: styd on again fnl 2f) ............... 2½.10
290² Holiday Island (72) *(CEBrittain)* 9-4 MRoberts (17) (led after 2f tl over 6f out: lost pl fnl 3f) ............... ½.11
Dramatic Pass (IRE) (58) *(MrsGRReveley)* 8-4 KDarley (8) (bit bkwd: bhd & hrd rdn appr st) ............... s.h.12
256² Lady St Lawrence (USA) (60) *(SirMarkPrescott)* 8-6 GDuffield (1) (lw: hdwy & prom appr st: wknd fnl 3f) ............... ½.13
Pharlander (IRE) (54) *(MHEasterby)* 7-9 ‡⁵SMaloney (3) (sn bhd & drvn along) 1.14
Tricycle (IRE) (47) *(JWWatts)* 7-7 GBardwell (11) (b.off hind: chsd ldrs tl lost pl over 3f out) ............... ¾.15
Noble Vienna (USA) (53) *(RHollinshead)* 7-6[6] ‡⁷MHumphries (5) (bit bkwd: a in rr) ............... 15.16
Ballyranter (59) *(HJCollingridge)* 8-5 JQuinn (6) (wl bhd fnl 2f) ............... 8.17
Jubal Early (IRE) (55) (v) *(CNAllen)* 8-1 WHind (18) (led 2f: chsd ldrs tl wknd qckly over 3f out: sn wl bhd) ............... 15.18
LONG HANDICAP: Mayo Man (IRE) 7-6, Noble Vienna 7-6.

**3/1** FASSFERN (USA)(7/2—5/1), Romansh, **8/1** Holiday Island, **9/1** Lady St Lawrence (USA), **10/1** Jack Button (IRE), **11/1** Dramatic Pass (IRE), **14/1** Anar (IRE), **16/1** Pharlander (IRE), Elsharh (IRE), Tricycle (IRE), **20/1** Eleganza (IRE), Ballyranter, Thor Power, Mr News, **25/1** Jubal Early (IRE), Noble Vienna (USA), Mr News (IRE), **33/1** Ors. CSF £66.44, CT £196.50. Tote £3.30: £1.40 £4.90 £1.80 £3.40 (£74.10). Mr George L. Ohrstrom (NEWMARKET) bred by George Ohrstrom in USA. 18 Rn
2m 52.7 (18.7)

**370** SPA WELTER MEDIAN AUCTION GRADUATION STKS (3-Y.O) £2480.80 (£688.40: £330.40) 1m 1f                          5-00 (5-08)

**Deer Hunt** *(PJMakin)* 8-10 TQuinn (17) (a chsng ldrs: led jst ins fnl f: r.o wl nr fin) ............... —1
Inner City (IRE) *(Fav)* *(LMCumani)* 9-0 LDettori (3) (gd sort: bit bkwd: hld up & bhd: hdwy appr st: disp ld 1f out: nt qckn nr fin) ............... ½.2
Double Flutter *(MRChannon)* 8-2 CRutter (11) (hdwy over 2f out: shkn up & r.o fnl f) ............... 2.3

Jato *(WJHaggas)* 8-10 MHills (15) (cmpt: scope: led after 1f tl jst ins fnl f: sn wknd) ......................................................................... 2¹/₂.4

295² Nicely Thanks (USA) **(73)** *(TDBarron)* 8-11 AlexGreaves (12) (hdwy over 3f out: kpt on u.p fnl 2f: nvr able to chal) .............................. 1¹/₂.5

235⁴ Buzzards Bellbuoy **(72)** *(HJCollingridge)* 8-7 JQuinn (16) (trckd ldrs: effrt over 2f out: kpt on) ................................................................ s.h.6

Cultured *(MRStoute)* 9-0 RCochrane (14) (lw: mid div: styd on fnl 2f: nrp) .. nk.7

Usaidit *(WCarter)* 8-10 JReid (5) (lw: hld up: stdy hdwy over 2f out: nvr plcd to chal) .................................................................................... 6.8

Port in a Storm *(WJarvis)* 9-0 MTebbutt (2) (sn bhd: gd hdwy on outside appr st: sn ev ch: wknd over 2f out) .................................................. 5.9

Bashamah (IRE) *(CEBrittain)* 8-5 MRoberts (19) (sn bhd: hdwy 3f out: sn wknd) 2.10

289 Treasure Beach *(MBrittain)* 8-7 KDarley (1) (hld up & wl bhd: hdwy fnl 2f: styd on) ................................................................................. 1¹/₂.11

Liability Order **(70)** *(RBoss)* 8-11 BRaymond (7) (chsd ldrs tl wknd 3f out) ....... 2.12

Coastal Express **(62)** *(EWeymes)* 8-11 DaleGibson (8) (plld hrd: trckd ldrs 3f: sn lost pl) ................................................................................. 4.13

Safari Park *(BSRothwell)* 8-5 RFox (13) (plld hrd: c wd st: sn bhd) ................... 6.14

302⁶ Tajigrey *(BWLunness)* 8-2 JLowe (9) (plld hrd: in tch tl lost pl over 3f out) .... s.h.15

Manbaa (IRE) *(HThomsonJones)* 8-9 RHills (18) (led 1f: chsd ldrs tl lost pl over 3f out) ...................................................................................... nk.16

238 Cellist *(RThompson)* 8-10 AProud (10) (chsd ldrs tl lost pl appr st: sn bhd) .. 1¹/₂.17

Dragon Spirit **(71)** *(AHide)* 8-10 WRyan (6) (prom to st: sn bhd) ...................... 1¹/₂.18

**11/4** Inner City (IRE)(7/4—3/1), **4/1** Nicely Thanks (USA)(op 6/1), **8/1** DEER HUNT(tchd 5/1), Double Flutter, **10/1** Usaidit, Manbaa (IRE), **11/1** Cultured, **12/1** Port in a Storm, **14/1** Buzzards Bellbuoy, **16/1** Jato, Liability Order, **25/1** Dragon Spirit, Bashamah (IRE), **33/1** Ors. CSF £31.95, Tote £11.80: £3.70 £2.00 £1.70 (£25.90). Mrs P. J. Makin (MARLBOROUGH) bred by Mrs J. H. Weller-Poley. 18 Rn                    2m 4.2 (14)

T/Plpt: £119.70 (21.2 Tckts).                                                                        WG

## 323—HAMILTON (R-H)

**Thursday, April 9th [Good to soft, Soft patches]**

Going Allowance: 0.70 sec per fur (Y)                          Wind: slt half bhd

Stalls: low

**371**          EARN CLAIMING STKS (2-Y-O) £2128.00 (£588.00: £280.00)    **5f 4y**    2-15 (2-16)

**Purchased by Phone (IRE)** *(DMoffatt)* 7-8 ‡⁷DarrenMoffatt (1) (unf: lw: chsd ldrs: led over 1f out: styd on wl) ..................................... —1

231* Classic Storm *(JBerry)* 8-4 GCarter (3) (led tl hdd over 1f out: no ex) ........ 3.2

286* Shadow Jury (Fav) *(MrsGRReveley)* 8-11 KDarley (4) (lw: a chsng ldrs: rdn ¹/₂-wy: kpt on one pce) ................................................................ hd.3

286 Take Your Partner (IRE) *(MJohnston)* 8-1 RPElliott (6) (a.p: effrt ¹/₂-wy: rdn & nt qckn) ...................................................................................... 2¹/₂.4

Babytalker *(NACallaghan)* 8-6 TLucas (2) (leggy: s.i.s: shkn up ¹/₂-wy: n.d) ...... 5.5

All Baileys *(MJohnston)* 8-4 JLowe (5) (small: outpcd fr ¹/₂-wy) .................... hd.6

**10/11** Shadow Jury, **7/4** Classic Storm, **10/1** PURCHASED BY PHONE, **14/1** Babytalker(op 8/1), **20/1** Take Your Partner (IRE)(op 7/1), **50/1** All Baileys. CSF £26.31, Tote £6.30: £1.60 £1.70 (£13.20). Mr L. N. Sloan (CARTMEL) bred by Miss V. Charlton in Ireland. 6 Rn; Purchased by Phone (IRE) clmd A Dinsmore £5,505

63.4 sec (6)

SF—30/28/34/14/—/—

**372**          GLEN H'CAP (3-Y-O) (0-70) £2186.80 (£604.80: £288.40)    **6f 5y**    2-45 (2-47)

298 **Abigails Boy (HOL) (53)** *(DrJDScargill)* 8-1 ‡³JFanning (1) (chsd ldrs: disp ld ¹/₂-wy: styd on wl appr fnl f) ........................................... —1

242³ Double Feature (IRE) **(64)** (Fav) *(MrsJRRamsden)* 8-8 ‡⁷JWeaver (4) (lw: wnt rt s: hung rt most of wy: redw wy: r.o nr fin) .............................. ³/₄.2

269⁴ Palacegate King **(58)** *(JBerry)* 8-9 GCarter (9) (lw: cl up: disp ld ¹/₂-wy tl rdn & btn appr fnl f) ....................................................................... 2.3

242 Buddy (IRE) **(63)** *(MBell)* 9-0 MHills (6) (lw: a in tch: kpt on one pce fnl 2f) 6.4

High Principles **(57)** *(JBerry)* 8-1 ‡⁷PRoberts (5) (hmpd s: hdwy to jn ldrs ¹/₂-wy: btn over 1f out) ......................................................................... nk.5

Denim Blue **(63)** *(CWThornton)* 9-0 MBirch (2) (a chsng ldrs: shkn up ¹/₂-wy: sn btn) ............................................................................................ 3.6

Spanish Express **(70)** *(RBoss)* 9-7 MRoberts (3) (bit bkwd: spd over 3f) ............ 5.7

　　　Summoned by Bells **(55)** *(MJohnston)* 8-6 RPElliott (7) (bit bkwd: outpcd fr
　　　　¹/₂-wy) ............................................................................... 12.8

218 Shadaylou (IRE) **(59)** (bl) *(MrsJJordan)* 8-10 KFallon (10) (led to ¹/₂-wy: wknd
　　　　qckly) ................................................................................ 12.9

　　　Indian Guest **(46)** (v) *(FHLee)* 7-6⁽⁴⁾ ‡⁵NKennedy (8) (bit bkwd: sn bhd: t.o) ........ **10**

**5/2** Double Feature (IRE), **4/1** Spanish Express, **6/1** Denim Blue, **8/1** Buddy (IRE), Palacegate King, **12/1**
ABIGAILS BOY (HOL), **14/1** Summoned by Bells, **20/1** Indian Guest, **25/1** Ors. CSF £38.03, CT £231.12. Tote
£13.10: £2.20 £2.00 £1.80 (£21.40). Mr Derek W. Johnson (NEWMARKET) bred by Stal de Kraal in Holland. 10
Rn　　　　　　　　　　　　　　　　　　　　　　　　　　　　　　　　　　　　1m 17.5 (7.5)
　　　　　　　　　　　　　　　　　　　　　　　　　　　　　　　　　　SF—21/25/18/–/–/–

## 373　　STANDARD LIFE H'CAP (0-80) £2709.00 (£749.00: £357.00)　**1m 65y**　　3-15 (3-17)

250* **Majed (IRE) (69)** *(NACallaghan)* 4-9-3 ‡⁷JWeaver (8) (a.p: rdn to ld over 1f out:
　　　　sn clr) ................................................................................ —1

225 Rose Glen **(60)** *(ABailey)* 6-8-10 ‡⁵ATucker (3) (hld up: effrt 3f out: styd on: nt
　　　　pce to chal) .......................................................................... 5.2

　　　Blue Grit **(44)** (bl) *(MDods)* 6-7-13 LCharnock (2) (bit bkwd: cl up: led over 4f
　　　　out tl over 1f out: wknd) .......................................................... 2.3

285² Laurel Queen (IRE) **(61)** (Fav) *(JBerry)* 4-9-2 GCarter (6) (b.hind: hld up: effrt
　　　　on outside 3f out: rdn & no imp fnl 2f) ........................................ 2.4

277* Solid (IRE) **(54)** *(JRJenkins)* 4-8-9 SWhitworth (5) (lw: bhd & pushed along ent
　　　　st: sme hdwy 3f out: no imp) .................................................. ¹/₂.5

158 Mofador (GER) **(60)** *(FHLee)* 8-8-10 ‡⁵NKennedy (7) (lw: led tl hdd over 4f out:
　　　　grad wknd) ........................................................................ 3¹/₂.6

　　　Skipper to Bilge **(72)** *(MAJarvis)* 5-9-13 BRaymond (4) (chsd ldrs tl wknd over
　　　　3f out) ................................................................................. 5.7

50 Fair Dare **(48)** *(CBBooth)* 4-8-3⁽²⁾ ACulhane (1) (hdwy to jn ldrs ent st: wknd
　　　　3f out) ................................................................................. 12.8

**5/2** Laurel Queen (IRE), **4/1** Rose Glen, **5/1** Skipper to Bilge, MAJED (IRE), **11/2** Solid (IRE), **12/1** Mofador (GER),
**25/1** Fair Dare, **33/1** Blue Grit. CSF £22.87, CT £520.53. Tote £7.30: £2.60 £2.20 £5.30 (£13.60). Mr N. A.
Callaghan (NEWMARKET) bred by Rowlane Investments in Ireland. 8 Rn　　　　　　1m 52.4 (9.1)
　　　　　　　　　　　　　　　　　　　　　　　　　　　　　　　　　　SF—53/31/14/25/16/6

## 374　　STANDARD LIFE STKS (Mdn 3-Y.O) £2147.60 (£593.60: £282.80)
　　　　**1m 65y**　　　　　　　　　　　　　　　　　　　　　　3-45 (3-46)

　　　**St James's Antigua (IRE)** *(WJHaggas)* 8-9 MHills (1) (hld up: stdy hdwy to ld
　　　　over 2f out: easily) ................................................................ —1

235 Houlston's Will (Fav) *(MrsJRRamsden)* 8-9 TLucas (7) (lw: hld up: hdwy over 3f
　　　　out: effrt & hung rt 2f out: nt pce of wnr) .................................. 3.2

296⁵ Chipper *(RBoss)* 9-0 MRoberts (5) (lw: pushed along appr st: hdwy 3f out: styd
　　　　on wl) ................................................................................. 2¹/₂.3

　　　The Dandy Don (IRE) *(DenysSmith)* 9-0 BRaymond (3) (bit bkwd: chsd ldr: kpt
　　　　on one pce fnl 3f) ................................................................. 2¹/₂.4

242 Stoproveritate **(63)** *(SGNorton)* 8-2 ‡⁷OPears (8) (in tch: effrt over 3f out: no
　　　　imp) .................................................................................... 8.5

324⁶ Crimson Consort (IRE) **(40)** *(DonEnricoIncisa)* 9-0 KimTinkler (4) (nvr nr to chal) 7.6

　　　Siolfor (USA) *(MrsJRRamsden)* 9-0 KFallon (6) (neat: s.s: t.o tl sme late hdwy) . 6.7

　　　Allimac Nomis *(NACallaghan)* 9-0 GCarter (2) (bit bkwd: led: clr ent st: hdd over
　　　　2f out: wknd qckly) ............................................................. ³/₄.8

**5/4** Houlston's Will, **6/4** ST JAMES'S ANTIGUA (IRE)(op Evens), **5/1** Chipper, **20/1** Stoproveritate, **25/1** The
Dandy Don (IRE), **33/1** Siolfor (USA), **100/1** Allimac Nomis, Crimson Consort (IRE). CSF £3.68, Tote £2.00:
£1.20 £1.20 £1.10 (£2.60). Sheikh Amin Dahlawi (NEWMARKET) bred by Barronstown Stud in Ireland. 8 Rn
　　　　　　　　　　　　　　　　　　　　　　　　　　　　　　　　　　1m 53 (9.7)
　　　　　　　　　　　　　　　　　　　　　　　　　　　　　　　　　　SF—37/28/25/17/–/–

## 375　　CALDER H'CAP (3-Y.O) (0-70) £2343.60 (£649.60: £310.80)　**1m 1f 36y**　4-15 (4-16)
　　　　　　　　　　　　　　　　(Weights raised 1 lb)

313* Philgun **(57)** (Fav) *(CWCElsey)* 8-7 (5x) ‡⁵SMaloney (11) (a cl up: led 3f out:
　　　　styd on strly) ........................................................................ —1

　　　Kadari **(58)** *(AHarrison)* 8-13 KFallon (9) (bit bkwd: cl up: outpcd over 3f out:
　　　　styd on wl fnl f) ..................................................................... 5.2

　　　Double the Stakes (USA) **(50)** *(FHLee)* 8-5 GCarter (5) (led tl hdd 3f out: kpt on
　　　　wl) ...................................................................................... ¹/₂.3

　　　Roger Rabbit (FR) **(48)** *(RBoss)* 8-3⁽¹⁾ MRoberts (4) (a in tch: hdwy on outside
　　　　& ev ch 3f out: rdn & one pce) ............................................... ¹/₂.4

281 Bartolomeo (USA) **(60)** *(MrsJRRamsden)* 9-1 NConnorton (1) (hld up & bhd: hdwy on ins whn nt clr run over 1f out: swtchd & styd on) .. 1.5
*215* Debsy Do (USA) **(65)** *(SGNorton)* 8-13 ‡7OPears (8) (lw: prom tl outpcd fnl 2f) . 6.6
*168⁵* Victor Romeo **(62)** *(WJPearce)* 9-3 DNicholls (10) (in tch tl wknd over 2f out) .... 2.7
Millfit (USA) **(66)** *(BHanbury)* 9-7 BRaymond (6) (bit bkwd: hld up: sme hdwy 4f out: n.d) 1½.8
Rap Up Fast (USA) **(54)** *(CWThornton)* 8-2 ‡7KSked (7) (bit bkwd: in tch tl wknd over 3f out) 3½.9
281³ Galley Gossip **(62)** *(MrsJRRamsden)* 9-3 TLucas (2) (lw: dwlt: hld up & bhd: n.d) 10

**100/30** PHILGUN, **7/2** Roger Rabbit (FR)(op 7/1), **11/2** Galley Gossip(4/1—6/1), **7/1** Kadari, **8/1** Millfit (USA)(op 9/2), **10/1** Double the Stakes (USA), **12/1** Debsy Do (USA)(op 8/1), **20/1** Victor Romeo, Bartolomeo (USA), **25/1** Rap Up Fast (USA). CSF £24.24, CT £188.69. Tote £3.30: £1.10 £2.00 £6.50 (£14.40). Mr C. D. Barber-Lomax (MALTON) bred by Mrs M. Morley. 10 Rn 2m 5.3 (11)
SF—23/14/4/–/9/–

**376**  DUNWAN STKS (Mdn 3-Y.O) £1932.00 (£532.00: £252.00)  **1m 3f 16y**  4-45 (4-45)

Lady Lydia *(MAJarvis)* 8-9 MHills (5) (mde most: kpt on wl fnl 2f) ...................... —1
Saif Al Adil (IRE) *(BHanbury)* 9-0 BRaymond (2) (cl up: disp ld over 3f out tl wknd ins fnl f) 2½.2
Five to Seven (USA) **(Fav)** *(SGNorton)* 9-0 AProud (4) (a.p: outpcd over 2f out: styd on wl fnl f) nk.3
296⁴ Rock Hard *(WJarvis)* 9-0 MTebbutt (1) (trckd ldrs gng wl: chal over 2f out: rdn & r.o one pce) hd.4
230⁴ Illuminating **(65)** *(MrsJRRamsden)* 8-9 TLucas (3) (hld up: effrt 5f out: wknd 3f out) 8.5
*136⁶* Elgin **(47)** (bl) *(ABailey)* 8-7 ‡7PBowe (6) (plld hrd: sddle slipped: cl up to st: t.o) dist.6

**6/4** Five to Seven (USA), **5/2** Rock Hard, **7/2** Illuminating, **5/1** Saif Al Adil (IRE), **14/1** LADY LYDIA, **40/1** Elgin. CSF £72.86, Tote £20.20: £1.30 £4.00 (£30.50). Mr K. G. Powter (NEWMARKET) bred by Dana Stud Ltd and Sussex Stud Ltd. 6 Rn 2m 33.4 (14.4)
SF—28/28/27/26/5/–

**377**  LEVY BOARD H'CAP (0-70) £2284.80 (£632.80: £302.40)  **1m 5f 9y**  5-15 (5-18)

328* **Sillars Stalker (IRE) (36) (Fav)** *(MrsJRRamsden)* 4-7-7 NCarlisle (1) (bhd: hdwy 4f out: led 1f out: r.o wl) ..................................................... —1
*139⁵* Hamilton Lady (IRE) **(40)** *(DMoffatt)* 4-7-4 ‡7DarrenMoffatt (4) (chsd ldrs: outpcd over 2f out: r.o wl fnl f) 3.2
358⁵ Sharp Top **(45)** *(MJRyan)* 4-7-13 (4x) ‡3DBiggs (5) (w ldrs: led 2f out: wandered & hdd 1f out: no ex) ½.3
Samain (USA) **(35)** *(JAGlover)* 5-7-8⁽¹⁾ JQuinn (7) (bit bkwd: in tch: effrt over 3f out: one pce fnl 2f) 4.4
229 Grey Power **(69)** *(MrsSPReveley)* 5-9-7 JWeaver (12) (lw: led tl hdd 9f out: led over 4f out: hung lft 3f out: hdd 2f out: one pce) 1½.5
Derry Reef **(39)** *(MDods)* 5-7-12 LCharnock (3) (chsd ldrs: ev ch over 3f out: rdn & wknd 2f out) 2½.6
312 Brusque (USA) **(35)** *(DonEnricoIncisa)* 8-7-8 KimTinkler (6) (nvr plcd to chal) .. ½.7
Persuasive **(63)** *(MissLAPerratt)* 5-9-8 DaleGibson (15) (hld up & bhd: effrt 4f out: nvr rchd ldrs) ½.8
328³ Needwood Poppy **(36)** *(BCMorgan)* 4-7-7 JLowe (2) (outpcd & bhd: hdwy u.p 4f out: n.d) nk.9
312 Buckingham Band (USA) **(54)** (v) *(FHLee)* 4-8-11 MRoberts (9) (lw: a bhd) ...... 8.10
Julietski **(43)** *(MDHammond)* 4-8-0 GCarter (11) (led 9f out tl over 4f out: wknd) 1.11
326 Master Plan (FR) **(41)** *(MissLAPerratt)* 6-7-7⁽⁷⁾ ‡7RHavlin (14) (cl up tl wknd 4f out) 12
328 Arrow Dancer **(45)** *(JJO'Neill)* 6-8-4 MBirch (13) (prom to st: sn bhd) ................ 13
Red Tempest (IRE) **(44)** (bl) *(LLungo)* 4-7-12 ‡3JFanning (8) (a bhd) ................ 14
LONG HANDICAP: Sillars Stalker (IRE) 7-6, Needwood Poppy 7-0, Master Plan (FR) 7-6.

**11/8** SILLARS STALKER (IRE), **9/2** Sharp Top, **7/1** Grey Power, **9/1** Needwood Poppy, **16/1** Julietski(10/1—20/1), Persuasive, Buckingham Band (USA), **20/1** Derry Reef(op 12/1), Samain (USA), **33/1** Hamilton Lady (IRE), Arrow Dancer, **50/1** Ors. CSF £42.53, CT £158.55. Tote £2.50: £1.10 £5.80 £1.80 (£70.30). Sillars Civil Engineering (THIRSK) bred by Martyn J. McEnery in Ireland. 14 Rn 3m 0.9 (15.2)
SF—18/9/17/4/28/–

T/Plpt: £255.10 (13 Tckts). AA

## 283a—SAINT-CLOUD (L-H)
**Tuesday, March 31st [Heavy]**
Going Allowance: 1.00 sec per fur (S)

**378a**    PRIX EDMOND BLANC (Gp 3)    £20640.00    **1m**

      **Exit To Nowhere (USA)** *(France)* 4–8–11 FHead ............................................. —**1**
13a\* Zanadiyka (FR) *(France)* 4–8–8 WMongil ............................................................ nk.**2**
      Goofalik (USA) *(France)* 5–9–4 CAsmussen ............................................... 2¹/₂.**3**
Tote 8.40f: 2.40f 1.50f 1.50f (22.40f). Mr S.Niarchos (F.Boutin,FRANCE) bred by Flaxman Holdings Ltd in USA.
11 Rn                                                                                                         1m 53.2 (14.6)

**379a**    PRIX RONDE DE NUIT (listed race) (3-Y.O.F) £12384.00    **1¹/₄m 110y**

      **Daltawa (IRE)** *(France)* 3–8–9 WMongil ................................................................ —**1**
      Berceau (IRE) *(France)* 3–8–9 PatEddery ........................................................... 2.**2**
      Garendare *(France)* 3–8–9 DBoeuf ................................................................. 1¹/₂.**3**
Tote 3.00f: 1.50f 1.60f (SF: 7.80f). H.H.Aga Khan (A.de Royer Dupre,FRANCE) bred by H.H.Aga Khan in Ireland.
7 Rn                                                                                                                2m 28.7

## 13a—EVRY (R-H)
**Wednesday, April 1st [Heavy]**

**380a**    PRIX DE COLOMBES (3-Y.O.F) £8256.00    **7f 110y**

      **Hydro Calido (USA)** *(France)* 3–9–2 FHead .......................................................... —**1**
      Royale Bobbe (FR) *(France)* 3–9–2 CLeScrill ..................................................... nk.**2**
      Carezza (USA) *(France)* 3–9–2 CAsmussen ........................................................ 3.**3**
Tote 2.70f: 1.50f 1.90f 1.80f (17.70f). Mr S. Niarchos (F.Boutin,FRANCE) bred by Flaxman Holdings Ltd in USA.
8 Rn                                                                                                                1m 41.7

## DUSSELDORF (R-H)
**Saturday, April 4th [Soft]**

**381a**    PHILIPP HOLZMANN-PREIS DER DREIJAHRIGEN (listed race) (3-Y.O) £21127.00
      **7f 110y**

      **Platini (GER)** *(Germany)* 3–9–2 MRimmer ............................................................. —**1**
175a\* Wedding Ring (IRE) *(France)* 3–8–12 MBoutin ................................................ 2.**2**
      Montepulciano (USA) *(Germany)* 3–9–2 THellier ............................................ 2¹/₂.**3**
      SYLVAN SABRE (IRE) *(PMitchell)* 3–9–2 MRoberts (btn more than further 3³/₄l) .... **9**
Tote 19DM: 12DM 18DM 20DM (SF: 93DM). Stall Steigenberger (B.Schutz,GERMANY) bred by Frau E & A
Steigenberger in Germany. 9 Rn                                                                                1m 36.6

## LONGCHAMP (R-H)
**Sunday, April 5th [Heavy]**
Going Allowance: 0.50 sec per fur (Y)

**382a**    PRIX D'HARCOURT (Gp 2)    £25800.00    **1¹/₄m (Moyenne)**

283a\* **Fortune's Wheel (IRE)** *(France)* 4–8–12 MBoutin (lw: bhd tl gd hdwy 2f out: r.o
      wl to ld nr fin) ........................................................................................... —**1**
      Pistolet Bleu (IRE) (Jt-Fav) *(France)* 4–9–1 DBoeuf (swtg: trckd ldr tl led 2f out:
      ct nr fin) ..................................................................................................... 1.**2**
      Art Bleu (Jt-Fav) *(France)* 5–8–12 AGoldsztejn (led 8f: sn hdd: r.o gamely) ...... 1¹/₂.**3**
283a³ Glity (USA) *(France)* 4–9–1 ELegrix (a cl up: effrt 2f out: outpcd fnl f) ........... nose.**4**
      Passing Sale (FR) *(France)* 5–9–4 ALequeux (5th st: nvr able to chal) ............... 2.**5**
      Arcangues (USA) (Jt-Fav) *(France)* 4–9–1 TJarnet (7th st: hdwy 2f out: one pce
      appr fnl f) .................................................................................................... nk.**6**
      Wiorno (Jt-Fav) *(France)* 4–9–1 PatEddery (6th st: no hdwy fnl 2f) ..................... 3.**7**
283a² Michel Georges *(France)* 4–8–12 CLeScrill (a bhd) ........................................ s.h.**8**
      SIKESTON (USA) *(CEBrittain)* 6–9–4 MRoberts (3rd st: ev ch 2f out: wknd qckly
      appr fnl f) ..................................................................................................... 1.**9**

**2/5** Arcangues (USA), Wiorno, Pistolet Bleu (IRE), Art Bleu, **54/10** FORTUNE'S WHEEL (IRE), **76/10** Passing Sale (FR), **83/10** Michel Georges, **102/10** Sikeston (USA), **103/10** Glity (USA). Tote 6.40f: 1.60f 1.10f 5.00f (8.20f). Mr R.C.Strauss (R. Collet,FRANCE) bred by Kilrush Stud Ltd in Ireland. 9 Rn      2m 10.4 (7.4)

SF—74/75/69/71/70/66/60

# NEWBURY (L-H)
## Friday, April 10th [Good to soft, Soft patches back st]
Going Allowance: 0.80 sec per fur (Y)                Wind: almost nil

Stalls: centre

**383**    E.B.F. BECKHAMPTON STKS (Mdn 2-Y.O) £3980.00 (£1190.00: £570.00: £260.00)
        5f 34y                                      2-10 (2-12)

323² **Sabre Rattler** *(JBerry)* 9-0 PatEddery (8) (lw: mde all: rdn out) .......................... —1
    Conspicuous (IRE) *(Fav) (PFICole)* 9-0 AMunro (13) (w'like: bit bkwd: a.p: chsd
        wnr over 1f out: r.o) ..................................................................... 2.2
    Simply Sooty *(BRMillman)* 8-9 GBaxter (3) (scope: bkwd: gd hdwy over 1f out:
        r.o ins fnl f) .............................................................................. 1½.3
  329 Bird Hunter *(NACallaghan)* 9-0 DHolland (14) (hdwy over 2f out: rdn over 1f
        out: unable qckn) ...................................................................... hd.4
    Aradanza *(MRChannon)* 9-0 JWilliams (4) (w'like: bit bkwd: outpcd: hdwy fnl f:
        r.o) ........................................................................................ 3½.5
    Grand Applause (IRE) *(RSimpson)* 8-9 ‡⁵ATucker (10) (leggy: bit bkwd: rdn
        over 3f out: nvr nr to chal) ......................................................... 2½.6
    Crusade (IRE) *(RHannon)* 9-0 JReid (11) (unf: spd over 3f) .......................... ¾.7
    Beaver Brook *(RHannon)* 9-0 BRaymond (6) (leggy: lt-f: hdwy over 2f out:
        wknd over 1f out) ...................................................................... 2½.8
    Midwinter Dream *(DRCElsworth)* 9-0 SCauthen (2) (w'like: scope: dwlt: hdwy
        3f out: eased whn btn over 1f out) .............................................. 3½.9
    Ansellman *(MJHaynes)* 9-0 BRouse (1) (str: bkwd: a bhd) ........................... 3.10
    Kintwyn *(DRLaing)* 9-0 SWhitworth (12) (w'like: bhd fnl 2f) ......................... hd.11
    Coppot Tel (IRE) *(CEBrittain)* 9-0 MRoberts (7) (leggy: bit bkwd: spd over 2f) ½.12
    Shades of Croft *(MDIUser)* 9-0 CRutter (9) (scope: bit bkwd: s.s: a wl bhd) 3½.13
    Wickins *(GLewis)* 9-0 PaulEddery (5) (leggy: bit bkwd: prom over 2f) .............. ¾.14

**2/1** Conspicuous (IRE)(6/4—9/4), **100/30** SABRE RATTLER, **10/1** Midwinter Dream(6/1—12/1), Beaver Brook(op 5/1), **12/1** Aradanza(16/1—10/1), Simply Sooty(7/1—14/1), **14/1** Wickins(op 6/1), Crusade (IRE)(op 8/1), Bird Hunter(25/1—33/1), **16/1** Coppot Tel (IRE)(10/1—20/1), **25/1** Shades of Croft, Kintwyn, **33/1** Ors. CSF £10.59, Tote £3.20: £1.50 £1.60 £3.30 (£4.10). Mr H. B. Hughes (COCKERHAM) bred by H. B. Hughes. 14 Rn      67.42 sec (6.72)

SF—46/38/27/31/17/2

**384**    SPRING STKS (Mdn 3-Y.O) £3494.25 (£1044.00: £499.50: £227.25)
        1m 3f 5y                                     2-40 (2-41)

**Tapis Rouge (IRE)** *(HRACecil)* 9-0 SCauthen (2) (scope: 4th st: led wl over 1f
        out: r.o wl) .............................................................................. —1
    Greek Tycoon (IRE) *(Fav) (PFICole)* 9-0 TQuinn (7) (2nd st: led over 3f out tl wl
        over 1f out: unable qckn) ........................................................... 2.2
    Ambiguously Regal (USA) *(MrsJCecil)* 9-0 PaulEddery (3) (leggy: 3rd st: rdn
        over 2f out: one pce) ................................................................. 4.3
    Silvernesian (USA) *(JLDunlop)* 9-0 WCarson (4) (5th st: one pce fnl 3f) ............ 4.4
    Poinciana *(RHannon)* 9-0 PatEddery (9) (nvr nr to chal) .............................. 7.5
    Landed Gentry (USA) *(PWChapple-Hyam)* 9-0 LDettori (10) (bit bkwd: a bhd) .. 2.6
    Paradise Navy *(CEBrittain)* 9-0 MRoberts (1) (leggy: bit bkwd: led over 7f: wkng
        whn hmpd on ins 3f out) ............................................................ 8.7
    Pyare Square *(IABalding)* 9-0 JReid (8) (unf: a bhd) .................................. ½.8
    Secret Picnic (USA) *(BHanbury)* 9-0 BRaymond (5) (leggy: scope: 6th st: wknd
        over 2f out) ............................................................................. nk.9
    Whitehall (IRE) *(CRNelson)* 9-0 DHolland (6) (str: bkwd: prom over 5f: virtually
        p.u over 3f out: t.o) ................................................................... 10

**11/8** Greek Tycoon (IRE), **11/4** TAPIS ROUGE (IRE)(9/4—7/2), **8/1** Pyare Square(op 5/1), **9/1** Silvernesian (USA), **14/1** Ambiguously Regal (USA), Poinciana, Paradise Navy, **20/1** Ors. CSF £7.09, Tote £3.00: £1.20 £1.20 £4.60 (£2.30). Sheikh Mohammed (NEWMARKET) bred by Newton Stud Farm Inc in Ireland. 10 Rn      2m 29.37 (13.37)

SF—54/50/42/34/20/16

**385** GAINSBOROUGH STUD FRED DARLING STKS (Gp 3) (3-Y.O.F) £18353.40 (£6804.22: £2278.19 each) **7f 64y**
3-10 (3-12)

**Musicale (USA) (117)** (Fav) *(HRACecil)* 9-0 PatEddery (1) (lw: 3rd st: rdn 3f out: swtchd rt 2f out: squeezed thro to ld ins fnl f: r.o wl) .... —1
Wiedniu (USA) *(LordHuntingdon)* 9-0 MRoberts (6) (6th st: led wl over 1f out tl ins fnl f: r.o) .................................................................. 1.2
Central City *(RHannon)* 9-0 BRaymond (2) (led over 1f: 2nd st: ev ch over 1f out: unable qckn) .......................................................... 2½.3
Culture Vulture (USA) **(114)** *(PFICole)* 9-0 TQuinn (4) (bit bkwd: 5th st: rdn over 1f out: one pce) ................................................... d.h.3
Oumaldaaya (USA) **(100)** *(JLDunlop)* 9-0 WCarson (3) (led 6f out tl wl over 1f out: sn wknd) ........................................................ 8.5
Rose Indien (FR) *(MMoubarak)* 9-0 LDettori (5) (4th st: wknd over 2f out) ......... 7.6

**8/11** MUSICALE (USA), **7/2** Culture Vulture (USA), **6/1** Rose Indien (FR), **10/1** Central City(8/1—12/1), **14/1** Oumaldaaya (USA)(10/1—16/1), **16/1** Wiedniu (USA). CSF £11.58, Tote £1.70: £1.10 £6.90 (£12.80). Mr R. E. Sangster (NEWMARKET) bred by Swettenham Stud in USA. 6 Rn
1m 35.22 (7.92)
SF—68/65/57/57/33/12

**386** NEWBURY TRADE STANDS H'CAP (0-100) £5020.00 (£1510.00: £730.00: £280.00) **5f 34y**
3-40 (3-45)

241⁴ **Stack Rock (88)** (Fav) *(EJAlston)* 5-9-5 KFallon (5) (lw: chsd ldr: led 1f out: pushed out) .................................................................. —1
Macfarlane **(75)** *(MJFetherston-Godley)* 4-8-6 WCarson (8) (hdwy over 1f out: r.o ins fnl f) ................................................................ 2.2
So Rhythmical **(72)** *(GHEden)* 8—8-3 NCarlisle (2) (b.off hind: hdwy 2f out: r.o ins fnl f) .............................................................. ?.3
Touch of White **(85)** *(JEBanks)* 6–8-11 ‡⁵LNewton (11) (led: hung bdly lft 2f out: hdd 1f out: unable qckn) .......................................... ¾.4
Tino Tere **(96)** *(JBerry)* 3–9-1 PatEddery (6) (hdwy over 2f out: one pce) ........ hd.5
Prenonamoss **(88)** *(DWPArbuthnot)* 4–9-5 TQuinn (4) (hdwy fnl f: r.o) ............. nk.6
236 Miami Banker **(79)** (bl) *(WRMuir)* 6–8-10 MRoberts (12) (spd over 3f) .......... nk.7
Love Legend **(86)** *(DWPArbuthnot)* 7–9-3 AMunro (3) (prom over 2f) ............... hd.8
Aughfad **(81)** *(TCasey)* 6–8-12 JReid (9) (outpcd) .......................................... hd.9
Choir Practice **(90)** *(WJHaggas)* 5–9-7 LPiggott (7) (prom 3f) ........................ 2.10
294★ Misdemeanours Girl (IRE) **(67)** *(MRChannon)* 4–7-7⁽⁴⁾ ‡⁵BDoyle (1) (lw: prom 3f) 3.11

**9/2** STACK ROCK, **11/2** Macfarlane, **13/2** Tino Tere, Choir Practice, **15/2** Misdemeanours Girl (IRE), **9/1** So Rhythmical, **10/1** Miami Banker(8/1—12/1), **11/1** Prenonamoss, Love Legend, **16/1** Aughfad, **20/1** Touch of White. CSF £27.87, CT £196.39. Tote £5.00: £2.00 £1.70 £3.00 (£9.10). Castle Racing (PRESTON) bred by Collinstown Stud Farm Ltd. 11 Rn
67.19 sec (6.49)
SF—55/34/23/28/31/34

**387** STROUD GREEN H'CAP (3-Y.O) (0-100) £4175.00 (£1250.00: £600.00: £275.00) **1m (st)**
4-10 (4-13)

**Amaze (90)** *(LadyHerries)* 9-4 SWhitworth (1) (b: a.p: led over 3f out: clr 2f out: comf) ............................................................................... —1
242★ Big Leap (IRE) **(87)** (Fav) *(MMoubarak)* 9-1 LDettori (13) (hdwy over 2f out: chsd wnr over 1f out: no imp) ............................................ 8.2
Vanborough Lad **(74)** *(MJHaynes)* 7-13 ‡³DBiggs (18) (a.p: one pce fnl 2f) ....... 2.3
Bold Stroke **(88)** *(JLDunlop)* 9-2 BRaymond (11) (swtchd rt over 2f out: hdwy over 1f out: r.o) .......................................................... 2.4
160³ By Hand **(80)** *(WJHaggas)* 8-8 LPiggott (5) (led over 4f: eased whn btn over 1f out) .................................................................... 4.5
Major Bugler (IRE) **(78)** *(GBBalding)* 8-6 JWilliams (4) (bit bkwd: stdy hdwy fnl 2f: r.o) ................................................................... ½.6
Khazar (USA) **(76)** *(SirMarkPrescott)* 8-4 CNutter (6) (bit bkwd: prom 6f) ....... 3½.7
3a² Jairzinho (USA) **(93)** *(RHannon)* 9-2 ‡⁵RPerham (14) (nvr nr to chal) .............. 2½.8
Confronter **(81)** *(PFICole)* 8-9 TQuinn (7) (bit bkwd: hdwy over 2f out: wknd over 1f out) ................................................................ 1.9
242² Eastleigh **(72)** *(RHollinshead)* 8-0 WCarson (10) (a mid div) ......................... 2.10
Salisong **(78)** *(PFICole)* 8-6 CRutter (2) (bit bkwd: prom 4f) ......................... 2½.11
Sharp Prince **(93)** *(HRACecil)* 9-7 PatEddery (8) (prom 5f) ........................... 1.12
Constructivist (IRE) **(74)** *(BWHills)* 8-2 DHolland (12) (bit bkwd: prom 4f) ...... 2½.13
Lobinda **(80)** *(JLDunlop)* 8-8 JReid (3) (nt grwn: outpcd) ............................ nk.14
Shakreen (USA) **(71)** *(MrsLPiggott)* 7-13 AMunro (17) (bit bkwd: prom over 3f) hd.15
Miss Doody **(70)** (v) *(MRChannon)* 7-7⁽⁴⁾ ‡⁵BDoyle (16) (bit bkwd: s.s: a bhd) 15.16
Mogwai (IRE) **(75)** *(RFJohnsonHoughton)* 8-3 PaulEddery (9) (bit bkwd: outpcd) ............................................................................... ½.17

5/2 Big Leap (IRE), 11/2 Sharp Prince, 8/1 Jairzinho (USA)(10/1—12/1), 10/1 Confronter, Constructivist (IRE), Eastleigh, Shakreen (USA), 12/1 Salisong, 14/1 Khazar (USA), By Hand, 16/1 Lobinda, Miss Doody, 20/1 Major Bugler (IRE), Mogwai (IRE), Vanborough Lad, 25/1 AMAZE & Ors. CSF £94.75, CT £1,282.66. Tote £55.30: £8.90 £1.50 £6.00 £5.50 (£55.30). Lady Katharine Phillips (LITTLEHAMPTON) bred by Lavinia Duchess of Norfolk. 17 Rn                                                       1m 46.75 (9.75)
SF—54/27/5/16/–/–

### 388
THATCHAM H'CAP (0-100) £3980.00 (£1190.00: £570.00: £260.00)    2m   4-40 (4-41)

|  | | | |
|---|---|---|---|
| | Go South (71) (bl) (JRJenkins) 8-8-6[1] PatEddery (14) (hdwy over 3f out: edgd rt & bmpd over 2f out: led 1f out: rdn out) | ................ | —1 |
| 234 | Prince Sobur (59) (MBlanshard) 6-7-8[1] NCarlisle (6) (hdwy over 3f out: hrd rdn over 1f out: r.o ins fnl f) | ................ | 2.2 |
| | Satin Lover (80) (Fav) (RAkehurst) 4-8-11 SCauthen (2) (hdwy 5f out: 6th st: led 2f out to 1f out: unable qckn) | ................ | ³/₄.3 |
| 301⁴ | Shoofe (USA) (77) (DMorley) 4-8-8 LDettori (9) (hdwy 3f out: one pce fnl 2f) | . 3¹/₂.4 |
| | Moving Out (80) (SirMarkPrescott) 4-8-11 AMunro (3) (led 14f: one pce) | ..... nk.5 |
| 234 | Farsi (77) (RHollinshead) 4-8-8 WCarson (13) (hrd rdn & hdwy 2f out: nvr nrr) | 10.6 |
| 301* | Army of Stars (86) (CEBrittain) 7-9-7 MRoberts (18) (lw: 2nd st: wknd 2f out) | ³/₄.7 |
| | Subsonic (IRE) (78) (JLDunlop) 4-8-9 JWilliams (10) (nvr nr to chal) | ........... ³/₄.8 |
| | Brandon Prince (IRE) (84) (bl) (IABalding) 4-9-1 JReid (16) (a mid div) | ...... 1¹/₂.9 |
| | Beebob (80) (MCPipe) 4-8-11 PaulEddery (1) (hdwy 3f out: nvr nr to chal) .. s.h.10 |
| 342⁶ | Crabby Bill (63) (v) (MissBSanders) 5-7-7[5] ‡5BDoyle (17) (3rd st: wkng whn bmpd over 2f out) | ............ 3¹/₂.11 |
| | Sonic Signal (63) (MJHaynes) 6-7-9[5] ‡3DBiggs (11) (nvr nrr) | ............... 2¹/₂.12 |
| | Buonarroti (83) (JABOld) 5-9-4 BRaymond (7) (4th st: wknd 3f out) | ............ ³/₄.13 |
| 234 | Patroclus (60) (RVoorspuy) 7-7-9[2] SDawson (5) (b: a bhd) | ................ 5.14 |
| 234 | Honey Dancer (62) (MissAJWhitfield) 8—7-11 NAdams (12) (5th st: wknd over 4f out) | ................ 12.15 |
| | Haitham (93) (RAkehurst) 5–10-0 LPiggott (4) (a bhd) | .................. 10.16 |
| | Blushing Belle (72) (PFICole) 4-8-3 TQuinn (8) (bit bkwd: prom 10f) | ......... 1¹/₂.17 |
| | Wide Support (75) (AMoore) 7–8-10 BRouse (15) (prom over 9f) | ............. hd.18 |
| | Beauchamp Fizz (70) (NACallaghan) 4-8-1 DHolland (19) (prom 11f: virtually p.u over 3f out: t.o) | ................ 19 |

LONG HANDICAP: Prince Sobur 7-1, Crabby Bill 6-6, Sonic Signal 6-4, Patroclus 6-3.

100/30 Satin Lover, 11/2 Shoofe (USA)(8/1—5/1), 15/2 Army of Stars, 9/1 Moving Out, 10/1 Beebob(8/1—12/1), Farsi(8/1—12/1), 12/1 GO SOUTH, 14/1 Brandon Prince (IRE), Subsonic (IRE)(10/1—16/1), 20/1 Buonarroti(16/1—25/1), Crabby Bill(op 33/1), 25/1 Haitham, Blushing Belle, 33/1 Beauchamp Fizz, Honey Dancer, Prince Sobur, Wide Support, 50/1 Ors. CSF £317.85, CT £1,477.97. Tote £17.20: £3.00 £3.20 £1.60 £1.80 (£232.20). Mr Rex Joachim (ROYSTON) bred by M. E. Wates. 19 Rn                3m 45.53 (18.83)
SF—32/18/34/27/29/16

T/Trio: Race 4: £40.70 (40.9 Tckts). T/Jkpt: £73,440.80 (0.2 Tckts); £79,395.50 to Newbury 11/4/92. T/Plpt: £15.70 (558.8 Tckts).                                                                         AK

## NEWBURY (L-H)
### Saturday, April 11th [Good to soft, Soft patches back st]
Going Allowance: 0.70 sec per fur (Y)                                              Wind: nil

Stalls: centre 3rd, 5th & 6th, remainder low

### 389
BURGHCLERE STKS (3-Y.O) £6342.00 (£1896.00: £908.00: £414.00)
1m 3f 5y                                                              2-00 (2-00)

|  | | | |
|---|---|---|---|
| | Beyton (USA) (98) (RHannon) 9-1 BRaymond (3) (lw: 6th st: hrd rdn over 1f out: led ins fnl f: r.o wl) | ................ | —1 |
| | Feminine Wiles (IRE) (106) (PWChapple-Hyam) 8-5[1] LDettori (2) (bkwd: led tl ins fnl f: r.o) | ................ | 1.2 |
| | Pabouche (USA) (Fav) (HRACecil) 8-9 SCauthen (1) (5th st: rdn over 3f out: n.m.r over 2f out: r.o one pce) | ................ | 3¹/₂.3 |
| | Captain Horatius (IRE) (109) (JLDunlop) 9-1 WCarson (4) (2nd st: wknd over 1f out: eased whn btn) | ................ | 8.4 |
| | Royal Seaton (90) (BRMillman) 8-9 GBaxter (5) (4th st: wknd wl over 1f out) .. 3¹/₂.5 |
| 330² | Boloardo (CEBrittain) 8-9 MRoberts (6) (a bhd) | ................ | 2¹/₂.6 |
| | Alcoy (IRE) (62) (PAKelleway) 8-9 CAsmussen (7) (3rd st: wknd over 2f out) .. hd.7 |

Evens Pabouche (USA)(5/4—4/5), 3/1 Captain Horatius (IRE)(2/1—7/2), 5/1 Feminine Wiles (IRE), 14/1 Boloardo, BEYTON (USA)(op 8/1), 20/1 Alcoy (IRE), 33/1 Royal Seaton. CSF £72.63, Tote £16.60: £4.20 £1.80 (£36.30). Mr D. F. Cock (MARLBOROUGH) bred by Side Hill Stud & Floors Farming in USA. 7 Rn
2m 29.35 (13.35)
SF—45/33/30/20/7/2

**390**
LANES END JOHN PORTER E.B.F. STKS (Gp 3) £18873.60 (£7003.63: £3314.32: £1389.45) 1½m 5y
2-30 (2-31)

**Saddlers' Hall (IRE)** (119) *(Fav)* *(MRStoute)* 4-8-13 PatEddery (4) (2nd st: led wl over 1f out: sn clr) ........................................... —1

11a Shambo (107) *(CEBrittain)* 5-8-12 MRoberts (11) (bit bkwd: rdn 3f out: 5th st: r.o one pce fnl 2f) ................................................. 10.2

Parting Moment (USA) (102) *(IABalding)* 5-8-12 BRaymond (2) (led tl wl over 1f out) ................................................................... 3½.3

240⁵ Linpac West (96) *(CWCElsey)* 6-8-12 LDettori (6) (hdwy 3f out: one pce fnl 2f) hd.4

Corrupt (USA) (117) *(NACallaghan)* 4-8-13 TJarnet (7) (bit bkwd: 4th st: ev ch over 2f out: wknd over 1f out) ........................... 1.5

Oh so Risky *(DRCElsworth)* 5-8-12 JWilliams (9) (lw: wl bhd tl r.o fnl 2f) .......... ½.6

343⁵ Hateel (109) *(PTWalwyn)* 6-8-12 WCarson (10) (hdwy 4f out: n.m.r: wknd over 2f out) ..................................................................... 10.7

Jura (101) *(HRACecil)* 4-8-10 SCauthen (3) (lw: rdn 3f out: no hdwy) .............. 4.8

Young Buster (IRE) (117) *(GWragg)* 4-8-10 WRSwinburn (5) (lw: hdwy & 6th st: ev ch over 2f out: wknd over 1f out) .............................. 15.9

239⁵ Man From Eldorado (USA) (100) *(GHarwood)* 4-8-10 RCochrane (8) (bhd fnl 3f) ......................................................................... 10.10

228³ Lift and Load (USA) (94) *(RHannon)* 5-8-12 BRouse (1) (3rd st: wknd over 3f out) ........................................................................ 2½.11

**9/4** SADDLERS' HALL (IRE)(6/4—5/2), **3/1** Corrupt (USA), **9/2** Young Buster (IRE), **15/2** Jura, **8/1** Hateel, **14/1** Man From Eldorado (USA), **16/1** Shambo, **20/1** Lift and Load (USA), **25/1** Linpac West, **33/1** Oh so Risky, **50/1** Parting Moment (USA). CSF £35.69, Tote £3.20: £1.60 £4.40 £8.20 (£38.10). Lord Weinstock (NEWMARKET) bred by Ballymacoll Stud Farm Ltd in Ireland. 11 Rn
2m 41.70 (12)
SF—63/42/35/34/33/31

**391**
SINGER & FRIEDLANDER GREENHAM STKS (Gp 3) (3-Y.O.C & G) £18558.00 (£6882.65: £3253.83: £1360.52) 7f
3-00 (3-01)

**Lion Cavern (USA)** *(AFabre,France)* 9-0 SCauthen (1) (lw: hld up in rr: hdwy 2f out: hrd rdn over 1f out: r.o to ld last stride) ................ —1

River Falls (117) *(RHannon)* 9-0 BRaymond (8) (lw: led tl last stride) .............. hd.2

Swing Low (110) *(RHannon)* 9-0 WRSwinburn (5) (a.p: hrd rdn over 1f out: r.o) 1.3

Rodrigo de Triano (120) *(Fav)* *(PWChapple-Hyam)* 9-0 WCarson (2) (swtg: hld up: hdwy 2f out: ev ch over 1f out: nt qckn) ..... 1½.4

Alflora (IRE) (94) *(CEBrittain)* 9-0 MRoberts (4) (lw: w ldrs tl wknd over 1f out) 2½.5

Spanish Storm (IRE) (100) *(AHide)* 9-0 WRyan (6) (bit bkwd: w ldrs tl wknd wl over 1f out) .............................................................. 3.6

Alhijaz (110) *(JLDunlop)* 9-0 LDettori (3) (bhd fnl 2f) .................................. 3½.7

Magic Ring (IRE) (118) *(PFICole)* 9-0 AMunro (7) (prom tl wknd qckly wl over 1f out) ....................................................................... ¾.8

**15/8** Rodrigo de Triano (USA), **9/4** LION CAVERN (USA), **100/30** Magic Ring (IRE)(9/4—7/2), **9/1** Swing Low(14/1—8/1), **16/1** River Falls(12/1—20/1), **20/1** Alhijaz, **50/1** Alflora (IRE), **100/1** Spanish Storm (IRE). CSF £30.66, Tote £3.60: £1.20 £2.60 £1.20 (£23.00). Sheikh Mohammed (FRANCE) bred by Dr W. O. Reed in USA. 8 Rn
1m 32.04 (7.54)
SF—61/60/57/52/44/35

**392**
LADBROKES SPRING H'CAP (0-110) £18075.00 (£5475.00: £2675.00: £1275.00) 1m 7y (rnd)
3-30 (3-33)

**Rudimentary (USA)** (103) *(HRACecil)* 4-10-0 PatEddery (2) (lw: 3rd st: led over 1f out: r.o wl) ....................................................... —1

240 Roseate Lodge (78) *(RWArmstrong)* 6-8-3 MRoberts (3) (gd hdwy over 1f out: fin wl) ......................................................................... 7.2

Sharp N' Smooth (72) *(RHannon)* 5-7-11 WCarson (5) (6th st: r.o one pce fnl 2f) ..................................................................... s.h.3

Berlin Wall (IRE) (82) *(PWChapple-Hyam)* 4-8-7 WRSwinburn (19) (bit bkwd: 7th st: ev ch over 1f out: nt qckn) ................................. 1½.4

Troupe (84) *(BWHills)* 4-8-9(1) SCauthen (14) (lw: 8th st: ev ch wl over 1f out: wknd fnl f) ................................................................. 5.5

Conquista (82) *(LadyHerries)* 4-8-7 JWilliams (4) (nvr nr to chal) ................... ½.6

293² Langtry Lady (86) *(MJRyan)* 6-8-11 RCochrane (17) (s.s: hdwy & hmpd 2f out: nt rcvr) ................................................................ 2½.7

233² State Dancer (USA) (90) *(MMoubarak)* 5-9-1 LDettori (6) (4th st: led over 2f out tl wknd over 1f out) ..................................... 2.8

240² Mudaffar (IRE) (88) *(Fav)* *(RWArmstrong)* 4-8-13 CAsmussen (20) (rdn 3f out: no hdwy) ........................................................... ½.9

Pay Homage (96) *(IABalding)* 4-9-4 ‡³SO'Gorman (7) (9th st: nvr trbld ldrs) 1½.10

Bowden Boy (IRE) **(73)** *(NACallaghan)* 4–7-7 ‡5BDoyle (15) (bit bkwd: n.d) ...... **1.11**
Cheveux Mitchell **(77)** (v) *(MRChannon)* 5–8-2 CRutter (13) (bit bkwd: 2nd st: wknd 2f out) ........ ½.**12**
*202*6 Wingfield (USA) **(79)** *(DRCElsworth)* 4–8-4 WNewnes (12) (s.s: n.d) ............ 2½.**13**
233 Lord Oberon (IRE) **(77)** *(RJO'Sullivan)* 4–7-13 ‡3DBiggs (16) (n.d) .................. ¾.**14**
335* Two Left Feet **(93)** *(SirMarkPrescott)* 5–9-4 GDuffield (18) (n.d) ...................... ½.**15**
Halston Prince **(88)** *(RFJohnsonHoughton)* 5–8-13 TQuinn (9) (led tl wknd over 2f out) ........ 2½.**16**
Hard to Figure **(95)** *(RJHodges)* 6–9-1 ‡5TSprake (8) (bkwd: 5th st: wknd 3f out) 2.**17**
Beyond Our Reach **(74)** *(RJHodges)* 4–7-8 ‡5FNorton (1) (n.d) ......................... 3.**18**
240 Rise Up Singing **(83)** (bl) *(RHannon)* 4–8-3 ‡5RPerham (11) (t.o) .................... nk.**19**

**9/2** Mudaffar (IRE)(7/1—4/1), **11/2** State Dancer (USA), **10/1** Troupe(12/1—8/1), Roseate Lodge, **11/1** Berlin Wall (IRE)(8/1—12/1), Sharp N' Smooth, **12/1** Langtry Lady, Two Left Feet, RUDIMENTARY (USA), **16/1** Conquista, **20/1** Rise Up Singing, Beyond Our Reach, Bowden Boy (IRE), Pay Homage, **25/1** Wingfield (USA), **33/1** Ors. CSF £119.79, CT £1,242.27. Tote £13.60: £2.80 £2.00 £2.10 £3.40 (£59.20). Lord Howard de Walden (NEWMARKET) bred by Lord Howard de Walden in USA. 19 Rn 1m 43.27 (7.27)
SF—88/42/35/40/27/23

## 393 BRIDGET STKS (Mdn 3-Y.O. F) £3850.00 (£1150.00: £550.00: £250.00)
**7f** 4-00 (4-05)

**Lost Reputation (IRE)** *(BWHills)* 8-11 AMunro (15) (w'like: gd hdwy over 1f out: led wl ins fnl f: r.o) ........ —**1**
Dizzy Penny *(PFICole)* 8-11 TQuinn (12) (w'like: bit bkwd: a.p: led over 1f out tl wl ins fnl f) ........ 1½.**2**
Avila (Fav) *(JHMGosden)* 8-11 SCauthen (13) (w'like: scope: hdwy over 2f out: r.o ins fnl f) ........ ¾.**3**
Queen Warrior *(PTWalwyn)* 8-11 PatEddery (2) (w'like: a.p: rdn over 1f out: nt qckn) ........ 3½.**4**
She Looks on High (USA) *(BHanbury)* 8-11 BRaymond (3) (w'like: scope: bit bkwd: led tl wknd over 1f out) ........ ¾.**5**
Gong *(PTWalwyn)* 8-11 RCochrane (10) (w'like: nvr nrr) ........ 3½.**6**
Star Goddess (USA) *(MRChannon)* 8-11 BRouse (7) (w'like: scope: bit bkwd: prom over 5f) ........ 3.**7**
Tlaad (USA) *(MRStoute)* 8-11 GDuffield (4) (unf: scope: hdwy over 2f out: wknd over 1f out) ........ hd.**8**
Royal Glint *(IABalding)* 8-11 LDettori (14) (w'like: bit bkwd: n.d) ........ 3½.**9**
Tafrah (IRE) *(MajorWRHern)* 8-11 WCarson (5) (wl grwn: bit bkwd: a bhd) ..... nk.**10**
Do Run Run *(RHannon)* 8-11 MRoberts (8) (unf: scope: bit bkwd: w ldrs over 4f) ........ 2.**11**
Killshandra (IRE) *(MrsBarbaraWaring)* 8-11 NHowe (6) (unf: n.d) ........ ½.**12**
Cee Beat (v) *(EAWheeler)* 8-11 SWhitworth (11) (unf: scope: lft s: a wl bhd) .... 4.**13**
Anima *(MajorWRHern)* 8-11 WRSwinburn (9) (w'like: w ldrs tl wknd qckly 2f out) **14**
Hazy Prospect *(DRCElsworth)* 8-11 JWilliams (1) (wl grwn: bit bkwd: a bhd) ...... **15**

**11/4** Avila(2/1—3/1), **3/1** Tafrah (IRE), **8/1** LOST REPUTATION (IRE), **12/1** Gong, Tlaad (USA)(op 8/1), She Looks on High (USA)(8/1—14/1), Queen Warrior, **14/1** Royal Glint, Anima, **16/1** Dizzy Penny(12/1—20/1), **20/1** Do Run Run(op 12/1), Star Goddess (USA), **33/1** Ors. CSF £122.78, Tote £11.10: £2.80 £2.80 £2.00 (£65.50). Mr R. E. Sangster (LAMBOURN) bred by Seahorse Investments in Ireland. 15 Rn 1m 33.42 (8.92)
SF—37/32/30/19/17/6

## 394 COMPTON STKS (Mdn 3-Y.O) £3874.50 (£1161.00: £558.00: £256.50)
**1m (st)** 4-30 (4-40)

**River Defences (USA)** *(PWChapple-Hyam)* 9-0 LDettori (15) (a.p: led wl over 1f out: r.o wl) ........ —**1**
2382 Rebel Call *(RHannon)* 9-0 BRaymond (20) (hdwy 2f out: r.o ins fnl f) ........ 4.**2**
Majboor (IRE) *(PTWalwyn)* 9-0 RCochrane (24) (a.p: led 3f out tl wl over 1f out) ¾.**3**
Thamestar (IRE) *(JLDunlop)* 9-0 TQuinn (11) (leggy: nvr nrr) ........ 4.**4**
Rajai (IRE) *(JLDunlop)* 9-0 WCarson (14) (bit bkwd: hdwy 2f out: nrst fin) ....... 1½.**5**
The Power of One *(RSimpson)* 9-0 GDuffield (6) (nvr nr to chal) ........ nk.**6**
Hatta's Mill (Fav) *(HRACecil)* 9-0 MRoberts (22) (a.p: hrd rdn 3f out: wknd 2f out) ........ 6.**7**
Polish Blue (USA) *(MRStoute)* 9-0 PatEddery (7) (bit bkwd: no hdwy fnl 3f) ...... ½.**8**
Banish *(BWHills)* 8-7 ‡7CMunday (18) (bit bkwd: prom over 5f) ........ ¾.**9**
Thunderbird One (USA) *(CRNelson)* 8-7 ‡7DThompson (16) (leggy: prom 5f) . ¾.**10**
Santana Lady (IRE) *(MJHeaton-Ellis)* 8-9 SRaymont (12) (prom 5f) ........ 1.**11**
Maple Bay (IRE) *(PJMakin)* 9-0 CAsmussen (10) (bit bkwd: n.d) ........ ¾.**12**
Louisville Belle (IRE) *(MDIUsher)* 8-9 CRutter (21) (n.d) ........ s.h.**13**
334 Odoen (USA) *(MRChannon)* 9-0 BRouse (1) (n.d) ........ 2.**14**
Wakil (IRE) *(CJBenstead)* 9-0 JWilliams (2) (bit bkwd: a bhd) ........ 1½.**15**

Bel Baraka (IRE) *(DRCElsworth)* 9-0 SCauthen (13) (led tl wknd 3f out) .......... ¹/₂.**16**
Sir Mark Sykes (IRE) *(JRFanshawe)* 9-0 WRSwinburn (4) (w'like: scope: bit
    bkwd: n.d) ..................................................................................... **17**
Shirley's Train (USA) *(LordHuntingdon)* 9-0 AMunro (3) (wl grwn: bit bkwd: n.d) **18**
Thakawah *(RWArmstrong)* 9-0 BCrossley (5) (leggy: s.s: a bhd) ........................ **19**
Gentle Secret (IRE) *(IABalding)* 9-0 GBaxter (19) (w'like: scope: prom 5f) .......... **20**
Marpatann (IRE) *(ASReid)* 9-0 WRyan (9) (a bhd) ......................................... **21**
348 Mastamist *(RVoorspuy)* 9-0 SDawson (8) (a bhd) .......................................... **22**
Boring (USA) *(NACallaghan)* 9-0 TJarnet (17) (wl grwn: a bhd) ........................ **23**
Andes *(WGRWightman)* 9-0 WNewnes (23) (bit bkwd: prom over 3f) .................. **24**

**11/8** Hatta's Mill, **15/2** Rebel Call, **8/1** Rajai (IRE)(op 3/1), **9/1** RIVER DEFENCES (USA)(12/1—8/1), **10/1** Polish
Blue (USA), Thamestar (IRE)(7/1—12/1), **20/1** Boring (USA)(op 10/1), **25/1** Shirley's Train (USA), Sir Mark
Sykes (IRE), Majboor (IRE), **33/1** Santana Lady (IRE), Thakawah, Gentle Secret (IRE), Bel Baraka (IRE), **50/1** Ors.
CSF £72.80, Tote £12.50: £3.40 £2.00 £8.10 (£36.90). Mr R. E. Sangster (MARLBOROUGH) bred by
Swettenham Stud in USA. 24 Rn                                                    1m 46.85 (9.85)
                                                                        SF—37/25/23/11/6/5

**395**  LEVY BOARD SEVENTH RACE H'CAP (3-Y.O) (0-90) £4077.50 (£1220.00: £585.00:
        £267.50)   1¹/₄m 6y                                              5-00 (5-12)

**Ecliptic (IRE) (66)** *(PWChapple-Hyam)* 7-6⁽¹⁾ ‡⁵FNorton (15) (2nd st: led 4f out:
    sn clr: unchal) ................................................................................. —**1**
235 Desert Force (IRE) **(83)** *(MMoubarak)* 9-0 LDettori (7) (lw: 6th st: hrd rdn over 3f
    out: styd on: nt rch wnr) ............................................................... 3¹/₂.**2**
Judge and Jury **(73)** *(MJFetherston-Godley)* 8-4⁽¹⁾ TQuinn (17) (bit bkwd:
    hdwy 3f: nvr nr) ................................................................................ 1.**3**
Princess of Orange **(63)** *(CCElsey)* 7-8 JQuinn (18) (4th st: r.o one pce fnl 3f)  s.h.**4**
Jasoorah (IRE) **(80)** (Fav) *(ACStewart)* 8-11 MRoberts (16) (3rd st: one pce fnl
    3f) ................................................................................................ 2.**5**
Maestroso (IRE) **(76)** *(RFJohnsonHoughton)* 8-7 RCochrane (10) (bit bkwd:
    nvr nr to chal) .............................................................................. s.h.**6**
Classical Charmer **(66)** *(BRMillman)* 7-8⁽¹⁾ ‡³DBiggs (1) (hdwy over 2f out: hung
    bdly rt over 1f out: nt rcvr) ........................................................... 1.**7**
Cosmic Future **(75)** *(AHide)* 8-6 BRouse (8) (no hdwy fnl 3f) ...................... 1¹/₂.**8**
Leap in the Dark (IRE) **(76)** *(JLDunlop)* 8-7 WCarson (9) (5th st: wknd over 1f
    out) .............................................................................................. ³/₄.**9**
Ripsnorter (IRE) **(74)** *(SirMarkPrescott)* 8-5 GDuffield (3) (n.d) ................. 3.**10**
350★ Grog (IRE) **(81)** *(MRChannon)* 8-7 ‡⁵BDoyle (5) (led 6f) ...................... s.h.**11**
341 Vivitz (IRE) **(63)** *(GBBalding)* 7-8 DaleGibson (6) (n.d) ....................... 1¹/₂.**12**
242 Major's Law (IRE) **(85)** *(CEBrittain)* 8-13 ‡³RonHillis (22) (n.d) ........... 1¹/₂.**13**
Sports View **(65)** *(RJHolder)* 7-10 NAdams (2) (bit bkwd: n.d) ................... 2.**14**
National Emblem (FR) **(85)** *(PFICole)* 9-2 AMunro (20) (n.d) ....................... 5.**15**
Grand Vitesse (IRE) **(80)** *(RHannon)* 8-11 BRaymond (19) (n.d) ................... 5.**16**
216★ Mad Militant (IRE) **(90)** *(RHollinshead)* 9-7 WRyan (21) (lw: n.d) ........... 5.**17**
147⁵ Dublin Indemnity (USA) **(82)** *(NACallaghan)* 7-0 ‡⁷CHawksley (13) (n.d) ......... 18
Bold Surprise **(73)** *(RWArmstrong)* 8-4 BCrossley (12) (n.d) ....................... 19
Khalloof (IRE) **(80)** *(MAJarvis)* 8-11 SCauthen (11) (bit bkwd: prom 5f: wknd
    qckly) ............................................................................................. 20
Sterling Prospect **(74)** *(WCarter)* 8-5 WNewnes (14) (reluctant to r: a t.o) .......... 21

**7/2** Jasoorah (IRE), **7/1** Cosmic Future(tchd 14/1), **15/2** Leap in the Dark (IRE)(9/1—6/1), **8/1** National Emblem
(FR), **9/1** ECLIPTIC (IRE), **10/1** Grog (IRE), **12/1** Desert Force (IRE), **14/1** Grand Vitesse (IRE), **16/1** Mad Militant
(IRE), Ripsnorter (IRE), **20/1** Bold Surprise, Khalloof (IRE), Dublin Indemnity (USA), **25/1** Judge and Jury, **33/1**
Ors. CSF £108.08, CT £2,364.85. Tote £14.60: £2.80 £3.50 £3.80 £12.60 (£139.40). Mr R. E. Sangster
(MARLBOROUGH) bred by Swettenham Stud in Ireland. 21 Rn                      2m 17.76 (14.76)
                                                                        SF—1/16/4/–/6/1

T/Trio: Race 4: £194.80 (13.5 Tckts). T/Jkpt: Not won; £111,051.00 to Newmarket 14/4/92. T/Plpt: £1,593.00
(6.9 Tckts).                                                                            Hn

# THIRSK (L-H)
**Friday, April 10th [Good, Good to firm back st]**
Going Allowance: nil sec per fur (G)                                    Wind: almost nil

Stalls: high

**396**  E.B.F. BRITON STKS (Mdn 2-Y.O) £2629.70 (£729.20: £349.10)   **5f**    2-20 (2-23)

266⁴ **Sison (IRE)** *(RMWhitaker)* 9-0 ACulhane (2) (w ldrs: led ¹/₂-wy: rdn & r.o wl fnl f)  —**1**
339 Heber Spring (IRE) (Fav) *(RHannon)* 9-0 AMcGlone (7) (chsd ldrs: rdn to chal
    appr fnl f: hung bdly lft: nt qckn nr fin) ............................................. 2.**2**

Preston Guild (IRE) *(JBerry)* 9-0 NConnorton (8) (w'like: cmpt: lw: hung lft most of wy: w ldrs to ½-wy: kpt on same pce fnl f) .......................... 3½.3

Bonus Point *(MrsGRReveley)* 9-0 KDarley (10) (wl grwn: scope: bit bkwd: s.i.s & rn green: hdwy over 1f out: styd on wl nr fin) .................. s.h.4

Argyle Cavalier (IRE) *(FHLee)* 9-0 GCarter (6) (lt-f: unf: s.i.s: effrt & hdwy ½-wy: edgd lft & r.o fnl f) .......................... ¾.5

292² So so *(TDBarron)* 8-9 AlexGreaves (5) (swtg: slt ld to ½-wy: sn rdn & grad lost pl) .......................... 2.6

Warkworth (USA) *(JWWatts)* 9-0 JLowe (1) (neat: s.i.s: sn drvn along: nvr wnt pce) .......................... ¾.7

Penny Banger (IRE) *(MJohnston)* 8-9 RPElliott (3) (w'like: bit bkwd: prom on outside 3f) .......................... 8

Breakfast Boogie *(JRFanshawe)* 8-9 GDuffield (4) (unf: s.i.s: sn rcvrd to chase ldrs: hung lft after 2f: wknd wl over 1f out) .......................... 9

287 Great Mashhor *(JSWainwright)* 9-0 WNewnes (9) (bit bkwd: a bhd) .................. 10

3/1 Heber Spring (IRE), 7/2 Preston Guild (IRE), 4/1 Breakfast Boogie, 5/1 So so, 8/1 Warkworth (USA), 9/1 SISON (IRE), 10/1 Bonus Point, 14/1 Argyle Cavalier (IRE), Penny Banger (IRE), 25/1 Great Mashhor. CSF £38.15, Tote £12.60: £2.40 £1.10 £1.60 (£20.70). Mrs Carol A. Wyatt (WETHERBY) bred by A. P. Tierney in Ireland. 10 Rn
61.2 sec (3.5)
SF—30/22/8/7/4/−

**397**    KNAYTON (S) STKS    £2500.40 (£694.40: £333.20)    **7f**      2-50 (2-51)

178 **Lombard Ships (59)** *(MO'Neill)* 5-9-7 JFortune (1) (lw: chsd ldrs: led over 2f out: hrd rdn & hld on wl fnl f) .......................... —1

264² Mca Below the Line (65) (bl) (Jt-Fav) *(WJPearce)* 4-9-12 DNicholls (4) (chsd ldrs: rdn to chal over 1f out: r.o wl nr fin) .......................... nk.2

278 Between Two Fires (52) *(JBerry)* 3-8-6 GCarter (8) (a chsng ldrs: effrt 2f out: swtchd ins fnl f: styd on wl nr fin) .......................... hd.3

Plan Ahead (66) *(GLewis)* 3-7-10 ‡5FNorton (11) (in tch: effrt & hdwy on outside 2f out: sn ev ch: hung lft & no ex appr fnl f) .......................... 2.4

172 Yonge Tender (59) (bl) *(JWharton)* 5-9-4 ‡3JFanning (3) (bit bkwd: mid div: effrt 3f out: kpt on: nt rch ldrs) .......................... 2½.5

215 Pop to Stans (83) *(TDBarron)* 3-8-11 AlexGreaves (7) (w ldr: hrd rdn 3f out: wandered u.p: btn fnl f) .......................... ½.6

Penando (42) *(OO'Neill)* 4-9-7 AClark (2) (nvr rchd ldrs) .......................... 3.7

158⁵ Green's Seago (USA) *(JLHarris)* 4-9-12 RCochrane (9) (mid div: effrt over 2f out: n.d) .......................... ½.8

326² Dawn's Delight (45) *(KTIvory)* 14-9-12 MWigham (13) (b.hind: n.d) .................. 2½.9

264* Emerald Ears (60) *(EWeymes)* 3-8-6 GHind (6) (prom tl rdn & wknd over 2f out) 1½.10

Thornton Gate (64) *(MHEasterby)* 3-8-11 MBirch (5) (led tl hung rt & hdd over 2f out) .......................... 1.11

269 Too Eager (62) (bl) *(MWEasterby)* 4-9-2 KDarley (10) (lw: nvr nr ldrs) .......... ¾.12

333 Dashing April (48) (v) *(DTThom)* 4-9-2 JQuinn (12) (s.s: a in rr) .......... nk.13

Turbulent River (USA) (67) *(NTinkler)* 4-9-12 KimTinkler (14) (s.s: a bhd) ...... 14

Angel Train (IRE) *(JParkes)* 4-9-0 ‡7JWeaver (15) (chsd ldrs to st: t.o) .......... 15

351 Helawe (69) (bl) (Jt-Fav) *(SirMarkPrescott)* 9-9-12 GDuffield (14) (bhd: effrt over 3f out: sn btn: t.o) .......................... 16

9/2 Mca Below the Line, Helawe, 5/1 Plan Ahead, 6/1 Pop to Stans(op 4/1), 8/1 Yonge Tender, 9/1 Too Eager, 12/1 Emerald Ears, Thornton Gate, 14/1 Turbulent River (USA), 16/1 Between Two Fires, Dawn's Delight, LOMBARD SHIPS, 20/1 Green's Seago (USA), 25/1 Dashing April, 33/1 Ors. CSF £92.37, Tote £20.70: £3.80 £2.90 £5.10 (£314.10). Lombard Shipping Ltd (LYDIATE) bred by J. Ward. 16 Rn; No bid
1m 28.1 (4.8)
SF—35/39/18/2/16/7

**398**    BIRDFORTH H'CAP (0-90) £2941.00 (£816.00: £391.00)    **7f**      3-20 (3-24)

233 Just a Step (80) *(MMcCormack)* 6-9-7 WNewnes (3) (led 2f: chsd ldr: rdn to chal over 2f out: led over 1f out: r.o wl u.p) .......................... —1

325* Cronk's Courage (70) (v) *(EJAlston)* 6-8-11 (5x) MHills (11) (led after 2f: hdd over 1f out: kpt on gamely ins fnl f) .......................... nk.2

233³ Abso (68) (Fav) *(RHannon)* 4-8-9 RHills (5) (hdwy on ins over 2f out: ev ch appr fnl f: hung lft & nt qckn nr fin) .......................... nk.3

225 Ikteshaf (72) *(BHanbury)* 4-8-6 ‡7VBray (2) (a in tch: effrt over 2f out: styd on wl ins fnl f: n.m.r & hmpd nr fin) .......................... hd.4

240 Sharpalto (75) *(MrsGRReveley)* 5-9-2 GHind (6) (hdwy over 2f out: kpt on: nt pce to chal) .......................... 2½.5

Hamadryad (IRE) (64) *(WCarter)* 4-8-5 GCarter (4) (lw: bhd: effrt 3f out: nvr nrr) 5.6

196* Super Benz (82) *(TFairhurst)* 6-9-6 ‡3JFanning (7) (chsd ldrs: rdn over 3f out: wknd over 1f out) .......................... 2½.7

285 Duckington **(75)** *(MHEasterby)* 8-9-2 MBirch (9) (bit bkwd: chsd ldrs tl grad
    lost pl fnl 2f) ............................................................. ¹/₂.**8**

233 Northern Printer **(68)** *(MO'Neill)* 5-8-8 JFortune (14) (bit bkwd: effrt & hdwy
    over 2f out: n.d) ............................................................. nk.**9**

265⁵ Orient Air **(63)** (bl) *(TDBarron)* 4–8-4 AlexGreaves (12) (in tch to st: sn lost pl) 2¹/₂.**10**

Jazilah (FR) **(68)** *(MPNaughton)* 4–8-9 LCharnock (2) (bit bkwd: sn bhd &
    pushed along: n.d) ......................................................... 1¹/₂.**11**

285 Arabian King **(69)** *(MBrittain)* 4–8-10 KDarley (15) (s.s: a in rr) ............ ¹/₂.**12**

325² Toshiba Comet **(74)** (bl) *(WJPearce)* 5–9-1 DNicholls (13) (chsd ldrs tl rdn &
    wknd over 2f out) ..........................................................**13**

293 Tusky **(87)** *(MJCamacho)* 4–10-0 NConnorton (8) (bit bkwd: s.i.s: a in rr) ........**14**

293 Cashtal Dazzler **(67)** *(NTinkler)* 5–8-8 KimTinkler (16) (a bhd) ................**15**

Master Pokey **(77)** *(MWEasterby)* 8–9-4 TLucas (10) (b: bit bkwd: prom to
    ¹/₂-wy: sn lost pl) .............................................................**16**

**5/1** Abso, **7/1** Sharpalto, JUST A STEP, Hamadryad (IRE)(12/1—14/1), **17/2** Super Benz, **9/1** Cronk's
Courage(op 6/1), **10/1** Toshiba Comet, **11/1** Duckington(op 7/1), **12/1** Ikteshaf, **16/1** Arabian King(op 25/1),
Master Pokey, **20/1** Orient Air(op 12/1), Cashtal Dazzler, **25/1** Jazilah (FR), **33/1** Ors. CSF £67.03, CT £320.69.
Tote £9.80: £2.80 £3.00 £1.30 £3.00 (£111.80). Mrs M. E. Cooke (WANTAGE) bred by John Davison. 16 Rn
            1m 27.3 (4)
            SF—47/36/33/29/31/5

**399**     HAMBLETON GRADUATION STKS (3-Y.O) £2774.40 (£768.40: £367.20)
        **5f**                                3-50 (3-51)

**My Sovereign (USA)** *(JRFanshawe)* 8-9 GDuffield (3) (lw: wnt rt & bmpd s:
    trckd ldrs: rdn over 1f out: styd on gamely to ld nr fin) ........ —**1**

Threepence **(86)** (bl) *(JBerry)* 9-7 GCarter (5) (chsd ldr: led wl over 1f out: sn
    hrd drvn: hdd & no ex nr fin) .......................................... nk.**2**

Black Coral (IRE) *(CFWall)* 8-9 ROuchrane (4) (hmpd s: in tch: offrt & owtohd
    outside over 1f out: kpt on one pce) ................................. 2.**3**

Hot Lavender (CAN) *(CFWall)* 8-9 JQuinn (2) (led tl hdd & wknd wl over 1f out) 4.**4**

Swellegant **(85)** (Fav) *(WJHaggas)* 9-2 MHills (1) (b.nr hind: sn pushed along:
    outpcd after 2f: eased whn btn fnl f) ............................... 6.**5**

**4/5** Swellegant, **7/2** Threepence, **4/1** MY SOVEREIGN (USA), **8/1** Black Coral (IRE), **16/1** Hot Lavender (CAN).
CSF £16.81, Tote £4.30: £2.60 £2.20 (£6.10). Mr B. E. Nielsen (NEWMARKET) bred by Crescent Farm in USA. 5
Rn                                 61.3 sec (3.6)
            SF—23/34/14/–/–

**400**     SOWERBY STKS (3-Y.O) £2560.20 (£707.20: £336.60)    **1¹/₂m**      4-20 (4-21)

280✶ **Goldsmiths' Hall (83)** *(GWragg)* 9-2 RHills (1) (lw: mde all: shkn up & r.o strly
    fnl 2f) ....................................................................... —**1**

314✶ Viardot (IRE) (Fav) *(MRStoute)* 9-2 RCochrane (4) (lw: hdwy to chase wnr 5f
    out: hrd rdn over 3f out: hung lft & btn 2f out) .................. 6.**2**

230² In the Money (IRE) **(73)** *(RHollinshead)* 8-11 WRyan (3) (prom tl wl outpcd fnl
    4f) ............................................................................. 12.**3**

296³ Legendary (IRE) *(PWChapple-Hyam)* 8-11 MHills (2) (prom tl wknd qckly 5f out) 10.**4**

**8/13** Viardot (IRE), **7/2** GOLDSMITHS' HALL(op 2/1), **7/1** In the Money (IRE), **17/2** Legendary (IRE). CSF £5.81,
Tote £3.50 (£2.00). Sheikh Mohammed (NEWMARKET) bred by White Lodge Stud Ltd. 4 Rn  2m 35.3 (5.3)
            SF—49/37/8/–

**401**     OAKSTRIPE H'CAP (3-Y.O) (0-80) £3060.00 (£850.00: £408.00)   **7f**    4-50 (4-55)
                        (Weights raised 1 lb)

242 **Try Leguard (IRE) (74)** *(WCarter)* 9-2 GCarter (2) (lw: a.p: led wl over 1f out:
    drvn clr ins fnl f) ........................................................ —**1**

295 Daaris (USA) **(65)** *(DMorley)* 8-7 KDarley (9) (sn led: rdn over 2f out: hdd wl
    over 1f out) ................................................................. 5.**2**

105³ Jefferson Davis (IRE) **(71)** *(WJPearce)* 8-13 DNicholls (6) (lw: chsd ldrs: effrt
    over 2f out: kpt on same pce) ........................................ 1¹/₂.**3**

Olette **(74)** (bl) *(GWragg)* 9-2 RCochrane (4) (led over 1f: chsd ldr tl wknd over
    1f out) ....................................................................... 1¹/₂.**4**

37✶ General John (IRE) **(76)** *(PCHaslam)* 9-4 DaleGibson (1) (in tch: effrt over 2f
    out: nt pce to chal) ..................................................... 2.**5**

Big Hand (IRE) **(71)** (Fav) *(JWWatts)* 8-13 NConnorton (14) (lw: mid div: effrt &
    hdwy over 2f out: nvr able to rch ldrs) ............................. 1¹/₂.**6**

265 Hob Green **(60)** *(MrsJRRamsden)* 8-2 AMackay (7) (hdwy 3f out: hmpd 2f out:
    kpt on) ...................................................................... 1¹/₂.**7**

Abeloni **(68)** *(AAScott)* 8-10 JFortune (3) (b.nr hind: chsd ldrs tl wknd 2f out) . nk.**8**

Lowlands Boy **(65)** *(TFairhurst)* 8-4 ‡³JFanning (16) (stdd s: hld up & wl bhd tl
    styd on strly fnl 2f) ..................................................... ¹/₂.**9**

Redisham (79) (JHMGosden) 9-7 GHind (8) (in tch to st: hung lft u.p 2f out: sn btn) ............................................................................ 6.10

Molten Copper (IRE) (70) (MWEasterby) 8-5 ‡7JMarshall (5) (bit bkwd: nvr rchd ldrs) ...................................................................... hd.11

Personal Hazard (78) (MHEasterby) 9-6 MBirch (13) (a in rr) .................. 1.12

Essayeffsee (59) (bl) (MHEasterby) 7-10 ‡5SMaloney (12) (b.hind: bit bkwd: plld hrd: prom 4f) ............................................................ 1.13

298⁵ Stormswept (USA) (67) (PWChapple-Hyam) 8-2 ‡7BThomas (11) (dwlt: hdwy & c wd st: wknd 2f out) ...................................... ½.14

277⁶ Boulabas (IRE) (69) (MO'Neill) 8-11 JLowe (10) (a in rr) ...................... 5.15

My Jersey Pearl (IRE) (69) (DonEnricoIncisa) 8-11 KimTinkler (15) (a bhd) ... 2½.16

**4/1** Big Hand (IRE)(6/1—13/2), **5/1** Olette, **6/1** Stormswept (USA), **10/1** Hob Green, General John (IRE), Redisham, **12/1** Personal Hazard, Jefferson Davis (IRE), Daaris (USA), **14/1** Abeloni, **16/1** Boulabas (IRE), Essayeffsee, TRY LEGUARD (IRE), **25/1** Molten Copper (IRE), **33/1** Lowlands Boy, **50/1** My Jersey Pearl (IRE). CSF £189.88, CT £2,192.09. Tote £20.80: £3.50 £2.60 £2.30 £2.30 (£52.10). Mr J. P. Devaney (EPSOM) bred by D. P. McConnell in Ireland. 16 Rn                                        1m 27.3 (4)
SF—42/18/19/17/15/5

T/Plpt: £225.30 (9.85 Tckts).                                                                                      O'R

# THIRSK (L-H)

## Saturday, April 11th [St course Good, Rnd Good to firm]

Going Allowance: nil sec per fur (G)                                            Wind: slt half bhd

Stalls: high

**402**        CLIFTON STKS (2-Y.O) £2584.00 (£714.00: £340.00)        **5f**        2-15 (2-15)

282a★ **Sober Lad (IRE)** (Fav) (JBerry) 9-4 GCarter (4) (lw: mde all: shkn up over 1f out: r.o strly) ........................................................ —1

329★ Moodiesburn (IRE) (ABailey) 8-13 AMackay (6) (lw: unruly stalls: s.i.s: hdwy ½-wy: ev ch whn rdn 1f out: nt qckn) ................................. 2.2

287 Arkendale Diamond (USA) (WJPearce) 8-11 DNicholls (2) (chsd ldrs: rdn & hung bdly rt over 1f out: sn wknd) ................................... 5.3

339³ Gaynor Goodman (IRE) (JSMoore) 8-6 PaulEddery (5) (lw: trckd ldrs: effrt 2f out: sn btn) .............................................................. 2½.4

Samanthas Joy (TFairhurst) 8-3 ‡3JFanning (1) (lengthy: unf: s.i.s: sn outpcd) 2½.5

Gone for a Song (MWEasterby) 8-11 KDarley (3) (leggy: scope: bit bkwd: s.s: a wl bhd) ................................................................ 10.6

**6/4** SOBER LAD (IRE), **7/4** Moodiesburn (IRE), **5/1** Gaynor Goodman (IRE)(6/1—4/1), **12/1** Gone for a Song, **20/1** Ors. CSF £4.26, Tote £2.30: £1.20 £1.70 (£1.70). Mr F. Viner (COCKERHAM) bred by John Kent in Ireland. 6 Rn                                                                     60.5 sec (2.8)
SF—48/35/13/—/—/—

**403**        MICHAEL FOSTER MEMORIAL STKS        £6004.00 (£1792.00: £856.00: £388.00)
        **6f**                                                            2-45 (2-46)

**Prince Ferdinand (110)** (Jt-Fav) (MMcCormack) 3–9-1 JReid (6) (lw: hdwy & nt clr run over 2f out: swtchd ins over 1f out: r.o strly to ld fnl f) —1

254★ Arctic Appeal (IRE) (89) (JBerry) 3–7-11 NCarlisle (7) (led: edgd lft u.p & hdd ins fnl f) ................................................................... 2.2

241⁵ **Duplicity (IRE) (100)** (Jt-Fav) (LJHolt) 4–9-1 AMcGlone (3) (lw: sn drvn along: hdwy ½-wy: kpt on same pce fnl 2f) ............................... 1½.3

Norton Challenger (108) (MHEasterby) 5–10-0 MBirch (1) (bit bkwd: w ldr: rdn & nt qckn fnl f) ................................................... ¾.4

285 Corn Futures (68) (JPLeigh) 4–8-10 KDarley (4) (chsd ldr: n.m.r & wknd over 1f out) ................................................................... 5.5

241 The Auction Bidder (91) (RHollinshead) 5–9-1 PaulEddery (5) (chsd ldrs tl wknd 2f out) ......................................................... 3½.6

Gentle Hero (USA) (93) (MPNaughton) 6–10-0 GHind (2) (blind off eye: bkwd: outpcd fr ½-wy) ......................................................... ½.7

**9/4** Duplicity (IRE), PRINCE FERDINAND, **5/1** Arctic Appeal (IRE), **11/2** Norton Challenger, **12/1** The Auction Bidder, **20/1** Gentle Hero (USA), **33/1** Corn Futures. CSF £12.28, Tote £2.30: £1.90 £2.10 (£5.20). Miss J. Winch (WANTAGE) bred by Greensward Racing Ltd. 7 Rn                                        1m 12.7 (2.5)
SF—51/25/37/47/9/—

**404**        TETLEY BITTER CLASSIC TRIAL (Stks) (3-Y.O) £7570.00 (£2260.00: £1080.00: £490.00)
        **1m**                                                            3-15 (3-16)

341³ **Jeune (101)** (GWragg) 8-11 JReid (4) (lw: hdwy over 2f out: hrd rdn over 1f out: styd on to ld last strides) ............................................ —1

Zaahi (USA) (Fav) *(HThomsonJones)* 8-11 RHills (2) (lw: led over 6f out: clr ent
st: rdn over 1f out: jst ct) ................................................................. hd.2
Big Blue *(CEBrittain)* 8-6 GCrealock (5) (lw: effrt on outside 3f out: r.o same
pce) ................................................................................................... 5.3
239³ My Memoirs (99) *(RHannon)* 9-2 AMcGlone (6) (lw: led after 1f: sn hdd: chsd
wnr tl rdn & wknd 2f out) ............................................................... 2¹/₂.4
Greetland Folly (90) *(RMWhitaker)* 8-6 AColhane (3) (led 1f: sn drvn along: lost
pl ¹/₂-wy: n.d after) ............................................................................. 7.5
Ruhr (IRE) (109) (bl) *(BWHills)* 8-11 DHolland (1) (bit bkwd: s.i.s: effrt appr st:
sn rdn along: lost pl 2f out: eased whn no ch) ................... 12.6

**6/4** Zaahi (USA), **5/2** Ruhr (IRE), **100/30** JEUNE, **7/1** My Memoirs, **12/1** Big Blue, **33/1** Greetland Folly. CSF
£8.64, Tote £4.00: £2.10 £1.50 (£4.70). Sir Robin McAlpine (NEWMARKET) bred by Sir Robin McAlpine. 6 Rn
1m 39.3 (3.3)
SF—47/46/26/26/–/–

**405**    STRAIGHTLACE H'CAP (0-80) £3210.00 (£960.00: £460.00: £210.00)
1¹/₂m
3-45 (3-47)

315 **I Perceive (61)** (Jt-Fav) *(FHLee)* 5–8-9 PaulEddery (9) (lw: hld up: stdy hdwy 4f
out: led 1f out: drvn out) .................................................................. —1
Comstock (80) *(JGFitzGerald)* 5–10-0 KFallon (11) (chsd ldrs: drvn along
¹/₂-wy: led 2f out to 1f out: r.o wl nr fin) .................................... s.h.2
234 Carlingford (USA) (53) (Jt-Fav) *(MPNaughton)* 6–8-1 LCharnock (1) (lw: led to
2f out: one pce) ............................................................................... 8.3
Just My Bill (70) (Jt-Fav) *(CWCElsey)* 6–9-4 JLowe (6) (hld up gng wl: smooth
hdwy appr st: ev ch over 2f out: sn rdn & no rspnse) ....... 3¹/₂.4
326 Fen Princess (IRE) (55) *(PCHaslam)* 4–8-1 KDarley (4) (sn bhd & drvn along:
hdwy 3f out: wknd over 1f out) ...................................................... 6.5
Sharquin (45) *(MBrittain)* 5–7-7 GBardwell (13) (bit bkwd: wnt prom ¹/₂-wy: rdn
& wknd 2f out) ............................................................................ 1¹/₂.6
267 Smoke (46) *(JParkes)* 6–7-8 NCarlisle (14) (bit bkwd: sn wl bhd: hdwy over 2f
out: nvr nrr) ..................................................................................... hd.7
J P Morgan (56) *(MPNaughton)* 4–8-2 GHind (5) (sn bhd: effrt u.p appr st: nvr nr
to chal) ............................................................................................ 4.8
Roberty Lea (69) *(TFairhurst)* 4–8-12 ‡3JFanning (3) (swtg: w ldr tl wknd over 2f
out) ................................................................................................... hd.9
27⁶ Talish (53) *(TDBarron)* 4–7-8 ‡⁵SMaloney (2) (a in rr) .......................... ¹/₂.10
Bold Elect (73) *(PWigham)* 4–9-5 MWigham (7) (bit bkwd: chsd ldrs tl grad
wknd fnl 3f) .................................................................................. 2¹/₂.11
Cheeky Pot (62) (v) *(DenysSmith)* 4–8-8 DHolland (12) (chsd ldrs tl rdn & wknd
2f out) .............................................................................................. nk.12
244⁴ Le Temeraire (69) *(NTinkler)* 6–9-3 KimTinkler (10) (lw: bhd: sme hdwy 3f out:
sn wknd) .......................................................................................... 5.13
Fassadinin (45) *(WLBarker)* 11–7-7 SWood (8) (b: bit bkwd: chsd ldrs tl wknd 3f
out) ............................................................................................... 1¹/₂.14
Vasiliev (76) *(JPLeigh)* 4–9-8 JReid (15) (reluctant to r: a wl bhd) ....................... 15
LONG HANDICAP: Sharquin 7-2, Fassadinin 6-11.

**11/2** Just My Bill, I PERCEIVE, Carlingford (USA), **7/1** Smoke, Roberty Lea, **8/1** Vasiliev, **12/1** Cheeky Pot,
Comstock, **14/1** Talish, **16/1** Sharquin, Le Temeraire, **20/1** Bold Elect, J P Morgan, Fen Princess (IRE), **50/1**
Fassadinin. CSF £68.97, CT £359.90. Tote £4.80: £2.40 £4.70 £2.20 (£47.40). Mr F. H. Lee (WILMSLOW) bred
by R. Hodgins. 15 Rn
2m 34.7 (4.7)
SF—48/66/23/33/4/–

**406**    BYLAND MEDIAN AUCTION STKS (Mdn 3-Y.O) £2461.20 (£683.20: £327.60)
7f
4-15 (4-18)

**Ships Lantern** *(CFWall)* 8-2 NCarlisle (4) (lw: trckd ldrs: led over 1f out: pushed
out) ................................................................................................... —1
Mainly Me (84) (Fav) *(MrsJCecil)* 8-2 PaulEddery (6) (b.nr fore: lw: trckd ldrs:
effrt ov ch & rdn 1f out: nt qckn) ............................................... 1¹/₂.2
Nimble Deer *(BWHills)* 8-5 DHolland (5) (led tl over 1f out: one pce) .................. 3.3
289⁵ Canaan Lane *(AHarrison)* 8-7 KFallon (11) (sn chsng ldrs: kpt on same pce fnl
2f) ...................................................................................................... 1.4
Turtle Beach *(AAScott)* 9-0 JFortune (12) (in tch: effrt u.p over 2f out: kpt on: nvr
able to chal) ................................................................................. 1¹/₂.5
252⁵ Hugging (65) *(MMcCormack)* 8-5 MBirch (9) (lw: chsd ldrs: ev ch tl rdn & wknd
over 1f out) .................................................................................. 1¹/₂.6
Speedy Sioux *(CWThornton)* 7-13 ‡3JFanning (8) (bit bkwd: in tch: drvn along
appr st: wknd over 1f out) ............................................................ 2¹/₂.7
Villa Capri *(CEBrittain)* 8-2 GCrealock (1) (bit bkwd: chsd ldrs tl wknd 2f out) .. hd.8

Katie's Dream (IRE) (43) (PSFelgate) 8-2 JLowe (7) (hld up: a in rr) .................. 2½.9
2163 Forza Azzurri (IRE) (52) (MrsNMacauley) 8-7 NDay (3) (nvr nr ldrs) .................. 3.10
264 Super Marco (54) (WWHaigh) 8-10 AMcGlone (14) (hld up & a bhd) .................. 1.11
Cherry Bob (CWThornton) 7-9 ‡7KSked (10) (bit bkwd: s.s: hmpd after 1f: n.d) 1½.12
2765 Preamble (65) (MrsJRRamsden) 8-9 TLucas (13) (rdn over 2f out: a bhd) ...... ¾.13
Jester's Gem (42) (BWMurray) 8-2 KDarley (2) (bit bkwd: a in rr) .................. 2½.14

**11/10** Mainly Me, **4/1** Nimble Deer, **6/1** Hugging(10/1—5/1), **9/1** Turtle Beach, **12/1** SHIPS LANTERN, **16/1** Villa Capri, **20/1** Preamble, **33/1** Canaan Lane, Forza Azzurri (IRE), Super Marco, **50/1** Katie's Dream (IRE), **66/1** Ors. CSF £24.92, Tote £15.50: £2.40 £1.10 £1.50 (£12.80). Mr S. S. De Chair (NEWMARKET) bred by Somerset and Lady Juliet de Chair. 14 Rn
1m 27.3 (4)
SF—28/23/17/16/18/4

## 407      THOMAS LORD H'CAP (0-70) £2382.80 (£660.80: £316.40)      5f      4-45 (4-48)

2196 **Slades Hill (54)** (TDBarron) 5-9-0 AlexGreaves (16) (chsd ldr: r.o wl u.p to ld
last strides) ........................................................ —1
253 The Noble Oak (IRE) (48) (bl) (MMcCormack) 4-8-8 JReid (7) (led: clr 2f out:
wknd ins fnl f: jst ct) ........................................ hd.2
2792 Strip Cartoon (IRE) (52) (bl) (SRBowring) 4-8-5 ‡7MHarris (1) (lw: racd far side:
kpt on u.p fnl 2f: nvr nr to chal) ............................ 4.3
1744 Drummer's Dream (IRE) (43) (MrsNMacauley) 4-8-3 DHolland (21) (sn chsng
ldrs: outpcd & n.m.r ½-wy: swtchd & styd on) .......... 1½.4
2942 Drum Sergeant (54) (JParkes) 5-9-0 NCarlisle (18) (lw: dwlt: bhd tl r.o fnl
f) ............................................................. 1.5
279 Uppance (33) (DWChapman) 4-7-7 SWood (6) (chsd ldrs tl wknd over 1f out) s.h.6
2945 Sully's Choice (USA) (52) (bl) (DWChapman) 11-8-12 JFortune (14) (lw: chsd
ldrs: rdn 2f out: sn wknd) .................................. s.h.7
Best Effort (52) (MPNaughton) 6-8-12 GHind (8) (bkwd: styd on fnl 2f: nvr nr to
chal) ......................................................... s.h.8
269 Miss Brightside (35) (ASmith) 4-7-9 JLowe (17) (lw: mid div: hdwy ½-wy:
swtchd & styd on u.p) ...................................... s.h.9
2695 Par de Luxe (39) (bl) (BWMurray) 5-7-13 AMackay (19) (s.i.s: sn wl outpcd:
hdwy u.p over 1f out: n.d) ................................. ½.10
3594 Minizen Music (IRE) (41) (MBrittain) 4-8-1 KDarley (5) (lw: chsd ldrs 3f: sn lost
pl) ........................................................... 1.11
Samsolom (68) (JBalding) 4-10-0 AClark (4) (bit bkwd: chsd ldrs tl wknd wl
over 1f out) .................................................. ¾.12
294 Hinari Video (50) (MJohnston) 7-8-10 RPElliott (10) (lw: chsd ldrs to ½-wy:
grad wknd) ................................................... ½.13
3002 Hotfoot Hannah (IRE) (50) (PSFelgate) 4-8-5 ‡5RPrice (15) (b: nvr nr ldrs) ...... ¾.14
Silver Stone Boy (50) (WJPearce) 4-8-10 SWebster (2) (bit bkwd: racd far side:
outpcd fr ½-wy) ............................................. 1½.15
Here Comes a Star (56) (bl) (JMCarr) 4-9-2 SMorris (9) (sn outpcd) ................. 2.16
265 Brisas (56) (bl) (TFairhurst) 5-8-13 ‡3JFanning (13) (a outpcd) .................. 17
Lady's Mantle (USA) (50) (RBastiman) 8-8-10 LCharnock (12) (bit bkwd: swtg:
in tch to ½-wy: eased whn btn) ............................ 18
2193 Beckingham Ben (45) (JPLeigh) 4-8-5 KFallon (11) (chsd ldrs: drvn along
½-wy: sn lost pl) ............................................ 19
277 Company Cash (55) (bl) (RBastiman) 4-8-8 ‡7HBastiman (20) (s.s: a wl bhd) ..... 20

**11/2** Drum Sergeant, **13/2** Drummer's Dream (IRE), **8/1** The Noble Oak (IRE), **11/1** Strip Cartoon (IRE), **12/1** Minizen Music (IRE), Sully's Choice (USA), Par de Luxe(op 8/1), **14/1** Hotfoot Hannah (IRE), Hinari Video, Best Effort, Beckingham Ben, Company Cash, Brisas, SLADES HILL, **16/1** Lady's Mantle (USA), **20/1** Miss Brightside, **25/1** Silver Stone Boy, **33/1** Samsolom, Here Comes a Star, **50/1** Uppance. CSF £122.90, CT £1,203.40. Tote £19.00: £4.80 £3.80 £5.80 £2.10 (£245.00). Mr James E. Greaves (THIRSK) bred by Courtown Stud Co. 20 Rn
60.1 sec (2.4)
SF—52/45/26/18/25/3

T/Plpt: £41.20 (66.25 Tckts).
WG

## 329—BRIGHTON (L-H)

### Monday, April 13th [Good to firm]
Going Allowance: minus 0.05 sec per fur (F)
Wind: str half bhd

Stalls: low

## 408      ORLEANS STKS (Mdn 3-Y.O.F) £1932.00 (£532.00: £252.00)      5f 213y      2-00 (2-03)

**Mathaayl (USA)** (HThomsonJones) 8-11 NCarlisle (7) (plld hrd: hdwy over 2f
out: led over 1f out: easily) ............................... —1
Oh so Rosy (PFICole) 8-11 TQuinn (5) (6th st: rdn over 1f out: unable qckn) ..... 5.2

    Ahbab (IRE) *(Fav) (PTWalwyn)* 8-11 WCarson (8) (h.d.w: bit bkwd: bmpd over
        3f out: hdwy on ins over 2f out: hmpd 1f out: r.o wl) .......... ¾.**3**

    Sharling *(JHMGosden)* 8-11 WRSwinburn (9) (5th st: one pce fnl 2f) ............. 1½.**4**

    Pleasuring **(65)** *(MMcCormack)* 8-11 JReid (3) (bit bkwd: led 4f out tl hung lft &
        hdd over 1f out: sn wknd) ...................................... ¾.**5**

    Mabonne **(64)** *(JLDunlop)* 8-11 GDuffield (11) (outpcd: gd hdwy fnl f: fin wl) .. 2½.**6**

    Rockbourne **(55)** *(DRCElsworth)* 8-11 JWilliams (4) (bkwd: 4th st: wknd 2f out) 1½.**7**

2703  Tulapet **(55)** *(SDow)* 8-11 MRoberts (12) (nvr nr to chal) .................................. s.h.**8**

    Ballycastle Mary (IRE) *(TJNaughton)* 8-11 AMunro (10) (b.nr hind: w'like: lw:
        s.s: nvr nrr) ........................................................ 1½.**9**

    Kindred Cameo *(GLewis)* 8-11 BRouse (13) (a bhd) ................................. ¾.**10**

    Mint Addition **(60)** *(RHannon)* 8-11 AMcGlone (1) (nt grwn: spd 3f) ................ 2.**11**

3475  Freni **(41)** *(MDIUsher)* 8-11 CRutter (15) (a bhd) .................................. 3.**12**

    Bells of Longwick **(60)** *(DRLaing)* 8-11 SWhitworth (2) (led 2f: 3rd st: wknd over
        2f out) ............................................................ nk.**13**

2705  Placid Lady (IRE) **(48)** *(WCarter)* 8-6 ‡5NGwilliams (6) (2nd st: wknd over 2f out)2½.**14**

296  Lady Reem (USA) *(MMoubarak)* 8-11 LDettori (14) (bhd fnl 2f) ................ ½.**15**
        *Stewards Enquiry: Reid suspended 22-25/4/92 (careless riding).*

**13/8** Ahbab (IRE)(5/2—6/4), **2/1** MATHAAYL (USA)(5/4—5/2), **8/1** Pleasuring, **10/1** Oh so Rosy, **14/1** Lady
Reem (USA)(op 8/1), **16/1** Mabonne(10/1—20/1), **20/1** Ballycastle Mary (IRE)(op 8/1), Tulapet, Kindred
Cameo(op 8/1), Mint Addition, **25/1** Placid Lady (IRE), **33/1** Bells of Longwick, Rockbourne, Sharling, **50/1** Freni.
CSF £24.79, Tote £2.70: £1.10 £2.00 £2.80 (£37.60). Mr Hamdan Al-Maktoum (NEWMARKET) bred by
Hamdan Al Maktoum in USA. 15 Rn                  1m 11.7 (3.3)
                                               SF—25/5/2/–/–/–

**409**   TOWN PURSE H'CAP (0-70) £2480.80 (£688.80: £151.20 each)
       **1m 3f 196y**                            2-30 (2-40)
                         *(Weights raised 1 lb)*

2724  **Abingdon Flyer (IRE) (56)** (bl) *(RHannon)* 4-8-13 JReid (6) (hdwy 5f out: 4th
        st: hrd rdn over 1f out: led wl ins fnl f: all out) ........................ —**1**

    Checkpoint Charlie **(56)** *(JMPEustace)* 7-9-1 RCochrane (5) (s.s: hdwy 5f out:
        6th st: led over 2f out tl wl ins fnl f: r.o wl) ........................ hd.**2**

2732  Tiger Claw (USA) **(55)** *(Fav) (RJHodges)* 6-9-0 WCarson (1) (7th st: n.m.r on
        ins over 2f out: r.o one pce) ...................................... 2½.**3**

3312  Absolutely Right **(52)** *(RAkehurst)* 4-8-9 TQuinn (12) (b.nr hind: hdwy 3f out:
        one pce fnl f) .................................................. d.h.**3**

193*  Classic Account **(44)** *(JAkehurst)* 4-8-1 AMunro (15) (2nd st: ev ch over 2f out:
        wknd over 1f out) ................................................ 4.**5**

288  Bold Resolution (IRE) **(46)** *(CACyzer)* 4-7-10 ‡7AMorris (16) (nvr nr to chal) .... 3½.**6**

    Camden's Ransom (USA) **(64)** *(DRCElsworth)* 5-9-9 JWilliams (19) (3rd st: led
        over 3f out tl over 2f out: sn wknd) ................................ 1½.**7**

2733  Joli's Great **(52)** *(MJRyan)* 4-8-6 ‡3DBiggs (17) (5th st: wknd over 2f out) ...... 1½.**8**

    Podrida **(52)** *(RJO'Sullivan)* 6-8-11 AClark (3) (hdwy fnl 2f: nvr nrr) ............. 3½.**9**

331  Midday Show (USA) **(65)** *(JRJenkins)* 5-9-10 SWhitworth (7) (s.s: hdwy 4f out:
        nvr nrr) ........................................................ 2.**10**

2723  Ramble (USA) **(47)** *(JABOld)* 5-8-6 RFox (4) (prom 6f) ......................... ¾.**11**

155  Red Dollar **(45)** *(BGubby)* 7-8-4 NCarlisle (5) (8th st: wknd 3f out) ............ hd.**12**

331  Romanian (IRE) **(50)** *(ARDavison)* 4-8-7 CandyMorris (18) (prom 7f: 9th &
        wkng st) ........................................................ 2½.**13**

166  Wise Friend (USA) **(40)** *(CPWildman)* 4-7-11(4) CRutter (13) (bhd fnl 4f) ....... 2½.**14**

2025  Carlowitz (USA) **(41)** *(AMoore)* 4-7-12 NAdams (9) (led over 8f) ................. 3.**15**

358  Boogy Lady (IRE) **(46)** *(ICampbell)* 4-8-3 AMackay (14) (bhd fnl 4f) ............. 2.**16**

    Victory Gate (USA) **(44)** *(AMoore)* 7-7-12 ‡5ATucker (11) (b: a bhd) ............. nk.**17**

    As Always (IRE) **(53)** *(GLewis)* 4-8-3 ‡7BRussell (10) (bkwd: bhd fnl 6f) ......... 1½.**18**

90  Striking Distance **(40)** *(JFitch-Heyes)* 5-7-13 SDawson (20) (bhd fnl 4f) ......... 2.**19**

    Gaily Dance **(43)** *(RJHodges)* 4-7-7(7) ‡7BThomas (2) (a bhd) .................. 6.**20**
        *LONG HANDICAP: Wise Friend (USA) 6-11, Gaily Dance 7-1.*

**9/2** Tiger Claw (USA), **5/1** Classic Account, **6/1** Camden's Ransom (USA), **13/2** Absolutely Right, **7/1** Joli's
Great, **14/1** Checkpoint Charlie, Boogy Lady (IRE), Bold Resolution (IRE), **16/1** ABINGDON FLYER (IRE),
Carlowitz (USA), **25/1** As Always (IRE), Romanian (IRE), Striking Distance, **33/1** Ramble (USA), Red Dollar,
Podrida, Midday Show (USA), **66/1** Ors. CSF £212.51, CT w TC £542.07; w AR £737.26. Tote £13.30: £3.40
£3.30 TC £1.50 AR £1.50 (£69.40). Mr J. A. Nichols (MARLBOROUGH) bred by Grange Thoroughbreds in
Ireland. 20 Rn                                     2m 32.7 (flag) (5.7)
                                       SF—36/37/31/26/10/–

**410**   PRINCE OF WALES GRADUATION STKS (3-Y.O) £6248.00 (£1728.00: £824.00)
       **1m 1f 209y**                            3-00 (3-04)

    **Beldi (USA) (86)** *(CEBrittain)* 8-11 MRoberts (3) (3rd st: led wl over 1f out: all
        out) ............................................................... —**1**

Anchorite (110) (Fav) (PTWalwyn) 9-4 RCochrane (1) (led over 8f: hrd rdn & ev ch fnl f: r.o wl) .................................................................. s.h.2

330* Desert Zone (USA) (100) (PFICole) 9-4 AMunro (2) (2nd st: ev ch over 2f out: unable qckn) ..................................................................... 2½.3

10/11 Anchorite, **Evens** Desert Zone (USA), 14/1 BELDI (USA)(op 8/1). CSF £24.23, Tote £5.30 (£2.50). Mr Luciano Gaucci (NEWMARKET) bred by Jayeff B. Stables in USA. 3 Rn
2m 4.5 (6.5)
SF—27/33/28

# 411

PETWORTH H'CAP (0-70) £2598.40 (£722.40: £347.20)   **7f 214y**   3-30 (3-35)

273⁵ Marzocco (50) (JFfitch-Heyes) 4-8-9 AMackay (7) (lw: hdwy 2f out: led over 1f out: r.o wl) ............................................................ —1
344 Saafend (65) (JSutcliffe) 4-9-10 WRSwinburn (11) (hdwy 2f out: r.o ins fnl f) .. 1½.2
112² El Volador (56) (RJO'Sullivan) 5-9-1 LDettori (8) (hdwy fnl 2f: r.o) ................... nk.3
270² Prince Rodney (70) (Fav) (RHannon) 3-8-13 WCarson (12) (3rd st: ev ch over 1f out: unable qckn) ....................................................... 2.4
351³ Sarum (56) (CPWildman) 6-9-1 CRutter (9) (hdwy over 2f out: r.o one pce) ....... 1.5
277 Tender Moment (IRE) (62) (CEBrittain) 4-9-7 MRoberts (14) (lw: 2nd st: led 3f out tl over 1f out: wn wknd) ............................................. 2.6
299 Devil's Soul (57) (RAkehurst) 4-9-2 AMunro (13) (nvr nr to chal) ................... hd.7
250⁵ Breezed Well (68) (CNAllen) 6-9-6 ‡7MichaelDenaro (16) (hdwy 4f out: 5th st: ev ch 2f out: wknd over 1f out) ........................................... 2½.8
207⁵ Precious Air (IRE) (52) (AMoore) 4-8-11 BRouse (2) (rdn over 3f out: hdwy on ins 2f out: wknd over 1f out) ........................................... ½.9
Ivanov (USA) (62) (PMitchell) 4-9-7 JWilliams (17) (lw: nvr nrr) ................. 1½.10
Debjanjo (51) (JRJenkins) 4-8-10 SWhitworth (5) (nvr nrr) ........................ 2.11
Charmed Knave (52) (DRLaing) 7-8-4 ‡7PBowe (4) (bit bkwd: outpcd) ........... nk.12
253 Kissavos (56) (CCElsey) 6-9-1 TRogers (10) (6th st: wknd 2f out) ............ 1.13
Lamastre (68) (RJHodges) 3-8-11 ADicks (3) (s.s: a bhd) ....................... 1.14
Kirriemuir (50) (KOCunningham-Brown) 4-8-9 JReid (15) (4th st: wknd over 2f out) ............................................................................. nk.15
Juvenara (53) (CJHill) 6-8-12 NAdams (6) (bit bkwd: led 5f) ................... 15.16
340 Tendresse (IRE) (50) (DRTucker) 4-8-6 ‡3DBiggs (6) (a bhd) ................. 3.17

5/1 Prince Rodney, 11/2 El Volador, 6/1 Saafend, 7/1 Sarum, 8/1 Devil's Soul, 12/1 Kissavos, 14/1 Tender Moment (IRE), Juvenara, 16/1 Breezed Well(12/1—20/1), MARZOCCO, Precious Air (IRE), Charmed Knave, 20/1 Tendresse (IRE), 25/1 Lamastre, 33/1 Ivanov (USA), Debjanjo, 50/1 Kirriemuir. CSF £105.92, CT £560.81. Tote £33.50: £4.10 £2.60 £2.00 £1.60 (£218.20). Mr Chris Steward (LEWES) bred by R. H. Cowell. 17 Rn
1m 36.9 (4.7)
SF—19/29/19/11/10/10

# 412

LEVY BOARD STKS (Mdn) £2520.00 (£700.00: £336.00)   **7f 214y**   4-00 (4-09)

**Kitaab (USA)** (ACStewart) 3-8-8 MRoberts (13) (str: hdwy over 2f out: led ins fnl f: pushed out) ................................................................. —1
Nashville Blues (IRE) (JWHills) 3-8-3 SWhitworth (4) (3rd st: led 2f out tl ins fnl f: r.o) ..................................................................... ½.2
Bayaireg (USA) (AAScott) 3-8-8 WRSwinburn (2) (hdwy 4f out: 6th st: rdn over 1f out: r.o one pce) .................................................... 1½.3
Fusion (USA) (PFICole) 3-8-8 AMunro (12) (wl grwn: bit bkwd: 5th st: r.o one pce fnl 2f) ................................................................... ½.4
Combative (IRE) (v) (JHMGosden) 3-8-8 LDettori (9) (leggy: lost pl over 4f out: rallied over 1f out: r.o) ................................................... 2.5
Top Royal (JLDunlop) 3-8-8 TQuinn (11) (4th st: ev ch 2f out: eased whn btn over 1f out) .............................................................. 4.6
Day of History (IRE) (CACyzer) 3-7-11(1) ‡7AMorris (1) (w'like: bkwd: outpcd: hdwy 2f out: nvr nrr) ...................................................... 3½.7
Forgetful (RHannon) 3-8-3 AMcGlone (5) (2nd st: led 3f out to 2f out: sn wknd) 1½.8
Bellatrix (CEBrittain) 4-9-2 ‡3RonHillis (14) (bit bkwd: led 5f) .................. 1.9
235² Glasgow (Fav) (BWHills) 3-8-8 WCarson (7) (rdn over 2f out: no rspnse) ......... hd.11
Agincourt Song (USA) (JLDunlop) 3-8-8 JReid (10) (lw: outpcd) ............... 3.12
Philostra (AndrewTurnell) 4-9-0 ‡5ATucker (6) (unf: scope: lw: a bhd) .......... 3.12
Reina (JDBethell) 4-9-5 GDuffield (3) (lw: bhd fnl 4f) ....................... 2.13
302 Barjonal (40) (bl) (JJBridger) 3-8-3 NAdams (8) (lw: a bhd) ................ 15.14
Suemax (IRE) (RJHodges) 4-9-5 ADicks (15) (w'like: scope: prom 4f) ......... 3.15

**Evens** Glasgow(6/4—7/4), 100/30 Fusion (USA), 6/1 KITAAB (USA)(3/1—7/1), 10/1 Bayaireg (USA)(op 6/1), 14/1 Combative (IRE), Agincourt Song (USA)(op 6/1), 16/1 Forgetful, 20/1 Nashville Blues (IRE)(op 12/1), 25/1 Top Royal, 33/1 Day of History (IRE), Bellatrix, 50/1 Philostra, Reina, 100/1 Ors. CSF £116.65, Tote £9.30: £2.30 £2.30 £3.80 (£322.60). Mr Hamdan Al-Maktoum (NEWMARKET) bred by Fittocks Stud Farm in USA. 15 Rn
1m 36.1 (3.9)
SF—29/22/22/20/14/–

**413** SIDNEY THOMPSON MEMORIAL STKS £2406.00 (£666.00: £318.00)
6f 209y 4-30 (4-32)

**Gotcha (BAR) (83)** *(RHannon)* 3–7-13 WCarson (2) (rdn thrght: 5th st: hrd rdn
over 1f out: led ins fnl f: r.o wl) .................................... —1
2394 Soleil Dancer (IRE) **(98)** *(Fav) (MMcCormack)* 4–9-10 JReid (1) (lw: led: bmpd
2f out: hdd ins fnl f: unable qckn) ............................... 2¹/₂.2
3514 Invocation *(AMoore)* 5–9-0 NAdams (3) (2nd st: ev ch whn edgd lft & bmpd 2f
out: one pce) ................................................ 4.3
Walk in the Park **(91)** *(RSimpson)* 3–7-10(3) ‡5ATucker (5) (3rd st: wknd over 1f
out) ...................................................... 5.4
182 Spectacle Jim *(JO'Donoghue)* 3–7-10 ‡3DBiggs (4) (4th st: wknd 3f out) ......... 20.5

**10/11** Soleil Dancer (IRE), **9/4** GOTCHA (BAR), **6/1** Walk in the Park(op 7/2), **10/1** Invocation(7/1—14/1), **66/1**
Spectacle Jim. CSF £4.40, Tote £2.50 £2.00 £1.20 (£2.40). Mr David Seale (MARLBOROUGH) bred by C. D.
Seale in Barbados. 5 Rn
1m 22.8 (2.8)
SF—38/55/33/–/–

**414** CONFLANS H'CAP (0-80) £2448.00 (£678.00: £324.00) **5f 59y** 5-00 (5-01)

3493 **Plain Fact (75)** *(Fav) (SirMarkPrescott)* 7–10-0 GDuffield (6) (hdwy over 2f out:
led over 1f out: comf) ........................................ —1
3442 Across the Bay **(69)** (v) *(SDow)* 5–9-8 TQuinn (10) (6th st: hdwy over 1f out: r.o
ins fnl f) .................................................. 4.2
Belfort Ruler **(68)** *(BGubby)* 5–9-7 JReid (9) (5th st: one pce fnl 2f) ............... s.h.3
344 How's Yer Father **(70)** *(RJHodges)* 6–9-9 WCarson (5) (hrd rdn 2f out: hdwy
over 1f out: r.o ins fnl f) ..................................... ¹/₂.4
349 Restore **(56)** (bl) *(RVoorspuy)* 9–8-9 SDawson (1) (4th st: one pce fnl 2f) ......... ³/₄.5
2704 Savalaro **(54)** *(JFfitch-Heyes)* 3–7-9 AMackay (11) (led 4f) ....................... 2.6
Battling Bella (USA) **(68)** *(JSutcliffe)* 3–8-9 BRouse (3) (bkwd: swtg: s.i.s: nvr nrr) .7
188 Greetland Rock **(52)** *(PHowling)* 4–8-5 JMurray (2) (swtg: a bhd) ................... 1¹/₂.8
1305 Slip-a-Snip **(70)** *(GBBalding)* 5–9-2 ‡7TraceyPurseglove (12) (lw: 3rd st: wknd
over 1f out) ............................................... ³/₄.9
2476 Saruk (IRE) **(52)** *(JJBridger)* 3–7-7 RFox (8) (2nd st: wknd 3f out) ............... 1¹/₂.10
217 Sports Post Lady **(65)** *(CJHill)* 4–9-4 NAdams (7) (lw: bhd fnl 2f) ............... 6.11
LONG HANDICAP: Saruk (IRE) 6-8.

**9/4** PLAIN FACT, **4/1** Across the Bay, **9/2** How's Yer Father(4/1—6/1), **13/2** Battling Bella (USA), **8/1** Sports
Post Lady (IRE), **11/1** Slip-a-Snip(8/1—12/1), **20/1** Restore(op 12/1), **33/1** Greetland Rock, **50/1** Belfort Ruler,
Savalaro, **100/1** Saruk (IRE). CSF £10.71, CT £302.79. Tote £3.00 £1.60 £1.20 £7.80 (£2.90). Mr W. E. Sturt
(NEWMARKET) bred by Clanville Lodge Stud. 11 Rn
62.1 sec (1.8)
SF—73/51/49/32/10

T/Plpt: £1,110.00 (2 Tckts). AK

# EDINBURGH (R-H)
## Monday, April 13th [Good, Good to firm patches]
Going Allowance: St: 0.20 sec; Rnd: nil sec per fur (G) Wind: fresh against

Stalls: high

**415** NORTH BERWICK STKS (Mdn 3-Y.O) £1500.50 (£418.00: £201.50) **5f** 2-10 (2-12)

**Stonewall Jackson (IRE)** *(Fav) (WJPearce)* 9-0 DNicholls (9) (a chsng ldrs:
led wl over 1f out: r.o) ...................................... —1
3633 Rural Lad *(MrsJRRamsden)* 9-0 TLucas (7) (lw: hld up & bhd: gd hdwy 2f out:
ev ch ins fnl f: r.o) ......................................... 1.2
363 Tagetes *(JPearce)* 8-4 ‡5RPrice (8) (w ldrs: rdn & ev ch appr fnl f: nt qckn) ..... 1¹/₂.3
2764 Murray's Mazda (IRE) **(58)** *(JBerry)* 9-0 GCarter (1) (lw: led tl hdd wl over 1f out:
no ex) .................................................... 1¹/₂.4
2763 We're All Game **(58)** *(BCMorgan)* 8-9 JLowe (2) (hdwy ¹/₂-wy: rdn & no imp fnl
2f) ...................................................... 3¹/₂.5
363 Ipsilante *(ASReid)* 8-9 MBirch (3) (b: chsd ldrs: effrt 2f out: sn btn) .............. nk.6
Long Last *(DWChapman)* 8-9 SWood (5) (w'like: bit bkwd: in tch tl wknd 2f out) 4.7
224 Persian Anthem (IRE) *(GWragg)* 8-4 ‡5FNorton (4) (lw: bhd fr ¹/₂-wy) ........... 5.8
324 Ebony Isle *(PMonteith)* 8-6 ‡3JFanning (6) (dwlt: a in rr) ..................... 5.9
3136 Bantel Brigadier **(45)** *(RAllan)* 9-0 SWebster (10) (gd spd tl wknd qckly ¹/₂-wy) 1.10

**7/4** STONEWALL JACKSON (IRE), **9/4** Rural Lad(op 5/4), **6/1** Tagetes, **9/1** Murray's Mazda (IRE), **10/1** We're All
Game, **11/1** Persian Anthem (IRE)(op 7/1), **20/1** Long Last(op 12/1), Ipsilante(op 12/1), **66/1** Ebony Isle, **200/1**
Bantel Brigadier. CSF £6.09, Tote £3.40: £1.80 £2.10 £1.80 (£4.80). The Confederacy (HAMBLETON) bred by
Noel O'Callaghan in Ireland. 10 Rn
62.1 sec (4.4)
SF—32/28/12/16/–/–

## 416 CARBERRY AUCTION STKS (Mdn 2-Y.O) £1563.50 (£436.00: £210.50) 5f 2-40 (2-44)

237 **Two Moves in Front (IRE)** *(JBerry)* 8-8 GCarter (10) (lw: a w ldrs: led 2f out: r.o) —1
Peedie Peat *(JJO'Neill)* 8-12 TLucas (7) (leggy: bit bkwd: in tch: rdn & outpcd ½-wy: r.o wl fnl f) ........................ ¾.2
2873 Royal Folly (IRE) *(CWCElsey)* 7-12 JLowe (8) (chsd ldrs: outpcd ½-wy: styd on ins fnl f) ........................ nk.3
Dead Calm *(CTinkler)* 8-4 MBirch (3) (neat: bit bkwd: w ldrs: ev ch 2f out: nt qckn) ........................ 2.4
2872 Stardust Express (Fav) *(MJohnston)* 8-7 RPElliott (4) (led tl hdd 2f out: no ex) 2½.5
2973 Not so Generous (IRE) *(WGMTurner)* 7-6 ‡7TWilson (9) (bhd: hdwy & hung lft ½-wy: rdn & btn appr fnl f) ........................ 2½.6
2632 Annie Rose *(TDBarron)* 8-2 AlexGreaves (1) (lw: in tch: drvn along 2f out: sn wknd) ........................ 1½.7
Sea-Ayr (IRE) *(MissLAPerratt)* 7-11 ‡3JFanning (2) (neat: bit bkwd: sn bhd) ....... 5.8
2316 Mantlepiece (IRE) *(TDBarron)* 8-1 KDarley (5) (gd spd tl wknd qckly ½-wy) ..... 2.9
Our Price *(GMMoore)* 8-4 KFallon (6) (unf: leggy: bit bkwd: a wl in rr) ......... s.h.10

3/1 Stardust Express, 4/1 Peedie Peat, 5/1 TWO MOVES IN FRONT (IRE), 11/2 Annie Rose(op 3/1), 6/1 Dead Calm, 8/1 Royal Folly (IRE), 12/1 Not so Generous (IRE), 14/1 Sea-Ayr (IRE), 20/1 Our Price(op 10/1), 33/1 Mantlepiece (IRE). CSF £25.32, Tote £6.70: £2.00 £2.30 £2.00 (£45.30). Mr Robert Aird (COCKERHAM) bred by Newlands House Stud in Ireland. 10 Rn
62.2 sec (4.5)
SF—24/25/10/8/1/–

## 417 TENNENTS SPRING H'CAP (0-80) £1640.50 (£458.00: £221.50)
1½m 31y 3-10 (3-10)

(Weights raised 2 lb)
315* El Nido (59) (Fav) *(MJCamacho)* 4-9-4 NConnorton (6) (lw: plld hrd early: prom: led appr fnl f: styd on) ........................ —1
3124 K-Brigade (49) (bl) *(CWCElsey)* 7-8-10 KFallon (5) (hld up in tch: n.m.r appr fnl f: r.o nr fin) ........................ 1.2
267* Glastondale (39) *(TDBarron)* 6-8-0 DaleGibson (3) (led & set mod pce: hdd appr fnl f: kpt on) ........................ 1.3
2676 Not Yet (40) *(EWeymes)* 8-7-8 ‡7AGarth (7) (in tch: effrt & n.m.r appr fnl f: styd on) ........................ ¾.4
1615 Margs Girl (56) *(TFairhurst)* 5-9-0 ‡3JFanning (1) (chsd ldr: ev ch & rdn 2f out: nt qckn) ........................ 2.5
3285 Long Furlong (60) *(RAkehurst)* 4-9-0 ‡5FNorton (4) (hld up & bhd: hdwy to disp ld over 2f out: sn wknd & no ex) ........................ 1½.6
1795 Starlight Wonder (43) *(REBarr)* 6-8-4 SWebster (8) (in tch: effrt & no imp fnl 2f) hd.7
Royal Borough (63) *(MPNaughton)* 7-9-10 GHind (2) (chsd ldrs: rdn & ev ch over 2f out: sn btn) ........................ 1.8

11/8 EL NIDO, 7/2 Glastondale, 5/1 K-Brigade, 7/1 Long Furlong(op 4/1), 10/1 Margs Girl, 20/1 Royal Borough, 25/1 Not Yet, 50/1 Starlight Wonder. CSF £8.21, CT £17.42. Tote £2.50: £1.70 £1.10 £1.80 (£4.70). Mr H. Roberts (MALTON) bred by M. J. Camacho. 8 Rn
2m 41.2 (8.7)
SF—17/7/–/–/–/–

## 418 INVERESK STKS (Mdn 3 & 4-Y.O) £1563.50 (£436.00: £210.50)
1½m 31y 3-40 (3-41)

3305 Landowner (IRE) (68) (Fav) *(JHMGosden)* 3-8-4 GHind (5) (led 3f: cl up: led 3f out: edgd lft 2f out: hld on wl fnl f) ........................ —1
3142 White Willow *(BHanbury)* 3-8-4 AShoults (6) (lw: a w ldrs: disp ld 2f out: r.o wl fnl f) ........................ hd.2
2305 Northern Kingdom (USA) *(SGNorton)* 3-8-4 NConnorton (1) (prom: rdn over 2f out: styd on wl fnl f) ........................ 2½.3
Naseem Elbarr (USA) *(ACStewart)* 4-9-12 MBirch (4) (bit bkwd: cl up: led after 3f: hdd 3f out: no ex fnl 2f) ........................ ¾.4
Native Crown (IRE) *(MissLAPerratt)* 4-9-5 ‡7RHavlin (8) (in tch: effrt 3f out: nt qckn) ........................ 3.5
Father Hayes (USA) *(WJPearce)* 4-9-12 DNicholls (3) (bit bkwd: bhd: styd on fnl 2f: n.d) ........................ 3.6
120 Belarius (45) *(REBarr)* 4-9-12 SWebster (9) (a bhd) ........................ 15.7
243 Tumbling (USA) *(RAllan)* 4-9-12 JLowe (7) (lost tch ent st) ........................ 8.8
First Crusade (FR) *(RAllan)* 4-9-5 ‡7JWeaver (2) (bit bkwd: chsd ldrs: 6th & btn whn broke knee & p.u fnl f: dead) ........................ 0

5/4 LANDOWNER (IRE)(op 4/5), 2/1 White Willow, 9/2 Northern Kingdom (USA), 9/1 Naseem Elbarr (USA), 20/1 Father Hayes (USA), 33/1 Tumbling (USA), First Crusade (FR), 40/1 Native Crown (IRE), 150/1 Belarius. CSF £4.22, Tote £1.90: £1.50 £1.60 £2.10 (£2.30). Sheikh Mohammed (NEWMARKET) bred by Sheikh Mohammed bin Rashid al Maktoum in Ireland. 9 Rn
2m 41.7 (9.2)

**419**      ABERLADY (S) H'CAP (0-60) £1549.50 (£432.00: £208.50)    **1m 16y**    4-10 (4-11)

(Weights raised 9 lb)

326   **Lazy Rhythm (USA) (42)** *(RAkehurst)* 6–9-0 ‡⁵FNorton (7) (in tch: hdwy to ld
over 1f out: r.o) ......................................................................................... —1
364²   **Errema (42)** (Fav) *(CTinkler)* 7–9-5 MBirch (13) (mid div: hdwy ent st: swtchd
ins appr fnl f: r.o) ......................................................................................... hd.2
359⁶   Station Express (IRE) **(35)** *(BEllison)* 4–8-5 ‡⁷JWeaver (12) (hdwy 3f out: effrt 2f
out: kpt on) ................................................................................................. 1¹/₂.3
328   Tequila Gold **(34)** *(JJO'Neill)* 4–8-11 DaleGibson (16) (bhd: hdwy over 2f out:
styd on fnl f: nrst fin) ................................................................................... ¹/₂.4
397³   Between Two Fires **(52)** *(JBerry)* 3–8-13 GCarter (1) (w ldrs: rn wd ent st: ev ch
2f out: no ex) .............................................................................................. ¹/₂.5
232   Golden Beau **(28)** *(AHarrison)* 10–8-5 KFallon (15) (bhd: hdwy 2f out: styd on:
nvr able to chal) ......................................................................................... 3¹/₂.6
208⁵   Say You Will **(36)** (v) *(MPNaughton)* 8–8-13 GHind (3) (chsd ldrs: rdn & no imp
fnl 2f) ......................................................................................................... 3¹/₂.7
364   The Devil's Music **(42)** *(MrsJRRamsden)* 8–9-5 TLucas (11) (bhd: effrt ent st:
one pce fnl 2f) ............................................................................................. 1¹/₂.8
Rostovol **(40)** (v) *(DRFranks)* 7–9-0 ‡³JFanning (4) (bhd: effrt ent st: n.d) ....... 1¹/₂.9
359⁵   Miss Knight **(47)** *(RBastiman)* 5–9-10 NConnorton (9) (nvr bttr than mid div) . hd.10
173   Our Amber **(33)** *(DWChapman)* 5–8-10 SWood (5) (bhd whn rn wd ent st: n.d) 2¹/₂.11
333⁵   Internal Affair **(41)** *(JPearce)* 4–8-13 ‡⁵RPrice (8) (cl up: led ent st: hdd over 1f
out: sn wknd) ............................................................................................... ¹/₂.12
377   Master Plan (FR) **(30)** *(MissLAPerratt)* 6–8-0 ‡⁷RHavlin (6) (sn led: hdd ent st:
wknd qckly) ................................................................................................. nk.13
Fait Accompli (FR) **(55)** (bl) *(JJO'Neill)* 3–9-2 DNicholls (14) (s.i.s: a bhd) ....... nk.14
326⁴   Stormy Praise (USA) **(41)** (bl) *(WGMTurner)* 8–9-4 JLowe (2) (prom: rn wd ent
st: wknd qckly over 2f out) ........................................................................... 2.15
Dangina **(35)** *(ASReid)* 3–7-10 LCharnock (10) (led early: cl up u wknd 3f out) nk.16

**7/2** Errema, **4/1** Station Express (IRE)(op 8/1), **5/1** Between Two Fires, LAZY RHYTHM (USA), **10/1** Say You Will,
Miss Knight, **12/1** Stormy Praise (USA)(op 8/1), Internal Affair, Golden Beau, **16/1** Master Plan (FR), The Devil's
Music, Rostovol, Tequila Gold, **25/1** Fait Accompli (FR), **40/1** Dangina, **66/1** Our Amber. CSF £25.63, CT
£78.90. Tote £15.60: £4.10 £1.30 £2.30 £3.30 (£20.50). Miss S. A. Hamilton (EPSOM) bred by Donald T.
Johnson in USA. 16 Rn; Bt in 2,000 gns                     1m 43.7 (5.1)
                                               SF—24/28/16/13/13/–

---

**420**      DALMENY H'CAP (0-70) £1735.00 (£485.00: £235.00)    **7f 15y**    4-40 (4-43)

(Weights raised 2 lb)

285³   **Euroblake (53)** (Fav) *(TDBarron)* 5–8-13 AlexGreaves (3) (a chsng ldrs: led
appr fnl f: hld on wl) ................................................................................... —1
269   Kawwas **(33)** *(WHolden)* 7–7-7 JLowe (6) (bhd: gd hdwy over 2f out: ev ch ins
fnl f: styd on) ............................................................................................. hd.2
269   Cool Enough **(38)** *(MrsJRRamsden)* 11–7-9 ‡³FNorton (12) (hdwy 2f out: styd
on fnl f: nt rch ldrs) ..................................................................................... 3.3
265⁴   In a Whirl (USA) **(49)** *(DWChapman)* 4–8-9 GCarter (10) (lw: mde most tl hdd
appr fnl f: no ex) ......................................................................................... 4.4
Cornhill Melody **(42)** *(JLSpearing)* 4–9-7⁽⁹⁾ ‡⁷AGarth (14) (hdwy appr st: rdn
over 2f out: one pce) .................................................................................... 1¹/₂.5
Nevada Mix **(51)** *(MissLAPerratt)* 8–8-11 DaleGibson (4) (mid div: hdwy 3f out:
sn rdn: btn wl over 1f out) ............................................................................ s.h.6
333★   Daisy Grey **(49)** (bl) *(ASReid)* 4–8-2 ‡⁷PMcCabe (9) (w ldrs: rdn ent st: wknd 2f
out) ............................................................................................................. ³/₄.7
Manuleader **(66)** *(WJPearce)* 3–8-11 DNicholls (5) (mid div: styd on fnl 2f: n.d) nk.8
Revel **(45)** (bl) *(LLungo)* 4–8-5⁽³⁾ KFallon (13) (b.off hind: chsd ldrs tl wknd 2f
out) ............................................................................................................. ³/₄.9
325   Castle Cary **(39)** *(TCraig)* 6–7-13 LCharnock (1) (plld hrd: hld up & bhd: n.d) 2¹/₂.10
Fair Flyer (IRE) **(61)** *(PMonteith)* 3–8-3 ‡³JFanning (7) (in tch: effrt ent st: btn wl
over 2f out) ................................................................................................. ³/₄.11
Flying Down to Rio (IRE) **(64)** *(MPNaughton)* 4–9-10 GHind (11) (a bhd) ......... 1¹/₂.12
315   Aussie Aisle (IRE) **(47)** *(DMoffatt)* 4–8-0 ‡⁷DarrenMoffatt (2) (a in rr) ............... nk.13
70   Kabera **(33)** *(DWChapman)* 4–7-7 SWood (8) (prom whn rn wd ent st: sn bhd) 5.14

LONG HANDICAP: Kawwas 7-6.

**3/1** EUROBLAKE, **5/1** In a Whirl (USA), **6/1** Nevada Mix, Cool Enough, **7/1** Kawwas, **9/1** Daisy Grey, **14/1**
Manuleader, **20/1** Fair Flyer (IRE), **25/1** Revel, **33/1** Aussie Aisle (IRE), Cornhill Melody,
Kabera, **50/1** Castle Cary. CSF £22.99, CT £110.80. Tote £4.70: £3.40 £2.20 £3.00 (£21.10). Mr W. G. Swiers
(THIRSK) bred by Viscount Leverhulme. 14 Rn                           1m 30.3 (4.1)
                                              SF—38/17/10/12/–/8

T/Plpt: £18.00 (85 Tckts).                                                    GB

# NOTTINGHAM (L-H)

## Monday, April 13th [Good, Good to soft patches]

Going Allowance: St: 0.65 sec (Y); Rnd: 0.20 sec per fur (G)      Wind: fresh half against

Stalls: high

**421**      FELSTEAD CLAIMING STKS      £2441.60 (£677.60: £324.80)      **5f 13y**      2-15 (2-21)

300³ **Fangio** *(WGMTurner)* 3-8-0 ‡⁵TSprake (11) (b.off hind: led tl wl ins fnl f: hrd rdn to ld nr fin) ......................... —1

221 Last Straw (33) *(AWJones)* 4-8-12 GBaxter (10) (a.p: led wl ins fnl f: hdd cl home) ........................ nk.2

Stormbuster (56) *(PSFelgate)* 3-8-5 WRyan (7) (hdwy over 1f out: squeezed thro ins fnl f: r.o) ................. 1.3

Whippet (85) *(JABennett)* 8-9-7 DHolland (14) (bkwd: a.p: r.o ins fnl f) .......... hd.4

Cumbrian Cavalier (56) *(KGWingrove)* 3-8-1 RHills (1) (w'like: bkwd: w ldrs: ev ch over 1f out: edgd lft & wknd ins fnl f) ...... ¹/₂.5

357 Ever so Lonely (70) *(ABailey)* 3-8-1 GBardwell (3) (swtg: nvr nr to chal) ........ 1¹/₂.6

22¹³ Morpick (48) (bl) *(JPLeigh)* 5-9-4 ACulhane (4) (lw: a.p: btn whn bmpd ins fnl f) ³/₄.7

298⁶ Summer Express (67) *(JLSpearing)* 3-8-6 PaulEddery (15) (w ldrs 3f) ............ 1¹/₂.8

236 Tigani (86) (bl) *(DWChapman)* 6-9-11 JFortune (13) (dwlt: n.d) ..................... hd.9

247⁵ Cranfield Comet (74) (bl) *(JBerry)* 3-8-11 MHills (9) (s.s: hdwy 3f out: ev ch over 1f out: wknd fnl f) ............... nk.10

King Victor (IRE) (45) *(RO'Leary)* 4-8-9 ‡⁵SMaloney (12) (bit bkwd: n.d) ......... 2.11

253 Red Verona (55) *(EAWheeler)* 3-7-7⁽⁵⁾ ‡⁷DHarrison (2) (spd over 2f) ............ 1.12

Bassetlaw Belle *(SRBowring)* 3-7-12 AProud (5) (lt-f: s.i.s: outpcd) ............... ¹/₂.13

279 Carnfield (33) (v) *(JAGlover)* 4-8-0 ‡⁷CHawksley (8) (n.d) ........................ ¹/₂.14

Beljinski (34) *(BJMcMath)* 4-8-7 JQuinn (6) (n.d) ........................... 2¹/₂.15

2/1 Cranfield Comet, 7/2 Summer Express, 9/2 FANGIO(op 8/1), 10/1 Ever so Lonely(op 6/1), 12/1 Morpick, 16/1 King Victor (IRE), Tigani, Whippet(op 7/1), 20/1 Cumbrian Cavalier, Stormbuster, 33/1 Beljinski, Carnfield, Red Verona, 66/1 Ors. CSF £209.36, Tote £6.40: £2.00 £48.00 £6.00 (£173.20). Mr Simon Swift (SHERBORNE) bred by Melbury Park Stud. 15 Rn
65.4 sec (6.7)
SF—17/28/17/32/10/4

**422**      CORONACH H'CAP (0-70) £2774.80 (£772.80: £372.40)      **1m 1f 213y**      2-45 (2-55)

225* **Mr Confusion (IRE)** (70) (Fav) *(SGNorton)* 4-10-0 JFortune (16) (hld up: 6th st: led 2f out: rdn out) ................ —1

Swift Silver (50) *(WJMusson)* 5-8-8 MWigham (4) (b: hdwy on ins 3f out: nt clr run & plld out over 1f out: r.o wl) ............ 2.2

364⁵ Execution Only (IRE) (53) (v) *(JWWatts)* 4-8-11 SCauthen (18) (lw: 7th st: hdwy 3f out: r.o one pce fnl 2f) ........... 1¹/₂.3

225 Golden Torque (65) *(RBastiman)* 5-9-2 ‡⁷HBastiman (20) (bit bkwd: s.s: gd hdwy over 1f out: fin wl) .............. 1¹/₂.4

Modest Hope (USA) (56) *(GHEden)* 5-9-0 JQuinn (8) (b.hind: bit bkwd: hdwy over 2f out: r.o ins fnl f) ........... 1¹/₂.5

364 Friendlypersuasion (IRE) (46) *(RHollinshead)* 4-8-4⁽¹⁾ WRyan (3) (bhd tl hdwy 4f out: nt clr run over 1f out: nt rcvr) .......... 1¹/₂.6

299 Weekday Cross (IRE) (50) *(JRJenkins)* 4-8-8 GBaxter (21) (4th st: wknd 2f out) 3.7

Presque Noir (60) *(HCandy)* 4-9-4 WNewnes (14) (bkwd: led 8f) ................. 1¹/₂.8

Chew it Over (IRE) (54) *(CASmith)* 4-8-12 MTebbutt (5) (bkwd: nvr nrr) .......... nk.9

Mabthul (USA) (50) *(MJHeaton-Ellis)* 4-8-8 BRaymond (15) (5th st: wknd over 2f out) ................ 1¹/₂.10

342 Modesto (USA) (63) *(KOCunningham-Brown)* 4-9-7 MHills (22) (b: chsd ldr: 2nd st: wknd 3f out) ........... 1¹/₂.11

Dancing Sensation (USA) (50) *(JWharton)* 5-8-8 DHolland (19) (hdwy 6f out: wknd 3f out) ................ 1¹/₂.12

Sir George Chuffy (IRE) (65) *(FHLee)* 4-9-9 PaulEddery (9) (3rd st: wknd 2f out) ³/₄.13

New Mexico (70) *(DMorley)* 8-10-0 RHills (2) (bkwd: bhd fnl 3f) ................. nk.14

405⁶ Sharquin (40) *(MBrittain)* 5-7-12 GBardwell (6) (bkwd: bhd fnl 3f) .......... hd.15

277 Jolizal (42) *(DMorris)* 4-8-0 BCrossley (7) (n.d) ........................ 1¹/₂.16

Yimkin Bookra (62) *(WRMuir)* 4-8-13 ‡⁷KimMcDonnell (11) (bkwd: n.d) .......... 1.17

Mezaaj (USA) (46) *(BPreece)* 4-7-11 ‡⁷MHumphries (13) (bkwd: n.d) .......... 3¹/₂.18

Rapid Lad (48) *(JLSpearing)* 14-7-13⁽³⁾ ‡⁷DCarson (10) (bkwd: n.d) .......... 1¹/₂.19

Question of Honor (48) *(AWJones)* 4-7-13⁽⁸⁾ ‡⁷JDennis (1) (n.d) ................. 1.20

Thimbalina (51) *(DAWilson)* 6-8-2 ‡⁷OPears (23) (a bhd) ..................... 1.21

187 Foursingh (33/1) Withdrawn (lame at s) : not under orders

**9/2** MR CONFUSION (IRE), **13/2** Golden Torque, **8/1** Friendlypersuasion (IRE), **9/1** Execution Only (IRE)(op 6/1), **10/1** Swift Silver, **11/1** Presque Noir(6/1—12/1), Modest Hope (USA)(tchd 20/1), **12/1** Sharquin(op 20/1), **14/1** Dancing Sensation (USA), **16/1** Thimbalina, Mabthul (USA), Sir George Chuffy (IRE), Modesto (USA), **20/1** Weekday Cross (IRE), New Mexico, **33/1** Chew it Over (IRE), Mezaaj (USA), Rapid Lad, Jolizal, Yimkin Bookra, **50/1** Question of Honor. CSF £51.15, CT £383.21. Tote £8.50: £2.90 £3.20 £2.40 £2.00 (£16.50). Mr R. Fenwick-Gibson (BARNSLEY) bred by D. P. O'Brien in Ireland. 21 Rn
2m 11.6 (9.1)
SF—43/19/19/21/16/3

**423**      ABOYEUR (S) STKS (2-Y-O) £2578.80 (£716.80: £344.40)     **5f 13y**     3-15 (3-27)

286³   **Ruby Cooper** (Jt-Fav) *(JWharton)* 8-6 DHolland (8) (mde all: hung lft over 1f
        out: r.o wl) ......................................................................................... —1
323⁶   Plum First (bl) *(NBycroft)* 8-11 NDay (18) (a.p: ev ch over 1f out: r.o wl cl home) hd.2
329³   Awesome Risk (Jt-Fav) *(GLewis)* 8-6 PaulEddery (11) (hld up: rdn over 1f out:
        one pce) .............................................................................................. 5.3
      Total Truth *(JWhite)* 7-13 ‡⁷CAvery (16) (small: bit bkwd: hdwy 2f out: one pce
        fnl f) ................................................................................................ ¾.4
231   Genesis Four (bl) *(JRJenkins)* 8-11 GBaxter (14) (no hdwy fnl 2f) ................ 3.5
      Grey Runner *(BPalling)* 8-6 RHills (2) (small: bkwd: prom: hung lft after 1f: racd
        alone far side: wknd over 1f out) ......................................................... hd.6
352   The Cut *(MJohnston)* 8-6 BRaymond (17) (prom over 3f) ............................... 2.7
265⁵   Never in Touch *(MBrittain)* 7-13 ‡⁷DWright (13) (nvr trbld ldrs) ................... hd.8
352   Stay Great *(WCarter)* 8-11 WRyan (10) (nvr trbld ldrs) ............................ 1½.9
286   Craigie Boy *(JPLeigh)* 8-11 JQuinn (6) (s.s: n.d) ..................................... 1.10
263   Canazei *(DonEnricoIncisa)* 8-6 KimTinkler (5) (bkwd: n.d) ...................... 1½.11
286   Red Ronnie *(JBerry)* 8-6 BCrossley (3) (spd 3f) .................................... 1½.12
      Twitcher *(GBlum)* 8-6 GBardwell (4) (unf: dwlt: hdwy over 3f out: wknd 2f out) 2.13
329   Arogant Fool *(DAWilson)* 8-11 JFortune (15) (n.d) ................................... nk.14
      Grand Game *(DHaydnJones)* 8-11 MHills (1) (lt-f: s.s: a bhd) ..................... ½.15
      Pfaff's Cellar (bl) *(WGMTurner)* 8-6 WNewnes (12) (lt-f: unf: n.d) ............... s.h.16
352⁴   Silly Sally *(WGMTurner)* 8-1 ‡⁵TSprake (7) (prom 3f) ............................... ½.17
      Dazzling Baby *(MDods)* 8-1 ‡⁵SMaloney (9) (neat: bkwd: prom 3f) ............. ½.18

**7/2** Awesome Risk(op 5/4), RUBY COOPER, **7/1** Twitcher(op 12/1), Stay Great, **8/1** Silly Sally, **9/1** Never in Touch, **12/1** The Cut(op 8/1), Total Truth, **14/1** Red Ronnie(10/1—16/1), Craigie Boy, Plum First, **16/1** Pfaff's Cellar, **20/1** Genesis Four, **33/1** Arogant Fool, Grey Runner, Canazei, Grand Game, **66/1** Dazzling Baby. CSF £58.30, Tote £5.10: £1.50 £2.80 £1.80 (Wnr or 2nd w any £2.00). Mr J. Rose (MELTON MOWBRAY) bred by Eric Saunders. 18 Rn; Bt in 3,400 gns
66.2 sec (7.5)
SF—7/11/-/-/-/-

**424**      SLIP ANCHOR STKS (3-Y.O.C) £3289.50 (£981.00: £468.00: £211.50)
     **1m 54y**                                  3-45 (3-52)

      Deserve (Fav) *(HRACecil)* 9-5 SCauthen (1) (lw: mde all: rdn over 1f out: r.o wl) —1
      Tawafij (USA) *(HThomsonJones)* 9-0 RHills (3) (bit bkwd: chsd wnr: 2nd st: ev
        ch 2f out: nt qckn ins fnl f) ............................................................... ¾.2
      Very Evident (IRE) *(BWHills)* 9-0 DHolland (5) (bkwd: 4th st: rdn over 2f out: one
        pce) ................................................................................................ 4.3
230   The Titan Ghost *(BAMcMahon)* 9-0 WRyan (2) (bit bkwd: last st: a bhd) ....... 3.4
      Sir Norman Holt (IRE) *(FHLee)* 9-0 PaulEddery (4) (3rd st: rdn over 3f out: wknd
        over 2f out) ..................................................................................... 4.5

**4/7** DESERVE(op 1/4), **9/4** Tawafij (USA), **8/1** Very Evident (IRE), **25/1** Sir Norman Holt (IRE), **100/1** The Titan Ghost. CSF £2.19, Tote £1.10: £1.10 £1.50 (£1.60). Sheikh Mohammed (NEWMARKET) bred by Sheikh Mohammed bin Rashid al Maktoum. 5 Rn
1m 47.6 (8)
SF—9/2/-/-/-

**425**      OH SO SHARP STKS (3-Y.O.F) £3201.75 (£954.00: £454.50: £204.75)
     **1m 1f 213y**                                4-15 (4-18)

      All At Sea (USA) (Fav) *(HRACecil)* 9-0 WRyan (2) (hld up: 3rd st: qcknd to ld 2f
        out: clr whn edgd rt ins fnl f: easily) ...................................................... —1
      Niodini (USA) (98) *(MRStoute)* 9-0 SCauthen (3) (swtg: hld up: 4th st: ev ch 2f
        out: one pce) .................................................................................... 5.2
      Kirsten *(WJarvis)* 8-8 BRaymond (4) (led over 7f: one pce) ......................... ¾.3
      Up Anchor (IRE) (78) *(PFICole)* 9-0 PaulEddery (5) (chsd ldr: 2nd st: led over 2f
        out: sn hdd & btn) ............................................................................. 3½.4
      Glacial Moon (USA) *(BWHills)* 8-8 DHolland (1) (still unf: nt grwn: last & outpcd
        st: rdn 4f out: a bhd) ......................................................................... 6.5

**13/8** ALL AT SEA (USA), **2/1** Niodini (USA)(op 5/4), **11/2** Glacial Moon (USA)(op 3/1), **6/1** Up Anchor (IRE)(tchd 10/1), **8/1** Kirsten(7/1—12/1). CSF £5.14, Tote £2.90: £1.40 £1.50 (£2.00). Mr K. Abdulla (NEWMARKET) bred by Juddmonte Farms Incorporated in USA. 5 Rn
2m 11.4 (8.9)
SF—31/21/13/12/–

**426**      CALL BOY H'CAP (0-70) £2657.20 (£739.20: £355.60)      **1¾m 15y**      4-45 (4-48)
(Weights raised 2 lb)

|  | Avro Anson **(44)** (Fav) *(MJCamacho)* 4–8-4  DHolland (15) (a.p: rdn over 5f out: 4th st: led wl over 1f out: rdn out) | —1 |
| 299⁵ | Lookingforarainbow (IRE) **(52)** *(BobJones)* 4–8-12  VSmith (20) (hld up & bhd: gd hdwy 3f out: chsd wnr over 1f out: hung lft & no ex ins fnl f) | 2½.2 |
|  | Fanlight **(47)** *(RAkehurst)* 4–8-7  HHills (4) (hld up: 6th st: r.o one pce fnl 2f) | 2½.3 |
| 225 | Westfield Moves (IRE) **(57)** *(HJCollingridge)* 4–9-3  JQuinn (2) (9th st: styd on u.p fnl 2f) | 1.4 |
|  | Good for a Loan **(57)** *(RLee)* 5–9-6  PaulEddery (18) (a.p: 2nd st: led 3f out tl wl over 1f out: wknd fnl f) | 1½.5 |
| 331⁴ | Clear Idea (IRE) **(43)** *(CRNelson)* 4–7-12 ‡⁵SMaloney (13) (b: led 11f) | 1.6 |
| 354⁴ | Famous Beauty **(49)** *(RHollinshead)* 5–8-5 ‡⁷EHusband (16) (hld up: hdwy 7f out: 8th st: wknd 3f out) | 1½.7 |
| 354⁶ | Franciscan **(51)** *(BPreece)* 5–9-0  WRyan (10) (7th st: wknd over 3f out) | ¾.8 |
|  | White River **(44)** *(DHaydnJones)* 6–8-7  MHills (6) (b.off hind: bit bkwd: 3rd st: wknd 2f out) | 1.9 |
|  | Shawwal (USA) **(49)** *(RO'Leary)* 5–8-12  ACulhane (5) (bkwd: n.d) | nk.10 |
| 342 | Moot Point (USA) **(63)** *(JRJenkins)* 4–9-9  WNewnes (14) (n.d) | ½.11 |
| 220 | Pondered Bid **(46)** (bl) *(PatMitchell)* 8–8-4⁽⁶⁾ ‡⁵RPerham (8) (rdn 6f out: a bhd) | 1½.12 |
| 243⁶ | Conjuring (USA) **(64)** (bl) *(GThorner)* 4–9-10  RWernham (12) (s.i.s: a bhd) | 1.13 |
| 299⁴ | Muddy Lane **(43)** *(BRMillman)* 4–8-3  GBaxter (17) (hdwy 6f out: 7th st: wknd over 3f out) | 3.14 |
|  | Bushfire Moon **(50)** *(CNWilliams)* 4–8-10  BRaymond (1) (prom 8f) | 3.15 |
|  | Smilingatstrangers **(44)** *(MrsBarbaraWaring)* 4–8-4  NHowe (7) (bit bkwd: swtg: a bhd) | 3½.16 |
|  | Lowawatha **(50)** *(DMorris)* 4–8-10  MTebbutt (19) (bit bkwd: bhd fnl 5f) | 2.17 |
|  | Jarras **(53)** *(CASmith)* 7–9-2  MWigham (3) (bkwd: rdn 8f out: a bhd) | nk.18 |
| 331⁶ | Greenwich Bambi **(58)** *(WCarter)* 4–9-4  SCauthen (9) (t.o) | 19 |
| 342 | Sweet Request **(62)** *(JRBostock)* 4–9-8  NDay (11) (lw: a bhd: t.o) | 20 |

**7/4** AVRO ANSON, **9/1** Lookingforarainbow (IRE)(op 6/1), Clear Idea (IRE)(tchd 16/1), **10/1** Greenwich Bambi(6/1—11/1), Famous Beauty(7/1—11/1), **12/1** Fanlight, Westfield Moves (IRE)(op 8/1), **14/1** Muddy Lane(10/1—16/1), Lowawatha, White River, **16/1** Moot Point (USA), **25/1** Good for a Loan, **33/1** Bushfire Moon, Pondered Bid, Shawwal (USA), **50/1** Ors. CSF £19.26, CT £149.48. Tote £2.60: £1.10 £2.60 £5.00 £2.10 (£70.20). Mr B. P. Skirton (MALTON) bred by B. P. Skirton and Mrs S. Camacho. 20 Rn
3m 10.9 (12.4)
T/Plpt: £176.80 (6.25 Tckts).      KH

# NEWMARKET  (R-H) Rowley Mile
## Tuesday, April 14th [Good to firm]
Going Allowance: minus 0.05 sec per fur (G)      Wind: str across

Stalls: low 2nd, 3rd & 4th, remainder high

**427**      CONSTANT SECURITY STKS (Mdn 3-Y.O) £2950.00 (£880.00: £420.00: £190.00)      **1½m**      2-00 (2-05)

|  | Iywaan (IRE) *(PTWalwyn)* 9-0  WCarson (7) (chsd ldrs: hmpd over 3f out: swtchd ins 2f out: r.o strly to ld cl home) | —1 |
|  | Alhamad (Fav) *(HRACecil)* 9-0  PatEddery (6) (lw: a.p: led ½-wy: shkn up 2f out: hdd & no ex nr fin) | ½.2 |
|  | Hidden Light (IRE) *(MAJarvis)* 9-0  BRaymond (2) (plld hrd: hld up: hdwy 2f out: edgd rt & nt qckn ins fnl f) | 2½.3 |
|  | Glaisdale *(HRACecil)* 9-0  SCauthen (1) (bit bkwd: hld up & bhd: stdy hdwy 4f out: rdn appr fnl f: eased whn btn fnl f) | 1.4 |
|  | Acrobate (USA) *(PAKelleway)* 9-0  TQuinn (8) (chsd ldrs: rdn over 3f out: kpt on) | nk.5 |
|  | Dime Bag *(BWHills)* 8-9  DHolland (5) (hld up: jnd ldr 4f out: hung rt & wknd over 1f out) | nk.6 |
|  | Prince Pericles (IRE) *(HCandy)* 9-0  CRutter (10) (lw: prom tl grad wknd fnl 2f) | 3½.7 |
|  | Ragamuffin Romeo *(NCWright)* 9-0  GDuffield (4) (led to ½-wy: wknd wl over 2f out) | 7.8 |
|  | Lobilio (USA) *(CEBrittain)* 9-0  MRoberts (9) (lw: hld up & bhd: shkn up over 3f out: no imp) | 1.9 |

251 Baher (USA) *(NACallaghan)* 9-0 LPiggott (3) (b: hld up: hdwy 4f out: wknd wl
over 1f out) ....................................................................... nk.**10**
Quadrireme *(MajorWRHern)* 9-0 WRSwinburn (11) (hld up: prom 6f: bhd fnl 3f) 4.**11**

**1/2** Alhamad, **8/1** Hidden Light (IRE), **12/1** IYWAAN (IRE)(op 6/1), **14/1** Glaisdale (IRE)(op 8/1), **20/1** Lobilio
(USA), Dime Bag(op 12/1), **25/1** Prince Pericles (IRE), **33/1** Quadrireme, Baher (USA), **50/1** Ors. CSF £17.12,
Tote £12.00: £1.90 £1.10 £1.70 (£4.60). Mr Hamdan Al-Maktoum (LAMBOURN) bred by Il Mariano SRL in
Ireland. 11 Rn                                                                          2m 32.79 (3.49)
                                                                      SF—59/58/53/51/50/44

---

**428**    STETCHWORTH STKS (Mdn 3-Y-O) £3054.00 (£912.00: £436.00: £198.00)
         **6f**                                                          2-35 (2-39)

**Garah** (Fav) *(HRACecil)* 8-9 SCauthen (1) (gd sort: dwlt: sn rcvrd: led over 3f
out: rdn & r.o gamely fnl f) ................................................ —**1**
Claybank (USA) *(BWHills)* 9-0 DHolland (10) (lw: a.p: ev ch 1f out: hrd rdn & r.o) hd.**2**
Venture Capitalist *(RHannon)* 9-0 JReid (6) (hdwy over 2f out: ev ch ins fnl f: no
ex nr fin) ....................................................................... 2.**3**
310² Saddlehome (USA) **(82)** *(RMWhitaker)* 9-0 MRoberts (9) (swtg: chsd ldrs: kpt
on u.p ins fnl f) .............................................................. 2.**4**
Forest Law (USA) *(PFICole)* 9-0 AMunro (3) (s.i.s: pushed along thrght: nvr
able to chal) ................................................................. 3½.**5**
Mufid (USA) *(MajorWRHern)* 9-0 WCarson (11) (w'like: leggy: s.s: bhd tl styd
on fnl 2f) ..................................................................... 4.**6**
Rock Band (IRE) *(LMCumani)* 9-0 LDettori (8) (w'like: scope: spd over 4f) ......... 7.**7**
Lord Leitrim (IRE) **(60)** *(NACallaghan)* 9-0 WNewnes (5) (outpcd) ............ ½.**8**
2484 Jaromic **(52)** *(PFTulk)* 9-0 WRyan (2) (b: unruly s: a in r) ................ hd.**9**
341 Baharlilys **(69)** (bl) *(NCWright)* 9-0 GDuffield (4) (chsd ldrs: sn pushed along:
bhd fr ½-wy) .................................................................. 3.**10**
Very Good (PHowling) 8-3(1) ‡7DebbieBiggs (7) (led over 2f: wknd qckly appr fnl
f) .............................................................................. **11**

**11/4** GARAH(6/4—3/1), **3/1** Venture Capitalist, **7/1** Mufid (USA)(4/1—8/1), Claybank (USA)(op 4/1), **8/1** Forest
Law (USA)(op 4/1), Saddlehome (USA), **10/1** Rock Band (IRE)(op 9/2), **14/1** Baharlilys(33/1—12/1), **33/1**
Jaromic, Lord Leitrim (IRE), **66/1** Very Good. CSF £21.71, Tote £3.90: £1.90 £2.70 £1.70 (£36.20). Prince A. A.
Faisal (NEWMARKET) bred by Nawara Stud Co Ltd. 11 Rn                           1m 12.83 (1.43)
                                                                      SF—60/64/56/48/34/18

---

**429**    SHADWELL STUD NELL GWYN STKS (Gp 3) (3-Y-O.F) £22869.00 (£8488.95: £4019.48:
         £1687.57)      **7f**                                          3-10 (3-11)

**A-to-Z (IRE) (98)** *(MBell)* 8-9 MHills (9) (h.d.w: hld up: hdwy over 2f out: r.o to ld
wl ins fnl f) ................................................................... —**1**
Perfect Circle **(100)** *(MRStoute)* 8-9 WRSwinburn (10) (h.d.w: a.p: led appr fnl f
tl wl ins fnl f) ................................................................ ¾.**2**
Soiree (IRE) **(102)** *(BWHills)* 8-9 DHolland (1) (hld up: effrt & n.m.r over 2f out:
r.o wl fnl f) ................................................................... 1.**3**
Harvest Girl (IRE) **(106)** *(GAPritchard-Gordon)* 8-9 AMunro (5) (chsd ldrs: effrt
over 1f out: unable qckn nr fin) ....................................... nk.**4**
Herora (IRE) **(95)** *(NAGraham)* 8-9 RCochrane (3) (plld hrd: chsd ldrs: outpcd
2f out: styd on ins fnl f) ................................................. ½.**5**
Red Slippers (USA) **(106)** *(LMCumani)* 8-9 LDettori (8) (lw: prom: chal 2f out:
kpt on same pce fnl f) .................................................... hd.**6**
Skimble (USA) *(HRACecil)* 8-9 PatEddery (2) (lw: led tl hdd wl over 1f out: no ex
fnl f) .......................................................................... hd.**7**
Miznah (IRE) *(JSBolger,Ireland)* 8-9 CRoche (4) (prom: hrd rdn over 2f out:
grad wknd) ................................................................... 2½.**8**
Midnight Air (USA) **(114)** (Fav) *(HRACecil)* 8-12 SCauthen (7) (chsd ldrs over 4f) 2.**9**
Cambrian Hills (IRE) **(107)** *(PWChapple-Hyam)* 8-9 PaulEddery (11) (a bhd) 3½.**10**

**9/4** Midnight Air (USA), **4/1** Skimble (USA)(5/2—9/2), **5/1** Soiree (IRE)(op 3/1), **8/1** Red Slippers (USA), A-TO-Z
(IRE)(14/1—16/1), **9/1** Miznah (IRE), Cambrian Hills (IRE), **12/1** Perfect Circle, **33/1** Ors. CSF £90.56, Tote
£11.40: £2.20 £2.70 £2.20 (£95.40). Mr Brian Cooper (NEWMARKET) bred by D. P. O'Brien in Ireland. 10 Rn
                                                                              1m 27.09 (3.09)
                                                                      SF—44/42/39/38/36/35

---

**430**    ABERNANT STKS (listed race) £10234.00 (£3052.00: £1456.00: £658.00)
         **6f**                                                          3-40 (3-54)

241* **Fylde Flyer (96)** *(JBerry)* 3-8-10 LPiggott (5) (lw: w ldrs: led over 1f out: hld on
gamely u.p cl home) ....................................................... —**1**

Case Law **(112)** *(SirMarkPrescott)* 5-9-9 GDuffield (8) (lw: led tl over 1f out: rallied gamely u.p nr fin) .................................................................. s.h.2
Sir Harry Hardman **(101)** (bl) *(FHLee)* 4-9-6 MRoberts (2) (bit bkwd: hld up: gd hdwy over 1f out: rdn & r.o) ............................................................. 1.3
Snaadee (USA) **(107)** *(MRStoute)* 5-9-9 PatEddery (7) (lw: unruly bef s: prom over 4f) .......................................................................................... 4.4
Chicarica (USA) **(114)** (Fav) *(JHMGosden)* 4-9-7 SCauthen (4) (swtg: chsd ldrs over 4f) ................................................................................. 1½.5
Lee Artiste **(102)** *(PFICole)* 4-9-4 TQuinn (6) (a chsng ldrs: no imp fnl 2f) .......... 7.6
Power Lake **(108)** *(RHannon)* 3-8-3 WCarson (1) (w ldrs 4f: wknd qckly: t.o) .. 20.7
241³ Letsbeonestaboutit **(94)** (bl) *(MrsNMacauley)* 6-9-6 DHolland (3) (s.i.s: sn bhd & outpcd: t.o) ....................................................................................... s.h.8

**15/8** Chicarica (USA), **9/2** Snaadee (USA), Power Lake(3/1—5/1), Case Law, **9/1** FYLDE FLYER(12/1—8/1), **16/1** Lee Artiste, **20/1** Letsbeonestaboutit(op 33/1), **33/1** Sir Harry Hardman. CSF £44.38, Tote £6.80: £1.40 £2.00 £5.20 (£21.00). Blackpool Gazette & Herald Ltd (COCKERHAM) bred by W. L. Caley. 8 Rn
1m 12.76 (1.36)
SF—63/75/68/55/47/16

**431**  LADBROKE H'CAP (0-100) £7635.00 (£2280.00: £1090.00: £495.00)
1¼m                                                                                          4-10 (4-23)

299★ Myfontaine **(65)** *(KTIvory)* 5-7-7 GBardwell (2) (hld up: stdy hdwy 3f out: led appr fnl f: r.o wl) .................................................................................. —1
Laburnum **(79)** *(LMCumani)* 4-8-7 LDettori (1) (hld up & bhd: hdwy over 3f out: str chal fnl f: r.o wl) .................................................................... nk.2
225⁴ Rive-Jumelle (IRE) **(68)** (Fav) *(MBell)* 4-7-10 WCarson (11) (a.p: effrt & rdn appr fnl f: unable qckn) .................................................... 1½.3
373★ Majed (IRE) **(74)** *(NACallaghan)* 4-7-13 (5x) ‡⁹FNorton (6) (hld up in tch: styd on fnl 2f: nvr nrr) ..................................................................... 1.4
299⁶ Latour **(72)** *(CEBrittain)* 4-8-0 GCrealock (4) (lw: led 1f: prom tl outpcd appr fnl f) ............................................................................................... 1.5
Grand Hawk (USA) **(82)** *(MMoubarak)* 4-8-10 TQuinn (3) (hld up & bhd: stdy hdwy fnl 3f: nrst fin) ......................................................................... s.h.6
Pharly Story **(93)** *(MCPipe)* 4-9-7 SCauthen (5) (lw: prom: led 3f out tl hdd & wknd appr fnl f) ................................................................................ nk.7
Scenic Dancer **(68)** *(AHide)* 4-7-10 DaleGibson (13) (nvr trbld ldrs) ............... 1½.8
Moonlight Quest **(80)** *(BHanbury)* 4-8-8 BRaymond (5) (b: b.hind: hld up & bhd: nvr plcd to chal) .......................................................................... 2.9
Prince Hannibal **(83)** *(JLDunlop)* 5-8-11 WRSwinburn (8) (led after 1f to 3f out: ev ch tl wknd appr fnl f) ...................................................................... nk.10
Widyan (USA) **(100)** *(PFICole)* 4-10-0 AMunro (10) (lw: chsd ldrs over 6f) .... 3½.11
St Patrick's Day **(68)** *(CEBrittain)* 4-7-5⁽¹⁾ ‡⁵BDoyle (9) (plld hrd: prom over 7f) nk.12
Statajack (IRE) **(77)** (bl) *(DRCEIsworth)* 4-8-5 JWilliams (12) (bhd fnl 3f) ............. 13
*Stewards Enquiry: Obj. to Myfontaine by Dettori overruled.*

**4/1** Rive-Jumelle (IRE), **13/2** Majed (IRE), Laburnum, Grand Hawk (USA), **8/1** Pharly Story, **9/1** Statajack (IRE), **10/1** MYFONTAINE, **14/1** Latour, Widyan (USA), **16/1** Prince Hannibal, **20/1** Moonlight Quest, St Patrick's Day, **25/1** Scenic Dancer. CSF £69.19, CT £280.63. Tote £12.10: £2.80 £2.90 £1.60 (£45.80). Mr K. T. Ivory (RADLETT) bred by Farmleigh Partners. 13 Rn
2m 4.68 (2.08)
SF—53/66/52/53/52/61/71

**432**  CHRIS BLACKWELL MEMORIAL H'CAP (3-Y.O) (0-100) £5481.00 (£1638.00: £784.00: £357.00)   7f                                                         4-40 (4-59)

Beware of Agents **(90)** *(MJohnston)* 9-4 RPElliott (4) (h.d.w: hld up: a.p: led ins fnl f: r.o u.p) .................................................................................... —1
Spanish Miner (USA) **(88)** *(AAScott)* 9-2 BRaymond (1) (swvd lft s: bhd tl hdwy over 2f out: str chal fnl f: r.o) .............................................................. s.h.2
Showgi (USA) **(87)** *(JRFanshawe)* 9-1 WRSwinburn (10) (a.p: led appr fnl f tl hdd & no ex ins fnl f) ........................................................................... 2.3
Marabella Star (USA) **(93)** (Fav) *(HRACecil)* 9-7 SCauthen (6) (lw: hld up: effrt & n.m.r 2f out: styd on ins fnl f) .................................................. nk.4
215³ Sand Table **(86)** *(LordHuntingdon)* 9-0 WRyan (8) (lw: hld up: stdy hdwy fnl 2f: nrst fin) ..................................................................................... 1½.5
298★ Sovereign Rock (IRE) **(75)** *(RHannon)* 8-3 WCarson (9) (prom: led 3f out tl appr fnl f: one pce) .................................................................................. ¾.6
Sybaritic Sam (IRE) **(71)** *(NACallaghan)* 7-13 DaleGibson (7) (s.s: bhd tl styd on wl fnl 2f) ........................................................................................... 1½.7
May Hills Legacy (IRE) **(80)** *(DWPArbuthnot)* 8-8 TQuinn (12) (b: hdwy 2f out: sn ev ch: wknd fnl f) ............................................................................ ¾.8

Walking on Water **(86)** (bl) *(RFJohnsonHoughton)* 9-0　LDettori (5) (chsd ldrs over 5f) ............................................................. nk.9
Risk Master **(74)** *(CAHorgan)* 8-2　AMcGlone (14) (hld up & bhd: hdwy 2f out: nvr plcd to chal) ....................................................... 1.10
Fragonard (IRE) **(74)** *(GAPritchard-Gordon)* 8-2　NCarlisle (3) (b.hind: a in rr) .. 1.11
Yousefia (USA) **(86)** *(MRStoute)* 9-0　PatEddery (13) (lw: bhd: gd hdwy whn hmpd 3f out: effrt 2f out: wknd appr fnl f) ...................... 1¹/₂.12
275⁴ Appealing Times (USA) **(78)** *(WAO'Gorman)* 8-1 ‡⁵EmmaO'Gorman (2) (racd centre: nvr nr ldrs) ........................................................ ³/₄.13
332⁴ Libra Legend (USA) **(69)** *(CEBrittain)* 7-6⁽³⁾ ‡⁵BDoyle (15) (lw: led 1f: wknd wl over 2f out) ................................................................. hd.14
Neo-Classical **(90)** *(BWHills)* 9-4　DHolland (11) (led after 1f to 3f out: sn wknd) 4.15

**9/4** Marabella Star (USA)(op 6/4), **9/2** Yousefia (USA), **5/1** Sand Table, **6/1** Sovereign Rock (IRE), **14/1** Libra Legend (USA)(tchd 25/1), **16/1** Showgi (USA)(12/1—20/1), Neo-Classical, Walking on Water(20/1—33/1), **20/1** Appealing Times (USA), **25/1** Fragonard (IRE), BEWARE OF AGENTS, Spanish Miner (USA), **33/1** Sybaritic Sam (IRE), May Hills Legacy (IRE), **50/1** Risk Master. CSF £472.47, CT £8,891.56. Tote £17.40: £3.20 £9.00 £3.80 (£309.00). Brian Yeardley Continental Ltd (MIDDLEHAM) bred by Kiplingcotes Stud. 15 Rn
　　　　　　　　　　　　　　　　　　　　　　　　　　　　　1m 26.48 (2.48)
　　　　　　　　　　　　　　　　　　　　　　　　　　SF—62/59/52/57/45/32

**433**　　MUSEUM STKS (Mdn 3-Y.O) £3366.00 (£1008.00: £484.00: £222.00)
　　　　1¹/₄m　　　　　　　　　　　　　　　　　　　5-10 (5-31)

Sayh *(MAJarvis)* 9-0　AMunro (9) (w'like: a.p: pushed along 3f out: styd on to ld cl home) ................................................................... —1
Yildiz *(BWHills)* 8-9　MHills (4) (bhd: hdwy over 2f out: r.o wl ins fnl f) ............... nk.2
Belgran (USA) *(HRACecil)* 9-0　PatEddery (15) (str: scope: bit bkwd: a.p: led over 3f out tl ct cl home) ........................................... s.h.3
Tradition *(MajorWRHern)* 8-9　JReid (11) (lw: chsd ldrs: chal 3f out: wknd wl over 1f out) .................................................................. 6.4
Sovereign Page (USA) *(BHanbury)* 9-0　BRaymond (2) (hdwy 2f out: kpt on fnl f: nvr nrr) ............................................................................. 4.5
Blessington (USA) *(JHMGosden)* 9-0　SCauthen (3) (leggy: scope: chsd ldrs 8f) 1.6
Robenko (USA) *(CEBrittain)* 9-0　MRoberts (1) (gd sort: bkwd: mid div tl styd on appr fnl f) ....................................................................... 1¹/₂.7
251⁵ American Boogie (FR) *(CEBrittain)* 8-9 ‡⁵BDoyle (10) (led 2f: wknd over 2f out) hd.8
Chief Minister (IRE) *(LMCumani)* 9-0　LDettori (16) (effrt ¹/₂-wy: nvr nr to chal) ... ¹/₂.9
Don't Forsake Me **(63)** *(DMorley)* 8-9　MBirch (6) (nvr nr to chal) ..................... 1¹/₂.10
Russian Vision *(AAScott)* 9-0　WRSwinburn (7) (b.hind: w'like: dwlt: sn prom: wknd over 2f out) ..................................................................... nk.11
Dancing Dancer *(NCWright)* 8-9　GDuffield (12) (effrt 4f out: n.d) ...................... 3.12
Captain Marmalade *(DTThom)* 9-0　CDwyer (14) (neat: a bhd) ........................... 1.13
Rainridge *(JLDunlop)* 9-0　LPiggott (8) (lw: mid div: effrt & bhd 3f out: no imp) .. 1.14
Leif the Lucky (Fav) *(WJarvis)* 9-0　WCarson (1) (led after 2f tl over 2f out: wknd qckly) ............................................................................... nk.15
Steel Mirror *(MrsJCecil)* 9-0　PaulEddery (13) (prom 7f) ................................... 1.16

**5/2** Leif the Lucky (USA), **11/2** Blessington (USA), **6/1** Yildiz(op 4/1), **13/2** Belgran (USA), **7/1** Robenko (USA)(10/1—14/1), **9/1** Steel Mirror, **12/1** Rainridge, **16/1** Tradition, Captain Marmalade(8/1—20/1), **20/1** Chief Minister (IRE)(op 12/1), SAYH, **25/1** Sovereign Page (USA), Russian Vision, **33/1** Ors. CSF £140.18, Tote £29.80: £5.90 £2.40 £2.90 (£239.10). Sheikh Ahmed Al Maktoum (NEWMARKET) bred by Enterprise Bloodstock. 16 Rn　　　　　　　　　　　　　　　　　　　　　　2m 7.87 (5.27)
　　　　　　　　　　　　　　　　　　　　　　SF—42/36/40/23/20/18

T/Trio: Race 3: £183.80 (5.1 Tckts); Race 5: £60.00 (19.8 Tckts). T/Jkpt: Not won; £195.497.05 to Newmarket 15/4/92. T/Plpt: £2,684.60 (4.45 Tckts).　　　　　　　　　　　　　　　　　IM

## NEWMARKET (R-H) Rowley Mile

## Wednesday, April 15th [Good to soft becoming Good]
Going Allowance: 5f: minus 0.10 sec (F); Rest: 0.15 sec per fur (G)　　　Wind: str half bhd

Stalls: 3rd, 4th & 6th high, remainder low

**434**　　GEOFFREY BARLING STKS (Mdn 3-Y.O.F) £2950.00 (£880.00: £420.00: £190.00)
　　　　7f　　　　　　　　　　　　　　　　　　　　2-00 (2-03)

302² **Juniper Berry (IRE)** *(PWChapple-Hyam)* 8-11　PatEddery (2) (a.p: rdn to ld ins fnl f: r.o wl) ............................................................... —1
Petal Girl *(RHannon)* 8-11　LPiggott (9) (led after 1f tl ins fnl f: r.o one pce) ...... 1¹/₂.2
334⁴ Sunley Silks *(MRChannon)* 8-11　CRutter (7) (led 1f: cl up: ev ch over 1f out: nt qckn nr fin) ............................................................ 1¹/₂.3

Just a Mirage (Fav) *(AAScott)* 8-11 WCarson (3) (b.hind: trckd ldrs: swtchd & effrt 2f out: rdn & nt qckn) .......................................... 1½.4
Shalabia *(MMoubarak)* 8-11 TQuinn (10) (b: lt-f: unf: a in tch: outpcd over 2f out: styd on wl nr fin) ........................................ s.h.5
Born to Dance *(MRStoute)* 8-11 BRaymond (6) (leggy: scope: bhd: stdy hdwy 2f out: r.o) ...................................................... s.h.6
Miliyel *(BHanbury)* 8-11 WRSwinburn (8) (chsd ldrs tl wknd fnl 2f) ........ 1½.7
Lysirra (USA) *(BWHills)* 8-11 SCauthen (5) (outpcd fnl 3f) .................. 5.8
Euridice (IRE) *(LMCumani)* 8-11 LDettori (1) (w'like: unf: a bhd) ......... 4.9
Trainee (USA) *(WJHaggas)* 8-11 NDay (4) (sn pushed along: a bhd) ...... 2½.10

7/4 Just a Mirage, **3/1** JUNIPER BERRY (IRE)(op 2/1), **5/1** Petal Girl(op 3/1), **10/1** Shalabia(4/1—12/1), Euridice (IRE)(op 5/1), **12/1** Born to Dance, **14/1** Sunley Silks, **20/1** Lysirra (USA)(op 12/1), Miliyel, **33/1** Trainee (USA). CSF £18.33, Tote £3.20: £1.20 £1.80 £2.60 (£4.50). Mr R. E. Sangster (MARLBOROUGH) bred by Swettenham Stud in Ireland. 10 Rn                                          1m 29.39 (5.39)
                                                                    SF—32/27/22/17/16/15

**435**    JEYES BLOO H'CAP (0-100) £5481.00 (£1638.00: £784.00: £357.00)
           1¾m                                                       2-35 (2-39)

301² **Gulf Palace (USA) (90)** *(RAkehurst)* 7-9-9 TQuinn (13) (hld up: hdwy 3f out: led ins fnl f: r.o wl) ........................................ —1
354* Al Mutahm (USA) **(84)** *(JABOld)* 4-9-0 (4x) LDettori (14) (in tch: drvn along over 3f out: r.o wl fnl f: nrst fin) ...................... 1½.2
Castle Courageous **(83)** *(LadyHerries)* 5-9-2 JReid (7) (a cl up: chal 4f out: outpcd over 2f out: r.o wl fnl f) ........................... hd.3
Sean's Scholar (USA) **(60)** *(CNAllen)* 5-7-0 ‡⁷CHawksley (8) (bhd: hdwy 4f out: styd on wl nr fin) ...................................... 2½.4
234⁴ Dom Wac **(78)** *(MBell)* 4-8-8 MHills (11) (hld up: smooth hdwy to ld over 2f out & qcknd: hdd & wknd ins fnl f) ...................... ½.5
228 Uluru (IRE) **(93)** *(MrsJRRamsden)* 4-9-9 BRaymond (12) (lw: stdy hdwy 3f out: r.o: nvr plcd to chal) .................................. 2.6
301⁵ Jackson Flint **(92)** *(HThomsonJones)* 4-9-8 RHills (9) (a.p: led 3f out: sn hdd & one pce) ................................................ ½.7
234* Coleridge **(77)** *(DShaw)* 4-8-7 GCarter (2) (effrt over 4f out: no imp) ... 4.8
Witness Box (USA) **(90)** *(JHMGosden)* 5-9-9 SCauthen (10) (lw: chsd ldrs tl outpcd fnl 3f) ........................................... 5.9
243³ Equity Card (IRE) **(72)** *(GAPritchard-Gordon)* 4-8-2 WCarson (17) (nvr trbld ldrs) ........................................................ nk.10
342⁴ Eire Leath-Sceal **(63)** *(MBrittain)* 5-7-10 GBardwell (4) (led tl hdd & wknd 4f out) ......................................................... 2½.11
342 Mubin (IRE) **(71)** *(CCElsey)* 4-8-1 JQuinn (16) (a.p: led 4f out tl hdd & wknd 3f out) ......................................................... 4.12
Deposki **(98)** *(MRStoute)* 4-10-0 WRSwinburn (5) (n.d) ................... ¾.13
Gondolier **(86)** *(HRACecil)* 4-9-2 PatEddery (5) (cl up: chal 7f out: wknd over 3f out) ............................................................. 14
Regent's Folly (IRE) **(96)** *(WJarvis)* 4-9-12 AMunro (3) (n.d) ............. 15
Madagans Grey **(86)** (bl) *(RBoss)* 4-9-2 MRoberts (15) (cl up tl wknd 4f out) . 16
                         LONG HANDICAP: Sean's Scholar (USA) 7-0.

9/4 Al Mutahm (USA), **8/1** Dom Wac(6/1—10/1), Witness Box (USA), **10/1** GULF PALACE (USA), **11/1** Gondolier(8/1—12/1), **12/1** Jackson Flint, Uluru (IRE), **14/1** Equity Card (IRE), Deposki, **20/1** Coleridge(16/1—25/1), **25/1** Mubin (IRE), Regent's Folly (IRE), Madagans Grey, Castle Courageous, Eire Leath-Sceal, **33/1** Sean's Scholar (USA). CSF £31.31, CT £529.51. Tote £13.30: £2.90 £1.30 £2.80 £4.50 (£14.70). Mr G. Burrell (EPSOM) bred by New Gate Stud Farm, Inc in USA. 16 Rn             3m 6.35 (10.35)
                                                                    SF—27/15/16/—/2/13

**436**    EARL OF SEFTON E.B.F. STKS (Gp 3)    £18990.00 (£7048.25: £3336.63: £1400.12)
           1m 1f                                                     3-05 (3-11)

**Sure Sharp (USA) (103)** *(BWHills)* 5-8-10 SCauthen (4) (lw: a cl up: led 3f out: sn hdd: led ins fnl f: r.o wl) ............................. —1
Adam Smith *(LMCumani)* 4-8-10 LDettori (6) (lw: hld up: effrt 3f out: led over 2f out tl ins fnl f: r.o) ........................................ 1½.2
Flashfoot **(111)** *(IABalding)* 4-8-10 BRaymond (8) (a.p: effrt 3f out: r.o: nt pce to chal) ......................................................... 2½.3
Star of Gdansk (USA) *(JSBolger,Ireland)* 4-8-13 CRoche (5) (lw: a cl up: chal 3f out: wknd ins fnl f) ............................................ nk.4
Desert Sun **(110)** (Jt-Fav) *(HRACecil)* 4-8-10 PatEddery (9) (h.d.w: hld up: stdy hdwy 3f out: chal 2f out: wknd ins fnl f) ........... 1½.5
Lahib (USA) *(JLDunlop)* 4-8-10 WCarson (2) (chsd ldrs tl outpcd fnl 2f out) 2½.6

Gai Bulga **(108)** *(GWragg)* 4–8-7 WRSwinburn (7) (led tl hdd 3f out: sn rdn & btn) ............................................................................................. 5.7
Cruachan (USA) **(120)** (Jt-Fav) *(GHarwood)* 4–8-10 RCochrane (1) (chsd ldrs 6f: sn wknd) ............................................................................... 1.8

**5/2** Desert Sun, Cruachan (USA), **5/1** Adam Smith, **7/1** Star of Gdansk (USA), **9/1** SURE SHARP (USA)(14/1—8/1), **12/1** Gai Bulga, **14/1** Lahib (USA), **16/1** Flashfoot. CSF £49.35, Tote £18.30: £3.10 £1.80 £3.60 (£48.20). Sheikh Mohammed (LAMBOURN) bred by Pillar Stud, Inc. in USA. 8 Rn    1m 52.05 (2.05)
SF—86/81/73/75/67/59/41

**437**    EUROPEAN FREE H'CAP (listed race) (3-Y.O) £16030.50 (£4794.00: £2297.00 £1048.50)
7f                                              3-35 (3-39)
(Weights raised 20 lb)
**Pursuit of Love (104)** *(HRACecil)* 9-1 PatEddery (1) (lw: a gng wl: led over 2f out: qcknd clr: r.o) ...................................................... —1
Steinbeck (USA) (Fav) *(AFabre,France)* 9-1 SCauthen (8) (gd sort: neat: a.p: effrt & ev ch 2f out: rdn & nt qckn) ......................................... 2.2
Wolfhound (USA) *(JHMGosden)* 9-4 WCarson (2) (in tch: effrt 3f out: styd on nr fin: fin 4th, 3l: plcd 3rd) ............................................ 3
Artic Tracker (USA) **(109)** *(CRNelson)* 9-6 JReid (9) (hld up: hdwy 3f out: ch 2f out: sn rdn & no ex: fin 5th, s.h: plcd 4th) ......................... 4
19a Fair Crack (IRE) **(110)** *(RHannon)* 9-7 BRaymond (3) (bhd: nt clr run over 2f out: r.o nr fin: fin 6th, 1½l: plcd 5th) .................... 5
Taylor Quigley **(104)** *(CNAllen)* 9-1 RCochrane (5) (chsd ldrs over 5f) ... nk.7
341⁴ Bobzao (IRE) **(105)** *(WCarter)* 9-2 MRoberts (4) (lw: led tl hdd over 2f out: sn wknd) ......................................................... hd.8
Master of Passion **(106)** *(JMPEustace)* 9-3 LPiggott (7) (lw: disp tl early: cl up tl wknd 2f out: eased ins fnl f) ........................... 1.9
Wilde Rufo **(105)** *(PAKelleway)* 9-2 TQuinn (6) (hld up: hdwy over 2f out: styd on: nt pce to chal: fin 2nd, d.h. disq. plcd last) ........................... 0
*Stewards Enquiry: Obj. by Clerk of Scales to Wilde Rufo sustained. Wilde Rufo disq. (carried incorrect weight).*

**5/2** PURSUIT of LOVE(2/1—3/1), **5/1** Wolfhound (USA), **11/2** Artic Tracker (USA), **15/2** Fair Crack (IRE), **16/1** Master of Passion, Taylor Quigley (USA), **33/1** Ors. CSF £9.67, CT £27.91. Tote £3.80: £1.60 £1.40 £2.00 (£3.60). Lord Howard de Walden (NEWMARKET) bred by Lord Howard de Walden. 9 Rn    1m 26.55 (2.55)
SF—79/79/74/67/66/62/55

**438**    LADBROKE RACING H'CAP (0-105) £7895.00 (£2360.00: £1130.00: £515.00)
7f                                              4-10 (4-13)
(Weights raised 8 lb)
233⁶ **Mango Manila (78)** (Jt-Fav) *(CAHorgan)* 7–8-12 CAsmussen (3) (b: bhd: hdwy 2f out: str burst to ld wl ins fnl f: sn clr) ............ —1
233* King of Chance (IRE) **(73)** *(MrsJRRamsden)* 4–8-0‡7JWeaver (13) (hdwy ½-wy: led ins fnl f: sn hdd & no ch w wnr) ......................... 2.2
240 Domicksky **(81)** *(MJRyan)* 4–9-1 NDay (18) (in tch: hdwy over 2f out: styd on one pce fnl f) ...................................... 3.3
233 Pytchley Night **(75)** *(DMorris)* 5–8-2 ‡7StephenDavies (14) (cl up: led over 1f out: sn hdd & one pce) .......................... 2.4
364³ Doulab's Image **(68)** (bl) *(JAGlover)* 5–8-2 JQuinn (7) (bhd tl r.o fnl 2f) ... 1½.5
240 Languedoc **(76)** *(MPNaughton)* 5–8-10 LCharnock (20) (a chsng ldrs: one pce fnl 2f) ....................................................... nk.6
221* African Chimes **(73)** *(WAO'Gorman)* 5–8-2(3) ‡5EmmaO'Gorman (5) (w ldrs: led ½-wy tl over 1f out: hung lft & sn btn) ................. ½.7
285* Colossus **(69)** (Jt-Fav) *(CEBrittain)* 4–8-3 MRoberts (15) (led to ½-wy: w ldrs tl wknd over 1f out) .................................. 2.8
Shining Jewel **(72)** *(MrsLPiggott)* 5–7-13 ‡7GMilligan (8) (cl up over 5f) ...... s.h.9
Annabelle Royale **(82)** *(MrsNMacauley)* 6–9-2 BCrossley (9) (lw: prom 5f) ...... ¾.10
344* Nordic Brave **(72)** *(MBrittain)* 6–8-6 PatEddery (4) (spd 5f) ...................... 1½.11
Superoo **(78)** *(JSutcliffe)* 6–8-12 PaulEddery (12) (bhd: sme hdwy over 1f out: n.d) .................................................. 1.12
Lamarsh (IRE) **(88)** *(JHMGosden)* 4–9-8 SCauthen (6) (prom tl rdn & wknd 2f out) ....................................................... 1½.13
Mahsul (IRE) **(62)** *(CJBenstead)* 4–7-10 WCarson (4) (lw: n.d) ...................... hd.14
Dry Point **(73)** *(JARToller)* 6–8-7 DaleGibson (2) (b: bit bkwd: outpcd fr ½-wy) .. 15
Field of Honour **(86)** *(LMCumani)* 4–9-6 LDettori (17) (bhd fr ½-wy) ............... 16
Saluting Walter (USA) **(72)** *(ICampbell)* 4–8-6 AClark (19) (sn wl bhd) ............ 17

**6/1** MANGO MANILA, Colossus, **7/1** King of Chance (IRE), **10/1** Nordic Brave, Pytchley Night, **11/1** Domicksky, **12/1** Saluting Walter (USA)(20/1—25/1), Field of Honour, **14/1** Mahsul (IRE), **16/1** African Chimes, Doulab's Image, Superoo, Languedoc, Lamarsh (IRE), **33/1** Ors. CSF £45.59, CT £415.89. Tote £5.60: £2.00 £2.30 £2.50 £3.00 (£16.70). Mr R. Del Rosario (BILLINGBEAR) bred by Arthur E. Smith. 17 Rn    1m 26.75 (2.75)
SF—73/55/61/42/37/44/34

**439** E.B.F. BARTLOW STKS (Mdn 2-Y.O.F) £3028.00 (£904.00: £432.00: £196.00)
5f

4-45 (4-47)

    **Ancestral Dancer** *(MBell)* 8-11 MHills (10) (neat: a:p: led 1f out: r.o wl) ............. —1
345² Defenceless *(Fav)* *(RHannon)* 8-11 BRouse (8) (lw: led tl hdd 1f out: kpt on same pce) ............. 1½.2
    Hawayah (IRE) *(BHanbury)* 8-11 WRSwinburn (7) (small: in tch: hdwy 2f out: styd on wl) ............. 2.3
    Northern Bird *(BWHills)* 8-11 DHolland (5) (b.hind: lt-f: unf: dwlt: hdwy 2f out: r.o) ............. s.h.4
    Crested Wave (IRE) *(PWChapple-Hyam)* 8-11 PaulEddery (9) (leggy: scope: chsd ldrs tl wknd appr fnl f) ............. 4.5
    Zany Zanna (IRE) *(GAPritchard-Gordon)* 8-11 AMunro (2) (unf: in tch tl outpcd appr fnl f) ............. 2½.6
    Simmering *(GWragg)* 8-11 SCauthen (4) (w'like: sn in tch: shkn up ½-wy: no rspnse) ............. 1½.7
    Duchess de Belfort *(JBerry)* 8-11 PatEddery (11) (neat: hung rt most of wy: prom tl wknd & eased appr fnl f) ............. 2.8
286⁴ Grand Dancer (IRE) *(RJRWilliams)* 8-11 RCochrane (1) (cmpt: unf: dwlt: nt rcvr) 1½.9
    The Wend (v) *(DTThom)* 8-11 JQuinn (3) (cmpt: spd to ½-wy: sn wknd) ............. 10
    Jasmin Isle *(ICampbell)* 8-11 AMackay (6) (neat: dwlt: a outpcd & bhd) ............. 11

**3/1** Defenceless, **4/1** Simmering(2/1—9/2), **6/1** ANCESTRAL DANCER, **8/1** Grand Dancer (IRE)(10/1—14/1), Duchess de Belfort(3/1—10/1), Hawayah (IRE)(tchd 14/1), Northern Bird(tchd 14/1), **12/1** Crested Wave (IRE)(op 5/1), **33/1** Ors. CSF £23.35, Tote £10.70: £2.90 £1.10 £2.80 (£14.50). Innlaw Racing (NEWMARKET) bred by Hillfields Stud. 11 Rn
60.93 sec (1.53)
SF—56/50/42/41/25/15

**440** WOOD DITTON STKS (Mdn 3-Y.O) £5617.50 (£1680.00: £805.00: £367.50)
1m

5-15 (5-27)

    **Muhayaa** (USA) *(AAScott)* 9-0 WRSwinburn (5) (str: mde most: shkn up & r.o wl fnl f) ............. —1
    Ivana (IRE) *(WJarvis)* 8-9 AMunro (7) (w'like: leggy: a chsng ldrs: hdwy 2f out: slt ld ins fnl f: sn hdd & no ex) ............. ½.2
    Barahin (IRE) *(JLDunlop)* 9-0 WCarson (12) (neat: unf: hld up: effrt over 2f out: r.o wl nr fin) ............. ½.3
    Coniston Water (USA) *(Fav)* *(JHMGosden)* 9-0 SCauthen (1) (gd sort: bit bkwd: hld up: stdy hdwy 3f out: ev ch over 1f out: eased ins fnl f) ............. 1½.4
    Highland Fantasy (USA) *(BWHills)* 8-9 DHolland (16) (leggy: scope: in tch: effrt over 2f out: styd on u.p) ............. 1.5
    Jathaab (IRE) *(MRStoute)* 9-0 RCochrane (20) (w'like: scope: mid div & rdn over 2f out: swtchd rt & r.o wl nr fin) ............. nk.6
    Hideyoshi (USA) *(DRCElsworth)* 9-0 CAsmussen (2) (gd sort: trckd ldrs: smooth hdwy to chal wl over 1f out: wknd ins fnl f) ............. nk.7
    Vagrancy *(BWHills)* 8-9 PatEddery (4) (w'like: lw: cl up tl grad wknd appr fnl f) ............. 2.8
    Cambrian *(MrsJCecil)* 9-0 PaulEddery (6) (cmpt: scope: a in tch: kpt on same pce fnl 2f) ............. 1.9
    Kalko *(CEBrittain)* 9-0 MRoberts (10) (cmpt: bit bkwd: s.s: hdwy u.p ½-wy: nvr trbld ldrs) ............. 1½.10
    Iftakhaar (USA) *(MajorWRHern)* 9-0 JReid (18) (w'like: scope: chsd ldrs 6f) ... nk.11
    Rolling the Bones (USA) *(JRFanshawe)* 9-0 GCarter (15) (w'like: scope: cl up 6f) ............. ¾.12
    Wafi (USA) *(BHanbury)* 9-0 BRaymond (21) (cmpt: scope: w ldrs tl wknd 2f out) nk.13
    Alycida (USA) *(LMCumani)* 9-0 LDettori (19) (gd sort: chsd ldrs 6f) ............. 1.14
    Turret Gates *(JARToller)* 9-0 TQuinn (13) (cmpt: bit bkwd: spd over 5f) ............. ¾.15
    Sahara Shield *(AAScott)* 9-0 AClark (14) (cmpt: bkwd: s.s: n.d) ............. ½.16
    Bold Boss *(BHanbury)* 9-0 AShoults (3) (w'like: leggy: outpcd fr ½-wy) ............. nk.17
    Pompion (USA) *(JHMGosden)* 9-0 GHind (11) (w'like: leggy: n.d) ............. s.h.18
    Maraady (USA) *(MRStoute)* 9-0 RHills (17) (w'like: scope: n.d) ............. 3.19
    Quadrant *(BWHills)* 9-0 MHills (9) (w'like: s.s: a bhd) ............. 20
    *General Dixie (USA) (16/1) Withdrawn (ref to ent stalls) : not under orders*

**11/4** Coniston Water (USA), **6/1** Barahin (IRE)(op 4/1), Hideyoshi (USA)(10/1—11/2), **8/1** Vagrancy(6/1—10/1), **10/1** MUHAYAA (USA)(op 5/1), **12/1** Jathaab (IRE)(tchd 20/1), **14/1** Iftakhaar (USA)(10/1—20/1), Rolling the Bones (USA), Alycida (USA), **16/1** Cambrian, **20/1** Maraady (USA), **25/1** Ors. CSF £231.72, Tote £14.70: £3.70 £9.10 £3.20 (£694.00). Maktoum Al Maktoum (NEWMARKET) bred by J. D. Wimpfheimer & Gilman Investment Co. in USA. 20 Rn
1m 41.89 (4.59)
SF—49/42/45/40/30/34/33

T/Trio: Races 3 & 5: £258.80 & £74.80 (2.2 & 13.5 Tckts). T/Jkpt: £248.435.30 (0.15 Tckts); £285.364.93 to Newmarket 16/4/92. T/Plpt: £322.00 (49.15 Tckts).
AA

# NEWMARKET (R-H) Rowley Mile
## Thursday, April 16th [Good]
Going Allowance: minus 0.05 sec per fur (G)

Wind: mod half bhd

Stalls: 3rd & 4th low, remainder high

**441**  GRANBY STKS (Mdn 3-Y.O.C & G) £3080.00 (£920.00: £440.00: £200.00)
7f
2-00 (2-02)

**King Olaf (IRE)** *(PWChapple-Hyam)* 9-0 PatEddery (3) (a.p: led wl over 1f out: hrd rdn & r.o) ................................................................. —1

**Hamas (IRE) (Fav)** *(PTWalwyn)* 9-0 WCarson (5) (leggy: unf: scope: a.p: chal over 1f out: r.o u.p) ........................................ nk.2

**Talb (USA)** *(JLDunlop)* 9-0 JReid (4) (gd sort: lw: in tch: hdwy 2f out: r.o) ...... 3½.3

**Zalon (IRE)** *(JHMGosden)* 9-0 SCauthen (12) (a cl up: ev ch 2f out: nt qckn) ... ¾.4

**Retender (USA)** *(LMCumani)* 9-0 (b.hind: w'like: leggy: a in tch: effrt over 2f out: kpt on) ............................................ 3½.5

**Young Max** *(DRCElsworth)* 9-0 TQuinn (13) (bit bkwd: led tl hdd wl over 1f out: grad wknd) ............................................ 1.6

**Desired Guest** *(MRStoute)* 9-0 PD'Arcy (15) (chsd ldrs over 5f) .............. nk.7

**Hopeful Bid (IRE)** *(RHannon)* 9-0 BRaymond (2) (lw: hld up: hdwy 3f out: wknd over 1f out) ............................................ 2.8

**Colonsay** *(JRFanshawe)* 9-0 GDuffield (14) (leggy: unf: s.i.s: pushed along & hdwy ½-wy: n.d) ....................................... nk.9

**Nasseer** *(ACStewart)* 9-0 MRoberts (6) (s.i.s: nvr wnt pce) ................ 2½.10

**Nael (IRE)** *(CJBenstead)* 9-0 RCochrane (8) (lw: s.i.s: n.d) .............. 2.11

**Chummy's Child (IRE)** *(BWHills)* 9-0 DHolland (7) (w'like: sn pushed along: a bhd) .............................................. 1½.12

**Nominoo Prinoo** *(RGuest)* 9-0 JQuinn (10) (a bhd) .................... 7.13

**Emigrator** *(RGuest)* 9-0 GBaxter (11) (unf: prom to ½-wy) ............ hd.14

**Boethius (USA)** *(JRFanshawe)* 9-0 WRSwinburn (1) (wl grwn: bkwd: sn bhd) ... 15

5/2 Hamas (IRE), 11/4 KING OLAF (IRE)(op 7/4), 6/1 Zalon (IRE)(op 7/2), 11/1 Talb (USA)(7/1—12/1), 12/1 Retender (USA), Boethius (USA)(8/1—14/1), Colonsay, Desired Guest(op 8/1), 16/1 Hopeful Bid (IRE), 20/1 Young Max, 25/1 Chummy's Child (IRE), Emigrator, 33/1 Ors. CSF £10.77, Tote £3.20: £1.10 £1.70 £4.80 (£4.20). Mr R. E. Sangster (MARLBOROUGH) bred by Regiura Syndicate in Ireland. 15 Rn   1m 27.67 (3.67)
SF—40/39/28/26/15/12

**442**  BABRAHAM H'CAP (0-105) £5481.00 (£1638.00: £784.00: £357.00)
1½m
2-35 (2-39)

**Close Friend (IRE) (95) (Fav)** *(BWHills)* 4-9-7 DHolland (7) (lw: a cl up: led 2f out: hung rt u.p: r.o) ...................................... —1

331 **Line Drummer (USA) (72)** *(PAKelleway)* 4-7-9(3) ‡3DBiggs (4) (b: hdwy ½-wy: chal over 1f out: r.o: no ex nr fin) ......................... nk.2

**Kimbers (IRE) (102)** *(CRNelson)* 4-10-0 JReid (1) (cl up: led 3f out to 2f out: r.o one pce) ............................................ 3.3

**Castoret (72)** *(JWHills)* 6-7-13 SDawson (5) (hld up & bhd: stdy hdwy 4f out: shkn up & edgd rt 2f out: nt qckn) ........................ ¾.4

**Seal Indigo (IRE) (92)** *(RHannon)* 4-8-13 ‡5RPerham (2) (hld up: hdwy 4f out: nt qckn fnl 2f) ............................................ 5.5

360⁴ **Swift Sword (97)** *(MrsGRReveley)* 4-9-9 RCochrane (10) (bhd: effrt 4f out: sn hrd rdn & nvr able to chal) .............................. 2.6

**Irish Emerald (79)** *(GCBravery)* 5-8-6 MHills (12) (bhd: sme hdwy 3f out: nvr nr to chal) ............................................ ½.7

**Farat (USA) (83)** *(JLDunlop)* 4-8-9 TQuinn (14) (lw: dwlt: effrt 4f out: no imp) .... 5.8

360³ **Kansk (94)** *(JHMGosden)* 4-9-6 SCauthen (6) (led tl hdd 3f out: wknd over 1f out) ............................................ ½.9

335² **Sea Goddess (76)** *(WJarvis)* 4-8-2 WCarson (13) (chsd ldrs tl wknd 2f out) .. 10.10

**Kiveton Kabooz (86)** *(LMCumani)* 4-8-12 LDettori (9) (swtg: bhd: pushed along 4f out) ...................................... nk.11

**Niani (IRE) (96)** *(JLDunlop)* 4-9-8 WRSwinburn (11) (lost tch fnl 4f) ......... 2½.12

**Libk (102)** *(HThomsonJones)* 4-10-0 RHills (8) (bit bkwd: chsd ldrs tl wknd 3f out) ............................................ ¾.13

**James Is Special (IRE) (67)** *(HJCollingridge)* 4-7-7 JQuinn (3) (in tch: rdn 4f out: sn outpcd) ...................................... 4.14

LONG HANDICAP: James Is Special (IRE) 7-1.

11/2 Kiveton Kabooz, Kansk, 7/1 CLOSE FRIEND (IRE), 8/1 Seal Indigo (IRE), 9/1 Sea Goddess, 10/1 Castoret, Irish Emerald, 12/1 James Is Special (IRE), Swift Sword, 14/1 Farat (USA), 16/1 Libk, 20/1 Niani (IRE), 33/1 Ors. CSF £177.19, CT £6,279.44. Tote £10.20: £2.90 £7.80 £13.30 (£139.70). Mr Wafic Said (LAMBOURN) bred by Roehart Ltd in Ireland. 14 Rn
2m 35.60 (6.30)
SF—38/11/38/7/11/17

### 443

FEILDEN STKS (listed race) (3-Y.O) £10416.00 (£3108.00: £1484.00: £672.00)
1m 1f
3-05 (3-13)

**Twist and Turn (111)** (Fav) *(HRACecil)* 8-11 SCauthen (1) (led tl hdd ins fnl f: rallied to ld cl home) ............................................................. —1

Young Senor (USA) **(111)** *(GWragg)* 9-2 WRSwinburn (5) (h.d:w: unruly s: trckd ldrs: effrt 2f out: slt ld ins fnl f: nt qckn nr fin) ......... hd.2

347* Thyer (USA) **(105)** *(JSBolger,Ireland)* 9-0 CRoche (8) (lw: cl up: effrt over 2f out: r.o one pce) ............................................................. 3.3

Distinct Thatcher (USA) *(RHannon)* 8-11 BRaymond (7) (lw: cl up tl outpcd appr fnl f: kpt on u.p) ...................................................... s.h.4

341⁵ Spartan Shareef (IRE) *(CEBrittain)* 8-11 MRoberts (4) (s.i.s: sn in tch: effrt 3f out: r.o one pce) ................................................... 3¹/₂.5

387* Amaze **(90)** *(LadyHerries)* 8-11 SWhitworth (3) (b: chsd ldrs tl outpcd over 2f out) ................................................................... 2¹/₂.6

Mack the Knife **(113)** *(MajorWRHern)* 8-11 WCarson (2) (trckd ldrs: effrt 3f out: sn rdn & btn) ................................................. 6.7

Ninja Dancer (USA) **(108)** *(MrsJCecil)* 9-5 LPiggott (6) (hld up & bhd: shkn up 3f out: n.d) ...................................................... 2¹/₂.8

**11/4** TWIST AND TURN, **7/2** Mack the Knife, **4/1** Thyer (USA), **13/2** Amaze, **7/1** Young Senor (USA), **10/1** Spartan Shareef (IRE)(op 20/1), **14/1** Ors. CSF £20.76, Tote £3.80: £1.30 £1.90 £1.90 (£15.70). Sheikh Mohammed (NEWMARKET) bred by Sheikh Mohammed bin Rashid al Maktoum. 8 Rn    1m 51.95 (1.95)
SF—61/65/54/50/39/31

### 444

CRAVEN STKS (Gp 3) (3-Y.O.C & G) £18801.00 (£6975.80: £3300.40: £1382.80)
1m
3-40 (3-42)

**Alnasr Alwasheek (109)** *(MRStoute)* 8-9 SCauthen (8) (h.d:w: hld up & bhd: stdy hdwy over 2f out: led over 1f out: qcknd: comf) .......... —1

Dr Devious (IRE) **(113)** *(PWChapple-Hyam)* 9-0 CAsmussen (2) (h.d:w: chsd ldrs: n.m.r 2f out: hdwy over 1f out: r.o wl: nt pce of wnr) 1¹/₂.2

Irish Memory *(JSBolger,Ireland)* 8-9 CRoche (3) (gd sort: lw: mde most tl hdd over 1f out: no ex) ............................................ 2¹/₂.3

Muhtarram (USA) *(JHMGosden)* 8-9 WCarson (6) (h.d:w: bit bkwd: trckd ldrs: ev ch ¹/₂-wy tl rdn & btn over 1f out) ............................ 2.4

Badie (USA) *(JLDunlop)* 8-9 JReid (4) (chsd ldrs tl rdn & btn appr fnl f) ............ ³/₄.5

Bold Pursuit (IRE) *(RHannon)* 8-9 LPiggott (1) (w ldr tl wknd over 2f out) ...... 8.6

Torrey Canyon (USA) **(110)** *(RCharlton)* 8-9 PatEddery (7) (bit bkwd: hld up: effrt 3f out: sn rdn & btn) ..................................... 5.7

238* Forest Tiger (USA) **(101)** (Fav) *(MMoubarak)* 8-9 LDettori (5) (plld hrd: hld up: effrt 3f out: sn btn) .................................... 10.8

**11/4** Forest Tiger (USA), **7/2** Dr Devious (IRE), **5/1** ALNASR ALWASHEEK, Muhtarram (USA), **6/1** Bold Pursuit (IRE), **15/2** Torrey Canyon (USA), **16/1** Irish Memory, **33/1** Badie (USA). CSF £21.84, Tote £6.60: £1.90 £1.10 £2.40 (£8.80). Sheikh Ahmed Al Maktoum (NEWMARKET) bred by Meon Valley Stud. 8 Rn  1m 37.39 (0.09)
SF—88/88/75/69/67/43

### 445

LADBROKES BOLDBOY SPRINT H'CAP (3-Y.O) (0-100) £7570.00 (£2260.00: £1080.00: £490.00)   6f
4-10 (4-16)
(Weights raised 1 lb)

**Heather Bank (80)** *(JBerry)* 8-6 PatEddery (13) (cl up: led over 2f out: r.o wl appr fnl f: sn clr) ....................................... —1

215 Master Planner **(83)** *(CACyzer)* 8-9 GCarter (3) (in tch: hdwy 2f out: hung bdly lft fnl f: no ch w wnr) .......................... 6.2

Euro Festival **(75)** *(MissLCSiddall)* 8-1 AMunro (7) (s.s: hdwy 2f out: r.o) ..... 1¹/₂.3

Isaiah **(95)** *(MJohnston)* 9-7 TQuinn (1) (h.d.w: a chsng ldrs: rdn 2f out: r.o one pce) ......................................................... ³/₄.4

Sir Boudle (IRE) **(83)** *(CRNelson)* 8-9 JReid (9) (hdwy 2f out: styd on: no imp) . 1.5

254³ Freddie Lloyd (USA) **(88)** *(NACallaghan)* 9-0 WCarson (14) (b.off fore: spd 4f) nk.6

Holetown **(86)** *(RHannon)* 8-7 ⁺5RPerham (11) (lw: prom over 3f) ................. nk.7

Walking Possession **(81)** (bl) *(RBoss)* 8-7 MRoberts (8) (led tl hdd over 2f out: sn btn) ............................................................ 2.8

227* Cindora (IRE) **(90)** *(MHTompkins)* 9-2 RHills (15) (prom over 4f) .............. hd.9

275* Ponsardin **(88)** (Fav) *(SirMarkPrescott)* 9-0 GDuffield (2) (effrt ¹/₂-wy: n.d) ..... 5.10

Splice **(88)** *(JRFanshawe)* 9-0 WRSwinburn (10) (outpcd fr ¹/₂-wy) ............... 1.11

348 Mansber (IRE) **(67)** *(PatMitchell)* 7-0 ⁺7CHawksley (4) (unruly stalls: s.i.s: n.d) nk.12

348 Peerage Prince **(76)** *(PatMitchell)* 7-13 ⁺3SO'Gorman (5) (lw: chsd ldrs 4f: wknd qckly) .......................................... 1.13

Kilmelford **(70)** *(JARToller)* 7-10 DaleGibson (6) (n.d) ............................... 1.14

Memu (USA) **(88)** *(DRCElsworth)* 9-0 LPiggott (12) (gd spd over 3f: eased whn btn) ............................................................. hd.15

LONG HANDICAP: Mansber (IRE) 6-8.

**9/2** Ponsardin, **6/1 HEATHER BANK**, **15/2** Cindora (IRE), **8/1** Isaiah, Splice, **9/1** Freddie Lloyd (USA), **10/1** Walking Possession, **12/1** Holetown, **14/1** Memu (USA), **14/1** Sir Boudle (IRE), **25/1** Master Planner, Euro Festival, Kilmelford, Peerage Prince, **100/1** Mansber (IRE). CSF £126.36, CT £3,146.49. Tote £5.70: £2.60 £6.80 £4.20 (£161.70). Mr Norman Harper (COCKERHAM) bred by Castle Farm Stud. 15 Rn   1m 14.04 (2.64)
SF—33/12/—/15/—/3

**446**     E.B.F. STUNTNEY STKS (Mdn 2-Y.O.C & G) £3132.00 (£936.00: £448.00: £204.00)
        **5f**                                                    4-45 (4-47)

Kharaj *(AAScott)* 9-0 WCarson (1) (neat: a cl up: led ¹/₂-wy: pushed along & r.o
wl fnl f) ......................................................................................... —1
Pistol (IRE) *(PFICole)* 9-0 TQuinn (10) (w'like: a:p: effrt 2f out: sn ev ch: r.o) ...... 3.2
Joyofracing *(Fav)* *(WAO'Gorman)* 9-0 DHolland (2) (str: cmpt: bit bkwd: a:p:
effrt 2f out: r.o: nt pce to chal) ................................................. 3¹/₂.3
White Crown (USA) *(BHanbury)* 9-0 WRSwinburn (11) (w'like: scope: bit bkwd:
chsd ldrs: effrt ¹/₂-wy: r.o one pce) ............................................... 2¹/₂.4
Darenot (IRE) *(CEBrittain)* 9-0 MRoberts (8) (leggy: scope: a.p: kpt on one pce
fnl 2f) ............................................................................................. 3.5
Kingston Brown *(JBerry)* 9-0 PatEddery (7) (str: cmpt: lw: a chsng ldrs: outpcd
fnl 2f) ............................................................................................. nk.6
339  Threeofus *(KTIvory)* 9-0 MWigham (4) (s.i.s: styd on fr ¹/₂-wy: nvr able to chal) ¹/₂.7
Soleil D'Or *(MMcCormack)* 9-0 JReid (13) (neat: led to ¹/₂-wy: wknd wl over 1f
out) ............................................................................................... s.h.8
Legal Dancer *(RJRWilliams)* 9-0 RCochrane (6) (w'like: lw: in tch: effrt ¹/₂-wy: sn
wknd) ............................................................................................. ³/₄.9
Roger the Butler (IRE) *(MBell)* 9-0 MHills (9) (w'like: scope: s.i.s: nvr nr ldrs) .. hd.10
Cashable *(JRJenkins)* 9-0 SWhitworth (12) (neat: spd 3f) ....................... 1¹/₂.11
Wahem (IRE) *(NACallaghan)* 9-0 RRaymond (5) (lt-f: unf: s.s: n.d) ............... nk.12
339  Aberdeen Heather *(DRCElsworth)* 9-0 SCauthen (3) (dwlt: hdwy ¹/₂-wy: sn
wknd & eased) ................................................................................ 1¹/₂.13

**9/4** Joyofracing(2/1—3/1), **5/1** Kingston Brown(6/1—4/1), **13/2** Aberdeen Heather(5/1—10/1), **8/1** Roger the Butler (IRE)(op 5/1), **10/1** KHARAJ, **11/1** Pistol (IRE)(8/1—12/1), **12/1** Darenot (IRE), **16/1** Wahem (IRE)(12/1—20/1), White Crown (USA), Soleil D'Or, **33/1** Ors. CSF £106.01, Tote £7.40: £2.70 £4.60 £1.80 (£53.90). Mr Hamdan Al-Maktoum (NEWMARKET) bred by Home Stud Ltd. 13 Rn       62.68 sec (3.28)
SF—30/18/4/—/—/—

T/Trio: Race 2: any 2 fr 1st 3 £26.20 (38.4 Tckts)., Race 5: £376.40 (3 Tckts)., T/Jkpt: £115,935.80 (2.95 Tckts). T/Plpt: £980.30 (24.45 Tckts).                                    AA

**358—PONTEFRACT (L-H)**
## Wednesday, April 15th [Soft, Heavy patches]
Going Allowance: 5f-6f: 0.60 sec (Y); Rest: 0.80 sec per fur (S)        Wind: str half bhd

Stalls: low

**447**     STRAWBERRY HILL STKS (2-Y.O) £1478.00 (£408.00: £194.00)    **5f**    2-45 (2-47)

361* Isotonic *(Fav)* *(GMMoore)* 8-13 KFallon (4) (lw: mde all: rdn & hung bdly rt over
1f out: drvn out) ............................................................................ —1
287* Calisar *(WGMTurner)* 8-13 ‡5TSprako (3) (lw: chsd ldrs: effrt ¹/₂-wy: styd on fnl f) 1¹/₂.2
Our Mica *(JBerry)* 8-11 MBirch (5) (w'like: scope: w ldrs: effrt over 1f out: kpt on
same pce) ...................................................................................... 1¹/₂.3
323⁴ Principal Player (USA) *(WBentley)* 8-11 JLowe (1) (lw: a chsng ldrs: hung rt &
styd on same pce u.p fnl 2f) ......................................................... 2.4
297² Stormy Heights *(JRJenkins)* 8-6 SWhitworth (7) (w ldrs tl wknd over 1f out) .... 1¹/₂.5
Ann Hill (IRE) *(RHollinshead)* 8-6 WRyan (2) (neat: bit bkwd: s.i.s: a outpcd) ..... 5.6
Meadow View (IRE) *(CJHill)* 8-6 NAdams (6) (str: cmpt: s.s: a wl bhd) ............. 8.7

**11/10** ISOTONIC, **5/2** Our Mica, **13/2** Stormy Heights, **9/1** Principal Player (USA), **12/1** Calisar(op 8/1), **20/1** Meadow View (IRE), **25/1** Ann Hill (IRE). CSF £13.57, Tote £1.80: £1.40 £2.80 (£8.50). Mr J. Burgess (MIDDLEHAM) bred by Mrs S. M. Sands and M. Yiapatos. 7 Rn       67.4 sec (5.9)
SF—41/35/27/19/8/—

**448**     OSSETT (S) STKS (3 & 4-Y.O) £1884.00 (£524.00: £252.00)    **1m 4y**    3-15 (3-18)

326* Tynron Doon (61) *(Fav)* *(JBerry)* 3-8-5 GDuffield (1) (lw: trckd ldrs: led over 2f
out: sn clr: drvn out) ...................................................................... —1
355² Ready to Draw (IRE) (63) *(RonaldThompson)* 3-8-5 NConnorton (5) (sn bhd &
rdn along: hdwy over 3f out: styd on appr fnl f: no ch w wnr) 4.2

221⁵ Prime Mover (bl) *(DBurchell)* 4–9-2 ‡⁵RPrice (10) (lw: a chsng ldrs: hrd rdn over 2f out: one pce) .................................................................. 8.3

366 Brotherlyaffection (59) *(RHollinshead)* 3–8-5 WRyan (21) (lw: chsd ldrs: rdn & no imp fnl 2f) .......................................................... 1¹⁄₂.4

375 Galley Gossip (62) *(MrsJRRamsden)* 3–7-11 ‡³FNorton (12) (hld up: stdy hdwy over 3f out: kpt on same pce fnl 2f) ......................... 1¹⁄₂.5

397 Angel Train (IRE) (bl) *(JParkes)* 4–9-2 SWhitworth (2) (lw: led tl over 2f out: wknd over 1f out) ................................................ 3¹⁄₂.6

King Optimist (42) *(ASmith)* 3–8-0 SWood (9) (bit bkwd: chsd ldrs: rdn 3f out: wknd 2f out) ........................................................... 6.7

366 Stag Night (55) *(CTinkler)* 3–8-0 KDarley (14) (bhd & rdn along 6f out: sme hdwy over 2f out: sn wknd) .................................. 1¹⁄₂.8

158⁴ Chloes Diamond (IRE) (58) *(JLSpearing)* 4–8-13 ‡³JFanning (22) (chsd ldrs tl wknd 2f out) ............................................................. 2¹⁄₂.9

264 Rowandene (IRE) *(MHEasterby)* 3–7-9 ‡⁵SMaloney (11) (nvr nr ldrs) ............ 2¹⁄₂.10

The Dominant Gene (36) *(JRJenkins)* 3–8-0 NAdams (15) (sn bhd) ½.11

278⁶ Hanjessdan (40) *(DHaydnJones)* 4–9-2 JWilliams (19) (lw: mid div: drvn along ½-wy: n.d) ...................................................... 12

Blue Cross *(PSFelgate)* 3–7-9 JLowe (3) (sn t.o) .............................. 13

356 Hot Sound *(BWLunness)* 3–7-9 RFox (13) (bit bkwd: a in rr) ............... 14

327 Johnston's Express (IRE) *(EJAlston)* 4–9-2 KFallon (8) (bit bkwd: bhd: swtchd outside ½-wy: n.d) ....................................... 15

366 Lady Randolph (60) *(ICampbell)* 3–7-9⁽⁷⁾ ‡⁷GMitchell (17) (sn wl bhd) ...... 16

333⁴ Tapestry Dancer (43) *(MJHaynes)* 4–8-13 ‡³DBiggs (20) (lw: in tch 5f: sn bhd) ... 17

Champagne Break *(MWEllerby)* 3–8-0 SMorris (6) (in tch over 4f: sn bhd) ....... 18

Del's Fargo *(JLHarris)* 3–8-0 NCarlisle (7) (chsd ldrs ½-wy: t.o) .................. 19

397 Turbulent River (USA) (67) *(NTinkler)* 4–9-7 KimTinkler (16) (prom early: sn bhd: t.o) ................................................................. 20

*Stewards Enquiry: Price suspended 24-25/4/92 (excessive use of whip).*

**3/1** TYRNON DOON, **6/1** Ready to Draw (IRE), Prime Mover, Galley Gossip(op 7/2), **11/1** Rowandene (IRE)(op 7/1), **12/1** Brotherlyaffection, Chloes Diamond (IRE), **14/1** Stag Night, **16/1** Tapestry Dancer, Turbulent River (USA), Lady Randolph, **20/1** Johnston's Express (IRE), **25/1** King Optimist, **33/1** Ors. CSF £22.36, Tote £3.50: £2.10 £1.60 £1.80 (£6.60). Mr D. G. Rogers (COCKERHAM) bred by Mrs C. A. Dickson. 20 Rn; Sld G Wiltshire 6,000 gns                                                                 1m 53 (11.4)

SF—16/4/–/–/–/–

**449**    ST GILES H'CAP (0-80) £2742.00 (£762.00: £366.00)    **6f**    3-45 (3-51)

344⁵ Pharoah's Dancer (55) *(EAWheeler)* 5–8-1 ‡³FNorton (5) (lw: trckd ldr: led ½-wy: hld on wl) .................................................................. —1

Densben (57) *(DenysSmith)* 8–8-6 KFallon (1) (a chsng ldrs: r.o wl u.p ins fnl f) ³⁄₄.2

Lochsong (72) *(IABalding)* 4–9-0 ‡⁷FArrowsmith (3) (lw: trckd ldrs gng wl: r.o fnl f) ....................................................................... ½.3

344⁶ Darakah (63) (Fav) *(CJHill)* 5–8-9 ‡³DBiggs (4) (in tch: outpcd over 2f out: swtchd outside: r.o wl ins fnl f) ............................ ½.4

Arc Lamp (55) *(JAGlover)* 6–8-4 JFortune (2) (led to ½-wy: wknd over 1f out) 10.5

344 Malunar (65) (v) *(MHTompkins)* 7–8-7 ‡⁷MGodsafe (8) (lw: effrt over 2f out: nvr nr ldrs) .......................................................... 1.6

277 Sandmoor Denim (54) *(SRBowring)* 5–8-3⁽¹⁾ SWebster (11) (nvr trbld ldrs) ..... 2¹⁄₂.7

35f5 Gorytus Star (54) *(DHaydnJones)* 6–8-3 JLowe (18) (racd wd: nvr nr to chal) . 12.8

357 Fay Eden (IRE) (60) *(RJHodges)* 4–8-9 NCarlisle (10) (chsd ldrs tl wknd over 2f out) ........................................................................ hd.9

397 Too Eager (62) (bl) *(MWEasterby)* 6–8-11 KDarley (16) (sn drvn along: nvr wnt pce) ............................................................................. ³⁄₄.10

344 Beatle Song (70) *(RJHodges)* 4–9-0 ‡⁵TSprake (6) (w ldrs over 3f: sn wknd) . hd.11

The Can Can Man (72) *(MJohnston)* 5–9-4 ‡³JFanning (14) (lw: broke wl: sn outpcd: sme hdwy over 2f out: sn wknd) ......................... ³⁄₄.12

Granny Mc (50) *(EJAlston)* 5–7-8 ‡⁵NKennedy (17) (bit bkwd: w ldrs on outside tl wknd 2f out) ....................................................... 1¹⁄₂.13

Victoria Road (IRE) (79) *(MHEasterby)* 4–10-0 MBirch (12) (bit bkwd: hld up: a in rr) ............................................................................ 1¹⁄₂.14

Glenfield Greta (69) *(PSFelgate)* 4–8-13 ‡⁵RPrice (9) (bit bkwd: a bhd) ............ 5.15

Filicaia (54) *(DonEnricoIncisa)* 6–8-3 KimTinkler (13) (bkwd: s.i.s: a wl bhd: t.o) 16

Welsh Secret (75) *(MrsJRRamsden)* 4–9-10 TLucas (15) (w ldrs on outside tl wknd qckly over 2f out: sn bhd: t.o) .................................. 17

**9/2** Darakah, **5/1** Lochsong, **11/2** PHAROAH's DANCER, **9/1** Malunar, Gorytus Star, **10/1** Densben, **14/1** Too Eager, The Can Can Man, **16/1** Glenfield Greta, **20/1** Granny Mc, Victoria Road (IRE), Sandmoor Denim, Welsh Secret(op 8/1), Beatle Song, Arc Lamp, **33/1** Ors. CSF £58.93, CT £275.98. Tote £6.00: £1.30 £2.80 £1.40 £2.10 (£30.70). Mr James Devaney (LAMBOURN) bred by Heinz Pollmeier. 17 Rn

1m 20.6 (6.6)

SF—27/29/35/28/–/–

**450**  BAUGH FELL H'CAP  *(2m 1f 22y)* 4-15 - **Abandoned**—Waterlogged

**451**  LADY BALK STKS (Mdn 3-Y-O) £1674.00 (£464.00: £222.00)  1¼m 6y  4-50 (4-51)

**Peto** (Fav) *(HRACecil)* 9-0 WRyan (2) (w'like: scope: bit bkwd: hmpd bnd after 2f: shkn up to chal 1f out: sn led: r.o) ........................................ —1
Courtline Jester *(MAJarvis)* 9-0 GCrealock (1) (bit bkwd: reard s: sn trckng ldrs: chal 2f out: rdn & hung lft ins fnl f: r.o) ........................................ ½.2
167 Basilica **(75)** *(CEBrittain)* 8-11 ‡³RonHillis (3) (led tl jst ins fnl f: one pce) ........ 2½.3
Eden's Close *(MHTompkins)* 9-0 MBirch (6) (lw: sn chsng ldrs: shkn up & wknd over 2f out) ........................................ 25.4
Barton Pride (IRE) *(RHollinshead)* 8-7 ‡⁷JFordham (9) (sn bhd: sme late hdwy) . 8.5
330³ Esbooain (FR) **(80)** *(LMCumani)* 9-0 JFortune (8) (lw: gd hdwy 4f out: swtchd outside & effrt over 2f out: sn wknd) ........................................ 1.6
Wilkins *(JRFanshawe)* 9-0 GDuffield (12) (in tch tl lost pl over 2f out: sn wknd) . 10.7
235³ Sudanor (IRE) *(MJHeaton-Ellis)* 9-0 WNewnes (5) (lw: chsd ldrs tl wknd over 2f out) ........................................ 2.8
274³ Dexter Chief *(IABalding)* 8-11 ‡³SO'Gorman (7) (lw: mid div: drvn along ½-wy: lost pl 3f out) ........................................ 9
Neltegrity **(53)** *(THCaldwell)* 9-0 CDwyer (13) (bit bkwd: hld up & a bhd) ............ 10
Manair (IRE) (v) *(ACStewart)* 9-0 KDarley (11) (str: cmpt: sn drvn along: bhd fnl 4f) ........................................ 11
Monaafis *(AAScott)* 8-9 ‡⁵LNewton (10) (bit bkwd: sn bhd: wl t.o) ........................ 12

**9/4** PETO, **4/1** Courtline Jester(op 5/2), **5/1** Eden's Close, **6/1** Esbooain (FR), **8/1** Dexter Chief, **9/1** Sudanor (IRE), **14/1** Manair (IRE), **20/1** Wilkins, **33/1** Basilica, Monaafis, **100/1** Ors. CSF £11.51, Tote £2.60: £1.80 £2.10 £8.70 (£9.20). Sheikh Muhammed (NEWMARKET) bred by P. T. Tollwright. 12 Rn  2m 21.3 (13)
SF—47/45/37/–/–/–

**452**  GARFORTH H'CAP (3-Y-O) (0-70) £1758.00 (£488.00: £234.00)  5f  5-20 (5-24)
(Weights raised 1 lb)

324* **Double Blue (65)** (Fav) *(MJohnston)* 9-3 GDuffield (4) (lw: mde all: shkn up & qccknd over 1f out: sn clr) ........................................ —1
279 Fighter Squadron **(50)** (v) *(JAGlover)* 8-2 JFortune (2) (in tch: effrt over 2f out: styd on: no ch w wnr) ........................................ 7.2
264 Who's That Lady **(54)** *(MHEasterby)* 8-6 MBirch (1) (a chsng ldrs: kpt on same pce fnl 2f) ........................................ ½.3
Amoureuse (IRE) **(56)** *(EHOwenjun)* 8-8⁽²⁾ CDwyer (10) (bit bkwd: w wnr tl wknd over 1f out) ........................................ 4.4
353 Palacegate Gold (IRE) **(63)** *(RJHodges)* 8-10 ‡⁵TSprake (3) (chsd ldrs tl wknd 2f out) ........................................ 1½.5
Auction King (IRE) **(62)** *(ASmith)* 9-0 SWebster (7) (bit bkwd: chsd ldrs tl rdn & wknd over 2f out) ........................................ 2½.6
332 Cheshire Annie **(60)** *(WCarter)* 8-12 WRyan (6) (lw: hld up: effrt ½-wy: no imp) ........................................ 2½.7
Just Bob **(69)** *(SEKettlewell)* 9-4 ‡³JFanning (14) (s.i.s: bhd tl hdwy over 2f out: wknd 1f out) ........................................ ¾.8
Battuta **(56)** *(REarnshaw)* 8-3 ‡⁵SMaloney (16) (sn bhd & drvn along: sme late hdwy) ........................................ ½.9
Miss Movie World **(49)** *(NBycroft)* 8-1 JLowe (18) (bit bkwd: hld up & bhd: sme hdwy over 2f out: n.d) ........................................ ½.10
Premier Envelope (IRE) **(55)** *(NTinkler)* 8-7 KimTinkler (5) (sn bhd & pushed along) ........................................ s.h.11
227 Doesyoudoes **(62)** *(DTThom)* 9-0 JWilliams (17) (s.i.s: a bhd) ........................ 2½.12
Capital Idea (IRE) **(62)** (bl) *(RonaldThompson)* 9-0 DNicholls (11) (n.d) .......... 1.13
174⁶ Petaurista **(49)** *(MJohnston)* 8-1 NAdams (13) (a bhd) ........................ 3.14
276 Grubby **(49)** *(RHollinshead)* 7-8 ‡⁷AGarth (9) (lw: sn wl outpcd) ........................ ¾.15
151² Grand Time **(64)** *(CJHill)* 8-13 ‡³DBiggs (15) (lw: chsd ldrs to ½-wy: sn wknd) 4.16
Ahkam (IRE) **(53)** *(HThomsonJones)* 8-5 NCarlisle (12) (a outpcd) ........................ 2½.17

**7/4** DOUBLE BLUE, **10/1** Ahkam (IRE)(8/1—14/1), **12/1** Cheshire Annie (IRE), Who's That Lady(op 6/1), Premier Envelope (IRE), Grand Time(op 6/1), **14/1** Petaurista, Fighter Squadron, **16/1** Capital Idea (IRE)(op 10/1), Auction King (IRE), Doesyoudoes, Just Bob, Amoureuse (IRE), **20/1** Miss Movie World, **25/1** Ors. CSF £28.52, CT £228.45. Tote £2.10: £1.70 £4.00 £1.80 £3.80 (£29.10). Mr R. W. Huggins (MIDDLEHAM) bred by The Queen. 17 Rn  67.5 sec (6)
SF—43/–/2/–/–/–

T/Plpt: £10.90 (202.7 Tckts).

WG

## 365—**RIPON (R-H)**

**Thursday, April 16th [Soft, Heavy patches]**

Going Allowance: 0.90 sec per fur (S)

Wind: almost nil

Stalls: low

**453**  MILBY CLAIMING STKS  £2402.40 (£666.40: £319.20)  1¼m  2-10 (2-15)

**Henpot (IRE)** (Fav) *(HRACecil)* 4–8–4 WRyan (8) (lengthy: unf: bit bkwd: trckd ldrs: chal 2f out: sn led & clr: eased nr fin) ............................ —1
Pennine Star (IRE) *(CWCElsey)* 5–9–0 ‡SMaloney (9) (mid div: rdn over 3f out: hung rt: styd on wl nr fin) ................................................ 3½.2
335⁴ Metternich **(69)** *(MHTompkins)* 7–8–3 MBirch (1) (chsd ldr: chal over 3f out: slt ld over 2f out: sn hdd & no ex) ........................................ ¾.3
214² Paper Craft (bl) *(MJohnston)* 5–8–3 PaulEddery (2) (led: rdn over 3f out: hdd over 2f out: one pce) ........................................ ¾.4
398 Tusky **(87)** *(MJCamacho)* 4–9–0 NConnorton (11) (hld up in tch: effrt on ins 3f out: kpt on fnl f: nt pce to chal) ...................... 1½.5
335³ Taunting (IRE) **(78)** *(MBlanshard)* 4–9–0 CRutter (5) (chsd ldrs tl rdn & wknd wl over 2f out) ...................................... 10.6
Lambson **(30)** *(RMWhitaker)* 5–8–9 ACulhane (10) (bhd: sme hdwy 3f out: n.d) . 3.7
Sayant *(WClay)* 7–8–3 JLowe (4) (mid div: effrt over 3f out: sn btn) .............. 1½.8
Whiskey Blues *(BRichmond)* 7–8–5⁽¹⁾ ‡7SWilliams (7) (b: hdwy 4f out: sn wknd) ½.9
327★ Saint Bene't (IRE) **(53)** *(PCHaslam)* 4–8–4 KDarley (3) (chsd ldrs tl rdn & wknd wl over 2f out) .............................. ¾.10
315 Kind Style (IRE)**(33)** *(RHollinshead)* 4–8–4 NCarlisle (6) (rdn & lost tch fnl 3f: t.o) 10.11
288 Nishara *(NBycroft)* 4–8–10 LCharnock (12) (a bhd: t.o) ..................... ½.12

11/8 HENPOT (IRE), 5/1 Saint Bene't (IRE), Paper Craft, 7/1 Tusky, 8/1 Metternich, 20/1 Pennine Star (IRE), 25/1 Kind Style (IRE), Lambson, 33/1 Nishara, 50/1 Ors. CSF £29.54, Tote £1.90: £1.30 £5.30 £1.50 (£24.90). H.E. Lhendup Dorji (NEWMARKET) bred by Dan Mangan in Ireland. 12 Rn
2m 17.7 (14.2)
SF—38/26/28/26/34/14

**454**  HACKFALL APP'CE STKS (3-Y-O) £2265.20 (£627.20: £299.60)  6f  2-40 (2-44)

363★ **The Old Chapel (59)** *(BAMcMahon)* 9–4 SSanders (6) (lw: a.p: rdn 2f out: led jst ins fnl f: r.o) ...................................... —1
Mamma's Too **(105)** (Fav) *(JBerry)* 9–2 SHaworth (8) (lw: led: rdn wl over 1f out: hdd jst ins fnl f: nt qckn cl home) ........................ nk.2
Afif **(94)** *(MrsJCecil)* 9–7 PTurner (5) (a.p: rdn over 2f out: one pce) ............... 2.3
Shati (IRE) **(102)** *(HThomsonJones)* 9–4 GForster (2) (chsd ldrs: nt qckn over 1f out) .............................. 1½.4
242 Pageboy **(85)** *(PCHaslam)* 9–4 NicolaHowarth (4) (s.s: wl bhd tl hdwy 2f out: r.o wl fnl f: nrst fin) ...................... 5.5
Wave Hill **(103)** *(HRACecil)* 9–7 StephenDavies (3) (lw: chsd ldrs: rdn over 2f out: wknd fnl f) ........................ hd.6
310⁴ Sally Tadpole *(NTinkler)* 8–6 GParkin (1) (dwlt: sn drvn along: nvr rchd ldrs) .... hd.7
Castlerea Lad **(80)** *(RHollinshead)* 9–4 DCarson (7) (sn outpcd) ............... 2½.8

13/8 Mamma's Too, 4/1 Afif, 11/2 Wave Hill, 6/1 Shati (IRE), 8/1 THE OLD CHAPEL, 17/2 Pageboy, 20/1 Castlerea Lad, 50/1 Sally Tadpole. CSF £20.73, Tote £10.10: £1.80 £1.30 £1.80 (£12.90). R. A. Holdings Ltd (TAMWORTH) bred by Roldvale Ltd. 8 Rn
1m 19.9 (8.2)
SF—48/45/42/33/13/15

**455**  MARKINGTON H'CAP (0-100) £3720.00 (£1110.00: £530.00: £240.00)  6f 3-15 (3-16)

325⁴ **Sea Devil (75)** (Fav) *(MJCamacho)* 6–8–10 NConnorton (1) (chsd ldrs: rdn over 2f out: styd on wl to ld ins fnl f: wnt rt & hld on nr fin) .. —1
344 Luna Bid **(63)** *(MBlanshard)* 9–7–12 CRutter (7) (sn bhd: drvn along ½-wy: gd hdwy over 1f out: edgd rt & nt qckn cl home) ............... ½.2
265★ Furiella **(59)** *(PCHaslam)* 4–7–5 ‡3JFanning (5) (prom: led wl over 1f out: hdd ins fnl f: no ex) ........................ 2½.3
420⁴ In a Whirl (USA) **(58)** *(DWChapman)* 4–7–7 SWood (4) (a cl up: rdn ½-wy: outpcd over 1f out: kpt on wl ins fnl f) ............... hd.4
359 Ballad Dancer **(61)** *(EJAlston)* 7–7–7⁽³⁾ ‡3FNorton (2) (lw: sn pushed along: nvr trbld ldrs) .............................. 4.5
311★ Amron **(89)** *(JBerry)* 5–9–10 NCarlisle (6) (chsd ldrs: drvn along ½-wy: wknd wl over 1f out) ........................ 3.6

Adwick Park **(93)** *(TDBarron)* 4–10-0 AlexGreaves (3) (h.d.w: nvr nr to chal) ...... 1.7
236⁴ Gondo **(71)** (v) *(EJAlston)* 5–8-1 ‡⁵NKennedy (8) (led tl hdd & wknd wl over 1f
out) ............................................................................................................... 5.8
LONG HANDICAP: In a Whirl (USA) 6-12, Ballad Dancer 7-5.

**5/2** SEA DEVIL, **3/1** Amron, **9/2** Furiella, **5/1** Gondo, **8/1** Luna Bid, **16/1** Ballad Dancer, In a Whirl (USA), **25/1**
Adwick Park. CSF £20.65, CT £76.81. Tote £3.00: £1.20 £2.70 £1.40 (£9.80). Mr E. G. Noble (MALTON) bred
by A. L. Goacher and E. G. Noble. 8 Rn
1m 18.9 (7.2)
SF—60/46/29/30/14/33

**456**    KIRBY HILL H'CAP (0-80) £3096.90 (£858.40: £410.70)    **1m**    3-45 (3-52)
(Weights raised 4 lb)
**Tolls Choice (IRE) (59)** *(MWEasterby)* 3–7-10 JLowe (7) (bit bkwd: stdd s: hld
up & bhd: stdy hdwy 3f out: led ins fnl f: sn clr) ................. —1
Causley **(70)** *(BAMcMahon)* 7–9-8 MBirch (14) (led & sn clr: rdn over 2f out:
hdd ins fnl f: no ch w wnr) ....................................................... 3½.2
198★ Qualitair Rhythm (IRE) **(45)** (bl) *(ICampbell)* 4–7-8 ‡³FNorton (13) (in tch:
effrt & hdwy 3f out: hung rt & nt qckn over 1f out) ................. 1.3
285 Pimsboy **(52)** (bl) *(PABlockley)* 5–8-4 GHind (12) (hdwy over 3f out: kpt on fnl
2f: nt pce to chal) .................................................................... 1½.4
277 Quietly Impressive (IRE) **(59)** *(MBell)* 4–8-4 ‡⁷PTurner (8) (lw: hdwy on outside
3f out: styd on fnl 2f: nrst fin) ................................................. 1½.5
Star Connection **(63)** *(RMWhitaker)* 4–9-1 ACulhane (9) (bit bkwd: bhd: stdy
hdwy fnl 2f: r.o nr fin) .............................................................. 2.6
364⁴ Veloce (IRE) **(56)** *(MO'Neill)* 4–8-8 JFortune (3) (chsd ldrs tl rdn & wknd over 2f
out) .......................................................................................... ³/₄.7
373⁶ Mofador (GER) **(60)** *(FHLee)* 8–8-7 ‡⁵NKennedy (6) (lw: chsd ldrs: rdn 3f out:
wknd wl over 1f out) ................................................................ 1½.8
240 Barford Lad **(73)** *(JRFanshawe)* 5–9-3 ‡⁷NVarley (5) (prom tl grad lost pl fnl 2f) 1½.9
Sie Amato (IRE) **(57)** *(CaptJWilson)* 3–7-1(t) ‡⁷DarrenMoffatt (11) (bit bkwd: n.d) 6.10
401 Molten Copper (IRE) **(70)** *(MWEasterby)* 3–8-7 TLucas (2) (bit bkwd: a bhd) . nk.11
315 Be the Best **(50)** *(MPNaughton)* 4–8-2 LCharnock (1) (prom to st: lost pl over 3f
out) .......................................................................................... 1½.12
Affordable **(72)** *(WCarter)* 4–9-10 PaulEddery (4) (bit bkwd: effrt over 3f out:
wknd over 2f out: eased whn btn) ............................................ hd.13
Vite Vite **(41)** *(RCSpicer)* 6–7-7 NCarlisle (10) (bit bkwd: chsd ldrs tl wknd wl
over 2f out) .............................................................................. 1½.14
LONG HANDICAP: Sie Amato (IRE) 7-5, Vite Vite 6-10.

**4/1** Qualitair Rhythm (IRE), **5/1** Causley, Quietly Impressive (IRE), **11/2** Veloce (IRE), **7/1** Barford Lad, **12/1**
Mofador (GER), **14/1** Affordable, Molten Copper (IRE), **20/1** Pimsboy, Star Connection, **25/1** Be the Best, TOLLS
CHOICE (IRE), **33/1** Sie Amato (IRE), **50/1** Vite Vite. CSF £137.64, CT £566.58. Tote £75.80: £7.60 £2.20 £1.80
(£56.80). Mr T. A. Hughes (SHERIFF HUTTON) bred by John Irish in Ireland. 14 Rn
1m 49.1 (11.4)
SF—19/34/3/8/3/8

**457**    LANGTHORPE H'CAP (3-Y.O) (0-70) £2500.40 (£694.40: £333.20)    4-20 (4-22)
1½m 60y
(Weights raised 2 lb)
355★ **Firefighter (62)** (Fav) *(RHollinshead)* 9-4 (5x) WRyan (3) (hdwy on outside
over 3f out: chal 2f out: hung rt & sn led: drvn clr ins fnl f) ... —1
369⁶ Thor Power (IRE) **(49)** *(DTThom)* 8-2 ‡³FNorton (13) (in tch: hdwy 3f out: kpt on
u.p fnl f) .................................................................................. 1½.2
375³ Double the Stakes (USA) **(50)** *(FHLee)* 8-6 PaulEddery (11) (chsd ldrs: rdn to ld
over 2f out: bmpd & sn hdd: edgd rt & no ex fnl f) ............ 2½.3
369 Mayo Man (IRE) **(46)** *(MrsGRReveley)* 8-2 JLowe (8) (s.s: rdn along thrght:
hdwy 3f out: kpt on same pce fnl 2f) ....................................... 6.4
281⁵ North Flyer **(45)** *(BAMcMahon)* 8-2 GHind (5) (chsd ldr tl wknd wl over 2f out) .. 3.5
Split Second **(50)** (v) *(JWWatts)* 8-6 NConnorton (1) (in tch: effrt & hdwy 3f out:
sn rdn & no imp) .................................................................... nk.6
256⁴ Amazon Express **(60)** *(CEBrittain)* 8-13 ‡³RonHillis (6) (led tl hdd & wknd over 2f
out: eased whn btn fnl f) .......................................................... hd.7
Newton Point **(61)** *(GAPritchard-Gordon)* 9-3 AClark (10) (hdwy ent st: effrt
over 3f out: eased over 1f out) ................................................ 4.8
366 Reach for Glory **(58)** *(RMWhitaker)* 9-0 ACulhane (4) (effrt ent st: n.d) ........... 1.9
369⁵ Mr News (IRE) **(62)** *(WJPearce)* 9-4 DNicholls (2) (lw: hld up gng wl: smooth
hdwy over 3f out: rdn & wknd wl over 1f out) ................. s.h.10
Broughpark Azalea **(55)** *(JJO'Neill)* 8-11 TLucas (7) (a in rr) ............................ 8.11
230 Tees Gazette Girl **(51)** *(MrsGRReveley)* 8-7 KDarley (14) (a in rr) ................... 2.12
Princess Tamar **(40)** *(PCHaslam)* 7-7 ‡³JFanning (12) (bhd fnl 3f: t.o) ................ 13
Yaakum **(65)** *(BHanbury)* 9-0 ‡⁷VBray (9) (bit bkwd: prom: racd wd: rdn & wknd
over 3f out: eased whn btn: t.o) ................................................ 14
*Stewards Enquiry: Hillis fined £105 under rule 151 (ii) (failure to ensure best possible placing).*

**100/30** FIREFIGHTER, **5/1** Amazon Express, Double the Stakes (USA), **8/1** Mr News (IRE), **9/1** Newton Point, Mayo Man (IRE), **10/1** Split Second, **12/1** Thor Power (IRE), Yaakum, **14/1** Reach for Glory, **16/1** North Flyer, **20/1** Tees Gazette Girl, **25/1** Ors. CSF £43.80, CT £193.09. Tote £3.50: £1.40 £3.40 £2.00 (£23.80). Mrs B. Facchino (UPPER LONGDON) bred by Sir Stephen Hastings. 14 Rn     2m 55.5 (21.5)

### 458

ALDBOROUGH STKS (Mdn 3-Y.O.C & G) £2284.80 (£632.80: £302.40)
1m                                      4-50 (4-54)

**Asaasy (USA)** *(MRStoute)* 9-0 MBirch (8) (led: hdd over 1f out: rn green & edgd lft: rallied to ld nr fin) ..................................... —1
Mr Flood (USA) (Jt-Fav) *(MrsJCecil)* 9-0 PaulEddery (6) (lw: trckd ldrs: rdn to ld over 1f out: hdd wl ins fnl f: r.o) ................................ s.h.2
Intent (Jt-Fav) *(HRACecil)* 9-0 WRyan (3) (chsd ldrs: effrt u.p wl over 3f out: nt pce to chal) ................................ 6.3
2745 Alkarif (USA) (72) *(AAScott)* 9-0 JFortune (2) (hld up in tch: effrt on outside 3f out: wknd 2f out) ................................ 1½.4
Charioteer *(PCHaslam)* 9-0 KDarley (5) (lengthy: scope: bit bkwd: bhd: hdwy ent st: nvr trbld ldrs) ................................ 15.5
Blimpers Disco *(EHOwenjun)* 9-0 CDwyer (1) (bit bkwd: prom tl rdn & grad wknd fnl 3f) ................................ 2½.6
Desert Power *(BHanbury)* 8-7 ‡7VBray (4) (w'like: bit bkwd: bhd: sme hdwy 4f out: sn wknd) ................................ 2½.7
374 Siolfor (USA) *(MrsJRRamsden)* 9-0 TLucas (7) (bit bkwd: a last) ................ 1½.8
*Stewards Enquiry: Birch suspended 25-28/4/92 (improper use of whip).*

**15/8** Mr Flood (USA), Intent, **100/30** ASAASY (USA), **11/1** Alkarif (USA), **14/1** Desert Power, **33/1** Charioteer, Siolfor (USA), **50/1** Blimpers Disco. CSF £9.64, Tote £4.60: £1.50 £1.30 £1.10 (£4.90). Maktoum Al Maktoum (NEWMARKET) bred by Gainsborough Farm Incorporated in USA. 8 Rn     1m 49.6 (11.9)
                                                 SF—29/28/10/5/–/–

T/Plpt: £13.70 (191.65 Tckts).                                                  O'R

## 378a—SAINT-CLOUD (L-H)

### Tuesday, April 7th [Heavy]
Going Allowance: 0.95 sec per fur (S)

### 459a

PRIX OMNIUM II (listed race) (3-Y.O.C) £12384.00   1m

**Arazi (USA)** *(France)* 3-9-2 SCauthen ................................ —1
Supermec (USA) *(France)* 3-9-2 DBoeuf ................................ 5.2
River Majesty (USA) *(France)* 3-9-2 CAsmussen ................................ 2½.3
Tote 1.20f: 1.10f 1.10f 1.10f (6.20f). Sheikh Mohammed (F.Boutin,FRANCE) bred by Ralph Wilson Jnr in USA. 8 Rn     1m 48 (9.4)
                                                 SF—75/60/52

## 284a—MAISONS-LAFFITTE (L-H)

### Friday, April 10th [Good to soft]
Going Allowance: nil sec per fur (G)

### 460a

PRIX DJEBEL (listed race) (3-Y.O.C) £12384.00   7f

**Cardoun (FR)** *(France)* 3-9-2 DBoeuf ................................ —1
Vogeluga *(France)* 3-9-2 CBlack ................................ 1.2
Africanus (FR) *(France)* 3-9-2 SCoffigny ................................ hd.3
Tote 1.90f: 1.20f 3.70f 2.50f (27.00f). Mr E.Zorbibe (E.Lellouche,FRANCE) bred by SNC de Chambure in France. 9 Rn     1m 26.4 (3.7)
                                                 SF—46/43/42

### 461a

PRIX IMPRUDENCE (listed race) (3-Y.O.F) £12384.00   7f

**Kenbu (FR)** *(France)* 3-9-2 FHead ................................ —1
Hatoof (USA) *(France)* 3-9-2 WRSwinburn ................................ nk.2
Plume Magique *(France)* 3-9-2 CBlack ................................ 2½.3
Tote 3.30f: 1.10f 1.10f (SF: 3.60f). Mr T. Wada (F.Boutin,FRANCE) bred by T. Wada in France. 6 Rn     1m 27.9 (5.2)
                                                 SF—24/23/15

## CURRAGH (R-H)
### Saturday, April 11th [Heavy]
Going Allowance: 1.00 sec per fur (S)

**462a**    GLADNESS STKS (Gp 3)    £11500.00    7f

Bezelle *(Ireland)* 3-8-7 PShanahan (hld up: hdwy 3f out: chal & led 1f out: kpt
   on u.p) ............................................................................................. —1
NORWICH *(BWHills)* 5-9-9 MHills (led tl hdd 1f out: rallied nr fin) ................... nk.2
Street Rebel (CAN) *(Ireland)* 4-9-9 RHughes (s.s: hld up: hdwy on outside over
   2f out: ev ch over 1f out: no ex fnl f) .................................................. ½.3
St Jovite (USA) *(Fav)* *(Ireland)* 3-8-10 CRoche (prom: pushed along & lost pl 4f
   out: styd on fnl f) .............................................................................. 8.4
CARDINAL POINT (USA) *(JHMGosden)* 4-9-9 MJKinane (cl up tl wknd 2f out) . ½.5
Thornberry (USA) *(Ireland)* 4-9-9 JPMurtagh (chsd ldr tl wknd over 2f out) ........ 5.6
Classic Venture (IRE) *(Ireland)* 4-9-9 PVGilson (n.d) ...................................... 3½.7

**8/11** St Jovite (USA), **5/1** BEZELLE, **11/2** Norwich, **8/1** Cardinal Point (USA), **12/1** Thornberry (USA), **14/1**
Classic Venture (IRE), **20/1** Street Rebel (CAN). Tote £6.30: £2.70 £5.10 (£27.30). Mr James McNeil
(C.Collins,IRELAND) bred by D.A & Mrs Hicks. 7 Rn                                    1m 32.6 (9.4)
                                                                                                        SF—57/72/70/33/44


## HAYDOCK (L-H)
### Saturday, April 18th [Good to soft, Soft patches]
Going Allowance: St: 1.40 sec; Rnd: 1.00 sec per fur (S)                    Wind: fresh against

Stalls: high

**463**    PHILIP CORNES NICKEL ALLOYS STKS (Mdn 2-Y.O) £2363.20 (£655.20: £313.60)
           5f                                                                        2-00 (2-01)

Norstano *(Fav)* *(MHEasterby)* 9-0 MBirch (6) (neat: cmpt: a.p: led over 2f out:
   rdn out) ............................................................................................. —1
Mad Mytton *(ABailey)* 9-0 AMackay (4) (lt-f: lw: s.s: hdwy 2f out: rdn & no ex nr
   fin) ................................................................................................... 1.2
Contract Elite (IRE) *(CWThornton)* 9-0 MHills (2) (w'like: scope: bkwd: a.p: rdn
   over 1f out: one pce) ......................................................................... 2½.3
Clangold *(JBerry)* 8-9 JCarroll (1) (leggy: lt-f: a.p: shkn up over 1f out: one pce) nk.4
Matthew David *(MBrittain)* 9-0 MWigham (3) (small: lt-f: spd over 3f) ................ 2.5
Zinjaal (IRE) *(BHanbury)* 9-0 BRaymond (5) (small: bit bkwd: led over 2f: wkng
   whn hmpd appr fnl f) ......................................................................... 10.6

**2/1** NORSTANO, **4/1** Zinjaal (IRE), Clangold, **9/2** Contract Elite (IRE)(6/1—4/1), **6/1** Mad Mytton, **20/1** Matthew
David. CSF £12.63, Tote £3.30: £1.60 £2.40 (£11.70). Mr A. M. Wragg (MALTON) bred by A. M. Wragg. 6 Rn
                                                                                            69.41 sec (10.41)
                                                                                                        SF—32/28/18/11/8/–


**464**    HOLIDAY CLUB PONTINS H'CAP (3-Y.O) (0-100) £4464.00 (£1332.00: £636.00: £288.00)
           1m 30y                                                                    2-30 (2-34)

                                      (Weights raised 15 lb)
332* **Magnificent (74)** *(MAJarvis)* 8-5 ‡7KRutter (7) (hld up: hdwy to ld 3f out: r.o wl) —1
295* Doyce (67) *(Fav)* *(JEtherington)* 8-5 NConnorton (8) (lw: hld up & bhd: hdwy 3f
   out: ev ch fnl 2f: unable qckn nr fin) .................................................... ½.2
395 Mad Militant (IRE) **(83)** *(RHollinshead)* 9-7 AClhane (5) (s.i.s: bhd: hdwy 3f
   out: hrd rdn & ev ch over 1f out: one pce) ............................................ 2.3
Devon Dancer **(80)** *(MHEasterby)* 9-4 MBirch (9) (chsd ldrs: 4th st: no hdwy fnl
   2f) ..................................................................................................... 6.4
325 She's Special **(76)** (v) *(MissLAPerratt)* 9-0 BRaymond (3) (swtg: prom: 3rd st:
   rdn over 2f out: sn btn) ...................................................................... 8.5
242 Reel of Tulloch (IRE) **(81)** *(PCHaslam)* 9-5 DaleGibson (6) (lw: 2nd st: wknd wl
   over 3f out) ....................................................................................... 4.6
387⁵ By Hand **(79)** *(WJHaggas)* 9-3 MHills (1) (5th st: styd far side: btn over 2f out) .. 2.7
Mindomica **(75)** *(MBell)* 8-13 RHills (4) (still unf: led 5f: sn rdn & wknd) ............ 6.8
215 Bassio (BEL) **(73)** *(CNAllen)* 8-4 ‡7GForster (2) (hld up: 6th st: styd far side: t.o
   fnl 3f) ................................................................................................ 25.9

**5/2** Doyce, **3/1** MAGNIFICENT, **5/1** Mindomica, **15/2** By Hand, **9/1** Reel of Tulloch (IRE), **11/1** Devon
Dancer(16/1—10/1), **16/1** Ors. CSF £10.63, CT £92.13. Tote £3.60: £1.70 £1.20 £3.20 (£4.40). Mrs P. L.
Yong (NEWMARKET) bred by Nasrullah Holdings. 9 Rn                                    1m 53.89 (13.49)
                                                                                                        SF—9/7/17/–/–/–

**465**  BEAMISH IRISH STOUT FIELD MARSHAL STKS (listed race)  £8893.75 (£2650.00:
£1262.50: £568.75)  **5f**  3-00 (3-01)

**Paris House (115)** *(JBerry)* 3-9-1 JCarroll (1) (lw: a.p: led 3f out: shkn up & r.o
nr fin) ..................................................................................................................... —1
386★ Stack Rock **(96)** *(EJAlston)* 5–8-9 KFallon (7) (lw: led 2f: rallied fnl f: r.o) ........... 1.2
430³ Sir Harry Hardman **(101)** (bl) *(FHLee)* 4–9-0 JWilliams (3) (lw: chsd ldrs: effrt wl
over 1f out: sn rdn: unable qckn) ....................................................................... 2.3
241² Notley **(111)** (Fav) *(RHannon)* 5–9-5 BRaymond (4) (lw: a.p: rdn 2f out: ev ch
over 1f out: unable qckn) ................................................................................... 1½.4
El Yasaf (IRE) **(86)** *(GHEden)* 4–9-0 GBaxter (6) (bit bkwd: chsd ldrs: kpt on u.p
ins fnl f) .............................................................................................................. hd.5
Tamim (USA) **(104)** *(HThomsonJones)* 3–8-8 RHills (8) (nt grwn: spd to ½-wy:
sn outpcd) ........................................................................................................... 1.6
Food of Love *(JBerry)* 4–8-9 MBirch (5) (bit bkwd: spd 3f) .................................. 2½.7
284a³ Medaille D'Or **(102)** (v) *(JWPayne)* 4–9-0 MHills (2) (lw: outpcd: t.o fnl 2f: nt
resolute) ............................................................................................................. 7.8

**9/4** Notley, **3/1** PARIS HOUSE, **6/1** Sir Harry Hardman, Stack Rock, **17/2** Medaille D'Or, **9/1** Food of Love, **10/1**
Tamim (USA), **66/1** El Yasaf (IRE). CSF £19.71, Tote £3.20: £1.60 £1.90 £1.50 (£9.70). Mr P. E. T. Chandler
(COCKERHAM) bred by Hillwood Stud. 8 Rn
66.86 sec (7.86)
SF—84/74/71/70/64/54

**466**  MATTHEW PEACOCK STKS (Mdn 3-Y.O) £3406.50 (£1017.00: £486.00: £220.50)
**1¼m 120y**  3-30 (3-35)

**Inchcailloch (IRE)** (Fav) *(RCharlton)* 9-0 SRaymont (1) (bit bkwd: hld up &
bhd: smooth hdwy 3f out: led over 1f out: shkn up nr fin) ... —1
Viva Darling *(BAMcMahon)* 8-7 ‡⁷SSanders (9) (6th st: led over 2f out tl over 1f
out: one pce) ...................................................................................................... 2½.2
Iron Baron (IRE) *(RHollinshead)* 9-0 ACulhane (6) (hld up & bhd: hdwy over 2f
out: one pce fnl 2f) ............................................................................................. 2½.3
235 High Mind (FR) *(MissLCSiddall)* 9-0 MBirch (8) (s.i.s: sn prom: 3rd st: ev ch
over 2f out: grad wknd) ...................................................................................... 10.4
Toss the Dice *(MAJarvis)* 9-0 MHills (8) (bkwd: chsd ldrs: 5th st: ev ch over 2f
out: sn rdn & btn) ............................................................................................... ½.5
384 Secret Picnic (USA) *(BHanbury)* 9-0 BRaymond (3) (lw: led tl hdd & wknd over
3f out) ................................................................................................................. 7.6
Princess Maxine (IRE) **(60)** *(MissLAPerratt)* 8-9 DaleGibson (5) (prom: 2nd st:
led over 3f out tl over 2f out: sn btn) .................................................................. ½.7
Robert Thomas (IRE) *(MO'Neill)* 9-0 JFortune (4) (leggy: unf: s.s: sn chsng
ldrs: 4th st: wknd 3f out: t.o) ............................................................................. 6.8
355 Sabzy *(PDEvans)* 8-4 ‡⁵LNewton (7) (a bhd: t.o fnl 3f) ...................................... 30.9

**Evens** INCHCAILLOCH (IRE), **5/2** Toss the Dice, **13/2** Secret Picnic (USA), **16/1** Iron Baron (IRE), Robert Thomas
(IRE), Viva Darling, **33/1** Princess Maxine (IRE), **50/1** Ors. CSF £16.40, Tote £1.80: £1.10 £2.90 £2.70 (£12.50).
Sir Philip Oppenheimer (BECKHAMPTON) bred by Hascombe and Valiant Studs in Ireland. 9 Rn
2m 28.98 (17.28)
SF—32/20/22/2/1/–/–

**467**  FARNWORTH VETERANS RACE CLUB H'CAP (0-90) £3785.00 (£1130.00: £540.00:
£245.00)  **1m 3f 200y**  4-00 (4-04)

301³ Saffaah (USA) **(64)** *(WRMuir)* 5–8-2⁽²⁾ SWhitworth (3) (lw: plld hrd: led after 2f:
r.o strly fnl f) ....................................................................................................... —1
229 Lord Hastie (USA) **(74)** *(SGNorton)* 4–8-11 DNicholls (2) (chsd ldrs: 3rd st: ev
ch 2f out: no ex fnl f) ......................................................................................... 3½.2
Bollin Patrick **(70)** *(MHEasterby)* 7–8-8 MBirch (4) (chsd ldrs: 5th st: nt clr
run over 2f out: styd on ins fnl f) ........................................................................ 3.3
Beau Quest **(58)** *(RMWhitaker)* 5–7-10 AMackay (5) (bhd: styd on fnl 2f: nrst
fin) ...................................................................................................................... 2½.4
405⁴ Just My Bill **(70)** (v) *(CWCElsey)* 6–8-9 DaleGibson (6) (lw: hld up: 6th st: kpt on
same pce fnl 2f) .................................................................................................. 2½.5
354 Hillzah (USA) **(82)** *(RBastiman)* 4–9-5 RHills (8) (prom: 2nd st: wknd over 2f out) 1½.6
Flockton's Own **(80)** *(MrsJRRamsden)* 6–9-4 BRaymond (9) (b: bit bkwd: hld
up & bhd: effrt 3f out: nt rch ldrs) ...................................................................... hd.7
Travelling Light **(88)** *(MrsJRRamsden)* 7–8-8 ‡⁷JWeaver (7) (bkwd: hld up: a bhd) 4.8
377⁵ Grey Power **(68)** *(MrsGRReveley)* 5–8-6 MHills (10) (hld up: hdwy wknd over 3f out:
wknd over 2f out) ............................................................................................... 2.9

228 Sarwan (IRE) **(80)** *(APStringer)* 4–9-3 JFortune (1) (bit bkwd: led 2f: 4th & wkng
　　st: sn t.o) ............................................................................................... **10**

**5/2** Bollin Patrick, **9/2** SAFFAAH (USA), **5/1** Lord Hastie (USA), **13/2** Just My Bill, **8/1** Grey Power(6/1—9/1),
Hillzah (USA), **14/1** Sarwan (IRE)(op 8/1), Beau Quest, **20/1** Flockton's Own, **25/1** Travelling Light. CSF £26.28,
CT £62.85. Tote £5.70: £2.00 £1.60 £1.80 (£11.30). Mrs H. Levy (LAMBOURN) bred by Mr. and Mrs. John C.
Mabee in USA. 10 Rn　　　　　　　　　　　　　　　　　　　　　　　　　　　2m 44.08 (16.08)
　　　　　　　　　　　　　　　　　　　　　　　　　　　　　　　　　　SF—47/49/40/23/30/38

---

**468**　　WEST LANCASHIRE EVENING GAZETTE CLAIMING STKS (3-Y.O) £2511.00 (£696.00:
　　　　　£333.00)　　**6f**　　　　　　　　　　　　　　　　　　　　　4-30 (4-36)

**Love Jazz (USA) (94)** *(TDBarron)* 9-3 BRaymond (9) (bit bkwd: mid div: rdn
　　½-wy: hdwy over 1f out: str run to ld nr fin) .............................. —**1**
242⁴ Early Star **(79)** (Fav) *(TDBarron)* 8-7 AlexGreaves (10) (hdwy ½-wy: led over 1f
　　out: rdn & edgd lft: ct cl home) ................................................. 1½.**2**
242 Lombard Ocean **(67)** *(MO'Neill)* 8-6 JFortune (12) (a.p: ev ch fnl f: r.o) .......... ½.**3**
Speedy Classic (USA) *(CTinkler)* 8-12 MBirch (6) (w'like: bkwd: hdwy appr fnl f:
　　fin wl) ..................................................................................... 2½.**4**
276 Rivet *(MBlanshard)* 8-9 SWhitworth (4) (bit bkwd: styd on fnl 2f: nvr nrr) .......... 5.**5**
332 Risk Zone **(56)** (bl) *(RHannon)* 8-7 RHills (13) (lw: led over 4f: sn rdn & wknd) .. 2.**6**
401 Boulabas (IRE) **(64)** *(MO'Neill)* 8-1 SWood (11) (nvr trbld ldrs) .......... 4.**7**
195⁴ Monti Beppo **(54)** *(LJBarratt)* 7-11 AProud (3) (w ldrs 4f) .......... 5.**8**
278 Weekend Girl **(30)** *(WMBrisbourne)* 7-4 ‡⁷CHawksley (2) (outpcd) .......... 5.**9**
105⁶ Palacegate Racing **(78)** *(JBerry)* 8-9 JCarroll (7) (lw: w ldrs 4f) .......... ¾.**10**
Baie Petite *(AWJones)* 8-0 BCrossley (1) (b. nr hind: w'like: cmpt: bkwd: dwlt: a
　　outpcd) ................................................................................. 1.**11**
279³ Peggy Mainwaring **(55)** *(RJHolder)* 8-4 MHills (5) (outpcd: t.o) .......... 10.1**2**
363 Bright Paragon (IRE) **(BRichmond)** 8-7 KFallon (8) (bkwd: outpcd: t.o) .......... 3½.1**3**

**5/2** Early Star, **5/1** Palacegate Racing, **6/1** Risk Zone, LOVE JAZZ (USA), **8/1** Lombard Ocean, Peggy
Mainwaring, **12/1** Monti Beppo, Boulabas (IRE), **16/1** Speedy Classic (op 10/1), **25/1** Rivet, **33/1** Bright
Paragon (IRE), **50/1** Ors. CSF £21.47, Tote £4.80: £1.90 £1.70 £2.30 (£5.20). Mr P. D. Savill (THIRSK) bred by
Marian Conrad and Jim Herbener in USA. 13 Rn　　　　　　　　　　　　1m 22.81 (11.11)
　　　　　　　　　　　　　　　　　　　　　　　　　　　　　　　　SF—49/33/30/26/3/–

---

**469**　　HORSERACE BETTING LEVY BOARD APP'CE H'CAP (0-70) £2385.00 (£660.00: £315.00)
　　　　　**1¼m 120y**　　　　　　　　　　　　　　　　　　　　　　5-00 (5-04)

368 **Admirals Seat (55)** (Fav) *(MrsJRRamsden)* 4–9-9 RHavlin (6) (a.p: 4th st: led 2f
　　out: r.o strly) ......................................................................... —**1**
299 Tanoda **(48)** *(MBrittain)* 6–8-11 ‡⁵DWright (11) (hdwy 3f out: hrd rdn & kpt on ins
　　fnl f: no ch w wnr) ................................................................. 3½.**2**
Lidanzia **(42)** *(RJHolder)* 4–8-10 SDrowne (4) (swtg: lw: stdy hdwy ½-wy: 6th
　　st: r.o wl fnl f) ....................................................................... 4.**3**
340² Always Ready **(42)** *(RLee)* 6–8-10 EHusband (12) (b: chsd ldrs: 5th st: rdn 2f
　　out: one pce) .......................................................................... 4.**4**
340³ Princess Roxanne **(56)** (bl) *(ABailey)* 5–9-10 PBowe (9) (hld up: styd on fnl 3f:
　　nt pce to chal) ........................................................................ 1½.**5**
223³ La Reine Rouge (IRE) **(47)** *(PJMakin)* 4–8-10 ‡⁵DMiddleton (10) (chsd along in
　　mid div: nvr trbld ldrs) ............................................................. 1½.**6**
Honey Boy Simba **(47)** (v) *(MO'Neill)* 6–8-10 ‡⁵WFrost (8) (nvr nr to chal) .......... 7
115 Always Alex **(40)** (bl) *(PDEvans)* 5–8-8 SSanders (5) (a in rr) .......... 8
453 Saint Bene't (IRE) **(53)** *(PCHaslam)* 4–9-2 ‡⁵NicolaHowarth (3) (plld hrd: prom:
　　3rd st: led over 3f out tl over 2f out: sn wknd) ............................ 9
422⁶ Friendlypersuasion (IRE) **(44)** *(RHollinshead)* 4–8-7 ‡⁵JFordham (1) (prom:
　　2nd st: led over 2f out: sn hdd & wknd) ..................................... **10**
220³ Tempering **(60)** *(DWChapman)* 6–9-9 ‡⁵GCoogan (7) (led tl hdd & wknd over 3f
　　out) ....................................................................................... **11**
264⁶ Chance Report **(42)** *(FHLee)* 4–8-10 GParkin (2) (b.hind: s.i.s: rdn ½-wy: sn
　　lost tch: t.o) .......................................................................... **12**

**9/4** ADMIRALS SEAT(tchd 7/2), **6/1** Tanoda, Always Ready, **13/2** Princess Roxanne, **9/1** Saint Bene't (IRE), La
Reine Rouge (IRE)(op 6/1), Friendlypersuasion (IRE), **14/1** Tempering, Always Alex, **16/1** Chance Report,
Lidanzia(op 10/1), **20/1** Honey Boy Simba. CSF £17.98, CT £179.29. Tote £4.30: £1.60 £2.60 £5.20 (£24.70).
Mr Nicholas De Savary (THIRSK) bred by E. G. P. St George and Mrs O. Fox-Pitt. 12 Rn　2m 28.82 (17.12)
　　　　　　　　　　　　　　　　　　　　　　　　　　　　　　　SF—43/24/15/7/18/1

T/Plpt: £36.70 (178.35 Tckts).　　　　　　　　　　　　　　　　　　　　　　　　IM

339—**KEMPTON (R-H)**

**Saturday, April 18th [Good to soft]**

Going Allowance: St: 0.90 sec (S); Rest: 0.70 sec per fur (Y)          Wind: almost nil

Stalls: centre

**470**     E.B.F. REDFERN STKS (Mdn 2-Y.O.C & G) £3003.00 (£833.00: £399.00)
5f                                                                                    2-10 (2-12)

| | |
|---|---|
| **Pips Pride** (RHannon) 9-0 WCarson (7) (leggy: scope: bit bkwd: a.p: led over 2f out: r.o wl) | —1 |
| Heathfield (USA) (Fav) (PFICole) 9-0 TQuinn (11) (unf: scope: bit bkwd: a.p: ev ch over 2f out: hrd rdn over 1f out: unable qckn) | 8.2 |
| 339 Toff Sundae (GLewis) 9-0 PaulEddery (1) (a.p: hrd rdn over 1f out: one pce) | 1.3 |
| Shynon (MHTompkins) 8-9 ‡5CHodgson (4) (neat: bit bkwd: outpcd: hdwy fnl f: r.o) | 1½.4 |
| Without a Flag (USA) (CACyzer) 9-0 AMunro (9) (w'like: bkwd: dwlt: hdwy 2f out: one pce) | hd.5 |
| 339 Chinnery (IRE) (JMPEustace) 9-0 RCochrane (8) (led over 2f: wknd fnl f) | ¾.6 |
| 3395 Glowing Dancer (JRJenkins) 9-0 MRoberts (6) (prom over 3f) | 1.7 |
| Anaheim (IRE) (RHannon) 9-0 JReid (2) (unf: swtchd rt over 3f out: prom 3f) | 1.8 |
| Mr Nevermind (IRE) (GLewis) 9-0 BRouse (3) (cmpt: bit bkwd: s.s: a bhd) | 3½.9 |
| Risky Number (JSMoore) 8-9 ‡5RPerham (10) (unf: bit bkwd: a bhd) | 2½.10 |
| Lucayan Treasure (JBerry) 9-0 PatEddery (12) (unf: bit bkwd: a bhd) | 1½.11 |

**100/30** Heathfield (USA), **7/2** Lucayan Treasure, **11/2** PIPS PRIDE(4/1—6/1), Glowing Dancer(4/1—6/1), **8/1** Anaheim (IRE)(5/1—10/1), **11/1** Risky Number(16/1—10/1), **12/1** Toff Sundae(op 8/1), Chinnery (IRE)(op 7/1), **16/1** Mr Nevermind (IRE)(8/1—20/1), **33/1** Shynon. CSF £24.03,
Tote £6.80: £2.20 £1.70 £3.80 (£12.80). Mrs V. S. Grant (MARLBOROUGH) bred by R. A. and J. H. Popely. 11
Rn                                                                                66.53 sec (7.53)
                                                                                SF—40/8/4/–/–/–

**471**     CHATSWORTH H'CAP (3-Y.O) (0-90) £3236.00 (£968.00: £464.00: £212.00)
1¼m                                                                              2-40 (2-44)

(Weights raised 3 lb)

| | |
|---|---|
| 191* **Fengari** (70) (PTWalwyn) 8-6 AMunro (2) (lw: a.p: led over 3f out: drvn out) | —1 |
| 3693 Romansh (77) (Fav) (GWragg) 8-13 SCauthen (13) (lw: hdwy over 2f out: hrd rdn & ev ch ins fnl f: r.o wl) | ½.2 |
| 251* In the Picture (IRE) (70) (RHannon) 7-13 ‡7MarkDenaro (10) (hdwy & hmpd over 2f out: nt clr run fnl f: r.o) | 1½.3 |
| Arctic Circle (IRE) (65) (MissAJWhitfield) 8-1 NAdams (5) (rdn over 7f out: hdwy 4f out: 5th st: one pce fnl 2f) | 3.4 |
| Three Wells (83) (JLDunlop) 9-5 JReid (3) (4th st: one pce fnl 2f) | ½.5 |
| Sastago (USA) (85) (JHMGosden) 9-7 PatEddery (1) (3rd st: wknd wl over 1f out) | 2½.6 |
| Murasil (USA) (73) (MajorWRHern) 8-9 WCarson (9) (bit bkwd: dropped rr over 4f out: stdy hdwy over 1f out: r.o) | 3½.7 |
| 3873 Vanborough Lad (74) (MJHaynes) 8-7 ‡3DBiggs (12) (6th st: wknd 2f out) | 4.8 |
| Lady of Sardinia (BEL) (78) (JWPayne) 9-0 RCochrane (11) (a bhd) | 1½.9 |
| Erlemo (60) (CJBenstead) 7-10 JQuinn (8) (bit bkwd: bhd fnl 5f) | 1½.10 |
| Douraj (IRE) (70) (CEBrittain) 8-6 MRoberts (4) (bit bkwd: led over 6f: 2nd st: wknd over 2f out) | 1½.11 |
| Caithness Rock (72) (MAJarvis) 8-8 PaulEddery (7) (bit bkwd: bhd fnl 5f) | s.h.12 |
| 3505 Mr Ziegfeld (USA) (83) (SirMarkPrescott) 9-5 CNutter (6) (prom over 6f) | 4.13 |
| *Lake Dominion (20/1) Withdrawn (spread plate at s) : not under orders* | |

**4/1** Romansh, **6/1** In the Picture (IRE), **8/1** Murasil (USA), Sastago (USA), **9/1** Vanborough Lad, FENGARI, **10/1** Caithness Rock, Lady of Sardinia (BEL), Three Wells, Erlemo, **14/1** Mr Ziegfeld (USA), Douraj (IRE), **25/1** Arctic Circle (IRE). CSF £45.36, CT £223.46. Tote £8.50: £2.60 £1.90 £2.10 (£16.70). Fairly Stable (LAMBOURN) bred by Hesmonds Stud Ltd. 13 Rn                                                    2m 15.87 (13.87)
                                                                                SF—23/29/12/8/25/22

**472**     QUEEN ELIZABETH H'CAP (3-Y.O) (0-90) £3496.00 (£1048.00: £504.00: £232.00)
6f                                                                               3-10 (3-15)

(Weights raised 1 lb)

| | |
|---|---|
| 452* **Double Blue** (71) (Fav) (MJohnston) 8-4 (6x) MRoberts (5) (lw: racd stands' side: mde virtually all: pushed out) | —1 |
| Don't Smile (72) (MHTompkins) 7-12 ‡7SMulvey (6) (racd stands' side: dwlt: gd hdwy over 1f out: r.o ins fnl f) | 3½.2 |

*136* Boogie Bopper (IRE) **(70)** *(MBell)* 8-3 JQuinn (8) (lw: racd stands' side: gd hdwy over 1f out: r.o) .................. ¹/₂.3

Windpower (IRE) **(76)** *(JBerry)* 8-9 DHolland (18) (bit bkwd: a.p: ev ch ins fnl f: unable qckn) ...................... 1.4

275⁵ Truthful Image **(70)** (bl) *(MJRyan)* 8-3 AMunro (19) (a.p: ev ch 1f out: wknd ins fnl f) ............................ 1¹/₂.5

332 Christian Warrior **(78)** *(RHannon)* 8-6 ‡⁵RPerham (20) (no hdwy fnl 2f) ............ 1¹/₂.6

273³ Duty Sergeant (IRE) **(66)** *(MPMuggeridge)* 7-10 ‡³DBiggs (2) (b.hind: racd stands' side: prom over 4f) ....... 5.7

332⁶ Another Vintage **(61)** *(PDCundell)* 7-8⁽¹⁾ EJohnson (22) (hdwy & nt clr run over 1f out: nt rcvr) ............... 1.8

387 Confronter **(79)** *(PFICole)* 8-12 TQuinn (4) (lw: racd stands' side: rdn thrght: hdwy over 2f out: wknd over 1f out) ......... nk.9

Night Asset **(62)** (bl) *(GLewis)* 7-9 GBardwell (3) (racd stands' side: spd over 4f) nk.10

So Superb **(75)** *(JLDunlop)* 8-8 LDettori (5) (bit bkwd: racd stands' side: prom over 4f) ..................... ¹/₂.11

Morocco (IRE) **(76)** *(RCharlton)* 8-9 PaulEddery (14) (bit bkwd: hdwy over 4f out: eased whn btn fnl f) ......... 1¹/₂.12

298² Sonderise **(71)** *(NTinkler)* 8-4 WCarson (13) (prom over 4f: eased whn btn fnl f) 1.13

215⁵ Empeeka (USA) **(74)** (h) *(WAO'Gorman)* 8-2⁽²⁾ ‡⁵EmmaO'Gorman (17) (lw: outpcd) ........................ ¹/₂.14

Courageous Knight **(79)** *(RHannon)* 8-12 PatEddery (21) (prom over 4f) ....... hd.15

Court Minstrel **(60)** *(LJHolt)* 7-7 NAdams (11) (bit bkwd: outpcd) ................ ³/₄.16

387 Salisong **(75)** *(PFICole)* 8-8 CRutter (16) (bhd fnl 3f) ................ 5.17

413⁴ Walk in the Park **(88)** *(RSimpson)* 9-2 ‡⁵ATucker (9) (swtchd rt s: prom over 3f) 2.18

Paradise Forum **(80)** *(CAHorgan)* 8-13 SCauthen (7) (racd stands' side: spd over 3f) ........................ 6.19

*186²* In the Game (IRE) **(61)** *(MissAJWhitfield)* 7-8 NCarlisle (15) (bhd fnl 3f) ........... 1.20

29⁸ Flammalina (IRE) **(77)** *(CFWall)* 8-10 NDay (12) (a bhd) ................ 1¹/₂.21

Gemini Bay **(85)** (bl) *(RVoorspuy)* 9-4 SDawson (10) (racd stands' side: prom over 3f) ......................... 1.22

LONG HANDICAP: Another Vintage 7-1, Court Minstrel 7-3.

**5/2** DOUBLE BLUE, **7/1** Sonderise, **10/1** Windpower, Confronter(8/1—12/1), **12/1** Truthful Image(op 8/1), Empeeka (USA), **14/1** Courageous Knight, **16/1** Paradise Forum, Duty Sergeant (IRE), Night Asset, Don't Smile, **20/1** Salisong, In the Game (IRE), **33/1** Ors. CSF £40.02, CT £968.51. Tote £3.30: £1.40 £3.40 £7.80 £1.90 (£47.20). Mr R. W. Huggins (MIDDLEHAM) bred by The Queen. 22 Rn      1m 17.91 (6.61)
SF—66/42/45/47/35/32

---

**473**      BONUSPRINT MASAKA STKS (3-Y.O.F) £9910.00 (£2980.00: £1440.00: £670.00)
1m **(J.C)**                                                              3-40 (3-43)

**Cloud of Dust (100)** *(JLDunlop)* 8-9 TQuinn (6) (3rd st: led 2f out tl over 1f out: led ins fnl f: r.o wl) ................... —1

Armarama *(CEBrittain)* 8-5 MRoberts (1) (bit bkwd: 2nd st: led over 1f out tl ins fnl f: r.o) .................. ¹/₂.2

Venturina (IRE) **(92)** *(BWHills)* 8-9 DHolland (3) (led 6f) ................. 7.3

302★ Waterfowl Creek (IRE) (Fav) *(GWragg)* 8-9 PatEddery (4) (lw: 5th st: rdn over 2f out: one pce) .......... s.h.4

Clytie (USA) *(HCandy)* 8-5 CRutter (5) (4th st: wknd over 2f out) ........... 7.5

**4/5** Waterfowl Creek (IRE), **5/1** Clytie (USA), **11/2** Venturina (IRE)(7/2—6/1), **6/1** CLOUD OF DUST, **9/1** Armarama. CSF £41.97, Tote £6.20: £2.00 £3.00 (£26.30). Miss Peggy Kwoh (ARUNDEL) bred by The Duke of Marlborough. 5 Rn      1m 45.07 (8.47)
SF—51/45/28/27/2

---

**474**      BONUSPRINT EASTER STKS (listed race) (3-Y.O.C & G) £12793.75 (£3850.00: £1862.50: £868.75) 1m **(J.C)**                                        4-10 (4-10)

**Lucky Lindy (IRE)** *(RHannon)* 8-6 JReid (4) (bit bkwd: rdn 5f out: 3rd st: led ins fnl f: r.o wl) ............. —1

Ezzoud (IRE) (Fav) *(MRStoute)* 8-10 PatEddery (6) (lw: rdn 5f out: 4th st: hrd rdn over 2f out: ev ch ins fnl f: r.o wl) ..... s.h.2

Silver Wisp (USA) **(107)** *(GLewis)* 8-10 PaulEddery (1) (bit bkwd: 2nd st: led 2f out: wandered: hdd ins fnl f: unable qckn) .... 2.3

L'Hermine **(85)** (bl) *(HCandy)* 8-10 RCochrane (3) (bit bkwd: led 6f) ............... 6.4

Al Sadi *(CEBrittain)* 8-6 MRoberts (5) (6th st: a bhd) ................... 6.5

Wesaam **(102)** *(MajorWRHern)* 8-10 WCarson (2) (lw: 5th st: a bhd) ........... 2.6

**5/2** Ezzoud (IRE), **3/1** LUCKY LINDY (IRE), **100/30** Wesaam (9/2—3/1), **5/1** Silver Wisp (USA), **15/2** L'Hermine, **14/1** Al Sadi. CSF £10.28, Tote £3.20: £1.70 £1.90 (£5.40). Mr G. Howard-Spink (MARLBOROUGH) bred by Broguestown Stud Ltd. in Ireland. 6 Rn      1m 44.66 (8.06)
SF—55/58/52/34/12/10

**475**      QUEEN'S PRIZE (H'cap) (0-100) £7115.00 (£2120.00: £1010.00: £455.00)
        2m                                               4-40 (4-41)

243* **Star Quest (77)** *(JRJenkins)* 5–9-12 PatEddery (7) (lw: hdwy over 7f out: 4th st: led over 1f out: rdn out) ................................................ —1
234² Bardolph (USA) **(75)** *(PFICole)* 5–9-10 TQuinn (9) (b.off hind: 2nd st: led wl over 1f out: sn hdd: r.o) ................................................ 1.2
388 Subsonic (IRE) **(77)** *(JLDunlop)* 4–9-8 WCarson (8) (hdwy over 3f out: 6th st: hrd rdn over 2f out: r.o ins fnl f) ................................ ¾.3
229² Welshman **(58)** (Fav) *(MBlanshard)* 6–8-7 RCochrane (4) (led over 14f: unable qckn) ................................................................ s.h.4
High Grade **(55)** *(SDow)* 4–8-0 JQuinn (2) (hdwy over 4f out: 5th st: hrd rdn over 1f out: nt r.o) ................................................ 3½.5
362³ Tactical Mission (IRE) **(68)** *(JAkehurst)* 4–8-13 MRoberts (3) (lw: 3rd st: wknd 2f out) ................................................ 5.6
388⁴ Shoofe (USA) **(77)** *(DMorley)* 4–9-8 LDettori (6) (bhd fnl 4f) ................ 6.7
435 Coleridge **(77)** (v) *(DShaw)* 4–9-8 AClark (1) (bhd fnl 7f) ................ 2½.8
Beldale Star **(69)** *(RAkehurst)* 9–8-13 ‡⁵RPerham (5) (b: hdwy over 4f out: wknd over 3f out) ................................................ 2.9

**100/30** Welshman(9/2—3/1), **5/1** Subsonic (IRE), Shoofe (USA), **11/2** Bardolph (USA)(4/1—6/1), Tactical Mission (IRE), **13/2** STAR QUEST, **12/1** Beldale Star(op 8/1), **16/1** Coleridge, **20/1** High Grade. CSF £39.54, CT £177.11. Tote £6.60: £3.00 £1.70 £2.10 (£16.40). Mr A. Escudero (ROYSTON) bred by Juddmonte Farms. 9 Rn
                                                   3m 40.07 (15.67)
                                            SF—67/64/61/45/34/42

T/Trio: Race 3: £947.80 (2.1 Tckts). T/Jkpt: Not won; £3,788.05 to Kempton 20/4/92. T/Plpt: £314.70 (28.6 Tckts).                                                  AK

## KEMPTON (R-H)

### Monday, April 20th [Good to soft]
Going Allowance: 0.20 sec per fur (G)                                  Wind: almost nil

Stalls: centre
**476**      REDSHANK STKS (Mdn 2-Y.O.F) £2637.00 (£732.00: £351.00)    **5f**      2-00 (2-04)

345 **Sheila's Secret (IRE)** *(WCarter)* 8-11 JReid (18) (racd far side: mde virtually all: r.o wl) ................................................ —1
383³ Simply Sooty (Jt-Fav) *(BRMillman)* 8-11 GBaxter (7) (a.p: hrd rdn over 1f out: r.o) ................................................ 1.2
339⁴ Hung Parliament (Jt-Fav) *(BWHills)* 8-11 DHolland (2) (a.p: hrd rdn over 1f out: r.o) ................................................ hd.3
Rain Splash *(RHannon)* 8-11 MRoberts (13) (leggy: racd far side: hld up: gd hdwy on ins over 1f out: r.o wl: bttr for r) ........................ 1.4
Hawaii Star (IRE) *(GLewis)* 8-11 BRouse (16) (neat: bit bkwd: racd far side: a.p: rdn over 2f out: one pce) ........................ s.h.5
Perfect Passion *(JJBridger)* 8-11 DaleGibson (19) (leggy: racd far side: a.p: one pce fnl 2f) ........................ ½.6
Sweet Disorder (IRE) *(GAPritchard-Gordon)* 8-11 WHood (15) (leggy: lt-f: racd far side: outpcd: hdwy over 1f out: r.o) ........................ ¾.7
De Chine *(JSMoore)* 8-8 ‡³DBiggs (17) (neat: bit bkwd: racd far side: nvr nr to chal) ........................ 1.8
Sea Exhibition (IRE) *(MBlanshard)* 8-11 RCochrane (14) (neat: bit bkwd: racd far side: prom over 3f) ........................ ½.9
Moving Image (IRE) *(MBell)* 8-11 LDettori (3) (b.hind: leggy: prom over 3f) .... nk.10
Risk a Little *(MJHeaton-Ellis)* 8-4 ‡⁷JWeaver (4) (leggy: prom over 3f) ........... 1½.11
Strike-a-Pose *(CNWilliams)* 8-11 JQuinn (8) (leggy: lt-f: prom over 3f) ......... 1½.12
Nicki-J (IRE) *(RHannon)* 8-11 WCarson (10) (leggy: bkwd: prom over 3f) ...... ¾.13
Gypsy Legend *(WGMTurner)* 8-11 AClark (1) (neat: bkwd: bhd fnl 3f) ......... 2½.14
Scenic Reef (IRE) *(JMPEustace)* 8-11 CDwyer (9) (leggy: s.s: a bhd) ......... 2½.15
Fleur Power (IRE) *(BPalling)* 8-11 WRyan (12) (leggy: lt-f: racd far side: s.s: a bhd) ........................ hd.16
Hills Raceaid (IRE) *(JBerry)* 8-11 LPiggott (11) (scope: bit bkwd: racd far side: bhd fnl 2f) ........................ 1½.17
Gabhadera *(BGubby)* 8-11 CRutter (5) (neat: a wl bhd) ........................ 8.18
Pretty Sure *(BGubby)* 8-11 NCarlisle (6) (neat: a wl bhd) ........................ 8.19

**7/2** Hung Parliament(op 9/4), Simply Sooty, **4/1** Moving Image (IRE)(5/2—9/2), **8/1** Hills Raceaid (IRE), **9/1** Nicki-J (IRE), **12/1** SHEILA'S SECRET (IRE), Rain Splash(8/1—14/1), **14/1** Sea Exhibition (IRE), **20/1** Risk a Little, Hawaii Star (IRE), De Chine, Fleur Power (IRE), **33/1** Ors. CSF £56.25, Tote £30.30: £5.20 £2.00 £1.90 (£49.90). Sherwoods Transport Ltd (EPSOM) bred by A. F. O'Callaghan in Ireland. 19 Rn    63.68 sec (4.68)
                                                      SF—23/19/18/14/13/11

**477**　　　DURANTE H'CAP (0-100) £3002.00 (£896.00: £428.00: £194.00)　　1m 1f　2-35 (2-38)

456 **Barford Lad (72)** (bl) *(JRFanshawe)* 5–8–7 LDettori (12) (3rd st: hrd rdn over 1f
　　　out: led wl ins fnl f: r.o wl) .................................................. —1
3685 **Crossillion (79)** *(GWragg)* 4–8–11 ‡³FNorton (13) (led: hrd rdn over 1f out: hdd
　　　wl ins fnl f: r.o) .................................................. nk.2
392 **Wingfield (USA) (75)** *(DRCElsworth)* 4–8–10 JReid (14) (4th st: hrd rdn over 1f
　　　out: r.o wl ins fnl f) .................................................. ¾.3
392 **Langtry Lady (85)** (Fav) *(MJRyan)* 6–9–6 RCochrane (4) (hdwy over 1f out: r.o
　　　one pce) .................................................. 3.4
212 **Champenoise (59)** *(MBell)* 4–7–8 JQuinn (7) (swtg: 5th st: hrd rdn over 1f out:
　　　one pce) .................................................. nk.5
　　　**Self Expression (93)** *(IABalding)* 4–9–11 ‡³SO'Gorman (11) (nvr nr to chal) ..... 3½.6
　　　**Gilderdale (87)** *(JWHills)* 10–9–8 DHolland (1) (bit bkwd: nvr nrr) .................................................. 1½.7
3404 **Ballerina Bay (59)** (v) *(DTThom)* 4–7–8(1) DaleGibson (10) (a bhd) .................................................. 1½.8
2492 **Awesome Power (63)** *(CRNelson)* 6–7–9 ‡³DBiggs (2) (6th st: wknd 2f out) ...... 2½.9
　　　**Danzarin (IRE) (85)** *(RHannon)* 4–9–6 WCarson (5) (bit bkwd: bhd fnl 3f) ........ 4.10
　　　**Petoski's Choice (70)** *(MJRyan)* 4–8–5 MRoberts (9) (2nd st: wknd over 2f out) 1.11
　　　**Mulciber (82)** *(GHarwood)* 4–9–3 AClark (3) (a bhd) .................................................. 1.12
3355 **Secretary of State (78)** *(PFICole)* 6–8–6 ‡⁷JDSmith (6) (a bhd) .................................................. 2.13
　　　　　　　LONG HANDICAP: Ballerina Bay 7-5.
　　*392 Bowden Boy (IRE) (9/1) Withdrawn (struck into on wy to s) : not under orders*

**4/1** Langtry Lady, **5/1** Crossillion, Awesome Power, **7/1** Barford Lad, **8/1** Ballerina Bay, Gilderdale, **10/1**
Danzarin (IRE), Secretary of State, **12/1** Petoski's Choice, **20/1** Ors. CSF £42.08, CT £610.45. Tote £9.30: £2.70
£2.70 £6.40 (£34.20). Mrs Christine Handscombe (NEWMARKET) bred by W. L. Caley. 13 Rn
　　　　　　　　　　　　　　　　　　　　　　　　　　　　1m 57.18 (7.18)
　　　　　　　　　　　　　　　　　　　　　　　　　　　　SF—12/15/12/13/–/6

**478**　　　QUAIL STKS　£5299.00 (£1582.00: £756.00: £340.00)　　6f　　3-05 (3-09)

　　　**Miss Nosey Parker (IRE) (98)** *(RHannon)* 3–8–4 MRoberts (6) (racd far side:
　　　　mde all: pushed out) .................................................. —1
　　　**Amigo Menor (108)** *(DJGMurray-Smith)* 6–9–10 CRutter (1) (bit bkwd: outpcd:
　　　　gd hdwy over 1f out: r.o wl ins fnl f) .................................................. 1½.2
3982 **Cronk's Courage (72)** (v) *(EJAlston)* 6–9–5 LPiggott (2) (a.p: hrd rdn over 1f
　　　　out: unable qckn) .................................................. ¾.3
　　　**Sunday's Hill (105)** *(MBlanshard)* 3–8–9 JReid (4) (bkwd: a.p: rdn over 2f out:
　　　　one pce) .................................................. 1.4
4135 **Spectacle Jim** *(JO'Donoghue)* 3–7–13 ‡³FNorton (8) (racd far side: no hdwy fnl
　　　　2f) .................................................. 4.5
4304 **Snaadee (USA) (107)** (Fav) *(MRStoute)* 5–9–7 RCochrane (3) (spd over 3f) ....... 3.6
　　　**A Prayer for Wings** *(JSutcliffe)* 8–9–7 LDettori (5) (bit bkwd: swtchd lft 5f out:
　　　　hdwy over 2f out: wknd over 1f out) .................................................. 1½.7
　　　**Mujadil (USA) (105)** *(RWArmstrong)* 4–9–0 WCarson (5) (a bhd) .................................................. 12.8

**7/4** Snaadee (USA), **100/30** MISS NOSEY PARKER (IRE), **7/2** Mujadil (USA), **6/1** Sunday's Hill, **12/1** Amigo
Menor, **14/1** A Prayer for Wings, Cronk's Courage, **100/1** Spectacle Jim. CSF £37.23, Tote £4.30: £1.50 £1.90
£1.50 (£16.10). Mr T. S. M. Cunningham (MARLBOROUGH) bred by John Kent in Ireland. 8 Rn
　　　　　　　　　　　　　　　　　　　　　　　　　　　　1m 16.29 (4.99)
　　　　　　　　　　　　　　　　　　　　　　　　　　　　SF—14/28/20/6/–/–

**479**　　　ROSEBERY H'CAP (0-105) £10950.00 (£3300.00: £1600.00: £750.00)
　　　1¼m　　　　　　　　　　　　　　　　　　　　　　3-40 (3-41)

368★ **Revif (FR) (82)** (Fav) *(ACStewart)* 4–8–10 MRoberts (10) (lw: 4th st: led wl over
　　　　1f out: comf) .................................................. —1
368 **No Submission (USA) (80)** *(CRNelson)* 6–8–8 DHolland (7) (lw: led over 8f:
　　　　unable qckn) .................................................. 4.2
3436 **Fire Top (91)** *(RAkehurst)* 7–9–5 RCochrane (1) (3rd st: rdn over 2f out: one
　　　　pce) .................................................. 3.3
　　　**Port Sunlight (IRE) (78)** *(RHannon)* 4–8–6 BRouse (4) (2nd st: hrd rdn over 1f
　　　　out: one pce) .................................................. 1½.4
343 **Green's Ferneley (IRE) (100)** *(RCharlton)* 4–9–7 ‡⁷JWeaver (3) (hdwy over 2f
　　　　out: one pce) .................................................. 2.5
　　　**Knock Knock (84)** *(IABalding)* 7–8–9 ‡³SO'Gorman (12) (bit bkwd: rdn 4f out:
　　　　nvr nr to chal) .................................................. 3.6
342★ **Western Dynasty (71)** *(MJRyan)* 6–7–10 ‡³DBiggs (14) (5th st: wknd over 2f out) 1.7
　　　**Wild Sable (IRE) (90)** *(MRStoute)* 4–9–4 JReid (8) (nvr nrr) .................................................. ¾.8
3434 **Busted Rock (88)** *(MrsLPiggott)* 7–9–2 LPiggott (2) (nvr nrr) .................................................. d.h.8
273★ **Double Echo (IRE) (75)** *(JDBethell)* 4–8–3 WCarson (9) (lw: 6th st: wknd wl over
　　　　1f out) .................................................. s.h.10

Virkon Venture (IRE) **(77)** *(MHTompkins)* 4–7-12 ‡7SMulvey (6) (bhd fnl 2f) ... 1½.**11**
299² Eastern Magic **(70)** *(JAkehurst)* 4–7-12 CRutter (13) (bhd fnl 3f) .............. 2½.**12**
431 Scenic Dancer **(68)** *(AHide)* 4–7-10 DaleGibson (5) (b.off fore: s.s: a wl bhd) .. 2.**13**
Lucky Guest **(99)** *(JLDunlop)* 5–9-13 LDettori (11) (a bhd) .......................... 10.**14**

**6/4** REVIF (FR), **6/1** Double Echo (IRE), **9/1** Busted Rock, **10/1** Fire Top, Western Dynasty, **12/1** Wild Sable (IRE), No Submission (USA), **16/1** Virkon Venture (IRE), **20/1** Port Sunlight (IRE), Eastern Magic, Lucky Guest, **25/1** Scenic Dancer, **33/1** Ors. CSF £20.68, CT £135.02. Tote £2.30: £1.50 £3.50 £3.50 (£13.00). S. Corman Ltd (NEWMARKET) bred by Petra Bloodstock Ltd in France. 14 Rn
2m 6.99 (4.99)
SF—66/56/61/45/56/38

### 480

TEAL H'CAP (0-90) £2872.00 (£856.00: £408.00: £184.00)     **5f**          4-10 (4-13)

344 **Olifantsfontein (68)** (bl) *(RSimpson)* 4–8-11 WRyan (8) (racd far side: mde virtually all: clr 2f out: r.o wl) ........................................ —**1**
236 Ski Captain **(60)** *(PHowling)* 8–8-3 NCarlisle (10) (racd far side: rdn over 2f out: unable qckn) ........................................... 6.**2**
414 Greetland Rock **(53)** *(PHowling)* 4–7-7(1) ‡3FNorton (11) (swtg: racd far side: lost pl over 3f out: hdwy over 1f out: r.o) ................. 1½.**3**
414² Across the Bay **(69)** (v) *(SDow)* 5–8-12 WCarson (5) (outpcd: gd hdwy over 1f out: r.o) ........................................................ ¾.**4**
455 Gondo **(71)** (v) *(EJAlston)* 5–9-0 LPiggott (6) (a.p: one pce fnl 2f) ............... s.h.**5**
344⁴ Baysham (USA) **(80)** (bl) *(BRMillman)* 6–9-9 GBaxter (3) (lw: dwlt: nvr nr to chal) ½.**6**
349* Wanda **(72)** (Fav) *(KRBurke)* 5–9-1 DHolland (1) (b.off hind: gd spd over 3f) .. s.h.**7**
Cash a Million (FR) **(55)** *(PDCundell)* 4–7-12 EJohnson (4) (a bhd) ............... 1½.**8**
386 Miami Banker **(79)** (bl) *(WRMuir)* 6–9-8 MRoberts (7) (racd far side: prom 3f) ... ¾.**9**
386⁴ Touch of White **(85)** *(JEBanks)* 6–9-9 ‡5LNewton (2) (gd spd 3f) .............. ½.**10**
Forlorn Diver **(56)** *(BGubby)* 4–7-13 JQuinn (9) (racd far side: a bhd) . 3½.**11**

**4/1** Wanda, **9/2** Across the Bay, **5/1** Baysham (USA), Touch of White, **7/1** Miami Banker, Gondo, **16/1** Ski Captain, **20/1** OLIFANTSFONTEIN, **25/1** Cash a Million (FR), **33/1** Ors. CSF £254.57, CT £9,012.95. Tote £25.60: £4.20 £2.90 £6.50 (£105.50). Mr Trevor Painting (FOXHILL) bred by Whitsbury Manor Stud. 11 Rn
61.21 sec (2.21)
SF—73/41/25/41/42/49

### 481

FIFIELD STKS (Mdn 3-Y.O) £2658.00 (£738.00: £354.00)     **1¼m**          4-40 (4-43)

**Allegan (USA)** (Fav) *(HRACecil)* 9-0 WRyan (6) (w'like: scope: 2nd st: led 3f out: clr over 1f out: easily) .................................... —**1**
Rain Rider *(JLDunlop)* 9-0 LPiggott (11) (wl bhd 7f: hrd rdn over 2f out: rapid hdwy over 1f out: fin wl) .................................. 10.**2**
Sun Seeker (IRE) *(MRStoute)* 9-0 WCarson (4) (w'like: scope: led over 5f out to 3f out: one pce fnl 2f) .......................................... 1.**3**
Tunbridge Wells (IRE) *(JHMGosden)* 9-0 RCochrane (12) (bkwd: hdwy over 5f out: 4th st: one pce fnl 2f) ................................ 1½.**4**
471 Lake Dominion **(80)** *(PWHarris)* 9-0 BRouse (7) (bkwd: hdwy over 3f out: one pce fnl 2f) .......................................... 2.**5**
Not in Doubt (USA) *(HCandy)* 9-0 CRutter (10) (bit bkwd: nvr nr to chal) ........ 2½.**6**
King's Treasure (USA) *(IABalding)* 9-0 JReid (5) (bit bkwd: s.s: a bhd) ............... 8.**7**
Snow Board *(BWHills)* 9-0 DHolland (3) (5th st: wknd over 2f out) .......... 2½.**8**
Host (IRE) *(CEBrittain)* 9-0 MRoberts (9) (w'like: scope: bit bkwd: 6th st: wknd over 2f out) .......................................... 4.**9**
Surely Gifted (IRE) *(WRMuir)* 9-0 JQuinn (1) (led over 4f: 3rd st: wknd over 2f out) .......................................... 3½.**10**
Royal Circus *(PWHarris)* 9-0 AClark (8) (bhd fnl 5f) ....................... 10.**11**
Private Practice (20/1) Withdrawn (bolted & inj on wy to s) : not under orders

**13/8** ALLEGAN (USA), **100/30** Sun Seeker (IRE), **7/2** Tunbridge Wells (IRE), **12/1** Rain Rider, Host (IRE), **14/1** Lake Dominion, **20/1** Snow Board, **25/1** King's Treasure (USA), Surely Gifted (IRE), **33/1** Ors. CSF £21.45, Tote £2.60: £1.20 £2.50 £1.70 (£17.60). Mr K. Abdulla (NEWMARKET) bred by Juddmonte Farms, Inc. in USA. 11 Rn
2m 7.70 (5.70)
SF—63/43/41/38/34/29

### 482

MIDDLESEX H'CAP (3-Y.O) (0-90) £3522.00 (£1056.00: £508.00: £234.00)
**1m (rnd)**                                              5-10 (5-19)

(Weights raised 7 lb)
369 **Holiday Island (70)** *(CEBrittain)* 8-8 MRoberts (13) (hdwy over 1f out: rdn fnl f: led last strides) .................................. —**1**
Red Kite **(62)** *(MBell)* 8-0 JQuinn (3) (lw: hdwy over 2f out: led over 1f out: hrd rdn ins fnl f: hdd last strides) ..................... s.h.**2**

341 Thinking Twice (USA) *(72) (PWHarris)* 8-10 WRyan (17) (s.s: gd hdwy over 1f
out: r.o wl ins fnl f) ............................................................ ¾.3
Zamirah (IRE) *(76) (GWragg)* 9-0 RCochrane (8) (hdwy over 1f out: r.o ins fnl f) ½.4
Systematic *(62) (RHannon)* 7-7 ‡⁷AWhelan (9) (hdwy on ins over 2f out: r.o ins
fnl f) ............................................................................ 2.5
332³ Parlemo (IRE) *(70) (JDBethell)* 8-8 DHolland (15) (hdwy over 4f out: 6th st:
wknd over 1f out) ............................................................ 3½.6
Walking the Plank *(79) (PTWalwyn)* 9-3 LDettori (11) (4th st: ev ch over 1f out:
wknd fnl f) .................................................................. nk.7
334² Baluga *(73)* (Fav) *(GHarwood)* 8-11 AClark (12) (lw: led 6f out tl over 2f out:
wknd over 1f out) ............................................................ 2½.8
348 Coniston Lake (IRE) *(66) (GLewis)* 8-1 ‡³FNorton (16) (led 7f out to 6f out: 2nd
st: led over 2f out tl over 1f out: sn wknd) ............................ ¾.9
401★ Try Leguard (IRE) *(83) (WCarter)* 9-7 JReid (6) (lw: led 1f: 5th st: wknd over 1f
out) ........................................................................... ½.10
Shujan (USA) *(83) (RWArmstrong)* 9-7 WCarson (7) (bit bkwd: nvr nrr) ......... 7.11
215⁶ Native Idol (USA) *(81) (JRFanshawe)* 9-5 DavidEddery (1) (3rd st: ev ch over 1f
out: wknd fnl f) ............................................................. 1½.12
Cretoes Dancer (USA) *(70) (WRMuir)* 8-8 CRutter (2) (bit bkwd: a bhd) ........ 1½.13
387 Khazar (USA) *(74) (SirMarkPrescott)* 8-12 CNutter (5) (prom over 4f) ......... ¾.14
Karen Louise *(77) (MissHCKnight)* 9-1 LPiggott (10) (bhd fnl 4f) .............. 4.15
334³ Precious Wonder *(65) (PButler)* 8-0 ‡³DBiggs (18) (swtg: hdwy over 3f out:
eased whn btn over 1f out) ................................................. ¾.16
Walk That Walk *(77) (NCWright)* 9-1 BRouse (14) (prom 4f) ................. 1½.17
370 Manbaa (IRE) *(69) (HThomsonJones)* 8-7 NCarlisle (4) (bhd fnl 3f) .......... 2.18

5/1 Baluga(op 8/1), 8/1 Shujan (USA), Try Leguard (IRE), Parlemo (IRE), 9/1 Walking the Plank, Zamirah (IRE),
10/1 Red Kite, 11/1 Khazar (USA), 12/1 Thinking Twice (USA), HOLIDAY ISLAND, Coniston Lake (IRE), Precious
Wonder, 14/1 Native Idol (USA), Karen Louise, 16/1 Systematic, 20/1 Manbaa (IRE), 25/1 Ors. CSF £136.98, CT
£1,389.62. Tote £15.80: £4.00 £1.80 £3.20 £3.20 (£16/.80). Mrs C. E. Brittain (NEWMARKET) bred by L. H. J.
Ward. 18 Rn                                                                       1m 42.76 (5.56)
                                                                      SF—34/35/33/35/8/12

T/Trio: Race 4: £120.70 (21.2 Tckts). T/Jkpt: Not won; £8,252.80 to Sandown 24/4/92. T/Plpt: £857.80 (13.9
Tckts).                                                                                      AK

## 310—NEWCASTLE (L-H)
### Saturday, April 18th [Heavy]
Going Allowance: St: 1.50 sec (Hvy); Rnd: 0.65 sec per fur (Y)          Wind: str against

Stalls: high

**483**    ST JOHN (NORTHUMBERLAND) H'CAP (0-80) £2070.00 (£570.00: £270.00)
       5f                                                                2-20 (2-21)

357★ No Quarter Given *(69)* (Fav) *(PSFelgate)* 7–9-3 JLowe (4) (lw: trckd ldrs gng
wl: shkn up to ld over 1f out: r.o) ........................................ —1
Consulate *(65) (JBalding)* 6–8-13 KDarley (6) (trckd ldrs: effrt 2f out: nt qckn ins
fnl f) ........................................................................ 2½.2
407 Best Effort *(53) (MPNaughton)* 6–8-1⁽¹⁾ GHind (1) (a chsng ldrs: one pce fnl 2f) 1.3
407 Minizen Music (IRE) *(45) (MBrittain)* 4–7-7 LCharnock (2) (disp ld tl led ½-wy:
hdd over 1f out: no ex) .................................................... s.h.4
359 The Right Time *(51)* (bl) *(JParkes)* 7–7-10 ‡³FNorton (3) (s.i.s: styd on fnl f: nvr
rchd ldrs) ................................................................... ¾.5
Snowgirl (IRE) *(78) (JBerry)* 4–9-5 ‡⁷SGiles (5) (disp ld to ½-wy: wknd over 1f
out) ......................................................................... ½.6
LONG HANDICAP: Minizen Music (IRE) 7-1.

11/8 NO QUARTER GIVEN, 3/1 Snowgirl (IRE), 9/2 Best Effort, 9/1 Consulate, 12/1 The Right Time, 14/1 Minizen
Music (IRE). CSF £11.96, Tote £1.70: £1.20 £2.70 (£7.00). Mr P. S. Felgate (MELTON MOWBRAY) bred by Sean
Madigan. 6 Rn                                                             68.63 sec (10.23)
                                                                      SF—49/35/19/10/10/31

**484**    ST JOHN (DURHAM) CLAIMING STKS (2-Y.O) £2070.00 (£570.00: £270.00)
       5f                                                                2-50 (2-52)

383⁴ **Bird Hunter** *(NACallaghan)* 8-5 ‡⁷JTate (5) (s.i.s: hdwy to ld over 1f out: sn hdd:
styd on to ld wl ins fnl f) ............................................... —1
365 Riston Lady (IRE) *(BSRothwell)* 8-0 RFox (4) (swtchd & hdwy 2f out: led ins fnl f:
no ex nr fin) ............................................................... ½.2

Kiss in the Dark *(MrsGRReveley)* 7-8 JLowe (7) (leggy: unf: s.i.s: swtchd & effrt
  ½-wy: styd on: no imp) ............................................................................... 2.3
Prawn Cracker (IRE) *(CTinkler)* 7-7 LCharnock (2) (neat: bit bkwd: w ldrs: led 2f
  out tl over 1f out: sn btn) ......................................................................... 5.4
371[6] All Baileys *(MJohnston)* 7-4 ‡3JFanning (8) (chsd ldrs tl rdn & btn over 1f out) 1½.5
323[3] Boldville Bash (IRE) (Fav) *(TDBarron)* 8-7 KDarley (6) (lw: led 3f: wandered u.p:
  wknd 1f out) ............................................................................................... 1.6
345[6] Ballaindy *(WGMTurner)* 7-7(1) ‡3FNorton (9) (lw: trckd ldrs: effrt & continually
  hmpd fnl 2f: nt rcvr) .................................................................................. 4.7

**8/11** Boldville Bash (IRE)(op 5/4), **5/2** BIRD HUNTER(7/4—11/4), **5/1** Ballaindy(op 3/1), **14/1** Kiss in the
Dark(op 7/1), **16/1** All Baileys, **20/1** Ors. CSF £40.79, Tote £3.20: £1.90 £4.10 (£25.40). Mr Yahya Nasib
(NEWMARKET) bred by Hamilton Bloodstock (UK) Ltd. 7 Rn                         69.95 sec (11.55)
                                                                                          SF—10/3/–/–/–/–

**485**     ST JOHN AMBULANCE H'CAP (0-90) £3200.00 (£950.00: £450.00: £200.00)
           7f                                                                                   3-20 (3-22)

398[5] **Sharpalto (74)** *(MrsGRReveley)* 5–9-5 JLowe (5) (lw: hld up & bhd: hdwy 2f
  out: n.m.r ins fnl f: qcknd to ld nr fin) .................................................... —1
Sagebrush Roller (73) (Fav) *(JWWatts)* 4–9-4 WRSwinburn (3) (lw: trckd ldrs:
  led ins fnl f: edgd rt: no ex cl home) ....................................................... ½.2
242 Misunderstanding (IRE) **(87)** *(MrsJRRamsden)* 3–8-13 ‡5RPrice (7) (lw: hld up:
  hdwy over 2f out: led over 1f out tl ins fnl f: nt qckn nr fin) .. ½.3
State Flyer (63) (v) *(CBBooth)* 4–8-8 AMcGlone (2) (a in tch: effrt 2f out: r.o
  one pce) ................................................................................................... 3.4
407 Silver Stone Boy (51) *(WJPearce)* 4–7-7(3) ‡3FNorton (6) (cl up: led 3f out tl over
  1f out: one pce) ........................................................................................ 1.5
398* Just a Step (83) *(MMcCormack)* 6–10-0 WNewnes (9) (led 4f: cl up tl wknd 1f
  out) ........................................................................................................... 3.6
398 Jazilah (FR) (65) *(MPNaughton)* 4–8-10 LCharnock (4) (hld up & bhd: nvr trbld
  ldrs) ........................................................................................................... 5.7
398 Master Pokey (73) *(MWEasterby)* 8–9-4 TLucas (8) (b: prom 5f) ................... 1½.8
109[3] Ringland (USA) (80) *(PCHaslam)* 4–9-11 KDarley (1) (lw: chsd ldrs 5f) .............. 2.9

**13/8** Sagebrush Roller, **9/2** SHARPALTO, **5/1** Just a Step, **15/2** Ringland (USA), **9/1** Misunderstanding (IRE),
**12/1** State Flyer, **16/1** Master Pokey, **20/1** Jazilah (FR), **25/1** Silver Stone Boy. CSF £11.77, CT £56.89. Tote
£4.00: £1.60 £1.30 £2.60 (£4.10). Millprew Bloodstock (SALTBURN) bred by E. A. Badger. 9 Rn
                                                                                          1m 37.43 (13.13)
                                                                                          SF—66/63/56/42/24/50

**486**     ORDER OF ST JOHN STKS (Mdn 3-Y.O.F) £2070.00 (£570.00: £270.00)
           1m                                                                                   3-50 (3-53)

**Fetish** (Fav) *(HRACecil)* 8-11 AMcGlone (2) (lw: trckd ldrs: led over 2f out: drvn
  clr: eased nr fin) ...................................................................................... —1
Clear Sound *(GWragg)* 8-8 ‡3FNorton (4) (outpcd appr st: styd on fnl 2f: no ch w
  wnr) .......................................................................................................... 8.2
314[5] Massiba (IRE) *(BHanbury)* 8-11 WRSwinburn (1) (led tl hdd over 2f out: sn rdn
  & wknd) ..................................................................................................... 3.3
302[3] Edge of Darkness *(JWHills)* 8-11 WNewnes (3) (last & pushed along appr st:
  n.d) ........................................................................................................... 2.4

**8/13** FETISH, **3/1** Edge of Darkness(op 2/1), **4/1** Massiba (IRE), **12/1** Clear Sound(op 7/1). CSF £6.80, Tote
£1.50 (£5.90). Mr K. Abdulla (NEWMARKET) bred by Juddmonte Farms. 4 Rn         1m 51.44 (12.44)

**487**     ST JOHN (NEWCASTLE) STKS (Mdn) £2070.00 (£570.00: £270.00)
           1¼m 32y                                                                             4-20 (4-25)

**Kaisar (GER)** (Fav) *(HRACecil)* 3–8-8 AMcGlone (5) (neat: led early: led 5f out:
  drvn out) .................................................................................................. —1
296[2] West Stow *(MRStoute)* 3–8-8 WRSwinburn (1) (lw: a.p: chsd wnr fnl 4f: rdn over
  2f out: styd on nr fin) ............................................................................... 1½.2
Free Transfer (IRE) *(PFTulk)* 3–8-8 AShoults (4) (dwlt: bhd tl styd on fnl 3f: n.d) 20.3
314[3] Linpac Express *(CWCElsey)* 3–8-8 ‡5SMaloney (6) (chsd ldrs: outpcd ent st: n.d
  after) ........................................................................................................ 3½.4
418 Tumbling (USA) *(RAllan)* 4–9-12 SWebster (7) (bhd: sme hdwy over 3f out: n.d) 6.5
394 Boring (USA) *(NACallaghan)* 3–8-8 WNewnes (3) (effrt appr st: sn btn) ........... 25.6
Grey Decision *(MBrittain)* 3–8-8 KDarley (2) (sn led tl hdd 5f out: wknd qckly) . 15.7

**5/4** KAISAR (GER)(op 4/6), **6/4** West Stow, **9/2** Linpac Express(op 7/1), **20/1** Boring (USA), **33/1** Tumbling (USA), **50/1** Ors. CSF £3.42, Tote £2.10: 1.30 £1.10 (£1.80). Sheikh Mohammed (NEWMARKET) bred by Gestut Zoppenbroich in Germany. 7 Rn
2m 18.27 (11.57)
SF—43/40/–/–/–/–/

**488**      ST JOHN H'CAP (3-Y.O) (0-70) £2070.00 (£570.00: £270.00)    1¼m 32y   4-50 (4-55)
(Weights raised 5 lb)

| | | |
|---|---|---|
| 223 | **Trump (54)** *(SirMarkPrescott)* 8-10 GDuffield (3) (in tch: effrt 2f out: styd on to ld wl ins fnl f: edgd lft) | —1 |
| 369 | Dramatic Pass (IRE) **(54)** *(MrsGRReveley)* 8-10 KDarley (1) (led: clr appr st: hdd wl ins fnl f: kpt on) | nk.2 |
| 375² | Kadari **(59)** *(AHarrison)* 9-2 ‡⁵SMaloney (6) (a chsng ldrs: rdn 2f out: styd on wl nr fin) | hd.3 |
| 375* | Philgun **(65)** *(CWCElsey)* 9-1 WRSwinburn (7) (a.p: effrt over 2f out: hrd rdn appr fnl f: kpt on same pce) | nk.4 |
| 375⁵ | Bartolomeo (USA) **(60)** *(MrsJRRamsden)* 8-9 ‡⁷JTate (2) (hld up & bhd: sme hdwy over 2f out: n.d) | 10.5 |
| 366 | Mummys Rocket *(MO'Neill)* 7-12 JLowe (4) (nvr nr ldrs) | 3½.6 |
| | Shanti Flyer (IRE) **(60)** *(AHide)* 9-2 WNewnes (5) (chsd ldrs to st: sn wknd) | 3½.7 |
| 194 | Native Lass (IRE) **(40)** *(JBalding)* 7-3⁽³⁾ ‡⁷ClaireBalding (8) (a bhd) | 10.8 |

LONG HANDICAP: Native Lass (IRE) 7-6.

**5/2** Philgun(op 6/4), **7/2** Kadari, TRUMP, **6/1** Bartolomeo (USA)(op 4/1), **10/1** Shanti Flyer (IRE), **12/1** Dramatic Pass (IRE), **20/1** Mummys Rocket, **33/1** Native Lass (IRE). CSF £36.94, CT £138.18. Tote £3.70: £1.80 £5.30 £1.10 (£62.50). Mrs David Thompson (NEWMARKET) bred by Cheveley Park Stud Ltd. 8 Rn
2m 18.84 (12.14)
SF—40/39/43/43/16/–

T/Plpt: £62.00 (35.75 Tckts).                                                     AA

# NEWCASTLE (L-H)

**Monday, April 20th [Soft]**                                       Wind: mod across
Going Allowance: St: 0.35 sec; Rnd: 0.10 sec per fur (G)

Stalls: high                                 *Race 1: No Tote dividends - technical fault*

**489**      NORTHERN H'CAP (3-Y.O) (0-80) £3557.50 (£1060.00: £505.00: £227.50)
       7f                                        2-20 (2-24)

| | | |
|---|---|---|
| 452³ | **Who's That Lady (54)** *(MHEasterby)* 7-8 ‡⁵SMaloney (4) (trckd ldrs: led wl over 2f out: shkn up & r.o wl) | —1 |
| 464⁵ | She's Special **(76)** (v) *(MissLAPerratt)* 9-7 JCarroll (2) (lw: in tch: effrt over 2f out: styd on wl: no ch w wnr) | 6.2 |
| 401³ | Jefferson Davis (IRE) **(71)** (Fav) *(WJPearce)* 9-2 DNicholls (5) (plld hrd: cl up: ev ch 2f out: rdn & nt qckn) | ½.3 |
| 374⁵ | Stoproveritate **(57)** (v) *(SGNorton)* 8-2 KDarley (1) (led over 4f: sn outpcd) | 3.4 |
| 242⁵ | Crept Out (IRE) **(67)** *(MissSEHall)* 8-12 NConnorton (3) (b.nr hind: hld up: effrt 3f out: sn rdn & btn) | 10.5 |

**2/1** Jefferson Davis (IRE), **5/2** WHO'S THAT LADY, **4/1** Stoproveritate, Crept Out (IRE), **12/1** She's Special(op 6/1). CT £22.13. Mr Jonathan Gill (MALTON) bred by Cheveley Park Stud Ltd. 5 Rn
1m 32.54 (8.24)

**490**      KILLINGWORTH MEDIAN AUCTION STKS (Mdn 3-Y.O) £2072.00 (£572.00: £272.00)
       7f                                          2-50 (2-52)

| | | |
|---|---|---|
| | **Cool Luke (IRE)** *(GMMoore)* 9-0 JCarroll (3) (w'like: cl up: led wl over 1f out: styd on wl) | —1 |
| 406⁶ | Hugging **(67)** *(MMcCormack)* 8-9 MBirch (7) (effrt 3f out: r.o fnl f: nrst fin) | 1½.2 |
| 440 | Bold Boss *(BHanbury)* 9-0 AShoults (8) (chsd ldrs tl outpcd over 2f out: r.o fnl f) | hd.3 |
| 406⁴ | Canaan Lane *(AHarrison)* 9-0 KFallon (9) (a w ldrs: edgd lft & no ex ins fnl f) | ¾.4 |
| 406⁵ | Turtle Beach *(AAScott)* 9-0 JFortune (4) (led tl hdd wl over 1f out: grad wknd) | 1.5 |
| 415² | Rural Lad (Fav) *(MrsJRRamsden)* 9-0 TLucas (1) (trckd ldrs: effrt & hung lft 2f out: sn btn & eased) | 8.6 |
| | Express Gift *(MrsGRReveley)* 9-0 KDarley (6) (in tch 4f) | 10.7 |
| | Noggings (IRE) **(68)** *(NTinkler)* 9-0 KimTinkler (2) (a bhd) | 7.8 |
| | Noel (IRE) *(GAPritchard-Gordon)* 9-0 NDay (5) (prom early: sn outpcd & bhd) | 10.9 |

**5/4** Rural Lad(7/4—Evens), **11/4** Turtle Beach, **5/1** Noel (IRE)(op 3/1), **7/1** COOL LUKE (IRE)(op 14/1), **10/1** Canaan Lane, **12/1** Hugging, **14/1** Bold Boss(10/1—16/1), **16/1** Express Gift, **20/1** Noggings (IRE). CSF £84.70, Tote £17.30: £2.20 £2.70 £1.90 (£71.00). Mr B. Batey (MIDDLEHAM) bred by Lodge Park Stud in Ireland. 9 Rn
1m 30.78 (6.48)
SF—40/30/34/32/29/5

**491**     E.B.F. BLANCHLAND STKS (Mdn 2-Y.O) £2782.50 (£770.00: £367.50)    **5f** 3-20 (3-21)

      **Whitley Gorse** *(JEtherington)* 9-0 TLucas (3) (cmpt: scope: w ldrs: led ins fnl f:
          r.o) ..................................................................................................... —1
361⁵ **Duke of Dreams** *(MrsGRReveley)* 9-0 KDarley (1) (a cl up: ev ch & rdn ins fnl f:
          r.o) .................................................................................................. nk.2
      **Make it Happen** (IRE) *(JBerry)* 9-0 JCarroll (5) (neat: scope: mde most tl hdd
          ins fnl f: kpt on same pce) ................................................................. ½.3
      **Public Way** (IRE) (Fav) *(MHEasterby)* 9-0 MBirch (6) (neat: a chsng ldrs: shkn
          up 2f out: nt qckn) ........................................................................... 1½.4
      **My Godson** *(WJPearce)* 9-0 DNicholls (8) (cmpt: bit bkwd: dwlt: hdwy 2f out:
          nvr nr to chal) ................................................................................. ½.5
      **Robix** (IRE) *(CTinkler)* 9-0 PBurke (2) (cmpt: scope: prom over 3f) ................. 2½.6
      **Make Mine a Double** *(MissSEHall)* 9-0 NConnorton (7) (cmpt: bit bkwd: spd
          over 3f: sn rdn & wknd) ...................................................................... 6.7
      **Coconut Johnny** *(GMMoore)* 9-0 KFallon (4) (str: cmpt: bkwd: bhd fr ½-wy) .... 12.8

**6/4** Public Way (IRE), **9/4** Make it Happen (IRE), **6/1** Duke of Dreams, **7/1** Robix (IRE), **12/1** Make Mine a Double,
**16/1** My Godson, **20/1** WHITLEY GORSE & Ors. CSF £124.76, Tote £16.10: £4.30 £1.80 £1.60 (£152.70). Mrs
G. Liversidge (MALTON) bred by Stud-On-The-Chart. 8 Rn                   65.18 sec (6.78)

**492**     NEWCASTLE H'CAP (0-100) £7245.00 (£2160.00: £1030.00: £465.00)
       **1m**                                           3-55 (3-58)

453⁵ **Tusky** (82) (v) *(MJCamacho)* 4–9-2 SMorris (6) (mde virtually all: edgd rt & kpt
          on wl nr fin) .......................................................................................... —1
364⁶ **Golden Chip** (IRE) (65) *(APStringer)* 4–7-8 ‡⁵SMaloney (4) (hld up & bhd: gd
          hdwy on ins 2f out: chal wl ins fnl f: no ex nr fin) .............................. hd.2
392 **Two Left Feet** (91) *(SirMarkPrescott)* 5–9-4 ‡⁷KRutter (1) (ln tch: effrt & swtchd
          over 2f out: r.o wl nr fin) .................................................................. hd.3
240⁴ **Ashdren** (83) *(AHarrison)* 5–9-3 KFallon (3) (lw: trckd ldrs: effrt 2f out: nt qckn) . 5.4
438³ **Domicksky** (81) (Fav) *(MJRyan)* 4–9-1 NDay (7) (lw: hld up: jnd ldrs appr st:
          outpcd fnl 2f) ................................................................................. 1½.5
348² **Sebosan** (80) *(AHide)* 3–7-13 PBurke (5) (lw: prom: effrt over 2f out: one pce) .. 1.6
293 **Matts Boy** (70) *(MissSEHall)* 4–8-4 NConnorton (2) (b.hind: effrt appr st: nvr
          rchd ldrs) ...................................................................................... 1.7
368 **Jalmusique** (94) *(MHEasterby)* 6–10-0 MBirch (8) (hdwy & prom appr st: grad
          wknd fnl 2f) .................................................................................. 2½.8
285⁶ **Martini Executive** (70) *(WJPearce)* 4–8-4 JCarroll (9) (lost tch fnl 3f) ................. 12.9

**11/4** Domicksky, **4/1** Ashdren, Two Left Feet, **8/1** Martini Executive, **9/1** Matts Boy, **10/1** Golden Chip (IRE),
Sebosan, **14/1** Jalmusique, **20/1** TUSKY. CSF £177.52, CT £876.06. Tote £17.40: £4.90 £2.50 £1.80
(£130.90). Lord Matthews (MALTON) bred by Lord Victor Matthews. 9 Rn       1m 44.16 (5.16)
                                                   SF—36/13/36/20/13/–

**493**     MELDON APP'CE STKS (Mdn 3-Y.O) £2072.00 (£572.00: £272.00)    **1m**   4-30 (4-32)

      **Teslemi** (USA) *(BHanbury)* 8-4 ‡⁵VBray (1) (leggy: unf: sn led: r.o wl fnl 2f) ........ —1
      **Bigwheel Bill** (IRE) *(JWWatts)* 9-0 KHusband (3) (lw: trckd ldrs: effrt 2f out: r.o) ½.2
374² **Houlston's Will** *(MrsJRRamsden)* 8-9 StephenDavies (4) (lw: a.p: effrt 2f out:
          hung rt & nt qckn) ........................................................................... 6.3
274² **Dune River** (79) (Fav) *(SirMarkPrescott)* 9-0 CMunday (2) (lw: led early: cl up tl
          outpcd fnl 2f) ................................................................................. ½.4
252⁶ **Grey Cphas** *(MMcCormack)* 9-0 HBastiman (2) (in tch: hrd drvn 3f out: no imp) 6.5
415 **Ebony Isle** *(PMonteith)* 8-9 RHavlin (5) (a bhd) .......................................... 3.6
363 **Yazaly** (USA) *(AAScott)* 9-0 EBentley (7) (outpcd 4f out: bhd after) ................. 5.7

**13/8** Dune River, **5/2** Houlston's Will, **5/1** Bigwheel Bill (IRE), **11/2** Yazaly (USA), **8/1** TESLEMI (USA)(op 5/1),
**16/1** Grey Cphas, **25/1** Ebony Isle. CSF £44.71, Tote £8.80: £3.00 £2.50 (£15.90). Mr Muttar Salem
(NEWMARKET) bred by Miller & West in USA. 7 Rn               1m 45.54 (6.54)
                                                 SF—4/12/–/–/–/–

**494**     FOREST HALL H'CAP (0-70) £2469.00 (£684.00: £327.00)    **1½m 93y**    5-00 (5-00)

417* **El Nido** (61) (Fav) *(MJCamacho)* 4–9-6 (3x) NConnorton (3) (a gng wl: led wl
          over 2f out: sn clr: easily) .................................................................. —1
422⁴ **Golden Torque** (65) *(RBastiman)* 5–9-4 ‡⁷HBastiman (1) (hld up & bhd: hdwy
          ent st: styd on wl: no ch w wnr) ......................................................... 4.2
417² **K-Brigade** (49) (bl) *(CWCElsey)* 7–8-9 JCarroll (7) (lw: hdwy appr st: sn chsng
          ldrs: rdn & one pce fnl 2f) ................................................................. 1½.3

328[4] Grey Commander **(42)** *(MBrittain)* 4–8-1[(2)] KDarley (6) (a cl up: chal 3f out: rdn & one pce) ............ 1$\frac{1}{2}$.**4**

417[3] Glastondale **(39)** *(TDBarron)* 6–7-13 AShoults (2) (led tl hdd wl over 2f out: sn btn) ............ 1$\frac{1}{2}$.**5**

358 Mingus (USA) **(60)** *(MrsJRRamsden)* 5–9-6 TLucas (5) (prom tl rdn & btn over 2f out) ............ 4.**6**

377 Needwood Poppy **(40)** *(BCMorgan)* 4–7-8[(6)] ‡[5]SMaloney (10) (prom tl outpcd fnl 3f) ............ 7.**7**

*138* Dale Park **(45)** *(NTinkler)* 6–8-5 KimTinkler (8) (cl up to st: sn lost pl) ............ 2.**8**

405 Cheeky Pot **(61)** (v) *(DenysSmith)* 4–9-6 KFallon (4) (lw: pushed along & lost tch appr st: n.d after) ............ 8.**9**

342 Buzzards Crest **(36)** *(BobJones)* 7–7-10[(2)] PBurke (9) (b.off fore: n.d) ............ 10.**10**

LONG HANDICAP: Needwood Poppy 7-2.

**6/4** EL NIDO, **7/2** K-Brigade, **6/1** Golden Torque(op 7/2), **8/1** Glastondale, **9/1** Mingus (USA), **14/1** Grey Commander, **16/1** Buzzards Crest, Cheeky Pot, **20/1** Dale Park, **25/1** Needwood Poppy. CSF £11.54, CT £27.17. Tote £2.90: £2.10 £1.60 £1.60 (£14.70). Mr H. Roberts (MALTON) bred by M. J. Camacho. 10 Rn
2m 45.04 (6.54)
SF—53/43/31/20/15/28

T/Plpt: £827.80 (1 Tckt).

AA

---

## 421—NOTTINGHAM (L-H)
### Monday, April 20th [Good to soft]
Going Allowance: St: 0.70 sec per fur; Rnd: 0.60 sec per fur (Y)       Wind: mod across

Stalls: high

**495**   ROBIN HOOD STKS (Mdn) £1932.00 (£532.00: £252.00)   **6f 15y**   2-10 (2-16)

**Bunty Boo (80)** (Fav) *(BAMcMahon)* 3–8-9 JLowe (12) (bit bkwd: mde all: clr over 1f out: unchal) ............ —**1**

Will of Steel *(HCandy)* 3–9-0 AMunro (17) (w'like: cmpt: bkwd: chsd ldrs: kpt on ins fnl f: no ch w wnr) ............ 3$\frac{1}{2}$.**2**

Sahel (IRE) *(JHMGosden)* 4–9-12 GHind (6) (bit bkwd: chsd ldrs: kpt on one pce fnl 2f) ............ 1$\frac{1}{2}$.**3**

406 Forza Azzurri (IRE) **(52)** (bl) *(MrsNMacauley)* 3–8-7 ‡[7]SWilliams (3) (racd alone far side: a.p: rdn over 1f out: unable qckn) ............ 1.**4**

348[5] Efra *(RHannon)* 3–8-9 ‡[5]RPerham (2) (prom: rdn over 1f out: sn btn) ............ 8.**5**

Miss Debonair *(DMorley)* 3–8-9 MTebbutt (15) (b.off hind: sme hdwy fnl 2f: nvr nrr) ............ $\frac{1}{2}$.**6**

356 Princess Dechtra (IRE) *(RHollinshead)* 3–8-9 ACulhane (7) (chsd ldrs over 4f) ............ 2$\frac{1}{2}$.**7**

Bear With Me (IRE) *(MBell)* 3–8-9 MHills (14) (b.hind: spd to '$\frac{1}{2}$-wy) ............ $\frac{1}{2}$.**8**

238 Our Eileen *(ASReid)* 3–8-9 LCharnock (13) (nvr trbld ldrs) ............ 1.**9**

Hataal (IRE) **(42)** *(JBalding)* 3–8-2 ‡[7]ClaireBalding (16) (swtg: m.n.s) ............ hd.**10**

Milton Rooms (IRE) *(CBBBooth)* 3–9-0 GOldroyd (9) (bit bkwd: s.s: effrt 2f out: nvr nr to chal) ............ nk.**11**

Superlativemaximus (IRE) *(JABennett)* 4–9-12 AProud (5) (wl grwn: bkwd: spd over 3f) ............ 12

Rue de Remarque (IRE) *(MBell)* 4–9-7 RPElliott (4) (m.n.s) ............ 13

Desert Champ (USA) *(AAScott)* 3–9-0 BRaymond (11) (b.off hind: w'like: bit bkwd: nvr nr ldrs: fin lame) ............ 14

277 Travel Token **(49)** *(LJHolt)* 4–9-12 NAdams (8) (outpcd: t.o) ............ 15

300[5] Blazing Sensation *(DWPArbuthnot)* 4–9-12 BProcter (10) (bit bkwd: outpcd: t.o) ............ 16

360 Sizzling Sarah *(BobJones)* 4–9-12 VSmith (1) (leggy: s.s: a outpcd: t.o) ............ 17

**2/1** BUNTY BOO(op 7/2), **11/2** Will of Steel(4/1—13/2), **13/2** Sahel (IRE), Desert Champ (USA)(op 7/2), **7/1** Efra, **17/2** Princess Dechtra (IRE), **10/1** Miss Debonair(op 5/1), **16/1** Bear With Me (IRE), Blazing Sensation, **25/1** Our Eileen, **33/1** Ors. CSF £14.67, Tote £2.90: £1.10 £2.10 £3.00 (£16.60). Mrs R. C. Mayall (TAMWORTH) bred by Mrs J. McMahon. 17 Rn
1m 18.9 (7.9)
SF—21/12/18/–/–/–

**496**   'FAMILY DAY OUT' H'CAP (0-70) £2676.80 (£744.80: £358.40)   **6f 15y**   2-40 (2-46)

407[3] **Strip Cartoon (IRE) (53)** (bl) *(SRBowring)* 4–8-4[(1)] ‡[7]MHarris (23) (mde all stands' side: hld on gamely nr fin) ............ —**1**

344 Lord High Admiral (CAN) **(67)** *(RHannon)* 4–9-6 ‡[5]RPerham (6) (hdwy '$\frac{1}{2}$-wy: str run fnl f: r.o) ............ $\frac{1}{2}$.**2**

357[3] Verro (USA) **(43)** (bl) *(JABennett)* 5–8-1[(4)] GHind (2) (lw: led far side: rdn 2f out: r.o) ............ 1$\frac{1}{2}$.**3**

My Ruby Ring **(43)** *(DRLaing)* 5–8–1 TyroneWilliams (22) (b: a:p: str chal 1f out: unable qckn fnl f) ............................................................ 1½.**4**
351 Zinbaq **(41)** *(CJBenstead)* 6–7–13 AMunro (17) (hdwy 2f out: r.o wl ins fnl f) ... 1½.**5**
253⁵ Domiana **(40)** *(MBlanshard)* 4–7–5 ‡7AntoinetteArmes (14) (in tch: effrt over 1f out: nrst fin) ....................................................................... ½.**6**
359³ Count Me Out **(43)** *(JPearce)* 7–7–8 ‡7CHawksley (12) (in tch: effrt 2f out: nt pce to chal) ........................................................................... 3½.**7**
Harry's Coming **(64)** *(Fav)* *(RJHodges)* 8–9–3 ‡5TSprake (20) (bit bkwd: chsd ldrs stands' side over 4f) ...................................................... 1.**8**
407 Miss Brightside **(35)** *(ASmith)* 4–7–0 ‡7DarrenMoffatt (7) (dwlt: sn chsng ldrs: no hdwy fnl 2f) ..................................................................... 2.**9**
Green's Stubbs **(46)** *(ABarrow)* 5–7–11⁽⁸⁾ ‡7SSanders (16) (m.n.s) ................ s.h.**10**
325⁶ Pretonic **(65)** *(MJohnston)* 4–9–9 RPElliott (21) (spd 4f) ............................... nk.**11**
Fair Reason (IRE) **(50)** *(DJSCosgrove)* 4–8–1 ‡7DHarrison (10) (bit bkwd: m.n.s) 3.**12**
349² Coppermill Lad **(49)** *(LJHolt)* 9–8–7 NAdams (3) (dwlt: swtchd rt sn after s: nvr trbld ldrs) ......................................................................... ½.**13**
485⁵ Silver Stone Boy **(48)** *(WJPearce)* 4–8–6 SWebster (15) (outpcd) ................. 2.**14**
253 Liffey River (USA) **(61)** *(MrsLPiggott)* 4–9–5 MTebbutt (8) (b: bit bkwd: bhd fnl 2f) ........................................................................................ 1½.**15**
420 Kabera **(35)** *(DWChapman)* 4–7–7 SWood (1) (racd far side: rdn & btn ½-wy) s.h.**16**
325³ Wellsy Lad (USA) **(53)** *(DWChapman)* 5–8–11 MHills (5) (chsd ldrs 4f) ......... 1½.**17**
344 Fivesevenfiveo **(64)** *(RJHodges)* 4–9–1 ‡7TThompson (19) (m.n.s) .............. nk.**18**
194* Swinging Lady **(54)** *(WWHaigh)* 4–8–12 BRaymond (13) (outpcd) ................ ¾.**19**
Ceatharlach **(49)** *(RJHolder)* 3–7–9 AProud (9) (bkwd: bhd fr ½-wy) ............ nk.**20**
Bernstein Bette **(69)** *(PSFelgate)* 6–9–13 JLowe (18) (bkwd: s.s: a bhd) ............ **21**
374 Allimac Nomis **(52)** *(NACallaghan)* 3–7–12 LCharnock (11) (outpcd) ................ **22**
LONG HANDICAP: Miss Brightside 7-6, Kabera 7-5.

**6/1** Harry's Coming, **7/1** STRIP CARTOON (IRE), Zinbaq, **15/2** Pretonic(op 7/1), **9/1** Coppermill Lad, **11/1** Swinging Lady, **12/1** Lord High Admiral (CAN), **14/1** Bernstein Bette, Wellsy Lad (USA), Count Me Out, My Ruby Ring, Fivesevenfiveo, Liffey River (USA), Domiana, **16/1** Verro (USA), Silver Stone Boy, **20/1** Ceatharlach, Allimac Nomis, Green's Stubbs, **25/1** Fair Reason (IRE), **33/1** Ors. CSF £100.00, CT £1,263.67. Tote £8.50: £1.80 £5.40 £8.00 £5.10 (£54.10). Mrs Irene Pryce (EDWINSTOWE) bred by John Kelly in Ireland. 22 Rn
1m 18.3 (7.3)
SF—28/42/17/11/3/–

---

**497**　　'THREE BEARS PICNIC' CLAIMING STKS (3-Y.O) £2284.80 (£632.80: £302.40)
**1m 54y**　　　　　　　　　　　　　　　　　　　　　　　　3-10 (3-12)

397⁴ **Plan Ahead (61)** *(GLewis)* 7-6 ‡7DHarrison (7) (lw: chsd ldrs: 4th st: led 2f out: clr fnl f) ......................................................................... —**1**
313² Silver Samurai **(65)** *(RHollinshead)* 8-13 ACulhane (2) (lw: hld up: 5th st: effrt u.p over 1f out: kpt on) ......................................................... 3½.**2**
Blockade (USA) **(82)** *(MBell)* 9-0 MHills (4) (t: b: chsd ldr: 2nd st: led over 2f out: sn hdd: one pce fnl f) ..................................................... hd.**3**
Mr Poppleton *(DWPArbuthnot)* 8-11 BRaymond (1) (b: wl grwn: bit bkwd: 6th st: hrd drvn 2f out: styd on) ............................................... 3.**4**
365⁵ Lyn's Return (IRE) **(54)** *(RSimpson)* 8-4 ‡5TSprake (3) (lw: led tl hdd over 2f out: wknd appr fnl f) ................................................................. 2.**5**
376⁵ Illuminating *(MrsJRRamsden)* 8-2 AMunro (5) (lw: 8th st: a bhd) ................. ½.**6**
268⁵ Queen of Pendona **(34)** *(DMoffatt)* 7-6 ‡7DarrenMoffatt (6) (prom: 3rd st: wknd over 2f out) .................................................................... 2.**7**
353 Gunmaker *(RJHolder)* 8-5 NAdams (8) (swtg: s.s: 7th st: a bhd) ................ 6.**8**

**6/5** Blockade (USA), **100/30** Illuminating, **4/1** PLAN AHEAD, **5/1** Silver Samurai, **14/1** Lyn's Return (IRE), **20/1** Mr Poppleton, **25/1** Gunmaker, **33/1** Queen of Pendona. CSF £24.16, Tote £4.80: £1.20 £1.30 £1.40 (£7.10). Planflow (Leasing) Ltd (EPSOM) bred by R. F. and Mrs Knipe. 8 Rn
1m 49.3 (9.7)
SF—4/14/14/2/–/–

---

**498**　　EASTER BUNNY H'CAP (3-Y.O) (0-70) £2637.60 (£733.60: £352.80)
**1m 1f 213y**　　　　　　　　　　　　　　　　　　　　　3-45 (3-50)

(Weights raised 1 lb)
334 **Dare to Dream (IRE) (49)** *(GLewis)* 7-8 ‡7DHarrison (1) (lw: hld up: 7th st: led appr fnl f: r.o wl) ..................................................................... —**1**
Glide Path (USA) **(67)** *(Fav)* *(JWHills)* 9-5 MHills (13) (hld up: hdwy 5f out: 4th st: rdn over 1f out: styd on) ........................................................ 2.**2**
355⁴ Holy Wanderer (USA) **(53)** *(DWPArbuthnot)* 8-5 BProcter (15) (hld up: hdwy over 2f out: styd on u.p fnl f) ......................................................... s.h.**3**
Stapleton (IRE) **(68)** *(JWWatts)* 9-6 JLowe (4) (bit bkwd: hld up: hdwy 3f out: rdn & r.o ins fnl f) ........................................................................ nk.**4**

375⁴ Roger Rabbit (FR) **(49)** *(RBoss)* 8-1[2] GHind (6) (chsd ldr: 2nd st: led over 3f out tl appr fnl f: sn wknd) ............................................ 5.5

Cappahoosh (IRE) **(65)** *(HJCollingridge)* 9-3 VSmith (3) (in tch: effrt u.p 2f out: nvr able to chal) ............................................ 1.6

Positive Aspect **(52)** *(JPearce)* 7-11 ‡7CHawksley (17) (s.s: sn chsng ldrs: wknd over 2f out) ............................................ 1½.7

315³ Miss Hyde (USA) **(62)** (v) *(JAGlover)* 9-0 AMunro (7) (6th st: wknd wl over 1f out) ............................................ s.h.8

366* Futures Gift (IRE) **(60)** *(AWPotts)* 8-12 AProud (10) (mid div: rdn over 2f out: no imp) ............................................ 2.9

290⁴ Ferdia (IRE) **(65)** *(RHollinshead)* 9-3 ACluhane (5) (swtg: a in rr) ............................................ 4.10

296 Tahitian **(60)** *(MrsJRRamsden)* 8-12 MTebbutt (2) (a bhd) ............................................ hd.11

395 Sports View **(59)** *(RJHolder)* 8-11 NAdams (16) (bit bkwd: s.i.s: a bhd) ............................................ 12

295⁵ Miss Kingfisher (USA) **(58)** *(SGNorton)* 8-3 ‡7OPears (11) (chsd ldrs: 3rd st: wknd 3f out) ............................................ 13

Thewaari (USA) **(60)** *(AAScott)* 8-12 BRaymond (14) (swtg: hld up in rr: shkn up 3f out: no rspnse) ............................................ 14

370 Tajigrey **(53)** *(BWLunness)* 7-12[10] ‡7SSanders (8) (led tl hdd & wknd over 3f out) ............................................ 15

274⁶ Bella Run **(50)** *(RJHodges)* 7-11 ‡5TSprake (9) (swtg: chsd ldrs: 5th st: sn wknd) ............................................ 16

**3/1** Glide Path (USA)(op 7/1), **5/1** Roger Rabbit (FR), **13/2** Stapleton (IRE), Miss Hyde (USA), **8/1** Futures Gift (IRE)(op 5/1), **10/1** Ferdia (IRE), DARE TO DREAM (IRE)(tchd 20/1), Thewaari (USA), Holy Wanderer (USA), **12/1** Miss Kingfisher (USA), Tahitian(op 7/1), **14/1** Positive Aspect, **20/1** Sports View, Cappahoosh (IRE), Bella Run, **25/1** Tajigrey. CSF £47.36, CT £319.92. Tote £24.20: £4.80 £1.50 £3.60 £1.70 (£527.50). Mrs Shirley Robins (EPSOM) bred by Bhima Breeding Partnership in Ireland. 16 Rn                2m 14 (11.5)
SF—25/46/31/45/16/30

**499**  LITTLE JOHN STKS (3-Y.O) £3289.50 (£981.00. £400.00: £211.60)
1m 54y                                                                4-15 (4-20)

**Killy (92)** *(FHLee)* 9-5 MHills (3) (h.d.w: hld up: 3rd st: led over 2f out: sn clr: hld on wl) ............................................ —1

Sasparella **(79)** *(WJarvis)* 8-13 AMunro (1) (hld up & bhd: 4th st: effrt appr fnl f: fin wl) ............................................ 1.2

274* Sky Hunter (USA) **(85)** (Fav) *(RHannon)* 9-3 BRaymond (4) (lw: plld hrd: led after 1f tl over 2f out: rallied u.p fnl f: no ex nr fin) ............................................ nk.3

Penny Orchid (IRE) **(87)** *(WJPearce)* 8-13 LCharnock (2) (swtg: prom: led 1f: 2nd st: wknd 2f out: eased whn btn) ............................................ 25.4

**8/11** Sky Hunter (USA), **7/2** Penny Orchid (IRE), **5/1** KILLY, **6/1** Sasparella. CSF £24.60, Tote £3.70 (£10.00). Mr Peter Barr (WILMSLOW) bred by Stowell Hill Ltd. 4 Rn                1m 51 (11.4)
SF—24/15/18/–

**500**  EASTER BONNET GRADUATION STKS (3-Y.O) £3577.50 (£990.00: £472.50)
1m 1f 213y                                                            4-45 (4-46)

**Profusion** *(PFICole)* 9-4 AMunro (1) (h.d.w: led 1f: 3rd st: led wl over 1f out: rdn out) ............................................ —1

Maji *(DMorley)* 8-6 MTebbutt (2) (nt grwn: s.i.s: led after 1f tl wl over 1f out: rdn appr fnl f: one pce) ............................................ 2½.2

Tik Fa (USA) **(108)** (Fav) *(BHanbury)* 9-4 BRaymond (4) (lw: hld up: 2nd st: shkn up over 2f out: no rspnse) ............................................ 12.3

**5/6** Tik Fa (USA), **13/8** PROFUSION, **6/1** Maji(op 7/2). CSF £7.08, Tote £2.50 (£2.90). Mr Fahd Salman (WHATCOMBE) bred by Dr F. Krief. 3 Rn                2m 15.4 (12.9)
SF—35/18/6

**501**  SHERWOOD H'CAP (0-70) £2657.20 (£739.20: £355.60)        1¾m 15y      5-15 (5-17)

**Lady Electric (41)** *(RJHodges)* 6-7-11[6] ‡5TSprake (8) (bit bkwd: a.p: 4th st: led 3f out: sn clr: styd on strly) ............................................ —1

377* Sillars Stalker (IRE) **(42)** (Fav) *(MrsJRRamsden)* 4-8-1 AMunro (11) (hld up: brought wd & hdwy 2f out: r.o wl fnl f) ............................................ 2½.2

426² Lookingforarainbow (IRE) **(52)** *(BobJones)* 4-8-11 VSmith (4) (hld up: stdy hdwy 3f out: chsd nr fnl 2f: kpt on) ............................................ nk.3

405³ Carlingford (USA) **(53)** *(MPNaughton)* 6-9-0 LCharnock (5) (w ldrs: 5th st: rdn 2f out: one pce) ............................................ 8.4

Nikitas **(54)** *(MissAJWhitfield)* 7-9-1 MHills (9) (mde most tl hdd over 3f out: sn rdn & btn) ............................................ 3½.5

Intrepid Lass **(52)** *(HCandy)* 5–8-13 JLowe (10) (bit bkwd: prom: 2nd st: led over 3f out: sn hdd: wknd over 1f out) .................. 2.6

*193²* Kovalevskia **(37)** *(DAWilson)* 7–7-12 TyroneWilliams (12) (chsd ldrs: 3rd st: wknd 2f out) .................. nk.7

229⁵ Paper Dance **(62)** *(RJHolder)* 4–9-7 NAdams (15) (reard s: hdwy ent st: nt trble ldrs) .................. 1.8

Lord Future (IRE) **(37)** *(AWPotts)* 4–7-10 AProud (7) (chsd ldrs: rdn over 3f out: sn btn) .................. ½.9

Shareef Star **(40)** *(MBlanshard)* 4–7-6⁽²⁾ ‡7DHarrison (14) (prom: 6th st: wknd over 2f out) .................. nk.10

426 Pondered Bid **(42)** (bl) *(PatMitchell)* 8–7-10⁽¹⁾ ‡7RTurner (2) (swtg: nvr plcd to chal) .................. ½.11

377 Buckingham Band (USA) **(49)** *(FHLee)* 4–8-8 MTebbutt (3) (m.n.s) .................. 1.12

Merton Mill **(63)** *(DMorley)* 5–9-10 BRaymond (1) (bit bkwd: a in rr) .................. hd.13

Suivez Moi **(35)** *(CNAllen)* 8–7-3 ‡7CHawksley (13) (chsd ldrs 10f) .................. 1.14

267 Brora Rose (IRE) **(42)** *(JDBethell)* 4–7-8 ‡7KateDovey (16) (a bhd) .................. ½.15

291 One for the Chief **(36)** (v) *(RMWhitaker)* 4–7-9 SWood (6) (bit bkwd: in tch over 9f: sn wknd) .................. 16

**15/8** Sillars Stalker (IRE), **3/1** Lookingforarainbow (IRE)(op 6/1), **8/1** Paper Dance, **10/1** Nikitas, Carlingford (USA), **11/1** Kovalevskia, **12/1** Merton Mill, **14/1** Shareef Star, **20/1** Intrepid Lass, Suivez Moi, LADY ELECTRIC, Lord Future (IRE), Brora Rose (IRE), **33/1** Ors. CSF £62.90, CT £149.87. Tote £18.80: £3.80 £3.10 £1.10 £1.90 (£28.30). Mr A. J. Coombes (SOMERTON) bred by P. P. Thorman. 16 Rn          3m 13.9 (15.4)

SF—13/12/21/8/2/–

T/Plpt: £462.70 (3.85 Tckts).          IM

## 297–WARWICK (L-H)
### Monday, April 20th [Good to soft]
Going Allowance: 5f-6f: 0.30 sec (G); Rest: 0.45 sec per fur (Y)          Wind: slt bhd

Stalls: low

**502**          LIONS CLUB INTERNATIONAL STKS (Mdn 3-Y.O.F) £1380.00 (£380.00: £180.00)
1m          1-45 (1-51)

**Valley of Fire** *(JRFanshawe)* 8–11 GDuffield (5) (w'like: unf: chsd ldrs: rdn & 7th st: plld out 2f out: r.o to ld ins fnl f) .................. —1

Petite Sonnerie **(82)** *(GLewis)* 8–11 PaulEddery (12) (chsd ldrs: 6th st: ev ch ins fnl f: no ex nr fin) .................. 2.2

Sea Dune *(RCharlton)* 8-8 ‡3JFanning (7) (chsd ldr: 2nd st: led wl over 1f out tl ins fnl f: one pce) .................. ½.3

Encore Une Fois (IRE) *(PWChapple-Hyam)* 8–11 SWhitworth (19) (bit bkwd: r.o fnl 2f: nrst fin) .................. 1¼.4

Twilight Secret *(JWHills)* 8–11 WNewnes (1) (prom: 4th st: sn rdn & btn) .................. sh.5

Just Hannah *(MrsBarbaraWaring)* 8–11 NHowe (4) (scope: bit bkwd: in tch: kpt on fnl 2f: no imp) .................. hd.6

363² Scarlatine (IRE) (Fav) *(JHMGosden)* 8–11 GCarter (13) (chsd ldrs: 5th st: one pce appr fnl f) .................. 1½.7

River Anchor *(RCharlton)* 8–11 SRaymont (16) (unf: scope: bkwd: bhd: r.o fnl 3f: nvr able to chal) .................. 1.8

Emaura *(DRCElsworth)* 8–11 JWilliams (10) (led tl hdd wl over 1f out: sn btn) ... ¾.9

Spectacular Dawn *(JLDunlop)* 8–11 TQuinn (22) (n.d) .................. nk.10

Kelimutu *(CFWall)* 8–11 GBardwell (11) (lw: a bhd) .................. 5.11

Gerish (IRE) *(JPearce)* 8-6 ‡5RPrice (6) (w'like: bit bkwd: bhd fnl 3f) .................. ½.12

Taurian Princess *(ANLee)* 8–11 RFox (8) (leggy: unf: bit bkwd: a bhd) .................. nk.13

Virginia Cottage *(BAMcMahon)* 8-4 ‡7JBramhill (14) (prom: 3rd st: sn wknd) .................. s.h.14

Athar (IRE) *(PTWalwyn)* 8–11 AMackay (18) (lw: chsd ldrs: rdn & 8th st: sn wknd) .................. 6.15

La Kermesse (USA) *(JHMGosden)* 8-5⁽¹⁾ ‡7DDunnachie (3) (leggy: scope: s.v.s: nt rcvr) .................. 3.16

Mamzooj (IRE) *(HThomsonJones)* 8–11 RHills (20) (lengthy: scope: bit bkwd: bhd fnl 3f) .................. s.h.17

Mayaasa (USA) *(RWArmstrong)* 8–11 BCrossley (17) (lengthy: bkwd: bhd fnl 3f) .................. 5.18

Christian Flight (IRE) *(RHannon)* 8-4 ‡7DGibbs (2) (rangy: scope: bit bkwd: a bhd) .................. hd.19

Gay Ming *(RHollinshead)* 8-4 ‡7AGarth (21) (bhd fnl 3f) .................. 3.20

Forelino (USA) *(JLDunlop)* 8–11 AMcGlone (15) (chsd ldrs tl wknd qckly over 3f out) .................. 3½.21

**2/1** Scarlatine (IRE)(op 5/4), **7/1** Petite Sonnerie(op 16/1), Encore Une Fois (IRE)(12/1—6/1), **8/1** Sea Dune(op 16/1), **9/1** Mamzooj (IRE), **12/1** Spectacular Dawn(op 8/1), **14/1** Twilight Secret(op 8/1), Athar (IRE), **16/1** River Anchor, Mayaasa (USA)(op 8/1), **20/1** La Kermesse (USA), VALLEY OF FIRE(op 12/1), **25/1** Forelino (USA), **33/1** Christian Flight (IRE), Kelimutu, **50/1** Emaura, Virginia Cottage, **66/1** Ors. CSF £155.47, Tote £18.50: £4.10 £2.50 £3.80 (£67.70). Sheikh Mohammed (NEWMARKET) bred by Sheikh Mohammed bin Rashid al Maktoum.
21 Rn                                                                                            1m 45.1 (8.1)
                                                                                            SF—29/23/18/16/15/14

---

**503**     PERSONAL NETWORKING GRADUATION STKS (3-Y.O) £3003.00 (£833.00: £399.00)
            **6f**                                                                          2-15 (2-16)

399² **Threepence (87)** *(JBerry)* 9-4 GCarter (5) (mde all: rdn clr appr fnl f: eased nr
            fin) ............................................................................................... —1
      Hazm (USA) *(HThomsonJones)* 9-4 RHills (6) (bit bkwd: sn chsng wnr: 2nd st:
            ev ch 2f out: no ex appr fnl f) ......................................................... 3.2
      Pure Formality **(Fav)** *(DRCElsworth)* 8-13 JWilliams (2) (bhd: 5th & outpcd st:
            r.o wl appr fnl f: nvr nr) .................................................................. 1½.3
254² Allthruthenight (IRE) **(84)** *(LJHolt)* 9-4 AMcGlone (4) (in tch: 4th st: rdn & kpt on
            fnl 2f) ............................................................................................ hd.4
      Orthorhombus **(89)** *(GLewis)* 9-4 PaulEddery (1) (prom: 3rd st: one pce fnl 2f) hd.5
      Waveband *(BWHills)* 8-13 GDuffield (3) (a bhd) ............................................. 12.6

**9/4** Pure Formality(op 7/2), **5/2** Hazm (USA), **4/1** Orthorhombus(op 5/2), THREEPENCE, **10/1** Allthruthenight (IRE), **12/1** Waveband. CSF £14.05, Tote £3.90: £1.50 £2.20 (£7.30). Mr R. E. Sangster (COCKERHAM) bred by The Overbury Stud. 6 Rn                                                                    1m 16.9 (4.9)
                                                                                            SF—42/30/19/23

---

**504**     JOHN D. TUPPER H'CAP (0-80) £3248.00 (£903.00: £434.00)     1¼m 169y 2-45 (2-47)
            (Weights raised 2 lb)
358★ **Katy's Lad (69)** *(BAMcMahon)* 5-9-7 TQuinn (16) (lw: mde all: rdn out) ............ —1
      Woodurather **(67)** *(MCPipe)* 6-9-5 RHills (12) (a.p: 2nd st: rdn & r.o fnl f: nt rch
            wnr) ............................................................................................... 1.2
417⁵ Margs Girl **(56)** *(TFairhurst)* 5-8-5 ‡³JFanning (2) (lw: bhd: rdn 6f out: gd hdwy &
            3rd st: no ex appr fnl f) .................................................................. 2½.3
      Queens Tour **(41)** *(MBrittain)* 7-7-7 GBardwell (6) (b: lw: r.o fnl 2f: nrst fin) ..... 2½.4
      Thin Red Line **(53)** (v) *(JRJenkins)* 8-8-5⁽³⁾ SWhitworth (10) (chsd ldrs: hmpd
            over 3f out: 6th st: one pce fnl 2f) ................................................... ¾.5
342  Full Quiver **(60)** (v) *(MrsBarbaraWaring)* 7-8-12 NHowe (3) (b: prom: 4th st: rdn
            2f out: sn btn) ................................................................................ 5.6
354⁵ Saint Ciel (USA) **(72)** *(FJordan)* 4-9-10 WNewnes (5) (lw: wl bhd tl r.o fnl 3f) .... hd.7
331  Mysterious Maid **(66)** *(JPearce)* 5-8-13 ‡⁵RPrice (9) (nvr nrr) ........................... 1.8
      Super Morning **(64)** *(GBBalding)* 6-9-2 PaulEddery (8) (wl bhd tl sme late
            hdwy) ............................................................................................ 1½.9
409  Camden's Ransom (USA) **(64)** *(DRCElsworth)* 5-9-2 JWilliams (7) (lw: chsd
            ldrs tl 7th & btn st) ......................................................................... 7.10
328² Santaray **(52)** **(Fav)** *(JMackie)* 6-8-4 GCarter (13) (chsd ldrs: rdn 4f out: wkng &
            8th st) ........................................................................................... 8.11
222² Loudest Whisper **(63)** *(KSBridgwater)* 4-8-10 ‡⁵ATucker (11) (prom: rdn 4f out:
            9th & wkng st) ................................................................................ 2.12
422  Rapid Lad **(45)** *(JLSpearing)* 14-7-11 RFox (4) (bkwd: a bhd) ........................... 3.13
233  Capital Bond (IRE) **(66)** *(RJHolder)* 4-8-11 ‡⁷SDrowne (15) (lw: a bhd) ........... ¾.14
      Walking Saint **(50)** *(GraemeRoe)* 5-7-9 ‡⁷DGibbs (14) (b: bit bkwd: chsd ldrs
            over 6f) .......................................................................................... 2.15
      Ushak **(58)** *(HCandy)* 4-8-10 GDuffield (1) (prom 5f: sn rdn & wknd) ........... 1½.16
221  Northern Vision **(50)** (bl) *(PABlockley)* 5-7-9 ‡⁷JDennis (17) (plld hrd: prom 5f:
            t.o fnl 3f) ....................................................................................... 20.17
            LONG HANDICAP: Queens Tour 7-3.

**5/2** Santaray, **7/2** KATY'S LAD(op 7/1), **7/1** Woodurather(op 4/1), **10/1** Super Morning, Camden's Ransom (USA), **14/1** Full Quiver, Margs Girl, **16/1** Capital Bond (IRE), Mysterious Maid (USA), **20/1** Loudest Whisper, **25/1** Ushak, Thin Red Line, **33/1** Walking Saint, Rapid Lad, **50/1** Ors. CSF £29.04, CT £298.36. Tote £4.90: £1.30 £2.50 £2.60 £7.80 (£15.60). Mr J. W. Butler (TAMWORTH) bred by Peter Doyle. 17 Rn                                                                                2m 24.2 (10.7)
                                                                                            SF—49/45/26/9/19/16

---

**505**     HIGH TENSILE BOLTS (S) STKS     £1828.00 (£508.00: £244.00)
            **1¼m 169y**                                                                     3-15 (3-19)

335  **Molly Splash (42)** *(CACyzer)* 5-8-6 GCarter (11) (lost pl 7f out: gd hdwy over 2f
            out: led post) ................................................................................. —1

| | | | |
|---|---|---|---|
| *120* | Misty Goddess (IRE) **(51)** *(MAJarvis)* 4–8–6 GDuffield (18) (bhd: hdwy 3f out: led ins fnl f: ct post) | | s.h.**2** |
| | Shoehorn *(MCPipe)* 5–8–11 AMcGlone (1) (prom: 5th st: ev ch ins fnl f: no ex nr fin) | | nk.**3** |
| | Gin and Orange *(JRJenkins)* 6–8–11 SWhitworth (8) (hdwy 4f out: 7th st: ev ch ins fnl f: sn btn: fin 5th, 2l: plcd 4th) | | **4** |
| *272²* | Kirby Opportunity **(48)** *(JPearce)* 4–8–1 ‡⁵RPrice (6) (lw: prom: 4th st: ev ch 1f out: one pce: fin 6th, hd: plcd 5th) | | **5** |
| | Rocquaine Bay **(35)** *(MJBolton)* 5–8–6 WNewnes (17) (bhd: hdwy & 8th st: no imp fnl 2f) | | **5.7** |
| *271⁵* | Pims Classic **(58)** *(WJHaggas)* 4–8–11 RHills (2) (bhd: hdwy & 7th st: no ex appr fnl f) | | 1½.**8** |
| *358⁴* | Royal Acclaim **(49)** (v) *(JMBradley)* 7–8–11 JWilliams (20) (nvr nrr) | | 3.**9** |
| | Miss Cookie *(MCPipe)* 4–8–6 BCrossley (12) (hdwy & 2nd st: wknd over 1f out) | | 2.**10** |
| | Stradbroke **(34)** *(MBJames)* 5–8–11 AMackay (14) (sn t.o: r.o fnl 3f: nrst fin) .. | ½.**11** |
| | Primera Ballerina *(JRBosley)* 4–8–6 RStreet (5) (bit bkwd: nvr nr to chal) | | nk.**12** |
| *453⁴* | Paper Craft (bl) *(MJohnston)* 5–8–11 PaulEddery (9) (lw: prom: led 6f out to 4f out: 3rd st: wknd qckly) | | hd.**13** |
| *278⁴* | Noushy **(43)** *(KSBridgwater)* 4–8–1 ‡⁵ATucker (4) (led 2f: wknd 4f out) | | 3.**14** |
| *291²* | Hand Painted **(52)** *(CRBeever)* 8–8–4 ‡⁷GForster (7) (b: nvr trbld ldrs) | | 3.**15** |
| *224²* | Tipperary Azul (IRE) (v) *(MHTompkins)* 4–8–6 ‡⁵CHodgson (3) (bhd fnl 3f) | | 5.**16** |
| *359* | Blazing Pearl **(35)** *(JLHarris)* 4–8–3 ‡³JFanning (19) (bhd fnl 3f) | | ½.**17** |
| *250* | Rushluan **(56)** *(RJHodges)* 8–8–11 ADicks (16) (a bhd) | | nk.**18** |
| *326* | Lucky Barnes **(49)** (bl) *(PABlockley)* 5–8–11 NHowe (15) (led after 2f: hdd 6f out: sn wknd: t.o) | | 12.**19** |
| | Highland Ruby *(PABlockley)* 4–8–6 GBardwell (10) (a bhd: t.o) | | 1.**20** |
| *388* | Blushing Belle **(69)** (bl) *(PFICole)* 4–8–6 TQuinn (13) (lw: prom: led 4f out: clr 1f out: hdd & no ex ins fnl f: fin 4th, hd: plcd last) | | **0** |

*Stewards Enquiry: Obj. by Clerk of the Scales sustained. Blushing Belle disq (failed to weigh in). Quinn fined £185.*

2/1 Blushing Belle, 8/1 Kirby Opportunity, Paper Craft, 9/1 Miss Cookie, 11/1 Hand Painted, 12/1 Pims Classic, 16/1 Misty Goddess (IRE), 20/1 Tipperary Azul (IRE), Royal Acclaim, 25/1 Gin and Orange, Highland Ruby, Rushluan, Shoehorn, MOLLY SPLASH, 33/1 Noushy, Primera Ballerina, Rocquaine Bay, Blazing Pearl, 50/1 Ors. CSF £350.35, Tote £38.60: £9.70 £6.30 £10.40 (£190.90). Mr R. M. Cyzer (HORSHAM) bred by S. Wingfield Digby. 20 Rn; No bid

2m 26.3 (12.8)

SF—13/12/16/10/9/–

---

**506**  P.J. ROWAN H'CAP (0-80) £2250.00 (£625.00: £300.00)  **5f**  3-45 (4-01)

(Weights raised 1 lb)

| | | | |
|---|---|---|---|
| *236* | **Breezy Day (75)** *(BAMcMahon)* 6–9–10 TQuinn (3) (w ldr tl led 2f out: rdn out) . | | —**1** |
| *201* | Hitchin a Ride **(60)** *(MPMuggeridge)* 5–8–9 JWilliams (5) (gd hdwy over 1f out: r.o wl: nt rch wnr) | | ¾.**2** |
| *357* | Lucy Dancer (IRE) **(55)** *(CGCox)* 4–7–13 ‡⁵ATucker (16) (a.p: ev ch wl over 1f out: one pce) | | 2.**3** |
| *414* | Slip-a-Snip **(70)** *(GBBalding)* 5–8–12 ‡⁷TraceyPurseglove (2) (hdwy over 1f out: no ex ins fnl f) | | nk.**4** |
| *357⁶* | Iron King **(62)** (Fav) *(JLSpearing)* 6–8–11 NHowe (6) (hdwy 2f out: nrst fin) | | s.h.**5** |
| | Petitesse **(57)** *(GBlum)* 4–8–6 RFox (17) (led 3f) | | nk.**6** |
| | Soba Guest (IRE) **(80)** *(JBerry)* 3–9–4 GCarter (9) (lw: prom: no hdwy fnl 2f) | | ½.**7** |
| | Let's Go Lochy **(48)** *(CJHill)* 6–7–11 AMackay (15) (nvr plcd to chal) | | ¾.**8** |
| *407* | Hotfoot Hannah (IRE) **(48)** *(PSFelgate)* 4–7–8 ‡³JFanning (11) (prom over 3f) | | ¾.**9** |
| *300* | Unveiled **(70)** *(RJHodges)* 4–8–12 ‡⁷SDrowne (1) (nvr trbld ldrs) | | ¾.**10** |
| *407* | Hinari Video **(48)** *(MJohnston)* 7–7–4 ‡⁷MBaird (19) (chsd ldrs 3f) | | s.h.**11** |
| | Rays Mead **(56)** *(LJHolt)* 4–7–12⁽³⁾ ‡⁷CAvery (12) (bit bkwd: chsd ldrs 3f: sn wknd) | | nk.**12** |
| | Grey Charmer **(69)** *(CJames)* 3–8–7 SWhitworth (18) (bit bkwd: nvr nr to chal) | | nk.**13** |
| | Cromer's Express **(61)** (v) *(MissLCSiddall)* 3–7–13⁽¹⁾ BCrossley (14) (lw: in tch: rdn over 2f out: sn btn) | | hd.**14** |
| *209* | Goody Four Shoes **(62)** *(DRTucker)* 4–8–6 ‡⁵RPrice (7) (spd over 2f) | | ½.**15** |
| *159⁶* | Miss Bell Ringer **(47)** *(CJHill)* 4–7–10 RStreet (4) (s.i.s: a bhd) | | 2.**16** |
| | Banbury Flyer **(68)** *(MrsALMKing)* 4–9–3 RHills (20) (bit bkwd: nvr nr) | | 1½.**17** |
| *357* | Factuelle **(47)** *(DRTucker)* 5–7–10 GBardwell (10) (a bhd) | | nk.**18** |
| | Madam Petoski **(63)** *(FHLee)* 3–8–1 GDuffield (8) (lw: hmpd & lost pl over 2f out: nt rcvr) | | ½.**19** |

11/2 Iron King, 6/1 Petitesse(op 16/1), 13/2 Soba Guest (IRE), 10/1 BREEZY DAY, 12/1 Madam Petoski, 14/1 Cromer's Express, Slip-a-Snip, Hinari Video, Hotfoot Hannah (IRE), 20/1 Factuelle, Rays Mead, 25/1 Lucy Dancer (IRE), Goody Four Shoes, Hitchin a Ride, Grey Charmer (IRE), Unveiled, Banbury Flyer, Miss Bell Ringer, 33/1 Let's Go Lochy. CSF £208.58, CT £5,388.75. Tote £13.80: £3.90 £7.60 £4.40 £4.40 (£230.50). Mrs J. McMahon (TAMWORTH) bred by John I. O'Byrne. 19 Rn

62.7 sec (4.7)

SF–46/28/10/22/20/14

**507**　　PEARL RUN H'CAP (0-90) £3552.75 (£1062.00: £508.50: £231.75)
　　　　1¾m 194y　　　　　　　　　　　　　　　　　　　4-15 (4-26)

(Weights raised 2 lb)

388⁵ **Moving Out (80)** (Fav) *(SirMarkPrescott)* 4–9-7 GDuffield (1) (lw: mde all: rdn &
　　　　hld on wl appr fnl f) ............................................................... —1
　　　Western Dancer (55) *(CAHorgan)* 11–7-12⁽¹⁾ AMcGlone (6) (chsd ldrs: 6th st:
　　　　rdn & r.o appr fnl f: nt trble wnr) ............................................. 2.2
291⁴ Don't Cry (58) *(JDBethell)* 4–7-8⁽⁶⁾ ‡5BDoyle (2) (a.p: 3rd st: rdn & ev ch 2f out:
　　　　nt qckn appr fnl f) .......................................................... ¾.3
388 Sonic Signal (50) *(MJHaynes)* 6–7-7 RFox (5) (bhd: r.o fnl 3f: nt rch ldrs) ....... 1½.4
234 Wings of Freedom (IRE) (61) *(JRJenkins)* 4–7-11⁽⁹⁾ ‡5RPrice (3) (hld up: 7th st:
　　　　kpt on: nvr able to chal) ...................................................... 4.5
　　　Cardinal Bird (USA) (54) *(SMellor)* 5–7-11 DanaMellor (10) (lw: chsd ldrs: 4th
　　　　st: sn btn) ................................................................. 1½.6
405⁵ Fen Princess (IRE) (54) *(PCHaslam)* 4–7-6 ‡3JFanning (7) (chsd ldrs 11f) ........ 5.7
409 Podrida (52) *(RJO'Sullivan)* 6–7-9 GBardwell (9) (sn pushed along: bhd fnl 4f) . 8.8
　　　Janiski (63) (v) *(MrsBarbaraWaring)* 9–8-6 NHowe (11) (in tch: effrt & 5th st: sn
　　　　btn) ....................................................................... 5.9
　　　Cruise Party (IRE) (83) *(MrsDHaine)* 4–9-10 RHills (8) (lw: chsd ldr: 2nd st: sn
　　　　wknd) ...................................................................... 1½.10
　　　Hawwar (USA) (55) *(MrsALMKing)* 5–7-5⁽⁵⁾ ‡7TWilson (12) (bit bkwd: wl bhd fnl
　　　　8f) ......................................................................... 8.11
　　　Lady Westgate (51) *(GBBalding)* 5–7-8⁽¹⁾ RStreet (4) (in tch: rdn 6f out: sn bhd)1½.12
　　　LONG HANDICAP: Don't Cry 7-0, Sonic Signal 6-12, Hawwar (USA) 7-1, Lady Westgate 5-13.

**13/8** MOVING OUT, **11/2** Cardinal Bird (USA)(3/1—6/1), **7/1** Cruise Party (IRE), **8/1** Wings of Freedom (IRE),
**10/1** Western Dancer, Fen Princess (IRE), Janiski, **14/1** Don't Cry, **20/1** Don't Cry, **33/1** Sonic Signal, Hawwar
(USA), **50/1** Lady Westgate. CSF £18.37, CT £233.26. Tote £2.70: £1.60 £2.80 £3.00 (£17.60). Mr Fahd
Salman (NEWMARKET) bred by Newgate Stud Ltd. 12 Rn　　　　　　　　　　3m 22.3 (13.3)
　　　　　　　　　　　　　　　　　　　　　　　　　　　　　　　Cf　41/16/11/8/8/6

---

**508**　　B.B.C. C.W.R. H'CAP (0-70) £2512.50 (£700.00: £337.50)　**1m**　　4-45 (5-02)

178³ **Tyrian Purple (IRE) (48)** *(RHollinshead)* 4–7-13 ‡7MHumphries (20) (lw: mde
　　　　virtually all: rdn & hld on wl fnl f) ......................................... —1
340⁵ Salbyng (56) *(JWHills)* 4–9-0 RHills (11) (bit bkwd: chsd ldrs: 5th st: rdn to chal
　　　　over 1f out: no ex fnl f) .................................................... ¾.2
330 Dominant Serenade (62) *(PWHarris)* 3–8-5⁽²⁾ SWhitworth (17) (hdwy over 2f
　　　　out: r.o fnl f: nrst fin) ...................................................... hd.3
364 Sooty Tern (46) *(JMBradley)* 5–7-11⁽⁴⁾ ‡7MichaelBradley (15) (a.p: 4th st: one
　　　　pce fnl 2f) ................................................................. 1½.4
422 Chew it Over (IRE) (54) *(CASmith)* 4–8-12 MWigham (25) (hdwy & 8th st: nt rch
　　　　ldrs) ...................................................................... 1½.5
246⁴ Rising Tempo (60) *(CACyzer)* 4–8-11 ‡7TMcLaughlin (12) (prom: jnd wnr
　　　　4f out: 2nd st: wknd over 1f out) ........................................... 2½.6
340 Lady Lacey (49) (v) *(GBBalding)* 5–8-7 JWilliams (6) (bhd: hdwy 2f out: nrst fin) ¾.7
359 Mystic Panther (47) (bl) *(RJHolder)* 4–8-5⁽¹⁾ ADicks (5) (hdwy 3f out: wknd over
　　　　1f out) .................................................................... ¾.8
　　　Tara's Girl (69) *(PABlockley)* 5–9-13 NHowe (19) (lw: dwlt: nvr nrr) ............... 3.9
344 Foolish Touch (50) *(WJMusson)* 10–8-8 ‡7PBowe (2) (b: s.s: nvr nrr) ......... 1½.10
397 Dawn's Delight (47) *(KTIvory)* 14–8-5 GBardwell (3) (b.hind: s.i.s: nvr rchd ldrs) nk.11
411³ El Volador (56) (Fav) *(RJO'Sullivan)* 5–9-0 GCarter (13) (hdwy & 6th st: c wd &
　　　　rdn: wknd over 1f out) ..................................................... 1½.12
285 Sir Arthur Hobbs (55) *(FHLee)* 5–8-8 ‡5NKennedy (7) (rdn 4f out: n.d) ............ hd.13
　　　Now Boarding (43) *(RJHodges)* 5–8-1 BCrossley (16) (bit bkwd: effrt & 7th st:
　　　　wknd 2f out) .............................................................. 3.14
326⁶ Golden Ancona (48) *(MBrittain)* 9–8-6 TQuinn (4) (lw: a bhd) .............. s.h.15
　　　Radio Caroline (52) *(MTate)* 4–8-5 ‡5ATucker (10) (prom 4f) ................ 1.16
208 Mushy Boff (51) *(CJHill)* 4–8-9 AMackay (23) (a bhd) ...................... 1½.17
　　　Dollar Wine (IRE) (67) *(RHannon)* 3–8-10 SRaymont (18) (bit bkwd: bhd fnl 3f) 1½.18
　　　Kellys Kingdom (IRE) (61) *(RABennett)* 4–9-5 WNewnes (8) (b: prom 4f: wknd
　　　　qckly) .................................................................... 6.19
411 Lamastre (68) *(RJHodges)* 3–8-4 ‡7SDrowne (21) (lw: bhd fnl 3f) ............. nk.20
　　　Colsan Boy (41) *(CGCox)* 5–7-10 ‡3JFanning (14) (bkwd: prom: 3rd st: wknd
　　　　qckly) .................................................................... 1½.21
344 Armaiti (69) *(DRTucker)* 4–9-8 ‡5CHodgson (1) (s.i.s: a bhd) ............... 1½.22
331 Paint the Lily (44) *(DCJermy)* 4–7-11⁽²⁾ ‡5RPrice (24) (bhd fnl 4f: t.o) ......... 6.23
　　　Ganeshaya (58) *(MFBarraclough)* 3–8-1 AMcGlone (22) (bhd fnl 4f: t.o) .......... 7.24

9/2 El Volador, **6/1** Salbyng, **8/1** Lady Lacey, **12/1** Sooty Tern, Rising Tempo (IRE), **14/1** Foolish Touch, Sir Arthur Hobbs, Dollar Wine (IRE), **16/1** Radio Caroline, **20/1** Dawn's Delight, Lamastre, Mystic Panther, **25/1** Now Boarding, Tara's Girl, Kellys Kingdom (IRE), Chew it Over (IRE), TYRIAN PURPLE (IRE), Golden Ancona, Mushy Boff, Colsan Boy, **33/1** Paint the Lily, **40/1** Dominant Serenade, Ganeshaya, **50/1** Armaiti. CSF £165.79, CT £5,477.13. Tote £32.50: £5.30 £1.90 £19.20 £2.70 (£121.90). Rykneld Thoroughbred Co Ltd (UPPER LONGDON) bred by Niels Schibbye in Ireland. 24 Rn                                          1m 45.4 (8.4)
SF—13/26/16/3/13/4

T/Plpt: Not won; £3,228.80 to Warwick 21/4/92.                                                                          Dk

# WARWICK (L-H)
## Tuesday, April 21st [Good to soft]
Going Allowance: 0.10 sec per fur (G)                                                   Wind: mod half bhd

Stalls: low

**509**   WARWICK CASTLE STKS (I) (Mdn 3-Y.O.C & G) £2324.00 (£644.00: £308.00)
1m                                                                                              1-45 (1-50)

| | | |
|---|---|---|
| **Handsome Gent** *(LordHuntingdon)* 9-0 JReid (4) (unf: scope: chsd ldrs: 4th st: led wl ins fnl f: r.o) | | —1 |
| Set Table (USA) *(JHMGosden)* 9-0 RCochrane (2) (w'like: scope: s.i.s: hdwy ½-wy: r.o wl ins fnl f) | | 2½.2 |
| Green Lane (IRE) (Fav) *(RCharlton)* 9-0 LDettori (3) (bit bkwd: a.p: 2nd st: styd on one pce ins fnl f) | | 1½.3 |
| Prince of Darkness (IRE) *(SirMarkPrescott)* 9-0 GDuffield (10) (w'like: bkwd: led tl hdd & wknd wl ins fnl f) | | 1½.4 |
| Bid for Six (USA) *(RHannon)* 8-9 ‡⁵RPerham (8) (hdwy ½-wy: 3rd st: wknd fnl f) | | 2.5 |
| Boldrullah *(DWPArbuthnot)* 9-0 TQuinn (6) (b: lt-f: unf: styd on fnl 2f: nvr nrr) | | 8.6 |
| 394  Thunderbird One (USA) *(CRNelson)* 8-7 ‡⁷DThompson (9) (nvr plcd to chal) | | 1½.7 |
| Masrur (USA) *(RWArmstrong)* 9-0 WCarson (13) (lt-f: hld up mid div: nvr trbld ldrs) | | ½.8 |
| Clifton Chase *(MAJarvis)* 9-0 BRaymond (5) (prom tl 6th & wkng st) | | 4.9 |
| Mma International (IRE) *(BRMillman)* 9-0 GBaxter (11) (cmpt: bit bkwd: m.n.s) | | s.h.10 |
| Back Billy (IRE) *(CEBrittain)* 9-0 PatEddery (1) (leggy: bit bkwd: s.s: a bhd) | | s.h.11 |
| Woodlands Legend *(DCTucker)* 9-0 ADicks (12) (bkwd: a bhd) | | 1½.12 |
| Red Archer *(PJMakin)* 9-0 WRSwinburn (14) (prom tl 5th & wkng st) | | 1½.13 |
| 348³  Grand Fellow (IRE) *(JDBethell)* 9-0 AMunro (7) (bit bkwd: chsd ldrs 4f: wknd qckly) | | 2½.14 |
| Spender *(PWHarris)* 9-0 WNewnes (15) (small: bit bkwd: s.s: a bhd) | | s.h.15 |

**15/8** Green Lane (IRE), **11/2** Bid for Six (USA), **13/2** Grand Fellow (IRE), **8/1** Prince of Darkness (IRE)(op 14/1), **10/1** Masrur (USA), Set Table (USA)(op 4/1), **16/1** HANDSOME GENT, Back Billy (IRE), **20/1** Clifton Chase, **25/1** Boldrullah, Thunderbird One (USA), **33/1** Spender, Mma International (IRE), Red Archer, **150/1** Woodlands Legend. CSF £156.09, Tote £21.30: £3.90 £2.20 £1.60 (£41.80). Mr K. H. Fischer (WEST ILSLEY) bred by Aldershawe Stud Farm. 15 Rn                                                       1m 42.7 (5.7)
SF—26/18/13/8/–/–

**510**   ROYAL PRIORS CLAIMING STKS (3-Y.O) £2598.40 (£722.40: £347.20)      **7f** 2-15 (2-25)

| | | |
|---|---|---|
| 300⁶  Certain Lady (60) *(GBlum)* 7-7 ‡⁷CHawksley (6) (chsd ldrs: led 3f out to 2f out: rallied u.p to ld ins fnl f: gamely) | | —1 |
| 123  Hand on Heart (IRE) *(WJHaggas)* 8-3 MHills (13) (hdwy ½-wy: 2nd st: led 2f out tl ins fnl f) | | 2.2 |
| 353²  Man of the Season (USA) (60) (Fav) *(JAkehurst)* 8-13 PatEddery (8) (hdwy 4f out: 6th st: rdn appr fnl f: edgd lft: styd on nr fin) | | 1½.3 |
| Monorose (70) *(DHaydnJones)* 8-8 DHolland (5) (bit bkwd: chsd ldrs: styd on u.p ins fnl f) | | 8.4 |
| 355⁶  Leigh Crofter (73) *(RJHolder)* 8-13 NAdams (2) (chsd ldrs: 3rd st: wknd over 1f out) | | 5.5 |
| 332  Rock Song (IRE) (55) *(PFICole)* 8-4 TQuinn (14) (prom: 5th st: ev ch 2f out: sn rdn & wknd) | | ½.6 |
| Crackling (60) *(DMarks)* 8-5 ‡⁷KRutter (4) (nvr plcd to chal) | | nk.7 |
| Trial Times (USA) (75) *(WAO'Gorman)* 9-2 ‡⁵EmmaO'Gorman (9) (bit bkwd: in tch: no hdwy fnl 2f) | | ¾.8 |
| Brush Wolf (USA) *(JMBradley)* 8-5 TyroneWilliams (16) (small: cmpt: n.d) | | ¾.9 |
| 281  Master Shikari (47) *(JEBanks)* 8-0 ‡⁷JSwinnerton (11) (nvr trbld ldrs) | | s.h.10 |
| 411⁴  Prince Rodney (70) *(RHannon)* 9-3 WCarson (7) (prom 4f: sn lost tch) | | ½.11 |
| 421  Red Verona (50) *(EAWheeler)* 7-11 ‡⁷DHarrison (19) (n.d) | | 2.12 |
| Our Emma *(MrsBarbaraWaring)* 8-10 NHowe (1) (prom 4f) | | 4.13 |

Rumbelow *(JRJenkins)* 8-11  SWhitworth (10) (swtg: dwlt: t.o) ........................ 7.14
Wise Portia *(HCandy)* 9-2  CRutter (15) (bit bkwd: t.o) ........................ 1½.15
332 Roly Wallace **(61)** *(KTIvory)* 8-11  GBardwell (20) (bit bkwd: a bhd: t.o) ........... 6.16
363 Dancing Gem *(JMBradley)* 8-5  AClark (3) (s.i.s: a bhd: t.o) ........................ 4.17
353 Morjinski Dancer *(RSimpson)* 7-11[4] ‡5ATucker (17) (t.o) ........................ 3½.18
*136* Loose Zeus (USA) **(40)** (bl) *(CFWall)* 8-12  NDay (12) (lw: led 4f: 4th & wkng st:
t.o) ........................ 4.19
Miss Shun Lee *(DRTucker)* 7-12[1] ‡5RPrice (18) (lt-f: unruly bef s: a bhd: t.o) 20.20

**5/2** Man of the Season (USA), **3/1** Prince Rodney, **5/1** Rock Song (IRE)(4/1—8/1), **17/2** Hand on Heart
(IRE)(5/1—9/1), **12/1** Trial Times (USA)(op 6/1), Leigh Crofter, Loose Zeus (USA), **16/1** Rumbelow(op 10/1),
**20/1** Monorose, CERTAIN LADY, **25/1** Crackling, Roly Wallace, **33/1** Our Emma, Master Shikari, Wise Portia,
Morjinski Dancer, **50/1** Ors. CSF £188.14, Tote £17.60: £3.90 £2.50 £1.80 (£75.80). Mrs Bridget Blum
(NEWMARKET) bred by Dunchurch Lodge Stud. 20 Rn
1m 28.9 (4.7)
SF—19/23/28/–/–/–

**511**    WARWICK CASTLE STKS (II) (Mdn 3-Y.O.C & G) £2304.40 (£638.40: £305.20)
1m    2-45 (2-55)

394³ **Majboor (IRE)** (Fav) *(PTWalwyn)* 9-0  WCarson (15) (lw: mde all: drvn clr 1f out:
v.easily) ........................ —1
394 Polish Blue (USA) *(MRStoute)* 9-0  PatEddery (13) (chsd wnr: 2nd st: eased
whn btn fnl f) ........................ 6.2
Unforgiving Minute *(PWHarris)* 9-0  PaulEddery (11) (bit bkwd: prom: 4th & rdn
st: kpt on same pce) ........................ 5.3
394 Maple Bay (IRE) *(PJMakin)* 9-0  WRSwinburn (4) (hdwy & 5th st: one pce fnl 2f) 5.4
394 Shirley's Train (USA) *(LordHuntingdon)* 9-0  DaleGibson (3) (chsd ldrs: 7th st:
nvr able chal) ........................ 1½.5
Gold Blade *(NACallaghan)* 9-0  RCochrane (12) (nvr nr to chal) ........................ s.h.6
Nectar Collector *(CFWall)* 9-0  NDay (10) (bit bkwd: nvr nr ldrs) ........................ ½.7
Trooping (IRE) *(GHarwood)* 9-0  AClark (6) (bit bkwd: hdwy & 3rd st: sn rdn:
wknd 2f out) ........................ 1½.8
235 Regal Lover (IRE) *(MBell)* 9-0  MHills (7) (chsd ldrs: 6th & btn st) ........................ ½.9
Southwold Air *(JLDunlop)* 9-0  AMcGlone (9) (bit bkwd: a bhd) ........................ 2½.10
Dominant Force *(RHannon)* 9-0  JReid (8) (unf: a in rr) ........................ ¾.11
Royal Print (IRE) *(WRMuir)* 9-0  SWhitworth (14) (prom 4f: sn lost tch) ........................ 1.12
37⁵ Serious Action *(SirMarkPrescott)* 9-0  GDuffield (2) (bkwd: s.s: a bhd) ........................ 5.13
Flash of Straw (IRE) *(GLewis)* 9-0  RaymondBerry (5) (w'like: bkwd: s.s: a bhd) 2.14
Washington Red *(MFBarraclough)* 9-0  JQuinn (1) (bhd fr ½-wy: t.o) ........................ 25.15

**Evens** MAJBOOR (IRE), **6/1** Polish Blue (USA)(op 3/1), **8/1** Trooping (IRE), **12/1** Nectar Collector(op 8/1), **14/1**
Shirley's Train (USA), Regal Lover (IRE), **16/1** Unforgiving Minute, **20/1** Maple Bay (IRE), **25/1** Serious Action,
Dominant Force, **33/1** Flash of Straw (IRE), Gold Blade, Royal Print (IRE), Southwold Air, **100/1** Washington Red.
CSF £8.09, Tote £2.30: £1.30 £2.00 £3.50 (£4.00). Mr Hamdan Al-Maktoum (LAMBOURN) bred by Shadwell
Estate Company Limited in Ireland. 15 Rn
1m 41.4 (4.4)
SF—46/28/13/–/–/–

**512**    COURIER STKS (Mdn C & G) £2520.00 (£700.00: £336.00)    1¼m 169y    3-15 (3-21)

**Nuez** *(CEBrittain)* 3-8-8  MRoberts (14) (cmpt: chsd ldr: led 3f out: clr fnl f) ........ —1
Hebridean *(HCandy)* 5–10-0  CRutter (1) (bkwd: chsd ldrs: 5th st: styd on strly
fnl f) ........................ 2.2
Pavonis (Fav) *(HRACecil)* 3–8-8  LPiggott (12) (bit bkwd: a.p: 3rd & rdn st: one
pce) ........................ 8.3
Inan (USA) *(JLDunlop)* 3–8-8  TQuinn (9) (bit bkwd: hld up & bhd: hdwy 4f out:
styd on fnl 2f: nvr nr) ........................ 1½.4
Indian Decision *(JLDunlop)* 3–8-8  LDettori (11) (chsd ldrs: 6th st: no hdwy fnl 2f) hd.5
Cryptic Clue (USA) *(MJHeaton-Ellis)* 3–8-8  JReid (6) (lt-f: sme hdwy fnl 2f: nvr
nrr) ........................ 4.6
Pinkjinski (IRE) **(69)** *(RHannon)* 3-8-3 ‡5RPerham (2) (chsd ldrs 6f) ........................ ½.7
Yaafoor (USA) *(AAScott)* 3–8-8  BRaymond (3) (bit bkwd: led to 3f out: 2nd st:
wknd 2f out) ........................ 3.8
Haut-Brion (IRE) *(PWChapple-Hyam)* 3–8-8  PaulEddery (13) (bit bkwd: chsd
ldrs: effrt & 4th st: eased whn btn appr fnl f) ........................ 1½.9
343 Meqdaam (USA) *(RAkehurst)* 3–8-8  RCochrane (7) (a bhd) ........................ 2.10
394 Thakawah *(RWArmstrong)* 3–8-8  WCarson (8) (hld up: a bhd) ........................ 2½.11
Schillachi (IRE) *(BAMcMahon)* 4–10-0  WRyan (4) (a bhd: t.o) ........................ 25.12
Court Rise (USA) *(RWArmstrong)* 3–8-8  BCrossley (5) (cmpt: bkwd: s.s: a bhd:
t.o) ........................ 12.13
Salmon Dancer (IRE) **(50)** *(MFBarraclough)* 3–8-5 ‡3FNorton (10) (bkwd: chsd
ldrs over 6f: sn wknd: t.o) ........................ 1.14

4/9 Pavonis, 7/1 Yaafoor (USA)(op 4/1), 14/1 Thakawah, NUEZ, Indian Decision, 16/1 Schillachi (IRE)(op 100/1), 20/1 Haut-Brion (IRE), 25/1 Cryptic Clue (USA), Pinkjinski (IRE), 33/1 Meqdaam (USA), Court Rise (USA), Inan (USA), Hebridean, 50/1 Salmon Dancer (IRE). CSF £352.50, Tote £8.80: £2.10 £7.50 £1.10 (£125.20). Sheikh Mohammed (NEWMARKET) bred by Sheikh Mohammed bin Rashid al Maktoum. 14 Rn
2m 23 (9.5)
SF—10/26/–/–/–/–

**513** BRADFORD & BINGLEY ENGLAND'S HISTORIC HEARTLAND H'CAP (0-100) £3115.35
(£928.80: £442.90: £199.95) 1½m 115y 3-45 (3-46)
(Weights raised 5 lb)

**Matador (USA) (85)** *(RCharlton)* 4-9-10 PatEddery (2) (lw: chsd ldrs: 2nd st: led over 1f out: rdn out) .......................................................... —1
211 Merry Marigold (58) *(JDRoberts)* 6–7–8[(4)] ‡³FNorton (6) (hdwy & 6th st: rdn & r.o ins fnl f) ........................................................... 1½.2
229 Clear Light (60) *(CASmith)* 5–7–6‡7DHarrison (9) (led tl hdd over 1f out: rdn & no ex fnl f) ............................................................ hd.3
Elaine Tully (IRE) (77) *(MJHeaton-Ellis)* 4-9-1 JReid (1) (bit bkwd: hdwy & 4th st: kpt on fnl f) ............................................ 1½.4
Zealous Kitten (USA) (55) *(RJPrice)* 4–7-7 GBardwell (5) (chsd ldrs: 5th st: sn outpcd) ............................................................ 12.5
342² Rare Detail (IRE) (76) (Fav) *(MrsLPiggott)* 4-9-0 LPiggott (8) (prom: 3rd st: rdn 2f out: eased whn btn) ................................................... 1.6
335 Empire Blue (82) *(PFICole)* 9–9-7 TQuinn (7) (b: bit bkwd: a bhd) ................. s.h.7
388 Beebob (79) *(MCPipe)* 4–9-3 PaulEddery (3) (hld up: effrt ent st: no imp) ........ hd.8
388 Army of Stars (84) *(CEBrittain)* 7–9-9 MRoberts (4) (chsd ldr 9f: wknd qckly) .. 1½.9
LONG HANDICAP: Merry Marigold 7-5, Zealous Kitten (USA) 7-0.

9/4 Rare Detail (IRE), 4/1 MATADOR (USA), 5/1 Army of Stars, 8/1 Beebob, Zealous Kitten (USA), 10/1 Empire Blue, Elaine Tully (IRE), 14/1 Clear Light, 20/1 Merry Marigold. CSF £65.92, CT £930.61. Tote £5.90: £2.00 £2.90 £3.00 (£32.90). Mr K. Abdulla (BECKHAMPTON) bred by Flaxman Holdings Limited in USA. 9 Rn
2m 48.4 (10.9)
SF—13/–/–/–/–/–

**514** E.B.F. HATTON COUNTRY WORLD STKS (Mdn 2-Y.O.C & G) £2633.60 (£729.60: £348.80)
5f 4-15 (4-19)

345⁴ **Zuno Warrior** *(GLewis)* 9-0 PaulEddery (2) (mde all: rdn & qcknd 1f out: hld on) —1
383 Crusade (IRE) (Fav) *(RHannon)* 9-0 WCarson (5) (lw: chsd ldrs: rdn ½-wy: swtchd lft 1f out: fin wl) ....................................... hd.2
Daytona Beach (IRE) *(RHollinshead)* 9-0 KDarley (13) (w'like: bit bkwd: chsd ldrs: kpt on u.p ins fnl f) .................................... 1½.3
Bourbon Jack *(JWPayne)* 9-0 RCochrane (11) (w'like: bkwd: hdwy 2f out: rdn & r.o ins fnl f) ...................................................... hd.4
345⁵ Pilgrim Bay (IRE) *(JBerry)* 9-0 JCarroll (14) (prom: ev ch whn faltered 1f out: sn btn) ......................................................... 2.5
Pirates Gold (IRE) *(MJHeaton-Ellis)* 9-0 JReid (7) (unf: scope: hdwy appr fnl f: kpt on) ................................................................ 1½.6
Run on Rebel (IRE) *(PFICole)* 9-0 TQuinn (3) (unf: bkwd: spd 3f) ........................ 5.7
Quick Silver Boy *(DBurchell)* 9-0 MRoberts (6) (leggy: bit bkwd: outpcd) ........ 1½.8
Strephon (IRE) *(MHTompkins)* 8-9 ‡⁵CHodgson (1) (unf: bkwd: outpcd) ........... 7.9
Barsley *(JRJenkins)* 9-0 SWhitworth (10) (small: lt-f: outpcd) ........................ ¾.10
Spanish Tower *(RJHolder)* 9-0 JWilliams (4) (cmpt: bkwd: chsd ldrs to ½-wy: wknd qckly) ................................................... hd.11
Buckski Echo *(TMJones)* 9-0 NAdams (8) (w'like: cmpt: bkwd: s.s: a bhd) . s.h.12
Young Absalom *(LGCottrell)* 9-0 TRogers (8) (unf: bkwd: outpcd) .................... 2.13
World Express (IRE) *(BRMillman)* 9-0 GBaxter (9) (unf: bkwd: swvd lft s: a bhd & outpcd: t.o) ............................................ dist.14

2/1 Crusade (IRE)(3/1—4/1), 5/1 Pilgrim Bay (IRE)(op 3/1), ZUNO WARRIOR(7/2—11/2), 6/1 Run on Rebel (IRE), Pirates Gold (IRE)(op 4/1), 14/1 Young Absalom, Daytona Beach (IRE), 16/1 Spanish Tower, 20/1 Bourbon Jack, 25/1 Strephon (IRE), World Express (IRE), Quick Silver Boy, 33/1 Barsley, 50/1 Buckski Echo. CSF £16.35, Tote £7.60: £2.50 £1.80 £2.50 (£8.60). Mr Vic Fatah (EPSOM) bred by Stowell Hill Ltd. 14 Rn
62 sec (4)
SF—30/29/23/22/14/8

**515** N.A.C. EVENTS AND EXHIBITIONS H'CAP (0-70) £2657.20 (£739.20: £355.60)
7f 4-45 (4-53)

411⁶ **Tender Moment (IRE) (62)** *(CEBrittain)* 4-9-6 MRoberts (17) (chsd ldrs: 2nd st: c stands' side: rdn to ld 2f out: sn clr) .......................... —1
456⁴ Pimsboy (52) (bl) *(PABlockley)* 5-8-10 JCarroll (15) (hdwy 3f out: n.m.r over 1f out: styd on nr fin) ............................................. 7.2

```
        Old Comrades (57) (LGCottrell) 5-9-1 TRogers (20) (a.p: 3rd st: sn ev ch: rdn &
              no ex ins fnl f) .................................................................................................... 2.3
        Scottish Bambi (65) (RHannon) 4-9-4 ‡5PPerham (5) (a.p: 5th st: one pce fnl f) nk.4
449*    Pharaoh's Dancer (60) (EAWheeler) 5-9-1 (5x) ‡3FNorton (2) (hdwy
              ½-wy: nt rch ldrs) ............................................................................................. 3.5
        Prepare (IRE) (50) (RJHolder) 4-8-8 JWilliams (3) (bkwd: hdwy fnl 2f: nvr nrr) ... 1.6
213     Faynaz (53) (bl) (WRMuir) 6-8-11 SWhitworth (16) (led & sn clr: hdd & wknd 2f
              out) .................................................................................................................. 1.7
351²    Sally's Son (66) (WAO'Gorman) 6-9-5 ‡5EmmaO'Gorman (18) (chsd ldrs: 4th
              st: wknd appr fnl f) ......................................................................................... ¾.8
        Sugemar (56) (JARToller) 6-9-0 WRSwinburn (8) (bkwd: in tch tl wknd wl over
              1f out) .............................................................................................................. ¾.9
        Scarlet Princess (51) (RJHodges) 4-8-4 ‡5TSprake (14) (prom over 4f) ........... ½.10
199⁴    Quinzii Martin (51) (DHaydnJones) 4-8-9 JReid (7) (n.d) ................................. 2.11
273     Neroli (60) (APJones) 4-9-4 DHolland (9) (a bhd) ........................................... 2.12
344     Grey Illusions (52) (LJHoll) 4-8-10 NAdams (10) (s.s: a bhd) ........................ 2¹/₂.13
364     Spring to the Top (61) (JWPayne) 5-9-5 RCochrane (1) (n.d) ......................... 2¹/₂.14
344     Highland Magic (IRE) (62) (MJFetherston-Godley) 4-9-6 TQuinn (11) (n.d) ...... 2.15
359     Erris Express (55) (bl) (KTIvory) 7-8-8 ‡5CHodgson (19) (b: lw: hdwy 4f out: 6th
              st: sn wknd) .................................................................................................... ½.16
        Surrey Racing (70) (GLewis) 4-10-0 PaulEddery (4) (bit bkwd: a bhd) ......... 1.17
        Dickens Lane (65) (RJHodges) 5-9-2⁽¹⁾ ‡7TThompson (12) (bkwd: a bhd) ...... ½.18
        Susanna's Secret (53) (WCarter) 4-8-11 GCarter (13) (bkwd: a bhd) ............. nk.19
232     King Ferdinand (63) (DRTucker) 5-9-7 GBardwell (2) (a bhd) ....................... nk.20
```

**4/1** Pharaoh's Dancer(op 6/1), **9/2** TENDER MOMENT (IRE)(op 10/1), **9/1** Spring to the Top, **10/1** Sally's Son, **12/1** Pimsboy(op 8/1), **14/1** Old Comrades, Quinzii Martin, Scottish Bambi(op 8/1), **16/1** Sugemar, Highland Magic (IRE), Surrey Racing, **20/1** Faynaz, Susanna's Secret, Prepare (IRE), **25/1** Scarlet Princess, Erris Express, Dickens Lane, **33/1** Ors. CSF £57.95, CT £665.43. Tote £7.60: £2.00 £3.40 £4.80 £3.40 £3.40. Mr Ray Richards (NEWMARKET) bred by Berkshire Equestrian Services Ltd in Ireland. 20 Rn 1m 28.4 (4.2)

SF—53/22/21/23/11/1

T/Plpt: £67.40 (112.3 Tckts).                                                                    IM

## 263—CATTERICK (L-H)
### Wednesday, April 22nd [Good]
Going Allowance: 5f: 0.10 sec per fur; Rest: 0.40 sec per fur (G)          Wind: almost nil

Stalls: low

**516**     ASPIRING JOCKEYS' APP'CE H'CAP (0-70) £2304.40 (£638.40: £305.20)
            5f                                                                          2-00 (2-02)

```
357²    Penny Hasset (54) (MWEasterby) 4-9-11 ‡5JMarshall (9) (a chsng ldrs: edgd lft
              1f out: r.o u.p to ld cl home) ........................................................................ —1
407²    The Noble Oak (IRE) (55) (bl) (PW) (MMcCormack) 4-9-7 JWeaver (5) (lw: led
              over 3f out: qcknd over 1f out: wknd & hdd nr fin) ................................... ¾.2
143     Sobering Thoughts (40) (DWChapman) 6-8-1 ‡5OPears (2) (swtg: chsd
              ldrs: ev ch 2f out: styd on ins fnl f) ............................................................. nk.3
407⁵    Drum Sergeant (54) (v) (JParkes) 5-9-1 ‡5MichaelDenaro (10) (lw: s.i.s: bhd tl
              hdwy over 1f out: swtchd rt: nt rch ldrs) .................................................... ¾.4
449⁵    Arc Lamp (55) (JAGlover) 6-9-2 ‡5SWilliams (3) (lw: a chsng ldrs: kpt on fnl 2f) ¾.5
372³    Palacegate King (57) (bl) (JBerry) 3-8-7 ‡5SHaworth (1) (sn outpcd: hdwy over
              1f out: styd on nr fin) ..................................................................................... 1½.6
506     Hinari Video (48) (MJohnston) 7-8-6 ‡8MBaird (7) (lw: swtchd rt s: racd wd:
              hdwy out: styd on nr fin) ................................................................................ ½.7
407⁶    Uppance (33) (DWChapman) 4-7-8 ‡5DarrenMoffatt (13) (racd wd: styd on u.p
              appr fnl f: nvr nr ldrs) .................................................................................... 1.8
357     It's Only Money (60) (THCaldwell) 3-9-1 NKennedy (12) (chsd ldrs 3f: sn wknd) 4.9
452     Just Bob (69) (SEKettlewell) 3-9-10 JFanning (4) (lw: hld up: hdwy over 1f out:
              nvr nr to chal) ................................................................................................. 1½.10
        Barnsview (47) (MWEllerby) 3-8-2 SMaloney (6) (bit bkwd: led over 1f: lost pl 2f
              out) ................................................................................................................... nk.11
452     Grubby (49) (RHollinshead) 3-7-10 ‡8JDennis (8) (sn outpcd) ....................... 1½.12
        Midnight Lass (51) (bl) (WJPearce) 4-8-12 ‡5GParkin (11) (chsd ldrs to ½-wy:
              sn wknd) ........................................................................................................... 2½.13
```

**5/2** The Noble Oak (IRE), **5/1** PENNY HASSET, **13/2** Palacegate King, **11/2** Drum Sergeant, **8/1** Just Bob, **12/1** Hinari Video, **16/1** Uppance, **20/1** It's Only Money, **25/1** Midnight Lass, Sobering Thoughts, **33/1** Ors. CSF £17.43, CT £265.27. Tote £5.30: £1.70 £1.60 £4.40 (£7.20). Mrs Anne Henson (SHERIFF HUTTON) bred by Mrs Anne Henson. 13 Rn                                                          60.9 sec (3.4)

SF—43/46/25/36/34/19

**517**    RICHMOND STKS (2-Y.O) £2476.80 (£684.80: £326.40)    **5f**    2-30 (2-31)

266* **Lucky Parkes** (Fav) *(JBerry)* 8-13 JCarroll (1) (lw: mde all: clr 2f out: eased nr
       fin) ....................................................................... —1
361² Nominator *(RHollinshead)* 8-11 WCarson (3) (lw: sn wl outpcd & drvn along:
       styd on appr fnl f: no ch w wnr) .................................... 1½.2
447* Isotonic *(GMMoore)* 8-9 ‡7JWeaver (2) (lw: w wnr: rdn ½-wy: wknd over 1f out) ½.3

**5/6** LUCKY PARKES, **2/1** Isotonic, **4/1** Nominator. CSF £3.63, Tote £1.50 (£2.10). Mr Joseph Heler
(COCKERHAM) bred by Joseph Heler. 3 Rn                                    60.8 sec (3.3)
                                                                          SF–43/35/31

**518**    'WIN WITH THE TOTE' H'CAP (0-80) £3080.00 (£920.00: £440.00: £200.00)
           **1m 5f 175y**                                                 3-00 (3-00)

                                  (Weights raised 2 lb)
138  **Malenoir (USA) (56)** (v) *(WJPearce)* 4–8-4 LCharnock (7) (lw: led 2f out: outpcd 5f
       out: hrd rdn & drvn along 2f out: hung lft: led nr fin) ............... —1
405  Vasiliev (76) (v) *(JPLeigh)* 4–9-10 DNicholls (6) (lw: reluctant to r: bhd 3f: hdwy
       & jnd ldrs 4f out: led 2f out: rdn & jst ct) ...................... s.h.2
     Easy Over (USA) (52) (Fav) *(RDEWoodhouse)* 6–8-2 WCarson (2) (swtg: led
       after 2f to 2f out: one pce) ...................................... 3.3
     Sovereign Niche (IRE) (48) *(NMiller)* 4–7-10 SWood (3) (lw: outpcd & lost pl 5f
       out: styd on fnl 2f: nt rch ldrs) ................................. 6.4
     Media Star (49) *(TKersey)* 7–7-8(6) ‡5SMaloney (5) (b: chsd ldrs: disp ld 5f out tl
       wknd over 2f out) ................................................ 3.5
     Rexy Boy (43) *(WLBarker)* 5–7-7 JLowe (4) (bkwd: wnt prom 7f out: wknd over
       3f out) .......................................................... 5.6
417  Starlight Wonder (45) *(REBarr)* 6–7-9(2) PBurke (8) (jnd ldr 6f out: lost pl over 3f
       out) ............................................................. 7.7
405  Talish (49) *(TDBarron)* 4–7-8 ‡3JFanning (9) (plld hrd & sddle slipped: bhd: effrt
       4f out: sn wknd) ................................................. 3.8
                  LONG HANDICAP: Media Star 6-7, Rexy Boy 7-2.

**100/30** Easy Over (USA), **4/1** MALENOIR (USA), **9/2** Talish, **6/1** Sovereign Niche (IRE), **8/1** Vasiliev, **9/1** Starlight
Wonder, Rexy Boy, **20/1** Media Star. CSF £30.84, CT £102.14. Tote £4.90: £1.80 £2.00 £1.10 (£15.90). Mr
John Purcell (HAMBLETON) bred by King Ranch Inc in USA. 8 Rn                3m 8 (12.8)
                                                                          SF–18/37/9/–/–/–

**519**    JOCKEY CAP (S) STKS (3-Y.O) £2147.60 (£593.60: £282.80)    **1½m 44y**    3-30 (3-31)

369  **Lady St Lawrence (USA) (59)** (bl) (Fav) *(SirMarkPrescott)* 8-5 JLowe (8) (lw:
       trckd ldrs: led 4f out: sn clr: styd on u.p) ...................... —1
366⁴ Stratford Lady (49) *(JAGlover)* 8-5 JFortune (2) (s.i.s: effrt 5f out: chsd wnr fnl
       2f: hung lft: rdn & no imp) ...................................... 1½.2
191  Major Risk (53) *(PAKelleway)* 8-10 JCarroll (7) (chsd ldrs tl outpcd 4f out: kpt
       on u.p) .......................................................... 5.3
375  Victor Romeo (58) (bl) *(WJPearce)* 8-10 DNicholls (4) (lw: hld up: gd hdwy &
       prom 5f out: wknd over 2f out) ................................... 3.4
376⁶ Elgin (47) (bl) *(ABailey)* 8-10 KFallon (9) (swtg: led to 4f out: sn wknd) ...... 5.5
     Great Oration (IRE) *(FWatson)* 8-10 LCharnock (5) (bit bkwd: unruly & reard s:
       bhd fnl 5f) ...................................................... 30.6
448⁴ Brotherlyaffection (56) *(RHollinshead)* 9-0 WCarson (1) (lw: mid div & drvn
       along 7f out: lost pl over 3f out: eased whn no ch) .............. 2.7
448  Del's Fargo (v) *(JLHarris)* 8-10 DHolland (6) (chsd ldrs: drvn along 6f out: sn
       wknd & bhd) ...................................................... 1½.8
     Hasty Amy *(MWEllerby)* 8-5 SMorris (3) (bit bkwd: chsd ldrs tl lost pl over 6f out:
       sn wl bhd) ....................................................... 25.9

**13/8** LADY ST LAWRENCE (USA), **3/1** Stratford Lady(op 2/1), **5/1** Brotherlyaffection, **10/1** Major Risk, Great
Oration (IRE), **12/1** Victor Romeo(op 8/1), **20/1** Elgin, **33/1** Hasty Amy, **50/1** Del's Fargo. CSF £6.64, Tote
£2.70: £1.10 £1.50 £2.40 (£3.40). Hesmonds Stud (NEWMARKET) bred by Hesmonds Stud Ltd in USA. 9 Rn; Bt
in 6,200 gns                                                              2m 46.5 (12.5)
                                                                          SF–14/12/7/1/–/–

**520**    SPRING H'CAP (I) (3-Y.O) (0-70) £2343.00 (£648.00: £309.00)    **7f**    4-00 (4-01)

366  **Kick on Majestic (IRE) (42)** (bl) *(NBycroft)* 7-10 SWood (4) (sn chsng ldrs: rdn
       to ld 2f out: jst hld on) ........................................ —1
     Act of Union (IRE) (67) *(WJPearce)* 9-7 DNicholls (6) (bit bkwd: hld up: effrt
       over 1f out: sn rdn: ev ch ins fnl f: r.o nr fin) ................ s.h.2

242 First Gold **(58)** *(JWharton)* 8-9 ‡³JFanning (7) (effrt ½-wy: outpcd over 2f out:
     styd on wl u.p fnl f) ...................................................... 2½.3

332² Bold Setko (IRE) **(65)** (Fav) *(JMPEustace)* 9-5 DHolland (1) (led: rn wd ent st:
     hdd over 2f out: sn hrd rdn: ev ch tl wknd jst ins fnl f) ....... 1½.4

369 Jubal Early (IRE) **(51)** (bl) *(CNAllen)* 7-12 ‡⁷GForster (2) (lw: sn chsng ldrs: led
     over 2f out: sn hdd: hrd rdn & wknd) .................................. 6.5

264³ Miss Parkes **(57)** *(JBerry)* 8-11 JCarroll (3) (lw: chsd ldrs tl wknd over 2f out) .... 7.6

406 Jester's Gem **(46)** (bl) *(BWMurray)* 7-9⁽⁴⁾ ‡⁵SMaloney (8) (swtg: sn chsng ldrs:
     wknd 3f out) ................................................................. 8.7

Shylou **(44)** *(JWHills)* 7-12 JLowe (5) (still unf: s.i.s: a bhd) ................................. 3.8
*Stewards Enquiry: Forster suspended 1-2/5/92 (improper use of whip).*

**11/10** Bold Setko (IRE), **7/2** Act of Union (IRE), **5/1** Miss Parkes, **8/1** First Gold(tchd 16/1), **10/1** Jubal Early
(IRE)(8/1—12/1), **16/1** KICK ON MAJESTIC (IRE), **25/1** Shylou, **50/1** Jester's Gem. CSF £67.95, CT £448.20.
Tote £20.70: £2.30 £1.50 £2.10 (£28.00). Mr J. G. White (BRANDSBY) bred by Lt-Col and Mrs Palmer in Ireland.
8 Rn                                                1m 30.5 (7.3)
                                                SF—15/39/19/24/–/–

---

**521**      SEDBURY STKS (Mdn) £2284.80 (£632.80: £302.40)    **7f**      4-30 (4-31)

363 **Pridian (IRE)** *(GWragg)* 3-8-10 RCochrane (9) (lw: mde all: edgd lft jst ins fnl f:
     styd on wl) ................................................................... —1

298⁴ Hawa Layaam (IRE) **(74)** (Fav) *(AAScott)* 3–8-10 WRSwinburn (4) (b.off hmp:
     lw: trckd ldrs: effrt, hmpd & swtchd ins fnl f: sn rdn & no
     imp) ............................................................................ 1½.2

393 Tlaad (USA) *(MRStoute)* 3-8-5 WCarson (7) (swtg: chsd ldrs tl wknd over 1f out) 7.3

Salda *(RMWhitaker)* 3–8-10 ACulhane (3) (bit bkwd: s.s: hdwy ½-wy: kpt on wl
     fnl 2f) ......................................................................... ½.4

Thisonesforalice *(WJPearce)* 4–9-10 DNicholls (8) (bkwd: s.s: stdy hdwy
     ½-wy: nvr trbld ldrs) ...................................................... 4.5

364 I'M Electric **(41)** *(RCurtis)* 6–9-10 NDay (2) (nvr nr ldrs) ............................. 2.6

Priceless Holly *(MAvison)* 4–9-10 JLowe (6) (bit bkwd: a in rr) ...................... 2.7

406 Preamble **(65)** *(MrsJRRamsden)* 3–8-5 TLucas (6) (hld up: nvr plcd to chal) .... 2.8

294 Bracken Bay **(30)** *(TKersey)* 5–9-5 SWebster (1) (b: w ldrs tl wknd over 2f out:
     sn bhd) ........................................................................ 8.9

**5/4** Hawa Layaam (IRE), **5/2** Tlaad (USA), **4/1** PRIDIAN (IRE), **9/1** Salda, **20/1** Preamble(op 12/1), **50/1**
Thisonesforalice, I'M Electric, **100/1** Bracken Bay. CSF £8.87, Tote £4.60: £1.30 £1.30 £1.20 (£3.40). Mollers
Racing (NEWMARKET) bred by Whitechurch Stud in Ireland. 9 Rn             1m 29.6 (6.4)
                                               SF—42/37/11/14/16/10

---

**522**      SPRING H'CAP (II) (3-Y.O) (0-70) £2322.00 (£642.00: £306.00)    **7f**    5-00 (5-01)
                                  (Weights raised 3 lb)

375⁶ **Debsy Do (USA) (61)** *(SGNorton)* 8-8 ‡⁷OPears (9) (lw: trckd ldrs: led 1f out: r.o
     wl) ............................................................................. —1

Brambles Way **(57)** *(WLBarker)* 8-11 KDarley (2) (bit bkwd: w ldrs: led 4f out to
     1f out: kpt on wl) .......................................................... 1.2

401² Daaris (USA) **(67)** (Fav) *(DMorley)* 9-7 WCarson (6) (lw: sn led: hdd 4f out: one
     pce fnl 2f) .................................................................... 2.3

295³ Malcesine (IRE) **(51)** *(CaptJWilson)* 8-5 JFortune (3) (lw: effrt u.p over 2f out:
     kpt on: nvr able to chal) .................................................. 2.4

Countercheck (IRE) **(55)** *(CFWall)* 8-9 NDay (4) (bit bkwd: w ldrs tl rdn & outpcd
     ½-wy: kpt on fnl 2f: n.d) ................................................. 1½.5

452 Battuta **(56)** *(REarnshaw)* 8-5 ‡⁵SMaloney (1) (swtg: prom tl rdn & wknd 3f out) 8.6

Joyful Thought **(54)** *(MrsJRRamsden)* 8-8 TLucas (7) (plld hrd: trckd ldrs tl
     grad wknd over 2f out) ..................................................... 1½.7

Tree Owl **(41)** *(MWEllerby)* 7-9⁽²⁾ PBurke (5) (bit bkwd: led early: sn lost pl &
     bhd) ........................................................................... 2.8

356 Briginski **(39)** *(KRBurke)* 7-7 JLowe (8) (swtg: racd wd: prom tl wknd ½-wy: sn
     bhd & eased) ................................................................ 9
                LONG HANDICAP: Tree Owl 7-5, Briginski 7-1.

**13/8** Daaris (USA), **7/2** Malcesine (IRE), **5/1** Countercheck (IRE), **8/1** Joyful Thought, DEBSY DO (USA), **12/1**
Battuta, **25/1** Brambles Way, **33/1** Ors. CSF £140.91, CT £432.54. Tote £10.00: £2.10 £3.00 £1.50 (£249.20).
Mr S. G. Norton (BARNSLEY) bred by Cambus Kenneth Farm in USA. 9 Rn          1m 30.8 (7.6)
                                               SF—22/22/26/4/3/–

T/Plpt: £57.40 (41.85 Tckts).                                                WG

303—**FOLKESTONE (R-H)**
**Wednesday, April 22nd [Good]**
Going Allowance: St: minus 0.40 sec; Rnd: minus 0.30 sec (F)          Wind: slt half bhd

Stalls: low

**524**      WALMER H'CAP (3-Y.O) (0-70) £2422.00 (£672.00: £322.00)
         1m 1f 149y                                           1-45 (1-47)

332 **Googly (45)** *(WGRWightman)* 7-10  GBardwell (7) (lw: rdn & hdwy over 3f out:
         6th st: hrd rdn over 1f out: led ins fnl f: r.o wl) ............... —1
355 Miss Pin Up **(47)** *(PatMitchell)* 7-9(4) ‡3DBiggs (5) (hdwy 2f out: r.o ins fnl f) .... 2½.2
    King's Guest (IRE) **(60)** *(GAPritchard-Gordon)* 8-11  AMcGlone (15) (bit bkwd:
         2nd st: led over 1f out tl ins fnl f: unable qckn) ................... ½.3
    My Senor **(45)** *(MMadgwick)* 7-10  JQuinn (9) (bit bkwd: hdwy 2f out: r.o ins fnl
         f) .................................................................. 2½.4
    Blackpatch Hill **(65)** *(JLDunlop)* 8-9 ‡7KateAhern (12) (bit bkwd: gd hdwy fnl f:
         r.o wl) ............................................................ 1.5
428 Lord Leitrim (IRE) **(60)** *(NACallaghan)* 8-11  WNewnes (10) (lw: nvr nr to chal) ... 2.6
252 Lindeman **(55)** *(SDow)* 8-6  TQuinn (1) (hdwy over 3f out: one pce fnl 2f) ...... s.h.7
395 Ripsnorter (IRE) **(70)** (Jt-Fav) *(SirMarkPrescott)* 9-7  GDuffield (6) (hdwy over 3f
         out: 4th st: wknd over 1f out) ................................... ½.8
448 The Dominant Gene **(44)** *(JRJenkins)* 7-9(2)  NCarlisle (2) (nvr nrr) ........... s.h.9
251⁴ Bernie Silvers **(60)** *(GLewis)* 8-11  PaulEddery (13) (led: clr 7f out: hdd over 1f
         out: sn wknd) .................................................... 2.10
251² Mujid (IRE) **(65)** (Jt-Fav) *(HThomsonJones)* 9-2  RHills (3) (lw: rdn 4f out: bhd fnl
         3f) .............................................................. hd.11
394 Odoen (USA) **(50)** *(MRChannon)* 8-1  CRutter (4) (lw: hdwy 1f out: hmpd ins fnl
         f: nt rcvr) ...................................................... hd.12
332 Confound (IRE) **(47)** *(JAkehurst)* 7-12  NAdams (11) (5th st: wknd over 1f out) .... 2.13
330⁶ Storm Drum **(67)** *(PJMakin)* 9-4  BRaymond (8) (a bhd) .................... s.h.14
  91 Red for Danger **(52)** (v) *(AMoore)* 7-12 ‡5ATucker (14) (3rd st: wknd over 1f out) s.h.15
                     LONG HANDICAP: The Dominant Gene 7-1.

**5/2** Ripsnorter (IRE), Mujid (IRE), **15/2** Bernie Silvers(7/2—8/1), **12/1** Storm Drum, Miss Pin Up(op 7/1), **14/1**
Odoen (USA)(op 7/1), Red for Danger, Lord Leitrim (IRE), **16/1** King's Guest (IRE), Blackpatch Hill(op 10/1),
**25/1** Lindeman, **33/1** The Dominant Gene, My Senor, **40/1** GOOGLY & Ors. CSF £429.56, CT £7,044.16. Tote
£18.00: £3.70 £2.80 £12.30 (£358.00). Mr A. G. Lansley (UPHAM) bred by W. G. R. Wightman and Mrs J. A.
Thomson. 15 Rn                                                         2m 5 (7.3)


**525**      TIM FREEMAN CLAIMING STKS      £2480.80 (£688.80: £330.40)
         1m 1f 149y                                           2-15 (2-18)

453³ **Metternich** *(MHTompkins)* 7-8-6 ‡5CHodgson (15) (lw: mde virtually all: drvn
         out) ............................................................. —1
409³ Absolutely Right **(52)** (Fav) *(RAkehurst)* 4-8-11  TQuinn (4) (b.nr hind: lw: hdwy
         on ins over 3f out: 5th st: hrd rdn fnl f: r.o wl) ................ ½.2
419 Internal Affair **(41)** *(JPearce)* 4-8-3 ‡5RPrice (9) (hdwy over 2f out: r.o ins fnl f) 2½.3
250 Lady Baraka (IRE) **(41)** *(ICampbell)* 4-8-5  AMackay (7) (hdwy over 1f out: r.o
         one pce) ......................................................... 2.4
422⁵ Modest Hope (USA) **(56)** *(GHEden)* 5-8-12  JQuinn (3) (b.hind: hdwy 5f out:
         2nd st: hrd rdn over 1f out: wknd fnl f) ......................... s.h.5
203 Conjurer **(66)** *(RSimpson)* 5-8-7 ‡5ATucker (14) (nvr nr to chal) ............ 1½.6
    Loki (IRE) **(77)** *(GLewis)* 4-9-7  PaulEddery (3) (hdwy over 3f out: 6th st: wknd
         over 1f out) ..................................................... 1½.7
  81 Gibbot **(36)** *(PHowling)* 7-8-11  JMurray (4) (4th st: wknd over 1f out) ........ 12.8
331 Manaolana **(37)** *(AMoore)* 4-8-6  BRouse (12) (3rd st: wknd over 1f out) ......... hd.9
127 Saysana **(31)** *(AMoore)* 5-8-8  JWilliams (5) (a bhd) ..................... nk.10
    Cordillero *(AMoore)* 6-8-12  CandyMorris (10) (b: a bhd) ................ ½.11
    Temple Island (IRE) **(35)** *(PJMakin)* 4-8-7  BRaymond (11) (prom 6f) ........ 3½.12
    Prince Jakatom **(61)** *(DWPArbuthnot)* 5-8-10  AMcGlone (2) (a bhd) ........ 13
273 Deepwood Nanusket **(23)** *(MMadgwick)* 6-8-6  SDawson (13) (lw: bhd fnl 4f) ..... 14
    Heard it Before (FR) *(RPCHoad)* 7-8-10  NAdams (8) (b: w wnr over 5f) .......... 15

**7/4** Absolutely Right, **3/1** Loki (IRE), **6/1** METTERNICH, **7/1** Modest Hope (USA), **10/1** Prince Jakatom, **16/1**
Lady Baraka (IRE), **20/1** Manaolana, Saysana, Conjurer, **25/1** Cordillero, Internal Affair, **33/1** Ors. CSF £17.68,
Tote £6.30: £1.70 £1.80 £3.00 (£9.30). Mr Ian Lochhead (NEWMARKET) bred by Juddmonte Farms. 15 Rn
                                                                       2m 4.4 (6.7)

**526** LEVY BOARD APP'CE STKS (Mdn) £2382.80 (£660.80: £316.40) **7f** 2-45 (2-47)

408³ **Ahbab (IRE)** (Fav) *(PTWalwyn)* 3–8-5 EHusband (10) (lw: chsd ldr: led over 2f out: clr over 1f out: easily) .......... —1
Morsun (79) *(DMorley)* 3–8-10 EBentley (12) (3rd st: hrd rdn over 1f out: unable qckn) .......... 6.2
Fen Dance (IRE) *(PJMakin)* 3–8-0 ‡5CWebb (7) (hdwy over 1f out: one pce) ..... 1¹/₂.3
Indian Style (IRE) *(RGuest)* 3–8-5 StephenDavies (2) (hdwy over 1f out: one pce) .... s.h.4
Miss Magenta (IRE) *(RThompson)* 4–9-0 ‡5LCarter (11) (nvr nr to chal) ......... s.h.5
Millsolin (IRE) (55) *(ARDavison)* 4–9-10 BRussell (6) (5th st: one pce fnl 2f) ..... hd.6
Minoan Light (IRE) *(RHannon)* 3–8-5 ‡5MarkDenaro (4) (nvr nrr) ........... ³/₄.7
274⁴ Silica (USA) *(JHMGosden)* 3–8-5 DDunnachie (3) (s.s: hdwy 4f out: wknd over 2f out) .......... ¹/₂.8
333 Miss Precocious (34) *(DShaw)* 4–9-5 CHawksley (5) (lw: hdwy over 3f out: 4th st: wkng whn hung lft over 1f out) .......... 2¹/₂.9
428⁵ Forest Law (USA) *(PFICole)* 3–8-10 JDSmith (9) (6th st: wknd 2f out) ......... 2¹/₂.10
254⁵ Ednego Bay (IRE) (v) *(MMcCormack)* 4–9-10 BThomas (8) (led tl rn wd bnd & hdd over 2f out: 2nd st: wkng whn hung bdly lft over 1f out)2¹/₂.11
Wild Persian (IRE) *(PatMitchell)* 3–8-0 ‡5RTurner (1) (prom over 3f) ........... 8.12

**4/6** AHBAB (IRE), **5/1** Forest Law (USA)(3/1—11/2), **7/1** Fen Dance (IRE)(6/1—9/1), **10/1** Morsun(8/1—12/1), **11/1** Silica (USA)(4/1—12/1), **16/1** Indian Style (IRE), **33/1** Minoan Light (IRE), **50/1** Ors. CSF £8.73, Tote £1.60: £1.40 £2.90 £2.00 (£9.80). Mr Hamdan Al-Maktoum (LAMBOURN) bred by Shadwell Estate Company Limited in Ireland. 12 Rn
1m 23.1 (1.5)
SF—37/24/9/2/10/19

**527** FOLKESTONE STKS £2322.00 (£642.00: £306.00) **5f** 3-15 (3-16)

430 **Power Lake (108)** (Fav) *(RHannon)* 3–8-12 PatEddery (7) (w ldr: led 2f out: hrd rdn ins fnl f: r.o wl) .......... 1
403² Arctic Appeal (IRE) (92) *(JBerry)* 3–8-7 GCarter (1) (led 3f: hrd rdn over 1f out: r.o wl ins fnl f) .......... nk.2
Love Returned (83) *(WJarvis)* 5–9-4 MTebbutt (3) (lw: hdwy over 1f out: hrd rdn ins fnl f: r.o) .......... ³/₄.3
Regal Chimes (104) *(BAMcMahon)* 3–9-1 AMunro (2) (lw: a.p: rdn over 1f out: unable qckn) .......... 2.4
403³ Duplicity (IRE) (97) (bl) *(LJHolt)* 4–9-9 AMcGlone (5) (lw: prom over 2f) .......... 4.5
Lady Sabo (69) *(GLewis)* 3–8-7 PaulEddery (4) (lw: s.s: a bhd) .......... 3¹/₂.6
408 Kindred Cameo *(GLewis)* 3–7-11 ‡³FNorton (6) (a bhd) .......... 1¹/₂.7

**9/4** POWER LAKE(op 6/4), **3/1** Regal Chimes, **7/2** Arctic Appeal (IRE)(op 6/1), **9/2** Duplicity (IRE), **12/1** Love Returned, **66/1** Ors. CSF £9.26, Tote £2.60: £1.50 £2.00 (£3.30). A. F. Budge (Equine) Limited (MARLBOROUGH) bred by Sir Stanley Grinstead. 7 Rn
59.9 sec (1.1)
SF—36/30/38/27/19/–

**528** GLOVER INSURANCE SERVICES CHALLENGE CUP (Stks) (2-Y.O) £2364.00 (£654.00: £312.00) **5f** 3-45 (3-47)

383★ **Sabre Rattler** (Fav) *(JBerry)* 9-4 PatEddery (5) (lw: mde all: pushed out) .......... —1
365★ Greenwich Chalenge *(WCarter)* 9-4 AMunro (4) (b.hind: chsd wnr: ev ch over 1f out: r.o) .......... ¹/₂.2
352★ Luckifosome *(PDEvans)* 8-8 ‡5LNewton (1) (a.p: hrd rdn 2f out: wknd over 1f out) .......... 10.3
The Atheling (IRE) *(MHTompkins)* 8-11 RHills (6) (cmpt: bkwd: lost pl over 2f out: r.o one pce fnl f) .......... s.h.4
School of Science *(RPCHoad)* 8-11 NAdams (2) (w'like: bkwd: s.s: a bhd) ........ 8.5
Rouwi (IRE) *(NACallaghan)* 7-13 ‡7JTate (3) (b.nr hind: lt-f: bkwd: s.s: a bhd) ..... 6.6

**1/2** SABRE RATTLER, **4/1** Greenwich Chalenge, **9/1** Luckifosome(op 6/1), **12/1** The Atheling (IRE)(op 6/1), **33/1** Rouwi (IRE), **50/1** School of Science. CSF £2.80, Tote £1.30: £1.10 £1.80 (£1.70). Mr H. B. Hughes (COCKERHAM) bred by H. B. Hughes. 6 Rn
60 sec (1.2)
SF—40/38/–/–/–/–

**529** BARHAM STKS (Mdn 3-Y.O) £1932.00 (£532.00: £252.00) **1¹/₂m** 4-15 (4-18)

**Truben (USA)** (Fav) *(HRACecil)* 8-9 PatEddery (6) (4th st: led over 1f out: pushed out) .......... —1
Sure Haven (IRE) *(SirMarkPrescott)* 9-0 GDuffield (5) (bit bkwd: 2nd st: hrd rdn over 1f out: unable qckn) .......... 3¹/₂.2
Wand (IRE) *(HRACecil)* 8-9 WRyan (8) (lw: led over 10f: one pce) .......... 1.3
Sir Pageant *(PFICole)* 9-0 TQuinn (1) (3rd st: rdn over 1f out: one pce) .......... 2¹/₂.4

    Farmer's Pet *(GAPritchard-Gordon)* 8-9 GCarter (2) (prom 8f: 5th st: bhd fnl 2f)  8.5
280³ Line of Kings *(DMorley)* 8-7 ‡⁷EBentley (7) (6th st: a bhd) ............................... nk.6
    No Islands *(MRStoute)* 8-9 WNewnes (3) (unf: scope: s.s: a bhd) ....................... 8.7
394 Marpatann (IRE) *(ASReid)* 8-7 ‡⁷KRutter (4) (a bhd) ........................................ 15.8

**11/8 TRUBEN (USA)**(op 4/6), **7/2** Sir Pageant, Sure Haven (IRE)(tchd 7/1), **8/1** Wand (IRE), **10/1** No Islands,
**33/1** Line of Kings, **50/1** Ors. CSF £6.33, Tote £1.70: £1.10 £1.30 £2.90 (£3.60). Mr Edward St George
(NEWMARKET) bred by Edward A. Seltzer in USA. 8 Rn                                           2m 37 (3.5)
                                                                                    SF—24/22/15/15/–/–

**530**      DOVER H'CAP (0-70) £2324.00 (£644.00: £308.00)    1½m          4-45 (4-48)

409⁶ **Bold Resolution (IRE) (46)** *(CACyzer)* 4–8-4 GCarter (14) (lost pl 7f out: rallied
         3f out: 6th st: hrd rdn over 1f out: led nr fin) ............................. —1
    Petavious (59) *(LadyHerries)* 7–9-4 PaulEddery (11) (lw: 4th st: ev ch wl ins fnl f:
         r.o) .................................................................................... ¾.2
422² Swift Silver (50) (Fav) *(WJMusson)* 5–8-9 MWigham (1) (b: 3rd st: led over 1f
         out: hrd rdn & hung lft ins fnl f: hdd nr fin) ................................. s.h.3
388 Beauchamp Fizz (66) *(NACallaghan)* 4–9-10 PatEddery (6) (lw: hdwy over 3f
         out: hrd rdn over 1f out: one pce fnl f) ....................................... 6.4
    Scent of Battle (38) *(MJHaynes)* 4–7-7 ‡³FNorton (9) (lw: a.p: led over 2f out tl
         over 1f out: 2nd & btn whn bdly hmpd ins fnl f) ........................ 1½.5
    Incola (46) *(HCandy)* 6–8-5 CRutter (8) (hdwy over 1f out: nvr nrr) ................... 1½.6
    The Yomper (FR) (39) *(RCurtis)* 10–7-12 GBardwell (13) (led after 1f tl over 2f
         out: 2nd st: wknd over 1f out) .................................................. 2.7
469 Always Alex (41) *(PDEvans)* 5–7-9⁽¹⁾ ‡⁵LNewton (16) (led 1f: 5th st: wknd over 1f
         out) ................................................................................... ½.8
    Nidomi (45) *(GPEnright)* 5–8-4 JQuinn (7) (no hdwy fnl 3f) ............................ 1.9
    Petmer (48) *(GBBalding)* 5–8-7 JWilliams (12) (bhd fnl 3f) ......................... 1½.10
250⁶ Jaeger (USA) (59) *(JRJenkins)* 5–8-4 SWhitworth (15) (t: lw: a bhd) ............... s.h.11
250 Run Free (39) *(PatMitchell)* 7–9-1⁽¹⁾ ‡³DBiggs (10) (b: bhd fnl 4f) .............. 3.12
229 Julfaar (USA) (69) *(JPearce)* 5–9-9 ‡⁵RPrice (5) (a bhd) ....................... 4.13
409 As Always (IRE) (53) *(GLewis)* 4–8-4 ‡⁷BRussell (4) (bhd fnl 4f) .................. 4.14
272⁶ Singing Reply (USA) (50) *(DMarks)* 4–8-1 ‡⁷KRutter (2) (sddle slipped: a bhd) .... 15
    272 Adjacent (IRE) (20/1) Withdrawn (lame at s) : not under orders

**7/2** Swift Silver, **9/2** Petavious(tchd 7/1), **6/1** Incola, **13/2** Scent of Battle(5/1—8/1), **8/1** Beauchamp Fizz, **12/1**
Petmer, As Always (IRE)(op 8/1), **16/1** BOLD RESOLUTION (IRE)(10/1—20/1), **20/1** Jaeger (USA)(op 12/1),
Singing Reply (USA), **25/1** Always Alex, **33/1** Ors. CSF £81.55, CT £285.13. Tote £13.50: £2.50 £1.90 £2.10
(£42.10). Mr R. M. Cyzer (HORSHAM) bred by G. O'Brien in Ireland. 15 Rn                        2m 37.4 (3.9)
                                                                                    SF—3/11/1/4/–/–

T/Plpt: £204.10 (10.95 Tckts).                                                                     AK

## 285—**BEVERLEY  (R-H)**

### Thursday, April 23rd [Good, Good to firm back st]
Going Allowance: 5f: 0.15 sec (G); Rest: minus 0.20 sec per fur (F)          Wind: almost nil

Stalls: high

**531**      ALD. WILLIAM HODGSON STKS (Mdn) £2284.80 (£632.80: £302.40)
          1m 100y                                                    2-15 (2-15)

341⁶ **Haroldon (IRE) (90)** (Fav) *(BPalling)* 3–8-13 RHills (2) (lw: mde all: rdn over 2f
         out: hld on gamely u.p ins fnl f) ................................................. —1
    Garden of Heaven (USA) *(CEBrittain)* 3–8-13 MRoberts (5) (small: lengthy:
         chsd ldr: chal over 2f out: edgd lft u.p: styd on wl nr fin) .............. ½.2
440⁶ Jathaab (IRE) *(MRStoute)* 3–8-13 WRSwinburn (6) (trckd ldrs: effrt on ins over
         2f out: n.m.r over 1f out: kpt on) ............................................... ½.3
412⁵ Combative (IRE) (v) *(JHMGosden)* 3–8-13 RCochrane (10) (trckd ldrs: rdn 3f
         out: styd on same pce) ............................................................. 4.4
412 Bellatrix *(CEBrittain)* 4–9-4 ‡⁵BDoyle (7) (in tch: rdn 3f out: nt rch ldrs) .......... 6.5
    Town Flower *(LMCumani)* 3–8-8 JFortune (3) (cmpt: bit bkwd: chsd ldrs: rn
         sltly wd ent st: wknd 2f out) ...................................................... ¾.6
    Sugar Loaf (IRE) *(NAGraham)* 3–8-8 BRaymond (4) (lengthy: unf: bit bkwd:
         n.d) ................................................................................... 3½.7
    Doughman *(JEtherington)* 3–8-13 NConnorton (9) (in tch tl wknd over 2f out) . nk.8
    Tate Express (IRE) (73) *(NAGraham)* 3–8-13 JQuinn (8) (hld up: effrt ent st: sn
         btn) ................................................................................... 4.9
    Velveteen Boy *(BWLunness)* 4–10-0 AClark (1) (str: bkwd: s.s: a bhd) .......... 10.10

BEVERLEY, April 23, 1992

**7/4** HAROLDON (IRE), **15/8** Jathaab (IRE)(op 5/4), **9/2** Garden of Heaven (USA), **10/1** Combative (IRE), Town Flower, **14/1** Sugar Loaf (IRE), **20/1** Tate Express (IRE), **33/1** Ors. CSF £10.89, Tote £3.20: £1.20 £1.60 £1.30 (£12.60). Lamb Brook Associates (COWBRIDGE) bred by Owen Bourke in Ireland. 10 Rn     1m 46.7 (4)
SF—15/13/1/–/–/–

**532**     BRIAN BOYES CLAIMING STKS     £2402.40 (£666.40: £319.20)     1m 100y 2-45 (2-46)

373⁴ **Laurel Queen (IRE) (58)** *(JBerry)* 4–9-0 JCarroll (13) (chsd ldrs: led 2f out: jst
hld on) .......... —1
397⁵ Yonge Tender **(56)** (bl) *(JWharton)* 5–8-12 JWilliams (11) (hdwy ent st: rdn 2f
out: styd on strly nr fin: jst failed) .......... s.h.2
431⁴ Majed (IRE) **(77)** (Fav) *(NACallaghan)* 4–9-5 ‡7JWeaver (1) (lw: s.s: sn drvn
along: hdwy ent st: sn prom: edgd rt & kpt on wl u.p fnl f) .......... s.h.3
448⁶ Angel Train **(40)** (bl) *(JParkes)* 4–8-9 SWhitworth (8) (a chsng ldrs: rdn &
nt qckn over 1f out) .......... 2.4
373 Skipper to Bilge **(71)** *(MAJarvis)* 5–9-11 BRaymond (15) (prom: effrt over 2f
out: no ex) .......... 4.5
351 Concert Pitch **(29)** *(BPalling)* 13–9-0 RHills (9) (bit bkwd: trckd ldrs gng wl: led
over 2f out: sn hdd & grad lost pl) .......... 3¹/₂.6
Ace Girl **(57)** *(SRBowring)* 3–7-13 JLowe (4) (swtg: prom tl wknd 3f out: faltered
& eased over 1f out) .......... 2.7
359 Super Ted **(35)** *(WJMusson)* 5–9-2 RCochrane (10) (b: nvr bttr than mid div) .......... ³/₄.8
351 Kay's Dilemma (IRE) **(43)** *(PAKelleway)* 4–8-6 ‡3DBiggs (7) (chsd ldrs tl lost pl
appr st) .......... ¹/₂.9
243 Cardea Castle (IRE) **(36)** (bl) *(BEllison)* 4–8-9 NCarlisle (5) (nvr trbld ldrs) .......... 2¹/₂.10
453 Kind Style (IRE) **(33)** *(RHollinshead)* 4–9-2 WRyan (16) (hld up: effrt appr st:
n.d) .......... 1¹/₂.11
453 Sayant *(WClay)* 7–9-1 PaulEddery (6) (mid div: effrt 3f out: sn wknd) .......... 1¹/₂.12
326⁵ Diving (USA) **(44)** (bl) *(MrsVAAconley)* 4–9-3 PBurke (3) (swtg: cl up tl wknd
over 2f out) .......... 5.13
458 Siolfor (USA) *(MrsJRRamsden)* 3–8-6 KFallon (2) (sn wl bhd: hdwy over 2f out:
hmpd over 1f out: nt rcvr) .......... ³/₄.14
Magdalene (IRE) *(TFairhurst)* 4–8-7 ‡3JFanning (14) (led tl hdd over 2f out:
wknd qckly) .......... 1¹/₂.15
Blanc Seing (FR) *(MWEasterby)* 5–9-9 TLucas (12) (b: bkwd: sn t.o) .......... ¹/₂.16

**2/1** Majed (IRE), **5/2** LAUREL QUEEN (IRE), **7/1** Skipper to Bilge, **8/1** Yonge Tender, **14/1** Blanc Seing (FR), **16/1** Kay's Dilemma (IRE), Siolfor (USA), Ace Girl, **25/1** Diving (USA), Angel Train, Super Ted, **33/1** Concert Pitch, Magdalene (IRE), Kind Style (IRE), **50/1** Ors. CSF £23.99, Tote £3.70: £1.40 £2.10 £1.40 (£10.40). Laurel (Leisure) Limited (COCKERHAM) bred by E. Lonergan in Ireland. 16 Rn     1m 48.6 (5.9)

**533**     BRIAN OUGHTRED H'CAP (0-80) £2929.50 (£812.00: £388.50)
1m 1f 207y     3-15 (3-18)

(Weights raised 2 lb)
358² **Supertop (52)** *(PWHarris)* 4–8-6 PaulEddery (5) (chsd ldrs: rdn & hdwy 2f out:
led ins fnl f: jst hld on) .......... —1
358⁶ Floating Line **(58)** *(PWigham)* 4–8-12 MWigham (6) (a.p: rdn to ld over 1f out:
hdd ins fnl f: rallied u.p nr fin: jst failed) .......... s.h.2
405 Smoke **(45)** *(JParkes)* 6–7-13 NCarlisle (2) (sn bhd: nt clr run 2f out: hdwy over
1f out: styd on strly fnl f) .......... 1¹/₂.3
368³ Rousitto **(70)** (Fav) *(RHollinshead)* 4–9-10 RCochrane (7) (lw: bhd: hdwy on
outside over 2f out: one pce ins fnl f) .......... s.h.4
Watch Me Go (IRE) **(60)** (v) *(BobJones)* 3–7-10 JQuinn (9) (led & sn clr: hdd
over 1f out: hung rt & no ex) .......... 5.5
456* Tolls Choice (IRE) **(64)** *(MWEasterby)* 3–7-9 (5x) ‡5SMaloney (1) (bhd: hdwy on
outside over 2f out: no imp fnl f) .......... 2¹/₂.6
368 Touch Above **(57)** *(TDBarron)* 6–8-11 AlexGreaves (11) (bit bkwd: hld up &
bhd: nt clr run 2f out: swtchd ins fnl f: n.d) .......... 2¹/₂.7
Who's Tef (IRE) **(62)** *(MHEasterby)* 4–9-2 MBirch (8) (bit bkwd: in tch tl wknd
over 2f out) .......... ³/₄.8
422 Sharquin **(40)** *(MBrittain)* 5–7-8 JLowe (10) (lw: bhd: hdwy & bmpd 2f out: nt
rcvr) .......... 4.9
362 Take One **(52)** *(RRLamb)* 6–8-6 MRoberts (12) (chsd clr ldr: rdn 3f out: sn lost
pl) .......... nk.10
Nobby **(60)** (bl) *(TFairhurst)* 6–8-11 ‡3JFanning (3) (in tch to st) .......... 12.11
368 Vague Dancer **(66)** *(MrsJRRamsden)* 6–9-6 TLucas (4) (lw: chsd ldrs tl wknd 3f
out: hung rt & bmpd 2f out) .......... ¹/₂.12

9/4 Rousitto, 7/2 Tolls Choice (IRE), 5/1 SUPERTOP, 10/1 Vague Dancer(op 9/2), 12/1 Touch Above(op 8/1), Watch Me Go (IRE)(op 20/1), 14/1 Smoke, 16/1 Sharquin, Who's Tef (IRE), 33/1 Ors. CSF £126.78, CT £1,937.77. Tote £6.20: £1.80 £6.00 £2.10 (£74.60). Mrs G. A. Godfrey (BERKHAMSTED) bred by Limestone Stud. 12 Rn
2m 6 (4)
SF—32/37/21/45/7/1

**534**        CHARLES GREIG H'CAP (0-80) £2856.00 (£791.00: £378.00)     **7f 100y**     3-45 (3-46)
(Weights raised 7 lb)

438  **Colossus (69)** (CEBrittain) 4–9-10 MRoberts (7) (lw: a.p: chal over 2f out: led cl home) ........................................................................................ —1

277  Obsidian Grey **(60)** (BAMcMahon) 5–9-1 BRaymond (8) (led tl disp ld over 2f out: styd on gamely: hdd nr fin) ................................................. s.h.2

Chain Shot **(49)** (MHEasterby) 7–8-4 MBirch (10) (dwlt: hdwy & nt clr run over 2f out: rdn & kpt on wl over 1f out) ......................................... 1.3

420*  Euroblake **(58)** (TDBarron) 5–8-13 (5x) AlexGreaves (11) (lw: hld up: nt clr run 2f out: n.m.r fnl f: styd on strly) ................................... nk.4

464²  Doyce **(67)** (Fav) (JEtherington) 3–8-8 NConnorton (4) (lw: chsd ldrs: bdly hmpd 3f out: kpt on u.p appr fnl f) .............................. 1¹/₂.5

438⁵  Doulab's Image **(68)** (JAGlover) 5–9-2 ‡7SWilliams (5) (bhd: hdwy & n.m.r over 1f out: styd on) ....................................................... 1.6

269⁶  Spanish Verdict **(53)** (DenysSmith) 5–8-8 AMunro (3) (in tch: rdn over 1f out: no ex) ........................................................................ hd.7

373³  Blue Grit **(43)** (bl) (MDods) 6–7-12 LCharnock (2) (lw: chsd ldrs: effrt on outside over 2f out: sn rdn & grad lost pl) ......................... 4.8

398  Arabian King **(66)** (MBrittain) 4–9-7 KDarley (6) (hld up: effrt & nt clr run over 2f out: n.d) .................................................................. 1¹/₂.9

Supreme Boy **(63)** (PWHarris) 3–8-4 CRutter (1) (sn chsng ldrs: rn wd appr st: sn lost pl) ....................................................................... 1¹/₂.10

327⁶  Yours Or Mine (IRE) **(45)** (DWChapman) 4–8-0 SWood (9) (swtg: plld hrd: prom tl rdn & wknd fnl 2f) ............................................... 6.11

11/4 Doyce, 100/30 COLOSSUS, 6/1 Euroblake, Doulab's Image, 13/2 Spanish Verdict(10/1—6/1), 12/1 Blue Grit, 14/1 Supreme Boy, Arabian King, Obsidian Grey, 20/1 Chain Shot, 33/1 Yours Or Mine (IRE). CSF £47.23, CT £766.94. Tote £4.40: £1.60 £4.00 £11.80 (£47.50). Capt. M. Lemos (NEWMARKET) bred by Flinders Enterprises S A. 11 Rn
1m 34.3 (4.1)
SF—28/18/3/11/1/6

**535**        GEORGE CULLINGTON H'CAP (0-70) £3027.50 (£840.00: £402.50)     **5f**     4-15 (4-17)
(Weights raised 4 lb)

472*  **Double Blue (72)** (Fav) (MJohnston) 3–10-0 (7x) MRoberts (5) (lw: a.p: rdn & edgd lft over 1f out: styd on wl to ld nr fin) .................... —1

Absolutely Nuts **(68)** (BAMcMahon) 3–9-10 BRaymond (4) (bit bkwd: led: rdn over 1f out: hdd & no ex nr fin) ................................ ³/₄.2

421²  Last Straw **(33)** (AWJones) 4–8-0 JQuinn (8) (a chsng ldrs: rdn & ev ch over 1f out: kpt on) ........................................................ ³/₄.3

B Grade **(43)** (JBalding) 7–8-3 ‡7ClaireBalding (9) (swtchd outside & hdwy wl over 1f out: nt qckn ins fnl f) ................................... 2.4

407  Here Comes a Star **(53)** (JMCarr) 4–9-6 SMorris (12) (hdwy ¹/₂-wy: styd on wl ins fnl f) ....................................................................... hd.5

324⁵  Don't Run Me Over **(46)** (BCMorgan) 3–8-2 JLowe (14) (plld hrd early: effrt & bmpd wl over 1f out: styd on same pce u.p) ........... hd.6

483⁵  The Right Time **(51)** (bl) (JParkes) 7–9-4 NConnorton (6) (lw: prom: carried lft & wknd over 1f out) .......................................... 2¹/₂.7

452²  Fighter Squadron **(50)** (v) (JAGlover) 3–8-6 JFortune (3) (nvr trbld ldrs) ............. ¹/₂.8

407  Par de Luxe **(37)** (bl) (BWMurray) 5–8-1 ‡3JFanning (13) (stumbled leaving stalls: nvr nr to chal) ................................................... hd.9

483⁴  Minizen Music (IRE) **(39)** (MBrittain) 4–8-6 KDarley (7) (chsd ldrs: bmpd wl over 1f out: sn wknd) .......................................... ¹/₂.10

407  Lady's Mantle (USA) **(43)** (RBastiman) 8–8-8 ‡7HBastimAn (11) (bit bkwd: swtg: mid div whn bmpd wl over 1f out: sn wknd) ........ ¹/₂.11

455⁴  In a Whirl (USA) **(49)** (DWChapman) 4–9-2 SWood (1) (lw: spd over 3f) ........ nk.12

496*  Strip Cartoon (IRE) **(59)** (bl) (SRBowring) 4–9-5 (7x) ‡7MHarris (10) (lw: chsd ldrs: rdn ¹/₂-wy: grad lost pl) ............................... nk.13

Miss Siham (IRE) **(64)** (JBalding) 3–9-6 AClark (2) (bkwd: dwlt: a in rr) .......... 7.14

8/13 DOUBLE BLUE, 17/2 Don't Run Me Over(op 7/1), 11/1 Strip Cartoon (IRE), Last Straw(op 7/1), 12/1 Fighter Squadron, 16/1 Minizen Music (IRE), Par de Luxe, 20/1 Absolutely Nuts, The Right Time, In a Whirl (USA), Lady's Mantle (USA), 33/1 Ors. CSF £17.88, CT £94.23. Tote £1.60: £1.40 £3.40 £2.20 (£19.70). Mr R. W. Huggins (MIDDLEHAM) bred by The Queen. 14 Rn
65.4 sec (3.9)
SF—51/44/17/12/28/23

**536**    CAPTAIN STORIE STKS (Mdn 3 & 4-Y.O.F) £2186.80 (£604.80: £288.40)
1m 3f 216y      4-45 (4-46)

| | | |
|---|---|---|
| **Miss Plum** *(Fav)* *(HRACecil)* 3-8-3 WRyan (1) (lw: mde all: styd on strly fnl 2f: unchal) | —1 | |
| 425³ Kirsten *(WJarvis)* 3-8-3 AMunro (6) (lw: prom: chsd wnr fnl 5f: no imp fnl 2f) | 6.2 | |
| Nina's Chocolates (USA) *(CEBrittain)* 3-8-3 MRoberts (3) (lengthy: unf: chsd wnr tl outpcd 5f out: rdn 3f out: styd on same pce) | 8.3 | |
| Docket (USA) *(BHanbury)* 4-9-10 BRaymond (2) (unf: scope: bit bkwd: bhd: effrt over 3f out: sn wl outpcd) | 5.4 | |
| Wedding Vow (USA) *(JHMGosden)* 4-9-10 RCochrane (4) (b.hind: lengthy: unf: bit bkwd: pushed along 5f out: sme hdwy ent st: sn btn) | 5.5 | |
| Motley *(WGMTurner)* 4-9-5 ‡STSprake (5) (hdwy to chase ldrs 5f out: wknd over 2f out) | 6.6 | |

8/11 MISS PLUM, 9/4 Kirsten, 8/1 Wedding Vow (USA), 10/1 Nina's Chocolates (USA)(op 6/1), 16/1 Docket (USA), 50/1 Motley. CSF £2.91, Tote £1.80: £1.30 £1.50 (£1.90). Mr Edward St George (NEWMARKET) bred by E. G. P. St George. 6 Rn    2m 36.7 (5.1)
SF—13/1/–/–/–/–

T/Plpt: £49.90 (88.15 Tckts).      O'R

## 382a—LONGCHAMP (R-H)

### Thursday, April 16th [Good to soft]
Going Allowance: 0.60 sec per fur (Y)

**537a**    PRIX DE GUICHE (Gp 3) (3-Y.O.C) £20639.00    1m 1f 55y (Grande)

| | |
|---|---|
| **Homme de Loi (IRE)** *(France)* 3-9-2 TJarnet | 1 |
| Kitwood (USA) *(France)* 3-9-2 MBoutin (fin 3rd, ¾l: plcd 2nd) | 2 |
| Luazur (FR) *(France)* 3-9-2 FHead (fin 4th, hd: plcd 3rd) | 3 |
| Calling Collect (USA) *(France)* 3-9-2 DBoeuf (fin 2nd, ½l: disq: plcd 4th) | 4 |

Tote 3.20f: 1.80f 3.50f (SF: 18.80f). Mr Paul de Moussac (A. Fabre,FRANCE) bred by Mrs E. Mulhern in Ireland. 6 Rn    2m 0.6 (7.3)
SF—73/71/69/68

## AQUEDUCT (L-H)

### Saturday, April 18th [Good]

**538a**    WOOD MEMORIAL STKS (Grade 1) (3-Y.O) £160428.00    1m 1f (dirt)

| | |
|---|---|
| **Devil His Due (USA)** *(America)* 3-9-0 MSmith | —1 |
| West by West (USA) *(America)* 3-9-0 J-LSamyn | 1.2 |
| 347² ROKEBY *(IABalding)* 3-9-0 JRVelazquez | 2.3 |
| Snappy Landing (USA) *(America)* 3-9-0 KDesormeaux | nk.4 |

Tote 7.60 (1-2) 5.40 22.20 (1-2-3) 4.60 13.80 6.00 (Perfecta (2 Dol) 209.80). Lion Crest Stable (H.Allen Jerkens,AMERICA) bred by Peter E Blum in USA. 12 Rn    1m 49.3

## 282a—LEOPARDSTOWN (L-H)

### Saturday, April 18th [Good to soft]
Going Allowance: St: 0.50 sec per fur; Rnd: 0.70 sec per fur (Y)

**539a**    LEOPARDSTOWN 2,000 GUINEAS TRIAL (Stks) (listed race) (3-Y.O.C) £8280.00    7f

| | |
|---|---|
| **Portico (USA)** *(Ireland)* 3-8-10 LPiggott | —1 |
| Brief Truce (USA) *(Ireland)* 3-8-10 MJKinane | nk.2 |
| Polar Wind *(Ireland)* 3-8-10 JPMurtagh | 8.3 |

Tote £1.40 (£2.80). Mrs M.V.O'Brien (D.K.Weld,IRELAND) bred by Ballydoyle Stud in USA. 4 Rn    1m 33.4 (8.4)
SF—44/43/19

**540a**    LEOPARDSTOWN 1,000 GUINEAS TRIAL (Stks) (listed race) (3-Y.O.F) £8280.00    7f

| | |
|---|---|
| **Gdansk's Honour (USA)** *(Ireland)* 3-8-10 CRoche | —1 |
| Track Twenty Nine (IRE) *(Ireland)* 3-8-10 WJO'Connor (fin 3rd, 4l: plcd 2nd) | 2 |
| Khanata (USA) *(Ireland)* 3-8-10 JPMurtagh (fin 2nd, ½l: disq: plcd 3rd) | 3 |
| Misako Togo *(Ireland)* 3-9-1 PShanahan | 6.4 |

*Stewards Enquiry: Khanata (USA) disq. (interference to Track Twenty Nine (IRE)).*

Tote £1.40: £1.10 £2.80 (£3.60). Mr Henry De Kwiakowski (J.S.Bolger,IRELAND) bred by Kennelot Stables Ltd in USA. 6 Rn
1m 32.5 (7.5)
SF—57/56/44/33

## CARLISLE (R-H)
### Friday, April 24th [Good to soft, Good patches]
Going Allowance: 5f-6f: 0.65 sec (Y); Rest: 0.40 sec per fur (G)　　　　Wind: str half against

Stalls: high

**541**　　　PEREGRINE FALCON H'CAP (0-70) £2363.20 (£655.20: £313.60)　　**5f 207y** 2-15 (2-16)

516* **Penny Hasset (54)** (MWEasterby) 4-9-3 TLucas (11) (lw: sn chsng ldrs: hdwy on ins to ld jst ins fnl f: edgd lft u.p: styd on) ............ —1
　　Coolaba Prince (IRE) **(53)** (FHLee) 3-7-13 ‡5NKennedy (4) (bit bkwd: w ldrs: rdn over 2f out: styd on wl nr fin) ............ nk.2
359* Twilight Falls **(52)** (Fav) (MJCamacho) 7-9-1 NConnorton (14) (lw: sn chsng ldrs: rdn ½-wy: sn wl outpcd: styd on strly fnl f) ............ ½.3
3575 Educated Pet **(44)** (MJohnston) 3-7-9 JLowe (1) (lw: w ldrs: led over 2f out tl jst ins fnl f: sn wknd) ............ 3.4
325 Crail Harbour **(61)** (PCHaslam) 6-9-10 DMcKeown (12) (bhd tl styd on wl fnl 2f) 3.5
351* Ain'tlifelikethat **(54)** (bl) (TJNaughton) 5-9-0 ‡3JFanning (2) (s.s: hdwy on bit ½-wy: ev ch whn rdn, wnt rt & wknd over 1f out) ............ hd.6
4492 Densben **(57)** (DenysSmith) 8-9-6 KFallon (3) (lw: sn bhd: hdwy u.p over 1f out: nvr rchd ldrs) ............ 2½.7
398 Orient Air **(60)** (bl) (TDBarron) 4-9-2 ‡7VHalliday (6) (dwlt: effrt ½-wy: n.d) ............ 10.8
265 Oyston's Life **(54)** (bl) (JBerry) 3-8-5 JCarroll (10) (s.i.s: hdwy & prom ½-wy: sn wknd) ............ 1½.9
264 Damaaz (IRE) **(32)** (v) (JSWainwright) 4-7-9 LCharnock (13) (led tl over 2f out: sn wknd) ............ 2.10
496 Kabera **(33)** (DWChapman) 4-7-10 SWood (7) (bhd fr ½-wy) ............ 2.11
285 Jovial Kate (USA) **(43)** (BEllison) 5-8-6 NCarlisle (9) (chsd ldrs tl wknd 2f out) s.h.12
3592 Chaplins Club (USA) **(50)** (bl) (DWChapman) 12-8-13 KDarley (5) (sn bhd & drvn along) ............ 3.13
420 Revel **(42)** (bl) (LLungo) 4-8-5 JQuinn (8) (b.off hind: chsd ldrs tl lost pl over 2f out: sn bhd) ............ 5.14

**6/4** Twilight Falls, **9/2** PENNY HASSET(3/1—5/1), **11/2** Densben, **10/1** Crail Harbour, Educated Pet, Chaplins Club (USA), **11/1** Ain'tlifelikethat, **12/1** Oyston's Life(op 8/1), **14/1** Orient Air, **16/1** Coolaba Prince (IRE), **20/1** Jovial Kate (USA), **25/1** Revel, **33/1** Kabera, **50/1** Damaaz (IRE). CSF £78.44, CT £152.60. Tote £4.80: £1.40 £6.30 £1.60 (£167.70). Mrs Anne Henson (SHERIFF HUTTON) bred by Mrs Anne Henson. 14 Rn
1m 18.6 (6.3)
SF—55/36/50/18/35/24

**542**　　　KESTREL CLAIMING STKS　　£2206.40 (£610.40: £291.20)　　**5f 207y**　　2-45 (2-55)

2944 **Dokkha Oyston (IRE) (77)** (JBerry) 4-8-11 JCarroll (3) (lw: trckd ldr: led over 2f out: clr over 1f out: rdn & jst hld on) ............ —1
3112 Never so Sure **(79)** (Fav) (MrsJRRamsden) 4-8-8 ‡7JWeaver (6) (lw: trckd ldrs: effrt & rdn over 1f out: edgd lft: styd on wl nr fin) ............ hd.2
359 Foxes Diamond **(36)** (BEllison) 4-7-10 NCarlisle (2) (reard s: hdwy over 2f out: n.m.r: kpt on u.p fnl f) ............ 2.3
　　Yes **(50)** (DTThom) 4-8-4 JLowe (8) (hld up & bhd: effrt over 2f out: nvr nr to chal) ............ 6.4
　　Stand At Ease **(39)** (WStorey) 7-8-5 SWebster (5) (b: led tl over 2f out: grad wknd) ............ 3.5
　　Bold Cookie **(MissSEHall)** 4-7-10 JQuinn (9) (bit bkwd: unruly & bolted bef s: hdwy ½-wy: no imp whn n.m.r 1f out: eased) ............ s.h.6
421 Tigani **(86)** (bl) (DWChapman) 6-8-11 SWood (7) (chsd ldrs tl rdn & wknd 2f out) ¾.7
4206 Nevada Mix **(51)** (MissLAPerratt) 8-8-4 ‡3JFanning (1) (s.i.s: a bhd & sn drvn along) ............ 3.8
449 Victoria Road (IRE) **(79)** (MHEasterby) 4-9-1 MBirch (4) (trckd ldrs tl grad wknd fnl 2f) ............ 3.9

**Evens** Never so Sure(op 6/4), **9/4** DOKKHA OYSTON (IRE), **9/1** Tigani, **11/1** Bold Cookie, **12/1** Victoria Road (IRE)(op 8/1), **20/1** Stand At Ease, Yes, Nevada Mix, **33/1** Foxes Diamond. CSF £5.06, Tote £2.90: £1.20 £1.10 £6.30 (£2.50). Mr Murray Grubb (COCKERHAM) bred by R. Oyston and Partners in Ireland. 9 Rn; Never so Sure clmd H O'Donnell £10,800
1m 19.2 (6.9)
SF—37/33/13/–/–/–

**543**     E.B.F. BUZZARD STKS (Mdn 2-Y.O) £2499.50 (£692.00: £330.50)    **5f**    3-20 (3-20)

     **Tarnside Rosal** *(JEtherington)* 8-9 TLucas (4) (neat: scope: rn green & sn
         pushed along: hdwy ½-wy: led 1f out: r.o wl) ..................... —1
     General Brooks (IRE) **(Fav)** *(JBerry)* 9-0 JCarroll (5) (str: neat: chsd ldrs: rdn to
         ld 1f out: sn hdd & no ch w wnr) ................................ 3.2
   396 Penny Banger (IRE) *(MJohnston)* 8-9 DMcKeown (2) (lw: led tl over 1f out) ....... 4.3
   352³ Heathyards Gem *(RHollinshead)* 8-9 BRaymond (6) (lw: w ldr tl wknd 2f out)   2½.4
     Jarabosky *(MWEllerby)* 9-0 SMorris (1) (neat: unf: bit bkwd: swvd lft s: a
         outpcd) ........................................................ 1.5
   361 Mrs Dawson *(DrJDScargill)* 8-9 JQuinn (3) (unruly & reard s: a wl bhd) ........... 25.6

**15/8** General Brooks (IRE)(5/4—2/1), **9/4** TARNSIDE ROSAL(3/1—2/1), **11/4** Heathyards Gem(op 7/4), **8/1**
Mrs Dawson, Penny Banger, (IRE), **33/1** Jarabosky. CSF £6.99, Tote £4.50: £2.10 £1.40 (£9.00). Mrs Ann
Lockhart (MALTON) bred by R. G. Percival. 6 Rn             67.1 sec (6.9)
                                              SF—23/16/–/–/–/–

**544**     LEVY BOARD STKS (Mdn 3-Y.O.C & G) £2049.60 (£565.60: £268.80)
       **6f 206y**                                                    3-50 (3-51)

   441 **Desired Guest** **(Fav)** *(MRStoute)* 9-0 PD'Arcy (3) (chsd ldr: effrt over 2f out: led
         over 1f out: sn clr: eased nr fin) ................................ —1
   457 Yaakum **(65)** *(BHanbury)* 9-0 BRaymond (4) (lw: reminders early: set str pce &
         sn clr: wknd & hdd over 1f out) ................................. 7.2
   415 Bantel Brigadier **(45)** *(RAllan)* 9-0 SWebster (2) (sn wl outpcd) ........................ 15.3

**1/5** DESIRED GUEST, **9/2** Yaakum, **25/1** Bantel Brigadier. CSF £1.38, Tote £1.10 (£1.10). Mrs V. Hue-Williams
(NEWMARKET) bred by Mrs & Exors of the late Col F. R. Hue-Williams. 3 Rn      1m 35.4 (10.2)

**545**     GOLDEN EAGLE H'CAP (3-Y.O) (0-80) £2382.80 (£660.80: £316.40)
       **7f 214y**                                                    4-20 (4-25)

                              (Weights raised 3 lb)
     **Trafalgar Boy (USA) (77)** *(JEtherington)* 9-0 ‡7JWeaver (7) (h.d.w: lw: trckd
         ldrs: led 1f out: hld on wl u.p nr fin) ........................... —1
   353* Karamoja **(70)** **(Fav)** *(NAGraham)* 9-0 JQuinn (1) (lw: trckd ldrs: effrt over 2f out:
         r.o wl u.p fnl f: nt qckn nr fin) ................................ ½.2
   401 Personal Hazard **(73)** *(MHEasterby)* 9-3 MBirch (6) (led: qcknd over 4f out: hdd
         1f out: kpt on wl) ............................................. 1½.3
   401 Lowlands Boy **(64)** *(TFairhurst)* 8-5 ‡3JFanning (3) (lw: hld up: effrt & n.m.r over
         2f out: nvr able to chal) ....................................... 7.4
   370 Coastal Express **(60)** *(EWeymes)* 8-4 DaleGibson (4) (trckd ldrs: outpcd ½-wy:
         n.d after) ..................................................... 2½.5
   370⁵ Nicely Thanks (USA) **(73)** *(TDBarron)* 9-3 AlexGreaves (2) (lw: sn bhd: effrt
         ½-wy: n.d) ................................................... s.h.6
   366² Akura (IRE) **(58)** *(MJohnston)* 8-2 RPElliott (5) (trckd ldrs tl lost pl over 2f out) 10.7

**2/1** Karamoja(6/4—9/4), **5/2** Nicely Thanks (USA), **6/1** Lowlands Boy, **7/1** Akura (IRE), TRAFALGAR BOY
(USA), **10/1** Personal Hazard, **16/1** Coastal Express. CSF £20.84, Tote £10.80: £3.10 £1.20 (£11.20). Mr W. L.
Armitage (MALTON) bred by R. Alex Rankin & John K. Sanderlin in USA. 7 Rn      1m 46.2 (7.5)
                                              SF—36/34/32/–/–/–

**546**     SPARROW HAWK MEDIAN AUCTION STKS (Mdn 3-Y.O.F) £2369.30 (£654.80: £311.90)
       **7f 214y**                                                    4-55 (4-55)

     **Ma Bella Luna** **(Fav)** *(JLDunlop)* 8-11 BRaymond (3) (lw: mde all: clr over 1f
         out: easily) .................................................. —1
   489⁴ Stoproveritate **(57)** *(SGNorton)* 8-11 LCharnock (1) (effrt 3f out: styd on u.p fnl
         f: no ch w wnr) ............................................... 10.2
   348⁴ Allmosa *(TJNaughton)* 8-8 ‡3JFanning (2) (lw: w wnr: rdn over 2f out: wknd over
         1f out) ....................................................... 2½.3
     Maid of Ice *(DrJDScargill)* 8-11 JQuinn (5) (bit bkwd: chsd ldrs: drvn along
         ½-wy: wknd over 2f out) ....................................... 6.4
   280⁴ My Grain **(40)** *(RHollinshead)* 8-11 KDarley (4) (swtg: lost pl 5f out: sn bhd) .... 15.5

**8/13** MA BELLA LUNA, **7/2** Allmosa, **13/2** Stoproveritate, **10/1** Maid of Ice(op 6/1), **20/1** My Grain. CSF £4.87,
Tote £1.70: £1.10 £2.40 (£6.00). Mr J. L. Dunlop (ARUNDEL) bred by J. Dunlop. 5 Rn    1m 48 (9.3)
                                              SF—5/–/4/–/–

**547**     MERLIN H'CAP (3-Y.O) (0-70) £2402.40 (£666.40: £319.20)    **1½m**    5-25 (5-27)
                               (Weights raised 1 lb)
   366³ **Eurotwist (51)** *(TDBarron)* 8-3 AlexGreaves (4) (lw: hld up: smooth hdwy 3f
         out: qcknd to ld wl over 1f out: sn clr: easily) ................... —1

346* Perforate (60) *(SirMarkPrescott)* 8-12 MBirch (8) (b.hind: lw: led tl hdd wl over 1f out: kpt on: no ch w wnr) .......... 10.2

268² Salu (65) *(JEtherington)* 8-10 ‡7JWeaver (4) (lw: trckd ldrs: effrt over 2f out: r.o one pce) .......... ¾.4.3

457² Thor Power (IRE) (49) (v) *(DTThom)* 8-1 JQuinn (3) (lw: w ldr tl rdn & wknd over 1f out) .......... 7.4

296 Escadaro (USA) (47) *(SGNorton)* 7-13 LCharnock (5) (sn bhd & drvn along: reminders ½-wy: kpt on fnl 3f: n.d) .......... 1½.5

376² Saif Al Adil (IRE) (69) *(BHanbury)* 9-7 BRaymond (6) (lw: effrt & drvn along 5f out: hung rt u.p: nvr rchd ldrs) .......... 3.6

457* Firefighter (74) *(RHollinshead)* 9-5 (5x) ‡7EHusband (9) (lw: trckd ldrs: effrt over 3f out: wknd over 2f out) .......... 2½.7

Litho Bold Flasher (57) *(WJPearce)* 8-9 TLucas (7) (bit bkwd: effrt 4f out: lost pl over 2f out) .......... 1½.8

330 Timurid (FR) (67) (Fav) *(JLDunlop)* 9-5 DMcKeown (1) (lw: hdwy 8f out: outpcd & lost pl 5f out: sn btn) .......... 2½.9

7/4 Timurid (FR), 6/1 Perforate, Thor Power (IRE), 13/2 Saif Al Adil (IRE), 7/1 Salu, 11/1 Firefighter, 12/1 EUROTWIST, 14/1 Escadaro (USA)(op 50/1), 25/1 Litho Bold Flasher. CSF £75.11, CT £496.39. Tote £10.90: £2.90 £3.40 £4.20 (£13.90). Mr W. G. Swiers (THIRSK) bred by Waresley Park Stud Ltd. 9 Rn  2m 43.4 (13.9)
T/Plpt: £6.30 (201 Tckts).                                                                                    WG

## SANDOWN  (R-H)

**Friday, April 24th [Good becoming Good to soft]**

Going Allowance: 0.25 sec per fur (G)                                         Wind: mod across

Stalls: 1st & 3rd low, remainder high

**548**  GARDNER MERCHANT STKS (Mdn 2-Y.O.F) £2343.00 (£648.00: £309.00)
5f 6y                                                                         2-00 (2-04)

**Risk Me's Girl** *(RHannon)* 8-11 WRSwinburn (7) (unf: scope: led 3f out: r.o wl) —1

Holly Golightly *(RHannon)* 8-11 MRoberts (1) (cmpt: a.p: ev ch fnl f: r.o) .......... ¾.2

Princess Oberon (IRE) (Fav) *(MBell)* 8-11 MHills (8) (unf: a.p: ev ch fnl f: r.o) .. nk.3

Margaret's Gift *(JBerry)* 8-11 PatEddery (4) (cmpt: lw: hld up: shkn u.p over 1f out: nt qckn) .......... 3.4

Sedgy's Sister *(PJJones)* 8-11 AMcGlone (3) (unf: scope: hdwy over 1f out: one pce fnl f) .......... 1½.5

Full Exposure *(WJarvis)* 8-11 MTebbutt (2) (neat: no hdwy fnl 2f) .......... hd.6

Poco Pierna (IRE) *(WCarter)* 8-11 LDettori (6) (lt-f: led 2f: wknd 2f out) .......... 4.7

Brief Habit (IRE) *(MRChannon)* 8-11 BRouse (5) (leggy: spd 3f) .......... nk.8

255² Always Risky *(PAKelleway)* 8-11 CAsmussen (10) (lw: prom 3f) .......... 1.9

352 Easy Touch *(MDIUsher)* 8-11 CRutter (9) (bhd fnl 3f) .......... 4.10

5/2 Princess Oberon (IRE), 9/2 Always Risky(3/1—11/2), 5/1 Margaret's Gift(op 9/4), Holly Golightly, 12/1 Brief Habit (IRE), RISK ME'S GIRL(5/1—14/1), 16/1 Poco Pierna (IRE)(op 8/1), Full Exposure(op 10/1), 33/1 Ors. CSF £63.25, Tote £15.60: £2.90 £1.90 £1.40 (£43.90). Roldvale Limited (MARLBOROUGH) bred by Mrs J. Everitt. 10 Rn                                                   64.19 sec (4.69)
SF—28/25/24/12/6/5

**549**  HARVESTER GRADUATION STKS (3-Y.O) £4081.00 (£911.00 each: £277.00)
1m 14y                                                                        2-35 (2-37)

441² **Hamas (IRE)** *(PTWalwyn)* 8-11 WCarson (4) (4th st: led over 2f out: pushed out) .......... —1

443⁴ Distinct Thatcher (USA) (104) (Fav) *(RHannon)* 9-5 PatEddery (9) (3rd st: ev ch 2f out: hrd rdn: nt qckn) .......... 2½.2

Jitterbugging (100) *(BWHills)* 9-2 DHolland (3) (5th st: hdwy on ins & hrd rdn over 1f out: nt qckn fnl f) .......... d.h.2

Binkhaldoun (USA) *(HThomsonJones)* 9-2 RHills (1) (b: bkwd: 6th st: hdwy over 2f out: rdn over 1f out: sn btn) .......... ½.4

404³ Big Blue *(CEBrittain)* 8-11 MRoberts (7) (2nd st: led 3f out: sn hdd & btn) ....... 2½.5

Sadler's Way *(GLewis)* 8-11 PaulEddery (2) (bit bkwd: nvr nrr) .......... 3½.6

Sir Oliver (IRE) *(RJHodges)* 8-11 RCochrane (6) (a bhd) .......... 4.7

Cannonale (IRE) *(JPearce)* 8-11 WNewnes (8) (led 5f) .......... 25.8

11/8 Distinct Thatcher (USA), 5/2 HAMAS (IRE), 7/1 Big Blue, 8/1 Binkhaldoun (USA)(op 5/1), Jitterbugging, 33/1 Sir Oliver (IRE), 50/1 Sadler's Way, 100/1 Cannonale (IRE). CSF wD T £2.92, w J £9.93, Tote £3.20: £1.30 DT £1.10 J £1.70 (w DT £1.30, w J £6.90). Mr Hamdan Al-Maktoum (LAMBOURN) bred by Hullin Co N V (International) in Ireland. 8 Rn                                                  1m 44.23 (5.03)
SF—52/52/48/43/30/19

**550**   FORTE POSTHOUSE H'CAP (0-105) £4614.00 (£1392.00: £676.00: £318.00)
5f 6y

3-05 (3-12)

480* **Olifantsfontein (74)** (bl) (Fav) (RSimpson) 4–8-3 (6x) WRyan (5) (mde all: r.o wl) —1
236⁶ Terrhars (IRE) **(99)** (RHannon) 4–9-9 ‡⁵RPerham (6) (chsd wnr: hrd rdn over 1f
out: r.o) ................................................................................................ ¾.2
386² Macfarlane **(78)** (MJFetherston-Godley) 4–8-7 WCarson (20) (hdwy & hrd rdn
2f out: nt qckn fnl f) ....................................................................... 2½.3
386 Misdemeanours Girl (IRE) **(69)** (MRChannon) 4–7-7⁽⁵⁾ ‡⁵BDoyle (16) (hdwy 2f
out: ev ch 1f out: nt qckn) ............................................................... ¾.4
414* Plain Fact **(81)** (SirMarkPrescott) 7–8-10 (6x) GDuffield (3) (a.p: nt qckn fnl f) ... 7½.5
Green Dollar **(87)** (EAWheeler) 9–8-9 ‡⁷DHarrison (1) (bit bkwd: nvr nrr) ............ 2.6
386 Love Legend **(86)** (DWPArbuthnot) 7–9-1 AMunro (10) (nrst fin) .................... 1½.7
Bold Lez **(97)** (MJHaynes) 5–9-12 JWilliams (15) (nvr nr to chal) ..................... ¾.8
392 Hard to Figure **(95)** (RJHodges) 6–9-10 TQuinn (2) (nvr trbld ldrs) ................ nk.9
465⁵ El Yasaf (IRE) **(86)** (GHEden) 4–9-1 DHolland (11) (gd spd over 3f) ............... 1.10
386 Aughfad **(81)** (v) (TCasey) 6–8-10 MRoberts (4) (lw: n.d) ............................ ¾.11
Lucedeo **(85)** (JLSpearing) 8–8-7 ‡⁷AGarth (8) (bit bkwd: s.s: n.d) ................ hd.12
480² Ski Captain **(67)** (PHowling) 8–7-7⁽³⁾ ‡³FNorton (14) (n.d) ......................... 1½.13
Ashtina **(73)** (RJHodges) 7–8-2 AMcGlone (12) (gd spd 3f) .......................... 1.14
Amber Mill **(91)** (JBerry) 4–9-6 PatEddery (19) (gd spd 3f) ......................... ½.15
Beau Venture (USA) **(83)** (FHLee) 4–8-12 GCarter (18) (n.d) ........................ 2.16
Rhythmic Dancer **(80)** (JLSpearing) 4–8-9 RFox (17) (swtg: n.d) .................. 1½.17
Masnun (USA) **(92)** (RJO'Sullivan) 7–9-4 ‡³DBiggs (13) (n.d) ....................... s.h.18
Mu-Arrik **(64)** (DAWilson) 4–7-0 ‡⁷CHawksley (7) (n.d) .............................. s.h.19
386 Choir Practice **(89)** (WJHaggas) 5–9-4 LPiggott (9) (bolted bef s: n.d) ........... 1.20
LONG HANDICAP: Misdemeanours Girl (IRE) 7-6, Ski Captain 7-3, Mu-Arrik 6-12.

6/1 Olifantsfontein. 7/1 Macfarlane, 8/1 Plain Fact, 9/1 El Yasaf (IRE), Amber Mill, 10/1 Aughfad, 12/1
Terrhars (IRE), 14/1 Choir Practice, 16/1 Love Legend, 20/1 Bold Lez, Ski Captain, 25/1 Misdemeanours Girl
(IRE), Hard to Figure, Lucedeo, Beau Venture (USA), Ashtina, 33/1 Rhythmic Dancer, Masnun (USA), Green
Dollar, 100/1 Mu-Arrik. CSF £69.43, CT £478.16. Tote £7.20: £2.30 £3.40 £1.40 £5.40 (£105.60). Mr Trevor
Painting (FOXHILL) bred by Whitsbury Manor Stud. 20 Rn
                                                                                         62.17 sec (2.67)
                                                                                    SF—61/78/52/35/50/41/41

**551**   FORTE MILE (Stks) (Gp 2) £39885.00 (£14863.75: £7086.88: £3029.37)
1m 14y

3-40 (3-45)

392* **Rudimentary (USA)** (Fav) (HRACecil) 4–9-0 SCauthen (4) (lw: 5th st: led ins fnl
f: drvn out) ....................................................................................... —1
Zoman (USA) (PFICole) 5–9-4 AMunro (10) (lw: w ldr: 2nd st: led 3f out tl ins fnl
f: r.o) .............................................................................................. 1½.2
436⁵ Desert Sun (HRACecil) 4–9-0 PatEddery (3) (hdwy over 2f out: hrd rdn over 1f
out: nt qckn fnl f) ............................................................................. 1.3
Lovealoch (IRE) (MBell) 4–8-11 MHills (9) (4th st: ntr over 2f out: r.o one pce) ¾.4
436³ Flashfoot (IABalding) 4–9-0 RCochrane (11) (lw: 6th st: no hdwy fnl 2f) ......... 3.5
Military Fashion (LMCumani) 6–9-0 LDettori (2) (nvr nrr) ............................. 3.6
Environment Friend (JRFanshawe) 4–9-0 GDuffield (1) (bit bkwd: 7th st: nvr nr
to chal) ......................................................................................... 1½.7
Fair Average (HCandy) 4–9-0 WNewnes (6) (nvr nr ldrs) ............................. 1½.8
Mukaddamah (USA) (PTWalwyn) 4–9-4 WCarson (7) (swtg: 3rd st: ev ch over
2f out: sn wknd) ............................................................................. 1.9
382a Sikeston (USA) (CEBrittain) 6–9-6 MRoberts (12) (led tl wknd 3f out) ............. 3.10
Enharmonic (USA) (LordHuntingdon) 5–9-0 WRyan (5) (a bhd) .................... 1½.11

2/1 Rudimentary (USA), 7/2 Desert Sun, 9/1 Flashfoot, 10/1 Sikeston (USA), Mukaddamah (USA)(op 6/1),
12/1 Zoman (USA), Environment Friend(op 8/1), 16/1 Lovealoch (IRE), 25/1 Military Fashion, 33/1 Ors. CSF
£23.43, Tote £2.90: £1.20 £2.70 £2.00 (£12.00). Lord Howard de Walden (NEWMARKET) bred by Lord Howard
de Walden in USA. 11 Rn
                                                                                         1m 42.09 (2.89)
                                                                                    SF—86/85/78/73/67/58/59

**552**   AMERICAN EXPRESS H'CAP (0-100) £4328.00 (£1304.00: £632.00: £296.00)
1¾m

4-10 (4-13)

299 **Hello My Darling (IRE) (65)** (WRMuir) 4–7-6 ‡³FNorton (1) (mde all: drvn clr 3f
out: hld on wl) ............................................................................... —1
388³ Satin Lover **(81)** (Fav) (RAkehurst) 4–8-11 SCauthen (2) (lw: hdwy & 5th st:
chsd wnr fnl 2f: r.o wl ins fnl f) ....................................................... ½.2
390 Lift and Load (USA) **(94)** (RHannon) 5–9-12 MRoberts (7) (swtg: hdwy & 4th st:
r.o one pce fnl 2f) ........................................................................... 4.3

Star Player **(88)** *(RJBaker)* 6–9-6 RCochrane (6) (nvr nrr) ................................. s.h.**4**
Chucklestone **(61)** *(JSKing)* 9-7-7 GBardwell (4) (3rd & rdn st: one pce fnl 3f) .. 6.**5**
388 Honey Dancer **(61)** *(MissAJWhitfield)* 8–7-7 NAdams (3) (lw: 2nd st: wknd 2f out) 3.**6**
405² Comstock **(85)** *(JGFitzGerald)* 5–9-3 WCarson (8) (lw: prom 10f) ..................... ¾.**7**
Mrs Barton (IRE) **(70)** *(BWHills)* 4–8-0 DHolland (5) (a wl bhd) ............................ ¾.**8**
229 Run High **(66)** *(PMitchell)* 9–7-9⁽⁵⁾ ‡³SO'Gorman (9) (lw: 6th st: wknd 3f out) ..... 5.**9**
LONG HANDICAP: Chucklestone 7-4, Honey Dancer 7-3, Run High 7-5.

**11/8** Satin Lover, **7/2** Comstock, **6/1** Lift and Load (USA), **15/2** Mrs Barton (IRE)(12/1—7/1), **10/1** HELLO MY
DARLING (IRE), **12/1** Star Player, **33/1** Run High, **40/1** Honey Dancer, **50/1** Chucklestone. CSF £22.81, CT
£83.75. Tote £10.20: £1.90 £1.30 £1.90 (£9.70). Fayzad Thoroughbred Limited (LAMBOURN) bred by
Swettenham Stud in Ireland. 9 Rn                                                      3m 7.60 (12.90)

**553** FORTE AIRPORT SERVICES STKS (Mdn 3-Y.O.F) £2469.00 (£684.00: £327.00)
1¼m 7y                                                                4-45 (4-50)

**User Friendly** *(CEBrittain)* 8-7 GDuffield (14) (leggy: scope: gd hdwy over 2f
out: led over 1f out: drvn out) ................................................ —**1**
Shirley Valentine *(HRACecil)* 8-11 PatEddery (6) (2nd st: led 3f out tl over 1f out:
hrd rdn & r.o) ..................................................................... 2½.**2**
Jood (USA) **(Fav)** *(MRStoute)* 8-11 WRSwinburn (7) (lw: 5th st: ev ch over 1f
out: nt qckn) ...................................................................... 2½.**3**
Party Cited (USA) **(105)** *(PAKelleway)* 8-11 CAsmussen (5) (3rd st: ev ch 2f out:
wknd fnl f) ......................................................................... 6.**4**
Marabou *(LMCumani)* 8-7 LDettori (10) (w'like: scope: nvr nrr) .............. 5.**5**
Donia (USA) *(PFICole)* 8-7 AMunro (8) (w'like: scope: lw: 6th st: no hdwy) ...... ¾.**6**
Barga *(DRCEIsworth)* 8-7 JWilliams (11) (unf: scope: bit bkwd: hdwy over 1f
out: r.o) ............................................................................ nk.**7**
Top Table *(MRStoute)* 8-7 DHolland (15) (w'like: bit bkwd: nvr nr to chal) ....... nk.**8**
Vernonia *(JHMGosden)* 8-11 SCauthen (3) (nvr trbld ldrs) ...................... 1½.**9**
Anghaam *(ACStewart)* 8-7 MRoberts (1) (w'like: scope: bit bkwd: 7th st:
hdwy over 2f out: wknd over 1f out) ......................................... 1.**10**
393⁶ Gong *(PTWalwyn)* 8-11 RCochrane (13) (4th st: wknd over 2f out) ........ 2.**11**
Beauchamp Grace *(JLDunlop)* 8-7 AMcGlone (12) (w'like: scope: a bhd) ....... ½.**12**
412 Day of History (IRE) *(CACyzer)* 8-11 GCarter (9) (led tl wknd 3f out) .......... 6.**13**
Change the Will *(MDIUsher)* 8-7 CRutter (4) (w'like: scope: lw: n.d) ............. 1½.**14**
Kentucky Starlet (USA) **(68)** *(RHannon)* 8-11 WCarson (2) (bit bkwd: mid div
whn hmpd 7f out: sn bhd: t.o) ................................................ 25.**15**

**2/1** Jood (USA), **3/1** Shirley Valentine, **9/2** Party Cited (USA), **8/1** Gong, **12/1** Anghaam (USA), **20/1** Vernonia(op
12/1), Marabou (USA)(op 12/1), Kentucky Starlet (USA), **25/1** Top Table, Donia (USA), USER FRIENDLY, **33/1**
Change the Will, Barga, Beauchamp Grace, **50/1** Day of History (IRE). CSF £99.19, Tote £40.00: £5.80 £1.50
£1.60 (£45.60). Mr W. J. Gredley (NEWMARKET) bred by Stetchworth Park Stud Ltd. 15 Rn  2m 10.23 (5.93)
                                                                       SF—59/58/53/41/27/25

**554** RING & BRYMER H'CAP (3-Y.O) (0-105) £3465.25 (£1042.00: £503.50: £234.25)
1¼m 7y                                                                5-20 (5-23)
(Weights raised 8 lb)
387⁴ **Bold Stroke (86)** Jt-Fav) *(JLDunlop)* 9-3 WCarson (5) (led to 3f out: led ins fnl
f: rdn out) ......................................................................... —**1**
Modernise (USA) **(90)** Jt-Fav) *(RCharlton)* 9-7 PatEddery (1) (lw: 4th st: qcknd
to ld 3f out: hdd ins fnl f: r.o) .............................................. nk.**2**
395 National Emblem (FR) **(80)** *(PFICole)* 8-11 AMunro (3) (2nd st: wknd wl over 1f
out) ................................................................................. 12.**3**
290⁵ Wild Fire **(80)** *(GWragg)* 8-11 WRSwinburn (2) (5th st: hdwy over 2f out: wknd
over 1f out) ....................................................................... 2.**4**
387 Jairzinho (USA) **(90)** *(RHannon)* 9-6 MRoberts (4) (3rd st: wknd over 2f out) ..... 8.**5**
Stewards Enquiry: Eddery suspended 3-6/5/92 (careless riding).

**2/1** BOLD STROKE, Modernise (USA), **4/1** Jairzinho (USA), **6/1** National Emblem (FR)(7/1—9/1), **9/1** Wild Fire.
CSF £6.11, Tote £2.90: £1.60 £1.50 (£2.90). Mr Tom Wilson (ARUNDEL) bred by Bloodstock Enterprises Ltd. 5
Rn                                                                          2m 10.35 (6.05)
                                                                       SF—67/70/36/32/26

T/Trio: Races 3 & 4: £116.30 & £14.80 (14.1 & 80.1 Tckts). T/Jkpt: Not won; £13,721 to Sandown 25/4/92.
T/Plpt: £13.40 (706.5 Tckts).                                                              Hn

## SANDOWN (R-H)
### Saturday, April 25th [Good to soft]
Going Allowance: St: 0.40 sec per fur; Rnd: 0.20 sec per fur (G)     Wind: almost nil

Stalls: low

**555**     PIZZA HUT STKS (Mdn 2-Y.O.C & G) £2469.00 (£684.00: £327.00)     **5f 6y**     2-25 (2-29)

      **Power of Polly (USA)** *(PFICole)* 9-0  TQuinn (7) (neat: rdn thrght: a.p: led ins fnl
              f: r.o wl) ................................................................................ —1
446³ Joyofracing (Jt-Fav) *(WAO'Gorman)* 9-0  PatEddery (8) (a.p: led over 1f out tl
              ins fnl f: unable qckn) ............................................................ 3.2
383⁵ Aradanza *(MRChannon)* 9-0  JWilliams (9) (hld up: rdn over 1f out: r.o wl ins fnl
              f) ............................................................................................ nk.3
      Zimzalabim *(BWHills)* 9-0  DHolland (1) (leggy: bit bkwd: outpcd: gd hdwy over
              1f out: r.o wl ins fnl f) ........................................................... s.h.4
383 Ansellman *(MJHaynes)* 9-0  SCauthen (2) (hld up: rdn over 2f out: r.o ins fnl f)  nk.5
      Elle Shaped (IRE) *(RHannon)* 9-0  MRoberts (10) (unf: bit bkwd: led over 3f) ...... 5.6
      Rock Symphony (Jt-Fav) *(AAScott)* 9-0  BRaymond (11) (leggy: bit bkwd: chsd
              ldr: ev ch over 1f out: sn wknd) ............................................ nk.7
      Perigord (IRE) *(WRMuir)* 9-0  SWhitworth (6) (neat: outpcd) ....................... s.h.8
226⁶ Sharro *(PAKelleway)* 9-0  CAsmussen (4) (outpcd) ...................................... 2.9
      Brigg Fair *(RHannon)* 8-9 ‡5RPerham (5) (leggy: bit bkwd: s.s: outpcd) ........ 2¹/₂.10
      Jaybee-Jay *(MJHaynes)* 9-0  RCochrane (3) (w'like: bkwd: a wl bhd) .............. 10.11

**2/1** Rock Symphony, Joyofracing(5/4—3/1), **7/1** Aradanza, **9/1** POWER OF POLLY (USA)(op 5/1), **12/1**
Zimzalabim(8/1—14/1), **14/1** Brigg Fair, Elle Shaped (IRE)(op 8/1), **16/1** Perigord (IRE), **20/1** Sharro(op 12/1),
**33/1** Ors. CSF £27.78, Tote £9.50: £2.60 £1.30 £2.20 (£13.20). Mr G. J. Beck (WHATCOMBE) bred by
Gainesway Thoroughbreds Limited in USA. 11 Rn     63.89 sec (4.39)
                                                SF—52/40/39/38/37/17

---

**556**     THRESHER CLASSIC TRIAL (Stks) (Gp 3) (3-Y.O) £32040.00 (£11912.00: £5656.00:
      £2392.00)     **1¹/₄m 7y**     3-00 (3-03)

341★ **Pollen Count (USA)** *(JHMGosden)* 8-11  SCauthen (6) (lw: 4th st: led 2f out to
              1f out: led wl ins fnl f: rdn out) ............................................. —1
      Aljadeer (USA) (Fav) *(HRACecil)* 8-11  PatEddery (8) (lw: 3rd st: led 1f out tl wl
              ins fnl f: r.o wl) ..................................................................... hd.2
      Assessor (IRE) (111) *(RHannon)* 8-11  WRSwinburn (9) (6th st: rdn over 2f out:
              r.o one pce) ........................................................................... 5.3
389★ Beyton (USA) (98) *(RHannon)* 8-11  BRaymond (4) (2nd st: led 3f out to 2 out:
              wknd fnl f) .............................................................................. 1.4
      Bonny Scot (IRE) (108) *(LMCumani)* 8-11  LDettori (10) (bit bkwd: s.s: rdn 3f
              out: no hdwy fnl 2f) ............................................................... 3.5
3a★ Jape (USA) *(PFICole)* 9-2  AMunro (2) (5th st: wknd 2f out) ...................... 1¹/₂.6
391⁵ Alflora (IRE) (94) *(CEBrittain)* 8-11  MRoberts (1) (lw: hdwy over 2f out: wknd wl
              over 1f out) ............................................................................. hd.7
      John Rose (108) *(PAKelleway)* 8-11  CAsmussen (7) (bhd fnl 6f) ................... 10.8
239⁵ Daros *(MrsJRRamsden)* 8-11  TQuinn (3) (a bhd) .......................................... s.h.9
410² Anchorite (110) *(PTWalwyn)* 8-11  RCochrane (5) (led 7f: wkng whn hmpd on
              ins over 2f out) ...................................................................... 2.10

**3/1** Aljadeer (USA), **4/1** Bonny Scot (IRE), **5/1** POLLEN COUNT (USA)(7/2—11/2), **13/2** Beyton (USA), Assessor
(IRE), **10/1** Anchorite, **16/1** Daros, **20/1** Alflora (IRE), **25/1** Jape (USA), **33/1** John Rose. CSF £18.84, Tote
£4.20: £1.70 £1.40 £2.10 (£5.30). Sheikh Mohammed (NEWMARKET) bred by Muckler Stables Incorporated
USA. 10 Rn     2m 7.85 (3.55)
                                                SF—82/81/71/69/63/65/59

---

**557**     T.G.I. FRIDAY'S GORDON RICHARDS E.B.F. STKS (Gp 3) £23328.00 (£8664.90: £4107.45:
      £1729.65)     **1¹/₄m 7y**     3-30 (3-38)

      **Dear Doctor (FR)** *(JEHammond,France)* 5-9-1  CAsmussen (2) (hdwy over 2f
              out: led 1f out: r.o wl) ............................................................ —1
343★ Red Bishop (USA) (106) *(JHMGosden)* 4-8-10  SCauthen (7) (b.nr hind: rdn
              over 5f out: led 2f out to 1f out: r.o) .................................. 1¹/₂.2
      Opera House (111) *(MRStoute)* 4-8-10  RCochrane (13) (s.s: hmpd over 4f out:
              nt clr run 3f out & over 2f out: hdwy over 1f out: r.o) .......... hd.3
      Perpendicular (112) (Fav) *(HRACecil)* 4-8-10  PatEddery (5) (5th st: hrd rdn &
              ev ch over 1f out: unable qckn) ............................................. 2¹/₂.4

Mohican Girl **(103)** *(JRFanshawe)* 4–8-7 WRSwinburn (6) (3rd st: led 3f out to 2f out: wknd over 1f out) ............................................................. 4.5
Half a Tick (USA) **(107)** *(PFICole)* 4–8-10 TQuinn (4) (swtg: bit bkwd: 6th st: no hdwy fnl 3f) ........................................................................... 2.6
Secret Haunt (USA) **(105)** *(LMCumani)* 4–8-10 LDettori (9) (lw: hdwy over 2f out: wknd over 1f out) ................................................................. s.h.7
Jaffa Line **(109)** *(DRCElsworth)* 4–8-7 JWilliams (3) (swtg: bit bkwd: nvr nr to chal) ........................................................................................ ¾.8
343³ Ile de Chypre **(108)** *(GHarwood)* 7–8-10 AClark (8) (swtg: 4th st: bmpd 3f out: sn wknd) ................................................................................ 7.9
Gussy Marlowe **(118)** *(CEBrittain)* 4–8-10 MRoberts (1) (bit bkwd: 2nd st: bmpd 3f out: sn wknd) ........................................................... 10.10
343 Prince Russanor **(102)** *(JLDunlop)* 4–8-10 BRaymond (11) (led tl bmpd 3f out: wknd qckly over 2f out) ................................................. 1½.11
436★ Sure Sharp (USA) **(103)** *(BWHills)* 5–8-13 DHolland (12) (swtg: bhd fnl 2f) ... 2½.12

**3/1** Perpendicular, **11/2** Red Bishop (USA), **6/1** DEAR DOCTOR (FR), **13/2** Sure Sharp (USA), **15/2** Gussy Marlowe, **8/1** Opera House, **10/1** Secret Haunt (USA), **14/1** Mohican Girl, Ile de Chypre, **20/1** Jaffa Line, **33/1** Half a Tick (USA), **50/1** Prince Russanor. CSF £37.39, Tote £6.00: £2.00 £2.10 £3.00 (£11.80). Mr Henri Chalhoub (FRANCE) bred by Amerigroup Leasing in France. 12 Rn      2m 7.42 (3.12)
SF—90/82/81/76/65/64/63

**558**     COUNTRY CLUB HOTELS H'CAP (3-Y.O) (0-110) £10820.00 (£3260.00: £1580.00: £740.00)   **1m 14y**                   4-40 (4-45)

(Weights raised 3 lb)
348★ Irek **(82)** (Fav) *(LordHuntingdon)* 8-5 MRoberts (9) (lw: 3rd st: led over 1f out: r.o wl) ................................................................................ —1
394⁶ The Power of One **(75)** *(RSimpson)* 7-12⁽¹⁾ AMunro (8) (lw: 6th st: rdn over 1f out: r.o wl ins fnl f) ........................................................ ½.2
Sharpitor (IRE) **(88)** *(WJarvis)* 8-11 BRaymond (3) (ev ch ins fnl f: r.o) .. nk.3
432³ Showgi (USA) **(88)** *(JRFanshawe)* 8-11 WRSwinburn (1) (swtg: 2nd st: led 2f out tl over 1f out: unable qckn) .................................................. 2½.4
Hadaad (USA) **(80)** *(AAScott)* 8-3 JFortune (5) (lw: 5th st: rdn over 2f out: one pce) ........................................................................... 1½.5
395 Major's Law (IRE) **(80)** *(CEBrittain)* 7-12 ‡5BDoyle (7) (hdwy on ins over 2f out: one pce) ................................................................. ¾.6
Strong Suit (IRE) **(98)** *(RHannon)* 9-2 ‡5RPerham (7) (swtg: a bhd) ............... 1½.7
290³ Majal (IRE) **(88)** *(BHanbury)* 8-11 RCochrane (2) (lw: a bhd) ....................... 2.8
468★ Love Jazz (USA) **(95)** *(TDBarron)* 9-4 LDettori (4) (lw: 4th st: hrd rdn over 2f out: wknd over 1f out) ....................................................... s.h.9
432 Sybaritic Sam (IRE) **(70)** *(NACallaghan)* 7-7 NCarlisle (10) (a bhd) ............. 2.10

**15/8** IREK, **5/1** Sharpitor (IRE), **13/2** The Power of One, **8/1** Love Jazz, **11/1** Majal (IRE), **12/1** Hadaad (USA), **16/1** Sybaritic Sam (IRE), **20/1** Strong Suit, **33/1** Major's Law (IRE). CSF £14.21, CT £49.43. Tote £2.50: £1.50 £2.10 £2.40 (£8.80). Sheikh Mohammed (WEST ILSLEY) bred by Somerhall Bloodstock Ltd. 10 Rn                1m 45.27 (6.07)
SF—24/15/27/19/6/–

**559**     LANSBURY HOTELS H'CAP (3-Y.O) (0-100) £3715.50 (£1119.00: £542.00: £253.50)   **5f 6y**                      5-15 (5-21)

445⁶ Freddie Lloyd (USA) **(87)** *(NACallaghan)* 8-4 ‡7JTate (3) (b.off fore: led 3f: led over 1f out: all out) ........................................................ —1
Silca-Cisa **(84)** *(MRChannon)* 8-8 JWilliams (4) (lw: hdwy over 1f out: rdn fnl f: r.o wl) ....................................................................... hd.2
399★ My Sovereign (USA) **(76)** (Fav) *(JRFanshawe)* 8-0 AMunro (2) (lw: hld up: rdn over 1f out: r.o one pce) ................................................. 3.3
445⁴ Isaiah **(95)** *(MJohnston)* 9-5 MRoberts (13) (hdwy over 2f out: one pce) ......... s.h.4
Ned's Bonanza **(75)** *(RMWhitaker)* 7-13 NCarlisle (5) (led 2f out tl over 1f out: wknd fnl f) ............................................................... 1.5
Tate Dancer (IRE) **(84)** *(RWArmstrong)* 8-8 LDettori (14) (lw: gd spd over 3f) ..... 1.6
254⁴ Isdar (IRE) **(89)** *(HThomsonJones)* 8-13 RHills (12) (hdwy over 1f out: one pce) nk.7
Walstead (IRE) **(77)** *(WJarvis)* 8-1 DHolland (10) (bit bkwd: outpcd) ................ nk.8
Verde Alitalia (IRE) **(80)** *(JLDunlop)* 8-4 TQuinn (7) (lw: prom over 3f) ............. 1.9
445 Holetown **(86)** *(RHannon)* 8-5 ‡5RPerham (8) (prom 3f) ............................. 1.10
227² Echo-Logical **(97)** *(JBerry)* 9-7 PatEddery (11) (lw: prom over 3f) .............. 1½.11
276★ Uccello **(75)** *(LJHolt)* 7-13 NAdams (9) (s.s: outpcd) ............................. 1½.12
215 Wild Honour (IRE) **(88)** *(WRMuir)* 8-12 SWhitworth (6) (prom 3f) ................. nk.13

**3/1** My Sovereign (USA), **7/2** Echo-Logical(11/2—11/4), **5/1** Isaiah(7/1—9/2), **8/1** Uccello, **10/1** Verde Alitalia (IRE), **12/1** Isdar (USA), **14/1** Holetown, FREDDIE LLOYD (USA), **20/1** Ors. CSF £235.68, CT £953.84. Tote £30.30: £5.30 £4.50 £1.60 (£136.80). Mr Michael Hill (NEWMARKET) bred by Jerry M. Cutrona Snr in USA. 13 Rn                    63.28 sec (3.78)

SF—54/57/37/55/31/36/40

T/Trio: Race 6: £197.00 (9.4 Tckts). T/Jkpt: Not won; £30,767.10 to Ascot 29/4/92. T/Plpt: £36.60 (528.05 Tckts).

**Other races under Rules of National Hunt racing.**                               AK

## 316—LEICESTER (R-H)

### Saturday, April 25th [Good, Good to soft patches]

Going Allowance: St: nil sec per fur; Rnd: 0.10 sec per fur (G)          Wind: mod across

Stalls: high

**560**          REDMILE STKS (I) (Mdn 3-Y-O) £2072.00 (£572.00: £272.00)     **1m 1f 218y** 2-20 (2-23)

**Aremef (USA)** *(MrsJCecil)* 9-0  PaulEddery (7) (mde all: rdn over 1f out: r.o wl) . —1
394[5] Rajai (IRE) (Jt-Fav) *(JLDunlop)* 9-0  WNewnes (9) (s.i.s: hdwy & 4th st: swtchd lft
          & rdn over 2f out: r.o ins fnl f) .................................................. ¾.2
Summer Cruise (Jt-Fav) *(HRACecil)* 9-0  WRyan (10) (3rd st: ev ch 2f out: eased
          whn btn ins fnl f) ................................................................ 3.3
Milanese *(DMorley)* 8-3[(1)] ‡7EBentley (8) (plld hrd: 2nd st: one pce fnl 2f) .......... 3.4
Restless Minstrel (USA) *(LMCumani)* 8-7 ‡7JWeaver (3) (scope: bkwd: 7th st:
          hdwy over 3f out: one pce fnl 2f) .............................................. 1.5
Bentico *(MAJarvis)* 9-0  GCrealock (5) (a bhd) ............................................ 10.6
Apollo Red *(PWHarris)* 9-0  GDuffield (1) (cmpt: bit bkwd: dwlt: 6th st: bhd fnl 3f:
          t.o) ............................................................................ 10.7
Highland Flame *(ANLee)* 9-0  JQuinn (2) (leggy: bkwd: bhd fnl 4f: t.o) ................ 5.8
Canadian Boy (IRE) *(DShaw)* 8-7 ‡7SWilliams (4) (lengthy: bit bkwd: dwlt: a bhd:
          t.o) ............................................................................ nk.9
Vis-a-Vis *(DBurchell)* 9-0  GCarter (6) (bit bkwd: plld hrd: 5th, rdn & wkng st: t.o) 7.10

**6/4** Summer Cruise, Rajai (IRE)(op 4/6), **8/1** AREMEF (USA), **12/1** Restless Minstrel (USA)(op 4/1), **20/1** Milanese(op 8/1), **33/1** Apollo Red, Bentico, **50/1** Canadian Boy (IRE), Highland Flame, **80/1** Vis-a-Vis. CSF £18.98, Tote £18.00: £3.00 £1.20 £1.00 (£11.70). Lord Petersham (NEWMARKET) bred by J. Menditeguy, T. Zuylen, A. Hancock, et al in USA. 10 Rn                    2m 9.6 (6.9)

SF—41/39/33/16/11/5

**561**          GADSBY (S) STKS (2-Y-O) £2461.20 (£683.20: £327.60)          **5f 2y** 2-50 (3-00)

423★ **Ruby Cooper** *(JWharton)* 8-11  WNewnes (6) (a.p: led over 1f out: rdn out) ...... —1
470[3] Toff Sundae (Fav) *(GLewis)* 8-11  PaulEddery (4) (lw: a.p: rdn over 2f out: ev ch
          fnl f: r.o) ................................................................... ¾.2
Walid's Princess (IRE) *(JWharton)* 8-2[(3)] ‡7KRutter (1) (unf: bkwd: s.s: hdwy
          over 1f out: fin wl) .......................................................... ½.3
Spring Sunrise *(MBlanshard)* 8-6  WRyan (2) (lt-f: unf: hdwy 2f out: one pce fnl f) 1½.4
423[6] Grey Runner *(BPalling)* 8-6  NDay (10) (prom: ev ch over 1f out: wknd fnl f) .... 2½.5
Abilene *(JARToller)* 8-6  DaleGibson (12) (scope: bit bkwd: dwlt: nvr nrr) .......... ½.6
484   Ballaindy *(WGMTurner)* 8-1 ‡5TSprake (9) (led over 3f) ......................... 1½.7
286   Hazy Dazy *(WGMTurner)* 8-3 ‡3DBiggs (7) (n.d) ................................. ½.8
Andrea's Girl *(JBerry)* 8-6  GCarter (11) (w'like: scope: s.s: n.d) ................... 1½.9
Rythmic Rascal *(MBrittain)* 8-11  MWigham (8) (leggy: bit bkwd: bhd fnl 2f) ..... ¾.10
423   Grand Game *(DHaydnJones)* 8-11  TyroneWilliams (5) (b.hind: bhd fnl 2f) .... 1½.11
484[4] Prawn Cracker (IRE) *(CTinkler)* 8-6  GDuffield (14) (spd 3f) ..................... ¾.12
Becky Boo *(DBurchell)* 8-7[(1)] MTebbutt (13) (lt-f: unf: bit bkwd: s.i.s: t.o) ...... 10.13
286   Farabout *(JPLeigh)* 8-6  JQuinn (3) (s.i.s: t.o) .................................. 2.14

**9/4** Toff Sundae, **4/1** RUBY COOPER(5/2—9/2), Spring Sunrise(7/2—6/1), **13/2** Andrea's Girl, **10/1** Ballaindy, Prawn Cracker (IRE)(7/1—12/1), **16/1** Abilene(12/1—20/1), **20/1** Grey Runner, **25/1** Rythmic Rascal, **33/1** Hazy Dazy, Walid's Princess (IRE), **50/1** Grand Game, **66/1** Ors. CSF £13.37, Tote £3.40: £1.10 £1.70 £13.40 (£4.40). Mr J. Rose (MELTON MOWBRAY) bred by Eric Saunders. 14 Rn; No bid          61.9 sec (3.2)

SF—33/30/19/21/11/9

**562**          MADAGANS H'CAP (3-Y-O) (0-90) £3106.00 (£928.00: £444.00: £202.00)
          **1m 3f 183y**                                                      3-20 (3-21)
          (Weights raised 7 lb)
**Simply-H (IRE) (60)** *(MBell)* 7-11 ‡7PTurner (2) (hld up: 3rd st: led 3f out: qcknd
          clr over 1f out: easily) ...................................................... —1

424⁴ The Titan Ghost **(59)** *(BAMcMahon)* 8-3 GCarter (3) (4th st: chsd wnr fnl 3f: no imp) .................................................................................................. 10.2

400³ In the Money (IRE) **(73)** *(RHollinshead)* 9-3 WRyan (7) (lw: 5th st: rdn & r.o one pce fnl 2f) .................................................................................................. 1.3

370 Liability Order **(65)** *(RBoss)* 8-9 MTebbutt (4) (6th st: rdn over 3f out: no hdwy) 2.4

471 Mr Ziegfeld (USA) **(77)** *(SirMarkPrescott)* 9-7 GDuffield (5) (hld up: last st: c wd & rdn 4f out: n.d) ........................................................................ 10.5

369* Fassfern (USA) **(74)** *(Fav)* *(MrsJCecil)* 9-4 PaulEddery (6) (lw: led 9f) .............. ½.6

376* Lady Lydia **(68)** *(MAJarvis)* 8-5 ‡⁷KRutter (1) (w ldr: 2nd st: rdn & wknd 3f out: t.o) .................................................................................................. 7.7

**11/10** Fassfern (USA), **7/2** Lady Lydia, **6/1** SIMPLY-H (IRE), In the Money (IRE), **12/1** The Titan Ghost(op 8/1), **14/1** Ors. CSF £61.93, Tote £5.90: £2.60 £2.80 (£37.90). Mr G. L. H. Lederman (NEWMARKET) bred by E. J. Loder in Ireland. 7 Rn　　　　　　　　　　　　　　　　　　　　　　　2m 35.3 (6.5)
SF—30/16/28/16/8/3

**563**　　　MADAGANS LEICESTERSHIRE STKS (listed race)　　£9381.25 (£2800.00: £1337.50: £606.25)　　**7f 9y**　　　　　　　　　　　　　　　　　　　3-50 (3-51)

23a⁴ **Shalford (IRE) (117)** *(RHannon)* 4—9-4 BRouse (2) (hld up: qcknd to ld 2f out: sn clr: pushed out) ........................................................................ —1

403⁴ Norton Challenger **(108)** *(MHEasterby)* 5—9-1 GCarter (11) (rdn & hdwy 3f out: chsd wnr over 1f out: no imp) ........................................................ 5.2

20a Susurration (USA) **(111)** *(Fav)* *(JHMGosden)* 5—8-13 WRyan (14) (a.p: one pce fnl 2f) .................................................................................................. 2½.3

403⁵ Corn Futures **(72)** (bl) *(JPLeigh)* 4—8-7 JWeaver (10) (prom: hung rt 2f out: one pce) .................................................................................................. 1.4

Arany **(88)** *(MHTompkins)* 5 8-12 CHodgson (1) (lw: wl bhd tl r.o fnl 2f: nrst fin) 1.5

413² Soleil Dancer (IRE) **(94)** (v) *(MMcCormack)* 4—8-12 WNewnes (4) (lw: led 5f) .... 2.6

Sylva Honda **(105)** *(CEBrittain)* 4—9-4 GCrealock (3) (dwlt: nvr trbld ldrs) ...... ½.7

515² Pimsboy **(51)** (bl) *(PABlockley)* 5—8-12 JQuinn (6) (n.d) ................................ nk.8

Pfalz **(104)** *(MRStoute)* 4—8-10 PaulEddery (8) (no hdwy fnl 3f) ...................... ¾.9

430 Letsbeonestaboutit **(94)** (bl) *(MrsNMacauley)* 6—8-12 NDay (5) (chsd ldr tl hrd rdn & wknd 3f out) ........................................................................ 1.10

Appledorn **(85)** *(BAMcMahon)* 5—8-7 GDuffield (9) (hdwy 3f out: wknd over 1f out) .................................................................................................. ½.11

Night Jar **(96)** *(LordHuntingdon)* 5—8-7 DaleGibson (13) (lw: prom over 4f) ..... 3.12

Knight of Mercy **(102)** *(RHannon)* 6—8-12 AMcGlone (12) (bkwd: a bhd: t.o) .... 8.13

**9/4** Susurration (USA), **4/1** SHALFORD (IRE)(op 9/4), **9/2** Norton Challenger, **8/1** Pfalz(5/1—9/1), **9/1** Night Jar(6/1—10/1), **12/1** Soleil Dancer (IRE), Knight of Mercy(10/1—16/1), **16/1** Sylva Honda, **33/1** Appledorn, Arany, Letsbeonestaboutit, **66/1** Ors. CSF £21.05, Tote £6.10: £2.90 £1.20 £1.70 (£15.60). Mr D. F. Cock (MARLBOROUGH) bred by D. M. Dick in Ireland. 13 Rn　　　　　　　　　　　　　1m 24.8 (2.5)
SF—67/49/39/30/32/26

**564**　　　WOOLSTHORPE STKS (Mdn 2-Y-O) £2072.00 (£572.00: £272.00)　　**5f 2y**　　4-20 (4-27)

**Carranita (IRE)** *(BPalling)* 8-9 PaulEddery (2) (leggy: hdwy 2f out: rdn to ld wl ins fnl: r.o) ........................................................................ —1

423 Craigie Boy *(JPLeigh)* 8-7 ‡⁷JWeaver (1) (hdwy 2f out: ev ch ins fnl f: r.o) ........ nk.2

365⁴ Two Times Twelve (IRE) (bl) *(JBerry)* 9-0 GCarter (7) (lw: led & sn clr: wandered over 1f out: hdd wl ins fnl f) ........................................................ 1½.3

446 Wahem (IRE) *(NACallaghan)* 9-0 GDuffield (8) (lw: prom: outpcd 2f out: r.o ins fnl f) .................................................................................................. ¾.4

Victoria Hall *(WGMTurner)* 8-4 ‡⁵TSprake (3) (lengthy: bkwd: nvr nr to chal) ...... 2.5

Caps Ninety-Two (IRE) *(DrJDScargill)* 9-0 MTebbutt (5) (scope: bit bkwd: nvr nrr) 1.6

439² Defenceless *(Fav)* *(RHannon)* 8-9 BRouse (4) (lw: prom 3f) .................................. 3.7

Expo Mondial (IRE) *(JMPEustace)* 9-0 MTebbutt (10) (neat: w'like: bkwd: a bhd) 5.8

Stately Run (USA) *(MBrittain)* 9-0 MWigham (11) (unf: scope: spd 3f) .................. ¾.9

Admiral Frobisher (USA) *(CFWall)* 9-0 NDay (9) (leggy: scope: outpcd) ........... ½.10

383 Shades of Croft *(MDIUsher)* 9-0 GBaxter (6) (lw: s.s) ...................................... ½.11

Trepidation (IRE) *(MJFetherston-Godley)* 9-0 WNewnes (12) (cmpt: bkwd: s.s: r.o) .................................................................................................. 8.12

**4/6** Defenceless(tchd 5/4), **11/2** Two Times Twelve (IRE), **10/1** Expo Mondial (IRE), Wahem (IRE)(op 6/1), **12/1** CARRANITA (IRE), **14/1** Trepidation (IRE)(op 8/1), Admiral Frobisher (USA)(op 8/1), **20/1** Shades of Croft, **25/1** Stately Run (USA), Caps Ninety-Two (IRE), **33/1** Ors. CSF £294.65, Tote £9.80: £1.40 £4.30 £1.80 (£238.50). Lamb Lane Associates (COWBRIDGE) bred by Mrs Anita Quinn in Ireland. 12 Rn　　　　62 sec (3.3)
SF—29/26/27/24/6/7

**565**    SPRING H'CAP (0-70) £2742.00 (£762.00: £366.00)    **1m 1f 218y**    4-55 (4-57)

3684 **Surrey Dancer (60)** (Fav) *(BHanbury)* 4-9-5 WRyan (15) (lw: a gng wl: 3rd st: shkn up to ld 1f out: pushed out) ......................................... —1
409 Joli's Great **(50)** *(MJRyan)* 4-8-6 ‡3DBiggs (13) (5th st: rdn over 1f out: r.o ins fnl f) ......................................... 1½.2
3406 Broughton Blues (IRE) **(39)** *(WJMusson)* 4-7-12 AMackay (1) (lw: hdwy & 7th st: led over 2f out tl over 1f out: one pce) ......................................... 1½.3
Reklaw **(38)** *(MDHammond)* 5-7-11 JQuinn (5) (bit bkwd: hdwy 3f out: r.o fnl f) 1.4
422 Presque Noir **(55)** *(HCandy)* 4-9-0 WNewnes (3) (lw: hdwy 3f out: one pce fnl f) ¾.5
4692 Tanoda **(50)** *(MBrittain)* 6-8-9 GCarter (8) (lw: hdwy 3f out: hrd rdn over 1f out: one pce) ......................................... 2½.6
354 Vallance **(66)** *(PWHarris)* 4-9-11 PaulEddery (2) (hld up: 6th st: led 3f out: sn hdd: wknd over 1f out) ......................................... 3½.7
Thunder Bug (USA) **(54)** *(APJames)* 4-8-13 SDawson (9) (bit bkwd: prom 5f) 1½.8
Eagle Feather (IRE) **(69)** *(JLDunlop)* 4-10-0 AMcGlone (4) (bit bkwd: nvr nr to chal) ......................................... 1½.9
King of Mileen **(50)** *(DShaw)* 6-8-9 BRouse (7) (b: bit bkwd: a bhd) ............. 1½.10
273 Tenayestelign **(47)** *(DMarks)* 4-8-6 GBaxter (6) (a bhd) ......................................... 2.11
Indian Sovereign **(40)** *(RLee)* 8-7-13 DaleGibson (14) (bit bkwd: a bhd: t.o) ... 6.12
335 Marjons Boy **(35)** (bl) *(CDBroad)* 5-7-8(1) EJohnson (10) (4th st: wknd over 3f out: t.o) ......................................... 2½.13
3583 Taylors Prince **(59)** *(HJCollinridge)* 5-8-11 ‡7CHawksley (11) (lw: led 2f: 2nd st: led 4f out to 3f out: sn wknd: t.o) ......................................... 6.14
Serious Time **(53)** *(SirMarkPrescott)* 4-8-12 GDuffield (12) (bit bkwd: led after 2f to 4f out: sn wknd: t.o) ......................................... 12.15
LONG HANDICAP: Marjons Boy 7-5.

**7/4** SURREY DANCER, **5/1** Tanoda, **11/2** Presque Noir, **8/1** Taylors Prince, **9/1** Joli's Great, **10/1** Eagle Feather (IRE)(7/1—12/1), **14/1** Broughton Blues (IRE), **20/1** Thunder Bug (USA), Serious Time(op 12/1), Vallance, Tenayestelign, **33/1** Indian Sovereign, Reklaw, **50/1** Ors. CSF £19.54, CT £174.58. Tote £3.20: £1.70 £3.60 £3.10 (£55.10). Cronk Thoroughbred Racing Ltd (NEWMARKET) bred by Fonthill Stud. 15 Rn   2m 9.8 (7.1)
SF—44/28/17/14/29/19

**566**    REDMILE STKS (II) (Mdn 3-Y.O) £2072.00 (£572.00: £272.00)
**1m 1f 218y**    5-25 (5-28)

**Kaiser Wilhelm** (Fav) *(HRACecil)* 9-0 WRyan (8) (leggy: scope: 3rd st: led over 2f out: rdn over 1f out: r.o) ......................................... —1
Garden District *(RCharlton)* 9-0 SRaymont (6) (unf: scope: bit bkwd: s.s: reminder after 2f: hdwy 2f out: swtchd 1f out: fin wl) ............. 1.2
Al Haal (USA) *(PTWalwyn)* 9-0 GBaxter (4) (led wl over 7f: hrd rdn over 1f out: no ex ins fnl f) ......................................... 2.3
Repledge (IRE) *(PFICole)* 9-0 PaulEddery (9) (4th st: r.o one pce fnl 2f) ......... ½.4
440 Rolling the Bones (USA) *(JRFanshawe)* 9-0 GCarter (3) (dwlt: rdn & hdwy fnl 2f: nvr nrr) ......................................... 2½.5
First Heiress (IRE) *(MRStoute)* 8-9 GDuffield (10) (chsd ldr: 2nd st: wknd over 3f out) ......................................... 8.6
Striking Image (IRE) **(77)** *(RHannon)* 8-9 BRouse (7) (5th st: wknd 3f out) ...... 2½.7
Aislabie Airborne *(MrsNMacauley)* 9-0 NDay (2) (6th st: wknd 4f out: t.o) ........ 25.8
Petty Cash *(DrJDScargill)* 8-9 WNewnes (5) (b.hind: a bhd: t.o) ......................................... 2.9
After the Fire *(ANLee)* 9-0 JQuinn (1) (lt-f: scope: bkwd: lost tch 5f out: t.o) ... 20.10

**11/8** KAISER WILHELM(4/5—6/4), **7/2** Repledge (IRE), **6/1** First Heiress (IRE)(4/1—7/1), **7/1** Garden District, **11/1** Striking Image(IRE)(8/1—12/1), **12/1** Rolling the Bones (USA)(op 6/1), **14/1** Al Haal (USA)(op 8/1), **50/1** Ors. CSF £11.45. Tote £2.20: £1.30 £1.70 £4.10 (£9.40). Mr Charles H. Wacker III (NEWMARKET) bred by C. Wacker III. 10 Rn   2m 10.5 (7.8)
SF—32/30/26/25/20/–

T/Plpt: £453.80 (5 Tckts).                             KH

### 453—RIPON (R-H)
### Saturday, April 25th [Good]
Going Allowance: St: 0.05 sec; Rnd: 0.40 sec per fur (G)      Wind: almost nil

Stalls: low

**567**    FORGET-ME-NOT APPEAL (S) STKS (3-Y.O) £2245.60 (£621.60: £296.80)
**1¼m**    2-10 (2-15)

4482 **Ready to Draw (IRE) (62)** (Fav) *(RonaldThompson)* 8-12 ‡7MichaelDenaro (5) (lw: in tch: led wl over 1f out: r.o wl) ......................................... —1

419⁵ Between Two Fires **(58)** *(JBerry)* 9-0 JCarroll (8) (b: lw: prom: chal 3f out: rdn & r.o one pce) ............................................................................................ 10.2

Tyrone Flyer **(59)** *(GHEden)* 9-0 CDwyer (13) (swtg: led: edgd lft 4f out: hdd wl over 1f out: no ex) ...................................................................... s.h.3

Floral Bouquet *(MJCamacho)* 8-9 NConnorton (4) (bit bkwd: in tch: effrt 4f out: styd on: no imp) ................................................................ 5.4

353⁴ Speed Oil **(54)** *(RBastiman)* 8-7 ‡⁷HBastiman (11) (b: lw: hld up & bhd: hdwy on outside over 3f out: edgd rt & no imp fnl 2f) ........ 2¹/₂.5

519⁴ Victor Romeo **(58)** (bl) *(WJPearce)* 9-5 DNicholls (10) (plld hrd: a.p: effrt 4f out: btn over 2f out) ................................................................ 3.6

295 Syke Lane **(43)** *(RMWhitaker)* 9-0 ACulhane (14) (a in tch: effrt over 3f out: btn over 2f out) ............................................................. nk.7

419 Dangina **(28)** *(ASReid)* 9-0 LCharnock (12) (styd on fnl 3f: nvr trbld ldrs) .......... ³/₄.8

278 Dots Dee **(30)** *(JMBradley)* 8-4 ‡⁵ATucker (9) (bhd tl sme late hdwy) ................ ¹/₂.9

353 Nun the Wiser (IRE) **(44)** *(BAMcMahon)* 8-9 MHills (7) (chsd ldrs tl wknd 3f out) 3.10

406 Super Marco **(54)** *(WWHaigh)* 9-0 GHind (3) (lw: cl up tl wknd 3f out) ........ 12.11

Sharp as You Like **(59)** *(JEtherington)* 9-0 KDarley (2) (prom tl wknd 4f out) .. 4.12

374⁶ Crimson Consort (IRE) **(37)** *(DonEnricoIncisa)* 9-0 KimTinkler (6) (lw: a bhd) .. 5.13

327 Sunrays (IRE) *(CWCElsey)* 8-4 ‡⁵SMaloney (1) (cl up to st: sn wknd) ............... 1.14

**15/8** READY TO DRAW (IRE)(3/1—7/4), **7/2** Between Two Fires(9/4—4/1), **7/1** Sharp as You Like, **10/1** Syke Lane, **12/1** Tyrone Flyer, **14/1** Speed Oil, Floral Bouquet, **16/1** Super Marco(op 10/1), Victor Romeo, **20/1** Nun the Wiser (IRE), **33/1** Sunrays (IRE), **50/1** Ors. CSF £8.88. Tote £3.00: £1.20 £1.80 £3.20 (£3.40). M. D. M. Racing (Thoroughbreds) Limited (DONCASTER) bred by Aidan Sexton in Ireland. 14 Rn; No bid  2m 15.1 (11.6)

SF—22/4/3/–/–/–

---

**568**　　SKYLINE RACING STKS (Mdn 2-Y.O.F) £2415.00 (£665.00: £315.00)　　**5f**　 2-40 (2-46)

Peperonata (IRE) *(NTinkler)* 8-11 KDarley (9) (b.off hind: w'like: w ldrs: led wl over 1f out: qcknd: comf) ............................................. —1

Panic Button (IRE) *(MHEasterby)* 8-6 ‡⁵SMaloney (4) (rangy: scope: outpcd tl hdwy ¹/₂-wy: r.o: nrst fin) ........................................................ 2.2

Just Baileys *(MJohnston)* 8-11 RPElliott (7) (unf: a chsng ldrs: edgd rt u.p over 1f out: nt qckn) ............................................................ 3.3

Pride's Desire *(TDBarron)* 8-11 AlexGreaves (3) (lt-f: scope: sn outpcd & bhd: hdwy 2f out: r.o nr fin) ...................................................... s.h.4

287⁵ Colfax Starlight *(BSRothwell)* 8-11 RFox (12) (lw: cl up tl rdn & btn over 1f out) 1¹/₂.5

Peaceful Air *(EWeymes)* 8-11 GHind (5) (rangy: scope: sn outpcd & bhd: styd on wl fnl f) .......................................................... 2¹/₂.6

Lucky Mill *(FHLee)* 8-11 MHills (10) (neat: scope: bit bkwd: gd spd over 3f) ... 2¹/₂.7

367² Local Heroine (Fav) *(JBerry)* 8-11 JCarroll (8) (led over 3f: sn wknd) ............ 3.8

April Point (IRE) *(RHollinshead)* 8-11 ACulhane (1) (lengthy: scope: s.s: nt rcvr) 1¹/₂.9

Beckswhite Abbey *(WJPearce)* 8-11 DNicholls (6) (w'like: str: bit bkwd: dwlt: sn drvn along: n.d) ......................................................... 2.10

Green Vote *(MPNaughton)* 8-11 NConnorton (2) (lt-f: unf: sn outpcd & bhd) . nk.11

Lady Lawn *(JMCarr)* 8-11 SMorris (11) (unf: bit bkwd: s.s: a bhd) ...................... 12

**3/1** Local Heroine(op 2/1), **100/30** Panic Button (IRE)(op 7/1), **9/2** PEPERONATA (IRE), **6/1** Lucky Mill, **7/1** Just Baileys, **8/1** Colfax Starlight, **12/1** April Point (IRE), Peaceful Air, **16/1** Pride's Desire, **20/1** Green Vote, **25/1** Ors. CSF £21.95. Tote £8.00: £3.40 £1.80 £1.20 (£23.10). Skyline Racing Ltd (MALTON) bred by R. G. Percival in Ireland. 12 Rn　　　　　　　　　　　　　　　　　　　62 sec (3.4)

SF—34/21/14/13/7/–

---

**569**　　C. B. HUTCHINSON MEMORIAL CHALLENGE CUP (H'cap) (0-100) £7375.00 (£2200.00: £1050.00: £475.00)　　**2m**　　　　　　　　　3-10 (3-11)

(Weights raised 2 lb)

Good Hand (USA) **(80)** *(JWWatts)* 6-9-5 NConnorton (4) (bit bkwd: bhd: hdwy over 3f out: led 1f out: r.o) ......................................... —1

Our Aisling **(66)** *(SGNorton)* 4-7-12 ‡³FNorton (1) (lw: hld up: hdwy 4f out: led over 2f out tl hdd 1f out: nt qckn) ........................... 2.2

467³ Bollin Patrick **(70)** (Fav) *(MHEasterby)* 7-8-4 ‡⁵SMaloney (5) (trckd ldrs: smooth hdwy to disp ld over 2f out: shkn up & nt qckn appr fnl f) ........................................................... 5.3

267³ Steppey Lane **(71)** *(WWHaigh)* 7-8-10 ACulhane (3) (lw: led: clr after 4f tl hdd over 2f out: wknd over 1f out) ........................ 2¹/₂.4

435⁴ Sean's Scholar (USA) **(55)** *(CNAllen)* 5-7-8 GBardwell (7) (lw: chsd ldrs: drvn along appr st: sn outpcd & no imp after) ............ 1¹/₂.5

467 Travelling Light **(85)** *(MrsJRRamsden)* 6-9-10 MHills (6) (bit bkwd: hld up & bhd: shkn up 3f out: nvr nr to chal) ......................... 2.6

362⁴ Yorkshire Holly **(57)** *(MAvison)* 9-7-10 JLowe (2) (chsd ldr tl rdn & wknd 4f out) nk.7

**2/1** Bollin Patrick, **9/4** Sean's Scholar (USA), **6/1** Steppey Lane, Our Aisling, **12/1** GOOD HAND (USA)(op 8/1) & Ors. CSF £72.64, Tote £13.70: £3.80 £3.40 (£48.10). Mrs M. M. Haggas (RICHMOND) bred by Tauner Dunlap, Jr. and Brereton C. Jones in USA. 7 Rn
3m 36.8 (11.8)
SF—51/28/29/32/14/42

## 570
YORKSHIRE TELEVISION H'CAP (0-80) £2560.00 (£760.00: £360.00: £160.00)
**6f**
3-45 (3-47)

455³ Furiella (58) **(Fav)** *(PCHaslam)* 4–8–6 KDarley (10) (lw: mde all: clr 2f out: r.o wl) —1
Profilic (78) *(CaptJWilson)* 7–9–12 JLowe (6) (a.p: styd on u.p: hung rt ins fnl f) 3¹/₂.2
397⁶ Pop to Stans (70) *(TDBarron)* 3–8–6 AlexGreaves (8) (lw: a chsng ldrs: nt qckn fnl 2f) hd.3
407 Sully's Choice (USA) (52) (bl) *(DWChapman)* 11–8–0 SWood (12) (lw: racd alone far side: a.p: rdn & no imp fnl 2f) 4.4
Crystal Jack (FR) (72) *(FHLee)* 4–9–1 ‡⁵NKennedy (7) (in tch: hdwy ¹/₂-wy: no imp) ³/₄.5
438⁶ Languedoc (74) *(MPNaughton)* 5–9–5 ‡3JFanning (11) (lw: chsd ldrs: effrt ¹/₂-wy: grad wknd) 2¹/₂.6
506⁵ Iron King (62) *(JLSpearing)* 6–8–10 NHowe (2) (in tch: effrt over 2f out: sn btn) nk.7
Simmie's Special (72) *(RHollinshead)* 4–9–6 ACulhane (3) (bit bkwd: spd 4f) 5.8
Red Rosein (79) *(CaptJWilson)* 6–9–13 JCarroll (9) (b.off hind: bit bkwd: s.i.s: sme hdwy 2f out: nvr nr to chal) ¹/₂.9
449 Glenfield Greta (69) *(PSFelgate)* 4–9–0 ‡3FNorton (14) (lw: nvr trbld ldrs) s.h.10
449 Filicaia (54) *(DonEnricoIncisa)* 4–9–0 ‡6–8-2 KimTinkler (13) (bit bkwd: nvr wnt pce) ¹/₂.11
485 Master Pokey (71) *(MWEasterby)* 8–9–5 TLucas (4) (b: nvr plcd to chal) ¹/₂.12
196⁵ Asterix (79) *(JMBradley)* 4–9–8 ‡⁵ATucker (5) (sn outpcd & bhd) nk.13
506⁶ Petitesse (79) *(GBlum)* 4–8–5 RFox (1) (spd to ¹/₂-wy: sn wknd) ¹/₂.14

**3/1** FURIELLA, **6/1** Iron King, Languedoc, **8/1** Petitesse, **10/1** Master Pokey, **12/1** Pop to Ctans, **14/1** Cully'o Choice (USA), Glenfield Greta, **16/1** Profilic, Red Rosein, Simmie's Special, **20/1** Crystal Jack (FR), **25/1** Ors. CSF £47.39, CT £469.23. Tote £3.30: £1.90 £4.90 £2.70 (£28.50). Mr W. J. Hall (MIDDLEHAM) bred by Langham Hall Bloodstock. 14 Rn
1m 14.1 (2.4)
SF—50/56/35/13/25/19

## 571
CSI STKS (Mdn 2-Y.O.C & G) £2415.00 (£665.00: £315.00)  **5f**
4-15 (4-16)

Huffa (USA) **(Fav)** *(WJHaggas)* 9-0 MHills (8) (lengthy: scope: lw: a cl up: led 2f out: shkn up & r.o) —1
396 Warkworth (USA) (bl) *(JWWatts)* 9-0 JLowe (11) (a chsng ldrs: rdn 2f out: styd on nr fin) 3.2
Creagmhor *(JBerry)* 9-0 JCarroll (6) (neat: scope: a chsng ldrs: chal ins fnl f: nt qckn ins fnl f) hd.3
402³ Arkendale Diamond (USA) *(WJPearce)* 9-0 DNicholls (12) (led 3f: kpt on u.p) nk.4
416⁴ Dead Calm *(CTinkler)* 9-0 PBurke (3) (lw: a in tch: no imp fr ¹/₂-wy) 5.5
Legendary Hero *(TDBarron)* 9-0 KDarley (10) (str: cmpt: bit bkwd: sn cl up: edgd rt ¹/₂-wy: grad lost pl fnl 2f) s.h.6
Vardy (IRE) *(PCHaslam)* 8-11 ‡3JFanning (7) (str: scope: bit bkwd: sn drvn along: nvr trbld ldrs) nk.7
Doc Spot *(CaptJWilson)* 9-0 SWood (1) (neat: nvr plcd to chal) 1¹/₂.8
Jersey Bob (IRE) *(JSWainwright)* 9-0 LCharnock (9) (leggy: scope: nvr wnt pce) 2.9
Red Red Wine *(MHEasterby)* 8-9 ‡⁵SMaloney (2) (rangy: bit bkwd: dwlt: a bhd) 3¹/₂.10
Ttyfran *(FHLee)* 9-0 ACulhane (5) (str: cmpt: s.s: nt rcvr) 2.11
Brackenthwaite *(TDBarron)* 9-0 KFallon (4) (w'like: bit bkwd: dwlt: sn t.o) 12

**4/5** HUFFA (USA)(op 5/4), **6/1** Creagmhor(op 4/1), **7/1** Warkworth (USA)(op 12/1), **10/1** Dead Calm, Arkendale Diamond (USA), Legendary Hero, **12/1** Ttyfran, **14/1** Red Red Wine, **33/1** Ors. CSF £8.59, Tote £2.00: £1.40 £2.60 £1.90 (£8.30). Mr B. Haggas (NEWMARKET) bred by Samuel D. Hinkle, IV & C. P. Kimmel in USA. 12 Rn
62.1 sec (3.5)
SF—35/23/22/21/1/–

## 572
RUSHLEVEL CONSTRUCTION H'CAP (0-70) £2415.00 (£665.00: £315.00)
**1m**
4-50 (5-05)
(Weights raised 1 lb)

Forever Diamonds (53) *(MHEasterby)* 5–8–12 KDarley (11) (trckd ldrs gng wl: shkn up to ld ins fnl f: r.o) —1
419² Errema (49) **(Jt-Fav)** *(CTinkler)* 7–8–3 ‡⁵SMaloney (4) (lw: chsd ldrs: led wl over 1f out tl ins fnl f: kpt on) 1¹/₂.2
456⁶ Star Connection (62) *(RMWhitaker)* 4–9–7 ACulhane (20) (lw: a in tch: effrt & n.m.r 2f out: r.o nr fin) ³/₄.3
315⁶ Puffy (48) (bl) *(GMMoore)* 5–8–7⁽¹⁾ KFallon (12) (cl up: chal 3f out: nt qckn ins fnl f) hd.4

Young Jason (54) *(FHLee)* 9-8-8 ‡5NKennedy (14) (bit bkwd: hld up: effrt 3f out: styd on wl nr fin) .................................................................. 1.5

477 Ballerina Bay (54) *(DTThom)* 4-8-6 ‡7DHarrison (5) (bhd whn hmpd & rn wd appr st: hdwy 3f out: r.o) ............................ hd.6

293★ Habeta (USA) (65) *(Jt-Fav) (JWWatts)* 6-9-10 JLowe (4) (lw: hld up: effrt & n.m.r over 2f out: nvr able to chal) ......................... 2.7

420³ Cool Enough (38) *(MrsJRRamsden)* 11-7-11 LCharnock (15) (lw: hld up: effrt on ins 3f out: n.m.r: styd on) ........................ ³/₄.8

China Sky (48) *(CNAllen)* 4-8-0 ‡7GForster (2) (chsd ldrs: nt qckn appr fnl f) ... s.h.9

420⁵ Cornhill Melody (39) *(JLSpearing)* 4-7-5⁽⁵⁾ ‡7AGarth (7) (chsd ldrs: outpcd 2f out: styd on fnl f) ........................ hd.10

315⁵ Colonel Fairfax (37) *(JWWatts)* 4-7-10 RFox (6) (led tl hdd wl over 1f out: eased whn btn ins fnl f) ........................ 3.11

419³ Station Express (IRE) (39) *(BEllison)* 4-7-9 ‡3FNorton (17) (in tch: effrt over 3f out: grad wknd) ........................ 2.12

420 Flying Down to Rio (IRE) (59) *(MPNaughton)* 4-9-1 ‡3JFanning (3) (n.d) ....... 1¹/₂.13

364 No Decision (52) *(MWEasterby)* 5-8-11 TLucas (9) (a bhd) ........................ 1.14

Persian Dynasty (42) *(JMBradley)* 8-7-10⁽²⁾ ‡5ATucker (16) (lw: in tch: effrt u.p ¹/₂-wy: sn btn) ........................ 1¹/₂.15

364 Deputy Tim (51) *(RBastiman)* 9-8-3 ‡7HBastiman (1) (swtg: bit bkwd: hmpd & rn wd appr st: a bhd) ........................ ³/₄.16

328 Bobby on the Bank (34) *(SGPayne)* 6-7-7 SWood (8) (n.d) ........................ hd.17

419 Miss Knight (45) *(RBastiman)* 5-8-4 NConnorton (10) (lw: chsd ldrs to ¹/₂-wy: sn wknd) ........................ 2.18

Hold Fast (IRE) (43) *(HCandy)* 4-8-2 CRutter (13) (lw: plld v.hrd: prom to st: sn bhd) ........................ 19

LONG HANDICAP: Cornhill Melody 7-6, Bobby on the Bank 6-7.
*Must Be Magical (USA) (50/1) Withdrawn (broke out of stalls) : not under orders*

6/1 Puffy, Habeta (USA), Errema, 9/1 FOREVER DIAMONDS, 11/1 Star Connection, Cool Enough, 12/1 Station Express (IRE), China Sky, 14/1 Ballerina Bay, No Decision, 16/1 Young Jason, Miss Knight, Hold Fast (IRE), Colonel Fairfax, 20/1 Persian Dynasty, 25/1 Flying Down to Rio (IRE), Cornhill Melody, Deputy Tim, 50/1 Bobby on the Bank. CSF £63.92, CT £578.26. Tote £8.70: £2.40 £1.90 £2.90 £1.70 (£26.30). Mrs J. B. Russell (MALTON) bred by J. B. Russell. 19 Rn
1m 44.8 (7.1)
SF—39/25/41/26/24/21

**573**   YORKSHIRE CHILDRENS HOSPITAL TRUST STKS (Mdn 3-Y.O) £2265.20 (£627.20: £299.60)   1¹/₄m
5-25 (5-35)

Folia *(Jt-Fav) (HRACecil)* 8-2 ‡7StephenDavies (1) (lw: chsd ldr: led 3f out: hung lft: r.o wl) ........................ —1

Seekin Cash (USA) *(JWWatts)* 9-0 JLowe (5) (wl grwn: scope: a.p: effrt & ev ch 3f out: rn green: r.o) ........................ 3¹/₂.2

Brier Creek (USA) *(Jt-Fav) (JHMGosden)* 9-0 GHind (2) (a.p: ev ch 3f out: nt qckn appr fnl f) ........................ 3.3

466³ Iron Baron (IRE) *(RHollinshead)* 9-0 ACulhane (8) (lw: hld up: hdwy over 3f out: sn rdn: btn 2f out) ........................ 8.4

433 Steel Mirror *(MrsJCecil)* 9-0 JCarroll (3) (lw: led tl hdd 3f out: sn wknd) ............ 3.5

Kasisi (IRE) *(ACStewart)* 8-9 KDarley (6) (bit bkwd: hld up: effrt 4f out: rdn & btn 3f out) ........................ 6.6

Mypeto *(PCalver)* 9-0 DNicholls (7) (rangy: scope: bit bkwd: chsd ldrs tl wknd over 3f out: t.o) ........................ 7

*369² Eleganza (IRE) (4/1) Withdrawn (ref to ent stalls) : not under orders — Rule 4 applies*

7/4 FOLIA, Brier Creek (USA), 12/1 Steel Mirror(op 7/1), 14/1 Seekin Cash (USA), 16/1 Kasisi (IRE)(op 10/1), 20/1 Iron Baron (IRE)(op 12/1), 33/1 Mypeto. CSF £16.07, Tote £2.60: £2.00 £1.50 (£20.70). Sheikh Mohammed (NEWMARKET) bred by Sheikh Mohammed bin Rashid al Maktoum. 7 Rn
2m 13.8 (10.3)
SF—25/30/24/8/2/–

T/Plpt: £1,775.70 (2 Tckts).
AA

447—**PONTEFRACT (L-H)**

**Monday, April 27th [Good, Good to firm fnl 6f]**

Going Allowance: minus 0.05 sec per fur (F)
Wind: mod half bhd

Stalls: low

**574**   TOTE PLACEPOT AUCTION STKS (Mdn 2-Y.O) £2868.00 (£798.00: £384.00)   5f
2-45 (2-50)

439⁵ **Crested Wave (IRE)** *(Fav) (PWChapple-Hyam)* 7-13 AMunro (4) (lw: mde most: rdn & styd on wl fnl f) ........................ —1

Swiftlet (IRE) *(MBell)* 7-9 SWood (10) (b.hind: neat: a cl up: rdn to chal over 1f
out: nt qckn) .................................................................... 2.2

423² Plum First (bl) *(NBycroft)* 8-0 LCharnock (1) (lw: a cl up: rdn 2f out: one pce
appr fnl f) ........................................................................ 1¹/₂.3

365 Nicky Mygirl *(MBrittain)* 7-9 NCarlisle (3) (a chsng ldrs: hdwy wl over 1f out: one
pce fnl f) ......................................................................... ¹/₂.4

Niteowlady *(SGNorton)* 7-11 AProud (7) (leggy: unf: chsd ldrs: effrt 2f out: kpt
on same pce) .................................................................... nk.5

Mdm Racer (IRE) *(JBerry)* 8-4 GCarter (2) (str: cmpt: s.i.s: hdwy to chase ldrs
¹/₂-wy: nt qckn appr fnl f) ...................................................... 2.6

Manor Adventure *(BAMcMahon)* 7-9 JLowe (5) (unf: scope: chsd ldrs: wkng
whn sltly hmpd ent st) ........................................................... nk.7

Hi Nod *(MJCamacho)* 8-0 NConnorton (8) (unf: scope: prom tl grad wknd appr
fnl f) .............................................................................. 1.8

The Sharp Bidder (IRE) *(RHollinshead)* 8-1(1) PaulEddery (12) (w'like: scope:
bhd: sme hdwy 2f out: nvr nr to chal) ......................................... 2.9

470⁴ Shynon *(MHTompkins)* 8-0 RHills (6) (s.i.s: nvr trbld ldrs) .................... ³/₄.10

Pretzel (IRE) *(NTinkler)* 8-3 KDarley (15) (neat: str: bit bkwd: s.i.s: nvr nr to chal) ³/₄.11

Hot Off the Press *(RMWhitaker)* 8-2(2) ACulhane (13) (w'like: s.s: bhd tl sme late
hdwy) ............................................................................. nk.12

Amerigue *(MissSEHall)* 7-10(1) PBurke (11) (lengthy: scope: bit bkwd: s.s: sme
late hdwy) ....................................................................... s.h.13

423 Never in Touch *(MBrittain)* 7-9 GBardwell (9) (s.i.s: a bhd) .................... ³/₄.14

Westmead Nick *(JBerry)* 8-2(2) GDuffield (14) (lengthy: scope: s.i.s: a bhd) ..... 1.15

**9/4** CRESTED WAVE (IRE)(op 6/4), **11/2** Plum First, **6/1** Shynon, **7/1** Swiftlet (IRE), **8/1** Mdm Racer (IRE)(op
5/1), **10/1** Niteowlady, Manor Adventure, **14/1** Westmead Nick, Hi Nod, **16/1** The Sharp Bidder (IRE), **33/1** Ors.
CSF £19.41, Tote £2.90: £1.60 £2.40 £1.90 (£16.00). Mr Luciano Gaucci (MARLBOROUGH) bred by
Ballymacoll Stud Farm Ltd in Ireland. 15 Rn ....................................... 64.5 sec (3)
 ɔℾ—ƹ0/0/7/–/1/–

---

**575** TOTE CREDIT (S) H'CAP (3 & 4-Y.O) (0-60) £2539.60 (£705.60: £338.80)
1¹/₂m 8y
3-15 (3-26)

(Weights raised 2 lb)

**Sea Paddy (41)** *(RBastiman)* 4–8–4(2) ‡⁷HBastiman (3) (bhd: drvn along 7f out:
gd hdwy 3f out: led ins fnl f: r.o wl) ........................................... —1

494⁴ Grey Commander (40) (Fav) *(MBrittain)* 4–8-10 KDarley (13) (lw: chsd ldrs: rdn
6f out: led wl over 2f out tl ins fnl f: no ex) ................................... 3.2

232 Carrolls Marc (IRE) *(PJFeilden)* 4–9-3 RCochrane (1) (hdwy ¹/₂-wy: sn
chsng ldrs: nt qckn appr fnl f) ................................................. 3¹/₂.3

505² Misty Goddess (IRE) *(MAJarvis)* 4–9-7 GDuffield (14) (in tch: effrt 3f out:
one pce) ......................................................................... 8.4

267 Bonny's Game (32) *(CWCElsey)* 4–7-11 ‡⁵SMaloney (10) (bhd tl styd on fnl 4f:
nrst fin) ......................................................................... 6.5

Drinks Party (IRE) (38) *(JWharton)* 4–8-1 ‡⁷GForster (17) (s.i.s: wnt prom after
4f: ev ch 4f out: wknd 2f out) .................................................. nk.6

406 Cherry Bob (47) *(CWThornton)* 3–7-4 ‡⁷KSked (7) (chsd ldrs: chal 4f out: wknd
over 2f out) ..................................................................... 1¹/₂.7

291 Spring Tern (USA) (54) (bl) *(RO'Leary)* 4–9-10 DNicholls (12) (nvr trbld ldrs) ... nk.8

457 Broughpark Azalea (53) (bl) *(JJO'Neill)* 3–8-3(1) MRoberts (5) (led tl hdd wl
over 2f out: sn wknd) ........................................................... 5.9

251 Midnight Galaxy (46) *(ANLee)* 3–7-5(3) ‡⁵NKennedy (4) (bhd: sme hdwy 4f out:
n.d) ............................................................................. 2.10

469 Saint Bene't (IRE) (50) *(PCHaslam)* 4–9-6 LPiggott (18) (lw: s.i.s: sn wknd) .... 3.11

Siberian King (52) *(ASmith)* 3–8-2 JLowe (8) (bit bkwd: in tch tl wknd 4f out) 2¹/₂.12

327 Statia (IRE) (42) *(DonEnricoIncisa)* 4–8-12 KimTinkler (9) (a bhd) ............. 12.13

210 Yeoman Bound (28) *(KTIvory)* 4–7-12 GBardwell (2) (chsd ldrs: effrt 4f out: sn
wknd) ........................................................................... 6.14

369 Elsharh (IRE) (50) (bl) *(JAGlover)* 3–7-7 ‡⁷CHawksley (6) (in tch tl wknd 5f out) 6.15

418 Belarius (45) (v) *(REBarr)* 4–9-1 SWebster (15) (cl up tl wknd 6f out: sn t.o) .. 16

LONG HANDICAP: Midnight Galaxy 7-4.

*138 Atlantic Way (13/2) Withdrawn (uns rdr & bolted bef s) : not under orders*

**100/30** Grey Commander(9/2–3/1), **9/2** Misty Goddess (IRE), **13/2** Drinks Party (IRE), **8/1** SEA PADDY(op
14/1), Saint Bene't (IRE), Carrolls Marc (IRE), **10/1** Elsharh (IRE), **14/1** Cherry Bob, **16/1** Broughpark Azalea(op
10/1), Spring Tern (USA), **20/1** Bonny's Game, **25/1** Ors. CSF £35.67, CT £208.16. Tote £9.00: £1.50 £1.10
£3.20 £1.40 (£11.50). Mr Greg Lancaster (WETHERBY) bred by Ferry Farm Co. 16 Rn; Bt in 4,000 gns
2m 41.8 (7.3)
SF—11/11/13/1/–/–

**576** TOTE DUAL FORECAST H'CAP (3-Y.O) (0-90) £3785.00 (£1130.00: £540.00: £245.00)
6f
3-45 (3-52)

(Weights raised 4 lb)

472⁴ **Windpower (IRE) (78)** *(JBerry)* 9-0 GCarter (7) (lw: cl up: led 2f out: qcknd clr
appr fnl f: easily) ......................................................................... —1
454⁵ Pageboy **(85)** *(PCHaslam)* 9-7 LPiggott (9) (led 4f: r.o one pce) .................. 3¹/₂.2
310* Taufan Blu (IRE) **(84)** *(MJohnston)* 9-6 DMcKeown (11) (lw: a chsng ldrs: kpt
on same pce fnl 2f) ..................................................................... 1¹/₂.3
387 Eastleigh **(69)** *(RHollinshead)* 8-5 PaulEddery (10) (a.p: effrt 2f out: r.o fnl f) ... s.h.4
387 Mogwai (IRE) **(69)** *(RFJohnsonHoughton)* 8-5 KDarley (14) (in tch: effrt over 2f
out: styd on: no imp) .................................................................. 1¹/₂.5
Waders Dream (IRE) **(72)** *(JEBanks)* 8-3 ‡⁵LNewton (5) (trckd ldrs tl grad lost pl
fnl 2f) ........................................................................................ ¹/₂.6
Philidor **(78)** *(JMPEustace)* 9-0 RCochrane (15) (bit bkwd: mid div: shkn up
¹/₂-wy: no imp) ............................................................................ ¹/₂.7
445³ Euro Festival **(75)** *(MissLCSiddall)* 8-11 AMunro (12) (lw: s.i.s & hmpd s: nvr
trbld ldrs) ................................................................................... hd.8
372* Abigails Boy (HOL) **(58)** *(DrJDScargill)* 7-5 ‡³JFanning (3) (chsd ldrs 4f) ......... s.h.9
472 Sonderise **(69)** *(NTinkler)* 8-5 GDuffield (1) (lw: hdwy whn nt clr run over 1f out:
n.d) .......................................................................................... 1¹/₂.10
472² Don't Smile **(75)** (Fav) *(MHTompkins)* 8-4 ‡⁷SMulvey (6) (nt clr run & hmpd after
2f to 2f out: nt rcvr) ................................................................... 1¹/₂.11
363⁶ Sammy Slew (USA) **(74)** *(SGNorton)* 8-10 DNicholls (4) (lw: plld hrd: hmpd
¹/₂-wy: n.d after) ............................................................................ 4.12
Thrie-Na-Helah (IRE) **(77)** *(RMWhitaker)* 8-13 ACulhane (8) (bit bkwd: nt clr run
after 2f & bdly hmpd: bhd after) .................................................... 3.13

5/2 Don't Smile, 5/1 Taufan Blu (IRE), 11/2 Sammy Slew (USA), 6/1 WINDPOWER (IRE), 10/1 Euro Festival,
Pageboy, Eastleigh, 11/1 Abigails Boy (HOL), 12/1 Sonderise, 14/1 Philidor, 16/1 Waders Dream (IRE), 25/1
Ors. CSF £67.68, CT £306.63. Tote £5.40: £2.20 £3.20 £1.90 (£38.10). Mr R. E. Sangster (COCKERHAM) bred
by Swettenham Stud in Ireland. 13 Rn                                           1m 16.4 (2.4)
SF—46/39/32/16/10/6

**577** TOTE PLACE ONLY STKS (Mdn 3-Y.O) £2490.00 (£690.00: £330.00)
1¹/₄m
4-15 (4-16)

**Duke of Eurolink** *(LMCumani)* 9-0 LDettori (1) (lw: hld up & bhd: effrt 2f out: str
run to ld nr fin) ............................................................................ —1
Suez Canal (IRE) *(PWChapple-Hyam)* 9-0 LPiggott (4) (swtg: a.p: led & qcknd
over 1f out: r.o: jst ct) ................................................................ nk.2
Mootawel (USA) *(HThomsonJones)* 9-0 RHills (3) (lw: chsd ldrs: effrt 3f out: r.o) 3.3
440 Sahara Shield *(AAScott)* 9-0 SCauthen (2) (b.off fore: mid div: effrt appr st: styd
on) ............................................................................................ 2¹/₂.4
466² Viva Darling *(BAMcMahon)* 9-0 BRaymond (6) (cl up early: stdd 5f out: hdwy
ent st: no imp) ............................................................................ 2¹/₂.5
406² Mainly Me **(82)** (Fav) *(MrsJCecil)* 8-9 PaulEddery (12) (hdwy 6f out: sn prom:
wknd 2f out) ............................................................................... 2.6
370⁴ Jato *(WJHaggas)* 9-0 MHills (5) (lw: led tl hdd over 1f out: eased whn btn) ..... 1¹/₂.7
Ler Cru (IRE) *(CEBrittain)* 9-0 MRoberts (8) (bit bkwd: chsd ldrs tl wknd 3f out) 3¹/₂.8
235 Northern Blade (IRE) **(64)** *(RHollinshead)* 9-0 RCochrane (9) (bhd: effrt appr st:
n.d) .......................................................................................... 1¹/₂.9
Hanley's Hands (IRE) *(MHTompkins)* 8-7 ‡⁷SMulvey (7) (unf: scope: bit bkwd:
hld up & a bhd) .......................................................................... hd.10
Kentucky Chicken (USA) *(MissLCSiddall)* 8-9 DMcKeown (10) (bit bkwd: a
bhd) .......................................................................................... s.h.11
Clifton Cruiser (USA) *(CRNelson)* 8-11 ‡³DBiggs (11) (cl up tl wknd qckly 4f out) 12

3/1 Mainly Me, 4/1 Jato, 9/2 Suez Canal (IRE), 5/1 DUKE OF EUROLINK, 11/2 Ler Cru (IRE), 8/1 Mootawel
(USA), 14/1 Viva Darling, 16/1 Sahara Shield, 25/1 Clifton Cruiser (USA), 50/1 Northern Blade (IRE), Hanley's
Hands (IRE), 66/1 Kentucky Chicken (USA). CSF £28.08, Tote £6.00: £1.80 £1.80 £3.70 (£19.20). Eurolink
Computer Services Ltd (NEWMARKET) bred by A. G. Antoniades. 12 Rn               2m 14.4 (6.1)
SF—34/33/27/22/17/8

**578** TOTE MARATHON H'CAP (0-70) £2511.00 (£696.00: £333.00)
2m 5f 122y
4-45 (4-47)

(Weights raised 1 lb)

388 **Patroclus (40)** *(RVoorspuy)* 7-8-9 PaulEddery (2) (b: lw: bhd: hdwy 8f out:
styd on to ld ins fnl f) ................................................................. —1
Premier Princess **(34)** (Fav) *(GAHam)* 6-8-3 SWood (14) (lw: a.p: shkn up to ld
3f out: hdd ins fnl f: kpt on one pce) ............................................ 1¹/₂.2

501 Suivez Moi (35) *(CNAllen)* 8–7–11 ‡⁷GForster (7) (wnt prom 12f out: outpcd 7f
out: hdwy 3f out: styd on) ........................................................... 4.3

Trojan Envoy (35) *(WCarter)* 4–7–12 JLowe (1) (lw: chsd ldrs: ev ch 4f out: one
pce) ................................................................................... hd.4

362 Ragtime (38) *(ASReid)* 5–8–0 ‡⁷StephenDavies (5) (chsd ldrs tl drdn & btn appr st) nk.5

501 Kovalevskia (37) *(DAWilson)* 7–8–6 GCarter (8) (swtg: bhd: effrt 6f out: nvr rchd
ldrs) ................................................................................. 10.6

501 One for the Chief (36) *(RMWhitaker)* 4–7–13 PBurke (11) (lw: bhd: sme hdwy 6f
out: nvr trbld ldrs) ................................................................. 8.7

362★ Dodger Dickins (41) *(RHollinshead)* 5–8–10 NCarlisle (4) (lw: bhd: effrt 7f out:
n.d) ................................................................................... 7.8

362² Carefree Times (52) *(JNorton)* 5–9–2 ‡⁵SMaloney (12) (lw: prom: rdn to ld 4f out:
hdd 3f out: sn wknd) .......................................................... 2¹/₂.9

234 Aberfoyle (IRE) (51) (bl) *(MissGayKelleway)* 4–8–11 ‡³DBiggs (3) (led tl hdd 10f
out: wknd 5f out) ................................................................. 2.10

501 Buckingham Band (USA) (49) (v) *(FHLee)* 4–8–12 DMcKeown (6) (swtg: cl up:
led 10f out to 4f out: sn lost pl) ......................................... 1.11

Isobar (27) *(MCChapman)* 6–7–3 ‡⁷CHawksley (16) (in tch tl wknd 7f out) ..... 4.12

288³ Pink Gin (55) *(MissSEHall)* 5–9–10 SCauthen (13) (bhd & pushed along ¹/₂-wy:
n.d) ................................................................................... 8.13

507 Hawwar (USA) (44) *(MrsALMKing)* 5–8–13 KFallon (10) (a bhd) ........................ 5.14

291³ Fit for Life (IRE) (48) (bl) *(MrsNMacauley)* 4–8–11 BRaymond (9) (t.o after 7f) ..... 15

**100/30** Premier Princess, **11/2** Pink Gin, Dodger Dickins(op 9/1), **13/2** PATROCLUS, **9/1** Carefree Times, **10/1** Fit for Life (IRE), **14/1** Trojan Envoy, Kovalevskia, **16/1** Suivez Moi, Ragtime, **25/1** Isobar, Aberfoyle (IRE), Buckingham Band (USA), **50/1** One for the Chief. CSF £28.02, CT £318.90. Tote £7.40: £2.10 £2.30 £11.20 (£12.40). Miss J. Newell (POLEGATE) bred by Sir Gerald Glover. 15 Rn       5m 0.8 (21.3)

**579**    TOTE BOOKMAKERS STKS    £2924.00 (£872.00: £416.00: £188.00)
1m 4y                                                              5-15 (5-15)

Badawi (USA) *(JHMGosden)* 4–8–9 RCochrane (6) (lw: hld up: hdwy over 2f
out: led ins fnl f: r.o wl) .................................................... —1

Safa (99) (Fav) *(AAScott)* 4–8–9 SCauthen (4) (bit bkwd: led: qcknd 2f out: hdd
& no ex ins fnl f) ................................................................ 3.2

239² Tanfith (CAN) (99) *(JEBanks)* 5–8–13 ‡⁵LNewton (5) (lw: a.p: hdwy 2f out: rdn &
nt qckn appr fnl f) ......................................................... 2¹/₂.3

St Ninian (101) *(MHEasterby)* 6–9–10 LPiggott (1) (bit bkwd: trckd ldrs: hdwy
over 2f out: rdn & btn over 1f out) ..................................... 1¹/₂.4

Shu Fly (NZ) *(MrsSOliver)* 8–9–3 ‡⁷TWilson (3) (bhd: hdwy over 2f out: nvr nr to chal) 4.5

531 Velveteen Boy *(BWLunness)* 4–8–7 GDuffield (2) (bit bkwd: chsd ldr tl wknd
over 2f out) ....................................................................... 15.6

Clifton Charlie (USA) *(CRNelson)* 4–9–0 PaulEddery (7) (bit bkwd: cl up tl wknd
3f out) .............................................................................. nk.7

**9/4** Safa, **5/2** St Ninian, **3/1** Tanfith (CAN), **5/1** BADAWI (USA), **8/1** Clifton Charlie (USA), **50/1** Shu Fly (NZ), **100/1** Velveteen Boy. CSF £16.05, Tote £4.50: £2.40 £1.40 (£4.60). Sheikh Mohammed (NEWMARKET) bred by Mill Ridge Farm Ltd in USA. 7 Rn       1m 44.2 (2.6)
SF—50/41/37/43/24/–

T/Plpt: £211.90 (17.25 Tckts).                                              AA

# WINDSOR  (Fig.8)
## Monday, April 27th [Good]
Going Allowance: 5f: minus 0.55 sec; Rest: minus 0.15 sec (F)          Wind: almost nil

Stalls: high

**580**    TORRISH CLAIMING STKS    £1758.60 (£489.60: £235.80)    1¹/₄m 7y    5-50 (5-52)

409★ **Abingdon Flyer (IRE) (60)** (bl) (Fav) *(RHannon)* 4–8–12 JReid (11) (6th st:
edgd rt: led wl ins fnl f: drvn out) ..................................... —1

505³ Shoehorn *(MCPipe)* 5–8–8 AMunro (16) (led tl wl ins fnl f) ...................... nk.2

Vanroy (70) *(JRJenkins)* 8–8–13 TQuinn (5) (b: bit bkwd: hdwy on ins 2f out:
one pce fnl f) ..................................................................... 5.3

525⁶ Conjurer (66) *(RSimpson)* 5–8–2 ‡⁵ATucker (17) (5th st: hrd rdn over 2f out: one
pce) ................................................................................... 4.4

505 Pims Classic (58) *(WJHaggas)* 4–8–9 NDay (14) (mid div tl rdn & styd on fnl 3f) ³/₄.5

273 Anne's Bank (IRE) (42) *(AMoore)* 4–8–4⁽¹⁾ BRouse (1) (wl bhd tl stdy hdwy fnl
3f) ..................................................................................... s.h.6

Armashocker *(DSasse)* 4–8–10 GBaxter (7) (swtg: nvr nr to chal) ........................ 2.7

504 Super Morning **(64)** *(GBBalding)* 6-9-2 WRSwinburn (9) (hdwy 4f out: ev ch 2f out: sn wknd) ........................................................ 5.8
Sporting Weekend (FR) *(DSasse)* 5-9-3 ‡7JWeaver (4) (bit bkwd: nvr trbld ldrs) 2.9
Bronze Runner **(45)** (bl) *(EAWheeler)* 8-8-7 ‡7BThomas (10) (2nd st: wknd over 2f out) ............................................................ 1½.10
249⁶ Mardior **(30)** *(WGRWightman)* 4-7-12 TyroneWilliams (15) (3rd st: wknd 3f out) 5.11
250 Monte Bre **(40)** *(RAkehurst)* 6-8-10 NAdams (8) (lw: 4th st: ev ch 3f out: sn wknd) ................................................................ 1½.12
Striding Edge *(JRJenkins)* 7-8-6 ‡7MichaelDenaro (6) (b: n.d) ...................... nk.13
409 Red Dollar **(42)** *(BGubby)* 7-8-4 ‡5CHodgson (12) (bhd fnl 4f) ................. 2.14
Lord's Final *(CRBarwell)* 5-9-1 TLang (13) (prom 5f) ................................ 1½.15
169 Trendy Auctioneer (IRE) **(42)** *(MCPipe)* 4-8-1 ‡7KRutter (2) (n.d) ............ d.h.15
Countess Brussels *(KGWingrove)* 4-7-12 RStreet (3) (rn v.wd thrght: t.o fnl 5f) 30.17

**11/4** ABINGDON FLYER (IRE), **9/2** Super Morning(op 3/1), **5/1** Shoehorn(op 3/1), **6/1** Conjurer(op 4/1), **15/2** Vanroy, **14/1** Monte Bre, Pims Classic, Bronze Runner, **16/1** Trendy Auctioneer (IRE), **20/1** Countess Brussels(op 12/1), Red Dollar, Striding Edge(op 10/1), Sporting Weekend (FR), **33/1** Ors. CSF £18.90, Tote £3.60: £1.40 £1.70 £2.50 (£5.90). Mr J. A. Nichols (MARLBOROUGH) bred by Grange Thoroughbreds in Ireland. 17 Rn
2m 6.5 (3.5)
SF—48/43/38/19/24/18

### 581

E.B.F. BLUE CHARM STKS (Mdn 2-Y.O) £1845.60 (£511.60: £244.80)
**5f 10y**
6-15 (6-20)

**Niche** *(RHannon)* 8-9 JReid (5) (neat: w ldr: led over 2f out: hung lft: drvn out) . —1
Tioman Island *(PFICole)* 9-0 TQuinn (11) (leggy: bit bkwd: a.p: ev ch fnl f: r.o) nk.2
The Informer *(PFICole)* (Fav) 9-0 AMunro (13) (cmpt: dwlt: hdwy over 3f out: rdn over 1f out: r.o ins fnl f) .................................. nk.3
Jonsalan *(WCarter)* 9-0 LDettori (2) (leggy: hdwy over 2f out: rdn over 1f out: r.o one pce) ............................................ 1½.4
297 Lochore *(RIngram)* 8-7 ‡7JWeaver (3) (hrd rdn & no hdwy fnl 2f) ............... 7.5
352⁵ Trentesimo (IRE) *(JBerry)* 9-0 JCarroll (10) (led over 2f: edgd bdly lft & wknd over 1f out) ...................................................... 1.6
339 Moonstruck Bard *(AHide)* 9-0 BRouse (7) (spd over 3f) ........................... 3½.7
383 Wickins *(GLewis)* 9-0 RaymondBerry (6) (nvr nrr) ................................ hd.8
C D Shareplan (USA) *(MRChannon)* 9-0 CRutter (8) (unf: bit bkwd: nvr nr to chal) ....................................................... 1.9
476 Gypsy Legend *(WGMTurner)* 8-2 ‡7KRutter (1) (bit bkwd: prom 3f) ............. hd.10
Second Colours (USA) *(PSFelgate)* 9-0 AMackay (4) (cmpt: bkwd: s.s: a bhd) 2.11
Heroic Deed *(MHTompkins)* 8-9 ‡5CHodgson (9) (cmpt: a bhd) .................. 2½.12
Raw Health *(MJHeaton-Ellis)* 9-0 MRoberts (14) (neat: bkwd: dwlt: a bhd) ... 4.13
Nordic Spirit (IRE) *(CFWall)* 9-0 NDay (12) (unf: bit bkwd: a bhd) ............. 3.14

**9/4** The Informer (USA), **11/2** Trentesimo (IRE)(op 3/1), Tioman Island(op 3/1), **8/1** Moonstruck Bard, NICHE(op 5/2), **10/1** C D Shareplan (USA)(6/1—12/1), Raw Health(6/1—12/1), **12/1** Jonsalan(op 8/1), **16/1** Lochore(op 10/1), Wickins(op 8/1), **20/1** Heroic Deed(op 12/1), Nordic Spirit (IRE)(op 10/1), Second Colours (USA), **33/1** Gypsy Legend. CSF £54.76, Tote £7.60: £1.80 £2.50 £1.50 (£33.00). Lord Carnarvon (MARLBOROUGH) bred by Highclere Stud Ltd. 14 Rn
59.2 sec (0.2)
SF—36/40/39/33/—/—

### 582

JOCK SCOTT H'CAP (3-Y.O) (0-80) £2110.00 (£585.00: £280.00)    **5f 10y**    6-40 (6-45)
(Weights raised 2 lb)

472⁵ **Truthful Image (70)** (bl) *(MJRyan)* 8-13 AMunro (7) (a.p: led wl over 1f out: r.o wl) ....................................................... —1
421⁵ Cumbrian Cavalier **(55)** *(KGWingrove)* 7-12(1) TyroneWilliams (14) (a.p: hrd rdn over 1f out: r.o ins fnl f) ................................ 2.2
472 Court Minstrel **(56)** *(LJHolt)* 7-13 NAdams (12) (hrd rdn & gd hdwy fnl 2f: nrst fin) ......................................................... nk.3
300 Super Rocky **(77)** *(JBerry)* 9-6 JCarroll (5) (a.p: ev ch 1f out: wknd nr fin) ...... s.h.4
Fourofus **(63)** *(RBoss)* 8-6 MRoberts (4) (bit bkwd: nrst fin) ..................... ½.5
298 Sea Crusader **(57)** *(MBlanshard)* 8-0 CRutter (10) (a.p: one pce fnl 2f) .......... s.h.6
452 Cheshire Annie (IRE) **(58)** *(WCarter)* 7-10(1) ‡5NGwilliams (2) (lw: nvr nr to chal) 1.7
399⁴ Hot Lavender (CAN) **(70)** *(CFWall)* 8-13 WRSwinburn (8) (led over 3f) ........... ¾.8
414 Battling Bella **(66)** *(JSutcliffe)* 8-9 BRouse (1) (swtg: stdy hdwy fnl 2f: r.o) ½.9
472 Paradise Forum **(78)** *(CAHorgan)* 9-0 ‡7JWeaver (11) (swtg: nvr trbld ldrs) ..... ¾.10
359 Golden Proposal **(54)** (bl) *(MBell)* 7-4(3) ‡7DHarrison (13) (n.d) ................. ½.11
219★ Creche **(76)** (bl) (Fav) *(MrsNMacauley)* 9-5 NDay (15) (lw: w ldr over 2f: sn rdn & wknd) ...................................................... ½.12
Chance to Dream **(58)** *(RHannon)* 8-1 SRaymont (6) (s.s: t.o tl r.o fnl f) ...... 1½.13
421³ Stormbuster **(57)** *(PSFelgate)* 8-0 AMackay (9) (n.d) .......................... hd.14
334⁶ Rio Trusky **(50)** *(MDIUsher)* 7-7 GBardwell (3) (a bhd) ........................ 2.15

**7/2** Creche, **9/2** TRUTHFUL IMAGE(3/1—5/1), **13/2** Hot Lavender (CAN), **8/1** Super Rocky(6/1—9/1), Stormbuster, **12/1** Court Minstrel, **14/1** Golden Proposal, Fourofus, Chance to Dream, Paradise Forum, **16/1** Battling Bella (USA)(10/1—20/1), **20/1** Cumbrian Cavalier, Cheshire Annie (IRE), **25/1** Ors. CSF £88.16, CT £951.01. Tote £5.20: £2.10 £6.70 £2.80 (£107.90). Mrs Margaret Baxter (NEWMARKET) bred by A. Bromley. 15 Rn
59.5 sec (0.5)
SF—34/11/11/31/15/8

**583**    'RACEGOERS ENCYCLOPAEDIA' H'CAP (3-Y.O) (0-90) £2880.50 (£798.00: £381.50)
1m 3f 135y                                                                          7-10 (7-12)

(Weights raised 2 lb)

562* **Simply-H (IRE)** (65) (Fav) (MBell) 7-11 (5x) ‡7PTurner (12) (lw: 4th st: led over 2f
out: sddle slipped: edgd lft: drvn out) ......................................... —1
370* Deer Hunt (82) (PJMakin) 9-7 TQuinn (7) (lw: 3rd st: ev ch fnl 2f: r.o) ............... s.h.2
374³ Chipper (65) (RBoss) 8-4 MRoberts (10) (lw: 5th st: r.o one pce fnl 2f) ............... 4.3
369⁴ Jack Button (IRE) (72) (BobJones) 8-11 NDay (4) (2nd st: led over 3f out tl over 2f
out) ................................................. ½.4
498* Dare to Dream (IRE) (54) (GLewis) 7-7 (5x) NAdams (5) (lw: hdwy 4f out: ev ch
over 2f out: sn wknd) ......................................... ¾.5
Cov Tel Lady (68) (MHTompkins) 8-2⁽³⁾ ‡5CHodgson (3) (nvr nr to chal) ............... 4.6
356³ Hymn Book (IRE) (76) (MRStoute) 9-1 WRSwinburn (6) (led tl wknd over 3f out) ...... 3.7
Mohana (70) (JLDunlop) 8-9 JReid (9) (nvr trbld ldrs) ............................. hd.8
Andy Jack (69) (MJHeaton-Ellis) 8-8 MHills (8) (hdwy 4f out: wknd 3f out) ............... 2.9
Last Conquest (IRE) (70) (PFICole) 8-9 AMunro (2) (n.d) ........................ 1½.10
Elite Reg (62) (PFICole) 8-1 CRutter (1) (6th st: wknd 3f out) ................... nk.11
471 Erlemo (56) (CJBenstead) 7-9 GBardwell (11) (lw: n.d) ...................... 3.12

**5/4** SIMPLY-H (IRE), **7/2** Deer Hunt, **6/1** Dare to Dream (IRE)(9/2—8/1) Hymn Book (IRE)(5/1—8/1), **10/1** Chipper, **25/1** Cov Tel Lady, Jack Button (IRE), Last Conquest (IRE), Mohana, Erlemo, **33/1** Ors. CSF £6.71, CT £30.75. Tote £2.40: £1.50 £2.20 £1.30 (£4.60). Mr G. L. H. Lederman (NEWMARKET) bred by E. J. Loder in Ireland. 12 Rn
2m 31.4 (8.9)

**584**    LADY CAROLINE STKS (2-Y.O.F) £2005.00 (£555.00: £265.00)    5f 10y    7-40 (7-42)

**Lyric Fantasy (IRE)** (RHannon) 8-8 MRoberts (4) (neat: a.p: hrd rdn over 1f
out: led ins fnl f: r.o) ............................................ —1
439* Ancestral Dancer (Fav) (MBell) 8-13 MHills (7) (dwlt: hdwy over 2f out: led wl
over 1f out tl ins fnl f) ............................................ ½.2
476* Sheila's Secret (IRE) (WCarter) 8-13 JReid (2) (led over 3f) ...................... 3.3
Miss Whittingham (IRE) (JBerry) 8-8 JCarroll (5) (cmpt: spd over 2f) ............... 12.4
476⁶ Perfect Passion (JJBridger) 8-8 DaleGibson (3) (lw: spd over 2f) ............... 6.5
Sterling Princess (JRJenkins) 8-8 GBaxter (1) (neat: bit bkwd: spd 2f) ............ 10.6
Freebyjove (PButler) 8-8 AProud (6) (b: neat: s.s: a wl bhd) ................... 12.7

**Evens** Ancestral Dancer, **3/1** LYRIC FANTASY (IRE)(6/4—4/1), **9/2** Sheila's Secret (IRE)(op 5/2), **6/1** Miss Whittingham (IRE)(tchd 9/1), **25/1** Perfect Passion, Sterling Princess, **33/1** Freebyjove. CSF £6.46, Tote £4.50: £2.30 £1.40 (£3.00). Lord Carnarvon (MARLBOROUGH) bred by Minch Bloodstock in Ireland. 7 Rn
59.4 sec (0.4)
SF—31/34/20/–/–/–

**585**    MAR LODGE MEDIAN AUCTION GRADUATION STKS (3-Y.O.C & G) £1632.00 (£452.00:
£216.00) 1¼m 7y                                                                    8-10 (8-11)

451* **Peto** (HRACecil) 9-10 SCauthen (2) (lw: 3rd st: led over 2f out: r.o wl) ................. —1
511* Majboor (IRE) (Fav) (PTWalwyn) 9-10 WCarson (4) (lw: 2nd st: led 3f out: sn
hdd: nt qckn) .................................................. 3½.2
348 First Century (IRE) (96) (PFICole) 9-10 TQuinn (7) (4th st: one pce fnl 3f) ............. 2½.3
Sirtelimar (IRE) (BobJones) 9-0 VSmith (1) (led to 3f out: one pce) ................... nk.4
Tooley's Boy (MrsBarbaraWaring) 9-0 NHowe (8) (6th st: nvr nr ldrs) ............... 5.5
Mediator (bl) (AMoore) 9-0 NAdams (5) (bit bkwd: 5th st: nvr nr to chal) ............... nk.6
441 Chummy's Child (IRE) (BWHills) 9-0 MHills (3) (lw: a bhd) ................... nk.7
Jorrocks (MDixon) 9-0 DaleGibson (6) (w'like: bkwd: a bhd: t.o) ................ 20.8

**10/11** Majboor (IRE), **5/2** PETO, **3/1** First Century (IRE)(5/2—5/1), **25/1** Chummy's Child (IRE), **66/1** Sirtelimar (IRE), **100/1** Ors. CSF £4.90, Tote £2.90: £1.10 £1.20 £1.40 (£1.60). Sheikh Mohammed (NEWMARKET) bred by P. T. Tellwright. 8 Rn
2m 9.2 (6.2)
SF—33/26/21/10/–/–

T/Plpt: £17.80 (81.75 Tckts).                                                          Hn

## 352—WOLVERHAMPTON (L-H)
### Monday, April 27th [Good]
Going Allowance: 5f: minus 0.30 (F); Rest: 0.05 sec per fur (G)          Wind: str bhd

Stalls: high

**586**     RUGELEY CLAIMING STKS (I)   £2343.60 (£649.60: £310.80)   1½m 70y   2-00 (2-01)

**Prosequendo (USA)** *(72) (MDixon)* 5–8–6 DaleGibson (12) (hld up & bhd: hdwy 4f out: rdn over 2f out: hung lft: led ins fnl f: r.o wl) .................—1
504² Woodurather *(67) (MCPipe)* 6–9–10 DHolland (10) (chsd ldr: 3rd st: led over 3f out tl ins fnl f) ...............................2½.2
505* Molly Splash *(42) (CACyzer)* 5–8–5 JFortune (8) (lw: hdwy & 6th st: hrd rdn & ev ch over 2f out: one pce) .....................3½.3
504⁴ Queens Tour *(37) (MBrittain)* 7–8–6 JQuinn (6) (b: bit bkwd: 5th st: hrd rdn over 2f out: no hdwy) ..................5.4
335 Prince Lyphard *(RAkehurst)* 6–9–1 ‡³FNorton (1) (nvr nr ldrs) ..................10.5
505 Hand Painted *(57) (CRBeever)* 8–7–13 ‡⁷MHumphries (9) (b: 7th & wkng st) ...........3.6
358 Great Impostor *(47) (RJHodges)* 4–8–1 ‡⁵TSprake (2) (lw: 2nd st: wknd 3f out) .....2½.7
453* Henpot (IRE) *(Fav) (HRACecil)* 4–8–9 PatEddery (5) (hld up: 4th st: rdn & wknd over 3f out) ..............................1½.8
422 Mabthul (USA) *(44) (MJHeaton-Ellis)* 4–8–3 ‡⁷JWeaver (4) (bit bkwd: led: clr 9f out: hdd over 3f out: wknd qckly) ..................3½.9
Doctor's Remedy *(30) (MrsJJordan)* 6–8–5² ‡⁷DThompson (11) (a bhd) ..................½.10
Beaufan *(CFCJackson)* 5–8–8 AMcGlone (3) (bhd most of wy) ..................2.11
Attic Wit (FR) *(RJHolder)* 6–8–10 ADicks (7) (bit bkwd: a bhd) ..................1½.12

**1/2 Henpot (IRE), 9/2 Woodurather**(3/1—5/1), **12/1 PROSEQUENDO (USA)**(op 6/1), **16/1 Molly Splash, 20/1** Hand Painted, Prince Lyphard, **25/1** Great Impostor, Queens Tour, **33/1** Mabthul (USA), **80/1** Doctor's Remedy, **100/1** Ors. CSF £61.94, Tote £13.90: £2.60 £1.40 £3.90 (£29.50). Mr J. Daniels (EPSOM) bred by H. Turney McKnight and June H. McKnight in USA. 12 Rn; Henpot (IRE) clmd D Walker £12,100          2m 41.6 (9.9)

**587**     ATHERSTONE H'CAP (3 & 4-Y.O.F) (0-70) £2598.40 (£722.40: £347.20)   7f   2-30 (2-34)

375 **Millfit (USA)** *(63) (BHanbury)* 3–8–0 ‡⁷VBray (6) (hdwy on ins 4f out: led ins fnl f: comf) ..............................—1
522* Debsy Do (USA) *(68) (SGNorton)* 3–8–5 (7x) ‡⁷OPears (11) (3rd st: led wl over 1f out: hdd ins fnl f) ..............................¾.2
387 Miss Doody *(66) (v) (MRChannon)* 3–8–10 PatEddery (2) (hdwy over 2f out: hrd rdn over 1f out: r.o ins fnl f) .............s.h.3
Oak Apple (USA) *(60) (BHanbury)* 3–8–4 WRyan (7) (b: still unf: 5th st: lost pl 3f out: rallied over 1f out: r.o) ....................1½.4
448 Chloes Diamond (IRE) *(54) (JLSpearing)* 4–8–12 JWilliams (8) (hdwy over 2f out: one pce fnl f) .............6.5
505 Miss Cookie *(58) (MCPipe)* 4–9–2 BCrossley (13) (nvr nr to chal) ..................1½.6
506 Unveiled *(70) (RJHodges)* 4–9–9 ‡⁵TSprake (1) (lw: no hdwy fnl 2f) ..................2.7
Ushba (FR) *(62) (CGCox)* 4–9–6 AClark (9) (bit bkwd: led over 5f: eased whn btn fnl f) .............s.h.8
Time Lapse *(62) (PJMakin)* 3–8–6 DHolland (15) (4th st: wknd over 2f out) ..................½.9
508 Mushy Boff *(51) (CJHill)* 4–8–2 ‡⁷JWeaver (5) (n.d) ..................¾.10
278 Princess Jestina (IRE) *(47) (GHYardley)* 4–8–5 SWhitworth (14) (m.n.s) ..................hd.11
412 Forgetful *(62) (RHannon)* 3–8–6 AMcGlone (16) (m.n.s) ..................¾.12
407⁴ Drummer's Dream (IRE) *(43) (MrsNMacauley)* 4–7–12 ‡³FNorton (3) (chsd ldr: 2nd st: wknd over 2f out) ..................1.13
449 Fay Eden (IRE) *(57) (RJHodges)* 4–9–1 JQuinn (9) (bhd fnl 3f) ..................½.14
408⁶ Mabonne *(64) (Fav) (JLDunlop)* 3–8–8 WCarson (12) (6th st: bhd fnl 3f) ..................¾.15
411 Tendresse (IRE) *(45) (DRTucker)* 4–7–12 ‡⁵RPrice (10) (t.o) ..................10.16
333 Swift Stream *(46) (ABarrow)* 4–8–4 NAdams (17) (t.o) ..................17

**100/30 Mabonne**(9/2—3/1), **15/2 Debsy Do (USA), 8/1 Miss Doody**(6/1—9/1), **10/1 Time Lapse, 11/1** Oak Apple (USA), Forgetful(op 7/1), **12/1 Miss** Cookie, Drummer's Dream (IRE), **14/1** Fay Eden (IRE)(10/1—20/1), Unveiled, **16/1** MILLFIT (USA), **20/1** Mushy Boff, **25/1** Tendresse (IRE), **33/1** Chloes Diamond (IRE), Ushba (FR), **50/1** Ors. CSF £121.05, CT £949.44. Tote £20.50: £3.40 £1.20 £2.50 £4.50 (£345.00). Mr Hilal Salem (NEWMARKET) bred by Heronwood Farm in USA. 17 Rn          1m 27.7 (3.4)
SF—40/43/47/36/26/25

**588**     TAMWORTH (S) STKS (2-Y.O) £2520.00 (£700.00: £336.00)   5f   3-00 (3-06)

329⁵ **Petite Lass** *(WCarter)* 8-1 ‡⁵NGwilliams (4) (a.p: led over 1f out: edgd lft fnl f: r.o) —1

| | | |
|---|---|---|
| | Convenient Moment *(JBerry)* 8-6 DHolland (12) (small: bit bkwd: led over 3f: r.o) | nk.2 |
| | Tudela *(MJHaynes)* 8-6 WCarson (5) (lt-f: bit bkwd: s.i.s: hdwy 2f out: r.o fnl f) .. | 1.3 |
| | Over the Dec *(BAMcMahon)* 8-6 JFortune (11) (lt-f: a.p: r.o ins fnl f) | hd.4 |
| 423 | Silly Sally *(WGMTurner)* 8-1 ‡5TSprake (2) (no hdwy fnl 2f) | 2.5 |
| 423 | Pfaff's Cellar *(WGMTurner)* 8-1 ‡5RPrice (14) (nrst fin) | 2½.6 |
| 423⁴ | Total Truth *(JWhite)* 7-13 ‡7CAvery (6) (spd over 3f) | hd.7 |
| 352² | Ukam's Lady (Fav) *(RHannon)* 8-6 PatEddery (7) (prom over 2f) | nk.8 |
| 329⁶ | Huesca *(JRJenkins)* 8-6 WNewnes (3) (s.s: n.d) | 2.9 |
| 361 | Surprise Partner *(MJohnston)* 8-11 RPElliott (8) (m.n.s) | ¾.10 |
| | Hawke Bay *(DHaydnJones)* 8-11 JWilliams (16) (w'like: bkwd: nvr plcd to chal) | nk.11 |
| 463⁵ | Matthew David *(MBrittain)* 8-11 JQuinn (13) (m.n.s) | ¾.12 |
| | Secret Tale *(GBlum)* 8-6 SWhitworth (1) (scope: outpcd) | ¾.13 |
| 423 | Twitcher *(GBlum)* 8-6 AShoults (10) (spd 3f) | 1½.14 |
| 447 | Meadow View (IRE) *(CJHill)* 8-6 AClark (9) (s.i.s: a bhd) | 1½.15 |
| 339 | Madame Cresson *(GAPritchard-Gordon)* 8-6 AMcGlone (15) (spd over 2f) | 4.16 |

7/4 Ukam's Lady, 11/2 Total Truth, 7/1 Matthew David(tchd 11/1), 8/1 Convenient Moment(op 9/2), 11/1 Madame Cresson, 12/1 PETITE LASS(op 8/1), 14/1 Twitcher(op 8/1), Surprise Partner(op 8/1), 16/1 Tudela, 25/1 Over the Dec, Silly Sally, 33/1 Hawke Bay, Huesca, Secret Tale, 40/1 Meadow View (IRE), 50/1 Pfaff's Cellar. CSF £102.25, Tote £23.80: £2.90 £2.60 £3.90 (£48.40). T. G. Mills Limited (EPSOM) bred by Mrs T. G. Mills. 16 Rn; No bid                                                        60.9 sec (3.6)

**589**      WATLING STREET STKS (3-Y-O) £2186.80 (£604.80: £288.40)      **1m 200y**   3-30 (3-32)

| | | |
|---|---|---|
| 356* | Rockawhile (IRE) (Fav) *(HRACecil)* 8-10 PatEddery (3) (2nd tl led 2f out: edgd lft 1f out: rdn out) | —1 |
| 413* | Gotcha (BAR) (87) *(RHannon)* 9-1 WCarson (1) (led 7f: rdn & r.o wl fnl f) | s.h.2 |
| | Spot the Dove *(RJPrice)* 8-7⁽¹⁾ JWilliams (2) (w'like: bkwd: 3rd st: one pce fnl 4f) | 8.3 |

4/11 ROCKAWHILE (IRE), 5/2 Gotcha (BAR), 66/1 Spot the Dove. CSF £1.41, Tote £1.10 (£1.10). Mr L. Marinopoulos (NEWMARKET) bred by Swettenham Stud in Ireland. 3 Rn                        1m 56.9 (8.4)

**590**      RUGELEY CLAIMING STKS (II)      £2343.60 (£649.60: £310.80)      **1½m 70y**   4-00 (4-04)

| | | |
|---|---|---|
| | Discord (63) (Fav) *(LordHuntingdon)* 6-9-0 PatEddery (8) (hld up: hdwy ½-wy: 7th st: led over 1f out: comf) | —1 |
| 513 | Empire Blue (82) *(PFICole)* 9-9-0 WCarson (7) (b: chsd ldrs: 4th st: rdn & ev ch 2f out: styd on ins fnl f) | 1½.2 |
| 505 | Rushluan (56) *(RJHodges)* 8-8-1 ‡5TSprake (3) (chsd ldrs: 3rd st: led before 2f out tl over 1f out: unable qckn fnl f) | 1.3 |
| 220⁶ | Erevnon (59) *(JLHarris)* 5-8-6 DHolland (5) (lw: chsd ldr: 2nd st: wknd over 1f out) | 12.4 |
| 244 | Billy Lomond (IRE) (42) (bl) *(CACyzer)* 4-8-6 JFortune (2) (hdwy & 6th st: wknd wl over 1f out) | 1½.5 |
| | Playful Juliet (CAN) *(BRCambidge)* 4-8-2 ‡5RPrice (9) (hld up: styd on fnl 2f: nvr nrr) | 2½.6 |
| | Beija Flor *(FJordan)* 5-9-0 WNewnes (1) (bit bkwd: led & sn clr: hdd over 2f out: wknd qckly) | 8.7 |
| | Mahaasin *(LJCodd)* 4-8-2 ‡7RMitchell (6) (chsd ldrs 8f: sn lost tch) | 1½.8 |
| | Gulfland (31) *(GAPritchard-Gordon)* 11-8-9 ‡7AntoinetteArmes (4) (bkwd: s.s: a bhd) | 1½.9 |
| | Saint Vending *(MBrittain)* 4-8-6 JQuinn (11) (a bhd: t.o) | 25.10 |
| | Logarithm (36) *(PJMakin)* 4-8-5 WRyan (10) (bit bkwd: prom: 5th & wkng st: t.o) | 7.11 |
| 106 | Little Miss Polly *(CJHill)* 4-8-1 SDawson (12) (s.i.s: in rr tl p.u over 3f out: lame) | 0 |

13/8 DISCORD, 5/2 Empire Blue, 8/1 Beija Flor(6/1—9/1), 20/1 Gulfland(op 12/1), Mahaasin(op 7/1), Rushluan, 25/1 Erevnon, 33/1 Saint Vending, Logarithm, Billy Lomond (IRE), 66/1 Ors. CSF £5.07, Tote £2.50: £1.60 £1.80 £1.10 (£5.20). Mrs Evan Williams (WEST ILSLEY) bred by Knockaney Stud. 12 Rn      2m 43.4 (11.7)

**591**      LICHFIELD MEDIAN AUCTION STKS (Mdn 3-Y-O) £2304.40 (£638.40: £305.20)      **5f**   4-30 (4-35)

| | | |
|---|---|---|
| | Cradle Days (79) (Fav) *(RHannon)* 9-0 WCarson (1) (lw: mde all centre: shkn up 1f out: r.o wl) | —1 |
| 415⁵ | We're All Game (57) *(BCMorgan)* 8-9 DHolland (5) (a chsng wnr: effrt over 1f out: r.o) | 2.2 |
| 372⁵ | High Principles (54) *(JBerry)* 8-7 ‡7PRoberts (3) (chsd ldrs: edgd rt over 1f out: one pce) | 6.3 |
| | Our Rita *(PAKelleway)* 8-9 AClark (6) (lengthy: unf: bit bkwd: s.s: sn rcvrd: one pce fnl 2f) | s.h.4 |

     Casting Shadows *(RDickin)* 8-9 SDawson (4) (w'like: bit bkwd: spd over 3f) ... 3½.5
363[5]  Dandy Desire *(BCMorgan)* 9-0 SWhitworth (9) (outpcd) ..................... 1½.6
495  Our Eileen *(ASReid)* 8-9 SMorris (2) (s.s: outpcd) ...................................... nk.7
372  Spanish Express *(66)* *(RBoss)* 9-0 PatEddery (7) (chsd ldrs 3f: sn outpcd) ........ 4.8
276[2]  Nigals Friend *(70)* *(DHaydnJones)* 9-0 JWilliams (10) (outpcd) ............... 1½.9
     The Dream Maker (IRE) *(MrsNMacauley)* 8-9 AMcGlone (11) (bhd fr ½-wy) .... 3.10
     Ballymust (IRE) *(JWhite)* 8-4 ‡5RPrice (8) (bkwd: s.i.s: a outpcd: t.o) ............. 20.11

**15/8** CRADLE DAYS, **4/1** Spanish Express, **5/1** Nigals Friend(op 3/1), **10/1** We're All Game, **11/1** Dandy Desire(8/1—12/1), High Principles(8/1—12/1), **16/1** Our Rita(op 10/1), **20/1** Our Eileen(op 12/1), **33/1** Casting Shadows, **50/1** Ors. CSF £19.00, Tote £3.50: £2.20 £2.70 £3.00 (£8.50). Mr T. A. Johnsey (MARLBOROUGH) bred by T. A. Johnsey. 11 Rn
                                            58.6 sec (1.3)
                                          SF—44/31/5/6/–/–

## 592    MIDLAND SPRING H'CAP (0-80) £2480.80 (£688.80: £330.40)  **1m**    5-00 (5-07)

508  Lady Lacey *(49)* (v) *(GBBalding)* 5—7-12 DaleGibson (16) (hld up: hdwy over 2f out: rdn to ld wl ins fnl f: r.o) ..................... —1
508  Foolish Touch *(57)* *(WJMusson)* 10—8-6 JHBrown (3) (b: lw: dwlt: hld up & bhd: gd hdwy wl over 1f out: fin fast) ................... ½.2
456  Veloce (IRE) *(55)* *(MO'Neill)* 4—8-4 JFortune (12) (7th st: led 2f out: sn rdn clr: ct wl ins fnl f) ......................... nk.3
277[3]  On Y Va (USA) *(70)* *(RJRWilliams)* 5—9-5 DHolland (8) (hld up: hdwy 2f out: styd on ins fnl f: nvr nrr) ........................... 4.4
398  Northern Printer *(63)* *(MO'Neill)* 7—8-12 PatEddery (15) (hld up: hdwy over 3f out: rdn over 1f out: one pce) ..................... 2.5
     Tartar's Bow *(59)* *(RJHolder)* 5—8-8 JWilliams (10) (lw: nvr nr to chal) ............ 3½.6
456[2]  Causley *(71)* (Fav) *(BAMcMahon)* 7—9-6 WRyan (14) (led after 1f to 2f out: sn rdn & btn) ........................ 1½.7
     Melodic Habit *(45)* *(MrsAKnight)* 5—7-8(1) JQuinn (18) (lw: 9th st: effrt 3f out: sn wknd) ...................... 2½.8
     Dawning Street (IRE) *(79)* *(JLDunlop)* 4—10-0 WNewnes (2) (dwlt: nvr plcd to chal) ....................... hd.9
     Cartel *(61)* *(JLHarris)* 5—8-5 ‡5BDoyle (17) (lw: s.i.s: effrt 2f out: n.d) ............. s.h.10
508*  Tyrian Purple (IRE) *(54)* *(RHollinshead)* 4—7-10 (6x) ‡7MHumphries (7) (led 1f: 3rd st: wknd over 2f out) ................ ½.11
515[4]  Scottish Bambi *(65)* *(RHannon)* 4—9-0 WCarson (1) (prom: 2nd st: wknd over 2f out) ....................... 1½.12
496  Green's Stubbs *(44)* *(ABarrow)* 5—7-7 RFox (20) (a bhd) ......................... ¾.13
508  Radio Caroline *(53)* *(MTate)* 4—8-2(1) GHind (19) (hdwy & 6th st: wknd wl over 2f out) ...................... ½.14
     Aldahe *(49)* *(BRMillman)* 7—7-12 AMcGlone (6) (5th st: rdn 3f out: sn wknd) .......... 5.15
508  Tara's Girl *(69)* *(PABlockley)* 5—9-4 NHowe (4) (chsd ldrs: 8th st: wknd over 2f out) ...................... 1½.16
57  Notanotherone (IRE) *(49)* *(JLHarris)* 4—7-12(2) BCrossley (13) (a bhd) ............... 1½.17
56  Foreign Assignment (IRE) *(54)* *(JWhite)* 4—7-12(3) ‡5RPrice (11) (a bhd) ............... ½.18
106  Top One *(56)* *(CJHill)* 7—8-5(3) AClark (9) (4th st: wknd 3f out: t.o) ........................ 20.19
                LONG HANDICAP: Green's Stubbs 7-1.

**11/2** Causley, **6/1** Tyrian Purple (IRE), **13/2** On Y Va (USA), **8/1** Scottish Bambi, **10/1** LADY LACEY, Veloce (IRE), **12/1** Foolish Touch, Northern Printer(op 8/1), **16/1** Tartar's Bow, Dawning Street (IRE), Tara's Girl(12/1—20/1), **25/1** Cartel, Radio Caroline, Aldahe, **33/1** Foreign Assignment (IRE), Top One, Melodic Habit, **50/1** Green's Stubbs, **66/1** Notanotherone (IRE). CSF £116.30, CT £1,137.54. Tote £7.00: £2.00 £3.50 £1.20 £2.70 (£41.60). Mrs K. L. Perrin (DORCHESTER) bred by Collinstown Stud Farm Ltd. 19Rn
                                          1m 41.5 (4.2)
                                    SF—27/33/30/33/20/5

## 593    LEVY BOARD SEVENTH RACE H'CAP (0-70) £2650.60 (£736.60: £353.80)
       **1¾m 134y**                                5-30 (5-36)
                     (Weights raised 2 lb)
513[5]  **Zealous Kitten (USA)** *(48)* *(RJPrice)* 4—8-7 ‡5TSprake (3) (hld up: hdwy 3f out: rdn to ld over 1f out: r.o strly) ................... —1
342[3]  Broom Isle *(48)* *(MrsAKnight)* 4—8-9 ‡3FNorton (2) (lw: hld up in tch: led over 2f out tl over 1f out: one pce) ......................... 5.2
312*  Needwood Muppet *(54)* (Fav) *(BCMorgan)* 5—9-6 WCarson (10) (hld up & bhd: hdwy on ins 4f out: hmpd: styd on u.p ins fnl f) ......................2½.3
103  Enfant du Paradis (IRE) *(PDEvans)* 4—8-2 ‡7AGarth (5) (styd on fnl 3f: nrst fin) ........ hd.4
426  Famous Beauty *(51)* *(RHollinshead)* 5—8-10 ‡7DCarson (1) (lw: chsd ldrs: 7th st: no hdwy fnl 2f) ..................... ½.5
422  Yimkin Bookra *(56)* *(WRMuir)* 4—9-6 SWhitworth (11) (hdwy 8f out: 6th st: led 3f out: sn hdd & btn) ..................... 10.6

   Peacock Feather **(52)** *(KRBurke)* 4–9-2 AShoults (8) (a bhd) .............. 8.7
271⁴ Amphigory **(56)** *(LordHuntingdon)* 4–9-6 WRyan (14) (prom: 2nd st: led 4f out
      to 3f out: sn wknd) .............. 2¹/₂.8
426⁴ Westfield Moves (IRE) **(57)** *(HJCollingridge)* 4–9-7 JQuinn (12) (prom: 3rd st:
      wknd over 3f out) .............. hd.9
426 Moot Point (USA) **(60)** *(JRJenkins)* 4–9-10 WNewnes (6) (prom: 5th st: bmpd 4f
      out: sn lost pl) .............. s.h.10
426 Franciscan **(48)** *(BPreece)* 5–8-7 ‡⁷EHusband (13) (chsd ldrs: hdwy & 4th st:
      wknd 3f out) .............. 1¹/₂.11
426 Jarras **(49)** *(CASmith)* 7–9-1 MWigham (4) (led to 4f out: sn wknd) .............. 12
594 Shadowland (IRE) **(56)** *(MJCharles)* 4–9-6 GHind (9) (hdwy 7f out: wknd ent st:
      sn t.o) .............. 13
   Access Supreme **(55)** *(RBoss)* 4–9-5 PatEddery (7) (broke down & p.u after 2f:
      dead) .............. 0

**11/8** Needwood Muppet, **4/1** Yimkin Bookra, **10/1** Westfield Moves (IRE), Amphigory, **11/1** Broom Isle(op 7/1), **14/1** Famous Beauty, **16/1** ZEALOUS KITTEN (USA), **20/1** Access Supreme, **25/1** Moot Point (USA), **33/1** Shadowland (IRE), **50/1** Peacock Feather, Franciscan, Enfant du Paradis (IRE), **66/1** Jarras. CSF £161.20, CT £365.13. Tote £23.00: £2.40 £4.80 £1.10 (£68.10). Mr M. F. Oseman (LEOMINSTER) bred by Sterlingbrook Farm in USA. 14 Rn
                                 3m 15.3 (9.3)
                                        SF—7/-/-/-/-/-

T/Plpt: £145.00 (10.4 Tckts).
                                            KH/IM

# BATH (L-H)
## Tuesday, April 28th [Good to soft]
Going Allowance: 0.45 sec per fur (Y)           Wind: fresh half against

Stalls: low

**594**     SPA (S) STKS (3-Y-O) £2355.00 (£655.00: £315.00)   **5f 11y**    2-00 (2-03)

411⁶ Savalaro **(51)** *(JFfitch-Heyes)* 8-2 AMackay (13) (lw: mde all: drvn out) .............. —1
252 Life's a Breeze **(59)** *(MRChannon)* 8-7 TQuinn (15) (a.p: r.o one pce fnl f) .......... 2.2
353 Orchard Bay **(46)** *(DRTucker)* 8-2 ‡⁵ATucker (5) (nt clr run 1f out: gd hdwy on
      ins fnl f: fin fast) .............. nk.3
524 Bernie Silvers **(60)** *(GLewis)* 8-7 PaulEddery (12) (a.p: nt qckn ins fnl f) .......... s.h.4
472 Another Vintage **(54)** (bl) *(PDCundell)* 8-7 AMunro (8) (hld up on ins: hdwy fnl f:
      r.o) .............. nk.5
353³ Little Nod **(60)** *(JWhite)* 8-0 ‡⁷CAvery (14) (lw: hdwy fnl f: nrst fin) .......... s.h.6
421⁶ Ever so Lonely **(59)** (bl) *(ABailey)* 8-7 GBardwell (2) (nvr nr to chal) .............. 1¹/₂.7
520⁵ Jubal Early (IRE) **(51)** (bl) *(CNAllen)* 8-12 RCochrane (9) (nvr nrr) .............. 1.8
359 Cashtal Queen **(52)** (Fav) *(JBerry)* 8-7 PatEddery (6) (b: lw: hdwy 2f out: rdn
      over 1f out: wknd fnl f) .............. nk.9
408 Mint Addition **(60)** *(RHannon)* 8-2 SRaymont (8) (n.d) .............. 2.10
468 Weekend Girl **(30)** (bl) *(WMBrisbourne)* 7-9 ‡⁷CHawksley (7) (n.d) .............. ¹/₂.11
452⁵ Palacegate Gold (IRE) **(58)** (bl) *(RJHodges)* 8-7 ‡⁵TSprake (16) (n.d) .......... ¹/₂.12
452 Grand Time **(62)** *(CJHill)* 8-12 DHolland (18) (prom: rdn over 2f out: eased whn
      btn fnl f) .............. nk.13
357 Injaka Boy **(46)** (v) *(KWhite)* 8-7 JWilliams (17) (n.d) .............. 3.14
247⁴ Corley Flower **(47)** *(PDCundell)* 8-2 EJohnson (4) (spd 3f) .............. ³/₄.15
   Reach Forward **(44)** *(RJHolder)* 8-2 NAdams (10) (swtg: n.d) .............. 2¹/₂.16
300 I Broke the Rules (IRE) **(35)** *(AJChamberlain)* 7-9 ‡⁷GMilligan (3) (b: bhd fnl 2f) ³/₄.17
414 Saruk (IRE) **(39)** *(JJBridger)* 8-2 TyroneWilliams (19) (spd over 2f: t.o) .......... 12.18

**7/2** Cashtal Queen, **6/1** Ever so Lonely(10/1—5/1), **13/2** Life's a Breeze(6/1—9/1), **8/1** Another Vintage, **9/1** Mint Addition, **10/1** Bernie Silvers, Grand Time, **14/1** Jubal Early (IRE)(10/1—16/1), Palacegate Gold (IRE), Little Nod, SAVALARO, **20/1** Corley Flower(op 10/1), **25/1** Reach Forward, Injaka Boy, **50/1** Saruk (IRE), Weekend Girl, **66/1** Ors. CSF £101.58, Tote £37.60: £9.60 £2.30 £12.60 (£294.10). Mr John Ffitch-Heyes (LEWES) bred by R. and Mrs J. Digby-Ware. 18 Rn; No bid           68 sec (7.5)

**595**     E.B.F. HODCOTT STKS (Mdn 2-Y-O) £2929.50 (£812.00: £388.50)   **5f 11y**  2-30 (2-36)

   **Jeremiahs Boy** *(RJHodges)* 8-9 ‡⁵TSprake (13) (leggy: scope: bit bkwd: hdwy
      2f out: led wl ins fnl f: r.o) .............. —1
237⁴ Night Melody (IRE) *(RHannon)* 9-0 KDarley (2) (led: edgd rt 2f out: hdd wl ins fnl
      f) .............. nk.2
297⁵ Duchess Dianne (IRE) *(RJHolder)* 8-9 JWilliams (5) (gd hdwy fnl f: fin wl) .......... 1.3
   Bold Acre *(DRLaing)* 9-0 TyroneWilliams (1) (leggy: unf: a chsng ldrs: r.o one
      pce fnl f) .............. 1¹/₂.4
446² Pistol (IRE) (Fav) *(PFICole)* 9-0 TQuinn (8) (a.p: ev ch 2f out: nt qckn fnl f) ..... s.h.5

514 World Express (IRE) *(BRMillman)* 9-0 GBaxter (9) (lw: no hdwy fnl 2f) ............. 2½.6
Wealthywoo *(JSMoore)* 8-9 BRouse (4) (str: scope: nrst fin) ............................. 1½.7
514⁶ Pirates Gold (IRE) *(MJHeaton-Ellis)* 9-0 JReid (14) (lw: w ldrs over 3f) ............ 3½.8
Royal Deed (USA) *(GLewis)* 8-9 PaulEddery (6) (w'like: w ldrs: bmpd 2f out: sn
wknd) ...................................................................................... 3.9
Both Barrels *(RJHolder)* 9-0 NAdams (12) (str: s.i.s: a bhd) ......................... ½.10
Ambivalentattitude *(MDIUsher)* 9-0 RCochrane (3) (neat: bit bkwd: outpcd) .. 1½.11
Sefio *(JBerry)* 9-0 PatEddery (10) (w'like: scope: dwlt: a bhd) ..................... nk.12
Persian Noble *(CJHill)* 9-0 AClark (11) (leggy: scope: bit bkwd: a bhd: t.o) .... 20.13

**Evens** Pistol (IRE)(tchd 13/8), **5/2** Night Melody (IRE), **6/1** Pirates Gold (IRE), **9/1** Sefio, **12/1** Royal Deed
(USA)(10/1—16/1), **20/1** Duchess Dianne (IRE), **33/1** Persian Noble, JEREMIAHS BOY, Bold Acre, **50/1** Ors.
CSF £116.81, Tote £40.30: £5.90 £1.70 £3.30 (£290.60). Mr J. Barber (SOMERTON) bred by L. H. Small and
Sons. 13 Rn                                                                            68.5 sec (8)

## 596
TRIPLEPRINT H'CAP (0-90) £2960.00 (£890.00: £430.00: £200.00)     5f 11y 3-00 (3-04)

1135 Cee-En-Cee (61) (bl) *(MMcCourt)* 8-8-6 TQuinn (13) (gd hdwy on ins wl over 1f
out: r.o to ld last strides) .......................................................... —1
550* Olifantsfontein (74) (bl) (Fav) *(RSimpson)* 4-9-5 (6x) PatEddery (11) (a.p: led
over 2f out: clr over 1f out: ct fnl strides) ........................................ hd.2
414⁴ How's Yer Father (70) *(RJHodges)* 6—8-10 ‡⁵TSprake (1) (a.p: r.o wl ins fnl f) ..... nk.3
496 Fivesevenfiveo (64) *(RJHodges)* 4-8-9 JReid (3) (chsd ldrs: no hdwy fnl 2f) ....... 6.4
550⁴ Misdemeanours Girl (IRE) (63) *(MRChannon)* 4-8-8 AMunro (4) (nvr nrr) ............. nk.5
506 Banbury Flyer (68) *(MrsALMKing)* 4-8-13 RCochrane (5) (hdwy over 2f out: rdn
over 1f out: one pce) .................................................................. 1½.6
Dominuet (82) *(JLSpearing)* 7-9-13 RFox (7) (s.s: nrst fin) ......................... nk.7
506² Hitchin a Ride (60) *(MPMuggeridge)* 5-8-5 JWilliams (2) (spd 3f) ................. 1½.8
421⁴ Whippet (77) (bl) *(JABennett)* 8-9-1 ‡⁷JWeaver (10) (lw: a bhd) .................. 1½.9
279 Barbara's Cutie (48) *(MBlanshard)* 4-7-7 NAdams (6) (led over 2f: t.o) ........... 7.10
414 Sports Post Lady (IRE) (63) *(CJHill)* 4—8-8 DHolland (9) (a bhd: t.o) ............ 1½.11
506³ Lucy Dancer (IRE) (55) *(CGCox)* 4-7-9 ‡⁵ATucker (12) (spd over 2f: t.o) ......... ¾.12
LONG HANDICAP: Barbara's Cutie 7-2.

**6/4** Olifantsfontein, **5/1** How's Yer Father(4/1—6/1), **6/1** Misdemeanours Girl (IRE), Hitchin a Ride(op 4/1),
**12/1** Sports Post Lady (IRE), Lucy Dancer (IRE), **14/1** CEE-EN-CEE, **20/1** Dominuet, Fivesevenfiveo(op
12/1), **25/1** Banbury Flyer, Whippet, **33/1** Barbara's Cutie. CSF £35.73, CT £121.58. Tote £11.80: £2.70
£1.30 £2.00 (£12.40). Mr D. N. Humphreys (WANTAGE) bred by Thomas Moore. 12 Rn          66.4 sec (5.9)
                                                                        SF—19/31/21/–/–/–

## 597
BLATHWAYT STKS (Mdn 3-Y.O) £2267.50 (£630.00: £302.50)
1m 3f 144y                                                              3-30 (3-34)

Antiguan Flyer (Fav) *(BWHills)* 9-0 PatEddery (6) (2nd st: qcknd to ld wl over 1f
out: pushed out) ...................................................................... —1
White Wedding (70) *(PFICole)* 8-9 AMunro (4) (plld hrd: 4th & rdn st: styd on fnl
f) .................................................................................... 4.2
Dolly Madison (IRE) *(BWHills)* 8-9 DHolland (5) (bit bkwd: dwlt: hdwy 6f out: 5th
st: ev ch 2f out: one pce) ........................................................... 3½.3
529⁴ Sir Pageant *(PFICole)* 9-0 TQuinn (8) (lw: led: hrd rdn & hdd wl over 1f out:
wknd fnl f) .......................................................................... nk.4
330⁴ Oco Royal (68) (bl) *(JFfitch-Heyes)* 9-0 GBaxter (1) (lw: last st: a bhd) ......... 6.5
Spontaneous (IRE) *(RCharlton)* 8-9 SRaymont (2) (unf: 6th st: a bhd) ............... 2.6
268³ Natral Exchange (IRE) (72) *(JWHills)* 9-0 MHills (4) (3rd st: rdn 3f out: wknd 2f
out) ................................................................................. 10.7
512 Pinkjinski (IRE) (69) *(RHannon)* 8-9 ‡⁵RPerham (3) (uns rdr & bolted bef s: 7th &
wkng st: t.o) ........................................................................ 20.8

**6/4** ANTIGUAN FLYER, **4/1** Sir Pageant, **9/2** Dolly Madison (IRE)(6/1—10/1), **7/1** Natral Exchange (IRE), **8/1**
Spontaneous (IRE), **12/1** White Wedding(8/1—14/1), **20/1** Pinkjinski (IRE)(op 10/1), **33/1** Oco Royal. CSF
£18.27, Tote £2.40: £1.30 £2.30 £1.70 (£8.50). Mr K. Abdulla (LAMBOURN) bred by Crest Stud Ltd. 8 Rn
                                                                        2m 38.5 (11.8)
                                                                        SF—34/21/14/18/6/–

## 598
EMPIRE H'CAP (0-80) £2901.50 (£872.00: £421.00: £195.50)
1m 3f 144y                                                              4-00 (4-02)

Easy Purchase (55) *(RJHolder)* 5-8-7 JWilliams (13) (hld up: stdy hdwy 6f out:
led ins fnl f: rdn out) ............................................................... —1
504⁵ Thin Red Line (54) (v) *(JRJenkins)* 8-8-6(4) PatEddery (8) (hld up: stdy hdwy 5f
out: r.o fnl f: nt rch wnr) ........................................................... 1½.2

225 Hills of Hoy **(56)** *(KCBailey)* 6–8-1 ‡7CMunday (7) (lw: 2nd tl led wl over 2f out: sn hrd rdn: hdd ins fnl f) .................... nk.3

513[2] Merry Marigold **(52)** (Fav) *(JDRoberts)* 6–8-4 GBaxter (9) (lw: 3rd st: wknd over 1f out) .................... 6.4

299 Horizon (IRE) **(65)** *(TThomsonJones)* 4–9-2 SWhitworth (10) (led: hrd rdn & hdd wl over 2f out: wknd 1f out) .................... 2.5

Master Line **(52)** *(HCandy)* 11–7-11 ‡7SDrake (5) (bit bkwd: 4th st: wknd 3f out) 7.6

Grove Serendipity (IRE) **(65)** (v) *(AHide)* 4–9-2 RCochrane (11) (6th st: wknd 3f out) .................... 4.7

211 El Dominio **(64)** *(KOCunningham-Brown)* 4–9-1 TQuinn (6) (lw: a bhd) .......... 1½.8

426 Muddy Lane **(42)** *(BRMillman)* 4–7-0 ‡7CHawksley (1) (dwlt: a bhd) .................... 2.9

525 Loki (IRE) **(77)** *(GLewis)* 4–10-0 PaulEddery (3) (7th & rdn st: a bhd) .................... ¾.10

210[5] Mai Pen Rai **(47)** *(CJHill)* 4–7-12 TyroneWilliams (4) (bit bkwd: a in rr: t.o fnl 3f) 20.11

Just Ready (IRE) **(47)** *(GAHam)* 4–7-12 SDawson (2) (prom 6f: t.o) .................... 6.12

LONG HANDICAP: Muddy Lane 7-5.

**3/1** Merry Marigold, **9/2** Thin Red Line, **6/1** Loki (IRE), **13/2** Horizon (IRE), **9/1** Grove Serendipity (IRE), **12/1** Hills of Hoy, Muddy Lane(8/1—14/1), **16/1** Mai Pen Rai, El Dominio, EASY PURCHASE, **25/1** Ors. CSF £81.77, CT £823.50. Tote £15.60: £3.70 £1.80 £2.20 (£26.20). Mr Ian Purchase (BRISTOL) bred by S. F. Strong. 12 Rn
2m 39.9 (13.2)
SF—24/20/14/5/13/–

**599**    ILCHESTER H'CAP (3-Y.O) (0-80) £3135.50 (£944.00: £457.00: £213.50)
1¼m 46y                   4-30 (4-36)

425[4] Up Anchor (IRE) **(78)** (Fav) *(PFICole)* 9-5 AMunro (15) (2nd st: rdn to ld wl over 1f out: sn clr) .................... —1

Notable Exception **(59)** *(JWHills)* 8-0 DHolland (16) (hdwy 5f out: 4th st: r.o one pce fnl 2f) .................... 8.2

471[2] Romansh **(80)** *(GWragg)* 9-7 MHills (1) (lw: led over 8f: one pce) .................... ⁹/₄.3

395[6] Maestroso (IRE) **(75)** *(RFJohnsonHoughton)* 9-2 RCochrane (3) (hdwy fnl 2f: nt rch ldrs) .................... 6.4

Trumpet **(70)** *(LordHuntingdon)* 8-11 DaleGibson (14) (nvr trbld ldrs) .................... ½.5

395[4] Princess of Orange **(65)** *(CCElsey)* 8-6 JReid (7) (lw: 5th st: rdn over 2f out: no hdwy) .................... s.h.6

Mexican Dancer **(70)** *(RJHolder)* 8-11 JWilliams (12) (nvr nr to chal) .................... 3¹/₂.7

Rocality **(78)** *(RHannon)* 9-0 ‡5RPerham (17) (bit bkwd: 3rd st: wknd over 2f out) ½.8

356[5] Eleckydo **(61)** *(RJHodges)* 7-11[(4)] ‡5TSprake (10) (bhd fnl 4f) .................... ¾.9

341 Probation **(55)** *(BRMillman)* 7-10 AMackay (4) (6th st: wknd over 2f out) .................... ½.10

Persian Fantasy **(74)** *(JLDunlop)* 9-1 PatEddery (8) (dwlt: a bhd) .................... nk.11

471[4] Arctic Circle (IRE) **(63)** (bl) *(MissAJWhitfield)* 8-4 NAdams (9) (lw: hdwy 8f out: wknd 4f out) .................... 5.12

400[4] Legendary (IRE) **(68)** *(PWChapple-Hyam)* 8-9 PaulEddery (2) (sn prom: rdn 7f out: 7th & wkng st: t.o) .................... 13

Hidden Flower **(52)** *(JDRoberts)* 7-7 NCarlisle (5) (t.o fnl 5f) .................... 14

**7/2** UP ANCHOR (IRE)(9/2—3/1), **5/1** Romansh, **13/2** Legendary (IRE), **8/1** Princess of Orange, **9/1** Rocality, **10/1** Maestroso (IRE), Persian Fantasy(8/1—12/1), Eleckydo, Arctic Circle (IRE), **14/1** Trumpet(8/1—16/1), **20/1** Mexican Dancer, **25/1** Probation, **33/1** Notable Exception, **50/1** Hidden Flower. CSF £101.44, CT £550.66. Tote £4.60: £1.70 £7.10 £2.60 (£198.50). Mr Fahd Salman (WHATCOMBE) bred by Universal Stables in Ireland. 14 Rn
2m 18.2 (10.5)
SF—45/10/29/12/6/–

T/Plpt: £907.20 (5.5 Tckts).                                                         KH

## 495—NOTTINGHAM (L-H)

### Tuesday, April 28th [Good to firm, Good patches]

Going Allowance: St: 0.30 sec (G); Rnd: minus 0.20 sec per fur (F)      Wind: slt half against

Stalls: high

**600**    OVAL STKS (Mdn 3-Y.O.C & G) £1932.00 (£532.00: £252.00)   **1m 1f 213y**  2-15 (2-18)

433[3] Belgran (USA) (Fav) *(HRACecil)* 9-0 WRyan (2) (led tl appr fnl f: rallied u.p to ld cl home) .................... —1

Dress Sense (IRE) *(LMCumani)* 9-0 LDettori (8) (leggy: scope: bit bkwd: s.i.s: 5th st: hdwy 2f out: led appr fnl f tl cl home) .................... nk.2

Ajo (IRE) *(MRStoute)* 9-0 SCauthen (7) (bit bkwd: a.p: 4th st: ev ch 3f out: styd on ins fnl f) .................... 2.3

394 Sir Mark Sykes (IRE) *(JRFanshawe)* 9-0 GDuffield (1) (bit bkwd: a.p: 3rd st: rdn over 1f out: one pce) .................... nk.4

427 Lobilio (USA) *(CEBrittain)* 9-0 MRoberts (3) (chsd wnr: 2nd st: wknd 2f out) ... 1½.5
Bitter Aloe *(JLDunlop)* 9-0 WCarson (6) (wl grwn: scope: bit bkwd: s.v.s: a bhd) 7.6
235 Amber Glow (IRE) *(LJCodd)* 8-7 ‡7RMitchell (4) (6th st: sn rdn & btn: t.o) ......... 25.7
363 Mash the Tea (IRE) (v) *(HJCollingridge)* 9-0 JQuinn (5) (bit bkwd: 7th st: a bhd:
t.o) ...................................................................................... 10.8

**2/5** BELGRAN (USA), **6/1** Dress Sense (IRE), **9/1** Ajo (IRE)(5/1—10/1), Lobilio (USA)(op 16/1), **16/1** Bitter Aloe, **25/1** Sir Mark Sykes (IRE), **50/1** Mash the Tea (IRE), **100/1** Amber Glow (IRE). CSF £3.81, Tote £1.50: £1.10 £1.20 £1.30 (£3.10). Mr S. Khaled (NEWMARKET) bred by Camelot Thoroughbred II in USA. 8 Rn   2m 7.2 (4.7)
SF—33/32/28/27/24/10

**601**    HEADINGLEY STKS (3-Y.O) £3261.30 (£974.40: £466.20: £212.10)    **6f 15y**   2-45 (2-46)

428* **Garah (90)** (Fav) *(HRACecil)* 8-10 SCauthen (5) (chsd ldr: qcknd to ld over 1f
out: comf) ........................................................................... —1
Dancing Boy (USA) **(96)** *(MrsJCecil)* 9-1 MRoberts (6) (bit bkwd: led tl hdd over
1f out: kpt on u.p nr fin) ...................................................... 2.2
527* Power Lake **(108)** *(RHannon)* 9-1 WCarson (9) (hld up: hdwy 2f out: one pce ins
fnl f) ................................................................................ 1½.3
454⁴ Shati (IRE) **(97)** *(HThomsonJones)* 8-11 RHills (2) (spd on outside: rdn & no ex
fnl f) ................................................................................ 1½.4
437 Bobzao (IRE) **(100)** *(WCarter)* 8-11 LDettori (3) (lw: spd 4f: sn outpcd) ......... 6.5
454* The Old Chapel **(97)** *(BAMcMahon)* 8-11 BRaymond (4) (gd spd over 3f) ............ 1½.6
Executive Spirit *(DSasse)* 9-1 GDuffield (8) (lt-f: s.s: a bhd) .................. hd.7
Langtonian **(95)** *(JBerry)* 9-1 JCarroll (1) (bkwd: swtg: outpcd: a bhd) ........ 3.8

**6/4** GARAH, **11/4** Power Lake(op 6/4), **6/1** Shati (IRE), **7/1** Bobzao (IRE), Dancing Boy (USA), **8/1** The Old Chapel, **12/1** Langtonian, **50/1** Executive Spirit. CSF £13.35, Tote £2.60: £1.30 £2.00 £1.20 (£9.40). Prince A. A. Faisal (NEWMARKET) bred by Nawara Stud Co Ltd. 8 Rn   1m 15.2 (4.2)
SF—48/45/39/29/5/–

**602**    OLD TRAFFORD STKS (Mdn 2-Y.O) £1932.00 (£532.00: £252.00)    **5f 13y**   3-15 (3-16)

439 **Simmering** *(GWragg)* 8-9 RHills (1) (a.p: led 1f out: jst hld on) ................ —1
Kensworth Lady *(MBlanshard)* 8-9 CRutter (6) (small: unf: bkwd: bhd: gd hdwy
appr fnl f: fin wl) .............................................................. hd.2
237⁵ Moscatop (IRE) *(RHollinshead)* 9-0 WRyan (5) (hdwy over 1f out: nrst fin) ...... 2½.3
Lord Olivier (IRE) *(WJarvis)* 9-0 BRaymond (2) (w'like: scope: bit bkwd: led
½-wy to 1f out: wknd fnl f) ..................................................... 1.4
Folly Vision (IRE) (Jt-Fav) *(RHannon)* 8-9 MRoberts (7) (cmpt: bit bkwd: led to
½-wy: wknd over 1f out) ......................................................... ¾.5
Daring King *(DSasse)* 9-0 GDuffield (3) (w'like: bkwd: outpcd: t.o) ............. 7.6
Safe to Say *(MrsJRRamsden)* 8-9 TLucas (4) (w'like: bkwd: bhd fr ½-wy: t.o) ... 4.7
292⁶ Price Rumpus (IRE) (Jt-Fav) *(JBerry)* 9-0 JCarroll (8) (lw: spd 3f: sn wknd: t.o:
b.b.v) ........................................................................... 25.8

**3/1** Price Rumpus (IRE), Folly Vision (IRE), **4/1** Lord Olivier (IRE), **9/2** Moscatop (IRE)(op 5/2), **5/1** SIMMERING, **9/1** Safe to Say(6/1—10/1), **16/1** Kensworth Lady(25/1—33/1), **40/1** Daring King. CSF £68.31, Tote £9.20: £2.30 £1.70 £1.10 (£140.20). Mrs G. Wragg (NEWMARKET) bred by P. D. and Mrs Player. 8 Rn   63 sec (4.3)
SF—39/38/33/29/21/–

**603**    TAVERN (S) STKS (3-Y.O) £2363.20 (£655.20: £313.60)    **1m 1f 213y**   3-45 (3-55)

497⁵ **Lyn's Return (IRE) (54)** (Jt-Fav) *(RSimpson)* 8-10 LDettori (3) (lw: a.p: 3rd st:
led wl over 1f out: rdn out) ................................................... —1
355 Fly for Gold (IRE) *(DWPArbuthnot)* 8-10 ‡5RPrice (12) (hdwy 3f out: sustained
chal ins fnl f: r.o) ............................................................ ¾.2
510 Roly Wallace **(61)** (bl) *(KTIvory)* 9-7 GDuffield (14) (chsd ldrs: 7th st: styd on ins
fnl f) .......................................................................... hd.3
457⁵ North Flyer **(43)** *(BAMcMahon)* 8-10 GHind (8) (led: clr 3f out: wknd & hdd wl
over 1f out) .................................................................... 4.4
Rich Pickings *(CACyzer)* 8-5 GCarter (15) (nt grwn: in tch: 8th st: kpt on fnl 3f: nt
rch ldrs) ....................................................................... 4.5
496 Allimac Nomis **(52)** *(NACallaghan)* 8-10 WNewnes (9) (bhd tl styd on fnl 2f: nrst
fin) ............................................................................. 2.6
519² Stratford Lady **(49)** (bl) *(JAGlover)* 8-5 JFortune (10) (prom: 2nd st: wknd over
2f out) ......................................................................... ¾.7
451 Manair (IRE) (v) *(ACStewart)* 8-10 MRoberts (6) (chsd ldrs: 4th st: rdn & wknd
over 2f out) .................................................................... 3½.8

370 Treasure Beach *(MBrittain)* 8-10  MWigham (5) (chsd ldrs: rn wd & 6th st: wknd
    over 2f out) ............................................................................................... 1.9
    Breakdancer (IRE) (Jt-Fav) *(MrsJRRamsden)* 8-10  TLucas (7) (unf: bit bkwd:
    chsd ldrs: 5th st: wknd over 2f out) ............................................... 1¹/₂.10
512 Salmon Dancer (IRE) **(50)** *(MFBarraclough)* 8-7 ‡3FNorton (13) (a bhd) .......... ¾.11
502 Gay Ming *(RHollinshead)* 8-5  WRyan (8) (swtg: s.i.s: a bhd) ........................ 1¹/₂.12
    Princess Proudfoot *(MissLCSiddall)* 8-5  DMcKeown (11) (bit bkwd: swtg: plld
    hrd: chsd ldrs 6f: sn lost tch) ....................................................... 2¹/₂.13
164² Mykindofmusic **(59)** (bl) *(MJHaynes)* 8-9 ‡7DToole (2) (s.i.s: a bhd) ............... 4.14
448 Blue Cross **(35)** *(PSFelgate)* 8-5  JLowe (4) (t.o) ........................................ dist.15

**5/2 LYN'S RETURN (IRE)**(7/2—2/1), Breakdancer (IRE)(6/1—10/1), **4/1** Stratford Lady(op 9/4), **8/1** North
Flyer(op 5/1), **12/1** Mykindofmusic(op 8/1), **14/1** Treasure Beach(20/1—12/1), Manair (IRE)(op 5/1), **20/1** Fly
for Gold (IRE)(33/1—16/1), Roly Wallace, Rich Pickings, **25/1** Blue Cross, Gay Ming, Princess Proudfoot, **33/1**
Ors. CSF £55.37, Tote £4.30: £1.50 £5.30 £8.30 (£244.90). Mr Rod Simpson (FOXHILL) bred by Hamwood
Stud in Ireland. 15 Rn; Bt in 4,400 gns
                                         2m 9.7 (7.2)
                                         SF—4/–/12/–/–/–

## 604

LORDS H'CAP (3-Y-O) (0-70) £2716.00 (£756.00: £364.00)   **1m 54y**   4-15 (4-26)
                      (Weights raised 2 lb)

350³ **Elizabethan Air (47)** *(ANLee)* 8-0  JQuinn (4) (chsd ldr: 2nd st: led ins over 2f out:
    jst hld on) ................................................................................................ —1
348⁶ Will Soon **(68)** (Fav) *(HCandy)* 9-2  CRutter (13) (dwlt: effrt & n.m.r 3f out: str
    burst fnl f: fin fast) ................................................................................ s.h.2
    Moon Spin **(63)** *(MajorWRHern)* 9-2  BProcter (7) (hdwy over 3f out: swtchd lft
    appr fnl f: n.m.r ins fnl f: nt rcvr) ......................................................... ¹/₂.3
498⁵ Roger Rabbit (FR) **(47)** *(RBoss)* 7-11 ‡3DBiggs (8) (prom: 3rd st: wknd over 1f
    out) ...................................................................................................... 1¹/₂.4
433 Don't Forsake Me **(63)** *(DMorley)* 9-2  LDettori (12) (hdwy & 6th st: one pce fnl
    2f) ......................................................................................................... 2.5
    Tiffany's Case (IRE) **(52)** *(CAHorgan)* 8-5  RHills (11) (bkwd: styd on fnl 2f: nt rch
    ldrs) ..................................................................................................... 2¹/₂.6
268⁴ Drummer Hicks **(62)** *(EWeymes)* 9-1  DMcKeown (3) (styd on fnl 2f: nvr nrr) ..... ¹/₂.7
401 Abeloni **(66)** *(AAScott)* 9-5  BRaymond (20) (chsd ldrs: ev ch 3f out: sn rdn &
    wknd) .................................................................................................. 1¹/₂.8
401 Hob Green **(58)** *(MrsJRRamsden)* 8-11  TLucas (15) (nvr trbld ldrs) ..................... 1.9
498 Ferdia (IRE) **(65)** *(RHollinshead)* 9-4  WRyan (19) (lw: nvr nr ldrs) ...................... ¹/₂.10
    Horizontale **(54)** *(CEBrittain)* 8-2 ‡5BDoyle (16) (chsd ldrs: 4th st: wknd 3f out) .. hd.11
    Sea Prodigy **(64)** *(MBlanshard)* 9-3  MRoberts (2) (bit bkwd: led tl hdd over 2f
    out: sn wknd) ......................................................................................... hd.12
482⁵ Systematic **(62)** *(RHannon)* 9-1  AMcGlone (10) (n.d) ........................................ ¾.13
    Missy-S (IRE) **(52)** *(GAPritchard-Gordon)* 8-5  JLowe (14) (n.d) ....................... 1¹/₂.14
295 Mill Burn **(48)** *(ICampbell)* 8-1⁽¹⁾  GDuffield (1) (chsd ldrs: 5th st: wknd 3f out) .. hd.15
520³ First Gold **(58)** *(JWharton)* 8-8 ‡3JFanning (9) (a bhd) .................................... hd.16
456 Molten Copper (IRE) **(66)** *(MWEasterby)* 8-12 ‡7JMarshall (6) (a bhd) ............. ¾.17
    Leonadis Polk **(66)** *(WJPearce)* 9-5  DNicholls (18) (bit bkwd: a bhd) ............ nk.18
412⁶ Top Royal **(64)** *(JLDunlop)* 9-3  WCarson (5) (s.s: a bhd) ............................... nk.19
332 Lonesome Train (USA) **(62)** (v) *(JHMGosden)* 9-1  GHind (17) (lw: s.s: a bhd) . 2.20

**5/1 Will Soon, 6/1** Don't Forsake Me, Systematic(4/1—7/1), **15/2** Top Royal(5/1—8/1), **10/1** Drummer Hicks,
Hob Green(op 5/1), **ELIZABETHAN AIR**(tchd 5/1), Roger Rabbit, (FR), **14/1** Tiffany's Case (IRE), Mill Burn, Molten
Copper (IRE), Abeloni, Moon Spin, **16/1** Sea Prodigy, Missy-S (IRE)(op 33/1), Lonesome Train (USA), **20/1** Ors.
CSF £68.94, CT £689.05. Tote £9.20: £2.70 £1.10 £5.70 £2.70 (£95.10). Mr R. A. Clowes (NEWMARKET) bred
by H. F. Craig Harvey. 20 Rn
                                               1m 44.6 (5)

## 605

TRENT BRIDGE H'CAP (0-85) £2551.30 (£706.80: £337.90)   **2¹/₄m 18y**   4-45 (4-53)
                      (Weights raised 1 lb)

    **Creeager (60)** *(JWharton)* 10–8-6 ‡3JFanning (1) (hld up in tch: 5th st: led ins
    fnl f: jst hld on) ....................................................................................... —1
426³ Fanlight **(52)** (Fav) *(RAkehurst)* 4–7-7⁽³⁾ ‡3FNorton (11) (in tch: hwdy & 3rd st:
    led 3f out tl ins fnl f: r.o) ......................................................................... s.h.2
435 Equity Card (IRE) **(70)** *(GAPritchard-Gordon)* 4–9-0  GCarter (8) (hld up: hdwy
    ¹/₂-wy: 4th st: ev ch fnl 2f: no ex nr fin) .................................................. 3.3
507⁴ Sonic Signal **(49)** *(MJHaynes)* 6–7-9⁽⁵⁾ ‡3DBiggs (2) (hld up in rr: hdwy & 6th st:
    nt pce to chal) ........................................................................................ ¹/₂.4
    Sagaman (GER) **(55)** *(LJCodd)* 6–8-4  MRoberts (6) (bkwd: hld up & bhd: hdwy
    3f out: wknd wl over 1f out) ................................................................... 2.5
501 Shareef Star **(53)** *(MBlanshard)* 8–7-4⁽⁴⁾ ‡7DHarrison (9) (prom: 2nd st: wknd
    over 2f out: t.o) ..................................................................................... 15.6
426 Sweet Request **(57)** (bl) *(JRBostock)* 4–8-1  JLowe (4) (lw: chsd ldrs 10f: sn lost
    tch: t.o) ................................................................................................. 20.7

Shentit (FR) **(74)** *(JLDunlop)* 4–9-4 WCarson (5) (bkwd: chsd ldr 11f: sn wknd: t.o) ...................................................................................................... s.h.**8**

362 Sailor Boy **(57)** (bl) *(ASReid)* 6–8-6 WRyan (3) (led & sn clr: hdd 3f out: sn wknd: t.o) ...................................................................................... 2¹/₂.**9**

LONG HANDICAP: Fanlight 7-6, Sonic Signal 7-4, Shareef Star 6-10.

**9/4** Fanlight, **11/4** Shentit (FR), **3/1** Sagaman (GER)(op 6/4), **6/1** Sonic Signal, Equity Card (IRE), **14/1** Sailor Boy, **25/1** CREEAGER, **33/1** Ors. CSF £83.42, CT £371.84. Tote £20.30: £2.90 £1.70 £1.70 (£39.90). Mr J. M. Berry (MELTON MOWBRAY) bred by Exors of the late H. Betteridge. 9 Rn                3m 59.1 (7.6)

## 606
EDGBASTON H'CAP (0-70) £2794.40 (£778.40: £375.20)        **1m 1f 213y**        5-15 (5-32)

4711³ **In the Picture (IRE) (71)** (Fav) *(RHannon)* 3–9-2 WCarson (11) (hld up: hdwy 3f out: led over 1f out: sn clr: easily) ...................................................... —**1**

Bescaby Boy **(63)** *(JWharton)* 6–9-9 ‡3JFanning (2) (bit bkwd: chsd ldrs: 5th st: led wl over 1f out: sn hdd: no ch w wnr) ...................................... 4.**2**

342 Samurai Gold (USA) **(48)** (v) *(PTWalwyn)* 4–8-11 LDettori (5) (a.p: 4th st: led 3f out tl wl over 1f out: one pce) .............................................. hd.**3**

508⁶ Rising Tempo (IRE) **(60)** *(CACyzer)* 4–9-9 GCarter (17) (lw: hld up: hdwy u.p 3f out: r.o fnl f) ................................................................................. hd.**4**

377⁴ Samain (USA) **(34)** *(JAGlover)* 5–7-11 JQuinn (6) (chsd ldrs: 6th st: one pce fnl 2f) .............................................................................................. 2¹/₂.**5**

457 Amazon Express **(58)** *(CEBrittain)* 3–8-3 MRoberts (4) (led 2f: 3rd st: wknd 2f out) ....................................................................................... 6.**6**

417⁴ Not Yet **(40)** *(EWeymes)* 8–7-10 ‡7AGarth (1) (hld up: styd on nr fin: nvr nrr) .... ³/₄.**7**

424⁵ Sir Norman Holt (IRE) **(59)** *(FHLee)* 3–8-4 GDuffield (13) (sme hdwy fnl 2f: nvr nrr) ...................................................................................... 2¹/₂.**8**

Wheeler's Wonder (IRE) **(52)** *(NCWright)* 3–7-8(4) ‡3FNorton (8) (still unf: hdwy 3f out: nt rch ldrs) .......................................................... 1¹/₂.**9**

358 Enchanted Flyer **(36)** (bl) *(TWDonnelly)* 5–7-13 PBurke (1) (led after 2f to 3f out: wknd qckly) .................................................................. 2.**10**

Parr (IRE) **(63)** *(JMackie)* 4–9-12 WNewnes (16) (bit bkwd: nvr nr ldrs) .......... 2.**11**

422 New Mexico **(65)** *(DMorley)* 8–10-0 RHills (19) (n.d) ................................... s.h.**12**

488⁵ Bartolomeo (USA) **(57)** *(MrsJRRamsden)* 3–8-2 JCarroll (12) (n.d) ............... hd.**13**

153 Mazin **(35)** *(CJBenstead)* 4–7-12(3) AMcGlone (21) (n.d) .............................. nk.**14**

Rasco **(61)** *(JEtherington)* 3–8-6 NConnorton (10) (bkwd: hdwy 3f out: wknd 2f out) .............................................................................................. ¹/₂.**15**

358 Sally Forth **(46)** *(JRBostock)* 6–8-4 ‡5RPrice (9) (n.d) ............................... hd.**16**

508 Golden Ancona **(48)** *(MBrittain)* 9–8-11 MWigham (14) (n.d) ...................... 2.**17**

Northern Gallery (IRE) **(34)** *(WJMusson)* 4–7-11 JLowe (15) (bkwd: n.d) ...... 2¹/₂.**18**

Tibby Head (IRE) **(51)** *(JMackie)* 4–9-0 GHind (20) (prom: 2nd st: wknd 3f out) 1¹/₂.**19**

Broad Appeal **(60)** *(WJPearce)* 4–9-9 DNicholls (22) (bit bkwd: bhd fr ¹/₂-wy: t.o) ................................................................................................. 12.**20**

395 Sterling Prospect **(69)** (bl) *(WCarter)* 3–8-9 ‡5NGwilliams (7) (reluctant to r: a t.o) 25.**21**

**2/1** IN THE PICTURE (IRE)(op 3/1), **4/1** Samurai Gold (USA)(7/1—8/1), **9/1** Amazon Express, **10/1** Rising Tempo (IRE), **12/1** Sir Norman Holt (IRE), **14/1** Samain (USA), Not Yet, Bartolomeo (USA)(op 5/1), **16/1** Bescaby Boy, Rasco, **20/1** New Mexico, Sterling Prospect, **25/1** Golden Ancona, **33/1** Parr (IRE), Northern Gallery (IRE), **50/1** Ors. CSF £36.66, CT £121.28. Tote £2.90: £1.20 £2.40 £1.80 £2.10 (£14.10). Mrs Diana Attwood (MARLBOROUGH) bred by Barronstown Stud in Ireland. 21 Rn                2m 5.9 (3.4)

SF—48/47/34/45/28/22

T/Plpt: £104.20 (17.45 Tckts).                                                                              IM

# ASCOT (R-H)
## Wednesday, April 29th [Good to soft]
Going Allowance: St: 0.50 sec; Rnd: 0.70 sec per fur (Y)                    Wind: almost nil

Stalls: low

## 607
INSULPAK GRADUATION STKS (3-Y.O.F) £9672.00 (£2886.00: £1378.00: £624.00)
**1m (rnd)**                                                                    2-00 (2-02)

**Arbusha (USA)** *(LordHuntingdon)* 8-11 AMunro (3) (lw: 4th st: led 1f out: r.o wl) —**1**

Never a Care (USA) (Fav) *(BWHills)* 9-3 PatEddery (4) (h.d.w: lw: 3rd st: rdn over 2f out: r.o ins fnl) .................................................................. 3¹/₂.**2**

434⁴ Just a Mirage *(AAScott)* 8-11 WCarson (5) (b.hind: led 7f: unable qckn) .......... 2.**3**

493* Teslemi (USA) *(BHanbury)* 8-11 WRSwinburn (6) (b.off hind: 2nd st: wknd wl over 1f out) ........................................................................... 1¹/₂.**4**

Lamore Ritorna *(KOCunningham-Brown)* 8-11 MRoberts (1) (5th st: no hdwy fnl 2f) .............................................................................................. hd.**5**

Phyliel (USA) *(MRStoute)* 9-3 GDuffield (2) (6th st: wknd over 2f out: t.o) ........ dist.**6**

**6/5** Never a Care (USA), **4/1** Teslemi (USA), **9/2** ARBUSHA (USA), **6/1** Just a Mirage(4/1—13/2), **13/2** Phyliel (USA)(9/2—7/1), **66/1** Lamore Ritorna. CSF £10.04, Tote £6.00: £2.00 £1.30 (£5.20). Mr Henryk De Kwiatkowski (WEST ILSLEY) bred by Kennelot Stables Ltd in USA. 6 Rn  
1m 47.32 (7.72)  
SF—64/59/47/42/41/–

---

**608**　INSULPAK SAGARO E.B.F. STKS (Gp 3)　£29988.00 (£11125.40: £5262.70: £2203.90)  
　2m 45y　　　　　　　　　　　　　　　　　　　　　　　　　　　　　　2-30 (2-31)

435² **Al Mutahm (USA) (80)** *(JABOld)* 4-8-8 LDettori (7) (lw: rdn over 5f out: 3rd st: led wl ins fnl f: r. o wl) ................................................ —1  
　Supreme Choice (USA) **(108)** *(BWHills)* 4-8-8 DHolland (4) (5th st: led over 1f out tl wl ins fnl f: r.o) ............................................................ nk.2  
390² Shambo **(107)** *(CEBrittain)* 5-8-12 MRoberts (1) (lw: rdn 4f out: hdwy 3f out: ev ch fnl f: unable qckn: in 4th, 1½l: plcd 3rd) ...................... 3  
　Clare Heights *(JRFanshawe)* 4-8-5 GDuffield (6) (a.p: led 3f out tl over 1f out: btn whn hmpd ins fnl f: fin 5th, 3½l: plcd 4th) ...................... 4  
390³ Parting Moment (USA) **(102)** *(IABalding)* 5-9-1 BRaymond (5) (4th st: wkng whn hmpd over 2f out: fin 6th, 6l: plcd 5th) .......................... 5  
442³ Kimbers (IRE) **(102)** *(CRNelson)* 4-8-8 JReid (10) (a bhd) ...................... 4.7  
228⁴ Arcadian Heights **(103)** *(GWragg)* 4-8-8 WRSwinburn (8) (lw: prom 12f) ..... 1½.8  
　Victoire Bleue (Fav) *(AFabre,France)* 5-9-1 TJarnet (3) (b: rdn over 3f out: bhd fnl 2f) ............................................................................. 7.9  
　Hawait Al Barr **(96)** *(MRStoute)* 4-8-5 PatEddery (9) (led 13f) ................. 10.10  
390 Hateel **(105)** *(PTWalwyn)* 6-8-12 WCarson (2) (hdwy 3f out: n.m.r over 1f out: swtchd fnl f: r.o: fin 3rd, hd: disq: plcd last) ..................... 0  

*Stewards Enquiry: Hateel disq. (interference to Clare Heights). Carson suspended 8-11/5/92 (careless riding).*

**15/8** Victoire Bleue, **4/1** Shambo, **9/2** Supreme Choice (USA), **13/2** Hawait Al Barr(10/1—6/1), **14/1** Hateel, **20/1** Arcadian Heights, **25/1** Kimbers (IRE), Clare Heights, Parting Moment (USA), **33/1** AL MUTAHM (USA). CSF £154.97, Tote £17.50: £3.50 £2.00 £1.30 (£79.30). Mr W. E. Sturt (WROUGHTON) bred by John Valentine and Mary Bradley in USA. 10 Rn  
3m 39.36 (12.86)  
SF—77/76/79/77/66/70/59

---

**609**　WHITE ROSE STKS (3-Y.O) £9503.00 (£2834.00: £1352.00: £611.00)  
　1¼m　　　　　　　　　　　　　　　　　　　　　　　　　　　　　　　3-05 (3-05)

　**Top Register (USA)** *(LordHuntingdon)* 8-9 WRSwinburn (4) (h.d.w: hdwy over 2f out: led & edgd rt over 1f out: rdn out) ................................. —1  
　Riszard (USA) *(JSBolger,Ireland)* 9-0 CRoche (3) (3rd st: led 2f out tl over 1f out: ev ch fnl f: r.o wl) ....................................................... hd.2  
　Powerful Edge *(IABalding)* 9-0 RCochrane (6) (lw: 5th st: rdn over 1f out: r.o one pce) ............................................................................. 3.3  
389³ Pabouche (USA) (Fav) *(HRACecil)* 9-0 SCauthen (5) (lw: 6th st: n.m.r over 1f out: one pce) ............................................................... nk.4  
389⁶ Boloardo *(CEBrittain)* 8-9 MRoberts (1) (chsd ldr: led over 3f out to 2f out: one pce) .............................................................................. ¾.5  
175a⁶ Flight Lieutenant (USA) *(PMitchell)* 8-9 AClark (2) (rdn 3f out: nvr nr to chal) ... 1½.6  
499★ Killy **(92)** *(FHLee)* 9-0 MHills (8) (4th st: wknd over 2f out) ................. 20.7  
347³ Hero's Light **(90)** *(PFICole)* 9-0 AMunro (7) (led over 6f: 2nd st: wknd over 2f out) ................................................................ 3½.8  

**7/4** Pabouche (USA), **5/2** TOP REGISTER (USA)(7/4—11/4), **6/1** Hero's Light (USA), **8/1** Riszard (USA)(op 12/1), **9/1** Powerful Edge, **16/1** Killy, **25/1** Ors. CSF £20.40, Tote £2.80: £1.30 £2.10 £2.30 (£17.10). The Queen (WEST ILSLEY) bred by The Queen in USA. 8 Rn  
2m 15.76 (11.36)  
SF—51/55/49/48/41/38

---

**610**　INSULPAK VICTORIA CUP (H'cap) (0-115) £20712.50 (£6200.00: £2975.00: £1362.50)  
　7f　　　　　　　　　　　　　　　　　　　　　　　　　　　　　　　　3-40 (3-43)

　**Band on the Run (87)** *(BAMcMahon)* 5-9-0 TQuinn (20) (a.p: hrd rdn over 1f out: led wl ins fnl f: r.o wl) ................................................ —1  
240★ High Low (USA) **(84)** *(WJHaggas)* 4-8-11 PatEddery (12) (swtg: a.p: led 2f out tl wl ins fnl f: r.o wl) ...................................................... nk.2  
438★ Mango Manila **(89)** (Fav) *(CAHorgan)* 7-9-2 SCauthen (16) (b: gd hdwy 2f out: ev ch fnl f: r.o) .................................................... 2.3  
392³ Sharp N' Smooth **(72)** *(RHannon)* 5-7-13 WCarson (14) (swtg: hrd rdn & hdwy over 1f out: r.o) ........................................................ 1½.4  
515★ Tender Moment (IRE) **(69)** *(CEBrittain)* 4-7-5(3) (6x) ‡5BDoyle (21) (a.p: ev ch over 1f out: one pce) .......................................... ¾.5  
344 Piquant **(77)** *(LordHuntingdon)* 5-8-4 MRoberts (19) (no hdwy fnl 2f) ..... 3.6  
240 Maggie Siddons **(84)** *(CJHill)* 4-8-11 JReid (11) (hdwy wl over 1f out: nvr nrr) 1½.7

438² King of Chance (IRE) **(79)** *(MrsJRRamsden)* 4–7–13⁽²⁾ ‡⁷JWeaver (17) (hdwy over 1f out: nvr nrr) ............................................................ 1.8
344 Go Executive **(86)** *(CEBrittain)* 4–8–13 GCrealock (6) (swtg: nvr nr to chal) ....... ¾.9
386³ So Rhythmical **(72)** *(GHEden)* 8–7–13 AMunro (1) (b.off hind: swtg: prom 5f) hd.10
492* Tusky **(77)** (v) *(MJCamacho)* 4–8–4 (6x) SMorris (18) (swtg: led over 3f: led over 2f out: sn hdd & wknd) ........................................... 2½.11
485* Sharpalto **(77)** *(MrsGRReveley)* 5–8–4 JLowe (13) (lw: outpcd) ...................... ½.12
Deprecator (USA) **(92)** *(JHMGosden)* 4–9–5 RCochrane (5) (b.hind: lw: spd 5f) nk.13
Caroles Express **(86)** *(RAkehurst)* 4–8–13 LDettori (15) (w ldr: led over 3f out tl over 2f out: sn wknd) ........................................ s.h.14
Takenhall **(66)** *(MJFetherston-Godley)* 7–7–7 NAdams (8) (bit bkwd: rdn 3f out: hdwy 2f out: wknd fnl f) ...................................... 1.15
Savoyard **(101)** *(MAJarvis)* 4–10–0 BRaymond (9) (lw: prom over 4f) .................. 5.16
392 Cheveux Mitchell **(74)** (v) *(MRChannon)* 5–8–1 RHills (2) (gd spd 5f) ............... ½.17
485² Sagebrush Roller **(75)** *(JWWatts)* 4–8–2 GDuffield (4) (a bhd) ........................ 1.18
285 Usa Dollar **(66)** (bl) *(BGubby)* 5–7–7 JQuinn (10) (prom 5f) ........................ ¾.19
477* Barford Lad **(74)** (bl) *(JRFanshawe)* 5–8–1 (6x) GCarter (3) (bhd fnl 3f) .......... 8.20
Prince of the Sea (IRE) **(90)** *(DWPArbuthnot)* 4–9–3 MHills (7) (b: bhd fnl 4f) 2½.21
LONG HANDICAP: Tender Moment (IRE) 7-5, Takenhall 7-6, Usa Dollar 7-4.

**6/1** Mango Manila, **15/2** Tender Moment (IRE), **8/1** Sharpalto, Sharp N' Smooth, **10/1** High Low (USA), **11/1** King of Chance (IRE), **14/1** Maggie Siddons, Piquant, Tusky, Sagebrush Roller, **16/1** BAND ON THE RUN, Deprecator (USA), **20/1** Caroles Express, Barford Lad, So Rhythmical, **25/1** Savoyard, **33/1** Prince of the Sea (IRE), Go Executive, Cheveux Mitchell, Takenhall, **50/1** Usa Dollar. CSF £162.14, CT £997.10. Tote £19.60: £3.80 £2.60 £1.70 £2.10 (£96.70). Mr D. J. Allen (TAMWORTH) bred by Mrs J. R. Hine and Miss J. Bunting. 21 Rn                                                                                                 1m 32.01 (5.51)
SF—70/66/65/43/24/28

**611** GARTER GRADUATION STKS (2-Y.0) £7029.00 (£1944.00: £927.00)    5f    4-10 (4-10)

470* **Pips Pride** *(RHannon)* 9-4 PatEddery (2) (mde all: rdn out) .............................. —1
446* Kharaj *(AAScott)* 9-4 WCarson (1) (hdwy 2f out: rdn & ev ch over 1f out: unable qckn) ............................................................. 2.2
Lord President (USA) (Fav) *(PFICole)* 8-12 AMunro (3) (w'like: scope: w wnr: ev ch over 1f out: one pce) ......................................... ½.3

**11/8** Lord President (USA), **2/1** PIPS PRIDE, **9/4** Kharaj(op 6/4). CSF £5.52, Tote £2.80 (£2.10). Mrs V. S. Grant (MARLBOROUGH) bred by R. A. and J. H. Popely. 3 Rn                        65.29 sec (4.79)
SF—58/50/40

**612** CHOBHAM APP'CE H'CAP (0-100) £3492.50 (£1040.00: £495.00: £222.50)
1½m                                                                             4-40 (4-41)

(Weights raised 3 lb)
229* **Whitechapel (USA) (73)** (Fav) *(LordHuntingdon)* 4-8-5 ‡³DHarrison (2) (lw: mde virtually all: clr 2f out: v.easily) ..................... —1
Kinematic (USA) **(89)** *(JHMGosden)* 4-9-4 ‡⁶DDunnachie (5) (rdn over 4f out: 3rd st: one pce fnl 3f) ...................................... 1½.2
Ivors Guest **(57)** (v) *(RLee)* 6-7-4 ‡³CHawksley (3) (2nd st: rdn over 2f out: one pce) ............................................................. nk.3
431⁵ Latour **(71)** *(CEBrittain)* 4-8-3 ‡³BDoyle (4) (s.s: 4th st: wknd over 2f out) ........ 20.4
Spring Forward **(57)** (bl) *(REPeacock)* 8-7-7 FNorton (1) (s.s: hdwy 9f out: wknd 6f out: t.o fnl 5f) ................................ dist.5
LONG HANDICAP: Ivors Guest 7-5, Spring Forward 5-11.

**5/6** WHITECHAPEL (USA), **5/2** Latour(7/2—9/4), **4/1** Kinematic (USA)(5/2—9/2), **20/1** Spring Forward, **33/1** Ivors Guest. CSF £4.40, Tote £1.80: £1.20 £2.10 (£2.70). The Queen (WEST ILSLEY) bred by The Queen in USA. 5 Rn                                                                                              2m 43.84 (14.34)
SF—32/42/13/8/–

T/Trio: Race 4: £205.80 (14.5 Tckts). T/Jkpt: £44,770.80 (0.25 Tckts); £45,375.90 to Newmarket 30/4/92. T/Plpt: £73.90 (155.56 Tckts).                                                               AK

# REDCAR (L-H)
## Thursday, April 30th [Good to firm]
Going Allowance: St: minus 0.50 sec; Rnd: minus 0.10 sec (F)        Wind: fresh half bhd

Stalls: high

**613** HUNTCLIFFE H'CAP (0-80) £2750.60 (£761.60: £363.80)    5f    2-05 (2-06)

236 **Sir Tasker (72)** *(JLHarris)* 4-9-2 ‡⁷SWilliams (4) (lw: led after 1f: drvn out) ......... —1

541　Jovial Kate (USA) **(43)** *(BEllison)* 5–7–8　JLowe (1) (w ldrs: kpt on wl fnl f) ......... nk.2
　　Catherines Well **(62)** *(MWEasterby)* 9–8–13　TLucas (6) (hld up: hdwy on
　　outside 2f out: r.o wl ins fnl f) ............................................. hd.3
407　Samsolom **(66)** *(JBalding)* 4–8–9　KDarley (8) (lw: trckd ldrs: effrt & nt clr run
　　over 1f out: r.o wl nr fin) ...................................................... s.h.4
311⁵　Real Stunner **(73)** *(MPNaughton)* 5–9–10　GHind (7) (chsd ldrs: effrt & nt clr run
　　1f out: styd on nr fin) ........................................................... nk.5
407★　Slades Hill **(62)** (Fav) *(TDBarron)* 5–8–13　AlexGreaves (5) (lw: swtg: chsd ldrs:
　　effrt over 1f out: nvr able to chal) ..................................... 1.6
294　Barrys Gamble **(76)** (bl) *(TFairhurst)* 6–9–10　‡3JFanning (9) (hld up: nt clr run fr
　　¹/₂-wy: nt rcvr) ................................................................ s.h.7
407　Beckingham Ben **(45)** *(JPLeigh)* 8–7–7⁽³⁾ ‡³FNorton (3) (led 1f: wknd over 1f out) hd.8
　　Rednet **(56)** *(PDEvans)* 5–8–7　KFallon (2) (b: bit bkwd: chsd ldrs: wkng whn
　　squeezed ins fnl f) ...................................................... ³/₄.9

**9/4** Slades Hill, **4/1** Samsolom, **6/1** Real Stunner, **7/1** Barrys Gamble, **10/1** Catherines Well, **11/1** Beckingham
Ben, SIR TASKER(7/1—12/1), **16/1** Jovial Kate (USA), **33/1** Rednet. CSF £136.24, CT £1,619.47. Tote £14.00:
£3.00 £1.70 £2.30 (£42.40). Mr J. F. Coupland (MELTON MOWBRAY) bred by W. H. Joyce. 9 Rn
　　　　　　　　　　　　　　　　　　　　　　　　　　　　　　　　　58.1 sec (1.4)
　　　　　　　　　　　　　　　　　　　　　　　　　　　　　　SF—24/1/19/22/28/13

**614**　　KILTON CLAIMING STKS (3-Y.O) £2578.80 (£716.80: £344.40)　　**6f**　　2-35 (2-38)

570³　Pop to Stans **(70)** *(TDBarron)* 8–6　AlexGreaves (13) (a.p: led over 1f out: sn clr) —1
　　Spanish Performer **(48)** *(TFairhurst)* 7–8 ‡³JFanning (18) (w ldrs: led over 2f out
　　tl over 1f out: no ch w wnr) ........................................... 6.2
415³　Tagetes **(65)** *(JPearce)* 7–11 ‡⁵RPrice (3) (lw: chsd ldrs: ev ch & rdn over 2f out:
　　r.o same pce) ............................................................. ³/₄.3
468⁴　Speedy Classic (USA) (Fav) *(CTinkler)* 8–12　MBirch (11) (chsd ldrs: rdn ¹/₂-wy:
　　kpt on fnl f) ............................................................... ³/₄.4
516⁶　Palacegate King **(57)** *(JBerry)* 8–6　JCarroll (19) (sn bhd: hdwy over 1f out: nt
　　rch ldrs) .................................................................. 2.5
452　Premier Envelope (IRE) **(53)** *(NTinkler)* 8–4　KimTinkler (8) (a chsng ldrs: kpt on
　　wl fnl 2f) ................................................................ nk.6
510★　Certain Lady **(60)** *(GBlum)* 7–6 ‡⁷CHawksley (16) (styd on appr fnl f: nt rch ldrs) 1.7
366　Chester Belle **(43)** *(PCHaslam)* 7–5⁽¹⁾ ‡⁵NKennedy (15) (swtg: hdwy over 1f out:
　　nvr nr to chal) ........................................................ ¹/₂.8
452　Capital Idea (IRE) **(60)** (bl) *(RonaldThompson)* 8–4　RPElliott (17) (led tl over 2f
　　out: wknd over 1f out) ................................................ nk.9
510　Loose Zeus (USA) **(40)** (bl) *(CFWall)* 8–4　SWebster (5) (lw: nvr trbld ldrs) ........ 1.10
363　Don't Worry **(57)** *(MHTompkins)* 8–1　DaleGibson (4) (nvr nrr) ............... s.h.11
　　Dame Helene (USA) *(PCHaslam)* 7–3 ‡⁷NicolaHowarth (7) (bit bkwd: n.d) ...... nk.12
535　Miss Siham (IRE) **(64)** *(JBalding)* 7–10 ‡⁷ClaireBalding (14) (bit bkwd: w ldrs tl
　　wknd over 2f out) ..................................................... 1¹/₂.13
421　Bassetlaw Belle *(SRBowring)* 7–13　AProud (1) (nvr plcd to chal) .............. 1¹/₂.14
452　Petaurista **(47)** *(MJohnston)* 7–9　JLowe (9) (s.s: a bhd) ................... 1¹/₂.15
330　And Me **(43)** (v) *(DTThom)* 7–8 ‡³FNorton (6) (s.i.s: sn chsng ldrs: lost pl ¹/₂-wy) hd.16
　　Live and Let Fly *(SEKettlewell)* 8–8　JFortune (12) (unf: bit bkwd: wknd) ...... 17
　　Another Ryton *(MWEllerby)* 8–6　SMorris (10) (bit bkwd: t.o) ................. 18
594　Jubal Early (IRE) **(51)** (bl) *(CNAllen)* 8–0　GBardwell (2) (lw: bhd & rdn ¹/₂-wy: t.o) 19

**5/2** Speedy Classic (USA), **7/2** POP TO STANS, **13/2** Certain Lady, **8/1** Palacegate King, **10/1** Don't Worry (IRE),
Tagetes, **14/1** Spanish Performer, **16/1** Capital Idea (IRE)(12/1—20/1), Miss Siham (IRE), Loose Zeus (USA),
**25/1** Petaurista, **33/1** Chester Belle, Premier Envelope (IRE), Jubal Early (IRE), **50/1** Bassetlaw Belle, And Me,
Dame Helene (USA), Live and Let Fly, **100/1** Another Ryton. CSF £53.70, Tote £5.60: £2.80 £3.60 £3.40
(£55.30). Mr W. G. Spink (THIRSK) bred by Lincoln Collins. 19 Rn; Pop to Stans clmd J Pearce £8,503
　　　　　　　　　　　　　　　　　　　　　　　　　　　　　　　　1m 9.5 (0.2)
　　　　　　　　　　　　　　　　　　　　　　　　　　　　　　SF—28/–/–/–/–/–

**615**　　ESTON H'CAP (0-70) £2402.40 (£666.40: £319.20)　　**7f**　　3-05 (3-09)

232　**Rag Time Belle (30)** *(MWEckley)* 6–7–0 ‡⁷DarrenMoffatt (2) (sn chsng ldrs: r.o
　　u.p fnl 2f: led last stride) ........................................... —1
534　Spanish Verdict **(53)** *(DenysSmith)* 5–8–9 ‡⁷CTeague (13) (w ldrs: led over 2f
　　out: jst ct) ............................................................. s.h.2
526⁵　Miss Magenta (IRE) **(30)** *(RThompson)* 4–7–0 ‡⁷CHawksley (8) (lw: s.s: bhd: gd
　　hdwy & nt clr run over 1f out: r.o fnl fin) ......................... ¹/₂.3
449　Granny Mc **(50)** *(EJAlston)* 5–8–13　KFallon (11) (lw: hdwy over 2f out: ev ch
　　over 1f out: kpt on) .................................................. 1¹/₂.4
449　Sandmoor Denim **(52)** *(SRBowring)* 5–8–8 ‡⁷MHarris (16) (lw: sn bhd: gd hdwy
　　2f out: r.o) ............................................................ nk.5

534³ Chain Shot **(49)** (Fav) *(MHEasterby)* 7–8–12 MBirch (15) (lw: w ldrs tl rdn & wknd over 1f out) ............................................................. 2.6

    Falcons Dawn **(57)** (v) *(MO'Neill)* 5–9–6 JFortune (17) (swtg: led tl over 2f out: wknd over 1f out) ............................................................. 1.7

485⁴ State Flyer **(62)** (v) *(CBBBooth)* 4–9–11 GOldroyd (12) (lw: s.i.s: sn bhd: hdwy 2f out: r.o) ..................................................... ¹/₂.8

419 Say You Will **(34)** (v) *(MPNaughton)* 8–7–8 ‡³JFanning (9) (w ldrs: outpcd over 2f out: n.m.r over 1f out: sn wknd) ........................ 1¹/₂.9

420 Castle Cary **(34)** *(TCraig)* 6–7–11 LCharnock (14) (sn bhd & drvn along: sme hdwy 2f out: n.d) ..................................... s.h.10

    Farmer Jock **(65)** *(MrsNMacauley)* 10–9–7 ‡7SWilliams (3) (bit bkwd: w ldrs tl wknd over 1f out: eased whn btn) .................... ¹/₂.11

532⁴ Angel Train (IRE) **(40)** (bl) *(JParkes)* 4–8–3 DaleGibson (7) (in tch: effrt u.p ¹/₂-wy: n.d) ........................................ 1¹/₂.12

496 Silver Stone Boy **(48)** *(WJPearce)* 4–8–11 SWebster (5) (chsd ldrs tl wknd over 2f out) .................................... 1¹/₂.13

532 Cardea Castle (IRE) **(39)** (v) *(BEllison)* 4–8–2⁽³⁾ GHind (4) (sn bhd & drvn along) 1¹/₂.14

    Pavers Good Shoes **(30)** *(MBrittain)* 4–7–7 JLowe (1) (bit bkwd: a bhd: t.o) ........ 15

    Blade of Fortune **(40)** *(FHLee)* 4–8–3 DMcKeown (6) (b.hind: bit bkwd: sn bhd: t.o) ............................................. 16

    Breezy Sailor **(30)** (v) *(RThompson)* 6–7–7 DanaMellor (18) (chsd ldrs tl lost pl ¹/₂-wy: t.o) ..................................... 17

119 Hinari Hi Fi **(43)** *(PDEvans)* 7–8–3 ‡³FNorton (10) (virtually p.u over 1f out: wl t.o) ... 18
                  LONG HANDICAP: Pavers Good Shoes 7-2.

**3/1** Chain Shot, **9/1** Sandmoor Denim, Angel Train (IRE), State Flyer, Spanish Verdict, **10/1** Falcons Dawn, RAG TIME BELLE(op 25/1) Miss Magenta (IRE), **16/1** Say You Will, Silver Stone Boy(op 50/1), **20/1** Granny Mc, **25/1** Hinari Hi Fi, Castle Cary, Farmer Jock, **33/1** Blade of Fortune, **50/1** Ors. CSF £90.98, CT £1,003.23. Tote £10.10: £1.80 £3.70 £1.80 £6.90 (£75.20). Mr R. A. Hughes (LUDLOW) bred by L. V. Wadge. 18 Rn
                                         1m 23.3 (1.1)
                                    SF—–/25/–/22/16/14

**616**      LADY JOCKEYS ASSOCIATION H'CAP (0-70) £2226.00 (£616.00: £294.00)
            1m 1f
                                                 3-35 (3-37)

                         (Weights raised 2 lb)
    **Sweet Mignonette (32)** (Fav) *(MrsGRReveley)* 4–7–10 JakiHouston (1) (lw: hld up: hdwy over 3f out: squeezed thro to ld over 2f out: rdn clr fnl f) —1

    Cool Parade (USA) **(52)** (bl) *(GMMoore)* 4–9–2 LisaCropp (2) (in tch: effrt 3f out: ev ch 3f out: hung lft: nt qckn) ........................... 8.2

232² Phil-Blake **(41)** *(SMellor)* 5–8–5 DanaMellor (7) (lw: led tl over 2f out: one pce) nk.3

572⁶ Ballerina Bay **(54)** (v) *(DTThom)* 4–8–11 ‡7BeverleyBrett (6) (dwlt: bhd: c wd ent st: styd on fnl 2f: nt rch ldrs) ......................... 1¹/₂.4

456 Be the Best **(45)** *(MPNaughton)* 4–8–2 ‡7CarolDavison (4) (in tch: effrt 3f out: sn wknd) ..................................... 5.5

534 Blue Grit **(43)** (bl) *(MDods)* 6–8–7 AlexGreaves (3) (chsd ldrs tl lost pl over 2f out) ..................................... ¹/₂.6

373² Rose Glen **(60)** *(ABailey)* 6–9–3 ‡7DonnaHayman (5) (lw: plld hrd: n.m.r: swtchd rt & lost pl over 2f out) ........................ 3¹/₂.7

422 Foursingh **(52)** (bl) *(CBBBooth)* 4–9–2 KimTinkler (8) (bhd fnl 3f) .................. 4.8

**3/1** SWEET MIGNONETTE(op 5/1), **9/2** Rose Glen, **5/1** Blue Grit, Phil-Blake, Ballerina Bay, **11/2** Cool Parade (USA), **12/1** Foursingh, **20/1** Be the Best. CSF £19.45, CT £74.20. Tote £4.40: £1.50 £1.70 £1.20 (£27.20). Mr M. J. Ogden (SALTBURN) bred by Countess of Durham. 8 Rn
                                         1m 52.2 (3.2)
                                    SF—20/16/4/5/–/–

**617**      MACKINLAY MEMORIAL H'CAP (0-80) £2954.00 (£819.00: £392.00)
            1m 3f
                                                 4-05 (4-07)

    **Young George (56)** *(MDods)* 5–8–8 KFallon (4) (hld up: gd hdwy 4f out: rdn & swvd lft 1f out: led ins fnl f: drvn out) —1

409² Checkpoint Charlie **(59)** (Jt-Fav) *(JMPEustace)* 7–8–11 MTebbutt (2) (lw: s.i.s: hdwy 4f out: led 2f out: hdd & nt qckn nr fin) ............... nk.2

504³ Margs Girl **(54)** (Jt-Fav) *(TFairhurst)* 5–8–3 ‡³JFanning (6) (a chsng ldrs: rdn 2f out: edgd lft: r.o one pce) ......................... 2¹/₂.3

533 Sharquin **(41)** *(MBrittain)* 5–7–7 GBardwell (7) (lw: w ldrs: led over 3f out to 2f out: kpt on same pce) ........................... s.h.4

405* I Perceive **(67)** (Jt-Fav) *(FHLee)* 5–9–5 DMcKeown (12) (lw: trckd ldrs: ev ch 3f out: sn rdn: wknd 2f out) ......................... 6.5

    Tarda **(58)** *(MrsGRReveley)* 5–8–10 JLowe (8) (hld up: effrt over 3f out: wknd over 1f out) ............................................ 2¹/₂.6

Marandisa (57) *(MPNaughton)* 5–8-9 LCharnock (5) (hld up: hdwy u.p & ev ch 3f out: sn wknd) ............................................... 8.7

Major Ivor (63) *(MrsGRReveley)* 7–8-8 ‡⁷SCopp (9) (a in rr) ............................ 1¹/₂.8

518 Talish (49) *(TDBarron)* 4–8-1 AlexGreaves (11) (hld up: bhd fnl 3f) ................. 3¹/₂.9

American Hero (72) *(CTinkler)* 4–9-10 MBirch (1) (bit bkwd: led: clr 8f out: hdd over 3f out: sn wknd & eased) ........................................... 10

Gods Law (45) *(REarnshaw)* 11–7-11⁽⁴⁾ AProud (10) (b.hind: bit bkwd: chsd ldrs tl lost pl over 3f out: sn bhd) ................................. 11

LONG HANDICAP: Sharquin 7-2, Gods Law 7-6.

**7/2** I Perceive, Checkpoint Charlie, Margs Girl, **4/1** Tarda, **12/1** YOUNG GEORGE, **14/1** Marandisa, Sharquin, **20/1** American Hero(op 10/1), **25/1** Major Ivor, Talish, **50/1** Gods Law. CSF £51.95, CT £167.50. Tote £29.20: £3.40 £1.40 £1.40 (£76.80). Mr J. A. Wynn-Williams (DARLINGTON) bred by Stephen Moloney. 11 Rn
2m 19.6 (3.9)
SF—44/46/33/22/36/26

# 618

DANBY STKS (Mdn) £1932.00 (£532.00: £252.00) 7f 4-35 (4-39)

440 **Alycida** (USA) *(LMCumani)* 3–8-10 JFortune (6) (lw: w ldrs: led over 1f out: edgd lft u.p: r.o wl) .................................................. —1

495³ Sahel (IRE) (Fav) *(JHMGosden)* 4–9-10 GHind (5) (lw: trckd ldrs: effrt & rdn over 2f out: nt qckn ins fnl f) ............................... 1.2

Scandalmonger (USA) *(BWHills)* 3–8-10 RStreet (10) (trckd ldrs: led & swtchd rt ¹/₂-wy: hdd over 1f out: unable qckn ins fnl f) ................. ³/₄.3

428⁴ Saddlehome (USA) (83) *(RMWhitaker)* 3–8-10 ACulhane (14) (lw: trckd ldrs: effrt 2f out: edgd lft u.p: r.o same pce) ........................ ¹/₂.4

Ty High (IRE) *(TDBarron)* 4–9-5 AlexGreaves (9) (lengthy: scope: bit bkwd: s.i.s: sn bhd: hdwy over 1f out: r.o nr fin) ................... 8.5

450⁵ Charioteer *(PCHaslam)* 3–8-10 DMcKeown (13) (bit bkwd: stdy hdwy over 2f out: nvr plcd to chal) ..................................... s.h.6

238⁵ Mashakel (USA) (bl) *(BHanbury)* 3–8-3 ‡⁷VBray (8) (b: chsd ldrs: rdn over 2f out: sn wknd) ............................................ ¹/₂.7

495⁶ Miss Debonair *(DMorley)* 3–8-6⁽¹⁾ MTebbutt (2) (chsd ldrs tl wknd over 2f out) 2¹/₂.8

Primo Pageant *(MJCamacho)* 3–8-10 NConnorton (7) (wl grwn: rangy: bkwd: sn bhd & drvn along) ........................................... 1¹/₂.9

522² Brambles Way (57) *(WLBarker)* 3–8-10 KDarley (4) (led to ¹/₂-wy: wknd over 2f out) ..................................................... nk.10

238⁶ Canon Kyle (IRE) *(MHEasterby)* 3–8-10 MBirch (12) (in tch: sltly hmpd ¹/₂-wy: grad wknd) ............................................... s.h.11

Lillah Darak (USA) *(PDEvans)* 4–9-7 ‡³FNorton (3) (w'like: bit bkwd: sme hdwy ¹/₂-wy: wknd over 2f out) ............................... s.h.12

Royal Girl *(MissSEHall)* 5–9-5 SWebster (11) (bit bkwd: in tch: rdn ¹/₂-wy: hung lft & grad wknd) ......................................... 1¹/₂.13

495 Milton Rooms (IRE) *(CBBooth)* 3–8-10 GOldroyd (16) (bit bkwd: sn wl outpcd) ............................................................... nk.14

Crestwood Lad (USA) (63) *(MrsGRReveley)* 3–8-10 JLowe (1) (h.d.w: bit bkwd: chsd ldrs tl wknd over 2f out) ................................. 2.15

Scherzo Impromptu *(TFairhurst)* 3–8-2 ‡³JFanning (15) (w'like: bkwd: t.o) ......... 16

**Evens** Sahel (IRE), **9/2** ALYCIDA (USA), **6/1** Scandalmonger (USA), **8/1** Saddlehome (USA)(op 5/1), **14/1** Mashakel (USA), **20/1** Miss Debonair, Canon Kyle (IRE), Primo Pageant, **25/1** Scherzo Impromptu, Brambles Way, **33/1** Charioteer, Crestwood Lad (USA), **50/1** Ty High (IRE), Lillah Darak (USA), Royal Girl, **100/1** Milton Rooms (IRE). CSF £9.66, Tote £7.60: £2.30 £1.30 £2.00 (£3.50). Sheikh Mohammed (NEWMARKET) bred by Echo Valley Horse Farm Incorporated in USA. 16 Rn
1m 22.5 (0.3)
SF—39/50/34/32/17/7

# 619

E.B.F. AYTON STKS (Mdn 2-Y-O) £2507.90 (£694.40: £331.70) 5f 5-05 (5-08)

396⁴ **Bonus Point** (Fav) *(MrsGRReveley)* 9-0 KDarley (3) (lw: chsd ldrs: reminders ¹/₂-wy: led wl over 1f out: r.o strly) ........................... —1

Marina Park *(MJohnston)* 8-9 DMcKeown (1) (neat: unf: sn chsng ldrs: rn green ¹/₂-wy: styd on fnl f: nt rch wnr) ........................... 1.2

491 Make Mine a Double *(MissSEHall)* 9-0 NConnorton (9) (a chsng ldrs: rdn & nt qckn fnl f) ..................................................... ¹/₂.3

447⁴ Principal Player (USA) *(WBentley)* 9-0 TLucas (8) (lw: chsd ldrs tl outpcd ¹/₂-wy: n.m.r, edgd lft & styd on wl fnl f) ....................... nk.4

396⁵ Argyle Cavalier (IRE) *(FHLee)* 9-0 ACulhane (2) (swvd lft s: hdwy ¹/₂-wy: kpt on: nvr rchd ldrs) ........................................... 1¹/₂.5

491⁵ My Godson *(WJPearce)* 9-0 DNicholls (4) (chsd ldrs tl rdn & wknd over 1f out) . 1.6

491 Coconut Johnny (bl) *(GMMoore)* 9-0 KFallon (7) (led over 3f: sn wknd) ........... hd.7

447³ Our Mica *(JBerry)* 9-0 JCarroll (11) (lw: hld up: hung lft thrght: sme hdwy ¹/₂-wy: n.d) ...................................................... ³/₄.8

4916 Robix (IRE) *(CTinkler)* 9-0 MBirch (10) (lw: sn outpcd) .................... 3½.9
286 Dardanelle *(TFairhurst)* 8-6 ‡3JFanning (5) (chsd ldrs over 3f: wknd qckly) ......... 10
Private Liner *(RonaldThompson)* 9-0 RPElliott (6) (lengthy: scope: bit bkwd:
s.i.s: wl outpcd & rn green) ............................. 11

11/8 BONUS POINT, 5/2 Our Mica, 13/2 My Godson, 7/1 Argyle Cavalier (IRE), 10/1 Principal Player (USA), 11/1 Robix (IRE)(op 6/1), 14/1 Marina Park(op 8/1), 16/1 Make Mine a Double, 33/1 Coconut Johnny, 50/1 Ors. CSF £23.26, Tote £3.00: £1.90 £3.30 £3.50 (£50.90). Mr P. D. Savill (SALTBURN) bred by R. M. West. 11 Rn
58.8 sec (2.1)
SF—8/–/–/–/–/–
T/Plpt: £870.50 (2.55 Tckts).                                                                                    WG

# SALISBURY (R-H)
## Thursday, April 30th [Good to soft, Soft fnl 2f]
Going Allowance: 0.45 sec per fur (Y)                                          Wind: almost nil

Stalls: low
**620**          LEVY BOARD STKS (Mdn 3-Y.0) £2539.60 (£705.60: £338.80)     **6f**      2-20 (2-25)

**Regal Racer** *(DRCElsworth)* 9-0 JWilliams (1) (hdwy over 2f out: led over 1f
out: all out) ................................................. —1
4283 Venture Capitalist **(89)** *(RHannon)* 9-0 JReid (14) (lw: a.p: led wl over 1f
out: sn hrd rdn & hdd: r.o) ................................. ½.2
393 Do Run Run *(RHannon)* 8-4 ‡5RPerham (9) (hdwy fnl 2f: nvr nrr) .............. 3½.3
Noble Pet **(70)** *(PJMakin)* 8-9 ‡5TSprake (12) (bit bkwd: a.p: ev ch wl over 1f out:
one pce fnl f) ............................................. ½.4
Bodari *(DAWilson)* 9-0 BRouse (7) (bkwd: w ldr: led over 2f out tl wl over 1f out)  7.5
Arboretum (IRE) *(RCharlton)* 8-9 WRyan (10) (led wl 2f) ....................... 3.6
394 Louisville Belle (IRE) *(MDIUsher)* 8-9 AMcGlone (4) (b.nr hind: hrd rdn over 2f
out: nvr nr to chal) ....................................... hd.7
Hinton Harry (IRE) *(SMellor)* 9-0 GBaxter (5) (leggy: bit bkwd: s.s: w bhd) ... 1½.8
Elwazir (USA) *(PTWalwyn)* 9-0 GCarter (8) (bit bkwd: no hdwy fnl 2f) ......... ½.9
428 Rock Band (IRE) *(LMCumani)* 9-0 LDettori (2) (outpcd) ....................... nk.10
Sure Shot Norman **(60)** *(JSutcliffe)* 9-0 BCrossley (6) (prom 3f) ............... 2½.11
Suzie Sue (IRE) *(DWPArbuthnot)* 8-9 BProcter (13) (b.hind: lw: s.s: a wl bhd)  ¾.12
Fisianna *(ARDavison)* 8-9 CandyMorris (3) (cmpt: bit bkwd: s.s: a wl bhd) ... ¾.13

4/7 Venture Capitalist(tchd Evens), 7/1 Arboretum (IRE)(4/1—8/1), 8/1 Rock Band (IRE)(6/1—10/1), 9/1 REGAL RACER(5/1—10/1), 14/1 Elwazir (USA)(10/1—16/1), Noble Pet, 20/1 Bodari, Do Run Run, 33/1 Ors. CSF £15.24, Tote £16.10: £3.50 £1.10 £5.90 (£7.40). Mr J. C. Smith (WHITSBURY) bred by Littleton Stud. 13 Rn
1m 17.80 (5.50)
SF—44/42/18/21/–/–

**621**          ALMOND APP'CE H'CAP (3-Y.0) (0-70) £2480.80 (£688.80: £330.40)
6f 212y                                                                 2-50 (2-53)

**Aragona (48)** *(PDCundell)* 7-10 ‡3DGibbs (2) (hdwy 2f out: led ins fnl f: r.o wl) .. —1
Gold Jubilee **(65)** *(PJMakin)* 8-11 ‡5CWebb (10) (led over tl ins fnl f) ..... 1½.2
508 Dollar Wine (IRE) **(67)** *(RHannon)* 8-13 ‡5AWhelan (6) (lw: prom 3f: styd on fnl
2f) .......................................................... 5.3
4416 Young Max **(77)** *(DRCElsworth)* 10-0 JHunter (12) (led 4f) ................. ¾.4
5942 Life's a Breeze **(56)** *(MRChannon)* 8-4 ‡3LMahoney (1) (lw: a.p: ev ch over 1f
out: wknd fnl f) ........................................... 1.5
Green's Exhibit **(55)** *(KOCunningham-Brown)* 8-6 PTurner (5) (nvr nr to chal)  1½.6
472 Duty Sergeant (IRE) **(64)** *(MPMuggeridge)* 9-1 BThomas (3) (hdwy over
2f out: wknd fnl f) ........................................ hd.7
498 Bella Run **(52)** *(RJHodges)* 8-0(2) ‡3SDrowne (8) (lw: hrd rdn over 3f out: no
rspnse) .................................................... 4.8
252 Yatoo (IRE) **(69)** *(RHannon)* 9-3 ‡3MarkDenaro (4) (lw: led 3f out: sn hrd rdn &
hdd) ....................................................... ¾.9
251 Lord Belmonte (IRE) **(45)** *(CACyzer)* 7-10(1) TMcLaughlin (13) (n.d) ........... 1½.10
Nomadic Rose **(63)** *(BWHills)* 8-9 ‡5SMcCarthy (7) (bit bkwd: n.d) ............ 4.11
582 Chance to Dream **(58)** *(RHannon)* 8-6 ‡3MRHunt (9) (hdwy 3f out: wknd qckly
over 1f out) ............................................... 1.12
Sea Cloud (USA) **(47)** *(MBlanshard)* 7-12 CAvery (11) (n.d) ..................... 1½.13

7/2 Duty Sergeant (IRE), 9/2 Life's a Breeze(3/1—5/1), 6/1 Young Max, 13/2 Nomadic Rose(op 4/1), 9/1 Yatoo (IRE), 10/1 Dollar Wine (IRE)(8/1—12/1), Chance to Dream, Sea Cloud (USA)(op 25/1), 14/1 Green's Exhibit, Gold Jubilee, 16/1 ARAGONA, 20/1 Lord Belmonte (IRE), 33/1 Bella Run. CSF £210.93, CT £2,154.34. Tote £23.80: £3.70 £2.80 £5.20 (£116.00). Lord Carrick (NEWBURY) bred by Sexton Enterprises. 13 Rn
1m 34.98 (9.28)

**622—624**

**622**     DOUGLAS STKS     £4337.50 (£1300.00: £625.00: £287.50)     1¾m     3-20 (3-20)

Le Corsaire (USA) (109) (Fav) (LMCumani) 4-9-2 LDettori (2) (lw: chsd ldr: led
wl over 1f out: drvn out) ............................................................................. —1
Piper's Son (MBradstock) 6-8-12 WNewnes (6) (b: lw: led tl wl over 1f out: r.o
wl ins fnl f) ................................................................................................. ½.2
Romany Rye (97) (GWragg) 4-9-2 JReid (3) (hld up: rdn 3f out: r.o one pce) . 2½.3
Kashan (IRE) (NJHenderson) 4-9-8 WRyan (4) (nvr nr to chal) ........................ 3.4
435★ Gulf Palace (USA) (96) (RAkehurst) 7-9-10 JWilliams (1) (lw: prom tl rdn &
wknd over 2f out) ........................................................................................ 10.5
Neologist (JO'Donoghue) 6-8-12 NAdams (5) (bit bkwd: hrd rdn 6f out: wknd
4f out) ........................................................................................................ 25.6

**11/8** LE CORSAIRE (USA), **5/2** Romany Rye, **11/4** Gulf Palace (USA), **15/2** Kashan (IRE), **20/1** Piper's Son, **66/1**
Neologist. CSF £21.32, Tote £2.70: £1.90 £2.00 (£25.90). Sheikh Mohammed (NEWMARKET) in USA. 6 Rn
Tree Stable in USA. 6 Rn
SF—9/2/3/3/—/—

**623**     PENTLAND STKS (I) (Mdn 3-Y.O)     £2245.60 (£621.60: £296.80)     3-50 (3-52)
       **1m 1f 209y**

Jezebel Monroe (USA) (RCharlton) 8-9 WRyan (4) (hdwy 4f out: led 2f out: r.o
wl) ............................................................................................................... —1
341 Hierarch (USA) (Fav) (LordHuntingdon) 9-0 LDettori (5) (lw: a.p: hrd rdn fnl 3f:
ev ch 1f out: r.o) ........................................................................................ 2½.2
Sheringa (GBBalding) 8-9 JWilliams (3) (bit bkwd: hdwy fnl 2f: nvr nrr) .......... 1½.3
Second Call (HCandy) 8-9 WNewnes (1) (str: led to 2f out: r.o one pce) ......... ¾.4
394 Santana Lady (IRE) (65) (MJHeaton-Ellis) 8-2 ‡7JWeaver (9) (chsd ldr over 6f) .. 5.5
Rushing Storm (USA) (JRFanshawe) 8-9 GCarter (11) (lengthy: nvr nr to chal) . 7.6
Sharp Dance (BSmart) 8-9 NAdams (2) (ev ch 4f out: wknd 3f out) ................. 2½.7
Shesadelight (JLDunlop) 8-9 JReid (8) (unf: scope: bit bkwd: a bhd) ............... 4.8
394 Gentle Secret (IRE) (IABalding) 8-11 ‡3SO'Gorman (6) (lw: nvr trbld ldrs) ...... 1½.9
509 Woodlands Legend (DCTucker) 9-0 ADicks (7) (t.o) ................................... 10.10
509 Mma International (IRE) (BRMillman) 9-0 GBaxter (10) (t.o) ...................... 20.11

**Evens** Hierarch (USA), **4/1** JEZEBEL MONROE (USA), Blushing Storm (USA)(op 2/1), **8/1** Shesadelight, **10/1**
Second Call(op 6/1), **11/1** Sheringa(8/1—12/1), **14/1** Gentle Secret (IRE), **33/1** Ors. CSF £9.33, Tote £5.80:
£1.40 £1.40 £1.90 (£4.70). Mr S. S. Niarchos (BECKHAMPTON) bred by Flaxman Holdings Ltd. in USA. 11 Rn
2m 15.73 (11.03)
SF—30/30/22/3/—/—

**624**     SUTHERLAND H'CAP (0-80)     £3392.00 (£1016.00: £488.00: £224.00)     6f     4-20 (4-23)

4806 Baysham (USA) (80) (bl) (BRMillman) 6-9-7 ‡7JWeaver (17) (led over 2f out: sn
clr: jst hld on) ........................................................................................... —1
Garth (76) (PJMakin) 4-9-10 LDettori (6) (swtg: hdwy 2f out: r.o wl ins fnl f) .... hd.2
Neither Nor (71) (RJHolder) 3-8-7 JWilliams (2) (rapid hdwy over 1f out: fin wl) ½.3
4804 Across the Bay (69) (v) (SDow) 5-9-3 GBaxter (1) (a.p: nt qckn fnl f) .......... 2.4
1722 Grand Guignol (70) (GWragg) 4-8-11 ‡7NHall (5) (a.p: ev ch 1f out: nt qckn) .. 1½.5
472 Morocco (IRE) (74) (RCharlton) 3-8-10 SRaymont (18) (swtchd lft s: hdwy over
1f out: hrd rdn: r.o) ................................................................................... s.h.6
506 Grey Charmer (IRE) (69) (CJames) 3-8-5 SWhitworth (13) (nvr nr to chal) ..... 1.7
Premier Prince (57) (LGCottrell) 6-7-12 ‡7CAvery (15) (bit bkwd: nvr trbld ldrs) nk.8
253 Teanarco (IRE) (61) (RJHolder) 4-8-9 NAdams (10) (nvr nr ldrs) .................. ¾.9
3443 Paddy Chalk (76) (LJHolt) 6-9-10 JReid (3) (b: n.d) ................................. 2½.10
Jaldi (IRE) (55) (JSutcliffe) 4-8-3 BCrossley (16) (prom over 3f) ..................... 2.11
449 Beatle Song (67) (RJHodges) 4-8-10 ‡5TSprake (4) (spd 3f) ..................... nk.12
496 Harry's Coming (64) (RJHodges) 8-8-12 AMcGlone (19) (led over 3f) ......... 1½.13
4552 Luna Bid (65) (MBlanshard) 9-8-13 WRyan (12) (lw: n.d) ......................... ½.14
Face North (IRE) (55) (ARDavison) 4-8-7 CandyMorris (8) (n.d) ..................... 1½.15
Aedean (77) (CCElsey) 3-8-13 WNewnes (14) (lw: n.d) ................................ ¾.16
480 Cash a Million (FR) (55) (PDCundell) 4-8-3 EJohnson (9) (n.d) ................... ¾.17
4494 Darakah (63) (CJHill) 5-8-8 ‡3DBiggs (20) (outpcd) ................................ 2.18
4145 Restore (56) (bl) (RVoorspuy) 9-8-4 SDawson (11) (spd 3f) ..................... 3.19
550 Mu-Arrik (55) (DAWilson) 4-8-3 GCarter (7) (spd 3f) ............................. hd.20

**9/2** Across the Bay(7/1—4/1), **6/1** Paddy Chalk, **15/2** BAYSHAM (USA), **9/1** Darakah(6/1—10/1), **10/1** Luna
Bid(7/1—12/1), **12/1** Grand Guignol, Beatle Song, Harry's Coming(7/1—14/1), Neither Nor, **14/1** Premier
Prince, Garth, **20/1** Restore, Teanarco (IRE), Morocco (IRE), **25/1** Grey Charmer (IRE), Cash a Million (FR), **33/1**
Ors. CSF £108.00, CT £1,161.84. Tote £9.40: £2.40 £3.40 £3.50 £1.90 (£150.10). Mr W. J. Butt
(CULLOMPTON) bred by Juddmonte Farms, Incorporated in USA. 20 Rn
1m 18.25 (5.95)
SF—42/44/25/27/18/16

**625**     MORRISTON STKS (Mdn 3-Y.O) £2265.20 (£627.20: £299.60)    1½m    4-50 (4-52)

433 **Chief Minister (IRE)** *(LMCumani)* 9-0 LDettori (10) (lw: hdwy 5f out: hrd rdn
over 2f out: led wl ins fnl f: r.o) ............................................ —1
384⁴ Silvernesian (USA) (Fav) *(JLDunlop)* 9-0 JReid (9) (hld up: led & hung lft over 2f
out: veered lft over 1f out: hdd wl ins fnl f) .................... ½.2
Awol *(HRACecil)* 8-9 WRyan (6) (w'like: scope: led: rdn along & hdd over 2f out:
styd on) ........................................................ 2½.3
Cantanta *(RCharlton)* 8-9 AMcGlone (1) (w'like: scope: jnd ldrs 6f out: hmpd
over 2f out: one pce) ........................................ 8.4
502 Athar (IRE) *(PTWalwyn)* 8-9 BRouse (11) (lw: hdwy 5f out: ev ch over 2f out: sn
wknd) .......................................................... 7.5
Bayadere (USA) *(MRStoute)* 8-9 PD'Arcy (3) (lw: nvr nr to chal) ...................... d.h.5
Sandro *(JRFanshawe)* 9-0 GCarter (5) (a bhd) .......................................... 6.7
230⁶ Tree Frog (IRE) *(LordHuntingdon)* 8-9 JWilliams (8) (w ldr tl wknd 5f out) ............ ¾.8
Kajaani (IRE) *(PFICole)* 8-9 GBaxter (4) (prom tl rdn & wknd 4f out) ................... 3.9
511 Dominant Force *(RHannon)* 8-9 ‡5RPerham (2) (t.o) ....................................... 12.10
412 Barjonal (39) *(JJBridger)* 8-9 NAdams (2) (t.o fnl 5f) .................................. 20.11

**9/4** Silvernesian (USA), **5/2** Awol(2/1—3/1), **6/1** Cantanta, **13/2** Kajaani (IRE)(5/2—7/1), **9/1** Athar
(IRE)(6/1—10/1), **10/1** Bayadere (USA)(op 6/1), **11/1** Tree Frog (IRE), **14/1** CHIEF MINISTER (IRE), Dominant
Force, **16/1** Sandro(op 10/1), **50/1** Barjonal. CSF £49.30, Tote £8.20: £2.00 £1.50 £1.20 (£18.80). Mr David
Thompson (NEWMARKET) bred by The Mount Coote Partnership in Ireland. 11 Rn    2m 42.63 (10.03)
SF—54/52/42/26/12/12

**626**     LAUDERDALE H'CAP (0-85) £3340.00 (£1000.00: £480.00: £220.00)    1m   5-20 (5-26)
                      (Weights raised 3 lb)

364 **Little Rousillon (60)** *(ACStewart)* 4-8-8 SWhitworth (1) (hdwy over 2f out: led
ins fnl f: r.o wl) ............................................ —1
Cape Pigeon (USA) (72) *(LGCottrell)* 7-8-13 ‡7CAvery (16) (lw: led 4f out tl ins
fnl f: r.o) ..................................................... ¾.2
387⁶ Major Bugler (IRE) (77) *(GBBalding)* 3-8-10 JWilliams (4) (lw: hdwy 2f out: r.o
ins fnl f) ...................................................... ½.3
456⁵ Quietly Impressive (IRE) (58) *(MBell)* 4-7-13 ‡7PTurner (6) (lw: w ldr: ev ch 1f
out: wknd ins fnl f) .......................................... 5.4
Hamanaka (USA) (72) (Fav) *(JRFanshawe)* 3-8-5 GCarter (3) (swtg: a.p: nt
qckn fnl f) ................................................... hd.5
398³ Abso (69) *(RHannon)* 4-9-3 JReid (11) (nrst fin) ...................................... 5.6
508² Salbyng (56) *(JWHills)* 4-8-4 WNewnes (14) (no hdwy fnl 2f) ...................... s.h.7
Marine Diver (69) *(BRMillman)* 6-9-3 AMackay (12) (prom tl rdn & wknd 2f out) 3.8
504 Capital Bond (IRE) (66) *(RJHolder)* 4-9-0 NAdams (8) (nvr nr to chal) .............. ¾.9
411 Devil's Soul (56) *(RAkehurst)* 4-8-4 SDawson (2) (s.s: nrst fin) ................... hd.10
Cru Exceptionnel (74) *(PJMakin)* 4-9-8 LDettori (9) (nvr bttr than mid div) ...... nk.11
411 Ivanov (USA) (55) *(PMitchell)* 4-8-0 ‡3SO'Gorman (13) (lw: a bhd) ................. hd.12
Lucknam Style (69) *(MrsBarbaraWaring)* 4-9-3 BCrossley (18) (n.d) ............... ¾.13
Neptune's Pet (72) *(GLewis)* 4-9-6 BRouse (15) (bit bkwd: a bhd) ............... s.h.14
411⁵ Samarni (54) *(CPWildman)* 6-7-13 ‡3DBiggs (5) (led 4f: wknd 2f out) .............. ¾.15
344 Candle King (IRE) (61) *(MJFetherston-Godley)* 4-8-9 WRyan (7) (a bhd) ........... ¾.16
Lucknam Dreamer (76) *(MrsBarbaraWaring)* 4-9-10 NHowe (10) (n.d) ........... ½.17
Knockavon (69) *(RJBaker)* 4-8-12 ‡5ATucker (17) (t.o fnl 3f) ......................... 18

**7/2** Hamanaka (USA), **6/1** Devil's Soul(8/1—10/1), **13/2** Salbyng, Abso, **8/1** Major Bugler (IRE), **9/1** Cru
Exceptionnel(8/1—12/1), **10/1** Marine Diver, Quietly Impressive (IRE), LITTLE ROUSILLON(8/1—12/1), **11/1**
Sarum(8/1—12/1), **12/1** Capital Bond (IRE)(op 8/1), **14/1** Knockavon, Candle King (IRE), Cape Pigeon (USA),
**20/1** Neptune's Pet, Lucknam Dreamer, Lucknam Style, **25/1** Ivanov (USA). CSF £166.37, £1,133.08. Tote
£8.80: £1.90 £3.90 £2.10 £2.60 (£159.60). Fayzad Thoroughbred Limited (NEWMARKET) bred by Normanby
Stud Ltd. 18 Rn    1m 48.11 (8.81)
SF—16/19/14/—/—/—

**627**     PENTLAND STKS (II) (Mdn 3-Y.O) £2245.60 (£621.60: £296.80)
1m 1f 209y                             5-50 (6-00)

**Matching Green** *(GBBalding)* 8-9 JWilliams (1) (a.p: styd on to ld nr fin) .......... —1
384 Pyare Square (bl) (Fav) *(IABalding)* 9-0 JReid (7) (chsd ldr: led over 2f out tl nr
fin) .......................................................... 2.2
394 Bel Baraka (IRE) *(DRCElsworth)* 9-0 LDettori (6) (plld hrd: led tl over 2f out) ...... 5.3
Temple Knight *(CACyzer)* 9-0 GCarter (8) (leggy: ev ch 3f out: wknd over 1f out) hd.4
440 General Dixie (USA) *(RHannon)* 9-0 ‡5RPerham (5) (w'like: scope: a.p: ev ch
over 2f out: sn wknd) .......................................... ½.5
Scultore (USA) *(MRChannon)* 9-0 WNewnes (4) (nvr nrr) ............................... 2½.6
Sizzling Thoughts *(GLewis)* 9-0 AClark (10) (leggy: bit bkwd: a bhd) ............... 12.7

Morgans Ace *(BRMillman)* 9-0 GBaxter (3) (w'like: bit bkwd: bhd fnl 3f) ............ 2.**8**
Utamaro *(BWHills)* 8-9 BRouse (2) (w'like: scope: bit bkwd: bhd fnl 3f) ............. 6.**9**
440 Maraady (USA) *(MRStoute)* 9-0 PD'Arcy (9) (prom tl wknd qckly 3f out) .......... 3.**10**

**15/8** Pyare Square, **3/1** General Dixie (USA), **4/1** Maraady (USA)(op 6/1), Bel Baraka (IRE)(6/1—8/1), **9/1** Utamaro(4/1—10/1), **12/1** Scultore (USA), **14/1** Morgans Ace(8/1—20/1), Sizzling Thoughts(10/1—20/1), MATCHING GREEN(8/1—16/1), **16/1** Temple Knight. CSF £46.89, Tote £12.40: £2.30 £1.40 £1.90 (£14.10). Miss B. Swire (DORCHESTER) bred by Miss B. Swire. 10 Rn                    2m 15.99 (11.29)
SF—27/28/18/17/10/10

T/Plpt: £264.20 (8.4 Tckts).                                                      Hn

427—**NEWMARKET (R-H)** Rowley Mile
**Thursday, April 30th [Good]**
Going Allowance: 2m: nil sec per fur; Rest: 0.10 sec per fur (G)          Wind: mod across

Stalls: 3rd & 4th low, remainder high

**628**     MAY STKS (3-Y.O) £4980.50 (£1484.00: £707.00: £318.50)   1¼m     2-00 (2-07)

4435 **Spartan Shareef (IRE)** *(CEBrittain)* 8-10 MRoberts (4) (trckd ldrs: effrt 2f out:
sn ev ch: r.o to ld nr fin) ............................................................ —**1**
3942 Rebel Call *(RHannon)* 8-10 BRaymond (3) (lw: cl up: led 2f out: hung rt ins fnl f:
no ex nr fin) ................................................................ s.h.**2**
4272 Alhamad **(Fav)** *(HRACecil)* 8-10 PatEddery (5) (lw: led: hung bdly lft & hdd 2f
out: sn rdn & btn) .......................................................... 5.**3**
389 Alcoy (IRE) **(62)** *(PAKelleway)* 8-10 TQuinn (2) (pushed along & outpcd 5f out:
eased fnl 3f) ............................................................... dist.**4**
*Cezanne (7/1) Withdrawn (una rdr & bolted bef s) · not under orders*

**5/4** Alhamad, **7/4** SPARTAN SHAREEF (IRE), **3/1** Rebel Call, **25/1** Alcoy (IRE). CSF £6.59, Tote £2.80: £2.60 (£3.50). Mr C. T. Olley (NEWMARKET) bred by Melchester Ltd in Ireland. 4 Rn     2m 7.97 (5.37)
SF—52/51/41/–

**629**     BRETBY H'CAP (0-105) £6420.00 (£1920.00: £920.00: £420.00)   **6f**     2-30 (2-41)

5506 **Green Dollar (87)** *(EAWheeler)* 9-8-8 ‡7DHarrison (16) (hdwy ½-wy: led ins fnl
f: r.o wl) ................................................................. —**1**
455* Sea Devil **(79)** *(MJCamacho)* 6-8-7 RCochrane (10) (lw: chsd ldrs: chal 2f out:
hung rt ins fnl f: r.o) ........................................................ nk.**2**
4962 Lord High Admiral (CAN) **(67)** *(RHannon)* 4-7-9 NCarlisle (7) (cl up: disp ld
over 1f out: nt qckn ins fnl f) .............................................. hd.**3**
344 Merryhill Maid (IRE) **(69)** *(JLHarris)* 4-7-6(4) ‡5BDoyle (11) (chsd ldrs: outpcd 2f
out: styd on wl nr fin) ...................................................... 1.**4**
Petraco (IRE) **(78)** **(Fav)** *(LJCodd)* 4-8-6 DHolland (5) (cl up: led 2f out tl ins fnl
f: no ex) .................................................................. ½.**5**
4783 Cronk's Courage **(72)** (v) *(EJAlston)* 6-8-0 AMunro (6) (led 4f: grad wknd) ..... 3½.**6**
438 Dry Point **(71)** *(JARToller)* 6-7-13 WCarson (15) (a chsng ldrs: rdn 2f out: r.o
one pce) .................................................................. ¾.**7**
2072 Mac's Fighter **(90)** (bl) *(WAO'Gorman)* 7-8-13 ‡5EmmaO'Gorman (2) (hdwy
over 2f out: styd on nr fin) ................................................. 1½.**8**
550 Choir Practice **(89)** *(WJHaggas)* 5-9-3 NDay (8) (dwlt: bhd tl r.o appr fnl f) ...... nk.**9**
403 Gentle Hero (USA) **(93)** *(MPNaughton)* 6-9-7 MRoberts (1) (effrt ½-wy: nvr
trbld ldrs) ................................................................ 1½.**10**
4143 Belfort Ruler **(68)** *(BGubby)* 5-7-10 JQuinn (12) (chsd ldrs tl outpcd fnl 2f) ...... 1.**11**
4556 Amron **(89)** *(JBerry)* 5-9-3 CRoche (9) (prom 4f) ................................ ¾.**12**
4836 Snowgirl (IRE) **(72)** *(JBerry)* 4-8-6 PatEddery (13) (cl up 4f: sn btn) ............. 2½.**13**
Spaniards Close **(100)** *(PJMakin)* 4-10-0 BRaymond (14) (chsd ldrs 4f) ...... 1½.**14**
Thornfield Boy **(85)** *(RJHolder)* 6-8-13 LPiggott (18) (dwlt: nt rcvr) ................ ¾.**15**
455 Adwick Park **(93)** *(TDBarron)* 4-9-7 GDuffield (19) (s.s: a bhd) ................ ¾.**16**
5702 Profilic **(78)** *(CaptJWilson)* 7-8-6 RHills (17) (lw: gd spd 4f) .................... s.h.**17**
Fabled Orator **(72)** *(PHowling)* 7-8-0(7) CRutter (3) (n.d) ..................... ¾.**18**
4036 The Auction Bidder **(90)** *(RHollinshead)* 5-9-4 PaulEddery (20) (lw: spd 4f: sn
lost pl) .................................................................... ¾.**19**
LONG HANDICAP: Merryhill Maid (IRE) 7-6, Fabled Orator 6-11.

**7/1** Petraco (IRE)(14/1—5/1), **15/2** Lord High Admiral (CAN), **9/1** Dry Point, **10/1** Profilic, Snowgirl (IRE)(7/1—11/1), Cronk's Courage, Sea Devil(7/1—11/1), **12/1** GREEN DOLLAR, **14/1** Amron, Merryhill Maid (IRE), Gentle Hero (USA), Spaniards Close, **20/1** Belfort Ruler, **25/1** Mac's Fighter, Choir Practice, **33/1** Thornfield Boy, Adwick Park, The Auction Bidder, **100/1** Fabled Orator. CSF £117.18, CT £887.92. Tote £13.90: £2.90 £2.00 £1.70 £4.70 (£77.90). Mr B. Azemoudeh (LAMBOURN) bred by Brian Gubby Ltd. 19 Rn     1m 12.92 (1.52)
SF—78/76/63/54/66/46/42

**630**  MADAGANS PRETTY POLLY STKS (listed race) (3-Y.O.F) £13710.00 (£4080.00: £1940.00: £870.00)  1¼m
3-00 (3-09)

425★ **All At Sea** (USA) (Fav) *(HRACecil)* 8-10 PatEddery (3) (hld up & bhd: swtchd outside 4f out: led over 2f out: shkn up & r.o v.wl) ...................... —1

473² Armarama *(CEBrittain)* 8-10 MRoberts (2) (cl up: led over 3f out tl over 2f out: hung rt & nt qckn) ....................................... 5.2

Mystery Play (IRE) **(110)** *(BWHills)* 8-10 SCauthen (1) (lw: trckd ldrs: effrt 3f out: sn rdn & outpcd: r.o fnl f) ....................................... 2½.3

Al Guswa *(JSBolger,Ireland)* 8-10 CRoche (4) (w'like: leggy: hld up: effrt over 3f out: nt qckn appr fnl f) ....................................... 3½.4

553⁴ Party Cited (USA) **(105)** *(PAKelleway)* 8-10 TQuinn (6) (cl up tl outpcd over 2f out) ....................................... 3½.5

389² Feminine Wiles (IRE) **(100)** *(PWChapple-Hyam)* 8-10 LPiggott (5) (plld hrd: led tl hdd over 3f out: sn btn) ....................................... 2.6

**Evens** ALL AT SEA (USA), **11/4** Mystery Play (IRE)(7/4—3/1), **13/2** Feminine Wiles (IRE), **8/1** Armarama, **20/1** Al Guswa(op 12/1), **33/1** Party Cited (USA). CSF £8.29, Tote £1.90: £1.20 £2.70 (£8.80). Mr K. Abdulla (NEWMARKET) bred by Juddmonte Farms Incorporated in USA. 6 Rn  2m 5.61 (3.01)
SF—76/66/61/54/47/43

**631**  GENERAL ACCIDENT 1,000 GUINEAS STKS (Gp 1) (3-Y.O.F) £111387.00 (£41133.00: £19666.50: £7957.50: £3078.75: £1127.25)  1m
3-40 (3-48)

461a² **Hatoof** (USA) *(MrsCHead,France)* 9-0 WRSwinburn (12) (gd sort: lw: trckd ldrs: effrt 2f out: hung lft: led ins fnl f: all out) ...................... —1

Marling (IRE) *(GWragg)* 9-0 SCauthen (9) (h.d.w: hld up: nt clr run 2f out: hdwy & swtchd over 1f out: fin wl) ....................................... hd.2

461a★ Kenbu (FR) *(FBoutin,France)* 9-0 FHead (2) (neat: a.p: led & qcknd wl over 1f out: hdd ins fnl f: kpt on) ....................................... ¾.3

429² Perfect Circle *(MRStoute)* 9-0 RCochrane (5) (lw: hld up: effrt over 2f out: nt clr run: hdwy over 1f out: bmpd ins fnl f: r.o) ....................................... ½.4

385³ Culture Vulture *(PFICole)* 9-0 TQuinn (6) (lw: prom: effrt & nt clr run 2f out: one pce appr fnl f) ....................................... 8.5

429³ A-to-Z (IRE) *(MBell)* 9-0 MHills (3) (trckd ldrs: effrt & nt clr run over 2f out: hdwy over 1f out: no imp) ....................................... ¾.6

Pearl Angel *(MissBSanders)* 9-0 LPiggott (10) (hld up & bhd: styd on fnl 2f: nrst fin) ....................................... ½.7

429³ Soiree (IRE) *(BWHills)* 9-0 DHolland (8) (lw: chsd ldrs tl outpcd fnl 2f) ....................................... s.h.8

385★ Musicale (Fav) *(HRACecil)* 9-0 MRoberts (4) (lw: cl up: led over 3f out tl wl over 1f out: btn whn hmpd over 1f out) ....................................... 1.9

429⁴ Harvest Girl (IRE) *(GAPritchard-Gordon)* 9-0 AMunro (8) (prom 6f) ....................................... nk.10

429 Skimble (USA) *(HRACecil)* 9-0 PatEddery (11) (plld hrd: bhd: effrt 3f out: rdn & btn over 2f out) ....................................... 2.11

Mahasin (USA) *(JLDunlop)* 9-0 WCarson (1) (unruly in stalls: led tl hdd over 3f out: edgd rt & grad wknd) ....................................... 5.12

385³ Central City *(RHannon)* 9-0 BRaymond (13) (prom over 5f: sn wknd & eased) 1½.13

406³ Nimble Deer *(BWHills)* 9-0 GDuffield (14) (hld up & bhd: lost tch fnl 3f) ....................................... 8.14

**7/2** Musicale (USA), **5/1** Marling (IRE), HATOOF (USA), **13/2** Soiree (IRE), **10/1** A-to-Z (IRE), **11/1** Kenbu (FR), **12/1** Perfect Circle, **14/1** Culture Vulture (USA), **16/1** Mahasin (USA), **25/1** Skimble (USA), **33/1** Central City, **40/1** Harvest Girl (IRE), **100/1** Pearl Angel, **150/1** Nimble Deer. CSF £27.27, Tote £6.10: £2.10 £2.50 £3.20 (£11.60). Maktoum Al Maktoum (FRANCE) bred by Gainsborough Farm, Inc. in USA. 14 Rn  1m 39.45 (2.15)
SF—80/79/77/75/51/49/47

**632**  MADAGANS H'CAP (0-105) £6985.00 (£2080.00: £990.00: £445.00)  2m  4-15 (4-28)
(Weights raised 7 lb)

435 **Witness Box** (USA) **(89)** *(JHMGosden)* 5-9-8 SCauthen (3) (lw: mde most: rdn & r.o wl fnl 2f) ...................... —1

388⁶ Farsi **(76)** *(RHollinshead)* 4-8-5 WCarson (2) (cl up: chal over 2f out: wandered u.p: styd on nr fin) ....................................... ½.2

435³ Castle Courageous **(86)** (Jt-Fav) *(LadyHerries)* 5-9-5 PaulEddery (4) (chsd ldrs: chal over 2f out: nt qckn u.p fnl f) ....................................... 1.3

435 Jackson Flint **(90)** *(HThomsonJones)* 4-9-5 RHills (1) (hld up & bhd: stdy hdwy 5f out: effrt 3f out: sn btn & eased) ....................................... 25.4

Gay Glint **(91)** *(NAGraham)* 5-9-10 TQuinn (6) (chsd ldrs: disp ld 6f out tl wknd qckly over 3f out) ....................................... 8.5

475★ Star Quest **(82)** (Jt-Fav) *(JRJenkins)* 5-9-1 PatEddery (5) (lw: hld up: effrt 5f out: sn btn) ....................................... 20.6

**3/1** Star Quest, Castle Courageous(op 2/1), **9/2** WITNESS BOX (USA)(op 3/1), Jackson Flint, **13/2** Farsi, **15/2** Gay Glint(12/1—7/1). CSF £28.34, Tote £4.90: £2.50 £2.40 (£13.80). Sheikh Mohammed (NEWMARKET) bred by Hill 'N' Dale Farms and Gainesway Farm in USA. 6 Rn　　3m 27.09 (3.79)
SF—70/52/65/40/37/8

**633**　　REX COHEN MEMORIAL STKS (Mdn 3-Y.O) £5344.50 (£1596.00: £763.00: £346.50)
1m　　4-45 (4-58)

| | | |
|---|---|---|
| 441[4] | **Zalon (IRE)** *(Fav)* *(JHMGosden)* 9-0 SCauthen (5) (chsd ldrs: led wl over 2f out: rdn & r.o wl) | —1 |
| 458[2] | Mr Flood (USA) *(MrsJCecil)* 9-0 PaulEddery (4) (lw: pushed along ½-wy: hdwy 3f out: ev ch over 1f out: r.o wl) | ½.2 |
| | Exclusion *(HCandy)* 9-0 CRutter (7) (h.d.w: led tl hdd wl over 2f out: r.o one pce) | 3½.3 |
| | Calpella *(JARToller)* 8-9 WRSwinburn (8) (leggy: scope: bhd: hdwy fr ½-wy: nt qckn fnl 2f) | 3.4 |
| | Post Impressionist (IRE) *(BWHills)* 8-9 DHolland (6) (chsd ldrs tl wknd 2f out) | 4.5 |
| | Montagne *(HCandy)* 8-9 GDuffield (2) (prom tl outpcd ½-wy: sme hdwy over 2f out: no imp) | 6.6 |
| | Hurricane Toke (IRE) *(ACStewart)* 9-0 MRoberts (1) (w'like: leggy: s.i.s: sn prom: rdn over 3f out: sn btn) | ¾.7 |
| | Isle of Innisfree (USA) *(HRACecil)* 8-7 ‡7StephenDavies (3) (str: scope: bkwd: chsd ldrs: drvn along ½-wy: wknd wl over 2f out) | ¾.8 |

**11/8** ZALON (IRE)(Evens—6/4), **5/2** Mr Flood (USA), **9/1** Isle of Innisfree (USA)(8/1—12/1), **11/1** Exclusion(8/1—14/1), **12/1** Hurricane Toke (IRE)(8/1—14/1), Post Impressionist (IRE)(op 8/1), Calpella, **16/1** Montagne(12/1—20/1). CSF £5.28, Tote £2.10: £1.40 £1.50 £2.30 (£2.70). Sheikh Mohammed (NEWMARKET) bred by Mrs A. Whitehead in Ireland. 8 Rn　　1m 40.89 (3.59)
SF—58/56/45/31/19/1

**634**　　PORTLAND LODGE STKS (Mdn 3-Y.O.F) £3752.50 (£1120.00: £535.00: £242.50)
7f　　5-15 (5-26)

| | | |
|---|---|---|
| 356[6] | **Flute (USA)** *(CEBrittain)* 8-11 MRoberts (3) (lw: mde most: kpt on gamely nr fin) | —1 |
| 440[2] | Ivana (IRE) *(WJarvis)* 8-11 AMunro (6) (trckd ldrs: effrt 2f out: disp ld ins fnl f: no ex nr fin) | hd.2 |
| | Jade Vale *(JWHills)* 8-11 RHills (1) (w'like: lw: a chsng ldrs: rdn over 2f out: kpt on same pce) | 1½.3 |
| 393[5] | She Looks on High (USA) *(BHanbury)* 8-11 BRaymond (5) (a chsng ldrs: effrt over 2f out: kpt on one pce) | ½.5 |
| | Badawiah *(WAO'Gorman)* 8-11 RCochrane (2) (b: lw: s.s: effrt 3f out: styd on: no imp) | 3½.5 |
| 393[3] | Avila *(Fav)* *(JHMGosden)* 8-11 SCauthen (8) (in tch: pushed along over 3f out: btn 2f out) | 4.6 |
| | Ithkurni (USA) *(BHanbury)* 8-11 WRSwinburn (7) (nvr nr to chal) | 3.7 |
| 482 | Karen Louise (77) *(MissHCKnight)* 8-11 LPiggott (4) (chsd wnr over 4f: sn wknd) | 2.8 |

**Evens** Avila, **9/4** Ivana, **8/1** She Looks on High (USA), **14/1** Ithkurni (USA), **16/1** Karen Louise, **33/1** Ors. CSF £44.39, Tote £12.40: £2.00 £1.60 £3.70 (£20.10). Sheikh Mohammed (NEWMARKET) bred by Tobeko Thoroughbreds Incorporated in USA. 8 Rn　　1m 27.60 (3.60)
SF—54/53/48/46/35/23

T/Trio: Races 2 & 4: £74.30 & £53.50 (20.6 & 42.1 Tckts). T/Jkpt: £26,933.10 (2.2 Tckts). T/Plpt: £248.30 (58.5 Tckts).　　AA

## 537a—LONGCHAMP (R-H)

### Monday, April 20th
Going Allowance: 0.10 sec per fur (G)

**635a**　　PRIX NOAILLES (Gp 2) (3-Y.O.C & F) £25800.00　　**1m 3f (Grande)**

| | | |
|---|---|---|
| | **Grand Plaisir (IRE)** *(France)* 3-9-2 FHead (mde virtually all: qcknd st: hld on wl) | —1 |
| | Modhish (IRE) *(France)* 3-9-2 TJarnet (cl up: outpcd & hrd rdn st: fin wl) | 1½.2 |
| | Glaieul (USA) *(Fav)* *(France)* 3-9-2 DBoeuf (2nd st: chal 1f out: r.o one pce) | s.h.3 |
| | Dadarissime (FR) *(France)* 3-9-2 RBriard (hrd rdn over 1f out: r.o one pce) | s.nk.4 |
| | Dissimulateur (FR) *(France)* 3-9-2 SCauthen (hld up: last st: styd on one pce) | s.h.5 |

**4/5** Glaieul (USA), **24/10** Dadarissime (FR), **27/10** Dissimulateur (FR), Modhish (IRE), **46/10** GRAND PLAISIR (IRE). Tote 5.60f: 2.60f 3.20f (SF: 32.90f). Mr T.Fujishima (J-C.Cunnington,FRANCE) bred by Marystead Farm in Ireland. 5 Rn　　2m 28.4 (12.1)

## 636a  PRIX DE FONTAINEBLEAU (Gp 3) (3-Y.O.C) £20640.00  **1m (Grande)**

Rainbow Corner (Fav) *(France)* 0 0 0 PatEddery ....................................... —1
Highest Ody (FR) *(France)* 3–9-2 ELegrix ...................................... nk.2
Judge Decision (FR) *(France)* 3–9-2 WRSwinburn ................................ 2.3
Tote 2.30f: 1.30f 1.90f 3.00f (7.40f). Mr K.Abdullah (A.Fabre,FRANCE) bred by Juddmonte Farms. 10 Rn
1m 41.1 (3.4)
SF—63/62/56

## 459a—SAINT-CLOUD (L-H)

### Tuesday, April 21st [Good]
Going Allowance: 0.10 sec per fur (G)

## 637a  PRIX PENELOPE (Gp 3) (3-Y.O.F) £20640.00  **1¼m 110y**

Trampoli (USA) *(France)* 3–8-11 SGuillot ...................................... —1
379a* Daltawa (IRE) *(France)* 3–8-11 WMongil ....................................... nk.2
Good to Dance (IRE) *(France)* 3–8-11 TJarnet ................................ 2½.3
Tote 5.80f: 8.30f 1.20f (15.60f). Mr P. de Moussac (A.Fabre,FRANCE) bred by Mayland Stud in USA. 10 Rn
2m 18.7 (8.4)
SF—23/22/17

## 635a—LONGCHAMP (R-H)

### Thursday, April 23rd [Good]
Going Allowance: 0.25 sec per fur (G)

## 638a  PRIX D'HEDOUVILLE (Gp 3)  £20640.00  **1½m (Grande)**

Vert Amande (FR) *(France)* 4–8-11 DBoeuf ...................................... —1
Northern Park (USA) *(France)* 4–8-11 TJarnet ................................. ½.2
Flanaghan Cocktail (IRE) *(France)* 4–9-0 CAsmussen ............................ 1.3
Tote 11.80f: 2.40f 2.20f (27.60f). Mr E.Sarasola (E.Lellouche,FRANCE) bred by Baron Guy de Rothschild in
France. 4 Rn
2m 39.8 (9.8)
SF—29/25/27

## 11a—CAPANNELLE (R-H)

### Saturday, April 25th [Good]

## 639a  PREMIO REGINA ELENA (Gp 2) (3-Y.O.F) £41860.00  **1m**

Treasure Hope (IRE) *(Ireland)* 3–8-11 WJSupple .............................. —1
Without Delay (IRE) *(Italy)* 3–8-11 EBotti (fin 3rd, 1½l: plcd 2nd) ................. 2
Penny's Valentine (USA) *(France)* 3–8-11 ESaint-Martin (fin 4th, hd: plcd 3rd) ...... 3
385⁵ OUMALDAAYA (USA) *(JLDunlop)* 3–8-11 WCarson (fin 2nd, nose: disq: plcd 4th) 4
*Stewards Enquiry: Oumaldaaya (USA) disq. (interference to Penny's Valentine (USA)).*
Tote 37L: 18L 24L 27L (220L). A.J.B (J.S.Bolger,IRELAND) bred by St Simon Foundation in Ireland. 16 Rn
1m 38.5

## 462a—CURRAGH (R-H)

### Saturday, April 25th [Heavy]
Going Allowance: 5f: 1.10 sec (S); Rest: 1.30 sec per fur (Hvy)

## 640a  DERMOT McCALMONT TETRARCH STKS (Gp 3) (3-Y.O.C & F) £11500.00  **7f**

444³ **Irish Memory** (Fav) *(Ireland)* 3–8-9 CRoche (sn led: rdn clr wl over 1f out: r.o) . —1
432* BEWARE OF AGENTS *(MJohnston)* 3–8-9 DMcKeown (in tch: wnt 2nd ½-wy:
effrt 3f out: rdn over 2f out: no ex & wknd over 1f out) ........ 9.2
Vaganova (IRE) (bl) *(Ireland)* 3–8-9 KJManning (bhd: last over 1f out: kpt on ins
fnl f) ...................................... 6.3
Tarwiya (IRE) *(Ireland)* 3–8-9 JPMurtagh (in tch: 3rd & no ex wl over 1f out:
wknd) ...................................... 1½.4
Rosie's Mac (IRE) *(Ireland)* 3–8-9 RHughes (in tch: 4th & no imp wl over 1f out:
wknd) ...................................... ¾.5
Safety Tactic (IRE) *(Ireland)* 3–8-9 MJKinane (cl up: 3rd ½-wy: rdn & no imp 2f
out) ...................................... 8.6

8/11 IRISH MEMORY, **5/2** Tarwiya (IRE), **5/1** Safety Tactic (IRE), **8/1** Beware of Agents, **14/1** Rosie's Mac (IRE),
**20/1** Vaganova (IRE). Tote £1.50: £1.30 £1.60 (£4.40). Mr D.H.W.Dobson (J.S.Bolger,IRELAND) bred by
R.P.Williams. 6 Rn
1m 33.4 (10.2)
SF—78/51/35/28/26

### 637a—SAINT-CLOUD (L-H)
**Saturday, April 25th [Good]**
Going Allowance: 0.25 sec per fur (G)

**641a**     PRIX CORRIDA (Gp 3) (F & M) £20640.00    1¼m 110y

  12a★ **Fabulous Hostess (USA)** *(France)* 4-9-2 CBlack ............................ —1
  22a★ La Tirana (FR) *(France)* 5-8-11 WMongil ........................................ 1.2
         Salaam (SPA) *(France)* 4-8-11 ODoleuze ................................... nk.3
Tote 2.90f: 1.70f 1.50f 6.00f (9.50f). Mr J. Wertheimer (Mrs C.Head,FRANCE) bred by Wertheimer & Frere in
USA. 11 Rn                                        2m 15.3 (5)
                                                 SF—77/70/69

### 638a—LONGCHAMP (R-H)
**Sunday, April 26th [Good]**
Going Allowance: 0.05 sec per fur (G)

**642a**     PRIX GREFFULHE (Gp 2) (3-Y.O.C & F) £25800.00    1⅛m 110y (Grande)

    **Apple Tree (FR)** *(France)* 3-9-2 TJarnet (3rd st: hdwy wl over 1f out: led 1f out:
                r.o wl) ................................................................................. —1
    Break Bread (USA) *(France)* 3-9-2 CAsmussen (4th st: hdwy wl over 1f out: ev
                ch ins fnl f: one pce) ........................................................... 2.2
    Silver Kite (USA) *(France)* 3-9-2 FHead (mid div: outpcd over 1f out: styd on wl
                fnl f) ................................................................................... hd.3
    Standiford (USA) *(France)* 3-9-2 PatEddery (hdwy 2f out: rdn & one pce fnl f)   1.4
    Cristofori (USA) (Fav) *(France)* 3-9-2 SCauthen (cl up: led 2f out: hdd 1f out &
                one pce) ............................................................................... ½.5
    Adieu Au Roi (IRE) *(France)* 3-9-2 MBoutin (bhd: nvr nr to chal) ................... s.nk.6
    In-Quarto (bl) *(France)* 3-9-2 ALequeux (led tl hdd 2f out: sn wknd) .......... 1½.7
**Evens** Cristofori (USA), **13/4** Break Bread (USA), **4/1** Silver Kite (USA), **69/10** APPLE TREE (FR), **15/2** Standiford
(USA), **14/1** In-Quarto, **18/1** Adieu Au Roi (IRE). Tote 7.90f: 3.00f 2.50f (SF: 42.20f). Mr P. de Moussac
(A.Fabre,FRANCE) bred by Paul de Moussac in France. 7 Rn                 2m 14.7 (5.1)
                                       SF—57/53/52/50/49/48/43

**643a**     PRIX DE LA GROTTE (Gp 3) (3-Y.O.F) £20840.00    1m (Grande)

    **Absurde (FR)** *(France)* 3-9-2 FHead .................................................. —1
    Guislaine (FR) *(France)* 3-9-2 CAsmussen ......................................... nose.2
    Verveine (USA) *(France)* 3-9-2 ALequeux ........................................... s.nk.3
Tote 5.90f: 1.40f 1.40f 1.10f (11.90f). Mrs A.O'Reilly (F.Boutin,FRANCE) bred by Mrs & Dr G.Sander in France. 8
Rn                                                 1m 41.9 (4.2)
                                               SF—45/44/43

### SAN SIRO (R-H)
**Sunday, April 26th [Good to firm]**

**644a**     COPPA D'ORO DI MILANO (Gp 3)    £32558.00    1m 7f

  10a **DRUM TAPS (USA)** *(LordHuntingdon)* 6-8-11 LDettori ................................ —1
       Proud Panther (FR) *(France)* 6-8-11 ABadel .......................................... 3½.2
       Persian Halo (IRE) *(Ireland)* 4-8-11 WJO'Connor ................................... s.nk.3
228⁶ PER QUOD (USA) *(BHanbury)* 7-8-11 GDettori ..................................... 1.4
Tote 21L: 14L 16L 21L (41L). Mr Y. Asakawa (WEST ILSLEY) bred by J.Ward Ramos in USA. 11 Rn   3m 10.4

### NEWMARKET (R-H) Rowley Mile
**Friday, May 1st [Good]**
Going Allowance: minus 0.25 sec per fur (F)                          Wind: mod bhd

Stalls: high 2nd, 3rd & 5th, low remainder

**645**     ARLINGTON AUCTION STKS (2-Y.O) £4012.50 (£1200.00: £575.00: £262.50)
      5f                                                         2-00 (2-03)
  292★ **Toocando (IRE)** (Fav) *(CNAllen)* 8-7 RCochrane (2) (trckd ldrs: qcknd to ld ins
               fnl f: r.o wl) ....................................................................... —1

555³ Aradanza *(MRChannon)* 8-7 PatEddery (8) (disp ld tl hdd ins fnl f: kpt on) ......... 2.2
339 Surprise Offer *(RHannon)* 8-11 JReid (15) (lw: disp ld tl hdd fnl f: kpt on same
     pce) ................................................................................................................... nk.3
514⁴ Bourbon Jack *(JWPayne)* 8-11 AMunro (13) (a chsng ldrs: rdn 2f out: nt qckn) . 5.4
528⁴ The Atheling (IRE) *(MHTompkins)* 9-1 PRobinson (4) (a chsng ldrs: shkn up
     ¹/₂-wy: no imp) ............................................................................................ 2¹/₂.5
Marius (IRE) *(BWHills)* 8-7 DHolland (7) (cmpt: leggy: b.hind: mid div & drvn
     along ¹/₂-way: styd on: no imp) ........................................................................ hd.6
476 Sweet Disorder (IRE) *(GAPritchard-Gordon)* 8-2 GCarter (1) (in tch tl outpcd fnl
     2f) .................................................................................................................... ¹/₂.7
My Ballyboy *(ABailey)* 8-0 ‡7PBowe (12) (cmpt: scope: outpcd fr ¹/₂-wy) ........... 5.8
Midget Gem *(MissLCSiddall)* 8-11 DMcKeown (10) (neat: outpcd after 2f: n.d
     after) .......................................................................................................... 1¹/₂.9
Mister Blake *(WAO'Gorman)* 8-4⁽²⁾ ‡5EmmaO'Gorman (11) (w'like: scope: bit
     bkwd: nvr wnt pce) ......................................................................................... s.h.10
Primo Prince *(PFICole)* 8-11 TQuinn (9) (cmpt: s.i.s: n.d) ................................... 1¹/₂.11
Our Nikki *(GBlum)* 8-2 AShoults (3) (leggy: unf: a outpcd & bhd) ..................... 3.12
Miss Ribbons *(PatMitchell)* 7-13 ‡3SO'Gorman (14) (leggy: a outpcd & bhd) . 2¹/₂.13
588 Secret Tale *(GBlum)* 8-2 GBardwell (6) (a outpcd & bhd) ............................... 5.14
*339 Runnett Dancer (IRE) (14/1) Withdrawn (lame) : not under orders*

**13/8** TOOCANDO (IRE), **9/2** Aradanza, **7/1** Surprise Offer, Bourbon Jack, **9/1** Sweet Disorder (IRE), **10/1** Primo
Prince, Marius (IRE), **20/1** The Atheling (IRE), Midget Gem, **50/1** Ors. CSF £9.75, Tote £2.50: £1.50 £1.90 £2.00
(£3.60). Acorn Bloodstock (NEWMARKET) bred by Tim Corridan in Ireland. 14 Rn
                                                        60.24 sec (0.84)
                                                       SF—51/43/46/26/20/11

---

**646**
EASTERN ELECTRICITY H'CAP (3-Y.O) (0-105) £6056.00 (£1808.00: £864.00: £392.00)
1m
                                           2-35 (2-37)

*(Weights raised 12 lb)*
**Good Reference (IRE) (85)** *(MBell)* 9-2 MHills (3) (a cl up: chal 2f out: r.o wl
     towards fin: fin 2nd, s.h: awrdd r) ................................................................... —1
Magnified (USA) **(86)** *(BWHills)* 9-3 PatEddery (5) (lw: hld up: effrt over 2f out:
     hrd rdn & hmpd appr fnl f: fin 3rd, nk: plcd 2nd) ......................................... 2
387 Sharp Prince **(90)** *(HRACecil)* 9-7 MRoberts (7) (lw: cl up: led over 2f out: hung
     rt: all out: fin 1st: disq: plcd 3rd) ..................................................................... 3
451⁴ Eden's Close **(78)** *(MHTompkins)* 8-9 PRobinson (6) (led tl hdd over 2f out: r.o
     one pce) ....................................................................................................... 2.4
589² Gotcha (BAR) **(87)** (Fav) *(RHannon)* 9-4 WRSwinburn (4) (prom: rdn ¹/₂-wy: no
     imp after) ...................................................................................................... 1¹/₂.5
Wild Strawberry **(82)** *(JMPEustace)* 8-13 MTebbutt (2) (prom tl outpcd over 2f
     out) ............................................................................................................... 2¹/₂.6
Fair American (USA) **(86)** *(MRStoute)* 9-3 SCauthen (1) (lw: hld up: hdwy 3f
     out: rdn & wknd wl over 1f out) ...................................................................... 5.7
*Stewards Enquiry: Sharp Prince disq. (interference to Magnified). Roberts suspended 10-13/5/92 (careless riding).*

**5/2** Gotcha (BAR), **7/2** Fair American (USA), Eden's Close, **7/1** Magnified (USA), **8/1** Sharp Prince(op 5/1), **9/1**
GOOD REFERENCE (IRE), **12/1** Wild Strawberry(20/1 —10/1). CSF £60.72, Tote £13.80: £4.40 £3.00 (£31.10).
Mr Alan Lillingston (NEWMARKET) bred by Mount Coote Stud in Ireland. 7 Rn         1m 40.88 (3.58)
                                                       SF—23/17/17/3/7/–

---

**647**
NEWMARKET STKS (listed race) (3-Y.O) £10770.00 (£3210.00: £1530.00: £690.00)
1¹/₄m
                                           3-05 (3-19)

389⁴ **Captain Horatius (IRE) (109)** *(JLDunlop)* 8-13 WCarson (1) (hld up: stdy
     hdwy to ld over 1f out: hung rt: rdn & r.o) .................................................... —1
Shuailaan (USA) (Fav) *(ACStewart)* 8-13 MRoberts (3) (lw: a cl up: led over 2f
     out tl over 1f out: no ex) ................................................................................ 2.2
404* Jeune **(102)** *(GWragg)* 8-13 WRSwinburn (5) (led tl hdd over 2f out: kpt on one
     pce) .............................................................................................................. ¹/₂.3
437 Taylor Quigley (USA) **(103)** *(CNAllen)* 8-10 RCochrane (4) (chsd ldrs tl wknd
     over 2f out) .................................................................................................... 10.4
474⁴ L'Hermine **(92)** (bl) *(HCandy)* 8-10 LPiggott (2) (lw: hld up: effrt over 4f out: sn
     rdn & btn) ...................................................................................................... 7.5
Kingdom of Spain (USA) *(HRACecil)* 8-10 SCauthen (6) (h.d.w chsd ldrs: rdn
     over 3f out: sn wknd) ..................................................................................... 15.6

**6/5** Shuailaan (USA), **4/1** Jeune, **5/1** CAPTAIN HORATIUS (IRE), **7/1** Kingdom of Spain (USA)(op 4/1), **10/1**
Taylor Quigley (USA)(tchd 16/1), **12/1** L'Hermine. CSF £10.97, Tote £6.00: £2.90 £1.40 (£4.70). Mr D. R.
Hunnisett (ARUNDEL) bred by B. W. Hills and Mrs V. Shaw in Ireland. 6 Rn         2m 5.13 (2.53)
                                                       SF—49/45/44/21/7/–

**648**　GENERAL ACCIDENT JOCKEY CLUB STKS (Gp 2)　£34254.00 (£12760.70: £6080.35: £2594.95)　1½m
3-40 (3-51)

**Sapience** *(DRCElsworth)* 6-8-12 RCochrane (6) (mde all: qcknd over 4f out: r.o wl) ............................................................................ —1

228* Luchiroverte (IRE) *(CEBrittain)* 4-8-9 MRoberts (1) (lw: a clp up: chsd wnr fnl 4f: r.o wl: nt pce to chal) .................................................. 3.2

Toulon (Fav) *(AFabre,France)* 4-9-0 PatEddery (7) (lw: hld up: hdwy 4f out: prom & hrd rdn over 2f out: nt qckn) ......................... 1½.3

Always Friendly *(HCandy)* 4-8-6 AMunro (8) (plld hrd: in tch tl outpcd over 4f out: hdwy 2f out: styd on wl) ..................................... 1.4

10a Rock Hopper *(MRStoute)* 5-8-12 WRSwinburn (5) (lw: hld up: effrt over 4f out: hrd rdn & no imp fnl 2f) ........................................ hd.5

Surrealist (IRE) *(BWHills)* 4-8-9 WCarson (9) (chsd ldrs tl outpcd over 3f out: n.d after) ................................................................ 15.6

390⁵ Corrupt (USA) *(NACallaghan)* 4-8-12 LPiggott (4) (cl up tl wknd over 3f out) ..... 4.7

Marcus Thorpe (USA) *(PAKelleway)* 4-8-9 TQuinn (3) (b.off hind: hdwy & prom ½-wy: wknd 4f out) ......................................... s.h.8

Possessive Dancer *(AAScott)* 4-8-11 SCauthen (2) (hld up: effrt 4f out: a bhd) nk.9

**Evens** Toulon, **9/2** Rock Hopper(op 3/1), **10/1** Corrupt (USA), Luchiroverte (IRE), Possessive Dancer, **11/1** Surrealist (IRE), **20/1** Always Friendly, **40/1** SAPIENCE, **50/1** Marcus Thorpe (USA). CSF £327.15, Tote £64.30: £7.90 £2.20 £1.20 (£147.50). Mr W. H. O'Gorman (WHITSBURY) bred by George Strawbridge and partners. 9 Rn
2m 32.13 (2.83)
SF—40/31/33/23/28/–

---

**649**　BURWELL H'CAP (3-Y.O) (0-100) £4581.00 (£1368.00: £654.00: £297.00)
6f
4-10 (4-21)

445² **Master Planner (86)** *(CACyzer)* 8-12 TQuinn (7) (cl up: led over 2f out: hld on wl) .............................................................. —1

576 Euro Festival **(75)** *(MissLCSiddall)* 8-1 AMunro (6) (s.i.s: hdwy ½-wy: chal ins fnl f: edgd rt & no ex nr fin) ........................... nk.2

432 Risk Master **(72)** *(CAHorgan)* 7-12(1) AMcGlone (8) (lw: a chsng ldrs: ev ch over 1f out: kpt on) ......................................... 1½.3

445 Splice **(88)** *(JRFanshawe)* 8-7 ‡⁷NVarley (2) (s.i.s: swtchd rt ½-wy: r.o: nrst fin) 1.4

559⁴ Isaiah **(95)** (Fav) *(MJohnston)* 9-7 DMcKeown (1) (lw: cl up: drvn along ½-wy: lost pl 2f out: kpt on: no imp) ......................... 3½.5

468² Early Star **(79)** *(TDBarron)* 8-5 AlexGreaves (9) (in tch: effrt ½-wy: rdn & no imp) 1½.6

503* Threepence **(94)** *(JBerry)* 9-6 (7x) PatEddery (14) (led over 3f: edgd lft: btn appr fnl f) ............................................ hd.7

503⁵ Orthorhombus **(89)** *(GLewis)* 9-1 PaulEddery (4) (lw: in tch: effrt over 2f out: hung rt most of wy: no imp) ......................... ¾.8

Milagro **(85)** *(RHannon)* 8-6 ‡⁵RPerham (3) (chsd ldrs over 4f) ...................... 1½.9

Arabellajill **(82)** *(RHannon)* 8-8 WCarson (3) (nvr trbld ldrs) ...................... 3½.10

Jazz **(83)** *(LMCumani)* 8-9 LDettori (10) (h.d.w: outpcd after 2f) ............ nk.11

445 Peerage Prince **(73)** *(PatMitchell)* 7-10 ‡³SO'Gorman (13) (prom centre over 3f) ½.12

Nobby Barnes **(70)** *(RWArmstrong)* 7-10 BCrossley (12) (prom centre over 3f) 5.13

**4/1** Isaiah, **9/2** Threepence(3/1—5/1), **7/1** Orthorhombus, **8/1** MASTER PLANNER, Jazz, **9/1** Arabellajill(op 6/1), **10/1** Early Star, Euro Festival, **11/1** Splice(10/1—16/1), **16/1** Risk Master, **20/1** Milagro, **33/1** Ors. CSF £80.96, CT £1,144.48. Tote £10.50: £2.30 £3.30 £8.00 (£30.70). Mr R. M. Cyzer (HORSHAM) bred by C. A. Cyzer. 13 Rn
1m 12.05 (0.65)
SF—55/43/34/39/39/17

---

**650**　E.B.F. WILBRAHAM STKS (Mdn 2-Y.O.F) £3557.50 (£1060.00: £505.00: £227.50)
5f
4-40 (4-49)

476⁴ **Rain Splash** *(RHannon)* 8-11 MRoberts (4) (s.i.s: sn chsng ldrs: rdn to ld 1f out: r.o) ....................................................... —1

Nuryandra *(GWragg)* 8-11 PatEddery (5) (neat: unf: chsd ldrs: led over 1f out: hdd 1f out: r.o) ............................................. 1.2

439³ Hawayah (IRE) (Fav) *(BHanbury)* 8-11 WRSwinburn (1) (trckd ldrs: effrt & ev ch over 1f out: r.o) ............................... hd.3

Hairraising *(NACallaghan)* 8-11 WCarson (2) (leggy: unf: sn bhd: hdwy over 1f out: styd on wl nr fin) .......................... 5.4

Anonymous *(CEBrittain)* 8-6 ‡⁵BDoyle (7) (w'like: scope: bkwd: cl up tl hung bdly lft & wknd over 1f out) ......................... ½.5

476⁵ Hawaii Star (IRE) *(GLewis)* 8-11 PaulEddery (10) (nvr trbld ldrs) ................ 1.6

476 Sea Exhibition (IRE) *(MBlanshard)* 8-11 RCochrane (6) (led over 3f: wknd) ...... ½.7

    Tee Gee Jay *(CNWilliams)* 8-11 BRaymond (9) (w'like: scope: nvr wnt pce) ...... 2.8
    Bergliot *(JBerry)* 8-11 GCarter (8) (cmpt: scope: dwlt: a bhd) ......................... 2¹/₂.9
    Diamond Lucy *(WAO'Gorman)* 8-6 ‡⁵EmmaO'Gorman (3) (leggy: b.hind: dwlt:
        a bhd) ................................................................................................ ³/₄.10

**11/4** Hawayah (IRE)(3/1—5/1), **3/1** RAIN SPLASH, **7/2** Nuryandra, **8/1** Hawaii Star (IRE)(op 4/1), **9/1** Anonymous(4/1—10/1), **10/1** Sea Exhibition (IRE)(op 5/1), **12/1** Bergliot(op 8/1), **14/1** Hairraising, **25/1** Ors. CSF £14.42, Tote £3.40: £1.90 £2.10 £1.90 (£5.20). Mr R. A. Bernard (MARLBOROUGH) bred by Lady Joanna Wellesley. 10 Rn                             61.09 sec (1.69)
                                                SF—38/34/33/13/6/7

## 651    NEWMARKET CHALLENGE WHIP (Mdn 3-Y.O) **1m**      5-10 (5-13)

393⁴ **Queen Warrior** *(Fav)* *(PTWalwyn)* 8-9 PatEddery (3) (trckd ldr: led wl over 1f
    out: shkn up & r.o wl) ............................................................................ —1
    Belated *(HThomsonJones)* 8-9 RHills (1) (w'like: hld up: hdwy & ev ch ins fnl f:
    no ex) ................................................................................................ 3¹/₂.2
    La Cousine *(CEBrittain)* 8-4 ‡⁵BDoyle (2) (led tl hdd wl over 1f out: sn btn) ........ 5.3

**1/3** QUEEN WARRIOR(tchd 1/2), **11/4** Belated(op 6/4), **10/1** La Cousine(5/1—12/1). CSF £1.66, Tote £1.30 (£1.20). Mr Christopher Spence (LAMBOURN) bred by C. J. Spence and P. T. Walwyn. 3 Rn   1m 40.41 (3.11)
                                                  SF—18/7/—

T/Trio: Race 5: £792.60 (2 Tckts). T/Jkpt: Not won; £3,052.20 to Newmarket 2/5/92. T/Plpt: £212.60 (38.85 Tckts).                                               AA

# NEWMARKET (R-H) Rowley Mile
## Saturday, May 2nd [Good]
Going Allowance: 5f: minus 0.15 sec; Rest: nil sec per fur (G)            Wind: fresh bhd

Stalls: high 1st & 3rd, low 4th & 5th, remainder centre

## 652    CULFORD STKS (3-Y.O) £4230.00 (£1260.00: £600.00: £270.00)    **1¹/₂m**   2-00 (2-01)

481* **Allegan** (USA) *(Fav)* *(HRACecil)* 9-4 PatEddery (3) (lw: hld up: hdwy 4f out: hrd
    rdn 2f out: styd on wl) ........................................................................ —1
427* Iywaan (IRE) *(PTWalwyn)* 9-4 WCarson (1) (cl up: slt ld 7f out: qcknd 3f out: hdd
    & no ex ins fnl f) .............................................................................. 1¹/₂.2
433* Sayh *(MAJarvis)* 9-4 SCauthen (2) (lw: led tl hdd 7f out: cl up tl outpcd wl over 2f
    out) .................................................................................................. 7.3
427⁵ Acrobate (USA) *(PAKelleway)* 8-11 BRaymond (4) (chsd ldrs tl rdn & btn 3f out) 10.4

**1/3** ALLEGAN, (USA), **6/1** Iywaan (IRE), **13/2** Sayh, **33/1** Acrobate (USA). CSF £2.50, Tote £1.30 (£2.00). Mr K. Abdulla (NEWMARKET) bred by Juddmonte Farms, Inc. in USA. 4 Rn               2m 34.85 (5.55)
                                                SF—49/46/32/5

## 653    MAYER PARRY H'CAP (3-Y.O) (0-110) £7375.00 (£2200.00: £1050.00: £475.00)
       **7f**             (Weights raised 9 lb)             2-30 (2-32)

499³ **Sky Hunter** (USA) **(84)** (v) *(RHannon)* 8-9 MJKinane (8) (lw: s.s: hdwy over 2f
    out: r.o u.p to ld cl home) .................................................................. —1
502² Petite Sonnerie **(79)** *(GLewis)* 8-4 PaulEddery (7) (lw: chsd ldrs: rdn to ld ins fnl
    f: nt qckn nr fin) .............................................................................. nk.2
445⁵ Sir Boudle (IRE) **(83)** *(CRNelson)* 8-8 JReid (5) (a cl up: led over 1f out tl ins fnl f:
    kpt on) ........................................................................................... ¹/₂.3
454³ Afif **(95)** *(MrsJCecil)* 9-1 ‡⁵DHarrison (1) (led tl hdd over 1f out: one pce) ........... 6.4
    Najeb (USA) **(84)** *(BHanbury)* 8-9 BRaymond (3) (lw: cl up tl rdn & outpcd 3f
    out: no imp after) .............................................................................. 2.5
    Mutabahi (CAN) **(96)** *(RWArmstrong)* 9-7 WCarson (2) (bit bkwd: prom: drvn
    along ¹/₂-wy: no imp fnl 3f) .............................................................. hd.6
404⁵ Greetland Folly **(87)** *(RMWhitaker)* 8-12 ACulhane (4) (w ldrs tl wknd appr fnl f) ¹/₂.7
 432 Walking on Water **(83)** (bl) *(RFJohnsonHoughton)* 8-8 PatEddery (9) (chsd
    ldrs: ev ch & rdn 2f out: nt qckn) ...................................................... 1¹/₂.8
432² Spanish Miner (USA) **(93)** *(Fav)* *(AAScott)* 8-13 ‡⁵LNewton (6) (trckd ldrs: effrt
    u.p 2f out: sn btn) ........................................................................... ³/₄.9

**3/1** Spanish Miner (USA), **5/1** Afif, **11/2** SKY HUNTER (USA), Petite Sonnerie, **6/1** Sir Boudle (IRE), **10/1** Walking on Water(8/1—12/1), **14/1** Najeb (USA), Mutabahi (CAN), **25/1** Greetland Folly. CSF £32.02, CT £167.21. Tote £5.20: £1.70 £1.80 £1.90 (£14.70). A. F. Budge (Equine) Limited (MARLBOROUGH) bred by Mrs Lucy G. Bassett in USA. 9 Rn                                  1m 26.77 (2.77)
                                              SF—53/47/49/38/26/37

**654**    PHILIP CORNES NICKEL ALLOYS STKS (Mdn 2-Y.O) £4386.00 (£1308.00: £624.00: £282.00)  **5f**

3-00 (3-04)

**Silver Wizard (USA)** *(GLewis)* 9-0 PaulEddery (4) (wl grwn: bit bkwd: disp ld tl led 2f out: r.o wl) ................................................................ —1
Ardkinglass *(Fav)* *(HRACecil)* 9-0 PatEddery (3) (lt-f: leggy: a cl up: effrt 2f out: r.o wl) ....................................................................... nk.2
Splendent *(USA)* *(PFICole)* 9-0 AMunro (6) (cmpt: bkwd: sn chsng ldrs: outpcd 2f out: r.o wl nr fin) .................................................... 2.3
555 Rock Symphony *(AAScott)* 9-0 BRaymond (7) (disp ld 3f: wknd ins fnl f) ........ 2½.4
Son Pardo *(RHannon)* 9-0 MJKinane (5) (w'like: scope: lw: s.i.s: bhd tl styd on wl fnl 2f) ................................................................... 3.5
Never so Lost *(BWHills)* 9-0 WCarson (8) (w'like: scope: sn prom: pushed along ½-wy: grad wknd) ........................................ 1.6
491³ Make it Happen (IRE) *(JBerry)* 9-0 JCarroll (2) (lw: nvr wnt pce) .................... 8.7
Spanish Thread *(GAPritchard-Gordon)* 8-9 RCochrane (1) (neat: s.i.s: a bhd) ... 1.8

**7/4** Ardkinglass(11/10—2/1), **11/4** Splendent (USA)(5/1—5/2), **7/1** Rock Symphony, Make it Happen (IRE), **10/1** Never so Lost, **12/1** Son Pardo(op 7/1), Spanish Thread(20/1—12/1), **14/1** SILVER WIZARD (USA)(op 8/1). CSF £38.43, Tote £22.60: £3.70 (£39.70). Mrs Shirley Robins (EPSOM) bred by Bounding Basque Breeding Syndicate in USA. 8 Rn
60.77 sec (1.37)
SF—58/57/49/39/27/23

**655**    GENERAL ACCIDENT 2,000 GUINEAS STKS (Gp 1) (3-Y.O.C & F) £113736.00 (£42024.00: £20112.00: £8160.00: £3180.00: £1188.00)  **1m**

3-40 (3-50)

391⁴ **Rodrigo de Triano (USA)** *(PWChapple-Hyam)* 9-0 LPiggott (3) (h.d.w: s.i.s: hld up & bhd: hdwy 3f out: led & qcknd 1f out: r.o wl) ......... —1
474* Lucky Lindy (IRE) *(RHannon)* 9-0 MJKinane (9) (a chsng ldrs: rdn over 2f out: r.o wl fin) ............................................................ 1½.2
437* Pursuit of Love *(HRACecil)* 9-0 MRoberts (13) (lw: a.p: hdwy to ld 2f out: hdd 1f out: r.o) ................................................................ ½.3
474³ Silver Wisp (USA) *(GLewis)* 9-0 PaulEddery (8) (hld up: effrt 3f out: styd on wl: nrst fin) ..................................................................... hd.4
444⁴ Muhtarram (USA) *(JHMGosden)* 9-0 WCarson (1) (hld up & bhd: hdwy 3f out: n.m.r 2f out: r.o wl nr fin) .................................... ½.5
Tertian (USA) *(AFabre,France)* 9-0 PatEddery (10) (a.p: effrt & wnt lft over 2f out: wandered u.p appr fnl f: nt qckn) ............................ 1½.6
Thourios *(GHarwood)* 9-0 RCochrane (6) (h.d.w: led tl hdd 2f out: r.o one pce) ³/₄.7
391³ Swing Low *(RHannon)* 9-0 WRSwinburn (16) (chsd ldrs centre: effrt & ev ch over 2f out: wknd) ................................................. 2.8
444* Alnasr Alwasheek *(Fav)* *(MRStoute)* 9-0 SCauthen (4) (lw: hld up: effrt over 3f out: hrd rdn 2f out: nt qckn) ...................................... 2½.9
444⁵ Badie (USA) *(JLDunlop)* 9-0 LDettori (2) (lw: in tch: effrt 3f out: nt pce to chal) nk.10
437² Steinbeck (USA) *(AFabre,France)* 9-0 TJarnet (7) (lw: effrt 3f out: sn rdn & btn) hd.11
460a* Cardoun (FR) *(ELellouche,France)* 9-0 DBoeuf (12) (gd sort: chsd ldrs tl wknd 2f out) .................................................................... 1.12
437 Wilde Rufo *(PAKelleway)* 9-0 TQuinn (11) (prom centre 5f) ........................ 1½.13
391² River Falls *(RHannon)* 9-0 BRaymond (14) (lw: led centre tl wknd 3f out) ......... 3.14
Dilum (USA) *(PFICole)* 9-0 AMunro (15) (lw: prom centre 5f: sn wknd) .......... 5.15
437⁴ Artic Tracker (USA) (bl) *(CRNelson)* 9-0 JReid (12) (racd centre: s.i.s: hld up: effrt 3f out: sn btn) ........................................... 1½.16

**5/2** Alnasr Alwasheek, **9/2** Pursuit of Love, **6/1** RODRIGO DE TRIANO (USA), **8/1** Cardoun (FR), **12/1** Tertian (USA), **14/1** Dilum (USA), **16/1** Steinbeck (USA)(20/1—12/1), **20/1** Swing Low, River Falls, **25/1** Muhtarram (USA), Silver Wisp (USA), **50/1** Lucky Lindy (IRE), Thourios, **66/1** Artic Tracker (USA), Badie (USA), **100/1** Wilde Rufo. CSF £209.22, Tote £6.10: £2.50 £6.10 £2.00 (£186.70). Mr R. E. Sangster (MARLBOROUGH) bred by Swettenham Stud in USA. 16 Rn
1m 38.37 (1.07)
SF—84/79/77/76/74/69/67

**656**    PALACE HOUSE STKS (Gp 3) £15654.00 (£5797.20: £2733.60: £1135.20)  **5f**

4-15 (4-21)

**Monde Bleu** *(AFabre,France)* 4–8-10 TJarnet (5) (gd sort: a.p: hdwy 2f out: led ins fnl f: r.o wl) ..................................................... —1
465* Paris House (115) *(Fav)* *(JBerry)* 3–8-0 JCarroll (4) (lw: led tl hdd ins fnl f: r.o) .. 1.2
Blyton Lad (113) *(WJPearce)* 6–8-10 SWebster (3) (lw: chsd ldr tl rdn & outpcd ½-wy: no imp after) .................................................. 5.3
465 Food of Love *(JBerry)* 4–8-7 TQuinn (1) (b.hind: sn pushed along & bhd: sme hdwy 2f out: n.d) ..................................................... 2.4

465³ Sir Harry Hardman **(101)** *(FHLee)* 4–8–10 MRoberts (6) (spd 3f: sn wknd) ...... 2¹/₂.**5**
    478* Miss Nosey Parker (IRE) *(9/2)* Withdrawn (lame at s) : not under orders

**4/5** Paris House, **8/1** MONDE BLEU, Blyton Lad, **10/1** Food of Love(op 20/1), **14/1** Sir Harry Hardman. CSF
£12.90, Tote £6.40: £2.10 £1.10 (£2.40). Mr Daniel Wildenstein (FRANCE) bred by Dayton Ltd. 5 Rn
                                                     59.44 sec (0.04)
                                              SF—80/66/56/45/38

**657**     LADBROKES H'CAP (0-110) £11355.00 (£3390.00: £1620.00: £735.00)
         1¹/₄m                                           4-45 (4-49)

     **Mashaallah (USA) (96)** *(JHMGosden)* 4–9–5 SCauthen (11) (h.d.w: a.p: led
                       over 2f out: r.o wl) ................................................... —**1**
431² Laburnum **(82)** (Fav) *(LMCumani)* 4–8–5 LDettori (10) (hld up: hdwy & prom
                   ¹/₂-wy: rdn & outpcd 2f out: r.o nr fin) .............................. 3.**2**
431* Myfontaine **(70)** *(KTIvory)* 5–7–7 GBardwell (12) (hld up & bhd: stdy hdwy
                   ¹/₂-wy: ev ch 2f out: rdn & nt qckn) ............................ ¹/₂.**3**
 343 Cooley's Valve (IRE) **(91)** *(BWHills)* 4–9–0 PatEddery (7) (bhd: hdwy 3f out:
                   styd on wl) ........................................................ 2.**4**
 479 Lucky Guest **(94)** *(JLDunlop)* 5–9–3 LPiggott (9) (hld up & bhd: hdwy over 1f
                   out: r.o) .......................................................... ³/₄.**5**
 477 Danzarin (IRE) **(83)** *(RHannon)* 4–8–6 MRoberts (6) (chsd ldr: led 3f out tl over
                   2f out: grad wknd) ................................................ 4.**6**
 343 Heart of Darkness **(105)** *(IABalding)* 4–10–0 JReid (4) (lw: hld up: hdwy & ev ch
                   3f out: wknd wl over 1f out) ...................................... nk.**7**
532³ Majed (IRE) **(74)** *(NACallaghan)* 4–7–6 ‡⁵DHarrison (1) (in tch: effrt 3f out: no
                   imp) ............................................................. ³/₄.**8**
 392 Halston Prince **(83)** *(RFJohnsonHoughton)* 5–8–6 TQuinn (5) (bhd: hdwy 4f
                   out: rdn & wknd 2f out) ........................................... 2.**9**
 225 Chatham Island **(74)** *(CEBrittain)* 4–7–6⁽⁴⁾ ‡⁵BDoyle (8) (chsd ldrs tl wknd over 2f
                   out) ............................................................. nk.**10**
     Corcina **(83)** *(MBell)* 4–8–6 JCarroll (3) (b: b.hind: led tl hdd 3f out: sn wknd) .. 4.**11**
     King Athelstan (USA) **(103)** *(JHMGosden)* 4–9–12 WCarson (2) (b.hind: prom tl
                   wknd 3f out) ...................................................... 15.**12**
                 LONG HANDICAP: Chatham Island 7-6.

**2/1** Laburnum, **100/30** MASHAALLAH (USA), **8/1** Myfontaine, Majed (IRE), **10/1** Lucky Guest, **11/1** Cooley's
Valve (IRE), **12/1** King Athelstan (USA), **16/1** Danzarin (IRE), **20/1** Corcina, Heart of Darkness, **25/1** Chatham
Island, **33/1** Halston Prince. CSF £10.51, CT £47.48. Tote £4.10: £1.90 £1.30 £2.40 (£4.20). Sheikh Ahmed Al
Maktoum (NEWMARKET) bred by W.S.Farish, W.T.Carter & E.J.Hudson Jnr in USA. 12 Rn    2m 5.40 (2.80)
                                              SF—77/57/44/61/62/43

**658**     CHIPPENHAM PARK STKS (Mdn 3-Y.O.C & G) £3590.00 (£1070.00: £510.00: £230.00)
         7f                                             5-15 (5-19)

428² **Claybank (USA) (91)** (Fav) *(BWHills)* 9-0 PatEddery (6) (lw: a cl up: slt ld wl
                   over 1f out: r.o up) ................................................ —**1**
509⁵ Bid for Six (USA) *(RHannon)* 9-0 MJKinane (4) (effrt 3f out: sn hrd rdn: r.o wl:
                   nrst fin) ......................................................... ¹/₂.**2**
474⁵ Al Sadi *(CEBrittain)* 9-0 MRoberts (3) (lw: led: rdn over 3f out: hdd wl over 1f out:
                   kpt on wl) ........................................................ s.h.**3**
     Bravura *(WJHaggas)* 9-0 MHills (8) (a w ldrs: effrt 3f out: nt qckn ins fnl f) ........ nk.**4**
 440 Turret Gates *(JARToller)* 9-0 TQuinn (7) (lw: a.p: effrt 3f out: nt qckn appr fnl f) . 3.**5**
     Dawaahi (USA) *(JHMGosden)* 9-0 SCauthen (5) (w'like: b.nr hind: hld up: hdwy
                   4f out: lost pl 3f out: stdy hdwy 1f out: fin wl) .................... hd.**6**
     Mizoram (USA) *(HRACecil)* 9-0 AMcGlone (1) (w'like: scope: s.i.s: effrt u.p 4f
                   out: sn btn) ...................................................... 15.**7**
487⁶ Boring (USA) *(NACallaghan)* 9-0 BRaymond (9) (a bhd) .......................... 1.**8**
     Ramaas (USA) *(AAScott)* 9-0 WRSwinburn (2) (chsd ldrs 4f: sn wknd) .............. ³/₄.**9**

**2/1** CLAYBANK, **3/1** Bravura(op 5/1), **9/2** Dawaahi (USA)(op 2/1), **9/1** Al Sadi, Ramaas (USA)(op 5/1),
**11/1** Mizoram (USA)(5/1—12/1), **14/1** Bid for Six (USA)(op 7/1), **33/1** Ors. CSF £26.90, Tote £2.80: £1.30
£3.70 £2.00 (£16.30). Mr D. F. Smurfit (LAMBOURN) bred by Welcome Farm in USA. 9 Rn   1m 26.99 (2.99)
                                              SF—55/53/52/51/42/41

T/Trio: Races 2 & 4: £163.10 & £12.00 (28.4 & 198.5 Tckts). T/Jkpt: Not won; £11,065.75 to Kempton 4/5/92.
T/Plpt: £19.00 (767.3 Tckts).                                                 AA

371—**HAMILTON (R-H)**
**Friday, May 1st [Soft, Heavy patches]**
Going Allowance: St: 1.20 sec per fur; Rnd: 0.95 sec per fur (S)    Wind: fresh almost across

Stalls: low

**659**    E.B.F. PLUMB CENTER & I.M.I. YORKSHIRE FITTINGS STKS (Mdn 2-Y.O) £2499.50
(£692.00: £330.50)    **5f 4y**                                              2-15 (2-23)

**Daaniera (IRE)** *(JBerry)* 9-0 JCarroll (8) (neat: scope: lw: a cl up: rdn ½-wy: led
    appr fnl f: r.o wl) ..................................................................... —1
564⁴ Wahem (IRE) *(NACallaghan)* 9-0 GDuffield (5) (w ldrs: rdn whn squeezed out &
    swtchd wl over 1f out: styd on) ............................................. 3.2
Dayjuz (IRE) *(FHLee)* 9-0 SWebster (4) (cl cpld: leggy: bit bkwd: led tl hdd appr
    fnl f: no ex) ........................................................................ nk.3
Hod-Mod (IRE) (Jt-Fav) *(ABailey)* 9-0 AMackay (7) (small: chsd ldrs: drvn along
    ½-wy: one pce appr fnl f) ....................................................... 1.4
491² Duke of Dreams (Jt-Fav) *(MrsGRReveley)* 9-0 KDarley (3) (lw: prom: rdn 2f out:
    no imp) ............................................................................... 1.5
Oscars Quest *(JBerry)* 9-0 LCharnock (2) (cmpt: bit bkwd: cl up tl wknd wl over
    1f out) ................................................................................ 3.6
Lucky Owl *(PMonteith)* 8-6 ‡3JFanning (6) (neat: bit bkwd: s.s: a bhd) ............... 3.7
Onewithwhitepaw *(ABailey)* 9-0 KFallon (1) (neat: scope: bit bkwd: sn drvn
    along & outpcd) .................................................................. 2½.8

5/2 Hod-Mod (IRE), Duke of Dreams(3/1—2/1), **9/2** Wahem (IRE), **5/1** DAANIERA (IRE)(op 5/2), **10/1**
Onewithwhitepaw(op 5/1), **12/1** Dayjuz (IRE), **20/1** Ors. CSF £26.42, Tote £3.80: £1.30 £1.30 £7.90 (£4.50).
Mrs Seamus Purcell (COCKERHAM) bred by Andrew Dannon in Ireland. 8 Rn    69.4 sec (10.1)
                                           SF—18/6/5/1/–/–

**660**    PLUMB CENTER & DANFOSS RANDALL (S) STKS (3 & 4-Y.O) £2448.00 (£678.00:
£324.00)    **5f 4y**                                                   2-45 (2-48)

**Francis Ann (44)** *(MissLAPerratt)* 4-8-4 ‡7RHavlin (2) (in tch: hdwy 2f out: led
    ins fnl f: styd on) ................................................................ —1
594 Palacegate Gold (IRE) **(58)** *(RJHodges)* 3-8-8 ‡5TSprake (1) (sn led: hdd ½-wy:
    led appr fnl f: hdd & nt qckn ins fnl f) ................................... 2½.2
542³ Foxes Diamond **(36)** *(BEllison)* 4-8-11 NCarlisle (3) (chsd ldrs: rdn ½-wy: nt
    qckn appr fnl f) .................................................................. 2½.3
198⁴ Danzig Lad (USA) *(MPNaughton)* 4-9-2 GHind (9) (prom: effrt ½-wy: no ex
    appr fnl f) .......................................................................... hd.4
468 Palacegate Racing **(74)** *(JBerry)* 3-8-13 JCarroll (4) (cl up: led ½-wy tl hdd
    appr fnl f: sn btn) .............................................................. 2½.5
355⁵ Jiggerak **(59)** (v) *(SGNorton)* 3-8-1 ‡7OPears (6) (w ldrs: effrt ½-wy: wknd
    wl over 1f out) ................................................................... 2½.6
544³ Bantel Brigadier **(40)** (bl) *(RAllan)* 3-8-6 SWebster (8) (a in rr) .................. ½.7
415 Long Last *(DWChapman)* 3-8-1 SWood (7) (prom 3f: sn wknd) ...................... 5.8
532 Magdalene (IRE) **(29)** *(TFairhurst)* 4-8-8 ‡3JFanning (5) (a bhd) ................. 8.9

3/1 Jiggerak(op 2/1), **7/2** Palacegate Racing, **4/1** Palacegate Gold (IRE), Foxes Diamond, **14/1** Long Last, **20/1**
FRANCIS ANN(op 12/1), Danzig Lad (USA)(op 12/1), **25/1** Magdalene (IRE), **66/1** Bantel Brigadier. CSF £85.50,
Tote £22.20: £4.10 £1.90 £2.20 (£115.00). Mrs M. Gray (AYR) bred by Mrs H. T. Jones. 9 Rn; No bid
                                         67.2 sec (8.9)
                                     SF—32/26/19/23/10/–

**661**    LANGS SUPREME SCOTCH WHISKY H'CAP (0-70) £2807.00 (£777.00: £371.00)
**5f 4y**                                                             3-15 (3-16)

(Weights raised 2 lb)
496³ **Verro (USA) (39)** (bl) *(JABennett)* 5-8-2 NCarlisle (4) (hld up: hdwy 2f out: led
    ins fnl f: rdn out) ................................................................ —1
421* Fangio **(60)** *(WGMTurner)* 3-8-8 ‡5TSprake (8) (led: qcknd appr fnl f: hdd ins fnl
    f: styd on nr fin) ................................................................. nk.2
487⁵ Tumbling (USA) **(47)** *(RAllan)* 4-8-10 SWebster (2) (racd stands' side: w ldrs:
    effrt ½-wy: styd on same pce) .............................................. 4.3
541⁵ Crail Harbour **(61)** *(PCHaslam)* 6-9-10 KDarley (7) (drvn along ½-wy: styd on
    fnl f: nt rch ldrs) ............................................................... ¾.4
541² Coolaba Prince (IRE) **(53)** (v) (Fav) *(FHLee)* 3-8-1 ‡5NKennedy (5) (cl up: ev ch
    appr fnl f: nt qckn) ........................................................... s.h.5
483³ Best Effort **(52)** *(MPNaughton)* 6-9-1 GHind (3) (w ldrs: rdn 2f out: btn appr fnl f) 1½.6
279⁵ Chateau Nord **(59)** *(JBerry)* 3-8-12 JCarroll (6) (nvr trbld ldrs) .................... 3.7

516³ Sobering Thoughts **(40)** (bl) *(DWChapman)* 6-8-3 SWood (1) (gd spd stands' side: rdn & wknd 2f out) ............................ 1½.**8**
535⁶ Don't Run Me Over **(46)** *(BCMorgan)* 3-7-13 JLowe (9) (w ldrs tl wknd qckly wl over 1f out) ............................ 2½.**9**

**100/30** Coolaba Prince (IRE), **5/1** VERRO (USA), **6/1** Chateau Nord, **7/1** Don't Run Me Over, Best Effort, **8/1** Fangio, Crail Harbour, **9/1** Sobering Thoughts, **20/1** Tumbling (USA). CSF £39.99, CT £662.62. Tote £5.90: £2.00 £2.00 £5.70 (£13.50). Mr P. D. Purdy (WANTAGE) bred by Juddmonte Farms in USA. 9 Rn
66.9 sec (8.6)
SF—36/41/27/38/14/22

**662**    PLUMB CENTER & IDEAL STANDARD H'CAP (3-Y.O) (0-70) £2709.00 (£749.00 (£357.00)
**1m 65y**                                                    3-50 (3-51)

482² Red Kite **(62)** (Fav) *(MBell)* 9-0 GDuffield (3) (in tch: rdn along ent st: styd on u.p to ld cl home) ............................ —**1**
466 Princess Maxine (IRE) **(47)** *(MissLAPerratt)* 7-13 DaleGibson (5) (led: drvn along 2f out: hdd nr fin: kpt on) ............................ nk.**2**
374⁴ The Dandy Don (IRE) **(59)** *(DenysSmith)* 8-11 KFallon (8) (cl up: outpcd wl over 2f out: hdwy & ev ch ins fnl f: nt qckn nr fin) ............................ 1½.**3**
216⁶ Qualitair Idol **(50)** (v) *(JFBottomley)* 8-2 JLowe (1) (hld up & bhd: hdwy u.p to chase ldrs 2f out: wknd ins fnl f) ............................ 2½.**4**
350⁴ Eriny (USA) **(69)** *(SGNorton)* 9-0 ‡7OPears (4) (prom: chal on bit over 2f out: sn rdn & wknd) ............................ 1.**5**
395 Dublin Indemnity (USA) **(54)** *(NACallaghan)* 7-13 ‡7JTate (2) (bhd & pushed along ½-wy: nvr trbld ldrs) ............................ 2½.**6**
420 Fair Flyer (IRE) **(61)** (v) *(PMonteith)* 8-10 ‡3JFanning (7) (w ldrs: rdn 4f out: sn wknd) ............................ 5.**7**
456 Sie Amato (IRE) **(52)** *(CaptJWilson)* 8-4 JCarroll (6) (prom tl rdn & wknd wl over 3f out) ............................ 3½.**8**

**5/4** RED KITE, **6/1** The Dandy Don (IRE), Princess Maxine (IRE)(8/1—5/1), Eriny (USA)(op 3/1), **9/1** Qualitair Idol(14/1—16/1), Dublin Indemnity (USA), **14/1** Fair Flyer (IRE), **33/1** Sie Amato (IRE). CSF £9.11, CT £30.60. Tote £1.70: £1.00 £2.50 £2.50 (£16.60). Mr Robert Baker (NEWMARKET) bred by Bobby Donworth and Honora Corridan. 8 Rn
1m 58.7 (15.4)

**663**    PLUMB CENTER & MARLEY EXTRUSIONS CLAIMING STKS (Mdn 3 & 4-Y.O) £2427.00
(£672.00: £321.00)    **1m 3f 16y**                              4-20 (4-21)

565² **Joli's Great (50)** (Fav) *(MJRyan)* 4-8-9 ‡3DBiggs (6) (chsd ldrs: hdwy to ld over 1f out: sn drew clr: comf) ............................ —**1**
536⁴ Docket (USA) *(BHanbury)* 4-9-0 ‡7VBray (9) (hld up & bhd: stdy hdwy on outside 2f out: styd on: nvr able to chal) ............................ 7.**2**
405 J P Morgan **(54)** (v) *(MPNaughton)* 4-9-5 GHind (5) (led tl hdd over 3f out: one pce fnl 2f) ............................ 3.**3**
327² Grey Record **(51)** *(MrsGRReveley)* 4-8-12 ‡7DarrenMoffatt (3) (prom: rdn ent st: one pce fnl 4f) ............................ 3.**4**
524 Ripsnorter (IRE) **(70)** *(SirMarkPrescott)* 3-8-8 GDuffield (10) (chsd ldr: led over 3f out: hdd over 1f out: sn wknd) ............................ 10.**5**
536⁶ Motley *(WGMTurner)* 4-8-11 ‡5TSprake (7) (prom: rdn ent st: sn btn) ............................ nk.**6**
507 Fen Princess (IRE) **(54)** *(PCHaslam)* 4-8-8 ‡3JFanning (8) (mid div & rdn along ent st: n.d) ............................ ½.**7**
497 Queen of Pendona **(37)** *(DMoffatt)* 3-7-5⁽³⁾ ‡5NKennedy (4) (chsd ldrs tl rdn 4f out: sn wknd) ............................ 1½.**8**
97 I'M Special (IRE) **(40)** (v) *(AHarrison)* 4-8-11 KFallon (1) (bhd & drvn along ent st: n.d) ............................ ½.**9**
Aragon Ayr *(PMonteith)* 4-9-5 ‡7ADobbin (2) (a bhd: t.o fnl 3f) ............................ 25.**10**

**13/8** JOLI'S GREAT, **5/2** Ripsnorter (IRE), **7/1** Docket (USA), **10/1** Grey Record, **14/1** Fen Princess (IRE), **16/1** J P Morgan, **25/1** Aragon Ayr, I'M Special (IRE), **33/1** Queen of Pendona, **50/1** Motley. CSF £12.32, Tote £3.00: £1.30 £2.80 £7.00 (£15.30). Enterprise Markets Ltd (NEWMARKET) bred by Mrs M. A. Ryan. 10 Rn
2m 37.2 (18.2)
SF—18/9/8/–/–/–

**664**    PLUMB CENTER & STELRAD H'CAP (0-70) £2574.00 (£714.00: £342.00)
**1½m 17y**                                                    4-50 (4-52)

547∗ Eurotwist **(56)** *(TDBarron)* 3-7-7 (5x) ‡3JFanning (4) (hld up: hdwy ent st: led over 1f out: r.o wl) ............................ —**1**

494★ El Nido (68) (Fav) (MJCamacho) 4–9-13 (5x) NConnorton (7) (trckd ldrs: led on bit over 2f out: shkn up & hdd over 1f out: no ch w wnr) ..... 6.2

501★ Lady Electric (43) (RJHodges) 6–7-11(3) (5x) ‡5TSprake (1) (cl up: ev ch 2f out: sn rdn & nt qckly) ........................................................ 3.3

377 Brusque (USA) (35) (DonEnricoIncisa) 8–7-8(1) KimTinkler (5) (hld up & bhd: hdwy 3f out: no imp fnl 2f) ............................................. 3.4

518³ Easy Over (USA) (52) (bl) (RDEWoodhouse) 6–8-11 SWhitworth (8) (led tl hdd over 2f out: sn wknd) ..................................................... 2¹/₂.5

586⁴ Queens Tour (37) (MBrittain) 7–7-10 LCharnock (3) (chsd ldrs: ev ch over 2f out: wknd qckly) ......................................................... ¹/₂.6

211 Lord Advocate (48) (v) (MPNaughton) 4–8-7 GHind (6) (in tch tl wknd ent st) .... 5.7
Newark Antiquefair (36) (BCMorgan) 4–7-9 JLowe (2) (a bhd) ....................... 1¹/₂.8
Dizzy (USA) (69) (PMonteith) 4–9-7 ‡7ADobbin (9) (prom tl rdn & wknd ent st) ... 4.9

LONG HANDICAP: Brusque (USA) 7-3.

13/8 El Nido, 11/4 Lady Electric, 3/1 EUROTWIST, 10/1 Queens Tour, Dizzy (USA), 16/1 Easy Over (USA), 25/1 Lord Advocate, 50/1 Ors. CSF £8.38, CT £13.25. Tote £3.90: £1.60 £1.40 £1.40 (£5.20). Mr W. G. Swiers (THIRSK) bred by Waresley Park Stud Ltd. 9 Rn
2m 48.3 (16.3)
SF—30/52/16/7/19/3

T/Plpt: £70.00 (37.75 Tckts).
GB

## 396—THIRSK (L-H)
### Saturday, May 2nd [Good]
Going Allowance: St: 0.40 sec; Rnd: 0.30 sec per fur (G)          Wind: fresh half against

Stalls: high

**665**     MARKET PLACE MEDIAN AUCTION STKS (Mdn 2-Y.O) £2382.80 (£660.80: £316.40)
5f                                                            2-15 (2-18)

Nitouche (PatMitchell) 7-13 ‡3SO'Gorman (5) (lengthy: bit bkwd: hdwy 2f out: styd on to ld jst ins fnl f: r.o strly) ............................... —1

571⁴ Arkendale Diamond (USA) (WJPearce) 8-7 DNicholls (14) (a.p: rdn ¹/₂-wy: ev ch 1f out: unable qckn) ................................................... 2¹/₂.2

571⁶ Legendary Hero (TDBarron) 8-7 KDarley (2) (lw: led: rdn wl over 1f out: hung lft & hdd jst ins fnl f) ........................................................ 2¹/₂.3

Tanagome (USA) (SGNorton) 8-3 ‡7OPears (7) (w'like: lengthy: bit bkwd: hdwy on outside ¹/₂-wy: kpt on u.p fnl f) .................................... 1.4

Girl Next Door (NAGraham) 8-2 JQuinn (3) (small: neat: chsd ldrs: effrt & bmpd over 1f out: no ex fnl f) ....................................................... ³/₄.5

A Bridge Too Far (IRE) (WJPearce) 8-2 LCharnock (6) (small: leggy: s.s: rn green: hdwy 2f out: hmpd appr fnl f: fin strly) ..................... hd.6

571⁵ Dead Calm (CTinkler) 8-7 PBurke (10) (hdwy ¹/₂-wy: nvr trbld ldrs) .............. ³/₄.7

365³ Puenta Aguila (Fav) (MHEasterby) 8-2 ‡5SMaloney (9) (prom tl rdn & outpcd fnl 2f) ............................................................................... 3.8

Indian Secret (IRE) (PCalver) 8-7 DMcKeown (8) (small: lengthy: prom tl rdn & grad wknd wl over 1f out) ........................................... 1¹/₂.9

Say Sunpak (MrsVAAconley) 8-5 JFortune (12) (small: lengthy: unf: chsd ldrs: rdn over 2f out: bdly hmpd over 1f out: nt rcvr) ............. nk.10

287 Common Gain (IRE) (JBerry) 8-10 GCarter (1) (lw: chsd ldrs tl wknd u.p over 1f out) ................................................................................ hd.11

Greystyle (MBrittain) 8-7 GDuffield (4) (lengthy: unf: s.i.s: a bhd) ............ s.h.12

Shy Romance (PMMcEntee) 7-13 ‡3JFanning (13) (unf: bkwd: chsd ldrs: hung bdly lft wl over 1f out: sn lost pl) .......................................... 3.13

Apollo's Sister (MrsJJordan) 8-5 NAdams (11) (lt-f: unf: s.i.s: a bhd) ......... 6.14

3/1 Puenta Aguila, 7/2 Legendary Hero(op 8/1), 9/2 Arkendale Diamond (USA), 5/1 Girl Next Door, 7/1 Common Gain (IRE), 8/1 Tanagome (USA), 12/1 Dead Calm(op 7/1), 16/1 Greystyle, Indian Secret (IRE), A Bridge Too Far (IRE), 20/1 NITOUCHE, 25/1 Apollo's Sister, 33/1 Ors. CSF £118.44, Tote £37.10: £9.30 £1.70 £2.40 (£61.20). Miss L. J. Ward (NEWMARKET) bred by Old Mill Stud. 14 Rn
62.6 sec (4.9)
SF—27/24/14/6/2/1

**666**     MAY CLAIMING STKS (3-Y.O) £2284.80 (£632.80: £302.40)   1¹/₂m
2-45 (2-47)

519★ **Lady St Lawrence (USA) (57)** (bl) (SirMarkPrescott) 8-5 GDuffield (5) (led: hdd 2f out: sn led again: r.o gamely u.p) ....................................... —1

567★ Ready to Draw (IRE) (70) (Fav) (RonaldThompson) 8-6 ‡7MichaelDenaro (2) (lw: chsd ldrs: hdwy 3f out: led 2f out: sn rdn & hdd: one pce fnl f) ..... ³/₄.2

497² Silver Samurai **(67)** *(RHollinshead)* 8-6 ‡⁷EHusband (4) (lw: dwlt: sddle slipped
after 2f: sn cl up: wknd fnl 3f) ............................................................ 25.3
Pass the Key (IRE) **(75)** *(NTinkler)* 9-7 KimTinkler (3) (bit bkwd: hld up & bhd:
effrt 3f out: n.d) .................................................................................. 2¹/₂.4
355 Tender Look (IRE) **(75)** *(ANLee)* 7-9 ‡³JFanning (6) (chsd ldrs tl lost pl over 3f out) . 10.5
Blushing Gold *(MrsJJordan)* 8-12 NAdams (1) (lengthy: bit bkwd: drvn along 7f
out: sn wl bhd) ................................................................................... 5.6

*Stewards Enquiry: Denaro suspended 11-12/5/92 (excessive use of whip).*

**13/8** Ready to Draw (IRE), **2/1** LADY ST LAWRENCE (USA), **3/1** Silver Samurai, **8/1** Pass the Key (IRE), **25/1**
Tender Look (IRE), **33/1** Blushing Gold. CSF £5.58, Tote £2.40: £1.40 £1.60 (£2.80). Hesmonds Stud
(NEWMARKET) bred by Hesmonds Stud Ltd in USA. 6 Rn; Lady St Lawrence clmd H Inskip £6,650
2m 39.4 (9.4)
SF—33/32/–/–/–/–

**667**     THIRSK HUNT CUP (H'cap) (0-110) £10575.00 (£3150.00: £1500.00: £675.00)
1m                                                           3-20 (3-21)

(Weights raised 7 lb)
572³ **Star Connection (64)** *(RMWhitaker)* 4-7-4 ‡³JFanning (2) (a.p: led 2f out: drvn
clr: jst hld on) ..................................................................................... —1
392 Mudaffar (IRE) **(87)** (Fav) *(RWArmstrong)* 4-9-2 BCrossley (3) (lw: hld up in tch:
effrt 3f out: swtchd & styd on wl over 1f out: jst btn) .......... nk.2
165³ Dorset Duke **(87)** *(GWragg)* 5-9-2 GDuffield (4) (lw: bhd: effrt over 3f out:
swtchd ins & styd on wl fnl f) ............................................................. 4.3
392 Pay Homage **(94)** *(IABalding)* 4-9-6 ‡³SO'Gorman (8) (led 3f: cl up: rdn over 2f
out: one pce appr fnl f) ...................................................................... 1¹/₂.4
High Premium **(88)** *(MrsJRRamsden)* 4-8-10 ‡⁷JWeaver (5) (hld up: hdwy over
2f out: edgd rt & unable qckn over 1f out) ....................................... s.h.5
492 Jalmusique **(92)** *(MHEasterby)* 6-9-2 ‡⁵SMaloney (1) (cl up: led 5f out tl hdd &
wknd 2f out) ....................................................................................... 2¹/₂.6
592⁵ Northern Printer **(64)** *(MO'Neill)* 7-7-7 JQuinn (6) (chsd ldrs: effrt 3f out: wknd
u.p over 1f out) .................................................................................. nk.7
Sabotage (FR) **(95)** *(MRStoute)* 6-9-5 ‡⁵RPerham (7) (b.nr hind: chsd ldrs tl
hung rt & lost pl appr st: sn rdn & btn) ............................................. 3.8
LONG HANDICAP: Star Connection 7-6, Northern Printer 7-6.

**4/1** Mudaffar (IRE), **5/1** Jalmusique, Sabotage (FR), **11/2** Pay Homage, High Premium, Dorset Duke, **8/1** STAR
CONNECTION, **25/1** Northern Printer. CSF £36.87, CT £172.96. Tote £10.60: £1.90 £1.80 £1.40 (£18.50). Mr A.
F. S. Bridgwood (WETHERBY) bred by Roldvale Ltd. 8 Rn
1m 40.1 (4.1)
SF—50/75/63/62/51/49

**668**     THORNTON H'CAP (0-70) £2500.40 (£694.40: £333.20)     6f     3-50 (3-52)

515⁵ **Pharaoh's Dancer (59)** *(EAWheeler)* 5-9-3 MWigham (5) (lw: racd far side:
s.i.s: sn chsng ldrs: led wl over 1f out: r.o) .................................... —1
541 Densben **(58)** *(DenysSmith)* 8-9-2 NConnorton (8) (in tch: hdwy wl over 1f out:
rdn to ld stands' side ins fnl f: edgd lft: r.o) .................................... 2¹/₂.2
496 Pretonic **(62)** *(MJohnston)* 4-9-6 DMcKeown (19) (hdwy over 2f out: ev ch over
1f out: unable qckn) ........................................................................... 1.3
541* Penny Hasset **(58)** (Jt-Fav) *(MWEasterby)* 4-9-2 TLucas (4) (lw: swtchd rt after
s: w ldrs: led wl over 1f out tl wknd ins fnl f) ................................... nk.4
496 Miss Brightside **(35)** *(ASmith)* 4-7-7 JQuinn (16) (mde most stands' side tl hdd
wl over 1f out: grad wknd) ................................................................. 2.5
Tongue Tied **(62)** *(JWharton)* 4-9-3 ‡³JFanning (17) (bit bkwd: trckd ldrs: effrt 2f
out: nt clr run & nt pce to chal fnl f) ................................................. 2.6
570* Furiella **(67)** *(PCHaslam)* 4-9-11 KDarley (2) (racd far side: mde most tl wknd wl
over 1f out) ......................................................................................... 1.7
516 Uppance **(35)** *(DWChapman)* 4-7-7 SWood (7) (chsd ldrs: rdn & hung lft over
2f out: wknd) ...................................................................................... 1¹/₂.8
570⁴ Sully's Choice (USA) **(50)** (bl) *(DWChapman)* 11-8-8 GBaxter (18) (lw:
chsd ldrs: rdn ¹/₂-wy: grad wknd) ...................................................... nk.9
541 Orient Air **(57)** (bl) *(TDBarron)* 4-9-1 AlexGreaves (9) (prom: rdn along ¹/₂-wy:
wknd wl over 1f out) .......................................................................... ³/₄.10
535⁴ B Grade **(43)** *(JBalding)* 7-7-8 ‡⁷ClaireBalding (11) (lw: n.d) ........................ 3.11
535 Par de Luxe **(36)** *(BWMurray)* 5-7-8⁽¹⁾ AMackay (14) (hrd rdn over 2f out: nt rch
ldrs) ..................................................................................................... ³/₄.12
Long Lane Lady **(50)** *(JMackie)* 6-8-8 DNicholls (10) (nvr trbld ldrs) ................ ³/₄.13
Hemsworth Lad (IRE) **(65)** *(PCalver)* 3-8-12 GDuffield (15) (bit bkwd: a bhd) 3¹/₂.14
535 Lady's Mantle (USA) **(46)** *(RBastiman)* 8-8-4 LCharnock (3) (swtg: racd far
side: w ldr over 3f) ............................................................................. 1¹/₂.15

567 Sunrays (IRE) **(51)** *(CWCElsey)* 3–7-7(5) ‡5SMaloney (12) (a bhd) .................. 6.16
Never Late **(61)** *(MHEasterby)* 3–8-5 ‡3DBiggs (6) (gd spd to ¹/₂-wy) .............. 3.17
295 Parisienne King (USA) **(53)** (bl) *(FHLee)* 3–8-0 GCarter (1) (racd far side: wl bhd
fnl 2f) ...................................................................................................... 4.18

LONG HANDICAP: Miss Brightside 7-3, Uppance 7-2, Par de Luxe 7-6, Sunrays (IRE) 7-1.

**11/2** Sully's Choice (USA), Penny Hasset, **6/1** Furiella, **8/1** PHARAOH'S DANCER, **9/1** Tongue Tied, **10/1**
Pretonic, **12/1** Never Late, Densben, B Grade, **16/1** Orient Air, Lady's Mantle (USA), Uppance, **20/1** Miss Brightside, Par de
Luxe, Long Lane Lady, **25/1** Hemsworth Lad (IRE), **33/1** Parisienne King (USA), **50/1** Sunrays (IRE).
CSF £99.43, CT £911.71. Tote £8.00: £1.90 £3.00 £2.00 £1.50 (£281.70). Mr James Devaney (LAMBOURN)
bred by Heinz Pollmeier. 18 Rn
1m 15.6 (5.4)
SF—43/32/32/27/–/13

**669**     MILLGATE STKS (Mdn 3-Y.O) £2167.20 (£599.20: £285.60)     **5f**     4-25 (4-27)

5352 **Absolutely Nuts (73)** (Fav) *(BAMcMahon)* 8-9 GDuffield (11) (mde all: easily) .. —1
4526 Auction King (IRE) **(62)** *(ASmith)* 9-0 JQuinn (6) (lw: a cl up: rdn 2f out: rdr
dropped whip appr fnl f: no ch w wnr) ................................... 2¹/₂.2
3242 Music Dancer *(JBerry)* 9-0 GCarter (8) (unruly stalls: chsd ldrs: rdn & styd on
same pce over 1f out) ...................................................... ¹/₂.3
420 Manuleader **(63)** (bl) *(WJPearce)* 9-0 DNicholls (4) (prom: hrd drvn wl over 1f
out: no ex fnl f) ..................................................................... 2.4
Boy Martin *(MJohnston)* 9-0 DMcKeown (3) (w'like: str: bit bkwd: rn green on
outside: hdwy ¹/₂-wy: nt pce to chal) ................................ 1¹/₂.5
506 Cromer's Express **(60)** (v) *(MissLCSiddall)* 9-0 BCrossley (5) (chsd ldrs: hrd
rdn 2f out: wknd fnl f) ............................................................ nk.6
353 Our John **(48)** (v) *(RonaldThompson)* 9-0 RPElliott (2) (prom tl wknd wl over 1f
out) ........................................................................................ 1 7
Chocolate Mint *(CWThornton)* 8-9 KDarley (9) (lengthy: unf: scope: bit bkwd:
s.s: bhd tl sme late hdwy) ................................................. hd.8
Throw Away Line *(JEtherington)* 8-9 NConnorton (1) (chsd ldrs over 3f) ....... 2¹/₂.9
Slumber Thyme (IRE) *(JGFitzGerald)* 8-2 ‡7MHunt (7) (a outpcd) ................ hd.10
372 Shadaylou (IRE) **(54)** (bl) *(MrsJJordan)* 8-8 NAdams (10) (hrd rdn & outpcd fr
¹/₂-wy) ................................................................................... 8.11

**4/7** ABSOLUTELY NUTS, **4/1** Music Dancer, **12/1** Manuleader, Cromer's Express(op 8/1), **16/1** Boy Martin(op
10/1), Auction King (IRE), **20/1** Throw Away Line, **33/1** Shadaylou (IRE), Slumber Thyme (IRE), Chocolate Mint,
**50/1** Our John. CSF £12.37, Tote £1.80: £1.20 £3.80 £1.20 (£12.00). Mr J. W. Hall (TAMWORTH) bred by M. P.
Allen. 11 Rn
62.5 sec (4.8)
SF—39/34/32/24/18/17

**670**     COXWOLD H'CAP (0-90) £3752.50 (£1120.00: £535.00: £242.50)     **7f**     4-55 (4-57)

293 **Brown Fairy (USA) (65)** *(MrsNMacauley)* 4–8-1 ‡3DBiggs (10) (bhd: hdwy on
outside over 2f out: styd on strly to ld last strides) ........................... —1
269 Wild Prospect **(66)** *(CTinkler)* 4–8-5 KDarley (8) (lw: cl up: led over 2f out tl nr
fin) ........................................................................................ nk.2
4853 Misunderstanding (IRE) **(88)** *(MrsJRRamsden)* 3–8-8 ‡7JWeaver (1) (lw: led tl
hdd over 2f out: rallied over 1f out) ................................... ¹/₂.3
5344 Euroblake **(59)** (Fav) *(TDBarron)* 5–7-7 ‡5SMaloney (6) (swtg: bhd: gd hdwy to
chal 2f out: sltly hmpd wl over 1f out: edgd lft & no ex) ...... ¹/₂.4
482 Try Leguard (IRE) **(81)** *(WCarter)* 3–8-8 GCarter (3) (chsd ldrs: effrt 3f out: nt
qckn appr fnl f) ...................................................................... 2.5
1092 Bold Habit **(89)** *(WJPearce)* 7–10-0 DNicholls (4) (hld up: hdwy on bit over 2f
out: nt clr run appr fnl f: nvr plcd to chal) ........................... s.h.6
5706 Languedoc **(72)** *(MPNaughton)* 5–8-11 LCharnock (2) (lw: chsd ldrs: nt clr run
over 2f out: swtchd wl over 1f out: sn rdn & btn) ................. nk.7
449 The Can Can Man **(72)** *(MJohnston)* 5–8-11 DMcKeown (7) (hdwy & rn sltly wd
ent st: sn rdn & nvr able to chal) ........................................ s.h.8
397* Lombard Ships **(59)** *(MO'Neill)* 5–7-12 JQuinn (5) (chsd ldrs: rdn 3f out: wkng
whn hmpd over 1f out: eased) ........................................... 10.9
570 Master Pokey **(69)** *(MWEasterby)* 8–8-8 TLucas (9) (b: hld up & a bhd) .......... 2.10

**11/4** Euroblake, **3/1** Try Leguard (IRE), **5/1** Misunderstanding (IRE), **15/2** Lombard Ships, **8/1** The Can Can Man,
Languedoc, **9/1** Bold Habit, **12/1** Wild Prospect(op 8/1), BROWN FAIRY (USA), **25/1** Master Pokey. CSF
£139.83, CT £755.58. Tote £14.60: £4.10 £2.70 £2.00 (£57.20). Mrs Carole Biggs (MELTON MOWBRAY) bred
by Peter McBean in USA. 10 Rn
1m 28.4 (5.1)
SF—42/45/46/29/38/57

T/Plpt: £50.10 (60.8 Tckts).
O'R

463—**HAYDOCK (L-H)**

## Saturday, May 2nd [Good to soft, Soft patches]

Going Allowance: 0.60 sec per fur (Y)                                    Wind: nil

Stalls: high 6th, remainder low

**671**     DOULTON ALLIED INSULATORS H'CAP (3-Y.O) (0-100) £3947.50 (£1180.00: £565.00:
            £257.50)   1¼m 120y   (Weights raised 2 lb)                        1-00 (1-02)

451² **Courtline Jester (76)** *(MAJarvis)* 8-9 MHills (5) (5th st: led 2f out: r.o wl) .......... —1
486★ Fetish (80) (Fav) *(HRACecil)* 8-13 WRyan (9) (hdwy over 2f out: ev ch over 1f
            out: r.o) ....................................................................... ¾.2
502⁴ Encore Une Fois (IRE) *(PWChapple-Hyam)* 8-5 ‡³FNorton (10) (hdwy over 2f
            out: r.o wl ins fnl f) ......................................................... 2.3
545★ Trafalgar Boy (USA) (80) *(JEtherington)* 8-13 CRutter (7) (hdwy over 2f out: rdn
            over 1f out: r.o one pce) .................................................... 1½.4
488⁴ Philgun (65) *(CWCElsey)* 7-7 ‡⁵NKennedy (8) (4th st: hrd rdn 2f out: one pce) 1½.5
      Mahool (USA) (85) *(AAScott)* 9-4 WRSwinburn (4) (lw: led to 2f out: wknd fnl f)  6.6
      Sword Master (88) *(BobJones)* 9-7 VSmith (3) (2nd st: wknd 2f out) ................ 2.7
493³ Houlston's Will (65) *(MrsJRRamsden)* 7-12 JLowe (6) (a bhd) ................. nk.8
464⁴ Devon Dancer (78) *(MHEasterby)* 8-11 MBirch (2) (3rd st: wknd over 2f out) .. 1½.9
412★ Kitaab (USA) (80) *(ACStewart)* 8-13 RHills (1) (lw: 6th st: wknd over 2f out) ........ 10

**11/4** Fetish, **100/30** COURTLINE JESTER, **13/2** Kitaab (USA), **8/1** Mahool (USA), **9/1** Houlston's Will, Trafalgar
Boy (USA), **11/1** Encore Une Fois (IRE), **14/1** Philgun, **20/1** Devon Dancer, **33/1** Sword Master. CSF £12.25, CT
£80.89. Tote £4.90: £1.70 £1.50 £2.70 (£6.30). Mr Jerry Sung (NEWMARKET) bred by Jerry Sung. 10 Rn
                                                                          2m 21.81 (10.11)
                                                                          SF—57/59/47/52/29/42

**672**     SIR RICHARD FAIREY MEMORIAL STKS (3-Y.O.F) £3427.50 (£1020.00: £485.00: £217.50)
            7f 30y                                                             1-30 (1-30)

406★ **Ships Lantern (85)** *(CFWall)* 8-13 WRSwinburn (3) (lw: mde all: r.o wl) ............ —1
356² Flourishing (IRE) (94) *(GWragg)* 8-11 ‡³FNorton (4) (3rd st: squeezed thro 2f
            out: hrd rdn: no imp) .......................................................... 4.2
393★ Lost Reputation (IRE) (Fav) *(BWHills)* 9-2 RHills (2) (2nd st: lost pl over 2f out:
            no ch after) ................................................................... 2.3
429   Cambrian Hills (IRE) (107) *(PWChapple-Hyam)* 9-7 MHills (1) (4th st: ev ch 2f
            out: sn wknd) ................................................................. ½.4

**11/8** Lost Reputation (IRE), **5/2** Cambrian Hills (IRE)(6/4—11/4), **4/1** SHIPS LANTERN(6/1—7/2), **9/2**
Flourishing (IRE). CSF £17.09, Tote £4.70 (£10.90). Mr S. S. De Chair (NEWMARKET) bred by Somerset and
Lady Juliet de Chair. 4 Rn                                                  1m 35.92 (8.62)
                                                                          SF—33/19/18/21

**673**     FAIREY GROUP SPRING TROPHY (Stks) (listed race) £10867.50 (£3240.00: £1545.00:
            £697.50)   7f 30y                                                  2-00 (2-01)

      **Night Manoeuvres (98)** *(HCandy)* 3-8-5 CRutter (4) (5th st: hdwy 2f out: led 1f
            out: r.o wl) ................................................................... —1
563   Night Jar (95) *(LordHuntingdon)* 5-8-12 WRyan (3) (7th st: hdwy 2f out: ev ch
            fnl f: r.o) .................................................................... 1.2
      Ajaad (USA) (110) *(MRStoute)* 4-9-3 WRSwinburn (7) (4th st: rdn over 1f out: nt
            qckn) ......................................................................... 2.3
241⁶ Montendre (110) *(MMcCormack)* 5-9-7 WNewnes (6) (6th st: hdwy 2f out: hrd
            rdn: nt qckn fnl f) ........................................................... nk.4
563★ Shalford (IRE) (117) (Fav) *(RHannon)* 4-9-10 BRouse (5) (lw: plld hrd: led after
            2f to 1f out: eased whn btn) ................................................. 3.5
563² Norton Challenger (106) *(MHEasterby)* 5-9-7 MBirch (2) (2nd st: hrd rdn over
            2f out: sn wknd) ............................................................. 6.6
437   Master of Passion (105) (bl) *(JMPEustace)* 3-8-5 RHills (1) (led 2f: 3rd st: wknd
            over 2f out) .................................................................. 7

**11/10** Shalford (IRE), **7/2** Ajaad (USA), **8/1** Norton Challenger, Montendre, **12/1** Night Jar(op 8/1), Master of
Passion(op 8/1), **14/1** NIGHT MANOEUVRES. CSF £131.81, Tote £13.50: £3.40 £4.70 (£41.90). Mr P. G.
Goulandris (WANTAGE) bred by Shutford Stud. 7 Rn                            1m 33.60 (6.30)
                                                                          SF—58/62/61/64/58/37

**674**     DARWEN STKS (Mdn 3-Y.O.F) £2856.00 (£791.00: £378.00)   1m 30y   2-35 (2-36)

434⁶ **Born to Dance** (Fav) *(MRStoute)* 8-11 DHolland (6) (lw: hld up: 4th st: led ins fnl
            f: easily) .................................................................... —1

560[4] Milanese *(DMorley)* 8-11 GHind (1) (plld hrd: 3rd st: led over 2f out tl ins fnl f: no
       ch w wnr) .................................................................................. 1.2
       Irish Honey (IRE) *(BHanbury)* 8-11 WRyan (2) (bit bkwd: 6th st: styd on fnl 2f) 12.3
       Speedy Beauty *(BHanbury)* 8-4 ‡7VBray (3) (w'like: bit bkwd: led after 2f tl over
       2f out: sn btn) .......................................................................... nk.4
  502 Gerish (IRE) *(JPearce)* 8-6 ‡5RPrice (4) (b.hind: 5th st: outpcd over 2f out) ........ 3.5
  502 Virginia Cottage *(BAMcMahon)* 8-11 JLowe (5) (led 2f: 2nd st: rdn & wknd 3f
       out) ....................................................................................... 4.6

**4/5** BORN TO DANCE, **11/4** Milanese, **8/1** Speedy Beauty, **11/1** Irish Honey (IRE), **20/1** Ors. CSF £3.29, Tote
£1.60: £1.20 £1.70 (£2.10). Cheveley Park Stud (NEWMARKET) bred by Cheveley Park Stud Ltd. 6 Rn
                                                                           1m 49.72 (9.32)
                                                                           SF—29/26/–/–/–/–

## 675

BOTANY BAY H'CAP (0-70) (Amateurs) £3052.00 (£847.00: £406.00)
**2m 45y**                                                              3-05 (3-10)

       **Aswamedh (57)** *(PJHobbs)* 4–10-7 MrsSHobbs (11) (a.p: 2nd st: led ins fnl f: r.o) —1
467[5] Just My Bill **(68)** *(CWCElsey)* 6–11-7 MrSSwiers (13) (hdwy 3f out: ev ch ins fnl
       f: nt qckn) ............................................................................... 1.2
       Bay Tern (USA) **(42)** *(MHEasterby)* 6-9-9 MissAHarwood (6) (led tl hdd ins fnl f:
       unable qckn) ............................................................................. hd.3
       Torwada **(53)** (Fav) *(BJCurley)* 9-10-6 MrsLyons (1) (chsd ldrs: 4th st: one pce
       over 1f out) ............................................................................. 2.4
507[6] Cardinal Bird (USA) **(49)** *(SMellor)* 5–10-2 MrsEMellor (15) (mid div tl styd on
       over 2f out) ............................................................................ 15.5
501[4] Carlingford (USA) **(53)** *(MPNaughton)* 6–10-2 ‡4MrRGreen (5) (5th st: one pce
       fnl 2f) .................................................................................... nk.6
  84[4] Balaat (USA) **(59)** *(MCChapman)* 4–10-5 ‡4MrMChapman (10) (wl bhd fr 1/2-wy) 11/2.7
  505 Stradbroke **(34)** *(MBJames)* 5–9-1 MissLWallace (14) (nvr nr to chal) ............. 2.8
501[5] Nikitas **(53)** *(MissAJWhitfield)* 7–10-2 ‡4MissJRussell (4) (b.nr fore: chsd ldr 12f:
       3rd st: wknd 3f out) ................................................................... 5.9
  507 Lady Westgate **(36)** *(GBBalding)* 8–8-13(3) ‡4MissCBalding (12) (nvr nr ldrs) .... 2.10
211[4] North-West One (IRE) **(36)** *(HJCollingridge)* 4–9-0 MrPClose (2) (bhd fnl 7f) .... 1.11
291[5] Polyplate **(42)** *(MJRyan)* 4–9-6 MrsTPearce (8) (a bhd) ......................... nk.12
       King William **(34)** *(JLSpearing)* 7-9-1 MissTSpearing (16) (effrt 1/2-wy: sn btn) hd.13
501[3] Lookingforarainbow (IRE) **(56)** *(BobJones)* 4–10-6 MissDianaJones (3) (lw:
       6th st: wknd qckly 3f out) ............................................................ 2.14
  501 Merton Mill **(60)** *(DMorley)* 5–10-9 ‡4MissLPeate (9) (a bhd: t.o) ................. 15
       LONG HANDICAP: Lady Westgate 8-9, North-West One (IRE) 8-13.

**2/1** Torwada(op 7/1), **5/1** Bay Tern (USA), **6/1** Lookingforarainbow (IRE), **7/1** Nikitas, **8/1** ASWAMEDH(6/1—
10/1), **11/1** Just My Bill, **12/1** Carlingford (USA), Polyplate(8/1—14/1), **14/1** Cardinal Bird (USA), **16/1** King
William, Balaat (USA), Merton Mill, **20/1** Lady Westgate, **25/1** North-West One (IRE), **33/1** Stradbroke. CSF
£111.93, CT £526.39. Tote £20.50: £5.10 £3.80 £2.30 (£87.50). Mr O. Zawawi (MINEHEAD) bred by Dr O.
Zawawi. 15 Rn                                                            3m 48.18 (20.98)

## 676

PENNY LANE H'CAP (0-90) £3002.00 (£896.00: £428.00: £194.00)    **5f**    3-35 (3-36)
                          (Weights raised 1 lb)
516[4] **Drum Sergeant (54)** (v) *(JParkes)* 5–7-7 NCarlisle (8) (lw: hdwy over 2f out: led
       ins fnl f: r.o) ............................................................................ —1
480[5] Gondo **(69)** (v) (Jt-Fav) *(EJAlston)* 5–8-8 KFallon (7) (led tl hdd ins fnl f: unable
       qckn) ................................................................................... 11/2.2
       Pallium (IRE) **(77)** *(MPNaughton)* 4–9-2 GHind (1) (bhd: hdwy over 2f out: r.o
       one pce fnl f) .......................................................................... nk.3
221[2] Gorinsky (IRE) **(76)** (bl) *(JBerry)* 4–9-1 RHills (4) (r.o u.p fnl 2f: nvr nrr) ....... nk.4
483★ No Quarter Given **(75)** *(PSFelgate)* 7–9-0 JLowe (3) (lw: chsd ldrs tl rdn
       & wknd over 1f out) .................................................................. 3.5
  570 Simmie's Special **(72)** *(RHollinshead)* 4–8-11 WRyan (5) (w ldr 2f: rdn & wknd
       over 1f out) ........................................................................... 21/2.6
527[3] Love Returned **(85)** *(WJarvis)* 5–9-10 MTebbutt (2) (prom tl wknd over 1f out:
       eased whn btn) ....................................................................... 2.7
483[2] Consulate **(66)** *(JBalding)* 6–8-5 MBirch (6) (bhd: rdn & wknd 1/2-wy) ........... hd.8
       LONG HANDICAP: Drum Sergeant 7-6.

**4/1** Gondo, No Quarter Given, **9/2** Love Returned, **5/1** Consulate, **15/2** DRUM SERGEANT, Gorinsky (IRE), **12/1**
Simmie's Special, **14/1** Pallium (IRE). CSF £34.13, CT £368.53. Tote £7.20: £1.70 £1.60 £5.80 (£10.40). Mr W.
A. Sellers (MALTON) bred by Snarehill Stud Co. 8 Rn                        64.22 sec (5.22)
                                                                           SF—35/44/51/49/36/23

T/Plpt: £958.40 (4.85 Tckts).                                              Hn/J

## 463—HAYDOCK (L-H)

**Monday, May 4th [Good, Good to soft patches]**
Going Allowance: 0.15 sec per fur (G)                    Wind: almost nil

Stalls: high

**677**       E.B.F. MORNINGTON CANNON STKS (Mdn 2-Y.O.F) £2684.50 (£742.00: £353.50)
              **5f**                                              12-50 (12-53)

    **Star Family Friend (IRE)** *(MHTompkins)* 8-11 PRobinson (9) (unf: dwlt: hdwy
        2f out: hrd rdn to ld ins fnl f: veered rt: r.o) ......................... —1
    Cynic *(Fav)* *(JWWatts)* 8-11 SCauthen (2) (scope: a.p: ev ch 1f out: edgd lft:
        unable qckn fnl f) .......................................................... 2.2
5645 Victoria Hall *(WGMTurner)* 8-8 ‡3DBiggs (3) (led over 1f: rdn & hmpd ins fnl f: nt
        rcvr) ............................................................................ hd.3
  574 Manor Adventure *(BAMcMahon)* 8-11 JLowe (4) (bit bkwd: led over 3f out tl
        wknd ins fnl f) .............................................................. 1½.4
2636 Glow of Hope *(EJAlston)* 8-11 KFallon (1) (spd over 3f) ..................... 7.5
    Last Typhoon *(EHOwenjun)* 8-11 CDwyer (8) (leggy: lt-f: outpcd) ............ 1.6
    Spring Flyer (IRE) *(MO'Neill)* 8-11 WRSwinburn (6) (leggy: outpcd) ......... 3½.7
2925 Fanfan (IRE) *(MHEasterby)* 8-11 TLucas (5) (outpcd) ......................... ½.8
    Miss Otter (IRE) *(GAPritchard-Gordon)* 8-11 WHood (7) (lt-f: dwlt: outpcd) ...... nk.9

**7/4** Cynic, **5/1** Manor Adventure(6/1—4/1), **13/2** Spring Flyer (IRE), STAR FAMILY FRIEND (IRE), **8/1** Victoria
Hall, Fanfan (IRE)(6/1—9/1), **14/1** Glow of Hope, Miss Otter (IRE)(10/1—16/1), **16/1** Last Typhoon. CSF
£18.25, Tote £8.40: £1.50 £1.50 £1.60 (£6.60). Sheffield Newspapers Limited (NEWMARKET) bred by Mrs J.
Corcoran in Ireland. 9 Rn                                          63.06 sec (4.06)
                                                                   SF—31/23/19/16/–/–

**678**       TADHG MEEHAN H'CAP (3-Y.O) (0-90) £3622.50 (£1080.00: £515.00: £232.50)
              **6f**                                              1-25 (1-26)

                (Weights raised 7 lb)
  576 **Sonderise (69)** *(NTinkler)* 8-13 WNewnes (7) (s.i.s: gd hdwy over 1f out: r.o to
        ld cl home) .................................................................. —1
    Petite-D-Argent *(77)* *(MissLAPerratt)* 9-0 ‡7RHavlin (2) (a.p: led 2f out: rdn & wnt
        lft fnl f: hdd nr fin) ......................................................... ½.2
3325 Battle Colours (IRE) *(74)* *(SirMarkPrescott)* 9-4 JLowe (4) (lw: a.p: ev ch 1f out:
        r.o) ............................................................................. ¾.3
  576 Don't Smile *(75)* *(Fav)* *(MHTompkins)* 9-5 PRobinson (6) (lw: a.p: rdn 1f out:
        unable qckn) ................................................................. 2.4
  363 Nest *(64)* *(LordHuntingdon)* 8-8 DMcKeown (8) (swtg: nvr nr to chal) ........ 1½.5
  576 Abigails Boy (HOL) *(58)* *(DrJDScargill)* 7-13 ‡3JFanning (3) (outpcd) ............ 1½.6
  559 Walstead (IRE) *(75)* *(WJarvis)* 9-5 SCauthen (1) (spd over 3f) ............... 1½.7
4683 Lombard Ocean *(75)* *(MO'Neill)* 9-5 WRSwinburn (5) (led 4f: rdn & wknd over
        1f out) ........................................................................ 1½.8
  472 So Superb *(72)* *(JLDunlop)* 9-2 PaulEddery (9) (outpcd: t.o) ................ 6.9

**13/8** Don't Smile, **9/2** Battle Colours (IRE), **13/2** SONDERISE, **8/1** Walstead (IRE), **9/1** Lombard Ocean, Nest(op
6/1), **11/1** Abigails Boy (HOL)(8/1—12/1), So Superb, **16/1** Petite-D-Argent. CSF £90.25, CT £474.05. Tote
£8.40: £2.10 £3.40 £1.60 (£53.50). Mrs D. Wright (MALTON) bred by Doublet Ltd. 9 Rn    1m 15.25 (3.55)
                                                                   SF—46/45/46/39/22/7

**679**       WIGAN STKS (3-Y.O) £3357.00 (£927.00: £441.00)    1¼m 120y    2-30 (2-30)

4002 **Viardot (IRE) (80)** *(MRStoute)* 9-2 WRSwinburn (1) (hld up: 3rd st: led on bit
        ins fnl f: v.easily) ........................................................... —1
560* Aremef (USA) *(MrsJCecil)* 9-2 PaulEddery (2) (led 6f out tl ins fnl f: no ch w wnr) .. 3.2
487* Kaisar (GER) *(85)* *(HRACecil)* 9-2 SCauthen (3) (b: lw: led over 4f: 2nd st:
        rdn 3f out: sn lost tch) ...................................................... dist.3

**5/4** Kaisar (GER), **15/8** Aremef (USA), **11/4** VIARDOT (IRE). CSF £6.72, Tote £2.90 (£2.80). Sheikh Mohammed
(NEWMARKET) bred by Barronstown Stud in Ireland. 3 Rn               2m 18.34 (6.64)
                                                                   SF—52/46/–

**680**       MANCHESTER STKS (Mdn 3-Y.O) £2385.00 (£660.00: £315.00)
              **1¼m 120y**                                        3-00 (3-02)

5112 **Polish Blue (USA) (88)** *(MRStoute)* 9-0 WRSwinburn (3) (led tl over 2f out: led
        appr fnl f: clr fnl f) ......................................................... —1

490³ Bold Boss *(BHanbury)* 9-0 AShoults (1) (lw: chsd ldrs: 4th st: led 2f out: sn hdd: one pce) .................................................................. 5.2

Queen Caroline (USA) (Fav) *(HRACecil)* 8-9 SCauthen (8) (unf: scope: dwlt: 6th st: effrt & ev ch over 2f out: unable qckn fnl f) ............ 1¹⁄₂.3

Lady Dundee (USA) *(MrsJCecil)* 8-9 PaulEddery (6) (hdwy & 2nd st: kpt on one pce appr fnl f) .................................................... 2.4

433 Rainridge (bl) *(JLDunlop)* 9-0 PRobinson (2) (swtg: w ldrs: 5th st: led over 2f out: sn hdd: rdn & btn appr fnl f) ............................. ³⁄₄.5

562² The Titan Ghost (57) *(BAMcMahon)* 9-0 JLowe (4) (swtg: 3rd st: wknd over 2f out: t.o) ...................................................... 15.6

466 Robert Thomas (IRE) *(MO'Neill)* 9-0 KFallon (5) (a bhd: 7th st: t.o) ................. 10.7

577 Kentucky Chicken (USA) *(MissLCSiddall)* 8-9 DMcKeown (7) (a bhd: 8th st: t.o) 7.8

**5/4** Queen Caroline (USA), **9/4** POLISH BLUE (USA), **6/1** Rainridge, **8/1** Bold Boss, **14/1** The Titan Ghost, **16/1** Lady Dundee (USA), **50/1** Ors. CSF £19.13, Tote £3.50: £1.40 £1.60 £1.10 (£10.40). Mr Mana Al Maktoum (NEWMARKET) bred by John and Mrs C. Mabee in USA. 8 Rn     2m 17.58 (5.88)
SF—57/47/39/35/38/8

**681**     TRAFFORD PARK H'CAP (0-90) £2924.00 (£872.00: £416.00: £188.00)
    1m 3f 200y            3-30 (3-33)

**Quick Ransom (70)** *(MJohnston)* 4-9-3 DMcKeown (7) (chsd ldrs: 5th st: led wl over 1f out: sn clr) ..................................................... —1

442 Sea Goddess (73) *(WJarvis)* 4-9-6 SCauthen (9) (lw: led tl over 2f out: hmpd appr fnl f: kpt on u.p nr fin) ........................................ 3.2

469* Admirals Seat (62) (Fav) *(MrsJRRamsden)* 4-8-2 ‡⁷RHavlin (10) (a.p: 2nd st: led over 2f out: sn hdd: hung lft appr fnl f: one pce) ........ ¹⁄₂.3

467² Lord Hastie (USA) (76) (v) *(SGNorton)* 4-9-2 ‡⁷OPears (3) (lw: chsd ldrs: 6th st: rdn 2f out: nvr able chal) ......................................... ¹⁄₂.4

470 Western Dynasty (70) *(MJRyan)* 6-9-3 PRobinson (8) (prom: 4th st: rdn over 2f out: wknd btn) ...................................................... 5.5

193 Emperor Chang (USA) (48) *(PABlockley)* 5-7-9 JLowe (5) (bit bkwd: nvr nr to chal) ..................................................................... 7.6

Westholme (USA) (79) *(MHEasterby)* 4-9-12 TLucas (4) (bkwd: a in rr) ............ 6.7

442 Farat (USA) (81) *(JLDunlop)* 4-10-0 WRSwinburn (6) (b.nr fore: lw: chsd ldrs: 3rd st: wknd over 2f out) ............................................. s.h.8

High Savannah (70) *(MAJarvis)* 4-8-10 ‡⁷KRutter (1) (bit bkwd: dwlt: a bhd) ... 2¹⁄₂.9

467 Flockton's Own (80) *(MrsJRRamsden)* 6-9-13 KFallon (2) (b: bkwd: in tch 7f: grad wknd) ................................................................... 1¹⁄₂.10

**13/8** Admirals Seat, **11/2** Lord Hastie (USA), **6/1** Western Dynasty, **15/2** Sea Goddess, Farat (USA)(op 5/1), **10/1** High Savannah, **12/1** Flockton's Own, **14/1** QUICK RANSOM, Westholme (USA), **33/1** Emperor Chang (USA). CSF £108.75, CT £242.60. Tote £21.10: £3.70 £1.80 £1.50 (£51.70). Mr J. S. Morrison (MIDDLEHAM) bred by Benham Stud. 10 Rn     2m 36.44 (8.44)
SF—37/34/15/27/18/–

T/Plpt: £158.10 (30.05 Tckts).
**Other race under Rules of National Hunt Racing.**        IM

## 574—PONTEFRACT (L-H) Transferred from Doncaster

### Monday, May 4th [Good to firm, Firm fnl 2f]
Going Allowance: minus 0.20 sec per fur (F)        Wind: almost nil

Stalls: low

**682**     WISETON AUCTION STKS (Mdn 2-Y-O) £2637.00 (£732.00: £351.00)    **5f**   2-20 (2-24)

**My Bonus** *(DJSCosgrove)* 7-6 ‡⁵DHarrison (9) (leggy: scope: bit bkwd: trckd ldrs gng wl: led over 1f out: rdn & r.o ins fnl f) ...................... —1

Juliet Bravo *(WJPearce)* 8-0 LCharnock (7) (lengthy: scope: a in tch: r.o wl u.p fnl f) ........................................................................ ¹⁄₂.2

416³ Royal Folly (IRE) *(CWCElsey)* 7-7(1) ‡⁵SMaloney (6) (led over 3f: kpt on wl) ... ¹⁄₂.3

574 Hi Nod *(MJCamacho)* 8-2 NConnorton (1) (chsd ldrs: outpcd wl over 1f out: kpt on fnl f) .................................................................... 4.4

568⁵ Colfax Starlight *(BSRothwell)* 7-11 RFox (15) (a in tch: styd on fnl f) ............ ³⁄₄.5

Wentbridge Lad (IRE) *(BAMcMahon)* 8-5 JFortune (8) (lengthy: scope: s.s: bhd & drvn along tl r.o wl over 1f out) ..................................... s.h.6

574⁵ Niteowlady *(SGNorton)* 8-0 NCarlisle (10) (lw: a in tch: effrt 2f out: nt qckn) ..... hd.7

543³ Penny Banger (IRE) *(MJohnston)* 7-11 DaleGibson (4) (lw: chsd ldrs: rdn ¹⁄₂-wy: grad wknd) ................................................. 1¹⁄₂.8

Pine Ridge Lad (IRE) *(WJPearce)* 9-0 DNicholls (14) (str: scope: bit bkwd: sn bhd: hdwy over 1f out: nvr nr to chal) ................................ nk.9

476 Scenic Reef (IRE) *(JMPEustace)* 8-0 JQuinn (5) (sn outpcd: nvr trbld ldrs) ..... ½.**10**
    Duplicate *(MHEasterby)* 8-11 MBirch (11) (w'like: scope: bit bkwd: sn outpcd &
        bhd: n.d) ......................................................... 1½.**11**
286 Nellie's Gamble *(APStringer)* 7-11 ‡³FNorton (2) (prom over 3f) ...................... nk.**12**
    Crab 'n Lobster (IRE) *(MrsJRRamsden)* 8-0 ‡³DBiggs (12) (lt-f: unf: s.s: a bhd) 1½.**13**
574² Swiftlet (IRE) *(Fav) (MBell)* 7-9 ‡⁵NKennedy (3) (b.hind: swtg: chsd ldrs: drvn
        along ½-wy: sn wknd) .............................. 2½.**14**
574 Pretzel (IRE) *(NTinkler)* 8-8 KDarley (13) (s.s: a bhd) ..................... 2½.**15**

**9/4** Swiftlet (IRE), **7/1** Penny Banger (IRE)(6/1–9/1), **8/1** Niteowlady, Juliet Bravo(20/1–7/1), Royal Folly
(IRE), **9/1** Hi Nod, **10/1** MY BONUS(op 5/1), **12/1** Wentbridge Lad (IRE), **14/1** Duplicate, **16/1** Scenic Reef (IRE),
**20/1** Crab 'n Lobster (IRE)(op 12/1), Colfax Starlight, **33/1** Ors. CSF £88.10, Tote £8.60: £2.50 £2.90 £2.70
(£41.20). Crazy Horse Bloodstock (NEWMARKET) bred by Edmond and Richard Kent. 15 Rn    63.5 sec (2)
                                                                                SF—18/24/15/8/–/–

**683**        INTAKE H'CAP (0-70) £2616.00 (£726.00: £348.00)    **2m 1f 22y**    2-50 (2-50)

166² Jawani (IRE) (47) (v) *(DrJDScargill)* 4-8-12 JQuinn (7) (a.p: led 5f out & sn
        qcknd clr: styd on u.p fnl 2f) ....................................... —**1**
501² Sillars Stalker (IRE) (46) *(Fav) (MrsJRRamsden)* 4-8-4 ‡⁷JWeaver (10) (lw: in
        tch: outpcd 4f out: hdwy 2f out: r.o wl) .......................... 1½.**2**
518* Malenoir (USA) (59) (v) *(WJPearce)* 4-9-10 DNicholls (12) (a in tch: hdwy 5f
        out: chsd wnr 2f out: rdn & nvr able to chal) ........................... 3.**3**
569 Yorkshire Holly (53) *(MAvison)* 9-9-7 MBirch (1) (hld up: stdy hdwy ½-wy: effrt
        4f out: one pce fnl 2f) ...................................... 2.**4**
    Enkindle (32) *(BWMurray)* 5-8-0 AMackay (11) (hdwy 7f out: rdn & no imp fnl 3f) 1.**5**
    Cost Effective (32) *(MBrittain)* 5-7-9 ‡⁵SMaloney (6) (w ldrs tl outpcd 4f out:
        grad wknd) ..................................... 7.**6**
586⁶ Hand Painted (51) *(CRBeever)* 8-9-2 ‡³FNorton (2) (b: chsd ldrs tl outpcd fnl 4f) 1.**7**
    Welcoming Arms (45) *(PCalver)* 5-8-13 ACulhane (9) (hld up: hdwy 6f out: nvr
        able to chal: eased fnl f) ............................... 1.**8**
578 Dodger Dickins (41) *(RHollinshead)* 5-8-9 KDarley (5) (lw: bhd: effrt 7f out: n.d) 1½.**9**
578 Buckingham Band (USA) (45) (v) *(FHLee)* 4-8-7 ‡³DBiggs (3) (led tl hdd 5f out:
        sn wknd) ...................................... 10
362⁵ Mandalay Prince (38) *(TKersey)* 8-8-6 DaleGibson (14)(b: lw: rdn & lost tch ½-wy) 11
    Qualitair Promise (38) *(GMMoore)* 4-8-3 NConnorton (8) (prom tl wknd 7f out) . 12
291 Elissa (32) *(GPKelly)* 6-7-9 ‡⁵NKennedy (4) (swtg: bhd fr ½-wy) ................ 13
    362 Topcliffe (12/1) Withdrawn (lame at s) : not under orders  — Rule 4 applies

**85/40** Sillars Stalker (IRE), **5/1** JAWANI (IRE), **8/1** Malenoir (USA), Dodger Dickins, **12/1** Yorkshire Holly,
Welcoming Arms, **16/1** Mandalay Prince, **20/1** Hand Painted, Cost Effective, Enkindle, **33/1** Buckingham Band
(USA), **50/1** Qualitair Promise, **66/1** Elissa. CSF £13.56, CT £65.39. Tote £4.30: £1.50 £1.50 £3.40 (£4.90). Mr
G. Hardman (NEWMARKET) bred by Barronstown Bloodstock Ltd in Ireland. 13 Rn    3m 46.3 (6.3)

**684**        SUE LINDSAY CELEBRATION STKS (0-80) £3106.00 (£928.00: £444.00: £202.00)
                **1m 4y**                                                3-20 (3-21)
                (Weights raised 2 lb)
572 **Habeta** (USA) (64) *(JWWatts)* 6-9-5 BRaymond (5) (lw: hld up: effrt 2f out:
        qcknd to ld wl ins fnl f) .................................... —**1**
592³ Veloce (IRE) (55) *(MO'Neill)* 4-8-10 JFortune (14) (a.p: rdn to ld 1f out: hdd &
        no ex nr fin) ...................................... 1½.**2**
572⁵ Young Jason (54) *(FHLee)* 9-8-4 ‡⁵NKennedy (6) (hld up & bhd: nt clr run 3f
        out: r.o fnl 2f: nrst fin) ................................ 1½.**3**
534² Obsidian Grey (63) *(BAMcMahon)* 8-8-13 ‡⁵SMaloney (3) (lw: led tl hdd 1f out:
        kpt on same pce) ................................. ½.**4**
572* Forever Diamonds (59) *(MHEasterby)* 5-9-0 MBirch (10) (lw: hld up & bhd:
        stdy hdwy ½-wy: nvr plcd to chal) ...................... 3½.**5**
438 Shining Jewel (69) *(MrsLPiggott)* 5-9-10 LPiggott (2) (lw: trckd ldrs: effrt on ins
        whn hmpd over 1f out: nt rcvr) .......................... nk.**6**
515 Sugemar (53) *(JARToller)* 6-8-8 DaleGibson (13) (swtg: prom: effrt appr st: nt
        qckn appr fnl f) ..................................... hd.**7**
492² Golden Chip (IRE) (69) *(APStringer)* 4-9-10 JQuinn (1) (hld up & bhd tl sme late
        hdwy) ........................................... 1.**8**
524² Miss Pin Up (56) *(PatMitchell)* 3-7-9⁽⁵⁾ ‡³DBiggs (12) (chsd ldr tl wknd wl over 1f
        out) ............................................ ¾.**9**
364 Sally Fay (IRE) (55) *(TKersey)* 4-8-10 DNicholls (7) (chsd ldrs tl wknd over 1f
        out) ............................................ ½.**10**
482² Zamirah (IRE) (76) *(Fav) (GWragg)* 3-9-1 ‡³FNorton (4) (swtg: lw: mid div: effrt
        whn nt clr run 3f out: n.d) ............................. 1.**11**

Batabanoo **(72)** *(MrsGRReveley)* 3–9-0 KDarley (9) (bit bkwd: hld up & bhd: nvr plcd to chal) ............................................................................................ hd.12

372² Double Feature (IRE) **(66)** *(MrsJRRamsden)* 3–8-3 ‡⁵DHarrison (8) (nvr nr to chal) ............................................................................................................... 3.13

521 Priceless Holly **(47)** *(MAvison)* 4–8-2 PBurke (11) (a bhd) ......................... 14
LONG HANDICAP: Miss Pin Up 7-5.

**9/2** Zamirah (IRE), **6/1** Forever Diamonds, **8/1** Veloce (IRE), Shining Jewel, Double Feature (IRE), **9/1** Sugemar, Obsidian Grey, **10/1** HABETA (USA), Young Jason, **14/1** Batabanoo, Golden Chip (IRE), **20/1** Miss Pin Up, **50/1** Sally Fay (IRE), **66/1** Priceless Holly. CSF £83.04, CT £759.72. Tote £12.00: £2.70 £3.20 £2.50 (£38.80). Mr R. D. Bickenson (RICHMOND) bred by Spendthrift Farm, Inc in USA. 14 Rn
1m 43.8 (2.2)
SF—48/34/23/30/20/29

---

**685**     BAWTRY CLAIMING STKS     £2490.00 (£690.00: £330.00)    **5f**     3-55 (3-57)

661² **Fangio (60)** *(WGMTurner)* 3–8-7 ‡³DBiggs (8) (b.off hind: lw: w ldr: led over 1f out: r.o) ............................................................................................................... —1

582⁴ Super Rocky **(77)** (Fav) *(JBerry)* 3–8-7 JCarroll (2) (led tl hdd over 1f out: sn btn) ..................................................................................................................... 4.2

516² The Noble Oak (IRE) **(56)** (bl) *(MMcCormack)* 4–9-2 WNewnes (3) (sn chsng ldrs: effrt 2f out: nt pce to chal) ...................................................................... 1.3

613⁵ Real Stunner **(73)** *(MPNaughton)* 5–9-0 LPiggott (1) (lw: chsd ldrs: shkn up ent st: sn btn) .................................................................................................... 3.4

Easy Line **(95)** *(PJFeilden)* 9–9-7 BRaymond (6) (b: bit bkwd: sn outpcd & bhd: sme hdwy fnl 2f: nrst fin) ................................................................................ 1½.5

Baladee Pet **(63)** *(MrsVAAconley)* 3–8-4 PBurke (9) (hld up & bhd: hdwy ½-wy: nvr nr to chal) ........................................................................................ hd.6

516 Just Bob **(65)** *(SEKettlewell)* 3–8-8 ‡³JFanning (7) (lw: nvr plcd to chal) ............. ½.7

Masaken *(TKersey)* 4–8-6 DaleGibson (5) (bit bkwd: outpcd fr ½-wy) ............. 8.8

468 Boulabas (IRE) **(59)** (v) *(MO'Neill)* 3–8-7 JFortune (4) (outpcd & bhd fr ½-wy) . ½.9

**6/4** Super Rocky, **3/1** Real Stunner, **4/1** Easy Line(op 5/2), **8/1** The Noble Oak (IRE)(op 12/1), **10/1** FANGIO, **20/1** Just Bob, **25/1** Boulabas (IRE), **33/1** Baladee Pet, **100/1** Masaken. CSF £24.64, Tote £7.30: £1.60 £1.30 £1.50 (£11.60). Mr Simon Swift (SHERBORNE) bred by Melbury Park Stud. 9 Rn; Super Rocky clmd A W A Bates £6,030.00
62.5 sec (1)
SF—53/37/42/28/29/11

---

**686**     COAL MINER H'CAP (0-100) £3525.00 (£1050.00: £500.00: £225.00)    **5f**     4-25 (4-26)

300 **Eager Deva (90)** *(RHollinshead)* 5–9-4 LPiggott (2) (lw: trckd ldrs: led wl ins fnl f: rdn out) ................................................................................................. —1

311⁴ Sigama (USA) **(80)** (Fav) *(FHLee)* 6–8-3 ‡⁵NKennedy (1) (led: qcknd wl over 1f out: hdd wl ins fnl f: no ex) ....................................................................... 1.2

Viceroy **(92)** *(WJPearce)* 5–9-6 DNicholls (5) (hld up: hdwy & ev ch ins fnl f: nt qckn) .......................................................................................................... nk.3

Cumbrian Waltzer **(100)** *(MHEasterby)* 7–10-0 MBirch (3) (swtg: bit bkwd: hld up: hdwy whn nt clr run appr fnl f: nvr plcd to chal) .................................. 1.4

Singing Star **(83)** *(JBalding)* 6–8-11 KDarley (8) (a chsng ldrs: rdn & nt qckn appr fnl f) ................................................................................................. 1½.5

Poets Cove **(83)** *(MMcCormack)* 4–8-11 WNewnes (6) (lw: chsd ldrs: sn pushed along: no imp fnl 2f) .................................................................... hd.6

542* Dokkha Oyston (IRE) **(77)** *(JBerry)* 4–8-5 JCarroll (4) (lw: s.s: hdwy 2f out: n.d) 3.7

550 Lucedeo **(83)** *(JLSpearing)* 8–8-11 BRaymond (7) (effrt ½-wy: nvr nr to chal) .. ¾.8

**3/1** Sigama (USA), **7/2** EAGER DEVA, **11/2** Dokkha Oyston (IRE), **6/1** Lucedeo, **8/1** Viceroy, **11/1** Cumbrian Waltzer, **12/1** Ors. CSF £13.24, CT £66.92. Tote £4.00: £1.50 £1.60 £1.50 (£5.60). Mrs E. G. Faulkner (UPPER LONGDON) bred by Longdon Stud Ltd. 8 Rn
62.5 sec (1)
SF—64/45/61/65/42/41

---

**687**     CARR HILL STKS (Mdn 3-Y.O) £2343.00 (£648.00: £309.00)    **1½m 8y**     4-55 (4-56)

427⁴ Glaisdale (IRE) *(HRACecil)* 9-0 AMcGlone (7) (lw: cl up: led 7f out: hld on wl fnl 2f) ........................................................................................................... —1

384³ Ambiguously Regal (USA) (Fav) *(MrsJCecil)* 9-0 PaulEddery (1) (lw: in tch: bmpd over 3f out: hdwy & ev ch over 1f out: styd on u.p) .. 1½.2

Kiveton Tycoon (IRE) (bl) *(JAGlover)* 9-0 DNicholls (3) (w'like: chsd ldrs: chal 3f out: wknd wl over 1f out) ........................................................................ 5.3

427³ Hidden Light (IRE) *(MAJarvis)* 9-0 BRaymond (4) (lw: effrt & nt clr run over 3f out: no imp fnl 2f) ............................................................................................ 1½.4

376³ Five to Seven (USA) **(63)** *(SGNorton)* 9-0 LPiggott (6) (lw: led tl hdd 7f out: outpcd fnl 4f) .......................................................................... ¾.5

466⁴ High Mind (FR) *(MissLCSiddall)* 9-0 MBirch (2) (chsd ldrs tl wknd 4f out) .......... 4.6

369 Noble Vienna (USA) **(46)** *(RHollinshead)* 9-0 KDarley (5) (lost tch fr ½-wy) ....... 5.7

**7/4** Ambiguously Regal (USA), Hidden Light (IRE), **5/2** GLAISDALE (IRE), **17/2** Five to Seven (USA), **25/1** High Mind (FR), **40/1** Kiveton Tycoon (IRE), **150/1** Noble Vienna (USA). CSF £6.81, Tote £3.90: £2.00 £1.40 (£3.20). Sheikh Mohammed (NEWMARKET) bred by Ron Con Ltd in Ireland. 7 Rn       2m 38.4 (3.9)
SF—37/36/26/23/22/14

**688** MAY DAY HOLIDAY H'CAP (0-90) £2976.00 (£888.00: £424.00: £192.00)
1¼m 6y                                                                5-25 (5-25)

565* **Surrey Dancer (66)** *(Fav)* *(BHanbury)* 4-8-11 BRaymond (3) (lw: trckd ldrs: swtchd over 1f out: r.o wl to ld nr fin) ....................................... —1

479⁶ Knock Knock **(83)** *(IABalding)* 7-9-11 ‡SO'Gorman (8) (lw: trckd ldrs: led & qcknd over 1f out: r.o wl: jst ct) ......................................... hd.2

368⁶ Mardessa **(64)** *(FHLee)* 4-8-9 PaulEddery (4) (swtg: lw: hdwy 2f out: squeezed thro on ins to chal fnl f: r.o) ............................................ 1½.3

533 Vague Dancer **(64)** *(MrsJRRamsden)* 6-8-3 ‡7JWeaver (1) (lw: hld up: effrt appr st: r.o fnl f) ................................................................. 1½.4

453² Pennine Star (IRE) **(65)** *(CWCElsey)* 4-8-5 ‡5SMaloney (7) (led: qcknd 4f out: hdd over 1f out: no ex) ............................................... hd.5

572 Flying Down to Rio (IRE) **(53)** *(MPNaughton)* 4-7-9 ‡3JFanning (6) (hld up: hdwy appr st: ev ch over 1f out: nt qckn ins fnl f) ................ ¾.6

518² Vasiliev **(79)** (bl) *(JPLeigh)* 4-9-10 DNicholls (2) (lw: bhd: hdwy 2f out: sn btn) ..... 7

Bold Ambition **(78)** *(TKersey)* 5-9-4 DaleGibson (5) (bit bkwd: swtg: chsd ldrs tl wknd qckly 2f out: t.o) ............................................... 8

**7/4** SURREY DANCER, **3/1** Mardessa, **11/2** Knock Knock, **10/1** Vague Dancer, **12/1** Pennine Star (IRE), Vasiliev, **14/1** Flying Down to Rio (IRE), **50/1** Bold Ambition. CSF £10.55, CT £21.48. Tote £2.80: £1.40 £1.40 £1.30 (£7.70). Cronk Thoroughbred Racing Ltd (NEWMARKET) bred by Fonthill Stud. 8 Rn       2m 16.6 (8.3)
T/Plpt: £135.40 (26.8 Tckts).                                                    AA

470—**KEMPTON (R-H)**
**Monday, May 4th [Good]**
Going Allowance: St: 0.15 sec per fur; Rnd: 0.40 sec per fur (G)              Wind: almost nil

Stalls: low

**689** SYON PARK STKS (Mdn 3-Y.O.F) £2448.00 (£678.00: £324.00)      **1m (J.C)** 2-10 (2-12)

**Muhit (USA)** *(PTWalwyn)* 8-11 WCarson (6) (led over 6f out to 3f out: led over 1f out: rdn out) ........................................................... —1

490² Hugging **(72)** *(MMcCormack)* 8-11 JReid (7) (swtg: plld hrd: hdwy on ins over 2f out: r.o ins fnl f) ...................................................... ¾.2

Cachou (USA) *(JHMGosden)* 8-11 GHind (5) (cmpt: lw: 6th st: r.o one pce fnl 2f) ....................................................................................... 1½.3

Up All Night *(JWHills)* 8-11 RHills (2) (lw: 3rd st: hrd rdn over 2f out: one pce fnl f) ......................................................................... 2½.4

Cunning *(Fav)* *(LMCumani)* 8-11 LDettori (8) (unf: scope: lw: rdn over 3f out: 4th st: n.m.r over 1f out: one pce) .......................... 1.5

502⁶ Just Hannah *(MrsBarbaraWaring)* 8-11 NHowe (4) (rdn over 3f out: nvr nr to chal) ....................................................................... ½.6

Agnes Flemming (USA) *(PWHarris)* 8-11 TQuinn (3) (leggy: scope: bit bkwd: 5th st: wknd over 2f out) .................................................. 5.7

Ustka *(MRStoute)* 8-11 RCochrane (1) (leggy: led over 1f: 2nd st: led 3f out tl over 1f out: sn wknd) ........................................... nk.8

**11/4** Cunning, **9/2** Just Hannah(tchd 7/1), **6/1** Ustka(op 3/1), MUHIT (USA), **13/2** Cachou (USA)(op 3/1), **7/1** Up All Night(8/1—12/1), **8/1** Hugging, **16/1** Agnes Flemming (USA)(op 10/1). CSF £47.11, Tote £5.10: £1.70 £2.00 £3.00 (£21.50). Mr Hamdan Al-Maktoum (LAMBOURN) bred by Shadwell Farm Incorporated in USA. 8 Rn
1m 44.39 (7.79)
SF—28/26/21/13/10/8

**690** APPLEDORE H'CAP (3-Y.O) (0-90) £3054.00 (£912.00: £436.00: £198.00)
5f                                                                          2-40 (2-44)

(Weights raised 5 lb)

298³ **Inherent Magic (IRE) (71)** *(MMcCormack)* 8-7 AClark (2) (lw: w ldr: led 2f out tl over 1f out: hrd rdn fnl f: led last strides) .............................. —1

**691—693**

559 Wild Honour (IRE) **(84)** *(WRMuir)* 9-6 AMunro (7) (a.p: led over 1f out: hrd rdn fnl f: hdd last strides) .................................................. hd.2

559⁵ Ned's Bonanza **(75)** *(Jt-Fav)* *(MDods)* 8-11 WCarson (6) (led 3f: ev ch ins fnl f: r.o) .................................................. ¾.3

582 Hot Lavender (CAN) **(70)** *(CFWall)* 8-6 LDettori (4) (a.p: ev ch ins fnl f: r.o) ...... nk.4

472 Walk in the Park **(85)** *(RSimpson)* 9-2 ‡5ATucker (5) (swtg: hdwy over 1f out: r.o ins fnl f) .................................................. nk.5

559 Verde Alitalia (IRE) **(78)** *(JLDunlop)* 9-0 MRoberts (10) (lw: stdy hdwy over 1f out: r.o) .................................................. 2¹/₂.6

Canadian Capers **(84)** *(MRChannon)* 9-6 TQuinn (8) (swtg: prom over 3f) ...... 3¹/₂.7

527⁶ Lady Sabo **(69)** *(GLewis)* 8-5 BRouse (4) (outpcd) .................................................. 1.8

582² Cumbrian Cavalier **(62)** *(KGWingrove)* 7-7⁽⁵⁾ ‡5BDoyle (9) (s.s: a bhd) ............. 12.9

503⁴ Allthruthenight (IRE) **(84)** *(LJHolt)* 9-6 JReid (11) (lw: racd centre: prom over 2f) 1.10

399⁵ Swellegant **(84)** *(WJHaggas)* 9-6 NDay (12) (b.hind: swtg: racd centre: outpcd) nk.11

428 Very Good **(57)** *(PHowling)* 7-7 GBardwell (13) (racd centre: spd over 2f) ...... 2.12

LONG HANDICAP: Cumbrian Cavalier 7-4, Very Good 7-4.

**5/1** Verde Alitalia (IRE), Ned's Bonanza, **7/1** INHERENT MAGIC (IRE), **15/2** Allthruthenight (IRE), **8/1** Swellegant, **10/1** Cumbrian Cavalier, Hot Lavender (CAN)(8/1—12/1), **12/1** Lady Sabo, **14/1** Canadian Capers, Wild Honour (IRE), **16/1** Walk in the Park, **25/1** Very Good. CSF £87.61, CT £483.73. Tote £10.10: £2.30 £3.60 £1.70 (£109.60). Orchid Racing & Bloodstock Limited (WANTAGE) bred by Mrs M. McStay in Ireland. 12 Rn

62.13 sec (3.13)

SF–45/57/45/39/48/36

**691**  SKYLARK GRADUATION STKS (3-Y.O.F) £2872.00 (£856.00: £408.00: £184.00)
**6f**                                                                          3-10 (3-12)

**Vailmont (USA) (95)** *(IABalding)* 9-3 RCochrane (3) (lw: plld hrd: hdwy over 1f out: led ins fnl f: rdn out) .................................................. —1

559² Silca-Cisa **(89)** *(MRChannon)* 9-3 BRouse (4) (chsd ldr: led 2f out tl ins fnl f: r.o) nk.2

526* Ahbab (IRE) **(88)** *(Fav)* *(PTWalwyn)* 8-10 WCarson (2) (led 4f) .................................................. 4.3

408* Mathaayl (USA) *(HThomsonJones)* 9-3 RHills (1) (bhd fnl 2f) .................................................. 12.4

**11/10** Ahbab (IRE), **100/30** Silca-Cisa, **7/2** Mathaayl (USA), **11/2** VAILMONT (USA). CSF £19.51, Tote £7.00 (£9.60). Mr George Strawbridge (KINGSCLERE) bred by George Strawbridge Jnr in USA. 4 Rn

1m 14.56 (3.26)

SF–56/55/32/–

**692**  JUBILEE H'CAP (0-105) £13940.00 (£4220.00: £2060.00: £980.00)
**1m (J.C)**                                                                  3-40 (3-42)

**Venus Observed (88)** *(HCandy)* 4–9-1 ‡7AntoinetteArmes (4) (2nd st: led over 2f out: r.o) .................................................. —1

610⁴ Sharp N' Smooth **(72)** *(Fav)* *(RHannon)* 5–8-6 WCarson (10) (rdn & hdwy on ins over 2f out: ev ch ins fnl f: unable qckn) .................................................. 1¹/₂.2

392² Roseate Lodge **(78)** *(RWArmstrong)* 6–8-12 MRoberts (1) (hdwy 2f out: r.o ins fnl f) .................................................. 2¹/₂.3

477 Gilderdale **(85)** *(JWHills)* 10–9-5 RHills (11) (5th st: ev ch 2f out: one pce) ....... nk.4

438 Field of Honour **(84)** *(LMCumani)* 4–9-4 LDettori (5) (lw: 4th st: one pce fnl 2f) nk.5

492⁵ Domicksky **(79)** *(MJRyan)* 4–8-13 NDay (7) (hdwy wl over 1f out: wknd fnl f) ...... 4.6

411² Saafend **(67)** *(JSutcliffe)* 4–8-1 AMunro (12) (nvr nrr) .................................................. 1.7

477 Bowden Boy (IRE) **(71)** *(NACallaghan)* 4–7-12 ‡7JTate (6) (3rd st: wknd over 2f out) .................................................. s.h.8

492⁴ Ashdren **(82)** *(AHarrison)* 5–9-2 TQuinn (8) (a bhd) .................................................. 3¹/₂.9

Santi Sana **(72)** *(LadyHerries)* 4–8-6⁽²⁾ RCochrane (9) (dwlt: a bhd) .................................................. ¾.10

477⁶ Self Expression **(91)** *(IABalding)* 4–9-11 JReid (3) (6th st: wknd over 2f out) .. hd.11

Croupier **(93)** *(CEBrittain)* 5–9-8 ‡5BDoyle (2) (led over 5f) .................................................. s.h.12

**7/2** Sharp N' Smooth, **4/1** Roseate Lodge, **7/1** Domicksky, **8/1** Saafend(6/1—10/1), **9/1** Ashdren, **10/1** Field of Honour, **12/1** Gilderdale, Bowden Boy (IRE), **14/1** VENUS OBSERVED, Self Expression, **25/1** Santi Sana, **33/1** Croupier. CSF £59.07, CT £217.92. Tote £11.40: £2.40 £1.80 £1.90 (£24.20). Mrs C. E. Gross (WANTAGE) bred by Wheelersland Stud. 12 Rn

1m 42.02 (5.42)

SF–68/54/52/58/56/39

**693**  WINDSOR PARK STKS (Mdn 3-Y.O.C & G) £2553.00 (£708.00: £339.00)
**1m (J.C)**                                                                  4-10 (4-14)

440 **Cambrian** *(MrsJCecil)* 9-0 JReid (2) (lw: led 1f: led over 3f out: r.o wl) .................................................. —1

394⁴ Thamestar (IRE) *(Fav)* *(JLDunlop)* 9-0 TQuinn (14) (rdn over 3f out: 4th st: chsd wnr fnl 2f: r.o) .................................................. 1¹/₂.2

511　Trooping (IRE) *(GHarwood)* 9-0 AClark (12) (5th st: rdn 2f out: r.o ins fnl f) ...... hd.3
627⁵ General Dixie (USA) *(RHannon)* 9-0 GBardwell (5) (6th st: rdn over 2f out: r.o
　　　 ins fnl f) ....................................................................................................... 1.4
440　Kalko *(CEBrittain)* 9-0 MRoberts (3) (3rd st: one pce fnl 2f) ............................ 2.5
549⁶ Sadler's Way **(82)** *(GLewis)* 9-0 NDay (16) (lw: hdwy 2f out: nvr nr to chal) ...... 4.6
　　　 Master of the Rock *(PJMakin)* 9-0 LDettori (6) (w'like: bit bkwd: nvr nrr) ......... 7.7
　　　 Majjra (USA) *(JHMGosden)* 9-0 RCochrane (1) (unf: scope: bit bkwd: s.s: nvr
　　　 nrr) ....................................................................................................... ½.8
　　　 Gachette *(JSutcliffe)* 8-9 ‡ATucker (4) (bit bkwd: a mid div) ......................... ½.9
252　Formal Invitation (IRE) *(GLewis)* 9-0 RichardBerry (7) (s.i.s: nvr nrr) ............... 1.10
509⁶ Boldrullah *(DWPArbuthnot)* 9-0 BProcter (15) (b: prom 5f) ........................... 7.11
509　Spender *(PWHarris)* 9-0 GHind (13) (led 7f out tl over 3f out: sn wknd) ....... hd.12
　　　 Rose Edge *(JWHills)* 9-0 RHills (17) (unf: bit bkwd: prom over 4f) ................ ½.13
　　　 Slanderinthestrand (IRE) *(MJHaynes)* 9-0 BRouse (8) (bhd fnl 3f) .............. 15.14
　　　 Quixotic *(PWHarris)* 9-0 MWigham (10) (w'like: bkwd: s.s: a bhd) ............... 2.15
341　Brooks Express (FR) *(RAkehurst)* 9-0 AMunro (11) (bit bkwd: a bhd) ............... 16
441　Nael (IRE) *(CJBenstead)* 9-0 WCarson (9) (prom tl struck into & p.u 3f out:
　　　 dead) ...................................................................................................... 0

**5/2** Thamestar (IRE)(op 6/4), **5/1** Majjra (USA), **6/1** CAMBRIAN, **7/1** Kalko, General Dixie (USA), **16/1** Nael (IRE), Trooping (IRE), Sadler's Way, **20/1** Master of the Rock, **25/1** Quixotic, **33/1** Rose Edge, Boldrullah, Brooks Express (FR), **50/1** Spender, Gachette, **66/1** Ors. CSF £20.32, Tote £7.50: £2.40 £1.60 £4.20 (£8.70). Sheikh Mohammed (NEWMARKET) bred by Sheikh Mohammed bin Rashid al Maktoum. 17 Rn　　1m 43.64 (7.04)
　　　　　　　　　　　　　　　　　　　　　　　　　　　　　　　　　　SF—43/38/37/34/28/16

**694**　　　PARTH CLAIMING STKS (3-Y-O) £2364.00 (£654.00: £312.00)　1½m　4-40 (4-41)

562⁵ **Mr Ziegfeld (USA) (70)** *(Fav)* *(SirMarkPrescott)* 8-10 MRoberts (7) (lw: hld up:
　　　 6th st: led over 1f out: r.o wl) .................................................................. —1
256　A a Bamba **(60)** *(NACallaghan)* 8-3 AMunro (6) (rdn over 3f out: 5th st: ev ch
　　　 over 1f out: r.o) ...................................................................................... nk.2
497⁴ Mr Poppleton *(DWPArbuthnot)* 8-13 RCochrane (1) (b: led 11f out to 9f out: led
　　　 over 2f out tl over 1f out: unable qckn) ...................................................... 4.3
433　Dancing Dancer *(NCWright)* 7-12 ‡⁵BDoyle (3) (4th st: rdn over 1f out: one pce) nk.4
603⁶ Lyn's Return (IRE) **(54)** *(RSimpson)* 8-1 ‡⁵ATucker (2) (lw: plld hrd: led 8f out tl
　　　 hung bdly lft 2f out: sddle & bit slipped: nt rcvr) ........................................ nk.5
585⁵ Tooley's Boy *(MrsBarbaraWaring)* 8-8 NHowe (4) (swtg: 3rd st: wknd over 2f
　　　 out) ....................................................................................................... 15.6
346³ Beam Me Up Scotty (IRE) **(59)** *(PMitchell)* 8-6 AClark (5) (led 1f: wknd 4f out) . hd.7

**7/2** MR ZIEGFELD (USA)(tchd 6/1), **4/1** A a Bamba, Lyn's Return (IRE), **11/2** Mr Poppleton, **6/1** Beam Me Up Scotty (IRE)(op 4/1), **8/1** Dancing Dancer(14/1—7/1), **14/1** Tooley's Boy. CSF £15.96, Tote £5.40: £3.10 £2.30 (£7.70). Capt. J. Macdonald-Buchanan (NEWMARKET) bred by Robert S. West, Jnr. in USA. 7 Rn
　　　　　　　　　　　　　　　　　　　　　　　　　　　　　　　　　　2m 43.38 (13.18)
　　　　　　　　　　　　　　　　　　　　　　　　　　　　　　　　　　SF—12/4/6/–/–/–

**695**　　　SAXON HOUSE H'CAP (3-Y-O) (0-80) £3418.00 (£1024.00: £492.00: £226.00)
　　　　　1m 1f　　　　　　　　　　　　　　　　　　　　　　　　　　5-10 (5-13)

(Weights raised 6 lb)

524★ Googly **(52)** *(WGRWightman)* 7-13 GBardwell (2) (6th st: led over 1f out: rdn
　　　 out) ....................................................................................................... —1
587³ Miss Doody **(66)** (v) *(MRChannon)* 8-13 TQuinn (14) (5th st: rdn & edgd rt 1f
　　　 out: bmpd ins fnl f: r.o: fin 2nd,½: plcd 2nd) ........................................... 2
545² Karamoja **(72)** *(Fav)* *(NAGraham)* 9-5 LDettori (16) (lw: 4th st: hrd rdn 1f out:
　　　 bmpd ins fnl f: r.o: fin 1st,1½: plcd 3rd) ................................................... 3
　　　 Crystal Cross (USA) **(71)** *(IABalding)* 9-4 JReid (10) (lw: hdwy over 1f out: r.o) 3½.3
511　Nectar Collector **(71)** *(CFWall)* 9-4 NDay (4) (hdwy over 1f out: nvr nrr) ........... 3.5
　　　 Kingchip Boy **(57)** *(MJRyan)* 8-4 GHind (1) (led over 3f out tl over 1f
　　　 out: sn wknd) ......................................................................................... ½.6
587　Forgetful **(62)** *(RHannon)* 8-4 ‡⁵BDoyle (15) (led over 7f out tl over 3f out: 2nd st:
　　　 wknd 2f out) ........................................................................................... hd.7
471　Lady of Sardinia (BEL) **(74)** *(JWPayne)* 9-7 RCochrane (5) (nvr nr to chal) ...... ¾.8
　　　 Distant Memory **(73)** *(JWHills)* 9-6 RHills (12) (prom 6f) .............................. ¾.9
　　　 Roberto's Gal **(68)** *(NCWright)* 9-1 BRouse (11) (a mid div) ......................... ¾.10
394　Wakil (IRE) **(60)** *(CJBenstead)* 8-7 WCarson (9) (prom 5f) ............................ 2.11
526　Minoan Light (IRE) **(65)** (bl) *(RHannon)* 8-12 MWigham (9) (rdn 7f out: a bhd) ½.12
482⁶ Holiday Island **(67)** *(CEBrittain)* 9-7 MRoberts (6) (lw: a bhd) ....................... 1.13
482⁶ Parlemo (IRE) **(67)** *(JDBethell)* 9-0 AMunro (3) (lw: a bhd) ......................... 1½.14
　　　 Roca Murada (IRE) **(61)** *(MJRyan)* 8-8 AClark (13) (a bhd) .......................... 5.15
524⁶ Lord Leitrim (IRE) **(57)** *(NACallaghan)* 7-11 ‡⁷JTate (7) (lw: 3rd st: wknd over 2f
　　　 out) ....................................................................................................... 6.16

*Stewards Enquiry: Karamoja disq. (interference to Miss Doody). Dettori suspended 13-16/5/92 (careless riding).*

7/2 Karamoja, **5/1** Holiday Island, **6/1** Miss Doody, **15/2** Lady of Sardinia (BEL), **10/1** Parlemo (IRE), GOOGLY, Nectar Collector, **12/1** Crystal Cross (USA), **16/1** Mukall (IRE), **20/1** Lord Leitrim (IRE)(op 12/1), Kingchip Boy, Minoan Light (IRE), Distant Memory, **33/1** Ors. CSF £69.09, CT £236.41. Tote £10.50: £1.80 £1.80 £1.90 £2.40 (£19.60). Mr A. G. Lansley (UPHAM) bred by W. G. R. Wightman and Mrs J. A. Thomson. 16 Rn
1m 57.59 (7.59)
SF—25/40/32/26/17/1

T/Trio: Race 4: £25.30 (90.7 Tckts). T/Jkpt: Not won; £18,443.45 to Chester 5/5/92. T/Plpt: £721.40 (11.8 Tckts).
AK

## 502—**WARWICK** (L-H)

### Monday, May 4th [Good to firm]

Going Allowance: nil sec per fur (G)　　　　　　　　　　　Wind: slt bhd

Stalls: low

**696**　　LEVY BOARD APP'CE H'CAP (0-70) £2559.20 (£711.20: £341.60)　　**1m**　1-45 (1-51)

497* **Plan Ahead (61)** (Fav) (GLewis) 3-8-1 ‡⁵BRussell (16) (lw: hdwy & 5th st: led 2f out: sn clr) ..................................................................................................... —1
508⁴ Sooty Tern **(46)** (JMBradley) 5-7-13 ‡⁵MichaelBradley (18) (hdwy over 1f out: r.o wl) ................................................................................................................. 3.2
592* Lady Lacey **(55)** (v) (GBBalding) 5-8-13 (7x) TraceyPurseglove (20) (lw: gd hdwy over 1f out: fin wl) ......................................................................................... nk.3
Irish Groom **(42)** (bl) (JPSmith) 5-7-9⁽⁷⁾ ‡⁵DCarson (13) (bit bkwd: hdwy 2f out: one pce fnl f) ............................................................................................................ 1.4
592 Radio Caroline **(47)** (bl) (MTate) 4-8-0 ‡⁵SMulvey (7) (3rd st: one pce fnl 2f) ...... 3.5
572 Persian Dynasty **(39)** (JMBradley) 8-7-11 BThomas (17) (nvr nr to chal) ............ ³/₄.6
592 Tyrian Purple (IRE) **(55)** (HHollinshead) 4-8-13 MHumphries (2) (led 0f) ............ ¹/₂.7
508⁵ Chew it Over (IRE) **(52)** (CASmith) 4-8-10 PBowe (10) (no hdwy fnl 2f) ............ 1¹/₂.8
572 Station Express (IRE) **(43)** (BEllison) 4-7-10⁽⁶⁾ ‡⁵MHunt (12) (nvr trbld ldrs) ...... 2.9
Faryal **(55)** (JLSpearing) 3-8-0 AGarth (19) (bkwd: n.d) ....................................... ³/₄.10
525 Gibbot **(36)** (PHowling) 7-7-8 CAvery (5) (s.s: nrst fin) ...................................... nk.11
Corrin Hill **(70)** (BWHills) 5-9-9 ‡⁵SLanigan (3) (b: bit bkwd: a mid div) ............... nk.12
615* Rag Time Belle **(37)** (MWEckley) 6-7-9 (7x) DarrenMoffatt (24) (prom tl 6th & wkng st) ............................................................................................................... 2.13
Prima Aurora **(40)** (CPEBrooks) 4-7-12 JDSmith (11) (b.nr hind: prom tl hrd rdn & wknd 4f out) ......................................................................................................... 1.14
504 Walking Saint **(47)** (GraemeRoe) 5-8-5 DGibbs (15) (b.hind: n.d) ..................... ³/₄.15
565 Indian Sovereign **(40)** (RLee) 8-7-7⁽⁵⁾ ‡⁵MadeleineSmith (6) (n.d) .................... s.h.16
333 Gemdoubleyou **(40)** (FJordan) 4-7-12 SDrowne (9) (n.d) .................................. s.h.17
56 Night Transaction **(47)** (AHide) 5-8-5 CHawksley (23) (bit bkwd: bhd fnl 3f) ....... 4.18
477⁵ Champenoise **(58)** (MBell) 4-8-11 ‡⁵ACairns (25) (4th st: wknd qckly 2f out) . hd.19
592 Cartel **(61)** (JLHarris) 5-9-0 ‡⁵MHarris (4) (bit bkwd: w ldr: 2nd st: wknd qckly 2f out) ..................................................................................................................... ³/₄.20
397 Penando **(42)** (OO'Neill) 4-7-9 ‡⁵DWilliams (22) (n.d) ....................................... 2.21
532 Super Ted **(35)** (JMusson) 5-7-7 TWilson (21) (n.d) ........................................... ¹/₂.22
526 Miss Precocious **(45)** (v) (DShaw) 4-8-3⁽¹⁰⁾ LMahoney (14) (n.d) ..................... ³/₄.23
508 Armaiti **(62)** (DRTucker) 4-9-1 ‡⁵JFordham (8) (a bhd) ..................................... 1¹/₂.24
333³ Beechwood Cottage **(44)** (bl) (ABailey) 9-7-11⁽¹⁾ ‡⁵WHollick (1) (s.s: t.o) ...... 15.25
LONG HANDICAP: Irish Groom 7-2, Miss Precocious 7-6.

**9/2** PLAN AHEAD(11/2—7/2), **6/1** Rag Time Belle, **8/1** Champenoise, **10/1** Sooty Tern, Persian Dynasty, **12/1** Lady Lacey, **14/1** Tyrian Purple (IRE), Chew it Over (IRE), Super Ted, Cartel, Corrin Hill, **16/1** Faryal, Station Express (IRE), Beechwood Cottage, Radio Caroline, **25/1** Night Transaction, Gibbot, Penando, Gemdoubleyou, **33/1** Ors. CSF £53.41, CT £497.74. Tote £4.20: £1.90 £2.40 £4.10 £11.30 (£28.80). Planflow (Leasing) Ltd (EPSOM) bred by R. F. and Mrs Knipe. 25 Rn
1m 40.3 (3.3)
SF—37/26/39/18/14/9

**697**　　OFFCHURCH BURY POLO CLUB H'CAP (3-Y.O) (0-80) £3366.00 (£1008.00: £484.00: £222.00)　**7f**　　　　　　　　　　　　　　　　　　2-15 (2-19)

(Weights raised 2 lb)
412² **Nashville Blues (IRE) (69)** (Fav) (JWHills) 8-12 MHills (8) (4th st: led 1f out: sn clr) .................................................................................................................... —1
Ghurrah (IRE) **(63)** (CJBenstead) 8-6⁽³⁾ JWilliams (16) (bkwd: s.i.s: gd hdwy over 1f out: r.o) ......................................................................................................... 5.2
522⁵ Countercheck (IRE) **(53)** (CFWall) 7-10⁽¹⁾ TyroneWilliams (19) (3rd st: r.o one pce fnl 2f) ............................................................................................................... nk.3
472³ Boogie Bopper (IRE) **(72)** (MBell) 9-1 GDuffield (13) (hdwy 2f out: r.o ins fnl f) . ³/₄.4
521² Hawa Layaam (IRE) **(74)** (AAScott) 8-12 ‡⁵LNewton (14) (5th st: no hdwy fnl 2f) 1¹/₂.5
366⁶ Kipini **(52)** (WJMusson) 7-2⁽²⁾ ‡⁷CHawksley (6) (7th st: no hdwy fnl 2f) ............... 1.6

Sure Lord (IRE) **(74)** *(WRMuir)* 9-3 SWhitworth (1) (bit bkwd: a.p: led 3f out: hdd & wknd 1f out) ............ ¹/₂.7

472⁶ Christian Warrior **(78)** *(RHannon)* 9-2 ‡⁵RPerham (11) (nvr trbl ldrs) ............ nk.8

363 Hester Stanhope **(65)** *(PWHarris)* 8-8 GCarter (12) (n.d) ............ hd.9

395 Bold Surprise **(65)** (bl) *(RWArmstrong)* 8-8 BCrossley (3) (a mid div) ............ ³/₄.10

458⁶ Blimpers Disco **(55)** *(EHOwenjun)* 7-5⁽⁵⁾ ‡⁵GMilligan (9) (n.d) ............ ³/₄.11

549 Cannonale (IRE) **(59)** *(JPearce)* 7-11⁽⁴⁾ ‡⁵RPrice (7) (n.d) ............ 12

432 Libra Legend (USA) **(65)** *(CEBrittain)* 8-8 GCrealock (15) (n.d) ............ 13

594⁵ Another Vintage **(54)** (v) *(PDCundell)* 7-11 NAdams (18) (n.d) ............ 14

324⁴ Cocos Island (USA) **(69)** *(PWChapple-Hyam)* 8-12 WRyan (17) (led 4f: 2nd st: wknd qckly 2f out) ............ 15

David's Own **(60)** *(SMellor)* 8-3 DanaMellor (5) (bit bkwd: a bhd) ............ 16

468⁵ Rivet **(65)** *(MBlanshard)* 8-8 CRutter (4) (prom: 6th & wknd st: t.o) ............ 17

408 Placid Lady (IRE) **(58)** *(WCarter)* 7-10⁽⁸⁾ ‡⁵NGWilliams (2) (s.s: t.o) ............ 18

LONG HANDICAP: Kipini 7-2, Blimpers Disco 7-3, Placid Lady (IRE) 7-3.

**4/1** NASHVILLE BLUES (IRE), **9/2** Boogie Bopper (IRE), **6/1** Hawa Layaam (IRE), **15/2** Christian Warrior, **8/1** Sure Lord (IRE)(tchd 12/1), Cocos Island (USA), **12/1** Hester Stanhope, Libra Legend (USA)(8/1—14/1), **14/1** Bold Surprise, Another Vintage, **16/1** Countercheck (IRE), Rivet, **20/1** Ghurrah (IRE), Cannonale (IRE), **25/1** Blimpers Disco, Kipini, **33/1** Ors. CSF £88.91, CT £1,145.84. Tote £4.60: £1.10 £9.80 £9.10 £1.80 (£98.50). Mrs S. Bosher (LAMBOURN) bred by Mrs Larry Walsh in Ireland. 18 Rn 　　1m 27.1 (2.9)

SF—54/33/22/39/31/4

**698**　　STONEBRIDGE STKS (Mdn 3-Y.O) £1932.00 (£532.00: £252.00)　　**7f**　　2-45 (2-52)

502³ **Sea Dune** (Fav) *(RCharlton)* 8-9 MHills (2) (lw: hld up: 4th st: led wl over 1f out: easily) ............ —1

412 Agincourt Song (USA) **(70)** *(JLDunlop)* 9-0 GDuffield (11) (5th st: hrd rdn over 1f out: r.o ins fnl f: no ch w wnr) ............ 4.2

440 Wafi (USA) *(BHanbury)* 9-0 WRyan (12) (lw: hdwy over 1f out: hrd rdn & r.o ins fnl f) ............ nk.3

509 Red Archer *(PJMakin)* 8-9 ‡⁵TSprake (4) (hdwy over 1f out: n.m.r & swtchd rt ins fnl f: nrst fin: fin 5th, 2l: plcd 4th) ............ 4

Sirmoor (IRE) *(RHannon)* 9-0 SRaymont (6) (bkwd: 6th st: no hdwy fnl 2f) ............ 2.6

498 Tajigrey **(43)** *(RCurtis)* 8-9 GCarter (1) (lw ldr: led over 2f out tl wknd wl over 1f out) ............ 3.7

585 Chummy's Child (IRE) *(BWHills)* 9-0 DHolland (9) (prom over 3f) ............ 6.8

577 Hanley's Hands (IRE) *(MHTompkins)* 8-9 ‡⁵CHodgson (14) (a bhd) ............ 3.9

509 Masrur (USA) *(RWArmstrong)* 9-0 BCrossley (3) (a bhd) ............ ³/₄.10

Tommy Tempest *(KRBurke)* 9-0 TyroneWilliams (10) (small: bkwd: led over 4f: 2nd st: wknd qckly 2f out) ............ 1¹/₂.11

Bishopstone Bill **(46)** *(SMellor)* 9-0 DanaMellor (8) (bkwd: bhd fnl 3f: t.o) ............ 12

Sennon Cove *(MJCharles)* 8-9 NAdams (7) (w'like: bkwd: a bhd: t.o) ............ 13

458⁴ Alkarif (USA) **(72)** *(AAScott)* 8-9 ‡⁵LNewton (5) (plld hrd: 3rd st: one pce fnl 2f: fin 4th, ¹/₂l: disq: plcd last) ............ 0

*Stewards Enquiry: Obj. to Alkarif (USA) by Clerk of Scales sustained. Newton fined £125 (failure to weigh-in).*

**4/5** SEA DUNE(op 5/4), **5/1** Wafi (USA), **11/2** Agincourt Song (USA), **8/1** Alkarif (USA), **12/1** Masrur (USA), **14/1** Chummy's Child (IRE), Sirmoor (IRE), **20/1** Hanley's Hands (IRE), **33/1** Ors. CSF £7.13, Tote £1.60: £1.30 £1.80 £2.00 (£4.30). Mr Jocelyn Hambro (BECKHAMPTON) bred by Waverton Stud Ltd. 13 Rn 　1m 27.9 (3.7)

SF—39/32/31/24/18/17

**699**　　ALVESTON STKS (Mdn 3-Y.O.F) £1932.00 (£532.00: £252.00)　　**1m**　　3-15 (3-22)

**Rafah** *(BHanbury)* 8-11 WRyan (2) (unf: hld up & bhd: rdn & hdwy 2f out: led ins fnl f: all out) ............ —1

Jade Green *(PJMakin)* 8-6 ‡⁵TSprake (3) (b.hind: 5th st: ev ch 1f out: hrd rdn: r.o) ............ ³/₄.2

Rose Elegance (Jt-Fav) *(WRMuir)* 8-4 ‡⁷KimMcDonnell (9) (bit bkwd: hld up & plld hrd: swtchd rt & gd hdwy fnl f: fin wl) ............ s.h.3

Waseela (IRE) (Jt-Fav) *(AAScott)* 8-6 ‡⁵LNewton (10) (bit bkwd: hld up: 6th st: hdwy 2f out: ev ch 1f out: nt qckn) ............ 2.4

553 Change the Will *(MDIUsher)* 8-11 CRutter (6) (a.p: led over 2f out tl ins fnl f) ............ ³/₄.5

502 Kelimutu *(CFWall)* 8-11 SWebster (5) (2nd st: ev ch over 1f out: one pce) ............ ³/₄.6

Laughing Falcon *(JLDunlop)* 8-11 GDuffield (7) (no hdwy fnl 2f) ............ 3.7

589³ Spot the Dove *(RJPrice)* 8-6 ‡⁵NGWilliams (8) (4th st: ev ch whn hung rt 2f out: sn wknd) ............ s.h.8

Mariette Larkin *(GBBalding)* 8-11 JWilliams (11) (bit bkwd: prom over 3f) ............ 2¹/₂.9

Kaytura *(MHTompkins)* 8-6 ‡⁵CHodgson (13) (w'like: bkwd: a bhd) ............ ¹/₂.10

434 Lysirra (USA) *(BWHills)* 8-11 DHolland (12) (bit bkwd: a bhd) ...................... hd.**11**
502 Christian Flight (IRE) *(RHannon)* 8-11 SRaymont (4) (led over 5f: 3rd st: wknd 2f
　　out) .................... 3¹/₂.**12**
　　Winnie Reckless *(CEBrittain)* 8-11 GCrealock (1) (neat: s.s: t.o) ................... 20.**13**

**7/2** Rose Elegance, Waseela, (IRE), **6/1** Lysirra (USA), **8/1** Mariette Larkin(op 20/1), RAFAH(op 4/1), Winnie
Reckless(op 5/1), Spot the Dove, **10/1** Laughing Falcon, **14/1** Jade Green, Kaytura, **16/1** Kelimutu(op 10/1),
**20/1** Christian Flight (IRE), **33/1** Change the Will. CSF £135.32, Tote £12.20: £2.80 £3.00 £1.80 (£35.40). Mr
Hilal Salem (NEWMARKET) bred by Gainsborough Stud Management Ltd. 13 Rn
1m 42.6 (5.6)
SF—13/6/3/–/–/–

**700**　　EVENING TELEGRAPH H'CAP (3-Y.O) (0-80) £2929.50 (£812.00: £388.50)
　　　　1¹/₂m 115y　　　　　　　　　　　　　　　　　　　　　　　3-45 (3-46)

(Weights raised 3 lb)
　　**Pica (71)** *(HRACecil)* 9-1 WRyan (2) (hld up: stdy hdwy 5f out: 4th st: swtchd rt
　　　　over 1f out: led ins fnl f: easily) ................................................ —**1**
498 Sports View **(54)** *(RJHolder)* 7-12 NAdams (3) (5th st: hdwy 2f out: r.o: no ch w
　　wnr) ............................................... 5.**2**
524⁴ My Senor **(57)** *(MMadgwick)* 7-8(8) ‡⁷CAvery (5) (bhd tl gd hdwy over 4f out: r.o) 1¹/₂.**3**
529² Sure Haven (IRE) **(77)** *(SirMarkPrescott)* 9-7 GDuffield (1) (rdn & lost pl over 4f
　　out: styd on over 1f out) ............................................... 1.**4**
512⁴ Inan (USA) **(72)** (Fav) *(JLDunlop)* 9-2 MHills (8) (hld up: 2nd st: led over 1f out tl
　　ins fnl f) ............................................... hd.**5**
　　Citiqueen (IRE) **(75)** *(HRACecil)* 8-12 ‡⁷StephenDavies (6) (bit bkwd: rdn 7f out:
　　6th st: no hdwy) ............................................... 1.**6**
376⁴ Rock Hard **(63)** *(WJarvis)* 8-7 MTebbutt (4) (chsd ldr: led over 3f out tl over 1f
　　out: wknd fnl f) ............................................... ³/₄.**7**
384⁶ Landed Gentry (USA) **(68)** *(PWChapple-Hyam)* 0 1Ω DHolland (0) (hld up:
　　hdwy 6f out: wknd over 3f out: t.o) ............................................... 12.**8**
512 Yaafoor (USA) **(63)** *(AAScott)* 8-2 ‡⁵LNewton (7) (led 9f: 3rd st: wknd 2f out: t.o) 1.**9**
LONG HANDICAP: My Senor 7-3.

**11/4** Inan (USA)(op 11/2), **7/2** Landed Gentry (USA), Sure Haven (IRE), **6/1** Citiqueen (IRE),
**8/1** Rock Hard, Yaafoor (USA), **20/1** Ors. CSF £73.14, CT £1,369.04. Tote £3.20: £1.40 £10.50 £5.10
(£113.10). Sheikh Mohammed (NEWMARKET) bred by Sheikh Mohammed bin Rashid al Maktoum. 9 Rn
2m 44.9 (7.4)
SF—27/–/–/18/12/6

**701**　　E.B.F. PRIMROSE STKS (Mdn 2-Y.O.F) £2588.80 (£716.80: £342.40)　　**5f**　4-15 (4-17)

　　**Laurel Delight** *(JBerry)* 8-11 GCarter (3) (w'like: led over 3f: led ins fnl f: r.o) .... —**1**
　　Rahon (IRE) (Fav) *(PWChapple-Hyam)* 8-11 WRyan (4) (lt-f: a.p: rdn over 2f
　　out: r.o fnl f) ............................................... nk.**2**
287 Be Polite (IRE) *(MBell)* 8-11 MHills (5) (a chsng ldrs: r.o ins fnl f) ................... 1¹/₂.**3**
　　Magic Orb *(JLSpearing)* 8-11 JWilliams (2) (w'like: bkwd: w ldrs: led wl over 1f
　　out tl ins fnl f) ............................................... ³/₄.**4**
602⁵ Folly Vision (IRE) *(RHannon)* 8-11 SRaymont (1) (w ldrs tl rdn & wknd over 1f
　　out) ............................................... 2¹/₂.**5**
　　Nikki Noo Noo *(CJHill)* 8-11 NAdams (6) (nt: bkwd: no hdwy fnl 2f) ................. hd.**6**
　　Formaestre (IRE) *(MHTompkins)* 8-6 ‡⁹CHodgson (8) (lt-f: scope: swtchd rt s:
　　outpcd tl sme late hdwy) ............................................... ¹/₂.**7**
　　Dorazine *(CJHill)* 8-11 SWhitworth (7) (leggy: bhd fnl 2f) ........................... ¹/₂.**8**

**2/1** Rahon (IRE)(Evens—9/4), **9/4** LAUREL DELIGHT(3/1—2/1), **7/2** Folly Vision (IRE), **6/1** Magic Orb(op 9/1),
**9/1** Be Polite (IRE), **16/1** Formaestre (IRE)(op 10/1), **20/1** Nikki Noo Noo, **25/1** Dorazine. CSF £7.67, Tote £2.70:
£1.20 £1.60 £2.00 (£4.50). Laurel (Leisure) Limited (COCKERHAM) bred by G. Blum and Ridge Barn Farm Ltd. 8
Rn
61.4 sec (3.4)
SF—29/28/22/19/9/8

**702**　　WARWICK SPRING H'CAP (0-70) £3574.00 (£1072.00: £516.00: £238.00)
　　　　1¹/₄m 169y　　　　　　　　　　　　　　　　　　　　　　　4-45 (4-47)

505⁴ Gin and Orange **(52)** *(JRJenkins)* 6–8-12 SWhitworth (1) (dwlt: stdy hdwy 4f
　　out: r.o strly to ld fnl strides) ............................................... —**1**
271 Predestine **(53)** *(MMadgwick)* 7–8-13 GBaxter (18) (b: 3rd st: led over 1f out tl
　　hdd last strides) ............................................... hd.**2**
572 Cornhill Melody **(34)** *(JLSpearing)* 4–7-1(1) ‡⁷CHawksley (12) (lw: led after 2f st
　　over 3f out: 2nd st: ev ch 1f out: nt qckn) ............................................... 2.**3**
471 Murasil (USA) **(68)** *(MajorWRHern)* 3–8-10 WRyan (3) (hld up: hdwy fnl 2f: r.o) hd.**4**

299 Premier Dance **(41)** *(DHaydnJones)* 5–8-1 TyroneWilliams (15) (lw: 5th st: no
 hdwy fnl 2f) ...................................................................... 1¹/₂.5
530* Bold Resolution (IRE) **(51)** (Fav) *(CACyzer)* 4–8-11 GCarter (6) (lw: 6th st: hrd
 rdn 2f out: no hdwy) ...................................................................... 1¹/₂.6
 Lawnswood Junior **(40)** *(JLSpearing)* 5–8-0 SWood (14) (w ldr: led over 3f out
 tl over 1f out: wknd fnl f) ...................................................................... 2¹/₂.7
4536 Taunting (IRE) **(65)** *(MBlanshard)* 4–9-11 CRutter (10) (nvr nr to chal) ............ 1¹/₂.8
243 Shrewd Girl (USA) **(67)** *(BWHills)* 4–9-13 DHolland (8) (s.i.s: nvr trbld ldrs) ....... 1¹/₂.9
505 Royal Acclaim **(49)** (v) *(JMBradley)* 7–8-2 ‡7MichaelBradley (4) (nvr nr ldrs) .. 2¹/₂.10
530 Singing Reply (USA) **(49)** *(DMarks)* 4–8-9 MHills (7) (n.d) .................................... nk.11
565 Marjons Boy **(41)** (bl) *(CDBroad)* 5–7-8(8) ‡7BThomas (11) (bhd fnl 2f) .......... s.h.12
 Millador **(62)** *(MHTompkins)* 3–7-11(5) ‡7SMulvey (8) (n.d) ........................... 1¹/₂.13
 Times Are Hard **(44)** *(CASmith)* 8–7-11(3) ‡7PBowe (17) (n.d) ...................... 1¹/₂.14
 Captain My Captain (IRE) **(60)** *(GBBalding)* 4–9-6 JWilliams (9) (bit bkwd: a bhd)s.h.15
435 Mubin (IRE) **(68)** *(CCElsey)* 4–10-0 GDuffield (19) (lw: prom 6f) .................... 2¹/₂.16
 Gina's Choice **(33)** *(PAPritchard)* 6–7-7 RStreet (20) (bkwd: 4th st: wknd qckly
 2f out) ...................................................................... ¹/₂.17
598 Mai Pen Rai **(47)** *(CJHill)* 4–8-2 ‡5RPrice (16) (a in rr) ...................................... ¹/₂.18
 La Raptotte **(35)** (bl) *(MJCharles)* 5–7-9(1) NAdams (3) (n.d) .......................... 2¹/₂.19
553 Kentucky Starlet (USA) **(68)** *(RHannon)* 3–8-10 SRaymont (5) (bit bkwd: led 2f:
 7th & wkng st) ...................................................................... 6.20

LONG HANDICAP: Marjons Boy 7-1, Gina's Choice 7-1.

**7/2** Bold Resolution (IRE), **11/2** Murasil (USA), **6/1** Shrewd Girl (USA), **8/1** Mubin (IRE), Kentucky Starlet (USA),
Premier Dance(10/1—16/1), **10/1** La Raptotte, **12/1** Captain My Captain (IRE), **14/1** Times Are Hard, Royal
Acclaim, **16/1** Singing Reply (USA), Taunting (IRE), Lawnswood Junior, Cornhill Melody, **20/1** Millador, Mai Pen
Rai, Predestine, GIN AND ORANGE, **25/1** Marjons Boy, **33/1** Gina's Choice. CSF £405.09, CT £5,872.65. Tote
£14.10: £2.70 £4.60 £4.00 £1.90 (£473.50). Mr Paul Walker (ROYSTON) bred by R. E. A. Bott (Wigmore Street)
Ltd. 20 Rn                                                                         2m 20.9 (7.4)
                                                                     SF—24/24/–/16/4/11

T/Plpt: £30.40 (75.7 Tckts).                                                              KH

---

548—**SANDOWN (R-H)**

**Tuesday, May 5th [St Good to soft, Soft patches, Rnd Good, Good to
soft patches]**

Going Allowance: 0.25 sec per fur (G)                                        Wind: nil

Stalls: high

**703**  'SANDOWNER' AUCTION STKS (Mdn 2-Y.O) £2679.00 (£744.00: £357.00)
         **5f 6y**                                                              5-50 (5-57)

4394 **Northern Bird** (Fav) *(BWHills)* 8-1 WCarson (14) (b: b.hind: lw: mde all: qcknd
 over 1f out: r.o) ...................................................................... —1
 No Reservations (IRE) *(RFJohnsonHoughton)* 7-7 ‡5DHarrison (13) (unf: a.p:
 ev ch over 1f out: nt qckn) ...................................................................... 2¹/₂.2
 Sure Risk *(RHannon)* 8-2 ‡5RPerham (4) (unf: scope: hdwy 2f out: rdn over 1f
 out: r.o) ...................................................................... 2.3
5814 Jonsalan *(WCarter)* 8-6 LDettori (7) (rdn along: a.p: one pce fnl 2f) ................... 2.4
 Chili Heights *(GBBalding)* 8-5(2) JWilliams (9) (b.nr hind: w'like: bkwd: a.p: one
 pce fnl 2f) ...................................................................... 1.5
4396 Zany Zanna (IRE) *(GAPritchard-Gordon)* 7-12 NCarlisle (8) (s.s: hdwy & nt clr
 run over 1f out: nrst fin) ...................................................................... 1.6
548 Always Risky *(PAKelleway)* 7-12 JQuinn (2) (lw: gd spd 3f) ........................... 2¹/₂.7
339 Second Chance (IRE) *(PMitchell)* 8-0 ‡3SO'Gorman (10) (gd spd 3f) ............. 1¹/₂.8
 Hallorina *(WGRWightman)* 7-12 GBardwell (5) (w'like: bkwd: s.s: a bhd) ......... s.h.9
5613 Walid's Princess (IRE) *(JWharton)* 7-9 ‡3JFanning (12) (outpcd) ................ ³/₄.10
470 Mr Nevermind (IRE) *(GLewis)* 8-4(1) BRouse (15) (n.d) ................................ ¹/₂.11
 Don't Tell Dick *(DRLaing)* 8-1 TyroneWilliams (11) (unf: bkwd: s.s: a bhd) ..... nk.12
 All Promises *(PButler)* 7-12 AProud (6) (lt-f: bit bkwd: a bhd) ...................... 3¹/₂.13
 Five Clubs (IRE) *(DTTThom)* 7-12 JLowe (1) (w'like: s.s: a bhd) .................... s.h.14
514 Buckski Echo *(TMJones)* 8-3 NAdams (3) (t.o) ............................................ 2¹/₂.15

**11/8** NORTHERN BIRD, **3/1** Jonsalan, **13/2** Walid's Princess (IRE), **9/1** Sure Risk(6/1—10/1), **12/1** Mr
Nevermind (IRE)(op 7/1), **14/1** Second Chance (IRE), No Reservations (IRE), Always Risky, **16/1** Zany Zanna
(IRE)(12/1—20/1), **20/1** Chili Heights, **25/1** Don't Tell Dick, Hallorina, Five Clubs (IRE), **50/1** Ors. CSF £25.61,
Tote £2.60: £1.30 £3.90 £3.20 (£14.70). Mr John E. Bradley (LAMBOURN) bred by S. Wingfield Digby. 15 Rn
                                                                           63.02 sec (3.52)
                                                                     SF—42/24/25/21/16/5

**704**  LBC MICHAEL PARKINSON GRADUATION STKS (3-Y.O) £2714.00 (£754.00: £362.00)
1m 14y                                                        6-20 (6-24)

474² **Ezzoud (IRE)** (bl) *(Fav) (MRStoute)* 9-4 WRSwinburn (5) (lw: 4th st: led 1f out:
drvn out) ................................................................. —1
549* Hamas (IRE) **(100)** *(PTWalwyn)* 9-4 WCarson (7) (plld hrd: 3rd st: led 2f out to 1f
out: r.o) ................................................................. 2¹/₂.2
443⁶ Amaze **(100)** *(LadyHerries)* 9-4 LDettori (1) (b: 2nd st: one pce fnl 2f) ....... 2.3
458* Asaasy (USA) **(90)** *(MRStoute)* 9-4 BRaymond (3) (7th st: nrst fin) .......... nk.4
444⁶ Bold Pursuit (IRE) **(100)** *(RHannon)* 9-4 JReid (2) (5th st: hdwy & rdn over 2f
out: sn wknd) ................................................................. 2.5
531* Haroldon (IRE) **(90)** *(BPalling)* 9-4 RCochrane (4) (lw: 6th st: nvr nr to chal) .. 3.6
Berseto (USA) *(HRACecil)* 9-4 WRyan (6) (bit bkwd: led tl wknd 2f out) ........... 5.7

**13/8** EZZOUD (IRE), **5/2** Hamas (IRE), **5/1** Berseto (USA)(4/1—6/1), **7/1** Bold Pursuit (IRE), **10/1**
Amaze(8/1—12/1), **20/1** Asaasy (USA), **25/1** Haroldon (IRE). CSF £5.89, Tote £2.40: £1.70 £1.70 (£3.00).
Maktoum Al Maktoum (NEWMARKET) bred by T. J. Monaghan in Ireland. 7 Rn       1m 43.51 (4.31)
                                                          SF—69/61/55/54/48/39

**705**  LBC MIKE CARLTON H'CAP (0-100) £2862.50 (£860.00: £415.00: £192.50)
1m 14y                                                        6-50 (6-53)

354 **Jimlii (76)** *(BPalling)* 4-8-9 WRyan (7) (7th st: hdwy 2f out: led ins fnl f: all out) —1
Aitch N'Bee **(74)** *(LadyHerries)* 9-8-7 LDettori (1) (gd hdwy over 1f out: ev ch
ins fnl f: r.o) ................................................................. nk.2
479⁴ Port Sunlight (IRE) **(78)** *(Fav) (RHannon)* 4-8-11 RCochrane (9) (lw: 3rd st: led
over 2f out tl ins fnl f) ................................................................. 1.3
438 Mahsul (IRE) **(60)** *(CJBenstead)* 4-7-7 JLowe (8) (nvr nrr) ................... 2¹/₂.4
563⁶ Bold Bostonian **(FR)** **(83)** *(PJTIbbbs)* 4-9-2 JWilliams (2) (6th st: one pce fnl 2f) 4.5
Soleil Dancer (IRE) **(93)** *(MMcCormack)* 4-9-12 JReid (5) (lw: 2nd st: hdwy
over 2f out: sn wknd) ................................................................. hd.6
477 Petoski's Choice **(67)** *(MJRyan)* 4-8-0 GCarter (3) (5th st: wknd 2f out) ...... 1¹/₂.7
Arak (USA) **(80)** *(RWArmstrong)* 4-8-13 WCarson (6) (4th st: grad wknd) ........ ³/₄.8
Daswaki (CAN) **(87)** *(RHannon)* 4-9-6 BRouse (4) (swtg: led over 5f) .......... 2.9

**3/1** Port Sunlight (IRE), **6/1** Soleil Dancer (IRE)(op 4/1), **8/1** Daswaki (CAN), **13/2** JIMLII, **8/1** Bold Bostonian (FR),
Arak (USA), Mahsul (IRE), Aitch N'Bee, **14/1** Petoski's Choice. CSF £52.13, CT £170.79. Tote £9.30: £2.40
£3.50 £1.40 (£49.50). Mr James F. Knowles (COWBRIDGE) bred by R. S. A. Urquhart. 9 Rn    1m 44.04 (4.84)
                                                          SF—53/50/51/25/36/45

**706**  LBC ANGELA RIPPON H'CAP (0-80) £2735.00 (£760.00: £365.00)    5f 6y   7-20 (7-23)
(Weights raised 4 lb)

**Dawes of Nelson (38)** *(MJBolton)* 7-7-11 WCarson (13) (a.p: led over 1f out:
drvn out) ................................................................. —1
Martina **(58)** *(JWharton)* 4-9-3 JWilliams (9) (lw: a.p: ev ch fnl f: r.o) ........... ¹/₂.2
524* Yes **(50)** *(Fav) (DTThom)* 4-8-9 JLowe (12) (a.p: hmpd 1f out: r.o ins fnl f) ...... 1.3
L'Ete (IRE) **(58)** *(PMitchell)* 4-9-0 ‡3SO'Gorman (11) (led over 3f) ........... 2¹/₂.4
349 Frimley Parkson **(40)** *(PHowling)* 8-7-13 NAdams (7) (hdwy over 1f out: nvr
nrr) ................................................................. ³/₄.5
596⁵ Misdemeanours Girl (IRE) **(65)** *(MRChannon)* 4-9-5 ‡5BDoyle (8) (nvr nr to chal) s.h.6
58 Tachyon Park **(48)** *(PHowling)* 10-8-7 JQuinn (10) (bit bkwd: spd over 3f) 2¹/₂.7
480³ Greetland Rock **(51)** *(PHowling)* 4-8-7 ‡3FNorton (6) (b: no hdwy fnl 2f) ....... ³/₄.8
661⁶ Best Effort **(52)** *(MPNaughton)* 6-8-11 MRoberts (1) (outpcd) ................. 1¹/₂.9
Miramede **(43)** *(RJHodges)* 4-8-2 TyroneWilliams (4) (swtg: plld hrd: nvr nr ldrs)hd.10
515 Dickens Lane **(62)** *(RJHodges)* 5-9-2 ‡5TSprake (3) (lw: outpcd) ........... ¹/₂.11
Profit a Prendre **(54)** *(DAWilson)* 8-8-13 BRouse (5) (bit bkwd: a bhd) ......... 2.12
Albert **(54)** *(DAWilson)* 5-8-13 GCarter (2) (bit bkwd: a bhd) ............... 6.13

**7/2** Yes, **5/1** Misdemeanours Girl (IRE), **6/1** DAWES OF NELSON, **7/1** Greetland Rock, **15/2** Best Effort, **10/1**
Martina(8/1—12/1), **12/1** Tachyon Park, **14/1** L'Ete (IRE), **16/1** Profit a Prendre, Frimley Parkson, **20/1** Dickens
Lane, **33/1** Ors. CSF £60.39, CT £221.25. Tote £7.40: £2.30 £3.10 £1.80 (£44.00). Mr A. R. M. Galbraith
(SHREWTON) bred by D. Cornwall. 13 Rn                                  63.30 sec (3.80)
                                                          SF—32/50/38/33/15/34

**707**  LBC NEWSTALK 97.3 FM STKS (Mdn 3-Y.O.F) £2511.00 (£696.00: £333.00)
1¹/₄m 7y                                                      7-50 (7-54)

**Cottonwood** *(LordHuntingdon)* 8-11 AMunro (11) (5th st: led over 1f out: drvn
out) ................................................................. —1
553² Shirley Valentine *(Fav) (HRACecil)* 8-11 WRyan (5) (hdwy & brght v.wd st: r.o 2f
out: ev ch fnl f: no ex) ................................................................. 1¹/₂.2
Fleeting Rainbow *(JLDunlop)* 8-11 TQuinn (13) (lw: hdwy fnl 2f: nvr nrr) ........ 2¹/₂.3

Themeda *(CRNelson)* 8-11 MHills (14) (w'like: scope: gd hdwy fnl f: fin wl) ...... ½.4
Alessandrina (USA) *(MRStoute)* 8-11 RCochrane (7) (led tl over 2f out: r.o one
pce) ................................................................................ 1.5
Continuity *(GHarwood)* 8-11 AClark (8) (w'like: bkwd: 6th st: led over 2f out tl
wknd over 1f out) .................................................... 1½.6
5736 Kasisi (IRE) *(ACStewart)* 8-11 MRoberts (3) (lw: 2nd st: ev ch over 2f out: sn
wknd) .................................................................... 2.7
Shameem (USA) *(MRStoute)* 8-11 WRSwinburn (2) (w'like: scope: hdwy 3f out:
wknd over 1f out) ..................................................... s.h.8
Just Julia *(MRChannon)* 8-11 CRutter (10) (unf: scope: s.s: nrst fin) ............... ½.9
Rose of Macmillion *(MrsBarbaraWaring)* 8-11 NHowe (12) (4th st: wknd over 2f
out) ........................................................................ ½.10
Magnetic Point (USA) *(AAScott)* 8-11 BRaymond (4) (lw: 3rd st: wknd 2f out) .. 2.11
393 Royal Glint *(IABalding)* 8-11 JReid (6) (n.d) ........................................ ¾.12
On the Rampage *(RHannon)* 8-6 ‡5RPerham (9) (unf: scope: n.d) ................. 2½.13
393 Tafrah (IRE) *(MajorWRHern)* 8-11 WCarson (1) (7th st: wknd 3f out) ............. 3½.14

5/6 Shirley Valentine, 5/1 Tafrah (IRE), 6/1 COTTONWOOD(10/1—12/1), 9/1 Shameem (USA)(7/2—10/1),
14/1 Magnetic Point (USA), 16/1 Alessandrina (USA), 20/1 Royal Glint, On the Rampage, 25/1 Fleeting
Rainbow, Just Julia, Kasisi (IRE), 33/1 Ors. CSF £12.24, Tote £6.60: £1.80 £1.20 £7.30 (£5.50). Lord Carnarvon
(WEST ILSLEY) bred by Highclere Stud Ltd. 14 Rn                                      2m 13.27 (8.97)
                                                                     SF—32/29/24/23/21/18

**708**    LBC ANDREW NEIL H'CAP (0-90) £3077.00 (£926.00: £448.00: £209.00)
           1¾am                                                          8-20 (8-24)

2204 **Aude la Belle (FR) (59)** *(MrsAKnight)* 4-8-0 ‡3FNorton (13) (6th st: led & qcknd
clr over 2f out: eased ins fnl f) ................................ —1
Marine Society **(72)** *(PTWalwyn)* 4-9-2 AMunro (12) (bit bkwd: mid div tl styd
on fnl 2f) ............................................................ 2½.2
Zuhal **(59)** *(HThomsonJones)* 4-9-6 RHills (4) (gd hdwy on ins 2f out: nvr nrr) . ½.3
Holy Zeal **(82)** *(DWPArbuthnot)* 6-9-13 TQuinn (5) (b: bit bkwd: wl bhd tl gd
hdwy fnl 2f) ......................................................... ¾.4
4424 Castoret **(72)** (Fav) *(JWHills)* 6-9-3 MHills (9) (hdwy & rdn 3f out: r.o one pce) ¾.5
342 Mahrajan **(65)** *(CJBenstead)* 8-8-10 RCochrane (11) (lw: nrst fin) ............... ½.6
5073 Don't Cry **(53)** *(JDBethell)* 4-7-6(4) ‡5BDoyle (2) (a mid div) ..................... nk.7
3882 Prince Sobur **(60)** *(MBlanshard)* 6-8-5 NCarlisle (8) (nvr nr to chal) ............. hd.8
552* Hello My Darling (IRE) **(70)** *(WRMuir)* 4-9-0 SWhitworth (1) (lw: led 4f; 2nd st:
led over 3f out tl over 2f out) .................................. 1.9
Dutyful **(53)** *(MJHaynes)* 6-7-9(2) ‡3DBiggs (6) (n.d) ............................. 6.10
Mull House **(64)** *(FJO'Mahony)* 5-8-9 WRSwinburn (7) (n.d) ................... hd.11
5695 Sean's Scholar (USA) **(53)** *(CNAllen)* 5-7-12 GBardwell (3) (lw: 4th st: wknd
over 2f out) .......................................................... nk.12
475 Beldale Star **(66)** *(RAkehurst)* 9-8-6 ‡5RPerham (14) (b: 5th st: wknd over 2f out) 2.13
Arrastra **(70)** *(IABalding)* 4-9-0 JReid (10) (3rd st: ev ch over 2f out: wknd qckly) 4.14
Access Ski **(83)** *(RBoss)* 5-10-0 BRaymond (15) (lw: led after 4f tl wknd qckly
over 3f out) ......................................................... 15

LONG HANDICAP: Don't Cry 7-6.

100/30 Castoret, 9/2 Hello My Darling (IRE), 6/1 Sean's Scholar (USA), 7/1 Prince Sobur, 8/1 Beldale Star(op
20/1), 10/1 Mahrajan, 12/1 Arrastra, Don't Cry, 16/1 AUDE LÀ BELLE (FR), 20/1 Ors. CSF £277.61, CT
£5,624.55. Tote £23.80: £4.40 £11.10 £8.20 (£1,242.60). Mrs Val Rapkins (CULLOMPTON) bred by J. P. de
Gaste in France. 15 Rn                                                                3m 5.84 (11.14)
                                                                     SF—10/21/7/29/17/9

T/Plpt: £366.70 (8.55 Tckts).                                                        Hn

# CHESTER (L-H)
## Tuesday, May 5th [Good]
Going Allowance: minus 0.25 sec per fur (F)                          Wind: almost nil

Stalls: low

**709**    LILY AGNES STKS (2-Y.O) £5530.00 (£1660.00: £800.00: £370.00)
           5f 16y                                                       2-15 (2-18)

517* **Lucky Parkes** (Fav) *(JBerry)* 8-6 JCarroll (1) (mde all: r.o wl fnl f) ................. —1
548* Risk Me's Girl *(RHannon)* 8-6 WRSwinburn (3) (chsd wnr: ev ch over 1f out: r.o
nr fin) ................................................................... ¾.2
571* Huffa (USA) *(WJHaggas)* 8-11 MHills (2) (trckd ldrs: chal 1f out: rdn & nt qckn) 1½.3
4022 Moodiesburn (IRE) *(ABailey)* 8-6 AMackay (4) (trckd ldrs: effrt over 1f out: sn
rdn & btn) ............................................................ 1½.4

602* Simmering *(GWragg)* 8-6 RHills (5) (lw: chsd ldrs tl rdn & btn wl over 1f out) .. 3¹/₂.5
484* Bird Hunter *(NACallaghan)* 8-11 MRoberts (6) (dwlt: a outpcd & bhd) ............... 1.6

**Evens** LUCKY PARKES(6/4—10/11), **4/1** Huffa (USA)(5/2—9/2), **6/1** Risk Me's Girl, **7/1** Moodiesburn (IRE), **10/1** Simmering, **20/1** Bird Hunter. CSF £6.89, Tote £1.90: £1.50 £1.90 (£3.20). Mr Joseph Heler (COCKERHAM) bred by Joseph Heler. 6 Rn
61.32 sec (0.72)
SF—52/49/48/37/23/24

**710** CRABWALL MANOR HOTEL STKS (Mdn 3-Y.O) £7096.00 (£2128.00: £1024.00: £472.00)
1¹/₄m 75y
2-45 (2-46)

394 Hatta's Mill *(HRACecil)* 9-0 WRyan (4) (mde all: shkn up ent st: r.o wl) ............. —1
433² Yildiz *(BWHills)* 8-9 MHills (6) (trckd ldrs: effrt over 2f out: ev ch ins fnl f: r.o wl) 1.2
440 Iftakhaar (USA) *(MajorWRHern)* 9-0 WCarson (1) (rn in snatches: a in tch: hdwy
u.p over 2f out: nt qckn ins fnl f) ............. 3.3
509² Set Table (USA) (Fav) *(JHMGosden)* 9-0 SCauthen (5) (lw: trckd wnr: rdn. 2f
out: one pce) ............. ¹/₂.4
Eightandahalf (IRE) *(PWChapple-Hyam)* 9-0 PaulEddery (2) (bit bkwd: hld up:
effrt 3f out: nvr trbld ldrs) ............. 1¹/₂.5
433 American Boogie (FR) *(CEBrittain)* 9-0 MRoberts (3) (lw: a chsng ldrs: rdn over
2f out: no imp) ............. s.h.6
Two and Sixpence (USA) *(BWHills)* 8-9 WRSwinburn (7) (b.off hind: effrt u.p 3f
out: n.d) ............. 8.7
356 Alizarin *(BCMorgan)* 8-9 DMcKeown (8) (a bhd) ............. 12.8

**11/4** Set Table (USA), **3/1** Yildiz(op 2/1), **4/1** HATTA'S MILL, Iftakhaar (USA), **8/1** Eightandahalf (IRE), **20/1** Two and Sixpence (USA), **33/1** American Boogie (FR), **200/1** Alizarin. CSF £14.94, Tote £5.70: £2.00 £1.40 £1.40 (£6.00). Cliveden Stud (NEWMARKET) bred by Cliveden Stud. 8 Rn
2m 13.32 (3.32)
SF—41/34/33/32/29/28

**711** DALHAM CHESTER VASE (Stks) (Gp 3) (3-Y.O) £29808.00 (£11056.40: £5228.20:
£2187.40) 1¹/₂m 66y
3-15 (3-15)

443* **Twist and Turn (111)** (Fav) *(HRACecil)* 8-11 SCauthen (4) (lw: chsd ldr: rdn to
ld ins fnl f: r.o) ............. —1
556⁶ Jape (USA) *(PFICole)* 8-11 AMunro (5) (a.p: effrt 3f out: r.o wl u.p fnl f) ............. ³/₄.2
443 Mack the Knife (113) *(MajorWRHern)* 8-11 WCarson (3) (led: qcknd 4f out: hrd
rdn & hdd ins fnl f: no ex) ............. ³/₄.3
556⁴ Beyton (108) *(RHannon)* 8-11 BRaymond (1) (chsd ldrs tl outpcd 3f out:
styd on wl nr fin) ............. 1¹/₂.4
394* River Defences (USA) *(PWChapple-Hyam)* 8-11 LPiggott (2) (lw: plld hrd: hld
up & bhd: effrt 3f out: sn rdn & no imp) ............. 7.5

**13/8** TWIST AND TURN(5/4—2/1), **9/4** River Defences (USA), **5/1** Mack the Knife, Beyton (USA)(op 8/1), **9/1** Jape (USA). CSF £13.28, Tote £2.50: £1.20 £3.10 (£14.60). Sheikh Mohammed (NEWMARKET) bred by Sheikh Mohammed bin Rashid al Maktoum. 5 Rn
2m 37.13 (0.53)
SF—61/59/57/54/40

**712** TOTE CREDIT TROPHY (H'cap) (0-110) £14020.00 (£4210.00: £2030.00: £940.00)
7f 122y
3-45 (3-49)

**Parliament Piece (94)** *(RMWhitaker)* 6–10-0 ACulhane (7) (lw: a chsng ldrs:
rdn to ld wl ins fnl f: all out) ............. —1
563⁵ Arany (89) *(MHTompkins)* 5–9-9 PRobinson (6) (lw: a cl up: effrt & hung rt over
1f out: r.o nr fin) ............. nk.2
534* Colossus (72) *(CEBrittain)* 4–8-6 MRoberts (4) (lw: led tl hdd wl ins fnl f: kpt on
wl) ............. hd.3
610 Sagebrush Roller (75) *(JWWatts)* 4–8-9 WRSwinburn (9) (hld up & bhd: nt clr
run ent st: hdwy ins fnl f: fin fast) ............. ¹/₂.4
477⁴ Langtry Lady (85) *(MJRyan)* 6–9-2 ‡³DBiggs (1) (hld up: effrt ent st: swtchd ins:
r.o) ............. nk.5
Selaah (93) *(MRStoute)* 5–9-10 ‡³FNorton (8) (bit bkwd: pushed along ¹/₂-wy:
hdwy ent st: no imp) ............. 1¹/₂.6
542² Never so Sure (80) *(ABailey)* 4–9-0 KFallon (3) (hld up: effrt over 2f out: nt qckn) 1¹/₂.7
392⁵ Troupe (83) (bl) (Fav) *(BWHills)* 4–9-3 SCauthen (5) (effrt 3f out: rdn & no imp
fnl 2f) ............. nk.8
563⁴ Corn Futures (85) (bl) *(JPLeigh)* 4–8-12 ‡⁷JWeaver (2) (chsd ldrs tl outpcd fnl
2f) ............. nk.9
Dream Carrier (IRE) (71) *(RHannon)* 4–8-5 RHills (10) (bkwd: prom: rdn ¹/₂-wy:
wknd ent st) ............. 10.10

**100/30** Troupe, **9/2** Colossus, Arany(op 3/1), **6/1** Langtry Lady, **10/1** Never so Sure, **12/1** Sagebrush Roller, Selaah, Corn Futures, **16/1** Dream Carrier (IRE), **20/1** PARLIAMENT PIECE. CSF £98.81, CT £439.59. Tote £27.10: £4.50 £2.20 £1.60 (£81.90). Mr G. A. Farndon (WETHERBY) bred by Patrick Headon. 10 Rn
1m 33.54 (0.84)
SF—72/66/48/49/55/58

**713**      GREAT CHESHIRE H'CAP (0-100) £7356.00 (£2208.00: £1064.00: £492.00)
1¼m 75y                                                                4-15 (4-18)

422 **Modesto (USA) (66)** *(KOCunningham-Brown)* 4-7-9(5) ‡3DBiggs (8) (b: lw: cl
up: led over 6f out: styd on wl fnl 2f) ............................................ —1
479 **Double Echo (IRE) (72)** *(JDBethell)* 4-8-4 AMunro (3) (a.p: effrt & ch 2f out:
styd on nr fin) ...................................................................... 1½.2
616 **Rose Glen (64)** *(ABailey)* 6—7-7(3) ‡3FNorton (7) (a chsng ldrs: ev ch over 1f out:
nt qckn) ............................................................................ hd.3
431 **Moonlight Quest (76)** *(BHanbury)* 4-8-8 MHills (2) (b: b.hind: bit bkwd: hdwy &
prom 4f out: rdn & no imp fnl 2f) ............................................. 3½.4
504* **Katy's Lad (74)** (Fav) *(BAMcMahon)* 5-8-6 TQuinn (4) (lw: led tl hdd over 6f out:
chsd ldrs tl rdn & btn 2f out) ................................................. 3½.5
479⁵ **Green's Ferneley (IRE) (95)** *(RCharlton)* 4—9-13 SCauthen (1) (chsd ldrs tl rdn
over 3f out: sn outpcd) ........................................................ nk.6
492³ **Two Left Feet (95)** *(SirMarkPrescott)* 5—9-13 GDuffield (6) (lw: bhd: effrt 4f out:
no imp) ............................................................................ 2½.7
**Andrath (IRE) (81)** *(CEBrittain)* 4-8-13 MRoberts (9) (bit bkwd: bhd: hrd drvn
appr st: n.d) ...................................................................... 3.8
485 **Jazilah (FR) (64)** *(MPNaughton)* 4—7-10 LCharnock (5) (outpcd 5f out: a bhd) 2½.9
368 **Admiralty Way (61)** *(MO'Neill)* 6—7-7 AMackay (10) (lw: prom tl wknd u.p 4f out:
sn bhd) ........................................................................... s.h.10
LONG HANDICAP: Modesto (USA) 7-3, Rose Glen 7-6, Admiralty Way 7-0.

**4/1** Katy's Lad, **9/2** Green's Ferneley (IRE), **11/2** Double Echo (IRE), **7/1** Admiralty Way, **15/2** Moonlight Quest, **8/1** Two Left Feet, **10/1** Rose Glen, **14/1** Andrath (IRE), **20/1** MODESTO (USA) & Ors. CSF £112.51, CT £1,056.00. Tote £31.30: £5.20 £2.10 £2.50 (£66.80). Mr D. Bass (STOCKBRIDGE) bred by Rhydian Morgan-Jones in USA. 10 Rn
2m 10.93 (0.93)
SF—46/52/40/48/39/59

**714**      PRINCE OF WALES H'CAP (3-Y.O) (0-105) £7044.00 (£2112.00: £1016.00: £468.00)
5f 16y                                                                4-45 (4-46)

445 **Cindora (IRE) (90)** *(MHTompkins)* 8-10 PRobinson (2) (chsd ldrs: led ins fnl f:
r.o u.p) ........................................................................... —1
559* **Freddie Lloyd (USA) (93)** *(NACallaghan)* 8-6 ‡7JTate (6) (swtg: chsd ldrs: racd
wd: hdwy & ev ch ins fnl f: kpt on) ......................................... hd.2
503² **Hazm (USA) (88)** (Fav) *(HThomsonJones)* 8-8 RHills (8) (lw: outpcd tl hdwy ent
st: styd on fnl f) ................................................................ 1½.3
445 **Walking Possession (81)** (bl) *(RBoss)* 8-1 MRoberts (5) (lw: w ldrs: hrd rdn over
1f out: nt qckn) ................................................................. ¾.4
454 **Castlerea Lad (79)** *(RHollinshead)* 7-13 AMunro (9) (bit bkwd: s.i.s: outpcd &
bhd tl r.o wl fnl f) ............................................................. 1½.5
506 **Soba Guest (IRE) (79)** *(JBerry)* 7-13 LCharnock (7) (lw: mde most tl hdd ins fnl
f: no ex) ......................................................................... 1½.6
386⁵ **Tino Tere (96)** *(JBerry)* 9-2 JCarroll (3) (lw: chsd ldrs: n.m.r ent st: sn btn) ....... ½.7
527⁴ **Regal Chimes (101)** *(BAMcMahon)* 9-7 TQuinn (4) (disp ld 3f: sn rdn & btn) ..... 5.8

**4/1** Hazm (USA), **9/2** Tino Tere(op 11/4), **11/2** Walking Possession, Soba Guest (IRE), **7/1** Freddie Lloyd (USA), Regal Chimes, **15/2** CINDORA (IRE), **14/1** Castlerea Lad. CSF £51.18, CT £214.64. Tote £9.60: £2.40 £2.20 £1.60 (£24.50). Mark Tompkins Racing (NEWMARKET) bred by P. Myerscough in Ireland. 8 Rn
61.51 sec (0.91)
SF—53/48/44/34/26/20

T/Trio: Race 4: £118.50 (20.1 Tckts). T/Jkpt: Not won; £39,484.55 to Chester 6/5/92. T/Plpt: £85.10 (133.94 Tckts).
AA

# CHESTER (L-H)
## Wednesday, May 6th [Good]
Going Allowance: minus 0.20 sec per fur (F)          Wind: fresh across    *Flag start: 4th race*

Stalls: low

**715**      SEFTON STKS (Mdn 3-Y.O.F) £6732.00 (£2016.00: £968.00: £444.00)
7f 122y                                                               2-15 (2-18)

502 **Scarlatine (IRE)** *(JHMGosden)* 8-11 RCochrane (3) (lw: a.p: led over 3f out to
1f out: rallied u.p to ld nr fin) ............................................. —1

434² Petal Girl (Fav) *(RHannon)* 8-11 LPiggott (2) (hmpd after s: hdwy & 2nd st: rdn to ld 1f out: hdd & no ex cl home) .................... hd.2
393 Anima *(MajorWRHern)* 8-11 MRoberts (6) (led 4f: 3rd & btn st) .................... 15.3
577⁶ Mainly Me **(82)** *(MrsJCecil)* 8-11 PaulEddery (4) (chsd ldr to ½-wy: 4th & wkng st) .................... 1½.4
Last Appearance *(MBell)* 8-11 MHills (5) (b.off hind: prom: pushed along ½-wy: sn btn: 5th st) .................... 2½.5
302⁵ Chatino **(72)** *(CEBrittain)* 8-11 SCauthen (1) (sn outpcd & bhd: 6th st: t.o) .................... 12.6

*Stewards Enquiry: Obj. to Scarlatine (IRE) by Piggott overruled. Paul Eddery suspended 15-18/5/92 (careless riding).*

**11/8** Petal Girl, **9/2** Last Appearance(8/1—4/1), **11/2** Mainly Me, **6/1** SCARLATINE (IRE)(op 4/1), **8/1** Chatino, **12/1** Anima. CSF £13.69, Tote £7.30: £2.50 £1.40 (£4.90). Lord Derby (NEWMARKET) bred by Rathbarry Stud in Ireland. 6 Rn　　　　　　　　　　　　　　　　　　　　　　　　　　1m 33.37 (0.67)
SF—64/63/18/14/5/–

---

**716**　　CHESHIRE REGIMENT H'CAP (3-Y.O) (0-105) £7148.00 (£2144.00: £1032.00: £476.00)
　　　　1½m 66y　　　　　　　　　　　　　　　　　　　　　　2-45 (2-46)

(Weights raised 4 lb)

471⁶ **Sastago (USA) (81)** *(JHMGosden)* 9-4 MHills (5) (mde all: sn clr: hrd rdn fnl f: hld on gamely) .................... —1
230* Touch Paper (USA) (Fav) *(BWHills)* 9-1 SCauthen (4) (lw: stdd s: wnt 2nd 3f out: ev ch fnl f: unable qckn) .................... ½.2
558⁶ Major's Law (IRE) **(77)** *(CEBrittain)* 9-0 MRoberts (1) (chsd wnr: rdn 4f out: 3rd st: kpt on one pce fnl f) .................... 2½.3
464³ Mad Militant (IRE) **(84)** *(RHollinshead)* 9-7 WRyan (3) (lw: hld up & bhd: hdwy 3f out: 4th st: nvr able to chal) .................... 2.4
440^ Tynron Doon **(70)** *(DJWintle)* 8-7 AMunro (2) (h: lost tch ½-wy: 5th & t.o st) ,,, 30.5

**10/11** Touch Paper (USA), **4/1** Major's Law (IRE)(op 7/1), SASTAGO (USA), **7/1** Mad Militant (IRE), **10/1** Tynron Doon. CSF £8.09, Tote £6.90: £2.20 £1.40 (£3.60). Mr K. Abdulla (NEWMARKET) bred by Oakcliff Thoroughbred Bloodstock Ltd '85 in USA. 5 Rn　　　　　　　　　　　　　　2m 40.3 (3.7)
SF—43/39/33/34/–

---

**717**　　SHADWELL STUD CHESHIRE OAKS (Stks) (listed race) (3-Y.O.F) £21996.25 (£6595.00: £3172.50: £1461.25)　　1m 3f 79y　　　　　　　　　3-15 (3-15)

**Aquamarine** *(BWHills)* 8-11 PaulEddery (4) (lw: chsd ldr: hrd drvn 4f out: 2nd st: led ins fnl f: r.o) .................... —1
434* Juniper Berry (IRE) *(PWChapple-Hyam)* 8-11 LPiggott (5) (hld up: effrt & 4th st: n.m.r & swtchd ins fnl f: fin fast) .................... ¾.2
433⁴ Tradition *(MajorWRHern)* 8-11 AMunro (5) (lw: led tl hdd ins fnl f: r.o) .................... nk.3
429 Midnight Air (USA) **(114)** (Fav) *(HRACecil)* 8-11 MRoberts (3) (hld up: hdwy & 3rd st: one pce fnl f) .................... 1½.4
374* St James's Antigua (IRE) **(76)** *(WJHaggas)* 8-11 MHills (2) (lw: chsd ldrs: lost pl & 5th st: sn bhd) .................... 12.5

*Stewards Enquiry: Munro suspended 15-18/5/92 (excessive use of whip).*

**4/6** Midnight Air (USA), **9/2** Juniper Berry (IRE), **8/1** AQUAMARINE(op 5/1), **9/1** St James's Antigua (IRE), **10/1** Tradition. CSF £35.83, Tote £8.50: £2.60 £1.50 (£14.60). Mr K. Abdulla (LAMBOURN) bred by Juddmonte Farms. 5 Rn　　　　　　　　　　　　　　　　　　　　　　2m 25.79 (1.79)
SF—57/55/54/51/27

---

**718**　　LADBROKE CHESTER CUP (H'cap) (0-115) £19250.00 (£5750.00: £2750.00: £1250.00)
　　　　2¼m 117y　　　　　　　　　　　　　　　　　　　3-45 (3-47)

(Weights raised 4 lb)

475⁴ **Welshman (58)** *(MBlanshard)* 6—7-8 JQuinn (6) (a.p: led over 5f out: styd on strly) .................... —1
475² Bardolph (USA) **(77)** *(PFICole)* 5–8-13 TQuinn (3) (b.off hind: a.p: 2nd st: hrd rdn & kpt on ins fnl f) .................... 3.2
442² Line Drummer (USA) **(74)** *(PAKelleway)* 4–8-3 ‡3DBiggs (9) (b: chsd ldrs: 3rd & ev ch ent st: unable qckn fnl f) .................... 1½.3
234³ Tamarpour (USA) **(75)** (v) *(MCPipe)* 5–8-11 MRoberts (7) (chsd ldrs: effrt & 5th st: nvr able to chal) .................... 6.4
467⁴ Beau Quest **(57)** (v) *(RMWhitaker)* 5–7-4 ‡3JFanning (11) (chsd ldrs: effrt & ev ch 4f out: 4th & wkng st) .................... 3½.5
569² Our Aisling **(68)** *(SGNorton)* 4–8-0 JLowe (5) (lw: bhd: hdwy 4f out: nvr nrr) .................... ¾.6

552⁴ Star Player **(88)** (Fav) *(RJBaker)* 6–9–10 RCochrane (16) (mid div: effrt 7f out: nvr trbld ldrs) ............................................................ 1½.7
569* Good Hand (USA) **(85)** (v) *(JWWatts)* 6–9–7 NConnorton (4) (lw: hld up: hdwy ½-wy: 6th st: sn rdn & wknd) ............................ nk.8
388* Go South **(74)** (bl) *(JRJenkins)* 8–8–10 NCarlisle (8) (nvr bttr than mid div) ........ 2.9
513 Beebob **(76)** *(MCPipe)* 4–8–8 PaulEddery (17) (lw: a in rr) ............................ 1½.10
632² Farsi **(76)** *(RHollinshead)* 4–8–8 WRyan (15) (lw: a bhd) ........................ 3½.11
569⁴ Steppey Lane **(68)** *(WWHaigh)* 7–8–4 DMcKeown (18) (a bhd) ............... 2.12
Golden **(60)** *(CWCElsey)* 5–7–10 LCharnock (2) (led over 8f: wknd 7f out: t.o) 25.13
507* Moving Out **(82)** *(SirMarkPrescott)* 4–9–0 AMunro (1) (led 10f out tl over 5f out: sn lost tch: t.o) .......................................................... 1.14
French Ivy (USA) **(88)** *(MrsALMKing)* 5–9–10 KFallon (14) (b: a bhd: t.o) ....... 2½.15
Dreaming Star **(60)** *(LJCodd)* 7–7–5(3) ‡5NKennedy (10) (b: lost pl ½-wy: t.o) 25.16
LONG HANDICAP: Dreaming Star 6-4.

**6/1** Star Player(4/1—13/2), **7/1** Tamarpour (USA), Bardolph (USA), **8/1** Go South, **9/1** Moving Out, Our Aisling, Farsi, **11/1** WELSHMAN, Good Hand (USA), **14/1** Beebob, **18/1** Line Drummer (USA), **20/1** Steppey Lane, Beau Quest, **33/1** French Ivy (USA), **50/1** Golden, **200/1** Dreaming Star. CSF £80.41, CT £1,135.41. Tote £7.80; £1.50 £2.50 £5.10 £1.80 (£32.80). Mr Brian Oxton (UPPER LAMBOURN) bred by Pinfold Stud and Farms Ltd. 16 Rn
3m 57.96 (U1.04)
SF—53/69/57/59/33/42/64

**719** SHEPHERD CONSTRUCTION H'CAP (3-Y.O.F) (0-100) £7304.00 (£2192.00: £1056.00: £488.00) **6f 18y** 4-15 (4-20)

408⁴ **Sharling (69)** *(JHMGosden)* 7-10(2) AMcGlone (3) (lw: chsd ldrs: hrd rdn wl over 1f out: r.o stly to ld ins fnl f) ....................................... —1
587² Debsy Do (USA) **(68)** (Jt-Fav) *(SGNorton)* 7-6(2) ‡3FNorton (6) (lw: a.p: led over 1f out tl ins fnl f) ......................................... 2.2
My Abbey **(73)** *(EJAlston)* 8-0 PBurke (1) (led tl over 1f out: r.o one pce) ........ 1½.3
452⁴ Amoureuse (IRE) **(70)** *(EHOwenjun)* 7-6(4) ‡5BDoyle (4) (hdwy ½-wy: r.o wl ins fnl f: nvr nrr) ............................................................ 1½.4
Indian Endeavour **(76)** *(RGuest)* 8-3 MRoberts (2) (chsd ldrs over 4f) ............. ½.5
576 Thrie-Na-Helah (IRE) **(77)** *(RMWhitaker)* 8-4 ACulhane (10) (bhd: hdwy over 1f out: nvr plcd to chal) ............................................ 1.6
495* Bunty Boo **(84)** (Jt-Fav) *(BAMcMahon)* 8-11 JLowe (11) (s.i.s: hdwy after 2f: nt rch ldrs) .................................................................. 1½.7
Nur (USA) **(78)** *(HThomsonJones)* 8-5 RHills (9) (nvr nr to chal) ................. 1½.8
527² Arctic Appeal (IRE) **(94)** *(JBerry)* 9-7 JCarroll (8) (outpcd: a bhd) .............. 1½.9
614³ Tagetes **(66)** *(JPearce)* 7-0 ‡7CHawksley (5) (in rr: rn v.wd ent st: a bhd) ........ 2.10
Pink'n Black (IRE) **(67)** *(GBlum)* 7-8 JQuinn (7) (chsd ldrs to ½-wy: sn lost pl: t.o) ........................................................................ 4.11
LONG HANDICAP: Debsy Do (USA) 7-6, Amoureuse (IRE) 6-9, Tagetes 7-6.

**5/1** Debsy Do (USA), Bunty Boo, **11/2** Arctic Appeal (IRE), **13/2** SHARLING, **7/1** My Abbey, **17/2** Indian Endeavour, **10/1** Thrie-Na-Helah (IRE), **14/1** Nur (USA), **16/1** Pink'n Black (IRE), Tagetes, **20/1** Amoureuse (IRE). CSF £35.98, CT £213.59. Tote £9.10: £2.80 £2.10 £2.20 (£21.50). Mr C. M. Watt (NEWMARKET) bred by Highclere Stud Ltd. 11 Rn
1m 14.43 (1.13)
SF—35/23/25/11/20/17

**720** RED DRAGON STKS (Mdn 2-Y.O.C.& G) £3590.00 (£1070.00: £510.00: £230.00) **5f 16y** 4-45 (4-48)

555⁶ **Elle Shaped (IRE)** (Fav) *(RHannon)* 9-0 MRoberts (4) (lw: mde all: clr fnl f: unchal) ................................................................. —1
514³ Daytona Beach (IRE) **(IRE)** *(RHollinshead)* 9-0 KDarley (7) (lw: in tch: effrt & rdn 2f out: kpt on fnl f) ...................................... 7.2
659⁴ Hod-Mod (IRE) *(ABailey)* 9-0 AMackay (8) (lw: s.s: bhd & outpcd tl r.o strly ins fnl f) ............................................................ 2½.3
Club Verge (IRE) *(EJAlston)* 9-0 KFallon (2) (cmpt: bkwd: s.s: wl bhd tl r.o ins fnl f) ........................................................................ nk.4
361 Tom Piper *(JBerry)* 9-0 JCarroll (3) (w wnr tl wknd wl over 1f out) ................... 1½.5
Cardinal Dogwood (USA) *(MBrittain)* 9-0 MWigham (1) (w'like: scope: bkwd: outpcd: sn wl bhd: t.o) ............................................... ½.6
Calcutta Flyer (IRE) *(PWChapple-Hyam)* 9-0 LPiggott (6) (lengthy: unf: scope: bit bkwd: chsd ldrs over 3f) ....................................... nk.7
287 Cracker Jack (bl) *(TFairhurst)* 8-11 ‡3JFanning (5) (lw: chsd ldrs 3f: wknd qckly) 2½.8

**9/4** ELLE SHAPED (IRE), **3/1** Daytona Beach (IRE), Calcutta Flyer (IRE), **8/1** Hod-Mod (IRE), Tom Piper, **14/1** Cardinal Dogwood (USA), **16/1** Club Verge (IRE), **25/1** Cracker Jack. CSF £9.47, Tote £3.40: £1.40 £1.40 £1.70 (£4.20). Mr J. E. Marsden (MARLBOROUGH) bred by Dan Daly in Ireland. 8 Rn   62.06 sec (1.46)
SF—49/21/11/10/4/2

T/Trio: 4th race: £123.70 (30.9 Tckts). T/Jkpt: £50,972.50 (1.1 Tckts). T/Plpt: £62.90 (217.15 Tckts).   IM

# CHESTER (L-H)
## Thursday, May 7th [Good to firm]
Going Allowance: minus 0.45 sec per fur (F)        Wind: mod half against

Stalls: low

### 721
E.B.F. SCEPTRE STKS (Mdn 2-Y.O.F) £4272.50 (£1280.00: £615.00: £282.50)
**5f 16y**        2-15 (2-24)

| | | |
|---|---|---|
| 548² | Holly Golightly (Fav) *(RHannon)* 8-11 MRoberts (3) (a.p: led appr fnl f: r.o wl) . | —1 |
| 365² | Magic Pearl *(EJAlston)* 8-11 LPiggott (2) (led tl over 1f out: rdn & no ex nr fin) | 1¹⁄₂.2 |
| 476³ | Hung Parliament *(BWHills)* 8-11 MHills (6) (chsd ldrs: kpt on u.p ins fnl f) | 1.3 |
| | Polar Moon *(BAMcMahon)* 8-11 AMunro (1) (leggy: scope: bit bkwd: s.s: bhd & outpcd tl r.o strly ins fnl f) | ¹⁄₂.4 |
| 548⁴ | Margaret's Gift *(JBerry)* 8-11 PatEddery (4) (spd over 3f) | ³⁄₄.5 |
| | General Chase *(RJHolder)* 8-11 GCarter (5) (small: cmpt: bkwd: sn outpcd: a bhd) | 8.6 |

*Stewards Enquiry: Pat Eddery fined £235 under Rule 151 (ii) (failure to ensure best possible placing).*

**10/11** HOLLY GOLIGHTLY, **4/1** Margaret's Gift, **9/2** Hung Parliament(op 11/4), **8/1** Magic Pearl, **12/1** Polar Moon(op 8/1), **33/1** General Chase. CSF £8.03, Tote £2.00: £1.40 £2.10 (£4.60). Mr Victor Behrens (MARLBOROUGH) bred by Thoroughbred Stock Investors Ltd. 6 Rn   61.62 sec (1.02)
SF—32/26/22/20/17/–

### 722
DEE STKS (listed race) (3-Y.O) £23377.50 (£7020.00: £3385.00: £1567.50)
**1¹⁄₄m 75y**        2-45 (2-48)

| | | |
|---|---|---|
| 404⁴ | My Memoirs (97) *(RHannon)* 9-2 JReid (2) (led over 3f: 6th st: r.o strly ins fnl f to ld last stride) | —1 |
| 500* | Profusion *(PFICole)* 8-12 AMunro (5) (lw: hld up: stdy hdwy 4f out: led ent st tl ct cl home) | s.h.2 |
| | Torrey Canyon (USA) (110) (v) (Fav) *(RCharlton)* 9-2 PatEddery (7) (lw: led over 6f out to 2f out: kpt on u.p) | 1¹⁄₂.3 |
| 556 | John Rose (108) *(PAKelleway)* 8-12 BRaymond (6) (bit bkwd: chsd ldr: effrt & 3rd st: one pce) | 1¹⁄₂.4 |
| | For Reg (IRE) (98) *(ACStewart)* 8-12 MRoberts (1) (lw: chsd ldrs: 5th st: no hdwy appr fnl f) | 2¹⁄₂.5 |
| 474⁶ | Wesaam (USA) (102) *(MajorWRHern)* 9-2 WCarson (4) (lw: w ldrs tl 4th & wkng st) | 6.6 |
| | Muharib (USA) (102) *(NACallaghan)* 9-2 LPiggott (3) (b.nr fore: bkwd: chsd ldrs 7f: wknd & 7th st: t.o) | 20.7 |

**11/4** Torrey Canyon (USA)(op 7/4), **3/1** Profusion(tchd 9/2), **9/2** Wesaam (USA), **11/2** Muharib (USA), **8/1** For Reg (IRE), **10/1** MY MEMOIRS, **16/1** John Rose. CSF £36.62, Tote £13.50: £3.70 £2.10 (£22.90). Amity Finance Ltd (MARLBOROUGH) bred by Mrs S. Smart and Mrs J. J. Hindley. 7 Rn   2m 9.29 (U.71)
SF—62/57/58/51/46/38

### 723
GRAHAMS MACHINERY SALES H'CAP (0-105) £6940.00 (£2080.00: £1000.00: £460.00)
**5f 16y**        3-15 (3-16)

| | | |
|---|---|---|
| 550 | Love Legend (84) (bl) *(DWPArbuthnot)* 7-9-2 AMunro (4) (hld up & bhd: hdwy wl over 1f out: led ins fnl f: sn clr) | —1 |
| 629⁶ | Cronk's Courage (80) (v) *(EJAlston)* 6-8-12 LPiggott (10) (led tl ins fnl f) | 1¹⁄₂.2 |
| 629⁵ | Petraco (IRE) (78) (Jt-Fav) *(LJCodd)* 4-8-10 WRSwinburn (5) (lw: hdwy 2f out: ev ch & hung rt 1f out: rdn & r.o) | hd.3 |
| | Never in the Red (96) (bl) *(JBerry)* 4-10-0 GCarter (8) (lw: a.p: jnd ldr ent st: unable qckn fnl f) | 2.4 |
| | Glenstal Princess (68) *(RHollinshead)* 5-8-0 RHills (6) (chsd ldrs: rdn wl over 1f out: sn btn) | 2.5 |
| 570⁵ | Crystal Jack (FR) (72) (v) *(FHLee)* 4-8-4 MRoberts (9) (chsd ldrs: ev ch over 1f out: wknd ins fnl f) | ¹⁄₂.6 |

506* Breezy Day **(80)** *(BAMcMahon)* 6–8-12 BRaymond (1) (lw: nvr gng wl: a bhd) .. **1.7**
550³ Macfarlane **(78)** (Jt-Fav) *(MJFetherston-Godley)* 4–8-10 WCarson (3) (a bhd) . **nk.8**
613* Sir Tasker **(79)** *(JLHarris)* 4–8-11 (7x) PatEddery (7) (gd spd over 3f: eased whn btn) ........................................................................ **1½.9**
Darussalam **(66)** *(RLee)* 5–7-12 CRutter (2) (b: spd 3f: sn lost tch) .................. **1.10**

**4/1** Petraco (IRE), Macfarlane, **5/1** Breezy Day, **7/1** LOVE LEGEND, **8/1** Crystal Jack (FR), **9/1** Sir Tasker, **10/1** Never in the Red, **14/1** Cronk's Courage, Darussalam, **20/1** Glenstal Princess. CSF £86.02, CT £403.09. Tote £7.70: £2.40 £3.40 £2.00 (£54.40). Mr George S. Thompson (COMPTON) bred by Hesmonds Stud Ltd. 10 Rn
60.53 sec (U.07)
SF—58/48/45/55/19/21

**724**    ORMONDE E.B.F. STKS (Gp 3)   £29421.00 (£10954.30: £5214.65: £2220.05)
1m 5f 89y                                                      3-45 (3-46)

390* **Saddlers' Hall (IRE) (119)** (Fav) *(MRStoute)* 4–9-2 PatEddery (6) (lw: a gng wl: led on bit over 2f out: sn clr: canter) ................................. **—1**
608 Arcadian Heights **(103)** *(GWragg)* 4–8-11 WRSwinburn (7) (lw: s.i.s: sn rcvrd: led 5f out tl over 2f out: 5th st: rallied u.p nr fin) ................ **10.2**
608⁵ Parting Moment (USA) **(102)** *(IABalding)* 5–8-11 BRaymond (5) (lw: hld up: effrt & 3rd st: styd on one pce fnl f) ......................... **1½.3**
435 Regent's Folly (IRE) **(96)** *(WJarvis)* 4–8-8 AMunro (1) (swtg: hld up & bhd: gd hdwy 4f out: 2nd st: sn outpcd) ........................................ **hd.4**
431 Pharly Story **(93)** *(MCPipe)* 4–8-11 LPiggott (9) (hld up & bhd: hdwy 3f out: 4th st: no imp) ........................................................ **nk.5**
442* Close Friend (IRE) **(95)** *(BWHills)* 4–8-11 MHills (4) (b.off fore: prom tl wknd & 6th st: t.o) ................................................. **12.6**
Dowland (USA) *(MKauntze,Ireland)* 4–8-11 WJO'Connor (3) (led over 8f: wknd qckly: 7th st: t.o) ...................................... **30.7**

**4/11** SADDLERS' HALL (IRE), **9/1** Arcadian Heights, Close Friend (IRE), **10/1** Dowland (USA), **14/1** Pharly Story, **16/1** Parting Moment (USA), **50/1** Regent's Folly (IRE). CSF £4.83, Tote £1.50: £1.30 £2.10 (£4.70). Lord Weinstock (NEWMARKET) bred by Ballymacoll Stud Farm Ltd in Ireland. 7 Rn                     2m 48.38 (U1.02)
SF—52/27/24/20/22/–

**725**    WYNN H'CAP (3-Y.O) (0-100) £5725.00 (£1720.00: £830.00: £385.00)
7f 2y                                                           4-15 (4-18)
(Weights raised 15 lb)
341 **Mizaaya (81)** (Fav) *(MRStoute)* 9-3 PatEddery (3) (hld up: hdwy 3f out: 3rd st: qcknd to ld ins fnl f) ............................................. **—1**
464 By Hand **(75)** *(WJHaggas)* 8-11 MHills (5) (hld up: hdwy & 2nd st: led 1f out: sn hdd: no ch w wnr) ........................................................ **2.2**
576² Pageboy **(85)** *(PCHaslam)* 9-7 LPiggott (1) (led to 1f out: r.o one pce) ........... **3½.3**
576⁴ Eastleigh **(69)** *(RHollinshead)* 8-5 AMunro (6) (hdwy u.p ent st: r.o ins fnl f: nvr nr to chal) .......................................................... **4.4**
554⁵ Jairzinho (USA) **(83)** (bl) *(RHannon)* 9-5 MRoberts (4) (chsd ldrs: 4th st: wknd over 1f out) ............................................................ **1½.5**
576 Sammy Slew (USA) **(74)** (v) *(SGNorton)* 8-10 BRaymond (7) (bdly hmpd after 2f: a bhd: 6th st) ........................................................ **12.6**
464 Mindomica **(70)** *(MBell)* 8-6 RHills (2) (chsd ldr over 5f: 5th & btn whn hmpd ent st) ........................................................................... **nk.7**
521* Pridian (IRE) **(77)** *(GWragg)* 8-13 WRSwinburn (8) (broke leg & fell after 2f: dead) ................................................................ **0**

**5/2** MIZAAYA, **5/1** Pridian (IRE), Pageboy, **13/2** By Hand, **15/2** Sammy Slew (USA), **8/1** Eastleigh, **9/1** Jairzinho (USA), **10/1** Mindomica. CSF £18.00, CT £68.85. Tote £3.60: £1.50 £2.00 £1.70 (£14.60). Maktoum Al Maktoum (NEWMARKET) bred by Cheveley Park Stud Ltd. 8 Rn           1m 25.27 (0.85 under best; U.93)
SF—70/58/57/29/38/–

**726**    EATON H'CAP (0-105) £7408.00 (£2224.00: £1072.00: £496.00)
1½m 66y                                                         4-45 (4-46)

513* **Matador (USA) (90)** *(RCharlton)* 5–9-4 PatEddery (5) (lw: led 1f: 2nd st: led over 1f out: r.o wl) ............................................... **—1**
Mellaby (USA) **(96)** *(MRStoute)* 4–9-10 WRSwinburn (4) (hld up & bhd: hdwy 3f out: 3rd st: r.o strly fnl f) ................................. **¾.2**
435 Gondolier **(84)** *(HRACecil)* 4–8-12 MRoberts (1) (led after 1f: sn hdd: led 4f out tl over 1f out: unable qckn) ................................. **1½.3**
442 Libk **(100)** *(HThomsonJones)* 4–10-0 RHills (7) (chsd ldrs: 4th & rdn st: sn btn) **7.4**

435⁵ Dom Wac **(78)** (Fav) *(MBell)* 4–8–6 MHills (3) (lw: hld up: hdwy 4f out: 5th st: nt rch ldrs) ............................................................................................................. 6.5
442⁵ Seal Indigo (IRE) **(91)** *(RHannon)* 4–9-5 JReid (10) (hld up: effrt 4f out: 6th st: nvr nr to chal) ..................................................................................................... 4.6
513³ Clear Light **(67)** (bl) *(CASmith)* 5–7-4⁽²⁾ ‡5DHarrison (8) (led after 2f to 4f out: wknd over 2f out) .................................................................................................. 3.7
590 Mahaasin **(69)** *(LJCodd)* 4–7–6⁽⁴⁾ ‡5NKennedy (9) (lw: lost pl & rdn ¹/₂-wy: sn bhd) ³/₄.8
Thomas Leng **(65)** *(MBrittain)* 7–7-7 GBardwell (6) (prom tl wknd 2f out: virtually p.u fnl f) ..................................................................................................... ³/₄.9
LONG HANDICAP: Clear Light 7-4, Mahaasin 6-6, Thomas Leng 7-5.

**100/30** Dom Wac, **7/2** MATADOR (USA), **9/2** Seal Indigo (IRE), **11/2** Gondolier, **8/1** Mellaby (USA)(op 5/1), Clear Light, **10/1** Libk, **16/1** Thomas Leng, **33/1** Mahaasin. CSF £29.39, CT £138.64. Tote £3.40: £1.50 £3.00 £2.00 (£16.00). Mr K. Abdulla (BECKHAMPTON) bred by Flaxman Holdings Limited in USA. 9 Rn
2m 34.75 (1.85)
SF—67/71/56/58/24/29

T/Trio: Race 3: £110.10 (24.3 Tckts). T/Jkpt: Not won; £5,468.75 to Lingfield 8/5/92. T/Plpt: £135.10 (92.65 Tckts).                                                                                         IM

## 620— **SALISBURY (R-H)**
### Wednesday, May 6th [Good]
Going Allowance: 5f-6f: 0.05 sec (G); Rest: minus 0.10 sec (F)                     Wind: nil

Stalls: high

**727**     WARMINSTER STKS (Mdn 3-Y,0) £2422.00 (£672.00: £322.00)   **6f**   2-00 (2-01)

620² **Venture Capitalist (89)** (Fav) *(RHannon)* 9-0 JReid (11) (a.p: led 3f out: rdn out) —1
Lady Roxanne *(LordHuntingdon)* 8-4 ‡5DHarrison (10) (hdwy 3f out: r.o wl ins fnl f) ..................................................................................................................... ¹/₂.2
Desert Dagger *(MajorWRHern)* 9-0 WRSwinburn (13) (unf: a.p: rdn 2f out: r.o ins fnl f) ................................................................................................................. hd.3
Super Serenade *(GBBalding)* 9-0 JWilliams (7) (bit bkwd: hdwy fnl 2f: nvr nrr) 2¹/₂.4
Red Sombrero **(59)** *(LGCottrell)* 9-0 TRogers (2) (nvr nr to chal) .....................:. 1.5
238 Hi-Tech Honda (IRE) *(CEBrittain)* 9-0 LDettori (4) (prom over 3f) ................. 2¹/₂.6
Beyond the Moon (IRE) *(MJFetherston-Godley)* 8-9 GCarter (14) (no hdwy fnl 2f) 2.7
Our Eddie *(BGubby)* 9-0 NAdams (6) (wl bhd tl sme late hdwy) ......................... 1.8
408⁴ Oh so Rosy *(PFICole)* 8-9 CRutter (12) (b.hind: led 3f) .................................. 4.9
Red Mirage (IRE) *(MMcCormack)* 8-9 WNewnes (8) (str: a bhd) ....................... hd.10
Jalore *(PABlockley)* 9-0 GHind (3) (lt-f: s.s: a bhd) ............................................ 1.11
Call to the Bar (IRE) *(CGCox)* 9-0 AClark (5) (leggy: a bhd) ............................ 1.12
Family Rose *(GHEden)* 9-0 KGing (1) (bit bkwd: s.s: a bhd) ........................... 2¹/₂.13
466⁶ Secret Picnic (USA) *(BHanbury)* 9-0 BRaymond (9) (spd 3f) ......................... nk.14

**8/11** VENTURE CAPITALIST, **7/1** Oh so Rosy, **10/1** Hi-Tech Honda (IRE), Desert Dagger(op 4), **12/1** Beyond the Moon (IRE)(10/1—16/1), Secret Picnic (USA), **16/1** Red Sombrero(12/1—20/1), Lady Roxanne(op 10/1), Red Mirage (IRE)(12/1—20/1), **20/1** Super Serenade(op 12/1), **33/1** Our Eddie, **50/1** Ors. CSF £16.29, Tote £1.80: £1.10 £6.10 £2.50 (£39.70). Mr D. K. Harris (MARLBOROUGH) bred by Brook Bloodstock Plc. 14 Rn
1m 16.68 (4.38)
SF—18/6/15/5/1/—

**728**     WEBSTERS YORKSHIRE BITTER H'CAP (3-Y.O) (0-75) £2889.00 (£804.00: £387.00)
**1m 1f 209y**     2-30 (2-36)

606* **In the Picture (IRE) (76)** (Fav) *(RHannon)* 9-8 (5x) WCarson (2) (hld up: hdwy 3f out: led over 1f out: r.o wl) ......................................................................... —1
395 Vivitz (IRE) **(59)** (v) *(GBBalding)* 8-5⁽¹⁾ JWilliams (18) (a.p: led 4f out tl over 1f out) ....................................................................................................................... 3¹/₂.2
412³ Bayaireg (USA) **(72)** *(AAScott)* 9-4 WRSwinburn (6) (hdwy 5f out: ev ch over 1f out: nt qckn) ................................................................................................. nk.3
Pride of Britain (CAN) **(49)** *(LGCottrell)* 7-9 RFox (14) (chsd ldr 5f: rallied over 1f out: r.o ins fnl f) ........................................................................................... s.h.4
242 Freephone (CAN) **(59)** (bl) *(JWHills)* 8-5⁽¹⁾ WNewnes (17) (led 6f: r.o one pce) . 3.5
502 Spectacular Dawn **(68)** *(JLDunlop)* 9-3 JReid (16) (hmpd 8f out: styd on fnl 2f) 2¹/₂.6
395 Classical Charmer **(64)** *(BRMillman)* 8-10 GBaxter (9) (lw: nvr nr to chal) ......... nk.7
Prince Mercury **(69)** *(JLDunlop)* 9-1 GCarter (5) (wl bhd tl r.o fnl 2f) ............... 2¹/₂.8
524 Lindeman **(52)** *(SDow)* 7-12 DaleGibson (4) (swtg: nvr nr ldrs) ..................... 2¹/₂.9

524 Odoen (USA) **(47)** *(MRChannon)* 7-0 ‡7AntoinetteArmes (13) (nrst fin) .......... nk.**10**
395³ Judge and Jury **(75)** *(MJFetherston-Godley)* 9-7 LDettori (10) (lw: prom 6f) . 1½.**11**
Socks and Shares **(75)** *(PWHarris)* 9-7 GHind (11) (bit bkwd: n.d) ................ hd.**12**
498³ Holy Wanderer (USA) **(56)** *(DWPArbuthnot)* 7-11(2) ‡5RPrice (1) (lw: n.d) .......... 2.**13**
498 Positive Aspect **(47)** *(JPearce)* 7-7 GBardwell (8) (hdwy 5f out: wknd 3f out) . hd.**14**
583 Erlemo **(56)** *(CJBenstead)* 8-2 NAdams (15) (lw: hrd rdn 5f out: ro rspnse) ... nk.**15**
*200*³ Witches Coven **(54)** *(MBell)* 8-0 CRutter (7) (prom 6f) ................................ nk.**16**
334⁵ Chinaman **(61)** *(WGRWightman)* 8-7 TyroneWilliams (12) (dwlt: a bhd) .......... ½.**17**
621 Sea Cloud (USA) **(50)** *(MBlanshard)* 7-5(3) ‡5DHarrison (3) (n.d) ...................... 3.**18**
LONG HANDICAP: Odoen (USA) 7-5, Positive Aspect 7-6.

**5/2** IN THE PICTURE (IRE), **6/1** Bayaireg (USA), Holy Wanderer (USA), **13/2** Witches Coven, **9/1** Judge and Jury, Spectacular Dawn(8/1—12/1), **16/1** Odoen (USA)(op 10/1), **20/1** Classical Charmer, Prince Mercury, **25/1** Erlemo, **33/1** Ors. CSF £88.66, CT £402.47. Tote £2.60: £1.50 £5.70 £1.70 £7.20 (£111.10). Mrs Diana Attwood (MARLBOROUGH) bred by Barronstown Stud in Ireland. 18 Rn 2m 11.02 (6.52)
SF—33/9/2/-/-/-

## 729 DRUIDS MEDIAN AUCTION STKS (2-Y.O) £2574.00 (£714.00: £342.00) **5f** 3-00 (3-12)

564★ **Carranita (IRE)** *(BPalling)* 8-11 GCarter (11) (unruly s: a.p: led ins fnl f: r.o wl) . —**1**
476² Simply Sooty (Fav) *(BRMillman)* 8-6 GBaxter (6) (lw: w ldr: ev ch 1f out: edgd lft: r.o) .................................................................................. nk.**2**
528² Greenwich Chalenge *(WCarter)* 9-2 JReid (10) (b.hind: lw: led tl ins fnl f) ........... 3.**3**
Visimotion (USA) *(MJHeaton-Ellis)* 8-11 WNewnes (4) (w'like: a.p: nt qckn fnl f) ½.**4**
Cop the Cash (USA) *(MBell)* 8-11 WRSwinburn (3) (leggy: lw: nvr nr to chal) ..... 3.**5**
564 Trepidation (IRE) *(MJFetherston-Godley)* 8-11 LDettori (8) (rdn along & prom over 2f) .................................................................................. 4.**6**
Ian's Ace *(BWHills)* 8-11 RStreet (9) (b.hind: str: bit bkwd: dwlt: nvr nrr) .......... nk.**7**
Remembrance Day (IRE) *(RHannon)* 8-11 WCarson (1) (w'like: scope: a bhd) .. 3.**8**
Southampton *(GBBalding)* 8-11 BRaymond (2) (w'like: bkwd: a bhd) ............. 1½.**9**
514 Young Absalom *(LGCottrell)* 8-11 TRogers (7) (bit bkwd: a bhd) .................... ½.**10**

**5/2** Simply Sooty, **11/4** Greenwich Chalenge, **5/1** Cop the Cash (USA)(4/1—6/1), **6/1** CARRANITA (IRE), **8/1** Remembrance Day (IRE)(op 5/1), **12/1** Visimotion (USA), **14/1** Ian's Ace(op 8/1), **33/1** Ors. CSF £20.84, Tote £8.20: £1.80 £1.40 £1.60 (£9.60). Lamb Lane Associates (COWBRIDGE) bred by Mrs Anita Quinn in Ireland. 10 Rn 63.27 sec (3.27)
SF—37/31/29/22/10/-

## 730 COURAGE TROPHY (H'cap) (0-90) £3817.50 (£1140.00: £545.00: £247.50) 1½m 3-30 (3-34)

(Weights raised 7 lb)

612★ **Whitechapel (USA) (73)** (Fav) *(LordHuntingdon)* 4-9-4 WRSwinburn (3) (a.p: led 3f out tl wl over 1f out: led 1f out: r.o wl) ........................ —**1**
467★ Saffaah (USA) **(69)** *(WRMuir)* 5-9-0 SWhitworth (2) (lw: a.p: led wl over 1f out to 1f out: r.o) .................................................................................. 1.**2**
513⁴ Elaine Tully (IRE) **(77)** *(MJHeaton-Ellis)* 4-9-8 JReid (7) (nvr nrr) ...................... 4.**3**
431 Prince Hannibal **(79)** *(JLDunlop)* 5-9-10 WCarson (4) (stdy hdwy 3f out: eased whn btn over 1f out) .................................................................................. ½.**4**
*246*² Caspian Beluga **(57)** *(MrsAKnight)* 4-7-11(2) ‡5RPrice (8) (led over 5f out to 3f out: wknd 2f out) .................................................................................. 3.**5**
Rock Legend **(61)** *(DShaw)* 4-8-6 BRouse (1) (a bhd) .................................... ¾.**6**
389⁵ Royal Seaton **(90)** *(BRMillman)* 3-9-2 GBaxter (6) (lw: hdwy on ins 4f out: ev ch 3f out: sn wknd) .................................................................................. ¾.**7**
504 Ushak **(54)** (bl) *(HCandy)* 4-7-13 CRutter (5) (plld hrd: led over 6f: nt resolute) dist.**8**

**4/7** WHITECHAPEL (USA), **6/1** Prince Hannibal(op 7/2), Saffaah (USA), **12/1** Caspian Beluga, Royal Seaton(8/1—14/1), Elaine Tully (IRE)(8/1—14/1), **20/1** Rock Legend, **33/1** Ushak. CSF £5.31, CT £22.76. Tote £1.60: £1.20 £1.50 £2.40 (£3.00). The Queen (WEST ILSLEY) bred by The Queen in USA. 8 Rn 2m 36.07 (3.47)
SF—57/51/51/52/19/26

## 731 FOSTERS H'CAP (0-70) £2721.00 (£756.00: £363.00) **6f** 4-00 (4-04)

596³ **How's Yer Father (70)** (Fav) *(RJHodges)* 6-10-0 WCarson (18) (a.p: led ins fnl f: all out) .................................................................................. —**1**
496 Coppermill Lad **(47)** *(LJHolt)* 9-7-12 ‡7CAvery (17) (lw: gd hdwy over 1f out: r.o wl ins fnl f) .................................................................................. nk.**2**
515³ Old Comrades **(56)** *(LGCottrell)* 5-9-0 TRogers (10) (hdwy 2f out: ev ch 1f out: r.o) .................................................................................. 1.**3**
Gone Savage **(70)** *(GBBalding)* 4-9-7 ‡7TraceyPurseglove (7) (a.p: led over 2f out tl ins fnl f) .................................................................................. ¾.**4**
Gallant Hope **(51)** (bl) *(LGCottrell)* 10-8-9 RFox (19) (lw: a.p: nt qckn fnl f) ..... 2½.**5**

Divine Pet **(64)** *(WGRWightman)* 7–9–8 JWilliams (9) (hdwy fnl 2f: nvr nrr) ........ ¾.6
Shikari's Son **(56)** *(JWhite)* 5–9–0 GCarter (6) (nvr nr to chal) ......................... 1.7
Looting (USA) **(51)** *(MDIUsher)* 6–8–4 ‡⁵CHodgson (12) (bit bkwd: nvr trbld ldrs) ½.8
Idir Linn (IRE) **(43)** *(DJGMurray-Smith)* 4–8–1 CRutter (1) (nvr nr ldrs) ............ ¾.9
*121* Flying Promise **(52)** *(RABennett)* 4–8–10 WNewnes (20) (lw: led over 3f) ...... 2½.10
*506* Let's Go Lochy **(48)** *(CJHill)* 6–8–6 JReid (2) (s.s: nvr nrr) ............................ ½.11
*587* Ushba (FR) **(62)** *(CGCox)* 4–9–6 AClark (15) (lw: chsd ldr 3f) ...................... ½.12
*592* Top One (USA) **(53)** *(CJHill)* 7–8–11 GHind (13) (n.d) ................................. 1.13
*515* Scarlet Princess **(49)** *(RJHodges)* 4–8–2 ‡⁵TSprake (11) (n.d) ................. 1½.14
*495* Travel Token **(46)** *(LJHolt)* 4–8–4 BRouse (3) (s.s: a bhd) ........................ ¾.15
Cronk's Quality **(51)** *(DCJermy)* 9–8–9 GBardwell (8) (spd 3f) ................... ¾.16
*496* Liffey River (USA) **(58)** *(MrsLPiggott)* 4–9–2 LDettori (4) (b: n.d) .............. s.h.17
*587* Fay Eden (IRE) **(57)** *(RJHodges)* 4–9–1 BRaymond (14) (lw: n.d) .............. hd.18
*412* Reina **(47)** *(JDBethell)* 4–8–5 SWhitworth (16) (prom 3f) ...................... ¾.19
*411* Juvenara **(50)** *(CJHill)* 6–8–8 NAdams (5) (n.d) ...................................... 6.20

**11/4** HOW'S YER FATHER, **11/2** Old Comrades, **10/1** Liffey River (USA), Divine Pet, Coppermill Lad, **12/1** Let's Go Lochy(op 8/1), **16/1** Juvenara, **20/1** Scarlet Princess, Ushba (FR), Fay Eden (IRE), **25/1** Top One, Flying Promise, Gallant Hope, Shikari's Son, Reina, Looting (USA), Gone Savage, **33/1** Ors. CSF £30.41, CT £136.92. Tote £2.30: £1.40 £2.00 £1.50 £12.80 (£15.60). Unity Farm Holiday Centre Ltd (SOMERTON) bred by Lord Edwin McAlpine. 20 Rn                                            1m 16.38 (4.08)
SF—38/7/19/23/1/11

---

**732**        WINCANTON STKS (Mdn 3-Y.O) £2284.80 (£632.80: £302.40)        1¼m        4-30 (4-32)

*481³* **Sun Seeker (IRE)** (Fav) *(MRStoute)* 9-0 WRSwinburn (4) (lw: stdy hdwy 3f out:
led 1f out: comf) ............................................................... —1
*280²* For Mog (USA) *(CEBrittain)* 9-0 LDettori (5) (chsd ldr: led over 2f out to 1f out: nt
qckn) ............................................................................... 2½.2
Winged Bayard *(RFJohnsonHoughton)* 9-0 JReid (7) (leggy: hdwy fnl 2f: nvr nrr) 2.3
*566³* Al Haal (USA) *(PIWalwyn)* 9-0 WCarson (1) (lw: a.p: ev ch 2f out: one pce) ... 1¼.4
*427* Prince Pericles (IRE) *(HCandy)* 9-0 CRutter (3) (lw: led tl over 2f out: sn btn) ... s.h.5
Dancing Years (USA) *(MRChannon)* 8-9 BRouse (6) (hdwy 3f out: one pce fnl
2f) ................................................................................... 1.6
Istanbullu *(MBell)* 9-0 WNewnes (8) (bit bkwd: prom tl wknd over 2f out) ....... 7.7
*585⁴* Sirtelimar (IRE) *(BobJones)* 9-0 VSmith (2) (lw: hdwy 4f out: wknd 2f out) ......... 6.8

**10/11** SUN SEEKER (IRE), **4/1** Al Haal (USA), **9/2** Prince Pericles (IRE), **8/1** For Mog (USA), **14/1** Sirtelimar (IRE), **16/1** Winged Bayard(12/1—20/1), **20/1** Istanbullu(op 12/1), **50/1** Dancing Years (USA). CSF £9.21, Tote £1.80: £1.10 £2.00 £2.40 (£8.70). Lord Weinstock (NEWMARKET) bred by Ballymacoll Stud Farm Ltd in Ireland.
8 Rn                                                                 2m 39.19 (6.59)
SF—22/17/13/7/6/–

T/Plpt: £3.40 (775.25 Tckts).                                                              Hn

---

**408—BRIGHTON (L-H)**

## Thursday, May 7th [Good to firm]

Going Allowance: minus 0.10 sec per fur (F)                          Wind: mod half bhd

Stalls: low

**733**        ST ANN'S WELLS STKS (Mdn 2-Y.O) £2226.00 (£616.00: £294.00)
**5f 59y**                                                              2-00 (2-02)

*595²* **Night Melody (IRE)** (Fav) *(RHannon)* 9-0 KDarley (5) (lw: 5th st: swtchd rt wl
over 1f out: led ins fnl f: pushed out) ....................................... —1
*470⁶* Chinnery (IRE) *(JMPEustace)* 9-0 RCochrane (3) (w ldr: led over 2f out tl ins fnl
f: r.o) ............................................................................... 1.2
*581⁵* Lochore *(RIngram)* 8-7 ‡⁷JWeaver (1) (lw: hdwy over 1f out: r.o) ...................... 4.3
*447⁵* Stormy Heights *(JRJenkins)* 8-9 GBaxter (2) (led 3f: unable qckn) ................. s.h.4
Water Diviner (bl) *(RFJohnsonHoughton)* 9-0 SWhitworth (7) (leggy: hdwy
over 1f out: nvr nrr) ............................................................. 1½.5
*383* Kintwyn *(DRLaing)* 9-0 TyroneWilliams (8) (4th st: wknd over 1f out) ................ 2.6
*564* Admiral Frobisher (USA) *(CFWall)* 9-0 NDay (6) (outpcd) ................................. nk.7
*514* Run on Rebel (IRE) *(PFICole)* 9-0 TQuinn (10) (lw: 3rd st: wknd wl over 1f out) . 3.8
Newington Butts (IRE) *(RAkehurst)* 8-6 ‡³FNorton (9) (neat: lw: a wl bhd) .......... 5.9
*561* Ballaindy *(WGMTurner)* 8-4 ‡⁵TSprake (4) (6th st: wknd 2f out) .................... hd.10

**8/11** NIGHT MELODY (IRE), **13/2** Run on Rebel (IRE), **7/1** Chinnery (IRE)(op 12/1), **8/1** Stormy Heights, **14/1** Newington Butts (IRE), **16/1** Water Diviner(8/1—20/1), **25/1** Lochore, Admiral Frobisher (USA), **33/1** Ors. CSF £6.87, Tote £1.60: £1.10 £1.90 £3.50 (£5.70). Mr P. D. Savill (MARLBOROUGH) bred by Leo Collins in Ireland.
10 Rn                                                                 63.3 sec (3)
SF—30/26/3/4/3/–

**734** HOLLINGBURY (S) STKS (3-Y.O) £2441.60 (£677.60: £324.80)    **7f 214y**    2-30 (2-34)

281 **Up the Punjab (63)** (Fav) *(SDow)* 8-9 TQuinn (1) (led 5f out: r.o wl) .................. —1
614 Don't Worry (IRE) **(57)** *(MHTompkins)* 8-4 ‡5CHodgson (17) (5th st: one pce fnl 2f) .................. 3½.2
510 Master Shikari **(47)** *(JEBanks)* 8-9 ‡5LNewton (16) (2nd st: hrd rdn over 2f out: one pce) .................. nk.3
145⁴ Betalongabill *(MMadgwick)* 9-0 JQuinn (13) (lost pl 5f out: r.o one pce fnl 2f) . 2½.4
355 Honey Vision **(61)** (bl) *(GHEden)* 8-9 JWilliams (6) (hmpd s: nvr nr to chal) ... 1½.5
355 Have a Nightcap **(60)** *(MAJarvis)* 8-7 ‡7KRutter (4) (swvd lft s: hdwy 2f out: one pce) .................. 2½.6
594⁶ Little Nod **(60)** *(JWhite)* 8-7 ‡7CAvery (12) (prom 4f) .................. 3½.7
510 Prince Rodney **(67)** *(RHannon)* 9-0 KDarley (7) (hmpd s: nvr nrr) .................. s.h.8
441 Nominee Prince **(52)** *(RGuest)* 9-0 GBaxter (10) (nvr nrr) .................. 1.9
353⁵ Simon Ellis (IRE) **(47)** *(DRLaing)* 9-0 SWhitworth (8) (lw: nvr nrr) .................. 1.10
524 Red for Danger **(44)** (v) *(AMoore)* 8-9 ‡5ATucker (9) (hmpd s: hdwy 5f out: wknd 3f out) .................. ½.11
510⁴ Monorose **(64)** *(DHaydnJones)* 8-9 TyroneWilliams (a mid div) .................. ½.12
366 Sizzling Rose **(45)** *(WCarter)* 8-4 ‡5NGwilliams (3) (4th st: wknd over 2f out) .. 10.13
577 Clifton Cruiser (USA) (bl) *(CRNelson)* 8-7 ‡7DThompson (14) (6th st: wknd 3f out) .................. 8.14
300 St Piran's Lass *(RJHolder)* 8-9 ADicks (2) (a bhd) .................. 8.15
531 Tate Express (IRE) **(62)** (bl) *(NAGraham)* 9-0 RCochrane (11) (a bhd) .................. nk.16
510³ Man of the Season (USA) **(65)** *(JAkehurst)* 9-0 PaulEddery (15) (lw: led 3f: 3rd st: wknd over 2f out: virtually p.u over 1f out: lame) ........ dist.17

**3/1** UP THE PUNJAB(tchd 5/1), **4/1** Prince Rodney, **5/1** Man of the Season (USA), **8/1** Tate Express (IRE)(tchd 12/1), **10/1** Don't Worry (IRE)(op 6/1), Have a Nightcap(8/1—12/1), **12/1** Monorose, **16/1** Little Nod, **20/1** Clifton Cruiser (USA)(op 12/1), Honey Vision, Nominee Prince, Betalongabill, **33/1** Ors. CSF £34.07, Tote £4.00: £2.10 £2.60 £2.10 (£68.10). Mr Ray Hawthorn (EPSOM) bred by Giles W. Pritchard-Gordon. 17 Rn; No bid
1m 37.2 (5)
SF—8/-/-/-/-/-

**735** COLDEAN H'CAP (0-70) £2284.80 (£632.80: £302.40)    **5f 59y**    3-00 (3-03)

570 **Iron King (60)** (v) *(JLSpearing)* 6–9-5 NHowe (3) (6th st: led over 1f out: rdn out) .................. —1
188 Pendor Dancer **(49)** (bl) *(BForsey)* 9–8-8 JWilliams (11) (hdwy 2f out: r.o ins fnl f) .................. 3.2
506 Factuelle **(43)** *(DRTucker)* 5–7-11 ‡5ATucker (10) (gd hdwy over 1f out: r.o wl ins fnl f) .................. nk.3
596⁶ Banbury Flyer **(66)** *(MrsALMKing)* 4–9-11 RCochrane (13) (hdwy over 2f out: one pce) .................. 2.4
525 Deepwood Nanusket **(37)** *(MMadgwick)* 6–7-10(3) SDawson (8) (hdwy over 1f out: r.o) .................. ½.5
496⁴ My Ruby Ring **(43)** (Jt-Fav) *(DRLaing)* 5–8-2 TyroneWilliams (5) (b: 3rd st: led over 2f out tl over 1f out: sn wknd) .................. ½.6
506 Rays Mead **(53)** *(LJHolt)* 4–8-5 ‡7CAvery (4) (4th st: wknd 2f out) .................. hd.7
706 Greetland Rock **(51)** (v) *(PHowling)* 4–8-7 ‡3FNorton (14) (swtg: nvr nr to chal) .. s.h.8
357 Stocktina **(43)** *(RJHodges)* 5–7-11 ‡5TSprake (16) (led 1f: 2nd st: wknd over 1f out) .................. ½.9
506⁴ Slip-a-Snip **(69)** (Jt-Fav) *(GBBalding)* 5–9-7 ‡7TraceyPurseglove (2) (lw: 5th st: wknd over 1f out) .................. 3½.10
527 Kindred Cameo **(58)** *(GLewis)* 3–8-7 PaulEddery (7) (outpcd) .................. ½.11
506 Goody Four Shoes **(58)** *(DRTucker)* 4–8-12 ‡5RPrice (1) (outpcd) .................. 1.12
525 Saysana **(34)** *(AMoore)* 5–7-7 NAdams (15) (a bhd) .................. ½.13
506 Miss Bell Ringer **(45)** *(CJHill)* 4–8-4 AMackay (6) (a bhd) .................. 1.14
245 Ever so Artistic **(49)** (bl) *(PHowling)* 5–8-8 JMurray (9) (b: led over 4f out tl over 2f out: sn wknd) .................. 1.15
LONG HANDICAP: Deepwood Nanusket 6-10, Saysana 7-4.

**6/1** My Ruby Ring(op 4/1), Slip-a-Snip(8/1—9/1), **7/1** Stocktina, **8/1** Banbury Flyer, IRON KING, Greetland Rock, **10/1** Ever so Artistic, **12/1** Factuelle, Pendor Dancer, **14/1** Kindred Cameo, Rays Mead, **20/1** Miss Bell Ringer, Saysana, **33/1** Ors. CSF £94.65, CT £1,052.77. Tote £10.10: £3.40 £3.40 £2.60 (£40.90). Mr Tom Coleman (ALCESTER) bred by L. Hutch. 15 Rn
62.1 sec (1.8)
SF—59/36/24/44/10/17

**736** JIM TAYLOR MEMORIAL H'CAP (0-70) £2553.00 (£708.00: £339.00)
**1m 1f 209y**    3-30 (3-33)

(Weights raised 6 lb)
342 **Dazzle the Crowd (IRE) (49)** *(CACyzer)* 4–9-3 TQuinn (8) (lw: hld up: 4th st: led over 2f out: hrd rdn over 1f out: r.o wl) .................. —1

508 El Volador **(56)** *(RJO'Sullivan)* 5-9-10 RCochrane (3) (hdwy 3f out: ev ch over 2f out: r.o) .................................................................................. ³/₄.**2**

409³ Tiger Claw (USA) **(56)** (Fav) *(RJHodges)* 6-9-5 ‡⁵TSprake (1) (rdn 4f out: 5th st: r.o one pce fnl 2f) ........................................................... 3.**3**

342 Indian Slave (IRE) **(53)** *(RGuest)* 4-9-7 GBaxter (7) (3rd st: led 3f out tl over 2f out: sn wknd) .................................................................... 2¹/₂.**4**

277 Crown Reserve **(40)** *(MJRyan)* 4-8-5 ‡³DBiggs (6) (6th st: wknd 2f out) ... 2.**5**

598² Thin Red Line **(50)** (v) *(JRJenkins)* 8-9-4 SWhitworth (9) (lw: hdwy on ins over 2f out: one pce) .......................................................... 2¹/₂.**6**

411* Marzocco **(55)** *(JFfitch-Heyes)* 4-9-9 AMackay (2) (lw: nvr nr to chal) .............. 2.**7**

546⁴ Maid of Ice **(44)** *(DrJDScargill)* 3-7-10 JQuinn (13) (7th st: wknd over 2f out) . 1¹/₂.**8**

250 Viceroy Gem (IRE) **(41)** *(RJHolder)* 4-8-9 JWilliams (14) (a bhd) .............. 1¹/₂.**9**

411 Precious Air (IRE) **(47)** *(AMoore)* 4-9-1 BRouse (5) (a bhd) ...................... ¹/₂.**10**

Mamalama **(43)** *(LJHolt)* 4-8-11 NAdams (11) (bit bkwd: a bhd) ............... 2¹/₂.**11**

565 Thunder Bug (USA) **(51)** *(APJames)* 4-9-5 SDawson (12) (led 7f) ............. 5.**12**

335 Al Skeet (USA) **(37)** *(AMoore)* 6-8-0 ‡⁵ATucker (10) (lw: dwlt: hdwy over 8f out: rdn over 4f out: 2nd st: wknd over 3f out) ..................................... 2.**13**

San Roque **(30)** *(SWoodman)* 7-7-7⁽⁵⁾ ‡⁵BDoyle (4) (a bhd) ...................... 12.**14**

LONG HANDICAP: San Roque 7-6.

**100/30** Tiger Claw (USA), **5/1** DAZZLE THE CROWD (IRE)(8/1—9/1), **11/2** Thin Red Line(4/1—6/1), **13/2** El Volador(5/1—8/1), **8/1** Marzocco(op 5/1), Indian Slave (IRE), **14/1** Thunder Bug (USA), Crown Reserve, **16/1** Viceroy Gem (IRE), **20/1** Maid of Ice, Precious Air (IRE), **25/1** San Roque, **33/1** Ors. CSF £37.28, CT £116.06. Tote £5.20: £2.60 £1.50 £1.30 (£18.60). Mr R. M. Cyzer (HORSHAM) bred by J. B. Clarke in Ireland. 14 Rn
2m 3.4 (5.4)
SF—39/44/33/30/10/18

**737**     VARDEAN STKS (Mdn) £1932.00 (£532.00: £252.00)    **1m 1f 209y**    4-00 (4-01)

**Young Frooman (USA)** *(GHarwood)* 3-8-8 RCochrane (3) (lw: dwlt: hdwy 4f out: 2nd st: led 3f out: easily) ............................................................ —**1**

500² Maji *(DMorley)* 3-8-3 SWhitworth (2) (3rd st: chsd wnr over 2f out: no imp) ....... 8.**2**

Zamaan Ya Zamaan (IRE) *(MAJarvis)* 3-8-8 JWilliams (4) (bit bkwd: 4th st: one pce fnl 3f) ..................................................................... s.h.**3**

Portree (Fav) *(HRACecil)* 3-8-3 WRyan (5) (chsd ldr: led over 4f out to 3f out: sn wknd) ..................................................................... 12.**4**

Chez Polly (bl) *(PRHedger)* 6-9-5 AClark (6) (6th st: a bhd) .......................... 15.**5**

340 Easter Term **(36)** *(RJHolder)* 4-9-5 NAdams (1) (led over 5f: 5th st: wknd over 3f out) ..................................................................... 12.**6**

**10/11** Portree, **5/4** YOUNG FREEMAN (USA), **12/1** Maji(8/1—16/1), **14/1** Zamaan Ya Zamaan (IRE), **100/1** Ors. CSF £14.01, Tote £2.30: £1.30 £3.30 (£6.80). Mr R. A. Kirstein (PULBOROUGH) bred by Allen E. Paulson in USA. 6 Rn
2m 2.7 (4.7)
SF—37/16/20/–/–/–

**738**     CORN EXCHANGE H'CAP (0-70) £2657.20 (£739.20: £355.60)    **6f 209y**    4-30 (4-32)

420² Kawwas **(38)** (Jt-Fav) *(WHolden)* 7-7-11 TyroneWilliams (3) (hdwy over 2f out: led 1f out: r.o wl) ............................................................ —**1**

Durneltor **(62)** *(RHannon)* 4-9-7 KDarley (18) (hdwy over 2f out: ev ch 1f out: unable qckn) ..................................................................... 2¹/₂.**2**

580 Monte Bre **(40)** *(RAkehurst)* 6-7-13 SDawson (13) (hdwy over 1f out: r.o ins fnl f) ..................................................................... nk.**3**

629 Belfort Ruler **(68)** *(BGubby)* 5-9-13 TQuinn (5) (6th st: n.m.r over 1f out: one pce) ..................................................................... ¹/₂.**4**

Martinosky **(51)** *(WGRWightman)* 6-8-10 JWilliams (7) (bit bkwd: s.s: hdwy fnl f: r.o) ..................................................................... 2.**5**

624 Beatle Song **(67)** *(RJHodges)* 4-9-7 ‡⁵TSprake (15) (rdn 3f out: nvr nr to chal) .. 1.**6**

592 Melodic Habit **(44)** *(MrsAKnight)* 5-8-0 ‡³FNorton (14) (3rd st: wknd 2f out) .. 1¹/₂.**7**

508 Lamastre **(61)** *(RJHodges)* 3-8-3 ‡⁵ATucker (11) (nvr nrr) ...................... ³/₄.**8**

117 Please Please Me (IRE) **(39)** *(KOCunningham-Brown)* 4-7-7⁽²⁾ ‡⁵BDoyle (10) (nvr nrr) ..................................................................... 1¹/₂.**9**

332 Tadora (IRE) **(54)** *(CJBenstead)* 3-8-1 JQuinn (9) (5th st: wknd 2f out) .......... ¹/₂.**10**

515 Quinzii Martin **(49)** (v) *(DHaydnJones)* 4-8-8 WRyan (1) (led 6f) ................ 1¹/₂.**11**

397 Helawe **(63)** (bl) (Jt-Fav) *(SirMarkPrescott)* 9-9-8 RCochrane (12) (2nd st: wknd over 2f out) ..................................................... hd.**12**

575 Proud Brigadier (IRE) **(55)** *(WCarter)* 4-8-9 ‡⁵NGWilliams (17) (4th st: wknd 2f out) ..................................................................... nk.**13**

333⁶ Foo Foo (IRE) **(35)** *(DMarks)* 4-9-7 ‡⁷AntoinetteArmes (16) (a bhd) .......... 1.**14**

620 Sure Shot Norman **(60)** *(JSutcliffe)* 3-8-7 BRouse (6) (a bhd) .................... ³/₄.**15**

Klairover **(45)** *(CJHill)* 5-8-4 NAdams (8) (s.s: a bhd) ............................... 1.**16**

Sam the Man **(54)** *(JFfitch-Heyes)* 5-8-13 AMackay (4) (a bhd) ..................... 2.**17**

411 Kirriemuir **(42)** *(KOCunningham-Brown)* 4-7-12 ‡³DBiggs (2) (prom 3f) ............ 8.**18**

**5/1** KAWWAS, Helawe, **13/2** Belfort Ruler, Quinzii Martin, **10/1** Tadora (IRE)(8/1—12/1), **11/1** Proud Brigadier (IRE), **12/1** Durneltor, **16/1** Klairover, Sure Shot Norman, Martinosky, **20/1** Foo Foo (IRE), Beatle Song, **25/1** Lamastre, Melodic Habit, Monte Bre, Sam the Man, Please Please Me (IRE), **33/1** Kirriemuir. CSF £63.28, CT £1,299.25. Tote £4.00: £1.60 £3.60 £6.70 £3.30 (£22.30). Whitting Commodities Ltd (NEWMARKET) bred by Michael Smurfit. 18 Rn    1m 23.4 (3.4)

SF—22/38/15/41/18/26

T/Plpt: £671.60 (3.7 Tckts).    AK

## 460a—MAISONS-LAFFITTE (L-H)
### Friday, May 1st [Good to soft]

**739a**    PRIX DE BARBEVILLE (Gp 3)    £20640.00    **1m 7f 110y**

|  |  |  |
|---|---|---|
| **Commendable (IRE)** (bl) *(France)* 4–8–11 JBoisnard | ....................... | —**1** |
| 9a²   Last King (FR) *(France)* 4–8–9 CLeScrill | ....................... | ¹/₂.**2** |
| River Test (USA) *(France)* 6–8–11 FHead | ....................... | 1¹/₂.**3** |

Tote 11.30f: 2.00f 1.40f 1.60f (17.20f). Mr K.Abdulla (H-A.Pantall,FRANCE) bred by Kilfrush Stud in Ireland. 9 Rn
3m 20.4

## 644a— SAN SIRO (R-H)
### Friday, May 1st [Good]

**740a**    PREMIO CERTOSA (Gp 3)    £27907.00    **5f**

|  |  |  |
|---|---|---|
| **Special Power** *(Italy)* 5–8–13 SSoto | ....................... | —**1** |
| Whittingham (IRE) *(Italy)* 3–8–6(1) LSorrentino | ....................... | 1.**2** |
| Diamond Mine (IRE) *(Italy)* 3–8–5 CBertolini (fin 4th, s.h: plcd 3rd) | ....................... | **3** |
| ANOTHER EPISODE (IRE) *(JBerry)* 3–8–5 GDettori (btn further 5¹/₂l) | ....................... | **9** |
| Manoftheyear *(Italy)* 5–8–13 MTellini (fin 3rd, 1l: disq: plcd last) | ....................... | **0** |

*Stewards Enquiry: Manoftheyear disq. & plcd last*

Tote 67L: 24L 18L 28L (199L). Stall Klosterneuburg (L.D'Auria,ITALY) bred by Corballis and Hamwood Studs
11 Rn    58.5 sec

## CHURCHILL DOWNS (L-H)
### Saturday, May 2nd [Fast]

**741a**    KENTUCKY DERBY (Grade 1) (3-Y.O.C & F) £390850.00    **1¹/₄m (dirt)**

|  |  |  |
|---|---|---|
| **Lil E.Tee (USA)** *(America)* 3–9–0 PDay | ....................... | —**1** |
| Casual Lies (USA) *(America)* 3–9–0 GStevens | ....................... | 1.**2** |
| Dance Floor (USA) *(America)* 3–9–0 CAntley | ....................... | 3¹/₄.**3** |
| 444²   DR DEVIOUS (IRE) *(PWChapple-Hyam)* 3–9–0 CMcCarron (btn further 4l) | ........... | **7** |
| 459a⋆ Arazi (USA) *(France)* 3–9–0 PValenzuela (btn over 8¹/₂l by wnr) | ........... | **8** |
| 443³ Thyer (USA) *(Ireland)* 3–9–0 CRoche (btn 20¹/₂l by wnr) | ........... | **13** |

Tote 35.60 (1-2) 12.60 22.00 (1-2-3) 7.60 11.60 12.80 (Exacta (2 dol) 854.40). Mr W.C.Partee
(L.Whiting,AMERICA) bred by L.Littman in USA. 18 Rn    2m 3

## 642a—LONGCHAMP (R-H)
### Sunday, May 3rd [Good to firm]
Going Allowance: minus 0.10 sec per fur (G)

**742a**    PRIX VANTEAUX (Gp 3) (3-Y.O.F) £20640.00    **1m 1f 55y (Grande)**

|  |  |  |
|---|---|---|
| **Sheba Dancer (FR)** *(France)* 3–9–2 DBoeuf | ....................... | —**1** |
| Symphorino (USA) *(France)* 3–9–2 TJarnet | ....................... | s.h.**2** |
| Renashaan (FR) *(France)* 3–9–2 CBlack | ....................... | ³/₄.**3** |

Tote 3.70f: 2.00f 1.90f (SF: 10.70f). Mr J.Sebag (E.Lellouche,FRANCE) bred by B.B.A. & M.R.Jacqueline in
France. 7 Rn    1m 55.7 (2.4)
SF—52/51/49

**743a**    PRIX GANAY (Gp 1)    £51600.00    **1¹/₄m 110y (Grande)**

|  |  |  |
|---|---|---|
| **Subotica (FR)** *(France)* 4–9–2 TJarnet (hld up: stdy hdwy 1f out: r.o wl to ld cl home) | ....................... | —**1** |

382a² Pistolet Bleu (IRE) *(France)* 4-9-2 DBoeuf (lw: cl up: led over 1f out: hdd & one pce cl home) ............ nk.2

Suave Dancer (USA) *(Fav) (France)* 4-9-2 CAsmussen (bkwd: hld up: 5th st: one pce fnl f) ............ 3.3

382a★ Fortune's Wheel (IRE) *(France)* 4-9-2 MBoutin (hld up: hdwy fr over 1f out: faltered cl home) ............ ½.4

382a³ Art Bleu (bl) *(France)* 5-9-2 CAubert (led tl over 1f out: grad wknd) ............ 2.5

382a⁵ Passing Sale (FR) *(France)* 5-9-2 ALequeux (outpcd thrght: nvr nr to chal) .... 1½.6

382a⁴ Glity (USA) *(France)* 4-9-2 ELegrix (cl up: 2nd st: wknd 1f out) ............ nk.7

**2/5** Suave Dancer (USA), **7/2** Pistolet Bleu (IRE), Art Bleu, **57/10** Fortune's Wheel (IRE), **74/10** SUBOTICA (FR), **24/1** Passing Sale (FR), **29/1** Glity (USA). Tote 8.40f: 3.10f 2.00f (SF: 30.00f). Mr O.Lecerf (A.Fabre,FRANCE) bred by M.P.de Moussac in France. 7 Rn
2m 9.3 (U.3)
SF—95/94/88/87/78/77

## 639a—CAPANNELLE (R-H)
### Sunday, May 3rd [Soft]

**744a**   PREMIO PARIOLI (Gp 1) (3-Y-O) £51163.00   **1m**

391 ALHIJAZ *(JLDunlop)* 3-9-2 WCarson ............ —1

Spendaccione (USA) *(Italy)* 3-9-2 VMezzatesta ............ 2.2

Glacial *(Italy)* 3-9-2 WRSwinburn ............ ¾.3

549² JITTERBUGGING *(BWHills)* 3-9-2 DHolland ............ 3.4

334★ SECRET THING (USA) *(CEBrittain)* 3-9-2 MRoberts ............ 3.5

Tote 29L: 18L 25L 21L (227L). Prince A.A.Faisal (ARUNDEL) bred by Nawara Stud Co Ltd. 10 Rn   1m 39.9

## 541—CARLISLE (R-H)
### Thursday, May 7th [Good to soft, Soft patches]
Going Allowance: 0.35 sec per (G)                                    Wind: str across

Stalls: high

**745**   LOWESWATER H'CAP (3-Y-O) (0-70) £2422.00 (£672.00: £322.00)   **1½m** 2-10 (2-14)
(Weights raised 4 lb)

281 Tronchetto (IRE) (52) *(SirMarkPrescott)* 8-8 GDuffield (7) (cl up: led 5f out: styd on wl) ............ —1

488³ Kadari (59) *(Fav) (AHarrison)* 9-1 KFallon (4) (hld up: hdwy to chal 3f out: rdn & no ex fnl f) ............ 5.2

369 Pharlander (IRE) (50) (bl) *(MHEasterby)* 8-6 MBirch (8) (bhd: hdwy 4f out: rdn & one pce fnl 2f) ............ 4.3

583⁶ Cov Tel Lady (65) *(MHTompkins)* 9-7 PRobinson (6) (lw: a.p: effrt 4f out: rdn & btn over 2f out) ............ 2.4

327 Sparkling Vision (52) (bl) *(MrsGRReveley)* 8-1 ‡7DarrenMoffatt (5) (s.i.s: sn rcvrd: led after 1f to 5f out: sn wknd) ............ 6.5

457⁴ Mayo Man (IRE) (44) *(MrsGRReveley)* 8-0 JLowe (2) (lw: s.i.s: sme hdwy whn bdly hmpd 6f out: nt rcvr) ............ 15.6

531 Doughman (57) *(JEtherington)* 8-13 NConnorton (1) (lw: hdwy & prom 6f out: wknd over 3f out) ............ 6.7

481 Royal Circus (47) *(PWHarris)* 8-3 RFox (3) (led 1f: chsd ldrs tl wknd 4f out) ....... 4.8

**13/8** Kadari, **9/2** Cov Tel Lady(op 11/4), **13/2** Mayo Man (IRE), **8/1** Royal Circus, Pharlander (IRE), Doughman, **10/1** TRONCHETTO (IRE), **50/1** Sparkling Vision. CSF £25.31, CT £126.09. Tote £6.20: £2.50 £1.10 £2.80 (£9.70). Lord Derby (NEWMARKET) bred by Stanley Estate and Stud Co in Ireland. 8 Rn   2m 43.1 (13.6)

**746**   ENNERDALE STKS (Mdn 3-Y.O.C & G) £2265.20 (£627.20: £299.60)
7f 214y                                                              2-40 (2-41)

600⁴ Sir Mark Sykes (IRE) *(JRFanshawe)* 9-0 GDuffield (1) (a.p: rdn to ld appr fnl f: styd on strly) ............ —1

531⁴ Combative (IRE) (v) *(JHMGosden)* 9-0 GHind (5) (led tl hdd over 1f out: sn btn) ............ 8.2

Triennium (USA) *(Fav) (LMCumani)* 9-0 LDettori (4) (str: scope: trckd ldrs: nt clr run & swtchd over 2f out: rdn & btn appr fnl f) ............ 1½.3

577⁵ Viva Darling *(BAMcMahon)* 9-0 JFortune (2) (outpcd ½-wy: hdwy u.p over 2f out: no imp) ............ 2.4

531³ Jathaab (IRE) *(MRStoute)* 9-0 MBirch (3) (chsd ldr tl rdn & btn over 2f out) ...... nk.5

Great North Road *(DenysSmith)* 9-0 NConnorton (6) (wl grwn: bit bkwd: lost tch fr ½-wy) ............ 30.6

**10/11** Triennium (USA), **11/4** Jathaab (IRE), **9/2** SIR MARK SYKES (IRE), **14/1** Combative (IRE)(op 8/1), **16/1** Viva Darling, **100/1** Great North Road. CSF £45.92, Tote £6.70: £1.80 £3.80 (£29.30). Lord White of Hull (NEWMARKET) bred by Associated Bloodstock Inc in Ireland. 6 Rn
1m 45.3 (6.6)
SF—43/19/14/8/7/–

### 747
BUTTERMERE CLAIMING STKS (I)    £2245.60 (£621.60: £296.80)
7f 214y
3-10 (3-12)

485[6]  **Just a Step (83)** (Fav) *(MMcCormack)* 6–8-10 WNewnes (7) (lw: mde all: drew clr fnl 2f: easily) ..................................................................... —1
    Claudia Miss (59) *(WWHaigh)* 5–7-13 DaleGibson (2) (bit bkwd: sn trckng ldrs: effrt over 2f out: no ch w wnr) ..................................................... 5.2
    Kagram Queen *(MrsGRReveley)* 4–7-10 JLowe (6) (hld up: effrt ent st: styd on: no imp) ................................................................................. 1½.3
532*  Laurel Queen (IRE) (60) *(JBerry)* 4–7-11 LCharnock (9) (lw: in tch: effrt u.p 3f out: nvr able to chal) ......................................................... s.h.4
327[3]  Acquisition (50) *(SGPayne)* 5–8-4[(4)] SWebster (4) (chsd ldrs: wnt 2nd over 2f out: rdn & btn appr fnl f) ................................................. 2.5
    Primino (FR) *(JJO'Neill)* 7–8-4 GDuffield (5) (bit bkwd: outpcd & bhd tl sme late hdwy) ...................................................................... 6.6
453  Nishara *(NBycroft)* 4–8-11 NConnorton (3) (sn pushed along & bhd: n.d) ......... 5.7
    Highbrook (USA) *(DonEnricoIncisa)* 4–8-3 KimTinkler (1) (bit bkwd: a bhd) ....... 1.8
90[5]  Soda Popinski (USA) (45) *(ICampbell)* 4–8-4 NCarlisle (8) (in tch: effrt 3f out: wknd wl over 1f out) ..................................................... 1½.9
    Moona (USA) (65) *(GMMoore)* 4–7-9 PBurke (10) (chsd wnr to st: sn wknd) ... 6.10

**3/1** JUST A STEP, **4/1** Laurel Queen (IRE), **13/2** Highbrook (USA), **7/1** Soda Popinski (USA)(op 20/1), **8/1** Moona (USA), **9/1** Primino (FR), **10/1** Claudia Miss, **14/1** Kagram Queen, **33/1** Acquisition, **200/1** Nishara. CSF £28.26, Tote £4.00: £1 60 £2.90 £4.80 (£348.60). Mrs M. E. Cooke (WANTAGE) bred by John Davison. 10 Rn, Highbrook (USA) clmd A Smith £12,501
1m 45.2 (6.5)
SF—40/14/6/6/7/–

### 748
BUTTERMERE CLAIMING STKS (II)    £2245.60 (£621.60: £296.80)
7f 214y
3-40 (3-43)

525*  **Metternich (63)** *(MHTompkins)* 7–8-1[(1)] PRobinson (6) (cl up: slt ld 3f out: hld on wl fnl f) ....................................................................... —1
    Henbury Hall (IRE) (84) *(MrsGRReveley)* 4–8-5 JLowe (3) (lw: a.p: chal 2f out: no ex wl ins fnl f) ........................................................... ¾.2
448[3]  Prime Mover (65) (v) *(DBurchell)* 4–8-0 DaleGibson (1) (in tch: outpcd over 2f out: hdwy over 1f out: nt qckn nr fin) ........................... 1½.3
670  Lombard Ships (59) *(MO'Neill)* 5–8-2 JFortune (4) (lw: led 1f: chsd ldrs: outpcd 2f out: styd on one pce fnl f) .................................. 1½.4
616[2]  Cool Parade (USA) (52) (bl) *(GMMoore)* 4–7-9 ‡5SMaloney (5) (lw: in tch: pushed along appr st: r.o one pce) ...................... 1½.5
492  Matts Boy (67) (Fav) *(MissSEHall)* 4–8-5 ‡3JFanning (8) (bhd: hdwy on ins 3f out: ev ch 2f out: wknd 1f out) ................................ 1.6
615  Cardea Castle (IRE) (30) (v) *(BEllison)* 4–7-9 NCarlisle (10) (led after 1f to 3f out: grad wknd) ................................................ ¾.7
    Borocay *(MJCamacho)* 4–8-0 NConnorton (7) (bit bkwd: hld up & bhd: nvr plcd to chal) ................................................................. nk.8
377  Red Tempest (IRE) (39) (bl) *(LLungo)* 4–7-7 ‡7RHavlin (2) (chsd ldrs to st: sn wknd) ............................................................... 7.9

**3/1** Matts Boy, **9/2** Henbury Hall (IRE), Prime Mover, METTERNICH, **6/1** Cool Parade (USA), Lombard Ships, **25/1** Borocay, **33/1** Cardea Castle (IRE), **50/1** Red Tempest (IRE). CSF £23.53, Tote £4.30: £1.70 £2.10 £1.80 (£9.40). Mr Ian Lochhead (NEWMARKET) bred by Juddmonte Farms. 9 Rn
1m 47.7 (9)

### 749
BASSENTHWAITE H'CAP (3-Y.O) (0-70) £2402.40 (£666.40: £319.20)
6f 206y
4-10 (4-13)

(Weights raised 7 lb)
490  **Express Gift (56)** *(MrsGRReveley)* 8-9 ‡7DarrenMoffatt (12) (a chsng ldrs: rdn wl over 1f out: styd on wl to ld cl home) ......................... —1
662[2]  Princess Maxine (IRE) (47) (Fav) *(MissLAPerratt)* 8-7 DaleGibson (8) (mde most: edgd lft fnl 3f: hdd & no ex nr fin) ..................... nk.2
545[5]  Coastal Express (56) *(EWeymes)* 9-2 GHind (14) (lw: a cl up: chal 2f out: ev ch tl one pce fnl f) ............................................. ½.3
522[4]  Malcesine (IRE) (50) *(CaptJWilson)* 8-10 JCarroll (4) (prom: ev ch over 2f out: sn rdn: btn & eased fnl f) .............................. 2½.4
489*  Who's That Lady (60) *(MHEasterby)* 9-1 ‡5SMaloney (13) (hld up: effrt on outside over 2f out: nvr rchd ldrs) ........................... 2.5

520★ Kick on Majestic (IRE) **(46)** (bl) *(NBycroft)* 8-6 MBirch (11) (chsd ldrs: rdn wl over 2f out: one pce) .................................................. 3.6

401 My Jersey Pearl (IRE) **(59)** *(DonEnricoIncisa)* 9-5 KimTinkler (15) (s.i.s: bhd tl r.o fnl f: n.d) ............................................................... 6.7

Aegaen Lady **(56)** *(JEtherington)* 9-2 LDettori (3) (prom tl rdn & wknd 2f out: sn eased) ........................................................................ 3¹/₂.8

372⁶ Denim Blue **(59)** *(CWThornton)* 9-5 WNewnes (2) (lw: s.i.s: bhd tl sme late hdwy: n.d) ...................................................................... 2¹/₂.9

Strangersinthenite **(50)** *(JSWainwright)* 8-10 LCharnock (9) (in tch tl wknd 4f out) ................................................................................. 1.10

521 Preamble **(61)** *(MrsJRRamsden)* 9-7 TLucas (7) (a bhd) ......................... 2.11

Ponte Cervo **(47)** *(GRichards)* 8-7 GDuffield (10) (nvr trbld ldrs) ............. 1¹/₂.12

Fletchinni (IRE) **(40)** *(MO'Neill)* 8-0 NCarlisle (6) (swtg: in tch to st) ........... s.h.13

223 Kashgar **(33)** *(DWChapman)* 7-7 SWood (5) (s.i.s: a bhd) ........................ 6.14

Gogolette **(48)** *(MO'Neill)* 8-8 JFortune (1) (dwlt: a bhd) ........................ 1¹/₂.15

LONG HANDICAP: Kashgar 7-4.

*Stewards Enquiry: Hind suspended 16-19/5/92 (excessive use of whip).*

**100/30** Princess Maxine (IRE), **7/2** Who's That Lady(op 2/1), **11/2** EXPRESS GIFT(op 12/1), **9/1** Kick on Majestic (IRE), **10/1** Denim Blue, Malcesine (IRE), **12/1** Coastal Express, Aegaen Lady, **16/1** Gogolette, **20/1** Ponte Cervo, Preamble, Strangersinthenite, **33/1** Fletchinni (IRE), **100/1** Ors. CSF £24.03, CT £202.94. Tote £15.10: £2.60 £3.10 £2.50 (£116.90). Mr H. Young (SALTBURN) bred by H. Young. 15 Rn          1m 33.3 (8.1)
SF—10/7/14/–/–/–

**750**     LEVY BOARD STKS (Mdn) £2108.40 (£582.40: £277.20)     **6f 206y**     4-40 (4-43)

**Straw Thatch (61)** *(MJohnston)* 3–8-12 DMcKeown (6) (w ldrs: led jst ins fnl f: rdn & r.o) ................................................................................. —1

Ace Reporter (Fav) *(MHTompkins)* 3–8-7 PRobinson (3) (w'like: lw: led: rdn appr fnl f: hdd ins fnl f: kpt on) ................................................. 1.2

618 Canon Kyle (IRE) *(MHEasterby)* 3–8-12 MBirch (2) (w ldr tl rdn & outpcd 2f out: r.o wl ins fnl f) .................................................................. 1.3

526 Silica (USA) **(70)** *(JHMGosden)* 3–8-7 GHind (4) (prom: ev ch & rdn over 2f out: rdr dropped whip wl over 1f out: styd on nr fin) ...................... s.h.4

Any Dream Would Do *(CWThornton)* 3–8-7 WNewnes (5) (b.hind: w'like: scope: s.i.s: hdwy ¹/₂-wy: styd on fnl 2f) ........................................ 2¹/₂.5

511 Serious Action *(SirMarkPrescott)* 3–8-12 GDuffield (1) (lw: bhd: drvn along & lost tch ¹/₂-wy: sme late hdwy) ............................................. ¹/₂.6

**11/10** Ace Reporter, **4/1** Silica (USA)(op 5/2), **13/2** Canon Kyle (IRE), **7/1** STRAW THATCH, Serious Action(op 16/1), **33/1** Any Dream Would Do. CSF £14.24, Tote £9.90: £4.70 £1.40 (£15.70). Mr David McKenzie (MIDDLEHAM) bred by Sheikh Mohammed bin Rashid al Maktoum. 6 Rn          1m 34.6 (9.4)

**751**     WASTWATER AUCTION STKS (Mdn 2-Y.O) £2324.00 (£644.00: £308.00)     **5f**          5-10 (5-15)

463³ **Contract Elite (IRE)** *(CWThornton)* 8-4 GDuffield (1) (lw: a cl up: rdn 2f out: styd on to ld wl ins fnl f) ....................................................... —1

574⁴ Nicky Mygirl *(MBrittain)* 7-7 LCharnock (3) (led: drvn along 2f out: hdd wl ins fnl f: kpt on) ...................................................................... ¹/₂.2

491⁴ Public Way (IRE) *(MHEasterby)* 7-12 JLowe (2) (racd wd: prom: rdn ¹/₂-wy: styd on one pce fnl 2f) ................................................................ 2.3

484² Riston Lady (IRE) *(BSRothwell)* 7-7 RFox (6) (lw: trckd ldrs gng wl: ev ch wl over 1f out: sn rdn: wknd fnl f) .................................................. 5.4

543² General Brooks (IRE) (Fav) *(JBerry)* 8-2 JCarroll (4) (lw: w ldr: rdn ¹/₂-wy: wknd wl over 1f out) ........................................................................ 8.5

Supreme Soviet *(JSHaldane)* 7-12 DaleGibson (5) (leggy: unf: s.i.s: a drvn along & bhd) ................................................................................ 5.6

**15/8** General Brooks (IRE), **9/4** Public Way (IRE), **4/1** CONTRACT ELITE (IRE), **6/1** Riston Lady (IRE), **12/1** Nicky Mygirl(op 8/1), **200/1** Supreme Soviet. CSF £36.84, Tote £4.00: £1.80 £4.40 (£10.60). Mr Brian Whitelaw (MIDDLEHAM) bred by J. Ryan in Ireland. 6 Rn          65.3 sec (5.1)
SF—23/10/7/–/–/–

**752**     CRUMMOCK WATER H'CAP (0-70) £2304.40 (£638.40: £305.20)     **5f**     5-40 (5-42)
(Weights raised 1 lb)

668⁴ Penny Hasset **(58)** (Jt-Fav) *(MWEasterby)* 4–9-10 TLucas (9) (lw: chsd ldrs: rdn 2f out: led ins fnl f: r.o) ......................................................... —1

516 Hinari Video **(46)** (Jt-Fav) *(MJohnston)* 7–8-12 DMcKeown (11) (a cl up: rdn & ev ch ins fnl f: kpt on) ......................................................... ³/₄.2

535 In a Whirl (USA) **(48)** *(DWChapman)* 4–9-0 SWood (12) (lw: a.p: effrt 2f out: styd on nr fin) .......................................................................... 1¹/₂.3

Jive Music **(33)** (bl) *(NBycroft)* 6–7–13  LCharnock (8) (lw: led: rdn wl over 1f out: hdd & wknd ins fnl f) .................................................. ³/₄.**4**

506 Hotfoot Hannah (IRE) **(45)** *(PSFelgate)* 4–8–8 ‡³JFanning (5) (prom: kpt on one pce fnl 2f) .................................................. ¹/₂.**5**

535³ Last Straw **(40)** *(AWJones)* 4–8–6  GDuffield (7) (chsd ldrs: nt qckn fnl 2f) .......... ¹/₂.**6**

535 The Right Time **(48)** (bl) *(JParkes)* 7–9–0  NConnorton (2) (in tch: drvn along ¹/₂-wy: sn wknd) .................................................. 1¹/₂.**7**

661★ Verro (USA) **(50)** (bl) *(JABennett)* 5–9–2 (7x)  NCarlisle (6) (in tch: drvn along after 2f: btn 2f out) .................................................. s.h.**8**

516⁵ Arc Lamp **(52)** *(JAGlover)* 6–9–4  DaleGibson (13) (prom: effrt over 2f out: no ex) s.h.**9**

357 R a Express **(41)** *(BAMcMahon)* 7–8–7  JLowe (3) (racd wd: spd over 3f: sn bhd) 5.**10**

Johanna Thyme **(45)** *(RBastiman)* 5–8–4⁽¹⁾ ‡⁷HBastiman (4) (a bhd: eased fr ¹/₂-wy) .................................................. hd.**11**

570 Filicaia **(52)** (v) *(DonEnricoIncisa)* 6–9–4  KimTinkler (1) (s.i.s: a bhd) ............... 3.**12**

541 Damaaz (IRE) **(32)** (v) *(JSWainwright)* 4–7–7⁽⁴⁾ ‡⁵SMaloney (10) (dwlt: a in rr) .. 5.**13**

**4/1** PENNY HASSET(3/1—9/2), Hinari Video, **9/2** Last Straw, **6/1** Verro (USA), **8/1** Arc Lamp(op 5/1), **9/1** The Right Time, **12/1** Hotfoot Hannah (IRE), **14/1** Filicaia, **16/1** In a Whirl (USA), R a Express, **20/1** Jive Music, **25/1** Johanna Thyme, **100/1** Damaaz (IRE). CSF £20.79, CT £223.08. Tote £5.90: £1.80 £1.80 £3.30 (£16.70). Mrs Anne Henson (SHERIFF HUTTON) bred by Mrs Anne Henson. 13 Rn
65.4 sec (5.2)
SF–41/26/22/4/11/7

T/Plpt: £157.20 (9.05 Tckts).
AA/GB

# CARLISLE (R-H) Friday, May 8th

753  **Abandoned**—Waterlogged

# 531–BEVERLEY (R-H)

## Friday, May 8th [Firm]

Going Allowance: St: 0.40 sec (G); Rnd: minus 0.20 sec per fur (F)        Wind: str against

Stalls: high

**759**     LUND (S) STKS (2-Y-O) £2598.40 (£722.40: £347.20)     **5f**     2-20 (2-24)

371² **Classic Storm** *(Fav)* *(JBerry)* 8-13  JCarroll (16) (lw: mde all: r.o u.p fnl 2f) ........ —**1**

619 Coconut Johnny (bl) *(GMMoore)* 8-4 ‡⁷JWeaver (17) (lw: chsd ldrs: rdn & swvd lft 2f out: wandered: kpt on ins fnl f) .................................................. 1.**2**

574 Amerigue *(MissSEHall)* 8-6  SWebster (13) (bit bkwd: hdwy ¹/₂-wy: styd on wl fnl f) ³/₄.**3**

Dailysportdutch *(PAKelleway)* 8-6  CRutter (12) (lt-f: chsd ldrs: effrt 2f out: kpt on one pce) .................................................. ¹/₂.**4**

First Option *(MHEasterby)* 8-11  KDarley (15) (w'like: scope: bit bkwd: chsd ldrs: ev ch whn bdly bmpd 2f out: edgd rt & wknd) .......... 2¹/₂.**5**

484³ Kiss in the Dark *(MrsGRReveley)* 7-13 ‡⁷DarrenMoffatt (1) (lw: s.i.s: sn bhd: styd on appr fnl f) .................................................. 5.**6**

588 Matthew David *(MBrittain)* 8-6 ‡⁵BDoyle (3) (in tch: no hdwy fnl 2f) ................... nk.**7**

571 Vardy (IRE) *(PCHaslam)* 8-11  DMcKeown (14) (in tch: effrt ¹/₂-wy: sn rdn & no imp) .................................................. nk.**8**

588⁴ Over the Dec *(BAMcMahon)* 8-6  AMunro (14) (chsd ldrs tl wknd 2f out) ........... 4.**9**

Libby-J *(MWEasterby)* 8-7⁽¹⁾  CDwyer (9) (neat: sn bhd: stdy hdwy ¹/₂-wy: r.o nr fin) .................................................. nk.**10**

352 The Rover's *(RonaldThompson)* 8-11  LCharnock (10) (s.i.s: sn bhd & drvn along: sme late hdwy) .................................................. 3.**11**

361⁶ Peak Fitness *(JAGlover)* 8-8 ‡³FNorton (4) (sn bhd) ........................................ ¹/₂.**12**

543⁵ Jarabosky *(MWEllerby)* 8-11  SMorris (5) (s.i.s: a bhd) ................................... 2.**13**

571 Red Red Wine *(MHEasterby)* 8-6 ‡⁵SMaloney (7) (sn outpcd: swtchd lft ¹/₂-wy: n.d) .................................................. 1.**14**

571 Brackenthwaite *(TDBarron)* 8-11  BCrossley (6) (a bhd) ..................................... ¹/₂.**15**

561 Prawn Cracker (IRE) (v) *(CTinkler)* 8-6  PBurke (8) (lw: chsd ldrs to ¹/₂-wy: sn wknd) .................................................. 7.**16**

619 Dardanelle *(TFairhurst)* 8-6  JQuinn (2) (outpcd ¹/₂-wy: sn bhd) ....................... ³/₄.**17**

**9/4** CLASSIC STORM, **7/2** First Option, **5/1** Over the Dec, **8/1** Vardy (IRE), Coconut Johnny, **9/1** Kiss in the Dark, **14/1** Amerigue, Dailysportdutch, **16/1** Libby-J, **20/1** Matthew David, Prawn Cracker (IRE), **25/1** Red Red Wine, Brackenthwaite, Jarabosky, Dardanelle, **33/1** Ors. CSF £25.11, Tote £3.40: £1.40 £2.60 £8.70 (£14.70). Mr D. J. Ayres (COCKERHAM) bred by Concorde Breeding and Racing International P'Ship. 17 Rn; Bt in 4,600 gns
67.2 sec (5.7)
SF–25/12/11/9/4/–

**760** SETTRINGTON H'CAP (0-80) £3106.00 (£928.00: £444.00: £202.00)
     2m 35y                                  2-50 (2-52)
                          (Weights raised 4 lb)

708* **Aude la Belle (FR) (63)** *(Fav) (MrsAKnight)* 4–8-13 (4x) ‡³FNorton (6) (lw: hld
         up: hdwy 5f out: led over 2f out: sn clr) ........................ —1

267⁴ Bridge Player **(42)** *(DMoffatt)* 5–7-5 ‡⁷DarrenMoffatt (4) (lw: trckd ldrs tl outpcd
         over 3f out: styd on fnl 2f: no ch w wnr) ...................... 5.2

475⁶ Tactical Mission **(IRE) (66)** *(JAkehurst)* 4–8-12 ‡⁷JWeaver (3) (lw: hld up: jnd ldr
         6f out: led over 3f out tl over 2 out: one pce) ............. ½.3

494⁶ Mingus **(USA) (57)** *(MrsJRRamsden)* 5–8-13 DMcKeown (8) (hld up & bhd:
         hdwy on outside 3f out: wknd over 1f out) ............... 1¹/₂.4

683⁶ Cost Effective **(37)** *(MBrittain)* 5–7-7 LCharnock (1) (chsd ldr: led over 5f out tl
         over 3f out: wknd 2f out) ....................................... 1¹/₂.5

405 Bold Elect **(70)** *(PWigham)* 4–9-9 MWigham (7) (chsd ldrs tl rdn & wknd over 1f
         out) ................................................................... ³/₄.6

122² Clifton Hampden **(71)** *(LadyHerries)* 4–9-10 WRSwinburn (5) (lw: led tl over 5f
         out: sn lost pl & wl bhd: kpt on ins fnl f) ................. 2¹/₂.7

578 Carefree Times **(52)** *(JNorton)* 5–8-3 ‡⁵SMaloney (2) (in tch tl outpcd over 3f
         out: sn bhd) ....................................................... ¹/₂.8
                LONG HANDICAP: Cost Effective 7-2.

**2/1** AUDE LA BELLE (FR), **9/2** Bridge Player, **11/2** Tactical Mission (IRE), **6/1** Clifton Hampden, **8/1** Mingus
(USA), **10/1** Bold Elect, Carefree Times, **16/1** Cost Effective. CSF £11.04, CT £38.38. Tote £2.90: £1.10 £1.80
£2.10 (£5.40). Mrs Val Rapkins (CULLOMPTON) bred by J. P. de Gaste in France. 8 Rn    3m 44.2 (13.5)

**761** BEVERLEY RUGBY CLUB H'CAP (0-70) £2637.00 (£732.00: £351.00)
     1m 3f 216y                                  3-20 (3-22)
                          (Weights raised 3 lb)

530² **Petavious (63)** *(LadyHerries)* 7–9-10 WRSwinburn (1) (lw: hld up gng wl: gd
         hdwy over 3f out: led over 1f out: drvn out) ............... —1

593² Broom Isle **(48)** *(MrsAKnight)* 4–8-6 ‡³FNorton (15) (chsd ldrs: ev ch over 2f out:
         styd on same pce fnl f) ......................................... 2.2

575* Sea Paddy **(45)** *(RBastiman)* 4–8-6 (6x) DMcKeown (9) (lw: hld up & bhd: gd
         hdwy over 3f out: nt qckn fnl f) ............................ 1.3

494⁵ Glastondale **(40)** *(TDBarron)* 6–8-1 [1] AlexGreaves (13) (lw: w ldrs: led over 2f
         out tl over 1f out: kpt on one pce) ........................ 1.4

533² Floating Line **(60)** *(PWigham)* 4–9-7 MWigham (14) (lw: chsd ldrs: drvn along
         6f out: one pce fnl 2f) ....................................... 2¹/₂.5

469³ Lidanzia **(42)** *(RJHolder)* 4–7-12 ‡⁵ATucker (3) (lw: hdwy 6f out: styd on u.p fnl
         2f: no imp) ........................................................ s.h.6

530⁶ Incola **(44)** *(Fav) (HCandy)* 6–8-5 CRutter (8) (hdwy 6f out: rdn & hung rt 2f out:
         n.d) ................................................................. 2¹/₂.7

312⁶ Deb's Ball **(59)** *(DMoffatt)* 6–8-13 ‡⁷DarrenMoffatt (11) (sn bhd & pushed along:
         reminders 6f out: styd on wl fnl 2f) ..................... 2.8

575 Statia **(IRE) (42)** *(DonEnricoIncisa)* 4–8-3 JakiHouston (4) (chsd ldrs: led over
         4f out tl over 2f out: grad wknd) ......................... hd.9

518 Starlight Wonder **(38)** *(REBarr)* 6–7-13 PBurke (5) (nvr nr to chal) ................... 3.10

     Crimson Cloud **(IRE) (47)** *(NTinkler)* 4–8-8 KimTinkler (7) (bit bkwd: sn bhd) ... 3.11

     First Exhibition **(39)** *(MrsAKnight)* 5–8-0 JQuinn (12) (b.off fore: chsd ldrs tl lost
         pl over 3f out) .................................................. 5.12

518⁶ Rexy Boy **(38)** (v) *(WLBarker)* 5–7-13 LCharnock (16) (led tl over 4f out: wknd 3f
         out) ................................................................. 4.13

422 Thimbalina **(45)** *(DAWilson)* 6–8-1 ‡⁵NKennedy (2) (a in rr) ....................... 3¹/₂.14

617 Gods Law **(40)** *(REarnshaw)* 11–8-1 AProud (10) (b.hind: bit bkwd: chsd ldrs tl
         wknd 5f out) ..................................................... ¹/₂.15

**4/1** Incola, **6/1** Sea Paddy, PETAVIOUS, **7/1** Deb's Ball, **17/2** Broom Isle, **9/1** Floating Line, **10/1** Glastondale,
Thimbalina, Lidanzia, **16/1** Crimson Cloud (IRE), **20/1** Rexy Boy, **25/1** First Exhibition, Starlight Wonder, **50/1**
Ors. CSF £55.70, CT £300.59. Tote £6.00: £2.10 £3.00 £1.80 (£20.00). Lady Herries (LITTLEHAMPTON) bred
by Lavinia Duchess of Norfolk. 15 Rn                                   2m 34.3 (2.7)
                                                   SF—59/37/35/28/43/19

**762** EVERINGHAM STKS (Mdn 3-Y.O) £2206.40 (£610.40: £291.20)   **7f 100y**   3-50 (3-52)

289⁴ **Scottish Park (70)** *(JPLeigh)* 8-2 ‡⁷JWeaver (4) (chsd ldr: shkn up to ld over 1f
         out: rdn out) ..................................................... —1

526² Morsun **(79)** *(Fav) (DMorley)* 9-0 WRSwinburn (2) (lw: led tl over 1f out: fnd
         little: eased whn btn nr fin) ................................ 5.2

512 Thakawah *(RWArmstrong)* 9-0 AMunro (7) (chsd ldrs: one pce fnl 2f) ............ 2.3

     Kateb **(IRE)** *(RWArmstrong)* 9-0 BCrossley (1) (str: lengthy: bit bkwd: s.s: sn wl
         bhd: hdwy & prom ¹/₂-wy: wknd over 2f out) ......... 8.4

614⁴ Speedy Classic **(USA)** *(CTinkler)* 9-0 KDarley (6) (lw: trckd ldrs tl wknd 2f out) s.h.5

     Dancing Pet *(WWHaigh)* 8-9 DMcKeown (3) (bit bkwd: wl bhd fnl 5f) ................ 8.6

466 Sabzy *(PDEvans)* 8-4 ‡⁵LNewton (5) (bhd fr ½-wy: t.o) ................................... dist.**7**

**8/11** Morsun, **4/1** Kateb (IRE)(op 9/4), **5/1** Speedy Classic (USA), **8/1** Thakawah, SCOTTISH PARK, **33/1** Ors. CSF £15.03, Tote £10.60: £3.10 £1.10 (£3.80). Mr K. G. Bridges (GAINSBOROUGH) bred by J. B. H. Stevens. 7 Rn
1m 33.1 (2.9)
SF—22/19/13/–/–/–

---

**763**      HUMBERSIDE APP'CE H'CAP (0-70) £2500.40 (£694.40: £333.20)
**1m 100y**                                                         4-20 (4-20)

**Overpower (50)** *(MHTompkins)* 8-8-5 ‡⁷MGodsafe (14) (bit bkwd: hdwy over 3f out: led over 1f out: edgd lft: hld on nr fin) ......................... —**1**
431 St Patrick's Day **(63)** *(CEBrittain)* 4-9-11 BDoyle (6) (bhd: hdwy on outside 2f out: r.o nr fin) ............................................................... ½.**2**
616★ Sweet Mignonette **(38)** (Fav) *(MrsGRReveley)* 4-8-0 (6x) DarrenMoffatt (13) (lw: sltly hmpd & carried wd over 2f out: swtchd rt 1f out: styd on same pce) ................................................. 1.**3**
Stelby **(59)** *(OBrennan)* 8-9-7 FNorton (4) (lw: hdwy 2f out: r.o u.p: nrst fin) ...... 1.**4**
615⁵ Sandmoor Denim **(52)** *(SRBowring)* 5-8-7 ‡⁷MHarris (8) (s.s: bhd: hdwy on ins over 2f out: nt clr run & swtchd ocver 1f out: styd on) ........ ½.**5**
Routing **(61)** *(MDHammond)* 4-9-2⁽³⁾ ‡⁷ADobbin (9) (hdwy fnl 2f: nt rch ldrs) ... nk.**6**
Chart Cross **(38)** *(KSBridgwater)* 6-8-0 ATucker (15) (led 1f: trckd ldrs: led 2f out: sn hdd & wknd) ......................................................... 3½.**7**
469 Honey Boy Simba **(43)** (v) *(MO'Neill)* 6-7-12 ‡⁷WFrost (12) (nvr rchd ldrs) ....... hd.**8**
606 Enchanted Flyer **(36)** (bl) *(TWDonnelly)* 5-7-12 TWilson (2) (b: prom: rn wd appr st: sn lost pl) ................................................................. 1½.**9**
572 Must Be Magical (USA) **(41)** *(FHLee)* 4-8-3 NKennedy (1) (bit bkwd: led after 1st: swvd lft over 2f out: sn hdd & wknd) ......................... 1½.**10**
Into the Future **(33)** *(APStringer)* 5-7-2⁽²⁾ ‡⁷DWright (10) (s.i.s: a in rr) ............. 3.**11**
572 Deputy Tim **(48)** *(RBastiman)* 9-8-10 HBastiman (3) (hld up & bhd) ............. s.h.**12**
572² Errema **(51)** *(CTinkler)* 7-8-13 SMaloney (5) (b.nr hind: lw: chsd ldrs tl lost pl over 2f out) .............................................................. 2½.**13**
193 Orchanda **(42)** *(MrsAKnight)* 4-7-11⁽⁴⁾ ‡⁷GParkin (7) (prom tl wknd appr st) ...... 3.**14**
25 Bold Answer **(31)** *(MCChapman)* 9-7-7 AntoinetteArmes (11) (sn t.o) ................. **15**
LONG HANDICAP: Into the Future 7-0, Bold Answer 6-9.

**10/11** Sweet Mignonette, **5/1** St Patrick's Day, **9/1** Errema, **12/1** Sandmoor Denim, **14/1** Honey Boy Simba, OVERPOWER, **16/1** Chart Cross, **20/1** Deputy Tim, Stelby(op 12/1), Routing, **33/1** Orchanda, Into the Future, Enchanted Flyer, **50/1** Must Be Magical (USA), **100/1** Bold Answer. CSF £131.36, CT £213.66. Tote £13.20: £3.00 £2.80 £1.20 (£38.90). Mr M. P. Bowring (NEWMARKET) bred by Barronstown Stud. 15 Rn
1m 46.9 (4.2)
SF—2/20/–/10/–/2

---

**764**      HOUGHTON STKS (Mdn) £1932.00 (£532.00: £252.00)    **5f**    4-50 (4-58)

618 **Lillah Darak (USA)** *(PDEvans)* 4-9-5 ‡⁵LNewton (6) (b: hdwy ½-wy: led jst ins fnl f: r.o) ................................................................. —**1**
Haunting Rhapsody (USA) *(JEtherington)* 3-8-9 KDarley (3) (lt-f: scope: chsd ldr: rn green ½-wy: effrt & ev ch 1f out: r.o) .......................... ¾.**2**
506 Madam Petoski **(61)** *(FHLee)* 3-8-9 AMunro (8) (chsd ldrs: ev ch over 1f out: sn wknd) .......................................................................... 2½.**3**
618⁴ Saddlehome (USA) **(83)** (Fav) *(RMWhitaker)* 3-9-0 WRSwinburn (7) (lw: w ldrs: rdn to ld wl over 1f out: hdd & wknd jst ins fnl f) ........ 1½.**4**
45 Call for Rooney **(53)** *(ASmith)* 4-9-10 CDwyer (10) (sn bhd: hdwy 2f out: r.o u.p) nk.**5**
591¹³ High Principles **(54)** *(JBerry)* 3-9-0 JCarroll (2) (lw: effrt ½-wy: hung rt: nvr nr to chal) .................................................................... ¾.**6**
Supreme Desire *(ASmith)* 4-9-5 SWebster (12) (b.off hind: w ldrs tl wknd wl over 1f out) ................................................................. 1½.**7**
516 Barnsview **(44)** *(MWEllerby)* 3-9-0 SMorris (11) (nvr rchd ldrs) ........................ 1½.**8**
Admirals Realm *(BAMcMahon)* 3-8-7 ‡⁷JBramhill (4) (lengthy: unf: chsd ldrs tl wknd 2f out) ............................................................... ¾.**9**
Lawnswood Prince (IRE) **(69)** *(JLSpearing)* 3-9-0 BCrossley (9) (led over 3f: sn wknd) .......................................................................... ½.**10**
*Rock Opera (IRE) (12/1) Withdrawn (burst from stalls) : not under orders — Rule 4 applies*
*669 Boy Martin (12/1) Withdrawn (ref to ent stalls) : not under orders*

**8/11** Saddlehome (USA)(op 5/4), **9/2** Haunting Rhapsody (USA)(5/1—7/1), **10/1** High Principles(op 5/1), **12/1** Madam Petoski, **16/1** Admirals Realm(op 10/1), Lawnswood Prince (IRE), **33/1** Call for Rooney, LILLAH DARAK (USA), Barnsview, **50/1** Supreme Desire. CSF £141.62, Tote £61.40: £8.70 £1.80 £1.50 (Wnr or 2nd w any £2.40). Mrs A. Swinbank (WELSHPOOL) bred by Gainsborough Farm, Inc. in USA. 10 Rn    67.4 sec (5.9)
SF—27/14/4/3/12/–

T/Plpt: £213.00 (13.65 Tckts).
                                                            WG

# BEVERLEY (R-H)
**Saturday, May 9th [Firm]**
Going Allowance: minus 0.35 sec per fur (F)       Wind: almost nil

Stalls: high

**765**    KIPLINGCOTE (S) STKS (3-Y.O) £2598.40 (£722.40: £347.20)    **7f 100y**    2-20 (2-24)

| | |
|---|---|
| 406 | **Katie's Dream (IRE) (43)** *(PSFelgate)* 8-2 JLowe (1) (hdwy over 2f out: nt clr run over 1f out: swtchd ins & styd on wl to ld nr fin) ............ —1 |
| | Rose Gem (IRE) **(66)** *(PCHaslam)* 8-2 DaleGibson (14) (plld hrd: led: rdn over 1f out: hdd & no ex cl home) .............................................. ¾.2 |
| 116 | Super-Sub **(59)** *(GFleming)* 8-2 PRobinson (6) (chsd ldr: rdn over 2f out: nt qckn appr fnl f) ................................................................... 2.3 |
| 520⁶ | Miss Parkes **(53)** *(Fav)* *(JBerry)* 8-2 JCarroll (12) (a in tch: effrt over 2f out: one pce appr fnl f) .................................................... ¾.4 |
| 567⁶ | Victor Romeo **(53)** (bl) *(WJPearce)* 9-0 DNicholls (11) (bhd: hdwy 2f out: styd on fnl f: nvr nrr) ......................................................... hd.5 |
| 448 | King Optimist **(42)** *(ASmith)* 8-7 SWebster (10) (hdwy ent st: r.o u.p appr fnl f) .. 1.6 |
| 495 | Hataal (IRE) **(44)** *(JBalding)* 7-13⁽²⁾ ‡5RPrice (2) (s.i.s: wl bhd tl styd on strly fnl 2f) .............................................................................. ¾.7 |
| 544² | Yaakum **(62)** (bl) *(BHanbury)* 8-7 BRaymond (3) (hdwy ½-wy: rdn & edgd rt 2f out: btn 1f out) .......................................................... s.h.8 |
| 82⁶ | Mississippi Queen **(40)** *(MrsNMacauley)* 7-9 ‡7MadeleineSmith (8) (prom: effrt & wandered bdly fnl 2f: wknd over 1f out) ...................... 1½.9 |
| 567 | Super Marco **(43)** *(WWHaigh)* 8-7 ACulhane (4) (lw: effrt on outside over 2f out: nt rch ldrs) ......................................................... 3.10 |
| 614 | Bassetlaw Belle *(SRBowring)* 8-2 AProud (15) (nvr trbld ldrs) ................... s.h.11 |
| 614 | Another Ryton *(MWEllerby)* 8-7 SMorris (16) (a bhd) ................................. 6.12 |
| 567 | Sharp as You Like **(50)** *(JEtherington)* 8-7 KDarley (13) (prom: rdn & wknd 2f out: btn whn hmpd over 1f out) ......................................... 1.13 |
| 397 | Emerald Ears **(58)** *(EWeymes)* 8-9 GHind (9) (in tch: effrt on ins over 2f out: wkng whn hmpd over 1f out: eased whn btn) ................... 1½.14 |
| | On the Hop (IRE) *(APStringer)* 8-2 JFortune (5) (t.o) ................................. 15 |
| | Whitrigg Lad *(WWHaigh)* 8-7 KFallon (7) (cmpt: bit bkwd: s.s: rn v.green: a t.o) . 16 |
| 487 | Grey Decision *(MBrittain)* 8-7 MBirch (17) (t.o) ....................................... 17 |

**11/4** Miss Parkes, **5/1** Yaakum(op 3/1), **6/1** Emerald Ears, **7/1** Rose Gem (IRE)(op 9/2), **8/1** KATIE'S DREAM (IRE)(op 12/1), **12/1** Super-Sub, Victor Romeo(op 8/1), Sharp as You Like, **20/1** Super Marco, Hataal (IRE), Whitrigg Lad, Mississippi Queen, **25/1** Grey Decision, King Optimist, **33/1** Ors. CSF £65.64, Tote £10.10: £2.30 £2.90 £3.40 (£43.40). Mr P. O'Malley (MELTON MOWBRAY) bred by Theodore Barry in Ireland. 17 Rn; Bt in 4,200 gns; Yaakum clmd D A Broadbent £5,081     1m 32.7 (2.5)

**766**    RAPID LAD H'CAP (0-80) £3817.50 (£1140.00: £545.00: £247.50)
     **1m 1f 207y**      2-50 (3-09)

(Weights raised 2 lb)

| | |
|---|---|
| 533 | **Touch Above (55)** *(TDBarron)* 6-9-2 AlexGreaves (12) (chsd ldrs: effrt & n.m.r over 2f out: swtchd & led over 1f out: hld on wl) ................. —1 |
| 370 | Cultured **(76)** *(Fav)* *(MRStoute)* 3-9-7 BRaymond (7) (in tch: hdwy over 2f out: rdn & styd on wl fnl f: jst failed) ........................................ hd.2 |
| 606² | Bescaby Boy **(63)** *(JWharton)* 6-9-10 MBirch (6) (lw: hdwy 2f out: kpt on u.p fnl f: nvr able to chal) ................................................................... 3½.3 |
| 533 | Who's Tef (IRE) **(60)** *(MHEasterby)* 4-9-2 ‡5SMaloney (4) (bit bkwd: chsd ldrs: rdn to ld 2f out: hdd over 1f out: no ex) ..................................... nk.4 |
| 617⁴ | Sharquin **(38)** *(MBrittain)* 5-7-13 GBardwell (3) (in tch: effrt on outside appr st: nt pce to chal) ...................................................................... 3½.5 |
| 533³ | Smoke **(45)** *(JParkes)* 6-8-6 NCarlisle (8) (s.i.s: hdwy 4f out: effrt & rdn over 2f out: nvr able to chal) ............................................................. 2.6 |
| 617* | Young George **(61)** *(MDods)* 5-9-8 KFallon (10) (lw: hld up & bhd: hdwy over 2f out: sn rdn & no imp: eased ins fnl f) ..................................... 1½.7 |
| 340 | Sauvignon (IRE) **(55)** *(RGuest)* 4-9-2 GBaxter (11) (w ldr tl wknd over 2f out) ... ½.8 |
| 464⁶ | Reel of Tulloch (IRE) **(76)** *(PCHaslam)* 3-9-7 KDarley (5) (in tch: sltly hmpd after 3f: effrt 3f out: wknd & eased appr fnl f) .............................. 2.9 |
| 457³ | Double the Stakes (USA) **(51)** *(FHLee)* 3-7-5⁽¹⁾ ‡5NKennedy (9) (plld hrd: led tl hdd 2f out: wknd over 1f out) ................................................ ¾.10 |
| 504 | Mysterious Maid (USA) **(63)** *(JPearce)* 5-9-5 ‡5RPrice (13) (a bhd) .............. nk.11 |
| 504 | Rapid Lad **(42)** *(JLSpearing)* 14-8-3 JLowe (2) (s.i.s: sn wl bhd) ................. 12 |

5/2 Cultured, 9/2 Smoke, 13/2 Bescaby Boy, 7/1 TOUCH ABOVE, 9/1 Young George, 10/1 Who's Tef (IRE), 12/1 Sharquin, Double the Stakes (USA), 16/1 Reel of Tulloch (IRE), Mysterious Maid (USA), 20/1 Sauvignon (IRE), 25/1 Rapid Lad. CSF £25.08, CT £115.47. Tote £7.00: £2.10 £1.80 £1.80 (£17.20). Mrs J. Hazell (THIRSK) bred by Crockfords Stud. 12 Rn

2m 5.4 (3.4)

SF—33/37/33/24/–/3

### 767    HYPAC H'CAP (3-Y.O) (0-90) £3915.00 (£1170.00: £560.00: £255.00)
1m 100y

3-20 (3-35)

| | | |
|---|---|---|
| 558[5] | **Hadaad (USA) (80)** (AAScott) 8-13 BRaymond (11) (trckd ldrs: led over 1f out: drvn out & r.o wl) | —1 |
| | Eid (USA) (77) (DMorley) 8-10 KDarley (4) (hdwy over 2f out: styd on wl u.p fnl f) | ¾.2 |
| 482[3] | Thinking Twice (USA) (74) (PWHarris) 8-7 WNewnes (6) (trckd ldrs: n.m.r over 1f out: swtchd & kpt on wl ins fnl f) | hd.3 |
| 545[6] | Nicely Thanks (USA) (70) (TDBarron) 8-3 AlexGreaves (1) (hdwy on outside 2f out: ev ch jst ins fnl f: wandered u.p: no ex) | 1.4 |
| 646[4] | Eden's Close (78) (v) (Fav) (MHTompkins) 8-11 PRobinson (12) (plld hrd: prom tl rdn & wknd over 1f out) | 1½.5 |
| 490* | Cool Luke (IRE) (81) (GMMoore) 8-7 ‡JWeaver (10) (chsd ldrs: ev ch 2f out: edgd lft u.p & sn btn) | 2½.6 |
| | Super Summit (60) (JPearce) 7-0 ‡CHawksley (9) (chsd ldrs: rdn over 2f out: wknd over 1f out) | d.h.6 |
| | North Esk (USA) (88) (JWWatts) 9-7 JLowe (8) (lw: hld up & bhd: stdy hdwy 2f out: swtchd ins fnl f: no imp) | ¾.8 |
| | Talented Ting (IRE) (66) (PCHaslam) 7-13 DaleGibson (7) (bit bkwd: cl up: led over 1f out: sn hdd & wknd) | 4.9 |
| 662[3] | The Dandy Don (IRE) (60) (DenysSmith) 7-0 ‡CTeague (2) (plld hrd: in tch: rn wd appr st: lost pl 2f out) | 3½.10 |
| 533[5] | Watch Me Go (IRE) (60) (BobJones) 7-7 GBardwell (14) (plld hrd: trckd ldrs: hmpd ent st: wknd wl over 1f out) | ½.11 |
| 558 | Majal (IRE) (84) (BHanbury) 9-3 AShoults (13) (led: rdn over 2f out: hdd & wknd over 1f out) | 1.12 |
| | Gold Belt (IRE) (66) (RHollinshead) 7-6[6] ‡MHumphries (3) (unruly stalls: hdwy on outside 3f out: sn btn) | 2.13 |
| 395 | Khalloof (IRE) (73) (MAJarvis) 8-6 JCarroll (5) (t.o fnl 3f) | 14 |

LONG HANDICAP: Super Summit 7-3, The Dandy Don (IRE) 7-6, Watch Me Go (IRE) 7-4, Gold Belt (IRE) 7-6.

3/1 Eden's Close, 9/2 Cool Luke (IRE), 5/1 HADAAD (USA), 17/2 Watch Me Go (IRE), Thinking Twice (USA), 9/1 Nicely Thanks (USA), 10/1 The Dandy Don (IRE), 11/1 Majal (IRE), 14/1 Khalloof (IRE), Eid (USA), 16/1 North Esk (USA), 20/1 Talented Ting (IRE), Gold Belt (IRE), 33/1 Super Summit. CSF £75.92, CT £563.04. Tote £5.00: £1.80 £7.90 £2.60 (£76.80). Maktoum Al Maktoum (NEWMARKET) bred by Gainsborough Stud Management Ltd in USA. 14 Rn

1m 46 (3.3)

SF—5/–/–/–/–/–.

### 768    HESSLE H'CAP (0-90) £2898.00 (£864.00: £412.00: £186.00)
7f 100y

3-50 (4-02)

| | | |
|---|---|---|
| | **Major Mouse (65)** (WWHaigh) 4-8-12 ACulhane (9) (in tch: hdwy to ld over 1f out: r.o wl) | —1 |
| | Genair (FR) (57) (MrsGRReveley) 7-8-4[1] KFallon (11) (lw: bhd: pushed along 4f out: hdwy 2f out: kpt on wl fnl f: nt rch wnr) | 1½.2 |
| 485 | Ringland (USA) (77) (PCHaslam) 4-9-10 KDarley (12) (a.p: ev ch 2f out: nt qckn appr fnl f) | nk.3 |
| 532[2] | Yonge Tender (57) (bl) (JWharton) 5-8-4 DaleGibson (2) (mid div: effrt & hdwy 2f out: hmpd over 1f out: styd on) | ¾.4 |
| 667 | Northern Printer (60) (MO'Neill) 7-8-7 JFortune (6) (bhd: hdwy 2f out: n.m.r over 1f out: styd on) | ¾.5 |
| 392[6] | Conquista (81) (bl) (LadyHerries) 4–10-0 BRaymond (7) (in tch: effrt & hdwy 2f out: sltly hmpd over 1f out: no ex) | 1.6 |
| 240[6] | Gabbiadini (76) (v) (Fav) (MHTompkins) 5-9-9 PRobinson (13) (prom tl rdn & wknd over 1f out) | hd.7 |
| 572[4] | Puffy (51) (bl) (GMMoore) 5-7-7[2] ‡‡SMaloney (1) (chsd ldrs: rdn 3f out: one pce fnl 2f) | hd.8 |
| 563 | Pimsboy (55) (bl) (PABlockley) 5-8-2 GHind (5) (chsd ldrs: effrt over 3f out: btn wl over 1f out) | ¾.9 |
| 496 | Bernstein Bette (68) (PSFelgate) 6-9-1 MRoberts (10) (nvr trbld ldrs) | 5.10 |
| 398 | Super Benz (80) (TFairhurst) 6–9-10 ‡JFanning (4) (chsd ldr: led 3f out tl hdd over 1f out: wknd) | 4.11 |
| 617 | American Hero (70) (CTinkler) 4-9-3 MBirch (8) (swtg: led tl hdd 3f out: sn btn) | 1½.12 |
| 676* | Drum Sergeant (59) (v) (JParkes) 5-8-6 NCarlisle (3) (lw: s.i.s: effrt & n.m.r over 2f out: sn wknd) | ¾.13 |

**4/1** Gabbiadini, **6/1** Yonge Tender, Conquista, Puffy(8/1—9/1), **7/1** Drum Sergeant, **8/1** Super Benz, Pimsboy, **9/1** Genair (FR), **12/1** Ringland (USA), American Hero, **14/1** Northern Printer, **16/1** MAJOR MOUSE, **20/1** Bernstein Bette. CSF £158.17, CT £1,671.52. Tote £25.00: £4.80 £3.60 £5.00 (£87.70). Mr N. Barber (MALTON) bred by Mrs V. Haigh. 13 Rn                                                                        1m 31.8 (1.6)
                                                                                                      SF—35/22/41/19/20/37

---

**769**      FILEY CLAIMING STKS (2-Y.O) £2441.60 (£677.60: £324.80)      **5f**      4-20 (4-31)

371* **Purchased by Phone (IRE)** *(Fav)* *(PCHaslam)* 8-4 MRoberts (14) (mde all: r.o
                strly) .....................................................................................................................  —1
371³ Shadow Jury *(MrsGRReveley)* 8-11 KDarley (10) (lw: a chsng wnr: rdn 2f out:
                wandered u.p & no ex fnl f) ..................................................................  1½.2
        Cloudy Reef *(RHollinshead)* 7-7 ‡⁷AGarth (6) (neat: bit bkwd: in tch: hdwy over
                1f out: kpt on fnl f) .............................................................................  4.3
561* Ruby Cooper *(JWharton)* 8-4 NNewnes (3) (prom: rdn 2f out: one pce fnl f) ..  1½.4
263³ Bright Gem *(TFairhurst)* 8-1 ‡³JFanning (4) (chsd ldrs tl rdn & wknd over 1f out)  1½.5
        Hodge Beck *(MHEasterby)* 8-5⁽⁶⁾ MBirch (13) (cmpt: in tch: effrt ½-wy: nt qckn
                appr fnl f) ...........................................................................................  hd.6
        Don't Jump (IRE) *(MHTompkins)* 8-1 PRobinson (12) (cmpt: unf: s.i.s: hdwy wl
                over 1f out: nvr nrr) ...............................................................................  2½.7
571  Jersey Bob (IRE) *(JSWainwright)* 7-11 ‡⁷GParkin (8) (nvr trbld ldrs) ..............  2.8
619  Private Liner *(RonaldThompson)* 8-9 SMorris (7) (bit bkwd: in tch tl grad lost pl
                fnl 2f) ...................................................................................................  3½.9
        Sweet Poppy *(JSWainwright)* 7-13 LCharnock (9) (small: n.d) .....................  2½.10
286⁶ Laxey Flyer *(JBerry)* 7-13 NCarlisle (11) (in tch over 3f) ...............................  nk.11
        Newgatesky *(BWMurray)* 8-2 JFortune (1) (leggy: unf: carried lft s: nvr nr ldrs)  1½.12
423  Dazzling Rahy *(MDods)* 7-12 JLowe (15) (bit bkwd: in tch tl hmpd ½-wy: sn lost
                pl) .........................................................................................................  1½.10
231  Cheltenham Windows *(MWEasterby)* 8-6 TLucas (2) (wnt lft s: a in rr) .............  ½.14
423  Canazei *(DonEnricoIncisa)* 7-12 KimTinkler (5) (s.s: a bhd) .............................  15

**5/4** PURCHASED BY PHONE (IRE), **11/4** Shadow Jury, **6/1** Ruby Cooper(op 4/1), **10/1** Hodge Beck, Bright Gem, **12/1** Laxey Flyer, **14/1** Don't Jump (IRE)(op 8/1), **20/1** Cloudy Reef(op 12/1), Private Liner, **25/1** Cheltenham Windows, **33/1** Ors. CSF £6.25, Tote £2.50: £1.50 £1.70 £11.50 (£4.50). Mr S. A. B. Dinsmore (MIDDLEHAM) bred by Miss V. Charlton in Ireland. 15 Rn                                                                        62.3 sec (0.8)
                                                                                                      SF—39/40/6/11/2/5

---

**770**      BYGOT WOOD MEDIAN AUCTION GRADUATION STKS (2-Y.O) £2595.00 (£720.00:
             £345.00)      **5f**                                                                          4-50 (5-01)

        **Whisperdales** *(MWEllerby)* 8-11 SMorris (12) (neat: unf: in tch: hdwy on ins
                over 1f out: styd on wl to ld nr fin) ......................................................  —1
564² Craigie Boy *(JPLeigh)* 8-4 ‡⁷JWeaver (14) (a.p: led over 1f out: hung lft: hdd &
                no ex nr fin) ..........................................................................................  ½.2
555  Sharro *(PAKelleway)* 8-11 PRobinson (4) (a.p: hrd rdn 2f out: kpt on fnl f) ......  1½.3
        Fort Vally *(BWMurray)* 8-6 GBaxter (2) (b.nr hind: leggy: lt-f: unf: racd wd in tch:
                rdn ½-wy: kpt on wl u.p fnl f) .................................................................  hd.4
543* Tarnside Rosal *(Fav)* *(JEtherington)* 8-13 TLucas (13) (trckd ldrs: n.m.r wl over
                1f out: hmpd over 1f out: styd on) ........................................................  1½.5
        Betrayed *(PCHaslam)* 8-6 EJohnson (9) (cmpt: leggy: led tl edgd lft & hdd over
                1f out: no ex ins fnl f) ...........................................................................  hd.6
        Paajib (IRE) *(CTinkler)* 8-11 MBirch (5) (w'like: cmpt: hdwy ½-wy: styd on: nt
                rch ldrs) ...............................................................................................  1½.7
365  Hawaymyson (IRE) *(APStringer)* 8-11 JFortune (8) (w ldr over 3f: no ex) ..........  nk.8
665  Greystyle *(MBrittain)* 8-11 KDarley (3) (nvr nr ldrs) .....................................  ½.9
        Bella Bambola (IRE) *(SGNorton)* 8-6 LCharnock (11) (cmpt: unf: sme hdwy
                ½-wy: nvr plcd to chal) ..........................................................................  hd.10
        Volunteer Point (IRE) *(MrsSABramall)* 8-11 SWood (10) (cmpt: bkwd: nvr nr
                ldrs) .....................................................................................................  1½.11
        Hotaria *(RMWhitaker)* 8-6 ACulhane (1) (small: neat: bit bkwd: s.s: hdwy to
                chase ldrs ½-wy: wknd appr fnl f) ..........................................................  s.h.12
        Blowedifiknow *(JWharton)* 8-11 WNewnes (7) (unf: bit bkwd: s.i.s: a bhd) .......  2.13
        Kentucky Dreams *(JBerry)* 8-11 JCarroll (6) (cmpt: leggy: bit bkwd: in tch over
                3f) .........................................................................................................  d.h.13

**8/11** Tarnside Rosal(op 5/4), **9/2** Craigie Boy, **12/1** Kentucky Dreams, **12/1** Sharro, **14/1** Hawaymyson (IRE), Hotaria, Bella Bambola (IRE), **16/1** Betrayed, Blowedifiknow, **25/1** WHISPERDALES & Ors. CSF £148.09, Tote £96.80: £11.80 £1.70 £2.80 (£109.10). Mrs H. J. Ellerby (PICKERING) bred by Mrs K. M. and A. Mack. 14 Rn                                                                        64.5 sec (3)
                                                                                                      SF—2/-/-/-/-/-/-

**771** LAMWORTH STKS (Mdn) £2343.60 (£649.60: £310.80) **1m 3f 216y** 5-20 (5-29)

    **Row Ree** *(PJHobbs)* 4–9-10 JCarroll (9) (bhd: pushed along 6f out: chsd ldrs
      ent st: chal wl over 1f out: led nr fin) .................................... —1
4184 Naseem Elbarr (USA) *(ACStewart)* 4–9-10 MRoberts (7) (lw: plld hrd: hdwy on
      outside appr st: brght wd: slt ld appr fnl f: hdd nr fin) ........ hd.2
5605 Restless Minstrel (USA) (Fav) *(LMCumani)* 3–8-5 JFortune (3) (trckd ldr: led wl
      over 2f out: sn drvn along: nt qckn ins fnl f) .................... 1½.3
    Tour Leader (NZ) *(TDBarron)* 3–8-5 AlexGreaves (1) (w'like: str: bit bkwd: s.s:
      wl bhd tl hdwy over 2f out: kpt on fnl f) .................... ¾.4
    Sherraa (USA) *(MAJarvis)* 3–8-0 GCrealock (5) (unf: in tch: effrt 5f out: one pce
      fnl 3f) .................................... 2½.5
    Helmsley Palace (bl) *(MrsJCecil)* 3–8-0 BCrossley (4) (led tl hdd & wknd wl
      over 2f out) .................................... 12.6
    Tremendous (USA) *(JNorton)* 4–9-10 ACulhane (2) (chsd ldrs tl wknd over 3f out) 3.7
    Give All *(BRichmond)* 6–9-5 ‡5SMaloney (6) (b: s.i.s: in rr tl effrt appr st: sn btn) 15.8
    Jane's Affair *(RonaldThompson)* 4–9-5 JLowe (8) (p.u after 3f) .................... 0

**13/8** Restless Minstrel (USA)(op 4/5), **4/1** Naseem Elbarr (USA), **5/1** ROW REE(op 10/1), **6/1** Helmsley Palace,
**8/1** Sherraa (USA), **20/1** Tour Leader (NZ), **33/1** Jane's Affair, **50/1** Ors. CSF £22.75, Tote £6.70: £1.60 £2.00
£1.20 (£15.60). Mr O. Zawawi (MINEHEAD) bred by Dr O. Zawawi. 9 Rn     2m 37.8 (6.2)
                                               SF—8/7/–/–/–/–

T/Plpt: £2,032.20 (1.8 Tckts).                                              O'R

## 345—LINGFIELD (L-H)

### Friday, May 8th [Turf Good, Good to firm back st, AWT Standard]
Going Allowance: AWT: minus 0.30 sec (FS); Turf: minus 0.15 sec (F)    Wind: fresh across

Stalls: high

**772** R. R. RICHARDSON STKS (Mdn 2-Y.O) £2324.00 (£644.00: £308.00)   **5f** 2-30 (2-34)

    **Fortune Cay (IRE)** (Fav) *(RHannon)* 9-0 AMcGlone (7) (unf: scope: lw: a.p: led
      2f out: clr 1f out: eased nr fin) .................................... —1
    Charity Express (IRE) *(JBerry)* 8-9 TQuinn (8) (unf: bit bkwd: a.p: led over 2f
      out: sn hdd: unable qckn) .................................... 3½.2
    Mr Dingle *(WJHaggas)* 9-0 NDay (4) (unf: scope: lw: dwlt: swtchd rt 4f out:
      n.m.r over 2f out: hdwy fnl f: rn green) .................... 3.3
    Madam Cyn's Risk *(NACallaghan)* 8-2 ‡7JTate (2) (lt-f: hdwy over 1f out: r.o) ... s.h.4
6026 Daring King *(DSasse)* 8-9 ‡5RPerham (9) (nvr nr to chal) .................... 2½.5
    War Requiem (IRE) *(GBBalding)* 9-0 JWilliams (11) (w'like: scope: bkwd: nvr
      nrr) .................................... s.h.6
    Aragrove *(LJHolt)* 9-0 JReid (5) (leggy: bit bkwd: s.s: nvr nrr) .................... s.h.7
    Le Couteau *(DWPArbuthnot)* 8-9 ‡5RPrice (3) (unf: bkwd: prom over 2f) .......... s.h.8
5954 Bold Acre *(DRLaing)* 9-0 TyroneWilliams (13) (rdn thrght: outpcd) .......... s.h.9
595 Royal Deed (USA) *(GLewis)* 8-9 PaulEddery (12) (prom over 2f) .................... 3.10
    Ombre Darme (IRE) *(JWPayne)* 9-0 RCochrane (6) (unf: lw: hdwy over 2f out:
      wknd over 1f out) .................................... 1.11
    Tee-Emm *(PHowling)* 9-0 JMurray (10) (unf: scope: bkwd: led over 2f) .......... 4.12

**6/5** FORTUNE CAY (IRE), **5/1** Bold Acre(7/1—9/2), **8/1** Royal Deed (USA), **9/1** Charity Express (IRE)(5/1—10/
1), **12/1** Mr Dingle, **14/1** Ombre Darme (IRE)(op 7/1), **20/1** Le Couteau, Daring King, **33/1** Ors. CSF £11.90, Tote
£2.50: £1.40 £1.50 £3.80 (£5.50). Mr Edward St George (MARLBOROUGH) bred by W. J. Byrne in Ireland. 12
Rn                                                        59.40 sec (2.40)
                                           SF—37/18/14/1/–/–

**773** HOLIDAY CLUB PONTINS CLAIMING STKS   £2422.00 (£672.00: £322.00)
    **1½m (AWT)**
                                                           3-00 (3-02)

586* **Prosequendo (USA)** (74) (Fav) *(MDixon)* 5–8-11 DaleGibson (13) (dwlt: hdwy
      over 4f out: hrd rdn fnl f: led nr fin) .................................... —1
505 Blushing Belle (67) (bl) *(PFICole)* 4–8-4 TQuinn (11) (a.p: ev ch fnl 2f: hrd rdn:
      r.o wl) .................................... hd.2
505 Paper Craft (55) (v) *(MJohnston)* 5–8-4 RPElliott (10) (led: hrd rdn fnl f: hdd nr
      fin) .................................... hd.3
4095 Classic Account (62) *(JAkehurst)* 4–8-4 ‡7KimMcDonnell (5) (chsd ldr 6f: one
      pce) .................................... 6.4
272 John Shaw (USA) (67) *(WJHaggas)* 4–8-7 NDay (8) (a.p: chsd ldr 6f out tl over
      2f out: one pce) .................................... 1½.5
598 Loki (IRE) (75) *(GLewis)* 4–8-13 PaulEddery (4) (a.p: rdn over 3f out: one pce) 2½.6

580[6] Anne's Bank (IRE) **(42)** *(AMoore)* 4–8-5[(1)] BRouse (2) (hdwy 6f out: nvr nr to chal) ............................................................................. 6.7

586[3] Molly Splash **(51)** *(CACyzer)* 5–7-13 ‡[7]TMcLaughlin (12) (b.nr hind: hrd rdn over 3f out: a mid div) ................................................ 2.8

    Tel E Thon *(PJJones)* 5–8-4 AMcGlone (1) (a bhd) .......................... ¾.9

273 Solid Steel (IRE) **(45)** *(AMoore)* 4–8-9 CandyMorris (6) (a bhd) ......... 8.10

580 Red Dollar **(45)** *(BGubby)* 7–8-6 NAdams (3) (b.hind: a bhd) ............ 1½.11

    Treasure Court *(PBurgoyne)* 5–8-9 RCochrane (7) (plld hrd: bhd fnl 7f: t.o) .. dist.12

**5/2** PROSEQUENDO (USA), **9/2** Blushing Belle, **5/1** Loki (IRE), **13/2** Classic Account, **8/1** John Shaw (USA), **9/1** Paper Craft, Molly Splash(op 6/1), **10/1** Anne's Bank (IRE), **25/1** Red Dollar, **33/1** Solid Steel (IRE), **50/1** Ors. CSF £14.67, Tote £3.60: £1.30 £2.30 £2.80 (£5.30). Mr J. Daniels (EPSOM) bred by H. Turney McKnight and June H. McKnight in USA. 12 Rn
2m 31.71 (2.31)
SF–38/30/29/17/17/18

## 774

SHARRON MURGATROYD CENTER PARCS H'CAP (0-70) (Ladies) £2560.00 (£760.00: £360.00: £160.00) **7f**
3-30 (3-35)

*(Weights raised 6 lb)*

616[4] **Ballerina Bay (54)** (v) *(DTThom)* 4–10-11 MissDianaJones (18) (hdwy over 2f out: led over 1f out: r.o wl) .................................................... —1

592[2] Foolish Touch **(54)** (Fav) *(WJMusson)* 10–10-11 MrsJCrossley (7) (b: s.s: wl bhd 5f: rapid hdwy over 1f out: str run fnl f: fin wl) .............. ¾.2

    Bill Moon **(43)** *(PJFeilden)* 6–10-0 MissJFeilden (11) (a.p: ev ch 1f out: r.o) ...... 1.3

340 Lucky Noire **(64)** *(GHarwood)* 4–11-7 MissAHarwood (8) (hdwy 2f out: r.o ins fnl f) ................................................................................. 1.4

    Quick Steel **(56)** *(TPMcGovern)* 4–10-13 MissABillot (9) (hdwy 2f out: r.o one pce) ........................................................................ hd.5

    Coral Flutter **(45)** (bl) *(JWPayne)* 5–10-2 MissJArmytage (16) (led over 5f: one pce) ...................................................................... nk.6

340★ Bengal Tiger (IRE) **(54)** (bl) *(JAkehurst)* 4–10-11 HRHThePrincessRoyal (13) (lw: lost pl over 3f out: r.o one pce fnl 2f) ............................... 2.7

615[3] Miss Magenta (IRE) **(35)** *(RThompson)* 4–9-6 MissJWinter (1) (hdwy over 2f out: one pce) .......................................................... ½.8

    Albert **(54)** *(DAWilson)* 5–10-11 MrsTBailey (14) (lw: nvr nr to chal) .......... ½.9

496[5] Zinbaq **(39)** *(CJBenstead)* 6–9-10 MrsJParris (4) (lw: a mid div) ........ nk.10

706 Profit a Prendre **(54)** *(DAWilson)* 8–10-0 MrsSBrook (15) (b: prom over 5f) ... ½.11

480 Forlorn Diver **(52)** *(BGubby)* 4–10-9 MissEJohnsonHoughton (17) (prom over 4f) ....................................................................... 2.12

696 Beechwood Cottage **(43)** (bl) *(ABailey)* 9–10-0 MissTBracegirdle (19) (outpcd) ¾.13

210 Sciacca **(35)** *(SMellor)* 5–9-6 MrsEMellor (20) (a mid div) ..................... 1.14

508 Now Boarding **(38)** *(RJHodges)* 5–9-9 MrsSHembrow (3) (a bhd) .......... 1.15

496[6] Domiana **(38)** *(MBlanshard)* 4–9-9 MissKMarks (2) (bhd fnl 2f) ........... 3.16

333[2] Sergeant Meryll **(38)** *(PHowling)* 8–9-9 MissYHaynes (5) (prom 5f) .......... s.h.17

358 Ackers Wood **(49)** *(KRBurke)* 4–10-6 MrsGRees (10) (prom over 4f) .......... 1.18

285[5] Hawaii Storm (FR) **(41)** *(MissAJWhitfield)* 4–9-12 MrsSCumani (6) (b.nr hind: bhd fnl 3f) ................................................................ 1½.19

**4/1** Foolish Touch(op 6/1), **6/1** BALLERINA BAY, **8/1** Bengal Tiger (IRE), **9/1** Profit a Prendre, **10/1** Bill Moon, **12/1** Zinbaq, Miss Magenta (IRE), **14/1** Lucky Noire, Sciacca, **16/1** Beechwood Cottage, Hawaii Storm (FR), Quick Steel, Sergeant Meryll, **20/1** Albert, **25/1** Forlorn Diver, Domiana, Coral Flutter, **33/1** Ackers Wood, **50/1** Now Boarding. CSF £30.92, CT £233.12. Tote £10.10: £2.30 £1.80 £3.70 £3.80 (£23.70). Mrs Carol Whitwood (NEWMARKET) bred by Mrs C. Whitwood and N. E. C Sherwood. 19 Rn
1m 25.67 (4.37)
SF–44/42/28/46/37/25

## 775

WESTMINSTER MOTOR TAXI INSURANCE H'CAP (0-80) £3236.00 (£968.00: £464.00: £212.00) **6f**
4-00 (4-05)

*(Weights raised 4 lb)*

624[4] **Across the Bay (69)** (v) *(SDow)* 5–9-8 TQuinn (6) (lw: hrd rdn over 3f out: hdwy 2f out: led ins fnl f: r.o wl) ................................................. —1

624 Luna Bid **(65)** *(MBlanshard)* 9–9-4 JReid (9) (lw: a.p: ev ch ins fnl f: r.o) .......... ¾.2

624 Cash a Million (FR) **(54)** *(PDCundell)* 4–8-7[(1)] TRogers (8) (hdwy 2f out: r.o one pce) ...................................................................... 2½.3

364 A Little Precious **(58)** *(JRBostock)* 6–8-11 SWhitworth (2) (hld up: stdy hdwy over 1f out: r.o wl) .............................................................. nk.4

349[5] Tauber **(62)** *(PatMitchell)* 8–8-12 ‡[3]SO'Gorman (3) (a.p: led over 2f out tl ins fnl f: one pce) ................................................................ nk.5

550 Ashtina **(71)** *(RJHodges)* 7–9-10 RCochrane (4) (led over 3f) ............... ½.6

495[5] Efra **(72)** *(RHannon)* 3–9-0 MRoberts (10) (a.p: one pce fnl 2f) ............ nk.7

515 Surrey Racing **(67)** *(GLewis)* 4–9-6 PaulEddery (7) (a bhd) ................... 1½.8

731[2] Coppermill Lad **(47)** (Fav) *(LJHolt)* 9–7-7 ‡[7]CAvery (5) (hdwy over 2f out: wknd wl over 1f out) .............................................................. nk.9

71 Kaths Choice **(43)** *(HJCollingridge)* 4–7–3 ‡[7]CHawksley (4) (s.s: a bhd) .......... ³/₄.**10**
Starchy Cove **(49)** *(BRCambidge)* 5–7–11[2] ‡[5]RPrice (1) (spd over 3f) ............. 3.**11**

**4/1** Coppermill Lad, **9/2** Efra, **5/1** Ashtina, **11/2** ACROSS THE BAY(4/1—6/1), **6/1** Surrey Racing, **8/1** Luna Bid, **9/1** Tauber, **12/1** A Little Precious, **25/1** Cash a Million (FR), **50/1** Ors. CSF £45.83, CT £922.76. Tote £6.10: £1.80 £2.90 £9.10 (£20.80). Mr J. A. Redmond (EPSOM) bred by Patrick McGrath and Liam Slattery. 11 Rn
1m 11.45 (2.85)
SF—33/26/5/8/8/18

**776**     HOLIDAY CLUB PONTINS (S) H'CAP (0-60) £2520.00 (£700.00: £336.00)
1¹/₄m (AWT)                                                                    4-30 (4-47)

355³ High Post **(49)** *(DMarks)* 3–8–6 TQuinn (6) (hdwy over 5f out: ev ch ins fnl f: r.o
wl: fin 2nd, s.h: awrdd r) ....................................................... —**1**
565 Serious Time **(48)** *(SirMarkPrescott)* 4–9–7 CNutter (11) (w ldr: led over 4f out:
edgd rt ins fnl f: all out: fin 1st: disq: plcd 2nd) ...................... **2**
154⁴ Pleasure Ahead **(47)** (Fav) *(MDixon)* 5–9–6 DaleGibson (2) (hdwy over 3f out:
r.o wl ins fnl f) ........................................................................ 2.**3**
335 Weapon Exhibition **(45)** *(GAHam)* 5–9–4 ADicks (1) (a.p: rdn over 2f out: unable
qckn) ...................................................................................... ³/₄.**4**
586 Great Impostor **(47)** *(RJHodges)* 4–9–6 RCochrane (12) (a.p: one pce fnl 2f) ...... 3.**5**
603⁶ Allimac Nomis **(45)** *(NACallaghan)* 3–8–2 MRoberts (10) (prom 8f) ................... 3.**6**
351⁶ Sareen Express (IRE) **(43)** *(MrsJCDawe)* 4–9–2 NHowe (14) (s.s: hdwy over 3f
out: wknd wl over 1f out) ...................................................... 2¹/₂.**7**
616 Foursingh **(53)** (bl) *(CBBBooth)* 4–9–12 GOldroyd (8) (lw: nvr nr to chal) ......... 1¹/₂.**8**
606 Northern Gallery (IRE) **(34)** *(WJMusson)* 4–8–7 AMackay (4) (b.hind: led over 5f) **8.9**
505 Blazing Pearl **(28)** (v) *(JLHarris)* 4–8–1 PaulEddery (7) (bhd fnl 4f) ............... 1¹/₂.**10**
508 Paint the Lily **(40)** (bl) *(DCJermy)* 4–8–8 ‡[5]RPrice (13) (bhd fnl 4f) ............... ³/₄.**11**
606 Mazin **(32)** *(CJBenstead)* 4–8–5 TyroneWilliams (5) (bhd fnl 3f) ..................... 2¹/₂.**12**
525 Manaolana **(31)** (bl) *(AMoore)* 4–8–4[1] BRouse (9) (bhd fnl 4f) ..................... 8.**13**
448 Hanjessdan (14/1) Withdrawn (bolted bef s) : not under orders
*Stewards Enquiry: Serious Time disq. (interference to High Post).*

**5/2** Pleasure Ahead, **5/1** HIGH POST, **11/2** Allimac Nomis, **8/1** Serious Time, Great Impostor, Sareen Express (IRE), **10/1** Manaolana, **12/1** Foursingh, **14/1** Northern Gallery (IRE), Mazin, **16/1** Blazing Pearl, **33/1** Ors. CSF £46.78, CT £117.61. Tote £5.10: £1.70 £3.20 £1.60 (£19.90). Mr V. Squeglia (UPPER LAMBOURN) bred by Gaberson Ltd. 13 Rn; No bid
2m 7.81 (4.81)
SF—29/13/23/19/15/—

**777**     TAXINEWS H'CAP (0-70) £2427.00 (£672.00: £321.00)     1¹/₂m (AWT)     5-00 (5-14)

469⁶ La Reine Rouge (IRE) **(43)** (Jt-Fav) *(PJMakin)* 4–7–10 ‡[5]TSprake (2) (lw: lost pl
over 5f out: rallied over 2f out: led 1f out: rdn out) ............... —**1**
206² Smiling Chief (IRE) **(52)** *(CACyzer)* 4–8–3 ‡[7]AMorris (8) (a.p: led over 4f out: hrd
rdn over 2f out: hdd 1f out: unable qckn) ......................... 1¹/₂.**2**
469⁵ Princess Roxanne **(63)** (bl) *(ABailey)* 5–9–7 JWilliams (3) (lw: hdwy over 4f out:
chsd ldr over 3f out tl over 1f out: one pce) ....................... 3¹/₂.**3**
479 Eastern Magic **(67)** *(JAkehurst)* 4–9–6 ‡[5]RPerham (5) (lw: nvr nr to chal) **7.4**
565 Tenayestelign **(52)** *(DMarks)* 4–8–10 TQuinn (4) (hdwy over 4f out: wknd 2f out) 3¹/₂.**5**
501 Brora Rose (IRE) **(47)** (v) *(JDBethell)* 4–8–5 PaulEddery (1) (a wl bhd) ............. 12.**6**
354 Plectrum **(50)** (bl) *(JLSpearing)* 4–8–8 MRoberts (4) (led over 6f) .................... 3.**7**
590⁴ Erevnon **(50)** *(JLHarris)* 5–8–8 RCochrane (6) (lw: chsd ldr: led over 5f out tl
over 4f out: sn wknd) ........................................................... 7.**8**

**7/2** Eastern Magic, LA REINE ROUGE (IRE), **9/2** Princess Roxanne(op 3/1), **11/2** Tenayestelign, **6/1** Smiling Chief (IRE), **8/1** Plectrum, **12/1** Brora Rose (IRE), **14/1** Erevnon. CSF £23.24, CT £87.26. Tote £7.30: £2.30 £1.20 £1.30 (£23.40). Mr D. M. Ahier (MARLBOROUGH) bred by Lodge Park Stud in Ireland. 8 Rn
2m 31.51 (2.11)
SF—25/29/40/25/8/—

**778**     McCALL GROUP STKS     £2950.00 (£880.00: £420.00: £190.00)     7f     5-30 (5-43)

610 **Deprecator (USA) (92)** (Fav) *(JHMGosden)* 4–9–10 RCochrane (7) (b.hind:
chsd ldr: led 2f out: r.o wl) .................................................... —**1**
549 Sir Oliver (IRE) *(RJHodges)* 3–8–5 MRoberts (9) (rdn 3f out: hdwy over 1f out:
r.o ins fnl f) ........................................................................... 4.**2**
601 Executive Spirit *(DSasse)* 3–8–7 ‡[5]RPerham (5) (rdn over 4f out: hdwy over 1f
out: r.o) ................................................................................ 1.**3**
Rasan **(93)** *(RWArmstrong)* 5–9–10 LPiggott (3) (lw: led 5f) ........................ 2.**4**
Alice's Mirror *(TPMcGovern)* 3–8–0 NAdams (8) (nvr nr to chal) ................... 2¹/₂.**5**
Simple Sound (IRE) *(MAJarvis)* 3–9–1 GCrealock (6) (prom 5f) ..................... s.h.**6**
495 Rue de Remarque *(MJHaynes)* 4–8–12 RPElliott (2) (a bhd) ...................... 1¹/₂.**7**

145 Camino a Ronda **(44)** *(PatMitchell)* 3–7–7 ‡7CHawksley (4) (b.hind: bhd fnl 5f) ... 2.8
In the Print *(MrsBarbaraWaring)* 4–9–3 NHowe (1) (s.s: a wl bhd) ..................... 5.9

**Evens** DEPRECATOR (USA)(op 4/6), **11/4** Rasan, **6/1** Simple Sound (IRE), **7/1** Sir Oliver (IRE)(10/1—12/1), **33/1** Executive Spirit, **50/1** Ors. CSF £7.99, Tote £2.00: £1.20 £1.50 £1.50 (£5.40). Ms Rachel D. S. Hood (NEWMARKET) bred by Dr Thomas F. Van Meter II in USA. 9 Rn                     1m 24.20 (2.90)
SF—50/19/18/29/–/14

T/Jkpt: Not won; £6,807.90 to Lingfield 9/5/92. T/Plpt: £20.40 (177.3 Tckts).                     AK

# LINGFIELD (L-H)

## Saturday, May 9th [Turf Good to firm becoming Good, AWT Standard]

Going Allowance: AWT: minus 0.20 sec (FS); Turf: 0.15 sec (G)          Wind: mod half bhd

Stalls: 5th race centre, remainder high

### 779
SLIP ANCHOR H'CAP (0-100) £6056.00 (£1808.00: £864.00: £392.00)
**6f**                                                                 11-55 (12-00)

550 **Bold Lez (95)** *(MJHaynes)* 5–10–0 SCauthen (2) (hld up: rdn over 2f out: led ins
fnl f: r.o wl) .................... —1
629³ Lord High Admiral (CAN) **(70)** *(Fav)* *(RHannon)* 4–8–3 MRoberts (8) (lw: a.p:
rdn over 2f out: r.o) ...... 1.2
Zeboim **(67)** (bl) *(WRMuir)* 6–7–7 ‡7KimMcDonnell (1) (a.p: rdn over 1f out: r.o) . 2.3
610 Maggie Siddons **(82)** *(CJHill)* 4–9–1 JReid (12) (hrd rdn & hdwy over 1f out: r.o) hd.4
207* Very Dicey **(78)** *(WRMuir)* 4–8–11 SWhitworth (7) (led tl ins fnl f: unable qckn) . ½.5
550 Hard to Figure **(93)** *(RJHodges)* 6–9–12 RCochrane (5) (hdwy over 1f out: r.o) nk 6
413³ Invocation **(76)** *(AMoore)* 5–8–9 NAdams (3) (b.hind: a.p: ev ch over 1f out: one
pce) ........................ ½.7
629³ Green Dollar **(91)** *(EAWheeler)* 9–9–5 ‡5DHarrison (10) (nvr nr to chal) .......... 1½.8
624 Paddy Chalk **(75)** *(LJHolt)* 6–8–8 LDettori (9) (b: outpcd) ........................ 1.9
624 Harry's Coming **(63)** *(RJHodges)* 8–7–7⁽²⁾ ‡3FNorton (11) (a bhd) ..................... ¾.10
596² Olifantsfontein **(81)** (bl) *(RSimpson)* 4–9–0 WRyan (13) (spd over 3f) ............. ¾.11
550 Masnun (USA) **(90)** *(RJO'Sullivan)* 7–9–9 GDuffield (6) (a bhd) ..................... 1.12
570 Red Rosein **(79)** *(CaptJWilson)* 6–8–7 ‡5ATucker (4) (b.off hind: s.s: a bhd) ..... 5.13
629 Fabled Orator **(61)** *(PHowling)* 7–7–8⁽¹⁾ JQuinn (14) (bhd fnl 3f) .................. 6.14
LONG HANDICAP: Fabled Orator 7-2.

**4/1** Lord High Admiral (CAN), **11/2** Maggie Siddons, **13/2** Olifantsfontein, Green Dollar, **9/1** Very Dicey, **10/1** Zeboim(op 20/1), **12/1** Harry's Coming, BOLD LEZ, Hard to Figure(8/1—14/1), Paddy Chalk, **20/1** Masnun (USA), **25/1** Red Rosein, **33/1** Invocation, **100/1** Fabled Orator. CSF £56.92, CT £468.32. Tote £20.30: £4.50 £1.60 £4.50 (£34.00). Ansells of Watford (EPSOM) bred by Hesmonds Stud Ltd. 14 Rn     1m 10.65 (2.05)
SF—91/62/44/65/59/73

### 780
DAILY STAR OAKS TRIAL (Stks) (listed race) (3-Y.O.F) £13840.00 (£4120.00: £1960.00: £880.00)     **1m 3f 106y**                                        12-30 (12-32)

553* **User Friendly** *(Fav)* *(CEBrittain)* 8-9 GDuffield (2) (3rd st: led 3f out: pushed out) —1
425² Niodini (USA) **(96)** *(MRStoute)* 8-9 SCauthen (3) (2nd st: ev ch 2f out: unable
qckn) ...................... 2½.2
473³ Venturina (IRE) **(92)** *(BWHills)* 8-9 JReid (5) (4th st: one pce fnl 3f) ................. 7.3
536* Miss Plum *(HRACecil)* 8-9 PatEddery (1) (lw: led over 8f) ........................... 10.4
Abbey Strand (USA) *(LordHuntingdon)* 8-9 LDettori (4) (5th st: wknd 3f out) ...... 15.5

**2/1** USER FRIENDLY, **5/2** Miss Plum(op 11/8), **7/2** Abbey Strand (USA), **9/2** Niodini (USA), **14/1** Venturina (IRE). CSF £9.91, Tote £3.20: £1.40 £1.60 (£7.70). Mr W. J. Gredley (NEWMARKET) bred by Stetchworth Park Stud Ltd. 5 Rn     2m 30.27 (8.27)
SF—30/25/11/–/–

### 781
MAXIMS CLUB DERBY TRIAL (Stks) (Gp 3) (3-Y.O) £35740.00 (£13392.00: £6446.00: £2822.00)     **1m 3f 106y**                                     1-00 (1-02)

556³ **Assessor (IRE) (111)** *(Fav)* *(RHannon)* 9-0 WRSwinburn (7) (lw: rdn 10f out:
hdwy 5f out: 3rd st: led 3f out: comf) ................. —1
384* Tapis Rouge (IRE) *(HRACecil)* 9-0 SCauthen (6) (lw: 2nd st: rdn over 2f out: no
imp) ...................... 7.2
556⁵ Bonny Scot (IRE) **(108)** *(LMCumani)* 9-0 LDettori (4) (rdn 7f out: 5th st: r.o one
pce fnl 2f) ............... 2½.3
400* Goldsmiths' Hall **(87)** *(GWragg)* 9-0 RHills (3) (led 8f out to 3f out: sn wknd) .... 4.4
556 Anchorite **(106)** *(PTWalwyn)* 9-0 RCochrane (5) (6th st: wknd over 2f out) ......... 6.5

628★ Spartan Shareef (IRE) *(CEBrittain)* 9-0 MRoberts (2) (bhd fnl 3f) ...................... 1½.6
647⁵ L'Hermine **(92)** *(HCandy)* 9-0 TQuinn (1) (led over 3f: 4th st: wknd over 3f out:
    t:o) ...................................................................................................................... 30.7

**9/4** ASSESSOR (IRE)(11/8—5/2), **3/1** Bonny Scot (IRE), Tapis Rouge (IRE), **4/1** Goldsmiths' Hall(op 6/1), **10/1**
Spartan Shareef (IRE), **16/1** Anchorite, **25/1** L'Hermine. CSF £9.57, Tote £3.20: £1.80 £2.10 (£4.10). Mr B. E.
Nielsen (MARLBOROUGH) bred by Airlie Stud in Ireland. 7 Rn              2m 31.65 (9.65)
                                                           SF—22/8/3/–/–/–

### 782
HOLIDAY CLUB PONTIN'S (S) STKS (2-Y.O) £3980.00 (£1190.00: £570.00: £260.00)
**6f**                                                     1-30 (1-33)

439 **Grand Dancer (IRE)** *(RJRWilliams)* 8-6 RCochrane (9) (mde all: rdn out) ............... —1
561⁴ Spring Sunrise *(MBlanshard)* 8-6 JReid (4) (chsd wnr: ev ch fnl 2f: r.o) ............. ½.2
371⁴ Take Your Partner (IRE) *(MJohnston)* 8-6 DMcKeown (7) (a.p: hrd rdn over 1f
    out: unable qckn) .......................................................................................... 3½.3
564⁶ Caps Ninety-Two (IRE) *(DrJDScargill)* 8-6 JQuinn (3) (lw: a.p: hrd rdn over 1f
    out: one pce) ................................................................................................... hd.4
581 Heroic Deed *(MHTompkins)* 8-6 ‡⁵CHodgson (5) (hdwy 3f out: hrd rdn over 2f
    out: one pce) ................................................................................................... 1.5
561 Andrea's Girl *(JBerry)* 8-6 AMackay (12) (nvr nr to chal) ................................ 1½.6
352 Burishki *(GAPritchard-Gordon)* 8-6 GDuffield (1) (prom over 4f) ..................... 4.7
548 Poco Pierna (IRE) *(WCarter)* 8-6 AMunro (11) (prom over 3f) ......................... ¾.8
423 Stay Great *(WCarter)* 8-6 ‡⁵NGwilliams (14) (nvr nrr) ..................................... ¾.9
Krayyan Dawn *(RVoorspuy)* 8-6 ‡⁵ATucker (15) (w'like: bkwd: s.s: nvr nrr) ..... hd.10
345 Buck the Tiger *(RHannon)* 8-11 SRaymont (6) (bhd fnl 3f) .............................. ½.11
528⁶ Rouwi (IRE) *(NACallaghan)* 7-13 ‡⁷JTate (10) (b.nr hind: outpcd) ................. nk.12
645 Primo Prince *(PFICole)* 8-11 TQuinn (2) (bhd fnl 3f) ...................................... 2½.13
584 Freebyjove *(PButler)* 8-3 ‡³FNorton (8) (swtg: a bhd) ..................................... 1.14
588 Huesca (bl) *(JRJenkins)* 8-1 ‡⁵DHarrison (14) (a bhd) .................................. 5.15
Victorian Star *(PButler)* 7-13 ‡⁷BRussell (13) (unf: scope: bhd fnl 3f) ............. 3½.16

**4/1** PLAN AHEAD (61) (Fav), **11/2** Spring Sunrise, Take Your Partner (IRE), GRAND DANCER (IRE), Caps Ninety-Two
(IRE), **8/1** Andrea's Girl, **9/1** Primo Prince, **14/1** Buck the Tiger, Heroic Deed, **16/1** Burishki, **20/1** Huesca, Rouwi
(IRE), **25/1** Stay Great, **33/1** Ors. CSF £39.31, Tote £8.40: £2.20 2.20 £2.30 (£52.00). Mr D. A. Johnson
(NEWMARKET) bred by E. O'Gorman in Ireland. 16 Rn; Bt in 5,200 gns           1m 14.07 (5.47)

### 783
VICTOR CHANDLER CUP FINAL H'CAP (3-Y.O) (0-90) £4815.00 (£1440.00: £690.00:
£315.00)   **7f 140y**                                          2-00 (2-04)

                        (Weights raised 2 lb)
696★ **Plan Ahead (61)** (Fav) *(GLewis)* 7-9 ‡⁵DHarrison (9) (rdn over 4f out: gd hdwy
    over 2f out: led over 1f out: pushed out) ............................................. —1
471 Vanborough Lad **(72)** *(MJHaynes)* 8-11 SCauthen (4) (hdwy over 2f out: ev ch
    over 1f out: unable qckn) ............................................................................ 2½.2
472 Confronter **(76)** (bl) *(PFICole)* 9-1 TQuinn (12) (lw: hld up: hrd rdn over 1f out:
    one pce) ........................................................................................................... 1½.3
370 Usaidit **(72)** *(WCarter)* 8-11 JReid (13) (w ldr: led over 3f out tl over 1f out: one
    pce) ................................................................................................................... 2.4
370⁶ Buzzards Bellbuoy **(69)** *(HJCollingridge)* 8-8 JQuinn (5) (a.p: hrd rdn over 3f
    out: one pce) ................................................................................................... 4.5
Master Hyde (USA) **(63)** *(PMitchell)* 7-13 ‡³SO'Gorman (1) (prom 5f) ............. nk.6
298 Mustahil (IRE) **(74)** *(RJHodges)* 8-13 RCochrane (2) (a.p: ev ch 2f out: wknd
    over 1f out) ...................................................................................................... ¾.7
509 Grand Fellow (IRE) **(68)** *(JDBethell)* 8-7 AMunro (6) (nvr nr to chal) ................ nk.8
482 Khazar (USA) **(69)** *(SirMarkPrescott)* 8-8 GDuffield (11) (lw: led 4f) ............... 2.9
697 Christian Warrior **(78)** *(RHannon)* 9-3 SRaymont (3) (s.s: a bhd) .................. hd.10
624 Aedean **(74)** *(CCElsey)* 8-10 ‡³FNorton (10) (bhd fnl 4f) .............................. 4.11
Naseer (USA) **(60)** *(NACallaghan)* 7-13 AMackay (8) (lw: a bhd) ...................... 2.12
348 Elton Ledger (IRE) **(82)** *(AAScott)* 9-2 ‡LNewton (7) (a bhd: t:o) ................. dist.13

**6/4** PLAN AHEAD, **13/2** Usaidit, **7/1** Vanborough Lad, **15/2** Confronter, **9/1** Buzzards Bellbuoy, Khazar (USA),
**12/1** Christian Warrior, **14/1** Grand Fellow (IRE), Naseer (USA), **16/1** Elton Ledger (IRE), **25/1** Mustahil (IRE),
**33/1** Ors. CSF £14.11, CT £63.83. Tote £2.30: £1.50 £2.10 £2.80 (£9.50). Planflow (Leasing) Ltd (EPSOM)
bred by R. F. and Mrs Knipe. 13 Rn                               1m 34.85 (6.35)

### 784
TURNELL CHILLED DISTRIBUTION STKS (Mdn 3-Y.O) £2427.00 (£672.00: £321.00)
**1¼m**                                                       2-30 (2-32)

609⁶ **Flight Lieutenant (USA)** *(PMitchell)* 9-0 LPiggott (5) (lw: led over 1f: 2nd st: led
    3f out: hrd rdn over 1f out: r.o wl) ....................................................... —1
Chief of Staff (Fav) *(PFICole)* 9-0 AMunro (6) (led over 8f out to 3f out: hrd rdn
    over 1f out: r.o ins fnl f) .............................................................................. 1.2

Anditisitis (USA) *(DWPArbuthnot)* 9-0 TQuinn (4) (w'like: scope: bit bkwd: 4th st: rdn over 2f out: r.o ins fnl f) .................................................. ³/₄.3
553　Vernonia *(JHMGosden)* 8-9 SCauthen (3) (3rd st: wknd 2f out) ........................ 10.4
627　Sizzling Thoughts *(GLewis)* 9-0 JReid (1) (5th st: wknd 3f out) ...................... 12.5
Space Camp *(RJHodges)* 9-0 RCochrane (2) (unf: scope: 6th st: wknd over 3f out) ....................................................................................................... 2.6

**6/4** Chief of Staff(op 4/6), **9/4** FLIGHT LIEUTENANT (USA), **5/2** Vernonia, **20/1** Ors. CSF £5.91, Tote £3.30: £1.70 £1.40 (£2.10). P. & S. Lever Partners (EPSOM) bred by Dale Barlage in USA. 6 Rn　2m 14.93 (11.93)

---

**785**　CST WHOLESALE MEAT SUPPLIES H'CAP (0-80) £2584.00 (£714.00: £340.00)
**1m (AWT)**　　　　　　　　　　　　　　　　　　　　　　　3-00 (3-02)

776　**Sareen Express (IRE) (44)** *(MrsJCDawe)* 4-7-10(1) ‡5ATucker (4) (dropped rr over 3f out: gd hdwy over 1f out: str run fnl f: led nr fin) ...... —1
626　**Sarum (64)** *(CPWildman)* 6-9-7 RCochrane (5) (hld up: led over 1f out: hrd rdn: hdd nr fin) ................................................................................................ 1¹/₂.2
692　Bowden Boy (IRE) **(71)** (bl) *(NACallaghan)* 4-10-0 JReid (2) (w ldr: ev ch fnl 2f: r.o) ................................................................................................................ nk.3
684⁶　Shining Jewel **(69)** (Fav) *(MrsLPiggott)* 5-9-12 LPiggott (6) (hld up: rdn over 2f out: unable qckn) ...................................................................................... 1¹/₂.4
203　Vuchterbacher **(61)** *(PFTulk)* 6-8-11 ‡7TWilson (3) (b: led over 6f) .................... 2¹/₂.5
93　Litmore Dancer **(53)** *(JDBethell)* 4-8-10 GDuffield (1) (rdn over 3f out: bhd fnl 2f) 4.6

**9/4** Shining Jewel(6/4—5/2), **3/1** Sarum, **4/1** Litmore Dancer, **11/2** Vuchterbacher, **6/1** Bowden Boy (IRE)(op 4/1), **9/1** SAREEN EXPRESS (IRE)(20/1—8/1). CSF £34.04, Tote £14.90: £2.60 £2.30 (£33.00). Mr Don Hazzard (BRIDGWATER) bred by Gestut Holsten Ag in Ireland. 6 Rn　　　1m 38.90 (2.20)
　　　　　　　　　　　　　　　　　　　　　　　　　　　　　SF—25/45/51/44/27/14

T/Jkpt: Not won; £9,202 to York 12/5/92. T/Plpt: £44.10 (109.65 Tckts).　　　　　　AK

---

594—**BATH (L-H)**
**Saturday, May 9th [Soft]**
Going Allowance: 5f 11y-5f 161y: 1.05 sec; Rest: 0.85 sec (S)　　　Wind: str against

Stalls: low

**786**　FRANCASAL (S) STKS (2-Y.O) £1660.00 (£460.00: £220.00)　**5f 11y**　2-10 (2-12)

476　**Nicki-J (IRE)** *(RHannon)* 8-6 AMcGlone (7) (a.p: led over 2f out: edgd lft: drvn out) .............................................................................................................. —1
Homemaker *(RJHolder)* 8-6 ADicks (12) (w'like: bkwd: gd hdwy over 1f out: r.o wl ins fnl f) ........................................................................................ ¹/₂.2
595　Wealthywoo *(JSMoore)* 8-6 BRouse (9) (hdwy & hung rt 2f out: hrd rdn: r.o) .. 1¹/₂.3
Mighty Miss Magpie (IRE) *(MRChannon)* 8-1 ‡5BDoyle (8) (leggy: s.s: stdy hdwy fnl 2f: nvr nrr) ...................................................................... 3¹/₂.4
588　Hawke Bay *(DHaydnJones)* 8-11 MWigham (10) (hrd rdn 2f out: nvr nr to chal) ³/₄.5
528⁵　School of Science *(RPCHoad)* 8-6 ‡5RPerham (5) (dwlt: hdwy over 3f out: one pce fnl 2f) ......................................................................................... 1¹/₂.6
588⁶　Pfaff's Cellar *(WGMTurner)* 8-3 ‡3TSprake (3) (spd over 3f) ............................ 2¹/₂.7
561²　Toff Sundae (Fav) *(GLewis)* 8-11 PaulEddery (2) (lw: led over 2f) ................... s.h.8
588⁵　Silly Sally *(WGMTurner)* 7-13 ‡7SMulvey (6) (outpcd) ...................................... s.h.9
588³　Tudela *(MJHaynes)* 8-6 TyroneWilliams (1) (spd over 3f) ............................... 2¹/₂.10
231　Purbeck Centenary *(MRChannon)* 8-11 CRutter (4) (lw: spd over 2f: t.o) ....... 30.11

**5/2** Toff Sundae, **3/1** NICKI-J (IRE), **Wealthywoo, 9/2** Tudela(op 3/1), **9/1** Mighty Miss Magpie (IRE)(6/1—10/1), **10/1** Purbeck Centenary, **14/1** School of Science, Homemaker(10/1—20/1), Pfaff's Cellar(10/1—16/1), Silly Sally, **16/1** Hawke Bay. CSF £50.26, Tote £5.00: £1.80 £6.20 £1.60 (£114.70). Mr Derek Joseph (MARLBOROUGH) bred by J. O'Regan in Ireland. 11 Rn; Bt in 3,800 gns　　　70.5 sec (10)

---

**787**　LEVY BOARD STKS (Mdn 3-Y.O.F) £2320.00 (£645.00: £310.00)　**1m 5y**　2-40 (2-44)

620³　**Do Run Run** (Jt-Fav) *(RHannon)* 8-6 ‡5RPerham (2) (2nd st: led over 2f out: edgd rt over 1f out: drvn out) ................................................................. —1
Zawaahy (USA) *(AAScott)* 8-11 WRSwinburn (8) (unf: scope: 7th st: hdwy 3f out: chsd wnr over 1f out: r.o) ........................................................ 3¹/₂.2
Dazzling Fire (IRE) **(74)** (Jt-Fav) *(BWHills)* 8-11 RHills (10) (6th st: one pce fnl 2f) ............................................................................................................... 3¹/₂.3
Edgeaway *(JWHills)* 8-11 MHills (1) (hdwy over 1f out: nvr nrr) ........................ 1¹/₂.4
Super Beauty *(GBBalding)* 8-11 JWilliams (6) (nvr nr to chal) ........................... 5.5
Sally Fast *(BPalling)* 8-4 ‡7StephenDavies (11) (neat: bit bkwd: 8th st: hdwy over 2f out: wknd fnl f) ..................................................................... hd.6

633⁶ Montagne *(HCandy)* 8-11 CRutter (5) (5th st: wknd over 2f out) ...................... s.h.7
  Afore Jane *(GHarwood)* 8-11 AClark (4) (leggy: scope: bit bkwd: 3rd st: wknd
    2f out) ........................................................................................................... ¹/₂.8
348 Spanish Glory *(IABalding)* 8-11 BRouse (9) (4th st: wknd 3f out) ....................... 2.9
  Shapely Deb *(DRLaing)* 8-11 TyroneWilliams (4) (led over 5f) ...................... nk.10
406 Villa Capri *(CEBrittain)* 8-6 ‡⁵BDoyle (12) (bhd fnl 4f) ................................... 2.11
  Fanny Burney (USA) *(PWHarris)* 8-11 PaulEddery (7) (leggy: lw: s.s: a bhd) ... ³/₄.12

**7/2 DO RUN RUN, Dazzling Fire (IRE), 5/1 Afore Jane, Zawaahy (USA)(op 2/1), 13/2 Edgeaway(op 4/1), 12/1**
Montagne, **16/1** Spanish Glory(12/1—20/1), Super Beauty(op 10/1), Villa Capri, **33/1** Fanny Burney (USA), **40/1**
Ors. CSF £21.06, Tote £3.90: £1.40 £1.70 £1.60 (£6.30). Mrs Henry Lopes (MARLBOROUGH) bred by J.
Weinfeld. 12 Rn                                                                                    1m 50.2 (10.9)
                                                                                    SF—31/25/14/9/–/–

---

**788**     JEAN MCINTOSH BIRTHDAY H'CAP (3-Y.O.F) (0-90) £3038.00 (£914.00: £442.00:
£206.00) **1¹/₄m 46y** Weights raised 4 lb

3-10 (3-15)

573★ **Folia (80)** *(Fav)* *(HRACecil)* 9-2 WRyan (1) (lw: led after 2f: rdn over 2f out: drvn
    out) ............................................................................................................ —1
  Choppy Choppy (USA) *(74)* *(BWHills)* 8-10 MHills (13) (2nd st: ev ch 1f out: hrd
    rdn & r.o) ................................................................................................... ¹/₂.2
356⁴ Humour (IRE) *(73)* *(CFWall)* 8-9 NDay (9) (hrd rdn & gd hdwy fnl 2f: nvr nrr) ..... 5.3
  Dubitable **(64)** *(HCandy)* 8-0 CRutter (12) (hdwy 5f out: 3rd st: one pce fnl 2f) 3¹/₂.4
  Brave the Wind **(70)** *(IABalding)* 8-6 JWilliams (10) (bit bkwd: hdwy over 2f out:
    nvr nr to chal) ............................................................................................. 7.5
167★ Khrisma **(75)** *(MrsJCecil)* 8-11 PaulEddery (5) (7th st: hdwy 3f out: one pce fnl
    2f) .......................................................................................................... 1¹/₂.6
566 Striking Image (IRE) **(70)** *(RHannon)* 8-6 AMcGlone (8) (lw: led 2f: 4th st: wknd
    3f out) ......................................................................................................... 1.7
  Sea Clover (IRE) **(85)** *(MajorWRHern)* 9-7 RHills (4) (lw: 6th st: wknd over 2f
    out) ............................................................................................................ 6.8
  Silken Words (USA) **(76)** *(WRMuir)* 8-12 SWhitworth (3) (bit bkwd: bhd fnl 4f:
    poor 9th st) .............................................................................................. 8.9
499² Sasparella **(80)** *(WJarvis)* 9-2 WRSwinburn (6) (8th st: bhd fnl 3f) .................. 2.10
  Arsaad (USA) **(70)** *(PTWalwyn)* 8-6 GCarter (7) (prom 3f: bhd fnl 4f: t.o) ........ 20.11
179★ Money Spinner (USA) **(71)** *(LordHuntingdon)* 8-7⁽¹⁾ PatEddery (11) (wl bhd fnl
    5f: t.o) ....................................................................................................... 2.12
  Grey But Rosy (IRE) **(61)** *(DRCElsworth)* 7-6⁽⁴⁾ ‡⁵BDoyle (2) (b.hind: chsd wnr 8f
    out: 5th & wkng st: t.o) ............................................................................. 20.13

**9/4 FOLIA, 4/1 Sea Clover (IRE)(8/1—12/1), 7/1 Money Spinner (USA)(op 3/1), 17/2 Choppy Choppy,**
**9/1 Sasparella(6/1—10/1), Khrisma(op 6/1), 10/1 Arsaad (USA), 12/1 Brave the Wind(16/1—10/1), 16/1**
Striking Image (IRE)(12/1—20/1), Dubitable, Humour (IRE), Grey But Rosy (IRE), **20/1** Silken Words (USA). CSF
£24.45, CT £258.03. Tote £3.70: £1.60 £3.50 £6.00 (£28.00). Sheikh Mohammed (NEWMARKET) bred by
Sheikh Mohammed bin Rashid al Maktoum. 13 Rn                                      2m 20.7 (13)
                                                                                    SF—57/50/39/23/15/17

---

**789**     WEST LITTLETON STKS (Mdn 3-Y.O) £1863.00 (£518.00: £249.00)
**1m 3f 144y**

3-40 (3-44)

509³ **Green Lane (IRE)** *(Fav)* *(RCharlton)* 9-0 PaulEddery (10) (lw: led 2f: 6th st: led
    wl over 1f out: pushed out) ................................................................... —1
481 King's Treasure (USA) *(IABalding)* 9-0 JWilliams (4) (lw: 9th st: hdwy over 2f
    out: chsd wnr over 1f out: r.o) ............................................................... 2.2
  Bar Billiards *(RFJohnsonHoughton)* 9-0 SWhitworth (2) (5th st: r.o one pce fnl
    2f) .......................................................................................................... 3.3
471⁵ Three Wells **(82)** *(JLDunlop)* 9-0 AClark (1) (4th st: nt clr run 2f out: r.o ins fnl f)
                                                                                    1¹/₂.4
566⁵ Rolling the Bones (USA) *(JRFanshawe)* 9-0 GCarter (5) (7th st: hrd rdn over 3f
    out: one pce) .......................................................................................... 7.5
  Simonov *(GHarwood)* 9-0 PatEddery (3) (bit bkwd: led after 2f tl wknd wl over 1f
    out) ........................................................................................................ 2.6
427⁶ Dime Bag *(BWHills)* 8-9 MHills (11) (2nd st: wknd 3f out) .............................. 2.7
487² West Stow *(MRStoute)* 9-0 WRSwinburn (6) (3rd st: ev ch 2f out: sn wknd) .... 2¹/₂.8
  Olej (USA) *(LordHuntingdon)* 9-0 RHills (7) (prom 6f) ..................................... 12.9
  Granache (IRE) *(MRChannon)* 9-0 BRouse (9) (w'like: scope: bit bkwd: sme
    hdwy 5f out: 8th st: sn wknd: t.o) ......................................................... 30.10
  Fighting Talk (USA) *(CRNelson)* 9-0 NAdams (8) (wl grwn: bkwd: a bhd: t.o) . 20.11

**2/1 GREEN LANE (IRE), 4/1 West Stow, 9/2 Dime Bag(op 3/1), 6/1 Simonov(3/1—7/1), 7/1 Rolling the Bones**
(USA)(6/1—10/1), Three Wells, **10/1** King's Treasure (USA)(op 6/1), **12/1** Olej (USA), **16/1** Granache (IRE),
**25/1** Ors. CSF £25.85, Tote £3.90: £1.40 £3.40 £8.10 (£22.60). Lord Weinstock (BECKHAMPTON) bred by
Ballymacoll Stud Farm Ltd in Ireland. 11 Rn                                       2m 42.8 (16.1)
                                                                                    SF—39/35/29/26/12/8

## 790

BOX H'CAP (0-70) £2742.00 (£762.00: £366.00)     2m 1f 34y     4-10 (4-12)

593★ **Zealous Kitten (USA) (53)** *(RJPrice)* 4–8–7 ‡⁷StephenDavies (2) (hdwy 7f out:
6th st: rdn over 2f out: led ins fnl f: r.o wl) ............................ —1
664³ Lady Electric **(44)** (Fav) *(RJHodges)* 6–8–5 ‡³TSprake (7) (8th st: hdwy over 2f
out: led wl over 1f out tl ins fnl f: r.o) ............................ nk.2
605² Fanlight **(54)** *(RAkehurst)* 4–9–1 RHills (1) (4th st: ev ch whn nt clr run & hmpd 2f
out: r.o ins fnl f) ............................ 1¹/₂.3
578★ Patroclus **(45)** *(RVoorspuy)* 7–8–9 PaulEddery (10) (b: 7th st: hdwy over 2f out:
ev ch over 1f out: unable qckn) ............................ ³/₄.4
426 White River **(41)** *(DHaydnJones)* 6–8–5 JWilliams (16) (5th st: one pce fnl 2f) .. 15.5
507² Western Dancer **(54)** *(CAHorgan)* 11–9–4 AMcGlone (11) (b: 2nd st: led over 2f
out tl wl over 1f out: sn wknd) ............................ 3¹/₂.6
507 Janiski **(58)** (v) *(MrsBarbaraWaring)* 9–9–8 NHowe (15) (hdwy 6f out: 3rd st:
wknd 2f out) ............................ 10.7
578⁴ Trojan Envoy **(35)** *(WCarter)* 4–7–10 JQuinn (9) (prom 11f: 9th & wkng st) ......... 8.8
501⁶ Intrepid Lass **(50)** *(HCandy)* 5–8–7 ‡⁷AntoinetteArmes (12) (t.o fnl 8f) ............ 7.9
675 Lady Westgate **(30)** *(GBBalding)* 8–7–8⁽¹⁾ NAdams (8) (led 8f out tl wknd over 2f
out) ............................ ¹/₂.10
525 Temple Island (IRE) **(35)** *(PJMakin)* 4–7–10 SDawson (5) (bhd fnl 6f: t.o) ....... 20.11
342 Sedgy Mead **(40)** *(PJJones)* 4–7–8 ‡⁷AWhelan (3) (a bhd: t.o) ............................ 8.12
409 Wise Friend (USA) **(36)** *(CPWildman)* 4–7–6⁽⁴⁾ ‡⁵BDoyle (6) (led over 9f: wknd 6f
out: t.o) ............................ dist.13
Nikolayevich **(45)** (bl) *(DCJermy)* 5–8–9 ADicks (13) (prom 8f: t.o) ............ 20.14
LONG HANDICAP: Lady Westgate 7-6, Wise Friend (USA) 7-1.

7/2 Lady Electric, 4/1 ZEALOUS KITTEN (USA), 5/1 Fanlight, 13/2 Western Dancer, 15/2 Patroclus(5/1—8/1),
8/1 White River, 10/1 Trojan Envoy, 12/1 Intrepid Lass, 20/1 Janiski, Temple Island (IRE), Lady Westgate, 50/1
Ors. CSF £19.04. CT £68.73. Tote £5.90: £2.20 1.60 2.20 (£7.60). Mr M. F. Oseman (LEOMINSTER) bred by
Sterlingbrook Farm in USA. 14 Rn                                        4m 9.2 (25.2)

## 791

PULTENEY AUCTION STKS (Mdn 2-Y.O) £1814.00 (£504.00: £242.00)
5f 11y     4-40 (4-44)

**Moon Over Miami** *(CJames)* 7-9 JQuinn (5) (w'like: hdwy 2f out: hrd rdn over
1f out: led wl ins fnl f) ............................ —1
Rough Guess (IRE) *(LordHuntingdon)* 7-4 ‡⁵DHarrison (12) (str: bit bkwd:
outpcd: rapid hdwy over 1f out: fin fast) ............................ 1¹/₂.2
396² Heber Spring (IRE) (Fav) *(RHannon)* 8-0 AMcGlone (14) (lw: led 3f out: clr over
1f out: ct wl ins fnl f) ............................ s.h.3
416⁶ Not so Generous (IRE) *(WGMTurner)* 7-9 PBurke (8) (a.p: one pce fnl 2f) ......... 8.4
Knyaz *(LGCottrell)* 8-0 RFox (13) (cmpt: bit bkwd: outpcd: nvr nrr) ......... ¹/₂.5
361 Border Dream *(WGMTurner)* 8-0 RHills (6) (a.p: hrd rdn 2f out: one pce) ...... hd.6
Spenmax (IRE) *(WGMTurner)* 7-11 ‡³TSprake (7) (unf: nvr nr to chal) ......... nk.7
595³ Duchess Dianne (IRE) *(RJHolder)* 7-9 NAdams (2) (prom whn hmpd on ins 3f
out: nt rcvr) ............................ 1¹/₂.8
365⁵ Field of Vision (IRE) *(MJohnston)* 8-0 RPElliott (14) (prom over 2f) ............ 2¹/₂.9
476 De Chine *(JSMoore)* 8-0 BRouse (1) (outpcd) ............................ hd.10
Infant Protege (USA) *(CEBrittain)* 7-6⁽²⁾ ‡⁵BDoyle (9) (scope: s.v.s: a wl bhd) . hd.11
Stanford Avenue *(BForsey)* 7-10⁽¹⁾ TyroneWilliams (3) (scope: s.s: a bhd) ...... ³/₄.12
574⁶ Mdm Racer (IRE) *(JBerry)* 8-0 GCarter (10) (led 2f: wknd 2f out) ............ s.h.13
Risky Rosie *(RVoorspuy)* 7-10⁽¹⁾ SDawson (4) (lt-f: outpcd: t.o) ............ 20.14

5/4 Heber Spring (IRE), 7/2 Duchess Dianne (IRE), 7/1 Rough Guess (IRE), 15/2 Mdm Racer (IRE)(5/1—8/1),
9/1 MOON OVER MIAMI(5/1—10/1), 14/1 De Chine(7/1—16/1), Field of Vision (IRE)(op 7/1), 16/1 Not so
Generous (IRE), Infant Protege (USA)(op 8/1), 20/1 Border Dream, 25/1 Spenmax (IRE), 33/1 Ors. CSF £76.67,
Tote £7.40: £3.00 2.50 1.50 (£204.80). Mr Barry J. Ross (NEWBURY) bred by Benham Stud. 14 Rn
69.8 sec (9.3)

## 792

CHAPEL FARM H'CAP (3-Y.O) (0-90) £2819.00 (£784.00: £377.00)
5f 161y     (Weights raised 1 lb)     5-10 (5-13)

**Ghalyoon (USA) (79)** *(PTWalwyn)* 9-2 WRSwinburn (3) (hdwy 2f out: led ins fnl
f: rdn out) ............................ —1
472 Salisong **(72)** *(PFICole)* 8-9 CRutter (4) (hrd rdn 2f out: hdwy over 1f out: r.o) ... 1.2
Jigsaw Boy **(78)** *(RJHolder)* 9-1 JWilliams (2) (hdwy over 1f out: r.o wl ins fnl f) nk.3
660² Palacegate Gold (IRE) **(57)** *(RJHodges)* 7-8 JQuinn (11) (a.p: led wl over 1f out
tl ins fnl f: unable qckn) ............................ 3¹/₂.4
576³ Taufan Blu (IRE) **(84)** *(MJohnston)* 9-7 DMcKeown (1) (mid div whn n.m.r &
hmpd wl over 1f out: rallied fnl f: r.o) ............................ s.h.5
Ben Bluff **(56)** *(LGCottrell)* 7-7 RFox (7) (lw: outpcd: hdwy fnl 2f: nvr nrr) ......... ³/₄.6
621⁵ Life's a Breeze **(59)** *(MRChannon)* 7-5⁽³⁾ ‡⁵BDoyle (10) (lw: spd 4f) ................... 3.7
690★ Inherent Magic (IRE) **(78)** *(MMcCormack)* 9-1 (7x) AClark (5) (lw: prom over 3f) ³/₄.8

591* Cradle Days **(79)** (Fav) *(RHannon)* 9-2 PatEddery (9) (lw: spd 4f) ..................... ¹/₂.9
582* Truthful Image **(76)** (bl) *(MJRyan)* 8-13 AMunro (8) (led 4f) ........................... 3¹/₂.10
582⁵ Fourofus **(63)** *(RBoss)* 8-0 RHills (6) (bhd fnl 2f) ............................................. 5.11
LONG HANDICAP: Ben Bluff 7-3.

**9/4** Cradle Days, **4/1** Taufan Blu (IRE), **5/1** Fourofus, **6/1** Truthful Image(op 7/2), **13/2** Jigsaw Boy, **10/1** Inherent Magic (IRE), **12/1** GHALYOON (USA), Palacegate Gold (IRE), **14/1** Life's a Breeze(10/1—16/1), Salisong, **33/1** Ben Bluff. CSF £162.81, CT £1,103.05. Tote £19.80: £5.30 £2.70 £1.60 (£70.70). Mr Hamdan Al-Maktoum (LAMBOURN) bred by Christiana Nursery Trust in USA. 11 Rn                    1m 17.6 (8.3)
SF—54/43/48/13/39/8

T/Plpt: £52.70 (57.9 Tckts).                                                                    LMc

## 659—HAMILTON (R-H)
### Monday, May 11th [Soft, Heavy patches]
Going Allowance: St: 0.80 sec per fur; Rnd: 0.90 sec per fur (S)          Wind: slt half bhd
Stalls: low                                          *Racing delayed 30 mins - bomb scare*

**793**    E.B.F. DRUMLOCH STKS (Mdn 2-Y.O.C & G) £2260.80 (£623.80: £296.40)
**5f 4y**                                                              2-00 (2-30)

    **Glowing Value (IRE)** (Fav) *(JBerry)* 9-0 JCarroll (2) (neat: scope: lw: mde
most: rdn & styd on wl appr fnl f) ............................................ —1
682 Pine Ridge Lad (IRE) *(WJPearce)* 9-0 DNicholls (1) (hld up: hdwy ¹/₂-wy: ev ch
1f out: nt qckn) .......................................................... 1¹/₂.2
665⁴ Tanagome (USA) *(SGNorton)* 9-0 KDarley (4) (bit bkwd: cl up: rdn 2f out: grad
wknd) ................................................................... 5.3
571³ Creagmhor *(JBerry)* 9-0 DMcKeown (3) (disp ld to ¹/₂-wy: sn rdn & btn) ......... 3¹/₂.4

**10/11** GLOWING VALUE (IRE), **3/1** Pine Ridge Lad (IRE), **4/1** Creagmhor(5/2—5/1), **11/2** Tanagome (USA). CSF £3.94, Tote £1.50 (£6.10). Mr F. Dunne (COCKERHAM) bred by Hamwood Stud in Ireland. 4 Rn   65.4 sec (7.1)
SF—38/32/12/–

**794**    AIRDRIE H'CAP (0-70) £2265.20 (£627.20: £299.60)      **6f 5y**      2-30 (3-01)

668* Pharoah's Dancer **(67)** (Fav) *(EAWheeler)* 5-9-9 ‡5DHarrison (1) (lw: trckd ldrs
gng wl: led over 1f out: shkn up & r.o) ...................................... —1
752³ In a Whirl (USA) **(48)** *(DWChapman)* 4–8-6 ‡3JFanning (5) (led tl hdd over 1f out:
kpt on same pce) .......................................................... 3¹/₂.2
449⁶ Malunar **(63)** *(MHTompkins)* 7–9-10 PRobinson (6) (lw: bhd: effrt ¹/₂-wy: styd
on wl nr fin) .............................................................. s.h.3
521⁵ Thisonesforalice **(55)** *(WJPearce)* 4–9-2 DNicholls (8) (a chsng ldrs: rdn 2f out:
r.o one pce) .............................................................. 1.4
660* Francis Ann **(53)** *(MissLAPerratt)* 4-8-7 ‡7RHavlin (3) (trckd ldrs: effrt over 2f
out: nt qckn) ............................................................. nk.5
668 B Grade **(41)** *(JBalding)* 7–7-9 ‡7ClaireBalding (10) (bhd: hdwy 2f out: edgd lft &
nvr able chal) ............................................................. 1¹/₂.6
668² Densben **(60)** *(DenysSmith)* 8–9-7 KFallon (7) (lw: chsd ldrs: outpcd ¹/₂-wy:
hdwy 2f out: sn btn) ....................................................... 5.7
615 Silver Stone Boy **(42)** *(WJPearce)* 4–8-3 SWebster (2) (spd to ¹/₂-wy: sn wknd) hd.8
Fabius Cunctator (IRE) **(48)** *(BJMcMath)* 3–7-12 LCharnock (11) (bit bkwd:
prom over 3f) ............................................................. hd.9
541 Chaplins Club (USA) **(48)** (bl) *(DWChapman)* 12–8-9 KDarley (4) (s.i.s: effrt &
hung rt over 2f out: a bhd) ................................................ 3¹/₂.10

**5/2** PHAROAH'S DANCER, **6/1** Francis Ann, Densben, **7/1** Malunar, **8/1** B Grade, **9/1** Thisonesforalice, In a Whirl (USA), **16/1** Chaplins Club (USA), **20/1** Silver Stone Boy, **100/1** Fabius Cunctator (IRE). CSF £22.18, CT £123.39. Tote £3.90: £1.40 £1.60 £3.70 (£10.50). Mr James Devaney (LAMBOURN) bred by Heinz Pollmeier. 10 Rn                                                                  1m 17.8 (7.8)
SF—49/18/35/23/13/–

**795**    COATBRIDGE AUCTION STKS (Mdn 2-Y.O) £1932.00 (£532.00: £252.00)
**6f 5y**                                                              3-00 (3-32)

    **Sudbury (IRE)** *(MHTompkins)* 8-2 PRobinson (7) (neat: s.i.s: bhd tl hdwy
¹/₂-wy: r.o to ld wl ins fnl f) ................................................ —1
703 Five Clubs (IRE) *(DTThom)* 7-11 ‡3FNorton (6) (a chsng ldrs: outpcd over 1f out:
kpt on nr fin) ............................................................. 1¹/₂.2
677³ Victoria Hall *(WGMTurner)* 7-13 ‡3DBiggs (1) (led: rdn clr appr fnl f: hung rt,
wknd & hdd wl ins fnl f) .................................................... s.h.3
396³ Preston Guild (IRE) *(JBerry)* 8-12 JCarroll (4) (a chsng ldrs: shkn up ¹/₂-wy: r.o
one pce) ................................................................. 5.4

682² Juliet Bravo (Fav) *(WJPearce)* 8-2 LCharnock (2) (lw: chsd ldrs: hrd drvn & swtchd ¹/₂-wy: eased whn btn appr fnl f) ............................ 8.5
682 Pretzel (IRE) *(NTinkler)* 8-9 KDarley (8) (prom tl outpcd fnl 2f) ........................ 3¹/₂.6
Apollo de Oriente *(JSWainwright)* 8-9 KFallon (5) (w'like: prom to ¹/₂-wy: sn bhd) 5.7
484⁵ All Baileys *(MJohnston)* 7-13 ‡³JFanning (3) (wl bhd fr ¹/₂-wy) ........................ 2.8

**6/4** Juliet Bravo(2/1—9/4), **5/2** Victoria Hall, **7/2** Preston Guild (IRE)(op 2/1), **10/1** Pretzel (IRE)(op 6/1), **12/1** SUDBURY (IRE)(op 5/1), **25/1** Five Clubs (IRE), Apollo de Oriente, **33/1** All Baileys. CSF £193.49, Tote £6.20: £2.40 £2.50 £1.30 (£122.90). Mr John Wimbs (NEWMARKET) bred by Ballykisteen Stud Ltd in Ireland. 8 Rn
1m 19.3 (9.3)

---

## 796
I.M.I. YORKSHIRE FITTINGS H'CAP (0-70) £2448.00 (£678.00: £324.00)
1m 65y

3-30 (4-02)

419* Lazy Rhythm (USA) **(49)** (Fav) *(RAkehurst)* 6-8-9 ‡³FNorton (6) (lw: effrt ¹/₂-wy: rdn to ld appr fnl f: r.o wl) ........................ —1
684⁵ Forever Diamonds **(59)** *(MHEasterby)* 5-9-8 KDarley (5) (lw: hld up: effrt 3f out: styd on wl nr fin) ........................ 1¹/₂.2
Manulife **(67)** *(WJPearce)* 3-9-3 DNicholls (10) (trckd ldrs: led over 2f out tl over 1f out: no ex) ........................ nk.3
590 Saint Vending **(51)** *(MBrittain)* 4-9-0 MWigham (2) (bhd: effrt ¹/₂-wy: styd on wl fnl f: nrst fin) ........................ 3¹/₂.4
Strength in Depth (IRE) **(48)** *(MJohnston)* 4-8-11 DMcKeown (4) (a cl up: r.o one pce fnl 3f) ........................ hd.5
615 State Flyer **(60)** (v) *(CBBBooth)* 4-9-0 GOldroyd (11) (lw: bhd tl styd on fnl 3f: nvr nrr) ........................ 1.6
587* Millfit (USA) **(68)** *(BHanbury)* 3-8-11 ‡⁷VBray (1) (cl up: led over 4f out tl over 2f out: grad wknd) ........................ 1¹/₂.7
663 Aragon Ayr **(46)** *(PMonteith)* 4-8-9 NConnorton (8) (bhd: hdwy 4f out: sn rdn & no imp) ........................ 3¹/₂.8
Diet **(65)** *(MissLAPerratt)* 6-9-7 ‡⁷RHavlin (9) (bit bkwd: led tl hdd over 4f out: wknd over 2f out) ........................ 8.9
419 Master Plan (FR) **(30)** *(MissLAPerratt)* 6-7-4 ‡³JFanning (7) (prom tl wknd 3f out) 6.10
615 Castle Cary **(30)** *(TCraig)* 6-7-7 LCharnock (3) (prom tl wknd 4f out) ............... 4.11
LONG HANDICAP: Master Plan (FR) 7-2.

**7/4** LAZY RHYTHM (USA), **5/2** Forever Diamonds, **5/1** Millfit (USA), **12/1** State Flyer, **16/1** Manulife, Strength in Depth (IRE), **20/1** Saint Vending, Diet, **25/1** Ors. CSF £6.58, CT £43.45. Tote £2.60: £1.90 £2.00 £4.80 (£3.70). Miss S. A. Hamilton (EPSOM) bred by Donald T. Johnson in USA. 11 Rn
1m 54.7 (11.4)
SF—35/43/37/23/19/28

---

## 797
BELLSHILL CLAIMING STKS (3-Y.O) £2167.20 (£599.20: £285.60)
1m 65y

4-00 (4-34)

Ballymoneyboy (Fav) *(MHTompkins)* 8-7 PRobinson (5) (lw: hld up: hdwy 4f out: led wl over 1f out: r.o strly) ........................ —1
434 Miliyel *(BHanbury)* 7-12 ‡⁷VBray (3) (lw: hld up: hdwy whn nt clr run 2f out: swtchd appr fnl f: no ch w wnr) ........................ 8.2
618 Milton Rooms (IRE) **(56)** (bl) *(CBBBooth)* 8-4 ACulhane (8) (lw: w ldrs: disp ld 4f out: one pce appr fnl f) ........................ 3.3
567² Between Two Fires **(58)** *(JBerry)* 7-13 NCarlisle (9) (mde most tl hdd wl over 1f out: sn btn) ........................ 1¹/₂.4
666⁴ Pass the Key (IRE) **(70)** *(NTinkler)* 8-7 KimTinkler (6) (bhd: rdn 4f out: nvr rchd ldrs) ........................ ¹/₂.5
406 Speedy Sioux **(61)** *(CWThornton)* 7-11 ‡³JFanning (2) (lw: prom tl wknd over 2f out) ........................ nk.6
314⁶ Tidal River **(43)** *(DenysSmith)* 7-5 ‡⁴CTeague (7) (w ldr tl wknd over 3f out) ... 10.7

**7/4** BALLYMONEYBOY, **2/1** Miliyel(op 5/4), **6/1** Between Two Fires, Speedy Sioux, **10/1** Pass the Key (IRE), **33/1** Ors. CSF £5.44, Tote £3.90: £2.00 £2.70 (£3.30). Mrs Anne Coughlan (NEWMARKET) bred by Brick Kiln Stud Farm. 7 Rn
1m 54.9 (11.6)
SF—31/–/–/–/–/–

---

## 798
AVON H'CAP (3-Y.O) (0-70) £2147.60 (£593.60: £282.80)
1¹/₂m 17y

4-30 (5-03)

488* Trump **(56)** (Fav) *(CParker)* 9-0 JCarroll (8) (lw: mde all: hld on wl fnl 3f) .......... —1
Moor Lodge (USA) **(63)** *(MHTompkins)* 9-7 PRobinson (7) (bhd: effrt 4f out: rdn to chal 1f out: no ex) ........................ 1.2
745² Kadari **(59)** *(AHarrison)* 9-3 KFallon (2) (trckd ldrs: effrt on ins 2f out: rdn & nt qckn) ........................ ¹/₂.3
547⁴ Thor Power (IRE) **(49)** *(DTThom)* 8-4 ‡³FNorton (3) (a cl up: chal 4f out: one pce fnl f) ........................ s.h.4

547⁶ Saif Al Adil (IRE) **(63)** (bl) *(BHanbury)* 9-0 VBray (6) (lw: cl up tl outpcd 3f out: sn wknd) ............ 20.5
Legitim **(45)** *(JMJefferson)* 8-3 JFortune (2) (in tch: rdn 4f out: sn btn) ........... 1¹/₂.6
567⁴ Floral Bouquet **(50)** (v) *(MJCamacho)* 8-8 NConnorton (1) (chsd ldrs tl hung rt & wknd over 3f out) .......... nk.7
606 Bartolomeo (USA) **(52)** *(MrsJRRamsden)* 8-3 ‡7RHavlin (4) (a bhd) ............... 30.8

**11/4** TRUMP, **4/1** Kadari, **6/1** Legitim, **7/1** Thor Power (IRE), Bartolomeo (op 4/1), **8/1** Ors. CSF £23.42, CT £80.55. Tote £3.10: £1.00 £10.30 £1.60 (£28.20). Mr Raymond Anderson Green (LOCKERBIE) bred by Cheveley Park Stud Ltd. 8 Rn
2m 50.7 (18.7)
SF—21/26/21/7/–/–

T/Plpt: £31.20 (69.9 Tckts). AA

580—**WINDSOR (Fig.8)**
**Monday, May 11th [Good]**
Going Allowance: minus 0.20 sec per fur (F) Wind: almost nil

Stalls: high

**799** 'OVER TO YOU JOHN' CLAIMING STKS (3 & 4-Y.O) £1683.00 (£468.00: £225.00)
1m 67y 6-15 (6-17)

240 **Take Two (75)** *(JWhite)* 4-9-10 TyroneWilliams (20) (lw: 4th st: hrd rdn over 2f out: r.o to ld cl home) ............ —1
392 Rise Up Singing **(79)** (bl) *(RHannon)* 4-9-2 ‡5RPerham (2) (led tl nr fin) ........... nk.2
Ibsen (Fav) *(PJMakin)* 4-9-6 LDettori (18) (6th st: hrd rdn over 2f out: r.o ins fnl f) .. 6.3
734* Up the Punjab **(63)** *(SDow)* 3-8-0 CRutter (10) (2nd st: ev ch over 1f out: nt qckn) ............ 2.4
657 Majed (IRE) **(73)** *(NACallaghan)* 4-9-10 PatEddery (13) (hdwy on ins 4f out: styd on one pce) ............ 4.5
508 Mystic Panther **(43)** *(RJHolder)* 4-9-1 ADicks (12) (no hdwy fnl 3f) ............ 2.6
Super Flyer (IRE) *(MrsAKnight)* 3-8-2(3) ‡5CHodgson (8) (bit bkwd: 5th st: hrd rdn over 2f out: sn wknd) ............ s.h.7
Count Robert (USA) *(MrsJSPerrin)* 4-9-10 JQuinn (19) (lw: nvr nr to chal) ...... 2¹/₂.8
580 Trendy Auctioneer (IRE) **(42)** *(MCPipe)* 4-9-2 RHills (9) (nvr trbld ldrs) ............ 4.9
411 Debjanjo **(47)** *(JRJenkins)* 4-9-6 SWhitworth (5) (n.d) ............ hd.10
525² Absolutely Right **(57)** *(JWhite)* 4-9-3 ‡7CAvery (11) (lw: s.s: nrst fin) ............ 1.11
587⁶ Miss Cookie **(52)** (bl) *(MCPipe)* 4-8-10 BCrossley (16) (3rd st: wknd 3f out) 1¹/₂.12
Savanga (USA) **(47)** *(MMcCormack)* 4-9-8 GBaxter (7) (n.d) ............ 1.13
586 Mabthul (USA) **(44)** *(MJHeaton-Ellis)* 4-9-6 RCochrane (6) (lw: n.d) ............ 1¹/₂.14
Daunt Not *(JWhite)* 4-8-13 AClark (14) (bit bkwd: n.d) ............ s.h.15
Cheren Boy *(BForsey)* 3-8-5 NHowe (3) (leggy: n.d) ............ ¹/₂.16
Express Signmaker (IRE) **(51)** *(JWhite)* 3-8-0 DaleGibson (4) (n.d) ............ ³/₄.17
Royal Opera Star *(JRBosley)* 3-8-3 RFox (17) (a bhd) ............ ³/₄.18
Dal Pascatore **(29)** *(FJYardley)* 4-8-11 ‡7TWilson (21) (n.d) ............ 1¹/₂.19
575 Yeoman Bound **(22)** (bl) *(KTIvory)* 4-8-8 ‡7CScally (15) (b.hind: 7th st: wknd 4f out: t.o) ............ 30.20

**9/4** Ibsen, **9/2** TAKE TWO, Majed (IRE)(3/1—5/1), **6/1** Rise Up Singing(op 3/1), Up the Punjab(3/1—13/2), **14/1** Absolutely Right, **16/1** Miss Cookie(10/1—20/1), **20/1** Trendy Auctioneer (IRE), **33/1** Mystic Panther, Royal Opera Star, Express Signmaker (IRE), Daunt Not, Cheren Boy, Super Flyer (IRE), Debjanjo, Mabthul (USA), Count Robert (USA), **50/1** Ors. CSF £34.19, Tote £4.60: £2.20 £1.70 £1.70 (£16.60). Mr Brian Gatensbury (WENDOVER) bred by Viscount Leverhulme. 20 Rn; Rise Up Singing clmd W Musson £9,555; Ibsen clmd M Spore £9,001.
1m 44 (2.4)
SF—50/41/27/1/13/–

**800** TRUVOX INTERNATIONAL H'CAP (0-80) £2092.00 (£582.00: £280.00)
1¹/₄m 7y 6-40 (6-52)

592 **Scottish Bambi (61)** *(RHannon)* 4-8-10 ‡5RPerham (18) (lw: 4th st: led 2f out: r.o wl) ............ —1
580³ Vanroy **(62)** *(JRJenkins)* 8-9-2 SWhitworth (8) (hdwy on ins over 2f out: styd on: nt rch wnr) ............ 3.2
533* Supertop **(55)** (Fav) *(PWHarris)* 4-8-9 PaulEddery (5) (gd hdwy over 2f out: hung rt over 1f out: r.o) ............ 1¹/₂.3
616³ Phil-Blake **(41)** *(SMellor)* 5-7-9 DanaMellor (20) (led to 2f out: r.o one pce) .... 1¹/₂.4
Tiger Shoot **(58)** *(PJFeilden)* 5-8-12 AShoults (10) (nvr nrr) ............ nk.5
Le Baron Perche (FR) **(76)** *(CJames)* 3-9-0 GBaxter (15) (7th st: rdn 4f out: one pce) ............ nk.6
249³ Beau Dada (IRE) **(54)** *(JWhite)* 4-8-8 DHolland (16) (2nd st: wknd 2f out) ...... hd.7
598 El Dominio **(60)** *(KOCunningham-Brown)* 4-9-0 LDettori (17) (lw: 5th & rdn st: one pce fnl 2f) ............ nk.8

544* Desired Guest **(76)** (bl) *(MRStoute)* 3–9-0 PD'Arcy (6) (b.off hind: hdwy 2f out:
　　　nt clr run ins fnl f: nt rch ldrs) ...................................................... hd.**9**
530 Petmer **(44)** *(GBBalding)* 5–7-12 CRutter (14) (nvr nrr) ................................ hd.**10**
565³ Broughton Blues (IRE) **(39)** (bl) *(WJMusson)* 4–7-0 ‡⁷CHawksley (13) (lw: n.d) 2¹/₂.**11**
438 Saluting Walter (USA) **(69)** *(lCampbell)* 4–9-9 AClark (12) (n.d) ...................... 1.**12**
504⁶ Full Quiver **(57)** (v) *(MrsBarbaraWaring)* 7–8-11 NHowe (9) (b.off fore: hdwy 4f
　　　out: hrd rdn 2f out: wknd fnl f) ........................................... 1¹/₂.**13**
240 Glassblower **(74)** *(RAkehurst)* 5–10-0 RCochrane (7) (lw: a bhd) .................. 1¹/₂.**14**
340 With Gusto **(45)** *(KOCunningham-Brown)* 5–7-13 SDawson(4)(b.hind: bhd fnl 4f) hd.**15**
210 Littledale **(45)** *(DJGMurray-Smith)* 6–7-13 DaleGibson (2) (a bhd) ...... 3¹/₂.**16**
　　Quiet Riot **(50)** *(JWhite)* 10–7-11⁽⁸⁾ ‡⁷LisaBateman (11) (bit bkwd: a bhd) ...... 1¹/₂.**17**
508 Dawn's Delight **(43)** *(KTIvory)* 14–7-11 GBardwell (3) (b.hind: t.o) .................. 5.**18**
　　Possessive Lady **(50)** *(MBell)* 5–8-4 MHills (1) (6th st: wknd qckly 3f out: t.o) 2¹/₂.**19**
580² Shoehorn **(62)** (bl) *(MCPipe)* 5–9-2 RHills (19) (plld hrd: 3rd st: wknd qckly 3f
　　　out: t.o) ...................................................................... nk.**20**

11/2 Supertop, 8/1 Full Quiver(op 14/1), Shoehorn, Desired Guest, 9/1 Tiger Shoot, Broughton Blues (IRE), 11/1
Vanroy, 12/1 SCOTTISH BAMBI, Littledale (USA), Possessive Lady, 14/1 Beau Dada (IRE), Glassblower, 16/1
Saluting Walter (USA), Petmer, 20/1 Phil-Blake, 25/1 El Dominio, 33/1 Le Baron Perche (FR), With Gusto,
Dawn's Delight, 50/1 Quiet Riot. CSF £141.99, CT £764.61. Tote £20.50: £4.00 £3.50 £1.70 £5.80 (£190.20).
Mr William J. Kelly (MARLBOROUGH) bred by Cheveley Park Stud Ltd. 20 Rn　　　　　2m 7.5 (4.5)
　　　　　　　　　　　　　　　　　　　　　　　　　　　　　　　　　　　　SF—31/31/21/4/20/21

**801**　　　JUNE ROSE H'CAP (3-Y.O) (0-80) £2045.80 (£568.80: £273.40)　　**5f 217y** 7-05 (7-22)

468⁶ **Risk Zone (56)** (bl) *(RHannon)* 7-12 AMcGlone (11) (a.p: led over 1f out: hrd
　　　rdn: r.o) ............................................................................ —**1**
472 Night Asset **(60)** (bl) *(GLewis)* 8-2 PaulEddery (3) (a.p: ev ch 1f out: r.o) .......... ³/₄.**2**
576⁵ Mogwai (IRE) **(67)** (bl) *(RFJohnsonHoughton)* 8-9 JReid (9) (hdwy 2f out: r.o
　　　one pce fnl f) ...................................................................... 4.**3**
363³ Sartigila **(62)** (Fav) *(JWPayne)* 8-4 AMunro (4) (a.p: r.o one pce fnl f) .............. s.h.**4**
624 Grey Charmer (IRE) **(67)** *(CJames)* 8-9 SWhitworth (14) (hrd rdn over 2f out: r.o
　　　fnl f) ................................................................................ 2.**5**
582³ Court Minstrel **(56)** *(LJHolt)* 7-12 NAdams (12) (nvr nrr) .............................. nk.**6**
478⁵ Spectacle Jim **(59)** *(JO'Donoghue)* 8-1 GBardwell (21) (unruly s: nvr nr to chal) 2¹/₂.**7**
　　Sandcastle City **(79)** *(RHannon)* 8-2 PatEddery (1) (no hdwy fnl 2f) ................ 2¹/₂.**8**
649 Peerage Prince **(69)** *(PatMitchell)* 8-8 ‡³SO'Gorman (13) (spd 4f) .................. 1.**9**
582 Cheshire Annie (IRE) **(56)** *(WCarter)* 7-12 JQuinn (16) (prom 4f) .................. 1.**10**
604 First Gold **(55)** *(JWharton)* 7-11 RFox (6) (nrst fin) ...................................... hd.**11**
690 Cumbrian Cavalier **(56)** *(KGWingrove)* 7-12 TyroneWilliams (17) (led over 4f
　　　out tl over 1f out) ............................................................ ¹/₂.**12**
582 Rio Trusky **(51)** (bl) *(MDIUsher)* 7-0 ‡⁷AntoinetteArmes (22) (nvr nrr) .............. nk.**13**
697 Another Vintage **(56)** (bl) *(PDCundell)* 7-7⁽²⁾ ‡⁵DHarrison (20) (lw: prom 3f) .... hd.**14**
468 Peggy Mainwaring **(54)** *(RJHolder)* 7-3 ‡⁷CHawksley (18) (n.d) .................. s.h.**15**
　　Pearly White **(62)** *(GBBalding)* 8-4 JWilliams (2) (a bhd) .............................. s.h.**16**
279 Queen's Tickle **(57)** *(APJarvis)* 7-13 WRadmore (7) (b.nr hind: s.s: a bhd) ..... nk.**17**
621 Duty Sergeant (IRE) **(62)** *(MPMuggeridge)* 8-4 AClark (15) (a bhd) .................. 2.**18**
372⁴ Buddy (IRE) **(62)** *(MBell)* 8-2 MHills (10) (lw: led over 1f: wknd qckly over 2f out) 2.**19**
582⁶ Sea Crusader **(57)** *(MBlansharsd)* 7-13 CRutter (8) (a bhd) ........................ 1¹/₂.**20**
503⁶ Waveband **(78)** *(BWHills)* 9-6 DHolland (5) (n.d) ........................................ 1¹/₂.**21**
　　　　　　　　　　　　　　　LONG HANDICAP: Rio Trusky 7-1.

5/1 Sartigila, 7/1 Night Asset, Court Minstrel, Another Vintage(10/1—6/1), 15/2 Queen's Tickle(14/1—7/1), 9/1
Grey Charmer (IRE), 10/1 Sandcastle City, 12/1 Mogwai (IRE)(7/1—3/1), 14/1 Duty Sergeant (IRE), Cumbrian
Cavalier(op 8/1), 16/1 Peggy Mainwaring, Buddy (IRE), RISK ZONE, 20/1 Spectacle Jim, Cheshire Annie (IRE),
First Gold, Pearly White, Waveband, 25/1 Sea Crusader, 33/1 Ors. CSF £138.34, CT £1,335.36. Tote £25.80:
£5.00 £1.40 £4.00 £2.10 (£51.90). Roldvale Limited (MARLBOROUGH) bred by Roldvale Ltd. 21 Rn
　　　　　　　　　　　　　　　　　　　　　　　　　　　　　　　　　　1m 11.6 (1.1)
　　　　　　　　　　　　　　　　　　　　　　　　　　　　　　SF—38/39/30/24/21/9

**802**　　　GEORGE A. MOORE H'CAP (3-Y.O) (0-90) £2110.00 (£585.00: £280.00)
　　　　　**1m 3f 135y**　　　　　　　　　　　　　　　　　　　　7-35 (7-46)

　　　　　　　　　　　　　(Weights raised 2 lb)
418* **Landowner (IRE) (68)** *(JHMGosden)* 8-9 RCochrane (4th st: led over 3f out:
　　　r.o wl) .............................................................................. —**1**
577* Duke of Eurolink **(80)** (Fav) *(LMCumani)* 9-7 LDettori (2) (lw: 6th st: hdwy 3f out:
　　　ev ch over 1f out: hrd rdn: nt qckn) ...................................... 2.**2**
599⁴ Maestroso (IRE) **(70)** (bl) *(RFJohnsonHoughton)* 8-11 JReid (4) (nvr nrr) .......... 3.**3**
554³ National Emblem (FR) **(75)** *(PFlCole)* 9-2 AMunro (1) (lw: 2nd st: ev ch 3f out:
　　　sn rdn: one pce) ............................................................ 10.**4**
　　Paper Clip **(66)** *(JDBethell)* 8-7 TyroneWilliams (7) (bit bkwd: nvr nr to chal) ... 20.**5**
　　The Karaoke King **(71)** *(RHannon)* 8-12 AMcGlone (3rd st: wknd 3f out) ............ 2.**6**

369 Anar (IRE) **(52)** *(WCarter)* 7-0 ‡7CHawksley (3) (lw: 5th st: wknd 4f out) ............ 3.7
481 Surely Gifted (IRE) **(60)** *(WRMuir)* 8-1 JQuinn (8) (led tl wknd qckly over 3f out:
 t.o) .................................................................................................................................. 20.8
LONG HANDICAP: Anar (IRE) 7-5.

**8/13** Duke of Eurolink, **5/1** LANDOWNER (IRE)(7/2—11/2), **10/1** Maestroso (IRE), Surely Gifted (IRE), National Emblem (FR), **14/1** The Karaoke King(10/1—16/1), **20/1** Paper Clip, **33/1** Anar (IRE). CSF £8.58, CT £28.63. Tote £4.20: £1.30 £1.30 £2.20 (£2.60). Sheikh Mohammed (NEWMARKET) bred by Sheikh Mohammed bin Rashid al Maktoum in Ireland. 8 Rn
2m 28.9 (6.4)
SF—8/16/-/-/-/-

---

### 803
HERBERT & PETER BLAGRAVE MEMORIAL STKS (2-Y.O) £1845.60 (£511.60: £244.80)
**5f 10y**
8-05 (8-09)

709² **Risk Me's Girl** (Fav) *(RHannon)* 8-13 WRSwinburn (8) (mde virtually all: r.o wl) —1
 The Seer *(BWHills)* 8-11 DHolland (5) (unf: gd hdwy over 1f out: r.o ins fnl f) . 3½.2
 Press the Bell *(JBerry)* 8-11 PatEddery (6) (unf: w wnr: ev ch over 1f out: wknd
 fnl f: eased nr fin) ....................................................................................... 1½.3
 650 Tee Gee Jay *(CNWilliams)* 8-6 JCurant (6) (b.hind: a.p: one pce fnl 2f) ............ 2.4
 Kingsdown Cavalier *(RHannon)* 8-11 BRouse (2) (cmpt: nvr nrr) ............... s.h.5
 Will's Legacy *(WCarter)* 8-11 JReid (3) (leggy: no hdwy fnl 2f) ...................... 2.6
 772⁶ War Requiem (IRE) *(GBBalding)* 8-11 JWilliams (7) (a bhd) ............................ 4.7
 Monet Order *(JRJenkins)* 8-6 GBaxter (9) (leggy: bit bkwd: prom over 2f) ........ ¾.8
 Petite Vino *(JJBridger)* 8-6 NAdams (1) (neat: bit bkwd: s.s: a wl bhd) ........... 4.9
 Walters Wonder *(JRJenkins)* 8-11 SWhitworth (10) (neat: bkwd: outpcd: t.o) .. 8.10

**4/6** RISK ME'S GIRL, **2/1** Press the Bell(6/4—9/4), **10/1** The Seer(op 6/1), **20/1** Kingsdown Cavalier, **25/1** War Requiem (IRE), **40/1** Ors. CSF £8.37, Tote £1.70: £1.20 £1.90 £1.60 (£5.80). Roldvale Limited (MARLBOROUGH) bred by Mrs J. Everitt. 10 Rn
61.3 sec (2.3)
SF—33/17/11/-/2/-

---

### 804
G.A.R. RICHARDSON STKS (Mdn 3-Y.O) £1720.80 (£478.80: £230.40)
**1¼m 7y**
8-35 (8-39)

370² **Inner City (IRE)** (Fav) *(LMCumani)* 9-0 LDettori (1) (lw: 8th st: led 2f out: hung
 rt: drvn out) ............................................................................................... —1
511³ Unforgiving Minute *(PWHarris)* 9-0 PaulEddery (10) (5th st: ev ch over 1f out:
 sltly hmpd & swtchd ins fnl f: edgd lft: no ex) ...................................... 1.2
 Big Easy (IRE) *(MrsJCecil)* 9-0 AClark (3) (bit bkwd: 6th st: ev ch over 1f out: nt
 qckn) ....................................................................................................... 2.3
 628 Cezanne *(MRStoute)* 9-0 WRSwinburn (4) (leggy: scope: hdwy 4f out: hrd rdn
 over 2f out: r.o one pce) ....................................................................... 2.4
 435⁵ Sovereign Page (USA) *(BHanbury)* 9-0 BRaymond (5) (lw: 2nd st: led over 2f
 out: sn hdd: nt qckn) ............................................................................. hd.5
 Magadeer (USA) **(78)** *(JLDunlop)* 8-9 JReid (20) (b.nr hind: nvr nrr) ............. 3½.6
 Busman (IRE) *(MajorWRHern)* 9-0 MHills (21) (nvr nr to chal) ..................... 2½.7
 Storm Dust *(JRFanshawe)* 9-0 GCarter (9) (w'like: nrst fr) ........................... s.h.8
 433 Russian Vision *(AAScott)* 9-0 WNewnes (17) (7th st: wknd 2f out) .................. 1.9
 465⁵ Toss the Dice *(MAJarvis)* 9-0 AMunro (4) (lw: 4th st: ev ch 2f out: sn wknd) . 2½.10
 573³ Brier Creek (USA) *(JHMGosden)* 9-0 RCochrane (9) (nvr nr ldrs) ................. 1.11
 560⁶ Bentico *(MAJarvis)* 9-0 GCrealock (22) (n.d) ............................................. 5.12
 607⁵ Lamore Ritorna *(KOCunningham-Brown)* 8-9 JWilliams (18) (led tl wknd over 2f
 out) ........................................................................................................ nk.13
 Field of Dreams *(CFWall)* 8-9 NDay (14) (bit bkwd: n.d) ............................... 2½.14
 424³ Very Evident (IRE) *(BWHills)* 8-9 PatEddery (7) (3rd st: wknd 3f out) ........... 3½.15
 451 Wilkins *(JRFanshawe)* 8-7 ‡7NVarley (15) (n.d) ...................................... 2.16
 502 River Anchor *(RCharlton)* 8-9 SRaymont (19) (lw: n.d) ............................... 4.17
 200⁴ Prove It's Gold *(TMJones)* 8-9 NAdams (11) (n.d) ...................................... 2½.18
 560 Highland Flame *(ANLee)* 9-0 JQuinn (8) (n.d) ............................................. 3½.19
 627⁶ Scultore (USA) *(MRChannon)* 9-0 BRouse (6) (a bhd) ................................... 4.20
 Turgenev (IRE) *(JHMGosden)* 9-0 GHind (12) (str: scope: bkwd: n.d) ............. nk.21
 Antique Song (IRE) *(CFWall)* 8-9 AMcGlone (16) (w'like: bit bkwd: n.d) .......... 1.22
*Stewards Enquiry: Obj. to Inner City (IRE) by Paul Eddery overruled.*

**6/4** INNER CITY (IRE), **5/1** Cezanne, **6/1** River Anchor, **7/1** Brier Creek (USA)(12/1—14/1), **8/1** Very Evident (IRE)(tchd 16/1), **9/1** Sovereign Page (USA), **12/1** Lamore Ritorna, **20/1** Magadeer (USA), **25/1** Busman (IRE), **50/1** Ors. CSF £98.02, Tote £2.70: £1.60 £6.20 £7.40 (£48.40). Sheikh Mohammed (NEWMARKET) bred by Ballynagran Bloodstock Ltd in Ireland. 22 Rn
2m 8 (5)
SF—30/28/24/20/19/7

---

T/Plpt: £38.60 (66.95 Tckts).
Hn

## 586—WOLVERHAMPTON (L-H)
### Monday, May 11th [St Course Good, Rnd Good to firm]
Going Allowance: 0.05 sec per fur (G)                                    Wind: mod half bhd

Stalls: high

**805**     PENN FIELDS H'CAP (0-70) £2676.80 (£744.80: £358.40)     **2m 201y**     2-15 (2-20)

Seldom In (39) *(JWharton)* 6–8-3 JQuinn (14) (swtg: hld up gng wl: hdwy to ld
     over 3f out: sn clr: styd on) ......................................................... —1
605* Creeager (63) *(JWharton)* 10–9-6 ‡7SWilliams (8) (hdwy 4f out: ev ch fnl f:
     unable qckn) ........................................................................... ¾.2
675 Merton Mill (57) *(DMorley)* 5–9-7 WRSwinburn (16) (hld up: hdwy over 2f out:
     rdn & no ex nr fin) ................................................................... 2.3
593³ Needwood Muppet (54) (Jt-Fav) *(BCMorgan)* 5–9-4 SCauthen (7) (chsd ldrs:
     effrt 3f out: sn rdn: one pce) ................................................... 2.4
501 Paper Dance (60) *(RJHolder)* 4–9-7 JWilliams (18) (hld up & bhd: gd hdwy over
     3f out: one pce appr fnl f) ....................................................... ¾.5
Grace Card (43) (Jt-Fav) *(MrsGRReveley)* 6–8-7 JLowe (12) (lw: hld up in rr:
     effrt & nt clr run over 2f out: nt rcvr) ...................................... 7.6
593⁴ Enfant du Paradis (IRE) *(PDEvans)* 4–8-5 GCarter (15) (prom: 2nd st: wknd 2f
     out) ........................................................................................ ¾.7
377² Hamilton Lady (IRE) (42) *(DMoffatt)* 4–7-10 ‡7DarrenMoffatt (19) (hdwy 9f out:
     wknd over 2f out) .................................................................... 2.8
Andrelot (46) (v) *(KWhite)* 5–8-3 ‡7AGarth (9) (b: nvr plcd to chal) ........ 1½.9
475⁵ High Grade (53) *(SDow)* 4–9-0 TQuinn (4) (bit bkwd: led over 14f: eased whn
     btn appr fnl f) ....................................................................... ¾.10
Classic Statement (64) *(RLee)* 6–9-9 ‡5RPrice (17) (hld up: hdwy 7f out: 4th st:
     wknd over 2f out) ................................................................... 1½.11
590³ Rushluan (52) *(RJHodges)* 8–8-13 ‡3TSprake (11) (hld up in tch: 8th st: wknd 3f
     out) ........................................................................................ 1.12
552⁵ Chucklestone (57) *(JSKing)* 9–9-7 PatEddery (3) (bit bkwd: chsd ldr: 3rd st:
     wknd 3f out) ........................................................................... 5.13
675⁵ Cardinal Bird (USA) (48) *(SMellor)* 5–9-3 DanaMellor (2) (n.d) ............... ½.14
708 Don't Cry (48) *(JDBethell)* 4–8-9 AMunro (1) (w ldrs: 5th st: wknd over 2f out) hd.15
578⁵ Ragtime (38) *(ASReid)* 5–8-2 BCrossley (13) (chsd ldrs: 7th st: wknd 3f out) . nk.16
530 As Always (IRE) (47) (bl) *(GLewis)* 4–8-8 PaulEddery (5) (lw: prom: rdn 6f out:
     6th st: sn wknd: t.o) ............................................................... 6.17
593 Peacock Feather (48) *(KRBurke)* 4–8-9 AShoults (20) (a bhd: t.o) ......... 8.18
Legal Win (USA) (53) (bl) *(FJordan)* 4–9-0 WNewnes (6) (a bhd: t.o) .......... 1½.19

**11/4** Grace Card, Needwood Muppet, **15/2** As Always (IRE)(12/1—6/1), **12/1** High Grade, **14/1** Merton Mill,
Creeager(op 8/1), **16/1** Rushluan, Chucklestone(op 10/1), Don't Cry, **20/1** Paper Dance, Hamilton Lady (IRE),
**25/1** Enfant du Paradis (IRE), Legal Win (USA), **33/1** Cardinal Bird (USA), Classic Statement, Ragtime, Andrelot,
**50/1** SELDOM IN & Ors. CSF £600.81, CT £8,959.22. Tote £33.90: £5.60 £4.90 £7.30 £1.60 (£249.20). Mrs V.
Craggs (MELTON MOWBRAY) bred by Bylon Farmers Ltd. 19 Rn                              3m 44.4 (7.7)
                                                                                      SF—20/36/35/30/32/11/8

**806**     GRAND UNION (S) STKS (3-Y-O) £2461.20 (£683.20: £327.60)     **1m 3f**     2-45 (2-50)

603² Fly for Gold (IRE) (Jt-Fav) *(DWPArbuthnot)* 8-9 TQuinn (6) (nt clr run over 6f
     out: hdwy over 3f out: hrd rdn to ld nr fin) ................................ —1
599⁶ Princess of Orange (60) *(CCElsey)* 8-9 JQuinn (1) (chsd ldrs: 6th st: rdn to ld
     over 2f out: ct last strides) .................................................... nk.2
Big Pat *(JPearce)* 8-9 ‡5RPrice (7) (rdn & hdwy 3f out: ev ch over 1f out: no ex fnl
     f) ........................................................................................... 4.3
674⁴ Speedy Beauty *(BHanbury)* 8-9 WRSwinburn (3) (hld up: hdwy over 2f out: nvr
     nrr) ........................................................................................ 3½.4
666² Ready to Draw (IRE) (67) (Jt-Fav) *(RonaldThompson)* 9-5 RPElliott (16) (hdwy
     ent st: r.o one pce fnl 2f) ...................................................... 2½.5
355 Elsa (43) *(RJHolder)* 8-2 ‡7SDrowne (5) (bhd: styd on fnl 2f: nrst fin) ......... 2.6
728 Odoen (USA) (45) *(MRChannon)* 9-0 BRouse (15) (chsd ldrs: 5th st: wknd 2f
     out) ........................................................................................ 1½.7
519³ Major Risk (52) *(PAKelleway)* 9-0 PaulEddery (11) (prom: 2nd st: ev ch 3f out:
     sn rdn & wknd) ...................................................................... ¾.8
577 Northern Blade (IRE) (57) *(RHollinshead)* 9-0 WRyan (13) (lw: led tl over 2f out:
     wknd qckly) ........................................................................... 1.9
510 Brush Wolf (USA) *(JMBradley)* 9-0 WNewnes (8) (a in rr) ......................... 2½.10
603⁵ Rich Pickings *(CACyzer)* 8-9 GCarter (2) (lw: prom: 4th st: sn wknd) ......... 2½.11
355 Magnetic Prince (37) *(GBlum)* 8-7 ‡7JWeaver (14) (a bhd) ...................... 1½.12
594 Injaka Boy (44) *(KWhite)* 9-0 NAdams (4) (a bhd) ................................... 4.13

177⁵ Albany Spark (bl) *(GHEden)* 9-0 AMunro (10) (prom: 3rd st: wknd 3f out) ........ 6.14
603 Salmon Dancer (IRE) **(36)** *(MFBarraclough)* 9-0 GDuffield (12) (hld up: 7th st: wknd 3f out: t.o) ...................................................... 2.15
567 Dangina **(28)** *(ASReid)* 9-0 BCrossley (9) (plld hrd: lost pl 5f out: t.o) ............. 30.16

**7/2** Ready to Draw (IRE), FLY FOR GOLD (IRE)(op 6/1), **5/1** Speedy Beauty, Princess of Orange(op 5/2), **13/2** Odoen (USA), **14/1** Rich Pickings, Major Risk, **16/1** Northern Blade (IRE), **20/1** Salmon Dancer (IRE), Albany Spark, **50/1** Ors. CSF £21.36, Tote £3.10: £1.20 £2.40 £8.90 (£3.70). Mr J. S. Gutkin (COMPTON) bred by Stonethorn Stud Farms Ltd. 16 Rn; Bt in 5,400 gns                                    2m 26.9 (11.9)

## 807

E.B.F. PENKRIDGE STKS (Mdn 2-Y.O) £2678.40 (£742.40: £355.20)   **5f**   3-15 (3-20)

352⁶ **Finmental (IRE)** *(ABailey)* 9-0 AMackay (7) (a.p: rdn over 1f out: qcknd to ld ins fnl f) ..................................................... —1
564³ Two Times Twelve (IRE) (bl) (Jt-Fav) *(JBerry)* 9-0 PatEddery (12) (led tl ins fnl f) ... 2.2
Galejade *(DHaydnJones)* 8-9 JReid (11) (lt-f: dwlt: hdwy wl over 1f out: nrst fin) 2¹/₂.3
564 Expo Mondial (IRE) *(JMPEustace)* 9-0 MTebbutt (3) (hdwy over 1f out: r.o wl ins fnl f) ....................................................... s.h.4
574 The Sharp Bidder (IRE) *(RHollinshead)* 9-0 PaulEddery (1) (gd spd over 3f) ... s.h.5
581 Second Colours (USA) *(PSFelgate)* 9-0 JLowe (2) (hdwy 2f out: kpt on wl ins fnl f) ............................................................. hd.6
Fierro *(CEBrittain)* 9-0 SCauthen (9) (neat: sn outpcd: effrt & hrd rdn over 1f out: one pce) ................................................. hd.7
Superensis *(WRMuir)* 9-0 SWhitworth (8) (cmpt: spd over 3f) .................... hd.8
Kind of Cute *(CCElsey)* 8-9 WNewnes (4) (lengthy: unf: s.s: outpcd) ............. 10.9
Caldervale *(ABailey)* 9-0 JQuinn (4) (lt-f: unf: dwlt: a bhd: t.o) ................ nk.10
602² Kensworth Lady (Jt-Fav) *(MBlanshard)* 8-9 CRutter (13) (a bhd: t.o) ............. ¹/₂.11
Form Secret (IRE) *(LJBarratt)* 8-9 NAdams (5) (lt-f: bit bkwd: outpcd: t.o) ....... 7.12
Salt N Vinegar (IRE) *(RonaldThompson)* 8-9 RPElliott (6) (lengthy: unf: outpcd: t.o) ................................................................ 12.13

**11/4** Kensworth Lady, Two Times Twelve (IRE), **3/1** Fierro(op 6/1), **6/1** FINMENTAL (IRE)(8/1—5/1), **10/1** Superensis(op 5/1), **16/1** Caldervale(op 10/1), **20/1** Kind of Cute, **25/1** Expo Mondial (IRE), The Sharp Bidder (IRE), **33/1** Ors. CSF £23.44, Tote £13.50: £4.50 £1.70 £3.10 (£17.40). Mrs M. O'Donnell (TARPORLEY) bred by E. Lonergan in Ireland. 13 Rn                                         60.6 sec (3.3)
SF—39/31/16/20/19/18

## 808

COMPTON STKS (3-Y.O) £2226.00 (£616.00: £294.00)   **7f**   3-45 (3-45)

403✶ **Prince Ferdinand (116)** (Fav) *(MMcCormack)* 9-7 JReid (5) (hld up: 3rd st: led ins fnl f: readily) ....................................... —1
239 Ernestan **(100)** *(MHEasterby)* 9-7 MBirch (2) (chsd ldrs: 2nd st: led over 2f out tl ins fnl f) ......................................................... 2¹/₂.2
624³ Neither Nor **(73)** *(RJHolder)* 8-6 JWilliams (4) (5th st: sn rdn & no imp) ............. 7.3
252³ Everybodys Talking *(CEBrittain)* 8-6 ‡5BDoyle (3) (chsd ldrs: 4th st: rdn over 3f out: sn outpcd) .......................................... 3¹/₂.4
Double Lark **(75)** *(RHollinshead)* 8-11 PaulEddery (1) (led tl hdd & wknd over 2f out) ...................................................... 12.5

**2/5** PRINCE FERDINAND, **9/2** Ernestan(op 3/1), **5/1** Everybodys Talking, **10/1** Neither Nor, **33/1** Double Lark. CSF £2.79, Tote £1.50: £1.10 £1.50 (£1.70). Miss J. Winch (WANTAGE) bred by Greensward Racing Ltd. 5 Rn
1m 28.3 (4)
SF—52/44/8/–

## 809

TELFORD H'CAP (0-80) £2402.40 (£666.40: £319.20)   **1m 200y**   4-15 (4-18)

422³ **Execution Only (IRE) (54)** (v) *(JWWatts)* 4-8-7 GHind (9) (5th st: shkn up 3f out: led wl over 1f out: sn clr) ............................. —1
696⁶ Persian Dynasty **(40)** *(JMBradley)* 8-7-7 NAdams (4) (lw: gd hdwy over 2f out: hrd rdn appr fnl f: no ch w wnr) ................................ 6.2
696³ Lady Lacey **(54)** (v) (Fav) *(GBBalding)* 5-8-4 JWilliams (18) (lw: hld up: hdwy 3f out: r.o ins fnl f: nvr nrr) ...................................... 2¹/₂.3
713³ Rose Glen **(58)** *(ABailey)* 6-8-6 ‡5ATucker (17) (4th st: led 2f out: sn hdd: one pce) ................................................................ ¹/₂.4
515⁶ Prepare (IRE) **(49)** *(RJHolder)* 4-7-11⁽¹⁾ ‡5RPrice (2) (chsd ldrs: 6th st: one pce appr fnl f) ............................................... ³/₄.5
684 Sally Fay (IRE) **(55)** *(TKersey)* 4-8-8 WRyan (1) (bhd: stdy hdwy fnl 3f: nvr nrr) .. 5.6
579⁵ Shu Fly (NZ) **(60)** *(MrsSOliver)* 8-8-13 PatEddery (3) (in rr: rdn ¹/₂-wy: nvr able chal) ................................................................ 6.7
Wheels of Weetman **(49)** *(MissSJWilton)* 5-7-11⁽⁹⁾ ‡5NGwilliams (5) (nvr plcd to chal) ................................................................ 1¹/₂.8

657 Chatham Island **(67)** *(CEBrittain)* 4–9-1 ‡⁵BDoyle (11) (chsd ldrs tl wknd over 2f out) ................................................................................ 1.9
684⁴ Obsidian Grey **(63)** *(BAMcMahon)* 5–9-2 TQuinn (7) (led 1f: 3rd st: led over 2f out: sn hdd & wknd) ........................................................ nk.10
696 Chew it Over (IRE) **(52)** *(CASmith)* 4–8-5 GCarter (14) (prom: 2nd st: ev ch 3f out: sn wknd) ................................................................... ¹/₂.11
570 Asterix **(75)** *(JMBradley)* 4–9-7 ‡⁷MichaelBradley (13) (n.d) ................. ³/₄.12
504 Loudest Whisper **(60)** *(KSBridgwater)* 4–8-13 GDuffield (16) (n.d) ........ 1.13
Woodlands Grey **(40)** *(PAPritchard)* 6–7-7 RStreet (2) (bit bkwd: a bhd) .. 1¹/₂.14
Birthdays' Child **(64)** *(JRFanshawe)* 4–9-3 WRSwinburn (10) (gd hdwy 3f out: wknd 2f out) ...................................................................... 2.15
504 Northern Vision **(44)** (bl) *(PABlockley)* 5–7-11 JLowe (8) (led after 1f tl wknd over 2f out: sn wknd) ......................................................... 3.16
587⁵ Chloes Diamond (IRE) **(50)** *(JLSpearing)* 4–8-3 AMackay (6) (n.d) ...... 1¹/₂.17
590 Beija Flor **(66)** *(FJordan)* 5–9-5 WNewnes (12) (prom tl 7th & wkng st: t.o) .... 30.18
LONG HANDICAP: Persian Dynasty 7-6, Wheels of Weetman 7-5, Woodlands Grey 6-8.

**4/1** Lady Lacey, **9/2** Shu Fly (NZ), **6/1** Rose Glen, **13/2** Birthdays' Child(10/1—6/1), **7/1** Prepare (IRE)(10/1—6/1), **10/1** Obsidian Grey, EXECUTION ONLY (IRE), **12/1** Beija Flor, **14/1** Persian Dynasty, **16/1** Chatham Island, Loudest Whisper, **20/1** Chloes Diamond (IRE), **33/1** Chew it Over (IRE), Asterix, **50/1** Sally Fay (IRE), Wheels of Weetman, Northern Vision, **100/1** Woodlands Grey. CSF £143.15, CT £614.05. Tote £10.50: £1.30 £2.60 £1.60 £2.10 (£195.70). Mr Jeremy J. Thompson (RICHMOND) bred by Hollyhill Stud in Ireland. 18 Rn                                           1m 53.8 (5.3)
SF—21/–/–/–/–/–

**810**     CANNOCK H'CAP (3-Y.O) (0-70) £2441.60 (£677.60: £324.80)
               1³/₄m 134y                                               4-45 (4-48)

(Weights raised 5 lb)
529⁵ **Farmer's Pet (53)** *(GAPritchard-Gordon)* 8-9 GCarter (13) (chsd ldr: 2nd st: led over 3f out: on olr: eqsily) ......................................... 1
191⁶ Child Star (FR) **(45)** *(DMarks)* 7-10 ‡⁵ATucker (2) (hdwy & 7th st: hrd rdn & chsd wnr fnl 3f: kpt on) ......................................................... 3.2
Yenoora (IRE) **(59)** *(PFICole)* 9-1 TQuinn (8) (swtg: chsd ldrs: 3rd st: hrd rdn 3f out: eased whn btn fnl f) ................................................. 12.3
547⁵ Escadaro (USA) **(43)** (v) *(SGNorton)* 7-6 ‡⁷AGarth (6) (hdwy 7f out: 4th st: wknd 3f out) ................................................................................. 6.4
547² Perforate **(60)** *(SirMarkPrescott)* 9-2 GDuffield (5) (b.hind: hdwy 6f out: nvr nr to chal) .............................................................................. 7.5
451⁵ Barton Pride (IRE) **(52)** *(RHollinshead)* 8-8 WRyan (1) (styd on fnl 3f: n.d) ...... ¹/₂.6
599 Eleckydo **(55)** *(RJHodges)* 8-8 ‡³TSprake (14) (chsd ldrs: effrt ¹/₂-wy: no imp fnl 3f) ........................................................................................ nk.7
Benefact (USA) **(48)** *(DWPArbuthnot)* 7-13 ‡⁵RPrice (3) (lw: nvr nr to chal) ...... 1¹/₂.8
547³ Salu **(65)** *(JEtherington)* 9-0 ‡⁷JWeaver (9) (lw: hdwy ¹/₂-wy: 5th st: wknd 3f out) 5.9
457⁶ Split Second **(49)** *(JWWatts)* 8-5 GHind (11) (chsd ldrs: 6th st: sn wknd) ......... 4.10
519⁵ Elgin **(47)** (bl) *(ABailey)* 8-3 AMackay (10) (swtg: led & sn wl clr: rdn 4f out: sn hdd & wknd: t.o) ...................................................................... 6.11
Mr Elk **(54)** *(MrsGRReveley)* 8-10 JLowe (12) (bkwd: a bhd: t.o) ................... 8.12
Ellafitzetty (IRE) **(65)** *(RFJohnsonHoughton)* 9-7 WNewnes (7) (chsd ldrs: rdn ¹/₂-wy: wknd 6f out: t.o) ...................................................... 2¹/₂.13
625 Tree Frog (IRE) **(60)** (v) (Fav) *(LordHuntingdon)* 9-2 SCauthen (4) (nvr gng wl: sn bhd: t.o) ........................................................................... 12.14

**7/2** Tree Frog (IRE), **9/2** Perforate(op 3/1), **5/1** Salu, **7/1** Yenoora (IRE), **11/1** FARMER'S PET(20/1—10/1), **12/1** Benefact (USA), **14/1** Barton Pride (IRE)(op 6/1), Split Second, Ellafitzetty (IRE), **16/1** Mr Elk, Escadaro (USA), **20/1** Eleckydo, **25/1** Ors. CSF £229.38, CT £1,874.97. Tote £20.50: £4.10 £6.60 £3.10 (£108.80). Mr D. R. Midwood (NEWMARKET) bred by Normanby Stud Ltd. 14 Rn                    3m 13.4 (7.4)
SF—28/9/4/–/–/–

T/Plpt: £236.40 (12.2 Tckts).                                                       IM

# YORK (L-H)
## Tuesday, May 12th [Good]
Going Allowance: nil sec per fur (G)                                     Wind: fresh half bhd

Stalls: high

**811**     E.B.F. ZETLAND STKS (Mdn 2-Y.O.F) £5848.00 (£1744.00: £832.00: £376.00)
               5f                                                   2-00 (2-00)

619² **Marina Park** *(MJohnston)* 8-11 DMcKeown (2) (lw: w ldrs: led ¹/₂-wy: drvn out) —1
677² Cynic *(JWWatts)* 8-11 SCauthen (1) (swtg: w ldrs: rdn & nt qckn fnl f) ............... 1.2

Poker Chip (Fav) *(IABalding)* 8-11 RCochrane (6) (w'like: scope: hmpd s: hdwy & prom ½-wy: rdn & hung lft 1f out: kpt on wl) .................. ¾.3

568 Lucky Mill *(FHLee)* 8-11 MHills (5) (hmpd s: swtchd outside ½-wy: sn prom: wknd over 1f out) ......... 2½.4

Express Mariecurie (IRE) *(PWChapple-Hyam)* 8-11 PaulEddery (4) (lengthy: scope: squeezed s: sn w ldrs: led over 3f out tl over 2f out: wknd) ......... 6.5

564 Defenceless *(RHannon)* 8-11 BRouse (3) (swtg: swvd rt s: led over 1f: rdn & wknd 2f out) ......... 1½.6

**11/10** Poker Chip, **9/2** Cynic, **5/1** Defenceless, **7/1** Express Mariecurie (IRE), MARINA PARK, **14/1** Lucky Mill. CSF £34.42, Tote £7.40: £2.40 £1.90 (£10.50). Laharna Ltd (MIDDLEHAM) bred by Laharna Ltd. 6 Rn
60.05 sec (2.55)
SF–46/42/39/29/5/–

**812**　LAMBSON GRADUATION STKS (3-Y.O) £5536.00 (£1648.00: £784.00: £352.00)
**1m 5f 194y**　2-35 (2-36)

687² Ambiguously Regal (USA) *(MrsJCecil)* 8-11 PaulEddery (2) (mde all: styd on wl fnl 2f) ......... —1

597* Antiguan Flyer **(81)** *(BWHills)* 9-4 PatEddery (1) (lw: hld up: hdwy 6f out: effrt u.p over 3f out: no imp) ......... 5.2

433 Robenko (USA) *(CEBrittain)* 8-11 LDettori (4) (prom tl rdn & outpcd 4f out: kpt on fnl 2f) ......... 1.3

609⁴ Pabouche (USA) (Fav) *(HRACecil)* 9-4 SCauthen (3) (lw: trckd wnr: effrt 4f out: sn rdn: hung lft 2f out: sn wknd) ......... ¾.4

**6/4** Pabouche (USA), **5/2** Antiguan Flyer, **7/2** AMBIGUOUSLY REGAL (USA), **11/2** Robenko (USA). CSF £10.78, Tote £4.50 (£4.10). Mr George L. Ohrstrom (NEWMARKET) bred by George L. Ohrstrom in USA. 4 Rn
3m 2.14 (8.54)
SF–12/9/–/5

**813**　PAUL CADDICK AND MACGAY SPRINT TROPHY (H'cap) (0-110) £12232.50 (£3660.00: £1755.00: £802.50)　**6f**　3-05 (3-07)

449³ Lochsong **(73)** (Fav) *(IABalding)* 4-7-12 WCarson (14) (lw: w ldrs gng wl: led over 1f out: drvn out) ......... —1

610 So Rhythmical **(71)** *(GHEden)* 8-7-7 ‡³FNorton (8) (b.off hind: swtg: bhd: hdwy 2f out: r.o wl ins fnl f: nt rch wnr) ......... 1½.2

686⁴ Cumbrian Waltzer **(100)** *(MHEasterby)* 7-9-11 MBirch (21) (sn chsng ldrs: effrt & edgd rt over 1f out: r.o nr fin) ......... 1.3

676⁴ Gorinsky (IRE) **(76)** (bl) *(JBerry)* 4-8-1 JCarroll (19) (led tl over 1f out: edgd rt & kpt on wl) ......... ½.4

527⁵ Duplicity (IRE) **(95)** *(LJHolt)* 4-9-6 JReid (18) (swtg: chsd ldrs: rdn 2f out: kpt on fnl f) ......... hd.5

550² Terrhars (IRE) **(103)** *(RHannon)* 4-9-9 ‡⁵RPerham (11) (lw: chsd ldrs tl wknd ins fnl f) ......... s.h.6

629 Profilic **(79)** *(CaptJWilson)* 7-8-4(1) WRyan (20) (lw: hld up & bhd: n.m.r over 1f out: r.o: nt rch ldrs) ......... hd.7

596 Dominuet **(82)** *(JLSpearing)* 7-8-7 RFox (16) (lw: s.i.s: gd hdwy over 2f out: bdly hmpd over 1f out: nt rcvr) ......... 1½.8

629 Amron **(86)** *(JBerry)* 5-8-11 NCarlisle (17) (prom: rdn ½-wy: grad wknd) ......... 1.9

629² Sea Devil **(82)** *(MJCamacho)* 6-8-7 NConnorton (7) (lw: chsd ldrs: rdn over 2f out: kpt on same pce) ......... ½.10

629 Choir Practice **(86)** *(WJHaggas)* 5-8-11 NDay (15) (bhd: styng on whn n.m.r over 1f out: n.d) ......... ¾.11

236² Panikin **(93)** *(JWharton)* 4-9-4 JWilliams (10) (nvr trbld ldrs) ......... hd.12

779 Green Dollar **(91)** *(EAWheeler)* 9-8-11 ‡⁵DHarrison (9) (lw: bhd: sme hdwy 2f out: n.d) ......... hd.13

676² Gondo **(70)** (v) *(EJAlston)* 5-7-6 ‡³JFanning (2) (w ldrs over 4f: sn wknd) ......... ½.14

670⁶ Bold Habit **(89)** *(WJPearce)* 7-9-0 DNicholls (1) (lw: hld up: gd hdwy over 1f out: n.m.r & eased ins fnl f) ......... hd.15

629 Adwick Park **(89)** *(TDBarron)* 4-9-0 LDettori (5) (lw: hdwy u.p ½-wy: wknd 2f out) ......... ½.16

438 Nordic Brave **(72)** *(MBrittain)* 6-7-11 JLowe (12) (chsd ldrs tl rdn & wknd 2f out) ......... ½.17

629 Gentle Hero (USA) **(91)** *(MPNaughton)* 6-9-2 GHind (13) (chsd ldrs tl rdn & wknd over 2f out) ......... 3½.18

629 The Auction Bidder **(86)** *(RHollinshead)* 5-8-11 PaulEddery (3) (nvr wnt pce) ......... nk.19

Broad Story (NZ) **(73)** *(PCalver)* 5-7-12 DaleGibson (4) (w ldrs to ½-wy: sn wknd) ......... 1½.20

Resolute Bay **(86)** *(RMWhitaker)* 6-8-11 ACulhane (9) (bit bkwd: bhd fr ½-wy) ......... hd.21

9/2 LOCHSONG, 9/1 Cumbrian Waltzer, 10/1 So Rhythmical, Sea Devil, Bold Habit, 12/1 Terrhars (IRE), 14/1 Panikin, Choir Practice, 16/1 Green Dollar, Profilic, 18/1 Gorinsky (IRE), Duplicity (IRE), 20/1 Gentle Hero (USA), Nordic Brave, 22/1 Gondo, Amron, 25/1 Resolute Bay, Dominuet, Adwick Park, 33/1 Ors. CSF £48.13, CT £371.14. Tote £4.40: £1.40 £2.60 £2.30 £4.10 (£18.60). Mr J. C. Smith (KINGSCLERE) bred by Littleton Stud.
21 Rn　　　　　　　　　　　　　　　　　　　　　　　　　　　　1m 10.84 (0.64)
　　　　　　　　　　　　　　　　　　　　　　　　　　　SF—71/60//88/62/80/82

**814**　　TATTERSALLS MUSIDORA STKS (Gp 3) (3-Y.O.F) £25902.00 (£9605.35: £4540.18:
　　　　£1897.47)　　1¹⁄₄m 85y　　　　　　　　　　　　　　　　　　3-40 (3-41)

630* All At Sea (USA) (Fav) (HRACecil) 8-8 PatEddery (5) (lw: trckd ldrs: shkn up to
　　　　ld over 1f out: qcknd & r.o strly) ........................... —1
631⁴ Perfect Circle (109) (MRStoute) 8-8 WRSwinburn (3) (lw: hld up: stdy hdwy 2f
　　　　out: shkn up over 1f out: r.o: nt pce of wnr) ........................... 1.2
630² Armarama (CEBrittain) 8-8 LDettori (1) (led: drvn along & hung rt 3f out: kpt on
　　　　wl fnl f) ........................... 1.3
630⁶ Feminine Wiles (IRE) (100) (PWChapple-Hyam) 8-8 PaulEddery (4) (lw: trckd
　　　　ldrs: effrt & rdn over 2f out: r.o one pce) ........................... 2¹⁄₂.4
　　　Super Sarena (IRE) (102) (DRCElsworth) 8-8 WCarson (2) (lw: outpcd & lost pl
　　　　over 3f out: sn wl bhd) ........................... 15.5

8/11 ALL AT SEA (USA), 13/8 Perfect Circle, 16/1 Armarama, 25/1 Super Sarena (IRE), 28/1 Feminine Wiles (IRE). CSF £2.15, Tote £1.60: £1.10 £1.20 (£1.30). Mr K. Abdulla (NEWMARKET) bred by Juddmonte Farms Incorporated in USA. 5 Rn　　　　　　　　　　　　　　　　　　　　　　2m 18.78 (11.28)

**815**　　YORKSHIRE TELEVISION H'CAP (0-100) £5481.00 (£1638.00: £570.50 each)
　　　　1m 3f 195y　　　　　　　　　　　　　　　　　　　　　4-10 (4-14)

390⁴ Linpac West (96) (CWCElsey) 6-9-13 BRaymond (6) (lw: pushed along 5f out:
　　　　r.o u.p fnl 3f: edgd lft 1f out: led wl ins fnl f) ........................... —1
　　　Rinja (USA) (01) (DWRArbuthnot) 5-8-12 TQuinn (2) (b.hind: chsd ldrs: led 2f
　　　　out: jst ct) ........................... hd.2
552 Comstock (82) (Jt-Fav) (JGFitzGerald) 5-8-13 KFallon (7) (chsd ldrs: drvn
　　　　along ¹⁄₂-wy: ev ch 2f out: one pce) ........................... 3¹⁄₂.3
435 Eire Leath-Sceal (62) (MBrittain) 5-7-7 JLowe (9) (b.off hind: led 3f: chsd ldrs:
　　　　wkng whn squeezed out jst ins fnl f) ........................... d.h.3
442 Kansk (96) (JHMGosden) 4-9-13 SCauthen (12) (lw: led after 3f: sn clr: hdd 2f
　　　　out: sn wknd) ........................... 3.5
　　　Opera Ghost (84) (PWHarris) 6-9-1 WRSwinburn (4) (hld up: stdy hdwy over 4f
　　　　out: wknd 2f out) ........................... nk.6
405 Roberty Lea (66) (TFairhurst) 4-7-8 ‡³JFanning (1) (swtg: effrt appr st: kpt on:
　　　　nvr nr to chal) ........................... 7
　　　Itqan (IRE) (88) (Jt-Fav) (BWHills) 4-9-5 WCarson (3) (hld up & bhd: hdwy 3f
　　　　out: r.o nr fin) ........................... 8
612⁴ Latour (68) (CEBrittain) 4-7-13 GCrealock (11) (chsd ldrs tl lost pl 3f out) ........................... 9
442 Kiveton Kabooz (84) (LMCumani) 4-9-1 LDettori (13) (sn bhd: sme hdwy 2f
　　　　out: n.d) ........................... 10
675 Balaat (62) (MCChapman) 4-7-0 ‡⁷AntoinetteArmes (5) (nvr nr ldrs) ........................... 11
　　　Aahsaylad (78) (FHLee) 6-8-4 ‡⁵NKennedy (8) (s.i.s: a in rr) ........................... 12
　　　Alilisa (USA) (78) (WJHaggas) 4-8-9 MHills (15) (b: a bhd) ........................... 13
552³ Lift and Load (USA) (94) (RHannon) 5-9-11 PatEddery (10) (lw: a in rr) ........................... 14
442 Niani (IRE) (93) (JLDunlop) 4-9-10 GDuffield (14) (lost pl 5f out: sn wl bhd) ........................... 15
　　　　　　LONG HANDICAP: Eire Leath-Sceal 7-6, Balaat (USA) 7-1.

13/2 Itqan (IRE), Comstock, 7/1 Lift and Load (USA), 15/2 LINPAC WEST, 8/1 Kansk, Kiveton Kabooz, 12/1 Roberty Lea, Rinja (USA), 16/1 Opera Ghost, Latour, Niani (IRE), 18/1 Alilisa (USA), 20/1 Eire Leath-Sceal, Aahsaylad, 100/1 Balaat (USA). CSF £85.26, CT LW, R & ELS £786.21; LW, R & C £282.41. Tote £7.70: £2.40 £3.90 ELS £2.50 C £1.30 (£55.70). Linpac Group Limited (MALTON) bred by Lin Pac Containers Ltd. 15 Rn
　　　　　　　　　　　　　　　　　　　　　　　　　2m 30.75 (3.75)
　　　　　　　　　　　　　　　　　　　　　　　SF—76/60/34/54/62/51

**816**　　SOTHEBY'S SLEDMERE H'CAP (3-Y.O) (0-105) £5754.00 (£1722.00: £826.00: £378.00)
　　　　1m 205y　　　　　　(Weights raised 3 lb)　　　　　　　　4-40 (4-46)

395* Ecliptic (IRE) (77) (PWChapple-Hyam) 8-3 DHolland (8) (lw: trckd ldrs: effrt &
　　　　n.m.r 2f out: swtchd ins fnl f: qcknd u.p to ld nr fin) ........................... —1
704⁴ Asaasy (USA) (89) (Fav) (MRStoute) 9-1 WRSwinburn (14) (chsd ldrs: rdn over
　　　　2f out: led wl over 1f out: sn hdd: nt qckn ins fnl f) ........................... 1.2
671⁴ Trafalgar Boy (USA) (80) (JEtherington) 8-6 RCochrane (4) (lw: chsd ldrs:
　　　　outpcd & rdn over 2f out: r.o same pce appr fnl f) ........................... nk.3
554² Modernise (USA) (95) (RCharlton) 9-7 PatEddery (3) (lw: effrt over 3f out: r.o
　　　　u.p to ld over 1f out: hdd wl ins fnl f) ........................... s.h.4
633* Zalon (IRE) (90) (JHMGosden) 9-2 SCauthen (1) (lw: effrt u.p over 3f out: kpt
　　　　on: nt rch ldrs) ........................... 3.5

670³ Misunderstanding (IRE) **(89)** *(MrsJRRamsden)* 8-8 ‡⁷JWeaver (2) (chsd ldrs: kpt on fnl 2f: nvr able chal) .......................................... 2¹/₂.**6**

Kinglow (USA) **(83)** *(MrsJCecil)* 8-9 PaulEddery (6) (bit bkwd: effrt & reminders over 3f out: stdy hdwy 2f out: r.o wl nr fin) ........................... 4.**7**

Stani (USA) **(85)** *(BHanbury)* 8-11 BRaymond (5) (lw: effrt over 3f out: nvr rchd ldrs) .......................................... nk.**8**

Al Ramis (IRE) **(81)** *(CEBrittain)* 8-7 AMunro (13) (lw: sme hdwy 3f out: n.d) .... nk.**9**

545⁴ Lowlands Boy **(67)** *(TFairhurst)* 7-4 ‡³JFanning (15) (led tl over 3f out: wknd over 1f out) .......................................... 2.**10**

627² Pyare Square **(77)** (bl) *(IABalding)* 8-3 GDuffield (11) (in tch: effrt over 3f out: sn wknd) .......................................... nk.**11**

646³ Sharp Prince **(94)** *(HRACecil)* 9-6 WRyan (12) (lw: w ldrs: led over 3f out: hdd wl over1f out: eased) .......................................... **12**

Kasikci **(90)** *(RHollinshead)* 9-2 MHills (9) (s.i.s: a in rr) .......................................... **13**

585³ First Century (IRE) **(92)** *(PFICole)* 9-4 TQuinn (7) (lw: a bhd) .......................................... **14**

171 Dance Scene (IRE) **(80)** *(DRCElsworth)* 8-6 JWilliams (10) (a in rr) .......................................... **15**

646⁵ Gotcha (BAR) **(87)** *(RHannon)* 8-13 JReid (19) (sn bhd) .......................................... **16**

653⁶ Mutabahi (CAN) **(92)** *(RWArmstrong)* 9-4 WCarson (16) (sn bhd & drvn along) .. **17**

554* Bold Stroke **(92)** *(JLDunlop)* 9-4 LDettori (18) (lw: chsd ldrs tl lost pl 3f out: eased whn btn) .......................................... **18**

545³ Personal Hazard **(73)** *(MHEasterby)* 7-8 ‡⁵SMaloney (17) (b.hind: sn drvn along: chsd ldrs tl lost pl 5f out: sn bhd) .......................................... **19**

LONG HANDICAP: Lowlands Boy 7-0.

**4/1** Asaasy (USA), **5/1** Zalon (IRE), **6/1** ECLIPTIC (IRE), **8/1** Stani (USA), **17/2** Modernise (USA), **9/1** Sharp Prince, **10/1** Bold Stroke, Misunderstanding (IRE), **14/1** Gotcha (BAR), Pyare Square, **16/1** Personal Hazard, Trafalgar Boy (USA), Kinglow (USA), **20/1** Al Ramis (IRE), Dance Scene (IRE), First Century (IRE), Mutabahi (CAN), **33/1** Kasikci, **50/1** Lowlands Boy. CSF £35.05, CT £378.35. Tote £7.20: £1.80 £1.70 £4.20 £2.00 (£14.80). Mr R. E. Sangster (MARLBOROUGH) bred by Swettenham Stud in Ireland. 19 Rn 1m 50.82 (1.82)
SF—62/71/61/75/61/45

T/Trio: Race 5: w ELS £156.10 (7 Tckts), w C £50.30 (21.6 Tckts). T/Jkpt: Not won; £20,443.65 to York 13/5/92. T/Plpt: £163.80 (71.8 Tckts).  WG

# YORK (L-H)

## Wednesday, May 13th [Good to firm, Good patches]

Going Allowance: minus 0.15 sec per fur (F)  Wind: fresh bhd

Stalls: high

**817**  DALTON STKS (2-Y.O) £5299.00 (£1582.00: £756.00: £343.00)  **6f**  2-00 (2-03)

555* Power of Polly (USA) (Fav) *(PFICole)* 9-3 TQuinn (6) (lw: cl up: rdn to ld wl ins fnl f: r.o wl) .......................................... —**1**

528* Sabre Rattler *(JBerry)* 9-3 JCarroll (4) (lw: led: rdn over 1f out: hdd wl ins fnl f: r.o) .......................................... nk.**2**

Icy South (USA) *(JHMGosden)* 8-8 SCauthen (3) (rangy: scope: chsd ldrs: rdn & outpcd 2f out: styd on wl ins fnl f) .......................................... nk.**3**

Salatin (USA) *(PTWalwyn)* 8-8 WCarson (5) (w'like: cmpt: s.i.s: shkn up ¹/₂-wy: swtchd over 1f out: r.o wl nr fin) .......................................... hd.**4**

Midhish *(BHanbury)* 8-8 WRSwinburn (9) (w'like: str: cmpt: bit bkwd: in tch: effrt over 2f out: kpt on ins fnl f) .......................................... 1¹/₂.**5**

514² Crusade (IRE) *(RHannon)* 8-11 JReid (7) (chsd ldrs: rdn over 2f out: edgd lft appr fnl f: no ex) .......................................... 1.**6**

602³ Moscatop (IRE) *(RHollinshead)* 8-11 WRyan (1) (in tch on outside over 3f: sn wl outpcd) .......................................... 15.**7**

226* Touch Silver *(BWHills)* 9-3 DHolland (8) (lw: unruly s: chsd ldrs: hmpd & sddle slipped after 2f: sn eased & wl bhd) .......................................... 3.**8**

517³ Isotonic *(GMMoore)* 8-12 KFallon (2) (chsd ldrs to ¹/₂-wy: sn btn) .......................................... 1¹/₂.**9**

**3/1** POWER OF POLLY (USA), **7/2** Sabre Rattler, **11/2** Touch Silver, Midhish, **6/1** Salatin (USA), **9/1** Icy South (USA), **10/1** Crusade (IRE)(op 6/1), **16/1** Isotonic, **25/1** Moscatop (IRE). CSF £13.89, Tote £3.90: £1.40 £1.60 £2.30 (£5.20). Mr G. J. Beck (WHATCOMBE) bred by Gainesway Thoroughbreds Limited in USA. 9 Rn 1m 11.61 (1.41)
SF—57/56/46/45/39/38

**818**  MIDDLETON GRADUATION STKS (3-Y.O.F) £5640.00 (£1680.00: £800.00: £360.00) 1¹/₄m 85y  2-35 (2-37)

631 Skimble (USA) (Jt-Fav) *(HRACecil)* 9-2 PatEddery (1) (lw: plld hrd: led 1f: hdwy on bit 2f out: led 1f out: shkn up: easily) .......................................... —**1**

Resounding Success (IRE) *(BWHills)* 8-11 DHolland (2) (jnd ldr 7f out: led over
3f out: drvn clr: hdd 1f out: no ch w wnr) ............................... 2.2

536³ Nina's Chocolates (USA) *(CEBrittain)* 8-11 SCauthen (3) (bhd: hdwy over 4f
out: rdn 3f out: kpt on same pce) ............................................ 5.3

Enaya (Jt-Fav) *(RWArmstrong)* 9-2 WCarson (5) (bit bkwd: hdwy ent st: drvn
along 3f out: wknd over 1f out) ............................................. 1¹/₂.4

Shakela (USA) *(BHanbury)* 8-11 WRSwinburn (4) (led after 1f: disp ld 7f out tl
wknd over 3 out) ................................................................ 20.5

**15/8** Enaya, SKIMBLE (USA), **9/2** Resounding Success (IRE), **15/2** Nina's Chocolates (USA), **11/1** Shakela
(USA). CSF £9.24, Tote £2.60: £1.50 £1.90 (£5.50). Mr K. Abdulla (NEWMARKET) bred by Juddmonte Farms
Incorporated in USA. 5 Rn
2m 11.48 (3.98)
SF—47/38/28/30/–

**819**     BOB GARDNER MEMORIAL SPRINT H'CAP (0-110) £11160.00 (£3330.00: £1590.00:
£720.00)    **5f**                           3-05 (3-07)

714² **Freddie Lloyd (USA) (93)** *(NACallaghan)* 3-8-7 PatEddery (2) (made all far
side: r.o wl ins fnl f) ...................................................... —1

311³ Macrobian **(90)** *(MHEasterby)* 8-9-0 MBirch (8) (led stands' side: rdn wl over 1f
out: kpt on wl) ................................................................ nk.2

550 Beau Venture (USA) **(81)** *(FHLee)* 4-8-5 PaulEddery (5) (bit bkwd: chsd wnr far
side: rdn over 1f out: nt qckn fnl f) ..................................... 2¹/₂.3

Farfelu **(95)** (bl) *(WRMuir)* 5-9-5 SWhitworth (6) (lw: prom stands' side: kpt on
u.p fnl f) ...................................................................... 1.4

550 El Yasaf (IRE) **(86)** *(GHEden)* 4-8-10 DHolland (12) (lw: prom stands' side tl rdn
& no ex appr fnl f) .......................................................... hd.5

686³ Viceroy **(92)** *(WJPearce)* 5-9-2 DNicholls (3) (trckd ldrs far side tl rdn & wknd
over 1f out) .................................................................. nk.6

723* Love Legend **(91)** (bl) *(DWPArbuthnot)* 7-9-1 (7x) AMunro (14) (drvn along
¹/₂-wy: nvr rchd ldrs) ......................................................... ³/₄.7

On Tiptoes **(104)** *(JPLeigh)* 4-9-7 ‡7JWeaver (7) (chsd ldrs: hrd rdn 2f out: grad
wknd) .......................................................................... ¹/₂.8

686⁵ Singing Star **(83)** *(JBalding)* 6-8-7 GDuffield (1) (lw: sn bhd & drvn along: hdwy
2f out: nt rch ldrs ldrs) .................................................. d.h.8

723³ Petraco (IRE) **(79)** (Fav) *(LJCodd)* 4-8-3 WCarson (4) (lw: chsd ldrs far side tl
rdn & wknd over 1f out) .................................................. 1¹/₂.10

550 Amber Mill **(88)** *(JBerry)* 4-8-12 JCarroll (11) (lw: spd over 3f) ................ nk.11

676³ Pallium (IRE) **(77)** *(MPNaughton)* 4-8-1 GHind (10) (nvr wnt pce) ........... 2¹/₂.12

676⁵ No Quarter Given **(74)** *(PSFelgate)* 7-7-12 JLowe (13) (lw: cl up stands' side
over 3f) ....................................................................... 1.13

613² Jovial Kate (USA) **(69)** *(BEllison)* 5-7-0 ‡7DarrenMoffatt (9) (bhd fr ¹/₂-wy) ...... 4.14
LONG HANDICAP: Jovial Kate (USA) 5-10.

**11/2** Petraco (IRE), **6/1** FREDDIE LLOYD (USA), **13/2** Love Legend, **8/1** Viceroy, **9/1** Macrobian, Amber Mill,
Pallium (IRE), **12/1** Farfelu, **14/1** No Quarter Given, Singing Star, On Tiptoes, **16/1** El Yasaf (IRE), **25/1** Beau
Venture (USA), **100/1** Jovial Kate (USA). CSF £54.81, CT £1,153.19. Tote £6.10: £2.10 £2.80 £7.70 (£34.00).
Mr Michael Hill (NEWMARKET) bred by Jerry M. Cutrona, Snr in USA. 14 Rn
57.73 sec (0.23)
SF—73/79/60/70/60/65/61

**820**     HOMEOWNERS DANTE STKS (Gp 2) (3-Y.O) £73554.00 (£27548.20: £13249.10:
£5788.70)    **1¹/₄m 85y**                   3-40 (3-45)

655 **Alnasr Alwasheek** *(MRStoute)* 9-0 SCauthen (2) (lw: mde all: qcknd 3f out: r.o
strly fnl f: readily) ........................................................ —1

Great Palm (USA) *(PFICole)* 9-0 AMunro (4) (h.d.w: bit bkwd: chsd wnr: rdn 3f
out: edgd lft over 1f out: no ex) ......................................... 3.2

556² Aljadeer (USA) (Fav) *(HRACecil)* 9-0 PatEddery (1) (lw: trckd ldrs: effrt over 3f
out: r.o same pce fnl 2f) ................................................. 2¹/₂.3

443² Young Senor (USA) *(GWragg)* 9-0 WRSwinburn (5) (stumbled bdly s: hld up in
tch: effrt 3f out: one pce appr fnl f) .................................. 1¹/₂.4

556 Alflora (IRE) *(CEBrittain)* 9-0 TQuinn (7) (lw: bhd: effrt on outside over 3f out: nt
pce to chal) ................................................................ 1¹/₂.5

609* Top Register (USA) *(LordHuntingdon)* 9-0 JReid (3) (trckd ldrs: rdn over 3f out:
wknd wl over 1f out) ........................................................ ¹/₂.6

El Cortes (USA) *(PWChapple-Hyam)* 9-0 PaulEddery (6) (h.d.w: swtg: bit
bkwd: in rr: effrt 4f out: sn rdn & btn) .................................. 15.7

**5/4** Aljadeer (USA), **7/2** ALNASR ALWASHEEK, **9/2** Young Senor (USA), **8/1** Great Palm (USA), **16/1** El Cortes
(USA), Top Register (USA), **66/1** Alflora (IRE). CSF £26.21, Tote £4.40: £2.50 £3.00 (£15.90). Sheikh Ahmed Al
Maktoum (NEWMARKET) bred by Meon Valley Stud. 7 Rn
2m 8.71 (1.21)
SF—73/67/62/59/56/55

**821**  SCARBOROUGH H'CAP (3-Y.O.F) (0-100) £5952.00 (£1776.00: £848.00: £384.00)
7f 202y
4-10 (4-14)

671² Fetish (82) **(Fav)** *(HRACecil)* 8-6 PatEddery (4) (effrt & hdwy over 2f out: disp ld
1f out: led cl home) ............ —1
697* Nashville Blues (IRE) **(74)** *(JWHills)* 7-12 (5x) WCarson (2) (trckd ldrs on ins:
squeezed thro to disp ld 1f out: hung lft: r.o: jst ct) ........... s.h.2
599 Rocality **(74)** *(RHannon)* 7-12 NCarlisle (5) (bhd: hdwy 2f out: styd on ins fnl f:
nrst fin) ............ 2.3
432 Yousefia (USA) **(84)** *(MRStoute)* 8-8 WRSwinburn (7) (led: disp ld over 3f out tl
hdd & wknd over 1f out) ............ ¾.4
La Dama Bonita (USA) **(84)** *(DWPArbuthnot)* 8-8 TQuinn (1) (cl up: chal over 3f
out: rdn & wknd over 1f out) ............ 3½.5
671 Devon Dancer **(74)** *(MHEasterby)* 7-7(1) ‡5SMaloney (3) (b.off hind: chsd ldrs:
rdn over 3f out: btn wl over 1f out) ............ s.h.6
Swallowcliffe **(97)** *(PTWalwyn)* 9-7 AMunro (12) (swtg: s.i.s: hld up & bhd:
hdwy 2f out: r.o fnl f: nrst fin) ............ s.h.7
534⁵ Doyce **(69)** *(JEtherington)* 7-4 ‡3JFanning (8) (chsd ldrs: effrt over 3f out: wknd
2f out) ............ 1.8
684 Zamirah (IRE) **(76)** *(GWragg)* 7-11 ‡3FNorton (9) (lw: a in rr) ............ 1.9
719⁶ Thrie-Na-Helah (IRE) **(77)** *(RMWhitaker)* 8-1 ACulhane (6) (chsd ldrs: rdn & ev
ch 3f out: btn 2f out) ............ 3½.10
Panchellita (USA) **(80)** *(DenysSmith)* 8-4 KFallon (10) (hld up: effrt over 3f out:
sn btn) ............ 5.11
695² Miss Doody **(69)** (v) *(MRChannon)* 7-7 JLowe (11) (bhd & rdn appr st: sn btn) ½.12
LONG HANDICAP: Miss Doody 7-6.

**11/4** FETISH, **3/1** Nashville Blues (IRE), **15/2** Yousefia (USA), **8/1** Zamirah (IRE), Thrie-Na-Helah (IRE), **10/1**
Rocality, **14/1** Miss Doody, **16/1** Doyce, **20/1** La Dama Bonita (USA), **25/1** Devon Dancer, **33/1** Ors. CSF
£11.15, CT £65.09. Tote £3.30: £1.70 £1.40 £3.30 (£3.40). Mr K. Abdulla (NEWMARKET) bred by Juddmonte
Farms. 12 Rn
1m 37.39 (1.39)
SF—53/44/38/46/35/19/46

**822**  WILKINSON MEMORIAL STKS (Mdn 3-Y.O) £5253.50 (£1568.00: £749.00: £308.00)
6f 214y
4-45 (4-45)

**Hazaam (USA)** **(Fav)** *(MRStoute)* 9-0 SCauthen (8) (w'like: lengthy: scope: sn
trckng ldrs: rdn to ld over 1f out: rn green: r.o) ............ —1
651* Queen Warrior *(PTWalwyn)* 8-9 DHolland (9) (a.p: led 2f out: hung lft: rdn over
1f out: nt qckn) ............ 1½.2
727⁶ Hi-Tech Honda (IRE) *(CEBrittain)* 9-0 MBirch (6) (prom tl outpcd 4f out: sn drvn
along: kpt on same pce fnl 2f) ............ 6.3
Elabjer (USA) *(HThomsonJones)* 9-0 RHills (4) (lengthy: scope: chsd ldrs: effrt
over 2 out: styd on same pce) ............ 2½.4
238 Boursin (IRE) *(PCalver)* 9-0 DMcKeown (1) (led tl hdd over 2f out: grad wknd) nk.5
658⁵ Turret Gates *(JARToller)* 9-0 TQuinn (3) (prom tl wknd over 2f out) ............ 6.6
238⁴ Open Agenda (IRE) *(BWHills)* 9-0 PatEddery (7) (trckd ldrs: led over 2 out: sn
hdd: faltered & eased fnl f) ............ 2.7
314⁴ Klingon (IRE) *(RHollinshead)* 9-0 PaulEddery (2) (swtg: s.s: sn pushed along: a
bhd) ............ 2.8

**5/4** HAZAAM (USA), **9/2** Open Agenda (IRE), Queen Warrior, **8/1** Turret Gates, **9/1** Elabjer (USA), **14/1** Hi-Tech
Honda (IRE), Klingon (IRE), **20/1** Boursin (IRE). CSF £7.60, Tote £2.10: £1.30 £1.30 £3.20 (£3.50). Sheikh
Mohammed (NEWMARKET) bred by Darley Stud Management Co Ltd in USA. 8 Rn
1m 23.57 (1.17)
SF—67/57/44/36/35/17

T/Trio: Races 3 & 5: £710.80 (4.1) & £22.90 (111.8 Tckts). T/Jkpt: £3,132.40 (10.15 Tckts). T/Plpt: £89.30
(186.85 Tckts).
O'R

# YORK (L-H)

## Thursday, May 14th [Good to firm]
Going Allowance: 5f-7f: minus 0.30 sec; Rest: minus 0.20 sec (F)     Wind: fresh half bhd

Stalls: high

**823**  GLASGOW GRADUATION STKS (3-Y.O.C & G) £5848.00 (£1744.00: £832.00: £376.00)
1¼m 85y
2-00 (2-01)

680* **Polish Blue (USA)** **(88)** *(MRStoute)* 9-1 PatEddery (2) (hld up & plld hrd early:
hdwy over 3f out: led 2f out: r.o wl: eased nr fin) ............ —1
549⁴ Binkhaldoun (USA) **(97)** *(HThomsonJones)* 9-1 RHills (4) (b: trckd ldrs: effrt &
edgd rt over 2f out: r.o wl nr fin) ............ ½.2

Tony San (IRE) *(CEBrittain)* 8-10 MRoberts (3) (led to 8f out: outpcd over 3f out: kpt on fnl f) ............ 6.3
652² Iywaan (IRE) *(Fav)* *(PTWalwyn)* 9-1 WCarson (6) (lw: hdwy to ld 8f out: hdd & wknd 2f out) ............ 1.4
628² Rebel Call *(RHannon)* 8-10 JReid (1) (lw: effrt & sltly hmpd ent st: n.m.r over 3f out: rdn & fnd nil over 2f out) ............ nk.5
573⁴ Iron Baron (IRE) *(RHollinshead)* 8-10 PaulEddery (5) (lost pl appr st: sn t.o) ... dist.6

15/8 Iywaan (IRE), 11/4 Rebel Call, 7/2 Binkhaldoun (USA), 9/2 POLISH BLUE (USA), 16/1 Tony San (IRE), 50/1 Iron Baron (IRE). CSF £18.41, Tote £4.20: £1.90 £2.50 (£10.10). Mr Mana Al Maktoum (NEWMARKET) bred by John and Mrs C. Mabee in USA. 6 Rn
2m 9.81 (2.31)
SF—57/56/39/42/36/–

**824** HAMBLETON H'CAP (0-115) £15270.00 (£4560.00: £2180.00: £990.00)
7f 202y
2-35 (2-36)

610★ **Band on the Run (92)** *(BAMcMahon)* 5-8-11 TQuinn (2) (lw: chsd ldrs: effrt on ins over 2f out: squeezed thro & r.o wl to ld ins fnl f) ............ —1
563 Sylva Honda **(105)** *(CEBrittain)* 4-9-10 MRoberts (3) (led: qcknd over 3f out: kpt on wl) ............ 1¹/₂.2
667³ Dorset Duke **(86)** (bl) *(GWragg)* 5-8-5 MHills (13) (swtg: chsd ldrs: rdn & swrvd rt ins fnl f: hung lft nr fin) ............ 1.3
579⁴ St Ninian **(101)** *(MHEasterby)* 6-9-6 MBirch (6) (lw: effrt over 3f out: styd on wl u.p fnl f) ............ hd.4
551⁶ Military Fashion **(101)** *(LMCumani)* 6-9-6 SCauthen (8) (chsd ldrs: kpt on same pce fnl 2f) ............ hd.5
712★ Parliament Piece **(99)** *(RMWhitaker)* 4-9-4 (5x) ACulhane (4) (lw: chsd ldrs: styng on one pce whn hmpd ins fnl f) ............ 1¹/₂.6
667⁵ High Premium **(86)** *(MrsJRRamsden)* 4-8-5 KDarley (1) (lw: hld up: stdy hdwy 2f out: r.o wl: nvr plcd to chal) ............ 1¹/₂ 7
667² Mudaffar (IRE) **(92)** *(RWArmstrong)* 4-8-11 LPiggott (5) (lw: hld up & bhd: hdwy 2f out: r.o nr fin) ............ 1.8
657 Heart of Darkness **(100)** *(IABalding)* 4-9-5 JReid (14) (dwlt: bhd tl sme hdwy fnl 2f: n.d) ............ 1.9
392² Berlin Wall (IRE) **(82)** (v) *(Fav)* *(PWChapple-Hyam)* 4-8-1 PaulEddery (11) (effrt on outside over 3f out: rdn & wnt rt over 2f out: wandered & sn wknd) ............ hd.10
712⁶ Selaah **(93)** *(MRStoute)* 5-8-12 PatEddery (7) (bhd tl r.o fnl f) ............ 1¹/₂.11
610 Savoyard **(98)** *(MAJarvis)* 4-9-3 BRaymond (9) (bit bkwd: sn drvn along: n.d) 1¹/₂.12
Gymcrak Premiere **(95)** *(MHEasterby)* 4-9-0 GCarter (15) (bit bkwd: s.i.s: a in rr) ............ 1¹/₂.13
579★ Badawi (USA) **(102)** *(JHMGosden)* 4-9-7 RCochrane (10) (chsd ldrs tl lost pl over 3f out) ............ 2.14
Rocton North (IRE) **(94)** *(RHannon)* 4-8-13 WRSwinburn (12) (chsd ldrs tl wknd over 2f out: sn bhd) ............ 3.15

4/1 Berlin Wall (IRE), 8/1 Mudaffar (IRE), 17/2 High Premium, 9/1 BAND ON THE RUN, 10/1 Military Fashion, Badawi (USA), 12/1 St Ninian, Heart of Darkness, Selaah, 14/1 Parliament Piece, Savoyard, 16/1 Dorset Duke, 20/1 Rocton North (IRE), Gymcrak Premiere, 33/1 Sylva Honda. CSF £229.58, CT £4,182.07. Tote £9.80: £3.10 £11.30 £4.70 (£203.80). Mr D. J. Allen (TAMWORTH) bred by Mrs J. R. Hine and Miss J. Bunting. 15 Rn
1m 35.98 (U.02)
SF—73/81/59/73/72/65

**825** NORWEST HOLST TROPHY (H'cap) (3-Y.0) (0-115) £19412.50 (£5800.00: £2775.00: £1262.50) 6f 214y
3-10 (3-12)

(Weights raised 3 lb)
725★ **Mizaaya (90)** *(Fav)* *(MRStoute)* 9-0 (9x) PatEddery (9) (lw: hld up: nt clr run ¹/₂-wy: several positions: squeezed thro to ld wl ins fnl f) .... —1
653★ Sky Hunter (USA) **(88)** *(RHannon)* 8-12 MRoberts (8) (hdwy ¹/₂-wy: sn rdn & edgd lft: led over 1f out: kpt on wl) ............ ¹/₂.2
520² Act of Union (IRE) **(71)** *(WJPearce)* 7-9 LCharnock (10) (lw: chsd ldrs: rdn & hung lft over 2f out: nt qckn fnl f) ............ 2.3
649² Euro Festival **(78)** *(MissLCSiddall)* 8-2 AMunro (5) (lw: dwlt: bhd tl r.o wl u.p fnl 2f) ............ nk.4
640a² Beware of Agents **(96)** *(MJohnston)* 9-6 DMcKeown (11) (lw: trckd ldrs: led over 2f out tl hdd & wknd over 1f out) ............ ³/₄.5
658⁴ Bravura **(84)** *(WJHaggas)* 8-8 MHills (2) (lw: led 2f: led 3f out: sn hdd: wkng whn bdly hmpd over 1f out) ............ 7.6
558 Love Jazz (USA) **(93)** *(TDBarron)* 9-3 KDarley (4) (hld up: effrt & nt clr run over 3f out: n.d after) ............ 1¹/₂.7
Seagull Hollow (IRE) **(83)** (v) *(MHEasterby)* 8-7 MBirch (1) (swrvd lft s: led after 2f to 3f out: sn wknd) ............ 6.8

432 May Hills Legacy (IRE) **(78)** *(DWPArbuthnot)* 8-2 JLowe (7) (b.nr fore: sn bhd & drvn along) ......................................................................... 2½.9
601⁶ The Old Chapel **(97)** *(BAMcMahon)* 9-7 TQuinn (6) (lw: chsd ldrs: wkng whn sltly hmpd over 2f out: eased whn no ch: t.o) ...................... 10

2/1 MIZAAYA, 5/1 Beware of Agents, 11/2 Bravura, 13/2 Sky Hunter (USA), 9/1 Euro Festival, 14/1 Act of Union (IRE), 16/1 May Hills Legacy (IRE), 20/1 Love Jazz (USA), 25/1 Ors. CSF £14.09, CT £124.40. Tote £2.50: £1.40 £2.20 £2.50 (£5.50). Maktoum Al Maktoum (NEWMARKET) bred by Cheveley Park Stud Ltd. 10 Rn
1m 22.59 (0.19)
SF—65/61/38/44/60/27

**826** POLO MINTS YORKSHIRE CUP (Gp 2) £52302.00 (£19494.10: £9297.05: £3976.85)
**1m 5f 194y**
3-40 (3-43)

648⁵ **Rock Hopper** (Jt-Fav) *(MRStoute)* 5-8-13 PatEddery (1) (lw: hld up & bhd: stdy hdwy over 3f out: r.o wl to ld ins fnl f) ................................ —1
648* Sapience *(DRCElsworth)* 6-8-13 RCochrane (5) (lw: led: qcknd over 3f out: edgd rt & kpt on wl fnl f) ................................................................. 1.2
11a* Snurge *(PFICole)* 5-9-1 TQuinn (3) (bit bkwd: trckd ldrs: rdn & outpcd over 2f out: edgd lft & r.o sme pce u.p fnl f) ............................................ 2½.3
648² Luchiroverte (IRE) *(CEBrittain)* 4-8-9 MRoberts (7) (lw: w ldr: disp ld 4f out to 2f out: wkng whn sltly hmpd ins fnl f) .......................................... 3.4
Further Flight (Jt-Fav) *(BWHills)* 6-8-10 MHills (8) (bit bkwd: hld up: styd on fnl 3f: nvr nr to chal) ......................................................................... ½.5
557 Jaffa Line *(DRCElsworth)* 4-8-6 JWilliams (6) (trckd ldrs tl lost pl over 3f out) .... 5.6
Mountain Kingdom (USA) *(NTinkler)* 8-8-13 WCarson (4) (lw: prom tl outpcd fnl 3f) ........................................................................................... 4.7
Nibbs Point (IRE) *(LMCumani)* 4-8-8⁽²⁾ SCauthen (2) (dwlt: wnt prom 6f out: sn lost pl & bhd: eased whn no ch) ................................................. 30.8

100/30 ROCK HOPPER, Further Flight, 7/2 Sapience, 5/1 Snurge, 11/2 Luchiroverte (IRE), 10/1 Nibbs Point (IRE), 20/1 Jaffa Line, 28/1 Mountain Kingdom (USA). CSF £14.95, Tote £3.90: £1.40 £1.90 £2.00 (£8.20). Maktoum Al Maktoum (NEWMARKET) bred by Gainsborough Stud Management Ltd. 8 Rn 2m 59.91 (6.31)
SF—8/6/3/–/–/–

**827** DUKE OF YORK STKS (Gp 3) £23220.00 (£8623.50: £4086.75: £1719.75)
**6f**
4-10 (4-12)

673⁵ **Shalford (IRE) (117)** *(RHannon)* 4-9-4 MRoberts (3) (trckd ldr: led over 2f out: r.o wl & drvn clr fnl f) ....................................................................... —1
Mr Brooks *(JSBolger,Ireland)* 5-9-6 LPiggott (1) (a chsng ldrs: ev ch & rdn 2f out: unable qckn fnl f) .......................................................................... 3½.2
478² Amigo Menor **(108)** (bl) *(DJGMurray-Smith)* 6-9-4 CRutter (8) (sn bhd: hdwy over 1f out: kpt on: nvr nr to chal) ..................................................... 1½.3
Colway Bold **(106)** *(JWWatts)* 3-8-3 WCarson (2) (led tl over 2f out: sn wknd) 1½.4
465² Stack Rock **(101)** *(EJAlston)* 5-8-11 KFallon (10) (made most stands' side: chsd ldrs tl outpcd fnl 2f) .................................................................... 1.5
673⁴ Montendre **(110)** *(MMcCormack)* 5-9-0 JReid (7) (effrt ½-wy: sn rdn & no imp) 1.6
430* Fylde Flyer **(109)** *(JBerry)* 3-8-3 JCarroll (11) (racd stands' side: chsd ldr: rdn over 2f out: edgd bdly lft ins fnl f) ................................................... 5.7
462a² Norwich (Fav) *(BWHills)* 5-9-4 SCauthen (5) (chsd ldrs: rdn over 2f out: sn wknd) ........................................................................................................ nk.8
Line Engaged (USA) *(PTWalwyn)* 4-9-0 RCochrane (9) (racd stands' side: bhd fr ½-wy) ....................................................................................................... 7.9

7/2 Norwich, 4/1 Mr Brooks, 9/2 Fylde Flyer, 6/1 SHALFORD (IRE), 8/1 Montendre, 17/2 Stack Rock, 10/1 Amigo Menor, 14/1 Colway Bold, 25/1 Line Engaged (USA). CSF £28.18, Tote £6.80: £1.90 £1.70 £2.70 (£12.00). Mr D. F. Cock (MARLBOROUGH) bred by D. M. Dick in Ireland. 9 Rn
1m 8.82 (1.08 under best; U1.38)
SF—96/84/76/55/62/55

**828** E.B.F. YORKSHIRE STKS (Mdn 2-Y-O) £6316.00 (£1888.00: £904.00: £412.00)
**6f**
4-45 (4-47)

654² **Ardkinglass** (Fav) *(HRACecil)* 9-0 SCauthen (5) (lw: led over 3f out: r.o wl fnl f: drvn out) ................................................................................................... —1
Geisway (CAN) *(RHannon)* 9-0 BRaymond (10) (w'like: scope: rn green & sn outpcd: hdwy over 2f out: ev ch over 1f out: kpt on) ......... 2½.2
581³ The Informer (USA) *(PFICole)* 9-0 AMunro (7) (lw: a chsng ldrs: nt qckn fnl 2f) nk.3
292³ Totally Unique (USA) *(MBell)* 9-0 TQuinn (2) (chsd ldrs tl wknd over 1f out) 6.4
Tychonic *(BWHills)* 9-0 PatEddery (3) (wl grwn: lengthy: scope: bkwd: trckd ldrs tl wknd over 1f out: eased) .............................................................. 5.5
619⁴ Principal Player (USA) *(WBentley)* 9-0 TLucas (4) (chsd ldrs tl wknd over 2f out) ½.6

Brown's (FR) *(NACallaghan)* 9-0 MRoberts (1) (w'like: scope: outpcd tl kpt on fnl 2f) ............................................................... hd.**7**
Finavon *(IABalding)* 9-0 RCochrane (9) (str: cmpt: bit bkwd: hld up: efft ½-wy: sn outpcd & bhd) .............................................. hd.**8**
White Creek (IRE) *(JBerry)* 9-0 JCarroll (6) (leggy: scope: s.s: nvr nr ldrs)' ........ ¾.**9**
463² Mad Mytton *(ABailey)* 9-0 AMackay (8) (lw: s.i.s: a in rr) ................................. 2.**10**
581 C D Shareplan (USA) *(MRChannon)* 9-0 CRutter (11) (sn bhd) ........................ 3.**11**
645 Midget Gem *(MissLCSiddall)* 9-0 JReid (12) (swtg: led over 2f: wknd qckly) .... 7.**12**

**4/5** ARDKINGLASS(5/4—11/8), **5/1** The Informer (USA), **6/1** Geisway (CAN)(op 3/1), **10/1** Tychonic(op 9/1), **14/1** Finavon(op 8/1), **16/1** Mad Mytton, White Creek (IRE)(op 8/1), Totally Unique (USA), Brown's (FR), **33/1** Principal Player (USA), C D Shareplan (USA), **50/1** Midget Gem. CSF £7.56, Tote £1.90: £1.20 £2.10 £1.60 (£5.40). Sir David Wills (NEWMARKET) bred by Sir H. D. H. Wills. 12 Rn     1m 10.76 (0.56)
SF—53/43/42/18/–/–

**829**    LEVY BOARD SEVENTH RACE (H'cap) (0-90) £4136.00 each (£912.00: £416.00)
       1¼m 85y                                        5-15 (5-17)

713 **Andrath (IRE)** (81) *(CEBrittain)* 4–9-7 MRoberts (4) (chsd ldr: led over 3f out: r.o u.p fnl f) ................................................................. —**1**
277 **Dawn Success** (60) *(DWChapman)* 6–8-0 SWood (2) (lw: chsd ldrs: effrt & disp ld over 1f out: kpt on u.p) ................................ —**1**
688² Knock Knock (83) (Fav) *(IABalding)* 7–9-9 RCochrane (16) (lw: s.v.s: bhd: gd hdwy 3f out: kpt on wl fnl f) ...................................... 3.**3**
617⁶ Tarda (55) *(MrsGRReveley)* 5–7-9 JLowe (5) (lw: hld up & plld hrd: effrt over 3f out: one pce fnl 2f) ......................................... 1½.**4**
688⁴ Vague Dancer (64) *(MrsJRRamsden)* 6–8-4 DMcKeown (3) (lw: hld up: hdwy 3f out: kpt on: nvr nr to chal) ..................................... 1.**5**
713² Double Echo (IRE) (72) *(JDBethell)* 4–8-12 AMunro (9) (lw: bhd tl styd on u.p fnl 2f) ................................................................... 2½.**6**
533⁴ Rousitto (70) *(RHollinshead)* 4–8-10 WCarson (7) (bhd: sme hdwy u.p 2f out: n.d) ................................................................... 12.**7**
688* Surrey Dancer (71) *(BHanbury)* 4–8-11 (5x) BRaymond (13) (lw: in tch: effrt u.p over 3f out: wknd 2f out) ........................................ 8.**8**
Chiefs Babu (77) *(RO'Leary)* 4–9-3 LPiggott (6) (led tl over 3f out: wknd over 1f out: eased) ................................................... 9.**9**
Doctor Roy (65) *(NBycroft)* 4–8-5 SWebster (12) (bit bkwd: chsd ldrs tl lost pl over 3f out) ....................................................... 10.**10**
Barbary Reef (IRE) (55) *(GHEden)* 4–7-9 JQuinn (10) (chsd ldrs: ev ch & rdn 3f out: sn wknd) ....................................................... 11.**11**
431³ Rive-Jumelle (IRE) (69) *(MBell)* 4–8-2 ‡⁷PTurner (8) (lw: hld up: sme hdwy 3f out: sn wknd) ..................................................... 12.**12**
612² Kinematic (USA) (88) *(JHMGosden)* 4–10-0 PatEddery (11) (chsd ldrs tl rdn & lost pl over 3f out: eased whn btn) ........................ 13.**13**
688 Bold Ambition (78) *(TKersey)* 5–9-4 GHind (15) (bit bkwd: s.i.s: a bhd: t.o) ........ 14.**14**

**5/1** Knock Knock, **6/1** Surrey Dancer, Rive-Jumelle (IRE), **7/1** Rousitto, Kinematic (USA), **15/2** Tarda, **8/1** Double Echo (IRE), **9/1** Vague Dancer, **16/1** ANDRATH (IRE), **20/1** Barbary Reef (IRE), Chiefs Babu, **33/1** DAWN SUCCESS, **50/1** Doctor Roy, **100/1** Bold Ambition. CSF A & DS £188.01; DS A & A £214.18, CT A, DS & KK £1,360.71; DS, A & KK £1,393.95. Tote A £15.10 DS £20.50: A £6.20 DS £8.40 KK £2.00 (£350.20). The Dowager Lady Beaverbrook (NEWMARKET) bred by Major V. McCalmont in Ireland. Mrs Jeanne Chapman (YORK) bred by Mrs T. V. Ryan. 14 Rn     2m 9.13 (1.63)
SF—70/49/66/35/42/45

T/Trio: Races 3, 5 & 7: £27.60, £45.70 & £815.50. (67.25, 36.5, 2.2 Tckts) T/Jkpt: £1,769.90 (2 Tckts). T/Plpt: £158.70 (91.25 Tckts).                                   WG

## 689—KEMPTON (R-H)

### Wednesday, May 13th [Good]

Going Allowance: nil sec per fur (G)                                          Wind: nil

Stalls: high

**830**    AMBITION APP'CE H'CAP (0-70) £2595.00 (£720.00: £345.00)    **7f (J.C)**    6-05 (6-06)

515 **Highland Magic (IRE)** (56) *(MJFetherston-Godley)* 4–8-12 ‡³DHarrison (12) (b.off hind: gd hdwy on ins over 2f out: led over 1f out: r.o) —**1**
738² Durneltor (62) *(RHannon)* 4–9-7 RPerham (5) (hdwy over 2f out: ev ch over 1f out: r.o ins fnl f) ......................................... 2.**2**
783* Plan Ahead (66) (Fav) *(GLewis)* 3–8-8 (5x) ‡⁵BRussell (2) (5th st: ev ch 2f out: r.o ins fnl f) ................................................. ½.**3**

| | | | |
|---|---|---|---|
| *127* | Nazare Blue **(43)** *(MrsBarbaraWaring)* 5–7-11 ‡5GParkin (6) (hdwy fnl 2f: nvr nrr) | 1.4 |
| *186* | Judgement Call **(67)** *(PHowling)* 5–9-7 ‡5TMcLaughlin (7) (led tl over 1f out) | hd.5 |
| *604* | Sea Prodigy **(60)** *(MBlanshard)* 3–8-7 CHodgson (3) (lw: 4th st: one pce fnl 2f) | ½.6 |
| *731* | Idir Linn (IRE) **(43)** *(DJGMurray-Smith)* 4–8-2 RPrice (8) (nrst fin) | 1½.7 |
| *24⁵* | Erik Odin **(45)** *(MrsLPiggott)* 5–7-13 ‡5WAldwinkle (9) (b: b.hind: 6th st: no hdwy) | nk.8 |
| *624* | Premier Prince **(56)** *(LGCottrell)* 6–9-1 ATucker (1) (lw: 2nd st: ev ch over 1f out: wknd f) | 2¹/₂.9 |
| *515* | Grey Illusions **(48)** *(LJHolt)* 4–8-2 ‡5CAvery (14) (nvr nrr) | nk.10 |
| *624* | Jaldi (IRE) **(53)** *(JSutcliffe)* 4–8-7 ‡5JTate (16) (nrst fin) | nk.11 |
| *592⁴* | On Y Va (USA) **(69)** *(RJRWilliams)* 5–9-9 ‡5GMitchell (15) (b.off hind: 3rd st: wknd over 2f out) | 2¹/₂.12 |
| | Petivara **(42)** *(SDow)* 5–7-10⁽²⁾ ‡5AMartinez (4) (n.d) | 2¹/₂.13 |
| *621★* | Aragona **(54)** *(PDCundell)* 3–7-10 ‡5DGibbs (11) (n.d) | nk.14 |
| *273* | Wileys Folly **(44)** *(SDow)* 6–7-12 ‡5MJermy (10) (lw: rdr lost iron s: a bhd: t.o) | .8.15 |

**9/4** Plan Ahead, **4/1** Premier Prince(6/1), **9/2** Durneltor, **8/1** Aragona(op 5/1), **10/1** On Y Va (USA), **12/1** HIGHLAND MAGIC (IRE), **20/1** Jaldi (IRE), Erik Odin, Idir Linn (IRE), **25/1** Nazare Blue, Grey Illusions, **33/1** Ors. CSF £64.05, CT £154.21. Tote £13.50: £3.40 £1.70 £1.10 (£34.80). Miss N. Carroll (EAST ILSLEY) bred by W. J. Burke in Ireland. 15 Rn
1m 27.96 (3.76)
SF—42/45/30/16/39/23

---

**831**  LBC NEWSTALK 97.3 FM RICHARD DALLYN H'CAP (0-80) £3314.00 (£992.00: £476.00: £218.00)) 1¹/₂m

6-35 (6-37)

| | | | |
|---|---|---|---|
| | **Kaytak (FR) (66)** *(JRJenkins)* 5–9-7 WNewnes (8) (gd hdwy over 1f out: qcknd to ld cl home) | —1 |
| *426⁵* | Good for a Loan **(57)** *(RLee)* 5–8-12 BRaymond (24) (6th st: rdn over 2f out: led over 1f out: ct nr fin) | 1¹/₂.2 |
| *565* | Taylors Prince **(55)** *(HJCollingridge)* 5–8-10 JQuinn (4) (hdwy over 2f out: ev ch ins fnl f: no ex) | ³/₄.3 |
| *513⁶* | Rare Detail (IRE) **(73)** *(MrsLPiggott)* 4–10-0 LPiggott (12) (lw: 3rd st: led over 2f out tl over 1f out) | 1.4 |
| *702²* | Predestine **(53)** *(MMadgwick)* 7–8-8 GBaxter (18) (b: lw: hdwy over 2f out: nrst fin) | s.h.5 |
| *708⁶* | Mahrajan **(65)** *(CJBenstead)* 8–9-6 RCochrane (2) (nvr nrr) | 2¹/₂.6 |
| *606⁴* | Rising Tempo (IRE) **(57)** *(Fav)* *(CACyzer)* 4–8-12 GCarter (16) (5th st: ev ch over 1f out: wknd fnl f) | 3.7 |
| *598⁴* | Merry Marigold **(55)** *(JDRoberts)* 6–8-10 JWilliams (7) (b: s.s: hdwy fnl 2f: r.o) | nk.8 |
| *598³* | Hills of Hoy **(56)** *(KCBailey)* 6–8-4 ‡7CMunday (17) (2nd st: wknd over 1f out) | 1.9 |
| *426* | Greenwich Bambi **(55)** *(WCarter)* 4–8-10 JReid (1) (lw: nvr nrr) | ½.10 |
| *530* | Run Free **(39)** *(PatMitchell)* 7–7-8⁽¹⁾ RFox (5) (b: nrst fin) | hd.11 |
| *271³* | Polistatic **(45)** *(CAHorgan)* 5–8-0 DaleGibson (6) (wl bhd tl r.o fnl 2f) | s.h.12 |
| | Case for the Crown (USA) **(47)** *(BJCurley)* 5–7-13 ‡3FNorton (15) (4th st: wknd over 2f out) | 2.13 |
| *708* | Hello My Darling **(70)** *(WRMuir)* 4–9-11 SWhitworth (10) (n.d) | nk.14 |
| *583⁴* | Jack Button (IRE) **(72)** *(BobJones)* 3–8-8 NDay (13) (n.d) | ³/₄.15 |
| *681⁵* | Western Dynasty **(70)** *(MJRyan)* 6–9-8 ‡3DBiggs (22) (prom tl wknd over 3f out) | ½.16 |
| | Shadow Bird **(56)** *(GAPritchard-Gordon)* 5–8-11 WRyan (3) (a bhd) | s.h.17 |
| | Waterlow Park **(67)** *(IABalding)* 10–9-5 ‡3SO'Gorman (21) (n.d) | ½.18 |
| *730⁶* | Rock Legend **(39)** *(DShaw)* 4–9-2 BRouse (19) (lw: led tl wknd over 2f out) | hd.19 |
| *612³* | Ivors Guest **(55)** (v) *(RLee)* 6–8-3 ‡7CHawksley (14) (hdwy 5f out: rdn & eased over 2f out) | s.h.20 |
| *695* | Roberto's Gal **(68)** *(NCWright)* 3–7-13 ‡5BDoyle (20) (prom tl wknd over 3f out) | 2¹/₂.21 |
| | Kanooz (IRE) **(54)** (bl) *(SMellor)* 4–8-9 DanaMellor (23) (bhd fnl 7f: t.o) | 7.22 |
| *90* | Valued Friend (USA) **(39)** *(JJBridger)* 4–7-8 NAdams (9) (t.o fnl 7f) | 23 |

LONG HANDICAP: Run Free 7-3.

**6/1** Rising Tempo (IRE), **7/1** Predestine, **15/2** Mahrajan, Hello My Darling (IRE), **9/1** Rare Detail (IRE), **11/1** Western Dynasty, **12/1** Case for the Crown (USA)(op 6/1), **14/1** KAYTAK (FR), Good for a Loan, Shadow Bird, **16/1** Hills of Hoy, Merry Marigold, Ivors Guest, **20/1** Jack Button (IRE), Polistatic, Rock Legend, Greenwich Bambi, **25/1** Waterlow Park, Taylors Prince, **33/1** Kanooz (IRE), Roberto's Gal, **50/1** Ors. CSF £204.62, CT £4,429.45. Tote £20.20: £3.90 £3.00 £8.70 £2.60 (£483.90). T. J. Myles & Co (Contractors) Ltd (ROYSTON) bred by H. H. Aga Khan in France. 23 Rn
2m 37.79 (7.59)
SF—31/19/15/31/10/17

---

**832**  KINGHORNS H'CAP (0-90) £3158.00 (£944.00: £452.00: £206.00) 1m (J.C)

7-05 (7-07)

| | | | |
|---|---|---|---|
| *592* | **Dawning Street (IRE) (77)** *(Fav)* *(JLDunlop)* 4–9-3 WNewnes (4) (plld hrd: hdwy over 2f out: led wl over 1f out: comf) | —1 |
| *610⁶* | Piquant **(75)** *(LordHuntingdon)* 5–9-1 WRSwinburn (1) (lw: hld up: hdwy over 2f out: rdn over 1f out: r.o) | 3¹/₂.2 |

Gueca Solo **(83)** *(HRACecil)* 4–9-9  PatEddery (11) (gd hdwy 2f out: nt qckn fnl f) ........................................................................ ¾.3

532⁵ Skipper to Bilge **(70)** *(MAJarvis)* 5–8-10  BRaymond (2) (6th st: bmpd over 1f out: one pce fnl f) ................................................... 2½.4

626 Lucknam Dreamer **(72)** *(MrsBarbaraWaring)* 4–8-12  NHowe (8) (4th st: one pce fnl 2f) ....................................................................... ½.5

712⁵ Langtry Lady **(85)** *(MJRyan)* 6–9-8  ‡³DBiggs (10) (nvr nr to chal) ........... ¾.6

477 Secretary of State **(71)** *(PFICole)* 6–8-4  ‡⁷JDSmith (5) (b: lw: hdwy 2f out: one pce fnl f) ............................................................... ¾.7

610 Takenhall **(63)** *(MJFetherston-Godley)* 7–8-3  NAdams (16) (lw: hdwy 2f out: nt clr run over 1f out: nvr nrr) ........................................... nk.8

583 Andy Jack **(69)** *(MJHeaton-Ellis)* 3–7-5⁽³⁾ ‡⁷DHarrison (6) (nvr trbld ldrs) ...... ¾.9

712 Dream Carrier (IRE) **(71)** (bl) *(RHannon)* 4–8-11  JReid (18) (lw: n.d) ............. 6.10

Celia Brady **(65)** *(HCandy)* 4–8-5  CRutter (15) (n.d) ................................. 2.11

March Bird **(77)** *(JSutcliffe)* 7–9-3  BRouse (7) (b: bit bkwd: wl bhd tl sme late hdwy) ................................................................................... ¾.12

610 Cheveux Mitchell **(71)** (v) *(MRChannon)* 5–8-11  LPiggott (17) (led tl wknd qckly wl over 1f out) ....................................................................... 1½.13

Akkazao (IRE) **(76)** *(WCarter)* 4–8-11  ‡⁵NGwilliams (12) (bit bkwd: 3rd st: wknd over 2f out) ............................................................................ 2.14

Rosietoes (USA) **(55)** *(LGCottrell)* 4–7-9  RFox (13) (2nd st: wknd 2f out) ........ 1.15

705 Arak (USA) **(80)** *(RWArmstrong)* 4–9-6  WCarson (14) (n.d) ......................... ¾.16

696 Gibbot **(57)** (v) *(PHowling)* 7–7-8⁽⁴⁾ ‡³FNorton (3) (lw: a wl bhd) .............. ¾.17

610 Prince of the Sea (IRE) **(88)** *(DWPArbuthnot)* 4–10-0  MHills (9) (b: 5th st: wknd over 2f out) ........................................................................... 4.18

LONG HANDICAP: Andy Jack 7-5, Gibbot 6-4.

**11/2** DAWNING STREET (IRE), **6/1** Langtry Lady, Gueca Solo, **13/2** Piquant, **9/1** Cheveux Mitchell, **11/1** Dream Carrier (IRE), Arak (USA), Celia Brady, **12/1** Takenhall(op 8/1), Skipper to Bilge, **20/1** Secretary of State, March Bird, Rosietoes (USA), 25/1 Akkazao (IRE), Prince of the Sea (IRE), 33/1 Lucknam Dreamer, Andy Jack, 66/1 Gibbot. CSF £42.09, CT £215.26. Tote £7.90: £2.40 £2.40 £1.50 £3.00 (£29.40). Windflower Overseas Holdings Inc (ARUNDEL) bred by Windflower Overseas in Ireland. 18 Rn
　　　　　　　　　　　　　　　　　　　　　　　1m 40.11 (3.51)
　　　　　　　　　　　　　　　　　　　　　　　SF—51/38/44/23/23/31

**833**　　WATERLOO STKS (Mdn 3-Y.O) £2532.00 (£702.00: £336.00)　**7f (rnd)**　7-35 (7-39)

658³ Al Sadi **(85)** (Fav) *(CEBrittain)* 9-0  WRSwinburn (1) (led 2f: led over 3f out: drvn out) ................................................................................... —1

495² Will of Steel *(HCandy)* 9-0  CRutter (3) (lw: 2nd st: ev ch over 2f out: r.o) ........... 3.2

Express Service *(PJMakin)* 9-0  AMunro (6) (bit bkwd: bhd & plld out over 2f out: rapid hdwy fnl f) ................................................................. ¾.3

Top Song *(RHannon)* 8-9  WCarson (4) (hdwy over 2f out: one pce fnl 2f) ....... 6.4

Poly Snip *(MissBSanders)* 8-9  BCrossley (9) (leggy: lt-f: nvr nrr) .................. 1.5

Heavyweight (IRE) *(CAHorgan)* 9-0  AMcGlone (8) (bkwd: nvr nr to chal) ...... 2½.6

Lord Neptune *(MAJarvis)* 9-0  BRaymond (2) (6th st: wknd 2f out) .................. 3.7

698⁵ Sirmoor (IRE) *(RHannon)* 9-0  JReid (5) (5th st: wknd 2f out) ..................... 3.8

434 Trainee (USA) *(WJHaggas)* 8-9  NDay (10) (a bhd) ................................... 1.9

Frankus **(50)** *(SMellor)* 9-0  DanaMellor (7) (4th st: wknd over 2f out) ............. 2½.10

727 Beyond the Moon (IRE) *(MJFetherston-Godley)* 8-9  PatEddery (11) (lw: led after 2f tl over 3f out: 3rd st: wknd over 1f out) .................................. 4.11

**15/8** AL SADI, **7/2** Will of Steel, **4/1** Express Service, **6/1** Top Song, **14/1** Beyond the Moon (IRE), Lord Neptune, **16/1** Sirmoor (IRE), **33/1** Poly Snip, Trainee (USA), Heavyweight (IRE), **50/1** Frankus. CSF £8.84, Tote £2.70: £1.30 £1.50 £1.70 (£4.70). Mr Mohamed Obaida (NEWMARKET) bred by Gainsborough Stud Management Ltd.
11 Rn
　　　　　　　　　　　　　　　　　　　　　　　1m 28.37 (4.37)
　　　　　　　　　　　　　　　　　　　　　　　SF—35/26/24/1/–/–

**834**　　RING & BRYMER STKS (3-Y.O) £3655.00 (£1090.00: £520.00: £235.00)
　　　　　　**5f**　　　　　　　　　　　　　　　　8-05 (8-08)

691★ Vailmont (USA) **(95)** (Jt-Fav) *(IABalding)* 8-13  RCochrane (2) (hld up: qcknd to ld 1f out: jst hld on) ..................................................... —1

Bold Memory **(94)** *(DRCElsworth)* 9-4  JWilliams (1) (hdwy over 1f out: r.o wl ins fnl f) ................................................................................. ½.2

601⁴ Shati (IRE) **(95)** *(HThomsonJones)* 9-4  RHills (5) (lw: hdwy over 1f out: r.o ins fnl f) ............................................................................... 1.3

454² Mamma's Too **(103)** *(JBerry)* 9-2  JCarroll (3) (lw: led over 3f) ................... 1½.4

601³ Power Lake **(103)** (Jt-Fav) *(RHannon)* 9-4  PatEddery (4) (chsd ldr: led over 1f out: sn hdd & wknd) ................................................................ 1½.5

**5/2** VAILMONT (USA), Mamma's Too, Power Lake, **9/2** Bold Memory, **14/1** Shati (IRE). CSF £12.31, Tote £2.70: £1.30 £2.90 (£8.00). Mr George Strawbridge (KINGSCLERE) bred by George Strawbridge Jnr in USA. 5 Rn
　　　　　　　　　　　　　　　　　　　　　　　61.25 sec (2.25)
　　　　　　　　　　　　　　　　　　　　　　　SF—54/57/53/45/41

### 835

KEMPTON BUSINESS CENTRE STKS (Mdn 3-Y.O) £2763.00 (£768.00: £369.00)
1m 1f (rnd)                                                      8-35 (8-37)

| | |
|---|---|
| **Balnibarbi** (*HRACecil*) 9-0 PatEddery (9) (w'like: scope: 2nd st: led 3f out: sn clr: r.o wl) | —1 |
| 600² Dress Sense (IRE) (Fav) (*LMCumani*) 9-0 RCochrane (1) (gd hdwy 2f out: r.o: nt rch wnr) | 7.2 |
| 502 Mayaasa (USA) (*RWArmstrong*) 8-9 WCarson (8) (bit bkwd: led to 3f out: r.o one pce) | ½.3 |
| 707⁵ Alessandrina (USA) (*MRStoute*) 8-9 WRSwinburn (7) (stdy hdwy fnl 2f: nvr nrr) | 5.4 |
| 625 Dominant Force (*RHannon*) 9-0 BRaymond (12) (5th st: no hdwy) | 1.5 |
| Biblical Times (*CRNelson*) 9-0 JReid (15) (leggy: scope: nrst fin) | 1½.6 |
| Gallant Jack (IRE) **(70)** (*DHaydnJones*) 9-0 MHills (13) (4th st: wknd 2f out) | ½.7 |
| Dizzy Dame (*MRChannon*) 8-9 CRutter (5) (unf: scope: nvr nrr) | nk.8 |
| Million in Mind (IRE) (*MrsJCecil*) 9-0 PaulEddery (6) (w'like: scope: nvr nr to chal) | 1½.9 |
| 560 Apollo Red (*PWHarris*) 9-0 AMunro (2) (3rd st: wknd over 2f out) | hd.10 |
| 490 Noel (IRE) (*GAPritchard-Gordon*) 9-0 WRyan (10) (n.d) | 2.11 |
| Mittenoski Pet (*TJNaughton*) 8-9 GCarter (14) (unf: scope: n.d) | s.h.12 |
| Believe it (*CEBrittain*) 9-0 GCrealock (4) (n.d) | ¾.13 |
| Be My Habitat (*NAGraham*) 9-0 JQuinn (11) (w'like: scope: 6th st: wknd over 2f out: t.o) | 14 |
| Trunk Call (USA) (*MrsJCecil*) 9-0 BCrossley (3) (wl grwn: bit bkwd: hdwy over 4f out: wknd 3f out: t.o) | 15 |

**6/4** Dress Sense (IRE)(op 9/4), **15/8** BALNIBARBI(5/4—2/1), **7/1** Alessandrina (USA), **8/1** Million in Mind (IRE), **16/1** Believe it, **20/1** Mayaasa (USA), **33/1** Mittenoski Pet, Gallant Jack (IRE), Noel (IRE), Trunk Call (USA), Be My Habitat, Biblical Times, Dominant Force, **50/1** Ors. CSF £5.38, Tote £2.80: £1.50 £1.40 £6.40 (£2.70). Mr K. Abdulla (NEWMARKET) bred by Juddmonte Farms. 15 Rn
1m 55.67 (5.67)
SF—15/–/–/–/–/–

T/Plpt: £64.80 (40.5 Tckts).                                                                Hn

---

### 742a—**LONGCHAMP (R-H)**

**Thursday, May 7th [Good]**
Going Allowance: minus 0.10 sec per fur (G)

### 836a

PRIX DE SAINT-GEORGES (Gp 3) (C & F) £20640.00    **5f**

| | |
|---|---|
| **ELBIO** (*PJMakin*) 5-8-11 SCauthen | —1 |
| 4a² Dream Talk (bl) (*France*) 5-9-2 CAsmussen | nk.2 |
| Mister Slippers (USA) (*France*) 3-8-4 TJarnet | 4.3 |

Tote 2.50f: 1.40f 1.30f 2.90f (SF: 3.70f). Mr B. Brackpool (MARLBOROUGH) bred by D. W. Samuel. 8 Rn
56.9 sec (U.1)
SF—89/93/65

---

### 641a—**SAINT-CLOUD (L-H)**

**Friday, May 8th [Good]**
Going Allowance: 0.35 sec per fur (G)

### 837a

PRIX CLEOPATRE (Gp 3) (3-Y.O.F) £20640.00    **1¼m 110y**

| | |
|---|---|
| 379a³ **Garendare** (*France*) 3-8-9 DBoeuf | —1 |
| Paix Blanche (FR) (*France*) 3-8-9 CAsmussen | hd.2 |
| Triple Tiara (USA) (*France*) 3-8-9 TJarnet | hd.3 |

Tote 2.20f: 3.50f 1.50f (SF: 61.00f). Mr D. Wildenstein (E. Lellouche,FRANCE) bred by Dayton Ltd. 7 Rn
2m 16.4 (6.1)
SF—71/70/69

### 838a

PRIX DU MUGUET (Gp 3)    £30960.00    **1m**

| | |
|---|---|
| 378a★ **Exit To Nowhere** (USA) (*France*) 4-9-0 FHead | —1 |
| Caerlina (IRE) (*France*) 4-9-1 ELegrix | 1½.2 |
| Star Of Cozzene (USA) (*France*) 4-9-0 CAsmussen | ½.3 |

Tote 2.20f: 1.40f 2.30f (SF: 11.40f). Mr S. Niarchos (F. Boutin,FRANCE) bred by Flaxman Holdings Ltd in USA. 7 Rn
1m 45.4 (7.2)
SF—34/30/27

## 539a—LEOPARDSTOWN (L-H)

**Saturday, May 9th [Good to soft]**
Going Allowance: 0.40 sec per fur (Y)

### 839a   IRISH MERCHANTS AMETHYST STKS (listed race) IR£8625.00   1m

539a² **Brief Truce (USA)** *(Ireland)* 3-8-9 MJKinane ........................................ —1
Tijara (IRE) *(Ireland)* 3-8-8⁽²⁾ JPMurtagh ......................................... 4.2
609² Riszard (USA) *(Ireland)* 3-8-9 CRoche ........................................ 4½.3
Tote £1.80: £1.10 £2.60 (£7.90). Moyglare Stud Farms Ltd (D. K. Weld,IRELAND) bred by Moyglare Stud Farms
Ltd in USA. 5 Rn                                                                                                   1m 43.5 (5.5)
                                                                                                                      SF—60/47/34

### 840a   DERRINSTOWN STUD DERBY TRIAL STKS (Gp 3) (3-Y.O.) IR£24000.00   1¼m

462a⁴ **St Jovite (USA)** *(Fav)* *(Ireland)* 3-9-0 CRoche (cl up: pushed along ½-wy: led
3f out: rdn over 1f out: r.o) ....................................................... —1
Firing Line (IRE) *(Ireland)* 3-8-11 SCraine (hld up: hdwy over 1f out: no imp fnl f) . 3.2
Garabagh (IRE) *(Ireland)* 3-8-11 JPMurtagh (hld up: sme hdwy 1f out: kpt on) . ½.3
Reported (IRE) *(Ireland)* 3-8-11 WJO'Connor (cl up: sme hdwy 2f out: sn btn) 1½.4
Bryan Station (USA) *(Ireland)* 3-8-11 WJSupple (led tl hdd over 3f out: sn lost
pl) ...................................................................................... 1½.5

**40/85** ST JOVITE (USA), **4/1** Firing Line (IRE), **7/1** Garabagh (IRE), **8/1** Reported (IRE), **20/1** Bryan Station (USA).
Tote £1.30: £1.10 £1.50 (£2.90). Mrs Virginia Kraft Payson (J. S. Bolger,IRELAND) bred by Virginia Kraft Payson
in USA. 5 Rn                                                                                                       2m 10.4 (6.4)
                                                                                                                      SF—76/67/66/63/60

### 841a   DERRINSTOWN STUD 1,000 GUINEAS TRIAL (listed race) (3-Y.O.F) IR£12500.00   1m

540a³ **Khanata (USA)** *(Ireland)* 3-8-9 JPMurtagh ...................................... —1
540a★ Gdansk's Honour (USA) (bl) *(Ireland)* 3-8-12 CRoche ........................... 2½.2
French Flair (USA) *(Ireland)* 3-8-9 SCraine ...................................... 5.3
Tote £1.70: £1.20 £1.70 £1.30 (£2.20). H. H. Aga Khan (J. Oxx,IRELAND) bred by H. H. Aga Khan in USA. 6 Rn
                                                                                                                      1m 46 (8)
                                                                                                                      SF—23/18/–

## 742a—LONGCHAMP (R-H)

**Sunday, May 10th [Good]**
Going Allowance: nil sec per fur (G)

### 842a   DUBAI POULE D'ESSAI DES POULAINS (Gp 1) (3-Y.O.C) £103200.00   1m (Grande)

**Shanghai (USA)** *(France)* 3-9-2 FHead (hld up: 8th st: rapid hdwy over 1f out:
led wl ins fnl f) ..................................................................... —1
636a★ Rainbow Corner *(Fav)* *(France)* 3-9-2 PatEddery (5th st: chal over 1f out: led 1f
out tl wl ins fnl f) ................................................................. s.nk.2
391★ Lion Cavern (USA) *(France)* 3-9-2 SCauthen (plld hrd early: stumbled after 2f:
6th st: hdwy to chal 1f out: wknd nr fin) .......................................... ¾.3
404² ZAAHI (USA) *(HThomsonJones)* 3-9-2 RHills (a.p: 4th st: r.o one pce fr over 1f
out) .................................................................................... 1.4
636a³ Judge Decision (FR) *(France)* 3-9-2 WRSwinburn (7th st: hdwy & hmpd over 1f
out: sn ev ch: one pce fnl f) ...................................................... s.h.5
Take Risks (FR) *(France)* 3-9-2 TJarnet (prom: 3rd st: one pce fnl f) ............ s.h.6
636a² Highest Ody (FR) *(France)* 3-9-2 ELegrix (al in rr: sme late hdwy) .......... s.h.7
Bakari (IRE) *(France)* 3-9-2 DBoeuf (2nd to 2f out: wknd qckly) ................ 6.8
Lucet (USA) *(France)* 3-9-2 CAubert (led to 1f out: sn btn) ..................... 3.9

**Evens** Rainbow Corner, **4/1** Lion Cavern (USA), Highest Ody (FR), **7/1** Lucet (USA), Bakari (IRE), **12/1**
SHANGHAI (USA), **17/1** Zaahi (USA), Judge Decision (FR), **18/1** Take Risks (FR). Tote 12.70f: 1.80f 1.10f 1.40f
(SF: 19.40f). Mr S. Niarchos (F. Boutin,FRANCE) bred by Flaxman Holdings Ltd in USA. 9 Rn   1m 38.2 (0.5)
                                                                                                                      SF—94/93/91/88/87/84/83

### 843a   PRIX HOCQUART (Gp 2) (3-Y.O.C & F) £38271.00   1½m (Grande)

642a⁶ **Adieu Au Roi (IRE)** *(France)* 3-9-2 WRSwinburn (hld up: last st: hdwy over 1f
out: led ins fnl f: r.o wl) ......................................................... —1
Glanville (USA) *(France)* 3-9-2 WMongil (hld up: 5th st: hdwy to ld over 1f out:
hdd ins fnl f: r.o) ................................................................. 1½.2
Prince Polino (USA) *(France)* 3-9-2 ELegrix (prom: 4th st: kpt on one pce) ..... nk.3
642a⁵ Cristofori (USA) *(Jt-Fav)* *(France)* 3-9-2 TJarnet (led tl over 1f out: grad wknd) .. 1.4

635a² Modhish (IRE) (Jt-Fav) *(France)* 3-9-2 SCauthen (2nd st: one pce fnl 2f) ........ s.h.**5**
Summer Ensign (USA) *(France)* 3-9-2 CAsmussen (3rd st: ev ch 2f out: sn btn) 4.**6**

**7/10** Cristofori (USA), Modhish (IRE), **11/4** Prince Polino (USA), Summer Ensign (USA), **11/1** Glanville (USA), **15/1** ADIEU AU ROI (IRE). Tote 15.70f: 4.30f 4.40f (SF: 129.50f). Mr D. Tsui (J. Lesbordes,FRANCE) bred by P. de Moussac in Ireland. 6 Rn
2m 37.2 (7.2)
SF—30/27/26/24/23/15

## 744a—CAPANNELLE (R-H)
### Sunday, May 10th [Good]

**844a** PREMIO CONTE FELICE SCHEIBLER (3-Y.O) £69767.00 **1m 3f**

    **MASAD (IRE)** *(LMCumani)* 3-9-2 LDettori ...................................................... —**1**
    Obereggen (ITY) *(Italy)* 3-9-2 JFreda .................................................................. 6.**2**
    Guado d'Annibale (IRE) *(Italy)* 3-9-2 MPhilipperon ........................................ 1.**3**
Tote 21L: 14L 31L 14L (294L). Scuderia Gabriella (NEWMARKET) bred by Azzienda Agricola San Jore in Ireland. 14 Rn
2m 15.7

## 381a—DUSSELDORF (R-H)
### Sunday, May 10th [Good to soft]

**845a** ARAG PREIS (Gp 2) (3-Y.O.F) £42105.00 **1m**

    **Princess Nana** *(Germany)* 3-8-11 MRimmer ................................................... —**1**
    Chesa Plana *(Germany)* 3-8-11 ABest ........................................................... nse.**2**
    Urban Sea (USA) *(France)* 3-8-11 MJKinane .................................................. nk.**3**
385² WIEDNIU (USA) *(LordHuntingdon)* 3-8-11 AMunro .................................... ¾.**4**
473* CLOUD OF DUST *(JLDunlop)* 3-8-11 TQuinn (btn further 8¾l) ................... **8**
    TWAFEAJ (USA) *(BHanbury)* 3-8-11 BRaymond (btn more than 9¾l by wnr) .... **13**
Tote 203DM: 74DM 88DM 76DM (SF: 2776DM). Stall Imperator (B. Schutz,GERMANY) bred by Shutford Stud.
13 Rn
1m 42.19

## MAGDEBURG (R-H)
### Sunday, May 10th [Good]

**846a** GROSSER IJSBOERKE PREIS VON MAGDEBURG £4119.00 **1m 110y**

    **Zend (POL)** *(Germany)* 5-8-7 LPyritz ............................................................. —**1**
    Karloff (GER) *(Germany)* 5-8-7 RKalmus ....................................................... 3.**2**
    Akademos (GER) *(Germany)* 6-9-11 FWerning .............................................. 6.**3**
532 KAY'S DILEMMA (IRE) *(PAKelleway)* 4-8-5 DBiggs ...................................... 10.**4**
Tote 28.10DM: 18DM 24DM 10DM (49.10DM). R.Wassibauer (J.Pall,GERMANY) bred by P.S.K.Moszna in Poland. 5 Rn
1m 58.1

## 383—NEWBURY (L-H)
### Friday, May 15th [Good]
Going Allowance: minus 0.20 sec per fur (F)                Wind: almost nil

Stalls: centre

**847** CROOKHAM MEDIAN AUCTION STKS (Mdn 2-Y.O) £3184.00 (£952.00: £456.00: £208.00)
    **5f 34y**                                        2-05 (2-07)

470² Heathfield (USA) *(PFICole)* 9-0 TQuinn (7) (mde all: rdn out) .......................... —**1**
    Rocket to the Moon (IRE) *(PWChapple-Hyam)* 9-0 WRSwinburn (8) (leggy: lw:
        a.p: ev ch over 1f out: r.o) ............................................................................. 1.**2**
    Sharp Prod (USA) *(LordHuntingdon)* 9-0 SCauthen (5) (neat: a.p: one pce fnl
        2f) ................................................................................................................... 3½.**3**
    Kahellan (FR) (Fav) *(LMCumani)* 9-0 RCochrane (2) (w'like: bit bkwd: a.p: ev ch
        2f out: eased whn btn ins fnl f: rn green) ............................ 2½.**4**
    Geoff's Risk *(GLewis)* 9-0 MHills (10) (w'like: bkwd: hdwy over 1f out: nvr nrr) .. ½.**5**
    Body Language *(IABalding)* 8-9 JReid (14) (w'like: no hdwy fnl 2f) ................... ½.**6**
    By Rubies *(BWHills)* 8-9 JWilliams (3) (unf: s.s: nvr nrr) ................................... 1½.**7**
    Rockover *(RHannon)* 8-9 ‡5RPerham (11) (neat: bit bkwd: dwlt: nvr nr to chal) 1½.**8**
339⁶ Tigerspike (IRE) *(MMcCormack)* 9-0 CRutter (9) (bit bkwd: outpcd) ............... nk.**9**
    Credit Squeeze *(RFJohnsonHoughton)* 9-0 SWhitworth (12) (leggy: prom over
        3f) ................................................................................................................. hd.**10**
    Coopers Delight *(GLewis)* 9-0 WNewnes (6) (w'like: bit bkwd: a bhd) ............. 1.**11**

514 Quick Silver Boy *(DBurchell)* 9-0 PatEddery (1) (prom over 2f) .................. hd.**12**
    Honey Juice *(MJFetherston-Godley)* 8-9 WCarson (4) (neat: bit bkwd: s.s: a
         bhd) .................................................................................... 12.**13**

**100/30** Kahellan (FR), **7/2** HEATHFIELD (USA), **4/1** Rocket to the Moon (IRE)(op 5/2), **8/1** Rockover(op 5/1),
Sharp Prod (USA), **9/1** Body Language(op 5/1), **12/1** Quick Silver Boy, Honey Juice, **16/1** By Rubies(op 10/1),
**20/1** Ors. CSF £19.18, Tote £3.80: £1.70 £1.90 £2.50 (£5.40). Sir George Meyrick (WHATCOMBE) bred by
Arthur B. Hancock III in USA. 13 Rn
                                          61.92 sec (1.22)
                                      SF—56/52/38/28/26/19

**848**    ERICSSON BUSINESSPHONE H'CAP (3-Y.O) (0-100) £4464.00 (£1332.00: £636.00:
         £288.00)    **1½m 5y**                            2-40 (2-42)

                          (Weights raised 5 lb)
600* **Belgran (USA) (87)** *(HRACecil)* 9-7 SCauthen (4) (2nd st: rdn over 3f out: led
                     over 2f out: hrd rdn & edgd lft ins fnl f: r.o wl) .................. —**1**
384⁵ Poinciana **(69)** *(RHannon)* 8-3 MRoberts (5) (3rd st: led 3f out tl over 2f out:
                     n.m.r on ins ins fnl f: r.o) .................................... ¾.**2**
466* Inchcailloch (IRE) **(83)** *(Fav)* *(RCharlton)* 9-3 PatEddery (3) (hdwy over 3f out:
                     hrd rdn over 1f out: r.o) ........................................ ¾.**3**
679² Aremef (USA) **(85)** *(MrsJCecil)* 9-5 JReid (2) (led 9f: unable qckn) .............. 1.**4**
395   Leap in the Dark (IRE) **(73)** *(JLDunlop)* 8-7 WCarson (7) (4th st: wknd 2f out) ... 8.**5**
      Lord Vivienne (IRE) **(78)** *(PFICole)* 8-12 TQuinn (6) (5th st: wknd over 1f out) 2½.**6**
471* Fengari **(75)** *(PTWalwyn)* 8-9 RCochrane (1) (6th st: wknd over 3f out) ........... ¾.**7**

**6/4** Inchcailloch (IRE), **100/30** BELGRAN (USA), **6/1** Leap in the Dark (IRE), **8/1** Fengari, Poinciana, **12/1** Ors.
CSF £26.38, Tote £3.90: £1.60 £2.80 (£15.70). Mr S. Khaled (NEWMARKET) bred by Camelot Thoroughbred II
in USA. 7 Rn
                                       2m 32.39 (2.69)
                                  SF—56/36/48/48/20/20

**849**    JUDDMONTE LOCKINGE STKS (Gp 2)    £41538.00 (£15460.40: £7355.20. £3120.40)
         **1m (st)**                                   3-10 (3-13)

      **Selkirk (USA)** *(IABalding)* 4-9-5 RCochrane (5) (h.d.w: lw: hdwy over 3f out:
                     led over 1f out: edgd rt: r.o) .................................. —**1**
436⁶ Lahib (USA) *(JLDunlop)* 4-9-0 TQuinn (2) (hdwy over 2f out: ev ch over 1f out:
                     r.o) .......................................................... 2½.**2**
551* Rudimentary (USA) *(Fav)* *(HRACecil)* 4-9-3 SCauthen (8) (led over 4f out tl over
                     1f out: unable qckn) ........................................... 2.**3**
      Flying Brave *(JLDunlop)* 4-9-3 JReid (3) (a.p: hrd rdn over 1f out: one pce) ...... 5.**4**
      Mystiko (USA) *(CEBrittain)* 4-9-5 MRoberts (6) (led over 3f: wknd over 2f out) .. 1.**5**
551   Fair Average *(HCandy)* 4-9-0 WNewnes (4) (nvr nr to chal) ......................... 1.**6**
      Leariva (USA) *(DSmaga,France)* 4-9-0 DBoeuf (9) (nvr nrr) ......................... 2½.**7**
551³ Desert Sun *(HRACecil)* 4-9-0 PatEddery (1) (lw: prom over 6f) ..................... 1½.**8**
551   Mukaddamah (USA) *(PTWalwyn)* 4-9-3 WCarson (7) (bhd fnl 2f) ..................... 3½.**9**
673³ Ajaad (USA) *(MRStoute)* 4-9-0 WRSwinburn (10) (a bhd) ......................... 15.**10**

**9/4** Rudimentary (USA), **5/2** SELKIRK (USA), **9/2** Desert Sun, **5/1** Mystiko (USA), **12/1** Ajaad (USA),
Mukaddamah (USA), **16/1** Leariva (USA), Lahib (USA), **33/1** Ors. CSF £40.18, Tote £3.70: £1.60 £4.70 £1.40
(£81.50). Mr George Strawbridge (KINGSCLERE) bred by George Strawbridge Jnr in USA. 10 Rn
                                       1m 36.99 (U.01)
                                  SF—81/68/65/50/49/46

**850**    VODAFONE GROUP TRIAL STKS (listed race) (3-Y.O.F) £10495.00 (£3160.00: £1530.00:
         £715.00)    **1¼m 6y**                            3-40 (3-43)

      **Saratoga Source (USA) (105)** *(IABalding)* 8-9 RCochrane (6) (lw: 5th st: led
                     ins fnl f: rdn out) ............................................ —**1**
623* Jezebel Monroe (USA) **(82)** *(RCharlton)* 8-9 PatEddery (2) (4th st: led over 1f
                     out tl ins fnl f: hrd rdn: r.o) ................................... nk.**2**
630³ Mystery Play (IRE) **(110)** *(Fav)* *(JLDunlop)* 8-6 SCauthen (1) (lw: 3rd st: led over
                     3f out tl over 1f out: hrd rdn: unable qckn ins fnl f) .............. 2.**3**
      Delve (IRE) *(JLDunlop)* 8-6 WCarson (7) (2nd st: ev ch 3f out: rdn over 2f out:
                     r.o one pce) .................................................. 1.**4**
715² Petal Girl *(RHannon)* 8-6 JReid (3) (hdwy over 1f out: r.o) ....................... 1.**5**
646⁵ Good Reference (IRE) **(89)** *(MBell)* 8-9 MHills (4) (led over 6f: one pce) ........ nk.**6**
780⁵ Abbey Strand (USA) *(LordHuntingdon)* 8-6 MRoberts (5) (6th st: a bhd: t.o) .... 25.**7**

**6/4** Mystery Play (IRE), **7/2** Jezebel Monroe (USA), **7/1** Delve (IRE), **15/2** Petal Girl, **8/1** Good Reference
(IRE)(6/1—9/1), **10/1** Abbey Strand (USA), **12/1** SARATOGA Source (USA). CSF £49.71, Tote £16.50: £5.40
£2.70 (£31.10). Mr George Strawbridge (KINGSCLERE) bred by Sarah Louise Smith in USA. 7 Rn
                                       2m 5.89 (2.89)
                                  SF—46/45/41/36/34/36

**851**   HUE-WILLIAMS STKS (3-Y.O) £5949.00 (£1782.00: £856.00: £393.00)
          6f 8y                                                    4-10 (4-13)

601* **Garah (107)** (Fav) (HRACecil) 8-8(2) SCauthen (1) (a.p: led over 2f out: easily) . —1
      High Sevens (96) (HCandy) 8-6 CRutter (2) (hld up: chsd wnr fnl 2f: no imp) .... 4.2
649 Threepence (93) (JBerry) 8-11 TQuinn (3) (lw: led over 1f: edgd lft over 1f out:
      one pce) ...................................................................................... 2.3
503³ Pure Formality (92) (DRCElsworth) 8-6 JWilliams (4) (outpcd: nvr nrr) ............ hd.4
478⁴ Sunday's Hill (105) (MBlanshard) 8-11 JReid (5) (nvr nr to chal) ............... 1¹/₂.5
      Basma (USA) (113) (MajorWRHern) 8-6 WCarson (6) (led over 4f out tl one over 2f
      out: 4th & btn whn hmpd over 1f out) ................................................. 5.6

**8/13** GARAH, **9/2** Basma (USA), **7/1** Sunday's Hill(op 4/1), **9/1** Threepence, **10/1** Pure Formality,
**14/1** High Sevens. CSF £9.68, Tote £1.60: £1.10 £4.80 (£11.30). Prince A. A. Faisal (NEWMARKET) bred by
Nawara Stud Co Ltd. 6 Rn                                            1m 11.83 (0.03)
                                                            SF—70/52/49/45/44/19

**852**   HATHERDEN STKS (Mdn 2-Y.O.F) £2924.00 (£872.00: £416.00: £188.00)
          6f 8y                                                    4-45 (4-52)

      **Lacerta (IRE)** (Fav) (PWChapple-Hyam) 8-11 SCauthen (6) (unf: scope: a.p:
      hrd rdn over 1f out: led ins fnl f: r.o wl) ............................. —1
      Love in the Mist (USA) (IABalding) 8-11 JReid (1) (scope: s.i.s: outpcd: hdwy 2f
      out: ev ch fnl f: r.o wl) ................................................. hd.2
650 Bergliot (JBerry) 8-11 TQuinn (8) (led tl ins fnl f: unable qckn) ............... 3.3
      Bichette (RHannon) 8-11 WCarson (9) (leggy: bit bkwd: hdwy 2f out: one pce
      fnl f) ................................................................. nk.4
      Actinella (USA) (RHannon) 8-11 MRoberts (7) (unf: bit bkwd: a.p: ev ch 2f out:
      one pce) ............................................................... 1.5
548⁵ Sedgy's Sister (PJJones) 8-11 JWilliams (10) (lw: a.p: one pce fnl 2f) ........... ³/₄.6
      Malzeta (IRE) (MJHeaton-Ellis) 8-11 WNewnes (4) (neat: lw: s.s: mid div whn
      bmpd over 1f out: nvr nr to chal) ...................................... 1.7
      Brigadore Gold (RHannon) 8-6 ‡5RPerham (2) (leggy: prom 3f) ............... ³/₄.8
      Astroid (WRMuir) 8-11 SWhitworth (3) (w'like: v.bkwd: a bhd: t.o) ........... dist.9
      548 Brief Habit (IRE) (20/1) Withdrawn (broke loose at s) : not under orders

**15/8** LACERTA (IRE), **5/2** Actinella (USA), **7/2** Love in the Mist (USA), **10/1** Sedgy's Sister(tchd 20/1),
Bergliot(8/1—14/1), Bichette(7/1—12/1), **20/1** Astroid, **25/1** Ors. CSF £9.44, Tote £3.20: £1.20 £1.50 £4.30
(£4.40). Mr R. E. Sangster (MARLBOROUGH) bred by Moygaddy Stud in Ireland. 9 Rn      1m 14.16 (2.36)
                                                            SF—26/25/13/12/8/5

T/Trio: Race 3: £35.40 (26 Tckts). T/Jkpt: Not won; £1,946.40 to Newbury 16/5/92. T/Plpt: £94.80 (63.1 Tckts).
                                                                                AK

# NEWBURY (L-H)
## Saturday, May 16th [Good to firm]
Going Allowance: St: minus 0.30 sec; Rnd: minus 0.40 sec (F)          Wind: slt bhd

Stalls: centre

**853**   WINCHESTER H'CAP (0-100) £5309.00 (£1592.00: £766.00: £353.00)
          6f 8y                                                    2-00 (2-04)

649 **Orthorhombus (87)** (bl) (GLewis) 3-8-1 ‡5DHarrison (7) (led over 3f out: clr 2f
      out: rdn out) ...................................................... —1
      Consigliere (82) (RCharlton) 4-8-11 SRaymont (13) (hdwy 2f out: chsd wnr
      over 1f out: r.o) .................................................. 2.2
386⁶ Prenonamoss (88) (Fav) (DWPArbuthnot) 4-9-3 SWhitworth (8) (b.off hind: hrd
      rdn 2f out: hdwy over 1f out: r.o) .................................. 3.3
731* How's Yer Father (74) (RJHodges) 6-8-0 ‡3TSprake (12) (outpcd: gd hdwy fnl f:
      fin wl) ........................................................... hd.4
629 Spaniards Close (99) (PJMakin) 4-10-0 BRaymond (1) (hdwy 2f out: one pce
      fnl f) ............................................................ nk.5
624* Baysham (USA) (84) (bl) (BRMillman) 6-8-8 ‡5RPrice (2) (swtg: lw: a.p: one pce
      fnl 2f) ........................................................... ¹/₂.6
801 Sandcastle City (79) (RHannon) 3-7-12 DHolland (14) (spd 4f) ............. 2.7
478 A Prayer for Wings (98) (JSutcliffe) 8-9-13 MRoberts (4) (b: rdn 3f out: nvr nr to
      chal) ............................................................. nk.8
      Morgannwg (IRE) (82) (RDickin) 4-8-11 JWilliams (10) (s.s: rdn 2f out: nvr nrr) ³/₄.9
      Seneca Reef (IRE) (88) (IABalding) 4-9-3 RCochrane (5) (prom 4f) ......... hd.10

706⁶ Misdemeanours Girl (IRE) **(64)** *(MRChannon)* 4–7-7 NAdams (15) (led over 2f: wknd 2f out) ....................................... ¾.11
550 Aughfad **(79)** *(TCasey)* 6–8-8 WNewnes (9) (spd 3f) ....................................... 1½.12
775² Luna Bid **(68)** *(MBlanshard)* 9–7-11⁽¹⁾ CRutter (6) (lw: outpcd) ....................................... ¾.13
Bertie Wooster **(86)** *(RJHolder)* 9–9-1 ADicks (16) (a bhd) ....................................... 3.14
LONG HANDICAP: Misdemeanours Girl (IRE) 7-6.

**6/1** Prenonamoss, **13/2** Seneca Reef (IRE), How's Yer Father, Baysham (USA), **8/1** Luna Bid, **9/1** ORTHORHOMBUS, **10/1** Sandcastle City, **12/1** Aughfad, **14/1** Misdemeanours Girl (IRE), A Prayer for Wings, Spaniards Close, **16/1** Consigliere, **20/1** Ors. CSF £133.52, CT £852.83. Tote £12.50: £3.10 £4.30 £2.30 (£294.60). Mr M. J. E. Thornhill (EPSOM) bred by Cliveden Stud. 14 Rn 1m 11.13 (U.67)
SF—65/67/61/43/70/48

**854**  LONDON GOLD CUP (H'cap) (0-100) £5114.00 (£1532.00: £736.00: £338.00)
1m 3f 5y      2-30 (2-32)

**Fragrant Hill (98)** *(IABalding)* 4–9-12 RCochrane (5) (lw: 5th st: hdwy 3f out: hrd rdn over 1f out: led nr fin) ....................................... —1
718³ Line Drummer (USA) **(76)** *(PAKelleway)* 4–8-4 WRyan (6) (b: lw: led: qcknd 5f out: clr 3f out: hrd rdn over 1f out: ct nr fin) ....................................... ½.2
240 Montpelier Boy **(84)** (Fav) *(LordHuntingdon)* 4–8-12 DHolland (1) (s.s: hdwy & 4th st: chsd ldr 3f out tl over 1f out: one pce) ....................................... 5.3
Hashar (IRE) **(94)** *(DRCElsworth)* 4–9-8 JWilliams (3) (lw: 2nd st: wknd over 2f out) ....................................... 3.4
705⁵ Bold Bostonian (FR) **(80)** *(PJHobbs)* 4–8-8 WNewnes (4) (rdn 5f out: 3rd st: wknd 3f out) ....................................... s.h.5

**11/8** Montpelier Boy, **7/2** FRAGRANT HILL, Line Drummer (USA), **7/1** Bold Bostonian (FR), **8/1** Hashar (IRE). CSF £14.27, Tote £4.20: £1.90 £1.90 (£7.50). Mr Paul Mellon (KINGSCLERE) bred by Paul Mellon. 5 Rn
?m 20.34 (4.34)
SF—25/2/–/4/–

**855**  ASTON PARK STKS (listed race) £11268.00 (£3384.00: £1632.00: £756.00)
1m 5f 61y      3-00 (3-02)

**Endoli (USA) (98)** *(CEBrittain)* 5–8-11 MRoberts (13) (7th st: hdwy 3f out: led 2f out: edgd lft: rdn out) ....................................... —1
657* Mashaallah (USA) **(105)** (Fav) *(JHMGosden)* 4–8-11 RCochrane (1) (lw: 8th st: hdwy 2f out: hrd rdn over 1f out: r.o ins fnl f) ....................................... 1.2
512² Hebridean *(HCandy)* 5–8-8 CRutter (10) (rdn & gd hdwy over 2f out: r.o one pce fnl f) ....................................... 1.3
360* Torchon **(105)** *(GWragg)* 4–8-11 WNewnes (7) (10th st: gd hdwy 3f out: ev ch over 1f out: unable qckn) ....................................... 1½.4
622* Le Corsaire (USA) **(106)** *(LMCumani)* 4–9-0 DHolland (5) (lw: 5th st: rdn over 4f out: one pce 3f) ....................................... 7.5
608 Kimbers (IRE) **(102)** *(CRNelson)* 4–9-4 SWhitworth (9) (2nd st: led 4f out tl over 2f out: sn wknd) ....................................... 1.6
435 Deposki **(97)** (v) *(MRStoute)* 4–8-11 WRyan (3) (hld up: 6th st: led over 2f out: sn hdd & wknd) ....................................... s.h.7
Run Don't Fly (USA) **(113)** *(PFICole)* 4–9-6 AClark (4) (rdn 3f out: nvr nr to chal) 2.8
228⁵ Spinning **(102)** *(IABalding)* 5–8-11 BRaymond (11) (4th st: ev ch 3f out: hung lft & wknd over 2f out: eased wl over 1f out) ....................................... 4.9
Flakey Dove *(RJPrice)* 6–8-3 JWilliams (6) (9th st: a bhd) ....................................... 1½.10
Fly Away Soon (USA) **(109)** *(PFICole)* 4–9-4 GBaxter (8) (3rd st: wknd qckly over 3f out: t.o) ....................................... 20.11
648 Marcus Thorpe (USA) **(109)** (bl) *(PAKelleway)* 4–8-8 NAdams (12) (led over 9f: wknd qckly: t.o) ....................................... 8.12

**10/11** Mashaallah (USA), **8/1** Torchon(op 5/1), **9/1** ENDOLI (USA), Spinning, Le Corsaire (USA)(op 6/1), **11/1** Fly Away Soon (USA), **12/1** Deposki, Run Don't Fly (USA), **20/1** Marcus Thorpe (USA), **25/1** Hebridean, **33/1** Ors. CSF £18.44, Tote £11.90: £3.00 £1.30 £4.80 (£9.50). The Dowager Lady Beaverbrook (NEWMARKET) bred by Sigma Group, Inc. in USA. 12 Rn 2m 45.15 (0.01 under best; U.55)
SF—50/48/43/43/32/34

**856**  MAY STKS (Mdn 2-Y.O.C & G) £3377.25 (£1008.00: £481.50: £218.25)
6f 8y      3-35 (3-36)

654⁵ Son Pardo (Fav) *(RHannon)* 9-0 MRoberts (4) (hmpd s: jnd ldr 5f out: led wl over 1f out: hrd rdn & r.o wl) ....................................... —1
Vladivostok *(BWHills)* 9-0 DHolland (3) (leggy: unf: hld up: ev ch over 1f out: r.o) ....................................... 2.2
555⁵ Ansellman *(MJHaynes)* 9-0 BRaymond (2) (led over 4f: unable qckn fnl f) ......... 1.3

Pair of Jacks (IRE) *(WRMuir)* 9-0 SWhitworth (1) (w'like: scope: rdn along & prom 4f) ........................................................................... 3½.4
729  Ian's Ace *(BWHills)* 9-0 JWilliams (5) (outpcd) ................................. 10.5

**4/6** SON PARDO, **9/2** Ansellman(op 5/2), **5/1** Vladivostok(op 2/1), **7/1** Pair of Jacks (IRE)(5/1—8/1), **14/1** Ian's Ace(7/1—16/1). CSF £4.50, Tote £1.80: £1.10 £1.90 (£2.90). N.T.C. (Racing) Limited (MARLBOROUGH) bred by R. T. and Mrs Watson. 5 Rn                                               1m 13.13 (1.33)
SF—38/30/26/12/–

---

**857**       SHAW STKS (Mdn 3-Y-O) £3366.00 (£1008.00: £484.00: £222.00)
1¼m 6y                                                                   4-05 (4-11)

**Surf** *(MrsJCecil)* 9-0 MRoberts (13) (6th st: led over 1f out: all out) ................. —1
Alum Bay *(HRACecil)* 9-0 WRyan (12) (gd sort: 8th st: hdwy 4f out: ev ch fnl f: r.o wl) ............................................................................................. hd.2
Scrutineer (USA) *(Fav)* *(JHMGosden)* 9-0 RCochrane (4) (b.hind: h.d.w: bit bkwd: led 1f: led over 4f out tl over 1f out: unable qckn) ..... 4.3
Greek Gold (IRE) *(MRStoute)* 9-0 PD'Arcy (7) (w'like: scope: 3rd st: one pce fnl 2f) ............................................................................................. 2.4
600⁶ Bitter Aloe *(JLDunlop)* 9-0 BRaymond (8) (hdwy 3f out: one pce fnl 2f) ........... 3.5
Spring *(JLDunlop)* 8-9 WNewnes (11) (w'like: scope: bit bkwd: gd hdwy fnl f: bttr for r) ..................................................................................... 2.6
Dajitus *(MJHeaton-Ellis)* 9-0 GBaxter (15) (b: lengthy: 4th st: wknd 2f out) ........ 2.7
623⁴ Second Call *(HCandy)* 8-9 CRutter (5) (led after 1f tl over 4f out: 2nd st: wknd 2f out) ........................................................................................ 2.8
Garachico (USA) *(GHarwood)* 9-0 AClark (1) (gd sort: scope: bit bkwd: 5th st: wknd over 2f out) ......................................................................... s.h.9
693  Master of the Rock *(PJMakin)* 8-11 ‡3TSprake (9) (a bhd) ............................ 1½.10
394  Andes *(WGRWightman)* 9-0 TRogers (3) (a bhd) ......................................... s.h.11
707  Rose of Macmillion *(MrsBarbaraWaring)* 8-9 NHowe (2) (9th st: bhd fnl 3f) ..... 2.12
Neviskia (USA) *(CFWall)* 8-9 NDay (6) (lt-f: unf: s.s: a bhd) ....................... 8.13
Folkboat *(BWHills)* 8-9 DHolland (10) (unf: scope: a bhd) ......................... 1½.14
428  Baharlilys *(NCWright)* 8-9 JWilliams (16) (7th st: wknd over 2f out) ......... nk.15
693  Rose Edge *(JWHills)* 9-0 SWhitworth (14) (swtg: bhd fnl 4f: t.o) ............... 15.16

**13/8** Scrutineer (USA), **3/1** SURF, **5/1** Alum Bay, **8/1** Second Call, **11/1** Greek Gold (IRE), **14/1** Folkboat(op 8/1), Garachico (USA)(op 8/1), **16/1** Bitter Aloe, **20/1** Spring, **50/1** Ors. CSF £19.30, Tote £4.70: £1.80 £2.60 £1.60 (£7.20). Grundy Bloodstock Limited (NEWMARKET) bred by Cotswold Bloodstock Ltd. 16 Rn  2m 5.58 (2.58)
SF—34/33/25/21/15/11

---

**858**       HEADLEY H'CAP (3-Y-O) (0-90) £3850.00 (£1150.00: £550.00: £250.00)
1m 7y (rnd)                                                               4-35 (4-43)

576  **Philidor** *(78)* *(JMPEustace)* 8-9 RCochrane (2) (5th st: led over 2f out: r.o wl) .. —1
658² Bid for Six (USA) *(85)* *(RHannon)* 9-2 MRoberts (6) (lw: 3rd st: hrd rdn to chase wnr over 1f out: no imp) ...................................................... 4.2
Wassl This Then (IRE) *(65)* *(DWPArbuthnot)* 7-10 NAdams (3) (led after 2f tl over 2f out: one pce) ........................................................... 3½.3
604² Will Soon *(72)* *(HCandy)* 8-3 CRutter (7) (outpcd: hrd rdn & hdwy over 2f out: nvr nrr) ............................................................................... 5.4
689* Muhit (USA) *(PTWalwyn)* 8-7 GBaxter (10) (4th st: no hdwy fnl 3f) .............. ¾.5
626³ Major Bugler (IRE) *(79)* *(GBBalding)* 8-10 JWilliams (1) (outpcd: hdwy fnl f: r.o) 1½.6
646  Fair American (USA) *(81)* *(MRStoute)* 8-12 BRaymond (8) (8th st: nvr nr to chal) ¾.7
704⁶ Haroldon (IRE) *(90)* *(BPalling)* 9-7 WRyan (9) (6th st: wknd over 2f out) ........ 4.8
511  Royal Print (IRE) *(62)* *(WRMuir)* 7-0 ‡7KimMcDonnell (4) (7th st: bhd fnl 3f) ...... 1.9
715* Scarlatine (IRE) *(82)* *(JHMGosden)* 8-13 DHolland (11) (reluctant s: led 2f: 2nd st: wknd over 2f out: eased whn btn over 1f out) ........... 1½.10

**5/2** Will Soon, **7/2** Bid for Six (USA), **5/1** Scarlatine (IRE), **6/1** Muhit (USA), **7/1** Fair American (USA), Major Bugler (IRE), **10/1** PHILIDOR, **12/1** Haroldon (IRE), Wassl This Then (IRE), **33/1** Royal Print (IRE). CSF £48.10, CT £412.99. Tote £13.30: £2.50 £2.10 £3.80 (£38.00). Mr J. C. Smith (NEWMARKET) bred by John A. Jones Morgan. 10 Rn                                              1m 34.91 (0.28 under best: U1.09)
SF—63/58/24/16/18/16

---

T/Trio: Race 3: £210.60 (8.4 Tckts). T/Jkpt: Not won; £4,816.85 to Goodwood 19/5/92. T/Plpt: £117.00 (77.2 Tckts).                                                                                       LMc

628—**NEWMARKET (R-H)** Rowley Mile
**Friday, May 15th [Good]**
Going Allowance: 5f: minus 0.20 sec; Rest minus 0.10 sec (G)          Wind: almost nil

Stalls: centre

**859**  DITCH MEDIAN AUCTION STKS (Mdn 2-Y.O.F) £3752.50 (£1120.00: £535.00: £242.50)
**5f**                                                                2-15 (2-18)

581* **Niche** (Fav) (RHannon) 8-11 LPiggott (2) (mde all: drew clr fnl f: comf) ............. —1
568* Peperonata (IRE) (NTinkler) 8-12 KDarley (4) (lw: w wnr: rdn over 1f out: one
      pce) ................................................................................................. 2½.2
      Aberlady (MAJarvis) 8-8 PRobinson (7) (cmpt: scope: prom: shkn up 2f out:
      styd on ins fnl f) ................................................................................. 4.3
      My Bonus (DJSCosgrove) 8-8 ‡5DHarrison (3) (s.i.s: chsd ldrs: rdn appr fnl f: sn
      outpcd) ........................................................................................... s.h.4
      Trundley Wood (GAPritchard-Gordon) 8-8 WHood (9) (leggy: scope: chsd
      ldrs: rdn ½-wy: no imp) ........................................................................ ½.5
      Dowreyna (MRStoute) 8-8 PD'Arcy (6) (lt-f: neat: outpcd tl sme hdwy fnl f) .... 2½.6
654   Spanish Thread (GAPritchard-Gordon) 8-8 NCarlisle (5) (s.i.s: a bhd) ......... 3½.7
7095  Simmering (GWragg) 8-8 ‡3FNorton (1) (lw: swvd lft s: a bhd) ...................... 1.8

**13/8** NICHE, **7/4** Peperonata (IRE), **11/2** My Bonus, **12/1** Dowreyna(op 6/1), Simmering(op 5/1), **20/1**
Aberlady(op 10/1), **33/1** Spanish Thread, **50/1** Trundley Wood. CSF £4.69, Tote £2.20: £1.10 £1.20 £3.60
(£2.50). Lord Carnarvon (MARLBOROUGH) bred by Highclere Stud Ltd. 8 Rn          60.28 sec (0.88)
                                                                    SF—59/49/29/28/26/16

**860**  BRANDON H'CAP (0-90) £3817.50 (£1140.00: £545.00: £247.50)    **7f**    2-45 (2-48)

610  **Go Executive** (83) (CEBrittain) 4–9-8 GCrealock (8) (led 4f: rallied to ld ins fnl f:
     r.o wl) ............................................................................................. —1
73⁵  Myasha (USA) (71) (MrsLPiggott) 3–7-5(2) ‡7GMilligan (7) (b.hind: plld hrd:
     hdwy to ld appr fnl f: hdd & no ex ins fnl f) ........................................... 1.2
774² Foolish Touch (61) (Fav) (WJMusson) 10–8-0 JQuinn (4) (b: dwlt: hdwy 2f out:
     rdn ins fnl f: r.o strly) ........................................................................ hd.3
     Kimberley Park (66) (DWPArbuthnot) 4–8-0 ‡5RPrice (1) (plld hrd: prom tl
     outpcd 2f out: rdn & r.o wl fnl f) ......................................................... s.h.4
     La Bamba (82) (GAPritchard-Gordon) 6–9-7 WHood (6) (hld up: gd hdwy 2f
     out: rdn & no ex fnl f) ........................................................................ hd.5
629  Mac's Fighter (88) (v) (WAO'Gorman) 7–9-8 ‡5EmmaO'Gorman (3) (lw: chsd
     ldrs: rdn 2f out: sn btn) .................................................................... 2½.6
696  Corrin Hill (70) (BWHills) 5–8-2 ‡7CMunday (10) (b: chsd ldrs over 4f) ......... nk.7
349⁶ Mitsubishi Video (IRE) (75) (DrJDScargill) 4–9-0 WRyan (9) (prom: ev ch 2f out:
     wknd appr fnl f) ................................................................................ nk.8
438  Superoo (77) (JSutcliffe) 6–9-2 BRouse (5) (lw: led 3f out tl appr fnl f: sn wknd) nk.9
624  Mu-Arrik (57) (DAWilson) 4–7-7(3) ‡3FNorton (2) (lw: prom over 4f) ............. 2½.10
     LONG HANDICAP: Mu-Arrik 7-5.
     *Stewards Enquiry: Obj. to Go Executive by Quinn overruled.*

**4/1** Foolish Touch, **5/1** GO EXECUTIVE, Superoo, **7/1** Kimberley Park, La Bamba, **10/1** Mac's Fighter, **14/1** Ors.
CSF £61.12, CT £274.81. Tote £6.40: £2.20 £3.00 £1.50 (£91.50). Mr Mike Dawes (NEWMARKET) bred by
Somerhall Bloodstock Ltd. 10 Rn                                      1m 28.06 (4.06)
                                                                    SF—36/2/10/9/29/24

**861**  JEYES FLUID H'CAP (0-105) £6160.00 (£1840.00: £880.00: £400.00)
         **1¾m**                                                      3-20 (3-22)

632³ **Castle Courageous** (87) (LadyHerries) 5–9-5 WRyan (1) (lw: hld up: hdwy 4f
     out: rdn to ld appr fnl f: styd on) ........................................................ —1
632* Witness Box (USA) (92) (Fav) (JHMGosden) 5–9-10 BRaymond (7) (disp ld:
     rdn 2f out: hdd appr fnl f: unable qckn) ................................................ 1½.2
681* Quick Ransom (74) (MJohnston) 4–8-5 (4x) DMcKeown (2) (lw: hld up in rr:
     hdwy 3f out: rdn over 1f out: kpt on) .................................................... 2½.3
632⁵ Gay Glint (86) (NAGraham) 5–9-1 ‡3FNorton (6) (chsd ldrs: rdn 3f out: sn btn) 10.4
632⁴ Jackson Flint (86) (HThomsonJones) 4–9-3 NCarlisle (4) (hld up in rr: effrt 4f
     out: sn rdn & btn) .............................................................................. 1.5
736  Thunder Bug (USA) (62) (APJames) 4–7-0 ‡7CHawksley (3) (w ldr tl rdn & wknd
     3f out: t.o) ....................................................................................... 15.6
     Tsunami (76) (CEBrittain) 4–8-7 GCrealock (5) (chsd ldrs 9f: sn wknd: t.o) ........ 5.7
     LONG HANDICAP: Thunder Bug (USA) 6-10.

**2/1** Witness Box (USA), **100/30** Quick Ransom, **7/2** CASTLE COURAGEOUS, **6/1** Jackson Flint, **8/1** Gay Glint, **25/1** Tsunami, **100/1** Thunder Bug (USA). CSF £9.95. Tote £4.50: £2.30 £1.70 (£4.00). Lady Mary Mumford (LITTLEHAMPTON) bred by Lady Mary Mumford. 7 Rn
2m 58.33 (2.33)
SF–68/70/46/36/36/–

**862**  KING CHARLES II STKS (3-Y.O) £7245.00 (£2160.00: £1030.00: £465.00)
7f
3-50 (3-53)

441* **King Olaf (IRE)** (Fav) *(PWChapple-Hyam)* 8-12 LPiggott (7) (a.p: led 2f out: styd on u.p fnl f) ............................... —1

347⁴ Balla Jidaal (USA) **(105)** *(MRStoute)* 8-12 BRaymond (2) (lw: led 5f: sn rdn: kpt on fnl f) ....................................... 1½.2

437⁵ Fair Crack (IRE) **(109)** *(RHannon)* 9-5 BRouse (3) (rdn & lost pl 3f out: rallied ins fnl f: fin wl) .......................... 2.3

7a⁴ Mougins (IRE) *(DRCElsworth)* 9-2 AProcter (5) (h.d.w: prom: ev ch wl over 1f out: wknd fnl f) ....................... 1.4

744a5 Secret Thing (USA) **(97)** *(CEBrittain)* 8-12 GCrealock (1) (racd alone stands' side: in tch 4f) ................... 2½.2.5

778⁶ Simple Sound (IRE) *(MAJarvis)* 8-12 PRobinson (4) (hmpd s: a bhd: t.o) ....................... 8.6

**15/8** KING OLAF (IRE), **5/2** Balla Jidaal (USA), **11/4** Fair Crack (IRE)(2/1—3/1), **13/2** Mougins (IRE), **14/1** Secret Thing (USA), **33/1** Simple Sound (IRE). CSF £6.73, Tote £2.40: £1.80 £1.40 (£3.00). Mr R. E. Sangster (MARLBOROUGH) bred by Regiura Syndicate in Ireland. 6 Rn
1m 26.02 (2.02)
SF–57/52/53/47/35/11

**863**  COWLINGE CLAIMING STKS (3-Y.O) £3184.00 (£952.00: £456.00: £208.00)
1m
4-20 (4-22)

734 **Prince Rodney (67)** *(RHannon)* 8-3 KDarley (10) (hld up: hdwy 3f out: led 1f out: r.o) .................. —1

510² Hand on Heart (IRE) **(61)** *(WJHaggas)* 7-12 JQuinn (6) (chsd ldrs: led wl over 1f out: sn hdd: no ex fnl f) .......... 2½.2

O'Donnell's Folly **(60)** (Fav) *(ABailey)* 7-12 ‡5BDoyle (12) (chsd ldrs: rdn 3f out: one pce appr fnl f) ............... 4.3

486³ Massiba (IRE) *(BHanbury)* 9-2 BRaymond (7) (s.s: hdwy 3f out: rdn wl over 1f out: one pce) .................... 1½.2.4

693 Gachette *(JSutcliffe)* 8-7 BRouse (2) (racd alone stands' side: kpt on one pce fnl 2f) ............................. ½.2.5

614 Certain Lady **(60)** *(GBlum)* 7-5 ‡7CHawksley (5) (lw: prom over 5f) ..................... 3.6

662⁶ Dublin Indemnity (USA) **(49)** (bl) *(NACallaghan)* 8-7 LPiggott (3) (hld up in rr: effrt over 2f out: nt rch ldrs) ....... nk.7

734⁶ Have a Nightcap **(60)** *(MAJarvis)* 8-3 PRobinson (4) (a in rr: t.o) ..................... 8.8

353⁶ Spareathought *(CNAllen)* 7-9 ‡3FNorton (9) (b.hind: prom: led over 3f out tl hdd & wknd wl over 1f out: t.o) ..... 4.9

697 Cannonale (IRE) **(55)** *(JPearce)* 8-2 ‡5RPrice (1) (a bhd: t.o) ...................... 5.10

567³ Tyrone Flyer **(57)** *(GHEden)* 8-7 CDwyer (8) (lw: fly-jumped s: sn led: hdd over 3f out: sn wknd: t.o) ......... d.h.10

**3/1** O'Donnell's Folly(12/1—14/1), **5/1** Massiba (IRE), Certain Lady(3/1—11/2), Hand on Heart (IRE)(4/1—6/1), **11/2** PRINCE RODNEY, **8/1** Gachette, Spareathought, **12/1** Dublin Indemnity (USA), Have a Nightcap(op 8/1), **25/1** Tyrone Flyer, **33/1** Cannonale (IRE). CSF £35.37, Tote £7.00: £2.30 £2.00 £2.30 (£11.20). Mr G. A. Bosley (MARLBOROUGH) bred by G. A. Bosley and H. Clarkin. 11 Rn 1m 39.43 (2.13)
SF–45/32/20/33/22/–

**864**  ASHLEY STKS (Mdn 3-Y.O) £3687.50 (£1100.00: £525.00: £237.50)
1½m
4-55 (4-59)

**Lemon's Mill (USA)** *(JHMGosden)* 8-9 MHills (5) (wl grwn: bit bkwd: chsd ldrs: led over 3f out: styd on strly) ........... —1

512³ Pavonis *(HRACecil)* 9-0 WRyan (2) (w ldrs: rdn over 1f out: unable qckn) ................. 3.2

553 Beauchamp Grace *(JLDunlop)* 8-9 BRaymond (4) (hld up: hdwy ½-wy: shkn up over 2f out: fin wl) ........... 1½.3

560² Rajai (IRE) (Fav) *(JLDunlop)* 9-0 LPiggott (6) (lw: chsd ldrs: effrt & ev ch 3f out: rdn & wknd fnl f) ....... ½.4

Alizari (USA) *(GHarwood)* 9-0 AClark (3) (gd sort: hld up: lost pl 5f out: styd on u.p fnl 2f) ........... s.h.5

Halley (USA) *(HRACecil)* 9-0 McGlone (7) (w'like: scope: bit bkwd: chsd ldrs 9f: sn wknd: t.o) ....... 15.6

693⁵ Kalko *(CEBrittain)* 9-0 GCrealock (1) (mde most tl over 3f out: sn wknd: t.o) ...... 8.7

Orienteer *(LMCumani)* 8-7 ‡7JWeaver (8) (gd sort: wl grwn: bit bkwd: s.s: hdwy after 4f: wknd 5f out: t.o) ......... 12.8

**7/4** Rajai (IRE)(5/4—2/1), **7/2** Kalko, **5/1** Pavonis(4/1—13/2), **13/2** Halley (USA)(14/1—6/1), **10/1** Alizari (USA)(op 4/1), **12/1** LEMON'S MILL (USA), **20/1** Ors. CSF £64.28, Tote £10.90: £2.60 £1.70 £3.10 (£27.70). Mr K. Abdulla (NEWMARKET) bred by Juddmonte Farms Incorporated in USA. 8 Rn 2m 34.53 (5.23)
SF—31/30/22/26/25/–

**865**    TUDDENHAM STKS (Mdn 3-Y.O.F) £3947.50 (£1180.00: £565.00: £257.50)
    1m                                              5-25 (5-28)

    **Anne Bonny** (Fav) *(JRFanshawe)* 8-11 WRSwinburn (6) (lw: hld up: stdy hdwy
                       3f out: led ins fnl f: r.o wl) ..................................... —1
502[5] Twilight Secret *(JWHills)* 8-11 MHills (3) (lw: a.p: led 3f out ti ins fnl f: one pce) 3$\frac{1}{2}$.2
    Avice Caro (USA) *(JHMGosden)* 8-11 WRyan (2) (cmpt: scope: s.i.s: hdwy 3f
                       out: styd on ins fnl f) ......................................... s.h.3
    Music in My Life (IRE) *(WJarvis)* 8-8 ‡[3]FNorton (5) (bhd: rdn 3f out: nvr plcd to
                       chal) ..................................................................... 6.4
    Romoosh *(NACallaghan)* 8-11 KDarley (1) (w'like: scope: hdwy $\frac{1}{2}$-wy: wknd wl
                       over 1f out) ............................................................. $\frac{1}{2}$.5
651[3] La Cousine *(CEBrittain)* 8-6 ‡[5]BDoyle (8) (chsd ldrs over 5f) ..................... 3$\frac{1}{2}$.6
 502 La Kermesse (USA) *(JHMGosden)* 8-11 AMcGlone (7) (led 5f: wknd wl over 1f
                       out) ......................................................................... 2.7
    Gizlaan (USA) *(BHanbury)* 8-11 BRaymond (4) (chsd ldrs: rdn 3f out: sn btn) .... 6.8

**11/10** ANNE BONNY(op 9/4), **7/2** Twilight Secret(op 2/1), **6/1** Avice Caro (USA)(op 3/1), **8/1** Gizlaan (USA)(op 5/1), **14/1** La Kermesse (USA), **16/1** La Cousine, Romoosh(10/1—20/1), **20/1** Music in My Life (IRE). CSF £5.54, Tote £1.90: £1.10 £1.10 £2.00 (£2.50). Mr David Thompson (NEWMARKET) bred by R. H. Cowell. 8 Rn 1m 39.77 (2.47)
SF—47/36/35/14/15/–

T/Trio: Race 5: £159.90 (8.1 Tckts). T/Plpt: £18.50 (222.2 Tckts).                  IM

# NEWMARKET (R-H) Rowley Mile
## Saturday, May 16th [Good to firm]
Going Allowance: minus 0.20 sec per fur (F)             Wind: mod across

Stalls: centre

**866**    CAMBRIDGE EVENING NEWS H'CAP (Celebrities) (0-60) £1952.50 (£540.00: £257.50)
    1m                                             1-40 (1-43)

 211 **Charming Gift (46)** *(RJRWilliams)* 5-11-0 EdwardHide (3) (chsd ldrs: led on bit
                       1f out: pushed clr fnl f) ....................................... —1
 572 China Sky (46) (Fav) *(CNAllen)* 4-11-0 GrevilleStarkey (2) (led tl hdd 1f out:
                       one pce) .................................................................. 7.2
    Jurran (59) *(HThomsonJones)* 7-11-13 StanMellor (9) (hld up & bhd: gd hdwy
                       over 2f out: one pce fnl f) .................................... nk.3
 766 Sauvignon (IRE) (50) *(RGuest)* 4-11-4 WalterSwinburnSnr (8) (hld up: effrt 3f
                       out: rdn over 1f out: nt rch ldrs) ......................... 4.4
 373 Fair Dare (42) *(CBBBooth)* 4-10-10 ClaireKing (4) (chsd ldrs tl wknd over 1f
                       out) ....................................................................... 1$\frac{1}{2}$.5
 776[2] Serious Time (48) *(SirMarkPrescott)* 4-11-2 TomO'Ryan (1) (lw: w ldrs: rdn
                       along $\frac{1}{2}$-wy: hmpd & outpcd 3f out: styd on fnl f) ......... 1$\frac{1}{2}$.6
 696 Night Transaction (44) *(AHide)* 5-10-12 RobinGray (7) (s.s: hdwy $\frac{1}{2}$-wy: kpt on
                       one pce fnl 2f) ....................................................... 1.7
 626[4] Quietly Impressive (IRE) (56) *(MBell)* 4-11-10 JackBerry (11) (lw: bhd $\frac{1}{2}$-wy:
                       sn rdn: no imp) ...................................................... 4.8
    Freaky Deaky (60) *(NACallaghan)* 5-12-0 JohnFrancome (12) (lw: a bhd) ........ 4.9
 779 Fabled Orator (53) *(PHowling)* 7-11-7 FrazerHines (5) (b.nr hind: plld hrd:
                       chsd ldrs 5f) ......................................................... 1.10
 137 Blake's Treasure (41) (bl) *(TThomsonJones)* 5-10-9 ElainMellor (10) (chsd
                       ldrs 5f) .................................................................. 1.11

**3/1** China Sky, **100/30** Serious Time, **7/2** Quietly Impressive (IRE), **15/2** Sauvignon (IRE), **10/1** CHARMING GIFT, **14/1** Blake's Treasure, Jurran, **20/1** Night Transaction, **25/1** Freaky Deaky, **33/1** Ors. CSF £37.95, CT £386.00. Tote £18.40: £3.10 £1.40 £2.70 (£14.80). Mr Colin G. R. Booth (NEWMARKET) bred by R. P. Ryan. 11 Rn 1m 40.94 (3.64)
SF—50/29/41/20/7/8

**867**    SUNLEY BUILDS AUCTION STKS (Mdn 2-Y.O) £3184.00 (£952.00: £456.00: £208.00)
    6f                                             2-10 (2-16)

555[4] **Zimzalabim** (Fav) *(BWHills)* 8-5 WCarson (9) (lw: hdwy to ld over 2f out:
                       pushed clr fnl f) .................................................... —1

Iommelli (IRE) *(PAKelleway)* 8-6 PRobinson (8) (cmpt: a.p: ev ch 2f out: kpt on ins fnl f) ........................................................ 2¹/₂.2

548³ Princess Oberon (IRE) *(MBell)* 8-5 MHills (3) (hmpd after 1f: hdwy over 2f out: rdn & no ex fnl f) ................................................ 3¹/₂.3

791 Infant Protege (USA) *(CEBrittain)* 7-9 ‡⁵BDoyle (5) (led tl over 2f out: kpt on one pce) .................................................... 3¹/₂.4

Erlking (IRE) *(LordHuntingdon)* 8-5 DMcKeown (4) (w'like: scope: outpcd tl r.o u.p appr fnl f) ............................................ ³/₄.5

795² Five Clubs (IRE) *(DTThom)* 8-0 JQuinn (7) (nvr trbld ldrs) ...................... 2.6

Nut Bush *(NACallaghan)* 8-5 AMcGlone (10) (w'like: scope: chsd ldrs tl wknd wl over 1f out) ........................................ 4.7

446 Cashable *(JRJenkins)* 8-13 JFortune (11) (chsd ldrs: rdn along ¹/₂-wy: sn wknd) ....................................................... 2¹/₂.8

In the Air *(GAPritchard-Gordon)* 8-0 NCarlisle (6) (cmpt: scope: bit bkwd: s.s: a bhd) ............................................. hd.9

677 Miss Otter (IRE) *(GAPritchard-Gordon)* 8-0 RFox (12) (lw: spd over 3f) ............ 2.10

772 Ombre Darme (IRE) *(JWPayne)* 8-6 GCarter (1) (chsd ldrs over 3f) ............ s.h.11

720³ Hod-Mod (IRE) *(ABailey)* 8-9 AMackay (2) (w ldrs: hrd rdn over 2f out: sn wknd: t.o) ................................................. 8.12

6/4 ZIMZALABIM, **13/8** Princess Oberon (IRE), **15/2** Hod-Mod (IRE), **14/1** Five Clubs (IRE), **16/1** Erlking (IRE)(7/1—20/1), **25/1** Iommelli (IRE), Nut Bush, In the Air, **33/1** Infant Protege (USA), Cashable, **40/1** Ombre Darme (IRE), **50/1** Miss Otter (IRE). CSF £36.84, Tote £2.30: £1.40 £4.70 £1.60 (£54.40). K. Al-Said (LAMBOURN) bred by Hesmonds Stud Ltd. 12 Rn ......... 1m 13.22 (1.82)
SF—31/22/7/–/–/–

**868** HAMBRO GUARDIAN CLAIMING STKS (3-Y.O) £3028.00 (£904.00: £432.00: £196.00)
1¹/₄m
2-40 (2-52)

618 **Mashakel (USA)** *(BHanbury)* 9-7 MHills (11) (b: lw: hld up: hdwy 3f out: led over 1f out: rdn out) ....................................... —1

562⁴ Liability Order (60) *(RBoss)* 8-11 PRobinson (1) (chsd ldrs: ev ch whn carried lft appr fnl f: r.o ins fnl f: unlucky) ................... 1¹/₂.2

603³ Roly Wallace (66) (bl) *(KTIvory)* 8-6 RFox (10) (a.p: ev ch whn carried lft over 1f out: swtchd rt & r.o fnl f) ....................... ¹/₂.3

666³ Silver Samurai (67) *(RHollinshead)* 8-7 WCarson (8) (s.s: hdwy 4f out: ev ch appr fnl f: one pce) .................................... nk.4

497³ Blockade (USA) (80) (Fav) *(MBell)* 8-4 ‡⁷PTurner (13) (t: b: led ¹/₂-wy: sn clr: hung lft 2f out: sn hdd & btn) ........................ 2¹/₂.5

Gone Bust (IRE) (70) *(RFJohnsonHoughton)* 8-5 RHills (12) (lw: in tch: effrt over 2f out: wknd appr fnl f) ........................ 6.6

Kojiki *(LMCumani)* 9-7 JFortune (6) (w'like: scope: bhd: rdn over 3f out: nvr nrr) 1¹/₂.7

734⁵ Honey Vision (56) (bl) *(GHEden)* 7-12 NCarlisle (3) (w ldrs: rdn 4f out: sn wknd: t.o) .......................................... 10.8

433 Captain Marmalade *(DTThom)* 9-1 CDwyer (2) (a in rr: t.o) .................. ¹/₂.9

Bit on the Side (IRE) *(WJMusson)* 8-0 JHBrown (7) (w'like: scope: s.s: a bhd: t.o) ......................................... 1¹/₂.10

695 Minoan Light (IRE) (59) (bl) *(RHannon)* 8-3 AMcGlone (4) (plld hrd: prom 6f: sn lost pl: t.o) ........................................ 2¹/₂.11

510 Wise Portia (bl) *(HCandy)* 7-5 ‡⁷AntoinetteArmes (5) (lw: led to ¹/₂-wy: wknd 3f out: t.o) ............................................. 20.12

6/4 Blockade (USA), **7/2** Silver Samurai, **8/1** Liability Order, **9/1** Roly Wallace, **10/1** Kojiki, **12/1** Honey Vision, **14/1** MASHAKEL (USA)(op 8/1), **20/1** Captain Marmalade, Minoan Light (IRE), Bit on the Side (IRE), **25/1** Ors. CSF £118.05, Tote £19.90: £4.20 £1.80 £2.40 (£59.10). Mr Muttar Salem (NEWMARKET) bred by Amerivest T'bred Prtnrs No. 3 & E. Seltzer in USA. 12 Rn ......... 2m 6.90 (4.30)
SF—44/31/24/25/17/6

**869** MALONEY & RHODES STKS (Mdn 3-Y.O) £3785.00 (£1130.00: £540.00: £245.00)
1m
3-10 (3-23)

658⁶ **Dawaahi (USA)** (Fav) *(JHMGosden)* 9-0 WCarson (7) (b.nr hind: chsd ldrs: led 2f out: hrd rdn fnl f: all out) ....................... —1

Little Bean *(GWragg)* 9-0 MHills (8) (gd sort: lw: dwlt: hdwy over 3f out: jnd wnr fnl f: hrd rdn: r.o) .................................. nk.2

Wellington Rock (USA) *(JARToller)* 9-0 PRobinson (1) (h.d.w: dwlt: hdwy ¹/₂-wy: rdn over 1f out: r.o ins fnl f) ..................... 2¹/₂.3

577 Jato *(WJHaggas)* 9-0 BRouse (9) (a.p: led over 3f out to 2f out: swtchd lft appr fnl f: r.o) ............................................. 1.4

606 Wheeler's Wonder (IRE) (48) *(NCWright)* 8-4 ‡⁵BDoyle (3) (bhd: sn pushed along: styd on fnl f: nvr nrr) .............................. 5.5

577 Ler Cru (IRE) *(CEBrittain)* 9-0 GCrealock (5) (lw: prom tl wknd over 2f out) ..... 2¹/₂.6
633 Isle of Innisfree (USA) *(HRACecil)* 9-0 AMcGlone (2) (lw: prom over 4f: sn lost
pl) ............................................................................................. 7.7
715⁵ Last Appearance *(MBell)* 8-2 ‡7ACairns (6) (b.nr hind: led over 4f: sn wknd) ....... 2.8

**8/13** DAWAAHI (USA), **4/1** Wellington Rock (USA), **10/1** Jato, **12/1** Little Bean(op 7/1), **14/1** Ler Cru (IRE)(op 8/1), **16/1** Isle of Innisfree (USA), **25/1** Last Appearance, **66/1** Wheeler's Wonder (IRE). CSF £8.83, Tote £1.60: £1.10 £1.60 £1.40 (£6.20). Sheikh Ahmed Al Maktoum (NEWMARKET) bred by Peter Fuller & Jayeff "B" Stables in USA. 8 Rn
1m 39.21 (1.91)
SF—47/46/38/35/10/12

---

**870**  CORAL H'CAP (3-Y.O) (0-115) £19087.50 (£5700.00: £2725.00: £1237.50)
6f
3-45 (3-55)

(Weights raised 6 lb)

649⁴ Splice (88) *(JRFanshawe)* 8-4 ‡7NVarley (7) (lw: hdwy 2f out: led ins fnl f: rdn
out) ........................................................................................ —1
535* Double Blue (85) *(MJohnston)* 8-8 DMcKeown (10) (lw: led tl ins fnl f: r.o) .... nk.2
649* Master Planner (90) *(CACyzer)* 8-13 WCarson (1) (lw: w ldrs: ev ch 3f out: rdn &
no ex fnl f) ............................................................................ ³/₄.3
678² Petite-D-Argent (80) *(Fav)* *(MissLAPerratt)* 8-3 NCarlisle (13) (lw: prom: ev ch
over 1f out: sn rdn & no ex) ................................................ 1.4
727* Venture Capitalist (85) *(RHannon)* 8-8 MHills (9) (dwlt: sn rcvrd: effrt over 1f
out: no ex ins fnl f) ........................................................ 2¹/₂.5
445* Heather Bank (98) *(JBerry)* 9-7 PRobinson (11) (gd spd over 3f) ..................... nk.6
454⁶ Wave Hill (98) *(HRACecil)* 9-0 ‡7StephenDavies (3) (nvr nr to chal) ............... 2.7
719⁵ Sharling (76) *(JHMGosden)* 7-13 AMcGlone (12) (lw: chsd ldrs: hung rt 2f out:
no imp) ............................................................................... s.h.8
719⁵ Indian Endeavour (76) *(RGuest)* 7-13 JQuinn (9) (spd 4f) ........................... s.h.9
576³ Windpower (IRE) (89) *(JBerry)* 8-12 GCarter (5) (in tch: sn pushed along: nvr
able to chal) ...................................................................... ³/₄.10
624⁶ Morocco (IRE) (73) *(RCharlton)* 7-5⁽¹⁾ ‡5BDoyle (4) (dwlt: a bhd) ................. ³/₄.11
691² Silca-Cisa (92) *(MRChannon)* 9-1 BRouse (6) (chsd ldrs 3f) ......................... 2.12
714³ Hazm (USA) (88) *(HThomsonJones)* 8-11 RHills (8) (in tch: rdn ¹/₂-wy: sn wknd) 5.13

**4/1** Petite-D-Argent(op 7/1), **9/2** Double Blue, **15/2** SPLICE(14/1—7/1), **8/1** Windpower (IRE), Sharling, Venture Capitalist, Silca-Cisa, **10/1** Heather Bank, Master Planner, Hazm (USA), **11/1** Morocco (IRE), **25/1** Indian Endeavour, **33/1** Wave Hill. CSF £43.80, CT £329.81. Tote £9.10: £3.20 £2.60 £2.50 (£53.50). Cheveley Park Stud (NEWMARKET) bred by Cheveley Park Stud Ltd. 13 Rn
1m 12.61 (1.21)
SF—42/45/47/33/28/40

---

**871**  SHADAYID STKS (3-Y.O.F) £7460.00 (£2060.00: £980.00)  6f
4-15 (4-20)

631 **Central City (106)** (Fav) *(RHannon)* 9-10 RHills (2) (chsd ldr: led over 2f out:
shkn up & r.o wl appr fnl f) ........................................... —1
631 Harvest Girl (IRE) (106) *(GAPritchard-Gordon)* 9-6 WCarson (1) (hld up: effrt &
chsd wnr 2f out: rdn over 1f out: no imp) ....................... 5.2
690 Canadian Capers (61) *(MRChannon)* 9-2 BRouse (3) (lw: led over 3f: sn outpcd) 5.3

**Evens** CENTRAL CITY, **11/10** Harvest Girl (IRE), **11/1** Canadian Capers. CSF £2.25, Tote £1.20 (£1.20). A. F. Budge (Equine) Limited (MARLBOROUGH) bred by E. Aldridge. 3 Rn
1m 13.41 (2.01)
SF—46/22/–

---

**872**  BURLINGTON PRESS H'CAP (0-90) £4464.00 (£1332.00: £462.00: £462.00)
5f
4-45 (4-47)

(Weights raised 8 lb)

668⁶ **Tongue Tied (62)** *(JWharton)* 4–8-8 WCarson (5) (lw: w ldr: led over 2f out: hld
on wl fnl f) ......................................................................... —1
270* Blake End (USA) (81) *(Fav)* *(WAO'Gorman)* 3–9-4 MHills (9) (lw: w ldrs: ev ch 1f
out: rdn & r.o) ................................................................... hd.2
706² Martina (60) *(JWharton)* 4–8-6 PRobinson (3) (chsd ldrs: ev ch over 1f out: no
ex fnl f) ........................................................................... ¹/₂.3
768 Drum Sergeant (59) (v) *(JParkes)* 5–8-5 NCarlisle (2) (hdwy over 1f out: r.o wl
nr fin) ................................................................................ d.h.3
731 Liffey River (USA) (54) *(MrsLPiggott)* 4–7-7 ‡7GMilligan (1) (b: outpcd tl r.o wl
appr fnl f) ........................................................................ 2¹/₂.5
712 Never so Sure (78) *(ABailey)* 4–9-3 ‡7PBowe (10) (dwlt: hdwy over 1f out: nvr
nrr) ..................................................................................... hd.6
620⁵ Bodari (75) *(DAWilson)* 3–8-12 BRouse (7) (bit bkwd: n.d) ......................... 1¹/₂.7
735⁴ Banbury Flyer (64) *(MrsALMKing)* 4–8-5 ‡5BDoyle (4) (prom tl wknd ins fnl f) .... ¹/₂.8
706³ Yes (50) *(DTThom)* 4–7-10 JQuinn (8) (chsd ldrs 3f) ................................... 1.9
550 Ski Captain (61) *(PHowling)* 8–8-0 ‡7TMcLaughlin (6) (led over 2f: sn wknd) .. nk.10

**7/2** Blake End (USA), **11/2** Martina, **6/1** TONGUE TIED, **7/1** Yes, **8/1** Liffey River (USA), Bodari, **9/1** Never so Sure, **10/1** Ors. CSF £27.18, CT TT, BE & M £54.16, TT, BE & DS £91.63. Tote £4.40: £1.60 £1.80 M £1.00 DS £1.80 (£8.90). Mrs R. T. Watson (MELTON MOWBRAY) bred by R. T. and Mrs Watson. 10 Rn
60.10 sec (0.70)
SF—60/69/55/54/32/56

**873** DALHAM HALL STUD STKS (Mdn 3-Y.O) £3427.50 (£1020.00: £485.00: £217.50)
1³/₄m 5-15 (5-17)

Faugeron *(GWragg)* 9-0 RHills (4) (leggy: scope: lw: hld up: plld out wl over 1f
out: qcknd & led ins fnl f: sn clr) ............................ —1
384 Paradise Navy *(CEBrittain)* 9-0 GCrealock (2) (lw: led tl hdd & unable qckn ins
fnl f) ............................ 3¹/₂.2
625⁴ Cantanta *(RCharlton)* 8-9 AMcGlone (1) (plld hrd: prom: rdn & ev ch over 1f out:
one pce fnl f) ............................ 1.3
536² Kirsten (Fav) *(WJarvis)* 8-9 WCarson (6) (a.p: ev ch over 1f out: sn btn) .......... 2¹/₂.4
694⁴ Dancing Dancer *(NCWright)* 8-9 JQuinn (5) (chsd ldrs tl wknd over 2f out) ...... 12.5
625⁵ Bayadere (USA) *(MRStoute)* 8-9 JFortune (3) (bhd fnl 5f) ............................ 4.6

**6/5** Kirsten, **100/30** Cantanta, **5/1** Paradise Navy, **6/1** FAUGERON, **10/1** Bayadere (USA)(8/1—14/1), **20/1** Dancing Dancer. CSF £31.67, Tote £5.90: £2.40 £2.30 (£12.30). Mr J. L. C. Pearce (NEWMARKET) bred by J. L. C. Pearce. 6 Rn
3m 6.78 (10.78)

T/Trio: Race 5: £250.70 (9.2 Tckts). T/Plpt: £143.80 (45.55 Tckts). IM/Dk

665—**THIRSK (L-H)**

**Friday, May 15th [Firm]**

Going Allowance: minus 0.40 sec per fur (F) Wind: slt half bhd

Stalls: high

**874** E.B.F. STATION ROAD STKS (Mdn 2-Y.O.C & G) £2499.50 (£692.00: £330.50)
5f 2-30 (2-30)

602⁴ Lord Olivier (IRE) *(WJarvis)* 9-0 MTebbutt (5) (trckd ldrs gng wl: shkn up to ld
over 1f out: pushed out) ............................ —1
654⁴ Rock Symphony (Fav) *(AAScott)* 9-0 JFortune (3) (lw: trckd ldrs: led wl over 1f
out: sn hdd & nt qckn) ............................ 1¹/₂.2
Garnock Valley *(JBerry)* 9-0 JCarroll (4) (cmpt: scope: bit bkwd: sn pushed
along: hdwy 2f out: r.o fnl f) ............................ 3¹/₂.3
807 Caldervale *(ABailey)* 9-0 AMackay (6) (chsd ldrs: no imp fr ¹/₂-wy) ............... 3.4
659³ Dayjuz (IRE) *(FHLee)* 9-0 SWebster (1) (unruly stalls: led tl wl over 1f out: hung
lft & sn wknd) ............................ ¹/₂.5
365 Bold Philip *(WJPearce)* 9-0 DNicholls (2) (sn chsng ldrs: lost pl 2f out) ............. 6.6
Eightofus *(GMMoore)* 9-0 KFallon (7) (leggy: scope: lost tch over 3f out: t.o
whn p.u over 1f out) ............................ 0

**Evens** Rock Symphony, **9/4** Garnock Valley, **7/1** LORD OLIVIER (IRE)(op 4/1), **8/1** Dayjuz (IRE), **25/1** Eightofus, **33/1** Ors. CSF £14.05, Tote £7.30: £3.10 £1.30 (£3.90). Miss V. R. Jarvis (NEWMARKET) bred by Michael Staunton in Ireland. 7 Rn
58.5 sec (0.8)
SF—44/38/24/12/10/–

**875** MOWBRAY (S) STKS £2461.20 (£683.20: £327.60) 1¹/₂m 3-00 (3-01)

505⁵ Kirby Opportunity (48) *(JPearce)* 4-8-11 DaleGibson (4) (lw: chsd ldrs: rdn
over 2f out: r.o wl to ld jst ins fnl f: sn clr) ............................ —1
Dancing Street (54) *(RMWhitaker)* 4-8-6 ACulhane (9) (lw: trckd ldrs: rdn to ld
wl over 1f out: hdd jst ins fnl f: nt pce of wnr) ............................ 4.2
683 Buckingham Band (USA) (45) (bl) *(FHLee)* 4-8-6 ‡5NKennedy (11) (outpcd &
bhd: hdwy u.p 5f out: hung lft & styd on fnl 2f) ............................ hd.3
773³ Paper Craft (v) *(MJohnston)* 5-9-2 RPElliott (10) (lw: led tl wl over 1f out: one
pce) ............................ ¹/₂.4
606 Not Yet (37) *(EWeymes)* 8-8-9 ‡7AGarth (14) (in tch: effrt over 2f out: nvr able to
chal) ............................ 1.5
525⁵ Modest Hope (USA) (52) (Fav) *(GHEden)* 5-8-11 JCarroll (12) (b.hind: hdwy
¹/₂-wy: ev ch over 2f out: wknd over 1f out) ............................ 1¹/₂.6
197 Mississippi Beat (USA) (v) *(MPNaughton)* 5-9-2 JakiHouston (17) (styd on
u.p fnl 2f: nt rch ldrs) ............................ 1¹/₂.7
Juris Prudence (IRE) (52) *(BAMcMahon)* 4-8-6 GCarter (16) (effrt appr st: no
imp) ............................ 2.8
Premier Venues (48) *(SGNorton)* 4-8-9 ‡7OPears (7) (in tch tl lost pl 3f out) ....... 4.9

| 420 | Aussie Aisle (IRE) **(43)** (v) *(DMoffatt)* 4–8–4 ‡7DarrenMoffatt (8) (hld up: effrt ent st: sn rdn & no imp) ............................................. s.h.**10** |
|---|---|
| 617 | Marandisa **(54)** *(MPNaughton)* 5–8–11  DHolland (6) (chsd ldrs tl wknd 3f out) hd.**11** |
|  | Lisalee (IRE) *(JParkes)* 4–8–1 ‡5SMaloney (5) (mid div & drvn along ½-wy: n.d) 2.**12** |
| 469 | Friendlypersuasion (IRE) **(40)** *(RHollinshead)* 4–9–2  RHills (18) (lw: nvr nr ldrs) nk.**13** |
| 533 | Nobby **(53)** (bl) *(TFairhurst)* 6–8–13 ‡3JFanning (1) (t.o) ......................... 15.**14** |
| 663 | I'M Special (IRE) **(40)** (bl) *(AHarrison)* 4–8–6  KFallon (13) (lw: chsd ldrs: sn drvn along: lost pl 7f out: t.o) ...................... **15** |
| 763 | Into the Future **(24)** (bl) *(APStringer)* 5–8–11  JFortune (3) (chsd ldrs tl hrd rdn & wknd appr st: t.o) ...................... **16** |
|  | Burmese Pearl *(PTDalton)* 4–8–6  PBurke (2) (b: a last: t.o) ...................... **17** |

**9/2** Modest Hope (USA), **5/1** KIRBY OPPORTUNITY, **11/2** Dancing Street, **6/1** Marandisa, **9/1** Paper Craft, Not Yet, **12/1** Juris Prudence (IRE), **14/1** Premier Venues, Friendlypersuasion (IRE), **20/1** Mississippi Beat (USA), I'M Special (IRE), Nobby, Into the Future, Buckingham Band (USA), **33/1** Aussie Aisle (IRE), **66/1** Ors. CSF £33.38, Tote £5.40: £1.60 £1.40 £9.70 (£11.40). Mr Peter Bradley (NEWMARKET) bred by Highfield Stud Ltd. 17 Rn; No bid
2m 31.9 (1.9)
SF—30/17/16/25/16/15

## 876

NORBY H'CAP (0-90) £2798.20 (£775.20: £370.60)     **5f**     3-30 (3-31)
(Weights raised 2 lb)

| 613 | **Barrys Gamble (76)** (bl) *(TFairhurst)* 6–9–0 ‡3JFanning (7) (lw: sn bhd: rdn ½-wy: swtchd lft over 1f out: r.o wl to ld wl ins fnl f) ............. —**1** |
|---|---|
| 686² | Sigama (USA) **(80)** *(FHLee)* 6–9-2 ‡5NKennedy (3) (led: pushed along 2f out: edgd rt & hdd wl ins fnl f: no ex) ............. 1½.**2** |
| 723 | Sir Tasker **(74)** *(JLHarris)* 4–9-1  DHolland (4) (chsd ldr: swtchd lft ins fnl f: r.o same pce) ............. ½.**3** |
| 669* | Absolutely Nuts **(73)** (Fav) *(BAMcMahon)* 3–8–4  GDuffield (8) (chsd ldrs: rdn over 1f out: kpt on) ............. 1½.**4** |
|  | Absolution **(83)** *(MPNaughton)* 8–9-10  GHind (5) (prom tl outpcd ½-wy: r.o fnl f) ¾.**5** |
| 613⁴ | Samsolom **(67)** *(JBalding)* 4–8-8  JCarroll (6) (lw: effrt ½-wy: kpt on same pce appr fnl f) ............. 1½.**6** |
| 676⁶ | Simmie's Special **(70)** *(RHollinshead)* 4–8–11  RHills (1) (chsd ldrs tl wknd 2f out) ............. 2½.**7** |
| 614 | Miss Siham (IRE) **(64)** *(JBalding)* 3–7–2(2) ‡7ClaireBalding (2) (sn outpcd: effrt ½-wy: n.d) ............. 1½.**8** |
|  | LONG HANDICAP: Miss Siham (IRE) 7-2 |

**6/4** Absolutely Nuts (USA), **4/1** Sigama (USA), **5/1** BARRYS GAMBLE, **11/2** Samsolom, **9/1** Sir Tasker, **14/1** Simmie's Special, **16/1** Absolution, **50/1** Miss Siham (IRE). CSF £23.90, CT £158.51. Tote £5.80: £1.10 £1.10 £2.70 (£11.20). North Cheshire Trading & Storage Ltd (MIDDLEHAM) bred by Gerald Carey. 8 Rn     57.4 sec (U.3)
SF—66/62/59/42/59/37

## 877

ROSEDALE MEDIAN AUCTION STKS (2-Y.O) £2559.20 (£711.20: £341.60)
**6f**     4-00 (4-01)

| 323* | **Key to My Heart (IRE)** *(DMoffatt)* 9-3  JFortune (8) (lw: trckd ldrs: swtchd lft 2f out: led jst ins fnl f: hrd rdn & r.o) ............. —**1** |
|---|---|
| 807* | Finmental (IRE) *(ABailey)* 9-3  AMackay (1) (w ldrs: led over 2f out: hdd jst ins fnl f: kpt on wl) ............. nk.**2** |
| 703* | Northern Bird (Fav) *(BWHills)* 8-12  DHolland (6) (b.hind: led tl over 2f out: rdn & nt qckn fnl f) ............. ¾.**3** |
| 659* | Daaniera (IRE) *(JBerry)* 9-3  JCarroll (12) (chsd ldrs: hung lft thrght: styd on u.p appr fnl f) ............. 2.**4** |
| 568² | Panic Button (IRE) *(MHEasterby)* 8-6  MBirch (5) (sn bhd: r.o wl fnl f) ............. 1.**5** |
| 665* | Nitouche *(PatMitchell)* 8-9 ‡3SO'Gorman (9) (chsd ldrs: rdn & wnt lft over 1f out: sn wknd) ............. nk.**6** |
| 517² | Nominator *(RHollinshead)* 8-11  RHills (3) (chsd ldrs: rdn ½-wy: wknd 2f out) ...... 3.**7** |
| 571² | Warkworth (USA) (bl) *(JWWatts)* 8-11  JLowe (4) (lw: w ldrs over 3f: sn wknd) . nk.**8** |
|  | Master Fiddler *(EWeymes)* 8-11  GHind (13) (leggy: sn outpcd) ............. 2.**9** |
|  | Ho-Joe (IRE) *(AHarrison)* 8-6 ‡5SMaloney (10) (unf: scope: sn bhd) ............. ½.**10** |
| 619 | Robix (IRE) *(CTinkler)* 8-11  TLucas (11) (s.i.s: a bhd) ............. 3½.**11** |
|  | Hallmote *(JGFitzGerald)* 8-11  SWebster (7) (scope: bit bkwd: outpcd ½-wy: sn bhd) ............. 2½.**12** |
| 416 | Our Price *(GMMoore)* 8-11  KFallon (2) (s.i.s: a bhd) ............. 2½.**13** |

**5/4** Northern Bird(op 2/1), **8/1** Panic Button (IRE)(op 5/1), Finmental (IRE)(12/1—7/1), Daaniera (IRE), KEY TO MY HEART (IRE), **9/1** Nominator, **10/1** Nitouche, **14/1** Warkworth (USA), **33/1** Hallmote, Robix (IRE), **50/1** Ors. CSF £67.86, Tote £9.00: £2.20 £2.60 £1.20 (£87.90). Mrs Maureen Pickering (CARTMEL) bred by Miss Fiona Meehan in Ireland. 13 Rn
1m 10.9 (0.6)
SF—43/42/34/31/16/18

**878**     GORDON FOSTER STKS (Mdn 3-Y.O) £2226.00 (£616.00: £294.00)    **1m**    4-30 (4-30)

674² **Milanese** (Fav) *(DMorley)* 8-9 GHind (8) (lw: hld up: effrt over 2f out: hung & ducked lft twice: hrd rdn to ld post) ..................................... —1
Remany *(JRFanshawe)* 8-9 GCarter (1) (lw: hld up: stdy hdwy over 2f out: led ins fnl f: r.o: hdd post) ................................ s.h.2
Vanart *(WWHaigh)* 9-0 ACulhane (5) (w'like: hld up: hdwy appr st: led wl over 1f out tl ins fnl f: kpt on wl) ............................ 1.3
699⁴ Waseela (IRE) *(AAScott)* 8-9 JFortune (3) (trckd ldrs: ev ch & rdn 2f out: wknd 1f out) ........................................ 2¹/₂.4
By Arrangement (IRE) **(72)** *(RGuest)* 8-9 NDay (2) (b.nr hind: chsd ldr tl wknd 2f out) ................................................ 3.5
606 Sir Norman Holt (IRE) **(54)** (bl) *(FHLee)* 9-0 GDuffield (4) (plld hrd: led: clr 5f out: hdd & wknd wl over 1f out) ............. ¹/₂.6
618 Scherzo Impromptu *(TFairhurst)* 8-6 ‡3JFanning (7) (chsd ldrs tl rdn & lost pl over 2f out: sn bhd) ........................ 15.7
Mac the Lad *(DenysSmith)* 9-0 KFallon (6) (unf: s.i.s: sn wl t.o & virtually p.u) ...... 8

**5/4** MILANESE, **3/1** Waseela (IRE), **5/1** Remany, **7/1** Sir Norman Holt (IRE), **8/1** By Arrangement (IRE), **20/1** Vanart, Mac the Lad, **33/1** Scherzo Impromptu. CSF £8.44, Tote £2.50: £1.10 £2.50 £3.10 (£8.60). Sir William McAlpine (NEWMARKET) bred by Mrs William McAlpine. 8 Rn      1m 38 (2)
SF—17/16/18/5/–/–

**879**     DISHFORTH STKS    £2655.40 (£734.40: £350.20)    **6f**      5-00 (5-00)

465 **Medaille D'Or (102)** (v) *(JWPayne)* 4-9-10 GDuffield (6) (lw: w ldrs: led over 1f out: r.o wl) ................................. —1
430⁶ Lee Artiste **(102)** *(PFICole)* 4-9-5 GBaxter (1) (chsd ldrs: outpcd ¹/₂-wy: hdwy over 1f out: kpt on wl) ...................... 2.2
656⁵ Sir Harry Hardman **(104)** (bl) *(FHLee)* 4 9-10 GCarter (8) (lw: w ldrs: shkn up to ld over 2f out: hdd over 1f out: edgd lft & wknd fnl f) ...... 2.3
465⁶ Tamim (USA) **(104)** (Fav) *(HThomsonJones)* 3-8-13 RHills (7) (lw: led: sn pushed along: hdd over 2f out: hung lft & wknd over 1f out) 2.4
Imperial Bid (FR) *(DenysSmith)* 4-9-10 KFallon (3) (lw: sn wl outpcd: hdwy over 1f out: eased nr fin) ......................... 1¹/₂.5
289 Lord Lambson *(RMWhitaker)* 3-8-6 ACulhane (5) (sn wl outpcd: sme hdwy 2f out: n.d) .................................. 2.6
601 Langtonian **(90)** *(JBerry)* 3-8-13 JACarroll (4) (rdn & outpcd ¹/₂-wy: sn bhd: eased whn no ch) ...................... 4.7

**6/4** Tamim (USA), **5/2** Sir Harry Hardman(op 6/4), **9/2** Lee Artiste, **7/1** MEDAILLE D'OR, **14/1** Langtonian, **33/1** Imperial Bid (FR), **40/1** Lord Lambson. CSF £34.19, Tote £8.60: £3.10 £1.80 (£12.30). Mr J. G. K. Borrett (NEWMARKET) bred by Mrs N. V. Fox. 7 Rn      1m 10.2 (equals standard)
SF—62/49/46/27/32/6

**880**     HELMSLEY H'CAP (0-80) £2869.60 (£795.60: £380.80)    **1¹/₂m**      5-30 (5-36)

617² **Checkpoint Charlie (63)** *(JMPEustace)* 7-8-4 ‡7AntoinetteArmes (10) (lw: hld up & bhd: stdy hdwy over 2f out: led 1f out: pushed out) .... —1
688 Vasiliev **(79)** (v) *(JPLeigh)* 4-9-13 DNicholls (2) (lw: hld up: stdy hdwy 3f out: ev ch ins fnl f: kpt on) ................... ¹/₂.2
First Bid **(45)** *(RMWhitaker)* 5–7-7 DaleGibson (6) (trckd ldr: one pce fnl 2f) ... 2¹/₂.3
289³ Arctic Splendour (USA) **(64)** *(PWChapple-Hyam)* 3–7-7 JLowe (4) (lw: trckd ldrs: effrt over 2f out: kpt on same pce) .......... nk.4
617 Talish **(45)** *(TDBarron)* 4–7-4 ‡3JFanning (1) (trckd ldrs: led over 2f out to 1f out: sn wknd) ................................ hd.5
Quip **(45)** *(MPNaughton)* 7–7-7 JakiHouston (8) (reluctant to go to s: led tl over 2f out: wknd over 1f out) .................... 6.6
504 Saint Ciel (USA) **(69)** (Fav) *(FJordan)* 4–9-3 JFortune (9) (lw: trckd ldrs: effrt over 2f out: sn rdn: wknd over 1f out) ...... 2¹/₂.7
Sinclair Lad (IRE) **(63)** *(RHollinshead)* 4–8-11 RHills (5) (hld up: sme hdwy over 2f out: sn wknd) ..................... 2¹/₂.8
688⁵ Pennine Star (IRE) **(65)** *(CWCElsey)* 4–8-13 JCarroll (7) (lw: prom tl lost pl over 4f out: sn wl bhd) ................. 15.9
LONG HANDICAP: First Bid 7-6, Arctic Splendour (USA) 7-0, Quip 6-13.
815³ *Eire Leath-Sceal (7/2)* Withdrawn (lame at s) : not under orders

**3/1** Saint Ciel (USA), **100/30** Arctic Splendour (USA), **7/2** CHECKPOINT CHARLIE, **13/2** Pennine Star (IRE), **11/1** Vasiliev, Sinclair Lad (IRE), **12/1** First Bid, **16/1** Talish, **25/1** Quip. CSF £37.13, CT £378.87. Tote £3.00: £1.10 £2.60 £2.90 (£16.70). Mrs T. R. H. Eustace (NEWMARKET) bred by Airlie Stud and V. O'Donoghue. 9 Rn
2m 32.2 (2.2)
SF—20/42/3/2/–/–

T/Plpt: £150.70 (17.25 Tckts).      WG

## THIRSK (L-H)
### Saturday, May 16th [Firm]
Going Allowance: minus 0.40 sec per fur (F)      Wind: slt half against

Stalls: high

**881**    ELMIRE STKS (Mdn 3-Y.O.F) £2846.00 (£848.00: £404.00: £182.00)
       1½m                             2-15 (2-15)

625³ Awol (Fav) *(HRACecil)* 8-11 KDarley (5) (trckd ldr: shkn up to ld 2f out: r.o wl) .. —1
553   Top Table *(MRStoute)* 8-11 MBirch (4) (hld up: hdwy to chal over 2f out: r.o: nt
                       pce of wnr) ............................................................ 1½.2
     Kate Labelle *(GWragg)* 8-8 ‡³FNorton (6) (lengthy: unf: hld up: effrt over 2f out:
                       r.o: nvr able chal) ................................................ 2.3
732⁶ Dancing Years (USA) (63) *(MRChannon)* 8-11 KFallon (2) (led tl hdd 2f out: kpt
                       on same pce) ..................................................... 1½.4
597³ Dolly Madison (IRE) *(BWHills)* 8-11 GDuffield (1) (lw: trckd ldrs: effrt & n.m.r
                       over 2f out: sn outpcd) ..................................... 1½.5

**8/13** AWOL, **9/2** Top Table, **11/2** Dolly Madison (IRE), **11/1** Kate Labelle, **16/1** Dancing Years (USA). CSF £3.66,
Tote £1.60: £1.20 £1.70 (£2.30). Lord Howard de Walden (NEWMARKET) bred by Lord Howard de Walden. 5 Rn
                                            2m 35.5 (5.5)

**882**    SKIPTON (S) STKS (2-Y.O) £2206.40 (£610.40: £291.20)   **5f**      2-45 (2-47)

759² **Coconut Johnny** (bl) (Jt-Fav) *(GMMoore)* 8-11 KFallon (11) (lw: mde all: clr
                       over 1f out: r.o) .................................................. —1
463⁴ Clangold (Jt-Fav) *(JBerry)* 8-6 JCarroll (10) (s.i.s: sn in tch: kpt on wl fnl f: nvr
                       able chal) ............................................................. 1½.2
665   Dead Calm (Jt-Fav) *(CTinkler)* 8-11 MBirch (4) (lw: in tch: effrt ½-wy: sn chsng
                       wnr & hrd drvn: nt qckn fnl f) ......................... 2.3
     Suitability (IRE) *(PCHaslam)* 8-6 KDarley (7) (cmpt: s.i.s: bhd tl hdwy 2f out: fin
                       strly) ...................................................................... 1.4
286⁵ Yeveed (IRE) *(MHEasterby)* 8-1 ‡⁵SMaloney (5) (mid div tl styd on fnl 2f) ......... nk.5
416   Annie Rose *(TDBarron)* 8-6 AlexGreaves (6) (swtg: chsd ldrs: hdwy u.p 2f out:
                       wknd over 1f out) ............................................. 2½.6
423   The Cut *(MJohnston)* 8-6 RPElliott (1) (spd over 3f) ................................................ 1½.7
323   Sensabo *(MissLAPerratt)* 7-13 ‡⁷RHavlin (2) (outpcd & bhd: sme hdwy fnl f:
                       n.d) ........................................................................ 1½.8
733   Ballaindy (bl) *(WGMReveley)* 8-3 ‡³JFanning (8) (spd 3f: sn wknd) ................. 1½.9
     Cupboard Love *(JBerry)* 8-6 GDuffield (9) (lt-f: unf: dwlt: wl bhd tl sme late
                       hdwy) ...................................................................... 2.10
588★ Petite Lass *(WCarter)* 8-8 ‡⁵NWilliams (3) (spd 3f: wknd qckly) ..................... nk.11

**3/1** Clangold, COCONUT JOHNNY, Dead Calm(op 5/1), **8/1** Annie Rose, Petite Lass, **12/1** Cupboard Love, **16/1**
Suitability (IRE), Yeveed (IRE), **25/1** The Cut, Ballaindy, **33/1** Sensabo. CSF £12.89, Tote £4.40: £1.60 £1.60
£1.40 (£4.50). Crestmart Ltd (MIDDLEHAM) bred by A. C. Birkle. 11 Rn; No bid      60.1 sec (2.4)
                                                 SF—9/–/–/–/–/–

**883**    EASINGWOLD H'CAP (0-90) £3817.50 (£1140.00: £545.00: £247.50)   **1m**   3-20 (3-22)

610   **King of Chance (IRE) (76)** (Fav) *(MrsJRRamsden)* 4-10-0 MBirch (3) (lw: in
                       tch: shkn up ent st: r.o to ld wl ins fnl f) ........ —1
398⁶ Hamadryad (IRE) (61) *(WCarter)* 4-8-13 JCarroll (6) (lw: led after 1f: rdn 2f out:
                       hdd & no ex wl ins fnl f) .................................. 1.2
615² Spanish Verdict (57) *(DenysSmith)* 5-8-9 KFallon (2) (led 1f: chsd ldrs: effrt
                       over 2f out: kpt on one pce) ........................... 1½.3
616⁶ Blue Grit (41) (bl) *(MDods)* 6-7-7 LCharnock (8) (chsd ldrs: rdn ent st: r.o one
                       pce) ....................................................................... 2½.4
670⁴ Euroblake (59) *(TDBarron)* 5-8-11 AlexGreaves (10) (swtg: hld up & bhd: effrt
                       ent st: r.o: too much to do) ............................ 2.5
111   Inseyab (59) *(PCHaslam)* 4-8-8 ‡³JFanning (9) (chsd ldr tl grad wknd fnl 2f) ... 1½.6
684   Batabanoo (70) *(MrsGRReveley)* 3-8-6 KDarley (13) (hld up: hdwy 2f out: too
                       much to do) ........................................................ 2.7
767   North Esk (USA) (86) *(JWWatts)* 3-9-12 JLowe (1) (lw: hld up & bhd: n.d) ........ 4.8
748⁶ Matts Boy (64) *(MissSEHall)* 4-8-13 ‡³FNorton (5) (lw: hld up & bhd: effrt ent st:
                       n.d) ........................................................................ ½.9
766   Reel of Tulloch (IRE) (70) *(PCHaslam)* 3-8-10 DaleGibson (7) (a rr div) .......... 2.10
315   Barney O'Neill (55) *(JJO'Neill)* 6-8-7 TLucas (11) (bit bkwd: mid div tl grad lost
                       pl fnl 3f) ............................................................... 3.11
                     LONG HANDICAP: Blue Grit 7-6.
       *Persian House Withdrawn (spread plate at s) : not under orders*

**4/1** KING OF CHANCE (IRE), **9/2** Hamadryad (IRE), **5/1** Euroblake, **13/2** Spanish Verdict, **8/1** Batabanoo, **12/1** Matts Boy, **14/1** North Esk (USA), **16/1** Inseyab, Blue Grit, **20/1** Reel of Tulloch (IRE), **25/1** Barney O'Neill. CSF £20.16, CT £101.78. Tote £4.80: £1.80 £1.80 £1.70 (£11.80). Mr David Thompson (THIRSK) bred by Ardenode Stud Ltd in Ireland. 11 Rn
1m 36.8 (0.8)
SF—54/36/27/3/15/7

**884**    DIBB LUPTON BROOMHEAD CUP (H'cap) (3-Y-O) (0-80) £4776.00 (£1428.00: £684.00: £312.00)  **7f**
(Weights raised 6 lb)
3-55 (3-58)

| | | |
|---|---|---|
| 678³ | **Battle Colours (IRE) (74)** (Fav) *(SirMarkPrescott)* 9-7 GDuffield (12) (lw: mid div & pushed along appr st: hdwy 2f out: r.o to ld ins fnl f) .. | —1 |
| 401⁶ | Big Hand (IRE) **(68)** *(JWWatts)* 9-1 JLowe (3) (lw: disp ld tl led 3f out: hdd ins fnl f: kpt on wl) | 1.2 |
| 534 | Supreme Boy **(59)** *(PWHarris)* 8-3 ‡³FNorton (6) (lw: mid div: effrt & n.m.r fnl 2f: styd on) | ¹⁄₂.3 |
| 762* | Scottish Park **(73)** *(JPLeigh)* 8-13 ‡⁷JWeaver (4) (a chsng ldrs: ev ch over 2f out: r.o one pce fnl f) | 1¹⁄₂.4 |
| | Breeze Away **(63)** *(RMWhitaker)* 8-10 ACulhane (1) (bit bkwd: a chsng ldrs: kpt on one pce fnl 3f) | 2¹⁄₂.5 |
| 482 | Manbaa (IRE) **(59)** *(HThomsonJones)* 8-6 MBirch (10) (bhd & pushed along appr st: styd on: nrst fin) | 1¹⁄₂.6 |
| | Petastra **(62)** *(MrsJRRamsden)* 8-9 TLucas (7) (bit bkwd: hld up: stdy hdwy 3f out: wknd over 1f out) | hd.7 |
| 591 | Spanish Express **(60)** *(RBoss)* 8-7 JCarroll (15) (effrt ent st: styd on: no imp) .. | hd.8 |
| 397 | Thornton Gate **(59)** *(MHEasterby)* 8-1 ‡⁵SMaloney (5) (chsd ldrs tl wknd over 2f out) | ¹⁄₂.9 |
| 498 | Tahitian **(55)** *(MrsJRRamsden)* 7-9 ‡⁷RHavlin (14) (stdd s: nvr nr to chal) | s.h.10 |
| 767 | Talented Ting (IRE) **(64)** *(PCHaslam)* 8-11 DaleGibson (16) (bit bkwd: a rr div) | 1¹⁄₂.11 |
| 618 | Brambles Way **(59)** *(WLBarker)* 7-13 ‡⁷VHalliday (2) (disp ld 4f: wknd 2f out) | 1.12 |
| 489² | She's Special **(74)** (v) *(MissLAPerratt)* 9-2 ‡⁵CHodgson (9) (chsd ldrs: hrd rdn ent st: sn wknd) | 1.13 |
| | Round by the River **(60)** *(WWHaigh)* 8-7 KFallon (11) (bit bkwd: effrt on ins whn bdly hmpd 2f out: nt rcvr) | 1.14 |

**11/4** BATTLE COLOURS (IRE), **9/2** Scottish Park, **5/1** Big Hand (IRE), **14/1** Spanish Express, Petastra, She's Special, Tahitian, Manbaa (IRE), Thornton Gate, **16/1** Talented Ting (IRE), Breeze Away, **20/1** Ors. CSF £17.04, CT £208.17. Tote £2.80: £1.60 £1.90 £4.80 (£3.50). Mr Garth Insoll (NEWMARKET) bred by Stackallan Stud in Ireland. 14 Rn
1m 24.5 (1.2)
SF—47/38/24/29/18/9

**885**    DICK PEACOCK SPRINT H'CAP (0-85) £3184.00 (£952.00: £456.00: £208.00)  **6f**
4-30 (4-31)

| | | |
|---|---|---|
| 668 | **Furiella (66)** (Fav) *(PCHaslam)* 4–9-3 KDarley (11) (lw: chsd ldrs: led wl over 1f out: hrd rdn & r.o: jst ct: fin 2nd, nk: awrdd r) | —1 |
| | Most Surprising (IRE) **(52)** *(RMWhitaker)* 3–7-7 DaleGibson (6) (a chsng ldrs: effrt & ev ch over 1f out: kpt on wl: fin 3rd, ¹⁄₂l: plcd 2nd) | 2 |
| 668³ | Pretonic **(62)** *(MJohnston)* 4–8-13 RPElliott (13) (lw: mid div: effrt whn hmpd wl over 1f out: r.o wl fnl f: fin 4th, hd: plcd 3rd) | 3 |
| 779 | Red Rosein **(77)** *(CaptJWilson)* 6–10-0 JCarroll (8) (prom ¹⁄₂-way: edgd rt over 1f out: r.o u.p to ld cl home: fin 1st: disq: plcd 4th) | 4 |
| 570 | Glenfield Greta **(66)** *(PSFelgate)* 4–9-0 ‡³FNorton (12) (mid div tl hdwy over 1f out: r.o nr fin) | nk.5 |
| | Great Lord (IRE) **(64)** *(JWWatts)* 3–8-5 JLowe (4) (h.d.w: outpcd after 2f: styd on fnl 2f: nvr rchd ldrs) | 1¹⁄₂.6 |
| | Prince Belfort **(69)** *(MPNaughton)* 4–8-13 ‡⁷JWeaver (14) (cl up: slt ld 2f out: sn hdd & grad wknd) | nk.7 |
| 613³ | Catherines Well **(63)** *(MWEasterby)* 9–9-0 TLucas (5) (a chsng ldrs: effrt ¹⁄₂-wy: outpcd fnl f) | 1¹⁄₂.8 |
| 542 | Nevada Mix **(49)** *(MissLAPerratt)* 8–7-7 ‡⁷RHavlin (3) (in tch: effrt ¹⁄₂-wy: sn btn) | 1¹⁄₂.9 |
| 668 | Orient Air **(54)** (v) *(TDBarron)* 4–8-5 AlexGreaves (9) (led 4f: sn wknd) | 1.10 |
| | Northern Spark **(71)** *(CWThornton)* 4–9-8 MBirch (2) (bit bkwd: n.d) | 1¹⁄₂.11 |
| 752 | Filicaia **(49)** *(DonEnricoIncisa)* 6–8-0 KimTinkler (7) (s.i.s: a bhd) | 1.12 |
| 615 | Farmer Jock **(65)** *(MrsNMacauley)* 10–9-2 MTebbutt (1) (sn bhd) | ³⁄₄.13 |
| 764³ | Madam Petoski **(61)** *(FHLee)* 3–8-2 ACulhane (10) (plld hrd: lost tch fr ¹⁄₂-wy) | 1¹⁄₂.14 |

LONG HANDICAP: Most Surprising (IRE) 7-6.

*Stewards Enquiry: Red Rosein disq. (interference to Pretonic). Carroll suspended 25-28/5/92 (careless riding).*

**7/2** FURIELLA, **4/1** Pretonic(op 5/2), Catherines Well, **10/1** Glenfield Greta, Madam Petoski, **12/1** Most Surprising (IRE), **16/1** Orient Air, Farmer Jock, Great Lord (IRE), Red Rosein, **20/1** Ors. Prince Belfort, **25/1** Nevada Mix, **33/1** Filicaia, Northern Spark, Farmer Jock. CSF £43.98, CT £161.10. Tote £5.60: £2.00 £3.30 £1.80 (£26.90). Mr W. J. Hall (MIDDLEHAM) bred by Langham Hall Bloodstock. 14 Rn
1m 11.3 (1.1)
SF—44/32/2/21/21/6/13

**886**    E.B.F. CARLTON MINIOTT STKS (Mdn 2-Y.O.F) £2542.90 (£704.40: £336.70)
       5f                                                  5-00 (5-05)

         **Petite Epaulette** *(WJarvis)* 8-11 MTebbutt (3) (cmpt: unf: lw: hld up: hdwy to ld
           wl over 1f out: rdn & r.o wl) ................................................. —1
         Willshe Gan *(DenysSmith)* 8-11 KFallon (1) (cmpt: scope: bit bkwd: a.p: effrt &
           ev ch over 1f out: r.o wl) ................................................. 2.2
         Palm Chat *(LMCumani)* 8-4 ‡7JWeaver (5) (cmpt: unf: a chsng ldrs: rdn over 2f
           out: r.o) ................................................. 3.3
    770 Hotaria *(RMWhitaker)* 8-11 ACulhane (8) (trckd ldrs: hdwy & ev ch wl over 1f
           out: hrd rdn & nt qckn) ................................................. 2.4
    701² Rahon (IRE) **(Fav)** *(PWChapple-Hyam)* 8-11 MBirch (2) (cl up: led over 2f out tl
           wl over 1f out: sn btn) ................................................. 2.5
         Sharisa *(JBerry)* 8-11 JCarroll (6) (lt-f: unf: cl up tl outpcd fnl 2f) ................. ¾.6
         Bluebella *(MrsPABarker)* 8-11 JLowe (7) (leggy: scope: bit bkwd: dwlt: a
           outpcd & bhd) ................................................. 2¹/₂.7
         Selvole *(MissLAPerratt)* 8-8 ‡3JFanning (4) (cmpt: bit bkwd: led tl hdd over 2f
           out: sn btn) ................................................. hd.8

**13/8** Rahon (IRE), **2/1** PETITE EPAULETTE, **7/1** Palm Chat, **8/1** Hotaria, Sharisa, **14/1** Willshe Gan, **50/1** Ors. CSF
£26.16, Tote £3.70: £1.50 £2.60 £1.80 (£50.70). Mrs F. G. Allen (NEWMARKET) bred by Mrs F. G. Allen. 8 Rn
                                                            59.6 sec (1.9)
                                                         SF—19/11/–/–/–/–

**887**    'BET WITH THE TOTE' H'CAP (0-100) £5299.00 (£1582.00: £756.00: £343.00)
       7f                                                  5-30 (5-35)

                          (Weights raised 15 lb)
         **Bold Angel (72)** *(MHEasterby)* 5–9-4 MBirch (9) (trckd ldrs: smooth hdwy to ld
           wl over 1f out: snkn up & r.o) ................................................. —1
         Spanish Grandee (USA) **(75)** *(PWChapple-Hyam)* 4–9-4 ‡3FNorton (5) (b.off
           hind: hld up: effrt over 2f out: styd on wl fnl f) ................................ 2.2
    398⁴ Ikteshaf **(73)** *(BHanbury)* 4–8-12 ‡7VBray (8) (b: hld up: c wd ent st: rdn 2f out:
           kpt on one pce) ................................................. 2.3
    670* Brown Fairy (USA) **(68)** *(MrsNMacauley)* 4–9-0 MTebbutt (1) (hld up & bhd:
           effrt on outside over 2f out: nvr rchd ldrs) ................................. ¾.4
    670² Wild Prospect **(68)** *(CTinkler)* 4–8-9 ‡5SMaloney (6) (lw: w ldr: rdn over 2f out:
           btn over 1f out) ................................................. ¹/₂.5
    667* Star Connection **(70)** **(Fav)** *(RMWhitaker)* 4–9-2 ACulhane (3) (chsd ldrs: rdn
           over 2f out: no imp) ................................................. 1¹/₂.6
    768 Super Benz **(78)** *(TFairhurst)* 6–9-7 ‡3JFanning (2) (lw: led tl hdd wl over 1f out:
           sn btn) ................................................. 5.7
         *Canaan Valley Withdrawn (ref to enter stalls) : not under orders*

**4/1** Star Connection, **9/2** Ikteshaf, Spanish Grandee (USA)(op 9/4), **5/1** Brown Fairy (USA), Wild Prospect, **13/2**
BOLD ANGEL, **10/1** Super Benz. CSF £32.06, CT £129.28. Tote £10.10: £3.30 £2.60 (£29.00). Mr A. M. Wragg
(MALTON) bred by A. M. Wragg. 7 Rn
                                                          1m 24.5 (1.2)
                                                 SF—44/38/26/26/19/21

T/Plpt: £42.30 (121.25 Tckts).                                                   AA

## 793—HAMILTON (R-H)

### Saturday, May 16th [Good, Good to soft patches]

Going Allowance: St: 0.05 sec per fur; Rnd: 0.20 sec per fur (G)        Wind: nil

Stalls: low

**888**    LEGGAT PLANT H'CAP (0-70) (Amateurs) £1716.00 (£476.00: £228.00)
       5f 4y                                                  6-45 (6-51)

                          (Weights raised 4 lb)
    685 **Just Bob (63)** (bl) *(SEKettlewell)* 3–10-3 ‡7MrsDKettlewell (11) (hdwy ¹/₂-wy: led
           2f out: r.o wl fnl f) ................................................. —1
    455⁵ Ballad Dancer **(54)** *(EJAlston)* 7–10-5 ‡5MrWilkinson (5) (s.i.s: bhd: hdwy 2f
           out: styd on fnl f) ................................................. 2.2
    748³ Prime Mover **(60)** (v) *(DBurchell)* 4–10-11 ‡5MrNMiles (8) (dwlt: bhd: gd
           hdwy 2f out: r.o ins fnl f) ................................................. ¹/₂.3
    661³ Tumbling (USA) **(44)** (Jt-Fav) *(RAllan)* 4–9-7 ‡7MissPRobson (9) (in tch: effrt 2f
           out: styd on: nt pce to chal) ................................................. 2¹/₂.4
    796 Diet **(65)** *(MissLAPerratt)* 6–11-0 ‡7MrRHale (13) (a cl up: rdn 2f out: nt qckn) .. hd.5
    660⁴ Danzig Lad (USA) **(43)** *(MPNaughton)* 4–9-6 ‡7MrRGreen (2) (drvn along &
           outpcd ¹/₂-wy: styd on fnl f: nt rch ldrs) ................................. 1¹/₂.6

7945 Francis Ann (53) *(MissLAPerratt)* 4–10-9 MissLPerratt (6) (cl up: ev ch 2f out: sn rdn & btn) .................................................. 1½.7

7524 Jive Music (37) (bl) *(NBycroft)* 6–9-0 ‡7MissABycroft (1) (cl up stands' side: rdn & wknd 2f out) .................................................. nk.8

7526 Last Straw (37) *(AWJones)* 4–9-7 MissIDWJones (4) (in tch: effrt 2f out: no imp) nk.9
Choice Lot (49) *(JJO'Neill)* 5–9-12 ‡7MissSNichol (12) (led tl hdd 2f out: sn wknd) .................................................. 1½.10

265 Saladan Knight (58) *(JGFitzGerald)* 7–10-9 ‡5MrsSEasterby (10) (chsd ldrs: rdn ½-wy: sn wknd) .................................................. 2.11

1886 Galaxy Express (42) *(GHEden)* 4–9-5 ‡7MrsSEden (3) (chsd ldrs to ½-wy: sn bhd) .................................................. ½.12

541 Revel (38) (bl) *(LLungo)* 4–9-3 ‡5MrsLLeggat (7) (in tch: bhd fr ½-wy: eased fnl f)2½.13

LONG HANDICAP: Jive Music 9-3.

**5/1** Prime Mover(op 8/1), Tumbling (USA), **11/2** Last Straw(8/1—5/1), **6/1** Francis Ann, **9/1** Ballad Dancer, **10/1** Jive Music, **11/1** Diet, **12/1** Saladan Knight(op 5/1), **14/1** Galaxy Express, **20/1** Danzig Lad (USA), JUST BOB, **33/1** Ors. CSF £170.50, CT £946.68. Tote £33.60: £11.90 £6.40 £2.20 (£54.30). Mr J. Fotherby (MIDDLEHAM) bred by Mrs D. Whittingham. 13 Rn
62.7 sec (4.4)
SF—34/28/32/4/24/–

**889** LUDDON CONSTRUCTION CLAIMING STKS (Mdn 2-Y.O) £1674.00 (£464.00: £222.00)
6f 5y 7-15 (7-18)

7593 **Amerigue** (Fav) *(MissSEHall)* 7-12 ‡5NKennedy (15) (racd far side: a chsng ldrs: hrd drvn to ld wl ins fnl f) .................................................. —1

Trevorsninepoints *(NTinkler)* 7-10(8) ‡7MHunt (13) (racd far side: mde most: hung bdly lft fr wl over 2f out: hdd & no ex cl home) .................................................. ½.2

Steven's Dream (IRE) *(JWhite)* 7-10 ‡5RPrice (5) (cl up: ev ch 2f out: nt qckn) 3½.3
759 Vardy (IRE) (bl) *(PCHaslam)* 8-5 DaleGibson (4) (chsd ldrs: rdn 2f out: one pce) 2.4
Kesanta *(WGMTurner)* 7-9 PBurke (14) (cl up far side: ev ch 2f out: no ex) ....... ½.5
759 Brackenthwaite *(TDBarron)* 8-1 AlexGreaves (8) (hdwy & swtchd 2f out: styd on: nt rch ldrs) .................................................. ½.6

561 Hazy Dazy *(WGMTurner)* 7-5(1) ‡7AGarth (9) (effrt & swtchd 2f out: no imp) ..... 2½.7
769 Jersey Bob (IRE) *(JSWainwright)* 8-0 ‡7GParkin (10) (chsd ldrs: rdn & one pce fr ½-wy) .................................................. 3½.8

6196 My Godson *(WJPearce)* 8-9(3) DNicholls (12) (in tch: drvn along ½-wy: sn btn) 4.9
Hohne Garrison *(JWhite)* 7-13 ‡7CAvery (7) (s.i.s: sme late hdwy: n.d) ............. ½.10
659 Lucky Owl *(PMonteith)* 7-6 ‡7DarrenMoffatt (11) (unruly s: dwlt: a bhd) ............. 3.11
6595 Duke of Dreams *(MrsGRReveley)* 8-10 KDarley (6) (in tch: drvn along 2f out: sn wknd) .................................................. ½.12

619 Our Mica *(JBerry)* 8-10 LCharnock (3) (sn pushed along: bhd fr ½-wy) ......... hd.13
759 Matthew David *(MBrittain)* 7-12 ‡7DWright (2) (s.i.s: a wl bhd: sddle slipped) .... 5.14

**2/1** AMERIGUE, **9/2** My Godson, **5/1** Duke of Dreams(op 3/1), **11/2** Steven's Dream (IRE), **7/1** Our Mica, **8/1** Hohne Garrison, **12/1** Vardy (IRE), **16/1** Matthew David, **20/1** Jersey Bob (IRE), **25/1** Lucky Owl, Hazy Dazy, Kesanta, **33/1** Trevorsninepoints, **66/1** Brackenthwaite. CSF £68.56, Tote £3.30: £1.60 £14.50 £2.60 (£217.60). Miss S. E. Hall (MIDDLEHAM) bred by Mrs T. Hall. 14 Rn
1m 15.7 (5.7)

**890** PETER YARWOOD STKS (Mdn 3-Y.O) £1660.00 (£460.00: £220.00) 6f 5y 7-45 (7-47)

6693 Music Dancer (Fav) *(JBerry)* 9-0 LCharnock (8) (a cl up: led wl over 1f out: drvn out) .................................................. —1

366 Optical (IRE) (60) *(MPNaughton)* 8-7 ‡7JWeaver (6) (cl up tl rdn & outpcd ½-wy: swtchd appr fnl f: styd on wl nr fin) .................................................. hd.2
Treasure Time (IRE) (54) *(JWhite)* 8-9 DaleGibson (2) (led to ½-wy: prom: kpt on u.p fnl f) .................................................. 2½.3

6856 Baladee Pet (61) *(MrsVAAconley)* 9-0 PBurke (4) (cl up: led ½-wy: hdd wl over 1f out: wknd ins fnl f) .................................................. 2.4
669 Chocolate Mint *(CWThornton)* 8-9 KDarley (7) (chsd ldrs: rdn & ev ch appr fnl f: one pce) .................................................. 1½.5
727 Jalore *(PABlockley)* 8-7 ‡7GParkin (3) (chsd ldrs: drvn along ½-wy: no ex fnl 2f) 1½.6
6694 Manuleader (60) (bl) *(WJPearce)* 9-0 DNicholls (10) (in tch: rdn ½-wy: ev ch 2f out: sn btn) .................................................. 2.7

468 Baie Petite *(AWJones)* 8-9 KFallon (1) (in tch: rdn & wknd ½-wy) .................................................. ½.8
7625 Speedy Classic (USA) *(CTinkler)* 9-0 MBirch (9) (drvn along ½-wy: wknd 2f out) 2½.9
560 Vis-a-Vis (USA) *(DBurchell)* 9-0 AlexGreaves (5) (in tch: bhd fnl 2f) .................................................. 1½.10

**15/8** MUSIC DANCER, **5/2** Speedy Classic (USA), **11/2** Manuleader, **13/2** Chocolate Mint, **12/1** Optical (IRE), **14/1** Treasure Time (IRE)(10/1—16/1), **16/1** Baladee Pet, **20/1** Vis-a-Vis, **33/1** Jalore, **100/1** Baie Petite. CSF £23.56, Tote £2.60: £1.50 £2.10 £3.90 (£9.20). Heathavon Stables Limited (COCKERHAM) bred by Heathavon Stables Ltd. 10 Rn
1m 16.9 (6.9)

**891**     DALLFIELD CONSTRUCTION (S) H'CAP (0-60) £1814.00 (£504.00: £242.00)
       1m 1f 36y

8-15 (8-17)

6886 **Flying Down to Rio (IRE) (51)** *(MPNaughton)* 4–9–3 ‡7JWeaver (6) (a chsng ldrs: led wl over 1f out: r.o wl fnl f) ............................................. —1

796 Aragon Ayr **(51)** *(PMonteith)* 4–9–3(5) ‡7ADobbin (8) (a.p: led wl over 3f out: hdd wl over 1f out: nt qckn) ............................................. 3½.2

4196 Golden Beau **(31)** *(AHarrison)* 10–8–4(5) KFallon (14) (hdwy to chase ldrs ent st: rdn over 2f out: styd on same pce) ............................................. 2½.3

763 Errema **(47)** *(CTinkler)* 7–9–6 MBirch (9) (bhd: stdy hdwy over 2f out: styd on: nvr able chal) ............................................. ½.4

6646 Queens Tour **(36)** *(MBrittain)* 7–8–2‡7DWright (13) (bhd tl styd on fnl 2f: nvr rchd ldrs) ............................................. 3½.5

7654 Miss Parkes **(51)** *(JBerry)* 3–8–10 LCharnock (17) (chsd ldrs: drvn along 3f out: sn wknd) ............................................. ½.6

5254 Lady Baraka (IRE) **(45)** (Fav) *(MissGayKelleway)* 4–9–4 AMackay (7) (mid div: rdn ent st: one pce fnl 2f) ............................................. 2½.7

505 Lucky Barnes **(42)** (bl) *(PABlockley)* 5–8–8 ‡7GParkin (10) (prom: rdn ent st: wknd 2f out) ............................................. 2½.8

Design Wise **(30)** *(DMoffatt)* 8–7–10 ‡7DarrenMoffatt (15) (nvr trbld ldrs) ............................................. 2½.9

Young India **(47)** *(DBurchell)* 5–9–6 AlexGreaves (12) (led tl hdd wl over 3f out: eased whn btn fnl f) ............................................. 1½.10

At Peace **(53)** *(JWhite)* 6–9–7 ‡5RPrice (16) (in tch tl rdn & wknd over 2f out) .. 2.11

7655 Victor Romeo **(55)** (bl) *(WJPearce)* 3–9–0 DNicholls (5) (in tch: drvn along 3f out: sn wknd) ............................................. nk.12

575 Saint Bene't (IRE) **(46)** *(PCHaslam)* 4–9–5 DaleGibson (11) (a bhd) ............... 1½.13

748 Cardea Castle (IRE) **(30)** (v) *(BEllison)* 4–7–10 ‡7MHunt (18) (a in rr) ............ 3½.14

448 Stag Night **(45)** (v) *(CTinkler)* 3–8–4 KDarley (3) (prom: rdn & ev ch 3f out: wknd qckly) ............................................. 4.15

748 Red Tempest (IRE) **(35)** (bl) *(LLungo)* 4–8–1 ‡7RHavlin (2) (prom tl wknd qckly ent st) ............................................. 16

Brilliant Disguise **(59)** *(PMonteith)* 3–8–13 ‡5NKennedy (1) (prom early: sn lost pl: t.o) ............................................. 17

6636 Motley **(43)** (bl) *(WGMTurner)* 4–9–2 PBurke (4) (w ldrs tl wknd qckly ent st: t.o) 18

9/2 Lady Baraka (IRE), 5/1 At Peace, 6/1 FLYING DOWN TO RIO (IRE)(op 4/1), Errema, 10/1 Miss Parkes(op 6/1), 12/1 Queens Tour, Golden Beau, Saint Bene't (IRE), 14/1 Cardea Castle (IRE), 16/1 Aragon Ayr, 20/1 Young India, Stag Night, Victor Romeo, 25/1 Red Tempest (IRE), 33/1 Design Wise, Brilliant Disguise, Motley, 50/1 Lucky Barnes. CSF £97.50, CT £1,056.83. Tote £9.50: £3.10 £6.20 £3.10 £2.30 (£160.30). Mr W. J. Kelly (RICHMOND) bred by Tsarina Stud in Ireland. 18 Rn; No bid
2m 1 (6.7)
SF—29/18/–/11/–/–

**892**     GEORGE JAMES PLANT MEDIAN AUCTION STKS (Mdn 3-Y.O) £1478.00 (£408.00: £194.00)    1½m 17y

8-45 (8-48)

4182 **White Willow** *(MrsGRReveley)* 8–10 KDarley (3) (mde all: r.o wl fnl 2f: clr whn eased nr fin) ............................................. —1

5772 Suez Canal (IRE) (Fav) *(PWChapple-Hyam)* 8–10 MBirch (2) (trckd wnr: rdn 3f out: nt qckn fnl 2f) ............................................. 3½.2

547 Litho Bold Flasher **(52)** *(WJPearce)* 8–7 LCharnock (1) (chsd ldrs: rdn 4f out: sn outpcd) ............................................. 4.3

1/3 Suez Canal (IRE), 95/40 WHITE WILLOW, 50/1 Litho Bold Flasher. CSF £3.41, Tote £2.80 (£1.10). Mrs H. North (SALTBURN) bred by Gainsborough Stud Management Ltd. 3 Rn
2m 45.4 (13.4)

**893**     CONTRACTORS MECHANICAL PLANT ENGINEERS (Glasgow Branch) H'CAP (0-70) £1861.00 (£516.00: £247.00)    1m 5f 9y

9-15 (9-17)

377 **Persuasive (60)** *(MissLAPerratt)* 5–9–4 DaleGibson (5) (hld up & bhd: hdwy ent st: led 2f out: jst hld on) ............................................. —1

7602 Bridge Player **(42)** (Fav) *(DMoffatt)* 5–7–7 ‡7DarrenMoffatt (3) (a chsng ldrs: chal appr fnl f: styd on: jst failed) ............................................. s.h.2

5752 Grey Commander **(43)** *(MBrittain)* 4–8–1 KDarley (2) (a.p: rdn & ev ch 2f out: kpt on same pce) ............................................. 1½.3

3125 Northants **(47)** *(WStorey)* 6–8–5 AlexGreaves (10) (hld up & bhd: rdn 3f out: styd on fnl 2f: nvr rchd ldrs) ............................................. 1.4

7614 Glastondale **(39)** *(TDBarron)* 6–7–11 AMackay (11) (led tl hdd 2f out: one pce) 1½.5

Lumberjack (USA) **(70)** *(JGFitzGerald)* 8–10–0 KFallon (12) (hld up & bhd: styd on fnl 3f: nt pce to chal) ............................................. ¾.6

664 Lord Advocate **(43)** *(MPNaughton)* 4–8–1 JakiHouston (8) (bhd: jnd ldrs ent st: ev ch wl over 2f out: sn rdn: btn wl over 1f out) ............................................. 3½.7

Mac Rambler **(35)** *(NBycroft)* 5-7-7 LCharnock (7) (bhd: effrt ent st: no imp fnl 3f) ......................................................................................... 2.8

358 Sunset Reins Free **(43)** (v) *(EJAlston)* 7-7-10 ‡⁵NKennedy (13) (bhd: sme hdwy u.p over 2f out: n.d) .............................................. nk.9

512 Haut-Brion (IRE) **(65)** *(PWChapple-Hyam)* 3-8-4⁽¹⁾ MBirch (4) (prom tl wknd over 2f out) ................................................ 6.10

683³ Malenoir (USA) **(58)** (v) *(WJPearce)* 4-9-2 DNicholls (9) (chsd ldrs: drvn along 3f out: wknd appr fnl f) .................................. nk.11

76 Free Minx **(52)** *(MrsVAAconley)* 6-8-10 PBurke (6) (a bhd) .......................................... 12

Alpha Helix **(42)** (v) *(MissLAPerratt)* 9-7-7⁽⁷⁾ ‡⁷RHavlin (1) (mid div: wknd ent st) . 13
LONG HANDICAP: Mac Rambler 7-0, Alpha Helix 7-5.

**11/4** Bridge Player, **11/2** Malenoir (USA), **6/1** Lumberjack (USA), **7/1** Glastondale, **9/1** PERSUASIVE(op 6/1), Haut-Brion (IRE), **12/1** Northants(op 9/2), Grey Commander, **14/1** Sunset Reins Free(8/1—16/1), **16/1** Free Minx, Lord Advocate, **20/1** Mac Rambler, **33/1** Alpha Helix. CSF £34.60, CT £290.74. Tote £18.90: £5.20 £1.40 £2.40 (£60.80). Mr W. G. McHarg (AYR) bred by Waverton Stud Ltd. 13 Rn
2m 56 (10.3)
SF—27/1/6/8/–/26

T/Plpt: £277.10 (5.35 Tckts). GB

---

## 772-LINGFIELD (L-H)
### Saturday, May 16th [Firm]
Going Allowance: minus 0.15 sec per fur (F) Wind: almost nil

Stalls: high

**894** CONFERENCE STKS (Mdn) £1380.00 (£380.00: £180.00) **6f** 6-10 (6-12)

242 **Lifetime Fame (70)** *(JWPayne)* 3-9-0 RCochrane (2) (a.p: led over 2f out: hrd rdn over 1f out: r.o wl) ..................................... —1

620⁴ Noble Pet **(75)** (Fav) *(PJMakin)* 3-9-0 BRaymond (9) (lw: a.p: hrd rdn over 1f out: unable qckn) ............................... 3.2

Sylvan Breeze **(90)** *(PMitchell)* 4-9-10 MRoberts (7) (led over 3f: nt r.o) ........... ¾.3

591⁴ Our Rita *(PAKelleway)* 3-8-9 PRobinson (4) (a.p: one pce fnl 2f) ................. ¾.4

445 Mansber (IRE) **(54)** *(PatMitchell)* 3-8-11 ‡³SO'Gorman (8) (nvr nr to chal) ...... 7.5

408 Tulapet *(SDow)* 3-8-4 ‡⁵RPerham (3) (spd 3f) ......................................... 1½.6

Flying Hen *(WJHaggas)* 3-8-9 NDay (5) (b.hind: leggy: bit bkwd: a bhd) .......... ½.7

Everglades (IRE) *(RCharlton)* 4-9-10 SRaymont (6) (prom 4f) ......................... ¾.8

Trioming *(APJones)* 6-9-10 SWhitworth (1) (bkwd: dwlt: a bhd) ....................... 1½.9

620 Hinton Harry (IRE) *(SMellor)* 3-9-0 DanaMellor (10) (a bhd) ....................... 3½.10

**7/4** Noble Pet, **7/2** Sylvan Breeze, **5/1** Everglades (IRE)(4/1—6/1), **13/2** LIFETIME FAME, **12/1** Our Rita, Flying Hen(op 6/1), **33/1** Tulapet, Trioming, **40/1** Hinton Harry (IRE), **50/1** Mansber (IRE). CSF £16.91, Tote £9.80: £2.10 £1.10 £1.80 (£9.10). Mr Ettore Landi (NEWMARKET) bred by Woodditton Stud Ltd. 10 Rn
1m 10.93 (2.33)
SF—36/24/31/13/–/–

**895** WILLIAM HILL RAPID RACELINE CLAIMING STKS £1884.00 (£524.00: £252.00)
1m 3f 106y 6-40 (6-40)

580* **Abingdon Flyer (IRE) (67)** (bl) (Fav) *(RHannon)* 4-8-11 MRoberts (10) (lw: 5th st: hrd rdn over 1f out: led wl ins fnl f: r.o wl) ..................... —1

Marchman **(44)** *(JSKing)* 7-9-0 TRogers (14) (bit bkwd: s.s: hdwy over 5f out: 3rd st: ev ch ins fnl f: unable qckn) ................. 2.2

708 Arrastra **(67)** *(IABalding)* 4-9-0 RCochrane (8) (lw: a.p: led 5f out: clr over 3f out: hdd ins fnl f: one pce) ......................... nk.3

The Last Empress (IRE) **(70)** *(PFICole)* 4-8-8 CRutter (2) (hdwy over 3f out: one pce fnl 2f) .................................................. 4.4

525 Cordillero *(AMoore)* 6-8-5 CandyMorris (6) (b: a.p: led over 5f out: sn hdd: 2nd st: wknd over 2f out) ................................... 2.5

800 Glassblower **(74)** *(RAkehurst)* 5-8-11 JWilliams (1) (lw: nvr nr to chal) ........... hd.6

586⁵ Prince Lyphard **(RAkehurst)** 6-8-4 ‡⁵RPerham (7) (led 6f: 4th st: wknd over 3f out) .......................................................... 4.7

Vision of Wonder **(25)** *(JSKing)* 8-8-7 DanaMellor (4) (nvr nrr) ....................... 2.8

580 Sporting Weekend (FR) *(DSasse)* 5-8-10 ‡⁷StephenDavies (12) (a bhd) ........... 1.9

Muirfield Village **(44)** *(SDow)* 6-7-13 ‡⁷MJermy (9) (bkwd: bhd fnl 4f) ............. hd.10

580 Armashocker *(DSasse)* 4-8-8 ‡³SO'Gorman (13) (6th st: wknd over 3f out) ... 3½.11

409 Midday Show (USA) **(63)** *(JRJenkins)* 5-8-11 SWhitworth (3) (prom 7f) ......... 2½.12

**13/8** ABINGDON FLYER (IRE), **11/2** Glassblower, Arrastra, **6/1** The Last Empress (IRE), **7/1** Midday Show (USA)(op 12/1), **20/1** Prince Lyphard, Muirfield Village, **25/1** Marchman, **33/1** Ors. CSF £36.64, Tote £2.60: £1.20 £9.00 £2.00 (£82.00). Mr J. A. Nichols (MARLBOROUGH) bred by Grange Thoroughbreds in Ireland. 12 Rn
2m 27.45 (5.45)
SF—26/25/24/10/3/8

**896**     WILLIAM BETCALL H'CAP (3-Y.O) (0-70) £2180.20 (£607.20: £292.60)
    **1¼m**     7-10 (7-12)

498[2]  **Glide Path (USA) (69)** (Fav) *(JWHills)* 9-6 MHills (13) (hdwy 4f out: 3rd st: led wl over 1f out: drvn out) .................................................................. —1

    **Deevee (43)** *(CJBenstead)* 7-8[(1)] TyroneWilliams (14) (bit bkwd: dwlt: hdwy 3f out: hrd rdn & ev ch ins fnl f: r.o) ...................................... 1.2

628[4]  Alcoy (IRE) (62) *(PAKelleway)* 8-13 DHolland (10) (5th st: n.m.r wl over 1f out: hrd rdn: unable qckn) ........................................................... 4.3

684  Miss Pin Up (49) *(PatMitchell)* 7-11 ‡3DBiggs (8) (hdwy over 2f out: one pce) .... 3.4

    Amatorial (69) *(SirMarkPrescott)* 9-6 CNutter (6) (swtg: nvr nr to chal) ............. ½.5

783[6]  Master Hyde (USA) (59) *(PMitchell)* 8-10 MRoberts (12) (2nd st: wknd over 2f out) ............................................................................................. 2½.6

604  Horizontale (50) *(CEBrittain)* 7-10 ‡5BDoyle (11) (led 7f out tl wl over 1f out: sn wknd) ........................................................................................ 2½.7

524[3]  King's Guest (IRE) (62) *(GAPritchard-Gordon)* 8-13 RCochrane (2) (led 2f: 6th st: wknd over 3f out) ................................................................... 2½.8

776★  High Post (49) *(DMarks)* 8-0 BCrossley (7) (rdn thrght: a bhd) ......................... 2.9

    Ragtime Song (50) *(RAkehurst)* 8-1 NAdams (1) (a bhd) .............................. 2.10

136★  Admirals Secret (USA) (60) *(CFWall)* 8-11 NDay (4) (lw: a bhd) ................ 1½.11

    Marvelous Molly (70) *(IABalding)* 9-4 ‡3SO'Gorman (5) (led 8f out to 7f out: 4th st: wknd over 3f out) ........................................................................ 7.12

          LONG HANDICAP: Deevee 7-5.

**9/4** GLIDE PATH (USA), **11/2** Alcoy (IRE), **7/1** High Post, **8/1** Admirals Secret (USA), Amatorial, **9/1** King's Guest (IRE), **10/1** Master Hyde (USA)(7/1—14/1), **12/1** Miss Pin Up, **14/1** Marvelous Molly, **33/1** Ors. CSF £63.72, CT £339.31. Tote £3.50: £1.40 £9.60 £1.90 (£165.00). The Jampot Partnership (LAMBOURN) bred by John T. L. Jones Jnr. & Robert S. Folsom in USA. 12 Rn
2m 7.70 (4.70)
SF—44/16/27/5/27/12

**897**     G.M.BENEFIT CONSULTANT H'CAP (0-70) £1730.00 (£480.00: £230.00)
    **5f**     7-40 (7-42)

121  **Catalani (48)** *(TJNaughton)* 7-8-6 DHolland (15) (b: b.nr hind: gd hdwy over 1f out: hrd rdn ins fnl f: led last strides) ............................................ —1

596  Lucy Dancer (IRE) (54) *(CGCox)* 4-8-12 AClark (14) (hdwy over 1f out: hrd rdn & ev ch wl ins fnl f: r.o wl) ............................................................. s.h.2

775[5]  Tauber (59) *(PatMitchell)* 8-9-0 ‡3DBiggs (3) (a.p: led over 1f out: hrd rdn: hdd last strides) ...................................................................................... hd.3

696  Miss Precocious (39) (v) *(DShaw)* 4-7-6[(4)] ‡5BDoyle (1) (b: s.s: hdwy over 1f out: r.o ins fnl f) .............................................................................. 1.4

    Fay's Song (IRE) (72) *(RAkehurst)* 4-9-9 ‡7LCarter (10) (swtg: hdwy 2f out: r.o ins fnl f) .......................................................................................... hd.5

731  Cronk's Quality (48) *(DCJermy)* 9-8-6 RCochrane (2) (hdwy over 1f out: r.o) .. nk.6

685[3]  The Noble Oak (IRE) (58) (bl) *(MMcCormack)* 4-9-2 WNewnes (4) (lw: a.p: hrd rdn & ev ch over 1f out: r.o) .......................................................... s.h.7

594★  Savalaro (56) *(JFfitch-Heyes)* 3-8-5 MRoberts (8) (led over 1f: rdn over 1f out: r.o) ...................................................................................................... nk.8

706[4]  L'Ete (IRE) (57) (Fav) *(PMitchell)* 4-8-12 ‡3SO'Gorman (11) (a.p: ev ch over 1f out: r.o) ............................................................................................ hd.9

570  Petitesse (55) *(GBlum)* 4-8-13 AShoults (12) (prom over 3f) ........................ 1½.10

735  Stocktina (41) *(RJHodges)* 5-7-10[(1)] ‡3TSprake (7) (prom over 3f) ................ s.h.11

735  Greetland Rock (48) *(PHowling)* 4-8-6 JWilliams (5) (outpcd) ....................... ½.12

    Kelly's Kite (35) *(HJCollingridge)* 4-7-7 NAdams (9) (outpcd) ..................... ¾.13

706  Tachyon Park (45) (v) *(PHowling)* 10-8-3 BCrossley (16) (lw: outpcd) ............ ¾.14

    Tippling (USA) (36) *(PBurgoyne)* 5-7-8[(1)] RFox (13) (swtg: outpcd) ............. ½.15

    Shades of Jade (50) *(JJBridger)* 4-8-8 SWhitworth (6) (w ldr: led over 3f out tl over 1f out: wknd) .......................................................................... ½.16

          LONG HANDICAP: Miss Precocious 7-6, Kelly's Kite 7-6, Tippling (USA) 7-6.

**4/1** L'Ete (IRE), **9/2** The Noble Oak (IRE), **7/1** Tauber, **15/2** Savalaro, **8/1** Petitesse, **9/1** Stocktina, **10/1** Tachyon Park, **12/1** Lucy Dancer (IRE), **14/1** Fay's Song, Greetland Rock, **20/1** CATALANI(16/1—25/1), **25/1** Cronk's Quality, Shades of Jade, **33/1** Ors. CSF £234.57, CT £1,693.66. Tote £36.20: £6.70 £3.70 £2.00 £9.00 (£158.60). Mrs P. Payne (EPSOM) bred by R. M. and Mrs P. J. Payne. 16 Rn
58.83 sec (1.83)
SF—40/45/46/20/50/32

**898**

WILLIAM HILL ACTION LINE H'CAP (3-Y.O) (0-90) £3158.00 (£452.00: £206.00)
7f
8-10 (8-11)

(Weights raised 1 lb)

|  | | | |
|---|---|---|---|
| | **Rocky Waters (USA) (80)** *(GLewis)* 9-4 BRouse (4) (gd hdwy over 1f out: led ins fnl f: r.o wl) | | —1 |
| 698* | Sea Dune (81) (Fav) *(RCharlton)* 9-5 MHills (3) (hld up: rdn 2f out: ev ch ins fnl f: unable qckn) | | 2.2 |
| 559⁶ | Tate Dancer (IRE) (83) *(RWArmstrong)* 9-7 MRoberts (1) (racd alone: led tl ins fnl f: one pce) | | 1½.3 |
| 432⁶ | Sovereign Rock (IRE) (75) *(RHannon)* 8-8 ‡5RPerham (5) (a.p: one pce rn 2fl) .. | | ½.4 |
| 697² | Ghurrah (IRE) (64) *(CJBenstead)* 8-2 WCarson (9) (hrd rdn over 1f out: nvr nr to chal) | | hd.5 |
| 296 | Owner's Dream (USA) (75) *(BHanbury)* 8-13 BRaymond (8) (prom 5f) | | 1½.6 |
| 792² | Salisong (74) *(PFICole)* 8-12 RCochrane (6) (prom 5f) | | hd.7 |
| 171⁵ | Clare Kerry Lass (70) *(TJNaughton)* 8-8 DHolland (2) (prom 5f) | | 2½.8 |

15/8 Sea Dune, 5/2 Ghurrah (IRE), 4/1 Salisong(6/1—3/1), 6/1 Sovereign Rock (IRE), 14/1 Tate Dancer (IRE), 16/1 Owner's Dream (USA), 20/1 ROCKY WATERS (USA) & Ors. CSF £57.05, CT £511.52. Tote £17.10: £3.00 £1.40 £2.10 (£35.50). Mr K. Higson (EPSOM) bred by Dan C. Pitts in USA. 8 Rn 1m 23.56 (2.26)
SF—54/49/46/31/24/30

**899**

C.J.ROOT STKS (Mdn) £1856.00 (£516.00: £248.00) 7f
8-40 (8-44)

|  | | | |
|---|---|---|---|
| 689 | Ustka *(MRStoute)* 3–8-5 RCochrane (2) (gd hdwy over 1f out: hrd rdn: led wl ins fnl f: r.o wl) | | —1 |
| | Sharptino *(RAkehurst)* 3–8-10 TQuinn (10) (unf: bit bkwd: a.p: rdn over 1f out: r.o) | | 1.2 |
| | Traders Dream (72) *(TThomsonJones)* 3–8-10 SWhitworth (6) (bit bkwd: a.p: led ins fnl f: sn hdd: r.o) | | hd.3 |
| 526 | Ednego Bay (IRE) (v) *(MMcCormack)* 4–9-7 JReid (13) (a.p: ev ch ins fnl f: r.o) | | s.h.4 |
| 698 | Masrur *(RWArmstrong)* 3–8-10 BCrossley (8) (lw: led tl ins fnl f: unable qckn) | | ¾.5 |
| | Beveled Edge *(BPalling)* 3–8-5 JWilliams (9) (prom over 5f) | | 12.6 |
| 707 | On the Rampage *(RHannon)* 3–8-5 SRaymont (14) (prom over 5f) | | 2½.7 |
| | Fighting Ajdal (IRE) (Fav) *(ACStewart)* 3–8-10 MRoberts (7) (unf: scope: rdn over 4f out: eased whn btn over 1f out: rn green) | | hd.8 |
| 762⁴ | Kateb (IRE) *(RWArmstrong)* 3–8-10, WCarson (11) (bit bkwd: bhd fnl 4f) | | s.h.9 |
| 778⁵ | Alice's Mirror *(TPMcGovern)* 3–7-12 ‡7DCarson (12) (a bhd) | | d.h.9 |
| 778 | Rue de Remarque *(MJHaynes)* 4–9-2 BRaymond (4) (a bhd) | | 2.11 |
| 585 | Jorrocks (bl) *(MDixon)* 3–8-10 AClark (3) (a bhd) | | 3.12 |
| | Mayles Lass (45) *(JJBridger)* 3–8-5 NAdams (1) (a bhd) | | 2.13 |

2/1 Fighting Ajdal (IRE), 7/2 Kateb (IRE), 11/2 Sharptino, 6/1 USTKA, 10/1 Traders Dream, 12/1 Alice's Mirror(16/1—25/1), 14/1 On the Rampage, 25/1 Masrur, 33/1 Ednego Bay (IRE), 50/1 Rue de Remarque, Beveled Edge, 66/1 Ors. CSF £36.93, Tote £7.30: £2.60 £1.90 £2.80 (£19.00). Mr James Wigan (NEWMARKET) bred by London Thoroughbred Services Ltd. 13 Rn 1m 24.40 (3.10)
SF—29/31/30/40/27/–

T/Plpt: £444.60 (4.6 Tckts).
AK

## 219—SOUTHWELL (L-H) Fibresand

## Saturday, May 16th [Standard]

Going Allowance: minus 0.20 sec per fur (FS)
Wind: slt half against

Stalls: high

**900**

TULIP STKS (Mdn 2-Y.O) £1725.00 (£475.00: £225.00) 5f **(AWT)**
6-15 (6-16)

|  | | | |
|---|---|---|---|
| | **Super Seve (IRE)** *(JBerry)* 9-0 DMcKeown (1) (w'like: w ldrs: rdn to ld over 1f out: drvn clr) | | —1 |
| 772⁴ | Madam Cyn's Risk *(NACallaghan)* 8-2 ‡7JTate (3) (a chsng ldrs: rdn ½-wy: styd on fnl f: no ch w wnr) | | 6.2 |
| 514⁵ | Pilgrim Bay (IRE) (Fav) *(JBerry)* 9-0 GCarter (4) (lw: disp ld tl hrd rdn & wknd over 1f out) | | 1½.3 |
| | Broadstairs Beauty (IRE) *(MCChapman)* 9-0 SWebster (6) (lt-f: disp ld tl hrd rdn & no ex over 1f out) | | ½.4 |
| 286 | Get Daily Sport *(PAKelleway)* 9-0 GDuffield (5) (a outpcd) | | 10.5 |
| 665 | Shy Romance *(RHollinshead)* 8-2 ‡7MHumphries (7) (outpcd fr ½-wy) | | 2½.6 |
| | Buy Sunday Sport *(MissGayKelleway)* 8-2 ‡7GForster (2) (b: unf: bkwd: nvr wnt pce) | | 3½.7 |

**11/8** Pilgrim Bay (IRE), **5/2** Madam Cyn's Risk, **11/2** SUPER SEVE (IRE), **11/1** Get Daily Sport, **14/1** Broadstairs Beauty (IRE), Shy Romance, **33/1** Buy Sunday Sport. CSF £18.06, Tote £4.90: £1.70 £1.40 (£6.70). Wentdale Const Ltd (COCKERHAM) bred by R. Duggan in Ireland. 7 Rn     62.1 sec (4.1)

## 901    BEGONIA (S) STKS    £2302.50 (£640.00: £307.50)    **5f (AWT)**    6-45 (6-48)

| | | |
|---|---|---|
| | **Spring High (45)** (bl) *(KTIvory)* 5–9-5 GBardwell (12) (a.p: slt ld 2f out: kpt on wl) | —1 |
| 535 | Fighter Squadron (48) (v) *(JAGlover)* 3–8-10 WRyan (2) (hdwy ½-wy: rdn over 1f out: styd on nr fin) | 1½.2 |
| 495 | Superlativemaximus (IRE) *(JABennett)* 4–9-0 ‡5ATucker (10) (a.p: ev ch over 2f out: nt qckn fnl f) | hd.3 |
| 421 | King Victor (IRE) (45) (bl) *(RO'Leary)* 4–9-5 NConnorton (5) (chsd ldrs: led 3f out to 2f out: rdn & unable qckn appr fnl f) | 1½.4 |
| 594⁴ | Bernie Silvers (55) *(MCChapman)* 3–8-10 SWebster (8) (in tch: hdwy u.p over 2f out: nt pce to chal) | 1½.5 |
| 421 | Cranfield Comet (67) *(JBerry)* 3–9-1 GCarter (13) (chsd ldrs: hrd rdn 2f out: wknd fnl f) | hd.6 |
| 660⁶ | Jiggerak (53) *(SGNorton)* 3–8-3 ‡7OPears (11) (hdwy over 1f out: n.d) | hd.7 |
| 660 | Long Last *(DWChapman)* 3–8-5 SWood (4) (prom 3f) | 1.8 |
| 204 | The Shanahan Bay (54) (bl) *(MrsNMacauley)* 7–9-0 DMcKeown (3) (b: s.i.s: racd alone far side: outpcd fr ½-wy) | 2.9 |
| 764 | Barnsview (44) *(MWEllerby)* 3–8-10 SMorris (4) (swtg: nvr nr ldrs) | 3½.10 |
| | Will-O-Bay *(JKCresswell)* 4–8-7 ‡7JDennis (17) (bit bkwd: a in rr) | nk.11 |
| | Print Finisher (v) *(BobJones)* 6–9-0 VSmith (15) (bkwd: a bhd) | 1.12 |
| 421 | Beljinski (33) *(BJMcMath)* 4–8-7 ‡7MHumphries (16) (n.d) | hd.13 |
| | Serious Hurry (80) (Fav) *(SirMarkPrescott)* 4–9-10 GDuffield (9) (bkwd: swtg: led 2f: sn rdn: wknd over 1f out) | nk.14 |
| 511 | Washington Red (bl) *(MFBarraclough)* 3–8-5 ‡5DHarrison (1) (bit bkwd: outpcd fr ½-wy) | 4.15 |
| 685 | Masaken (50) *(TKersey)* 4–9-0 AProud (6) (b: stumbled s: a bhd) | 6.16 |

**3/1** Serious Hurry, **7/2** Fighter Squadron, **9/2** Cranfield Comet, **8/1** Bernie Silvers, **17/2** The Shanahan Bay, **14/1** Jiggerak, Print Finisher, **16/1** King Victor (IRE), **20/1** SPRING HIGH, Superlativemaximus (IRE), **25/1** Will-O-Bay, **33/1** Washington Red, Long Last, **50/1** Ors. CSF £87.99, Tote £18.90: £5.50 £1.60 £8.30 (£41.10). Mr K. T. Ivory (RADLETT) bred by Mrs P. A. Brown. 16 Rn; No bid     61.4 sec (3.4)
SF—17/2/5/4/–/–

## 902    CAMELLIA STKS (Mdn 3-Y.O) £1725.00 (£475.00: £225.00)    **1½m (AWT)**    7-15 (7-16)

| | | |
|---|---|---|
| 700⁴ | Sure Haven (IRE) (75) (Jt-Fav) *(SirMarkPrescott)* 9-0 GDuffield (9) (lw: a.p: rdn to ld over 2f out: drvn clr) | —1 |
| 687⁵ | Five to Seven (USA) (65) *(SGNorton)* 9-0 AProud (2) (w ldr: effrt appr st: one pce fnl 2f) | 4.2 |
| | Receptionist (Jt-Fav) *(HRACecil)* 8-9 WRyan (4) (bit bkwd: mde most: rdn over 3f out: hdd over 2f out: styd on same pce) | s.h.3 |
| 224⁴ | Heniu (USA) *(LordHuntingdon)* 9-0 DMcKeown (8) (hld up in tch: smooth hdwy 6f out: sn chsng ldrs: rdn & no imp fnl 3f) | 2.4 |
| 583 | Hymn Book (IRE) (72) (v) *(MRStoute)* 8-9 GCarter (5) (chsd ldrs: hrd rdn 6f out: wknd appr st) | 6.5 |
| 553 | Day of History (IRE) *(CACyzer)* 8-9 AMorris (7) (bhd: hdwy 5f out: sn rdn & btn) | 15.6 |
| | Laughton Lady *(MrsNMacauley)* 8-2 ‡7MadeleineSmith (3) (bit bkwd: a bhd: t.o fnl 6f) | 7 |
| 502 | Taurian Princess *(ANLee)* 8-9 JQuinn (6) (chsd ldrs tl wknd 7f out: sn t.o) | 8 |
| 495 | Sizzling Sarah *(BobJones)* 8-9 VSmith (1) (a bhd: t.o fnl 8f) | 9 |

**11/4** Receptionist, SURE HAVEN (IRE), **7/2** Heniu (USA), **9/2** Hymn Book (IRE)(op 3/1), **6/1** Five to Seven (USA)(op 10/1), **33/1** Day of History (IRE), Taurian Princess, Sizzling Sarah, **50/1** Laughton Lady. CSF £18.79, Tote £3.70: £1.30 £1.50 £1.20 (£8.00). Mr Neil Greig (NEWMARKET) bred by Major V. McCalmont. 9 Rn
2m 38.9 (4.7)
SF—29/21/15/16/–/–

## 903    TED MARSDEN H'CAP (0-70) £2742.00 (£762.00: £366.00)    **7f (AWT)**    7-45 (7-52)

| | | |
|---|---|---|
| 738 | Quinzii Martin (52) (v) *(DHaydnJones)* 4–8-13 WRyan (15) (chsd ldrs: led 1f out: r.o u.p) | —1 |
| 190³ | Tara's Delight (59) (Fav) *(WAO'Gorman)* 5–9-1 ‡5EmmaO'Gorman (2) (b.hind: led tl hdd 1f out: no ex) | 1½.2 |
| 541⁶ | Ain'tlifelikethat (55) (bl) *(TJNaughton)* 5–9-2 GCarter (7) (in tch: hdwy over 2f out: hrd rdn & styd on same pce fnl f) | nk.3 |
| 785★ | Sareen Express (IRE) (48) *(MrsJCDawe)* 4–8-4 ‡5ATucker (8) (sltly hmpd after s & sn bhd: effrt & n.m.r 2f out: swtchd & fin fast u.p) | 1½.4 |

785⁵ Vuchterbacher **(59)** *(PFTulk)* 6–8–13 ‡⁷TWilson (6) (b: swtg: chsd ldrs: effrt appr st: nvr able chal) .................................................... ¹/₂.5

Verdant Boy **(54)** *(MPNaughton)* 9–9–1 NConnorton (13) (bit bkwd: prom tl rdn & wknd 2f out) ........................................................... 1¹/₂.6

731 Reina **(43)** *(JDBethell)* 4–8–4 DMcKeown (9) (chsd ldrs tl wknd over 2f out) .... 3¹/₂.7

702 Times Are Hard **(44)** *(CASmith)* 8–8–0 ‡⁵DHarrison (11) (dwlt: sme hdwy ent st: n.d) ...................................................................... 1.8

768 Pimsboy **(53)** (bl) *(PABlockley)* 5–9–0 JQuinn (14) (effrt on outside over 2f out: sn rdn & btn) ............................................................... 1¹/₂.9

496 Wellsy Lad (USA) **(65)** *(DWChapman)* 5–9–12 SWood (12) (lw: hmpd & lost pl after wl over 1f: c wd st: sn rdn & no imp) ...................... 6.10

407 Company Cash **(59)** (v) *(RBastiman)* 4–8–13 ‡⁷HBastiman (2) (lw: sn bhd) .... nk.11

357 Regal Tiger **(32)** *(MrsJCDawe)* 7–7–7 GBardwell (3) (chsd ldr to st: sn rdn & wknd) ............................................................................... 3.12

468 Monti Beppo **(52)** *(LJBarratt)* 3–7–13 ‡³FNorton (4) (chsd ldrs tl wknd wl over 2f out) ................................................................................. 13

580 Countess Brussels **(40)** *(KGWingrove)* 4–7–10⁽⁸⁾ ‡⁵LNewton (5) (a bhd) ............. 14

LONG HANDICAP: Regal Tiger 7-5, Countess Brussels 7-5.

**11/2** Tara's Delight, **6/1** Vuchterbacher, **7/1** Ain'tlifelikethat, Pimsboy, **8/1** Times Are Hard(op 20/1), Sareen Express (IRE), **9/1** Company Cash, **10/1** Verdant Boy, **12/1** QUINZII MARTIN(op 8/1), **14/1** Monti Beppo, **16/1** Wellsy Lad (USA), **33/1** Regal Tiger, Reina, **50/1** Countess Brussels. CSF £72.57, CT £463.47. Tote £15.10: £4.00 £1.70 £2.10 (£31.50). Monolithic Refractories Ltd (PONTYPRIDD) bred by Lord Fairhaven. 14 Rn
1m 29.2 (2.6)
SF—36/36/36/19/26/23

**904**  NATIONAL PLANT & TRANSPORT H'CAP (3-Y.O) (0-70) £2763.00 (£768.00: £369.00)
**1m (AWT)**  8 15 (8-19)

(Weights raised 3 lb)

662 **Sie Amato (IRE) (52)** *(CaptJWilson)* 8-6 GBardwell (4) (a cl up: disp ld over 2f out: hdd appr fnl f: rallied to ld nr fin) ........................ —1

604 Abeloni **(62)** *(AAScott)* 9-2 JFortune (1) (a.p: hrd rdn & chal over 2f out: led appr fnl f: hdd & no ex cl home) ................................... nk.2

498 Miss Hyde (USA) **(57)** (v) *(JAGlover)* 8-11 GCarter (6) (lw: a in tch: rdn & outpcd over 2f out: kpt on u.p fnl f) .................................. 1¹/₂.3

823 Invigilate **(56)** *(MPNaughton)* 8-5 ‡⁵DHarrison (5) (a.p: rdn & ev ch 2f out: unable qckn fnl f) ................................................................ hd.4

604 Mill Burn **(53)** *(ICampbell)* 8-7⁽¹⁾ MTebbutt (8) (sn wl bhd: hdwy ent st: kpt on fnl 2f) ....................................................................................... 2.5

567 Crimson Consort (IRE) **(39)** (v) *(DonEnricoIncisa)* 7-4 ‡³JFanning (10) (hmpd & lost pl after s: drvn along & wnt prom appr st: wknd over 1f out) ........................................................................................... ¹/₂.6

604★ Elizabethan Air **(52)** *(ANLee)* 8-6 JQuinn (2) (b.nr hind: chsd ldrs: effrt over 2f out: wknd over 1f out) ................................................ ³/₄.7

587⁴ Oak Apple (USA) **(60)** (Fav) *(BHanbury)* 9-0 WRyan (7) (b: hdwy ent st: sn rdn & nvr able chal) ........................................................ 1¹/₂.8

734³ Master Shikari **(47)** *(JEBanks)* 7-10 ‡⁵LNewton (3) (led tl hdd over 2f out: sn lost pl) .................................................................................... 1¹/₂.9

281⁶ Cold Shower (IRE) **(57)** (bl) *(JAGlover)* 8-11 GDuffield (13) (in tch: effrt on outside appr st: sn btn) .......................................... ¹/₂.10

295 Broughton's Tango (IRE) **(46)** *(WJMusson)* 8-0 JHBrown (9) (b: a bhd) ........ 2¹/₂.11

614⁵ Palacegate King **(67)** *(JBerry)* 9-7 JCarroll (12) (in tch to st) ................... 2.12

248³ High Success **(56)** (v) *(WAO'Gorman)* 8-10 DMcKeown (11) (in tch: drvn along after 3f: sn lost pl) ................................................... 13

LONG HANDICAP: Crimson Consort (IRE) 6-12.

**5/2** Oak Apple (USA)(4/1—9/2), **11/2** Elizabethan Air, **7/1** Cold Shower (IRE), **8/1** High Success, Palacegate King, Master Shikari, **10/1** Miss Hyde (USA), **14/1** Mill Burn, Abeloni, **16/1** Invigilate, Broughton's Tango (IRE), **20/1** SIE AMATO (IRE), **50/1** Crimson Consort (IRE). CSF £256.47, CT £2,696.87. Tote £24.80: £4.40 £4.60 £3.00 (£117.50). Red Rose Partnership (PRESTON) bred by Mrs M. Johnston in Ireland. 13 Rn  1m 43.7 (4.4)
SF—2/11/1/–/–/–

**905**  MAGNOLIA H'CAP (0-70) £2553.00 (£708.00: £339.00)  **1¹/₂m (AWT)**  8-45 (8-47)

590★ **Discord (60)** *(LordHuntingdon)* 6-9-4 DMcKeown (6) (lw: hld up gng wl: hdwy on bit appr st: led over 2f out: sn clr: v.easily) ...................... —1

155⁵ Mr Wishing Well **(51)** *(RJRWilliams)* 6-8-2 ‡⁷GMitchell (3) (rapid hdwy appr st: chal over 2f out: hung lft & no ch w wnr) ................... 5.2

761★ Petavious **(69)** (Fav) *(LadyHerries)* 7-9-13 WRyan (5) (hld up: hdwy 5f out: sn chsng ldrs: one pce fnl 2f) ........................................ 1¹/₂.3

312 Suluk (USA) **(50)** *(RHollinshead)* 7–8–1 ‡⁷MHumphries (11) (bhd: hdwy on
outside 3f out: r.o wl fnl f: nvr nrr) .................................................... s.h.4
Domain **(55)** (bl) *(RJWeaver)* 4–8–8 ‡⁵ATucker (9) (hrd rdn over 4f out: styd on
fnl 2f: n.d) ........................................................................................ 1¹/₂.5
Sweet Bubbles (IRE) **(55)** *(CACyzer)* 4–8–6 ‡⁷TMcLaughlin (12) (bit bkwd: effrt
u.p 5f out: sme late hdwy: n.d) ...................................................... 4.6
593 Jarras **(42)** (bl) *(CASmith)* 7–7–9 ‡⁵DHarrison (8) (hdwy 6f out: led over 4f out:
hdd over 2f out: wknd) .................................................................... nk.7
606⁵ Samain (USA) **(36)** (v) *(JAGlover)* 5–7–8⁽¹⁾ JQuinn (3) (dwlt: sn rcvrd: prom tl
wknd appr st: eased fnl f) ................................................................ 5.8
358 Salman (USA) **(46)** *(SGNorton)* 6–8–1 ‡¹³FNorton (4) (w ldr: led 5f out: sn hdd:
wknd 3f out) ...................................................................................... 1.9
683 Hand Painted **(57)** *(CRBeever)* 8–9–1 JCarroll (10) (b: a bhd) ...................... 3.10
586 Doctor's Remedy **(35)** *(MrsJJordan)* 6–7–7 GBardwell (13) (a in rr) ............... hd.11
578 Isobar **(35)** (bl) *(MCChapman)* 6–7–7 SWood (14) (chsd ldrs 7f) .................. 2¹/₂.12
225 Valatch **(54)** *(JLHarris)* 4–8–5 ‡⁷GForster (7) (led 7f: sn wknd) ................... 13
Tyrnippy **(57)** *(MBrittain)* 6–9–1 GDuffield (1) (bit bkwd: prom tl wknd u.p 6f out) 14
LONG HANDICAP: Samain (USA) 7-4, Doctor's Remedy 7-0, Isobar 6-13.

**7/4** Petavious, **4/1** DISCORD, **7/1** Valatch, **12/1** Mr Wishing Well, Suluk (USA), Salman (USA), **14/1** Samain
(USA), Sweet Bubbles (IRE), Tyrnippy, Hand Painted, **16/1** Doctor's Remedy, **20/1** Domain, **50/1** Ors. CSF
£51.86, CT £107.53. Tote £4.90: £2.10 £2.40 £1.70 (£22.40). Mrs Evan Williams (WEST ILSLEY) bred by
Knockaney Stud. 14 Rn                                                                          2m 38.9 (4.7)
                                                                                              SF—33/7/29/2/6/–

T/Plpt: £666.00 (1.9 Tckts).                                                                          O'R

---

## 786—BATH (L-H)

### Monday, May 18th [Firm]

Going Allowance: minus 0.40 sec per fur (F)                                         Wind: nil

Stalls: low

**906**   MILBOURNE STKS (Mdn 3-Y.O) £2390.00 (£665.00: £320.00)   **5f 11y**   2-15 (2-17)

727³ **Desert Dagger** (Fav) *(MajorWRHern)* 9-0 SCauthen (6) (rdn along: chsd ldr fr
2f out tl led nr fin: all out) ............................................................... —1
690⁴ Hot Lavender (CAN) **(69)** *(CFWall)* 8-9 RCochrane (10) (lw: dwlt: hdwy 2f out:
led wl ins fnl f tl cl home) ............................................................. nk.2
Temple Fortune (USA) **(66)** (bl) *(DRCEIsworth)* 8-9 TQuinn (9) (led: sn clr:
wknd & hdd wl ins fnl f) ................................................................. ³/₄.3
620 Rock Band (IRE) *(LMCumani)* 9-0 LDettori (2) (lw: nvr nrr) ......................... 2¹/₂.4
764 Lawnswood Prince (IRE) **(64)** *(JLSpearing)* 9-0 JWilliams (8) (no hdwy fnl 2f) ... 3.5
Musval *(RHannon)* 8-9 PatEddery (7) (nvr nr to chal) ............................... 1¹/₂.6
Orchid Valley (IRE) *(RMWhitaker)* 8-9 ACulhane (5) (nvr nr ldrs) ................. ¹/₂.7
728 Sea Cloud (USA) **(41)** *(MBlanshard)* 8-9 DHolland (3) (spd over 2f) ............. ¹/₂.8
Bridle Talk (IRE) **(52)** *(MMcCormack)* 8-9 JReid (1) (dwlt: a bhd) ................ 4.9
594 I Broke the Rules (IRE) **(35)** *(AJChamberlain)* 8-4 ‡⁵ATucker (4) (b: prom over
2f) ...................................................................................................... 1¹/₂.10

**Evens** DESERT DAGGER, **5/1** Hot Lavender (CAN), **13/2** Musval, **9/1** Rock Band (IRE), **10/1** Temple Fortune
(USA), **12/1** Orchid Valley (IRE), **33/1** Sea Cloud, Lawnswood Prince (IRE), Bridle Talk (IRE), **50/1** I Broke
the Rules (IRE). CSF £6.47, Tote £1.80: £1.30 £1.40 £2.00 (£3.80). Sheikh Ahmed Al Maktoum (LAMBOURN)
bred by Highclere Stud Ltd. 10 Rn                                                     61.8 sec (1.3)
                                                                                      SF—34/28/25/20/12/–

**907**   E.B.F. MONUMENT STKS (Mdn 2-Y.O) £3101.00 (£861.00: £413.00)
          **5f 11y**                                                            2-45 (2-50)

Darbonne (USA) *(GHarwood)* 9-0 SCauthen (11) (cmpt: bit bkwd: hdwy 2f out:
plld out 1f out: qcknd to ld ins fnl f: comf) .................................. —1
Windrush Boy *(MMcCormack)* 9-0 JReid (10) (unf: led tl ins fnl f: r.o) ............. 1¹/₂.2
729⁴ Visimotion (USA) *(MJHeaton-Ellis)* 9-0 WNewnes (12) (a.p: ev ch over 1f out:
r.o) ................................................................................................... 1.3
383 Beaver Brook (Fav) *(RHannon)* 9-0 BRaymond (2) (sn w ldr: hrd rdn over 1f out:
nt qckn) .......................................................................................... 2¹/₂.4
Bold Face (IRE) *(RFJohnsonHoughton)* 9-0 SWhitworth (8) (lt-f: unf: lw: chsd
ldrs: r.o one pce fnl 2f) .................................................................. ³/₄.5
Tahasun (IRE) *(HThomsonJones)* 9-0 RHills (4) (unf: scope: bkwd: prom over 3f) 1.6
Break My Heart *(PFICole)* 9-0 TQuinn (5) (gd sort: nvr nrr) ......................... ³/₄.7
Lowrianna (IRE) *(DHaydnJones)* 8-9 MHills (14) (w'like: bkwd: s.s: nrst fin) ....... 5.8

581 Wickins *(GLewis)* 9-0 AClark (1) (nvr nr to chal) ....................................... nk.9
Avril Etoile *(LJHolt)* 8-2 ‡⁷CAvery (16) (neat: n.d) ................................. ¾.10
Apifera *(RJHodges)* 8-6 ‡³TSprake (13) (scope: prom over 2f) ............ ½.11
Morning News (IRE) *(MHTompkins)* 9-0 PRobinson (6) (unf: lw: n.d) ........... 1.12
595 Both Barrels *(RJHolder)* 9-0 JWilliams (3) (n.d) ..................................... 2.13
Alaska Bay *(RJHolder)* 9-0 NAdams (15) (scope: bit bkwd: n.d) ............ 1½.14
Orchard Queen (IRE) *(JWhite)* 8-9 TyroneWilliams (7) (lengthy: scope: s.s: a wl
bhd) ...................................................................... 10.15
Frankie Goodman (IRE) *(JSMoore)* 9-0 BRouse (9) (w'like: stood still s: a t.o) . 8.16

11/4 Beaver Brook, 100/30 DARBONNE (USA), 13/2 Visimotion (USA), 7/1 Break My Heart(4/1—8/1),
Windrush Boy(6/1—10/1), 8/1 Tahasun (IRE)(op 5/1), 14/1 Morning News (IRE), Bold Face (IRE), 20/1 Alaska
Bay, 33/1 Wickins, Lowrianna (IRE), 50/1 Ors. CSF £27.27, Tote £4.50: £2.20 £2.80 £1.90 (£33.30). Sheikh
Mohammed (PULBOROUGH) bred by Hermitage Farm Inc in USA. 16 Rn
61.3 sec (0.8)
SF—44/38/34/24/21/17

**908**  MONKTON FARLEIGH H'CAP (3-Y.O) (0-80) £3071.00 (£856.00: £413.00)
1m 5f 22y
3-15 (3-16)

(Weights raised 8 lb)

583★ Simply-H (IRE) (72) *(MBell)* 9-0 ‡⁷PTurner (5) (lw: a gng wl: 4th st: led wl over 1f
out: easily) .................................................................... —1
695⁴ Crystal Cross (USA) (71) *(Fav)* *(IABalding)* 9-6 JReid (3) (6th st: ev ch wl one f out:
nt qckn) ...................................................................... 4.2
693 Formal Invitation (IRE) (58) *(GLewis)* 8-7 PatEddery (6) (hdwy 7f out: 7th st:
styd on fnl 2f) ................................................................ 1½.3
583 Last Conquest (IRE) (63) *(PFICole)* 8-12 TQuinn (9) (nvr nrr) ...................... 2½.4
625 Sandro (63) *(JRFanshawe)* 8-12 GCarter (1) (2nd st: ev ch 2f out: sn wknd) ...... ¾.5
783 Mustahil (IRE) (70) *(RJHodges)* 9-2 ‡³TSprake (7) (lw: nvr nr to chal) ............ 1.6
788³ Humour (IRE) (71) *(CFWall)* 9-6 LDettori (14) (5th st: wknd 2f out) ............ nk.7
524 Storm Drum (59) *(PJMakin)* 8-8 NNewnes (4) (nvr trbld ldrs) .................. s.h.8
290⁶ Simply George (RBoss) 9-5 BRaymond (2) (lw: led tl wknd qckly wl over 1f
out) ............................................................................ 1½.9
583 Elite Reg (55) (bl) *(PFICole)* 7-11 ‡⁷JDSmith (11) (3rd st: wknd over 2f out) .. 1½.10
700² Sports View (54) *(RJHolder)* 8-3 NAdams (15) (a bhd) ........................... ½.11
Winter Lightning (55) *(PTWalwyn)* 8-4 NHowe (10) (bhd fnl 8f) .................... 5.12
Heavenly Waters (62) *(RFJohnsonHoughton)* 8-11 RHills (13) (b.hind: bhd fnl
8f) ............................................................................. 3.13
694★ Mr Ziegfeld (USA) (69) *(SirMarkPrescott)* 9-4 MRoberts (12) (virtually p.u over
1f out: t.o) ................................................................... 14
802 Surely Gifted (IRE) (60) (bl) *(WRMuir)* 8-9 SWhitworth (2) (virtually p.u over 1f
out: t.o) ...................................................................... 15

11/4 Crystal Cross (USA), 7/2 SIMPLY-H (IRE), 11/2 Mr Ziegfeld (USA), 7/1 Formal Invitation (IRE), 10/1 Sports
View, 11/1 Humour (IRE), Simply George(8/1—12/1), 20/1 Storm Drum, Sandro, Last Conquest (IRE), 25/1
Heavenly Waters, Winter Lightning, Mustahil (IRE), 33/1 Ors. CSF £63.34, Tote £4.00: £2.20 £1.70 £2.20 £7.30
(£14.20). Mr G. L. H. Lederman (NEWMARKET) bred by E. J. Loder in Ireland. 15 Rn   2m 50 (2.3)
SF—25/23/7/7/5/7

**909**  MALMESBURY H'CAP (0-75) £3135.50 (£944.00: £457.00: £213.50)
5f 161y
3-45 (3-53)

596★ Cee-En-Cee (66) (bl) *(MMcCourt)* 8-9-8 TQuinn (11) (a.p: squeezed thro ins
fnl f: led cl home) ........................................................... —1
510⁵ Leigh Crofter (67) (bl) *(RJHolder)* 3-8-6 ‡⁷SDrowne (9) (a.p: ev ch fnl f: r.o) ..... nk.2
801² Night Asset (60) (bl) *(Fav)* *(GLewis)* 3-8-6 PatEddery (10) (lw: a.p: hrd rdn fnl 2f:
r.o) ........................................................................... hd.3
685★ Fangio (75) *(WGMTurner)* 3-9-4 ‡³TSprake (4) (led tl nr fin) .................... ¾.4
La Belle Vie (65) *(RJBaker)* 6-9-7 GCarter (6) (gd hdwy over 1f out: r.o ins fnl f) hd.5
344 Respectable Jones (71) *(GBBalding)* 6-9-13 JWilliams (7) (nvr nrr) .............. 4.6
738⁶ Beatle Song (64) *(RJHodges)* 4-9-3 ‡³DBiggs (12) (nvr nr to chal) ............... ½.7
731⁵ Gallant Hope (50) (bl) *(LGCottrell)* 10-8-6 RFox (5) (w ldr: bdly hmpd ins fnl f: nt
rcvr) ........................................................................... 1½.8
735² Pendor Dancer (51) (bl) *(BForsey)* 9-8-7 SWhitworth (15) (swtg: nvr trbld ldrs) nk.9
731 Juvenara (46) *(CJHill)* 6-8-2 NAdams (14) (n.d) ................................. hd.10
587 Unveiled (66) *(RJHodges)* 4-9-8 MRoberts (18) (rn v.wd over 3f out: no ch
after) ......................................................................... ½.11
731 Flying Promise (49) *(RABennett)* 4-8-5 WNewnes (13) (n.d) ..................... nk.12
582 Battling Bella (USA) (64) *(JSutcliffe)* 3-8-10 BRouse (16) (swtg: prom 3f) ....... ¾.13
592 Tara's Girl (66) *(PABlockley)* 5-9-1 ‡⁷GParkin (8) (s.s: n.d) ................... s.h.14
723 Darussalam (64) *(RLee)* 5-9-6 BRaymond (14) (n.d) ............................ nk.15
735 Goody Four Shoes (54) *(DRTucker)* 4-8-5 ‡⁵RPrice (1) (n.d) .................... 2½.16

278 Flying Petal **(41)** *(CJHill)* 4–7–8[(4)] ‡3FNorton (1) (bit bkwd: s.s: a bhd) .................. 17
735³ Factuelle **(45)** *(DRTucker)* 5–8–1 GBardwell (17) (s.s: a bhd) .............................. 18
LONG HANDICAP: Flying Petal 7-0.

*Subsequent Stewards Enquiry: Cee-En-Cee (originally disqualified for careless riding) was re-instated on appeal and the suspension of T. Quinn quashed. All bets settled on Leigh Crofter.*

**9/4** Night Asset(4/1—2/1), **5/1** Fangio, **9/1** CEE-EN-CEE(op 6/1), **10/1** Battling Bella (USA)(8/1—14/1), **11/1** Gallant Hope(8/1—12/1), **12/1** Factuelle(op 7/1), **14/1** Pendor Dancer(op 8/1), Respectable Jones, **20/1** Leigh Crofter, Darussalam, Unveiled, **25/1** Beatle Song, **33/1** Juvenara, Tara's Girl, La Belle Vie, **50/1** Ors. CSF £66.22, CT £253.31. Tote £24.70: £4.30 £1.10 £1.20 £12.80 (£98.40). Mr D. N. Humphreys (WANTAGE) bred by Thomas Moore. 18 Rn
1m 9.8 sec (0.5)
SF—52/35/34/43/45/35

## 910    BRISTOL STKS (I) (Mdn 3-Y.O) £2250.00 (£625.00: £300.00)    1¼m 46y    4-15 (4-26)

**Source of Light** (Jt-Fav) *(RCharlton)* 9-0 PatEddery (8) (scope: lw: hld up & bhd: gd hdwy to ld over 2f out: easily) ................ —1
Indian Jack (IRE) *(MajorWRHern)* 9-0 SCauthen (10) (w'like: 5th st: ev ch over 2f out: r.o one pce) ........................................... 8.2
Sky Train (IRE) **(70)** *(JLDunlop)* 9-0 AMcGlone (11) (swtg: shd st: led over 3f out tl over 2f out) ............................................... 3.3
804 Russian Vision *(AAScott)* 9-0 BRaymond (2) (stdy hdwy fnl 2f: nvr nrr) ........... s.h.4
Indian Territory **(66)** *(DHaydnJones)* 9-0 TyroneWilliams (3) (w'like: lft in ld over 4f out: wknd 3f out) ......................................... 2½.5
623³ Sheringa (Jt-Fav) *(GBBalding)* 8-9 JWilliams (9) (6th st: no hdwy) ............... ¾.6
Whatcomesnaturally (USA) *(JWHills)* 8-9 RHills (6) (4th st: wknd 3f out) .......... 10.7
Dave's Lass *(DBurchell)* 8-9 TQuinn (5) (lengthy: unf: a bhd) ...................... 2.8
Soft Note (IRE) *(MBell)* 9-0 MHills (7) (b.hind: w'like: 3rd st: wknd 3f out) ...... 4.9
784⁶ Space Camp *(RJHodges)* 8-11 ‡3TSprake (4) (racd v.wd: a bhd) .............. 8.10
627 Morgans Ace *(BRMillman)* 9-0 GBaxter (1) (led tl rn out & crashed thro rails over 4f out) ........................................................ 0

**9/4** SOURCE OF LIGHT, Sheringa, **11/2** Indian Jack (IRE), **7/1** Sky Train (IRE), **11/1** Soft Note (IRE)(8/1—12/1), Russian Vision(8/1—12/1), **14/1** Space Camp, **16/1** Whatcomesnaturally (USA), **33/1** Ors. CSF £15.72, Tote £3.00: £1.10 £2.40 £2.50 (£5.90). Mr K. Abdulla (BECKHAMPTON) bred by Juddmonte Farms. 11 Rn
2m 9.4 (1.7)
SF—43/27/16/20/15/8

## 911    BRISTOL STKS (II) (Mdn 3-Y.O) £2250.00 (£625.00: £300.00)    1¼m 46y    4-45 (4-54)

**Besotted** *(BWHills)* 8-9 PatEddery (4) (w'like: scope: 2nd st: led 2f out: r.o wl) . —1
633² Mr Flood (USA) *(MrsJCecil)* 9-0 MRoberts (2) (lw: led to 2f out: r.o) .......... 2.2
623⁶ Blushing Storm (USA) *(JRFanshawe)* 8-9 GCarter (10) (3rd st: r.o one pce fnl 2f) ...................................................................... 5.3
600³ Ajo (IRE) *(MRStoute)* 9-0 SCauthen (9) (lw: 4th st: rdn 3f out: one pce) ...... 1½.4
707⁴ Themeda *(CRNelson)* 8-9 JReid (3) (6th st: no hdwy fnl 2f) ................... 3½.5
Addicted to Love *(PJMakin)* 8-9 TQuinn (6) (w'like: bit bkwd: nvr nr to chal) ...... 3.6
689⁶ Just Hannah *(MrsBarbaraWaring)* 8-9 NHowe (1) (5th & wkng st) ............ 1½.7
Diciembre *(IABalding)* 9-0 RCochrane (7) (a bhd) ................................ 1½.8
Kandy Secret (USA) *(RHannon)* 9-0 AMcGlone (5) (swtg: a bhd) ................. 2.9
497 Gunmaker *(RJHolder)* 9-0 ADicks (8) (a bhd) ................................ 8.10
799 Royal Opera Star *(JRBosley)* 9-0 RFox (11) (a bhd) ......................... 10.11

**11/8** Mr Flood (USA), **5/2** Ajo (IRE), **3/1** BESOTTED, **9/2** Themeda(op 9/2), **11/1** Diciembre(op 5/1), **25/1** Blushing Storm (USA), **50/1** Ors. CSF £7.51, Tote £5.10: £1.60 £1.10 £3.40 (£5.80). Mr K. Abdulla (LAMBOURN) bred by Juddmonte Farms. 11 Rn
2m 10 (2.3)
SF—32/33/18/20/8/2

## 912    DOWNS H'CAP (0-70) £2827.50 (£790.00: £382.50)    1m 5y    5-15 (5-23)

504 **Camden's Ransom (USA) (61)** *(DRCElsworth)* 5–9–8 JWilliams (15) (7th st: led wl ins fnl f: r.o) ....................................................... —1
Eternal Flame **(57)** *(JWHills)* 4–9–4 RHills (16) (3rd st: led over 1f out tl wl ins fnl f: r.o) ...................................................... nk.2
626⁶ Abso **(67)** *(RHannon)* 4–10–0 JReid (2) (6th st: nt clr run 2f out: hung lft: r.o ins fnl f) ...................................................... 1.3
Jagged Edge **(43)** *(RJHolder)* 5–8–4 JQuinn (13) (hdwy fnl 2f: nvr nrr) .......... s.h.4
738 Melodic Habit **(40)** *(MrsAKnight)* 5–7–12 ‡3FNorton (6) (b.hind: 4th st: ev ch 1f out: nt qckn) .................................................. 1.5
697³ Countercheck (IRE) **(53)** *(CFWall)* 3–8–2 TyroneWilliams (11) (lw: 5th st: rdn 3f out: r.o one pce) .................................................. ¾.6

| | | | |
|---|---|---|---|
| 809 | Loudest Whisper (60) (v) (KSBridgwater) 4-9-2 ‡5BDoyle (5) (nrst fin) | s.h.7 |
| 774 | Bengal Tiger (IRE) (54) (bl) (JAkehurst) 4-9-1 DHolland (3) (nvr nr to chal) | 3.8 |
| 469⁴ | Always Ready (39) (RLee) 6-8-0 DaleGibson (14) (wl bhd tl r.o fnl 2f) | 3.9 |
| 598 | Just Ready (IRE) (42) (GAHam) 4-8-3 ADicks (12) (led 6f out tl wknd over 1f out) | 2.10 |
| | Set Up (39) (DBurchell) 4-8-0 NAdams (9) (n.d) | ½.11 |
| 738 | Lamastre (57) (RJHodges) 3-8-3‡³TSprake (7) (led 2f: 2nd st: wknd over 2f out) | nk.12 |
| 249⁵ | Texan Clamour (FR) (58) (JSMoore) 4-9-2 ‡³DBiggs (8) (b.off hind: n.d) | 2.13 |
| | Revoke (USA) (45) (CJHill) 5-8-1 ‡5ATucker (10) (bit bkwd: s.s: nrst fin) | 3½.14 |
| 696 | Armaiti (55) (DRTucker) 4-9-2 GBardwell (1) (n.d) | ¾.15 |
| 775³ | Cash a Million (FR) (52) (PDCundell) 4-8-13 TRogers (18) (n.d) | nk.16 |
| 587 | Tendresse (IRE) (42) (DRTucker) 4-7-12⁽¹⁾ ‡5RPrice (4) (n.d) | 2.17 |
| | Daily Sport Girl (58) (PABlockley) 3-8-0 ‡7GParkin (17) (n.d) | 18 |

**9/2** Countercheck (IRE)(4/1—6/1), **5/1** Abso(4/1—6/1), **7/1** Always Ready(5/1—8/1), **15/2** Bengal Tiger (IRE), **10/1** Eternal Flame, **12/1** Texan Clamour (FR)(7/1—14/1), Cash a Million (FR)(8/1—14/1), CAMDEN'S RANSOM (USA), **14/1** Revoke (USA)(10/1—20/1), **16/1** Tendresse (IRE), Jagged Edge, **20/1** Lamastre, **25/1** Melodic Habit, **33/1** Daily Sport Girl, **50/1** Ors. CSF £118.79, CT £623.44. Tote £10.20: £2.30 £2.40 £2.00 £2.50 (£27.00). Mr Bob Cullen (WHITSBURY) bred by Dr and Mrs Chris Elia and Phil Needham in USA. 18 Rn
1m 40.4 (1.1)
SF—43/38/45/20/11/13

T/Plpt: £28.70 (129.85 Tckts). Hn

---

415—**EDINBURGH (R-H)**

## Monday, May 18th [Good to firm]
Going Allowance: minus 0.35 sec per fur (F)
Stalls: high

Wind: almost nil

**913**  WIMPEY HOMES BRUNSTANE PARK (S) H'CAP (0-60) £2323.00 (£653.00: £319.00)
**1m 16y**  2-00 (2-04)

(Weights raised 2 lb)

| | | | |
|---|---|---|---|
| 702 | **Lawnswood Junior (37)** (Fav) (JLSpearing) 5-8-9 KDarley (16) (bhd: hdwy on ins ent st: chal 1f out: led nr fin) | —1 |
| 521⁶ | I'M Electric (41) (RCurtis) 6-8-13 NDay (6) (b: in tch: hdwy 3f out: led over 1f out: r.o: jst ct) | s.h.2 |
| 326 | Valley of Time (FR) (35) (TCraig) 4-8-0 ‡7DarrenMoffatt (14) (led tl hdd over 1f out: kpt on wl) | 1½.3 |
| 797⁴ | Between Two Fires (58) (bl) (JBerry) 4-8-9 JCarroll (15) (a chsng ldrs: rdn over 2f out: r.o one pce) | 6.4 |
| 696 | Station Express (IRE) (37) (BEllison) 4-8-4⁽³⁾ ‡5JWeaver (12) (a chsng ldrs: rdn 3f out: no imp fnl 2f) | 3½.5 |
| 572 | Miss Knight (41) (RBastiman) 5-8-6 ‡7HBastiman (8) (hdwy 3f out: sn rdn & nvr able chal) | 1½.6 |
| 542⁵ | Stand At Ease (39) (WStorey) 7-8-11 SWebster (4) (swtg: nvr bttr than mid div) | nk.7 |
| 809 | Chloes Diamond (IRE) (50) (JLSpearing) 4-9-5 ‡³JFanning (13) (lw: bhd: hdwy 3f out: nvr rchd ldrs) | 1½.8 |
| | Little Ivor (52) (v) (DenysSmith) 3-8-12 LCharnock (11) (in tch tl rdn & btn over 2f out) | 2.9 |
| 796⁵ | Strength in Depth (IRE) (48) (MJohnston) 4-9-6 DMcKeown (9) (bhd tl some late hdwy) | 1½.10 |
| 662 | Fair Flyer (IRE) (56) (bl) (PMonteith) 3-9-2 JFortune (5) (in tch: rdn & c wd st: sn btn) | 2.11 |
| 615 | Angel Train (IRE) (40) (bl) (JParkes) 4-8-12 NCarlisle (7) (lw: chsd ldrs tl rdn & btn over 2f out) | nk.12 |
| 606 | Broad Appeal (52) (WJPearce) 4-9-10 DNicholls (3) (a bhd) | 3½.13 |
| 572 | Cool Enough (36) (MrsJRRamsden) 11-8-8 TLucas (10) (chsd ldrs to st: sn wknd) | ½.14 |
| 326 | Brown as a Berry (36) (WStorey) 4-8-8 AlexGreaves (1) (hld up & a bhd) | ½.15 |
| 405 | Fassadinin (35) (v) (WLBarker) 11-8-0 ‡7VHalliday (2) (b: a bhd) | 1½.16 |

**5/1** LAWNSWOOD JUNIOR(4/1—6/1), **11/2** Cool Enough, Fair Flyer (IRE)(4/1—6/1), **7/1** Station Express (IRE), **8/1** Between Two Fires, **9/1** I'M Electric, **10/1** Brown as a Berry (IRE), **25/1** Little Ivor, **33/1** Stand At Ease, Broad Appeal, **100/1** Fassadinin. CSF £48.70, CT £560.68. Tote £5.40: £1.50 £2.10 £4.20 £2.10 (£106.30). Mr Graham Treglown (ALCESTER) bred by Chilcombe Manor Stud. 16 Rn; No bid  1m 40.8 (2.2)
SF—20/23/5/5/—/—

**914** WIMPEY HOMES HARLAWHILL GARDENS STKS (Mdn 3-Y.O.F) £2137.50 (£600.00: £292.50) **7f 15y** 2-30 (2-31)

**Sweet Lips** *(JGFitzGerald)* 8-11 KFallon (2) (bit bkwd: bhd: swtchd outside over 2f out: led ins fnl f: rn green: rdn & r.o) ....................... —1
7494 Malcesine (IRE) **(49)** *(CaptJWilson)* 8-11 JLowe (4) (trckd ldrs: led over 1f out tl ins fnl f) ............................................................................ nk.2
5264 Indian Style (IRE) **(Fav)** *(RGuest)* 8-11 NDay (3) (trckd ldrs: chal over 2f out: nt qckn wl ins fnl f) ................................................. 1½.3
Kirkby Belle **(54)** *(EWeymes)* 8-11 DMcKeown (5) (bit bkwd: led tl hdd over 1f out: nt qckn) .............................................................. 3.4
Palacegate Queen (IRE) *(JBerry)* 8-11 JCarroll (1) (bit bkwd: cl up tl wknd 2f out) ....................................................................................... 12.5

5/2 Indian Style (IRE), 11/4 Malcesine (IRE), 7/2 Kirkby Belle, 9/2 SWEET LIPS(op 8/1), 10/1 Palacegate Queen (IRE). CSF £14.84, Tote £6.00: £2.90 £2.00 (£9.70). The Kilroe Group Limited (MALTON) bred by T. Kilroe. 5 Rn
1m 28.7 (2.5)
SF—23/22/17/8/–

**915** WIMPEY HOMES WOODLAND PARK CLAIMING STKS £2295.00 (£645.00: £315.00) **1m 3f 32y** 3-00 (3-00)

6715 **Philgun (63)** **(Fav)** *(CWCElsey)* 3–8–0 ‡5SMaloney (4) (trckd ldrs: rn wd appr st: slt ld 2f out: hdd ins fnl f: rallied to ld cl home) ....................... —1
3135 Feeling Foolish (IRE) **(59)** (bl) *(TFairhurst)* 3–7-13 ‡3JFanning (2) (lw: hld up: hdwy appr st: chal 2f out: slt ld ins fnl f: r.o: jst ct) ............. hd.2
8105 Perforate **(60)** (bl) *(SirMarkPrescott)* 3–8-6 GDuffield (1) (b.hind: led tl hdd & outpcd 2f out: styd on fnl f) ............................................ 2½.3
603 Breakdancer (IRE) *(MrsJRRamsden)* 3–8-5 TLucas (6) (hld up & bhd: stdy hdwy ent st: snkn up 2f out: nvr plcd to chal) ..................... 2½.4
Rage **(65)** (bl) *(TCraig)* 5–9-5 LCharnock (3) (lw: cl up tl wknd 2f out) ............... 8.5
771 Tremendous (USA) *(JNorton)* 4–9-3 ‡7OPears (7) (chsd ldrs tl wknd appr st) .... 20.6
Buy Nordan *(FWatson)* 8–9-0 DNicholls (5) (bkwd: broke leg & p.u after 2f: dead) 0

11/10 PHILGUN(6/4—Evens), 2/1 Perforate, 15/2 Feeling Foolish (IRE), 12/1 Breakdancer (IRE)(op 3/1), 16/1 Rage, 33/1 Tremendous (USA), 100/1 Buy Nordan. CSF £8.86, Tote £2.50: £1.50 £1.90 (£7.90). Mr C. D. Barber-Lomax (MALTON) bred by Mrs M. Morley. 7 Rn
2m 24.2 (4.5)
SF—3/1/3/–/–/–

**916** EDINBURGH GOLD CUP (H'cap) (0-90) £3415.00 (£1030.00: £500.00: £235.00) **1½m 31y** 3-30 (3-31)

766 **Young George (59)** **(Fav)** *(MDods)* 5–8-5 KFallon (1) (hld up & bhd: hdwy to ld 2f out: hung rt: r.o: comf) ........................................... —1
Family Line **(82)** *(MissLAPerratt)* 4–10-0 NConnorton (2) (lw: chsd ldrs: chal 3f out: r.o: nt pce of wnr) ............................................. ¾.2
6633 J P Morgan **(52)** (v) *(MPNaughton)* 4–7-12 JakiHouston (3) (led & sn clr: hdd 2f out: one pce) ........................................................... 2½.3
760 Carefree Times **(47)** *(JNorton)* 5–7-7 JLowe (4) (lw: chsd ldr: ev ch over 2f out: sn rdn & outpcd) ...................................................... 2½.4

11/10 YOUNG GEORGE, 3/1 J P Morgan, 7/2 Carefree Times, 13/2 Family Line(op 4/1). CSF £6.86, Tote £1.50 (£3.20). Mr J. A. Wynn-Williams (DARLINGTON) bred by Stephen Moloney. 4 Rn
2m 37.3 (4.8)
SF—1/22/–/–

**917** E.B.F. PEOPLES' STKS (Mdn 2-Y.O) £2358.40 (£662.40: £323.20) **5f** 4-00 (4-03)

**Sabo Song** *(RAllan)* 8-9 SWebster (2) (w'like: scope: trckd ldrs: led appr fnl f: shkn up & r.o) ................................................................ —1
654 Make it Happen (IRE) (bl) **(Fav)** *(JBerry)* 9-0 JCarroll (3) (lw: cl up: led ½-wy tl appr fnl f: no ex) ........................................................... 1½.2
7512 Nicky Mygirl *(MBrittain)* 8-9 KDarley (1) (led: hung lft most of wy: hdd ½-wy: grad wknd) ...................................................................... 6.3
5683 Just Baileys *(MJohnston)* 8-9 DMcKeown (4) (s.i.s: sn chsng ldrs: rdn whn stumbled & fell ½-wy) ................................................... 0

11/8 Make it Happen (IRE)(Evens—6/4), 2/1 Just Baileys, 3/1 Nicky Mygirl, 14/1 SABO SONG(20/1—25/1). CSF £30.48, Tote £9.90 (£15.40). Mr James S. Kennerley (CORNHILL-ON-TWEED) bred by J. L. Woolford. 4 Rn
58.8 sec (1.1)
SF—38/37/8

**918** LOTHIAN APP'CE H'CAP (0-70) £2263.50 (£636.00: £310.50) **5f** 4-30 (4-37)

752★ **Penny Hasset (63)** **(Fav)** *(MWEasterby)* 4–9-8 JMarshall (2) (a.p: hdwy ½-wy: led ins fnl f: r.o) ............................................... —1

752　The Right Time (45) (bl) *(JParkes)* 7–8–4　VHalliday (7) (hdwy ½-wy: chal 1f out: r.o wl) ......................................................... ¾.2

888　Last Straw (37) (bl) *(AWJones)* 4–7–10　ClaireBalding (9) (a w ldrs: kpt on same pce fnl f) ......................................................... ¾.3

668　Lady's Mantle (USA) (44) *(RBastiman)* 8–8–3　HBastiman (10) (swtg: mde most tl hdd ins fnl f: kpt on) ......................................................... s.h.4

819　Jovial Kate (USA) (44) *(BEllison)* 5–8–3　RHavlin (11) (a w ldrs: kpt on one pce fnl f) ......................................................... s.h.5

735*　Iron King (69) *(JLSpearing)* 6–10–0　AGarth (6) (effrt ½-wy: styd on: nvr able chal) ......................................................... 1½.6

366　Lift Boy (USA) (48) *(DenysSmith)* 3–7–7 ‡5CTeague (5) (disp ld tl outpcd ins fnl f) ......................................................... ½.7

661　Chateau Nord (56) *(JBerry)* 3–8–1 ‡5ADaly (14) (lw: cl up tl wknd ins fnl f) ......................................................... ½.8

888　Saladan Knight (58) (bl) *(JGFitzGerald)* 7–9–3　MHunt (13) (styd on fnl 2f: nvr rchd ldrs) ......................................................... ½.9

North of Watford (49) *(MPNaughton)* 7–8–8　DCarson (4) (b.nr hind: disp ld tl wknd 1f out) ......................................................... 1½.10

Bee Dee Ell (USA) (51) *(MissLAPerratt)* 3–7–10 ‡5JScotland (8) (in tch 3f: rdr lost iron & sn wknd) ......................................................... 1½.11

407　Brisas (53) (bl) *(TFairhurst)* 5–8–12　OPears (1) (lw: sn outpcd) ......................................................... 6.12

Melody Anne (46) *(JSHaldane)* 3–7–5(2) ‡5GCoogan (12) (b.hind: sn outpcd & bhd) ......................................................... 13

*Minsk (66/1) Withdrawn (bolted two circuits bef s) : not under orders*

**4/1** PENNY HASSET, **5/1** The Right Time, **11/2** Iron King, **8/1** Lady's Mantle (USA), Last Straw, Chateau Nord, **9/1** Jovial Kate, **12/1** Brisas, **16/1** North of Watford, **20/1** Saladan Knight(op 12/1), **25/1** Melody Anne, **33/1** Lift Boy (USA), **50/1** Bee Dee Ell (USA). CSF £23.28, CT £142.36. Tote £5.80: £2.20 £4.10 £2.00 (£42.10). Mrs Anne Henson (SHERIFF HUTTON) bred by Mrs Anne Henson. 13 Rn　　　　58.7 sec (1)
SF—53/32/21/27/26/45

T/Plpt: £578.10 (3.35 Tckts).　　　　　　　　　　　　　　　　　　　　　　　　　　　AA

## 759—BEVERLEY (R-H)
### Tuesday, May 19th [Firm]
Going Allowance: minus 0.40 sec per fur (F)　　　　　　　　　　　　Wind: slt half bhd

Stalls: high

**919**　WINDMILL INN STKS (Mdn) £1932.00 (£532.00: £252.00)　　1m 100y　　2-30 (2-30)

**Gulf Sailor (IRE)** (Fav) *(MRStoute)* 4–9–7　WRSwinburn (4) (trckd ldrs: smooth hdwy over 2f out: chal on bit appr fnl f: sn led: pushed out) —1

698²　Agincourt Song (USA) (75) (Fav) *(JLDunlop)* 3–8–9　GDuffield (9) (led: rdn 2f out: hdd ins fnl f: kpt on u.p) ......................................................... ½.2

698　Hanley's Hands (IRE) *(MHTompkins)* 3–8–9　PRobinson (2) (lw: hdwy 3f out: hung rt over 1f out: nt pce of ldrs) ......................................................... 8.3

418⁶　Father Hayes (USA) *(WJPearce)* 4–9–7　DNicholls (1) (s.s: bhd tl hdwy on outside 2f out: n.d) ......................................................... 3.4

Lightning Spark *(MAvison)* 3–8–4　MBirch (8) (w'like: leggy: s.s: sn in tch: effrt wl over 2f out: sn outpcd) ......................................................... hd.5

Copper Trader *(KSBridgwater)* 3–8–4　KDarley (5) (in tch: effrt appr st: sn rdn & btn) ......................................................... 2½.6

Share Holder *(MissGayKelleway)* 4–8–11 ‡5BDoyle (6) (b: small: neat: cl up tl rdn & wknd over 2f out) ......................................................... 6.7

206　Lunagraphe (USA) *(BobJones)* 4–9–2　VSmith (3) (swtg: chsd ldrs tl rn wd appr st: sn lost pl) ......................................................... 4.8

600　Mash the Tea (IRE) (v) *(HJCollingridge)* 3–8–2 ‡7CHawksley (7) (lw: a bhd) ......................................................... 9

**8/11** Agincourt Song (USA)(11/10—4/6), **13/8** GULF SAILOR (IRE), **12/1** Father Hayes (USA), **20/1** Share Holder, Hanley's Hands (IRE)(op 12/1), **33/1** Ors. CSF £3.27, Tote £2.60: £1.10 £1.10 £2.30 (£1.50). Lord Weinstock (NEWMARKET) bred by Ballymacoll Stud Farm Ltd in Ireland. 9 Rn　　　1m 43.3 (0.6)
SF—47/33/9/12/–/–

**920**　GREEN DRAGON (S) STKS (2-Y.O) £2441.60 (£677.60: £324.80)　　5f　　3-00 (3-02)

769²　**Shadow Jury** (Fav) *(MrsGRReveley)* 9-2　KDarley (4) (lw: sltly hmpd after s: chsd ldrs: smooth hdwy 1f out: led ins fnl f: r.o wl) —1

882³　Dead Calm *(CTinkler)* 8–11　MBirch (11) (lw: led after 2f: sn drvn along: hdd ins fnl f: unable qckn) ......................................................... 1½.2

665⁶　A Bridge Too Far (IRE) *(WJPearce)* 8–6　LCharnock (7) (lw: hung lft after s: a cl up: rdn & kpt on same pce appr fnl f) ......................................................... 1.3

659⁶ Oscars Quest *(JBerry)* 8-11 JCarroll (2) (bit bkwd: sn outpcd & drvn along: hdwy over 1f out: r.o wl towards fin) ............................. hd.4
    Sunshine in Ramsey *(TFairhurst)* 8-3 ‡³JFanning (9) (lt-f: unf: s.s: hdwy 2f out: kpt on u.p: nrst fin) ................................................. 2.5
769 Private Liner *(RonaldThompson)* 8-11 RPElliott (5) (hld up: stdy hdwy over 1f out: nvr plcd to chal) ............................................. s.h.6
759 Libby-J *(MWEasterby)* 8-6 TLucas (10) (bhd: hdwy over 1f out: nt pce to chal) . 2.7
786 Pfaff's Cellar *(WGMTurner)* 8-11 ‡⁵RPrice (12) (swtg: led 2f: sn hrd rdn: wknd over 1f out) ...................................................... hd.8
365 Dunnington *(MWEasterby)* 7-13 ‡⁷JMarshall (1) (dwlt: nvr trbld ldrs) ............... 1½.9
    Arrochar *(JGFitzGerald)* 8-6 KFallon (6) (leggy: bhd & rdn along ½-wy: sme hdwy & swtchd over 1f out: no imp) ......................... 1½.10
602 Safe to Say *(MrsJRRamsden)* 8-6 NConnorton (3) (sltly hmpd sn after s: chsd ldrs over 3f) ...................................................... 8.11

1/3 SHADOW JURY(op 10/11), 6/1 Dead Calm, A Bridge Too Far (IRE), 14/1 Oscars Quest, 20/1 Arrochar, Safe to Say, 25/1 Libby-J, Private Liner, Sunshine in Ramsey, 33/1 Ors. CSF £4.55, Tote £1.50: £1.10 £1.40 £1.50 (£2.70). Mr P. D. Savill (SALTBURN) bred by J. S. Bell. 11 Rn; Bt in 8,400 gns     63.5 sec (2)
SF—22/11/2/6/–/–

**921**     BEVERLEY ARMS H'CAP (3-Y.O) (0-90) £3028.00 (£904.00: £432.00: £196.00)
      1m 1f 207y               3-30 (3-32)

(Weights raised 4 lb)
728³ Bayaireg (USA) **(72)** (Jt-Fav) *(AAScott)* 8-10 WRSwinburn (1) (lw: stdd s: hld up & plld hrd: smooth hdwy over 2f out: led over 1f out: sn clr) —1
599 Persian Fantasy **(70)** *(JLDunlop)* 8-8 GDuffield (2) (a.p: pushed along appr st: styd on same pce fnl 2f) ...................................... 3.2
395 Grog (IRE) **(78)** *(MRChannon)* 8-11 ‡⁵BDoyle (5) (lw: led tl hdd over 1f out: no ex ins fnl f) ............................................................. 2½.3
767² Eid (USA) **(80)** (Jt-Fav) *(DMorley)* 9-4 KDarley (4) (lw: in tch: effrt over 2f out: nt pce to chal) ................................................... 2.4
493² Bigwheel Bill (IRE) **(80)** *(JWWatts)* 9-4 JLowe (6) (s.i.s: hld up: hdwy 4f out: rdn & wl outpcd 3f out: styd on appr fnl f) ........................ ½.5
    Sweet Noble (IRE) **(57)** *(JGFitzGerald)* 7-6 ‡³JFanning (3) (chsd ldr tl wknd 2f out) ................................................................. ¾.6
716⁴ Mad Militant (IRE) **(83)** *(RHollinshead)* 9-7 MBirch (7) (lw: hld up: nt clr run over 2f out: swtchd outside: sn rdn & btn) ...................... s.h.7

7/2 Eid (USA), BAYAIREG (USA), 4/1 Persian Fantasy, Bigwheel Bill (IRE), 8/1 Ors. CSF £17.25, Tote £4.20: £2.20 £2.40 (£11.20). Maktoum Al Maktoum (NEWMARKET) bred by Mrs Nancy S. Dillman in USA. 7 Rn
2m 2.6 (0.6)
SF—50/42/40/43/42/14

**922**     ROYAL STANDARD STKS (Mdn 3-Y.O.F) £2284.80 (£632.80: £302.40)
      1m 1f 207y               4-00 (4-02)

    **Spikenard** *(PTWalwyn)* 8-11 MBirch (4) (prom: shkn up & outpcd over 2f out: styd on to ld 1f out: r.o) ...................................... —1
    Forest Dew (USA) *(MHTompkins)* 8-11 PRobinson (8) (unf: scope: hld up: swtchd outside & gd hdwy 2f out: led 1f out: sn hdd: r.o) .. ¾.2
486² Clear Sound *(GWragg)* 8-8 ‡³FNorton (5) (lw: led: disp ld 3f out: hdd & one pce over 1f out) ...................................................... 2½.3
680³ Queen Caroline (USA) (Fav) *(HRACecil)* 8-11 AMcGlone (1) (lw: a.wl plcd: wnt 2nd 5f out: chal 3f out: styd on same pce over 1f out) ... ½.4
    Sakbah (USA) *(JRFanshawe)* 8-11 WRSwinburn (7) (lt-f: trckd ldrs: effrt over 2f out: wknd appr fnl f) ............................................ 4.5
707 Just Julia *(MRChannon)* 8-11 CRutter (6) (effrt & rn sltly wd st: sn bhd) ............. 6.6
902 Sizzling Sarah (v) *(BobJones)* 8-11 VSmith (2) (s.s: drvn along to go prom wl over 1f: wknd qckly: t.o fnl 5f) .................................... 7
878 Scherzo Impromptu (100/1) Withdrawn (ref to ent stalls) : not under orders

4/9 Queen Caroline (USA), 7/1 Clear Sound, 9/1 Sakbah (USA), 11/1 Just Julia, SPIKENARD, 16/1 Forest Dew (USA)(op 10/1), 100/1 Sizzling Sarah. CSF £126.47, Tote £10.90: £2.50 £4.10 (£52.20). Lord Howard de Walden (LAMBOURN) bred by Lord Howard de Walden. 7 Rn
2m 4.7 (2.7)
SF—30/28/20/22/14/2

**923**     ROSE & CROWN APP'CE H'CAP (0-80) £2441.20 (£673.20: £319.60)
      1m 3f 216y               4-30 (4-31)

    **Nipotina (40)** *(RHollinshead)* 6-8-0 ‡⁷AGarth (4) (trckd ldrs: squeezed thro on ins to ld 2f out: r.o strly) ............................... —1

766[6] Smoke **(44)** (Fav) *(JParkes)* 6–8-11  FNorton (1) (lw: b: hld up in tch: hdwy on outside 2f out: ev ch 1f out: styd on u.p) .............................. 1.2

880 Eire Leath-Sceal **(61)** *(MBrittain)* 5–9-7 ‡7DMeredith (2) (led tl hdd 3f out: hrd rdn & hung lft over 2f out: styd on same pce) .............................. 3.3

Sarsta Grai **(52)** *(MHEasterby)* 4–9-5  SMaloney (3) (cl up: led 3f out : bmpd over 2f out: sn hdd & btn) ................................................... 1½.4

**11/8** Smoke, **7/4** Eire Leath-Sceal, **7/2** Sarsta Grai, **8/1** NIPOTINA. CSF £18.37, Tote £8.50 (£6.00). Miss Sarah Hollinshead (UPPER LONGDON) bred by R. G. Bonson. 4 Rn                    2m 39.1 (7.5)

---

**924**    ANGEL INN MEDIAN AUCTION STKS (Mdn 2-Y.O) £2324.00 (£644.00: £308.00)
5f                                                                        5-00 (5-03)

**Razaroo (USA)** *(JEtherington)* 8-10  TLucas (7) (w'like: scope: chsd ldrs: rn green & nt clr run 1f out: styd on wl to ld cl home) ...................... —1

769[3] Cloudy Reef *(RHollinshead)* 7-8 ‡7AGarth (4) (prom: led 3f out: rdn clr & edgd lft ins fnl f: ct nr fin) ......................................................... s.h.2

Canny Lad *(JGFitzGerald)* 8-6  KFallon (8) (lengthy: scope: disp ld 2f: styd prom: rdn wl over 1f out: edgd rt & r.o nr fin) ........................... s.h.3

665[3] Legendary Hero (Fav) *(TDBarron)* 8-6  KDarley (10) (chsd ldrs: nt clr run 2f out: rdn & hdwy appr fnl f: n.m.r & snatched up cl home) ............... 1.4

Cliburnel News (IRE) *(MHTompkins)* 8-5  PRobinson (2) (unf: scope: lw: rdn along & outpcd early: hdwy u.p over 1f out: styd on nr fin) ............ ½.5

Royal Interval *(WGMTurner)* 8-3 ‡3TSprake (6) (w'like: in tch: rdn & outpcd 2f out: kpt on fnl f) ................................................................. 2.6

770[4] Fort Vally *(BWMurray)* 8-1  JLowe (13) (b.nr hind: hdwy on ins whn bdly hmpd wl over 1f out: snatched up ins fnl f: n.d) .............................. nk.7

439 Jasmin Isle *(MissGayKelleway)* 8-5  AMackay (5) (w ldrs tl wknd over 1f out) ... 2½.8

Lancaster Pilot *(RMWhitaker)* 8-6  ACulhane (11) (cmpt: scope: bit bkwd: s.s: sn rcvrd: in tch over 3f out) ........................................... 2½.9

446[6] Kingston Brown *(JBerry)* 8-6  JCarroll (12) (bit bkwd: sn outpcd) .............. 1½.10

770 Hawaymyson (IRE) *(APStringer)* 8-10  JFortune (9) (disp ld 2f: sn hrd rdn & wknd) .......................................................................................... hd.11

Newinsky *(CTinkler)* 8-6  MBirch (1) (leggy: scope: s.i.s: nvr wnt pce) ......... hd.12

568 Beckswhite Abbey *(WJPearce)* 8-5  LCharnock (3) (hung lft & wl bhd fr ½-wy) ... 13

**5/2** Legendary Hero, **4/1** RAZAROO (USA), **11/2** Kingston Brown, Fort Vally, **8/1** Cloudy Reef, **10/1** Canny Lad, **12/1** Cliburnel News (IRE)(op 8/1), Royal Interval, **14/1** Lancaster Pilot(op 6/1), **16/1** Newinsky, Hawaymyson (IRE), **20/1** Jasmin Isle, **25/1** Beckswhite Abbey. CSF £39.86, Tote £6.10: £2.20 £3.00 £3.60 (£76.60). Mr J. R. Rowbottom (MALTON) bred by Hunter Farm in USA. 13 Rn                    63 sec (1.5)
                                                                    SF—26/9/20/16/13/3

T/Plpt: £1,816.90 (1.7 Tckts).                                                   O'R

---

# GOODWOOD  (R-H)
## Tuesday, May 19th [Good to firm]
Going Allowance: minus 0.10 sec per fur (F)

Wind: almost nil

Stalls: low

**925**    TREHEARNE & NORMAN STKS (Mdn 3-Y.O.C & G) £3590.00 (£1070.00: £510.00:
£230.00)  7f                                                             2-10 (2-11)

441 **Hopeful Bid (IRE) (76)** (Fav) *(RHannon)* 9-0  BRaymond (5) (4th st: rdn & nt clr run 2f out: swtchd rt over 1f out: led nr fin) ........................... —1

157 Efharisto **(77)** *(CEBrittain)* 9-0  MRoberts (1) (led over 1f: 2nd st: led over 2f out tl hdd nr fin) ...................................................................... nk.2

727[4] Super Serenade **(72)** *(GBBalding)* 9-0  JWilliams (4) (5th st: nt clr run fnl 3f: r.o) 1½.3

Nbaat (USA) *(CJBenstead)* 9-0  RCochrane (2) (neat: bit bkwd: dwlt: hdwy over 2f out: ev ch over 1f out: r.o) ................................................. hd.4

620 Elwazir (USA) *(PTWalwyn)* 9-0  WCarson (3) (3rd st: hrd rdn & ev ch 1f out: r.o) nk.5

727 Our Eddie *(BGubby)* 9-0  NAdams (7) (led over 5f out tl over 2f out: ev ch ins fnl f: unable qckn) ................................................................... hd.6

Tom's Apache *(WRWilliams)* 8-9 ‡5ATucker (6) (6th st: wknd over 1f out) .......... 7.7

**6/4** HOPEFUL BID (IRE), **5/2** Super Serenade, **5/1** Efharisto(9/4—11/2), **15/2** Nbaat (USA)(8/1—12/1), **9/1** Elwazir (USA)(6/1—10/1), **20/1** Our Eddie(op 10/1), **50/1** Tom's Apache. CSF £8.97, Tote £2.60: £1.70 £2.40 (£5.30). Mr N. Capon (MARLBOROUGH) bred by Cloghran Stud Farm Ltd and Mrs E. Burke in Ireland. 7 Rn
                                                                 1m 28.27 (3.57)
                                                            SF—35/34/29/28/27/26

**926** CHICHESTER FESTIVAL THEATRE H'CAP (0-95) £3687.50 (£1100.00: £525.00: £237.50)
1½m
2-40 (2-44)

736² El Volador (59) *(RJO'Sullivan)* 5–8-8 RCochrane (3) (swtg: hdwy 2f out: nt clr run over 1f out: led ins fnl f: r.o wl) ..................................... —1
713⁴ Moonlight Quest (73) *(BHanbury)* 4–9-8 LDettori (5) (2nd st: led over 1f out tl ins fnl f: unable qckn) ............................ 2.2
552 Run High (58) *(PMitchell)* 9–8-4 ‡3SO'Gorman (8) (4th st: rdn over 3f out: one pce fnl f) ....................... 1½.3
Monarda (66) *(PFICole)* 5–8-8 ‡7JDSmith (4) (5th st: lost pl over 2f out: rallied fnl f: r.o) ........................ 1.4
730⁴ Prince Hannibal (79) (Fav) *(JLDunlop)* 5–10-0 WCarson (6) (lw: 6th st: nt clr run 2f out: one pce) .................. 1½.5
805 Rushluan (52) *(RJHodges)* 8–8-1 JQuinn (1) (3rd st: wknd over 1f out) .......... s.h.6
368 Green Medina (IRE) (76) *(MBell)* 4–9-11 MHills (7) (led over 10f) ................ 1.7
Mahfil (67) *(RAkehurst)* 4–9-2 TQuinn (2) (hdwy 2f out: wknd fnl f) ................ hd.8

6/4 Prince Hannibal, 11/2 Moonlight Quest, Mahfil, 7/1 Monarda, EL VOLADOR, 11/1 Green Medina (IRE)(8/1—12/1), 20/1 Rushluan, 33/1 Run High. CSF £39.31, CT £1,050.31. Tote £5.30: £1.50 £1.10 £8.80 (£12.90). Mr I. A. Baker (BOGNOR REGIS) bred by L. and Mrs Hutch. 8 Rn 2m 38.17 (6.47)
SF—17/27/6/8/25/–

**927** A.R. DENNIS BOOKMAKERS PREDOMINATE STKS (listed race) (3-Y.O) £18600.00 (£5550.00: £2650.00: £1200.00) 1¼m
3-10 (3-15)

647³ Jeune (105) *(GWragg)* 8-12 MHills (5) (2nd st: led over 2f out: comf) ................. —1
710* Hatta's Mill *(HRACecil)* 8-12 WRyan (9) (lw: led over 7f: unable qckn) ................ 5.2
110* Beldi (USA) (92) *(CFBrittain)* 8-12 MRoberts (3) (hdwy 2f out: r.o one pce) ...... ¾.3
737* Young Freeman (USA) (Fav) *(GHarwood)* 8-12 RCochrane (2) (dwlt: rdn & hdwy 2f out: r.o one pce) ................ nk.4
443 Ninja Dancer (USA) (106) *(MrsJCecil)* 9-1 LPiggott (7) (4th st: one pce fnl 2f) .... s.h.5
722² Profusion *(PFICole)* 8-12 AMunro (4) (swtg: nvr nr to chal) ................. 1½.6
679* Viardot (IRE) (94) *(MRStoute)* 8-12 SCauthen (4) (3rd st: wknd over 1f out) ....... 2.7
609³ Powerful Edge *(IABalding)* 8-12 BRaymond (8) (6th st: wknd over 1f out) ....... 2½.8
538a³ Rokeby (bl) *(IABalding)* 9-1 LDettori (6) (lw: 5th st: wknd 3f out: t.o) ............... 25.9

11/8 Young Freeman (USA), 5/1 Profusion, 7/1 JEUNE, 15/2 Hatta's Mill, Viardot (IRE), 14/1 Powerful Edge, Ninja Dancer (USA), Rokeby, 33/1 Beldi (USA). CSF £53.15, Tote £7.90: £1.70 £2.80 £7.70 (£37.20). Sir Robin McAlpine (NEWMARKET) bred by Sir Robin McAlpine. 9 Rn 2m 8.45 (3.45)
SF—54/44/42/41/43/37

**928** GOODWOOD AERODROME CLAIMING STKS (Mdn 2-Y.O) £3817.50 (£1140.00: £545.00: £247.50) 6f
3-40 (3-45)

645⁴ Bourbon Jack (Fav) *(JWPayne)* 8-13 AMunro (13) (a.p: led over 1f out: all out) —1
682 Scenic Reef (IRE) *(JMPEustace)* 8-4 TQuinn (12) (a.p: hrd rdn & ev ch fnl f: r.o wl) .................. hd.2
733³ Lochore *(RIngram)* 8-11 ‡5JWeaver (8) (a.p: hrd rdn over 1f out: r.o) ............... nk.3
803⁵ Kingsdown Cavalier *(RHannon)* 9-2 BRouse (5) (lw: a.p: rdn over 2f out: bmpd wl over 1f out: r.o) ......... 1½.4
470 Glowing Dancer *(JRJenkins)* 9-3 MRoberts (7) (a.p: rdn over 2f out: bmpd wl over 1f out: unable qckn) ......... 1½.5
701³ Be Polite (IRE) *(MBell)* 8-4 MHills (4) (led over 4f: one pce) ................ ¾.6
786⁴ Mighty Miss Magpie (IRE) *(MRChannon)* 8-5 PaulEddery (16) (nvr nr to chal) .... 3.7
782⁴ Caps Ninety-Two (IRE) *(DrJDScargill)* 8-4 JQuinn (15) (a.p: ev ch over 1f out: wknd ins fnl f) ......... nk.8
Sabo's Express *(RHannon)* 9-2 JReid (3) (unf: nvr nrr) ................. ½.9
729⁶ Trepidation (IRE) (bl) *(MJFetherston-Godley)* 8-9 LDettori (11) (bhd fnl 2f) ...... ½.10
729 Southampton *(GBBalding)* 8-7 JWilliams (14) (nvr nrr) ................ hd.11
782 Burishki *(GAPritchard-Gordon)* 8-0 NCarlisle (10) (prom over 3f) ............ ¾.12
555 Jaybee-Jay *(MJHaynes)* 8-11 RCochrane (2) (bhd fnl 2f) ............ 1½.13
786³ Wealthywoo *(JSMoore)* 7-12 ‡3DBiggs (1) (a bhd) ................. 8.14
645 Miss Ribbons *(PatMitchell)* 8-3 ‡3SO'Gorman (6) (dwlt: outpcd) ............... ½.15
*Stewards Enquiry: Weaver suspended 28-30/5/92 (excessive use of whip).*

3/1 BOURBON JACK, 5/1 Kingsdown Cavalier, Be Polite (IRE), 8/1 Wealthywoo, Glowing Dancer(op 5/1), 10/1 Caps Ninety-Two (IRE), Sabo's Express, 16/1 Lochore, 20/1 Jaybee-Jay(op 12/1), Trepidation (IRE), 25/1 Southampton, Scenic Reef (IRE), Burishki, 50/1 Miss Ribbons. CSF £77.33, Tote £3.80: £1.60 £11.40 £3.40 (£281.70). Mr Ettore Landi (NEWMARKET) bred by Whitsbury Manor Stud. 15 Rn 1m 12.99 (2.59)
SF—35/25/31/30/25/9

**929**  FESTIVAL STKS (listed race)   £11062.50 (£3300.00: £1575.00: £712.50)
  1¼m                                                                      4-10 (4-14)

551⁵ **Flashfoot (107)** (Fav) *(IABalding)* 4–8-12 RCochrane (8) (lw: hld up: 5th st: rdn
  & swtchd lft 2f out: led ins fnl f: r.o wl) .................................... —1
390  Jura **(101)** *(HRACecil)* 4–8-12 WRyan (7) (s.s: hdwy over 1f out: hrd rdn: r.o wl
  ins fnl f) ............................................................................. hd.2
436  Gai Bulga **(108)** *(GWragg)* 4–8-10 MRoberts (6) (led tl ins fnl f: unable qckn) ... ¾.3
  Tetradonna (IRE) *(RHannon)* 4–8-7 LPiggott (5) (3rd st: hrd rdn over 1f out: one
  pce) ........................................................................................ 2.4
579³ Tanfith (CAN) **(99)** *(JEBanks)* 5–8-12 AMunro (3) (4th st: hrd rdn over 1f out:
  one pce) ................................................................................. 2.5
22a⁵ Knifebox (USA) **(108)** *(JHMGosden)* 4–9-1 WCarson (2) (2nd st: wknd over 1f
  out) ...................................................................................... 10.6
557⁶ Half a Tick (USA) **(105)** *(PFICole)* 4–9-1 TQuinn (9) (swtg: 7th st: wknd over 2f
  out) .................................................................................... 1½.7
390  Man From Eldorado (USA) *(GHarwood)* 4–9-1 JReid (1) (lw: a bhd) ................ hd.8
  Hailsham (CAN) **(112)** *(CEBrittain)* 4–9-7 SCauthen (4) (6th st: wknd over 2f
  out) .................................................................................... 1½.9

**7/4** FLASHFOOT, **4/1** Gai Bulga, **5/1** Jura, **7/1** Half a Tick (USA), **9/1** Hailsham (CAN), **12/1** Man From Eldorado
(USA), **14/1** Knifebox (USA), **16/1** Tanfith (CAN), **20/1** Tetradonna (IRE). CSF £11.03, Tote £2.80: £1.40 £1.80
£1.70 (£9.90). Mr J. C. Smith (KINGSCLERE) bred by Littleton Stud. 9 Rn        2m 7.09 (2.09)
                                                                      SF—67/66/62/55/56/39

**930**  NPI CELEBRATION H'CAP (3-Y.O) (0-90) £3720.00 (£1110.00: £530.00: £240.00)
  1m                                                                       4-45 (4-49)

482  **Baluga (71)** *(GHarwood)* 8-2(2) AClark (12) (lw: led 6f out tl over 2f out: led over
  1f out: r.o wl) ........................................................................ —1
783³ Confronter **(75)** (bl) *(PFICole)* 8-6 TQuinn (10) (2nd st: led over 2f out tl over 1f
  out: unable qckn ins fnl f) ..................................................... 1½.2
  Common Council **(74)** *(GAPritchard-Gordon)* 8-5 GCarter (1) (hdwy over 2f
  out: hrd rdn over 1f out: r.o ins fnl f) ..................................... hd.3
  Merlins Wish (USA) **(90)** *(RHannon)* 9-7 BRaymond (9) (4th st: one pce fnl 2f) .. 5.4
  Well Saddled (IRE) **(88)** *(DRCElsworth)* 9-5 JWilliams (3) (lw: hdwy over 1f out:
  r.o) ...................................................................................... ½.5
730  Royal Seaton **(86)** *(BRMillman)* 8-12 ‡5JWeaver (2) (hdwy over 1f out: nvr nrr) 2½.6
695* Googly **(62)** *(WGRWightman)* 7-7 GBardwell (13) (6th st: wknd 2f out) ......... 1.7
767³ Thinking Twice (USA) **(76)** *(PWHarris)* 8-7 PaulEddery (5) (a mid div) ......... ¾.8
  Severine (USA) **(65)** *(JLDunlop)* 7-10 NCarlisle (8) (nvr nr to chal) ........... 1.9
778² Sir Oliver (IRE) **(73)** *(RJHodges)* 8-4 WCarson (11) (led 2f: 3rd st: wknd over 1f
  out) ...................................................................................... 1.10
674* Born to Dance **(83)** *(MRStoute)* 9-0 SCauthen (4) (bhd fnl 3f) ................ 4.11
451³ Basilica **(75)** *(CEBrittain)* 8-6 MRoberts (6) (bhd fnl 3f) ................... 6.12
  Dordogne **(66)** *(RAkehurst)* 7-11 NAdams (7) (bit bkwd: 5th st: wknd over 2f
  out) ...................................................................................... 13
                              LONG HANDICAP: Googly 7-4.

**4/1** Born to Dance, **7/1** BALUGA, Sir Oliver (IRE), **15/2** Well Saddled (IRE), **8/1** Googly, **10/1** Basilica, Confronter,
**12/1** Merlins Wish (USA), Severine (USA), Thinking Twice (USA), **14/1** Royal Seaton, **20/1** Common Council,
**25/1** Dordogne. CSF £70.50, CT £1,228.18. Tote £11.90: £3.70 £5.10 £8.90 (£67.30). Mr J. C. Thompson
(PULBOROUGH) bred by K. J. and Mrs Buchanan. 13 Rn               1m 38.78 (1.18)
                                                                      SF—58/57/55/56/52/37

**931**  PANAMA HAT H'CAP (0-90) £3785.00 (£1130.00: £540.00: £245.00)
  1m 1f                                                                    5-20 (5-21)

705³ **Port Sunlight (IRE) (78)** *(RHannon)* 4–9-8 RCochrane (8) (hld up: swtchd rt wl
  over 1f out: led ins fnl f: drvn out) .......................................... —1
809* Execution Only (IRE) **(61)** (v) (Fav) *(JWWatts)* 4–8-5 (7x) MRoberts (7) (b.hind:
  3rd st: led 2f out tl ins fnl f: r.o) ............................................. nk.2
736³ Tiger Claw (USA) **(55)** (bl) *(RJHodges)* 6-7-13 WCarson (1) (6th st: rdn over 3f
  out: r.o ins fnl f) ..................................................................... 3½.3
692⁴ Gilderdale **(84)** *(JWHills)* 10–10-0 MHills (10) (5th st: rdn over 2f out: ev ch over
  1f out: unable qckn) .............................................................. ½.4
626  Neptune's Pet **(70)** *(GLewis)* 4–9-0 PaulEddery (5) (led 7f) ................ 7.5
692³ Roseate Lodge **(77)** *(RWArmstrong)* 6–9-7 LPiggott (3) (lw: 4th st: wknd 3f out) 1½.6
392  Lord Oberon (IRE) **(71)** *(RJO'Sullivan)* 4–8-12 ‡3DBiggs (9) (bhd fnl 3f) ...... ¾.7
  Altermeera **(70)** *(MrsBarbaraWaring)* 4–9-0 NHowe (6) (a bhd) ................... ¾.8
693³ Trooping (IRE) **(88)** *(GHarwood)* 3–9-4 AClark (4) (2nd st: wknd 2f out) .......... s.h.9
  Sonalto **(50)** *(DLWilliams)* 6–7-8(1) NAdams (2) (a bhd) ...................... 15.10
                              LONG HANDICAP: Sonalto 7-6.

**9/2** Execution Only (IRE), **5/1** Lord Oberon (IRE)(7/1—9/2), Roseate Lodge, **11/2** PORT SUNLIGHT (IRE), Gilderdale(4/1—6/1), **6/1** Tiger Claw (USA), **8/1** Neptune's Pet(12/1—14/1), **9/1** Trooping (IRE)(8/1—12/1), **25/1** Altermeera, **100/1** Sonalto. CSF £29.77, CT £142.90. Tote £6.20: £2.20 £1.50 £2.10 (£14.10). Mrs C. J. Powell (MARLBOROUGH) bred by Shanbally House Stud in Ireland. 10 Rn

1m 55.14 (4.44)
SF—29/10/–/21/–/–

T/Trio: Races 3 & 5: £438.70 (2 Tckts) & £251.80 (5 Tckts). T/Jkpt: Not won; £8,194.65 to Goodwood 20/5/92.
T/Plpt: £585.40 (13 Tckts).                                                                                   AK

## GOODWOOD (R-H)
### Wednesday, May 20th [Good to firm, Firm patches]
Going Allowance: 2m: minus 0.35 sec; Rest: minus 0.20 sec (F)                     Wind: almost nil

Stalls: low

**932**      FINNBOARD CLAIMING STKS (Mdn 3-Y.O) £3752.50 (£1120.00: £535.00: £242.50)
       1½m                                          2-10 (2-12)

5995 Trumpet (66) *(LordHuntingdon)* 9-0 WRSwinburn (9) (5th st: rdn over 2f out: led ins fnl f: edgd lft: r.o wl) ........................................................ —1
6943 Mr Poppleton *(DWPArbuthnot)* 8-7 BRaymond (2) (dwlt: rdn over 2f out: hdwy over 1f out: r.o wl ins fnl f) .......................................... hd.2
5974 Sir Pageant (70) *(PFICole)* 9-2 TQuinn (7) (lw: led over 8f: led over 2f out tl ins fnl f: r.o) ........................................................................ ½.3
457 Newton Point (58) *(GAPritchard-Gordon)* 8-8 RCochrane (3) (6th st: ev ch 1f out: edgd rt ins fnl f: r.o) ............................................. nk.4
5992 Notable Exception (60) *(JWHills)* 8-8 DHolland (5) (lw: 4th st: ev ch over 1f out: 4th & btn whn hmpd ins fnl f) ........................................ 2.5
7106 American Boogie (FR) (Fav) *(JWHills)* 9-0 MRoberts (10) (lw: rdn over 3f out: hdwy over 2f out: one pce) ........................................... 2½.6
8062 Princess of Orange (60) *(CCElsey)* 7-11 JQuinn (8) (2nd st: led over 3f out tl over 2f out: sn wknd) ................................................. 15.7
      Green Slippers *(GHarwood)* 8-4 AClark (6) (bhd fnl 6f) ........................................... 5.8
8063 Big Pat *(JPearce)* 8-2 WCarson (1) (bhd fnl 3f) ...................................................... 5.9
      Loviste Bay *(JFfitch-Heyes)* 7-10 AMackay (4) (3rd st: wknd over 3f out) ........ 8.10

**5/2** American Boogie (FR), **9/2** Princess of Orange, **7/1** Notable Exception, **8/1** Sir Pageant, TRUMPET, **9/1** Mr Poppleton(op 6/1), **10/1** Green Slippers, Big Pat, **11/1** Newton Point(8/1—12/1), **33/1** Loviste Bay. CSF £71.51, Tote £10.50: £2.30 £3.40 £3.00 (£61.60). The Queen (WEST ILSLEY) bred by The Queen. 10 Rn

2m 39.51 (7.81)

**933**      PAYNE & GUNTER STKS (Mdn 2-Y.O) £3687.50 (£1100.00: £525.00: £237.50)
       6f                                          2-40 (2-42)

      **Firm Pledge (USA)** (Fav) *(PFICole)* 9-0 AMunro (8) (unf: scope: lw: w ldr: led over 2f out: clr over 1f out: easily) ................................... —1
      Canaska Star *(PAKelleway)* 9-0 PRobinson (2) (unf: bit bkwd: led over 3f: unable qckn) ........................................................................... 7.2
      Cissbury Ring *(LadyHerries)* 9-0 LDettori (5) (w'like: rdn over 2f out: hdwy fnl f: r.o) ....................................................................................... 2.3
      Simply Finesse *(RAkehurst)* 9-0 RCochrane (7) (unf: a.p: one pce fnl 2f) ......... hd.4
      Well Suited *(RHannon)* 9-0 JReid (10) (unf: scope: s.s: hdwy over 4f out: one pce fnl 2f) ............................................................................ 1.5
      Heart of Spain *(PJMakin)* 9-0 WRSwinburn (4) (leggy: nvr nr to chal) ............... ½.6
      Savings Bank *(GAPritchard-Gordon)* 9-0 MRoberts (9) (neat: bit bkwd: prom over 3f) ....................................................................................... 5.7
      Young Ern *(SDow)* 9-0 TQuinn (3) (w'like: bkwd: prom over 3f) ........................... 1.8
      Regal Aura (IRE) *(GHarwood)* 9-0 AClark (1) (str: spd over 3f) ............................. 2.9
      Fir Copse *(PRHedger)* 8-9 JWilliams (6) (w'like: a bhd) ....................................... 5.10

**13/8** FIRM PLEDGE (USA), **5/1** Well Suited(7/2—6/1), **11/2** Cissbury Ring, **7/1** Heart of Spain(op 4/1), **8/1** Canaska Star(tchd 14/1), **12/1** Regal Aura (IRE)(op 7/1), Simply Finesse(8/1—16/1), **25/1** Savings Bank, Young Ern, **33/1** Fir Copse. CSF £14.78, Tote £2.50: £1.30 £3.90 £1.60 (£25.90). Mr Fahd Salman (WHATCOMBE) bred by Hermen Greenberg in USA. 10 Rn

1m 11.13 (0.73)
SF—61/33/25/24/20/18

**934**      LUPE STKS (listed race) (3-Y.O.F) £13840.00 (£4120.00: £1960.00: £880.00)
       1¼m                                          3-10 (3-12)

639a4 Oumaldaaya (USA) (100) *(JLDunlop)* 8-11 WCarson (2) (lw: mde all: pushed out) ................................................................................................... —1

780[2] Niodini (USA) **(102)** (Fav) *(MRStoute)* 8-11 SCauthen (5) (swtg: 2nd st: rdn over 3f out: r.o one pce fnl f) .................................................. 3.2

    Fern **(104)** *(LMCumani)* 8-11 LDettori (1) (hld up: 6th st: hrd rdn over 1f out: one pce) ........................................................ 2.3

607[2] Never a Care (USA) *(BWHills)* 8-11 PaulEddery (6) (5th st: wknd over 2f out) .... 7.4

717[2] Juniper Berry (IRE) *(PWChapple-Hyam)* 8-11 LPiggott (3) (3rd st: wknd 2f out) 1½.5

    Miss Bluebird (IRE) **(105)** *(PAKelleway)* 8-11 PRobinson (4) (4th st: wknd 3f out) 6.6

**5/2** Niodini (USA), **3/1** OUMALDAAYA (USA), **9/2** Never a Care (USA), Fern, Juniper Berry (IRE), **12/1** Miss Bluebird (IRE)(op 8/1). CSF £10.54, Tote £4.00: £2.20 £1.70 (£5.70). Mr Hamdan Al-Maktoum (ARUNDEL) bred by Shadwell Estate Company Ltd in USA. 6 Rn           2m 8.73 (3.73)

                                        SF—40/34/30/16/13/1

---

**935**      IRISH LIFE H'CAP (0-100) £5385.00 (£1605.00: £765.00: £345.00)    **6f**    3-40 (3-41)

649 **Milagro (83)** *(RHannon)* 3-8-10 MRoberts (7) (a.p: led over 2f out: all out) ........ —1

813[2] So Rhythmical **(71)** (Fav) *(GHEden)* 8-8-5 ‡[3F]Norton (8) (b.off hind: a.p: hrd rdn over 1f out: ev ch fnl f: r.o wl) ....................................... hd.2

779[6] Hard to Figure **(91)** *(RJHodges)* 6-10-0 TQuinn (1) (lw: rdn over 3f out: swtchd rt over 2f out: hdwy over 1f out: r.o wl) ................................. ¾.3

    Kayvee **(93)** *(GHarwood)* 3-9-6 AClark (3) (led over 3f: unable qckn) ........... 3.4

779 Masnun (USA) **(88)** *(RJO'Sullivan)* 7-9-8 ‡[3]DBiggs (6) (hld up: rdn over 2f out: one pce) .................................................................. nk.5

686[6] Poets Cove **(81)** *(MMcCormack)* 4-9-4 JReid (4) (gd spd over 3f) ............ 6.6

872[2] Blake End (USA) **(81)** *(WAO'Gorman)* 3-8-8 RCochrane (9) (plld hrd: bhd fnl 2f) hd.7

    813 *Green Dollar (7/1) Withdrawn (spread a plate) : not under orders*

**9/4** So Rhythmical, **5/2** Blake End (USA), **5/1** Hard to Figure, **11/2** Masnun (USA), **10/1** Kayvee, **12/1** MILAGRO & Ors. CSF £37.77, CT £142.23. Tote £12.20: £3.70 £2.10 (£21.60). Mrs D. Hammerson (MARLBOROUGH) bred by W. D. J. Ropner. 7 Rn                1m 10.71 (0.02 under best: 0.31)

                                        SF—66/60/80/60/62/33

---

**936**      PEUGEOT 309 GTI H'CAP (0-90) £3720.00 (£1110.00: £530.00: £240.00)
          **1m**                                    4-10 (4-15)

                         (Weights raised 1 lb)

692 **Saafend (64)** *(JSutcliffe)* 4-8-4 MRoberts (1) (2nd st: led 2f out: pushed out) ... —1

705 Daswaki (CAN) **(84)** *(RHannon)* 4-9-10 BRouse (9) (led 6f: unable qckn) 2½.2

626 Cru Exceptionnel **(72)** *(PJMakin)* 4-8-12 BRaymond (11) (lw: dwlt: 6th st: rdn over 1f out: r.o) ..................................................... ¾.3

626 Salbyng **(56)** *(JWHills)* 4-7-10 NCarlisle (3) (4th st: rdn over 1f out: one pce) ... ½.4

736 Marzocco **(55)** *(JFfitch-Heyes)* 4-7-9 AMackay (8) (b.nr hind: rdn over 5f out: nvr nr to chal) ................................................... 6.5

705[2] Aitch N'Bee **(76)** (Jt-Fav) *(LadyHerries)* 9-9-2 LDettori (2) (swtg: 5th st: wknd over 1f out) ................................................... hd.6

477[3] Wingfield (USA) **(79)** *(DRCElsworth)* 4-9-5 SCauthen (7) (hdwy 3f out: wknd 2f out) .......................................................... ½.7

705[4] Mahsul (IRE) **(59)** (Jt-Fav) *(CJBenstead)* 4-7-13 WCarson (6) (lw: a mid div) ... 1½.8

610 Usa Dollar **(60)** (v) *(BGubby)* 5-8-0 AMunro (5) (hdwy 3f out: wknd 2f out) ... nk.9

774[4] Lucky Noire **(66)** *(GHarwood)* 4-7-13[1] ‡[7]GayeHarwood (4) (a bhd) ................ ¾.10

626 Devil's Soul **(55)** *(RAkehurst)* 4-7-9[1] SDawson (12) (s.s: a bhd) ............... ¾.11

273[6] Castle Galah **(53)** *(SWoodman)* 5-7-7 JQuinn (10) (3rd st: wknd over 2f out) 20.12
              LONG HANDICAP: Castle Galah 5-7.

**5/1** Aitch N'Bee, Mahsul (IRE), **13/2** SAAFEND, **8/1** Cru Exceptionnel, Devil's Soul, Daswaki (CAN), Wingfield (USA), **12/1** Lucky Noire(op 8/1), Usa Dollar, **14/1** Salbyng, **20/1** Marzocco, **100/1** Castle Galah. CSF £52.61, CT £384.97. Tote £8.50: £2.60 £3.20 £3.30 (£21.30). J. B. R. Leisure Ltd (EPSOM) bred by Edwin Turner. 12 Rn                1m 39.38 (1.78)

                                        SF—39/51/37/19/—/20

---

**937**      KINCSEM H'CAP (0-80) £4045.00 (£1210.00: £580.00: £265.00)    **2m**    4-45 (4-46)

205 **Art Form (USA) (72)** *(CACyzer)* 5-9-3 ‡[7]TMcLaughlin (10) (2nd st: led over 2f out: rdn out) ............................................... —1

708 Mull House **(58)** *(FJO'Mahony)* 5-8-10 WRSwinburn (4) (4th st: hrd rdn over 1f out: unable qckn) ....................................... 5.2

805 Chucklestone **(57)** *(JSKing)* 9-8-9 TRogers (6) (led: clr after 3f: hdd over 2f out: one pce) ..................................................... 2½.3

590[2] Empire Blue **(69)** *(PFICole)* 9-9-7 TQuinn (1) (b: hdwy over 4f out: 5th st: one pce fnl 2f) ................................................... 1½.4

    Requested **(71)** *(RAkehurst)* 5-9-9 AMunro (3) (6th st: one pce fnl 3f) .............. 4.5

718[4] Tamarpour (USA) **(75)** (v) *(MCPipe)* 5-9-13 MRoberts (12) (b: hdwy over 2f out: one pce) ..................................................... ½.6

475³ Subsonic (IRE) **(78)** *(Fav)* *(JLDunlop)* 4–10-0 WCarson (16) (lw: nvr nr to chal) 1½.**7**
  Skisurf **(55)** *(CEBrittain)* 6–8-7 GCrealock (14) (bit bkwd: nvr nrr) ...... 3.**8**
475  Coleridge **(75)** (v) *(DShaw)* 4–9-11 GCarter (8) (nvr nrr) ...... 1.**9**
605⁵ Sagaman (GER) **(54)** *(LJCodd)* 6–8-6 WNewnes (5) (bhd fnl 8f) ...... 2½.**10**
  Jokers Patch **(62)** *(WRWilliams)* 5–9-0 NAdams (2) (swtg: a bhd) ...... 1½.**11**
  Kilcash (IRE) **(70)** (bl) *(PRHedger)* 4–9-6 JReid (11) (chsd ldr 12f: 3rd st: wknd over 3f out) ...... 2.**12**
205² Postage Stamp **(67)** *(JPearce)* 5–9-5 LPiggott (7) (bhd fnl 3f) ...... 7.**13**
790★ Zealous Kitten (USA) **(57)** *(RJPrice)* 4–8-0 ‡⁷StephenDavies (15) (a bhd) ...... ½.**14**
708² Marine Society **(74)** *(PTWalwyn)* 4–9-10 RCochrane (13) (prom 12f) ...... 7.**15**

**4/1** Subsonic (IRE), **11/2** Postage Stamp, **7/1** Marine Society, Tamarpour (USA), **8/1** Sagaman (GER)(6/1—9/1), **10/1** Requested, Zealous Kitten (USA), **14/1** Kilcash (IRE), ART FORM (USA), Empire Blue, **16/1** Mull House, **25/1** Coleridge, **33/1** Ors. CSF £202.39, CT £6,370.68. Tote £30.60: £2.00 £4.50 £11.50 (£227.20). Mr R. M. Cyzer (HORSHAM) bred by Morgan's Ford Farm and Elizabeth Thomas in USA. 15 Rn
3m 25.60 (3.09 under best; U1)
SF—57/45/41/51/49/52

**938**    BOXGROVE STKS (Mdn 3-Y.O.F) £3850.00 (£1150.00: £550.00: £250.00)
      **7f**                                 5-20 (5-36)

634³ Jade Vale *(JWHills)* 8-11 MHills (12) (2nd st: led over 3f out: all out) ...... —**1**
  Lady Debra Darley *(RHannon)* 8-11 MRoberts (8) (w'like: scope: bit bkwd: s.s: hdwy over 5f out: 4th st: rdn over 1f out: r.o wl) ...... s.h.**2**
634² Ivana (IRE) **(Fav)** *(WJarvis)* 8-11 AMunro (5) (hdwy over 2f out: hrd rdn 1f out: unable qckn) ...... 1½.**3**
689² Hugging **(72)** *(MMcCormack)* 8-11 JReid (6) (swtg: hdwy over 1f out: r.o) ...... 2½.**4**
  Thames Glow *(DRCElsworth)* 8-11 SCauthen (4) (unf: scope: bit bkwd: 6th st: one pec fnl 2f) ...... ¾.**5**
651² Belated *(HThomsonJones)* 8-11 RHills (3) (3rd st: ev ch 2f out: wknd fnl f) ...... hd.**6**
699⁵ Change the Will *(MDIUsher)* 8-11 CRutter (2) (b.off fore: led over 3f: wknd 2f out) ...... 2½.**7**
699  Mariette Larkin *(GBBalding)* 8-11 JWilliams (10) (5th st: wknd over 2f out) ...... hd.**8**
393  Hazy Prospect *(DRCElsworth)* 8-11 TQuinn (7) (dwlt: plld hrd: hdwy over 2f out: wknd over 1f out) ...... 2½.**9**
833⁵ Poly Snip *(MissBSanders)* 8-11 BCrossley (9) (a bhd) ...... 4.**10**
  Early Gales *(MMcCormack)* 8-11 WNewnes (1) (unf: a bhd) ...... 15.**11**
  *Rowan Empire (50/1) Withdrawn (broke loose bef s) : not under orders*

**6/4** Ivana (IRE), **3/1** JADE VALE(7/4—7/2), **7/1** Lady Debra Darley(8/1—12/1), **8/1** Thames Glow(5/1—10/1), **9/1** Belated, **12/1** Hugging(op 8/1), **25/1** Change the Will, **33/1** Ors. CSF £23.01, Tote £5.40: £2.00 £2.30 £1.20 (£18.20). Major Brijendra Singh (LAMBOURN) bred by Maj B. Singh. 11 Rn
1m 28.35 (3.65)
SF—21/20/15/7/5/4

T/Trio: Race 4: £257.50 (6 Tckts) & Race 5: Any 2 fr 1st 3 w any £64.40 (18.5 Tckts). T/Jkpt: Not won; £12,494.85 to Goodwood 21/5/92. T/Plpt: £3,725.30 (2.3 Tckts).      AK

# GOODWOOD (R-H)
## Thursday, May 21st [Firm]
Going Allowance: minus 0.30 sec per fur (F)          Wind: almost nil

Stalls: low

**939**    GOODWOOD PARK HOTEL GOLF AND COUNTRY CLUB CLAIMING STKS (3-Y.O) £3752.50 (£1120.00: £535.00: £242.50)   **6f**        2-10 (2-12)

690  **Lady Sabo (66)** *(GLewis)* 8-2 PaulEddery (10) (lw: a.p: led wl over 1f out: rdn out) ...... —**1**
690⁵ Walk in the Park **(84)** **(Fav)** *(RSimpson)* 8-8 ‡⁵ATucker (5) (lw: stumbled & bmpd s: hdwy over 2f out: hrd rdn over 1f out: r.o) ...... 2½.**2**
614  Loose Zeus (USA) **(45)** *(CFWall)* 7-9 ‡⁷TWilson (4) (bmpd s: swtchd rt 4f out: hdwy 3f out: led 2f out tl wl over 1f out: unable qckn) ...... 2½.**3**
599  Mexican Dancer **(66)** *(RJHolder)* 7-13 NAdams (8) (no hdwy fnl 2f) ...... 3.**4**
502  Emaura **(67)** *(DRCElsworth)* 8-1 WCarson (6) (gd spd over 4f) ...... s.h.**5**
678  Walstead (IRE) **(72)** *(WJarvis)* 8-13 LDettori (3) (spd over 4f) ...... 2.**6**
792  Life's a Breeze **(55)** *(MRChannon)* 8-2 CRutter (11) (led 4f) ...... 4.**7**
  Digger Doyle **(59)** *(CNAllen)* 7-13 ‡⁷GForster (9) (bit bkwd: prom 4f) ...... 4.**8**
  Excelled (IRE) *(BGubby)* 7-6 ‡⁵DHarrison (12) (prom over 3f) ...... 1½.**9**
278  Pace E Salute **(38)** (v) *(SDow)* 7-8 ‡³FNorton (1) (a bhd) ...... 1½.**10**
801  Pearly White **(62)** *(GBBalding)* 8-5 JWilliams (2) (spd 4f) ...... 1½.**11**
394  Mastamist *(RVoorspuy)* 8-2 SDawson (7) (a wl bhd) ...... 1½.**12**

**9/4** Walk in the Park(5/4—5/2), **7/2** Emaura, LADY SABO, **15/2** Walstead (IRE), **9/1** Mexican Dancer(6/1—12/1), **16/1** Life's a Breeze, **20/1** Pearly White, **33/1** Digger Doyle, **66/1** Ors. CSF £10.88, Tote £4.30: £1.50 £1.40 £16.30 (£5.20). Cronk Thoroughbred Racing Ltd (EPSOM) bred by Cheveley Park Stud Ltd. 12 Rn
1m 11.40 (1)
SF—32/28/–/–/–/–

**940** ROYAL SUSSEX REGIMENT H'CAP (3-Y.O) (0-90) £3785.00 (£1130.00: £540.00: £245.00)
1½m
2-40 (2-41)
(Weights raised 6 lb)

802* Landowner (IRE) **(74)** (Fav) *(JHMGosden)* 8-13 (6x) SCauthen (2) (lw: mde all: hrd rdn over 1f out: r.o wl) ...... —1

600⁵ Lobilio (USA) **(78)** *(CEBrittain)* 9-3 MRoberts (1) (2nd st: hrd rdn over 2f out: ev ch fns fnl f: r.o) ...... ¾.2

766² Cultured **(82)** *(MRStoute)* 9-7 RCochrane (6) (3rd st: hrd rdn over 2f out: unable qckn) ...... 10.3

583³ Chipper **(65)** *(RBoss)* 8-4 TQuinn (3) (nvr nr to chal) ...... 1½.4

558 Sybaritic Sam (IRE) **(65)** *(NACallaghan)* 8-4 AMackay (7) (6th st: nvr nrr) ...... 2½.5

728 Taroob (IRE) **(79)** *(JLDunlop)* 9-4 WCarson (5) (5th st: wknd over 2f out) ...... nk.7

Classical Charmer **(59)** *(BRMillman)* 7-12 RFox (4) (4th st: wknd over 2f out) .. nk.7

**7/4** LANDOWNER (IRE), **2/1** Cultured, **8/1** Taroob (IRE), Chipper, **9/1** Lobilio (USA), **20/1** Sybaritic Sam (IRE), **33/1** Classical Charmer. CSF £15.21, Tote £2.80: £2.00 £3.80 (£11.90). Sheikh Mohammed bred by Sheikh Mohammed bin Rashid al Maktoum in Ireland. 7 Rn
2m 37.35 (5.65)
SF—4/6/–/–/–/–

**941** KIDSONS IMPEY TROPHY (H'cap) (0-90) £3882.50 (£1160.00: £555.00: £252.50)
7f
3-10 (3-18)
(Weights raised 2 lb)

626² Cape Pigeon (USA) **(75)** *(LGCottrell)* 7-9-2 AMunro (12) (lw: 5th st: led over 2f out: clr 1f out: r.o wl) ...... —1

610⁵ Tender Moment (IRE) **(71)** (Fav) *(CEBrittain)* 4-8-12 MRoberts (13) (lw: 4th st: hrd rdn over 1f out: unable qckn) ...... 10.2

832 Cheveux Mitchell **(71)** (v) *(MRChannon)* 5-8-12 RHills (5) (3rd st: led 3f out tl over 2f out: one pce) ...... 2.3

738⁴ Belfort Ruler **(68)** *(BGubby)* 5-8-9 MRoberts (6) (hdwy fnl 2f: r.o) ...... ½.4

670 The Can Can Man **(69)** *(MJohnston)* 5-8-10 RPElliott (3) (lw: hdwy 4f out: nvr nrr) ...... s.h.5

779 Invocation **(74)** *(AMoore)* 5-9-1 NAdams (7) (b.nr hind: led 1f: 2nd st: ev ch 3f out: wknd 2f out) ...... 4.6

456 Affordable **(70)** *(WCarter)* 4-8-11 PaulEddery (1) (6th st: no hdwy fnl 3f) ...... 1½.7

785² Sarum **(55)** *(CPWildman)* 6-7-7⁽³⁾ ‡³FNorton (11) (slipped & lost pl bnd over 5f out: nt rcvr) ...... 3.8

731³ Old Comrades **(56)** *(LGCottrell)* 5-7-11 RFox (4) (nvr nr to chal) ...... 1½.9

725⁵ Jairzinho (USA) **(80)** (bl) *(RHannon)* 3-8-5 ‡⁵RPerham (15) (led 6f out to 3f out: sn wknd) ...... 2.10

792³ Jigsaw Boy **(79)** *(RJHolder)* 3-8-9 JWilliams (10) (lw: a bhd) ...... 1½.11

768 Gabbiadini **(75)** (v) *(MHTompkins)* 5-8-2 PRobinson (8) (a bhd) ...... 1½.12

253 Barlogan **(62)** *(CFWall)* 4-8-3⁽¹⁾ NDay (9) (bhd whn slipped bnd over 5f out) .. 8.13

610 Caroles Express **(83)** *(RAkehurst)* 4-9-10 TQuinn (2) (bhd fnl 3f) ...... nk.14

Fascination Waltz **(77)** *(DShaw)* 5-9-4 GCarter (14) (lw: s.s: hdwy fnl 3f out: wknd 3f out) ...... 2.15

LONG HANDICAP: Sarum 7-4.

**6/1** Tender Moment (IRE), **8/1** Cheveux Mitchell(op 12/1), **9/1** Gabbiadini, CAPE PIGEON (USA), **10/1** The Can Can Man, Jigsaw Boy, Old Comrades, **12/1** Sarum, Jairzinho (USA)(op 20/1), Caroles Express, **14/1** Belfort Ruler, **16/1** Barlogan, **20/1** Affordable, **25/1** Invocation, **33/1** Fascination Waltz. CSF £56.46, CT £413.57. Tote £7.90: £2.50 £2.20 £3.10 (£14.70). Mr E. J. S. Gadsden (CULLOMPTON) bred by Ashwood Thoroughbreds, Inc. in USA. 15 Rn
1m 25.61 (0.91)
SF—57/23/17/12/12/5

**942** SIS LIVE ACTION CLAIMING STKS (3-Y.O) £3590.00 (£1070.00: £510.00: £230.00)
1¼m
3-40 (3-45)

868⁵ Blockade (USA) **(80)** *(MBell)* 8-4 MHills (7) (b: led over 4f out: rdn out) ...... —1

783 Naseer (USA) **(55)** *(NACallaghan)* 8-5 JWilliams (2) (lw: 3rd st: r.o ins fnl f) ...... 2½.2

835⁵ Dominant Force **(70)** *(RHannon)* 8-7 MRoberts (4) (led 3f: lft in ld 5f out: sn hdd: 2nd st: hrd rdn 2f out: eased whn btn fnl f) ...... ½.3

695 Distant Memory **(70)** *(JWHills)* 8-9 RHills (1) (lw: bdly hmpd 5f out: 5th st: nt rcvr) ...... 15.4

734⁴ Betalongabill **(52)** *(MMadgwick)* 8-4 BRouse (3) (6th st: bhd fnl 4f) ...... ½.5

734 Red for Danger **(44)** (v) *(AMoore)* 8-3 CandyMorris (5) (hmpd 5f out: 4th st: bhd fnl 4f: dead) ...... 10.6

848⁶ Lord Vivienne (IRE) **(78)** (Fav) *(PFICole)* 8-6 TQuinn (6) (lw: plld hrd: led 7f out tl slipped & fell bnd 5f out) ...... 0

11/8 Lord Vivienne (IRE), 3/1 BLOCKADE (USA), 4/1 Dominant Force, 7/1 Distant Memory, 16/1 Naseer (USA), 20/1 Betalongabill, 50/1 Red for Danger. CSF £37.82, Tote £3.40: £1.80 £5.40 (£28.00). Mr A. M. Warrender (NEWMARKET) bred by Patricia C. Warrender in USA. 7 Rn                                  2m 12.11 (7.11)

**943**   CLIVE GRAHAM GRADUATION STKS (2-Y.O) £3590.00 (£990.00: £470.00)
          5f                                                                                    4-10 (4-11)

720* **Elle Shaped (IRE)** (Fav) *(RHannon)* 9-5 MRoberts (2) (mde all: rdn out) ........... —1
874* Lord Olivier (IRE) *(WJarvis)* 9-0 ‡JWeaver (1) (chsd wnr over 2f out: ev ch fnl 2f:
     r.o) .................................................................................................... ³/₄.2
703 Second Chance (IRE) *(PMitchell)* 8-11 SCauthen (3) (lw: chsd wnr over 3f:
    wknd fnl f) ........................................................................................ 3.3

2/7 ELLE SHAPED (IRE), 100/30 Lord Olivier (IRE), 16/1 Second Chance (IRE). CSF £1.52, Tote £1.30 (£1.10). Mr J. E. Marsden (MARLBOROUGH) bred by Dan Daly in Ireland. 3 Rn                            58.71 sec (1.11)
                                                                                                      SF—53/45/30

**944**   GOODWOOD HOUSE STKS (Mdn 3-Y.O) £3817.50 (£1140.00: £545.00: £247.50)
          1m 1f                                                                                 4-45 (4-47)

609⁵ **Boloardo** *(CEBrittain)* 9-0 MRoberts (1) (2nd st: hrd rdn over 1f out: led ins fnl f:
     r.o wl) ............................................................................................. —1
710⁴ Set Table (USA) (Fav) *(JHMGosden)* 9-0 SCauthen (4) (led: hrd rdn over 1f out:
     hdd ins fnl f: r.o) ............................................................................. ¹/₂.2
787² Zawaahy (USA) *(AAScott)* 8-9 WRSwinburn (7) (lw: 4th st: one pce fnl 2f) ........... 5.3
     Kabayil *(PTWalwyn)* 8-9 WCarson (9) (scope: bkwd: 6th st: r.o one pce fnl 2f) 3¹/₂.4
451 Dexter Chief *(IABalding)* 9-0 RCochrane (3) (hrd rdn over 2f out: nvr nrr) ........... ³/₄.5
    Ivor's Flutter *(DRCElsworth)* 9-0 JWilliams (5) (bit bkwd: nvr nr to chal) ............... 4.6
    Last Orders (47) *(RHannon)* 8-4 ‡⁵RPerham (8) (5th st: wknd over 2f out) 7.7
    June's Lear Fan (CAN) *(GHarwood)* 9-0 AClark (6) (ooope: 3rd st: wknd over 2f
    out) .................................................................................................... ³/₄.8
251³ Hawkish (USA) *(PMitchell)* 9-0 GCarter (2) (b: a bhd) ................................. s.h.9

11/8 Set Table (USA), 100/30 BOLOARDO, 4/1 Zawaahy (USA), 13/2 Kabayil, 14/1 Dexter Chief, 20/1 June's Lear Fan (CAN), 33/1 Ivor's Flutter, 50/1 Ors. CSF £8.02, Tote £4.90: £1.30 £1.20 £1.40 (£4.90). Mr B. H. Voak (NEWMARKET) bred by Grange Stud (UK). 9 Rn                                     1m 55.98 (5.28)

**945**   LEVIN DOWN APP'CE H'CAP (0-80) £3655.00 (£1090.00: £520.00: £235.00)
          5f                                                                                    5-20 (5-21)

596⁴ **Fivesevenfiveo (61)** *(RJHodges)* 4-8-10 TSprake (10) (a.p: led over 1f out:
     pushed out) ....................................................................................... —1
792 Cradle Days (77) (Fav) *(RHannon)* 3-8-10 ‡7AWhelan (3) (hdwy & hung rt wl
    over 1f out: edgd lft fnl f: r.o) ............................................................... 2.2
909³ Fangio (75) *(WGMTurner)* 3-9-1 KRutter (4) (a.p: hrd rdn over 1f out: unable
    qckn) ................................................................................................. 1¹/₂.3
853 Aughfad (79) (v) *(TCasey)* 6-10-0 SWilliams (6) (hdwy over 2f out: carried rt
    over 1f out: one pce) ............................................................................ 3¹/₂.4
596 Hitchin a Ride (62) (v) *(MPMuggeridge)* 5-8-11 RPerham (7) (no hdwy fnl 2f) 1¹/₂.5
735 Ever so Artistic (46) (bl) *(PHowling)* 5-7-9 BDoyle (5) (spd over 2f) ............... nk.6
794* Pharaoh's Dancer (74) *(EAWheeler)* 3-8-5 DHarrison (2) (lw: s.s: nvr nrr) ...... s.h.7
897 Greetland Rock (48) *(PHowling)* 4-7-11 FNorton (9) (outpcd) ....................... s.h.8
253 Pigalle Wonder (46) *(RJO'Sullivan)* 4-7-6 ‡³CHawksley (8) (lw: outpcd) ........... 1.9
    Mertola's Pet (78) *(LGCottrell)* 6-9-13 ATucker (1) (led over 3f) ..................... 4.10

100/30 Cradle Days, 4/1 Fangio, Pharaoh's Dancer(3/1—9/2), 6/1 Aughfad(4/1—13/2), 8/1 Mertola's Pet, 11/1 FIVESEVENFIVEO, 14/1 Hitchin a Ride, 25/1 Greetland Rock, Ever so Artistic, 33/1 Pigalle Wonder. CSF £43.48, CT £157.12. Tote £11.20: £2.20 £2.00 £1.70 (£31.90). Mr George W. Baker (SOMERTON) bred by Roger C. Denton. 10 Rn                                                       57.63 sec (0.03)
                                                                                                      SF—66/58/57/56/33/16

T/Trio: Race 3: £49.50 (40.7 Tckts). T/Jkpt: £3,778.50 (4.1 Tckts). T/Plpt: £15.00 (517.05 Tckts).    AK

## 516—CATTERICK (L-H)

**Thursday, May 21st [Good to firm, Firm patches]**
Going Allowance: minus 0.20 sec per fur (F)                                      Wind: almost nil

Stalls: low

**946**   MUKER STKS (Mdn 3-Y.O) £2280.00 (£630.00: £300.00)   **7f**        2-00 (2-01)

697⁵ **Hawa Layaam (IRE) (72)** (v) (Fav) *(AAScott)* 9-0 BRaymond (1) (b.nr hind: plld
     hrd: mde most: drew clr fnl 2f: easily) ................................................... —1

CATTERICK, May 21, 1992

522³ Daaris (USA) (65) (DMorley) 9-0 KDarley (5) (chsd wnr: rdn 2f out: sn btn) ...... 7.2
78⁵ Bilberry (CWCElsey) 8-9 JLowe (3) (led early: sn outpcd & lost tch) .............. 1½.3
765 Whitrigg Lad (WWHaigh) 9-0 SWebster (4) (bit bkwd: outpcd & bhd after 2f: n.d) ...... 1½.4

**4/7** HAWA LAYAAM (IRE), **15/8** Daaris (USA), **25/1** Bilberry, **100/1** Whitrigg Lad. CSF £1.76, Tote £1.30 (£1.10). Maktoum Al Maktoum (NEWMARKET) bred by Ballydoyle Stud in Ireland. 4 Rn    1m 25.8 (2.6)
SF—40/19/9/9

## 947
E.B.F. STAPLETON STKS (Mdn 2-Y-O) £2820.00 (£840.00: £400.00: £180.00)
**5f**    2-30 (2-30)

Bold County (MJohnston) 8-9 GDuffield (1) (lengthy: unf: scope: bit bkwd: dwlt: sn trckng ldrs: led wl over 1f out: sn clr) ...... —1
Hasta la Vista (MWEasterby) 9-0 TLucas (3) (cmpt: bit bkwd: outpcd to ½-wy: styd on wl fnl f: no ch w wnr) ...... 3.2
484⁶ Boldville Bash (IRE) (Fav) (TDBarron) 9-0 KDarley (4) (lw: w ldr: led after 2f tl wl over 1f out: rdn & one pce) ...... hd.3
263⁴ Pinkerton's Silver (MHEasterby) 9-0 MBirch (2) (led 2f: sn rdn & one pce) ...... hd.4
665 Say Sunpak (MrsVAAconley) 8-9 PBurke (5) (chsd ldrs tl rdn & btn over 1f out) 2.5
Summers Dream (BRichmond) 8-9 AProud (6) (unf: bit bkwd: dwlt: a outpcd & bhd) ...... 8.6

**13/8** Boldville Bash (IRE), **7/4** BOLD COUNTY, **9/2** Pinkerton's Silver, **11/1** Say Sunpak, **12/1** Hasta la Vista, **50/1** Summers Dream. CSF £18.09, Tote £2.50: £1.40 £3.60 (£17.30). The Fairyhouse 1992 Partnership (MIDDLEHAM) bred by Someries Stud. 6 Rn    60.5 sec (3)
SF—15/8/7/6/–/–

## 948
WILLIAM EDWIN NEESHAM MEMORIAL H'CAP (0-80) £2976.00 (£888.00: £424.00: £192.00)    **7f**    3-00 (3-02)

(Weights raised 1 lb)

883⁵ Euroblake (59) (TDBarron) 5-8-10 ‡JFanning (12) (swtg: hld up: effrt ent st: led over 1f out: rdn & r.o) ...... —1
397² Mca Below the Line (63) (bl) (WJPearce) 4-9-3 DNicholls (6) (bhd: hdwy over 2f out: r.o: nvr able to chal) ...... 2½.2
884 Brambles Way (59) (WLBarker) 3-8-2 KDarley (2) (in tch: hdwy ent st: styd on one pce fnl f) ...... nk.3
738* Kawwas (45) (Fav) (WHolden) 7-7-13 JLowe (5) (lw: hld up: hdwy over 2f out: nt pce to chal) ...... 2.4
670 Languedoc (70) (MPNaughton) 5-9-3 ‡AntoinetteArmes (8) (lw: cl up: led ent st: hdd over 1f out: sn btn) ...... hd.5
763⁴ Stelby (59) (OBrennan) 8-8-6 ‡OPears (4) (lw: s.s: r.o u.p fnl 2f) ...... 2½.6
774 Now Boarding (40) (RJHodges) 5-7-8(1) JQuinn (9) (chsd ldrs tl outpcd fnl 2f) . 2.7
794² In a Whirl (USA) (47) (DWChapman) 4-8-1 SWood (11) (lw: in tch: effrt on outside 2f out: rdn & no imp) ...... hd.8
508 Ganeshaya (54) (MFBarraclough) 3-7-6(2) ‡NKennedy (10) (led tl hdd ent st: grad wknd) ...... 2½.9
660³ Foxes Diamond (43) (BEllison) 4-7-11 NCarlisle (3) (effrt appr st: n.d) ...... 1.10
749 Preamble (55) (MrsJRRamsden) 3-7-12 PBurke (1) (nvr plcd to chal) ...... 1.11
749⁶ Kick on Majestic (IRE) (50) (bl) (NBycroft) 3-7-7 LCharnock (7) (chsd ldrs to st: sn wknd) ...... 2½.12
LONG HANDICAP: Now Boarding 7-1, Kick on Majestic (IRE) 7-2.

**4/1** Kawwas, **5/1** Stelby, EUROBLAKE, **6/1** Mca Below the Line, **8/1** Languedoc, In a Whirl (USA), **10/1** Foxes Diamond, **16/1** Kick on Majestic (IRE), Preamble(op 10/1), **25/1** Brambles Way, **33/1** Ors. CSF £32.93, CT £619.41. Tote £5.10: £2.50 £2.10 £3.30 (£14.60). Mr W. G. Swiers (THIRSK) bred by Viscount Leverhulme. 12 Rn    1m 25.4 (2.2)
SF—42/41/25/16/33/14

## 949
GRINTON H'CAP (3-Y.O) (0-80) £2954.00 (£819.00: £392.00)    **5f**    3-30 (3-38)

668 **Hemsworth Lad (IRE)** (61) (PCalver) 8-6 GDuffield (1) (chsd ldrs: styd on wl fnl f to ld cl home) ...... —1
685² Super Rocky (75) (RBastiman) 8-13 ‡HBastiman (6) (lw: led: hung lft ins fnl f: no ex nr fin) ...... hd.2
690³ Ned's Bonanza (75) (MDods) 9-6 GBaxter (8) (lw: trckd ldrs: effrt 2f out: nt qckn ins fnl f) ...... 2½.3
415* Stonewall Jackson (IRE) (76) (WJPearce) 9-7 DNicholls (9) (in tch: rdn ½-wy: styd on one pce) ...... 1½.4
792⁴ Palacegate Gold (IRE) (55) (RJHodges) 8-0 JQuinn (5) (in tch: effrt ½-wy: no imp) ...... 2.5

668 Never Late **(59)** *(MHEasterby)* 8-4⁽¹⁾ MBirch (10) (bit bkwd: chsd ldrs stands' side: rdn & no hdwy fnl 2f) .................... 1½.6
719³ My Abbey **(73)** (Jt-Fav) *(EJAlston)* 9-4 KFallon (3) (swtg: cl up 3f: sn outpcd) ... ½.8
186 Do the Business (IRE) **(49)** (bl) *(CNAllen)* 7-8 GBardwell (4) (outpcd & drvn along wl over 1f out: n.d) .................... ½.8
452 Miss Movie World **(48)** *(NBycroft)* 7-7 LCharnock (2) (nvr trbld ldrs) .............. nk.9
749 Kashgar **(48)** *(DWChapman)* 7-0 ‡7DarrenMoffatt (7) (dwlt: a bhd) ............... 1.10
133 Kalar **(48)** *(DWChapman)* 7-7 SWood (12) (racd stands' side: spd over 3f) .... hd.11
522 Joyful Thought **(50)** *(MrsJRRamsden)* 7-9 JLowe (14) (nvr wnt pce) .............. ½.12
614² Spanish Performer **(54)** *(TFairhurst)* 7-10 ‡3JFanning (11) (n.d) .................... 1.13
452 Ahkam (IRE) **(51)** *(HThomsonJones)* 7-10 NCarlisle (13) (sn outpcd & bhd) .... 7.14
LONG HANDICAP: Miss Movie World 7-6, Kashgar 5-12, Kalar 7-4.

**7/2** My Abbey, Ned's Bonanza, **11/2** Stonewall Jackson (IRE), **9/1** Joyful Thought, **10/1** Spanish Performer, **11/1** Super Rocky, **12/1** Palacegate Gold (IRE), **16/1** Never Late(op 10/1), HEMSWORTH LAD (IRE), **25/1** Ahkam (IRE), Do the Business (IRE), Miss Movie World, **33/1** Kalar, **200/1** Kashgar. CSF £163.09, CT £692.13. Tote £72.30: £11.70 £1.80 £1.80 (£207.80). Mrs C. Calver (RIPON) bred by Killarkin Stud in Ireland. 14 Rn
59.1 sec (1.6)
SF—40/46/43/38/9/7

**950**　PEN HILL CLAIMING STKS (3-Y.O) £2322.00 (£642.00: £306.00)
1½m 44y　　　　4-00 (4-01)

　Grouse-N-Heather *(MrsGRReveley)* 8-0 JLowe (2) (lw: shkn up & hdwy 5f out: styd on wl to ld ins fnl f: sn clr) .................... —1
658 Boring (USA) **(54)** *(WStorey)* 8-5 SWebster (8) (b: w ldr: led 7f out: wnt clr appr st: wknd & hdd ins fnl f) .................... 4.2
915² Feeling Foolish (IRE) **(59)** (bl) (Fav) *(TFairhurst)* 0-4 ‡7JFanning (6) (hld up: hdwy u.p ent st: sn chsng ldr: rdn & no imp appr fnl f) ........ 6.3
603 Stratford Lady **(53)** (v) *(JAGlover)* 7-10 JQuinn (5) (bhd: effrt 5f out: rdn & no imp) .................... 15.4
Judys Girl (IRE) **(40)** *(TFairhurst)* 7-10 SWood (4) (prom tl outpcd fnl 5f) ...... 3½.5
666⁶ Blushing Gold *(MrsJJordan)* 8-2 ACulhane (3) (chsd ldrs tl lost pl 7f out: n.d after) .................... 1½.6
Charlie Love *(WStorey)* 8-1 LCharnock (9) (leggy: s.s: plld hrd & wnt prom 7f out: wknd over 4f out) .................... 2.7
573 Mypeto *(PCalver)* 8-3 NCarlisle (7) (led tl hdd 7f out: cl up tl wknd 4f out) ...... 4.8

**8/11** Feeling Foolish (IRE), **5/2** Stratford Lady, **6/1** GROUSE-N-HEATHER(op 4/1), **14/1** Mypeto, **25/1** Boring (USA), **33/1** Judys Girl (IRE), **50/1** Charlie Love, **66/1** Blushing Gold. CSF £103.17, Tote £5.90: £1.10 £2.00 £1.10 (£72.40). Mr Robbie Cameron (SALTBURN) bred by R. A. Cameron. 8 Rn
2m 43.2 (9.2)

**951**　WENSLEY H'CAP (0-60) £2868.00 (£798.00: £384.00)　1m 5f 175y　4-30 (4-31)

291⁶ **Racing Raskal (31)** *(CaptJWilson)* 5–8-2⁽¹⁾ JCarroll (5) (prom: qcknd to ld over 4f out: sn clr: hld on wl cl home) .................... —1
575³ Carrolls Marc (IRE) **(47)** *(PJFeilden)* 4–9-4 KDarley (8) (hdwy u.p appr st: styd on wl to chal wl ins fnl f: kpt on) .................... ½.2
760⁴ Mingus (USA) **(55)** *(MrsJRRamsden)* 5–9-12 TLucas (2) (lw: hld up: hdwy 2f out: r.o nr fin) .................... 12.3
905 Doctor's Remedy **(28)** (bl) *(MrsJJordan)* 6–7-8 ‡5SMaloney (10) (a chsng ldrs: effrt over 4f out: one pce) .................... 2½.4
875* Kirby Opportunity **(52)** (Fav) *(JPearce)* 4–9-4 (4x) ‡9RPrice (1) (lw: hdwy 5f out: sn prom: rdn appr st: no imp) .................... s.h.5
683⁴ Yorkshire Holly **(50)** *(MAvison)* 9–9-7 MBirch (12) (effrt 6f out: rdn & nvr trbld ldrs) .................... 2½.6
Lapiaffe **(42)** *(RJHodges)* 8–8-13 JQuinn (4) (trckd ldrs: chal 6f out: rdn ent st: sn outpcd) .................... ½.7
358 Luks Akura **(34)** *(MJohnston)* 4–8-5 GDuffield (14) (outpcd & bhd over 7f out: n.d) .................... ¾.8
664 Newark Antiquefair **(30)** *(BCMorgan)* 4–8-5 LCharnock (15) (nvr nr ldrs) ........ 4.9
726 Mahaasin **(50)** *(LJCodd)* 4–9-0 ‡7RMitchell (16) (led tl hdd over 4f out: wknd 3f out) .................... ½.10
605 Sweet Request **(50)** *(JRBostock)* 4–9-7 JLowe (7) (a bhd) .................... 1.11
288⁵ See the Light **(41)** (v) *(MrsVAAconley)* 5–8-12 KFallon (3) (chsd ldrs tl wknd 5f out) .................... 2.12
875 Premier Venues **(48)** *(SGNorton)* 4–8-12 ‡7OPears (13) (a bhd) .................... 2.13
518⁵ Media Star **(29)** *(TKersey)* 7–7-9 ‡5NKennedy (11) (b: lw: bhd & drvn along 6f out: n.d) .................... 15.14

**9/4** Kirby Opportunity(op 7/2), **9/2** Lapiaffe, **10/1** Yorkshire Holly(8/1—12/1), RACING RASKAL, **12/1** Media Star, Mingus (USA)(op 8/1), **14/1** See the Light, **16/1** Carrolls Marc (IRE), Premier Venues, Newark Antiquefair(op 10/1), **25/1** Doctor's Remedy, Luks Akura, **33/1** Mahaasin, **50/1** Sweet Request. CSF £138.89, CT £1,751.28. Tote £12.40: £2.80 £5.30 £3.10 (£34.00). Mrs G. S. Rees (PRESTON) bred by John and Mrs McNamara. 14 Rn

3m 0.1 (4.9)
SF—11/26/10/–/–/–

T/Plpt: £430.10 (6 Tckts).
AA

## 640a—CURRAGH (R-H)

### Saturday, May 16th [Good to soft]
Going Allowance: 0.25 sec per fur (G)

**952a**　ORAL B MARBLE HILL E.B.F. STKS (listed race) (2-Y.O) £8725.00　**5f**

| | |
|---|---|
| **Tahdeed** (USA) (Ireland) 2-9-1 CRoche | —1 |
| Almond Flower (IRE) (Ireland) 2-8-10 WJSupple | 3½.2 |
| Hideout (IRE) (Ireland) 2-8-6 JReid | 2½.3 |
| 402* SOBER LAD (IRE) (JBerry) 2-9-1 LPiggott (further 10¾al) | 5 |

Tote £1.40: £1.10 £3.40 (£8.20). Maktoum Al Maktoum (J.S.Bolger,IRELAND) bred by Gainsborough Farm Inc. in USA. 5 Rn

63 sec (4.5)
SF—36/17/3/–/–

**953a**　AIRLIE/COOLMORE IRISH 2,000 GUINEAS (Gp 1) (3-Y.O.C & F) £120350.00　**1m**

| | |
|---|---|
| 655* **RODRIGO DE TRIANO** (USA) (Fav) (PWChapple-Hyam) 3-9-0 LPiggott (hld up & bhd: swtchd rt & gd hdwy over 1f out: qcknd to ld 1f out: r.o) | —1 |
| 704* EZZOUD (IRE) (bl) (MRStoute) 3-9-0 WRSwinburn (trckd ldrs: swtchd over 2f out: disp ld wl over 1f out: sn hdd: r.o nr fin) | 1.2 |
| 839a* Brief Truce (USA) (Ireland) 3-9-0 MJKinane (in tch: pushed along over 2f out: ev ch over 1f out: r.o) | 1½.3 |
| 655² LUCKY LINDY (IRE) (RHannon) 3-9-0 JReid (disp ld tl led ½-wy: u.p over 1f out: sn hdd: kpt on) | ½.4 |
| 640a* Irish Memory (Ireland) 3-9-0 CRoche (disp ld to ½-wy: rdn & btn 2f out) | 5.5 |
| 539a* Portico (USA) (Ireland) 3-9-0 SCauthen (trckd ldrs: rdn 2f out: sn wknd) | 3.6 |

**8/11** RODRIGO DE TRIANO (USA), **5/1** Ezzoud (IRE), **13/2** Lucky Lindy (IRE), **8/1** Portico (USA), **11/1** Brief Truce (USA), **20/1** Irish Memory. Tote £1.50: £1.30 £2.10 (£4.20). Mr R.E.Sangster (MARLBOROUGH) bred by Swettenham Stud in USA. 6 Rn

1m 41.7 (4.7)
SF—59/56/51/49/34/25

**954a**　TATTERSALLS ROGERS GOLD CUP (Gp 2)　£43125.00　**1¼m**

| | |
|---|---|
| 557³ **OPERA HOUSE** (MRStoute) 4-8-12 SCauthen (in tch: hdwy 2f out: sustained chal fr over 1f out: r.o to ld last stride) | —1 |
| 551² ZOMAN (USA) (Fav) (PFICole) 5-9-1 TQuinn (led: r.o u.p fnl f: hdd last stride) | s.h.2 |
| 436⁴ Star of Gdansk (USA) (bl) (Ireland) 4-9-3 CRoche (chsd ldrs: hrd rdn 2f out: kpt on) | 6.3 |
| Runyon (IRE) (Ireland) 4-8-12 SCraine (bhd: rdn & r.o 2f out: nvr able to chal) | 2.4 |
| 436² ADAM SMITH (LMCumani) 4-8-12 MJKinane (hld up: rdn 2f out: no hdwy) | 2½.5 |
| Nordic Soprano (IRE) (Ireland) 4-8-9 WJSupple (a bhd) | 8.6 |
| 724 Dowland (USA) (Ireland) 4-8-12 WJO'Connor (chsd ldr 4f: btn 3f out) | 2.7 |

**2/1** Zoman (USA), **5/2** OPERA HOUSE, **3/1** Adam Smith, **9/1** Star of Gdansk (USA), **12/1** Runyon (IRE), **25/1** Dowland (USA), **66/1** Nordic Soprano (IRE). Tote £2.70: £1.90 £1.50 (£2.50). Sheikh Mohammed (NEWMARKET) bred by Meon Valley Stud. 7 Rn

2m 6.4 (3.4)
SF—89/90/78/71/66/47/46

## 837a—SAINT-CLOUD (L-H)

### Saturday, May 16th [Good]
Going Allowance: 0.25 sec per fur (G)

**955a**　PRIX JEAN DE CHAUDENAY (Gp 2)　£30960.00　**1½m**

| | |
|---|---|
| 557* **Dear Doctor** (FR) (France) 5-9-6 CAsmussen (mde all: qcknd 2f out: hld on wl: cleverly) | —1 |
| 638a* Vert Amande (FR) (France) 4-9-2 DBoeuf (3rd st: n.m.r 1f out: fin wl) | ¾.2 |
| Lights Out (FR) (France) 6-9-2 WMongil (5th st: hdwy wl over 1f out: ev ch fnl f: one pce) | hd.3 |

Deja (USA) *(France)* 4–9–2 ODeleuze (hld up & last st: outpcd 2f out: r.o wl nr fin) .................................................................................................. s.h.4
Saganeca (USA) *(France)* 4–9–3 TJarnet (bhd early: 4th st: hdwy 1f out: fin wl & hmpd ins fnl f) ..................................................................... 1¹/₂.5
648³ Toulon (Fav) *(France)* 4–9–8 PatEddery (chsd wnr: 2nd st: grad wknd fr 2 out) nk.6

**9/10** Toulon, **23/10** DEAR DOCTOR (FR), **37/10** Deja (USA), **91/10** Vert Amande (FR), **13/1** Saganeca (USA), **17/1** Lights Out (FR). Tote 3.30f: 1.80f 3.20f (SF: 23.80f). Mr Henri Chalhoub (J.E.Hammond,FRANCE) bred by Amerigroup Leasing in France. 6 Rn
2m 40.4 (10.1)
SF—35/29/28/27/25/29

## 844a—CAPANNELLE (R-H)
### Sunday, May 17th [Good]

### 956a
PREMIO PRESIDENTE DELLA REPUBBLICA (Gp 1)    £51163.00    1¹/₄m

551 **SIKESTON (USA)** *(CEBrittain)* 6–9–2 MRoberts ........................................... —1
Sillery (USA) *(France)* 4–9–2 CBlack ................................................. ¹/₂.2
Lara's Idea *(Italy)* 4–8–13 DZarroli ..................................................... 1¹/₂.3
Tote 39L: 19L 13L (23L). Allevamento White Star (NEWMARKET) bred by John R.Gaines, H.Rodes Hart & William Simon in USA. 7 Rn
2m 1.4

## COLOGNE (R-H)
### Sunday, May 17th [Good]

### 957a
MEHL-MULHENS RENNEN (Gp 2) (3-Y.O.C & F) £51761.00    1m

381a★ **Platini (GER)** *(Germany)* 3–9–2 MRimmer (fin 2nd, hd: plcd 1st) ...................... —1
Konigslowe *(Germany)* 3–9–2 LMader (fin 3rd, 1¹/₂l: plcd 2nd) ........................ 2
549² DISTINCT THATCHER (USA) *(RHannon)* 3–9–2 RCochrane (fin 4th, hd: plcd 3rd)  3
744a★ ALHIJAZ *(JLDunlop)* 3–9–2 WCarson (fin 1st: disq: plcd 4th) .......................... 4
*Stewards Enquiry: Alhijaz disq (interference to Distinct Thatcher (USA)).*
Tote 16DM: 13DM 26DM 28DM (SF: 233DM). Stall Steigenberger (B.Schutz,GERMANY) bred by Frau E & A Steigenberger in Germany. 8 Rn
1m 36.3

## 842a—LONGCHAMP (R-H)
### Sunday, May 17th [Good]
Going Allowance: minus 0.20 sec per fur (F)

### 958a
DUBAI POULE D'ESSAI DES POULICHES (Gp 1) (3-Y.O.F) £103200.00    1m **(Grande)**

631⁵ **CULTURE VULTURE (USA)** *(PFICole)* 3–9–2 TQuinn (lw: hld up & bhd: gd hdwy fr 2f out to ld ins fnl f: r.o wl) ................................................. —1
380a★ Hydro Calido (USA) *(France)* 3–9–2 FHead (s.i.s & last early: stdy run on outside wl over 1f out: r.o) ......................................................... ¹/₂.2
643a² Guislaine (FR) *(France)* 3–9–2 CAsmussen (mid div: 3rd st: disp ld 2f out to 1f out: kpt on gamely) .................................................... ³/₄.3
643a★ Absurde (FR) *(France)* 3–9–2 ESaint-Martin (a cl up: 4th st: disp ld 2f out to 1f out: one pce) ..................................................................... nk.4
Euphonic (USA) *(France)* 3–9–2 PatEddery (mid div: sme hdwy & chal over 1f out: one pce fnl f) ..................................................................... nk.5
631³ Hatoof (USA) (Jt-Fav) *(France)* 3–9–2 WRSwinburn (cl up & 2nd st: outpcd & grad wknd fnl f) ........................................................... 1¹/₂.6
631³ Kenbu (FR) *(France)* 3–9–2 ALequeux (mid div: outpcd 2f out: grad wknd) ....... ¹/₂.7
742a² Symphorino (USA) *(France)* 3–9–2 TJarnet (in rr: outpcd st: n.d) ................... 2¹/₂.8
461a³ Plume Magique (Jt-Fav) *(France)* 3–9–2 BRaymond (led to 2f out: sn wknd) ... 2¹/₂.9

**7/4** Plume Magique, Hatoof (USA), **11/4** Hydro Calido (USA), **6/1** Guislaine (FR), **7/1** Euphonic (USA), **33/4** Symphorino (USA), **10/1** Absurde (FR), **11/1** Kenbu (FR), **13/1** CULTURE VULTURE (USA). Tote 14.10f: 4.10f 2.60f 2.50f (34.90f). Mr Christopher Wright (WHATCOMBE) bred by Holtsinger Inc. in USA. 9 Rn  1m 37 (U.7)
SF—88/86/84/83/82/76/74

### 959a
PRIX LUPIN (Gp 1) (3-Y.O.C & F) £51342.00    1¹/₄m 110y **(Grande)**

**Johann Quatz (FR)** *(France)* 3–9–2 FHead (lw: mde all: shkn up & qcknd wl over 1f out: hung lft & r.o wl cl home) ................................................. —1
19a★ Contested Bid (USA) *(France)* 3–9–2 PatEddery (mid div: 3rd st: hrd rdn & sltly hmpd 1f out: r.o wl) ..................................................................... 1.2

642a* Apple Tree (FR) (Fav) *(France)* 3-9-2 TJarnet (uns rdr bef s: 4th early: hdwy on outside 1f out: fin wl) .................................................... s.h.**3**
642³ Silver Kite (USA) *(France)* 3-9-2 WRSwinburn (a same pl: one pce) ............... 2½.**4**
722⁴ John Rose *(France)* 3-9-2 PRobinson (hld up: outpcd fr 2f out) .................. ¾.**5**
635³ Glaieul (USA) *(France)* 3-9-2 DBoeuf (a.p: 2nd st: wknd wl over 1f out) ......... 1½.**6**
Sharp Counsel (FR) *(France)* 3-9-2 ALequeux (a bhd: m.n.s) ............................ 3.**7**

**7/4** Apple Tree (FR), **9/4** Glaieul (USA), **32/10** JOHANN QUATZ (FR), **9/2** Silver Kite (USA), **9/1** Contested Bid (USA), **15/1** Sharp Counsel (FR), **29/1** John Rose. Tote 4.20f: 2.60f 4.70f (SF: 41.70f). Mr S. Niarchos (F.Boutin,FRANCE) bred by S. Niarchos in France. 7 Rn                                            2m 12.5 (2.9)
SF—52/50/49/44/42/39

# MUNICH (L-H)
## Sunday, May 17th [Good]

**960a**   GROSSER HERTIE-PRIES VON DEUTSCHLAND (Gp 2) (3-Y.O) £51761.00   **1m 3f**

647* **CAPTAIN HORATIUS (IRE)** *(JLDunlop)* 3-9-0 JReid ........................................ —**1**
Apis (GER) *(Germany)* 3-8-11 WNewnes .................................................... 1½.**2**
Greifvogel (bl) *(Germany)* 3-9-0 MHofer ................................................... 1½.**3**
Tote 48DM: 22DM 26DM 16DM (SF: 804DM). Mr D.R.Hunnisett (ARUNDEL) bred by B.W.Hills & Mrs V.Shaw in Ireland. 11 Rn                                            2m 17.7

# 682—PONTEFRACT (L-H)
## Friday, May 22nd [Good to firm]
Going Allowance: 5f-1m: minus 0.10 sec; Rest: minus 0.30 sec (F)
Stalls: low                          Wind: almost nil   Vis: fair, Race 6 poor

**961**   COURSE BOOKMAKERS GRADUATION STKS (2-Y.O) £2322.00 (£642.00: £306.00)
   5f                                                              6-45 (6-45)

677* **Star Family Friend (IRE)** (Fav) *(MHTompkins)* 8-12 PRobinson (3) (lw: hld up: smooth hdwy ½-wy: led over 1f out: pushed clr) ............... —**1**
491* Whitley Gorse *(JEtherington)* 9-3 TLucas (1) (lw: led: kpt on fnl f: no ch w wnr) . 5.**2**
770* Whisperdales *(MWEllerby)* 9-3 SMorris (2) (jnd ldr ½-wy: rdn & btn 2f out) ...... 6.**3**

**4/9** STAR FAMILY FRIEND (IRE), **5/1** Ors. CSF £2.38, Tote £1.40 (£1.50). Sheffield Newspapers Limited (NEWMARKET) bred by Mrs J. Corcoran in Ireland. 3 Rn                             64 sec (2.5)
SF—38/23/–

**962**   NARBOL CLAIMING STKS   £2784.00 (£774.00: £372.00)   **1m 4y**   7-10 (7-11)

763* **Overpower (54)** *(MHTompkins)* 8-8-11 PRobinson (16) (chsd ldrs: styd on u.p to ld ins fnl f: jst hld on) ......................................... —**1**
768⁴ Yonge Tender **(56)** (bl) *(JWharton)* 5-8-11 ‡³JFanning (14) (trckd ldrs: ev ch fnl f: r.o u.p) ..................................................... s.h.**2**
657 Halston Prince **(77)** (bl) *(RFJohnsonHoughton)* 5-8-10 JReid (17) (trckd ldrs: led over 2f out tl ins fnl f: no ex) ............................ 1½.**3**
748⁵ Cool Parade (USA) **(51)** (bl) *(GMMoore)* 4-8-9 KFallon (5) (bhd: hdwy u.p over 3f out: kpt on wl: nvr nr to chal) ........................ 4.**4**
785⁴ Shining Jewel **(67)** *(MrsLPiggott)* 5-9-4 LPiggott (8) (lw: chsd ldrs: ev ch over 2f out: one pce) ........................................... nk.**5**
684³ Young Jason **(54)** *(FHLee)* 9-8-6 ‡⁵NKennedy (7) (effrt over 3f out: styd on same pce fnl 2f: nvr able to chal) ........................ 1½.**6**
875 Friendlypersuasion (IRE) **(40)** *(RHollinshead)* 4-8-9 WRyan (3) (lw: hdwy 4f out: kpt on fnl 2f: n.d) ................................. 1½.**7**
696⁴ Irish Groom **(36)** (bl) *(JPSmith)* 5-8-3 ‡⁵ATucker (9) (hdwy & prom over 3f out: grad wknd fnl 2f) ................................. 1.**8**
606 Tibby Head (IRE) **(46)** *(JMackie)* 4-8-8 GHind (11) (nvr nr to chal) .............. 1.**9**
Randybay *(JMackie)* 7-8-10 MBirch (2) (b: bhd: sme hdwy 2f out: n.d) ............ ¾.**10**
875⁴ Paper Craft (v) *(MJohnston)* 5-8-9 RPElliott (18) (led tl hdd & wknd over 2f out) nk.**11**
411 Breezed Well **(64)** *(CNAllen)* 6-8-6 ‡⁷GForster (12) (nvr nr ldrs) ................ 1½.**12**
Gant Bleu (FR) **(45)** *(RMWhitaker)* 5-8-9 PBurke (4) (lw: hld up: a in rr) ......... 5.**13**
532 Sayant *(WClay)* 7-8-6 JLowe (10) (a bhd) ........................................... 1½.**14**
Really Honest *(MWEasterby)* 11-8-2 ‡⁷JMarshall (13) (b: lw: n.d) ................ hd.**15**
Serlby Connection **(50)** *(SRBowring)* 7-8-9 SWebster (6) (b: hld up: a bhd) ...... 1½.**16**
Quinta (IRE) **(50)** *(GPKelly)* 4-8-6 TLucas (15) (n.d) ................................ ¾.**17**
Glenderry **(21)** (bl) *(RLee)* 10-8-9 BRaymond (1) (b: chsd ldrs tl wknd qckly 4f out: sn bhd: t.o) ..................................................... 18

3/1 Halston Prince(op 8/1), 9/2 Yonge Tender, 5/1 Shining Jewel, 7/1 OVERPOWER, 15/2 Young Jason, 8/1 Breezed Well, 11/1 Paper Craft, 12/1 Cool Parade (USA), 25/1 Irish Groom, 33/1 Tibby Head (IRE), Serlby Connection, 40/1 Gant Bleu (FR), Friendlypersuasion (IRE), 50/1 Really Honest, Sayant, 100/1 Glenderry, Randybay, 200/1 Quinta (IRE). CSF £37.95, Tote £8.70: £3.00 1.90 1.50 (£22.40). Mr M. P. Bowring (NEWMARKET) bred by Barronstown Stud. 18 Rn; Halston Prince clmd J Ramsden £7,105, Yonge Tender clmd C Williams £6,153
1m 44.5 (2.9)
SF—41/30/34/21/29/12

**963**  TOTE H'CAP (3-Y.O) (0-80) £4305.00 (£1290.00: £620.00: £285.00)
1m 4y
7-35 (7-37)

749* **Express Gift (61)** (Fav) (MrsGRReveley) 7-10 ‡7DarrenMoffatt (13) (lw: trckd ldrs: led 2f out: r.o wl fnl f) .................................................................. —1

493 Yazaly (USA) (70) (v) (AAScott) 8-12 BRaymond (15) (lw: trckd ldrs: rdn appr st: disp ld over 1f out: nt qckn ins fnl f) ............................................ 1.2

313⁴ Sure to Win (IRE) (60) (DMorris) 8-2 PRobinson (6) (a chsng ldrs: r.o same pce appr fnl f) ......................................................................................... 2¹/₂.3

April Shadow (55) (CWThornton) 7-11 NCarlisle (8) (rr div: effrt & hdwy over 2f out: kpt on wl fnl f) ..................................................................................... 1¹/₂.4

604 Leonadis Polk (62) (WJPearce) 8-4 NConnorton (11) (bhd: hdwy over 2f out: r.o same pce appr fnl f) ................................................................................ hd.5

546² Stoproveritate (57) (SGNorton) 7-13 LCharnock (16) (led 4f: chsd ldrs tl wknd over 1f out) ............................................................................................. 1¹/₂.6

Pride of Pendle (60) (PCalver) 8-2 DaleGibson (14) (hld up: mid div tl styd on fnl 2f) .......................................................................................................... 1¹/₂.7

603 Treasure Beach (51) (MBrittain) 7-7 JLowe (4) (hmpd s: bhd: gd hdwy on outside over 1f out: nrst fin) ............................................................................ ¹/₂.8

604 Hob Green (57) (MrsJRRamsden) 7-10 ‡3FNorton (10) (mid div: effrt appr st: nvr nr to chal) ......................................................................................... hd.9

Kentucky Rain (67) (JGFitzGerald) 8-2 ‡7MHunt (9) (w ldr: led 4f out to 2f out: sn wknd) .......................................................................................... ¹/₂.10

Billy Blazer (79) (MHTompkins) 9-7 KDarley (1) (hld up & bhd: n.m.r over 1f out: nvr plcd to chal) ......................................................................................... ³/₄.11

Barmbrack (55) (RMWhitaker) 7-11 PBurke (12) (mid div whn n.m.r over 1f out: n.d) ......................................................................................................... ¹/₂.12

767⁴ Nicely Thanks (USA) (70) (TDBarron) 8-12 AlexGreaves (2) (hld up & bhd: hdwy over 2f out: hmpd over 1f out: sn wknd) .................................. 1¹/₂.13

508³ Dominant Serenade (66) (PWHarris) 8-8 SWhitworth (7) (n.d) ...................... 3¹/₂.14

816 Lowlands Boy (60) (TFairhurst) 7-13 ‡3JFanning (5) (swvd lft s: chsd ldrs tl wknd 2f out) .................................................................................................... 15

Clean Singer (51) (NBycroft) 7-7 SWood (3) (chsd ldrs tl wknd over 2f out: sn wknd) ........................................................................................................... 16

LONG HANDICAP: Treasure Beach 7-3, Clean Singer 7-0.

11/4 EXPRESS GIFT, 5/1 Hob Green(6/1—8/1), 13/2 Nicely Thanks (USA), 7/1 Sure to Win (IRE), 8/1 Billy Blazer, 10/1 Lowlands Boy, Dominant Serenade, 12/1 Yazaly (USA), 14/1 Stoproveritate, 20/1 Kentucky Rain, Leonadis Polk, Pride of Pendle, 33/1 Barmbrack, April Shadow, 50/1 Treasure Beach, 66/1 Clean Singer. CSF £37.62, CT £211.06. Tote £3.60: £1.70 1.80 1.90 6.00 (£30.00). Mr H. Young (SALTBURN) bred by H. Young. 16 Rn
1m 45 (3.4)
SF—19/32/11/1/7/–

**964**  WILLIAM HILL H'CAP (0-70) £2427.00 (£672.00: £321.00)  1¹/₂m 8y  8-05 (8-08)
(Weights raised 1 lb)

905 **Samain (USA) (32)** (JAGlover) 5-7-9 NCarlisle (5) (hld up & bhd: hmpd bnd after 4f: gd hdwy 4f out: led 2f out: drvn clr fnl f) .................................... —1

761² Broom Isle (51) (Jt-Fav) (MrsAKnight) 4-8-11 ‡3FNorton (7) (lw: chsd ldrs: hrd rdn to ld 3f out: hdd 2f out: no ch w wnr) .................................. 6.2

593⁵ Famous Beauty (50) (RHollinshead) 5-8-6 ‡7DCarson (11) (smooth hdwy over 3f out: sn wl outpcd: styd on ins fnl f) ................................. 1¹/₂.3

831 Ivors Guest (55) (RLee) 6-9-4 BRaymond (2) (chsd ldrs tl wl outpcd over 3f out: kpt on fnl f) .................................................................................. 10.4

Flying Connection (60) (WClay) 4-9-2 ‡7SWilliams (3) (lost pl 5f out: kpt on fnl f: n.d) ................................................................................................ 2.5

923³ Eire Leath-Sceal (61) (MBrittain) 5-9-10 KDarley (4) (chsd ldrs tl rdn & lost pl over 2f out) .............................................................................................. nk.6

736⁴ Indian Slave (IRE) (50) (Jt-Fav) (RGuest) 4-8-13 LPiggott (10) (jnd ldrs 5f out: wknd over 2f out: eased) ........................................................... 3.7

675⁶ Carlingford (USA) (50) (MPNaughton) 6-8-6 ‡5JWeaver (9) (led after 3f to 3f out: sn lost pl) .......................................................................................... 3.8

761 Rexy Boy (33) (WLBarker) 5-7-10 LCharnock (6) (a in rr) ....................................... 12.9

    Butlers Wharf **(47)** *(KWHogg)* 7–8–10  GHind (8) (sn bhd: sme hdwy 5f out: sn
      wknd) ............................................................................................................................ 3.10
809 Wheels of Weetman **(38)** *(MissSJWilton)* 5–7–10 ‡⁵NGwilliams (1) (led 3f: sn rdn
      & lost pl: t.o) ............................................................................................. 15.11
    *Access Cruise (USA) (11/1) Withdrawn (bolted 12f bef s) : not under orders*

**7/2** Indian Slave (IRE), Broom Isle, **5/1** Famous Beauty, **11/2** Carlingford (USA), Eire Leath-Sceal, **12/1** SAMAIN
(USA), **16/1** Ivors Guest, **20/1** Flying Connection, **25/1** Rexy Boy, **33/1** Wheels of Weetman, **50/1** Butlers Wharf.
CSF £50.64, CT £220.98. Tote £14.60: £2.50 £1.20 £2.50 (£41.00). Countrywide Classics Limited (WORKSOP)
bred by Stephen D. Peskoff in USA. 11 Rn                                    2m 35.7 (1.2)
                                             SF—33/37/29/21/15/22

**965**     CORAL H'CAP (0-70) £2679.00 (£744.00: £357.00)   **1¹⁄₄m 6y**    8-35 (8-35)
                            (Weights raised 2 lb)
498⁴ **Stapleton (IRE) (69)** (Fav) *(JWWatts)* 3–9–1  BRaymond (7) (lw: trckd ldr: shkn
      up 2f out: n.m.r: c thro on ins to ld ins fnl f: r.o wl) .............. —1
768 Puffy **(49)** (bl) *(GMMoore)* 5–8–10  KFallon (3) (lw: effrt & drvn along 4f out: styd
      on ins fnl f: hung lft: no ch w wnr) ............................................. 2.2
766 Rapid Lad **(32)** *(JLSpearing)* 14–7–7  JLowe (2) (lw: bhd & drvn 6f out: jnd ldrs 2f
      out: led over 1f out: hdd & wknd ins fnl f) ............................ 1.3
875⁵ Not Yet **(37)** *(EWeymes)* 8–7–12  DaleGibson (5) (bhd & drvn along 6f out: wnt
      prom 3f out: one pce) ...................................................................... hd.4
766* Touch Above **(61)** *(TDBarron)* 6–9–8  AlexGreaves (9) (led tl hdd & wknd over 1f
      out) .......................................................................................................... 1½.5
*158* Escape Talk **(33)** *(JDooler)* 5–7–5⁽¹⁾ ‡3JFanning (6) (nvr rchd ldrs) ................. 2.6
327 Sea Lord **(52)** *(KWHogg)* 3–7–5⁽⁵⁾ ‡⁷AGarth (4) (w ldr: lost pl over 2f out:
      wandered bdly u.p sn & sn bhd) .................................................. 6.7
880 Sinclair Lad (IRE) **(63)** *(RHollinshead)* 4–9–10  WRyan (8) (trckd ldrs tl lost pl
      over 2f out: sn bhd) ........................................................................ 3½.8
            LONG HANDICAP: Rapid Lad 7-5, Escape Talk 6-9, Sea Lord 6-13.

**9/4** STAPLETON (IRE), **100/30** Touch Above, **5/1** Not Yet, **6/1** Sinclair Lad (IRE), **7/1** Puffy, **14/1** Rapid Lad, **33/1**
Sea Lord, **66/1** Escape Talk. CSF £15.76, CT £136.86. Tote £2.70: £1.30 £1.80 £2.70 (£9.90). Sheikh
Mohammed (RICHMOND) bred by Seamus MacKenna in Ireland. 8 Rn                    2m 14.6 (6.3)
                                             SF—8/–/–/–/–/–

**966**     BROOKE GROUP STKS (Mdn 3-Y.O) £2448.00 (£678.00: £324.00)   **6f**   9-05 (9-06)
863⁴ **Massiba (IRE)** *(BHanbury)* 8–9  BRaymond (4) (mde all: qcknd over 2f out: sn
      clr: unchal) .......................................................................................... —1
764 Boy Martin *(MJohnston)* 9–0  RPElliott (1) (chsd ldrs: rdn over 2f out: kpt on fnl f:
      no ch w wnr) ...................................................................................... 3.2
697 Sure Lord (IRE) **(72)** (Fav) *(WRMuir)* 9–0  SWhitworth (2) (chsd ldrs: effrt u.p
      over 2f out: kpt on same pce) ...................................................... 1½.3
    Chantry Bellini *(CWThornton)* 8–9  NCarlisle (5) (bhd tl styd on u.p over 1f out:
      n.d) ......................................................................................................... 2½.4
669² Auction King (IRE) **(63)** *(ASmith)* 9–0  SWebster (7) (lw: chsd wnr tl outpcd fnl 2f) 2.5
879⁶ Lord Lambson *(RMWhitaker)* 9–0  ACulhane (9) (bhd: effrt u.p over 2f out: n.d) 2¹⁄.6
750² Ace Reporter *(MHTompkins)* 8–9  PRobinson (8) (lw: sn chsng ldrs: shkn up
      over 2f out: c wd ent st: sn wknd) ............................................ 4.7
    Secret Kin (IRE) *(OBrennan)* 8–7 ‡⁷OPears (6) (small: cmpt: bit bkwd: bhd fnl 2f) 12.8
    Stamshaw *(BAMcMahon)* 8–9  JFortune (3) (neat: scope: chsd ldrs: rdn ½-wy:
      sn lost pl) ............................................................................................. 3.9

**2/1** Sure Lord (IRE), **5/2** Ace Reporter, **9/2** MASSIBA (IRE)(op 8/1), **11/2** Boy Martin(8/1—5/1), **11/1** Lord
Lambson(16/1—9/1), **12/1** Auction King (IRE), **20/1** Stamshaw(14/1—33/1), **33/1** Chantry Bellini, **100/1**
Secret Kin (IRE). CSF £28.19, Tote £4.30: £1.50 £1.80 £1.60 (£13.70). Mr Muttar Salem (NEWMARKET) bred
by Gainsborough Stud Management Ltd in Ireland. 9 Rn                          1m 16.8 (2.8)
                                         SF—27/20/14/–/–/–

T/Plpt: £52.50 (61.25 Tckts).                                           WG

## 727—SALISBURY (R-H)
### Friday, May 22nd [Firm]
Going Allowance: minus 0.35 sec per fur (F)             Wind: almost nil

Stalls: high

**967**     LANGFORD APP'CE H'CAP (0-70) £2402.40 (£666.40: £319.20)   **6f**   2-10 (2-15)
735⁶ **My Ruby Ring (40)** *(DRLaing)* 5–7–12  KimMcDonnell (3) (b: led over 2f: hrd rdn
      over 1f out: led last stride) ........................................................... —1

624 Teanarco (IRE) **(59)** *(RJHolder)* 4–9-3 SDrowne (7) (a.p: hrd rdn over 2f out: r.o wl ins fnl f) ..................... s.h.**2**
7314 Gone Savage **(70)** (Fav) *(GBBalding)* 4–10-0 TraceyPurseglove (10) (lw: w ldr: led over 3f out: hrd rdn over 1f out: hdd last stride) .......... s.h.**3**
408 Bells of Longwick **(57)** *(DRLaing)* 3–8-5 PBowe (8) (hdwy 2f out: r.o ins fnl f) .... 1.**4**
My Czech Mate **(56)** *(RHannon)* 3–7-13 ‡5WendyJones (5) (no hdwy fnl 2f) ........ 5.**5**
Wessex Milord **(36)** *(JABennett)* 7–7-3(1) ‡5ClaireBalding (6) (b: nvr nr to chal)   nk.**6**
333 Tina's Angel **(37)** (bl) *(JCFox)* 5–7-9(2) DGibbs (9) (hrd rdn 4f out: a mid div) .... ¾.**7**
731 Scarlet Princess **(46)** *(RJHodges)* 4–8-4 CAvery (1) (nvr nrr) ..................... hd.**8**
738 Kirriemuir **(36)** *(KOCunningham-Brown)* 4–7-8 NVarley (12) (prom over 3f) ...... ½.**9**
300 Three Lucky (IRE) **(42)** *(MDIUsher)* 4–8-0 TMcLaughlin (4) (a bhd) .......... 6.**10**
8304 Nazare Blue **(43)** *(MrsBarbaraWaring)* 5–8-1 GParkin (2) (lw: hrd rdn 4f out: a bhd) ................... 6.**11**

LONG HANDICAP: Wessex Milord 7-2, Tina's Angel 7-2.

**5/2** Gone Savage, **4/1** Teanarco (IRE), **9/2** MY RUBY RING(op 3/1), **11/2** Nazare Blue(8/1—5/1), **9/1** Three Lucky (IRE), **11/1** Scarlet Princess, **12/1** My Czech Mate(op 8/1), **25/1** Bells of Longwick, **50/1** Ors. CSF £21.41, CT £48.41. Tote £4.30: £1.80 £1.60 £1.30 (£9.90). Mrs Marion Wickham (LAMBOURN) bred by Mrs Wickham.
11 Rn                                                          1m 13.48 (1.18)
SF—18/36/46/19/–/–

**968**     EDDIE REAVEY AUCTION STKS (I) (Mdn 2-Y-O) £2441.60 (£677.60: £324.80)
       **6f**                                                                 2-40 (2-42)

**Maybe Gold** *(DWPArbuthnot)* 8-4 PaulEddery (16) (b.nr hind: unf: a.p: led 2f out: drvn out) ..................... −**1**
339 Waterlord (IRE) *(CGCox)* 8-3(1) AClark (14) (b.hind: led 4f: hrd rdn over 1f out: btn whn swvd lft nr fin) ......................... nk.**2**
000 Lady Nellie *(RVeerapuy)* 7-9 SDawson (15) (hdwy 2f out: swtchd lft wl ins fnl f: r.o wl) ......................... nk.**3**
772 Bold Acre *(DRLaing)* 8-4 TyroneWilliams (7) (a.p: hrd rdn & ev ch 2f out: r.o ins fnl f: bmpd nr fin) ......................... nk.**4**
703 Hallorina *(WGRWightman)* 7-9 GBardwell (4) (a.p: ev ch 2f out: r.o: bmpd nr fin)   ½.**5**
3294 Christian Spirit (Fav) *(RHannon)* 8-2 AMcGlone (6) (hrd rdn & hdwy over 1f out: r.o ins fnl f) ......................... 4.**6**
Mena *(JWPayne)* 7-9 AMackay (3) (leggy: unf: no hdwy fnl 2f) ......................... hd.**7**
7216 General Chase *(RHannon)* 7-9 NAdams (9) (nvr nr to chal) ..................... s.h.**8**
7725 Daring King *(DSasse)* 8-4 ‡5RPerham (12) (prom 4f) ......................... 1½.**9**
Venture Prints *(RChampion)* 8-0 GCarter (1) (scope: bit bkwd: outpcd) ......... ½.**10**
Daisy James (IRE) *(JMPEustace)* 7-11 BCrossley (5) (scope: bkwd: outpcd) 1½.**11**
7916 Border Dream *(WGMTurner)* 7-11 ‡3TSprake (11) (lw: spd over 2f) ......... nk.**12**
Our Shadee (USA) *(KTIvory)* 8-2 GDuffield (2) (w'like: scope: bit bkwd: a bhd) 2.**13**
Miss Bridge (IRE) *(MBell)* 7-9 JQuinn (13) (neat: prom over 2f) ......... 2.**14**
5956 World Express (IRE) *(BRMillman)* 8-4 GBaxter (8) (lw: prom 3f) ......... ¾.**15**
Lady Argent (IRE) *(APJarvis)* 8-1 DHolland (10) (w'like: scope: bkwd: s.s: a bhd) ......................... 10.**16**

**5/2** Christian Spirit, **7/2** Miss Bridge (IRE)(5/2—4/1), **5/1** Bold Acre(op 3/1), **8/1** MAYBE GOLD(10/1—20/1), **10/1** Daring King(op 6/1), **12/1** Mena(op 7/1), Lady Argent (IRE)(8/1—20/1), **14/1** Border Dream(op 8/1), **16/1** Waterlord (IRE), World Express (IRE)(8/1—20/1), **20/1** Our Shadee (USA)(op 12/1), Venture Prints, Hallorina(op 12/1), Daisy James (IRE)(op 8/1), General Chase(op 12/1), **33/1** Lady Relko. CSF £137.19, Tote £10.10: £2.00 £5.10 £27.30 (£101.80). Mr George S. Thompson (COMPTON) bred by P. F. Boggis. 16 Rn    1m 14.99 (2.69)

**969**     REDENHAM CLAIMING STKS (3-Y-O) £2382.80 (£660.80: £316.40)    **1m**    3-10 (3-11)

863★ **Prince Rodney (63)** (Fav) *(RHannon)* 9-5 WCarson (4) (lw: a.p: led 2f out: pushed out) ..................... −**1**
788 Grey But Rosy (IRE) **(54)** *(DRCElsworth)* 8-9 RCochrane (3) (b.hind: lw: hrd rdn over 2f out: hdwy wl over 1f out: r.o) ......................... 2.**2**
7875 Super Beauty **(GBBalding)** 8-12 JWilliams (6) (lost pl over 3f out: rdn & rallied over 1f out: unable qckn) ......................... nk.**3**
801 Peggy Mainwaring **(54)** *(RJHoulder)* 8-3 ‡7SDrowne (5) (lw: a.p: hrd rdn over 2f out: one pce) ......................... 2½.**4**
Shafayif *(BHanbury)* 8-12 BRouse (7) (hld up: hrd rdn over 2f out: one pce) .... ¾.**5**
799 Super Flyer (IRE) **(57)** *(MrsAKnight)* 8-9 ‡5CHodgson (1) (led 6f: wknd fnl f) ..... hd.**6**
7845 Sizzling Thoughts *(GLewis)* 9-3 PaulEddery (8) (a bhd) ......................... 3½.**7**
5976 Spontaneous (IRE) *(RCharlton)* 8-8 DHolland (2) (bhd fnl 3f) ......................... 1½.**8**

**Evens** PRINCE RODNEY, **5/1** Super Beauty, Spontaneous (IRE), **10/1** Sizzling Thoughts, Shafayif(op 6/1), **12/1** Super Flyer (IRE)(op 6/1), Grey But Rosy (IRE), **16/1** Peggy Mainwaring(12/1—20/1). CSF £13.93, Tote £1.70: £1.20 £1.60 £1.60 (£7.80). Mr G. A. Bosley (MARLBOROUGH) bred by G. A. Bosley and H. Clarkin. 8 Rn
1m 43.63 (4.33)

**970**    TRYON H'CAP (3-Y.O) (0-90) £3915.00 (£1170.00: £560.00: £255.00)
      6f 212y                                                  3-40 (3-44)

   801★ **Risk Zone** (62) (bl) *(RHannon)* 7-11(1) (5x) AMcGlone (10) (mde all: clr over 1f out: easily) ......................................................................................... —1
   559   Holetown (83) (Jt-Fav) *(RHannon)* 9-4 WCarson (3) (a.p: chsd wnr fnl 2f: no imp) ........................................................................................................ 5.2
   482   Coniston Lake (IRE) (61) *(GLewis)* 7-5 ‡5DHarrison (2) (hdwy over 1f out: r.o one pce) ................................................................................................ 1½.3
   738   Tadora (IRE) (60) *(CJBenstead)* 7-9(2) TyroneWilliams (4) (lw: hrd rdn over 2f out: hdwy over 1f out: nvr nrr) ...................................................... 1½.4
   783   Khazar (USA) (65) *(SirMarkPrescott)* 8-0(1) GDuffield (5) (lw: a.p: rdn 3f out: one pce) ................................................................................................... 1.5
   620★ Regal Racer (86) (Jt-Fav) *(DRCElsworth)* 9-7 RCochrane (8) (prom over 5f) ... 1½.6
   6466 Wild Strawberry (80) *(JMPEustace)* 9-1 MTebbutt (9) (nvr nr to chal) ............. ¾.7
             Singers Image (72) *(GBBalding)* 8-7 JWilliams (7) (bhd fnl 2f) ....................... 2.8
   653   Greetland Folly (85) *(RMWhitaker)* 9-6 ACulhane (6) (a bhd) ....................... ½.9
   8713 Canadian Capers (81) *(MRChannon)* 9-2 PaulEddery (1) (bhd fnl 3f) ............. 6.10
                     LONG HANDICAP: Tadora (IRE) 7-0.

**4/1** Holetown, Regal Racer, **5/1** Coniston Lake (IRE), **6/1** RISK ZONE(op 4/1), Wild Strawberry, **13/2** Khazar (USA), **12/1** Greetland Folly, Canadian Capers(8/1—14/1), **25/1** Ors. CSF £29.41, CT £117.69. Tote £6.10: £2.40 £1.80 £2.10 (£12.40). Roldvale Limited (MARLBOROUGH) bred by Roldvale Ltd. 10 Rn
                                              1m 26.32 (0.62)
                                        SF—37/43/12/11/13/29

**971**    SALISBURY STKS (2-Y.O) £3622.50 (£1080.00: £515.00: £232.50)    5f    4-10 (4-11)

   654★ **Silver Wizard** (USA) (Fav) *(GLewis)* 9-2 PaulEddery (3) (mde all: clr over 1f out: comf) ................................................................................................... —1
   772★ Fortune Cay (IRE) *(RHannon)* 9-2 AMcGlone (5) (lw: chsd wnr over 2f out: no imp) ........................................................................................................ 6.2
   7334 Stormy Heights *(JRJenkins)* 8-6 GBaxter (1) (outpcd: nvr nr to chal) ........... 2½.3
   4024 Gaynor Goodman (IRE) *(JSMoore)* 8-6 BRouse (2) (chsd wnr over 2f) ............. 4.4
             Kill the Plague (USA) *(APJones)* 8-11 NAdams (4) (w'like: bit bkwd: s.s: a wl bhd) .......................................................................................................... 15.5

**8/11** SILVER WIZARD (USA), **6/5** Fortune Cay (IRE), **50/1** Stormy Heights, **66/1** Ors. CSF £1.80, Tote £1.60: £1.10 £1.20 (£1.10). Mrs Shirley Robins (EPSOM) bred by Bounding Basque Breeding Syndicate in USA. 5 Rn
                                              60.20 sec (0.20)
                                       SF—63/39/19/–/–

**972**    DURNFORD H'CAP (3-Y.O) (0-70) £2826.00 (£786.00: £378.00)
      1m 1f 209y                                          4-40 (4-47)

                           (Weights raised 2 lb)
             **Cool Society** (USA) (63) *(CRNelson)* 9-2 NAdams (17) (bit bkwd: a.p: hrd rdn over 1f out: led ins fnl f: drvn out) .............................................. —1
   697   Hester Stanhope (61) *(PWHarris)* 8-8 GDuffield (13) (swtchd lft over 2f out: hdwy wl over 1f out: hrd rdn: r.o wl ins fnl f) ...................................... nk.2
   7285 Freephone (CAN) (55) *(JWHills)* 8-8 WNewnes (3) (led 1f: led over 3f out tl ins fnl f: unable qckn) .................................................................... 2.3
   5835 Dare to Dream (IRE) (54) *(GLewis)* 8-7 PaulEddery (18) (hdwy 3f out: hrd rdn over 1f out: one pce) ................................................................... 3.4
             Affirmed's Destiny (USA) (50) *(JLDunlop)* 8-3 GCarter (4) (hdwy 3f out: r.o one pce fnl 2f) ....................................................................................... ½.5
   7282 Vivitz (IRE) (60) (v) *(GBBalding)* 8-13 JWilliams (15) (a.p: one pce fnl 2f) ........ 3½.6
   7003 My Senor (48) *(MMadgwick)* 8-1 JQuinn (14) (nvr nr to chal) ........................... 2½.7
   695   Wakil (IRE) (54) *(CJBenstead)* 8-7 WCarson (1) (lw: hdwy fnl 2f: nvr nrr) .......... nk.8
             Pie Hatch (42) *(SirMarkPrescott)* 7-4(2) ‡5DHarrison (9) (hrd rdn over 4f out: nvr nrr) .................................................................................. nk.9
   821   Miss Doody (68) (v) *(MRChannon)* 9-7 RCochrane (10) (nvr nrr) ..................... nk.10
   6043 Moon Spin (66) (Fav) *(MajorWRHern)* 9-5 BRouse (11) (prom 7f) ...................... hd.11
   745   Royal Circus (42) (bl) *(PWHarris)* 7-9(2) TyroneWilliams (16) (led 9f out tl over 3f out: sn wknd) ........................................................................................ 3.12
   7284 Pride of Britain (CAN) (49) *(LGCottrell)* 8-2 NHowe (6) (prom over 6f: wkng whn bmpd over 2f out) ................................................................................... 4.13
   6216 Green's Exhibit (52) *(KOCunningham-Brown)* 8-5 SDawson (7) (lw: bhd fnl 5f) 3½.14
   6255 Athar (IRE) (64) *(PTWalwyn)* 9-3 DHolland (12) (mid div whn bmpd over 2f out) 1.15
   700   Yaafoor (USA) (58) *(AAScott)* 8-11 AMcGlone (2) (prom whn rn wd bnd over 6f out: bhd fnl 4f) ........................................................................................... 16

623 Woodlands Legend **(50)** *(DCTucker)* 8-3 ADicks (8) (hrd rdn 5f out: a bhd: t.o
    fnl 4f) ............................................................................................ 17
            LONG HANDICAP: Pie Hatch (IRE) 7-4, Royal Circus 7-6.
        *Kathy Fair (IRE) (33/1) Withdrawn (bolted on wy to s) : not under orders*

**5/2** Moon Spin, **5/1** Dare to Dream (IRE), **13/2** Pride of Britain (CAN)(9/2—7/1), **9/1** Miss Doody, Vivitz
(IRE)(6/1—10/1), **10/1** My Senor(8/1—12/1), **12/1** Athar (IRE)(8/1—14/1), **14/1** Freephone (CAN), Hester
Stanhope, Affirmed's Destiny (USA)(op 8/1), **20/1** Yaafoor (USA), Pie Hatch (IRE), Wakil (IRE), Green's Exhibit,
**25/1** COOL SOCIETY (USA), **33/1** Royal Circus, **50/1** Woodlands Legend. CSF £339.46, CT £4,594.62. Tote
£94.60: £8.40 £6.80 £4.00 £1.20 (£248.70). Mr John W. Mitchell (UPPER LAMBOURN) bred by Brereton C.
Jones in USA. 17 Rn                                                              2m 6.52 (1.82)
                                                                          SF—49/46/36/29/24/27

**973**   EDDIE REAVEY AUCTION STKS (II) (Mdn 2-Y.O) £2441.60 (£677.60: £324.80)
          **6f**                                                                5-10 (5-16)

703[2] **No Reservations (IRE)** *(RFJohnsonHoughton)* 7-4 ‡[5]DHarrison (6) (a.p: led
    over 3f out: pushed out) ................................................... —1
721[3] Hung Parliament (Fav) *(BWHills)* 7-10[(1)] WCarson (7) (lw: led 4f out tl over 3f
    out: unable qckn fnl f) ....................................................... ³/₄.2
733[2] Chinnery (IRE) *(JMPEustace)* 8-9 RCochrane (13) (lw: a.p: hrd rdn over 1f out:
    one pce) ............................................................................ 2¹/₂.3
574 Hot Off the Press *(RMWhitaker)* 8-0 DHolland (12) (rdn 2f out: hdwy & edgd rt
    over 1f out: r.o ins fnl f) .................................................... 1¹/₂.4
703[6] Zany Zanna (IRE) *(GAPritchard-Gordon)* 7-12 JQuinn (4) (hdwy 3f out: one pce
    fnl 2f) ............................................................................... 1¹/₂.5
807 Superensis *(WRMuir)* 8-4 ‡[5]RPerham (8) (no hdwy fnl 2f) ...................... 4.6
803 Petite Vino *(JJBridger)* 7-9 NAdams (10) (bit bkwd: spd 3f) ..................... 4.7
    Manon Lescaut *(APJarvis)* 8-3 PaulEddery (3) (wl grwn: bkwd: outpcd: nvr nrr) ¹/₂.8
    Secret Formula *(ODDalling)* 0-0 AMcClone (1) (w'like: ecope: nvr nrr) ........ ³/₄.9
847 Tigerspike (IRE) *(MMcCormack)* 8-3[(1)] AClark (9) (a mid div) ................. nk.10
548 Easy Touch *(MDIUsher)* 7-13 CRutter (2) (a bhd) ............................... 3¹/₂.11
791 Stanford Avenue *(BForsey)* 7-10[(1)] TyroneWilliams (11) (bhd fnl 3f) ......... 3.12
791 Spenmax (IRE) *(WGMTurner)* 7-11 ‡[3]TSprake (5) (bhd fnl 2f) .................. nk.13
446 Threeofus *(KTIvory)* 8-11 GBardwell (15) (s.s: bhd fnl 3f) .................... 2.14
729 Young Absalom *(LGCottrell)* 9-0 TRogers (14) (led 2f: wknd 3f out) ........... 3¹/₂.15

**13/8** Hung Parliament(11/10—7/4), **100/30** NO RESERVATIONS (IRE), Chinnery (IRE), **10/1** Superensis, Zany
Zanna (IRE)(12/1—16/1), **16/1** Manon Lescaut, Tigerspike (IRE), **20/1** Hot Off the Press, **33/1** Ors. CSF £9.62,
Tote £4.30: £1.70 £1.70 £1.10 (£3.20). C. W. Sumner and Jim Short (DIDCOT) bred by R. Entenmann in Ireland.
15 Rn                                                                           1m 13.43 (1.13)
                                                                          SF—12/15/18/3/–/–

T/Plpt: £614.40 (4.55 Tckts).                                                              AK

**671—HAYDOCK (L-H)**
**Friday, May 22nd [Good to firm]**
Going Allowance: minus 0.30 sec per fur (F)                              Wind: slt half bhd

Stalls: high
**974**   BRITISH COAL APP'CE H'CAP (0-80) £2511.00 (£696.00: £333.00)
          **1¹/₄m 120y**                                                        2-00 (2-02)

904[3] *Miss Hyde (USA)* **(58)** (v) *(JAGlover)* 3-7-7 FNorton (4) (lw: mde all: rdn clr
    appr fnl f) ......................................................................... —1
766[5] Sharquin **(41)** *(MBrittain)* 5-7-7 BDoyle (1) (a.p: 3rd st: chsd wnr fnl 3f: no imp) 3¹/₂.2
891★ Flying Down to Rio (IRE) **(58)** *(MPNaughton)* 4-8-7 (7x) ‡[3]JWeaver (5) (lw: hdwy
    over 2f out: kpt on u.p fnl f) ................................................. ¹/₂.3
699[6] Kelimutu **(63)** *(CFWall)* 3-7-5 ‡[7]TWilson (8) (bhd: hdwy 3f out: hrd rdn appr fnl f:
    one pce) ........................................................................... 4.4
923★ Nipotina **(47)** *(RHollinshead)* 6-7-6 (7x) ‡[7]AGarth (13) (chsd ldrs: 6th st: no
    hdwy fnl 2f) ....................................................................... 6.5
688[3] Mardessa **(64)** (Fav) *(FHLee)* 9-9-2 NKennedy (11) (lw: dwlt: hdwy & 5th st: rdn
    2f out: nt pce to chal) ......................................................... hd.6
    Athene Noctua **(44)** *(BAMcMahon)* 7-7-3[(3)] ‡[7]JBramhill (3) (bit bkwd: prom: 4th
    st: wknd over 2f out) ........................................................... ³/₄.7
494 Cheeky Pot **(59)** (v) *(DenysSmith)* 4-8-4 ‡[7]CTeague (12) (nvr trbld ldrs) ......... 1¹/₂.8
565[4] Reklaw **(41)** *(MDHammond)* 5-7-7 JFanning (2) (a in rr) ....................... 3¹/₂.9
    Marowins **(70)** *(EJAlston)* 3-7-12[(12)] ‡[7]SKnott (7) (bkwd: s.i.s: a bhd) ............. 2.10
    Caromandoo (IRE) **(74)** *(ABarrow)* 4-9-5 ‡[7]JHunter (10) (b.nr hind: bit bkwd: a
    bhd) ............................................................................... 1¹/₂.11

675 Stradbroke **(43)** *(MBJames)* 5–7-9[2] SMaloney (6) (t: chsd ldrs 6f: sn lost tch) 2½.**12**
Killick **(44)** *(REPeacock)* 4–7-3[3] ‡7CHawksley (9) (bkwd: prom: 2nd st: wknd
over 3f out) ........................................................................ 6.**13**
LONG HANDICAP: Miss Hyde (USA) 7-6, Sharquin 7-3, Athene Noctua 7-1, Reklaw 7-4,
Marowins 6-13, Stradbroke 6-10, Killick 7-6.

2/1 Mardessa, 5/1 Reklaw, 11/2 Flying Down to Rio (IRE), 7/1 Nipotina, Kelimutu, 9/1 MISS HYDE (USA)(op
6/1), 12/1 Sharquin, 16/1 Killick, 20/1 Cheeky Pot, 25/1 Caromandoo (IRE), Athene Noctua, 50/1 Ors. CSF
£108.12, CT £602.68. Tote £18.30: £3.90 £3.10 £1.70 (£41.50). Hyde Sporting Promotions/Saddlehome Farm
(WORKSOP) bred by Saddle Home Farm in USA. 13 Rn                                         2m 14.82 (3.12)
                                                                                        SF—16/9/22/–/–/10

**975**      E.B.F. ERICSSON BUSINESSPHONE STKS (Mdn 2-Y.O.C & G) £2660.00 (£735.00:
             £350.00)   **5f**                                                        2-30 (2-31)

King Paris (IRE) *(MBell)* 9-0 MHills (1) (w'like: scope: s.s: hdwy ½-wy: led 1f
out: r.o wl) ...................................................................... —**1**
Mysterious Ways (FR) *(Fav)* *(MrsJCecil)* 9-0 MRoberts (5) (w'like: leggy: half
reard s: sn prom: led ½-wy to 1f out: rallied u.p nr fin) ....... ½.**2**
720[4] Club Verge (IRE) *(EJAlston)* 9-0 KFallon (4) (bit bkwd: led to ½-wy out:
unable qckn) .................................................................. 3.**3**
Northern Bluff *(JWWatts)* 9-0 SCauthen (3) (wl grwn: bit bkwd: chsd ldrs:
outpcd 2f out: sn btn) ...................................................... 3½.**4**
Umbubuzi (USA) *(FHLee)* 9-0 AMunro (2) (scope: bkwd: spd over 3f) ........... hd.**5**

11/10 Mysterious Ways (FR), 5/2 KING PARIS (IRE), 6/1 Northern Bluff(op 4/1), 7/1 Club Verge (IRE), 9/1
Umbubuzi (USA). CSF £5.60, Tote £4.60: £1.80 £1.30 (£3.20). Mrs Pauline Karpidas (NEWMARKET) bred by
Mrs P. Karpidas in Ireland. 5 Rn                                                           60.74 sec (1.74)
                                                                                          SF—35/33/21/7/6

**976**      BASS NORTH WEST H'CAP (0-100) £4347.00 (£1296.00: £618.00: £279.00)
             **1m 30y**                                                                3-00 (3-01)
                                   (Weights raised 8 lb)

832[2] Piquant **(75)** *(LordHuntingdon)* 5–8-13 AMunro (2) (lw: chsd ldr: 2nd st: shkn
up to ld jst ins fnl f: r.o) .................................................. —**1**
Eclipsing (IRE) **(78)** *(RCharlton)* 4–9-2 WRyan (3) (hld up: 3rd st: r.o ins fnl f: no
ch w wnr) .................................................................... 2.**2**
610 Tusky **(86)** (v) *(MJCamacho)* 4–9-10 SMorris (1) (led & sn clr: rdn over 1f out:
hdd jst ins fnl f: one pce) ................................................... ½.**3**
883* King of Chance (IRE) **(81)** *(Fav)* *(MrsJRRamsden)* 4–9-5 (5x) MBirch (4) (swtg:
s.i.s: 4th st: hdwy 3f out: rdn & wknd over 1f out) ............... 6.**4**

5/4 King of Chance (IRE)(op 2/1), 15/8 PIQUANT (op 11/2), 3/1 Eclipsing (IRE), 16/1 Tusky(op 10/1). CSF £7.03,
Tote £2.20 (£3.30). The Queen (WEST ILSLEY) bred by The Queen. 4 Rn                        1m 43.54 (3.14)

**977**      KNIGHTON GROUP STKS (3-Y.O) £4905.00   **1m 30y**                           3-30

609 Hero's Light (USA) **(85)** *(PFICole)* 9-4 AMunro (1) (walked over) ................ —**1**
             *Lead the Dance Withdrawn (lame gng to s) : not under orders*
Mr Fahd Salman (WHATCOMBE) bred by Ahmed Salman in USA.

**978**      PHURNACITE CLAIMING STKS   £2532.00 (£702.00: £336.00)   **6f**            4-00 (4-01)

685[5] Easy Line **(90)** *(Fav)* *(PJFeilden)* 9–9-4 BRaymond (1) (b: bit bkwd: hld up: led
ins fnl f: canter) ........................................................... —**1**
Finjan **(82)** *(MPNaughton)* 5–8-11 ‡5JWeaver (4) (bkwd: a.p: led over 2f out tl
ins fnl f: no ch w wnr) ..................................................... 1½.**2**
Military Expert **(72)** *(CaptJWilson)* 3–8-8 JLowe (5) (bkwd: led over 3f: wknd
over 1f out) ................................................................. 5.**3**
592 Green's Stubbs **(37)** *(ABarrow)* 5–8-6 ‡7JHunter (6) (swtg: sn rdn along: nvr wnt
pce) ......................................................................... 2.**4**
678 Lombard Ocean **(70)** *(MO'Neill)* 3–8-4 JFortune (2) (prom: rdn 2f out: sn btn) . nk.**5**
698 Tommy Tempest *(KRBurke)* 3–8-8 AShoults (3) (s.i.s: effrt 2f out: wknd appr fnl
f) ........................................................................... 1½.**6**

4/7 EASY LINE, 6/1 Finjan(op 4/1), Military Expert(op 5/2), Lombard Ocean, 50/1 Ors. CSF £4.32, Tote £1.60:
£1.20 £2.00 (£2.90). Mr C. A. Potter (NEWMARKET) bred by R. C. Bilborough. 6 Rn          1m 13.15 (1.45)
                                                                                         SF—39/26/3/–/–/–

**979**      FRENKEL TOPPING STKS (Mdn 3-Y.O) £2532.00 (£702.00: £336.00)
             **1m 3f 200y**                                                            4-30 (4-36)

625[2] Silvernesian (USA) *(Fav)* *(JLDunlop)* 9-0 MRoberts (2) (sn bhd & pushed
along: 5th st: hdwy to ld over 1f out: r.o wl) ......................... —**1**

573² Seekin Cash (USA) *(JWWatts)* 9-0  SCauthen (4) (led over 8f: rdn 2f out: kpt on)    4.2

560³ Summer Cruise *(HRACecil)* 9-0  WRyan (5) (lw: a.p: 2nd st: led over 3f out tl over
1f out: one pce) ................................................................ 2.3

577³ Mootawel (USA) *(HThomsonJones)* 9-0  RHills (1) (lw: prom: 3rd st: kpt on one
pce fnl 2f) ................................................................ ½.4

732³ Winged Bayard *(RFJohnsonHoughton)* 9-0  JReid (3) (lw: chsd ldrs: 4th st:
wknd wl over 2f out) ................................................................ 15.5

680⁶ The Titan Ghost (57) *(BAMcMahon)* 9-0  BRaymond (6) (swtg: a bhd: 6th st: t.o
fnl 2f) ................................................................ 12.6

**13/8** SILVERNESIAN (USA), **5/2** Summer Cruise, **9/2** Mootawel (USA), **6/1** Seekin Cash (USA), **7/1** Winged Bayard, **50/1** The Titan Ghost. CSF £10.85, Tote £2.60: £1.40 £2.20 (£6.00). Gerecon Italia (ARUNDEL) bred by Mark & Mrs Hardin in USA. 6 Rn                        2m 30.97 (2.97)

SF—34/26/22/21/–/–

---

**980**    SPINAL INJURIES ASSOCIATION H'CAP (0-100) £3289.50 (£981.00: £468.00: £211.50)
**5f**    5-00 (5-02)

813 **Gondo (70)** *(EJAlston)* 5-8-4  KFallon (9) (lw: chsd ldrs: qcknd to ld ins fnl f:
easily) ................................................................ —1

819³ Beau Venture (USA) **(81)** *(FHLee)* 4-9-1  AMunro (2) (a.p: led over 1f out tl hdd
& no ex ins fnl f) ................................................................ 1½.2

876⁵ Absolution **(83)** (Fav) *(MPNaughton)* 8-9-3  MRoberts (10) (disp ld: rdn over 1f
out: one pce) ................................................................ 3½.3

819 Pallium (IRE) **(77)** *(MPNaughton)* 4-8-6 ‡5JWeaver (3) (bhd: swtchd lft 2f out:
rdn & r.o) ................................................................ 1½.4

686⁎ Eager Deva **(94)** *(RHollinshead)* 5-10-0  LPiggott (4) (lw: led tl over 1f out: sn
rdn & btn) ................................................................ ¾.5

876⁎ Barrys Gamble **(83)** (bl) *(TFairhurst)* 6-9-0 (7x) ‡3JFanning (8) (chsd ldrs: rdn
wln n.m.r ins fnl f: sn htn) ................................................................ 1½.6

813 Dominuet **(82)** *(JLSpearing)* 7-9-2  RFox (7) (hld up: gd hdwy wln n.m.r 1f out:
nt rcvr) ................................................................ 1½.7

723 Breezy Day **(79)** *(BAMcMahon)* 6-8-6 ‡7SSanders (6) (lw: chsd ldrs: rdn along
2f out: sn btn) ................................................................ nk.8

872³ Drum Sergeant **(59)** (v) *(JParkes)* 5-7-7  NCarlisle (5) (lw: s.s: swtchd lft 2f out:
sn rdn & wknd) ................................................................ 2.9

Goodbye Mr Marks (IRE) **(67)** *(NBycroft)* 4-8-1  SWood (1) (bkwd: spd 3f) ...... 1.10

**3/1** Absolution(op 5/1), **9/2** Barrys Gamble, **11/2** Eager Deva(4/1—6/1), **6/1** Beau Venture (USA), **13/2** Drum Sergeant, **7/1** Dominuet, **10/1** Pallium (IRE), GONDO, **14/1** Breezy Day, **33/1** Goodbye Mr Marks (IRE). CSF £67.66, CT £209.53. Tote £12.00: £2.70 £1.70 £1.80 (£45.40). Mrs Helen O'Brien (PRESTON) bred by Trevor S. Child. 10 Rn                        59.09 sec (0.09)

SF—58/63/53/36/55/35

T/Jkpt: £900.90 (0.4 Tckts); £730.53 to Haydock 23/5/92. T/Plpt: £46.60 (126.85 Tckts).        IM

---

# HAYDOCK (L-H)
## Saturday, May 23rd [Good to firm]
Going Allowance: minus 0.30 sec per fur (F)        Wind: fresh bhd

Stalls: high

**981**    NATIONAL TYRES AND AUTOCARE STKS    £4347.00 (£1296.00: £618.00: £279.00)
**2m 45y**    2-00 (2-00)

622³ **Romany Rye (97)** *(GWragg)* 4-8-13  JReid (6) (lw: hld up: 7th st: jnd ldrs 2f out:
hrd rdn to ld ins fnl f) ................................................................ —1

608⁴ Clare Heights **(98)** (Fav) *(JRFanshawe)* 4-8-8  SCauthen (3) (hld up: 5th st: str
chal fr 2f out: n.m.r fnl f: r.o) ................................................................ ½.2

855⁵ Le Corsaire (USA) **(100)** *(LMCumani)* 4-8-13  LDettori (5) (lw: a.p: 3rd st: led
over 2f out: hrd rdn & hdd ins fnl f) ................................................................ ½.3

388 Haitham **(91)** *(RAkehurst)* 5-9-1  LPiggott (1) (led tl over 2f out: kpt on one pce)   6.4
Hondeghem *(CWCElsey)* 6-8-11  BRaymond (9) (chsd ldr: 2nd st: wknd 3f out)   6.5

826 Mountain Kingdom (USA) **(100)** *(NTinkler)* 8-9-7  PRobinson (7) (lw: hld up: 6th
st: lost tch 3f out) ................................................................ hd.6

622² Piper's Son *(MBradstock)* 6-8-11  GDuffield (8) (b: chsd ldrs: 4th st: wknd 3f
out: t.o) ................................................................ 20.7

796 Master Plan (FR) **(23)** *(MissLAPerratt)* 6-9-1  CDwyer (2) (a bhd: 8th st: t.o fnl 3f)  30.8

**2/1** Clare Heights, **9/4** ROMANY RYE, **3/1** Le Corsaire (USA), **15/2** Piper's Son, **14/1** Haitham, **16/1** Mountain Kingdom (USA), **40/1** Hondeghem, **100/1** Master Plan (FR). CSF £7.04, Tote £3.10: £1.10 £1.20 £1.40 (£3.80). Sir Philip Oppenheimer (NEWMARKET) bred by Hascombe and Valiant Studs. 8 Rn        3m 30.43 (3.23)

SF—19/13/17/13/3/12

**982**
SANDY LANE STKS (listed race) (3-Y.O) £11257.50 (£3360.00: £1605.00: £727.50)
6f
2-30 (2-34)

808* **Prince Ferdinand (116)** *(MMcCormack)* 8-11 JReid (1) (lw: hld up: swtchd rt over 1f out: rdn to ld ins fnl f: readily) .................... —1
871* Central City **(110)** *(RHannon)* 8-6 BRaymond (3) (a.p: led 1f out: sn hdd: unable qckn) .................... 2.2
655 Wilde Rufo **(101)** *(PAKelleway)* 8-11 PRobinson (4) (lw: s.s: hdwy u.p over 2f out: nvr nrr) .................... 3½.3
851* Garah **(113)** (Fav) *(HRACecil)* 8-8(2) SCauthen (6) (lw: led after 2f to 1f out: eased whn btn) .................... ½.4
827⁴ Colway Bold **(106)** *(JWWatts)* 9-0 LPiggott (5) (lw: chsd ldrs 4f: sn rdn & btn) 2½.5
719 Bunty Boo **(84)** *(BAMcMahon)* 8-6 GDuffield (7) (lw: spd over 4f) .................... 7.6
601² Dancing Boy (USA) **(104)** *(MrsJCecil)* 8-11 LDettori (2) (led 2f: rdn ½-wy: sn bhd: t.o) .................... 30.7

**8/13** Garah, **7/2** Central City, **9/2** PRINCE FERDINAND, **16/1** Colway Bold, **20/1** Dancing Boy (USA), **25/1** Wilde Rufo, **66/1** Bunty Boo. CSF £20.01, Tote £5.40: £2.30 £2.40 (£9.10). Miss J. Winch (WANTAGE) bred by Greensward Racing Ltd. 7 Rn
1m 10.85 (0.38 under best; U.85)
SF—78/65/56/51/47/11

**983**
TOTE CREDIT SILVER BOWL (H'cap) (3-Y.O) (0-115) £18275.00 (£5450.00: £2600.00: £1175.00) **1m 30y**
3-00 (3-04)

558³ **Sharpitor (IRE) (92)** *(WJarvis)* 9-0 JReid (4) (hld up: hdwy over 3f out: led 1f out: edgd lft fnl f: r.o wl) .................... —1
549⁵ Big Blue **(89)** (bl) *(CEBrittain)* 8-6 ‡⁵BDoyle (10) (lw: chsd ldrs: 4th st: kpt on u.p ins fnl f) .................... 1½.2
816⁴ Modernise (USA) **(99)** *(RCharlton)* 9-7 LDetton (3) (lw: a.p: 3rd st: ev ch ins fnl f: rdn & unable qckn) .................... s.h.3
767⁶ Cool Luke (IRE) **(79)** *(GMMoore)* 8-1 JCarroll (8) (2nd st: led 4f out to 1f out: n.m.r ins fnl f: one pce) .................... 3¼.4
432⁴ Marabella Star (USA) **(93)** (Fav) *(HRACecil)* 9-1 WRyan (1) (lw: led to ½-wy: wknd appr fnl f) .................... 4.5
432⁵ Sand Table **(86)** (v) *(LordHuntingdon)* 8-8 LPiggott (6) (plld hrd: 5th st: wknd over 2f out) .................... ½.6
558 Strong Suit (IRE) **(95)** *(RHannon)* 9-3 SRaymont (12) (swtg: nvr nr to chal) .................... 2½.7
767* Hadaad (USA) **(85)** *(AAScott)* 8-7 BRaymond (9) (s.i.s: hld up: a bhd) .................... 1½.8
746* Sir Mark Sykes (IRE) **(85)** *(JRFanshawe)* 8-7 GDuffield (11) (chsd ldrs: 6th st: wknd over 2f out) .................... 2½.9
693* Cambrian **(92)** *(MrsJCecil)* 9-0 SCauthen (2) (bhd fnl 3f: t.o) .................... 5.10
464* Magnificent **(79)** *(MAJarvis)* 8-1 PRobinson (5) (lw: a bhd: t.o) .................... ¾.11

**5/2** Marabella Star (USA), **6/1** Sand Table, **13/2** SHARPITOR (IRE), Sir Mark Sykes (IRE), **8/1** Modernise (USA), **9/1** Cambrian, **10/1** Magnificent, **11/1** Hadaad (USA), **16/1** Big Blue, **20/1** Strong Suit (IRE), **33/1** Cool Luke (IRE). CSF £92.84, CT £771.26. Tote £6.10: £2.40 £3.50 £2.40 (£39.50). Mr Henry Lopes (NEWMARKET) bred by Dr J. J. Ryan in Ireland. 11 Rn
1m 41.99 (1.59)
SF—40/27/41/10/12/3

**984**
BE FRIENDLY H'CAP (3-Y.O) (0-90) £3552.75 (£1062.00: £508.50: £231.75)
6f
3-30 (3-32)
(Weights raised 6 lb)

714⁵ **Castlerea Lad (77)** *(RHollinshead)* 9-0 WRyan (9) (a.p: led over 1f out: sn clr: jst hld on) .................... —1
870⁴ Petite-D-Argent **(80)** (Jt-Fav) *(MissLAPerratt)* 9-3 SCauthen (7) (lw: hdwy 2f out: hrd rdn fnl f: jst failed) .................... nk.2
719² Debsy Do (USA) **(70)** *(SGNorton)* 8-0 ‡⁷OPears (10) (led tl hdd over 1f out: no ex ins fnl f) .................... 1½.3
Jucea **(67)** *(DWPArbuthnot)* 7-13 ‡⁵RPrice (5) (bit bkwd: w ldrs: ev ch 1f out: unable qckn) .................... ½.4
894* Lifetime Fame **(81)** *(JWPayne)* 9-4 GDuffield (8) (lw: r.o ins fnl f: nvr nrr) .................... 1½.5
678* Sonderise **(73)** *(NTinkler)* 8-10 JReid (1) (lw: chsd ldrs: hrd rdn over 1f out: one pce) .................... 1.6
885⁶ Great Lord (IRE) **(63)** *(JWWatts)* 8-0 JLowe (2) (spd 4f) .................... nk.7
725³ Pageboy **(84)** (Jt-Fav) *(PCHaslam)* 9-7 LPiggott (4) (lw: prom over 3f) .................... 1½.8
719⁴ Amoureuse (IRE) **(64)** *(EHOwenjun)* 7-10 ‡⁵BDoyle (6) (a bhd: t.o) .................... 12.9

**7/2** Pageboy, Petite-D-Argent, **11/2** Lifetime Fame, Debsy Do (USA), **6/1** Great Lord (IRE), Sonderise, **10/1** CASTLEREA LAD, **12/1** Amoureuse (IRE), **25/1** Jucea. CSF £44.98, CT £200.69. Tote £15.50: £2.40 £1.50 £1.60 (£21.00). Mrs Tess Graham (UPPER LONGDON) bred by J. D. Hurd. 9 Rn
1m 12.20 (0.50)
SF—54/56/33/30/43/31

**985**     ROTHMANS ROYALS NORTH SOUTH CHALLENGE SERIES (H'cap) (3-Y.O) (0-90)
£5208.00 (£1554.00: £742.00: £336.00)    **7f 30y**     4-00 (4-00)

884★ **Battle Colours (IRE) (79)** (Fav) *(SirMarkPrescott)* 8-12 GDuffield (3) (lw: 3rd
    st: led over 1f out: easily) ......................................................... —1
821⁶ Devon Dancer **(70)** *(MHEasterby)* 7-12 ‡⁵SMaloney (1) (2nd st: led over 2f out tl
    over 1f out: one pce) ............................................................... ³/₄.2
816⁶ Misunderstanding (IRE) **(88)** *(MrsJRRamsden)* 9-7 TLucas (4) (swtg: hld up:
    4th st: nvr plcd to chal) ........................................................... 5.3
822³ Hi-Tech Honda (IRE) **(70)** (bl) *(CEBrittain)* 7-12 ‡⁵BDoyle (2) (led tl over 2f out:
    sn rdn & btn) ............................................................................ 5.4

**Evens** BATTLE COLOURS (IRE), Misunderstanding (IRE), **6/1** Devon Dancer. CSF
£6.23, Tote £1.90 (£3.60). Mr Garth Insoll (NEWMARKET) bred by Stackallan Stud in Ireland. 4 Rn
1m 29.85 (2.55)
SF—28/12/20/—

**986**     E.B.F. ST HELENS STKS (Mdn 2-Y.O.F) £2856.00 (£791.00: £378.00)    **5f**    4-30 (4-33)

    **Jervia** *(JWWatts)* 8-11 LPiggott (3) (w'like: hdwy over 1f out: rdn to ld cl home) —1
677⁴ Manor Adventure *(BAMcMahon)* 8-11 LDettori (1) (a.p: led 2f out tl ct nr fin) ..... ³/₄.2
    Satz (USA) (Fav) *(JHMGosden)* 8-11 SCauthen (7) (w'like: scope: bit bkwd: hld
    up: ev ch 1f out: rdn & nt qckn) ........................................... 1¹/₂.3
543⁴ Heathyards Gem *(RHollinshead)* 8-11 WRyan (2) (a.p: ev ch 1f out: unable
    qckn) ...................................................................................... hd.4
867⁴ Infant Protege (USA) *(CEBrittain)* 8-6 ‡⁵BDoyle (4) (lw: prom over 3f) .............. 5.5
859³ Aberlady *(MAJarvis)* 8-11 PRobinson (5) (led 3f: wknd wl over 1f out) .............. hd.6
677⁶ Last Typhoon *(EHOwenjun)* 8-11 CDwyer (8) (fell over 2f out) ............................ 0
    Melodys Daughter *(RFJohnsonHoughton)* 8-11 JReid (9) (lengthy: unf: dwlt:
    bhd wlin b.d over 2f out) ........................................................ 0
    Royal Liason (IRE) *(CWCElsey)* 8-6 ‡⁵SMaloney (6) (lt-f: b.d over 2f out: broke
    leg: dead) ............................................................................... 0

**2/1** Satz (USA)(op Evens), **3/1** Aberlady, **7/1** Manor Adventure, JERVIA, **8/1** Melodys Daughter, **9/1** Infant
Protege (USA), **20/1** Heathyards Gem, **25/1** Last Typhoon, **33/1** Royal Liason (IRE). CSF £49.73, Tote £5.70:
£1.70 £2.00 £1.30 (£17.80). Sheikh Mohammed (RICHMOND) bred by Sheikh Mohammed bin Rashid al
Maktoum. 9 Rn
60.59 sec (1.59)
SF—35/32/26/25/—/4

**987**     LEVY BOARD H'CAP (0-75) £3101.00 (£861.00: £413.00)    **1³/₄m**    5-00 (5-04)

681² **Sea Goddess (75)** (Fav) *(WJarvis)* 4-10-0 SCauthen (1) (lw: mde all: hrd rdn
    over 2f out: hld on gamely) ..................................................... —1
617⁵ I Perceive **(65)** *(FHLee)* 5-9-4 PRobinson (4) (lw: hld up: 6th st: str chal fnl f: r.o) ¹/₂.2
805★ Seldom In **(45)** *(JWharton)* 6-7-7⁽²⁾ ‡⁵SMaloney (13) (wnt 2nd ent st: ev ch fnl 2f:
    rdn & no ex nr fin) ................................................................... 2.3
    Magsood **(59)** *(SMellor)* 7-8-12 MWigham (9) (hld up: styd on fnl 2f: nvr nrr) .. 12.4
777² Smiling Chief (IRE) **(55)** *(CACyzer)* 4-8-8 GDuffield (10) (hdwy & 5th st: rdn
    over 2f out: sn btn) ................................................................. 1¹/₂.5
681⁶ Emperor Chang (USA) **(42)** *(PABlockley)* 5-7-2 ‡⁷ADaly (8) (bhd: effrt 3f out: nvr
    nr to chal) ............................................................................... hd.6
760⁵ Cost Effective **(44)** *(MBrittain)* 5-7-6⁽⁴⁾ ‡⁵BDoyle (6) (bhd: hdwy over 3f out: nt
    rch ldrs) ................................................................................. 1.7
895³ Arrastra **(67)** *(IABalding)* 4-9-6 WRyan (2) (lw: chsd ldrs: 6th st: wknd over 2f
    out) ....................................................................................... 2¹/₂.8
880⁶ Quip **(40)** *(MPNaughton)* 7-7-7 JakiHouston (3) (b.hind: bit bkwd: swtg: prom:
    4th st: wknd 3f out) ................................................................ 12.9
    Nicholas Mark **(65)** *(JGFitzGerald)* 8-9-4 TLucas (12) (lw: prom: 3rd st: wknd
    wl over 2f out: t.o) ................................................................. 15.10
681 Flockton's Own **(75)** (v) *(MrsJRRamsden)* 6-10-0 LDettori (5) (b: bkwd: swtg:
    chsd ldrs 8f: sn wknd: t.o) ....................................................... 15.11
342 Green's Van Goyen (IRE) **(66)** *(RAkehurst)* 4-9-5 LPiggott (7) (a in rr: eased
    whn btn 3f out: t.o) ................................................................ 12
761⁶ Lidanzia **(40)** *(RJHolder)* 4-7-0 ‡⁷DarrenMoffatt (11) (chsd ldrs tl fell 6f out) .......... 0
LONG HANDICAP: Cost Effective 6-11, Quip 7-4.

**2/1** SEA GODDESS(op 9/2), **5/1** Seldom In, I Perceive, **6/1** Arrastra(op 4/1), **8/1** Nicholas Mark, Smiling Chief
(IRE), **11/1** Green's Van Goyen (IRE), **14/1** Lidanzia, Flockton's Own, **16/1** Quip, **25/1** Ors. CSF £14.77, CT
£45.95. Tote £3.50: £1.60 £2.30 £2.00 (£8.70). Lord Howard de Walden (NEWMARKET) bred by Seend Stud.
13 Rn
3m 1.58 (3.08)
SF—41/30/1/—/—/—

T/Trio: Race 3: £74.10 (19.5 Tckts). T/Jkpt: Not won; £3,242.28 to Sandown 25/5/92. T/Plpt: £47.40 (182.05
Tckts).
IM

830—**KEMPTON (R-H)**

**Saturday, May 23rd [Good to firm]**

Going Allowance: St: minus 0.20 sec (F); Rest: nil sec per fur (G)          Wind: slt against

Stalls: high

**988**      NEW ENGLAND GRADUATION STKS (2-Y.O) £3106.00 (£928.00: £444.00: £202.00)
             **6f**                                                          2-10 (2-14)

   **New Capricorn (USA)** *(MAJarvis)* 8-7 RCochrane (6) (w'like: scope: hdwy 2f
     out: bmpd & ev ch ins fnl f: r.o: fin 2nd, s.h: awrdd r) ......... —1
   Green's Bid *(Fav) (PFICole)* 8-7 TQuinn (3) (unf: scope: led tl ins fnl f: edgd lft:
     led fnl strides: fin 1st: disq: plcd 2nd) ................................ 2
   Twice the Groom (IRE) *(PMitchell)* 8-7 MRoberts (11) (leggy: bit bkwd: a.p: led
     ins fnl f: hrd rdn: hdd last strides) ........................... hd.3
 733* Night Melody (IRE) *(RHannon)* 9-3 KDarley (2) (a.p: hrd rdn over 1f out: unable
     qckn ins fnl f) ................................................... 2.4
   Law Commission *(DRCEIsworth)* 8-7 JWilliams (4) (str: scope: lw: hdwy over 2f
     out: one pce: bttr for r) ..................................... 3$\frac{1}{2}$.5
   Skullcap *(DMorley)* 8-7 MTebbutt (7) (unf: bit bkwd: dwlt: nvr nr to chal) ......... $\frac{1}{2}$.6
   Special Risk (IRE) *(MBell)* 8-7 WNewnes (8) (leggy: lt-f: prom 3f) .............. 3.7
   Restart *(LordHuntingdon)* 8-7 AMunro (9) (leggy: scope: a bhd) ................. 2.8
 817 Touch Silver *(BWHills)* 9-3 DHolland (1) (prom 4f) ............................ $\frac{3}{4}$.9
 345* Polity Prince *(LJHolt)* 9-3 WCarson (5) (prom over 3f) ..................... 3.10
 564 Shades of Croft *(MDIUsher)* 8-11 CRutter (10) (bhd fnl 4f: t.o) ............ 30.11
    *Stewards Enquiry: Green's Bid disq. (interference to New Capricorn (USA)).*

**13/8** Green's Bid, **5/1** Night Melody (IRE), **11/2** Touch Silver(op 3/1), **9/1** Polity Prince, **10/1** NEW CAPRICORN
(USA)(tchd 16/1), **14/1** Twice the Groom (IRE), Restart, **16/1** Special Risk (IRE), **20/1** Law Commission, **33/1**
Ors. CSF £25.43, Tote £10.00: £2.40 £1.30 £2.40 (£12.40). Mr Kamal Bhatia (NEWMARKET) bred by
Stonereath Farms Inc. in USA. 11 Rn                                    1m 12.95 (1.65)
                                               SF—36/35/34/36/12/10

**989**      CALIFORNIAN STKS (Mdn 3-Y.O.F) £2700.00 (£750.00: £360.00)
             **1m (J.C)**                                                    2-40 (2-49)

 631 **Mahasin (USA)** *(JLDunlop)* 8-11 WCarson (4) (mde all: qcknd over 1f out: comf) —1
 822² Queen Warrior *(PTWalwyn)* 8-11 DHolland (11) (3rd st: chsd wnr fnl 2f: no imp) 3$\frac{1}{2}$.2
 689³ Cachou (USA) *(JHMGosden)* 8-11 AMcGlone (1) (2nd st: hrd rdn 2f out: one
     pce) ......................................................... 1$\frac{1}{2}$.3
 633⁴ Calpella *(JARToller)* 8-11 WNewnes (9) (6th st: one pce fnl 2f) ............ 2.4
   Raven Runner (USA) *(IABalding)* 8-11 RCochrane (12) (plld hrd: hdwy 3f out:
     one pce fnl 2f) ............................................... 3.5
   Rosina Mae *(LordHuntingdon)* 8-11 AMunro (10) (leggy: s.s: nvr nr to chal) .... $\frac{1}{2}$.6
   Sharriba **(78)** *(DRCEIsworth)* 8-11 JWilliams (3) (hdwy 3f out: wknd 2f out) .... 2.7
   Miss Haggis *(RBoss)* 8-11 MTebbutt (2) (unf: bit bkwd: nvr nrr) .............. hd.8
   Charolles *(Fav) (HRACecil)* 8-11 MRoberts (7) (lw: 5th st: wknd over 2f out) ... hd.9
   Flying Wind *(JSutcliffe)* 8-11 BRouse (5) (w'like: a bhd) ................... 4.10
   Selaginella *(MRChannon)* 8-11 CRutter (14) (lw: bhd fnl 2f) ................. $\frac{3}{4}$.11
 689 Agnes Flemming (USA) *(PWHarris)* 8-11 SWhitworth (8) (4th st: wknd over 2f
     out) ......................................................... $\frac{3}{4}$.12
   Mist of the Marsh (USA) *(JHMGosden)* 8-11 GHind (13) (unf: scope: bit bkwd:
     s.s: a bhd) ................................................... 10.13
   Bold Dancer (FR) *(PJMakin)* 8-11 TQuinn (6) (unf: bit bkwd: bhd fnl 5f) ...... s.h.14

**6/5** Charolles, **5/1** MAHASIN (USA)(2/1—11/2), **7/1** Queen Warrior, **8/1** Raven Runner (USA)(6/1—10/1), **12/1**
Cachou (USA), **14/1** Rosina Mae(op 8/1), **16/1** Mist of the Marsh (USA)(10/1—20/2), Sharriba, **20/1** Flying
Wind, Bold Dancer (FR)(op 12/1), Calpella, **33/1** Ors. CSF £41.46, Tote £4.80: £1.70 £2.00 £3.20 (£11.70). Mr
Hamdan Al-Maktoum (ARUNDEL) bred by Robert N. Clay & Richard L. Duchossois in USA. 14 Rn
                                               1m 38.63 (2.03)
                                         SF—67/56/51/45/36/34

**990**      CRAWLEY WARREN H'CAP (0-100) £10950.00 (£3300.00: £1600.00: £750.00)
             **2m**                                                          3-10 (3-11)

                        (Weights raised 2 lb)
 760* **Aude la Belle (FR) (69)** *(MrsAKnight)* 4-8-2 ‡³FNorton (3) (hdwy over 3f out:
     5th st: hrd rdn over 1f out: led last strides) .................... —1
 552² Satin Lover **(85)** *(RAkehurst)* 4-9-2 ‡⁵RPerham (11) (led 1f: 4th st: led over 1f
     out: hrd rdn ins fnl f: hdd last strides) ........................ hd.2
 718 Star Player **(86)** *(RJBaker)* 6–9-10 WCarson (5) (hdwy 4f out: 6th st: hrd rdn &
     wandered 1f out: eased whn btn nr fin) .......................... 6.3

726³ Gondolier (86) (Jt-Fav) (HRACecil) 4-9-8 MRoberts (2) (a.p: led 6f out tl over 3f out: one pce) .................................................................. s.h.4

708⁴ Holy Zeal (82) (Jt-Fav) (DWPArbuthnot) 6-9-6 AMunro (6) (b: 2nd st: led over 3f out tl over 1f out: one pce) ......................................... s.h.5

718² Bardolph (USA) (81) (PFICole) 5-9-5 TQuinn (8) (b.off hind: 3rd st: one pce fnl 2f) ................................................................................ s.h.6

726⁵ Dom Wac (75) (MBell) 4-8-11 WNewnes (4) (nvr nr to chal) ................. 8.7

388 Brandon Prince (IRE) (83) (bl) (IABalding) 4-9-5 RCochrane (1) (a bhd) ... ½.8
Officer Cadet (55) (RCurtis) 5-7-7 GBardwell (12) (bhd fnl 5f) ............ 1½.9

718 Beebob (74) (MCPipe) 4-8-10 DHolland (9) (a bhd) ........................... ½.10
Green Lane (USA) (81) (IABalding) 4-9-0 ‡SO'Gorman (10) (led after 1f to 6f out: wknd 4f out) ............................................................... 8.11

632⁶ Star Quest (82) (JRJenkins) 5-9-6 NDay (7) (bhd fnl 3f: t.o) ............... 12

LONG HANDICAP: Officer Cadet 7-4.

**5/1** Holy Zeal, Gondolier, **11/2** Satin Lover, **15/2** Bardolph (USA), Dom Wac, **8/1** AUDE LA BELLE (FR), **12/1** Brandon Prince (IRE), Star Player, **16/1** Star Quest, **20/1** Green Lane (USA), Beebob, **25/1** Officer Cadet. CSF £48.73, CT £485.19. Tote £8.40: £1.90 £1.90 £2.80 (£17.50). Mrs Val Rapkins (CULLOMPTON) bred by J. P. de Gaste in France. 12 Rn
3m 30.26 (5.86)
SF—30/43/45/42/39/37

**991** CRAWLEY WARREN HERON STKS (listed race) (3-Y.O) £14312.50 (£4300.00: £2075.00: £962.50) **1m (J.C)**
3-40 (3-41)

722³ **Torrey Canyon (USA) (103)** (RCharlton) 8-12 RCochrane (1) (3rd st: led over 2f out: drvn out) ................................................................. —1

655³ Pursuit of Love (117) (Fav) (HRACecil) 9-3 MRoberts (4) (lw: 5th st: hrd rdn over 1f out: unable qckn) ................................................ 2½.2

Casteddu (100) (JWPayne) 8-12 AMunro (6) (bit bkwd: 4th st: rdn over 1f out: wknd ins fnl f) ....................................................................... 2.0

Misterioso (102) (DRCElsworth) 8-12 WCarson (5) (swtg: 6th st: nvr nr to chal) 3½.4

391⁶ Spanish Storm (IRE) (100) (AHide) 8-12 BRouse (3) (led over 5f) ............. 2.5

3a Governor's Imp (USA) (103) (MBell) 8-12 WNewnes (2) (2nd st: wknd over 2f out: t.o) ................................................................................. 30.6

**8/13** Pursuit of Love, **5/1** Casteddu, **6/1** TORREY CANYON (USA), **10/1** Misterioso, **20/1** Governor's Imp (USA), **25/1** Spanish Storm (IRE). CSF £9.75, Tote £6.80: £1.70 £1.20 (£3.10). Mr K. Abdulla (BECKHAMPTON) bred by Juddmonte Farms Incorporated in USA. 6 Rn
1m 38.37 (1.77)
SF—71/68/57/46/40/–

**992** UNDERWRITING H'CAP (0-90) £3002.00 (£896.00: £428.00: £194.00) **6f** 4-10 (4-11)

909 **Cee-En-Cee (66)** (bl) (Fav) (MMcCourt) 8-8-8 TQuinn (11) (a.p: hrd rdn over 1f out: led nr fin) ...................................................................... —1

779 Paddy Chalk (73) (LJHolt) 6-9-1 AMunro (2) (b: hdwy 2f out: led ins fnl f: hrd rdn: hdd nr fin) ..................................................................... hd.2

853 Seneca Reef (IRE) (86) (IABalding) 4-10-0 RCochrane (8) (lw: led tl ins fnl f: unable qckn) ........................................................................ 2.3

830⁵ Judgement Call (66) (PHowling) 5-8-8 WNewnes (10) (a.p: rdn over 1f out: one pce) ............................................................................... nk.4

Princess Tara (79) (GLewis) 4-9-7 DHolland (7) (nvr nr to chal) ............ 5.5

Cashmiriana (IRE) (77) (MissHCKnight) 3-8-9 SWhitworth (5) (prom over 4f) ... ½.6

779³ Zeboim (67) (bl) (WRMuir) 6-8-2 ‡⁷KimMcDonnell (4) (prom over 4f) ..... nk.7

853 Sandcastle City (76) (RHannon) 3-8-8 MRoberts (9) (a bhd) ............... nk.8

779 Harry's Coming (60) (RJHodges) 8-8-2 WCarson (1) (a bhd) .................. 1.9

629 Thornfield Boy (80) (RJHolder) 6-9-8 JWilliams (6) (s.s: a bhd) ........... ¾.10

885³ Pretonic (64) (MJohnston) 4-8-6 RPElliott (3) (bhd fnl 2f) ................... 5.11

**3/1** CEE-EN-CEE, **6/1** Zeboim, **13/2** Pretonic, **7/1** Sandcastle City, Seneca Reef (IRE), **10/1** Harry's Coming (tchd 16/1), Judgement Call(op 6/1), **12/1** Paddy Chalk, Princess Tara, **20/1** Cashmiriana (IRE), **33/1** Thornfield Boy. CSF £35.36, CT £214.18. Tote £3.20: £1.50 £3.70 £2.10 (£30.60). Mr D. N. Humphreys (WANTAGE) bred by Thomas Moore. 11 Rn
1m 11.87 (0.57)
SF—59/65/70/49/42/28

**993** BROKING H'CAP (0-90) £3028.00 (£904.00: £432.00: £196.00) **1m 3f 30y**
4-40 (4-41)

Barrish (70) (RAkehurst) 6-8-10 TQuinn (3) (rdn 4f out: 6th st: swtchd lft over 1f out: led wl ins fnl f: r.o wl) ........................................... —1

829³ Knock Knock (83) (Jt-Fav) (IABalding) 7-9-6 ‡³SO'Gorman (8) (b: hdwy 3f out: led over 1f out tl wl ins fnl f: r.o) .................................. ½.2

Ambassador Royale (IRE) (79) (PFICole) 4-9-5 AMunro (7) (bit bkwd: hdwy over 2f out: hrd rdn over 1f out: unable qckn) ....................... 2.3

    Carousel Music **(57)** *(JAkehurst)* 5–7–11[(1)] AMcGlone (5) (2nd st: led over 2f
        out tl over 1f out: sn wknd) ......................................................... 3.4

800[5] Tiger Shoot **(58)** *(Jt-Fav)* *(PJFeilden)* 5–7–12[(1)] AShoults (6) (3rd st: wknd over
        1f out) ............................................................................. 2½.5

    Arabian Bold (IRE) **(86)** *(WJHaggas)* 4–9–12 NDay (1) (lw: led over 8f) ........... 2½.6

    Dovale **(71)** *(WJarvis)* 4–8–11 MTebbutt (2) (bit bkwd: plld hrd: 5th st: wknd
        over 2f out) ........................................................................ 3.7

702 Taunting (IRE) **(62)** *(MBlanshard)* 4–8–2 CRutter (4) (4th st: wknd over 2f out) s.h.8

**9/4** Tiger Shoot, Knock Knock, **6/1** Arabian Bold (IRE), **8/1** Ambassador Royale (IRE), BARRISH, **16/1**
Dovale(12/1—20/1), **20/1** Ors. CSF £24.70, CT £119.45. Tote £10.00: £2.60 £1.10 £2.00 (£10.70). Mr A. D.
Spence (EPSOM) bred by Sheikh Mohammed bin Rashid al Maktoum. 8 Rn        2m 24.46 (6.86)
                                        SF—27/36/31/3/–/22

T/Trio: Race 5: £81.70 (66.6 Tckts). T/Plpt: £102.00 (20.3 Tckts).                     AK

## 894—**LINGFIELD  (L-H)**

### Saturday, May 23rd [Firm]

Going Allowance: minus 0.30 sec per fur (F)                       Wind: almost nil

Stalls: high

**994**    HALL APP'CE MEDIAN AUCTION GRADUATION STKS (3-Y.O) £1534.00 (£424.00:
        £202.00)  **7f**                                   6-00 (6-02)

762[2] **Morsun (73)** *(Fav)* *(DMorley)* 8–12 EBentley (1) (lw: dropped rr 5f out: hrd rdn &
        hdwy wl over 1f out: r.o: fin 2nd, 1½zl: awrdd r) ...................—1

894[5] Mansber (IRE) **(54)** *(PatMitchell)* 8–7 ‡5RTurner (2) (hld up: hrd rdn & ev ch over
        2f out: unable qckn: fin 3rd, 6l: plcd 2nd) .............................. 2

370 Dragon Spirit **(70)** *(AHide)* 8–7 ‡5ALiggins (6) (prom 4f: fin 4th, 5l: plcd 3rd) ......... 3

778 Camino a Ronda **(44)** *(PatMitchell)* 8–2 ‡5BeverleyBrett (4) (b.hind: spd over 4f:
        fin 5th, 3½zl: plcd 4th) ......................................................... 4

801 Rio Trusky **(45)** *(MDIUsher)* 8–12 JHunter (7) (s.s: bhd fnl 3f: fin 6th, hd: plcd
        5th) ................................................................................... 5

775 Efra **(69)** *(RHannon)* 8–12 DGibbs (5) (mde all: qcknd over 1f out: r.o wl: fin 1st:
        disq: plcd last) .................................................................... 0

*Stewards Enquiry: Obj. by Clerk of Scales to Biggs sustained. Efra disq. (weighed in 10lbs light). Hannon fined £500*

**Evens** MORSUN, **6/4** Efra, **17/2** Dragon Spirit, **25/1** Mansber (IRE), **40/1** Rio Trusky, **50/1** Camino a Ronda. CSF
£17.91, Tote £1.90: £1.30 £2.40 (£8.90). Mr John B. Sunley (NEWMARKET) bred by Sunley Stud. 6 Rn
                                         1m 22.98 (1.68)
                                        SF—41/36/15/–/–/–

**995**    E.B.F. LINGFIELD STKS (Mdn 2-Y.O.F) £2232.50 (£620.00: £297.50)  **6f**    6-30 (6-40)

650[2] **Nuryandra** *(Fav)* *(GWragg)* 8–8 ‡3FNorton (6) (w ldr: led over 2f out: eased nr
        fin) ...................................................................................—1

650[5] Anonymous *(CEBrittain)* 8–11 MRoberts (3) (led over 3f: r.o) .................... 1½.2

    Welsh Pet *(PJMakin)* 8–8 ‡3TSprake (12) (neat: bit bkwd: hdwy over 1f out: r.o
        one pce) ........................................................................... 8.3

    Belle Soiree *(SDow)* 8–11 TQuinn (5) (str: bit bkwd: nvr nr to chal) ................ 4.4

329 Selectable *(MDIUsher)* 8–11 CRutter (11) (prom over 3f) .......................... 2½.5

    Generally *(PatMitchell)* 8–8 ‡3SO'Gorman (10) (unf: scope: s.s: a bhd) ........... 1.6

    Inonder *(MDIUsher)* 8–11 DHolland (1) (w'like: unf: scope: dwlt: a bhd) ......... d.h.6

    Lady of Shadows *(SDow)* 8–11 WNewnes (7) (scope: dwlt: a bhd) ................ 1.8

    Baileys Colours *(BJMcMath)* 8–11 AClark (9) (scope: bkwd: prom over 3f) ....... ¾.9

852 Brief Habit (IRE) (14/1) Withdrawn (uns rdr & bolted bef s twice) : not under orders — Rule 4
    applies

**1/2** NURYANDRA, **4/1** Anonymous(3/1—6/1), **12/1** Welsh Pet(op 5/1), **20/1** Belle Soiree(op 10/1), **33/1** Lady of
Shadows, Inonder, Selectable, **50/1** Ors. CSF £2.78, Tote £1.50: £1.10 £1.40 £1.80 (£1.70). Sir Philip
Oppenheimer (NEWMARKET) bred by Hascombe and Valiant Studs. 9 Rn        1m 11.59 (2.99)

**996**    ASHBOURNE WATER H'CAP (0-90) £2733.50 (£756.00: £360.50)  **5f**    7-00 (7-04)

897[3] **Tauber (60)** *(Fav)* *(PatMitchell)* 8–8–1 ‡3SO'Gorman (9) (hld up: led ins fnl f: rdn
        out) ..................................................................................—1

714[4] Walking Possession **(79)** (bl) *(RBoss)* 3–9–0 MRoberts (4) (rdn thrght: hrd rdn
        & hdwy over 1f out: r.o ins fnl f) ......................................... 1.2

    Fair Enchantress **(58)** *(JABennett)* 4–8–2 DHolland (8) (hdwy over 1f out: r.o ins
        fnl f) ................................................................................ nk.3

775[6] Ashtina **(68)** *(RJHodges)* 7–8–12 WCarson (5) (lw: a.p: ev ch over 1f out: r.o) . nk.4

876² Sigama (USA) **(81)** *(FHLee)* 6-9-8 ‡³DBiggs (7) (led tl ins fnl f: unable qckn) ..... ³/₄.5
236 Joe Sugden **(62)** *(PHowling)* 8-8-6 WNewnes (6) (lw: a:p: hrd rdn over 1f out: one pce) ............................................................................................. 1¹/₂.6
872 Ski Captain **(57)** *(PHowling)* 8-8-1 NCarlisle (1) (lw: rdn & no hdwy fnl 2f) ........ 1.7
217* Lady of the Fen **(52)** *(MrsNMacauley)* 4-7-7⁽³⁾ ‡³FNorton (3) (a.p: ev ch 2f out: eased whn btn fnl f) .............................................................................. 12.8
897 Shades of Jade **(49)** *(JJBridger)* 4-7-7 GBardwell (2) (a.p: ev ch 2f out: wknd over 1f out) ............................................................................................ s.h.9

LONG HANDICAP: Lady of the Fen 7-6, Shades of Jade 7-6.

**11/4 TAUBER, 3/1** Sigama (USA), **4/1** Walking Possession, **13/2** Ashtina, **10/1** Lady of the Fen, **12/1** Ski Captain, **14/1** Joe Sugden, **20/1** Shades of Jade, **33/1** Fair Enchantress. CSF £13.44, CT £264.18. Tote £3.90: £1.40 £1.70 £4.50 (£8.30). Mrs Catherine Reed (NEWMARKET) bred by Ivor Carroll. 9 Rn  58.03 sec (1.03)
SF—37/46/33/42/49/27

**997**     OASTWELL WINES H'CAP (0-70) £2103.20 (£585.20: £281.60)    **7f**    7-30 (7-34)

**Tea Dust (IRE) (60)** *(PJMakin)* 4-9-9 TQuinn (14) (led over 2f: led over 2f out: r.o wl) ................................................................................................ —1
684 Sugemar **(51)** *(JARToller)* 6-9-0 WNewnes (5) (a:p: ev ch over 1f out: unable qckn) ................................................................................................... 1¹/₂.2
903³ Ain'tlifelikethat **(52)** (bl) **(Fav)** *(TJNaughton)* 5-9-1 DHolland (20) (swtchd lft 3f out: hdwy over 1f out: r.o) ............................................................... nk.3
Jokist **(65)** *(WJarvis)* 9-10-0 MTebbutt (13) (hdwy 2f out: n.m.r over 1f out: swtchd rt: r.o wl ins fnl f) ............................................................................ ¹/₂.4
Harlequin Girl **(40)** *(KTIvory)* 4-8-3 GBardwell (18) (hdwy 2f out: one pce) ....... hd.5
Moving Force **(43)** *(EAWheeler)* 5-8-3 ‡³FNorton (10) (hld up: rdn 2f out: r.o one pce) ..................................................................................................... 2.6
774⁶ Coral Flutter **(43)** (bl) *(JWPayne)* 5-8-8 ASkingle (8) (rdn & no hdwy fnl 2f) ..... nk.7
626 Candle King (IRE) **(54)** (bl) *(MJFetherston-Godley)* 4-9-3 MRoberts (17) (nvr nr to chal) ...................................................................................................... nk.8
531⁵ Bellatrix **(60)** *(CEBrittain)* 4-9-6 ‡³RonHillis (1) (hdwy fnl 2f: nvr nrr) ................ 3.9
866 Fabled Orator **(51)** *(PHowling)* 7-9-0 JMurray (9) (b.nr hind: lw: a:p: ev ch 2f out: wknd fnl f) ......................................................................................... s.h.10
731 Looting (USA) **(48)** *(MDIUsher)* 6-8-6 ‡⁵CHodgson (16) (nvr nrr) ...................... 1¹/₂.11
Saifan **(69)** *(DMorris)* 3-9-0 ‡⁷StephenDavies (19) (swtchd lft 4f out: hdwy 2f out: wknd over 1f out) ........................................................................... 1¹/₂.12
Bo Knows Best (IRE) **(51)** *(JSutcliffe)* 3-8-3 GBaxter (12) (bhd fnl 4f) ................... ¹/₂.13
738³ Monte Bre **(41)** *(RAkehurst)* 6-8-4 SDawson (11) (lw: led over 4f out tl over 2f out: sn wknd) ....................................................................................... nk.14
621 Yatoo (IRE) **(65)** *(RHannon)* 3-9-3 WCarson (15) (a mid div) ............................ ³/₄.15
731 Shikari's Son **(53)** *(JWhite)* 5-9-2 AClark (6) (prom over 5f) ............................... ³/₄.16
Pine Glen Pepper **(40)** *(JAkehurst)* 4-7-12 ‡⁵ATucker (2) (bhd fnl 2f) ................ hd.17
Head Turner **(45)** *(CPWildman)* 4-8-8 CRutter (4) (a bhd) .................................. ¹/₂.18
Crimson Blade **(58)** *(PWHarris)* 3-8-10 GHind (7) (swtg: s.s: bhd fnl 3f) ............. 5.19

**9/2** Ain'tlifelikethat, **5/1** Candle King (IRE), **7/1** Moving Force, **8/1 TEA DUST (IRE)**, **17/2** Monte Bre, **9/1** Shikari's Son, Yatoo (IRE), **10/1** Sugemar(8/1—12/1), **14/1** Saifan, Jokist, Coral Flutter, Looting (USA), **25/1** Crimson Blade, Bo Knows Best (IRE), Bellatrix, Pine Glen Pepper, **33/1** Ors. CSF £92.58, CT £387.29. Tote £8.90: £2.50 £2.50 £1.60 £4.60 (£72.00). Mr R. P. Marchant (MARLBOROUGH) bred by John L. Moore in Ireland. 19 Rn
1m 22.95 (1.65)
SF—52/38/38/49/23/17

**998**     PATIO CLAIMING STKS    £1632.00 (£452.00: £216.00)    **5f**    8-00 (8-01)

676 **Love Returned (84)** *(WJarvis)* 5-9-5 MTebbutt (7) (hld up: led over 2f out: all out) ........................................................................................................... —1
939² Walk in the Park **(84)** **(Fav)** *(RSimpson)* 3-8-5 ‡⁵ATucker (5) (lw: a:p: ev ch ins fnl f: r.o wl) ................................................................................................. s.h.2
Nagida *(JARToller)* 3-8-0 NCarlisle (8) (near: hdwy 2f out: nvr rchd f: fin wl) .... ¹/₂.3
901³ Superlativemaximus (IRE) *(JABennett)* 4-8-12 GHind (4) (led over 2f: wknd over 1f out) ..................................................................................................... 5.4
901* Spring High **(30)** (bl) *(KTIvory)* 5-8-9 GBardwell (2) (prom over 3f) .................. 1¹/₂.5
Lime Street Lil **(30)** *(DAWilson)* 4-8-3 DHolland (6) (bit bkwd: spd over 2f) ....... 2.6
894 Trioming *(APJones)* 6-8-11 CRutter (9) (outpcd) ................................................ 2¹/₂.7
Mystery Cargo (USA) **(50)** *(JSutcliffe)* 4-8-13 MRoberts (1) (prom over 2f) ...... 3¹/₂.8
Wayward Son *(GLewis)* 3-8-4 ‡⁷RaymondBerry (3) (s.s: a wl bhd) .................. 1¹/₂.9

**5/4** Walk in the Park, **11/8** LOVE RETURNED, **9/1** Spring High, **12/1** Mystery Cargo (USA), **20/1** Superlativemaximus (IRE), **33/1** Nagida, **50/1** Ors. CSF £3.39, Tote £2.80: £1.20 £1.20 £4.20 (£1.80). Mr J. M. Ratcliffe (NEWMARKET) bred by Yeomanstown Lodge Stud. 9 Rn
58.10 sec (1.10)
SF—53/38/31/23/14/—

**999**          CORRIDOR H'CAP (3-Y.O) (0-90) £2902.40 (£806.40: £387.20)     1¼m     8-30 (8-32)
                                        (Weights raised 16 lb)
  728⁶ **Spectacular Dawn (65)** *(Fav)* *(JLDunlop)* 9-0 WCarson (5) (chsd ldr: led over
               6f out to 3f out: led over 1f out: rdn out) .............................. —1
  695⁵ Nectar Collector (70) *(CFWall)* 9-5 NDay (3) (lw: 3rd st: ev ch 1f out: r.o) .......... ½.2
  728 Socks and Shares (72) *(PWHarris)* 9-7 GHind (4) (led over 3f: 4th st: one pce fnl
               2f) .......................................................... ¾.3
  868³ Roly Wallace (66) (bl) *(KTIvory)* 9-1 GBardwell (1) (5th st: one pce fnl 2f) ....... 1½.4
         Stinger (71) *(CRNelson)* 9-6 AClark (2) (lw: 2nd st: led 3f out tl over 1f out: nt r.o) 2½.5

**Evens** SPECTACULAR DAWN, **3/1** Nectar Collector, **5/1** Stinger, Roly Wallace, **16/1** Socks and Shares. CSF
£4.44, Tote £2.00: £1.10 £1.90 (£2.00). Mr Peter S. Winfield (ARUNDEL) bred by Peter Winfield. 5 Rn
                                                                        2m 8.87 (5.87)
                                                                   SF—11/15/15/6/6

T/Plpt: £9.20 (235.65 Tckts).

                                                                        AK

**900—SOUTHWELL (L-H)** Fibresand
**Saturday, May 23rd [Standard]**
Going Allowance: minus 0.20 sec per fur (FS)                    Wind: mod across

Stalls: 1st high, remainder low

**1000**          GUNN H'CAP (3-Y.O) (0-70) £2364.00 (£654.00: £312.00)     5f (AWT)     6-30 (6-31)
                                        (Weights raised 6 lb)
  901² **Fighter Squadron (48)** (v) *(Fav)* *(JAGlover)* 8-8 JFortune (4) (a.p: led ins fnl f:
               drvn out) ......................................................... —1
  541¹⁴ Educated Pet (51) *(MJohnston)* 8-8 ‡³JFanning (2) (led ½-wy tl ins fnl f: r.o one
               pce) .......................................................... 2.2
         Sara Anne (IRE) (61) *(LJCodd)* 9-0 ‡7RMitchell (5) (lw: hdwy & hmpd ½-wy: r.o
               fnl f) ......................................................... 8.3
  765 Sharp as You Like (47) (v) *(JEtherington)* 8-7 JLowe (3) (led to ½-wy: sn btn) 1½.4
  495⁴ Forza Azzurri (IRE) (60) (bl) *(MrsNMacauley)* 8-13 ‡7SWilliams (1) (s.i.s: racd
               alone far side: no hdwy fnl 2f) ............................... s.h.5
  247* Cellito (IRE) (57) (bl) *(WAO'Gorman)* 8-12 ‡5EmmaO'Gorman (6) (lw: spd to
               ½-wy) ........................................................ 2½.6
  516 Grubby (50) *(RHollinshead)* 8-10 PaulEddery (8) (sn outpcd) ................ ½.7
  901 Long Last (39) *(DWChapman)* 7-13 SWood (7) (rdn ½-wy: sn bhd) ........... 3½.8

**3/1** FIGHTER SQUADRON, **4/1** Educated Pet, Cellito (IRE), **5/1** Forza Azzurri (IRE)(tchd 8/1), **6/1** Sharp as You
Like, **14/1** Long Last, Sara Anne (IRE), **16/1** Grubby. CSF £14.54, CT £128.73. Tote £3.40: £1.10 £1.50 £4.90
(£5.10). Claremont Management Services (WORKSOP) bred by Coxland Stud. 8 Rn      60.1 sec (2.1)
                                                                   SF—32/24/-/-/-/-

**1001**          BOTHAM (S) STKS (3 & 4-Y.O) £2250.00 (£625.00: £300.00)     7f (AWT)     7-00 (7-04)

         **Gallery Artist (IRE) (63)** *(RGuest)* 4-9-3 ‡7SEiffert (16) (a.p: 2nd st: r.o to ld wl
               ins fnl f: pushed out) ......................................... —1
  948² Mca Below the Line (63) (bl) *(Fav)* *(WJPearce)* 4-9-10 DNicholls (4) (chsd ldrs:
               5th st: rdn 3f out: r.o ins fnl f) ............................... hd.2
  904⁶ Crimson Consort (IRE) (36) (v) *(DonEnricoIncisa)* 3-8-10 SWood (3) (led: clr
               over 1f out: wknd & hdd ins fnl f) .............................. 1½.3
  545 Akura (IRE) (54) *(MJohnston)* 3-8-5 ‡³JFanning (5) (chsd ldrs: 4th st: r.o one
               pce fnl 2f) ...................................................... nk.4
  863⁶ Certain Lady (59) *(GBlum)* 3-8-3 ‡5JWeaver (15) (hdwy & c wd over 2f out: r.o
               u.p ins fnl f) .................................................. 1.5
  696 Penando (45) *(OO'Neill)* 4-9-7 JCarroll (10) (lw: prom: 3rd st: wknd over 1f out) 5.6
  600 Amber Glow (IRE) (LJCodd) 3-8-5⁽²⁾ ‡7RMitchell (7) (nvr nr to chal) ............ 2.7
  799 Miss Cookie (49) *(MCPipe)* 4-9-2 TyroneWilliams (2) (lw: n.d) ............... 2½.8
  594 Weekend Girl (30) *(WMBrisbourne)* 3-7-12 ‡7MHumphries (1) (lw: s.i.s: n.d) .. 1½.9
  765 Super Marco (3) *(WWHaigh)* 3-8-5 SWebster (14) (n.d) .................... nk.10
  912 Just Ready (IRE) (47) (v) *(GAHam)* 4-9-10 ADicks (9) (bhd fr ½-wy) ....... s.h.11
  901 Serious Hurry (75) *(SirMarkPrescott)* 4-9-10 GDuffield (11) (bit bkwd: a in rr) nk.12
  662² Qualitair Idol (48) (v) *(JFBottomley)* 3-8-5 JLowe (13) (lw: a bhd) ............ 3.13
  901 Beljinski (30) *(BJMcMath)* 4-9-2 WHood (6) (lw: chsd ldrs 3f) ............... 2.14
         Lady Risk Me *(KGWingrove)* 3-8-0 ‡5DHarrison (8) (bit bkwd: a bhd) ......... 8.15
  901 Will-O-Bay *(RHollinshead)* 4-8-9 ‡7JDennis (12) (prom tl 6th & wkng st) ...... 3.16

9/4 Mca Below the Line, **7/1** Certain Lady, **15/2** Miss Cookie, **8/1** Qualitair Idol, Akura (IRE)(op 5/1), Serious Hurry, **14/1** Crimson Consort (IRE), GALLERY ARTIST (IRE), **16/1** Just Ready (IRE), Amber Glow (IRE), **20/1** Super Marco, **25/1** Will-O-Bay, **33/1** Penando, **50/1** Ors. CSF £45.26, Tote £32.70: £7.70 £1.50 £3.70 (£68.30). Mr Rae Guest (NEWMARKET) bred by Viscount de Vesci in Ireland. 16 Rn; No bid　1m 30.1 (3.5)
SF—29/35/16/10/5/8

---

**1002**　　VOCE H'CAP (0-70) £2406.00 (£666.00: £318.00)　　1³/₄m (AWT)　　7-30 (7-31)

760³ **Tactical Mission (IRE) (70)** *(JAkehurst)* 4-9-9 ‡5JWeaver (6) (chsd ldr: 2nd st: led over 2f out: drvn out) ............................................................... —1
893³ **Grey Commander (35)** (v) *(MBrittain)* 4-7-7 JLowe (8) (led tl hdd over 2f out: rdn & r.o fnl f) ............................................................... 1¹/₂.2
905⁵ **Domain (53)** (bl) *(RJWeaver)* 4-8-11 LDettori (7) (lw: hld up: hdwy 6f out: 6th st: styd on fnl 2f: nt rch ldrs) ............................................................... 3.3
790⁵ **White River (37)** *(DHaydnJones)* 6—7-9 TyroneWilliams (4) (prom: 3rd st: wknd wl over 1f out) ............................................................... 1¹/₂.4
730* **Whitechapel (USA) (76)** (Fav) *(LordHuntingdon)* 4-10-1 ‡5DHarrison (1) (hld up & bhd: hdwy 6f out: 5th st: sn rdn & btn) ............................................................... 1¹/₂.5
905 **Hand Painted (52)** *(CRBeever)* 8—8-10 JCarroll (5) (effrt & 4th st: sn btn) ............ 2.6
893 **Malenoir (USA) (56)** (v) *(WJPearce)* 4-9-0 LCharnock (3) (lw: prom 8f) ............ 4.7
905⁴ **Suluk (USA) (49)** *(RHollinshead)* 7-8-0 ‡7MHumphries (2) (a bhd) .............. s.h.8
LONG HANDICAP: Grey Commander 7-6.

**11/10** Whitechapel (USA), **9/2** Suluk (USA), **7/1** Grey Commander, **8/1** TACTICAL MISSION (IRE), **10/1** Malenoir (USA), **11/1** Domain, **14/1** Hand Painted, **16/1** White River. CSF £57.53, CT £564.20. Tote £10.80: £2.50 £1.40 £2.60 (£16.10). Pharoahs Lodge Ltd (UPPER LAMBOURN) bred by Miss Eimear Haughey in Ireland. 8 Rn
3m 6.6 (7.3)
SF—8/—/—/—/—/

---

**1003**　　BROAD STKS (Mdn 3-Y.O.) £1725.00 (£475.00: £225.00)　　1¹/₈m (AWT)　　8-00 (8-01)

418³ **Northern Kingdom (USA)** (Fav) *(SGNorton)* 9-0 DNicholls (2) (chsd ldr: led 3f out: drvn out) ............................................................... —1
**Teddy's Play (USA) (85)** *(JWHills)* 9-0 RHills (3) (prom: 4th st: styd on u.p fnl f) 2¹/₂.2
**Alderbrook (USA)** *(MrsJCecil)* 9-0 PaulEddery (4) (lt-f: scope: hld up: effrt & 3rd st: r.o one pce fnl f) ............................................................... nk.3
562³ **In the Money (IRE) (70)** *(RHollinshead)* 9-0 LDettori (1) (lw: led 9f: 2nd st: wknd 2f out) ............................................................... 15.4
835 **Mittenoski Pet** *(TJNaughton)* 8-9 GCarter (5) (b: 5th & wkng st) ............ 7.5

**9/4** NORTHERN KINGDOM (USA), **11/4** In the Money (IRE), **3/1** Teddy's Play (USA), **7/2** Alderbrook, **20/1** Mittenoski Pet. CSF £8.56, Tote £3.10: £1.40 £1.60 (£5.80). Mr P. A. Deal (BARNSLEY) bred by Audley Farm Inc. in USA. 5 Rn
2m 38.6 (4.4)
SF—32/27/26/—/—

---

**1004**　　LARWOOD H'CAP (3-Y.O.) (0-70) £2616.00 (£726.00: £348.00)　　8-30 (8-32)
　　　　7f (AWT)　　(Weights raised 2 lb)

749³ **Coastal Express (58)** (Fav) *(EWeymes)* 9-0 LDettori (5) (mde all: r.o wl fnl f) .... —1
904⁴ **Invigilate (56)** *(MPNaughton)* 8-5 ‡7OPears (10) (lw: hdwy & 4th st: ev ch wl over 1f out: no ex fnl f) ............................................................... 3.2
904* **Sie Amato (IRE) (56)** *(CaptJWilson)* 8-12 JLowe (9) (a.p: 2nd st: wknd fnl f) .... 5.3
295 **Comiskey Park (IRE) (49)** *(DWChapman)* 8-5 SWood (6) (bit bkwd: hdwy fnl 2f: nt rchd ldrs) ............................................................... ¹/₂.4
**Spray of Orchids (53)** *(JEtherington)* 8-4 ‡5JWeaver (13) (bhd: styd on fnl 2f: n.d) ............................................................... 2¹/₂.5
587 **Time Lapse (59)** *(PJMakin)* 9-1 RHills (8) (hdwy & 6th st: sn btn) ............ 5.6
614⁶ **Premier Envelope (IRE) (53)** *(NTinkler)* 8-9 GCarter (11) (chsd ldrs: 5th st: wknd 2f out) ............................................................... 1¹/₂.7
904 **High Success (52)** (bl) *(WAO'Gorman)* 8-3 ‡5EmmaO'Gorman (12) (s.i.s: nrst fin) ............................................................... nk.8
904² **Abeloni (65)** *(AAScott)* 9-7 BRaymond (4) (lw: sn pushed along & prom: wknd over 1f out) ............................................................... ³/₄.9
**Roxy Music (IRE) (59)** *(GAPritchard-Gordon)* 8-10 ‡5DHarrison (1) (bit bkwd: prom over 3f) ............................................................... 2.10
783 **Grand Fellow (IRE) (64)** (bl) *(JDBethell)* 9-6 PaulEddery (2) (prom to ¹/₂-wy) 1¹/₂.11
591 **Our Eileen (50)** *(BSmart)* 8-6 LCharnock (7) (chsd ldrs: 3rd & wkng st) .......... 2.12

**4/1** COASTAL EXPRESS, **9/2** Abeloni, **7/1** Invigilate, **7/1** Sie Amato (IRE), Our Eileen(op 12/1), Time Lapse, **10/1** Premier Envelope (IRE), **12/1** High Success, Roxy Music (IRE), **14/1** Spray of Orchids, **20/1** Grand Fellow (IRE), **25/1** Comiskey Park (IRE). CSF £28.89, CT £156.70. Tote £5.40: £1.90 £2.40 £2.30 (£14.90). Mrs R. L. Heaton (MIDDLEHAM) bred by Bechmann Stud. 12 Rn
1m 28.7 (2.1)
SF—47/29/21/12/3/—

**1005**　　RANDALL STKS (Mdn) £1725.00 (£475.00: £225.00)　　**1m (AWT)**　　9-00 (9-02)

511⁵ **Shirley's Train (USA)** *(LordHuntingdon)* 3–8-9 LDettori (11) (hld up: 6th st:
shkn up to disp ld appr fnl f: led wl ins fnl f: cleverly) ........... —1
490⁵ Turtle Beach (75) *(AAScott)* 3–8-9 BRaymond (9) (lw: led 1f: 2nd st: led over 1f
out: sn rdn: hdd wl ins fnl f: no ex) ..................................... nk.2
823⁶ Iron Baron (IRE) (64) *(RHollinshead)* 3–8-9 PaulEddery (2) (sn pushed along &
prom: 3rd st: wknd over 1f out) ........................................ 10.3
868 Captain Marmalade *(DTThom)* 3–8-9 SWebster (12) (lw: hdwy fnl 2f: n.d) ...... nk.4
689⁴ Up All Night (Fav) *(JWHills)* 3–8-4 RHills (7) (chsd ldr: 4th st: wknd over 1f out) ½.5
157 Swynford Flyer *(JFBottomley)* 3–8-4 GCarter (6) (led after 1f tl over 1f out: wknd
qckly) ..................................................................... s.h.6
919⁴ Father Hayes (USA) *(WJPearce)* 4–9-7 DNicholls (1) (poor 7th st: no hdwy fnl 3f) 1.7
Shirley Ann *(RJWeaver)* 9–9-2 JLowe (4) (a in rr) ........................ 2½.8
895 Armashocker *(DSasse)* 4–9-2 ‡⁵JWeaver (10) (chsd ldrs tl 5th & wkng st) ........ hd.9
Gan Awry *(DWChapman)* 5–9-2 SWood (5) (s.i.s: a bhd) ................ d.h.9
Tickham Vixen (IRE) *(JDBethell)* 4–9-2 GDuffield (8) (bit bkwd: m.n.s) .......... 6.11
Gabesia *(HJCollingridge)* 4–9-2 VSmith (13) (bkwd: s.i.s: a bhd: t.o) .......... 3.12
Baman Powerhouse *(MScudamore)* 4–9-2 TyroneWilliams (3) (dwlt: t.o) ....... 20.13

7/4 Up All Night, 3/1 Turtle Beach, **7/2** SHIRLEY'S TRAIN (USA), 7/1 Iron Baron (IRE), 12/1 Father Hayes (USA),
16/1 Tickham Vixen (IRE)(op 10/1), 25/1 Shirley Ann, Gan Awry, Gabesia, 33/1 Baman Powerhouse, Captain
Marmalade, Armashocker, 50/1 Swynford Flyer. CSF £15.16, Tote £4.50: £2.00 £1.50 £1.80 (£4.70). Mr M. L.
Oberstein (WEST ILSLEY) bred by Maverick Production Ltd. in USA. 13 Rn　　　　　1m 42.8 (3.5)
SF—19/18/–/–/–/–

T/Plpt: £279.7 (4.6 Tckts).　　　　　　　　　　　　　　　　　　　　　　　　　　　　CR

## 696 – WARWICK (L-H)

### Saturday, May 23rd [Firm]

Going Allowance: minus 0.25 sec per fur (F)　　　　　　　Wind: slt across

Stalls: low

**1006**　　PACKWOOD MEDIAN AUCTION STKS (Mdn 3-Y.O) £1380.00 (£380.00: £180.00)
5f　　　　　　　　　　　　　　　　　　　　　　　6-15 (6-17)

764² **Haunting Rhapsody (USA)** (Fav) *(JEtherington)* 8-9 KDarley (3) (hld up: nt clr
run wl over 1f out: hdwy to ld ins fnl f: jst hld on) ................ —1
Swinging Tich *(BAMcMahon)* 8-2 ‡⁵SSanders (5) (lt-f: bkwd: outpcd: hdwy over
1f out: fin wl) ......................................................... hd.2
906⁶ Musval *(RHannon)* 8-4 ‡⁵RPerham (6) (a.p: led over 1f out tl hdd & wknd ins fnl f) 5.3
468 Bright Paragon (IRE) *(BRichmond)* 9-0 NAdams (4) (led over 3f) ................. 5.4
906⁵ Lawnswood Prince (IRE) (64) *(JLSpearing)* 9-0 JWilliams (2) (hdwy on ins 2f
out: btn whn n.m.r over 1f out) ...................................... ¾.5
151⁵ Shocking Times (64) *(RSimpson)* 8-9 SWhitworth (1) (w ldr 3f: sn wknd) ........ 2½.6
Fragrant Hackette *(AHide)* 8-9 DaleGibson (7) (bit bkwd: bhd fnl 2f) ........... 2½.7

4/6 HAUNTING RHAPSODY (USA), 11/4 Musval(op 6/1), 14/1 Shocking Times(op 8/1), Lawnswood Prince
(IRE)(op 8/1), 20/1 Fragrant Hackette, Swinging Tich, 100/1 Bright Paragon (IRE). CSF £12.41, Tote £1.50:
£1.30 £2.80 (£10.30). Mr David Wosskow (MALTON) bred by D. M. Kenney in USA. 7 Rn　　61.3 sec (3.3)
SF—4/–/–/–/–/–

**1007**　　COTTON END (S) STKS (2-Y.O) £1702.00 (£472.00: £226.00)　　**6f**　　6-45 (6-55)

782★ **Grand Dancer (IRE)** (Fav) *(RJRWilliams)* 8-6 RCochrane (4) (mde all: qcknd
clr 2f out: eased ins fnl f: v.easily) ................................. —1
867 Ombre Darme (IRE) (bl) *(JWPayne)* 8-11 AMunro (7) (6th st: hdwy over 1f out:
r.o ins fnl f) ......................................................... 2½.2
900² Madam Cyn's Risk *(NACallaghan)* 7-13 ‡⁷JTate (10) (5th st: chsd wnr over 1f
out: no imp) .......................................................... 3.3
Workingforpeanuts (IRE) *(CASmith)* 8-6 AProud (8) (leggy: unf: bhd tl hdwy
over 1f out: nvr nrr) ................................................. ¾.4
889⁵ Kesanta *(WGMTurner)* 8-6 PBurke (1) (nvr nr to chal) ....................... nk.5
782 Buck the Tiger (bl) *(RHannon)* 8-11 KDarley (2) (3rd & rdn st: wknd over 1f out) 6.6
Floodlight *(RJHolder)* 8-6 JWilliams (6) (unf: a bhd) ......................... ¾.7
900 Buy Sunday Sport *(MissGayKelleway)* 7-13 ‡⁷CHawksley (3) (b: a bhd) ...... 2½.8
803 Walters Wonder *(JRJenkins)* 8-11 SWhitworth (11) (chsd ldr: 2nd & rdn st:
wknd 2f out) ......................................................... 3.9
786 Silly Sally *(WGMTurner)* 7-13 ‡⁷PTurner (9) (4th st: & rn wd st: wknd 2f out) ....... 2½.10
Clare's Boy (50/1) Withdrawn (ref to ent stalls) : not under orders

**4/5** GRAND DANCER (IRE), **5/1** Madam Cyn's Risk(4/1—6/1), **15/2** Buck the Tiger(12/1—7/1), **8/1** Kesanta(20/1—7/1), **12/1** Ombre Darme (IRE), **16/1** Floodlight (IRE)(10/1—20/1), **20/1** Silly Sally, **25/1** Walters Wonder, **50/1** Ors. CSF £11.61, Tote £2.00: £1.20 £2.80 £1.60 (£10.10). Mr D. A. Johnson (NEWMARKET) bred by E. O'Gorman in Ireland. 10 Rn; Bt in 14,500 gns　　　　　　　1m 15.7 (3.7)

## 1008　　　DUDLEY H'CAP (0-70) £3052.00 (£847.00: £406.00)　1¼m 169y　7-15 (7-19)

| | | | |
|---|---|---|---|
| 800* | **Scottish Bambi (68)** (Fav) (RHannon) 4-9-8 ‡5RPerham (2) (hdwy 4f out: 2nd st: led over 1f out: drvn out) | —1 | |
| 7025 | Premier Dance **(41)** (DHaydnJones) 5-8-0 AMunro (6) (8th st: hdwy over 1f out: rdn & r.o ins fnl f) | 1½.2 | |
| 8004 | Phil-Blake **(39)** (SMellor) 5-7-12 DanaMellor (3) (led: sn clr: hdd over 1f out: r.o) | nk.3 | |
| 763 | Chart Cross **(36)** (KSBridgwater) 5-7-9 NAdams (9) (hld up & bhd: hdwy & 7th st: one pce fnl f) | 3.4 | |
| 702 | Royal Acclaim **(45)** (v) (JMBradley) 7-7-11 ‡7MichaelBradley (8) (4th st: no hdwy fnl 2f) | 2½.5 | |
| 155 | Little Big **(42)** (CDBroad) 5-7-10(2) ‡5RPrice (1) (5th st: no hdwy) | 1½.6 | |
| 7023 | Cornhill Melody **(35)** (JLSpearing) 4-7-1 ‡7CHawksley (5) (chsd ldr 9f: 6th & btn st) | ¾.7 | |
| 422 | Weekday Cross (IRE) **(45)** (JRJenkins) 4-8-4 SWhitworth (10) (hdwy 5f out: 3rd st: wknd 2f out) | 5.8 | |
| 6965 | Radio Caroline **(44)** (bl) (MTate) 4-7-10 ‡7SMulvey (4) (stumbled s: a in rr: t.o) | 12.9 | |
| | Persian Bud (IRE) **(45)** (JRBosley) 4-7-13 ‡5NGwilliams (7) (prom tl rdn & wknd 5f out: t.o) | 8.10 | |

**9/4** SCOTTISH BAMBI, **5/1** Premier Dance, Chart Cross, **7/1** Cornhill Melody(op 4/1), **8/1** Phil-Blake, **12/1** Weekday Cross (IRE), **14/1** Radio Caroline, **25/1** Ors. CSF £12.75, CT £66.03. Tote £3.00: £2.00 £2.20 £1.40 (£7.50). Mr William J Kelly (MARLBOROUGH) bred by Cheveley Park Stud Ltd. 10 Rn　　　2m 16.7 (3.2)
SF—49/22/19/10/7/3

## 1009　　　LEAM STKS (Amateurs) £2657.20 (£739.20: £355.60)　1m　　7-45 (7-53)

| | | | |
|---|---|---|---|
| | **Brilliant** (JPearce) 4-10-4 MrsLPearce (20) (wnt 2nd st: led over 1f out: sn clr: r.o wl) | —1 | |
| 7303 | Elaine Tully (IRE) **(77)** (Fav) (MJHeaton-Ellis) 4-9-13 ‡5MissFHaynes (1) (hdwy over 1f out: r.o ins fnl f) | 3½.2 | |
| 895* | Abingdon Flyer (IRE) **(69)** (RHannon) 4-10-12 ‡5MrRHannon (16) (lw: bhd tl hdwy fnl 2f: r.o) | s.h.3 | |
| 120 | Quinta Royale **(55)** (WGMTurner) 5-10-4 ‡5MrsJGault (12) (hdwy 4f out: 4th st: chsd wnr over 1f out: no imp) | s.h.4 | |
| | Sanawi (PDEvans) 5-10-4 ‡5MrWMcLaughlin (5) (nvr nrr) | 4.5 | |
| 505 | Primera Ballerina **(48)** (JRBosley) 4-9-13 ‡5MrsSBosley (2) (b.hind: nvr nr to chal) | 1½.6 | |
| 1842 | Thundering **(23)** (AWJones) 7-10-9 MissIDWJones (4) (3rd st: wknd over 1f out) | nk.7 | |
| | Susie Creamcheese (EJAlston) 5-9-13 ‡5MrWilkinson (9) (nrst fin) | nk.8 | |
| 799 | Dal Pascatore **(29)** (FJYardley) 4-10-4 ‡5MissHMcCaull (6) (n.d) | hd.9 | |
| 931 | Sonalto **(48)** (DLWilliams) 6-10-4 ‡5MrGLewis (11) (n.d) | 2.10 | |
| 5906 | Playful Juliet (CAN) **(48)** (BRCambidge) 4-10-4 MrJCambidge (14) (n.d) | nk.11 | |
| 830 | Petivara (SDow) 5-9-13 ‡5MrTCuff (10) (nrst fin) | 2.12 | |
| 422 | Jolizal **(36)** (DMorris) 4-9-13 ‡5MrsLCrofts (13) (n.d) | 2.13 | |
| 800 | Quiet Riot **(42)** (JWhite) 10-10-4 ‡5MrMMannish (25) (prom 4f) | 1.14 | |
| 799 | Savanga (USA) **(47)** (bl) (MMcCormack) 4-10-4 ‡5MissSFarrant (7) (led: sn clr: hdd over 1f out: wknd qckly) | 1½.15 | |
| 895 | Sporting Weekend (FR) (DSasse) 5-11-3(13) ‡5MrCRansom (22) (sddle slipped & 6th st: wknd 2f out) | 4.16 | |
| | No Comebacks (EJAlston) 4-10-1(2) ‡5MrsSBarclay (19) (n.d) | 1.17 | |
| | One of the Lads (BRCambidge) 10-10-4 ‡5MrsHNoonan (21) (a bhd) | 1.18 | |
| 586 | Attic Wit (FR) (RJHolder) 4-10-9 MrRFarrant (24) (prom 4f) | 1½.19 | |
| 587 | Princess Jestina (IRE) **(41)** (GHYardley) 4-9-13 ‡5MissAYardley (23) (prom: 5th & wkng st) | hd.20 | |
| | Amys Delight (AJChamberlain) 4-9-13 ‡5MrsCDunwoody (18) (n.d) | 3.21 | |
| 809 | Woodlands Grey **(27)** (v) (PAPritchard) 6-10-9 MrRDavis (8) (s.s: t.o) | 15.22 | |
| | Zafra (GFHCharles-Jones) 4-9-13 ‡5MissVSnowdon (3) (t.o) | 30.23 | |

**11/8** Elaine Tully (IRE), **11/4** Abingdon Flyer (IRE)(2/1—3/1), **6/1** BRILLIANT(op 4/1), **14/1** Sanawi, **16/1** No Comebacks, **20/1** Thundering(op 12/1), **25/1** Savanga (USA), **33/1** Quinta Royale, Quiet Riot, Playful Juliet (CAN), Jolizal, **50/1** Petivara, Primera Ballerina, Princess Jestina (IRE), Susie Creamcheese, Sonalto, Sporting Weekend (FR), **66/1** Woodlands Grey, **100/1** Ors. CSF £14.03, Tote £10.30: £3.20 £1.50 £1.60 (£12.50). Mr Arthur Old (NEWMARKET) bred by Stanley Estate and Stud Co. 23 Rn　　　1m 40.4 (3.4)
SF—37/21/33/24/12/2

**1010** RADWAY CLAIMING STKS (3-Y.O) £2110.00 (£585.00: £280.00) 7f 8-15 (8-19)

863² **Hand on Heart (IRE) (61)** (Fav) *(WJHaggas)* 7-13 JQuinn (7) (5th st: hdwy
over 1f out: led ins fnl f: r.o) ............................................................. —1
695 Forgetful (60) *(RHannon)* 7-11⁽²⁾ AMcGlone (9) (hdwy 4f out: 4th st: ev ch 1f
out: r.o) ................................................................................................. ¾.2
783 Aedean (69) (v) *(CCElsey)* 8-7 AMunro (2) (led 5f out tl ins fnl f) .............. 1.3
896 Horizontale (49) *(CEBrittain)* 7-6⁽⁴⁾ ‡⁵BDoyle (5) (6th st: styd on fnl 2f) ............ 1½.4
Agwa *(BHanbury)* 7-5 ‡⁷CHawksley (10) (cmpt: bkwd: hld up: hdwy 4f out: wnt
2nd st: wknd over 1f out) .......................................................................... 8.5
806 Injaka Boy (40) (v) *(KWhite)* 7-6 ‡⁷AGarth (3) (3rd st: wknd 2f out) ............ 5.6
727 Red Mirage (IRE) *(MMcCormack)* 7-10 RStreet (8) (led over 1f: 7th & wkng st) .. 7.7
278 Nicholas Star *(REPeacock)* 7-13 AProud (1) (prom tl wknd qckly over 3f out:
t.o) ......................................................................................................... 6.8
Ghosted Hassle *(GFHCharles-Jones)* 7-9 DanaMellor (4) (a bhd: t.o) ............. 2½.9

**2/1** HAND ON HEART (IRE), **3/1** Aedean, **7/2** Forgetful, **13/2** Agwa, **8/1** Red Mirage (IRE), Horizontale, **33/1**
Injaka Boy, Nicholas Star, **50/1** Ghosted Hassle. CSF £9.86, Tote £3.10: £1.40 £1.50 £1.50 (£3.90). Mrs M. M.
Haggas (NEWMARKET) bred by Kellsboro House Stud in Ireland. 9 Rn 1m 26.9 (2.7)
SF—18/14/21/1/–/–

**1011** BANBURY H'CAP (3-Y.O) (0-90) £3844.20 (£928.80) 1¾m 194y 8-45 (8-45)

810³ Yenoora (IRE) (56) *(PFICole)* 7-10 JQuinn (2) (mde all: rdn 2f out: r.o wl) ........ —1
908* Simply-H (IRE) (76) (Fav) *(MBell)* 8-9 (4x) ‡⁷PTurner (3) (hld up: rdn to chal over
1f out: one pce fnl f) ............................................................................. 3.2

**1/4** Simply-H (IRE)(op 1/7), **3/1** YENOORA (IRE)(op 5/1). Tote £2.50. Mr Reg Hester (WHATCOMBE) bred by
Binfield Manor Farms Ltd in Ireland. 2 Rn 3m 24.1 (15.1)
T/Plpt: £19.90 (78.25 Tckts). KH

## 225—DONCASTER (L-H)
### Saturday, May 23rd [Firm]
Going Allowance: St: minus 0.30 sec; Rnd: minus 0.15 sec (F) Wind: slt bhd

Stalls: high

**1012** FRICKLEY STKS (Mdn 3-Y.O) £2364.00 (£654.00: £312.00) 1m (rnd) 2-20 (2-23)

658 Mizoram (USA) *(HRACecil)* 8-7 ‡⁷StephenDavies (3) (mde all: rdn & r.o wl fnl 2f) —1
687³ Kiveton Tycoon (IRE) (bl) *(JAGlover)* 9-0 DNicholls (4) (lw: swtg: chsd ldrs:
hdwy 3f out: ev ch 2f out: r.o) ................................................................ ½.2
Reflecting (IRE) (Fav) *(JHMGosden)* 9-0 PatEddery (6) (neat: scope: a cl up:
chal over 3f out: sn rdn & btn wl over 1f out) ......................................... 5.3
707 Magnetic Point (USA) *(AAScott)* 8-9 JFortune (9) (swtg: unruly bef s: stdd s:
hdwy 3f out: r.o) .................................................................................... hd.4
Fairford *(JGFitzGerald)* 9-0 KFallon (8) (bit bkwd: bhd & pushed along ent st:
styd on: n.d) ......................................................................................... 8.5
899 Kateb (IRE) *(RWArmstrong)* 9-0 BCrossley (7) (lw: outpcd & bhd ent st: styd on
fnl 2f) ...................................................................................................... 1½.6
Young Musician (IRE) *(JGFitzGerald)* 9-0 MBirch (1) (bit bkwd: nvr trbld ldrs) .... 1.7
680 Robert Thomas (IRE) *(MO'Neill)* 9-0 JQuinn (5) (chsd ldrs tl rdn & wknd 4f out) 5.8
808⁵ Double Lark (70) *(RHollinshead)* 9-0 PaulEddery (2) (lw: chsd ldrs to ½-wy: sn
lost pl) .................................................................................................... 4.9

**5/4** Reflecting (IRE), **5/2** Kiveton Tycoon (IRE), **7/1** MIZORAM (USA), **10/1** Kateb (IRE), Magnetic Point (USA),
**14/1** Young Musician (IRE), **25/1** Double Lark, Fairford, **33/1** Robert Thomas (IRE). CSF £24.57, Tote £8.20:
£2.10 £1.10 £1.20 (£13.30). Sheikh Mohammed (NEWMARKET) bred by Bedford Farms, Skymarc Farm in USA.
9 Rn 1m 38.88 (2.58)
SF—36/41/26/20/1/–

**1013** THORNTON STUD RACING SCHOOLS APP'CE H'CAP (0-70) £2532.00 (£702.00:
£336.00) 7f 2-50 (2-54)

508 **Sir Arthur Hobbs (53)** *(FHLee)* 5-9-0 NKennedy (12) (hdwy 2f out: r.o wl to ld
post) ........................................................................................................ —1
794³ Malunar (63) *(MHTompkins)* 7-9-6 ‡⁴SMulvey (16) (lw: hdwy over 2f out: r.o wl
to ld cl home: jst ct) ............................................................................... s.h.2
Quiet Victory (42) *(MissLCSiddall)* 5-8-3 PTurner (15) (bit bkwd: a chsng ldrs:
hung lft 3f out: chal ins fnl f: r.o) ........................................................... hd.3
Leave it to Lib (55) *(PCalver)* 5-8-12 ‡⁴JTate (4) (bit bkwd: led tl ct cl home) .... hd.4

763⁵ Sandmoor Denim **(52)** *(SRBowring)* 5–8-9 ‡⁴MHarris (9) (lw: drvn along over 2f out: hdwy over 1fout: ev ch wl ins fnl f: no ex nr fin) ............ hd.5

774 Miss Magenta (IRE) **(34)** *(RThompson)* 4–7-5⁽¹⁾ ‡⁴NicolaHowarth (17) (lw: hdwy 2f out: r.o nr fin) ............................................ 1.6

883³ Spanish Verdict **(57)** (v) *(DenysSmith)* 5–8-10‡⁸CTeague (10) (lw: a chsng ldrs: hrd rdn 2f out: styd on fnl f) ............................ s.h.7

624 Darakah **(61)** (Fav) *(CJHill)* 5–9-8 DBiggs (3) (hdwy 3f out: styd on nr fin) ...... s.h.8

866² China Sky **(46)** *(CNAllen)* 4–8-7 MichaelDenaro (11) (lw: chsd ldrs: outpcd 3f out: styd on fnl f) ................................ ¾.9

696 Rag Time Belle **(35)** *(MWEckley)* 6–7-10 DHarrison (7) (chsd ldrs tl outpcd wl over 2f out) ................................................. 2¹/₂.10

Creselly **(66)** *(JGFitzGerald)* 5–9-13 JWeaver (14) (lw: cl up tl rdn & sltly hmpd 3f out: sn btn) ................................. hd.11

Hizeem **(34)** *(MPNaughton)* 6–7-5⁽¹⁾ ‡⁴AGarth (1) (effrt ¹/₂-wy: no imp) ......... s.h.12

419 The Devil's Music **(38)** *(MrsJRRamsden)* 8–7-9 ‡⁴RHavlin (13) (outpcd fr ¹/₂-wy) ¹/₂.13

830 On Y Va (USA) **(67)** *(RJRWilliams)* 5–9-10 ‡⁴GMitchell (8) (nvr trbld ldrs) .......... 1.14

Greatest of All (IRE) **(43)** *(RHannon)* 4–8-0⁽⁵⁾ ‡⁴MarkDenaro (n.d) .................... 1.15

Lust of Love **(61)** *(MrsVAAconley)* 6–9-8 FArrowsmith (6) (lw: dwlt: gd hdwy ¹/₂-wy: sn wknd) ...................................... 4.16

521 Bracken Bay **(34)** *(TKersey)* 5–7-5⁽²⁾ ‡⁴ClaireBalding (5) (b: t.o fr ¹/₂-wy) ............. 17

LONG HANDICAP: Bracken Bay 7-5.

**5/1** Darakah, **6/1** Creselly, **7/1** China Sky, **17/2** Spanish Verdict, **9/1** Malunar, Rag Time Belle, **10/1** Miss Magenta (IRE)(op 16/1), **12/1** Sandmoor Denim, **14/1** Lust of Love, On Y Va (USA), **16/1** Greatest of All (IRE), Leave it to Lib, SIR ARTHUR HOBBS, The Devil's Music, **20/1** Quiet Victory, **33/1** Hizeem, **66/1** Bracken Bay. CSF £152.66, CT £2,671.07. Tote £29.00: £4.60 £1.90 £4.50 £3.90 (£75.70). Mr John Hardman (WILMSLOW) bred by A. Tarry. 17 Rn

1m 24.90 (1.50)

SF–46/51/33/41/37/16

---

**1014**  PRIORY PLACE H'CAP (0-100) £3525.00 (£1050.00: £500.00: £225.00)
6f

3-20 (3-20)

723⁶ **Crystal Jack (FR) (70)** *(FHLee)* 4–8-12 PaulEddery (3) (chsd ldrs: led over 2f out: hung rt 1f out: r.o) ....................... —1

813 Sea Devil **(81)** *(MJCamacho)* 6–9-9 NConnorton (4) (lw: chsd ldrs: nt clr run 2f out: hdwy & ev ch ins fnl f: no ex nr fin) .................. 1.2

813 Resolute Bay **(84)** (v) *(RMWhitaker)* 6–9-12 ACulhane (5) (in tch: effrt over 2f out: ev ch whn hmpd ins fnl f: nt rcvr) ........................ 2.3

624² Garth **(79)** (Fav) *(PJMakin)* 4–9-7 PatEddery (2) (swtg: lw: a chsng ldrs: ev ch & rdn over 2f out: r.o one pce) ..................... ¹/₂.4

813 Profilic **(79)** *(CaptJWilson)* 7–9-7 GCarter (1) (lw: chsd ldrs: headway over 2f out: ev ch over 1f out: sn btn) .......................... 1¹/₂.5

712 Corn Futures **(81)** (v) *(JPLeigh)* 4–9-4 ‡⁵JWeaver (6) (led tl hdd over 2f out: sn wknd) ............................................ 3.6

**6/4** Garth, **2/1** Profilic, **6/1** Sea Devil, **9/1** CRYSTAL JACK (FR), Resolute Bay, **14/1** Corn Futures. CSF £52.86, Tote £11.00: £2.40 £2.10 (£21.90). Mrs B. Facchino (WILMSLOW) bred by Daniel Fernandez and Paul Vuillard in France. 6 Rn

1m 11.49 (0.49)

SF–52/59/54/47/41/26

---

**1015**  RIFLE BUTTS GRADUATION STKS (3-Y.O) £2898.00 (£864.00: £412.00: £186.00)
1¹/₄m 60y

3-50 (3-51)

823² **Binkhaldoun (USA) (97)** *(HThomsonJones)* 9-4 RHills (4) (b: hld up: squeezed thro to ld 1f out: r.o wl) .................... —1

781⁵ Anchorite **(96)** *(PTWalwyn)* 9-4 MBirch (2) (led: qcknd over 3f out: hdd 1f out: no ex) ..................................... 1¹/₂.2

857★ Surf **(98)** *(MrsJCecil)* 9-4 PaulEddery (3) (lw: hld up: effrt 3f out: sn ev ch: one pce fnl 2f) ...................................... 1.3

835★ Balnibarbi (Fav) *(HRACecil)* 9-4 PatEddery (1) (lw: chsd ldr: chal over 2f out: sn rdn & nt qckn) .............................. hd.4

**Evens** Balnibarbi, **9/4** Surf, **5/1** BINKHALDOUN (USA)(4/1—6/1), **8/1** Anchorite. CSF £22.78, Tote £6.00 (£11.50). Mr Hamdan Al-Maktoum (NEWMARKET) bred by Flaxman Holdings Ltd in USA. 4 Rn 2m 11 (4)

SF–49/46/44/43

---

**1016**  ROSEHILL H'CAP (0-80) £3028.00 (£904.00: £432.00: £196.00)  1¹/₂m 4-20 (4-20)

831³ **Taylors Prince (57)** *(HJCollingridge)* 5–8-6 JQuinn (2) (hld up: swtchd over 2f out: qcknd to ld ins fnl f: drvn out) ................... —1

718⁵ Beau Quest **(56)** (v) *(RMWhitaker)* 5–8-5 ACulhane (4) (chsd ldr: led over 2f out: hdd ins fnl f: hrd rdn & r.o) ........................ hd.2

Express Account **(64)** *(RJRWilliams)* 5-8-13  RHills (7) (hld up: smooth hdwy to chal over 1f out: n.m.r ins fnl f: r.o) .................................................. ¹/₂.3

Highflying **(79)** *(GMMoore)* 6-10-0  KFallon (3) (chsd ldrs tl outpcd fnl 2f) ......... 5.4

880★ Checkpoint Charlie **(63)** (Fav) *(JMPEustace)* 7-8-5 ‡7AntoinetteArmes (1) (hld up & bhd: sltly hmpd & swtchd 2f out: r.o: nvr able chal) .... 1.5

776 Foursingh **(46)** (bl) *(CBBBooth)* 4-7-9  LCharnock (5) (led tl hdd over 2f out: sn wknd) ......................................................................................... hd.6

Sultan's Son **(76)** *(MrsALMKing)* 6-9-11  JFortune (6) (stumbled s: hld up & bhd: n.d) ................................................................................................. 10.7

**9/4** Checkpoint Charlie, **3/1** Express Account, **7/2** Beau Quest, **5/1** TAYLORS PRINCE, **10/1** Highflying, **20/1** Ors. CSF £21.15, Tote £5.10: £2.20 £2.00 (£7.50). Mr H. J. Collingridge (NEWMARKET) bred by A. F. O'Callaghan. 7 Rn
2m 36.25 (5.65)
SF—18/16/23/28/3/–

---

## 1017

E.B.F. ZETLAND STKS (Mdn 2-Y.O) £2978.50 (£826.00: £395.50)     **6f**     4-50 (4-52)

828² Geisway (CAN) (Fav) *(RHannon)* 9-0  PaulEddery (8) (lw: chsd ldrs: effrt 2f out: disp ld 1f out: r.o wl u.p to ld nr fin) ..................................... —1

Kamaatera (IRE) *(AAScott)* 9-0  BRaymond (3) (w'like: scope: chsd ldrs gng wl: disp ld 1f out: ev ch nr fin: no ex nr fin) .................................. hd.2

817³ Icy South (USA) *(JHMGosden)* 9-0  PatEddery (9) (b.off fore: lw: led: hung lft fnl 2f: hdd 1f out: nt qckn) ................................................. 1¹/₂.3

619⁵ Argyle Cavalier (IRE) *(FHLee)* 9-0  ACulhane (7) (a chsng ldrs: nt qckn fnl 2f) .... 4.4

Sophie's Boy *(MHEasterby)* 9-0  MBirch (2) (neat: spd over 4f) ..................... 3¹/₂.5

770 Blowedifiknow *(JWharton)* 9-0  JQuinn (4) (dwlt: sn rcvrd & chsd ldrs: outpcd fr wl over 2f out) ............................................................................. 3¹/₂.6

Resolution Time *(MrsVAAconley)* 9-0  PBurke (1) (unf: bit bkwd: s.i.s: pushed along & in tch after 2f: wknd over 2f out) ....................................... ¹/₂.7

Mohican Brave (IRE) *(JGFitzGerald)* 9-0  KFallon (6) (unf: bit bkwd: scope: dwlt: a outpcd & bhd) ................................................................................ 3.8

**Evens** GEISWAY (CAN), **6/4** Icy South (USA), **7/1** Kamaatera (IRE), **20/1** Sophie's Boy, **25/1** Argyle Cavalier (IRE), **33/1** Mohican Brave (IRE), **50/1** Ors. CSF £8.62, Tote £2.00: £1.20 £1.10 £1.20 (£5.90). A. F. Budge (Equine) Limited (MARLBOROUGH) bred by Michael Byrne in Canada. 8 Rn
1m 12.35 (1.35)
SF—37/36/30/14/–/–

---

## 1018

GRESLEY H'CAP (0-80) £3052.00 (£847.00: £406.00)     **1m (rnd)**     5-20 (5-21)

768 **American Hero (68)** *(CTinkler)* 4-9-0 ‡5JWeaver (10) (mde all: clr ¹/₂-wy: hld on wl fnl f) ............................................................................. —1

768² Genair (FR) **(58)** *(MrsGRReveley)* 7-8-9  KFallon (1) (lw: a chsng ldrs: effrt 3f out: styd on wl nr fin) ........................................................... nk.2

866★ Charming Gift **(51)** (Fav) *(RJRWilliams)* 5-8-2  JQuinn (3) (lw: in tch: effrt & n.m.r over 2f out: r.o ins fnl f) ............................................................ ³/₄.3

766⁴ Who's Tef (IRE) **(60)** *(MHEasterby)* 4-8-11  MBirch (7) (lw: bhd: shkn up 3f out: r.o fnl 2f) ................................................................................. ¹/₂.4

768★ Major Mouse **(69)** *(WWHaigh)* 4-9-6  ACulhane (2) (lw: in tch: effrt over 2f out: styd on wl nr fin) ...................................................................... hd.5

684★ Habeta (USA) **(70)** *(JWWatts)* 6-9-0 ‡7EHusband (13) (lw: hld up: effrt 3f out: nvr rchd ldrs) ................................................................................... ³/₄.6

490⁶ Rural Lad **(71)** *(MrsJRRamsden)* 3-8-10  BRaymond (6) (hld up & bhd: effrt ¹/₂-wy: hung lft & nvr trbld ldrs) ......................................... 3.7

Regent Lad **(77)** *(MissLCSiddall)* 8-10-0  PatEddery (4) (bit bkwd: hld up: hdwy ¹/₂-wy: nt clr run: sn btn) .................................................................... hd.8

606 Rasco **(57)** *(JEtherington)* 3-7-10  LCharnock (5) (bhd & hmpd after 1f: hdwy whn n.m.r 3f out: sn bhd) ............................................................ 3.9

684² Veloce (IRE) **(58)** *(MO'Neill)* 4-8-9  JFortune (9) (lw: plld hrd: hld up & bhd: n.d)2¹/₂.10

962 Breezed Well **(64)** *(CNAllen)* 6-8-8 ‡7MichaelDenaro (11) (bhd: c wd & effrt 4f out: n.d) ....................................................................................... 5.11

456 Mofador (GER) **(57)** *(FHLee)* 8-8-3 ‡5NKennedy (8) (lw: chsd ldrs tl rdn & wknd after 3f: sn bhd) ........................................................................ 6.12

809⁶ Sally Fay (IRE) **(53)** *(TKersey)* 4-7-11⁽⁴⁾ ‡7JMarshall (12) (hmpd & fell after 1f) ........ 0

**4/1** Charming Gift, **9/2** Genair (FR), **6/1** Who's Tef (IRE), **7/1** Veloce (IRE), **15/2** Habeta (USA), **8/1** Major Mouse, **9/1** Regent Lad, **11/1** Rural Lad, **14/1** Mofador (GER), **16/1** AMERICAN HERO, Rasco, **20/1** Breezed Well, **50/1** Sally Fay (IRE). CSF £87.38, CT £327.74. Tote £39.60: £6.70 £2.40 £2.40 (£322.80). Mr G. Shiel (MALTON) bred by Sir Gordon White. 13 Rn
1m 38.88 (2.58)
SF—43/37/28/35/43/35

T/Plpt: £256.40 (16.7 Tckts).
AA

## 225—**DONCASTER (L-H)**
### **Monday, May 25th [Good to firm, Firm fnl 5f]**
Going Allowance: St: minus 0.30 sec; Rnd: minus 0.40 sec (F)            Wind: nil   Vis: hazy

Stalls: high

**1019**        RANSKILL STKS (2-Y.O) £3012.00 (£832.00: £396.00)    **6f**        2-10 (2-11)

856* **Son Pardo** (Jt-Fav) *(RHannon)* 9-4  KDarley (2) (mde all: shkn up & drew clr fnl
                 f) ........................................................................................................................ —1
611² Kharaj (Jt-Fav) *(AAScott)* 9-4  WRSwinburn (1) (chsd wnr: effrt over 1f out: no
                 imp) ..................................................................................................................... 3.2
447⁶ Ann Hill (IRE) *(RHollinshead)* 8-6  PaulEddery (3) (swtg: hld up: rdn appr fnl f:
                 kpt on) .............................................................................................................. hd.3

**Evens** Kharaj, SON PARDO, **12/1** Ann Hill (IRE)(op 20/1). CSF £2.22, Tote £1.90 (£1.10). N.T.C. (Racing)
Limited (MARLBOROUGH) bred by R. T. and Mrs Watson. 3 Rn                                1m 15.26 (4.26)

**1020**        SHADWELL STUD APP'CE SERIES H'CAP (0-70) £2579.00 (£714.00: £341.00)
                **5f**                                                                                      2-45 (2-46)

885 **Catherines Well (62)** *(MWEasterby)* 9-9-5 ‡⁵JMarshall (3) (swtg: chsd ldrs: led
                 wl over 1f out: rdn clr) ........................................................................................ —1
421 Morpick **(50)** (v) *(JPLeigh)* 5-8-12  StephenDavies (5) (swtg: a w ldrs: rdn &
                 unable qckn fnl f) .............................................................................................. 2.2
918² The Right Time **(45)** (bl) *(JParkes)* 7-8-2 ‡⁵VHalliday (6) (lw: dwlt: hdwy
                 over 2f out: led wl over 1f out: sn hdd: no ex ins fnl f) ........ nk.3
752² Hinari Video **(48)** *(MJohnston)* 7-8-5 ¹⁶NVarley (7) (lw: chsd ldrs: kpt on ins fnl f) 1.4
888 Jive Music **(33)** (bl) *(NBycroft)* 6-7-6 ‡³DarrenMoffatt (12) (w ldrs stands' side:
                 r.o one pce appr fnl f) ....................................................................................... hd.5
752 Arc Lamp **(49)** *(JAGlover)* 6-8-4 ‡⁷MHunt (11) (b.nr hind: hdwy appr fnl f: r.o wl) nk.6
661 Don't Run Me Over **(47)** *(BCMorgan)* 3-7-9⁽⁴⁾ ‡⁵SSanders (10) (chsd ldrs: rdn
                 along 2f out: no imp) ......................................................................................... 2.7
614 Capital Idea (IRE) **(60)** *(RonaldThompson)* 8-8-8⁽⁴⁾ ‡⁵SGiles (2) (outpcd) ......... 1.8
918⁴ Lady's Mantle (USA) **(44)** *(RBastiman)* 8-8-3 ‡³HBastiman (4) (swtg: disp ld:
                 rdn 2f out: sn btn) .......................................................................................... ¹/₂.9
180⁶ Glencroft **(62)** (bl) *(DWChapman)* 8-9-7 ‡³OPears (1) (lt: bit bkwd: racd alone far
                 side: mde most over 3f) ................................................................................... ¹/₂.10
613 Rednet **(56)** (bl) *(PDEvans)* 5-9-4  MichaelDenaro (8) (b: dwlt: a outpcd) ........... 2.11
668 Parisienne King **(47)** *(FHLee)* 3-8-0  NKennedy (9) (spd 3f) ............................... 1¹/₂.12

**9/2** The Right Time, **5/1** Lady's Mantle (USA), Hinari Video, **6/1** CATHERINES WELL(op 4/1), **13/2** Arc Lamp,
**11/1** Jive Music, Don't Run Me Over, **12/1** Rednet, **14/1** Morpick, **20/1** Capital Idea (IRE), Glencroft, **33/1**
Parisienne King (USA). CSF £78.82, CT £380.07. Tote £5.70: £2.00 £4.30 £1.80 (£58.80). Mr Robert Cox
(SHERIFF HUTTON) bred by R. J. Powell. 12 Rn                                                59.88 sec (1.18)
                                                                                             SF−51/36/25/24/10/21

**1021**        DURHAM H'CAP (3-Y.O) (0-100) £3687.50 (£1100.00: £525.00: £237.50)
                **7f**                                                                                      3-20 (3-22)

813 **Nordic Brave (70)** *(MBrittain)* 6-8-6  NConnorton (6) (led tl ins fnl f: rallied
                 gamely u.p to ld cl home) ................................................................................. —1
778* Deprecator (USA) **(89)** (Fav) *(JHMGosden)* 4-9-11  RCochrane (4) (b.hind:
                 swtg: chsd ldr: rdn to ld ins fnl f: hdd post) ...................................... hd.2
610 Sharpalto **(77)** *(MrsGRReveley)* 5-8-13  JLowe (3) (lw: hld up: gd hdwy 2f out:
                 ev ch fnl f: r.o) ................................................................................................... s.h.3
398 Duckington **(73)** *(MHEasterby)* 8-8-9  KDarley (1) (chsd ldrs: hrd rdn fnl f: r.o) 1¹/₂.4
941⁵ The Can Can Man **(69)** *(MJohnston)* 5-8-5  RPElliott (8) (lw: chsd ldrs: rdn appr
                 fnl f: nt pce to chal) ......................................................................................... hd.5
768 Bernstein Bette **(65)** *(PSFelgate)* 6-7-10 ‡⁵NKennedy (7) (lw: chsd ldrs: rdn
                 over 1f out: no ex fnl f) ..................................................................................... 3.6
821⁴ Yousefia (USA) **(85)** *(MRStoute)* 3-8-10  WRSwinburn (2) (prom tl rdn & wknd
                 appr fnl f: eased whn btn) ................................................................................. 1.7
860 Mitsubishi Video (IRE) **(72)** *(DrJDScargill)* 4-8-8  AMcGlone (5) (chsd ldrs: rdn
                 3f out: btn appr fnl f) ........................................................................................ 1.8

**9/4** Deprecator (USA), **3/1** Yousefia (USA), **5/1** The Can Can Man, **11/2** Sharpalto, **7/1** Duckington, **12/1** NORDIC
BRAVE, **20/1** Bernstein Bette, **25/1** Mitsubishi Video (IRE). CSF £37.74, CT £154.64. Tote £13.70: £2.90 £1.10
£2.70 (£18.70). Mr Mel Brittain (WARTHILL) bred by Tsarina Stud. 8 Rn                      1m 24.31 (0.91)
                                                                                             SF−47/65/52/43/38/20

**1022** HAREWOOD H'CAP (0-90) £3028.00 (£904.00: £432.00: £196.00)
2¼m
3-50 (3-51)

815 **Aahsaylad (75)** *(FHLee)* 6-8-13 ‡5NKennedy (6) (hld up: 6th st: styd on strly to ld fnl strides) .................................................. —1

718 Good Hand (USA) **(83)** (Fav) *(JWWatts)* 6-9-12 NConnorton (5) (chsd ldrs: 3rd st: led appr fnl f tl ins fnl f: rallied u.p cl home) ............. s.h.2

718 Farsi **(76)** (bl) *(RHollinshead)* 4-9-2 WRSwinburn (3) (chsd ldr: 2nd st: led over 2f out tl appr fnl f: led ins fnl f tl cl nr fin) ..................... hd.3

937 Sagaman (GER) **(54)** *(LJCodd)* 6-7-11 JLowe (1) (hld up: 4th st: n.m.r over 1f out: styd on fnl f) ...................................................... 2.4

718⁶ Our Aisling **(67)** *(SGNorton)* 4–8-0 ‡7OPears (4) (hld up: 5th st: rdn & ev ch 1f out: no ex nr fin) ............................................. 1.5

Crystal Spirit **(85)** *(IABalding)* 5–10-0 RCochrane (2) (led tl over 2f out: rallied u.p appr fnl f: btn whn hmpd ins fnl f) ........................ s.h.6

**3/1** Good Hand (USA), **7/2** Farsi, **4/1** Our Aisling, Crystal Spirit, **11/2** AAHSAYLAD, **8/1** Sagaman (GER). CSF £20.90, Tote £6.60: £2.20 £2.00 (£15.00). Mr M. Stapleton (WILMSLOW) bred by Blue Bear Stud Co Ltd. 6 Rn
3m 57.36 (4.66)

**1023** E.B.F. VYNER STKS (Mdn 2-Y.O) £2716.00 (£808.00: £384.00: £172.00)
5f
4-20 (4-22)

**Petardia** (Fav) *(GWragg)* 9-0 WRSwinburn (5) (w'like: scope: lw: hld up: led over 1f out: qcknd clr fnl f: impressive) ........................ —1

729⁵ Cop the Cash (USA) *(MBell)* 9-0 AMcGlone (2) (lw: led tl hdd over 1f out: sn outpcd) ................................................ 5.2

Chiltern Hundreds (USA) *(MrsJCecil)* 9-0 PaulEddery (3) (neat: bkwd: prom: rdn appr fnl f: sn btn) ................................... 6.3

Pressure Off *(APStringer)* 9-0 JFortune (4) (w'like: bkwd: s.s: a outpcd) ..................... 5.4

Shotley Again *(NBycroft)* 9-0 NConnorton (1) (w'like: leggy: bit bkwd: s.i.s: outpcd) ................................................ 1.5

**4/6** PETARDIA, **11/4** Chiltern Hundreds (USA), **5/1** Cop the Cash (USA), **16/1** Pressure Off, **33/1** Shotley Again. CSF £4.37, Tote £1.60 £1.10 £2.00 (£2.80). Mollers Racing (NEWMARKET) bred by Highfield Stud Ltd and The Glen Andred Stud. 5 Rn
60.21 sec (1.51)
SF—40/20/–/–/–

**1024** YORKSHIRE STAND STKS (Mdn 3-Y.O) £2238.00 (£618.00: £294.00)
1¾m 132y
4-50 (4-50)

864² **Pavonis** (Fav) *(HRACecil)* 9-0 AMcGlone (1) (lw: mde all: shkn up appr fnl f: styd on) ................................................ —1

789² King's Treasure (USA) *(IABalding)* 9-0 RCochrane (3) (lw: hld up: 2nd st: rdn along 3f out: one pce) .................................. 5.2

810⁶ Barton Pride (IRE) **(47)** *(RHollinshead)* 9-0 WRSwinburn (2) (a bhd: 3rd st: rdn 4f out: sn lost tch) ........................... 30.3

**10/11** PAVONIS, **11/10** King's Treasure (USA), **10/1** Barton Pride (IRE). CSF £2.17, Tote £1.80 (£1.20). Mr D. K. Harris (NEWMARKET) bred by Cheveley Park Stud Ltd. 3 Rn
3m 9.79 (6.19)

**1025** ARKSEY H'CAP (3-Y.O) (0-80) £3418.00 (£1024.00: £492.00: £226.00)
1¼m 60y
5-25 (5-29)

921★ **Bayaireg (USA) (77)** (Fav) *(AAScott)* 9-7 (5x) WRSwinburn (7) (lw: hld up: n.m.r 3f out: gd hdwy to ld 1f out: sn clr) ....................... —1

524 Mujid (IRE) **(61)** *(HThomsonJones)* 8-5 RHills (14) (hld up: hdwy to chal 2f out: styd on u.p ins fnl f) ................................. 2.2

788⁶ Khrisma **(70)** *(MrsJCecil)* 9-0 PaulEddery (13) (bhd: n.m.r 3f out: hdwy over 2f out: swtchd rt & r.o fnl f) ......................... 1.3

604 Drummer Hicks **(60)** *(EWeymes)* 8-4 ACulhane (15) (a chsng ldrs: 3rd st: led over 2f out to 1f out: one pce) ....................... 1.4

Sunderland Echo **(49)** *(MrsGRReveley)* 7-7 JLowe (2) (swtg: bit bkwd: dwlt: hdwy 3f out: kpt on ins fnl f) ........................... 2.5

451⁶ Esbooain (FR) **(75)** *(LMCumani)* 9-5 JFortune (12) (lw: hdwy u.p 3f out: nvr nrr) 2.6

488² Dramatic Pass (IRE) **(56)** *(MrsGRReveley)* 8-0(¹) KDarley (6) (prom: 2nd st: led over 2f out: sn hdd: one pce) ...................... 1.7

547 Timurid (FR) **(65)** *(JLDunlop)* 8-9 RPElliott (3) (swtg: hdwy 6f out: 5th st: rdn & wknd wl over 1f out) ......................... s.h.8

821 Doyce **(65)** *(JEtherington)* 8-9 NConnorton (5) (hdwy ½-wy: wknd wl over 1f out) 1.9

784⁴ Vernonia **(77)** *(JHMGosden)* 9-7 AMcGlone (8) (prom: 4th st: wknd over 2f out) 4.10

878⁶ Sir Norman Holt (IRE) **(57)** *(FHLee)* 7-10 ‡⁵NKennedy (1) (chsd ldrs: 3rd st: rdn & wknd 3f out) ............ 6.11
662* Red Kite **(66)** *(MBell)* 8-10 JQuinn (11) (lw: mid div tl wknd over 2f out) ............ 1.12
671 Houlston's Will **(60)** *(MrsJRRamsden)* 8-4 RLappin (10) (swtg: s.i.s: a bhd) .... ¹⁄₂.13
788⁵ Brave the Wind **(66)** *(IABalding)* 8-10 RCochrane (4) (led tl hdd & wknd over 2f out) ............ 3¹⁄₂.14
884 Petastra **(60)** *(MrsJRRamsden)* 8-4 MBirch (9) (prom tl wknd over 4f out: t.o) ..... 15
LONG HANDICAP: Sunderland Echo 7-4.

**15/8** BAYAIREG (USA), **7/1** Brave the Wind, **8/1** Red Kite, **9/1** Dramatic Pass (IRE)(12/1—8/1), **12/1** Esbooain (FR), Khrisma, **14/1** Timurid (FR), Doyce, Mujid (IRE), Petastra, Vernonia, **16/1** Houlston's Will, Drummer Hicks, Sir Norman Holt (IRE), **25/1** Sunderland Echo. CSF £31.45, CT £264.57. Tote £2.80: £1.50 £3.70 £3.30 (£18.60). Maktoum Al Maktoum (NEWMARKET) bred by Mrs Nancy S. Dillman in USA. 15 Rn  2m 8.09 (1.09)
SF—56/36/43/31/16/38

T/Plpt: £59.40 (62.25 Tckts).  IM

# CHEPSTOW (L-H)
## Monday, May 25th [Good to firm, Firm patches]
Going Allowance: minus 0.10 sec per fur (F)  Wind: almost nil

Stalls: high

**1026**  ST ARVANS STKS (Mdn 3-Y.O) £2402.40 (£666.40: £319.20)
1¹⁄₂m 23y  2-00 (2-02)

481⁶ **Not in Doubt (USA)** *(HCandy)* 9-0 SDawson (3) (4th st: rdn & lost pl 3f out: swtchd rt & rallied over 1f out: hrd rdn: led post) ............ —1
710⁵ Eightandahalf (IRE) **(79)** (Fav) *(PWChapple-Hyam)* 9-0 AMunro (4) (lw: hld up: 5th st: hdwy 4f out: led over 1f out: ct last stride) ............ s.h.2
789³ Bar Billiards *(RFJohnsonHoughton)* 9-0 SWhitworth (5) (lw: 3rd st: led over 2f out tl over 1f out: nt qckn) ............ 2¹⁄₂.3
732² For Mog (USA) *(CEBrittain)* 9-0 GCrealock (1) (led over 9f: nt qckn) ............ ¹⁄₂.4
710 Two and Sixpence (USA) *(BWHills)* 8-4 ‡⁵DHarrison (2) (2nd st: ev ch 2f out: wknd over 1f out) ............ 2¹⁄₂.5
707³ Fleeting Rainbow *(JLDunlop)* 8-9 WNewnes (2) (hld up: 6th st: hdwy 4f out: wknd over 1f out) ............ 2¹⁄₂.6
734 St Piran's Lass *(RJHolder)* 8-9 NAdams (6) (last st: t.o fnl 2f) ............ 15.7

**6/4** Eightandahalf (IRE), **13/8** Fleeting Rainbow, **11/2** Bar Billiards, **7/1** For Mog (USA), **20/1** NOT IN DOUBT (USA), Two and Sixpence (USA), **66/1** St Piran's Lass. CSF £49.61, Tote £17.20: £4.10 £1.70 (£26.60). Mrs David Blackburn (WANTAGE) bred by Gallagher's Stud in USA. 7 Rn  2m 38.9 (7.6)
SF—12/11/6/5/–/–

**1027**  NEWICK H'CAP (3-Y.O) (0-90) £2385.00 (£660.00: £315.00)  1¹⁄₂m 23y  2-30 (2-32)
(Weights raised 3 lb)

908³ **Formal Invitation (IRE) (58)** *(GLewis)* 7-10 ‡⁵DHarrison (3) (b: 3rd st: led over 2f out: r.o wl) ............ —1
802⁶ The Karaoke King **(66)** *(RHannon)* 8-6 ‡³RPerham (7) (chsd ldr: 2nd st: led 3f out: sn hdd: r.o one pce) ............ 2.2
728 Erlemo **(51)** (bl) *(CJBenstead)* 7-8⁽¹⁾ TyroneWilliams (1) (led: rdn 4f out: hdd 3f out: one pce) ............ 3¹⁄₂.3
908⁶ Mustahil (IRE) **(70)** *(RJHodges)* 8-10 ‡³TSprake (2) (4th st: no hdwy fnl 3f) ...... nk.4
802⁴ National Emblem (FR) **(70)** *(PFICole)* 8-13 AMunro (6) (hld up: 6th st: hdwy over 2f out: hung lft wl over 1f out: sn wknd) ............ ¹⁄₂.5
671³ Encore Une Fois (IRE) **(76)** (Fav) *(PWChapple-Hyam)* 9-2 ‡³FNorton (5) (swtg: last & rdn st: a bhd) ............ 1.6
Jupiter Moon **(78)** *(CEBrittain)* 9-7 GCrealock (4) (lw: 5th & rdn st: a bhd: t.o) ... 7.7
LONG HANDICAP: Erlemo 7-5.

**5/4** Encore Une Fois (IRE), **7/2** FORMAL INVITATION (IRE), **9/2** National Emblem (FR), **17/2** Jupiter Moon, **11/1** The Karaoke King, **12/1** Mustahil (IRE), **33/1** Erlemo. CSF £34.33, Tote £4.40: £2.90 £1.40 (£17.20). Mrs N. Lewis (EPSOM) bred by Patrick Eddery Ltd in Ireland. 7 Rn  2m 36.4 (5.1)
SF—19/25/6/21/23/24

**1028**  MERCURY H'CAP (0-100) £3590.00 (£107.00: £510.00: £230.00)
6f 16y  3-00 (3-02)

853⁴ **How's Yer Father (73)** (Fav) *(RJHodges)* 6-9-0 ‡³TSprake (3) (a.p: rdn to ld over 1f out: pushed out) ............ —1

909 Gallant Hope **(50)** (bl) *(LGCottrell)* 10–7-8 RFox (7) (w ldrs: led wl over 1f out: sn hdd: r.o) ............................................................ nk.2

853 Luna Bid **(65)** *(MBlanshard)* 9–8-9 WNewnes (1) (lw: sn outpcd: hdwy fnl f: r.o)  1.3

853 Morgannwg (IRE) **(80)** *(RDickin)* 4–9-10 AClark (5) (hld up in rr: hdwy over 2f out: nt qckn fnl f) ............................................................ nk.4

853 Bertie Wooster **(84)** *(RJHolder)* 9–9-7 ‡⁵SDrowne (2) (bhd: rdn over 2f out: nvr nrr) ............................................................ 1½.5

Noble Power (IRE) **(82)** *(BPalling)* 3–9-2 AMunro (4) (chsd ldr: led over 2f out tl wl over 1f out: wknd fnl f) ............................................................ 1.6

909 Darussalam **(64)** *(RLee)* 5–8-3 ‡⁵RPrice (6) (led over 3f) ............ 3½.7

**15/8** HOW'S YER FATHER, **7/2** Gallant Hope, **6/1** Noble Power (IRE), Morgannwg (IRE), **7/1** Luna Bid, **12/1** Ors. CSF £8.44, Tote £2.80: £1.80 £1.80 (£5.00). Unity Farm Holiday Centre Ltd (SOMERTON) bred by Lord Edwin McAlpine. 7 Rn        1m 11.1 (2.1)
SF—46/25/39/53/44/35

---

## 1029    ST BRIAVELS STKS (Mdn 3-Y.O) £1730.00 (£480.00: £230.00)    **1m 14y** 3-30 (3-37)

618³ **Scandalmonger (USA) (79)** (Jt-Fav) *(BWHills)* 8-11 ‡³TSprake (8) (lw: hld up & bhd: hdwy over 2f out: led 1f out: r.o) ............................ —1

472 Courageous Knight **(77)** *(RHannon)* 9-0 SWhitworth (2) (plld hrd: a.p: ev ch ins fnl f: r.o) ............................ s.h.2

412⁴ Fusion (USA) (Jt-Fav) *(PFICole)* 9-0 AMunro (3) (a.p: led 3f out to 1f out: nt qckn wl ins fnl f) ............................ ½.3

Eiras Mood *(RDickin)* 8-9 AClark (5) (lt-f: unf: s.s: rdn & hdwy 3f out: wknd wl over 1f out) ............................ 7.4

346⁴ Fine as Fivepence **(41)** *(MrsAKnight)* 8-4 ‡⁵DHarrison (7) (led 5f: wknd wl over 1f out) ............................ 1½.5

864 Kalko *(CEBrittain)* 9-0 GCrealock (1) (w ldrs over 5f) ............................ 4.6

Cavo Greco *(PFICole)* 8-11 ‡³FNorton (9) (swtg: a bhd) ............................ 3.7

806 Brush Wolf (USA) *(JMBradley)* 9-0 NAdams (6) (bhd fnl 3f) ............................ 5.8

Fairy Princess (IRE) *(RHollinshead)* 8-2 ‡⁷MHumphries (4) (lt-f: unf: s.s: plld hrd: sn prom: wknd 3f out: t.o) ............................ 12.9

**7/4** SCANDALMONGER (USA), Fusion (USA), **11/2** Kalko, **9/1** Courageous Knight, **16/1** Cavo Greco (USA), **33/1** Eiras Mood, Fairy Princess (IRE), Fine as Fivepence, **66/1** Brush Wolf (USA). CSF £16.34, Tote £2.70: £1.10 £2.10 £1.20 (£11.50). Mr R. E. Sangster (LAMBOURN) bred by Triple R Stables in USA. 9 Rn   1m 35.5 (3)
SF—40/42/40/14/4/2

---

## 1030    ST JOHN (S) H'CAP (0-60) £1786.00 (£496.00: £238.00)    **5f 16y**    4-00 (4-05)

738 **Klairover (42)** *(CJHill)* 5–8-10 NAdams (13) (a.p: led ins fnl f: r.o) ............................ —1

909 Pendor Dancer **(51)** (bl) *(BForsey)* 9–9-5 SWhitworth (16) (swtg: hld up: hdwy 2f out: ev ch fnl f: r.o) ............................ hd.2

897* Catalani **(50)** (Fav) *(TJNaughton)* 7–9-4 AMunro (14) (sn outpcd: hdwy over 1f out: r.o ins fnl f) ............................ 1½.3

897² Lucy Dancer (IRE) **(56)** *(CGCox)* 4–9-10 AClark (17) (hdwy 2f out: nt clr run over 1f out: rdn & r.o ins fnl f) ............................ nk.4

897 Tippling (USA) **(33)** *(PBurgoyne)* 5–8-1 RFox (6) (swtg: hdwy 2f out: one pce fnl f) ............................ 1.5

897 The Noble Oak (IRE) **(56)** (bl) *(MMcCormack)* 4–9-10 WNewnes (8) (led: sn clr: hdd & wknd ins fnl f) ............................ s.h.6

Nuclear Express **(58)** *(RLee)* 5–9-5 ‡⁷SDrowne (11) (a chsng ldrs: hrd rdn over 1f out: r.o one pce) ............................ ½.7

731 Fay Eden (IRE) **(53)** *(RJHodges)* 4–9-2 ‡⁵NGwilliams (4) (nvr trbld ldrs) ............................ ½.8

775 Starchy Cove **(45)** *(BRCambidge)* 5–8-8 ‡⁵RPrice (5) (n.d) ............................ nk.9

706 Dickens Lane **(59)** *(RJHodges)* 5–9-6 ‡⁷TThompson (15) (nvr plcd to chal) ............................ 1.10

706 Miramede **(40)** *(RJHodges)* 4–8-5 ‡³TSprake (9) (swtg: spd over 2f) ............................ 1.10

706⁵ Frimley Parkson **(37)** (bl) *(PHowling)* 8–8-5 JMurray (12) (swtg: b.hind: s.s: spd 3f) ............................ 1½.12

Royal Bear **(32)** *(JMBradley)* 10–7-7⁽⁷⁾ ‡⁷BThomas (3) (spd over 2f) ............................ ½.13

594 Reach Forward **(42)** *(RJHolder)* 3–7-10 ‡⁵ATucker (10) (swtg: n.d) ............................ 1.14

906 Sea Cloud (USA) **(41)** (bl) *(MBlanshard)* 3–7-11 ‡³FNorton (7) (prom over 2f) ............................ 2½.15

906 I Broke the Rules (IRE) **(36)** *(AJChamberlain)* 3–7-9⁽¹⁾ SDawson (2) (b: n.d) ............................ 1.16

Eidolon **(35)** *(MrsNSSharpe)* 5–8-3 AShoults (1) (t.o) ............................ 10.17

**9/2** Catalani, **5/1** KLAIROVER, The Noble Oak (IRE), **7/1** Lucy Dancer (IRE), **8/1** Pendor Dancer, **10/1** Nuclear Express(op 20/1), Frimley Parkson, **16/1** Miramede, Sea Cloud (USA), **20/1** Fay Eden (IRE), **25/1** Reach Forward, Starchy Cove, **33/1** Royal Bear, Tippling (USA), Dickens Lane, **50/1** Ors. CSF £43.70, CT £182.08. Tote £8.10: £1.50 £2.40 £1.50 £1.60 (£37.70). Mr C. John Hill (BARNSTAPLE) bred by Mrs J. McMahon. 17 Rn; Bt in 3,500 gns        59.5 sec (2.5)
SF—36/44/37/42/15/37

## 1031

BADMINTON STKS (3-Y.O) £1604.00 (£444.00: £212.00)    **7f 16y**    4-30 (4-31)

704² **Hamas (IRE) (104)** (Fav) *(PTWalwyn)* 9-4 AMunro (3) (chsd ldr: led wl over 1f out: comf) ............ —1

672² Flourishing (IRE) **(91)** *(GWragg)* 8-10 ‡³FNorton (2) (hld up: rdn over 1f out: chsd wnr fnl f: no imp) ............ 2.2

862⁵ Secret Thing (USA) **(94)** *(CEBrittain)* 9-4 GCrealock (1) (swtg: led over 5f: one pce) ............ 2½.3

**2/5 HAMAS (IRE), 4/1 Secret Thing (USA), 5/1 Flourishing (IRE).** CSF £2.46, Tote £1.20 (£1.50). Mr Hamdan Al-Maktoum (LAMBOURN) bred by Hullin Co N V (International) in Ireland. 3 Rn    1m 22.9 (2.4)
SF—57/43/43

## 1032

SEVERN H'CAP (0-70) £2390.00 (£665.00: £320.00)    **7f 16y**    5-00 (5-05)

830 **Jaldi (IRE) (50)** (bl) (Fav) *(JSutcliffe)* 4–8-1 ‡⁷JTate (16) (led 6f out: sn clr: r.o wl) ............ —1

411 Charmed Knave **(50)** *(DRLaing)* 7–8-8 TyroneWilliams (7) (rdn & hdwy over 2f out: r.o ins fnl f) ............ 1½.2

809² Persian Dynasty **(44)** *(JMBradley)* 8–8-2 NAdams (10) (lw: gd hdwy fnl 2f: r.o) nk.3

909 Juvenara **(46)** *(CJHill)* 6–7-13 ‡⁵ATucker (20) (a.p: nt qckn fnl f) ............ 2.4

997³ Ain'tlifelikethat **(52)** (bl) *(TJNaughton)* 5–8-5 ‡NGwilliams (13) (dwlt: sn rcvrd: hrd rdn over 1f out: nt qckn) ............ nk.5

830 Premier Prince **(53)** *(LGCottrell)* 6–8-11 AMunro (17) (lw: hdwy fnl 2f: nt rch ldrs) ¾.6

909 Beatle Song **(64)** *(RJHodges)* 4–9-5 ‡³TSprake (22) (rdn 3f out: r.o fnl f) ............ nk.7

696 Indian Sovereign **(36)** *(RLee)* 8–7-8⁽¹⁾ EJohnson (8) (dwlt: hrd rdn over 3f out: styd on fnl 2f) ............ s.h.8

912⁵ Melodic Habit **(40)** *(MrsAKnight)* 5–7-9 ‡³FNorton (9) (prom 5f) ............ ¾.9

978⁴ Green's Stubbs **(37)** *(ABarrow)* 5–7-9 DanaMellor (19) (swtg: prom over 4f) . s.h.10

800⁵ Prepare (IRE) **(47)** *(RJHolder)* 4–7-12 ‡⁷SDrowne (2) (w ldrs 5f) ............ 1½.11

832 Dream Carrier (IRE) **(68)** *(RHannon)* 4–9-9 ‡³RPerham (18) (n.d) ............ hd.12

232 Give Me Hope (IRE) **(44)** *(GHYardley)* 4–7-11⁽⁵⁾ ‡⁵RPrice (1) (n.d) ............ ¾.13

909⁴ La Belle Vie **(65)** *(RJBaker)* 4–9-9 AClark (12) (n.d) ............ ¾.14

903★ Quinzii Martin **(49)** (v) *(DHaydnJones)* 4–8-7 WNewnes (14) (swtg: led 1f: wknd 2f out) ............ s.h.15

931⁵ Neptune's Pet **(70)** (bl) *(GLewis)* 4–9-9 ‡⁵DHarrison (11) (w ldrs tl wknd qckly 3f out) ............ hd.16

773 Treasure Court **(35)** *(PBurgoyne)* 5–7-5 RFox (15) (dwlt: a bhd) ............ hd.17

912 Cash a Million (FR) **(52)** *(PDCundell)* 4–8-10 TRogers (6) (a bhd) ............ 2½.18

Eliza Wooding **(41)** *(CJHill)* 4–7-10 ‡³DBiggs (21) (a bhd) ............ 2½.19

738 Foo Foo (IRE) **(37)** *(DMarks)* 4–7-9⁽²⁾ SDawson (3) (t.o) ............ 10.20

LONG HANDICAP: Indian Sovereign 7-2, Foo Foo (IRE) 7-2.

**7/2 JALDI (IRE)**(op 8/1), 5/1 Juvenara, 7/1 Persian Dynasty, 10/1 Ain'tlifelikethat, Premier Prince, 11/1 La Belle Vie, 12/1 Charmed Knave, Quinzii Martin(op 7/1), Prepare (IRE), Neptune's Pet(op 8/1), 14/1 Melodic Habit, 16/1 Dream Carrier (IRE), Beatle Song(op 8/1), 20/1 Cash a Million (FR), 25/1 Eliza Wooding, 50/1 Ors. CSF £48.46, CT £276.06. Tote £5.80: £2.00 £2.90 £1.60 £3.90 (£102.30). Mr Albert Finney (EPSOM) bred by Albert Finney in Ireland. 20 Rn    1m 22.5 (2)
SF—46/48/41/32/37/41

T/Plpt: £69.90 (35.95 Tckts).        KH

## 560—LEICESTER (R-H)

### Monday, May 25th [Good]

Going Allowance: St: nil sec (G); Rnd: minus 0.20 sec per fur (F)      Wind: almost nil

Stalls: high

## 1033

GROBY STKS (Mdn 3-Y.O) £2072.00 (£572.00: £272.00)    **1m 1f 218y**    2-20 (2-22)

458³ **Intent** *(HRACecil)* 9-0 WRyan (8) (led 1f: 2nd st: led 3f out: rdn out) ............ —1

804 Turgenev (IRE) *(JHMGosden)* 9-0 GHind (7) (bit bkwd: prom: 3rd st: n.m.r on rails 2f out: pulled out & r.o wl fnl f) ............ ½.2

Pippin Park (USA) *(HCandy)* 8-9 CRutter (2) (unf: scope: dwlt: hdwy over 4f out: r.o fnl f) ............ ½.3

Diamond Wedding (USA) *(NAGraham)* 8-9 JQuinn (4) (hdwy & 7th st: ev ch over 1f out: wknd 3f in & no ex) ............ nk.4

717³ Tradition (Fav) *(MajorWRHern)* 8-9 JReid (1) (trckd ldrs: 4th st: rdn 3f out: swtchd 1f out: kpt on same pce) ............ 1.5

699 Kaytura *(MHTompkins)* 8-9 PRobinson (3) (bit bkwd: last st: styd on fnl 3f: nvr able to chal) ............ 1½.6

Weeheby (USA) *(AAScott)* 8-9 ‡LNewton (6) (lw: chsd ldrs: 5th st: rdn 3f out: one pce) ............ nk.7

835 Dizzy Dame *(MRChannon)* 8-9 GBaxter (9) (nvr nr to chal) ............... 1½.8
835³ Mayaasa (USA) *(RWArmstrong)* 8-9 NDay (11) (led after 1f tl hdd 3f out: wknd
　　　qckly over 1f out) ............................................... 15.9
531 Sugar Loaf (IRE) *(NAGraham)* 8-9 SRaymont (10) (chsd ldrs: 6th st: wknd over
　　　2f out) ......................................................... 10.10
710 Alizarin *(BCMorgan)* 8-4 ‡⁵CHodgson (5) (a bhd) ........................ 10.11

**4/6** Tradition, **9/2** INTENT(3/1—11/2), **13/2** Mayaasa (USA), **12/1** Weeheby (USA), **14/1** Pippin Park (USA), **20/1** Turgenev (IRE), **25/1** Kaytura, **33/1** Dizzy Dame, Sugar Loaf (IRE), Diamond Wedding (USA), **100/1** Alizarin. CSF £79.97, Tote £5.10: £1.60 £3.00 £2.50 (£32.70). Mr K. Abdulla (NEWMARKET) bred by Juddmonte Farms. 11 Rn 　　　　　　　　　　　　　　　　　　　　　　　　2m 7.3 (4.6)
　　　　　　　　　　　　　　　　　　　　　　　　　　　　　　SF—34/33/27/26/24/21

**1034**　　　ANSTEY (S) H'CAP (3 & 4-Y.O) (0-60) £2676.80 (£744.80: £358.40)
　　　　　　　**1m 1f 218y**　　　　　　　　　　　　　　　　　　2-50 (2-52)

(Weights raised 1 lb)

575⁴ **Misty Goddess (IRE) (48)** *(MAJarvis)* 4-9-3 ‡⁷KRutter (1) (bhd: hdwy 3f out: led
　　　ins fnl f: sn pushed clr) ........................................ —1
904 Cold Shower (IRE) **(51)** *(JAGlover)* 3-8-5 ‡⁷SWilliams (16) (led 3f: 2nd st: led
　　　over 3f out: hdd & no ex ins fnl f) ............................. 1½.2
776⁶ Allimac Nomis **(39)** *(NACallaghan)* 3-8-0 PBurke (8) (hdwy 4f out: ev ch over 2f
　　　out: one pce) .................................................. 2½.3
575⁶ Drinks Party (IRE) **(35)** *(JWharton)* 4-8-4 ‡⁷GForster (10) (hdwy over 2f out: nvr
　　　able to chal) .................................................. 1½.4
800 Broughton Blues (IRE) **(36)** *(WJMusson)* 4-8-12 MWigham (18) (hdwy over 3f
　　　out: one pce appr fnl f) ........................................ s.h.5
806 Rich Pickings **(43)** *(CACyzer)* 3-8-4 JQuinn (5) (lw: hdwy 3f out: one pce appr
　　　fnl f) .......................................................... 6.6
799 Trendy Auctioneer (IRE) **(39)** (bl) *(MCPipe)* 4-9-1 GBaxter (15) (prom: 3rd st:
　　　wknd over 1f out) .............................................. 3.7
799⁶ Mystic Panther **(43)** *(RJHolder)* 4-9-5 ADicks (17) (nvr nr to chal) .......... 2.8
Kinoko **(48)** *(KWHogg)* 4-9-10 ACulhane (13) (in tch: rdn over 2f out: wknd fnl f) hd.9
696 Gemdoubleyou **(33)** *(FJordan)* 4-8-2 ‡⁷CHawksley (14) (lw: s.i.s: hdwy over 4f
　　　out: wknd over 2f out) ......................................... ¾.10
912 Set Up **(39)** *(DBurchell)* 4-8-8 ‡⁷SMulvey (6) (lw: dwlt: bhd: effrt 3f out: sn no
　　　imp) ........................................................... 1½.11
448 Lady Randolph **(43)** *(ICampbell)* 3-8-4 GHind (9) (a bhd) ................... 1.12
776 Blazing Pearl **(28)** *(JLHarris)* 4-7-13 ‡⁵LNewton (4) (prom: 6th st: sn wknd) .. 2½.13
790 Temple Island (IRE) **(30)** (bl) *(PJMakin)* 4-8-6 WRyan (7) (swtg: chsd ldrs: 4th
　　　st: wknd 2f out) ............................................... ½.14
Catel Ring (IRE) **(46)** (Fav) *(ICampbell)* 3-8-0 ‡⁷GMitchell (19) (b.hind: led after
　　　3f tl over 3f out: sn wknd) .................................... 1½.15
575 Elsharh (IRE) **(44)** *(JAGlover)* 3-8-5 CRutter (12) (a bhd) ................... 1½.16
505 Noushy **(43)** (v) *(KSBridgwater)* 4-9-5 JReid (3) (a bhd) ................... 10.17
734² Don't Worry (IRE) **(53)** *(MHTompkins)* 3-9-0 PRobinson (11) (chsd ldrs: 5th st:
　　　wknd 3f out: t.o) .............................................. 5.18
998⁶ Lime Street Lil **(30)** *(DAWilson)* 4-8-6 MTebbutt (2) (swtg: a bhd: t.o) ...... 5.19

**5/2** Catel Ring (IRE), **6/1** Broughton Blues (IRE), **8/1** Don't Worry (IRE)(op 5/1), MISTY GODDESS (IRE), **12/1** Set Up, Temple Island (IRE), Trendy Auctioneer (IRE), Cold Shower (IRE)(op 8/1), Drinks Party (IRE), **14/1** Noushy(op 8/1), **16/1** Elsharh (IRE), Lady Randolph(op 10/1), **20/1** Lime Street Lil(op 12/1), Mystic Panther, Kinoko, **25/1** Rich Pickings, Allimac Nomis, **33/1** Ors. CSF £108.42, CT £2,173.65. Tote £8.20: £2.30 £2.30 £11.30 £3.00 (55.30). Mr J. R. Good (NEWMARKET) bred by A. P. Tierney in Ireland. 19 Rn; No bid
　　　　　　　　　　　　　　　　　　　　　　　　　　　　　2m 7.9 (5.2)
　　　　　　　　　　　　　　　　　　　　　　　　　　　　SF—31/16/6/7/14/–

**1035**　　　GREAT LEICESTERSHIRE H'CAP (3-Y.O) (0-100) £7635.00 (£2280.00: £1090.00:
　　　　　　　£495.00) **1m 8y**　　　　　　　　　　　　　　　　3-25 (3-27)

(Weights raised 5 lb)

646² **Magnified (USA) (90)** *(BWHills)* 9-5 JReid (4) (hld up & plld hrd: hdwy over 2f
　　　out: led ins fnl f: pushed out) ................................ —1
510 Trial Times (USA) **(70)** *(WAO'Gorman)* 7-13 CRutter (7) (plld hrd: w ldrs: led
　　　over 2f out: hdd & no ex ins fnl f) ............................ nk.2
Congress (IRE) **(83)** (Fav) *(MRStoute)* 8-12 WRyan (5) (lw: set slow pce: qcknd
　　　½-wy: hdd over 2f out: no ex) ................................. 5.3
697⁴ Boogie Bopper (IRE) **(71)** *(MBell)* 8-0 JQuinn (1) (lw: hld up: nvr nr to chal) ... 2.4
691³ Ahbab (IRE) **(85)** *(PTWalwyn)* 9-0 GBaxter (3) (hld up in tch: no imp fnl 2f) ...... hd.5
858² Bid for Six (USA) **(88)** *(RHannon)* 9-3 PRobinson (6) (plld hrd: trckd ldrs: rdn 3f
　　　out: sn btn) ................................................... 3.6
653 Spanish Miner (USA) **(92)** *(AAScott)* 9-2 ‡⁵LNewton (2) (lw: hld up: rdn 3f out: sn
　　　btn: t.o) ...................................................... 15.7

7/4 Congress (IRE), 7/2 Bid for Six (USA)(3/1—9/2), 9/2 MAGNIFIED (USA), 15/2 Boogie Bopper (IRE), 9/1 Ahbab (IRE), 12/1 Ors. CSF £45.70, Tote £4.60: £2.10 £3.30 (£16.30). Mr K. Abdulla (LAMBOURN) bred by Juddmonte Farms Incorporated in USA. 7 Rn
1m 38.6 (3.6)
SF—51/30/28/10/23/17

---

**1036**  EVERARDS TIGER BEST BITTER CLAIMING STKS (2-Y.O) £3158.00 (£944.00: £452.00: £206.00)  **5f 218y**  3-55 (4-02)

| | | | |
|---|---|---|---|
| 786* | Nicki-J (IRE) *(RHannon)* 8-11 NDay (7) (lw: chsd ldrs: led jst ins fnl f: rdn out) . | —**1** |
| 847 | By Rubies *(BWHills)* 8-9 JReid (6) (hdwy 2f out: r.o fnl f: nt rch wnr) ................ | 3.**2** |
| 795* | Sudbury (IRE) *(Fav)* *(MHTompkins)* 8-13 PRobinson (8) (lw: chsd ldrs: rdn & kpt on fnl f) ................ | 1½.**3** |
| 323⁵ | Costa Verde *(KWHogg)* 8-9 GHind (2) (led tl jst ins fnl f: sn wknd) ........... | nk.**4** |
| 645 | Mister Blake *(WAO'Gorman)* 8-13 ‡⁵EmmaO'Gorman (9) (r.o fnl 2f: nrst fin) ...... | ½.**5** |
| | Another Kingdom *(JWharton)* 8-5 ‡⁵KRutter (4) (neat: bit bkwd: spd 3f) ............. | 5.**6** |
| 786² | Homemaker *(RJHolder)* 8-8 ADicks (3) (dwlt: rdn 3f out: sn no imp) ............... f) | hd.**7** |
| | Miss Fitness *(DrJDScargill)* 8-4 CRutter (5) (neat: gd hdwy over 2f out: wknd fnl | nk.**8** |
| | True Story (IRE) *(RHannon)* 9-2 SRaymont (11) (unf: bit bkwd: s.i.s: a bhd) ... | 1½.**9** |
| 237 | Gold Desire *(MBrittain)* 9-2 MWigham (12) (dwlt: sn rcvd: rdn & wknd 2f out) | 2½.**10** |
| 769⁴ | Ruby Cooper *(JWharton)* 8-10 WRyan (10) (chsd ldrs over 3f) ............ | ¾.**11** |
| 759 | Over the Dec *(BAMcMahon)* 8-0 ‡⁷JBramhill (1) (gd spd over 3f) ........... | 8.**12** |

3/1 Sudbury (IRE), 5/1 Ruby Cooper, By Rubies(op 3/1), 6/1 Homemaker, 7/1 NICKI-J (IRE), 12/1 Costa Verde, 16/1 Miss Fitness, 20/1 True Story (IRE), 25/1 Mister Blake, Over the Dec, Another Kingdom, 33/1 Gold Desire. CSF £38.56, Tote £7.70: £2.40 £2.10 £2.10 (£26.20). Mr Derek Joseph (MARLBOROUGH) bred by J. O'Regan in Ireland. 12 Rn
1m 13.2 (3.2)
SF—33/19/17/12/14/–

---

**1037**  TIGERS APP CE H'CAP (0-70) £2500.40 (£004.40: £333.20)  **1m 3f 183y**  4-25 (4-27)
(Weights raised 7 lb)

| | | | |
|---|---|---|---|
| 456³ | Qualitair Rhythm (IRE) (45) *(Fav)* *(ICampbell)* 4-8-3 ‡⁷GMitchell (7) (lw: 5th st: hdwy to ld 2f out: r.o wl) ................ | —**1** |
| 565⁶ | Tanoda (48) *(MBrittain)* 6-8-10 ‡³GParkin (6) (prom: 3rd st: led over 3f out to 2f out: wandered, edgd rt & one pce fnl f) ................ | 4.**2** |
| 598⁶ | Master Line (46) *(HCandy)* 11–8-4 ‡⁷SDrake (4) (lw: chsd ldrs: 4th st: nvr able chal) ................ | 10.**3** |
| 776³ | Pleasure Ahead (40) *(MDixon)* 5–8-2 ‡³TWilson (1) (led 6f: 2nd st: wknd over 2f out) ................ | 6.**4** |
| 800 | Shoehorn (59) (bl) *(MCPipe)* 5–9-7 ‡³EHusband (3) (dwlt: sn prom: led 6f out tl over 3f out: sn wknd) ................ | 7.**5** |
| 273 | Rarfy's Dream (40) *(JEBanks)* 4–8-5 LNewton (5) (lw: dwlt: 6th st: bhd fnl 3f: t.o) | 12.**6** |
| | Tophard (40) *(RLee)* 6–8-2 ‡³CHawksley (2) (t.o fnl 7f) ................ | 2½.**7** |

3/1 QUALITAIR RHYTHM (IRE), 4/1 Pleasure Ahead, 5/1 Rarfy's Dream, Master Line, Tanoda, 6/1 Shoehorn, 20/1 Tophard. CSF £16.90, Tote £4.20: £2.00 £2.50 (£11.50). Mr M. J. Spore (NEWMARKET) bred by Brendan Powell in Ireland. 7 Rn
2m 33.9 (5.1)
SF—18/13/–/–/–/–

---

**1038**  LIONESS STKS (Mdn 2-Y.O.F) £2072.00 (£572.00: £272.00)  **5f 218y**  4-55 (4-58)

| | | | |
|---|---|---|---|
| | Mystic Goddess (USA) *(MRStoute)* 8-11 PD'Arcy (6) (gd sort: chsd ldrs: led 2f out: qcknd clr appr fnl f: easily) ................ | —**1** |
| 721⁴ | Polar Moon *(BAMcMahon)* 8-11 GHind (5) (rdn & hdwy 2f out: r.o fnl f: no ch w wnr) ................ | 4.**2** |
| 852⁴ | Bichette *(RHannon)* 8-11 JReid (3) (led 4f: one pce) ................ | hd.**3** |
| | Walsham Witch *(MHTompkins)* 8-11 PRobinson (9) (leggy: unf: in tch: kpt on fnl 2f) ................ | 1½.**4** |
| | Helvellyn (USA) *(Fav)* *(HRACecil)* 8-11 WRyan (7) (scope: dwlt: effrt & rn green 2f out: nvr able to chal) ................ | nk.**5** |
| 859⁵ | Trundley Wood *(GAPritchard-Gordon)* 8-11 WHood (1) (chsd ldrs: no hdwy fnl 2f) ................ | s.h.**6** |
| | Touch N' Glow *(RHannon)* 8-11 SRaymont (8) (lt-f: dwlt: nvr plcd to chal) ...... | 2½.**7** |
| | Umhambi *(BWHills)* 8-11 GBaxter (2) (leggy: bit bkwd: spd over 3f) ................ | 3½.**8** |
| | Desirable Miss *(MBrittain)* 8-11 MWigham (4) (lt-f: unf: spd 3f) ................ | ¾.**9** |

Evens Helvellyn (USA), 5/2 Bichette, 8/1 MYSTIC GODDESS (USA)(op 4/1), Polar Moon(op 5/1), 14/1 Walsham Witch(op 8/1), 16/1 Trundley Wood, Umhambi(op 8/1), 20/1 Touch N' Glow, 33/1 Desirable Miss. CSF £67.88, Tote £7.40: £2.10 £1.70 £1.40 (£19.80). Cheveley Park Stud (NEWMARKET) bred by Cheveley Park Stud in USA. 9 Rn
1m 13.6 (3.6)
SF—25/9/8/2/1/–

---

T/Plpt: £104.90 (21.9 Tckts).

Dk

## LEICESTER (R-H)
### Tuesday, May 26th [Good, Good to firm patches]
Going Allowance: St: minus 0.10 sec; Rnd: minus 0.20 sec (F)          Wind: mod half against

Stalls: high

**1039**    E.B.F. WOODHOUSE EAVES STKS (Mdn 2-Y.O.C & G) £2807.00 (£777.00: £371.00)
            5f 2y                                                    2-15 (2-18)

807 **Fierro** (Fav) *(CEBrittain)* 9-0 MRoberts (1) (mde all: sn clr: r.o wl ins fnl f) .......... —1
    Birchwood Sun *(RHollinshead)* 9-0 GHind (7) (cmpt: bit bkwd: dwlt: hdwy 2f
      out: r.o wl ins fnl f) ......................................................................... 1.2
    Soldiers Bay *(LordHuntingdon)* 9-0 WRSwinburn (8) (scope: bit bkwd: chsd
      ldrs: effrt u.p over 1f out: kpt on) ..................................................... 1.3
    Walnut Burl (IRE) *(LJHolt)* 9-0 JReid (9) (w'like: leggy: lw: dwlt: hdwy 2f out: nrst
      fin) ................................................................................................. 1½.4
867 Nut Bush *(NACallaghan)* 9-0 AMcGlone (3) (prom: rdn 2f out: wknd fnl f) ........ hd.5
    Awestruck *(WJHaggas)* 9-0 MHills (6) (lt-f: unf: chsd ldrs ovr 3f) .................. 2½.6
    No Extras (IRE) *(JSutcliffe)* 9-0 BRouse (4) (lt-f: unf: hdwy ½-wy: rdn 2f out: nt
      trble ldrs) ....................................................................................... 2.7
    Saseedo (USA) *(WAO'Gorman)* 9-0 RCochrane (5) (gd sort: chsd wnr 3f: sn
      rdn & wknd) .................................................................................... 2.8
    Junction Twentytwo *(CDBroad)* 9-0 MWigham (2) (leggy: lt-f: s.s: a outpcd &
      bhd) ................................................................................................. 5.9

**100/30** FIERRO, **7/2** Saseedo (USA), Soldiers Bay, **11/2** Awestruck, **9/1** Walnut Burl (IRE), **10/1** Nut Bush, **14/1**
No Extras (IRE)(8/1—16/1), **25/1** Birchwood Sun, **50/1** Junction Twentytwo. CSF £63.02, Tote £3.90: £1.70
£5.50 £1.70 (£32.30). Sheikh Mohammed (NEWMARKET) bred by Sheikh Mohammed bin Rashid al Maktoum. 9
Rn                                                                      61.5 sec (2.8)
                                                                      SF—34/30/26/20/19/9

**1040**    TOTE EACH WAY (S) STKS (3-Y.O) £2539.60 (£705.60: £338.80)
            5f 218y                                                  2-45 (2-49)

894⁴ **Our Rita** (Jt-Fav) *(PAKelleway)* 8-4 PRobinson (14) (hdwy ½-wy: led appr fnl f:
      r.o) ................................................................................................. —1
620 Fisianna *(ARDavison)* 8-4 CandyMorris (9) (swtg: hdwy over 2f out: rdn &
      unable qckn fnl f) ............................................................................. 2.2
884 She's Special (71) (v) (Jt-Fav) *(MissLAPerratt)* 8-9 WRSwinburn (4) (lw: hld up:
      gd hdwy appr fnl f: fin wl) ................................................................. s.h.3
949⁵ Palacegate Gold (IRE) (55) *(RJHodges)* 9-0 WCarson (6) (chsd ldrs: rdn over
      1f out: one pce) ............................................................................... 1½.4
684 Double Feature (IRE) (63) *(MrsJRRamsden)* 9-0 JReid (13) (hld up: effrt appr
      fnl f: rdn & no ex fnl f) ..................................................................... s.h.5
939 Digger Doyle (59) (v) *(CNAllen)* 8-2 ‡⁷GForster (15) (a.p: led appr fnl f: sn hdd:
      eased whn btn fnl f) ......................................................................... hd.6
765³ Super-Sub (54) *(GFleming)* 8-5⁽¹⁾ RCochrane (3) (spd 4f) ........................ 1½.7
    Red Ink (54) *(JSutcliffe)* 8-9 BRouse (2) (swtg: dwlt: sme hdwy fnl 2f: nvr nrr) .. ¾.8
719 Tagetes (61) *(JPearce)* 7-13 ‡⁵RPrice (10) (prom: hrd rdn 2f out: sn wknd) ..... 1½.9
295⁴ Thursley (55) *(HJCollingridge)* 9-0 JQuinn (18) (hdwy ½-wy: wknd over 1f out)1½.10
765 Mississippi Queen (40) *(MrsNMacauley)* 8-4 CRutter (11) (s.i.s: effrt 2f out: sn
      outpcd) ............................................................................................ ½.11
    Cledeschamps *(MWEllerby)* 8-4 NConnorton (5) (small: unf: n.d) ................. 1½.12
863 Spareathought *(CNAllen)* 8-4 GBardwell (8) (led tl appr fnl f: sn rdn & wknd) 1½.13
195 Moniaive *(WClay)* 8-9 JWilliams (17) (n.d) ........................................... ¾.14
    Missal (IRE) (47) *(PatMitchell)* 7-11 ‡⁷RTurner (7) (nt grwn: n.d) ................ 1½.15
719 Pink'n Black (IRE) (65) *(GBlum)* 8-9 GCarter (1) (w ldrs over 3f) ............... ¾.16
    Tender Monarch (IRE) (35) *(PJBevan)* 8-9 SWhitworth (16) (still unf: swtg: t.o) 6.17
    Princess Annie (41) *(GBlum)* 8-4 AShoults (12) (swtg: bhd fr ½-wy: t.o) ........ 10.18

**3/1** OUR RITA(op 5/1), She's Special, **8/1** Digger Doyle(tchd 25/1), Tagetes, Double Feature (IRE)(op 4/1), **11/1**
Palacegate Gold (IRE)(op 7/1), **14/1** Super-Sub(10/1—20/1), Pink'n Black (IRE), Thursley, **16/1**
Spareathought(12/1—33/1), **20/1** Red Ink(op 10/1), **33/1** Cledeschamps, Princess Annie, **50/1** Ors. CSF
£144.83, Tote £5.10: £1.50 £25.50 £1.60 (£662.40). Mr T. Brady (NEWMARKET) bred by Terry Brady. 18 Rn;
No bid                                                                  1m 13.7 (3.7)
                                                                      SF—4/-/-/-/-/-/-

**1041**    TOTE CREDIT H'CAP (3-Y.O) (0-70) £2973.00 (£828.00: £399.00)
            1m 1f 218y                                               3-15 (3-19)

942² **Naseer** (USA) (55) (Fav) *(NACallaghan)* 7-13 ‡⁷JTate (11) (a.p: 4th st: ev ch
      whn sltly hmpd ins fnl f: r.o: fin 2nd, nk: awrdd r) ................ —1

| | | |
|---|---|---|
| 896 | Admirals Secret (USA) **(55)** *(CFWall)* 8-6 NDay (18) (a.p: 3rd st: rdn, wnt lft & led wl ins fnl f: all out: fin 1st: disq: plcd 2nd) | **2** |
| 604⁵ | Don't Forsake Me **(60)** *(DMorley)* 8-11 LDettori (2) (hdwy ent st: styd on u.p ins fnl f) | 2¹/₂.**3** |
| 702⁴ | Murasil (USA) **(69)** *(MajorWRHern)* 9-6 WCarson (15) (lw: led tl wl ins fnl f) | 2.**4** |
| 788⁴ | Dubitable **(61)** *(HCandy)* 8-12 CRutter (16) (hdwy ¹/₂-wy: 6th st: styd on ins fnl f) | 1¹/₂.**5** |
| 787⁴ | Edgeaway **(68)** *(JWHills)* 9-5 MHills (19) (chsd ldrs: 5th st: rdn 2f out: nt pce to chal) | 2¹/₂.**6** |
| 804 | Brier Creek (USA) **(74)** *(JHMGosden)* 9-11 RCochrane (9) (hld up: effrt 2f out: nt rch ldrs) | ¹/₂.**7** |
| 804 | Bentico **(60)** *(MAJarvis)* 8-11 GCrealock (12) (styd on fnl 2f: nvr nrr) | 3¹/₂.**8** |
| 789⁵ | Rolling the Bones (USA) **(70)** *(JRFanshawe)* 9-7 WRSwinburn (14) (chsd ldr: 2nd st: eased whn btn fnl f) | 1¹/₂.**9** |
| | Tempelhof (IRE) **(65)** *(JWHills)* 9-2 RHills (10) (hld up: hdwy 3f out: sn rdn: nt rch ldrs) | nk.**10** |
| 699 | Laughing Falcon **(60)** *(JLDunlop)* 8-11 JReid (13) (bit bkwd: in tch 7f) | 2.**11** |
| 498⁶ | Cappahoosh (IRE) **(60)** *(HJCollingridge)* 8-11 JQuinn (3) (a mid div) | ³/₄.**12** |
| 519 | Brotherlyaffection **(52)** *(RHollinshead)* 7-10 ‡⁷MHumphries (1) (bhd: effrt u.p over 3f out: wknd 2f out) | 1.**13** |
| 698 | Chummy's Child (IRE) **(62)** *(BWHills)* 8-13 PatEddery (4) (chsd ldrs: 7th st: hrd rdn 3f out: sn wknd) | 3¹/₂.**14** |
| 868² | Liability Order **(72)** *(RBoss)* 9-9 MRoberts (5) (lw: a in rr) | 1¹/₂.**15** |
| | Borram (IRE) **(65)** *(DNicholson)* 9-2 JWilliams (8) (bit bkwd: s.i.s: a in rr: t.o) | 6.**16** |
| | Courtenay Bee **(68)** *(WJarvis)* 9-5 PaulEddery (17) (bit bkwd: a bhd: t.o) | 8.**17** |
| | Vital Voltage (IRE) **(54)** *(MWEllerby)* 8-5 NConnorton (7) (a bhd: t.o) | 12.**18** |
| | Findlays Choice **(59)** *(MJRyan)* 8-7 ‡³DBiggs (6) (a bhd: t.o) | 20.**19** |

*Stewards Enquiry: Admirals Secret disq. (interference to Naseer (USA) ins fnl f).*

**6/1** NASEER (USA)(op 4/1), **7/1** Murasil (USA), Rolling the Bones (USA), **8/1** Chummy's Child (IRE)(10/1—6/1), Brier Creek (USA), Admirals Secret (USA)(tchd 14/1), **10/1** Don't Forsake Me, **14/1** Dubitable, Edgeaway, Liability Order, **16/1** Courtenay Bee, Laughing Falcon(op 10/1), Cappahoosh (IRE), **25/1** Bentico, **33/1** Tempelhof (IRE), Findlays Choice, **50/1** Ors. CSF £53.10, CT £446.94. Tote £5.90: £2.60 £2.70 £3.00 £2.10 (£90.50). Mr N. A. Callaghan (NEWMARKET) bred by Universal Stables in USA. 19 Rn    2m 7.4 (4.7)
SF—17/25/25/30/19/21

---

**1042**   TOTE STKS (3-Y.O.F) £2846.00 (£848.00: £404.00: £182.00)
**5f 218y**   3-45 (3-47)

| | | |
|---|---|---|
| 876⁴ | **Absolutely Nuts (71)** *(BAMcMahon)* 8-11 LDettori (6) (mde all: qcknd ent fnl f: sn clr) | —**1** |
| | Forest Fairy **(80)** *(RBoss)* 8-7 MRoberts (3) (racd wd: chsd ldrs: rdn appr fnl f: one pce) | 5.**2** |
| 691⁴ | Mathaayl (USA) **(89)** (Jt-Fav) *(HThomsonJones)* 8-10 RHills (4) (s.s: hdwy 2f out: nt pce to chal) | 1¹/₂.**3** |
| | Parisien Singer **(85)** (Jt-Fav) *(IABalding)* 8-12 RCochrane (5) (b.nr hind: bit bkwd: w wnr tl wknd appr fnl f) | 1.**4** |

**7/4** Parisien Singer, Mathaayl (USA), **3/1** ABSOLUTELY NUTS(7/2—9/2), **5/1** Forest Fairy. CSF £14.51, Tote £3.80 (£4.30). Mr J. W. Hall (TAMWORTH) bred by M. P. Allen. 4 Rn    1m 15 (5)

---

**1043**   TOTE PLACEPOT STKS (3-Y.O) £3590.00 (£1070.00: £510.00: £230.00)
**7f 9y**   4-15 (4-15)

| | | |
|---|---|---|
| | **Pater Noster (USA)** *(MrsJCecil)* 9-2 PaulEddery (1) (hld up: led over 1f out: sn clr) | —**1** |
| | Mojave **(110)** (Fav) *(MRStoute)* 9-8 WRSwinburn (2) (bit bkwd: led: shkn up appr fnl f: hdd over 1f out: eased whn btn) | 4.**2** |
| 918 | Bee Dee Ell (USA) **(51)** *(MissLAPerratt)* 8-11 RCochrane (3) (prom over 4f: sn lost pl) | 12.**3** |
| | Specialist Dream (IRE) **(51)** *(LJCodd)* 8-11 VSmith (4) (bkwd: bhd & pushed along ¹/₂-wy: wknd u.p fnl 2f) | ³/₄.**4** |

**8/13** Mojave, **6/4** PATER NOSTER (USA), **50/1** Bee Dee Ell (USA), **100/1** Specialist Dream (IRE). CSF £2.55, Tote £2.10 (£1.10). Mr Martin Myers (NEWMARKET) bred by Stud Crown Ltd in USA. 4 Rn    1m 27.7 (5.4)
SF—10/4/–/–

---

**1044**   TOTE DUAL FORECAST H'CAP (0-70) £3150.00 (£875.00: £420.00)
**1m 3f 183y**   (Weights raised 3 lb)   4-45 (4-48)

| | | |
|---|---|---|
| | **Daisy Girl (50)** (Fav) *(JMackie)* 6-9-0 WCarson (8) (bit bkwd: hld up in rr: gd hdwy to ld appr fnl f: sn clr) | —**1** |

702⁶ Bold Resolution (IRE) **(51)** *(CACyzer)* 4–9-1 GCarter (14) (lw: wl bhd tl r.o fnl 2f: no ch w wnr) .......................... 6.2

Miss Witch **(54)** *(HCandy)* 4–8-11 ‡⁷AntoinetteArmes (3) (a.p: 2nd st: led over 3f out tl over 2f out: one pce) .......................... 1½.3

726 Thomas Leng **(60)** *(MBrittain)* 7–9-10 RCochrane (5) (b: lw: hld up: r.o appr fnl f: nvr nrr) .......................... 1½.4

800 Full Quiver **(53)** (v) *(MrsBarbaraWaring)* 7–9-3 NHowe (13) (b.off hind: in tch: effrt 2f out: styd on) .......................... 1½.5

895² Marchman **(51)** *(JSKing)* 7–9-1 TRogers (7) (dwlt: sn chsng ldrs: 6th st: led over 2f out tl appr fnl f: grad wknd) .......................... 1½.6

377³ Sharp Top **(48)** *(MJRyan)* 4–8-12 PRobinson (1) (prom: 3rd st: wknd wl over 1f out) .......................... 1.7

736 Mamalama **(38)** *(LJHolt)* 4–8-2 AMcGlone (6) (bit bkwd: in tch: no hdwy fnl 3f) 1½.8

598* Easy Purchase **(59)** *(RJHolder)* 5–9-9 JWilliams (2) (s.s: nvr nr to chal) .......................... 2½.9

702 Singing Reply (USA) **(40)** *(DMarks)* 4–8-1 ‡³DBiggs (4) (a in rr) .......................... 1½.10

Cold Blow **(45)** *(JWharton)* 5–8-9 AShoults (12) (bit bkwd: chsd ldrs: 5th st: wknd 3f out: t.o) .......................... 10.11

Casilla **(39)** *(HCandy)* 4–8-3 CRutter (10) (bit bkwd: prom: 4th st: wknd over 3f out: t.o) .......................... 7.12

964 Butlers Wharf **(47)** *(MrKWHogg)* 7–8-11 GHind (15) (s.s: a bhd: t.o) .......................... 3.13

737⁵ Chez Polly **(36)** (v) *(PRHedger)* 6–8-0 GBardwell (11) (led tl hdd & wknd over 3f out: t.o) .......................... 12.14

Hasty Spark **(40)** *(CFWall)* 4–8-4 JQuinn (9) (lw: t.o) .......................... 30.15

**9/2** DAISY GIRL, **5/1** Bold Resolution (IRE), **11/2** Marchman, **13/2** Easy Purchase, **9/1** Sharp Top, **11/1** Full Quiver, **12/1** Miss Witch, **14/1** Thomas Leng, **16/1** Mamalama(12/1—20/1), Hasty Spark, **20/1** Singing Reply (USA), **25/1** Casilla, **33/1** Chez Polly, **66/1** Ors. CSF £25.59, CT £233.43. Tote £4.40: £2.30 £2.60 £2.20 (£15.40). Mr S. Taberner (CHURCH BROUGHTON) bred by S. Taberner. 15 Rn   2m 32.3 (3.5)

SF—41/30/23/33/23/18

T/Plpt: £258.80 (16.25 Tckts).      IM

---

## 613—REDCAR (L-H)

### Monday, May 25th [Good to firm, Firm patches]

Going Allowance: minus 0.20 sec per fur (F)        Wind: almost nil

Stalls: high

### 1045      SANDHILLS CLAIMING STKS    £2108.40 (£582.40: £277.20)    **5f**    2-05 (2-06)

550⁵ Plain Fact **(80)** (Fav) *(SirMarkPrescott)* 7–9-3 GDuffield (4) (trckd ldrs: led over 1f out: qcknd: comf) .......................... —1

998⁵ Spring High **(30)** (bl) *(KTIvory)* 5–8-9 GBardwell (3) (led tl hdd over 1f out: kpt on one pce) .......................... 2½.2

Lord Magester (FR) *(MrsGRReveley)* 5–9-6 KFallon (1) (cl up: drvn along over 2f out: wknd over 1f out) .......................... 6.3

516 Midnight Lass **(47)** *(WJPearce)* 4–8-7 LCharnock (2) (spd 3f: sn btn) .......................... 10.4

**1/8** PLAIN FACT(op 1/5), **12/1** Spring High, **14/1** Lord Magester (FR), **16/1** Midnight Lass. CSF £2.48, Tote £1.10 (£1.80). Mr W. E. Sturt (NEWMARKET) bred by Clanville Lodge Stud. 4 Rn; Plain Fact clmd B Ramsden £8,259      58.3 sec (1.6)

SF—51/33/19/–

### 1046      SPRING BANK HOLIDAY AUCTION STKS (Mdn 2-Y.O) £2284.80 (£632.80: £302.40)    **5f**    2-35 (2-37)

886² Willshe Gan (Fav) *(DenysSmith)* 8-4 KFallon (9) (lw: mde all: shkn up over 1f out: r.o) .......................... —1

Sweetings Scampy (IRE) *(MHEasterby)* 8-4 MBirch (3) (unf: lw: chsd ldrs: styd on wl fnl f) .......................... 2.2

Spark (IRE) *(CWCElsey)* 7-10 ‡⁵SMaloney (5) (leggy: unf: a chsng ldrs: kpt on fnl f) .......................... s.h.3

Forest Flyer *(MBrittain)* 8-1 GBardwell (11) (small: neat: lw: cl up tl rdn & btn appr fnl f) .......................... 2½.4

Danny Blue (IRE) *(PAKelleway)* 8-6 GCarter (2) (cmpt: unf: lw: chsd ldrs tl rdn & btn over 1f out) .......................... 2.5

I'M a Dreamer (IRE) *(WWHaigh)* 8-6 DaleGibson (7) (w'like: scope: bit bkwd: hdwy ½-wy: nvr plcd to chal) .......................... ½.6

Emmandee *(MWEasterby)* 8-6 TLucas (8) (w'like: leggy: scope: bit bkwd: s.i.s: hdwy ½-wy: nvr nr to chal) .......................... s.h.7

793² Pine Ridge Lad (IRE) *(WJPearce)* 9-1 DNicholls (10) (prom tl grad wknd fnl 2f) ½.8

Moonshine Dancer *(MrsGRReveley)* 8-12 ‡3JFanning (6) (cmpt: dwlt: n.d) ......... **5.9**
Beat the Bagman (IRE) *(WJPearce)* 8-9 LCharnock (1) (cmpt: s.s: a bhd) ...... hd.**10**
Covent Garden Girl *(MWEasterby)* 8-1 GDuffield (4) (w'like: bkwd: s.i.s: a bhd) 2½.**11**

**Evens** WILLSHE GAN, **7/2** Danny Blue (IRE), **9/2** Pine Ridge Lad (IRE)(op 3/1), **14/1** Moonshine Dancer(op 8/1), **16/1** I'M a Dreamer (IRE), **20/1** Sweetings Scampy (IRE)(op 10/1), Covent Garden Girl, **25/1** Beat the Bagman (IRE), Emmandee, Spark (IRE), **66/1** Forest Flyer. CSF £22.29, Tote £2.30: £1.20 £3.00 £4.20 (£20.30). Mr Hamish Alexander (BISHOP AUCKLAND) bred by H. Alexander and R. E. Sangster. 11 Rn     59.1 sec (2.4)
SF—22/14/5/–/–/–

**1047**     ZETLAND GOLD CUP (H'cap) (0-115) £21930.00 (£6540.00: £3120.00: £555.00 each)
1¼m                                                                                           3-05 (3-07)
(Weights raised 6 lb)

**Rose Alto (81)** *(JRFanshawe)* 4-9-0 GDuffield (4) (lw: a cl up: led over 2f out: hld on gamely cl home) ....................................................................... —**1**
816² Asaasy (USA) **(94)** *(MRStoute)* 3–8-12 RHills (6) (lw: trckd ldrs: effrt over 2f out: styd on to chal wl ins fnl f: nt qckn nr fin) ........................... nk.**2**
681 Westholme (USA) **(76)** *(MHEasterby)* 4-8-9 MBirch (1) (hld up: effrt 4f out: n.m.r: styd on wl nr fin) .................................................... 1½.**3**
657⁵ Lucky Guest **(91)** *(Fav)* *(JLDunlop)* 5–9-10 LPiggott (7) (lw: cl up: chal over 3f out: nt qckn ins fnl f) ...................................................... ½.**4**
854² Line Drummer (USA) **(78)** *(PAKelleway)* 4-8-11 GCarter (8) (b: led tl hdd over 2f out: r.o one pce) ................................................. d.h.**4**
887⁶ Star Connection **(67)** *(RMWhitaker)* 4–7-11 ‡3JFanning (5) (hld up: effrt over 4f out: nt pce to chal) ........................................... 2.**6**
692 Self Expression **(88)** *(IABalding)* 4–9-4 ‡3SO'Gorman (2) (hld up: effrt over 3f out: wknd 2f out) ........................................... 15.**7**
657³ Myfontaine **(71)** *(KTIvory)* 5–8-4 GBardwell (3) (hld up & bhd: lost tch fnl 3f) .. 1½.**8**

**2/1** Lucky Guest, **11/4** Asaasy (USA), **9/2** Westholme (USA), **8/1** Self Expression, **9/1** Myfontaine, **10/1** ROSE ALTO, **12/1** Line Drummer (USA), **16/1** Star Connection. CSF £37.60, CT £133.50. Tote £0.00: £1.00 £1.70 £1.20 (£15.90). T. & J. Vestey (NEWMARKET) bred by T. R. G. Vestey. 8 Rn     2m 4.6 (2.1)
SF—59/56/50/64/51/33

**1048**     GLAISDALE H'CAP (3-Y.O) (0-80) £2607.80 (£720.80: £343.40)
1¾m 19y                                                                                     3-35 (3-35)

369 **Tricycle (IRE) (42)** *(JWWatts)* 7-8 GBardwell (5) (lw: trckd ldr: led 4f out: edgd rt 2f out: r.o) ....................................................................... —**1**
700⁵ Inan (USA) **(69)** *(JLDunlop)* 9-7 LPiggott (1) (trckd ldrs gng wl: smooth hdwy to chal over 2f out: hmpd & hung rt: rdn: fnd nil) ................... 1½.**2**
896⁵ Amatorial **(65)** *(Fav)* *(SirMarkPrescott)* 9-3 GDuffield (2) (hld up: slipped & lost pl st: hdwy 2f out: hung lft: nt qckn fnl f: fin lame) .............. ¾.**3**
902² Five to Seven (USA) **(65)** *(SGNorton)* 9-3 AProud (3) (lw: trckd ldrs tl rdn & btn 3f out) ....................................................................... 6.**4**
810 Mr Elk **(47)** *(MrsGRReveley)* 7-10 ‡3JFanning (6) (lw: prom tl rdn appr st: sn wknd) ....................................................................... 25.**5**
Northern Emperor (IRE) **(47)** *(MHEasterby)* 7-8 ‡5SMaloney (4) (led tl hdd 4f out) ....................................................................... 3.**6**

*Stewards Enquiry: Obj. to Tricycle (IRE) by Piggott overruled.*

**5/4** Amatorial, **9/4** Inan (USA), **5/2** Five to Seven (USA), **16/1** Northern Emperor (IRE)(op 10/1), **20/1** TRICYCLE (IRE)(op 10/1), **33/1** Mr Elk. CSF £62.90, Tote £17.20: £5.40 £1.50 (£21.40). Duke of Sutherland (RICHMOND) bred by D. Maher in Ireland. 6 Rn     3m 4 (6.4)

**1049**     BILLINGHAM STKS (Mdn 3-Y.O) £2245.60 (£621.60: £296.80)     1m 1f     4-05 (4-07)

693² **Thamestar (IRE)** *(Fav)* *(JLDunlop)* 9-0 LPiggott (3) (trckd ldr tl lost pl ent st: nt clr run & swtchd over 1f out: qcknd to ld nr fin) ................... —**1**
816 Pyare Square **(74)** *(IABalding)* 8-11 ‡3SO'Gorman (2) (led: rdn over 3f out: hdd & no ex wl ins fnl f) ....................................................... ½.**2**
490⁴ Canaan Lane **(75)** *(AHarrison)* 9-0 KFallon (4) (hld up: hdwy to chal 3f out: nt qckn ins fnl f) ....................................................... 2½.**3**
Olliver Duckett *(PCalver)* 9-0 DaleGibson (1) (w'like: hld up: stumbled bdly after 2f: qcknd to chal 5f out: wknd 2f out) ................... 6.**4**

**1/2** THAMESTAR (IRE), **9/4** Pyare Square, **10/1** Canaan Lane, **20/1** Olliver Duckett. CSF £2.03, Tote £1.40 (£1.40). Mr J. E. Nash (ARUNDEL) bred by Newton Stud Farm Inc in Ireland. 4 Rn     1m 55.8 (6.8)

**1050**     DUNDAS H'CAP (0-80) £2655.40 (£734.40: £350.20)     6f     4-35 (4-37)

794 **Densben (57)** *(DenysSmith)* 8–8-5 KFallon (7) (lw: trckd ldrs: led over 1f out: r.o wl) ....................................................................... —**1**

768³ Ringland (USA) **(77)** *(PCHaslam)* 4–9-11 LPiggott (4) (chsd ldrs: sn pushed along: ev ch over 1f out: r.o) ...................... 2.2

885⁴ Red Rosein **(80)** (Fav) *(CaptJWilson)* 6–10-0 GCarter (8) (b.off hind: hld up: gd hdwy to chal over 1f out: nt qckn) ...................... 2.3

725⁶ Sammy Slew (USA) **(70)** *(SGNorton)* 3–8-3 ‡⁵SMaloney (2) (w ldrs: led 2f out tl over 1f out: no ex) ...................... 1½.4

918⁵ Jovial Kate (USA) **(45)** *(BEllison)* 5–7-4 ‡³JFanning (3) (led tl hdd 2f out: grad wknd) ...................... 2.5

885² Most Surprising (IRE) **(55)** *(RMWhitaker)* 3–7-7 DaleGibson (1) (lw: unruly stalls: chsd ldrs tl rdn & wknd wl over 1f out) ...................... 3½.6

535⁵ Here Comes a Star **(53)** (bl) *(JMCarr)* 4–8-1 SMorris (6) (hld up: hdwy to chal 2f out: sn rdn & btn) ...................... ½.7

535 Minizen Music (IRE) **(45)** *(MBrittain)* 4–7-7 LCharnock (9) (chsd ldrs over 3f: sn wknd) ...................... 3.8

*219* Lets Go Sabo **(47)** *(DWChapman)* 4–7-9 SWood (5) (s.i.s: a outpcd & bhd) ...... 8.9

LONG HANDICAP: Jovial Kate (USA) 7-6, Most Surprising (IRE) 7-5, Minizen Music (IRE) 6-13.

**2/1** Red Rosein, **4/1** Most Surprising (IRE), **13/2** DENSBEN, **7/1** Ringland (USA), **8/1** Jovial Kate (USA)(op 5/1), **17/2** Here Comes a Star, **9/1** Sammy Slew (USA), **25/1** Minizen Music (IRE), **33/1** Lets Go Sabo. CSF £46.95, CT £112.04. Tote £6.90: £2.20 £3.00 £1.50 (£19.30). Mrs Janet M. Pike (BISHOP AUCKLAND) bred by D. W. Pike.
9 Rn    1m 10.4 (1.1)
SF—45/57/52/21/–/–

T/Plpt: £29.40 (75.4 Tckts).    AA

# REDCAR (L-H)
## Tuesday, May 26th [Firm, Good to firm patches]
Going Allowance: minus 0.20 sec per fur (F)    Wind: almost nil

Stalls: high

**1051**    DORMANSTOWN H'CAP (0-70) £2553.00 (£708.00: £339.00)    **1m 1f**    2-00 (2-00)

763³ **Sweet Mignonette (40)** (Fav) *(MrsGRReveley)* 4–8-4 KDarley (8) (lw: mid div: shkn up ent st: led appr fnl f: r.o wl) ...................... —1

702 Marjons Boy **(30)** (bl) *(CDBroad)* 5–7-8⁽¹⁾ NCarlisle (1) (hdwy 3f out: r.o fnl f: nrst fin) ...................... 2½.2

617 Major Ivor **(59)** *(MrsGRReveley)* 7–9-9 MBirch (2) (lw: trckd ldrs: rdn to chal 1f out: nt qckn) ...................... nk.3

696² Sooty Tern **(47)** *(JMBradley)* 5–8-11 NAdams (12) (lw: a.p: led over 2f out tl over 1f out: one pce) ...................... 3.4

469 Tempering **(55)** *(DWChapman)* 6–9-5 SWood (9) (swtg: led tl hdd over 2f out: grad wknd) ...................... 2½.5

974² Sharquin **(37)** *(MBrittain)* 5–7-10 ‡⁵SMaloney (4) (lw: trckd ldrs: effrt & chal 3f out: nt r.o fnl 2f) ...................... s.h.6

498 Miss Kingfisher (USA) **(54)** *(SGNorton)* 3–7-11 ‡⁷OPears (3) (in tch: nt qckn fnl 3f) ...................... 2.7

364 Wsom (IRE) **(53)** *(JMCarr)* 4–9-3 SMorris (11) (nvr trbld ldrs) ...................... ½.8

965 Sinclair Lad (IRE) **(60)** *(RHollinshead)* 4–9-10 WRyan (5) (bhd: nt clr run 2f out: nvr nr to chal) ...................... 5.9

765* Katie's Dream (IRE) **(54)** *(PSFelgate)* 3–8-4 JLowe (6) (a outpcd & bhd) .......... 5.10

883⁴ Blue Grit **(39)** (bl) *(MDods)* 6–8-3 GDuffield (10) (lw: prom tl wknd 3f out) ..... 2½.11

798⁶ Legitim **(43)** *(JMJefferson)* 3–7-4 ‡³JFanning (7) (cl up: rdn 4f out: sn wknd) 2½.12

LONG HANDICAP: Marjons Boy 7-5, Legitim 7-3.

**7/4** SWEET MIGNONETTE, **11/2** Sooty Tern, **6/1** Sharquin, **7/1** Katie's Dream (IRE), **10/1** Blue Grit, **20/1** Marjons Boy, Miss Kingfisher (USA)(op 12/1), Sinclair Lad (IRE), **25/1** Major Ivor, Tempering, **50/1** Ors. CSF £31.37, CT £576.26. Tote £2.60: £1.40 £3.80 £2.90 (£26.30). Mr M. J. Ogden (SALTBURN) bred by Countess of Durham.
12 Rn    1m 51.6 (2.6)
SF—24/6/34/13/13/–

**1052**    WILTON (S) H'CAP (3-Y.O) (0-60) £2441.60 (£677.60: £324.80)    **1¼m**    2-30 (2-33)

603 **Gay Ming (36)** *(RHollinshead)* 7-4 ‡⁷AGarth (10) (outpcd & bhd 4f out: hdwy 2f out: r.o wl to ld cl home) ...................... —1

457 Reach for Glory **(55)** *(RMWhitaker)* 9-2 ACulhane (6) (bhd & swtchd over 3f out: r.o wl to chal wl ins fnl f: no ex nr fin) ...................... hd.2

567 Dots Dee **(33)** *(JMBradley)* 7-8⁽¹⁾ NAdams (8) (hdwy 4f out: led 2f out: hung lft: ct cl home) ...................... nk.3

806⁶ Elsa **(42)** *(RJHolder)* 7-10 ‡⁷SDrowne (12) (a.p: nt clr run over 1f out: styd on) 1½.4

524 The Dominant Gene **(36)** *(JRJenkins)* 7-11  NCarlisle (17) (in tch: effrt u.p 3f out: hmpd 2f out: one pce) ............................................. ¹/₂.5

913 Fair Flyer (IRE) **(56)** *(PMonteith)* 8-12 ‡⁵JWeaver (9) (in tch: nt clr run & swtchd over 1f out: r.o nr fin) ......................................... ¹/₂.6

575 Cherry Bob **(43)** *(CWThornton)* 7-11 ‡⁷KSked (14) (in tch: effrt 4f out: one pce) ³/₄.7

913 Little Ivor **(52)** (v) *(DenysSmith)* 8-13  KFallon (1) (chsd ldrs tl hmpd & wknd over 1f out) ............................................................ 1¹/₂.8

765⁶ King Optimist **(45)** *(ASmith)* 8-6  SWebster (7) (rdn 4f out: no imp) .................. 1.9

766 Double the Stakes (USA) **(45)** *(Fav)* *(FHLee)* 8-6  WRyan (15) (chsd ldrs: led & qcknd over 3f out: hdd 2f out: sn btn) .................. 1.10

Desert Mist **(40)** *(SirMarkPrescott)* 8-1  GDuffield (4) (led 7f out tl over 3f out: btn whn hmpd over 1f out) ................................ 1.11

216 Turning Heads **(32)** *(CaptJWilson)* 7-7  JLowe (11) (dwlt: n.d) ......................... 8.12

806 Dangina **(38)** *(ASReid)* 7-6⁽⁶⁾ ‡⁷PMcCabe (3) (nvr trbld ldrs) .................... s.h.13

Lingdale Lass **(60)** *(MrsGRReveley)* 9-0 ‡⁷DarrenMoffatt (16) (in tch tl wknd over 3f out) ............................................................. 2.14

963 Treasure Beach **(47)** *(MBrittain)* 8-8  KDarley (5) (plld hrd early: effrt ent st: sn btn) ................................................................... ³/₄.15

457 Princess Tamar **(37)** *(PCHaslam)* 7-9 ‡³JFanning (13) (led 3f: racd wd: cl up tl wknd 4f out) ........................................................... 15.16

697 Placid Lady (IRE) **(46)** *(WCarter)* 8-2 ‡⁵NGwilliams (2) (dwlt: hdwy ent st: sn wknd) ...................................................................... 10.17

LONG HANDICAP: Dots Dee 7-5, Turning Heads 7-6, Dangina 7-3.

**3/1** Double the Stakes (USA), **4/1** The Dominant Gene, **6/1** Desert Mist(8/1—9/2), **9/1** Elsa, **10/1** Reach for Glory, **12/1** Treasure Beach, **14/1** King Optimist, **16/1** Fair Flyer (IRE), **20/1** Lingdale Lass, Turning Heads, GAY MING, **25/1** Little Ivor, **33/1** Placid Lady (IRE), Princess Tamar, **50/1** Ors. CSF £194.06, CT £8,593.14. Tote £53.50: £8.20 £3.20 £9.60 £1.20 (£407.50). Mr H. S. Yates (UPPER LOGDON) bred by H. S. Yates. 17 Rn; No bid
2m 7.4 (4.9)
3F—7/32/9/0/0/22

---

**1053**　　WILD TURKEY (101) BOURBON H'CAP (0-95) £2742.00 (£816.00: £388.00: £174.00)
　　　　**5f**　　　　　　　　　　　　　　　　　　　　3-00 (3-03)

872★ **Tongue Tied (65)** *(JWharton)* 4-8-4  WRyan (2) (lw: mde all: shkn up appr fnl f: r.o) ..................................................................... —1

918★ Penny Hasset **(63)** (Fav) *(MWEasterby)* 4-8-2  KDarley (1) (lw: a chsng wnr: rdn 2f out: r.o) ............................................................ 1.2

885 Prince Belfort **(67)** *(MPNaughton)* 4-8-1 ‡⁵JWeaver (7) (lw: chsd ldrs tl outpcd 2f out: r.o ins fnl f) ............................................. nk.3

819 Singing Star **(81)** *(JBalding)* 6-9-6  GDuffield (5) (lw: in tch: hdwy & ev ch over 1f out: rdn & no ex) ..................................... ¹/₂.4

Heaven-Liegh-Grey **(89)** *(MJohnston)* 4-10-0  RPElliott (6) (b.hind: chsd ldrs tl outpcd fnl 2f) ......................................... 1¹/₂.5

980⁶ Barrys Gamble **(81)** (bl) *(TFairhurst)* 6-9-3 ‡³JFanning (3) (s.s: nt rvcr) ............ 7.6

*Our Freddie (8/1) Withdrawn (ref to ent stalls) : not under orders — Rule 4 applies*

**13/8** Penny Hasset, **9/2** Singing Star, **11/2** TONGUE TIED, **6/1** Barrys Gamble, **8/1** Prince Belfort, **16/1** Heaven-Liegh-Grey. CSF £12.05, Tote £3.70: £2.40 £1.50 (£3.90). Mrs R. T. Watson (MELTON MOWBRAY) bred by R. T. and Mrs Watson. 6 Rn
58 sec (1.3)
SF—44/38/36/53/55/16

---

**1054**　　REDCAR H'CAP (Amateurs) (0-70) £2167.20 (£599.20: £285.60)　　**6f**　　3-30 (3-36)

615⁴ **Granny Mc (50)** *(EJAlston)* 5-9-11 ‡⁵MrRWilkinson (8) (lw: chsd ldrs: led appr fnl f: r.o) ............................................................... —1

888⁶ Danzig Lad (USA) **(41)** *(MPNaughton)* 4-9-7  MissPRobson (2) (lw: bolted gng to s: led tl hdd appr fnl f: kpt on wl) ......................... 1.2

774³ Bill Moon **(47)** *(PJFeilden)* 6-9-13  MissJFeilden (7) (hdwy ¹/₂-wy: styd on fnl f: nvr able to chal) ............................................ nk.3

918⁶ Iron King **(69)** (v) *(JLSpearing)* 6–11-2 ‡⁵MissTSpearing (6) (effrt ¹/₂-wy: sn prom: one pce fnl f) ................................... 1.4

774 Profit a Prendre **(52)** (Fav) *(DAWilson)* 8-10-4  MissJAllison (5) (b: lw: hdwy ¹/₂-wy: sn chsng ldrs: rdn & no ex appr fnl f) ................ 2.5

885 Nevada Mix **(46)** *(MissLAPerratt)* 8–9-12  MissLPerratt (1) (hdwy over 2f out: sn rdn & nvr trbld ldrs) ....................................... 1¹/₂.6

496 Count Me Out **(40)** (bl) *(JPearce)* 7-9-6  MrsLPearce (4) (effrt ¹/₂-wy: nvr nr to chal) ................................................................... 3¹/₂.7

534 Yours Or Mine (IRE) **(39)** *(DWChapman)* 4-9-5  MrsAFarrell (3) (plld hrd early: cl up tl wknd 2f out) ............................................ nk.8

**5/2** Profit a Prendre, **100/30** Bill Moon, **13/2** Iron King, **7/1** Nevada Mix, **8/1** Count Me Out, **9/1** GRANNY MC, **12/1** Danzig Lad (USA), **33/1** Yours Or Mine (IRE). CSF £87.68, CT £357.51. Tote £9.90: £3.10 £3.20 £1.50 (£52.00). Mrs S. Y. Alston (PRESTON) bred by Macbiehill Estates Ltd. 8 Rn
1m 12.3 (3)
SF—27/19/24/37/17/5

## 1055          KIRKLEATHAM STKS (Mdn 3-Y.O) £1932.00 (£532.00: £252.00)        7f      4-00 (4-03)

| | | |
|---|---|---|
| 8225 | **Boursin (IRE)** *(PCalver)* 9-0 WNewnes (3) (lw: mde all: shkn up 2f out: r.o) ...... | —1 |
| 869 | Isle of Innisfree (USA) *(HRACecil)* 9-0 WRyan (9) (a chsng ldrs: hung lft most of wy: rdn 3f out: kpt on) .................................................. | 3½.2 |
| | Patience Please *(MHEasterby)* 8-9 MBirch (5) (unf: bit bkwd: hld up & bhd: hdwy ½-wy: kpt on fnl f) ............................................. | 1½.3 |
| 412 | Glasgow (Fav) *(BWHills)* 9-0 DHolland (2) (sn cl up: rdn 3f out: one pce) ........ | nk.4 |
| | Alto *(JGFitzGerald)* 9-0 KFallon (6) (bit bkwd: effrt ½-wy: nvr trbld ldrs) ......... | 7.5 |
| 8783 | Vanart *(WWHaigh)* 9-0 ACulhane (8) (lw: plld hrd: effrt over 3f out: fnd nil) ...... | 4.6 |
| | Scottish Ruby **(64)** *(CTinkler)* 9-0 KDarley (4) (swtg: prom tl outpcd fr ½-wy) | 2½.7 |
| | Ferrovia *(JWWatts)* 8-9 GDuffield (7) (hld up: effrt ½-wy: n.d) .................... | 3.8 |

**9/4** Glasgow(op 6/4), **3/1** Vanart, **9/2** BOURSIN (IRE), **5/1** Ferrovia, Isle of Innisfree (USA), **20/1** Patience Please, **25/1** Alto, **33/1** Scottish Ruby. CSF £25.94, Tote £6.60: £1.50 £2.10 £2.20 (£17.40). Mr Kenneth MacPherson (RIPON) bred by K. Molloy in Ireland. 8 Rn
1m 24.4 (2.2)
SF—46/35/25/29/1/–

## 1056          E.B.F. SKELTON STKS (Mdn 2-Y.O) £2724.90 (£756.40: £362.70)        6f      4-30 (4-32)

| | | |
|---|---|---|
| 4464 | **White Crown (USA)** *(BHanbury)* 9-0 BRaymond (15) (lw: cl up: led ½-wy: hld on wl fnl f) ...................................................... | —1 |
| | Ten to Six *(EWeymes)* 8-9 WNewnes (14) (w'like: str: bit bkwd: s.i.s: stdy hdwy ½ wy: chal ins fnl f: nt qckn cl home) ............................ | ½.2 |
| 8032 | The Seer (Fav) *(BWHills)* 9-0 DHolland (6) (lw: trckd ldrs: chal 2f out: nt qckn wl ins fnl f) ........................................................ | hd.3 |
| 8074 | Expo Mondial (IRE) *(JMPEustace)* 9-0 MTebbutt (10) (a chsng ldrs: effrt over 2f out: nt qckn) ..................................................... | 3½.4 |
| | Mhemeanles *(MHEasterby)* 8-9 ‡5SMaloney (11) (w'like: scope: in tch: kpt on fnl 2f) ............................................................ | 3.5 |
| | Cutthroat Kid (IRE) *(SGNorton)* 9-0 KDarley (8) (w'like: str: scope: bit bkwd: s.i.s: hdwy 2f out: r.o nr fin) ....................................... | 1½.6 |
| | Yorkshire Rock *(MHEasterby)* 9-0 MBirch (7) (lengthy: scope: outpcd & bhd: hdwy 2f out: r.o) ................................................... | ¾.7 |
| 770 | Paajib (IRE) *(CTinkler)* 9-0 TLucas (3) (outpcd & bhd after 2f: sme late hdwy) ... | 3.8 |
| | El Guapo *(TFairhurst)* 8-11 ‡3JFanning (4) (wl grwn: lengthy: bit bkwd: s.i.s: gd hdwy ½-wy: wknd over 1f out) ..................................... | 1½.9 |
| | Sounds Risky *(GMMoore)* 8-9 ACulhane (13) (unf: in tch: rdn ½-wy: wknd 2f out) ............................................................ | ¾.10 |
| 877 | Hallmote *(JGFitzGerald)* 9-0 KFallon (9) (led to ½-wy: wknd 2f out) ................ | 2.11 |
| 770 | Greystyle *(MBrittain)* 9-0 GDuffield (5) (spd to ½-wy) .......................... | 1½.12 |
| 889 | Lucky Owl *(PMonteith)* 8-4 ‡5JWeaver (1) (unruly s: s.i.s: sn rcvrd: wknd over 2f out) ............................................................ | hd.13 |
| 769 | Newgatesky *(BWMurray)* 8-9 JFortune (12) (s.i.s: a bhd) ....................... | 15.14 |

**Evens** The Seer(op 6/4), **3/1** WHITE CROWN (USA)(9/4—7/2), **5/1** Expo Mondial (IRE), **16/1** Paajib (IRE), **20/1** Yorkshire Rock, **25/1** Ten to Six, Cutthroat Kid (IRE), **33/1** Sounds Risky, Greystyle, **50/1** Hallmote, El Guapo, **100/1** Ors. CSF £67.29, Tote £3.90: £1.40 £3.90 £1.40 (£98.40). Mr Saeed Suhail (NEWMARKET) bred by David Mowat & Fawn Leap Farm in USA. 14 Rn
1m 11.8 (2.5)
SF—26/19/23/9/–/–

T/Plpt: £349.20 (9.45 Tckts).                                                    AA

## 703—SANDOWN  (R-H)
### Monday, May 25th [Good to firm]
Going Allowance: nil sec per fur (G)
Wind: almost nil

Stalls: low                         *Rails on home bnd moved out 2 metres bef 4th race*

## 1057          COLLCHIMIE STKS (Mdn 2-Y.O.F) £2343.00 (£648.00: £309.00)        5f 6y      2-00 (2-02)

| | | |
|---|---|---|
| 8673 | **Princess Oberon (IRE)** (Fav) *(MBell)* 8-11 MHills (5) (mde all: rdn out) ............. | —1 |
| | Hamsah (IRE) *(DRCElsworth)* 8-11 SCauthen (3) (unf: scope: bit bkwd: a.p: chsd wnr fnl f: r.o) ................................................... | 2.2 |
| | Rich Midas (IRE) *(GLewis)* 8-4 ‡7BRussell (6) (leggy: a.p: rdn over 1f out: unable qckn) ............................................................ | 3.3 |

Page 384

852 Brigadore Gold *(RHannon)* 8-11 WCarson (9) (a.p: rdn over 2f out: one pce)   1½.4
Hello Hobson's (IRE) *(JAkehurst)* 8-11 DHolland (4) (w'like: bkwd: nvr nr to
chal) .................................................................. 5.5
Agil's Pet *(JSutcliffe)* 8-11 BRouse (7) (unf: bkwd: s.s: outpcd) ..................... 4.6
Brockton Dancer *(RHannon)* 8-11 PatEddery (2) (b.hind: unf: scope: s.s: a
bhd) .................................................................... 2½.7
Is She Quick *(MrsJCDawe)* 8-11 JWilliams (1) (leggy: scope: s.s: a wl bhd) ...... 5.8
Ascom Pager (IRE) *(PHowling)* 8-11 NCarlisle (8) (w'like: bkwd: bhd whn
stumbled over 2f out) .................................................... 6.9

2/1 PRINCESS OBERON (IRE), 5/2 Hamsah (IRE), 11/4 Brockton Dancer, 10/1 Brigadore Gold, 16/1 Agil's Pet,
20/1 Rich Midas (IRE), 33/1 Hello Hobson's (IRE), 50/1 Is She Quick, 66/1 Ascom Pager (IRE). CSF £7.03, Tote
£3.00: £1.10 £1.70 £4.00 (£4.80). Mr R. P. B. Michaelson (NEWMARKET) bred by E. O'Gorman in Ireland. 9 Rn
61.95 sec (2.45)
SF—48/40/21/22/2/–

**1058**      UNITED BREWERIES STKS (listed race) (F & M) £8646.50 (£2612.00: £1271.00:
£600.50)    **1m 14y**      2-35 (2-38)

563³ **Susurration (USA) (111)** *(JHMGosden)* 5–9-11 WCarson (8) (hdwy 2f out: led
1f out: all out) ........................................................... —1
845a Cloud of Dust **(104)** *(JLDunlop)* 3–8-8 DHolland (1) (swtg: s.s: hdwy over 1f
out: hrd rdn & ev ch fnl f: r.o wl) ....................................... s.h.2
551⁴ Loveloch (IRE) **(109)** (Fav) *(MBell)* 4–9-6 MHills (7) (4th st: led over 1f out: sn
hdd: unable qckn) ....................................................... 3.3
607✱ Arbusha (USA) *(LordHuntingdon)* 3–8-8 MRoberts (5) (lw: 5th st: ev ch over 1f
out: one pce) ........................................................... nk.4
Katakana (USA) **(100)** *(MRStoute)* 3–8-8 SCauthen (4) (lw: 3rd st: n.m.r on ins
2f out: one pce) ........................................................ 2.5
672✱ Ships Lantern **(97)** *(CFWall)* 3–8-8 LDettori (3) (b.off hind. 2nd st. ev ch 2f out.
wknd over 1f out) ....................................................... 2½.6
818✱ Skimble (USA) *(HRACecil)* 3–8-8 PatEddery (6) (lw: led over 6f) ............. 1½.7
239⁶ Shot Stopper **(64)** *(MJHeaton-Ellis)* 4–9-6 JWilliams (2) (6th st: wknd over 3f out) 4.8

3/1 Loveloch (IRE), 4/1 Skimble (USA), Katakana (USA), 6/1 Arbusha (USA)(tchd 10/1), 8/1 SUSURRATION
(USA)(op 9/2), 10/1 Cloud of Dust, 12/1 Ships Lantern, 100/1 Shot Stopper. CSF £68.26, Tote £8.90: £2.30
£2.70 £1.50 (£62.10). Pin Oak Stable (NEWMARKET) bred by Pin Oak Farm in USA. 8 Rn   1m 41.42 (2.22)
SF—78/60/63/50/44/36

**1059**      CEMENTONE BEAVER HENRY II E.B.F. STKS (Gp 3) £29196.00 (£10821.80: £5110.90:
£2131.30)    **2m 78y**      3-10 (3-12)

644a✱ **Drum Taps (USA) (119)** (Fav) *(LordHuntingdon)* 6–9-4 LDettori (4) (4th st: led
wl over 1f out: rdn out) ................................................. —1
724² Arcadian Heights **(103)** *(GWragg)* 4–8-10 MHills (3) (hmpd bnd 4f out: rdn over
3f out: gd hdwy fnl f: r.o wl) .......................................... 1½.2
Tyrone Bridge **(108)** *(MCPipe)* 6–8-12 PShanahan (6) (2nd st: rdn over 3f out:
unable qckn) ........................................................... 2½.3
608 Hateel **(109)** *(PTWalwyn)* 6–8-12 WCarson (8) (lw: 5th st: rdn over 2f out: one
pce) ................................................................... 1.4
826⁴ Luchiroverte (IRE) **(111)** *(CEBrittain)* 4–8-10 MRoberts (7) (lw: led: slipped bnd
4f out: hdd wl over 1f out: one pce) ................................... ¾.5
826⁶ Jaffa Line **(104)** *(DRCElsworth)* 4–8-10 SCauthen (2) (hld up: bhd whn slipped
bnd 4f out: nt rcvr) .................................................... 20.6
608² Supreme Choice (USA) **(108)** *(BWHills)* 4–8-10 DHolland (1) (lw: 6th & carried
wd st: rdn over 3f out: eased whn btn over 1f out) ..................... 15.7
608 Hawait Al Barr **(96)** *(MRStoute)* 4–8-7 PatEddery (5) (swtg: 3rd whn slipped
bdly bnd 4f out: nt rcvr: t.o) ......................................... dist.8

2/1 DRUM TAPS (USA), 7/2 Supreme Choice (USA), 5/1 Hateel, 6/1 Luchiroverte (IRE), 13/2 Hawait Al Barr,
12/1 Jaffa Line(op 20/1), 25/1 Arcadian Heights, 33/1 Tyrone Bridge. CSF £38.45, Tote £2.80: £1.50 £3.90
£3.10 (£23.40). Mr Yoshio Asakawa (WEST ILSLEY) bred by William Powell and Bates Newton in USA. 8 Rn
3m 32.75 (2.75)
SF—76/66/65/64/61/41

**1060**      UB GROUP TEMPLE STKS (Gp 2) £37260.00 (£13866.75: £6595.88: £2802.37)
**5f 6y**      3-40 (3-44)

478⁶ **Snaadee (USA)** *(MRStoute)* 5–9-3 PatEddery (6) (lw: mde all: rdn out) ............. —1
656³ Blyton Lad *(WJPearce)* 6–9-3 SWebster (4) (hdwy over 1f out: r.o wl ins fnl f) .... 2.2
879✱ Medaille D'Or (v) *(JWPayne)* 4–9-3 LDettori (3) (a.p: rdn over 1f out: unable
qckn) .................................................................. nk.3

836a★ Elbio (Fav) *(PJMakin)* 5-9-7 WCarson (9) (hld up: rdn over 1f out: one pce) .... nk.4
    Cardmania (USA) *(MrsMBollack-Badel,France)* 6-9-3 ALequeux (7) (a.p: rdn
    over 2f out: one pce) ........................................................................ 1.5
    Keen Hunter (USA) *(JHMGosden)* 5-9-10 SCauthen (5) (b.nr fore: bit bkwd:
    a.p: rdn over 1f out: eased whn btn wl ins fnl f) .................. nk.6
834² Bold Memory *(DRCElsworth)* 3-8-8 JWilliams (8) (a bhd) ............................ 4.7
819 On Tiptoes *(JPLeigh)* 4-9-0 MRoberts (2) (bhd fnl 2f) ......................... ¹/₂.8
827 Line Engaged (USA) *(PTWalwyn)* 4-9-3 BRaymond (1) (a bhd) ................. 5.9

**11/8 Elbio, 100/30 Keen Hunter (USA), 9/1 Blyton Lad, 12/1 Cardmania (USA), On Tiptoes, 14/1 Bold Memory, SNAADEE (USA), 20/1 Medaille D'Or(op 12/1), 50/1 Line Engaged (USA). CSF £111.69, Tote £16.60: £2.60 £2.40 £3.50 (£96.50). Maktoum Al Maktoum (NEWMARKET) bred by North Ridge Farm in USA. 9 Rn**
        60.30 sec (0.80)
SF—87/79/78/81/73/79

## 1061
KINGFISHER LAGER WHITSUN CUP (H'cap) (0-110) £14655.00 (£4440.00: £2170.00: £1035.00)   **1m 14y**                                 4-10 (4-25)

667⁴ Pay Homage (91) *(IABalding)* 4-9-4 MHills (9) (hdwy over 2f out: rdn over 1f
    out: led wl ins fnl f: r.o wl) ........................................................ —1
626 Marine Diver (68) *(BRMillman)* 6-7-9⁽¹⁾ AMackay (13) (4th st: rdn over 2f out:
    led ins fnl f: sn hdd: unable qckn) ............................................... 1.2
936² Daswaki (CAN) (84) (Fav) *(RHannon)* 4-8-11 BRouse (3) (swtg: 2nd st: led
    over 2f out tl ins fnl f: one pce) ............................................... 1¹/₂.3
692⁵ Field of Honour (83) *(LMCumani)* 4-8-10 LDettori (10) (lw: hdwy 2f out: one
    pce) ........................................................................................... 1¹/₂.4
824⁴ St Ninian (101) *(MHEasterby)* 6-10-0 PatEddery (14) (hdwy 2f out: r.o one pce) .2.5
692 Croupier (87) *(CEBrittain)* 5-8-9 ‡⁵BDoyle (6) (hdwy fnl 2f: nvr nrr) ......... ¹/₂.6
    Steerforth (IRE) (98) *(ACStewart)* 4-9-11 MRoberts (4) (bit bkwd: nvr nr to chal) s.h.7
936 Usa Dollar (67) (v) *(BGubby)* 5-7-8⁽¹⁾ NCarlisle (1) (nvr nrr) .................... ³/₄.8
832 Takenhall (71) *(MJFetherston-Godley)* 7-8-5⁽⁵⁾ ‡⁷AGarth (5) (nvr nrr) ......... s.h.9
    Pontenuovo (100) *(DRCElsworth)* 7-9-13 SCauthen (11) (led over 5f: wknd
    over 1f out) ............................................................................... 1¹/₂.10
832 Arak (USA) (73) *(RWArmstrong)* 4-8-0 BCrossley (12) (6th st: wknd 3f out) .. 1¹/₂.11
    Absonal (81) *(RHannon)* 5-8-8 JWilliams (8) (a bhd) .......................... hd.12
722⁶ Wesaam (USA) (97) (bl) *(MajorWRHern)* 3-8-12 WCarson (2) (lw: 5th st: wknd
    over 2f out) ............................................................................... 2.13
692★ Venus Observed (95) *(HCandy)* 4-9-1 ‡⁷AntoinetteArmes (7) (lw: 3rd st: wknd
    over 1f out) ............................................................................... 5.14
                LONG HANDICAP: Usa Dollar 7-1, Takenhall 7-2.

**5/1 Daswaki (CAN), 6/1 Swaam (USA), Field of Honour, 7/1 PAY HOMAGE, Venus Observed, 9/1 Steerforth (IRE), St Ninian, 10/1 Pontenuovo, 20/1 Marine Diver, Arak (USA), 25/1 Absonal, Takenhall, 33/1 Ors. CSF £121.68, CT £692.66. Tote £9.30: £3.10 £6.40 £2.10 (£92.40). Miss A. V. Hill (KINGSCLERE) bred by Cheveley Park Stud Ltd. 14 Rn**
                    1m 41.41 (2.21)
SF—71/45/56/50/62/41

## 1062
UB INTERNATIONAL H'CAP (3-Y.O) (0-90) £3601.75 (£1084.00: £524.50: £244.75)   **7f 16y**                                 4-45 (5-03)

825⁴ Euro Festival (77) (Jt-Fav) *(MissLCSiddall)* 8-8 PatEddery (10) (lw: 6th st: led
    over 1f out: hrd rdn: r.o wl) ......................................................... —1
699★ Rafah (75) *(BHanbury)* 8-6 BRaymond (11) (lw: led over 1f: 2nd st: ev ch 2f out:
    r.o one pce) ............................................................................... 2.2
985★ Battle Colours (IRE) (85) *(SirMarkPrescott)* 8-11 (6x) ‡⁵BDoyle (9) (4th st: hrd
    rdn 2f out: r.o ins fnl f) ............................................................. nk.3
620 Louisville Belle (IRE) (62) *(MDIUsher)* 7-7 RStreet (1) (b.nr hind: s.s: hdwy over
    1f out: r.o) ................................................................................. 3¹/₂.4
970³ Coniston Lake (IRE) (62) *(GLewis)* 7-0 ‡⁷AntoinetteArmes (6) (led over 5f out tl
    over 1f out: wknd fnl f) ............................................................. nk.5
725² By Hand (77) *(WJHaggas)* 8-8 MHills (2) (lw: nvr nr to chal) .................... 1.6
925³ Super Serenade (72) (Jt-Fav) *(GBBalding)* 8-3 JWilliams (3) (no hdwy fnl 2f) .. nk.7
830⁶ Sea Prodigy (66) *(MBlanshard)* 7-8⁽¹⁾ NCarlisle (4) (lw: 3rd st: wknd 2f out) .. 1.8
825² Sky Hunter (USA) (92) (Jt-Fav) *(RHannon)* 9-9 MRoberts (5) (a bhd) ............ 2.9
471 Douraj (IRE) (65) (bl) *(CEBrittain)* 7-10 AMackay (7) (swtg: bhd fnl 2f) ....... ³/₄.10
582 Paradise Forum (76) *(CAHorgan)* 8-2 ‡⁵JWeaver (8) (5th st: wknd 3f out) ......... 3.11
             LONG HANDICAP: Coniston Lake (IRE) 7-6, Sea Prodigy 7-3.

**5/1 Super Serenade, Sky Hunter (USA), EURO FESTIVAL, 11/2 Battle Colours (IRE), By Hand, 9/1 Rafah, 12/1 Coniston Lake (IRE)(op 6/1), 14/1 Douraj (IRE)(10/1—16/1), 20/1 Paradise Forum, 33/1 Ors. CSF £43.95, CT £228.25. Tote £6.40: £1.70 £3.20 £2.00 (£34.70). Mr Christopher Price (TADCASTER) bred by H. Alexander and R. E. Sangster. 11 Rn**
                  1m 29.72 (2.72)
SF—53/50/54/25/17/36

**1063** UB COATING H'CAP (0-80) £3715.50 (£1119.00: £542.00: £253.50)
1¼m 7y

5-20 (5-34)

831 **Rising Tempo (IRE) (55)** (Jt-Fav) *(CACyzer)* 4–8-3 MRoberts (10) (lw: 6th st:
led over 1f out: r.o wl) ................................................................... —1
606³ Samurai Gold (USA) **(47)** (v) *(PTWalwyn)* 4–7-9(1) AMackay (8) (led 1f: 2nd st:
led 2f out tl over 1f out: unable qckn) ........................... 1½.2
829 Barbary Reef (IRE) **(50)** *(GHEden)* 4–7-12 WCarson (9) (3rd st: rdn over 1f out:
one pce) ......................................................................... 2½.3
702 Captain My Captain (IRE) **(55)** *(GBBalding)* 4–8-3 JWilliams (7) (lw: hdwy over
2f out: r.o one pce) ................................................................... 4.4
763² St Patrick's Day **(66)** (Jt-Fav) *(CEBrittain)* 4–8-9 ‡⁵BDoyle (11) (led 9f out to 2f
out: sn wknd) .................................................................... 2.5
530³ Swift Silver **(54)** *(WJMusson)* 5–8-2 JHBrown (4) (b: nvr nr to chal) ............... 2.6
657⁶ Danzarin (IRE) **(80)** *(RHannon)* 4–9-7 ‡⁷DGibbs (1) (hdwy over 2f out: wknd
over 1f out) ......................................................................... ½.7
800 Petmer **(45)** *(GBBalding)* 5–7-7 NCarlisle (6) (lw: nvr nrr) ........................ 1½.8
774 Albert **(52)** *(DAWilson)* 5–8-0 BCrossley (2) (a bhd) ................................ 2½.9
Valiant Words **(70)** *(RAkehurst)* 5–9-4 BRouse (5) (5th st: wknd over 3f out) ...... 8.10
777⁴ Eastern Magic **(67)** *(JAkehurst)* 4–9-1 DHolland (3) (4th st: wknd over 2f out) 10.11
LONG HANDICAP: Petmer 7-4.

**9/2** St Patrick's Day, RISING TEMPO (IRE), 11/2 Barbary Reef (IRE), 7/1 Samurai Gold (USA), 9/1 Swift Silver,
**10/1** Danzarin (IRE), Valiant Words, Captain My Captain (IRE), 12/1 Eastern Magic(op 8/1), 25/1 Ors. CSF
£32.83, CT £157.29. Tote £5.70: £1.90 £2.00 £1.90 (£12.80). Mr R. M. Cyzer (HORSHAM) bred by Aramstone
Stud Co in Ireland. 11 Rn                                        2m 7.88 (3.58)
                                                                SF—53/42/40/37/39/28

T/Trio: Race 5: £180.70 (20.5 Tckts). T/Jkpt: Not won; £7,916.58 to Lingfield 30/5/92. T/Plpt: £850.90 (13.65
Ickts).                                                                                              ΔK

## SANDOWN (R-H)
### Tuesday, May 26th [Good to firm]
Going Allowance: St: minus 0.25 sec (F); Rnd: nil sec per fur (G)         Wind: almost nil

Stalls: 5f low, remainder high

**1064** RAILWAY CLAIMING STKS £2469.00 (£684.00: £327.00) **5f 6y** 6-20 (6-23)

**Tango Time (87)** (Fav) *(RHannon)* 4–8-4 MRoberts (4) (swtg: mde all: easily) ... —1
496 Fair Reason (IRE) **(47)** *(DJSCosgrove)* 4–7-9 ‡⁵DHarrison (5) (a.p: chsd wnr fnl
3f: no imp) ................................................................... 2.2
Blue Topaze *(RJHolder)* 4–8-0 ‡⁵ATucker (1) (s.s: hdwy over 2f out: r.o one pce) 2.3
872⁵ Liffey River (USA) **(53)** *(MrsLPiggott)* 4–9-0 JReid (7) (b: no hdwy fnl 2f) ........... 4.4
480 Miami Banker **(75)** *(PHowling)* 6–8-10 JMurray (6) (prom over 2f) ................. 1½.5
897 Tachyon Park **(41)** (v) *(PHowling)* 10–8-0 ‡³FNorton (3) (prom over 2f) ........... 2½.6
903 Regal Tiger **(25)** *(MrsJCDawe)* 7–7-11 ‡⁵BDoyle (3) (wl bhd fnl 3f) .............. 8.7

**4/7** TANGO TIME, 11/2 Miami Banker, Liffey River (USA), 14/1 Tachyon Park, 25/1 Fair Reason (IRE), 33/1 Blue
Topaze, 66/1 Regal Tiger. CSF £12.76, Tote £1.40: £1.20 £5.60 (£11.50). Mr R. J. Shannon (MARLBOROUGH)
bred by The Lavington Stud. 7 Rn; Tango Time clmd Mrs R Carter £10,702    60.09 sec (0.59)
                                                                          SF—53/36/33/31/21/1

**1065** LONDON RACING CLUB H'CAP (0-80) £3113.00 (£868.00: £419.00)
1¾m

6-50 (6-51)

**Wick Pound (42)** (bl) (Fav) *(JABOld)* 6–7-9 RFox (3) (4th st: led over 2f out:
v.easily) ......................................................................... —1
937² Mull House **(58)** *(FJO'Mahony)* 5–8-11 WRSwinburn (5) (hdwy 2f out: r.o fnl f:
no ch w wnr) ..................................................................... 3.2
773* Prosequendo (USA) **(64)** *(MDixon)* 5–9-3 DaleGibson (8) (hdwy over 2f out: hrd rdn:
r.o one pce) .............................................................. ¾.3
354² Belafonte **(65)** *(RJHolder)* 5–8-13 ‡⁵ATucker (11) (6th st: r.o one pce fnl 2f) ...... 3.4
926³ Run High **(58)** *(PMitchell)* 9–8-8 ‡³SO'Gorman (1) (hdwy & 5th st: one pce fnl 2f) nk.5
815 Alilisa **(74)** *(WJHaggas)* 4–9-13 MHills (10) (b: lw: led tl wknd over 2f out) 6.6
861 Tsunami **(72)** *(CEBrittain)* 4–9-11 MRoberts (9) (7th st: rdn over 2f out: no hdwy) 1.7
288² Shooting Lodge (IRE) **(67)** *(JRJenkins)* 4–9-6 PatEddery (2) (2nd tl wknd over
2f out) ......................................................................... s.h.8
501 Pondered Bid **(44)** *(PatMitchell)* 8–7-8(4) ‡³FNorton (7) (b: hdwy 6f out: 3rd st:
wknd 3f out) ..................................................................... 7.9
Bravo Star (USA) **(45)** *(PLeach)* 7–7-7(5) ‡⁵BDoyle (4) (a bhd: t.o) ................. 12.10
LONG HANDICAP: Pondered Bid 7-5, Bravo Star (USA) 7-0.

**100/30** WICK POUND, **4/1** Mull House, **5/1** Belafonte, **6/1** Prosequendo (USA), **7/1** Shooting Lodge (IRE), Run High, **11/1** Tsunami, **16/1** Alilisa (USA), **40/1** Ors. CSF £16.28, CT £68.57. Tote £5.10: £2.10 £1.70 £2.30 (£14.40). Mr K. R. Britten (WROUGHTON) bred by Wick-Dromdiah Investments Ltd. 10 Rn     3m 3.73 (9.03)

---

**1066**     BRIGADIER GERARD STKS (Gp 3) £17410.88 (£5895.08: £2779.04)
              1¼m 7y                                                           7-20 (7-23)

954a★ **Opera House (111)** (Fav) (MRStoute) 4–9–1  SCauthen (3) (lw: mde all: hrd rdn
              over 1f out: r.o wl) ...................................................... —1
382a  Wiorno (AFabre,France) 4–9–1  PatEddery (1) (swtg: 2nd st: rdn over 2f out: ev
              ch 1f out: r.o) ............................................................ 1.2
390   Young Buster (IRE) (117) (GWragg) 4–8–13  WRSwinburn (2) (lw: 3rd st: jnd wnr
              on bit 2f out: rdn & nt qckn over 1f out) ................................. 1½.3

**Evens** OPERA HOUSE, **5/2** Ors. CSF £3.30, Tote £1.80 (£1.70). Sheikh Mohammed (NEWMARKET) bred by Meon Valley Stud. 3 Rn                                                                 2m 8.68 (4.38)
                                                                                SF—57/55/50

---

**1067**     WINALOT NATIONAL STKS (2-Y-O) (listed race) £6863.75 (£2060.00: £992.50:
              £458.75)  5f 6y                                                   7-50 (7-54)

584★  **Lyric Fantasy (IRE)** (Fav) (RHannon) 8–7  MRoberts (2) (led 3f out: qcknd clr
              over 1f out: r.o wl) ...................................................... —1
      Hazy Kay (IRE) (PAKelleway) 8–4  PRobinson (4) (unf: scope: bit bkwd: a.p: wnt
              2nd over 1f out: no imp) ................................................. 6.2
584²  Ancestral Dancer (MBell) 8–7  MHills (1) (lw: led 2f: hrd rdn over 1f out: nt qckn)  1.3
709³  Huffa (USA) (WJHaggas) 8–12  PatEddery (5) (a.p: one pce fnl 2f) .............. hd.4
847²  Rocket to the Moon (IRE) (PWChapple-Hyam) 8–9  PaulEddery (6) (lw: rdn
              along & a bhd) ............................................................. 3.5
729★ Carranita (IRE) (10/1) Withdrawn (ref to ent stalls) : not under orders  — Rule 4 applies

**2/1** LYRIC FANTASY (IRE), **3/1** Ancestral Dancer, Rocket to the Moon (IRE), **5/1** Huffa (USA), **12/1** Hazy Kay (IRE)(20/1—10/1). CSF £17.35, Tote £2.50: £1.20 £2.90 (£12.20). Lord Carnarvon (MARLBOROUGH) bred by Minch Bloodstock in Ireland. 5 Rn                                                           59.62 sec (0.12)
                                                                                SF—65/38/37/41/26

---

**1068**     VICTOR CHANDLER H'CAP (3-Y-O) (0-90) £3571.00 (£1078.00: £524.00: £247.00)
              1m 3f 91y                                                         8-20 (8-23)

816   **Kinglow (USA) (80)** (MrsJCecil) 8–13  PaulEddery (8) (lw: 3rd st: led over 2f
              out: r.o wl) ................................................................ —1
728★  In the Picture (IRE) (84) (RHannon) 9–3  WCarson (2) (lw: 4th st: swtchd rt over
              2f out: ev ch fnl 2f: r.o) ................................................. 1½.2
784★  Flight Lieutenant (USA) (88) (PMitchell) 9–7  WRSwinburn (3) (5th st: ev ch over
              1f out: nt qckn) ........................................................... ¾.3
864★  Lemon's Mill (USA) (84) (Fav) (JHMGosden) 9–3  PatEddery (1) (dwlt: sn rcvrd:
              2nd st: hmpd & wknd over 2f out) ....................................... 6.4
816   Al Ramis (IRE) (78) (CEBrittain) 8–11  MRoberts (6) (7th st: nvr nr to chal) ...... 2.5
627³  Bel Baraka (IRE) (70) (DRCEllsworth) 8–3  JWilliams (4) (led: hung lft & hdd over
              2f out) .................................................................... 1.6
728   Judge and Jury (71) (MJFetherston-Godley) 8–1 ‡³FNorton (5) (a bhd: last st) ... 6.7
      Euroflight (66) (BWHills) 7–8 ‡⁵DHarrison (7) (swtg: 6th st: a bhd) .............. 6.8

**9/4** Lemon's Mill (USA), **5/2** In the Picture (IRE), **6/1** KINGLOW (USA), Euroflight, **8/1** Al Ramis (IRE)(tchd 14/1), **20/1** Judge and Jury, **25/1** Ors. CSF £19.63, CT £303.05. Tote £6.50: £1.80 £1.50 £1.80 (£11.90). Mr V. E. Barclay (NEWMARKET) bred by W. S. Farish & M. H. Cline in USA. 8 Rn                              2m 26.38 (4.68)
                                                                                SF—52/53/55/39/29/19

---

**1069**     LBC NEWSTALK 97.3 FM MIKE DICKIN STKS (Mdn 3-Y-O) £2595.00 (£720.00: £345.00)
              1¼m 7y                                                            8-50 (8-54)

804⁴  **Cezanne** (MRStoute) 9–0  WRSwinburn (1) (lw: 5th st: hrd rdn over 1f out: led wl
              ins fnl f: all out) ........................................................ —1
857³  Scrutineer (USA) (JHMGosden) 9–0  SCauthen (3) (lw: led tl wl ins fnl f) ......... ½.2
      Free Mover (IRE) (NAGraham) 9–0  RCochrane (4) (unf: scope: hdwy 2f out: r.o
              ins fnl f) ................................................................. 1½.3
      Legal Embrace (CAN) (JRFanshawe) 8–9  LDettori (8) (lw: gd hdwy over 1f out:
              nvr nrr) ................................................................... nk.4
857²  Alum Bay (Fav) (HRACecil) 9–0  PatEddery (7) (lw: chsd ldr: slipped 4f out: 2nd
              st: ev ch over 1f out: wknd fnl f) ....................................... 1½.5
804   Storm Dust (JRFanshawe) 9–0  GCarter (5) (hdwy 2f out: one pce fnl f) .......... s.h.6
869⁶  Ler Cru (IRE) (CEBrittain) 9–0  MRoberts (9) (lw: 4th st: wknd fnl f) .............. 1½.7

932⁶ American Boogie (FR) **(78)** (bl) *(CEBrittain)* 8-9 ‡5BDoyle (2) (6th st: wknd 2f out) .......... 3.8

Lady Buchan *(MrsJCecil)* 8-9 PaulEddery (3) (wl grwn: 3rd st: wknd over 1f out) .......... 3.9

Snappy's Boy Josh *(PJFeilden)* 9-0 RFox (6) (a bhd) .......... 8.10

**11/8** Alum Bay, **9/4** Scrutineer (USA), **5/1** Lady Buchan, **6/1** CEZANNE, **20/1** Legal Embrace (CAN)(op 12/1), **33/1** Free Mover (IRE), Ler Cru (IRE), Storm Dust, **50/1** American Boogie (FR), **100/1** Snappy's Boy Josh. CSF £19.41, Tote £7.70: £2.00 £1.30 £2.70 (£8.90). Sheikh Mohammed (NEWMARKET) bred by Meon Valley Stud.
10 Rn
2m 9.53 (5.23)
SF—48/47/44/38/40/39

T/Trio: Race 2: £18.80 (57.7 Tckts). T/Plpt: £53.90 (77.8 Tckts).
Hn

567—**RIPON (R-H)**

## Wednesday, May 27th [Good to firm]

Going Allowance: minus 0.30 sec per fur (F)

Wind: slt half against

Stalls: low

**1070**    RIPON CATHEDRAL TRUST APPEAL CLAIMING STKS (Mdn) £1518.10 (£421.60: £202.30)  **1m**
6-45 (6-52)

532 **Ace Girl (56)** *(SRBowring)* 3-7-7 ‡3FNorton (11) (mde most: rdn & kpt on wl fnl 3f) .......... —1

618⁶ Charioteer (Fav) *(PCHaslam)* 3-8-7 KDarley (19) (a in tch: effrt over 3f out: styd on u.p appr fnl f: nt pce of wnr) .......... 1.2

Highland Battle (USA) *(IABalding)* 3-8-6 RCochrane (18) (mid div: effrt over 3f out: swtchd & styd on wl ins fnl f) .......... 1½.3

669 Slumber Thyme (IRE) **(49)** *(JGFitzGerald)* 3-7-7⁽¹⁾ ‡5SMaloney (12) (in tch: hdwy 3f out: nt qckn u.p fnl 2f) .......... ½.4

1013³ Quiet Victory **(42)** *(MissLCSiddall)* 5-7-13 ‡7PTurner (15) (lw: a.p: rdn & ev ch over 2f out: one pce fnl f) .......... ½.5

Banana Cufflinks (USA) **(39)** *(MHTompkins)* 6-8-9 ‡5CHodgson (2) (s.i.s: hdwy on outside 2f out: nvr nr) .......... ½.6

Bobbie Bold *(RO'Leary)* 4-8-12 MBirch (9) (effrt 3f out: styd on: nvr trbld ldrs) . ½.7

497⁶ Illuminating *(MrsJRRamsden)* 3-7-6 ‡5DHarrison (5) (lw: effrt 4f out: nvr rchd ldrs) .......... 1½.8

Legend Dulac (IRE) *(JLHarris)* 3-8-4 PaulEddery (10) (w ldr: rn wd st: wknd 2f out) .......... 1.9

606 Parr (IRE) **(58)** *(JMackie)* 4-9-2 DNicholls (7) (n.d) .......... 2½.10

Heart Flutter **(55)** *(ASmith)* 3-7-12 PBurke (4) (in tch: sme hdwy over 3f out: sn rdn & wknd) .......... 1.11

Tauzio (IRE) *(JMackie)* 4-9-4 GHind (8) (dwlt: hdwy over 2f out: nvr rch ldrs) 1½.12

Dancing Wild *(MrsGRReveley)* 3-7-11 JLowe (6) (mid div: grad lost pl fnl 3f) . hd.13

919⁵ Lightning Spark *(MAvison)* 3-8-5⁽¹⁾ WRyan (3) (lw: nvr bttr than mid div) .......... 2.14

Auntie Lorna *(MrsPABarker)* 3-7-11 SWood (13) (leggy: bit bkwd: a in rr) .......... 5.15

Lady Ghislaine (FR) *(ASReid)* 5-7-12 ‡7PMcCabe (1) (chsd ldrs: rn wd st: sn rdn & btn) .......... 1½.16

Diamond Singh **(21)** *(SGNorton)* 5-8-12 LCharnock (14) (a in rr) .......... ½.17

806 Northern Blade (IRE) **(52)** *(RHollinshead)* 3-8-0 DaleGibson (17) (a bhd) .... 1½.18

950 Mypeto (v) *(PCalver)* 3-8-0 NCarlisle (16) (plld hrd early: sn bhd) .......... 19

*750 Any Dream Would Do (6/1) Withdrawn (ref to ent stalls) : not under orders — Rule 4 applies*

**7/2** Charioteer, **5/1** Highland Battle (USA)(tchd 9/1), Quiet Victory, **6/1** Illuminating, **16/1** Parr (IRE)(op 10/1), Banana Cufflinks (USA), ACE GIRL, **20/1** Slumber Thyme (IRE), **25/1** Diamond Singh, Northern Blade (IRE), Mypeto, Lightning Spark, Dancing Wild, **33/1** Tauzio (IRE), **50/1** Ors. CSF £59.25, Tote £18.70: £3.50 £1.70 £2.40 (£41.50). Mrs P. A. Barratt (EDWINSTOWE) bred by T. Barratt. 19 Rn
1m 41 (3.3)
SF—/5/—/—/—/—

**1071**    LISHMAN, SIDWELL, CAMPBELL AND PRICE STKS (Mdn 2-Y.O) £1173.00 (£323.00: £153.00)  **5f**
7-10 (7-18)

**Saint Express** *(RMWhitaker)* 9-0 ACulhane (2) (cmpt: scope: bit bkwd: a.p: led over 1f out: drvn clr) .......... —1

Nutty Brown *(SGNorton)* 9-0 KDarley (6) (w'like: chsd ldrs: effrt wl over 1f out: no ch w wnr) .......... 5.2

665 Indian Secret (IRE) *(BEWilkinson)* 8-11 ‡3JFanning (1) (a cl up: hrd rdn & kpt on same pce appr fnl f) .......... hd.3

807⁵ The Sharp Bidder (IRE) (Jt-Fav) *(RHollinshead)* 9-0 WRyan (4) (hdwy ½-wy: styd on fnl f) .......... ½.4

811⁵ Express Mariecurie (IRE) (Jt-Fav) *(PWChapple-Hyam)* 8-9 PaulEddery (5) (lw: outpcd & rdn along ½-wy: swtchd & styd on appr fnl f) .... nk.5

791 Field of Vision (IRE) (bl) *(MJohnston)* 9-0 RPElliott (12) (led tl hdd & wknd over 1f out) ............................................. 4.6

Steal a March *(MWEasterby)* 9-0 TLucas (14) (w'like: scope: bit bkwd: s.s: stdy hdwy 2f out: nvr plcd to chal) ............. 3.7

874⁶ Bold Philip *(WJPearce)* 9-0 DNicholls (7) (lw: in tch: effrt ½-wy: n.d) ........ 1.8

Alberstan *(MHEasterby)* 9-0 MBirch (10) (w'like: leggy: s.i.s: rn green & sn pushed along: sme hdwy ½-wy: grad wknd) ...... 1.9

886 Selvole *(MissLAPerratt)* 8-9 NConnorton (13) (hung rt virtually thrght: prom tl outpcd fr ½-wy) ................................ 2¹/₂.10

733⁵ Water Diviner (bl) *(RFJohnsonHoughton)* 9-0 SWhitworth (11) (lw: prom: rdn ½-wy: wknd wl over 1f out) ............... 1.11

886 Bluebella *(MrsPABarker)* 8-9 JLowe (8) (lw: tch 3f) ........................ 1.12

See You Jimmy *(RonaldThompson)* 9-0 LCharnock (3) (w'like: bit bkwd: s.i.s: nvr wnt pce) ......................... 2¹/₂.13

Free Market *(GMMoore)* 9-0 KFallon (9) (cmpt: str: bkwd: a outpcd) ............. hd.14

**4/1** The Sharp Bidder (IRE)(6/1—7/2), Express Mariecurie (IRE)(op 7/4), **6/1** Water Diviner, Alberstan(op 4/1), **8/1** Field of Vision (IRE)(12/1—7/1), SAINT EXPRESS(op 5/1), **9/1** Indian Secret (IRE), **12/1** Nutty Brown(op 8/1), **14/1** Free Market, **20/1** Steal a March, Selvole, **25/1** See You Jimmy, **33/1** Ors. CSF £99.58, Tote £14.40: £2.90 £3.50 £3.70 (£76.30). Mr M. G. St Quinton (WETHERBY) bred by R. M. Whitaker. 14 Rn  59.8 sec (1.2)
SF—46/26/22/23/17/6

---

**1072**  TOUCHE ROSS H'CAP STKS (3-Y.O) (0-80) £1518.00 (£418.00: £198.00)
1m  7-35 (7-44)

884 **Talented Ting (IRE) (60)** *(PCHaslam)* 8-9 KDarley (3) (lw: chsd ldrs: rdn to disp ld over 2f out: styd on gamely u.p fnl f) .................... —1

750* Straw Thatch **(72)** *(MJohnston)* 9-7 RPElliott (4) (a.p: rdn to disp ld over 2f out: no ex ins fnl f) ................................... nk.2

401 Essayeffsee **(56)** (bl) *(MHEasterby)* 8-5 MBirch (6) (b.hind: led: rdn 4f out: hdd over 2f out: kpt on u.p fnl f) ............ ³/₄.3

725⁴ Eastleigh **(66)** *(RHollinshead)* 9-1 WRyan (5) (plld hrd early: hdwy over 2f out: styd on wl u.p ins fnl f: nvr nrr) ........ hd.4

884 Tahitian **(51)** *(MrsJRRamsden)* 7-9 ‡⁵DHarrison (9) (lw: dwlt: bhd: rdn along 4f out: styd on wl appr fnl f) ........... 1¹/₂.5

Bonica **(61)** (Fav) *(JRFanshawe)* 8-10 WRSwinburn (1) (lw: in tch: effrt over 3f out: sn rdn & btn) ................... 7.6

749 My Jersey Pearl (IRE) **(53)** *(DonEnricoIncisa)* 7-13 ‡³JFanning (2) (lw: in tch: rdn over 3f out: sn wknd) ............ 7.7

963 Pride of Pendle **(60)** *(PCalver)* 8-9 DaleGibson (7) (lw: s.s: a bhd) ............ 8.8

978³ Military Expert **(72)** *(CaptJWilson)* 9-7 JLowe (8) (prom tl lost pl appr st: sn bhd) 1¹/₂.9

**11/4** Bonica, **3/1** Tahitian, **11/2** Eastleigh, **15/2** Military Expert, TALENTED TING (IRE), **8/1** Straw Thatch, **12/1** Essayeffsee, **14/1** Pride of Pendle, **20/1** My Jersey Pearl (IRE). CSF £61.04, CT £652.77. Tote £9.00: £2.00 £3.00 £2.60 (£32.10). Mr Martin Wickens (MIDDLEHAM) bred by R. A. Keogh in Ireland. 9 Rn  1m 40.1 (2.4)
SF—23/34/16/25/–/–

---

**1073**  FAIRCLOUGH H'CAP (0-85) £1518.00 (£418.00: £198.00)
1¹/₂m 60y  8-05 (8-10)

529* **Truben (USA) (79)** (Fav) *(HRACecil)* 3-8-7 WRyan (1) (lw: hld up in tch: hdwy 3f out: chal 2f out: kpt on wl u.p fnl f) ............... —1

681⁴ Lord Hastie (USA) **(76)** *(SGNorton)* 4-9-4 DNicholls (2) (lw: a.p: led wl over 2f out: sn chal: r.o gamely u.p) ........ nk.2

Sapphirine **(61)** *(RMWhitaker)* 5-8-7 DaleGibson (7) (in tch: effrt over 3f out: kpt on same pce fnl 2f) ........... 6.3

760⁶ Bold Elect **(66)** *(PWigham)* 4-8-12 MWigham (5) (lw: chsd ldrs: effrt & ev ch over 3f out: styd on same pce fnl 2f) ...... 4.4

417 Royal Borough **(60)** *(MPNaughton)* 7-8-6 GHind (8) (s.i.s: bhd: stdy hdwy over 3f out: wknd appr fnl f) ......... 1.5

815 Roberty Lea **(62)** *(TFairhurst)* 4-8-5 ‡³JFanning (6) (swtg: chsd ldrs tl outpcd over 5f out: n.d after) .......... 4.6

829 Chiefs Babu **(74)** *(RO'Leary)* 4-9-6 MBirch (3) (prom: hdwy to disp ld 9f out: led over 4f out: wknd over 2f out) ...... 3.7

916² Family Line **(82)** *(MissLAPerratt)* 4-10-0 NConnorton (4) (a in rr) ............. 7.8

83* Magic Secret **(70)** *(PCHaslam)* 4-9-2 KDarley (10) (bhd: hdwy on ins whn hmpd over 3f out: sn btn) .......... 2¹/₂.9

134⁴ In Truth **(51)** *(JPLeigh)* 4-7-11 LCharnock (9) (led: disp ld 9f out tl wknd over 4f out) ................... 5.10

**10/11** TRUBEN (USA), **7/1** Bold Elect(tchd 11/1), Roberty Lea, **10/1** Lord Hastie (USA), **12/1** Magic Secret, **14/1** Family Line, Chiefs Babu, Royal Borough, Sapphirine, **33/1** In Truth. CSF £11.42, CT £82.29. Tote £2.00: £1.20 £2.50 £2.80 (£12.00). Mr Edward St George (NEWMARKET) bred by Edward A. Seltzer in USA. 10 Rn
2m 36.1 (2.1)
SF—36/50/23/20/12/3

**1074**    PERSIMMON HOMES MEDIAN AUCTION STKS (3-Y.O) £1173.00 (£323.00: £153.00)
        1¹/₂m 60y
                                          8-35 (8-35)

781⁴ Goldsmiths' Hall (98) (Fav) (GWragg) 9-3 WRSwinburn (2) (lw: a gng wl trckd ldr: led over 3f out: easily) ......................................................... —1

892² Suez Canal (IRE) (74) (PWChapple-Hyam) 8-10 PaulEddery (4) (led: qcknd 4f out: sn hdd & no ch w wnr) ............................................... 6.2

Our Joey (JWharton) 8-7 MBirch (2) (w'like: leggy: s.s: chsd ldrs: rdn & wandered over 3f out: eased whn btn fnl f) ............................ 7.3

**1/5** GOLDSMITHS' HALL, **4/1** Suez Canal (IRE), **25/1** Our Joey. CSF £1.36, Tote £1.30 (£1.10). Sheikh Mohammed (NEWMARKET) bred by White Lodge Stud Ltd. 3 Rn
2m 43.2 (9.2)

**1075**    GLENFIDDICH PURE MALT WHISKY H'CAP (3-Y.O) (0-70) £1173.00 (£323.00: £153.00)
        6f
                                          9-05 (9-09)

801 **First Gold** (53) (bl) (JWharton) 8-5 MBirch (2) (lw: s.s: hdwy after 2f: n.m.r fr ¹/₂-wy: swtchd & led ins fnl f: edgd lft: r.o) ......................... —1

1004² Invigilate (50) (MPNaughton) 7-11 ‡5DHarrison (3) (a.p: disp ld 3f out tl hdd & kpt on u.p ins fnl f) ............................................... 1¹/₂.2

498 Thewaari (USA) (56) (AAScott) 8-8(1) WRSwinburn (8) (lw: a chsng ldrs: ev ch over 1f out: no ex nr fin) ......................................... 1¹/₂.3

1000² Educated Pet (12) (Fav) (MJohnston) 7-9 JLowe (9) (a.p: disp ld ¹/₈ wy: hdd ins fnl f: sltly hmpd nr fin) ............................... nk.4

949 Joyful Thought (50) (MrsJRRamsden) 8-2 KDarley (6) (lw: led to ¹/₂-wy: wknd over 1f out) ........................................................ 3.5

603⁴ North Flyer (50) (BAMcMahon) 8-2(1) GHind (12) (in tch: hdwy u.p 2f out: nt rch ldrs) ................................................................ 1¹/₂.6

614 Chester Belle (42) (PCHaslam) 8-4 DaleGibson (4) (swtg: bhd: hdwy over 2f out: nt pce to chal) ........................................ ¹/₂.7

591 The Dream Maker (IRE) (49) (MrsNMacauley) 8-1 NCarlisle (17) (spd on outside 4f) ..................................................................... ¹/₂.8

669 Throw Away Line (50) (JEtherington) 8-2 NConnorton (5) (in tch: effrt whn hmpd wl over 1f out: nt rcvr) ............................ 3¹/₂.9

Young Valentine (69) (RMWhitaker) 9-7 ACulhane (11) (lw: stdy hdwy over 1f out: n.d) ................................................................... ¹/₂.10

949 Spanish Performer (54) (TFairhurst) 8-3 ‡3JFanning (10) (chsd ldrs: sn pushed along: wknd over 1f out) ........................... 1.11

366 Hot Punch (53) (PCalver) 7-12 ‡7CAdamson (15) (spd centre to ¹/₂-wy) ...... s.h.12

Intrepid Fort (58) (BWMurray) 8-6 JFortune (7) (spd over 3f: grad lost pl) ...... hd.13

918 Lift Boy (USA) (48) (DenysSmith) 8-0 LCharnock (16) (spd 3f: sn lost pl) ........ 1.14

Pitch Black (IRE) (60) (MWEasterby) 8-12 TLucas (1) (a in rr) ........................ nk.15

890⁴ Baladee Pet (56) (MrsVAAconley) 8-8 PBurke (13) (prom tl outpcd fr ¹/₂-wy) ... 1.16

949 Kashgar (41) (DWChapman) 7-7 SWood (14) (t.o) ......................................... 17

LONG HANDICAP: Kashgar 6-5.

**9/4** Educated Pet, **6/1** Invigilate, **8/1** Thewaari (USA), **10/1** Spanish Performer, FIRST GOLD, **12/1** Pitch Black (IRE), **14/1** Throw Away Line, **16/1** Joyful Thought(op 8/1), Lift Boy (USA), North Flyer, Chester Belle, Young Valentine, Baladee Pet, **25/1** Intrepid Fort, The Dream Maker (IRE), **33/1** Hot Punch, **100/1** Kashgar. CSF £69.57, CT £480.30. Tote £15.10: £3.30 £1.70 £2.40 £1.40 (£37.40). Mr J. L. Ashby (MELTON MOWBRAY) bred by Messinger Stud Ltd. 17 Rn
1m 12.7 (1)
SF—35/21/25/11/7/1

T/Plpt: £909.40 (3.9 Tckts).
0'R

**733—BRIGHTON (L-H)**
## Wednesday, May 27th [Firm]
Going Allowance: minus 0.65 sec per fur (H)
                                                  Wind: fresh half bhd

Stalls: low

**1076**    WALLY COOMES H'CAP (3-Y.O) (0-80) £2684.50 (£742.00: £353.50)
        5f 59y
                                          2-00 (2-07)

801 **Cheshire Annie (IRE)** (52) (WCarter) 8-1 JQuinn (2) (2nd st: led over 2f out: drvn out) ............................................................................... —1

559 Uccello **(72)** *(LJHolt)* 9-7 JReid (5) (3rd st: ev ch fnl f: r.o) ................................. nk.2
897 Savalaro **(54)** *(JFfitch-Heyes)* 8-3 AMackay (6) (led 3f: wknd fnl f) ...................... 6.3
939 Life's a Breeze **(54)** *(MRChannon)* 8-3 CRutter (1) (lw: 5th st: nvr nr to chal) .. 1¹⁄₂.4
792 Fourofus **(61)** *(Fav)* *(RBoss)* 8-10 MRoberts (3) (lw: 4th st: wknd over 3f out) .... 8.5
899 Mayles Lass **(45)** *(JJBridger)* 7-8(1) NAdams (4) (6th st: a bhd) ............................ 5.6
LONG HANDICAP: Mayles Lass 7-3.

2/1 Fourofus, 7/2 Uccello(5/2—4/1), CHESHIRE ANNIE (IRE)(tchd 6/1), Savalaro(5/2—4/1), **10/1** Life's a Breeze(8/1—12/1), **50/1** Mayles Lass. CSF £14.69, Tote £5.30: £2.30 £2.20 (£8.50). Mr D. P. Delaney (EPSOM) bred by John and Mrs McNamara in Ireland. 6 Rn       60 sec (equals best; U3)
SF—28/47/5/–/–/–

**1077**    COOMES (S) STKS (2-Y-O) £2343.60 (£649.60: £310.80)    **5f 59y**    2-30 (2-32)

791⁴ **Not so Generous (IRE)** *(WGMTurner)* 8-3 ‡3DBiggs (5) (mde all: rdn out) ............... —1
Dark Eyed Lady (IRE) *(Jt-Fav)* *(DWPArbuthnot)* 8-6 TQuinn (6) (w'like: 4th st:
hrd rdn over 1f out: r.o) ............................................... 1.2
561⁵ Grey Runner *(BPalling)* 8-6 RHills (1) (6th st: r.o one pce fnl 2f) ...................... 5.3
900⁵ Get Daily Sport *(PAKelleway)* 8-6 CRutter (7) (2nd st: wknd over 1f out) ......... 2¹⁄₂.4
772 Royal Deed (USA) (bl) *(Jt-Fav)* *(GLewis)* 8-6 BRouse (3) (plld hrd: 3rd st: wknd
fnl f) ......................................................................... 1¹⁄₂.5
782 Victorian Star *(PButler)* 8-6 AProud (10) (nvr nr to chal) ............................. ¹⁄₂.6
786⁶ School of Science *(Jt-Fav)* *(RPCHoad)* 8-11 NAdams (9) (a bhd) ..................... 1.7
920 Pfaff's Cellar *(WGMTurner)* 8-3 ‡TSprake (2) (5th st: wknd over 2f out) ........... s.h.8
371⁵ Babytalker *(Jt-Fav)* *(NACallaghan)* 8-11 MRoberts (8) (rdn thrght: a bhd) ......... ¹⁄₂.9
791 Risky Rosie *(RVoorspuy)* 8-6 SDawson (4) w.lw bhd) ................................ 10

9/2 Royal Deed (USA), Babytalker(op 3/1), School of Science(op 9/2), Dark Eyed Lady (IRE), **5/1** Grey Runner, **7/1** NOT SO GENEROUS (IRE)(5/1—8/1), **12/1** Get Daily Sport(op 8/1), **16/1** Pfaff's Cellar(op 10/1), **33/1** Ors. CSF £37.15, Tote £6.80: £2.80 £1.50 £2.20 (£17.50). Mr E. Goody (SHERBORNE) bred by P. J. Foley in Ireland. 10 Rn; No bld       61.7 sec (1.4)

**1078**    COOMES H'CAP (F & M) (0-100) £4980.50 (£1484.00: £707.00: £318.50)
   **7f 214y**    3-05 (3-07)

821³ **Rocality (76)** *(Fav)* *(RHannon)* 3-8-8 WCarson (1) (mde all: rdn out) ................ —1
Hissma **(85)** *(HRACecil)* 3-9-3 PatEddery (5) (chsd wnr: hrd rdn 2f out: ev ch
ins fnl f: r.o) ............................................................. ¹⁄₂.2
832⁶ Langtry Lady **(84)** *(MJRyan)* 6-10-0 LDettori (3) (5th st: rdn over 1f out: unable
qckn) ...................................................................... 2¹⁄₂.3
972 Miss Doody **(65)** (v) *(MRChannon)* 3-7-11 CRutter (4) (3rd st: hrd rdn over 2f
out: one pce) ............................................................. 1.4
768⁶ Conquista **(79)** (bl) *(LadyHerries)* 4-9-9 JWilliams (2) (s.s: 4th st: wknd 2f out) . 5.5

5/4 ROCALITY, 7/2 Langtry Lady, **5/1** Hissma(3/1—11/2), **11/2** Conquista, **10/1** Miss Doody(8/1—12/1). CSF £6.92, Tote £2.10: £1.50 £2.10 (£4.20). Mr G. Z. Mizel (MARLBOROUGH) bred by Guest Leasing and Bloodstock Co. 5 Rn       1m 33.2 (1)
SF—1/8/10/–/–

**1079**    CATFORD STKS (Mdn 3 & 4-Y-O) £1932.00 (£532.00: £252.00)
   **1m 1f 209y**    3-40 (3-42)

680⁵ **Rainridge** (v) *(JLDunlop)* 3-8-9 WCarson (3) (led 9f out: clr over 1f out: comf) . —1
737² Maji *(DMorley)* 3-8-4 MRoberts (6) (3rd st: chsd wnr fnl 2f: no imp) ................ 5.2
440 Vagrancy *(Fav)* *(BWHills)* 3-8-5(1) PatEddery (8) (2nd st: rdn over 2f out: eased
whn btn wl over 1f out) ............................................... 5.3
707⁶ Continuity *(GHarwood)* 3-8-4 AClark (2) (rdn over 4f out: 4th st: one pce fnl 3f) 1.4
Betelgeuse *(HRACecil)* 3-8-4 AMcGlone (4) (leggy: unf: 5th st: no hdwy fnl 3f) ¹⁄₂.5
Asian Punter (IRE) *(AHide)* 3-8-9 JWilliams (5) (nvr nrr) ............................... 4.6
Baby Wizzard *(IABalding)* 3-8-6(2) JReid (7) (leggy: 6th st: wknd 3f out) .......... 1.7
693 Boldrullah *(DWPArbuthnot)* 3-8-9 TQuinn (9) (b.nr fore: a bhd) .................... 15.8
510 Morjinski Dancer *(RSimpson)* 3-7-13 ‡5ATucker (1) (led 1f: wknd over 5f out) .... 8.9

5/2 Vagrancy, 3/1 Maji(9/2—5/1), **9/2** Betelgeuse(op 5/2), **6/1** Continuity(4/1—8/1), **7/1** RAINRIDGE, **14/1** Baby Wizzard(op 6/1), **25/1** Asian Punter (IRE), **33/1** Boldrullah, **66/1** Morjinski Dancer. CSF £26.05, Tote £8.10: £1.70 £1.30 £1.80 (£10.50). Mr P. G. Goulandris (ARUNDEL) bred by Hesmonds Stud Ltd. 9 Rn
      1m 57.4 (U.6)
SF—36/21/12/9/8/5

**1080**    COOMES SENIOR CITIZENS MEDIAN AUCTION GRADUATION STKS (3-Y-O) £2514.00
   (£606.00)    **1m 3f 196y**    4-15 (4-16)

**Alphard (88)** *(HRACecil)* 9-7 PatEddery (2) (bit bkwd: mde all: clr over 1f out:
easily) ..................................................................... —1

802² Duke of Eurolink **(84)** (Fav) *(LMCumani)* 9-7 LDettori (1) (2nd st: rdn over 3f out: eased whn btn over 1f out) .......................................... 15.2

**4/7** Duke of Eurolink, **6/4** ALPHARD. Tote £2.20. Mr D. K. Harris (NEWMARKET) bred by Brook Bloodstock P L C.
**2 Rn**                                                                                    2m 28.9 (1.9)
                                                                                                    SF—10/–

**1081**   COOMES H'CAP (0-80) £2301.00 (£636.00: £303.00)   **1m 3f 196y**   4-45 (4-48)

926⁴ **Monarda (66)** *(PFICole)* 5-9-1 AMunro (1) (3rd st: hrd rdn over 1f out: led wl ins
fnl f: r.o wl) ............................................................................... —1
1009³ Abingdon Flyer (IRE) **(69)** (bl) *(RHannon)* 4-9-4 JReid (2) (5th st: hrd rdn over
1f out: led ins fnl f: sn hdd: r.o) ........................................................ nk.2
926⁵ Prince Hannibal **(79)** (Fav) *(JLDunlop)* 5-10-0 WCarson (4) (4th st: led over 2f
out tl ins fnl f: nt r.o) ..................................................................... 2¹/₂.3
Fitness Fanatic **(44)** *(JTGifford)* 4-7-7 JQuinn (5) (2nd st: led over 3f out tl over
2f out: sn wknd) ......................................................................... 10.4
271 Do the Right Thing **(64)** *(JABOld)* 4-8-13 WNewnes (3) (led over 8f) ............... 15.5
LONG HANDICAP: Fitness Fanatic 7-6.

**6/4** Prince Hannibal, **7/4** MONARDA, **3/1** Abingdon Flyer (IRE)(9/4—7/2), **20/1** Do the Right Thing(op 8/1), **33/1**
Fitness Fanatic. CSF £6.78, Tote £2.70: £1.40 £2.10 (£3.50). Mr Fahd Salman (WHATCOMBE) bred by Newgate
Stud Ltd. 5 Rn                                                                               2m 31 (4)

T/Plpt: £49.20 (62.8 Tckts).                                                                          AK

# BRIGHTON (L-H)
## Thursday, May 28th [Firm]
Going Allowance: minus 0.35 sec per fur (F)                                            Wind: slt across

Stalls: low

**1082**   REGENCY STKS (Mdn) £1932.00 (£532.00: £252.00)   **1m 3f 196y**   2-00 (2-02)

789⁶ **Simonov** *(GHarwood)* 3-8-6 AClark (5) (mde all: clr over 3f out: rdn over 1f out:
r.o) ........................................................................................ —1
789⁴ Three Wells **(78)** *(JLDunlop)* 3-8-6 WCarson (4) (lw: hld up: 6th st: rdn over 3f
out: chsd wnr over 1f out: r.o wl) ...................................................... hd.2
597² White Wedding **(70)** *(PFICole)* 3-8-1 CRutter (6) (4th st: one pce fnl 3f) ............ 7.3
788² Choppy Choppy (USA) **(79)** (Fav) *(BWHills)* 3-8-1 DHolland (1) (2nd st: wknd
over 1f out) .............................................................................. 12.4
771⁵ Sherraa (USA) *(MAJarvis)* 3-8-1 AMunro (3) (5th st: wknd 3f out) ..................... 2¹/₂.5
Unique Tribute *(CACyzer)* 3-8-6 AMorris (2) (unf: bkwd: 3rd st: wknd 3f out) ..... 5.6

**6/4** Choppy Choppy (USA), **5/2** Three Wells, **5/1** White Wedding, **7/1** SIMONOV, **10/1** Sherraa (USA)(8/1—14/
1), **33/1** Unique Tribute. CSF £22.69, Tote £7.20: £1.90 £1.60 (£7.70). Mr K. Abdulla (PULBOROUGH) bred by
Juddmonte Farms. 6 Rn                                                                     2m 28.1 (1.1)
                                                                                                    SF—39/38/19/–/–/–

**1083**   HELEN McLEOD-SMITH MEMORIAL CHALLENGE TROPHY (Stks) (App'ce) £2049.60
(£565.60: £268.80)   **1m 1f 209y**   2-30 (2-31)

832 **Secretary of State (69)** (Fav) *(PFICole)* 6-9-0 JDSmith (4) (b: 2nd st: led over
2f out: rdn & r.o wl) ..................................................................... —1
773² Blushing Belle **(62)** (bl) *(PFICole)* 4-9-2 SDrowne (1) (led: clr 9f out: hdd over 2f
out: unable qckn) ......................................................................... 4.2
Maryland Willie *(NACallaghan)* 5-9-2 ‡§WThomas (3) (b: 4th st: one pce fnl 3f) .. 5.3
736⁶ Thin Red Line **(50)** (v) *(JRJenkins)* 8-9-2 ‡§DCarson (2) (lw: 3rd st: wknd 3f out) 4.4

**5/4** SECRETARY OF STATE, **7/2** Thin Red Line(9/4—4/1), **5/1** Maryland Willie. CSF
£5.13, Tote £2.20 (£3.10). Mr W. H. Ponsonby (WHATCOMBE) bred by Greenville House Stud. 4 Rn
                                                                                                    2m 2.6 (4.6)
                                                                                                    SF—19/13/3/–

**1084**   FLANAGAN AND ALLEN H'CAP (0-70) £2322.00 (£642.00: £306.00)
**5f 213y**                                                                          3-00 (3-02)

**Caromish (USA) (60)** *(MDIUsher)* 5-9-8 MWigham (3) (mde virtually all: clr
over 1f out: comf) ....................................................................... —1
997 Shikari's Son **(53)** *(JWhite)* 5-9-1 CNutter (2) (hdwy & n.m.r on ins over 1f out:
r.o one pce) .............................................................................. 7.2
992⁴ Judgement Call **(66)** *(PHowling)* 5-10-0 JMurray (9) (2nd st: hrd rdn over 1f
out: one pce) ............................................................................. nk.3

897[6] Cronk's Quality (46) *(DCJermy)* 9-8-8 NHowe (5) (lw: hrd rdn over 2f out: hdwy over 1f out: r.o one pce) ..................... 1.4

967 Three Lucky (IRE) (42) *(MDIUsher)* 4-8-4 AMackay (1) (swtg: 5th st: one pce fnl 2f) .................... ¾.5

885 Farmer Jock (62) *(MrsNMacauley)* 10-9-10 CRutter (4) (b: 6th st: no hdwy fnl 3f) 3.6

967* My Ruby Ring (40) (Fav) *(DRLaing)* 5-8-2 TyroneWilliams (8) (b: 3rd st: hrd rdn 2f out: wknd over 1f out) ..................... 1½.7

735 Saysana (31) *(AMoore)* 5-7-7 NAdams (10) (4th st: wknd 2f out) ..................... 3.8

901 Print Finisher (45) (v) *(BobJones)* 6-8-7 VSmith (7) (bhd fnl 2f) ..................... 3.9

936 Castle Galah (31) *(SWoodman)* 5-7-7 RFox (6) (lw: a wl bhd) ..................... 2½.10

LONG HANDICAP: Castle Galah 7-1.

**15/8** My Ruby Ring, **4/1** Judgement Call, **11/2** Cronk's Quality, Farmer Jock, **7/1** Shikari's Son, **20/1** CAROMISH (USA)(op 12/1), **25/1** Saysana, Three Lucky (IRE), **50/1** Print Finisher, **66/1** Castle Galah. CSF £134.44, CT £613.07. Tote £13.60: £5.70 £2.90 £1.50 (£154.90). Mr John P. Pitt (EAST GARSTON) bred by Belvadere Stables, Inc. in USA. 10 Rn

1m 9.2 (0.8)

SF–50/15/27/3/–/4

---

## 1085

SEAFORD (S) H'CAP (3-Y.O) (0-60) £2422.00 (£672.00: £322.00)
**7f 214y**

3-30 (3-32)

1034[3] **Allimac Nomis (39)** *(NACallaghan)* 8-0 WCarson (13) (4th st: led over 1f out: rdn out) ..................... —1

728 Lindeman (46) (Fav) *(SDow)* 8-7 TQuinn (4) (rdn thrght: hdwy 3f out: r.o one pce fnl 2f) ..................... 2½.2

295 Walkonthemoon (55) *(MMcCormack)* 9-2 WNewnes (8) (lw: led 1f: led over 5f out tl over 1f out: one pce) ..................... 1½.3

734 Simon Ellis (IRE) (47) *(DRLaing)* 8-1 ‡7KimMcDonnell (12) (lw: n.m.r 2f out: swtchd rt & hdwy over 1f out: one pce) ..................... 5.4

355 Rocky Bay (47) *(DHaydnJones)* 8-8 DHolland (10) (led 7f tl over 5f out: 2nd st: wknd wl over 1f out) ..................... 7.5

863 Tyrone Flyer (50) *(GHEden)* 8-11 JWilliams (2) (6th st: wknd wl over 1f out) ..................... 2.6

621 Lord Belmonte (IRE) (40) *(CACyzer)* 8-1 AMorris (3) (lw: a mid div) ..................... nk.7

524 Confound (IRE) (40) (bl) *(JAkehurst)* 8-6 NAdams (6) (3rd st: wknd over 2f out) 2.8

Red Jack (IRE) (66) *(JAkehurst)* 9-6 ‡7MarkDenaro (1) (a bhd) ..................... 3.9

408 Freni (41) *(MDIUsher)* 8-2 RStreet (11) (bhd fnl 4f) ..................... 5.10

Cushty (42) *(JELong)* 8-3(2) MRoberts (5) (a bhd) ..................... ½.11

932 Loviste Bay (35) *(JFfitch-Heyes)* 7-10 AMackay (9) (a bhd) ..................... hd.12

787 Shapely Deb (41) *(DRLaing)* 8-12 TyroneWilliams (7) (5th st: wknd 3f out) ..................... ¾.13

**100/30** Lindeman, **4/1** ALLIMAC NOMIS, **11/2** Confound (IRE), **6/1** Rocky Bay, **13/2** Walkonthemoon, **8/1** Tyrone Flyer, **16/1** Red Jack (IRE)(10/1—20/1), Freni(12/1—20/1), **20/1** Cushty(op 12/1), Lord Belmonte (IRE)(op 12/1), Simon Ellis (IRE)(op 10/1), **33/1** Ors. CSF £18.10, CT £81.03. Tote £4.00: £1.80 £1.80 £1.70 (£6.00). Mrs J. Callaghan (NEWMARKET) bred by Mrs William McAlpine. 13 Rn; No bid

1m 34.4 (2.2)

SF–11/10/14/–/–/–

---

## 1086

SHOREHAM STKS (Mdn 3-Y.O) £1932.00 (£532.00: £252.00)
**6f 209y**

4-00 (4-01)

898[6] **Owner's Dream (USA) (72)** *(BHanbury)* 9-0 MRoberts (5) (lw: 2nd st: hrd rdn over 1f out: led ins fnl f: r.o wl) ..................... —1

620[6] Arboretum (IRE) (Fav) *(RCharlton)* 8-9 WRyan (1) (led tl ins fnl f: r.o) ..................... ½.2

865 La Kermesse (USA) *(JHMGosden)* 8-9 JWilliams (3) (3rd st: rdn over 1f out: r.o) 1.3

750[4] Silica (USA) (64) *(JHMGosden)* 8-9 WCarson (4) (nvr nr to chal) ..................... 5.4

967[4] Bells of Longwick (57) *(DRLaing)* 8-9 TyroneWilliams (6) (4th st: hrd rdn 2f out: wknd over 1f out) ..................... nk.5

899 Jorrocks *(MDixon)* 9-0 AClark (7) (6th st: a bhd) ..................... 10.6

408 Ballycastle Mary (IRE) *(TJNaughton)* 8-9 DHolland (2) (b.nr hind: 5th st: wknd 3f out) ..................... 3½.7

**13/8** Arboretum (IRE), **2/1** OWNER'S DREAM (USA), **7/2** Silica (USA)(op 2/1), **14/1** Ballycastle Mary (IRE), Bells of Longwick(10/1—20/1), **25/1** La Kermesse (USA), **66/1** Jorrocks. CSF £5.37, Tote £2.90: £1.60 (£3.70). Mr B. Hanbury (NEWMARKET) bred by Rogers Trust in USA. 7 Rn

1m 21.9 (1.9)

SF–35/28/25/10/9/–

---

## 1087

CLAYTON H'CAP (0-70) £2574.00 (£714.00: £342.00)
(Weights raised 2 lb)
**1m 1f 209y**

4-30 (4-33)

604 **Top Royal (59)** *(JLDunlop)* 3-8-5 WCarson (7) (2nd st: led ins fnl f: pushed out) —1

736* Dazzle the Crowd (IRE) (55) (Fav) *(CACyzer)* 4-9-2 TQuinn (10) (lw: rdn 6f out: hdwy 2f out: ev ch 1f out: unable qckn) ..................... 2.2

866[6] Serious Time (48) *(SirMarkPrescott)* 4-8-9 CNutter (6) (led: hrd rdn over 3f out: hdd ins fnl f: one pce) ..................... 3.3

800 Beau Dada (IRE) (52) *(JWhite)* 4-8-13 WRyan (2) (hdwy over 1f out: r.o) ..................... 2.4

809 Chatham Island **(63)** *(CEBrittain)* 4–9-10 MRoberts (1) (lw: 3rd st: ev ch 2f out: eased whn btn fnl f) .......................................................... nk.5
1041* Naseer (USA) **(62)** *(NACallaghan)* 3–8-1 (7x) ‡⁷JTate (11) (4th st: wknd over 2f out) ......................................................................... 2.6
580 Bronze Runner **(45)** (bl) *(EAWheeler)* 8–8-1 ‡⁵DHarrison (5) (nvr nr to chal) .... 2¹/₂.7
702 Shrewd Girl (USA) **(63)** *(BWHills)* 4–9-10 DHolland (4) (5th st: wknd over 2f out) 1.8
799 Debjanjo **(43)** *(JRJenkins)* 4–8-4 GBaxter (12) (lw: a bhd) ................................. ¹/₂.9
773 Anne's Bank (IRE) **(47)** *(AMoore)* 4–8-8 NAdams (3) (lw: 6th st: wknd over 2f out) ................................................................................................... 8.10
736 San Roque **(32)** (bl) *(SWoodman)* 7–7-7 JQuinn (8) (a bhd) ........................ 15.11
738 Sam the Man **(50)** *(JFfitch-Heyes)* 5–8-11 AMackay (9) (a bhd) ....................... 5.12

LONG HANDICAP: San Roque 6-13.

**2/1** Dazzle the Crowd (IRE), **7/2** Naseer (USA)(3/1—9/2), **5/1** TOP ROYAL, **8/1** Chatham Island, **10/1** Serious Time(7/1—12/1), **12/1** Shrewd Girl (USA)(7/1—14/1), Beau Dada (IRE)(10/1—16/1), **20/1** Anne's Bank (IRE)(op 12/1), Bronze Runner(op 12/1), **25/1** Debjanjo, **33/1** Sam the Man, **50/1** San Roque. CSF £15.46, CT £93.28. Tote £6.40: £2.10 £1.30 £1.80 (£6.70). Mr Aubrey Ison (ARUNDEL) bred by Miss G. Abbey. 12 Rn
1m 59.4 (1.4)
SF—42/49/36/36/46/19

T/Plpt: £222.20 (16.2 Tckts). AK

## 745—CARLISLE (R-H)
### Thursday, May 28th [Hard]
Going Allowance: minus 0.50 sec per fur (H)                    Wind: fresh almost across

Stalls: high

**1088**   WHITBREAD TROPHY (Stks) (Mdn 3-Y.O) £2128.00 (£588.00: £280.00)
1¹/₂m                                                              2-15 (2-17)

911² **Mr Flood (USA)** (Fav) *(MrsJCecil)* 9-0 PaulEddery (2) (trckd ldr: rdn 4f out: led wl over 1f out: sn pushed clr) ............................................................. —1
577⁴ Sahara Shield *(AAScott)* 9-0 BRaymond (1) (lw: led: qcknd over 4f out: hdd wl over 1f out: eased whn btn fnl f) .......................................... 5.2
Storm Gayle (IRE) *(MJohnston)* 8-9 DMcKeown (3) (w'like: scope: bit bkwd: s.i.s: rn green & outpcd 4f out: styd on wl fnl f) ................ 2¹/₂.5

**30/100** MR FLOOD (USA), **4/1** Sahara Shield, **9/1** Storm Gayle (IRE). CSF £1.75, Tote £1.30 (£1.20). Mr James H. Stone (NEWMARKET) bred by Edward A. Seltzer in USA. 3 Rn
2m 34.7 (5.2)

**1089**   HEINEKEN (S) HCAP (3, 4 & 5-Y.O) (0-60) £2520.00 (£700.00: £336.00)
7f 214y                                                           2-45 (2-46)

913* **Lawnswood Junior (44)** *(JLSpearing)* 5–9-0 (7x) KDarley (3) (lw: hld up & bhd: hdwy 3f out: swtchd appr fnl f: sn led: r.o wl) ...................... —1
469 Chance Report **(37)** *(FHLee)* 4–8-7 PaulEddery (12) (a chsng ldrs: rdn to ld wl over 1f out: hdd ins fnl f: kpt on) ........................................... 3¹/₂.2
962 Gant Bleu (FR) **(45)** *(RMWhitaker)* 5–9-1 ACulhane (8) (in tch: hdwy to disp ld wl over 1f out: sn rdn: nt qckn fnl f) .......................... 1¹/₂.3
615 Falcons Dawn **(55)** (v) *(MO'Neill)* 5–9-11 JFortune (10) (lw: w ldrs: rdn & ev ch appr fnl f: no ex) ............................................................... ³/₄.4
488⁶ Mummys Rocket **(35)** *(MO'Neill)* 3–7-7 SWood (13) (bhd: styd on fnl 2f: nt rch ldrs) ............................................................................... 2.5
532 Kind Style (IRE) **(30)** *(RHollinshead)* 4–8-0 NCarlisle (9) (chsd ldrs: rdn & outpcd over 2f out) ........................................................ 1¹/₂.6
913⁵ Station Express (IRE) **(35)** *(BEllison)* 4–8-5(1) KFallon (11) (lw: bhd: sme late hdwy: n.d) .................................................................... 3.7
765 Emerald Ears **(55)** *(EWeymes)* 3–8-13 GHind (15) (led: rdn 2f out: sn hdd: wknd appr fnl f) ..................................................................... ³/₄.8
1009 Savanga (USA) **(47)** (bl) *(MMcCormack)* 4–9-3 JReid (2) (lw: hdwy appr st: sn rdn & no imp) .......................................................... 1¹/₂.9
327⁵ Chiparopai (IRE) **(45)** *(WStorey)* 4–9-1 SWebster (7) (b: chsd ldrs: rdn 4f out: sn wknd) .............................................................................. nk.10
419 Fait Accompli (FR) **(51)** *(JJO'Neill)* 3–8-9 BRaymond (4) (nvr trbld ldrs) .......... ¹/₂.11
747³ Kagram Queen **(57)** *(MrsGRReveley)* 4–9-6 ‡⁷DarrenMoffatt (5) (lw: effrt on outside 4f out: sn btn) ......................................................... nk.12
875 Marandisa **(48)** *(MPNaughton)* 5–9-4 DNicholls (14) (in tch to st) ................ 1¹/₂.13
Sunnyside Rock (IRE) **(47)** *(JEtherington)* 4–9-3 TLucas (6) (prom 3f: sn wknd) 3.14

**11/2** Savanga (USA), **6/1** Falcons Dawn, **13/2** LAWNSWOOD JUNIOR, Chance Report, **7/1** Kagram Queen(5/1—8/1), **10/1** Sunnyside Rock (IRE)(op 16/1), **12/1** Gant Bleu (FR)(10/1—16/1), Station Express (IRE)(10/1—16/1), **14/1** Marandisa, **16/1** Emerald Ears(op 8/1), Fait Accompli (FR), Kind Style (IRE), Mummys Rocket, **20/1** Chiparopai (IRE). CSF £47.49, CT £465.98. Tote £6.00: £2.80 £2.50 £3.60 (£12.70). Mr Graham Treglown (ALCESTER) bred by Chilcombe Manor Stud. 14 Rn; No bid
1m 39.3 (0.6)
SF—31/13/16/24/–/–

---

**1090**  BODDINGTONS BITTER H'CAP (0-70) £2574.00 (£714.00: £342.00)
7f 214y

3-15 (3-17)

368 **Azureus (IRE) (65)** *(MrsGRReveley)* 4–9-3 ‡7DarrenMoffatt (11) (lw: s.i.s: sn in tch: swtchd appr fnl f: styd on to ld cl home) ..................... —1

1013 Spanish Verdict **(57)** (Fav) *(DenysSmith)* 5–9-2 BRaymond (8) (lw: a.p: led appr fnl f: sn rdn: hdd & no ex nr fin) ..................... s.h.2

913 Stand At Ease **(39)** *(WStorey)* 7–7-12 SWood (12) (swtg: cl up: led 4f out: hdd appr fnl f: one pce) ..................... 5.3

763[6] Routing **(58)** *(MDHammond)* 4–9-3 MBirch (5) (bhd: hdwy 3f out: rdn & one pce fnl 2f: btn whn hmpd over 1f out) ..................... hd.4

684 Golden Chip (IRE) **(67)** *(APStringer)* 4–9-12 JFortune (7) (chsd ldrs: drvn along 3f out: btn whn sltly hmpd appr fnl f) ..................... 2½.5

696 Tyrian Purple (IRE) **(52)** *(RHollinshead)* 4–8-4 ‡7MHumphries (9) (lw: led tl hdd 4f out: ev ch over 1f out: sn wknd) ..................... 1½.6

965[2] Puffy **(49)** (bl) *(GMMoore)* 5–8-8 KFallon (1) (in tch: drvn along 4f out: no imp) ..................... ¾.7

Sly Prospect (USA) **(69)** (v) *(KWhite)* 4–9-7 ‡7AGarth (2) (chsd ldr tl rdn & btn wl over 2f out) ..................... 1½.8

763 Honey Boy Simba **(40)** (v) *(MO'Neill)* 6–7-8 ‡5SMaloney (6) (bhd: effrt 4f out: n.d) ..................... 2½.9

891 Cardea Castle (IRE) **(42)** *(BEllison)* 4–8-1[(8)] GHind (3) (chsd ldrs: rdn & wknd over 3f out) ..................... ½.10

891[3] Golden Beau **(34)** (v) *(AHarrison)* 10–7-7 DaleGibson (10) (a outpcd & bhd) ... 8.11

LONG HANDICAP: Cardea Castle (IRE) 6-12, Golden Beau 7-3.

**7/2** Spanish Verdict, **5/1** Golden Chip (IRE), **11/2** Routing, **6/1** Puffy, **9/1** Tyrian Purple (IRE)(op 6/1), **10/1** AZUREUS (IRE), **14/1** Golden Beau, Honey Boy Simba, **16/1** Stand At Ease, **33/1** Sly Prospect (USA), **50/1** Cardea Castle (IRE). CSF £39.82, CT £496.69. Tote £15.80: £2.60 £1.70 £4.60 (£29.20). Mr J. C. Murdoch (SALTBURN) bred by Ballygoran Stud in Ireland. 11 Rn
1m 39 (0.3)
SF—38/36/3/21/22/–

---

**1091**  BODDINGTONS BITTER STKS (Mdn) £2385.00 (£660.00: £315.00)
5f 207y

3-45 (3-46)

825[3] **Act of Union (IRE) (71)** (Fav) *(WJPearce)* 3–9-0 DNicholls (5) (lw: cl up: led over 2f out: drvn along fnl f: edgd rt nr fin: styd on) ..................... —1

698 Alkarif (USA) **(72)** *(AAScott)* 3–9-0 BRaymond (4) (lw: led tl hdd over 2f out: kpt on wl u.p fnl f) ..................... hd.2

899[4] Ednego Bay (IRE) (v) *(MMcCormack)* 4–9-10 JReid (1) (lw: prom: outpcd over 2f out: styd on wl u.p fnl f) ..................... nk.3

Pipe Opener *(JLSpearing)* 4–9-5 KDarley (7) (lw: chsd ldrs: drvn along ½-wy: one pce) ..................... 2.4

Tellgas *(WStorey)* 3–9-0 SWebster (3) (w'like: s.i.s: bhd tl sme late hdwy: n.d) .. 4.5

918 Minsk **(20)** *(TCraig)* 6–9-5 LCharnock (2) (w ldrs to ½-wy: sn wknd) ..................... 7.6

Soul Intent *(WBentley)* 4–9-2 ‡3JFanning (6) (w ldrs tl wknd ½-wy: sn wl bhd) . 15.7

*Stewards Enquiry: Reid suspended 6-9/6/92 (excessive use of whip).*

**10/11** ACT OF UNION (IRE), **3/1** Alkarif (USA)(9/4—7/2), **4/1** Ednego Bay (IRE), **14/1** Pipe Opener, **50/1** Minsk, **66/1** Ors. CSF £3.71, Tote £1.90: £1.10 £2.10 (£2.20). Mr Derek Atkinson (HAMBLETON) bred by E. J. Loder in Ireland. 7 Rn
1m 13.9 (1.6)
SF—8/7/16/3/–/–

---

**1092**  HEINEKEN EXPORT AUCTION STKS (Mdn 2-Y.O) £2441.60 (£677.60: £324.80)
5f

4-15 (4-16)

Area Girl *(SirMarkPrescott)* 8-2 GDuffield (2) (neat: unf: lw: a w ldr: led appr fnl f: r.o wl) ..................... —1

720[2] Daytona Beach (IRE) (Fav) *(RHollinshead)* 8-7 KDarley (5) (lw: led tl hdd appr fnl f: kpt on) ..................... 2½.2

The Institute Boy *(KRBurke)* 8-7 AShoults (4) (cmpt: prom tl rdn & outpcd ½-wy: styd on fnl f) ..................... ¾.3

For the Present *(TDBarron)* 8-2 AlexGreaves (3) (w'like: lengthy: scope: bit bkwd: s.i.s: hdwy 2f out: styd on wl) ..................... hd.4

975[3] Club Verge (IRE) *(EJAlston)* 8-0 PBurke (7) (chsd ldrs: rdn ½-wy: one pce) ..... ½.5

665² Arkendale Diamond (USA) *(WJPearce)* 8-7 LCharnock (1) (cl up: rdn ½-wy: btn over 1f out) .................................................. **2.6**
Don't Be Saki (IRE) *(JEtherington)* 7-13 JLowe (9) (gd sort: bit bkwd: s.i.s: effrt ½-wy: n.d) ............................................... **2.7**
947² Hasta la Vista *(MWEasterby)* 8-11 TLucas (8) (in tch to ½-wy) ....................... 1½.**8**
Lady Adare (IRE) *(JJO'Neill)* 7-9 NCarlisle (6) (neat: unf: s.i.s: rdn ½-wy: a bhd) 1½.**9**

**3/1** Daytona Beach (IRE), **7/2** AREA GIRL, **4/1** Club Verge (IRE), **7/1** The Institute Boy(4/1—8/1), **8/1** Don't Be Saki (IRE), **9/1** Hasta la Vista, **10/1** Arkendale Diamond (USA), **20/1** For the Present, **50/1** Lady Adare (IRE). CSF £13.77, Tote £3.60: £1.30 £1.50 £2.80 (£6.30). Mr W. E. Sturt (NEWMARKET) bred by Edmond and Richard Kent. 9 Rn
61.6 sec (1.4)
SF—10/5/2/–/–/–

---

**1093**      MURPHYS STOUT H'CAP (0-70) £2500.40 (£694.40: £333.20)      **6f 206y** 4-45 (4-46)

**Kummel King (52)** *(EJAlston)* 4-8-11 KFallon (8) (a chsng ldrs: led 2f out: styd on strly) ................................................... —**1**
913 Cool Enough **(36)** *(MrsJRRamsden)* 11–7-9 JLowe (2) (lw: hld up & bhd: hdwy over 2f out: rdn & nt pce of wnr appr fnl f) ........................... **6.2**
948* Euroblake **(63)** (Fav) *(TDBarron)* 5–9-5 (6x) ‡³JFanning (1) (s.i.s & bhd: hdwy 3f out: sn rdn: one pce appr fnl f) ............................. 2½.**3**
723⁵ Glenstal Princess **(66)** *(RHollinshead)* 5–9-4 ‡⁷SWynne (5) (bhd tl styd on fnl 2f: nrst fin) ................................................ **3.4**
948 Foxes Diamond **(43)** *(BEllison)* 4-8-2 GHind (9) (led tl hdd 2f out: grad wknd) . ¾.**5**
Flashy's Son **(54)** *(MDHammond)* 4-8-13 MBirch (3) (chsd ldrs: rdn 3f out: sn btn) ...................................................... **3.6**
909 Tara's Girl **(66)** *(PABlockley)* 5–9-4 ‡⁷GParkin (6) (lw: prom tl rdn & wknd 3f out) **2.7**
883 Barney O'Neill **(48)** *(JJO'Neill)* 6–8-7 BRaymond (7) (chsd ldrs: rdn & hung lft 3f out: sn btn: ɢaɢɢd fnl f: broke leg: dead) .................... 2½.**8**
1013 The Devil's Music **(38)** (bl) *(MrsJRRamsden)* 8–7-11 NCarlisle (4) (lw: w ldr tl wknd over 3f out) ........................................ 1½.**9**

**2/1** Euroblake, **4/1** Glenstal Princess, **7/1** Cool Enough, **8/1** The Devil's Music, **10/1** Barney O'Neill, **12/1** Foxes Diamond, **20/1** KUMMEL KING, Tara's Girl, **33/1** Flashy's Son. CSF £125.99, CT £308.99. Tote £17.20: £2.20 £1.80 £1.60 (£171.80). Mr David Hall (PRESTON) bred by C. Arrand. 9 Rn
1m 26.6 (1.4)
SF—23/–/15/5/–/–

T/Plpt: £17.10 (157.95 Tckts).
GB

---

## 958a—LONGCHAMP (R-H)

### Thursday, May 21st [Good to firm]
Going Allowance: 0.10 sec per fur (G)

**1094a**      PRIX LA FORCE (Gp 3) (3-Y.O) £20640.00      **1¼m (Grande)**

642a² **Break Bread (USA)** *(France)* 3–8-11 CAsmussen ........................ —**1**
642a⁴ Standiford (USA) *(France)* 3–8-11 ODeleuze .......................... ½.**2**
Polytain (FR) *(France)* 3–8-11 WMongil ................................ nk.**3**
Tote 3.40f: 1.60f 4.70f 3.60f (25.90f). Lord Weinstock (D.Smaga,FRANCE) bred by Ballymacoll Stud Farm in USA. 9 Rn
2m 6.5 (3.3)
SF—74/73/72/70/68/66

---

## 952a—CURRAGH (R-H)

### Saturday, May 23rd [Good]
Going Allowance: 5f-1m: nil (G); minus 0.30 sec per fur (F)

**1095a**      HOTEL CONRAD SILVER RACE (Stks) (listed race) (3-Y.O) £8625.00      **1¼m**

**Ormsby (IRE)** *(Ireland)* 3-8-11 MJKinane ............................. —**1**
Andros Bay (USA) *(Ireland)* 3-8-11 PVGilson .......................... 1.**2**
839a² Tijara (IRE) *(Ireland)* 3-8-8 JPMurtagh ............................ nk.**3**
Tote £6.50: £1.70 £1.40 £1.30 (£12.80). Mr Peter Wetzel (D.K.Weld,IRELAND) bred by Mrs M.F.Weld. 8 Rn
2m 7 (4)
SF—27/25/21/23/19

---

**1096a**      DUNNE STORES GREENLANDS STKS (Gp 3)  £11500.00      **6f**

462a³ **Street Rebel (CAN)** *(Ireland)* 4–9-4 RHughes (s.s: sn rdn: hdwy 2f out: swtchd rt & chal jst ins fnl f: r.o to ld cl home) .................. —**1**
Maledetto (IRE) *(Ireland)* 3–8-6 CRoche (a.p: led u.p 1f out: hdd cl home: no ex) ½.**2**

430⁵ CHICARICA (USA) (Fav) *(JHMGosden)* 4–9-1 WRSwinburn (led tl hdd 1f out: sn no ex) ............................................................... 1.3

    Title Roll (IRE) *(Ireland)* 4–9-6 SCraine (in tch: effrt fr 2f out: ev ch over 1f out: sn rdn: no imp) ............................................ 1.4

    Milieu *(Ireland)* 7–9-4 MJKinane (cl up: rdn over 2f out: sn btn) ............... 3.5

**11/10** Chicarica (USA), **11/4** Maledetto (IRE), **4/1** Title Roll (IRE), **6/1** Milieu, **12/1** STREET REBEL (CAN). Tote £20.40: £5.00 £1.80 (£56.40). Mr P.Garvey (N.Meade,IRELAND) bred by Windfields Farm in Canada. 5 Rn
1m 14.8 (4.2)
SF—20/6/11/12/–

## 1097a      GOFFS IRISH 1,000 GUINEAS (Gp 1) (3-Y.O.F) £121000.00    1m

631² **MARLING (IRE)** (Fav) *(GWragg)* 3–9-0 WRSwinburn (hld up: nt clr run over 2f out: swtchd lft: wnt 3rd 2f out: qcknd & led fnl f) ................. —1

    Market Booster (USA) *(Ireland)* 3–9-0 MJKinane (led tl hdd & outpcd early fnl f: r.o wl) ....................................... 1.2

640a⁴ Tarwiya (IRE) *(Ireland)* 3–9-0 TJarnet (sn bhd: wnt rt over 2f out: swtchd lft & hdwy over 1f out: r.o: nrst fin) ............................ 1.3

631⁶ A-TO-Z (IRE) *(MBell)* 3–9-0 MHills (trckd ldrs: edgd lft 2f out: rdn & unable qckn fnl f) ........................................................ ¾.4

    Cattermole (USA) (bl) *(France)* 3–9-0 CAsmussen (in tch: rdn & no imp whn sltly hmpd 2f out: kpt on same pce) ........................... hd.5

841a★ Khanata (USA) *(Ireland)* 3–9-0 JPMurtagh (trckd ldr: hrd rdn over 1f out: sn btn) .. s.h.6

    Caurselle (IRE) *(Ireland)* 3–9-0 KJManning (bhd: hdwy on ins 2f out: wknd over 1f out) ................................................. 1½.7

841a² Gdansk's Honour (USA) (bl) *(Ireland)* 3–9-0 CRoche (chsd ldrs: rdn over2f out: sn btn) ...................................................... 8

462a★ Bezelle *(Ireland)* 3–9-0 PShanahan (in tch: rdn over 3f out: wkng whn sltly hmpd 2f out: sn bhd) ....................................... 9

**4/5** MARLING (IRE), **7/2** Bezelle, **10/1** Khanata (USA), **11/1** A-to-Z (IRE), **20/1** Market Booster (USA), Tarwiya (IRE), Cattermole (USA), Gdansk's Honour (USA), **100/1** Caurselle (IRE). Tote £2.00: £1.40 £2.90 £3.00 (£15.40). Mr E.J.Loder (NEWMARKET) bred by E.J.Loder. 9 Rn
1m 41.5 (4.5)
SF—33/30/27/25/24/23

### 1094a—LONGCHAMP (R-H)

## Sunday, May 24th [Good]
Going Allowance: minus 0.15 sec per fur (F)

## 1098a      PRIX SAINT-ALARY (Gp 1) (3-Y.O.F) £59257.00    1¼m (Grande)

    **Rosefinch (USA)** *(France)* 3–9-2 SCauthen (mid div: hdwy to ld wl over 1f out: r.o wl) ..................................................... —1

    Jolypha (USA) *(France)* 3–9-2 PatEddery (mid div: hdwy over 1f out: ev ch fnl f: r.o wl: jst failed) .......................................... s.h.2

643a³ Verveine (USA) (Jt-Fav) *(France)* 3–9-2 DBoeuf (hld up: hdwy fr wl over 1f out: styd on one pce) ........................................... hd.3

    Trishyde (USA) *(France)* 3–9-2 FHead (hld up: effrt fr 2f out: one pce: r.o cl home) ............................................................... ½.4

637a★ Trampoli (USA) *(France)* 3–9-2 SGuillot (a cl up: kpt on one pce fnl f) ............ 1½.5

637a³ Good to Dance (IRE) *(France)* 3–9-2 TJarnet (mid div: hdwy to ld 2f out: hdd & outpcd wl over 1f out) ....................................... hd.6

742a★ Sheba Dancer (FR) *(France)* 3–9-2 ALequeux (last st: sme hdwy fnl f: nrst fin) .. 4.7

    Winnetka (USA) *(France)* 3–9-2 CAsmussen (n.d) ....................... s.nk.8

    Shannkara (IRE) *(France)* 3–9-2 WMongil (cl up: grad wknd st) ....................... 5.9

    Irish Source *(France)* 3–9-2 ESaint-Martin (m.n.s) ....................... 2½.10

    Badiane (USA) (Jt-Fav) *(France)* 3–9-2 YTalamo (led to 2f out: wknd qckly) ........ 11

**3/1** Badiane (USA), Verveine (USA), **13/4** Jolypha (USA), Trishyde (USA), **21/4** Trampoli (USA), Good to Dance (IRE), **13/2** Sheba Dancer (FR), **27/4** Shannkara (IRE), **18/1** ROSEFINCH (USA), **25/1** Irish Source, **27/1** Winnetka (USA). Tote 19.20f: 3.50f 1.80f 1.60f (30.00f). Sheikh Mohammed (A.Fabre,FRANCE) bred by Darley Stud Management in USA. 11 Rn
2m 5 (1.8)
SF—69/68/67/66/63/62

## 1099a      PRIX VICOMTESSE VIGIER (Gp 2)    £25800.00    1m 7f 110y (Grande)

739a★ **Commendable (IRE)** (bl) *(France)* 4–8-11 PatEddery (cl up: chal ldr wl over 1f out: led ins fnl f: jst hld on) ................................. —1

739a² Last King (FR) *(France)* 4–8-11 CAsmussen (led tl ins fnl f: r.o again cl home) hd.2

    Mardonius (bl) (Jt-Fav) *(France)* 6–8-11 FHead (hld up: last st: r.o strly fnl f) ... nk.3

11a³ Turgeon (USA) (Jt-Fav) *(France)* 6-9-4 SCauthen (mid div: styd on one pce fr
2f out) .................................................................................... 2.4
608 Victoire Bleue (Jt-Fav) *(France)* 5-9-1 TJarnet (cl up: u.p & fnd nil 2f out: grad
wknd) ........................................................................................ 1½.5
739a³ River Test (USA) *(France)* 6-8-11 DBoeuf (in rr early: sn btn) ............................ 5.6

**7/4** Victoire Bleue, Turgeon (USA), Mardonius (IRE), **11/4** Last King (FR), **41/10** COMMENDABLE (IRE), **9/1**
River Test (USA). Tote 5.10f: 2.40f 2.10f (15.90f). Mr K.Abdulla (H.A.Pantall,FRANCE) bred by Kilfrush Stud in
Ireland. 6 Rn 3m 23.8 (4.8)
SF—27/26/25/29/24/16

## BADEN-BADEN  (L-H)
### Sunday, May 24th [Good]

**1100a** BADENER MEILE (Gp 3)  £26408.00  1m

Young Moon *(Norway)* 6-9-1 JMcLaughlin ............................................................. —1
Irish Stew (GER) *(Germany)* 4-9-7 OSchick ........................................................ nk.2
Andina (GER) *(Germany)* 4-8-10 KWoodburn ..................................................... 2½.3
849⁴ FLYING BRAVE *(JLDunlop)* 4-9-10 BRaymond (btn more than further 7l) ............ 9
Tote 370DM: 48DM 20DM 18DM (SF: 5,700DM). Stall Vic (D.Smith,NORWAY) bred by Pinfold Stud & Farms
Ltd. 11 Rn 1m 37.43

## 740a—SAN SIRO  (R-H)
### Sunday, May 24th [Good]

**1101a** OAKS D'ITALIA (Gp 1) (3-Y.O.F) £79070.00  1½m

Ivyanna (IRE) *(Ireland)* 3-8-11 CRoche ............................................................... —1
814³ ARMARAMA *(CEBrittain)* 3-8-11 MRoberts ................................................... 1.2
599★ UP ANCHOR (IRE) *(PFICole)* 3-8-11 AMunro ............................................... 1¼.3
814² FEMININE WILES (IRE) *(PWChapple-Hyam)* 3-8-11 PaulEddery (btn 4½l by wnr) 5
707★ COTTONWOOD *(LordHuntingdon)* 3-8-11 LDettori (btn 9l by wnr) ...................... 9
Tote 88L: 23L 14L 21L (97L). Mrs O.White (J.S.Bolger,IRELAND) bred by Kiltinan Farms in Ireland. 13 Rn
2m 29.8

## 925—GOODWOOD  (R-H)
### Friday, May 29th [Good to firm, Good patches]
Going Allowance: minus 0.05 sec per fur (G) Wind: slt across  Vis: mod race 5, poor race 6

Stalls: low

**1102** SEABEACH CLAIMING STKS (3-Y.O) £1900.00 (£525.00: £250.00)
1½m 6-30 (6-31)

694⁵ Lyn's Return (IRE) **(56)** (Fav) *(RSimpson)* 8-4 ‡⁵ATucker (1) (4th st: qcknd to ld
3f out: easily) .......................................................... —1
346² Alternation (FR) **(58)** *(PFICole)* 8-4 TQuinn (6) (2nd st: one pce fnl 3f) ............... 4.2
798⁵ Saif Al Adil (IRE) **(58)** *(BHanbury)* 8-5 WRyan (3) (lw: led 9f: one pce) ............... 2.3
Ideal Candidate **(57)** *(CACyzer)* 8-2 ‡⁷TMcLaughlin (2) (bit bkwd: rdn 7f out:
hdwy over 4f out: 3rd st: wknd over 4f out) ........................ 12.4
942⁴ Distant Memory **(70)** *(JWHills)* 9-0 RHills (4) (5th st: wknd 3f out) .................... 15.5
932 Green Slippers (bl) *(GHarwood)* 8-3 AClark (5) (s.i.s: chsd ldr 11f out to 6f out:
t.o fnl 4f) ........................................................................ 25.6

**5/2** LYN'S RETURN (IRE), **11/4** Distant Memory, **4/1** Alternation (FR), **9/2** Saif Al Adil (IRE), **14/1** Ideal
Candidate, **16/1** Green Slippers(op 7/1). CSF £11.12, Tote £3.10: £1.70 £2.00 (£4.30). Mr Rod Simpson
(FOXHILL) bred by Hamwood Stud in Ireland. 6 Rn 2m 39.98 (8.28)

**1103** E.B.F. PEP STKS (Mdn 2-Y.O) £3552.75 (£1062.00: £508.50: £231.75)
6f 7-00 (7-01)

Futurballa *(JLDunlop)* 9-0 WCarson (6) (w'like: scope: s.s: hdwy over 2f out:
led wl over 1f out: rdn out) ............................................. —1
Soleil Rayon (IRE) *(MMcCormack)* 9-0 JReid (7) (str: scope: led over 4f: unable
qckn fnl f) ........................................................................ 2½.2
847 Credit Squeeze *(RFJohnsonHoughton)* 9-0 SWhitworth (9) (a.p: hrd rdn over
1f out: r.o one pce) ....................................................... nk.3

470[5] Without a Flag (USA) *(CACyzer)* 9-0 TQuinn (8) (swtg: hld up: rdn over 2f out: r.o ins fnl f) ................................................................ s.h.4

Little Too Much (IRE) *(Fav)* *(GHarwood)* 9-0 AClark (2) (w'like: scope: w ldr over 4f: one pce) ........................................................ 1½.5

Embankment (IRE) *(RHannon)* 9-0 MRoberts (4) (w'like: scope: a.p: one pce fnl 2f) .................................................................. ½.6

Stevie's Wonder (IRE) *(WCarter)* 9-0 WNewnes (3) (w'like: scope: lw: s.s: hrd rdn 4f out: a bhd) ....................................................... 7.7

Coy Boy (IRE) *(GLewis)* 9-0 BRouse (1) (str: scope: bhd fnl 2f) ................ ½.8

Mouchez le Nez (IRE) *(JAkehurst)* 8-9 DHolland (5) (w'like: bkwd: bhd fnl 3f) .... 1.9

**8/11** Little Too Much (IRE), **3/1** FUTURBALLA, **13/2** Embankment (IRE)(2/1—7/1), **16/1** Without a Flag (USA)(10/1—20/1), Soleil Rayon (IRE)(10/1—20/1), **20/1** Credit Squeeze, **50/1** Ors. CSF £43.14, Tote £4.50: £1.30 £2.50 £3.20 (£37.60). Gerecon Italia (ARUNDEL) bred by J. L. Woolford. 9 Rn       1m 13.53 (3.13)
SF—32/22/21/20/14/12

**1104**    HALPERN AND WOOLF PARHAM BROTHERS CLAIMING STKS    £3406.50 (£1017.00: £486.00: £220.50)    **7f**        7-25 (7-28)

Talent (USA) (73) (v) *(LordHuntingdon)* 4-9-2 AMunro (4) (mde all: hrd rdn ins fnl f: r.o wl) ..................................................................... —1

898 Clare Kerry Lass (67) *(TJNaughton)* 3-7-7[(1)] ‡3FNorton (1) (swtg: rdn & hdwy over 1f out: ev ch ins fnl f: r.o) ................................. 1.2

998[2] Walk in the Park (86) *(Fav)* *(RSimpson)* 3-7-8[(2)] ‡5ATucker (2) (swtg: 5th st: ev ch wl over 1f out: hrd rdn: unable qckn) ..................... 2½.3

830[2] Durneltor (65) *(RHannon)* 4-8-11 WCarson (6) (3rd st: rdn 3f out: r.o one pce) ... hd.4

860 Corrin Hill (66) *(BWHills)* 5-8-11 DHolland (7) (6th st: one pce fnl 2f) ........... ¾.5

941[4] Belfort Ruler (68) *(BGubby)* 5-8-11 JReid (3) (2nd st: ev ch over 2f out: wknd over 1f out) ..................................................... nk.6

997 Fabled Orator (51) *(PHowling)* 7-8-9 JMurray (5) (lw: 4th st: wknd wl over 1f out) ............................................................ 5.7

**13/8** Walk in the Park, **7/2** Durneltor, **9/2** TALENT (USA), **5/1** Belfort Ruler, **7/1** Corrin Hill, **20/1** Clare Kerry Lass, **33/1** Fabled Orator. CSF £63.83, Tote £5.40: £2.30 £3.30 (£32.80). The Queen (WEST ILSLEY) bred by The Queen in USA. 7 Rn       1m 27.59 (2.89)
SF—53/27/20/36/34/33

**1105**    WILEY H'CAP (3-Y.O) (0-80) £3523.50 (£1053.00: £504.00: £229.50)    **1m**        7-55 (7-58)

(Weights raised 2 lb)

395 Grand Vitesse (IRE) (76) *(RHannon)* 9-7 MRoberts (2) (mde all: rdn out) ......... —1

858[3] Wassl This Then (IRE) (65) *(DWPArbuthnot)* 8-10 TQuinn (7) (rdn 4f out: 3rd st: ev ch ins fnl f: r.o) ......................................... ¾.2

698[4] Red Archer (66) (bl) *(PJMakin)* 8-11 JReid (1) (swtg: s.s: 6th st: hung rt over 1f out: r.o one pce) .................................................. 2.3

930* Baluga (76) *(Fav)* *(GHarwood)* 9-7 (7x) AClark (4) (lw: 2nd st: rdn 3f out: wknd over 1f out) ...................................................... 3.4

972 Kathy Fair (IRE) (50) *(RJBaker)* 7-9 RFox (5) (swtg: s.s: 5th st: a bhd) ........... 2½.5

970[4] Tadora (IRE) (51) *(CJBenstead)* 7-10 TyroneWilliams (6) (lw: 4th st: wknd over 1f out) ........................................................... 3.6

**6/4** Baluga, **11/4** Wassl This Then (IRE), **5/1** Red Archer, **11/2** GRAND VITESSE (IRE), **7/1** Tadora (IRE)(5/1—8/1), **50/1** Kathy Fair (IRE). CSF £19.68, Tote £5.00: £2.20 £1.70 (£7.00). Mr Robert Whitworth (MARLBOROUGH) bred by Mrs C. Martin Smith in Ireland. 6 Rn       1m 40.69 (3.09)
SF—55/42/37/38/4/–

**1106**    CELER et AUDAX H'CAP (0-80) £2180.00 (£605.00: £290.00)    **1m 1f**    8-25 (8-33)

832 Akkazao (IRE) (73) *(WCarter)* 4-9-3 ‡5NGwilliams (2) (led 8f out: rdn out) ......... —1

936[5] Marzocco (55) *(JFfitch-Heyes)* 4-8-4 TQuinn (1) (lw: gd hdwy 2f out: hrd rdn over 1f out: r.o) ....................................................... ½.2

913[2] I'M Electric (44) *(RCurtis)* 6-7-0 ‡7CHawksley (7) (swtg: 7th st: rdn over 2f out: r.o ins fnl f) ....................................................... ½.3

912* Camden's Ransom (USA) (67) *(DRCElsworth)* 5-9-2 (6x) JWilliams (13) (hdwy 2f out: rdn over 1f out: r.o ins fnl f) ................................ ½.4

1051[4] Sooty Tern (47) *(JMBradley)* 5-7-10 TyroneWilliams (4) (5th st: ev ch over 1f out: unable qckn) ................................................. 1½.5

936[4] Salbyng (56) *(JWHills)* 4-8-5 RHills (8) (3rd st: hrd rdn over 1f out: wknd fnl f) .. 5.6

830 Grey Illusions (44) (bl) *(LJHolt)* 4-7-7 NAdams (10) (6th st: ev ch 2f out: wknd over 1f out) ...................................................... hd.7

696 Champenoise (54) *(MBell)* 4-8-3 MHills (12) (swtg: rdn over 2f out: nvr nr to chal) ........................................................... 2.8

809 Asterix **(70)** *(JMBradley)* 4–9-5 WNewnes (11) (a bhd) ........................ 2¹/₂.9
477 Mulciber **(79)** *(GHarwood)* 4–10-0 AClark (6) (lw: led 1f: 2nd st: wknd 2f out) . ¹/₂.10
931³ Tiger Claw (USA) **(55)** (bl) **(Fav)** *(RJHodges)* 6–8-4 WCarson (3) (4th st: wknd
　　　　over 3f out) ........................ ³/₄.11
　　Hard to Snub **(53)** *(MMadgwick)* 4–7-9⁽⁹⁾ ‡⁷CAvery (5) (bit bkwd: rdn thrght: bhd
　　　　fnl 4f) ........................ 12.12
774 Ackers Wood **(47)** *(KRBurke)* 4–7-7⁽³⁾ ‡³FNorton (9) (t.o fnl 5f) ........................ 13
　　　　LONG HANDICAP: I'M Electric 7-4, Hard to Snub 7-3, Ackers Wood 7-6.
　　　　Stewards Enquiry: Obj. to Marzocco by J. Williams overruled.

**4/1** Tiger Claw (USA), **5/1** I'M Electric, Salbying, Camden's Ransom (USA), **10/1** Sooty Tern, Champenoise, **12/1**
AKKAZAO (IRE), **16/1** Marzocco(12/1—20/1), Grey Illusions, Mulciber(12/1—20/1), **33/1** Ackers Wood,
Asterix, **66/1** Hard to Snub. CSF £165.99, CT £987.06. Tote £21.70: £4.60 £4.10 £1.90 (£127.70). Mr Ernie
Penfold (EPSOM) bred by Red House Stud in Ireland. 13 Rn　　　　　1m 56.4 (hand) (5.7)
　　　　　　　　　　　　　　　　　　　　　　　　　　　　　　　SF—11/–/–/4/–/–

**1107**　　　CUCUMBER H'CAP (0-90) £2005.00 (£555.00: £265.00)　　**6f**　　　8-55 (9-04)

945⁴ Aughfad **(77)** (v) *(TCasey)* 6–9-3 JReid (6) (lw: mde all: rdn out) ........................ —1
970★ Risk Zone **(69)** (bl) *(RHannon)* 3–7-13 (7x) AMcGlone (5) (a.p: hrd rdn over 1f
　　　　out: unable qckn) ........................ 3.2
945★ Fivesevenfiveo **(61)** **(Fav)** *(RJHodges)* 4–8-1 WCarson (8) (a.p: ev ch over 1f
　　　　out: one pce) ........................ ¹/₂.3
819 Petraco (IRE) **(78)** (bl) *(LJCodd)* 4–9-4 DHolland (3) (a.p: hrd rdn over 1f out:
　　　　one pce) ........................ hd.4
819⁵ El Yasaf (IRE) **(84)** *(GHEden)* 4–9-10 AMunro (1) (hdwy 2f out: hrd rdn over 1f
　　　　out: one pce) ........................ ³/₄.5
　　Grand Prix **(84)** *(DRCElsworth)* 7–9-10 JWilliams (7) (s.i.s: gd hdwy 3f out:
　　　　wknd fnl f) ........................ 2.6
　　Baligay **(80)** *(RJHodges)* 7–9-3 ‡³TSprake (4) (prom over 4f) ........................ ³/₄.7
935⁵ Masnun (USA) **(88)** *(RJO'Sullivan)* 7–10-0 AClark (9) (s.i.s: a bhd) ........................ 2¹/₂.8
472 Gemini Bay **(83)** (bl) *(RVoorspuy)* 3–8-13 SDawson (2) (bhd fnl 4f: t.o) ........................ 20.9

**9/4** Fivesevenfiveo, **3/1** Risk Zone, **9/2** AUGHFAD, **8/1** Petraco (IRE)(10/1—6/1), **10/1** Masnun (USA)(6/1—11/1), El Yasaf (IRE), Grand Prix, **33/1** Ors. CSF £17.76, CT £33.89. Tote £5.50: £1.70 £1.50 £1.80 (£8.50). Mr M.
Mac Carthy (UPPER LAMBOURN) bred by M. Mac Carthy. 9 Rn　　　　1m 12.17 (1.77)
　　　　　　　　　　　　　　　　　　　　　　　　　　　　　SF—61/31/31/47/50/42

T/Trio: Race 5: £704.60 (2.1 Tckts). T/Plpt: £876.40 (3.8 Tckts).
　　　　　　　　　　　　　　　　　　　　　　　　　　　　　　　　　　　　AK

888—**HAMILTON** (R-H)
## Friday, May 29th [Good to firm, Firm patches]
Going Allowance: minus 0.20 sec per fur (F)　　　　　　　Wind: almost nil

Stalls: low

**1108**　　　SCOTTISH RIFLES H'CAP (0-70) £2363.20 (£655.20: £313.60)
　　　　　　1m 5f 9y　　　　　　　　　　　　　　　　　　　2-10 (2-13)

761³ Sea Paddy **(47)** *(RBastiman)* 4–8-3 ‡⁷HBastiman (10) (swtg: effrt on ins 4f out:
　　　　nt clr run & swtchd 2f out: r.o u.p to ld ins fnl f) ........................ —1
　　Brodessa **(61)** *(MrsGRReveley)* 6–9-10 LDettori (1) (lw: trckd ldrs: smooth
　　　　hdwy to ld 2f out: hdd & no ex ins fnl f) ........................ 1.2
951★ Racing Raskal **(35)** *(CaptJWilson)* 5–7-9⁽¹⁾ (4x) ‡³DBiggs (12) (lw: a cl up: chal
　　　　3f out: r.o one pce) ........................ 2¹/₂.3
694² A a Bamba **(60)** **(Fav)** *(NACallaghan)* 3–7-11 ‡⁷JTate (5) (a chsng ldrs: rdn over
　　　　2f out: r.o one pce) ........................ 1¹/₂.4
923² Smoke **(44)** *(JParkes)* 6–8-7 ACulhane (3) (b: hld up & bhd: hdwy on ins 3f out:
　　　　rdn & no ex appr fnl f) ........................ 1¹/₂.5
987⁶ Emperor Chang (USA) **(42)** *(PABlockley)* 5–8-5 JCarroll (9) (chsd ldrs: led 4f
　　　　out tl hdd 2f out: one pce) ........................ ¹/₂.6
893 Lord Advocate **(40)** *(MPNaughton)* 4–8-3 GHind (2) (chsd ldrs tl outpcd fnl 2f) ¹/₂.7
893 Alpha Helix **(33)** (v) *(MissLAPerratt)* 9–7-7 ‡³JFanning (7) (bhd: effrt 4f out: no
　　　　imp) ........................ s.h.8
664⁴ Brusque (USA) **(33)** *(DonEnricoIncisa)* 8–7-3⁽³⁾ ‡⁷ClaireBalding (4) (swtg: s.i.s:
　　　　bhd: effrt ent st: hung rt & n.d) ........................ 6.9
198³ Persuasius (IRE) **(54)** *(WJPearce)* 4–9-3 DNicholls (6) (bhd & slipped ent st: wl
　　　　bhd after) ........................ 8.10
166 Megan's Flight **(56)** *(THCaldwell)* 7–9-0 ‡⁵NKennedy (11) (led tl hdd 4f out: sn
　　　　wknd) ........................ 11

**7/2** A a Bamba, **4/1** Racing Raskal, **5/1** Smoke, **SEA PADDY**, **6/1** Brodessa, **14/1** Brusque (USA), **16/1** Lord Advocate, **20/1** Emperor Chang (USA), **25/1** Persuasius (IRE), **50/1** Megan's Flight, **100/1** Alpha Helix. CSF £31.26, CT £117.48. Tote £4.70: £2.30 £2.90 £1.40 (£15.00). Mr Greg Lancaster (WETHERBY) bred by Ferry Farm Co. 11 Rn
2m 50.7 (5)
SF—13/32/—/—/7/4

---

**1109**    BLENHEIM CLAIMING STKS    £2402.40 (£666.40: £319.20)
       1m 1f 36y                               2-40 (2-42)

451 **Neltegrity (53)** *(THCaldwell)* 3–7-13 ‡5NKennedy (11) (a chsng ldrs: rdn to ld over 1f out: styd on wl) ............... —1
912 Bengal Tiger (IRE) **(54)** (bl) *(JAkehurst)* 4–9-2 LDettori (9) (led tl hdd over 1f out: kpt on same pce) ............... ¾.2
797² Miliyel **(Fav)** *(BHanbury)* 3–7-0 ‡7CHawksley (5) (b: trckd ldrs: chal over 2f out: rdn & no ex appr fnl f) ............... ¾.3
962⁴ Cool Parade (USA) **(51)** (bl) *(GMMoore)* 4–8-12 JCarroll (10) (lw: hld up & bhd: gd hdwy on outside 3f out: rdn & no imp fnl 2f) ............... 3½.4
950³ Feeling Foolish (IRE) **(59)** (bl) *(TFairhurst)* 3–7-9 ‡3JFanning (6) (lw: in tch: effrt 4f out: no imp) ............... 3½.5
890⁶ Jalore *(PABlockley)* 3–8-4 GHind (12) (lw: effrt 4f out: nvr trbld ldrs) ............... hd.6
914³ Kirkby Belle **(54)** *(EWeymes)* 3–7-7 SWood (8) (prom tl outpcd fnl 2f) ............... 2½.7
891 Saint Bene't (IRE) **(43)** *(PCHaslam)* 4–8-12 TLucas (4) (effrt ½-wy: nvr bttr than mid div) ............... ½.8
962 Paper Craft **(55)** *(MJohnston)* 5–8-12 RPElliott (3) (mid div & rdn 3f out: n.d) ...... 3.9
891 Brilliant Disguise **(52)** *(PMonteith)* 3–7-6 ‡7RHavlin (2) (a bhd) ............... 1.10
Ziggy's Pearl (USA) *(WGMTurner)* 4–8-10 ‡3DBiggs (7) (swtg: bit bkwd: chsd ldrs to st) ............... 12.11
493⁶ Ebony Isle **(46)** *(PMonteith)* 3–8-3 NConnorton (1) (a wl bhd) ............... 25.12

**2/1** Miliyel, **5/1** Feeling Foolish (IRE)(7/2—11/2), Cool Parade (USA), **13/2** Bengal Tiger (IRE), **10/1** Kirkby Belle(op 6/1), **14/1** Ebony Isle, Brilliant Disguise, **20/1** Paper Craft, Saint Bene't (IRE), Jalore, **50/1** NELTEGRITY & Ors. CSF £316.89, Tote £39.10: £17.50 £1.30 £1.50 (£109.80). Mr T. J. Kenny (WARRINGTON) bred by Pearl Lawson Johnston. 12 Rn; Miliyel clmd W Monteith £6,010
1m 56.5 (2.2)
SF—25/40/8/23/—/3

---

**1110**    ROTHMANS ROYALS NORTH SOUTH CHALLENGE SERIES (H'cap) (0-80) £2872.00
       (£856.00: £408.00: £184.00)    **1m 65y**              3-10 (3-20)

887³ **Ikteshaf (72)** *(BHanbury)* 4–10-0 LDettori (2) (b: a cl up: led 2f out: rdn & r.o fnl f) ............... —1
903 Pimsboy **(53)** (v) *(PABlockley)* 5–8-9 JCarroll (5) (hld up: hdwy to chal over 1f out: no ex u.p ins fnl f) ............... 1½.2
Able Lassie **(70)** **(Fav)** *(MrsGRReveley)* 4–9-7 ‡5NKennedy (6) (set slow pce: qcknd over 4f out: hdd 2f out: kpt on same pce) ............... 4.3
883 Persian House **(60)** *(JMJefferson)* 5–9-2 NConnorton (4) (trckd ldrs & plld hrd: effrt ½-wy: kpt on one pce) ............... 1.4
891 Lucky Barnes **(37)** (bl) *(PABlockley)* 5–7-0 ‡7CHawksley (1) (s.i.s: hdwy to jn ldrs ent st: outpcd fnl 2f) ............... ¾.5
794⁴ Thisonesforalice **(53)** *(WJPearce)* 4–8-9 ACulhane (7) (hld up & bhd: effrt on ins 3f out: rdn & no imp) ............... ½.6
794 Silver Stone Boy **(38)** *(WJPearce)* 4–7-5 ‡3JFanning (8) (prom tl outpcd fnl 3f) . ¾.7
233 Stylish Gent **(66)** *(NTinkler)* 5–9-8 ABacon (3) (lw: hld up: outpcd over 3f out: n.d after) ............... nk.8

LONG HANDICAP: Lucky Barnes 7-6.

**7/4** Able Lassie(op 3/1), **15/8** IKTESHAF, **7/1** Thisonesforalice, **10/1** Pimsboy(8/1—12/1), **12/1** Stylish Gent(op 6/1), **14/1** Persian House(op 6/1), **33/1** Silver Stone Boy, **50/1** Lucky Barnes. CSF £18.28, CT £32.82. Tote £2.90: £1.40 £2.70 £1.10 (£32.10). Mr B. Hanbury (NEWMARKET) bred by The Sussex Stud. 8 Rn
1m 48.5 (5.2)
SF—12/—/—/—/—/—

---

**1111**    COURVOISIER COGNAC CLASSIC H'CAP (0-80) £2382.80 (£660.80: £316.40)
       **6f 5y**                                  3-40 (3-44)

888⁵ **Diet (63)** (v) **(Fav)** *(MissLAPerratt)* 6–8-12 ‡7RHavlin (5) (mde all: styd on wl fnl f) ............... —1
885 Filicaia **(47)** *(DonEnricoIncisa)* 6–7-10 ‡7ClaireBalding (4) (s.i.s: outpcd & bhd tl hdwy over 1f out: fin wl) ............... nk.2
1020⁴ Hinari Video **(48)** *(MJohnston)* 7–8-4 JCarroll (6) (a cl up: ev ch & rdn 2f out: nt qckn ins fnl f) ............... 1.3
706* Dawes of Nelson **(42)** *(MJBolton)* 7–7-9⁽¹⁾ ‡3DBiggs (1) (a chsng ldrs: rdn & one pce appr fnl f) ............... ¾.4

885⁵ Glenfield Greta (66) (PSFelgate) 4–9-8 LDettori (3) (a.p: effrt u.p 2f out: nt qckn
fnl f) ................................................................................................ 3.5
948⁵ Languedoc (70) (MPNaughton) 5–9-12 DNicholls (8) (spd over 4f) ................. 2.6
661⁴ Crail Harbour (58) (PCHaslam) 6–9-0 RPElliott (2) (lw: chsd ldrs tl wknd 2f out) 5.7
752 Johanna Thyme (42) (RBastiman) 5–7-7 ‡⁵NKennedy (7) (wl bhd fr ½-wy) ........ 7.8

3/1 DIET, 7/2 Hinari Video, 9/2 Glenfield Greta(op 3/1), 5/1 Dawes of Nelson, 7/1 Languedoc, 9/1 Crail
Harbour(op 5/1), 12/1 Johanna Thyme, 20/1 Filicaia. CSF £48.09, CT £199.34. Tote £4.40: £1.90 £5.50 £1.10
(£30.50). Mrs M. S. J. Clydesdale (AYR) bred by Rowcliffe Stud. 8 Rn                1m 11.1 (1.1)
SF—52/39/39/26/42/38

## 1112
E.B.F. MANDORA STKS (Mdn 2-Y.O) £2738.20 (£760.20: £364.60)
6f 5y
4-10 (4-11)

807⁶ **Second Colours (USA)** (Fav) (PSFelgate) 9-0 NConnorton (1) (trckd ldrs: led
over 1f out: rdn & r.o) .................................................................. —1
973⁴ Hot Off the Press (RMWhitaker) 9-0 ACulhane (4) (in tch: hdwy 2f out: r.o fnl f) . 1.2
828⁶ Principal Player (USA) (WBentley) 9-0 TLucas (1) (hld up: hung bdly lft most of
wy: hdwy over 1f out: nrst fin) .......................................... ½.3
924⁶ Royal Interval (WGMTurner) 8-11 ‡³DBiggs (3) (led tl hdd over 1f out: one pce) 1½.4
828 Brown's (FR) (NACallaghan) 9-0 LDettori (5) (in tch: effrt 2f out: r.o one pce u.p) . 2.5
Prime Painter (RFFisher) 9-0 DNicholls (8) (neat: bit bkwd: bhd: hdwy 2f out:
styd on) ............................................................................ s.h.6
682 Penny Banger (IRE) (MJohnston) 8-9 RPElliott (9) (spd 4f) ........................ 1.7
877 Ho-Joe (IRE) (AHarrison) 9-0 GHind (7) (cl up over 4f) ............................ 4.8
882 Sensabo (MissLAPerratt) 8-2 ‡⁷RHavlin (10) (prom 4f) .......................... 1½.9
571 Doc Spot (CaptJWilson) 9-0 JCarroll (2) (spd over 3f) .......................... 6.10
1056 El Guapo (TFairhurst) 8-11 ‡³JFanning (6) (lw: cl up tl wknd over 2f out) ....... 2½.11

7/4 SECOND COLOURS (USA)(up 7/2), 7/2 Hot Off the Press(op 5/1), 9/2 Brown's (FR), 7/1 Royal Interval, 8/1
Principal Player (USA), 11/1 Prime Painter, 20/1 El Guapo, Ho-Joe (IRE), Penny Banger (IRE), 33/1 Sensabo,
50/1 Doc Spot. CSF £8.92, Tote £4.50: £1.40 £2.00 £1.90 (£4.80). Mr P. D. Savill (MELTON MOWBRAY) bred
by Dinnaken Farm in USA. 11 Rn                1m 12.3 (2.3)
SF—30/26/24/15/10/6

## 1113
CAMERONIANS STKS (Mdn 3-Y.O) £1932.00 (£532.00: £252.00)          5f 4y     4-40 (4-41)

890² **Optical (IRE) (62)** (MPNaughton) 9-0 NConnorton (3) (cl up: led over 2f out:
r.o wl u.p fnl f) ................................................................ —1
966² Boy Martin (MJohnston) 9-0 RPElliott (4) (lw: chsd ldrs: ev ch 2f out: nt qckn ins
fnl f) ............................................................................ 1½.2
906⁴ Rock Band (IRE) (LMCumani) 9-0 LDettori (2) (lw: led tl hdd over 2f out: hrd rdn
& one pce) ...................................................................... 2½.3
906² Hot Lavender (CAN) (69) (Fav) (CFWall) 8-6 ‡³DBiggs (1) (s.s: gd hdwy 2f out:
nvr able to chal) ................................................................. hd.4

5/4 Hot Lavender (CAN), 2/1 Boy Martin, 5/2 Rock Band (IRE), 16/1 OPTICAL (IRE). CSF £42.96, Tote £6.50
(£6.70). Mrs H. H. Wane (RICHMOND) bred by Oliver Murphy in Ireland. 4 Rn                61.2 sec (2.9)
SF—22/16/6/–

T/Plpt: £234.40 (8.45 Tckts).                AA

## 483—NEWCASTLE (L-H)
### Friday, May 29th [Good to firm]
Going Allowance: minus 0.25 sec per fur (F)                Wind: fresh half bhd

Stalls: high

## 1114
3d 'NEW CARLISLE' ENVELOPE H'CAP (0-90) £3785.00 (£1130.00: £540.00: £245.00)
7f
2-20 (2-22)

1021³ **Sharpalto (77)** (Jt-Fav) (MrsGRReveley) 5–9-1 JLowe (3) (lw: hld up: gd hdwy
over 2f out: r.o wl u.p to ld ins fnl f) ................................. —1
667⁶ Jalmusique (90) (MHEasterby) 6–10-0 MBirch (5) (lw: mde most: drvn clr over
1f out: r.o u.p: hdd ins fnl f) ........................................... hd.2
860⁵ La Bamba (82) (GAPritchard-Gordon) 6–9-6 WHood (6) (s.i.s: hld up:
gd hdwy over 2f out: kpt on: nvr nr to chal) .......................... 6.3
887 Canaan Valley (72) (JGFitzGerald) 4–8-10 KFallon (9) (bit bkwd: sn trckng ldrs:
effrt over 2f out: styd on same pace) .................................. hd.4
706 Best Effort (55) (MPNaughton) 6–7-7 JakiHouston (1) (racd wd: edgd lft over 2f
out: n.d) ........................................................................ 10.5

903² Tara's Delight **(69)** *(WAO'Gorman)* 5-8-2[4] ‡5EmmaO'Gorman (8) (b.hind: chsd ldrs: rdn & edgd lft over 2f out: sn wknd) ................ 1¹/₂.6
903 Company Cash **(56)** *(RBastiman)* 4-7-8[1] JQuinn (4) (chsd ldrs over 4f: grad wknd) ......................................................................... 1¹/₂.7
Silver Haze **(64)** *(WAStephenson)* 8-8-2 GCarter (2) (sn bhd & drvn along) ..... hd.8
My Nominee **(67)** *(SEKettlewell)* 4-8-5 KDarley (7) (w ldrs tl wknd ¹/₂-wy: sn bhd) 4.9
LONG HANDICAP: Best Effort 7-2, Company Cash 7-3.

**11/4** La Bamba, SHARPALTO(2/1—3/1), **11/2** Tara's Delight(8/1—5/1), Jalmusique(op 4/1), **11/1** Canaan Valley, **20/1** My Nominee, **25/1** Best Effort, Company Cash, **33/1** Silver Haze. CSF £16.56, CT £35.44. Tote £3.50: £1.20 £1.80 £1.40 (£5.30). Millprew Bloodstock (SALTBURN) bred by E. A. Badger. 9 Rn
1m 24.90 (0.60)
SF—66/78/52/41/–/–

**1115** U.S.A. 'BOSCAWEN' PAID 5 CENTS STKS (Mdn) £2072.00 (£572.00: £272.00)
7f
2-50 (2-51)

884 **Round by the River (58)** *(WWHaigh)* 3-8-8 DMcKeown (5) (lw: mde most: drvn clr over 1f out: r.o wl) .......................................... —1
Rienroe (IRE) *(NAGraham)* 3-8-8 RCochrane (1) (leggy: unf: w wnr: rdn & nt qckn fnl f) ................................................................... 2¹/₂.2
963² Yazaly (USA) **(70)** (v) *(AAScott)* 3-8-13 BRaymond (4) (chsd ldrs: pushed along ¹/₂-wy: nt r.o) ..................................................... 10.3
618⁵ Ty High (IRE) *(TDBarron)* 4-9-5 AlexGreaves (2) (hld up & bhd: reminders ¹/₂-wy: sme hdwy over 1f out: nvr nr to chal) .................. 2¹/₂.4
919 Share Holder *(MissGayKelleway)* 4-9-5 KFallon (6) (b: b.hind: chsd ldrs: rdn & hung lft ¹/₂-wy: sn wknd) ............................................ 1¹/₂.5
363 Al-Dahlawia (IRE) **(49)** *(GAPritchard-Gordon)* 3-8-8 GCarter (3) (b.hind: chsd ldrs to ¹/₂-wy: sn wl bhd) .................................. 20.6

**11/8** Yazaly (USA), **3/1** Rienroe (IRE), **7/2** ROUND BY THE RIVER, **8/1** Ty High (IRE), **20/1** Al-Dahlawia (IRE), **25/1** Share Holder. CSF £13.01, Tote £5.20: £1.60 £2.00 (£6.00). Mr W. W. Haigh (MALTON) bred by Norton Court Stud Farm Ltd. 6 Rn
1m 26.49 (2.19)
SF—35/30/53/21/–

**1116** 2d TYRIAN PLUM CLAIMING STKS £2301.00 (£636.00: £303.00) 6f 3-20 (3-20)

978² Finjan **(82)** *(MPNaughton)* 5-8-7 KFallon (4) (lw: w ldr: led ¹/₂-wy: r.o wl fnl f) ... —1
978* Easy Line **(90)** (Fav) *(PJFeilden)* 9-8-9 BRaymond (1) (hld up: effrt over 1f out: sn rdn & unable qckn) ........................................ 2.2
860⁶ Mac's Fighter **(85)** (bl) *(WAO'Gorman)* 7-8-4 ‡5EmmaO'Gorman (3) (led to ¹/₂-wy: rdn & edgd lft: wknd 2f out) .............................. 2¹/₂.3

**2/5** Easy Line, **100/30** Mac's Fighter, **8/1** FINJAN. CSF £11.05, Tote £4.90 (£1.70). Mrs R. Olivier (RICHMOND) bred by Swettenham Stud. 3 Rn
1m 12.88 (1.38)
SF—35/29/14

**1117** 1856 BRITISH GUIANA 1 CENT H'CAP (3-Y.O) (0-110) £7180.00 (£2140.00: £1020.00: £460.00) 5f
(Weights raised 1 lb) 3-50 (3-52)

792⁵ Taufan Blu (IRE) **(82)** (bl) *(MJohnston)* 8-6 DMcKeown (4) (w ldrs: edgd rt & hmpd over 1f out: led 1f out: stumbled & kpt on u.p) .......... —1
949² Super Rocky **(75)** *(RBastiman)* 7-13 JQuinn (2) (lw: w ldrs: led 2f out to 1f out: nt qckn ins fnl f) ...................................... 1¹/₂.2
792 Truthful Image **(74)** (bl) *(MJRyan)* 7-12 GBardwell (5) (chsd ldrs: effrt ¹/₂-wy: styd on same pce) ........................................... 2¹/₂.3
949³ Ned's Bonanza **(75)** *(MDods)* 7-13 JLowe (7) (lw: hung lft thrght: led 3f: hdd 2f out: hmpd over 1f out: wknd ins fnl f) ............... ³/₄.4
935 Blake End (USA) **(83)** *(WAO'Gorman)* 8-7 PaulEddery (6) (lw: chsd ldrs: rdn ¹/₂-wy: sn btn) ................................................... 2.5
649⁵ Isaiah **(93)** *(MJohnston)* 9-3 BRaymond (3) (w ldrs early: sn outpcd: drvn along ¹/₂-wy: n.d) ............................................. 2¹/₂.6
834* Vailmont (USA) **(97)** (Fav) *(IABalding)* 9-7 RCochrane (1) (lw: hld up: hung lft thrght: effrt ¹/₂-wy: no rspnse) ......................... 6.7

**2/1** Vailmont (USA)(6/4—9/4), **11/2** TAUFAN BLU (IRE), **6/1** Super Rocky, **7/1** Isaiah, Blake End (USA), **9/1** Ors. CSF £32.32, Tote £7.10: £2.80 £2.10 (£14.70). Hambleton Lodge Equine Premix Ltd (MIDDLEHAM) bred by Mrs S. O'Riordan in Ireland. 7 Rn
59.62 sec (1.22)
SF—42/29/18/16/16/16

**1118** 'POST OFFICE' MAURITIUS 1d AND 2d COVER STKS (2-Y.O) £2322.00 (£642.00: £306.00) 5f
4-20 (4-21)

988⁴ Night Melody (IRE) (Fav) *(RHannon)* 9-0 KDarley (4) (trckd ldrs gng wl: smooth hdwy to ld just ins fnl f: easily) ................... —1

917* Sabo Song *(RAllan)* 8-9 SWebster (2) (lw: unruly s: w ldr: hung lft thrght: led ½-wy tl just ins fnl f: no ch w wnr) ...................................... 1½.2

882* Coconut Johnny (bl) *(GMMoore)* 9-0 KFallon (3) (lw: led to ½-wy: sn hrd drvn: nt qckn appr fnl f) ............................................................ 5.3

947* Bold County *(MJohnston)* 8-9 DMcKeown (1) (lw: s.s: hdwy to chase ldrs ½-wy: hung lft: sn wknd: eased whn no ch) ...................... 12.4

**4/6** NIGHT MELODY (IRE)(op Evens), **11/4** Bold County, **9/2** Sabo Song, **20/1** Coconut Johnny. CSF £3.78, Tote £1.60 (£3.50). Mr P. D. Savill (MARLBOROUGH) bred by Leo Collins in Ireland. 4 Rn    60.75 sec (2.35)
SF—28/17/2/–

## 1119
INDIA ½ ANNA SCARLET 'SCINDE DAWK' H'CAP (0-70) £2511.00 (£696.00: £333.00)
2m 19y     (Weights raised 3 lb)      4-50 (4-52)

964* **Samain** (USA) (35) *(JAGlover)* 5–8-0 (3x) NCarlisle (11) (lw: s.i.s: hld up: hdwy & nt clr run over 2f out: swtchd & r.o to ld ins fnl f) .............. —1

810³ Farmer's Pet (63) (Fav) *(GAPritchard-Gordon)* 3–8-6 GCarter (5) (lw: trckd ldr: led over 2f out tl ins fnl f: nt qckn) ....................................... 1½.2

805³ Merton Mill (58) *(DMorley)* 5–9-9 BRaymond (2) (hld up: effrt over 2f out: nt qckn over 1f out) ........................................................................ 1½.3

893⁴ Northants (47) *(WStorey)* 6–8-12 SWebster (3) (b: hld up & bhd: effrt appr 2f out: swtchd outside over 2f out: styd on: no imp ins fnl f) .......... ½.4

805 As Always (IRE) (41) (bl) *(GLewis)* 4–8-4 PaulEddery (8) (led tl over 2f out: wknd over 1f out) ................................................................................. 7.5

683⁵ Enkindle (29) *(BWMurray)* 5–7-8 PBurke (10) (lw: chsd ldrs tl lost pl over 2f out) 1½.6

My Desire (61) *(MrsGRReveley)* 4–9-3 ‡7DarrenMoffatt (6) (lw: chsd ldrs tl lost pl 6f out: effrt 3f out: n.d) ........................................................ 3½.7

Sexy Mover (28) *(WStorey)* 5–7-7 GBardwell (12) (chsd ldrs tl rdn & lost pl over 2f out) ........................................................................................ nk.8

683* Jawani (IRE) (51) (v) *(Dr.IDScargill)* 4–9-0 JQuinn (1) (lw: chsd ldrs: stumbled 11f out: hrd drvn 6f out: lost pl over 2f out) .......................... ½.9

987 Cost Effective (30) *(MBrittain)* 5–7-9 JLowe (7) (s.i.s: sn chsng ldrs: rdn & wknd over 3f out) ................................................................................ ½.10

916³ J P Morgan (52) (v) *(MPNaughton)* 4–9-1 JakiHouston (9) (effrt & prom 5f out: rdn & wknd over 3f out) ............................................................... hd.11

LONG HANDICAP: Sexy Mover 7-6.
*Austhorpe Sunset (20/1) Withdrawn (bolted bef s) : not under orders*

**4/1** Farmer's Pet, **5/1** SAMAIN (USA), **11/2** Jawani (IRE), **9/1** My Desire, **12/1** As Always (IRE), **14/1** Northants, Enkindle, **20/1** Cost Effective, J P Morgan, **50/1** Sexy Mover. CSF £22.23, CT £90.40. Tote £7.10: £2.20 £2.10 £1.90 (£14.30). Countrywide Classics Limited (WORKSOP) bred by Stephen D. Peskoff in USA. 11 Rn     3m 31.22 (5.72)

T/Plpt: £2,640 (0.7 Tckts); £1,070.52 to Lingfield 30/5/92.      WG

## 600—NOTTINGHAM (L-H)
### Friday, May 29th [Good to firm]
Going Allowance: St: 0.05 sec per fur; Rnd: 0.30 sec per fur (G) Wind: slt becoming mod bhd

Stalls: low
## 1120
CINDERHILL STKS (Mdn 2-Y.O.F) £1932.00 (£532.00: £252.00)    **5f 13y**    2-00 (2-01)

701 **Formaestre** (IRE) *(MHTompkins)* 8-11 PRobinson (2) (a.p: led 2f out: rdn out) —1

396 Breakfast Boogie *(JRFanshawe)* 8-11 GDuffield (4) (a.p: ev ch ins fnl f: no ex) .. 2.2

924² Cloudy Reef *(RHollinshead)* 8-4 ‡7AGarth (5) (gd spd over 3f) ......................... 5.3

650³ Hawayah (IRE) (Jt-Fav) *(BHanbury)* 8-11 WRSwinburn (8) (w ldrs 3f: wknd appr fnl f) ............................................................................................ 2.4

Cropton *(MHEasterby)* 8-6 ‡5SMaloney (7) (leggy: bkwd: prom: pushed along ½-wy: wknd over 1f out) ........................................................ 2½.5

701⁴ Magic Orb *(JLSpearing)* 8-11 JWilliams (1) (a bhd) ............................................ nk.6

Princess of Alar *(BPalling)* 8-11 MHills (3) (neat: bit bkwd: s.s: a outpcd) ......... 1½.7

703³ Sure Risk (Jt-Fav) *(RHannon)* 8-11 PatEddery (6) (lw: led 3f: wknd qckly over 1f out) ................................................................................................. nk.8

**6/4** Hawayah (IRE)(op Evens), Sure Risk, **11/1** Breakfast Boogie, **12/1** Magic Orb(op 7/1), **14/1** FORMAESTRE (IRE)(10/1—16/1), **16/1** Cloudy Reef(op 10/1), **25/1** Ors. CSF £131.65, Tote £27.00: £4.50 £3.30 £1.90 (wnr or 2nd w any £4.50). Saracen Racing (NEWMARKET) bred by James W. H. Hartley in Ireland. 8 Rn   61.7 sec (3)
SF—42/34/7/6/–/–

## 1121
BAGTHORPE (S) STKS (2-Y.O) £2480.80 (£688.80: £330.40)    **6f 15y**    2-30 (2-34)

920³ **A Bridge Too Far** (IRE) *(WJPearce)* 8-6 LCharnock (7) (lw: a.p: r.o to ld wl ins fnl f) .......................................................................................... —1

| | | | | |
|---|---|---|---|---|
| 882⁵ | Yeveed (IRE) *(MHEasterby)* 8-1 ‡⁵SMaloney (6) (lw: a.p: outpcd 2f out: rallied strly u.p ins fnl f) | hd.2 |
| 920² | Dead Calm (Fav) *(CTinkler)* 8-11 PatEddery (3) (mde most: clr over 1f out: wknd & hdd wl ins fnl f) | 1.3 |
| 682 | Nellie's Gamble *(APStringer)* 8-6 JFortune (5) (chsd ldrs: rdn ½-wy: sn btn) | 12.4 |
| 786⁵ | Hawke Bay *(DHaydnJones)* 8-11 JReid (4) (s.i.s: sn chsng ldrs: swtchd rt over 1f out: no imp) | ½.5 |
| 968 | Lady Argent (IRE) *(APJarvis)* 8-6 SWhitworth (10) (swtg: nvr plcd to chal) | ¾.6 |
| 703 | Walid's Princess (IRE) *(JWharton)* 8-8 (chsd ldrs 4f) | ¾.7 |
| 782 | Krayyan Dawn *(RVoorspuy)* 8-11 SDawson (1) (a bhd: t.o) | 10.8 |
| 971⁵ | Kill the Plague (USA) *(APJones)* 8-11 NAdams (2) (bit bkwd: outpcd: t.o) | 10.9 |
| | Ruled by Fashion *(JBalding)* 7-13 ‡⁷JEdmunds (9) (unf: bkwd: s.s: bhd most of wy: t.o) | 7.10 |

*Stewards Enquiry: Charnock suspended 7-10/6/92 (excessive use of whip).*

**11/8** Dead Calm(op 9/4), **7/2** Walid's Princess (IRE)(9/4—4/1), **5/1** Yeveed (IRE), A BRIDGE TOO FAR (IRE)(7/2—11/2), **9/1** Hawke Bay(op 6/1), **12/1** Nellie's Gamble, **16/1** Lady Argent (IRE), Krayyan Dawn(op 25/1), **33/1** Ors. CSF £32.07, Tote £6.50: £1.80 £2.40 £1.10 (£19.40). The Royal Partnership (HAMBLETON) bred by P. Tallis in Ireland. 10 Rn; No bid                                      1m 16.4 (5.4)

---

**1122**   AWEBB ELECTRICAL NETWORK H'CAP (3-Y.O) (0-70) £2814.00 (£784.00: £378.00)
1m 54y                                                                                3-00 (3-02)

| | | | |
|---|---|---|---|
| 746² | **Combative (IRE) (73)** (v) (Jt-Fav) *(JHMGosden)* 9-10 PatEddery (3) (a.p: 4th st: led ins fnl f: sn clr) | —1 |
| 767⁶ | Super Summit (56) *(JPearce)* 8-2 ‡⁵RPrice (16) (s.s: hdwy 2f out: fin wl) | 4.2 |
| 767 | The Dandy Don (IRE) (57) *(DenysSmith)* 8-8 JWilliams (6) (chsd ldrs: lost pl & 8th st: styd on ins fnl f) | 1.3 |
| 663⁵ | Ripsnorter (IRE) (60) *(SirMarkPrescott)* 8-11 GDuffield (2) (hmpd s: hdwy & 5th st: led 3f out tl hdd & wknd ins fnl f) | hd.4 |
| 835 | Gallant Jack (IRE) (66) *(DHaydnJones)* 9-3 MHills (1) (led 5f: wknd fnl f) | 2.5 |
| 696 | Faryal (57) *(JLSpearing)* 7-9 ‡⁷AGarth (11) (r.o 1f out: nvr nrr) | 2.6 |
| | Creego (48) *(JAGlover)* 7-8⁽¹⁾ ‡⁵SMaloney (9) (lw: hld up: sme hdwy fnl 2f: nt rch ldrs) | 2½.7 |
| 732 | Sirtelimar (IRE) (61) *(BobJones)* 8-12 VSmith (5) (lw: prom: 3rd st: wknd 2f out) | 7.8 |
| 621² | Gold Jubilee (68) *(PJMakin)* 9-5 JReid (15) (swtg: hld up: hdwy 4f out: wknd 1f out) | 2.9 |
| 695⁶ | Kingchip Boy (55) *(MJRyan)* 8-6 PRobinson (12) (chsd ldrs: 7th st: wknd 3f out) | nk.10 |
| | Premier Major (IRE) (52) *(WJPearce)* 8-3 LCharnock (14) (lw: a bhd) | 3.11 |
| 963⁴ | April Shadow (55) *(CWThornton)* 8-6 WCarson (10) (plld hrd: 6th st: wknd over 2f out) | 2½.12 |
| | Boon Hill (52) *(MWEllerby)* 8-3 SMorris (14) (a bhd) | 1.13 |
| 884 | Spanish Express (55) *(RBoss)* 8-6 AMunro (17) (lw: prom: 2nd st: wknd 3f out) | ¾.14 |
| 621³ | Dollar Wine (IRE) (64) (Jt-Fav) *(RHannon)* 9-1 WRSwinburn (7) (lw: a in rr) | s.h.15 |
| 715⁶ | Chatino (67) *(CEBrittain)* 9-4 SCauthen (4) (a bhd) | 2.16 |
| | Triple Trouble (55) *(HJCollingridge)* 8-6 DaleGibson (8) (swtg: bkwd: a bhd: t.o) | 8.17 |

**11/2** Dollar Wine (IRE)(4/1—6/1), COMBATIVE (IRE), **13/2** Gold Jubilee(op 7/2), **7/1** April Shadow, **8/1** Sirtelimar (IRE)(op 12/1), Ripsnorter (IRE), **10/1** The Dandy Don (IRE), Spanish Express, Chatino, **14/1** Gallant Jack (IRE), Super Summit, Kingchip Boy, **16/1** Creego, **25/1** Boon Hill, Premier Major (IRE), Faryal, **33/1** Triple Trouble. CSF £86.08, CT £730.36. Tote £7.20: £2.00 £4.50 £3.40 £2.20 (£107.60). Mr K. Abdulla (NEWMARKET) bred by Mrs Kiki Ward Platt in Ireland. 17 Rn                                      1m 45.9 (6.3)
SF—51/17/20/22/22/–

---

**1123**   LANGWITH APP'CE CLAIMING STKS (3-Y.O) £2382.80 (£660.80: £316.40)
1m 1f 213y                                                                            3-30 (3-31)

| | | | |
|---|---|---|---|
| 486⁴ | **Edge of Darkness** (Fav) *(JWHills)* 8-1 DHarrison (6) (a.p: 2nd st: led 3f out: pushed out) | —1 |
| 745⁴ | Cov Tel Lady (60) *(MHTompkins)* 7-10 ‡³SMulvey (4) (s.i.s: hdwy & 6th st: r.o 2f out: no ex ins fnl f) | 3.2 |
| 868⁴ | Silver Samurai (67) *(RHollinshead)* 8-3 ‡³MHumphries (8) (plld hrd: a.p: 4th st: rdn 2f out: kpt on) | 1.3 |
| 910 | Dave's Lass *(DBurchell)* 7-8 TWilson (1) (swtg: led 7f: wknd wl over 1f out) | 5.4 |
| 728 | Holy Wanderer (USA) (52) *(DWPArbuthnot)* 8-3 RPrice (3) (b.hind: hld up: 5th st: no imp fnl 2f) | 3.5 |
| | Misty View (72) *(MAJarvis)* 8-6 KRutter (5) (prom: 3rd st: wknd over 2f out) | nk.6 |
| 732 | Istanbullu *(MBell)* 8-1 ‡³ACairns (2) (lw: dwlt: 7th st: a bhd) | 6.7 |
| 966 | Secret Kin (IRE) *(OBrennan)* 7-13 OPears (7) (bit bkwd: a bhd: 8th st: t.o) | 25.8 |

**3/1** EDGE OF DARKNESS, **7/2** Cov Tel Lady, **4/1** Misty View(op 5/2), Silver Samurai, **9/1** Istanbullu, **10/1** Holy Wanderer (USA)(op 6/1), **25/1** Dave's Lass, **33/1** Secret Kin (IRE). CSF £12.93, Tote £2.70: £1.20 £1.60 £1.20 (£8.90). Mrs S. Bosher (LAMBOURN) bred by Mrs M. Tinkler. 8 Rn                                      2m 12.5 (10)
SF—17/6/11/–/–/–

## 1124

FLYING HORSE GRADUATION STKS (3-Y.O.F) £3318.75 (£990.00: £472.50: £213.75)
**1m 1f 213y**                                                                  4-00 (4-01)

850⁴ **Delve (IRE) (90)** *(JLDunlop)* 8-11 WCarson (1) (chsd ldr: 2nd st: hrd rdn to ld
nr fin) ........................................................................................... —1
865* Ardisia (USA) **(70)** *(PFlCole)* 8-11 AMunro (4) (swtg: led tl ct nr fin) ................. hd.2
      Anne Bonny *(JRFanshawe)* 9-4 WRSwinburn (3) (hld up: 3rd st: shkn up 3f out:
no rspnse) .................................................................................. 12.3
      Mount Helena **(Fav)** *(HRACecil)* 9-4 SCauthen (2) (lw: stdd s: 4th st: pushed
along 4f out: no imp fnl 2f) ........................................................ 12.4

**11/8** Mount Helena, **2/1** Anne Bonny, **9/4** DELVE (IRE)(op 6/4), **16/1** Ardisia (USA)(op 10/1). CSF £19.08, Tote
£2.50 (£10.70). Sir Robin McAlpine (ARUNDEL) bred by R. A. Collins in Ireland. 4 Rn          2m 9.8 (7.3)
SF—54/53/36/12

## 1125

FOREST H'CAP (0-70) £2618.00 (£728.00: £350.00)     **1³⁄₄m 15y**              4-30 (4-31)

675 **Lookingforararainbow (IRE) (55)** (Jt-Fav) *(BobJones)* 4–9-3 VSmith (13) (lw:
hld up: hdwy on ins 3f out: led over 2f out: clr fnl f) ............. —1
1002⁴ White River **(37)** (v) *(DHaydnJones)* 6–7-13 TyroneWilliams (7) (chsd ldrs: 6th
st: rdn & ev ch fr 3f out: styd on one pce) .......................... 3.2
964³ Famous Beauty **(50)** *(RHollinshead)* 5–8-5 ‡7DCarson (3) (lw: hld up: 4th st: ev
ch fr 3f out: outpcd appr fnl f) .................................. s.h.3
1065 Pondered Bid **(40)** (bl) *(PatMitchell)* 8–8-2⁽²⁾ GDuffield (6) (bhd: plld out 4f out:
styd on ins fnl f) ............................................... hd.4
895 Vision of Wonder **(31)** *(JSKing)* 8–7-0 ‡7AntoinetteArmes (12) (hdwy 10f out:
2nd st: styd on one pce fnl 2f) .................................. ³⁄₄.5
166⁴ Caroles Clown **(33)** *(MJHaynes)* 6–7-2⁽²⁾ ‡7DToole (5) (chsd ldrs tl lost pl ent st:
styd on fnl 2f) ................................................ 1¹⁄₂.6
964 Access Cruise (USA) **(50)** *(BAMcMahon)* 5–8-12 JFortune (1) (led tl hdd &
wknd over 2f out) ............................................. nk.7
267 Angelica Park **(50)** *(JWharton)* 6–8-5 ‡7SWilliams (10) (lw: hdwy 8f out: 3rd st:
rdn & wknd over 2f out) ....................................... 3¹⁄₂.8
761 Gods Law **(34)** *(REarnshaw)* 11–7-10⁽³⁾ AProud (8) (b.hind: bhd: effrt 6f out: nt
rch ldrs) ..................................................... hd.9
593 Moot Point (USA) **(55)** *(JRJenkins)* 4–9-3 SWhitworth (14) (effrt u.p 4f out: nt
trble ldrs) ................................................... ³⁄₄.10
605⁴ Sonic Signal **(46)** *(MJHaynes)* 6–8-3 ‡DHarrison (16) (m.n.s) ........... ³⁄₄.11
831 Polistatic **(40)** (Jt-Fav) *(CAHorgan)* 5–8-2 DaleGibson (2) (lost pl ¹⁄₂-wy: sn bhd) hd.12
805⁵ Paper Dance **(59)** (Jt-Fav) *(RJHolder)* 4–9-7 JWilliams (15) (hdwy ¹⁄₂-wy: 7th st:
wknd over 2f out) ............................................. 2¹⁄₂.13
951⁴ Doctor's Remedy **(37)** (bl) *(MrsJJordan)* 6–7-8⁽⁶⁾ ‡SMaloney (11) (prom: 5th
st: wknd 3f out) .............................................. 2.14
      Doolar (USA) **(62)** *(PTDalton)* 5–9-3 ‡7GForster (9) (b: bkwd: chsd ldrs tl 8th &
wkng st) ..................................................... 1¹⁄₂.15
831 Kanooz (IRE) **(50)** (v) *(SMellor)* 4–8-12 DanaMellor (4) (lw: bhd fr ¹⁄₂-wy: t.o) . 12.16
LONG HANDICAP: Vision of Wonder 7-1, Gods Law 7-6, Doctor's Remedy 7-4.

**11/2** Paper Dance, LOOKINGFORARARAINBOW (IRE)(op 7/2), Polistatic, **15/2** White River(5/1—8/1), **8/1** Sonic
Signal, Famous Beauty, **9/1** Angelica Park, **10/1** Access Cruise (USA), Pondered Bid(16/1—20/1), **16/1** Caroles
Clown, Moot Point (USA), Doctor's Remedy, **33/1** Ors. CSF £47.74, CT £310.63. Tote £8.20: £2.20 £2.70 £1.80
£3.00 (£70.40). Mr David S. Blake (NEWMARKET) bred by Red Sox Associates in Ireland. 16 Rn       3m 8.9 (10.4)
SF—41/17/22/18/–/–

T/Plpt: £513.50 (4.4 Tckts).                                                                      IM

## 913—**EDINBURGH (R-H)**

### Saturday, May 30th [Good to firm, Firm patches]
Going Allowance: minus 0.40 sec per fur (F)                              Wind: almost nil

Stalls: high

## 1126

FISHERROW STKS (Mdn) £2092.00 (£587.00: £286.00)     **1m 3f 32y**          2-10 (2-12)

767⁵ **Eden's Close (76)** (v) *(MHTompkins)* 3–8-9 PRobinson (4) (lw: trckd ldr:
led wl over 1f out: qcknd: comf) ................................ —1
771³ Restless Minstrel (USA) **(LMCumani)** 3–8-9 JFortune (7) (led tl hdd wl over 1f
out: no ch w wnr) ............................................. 3.2
771⁴ Tour Leader (NZ) *(TDBarron)* 3–8-9 AlexGreaves (6) (hld up: effrt 2f out: too
much to do) .................................................. 7.3

418⁵ Native Crown (IRE) *(MissLAPerratt)* 4–9-5 ‡⁷RHavlin (2) (swtg: a chsng ldrs: no
    imp fnl 3½f) .................................................. 1½.4
1043³ Bee Dee Ell (USA) **(48)** *(MissLAPerratt)* 3–8-9  GDuffield (3) (plld hrd: bhd: hdwy
    over 3f out: n.d) .................................................. 1.5
    Invisible Armour *(PCHaslam)* 3–8-9  DaleGibson (5) (hld up & a wl bhd) ............ 8.6
    Marian Evans *(TCraig)* 5–9-4 ‡³JFanning (1) (chsd ldrs to st: sn wknd) ............ 4.7

**Evens** EDEN'S CLOSE(5/4—4/5), **3/1** Restless Minstrel (USA), **7/2** Tour Leader (NZ), **12/1** Native Crown (IRE),
**33/1** Invisible Armour, Bee Dee Ell (USA), **100/1** Marian Evans. CSF £4.22, Tote £1.60: £1.10 £2.30 (£2.80).
Mrs M. Barwell (NEWMARKET) bred by Lariston Bloodstock. 7 Rn              2m 25.9 (6.2)

**1127**        OCHIL HILLS CLAIMING STKS (2-Y.O) £2200.50 (£618.00: £301.50)        5f 2-40 (2-42)

920⋆ **Shadow Jury** (Fav) *(MrsGRReveley)* 9-0  JFortune (4) (lw: trckd ldrs: hdwy 2f
    out: led 1f out: shkn up & styd on) .................................................. —1
920⁴ Oscars Quest *(JBerry)* 8-6  GDuffield (3) (led tl hdd 1f out: r.o one pce) .......... 2½.2
770⁶ Betrayed *(PCHaslam)* 8-0 ‡⁵NKennedy (2) (disp ld to ½-wy: sn outpcd) ......... 7.3
416 Sea-Ayr (IRE) *(MissLAPerratt)* 7-10 ‡³JFanning (1) (unruly bef s: spd to ½-wy:
    hung lft & sn lost pl) .................................................. 1½.4

**2/7** SHADOW JURY, **5/1** Betrayed, **11/2** Oscars Quest, **25/1** Sea-Ayr (IRE). CSF £2.58, Tote £1.20 (£1.80). Mr
P. D. Savill (SALTBURN) bred by J. S. Bell. 4 Rn; Shadow Jury clmd D Walker £12,869    59.8 sec (2.1)
                                                                                            SF—18/–/–/–

**1128**        GULLANE STKS (Mdn 3-Y.O.F) £2102.50 (£590.00: £287.50)        **1m 16y**   3-10 (3-11)

    **Only Royale (IRE)** (Fav) *(LMCumani)* 8-11  JFortune (3) (cmpt: s.s: sn rcvrd:
    led on bit wl over 1f out: shkn up & qcknd) .................................. —1
914³ Indian Style (IRE) *(RGuest)* 8-11  PRobinson (4) (led tl hdd wl over 1f out: no ch
    w wnr) .................................................. 2½.2
818⁵ Shakela (USA) (bl) *(BHanbury)* 8-11  GDuffield (5) (lw: trckd ldrs: effrt over 2f
    out: no rspnse) .................................................. 7.3
1001 Weekend Girl (30) *(WMBrisbourne)* 8-8 ‡³JFanning (1) (a outpcd & bhd) ......... 30.4

**1/3** ONLY ROYALE (IRE), **4/1** Shakela (USA)(tchd 6/1), **9/2** Indian Style (IRE)(3/1—5/1), **50/1** Weekend Girl.
CSF £2.56, Tote £1.30 (£1.70). Mr G. Sainaghi (NEWMARKET) bred by Barronstown Stud in Ireland. 4 Rn
                                                                                            1m 41.5 (2.9)
                                                                                            SF—6/–/–/–

**1129**        HIGHLAND SPRING H'CAP (0-90) £2660.00 (£735.00: £350.00)
                **1m 16y**                                                    3-40 (3-43)

1051 **Blue Grit** (39) (bl) *(MDods)* 6–7-10  PBurke (6) (a cl up: led wl over 1f out: rdn
    out) .................................................. —1
618⋆ Alycida (USA) (83) (Fav) *(LMCumani)* 3–10-0  JFortune (3) (lw: trckd ldr: rn wd
    appr st: sn rdn: hdwy over 1f out: r.o nr fin) .................................. nk.2
883⁶ Inseyab (57) *(PCHaslam)* 4–8-9 ‡⁵NKennedy (5) (trckd ldrs: hmpd appr st: ev
    ch 2f out: kpt on one pce) .................................................. nk.3
1013⁴ Leave it to Lib (57) *(PCalver)* 5–8-11 ‡³JFanning (4) (lw: led tl hdd wl over 1f out:
    sn outpcd) .................................................. 3.4
903⁶ Verdant Boy (60) *(MPNaughton)* 9–9-3  SWebster (7) (effrt 3f out: styd on: no
    imp) .................................................. ¾.5
    Anguish (IRE) (57) *(NACallaghan)* 3–8-2  GDuffield (2) (in tch tl outpcd wl over 2f) 7.6
981 Master Plan (FR) (36) (v) *(MissLAPerratt)* 6–7-7  DaleGibson (1) (s.i.s: a bhd) . 2½.7
                LONG HANDICAP: Master Plan (FR) 6-8.

**7/4** Alycida (USA), **2/1** Leave it to Lib, **7/1** Verdant Boy, Inseyab, **12/1** BLUE GRIT, **25/1** Anguish (IRE), **50/1**
Master Plan (FR). CSF £30.38, Tote £12.50: £3.70 £2.10 (£34.40). Mr C. Michael Wilson (DARLINGTON) bred
by Collinstown Stud Farm Ltd. 7 Rn                                            1m 40.4 (1.8)
                                                                                            SF—7/38/18/11/15/–

**1130**        DON'T BLINK (S) H'CAP (0-60) £2389.50 (£672.00: £328.50)        **7f 15y**   4-15 (4-23)

1093² **Cool Enough** (33) (Fav) *(MrsJRRamsden)* 11–8-3  PRobinson (6) (lw: hld up:
    qcknd to ld 1f out: r.o wl) .................................................. —1
913 Angel Train (IRE) (37) (bl) *(JParkes)* 4–8-7  AlexGreaves (10) (lw: mde most tl
    hdd 1f out: no ex) .................................................. 4.2
888 Choice Lot (47) *(JJO'Neill)* 5–9-3  JFortune (12) (lw: a chsng ldrs: chal over 1f
    out: hrd drvn & nt qckn) .................................................. 1½.3
765² Rose Gem (IRE) (56) *(PCHaslam)* 3–9-1  DaleGibson (1) (in tch tl rn wd appr st:
    styd on fnl 2f: nt pce to chal) .................................................. 1.4
866 Freaky Deaky (58) *(NACallaghan)* 5–10-0  GDuffield (4) (bhd tl styd on u.p fnl 3f:
    nrst fin) .................................................. 1½.5

1013 Hizeem **(33)** *(MPNaughton)* 6-8-3 SWebster (8) (bhd: hrd rdn & hdwy over 2f
out: nvr nrr) .................................................... ³/₄.6
Dreams Eyes **(33)** *(RBastiman)* 4-8-3 PBurke (5) (disp ld to st: wknd wl over 1f
out) ........................................................ ³/₄.7
Ravecino **(45)** *(JSHaldane)* 3-7-13 ‡⁵NKennedy (3) (chsd ldrs tl wknd over 2f
out) ........................................................ 2¹/₂.8
888 Francis Ann **(51)** *(MissLAPerratt)* 4-9-4 ‡³JFanning (7) (a bhd) ............ 2¹/₂.9
918 Melody Anne **(45)** *(JSHaldane)* 3-7-11⁽²⁾ ‡⁷RHavlin (2) (b.hind: in tch to st: sn
wknd) ...................................................... 10.10

**2/1** COOL ENOUGH, **7/2** Dreams Eyes(9/2—3/1), **4/1** Rose Gem (IRE), **10/1** Freaky Deaky, **11/1**
Hizeem(8/1—12/1), **12/1** Francis Ann(op 7/1), **14/1** Angel Train (IRE), **25/1** Choice Lot, Melody Anne, **33/1**
Ravecino. CSF £27.37, CT £498.30. Tote £4.30: £1.40 £1.90 £5.50 (£12.80). Mrs J. R. Ramsden (THIRSK)
bred by Miss Amanda Downes. 10 Rn; No bid                                    1m 27.1 (0.9)
                                                                    SF—33/25/30/25/33/6

---

**1131**    BLACKFORD H'CAP (3-Y.O.) (0-70) £2263.50 (£636.00: £310.50)
          1¹/₂m 31y                                              4-45 (4-48)

                      (Weights raised 11 lb)
950² Boring (USA) **(54)** *(WStorey)* 9-2 SWebster (7) (b: hld up: effrt 3f out: led wl
over 1f out) ................................................. —1
798 Bartolomeo (USA) **(47)** *(MrsJRRamsden)* 8-9 PRobinson (6) (a in tch: effrt over
2f out: styd on: nt pce of wnr) ................................. 3.2
745⁵ Sparkling Vision **(45)** (bl) *(MrsGRReveley)* 8-7 JFortune (5) (a chsng ldrs: rdn
over 2f out: r.o one pce) ...................................... ³/₄.3
745* Tronchetto (IRE) **(59)** (Fav) *(SirMarkPrescott)* 9-7 GDuffield (4) (lw: trckd ldrs:
rdn to ld 2f out: sn hdd & no ex) ............................. 1¹/₂.4
In No Doubt **(47)** *(JJO'Neill)* 8-6 ‡³JFanning (1) (led tl hdd 2f out: sn outpcd) 1¹/₂.5
296⁶ Glowing Devil **(58)** *(TDBarron)* 9-6 AlexGreaves (2) (lw: hld up & bhd: nvr plcd
to chal) ...................................................... 7.6
680 Kentucky Chicken (USA) **(45)** *(MissLCSiddall)* 8-7 DaleGibson (3) (t.o fnl 6f) .. dist.7

**5/6** Tronchetto (IRE)(6/4—4/5), **7/2** BORING (USA), **8/1** Bartolomeo (USA), **9/1** Glowing Devil, **14/1** Sparkling
Vision, **20/1** Ors. CSF £27.37, Tote £5.00: £2.50 £1.50 (£15.40). Mr W. Storey (CONSETT) bred by Marystead
Farm in USA. 7 Rn                                              2m 38.1 (5.6)
T/Plpt: £55.20 (40.65 Tckts).                                           AA

---

**894— LINGFIELD (L-H)**

## Saturday, May 30th [Good, Good to firm back st]

Going Allowance: 5f: minus 0.20 sec; Rest: nil sec per fur (F)        Wind: almost nil

Stalls: 5th race centre, remainder high

**1132**    DAILY MAIL H. H. & S. H'CAP (0-100) £5117.00 (£1526.00: £728.00: £329.00)
          1m 3f 106y                                            2-00 (2-02)

926 Mahfil **(63)** *(RAkehurst)* 4-7-8 ‡³FNorton (2) (2nd st: led over 2f out: hrd rdn
over 1f out: r.o wl) ........................................... —1
861³ Quick Ransom **(75)** *(MJohnston)* 4-8-9 DMcKeown (6) (lw: 4th st: rdn over 3f
out: r.o) .................................................... 1.2
832³ Gueca Solo **(83)** (Fav) *(HRACecil)* 4-9-3 LPiggott (1) (5th st: rdn over 2f out: r.o
one pce) ..................................................... 6.3
713* Modesto (USA) **(69)** *(KOCunningham-Brown)* 4-8-0 ‡³DBiggs (5) (b: led 9f) ... 3¹/₂.4
Retouch **(94)** *(PFICole)* 6-9-7 ‡⁷JDSmith (3) (b.off hind: nvr nr to chal) ........... ³/₄.5
926 Green Medina (IRE) **(72)** *(MBell)* 4-8-6 MHills (4) (3rd st: wknd over 2f out) ..... 12.6
708 Access Ski **(79)** *(RBoss)* 5-8-13 MTebbutt (4) (6th st: a bhd) ................ 15.7

**9/4** Gueca Solo(6/4—11/4), **11/4** MAHFIL, **100/30** Quick Ransom(5/1—3/1), **6/1** Modesto (USA), **14/1** Green
Medina (IRE)(10/1—16/1), **25/1** Access Ski, **33/1** Retouch. CSF £11.00, Tote £3.20: £2.00 £1.90 (£5.40). Mr
G. S. Beccle (EPSOM) bred by Derrinstown Stud Ltd. 7 Rn                     2m 28.08 (6.08)
                                                                    SF—19/32/28/4/23/—

**1133**    DAILY MAIL DREAM COTTAGE GAME H'CAP (0-110) £9240.00 (£2760.00: £1320.00:
          £600.00)    7f                                         2-30 (2-33)

941³ Cheveux Mitchell **(70)** (v) (Fav) *(MRChannon)* 5-8-7 RHills (15) (mde virtually
all: drvn out) ................................................ —1
860⁴ Kimberley Park **(66)** *(DWPArbuthnot)* 4-8-3 MHills (13) (a.p: ev ch fnl f: r.o) ..... ¹/₂.2

887* Bold Angel (79) (MHEasterby) 5-9-2 MBirch (11) (a.p: ev ch ins fnl f: unable qckn) ..................................................................................... 1½.3
610³ Mango Manila (89) (CAHorgan) 7-9-12 AMcGlone (12) (b: lw: hdwy over 1f out: one pce) ........................................................................... 4.4
935³ Hard to Figure (91) (RJHodges) 6-10-0 RCochrane (9) (a.p: rdn over 1f out: wknd fnl f) ........................................................................... ¾.5
1013 Darakah (60) (CJHill) 5-7-11 JQuinn (4) (nvr nr to chal) ................................ 1½.6
898* Rocky Waters (USA) (86) (GLewis) 3-8-12 BRouse (10) (hdwy 2f out: one pce) 1.7
860 Superoo (FR) (JSutcliffe) 6-8-11 DMcKeown (8) (a mid div) ......................... 2.8
997 Candle King (IRE) (59) (bl) (MJFetherston-Godley) 4-7-5(3) ‡5DHarrison (6) (a mid div) ...................................................................................... hd.9
Wild and Loose (86) (DRCElsworth) 4-9-9 SCauthen (14) (bit bkwd: a bhd) .... 6.10
930⁴ Merlins Wish (USA) (89) (RHannon) 3-9-1 LPiggott (7) (bhd fnl 3f) ............... 5.11
853⁶ Baysham (USA) (83) (bl) (BRMillman) 6-9-6 SWhitworth (2) (bhd fnl 3f) ........ 4.12
692⁶ Domicksky (75) (MJRyan) 4-8-12 WCarson (3) (prom over 3f) ....................... 2.13
858 Fair American (USA) (78) (MRStoute) 3-8-4 PaulEddery (1) (lw: bhd fnl 4f) .. 2½.14
LONG HANDICAP: Candle King (IRE) 7-5.

7/1 CHEVEUX MITCHELL, 15/2 Bold Angel, 8/1 Kimberley Park, Mango Manila, Merlins Wish (USA), 9/1 Rocky Waters (USA), Domicksky, 10/1 Hard to Figure, 12/1 Darakah(op 8/1), 14/1 Superoo, Wild and Loose, 20/1 Baysham (USA), 25/1 Ors. CSF £56.52, CT £391.13. Tote £6.50: £2.30 £2.80 2.00 (£20.80). Chitty Ltd (UPPER LAMBOURN) bred by Colby Bloodstock. 14 Rn
1m 22.72 (1.42)
SF−72/66/74/72/72/36

## 1134
DAILY MAIL LEISURE STKS (Listed Race) £13626.00 (£4068.00: £1944.00: £882.00)
6f
3-00 (3-03)

982² **Central City (108)** (Fav) (RHannon) 3-7-13 WCarson (1) (led 2f: led 2f out: rdn out) ................................................................................... —1
779* Bold Lez (100) (MJHaynes) 5-9-0 RCochrane (4) (lw: hld up: rdn over 2f out: r.o wl ins fnl f) ...................................................................... ½.2
827 Fylde Flyer (109) (JBerry) 3-8-9 JCarroll (3) (w wnr: led 4f out to 2f out: r.o) .... ¾.3
813³ Cumbrian Waltzer (100) (MHEasterby) 7-9-0 MBirch (6) (hld up: rdn over 2f out: nt clr run ins fnl f: r.o) ...................................................... ¾.4
851² High Sevens (96) (HCandy) 3-7-13 CRutter (2) (hld up: one pce fnl 2f) .......... 2.5
935 Green Dollar (90) (EAWheeler) 9-9-0 FNorton (7) (a bhd) ........................... 2½.6
853* Orthorhombus (96) (GLewis) 3-8-4 PaulEddery (8) (lw: bhd fnl 4f) ............... 1.7
Sarcita (108) (DRCElsworth) 4-8-9 SCauthen (5) (bit bkwd: a bhd) ............... 2.8

11/8 CENTRAL CITY, 5/1 Sarcita, 11/2 Bold Lez, 11/2 Cumbrian Waltzer, 10/1 Orthorhombus, 12/1 Fylde Flyer, 14/1 High Sevens, 50/1 Green Dollar. CSF £8.56, Tote £2.00: £1.10 £2.40 £3.20 (£7.50). A. F. Budge (Equine) Limited (MARLBOROUGH) bred by E. Aldridge. 8 Rn
1m 9.91 (1.31)
SF−59/76/68/70/47/52

## 1135
E.B.F. RACEMAIL STKS (Mdn 2-Y.O.C & G) £2542.90 (£704.40: £336.70)
5f
4-10 (4-12)

847⁴ **Kahellan (FR)** (Fav) (LMCumani) 9-0 RCochrane (2) (lw: mde all: clr over 1f out: r.o wl) ................................................................................ —1
907² Windrush Boy (MMcCormack) 9-0 JReid (6) (chsd wnr: rdn over 2f out: no imp) 4.2
Port Lucaya (RHannon) 9-0 WCarson (1) (cmpt: hdwy 2f out: r.o ins fnl f) ..... 3.3
907⁵ Bold Face (IRE) (RFJohnsonHoughton) 9-0 SWhitworth (7) (prom 3f) ............ 1½.4
772 Le Couteau (DWPArbuthnot) 8-9 ‡5RPrice (5) (nvr nr to chal) ..................... 1.5
Loch Patrick (LJHolt) 9-0 AMcGlone (8) (str: scope: outpcd: nvr nrr) ............ 3.6
733⁶ Kintwyn (DRLaing) 9-0 TyroneWilliams (3) (prom over 2f) ........................... 1.7
Right Will Prevail (GLewis) 9-0 BRouse (10) (w'like: scope: lw: a bhd) .......... 2½.8
847 Coopers Delight (GLewis) 9-0 PaulEddery (4) (b.hind: prom over 2f) ............ 1½.9
Silent Prince (MissBSanders) 9-0 NWewnes (9) (unf: lw: s.s: a wl bhd) .......... 2.10

15/8 KAHELLAN (FR), 2/1 Windrush Boy, 11/2 Port Lucaya(4/1—6/1), 13/2 Right Will Prevail, 12/1 Bold Face (IRE)(tchd 20/1), 25/1 Silent Prince, Le Couteau, Coopers Delight, 33/1 Ors. CSF £6.11, Tote £3.10: £1.20 £1.20 £1.80 (£3.20). Sultan Mohammed (NEWMARKET) bred by Manita Invest Corporation in France. 10 Rn
58.36 sec (1.36)
SF−53/37/25/19/15/8

## 1136
DAILY MAIL CLASSIFIED GRADUATION STKS £4503.00 (£1344.00: £642.00: £291.00)
7f 140y
4-40 (4-43)

822* **Hazaam (USA)** (Fav) (MRStoute) 3-8-11 SCauthen (1) (lw: hld up: plld out wl over 1f out: qcknd & led ins fnl f: r.o wl) ............................... —1
862⁴ Mougins (IRE) (100) (DRCElsworth) 3-8-11 RCochrane (2) (hmpd s: hld up: led over 1f out tl ins fnl f: unable qckn) ....................................... ¾.2

825⁵ Beware of Agents **(95)** *(MJohnston)* 3–9-0 DMcKeown (4) (lw: a.p: ev ch ins fnl
     f: one pce) ............................................................................................ ³/₄.3
832⁵ Lucknam Dreamer **(70)** *(MrsBarbaraWaring)* 4–9-9 NHowe (6) (led 6f: one pce) 1¹/₂.4
     Ajib (USA) *(JHMGosden)* 3–8-11 WCarson (5) (swtg: chsd ldr 6f) ...................... 8.5
778³ Executive Spirit *(DSasse)* 3–8-11 JQuinn (3) (swvd lft s: a bhd) ....................... 6.6
     704 Bold Pursuit (IRE) (7/1) Withdrawn (veterinary advice) : not under orders

**4/7** HAZAAM (USA), **4/1** Mougins (IRE), **6/1** Beware of Agents, **7/1** Ajib (USA), **33/1** Ors. CSF £3.56, Tote £1.40:
£1.10 £1.80 (£2.20). Sheikh Mohammed (NEWMARKET) bred by Darley Stud Management Co Ltd in USA. 6 Rn
                                        1m 30.98 (2.48)
                                     SF—60/58/59/63/27/9

**1137**     O.C.S. SPONSORED STKS (Ladies) £2831.50 (£784.00: £374.50)
        1m 3f 106y                                5-10 (5-12)

724⁵ **Pharly Story (93)** (Fav) *(MCPipe)* 4–10-10 MrsLPearce (4) (4th st: qcknd & led
     2f out: clr over 1f out: easily) ........................................................................ —1
993³ Ambassador Royale (IRE) **(80)** *(PFICole)* 4–10-10 MissMClark (7) (5th st: chsd
     wnr wl over 1f out: no imp) ......................................................................... 6.2
1027² The Karaoke King **(66)** *(RHannon)* 3–8-11 ‡³MrsJBoggis (1) (led over 9f out to 2f
     out: one pce) ............................................................................................. 1¹/₂.3
     Peace King **(74)** *(GHarwood)* 6–10-10 MissAHarwood (6) (2nd st: ev ch 2f out:
     wknd over 1f out) ....................................................................................... 6.4
1044 Singing Reply (USA) **(40)** *(DMarks)* 4–9-12 MissKMarks (8) (nvr nr to chal) ...... ³/₄.5
     Puff Puff **(55)** *(MissBSanders)* 6–10-5 MrsEMellor (3) (3rd st: wknd over 2f out) 6.6
526 Wild Persian (IRE) **(45)** *(PatMitchell)* 3–8-9⁽³⁾ ‡³MissLGlayzer (2) (led 2f: wknd 6f
     out: 6th st: t.o fnl 3f) ............................................................................... 30.7
1009 One of the Lads *(BRCambidge)* 10–10-3 MrsHNoonan (5) (b: t.o fnl 7f) .......... 15.8

**11/8** PHARLY STORY, **15/8** Ambassador Royale (IRE), **6/1** The Karaoke King, **7/1** Peace King(5/1—8/1), **14/1**
Puff Puff(10/1—16/1), **00/1** Ors. CCF £4.21, Tote £2.20: £1.10 £1.30 £1.60 (£2.60). Mr A. J. Lomas
(WELLINGTON) bred by Deepwood Farm Stud. 8 Rn                    2m 31.32 (9.32)
                                     SF—31/19/–/4/–/–

**1138**     DAILY MAIL CIRCULATION H'CAP (0-70) £2678.40 (£742.40: £355.20)
        5f                                    5-40 (5-43)

738⁵ **Martinosky (50)** *(WGRWightman)* 6–8-13 JWilliams (11) (a.p: led over 2f out:
     r.o wl) ....................................................................................................... —1
 80 Gabibti (IRE) **(60)** *(BGubby)* 4–9-4 ‡⁵DHarrison (9) (swtg: a.p: hrd rdn over 1f
     out: unable qckn) ....................................................................................... 6.2
897⁴ Miss Precocious **(38)** (v) *(DShaw)* 4–7-12 ‡³FNorton (13) (s.s: hdwy over 2f out:
     one pce) .................................................................................................... 1¹/₂.3
906 Bridle Talk (IRE) **(49)** *(MMcCormack)* 3–8-3 AClark (12) (hdwy 2f out: one pce) 2¹/₂.4
945⁵ Hitchin a Ride **(59)** (bl) *(MPMuggeridge)* 5–9-8 RCochrane (10) (a.p: one pce
     fnl 2f) ......................................................................................................... 2.5
996★ Tauber **(65)** *(PatMitchell)* 8–9-11 ‡³SO'Gorman (2) (nvr nr to chal) ................... 2¹/₂.6
897 Petitesse **(52)** *(GBlum)* 4–9-1 AShoults (6) (prom 3f) ....................................... hd.7
     Saint Systems **(49)** *(CJHill)* 6–8-12 TyroneWilliams (1) (bhd fnl 3f) ................ 1¹/₂.8
906³ Temple Fortune (USA) **(67)** (bl) (Fav) *(DRCElsworth)* 3–9-7 SCauthen (3)
     (swtg: led over 2f) ...................................................................................... ³/₄.9
996 Ski Captain **(53)** *(PHowling)* 8–9-2 WNewnes (5) (swtg: outpcd) ................... 2.10
872 Banbury Flyer **(61)** *(MrsALMKing)* 4–9-10 RHills (4) (prom over 2f) .................. 1.11
909 Factuelle **(43)** *(DRTucker)* 5–8-6 GBardwell (8) (a bhd) ................................. nk.12
     Belthorn **(43)** *(JJBridger)* 3–7-11 SDawson (7) (prom over 2f) ...................... 4.13

**100/30** Temple Fortune (USA)(op 9/2), **5/1** Tauber, Miss Precocious, **8/1** Hitchin a Ride, MARTINOSKY, **10/1** Ski
Captain, **12/1** Petitesse, Factuelle, **14/1** Banbury Flyer, **20/1** Gabibti (IRE), Saint Systems, Bridle Talk (IRE), **50/1**
Belthorn. CSF £140.37, CT £809.98. Tote £12.70: £3.40 £8.80 £1.60 (£221.10). Mr D. B. Clark (UPHAM) bred
by David B. Clark. 13 Rn                                      58.35 sec (1.35)
                                     SF—52/33/7/2/13/6

T/Trio: Race 2: £55.60 (38.6 Tckts). T/Jkpt: £7,869.30 (1 Tckt). T/Plpt: £49.70 (170.65 Tckts).     AK

## 805—**WOLVERHAMPTON (L-H)**

### Saturday, May 30th [Good to soft]
Going Allowance: 0.40 sec per fur (G)                              Wind: almost nil

Stalls: high

**1139**     BROSELEY MEDIAN AUCTION STKS (Mdn 3-Y.O) £1119.00 (£309.00: £147.00)
        1³/₄m 134y                                  6-15 (6-15)

566² Garden District (Fav) *(RCharlton)* 9-0 PatEddery (4) (bit bkwd: chsd ldr: rdn 6f
     out: 2nd st: led over 2f out: edgd rt fnl f: all out) .................. —1

728 Prince Mercury **(66)** *(JLDunlop)* 9-0 GCarter (2) (chsd ldrs: 3rd & rdn st: styd
on to chal 1f out: r.o) .................................................... ½.2
908 Elite Reg **(50)** *(PFICole)* 8-10 CRutter (1) (led tl hdd over 2f out: sn rdn & btn) .. 6.3
901 Washington Red *(MFBarraclough)* 8-10 KFallon (3) (a bhd: 4th st: t.o fnl 3f) .... 25.4

**2/9** GARDEN DISTRICT, **5/1** Prince Mercury, **16/1** Elite Reg(op 10/1), **100/1** Washington Red. CSF £1.62, Tote
£1.10 (£1.10). Mr K. Abdulla (BECKHAMPTON) bred by Sir Gordon Brunton. 4 Rn          3m 20.4 (14.4)
SF—15/14/–/–

**1140**    HIMLEY (S) STKS (2-Y.O) £1245.00 (£345.00: £165.00)    **5f**    6-45 (6-50)

786 Toff Sundae *(GLewis)* 8-11 GCarter (3) (lw: bhd & rdn along ½-wy: gd hdwy
over 1f out: str run to ld wl ins fnl f) ............................. —1
733 Admiral Frobisher (USA) **(Fav)** *(CFWall)* 8-11 NDay (1) (swtg: hdwy 2f out: led
ins fnl f: sn hdd: no ex) .............................................. 1½.2
1077³ Grey Runner *(BPalling)* 7-13 ‡7StephenDavies (8) (chsd ldrs: kpt on ins fnl f) ... 2.3
Alice Bay *(DHaydnJones)* 8-6 WRyan (6) (w'like: leggy: bit bkwd: outpcd tl r.o
wl ins fnl f: bttr for r) ................................................. 1.4
1036 Over the Dec *(BAMcMahon)* 7-13 ‡7SSanders (9) (a.p: led over 1f out: sn hdd &
wknd) ....................................................................... ¾.5
514 Spanish Tower *(RJHolder)* 8-11 JLowe (11) (bit bkwd: led tl hdd & wknd 1f out) .. ¾.6
889³ Steven's Dream (IRE) *(JWhite)* 8-1 ‡5RPrice (10) (w ldrs over 3f) .......... nk.7
463⁶ Zinjaal (IRE) *(BHanbury)* 8-11 PatEddery (5) (chsd ldrs: eased whn btn ins fnl f) ¾.8
Bell Lad (IRE) *(CASmith)* 8-12⁽¹⁾ MWigham (4) (w'like: bkwd: outpcd) ....... 3½.9
423⁵ Genesis Four (bl) *(JRJenkins)* 8-11 GBaxter (7) (lw: bhd fr ½-wy: t.o) ........... 7.10

**3/1** Admiral Frobisher (USA)(4/1—5/2), **4/1** Steven's Dream (IRE), **5/1** Spanish Tower(tchd 12/1), Zinjaal
(IRE)(7/2—11/2), **11/2** TOFF SUNDAE, **11/1** Grey Runner(op 7/1), **14/1** Over the Dec(10/1—16/1), **16/1** Alice
Bay(op 10/1), **20/1** Genesis Four, **33/1** Bell Lad (IRE). CSF £22.09, Tote £4.90: £1.60 £2.50 £2.50 (£13.80).
Roldvale Limited (EPSOM) bred by Mrs E. Rhind. 10 Rn; Bt in 2,000 gns          63.4 sec (6.1)
SF—15/9/14/–/–

**1141**    THREE SISTERS STKS (3-Y.O) £1576.00 (£436.00: £208.00)    **1m 3f**    7-15 (7-16)

585★ Peto **(100)** **(Fav)** *(HRACecil)* 9-1 WRyan (4) (lw: mde all: drew clr fnl 3f: eased nr
fin) .......................................................................... —1
910★ Source of Light *(RCharlton)* 9-1 PatEddery (2) (wnt 2nd 8f out: btn over 3f out) 20.2
816 Kasikci **(86)** *(RHollinshead)* 8-13 GCarter (1) (bhd: 4th st: hdwy 4f out: rdn &
one pce fnl f) ............................................................ 2.3
My Girl Friday *(WClay)* 8-6 JLowe (3) (chsd wnr 3f: 3rd & t.o ent st) .............. 20.4

**10/11** PETO, **11/10** Source of Light, **20/1** Kasikci(op 12/1), **125/1** My Girl Friday. CSF £2.06, Tote £1.80
(£1.20). Sheikh Mohammed (NEWMARKET) bred by P. T. Tellwright. 4 Rn          2m 28.9 (13.9)
SF—6/–/–/–

**1142**    MADELEY CLAIMING STKS (3-Y.O) £1266.00 (£351.00: £168.00)
**1m 200y**    7-45 (7-51)

547 Firefighter **(67)** *(RHollinshead)* 9-3 WRyan (14) (hdwy & 3rd st: jnd ldr 2f out:
rdn to ld over 1f out: r.o) ............................................ —1
921³ Grog (IRE) **(78)** **(Fav)** *(MRChannon)* 9-7 PatEddery (11) (led after 3f tl over 1f
out: hrd rdn & no ex fnl f) ........................................... 2.2
Winged Whisper (USA) **(67)** *(CWThornton)* 8-13 DMcKeown (12) (swtg: bit
bkwd: b.off hind: chsd ldrs: 6th st: styd on ins fnl f) ............... ¾.3
Handy Lass *(JWharton)* 8-7⁽¹⁾ NDay (9) (leggy: unf: bit bkwd: swtg: led 3f: 4th
st: kpt on one pce fnl 2f) ............................................. 2.4
357 Tina Meena Lisa **(42)** *(EHOwenjun)* 7-5 ‡7CHawksley (5) (in tch: styd on fnl 2f:
nvr nrr) .................................................................... 2½.5
919⁶ Copper Trader *(KSBridgwater)* 8-2 NAdams (8) (hmpd & lost pl after 2f: rallied
3f out: one pce fnl f) ................................................... ¾.6
915⁴ Breakdancer (IRE) *(MrsJRRamsden)* 8-12 JCarroll (4) (lw: prom: 5th st: rdn 2f
out: one pce) .......................................................... hd.7
974 Marowins **(50)** *(EJAlston)* 8-7 KFallon (2) (chsd ldrs: 7th st: rdn & wknd 2f out) s.h.8
Wrycrest *(RCharlton)* 8-6 SRaymont (3) (lw: bhd: effrt over 3f out: nvr able to
chal) ....................................................................... 1½.9
969⁴ Peggy Mainwaring **(51)** *(RJHolder)* 7-10⁽¹⁾ ‡7SDrowne (7) (mid div tl wknd 3f
out) ........................................................................ 4.10
Evening Stables *(JWharton)* 8-7 ‡3DBiggs (1) (leggy: unf: a bhd: t.o) ......... 12.11
510 Rumbelow **(55)** *(JRJenkins)* 8-13 SWhitworth (10) (swtg: a in rr: t.o) ............. hd.12
So Beguiling (USA) **(54)** *(MrsALMKing)* 8-2 JQuinn (6) (a bhd: t.o) ................... 1.13
863 Cannonale (IRE) **(45)** *(JPearce)* 8-11 GCarter (13) (lw: 2nd st: wknd over 3f out:
t.o) ......................................................................... 12.14

**5/2** Grog (IRE), **5/1** Wrycrest, FIREFIGHTER, **6/1** Breakdancer (IRE), **13/2** Winged Whisper (USA)(5/1—8/1), **14/1** Peggy Mainwaring(op 8/1), So Beguiling (USA), Copper Trader, **20/1** Rumbelow(op 10/1), **25/1** Cannonale (IRE), Evening Stables, **33/1** Marowins, **50/1** Ors. CSF £17.95, Tote £5.70: £1.90 £1.70 £3.70 (£4.20). Mrs B. Facchino (UPPER LONGDON) bred by Sir Stephen Hastings. 14 Rn
                                              1m 58.3 (9.8)
                                               SF—10/8/–/–/–/–

## 1143     AMATEUR RIDERS ASSOCIATION & LADY JOCKEYS ASSOCIATION H'CAP (Amateurs)
            (0–70) £1360.50 (£378.00: £181.50)     **1m 200y**      8-15 (8-16)
                                  (Weights raised 3 lb)

| | | |
|---|---|---|
| 1009 | **Thundering (28)** *(AWJones)* 7–9-8 MissIDWJones (5) (chsd ldrs: led over 1f out: r.o wl) | —1 |
| *1254* | Spanish Whisper **(34)** *(JRBostock)* 5–10-0 MrsLPearce (7) (lw: hld up: hdwy 2f out: fin wl) | 2.2 |
| 903 | Times Are Hard **(37)** *(CASmith)* 8–9-13 ‡4MrsDSmith (9) (a.p: 4th st: ev ch over 1f out: unable qckn) | 1.3 |
| 10095 | Sanawi **(53)** *(PDEvans)* 5–11-1 ‡4MrWMcLaughlin (3) (a.p: 5th st: led over 2f out tl over 1f out: one pce fnl f) | ½.4 |
| 893 | Sunset Reins Free **(39)** *(EJAlston)* 7–10-1 ‡4MrRWilkinson (8) (lw: bhd: hdwy 3f out: styd on ins fnl f) | nk.5 |
| | Talaton Flyer **(28)** *(PJHobbs)* 6–9-4 ‡4MrsSHobbs (13) (in tch: c wd 2f out: no imp) | 3½.6 |
| 8295 | Vague Dancer **(62)** *(Fav)* *(MrsJRRamsden)* 6–12-0 MrRHale (11) (hdwy 3f out: kpt on one pce fnl f) | nk.7 |
| | Just for Kicks **(37)** *(JJO'Neill)* 6–10-3(10) MrPCraggs (12) (bit bkwd: led 5f out: hdd over 2f out: wknd fnl f) | hd.8 |
| | Glen Finnan **(34)** *(JCFox)* 4–9-10 ‡4MissDPomeroy (15) (nvr nrr) | s.h.9 |
| 1032 | Give Me Hope (IRE) **(39)** *(GHYardley)* 4–10-1 ‡4MissAYardley (16) (lw: s.s: effrt ½-wy: nt rch ldrs) | s h 10 |
| 967 | Tina's Angel **(30)** *(JCFox)* 5–9-6 ‡4MissRHulme (17) (lw: prom: 2nd st: ev ch 3f out: wknd over 1f out) | 1.11 |
| 1013 | Rag Time Belle **(34)** *(MWEckley)* 6–9-10 ‡4MissJRussell (6) (led after 3f: sn hdd: 3rd st: wknd wl over 1f out) | ¾.12 |
| 1009 | Dal Pascatore **(28)** *(FJYardley)* 4–9-4 ‡4MrsCWalmsley (14) (a bhd) | 3.13 |
| 10096 | Primera Ballerina **(48)** *(JRBosley)* 4–10-10 ‡4MrsSBosley (2) (b.hind: chsd ldrs 5f: sn lost tch) | 3½.14 |
| 10094 | Quinta Royale **(55)** *(WGMTurner)* 5–11-3 ‡4MrsJGault (1) (bhd fnl 4f) | 2.15 |
| 912 | Armaiti **(48)** *(DRTucker)* 4–10-10 ‡4MissSRowe (10) (a bhd) | 2½.16 |
| *1001* | Just Ready (IRE) **(37)** *(GAHam)* 4–9-13 ‡4MissVSnowdon (4) (swtg: led 3f: 6th & wkng st) | hd.17 |

LONG HANDICAP: Just for Kicks 9-5.

**5/2** Vague Dancer, **9/2** Sunset Reins Free, **6/1** Talaton Flyer, **8/1** THUNDERING, Spanish Whisper, **10/1** Rag Time Belle, Quinta Royale, Sanawi, **12/1** Times Are Hard(op 20/1), **25/1** Just Ready (IRE), Primera Ballerina, Dal Pascatore, Just for Kicks, **33/1** Armaiti, Give Me Hope (IRE), **50/1** Ors. CSF £75.06, CT £732.73. Tote £6.70: £1.30 £1.70 £2.80 £3.50 (£17.70). Mr A. W. Jones (OSWESTRY) bred by L. K. McCreery. 17 Rn
                                              1m 59.1 (10.6)
                                       SF—3/3/–/13/–/–

## 1144     IRONBRIDGE H'CAP (3-Y.O) (0–70) £1255.50 (£348.00: £166.50)    **5f**    8-45 (8-46)
                                  (Weights raised 3 lb)

| | | |
|---|---|---|
| 10754 | **Educated Pet (42)** *(Fav)* *(MJohnston)* 7–10 JLowe (5) (chsd ldrs: rdn 2f out: qcknd to ld ins fnl f: r.o) | —1 |
| 678 | So Superb **(67)** (bl) *(JLDunlop)* 9–7 PatEddery (2) (lw: dwlt: led after 2f tl ins fnl f: r.o) | 2.2 |
| *9016* | Cranfield Comet **(62)** *(JBerry)* 9–2 JCarroll (3) (lw: s.s: hdwy ½-wy: rdn & ev ch appr fnl f: unable qckn) | 2.3 |
| 6746 | Virginia Cottage **(50)** *(BAMcMahon)* 8–4 JQuinn (4) (a.p: rdn over 1f out: one pce) | 3.4 |
| 698 | Bishopstone Bill **(46)** *(SMellor)* 8–0 DanaMellor (1) (lw: led 2f: wknd over 1f out) | 1.5 |
| 516 | It's Only Money **(57)** (v) *(THCaldwell)* 8–11 KFallon (6) (spd stands' side to ½-wy) | 3¾.6 |
| 10106 | Injaka Boy **(43)** (v) *(KWhite)* 7–4(3) ‡7AGarth (9) (nvr nr to chal) | 1½.7 |
| 10764 | Life's a Breeze **(53)** *(MRChannon)* 8–7 CRutter (7) (spd 3f) | 4.8 |

**2/1** EDUCATED PET, **3/1** So Superb, **5/1** Cranfield Comet, **13/2** Life's a Breeze(op 4/1), **7/1** Virginia Cottage, **14/1** It's Only Money, **20/1** Injaka Boy, **40/1** Bishopstone Bill. CSF £8.08, CT £22.59. Tote £2.90: £1.40 £2.10 £1.10 (£5.80). Mr Billy Morgan (MIDDLEHAM) bred by Highfield Stud Ltd. 8 Rn
                                           61.7 sec (4.4)
                                       SF—34/51/38/4/–/–

T/Plpt: £28.30 (46.8 Tckts).                                               IM

1033—**LEICESTER (R-H)**

**Monday, June 1st [Good to soft, Soft patches]**

Going Allowance: 5f-7f: 0.45 sec (Y); Rest: 0.25 sec per fur (G)          Wind: almost nil

Stalls: high

**1145**    GORDON WHITE & HOOD (S) STKS (3-Y.O) £2500.40 (£694.40: £333.20)
       **1m 8y**                                                    2-00 (2-04)

| | | |
|---|---|---|
| | **Norman Warrior** (DMorris) 8-11 MTebbutt (9) (hld up: stdy hdwy 4f out: led over 1f out: pushed out) | —1 |
| | Girton Degree **(53)** (RHannon) 8-6 MRoberts (4) (led over 6f: one pce) | 3.2 |
| 695 | Lord Leitrim (IRE) **(49)** (NACallaghan) 8-11 WCarson (20) (hld up: swtchd outside over 3f out: hdwy fnl 2f: r.o) | ¾.3 |
| 476 | Medbourne (IRE) **(37)** (JLHarris) 8-6 PaulEddery (12) (hdwy 3f out: one pce fnl 2f) | 3.4 |
| | Arjjil (MHTompkins) 8-11 PRobinson (11) (lt-f: unf: plld hrd: a.p: no hdwy fnl 2f) | 7.5 |
| 10295 | Fine as Fivepence **(41)** (MrsAKnight) 8-6 ‡5DHarrison (1) (no hdwy fnl 2f) | 4.6 |
| 7994 | Up the Punjab **(61)** (Fav) (SDow) 8-11 TQuinn (19) (prom 6f) | 1.7 |
| 799 | Cheren Boy **(339)** (BForsey) 8-11 NHowe (13) (nvr trbld ldrs) | nk.8 |
| 965 | Sea Lord **(39)** (KWHogg) 8-11 GHind (14) (no hdwy fnl 2f) | nk.9 |
| 734 | Nominee Prince **(49)** (v) (RGuest) 8-11 GBaxter (17) (prom 5f) | 1.10 |
| 9695 | Shafayif (BHanbury) 8-6 BRaymond (7) (prom over 5f) | hd.11 |
| 806 | Albany Spark **(40)** (v) (GHEden) 8-11 GCarter (5) (b: prom over 5f) | 5.12 |
| | Donald Stuart (MTate) 8-11 JWilliams (8) (wl grwn: bkwd: a bhd) | s.h.13 |
| 765 | Hataal (IRE) **(42)** (JBalding) 8-1 ‡§RPrice (16) (a bhd) | 1½.14 |
| 567 | Nun the Wiser (IRE) **(40)** (bl) (BAMcMahon) 8-6 JFortune (3) (spd 4f) | 1½.15 |
| 9696 | Super Flyer (IRE) **(55)** (MrsAKnight) 8-8 ‡‡FNorton (2) (prom 5f) | ½.16 |
| 765 | Bassetlaw Belle (SRBowring) 8-6 AProud (18) (spd over 4f) | nk.17 |
| 6665 | Tender Look (IRE) (ANLee) 8-6 JQuinn (15) (lw: t.o) | 12.18 |
| 10105 | Agwa (BHanbury) 8-11 WRyan (6) (bit bkwd: prom over 5f: t.o) | 25.19 |
| | Angel's Wing (RMWhitaker) 8-6 PBurke (10) (bit bkwd: w ldrs 5f: t.o) | d.h.19 |

**2/1** Up the Punjab, **7/1** Nominee Prince(10/1—6/1), Lord Leitrim (IRE), Shafayif, **8/1** Girton Degree(op 5/1), **9/1** Super Flyer (IRE), **10/1** Arjjil, **11/1** Agwa(7/1—12/1), **12/1** NORMAN WARRIOR, **16/1** Fine as Fivepence, **20/1** Hataal (IRE), **33/1** Ors. CSF 108.94, Tote £72.70: £22.70: £2.80 £3.00 (Wnr or 2nd w any £2.80). Mrs Patricia Lunn (NEWMARKET) bred by Mrs Caroline Berry. 20 Rn; Bt in 4,200 gns. Girton Degree clmd T Pearson £6,050
1m 41.9 (6.9)
SF—23/9/12/–/–/–

**1146**    ROTHMANS ROYALS NORTH SOUTH CHALLENGE SERIES H'CAP (3-Y.O)(0-80)
       £3366.00 (£1008.00: £484.00: £222.00)    **1m 8y**          2-30 (2-34)
                          (Weights raised 2 lb)

| | | |
|---|---|---|
| 904 | **Elizabethan Air (50)** (ANLee) 7-10 JQuinn (14) (hdwy 3f out: hrd rdn to ld wl ins fnl f: r.o) | —1 |
| 472 | Elanmatina (IRE) **(74)** (CFWall) 9-6 NDay (12) (lw: a.p: led over 2f out tl wl ins fnl f) | nk.2 |
| 8962 | Deevee **(48)** (CJBenstead) 7-8 TyroneWilliams (11) (hdwy 3f out: ev ch over 1f out: nt qckn) | 2½.3 |
| 804 | Toss the Dice **(60)** (MAJarvis) 8-6 AMunro (9) (prom: outpcd over 2f out: styd on fnl f) | s.h.4 |
| 6953 | Karamoja **(75)** (NAGraham) 9-7 LDettori (13) (lw: prom: hrd rdn over 2f out: r.o ins fnl f) | nk.5 |
| 10724 | Eastleigh **(65)** (RHollinshead) 8-11 WRyan (15) (hld up & plld hrd: hdwy over 2f out: r.o one pce fnl f) | 4.6 |
| 963 | Hob Green **(53)** (MrsJRRamsden) 7-13 BCrossley (16) (no hdwy fnl 2f) | 1½.7 |
| 5204 | Bold Setko (IRE) **(63)** (JMPEustace) 8-9 RCochrane (6) (lw: stdd s: nvr nr to chal) | nk.8 |
| 9633 | Sure to Win (IRE) **(59)** (DMorris) 8-5 PRobinson (1) (n.d) | s.h.9 |
| 604 | Systematic **(59)** (RHannon) 8-5 MRoberts (17) (racd alone far side: prom 5f) | s.h.10 |
| 10725 | Tahitian **(51)** (Fav) (MrsJRRamsden) 8-5 AMunro (2) (lw: n.d) | ¾.11 |
| 970 | Singers Image **(67)** (GBBalding) 8-13 JWilliams (5) (lw: n.d) | 3½.12 |
| 8985 | Ghurrah (IRE) **(63)** (CJBenstead) 8-9 WCarson (4) (lw: prom over 5f) | 5.13 |
| 963 | Dominant Serenade **(61)** (PWHarris) 8-9 PaulEddery (10) (led over 5f) | hd.14 |
| 788 | Sasparella **(75)** (WJarvis) 9-7 BRaymond (3) (a bhd) | 1.15 |
| 830 | Aragona **(53)** (PDCundell) 7-13 NAdams (7) (a bhd: t.o) | 6.16 |
| 5916 | Dandy Desire **(61)** (BCMorgan) 8-7 SWhitworth (8) (w ldr 5f: t.o) | ½.17 |

9/2 Tahitian, **5/1** Toss the Dice, **8/1** Systematic, ELIZABETHAN AIR(op 14/1), Deevee, Ghurrah (IRE), **9/1**
Karamoja, **10/1** Bold Setko (IRE), **12/1** Sure to Win (IRE), Eastleigh, Sasparella, **14/1** Aragona, **16/1** Hob
Green(op 10/1), Dominant Serenade, **20/1** Dandy Desire, **33/1** Ors. CSF £244.38, CT £2,044.95. Tote £16.10:
£3.80: £7.30 £2.90 £1.40 (£630.80). Mr R. A. Clowes (NEWMARKET) bred by H. F. Craig Harvey. 17 Rn
　　　　　　　　　　　　　　　　　　　　　　　　　　　　　　　　　1m 40.5 (5.5)
　　　　　　　　　　　　　　　　　　　　　　　　　　　　　　SF—29/52/18/29/43/21

---

**1147**　　BARNSDALE COUNTRY CLUB H'CAP (0-80) £3132.00 (£936.00: £448.00: £204.00)
　　　　　**1m 3f 183y**　　　　　　　　　　　　　　　　　　　　　3-00 (3-02)

926² **Moonlight Quest (75)** *(BHanbury)* 4–9-10 LDettori (5) (lw: chsd ldr: 2nd st: led
　　　3f out: r.o wl) ..............................................................................................—1
　831 Shadow Bird **(55)** *(GAPritchard-Gordon)* 5–7-13 ‡⁵DHarrison (9) (hld up: hdwy
　　　3f out: chsd wnr over 1f out: r.o) ..............................................................1¹/₂.2
831² Good for a Loan **(60)** *(RLee)* 5–8-9 BRaymond (4) (lw: 6th st: rdn over 2f out:
　　　one pce) ....................................................................................................3.3
730⁵ Caspian Beluga **(53)** *(MrsAKnight)* 4–7-13 ‡³FNorton (3) (hld up & plld hrd:
　　　hdwy 4f out: r.o one pce fnl 2f) ...........................................................hd.4
1063* Rising Tempo (IRE) **(59)** *(Fav)* *(CACyzer)* 4–8-8 (4x) MRoberts (11) (lw: 3rd st:
　　　wknd over 1f out) .......................................................................................nk.5
　696 Walking Saint **(45)** *(GraemeRoe)* 5–7-8⁽¹⁾ JQuinn (6) (led 9f: wknd over 1f out) . 2.6
1044⁴ Thomas Leng **(60)** *(MBrittain)* 7–8-9 RCochrane (2) (b: lw: hld up: hdwy & 5th
　　　st: hrd rdn 3f out: wknd 2f out) ..............................................................8.7
　　　Briggsmaid **(60)** *(JMPEustace)* 4–8-9 MTebbutt (7) (swtg: 8th st: wknd over 2f
　　　out) ...........................................................................................................2¹/₂.8
　　　Perfect Light **(61)** *(MrsSJSmith)* 3–7-8⁽¹⁾ RFox (1) (bkwd: hld up & plld hrd: a
　　　bhd) ..........................................................................................................1¹/₂.9
　　　Muzo (USA) **(79)** *(JMBradley)* 5–10-0 JWilliams (8) (a in rr) ..............................¹/₂.10
831³ Rare Detail (IRE) **(74)** *(MrsLPiggott)* 4–9-9 LPiggott (12) (7th st: wknd over 2f
　　　out) ............................................................................................................2.11
　702 Kentucky Starlet (USA) **(62)** (bl) *(RHannon)* 3–7-9 GBardwell (10) (4th st: wknd
　　　3f out: t.o) .................................................................................................30.12
　　　　　　LONG HANDICAP: Walking Saint 7-3, Perfect Light 7-3.

**4/1** Rising Tempo (IRE), **5/1** MOONLIGHT QUEST(4/1—6/1), **11/2** Good for a Loan, **6/1** Rare Detail (IRE),
Thomas Leng, **7/1** Shadow Bird, **10/1** Caspian Beluga, **12/1** Kentucky Starlet (USA), **16/1** Perfect Light, **20/1**
Briggsmaid, **33/1** Walking Saint, **50/1** Muzo (USA). CSF £38.89, CT £186.73. Tote £5.90: £1.40 £2.60 £2.40
(£47.80). Mrs John Lamb (NEWMARKET) bred by Raintree Stud. 12 Rn　　　　　　2m 38.7 (9.9)
　　　　　　　　　　　　　　　　　　　　　　　　　　　　　SF—41/13/17/6/14/–

---

**1148**　　DAVID WILSON HOMES STKS (3-Y.O.F) £2807.00 (£777.00: £371.00)
　　　　　**7f 9y**　　　　　　　　　　　　　　　　　　　　　　　3-30 (3-32)

989* **Mahasin (USA) (92)** *(Fav)* *(JLDunlop)* 8-12 WCarson (4) (mde all: clr over 2f
　　　out: canter) ..............................................................................................—1
　604 Missy-S (IRE) **(50)** *(GAPritchard-Gordon)* 8-7 GCarter (1) (rdn 4f out: chsd wnr
　　　over 1f out: hrd rdn: no imp) ....................................................................6.2
　623 Sharp Dance *(BSmart)* 8-7 WNewnes (4) (hdwy & bhd: hdwy 3f out: hrd rdn 2f
　　　out) ...........................................................................................................1¹/₂.3
　　　Silky Siren *(EAWheeler)* 8-7 SWhitworth (5) (cmpt: bkwd: no hdwy fnl 3f) ..........4.4
　　　Wishing Well *(MrsJCecil)* 8-7 PaulEddery (7) (bit bkwd: prom over 4f) ............1¹/₂.5
　699 Spot the Dove *(RJPrice)* 8-7 JWilliams (6) (chsd wnr 4f: sn wknd: t.o) ............15.6
　698 Sennon Cove *(MJCharles)* 8-7 NAdams (2) (bit bkwd: rdn over 2f out: sn bhd:
　　　t.o) .............................................................................................................3¹/₂.7

**1/14** MAHASIN (USA), **10/1** Wishing Well(op 5/1), **25/1** Spot the Dove, **33/1** Missy-S (IRE), **50/1** Silky Siren,
**100/1** Ors. CSF £5.54, Tote £1.10: £1.20 £3.00 (£8.10). Mr Hamdan Al-Maktoum (ARUNDEL) bred by Robert N.
Clay & Richard L. Duchossois in USA. 7 Rn　　　　　　　　　　　　　　1m 30.3 (8)
　　　　　　　　　　　　　　　　　　　　　　　　　　　　　SF—26/–/–/–/–/–

---

**1149**　　CORAH PLC CLAIMING STKS (2-Y.O) £2363.20 (£655.20: £313.60)
　　　　　**5f 218y**　　　　　　　　　　　　　　　　　　　　　4-00 (4-03)

803⁴ **Tee Gee Jay** *(Fav)* *(CNWilliams)* 8-9 JQuinn (2) (b.hind: hdwy over 2f out: led
　　　ins fnl f: rdn out) ......................................................................................—1
1036⁴ Costa Verde *(KWHogg)* 8-5 GHind (5) (hld up: hdwy 3f out: nt clr run & swtchd
　　　rt over 1f out: r.o) ....................................................................................¹/₂.2
　476 Fleur Power (IRE) *(BPalling)* 8-9 WRyan (4) (bit bkwd: a.p: ev ch over 1f out: nt
　　　qckn fnl f) ..................................................................................................3.3
　907 Break My Heart *(PFICole)* 9-0 AMunro (6) (b.nr fore: a.p: led 2f out: hdd & wknd
　　　ins fnl f) ......................................................................................................3.4

4472 Calisar *(WGMTurner)* 8-11 ‡3TSprake (7) (w ldrs: btn whn bmpd over 1f out) .. 1½.5
1036 True Story (IRE) *(RHannon)* 9-1 ‡3RPerham (10) (bit bkwd: nvr nr to chal) ........ hd.6
682 Crab 'n Lobster (IRE) *(MrsJRRamsden)* 8-0 ‡3DBiggs (9) (prom 5f) ................. 2½.7
Heavenly Body *(JWWatts)* 7-13 NAdams (3) (leggy: lt-f: unf: dwlt: nrst fin) ...... s.h.8
Atherton Green (IRE) *(JAGlover)* 8-7 ‡7SWilliams (8) (w'like: bkwd: prom 4f) ... ¾.9
10072 Ombre Darme (IRE) (bl) *(JWPayne)* 8-10 RCochrane (15) (lw: led 4f) ............... 3.10
973 Secret Formula *(GBBalding)* 8-4 JWilliams (13) (bhd fnl 2f) ..................... 1½.11
7596 Kiss in the Dark *(MrsGRReveley)* 7-12 ‡3FNorton (12) (spd over 3f) ............... 4.12
867 In the Air *(GAPritchard-Gordon)* 7-8 ‡5DHarrison (11) (dwlt: a bhd) ............ nk.13

**9/4** TEE GEE JAY, **5/2** Break My Heart(tchd 4/1), **9/2** Calisar(op 3/1), **10/1** Ombre Darme (IRE)(op 6/1), True Story (IRE), **14/1** Costa Verde, **16/1** Kiss in the Dark(op 10/1), **20/1** Crab 'n Lobster (IRE)(op 12/1), **33/1** Ors. CSF £31.91, Tote £3.10: £2.00 £2.10 £4.00 (£15.20). Mr A. N. Fiber (NEWMARKET) bred by Mrs R. D. Peacock. 13 Rn
1m 16 (6)
SF—29/23/15/8/–/–

**1150**  MEDISEARCH H'CAP (0-70) £2868.00 (£798.00: £384.00)  **1m 1f 218y**  4-30 (4-33)

11063 **I'M Electric (46)** *(RCurtis)* 6-8-4 NDay (4) (lw: hld up: 4th st: led 3f out: clr over 1f out: easily) ........................................................ —1
681 High Savannah (65) *(MAJarvis)* 4-9-4 ‡5KRutter (16) (dwlt: hdwy over 2f out: r.o: no ch w wnr) .................................................... 4.2
663* Joli's Great (54) (Fav) *(MJRyan)* 4-8-9 ‡3DBiggs (8) (swtg: hdwy over 3f out: one pce fnl 2f) ............................................. 1.3
Mizyan (IRE) (59) *(JEBanks)* 4-8-12 ‡5LNewton (14) (bit bkwd: hdwy 4f out: ev ch 2f out: one pce) ................................ 1½.4
10135 Sandmoor Denim (53) *(SRBowring)* 5-8-11 AProud (2) (s.i.s: nrst fin) ............. nk.5
10102 Forgetful (57) *(RHannon)* 3-8-2 MRoberts (15) (3rd st: wknd 2f out) .............. 4.6
10516 Sharquin (40) *(MBrittain)* 5-7-12 GBardwell (7) (b.hind: nvr nr to chal) ........ 2.7
479 Scenic Dancer (61) *(AHide)* 4-9-5 WRyan (19) (s.i.s: nvr trbld ldrs) ............. nk.8
580 Super Morning (54) *(GBBalding)* 6-8-12 JWilliams (18) (nvr nr ldrs) ............ 1½.9
1032 Melodic Habit (39) *(MrsAKnight)* 5-7-8 ‡3FNorton (1) (n.d) ....................... 1½.10
1034 Kinoko (48) *(KWHogg)* 4-8-6 GHind (11) (led 7f) ............................... s.h.11
8665 Fair Dare (42) *(CBBBooth)* 4-8-0 JQuinn (13) (a bhd) ........................... hd.12
Callipoli (USA) (66) *(RGuest)* 5-9-10 RCochrane (5) (swtg: bkwd: prom over 6f) 2.13
972* Cool Society (USA) (70) *(CRNelson)* 3-9-1 NAdams (12) (5th st: wknd 3f out) 2½.14
Make Me Proud (IRE) (56) *(RWArmstrong)* 3-8-1 BCrossley (5) (still unf: a bhd) 1.15
962 Friendlypersuasion (IRE) (40) *(RHollinshead)* 4-7-12 WCarson (9) (6th st: wknd over 2f out) ........................................ 2½.16
800 Littledale (USA) (40) (bl) *(DJGMurray-Smith)* 6-7-12 DaleGibson (10) (bhd fnl 3f: t.o) ............................................... 5.17
697 David's Own (55) *(SMellor)* 3-8-0 DanaMellor (6) (2nd st: rdn & wknd 4f out: t.o) 1.18

**7/2** Joli's Great(tchd 7/1), **7/1** Cool Society (USA), **15/2** Friendlypersuasion (IRE), **8/1** Super Morning, I'M ELECTRIC, Forgetful, **9/1** Scenic Dancer, Littledale (USA)(op 20/1), **12/1** Mizyan (IRE), **14/1** High Savannah, Callipoli (USA), **16/1** Sharquin, Sandmoor Denim, **20/1** Make Me Proud (IRE), **25/1** Melodic Habit, **33/1** Ors. CSF £123.91, CT £441.25. Tote £11.10: £2.40 £4.50 £1.70 £5.40 (Wnr or 2nd w any £2.60). Mr B. A. McGarrigle (EPSOM) bred by White Lodge Stud Ltd. 18 Rn
2m 11.3 (8.6)
SF—29/35/24/24/22/5

T/Plpt: £525.00 (5.5 Tckts).
KH

## 1045—REDCAR (L-H)

### Monday, June 1st [Firm, Good to firm patches]
Going Allowance: minus 0.20 sec per fur (F)  Wind: almost nil

Stalls: high

**1151**  JOHN BERRY (S) STKS (2-Y-O) £2343.60 (£649.60: £310.80)  **5f**  2-15 (2-16)

8892 **Trevorsninepoints** *(NTinkler)* 8-6 GDuffield (8) (lw: mde most: hung lft thrght: kpt on wl nr fin) ........................................... —1
10716 Field of Vision (IRE) (bl) *(MJohnston)* 8-11 DMcKeown (5) (lw: a cl up: disp ld ins fnl f: no ex nr fin) ........................................ hd.2
677 Fanfan (IRE) (bl) *(MHEasterby)* 8-6 KDarley (4) (a chsng ldrs: effrt & ev ch appr fnl f: nt qckn) .................................... 1½.3
770 Bella Bambola (IRE) *(SGNorton)* 8-6 LCharnock (3) (a chsng ldrs: kpt on one pce appr fnl f) ........................................ ½.4
8866 Sharisa *(JBerry)* 8-6 JCarroll (2) (a chsng ldrs: nt qckn fnl 2f) ................... ¾.5
9205 Sunshine in Ramsey (8-3 ‡3JFanning (1) (outpcd after 2f: styd on appr fnl: n.d) ...................................... 1½.6

Lettermore *(RMWhitaker)* 8-6 AGulhane (6) (leggy: s.i.s: outpcd & bhd tl sme late hdwy) .................... 3.7

920⁶ Private Liner (Fav) *(RonaldThompson)* 8-11 RPElliott (9) (lw: unruly s: s.s: hung lft & nt rcvr) .................... 1¹/₂.8

Archipellago Girl *(WJPearce)* 8-6 NConnorton (7) (small: sn outpcd & bhd: hung lft & n.d) .................... 1¹/₂.9

**3/1** Private Liner, **7/2** TREVORSNINEPOINTS, **4/1** Bella Bambola (IRE), Fanfan (IRE)(6/1—7/2), **7/1** Sharisa, **10/1** Sunshine in Ramsey, **12/1** Lettermore, **14/1** Field of Vision (IRE), **40/1** Archipellago Girl. CSF £47.44, Tote £3.00: £1.10 £2.90 £1.70 (£5.20). Captain F. M. E. Jacobsen (MALTON) bred by Peter Thomas. 9 Rn; No bid
60.1 sec (3.4)
SF—4/8/–/–/–/–

---

## 1152
BERYL BERRY H'CAP (3-Y.O) (0-80) £2905.00 (£805.00: £385.00)
1m 3f                                                         2-45 (2-46)

896★ **Glide Path (USA) (76)** *(JWHills)* 9-7 MHills (7) (lw: trckd ldrs: led over 2f out: qcknd: comf) .................... —1

883 Batabanoo **(68)** (Fav) *(MrsGRReveley)* 8-13 KDarley (3) (lw: hld up: effrt 3f out: nt clr run & swtchd over 1f out: r.o wl nr fin) .................... 1¹/₂.2

1131★ Boring (USA) **(59)** *(WStorey)* 8-4 (5x) SWebster (6) (b: lw: hld up: hdwy 3f out: rdn & effrt 2f out: rdr lost whip: nt qckn) .................... 2¹/₂.3

965★ Stapleton (IRE) **(73)** *(JWWatts)* 9-4 GDuffield (5) (lw: cl up: led 3f out: sn hdd & r.o one pce) .................... hd.4

1025 Sir Norman Holt (IRE) **(59)** *(FHLee)* 8-4⁽²⁾ MBirch (1) (in tch: effrt 3f out: nt pce to chal) .................... 7.5

810 Salu **(60)** *(JEtherington)* 8-0 ‡5JWeaver (4) (in tch: outpcd over 3f out: n.d) ..... s.h.6

963⁵ Leonadis Polk **(60)** *(WJPearce)* 8-2 LCharnock (2) (s.i.s: hld up & bhd: effrt over 0f out: n.d) .................... 1¹/₂.7

607⁴ Teslemi (USA) **(76)** *(BHanbury)* 9-7 WRSwinburn (8) (led tl hdd 3f out: sn lost pl) .................... 2.8

**11/4** Batabanoo, **9/2** Stapleton (IRE), Boring (USA), **5/1** GLIDE PATH (USA), **6/1** Teslemi (USA), **10/1** Leonadis Polk(8/1—12/1), **12/1** Sir Norman Holt (IRE), **16/1** Salu. CSF £18.41, CT £59.99. Tote £6.20: £1.70 £1.50 £1.50 (£19.30). The Jampot Partnership (LAMBOURN) bred by John T. L. Jones Jnr. & Robert S. Folsom in USA.
8 Rn                                                           2m 20.3 (4.6)
SF—39/28/14/27/–/–

---

## 1153
DICK GLARVEY H'CAP (0-90) £2782.50 (£770.00: £367.50)    **1m 1f**    3-15 (3-16)

931⁴ **Gilderdale (83)** *(JWHills)* 10-9-13 MHills (1) (lw: trckd ldrs: smooth hdwy to ld wl over 1f out: shkn up & qcknd) .................... —1

Tell No Lies **(84)** *(MHEasterby)* 5-10-0 MBirch (5) (lw: hld up: nt clr run 2f out: swtchd 1f out: fin wl) .................... 1¹/₂.2

868★ Mashakel (USA) **(83)** *(BHanbury)* 3-9-1 WRSwinburn (7) (b: hld up & bhd: gd hdwy over 1f out: r.o) .................... ³/₄.3

829⁴ Tarda **(53)** (Fav) *(MrsGRReveley)* 5-7-11 JLowe (6) (lw: hld up: smooth hdwy 3f out: led 2f out: hdd & nt qckn) .................... ³/₄.4

Richmond (IRE) **(56)** *(SGNorton)* 4-8-0 LCharnock (2) (led & clr to st: hdd 2f out: eased whn btn fnl f) .................... 4.5

766³ Bescaby Boy **(63)** *(JWharton)* 6-8-4 ‡3JFanning (4) (lw: a chsng ldrs: outpcd whn hmpd over 1f out: n.d after) .................... ¹/₂.6

Tancred Grange **(74)** *(MissSEHall)* 3-8-6 NConnorton (3) (prom tl outpcd fnl 2f) 2.7

796³ Manulife **(68)** *(WJPearce)* 3-8-0⁽¹⁾ GDuffield (8) (trckd ldrs: effrt over 2f out: sn btn) .................... ¹/₂.8

**15/8** Tarda, **9/2** Bescaby Boy, GILDERDALE, **8/1** Mashakel (USA)(op 5/1), Tell No Lies, **10/1** Manulife, **25/1** Ors. CSF £34.07, CT £233.56. Tote £4.70: £1.10 £3.10 £1.40 (£23.60). Abbott Racing Partners (LAMBOURN) bred by Mrs A. W. Kidd. 8 Rn
1m 52.7 (3.7)
SF—31/27/12/–/–/–

---

## 1154
IAN HERD CLAIMING STKS    £2265.20 (£627.20: £299.60)    **7f**    3-45 (3-59)

1050² **Ringland (USA) (77)** (Jt-Fav) *(PCHaslam)* 4-9-10 KDarley (11) (lw: a chsng ldrs: hdwy u.p 2f out: styd on wl to ld nr fin) .................... —1

1116★ Finjan **(80)** (Jt-Fav) *(MPNaughton)* 5-9-1 ‡5JWeaver (5) (lw: in tch: hdwy u.p to ld over 1f out: no ex cl home) .................... s.h.2

1001² Mca Below the Line **(64)** (bl) *(WJPearce)* 4-9-2 DNicholls (7) (a chsng ldrs: drvn along ¹/₂-wy: styd on: no imp) .................... 3.3

1050⁴ Sammy Slew (USA) **(70)** *(SGNorton)* 3-7-13 ‡7OPears (10) (led & sn clr: rdn 2f out: sn hdd & btn) .................... 1.4

888² Ballad Dancer **(55)** *(EJAlston)* 7-8-12 KFallon (9) (chsd ldrs: outpcd ¹/₂-wy: styd on wl fnl f) .................... ¹/₂.5

966[4] Chantry Bellini *(CWThornton)* 3–8-1 NCarlisle (4) (s.i.s: swtchd rt: styd on fnl 2f: n.d) .......................................................................................................... 8.6

Mbulwa **(65)** (bl) *(SEKettlewell)* 6–8-5 ‡5NKennedy (2) (b: hld up: outpcd ½-wy: n.d) ...................................................................................................... 1½.7

*1001* Super Marco **(43)** *(WWHaigh)* 3–8-6 DMcKeown (1) (lw: prom tl outpcd ½-wy: sn no ch) ....................................................................................... hd.8

747[4] Laurel Queen (IRE) **(58)** *(JBerry)* 4–9-3 JCarroll (8) (nvr nr ldrs) ...................... 4.9

614 Dame Helene (USA) *(PCHaslam)* 3–7-9 JLowe (3) (nvr wnt pce) .................... 1.10

747 Moona (USA) **(58)** *(GMMoore)* 4–8-7 ACulhane (6) (spd to ½-wy: sn rdn & wknd) ............................................................................................................. 1.11

1018 Rasco **(53)** (v) *(JEtherington)* 3–8-8 NConnorton (12) (spd to ½-wy: sn drvn along & bhd) ................................................................................................. 1.12

*Stewards Enquiry: Darley suspended 10-13/6/92 (excessive use of whip).*

**2/1** RINGLAND (USA), Finjan, **8/1** Mca Below the Line, **12/1** Sammy Slew (USA)(op 8/1), **14/1** Mbulwa, **16/1** Laurel Queen (IRE)(op 10/1), **25/1** Ballad Dancer, Rasco, Chantry Bellini, **33/1** Dame Helene (USA), **50/1** Moona (USA), **100/1** Super Marco. CSF £5.85, Tote £3.50: £1.70 £1.50 £1.60 (£4.00). Mr S. A. B. Dinsmore (MIDDLEHAM) bred by Robinson Farm in USA. 12 Rn
1m 24.1 (1.9)
SF−60/50/42/22/33/−

### 1155

JON CHARLTON H'CAP (3-Y.O) (0-70) £2284.80 (£632.80: £302.40)   **6f** 4-15 (4-25)

1075[2] **Invigilate (50)** (Fav) *(MPNaughton)* 8-1 ‡5JWeaver (6) (lw: chsd ldrs: nt clr run & swtchd over 1f out: r.o wl to ld cl home) ............................... —1

661[5] Coolaba Prince (IRE) **(65)** *(FHLee)* 8-6 ‡5NKennedy (3) (chsd ldrs: led over 1f out: wandered u.p: ct cl home) ........................................................... nk.2

1051 Legitim **(39)** *(JMJefferson)* 7-9 JLowe (4) (hdwy ½-wy: styd on u.p: nt pce to chal) .................................................................................................. 2.3

1020 Capital Idea (IRE) **(56)** (bl) *(RonaldThompson)* 8-12 RPElliott (1) (disp ld tl hdd over 1f out: edgd rt & nt qckn) ................................................... nk.4

890* Music Dancer **(63)** *(JBerry)* 9-5 JCarroll (7) (disp ld over 4f: grad wknd) ........ 1½.5

890 Manuleader **(56)** (bl) *(WJPearce)* 8-12 DNicholls (8) (s.i.s: shkn up ½-wy: styd on fnl f: nrst fin) ...................................................................................... ¾.6

984 Great Lord (IRE) **(61)** (v) *(JWWatts)* 9-3 WRSwinburn (2) (lw: disp ld: btn whn hmpd over 1f out) ......................................................................... 1.7

801 Queen's Tickle **(53)** *(APJarvis)* 8-9 MHills (5) (b.nr hind: hld up: effrt ½-wy: sn rdn & no imp) .......................................................................... nk.8

949* Hemsworth Lad (IRE) **(65)** *(PCalver)* 9-7 GDuffield (9) (chsd ldrs: edgd lft & outpcd ½-wy: sn no ch) ................................................................ 1½.9

**11/4** INVIGILATE, **7/2** Queen's Tickle, **5/1** Hemsworth Lad (IRE), **6/1** Music Dancer, Great Lord (IRE), **8/1** Coolaba Prince (IRE)(5/1− 10/1), **14/1** Manuleader, **25/1** Capital Idea (IRE), **33/1** Legitim. CSF £23.47, CT £544.58. Tote £4.00: £1.20 £1.70 £5.30 (£14 90). Mrs H. H. Wane (RICHMOND) bred by Bechmann Stud. 9 Rn
1m 11.9 (2.6)
SF−11/15/−/12/13/3

### 1156

HARRY RUDLAND STKS (Mdn 3-Y.O) £1932.00 (£532.00: £252.00)
**1¾m 19y**
4-45 (4-49)

**Best Gun** *(CWCElsey)* 9-0 JCarroll (4) (w'like: scope: bkwd: hld up: effrt st: led wl over 2f out: edgd lft & styd on wl) ................................. —1

873[3] Cantanta (Fav) *(RCharlton)* 8-9 PatEddery (2) (lw: swished tail repeatedly: hung fnl 5f: hdd wl over 2f out: nt resolute) ........................ 1½.2

922[5] Sakbah (USA) *(JRFanshawe)* 8-9 WRSwinburn (3) (chsd ldrs tl outpcd fnl 3f) .. 25.3

950[6] Blushing Gold *(MrsJJordan)* 8-6 ACulhane (1) (outpcd ent st: sn t.o) ............. dist.4

**1/3** Cantanta, **5/2** Sakbah (USA), **20/1** BEST GUN, **66/1** Blushing Gold. CSF £27.52, Tote £9.40 (£4.20). Mrs M. C. Butler (MALTON) bred by Mrs M. C. Butler and C. W. C. Elsey. 4 Rn
3m 4.8 (7.2)

### 1157

LEVY BOARD SEVENTH RACE H'CAP (0-80) (F & M) £2929.50 (£812.00: £388.50)
**7f**
5-15 (5-18)

912[2] **Eternal Flame (60)** *(JWHills)* 4–9-1 MHills (9) (hld up: effrt over 2f out: led ins fnl f: r.o u.p) ............................................................................... —1

668[5] Miss Brightside **(38)** *(ASmith)* 4–7-0 ‡7CHawksley (5) (led to ½-wy: led over 1f out tl ins fnl f: nt qckn: fin 3rd, 2l: plcd 2nd) ........................ 2

1013 Creselly **(64)** *(JGFitzGerald)* 5–9-5 MBirch (12) (lw: trckd ldrs: effrt over 2f out: styd on u.p: fin 4th, 1l: plcd 3rd) .................................... 3

747[2] Claudia Miss **(61)** *(WWHaigh)* 5–9-2 DMcKeown (8) (lw: in tch: hdwy & ev ch over 1f out: nt qckn: fin 5th, ¾l: plcd 4th) ......................... 4

899* Ustka **(68)** (Fav) *(MRStoute)* 3–8-13 WRSwinburn (13) (trckd ldrs: led ½-wy tl over 1f out: eased whn btn: fin 6th, 3½l: plcd 5th) ............. 5

1054* Granny Mc (55) *(EJAlston)* 5–8-10 (5x) KFallon (4) (lw: a chsng ldrs: btn whn hmpd appr fnl f) .................................................................... 1½.7
9843 Debsy Do (USA) (70) *(SGNorton)* 3–8-8 ‡7OPears (3) (chsd ldrs tl rdn 2f out: btn whn hmpd appr fnl f) .................................................................... hd.8
821 Ten High (IRE) (48) *(BEllison)* 3–7-4 ‡3JFanning (6) (nvr trbld ldrs) ...................... 1.9
821 Thrie-Na-Helah (IRE) (73) *(RMWhitaker)* 3–9-4 ACulhane (1) (prom over 4f) .... 2.10
1013 Lust of Love (58) *(MrsVAAconley)* 6–8-8 ‡5JWeaver (15) (b: chsd ldrs 4f) ....... nk.11
Jellyroll Blues (48) *(MrsGRReveley)* 3–7-7 JLowe (2) (lw: prom 4f) ................ nk.12
Fiction (64) *(MPNaughton)* 3–8-9 JakiHouston (10) (n.d) .................................. 1½.13
4994 Penny Orchid (IRE) (80) *(WJPearce)* 3–9-11 DNicholls (11) (swtg: hld up & bhd: n.d) ............................................................................................. 3.14
Grey Realm (43) *(REBarr)* 4–7-12 PBurke (14) (cl up 4f: wknd qckly) ............ 5.15
618 Royal Girl (52) *(MissSEHall)* 5–8-7 SWebster (7) (bhd: hdwy over 2f out: swtchd appr fnl f & r.o wl: fin 2nd, ½sl: disq: plcd last) ............. 0
LONG HANDICAP: Miss Brightside 7-0, Ten High (IRE) 7-2, Jellyroll Blues 7-4.
*Stewards Enquiry: Royal Girl disq. (interference to Granny Mc). Webster suspended 10-13/6/92 (careless riding).*

3/1 Ustka, 100/30 ETERNAL FLAME, 8/1 Debsy Do (USA), 10/1 Thrie-Na-Helah (IRE), Granny Mc, 11/1 Lust of Love(8/1–12/1), 12/1 Creselly, Claudia Miss, 20/1 Penny Orchid (IRE), 25/1 Jellyroll Blues, Fiction, 33/1 Royal Girl, Miss Brightside, 100/1 Urbs. CSF £91.96, CT £1,086.64. Tote £4.00: £2.10 £12.40 £4.00 (£89.00). Mr Cliffe Rowlands (LAMBOURN) bred by Stratford Place Stud. 15 Rn
1m 24.5 (2.3)
SF–45/8/38/33/28/–

T/Plpt: £481.40 (6.2 Tckts). 
AA

## 524—FOLKESTONE (R-H)

### Tuesday, June 2nd [Good to firm]

Going Allowance: St: minus 0.20 sec; Rest: minus 0.35 sec (F)      Wind: almost nil

Stalls: low

**1158**  BURLINGTON HOTEL (FOLKESTONE) STKS (Mdn 3-Y.O) £1932.00 (£532.00: £252.00)
1m 1f 149y                                                              1-45 (1-49)

**Lyphantastic (USA)** *(MRStoute)* 9-0 GDuffield (5) (w'like: scope: led over 1f: 2nd st: led over 1f out: rdn out) ............................................. —1
Desert Peace (IRE) *(PFICole)* 9-0 TQuinn (7) (str: scope: 3rd st: hrd rdn over 1f out: r.o wl) ..................................................... ½.2
427 Baher (USA) (Jt-Fav) *(NACallaghan)* 9-0 PatEddery (4) (led 8f out tl over 1f out: unable qckn) ................................................................ 2.3
787 Afore Jane *(GHarwood)* 8-9 AClark (3) (lw: 6th st: one pce fnl 2f) ................... 10.4
1033 Weeheby (USA) (Jt-Fav) *(AAScott)* 9-0 WRSwinburn (1) (lw: 4th st: wknd over 1f out) ....................................................................... s.h.5
River Hawk *(RFJohnsonHoughton)* 9-0 JReid (8) (w'like: bit bkwd: a bhd) ........ 8.6
707 Royal Glint (bl) *(IABalding)* 8-9 MHills (6) (hdwy 5f out: 5th st: wknd 2f out) ........ 7.7
566 After the Fire *(ANLee)* 8-11 ‡3JFanning (2) (t: a bhd) ..................................... 10.8

5/2 Baher (USA), Weeheby (USA)(op 4/1), 5/1 LYPHANTASTIC (USA)(op 5/2), Desert Peace (IRE)(op 7/4), 11/2 Afore Jane(6/1–12/1), 20/1 River Hawk(op 8/1), 25/1 Royal Glint, 50/1 After the Fire. CSF £28.07, Tote £4.60: £1.60 £1.60 £2.00 (£9.50). Miss Sandra H. Payson (NEWMARKET) bred by Sandra Payson in USA. 8 Rn
2m 1.7 (4)
SF–25/24/20/–/–/–

**1159**  KEITH SHIPTON MEMORIAL H'CAP (3-Y.O) (0-70) £2385.00 (£660.00: £315.00)
6f 189y                                                                 2-15 (2-17)

10753 **Thewaari (USA) (55)** (Fav) *(AAScott)* 8-6 WRSwinburn (5) (lw: hdwy 2f out: hrd rdn 1f out: led nr fin) .............................................................. —1
9126 Countercheck (IRE) (51) *(CFWall)* 8-2 NDay (11) (lw: led: hrd rdn over 1f out: hdd nr fin) ................................................................................ nk.2
495 Bear With Me (IRE) (60) *(MBell)* 8-11 MHills (10) (b.hind: 3rd st: rdn over 1f out: one pce) ............................................................................. 3½.3
8016 Court Minstrel (55) *(LJHolt)* 8-6(1) JReid (4) (hdwy over 1f out: r.o one pce) ..... ¾.4
930 Sir Oliver (IRE) (70) *(RJHodges)* 9-4 ‡3TSprake (3) (hdwy over 1f out: nvr nrr) .. nk.5
9026 Day of History (IRE) (45) *(CACyzer)* 7-10 NCarlisle (12) (4th st: wknd 1f out) ... nk.6
833 Frankus (50) *(SMellor)* 8-1 DanaMellor (1) (nvr nr to chal) ............................... 2½.7
939 Mastamint (42) (bl) *(RVoorspuy)* 7-7 NAdams (8) (no hdwy fnl 2f) ................... ½.8
587 Mabonne (61) *(JLDunlop)* 8-12 PatEddery (7) (5th st: wknd wl over 1f out) ....... 1.9
8015 Grey Charmer (IRE) (64) *(CJames)* 9-1 SWhitworth (2) (lw: 6th st: wknd over 1f out) ................................................................................................. nk.10
972 Royal Circus (43) (bl) *(PWHarris)* 7-8(1) GBardwell (9) (2nd st: wknd wl over 1f out) ................................................................................................. 4.11

997 Bo Knows Best (IRE) **(46)** *(JSutcliffe)* 7-11 DaleGibson (6) (a bhd) ............... 3½.**12**
LONG HANDICAP: Mastamist 7-5, Royal Circus 6-13.

**7/2** THEWAARI (USA), **9/2** Countercheck (IRE), **5/1** Mabonne, **8/1** Bear With Me (IRE), Court Minstrel, Grey Charmer (IRE), **10/1** Sir Oliver (IRE)(op 6/1), **12/1** Day of History (IRE), Bo Knows Best (IRE)(op 8/1), **20/1** Royal Circus, **33/1** Frankus, **50/1** Mastamist. CSF £19.44, CT £111.22. Tote £3.90: £1.60 £1.60 £3.50 (£7.30). Mr Saeed Suhail (NEWMARKET) bred by John Franks in USA. 12 Rn
1m 23.7 (2.1)
SF—24/19/21/14/25/2

**1160**      SELLINDGE (S) STKS    £2284.80 (£632.80: £302.40)    **6f**      2-45 (2-47)

1064⁴ **Liffey River (USA) (53)** (Fav) *(MrsLPiggott)* 4-9-6 LPiggott (4) (b: hld up: rdn over 1f out: led wl ins fnl f: r.o wl) ......................................... —**1**
830 Idir Linn (IRE) **(39)** *(DJGMurray-Smith)* 4-9-6 CRutter (5) (a.p: rdn over 1f out: led ins fnl f: sn hdd: r.o wl) ................................... s.h.**2**
1030 Dickens Lane **(59)** *(RJHodges)* 5-9-3 ‡³TSprake (6) (lw: a.p: led over 2f out tl ins fnl f: unable qckn) ....................................... 3.**3**
939⁵ Emaura **(63)** *(DRCElsworth)* 3-8-6 JWilliams (2) (led over 3f: wknd over 1f out) 2½.**4**
774 Domiana **(34)** *(MBlanshard)* 4-9-1 JReid (7) (no hdwy fnl 2f) ....................... ¾.**5**
1030 Fay Eden (IRE) **(53)** *(RJHodges)* 4-8-8 ‡⁷TMcLaughlin (3) (nvr nrr) ............... s.h.**6**
948⁶ Stelby **(58)** *(OBrennan)* 8-8-13 ‡⁷SWilliams (10) (nvr nrr) ........................... nk.**7**
1085 Freni **(41)** (bl) *(MDIUsher)* 3-8-6 RStreet (9) (s.s: a bhd) ........................... 5.**8**
1001 Beljinski **(33)** *(BJMcMath)* 4-9-1 AClark (8) (bhd fnl 2f) ........................... 10.**9**
799 Yeoman Bound **(22)** (bl) *(KTIvory)* 4-9-6 GBardwell (1) (spd over 3f) ............... 8.**10**

**11/4** LIFFEY RIVER (USA), **3/1** Emaura, **4/1** Stelby, **9/2** Dickens Lane, **10/1** Fay Eden (IRE)(8/1—12/1), **14/1** Domiana, Idir Linn (IRE)(op 8/1), **33/1** Ors. CSF £37.44, Tote £3.00: £1.40 £4.30 £1.90 (£26.80). Mrs Heather Hirschfeld (NEWMARKET) bred by Warren W. Rosenthal in USA. 10 Rn; Bt in 4,100 gns; Emaura clmd K Cunningham Brown £5,601
1m 13.4 (2.7)
SF—28/27/12/-/-/-

**1161**      WESTENHANGER MEDIAN AUCTION GRADUATION STKS (2-Y.O) £2343.00 (£648.00: £309.00)    **6f**      3-15 (3-17)

    **So Factual (USA)** (Fav) *(GHarwood)* 8-11 PatEddery (2) (str: scope: a.p: led over 1f out: comf) ......................................... —**1**
    Captain le Saux (IRE) *(MBell)* 8-11 MHills (11) (leggy: a.p: ev ch 2f out: unable qckn) ........................................... 3½.**2**
    Friendly Brave (USA) *(WCarter)* 8-11 JReid (5) (str: scope: rdn & hdwy wl over 1f out: r.o one pce) ....................................... 2.**3**
867 Cashable *(JRJenkins)* 8-11 SWhitworth (1) (led over 4f) ....................................... nk.**4**
988⁶ Skullcap *(DMorley)* 8-11 MTebbutt (6) (spd 4f) ........................................... ½.**5**
    Platinum Venture *(AHide)* 8-11 MWoods (7) (nvr nr to chal) ............................... 8.**6**
928★ Bourbon Jack *(JWPayne)* 9-4 AMunro (4) (prom over 3f) ............................... 1.**7**
928³ Lochore *(RIngram)* 8-11 GDuffield (10) (gd spd 4f) ....................................... 3.**8**
    Mac Tomb *(KOCunningham-Brown)* 8-11 JWilliams (3) (w'like: outpcd) ............... 6.**9**
    Galactic Fury *(BStevens)* 8-11 NAdams (8) (leggy: bhd whn b.d over 1f out) ........ 0
    Ascom Pager Too *(PHowling)* 8-6 JMurray (4) (b.hind: unf: mid div whn fell over 1f out) ............................................ 0

**4/5** SO FACTUAL (USA)(Evens—5/4), **5/1** Friendly Brave (USA)(12/1—14/1), **6/1** Lochore(op 3/1), **7/1** Bourbon Jack(op 3/1), **10/1** Skullcap(op 9/2), **14/1** Captain le Saux (IRE)(12/1—16/1), **40/1** Galactic Fury, Platinum Venture, **50/1** Ors. CSF £13.97, Tote £2.10: £1.10 £3.50 £2.20 (£16.80). Mr K. Abdulla (PULBOROUGH) bred by Juddmonte Farms Inc. in USA. 11 Rn
1m 13.8 (3.1)
SF—11/-/-/-/-/-

**1162**      HORNBY SPRINT H'CAP (0-70) £2206.40 (£610.40: £291.20)    **5f**      3-45 (3-47)

752⁵ **Hotfoot Hannah (IRE) (42)** *(PSFelgate)* 4-8-11 ‡³JFanning (5) (s.s: hdwy 3f out: led 2f out: hrd rdn & r.o wl) ................................. —**1**
1030³ Catalani **(50)** *(TJNaughton)* 7-9-8 DHolland (4) (b: hdwy 2f out: r.o wl ins fnl f) ¾.**2**
1045² Spring High **(43)** (bl) *(KTIvory)* 5-9-1 GBardwell (6) (a.p: ev ch 2f out: r.o) ....... hd.**3**
1020 Rednet **(56)** *(PDEvans)* 5-10-0 AMunro (8) (b: hrd rdn & hdwy over 1f out: r.o) 2½.**4**
735 Rays Mead **(50)** *(LJHolt)* 4-9-8 JReid (14) (a.p: one pce fnl 2f) ....................... ½.**5**
1020 Lady's Mantle (USA) **(44)** (Fav) *(RBastiman)* 8-8-9 ‡⁷HBastiman (13) (swtg: a.p: ev ch 2f out: one pce) ........................... hd.**6**
997 Pine Glen Pepper **(34)** *(JAkehurst)* 4-8-1 ‡⁵ATucker (9) (prom 3f) ................. ¾.**7**
1076³ Savalaro **(54)** *(JFfitch-Heyes)* 3-9-1 RPerham (12) (lw: led over 2f) ................. 3.**8**
    Village Pet **(47)** *(PJHobbs)* 4-9-5 JWilliams (7) (prom 3f) ........................... hd.**9**
1030 Miramede **(40)** *(RJHodges)* 4-8-9 ‡³TSprake (11) (swtg: outpcd) ................. 1½.**10**
945⁶ Ever so Artistic **(42)** (bl) *(PHowling)* 5-9-0 LPiggott (1) (a.p: led over 2f out: sn hdd & wknd) ....................................... ¾.**11**

909 Battling Bella (USA) **(61)** *(JSutcliffe)* 3–9–4 ‡[7]TMcLaughlin (2) (swtg: spd 3f) .. nk.**12**
888 Galaxy Express **(40)** *(GHEden)* 4–8–5 ‡[7]PTurner (3) (lw: prom 3f) .................. s.h.**13**
690 Very Good **(53)** *(PHowling)* 3–8–10 ‡[7]DebbieBiggs (10) (bhd fnl 2f) .................. 2.14

**7/2** Lady's Mantle (USA)(9/2—11/2), **9/2** Catalani, **11/2** Spring High, **9/1** Savalaro, Battling Belta (USA), **10/1** HOTFOOT HANNAH (IRE), Ever so Artistic, **12/1** Pine Glen Pepper(tchd 50/1), **14/1** Galaxy Express, Rays Mead, Village Pet, Rednet, **25/1** Miramede, **33/1** Very Good. CSF £56.56, CT £263.12. Tote £11.70: £2.80 £1.80 £1.90 (£19.20). Mr John S. Martin (MELTON MOWBRAY) bred by James Hender in Ireland. 14 Rn    61.2 sec (2.4)
SF—29/37/29/32/24/10

**1163**     CROWN INN (RYE) H'CAP (0-70) £2284.80 (£632.80: £302.40)    **1¹/₂m** 4-15 (4-16)

    **Snow Blizzard (46)** *(SDow)* 4–8-10 LPiggott (8) (mde all: r.o wl) ...................... —**1**
1065³ Prosequendo (USA) **(64)** *(MDixon)* 5–10-0 DaleGibson (1) (hdwy 3f out: hrd
      rdn over 1f out: r.o) .............................................. 3.**2**
1044 Mamalama **(38)** *(LJHolt)* 4–8-2 AMunro (2) (2nd st: one pce fnl 2f) .............. 1¹/₂.**3**
1044² Bold Resolution (IRE) **(51)** (Fav) *(CACyzer)* 4–9-1 PatEddery (11) (rdn over 4f
      out: 5th st: one pce fnl 2f) ...................................... 3.**4**
    Poppy Charm **(29)** *(RCurtis)* 5–7-7 GBardwell (3) (3rd st: wknd over 1f out) ...... 1.**5**
    Touching Star **(51)** (bl) *(PJHobbs)* 7–9-1 JWilliams (6) (swtg: 6th st: no hdwy fnl
      2f) ........................................................... nk.**6**
908 Heavenly Waters **(55)** *(RFJohnsonHoughton)* 3–8-3 MHills (7) (b.hind: nvr nrr) hd.**7**
    Cathos (FR) **(55)** *(DAWilson)* 7–9-5 MTebbutt (10) (b: a bhd) ....................... 3.**8**
761 Incola **(41)** *(HCandy)* 6–8-5 CRutter (4) (lw: 4th st: wknd wl over 1f out) ......... s.h.**9**
335 Singing Detective **(30)** *(RCurtis)* 5–7-5[1] ‡³JFanning (5) (bhd fnl 3f) .............. s.h.**10**
    Excelsis **(52)** *(JRJenkins)* 6–9-2 SWhitworth (9) (a bhd) ........................ 15.**11**
LONG HANDICAP: Singing Detective 7-3.

**6/4** Bold Resolution (IRE)(7/4—9/4), **3/1** Incola, **4/1** Prosequendo (USA), **7/1** Touching Star(12/1—6/1), **10/1** SNOW BLIZZARD, **14/1** Mamalama, **20/1** Excelsis(op 10/1), **25/1** Cathos (FR), Heavenly Waters, Poppy Charm, **33/1** Singing Detective. CSF £51.98, CT £538.16. Tote £8.70: £2.10 £1.40 £4.30 (£15.40). Mr M. F. Kentish (EPSOM) bred by M. F. Kentish. 11 Rn      2m 35 (1.5)
SF—39/51/22/29/5/26

T/Plpt: £80.80 (33.1 Tckts).                                          AK

## 847 — NEWBURY (L-H)

### Tuesday, June 2nd [Good]

Going Allowance: St: 0.20 sec per fur; Rnd: 0.10 sec per fur (G)       Wind: almost nil

Stalls: centre

**1164**     BOXFORD STKS (Mdn 2-Y.O.F) £3002.00 (£896.00: £428.00: £194.00)
      **5f 34y**                                          6-15 (6-18)

    **Amirati (USA)** (Fav) *(AAScott)* 8–11 WRSwinburn (9) (str: scope: hld up: qcknd
      to ld over 1f out: r.o wl) ....................................... —**1**
    Musical Prospect (USA) *(RHannon)* 8–11 MRoberts (8) (gd sort: dwlt: sn rcvrd:
      outpcd over 1f out: r.o ins fnl f) ................................. 3.**2**
729² Simply Sooty *(BRMillman)* 8–11 GBaxter (6) (lw: a.p: r.o one pce fnl f) ............. ³/₄.**3**
1057 Brockton Dancer *(RHannon)* 8–11 PatEddery (4) (lw: led 4f out tl over 1f out:
      one pce) ....................................................... 1¹/₂.**4**
    Tartouka *(GLewis)* 8–6 ‡⁵DHarrison (5) (unf: s.s: hdwy fnl f: r.o) ................ ³/₄.**5**
    Bodandere *(MJFetherston-Godley)* 8–11 AMunro (7) (unf: prom 4f) ................... 5.**6**
    Sui Generis (IRE) *(CGCox)* 8–11 AClark (2) (unf: led 1f: wknd over 2f out: t.o) . 15.**7**

**9/4** AMIRATI (USA), **5/2** Simply Sooty, **7/2** Brockton Dancer(op 6/4), **6/1** Musical Prospect (USA)(5/1—10/1), **12/1** Bodandere(5/1—14/1), **14/1** Tartouka(8/1—16/1), **20/1** Sui Generis (IRE). CSF £14.96, Tote £2.80: £1.60 £2.50 (£10.00). Maktoum Al Maktoum (NEWMARKET) bred by W. S. Farish III & W. S. Kilroy in USA. 7 Rn
65.25 sec (4.55)
SF—26/14/11/5/–/–

**1165**     BASINGSTOKE CLAIMING STKS (3-Y.O) £2924.00 (£872.00: £416.00: £188.00)
      **1¹/₂m 5y**                                         6-45 (6-47)

932★ **Trumpet (70)** *(LordHuntingdon)* 9-5 MRoberts (7) (4th st: rdn 2f out: r.o to ld wl
      ins fnl f) ..................................................... —**1**
583 Mohana **(65)** *(JLDunlop)* 8-8 WCarson (5) (led tl wl ins fnl f) ................... ³/₄.**2**
932⁴ Newton Point **(58)** *(GAPritchard-Gordon)* 9-3 RCochrane (4) (3rd st: ev ch fnl
      2f: r.o) ....................................................... nk.**3**
944⁶ Ivor's Flutter *(DRCElsworth)* 9-2 JWilliams (4) (7th st: hdwy over 1f out: r.o ins
      fnl f) ......................................................... 2.**4**

1102* Lyn's Return (IRE) **(56)** *(RSimpson)* 8-12 ‡5ATucker (6) (6th st: hdwy 4f out:
wknd over 1f out) .................................................................................. 8.5
911 Kandy Secret (USA) **(64)** *(RHannon)* 8-13 ‡3RPerham (2) (lw: 5th st: rdn 4f out:
bhd fnl 2f) .......................................................................................... 5.6
784² Chief of Staff **(87)** (Fav) *(PFICole)* 9-5 AMunro (3) (plld hrd: jnd ldr 6f out: 2nd st:
wknd qckly over 2f out: t:o) ..................................................... 10.7

**5/4** Chief of Staff, **5/1** Lyn's Return (IRE), **11/2** TRUMPET, **7/1** Mohana, **10/1** Ivor's Flutter(6/1—12/1), **12/1**
Newton Point, **14/1** Kandy Secret (USA)(10/1—16/1). CSF £37.47, Tote £4.40: £2.20 £2.80 (£19.90). The
Queen (WEST ILSLEY) bred by The Queen. 7 Rn; Mohana clmd A Lidderdale £4,521    2m 36.66 (6.96)
SF—47/34/42/37/17/8


**1166**  GEORGE GOULET PINK CHAMPAGNE H'CAP (3-Y.O) (0-100) £3752.50 (£1120.00:
£535.00: £242.50)  **7f 64y**                                            7-15 (7-16)

649³ **Risk Master (74)** *(CAHorgan)* 7-11⁽²⁾ AMcGlone (8) (mde all: clr over 1f out:
eased nr fin) ........................................................................ —1
787* Do Run Run **(78)** (Fav) *(RHannon)* 8-1 MRoberts (6) (chsd wnr: 2nd st: rdn over
2f out: no imp) .................................................................... 2¹/₂.2
870 Morocco (IRE) **(70)** *(RCharlton)* 7-7 DaleGibson (7) (6th st: hdwy over 2f out:
hrd rdn & hung lft over 1f out: nt qckn) ............................ ³/₄.3
930 Basilica **(72)** *(CEBrittain)* 7-9⁽²⁾ SDawson (3) (3rd st: rdn over 2f out: one pce) 1¹/₂.4
834³ Shati (IRE) **(97)** *(HThomsonJones)* 9-6 RHills (4) (last st: rdn over 2f out: nvr nr
to chal) ...................................................................... 1.5
341 Alsaarm (USA) **(98)** *(JLDunlop)* 9-7 WCarson (5) (4th st: rdn 2f out: eased whn
btn ins fnl f) .................................................................... 6.6
She's Pleased (USA) **(87)** *(LMCumani)* 8-8 LDettori (2) (5th st: a bhd) ............. ¹/₂.7
851⁴ Pure Formality **(90)** *(DRCElsworth)* 8-13 SCauthen (1) (lw: 5th st: wknd over 2f
out: t:o) .......................................................................... 8.8
LONG HANDICAP: Morocco (IRE) 7-6, Basilica 7-6.

**2/1** Do Run Run, **5/1** She's Pleased (USA)(op 3/1), **6/1** RISK MASTER, Pure Formality, **7/1** Shati (IRE), **8/1**
Alsaarm (USA), **10/1** Morocco (IRE), **14/1** Basilica. CSF £18.05, CT £108.90. Tote £9.10: £2.50 £1.30 £2.30
(£11.20). Mrs B. Sumner (BILLINGBEAR) bred by Arthur E. Smith. 8 Rn
SF—35/31/21/18/40/23


**1167**  KENNETH ROBERTSON H'CAP (0-80) £3262.00 (£976.00: £468.00: £214.00)
**6f 8y**                                                            7-45 (7-47)

1028 **Darussalam (61)** *(RLee)* 5-8-12 PatEddery (9) (a.p: led over 1f out: r.o wl) ....... —1
Rainbow Fleet **(53)** *(DMarks)* 4-8-4 GBaxter (12) (hdwy over 2f out: chsd wnr
fnl f: no imp) ............................................................ 2¹/₂.2
731⁶ Divine Pet **(62)** *(WGRWightman)* 7-8-13 WNewnes (14) (hdwy wl over 1f out:
r.o ins fnl f) ............................................................... 1.3
967² Teanarco (IRE) **(61)** *(RJHolder)* 4-8-5 ‡7SDrowne (13) (a.p: r.o one pce fnl f) .... 1.4
941 Fascination Waltz **(73)** *(DShaw)* 5-9-10 AClark (16) (s.s: hdwy over 1f out: fin wl) ³/₄.5
1054⁵ Iron King **(68)** *(JLSpearing)* 6-9-5 NHowe (17) (hdwy 2f out: r.o ins fnl f) ......... ³/₄.6
967³ Gone Savage **(72)** *(GBBalding)* 4-9-9 JWilliams (18) (hdwy over 1f out: r.o) ..... s.h.7
992* Cee-En-Cee **(70)** (bl) *(MMcCourt)* 8-9-7 TQuinn (11) (hdwy 2f out: one pce fnl f) ³/₄.8
1107* Aughfad **(84)** (v) *(TCasey)* 6-10-7 (7x) JReid (10) (prom over 4f) .................. nk.9
1032 Cash a Million (FR) **(48)** (bl) *(PDCundell)* 4-7-13 AMunro (6) (bhd fnl 2f: t:o) . 12.10
830³ Highland Magic (IRE) **(63)** *(MJFetherston-Godley)* 4-8-9 ‡5DHarrison (7) (hdwy
2f out: wknd qckly fnl f: t:o) ...................................... s.h.11
894 Everglades (IRE) **(75)** *(RCharlton)* 4-9-12 RCochrane (15) (dwlt: t:o) ............ s.h.12
946* Hawa Layaam (IRE) **(74)** (v) *(AAScott)* 3-9-2 WRSwinburn (2) (w ldr: led over 3f
out tl over 1f out: wknd qckly: t:o) .............................. s.h.13
945 Pharaoh's Dancer **(77)** (Fav) *(EAWheeler)* 5-10-0 MWigham (3) (lw: s.s: t:o) ...... 4.14
997 Yatoo (IRE) **(61)** *(RHannon)* 3-7-10 ‡7DGibbs (4) (bhd fnl 2f: t:o) ................... hd.15
75 Supreme Optimist **(43)** (bl) *(REPeacock)* 8-7-8⁽¹⁾ JLowe (8) (spd 3f: t:o) .......... 2.16
1028³ Luna Bid **(65)** *(MBlanshard)* 9-9-2 CRutter (5) (lw: chsd ldrs 4f: t:o) ............. s.h.17
992 Thornfield Boy **(75)** *(RJHolder)* 6-9-12 MRoberts (1) (led over 2f: wknd qckly
over 2f out: t:o) ....................................................... ¹/₂.18
LONG HANDICAP: Supreme Optimist 6-8.

**6/1** Pharaoh's Dancer, **7/1** Cee-En-Cee, **8/1** Highland Magic (IRE), Hawa Layaam (IRE), **10/1** Luna Bid, Divine
Pet, DARUSSALAM, Gone Savage, Aughfad, **14/1** Teanarco (IRE), **16/1** Iron King, Thornfield Boy, **20/1** Cash a
Million (FR), **25/1** Yatoo (IRE), Everglades (IRE), **33/1** Fascination Waltz, **50/1** Rainbow Fleet, **66/1** Supreme
Optimist. CSF £363.03, CT £4,601.75. Tote £13.20: £2.90 £21.10 £2.50 £2.90 (£901.40). Foxley Saddlery and
Countrywear (PRESTEIGNE) bred by Mrs I. M. Raine. 18 Rn    1m 15.03 (3.23)
SF—58/40/45/33/49/41

## 1168
HERMITAGE STKS    £4425.00 (£1320.00: £630.00: £285.00)
1¼m 6y
                                            8-15 (8-19)

|  |  |  |
|---|---|---|
| | **Sonus (IRE)** (*JHMGosden*) 3-8-8 WCarson (4) (4th st: rdn 2f out: r.o to ld nr fin) | —1 |
| 849[6] | Fair Average (104) (Jt-Fav) (*HCandy*) 4-9-11 WNewnes (2) (5th st: hdwy 2f out: led ins fnl f tl hdd nr fin) | ½.2 |
| 929[4] | Tetradonna (IRE) (*RHannon*) 4-9-2 MRoberts (3) (led tl ins fnl f) | 1½.3 |
| | Flaming Arrow (90) (*HRACecil*) 4-9-7 WRSwinburn (1) (hld up: 3rd st: ev ch over 1f out: wknd ins fnl f) | 2.4 |
| 579[2] | Safa (98) (*AAScott*) 4-9-2 BRaymond (8) (6th st: hld up: hdwy 3f out: wknd wl over 1f out) | 2.5 |
| 824 | Badawi (USA) (99) (*JHMGosden*) 4-9-2 RCochrane (7) (7th st: a bhd) | hd.6 |
| | Duc de Berry (USA) (96) (*GHarwood*) 4-9-11 AClark (6) (last st: a bhd) | 5.7 |
| 424* | Deserve (92) (Jt-Fav) (*HRACecil*) 3-8-12 SCauthen (5) (lw: chsd ldr: 2nd st: wknd 2f out) | 2.8 |

**11/4** Deserve, Fair Average, **5/1** SONUS (IRE)(op 3/1), **13/2** Badawi (USA), **15/2** Tetradonna (IRE), **10/1** Safa, **14/1** Flaming Arrow, **16/1** Duc de Berry (USA). CSF £18.42. Tote £4.40: £1.40 £1.40 £1.50 (£7.80). Sheikh Mohammed (NEWMARKET) bred by Ballydoyle Stud in Ireland. 8 Rn
                                                 2m 8.07 (5.07)
                                        SF—53/69/57/58/49/48

## 1169
NETHERAVON H'CAP (0-90) £3132.00 (£936.00: £448.00: £204.00)
1m 5f 61y
                                            8-45 (8-48)

|  |  |  |
|---|---|---|
| 987* | **Sea Goddess (81)** (Jt-Fav) (*WJarvis*) 4-9-5 PatEddery (4) (mde all: rdn out) | —1 |
| 708 | Prince Sobur (58) (*MBlanshard*) 6-7-10 NCarlisle (7) (6th st: hrd rdn over 1f out: edgd lft nr fin) | 3½.2 |
| 114[6] | Intricacy (60) (*CCElsey*) 4-7-12 JLowe (5) (lw: 8th st: hdwy on ins over 2f out: r.o ins fnl f) | ¾.3 |
| | Be a Honey (90) (*NAGraham*) 4-10-0 WCarson (1) (3rd st: r.o one pce fnl 2f) | nk.4 |
| 771[2] | Naseem Elbarr (USA) (65) (Jt-Fav) (*ACStewart*) 4-8-3 MRoberts (6) (lw: hld up: 5th st: one pce fnl f: btn whn hmpd nr fin) | nk.5 |
| 708[3] | Zuhal (60) (*HThomsonJones*) 4-7-12 RHills (3) (s.i.s: 9th st: stdy hdwy 3f out: wknd wl over 1f out) | 10.6 |
| 805 | Classic Statement (56) (*RLee*) 6-7-8 DaleGibson (9) (chsd ldr: 2nd st: rdn 3f out: wknd 2f out) | 4.7 |
| | High Beacon (80) (*KCBailey*) 5-9-4 RCochrane (10) (4th st: hrd rdn over 2f out: sn wknd) | 2.8 |
| | Shahdjat (IRE) (99) (*KCBailey*) 4-10-9 JReid (2) (dwlt: last st: a bhd) | 2.9 |
| 815 | Niani (IRE) (87) (*JLDunlop*) 4-9-11 SCauthen (8) (7th st: hdwy 3f out: wknd qckly 2f out: t.o) | 8.10 |

**3/1** SEA GODDESS, Naseem Elbarr (USA), **4/1** Zuhal, **13/2** Niani (IRE), **7/1** Prince Sobur, **8/1** High Beacon, **12/1** Be a Honey, **20/1** Intricacy, **25/1** Shahdjat (IRE), **40/1** Classic Statement. CSF £24.41, CT £339.40. Tote £3.20: £1.80 £2.40 £4.60 (£19.10). Lord Howard de Walden (NEWMARKET) bred by Seend Stud. 10 Rn
                                             2m 54.55 (8.85)
                                        SF—40/10/10/39/13/–

T/Plpt: £805.30 (4.65 Tckts).                                                  KH

# YARMOUTH (L-H)
## Tuesday, June 2nd [Good to firm]
Going Allowance: St: minus 0.20 sec; Rest: minus 0.40 sec (F)      Wind: slt half against

Stalls: high

## 1170
HOPTON AUCTION STKS (I) (Mdn 2-Y-O) £2072.00 (£572.00: £272.00)
6f 3y
                                            1-30 (1-33)

|  |  |  |
|---|---|---|
| 1038[4] | **Walsham Witch** (Fav) (*MHTompkins*) 8-0[(2)] PRobinson (7) (a.p: led over 2f out: rdn out) | —1 |
| 645 | Sweet Disorder (IRE) (*GAPritchard-Gordon*) 8-1 GCarter (1) (hld up & bhd: rapid hdwy appr fnl f: fin wl) | 1½.2 |
| | Formal Affair (*CACyzer*) 8-7 MRoberts (11) (lengthy: bkwd: s.i.s: sn rcvrd: ev ch fnl 2f: unable qckn) | ½.3 |
| | Red Ballet (*MrsNMacauley*) 7-12 ‡3DBiggs (10) (leggy: scope: a.p: ev ch 1f out: no ex ins fnl f) | 1.4 |
| | Midarida (IRE) (*RJRWilliams*) 8-9 RCochrane (6) (small: lt-f: hld up: hdwy ½-wy: kpt on one pce appr fnl f) | 1½.5 |
| 682 | Swiftlet (IRE) (*MBell*) 7-13 RHills (4) (swtg: rdn along thrght: chsd ldrs over 4f) | 2.6 |

Persian Traveller (IRE) *(CNAllen)* 7-11[(1)] ‡[7]GForster (9) (leggy: lw: chsd ldrs over 3f) ......................... ³/₄.7
Pickupadailysport *(MissGayKelleway)* 8-5 PaulEddery (3) (wl grwn: bkwd: a bhd) 3.8
995[6] Generally *(PatMitchell)* 7-9 ‡[3]FNorton (8) (led over 3f: sn rdn & wknd) ............... 5.9
928[2] Scenic Reef (IRE) *(JMPEustace)* 8-2 JQuinn (2) (prom: rdn ¹/₂-wy: sn lost tch) nk.10
645 Our Nikki *(GBlum)* 7-13 AShoults (5) (sn pushed along: a outpcd: t.o) ............ 8.11

**11/8** WALSHAM WITCH, **4/1** Scenic Reef (IRE)(5/2—5/1), **7/1** Persian Traveller (IRE)(10/1—6/1), Sweet Disorder (IRE)(op 4/1), **10/1** Midarida (IRE)(op 6/1), **12/1** Formal Affair(op 7/1), Swiftlet (IRE)(op 6/1), **16/1** Red Ballet, **25/1** Pickupadailysport, **50/1** Ors. CSF £12.12, Tote £2.60: £1.40 £3.70 £2.70 (£7.90). Mr J. H. Ellis (NEWMARKET) bred by J. R. Mitchell. 11 Rn
1m 13.4 (2.8)
SF—6/1/5/—/—/—

---

## 1171

HOPTON AUCTION STKS (II) (Mdn 2-Y.O) £2072.00 (£572.00: £272.00)
**6f 3y**
2-00 (2-01)

1046[3] **Spark (IRE)** *(CWCElsey)* 7-8 ‡[5]SMaloney (2) (mde all: rdn & r.o wl fnl f) ............ —1
703 Mr Nevermind (IRE) *(GLewis)* 8-8 BRouse (3) (lw: plld hrd: a.p: rdn 1f out: r.o) .. 2.2
Persian Revival (FR) *(Fav)* *(BAMcMahon)* 8-9 LDettori (7) (tall: bit bkwd: held up: gd hdwy ¹/₂-wy: jnd wnr 2f out: hrd rdn & nt qckn fnl f) ..... s.h.3
Hadeer's Dance *(RWArmstrong)* 9-5 BCrossley (10) (leggy: lt-f: bkwd: dwlt: outpcd tl r.o ins fnl f) ......................... 8.4
645 Secret Tale *(GBlum)* 7-12 JQuinn (8) (nvr trbld ldrs) ............................ 7.5
867[6] Five Clubs (IRE) *(DTThom)* 7-9 ‡[3]FNorton (6) (prom over 4f) .................... hd.6
Golden Klair *(CJHill)* 8-0 TyroneWilliams (9) (lengthy: unf: bkwd: s.s: a in rr) .. 2.7
968 Mena *(JWPayne)* 7-12 WCarson (5) (spd over 3f: rrn green appr fnl f: sn bhd) 2¹/₂.8
Big Gem *(MCChapman)* 8-4[(1)] SWebster (4) (lengthy: bkwd: s.s: a bhd) ...... s.h.9
968[3] Lady Relko *(RVoorspuy)* 7-12 SDawson (1) (chsd ldrs: rdn & wknd ¹/₂-wy) ...... 3.10

**7/4** Persian Revival (FR), **3/1** SPARK (IRE)(9/4—7/2), **11/2** Mena, **6/1** Lady Relko(op 4/1), Mr Nevermind (IRE)(op 10/1), **14/1** Five Clubs (IRE)(op 8/1), **20/1** Hadeer's Dance, **25/1** Golden Klair, **50/1** Ors. CSF £21.40, Tote £4.80: £1.90 £2.80 £1.10 (£24.70). Mr C. W. C. Elsey (MALTON) bred by W. and Mrs Whitehead in Ireland. 10 Rn
1m 13.4 (2.8)
SF—/6/6/—/—/—

---

## 1172

TOLHOUSE (S) H'CAP (0-60) £2676.80 (£744.80: £358.40) **1m 3y** 2-30 (2-34)
(Weights raised 5 lb)

731 **Top One** (46) *(CJHill)* 7-9-3 ‡[5]JWeaver (10) (hld up: a.p: led appr fnl f: sn wl clr: eased nr fin) ......................... —1
1009 Jolizal (36) (v) *(DMorris)* 4-8-5 ‡[7]StephenDavies (6) (led tl hdd appr fnl f: sn outpcd) ......................... 6.2
736[5] Crown Reserve (35) *(MJRyan)* 4-8-8 ‡[3]DBiggs (5) (a.p: ev ch wl over 1f out: sn btn) ......................... 1.3
897 Kelly's Kite (32) *(HJCollingridge)* 4-8-8 JQuinn (15) (hld up: hdwy appr fnl f: nrst fin) ......................... 2¹/₂.4
693 Slanderinthestrand (IRE) (47) *(MJHaynes)* 3-8-12 BRouse (20) (swtg: effrt over 1f out: nvr nrr) ......................... ¹/₂.5
1070[6] Banana Cufflinks (USA) (39) *(MHTompkins)* 6-9-1 PRobinson (11) (lw: chsd ldrs: no hdwy fnl 2f) ......................... 1¹/₂.6
Kate Royale (53) *(GCBravery)* 3-8-13 ‡[5]CHodgson (16) (lw: prom tl wknd over 2f out) ......................... 1¹/₂.7
997[5] Harlequin Girl (39) *(KTIvory)* 4-9-1 RCochrane (12) (bit bkwd: prom: rdn over 3f out: sn btn) ......................... s.h.8
1090 Golden Beau (30) *(AHarrison)* 10-8-6 KFallon (7) (sme hdwy & nt clr run over 2f out: eased whn btn fnl f) ......................... 2¹/₂.9
1013[6] Miss Magenta (IRE) (33) *(RThompson)* 4-8-2 ‡[7]CHawksley (4) (chsd ldrs to ¹/₂-wy) ......................... nk.10
901[5] Bernie Silvers (53) *(MCChapman)* 3-9-4 SWebster (18) (spd over 4f) ............... 5.11
1052 Placid Lady (IRE) (46) *(WCarter)* 3-8-6 ‡[5]NGwilliams (19) (s.s: sn chsng ldrs: wknd over 3f out) ......................... s.h.12
1085* Allimac Nomis (45) *(Fav)* *(NACallaghan)* 3-8-10 (6x) WCarson (17) (nvr plcd to chal) ......................... nk.13
875[6] Modest Hope (USA) (48) *(GHEden)* 5-9-7 ‡[3]FNorton (1) (b.hind: chsd ldrs 6f) ...... hd.14
969 Sizzling Thoughts (54) *(GLewis)* 3-9-5 PaulEddery (13) (m.n.s) ...................... hd.15
1013 China Sky (45) *(CNAllen)* 4-9-0 ‡[7]GForster (3) (lw: chsd ldrs: rdn 3f out: sn btn) ...... 1¹/₂.16
592 Foreign Assignment (IRE) (47) (bl) *(JWhite)* 4-9-9 MRoberts (14) (lw: m.n.s) . ¹/₂.17
1034[6] Rich Pickings (43) *(CACyzer)* 3-8-8 DMcKeown (8) (sn rdn & bhd: t.o) ......... 10.18
Clever Claude (37) *(KSBridgwater)* 6-8-8 ‡[5]BDoyle (9) (b: swtg: t.o) ................ 5.19
*Stewards Enquiry: Forster suspended 11-14/6/92 (excessive use of whip).*

7/2 Allimac Nomis, **4/1** China Sky, **9/2** Banana Cufflinks (USA)(6/1—4/1), **6/1** Harlequin Girl, **8/1** Jolizal(20/1—7/1), **9/1** Crown Reserve, **10/1** Miss Magenta (IRE), Modest Hope (USA), **12/1** TOP ONE(25/1—33/1), **14/1** Slanderinthestrand (IRE)(20/1—33/1), **16/1** Golden Beau, **20/1** Foreign Assignment (IRE), Kate Royale, **25/1** Sizzling Thoughts, Bernie Silvers, **33/1** Placid Lady (IRE), Rich Pickings, **50/1** Ors. CSF £121.53, CT £878.22. Tote £23.90: £3.50 £2.40 £4.20 £15.50 (£182.40). Mr C. John Hill (BARNSTAPLE) bred by R. O'Loghlen. 19 Rn; No bid
1m 38.3 (3)
SF—34/4/4/–/–/–

---

**1173**　　JOHN HOLDRICH STKS (Mdn 3-Y.O) £2072.00 (£572.00: £272.00)
　　　　　　**7f 3y**
　　　　　　　　　　　　　　　　　　　　　　　　　　　　　　　　3-00 (3-02)

|  |  |  |  |  |
|---|---|---|---|---|
| | **Robingo (IRE)** *(CEBrittain)* 9-0　MRoberts (4) (s.i.s: hdwy 3f out: led over 1f out: rdn out) | —1 |
| | Laura *(HThomsonJones)* 8-9　RHills (6) (lengthy: lt-f: hld up: effrt & n.m.r 2f out: str run fnl f: rn green: no ex) | 1½.2 |
| 869⁴ | Jato **(74)** (bl) *(WJHaggas)* 9-0　JQuinn (3) (a.p: ev ch 1f out: unable qckn) | ½.3 |
| 384 | Whitehall (IRE) *(CRNelson)* 8-11 ‡³FNorton (1) (bkwd: a.p: rdn appr fnl f: unable qckn) | 1.4 |
| | Little Park *(GAPritchard-Gordon)* 8-6 ‡³DBiggs (5) (chsd ldrs: rdn 2f out: nt pce to chal) | 1½.5 |
| 989³ | Cachou (USA) **(Fav)** *(JHMGosden)* 8-9　PaulEddery (7) (led tl hdd & wknd over 1f out) | 1.6 |
| 511 | Flash of Straw (IRE) *(GLewis)* 9-0　RaymondBerry (2) (bkwd: a bhd: rdn 2f out: no imp) | 1½.7 |

**4/5** Cachou (USA)(Evens—4/6), **5/2** Jato(tchd 6/4), **8/1** ROBINGO (IRE), **9/1** Laura, **33/1** Whitehall (IRE), Little Park, **50/1** Flash of Straw (IRE). CSF £63.95, Tote £5.80: £3.00 £2.20 (£10.70). Capt. M. Lemos (NEWMARKET) bred by J. J. Prendergast in Ireland. 7 Rn
1m 26.5 (3.7)
SF—24/14/17/11/1/1

---

**1174**　　POTTER HEIGHAM H'CAP (0-80) £3028.00 (£904.00: £432.00: £196.00)
　　　　　　**7f 3y**
　　　　　　　　　　　　　　　　　　　　　　　　　　　　　　　　3-30 (3-31)

|  |  |  |  |
|---|---|---|---|
| 997² | **Sugemar (52)** *(JARToller)* 6–8-0　MRoberts (6) (a.p: hrd rdn over 1f out: r.o to ld nr fin) | —1 |
| 1133 | Domicksky **(75)** *(MJRyan)* 4–9-6 ‡³DBiggs (10) (stdd s: rapid hdwy appr fnl f: fin wl) | ¾.2 |
| | Crystal Heights (FR) **(80)** *(WAO'Gorman)* 4–9-9 ‡⁵EmmaO'Gorman (1) (bkwd: mde most: qcknd clr over 1f out: wknd & ct ins fnl f) | ¾.3 |
| 948⁴ | Kawwas **(45)** *(WHolden)* 7–7-7　TyroneWilliams (11) (hdwy appr fnl f: r.o wl ins fnl f) | 1½.4 |
| 515 | Susanna's Secret **(53)** *(WCarter)* 5–7-10⁽²⁾ ‡⁵NGwilliams (7) (effrt 2f out: rdn & no ex ins fnl f) | 1½.5 |
| 860 | Mu-Arrik **(50)** (bl) *(DAWilson)* 4–7-9 ‡³FNorton (3) (swtg: chsd ldrs: rdn & ev ch 2f out: one pce) | 1.6 |
| 1032* | Jaldi (IRE) **(57)** (bl) **(Fav)** *(JSutcliffe)* 4–7-12 (7x) ‡⁷JTate (9) (hld up: effrt & hmpd several times fr ½-wy: nt rcvr) | 2.7 |
| 438 | Annabelle Royale **(80)** *(MrsNMacauley)* 6–10-0　LDettori (5) (prom: rdn 2f out: eased whn btn ins fnl f) | 1½.8 |
| | Seaside Minstrel **(46)** *(CJHill)* 4–7-8⁽¹⁾　AMackay (8) (swtg: nvr nr ldrs) | 2.9 |
| 783 | Elton Ledger (IRE) **(74)** *(AAScott)* 3–8-12　BRaymond (2) (disp ld 4f: hung bdly rt: grad wknd) | ¾.10 |
| 941 | Gabbiadini **(73)** *(MHTompkins)* 5–9-7　PRobinson (4) (a bhd) | 2.11 |

LONG HANDICAP: Kawwas 7-6, Seaside Minstrel 7-6.

**85/40** Jaldi (IRE), **5/1** Mu-Arrik(op 20/1), **11/2** SUGEMAR(7/2—6/1), **13/2** Domicksky, **15/2** Annabelle Royale, **9/1** Kawwas(op 6/1), **10/1** Gabbiadini, Elton Ledger (IRE)(12/1—8/1), **12/1** Crystal Heights (FR), **25/1** Ors. CSF £42.67, CT £389.57. Tote £6.10: £2.60 £2.60 £3.20 (£11.30). Mr B. S. McElney (NEWMARKET) bred by Rannerdale Trust. 11 Rn
1m 24.9 (2.1)
SF—34/52/53/18/16/12

---

**1175**　　CHARTER H'CAP (3-Y.O) (0-80) £3236.00 (£968.00: £464.00: £212.00)
　　　　　　**1¼m 21y**
　　　　　　　　　　　　　　　　　　　　　　　　　　　　　　　　4-00 (4-02)

|  |  |  |  |
|---|---|---|---|
| 554⁴ | **Wild Fire (73)** *(GWragg)* 9-2　MRoberts (2) (plld hrd: hld up & bhd: swtchd rt over 2f out: led over 1f out: sn wl clr) | —1 |
| 767 | Majal (IRE) **(78)** *(BHanbury)* 9-7　RCochrane (11) (stdd s: gd hdwy appr fnl f: no ch w wnr) | 3½.2 |
| 746⁴ | Viva Darling **(69)** *(BAMcMahon)* 8-12　LDettori (4) (gd hdwy fnl 2f: fin fast) | nk.3 |
| 725 | Mindomica **(66)** *(MBell)* 8-9　RHills (5) (hld up: gd hdwy to ld wl over 1f out: sn hdd: no ex fnl f) | 1½.4 |

| | | | |
|---|---|---|---|
| 1025³ | Khrisma **(70)** (Fav) *(MrsJCecil)* 8-13 PaulEddery (9) (led after 2f tl hdd wl over 1f out: sn rdn & btn) | 1¹/₂.5 |
| 695 | Roca Murada (IRE) **(55)** *(MJRyan)* 7-9 ‡³DBiggs (6) (plld hrd: 5th st: wknd 2f out) | 5.6 |
| 878⁴ | Waseela (IRE) **(68)** *(AAScott)* 8-11 BRaymond (12) (hdwy & 2nd st: rdn & wknd over 1f out) | ³/₄.7 |
| 974⁴ | Kelimutu **(58)** *(CFWall)* 8-1 PRobinson (8) (effrt 3f out: nvr able to chal) | 2¹/₂8 |
| 999⁵ | Stinger **(67)** *(CRNelson)* 8-7 ‡³FNorton (1) (nvr trbld ldrs) | 1¹/₂.9 |
| 783⁵ | Buzzards Bellbuoy **(65)** *(HJCollingridge)* 8-8 JQuinn (7) (mid div: 6th st: eased whn btn over 1f out) | 2¹/₂.10 |
| 804⁶ | Magadeer (USA) **(78)** *(JLDunlop)* 9-7 WCarson (13) (s.i.s: sn chsng ldrs: 3rd st: wknd over 2f out) | hd.11 |
| 999³ | Socks and Shares **(71)** *(PWHarris)* 9-0 GHind (3) (led 2f: 4th st: wknd 3f out) | hd.12 |
| 1102⁴ | Ideal Candidate **(57)** *(CACyzer)* 8-0 GCarter (10) (chsd ldrs to ¹/₂-wy: sn wknd) | 1.13 |

**Evens** Khrisma(op 2/1), **6/1** WILD FIRE(op 4/1), **15/2** Magadeer (USA), **9/1** Majal (IRE)(12/1—14/1), Socks and Shares, Waseela, (IRE), **10/1** Viva Darling, **14/1** Kelimutu, Buzzards Bellbuoy, **16/1** Stinger, Mindomica, **25/1** Ideal Candidate, **33/1** Roca Murada (IRE). CSF £65.91, CT £520.60. Tote £7.00: £2.70 £3.40 £2.90 (£29.80). Sir Philip Oppenheimer (NEWMARKET) bred by Hascombe and Valiant Studs. 13 Rn    2m 6.6 (2.2)
SF—40/38/38/22/23/–

**1176**    BLACKFRIARS STKS (Mdn 3-Y.O) £2072.00 (£572.00: £272.00)
      **1³/₄m 17y**                  4-30 (4-32)

| | | | |
|---|---|---|---|
| 481² | **Rain Rider** (Fav) *(JLDunlop)* 9-0 WCarson (2) (lw: led 9f out: hrd drvn over 2f out: styd on strly) | —1 |
| 812³ | Robenko (USA) *(CEBrittain)* 9-0 MRoberts (3) (led over 5f: 3rd st: styd on appr fnl f: no ch w wnr) | 8.2 |
| 896³ | Alcoy (IRE) **(62)** *(PAKelleway)* 9-0 PRobinson (1) (hld up: 4th st: gd hdwy over 2f out: one pce appr fnl f) | 1¹/₂.3 |
| 627⁴ | Temple Knight *(CACyzer)* 9-0 DMcKeown (4) (hld up: wnt 2nd st: rdn 3f out: btn appr fnl f) | 1¹/₂.4 |

**4/5** RAIN RIDER(op 1/2), **6/4** Robenko (USA)(op 9/4), **11/2** Alcoy (IRE)(12/1—5/1), **20/1** Temple Knight. CSF £2.51, Tote £1.50 (£1.30). Mrs E. M. H. Ogden White (ARUNDEL) bred by Ash Hill Stud. 4 Rn   3m 6.2 (8.2)
T/Plpt: £2,776.80 (0.45 Tckts);£2,063.90 to Yarmouth 3/6/92.          IM

# YARMOUTH (L-H)
## Wednesday, June 3rd [Good]
Going Allowance: St: 0.35 sec (G); Rest: minus 0.15 sec per fur (F)     Wind: fresh against

Stalls: 3rd, 4th & 5th low, remainder high

**1177**    HEYDON HALL APP'CE H'CAP (0-70) £2186.80 (£604.80: £288.40)
      **6f 3y**                    2-30 (2-31)

| | | | |
|---|---|---|---|
| 872 | Yes **(49)** *(DTThom)* 4–8-9 PBowe (7) (chsd ldrs: rdn to ld ins fnl f) | —1 |
| 885* | Furiella **(68)** *(PCHaslam)* 4–10-0 EHusband (2) (w ldr: led over 2f out: hdd & no ex ins fnl f) | 1¹/₂.2 |
| 775 | Kaths Choice **(39)** *(HJCollingridge)* 4–7-13 CHawksley (1) (s.i.s: hdwy 3f out: hmpd 2f out: r.o fnl f) | 3¹/₂.3 |
| 1084* | Caromish (USA) **(66)** *(MDIUsher)* 5–9-12 (6x) JHunter (6) (led tl hdd over 2f out: wknd appr fnl f) | 1¹/₂.4 |
| 801 | Cumbrian Cavalier **(53)** *(JRBostock)* 3–8-4 JTate (4) (chsd ldrs: hmpd 2f out: no ch after) | nk.5 |
| 863 | Dublin Indemnity (USA) **(49)** *(NACallaghan)* 3–8–0 DCarson (3) (lw: outpcd) | 1¹/₂.6 |
| 1064² | Fair Reason (IRE) **(47)** *(DJSCosgrove)* 4–8-7 MSimpson (5) (b: reard s: hdwy after 2f: ev ch whn fell 2f out) | 0 |

**4/5** Caromish (USA), **5/1** Furiella, **13/2** YES, Fair Reason (IRE), **11/1** Dublin Indemnity (USA), **16/1** Cumbrian Cavalier, **33/1** Kaths Choice. CSF £35.67, Tote £9.10: £3.40 £2.70 (£11.00). Mr W. F. Coleman (NEWMARKET) bred by R. Selby and Partners. 7 Rn     1m 15.9 (5.3)
SF—31/44/1/–/21/–

**1178**    FLEGGS (S) STKS (2-Y.O) £2324.00 (£644.00: £308.00)    **6f 3y**     3-00 (3-01)

| | | | |
|---|---|---|---|
| 928 | **Burishki** (bl) *(GAPritchard-Gordon)* 8-6 GCarter (6) (hld up: hdwy 2f out: hrd rdn to ld ins fnl f) | —1 |
| 782 | Poco Pierna (IRE) *(WCarter)* 8-1 ‡⁵NGwilliams (3) (led over 4f: ev ch ins fnl f: r.o) | 2.2 |
| 782⁵ | Heroic Deed *(MHTompkins)* 8-11 PRobinson (7) (lw: prom: led over 1f out: hdd & no ex ins fnl f) | nk.3 |

476 Strike-a-Pose *(CNWilliams)* 8-6 BCrossley (9) (dwlt: r.o appr fnl f: nrst fin) ......... 1.4
882⁴ Suitability (IRE) *(PCHaslam)* 8-6 DaleGibson (2) (dwlt: rdn & hdwy 2f out: nvr
able to chal) ................................................................ 1.5
1039⁵ Nut Bush (Fav) *(NACallaghan)* 8-11 AMcGlone (4) (chsd ldrs: rdn 2f out: no imp
appr fnl f) ................................................................ 1.6
Rose Flyer (IRE) *(MCChapman)* 8-6 GBaxter (5) (cmpt: bkwd: plld hrd: chsd
ldrs: rdn 3f out: sn btn) ................................................ 6.7
786 Tudela *(MJHaynes)* 8-3 ‡³FNorton (1) (dwlt: nvr trbld ldrs) ............................... nk.8
Heavenly Dream *(GBlum)* 8-6 AShoults (8) (w'like: bkwd: s.s: sn rdn along: t.o) ... 9

**7/4** Nut Bush(5/2—6/4), **9/4** Suitability (IRE), **9/2** Heroic Deed(op 3/1), **10/1** Strike-a-Pose(op 6/1), **12/1** Tudela(op 6/1), **14/1** Poco Pierna (IRE)(op 5/1), **25/1** Rose Flyer (IRE), **33/1** BURISHKI & Ors. CSF £355.34, Tote £23.70: £3.40 £3.80 £2.00 (£89.00). Mr Giles W. Pritchard-Gordon (NEWMARKET) bred by Giles W. Pritchard-Gordon. 9 Rn; No bid
1m 16.9 (6.3)
SF—8/–/4/–/–/–

**1179** ROYAL ANGLIAN REGIMENT H'CAP (0-80) £2733.50 (£756.00: £360.50)
1³/₄m 17y
3-30 (3-30)

831 **Greenwich Bambi (52)** *(WCarter)* 4–7-10⁽¹⁾ ‡⁵NGwilliams (5) (hld up: hdwy
over 3f out: led over 2f out: rdn out) .................................... —1
937 Skisurf **(51)** *(CEBrittain)* 6–8-0 GCrealock (4) (chsd ldr: 2nd st: lost pl over 3f
out: r.o appr fnl f) ........................................................ 1¹/₂.2
951 Sweet Request **(45)** (bl) *(JRBostock)* 4–7-1⁽¹⁾ ‡⁷CHawksley (2) (led tl hdd 2f out:
kpt on) ........................................................................ 1.3
1125* Lookingforarainbow (IRE) **(59)** *(BobJones)* 4–8-8 (4x) VSmith (1) (hld up: hdwy
& 3rd st: rdn 2f out: one pce) ........................................... ¹/₂.4
Nikatino **(47)** *(DrJDScargill)* 6–7-7 ‡³FNorton (9) (bit bkwd: hld up: rdn & kpt on
fnl 2f) ........................................................................ hd.5
861⁶ Thunder Bug (USA) **(44)** *(APJames)* 4–7-7 DaleGibson (3) (prom tl 6th & btn st) 2.6
937* Art Form (USA) **(79)** (Fav) *(CACyzer)* 5–9-7 ‡⁷TMcLaughlin (8) (chsd ldrs: 5th &
rn wd ent st: sn rdn & btn) ............................................... 4.7
Briggscare **(70)** *(WJarvis)* 6–8-12 ‡⁷StephenDavies (7) (b: bit bkwd: hld up &
bhd: effrt 5f out: wknd over 2f out) ................................... 5.8
St Athans Lad **(45)** *(RCurtis)* 7–7-8 GBardwell (6) (nvr plcd: prom: 4th st: wknd 3f
out) ........................................................................... 2¹/₂.9
LONG HANDICAP: Sweet Request 7-6.

**2/1** Art Form (USA), **5/2** Lookingforarainbow (IRE), **11/2** GREENWICH BAMBI(8/1—9/2), **8/1** Skisurf(op 5/1), Thunder Bug (USA)(op 16/1), **10/1** Briggscare, **16/1** Nikatino, **25/1** Sweet Request, **33/1** St Athans Lad. CSF £45.70, CT £929.72. Tote £7.40: £2.90 £3.30 £4.60 (£22.70). John Humphreys (Turf Accountants) Ltd (EPSOM) bred by Lord Bolton. 9 Rn
3m 6.9 (8.9)

**1180** RIVER YARE STKS (Mdn 3-Y.O.F) £2072.00 (£572.00: £272.00)
1m 3f 101y
4-00 (4-02)

**Bineyah (IRE)** *(MRStoute)* 8-11 DHolland (3) (unf: scope: chsd ldrs: 5th st: led
over 2f out: clr fnl f) ..................................................... —1
911³ Blushing Storm (USA) *(JRFanshawe)* 8-11 GCarter (7) (prom: 4th st: one pce
fnl 2f: no ch w wnr) ....................................................... 6.2
Funoon (IRE) *(MRStoute)* 8-11 PD'Arcy (6) (bit bkwd: led 1f: 2nd st: led wl over
2f out: sn hdd & no ex) ................................................... hd.3
Whisper's Shadow *(MHTompkins)* 8-11 PRobinson (2) (swtg: prom: 3rd st: btn
3f out) ........................................................................ 3.4
Iota *(MrsJCecil)* 8-11 AMcGlone (1) (led after 1f tl hdd & wknd wl over 2f out) ... 8.5
934³ Fern **(104)** (Fav) *(LMCumani)* 8-11 JFortune (8) (lw: hld up: poor 6th st: sn rdn
& no imp) .................................................................... 3¹/₂.6
922⁶ Just Julia *(MRChannon)* 8-11 WNewnes (5) (in tch tl 7th & btn st) ..................... 3.7
Shakinski **(51)** *(MJRyan)* 8-8 ‡³DBiggs (4) (in tch: lost tch & 8th st: t.o) ........... 25.8

**1/2** Fern, **4/1** Blushing Storm (USA)(op 2/1), **6/1** BINEYAH (IRE)(op 4/1), **10/1** Funoon (IRE), **14/1** Iota, **16/1** Whisper's Shadow(op 10/1), **33/1** Ors. CSF £31.36, Tote £10.90: £2.60 £1.20 £4.00 (£48.30). Maktoum Al Maktoum (NEWMARKET) bred by Swettenham Stud in Ireland. 8 Rn
2m 27.7 (3.7)
SF—43/31/30/24/8/1

**1181** RADIO NORFOLK H'CAP (0-90) £2898.00 (£864.00: £412.00: £186.00)
1¹/₄m 21y
4-30 (4-31)

919* **Gulf Sailor (IRE) (80)** (Fav) *(MRStoute)* 4–9-9 DHolland (4) (chsd ldr: 2nd st:
led 3f out: drvn out) ...................................................... —1
479 Busted Rock **(85)** *(MrsLPiggott)* 7–10-0 WNewnes (5) (hld up: last st: hdwy
over 3f out: ev ch over 1f out: kpt on) ................................ 1.2

Rival Bid (USA) *(59) (MAJarvis)* 4–8-2 GCrealock (6) (swtg: plld hrd: 6th st: plld out appr fnl f: rdn & r.o) ............ ¹/₂.3

1061 Arak (USA) *(73) (RWArmstrong)* 4–9-2 PRobinson (7) (lw: prom: 4th st: ev ch 2f out: one pce fnl f) ............ 1.4

829 Rive-Jumelle (IRE) *(67) (MBell)* 4–8-3 ‡⁷PTurner (3) (lw: prom: 3rd st: lost pl 3f out: r.o fnl f) ............ ¹/₂.5

Polonez Prima *(83) (JEBanks)* 5–9-7 ‡⁵LNewton (2) (bkwd: in tch: 5th st: rdn 3f out: sn wknd) ............ 7.6

1063³ Barbary Reef (IRE) *(53) (GHEden)* 4–7-7⁽³⁾ ‡³FNorton (5) (led over 7f: sn wknd) 6.7

**2/1** GULF SAILOR (IRE), **3/1** Barbary Reef (IRE), **9/2** Rive-Jumelle (IRE), **5/1** Busted Rock(op 3/1), **9/1** Rival Bid (USA), **14/1** Arak (USA), **20/1** Polonez Prima(op 10/1). CSF £11.72, Tote £2.10: £2.20 £1.50 (£5.50). Lord Weinstock (NEWMARKET) bred by Ballymacoll Stud Farm Ltd in Ireland. 7 Rn 2m 8.8 (4.4)
SF–50/53/26/38/22/26

**1182** SUFFOLK STKS (Mdn 3-Y-O) £2343.60 (£649.60: £310.80) **1m 3y** 5-00 (5-01)

869² **Little Bean** (Fav) *(GWragg)* 9-0 PRobinson (4) (w ldr: shkn up to ld ins fnl f) ..... —1

Wrets *(MRStoute)* 9-0 PD'Arcy (8) (chsd ldrs: r.o wl ins fnl f) ............ 1.2

Blue Sea *(MAJarvis)* 9-0 GCrealock (1) (leggy: unf: dwlt: sn prom: slt ld 2f out tl ins fnl f: no ex) ............ hd.3

Galactic Miss *(JLDunlop)* 8-9 AMcGlone (6) (leggy: unf: chsd ldrs: plld out over 1f out: r.o: nt rch ldrs) ............ 1¹/₂.4

Tafsir *(HThomsonJones)* 8-9 WRyan (7) (lengthy: unf: bit bkwd: bhd: r.o fnl 2f: nvr able to chal) ............ 3¹/₂.5

Hazaaf (USA) *(AAScott)* 9-0 JFortune (3) (w'like: scope: bkwd: hdwy over 2f out: wknd fnl f) ............ 4.6

Muktaar (USA) *(JRFanshawe)* 9-0 GCarter (2) (w'like: leggy: bkwd: prom 5f) .. 1¹/₂.7

Otter Bush *(GBlum)* 9-0 AShoults (5) (wl grwn: bkwd: s.s: a bhd) ............ 1¹/₂.8

Princess Evita (FR) *(RGuest)* 8-2 ‡⁷SEiffert (9) (led 6f: sn wknd) ............ 3.9

**8/13** LITTLE BEAN(tchd Evens), **4/1** Muktaar (USA), **5/1** Tafsir, **8/1** Hazaaf (USA), **12/1** Galactic Miss(op 7/2), **14/1** Blue Sea, **20/1** Wrets(op 10/1), **50/1** Ors. CSF £15.82, Tote £1.40: £1.10 £2.60 £2.80 (£13.80). Sir Philip Oppenheimer (NEWMARKET) bred by Hascombe and Valiant Studs. 9 Rn 1m 42.7 (7.4)
SF–31/28/27/17/6/–

**1183** BRECKLAND STKS (Mdn 3-Y-O) £2072.00 (£572.00: £272.00) **6f 3y** 5-30 (5-31)

**Toussaud** (USA) (Fav) *(JHMGosden)* 8-9 DHolland (7) (led after 1f: hit rail over 2f out: rdn out) ............ —1

998³ Nagida *(JARToller)* 8-9 WNewnes (3) (unruly s: dwlt: hdwy over 2f out: ev ch fnl f: nt qckn) ............ 1¹/₂.2

1091² Alkarif (USA) *(72) (AAScott)* 9-0 JFortune (1) (ld 1f: one pce fnl 2f) ............ 5.3

441 Emigrator *(GBlum)* 9-0 AShoults (2) (bit bkwd: spd 3f: sn wknd) ............ 8.4

Millyrous (IRE) *(RGuest)* 8-9 WWoods (6) (lt-f: unf: chsd ldrs 3f: sn bhd) ............ 4.5

Under the Bridge *(PWHarris)* 9-0 WRyan (4) (rangy: bkwd: unruly stalls: s.v.s: a t.o) ............ 15.6

**8/15** TOUSSAUD (USA), **4/1** Nagida(3/1—9/2), Alkarif (USA), **8/1** Under the Bridge(10/1—20/1), **25/1** Millyrous (IRE), **50/1** Emigrator. CSF £3.72, Tote £1.20: £1.10 £2.10 (£2.60). Mr K. Abdulla (NEWMARKET) bred by Juddmonte Farms Incorporated in USA. 6 Rn 1m 15.2 (4.6)
SF–45/39/24/–/–/–

T/Plpt: £2,426.20 (1.75 Tckts). Dk

919—**BEVERLEY (R-H)**

## Wednesday, June 3rd [Firm]

Going Allowance: minus 0.40 sec per fur (F) Wind: fresh bhd

Stalls: high

**1184** HURN APP'CE (S) H'CAP (0-60) £2559.20 (£711.20: £341.60) **1m 1f 207y** 6-45 (6-45)

(Weights raised 12 lb)

1034² **Cold Shower** (IRE) *(51) (JAGlover)* 3–9-4 SWilliams (11) (lw: trckd ldrs: led over 2f out: r.o u.p) ............ —1

965⁴ Not Yet *(35) (EWeymes)* 8–9-1 AGarth (6) (bhd: hdwy ent st: ev ch ins fnl f: nt qckn) ............ 1¹/₂.2

616⁵ Be the Best *(40) (MPNaughton)* 4–9-6 JWeaver (4) (lw: bhd: hdwy appr st: styd on wl nr fin) ............ 1¹/₂.3

880³ First Bid *(44) (RMWhitaker)* 5–9-10 OPears (2) (a chsng ldrs: ev ch over 2f out: one pce) ............ hd.4

11172[6] Banana Cufflinks (USA) **(39)** *(MHTompkins)* 6–9-5 CHodgson (9) (bhd & pushed along: hdwy ent st: nt qckn fnl f) .......................... 2¹/₂.5
  1090 Honey Boy Simba **(40)** (v) *(MO'Neill)* 6–9-6 DarrenMoffatt (7) (hdwy 3f out: kpt on: no imp) .......................... 1.6
    26 Corporate Type (IRE) **(20)** *(GPKelly)* 4–8-0 JMarshall (13) (lost pl 5f out & sn wl bhd: r.o fnl 2f) .......................... ³/₄.7
 1008[4] Chart Cross **(35)** (Fav) *(KSBridgwater)* 6–9-1 BDoyle (3) (b: trckd ldrs after 3f: effrt over 2f out: sn btn) .......................... 5.8
 1089[6] Kind Style (IRE) **(30)** *(RHollinshead)* 4–8-3 ‡7MHumphries (15) (cl up: led over 3f out tl over 2f out: sn wknd) .......................... 2.9
  1052 Turning Heads **(31)** *(CaptJWilson)* 3–7-12 AntoinetteArmes (8) (bhd: effrt appr st: n.d) .......................... 1.10
  891[6] Miss Parkes **(48)** *(JBerry)* 3–8-8 ‡7BethanPrys-Jones (10) (n.d) .......................... 2.11
       Ghylldale **(41)** *(RBastiman)* 4–9-7 HBastiman (1) (s.i.s: hdwy after 3f: c wd st: sn rdn & btn) .......................... 1¹/₂.12
  1034 Noushy **(43)** *(KSBridgwater)* 4–9-2 ‡7TArrand (16) (led tl hdd & wknd over 3f out) 7.13
   327 Shining Wood **(43)** *(JSWainwright)* 4–9-2 ‡7GParkin (12) (cl up tl wknd ent st) ³/₄.14
       Woodland Ride **(47)** *(JGFitzGerald)* 3–8-7 ‡7MHunt (14) (prom tl wknd 4f out) 15.15

**4/1** Chart Cross, **9/2** Not Yet, **13/2** COLD SHOWER (IRE), Ghylldale(op 8/1), **6/1** First Bid, **15/2** Banana Cufflinks (USA), **10/1** Be the Best, **12/1** Honey Boy Simba, **14/1** Shining Wood, Miss Parkes, **16/1** Kind Style, **25/1** Turning Heads, Woodland Ride, Noushy, **50/1** Corporate Type (IRE). CSF £31.62, CT £220.75. Tote £6.30: £2.10 £2.60 £3.20 (£10.50). Claremont Management Services (WORKSOP) bred by Leinster Stud in Ireland. 15 Rn; Bt in 4,200 gns                                                                      2m 5.3 (3.1)

SF—33/20/29/32/22/21

---

**1185**   SCARBOROUGH H'CAP (3-Y.O) (0-70) £2798.20 (£775.20: £370.60)
      **1m 100y**                                                      7-10 (7-11)

(Weights raised 6 lb)
 1012[6] **Kateb (IRE) (61)** *(RWArmstrong)* 9-4 BRaymond (3) (lw: hld up & bhd: gd hdwy ent st: led 1f out: r.o) .......................... —1
   884 Thornton Gate **(54)** (v) *(MHEasterby)* 8-11 MBirch (7) (swtg: led: clr over 2f out: hdd 1f out: no ex) .......................... 2¹/₂.2
  1145 Sea Lord **(40)** *(KWHogg)* 7-4⁽¹⁾ ‡7AGarth (8) (outpcd & wl bhd appr st: r.o wl fnl 2f) .......................... 6.3
 1004[5] Spray of Orchids **(53)** *(JEtherington)* 8-5 ‡5JWeaver (5) (chsd ldrs: effrt 3f out: one pce) .......................... 1¹/₂.4
  1051 Miss Kingfisher (USA) **(54)** (bl) *(SGNorton)* 8-11 KDarley (6) (swtg: chsd ldrs: drvn along appr st: no imp) .......................... 6.5
 1004[4] Comiskey Park (IRE) **(44)** *(DWChapman)* 8-1 SWood (1) (bhd: effrt u.p ent st: n.d) .......................... 3.6
       Noble Cause (IRE) **(59)** *(REarnshaw)* 9-2 JCarroll (10) (chsd ldrs to st: sn rdn & btn) .......................... 3.7
   767 Gold Belt **(57)** *(RHollinshead)* 8-7 ‡7MHumphries (2) (swtg: nvr trbld ldrs) nk.8
   963 Kentucky Rain **(64)** (Fav) *(JGFitzGerald)* 9-7 KFallon (4) (effrt appr st: sn btn) 1¹/₂.9
   963 Barmbrack **(51)** *(RMMWhitaker)* 8-8 ACulhane (9) (cl up to st: sn wknd) .......................... 3.10

**100/30** Kentucky Rain, **9/2** Thornton Gate, Spray of Orchids, **7/1** Comiskey Park (IRE), KATEB, **8/1** Noble Cause (IRE), **10/1** Gold Belt (IRE), Barmbrack, **12/1** Miss Kingfisher (USA), **20/1** Sea Lord. CSF £38.63, CT £565.44. Tote £6.80: £1.80 £2.30 £7.40 (£21.70). Mr Hamdan Al-Maktoum (NEWMARKET) bred by A. Tarry in Ireland. 10 Rn                                                          1m 45.5 (2.8)

SF—11/-/-/-/-/-

---

**1186**   HILARY NEEDLER TROPHY (Stks) (2-Y.O.F) £7050.00 (£2100.00: £1000.00: £450.00)
      **5f**                                                      7-35 (7-36)

   986★ **Jervia** *(JWWatts)* 8-10 BRaymond (3) (chsd ldrs: drvn along & wandered ¹/₂-wy: styd on u.p to ld cl home) .......................... —1
   721[2] Magic Pearl *(EJAlston)* 8-6 PRobinson (5) (led: edgd rt ins fnl f: jst ct) .......................... hd.2
  1046★ Willshe Gan *(DenysSmith)* 8-10 KFallon (7) (lw: outpcd early: hdwy whn n.m.r ¹/₂-wy: ev ch whn n.m.r ins fnl f) .......................... 1.3
  1057★ Princess Oberon (IRE) (Fav) *(MBell)* 8-10 MHills (2) (a chsng ldrs: rdn ¹/₂-wy: kpt on ins fnl f) .......................... ¹/₂.4
   886★ Petite Epaulette *(WJarvis)* 8-10 MTebbutt (1) (lw: trckd ldrs: effrt ¹/₂-wy: sn hrd drvn & styd on: no imp) .......................... s.h.5
  1092★ Area Girl *(SirMarkPrescott)* 8-10 GDuffield (6) (lw: chsd ldrs: outpcd whn hmpd ¹/₂-wy: n.d after) .......................... 1.6
   701★ Laurel Delight *(JBerry)* 8-10 JCarroll (4) (s.i.s: effrt u.p ¹/₂-wy: sn btn) .......................... 4.7

**11/4** Princess Oberon (IRE), **3/1** Petite Epaulette, **4/1** Area Girl, **9/2** JERVIA, **8/1** Willshe Gan, **12/1** Ors. CSF £46.53, Tote £5.10: £2.40 £3.90 (£19.80). Sheikh Mohammed (RICHMOND) bred by Sheikh Mohammed bin Rashid al Maktoum. 7 Rn                                                          63.2 sec (1.7)

SF—22/17/17/15/14/10

**1187**  GRP MASSEY SPRINT STKS  £3460.00 (£1030.00: £490.00: £220.00)
5f                                                                  8-05 (8-10)

**Branston Abby (IRE) (85)** *(JWharton)* 3-8-6 MBirch (4) (lw: stdd s: hdwy on bit to ld over 1f out: qcknd: comf) ............................. —**1**

872³ Martina (61) *(JWharton)* 4-8-9 PRobinson (7) (made most tl hdd over 1f out: kpt on wl) .............................................. 3.**2**

966⁵ Auction King (IRE) (63) *(ASmith)* 3-8-1 ‡⁵SMaloney (6) (lw: a chsng ldrs: kpt on one pce fnl 2f) ......................................... 3.**3**

685⁴ Real Stunner (72) *(MPNaughton)* 5-9-4 KFallon (3) (a.p: rdn ½-wy: no imp) 1½.**4**

719 Arctic Appeal (IRE) (90) (Fav) *(JBerry)* 3-8-10 JCarroll (2) (chsd ldrs 3f out: sn outpcd) .............................................. 3.**5**

1053³ Prince Belfort (67) *(MPNaughton)* 4-9-0 ‡JWeaver (5) (lw: disp ld to ½-wy: sn rdn & btn) ........................................... ½.**6**

1006* Haunting Rhapsody (USA) *(JEtherington)* 3-8-3 KDarley (1) (sn drvn along & bhd: n.d) ........................................... 2½.**7**

5/2 Arctic Appeal (IRE), **100/30** Martina, **9/2** Haunting Rhapsody (USA), **5/1** BRANSTON ABBY (IRE), **8/1** Real Stunner, **9/1** Prince Belfort, **16/1** Auction King (IRE). CSF £20.49, Tote £6.20: £3.50 1.90 (£17.70). Mr J. David Abell (MELTON MOWBRAY) bred by John David Abell in Ireland. 7 Rn  61.5 sec (equals standard)
SF—52/38/43/23/34/13/16

**1188**  DERBY NIGHT H'CAP (3-Y.O) (0-70) £2954.00 (£819.00: £392.00)
1m 3f 216y (Weights raised 6 lb)                                    8-35 (8-36)

798² **Moor Lodge (USA) (64)** *(MHTompkins)* 9-7 PRobinson (8) (hld up & bhd: stdy hdwy to ld appr fnl f: sn clr) ......................... —**1**

1052² Reach for Glory (55) *(RMWhitaker)* 8-12 AClhane (3) (lw: hld up: hdwy ent st: rdn to ld wl over 1f out: sn hdd & nt qcknd) ...... 2½.**2**

745³ Pharlander (IRE) (46) *(MHEasterby)* 7-12 ‡⁵SMaloney (2) (a chsng ldrs: rdn 3f out: r.o one pce) .................................. 2½.**3**

Stingray City (USA) (57) *(JEtherington)* 9-0 KDarley (4) (in tch: effrt ent st: no imp) .................................................... 3.**4**

880⁴ Arctic Splendour (USA) (58) (Fav) *(PWChapple-Hyam)* 9-1 MHills (7) (b.off hind: trckd ldrs: effrt & ev ch over 2f out: grad wknd) ...... hd.**5**

370 Bashamah (IRE) (58) *(CEBrittain)* 9-1 MBirch (6) (hmpd after 1f: jnd ldr 8f out: wknd 2f out) ...................................... 3½.**6**

798³ Kadari (59) *(AHarrison)* 9-2 KFallon (1) (lw: led after 2f tl hdd wl over 1f out: sn wknd) .............................................. hd.**7**

1052 Desert Mist (40) *(SirMarkPrescott)* 7-11 JLowe (9) (drvn along thrght: n.d) ..... 1½.**8**

963 Clean Singer (43) *(NBycroft)* 8-0 LCharnock (5) (bit bkwd: led 2f: chsd ldrs tl wknd 2f out) ...................................... 2½.**9**

3/1 Arctic Splendour (USA), **4/1** Pharlander (IRE), MOOR LODGE (USA), **11/2** Kadari, **13/2** Reach for Glory, **7/1** Stingray City (USA), **9/1** Bashamah (IRE), **12/1** Desert Mist, **33/1** Clean Singer. CSF £30.32, CT £104.75. Tote £5.90: £2.00 2.40 1.40 (£23.20). Mr B. Schmidt-Bodner (NEWMARKET) bred by Craig Singer in USA. 9 Rn
2m 36.9 (5.3)
SF—6/–/–/–/–/–

**1189**  WELTON STKS (Mdn) £2186.80 (£604.80: £288.40)  1m 100y  9-05 (9-05)

922² **Forest Dew (USA)** (Fav) *(MHTompkins)* 3-8-5 PRobinson (1) (a gng wl: hld up: hdwy on bit to ld ins fnl f: shkn up & qcknd) ......... —**1**

1012⁵ Fairford *(JGFitzGerald)* 3-8-10 KFallon (2) (lw: cl up: led wl over 2f out: sn rdn & r.o: nt pce of wnr wl ins fnl f) ................... 1½.**2**

Knight Pawn *(JPLeigh)* 3-8-5 ‡⁵JWeaver (5) (w'like: leggy: bit bkwd: cl up: rdn over 2f out: r.o) .......................................... 2.**3**

Qualitair Memory (IRE) *(JFBottomley)* 3-8-10 JLowe (3) (set slow pce: qcknd appr st: hdd wl over 2f out: sn outpcd) .............. 5.**4**

2/5 FOREST DEW (USA), **11/4** Fairford, **8/1** Knight Pawn, **20/1** Qualitair Memory (IRE). CSF £2.06, Tote £1.40 (£1.60). Ecurie Fustok (NEWMARKET) bred by Buckram Oak Farm in USA. 4 Rn  1m 53.6 (10.9)
T/Plpt: £312.90 (7.5 Tckts).                                            AA

# BEVERLEY (R-H)
## Thursday, June 4th [Good]
Going Allowance: 5f: 0.10 sec (G); Rnd: minus 0.10 sec per fur (F)        Wind: mod across
Stalls: high

**1190**  BRANTINGHAM H'CAP (0-70) £2964.80 (£822.80: £394.40)  **2m 35y**  2-20 (2-21)
(Weights raised 2 lb)

1119 **Cost Effective (32)** *(MBrittain)* 5-7-10 GBardwell (6) (lw: in tch: hdwy ent st: rdn to ld ins fnl f: styd on wl) ...................... —**1**

675 King William (31) *(JLSpearing)* 7-7-9 JLowe (4) (lw: hld up: hdwy 7f out: led 2f out tl ins fnl f: one pce) .................................................. 1½.2

1002³ Domain (55) (bl) *(RJWeaver)* 4-8-13 ‡⁵RPrice (3) (chsd ldrs: led 5f out to 2f out: one pce) .................................................. 1½.3

683 Topcliffe (41) (v) *(MrsVAAconley)* 5-8-5 LCharnock (2) (in tch: effrt ent st: one pce appr fnl f) .................................................. 2½.4

987 Lidanzia (40) *(RJHolder)* 4-8-3 JQuinn (5) (in tch: effrt 4f out: no imp fnl 2f) ...... ¾.5

951 Newark Antiquefair (31) *(BCMorgan)* 4-7-1(1) ‡⁷DarrenMoffatt (12) (bhd: reminders ½-wy: styd on fnl 3f: n.d) .................................................. 8.6

708 Beldale Star (60) *(RAkehurst)* 9-9-7 ‡³RPerham (13) (b: trckd ldrs: effrt appr st: wknd 3f out) .................................................. 1½.7

923⁴ Sarsta Grai (50) *(MHEasterby)* 4-8-13 MBirch (8) (lw: cl up: led ½-wy tl hdd 5f out: wknd 3f out) .................................................. 5.8

908⁵ Sandro (60) (Fav) *(JRFanshawe)* 3-8-4 GDuffield (11) (in tch: drvn along appr st: sn wknd) .................................................. 10.9

810⁴ Escadaro (USA) (50) *(SGNorton)* 3-7-1(1) ‡⁷CHawksley (9) (a bhd) .................................................. 2.10

974⁵ Nipotina (44) *(RHollinshead)* 6-8-1 ‡⁷AGarth (7) (bhd fr ½-wy) .................................................. 8.11

987 Quip (33) *(MPNaughton)* 7-7-11 JakiHouston (10) (b.hind: led to ½-wy: sn lost pl) .................................................. ½.12

893 Haut-Brion (IRE) (59) *(PWChapple-Hyam)* 3-8-3 DHolland (1) (lw: chsd ldr tl wknd appr st: eased fnl 2f) .................................................. 15.13

LONG HANDICAP: Newark Antiquefair 7-3, Escadaro (USA) 6-11.

**100/30** Sandro, **5/1** King William, **6/1** Sarsta Grai, **13/2** Beldale Star, **8/1** Nipotina, Lidanzia, **12/1** Topcliffe, **14/1** Domain, Haut-Brion (IRE), **16/1** Quip, COST EFFECTIVE, **20/1** Newark Antiquefair, **33/1** Escadaro (USA). CSF £93.80, CT £1,080.24. Tote £15.40: £4.80 £1.70 £10.90 (£69.10). Miss D. J. Woods (WARTHILL) bred by Miss S. Von Schilcher. 13 Rn
3m 39.2 (8.5)

**1191** ETTON CLAIMING 3TK3 (2-Y.O) £1100.00 (£004.00: ££00.40) **5f** £ 66 (£ 67)

769★ **Purchased by Phone (IRE)** (Fav) *(PCHaslam)* 8-6 DMcKeown (2) (led tl hdd ins fnl f: no ex: fin 2nd, 1½zl: awrdd r) .................................................. —1

Ban Ri (IRE) *(MHTompkins)* 8-3 PRobinson (1) (small: unf: trckd ldrs: effrt 2f out: nt qckn: fin 3rd, 1l: plcd 2nd) .................................................. 2

759★ Classic Storm *(JBerry)* 8-5 JCarroll (7) (chsd ldrs: outpcd whn hmpd over 1f out: no imp after: fin 4th, nk: plcd 3rd) .................................................. 3

1149² Costa Verde *(KWHogg)* 8-5 GHind (3) (lw: chsd ldrs: squeezed thro appr fnl f: led ins fnl f: fin 1st: disq: plcd 4th) .................................................. 4

574³ Plum First *(NBycroft)* 8-12 NDay (8) (chsd ldrs: outpcd ½-wy: n.m.r: swtchd & styd on) .................................................. 2.5

Cizard (IRE) *(AWPotts)* 8-6 AProud (6) (small: cmpt: nvr wnt pce) .................................................. 7.6

769 Cheltenham Windows *(MWEasterby)* 8-8 TLucas (5) (b.hind: sn outpcd & bhd) 10.7

Native Worth *(JMJefferson)* 8-8 JLowe (4) (cmpt: bkwd: s.s: a wl bhd) .................................................. 5.8

*Stewards Enquiry: Costa Verde disq. (interference to Classic Storm). Hind suspended 13-16/6/92 (careless riding).*

**4/7** PURCHASED BY PHONE (IRE), **9/2** Classic Storm, **15/2** Ban Ri (IRE), **10/1** Costa Verde(7/1—12/1), **20/1** Plum First, **25/1** Native Worth, **50/1** Ors. CSF £5.58, Tote £1.60: £1.10 £1.10 £1.40 (£3.80). Mr S. A. B. Dinsmore (MIDDLEHAM) bred by Miss V. Charlton in Ireland. 8 Rn; Purchased by Phone clmd D Walker £9,001
65 sec (3.5)
SF—31/26/19/20/19/–

**1192** GRP MASSEY TROPHY (Stks) (2-Y.O) £7050.00 (£2100.00: £1000.00: £450.00) **5f** 3-25 (3-26)

874² **Rock Symphony** *(AAScott)* 8-11 JFortune (8) (lw: mde most: qcknd 2f out: styd on u.p) .................................................. —1

1071★ Saint Express *(RMWhitaker)* 8-13 ACulhane (7) (a chsng ldrs: rdn 2f out: styd on nr fin) .................................................. 2.2

Satank (USA) *(JWWatts)* 8-11 GDuffield (4) (w'like: str: scope: a chsng ldrs: rdn 2f out: kpt on wl) .................................................. 2.3

943² Lord Olivier (IRE) (Fav) *(WJarvis)* 9-1 MTebbutt (2) (lw: w ldrs: rdn 2f out: wknd 1f out) .................................................. 1.4

Bob's Return (IRE) *(MHTompkins)* 8-11 PRobinson (3) (w'like: str: s.s: hdwy after 2f: nvr able to chal) .................................................. 4.5

793★ Glowing Value (IRE) *(JBerry)* 9-1 JCarroll (6) (disp ld tl grad wknd fr ½-wy) ...... nk.6

961³ Whisperdales *(MWEllerby)* 9-2 SMorris (5) (swtg: sn drvn along & nvr trbld ldrs) 6.7

463★ Norstano *(MHEasterby)* 9-1 MBirch (1) (sn outpcd & bhd) .................................................. 1½.8

**9/4** Lord Olivier (IRE), **100/30** Saint Express, **7/2** Bob's Return (IRE), **4/1** ROCK SYMPHONY, **8/1** Glowing Value (IRE), **10/1** Norstano, Satank (USA), **33/1** Whisperdales. CSF £18.83, Tote £6.60: £1.90 £1.10 £2.90 (£8.00). Sir Anthony Page-Wood (NEWMARKET) bred by J. R. and Mrs Haggas. 8 Rn
64.3 sec (2.8)
SF—51/45/35/35/15/18

**1193** SATURDAY MARKET H'CAP (0-80) £2703.00 (£748.00: £357.00)
7f 100y

4-00 (4-00)

10185 **Major Mouse (69)** *(WWHaigh)* 4-9-10 ACulhane (1) (lw: hld up: effrt over 2f out: r.o to ld ins fnl f) ...... —1
1018★ American Hero (71) *(CTinkler)* 4-9-7 ‡5JWeaver (3) (led tl hdd ins fnl f: kpt on wl) ¾.2
10722 Straw Thatch (72) *(MJohnston)* 3-9-3 DMcKeown (8) (trckd ldr: chal over 1f out: kpt on wl) ...... nk.3
1093★ Kummel King (58) (Fav) *(EJAlston)* 4-8-13 (6x) KFallon (4) (lw: a chsng ldrs: effrt over 2f out: r.o one pce) ...... 2½.4
1018 Veloce (IRE) (55) *(MO'Neill)* 4-8-10 JFortune (6) (lw: trckd ldrs: chal over 2f out: rdn & btn over 1f out) ...... 2.5
1090 Sly Prospect (USA) (69) (v) *(KWhite)* 4-9-3 ‡7AGarth (5) (bhd tl sme late hdwy) 2½.6
1032 Prepare (IRE) (47) *(RJHolder)* 4-8-2 JQuinn (2) (hld up: effrt ent st: n.d) ...... ¾.7
10893 Gant Bleu (FR) *(RMWhitaker)* 5-7-11 ‡3JFanning (9) (stdd s: plld hrd: hdwy ent st: sn rdn: wknd 2f out) ...... 2.8
10936 Flashy's Son (54) *(MDHammond)* 4-8-9 MBirch (7) (plld hrd: prom to st) ...... 12.9

11/4 Kummel King, 5/1 Straw Thatch, Veloce (IRE), American Hero, 7/1 MAJOR MOUSE, 9/1 Gant Bleu (FR), 10/1 Prepare (IRE), 25/1 Ors. CSF £38.57, CT £170.27. Tote £8.20: £2.10 £2.30 £1.60 (£29.10). Mr N. Barber (MALTON) bred by Mrs V. Haigh. 9 Rn
1m 34.3 (4.1)
SF—38/33/28/16/7/6/

**1194** WATT MEMORIAL STKS £3318.75 (£990.00: £472.50: £213.75)
1m 3f 216y

4-35 (4-35)

8554 **Torchon (103)** (Fav) *(GWragg)* 4-9-12 MHills (2) (a gng wl: led wl over 1f out: pushed along & sn qcknd clr) ...... —1
855 Spinning (100) *(IABalding)* 5-9-9 ‡3SO'Gorman (4) (led tl hdd wl over 1f out: no ch w wnr) ...... 7.2
1005 Shirley Ann *(RJWeaver)* 9-8-9 JLowe (3) (chsd ldrs: outpcd ent st: sn no ch) . 15.3
Master's Crown (USA) *(MCChapman)* 4-8-7 ‡7SWilliams (1) (disp ld after 4f tl wknd wl over 2f out) ...... 3½.4

4/9 TORCHON, 2/1 Spinning, 33/1 Master's Crown (USA), 100/1 Shirley Ann. CSF £1.56, Tote £1.40 (£1.20). Sir Robin McAlpine (NEWMARKET) bred by Sir Robin McAlpine. 4 Rn
2m 36.5 (4.9)
SF—51/34/–/–/

**1195** GRANDSTAND H'CAP (0-70) £3131.40 (£870.40: £418.20) 1m 1f 207y 5-10 (5-11)

**Sarah-Clare (51)** (Jt-Fav) *(RAkehurst)* 4-8-9 ‡3RPerham (9) (hdwy & prom 4f out: led over 1f out: r.o wl) ...... —1
963 Nicely Thanks (USA) (66) (Jt-Fav) *(TDBarron)* 3-9-0 AlexGreaves (16) (lw: s.i.s: hmpd after 2f: hdwy ent st: r.o wl fnl f) ...... 2½.2
Aardvark (67) *(RMWhitaker)* 6-10-0 ACulhane (2) (lw: mde most tl hdd over 1f out: edgd lft & nt qckn) ...... nk.3
10184 Who's Tef (IRE) (60) *(MHEasterby)* 4-9-2 ‡5SMaloney (18) (lw: a cl up: kpt on one pce fnl 2f) ...... 1½.4
1051 Sinclair Lad (IRE) (55) *(RHollinshead)* 4-9-2 MBirch (7) (prom: effrt ent st: nt qckn appr fnl f) ...... 1.5
761 Statia (IRE) (35) *(DonEnricoIncisa)* 4-7-10 JakiHouston (13) (cl up: rdn ent st: wknd over 1f out) ...... hd.6
7623 Thakawah (65) *(RWArmstrong)* 3-8-13 BCrossley (11) (a chsng ldrs: effrt 3f out: r.o one pce) ...... 2½.7
498 Futures Gift (IRE) (59) *(AWPotts)* 3-8-7 AProud (4) (lw: hmpd & lost pl after 2f: hdwy ent st: no imp) ...... 2½.8
974 Athene Noctua (35) *(BAMcMahon)* 7-7-10 GBardwell (15) (lw: bhd tl styd on fnl 2f) ...... ½.9
9636 Stoproveritate (54) *(SGNorton)* 3-8-2 LCharnock (12) (prom whn stumbled bdly after 2f: outpcd ent st: sn no ch) ...... hd.10
9463 Bilberry (52) *(CWCElsey)* 3-8-0 DaleGibson (10) (unruly gng to post: plld hrd: n.d) ...... ½.11
11104 Persian House (60) *(JMJefferson)* 5-9-7 JCarroll (5) (lw: hmpd after s: sn bhd: effrt appr st: sn wknd) ...... s.h.12
1150 Kinoko (48) *(KWHogg)* 4-8-9 GHind (14) (a bhd) ...... 1.13
9124 Jagged Edge (44) *(RJHolder)* 5-8-5 JQuinn (1) (mid div: effrt ent st: wknd 2f out) ...... ½.14
10512 Marjons Boy (32) (bl) *(CDBroad)* 5-7-7 NCarlisle (3) (a bhd) ...... ¾.15
913 Strength in Depth (IRE) (45) *(MJohnston)* 4-8-6 DMcKeown (17) (chsd ldrs to st) ...... hd.16
Top Scale (45) *(WWHaigh)* 6-8-6 NConnorton (6) (bit bkwd: hmpd after 2f: n.d) 5.17
LONG HANDICAP: Marjons Boy 7-2.

**4/1** SARAH-CLARE, Nicely Thanks (USA), **6/1** Who's Tef (IRE), **8/1** Marjons Boy, **9/1** Jagged Edge, **11/1** Thakawah, **12/1** Bilberry, **14/1** Athene Noctua, Stoproveritate, Top Scale, Persian House, **16/1** Sinclair Lad (IRE), Futures Gift (IRE), **20/1** Strength in Depth (IRE), **33/1** Ors. CSF £22.41, CT £462.54. Tote £3.20: £1.40 £1.10 £12.20 £1.90 (£12.10). Miss Clare Coyne (EPSOM) bred by M. F. Kentish. 17 Rn      2m 7.7 (5.7)

SF—28/28/41/26/24/3

T/Plpt: £34.60 (99.35 Tckts).      AA

# EPSOM (L-H)
## Wednesday, June 3rd [Good, Good to soft fnl 4f]
Going Allowance: nil sec per fur (G)      Wind: almost nil

Stalls: 5f high, remainder low

### 1196
SILVER SEAL WOODCOTE STKS (2-Y.O) £8415.00 (£2520.00: £1210.00: £555.00)
**6f**      2-15 (2-15)

| | | | |
|---|---|---|---|
| 988[2] | **Green's Bid** (PFICole) 8-11 TQuinn (3) (2nd st: led 2f out: r.o wl) | | —1 |
| | Ihtiraz (Fav) (HThomsonJones) 8-8 RHills (2) (unf: scope: lw: 4th st: ev ch fnl 2f: r.o) | | nk.2 |
| 1118* | Night Melody (IRE) (RHannon) 9-2 KDarley (5) (5th st: rdn 2f out: r.o one pce) | | 3½.3 |
| | Final Frontier (IRE) (RAkehurst) 8-8 WCarson (1) (cmpt: led 4f) | | 3½.4 |
| 416[4] | Two Moves in Front (IRE) (JBerry) 9-2 JCarroll (7) (lw: 6th st: no hdwy fnl 2f) | | 8.5 |
| 1039* | Fierro (CEBrittain) 9-2 SCauthen (4) (3rd st: wknd 2f out) | | 8.6 |
| | Hillsdown Boy (IRE) (SDow) 8-8 PaulEddery (6) (str: bit bkwd: s.s: a wl bhd) | | 2.7 |

**15/8** Ihtiraz, **9/4** GREEN'S BID(op 6/4), **9/2** Night Melody (IRE), **7/1** Fierro, **16/1** Two Moves in Front (IRE)(op 8/1), **Final Frontier** (IRE), **33/1** Hillsdown Boy (IRE). CSF £6.42, Tote £3.00: £1.90 £1.80 (£3.80). Richard Green (Fine Paintings) (WHATCOMBE) bred by Stud-On-The-Chart. 7 Rn      1m 10.64 (2.64)

SF—44/40/34/12/–/–

### 1197
DIOMED STKS (Gp 3) £19293.00 (£7164.40: £3394.70: £1427.90)
**1m 114y**      2-45 (2-48)

| | | | |
|---|---|---|---|
| 842a[4] | **Zaahi** (USA) (116) (Jt-Fav) (HThomsonJones) 3–8-5 RHills (4) (lw: 2nd st: led over 2f out: r.o wl) | | —1 |
| 991[4] | Misterioso (102) (DRCElsworth) 3–8-0 AMunro (2) (swtg: 6th st: hdwy 2f out: r.o: nt rch wnr) | | 2½.2 |
| 563 | Pfalz (104) (MRStoute) 4–8-13 WRSwinburn (5) (hdwy fnl 2f: nvr nrr) | | 1½.3 |
| 929* | Flashfoot (107) (IABalding) 4–9-4 RCochrane (6) (lw: 5th st: no hdwy fnl 2f) | | nk.4 |
| 557[5] | Mohican Girl (103) (JRFanshawe) 4–8-13 SCauthen (3) (4th st: hrd rdn over 2f out: r.o one pce) | | s.h.5 |
| 824[2] | Sylva Honda (105) (CEBrittain) 4–9-7 MRoberts (1) (lw: led tl over 2f out) | | 1½.6 |
| 862[3] | Fair Crack (IRE) (109) (RHannon) 3–8-5 MJKinane (8) (dwlt: a bhd) | | 5.7 |
| 1058* | Susurration (USA) (111) (Jt-Fav) (JHMGosden) 5–9-2 WCarson (9) (a bhd) | | hd.8 |
| 825* | Mizaaya (90) (MRStoute) 3–8-5 PatEddery (7) (lw: 3rd st: wknd 3f out) | | 10.9 |

**100/30** ZAAHI (USA), Susurration (USA), **4/1** Mizaaya, **8/1** Mohican Girl, **9/1** Flashfoot(op 6/1), **10/1** Fair Crack (IRE), Sylva Honda, **20/1** Misterioso, **33/1** Pfalz. CSF £53.34, Tote £3.90: £1.60 £3.50 £5.80 (£51.30). Mr Hamdan Al-Maktoum (NEWMARKET) bred by Shadwell Farm Incorporated in USA. 9 Rn      1m 43.50 (2.50)

SF—54/41/49/53/47/49

### 1198
EVER READY DERBY STKS (Gp 1) (3-Y.O.C & F) £355000.00 (£133000.00: £64000.00: £28000.00)
**1½m 10y**      3-45 (3-49)

| | | | |
|---|---|---|---|
| 741a | **Dr Devious** (IRE) (PWChapple-Hyam) 9-0 JReid (4) (b.off hind: 3rd st: led wl over 1f out: drvn out) | | —1 |
| 840a* | St Jovite (USA) (JSBolger,Ireland) 9-0 CRoche (2) (leggy: scope: rdn along: 4th st: r.o one pce fnl 2f) | | 2.2 |
| 655[4] | Silver Wisp (USA) (GLewis) 9-0 PaulEddery (5) (hdwy 3f out: rdn 2f out: edgd lft: r.o) | | s.h.3 |
| 655[5] | Muhtarram (USA) (JHMGosden) 9-0 WCarson (16) (lw: 7th st: r.o one pce fnl 2f) | | 3½.4 |
| 711* | Twist and Turn (HRACecil) 9-0 MJKinane (10) (lw: led after 2f tl wl over 1f out) | | 2½.5 |
| 820[5] | Alflora (IRE) (CEBrittain) 9-0 TQuinn (11) (lw: 8th st: one pce fnl 3f) | | 2½.6 |
| 820* | Alnasr Alwasheek (MRStoute) 9-0 SCauthen (18) (lw: 9th st: hrd rdn 2f out: no hdwy) | | hd.7 |
| 820[2] | Great Palm (USA) (PFICole) 9-0 AMunro (14) (lw: 2nd st: wknd 2f out) | | 1.8 |
| 953a* | Rodrigo de Triano (USA) (Fav) (PWChapple-Hyam) 9-0 LPiggott (19) (swtg: nvr nrr) | | 2.9 |
| 655 | Thourios (GHarwood) 9-0 MRoberts (7) (nvr nr to chal) | | 2½.10 |

842a² Rainbow Corner *(AFabre,France)* 9-0 PatEddery (3) (unf: scope: 6th st: wknd
3f out) ................................................ nk.11
930⁵ Well Saddled (IRE) *(DRCElsworth)* 9-0 JWilliams (1) (lw: a bhd) .................. 2.12
781★ Assessor (IRE) *(RHannon)* 9-0 WRSwinburn (13) (a wl bhd) ................... 6.13
873² Paradise Navy *(CEBrittain)* 9-0 GDuffield (6) (a wl bhd) ..................... 10.14
940² Lobilio (USA) *(CEBrittain)* 9-0 RHills (9) (lw: wl bhd fnl 6f) ................ 2.15
556★ Pollen Count (USA) *(JHMGosden)* 9-0 LDettori (17) (lw: plld hrd: led 2f: 5th st:
wknd over 3f out) ..................... 1½.16
927⁵ Ninja Dancer (USA) *(MrsJCecil)* 9-0 MHills (8) (lw: bhd fnl 3f) ............... ¾.17
927⁴ Young Freeman (USA) *(GHarwood)* 9-0 BRaymond (12) (lw: wl bhd fnl 6f) .... 20.18
820⁴ *Young Senor (USA)* (28/1) Withdrawn ( ref to ent stalls) : not under orders

**13/2** Rodrigo de Triano (USA), **8/1** DR DEVIOUS (IRE), **9/1** Alnasr Alwasheek, Assessor (IRE), Rainbow Corner,
Muhtarram (USA), **10/1** Great Palm (USA), **11/1** Silver Wisp (USA), **12/1** Twist and Turn, **14/1** Pollen Count
(USA), St Jovite (USA), **50/1** Thourios, **66/1** Young Freeman (USA), **100/1** Ninja Dancer (USA), **150/1** Well
Saddled (IRE), **200/1** Alflora (IRE), **250/1** Ors. CSF £91.72, CT £1,014.25. Tote £8.10: £2.70 £4.50 £2.40
(£82.80). Mr Sidney H. Craig (MARLBOROUGH) bred by Lyonstown Stud in Ireland. 18 Rn  2m 36.19 (1.19)
SF—88/84/83/76/71/66/65

**1199**    NIGHT RIDER H'CAP (0-105) £14330.00 (£4340.00: £2120.00: £1010.00)
5f                                                                    4-35 (4-38)

819⁶ **Viceroy (90)** (bl) *(WJPearce)* 5-9-1 RCochrane (17) (a.p: led wl over 1f out: r.o
wl) ............................................................. —1
819⁴ Farfelu **(95)** (bl) *(WRMuir)* 5-9-6 SWhitworth (4) (swtg: a.p: r.o ins fnl f) ......... 2½.2
996★ Ashtina **(68)** *(RJHodges)* 7-7-7 JQuinn (10) (swtg: w ldr: led over 2f out tl wl
over 1f out: edgd lft: nt qckn) .......................... ¾.3
998★ Love Returned **(83)** *(WJarvis)* 5-8-8 MTebbutt (3) (hdwy fnl 2f: nvr nrr) ......... ¾.4
779 Olifantsfontein **(79)** (bl) *(RSimpson)* 4-8-4 TQuinn (13) (lw: a.p: nt qckn fnl f) .. hd.5
1028² Gallant Hope **(68)** (bl) *(LGCottrell)* 10-7-7 RFox (1) (lw: hdwy fnl f: r.o) .......... ½.6
Loft Boy **(70)** (bl) *(JDBethell)* 9-7-9 SDawson (14) (s.s: hdwy over 1f out: r.o) s.h.7
980³ Absolution **(81)** (Fav) *(MPNaughton)* 8-8-6 MRoberts (18) (no hdwy fnl 2f) ....... 1.8
480 Touch of White **(83)** *(JEBanks)* 6-8-8 AMunro (7) (nvr nr to chal) ............. ¾.9
894³ Sylvan Breeze **(84)** *(PMitchell)* 4-8-9 MJKinane (12) (hdwy fnl f: nvr nrr) ........ nk.10
945 Mertola's Pet **(76)** *(LGCottrell)* 6-8-1 NCarlisle (15) (lw: led over 2f: dead) ... 1½.11
813⁶ Terrhars (IRE) **(103)** *(RHannon)* 4-9-11 ‡³RPerham (2) (n.d) ...................... hd.12
735 Slip-a-Snip **(71)** *(GBBalding)* 5-7-5⁽³⁾ ‡⁵DHarrison (19) (lw: n.d) ............... nk.13
1064⁵ Miami Banker **(75)** (bl) *(PHowling)* 6-8-0 NAdams (16) (n.d) ................... ¾.14
876³ Sir Tasker **(74)** *(JLHarris)* 4-7-13 WCarson (6) (n.d) ........................ nk.15
723⁴ Never in the Red **(94)** (bl) *(JBerry)* 4-9-6 JCarroll (11) (lw: n.d) ............... hd.16
1053⁵ Heaven-Liegh-Grey **(89)** *(MJohnston)* 4-9-0 DMcKeown (9) (lw: n.d) ........... nk.17
996⁶ Joe Sugden **(68)** (v) *(PHowling)* 8-7-7 Seb.WilliamsWilliams (8) (rdr lost irons ½-wy:
t.o) ............................................ 12.18

LONG HANDICAP: Gallant Hope 6-2, Slip-a-Snip 7-5, Joe Sugden 6-12.

**6/1** Absolution, **13/2** VICEROY, **15/2** Ashtina(12/1—7/1), **10/1** Mertola's Pet, Olifantsfontein(12/1—8/1), **11/1**
Slip-a-Snip, **12/1** Farfelu, **14/1** Never in the Red, Miami Banker, **16/1** Sir Tasker, Terrhars (IRE), Love Returned,
Sylvan Breeze, **20/1** Touch of White, Loft Boy, **25/1** Heaven-Liegh-Grey, **33/1** Ors. CSF £78.06, CT £555.11.
Tote £7.50: £2.00 £3.20 £3.00 £2.70 (£38.10). Mr Franco Gamma (HAMBLETON) bred by Jeremy Green and
Sons. 18 Rn                                                       55.69 sec (1.19)
SF—77/72/42/54/49/36/37

**1200**    BUTTERLEY BRICK H'CAP (0-110) £13550.00 (£4100.00: £2000.00: £950.00)
1¼m 18y                                                              5-10 (5-14)

854⁴ **Hashar (IRE) (89)** *(DRCElsworth)* 4-9-0 WCarson (2) (4th st: led over 2f out:
r.o wl) ............................................. —1
479³ Fire Top **(91)** (Fav) *(RAkehurst)* 7-9-2 TQuinn (3) (lw: 2nd st: led 3f out tl over 2f
out: r.o) .......................................... 1.2
829⁶ Double Echo (IRE) **(71)** *(JDBethell)* 4-7-10 TyroneWilliams (6) (lw: 5th st: ev ch
2f out: nt qckn) ................................... 12.3
929⁶ Knifebox (USA) **(103)** *(JHMGosden)* 4-9-10 SCauthen (1) (lw: led 7f) ............. nk.4
726² Mellaby (USA) **(100)** *(MRStoute)* 4-9-11 PatEddery (5) (lw: 6th st: a bhd) ......... 7.5
829★ Andrath (IRE) **(85)** *(CEBrittain)* 4-8-10 MRoberts (7) (swtg: 3rd st: wknd over 2f
out) .............................................. 5.6
887² Spanish Grandee (USA) **(78)** *(PWChapple-Hyam)* 4-8-3 PaulEddery (8) (b.nr
hind: in rr fnl 4f) ................................ 10.7

**5/2** Fire Top, **4/1** Mellaby (USA), **5/1** Andrath (IRE), **6/1** Spanish Grandee (USA), Double Echo (IRE), Knifebox
(USA), **14/1** HASHAR (IRE). CSF £46.49, CT £215.71. Tote £11.90: £4.10 £2.00 (£18.30). Mr W. J. Brown
(WHITSBURY) bred by H. H. Aga Khan in Ireland. 7 Rn                                2m 5.70 (1.20)
SF—88/88/44/75/58/33

## 1201

CRAVEN H'CAP (0-100) £7035.00 (£2130.00: £1040.00: £495.00)   **7f**  5-45 (5-49)

860* Go Executive **(87)** *(CEBrittain)* 4–9-3 MRoberts (1) (mde all: r.o wl) ................ —1
775 Surrey Racing **(66)** (Fav) *(GLewis)* 4–7-10(1) WCarson (3) (4th st: chsd wnr fnl
3f: r.o) ................................................................................................... 1.2
813 Bold Habit **(88)** *(WJPearce)* 7–9-4 DNicholls (7) (lw: gd hdwy 2f out: nt qckn ins
fnl f) ....................................................................................................... 1.3
42 Helios **(70)** *(RSimpson)* 4–7-9(6) ‡5ATucker (2) (hdwy fnl 2f: nvr nrr) .............. s.h.4
824(6) Parliament Piece **(98)** *(RMWhitaker)* 6–10-0 LPiggott (10) (lw: 3rd st: ev ch over
1f out: one pce) ..................................................................................... nk.5
941* Cape Pigeon (USA) **(87)** *(LGCottrell)* 7–9-3 AMunro (14) (lw: hdwy over 2f out:
one pce) ................................................................................................ nk.6
1028* How's Yer Father **(78)** *(RJHodges)* 6–8-5 (5x) ‡3TSprake (13) (hdwy 3f out: one
pce fnl 2f) ............................................................................................. nk.7
860(3) Foolish Touch **(63)** (v) *(WJMusson)* 10–7-7 JQuinn (4) (swtg: wl bhd tl r.o fnl 2f) 1.8
800(2) Vanroy **(66)** (v) *(JRJenkins)* 8–7-5(2) ‡5DHarrison (11) (hdwy over 2f out: wknd
over 1f out) ........................................................................................... hd.9
1032 Dream Carrier (IRE) **(68)** (bl) *(RHannon)* 4–7-5 ‡7AWhelan (5) (a mid div) ......... 1.10
1021(2) Deprecator (USA) **(89)** *(JHMGosden)* 4–9-5 RCochrane (9) (b.hind: lw: a bhd) s.h.11
747* Just a Step **(83)** *(MMcCormack)* 6–8-13 JReid (6) (6th st: wknd over 2f out) .... 3.12
941 Caroles Express **(80)** *(RAkehurst)* 4–8-10 TQuinn (12) (lw: 5th st: wknd over 2f
out) ...................................................................................................... 2.13
1021* Nordic Brave **(76)** *(MBrittain)* 6–8-6(1) (5x) PatEddery (8) (2nd st: wknd over 2f
out) .................................................................................................... ¾.14

LONG HANDICAP: Foolish Touch 7-5.

**5/1** Surrey Racing, **11/2** Cape Pigeon (USA), **6/1** Deprecator (USA)(op 7/2), **15/2** Bold Habit, **11/1** Parliament
Piece, **12/1** Just a Step, Vanroy, Foolish Touch, **14/1** Nordic Brave, GO EXECUTIVE, Caroles Express, **16/1** How's
Yer Father, **33/1** Dream Carrier (IRE), **66/1** Helios. CSF £75.67, CT £522.30. Tote £19.70: £4.60 £2.20 £2.70
(£45.50). Mr Mike Dawes (NEWMARKET) bred by Somerhall Bloodstock Ltd. 14 Rn                1m 23.53 (3.03)
                                                                        SF–58/34/53/29/61/49/36

T/Trio: Race 2: £411.70 (7.1 Tckts); Race 3: £232.80 (55.5. T/Jkpt: Not won; £25,709.70 to Epsom 4/6/92.
T/Plpt: £455.30 (83.15 Tckts).                                                                       Hn

## EPSOM (L-H)

### Thursday, June 4th [Good]

Going Allowance: nil sec per fur (G)                                        Wind: almost nil

Stalls: 5f high, remainder low

## 1202

STAFF INGHAM AUCTION STKS (2-Y.O) £3038.00 (£914.00: £442.00: £206.00)
**6f**                                                              2-00 (2-05)

867(2) Iommelli (IRE) (Fav) *(PAKelleway)* 8-8 MRoberts (1) (lw: 3rd st: plld out over 1f
out: qcknd to ld last strides) ................................................................. —1
817(6) Crusade (IRE) *(RHannon)* 9-0 JReid (4) (lw: led tl fnl strides) ...................... hd.2
973* No Reservations (IRE) *(RFJohnsonHoughton)* 7-13 ‡5DHarrison (5) (lw: 2nd st:
ev ch fnl 2f: r.o) ................................................................................... hd.3
1149(5) Calisar *(WGMTurner)* 8-6 ‡3TSprake (7) (s.s: 7th st: nrst fin) ........................ 6.4
423(3) Awesome Risk *(GLewis)* 7-8 ‡3FNorton (13) (nvr nrr) ................................. 2½.5
703 All Promises *(PButler)* 7-11 TyroneWilliams (9) (4th st: wknd over 2f out) ........ 4.6
446 Aberdeen Heather *(DRCElsworth)* 9-0 WCarson (3) (5th st: wknd over 2f out) .... hd.7
682(6) Wentbridge Lad (IRE) *(BAMcMahon)* 8-4(2) TQuinn (12) (nvr nr to chal) .......... nk.8
1039 No Extras (IRE) *(JSutcliffe)* 8-3(1) BRouse (6) (6th & hung rt st: wknd 3f out) ...... 2.9
907 Wickins *(GLewis)* 8-8 PaulEddery (11) (a bhd) ........................................ hd.10
Pondering *(SDow)* 8-2 WRyan (2) (cmpt: bit bkwd: a bhd) ......................... hd.11
339* Tuscan Dawn (8/1) Withdrawn (lame at s) : not under orders

**13/8** IOMMELLI (IRE), **7/2** No Reservations (IRE), Crusade (IRE), **9/1** Aberdeen Heather, **14/1** Wentbridge Lad
(IRE), **16/1** Awesome Risk, No Extras (IRE), **20/1** Pondering, Calisar, **25/1** Wickins, **50/1** All Promises. CSF
£8.22, Tote £2.30: £1.40 £1.60 £1.40 (£4.80). Mr G. Mazza (NEWMARKET) bred by Frank Barry in Ireland. 11
Rn                                                                             1m 11.53 (3.53)
                                                                        SF–23/28/12/–/–/–

## 1203

ARC H'CAP (0-90) £3533.50 (£1063.00: £514.00: £239.50)      **1m 114y**  2-35 (2-40)

1201 **Vanroy (64)** (v) *(JRJenkins)* 8–8-2 SWhitworth (2) (5th st: led ins fnl f: drvn out) —1
610 Barford Lad **(77)** *(JRFanshawe)* 5–9-1 WRSwinburn (3) (2nd st: led over 2f out
tl ins fnl f) ......................................................................................... 1½.2

Page 435

705* Jimlil **(79)** (Fav) *(BPalling)* 4-9-3 WRyan (1) (3rd st: nt clr run 2f out: r.o fnl f) .... 1.3
1061 Usa Dollar **(58)** *(BGubby)* 5-7-5(2) ‡5DHarrison (4) (wl bhd tl gd hdwy fnl 2f) ...... 3.4
887⁴ Brown Fairy (USA) **(67)** *(MrsNMacauley)* 4-8-2 ‡3DBiggs (7) (nvr nr to chal) ... 1¹/₂.5
*114* Northern Conqueror (IRE) **(73)** *(TJNaughton)* 4-8-11 PatEddery (5) (swtg: a
   bhd) ................................................................... 2¹/₂.6
997⁴ Jokist **(65)** *(WJarvis)* 9-8-3 WCarson (6) (6th st: ev ch 2f out: sn wknd) .......... nk.7
1063 Valiant Words **(70)** *(RAkehurst)* 5-8-8 BRouse (9) (led tl wknd over 2f out) ....... 1.8
824 Rocton North (IRE) **(90)** *(RHannon)* 4-10-0 BRaymond (8) (4th st: wknd over 2f
   out) ................................................................. 1¹/₂.9

**7/2** Jimlil, **9/2** Jokist, **7/1** VANROY, Barford Lad, **8/1** Northern Conqueror (IRE)(tchd 14/1), Brown Fairy (USA),
Usa Dollar, **10/1** Rocton North (IRE)(8/1—12/1), **16/1** Valiant Words. CSF £48.79, CT £179.86. Tote £8.00:
£2.10 £2.50 £1.30 (£38.90). Mr Derek Garrad (ROYSTON) bred by S. Taberner. 9 Rn    1m 46.28 (5.28)
SF—8/16/12/–/–/–

**1204**   STANLEY WOOTTON H'CAP (3-Y.O) (0-100) £4922.50 (£1480.00: £715.00: £332.50)
     **5f**                                                           3-05 (3-08)

690 Allthruthenight (IRE) **(82)** *(LJHolt)* 9-3 JReid (8) (hdwy over 1f out: r.o to ld last
   strides) .............................................................. —1
792 Inherent Magic (IRE) **(74)** *(MMcCormack)* 8-9 AClark (6) (lw: hdwy 2f out: led
   ins fnl f tl fnl strides) ............................................. s.h.2
872 Bodari **(72)** *(DAWilson)* 8-7 BRouse (2) (a.p: led over 1f out tl ins fnl f) ........... 1¹/₂.3
1042* Absolutely Nuts **(77)** (Fav) *(BAMcMahon)* 8-12 (6x) LDettori (7) (led over 3f) .. 2¹/₂.4
690² Wild Honour (IRE) **(86)** (v) *(WRMuir)* 9-7 SWhitworth (3) (a.p: ev ch 1f out: wknd
   nr fin) .............................................................. ³/₄.5
945² Cradle Days **(79)** *(RHannon)* 9-0 WCarson (4) (lw: hdwy 3f out: hmpd 2f out: nt
   rcvr) ................................................................ 2.6
996² Walking Possession **(81)** (bl) *(RBoss)* 9-2 MRoberts (1) (w ldr 3f: sn wknd) .... 3¹/₂.7
Memsahb **(86)** *(JBerry)* 9-7 PatEddery (5) (lw: hmpd s: hdwy 3f out: wknd over
   1f out) ............................................................. ¹/₂.8

**7/2** Absolutely Nuts, **4/1** Cradle Days, **5/1** Walking Possession, **11/2** Bodari, **6/1** Wild Honour (IRE), **10/1**
Memsahb, **14/1** ALLTHRUTHENIGHT (IRE) & Ors. CSF £149.50, CT £1,054.03. Tote £15.80: £3.60 £5.90 £1.80
(£75.50). Mr G. Steinberg (BASINGSTOKE) bred by Golden Vale Stud in Ireland. 8 Rn    56.15 sec (1.65)
SF—70/61/53/48/54/39

**1205**   HANSON CORONATION CUP (Stks) (Gp 1)   £90282.00 (£33590.60: £15970.30:
     £6777.10)   1¹/₂m 10y                                          3-45 (3-48)

724* Saddlers' Hall (IRE) **(Fav)** *(MRStoute)* 4-9-0 WRSwinburn (8) (lw: 4th st: led
   over 2f out: edgd lft over 1f out: hrd rdn: r.o) ...................... —1
826* Rock Hopper *(MRStoute)* 5-9-0 PatEddery (3) (lw: 7th st: chsd wnr fnl 2f: hrd
   rdn: r.o) ............................................................ ³/₄.2
10a Terimon *(CEBrittain)* 6-9-0 MRoberts (4) (3rd st: nt clr run & snatched up over
   2f out: r.o wl fnl f) ................................................. ³/₄.3
743a* Subotica (FR) *(AFabre,France)* 4-9-0 TJarnet (2) (5th st: hmpd over 2f out: r.o
   fnl f) ............................................................... nk.4
648⁴ Always Friendly *(HCandy)* 4-8-11 AMunro (6) (s.s: 6th st: r.o one pce fnl 2f) ... s.h.5
955a⁵ Saganeca (USA) *(ASpanu,France)* 4-8-11 WMongil (5) (8th st: nvr nr to chal) 2¹/₂.6
826³ Snurge *(PFICole)* 5-9-0 TQuinn (7) (lw: led 1f: led over 5f out tl over 2f out) .. ³/₄.7
826² Sapience *(DRCElsworth)* 6-9-0 RCochrane (1) (lw: 2nd st: hmpd & wknd over
   2f out) ............................................................. 2.8
1200⁵ Mellaby (USA) *(MRStoute)* 4-9-0 BRaymond (9) (lw: led after 1f tl wknd over 5f out:
   wknd qckly: t.o) .................................................... dist.9

**5/4** SADDLERS' HALL (IRE), **11/4** Subotica (FR), **7/1** Rock Hopper, **8/1** Snurge, **12/1** Terimon, **16/1** Sapience,
**25/1** Saganeca (USA), **40/1** Always Friendly, **150/1** Mellaby (USA). CSF £10.04, Tote £2.40: £1.20 £1.80 £2.10
(£3.80). Lord Weinstock (NEWMARKET) bred by Ballymacoll Stud Farm Ltd in Ireland. 9 Rn   2m 35.73 (0.73)
SF—93/91/89/88/84/79/80

**1206**   SEVEN SEAS H'CAP (3-Y.O) (0-90) £3692.75 (£1112.00: £538.50: £251.75)
     **7f**                                                          4-15 (4-25)

925² Efharisto **(74)** *(CEBrittain)* 8-6 MRoberts (5) (lw: 7th st: gd hdwy to ld over 1f
   out: all out) ........................................................ —1
894² Noble Pet **(75)** *(PJMakin)* 8-7 TQuinn (2) (lw: 8th st: gd hdwy over 1f out: ev ch
   ins fnl f: r.o) ....................................................... ¹/₂.2
1062* Euro Festival **(81)** (Fav) *(MissLCSiddall)* 8-13 (4x) PatEddery (4) (4th st: n.m.r
   2f out: r.o fnl f) .................................................... 3¹/₂.3
898³ Tate Dancer (IRE) **(82)** *(RWArmstrong)* 9-0 LDettori (6) (led tl wknd over 1f out) ³/₄.4
1133 Merlins Wish (USA) **(89)** *(RHannon)* 9-7 BRaymond (3) (6th st: nvr nr to chal) ... 1.5

909² Night Asset **(63)** (bl) *(GLewis)* 7-4⁽¹⁾ ‡5DHarrison (8) (5th st: wknd 2f out) .......... 1.6
783² Vanborough Lad **(74)** *(MJHaynes)* 8-3 ‡3DBiggs (1) (3rd st: nt clr run fnl f) .......... 1.7
939⁴ Mexican Dancer **(62)** *(RJHolder)* 7-8 NAdams (7) (2nd st: hrd rdn over 2f out:
sn wknd) ................................................................ 6.8

**11/4** Euro Festival, **3/1** Night Asset, **7/1** EFHARISTO, **8/1** Merlins Wish (USA), Tate Dancer (IRE), Vanborough Lad, **9/1** Noble Pet, **14/1** Mexican Dancer(10/1—16/1). CSF £58.43, CT £192.92. Tote £8.80: £1.60 £2.80 £1.40 (£48.60). The Dowager Lady Beaverbrook (NEWMARKET) bred by Barrettstown Stud Farms Ltd. 8 Rn
1m 24.32 (3.82)
SF—35/34/29/28/32/–

## 1207
NIGHTINGALL STKS (Mdn 3-Y.O) £2301.00 (£636.00: £303.00)
1¹/₄m 18y                                                             4-50 (5-00)

1069² **Scrutineer (USA)** (Fav) *(JHMGosden)* 9-0 RCochrane (5) (lw: 4th st: led over
2f out: hrd rdn over 1f out: r.o) .......................................... —1
Milzig (USA) **(92)** *(DRCElsworth)* 9-0 TQuinn (2) (3rd st: ev ch fnl f: r.o) .......... ¹/₂.2
Idoni (Fav) *(CEBrittain)* 9-0 LDettori (4) (w'like: scope: bit bkwd: 5th st: ev ch 1f
out: nt qckn) ........................................................ 3¹/₂.3
707 Shameem (USA) *(MRStoute)* 8-9 PatEddery (3) (lw: 2nd st: wknd over 2f out) .... 5.4
823⁵ Rebel Call *(RHannon)* 9-0 MRoberts (1) (led tl over 2f out: nt r.o) .......... 1¹/₂.5

**6/4** SCRUTINEER (USA), **15/8** Rebel Call, **6/1** Shameem (USA), **13/2** Milzig (USA), **14/1** Idoni. CSF £9.79, Tote £2.40: £1.90 £3.40 (£9.90). Sheikh Mohammed (NEWMARKET) bred by Luella M. Jensen & Kennelot Stables in USA. 5 Rn
2m 9.68 (5.18)
SF—48/47/40/25/27

T/Trio: Race 4: £20.60 (82 Tckts). T/Jkpt: £29,420.90 (0.3 Tckts); £27,830.64 to Epsom 5/6/92. T/Plpt: £133.60 (81.85 Tckts).
Hn

# EPSOM (L-H)
## Friday, June 5th [Good becoming Good to soft]
Going Allowance: 1st-3rd: 0.25 sec (G); Rest: 0.35 sec per fur (Y)

Wind: almost nil    Vis: poor 5th & 6th

Stalls: 1st high, remainder low

## 1208
E.B.F. FLEMINGTON STKS (Mdn 2-Y.O) £2782.50 (£770.00: £367.50)
5f                                                                   2-00 (2-09)

847³ **Sharp Prod (USA)** (Fav) *(LordHuntingdon)* 9-0 SCauthen (6) (mde virtually all:
easily) ................................................................. —1
995⁴ Belle Soiree *(SDow)* 8-9 WRSwinburn (8) (hdwy 2f out: r.o fnl f: no ch w wnr) 1¹/₂.2
Red Leader (IRE) *(PFICole)* 8-11 TQuinn (10) (cmpt: a.p: one pce fnl f) .......... 1.3
416⁵ Stardust Express *(MJohnston)* 9-0 MRoberts (12) (gd spd over 3f) .......... 3.4
852³ Bergliot *(JBerry)* 8-9 PatEddery (5) (w wnr tl wknd wl over 1f out) ........ ³/₄.5
Gangleader *(AHide)* 8-11 WWoods (2) (w'like: bit bkwd: nvr nrr) .......... 2.6
973 Petite Vino *(JJBridger)* 8-11 NAdams (7) (lw: nrst fin) .................. s.h.7
1057³ Rich Midas (IRE) *(GLewis)* 8-9 PaulEddery (1) (bhd fnl 2f) ................ s.h.8
1071 Water Diviner (bl) *(RFJohnsonHoughton)* 9-0 JReid (4) (a wl bhd) ........ 8.9
943³ Second Chance (IRE) (v) *(PMitchell)* 9-0 LPiggott (9) (lw: prom 2f: hung bdly lft:
t.o) ................................................................... 10.10
266 Gorodenka Boy (50/1) Withdrawn (rdr uns & inj) : not under orders
1135 Silent Prince (33/1) Withdrawn (ref to ent stalls) : not under orders

**13/8** SHARP PROD (USA), **6/1** Stardust Express(op 4/1), Rich Midas (IRE)(op 4/1), Bergliot(op 4/1), **8/1** Red Leader (IRE)(op 5/1), **10/1** Second Chance (IRE), **16/1** Water Diviner, Gangleader(12/1—20/1), Belle Soiree, **50/1** Petite Vino. CSF £26.13, Tote £2.50: £1.40 £4.40 £2.40 (£24.00). The Queen (WEST ILSLEY) bred by D. O. B. Syndicate in USA. 10 Rn
58.86 sec (4.36)
SF—38/27/25/16/8/2

## 1209
ALBERTA ROSE STKS (Mdn 3-Y.O.F) £2364.00 (£654.00: £312.00)
1m 114y                                                              2-35 (2-42)

938⁴ **Hugging (73)** *(MMcCormack)* 8-11 JReid (5) (4th st: led ins fnl f: all out) .......... —1
938² Lady Debra Darley (Fav) *(RHannon)* 8-11 MRoberts (2) (led tl ins fnl f: hrd rdn &
r.o) ................................................................... nk.2
865³ Avice Caro (USA) *(JHMGosden)* 8-11 SCauthen (4) (3rd & brought wd st: hrd
rdn & ev ch fnl 2f: nt qckn) .......................................... 1.3
989 Sharriba **(73)** *(DRCElsworth)* 8-11 JWilliams (3) (2nd st: wknd over 2f out) ........ 4.4
553⁶ Donia (USA) *(PFICole)* 8-11 AMunro (1) (5th st: wknd over 2f out) .......... 2.5
989 Flying Wind *(JSutcliffe)* 8-11 BRouse (6) (6th st: a bhd) .................. 8.6

**11/8** Lady Debra Darley, **5/2** Avice Caro (USA)(7/4—11/4), **5/1** Sharriba, **6/1** Donia (USA), **8/1** HUGGING, **25/1** Flying Wind. CSF £19.43, Tote £8.20: £1.70 £1.60 (£7.30). Mr Brian North (WANTAGE) bred by Marquess & Marchioness of Tavistock & Lord Howland. 6 Rn
1m 49.22 (8.22)
SF—4/3/–/–/–/–

## 1210

SUN LIFE OF CANADA H'CAP (3-Y.O) (0-100) £6970.00 (£2110.00: £1030.00: £490.00)
1¼m 18y
3-10 (3-13)

(Weights raised 10 lb)

930[6] **Royal Seaton (83)** *(BRMillman)* 9-0 JWilliams (9) (7th st: hdwy over 2f out: led wl ins fnl f: r.o) —1

804[3] Big Easy (IRE) **(82)** *(MrsJCecil)* 8-13 PaulEddery (4) (led tl wl ins fnl f) .......... 1½.2

502* Valley of Fire **(87)** *(JRFanshawe)* 9-4 SCauthen (8) (5th st: rdn over 2f out: r.o one pce) .......... 10.3

802[3] Maestroso (IRE) **(70)** (bl) *(RFJohnsonHoughton)* 7-10 ‡5DHarrison (2) (3rd st: wknd over 1f out) .......... 1½.4

835[4] Alessandrina (USA) **(78)** (Fav) *(MRStoute)* 8-9 WCarson (6) (lw: 4th st: rdn over 2f out: sn wknd) .......... 5.5

1069 Ler Cru (IRE) **(69)** *(CEBrittain)* 8-0 MRoberts (5) (lw: 2nd st: wknd over 2f out) 3½.6

471 Caithness Rock **(67)** *(MAJarvis)* 7-12 JQuinn (7) (lw: 6th st: wknd 3f out) .......... 7

**9/4** Alessandrina (USA), **4/1** Valley of Fire(op 5/2), **5/1** Ler Cru (IRE)(4/1—6/1), Big Easy (IRE), **8/1** ROYAL SEATON(op 12/1), **9/1** Maestroso (IRE), **10/1** Caithness Rock(8/1—12/1). CSF £42.91, CT £165.96. Tote £10.90: £2.90 £1.90 (£14.50). Axminster Carpets Limited (CULLOMPTON) bred by Mrs Nerys Dutfield. 7 Rn
2m 12.10 (7.60)
SF—49/45/30/5/8/–

## 1211

NORTHERN DANCER H'CAP (0-110) £14070.00 (£4260.00: £2080.00: £495.00)
1½m 10y
3-45 (3-55)

708[5] **Castoret (71)** *(JWHills)* 6-7-6 ‡5DHarrison (4) (hdwy 3f out: led wl ins fnl f: all out) —1

1132[2] Quick Ransom **(75)** (Fav) *(MJohnston)* 4-8-1 MRoberts (8) (lw: 2nd st: ev ch ins fnl f: r.o) s.h.2

1073[6] Roberty Lea **(67)** *(TFairhurst)* 4-7-7 NAdams (11) (swtg: led: drvn clr over 3f out: hdd wl ins fnl f) ½.3

815[5] Kansk **(94)** *(JHMGosden)* 4-9-6 SCauthen (9) (lw: 5th st: r.o one pce fnl 2f) ..... 4.4

815[6] Opera Ghost **(82)** *(PWHarris)* 6-8-8 PaulEddery (7) (8th st: styd on fnl 2f) ...... d.h.4

855 Deposki **(95)** (v) *(MRStoute)* 4-9-7 WRSwinburn (3) (hdwy 7f out: 4th st: grad wknd fnl 2f) 4.6

831* Kaytak (FR) **(72)** *(JRJenkins)* 5-7-12 TyroneWilliams (10) (nvr nr to chal) ...... 2½.7

993* Barrish **(75)** *(RAkehurst)* 6-8-1 WCarson (6) (3rd st: wknd wl over 1f out) ...... 1½.8

855[6] Kimbers (IRE) **(102)** *(CRNelson)* 4-10-0 PatEddery (3) (lw: nvr nrr) ............... 2½.9

815 Latour **(70)** *(CEBrittain)* 4-7-5[(3)] ‡5BDoyle (13) (n.d) ........ ¾.10

724[4] Regent's Folly (IRE) **(94)** *(WJarvis)* 4-9-6 AMunro (5) (swtg: 6th st: wknd 3f out) 1½.11

1016[3] Express Account **(68)** *(RJRWilliams)* 5-7-8 JQuinn (15) (7th st: wknd 3f out) . 10.12

726[4] Libk **(96)** *(HThomsonJones)* 4-9-8 RHills (2) (bhd most of wy: t.o) ............... 13

854[2] Fragrant Hill **(101)** *(IABalding)* 4-9-13 BRaymond (1) (lw: bhd fnl 5f: t.o) ....... 14

LONG HANDICAP: Roberty Lea 7-2, Latour 7-4.

773 Loki (IRE) (20/1) Withdrawn (uns & inj rdr on wy to s) : not under orders

**7/2** Quick Ransom, **13/2** CASTORET(op 12/1), **9/1** Deposki(7/1—12/1), **10/1** Barrish(7/1—12/1), Opera Ghost, **11/1** Latour(20/1—10/1), Express Account(8/1—12/1), Kaytak (FR), **12/1** Kansk, Fragrant Hill, Libk, Regent's Folly (IRE), **16/1** Kimbers (IRE), **33/1** Roberty Lea. CSF £29.30, CT £666.81. Tote £8.60: £3.00 £1.80 £5.60 (£14.40). Lady D'Avigdor-Goldsmid (LAMBOURN) bred by Mrs R. Owen-George. 14 Rn
2m 42 (7)
SF—50/58/49/68/54/31/31

## 1212

TOKYO TROPHY (H'cap) (0-100) £5842.00 (£1756.00: £848.00: £394.00)
6f
4-15 (4-31)

935[6] Poets Cove **(77)** *(MMcCormack)* 4-8-10 SCauthen (14) (5th st: led 1f out: r.o wl) —1

1134[6] Green Dollar **(90)** *(EAWheeler)* 9-9-9 LPiggott (5) (hdwy fnl f: r.o) .................... 2.2

819 Love Legend **(90)** *(DWPArbuthnot)* 7-9-9 AMunro (10) (late hdwy: nvr nrr) ....... ¾.3

813[4] Gorinsky (IRE) **(76)** (bl) *(JBerry)* 4-8-9 PatEddery (13) (led 5f) ........................... s.h.4

941[6] Invocation **(72)** *(AMoore)* 5-8-5 NAdams (12) (b.nr hind: 4th st: r.o one pce fnl 2f) .......... hd.5

775* Across the Bay **(73)** (v) (Jt-Fav) *(SDow)* 5-8-6 TQuinn (9) (gd hdwy fnl 2f: nrst fin) .......... 1½.6

563 Letsbeonestaboutit **(92)** (bl) *(MrsNMacauley)* 6-9-4 ‡7SWilliams (6) (6th st: hrd rdn 3f out: nt qckn) .......... 1.7

813[5] Duplicity (IRE) **(95)** *(LJHolt)* 4-10-0 JReid (7) (nvr nr to chal) ........................ s.h.8

1199[5] Olifantsfontein **(79)** (bl) *(RSimpson)* 4-8-12 WRyan (2) (2nd st: wknd over 1f out) ¾.9

992⁵ Princess Tara **(77)** *(GLewis)* 4–8-10 PaulEddery (4) (n.d) ............................ s.h.**10**
1201² Surrey Racing **(65)** (Jt-Fav) *(GLewis)* 4–7-12 WCarson (15) (rdn along: 3rd st:
　　　wknd 2f out) ......................................................................................... nk.**11**
1045★ Plain Fact **(85)** *(AHarrison)* 7–9-4 (5x) BRouse (3) (n.d) ...................... ³/₄.**12**
1199⁶ Gallant Hope **(60)** (bl) *(LGCottrell)* 10–7-7 RFox (8) (n.d) ................... ³/₄.**13**
1084³ Judgement Call **(65)** *(PHowling)* 5–7-12 JQuinn (11) (n.d) ............... 3¹/₂.**14**
　　　　　　　LONG HANDICAP: Gallant Hope 6-10.

**5/1** Across the Bay, Surrey Racing, **7/1** Gorinsky (IRE), **15/2** Olifantsfontein(12/1—7/1), **10/1** Green Dollar, **12/1** Princess Tara, Gallant Hope, Duplicity (IRE), Love Legend, **14/1** Plain Fact, POETS COVE, Judgement Call, **16/1** Letsbeonestaboutit, **25/1** Invocation. CSF £156.42, CT £1,816.69. Tote £21.90: £4.70 £2.10 £3.20 (£201.50).
Mr P. R. Cruden (WANTAGE) bred by P. R. Cruden. 14 Rn　　　　　　1m 12.08 (4.08)
　　　　　　　　　　　　　　　　　　　　　　　SF—56/61/58/43/38/33/41

**1213**　　KENTUCKY CLAIMING STKS (3-Y.O) £2979.50 (£896.00: £433.00: £201.50)
　　　　　1m 114y　　　　　　　　　　　　　　　　　4-45 (4-58)

830³ **Plan Ahead (68)** (Fav) *(GLewis)* 7-13 ‡5DHarrison (3) (gd hdwy over 2f out: led
　　　　1f out: easily) ....................................................................................... —**1**
870 Wave Hill **(94)** *(HRACecil)* 9-5 WRyan (6) (4th st: led 2f out to 1f out: r.o) ...... 1¹/₂.**2**
863⁵ Gachette **(61)** *(JSutcliffe)* 8-7 BRouse (5) (2nd st: led 3f out to 2f out: r.o one
　　　　　pce) .................................................................................................. s.h.**3**
1085² Lindeman **(46)** *(SDow)* 8-8 TQuinn (1) (led to 3f out: one pce fnl 2f) .................. 3.**4**
734 Clifton Cruiser (USA) *(CRNelson)* 8-6 SWhitworth (7) (nvr nr to chal) ................ 7.**5**
1122 Dollar Wine (IRE) **(64)** *(RHannon)* 8-11 MRoberts (8) (3rd st: wknd over 2f out) 3¹/₂.**6**
623 Mma International (IRE) *(BRMillman)* 8-11 AMackay (2) (rdn along & a bhd) .... hd.**7**
566⁶ First Heiress (IRE) *(MRStoute)* 9-0 JReid (10) (a bhd) ...................................... ³/₄.**8**
804 Lamore Ritorna **(60)** *(KOCunningham-Brown)* 8-11 PaulEddery (4) (5th st:
　　　　wknd 3f out) ....................................................................................... 1¹/₂.**9**
510 Crackling **(57)** *(DMarks)* 7-13 ‡7AntoinetteArmes (9) (prom tl wknd & 6th st: t.o) . 10

**5/4** PLAN AHEAD, **7/2** Wave Hill(2/1—4/1), **7/1** Gachette(op 12/1), **8/1** Lamore Ritorna, **9/1** Dollar Wine (IRE), First Heiress (IRE)(6/1—10/1), **14/1** Lindeman, **25/1** Clifton Cruiser (USA), Crackling, **50/1** Mma International (IRE). CSF £6.66, Tote £2.40: £1.20 £1.60 £3.00 (£3.30). Planflow (Leasing) Ltd (EPSOM) bred by R. F. and Mrs Knipe. 10 Rn　　　　　　　　　　　　　　　　1m 50.44 (9.44)

T/Dble: Races 4 & 5: £355.70 & £1,472.50 (5.2 & 1.1 Tckts). T/Trio: Races 4 & 5: £355.70 & £1,472.50 (5.2 & 1.1 Tckts). T/Jkpt: Not won; £39,934.84 to Epsom 6/6/92. T/Plpt: £1,758.60 (5.65 Tckts).　　　Hn

# EPSOM  (L-H)
## Saturday, June 6th [Good to soft]
Going Allowance: 0.25 sec per fur (G)　　　　　　　　　　Wind: almost nil

Stalls: high

**1214**　　EVER READY CLAIMING STKS (3-Y.O) £3018.50 (£908.00: £439.00: £204.50)
　　　　　7f　　　　　　　　　　　　　　　　　　2-15 (2-15)

1104² **Clare Kerry Lass (66)** *(TJNaughton)* 8-1 PaulEddery (1) (swtg: hdwy 3f out:
　　　　led over 1f out: comf) .............................................................................. —**1**
1040³ She's Special **(68)** (v) *(MissLAPerratt)* 7-12 WCarson (6) (lw: 2nd st: led
　　　　over 2f out tl over 1f out: unable qckn) ..................................................... 6.**2**
970 Canadian Capers **(75)** *(MRChannon)* 7-13 JQuinn (4) (led over 4f: one pce) .. 1¹/₂.**3**
816 First Century (IRE) **(88)** (bl) *(PFICole)* 8-11 TQuinn (5) (5th st: one pce fnl 2f) .. ³/₄.**4**
727⁵ Red Sombrero **(65)** *(LGCottrell)* 8-10 TRogers (9) (6th st: no hdwy fnl 3f) ....... 3¹/₂.**5**
1062⁵ Coniston Lake (IRE) **(60)** *(GLewis)* 8-4(1) BRouse (11) (swtg: nvr nr to chal) ... 2¹/₂.**6**
1107² Risk Zone **(74)** (bl) *(RHannon)* 8-11 AMcGlone (8) (swtg: lost pl over 4f out: no
　　　　hdwy fnl 3f) ......................................................................................... 5.**7**
939 Excelled (IRE) *(BGubby)* 7-10 NAdams (2) (3rd st: wknd over 2f out) ........... 2.**8**
164 Smudgemupum **(51)** *(MissBSanders)* 8-2 BCrossley (12) (a bhd) ..................... 1.**9**
894⁶ Tulapet *(SDow)* 8-1 MRoberts (7) (a bhd) ....................................................... ³/₄.**10**
1010³ Aedean **(66)** (v) *(CCElsey)* 8-8(1) LPiggott (10) (lw: bhd fnl 4f) ...................... 2.**11**
969² Grey But Rosy (IRE) **(54)** (bl) *(DRCElsworth)* 7-5 ‡5BDoyle (13) (b.hind: 4th st:
　　　　wknd over 2f out) .................................................................................. 1¹/₂.**12**
998 Wayward Son *(GLewis)* 8-1 ‡7BRussell (3) (s.s: a wl bhd) .............................. 1¹/₂.**13**

**4/1** She's Special, **9/2** Risk Zone, First Century (IRE)(op 5/2), **8/1** Canadian Capers, CLARE KERRY LASS, **12/1** Coniston Lake (IRE), Grey But Rosy (IRE), **14/1** Aedean(10/1—16/1), **16/1** Red Sombrero(op 10/1), **25/1** Tulapet, **33/1** Excelled (IRE), **50/1** Ors. CSF £36.42, Tote £8.90: £1.80 £1.50 £3.20 (£15.30). Mr T. O'Flaherty (EPSOM) bred by Hever Castle Stud Farm Ltd. 13 Rn; Clare Kerry Lass clmd W Smith £12,000, She's Special clmd A Merza £11,699　　　　　　　　　　　　　1m 24.41 (3.91)
　　　　　　　　　　　　　　　　　　　　SF—54/33/29/39/27/13

**1215**
BEAZER HOMES ACORN STKS (2-Y.O.F) £7318.00 (£2048.00: £994.00)
5f
2-45 (2-45)

995² **Anonymous** (CEBrittain) 8-8 MRoberts (3) (mde virtually all: hrd rdn ins fnl f: r.o wl) .... —1
367* Palacegate Episode (IRE) (Fav) (JBerry) 9-0 PatEddery (2) (b.off hind: lw: w wnr: hrd rdn & ev ch over 1f out: unable qckn ins fnl f) .... 1½.2
584³ Sheila's Secret (IRE) (WCarter) 9-0 RCochrane (1) (rdn thrght: outpcd: hdwy fnl f: nvr nrr) .... 1½.3

1/2 Palacegate Episode (IRE), 4/1 ANONYMOUS & Ors. CSF £6.07, Tote £4.00 (£1.60). Mrs J. L. Hislop (NEWMARKET) bred by J. L. and Mrs Hislop. 3 Rn
58.10 sec (3.60)
SF—47/47/41

**1216**
LONDON BRICK EBBISHAM H'CAP (3-Y.O.F) (0-100) £7100.00 (£2150.00: £1050.00: £500.00) 7f
3-15 (3-15)

984² **Petite-D-Argent** (83) (MissLAPerratt) 8-6(1) RCochrane (5) (swtg: led 1f: 2nd st: led over 3f out: clr over 2f out: r.o wl) .... —1
858⁵ Muhit (USA) (74) (PTWalwyn) 7-11(1) WCarson (4) (4th st: hrd rdn 2f out: r.o) ... 2.2
821² Nashville Blues (IRE) (80) (JWHills) 8-3 MHills (8) (5th st: rdn over 2f out: r.o) . nk.3
1078* Rocality (80) (RHannon) 8-3 JQuinn (1) (led 6f out tl over 3f out: unable qckn) 2½.4
653² Petite Sonnerie (82) (Fav) (GLewis) 8-5 PaulEddery (2) (lw: 6th st: rdn over 2f out: nvr nr to chal) .... 2½.5
1042² Forest Fairy (76) (RBoss) 7-13(1) RHills (6) (lw: 3rd st: wknd over 2f out) .... 6.6
821 Swallowcliffe (96) (PTWalwyn) 9-5 WRSwinburn (7) (lw: a bhd) .... 1½.7

3/1 Petite Sonnerie, 100/30 Nashville Blues (IRE), 5/1 PETITE-D-ARGENT, 11/2 Rocality(7/2—6/1), 6/1 Muhit (USA), 10/1 Swallowcliffe, 20/1 Forest Fairy. CSF £29.57, CT £89.37. Tote £5.20: £2.50 £2.80 (£14.50). Mr Daniel A. Couper (AYR) bred by Lord Haddington. 7 Rn
1m 24.01 (3.51)
SF—66/51/56/48/43/18

**1217**
GOLD SEAL OAKS STKS (Gp 1) (3-Y.O.F) £147500.00 (£55000.00: £26250.00: £11250.00) 1½m 10y
4-05 (4-07)

780* **User Friendly** (CEBrittain) 9-0 GDuffield (5) (lw: 2nd st: qcknd to ld over 3f out: drvn out) .... —1
814* All At Sea (USA) (Fav) (HRACecil) 9-0 PatEddery (3) (hld up: 4th st: chsd wnr 3f out: hrd rdn & ev ch 1f out: unable qckn) .... 3½.2
631 Pearl Angel (MissBSanders) 9-0 LPiggott (2) (lw: 7th st: nvr nr to chal) .... 20.3
850* Saratoga Source (USA) (IABalding) 9-0 RCochrane (7) (5th st: no hdwy fnl 3f) 2½.4
Shining Bright (AFabre,France) 9-0 TJarnet (4) (leggy: 6th st: wknd over 3f out) 1½.5
Fawaayid (USA) (JSBolger,Ireland) 9-0 CRoche (8) (gd sort: lw: led over 8f) .... 8.6
814² Perfect Circle (MRStoute) 9-0 WRSwinburn (1) (3rd st: wknd 2f out: t.o) .... 25.7

11/10 All At Sea (USA), 9/2 Perfect Circle, 5/1 USER FRIENDLY, 7/1 Fawaayid (USA), 20/1 Shining Bright, 33/1 Ors. CSF £9.74, Tote £4.70: £2.30 £1.50 (£3.90). Mr W. J. Gredley (NEWMARKET) bred by Stetchworth Park Stud Ltd. 7 Rn
2m 39.77 (4.77)
SF—82/75/35/30/27/11

**1218**
CRABTREE ELECTRICAL INDUSTRIES H'CAP (3-Y.O) (0-105) £10625.00 (£3200.00: £1550.00: £725.00) 1m 114y
4-40 (4-41)

983⁵ **Marabella Star** (USA) (92) (HRACecil) 9-7 WRyan (8) (4th st: swtchd rt over 2f out: led ins fnl f: hung lft: drvn out) .... —1
695 Parlemo (IRE) (64) (bl) (JDBethell) 7-7 TyroneWilliams (2) (hrd rdn over 2f out: hdwy over 1f out: r.o wl ins fnl f) .... 1.2
930² Confronter (77) (Fav) (PFICole) 8-6 TQuinn (3) (swtg: 2nd st: led over 3f out tl ins fnl f: unable qckn) .... 1½.3
858 Haroldon (IRE) (86) (BPalling) 9-1 RHills (10) (3rd st: hrd rdn & ev ch over 1f out: one pce) .... 2½.4
1142² Grog (IRE) (74) (MRChannon) 7-12 ⁵BDoyle (5) (led 5f: 3rd whn n.m.r over 1f out: wknd fnl f) .... 2½.5
944² Set Table (USA) (89) (JHMGosden) 9-4 RCochrane (6) (nvr nr to chal) .... 3½.6
Shrewd Partner (IRE) (84) (DRCElsworth) 8-13 MRoberts (3) (5th st: wknd over 2f out) .... 1.7
1029² Courageous Knight (77) (RHannon) 8-8 WCarson (7) (a bhd) .... ¾.8
558⁴ Showgi (USA) (88) (JRFanshawe) 9-3 WRSwinburn (11) (lw: a bhd) .... 5.9
558² The Power of One (80) (RSimpson) 8-9 GDuffield (9) (lw: rdn thrght: 6th st: wknd over 2f out) .... 1.10

4/1 Confronter, **9/2** The Power of One, **7/1** Grog (IRE), **MARABELLA STAR (USA)**, **15/2** Haroldon (IRE), **8/1** Set Table (USA), **9/1** Courageous Knight, **12/1** Showgi (USA), Shrewd Partner (IRE)(8/1—14/1), **20/1** Parlemo (IRE). CSF £110.79, CT £573.01. Tote £8.40: £2.20 £4.60 £2.10 (£79.00). Mr M. C. Samlalsingh (NEWMARKET) bred by Brereton C. Jones in USA. 10 Rn
1m 46.96 (5.96)
SF—50/19/27/28/3/12

**1219**    ABBOTS HILL H'CAP (3-Y.O) (0-90) £3783.75 (£1140.00: £552.50: £258.75)
6f
5-10 (5-11)

(Weights raised 4 lb)

| | | |
|---|---|---|
| 870 | **Hazm (USA) (86)** *(HThomsonJones)* 9-7 RHills (11) (lw: 3rd st: chsd ldr 3f out: hrd rdn over 1f out: led nr fin) | —1 |
| 1206[6] | Night Asset **(62)** (bl) *(GLewis)* 7-11 JQuinn (2) (lw: led: clr 3f out: hrd rdn 2f out: hdd nr fin) | ½.2 |
| 1076[2] | Uccello **(75)** *(Fav)* *(LJHolt)* 8-10 MRoberts (7) (hrd rdn & hung lft over 2f out: hdwy over 1f out: r.o wl) | nk.3 |
| 614* | Pop to Stans **(77)** *(JPearce)* 8-12 PatEddery (8) (lw: hdwy over 1f out: r.o wl ins fnl f) | 1½.4 |
| 714[6] | Soba Guest (IRE) **(76)** *(JBerry)* 8-11 MHills (5) (hdwy over 1f out: r.o) | hd.5 |
| 898 | Salisong **(73)** (bl) *(PFICole)* 8-8 TQuinn (4) (6th st: hrd rdn over 2f out: r.o one pce) | 1½.6 |
| 801 | Duty Sergeant (IRE) **(58)** *(MPMuggeridge)* 7-7 TyroneWilliams (1) (b.hind: nvr nrr) | 5.7 |
| 1028[6] | Noble Power (IRE) **(80)** *(BPalling)* 9-1 RCochrane (9) (s.s: nvr nrr) | 1½.8 |
| 984[4] | Jucea **(68)** *(DWPArbuthnot)* 7-12[2] ‡5RPrice (6) (lw: 2nd st: wknd 2f out) | nk.9 |
| 870 | Sharling **(74)** *(JHMGosden)* 8-9 AMcGlone (3) (5th st: wknd over 2f out) | 4.10 |
| 870 | Indian Endeavour **(73)** *(RGuest)* 8-8[1] LPiggott (10) (swtg: 4th st: wknd over 2f out) | 5.11 |

4/1 Uccello, 7/1 Pop to Stans, HAZM (USA), Night Asset, **15/2** Sharling, Salisong, **8/1** Jucea, **12/1** Indian Endeavour, Noble Power (IRE), **14/1** Soba Guest (IRE), **33/1** Duty Sergeant (IRE). CSF £50.19, CT £202.19. Tote £6.30: £2.50 £2.00 £2.00 (£18.10). Mr Hamdan Al-Maktoum (NEWMARKET) bred by Skara Glen Stables in USA. 11 Rn
1m 11.46 (3.46)
SF—68/42/54/50/48/39

**1220**    EPSOM H'CAP (3-Y.O) (0-90) £5800.00 (£1750.00: £850.00: £400.00)
1½m 10y
5-40 (5-42)

| | | |
|---|---|---|
| 908[2] | **Crystal Cross (USA) (73)** *(IABalding)* 8-8 RCochrane (5) (4th st: led 1f out: hrd rdn: r.o wl) | —1 |
| 716[3] | Major's Law (IRE) **(77)** *(CEBrittain)* 8-12 MRoberts (7) (swtg: 2nd st: qcknd to ld over 3f out: hdd 1f out: unable qcckn) | 6.2 |
| 1011* | Yenoora (IRE) **(60)** *(PFICole)* 7-9 JQuinn (3) (5th st: one pce fnl 3f) | 6.3 |
| 1025[2] | Mujid (IRE) **(64)** *(Fav)* *(HThomsonJones)* 7-13[1] RHills (4) (nvr nr to chal) | 3½.4 |
| 910[4] | Russian Vision **(69)** *(AAScott)* 8-4 JFortune (6) (6th st: wknd over 2f out) | 7.5 |
| 1026[3] | Bar Billiards **(78)** *(RFJohnsonHoughton)* 8-13 SWhitworth (9) (lw: rdn thrght: a bhd) | ½.6 |
| 805[3] | Paper Clip **(60)** *(JDBethell)* 7-9 TyroneWilliams (2) (a bhd) | 6.7 |
| 930 | Dordogne **(61)** (bl) *(RAkehurst)* 7-5 ‡5BDoyle (1) (lw: led over 8f) | nk.8 |
| 716* | Sastago (USA) **(86)** *(JHMGosden)* 9-7 PatEddery (8) (3rd st: wknd over 2f out) | 5.9 |

4/1 Mujid (IRE), **5/1** Russian Vision, Yenoora (IRE), Sastago (USA), **15/2** CRYSTAL CROSS (USA), **8/1** Major's Law (IRE), Dordogne, **12/1** Bar Billiards, **14/1** Paper Clip. CSF £59.88, CT £299.73. Tote £9.30: £2.30 £1.90 £2.10 (£25.60). Mr Paul Mellon (KINGSCLERE) bred by Paul Mellon in USA. 9 Rn
2m 42.60 (7.60)
SF—48/40/11/8/–/6

T/Trio: Race 5: £149.00 (18.4 Tckts). T/Jkpt: £55,170.00 (0.25 Tckts); £55,915.57 to Newbury 11/6/92. T/Plpt: £410.80 (40.5 Tckts).                                                                                        AK

## 1098a—**LONGCHAMP (R-H)**
### Thursday, May 28th [Soft]
Going Allowance: 0.20 sec per fur (G)

**1221a**    PRIX DE LA PORTE DE MADRID (listed race)    £12384.00    1½m (Grande)

| | | |
|---|---|---|
| 855[2] | **MASHAALLAH (USA)** *(JHMGosden)* 4–8-11 SCauthen | —1 |
| 743a | Glity (USA) *(France)* 4–8-11 CAsmussen | hd.2 |
| | Le Montagnard (FR) *(France)* 4–8-11 CJPhelippeau | 3.3 |

Tote 4.20f: 2.00f 1.60f 2.80f (8.10f). Sheikh Mohammed (NEWMARKET) bred by W.S.Farish et al in USA. 8 Rn
2m 35.2 (5.2)
SF—69/68/62

**1222a**     PRIX DU PALAIS-ROYAL (Gp 3)     £20640.00     **7f (Nouvelle)**

        **Robin des Pins (USA)** *(France)* 4–9–4 FHead ............................................ —1
378a² Zanadiyka (FR) *(France)* 4–9–1 WMongil ............................................ s.nk.2
655⁶ Tertian (USA) *(France)* 3–8–9 PatEddery ............................................ s.hd.3
Tote 4.80f: 2.50f 2.30f (SF: 18.50f). Mr S.Niarchos (F.Boutin,FRANCE) bred by Flaxmans Holdings Ltd in USA. 7
Rn                                             1m 22.7 (2.7)
                                            SF—84/80/73

956a—**CAPANNELLE  (R-H)**
**Saturday, May 30th [Good]**

**1223a**     PREMIO DELLA SPERANZA (listed race) (2-Y.O.C & G) £20930.00     **5f**

        **Mister Naif (USA)** *(Italy)* 2–8–11 FJovine ............................................ —1
        Golden Kabbuby (USA) *(Italy)* 2–8–11 VMezzatesta ............................................ 2.2
817★ POWER OF POLLY (USA) *(PFICole)* 2–8–11 TQuinn ............................................ s.h.3
Tote 29L: 16L 26L (88L). Scuderia Cieffedi (L.Brogi,ITALY) bred by Wimbledon Farm in USA. 6 Rn   57.8 sec

**1224a**     PREMIO BUONTALENTA (listed race) (3-Y.O.F) £20930.00     **1m**

        **Khai Tau (USA)** *(Italy)* 3–8–11 FJovine ............................................ —1
634★ FLUTE (USA) *(CEBrittain)* 3–8–7 MRoberts ............................................ 1.2
        Lavezzola (IRE) *(Italy)* 3–8–7 GDettori ............................................ s.nk.3
Tote 22L: 14L 17L (29L). Scuderia Cieffedi (L.Brogi,ITALY) bred by Dr W.O.Reed in USA. 6 Rn   1m 38.1

**1225a**     PREMIO LAZIO (listed race) (3-Y.O) £20930.00     **1¼m**

804★ **INNER CITY (IRE)** *(LMCumani)* 3–8–7 LDettori ............................................ —1
927⁶ PROFUSION *(PFICole)* 3–8–7 AMunro ............................................ nose.2
        Girolamo *(Italy)* 3–8–7 BJovine ............................................ 3½.3
Tote 38L: 13L 12L 18L (30L). Sheikh Mohammed (NEWMARKET) bred by Ballynagran Bloodstock Ltd in Ireland.
9 Rn                                           2m 1.5

**1226a**     PREMIO ELLINGTON (Gp 2)     £46512.00     **1½m**

557 **SECRET HAUNT (USA)** *(LMCumani)* 4–8–9 LDettori ............................................ —1
        Kohinoor (IRE) *(Italy)* 4–8–9 DZarroli ............................................ ½.2
        Jack Lang *(Italy)* 4–8–9 EBotti ............................................ 3½.3
855 MARCUS THORPE (USA) *(PAKelleway)* 4–8–9 FJovine ............................................ 1.4
724³ PARTING MOMENT (USA) *(IABalding)* 5–8–9 BRaymond ............................................ hd.5
Tote 17L: 12L 30L 20L (184L). Emdiem Ltd (NEWMARKET) bred by P.M.Brant in USA. 9 Rn   2m 26.7

**CAPANNELLE  (R-H)**
**Sunday, May 31st [Good]**

**1227a**     PREMIO NEARCO (listed race) (3-Y.O) £20930.00     **1m**

        **Stubass (IRE)** *(Italy)* 3–8–7 SSoto ............................................ —1
744a² Spendaccione (USA) *(Italy)* 3–8–11 VMezzatesta ............................................ 5.2
744a⁴ Jitterbugging *(Italy)* 3–8–7 LSorrentino ............................................ 1¾.3
983² BIG BLUE *(CEBrittain)* 3–8–7 MRoberts ............................................ nose.4
977★ HERO'S LIGHT (USA) *(PFICole)* 3–8–7 BRaymond ............................................ 3¼.5
Tote 59L: 18L 13L (37L). Scuderia Rencati (A.Botti,ITALY) bred by Joseph Crowley in Ireland. 6 Rn   1m 36.3

**1228a**     PREMIO MELTON-MEMORIAL TUDINI (Gp 2)     £46512.00     **6f**

836a² **Dream Talk** *(France)* 5–9–3 OPeslier ............................................ —1
        Reference Light *(Italy)* 5–9–3 MJKinane ............................................ hd.2
740a★ Special Power *(Italy)* 5–9–3 SSoto ............................................ 4½.3
1031³ SECRET THING (USA) *(CEBrittain)* 3–8–8 MRoberts (btn further 3¼l) ............................................ 5
Tote 20L: 14L 20L 17L (99L). Mr J.H.Metzger (N.Clement,FRANCE) bred by Prince Yazid Saud. 10 Rn
                                            68.8 sec

## 1229a
DERBY ITALIANO (Gp 1) (3-Y.O.C & F) £186046.00   1½m

    **In A Tiff (IRE)** *(Ireland)* 3–9–2  MJKinane ............................................................ —1
    Merzouk (USA) *(France)* 3–9–2  ESaint-Martin ..................................................... ½.2
844a★ MASAD (IRE) *(LMCumani)* 3–9–2  LDettori ................................................... nk.3
959a⁵ JOHN ROSE *(PAKelleway)* 3–9–2  PRobinson (btn further 10¼l) .............. 7
960a★ CAPTAIN HORATIUS (IRE) *(JLDunlop)* 3–9–2  WCarson (btn 14¼l by wnr) .......... 9
671⁴ COURTLINE JESTER *(MAJarvis)* 3–9–2  BRaymond (btn 17½l by wnr) ......... 10
781⁶ SPARTAN SHAREEF (IRE) *(CEBrittain)* 3–9–2  MBirch (btn 17¾l by wnr) ............. 11
927³ BELDI (USA) *(CEBrittain)* 3–9–2  MRoberts (btn 23¼l by wnr) ................. 12
Tote 144L: 32L 28L 14L (498L). C.A.M.M.A. Stable (D.K.Weld,IRELAND) bred by Michael Smurfit in Ireland. 13
Rn    2m 27.5

---

1221a— **LONGCHAMP (R-H)**
### Sunday, May 31st [Soft]
Going Allowance: 0.05 sec per fur (G)

## 1230a
PRIX JEAN PRAT (Gp 1) (3-Y.O.C & F) £51600.00   1m 1f (Grande)

537a² **Kitwood (USA)** *(France)* 3–9–2  SCauthen (cl up: 2nd st: wnt clr 2f out: hld on
    wl) ................................................................................................................. —1
953a⁴ LUCKY LINDY (IRE) *(RHannon)* 3–9–2  PatEddery (3rd & chsd ldrs: hdwy fr 2f
    out: wnt 2nd 1f out: r.o) ......................................................... s.nk.2
842a★ Shanghai (USA) *(Fav)* *(France)* 3–9–2  FHead (hld up: last st: gd hdwy fr wl over
    1f out: faltered cl home) .................................................... nk.3
537a⁴ Calling Collect (USA) *(France)* 3–9–2  DBoeuf (4th st: r.o one pce) ......... 2.4
    Heligoland (IRE) *(France)* 3–9–2  SGuillot (led tl 2f out: wknd qckly) ................... 6.5

**Evens** Shanghai (USA), **5/2** Heligoland (IRE), Calling Collect (USA), KITWOOD (USA), **13/4** Lucky Lindy (IRE).
Tote 3.50f: 2.00f 3.10f (SF: 21.10f). Sheikh Mohammed (A.Fabre,FRANCE) bred by Lazy Lane Farms in USA. 5
Rn    1m 58 (4.7)
    SF—39/38/37/31/13

## 1231a
PRIX D'ISPAHAN (Gp 1) (C & F) £51600.00   1m 1f (Grande)

954a² **ZOMAN (USA)** *(PFICole)* 5–9–2  AMunro (a cl up: 2nd st: wnt clr 2f out: hld on
    gamely: all out) ............................................................................. —1
382a⁶ Arcangues (USA) *(France)* 4–9–2  TJarnet (chsd ldrs: 3rd st: str chal fr wl over 1f
    out: kpt on) ......................................................................... nk.2
838a★ Exit To Nowhere (USA) *(France)* 4–9–2  FHead (hld up: last st: gd late hdwy fr wl
    over 1f out: one pce cl home) ................................................ 1½.4
    Funny Baby (FR) *(France)* 4–9–2  ALequeux (last early: hdwy & r.o wl fnl f) ...... 2½.4
    Tel Quel (FR) *(France)* 4–9–2  SCauthen (mid div: 4th st: r.o one pce fr 2 out) .. hd.5
849★ SELKIRK (USA) *(Fav)* *(IABalding)* 4–9–2  RCochrane (mid div: 6th st: hdwy fr 2
    out: nt qckn fnl f) ................................................................ 1½.6
10a² Magic Night (FR) *(France)* 4–8–13  ABadel (a mid div: one pce fnl 2f) ................. 2.7
849 Leariva (USA) *(France)* 5–8–13  CAsmussen (last st: m.n.s) ......................... 6.8
838a² Caerlina (IRE) *(France)* 4–8–13  ELegrix (a.p: wknd qckly st) ......................... 2.9
    Metal Storm (FR) *(France)* 4–9–2  PatEddery (mid div: n.d) ......................... 6.10
    L'Amour Fou (IRE) *(France)* 4–8–13  KVaillant (led to 2f out: wknd qckly) ........ 20.11

**6/4** Selkirk (USA), **17/4** Exit To Nowhere (USA), **6/1** Caerlina (IRE), **13/2** Magic Night (FR), L'Amour Fou (IRE),
**15/2** Tel Quel (FR), **12/1** ZOMAN (USA), **16/1** Leariva (USA), **17/1** Arcangues (USA), **26/1** Metal Storm (FR),
**32/1** Funny Baby (FR). Tote 13.30f: 2.90f 3.20f 2.20f (78.00f). Mr Fahd Salman (WHATCOMBE) bred by Harbor
View Farm in USA. 11 Rn    1m 54.6 (1.3)
    SF—89/88/83/75/74/69/60

---

1100a— **BADEN-BADEN (L-H)**
### Sunday, May 31st [Good]

## 1232a
GROSSER PREIS DER WIRTSCHAFT (Gp 2)   £56338.00   1m 3f

    **Hondo Mondo (IRE)** *(Germany)* 4–9–2  AHelfenbein ............................................. —1
    Lomitas *(Germany)* 4–9–7  ABoschert ..................................................... 1¼.2
    RUBY TIGER *(PFICole)* 5–9–0  TQuinn .................................................... ¾.3
24a KARINGA BAY *(GLewis)* 5–9–0  BRouse .................................................... hd.4
Tote 189DM: 27DM 12DM 16DM (SF: 442DM). Stall Marcassargues (U.Ostmann,GERMANY) bred by D.Von
Boetticher in Ireland. 9 Rn    2m 16.5

946—**CATTERICK (L-H)**
**Friday, June 5th [Good, Good to soft on bnds]**
Going Allowance: 0.55 sec per fur (Y)                    Wind: str half against

Stalls: low

**1233**    GILLING STKS (Mdn 2-Y.O.F) £2186.80 (£604.80: £288.40)    **5f**    2-20 (2-20)

772² **Charity Express (IRE)** *(JBerry)* 8-11 JCarroll (2) (lw: disp ld tl led over 1f out:
          r.o wl) ............................................................................................... —1
    476  Moving Image (IRE) *(MBell)* 8-11 PRobinson (1) (disp ld over 3f: r.o one pce) 2¹/₂.2
          Meconopsis *(TFairhurst)* 8-8 ‡³JFanning (6) (lt-f: dwlt: hdwy ¹/₂-wy: styd on one
          pce fnl f) .............................................................................................. 2¹/₂.3
  9476  Summers Dream *(BRichmond)* 8-11 KFallon (5) (s.i.s: outpcd & bhd tl styd on
          wl fnl 2f) .............................................................................................. 3¹/₂.4
    886⁴  Hotaria *(RMWhitaker)* 8-11 ACulhane (3) (lw: chsd ldrs: rdn ¹/₂-wy: grad wknd) 1¹/₂.5
          Simply Amiss (Fav) *(SirMarkPrescott)* 8-11 GDuffield (4) (leggy: scope: chsd
          ldrs: sn drvn along: wknd 2f out) ...................................................... 3.6
          Not Earsay *(EWeymes)* 8-11 WNewnes (7) (str: cmpt: bit bkwd: sn outpcd &
          bhd) ...................................................................................................... 2¹/₂.7

2/1 Simply Amiss, 5/2 CHARITY EXPRESS (IRE), 4/1 Moving Image (IRE), 5/1 Hotaria, 16/1 Meconopsis, 25/1
Not Earsay, 100/1 Summers Dream. CSF £11.57. Tote £2.40: £1.60 £2.80 (£5.80). Express Marie Curie Racing
Club (COCKERHAM) bred by Ennistown Stud in Ireland. 7 Rn                    64.4 sec (6.9)
                                                                          SF—14/4/–/–/–/–

**1234**    SCORTON CLAIMING STKS (3-Y.O) £2088.80 (£576.80: £274.40)
           **1m 5f 175y**                    2-50 (2-51)

          **Full Sight (IRE)** (53) *(MHTompkins)* 8-9 PRobinson (2) (trckd ldrs: hdwy on
          ins to ld over 1f out: easily) ............................................................ —1
    597  Natral Exchange (IRE) (66) (bl) *(JWHills)* 8-6 DHolland (6) (hld up: effrt 6f
          out: sn drvn along: hung lft 3f out: nvr able to chal) ...................... 4.2
  1048⁵  Mr Elk (48) *(MrsGRReveley)* 8-4⁽¹⁾ MBirch (1) (lw: disp ld: drvn along 5f out:
          hdd wl over 1f out: sn btn) ................................................................ ¹/₂.3
  1109⁵  Feeling Foolish (58) (bl) *(TFairhurst)* 8-6 ‡³JFanning (4) (in tch: effrt appr
          st: nt pce to chal) .............................................................................. 1¹/₂.4
    910  Soft Note (IRE) *(MBell)* 8-9 KFallon (5) (b.hind: trckd ldrs: effrt appr st: sn rdn &
          btn) ...................................................................................................... 6.5
    810  Split Second (42) (v) *(JWWatts)* 7-12 JLowe (3) (disp ld: drvn along:
          wknd 2f out) ........................................................................................ 1¹/₂.6

7/4 Natral Exchange (IRE), 9/4 FULL SIGHT (IRE), 9/2 Feeling Foolish (IRE)(op 9/4), 9/1 Soft Note (IRE)(op 7/2),
12/1 Split Second(op 8/1), 25/1 Mr Elk. CSF £5.96. Tote £3.10: £1.60 £1.50 (£2.30). Mr J. A. Fuller
(NEWMARKET) bred by Sean Gorman in Ireland. 6 Rn; Split Second clmd Mrs V Aconley £2,000
                                                                          3m 11.7 (16.5)
                                                                          SF—7/–/–/–/–/–

**1235**    LESLIE PETCH H'CAP (0-70) £2782.50 (£770.00: £367.50)    **5f 212y**    3-20 (3-21)

  1177²  **Furiella** (68) *(PCHaslam)* 4-9-9 ‡⁵JWeaver (5) (lw: chsd ldrs: led over 1f out: r.o
          wl) ........................................................................................................ —1
  1020²  Morpick (50) (v) *(JPLeigh)* 5-8-3 ‡⁷StephenDavies (3) (led tl hdd over 1f out: kpt
          on) ........................................................................................................ 1.2
  1130²  Angel Train (IRE) (37) (bl) *(JParkes)* 4-7-8 ‡³FNorton (1) (in tch: hdwy 2f out: no
          imp) ...................................................................................................... 5.3
  1020⁶  Arc Lamp (49) *(JAGlover)* 6-8-2 ‡⁷MHunt (6) (lw: rr div & hmpd appr st: hdwy 2f
          out: nvr able to chal) ........................................................................ 1¹/₂.4
  1020*  Catherines Well (62) (Fav) *(MWEasterby)* 9-9-8 TLucas (7) (lw: in tch tl lost pl
          over 2f out) ........................................................................................ 7.5
  1030  Nuclear Express (58) *(RLee)* 5-9-4 JCarroll (8) (lw: chsd ldrs 4f) ........ 5.6
    918  Brisas (50) (bl) *(TFairhurst)* 5-8-7 ‡³JFanning (4) (w ldr tl wknd 2f out) ........ 1.7
  1054²  Danzig Lad (USA) (41) *(MPNaughton)* 4-8-1 JakiHouston (2) (lw: rr div & effrt
          whn n.m.r & fell appr st) .................................................................. 0

13/8 Catherines Well, 4/1 FURIELLA, 9/2 Morpick, 8/1 Arc Lamp, 9/1 Nuclear Express, 11/1 Danzig Lad (USA),
20/1 Ors. CSF £20.80, CT £281.09. Tote £5.30: £1.30 £2.30 £2.90 (£20.00). Mr W. J. Hall (MIDDLEHAM) bred
by Langham Hall Bloodstock. 8 Rn                    1m 16.6 (6.1)
                                                    SF—53/29/–/2/–/–

**1236**     MERRYBENT MEDIAN AUCTION GRADUATION STKS (3-Y.O) £2108.40 (£582.40:
£277.20)     7f                                                    3-55 (3-55)

1055★ **Boursin (IRE)** *(PCalver)* 9-0 WNewnes (3) (lw: mde all: qcknd over 2f out:
easily) ....................................................................... —1
8844  Scottish Park (73) *(JPLeigh)* 8-1 ‡5JWeaver (4) (lw: a chsng wnr: one pce fnl 2f)   4.2
10312 Flourishing (IRE) (91) (Fav) *(GWragg)* 8-6 ‡3FNorton (2) (lw: hld up: effrt ent st:
sn rdn & no rspnse) ..................................................... hd.3
5214  Salda (76) *(RMWhitaker)* 8-11 ACulhane (1) (lw: dwlt: hld up & bhd: nvr plcd to
chal) ........................................................................ 1.4
9483  Brambles Way (59) *(WLBarker)* 8-4 JLowe (5) (hld up: hdwy to chal ent st: sn
rdn & btn) .................................................................. 2.5

**Evens** Flourishing (IRE), **9/4** BOURSIN (IRE), **9/2** Scottish Park, **14/1** Brambles Way, **16/1** Salda. CSF £11.30,
Tote £3.10: £2.10 £1.40 (£8.30). Mr Kenneth MacPherson (RIPON) bred by K. Molloy in Ireland. 5 Rn
1m 30.6 (7.4)
SF—47/22/26/28/15

**1237**     SCOTCH CORNER STKS (Mdn) £2382.80 (£660.80: £316.40)
1½m 44y                                                        4-25 (4-29)

789   West Stow (70) *(MRStoute)* 3–8-6 MBirch (1) (lw: mde all: easily) ................ —1
1009  Playful Juliet (CAN) *(BRCambidge)* 4–8-12 ‡5RPrice (5) (a.p: effrt u.p appr st: sn
chsng wnr: no imp) ....................................................... 15.2
9815  Hondeghem (Fav) *(CWCElsey)* 6–9-8 JCarroll (2) (lw: chsd wnr: pushed along
6f out: outpcd fnl 3f) ................................................... hd.3
Kalaberry *(WWHaigh)* 4–9-3 ACulhane (3) (hld up: hdwy 5f out: rdn ent st: sn
btn) ......................................................................... 15.4
9156  Tremendous (USA) *(JNorton)* 4–9-1 ‡7OPears (6) (wl bhd fnl 4f) ................ 6.5
O£O *Ivanov (USA) (12/1) Withdrawn (ref to ent stalls) · not under orders — Rule 4 applies*

**4/5** Hondeghem, **6/4** WEST STOW, **14/1** Kalaberry, **25/1** Playful Juliet (CAN), **100/1** Tremendous (USA). CSF
£19.93, Tote £2.20: £1.10 £4.90 (£5.10). Sheikh Mohammed (NEWMARKET) bred by White Lodge Stud Ltd. 5
Rn
2m 47.4 (13.4)
SF—24/–/9/–/–

**1238**     JERVAULX H'CAP (3-Y.O) (0-70) £2684.50 (£742.00: £353.50)     5f     4-55 (4-58)

1113★ **Optical (IRE) (69)** *(MPNaughton)* 9-8 (7x) ‡5JWeaver (4) (lw: trckd ldrs: led ins
fnl f: r.o u.p) ............................................................. —1
8903  Treasure Time (IRE) (53) *(JWhite)* 8-11 PRobinson (5) (lw: chsd ldrs: led appr
fnl f: sn hdd & nt qckn) ................................................ 1.2
7646  High Principles (54) *(JBerry)* 8-12 JCarroll (2) (s.i.s: hdwy 2f out: styd on wl nr
fin) .......................................................................... hd.3
1075  Baladee Pet (56) *(MrsVAAconley)* 9-0 KFallon (1) (hmpd s: hdwy ½-wy: ev ch
over 1f out: nt qckn) .................................................... 1½.4
11873 Auction King (IRE) (63) *(ASmith)* 9-7 ACulhane (9) (lw: hdwy u.p 2f out: nvr able
to chal) .................................................................... ½.5
1076★ Cheshire Annie (IRE) (59) (Fav) *(WCarter)* 9-3 (7x) WNewnes (6) (lw: led tl hdd
& wknd appr fnl f) ...................................................... 1½.6
582   Golden Proposal (50) (bl) *(MBell)* 8-5 ‡3FNorton (3) (b.hind: chsd ldrs over 3f:
sn wknd) ................................................................... 1½.7
949   Ahkam (IRE) (45) (bl) *(HThomsonJones)* 8-9 NCarlisle (8) (lw: nvr wnt pce) ...... 8.8
10064 Bright Paragon (IRE) (53) *(BRichmond)* 8-11 DHolland (7)(spd to ½-wy: sn wknd)7.9

**3/1** Cheshire Annie (IRE), **100/30** Treasure Time (IRE), **4/1** OPTICAL (IRE), **7/1** High Principles, **8/1** Auction King
(IRE), **14/1** Baladee Pet, Golden Proposal, **16/1** Ahkam (IRE), **33/1** Bright Paragon (IRE). CSF £16.40, CT
£79.92. Tote £3.50: £1.90 £1.40 £2.40 (£3.00). Mrs H. H. Wane (RICHMOND) bred by Oliver Murphy in Ireland.
9 Rn
63.9 sec (6.4)
SF—35/20/20/16/21/11

T/Plpt: £29.70 (45.95 Tckts).                                                       O'R

# CATTERICK (L-H)
## Saturday, June 6th [Good, Good to soft on bnds]
Going Allowance: 0.50 sec per fur (Y)                         Wind: slt half against
Stalls: low

**1239**     RIPON SELECT FOODS (S) STKS     £2304.40 (£638.40: £305.20)
1m 5f 175y                                                     2-25 (2-26)

8954  **The Last Empress (IRE) (66)** (Fav) *(PFICole)* 4-8-9 AClark (1) (lw: hld up gng
wl: smooth hdwy 5f out: hrd rdn to ld 1f out: wnt clr nr fin) .. —1

951² Carrolls Marc (IRE) **(54)** *(PJFeilden)* 4–8-11 ‡³JFanning (4) (stumbled bnd after 5f: hdwy over 6f out: led over 3f out to 1f out: no ex) .......... 6.2

1009 Quiet Riot **(40)** *(JWhite)* 10–8-11 ‡³FNorton (9) (in tch: effrt & hdwy 4f out: one pce fnl 2f) .......... 5.3

1119 J P Morgan **(49)** (v) *(MPNaughton)* 4–8-9 ‡⁵JWeaver (2) (lw: cl up: led after 5f: clr over 6f out: hdd over 3f out: wknd fnl 2f) .......... 7.4

875 Lisalee (IRE) *(JParkes)* 4–8-9 LCharnock (7) (bhd: hdwy 4f out: nvr nrr) .......... 7.5

362 Dari Sound (IRE) **(51)** *(JGFitzGerald)* 4–9-0 TLucas (10) (hld up: hdwy to chase ldrs over 6f out: rdn & wknd over 3f out) .......... ¾.6

1195 Strength in Depth (IRE) **(45)** *(MJohnston)* 4–8-9 RPElliott (3) (chsd ldrs tl rdn & wknd 4f out) .......... 2½.7

1034 Temple Island (IRE) **(25)** (bl) *(PJMakin)* 4–8-6 ‡³TSprake (12) (chsd ldrs tl wknd 5f out) .......... 20.8

Yorkshire Fisher (IRE) *(MissGayKelleway)* 4–9-0 AMunro (6) (b: a in rr: wl bhd fnl 6f) .......... 15.9

605 Sailor Boy **(50)** (bl) *(ASReid)* 6–8-7 ‡⁷PMcCabe (11) (led 5f: sn lost pl: lost tch 6f out) .......... 5.10

Emma Victoria *(TKersey)* 4–8-9 GHind (8) (b: sn bhd: t.o fnl 6f) .......... 25.11

**4/9** THE LAST EMPRESS (IRE)(op 4/6), **9/2** Carrolls Marc (IRE), **12/1** Dari Sound (IRE), J P Morgan (op 8/1), **14/1** Quiet Riot, Strength in Depth (IRE), **50/1** Temple Island (IRE), Sailor Boy, Yorkshire Fisher (IRE), **100/1** Ors. CSF £3.47, Tote £1.60: £1.10 £1.40 £3.30 (£2.20). Mr Reg Hester (WHATCOMBE) bred by Binfield Manor Farms Ltd in Ireland. 11 Rn; Bt in 10,600 gns

3m 8.1 (12.9)

SF—36/26/16/–/–/–

---

**1240** 'YORK HANDMADE BRICKS' STKS (2-Y.O) £2208.00 (£608.00: £288.00)
**5f 212y**

2-55 (2-56)

**Colyan (IRE)** (Fav) *(MRStoute)* 8-11 PD'Arcy (5) (unf: lw: chsd ldrs: bmpd after 1f: smooth hdwy to ld appr fnl f: sn clr: comf) .......... —1

1007* Grand Dancer (IRE) *(RJRWilliams)* 8-3 ‡³FNorton (6) (lw: sn led: rdn over 2f out: hdd 1f out: no ch w wnr) .......... 5.2

1127* Shadow Jury *(JSWainwright)* 9-4 WNewnes (1) (led early: pushed along & outpcd appr st: n.m.r & swtchd appr fnl f: styd on) .......... nk.3

900* Super Seve (IRE) *(JBerry)* 9-4 JCarroll (3) (prom: rdn to chal 2f out: wknd over 1f out) .......... ¾.4

769⁵ Bright Gem *(TFairhurst)* 8-10 ‡³JFanning (4) (cl up: rdn 2f out: hung rt u.p & wknd over 1f out) .......... 5.5

874 Eightofus *(GMMoore)* 8-11 PBurke (2) (nvr trbld ldrs) .......... 4.6

Charlies Reward *(WLBarker)* 8-11 LCharnock (3) (leggy: scope: bit bkwd: s.i.s: effrt ½-wy: sn outpcd) .......... 2½.7

**4/6** COLYAN (IRE)(op 5/4), **9/4** Grand Dancer (IRE)(op 5/4), **8/1** Super Seve(op 5/1), **16/1** Shadow Jury(op 10/1), **66/1** Bright Gem, **100/1** Eightofus, **200/1** Charlies Reward. CSF £2.40, Tote £2.00: £1.60 £1.70 (£2.00). Lord White of Hull (NEWMARKET) bred by Stackallan Stud in Ireland. 7 Rn

1m 17.7 (7.2)

SF—13/–/–/–/–

---

**1241** EUROPEAN LAND H'CAP (0-80) £2560.00 (£760.00: £360.00: £160.00)
**1m 7f 177y**

3-25 (3-27)

(Weights raised 6 lb)

1022⁵ Our Aisling **(66)** (Fav) *(SGNorton)* 4–9-0 ‡⁷OPears (8) (lw: hld up: stdy hdwy over 6f out: nt clr run 3f out: led jst ins fnl f: r.o wl) .......... —1

1119⁴ Northants **(48)** *(WStorey)* 6–8-4 AlexGreaves (12) (bhd: hdwy 6f out: rdn over 2f out: led briefly appr fnl f: hung lft & nt qckn) .......... 1.2

663 Fen Princess (IRE) **(43)** *(PCHaslam)* 4–7-9 ‡³JFanning (1) (chsd ldrs: led over 5f out: rdn clr 2f out: hdd appr fnl f: no ex) .......... 8.3

Latvian **(68)** *(RAllan)* 5–9-5 ‡⁵JWeaver (9) (trckd ldrs gng wl: bmpd appr st: wknd 2f out) .......... 4.4

964 Rexy Boy **(37)** *(WLBarker)* 5–7-7 LCharnock (7) (chsd ldrs: drvn along 4f out: wknd over 2f out) .......... nk.5

916⁴ Carefree Times **(44)** *(JNorton)* 5–8-0 AMunro (3) (in tch: outpcd 6f out: sme late hdwy) .......... 3½.6

South Cross (USA) **(43)** *(GMMoore)* 7–7-13 PBurke (10) (a in rr) .......... 30.7

1108⁴ A a Bamba **(59)** *(NACallaghan)* 3–7-2 ‡⁷CHawksley (11) (cl up: led after 7f: hdd over 5f out: sn wknd) .......... ½.8

987 Nicholas Mark **(60)** *(JGFitzGerald)* 8–9-2 TLucas (6) (led 7f: prom tl hmpd & wknd qckly 5f out) .......... 6.9

530⁴ Beauchamp Fizz **(62)** *(WStorey)* 4–9-3 SWebster (4) (a bhd: lost tch 7f out: t.o) **10**

LONG HANDICAP: Rexy Boy 6-12.

**13/8** OUR AISLING(5/2—6/4), **11/2** Northants, **13/2** A a Bamba(op 4/1), **8/1** Latvian, **10/1** Beauchamp Fizz, **11/1** Carefree Times, **14/1** Nicholas Mark, **25/1** South Cross (USA), **33/1** Fen Princess (IRE), **66/1** Rexy Boy. CSF £9.76, CT £168.05. Tote £2.60: £1.50 £1.80 £5.40 (£7.90). Mr A. K. Smeaton (BARNSLEY) bred by A. K. Smeaton. 10 Rn                                                              3m 36.5 (15.5)
SF—25/14/–/17/–/–

| **1242** | NICHOLAS MARK STKS (Mdn 3-Y.O.F) £2070.00 (£570.00: £270.00) |
|---|---|
| | 1½m 44y |

3-55 (3-55)

| 873[4] | **Kirsten** *(WJarvis)* 8-11  JCarroll (4) (trckd ldrs: led over 3f out: sn clr: drvn out) . —1 |
| 904 | Oak Apple (USA) **(58)** *(BHanbury)* 8-4 ‡[7]VBray (1) (b: hld up & bhd: hdwy over 2f out: styd on wl: nt rch wnr) . 7.2 |
| 1082[3] | White Wedding **(70)** *(PFICole)* 8-11  AClark (2) (prom: drvn along appr st: one pce fnl 2f) . 1½.3 |
| 881[2] | Top Table **(Fav)** *(MRStoute)* 8-11  AMunro (6) (chsd ldr: rdn along over 4f out: kpt on same pce fnl 2f) . ¾.4 |
| 908 | Humour (IRE) **(67)** (bl) *(CFWall)* 8-11  NDay (5) (reminders after s: led tl hdd over 3f out: wknd 2f out) . 3.5 |
| 922[3] | Clear Sound *(GWragg)* 8-8 ‡[3]FNorton (3) (lw: bhd: pushed along & outpcd 5f out: sn btn) . 15.6 |

**5/4** Top Table, **7/2** KIRSTEN, **9/2** Clear Sound, **7/1** Humour (IRE), White Wedding, **25/1** Oak Apple (USA). CSF £51.12, Tote £3.20: £1.80 £5.90 (£41.80). Lord Howard de Walden (NEWMARKET) bred by Miss K. Rausing and Lord Howard de Walden. 6 Rn                                                       2m 45.6 (11.6)
SF—41/20/24/22/16/–

| **1243** | YORKSHIRE TELEVISION H'CAP (0-70) £2560.00 (£760.00: £360.00: £160.00) |
|---|---|
| | 7f |

4-25 (4-27)

| 1093[3] | **Euroblake (65)** *(TDBarron)* 5-9-10 ‡[3]JFanning (7) (hld up: effrt 2f out: styd on u.p to ld nr fin) . —1 |
| 883[2] | Hamadryad (IRE) **(64)** **(Fav)** *(WCarter)* 4-9-12  JCarroll (13) (lw: chsd ldrs: led 2f out: edgd lft u.p: nt qckn & hdd nr fin) . nk.2 |
| 1129[3] | Inseyab **(57)** *(PCHaslam)* 4-9-0 ‡[5]JWeaver (1) (lw: a.p: rdn to chal wl over 1f out: no ex nr fin) . ½.3 |
| 1070[5] | Quiet Victory **(44)** *(MissLCSiddall)* 5-8-3 ‡[3]FNorton (8) (cl up: rdn over 2f out: styd on same pce fnl f) . 2½.4 |
| 1130[6] | Hizeem **(31)** *(MPNaughton)* 6-7-7  JakiHouston (3) (lw: bhd: styd on u.p fnl 2f: nvr nrr) . 2.5 |
| 948 | Kick on Majestic (IRE) **(45)** (bl) *(NBycroft)* 3-7-11  SWood (10) (chsd ldr tl outpcd appr fnl f) . nk.6 |
| 1130[3] | Choice Lot **(46)** *(JJO'Neill)* 5-8-8  LCharnock (4) (chsd ldrs: rdn appr st: grad wknd fnl 2f) . s.h.7 |
| 948 | Preamble **(51)** *(MrsJRRamsden)* 5-8-8  PBurke (12) (lw: hld up: nvr trbld ldrs) 1½.8 |
| 1130* | Cool Enough **(42)** *(MrsJRRamsden)* 11-8-4  AMunro (9) (stumbled s: bhd: effrt over 2f out: no imp: eased whn btn) . 5.9 |
| 1089 | Savanga (USA) **(40)** (v) *(MMcCormack)* 4-8-2  AClark (2) (lw: mde most tl wknd 2f out) . 3½.10 |
| 420 | Daisy Grey **(49)** (bl) *(ASReid)* 4-8-4 ‡[7]PMcCabe (5) (chsd ldrs over 4f) . 1.11 |

LONG HANDICAP: Hizeem 7-6.
*Stewards Enquiry: Houston suspended 5-8/6/92 (excessive use of whip).*

**3/1** Hamadryad (IRE)(op 9/2), **7/2** Cool Enough, **5/1** EUROBLAKE, Inseyab, **8/1** Quiet Victory, **12/1** Choice Lot, **14/1** Savanga (USA), **16/1** Preamble, **20/1** Daisy Grey, **25/1** Ors. CSF £20.31, CT £73.05. Tote £5.30: £1.70 £1.50 £1.90 (£11.60). Mr W. G. Swiers (THIRSK) bred by Viscount Leverhulme. 11 Rn      1m 31.3 (8.1)
SF—41/42/28/9/–/–

| **1244** | NORTHERN OCEAN SERVICES STKS (Mdn 3-Y.O) £2070.00 (£570.00: £270.00) |
|---|---|
| | 7f |

4-55 (4-55)

| 1029[3] | **Fusion (USA)** *(PFICole)* 9-0  AMunro (2) (lw: trckd ldrs: shkn up to ld appr fnl f: r.o wl) . —1 |
| | Ginger Flower **(Fav)** *(GWragg)* 8-6 ‡[3]FNorton (3) (unf: prom: led 4f out: rdn 2f out: hdd & nt qckn appr fnl f) . 3½.2 |
| 865 | Gizlaan (USA) *(BHanbury)* 8-2 ‡[7]VBray (4) (dwlt: led after 1f tl hdd 4f out: kpt on same pce fnl 2f) . 1½.3 |
| 1109 | Kirkby Belle **(49)** *(EWeymes)* 8-9  GHind (3) (led 1f: chal over 2f out: wknd over 1f out) . 2.4 |

**10/11** Ginger Flower, **11/10** FUSION (USA), **14/1** Gizlaan (USA)(op 8/1), **20/1** Kirkby Belle. CSF £2.44, Tote £1.70 (£1.40). Mr Fahd Salman (WHATCOMBE) bred by Edward A. Seltzer in USA. 4 Rn      1m 31.5 (8.3)
SF—28/9/–/1

T/Plpt: £15.70 (168.3 Tckts).                                                                0'R

974—**HAYDOCK (L-H)**

**Friday, June 5th [Good to soft]**

Going Allowance: St: 0.10; Rnd: 0.20 sec per fur (G)Wind: fresh half bhd    Vis: bad 5th & 6th

Stalls: high

## 1245

HALSALL STKS (Mdn 3-Y-O) £1884.00 (£524.00: £252.00)    1¹/₄m 120y 6-40 (6-43)

| | | |
|---|---|---|
| 1033² | **Turgenev (IRE)** *(JHMGosden)* 9-0 DHolland (2) (hld up: 6th st: led over 2f out: hld on gamely) | —1 |
| 857⁴ | Greek Gold (IRE) (Fav) *(MRStoute)* 9-0 PatEddery (8) (hld up: hdwy over 3f out: jnd wnr 1f out: hrd rdn & unable qckn nr fin) | ³/₄.2 |
| 746³ | Triennium (USA) *(LMCumani)* 9-0 LDettori (9) (lw: a.p: 3rd st: ev ch over 1f out: unable qckn) | 1¹/₂.3 |
| 944⁴ | Kabayil *(PTWalwyn)* 8-9 WCarson (1) (chsd ldrs: 4th st: kpt on one pce fnl 2f) | 1.4 |
| | Pharly Dancer *(WWHaigh)* 9-0 ACulhane (7) (styd on fnl 2f: nvr nrr) | 5.5 |
| | Mahairy (USA) *(AAScott)* 9-0 BRaymond (6) (bit bkwd: bhd: effrt u.p 3f out: nvr nr to chal) | ¹/₂.6 |
| 1012² | Kiveton Tycoon (IRE) (bl) *(JAGlover)* 9-0 DNicholls (5) (led tl hdd & wknd over 2f out) | ¹/₂.7 |
| 620 | Suzie Sue (IRE) *(DWPArbuthnot)* 8-9 BProcter (3) (b.hind: chsd ldrs: 5th st: wknd over 2f out) | 5.8 |
| | Dioman Shadeed (USA) *(JRFanshawe)* 9-0 WRSwinburn (4) (w'like: leggy: bit bkwd: s.v.s: a bhd: t.o) | 10.9 |
| | Venture Fourth (55) *(EJAlston)* 9-0 KFallon (3) (still unf: bhd fr ¹/₂-wy: t.o) | s.h.10 |
| 697 | Blimpers Disco (46) *(EHOwenjun)* 8-7 ‡7WBray (11) (bit bkwd: hdwy & 2nd st: rdn & wknd 3f out: t.o) | 20.11 |

**Evens** Greek Gold (IRE)(tchd 4/6), **5/1** Kiveton Tycoon (IRE), **7/1** TURGENEV (IRE), **15/2** Kabayil(5/1—8/1), **8/1** Triennium (USA), **14/1** Dioman Shadeed (USA), **25/1** Mahairy (USA), **50/1** Ors. CSF £13.95, Tote £6.90: £1.60 £1.30 £2.10 (£4.70). Sheikh Mohammed (NEWMARKET) bred by Paolo Tomei in Ireland. 11 Rn

2m 18.55 (6.85)

SF—52/50/47/40/35/34

## 1246

BURTONWOOD BREWERY H'CAP (3-Y-O) (0-85) £2978.50 (£826.00: £395.50)
1m 30y    7-10 (7-18)

(Weights raised 1 lb)

| | | |
|---|---|---|
| 1122★ | **Combative (IRE) (78)** (v) (Fav) *(JHMGosden)* 9-1 (6x) PatEddery (8) (lw: 6th st: rdn to ld ins fnl f: all out) | —1 |
| 816³ | Trafalgar Boy (USA) (84) *(JEtherington)* 9-2 ‡5JWeaver (1) (lw: a.p: 3rd st: c wd & racd alone: rdn over 2f out: kpt on gamely) | ¹/₂.2 |
| 930³ | Common Council (76) *(GAPritchard-Gordon)* 8-13 GCarter (5) (hld up: hdwy u.p 2f out: styd on fnl f) | 4.3 |
| 985² | Devon Dancer (73) (v) *(MHEasterby)* 8-10 MBirch (4) (swtg: led: clr ent st: hdd ins fnl f: sn btn) | 2¹/₂.4 |
| 825 | May Hills Legacy (IRE) (74) *(DWPArbuthnot)* 8-11 DHolland (7) (b: chsd ldrs: 4th st: wknd fnl 2f) | 8.5 |
| 801 | Buddy (IRE) (59) *(MBell)* 7-7³ ‡3FNorton (12) (hld up: styd on appr fnl f: nvr nrr) | 3.6 |
| 1072 | Military Expert (72) *(CaptJWilson)* 8-9 JLowe (10) (prom: 2nd st: wknd over 2f out) | 1.7 |
| 1091★ | Act of Union (IRE) (77) *(WJPearce)* 9-0 (6x) DNicholls (3) (lw: hld up: effrt 3f out: nvr nr to chal) | 2.8 |
| 984★ | Castlerea Lad (81) *(RHollinshead)* 9-4 WCarson (2) (chsd ldrs: 5th st: sn rdn & wknd) | hd.9 |
| 541 | Oyston's Life (56) *(JBerry)* 7-7 RFox (9) (sn pushed along: a bhd) | ³/₄.10 |
| | Chill Wind (57) *(NBycroft)* 7-5⁽¹⁾ ‡3JFanning (6) (bit bkwd: a bhd) | ¹/₂.11 |

LONG HANDICAP: Oyston's Life 7-0, Chill Wind 7-5.

**9/4** COMBATIVE (IRE), **9/2** Trafalgar Boy (USA), **11/2** Common Council, **9/1** Castlerea Lad, Act of Union (IRE), **12/1** May Hills Legacy (IRE), Buddy (IRE), Devon Dancer, **20/1** Military Expert, **33/1** Oyston's Life, **50/1** Chill Wind. CSF £12.08, CT £44.85. Tote £3.20: £1.80 £1.50 £1.90 (£6.30). Mr K. Abdulla (NEWMARKET) bred by Mrs Kiki Ward Platt in Ireland. 11 Rn

1m 46.45 (6.05)

SF—34/33/18/7/–/–

## 1247

CASSINI PARFUMS H'CAP (0-90) £3132.00 (£936.00: £448.00: £204.00)
6f    7-40 (7-44)

| | | |
|---|---|---|
| 1014★ | **Crystal Jack (FR) (75)** *(FHLee)* 4–9-3 BRaymond (5) (a.p: led 2f out: r.o wl) | —1 |
| 980 | Dominuet (80) *(JLSpearing)* 7–9-8 RFox (4) (hdwy ¹/₂-wy: ev ch fnl f: r.o) | 1.2 |
| 1050³ | Red Rosein (80) *(CaptJWilson)* 6–9-8 GCarter (1) (s.s: sn rdn along: hdwy wl over 1f out: nt rch ldrs) | 3.3 |

885 Northern Spark **(69)** *(CWThornton)* 4-8-11 DMcKeown (9) (hld up: hdwy 2f out: n.m.r over 1f out: nt rcvr) ............................................... nk.4
980* Gondo **(77)** *(EJAlston)* 5-9-5 KFallon (10) (lw: chsd ldrs: effrt & n.m.r appr fnl f: nt pce to chal) ............................................... ¹/₂.5
723 Macfarlane **(75)** *(MJFetherston-Godley)* 4-9-3 DHolland (12) (prom: rdn & edgd lft over 1f out: one pce) ............................................... hd.6
1014⁴ Garth **(77)** *(PJMakin)* 4-9-2 ‡³TSprake (2) (gd spd over 3f) ............................................... 1¹/₂.7
980⁴ Pallium (IRE) **(75)** *(MPNaughton)* 4-8-12 ‡⁵JWeaver (7) (lw: dwlt: nvr plcd to chal) ............................................... ³/₄.8
1093⁴ Glenstal Princess **(66)** *(RHollinshead)* 5-8-8 PatEddery (6) (outpcd: effrt wl over 1f out: no imp) ............................................... ³/₄.9
Playful Poet **(68)** *(MHEasterby)* 5-8-5 ‡⁵SMaloney (3) (bit bkwd: led 3f: sn wknd) hd.10
Final Shot **(74)** *(MHEasterby)* 5-9-2 MBirch (8) (bit bkwd: spd to ¹/₂-wy: grad wknd) ............................................... 1¹/₂.11

**7/2** Macfarlane, **5/1** Gondo, **11/2** Glenstal Princess, **13/2** Garth, **8/1** CRYSTAL JACK (FR), Pallium (IRE), **17/2** Red Rosein, **10/1** Dominuet, **14/1** Playful Poet, **16/1** Northern Spark, **20/1** Final Shot. CSF £81.39, CT £646.93. Tote £7.80: £2.40 £3.40 £2.60 (£98.70). Mrs B. Facchino (WILMSLOW) bred by Daniel Fernandez and Paul Vuillard in France. 11 Rn ............ 1m 14.27 (2.57)
SF—64/65/53/41/47/44/37

---

**1248**   RED ROSE H'CAP (0-70) (Amateurs) £1814.00 (£504.00: £242.00)
1¹/₄m 120y                                                        8-10 (8-15)

502 **Forelino (USA) (57)** *(JLDunlop)* 3-10-0 ‡³MissEJohnsonHoughton (7) (lost pl ¹/₂-wy: hdwy over 2f out: qcknd to ld wl ins fnl f) ............................... —1
232⁵ Lots of Luck **(47)** *(Fav)* *(JPearce)* 9-10-8 MrsLPearce (11) (a.p: 3rd st: led over 2f out: hrd rdn & hdd wl ins fnl f) ............................................... 4.2
075⁹ Buckingham Band (USA) **(40)** (hl) *(FHLee)* 4-10-1 MissIDWJones (16) (lw: a.p: 4th st: led over 3f out tl over 2f out: ev ch fnl f: r.o) ............ hd.3
1143⁵ Sunset Reins Free **(39)** (bl) *(EJAlston)* 7-9-11 ‡³MrWilkinson (17) (lw: hdwy 3f out: kpt on u.p ins fnl f) ............................................... 6.4
974³ Flying Down to Rio (IRE) **(57)** *(MPNaughton)* 4-11-4 MissPRobson (20) (lw: chsd ldrs: 6th st: rdn 2f out: one pce) ............................... 2¹/₂.5
1004 Abeloni **(62)** *(AAScott)* 3-10-5 ‡³MissTBracegirdle (18) (mde most over 7f: wknd wl over 1f out) ............................................... 8.6
Old Peg **(50)** (bl) *(MHEasterby)* 4-10-8 ‡³MrsSEasterby (12) (styd on fnl 2f: nvr nrr) ............................................... nk.7
974 Cheeky Pot **(52)** (v) *(DenysSmith)* 4-10-10 ‡³MissMCarson (6) (nvr nr to chal) ³/₄.8
1089 Marandisa **(48)** *(MPNaughton)* 5-10-6 ‡³MrRGreen (5) (prom: 5th st: rdn & wknd over 2f out) ............................................... hd.9
951 Mahaasin **(44)** *(LJCodd)* 4-10-2 ‡³MissCBurgess (19) (m.n.s) ............................ 1.10
Most Interesting **(38)** *(GHJones)* 7-9-10⁽²⁾ ‡³MissHMcCaull (4) (m.n.s) ............ 1¹/₂.11
763 Must Be Magical (USA) **(36)** *(FHLee)* 4-9-11 MissJWinter (2) (m.n.s) ............ 1.12
962³ Halston Prince **(65)** *(MrsJRRamsden)* 5-11-12 MrRHale (8) (2nd st: wknd 3f out)1¹/₂.13
Ben's Beauty **(40)** *(MrsSOliver)* 4-9-12⁽¹⁾ ‡³MrRBraham (14) (bit bkwd: m.n.s) 2¹/₂.14
1009 No Comebacks **(40)** *(EJAlston)* 4-10-5 ‡³MrsSBarclay (3) (swtg: s.s: a bhd) .... 3.15
761 First Exhibition **(34)** *(MrsAKnight)* 5-9-6 ‡³MrDSalter (1) (b.off hind: a bhd) .... 1¹/₂.16
1108⁵ Smoke **(46)** *(JParkes)* 6-10-7 MrsAFarrell (10) (m.n.s) ............................ 1¹/₂.17
Shadideen (USA) **(67)** *(MissLAPerratt)* 4-12-0 MissLPerratt (9) (bkwd: chsd ldrs over 5f) ............................................... 2.18
The Metropole (IRE) **(51)** *(AWPotts)* 3-9-8 ‡³MissSJudge (15) (b: bkwd: t.o) .. nk.19
*Ahsanta Sana Withdrawn not under orders (at 7/4 go to s) : not under orders*

**2/1** Lots of Luck(op 3/1), **6/1** Sunset Reins Free, Flying Down to Rio (IRE), **7/1** Halston Prince(op 4/1), **9/1** Smoke, **10/1** Old Peg, **14/1** Buckingham Band (USA), Cheeky Pot, Abeloni, **20/1** FORELINO (USA), **33/1** Mahaasin, Marandisa, No Comebacks, The Metropole (IRE), Shadideen (USA), Must Be Magical (USA), **50/1** Ors. CSF £62.68, CT £592.41. Tote £44.00: £4.70 £1.50 £2.90 £1.40 (£77.30). Mr P. G. Goulandris (ARUNDEL) bred by Hesmonds Stud Ltd in USA. 19 Rn ............ 2m 21.16 (9.46)
SF—40/40/32/16/32/3

---

**1249**   LANCASHIRE LIFE STKS (Mdn 2-Y-O) £1786.00 (£496.00: £238.00)      6f 8-40 (8-41)

**Humam (IRE) (Fav)** *(HThomsonJones)* 9-0 RHills (5) (gd sort: lw: a.p: led 1f out: pushed out) ............................................... —1
Shebl (USA) *(MRStoute)* 9-0 WRSwinburn (2) (gd sort: hld up: hdwy 2f out: rdn & ev ch fnl f: r.o) ............................................... 1¹/₂.2
Woodenville (USA) *(LMCumani)* 9-0 LDettori (7) (w'like: str: bit bkwd: led tl appr fnl f: one pce) ............................................... 2.3
933 Savings Bank *(GAPritchard-Gordon)* 9-0 GCarter (1) (b.nr hind: prom: rdn over 1f out: one pce) ............................................... 2¹/₂.4

Harpoon Louie (USA) *(MHEasterby)* 9-0 KDarley (6) (wl grwn: bkwd: hdwy ½-wy: kpt on ins fnl f: nt rch ldrs) ............................................... 2½.5

10174 Argyle Cavalier (IRE) *(FHLee)* 9-0 ACulhane (9) (s.i.s: hdwy 2f out: nvr nrr) .... 1½.6

Wufud (USA) *(JLDunlop)* 9-0 WCarson (3) (gd sort: chsd ldrs: drvn along over 2f out: nt pce to chal) ........................................................ ¾.7

Hawl (USA) *(AAScott)* 9-0 BRaymond (11) (w'like: str: bkwd: s.i.s: sn bhd & rdn along: n:d) ........................................................................ s.h.8

1017 Resolution Time *(MrsVAAconley)* 9-0 PBurke (10) (m.n.s) .................................... 3.9

Weaver George (IRE) *(MHEasterby)* 9-0 MBirch (4) (w'like: prom over 3f) ..... 1½.10

Knight of Shalot (IRE) *(PWChapple-Hyam)* 9-0 DHolland (8) (scope: s.i.s: sn rcvrd: spd over 3f) ..................................................................... 1½.11

**6/4** HUMAM (IRE)(op 9/4), **5/1** Hawl (USA), **11/2** Shebl (USA)(op 7/2), **6/1** Wufud (USA), **13/2** Knight of Shalot (IRE)(op 4/1), **8/1** Woodenville (USA), **14/1** Argyle Cavalier (IRE), **20/1** Savings Bank, **25/1** Weaver George (IRE), Harpoon Louie (USA), **33/1** Resolution Time. CSF £11.64, Tote £2.80: £1.30 £2.00 £2.90 (£6.80). Mr Hamdan Al-Maktoum (NEWMARKET) bred by Dene Investments N.V. in Ireland. 11 Rn     1m 15.44 (3.74)
SF—37/31/23/13/3/–

**1250**   WINWICK H'CAP (3-Y.O) (0-90) £2660.00 (£735.00: £350.00)   **2m 45y** 9-10 (9-10)
(Weights raised 18 lb)

831 **Jack Button (IRE) (68)** *(BobJones)* 9-7 NDay (2) (chsd ldr: 2nd st: led over 2f out: clr fnl f: eased nr fin) ................................................... —1

664* Eurotwist **(66)** (Fav) *(TDBarron)* 9-5 AlexGreaves (1) (hld up: 3rd st: chsd wnr fnl 2f: rdn over 1f out: r.o wl nr fin) ..................................... ¾.2

702 Millador **(55)** *(MHTompkins)* 8-8 PRobinson (3) (led & sn clr: rdn 3f out: sn hdd & btn: t.o) .................................................................... 25.3

**4/6** Eurotwist, **2/1** JACK BUTTON (IRE), **4/1** Millador. CSF £3.71, Tote £3.00 (£1.50). A. and B. Racing (NEWMARKET) bred by Empress Syndicate in Ireland. 3 Rn     3m 43.69 (16.49)

T/Dble: Race 3: £396.30 (3.1 Tckts). T/Trio: Race 3: £396.30 (3.1 Tckts). T/Plpt: £296.20 (14.4 Tckts). IM

# HAYDOCK (L-H)

## Saturday, June 6th [Good]

Going Allowance: St: nil sec per fur; Rnd: 0.10 sec per fur (G)     Wind: mod half bhd

Stalls: high

**1251**   PENNY LANE AUCTION STKS (Mdn 2-Y.O) £2679.00 (£744.00: £357.00)
**5f**                                                          2-00 (2-06)

9173 **Nicky Mygirl** *(MBrittain)* 7-11 JLowe (12) (mde all: wandered u.p fnl f: all out) .. —1

8745 Dayjuz (IRE) *(FHLee)* 9-0 DMcKeown (14) (a.p: ev ch fnl f: r.o) ........................ nk.2

10574 Brigadore Gold *(RHannon)* 8-0 KDarley (2) (a.p: ev ch ins fnl f: r.o) ................. s.h.3

7822 Spring Sunrise *(MBlanshard)* 7-6 ‡5DHarrison (11) (a chsng ldrs: rdn & unable qckn fnl f) ................................................................... nk.4

9862 Manor Adventure *(BAMcMahon)* 8-3 DHolland (15) (lw: a.p: nt clr run over 1f out: swtchd & r.o nr fin) ............................................... nk.5

Bold Seven (IRE) *(FHLee)* 8-3 RLappin (4) (scope: a.p: ev ch ins fnl f: unable qckn) ............................................................................ hd.6

Park Dance *(WJarvis)* 8-9 BRaymond (10) (small: chsd ldrs: no hdwy fnl f) ..... 1½.7

1017 Mohican Brave (IRE) *(JGFitzGerald)* 8-5 KFallon (7) (bit bkwd: prom over 3f) . 1½.8

867 Miss Otter (IRE) *(GAPritchard-Gordon)* 8-0 NCarlisle (9) (prom 3f: wknd qckly) s.h.9

Nancy (IRE) *(CWCElsey)* 7-7(1) ‡5SMaloney (5) (lt-f: s.s: r.o appr fnl f: nvr nrr) s.h.10

Sky Wish *(MissSEHall)* 8-2 NConnorton (1) (leggy: lt-f: bkwd: s.i.s: nvr nr ldrs) nk.11

476 Hills Raceaid (IRE) *(JBerry)* 8-3 GCarter (6) (spd over 3f) ............................... ½.12

Guv'nors Gift *(MHTompkins)* 7-10(6b) ‡7SMulvey (4) (lt-f: dwlt: outpcd) .......... 1½.13

10466 Sweetings Scampy (IRE) (Fav) *(MHEasterby)* 8-3 MBirch (13) (outpcd) ........... 1½.14

Rosie O'Reilly (IRE) *(EJAlston)* 8-0 CRutter (8) (lt-f: unf: outpcd: t.o) ................. 8.15

**3/1** Sweetings Scampy (IRE), **100/30** Manor Adventure(op 2/1), **13/2** Spring Sunrise, **7/1** Park Dance(op 4/1), **10/1** Brigadore Gold, NICKY MYGIRL, **12/1** Dayjuz (IRE), **16/1** Sky Wish, Nancy (IRE), Guv'nors Gift, **20/1** Mohican Brave (IRE), Bold Seven (IRE), **25/1** Hills Raceaid (IRE), Rosie O'Reilly (IRE), **33/1** Miss Otter (IRE). CSF £125.19, Tote £10.10: £2.30 £3.90 £2.90 (£59.10). Mr Jim Unsworth (WARTHILL) bred by Campbell Stud. 15 Rn     61.80 sec (2.80)
SF—27/43/28/19/29/28

**1252**   ECONOLOFT H'CAP (3-Y.O) (0-90) £5481.00 (£1638.00: £784.00: £357.00)
**1¼m 120y**                                                  2-30 (2-33)
(Weights raised 4 lb)

921 **Mad Militant (IRE) (77)** *(RHollinshead)* 9-1 LDettori (3) (hld up: hdwy 3f out: led 1f out: r.o wl) ...................................................... —1

911⁴ Ajo (IRE) (83) (MRStoute) 9-7 DHolland (7) (a.p: 2nd st: led over 2f out to 1f out: r.o u.p) .......................................................... 2¹/₂.2

921⁵ Bigwheel Bill (IRE) (77) (JWWatts) 9-1 JLowe (10) (chsd ldrs: 6th st: r.o u.p ins fnl f) ......................................................... nk.3

858⁴ Will Soon (70) (HCandy) 8-8 CRutter (2) (hdwy on ins over 2f out: n.m.r appr fnl f: r.o) ............................................................ nk.4

1025 Doyce (64) (JEtherington) 7-11 ‡5NKennedy (6) (hld up in tch: styd on fnl 2f: nvr plcd to chal) .................................................. 2¹/₂.5

974* Miss Hyde (USA) (63) (v) (JAGlover) 8-1 NCarlisle (4) (led tl over 2f out: sn wknd) ................................................................. 1.6

800⁶ Le Baron Perche (FR) (75) (CJames) 8-13 GBaxter (9) (swtg: nvr trbld ldrs) ...... 3.7

653⁵ Najeb (USA) (81) (BHanbury) 9-5 BRaymond (8) (lw: chsd ldrs: 4th st: wknd 2f out) ................................................................... 1¹/₂.8

1152² Batabanoo (68) (Fav) (MrsGRReveley) 8-6 KDarley (5) (lw: hld up: 5th st: rdn over 3f out: sn btn) ......................................... nk.9

99⁵ Quiet Miss (67) (MrsAKnight) 8-0 ‡5DHarrison (1) (bit bkwd: prom: 3rd st: wknd 3f out: t.o) ............................................................ 25.10

*Stewards Enquiry: Rutter fined £300 under Rule 151 (ii) (failure to ensure best possible placing).*

9/4 Batabanoo, 9/2 Will Soon, 13/2 Miss Hyde (USA), 15/2 Ajo (IRE), 8/1 Doyce(op 5/1), 9/1 Bigwheel Bill (IRE), 10/1 MAD MILITANT (IRE), 12/1 Najeb (USA), 16/1 Ors. CSF £78.53, CT £646.06. Tote £11.50: £2.40 £2.60 £3.00 (£44.00). Mrs B. Facchino (UPPER LONGDON) bred by Cloghran Stud Farm Co in Ireland. 10 Rn
2m 17.51 (5.81)
SF—53/54/47/39/23/25

## 1253 JOHN OF GAUNT STKS (listed race) £9218.75 (£2750.00: £1312.50: £593.75)
7f 30y
3-00 (3-01)

673⁶ **Norton Challenger (105)** (v) (MHEasterby) 5-9-4 MBirch (3) (lw: hdwy 2f out: str run u.p to ld last strides) ..................................... 1

927 Powerful Edge (98) (IABalding) 3-8-2 GBaxter (10) (lw: hld up: stdy hdwy 2f out: led ins fnl f tl ct last strides) .......................... nk.2

827⁵ Stack Rock (101) (EJAlston) 5-8-7 KFallon (8) (hld up: 5th st: ev ch fnl 2f: r.o) . ³/₄.3

824 Savoyard (95) (bl) (MAJarvis) 4-8-12 LDettori (2) (lw: 2nd st: led over 2f out tl ins fnl f) ............................................................... 1.4

563 Appledorn (85) (BAMcMahon) 5-8-7 PRobinson (6) (bit bkwd: prom: 4th st: wknd wl over 1f out) ...................................... 5.5

1028⁴ Morgannwg (IRE) (80) (RDickin) 4-8-9 JWilliams (9) (lw: s.s: 6th st: hdwy 3f out: sn ev ch: wknd fnl f) ......................................... 4.6

Sizzling Saga (IRE) (108) (JBerry) 4-9-4 GCarter (5) (lw: led tl hdd over 2f out: sn btn) .................................................................. 4.7

1043² Mojave (106) (Fav) (MRStoute) 3-8-5 DHolland (7) (prom: 3rd st: wknd over 1f out) ................................................................. s.h.8

*Stewards Enquiry: Birch suspended 15-18/6/92 (excessive use of whip).*

5/4 Mojave, 4/1 Stack Rock(op 2/1), 9/2 NORTON CHALLENGER, 8/1 Savoyard, 9/1 Powerful Edge, 12/1 Sizzling Saga (IRE), 14/1 Morgannwg (IRE), 33/1 Appledorn. CSF £40.75, Tote £6.00: £1.70 £2.10 £1.60 (£19.50). Maj J. S. Linley (MALTON) bred by Mrs P. J. Van Straubenzee and C. J. R. Trotter. 8 Rn
1m 30.31 (3.01)
SF—69/52/55/57/37/25

## 1254 LADBROKE RACING H'CAP (0-100) £7310.00 (£2180.00: £1040.00: £470.00)
1m 30y
3-30 (3-33)

1061² **Marine Diver (71)** (Jt-Fav) (BRMillman) 6-7-13 AMackay (2) (lw: 5th st: led ins fnl f: pushed out) ....................................... 1

712⁴ Sagebrush Roller (75) (Jt-Fav) (JWWatts) 4-8-3 DHolland (6) (lw: hld up & bhd: stdy hdwy 2f out: r.o strly ins fnl f) .......................... nk.2

713 Two Left Feet (93) (SirMarkPrescott) 5-9-7 JLowe (10) (hld up: 6th st: led over 1f out tl ins fnl f) ...................................... nk.3

1078³ Langtry Lady (83) (Jt-Fav) (MJRyan) 6-8-11 LDettori (4) (lw: hld up: hdwy 2f out: one pce appr fnl f) ......................................... 2¹/₄.4

1021⁵ The Can Can Man (67) (MJohnston) 5-7-9 NCarlisle (9) (lw: prom: 2nd st: wknd over 1f out) ...................................... 2.5

1078⁵ Conquista (77) (bl) (LadyHerries) 4-8-5 JWilliams (3) (plld hrd: prom: 4th st: wknd 3f out) ....................................... 4.6

976³ Tusky (85) (v) (MJCamacho) 4-8-13 SMorris (5) (led tl hdd & wknd over 1f out) nk.7

563 Knight of Mercy (100) (RHannon) 6-10-0 BRaymond (1) (bit bkwd: chsd ldrs: 3rd st: wknd 2f out) ....................................... 4.8

9/2 Langtry Lady, Sagebrush Roller, MARINE DIVER, 5/1 The Can Can Man, Two Left Feet, 11/2 Tusky, 11/1 Conquista, 14/1 Knight of Mercy. CSF £23.90, CT £95.70. Tote £4.00: £1.50 £1.60 £1.90 (£10.40). Merthyr Tydfil Car Auction Limited (CULLOMPTON) bred by Egmont Stud. 8 Rn
1m 44.37 (3.97)
SF—37/40/57/39/17/15

**1255**  JUDDMONTE CLAIMING STKS (Qualifier) £2616.00 (£726.00: £348.00)
1¼m 120y                                                           4-00 (4-02)

1142* **Firefighter (70)** *(RHollinshead)* 3-8-5 KDarley (8) (hld up: 5th st: led over 1f
out: rdn out) ........................................................................... —1

Rambo's Hall *(JAGlover)* 7-9-9 DMcKeown (6) (b: bkwd: hld up & bhd: hdwy 3f
out: r.o wl ins fnl f) .............................................................. nk.2

Light Hand **(75)** (Fav) *(MHTompkins)* 6-8-9 PRobinson (9) (bkwd: chsd ldrs:
4th st: ev ch 1f out: no ex ins fnl f) .................................. ¾.3

1102³ Saif Al Adil (IRE) **(53)** *(BHanbury)* 3-7-12 NCarlisle (11) (lw: led tl hdd over 1f
out: wknd fnl f) ...................................................................... 3.4

993 Taunting (IRE) **(57)** *(MBlanshard)* 4-8-8 ‡5DHarrison (4) (hdwy 3f out: kpt on:
nvr able to chal) ............................................................... 2½.5

1034* Misty Goddess (IRE) **(54)** *(MAJarvis)* 4-8-3 ‡5KRutter (7) (prom: 4th st: rdn &
wknd over 2f out) ................................................................. ½.6

1109* Neltegrity **(58)** *(THCaldwell)* 3-8-1 ‡5NKennedy (5) (lw: prom: 3rd st: wknd over
2f out) ................................................................................. 1½.7

232⁴ Panico **(35)** (v) *(MissSEHall)* 5-8-6 ‡5SMaloney (3) (bit bkwd: a bhd) .......... ½.8

1110 Stylish Gent **(61)** *(NTinkler)* 5-9-1 MBirch (2) (bit bkwd: stdd s: a bhd: t.o) ...... 12.9

964 Wheels of Weetman **(30)** *(MissSJWilton)* 5-8-11 KFallon (10) (wnt 2nd st: wknd
3f out: t.o) ........................................................................ 2½.10

1070 Lightning Spark *(MAvison)* 3-8-4 JLowe (1) (prom to ½-wy: sn lost pl: t.o) ..... 2.11

**9/4** Light Hand, **3/1** FIREFIGHTER, **5/1** Rambo's Hall, **6/1** Misty Goddess (IRE), **9/1** Saif Al Adil (IRE), **14/1**
Neltegrity, Stylish Gent, **20/1** Taunting (IRE), **25/1** Panico, **33/1** Ors. CSF £18.44, Tote £3.30: £1.40 £2.40 £1.40
(£9.60). Mrs B. Facchino (UPPER LONGDON) bred by Sir Stephen Hastings. 11 Rn    2m 17.73 (6.03)
SF—41/58/42/25/30/24

**1256**  HENRY IV H'CAP (0-100) £3817.50 (£1140.00: £545.00: £247.50)
1¾m                                                                4-30 (4-31)

1016⁴ **Highflying (76)** *(GMMoore)* 6-8-9 KFallon (8) (hld up: hdwy 3f out: led ins fnl f:
eased nr fin: jst hld on) ....................................................... —1

1169² Prince Sobur **(60)** *(MBlanshard)* 6-7-7 GBardwell (7) (chsd ldrs: 5th st: led over
2f out tl ins fnl f: rallied u.p nr fin) .................................... s.h.2

1016² Beau Quest **(60)** (v) *(RMWhitaker)* 5-7-7 DaleGibson (1) (hld up: hdwy 3f out:
hrd rdn & r.o fnl f) ............................................................. 1½.3

987² I Perceive **(70)** (Jt-Fav) *(FHLee)* 5-8-3 PRobinson (2) (hld up & bhd: hdwy on
ins over 2f out: hrd rdn & no ex fnl f) ................................... nk.4

861* Castle Courageous **(92)** (Jt-Fav) *(LadyHerries)* 5-9-11 BRaymond (6) (lw: hld
up: 6th st: plld outside & no hdwy fnl 2f) ............................. 5.5

475 Shoofe (USA) **(76)** *(DMorley)* 4-8-9 MBirch (4) (prom: 3rd st: wknd 2f out) ........ 2.6

937 Coleridge **(71)** *(DShaw)* 4-8-4 GCarter (11) (chsd ldr 8f: 4th st: wknd 3f out) ... nk.7

675 Nikitas **(61)** *(MissAJWhitfield)* 7-7-8⁽¹⁾ NCarlisle (10) (b.nr fore: led tl hdd over
2f out: sn btn) ..................................................................... 2.8

569⁶ Travelling Light **(83)** *(MrsJRRamsden)* 6-9-2 GBaxter (5) (a bhd) .................... hd.9

435⁶ Uluru (IRE) **(92)** ˙*(MrsJRRamsden)* 4-9-11 KDarley (9) (chsd ldrs: wnt 2nd st:
wknd over 2f out) ............................................................... 12.10

675² Just My Bill **(70)** *(NTinkler)* 6-8-3 JLowe (3) (a bhd: t.o) ..................................... 7.11

LONG HANDICAP: Prince Sobur 7-5, Nikitas 6-11.

**7/2** I Perceive, Castle Courageous, **6/1** Beau Quest, **13/2** Uluru (IRE)(op 4/1), **7/1** Just My Bill, **15/2** Prince Sobur,
**9/1** Travelling Light, **10/1** HIGHFLYING, Shoofe (USA), **12/1** Nikitas, **20/1** Coleridge. CSF £86.37, CT £464.98.
Tote £13.60: £3.70 £2.30 £2.60 (£49.00). Mr B. Batey (MIDDLEHAM) bred by Juddmonte Farms. 11 Rn
3m 4.20 (5.70)
SF—52/35/32/41/53/33

T/Trio: Race 3: £25.80 (39 Tckts). T/Plpt: £1,130.40 (9.05 Tckts).                                    IM

**1102—GOODWOOD (R-H)**
### Friday, June 5th [Rnd Good to firm, St Good]
Going Allowance: nil sec per fur (G)                          Wind: almost nil   Vis: bad

Stalls: low

**1257**  GOLDEN YEARS APPEAL CLAIMING STKS   £1725.00 (£475.00: £225.00)
1¼m                                                                6-35 (6-40)

240 **Pelorus (80)** *(DRCElsworth)* 7-8-13 ‡7JHunter (8) (6th st: led over 1f out: rdn
out) ...................................................................................... —1

King of Normandy (IRE) **(65)** *(RHannon)* 3–7-12 TyroneWilliams (3) (2nd st: led over 4f out tl over 1f out: rdn & r.o) .............. 1½.2

1029 Cavo Greco (USA) *(PFICole)* 3–7-12 JQuinn (6) (swtg: 7th st: rdn over 3f out: r.o one pce) ............... 6.3

10375 Shoehorn **(59)** *(MCPipe)* 5–8-11 AMunro (2) (3rd st: one pce fnl 2f) .............. nk.4

773 Molly Splash **(51)** *(CACyzer)* 5–8-6 JWilliams (7) (rdn 3f out: hdwy 2f out: eased whn btn ins fnl f) ............... 7.5

1123* Edge of Darkness (Fav) *(JWHills)* 3–7-8[(2)] ‡7JDSmith (5) (5th st: wknd over 2f out) ............... 1½.6

8315 Predestine **(55)** *(MMadgwick)* 7–8-6 ‡7CAvery (12) (b: lw: rdn 6f out: 9th st: nvr nr to chal) ............... hd.7

1041 Laughing Falcon **(60)** *(JLDunlop)* 3–7-11 AMcGlone (11) (4th st: wknd 3f out) nk.8

In the Spotlight (IRE) *(RCurtis)* 4–8-6 ‡5ATucker (1) (bit bkwd: a bhd) ............... 5.9

Broughton's Gold (IRE) **(40)** *(WJMusson)* 4–8-10 JHBrown (4) (lw: 8th st: bhd fnl 3f) ............... 8.10

Casniktony *(AMoore)* 3–7-13 NAdams (9) (a bhd) ............... 3.11

1085 Cushty **(41)** (bl) *(JELong)* 3–7-8[(1)] RStreet (10) (led over 5f: wknd qckly: t.o) . 20.12

**2/1** Edge of Darkness, **11/4** PELORUS(6/4—3/1), **13/2** Laughing Falcon, **9/1** Predestine, **11/1** Shoehorn, **14/1** Molly Splash, Cavo Greco (USA), King of Normandy (IRE), **50/1** Cushty, **66/1** Ors. CSF £36.82, Tote £3.60: £1.60 £4.80 £4.70 (£30.50). Mr George Ennor (WHITSBURY) bred by London Thoroughbred Services Ltd and partners. 12 Rn
2m 10.60 (5.60)
SF—43/25/13/25/6/–/

**1258** NEW HORIZONS CLAIMING STKS £1725.00 (£475.00: £225.00) **1m** 7-05 (7-14)

8324 **Skipper to Bilge (69)** (Fav) *(MAJarvis)* 5–9-3 MRoberts (8) (5th st: in ld ins fnl f: r.o wl) ............... —1

936 Devil's Soul **(51)** (bl) *(RAkehurst)* 4–9-3 AMunro (1) (lw: 7th st: in 2nd ins fnl f: unable qckn) ............... 1½.2

9425 Betalongabill **(52)** (bl) *(MMadgwick)* 3–8-2 JQuinn (6) (2nd st: lft in ld 4f out: in 3rd ins fnl f: one pce) ............... ¾.3

1044 Chez Polly **(37)** (v) *(PRHedger)* 6–8-6[(1)] JWilliams (4) (6th st: 4th & btn ins fnl f) 6.4

774 Forlorn Diver **(48)** *(BGubby)* 4–8-6 ‡5DHarrison (7) (8th st: 5th & btn ins fnl f) . 2½.5

1021 Mitsubishi Video (IRE) **(72)** *(DrJDScargill)* 4–8-9 WRyan (2) (b: 4th st: no ch fnl f) ............... 5.6

774 Sergeant Meryll **(36)** *(PHowling)* 4–8-3 ‡7TMcLaughlin (5) (3rd st: no ch fnl f) .... 4.7

1001 Miss Cookie **(49)** *(MCPipe)* 4–8-5 PaulEddery (3) (lw: led tl broke down & p.u 4f out: dead) ............... 0

**4/5** SKIPPER TO BILGE, **11/2** Mitsubishi Video (IRE)(4/1—6/1), **6/1** Devil's Soul, **8/1** Betalongabill(6/1—9/1), **14/1** Miss Cookie, **20/1** Sergeant Meryll, **25/1** Forlorn Diver, **50/1** Chez Polly. CSF £5.95, Tote £1.80: £1.20 £1.80 £1.50 (£5.40). Mrs J. R. Collins (NEWMARKET) bred by J. R. Collins. 8 Rn
1m 41.61 (4.01)
SF—43/37/20/6/–/–

**1259** BRITAX '21' CLUB STKS (Mdn 2-Y.O) £1725.00 (£475.00: £225.00) **6f** 7-30 (7-45)

**Marchwell Lad** *(MRChannon)* 9-0 MHills (3) (w'like: scope: a.p: led over 1f out: rdn out) ............... —1

9883 Twice the Groom (IRE) *(PMitchell)* 9-0 MRoberts (1) (led over 4f: rdn & r.o) .... 1½.2

Comanche Companion *(TJNaughton)* 8-4 ‡5DHarrison (16) (leggy: lt-f: lw: gd hdwy 2f out: unable qckn ins fnl f) ............... ½.3

Polar Storm (IRE) *(LadyHerries)* 8-9 JWilliams (7) (w'like: scope: bit bkwd: lost pl over 3f out: rallied fnl f: r.o) ............... 3½.4

Play Hever Golf *(TJNaughton)* 9-0 AMcGlone (15) (wl grwn: bit bkwd: gd hdwy over 1f out: nvr nrr) ............... 1.5

11034 Without a Flag (USA) *(CACyzer)* 9-0 JQuinn (8) (w ldr: ev ch over 2f out: wknd over 1f out) ............... 1½.6

The Executor *(RFJohnsonHoughton)* 9-0 AMunro (4) (w'like: bit bkwd: nvr nr to chal) ............... hd.7

10575 Hello Hobson's (IRE) *(JAkehurst)* 8-9 NAdams (2) (spd over 4f) ............... 1.8

Newbury Coat *(MMcCormack)* 9-0 JReid (6) (scope: prom over 4f) ............... 2.9

Koa *(MJHeaton-Ellis)* 9-0 SRaymont (5) (unf: scope: a mid div) ............... ¾.10

Mrs West (USA) (Fav) *(JLDunlop)* 8-9 TQuinn (13) (unf: outpcd) ............... nk.11

9752 Mysterious Ways (FR) *(MrsJCecil)* 9-0 PaulEddery (9) (spd over 4f) ............... nk.12

729 Remembrance Day (IRE) *(RHannon)* 8-11 ‡3RPerham (10) (s.i.s: outpcd) ............... 1.13

Linderhof (USA) *(MRStoute)* 9-0 PD'Arcy (12) (cmpt: s.s: a bhd) ............... 1.14

995 Lady of Shadows *(SDow)* 8-9 WRyan (14) (bhd fnl 2f) ............... 1½.15

Raging Thunder *(GLewis)* 9-0 BRouse (11) (str: scope: a wl bhd) ............... 2.16

**7/4** Mrs West (USA)(5/4—2/1), **11/4** Twice the Groom (IRE), **11/2** Mysterious Ways (FR), **7/1** Linderhof (USA), **16/1** Without a Flag (USA)(op 10/1), The Executor, Newbury Coat, **20/1** Raging Thunder, **25/1** Remembrance Day (IRE), Koa, MARCHWELL LAD, **33/1** Ors. CSF £96.05, Tote £61.20: £7.00 £1.70 £23.00 (£240.30). Mr C. C. Buckley (UPPER LAMBOURN) bred by Etchingham Stud. 16 Rn
1m 13.15 (2.75)
SF—45/39/27/18/19/13

**1260**    ORLANDO JEWELLERS H'CAP (3-Y.O) (0-80) £1725.00 (£475.00: £225.00)
1¾m                                                           8-00 (8-15)

908[4] Last Conquest (IRE) (60) (PFICole) 7-10 ‡[7]JDSmith (7) (3rd st: hrd rdn 2f out:
led ins fnl f: drvn out) .................................................................. —1
1003[2] Teddy's Play (USA) (72) (JWHills) 9-1 MHills (9) (4th st: led over 1f out tl ins fnl f:
unable qckn) .......................................................................... 2.2
1027[3] Erlemo (50) (bl) (CJBenstead) 7-7 TyroneWilliams (4) (lw: 2nd st: led 3f out tl
over 1f out: one pce) .............................................................. 2.3
1082[2] Three Wells (78) (Fav) (JLDunlop) 9-7 JReid (8) (lw: 9th st: shkn up & gd hdwy
over 1f out: fin wl) ................................................................. hd.4
932[2] Mr Poppleton (62) (DWPArbuthnot) 8-5 TQuinn (5) (5th st: one pce fnl 2f) ...... ½.5
908 Winter Lightning (51) (PTWalwyn) 7-8[(1)] AMackay (6) (6th st: no hdwy fnl 2f) ... 2.6
881[4] Dancing Years (USA) (63) (MRChannon) 8-6 BRouse (3) (7th st: bhd fnl 2f) ...... 7.7
1027* Formal Invitation (IRE) (63) (GLewis) 8-6 (5x) PaulEddery (1) (b: in ld 5f out:
hdd & wknd 3f out) ................................................................. 8.8
972 My Senor (50) (MMadgwick) 7-7 JQuinn (1) (8th st: bhd fnl 3f) ...................... 2½.9
LONG HANDICAP: Erlemo 7-5, My Senor 7-3.

**100/30** Three Wells, **4/1** Mr Poppleton, **9/2** Teddy's Play (USA), **5/1** Formal Invitation (IRE), **15/2** LAST
CONQUEST (IRE), My Senor, **12/1** Erlemo, **14/1** Dancing Years (USA), **50/1** Winter Lightning. CSF £38.72, CT
£366.55. Tote £10.10: £2.90 £1.70 £4.00 (£21.50). Mr Fahd Salman (WHATCOMBE) bred by Newgate Stud Co.
in Ireland. 9 Rn                                                    3m 5.37 (6.37)
SF—18/33/9/36/18/2

**1261**    STARMIN H'CAP (0-80) £1725.00 (£475.00: £225.00)    **7f**       8-30 (8-44)

1032[6] Premier Prince (53) (Fav) (LGCottrell) 6-8-1 AMunro (2) (6th over 2f out: hdwy
over 1f out: led wl ins fnl f: r.o wl) ............................................ —1
945 Pigalle Wonder (48) (RJO'Sullivan) 4-7-5[(3)] ‡[5]DHarrison (7) (2nd 5f out: rdn &
led over 1f out: hdd wl ins fnl f: r.o) ..................................... ½.2
774[5] Quick Steel (56) (bl) (TPMcGovern) 4-8-4 MRoberts (3) (4th over 2f out: unable
qckn fnl f) ............................................................................ 1½.3
997* Tea Dust (IRE) (66) (PJMakin) 4-9-0 TQuinn (6) (5th over 2f out: one pce fnl f) hd.4
1104[6] Belfort Ruler (67) (BGubby) 5-9-1 JWilliams (9) (8th over 2f out: styd on fnl f) 1½.5
1133* Cheveux Mitchell (77) (v) (MRChannon) 5-9-11 (7x) WRyan (10) (in ld 5f out:
hdd over 1f out: sn wknd) .................................................... ½.6
941 Affordable (66) (WCarter) 4-9-0 MHills (14) (7th over 2f out: one pce) ............. hd.7
41[5] Dance on Sixpence (68) (HJCollingridge) 4-9-2 JQuinn (12) (3rd over 2f out:
wknd over 1f out) ............................................................... 12.8
799[2] Rise Up Singing (77) (WJMusson) 4-9-11 BRouse (1) (9th st: btn over 2f out) 2½.9
939* Lady Sabo (70) (GLewis) 3-8-8 PaulEddery (13) (10th & no ch over 2f out) .. nk.10
1136[4] Lucknam Dreamer (70) (MrsBarbaraWaring) 4-9-4 NHowe (11) (13th & no ch
over 2f out) ......................................................................... ¾.11
565 King of Mileen (45) (DShaw) 6-7-7 NAdams (8) (b: 12th & no ch over 2f out) nk.12
Liu Liu San (IRE) (45) (bl) (PButler) 4-7-7 TyroneWilliams (5) (11th & no ch over
2f out) ................................................................................ 2½.13
LONG HANDICAP: Pigalle Wonder 7-6, Liu Liu San (IRE) 6-12.

**100/30** PREMIER PRINCE(5/1—3/1), **5/1** Tea Dust (IRE), **13/2** Cheveux Mitchell, Quick Steel, **7/1** Lucknam
Dreamer, **8/1** Affordable, **11/1** Belfort Ruler, **12/1** Lady Sabo, **14/1** Rise Up Singing, **16/1** Dance on Sixpence,
**25/1** Pigalle Wonder, **33/1** King of Mileen, **66/1** Liu Liu San (IRE). CSF £75.83, CT £489.00. Tote £5.50: £2.00
£3.90 £2.20 (£213.50). Mrs P. S. Boswell (CULLOMPTON) bred by Mrs I. A. Balding. 13 Rn     1m 27.95 (3.25)
SF—39/23/35/44/40/48/36

**1262**    LORDS TAVERNERS H'CAP (0-80) £1725.00 (£475.00: £225.00)    **5f**    9-00 (9-07)
(Weights raised 1 lb)

1030[6] The Noble Oak (IRE) (56) (bl) (MMcCormack) 4-8-13 JReid (4) (w ldr 2f out:
led over 1f out: rdn out) ..................................................... —1
1107[3] Fivesevenfive (67) (Fav) (RJHodges) 4-9-10 TQuinn (1) (3rd 2f out: unable
qckn fnl f) .......................................................................... 3½.2
996 Shades of Jade (44) (JJBridger) 4-8-1 TyroneWilliams (2) (in ld 2f out: hdd &
wknd over 1f out) ............................................................... 3.3
1006[3] Musval (59) (RHannon) 3-8-8 MRoberts (3) (bhd fnl 2f) ........................... 7.4

**13/8** Fivesevenfive(op 5/4), **7/4** THE NOBLE OAK (IRE), **11/4** Musval, **7/1** Shades of Jade. CSF £4.93, Tote
£2.70 (£2.60). Mr M. McCormack (WANTAGE) bred by Rosemount Stud in Ireland. 4 Rn    59.33 sec (1.73)
SF—64/61/26/5

T/Trio: Race 5: £210.10 (6.1 Tckts). T/Plpt: £1,214.40 (2.1 Tckts).

LMc

1000—**SOUTHWELL (L-H)** Fibresand
**Friday, June 5th [Standard]**
Going Allowance: minus 0.10 sec per fur (FS)

Wind: fresh half bhd   Vis: poor 6th

Stalls: high

## 1263
EATON H'CAP (0-80) £2265.20 (£627.20: £299.60)    5f (AWT)    2-30 (2-32)

660⁵ Palacegate Racing (67) *(JBerry)* 3–8-10 GCarter (13) (chsd ldrs: r.o wl to ld ins
   fnl f: drvn out) .................................................................. —1

1000* Fighter Squadron (54) (v) (Fav) *(JAGlover)* 3–7-11 NCarlisle (14) (hdwy ¹/₂-wy:
   r.o wl u.p fnl f: nt rch wnr) ...................................... ¹/₂.2

661 Sobering Thoughts (42) (bl) *(DWChapman)* 6–7-7 SWood (12) (w ldrs: led 2f
   out tl ins fnl f: no ex) ......................................... ¹/₂.3

Waverley Star (48) (bl) *(SGNorton)* 7-7-7 LCharnock (9) (effrt ¹/₂-wy: styd on
   u.p appr fnl f: nt rch ldrs) .......................................... 1.4

998⁴ Superlativemaximus (IRE) (54) *(JABennett)* 4–8-5 GHind (6) (w ldrs: rdn 2f out:
   r.o same pce) .................................................. ¹/₂.5

1111³ Hinari Video (60) *(MJohnston)* 7–8-11 DMcKeown (2) (chsd ldrs tl rdn &
   outpcd ¹/₂-wy: hdwy fnl f: nt rch ldrs) ............................ ³/₄.6

819 No Quarter Given (72) *(PSFelgate)* 7–9-4 ‡5CHodgson (3) (sn wl outpcd: hdwy
   fnl f: nrst fin) ................................................... 2.7

996 Lady of the Fen (63) *(MrsNMacauley)* 4–8-7 ‡7GForster (11) (led to 2f out: wknd
   1f out) ......................................................... ³/₄.8

1000³ Sara Anne (IRE) (57) *(LJCodd)* 3–7-9 ‡5NKennedy (7) (sn bhd: sme hdwy 1f
   out: n.d) ....................................................... ³/₄.9

752 R a Express (42) *(BAMcMahon)* 7-7-7 GBardwell (10) (sn drvn along: lost pl 3f
   out: cn bhd) ................................................... 5.10

1001 Serious Hurry (65) *(SirMarkPrescott)* 4–9-2 CNutter (1) (chsd ldrs tl lost pl
   ¹/₂-wy: sn bhd) ............................................... ³/₄.11

Justamanda (59) *(WHolden)* 3–8-2 SDawson (4) (bit bkwd: dwlt: a bhd) ......... 3.12
   LONG HANDICAP: Sobering Thoughts 7-3, R a Express 7-3.

**11/4** Fighter Squadron, **13/2** Hinari Video, **9/1** Lady of the Fen, No Quarter Given, **10/1** Superlativemaximus
(IRE), **11/1** Sara Anne (IRE), **12/1** PALACEGATE RACING, Sobering Thoughts(op 8/1), **14/1** Justamanda, **16/1**
Serious Hurry, **20/1** Waverley Star, **25/1** R a Express. CSF £40.47, CT £370.97. Tote £8.00: £1.60 £1.90 £2.50
(£25.10). Palacegate Corporation Ltd (COCKERHAM) bred by D. Rabey. 12 Rn            59.8 sec (1.8)
SF—50/35/29/31/35/38/37

## 1264
BELGRAVE (S) STKS (2-Y-O) £2343.60 (£649.60: £310.80)    6f (AWT)    3-00 (3-04)

889 **Matthew David** *(MBrittain)* 8-6 ‡5SMaloney (1) (mde all: clr ¹/₂-wy: rdn out) ....... —1

795⁶ Pretzel (IRE) (v) *(NTinkler)* 8-1 RDarley (2) (sn chsng wnr: hrd rdn over 2f out:
   kpt on: nvr able to chal) ...................................... 3.2

682 Niteowlady *(SGNorton)* 8-6 JFortune (6) (chsd ldrs: hung lft & kpt on u.p fnl 2f) 1¹/₂.3

1007³ Madam Cyn's Risk (Fav) *(NACallaghan)* 8-6 GHind (9) (chsd ldrs: rdn over 2f
   out: no imp) ................................................... ¹/₂.4

Russet Way *(MrsNMacauley)* 8-6 NDay (3) (lt-f: swtg: unruly stalls: s.s: sn wl
   bhd: t.o ¹/₂-wy: hdwy over 1f out: styd on) ........................ 5.5

759 Peak Fitness *(JAGlover)* 8-11 DMcKeown (12) (s.i.s: w chsng ldrs: wknd over
   2f out) ......................................................... 1.6

1077⁴ Get Daily Sport *(PAKelleway)* 8-6 CRutter (11) (chsd ldrs over 3f: sn lost pl) ...... 2.7

782⁶ Andrea's Girl *(JBerry)* 8-6 GCarter (4) (chsd ldrs tl rdn & wknd 2f out) ............ 1¹/₂.8

889 Hazy Dazy *(WGMTurner)* 8-3 ‡3TSprake (10) (nvr nr ldrs) .......................... 1¹/₂.9

588 Meadow View (IRE) *(CJHill)* 8-6 AProud (13) (n.d) ................................ 4.10

1036 Miss Fitness *(DrJDScargill)* 8-6 GBardwell (7) (dwlt: a bhd) ...................... 7.11

1007 Buy Sunday Sport(v) *(MissGayKelleway)* 8-6 NConnorton (8) (b.hind: sn bhd) 2¹/₂.12

I'Ll Risk it *(JBerry)* 7-13 ‡7PRoberts (5) (lt-f: unf: a bhd) ..................... 5.13

**4/1** Madam Cyn's Risk, **11/2** Niteowlady(3/1—6/1), **6/1** Miss Fitness(op 4/1), Pretzel (IRE)(op 4/1), **7/1**
Andrea's Girl, **8/1** I'Ll Risk it, **10/1** MATTHEW DAVID(op 16/1), **12/1** Hazy Dazy, **14/1** Get Daily Sport, **16/1**
Meadow View (IRE), Russet Way, **20/1** Peak Fitness, **33/1** Buy Sunday Sport. CSF £68.88, Tote £10.70: £3.10
£3.70 £1.60 (Wnr or 2nd w any £1.70). M. D. M. Racing (Thoroughbreds) Limited (WARTHILL) bred by MDM
Racing (Thoroughbreds) Ltd. 13 Rn; No bid            1m 17.5 (4.1)

## 1265
EAST MIDLANDS ELECTRICITY MEDIAN AUCTION STKS (Mdn 3-Y-O) £2206.40
(£610.40: £291.20)    1¹/₂m (AWT)    3-30 (3-32)

1048⁴ **Five to Seven (USA) (69)** *(SGNorton)* 9-0 KDarley (5) (chsd ldrs: led 4f out: sn
   clr: drvn out) .................................................. —1

1003³ Alderbrook (Fav) *(MrsJCecil)* 9-0 AClark (6) (b.off fore: chsd ldrs: hrd rdn 3f
out: no imp) ............................................................................... 12.2
896 King's Guest (IRE) (56) *(GAPritchard-Gordon)* 9-0 GCarter (2) (led to 4f out: sn
wknd) ........................................................................................ 10.3
804 Field of Dreams *(CFWall)* 8-9 NDay (5) (chsd ldrs: drvn along ¹/₂-wy: wknd over
3f out) .................................................................................. 1¹/₂.4
950⁴ Stratford Lady (48) (bl) *(JAGlover)* 8-9 NConnorton (1) (chsd ldrs tl rdn &
outpcd over 4f out: sn bhd) ................................................... 12.5
1034 Catel Ring (IRE) (46) *(ICampbell)* 9-0 MTebbutt (4) (b.hind: sn wl bhd) ......... 1¹/₂.6
911 Royal Opera Star *(JRBosley)* 8-9 ‡5NGwilliams (7) (sn wl bhd & drvn along: t.o
¹/₂-wy) ..................................................................................... 1¹/₂.7
370 Safari Park (46) *(BSRothwell)* 8-9 JFortune (8) (trckd ldrs tl drvn along & lost gd
over 5f out: sn bhd) ................................................................ s.h.8

**11/8** Alderbrook(4/5—7/4), **9/4** FIVE TO SEVEN (USA)(3/1—15/8), **8/1** King's Guest (IRE), **10/1** Field of
Dreams, **14/1** Stratford Lady, **16/1** Safari Park, Catel Ring (IRE)(op 7/1), **33/1** Royal Opera Star. CSF £5.48, Tote
£3.80: £1.10 £1.80 £1.60 (£2.10). The Five to Seven Partnership (BARNSLEY) bred by William A. Marquard in
USA. 8 Rn
2m 40.6 (6.4)
SF—24/–/–/–/–/–

## 1266

KPMG PEAT MARWICK H'CAP (0-70) £2343.60 (£649.60: £310.80)
7f (AWT)
4-05 (4-08)

774 **Hawaii Storm (FR) (43)** *(MissAJWhitfield)* 4-8-6 DaleGibson (7) (chsd ldrs:
led ins fnl f: r.o wl) ................................................................ —1
903 Wellsy Lad (USA) (60) *(DWChapman)* 5-9-9 SWood (12) (a chsng ldrs: led
over 1f out tl wl ins fnl f: no ex) ........................................... 2.2
1032⁵ Ain'tlifelikethat (56) (bl) *(TJNaughton)* 5-9-5 GCarter (6) (b: s.s: bhd tl hdwy
over 2f out: r.o wl fnl f) ...................................................... s.h.3
752 Verro (USA) (34) (bl) *(JABennett)* 5-7-11 GBardwell (3) (chsd ldr: led 2f
out: sn hdd: r.o same pce) ................................................ s.h.4
1008 Persian Bud (IRE) (39) *(JRBosley)* 4-7-11 ‡5NGwilliams (2) (b: chsd ldrs: sn
drvn along: kpt on same pce fnl 2f) ................................... 4.5
535 Strip Cartoon (IRE) (49) (bl) *(SRBowring)* 4-8-5 ‡7MHarris (11) (led tl hdd &
wknd 2f out) ....................................................................... nk.6
1129⁵ Verdant Boy (52) *(MPNaughton)* 9-9-1 NConnorton (5) (sn wl bhd:
sme late hdwy: n.d) ......................................................... nk.7
1032 Eliza Wooding (41) *(CJHill)* 4-8-4 AProud (8) (wl bhd tl hdwy u.p over 1f out:
nvr nr to chal) ................................................................... hd.8
1001⋆ Gallery Artist (IRE) (65) *(RGuest)* 4-9-7 ‡7SEiffert (13) (chsd ldrs tl wknd over 2f
out) ..................................................................................... 1¹/₂.9
Watermill Girl (37) *(DTThom)* 4-7-7 ‡7CHawksley (1) (bkwd: s.i.s: sn in tch: effrt
¹/₂-wy: wknd over ¹/₂-wy) ................................................. 2¹/₂.10
1013 On Y Va (USA) (59) *(RJRWilliams)* 5-9-8 KDarley (9) (a in rr) .................... 1¹/₂.11
997 Looting (USA) (49) *(MDIUsher)* 6-8-7 ‡5CHodgson (4) (b.off hind: chsd ldrs to
¹/₂-wy: sn wknd) ............................................................... 10.12
1005 Tickham Vixen (IRE) (47) *(JDBethell)* 4-8-10 DMcKeown (10) (in tch tl lost pce
¹/₂-wy: sn wl bhd) ............................................................ 2¹/₂.13

**5/1** Verdant Boy, Verro (USA)(op 5/2), **13/2** Ain'tlifelikethat(op 4/1), **8/1** Looting (USA)(op 14/1), **9/1** On Y Va
(USA), **10/1** Strip Cartoon (IRE), Gallery Artist (IRE), HAWAII STORM (FR), **12/1** Wellsy Lad (USA)(op 20/1),
Eliza Wooding(op 7/1), **20/1** Tickham Vixen (IRE), **25/1** Watermill Girl, **33/1** Persian Bud (IRE). CSF £112.39, CT
£767.39. Tote £10.00: £3.80 £2.50 £2.00 (£48.80). Mr Andreas Sofroniou (LAMBOURN) bred by Horse France
in France. 13 Rn
1m 30.2 (3.6)
SF—27/38/33/10/–/–

## 1267

GROSVENOR H'CAP (0-70) £2422.00 (£672.00: £322.00)
1m (AWT)
4-35 (4-38)

1150⁵ **Sandmoor Denim (43)** *(SRBowring)* 5-8-4⁽²⁾ ‡7MHarris (2) (trckd ldrs gng wl:
wnt 2nd 2f out: rdn to ld ins fnl f: sn clr) ........................... —1
210 Buddy's Friend (IRE) (52) *(RJRWilliams)* 4-9-6 KDarley (1) (w ldr: led 5f out tl
hdd & nt qckn ins fnl f) ...................................................... 2¹/₂.2
903⁴ Sareen Express (IRE) (48) *(MrsJCDawe)* 4-8-9 ‡7CHawksley (6) (s.i.s: bhd: gd
hdwy 2f out: r.o same pce fnl f) ......................................... 3¹/₂.3
1172 China Sky (45) *(CNAllen)* 4-8-13 GBardwell (7) (chsd ldrs: rdn 3f out: one pce) 4.4
1037⋆ Qualitair Rhythm (IRE) (54) (bl) (Fav) *(ICampbell)* 4-9-8 AClark (8) (chsd ldrs:
kpt on same pce fnl 3f) ...................................................... 2.5
866 Night Transaction (42) *(AHide)* 5-8-10 DaleGibson (14) (in tch: effrt over 3f out:
nvr able to chal) ................................................................ 6.6
912 Revoke (USA) (44) *(CJHill)* 5-8-7 ‡5SMaloney (12) (sn bhd: hdwy u.p 2f out:
n.d) ..................................................................................... 6.7
Edgewise (25) *(DMorris)* 9-7-7 SWood (4) (bkwd: sn wl bhd) ........................ 3.8

903 Reina (39) *(JDBethell)* 4–8-7 DMcKeown (13) (chsd ldr tl rdn & wknd 3f out) .... nk.**9**
Shaieef(IRE) (56) *(RJRWilliams)* 4–9-3 ‡7GMitchell (10) (bkwd: swtg: sn wl bhd)1½.**10**
615 Pavers Good Shoes (25) *(MBrittain)* 4–7-7 LCharnock (11) (chsd ldrs tl lost pl
4f out: sn bhd) ................................................................ ½.**11**
941 Barlogan (56) *(CFWall)* 4–9-10 NDay (9) (s.i.s: sn chsng ldrs: wknd over 3f out) hd.**12**
1040 Super-Sub (53) *(GFleming)* 3–8-10 GCarter (5) (led to 5f out: wknd over 3f out) 1.**13**

**2/1** Qualitair Rhythm (IRE)(tchd 3/1), **9/2** Sareen Express (IRE)(3/1—5/1), **11/2** SANDMOOR DENIM(4/1—6/1),
**8/1** Super-Sub(12/1—7/1), Revoke (USA)(op 3/1), **10/1** China Sky, Barlogan, **12/1** Reina, Buddy's Friend (IRE),
**20/1** Pavers Good Shoes, Night Transaction, **33/1** Ors. CSF £72.15, CT £306.88. Tote £4.90: £1.50 £3.10 £1.70
(£20.60). Mr E. H. Lunness (EDWINSTOWE) bred by Rathasker Stud. 13 Rn               1m 43 (3.7)
SF—23/31/15/7/10/–

---

**1268**  BLOOMSBURY STKS (Mdn 3-Y.O) £2363.20 (£655.20: £313.60)
7f **(AWT)**                                              5-05 (5-08)

1040[6] **Digger Doyle (55)** *(CNAllen)* 9-0 GBardwell (4) (chsd ldrs: styd on u.p to ld jst
ins fnl f) .......................................................................... —**1**
Nellie Dean *(JARToller)* 8-9 DaleGibson (6) (chsd ldrs: styd on same pce u.p fnl
f) .................................................................................... 1½.**2**
1005[4] Captain Marmalade (63) *(DTThom)* 9-0 SWebster (5) (bhd: hdwy 2f out: styd
on) ................................................................................ nk.**3**
509[4] Prince of Darkness (IRE) (Fav) *(SirMarkPrescott)* 9-0 GDuffield (9) (plld hrd: w
ldr: led over 3f out tl hdd & wknd jst ins fnl f) ...................... 4.**4**
218[6] Ingenuity *(LordHuntingdon)* 8-9 DMcKeown (7) (led tl over 3f out: ev ch tl wknd
over 1f out) ................................................................... nk.**5**
Arighi Boy *(JEBanks)* 8-7 ‡7JSwinnerton (8) (lengthy: scope: s.i.s: sn bhd: sme
hdwy over 1f out: n.d) ................................................... 4.**6**
Sanfoyt (USA) (bl) *(MrsNMacauley)* 9-0 AClark (1) (lt-f: s.i.s: bhd tl kpt on fnl 2f) 4.**7**
566 Aislabie Airborne *(MrsNMacauley)* 9-0 NDay (3) (s.i.s: a wl bhd) ...................... 12.**8**
764 Admirals Realm *(BAMcMahon)* 9-0 KDarley (10) (sn wl bhd) ............................ 2½.**9**
Padina Top *(CSmith)* 8-9 JFortune (2) (lt-f: unf: t.o) ................................... 10

**4/9** Prince of Darkness (IRE)(2/5—4/6), **6/1** Ingenuity, **7/1** Nellie Dean, **10/1** DIGGER DOYLE, **14/1** Captain
Marmalade, **20/1** Padina Top, **33/1** Admirals Realm, Sanfoyt, Arighi Boy, **50/1** Aislabie Airborne. CSF
£76.52, Tote £11.30: £2.00 £1.80 £2.30 (£38.80). Mr P. B. Doyle (NEWMARKET) bred by John Robson. 10 Rn
1m 31.1 (4.5)
SF—22/12/16/4/–/–/

T/Plpt: £1,110.30 (1 Tckt).                                               WG

---

1088—**CARLISLE (R-H)**

**Saturday, June 6th [Firm, Hard patches]**
Going Allowance: minus 0.60 sec per fur (H)                         Wind: fresh across

Stalls: high

**1269**  LANES CLAIMING STKS   £1562.00 (£432.00: £206.00)   1½m    6-30 (6-30)

1123[2] **Cov Tel Lady (62)** *(MHTompkins)* 3–8-3 PRobinson (2) (lw: trckd ldrs: str run
to ld over 1f out: sn clr: easily) .............................................. —**1**
748[2] Henbury Hall (IRE) (78) *(MrsGRReveley)* 4–9-10 KDarley (3) (mde most: rdn 3f
out: hdd over 1f out: no ch w wnr) ........................................ 8.**2**
Reilton *(JParkes)* 5–9-2 ‡5SMaloney (1) (hdwy to jn ldrs 4f out: rdn & edgd rt
over 2f out: one pce) ...................................................... 3.**3**
1009 Susie Creamcheese *(EJAlston)* 5–9-1 KFallon (5) (outpcd & drvn along 4f out:
n.d after) ...................................................................... 6.**4**
993[4] Carousel Music (56) (Fav) *(JAkehurst)* 5–9-0 DHolland (4) (sn trckng ldr: disp
ld 7f out to 3f out: sn hrd rdn & wknd) ................................ 5.**5**
Boogie Woogie Boy *(PBeaumont)* 5–9-10 PBurke (6) (bhd & drvn along 5f out:
sn t.o) ......................................................................... 15.**6**

**4/5** Carousel Music, **11/4** COV TEL LADY, **4/1** Henbury Hall (IRE), **14/1** Susie Creamcheese, **33/1** Reilton, **100/1**
Boogie Woogie Boy. CSF £13.06, Tote £3.50: £1.80 £1.70 (£4.00). Coventry Newspapers Limited
(NEWMARKET) bred by Mrs R. Owen-George. 6 Rn                              2m 33.2 (3.7)

**1270**  CARLISLE COURTS H'CAP (0-70) £1730.00 (£480.00: £230.00)
7f 214y                                                   7-00 (7-00)

1090[2] **Spanish Verdict (58)** *(DenysSmith)* 5–9-9 DHolland (9) (lw: trckd ldr: led over
2f out: r.o u.p) .............................................................. —**1**

962* Overpower **(61)** *(MHTompkins)* 8–9–12 PRobinson (5) (hld up: hdwy over 2f
out: ev ch 1f out: nt qckn ins fnl f) ................................ ³/4.2
1089* Lawnswood Junior **(52)** *(Fav)* *(JLSpearing)* 5–9–3 KDarley (1) (lw: trckd ldrs:
effrt over 2f out: rdn & nt qckn over 1f out) ...................... 3¹/2.3
1090³ Stand At Ease **(36)** *(WStorey)* 7–8–1 SWood (2) (bhd tl styd on fnl 2f) .............. 4.4
1090⁴ Routing **(56)** *(MDHammond)* 4–9–7 MBirch (4) (led tl over 2f out: sn wknd) ....... 8.5
748⁴ Lombard Ships **(59)** *(MO'Neill)* 5–9–5 ‡⁵SMaloney (7) (lw: chsd ldrs: rdn 3f out:
sn wknd) ...................................................... s.h.6
Perspicacity **(45)** *(MDods)* 5–8–10 JLowe (8) (a in rr) .......................... 2.7
1185³ Sea Lord **(41)** *(KWHogg)* 3–7–2⁽²⁾ ‡⁷AGarth (6) (in tch: rdn over 3f out: sn lost pl) nk.8

**11/4** Lawnswood Junior, **3/1** SPANISH VERDICT, **4/1** Overpower, **11/2** Routing, **8/1** Stand At Ease, **14/1** Sea
Lord, **16/1** Lombard Ships(op 10/1), **50/1** Perspicacity. CSF £14.18, CT £31.54. Tote £3.20: £1.10 £1.70 £1.50
(£7.40). Cox & Allen (Kendal) Ltd (BISHOP AUCKLAND) bred by Hyde Stud. 8 Rn
1m 38.1 (0.3 under best; U.6)
SF—46/47/27/13/9

---

**1271**     CARLISLE CASTLE H'CAP (0-70) £1618.00 (£448.00: £214.00)    **5f**    7-30 (7-30)
(Weights raised 3 lb)

1144* **Educated Pet (49)** *(Fav)* *(MJohnston)* 3–8–9 DMcKeown (4) (lw: hld up:
smooth hdwy 2f out: r.o wl to ld over 1f out: comf) ............. —1
764 Supreme Desire **(35)** *(ASmith)* 4–8–3⁽³⁾ SWebster (3) (a chsng ldrs: kpt on wl
u.p fnl f: no ch w wnr) ........................................ 1¹/2.2
1111² Filicaia **(49)** *(DonEnricoIncisa)* 6–8–10 ‡⁷ClaireBalding (7) (sn bhd: hdwy on
outside over 1f out: r.o nr fin) ................................ s.h.3
1020³ The Right Time **(47)** (bl) *(JParkes)* 7–8–10 ‡⁵SMaloney (6) (lw: mid div: rdn &
n.m.r ¹/2-wy: styd on same pce fnl f) ........................... 2.4
978⁵ Lombard Ocean **(64)** *(MO'Neill)* 3–9–10 KFallon (10) (outpcd tl styd on appr fnl f)1¹/2.5
1091⁶ Minsk **(27)** *(TCraig)* 6–7–9⁽²⁾ PBurke (1) (bhd tl kpt on fnl 2f: n.d) ................. s.h.6
796 Castle Cary **(26)** *(TCraig)* 6–7–8 LCharnock (2) (w ldrs tl wknd over 1f out) ...... hd.7
918 Chateau Nord **(53)** *(JBerry)* 3–8–13 JCarroll (9) (chsd ldrs 3f: sn wknd) ......... 1¹/2.8
1093⁵ Foxes Diamond **(40)** *(BEllison)* 4–8–8 NCarlisle (8) (chsd ldrs to ¹/2-wy: sn lost pl) 1¹/2.9
901⁴ King Victor (IRE) **(45)** (bl) *(RO'Leary)* 4–8–3 MBirch (11) (hld up: effrt & nt clr
run over 1f out: nt rcvr) ...................................... ¹/2.10
1020⁵ Jive Music **(32)** (bl) *(NBycroft)* 6–7–9 ‡⁵NKennedy (5) (led over 3f: sn wknd) .... 4.11
LONG HANDICAP: Minsk 7-2.

**11/4** EDUCATED PET, **9/2** Filicaia, **11/2** The Right Time, Castle Cary, **7/1** Chateau Nord, **8/1** Jive Music, **10/1**
Lombard Ocean, **12/1** King Victor (IRE), **14/1** Foxes Diamond, **25/1** Supreme Desire, **66/1** Minsk. CSF £62.68,
CT £290.65. Tote £3.50: £1.70 £2.70 £2.00 (£67.20). Mr Billy Morgan (MIDDLEHAM) bred by Highfield Stud
Ltd. 11 Rn
60.6 sec (0.4)
SF—27/15/21/13/21/—

---

**1272**     SANDS CENTRE MEDIAN AUCTION STKS (Mdn 3-Y.O) £1506.00 (£416.00: £198.00)
**5f 207y**                                      8-00 (8-00)

1113² **Boy Martin** *(Fav)* *(MJohnston)* 9-0 DMcKeown (3) (lw: led: hrd drvn over 2f out:
hdd over 1f out: styd on to ld ins fnl f) ....................... —1
415⁴ Murray's Mazda (IRE) **(66)** *(JBerry)* 9-0 JCarroll (2) (hld up: hdwy to ld over 1f
out: sltly hmpd, hdd & no ex ins fnl f) ......................... nk.2
1091⁵ Tellgas *(WStorey)* 9-0 SWebster (1) (w ldr: n.m.r & outpcd fnl f: swtchd & styd
on ins fnl f) .................................................. ³/4.3

**4/9** BOY MARTIN, **11/4** Murray's Mazda (IRE), **6/1** Tellgas. CSF £1.98, Tote £1.50 (£1.20). Laharna Ltd
(MIDDLEHAM) bred by Laharna Ltd. 3 Rn
1m 15.4 (3.1)

---

**1273**     E.B.F. CARLISLE STATION STKS (Mdn 2-Y.O) £1876.40 (£520.40: £249.20)
**5f 207y**                                      8-30 (8-33)

924⁵ **Cliburnel News (IRE)** *(MHTompkins)* 8-9 PRobinson (8) (lw: trckd ldrs: r.o wl
to ld jst ins fnl f: sn clr) .................................... —1
396⁶ So so *(TDBarron)* 8-9 AlexGreaves (1) (hld up & bhd: gd hdwy over 1f out: r.o wl
nr fin) ....................................................... 3¹/2.2
907⁶ Tahasun (IRE) *(HThomsonJones)* 9-0 NCarlisle (2) (lw: led: rdn & wandered
over 1f out: hdd & no ex jst ins fnl f) ......................... 1.3
1023² Cop the Cash (USA) *(Fav)* *(MBell)* 9-0 DMcKeown (4) (lw: chsd ldrs: ev ch & rdn
2f out: one pce) ............................................... 2¹/2.4
795⁴ Preston Guild (IRE) *(JBerry)* 9-0 JCarroll (6) (w ldrs tl rdn & wknd 2f out) ..... 7.5
Wishing Cap (USA) *(SirMarkPrescott)* 9-0 JLowe (7) (wl grwn: str: bit bkwd:
s.i.s: bhd: stdy hdwy over 1f out: nvr nr to chal) .............. ¹/2.6
Bardia *(DonEnricoIncisa)* 8-9 JakiHouston (3) (rangy: scope: bkwd: s.s: a wl
outpcd) ....................................................... 5.7

**7/4** Cop the Cash (USA), **11/4** CLIBURNEL NEWS (IRE), **4/1** Tahasun (IRE), **9/2** Wishing Cap (USA), **10/1** Preston Guild (IRE), **20/1** So so, **100/1** Bardia. CSF £41.56, Tote £3.90: £2.00 £3.40 (£15.40). East Lancs Newspapers Readers Club (NEWMARKET) bred by St Simon Foundation in Ireland. 7 Rn   1m 14.3 (2)

**1274** CARLISLE CATHEDRAL H'CAP (0-70) £1660.00 (£460.00: £220.00)
1½m                    (Weights raised 3 lb)                    9-00 (9-02)

| | | |
|---|---|---|
| 951 | **Luks Akura (30)** (v) (MJohnston) 4–7-0 ‡7MBaird (6) (mde all: sn clr: unchal) ... —1 |
| 951³ | Mingus (USA) **(55)** (Fav) (MrsJRRamsden) 5–9-4 TLucas (7) (lw: a chsng wnr: kpt on u.p fnl 2f: nvr able to chal) | 3½.2 |
| 1073³ | Sapphirine **(61)** (RMWhitaker) 5–9-10 ACulhane (1) (lw: hld up & bhd: hdwy over 2f out: styd on fnl f) | 2½.3 |
| 1195 | Kinoko **(44)** (KWHogg) 4–8-0 ‡7AGarth (9) (hld up & bhd: styd on fnl 2f: nrst fin) | ½.4 |
| | Mils Mij **(53)** (TAKCuthbert) 7–9-2 NCarlisle (5) (b: b.hind: chsd ldrs tl rdn, outpcd & lost pl 5f out: styd on fnl f) | 2½.5 |
| 1051 | Wsom (IRE) **(48)** (JMCarr) 4–8-11 SMorris (3) (bhd: kpt on fnl 3f: n.d) | 1½.6 |
| 880⁵ | Talish **(45)** (TDBarron) 4–8-8 AlexGreaves (4) (lw: hld up: effrt over 3f out: wknd 2f out) | 2.7 |
| 1008 | Cornhill Melody **(31)** (JLSpearing) 4–7-1 ‡7CHawksley (8) (chsd ldrs tl lost pl over 3f out) | 1½.8 |
| 950⋆ | Grouse-N-Heather **(60)** (MrsGRReveley) 3–8-7 JLowe (2) (trckd ldrs: effrt u.p 4f out: sn wknd & eased) | nk.9 |

**9/4** Mingus (USA)(op 7/2), **11/4** Grouse-N-Heather, **4/1** Mils Mij, **5/1** Sapphirine, **8/1** Cornhill Melody, **10/1** Talish, **33/1** Kinoko, **50/1** LUKS AKURA & Ors. CSF £156.30, CT £637.04. Tote £41.60: £4.50 £1.40 £1.90 (£97.10). Luks Ind Co (UK) Ltd (MIDDLEHAM) bred by Hesmonds Stud Ltd. 9 Rn   2m 31.5 (0.1 under best; 2)
T/Plpt: £58.8 (26.4 Tckts).                                                          WG

## 1145—LEICESTER (R-H)

### Saturday, June 6th [Good to soft, Good st]
Going Allowance: 0.20 sec per fur (G)                    Wind: mod across

Stalls: high

**1275** TIPSTERS TABLE MEDIAN AUCTION STKS (3-Y.O) £2040.00 (£565.00: £270.00)
1m 1f 218y                                              6-45 (6-47)

| | | |
|---|---|---|
| | **Clurican (IRE) (52)** (DNicholson) 8-9 JWilliams (3) (swtg: mde all: r.o wl) ......... —1 |
| 599³ | Romansh **(80)** (GWragg) 8-13 WRSwinburn (2) (lw: 4th st: chsd wnr 3f out: rdn over 1f out: no imp) | 3½.2 |
| 509⋆ | Handsome Gent (Fav) (LordHuntingdon) 8-13 LDettori (5) (bit bkwd: dwlt: hdwy 4f out: rdn 3f out: one pce) | 2½.3 |
| | Speedo Movement (BAMcMahon) 7-11 ‡7SSanders (7) (8th st: hdwy over 3f out: one pce fnl 2f) | ¾.4 |
| 1069⁶ | Storm Dust (JRFanshawe) 8-9 GCarter (8) (7th st: hdwy over 3f out: rdn 2f out: one pce) | nk.5 |
| 492⁶ | Sebosan **(77)** (AHide) 9-0 WWoods (1) (lw: 5th & rdn st: wknd 3f out) | 10.6 |
| 857 | Dajitus (MJHeaton-Ellis) 8-9 WNewnes (10) (b: lw: 6th & hmpd st: sn bhd) | nk.7 |
| 784³ | Anditisitis (USA) (DWPArbuthnot) 8-9 PaulEddery (4) (chsd wnr: 2nd st: wknd 3f out) | 3.8 |
| | Ay Beat **(44)** (EAWheeler) 8-4 ‡5DHarrison (6) (s.s: a bhd: t.o) | 25.9 |
| 1049⁶ | Thamestar (IRE) (JLDunlop) 8-13 WCarson (9) (lw: plld hrd: 3rd st: wknd qckly 3f out: t.o) | 2.10 |

**11/8** Handsome Gent, **7/2** Thamestar (IRE), **5/1** Romansh(op 5/2), **7/1** Storm Dust, **15/2** Anditisitis (USA)(op 5/1), **20/1** Sebosan, **25/1** Dajitus, **50/1** Speedo Movement, **66/1** CLURICAN (IRE), **100/1** Ay Beat. CSF £335.70, Tote £69.30: £7.20 £1.40 £1.30 (Wnr or 2nd w any £2.50). Mrs Claire Smith (STOW ON THE WOLD) bred by Capt. D. Foster and B. Corscadden in Ireland. 10 Rn   2m 11.2 (8.5)
SF—30/27/22/4/15/–

**1276** TELE-ADS (S) STKS (3-Y.O) £1856.00 (£516.00: £248.00)   7f 9y   7-15 (7-26)

| | | |
|---|---|---|
| 1001⁵ | **Certain Lady (59)** (GBlum) 8-6 ‡5DHarrison (16) (a.p: led over 3f out: clr 2f out: eased ins fnl f) | —1 |
| 1075 | Throw Away Line **(46)** (JEtherington) 8-6 NConnorton (1) (lw: a.p: wandered over 2f out: one pce) | 4.2 |
| 863 | Have a Nightcap **(49)** (bl) (MAJarvis) 8-11 BRaymond (17) (a.p: one pce fnl 2f) | nk.3 |
| 1172 | Bernie Silvers **(53)** (MCChapman) 8-11 LDettori (14) (led over 3f: wknd over 1f out) | 6.4 |
| 1145⁴ | Medbourne (IRE) **(37)** (JLHarris) 8-6 PaulEddery (9) (b.off hind: hdwy fnl 2f: nvr nrr) | nk.5 |
| 904 | Broughton's Tango (IRE) **(41)** (WJMusson) 8-11 JHBrown (13) (lw: nvr plcd to chal) | 3½.6 |

1040² Fisianna (ARDavison) 8-6  CandyMorris (7) (b.nr fore: chsd ldrs: nt clr run over
          2f out: sn btn) ................................................... 2.7
  1040 Missal (IRE) (45) (bl) (PatMitchell) 7-13 ‡⁷RTurner (19) (lw: prom 4f) ................. 2.8
      Swan Star (40) (GBlum) 8-6  RFox (6) (bit bkwd: nvr nr ldrs) ...................... nk.9
  1001 Amber Glow (IRE) (40) (LJCodd) 8-11  VSmith (12) (swtg: bhd fnl 3f) ............. ¾.10
   522 Briginski (33) (bl) (KRBurke) 8-6  GCarter (11) (prom 4f) ............................ s.h.11
  1040 Mississippi Queen (40) (MrsNMacauley) 7-13 ‡⁷MadeleineSmith (3) (reard s:
          rdn & hung rt 2f out: nt r.o) ................................... nk.12
      My Boy Buster (CJHill) 8-11  GDuffield (18) (lw: n.d) ............................... ½.13
   697 Rivet (59) (MBlanshard) 8-11  TQuinn (8) (a bhd) .................................... 5.14
  141⁵ Tamasha (60) (Fav) (CJHill) 8-6  NAdams (2) (bhd fnl 3f) ......................... 3½.15
      Tanana (61) (bl) (JGFitzGerald) 8-1⁽²⁾ ‡⁷MHunt (5) (bit bkwd: spd 4f) ...... 3½.16
  1154 Super Marco (43) (WWHaigh) 8-6 ‡⁵CHodgson (10) (lw: w ldr over 3f) .......... ¾.17
  1010 Nicholas Star (REPeacock) 8-11  AProud (4) (prom 3f: t.o) ....................... 20.18
  978⁶ Tommy Tempest (KRBurke) 8-11  AShoults (15) (t.o fnl 3f) ......................... 19

**5/1** Tamasha, **13/2** Fisianna, CERTAIN LADY, **7/1** Tanana, **8/1** Throw Away Line, Bernie Silvers, **10/1** Have a
Nightcap, Medbourne (IRE), **12/1** Broughton's Tango (IRE), **16/1** My Boy Buster, Rivet, Tommy Tempest(op
8/1), **20/1** Amber Glow (IRE), **33/1** Nicholas Star, Super Marco, Swan Star, Briginski, **50/1** Ors. CSF £60.30,
Tote £7.80: £2.90 £3.40 £3.50 (£21.90). Mrs Bridget Blum (NEWMARKET) bred by Dunchurch Lodge Stud. 19
Rn; Bt in 4,200 gns
                                                  1m 29.6 (7.3)
                                                   SF—6/-/-/-/-/-

**1277**    LEICESTER MERCURY H'CAP (3-Y.O) (0-80) £4240.00 (£1270.00: £610.00: £280.00)
         7f 9y                                        7-45 (7-49)

                 (Weights raised 2 lb)
   526³ **Fen Dance (IRE) (72)** (Fav) (PJMakin) 9-4  LDettori (8) (lw: hld up: hdwy 2f out:
          led ins fnl f: nt r.o wl) ................................................ —1
  697⁶ Kipini (47) (WJMusson) 7-7  RFox (12) (a.p: led over 1f out tl ins fnl f) ............ 2.2
  1122⁴ Ripsnorter (IRE) (60) (SirMarkPrescott) 8-6  GDuffield (5) (hld up: gd hdwy 2f
          out: nrst fin) ........................................................ 3½.3
  899⁵ Masrur (USA) (66) (RWArmstrong) 8-12  WCarson (11) (a.p: ev ch over 1f out:
          wknd fnl f) ........................................................... 2.4
   451 Sudanor (IRE) (67) (MJHeaton-Ellis) 8-13  WNewnes (6) (led: edgd rt & hdd
          over 1f out: sn wknd) ............................................. 1.5
   801 Peerage Prince (65) (PatMitchell) 8-8 ‡³SO'Gorman (4) (lw: led stands' side:
          wknd 2f out) ........................................................ 5.6
      Court Circular (75) (LordHuntingdon) 9-7  WRSwinburn (10) (bit bkwd: nvr trbld
          ldrs) .................................................................. s.h.7
  1051 Katie's Dream (IRE) (54) (PSFelgate) 7-9 ‡⁵DHarrison (2) (prom 4f) ............. nk.8
   591 Nigals Friend (67) (DHaydnJones) 8-13  JWilliams (7) (swtg: prom: wknd qckly
          over 2f out: t.o) ................................................... 15.9
  1035⁴ Boogie Bopper (70) (MBell) 9-2  TQuinn (3) (lw: prom over 4f: t.o) ........ s.h.10
  1062 Paradise Forum (71) (CAHorgan) 9-3  AMcGlone (1) (dwlt: hrd rdn 3f out: a
          bhd: t.o) ............................................................. 1½.11
                LONG HANDICAP: Kipini 7-5.

**7/2** FEN DANCE (IRE), **4/1** Ripsnorter (IRE), **11/2** Boogie Bopper (IRE), Sudanor (IRE), **8/1** Masrur (USA),
Peerage Prince, **9/1** Court Circular, **10/1** Katie's Dream (IRE), **20/1** Ors. CSF £65.83, CT £267.21. Tote £5.10:
£1.90 £6.00 £1.80 (£120.10). Mr D. M. Ahier (MARLBOROUGH) bred by Bobby Donworth and Honora Corridan
in Ireland. 11 Rn
                                                    1m 28 (5.7)
                                                 SF—39/8/10/10/8/–

**1278**    MERCURY RACE NIGHT H'CAP (0-70) £2721.00 (£756.00: £363.00)
         5f 218y                                      8-15 (8-17)

  1021⁶ **Bernstein Bette (62)** (Fav) (PSFelgate) 6–9-6  WRyan (3) (dwlt: nt clr run &
          swtchd lft over 1f out: r.o to ld post) ............................ —1
  1174⁶ Mu-Arrik (50) (bl) (DAWilson) 4–8-8  GCarter (4) (hdwy over 2f out: led over 1f
          out: ct post) ........................................................ s.h.2
  1030* Klairover (46) (CJHill) 5–8-4  NAdams (5) (lw: a.p: ev ch over 1f out: nt qckn fnl f) .. 2.3
   775 Coppermill Lad (47) (LJHolt) 9–7-12 ‡⁷CAvery (13) (rdn & hdwy fnl 2f: r.o) ...... 1½.4
  1155 Queen's Tickle (53) (APJarvis) 3–8-2  PaulEddery (10) (b.nr hind: led over 4f) ... 4.5
   967 Nazare Blue (44) (MrsBarbaraWaring) 5–8-2⁽³⁾ NHowe (3) (nvr nr to chal) ......... 2.6
  1030⁵ Tippling (USA) (35) (PBurgoyne) 5–7-7 (nvr nrr) ................................. 1½.7
   510 Red Verona (47) (EAWheeler) 3–7-5⁽²⁾ ‡⁵DHarrison (15) (dwlt: n.d) ............... 1.8
  1050 Minizen Music (IRE) (37) (MBrittain) 4–7-9  GBardwell (6) (lw: prom: hrd rdn 2f
          out: sn wknd) ...................................................... hd.9
   909 Goody Four Shoes (48) (DRTucker) 4–8-1 ‡⁵RPrice (1) (outpcd) ................. nk.10
   901 The Shanahan Bay (60) (v) (MrsNMacauley) 7–8-11 ‡⁷SWilliams (7) (b: lw: dwlt:
          sn rcvrd: wknd 2f out) ............................................ ¾.11
  1266⁴ Verro (USA) (43) (JABennett) 5–8-1  GHind (17) (lw: wl bhd fnl 2f) ............... 2½.12

948 Ganeshaya **(49)** *(MFBarraclough)* 3–7-12 AMunro (16) (spd over 3f) ............ 1½.**13**
909 Flying Promise **(44)** *(RABennett)* 4–8-2 JFortune (12) (lw: gd spd 4f) ............... 2.**14**
974 Killick **(40)** *(REPeacock)* 4–7-9(5) ‡³SO'Gorman (11) (lw: chsd ldrs 4f) ............ 1½.**15**
349 Everset (FR) **(66)** *(WJMusson)* 4–9-3 ‡⁷PBowe (lw: t.o) ............................. 10.**16**
LONG HANDICAP: Tippling (USA) 7-3.

**4/1** BERNSTEIN BETTE, **9/2** Klairover(4/1—6/1), Coppermill Lad, **8/1** Verro (USA), **10/1** Mu-Arrik, Nazare Blue, Minizen Music (IRE), **11/1** Ganeshaya, **12/1** Queen's Tickle(op 8/1), **14/1** Tippling (USA), Killick, Everset (FR), **20/1** The Shanahan Bay, **25/1** Flying Promise, **33/1** Ors. CSF £48.35, CT £185.98. Tote £5.70: £1.50 £3.40 £2.50 £1.50 (£25.10). Mr John Ford (MELTON MOWBRAY) bred by C. G. Reid. 16 Rn          1m 14.2 (4.2)
SF–46/33/21/9/1/–

**1279**      SPORTS MERCURY STKS (Mdn 2-Y.O.F) £1730.00 (£480.00: £230.00)
5f 218y                                                           8-45 (8-49)

**Just Speculation (IRE)** *(PFCole)* 8-11 TQuinn (6) (w'like: scope: bit bkwd: a.p: led 2f out: rdn out) ..................................................... —**1**
Moon Watch *(JRFanshawe)* 8-11 WRSwinburn (1) (unf: scope: bkwd: hdwy 3f out: ev ch fnl 2f: r.o) ....................................... 1½.**2**
Cinders Girl *(JMPEustace)* 8-11 MTebbutt (2) (neat: lt-f: hdwy 2f out: r.o ins fnl f) . 3.**3**
986³ Satz (USA) **(Fav)** *(JHMGosden)* 8-11 WCarson (9) (bit bkwd: plld hrd: ev ch 2f out: wknd fnl f) ............................................... 2½.**4**
1057 Is She Quick *(MrsJCDawe)* 8-11 JWilliams (11) (nvr nr to chal) ...................... 1½.**5**
Summit Fever (IRE) *(PFCole)* 8-11 AMunro (10) (w'like: lw: no hdwy fnl 2f) ...... 5.**6**
852 Malzeta (IRE) *(MJHeaton-Ellis)* 8-11 WNewnes (8) (led 4f) ............................. ½.**7**
Persian Fountain (IRE) *(BSRothwell)* 8-11 JFortune (4) (unf: bit bkwd: hrd rdn over 2f out: sn bhd) .................................... 3.**8**
1038 Desirable Miss *(MBrittain)* 8-11 GCarter (7) (prom over 3f) .......................... 1½.**9**
Petite Louie *(WCarter)* 8-6 ‡⁵NGwilliams (3) (unf: bkwd: bhd fnl 3f) ................. ½.**10**
807³ Galejade (8/1) *Withdrawn (ref to ent stalls) : not under orders*

**Evens** Satz (USA)(4/6—5/4), **5/1** Moon Watch(tchd 10/1), **6/1** Summit Fever (IRE)(op 5/2), **11/1** JUST SPECULATION (IRE), **12/1** Malzeta (IRE), **33/1** Cinders Girl, **50/1** Ors. CSF £49.18, Tote £11.70: £2.40 £1.50 £4.70 (£39.20). Mr Christopher Wright (WHATCOMBE) bred by Swettenham Stud in Ireland. 10 Rn          1m 15.5 (5.5)
SF–11/5/–/–/–/–

**1280**      LATE NIGHT EXTRA STKS      £2127.50 (£590.00: £282.50)      1m 3f 183y 9-15 (9-28)

652³ **Sayh (87)** *(MAJarvis)* 3–8-11 LDettori (10) (a.p: 3rd st: led 2f out: rdn out) ......... —**1**
1069* Cezanne **(Fav)** *(MRStoute)* 3–8-10 WRSwinburn (2) (lw: hld up: 4th st: led 3f out to 2f out: one pce) .................................. 3½.**2**
Wajeeb (USA) *(BHanbury)* 3–8-5 BRaymond (7) (tall: scope: dwlt: hdwy & 6th st: styd on fnl 2f) ...................................... 3.**3**
Ptolemy (FR) *(MissHCKnight)* 5–9-7 GDuffield (5) (bit bkwd: led 9f: wknd over 1f out) .................................................... 1.**4**
395 Cosmic Future **(72)** *(AHide)* 3–8-11 WWoods (4) (bit bkwd: 7th st: no imp fnl 4f) 3½.**5**
The Jones Boy (FR) **(60)** *(GHJones)* 5–9-11 WNewnes (a bhd) ......................... 12.**6**
1005 Gabesia *(HJCollingridge)* 4–9-2 VSmith (6) (chsd ldr: 2nd st: wknd over 3f out) 4.**7**
512 Court Rise (USA) *(RWArmstrong)* 3–8-5 BCrossley (1) (hdwy 8f out: 5th & wkng st) ............................................. 4.**8**
Cool Apollo (NZ) *(JCMcConnochie)* 5–9-7 JWilliams (3) (bit bkwd: a bhd) ...... s.h.**9**
Tinkosumtin *(PBurgoyne)* 6–9-2 MWigham (8) (a bhd) ..................................... 4.**10**

**10/11** Cezanne, **5/2** SAYH, **7/1** Wajeeb (USA), **9/1** Ptolemy (FR), **10/1** Cosmic Future, **20/1** The Jones Boy (FR), **50/1** Court Rise (USA), **100/1** Ors. CSF £5.14, Tote £4.10: £1.20 £1.40 £1.80 (£2.20). Sheikh Ahmed Al Maktoum (NEWMARKET) bred by Enterprise Bloodstock. 10 Rn          2m 42.8 (14)
T/Plpt: £255.80 (9.3 Tckts).                                                    KH

1120–**NOTTINGHAM (L-H)**
**Monday, June 8th [Good]**
Going Allowance: St: minus 0.15 sec (F); Rest: 0.15 sec per fur (G)          Wind: almost nil
Stalls: high

**1281**      RADCLIFFE APP'CE CLAIMING STKS (3-Y.O) £2245.60 (£621.60: £296.80)
6f 15y                                                           2-30 (2-31)

888* **Just Bob (69)** (bl) **(Fav)** *(SEKettlewell)* 9-1 MHumphries (8) (lw: a.p: led ½-wy: rdn clr fnl f) .......................................... —**1**

1144³ Cranfield Comet **(60)** *(JBerry)* 8-11 SHaworth (5) (led 2f: rdn over 1f out: one pce) ........................................................................... 2.2

1075 Hot Punch **(49)** *(PCalver)* 8-4 CAdamson (2) (chsd ldrs: kpt on ins fnl f: nvr nrr) 1.3

1012 Double Lark **(58)** (bl) *(RHollinshead)* 8-9 AGarth (7) (lw: led after 2f: sn hdd: rdn & wknd appr fnl f) ...................................................... ½.4

939³ Loose Zeus (USA) **(56)** *(CFWall)* 8-4 TWilson (1) (in tch: rdn 2f out: sn btn) .... nk.5

994² Mansber (IRE) **(55)** *(PatMitchell)* 8-9 RTurner (3) (chsd ldrs: rdn & drifted lft 2f out: no imp) ........................................................................ ½.6

890 Baie Petite *(AWJones)* 8-4 ClaireBalding (6) (b.nr hind: sn drvn along: nvr plcd to chal) .................................................................... 2½.7

**2/1** JUST BOB(6/4—5/2), **3/1** Loose Zeus (USA), **9/2** Cranfield Comet(op 3/1), **7/1** Double Lark(12/1—6/1), **8/1** Mansber (IRE), **16/1** Hot Punch, **33/1** Baie Petite. CSF £10.19, Tote £2.80: £1.70 £1.60 (£4.30). Mr J. Fotherby (MIDDLEHAM) bred by Mrs D. Whittingham. 7 Rn

1m 14.7 (3.7)
SF—9/–/–/–/–/–

---

# 1282

SANDIACRE H'CAP (0-70) £2343.60 (£649.60: £310.80)   **5f 13y**    3-00 (3-01)
(Weights raised 4 lb)

1162⁴ **Rednet (53)** *(PDEvans)* 5-9-4 AMunro (11) (b: chsd ldrs: rdn to ld ins fnl f: r.o) —1

Lincstone Boy (IRE) **(45)** (bl) *(WJPearce)* 4-8-10 SWebster (12) (swtg: hld up: effrt 2f out: hrd rdn fnl f: r.o) ........................................... nk.2

1263² Fighter Squadron **(49)** (v) *(Fav)* *(JAGlover)* 3-8-3 ‡³FNorton (10) (lw: led ½-wy: hung lft & hdd ins fnl f: unable qckn) ..................... ½.3

Young Shadowfax **(55)** *(CNAllen)* 5-9-6 MTebbutt (8) (bit bkwd: outpcd tl styd on ins fnl f) ................................................................ 1½.4

1162* Hotfoot Hannah (IRE) **(49)** *(PSFelgate)* 4-8-11 (7x) ‡³JFanning (7) (lw: chsd ldrs: btn whn hmpd over 1f out) ........................... 3½.5

1138 Petitesse **(50)** *(GBlum)* 4-9-1 AShoults (4) (in tch over 3f) .............. ¾.6

918³ Last Straw **(37)** (bl) *(AWJones)* 4-8-2 GBaxter (1) (swtg: dwlt: nvr nrr) ........ nk.7

1138 Saint Systems **(47)** *(CJHill)* 6-8-12 TyroneWilliams (9) (led to ½-wy: wknd wl over 1f out) ............................................................ hd.8

876 Miss Siham (IRE) **(57)** *(JBalding)* 4-8-9 ⁷ClaireBalding (2) (m.n.s) .......... ¾.9

996³ Fair Enchantress **(59)** *(JABennett)* 4-9-10 DHolland (5) (outpcd: hrd drvn ½-wy: no imp) ............................................................. hd.10

Vendredi Treize **(35)** *(SRBowring)* 9-8-0 NAdams (6) (b: bkwd: prom 3f) ...... ¾.11

1030⁴ Lucy Dancer (IRE) **(56)** *(CGCox)* 4-9-7 AClark (3) (a bhd) ................. 1½.12

**4/1** Fighter Squadron, **6/1** Hotfoot Hannah (IRE), **13/2** REDNET, **15/2** Saint Systems(5/1—8/1), **9/1** Lucy Dancer (IRE), Last Straw, **10/1** Fair Enchantress, **12/1** Petitesse(op 8/1), Lincstone Boy (IRE), **16/1** Young Shadowfax, **50/1** Ors. CSF £69.84, CT £313.57. Tote £6.40: £2.20 £3.50 £1.80 (£49.70). Mr John Fowden (WELSHPOOL) bred by Mrs D. M. Pollock. 12 Rn

60.8 sec (2.1)
SF—47/38/29/40/17/18

---

# 1283

E.B.F. PLUMTREE STKS (Mdn 2-Y-O) £2511.00 (£696.00: £333.00)
**5f 13y**
3-30 (3-32)

720⁵ **Tom Piper** *(JBerry)* 9-0 JCarroll (6) (mde all: rdn out) .................. —1

High Tycoon (IRE) *(Fav)* *(MrsJCecil)* 9-0 PaulEddery (7) (w'like: scope: s.s: hdwy ½-wy: hrd drvn & kpt on wl ins fnl f) .................... 2.2

The Fed *(RMWhitaker)* 9-0 ACulhane (9) (cmpt: lw: a.p: rdn & unable qckn ins fnl f) ................................................................... ¾.3

Jade Runner *(MrsNMacauley)* 8-9 LDettori (3) (leggy: unf: prom: rdn 2f out: kpt on one pce) ........................................................... 1.4

772 Aragrove *(LJHolt)* 9-0 AMunro (4) (swtg: chsd ldrs: hrd rdn over 1f out: one pce) ......................................................................... 1½.5

Prince Songline *(RBoss)* 9-0 TQuinn (5) (unf: scope: bit bkwd: swtchd centre ½-wy: a outpcd: t.o) .................................................. 10.6

Tajdif (USA) *(DMorley)* 9-0 WCarson (1) (cmpt: bkwd: effrt over 2f out: nvr able to chal: t.o) ............................................................ 5.7

Go Orange *(JLSpearing)* 8-9 NHowe (2) (lengthy: unf: bit bkwd: dwlt: a bhd: t.o) .......................................................................... 2½.8

Remember the Night *(JBalding)* 9-0 GDuffield (8) (str: bkwd: s.s: outpcd & bhd: t.o) .......................................................................... 1½.9

**8/11** High Tycoon (IRE), **13/2** Aragrove, **7/1** Tajdif (USA), TOM PIPER, **12/1** Jade Runner, The Fed(10/1—16/1), Prince Songline(10/1—16/1), **40/1** Go Orange, **50/1** Remember the Night. CSF £12.62, Tote £7.60: £1.60 £1.20 £3.30 (£4.10). Mr A. B. Atkins (COCKERHAM) bred by A. B. Atkins and B. V. Piper. 9 Rn

60.8 sec (2.1)
SF—43/35/32/23/22/–

**1284**    RIVER TRENT CLAIMING H'CAP (0-70) £2912.00 (£812.00: £392.00)
     1m 54y           4-00 (4-05)

(Weights raised 6 lb)

1106⁵ **Sooty Tern (45)** (JMBradley) 5–8-10 NAdams (3) (mde all: drew clr appr fnl f:
     v.easily) ...................................................... —1

1106 Grey Illusions (41) (LJHolt) 4–8-6⁽²⁾ LDettori (18) (swtg: gd hdwy over 2f out:
     rdn & kpt on ins fnl f: no ch w wnr) ........................ 2¹/₂.2

738 Please Please Me (IRE) (34) (KOCunningham-Brown) 4–7-10 ‡³FNorton (8)
     (hld up: hdwy 2f out: fin wl) ................................ 1¹/₂.3

1143⁴ Sanawi (53) (PDEvans) 5–9-4 AMunro (16) (lw: s.i.s: hdwy on outside 3f out: nt
     rch ldrs) ...................................................... 1.4

1177⁶ Dublin Indemnity (USA) (49) (NACallaghan) 3–8-3 PaulEddery (7) (lw: prom:
     3rd st: ev ch 3f out: kpt on one pce) ........................ hd.5

King's Shilling (USA) (52) (MrsSOliver) 5–9-3 WCarson (17) (prom: 4th st: one
     pce fnl 2f) .................................................. s.h.6

962 Irish Groom (38) (bl) (JPSmith) 5–7-10⁽²⁾ ‡⁷DCarson (5) (hld up: n.m.r 3f out: kpt
     on fnl f) ....................................................... ³/₄.7

1172* Top One (51) (Fav) (CJHill) 7–9-2 (5x) DHolland (14) (prom: 2nd st: ev ch 2f
     out: wandered rt & lft: sn btn) .............................. 1.8

1070 Parr (IRE) (53) (JMackie) 4–9-4 WNewnes (11) (lw: s.s: nvr nrr) ............... 1.9

796* Lazy Rhythm (USA) (53) (RAkehurst) 6–9-4 ADicks (9) (b: lw: nvr plcd to chal) hd.10

866 Quietly Impressive (IRE) (56) (MBell) 4–9-7 MHills (15) (lw: s.i.s: a bhd) .... ³/₄.11

884⁵ Breeze Away (60) (RMWhitaker) 3–9-0 ACulhane (1) (chsd ldrs: 6th st: n.m.r &
     wknd 2f out) ................................................. s.h.12

1013* Sir Arthur Hobbs (56) (FHLee) 5–9-2 ‡⁵NKennedy (4) (lw: chsd ldrs: 7th st: rdn &
     wknd 2f out) ................................................. 3¹/₂.13

366 Classic Exhibit (53) (AHide) 3–8-7 WWoods (10) (swtg: m.n.s) .............. s.h.14

Classics Pearl (IRE) (41) (NATwiston-Davies) 4–8-1⁽¹⁾ ‡⁵LNewton (13) (bit
     bkwd: m.n.s) ................................................. 1¹/₈.15

604⁴ Roger Rabbit (FR) (46) (RBoss) 3–8-0 JLowe (6) (a bhd) ................... hd.16

1051³ Major Ivor (59) (MrsGRReveley) 7–9-10 GDuffield (12) (chsd ldrs: 5th st: wknd
     over 2f out) ................................................. 1¹/₂.17

1025 Petastra (59) (MrsJRRamsden) 3–8-10 GBaxter (2) (lw: m.n.s) ............... hd.18

962 Serlby Connection (45) (SRBowring) 7–8-10 SWebster (19) (b: bit bkwd: prom
     to ¹/₂-wy: sn lost tch) ........................................ 19

**7/2** Top One(5/2—4/1), **8/1** Breeze Away(tchd 14/1), **9/1** Lazy Rhythm (USA)(9/2—10/1), Parr (IRE)(op 16/1),
Sanawi, **10/1** Sir Arthur Hobbs(7/1—12/1), Roger Rabbit (FR), SOOTY TERN(op 16/1), **11/1** Major Ivor, **12/1**
Quietly Impressive (IRE), King's Shilling (USA), **14/1** Classics Pearl (IRE), **16/1** Irish Groom, **20/1** Grey Illusions,
Dublin Indemnity (USA), Petastra, **33/1** Ors. CSF £202.76, CT £5,742.87. Tote £15.50: £3.30 £3.70 £15.10
£3.70 (£113.90). Mr J. M. Bradley (CHEPSTOW) bred by Sheikh Mohammed bin Rashid al Maktoum. 19 Rn
                                   1m 45.8 (6.2)
                                 SF—21/9/–/13/–/9

**1285**    LOUDHAM STKS (3-Y-O) £3608.00 (£872.00)    **1m 54y**      4-30 (4-32)

655 **Dilum (USA) (110)** (PFICole) 9-7 AMunro (1) (lw: plld hrd: hld up: 2nd st: led
     appr fnl f: qcknd clr) ........................................ —1

977 Lead the Dance (101) (Fav) (HRACecil) 9-0 WRyan (2) (lw: led: shkn up 2f out:
     hdd over 1f out: sn btn) ..................................... 3¹/₂.2

**4/6** Lead the Dance, **11/10** DILUM (USA). Tote £3.00. Mr Fahd Salman (WHATCOMBE) bred by RonCon Ltd 1 in
USA. 2 Rn
                                   1m 45.3 (5.7)
                                 SF—40/22

**1286**    BILBOROUGH H'CAP (3-Y-O) (0-70) £2520.00 (£700.00: £336.00)
     1³/₄m 15y           5-00 (5-01)

(Weights raised 3 lb)

896⁴ **Miss Pin Up (45)** (PatMitchell) 7-10 ‡³DBiggs (8) (hld up: hdwy & 4th st: led
     over 2f out: sn unchal) ...................................... —1

902 Laughton Lady (40) (MrsNMacauley) 7-8 NAdams (6) (lw: hdwy 8f out: kpt on
     fnl 2f: no ch w wnr) ......................................... 8.2

481 Snow Board (55) (BWHills) 8-9 MHills (7) (mid div: pushed along ¹/₂-wy: styd on
     fnl f) ........................................................ 3¹/₂.3

1102² Alternation (FR) (54) (PFICole) 8-8 TQuinn (2) (prom: led over 5f out tl over 2f
     out: sn btn) ................................................. 2¹/₂.4

532 Siolfor (USA) (45) (MrsJRRamsden) 7-8 ‡⁵NKennedy (11) (wl bhd tl styd on fnl
     2f) .......................................................... 1¹/₂.5

908 Storm Drum (54) (bl) (PJMakin) 8-8 WNewnes (4) (hdwy 8f out: 3rd st:
     ev ch 3f out: sn rdn: fnd nil) ............................... 3¹/₂.6

810 Ellafitzetty (IRE) (58) (RFJohnsonHoughton) 8-12 AClark (13) (nvr plcd to chal) 3.7

| | | |
|---|---|---|
| 10243 | Barton Pride (IRE) **(47)** *(RHollinshead)* 8-1 AMunro (16) (n.d) | 12.8 |
| 11312 | Bartolomeo (USA) **(47)** (v) *(MrsJRRamsden)* 8-1 GDuffield (14) (chsd ldrs: 5th st: rdn 3f out: sn wknd) | 3½.9 |
| 10274 | Mustahil (IRE) **(67)** *(RJHodges)* 9-7 WCarson (10) (a bhd: t.o) | 4.10 |
| 488 | Shanti Flyer (IRE) **(51)** *(AHide)* 8-5 WWoods (12) (chsd ldrs 8f: sn wknd: t.o) | ½.11 |
| 11315 | In No Doubt **(46)** (bl) *(JJO'Neill)* 7-11 ‡3JFanning (9) (led: clr 8f out: hdd over 5f out: 2nd st: wknd qckly: t.o) | 1½.12 |
| 908 | Simply George **(65)** *(RBoss)* 9-5 JCarroll (15) (lw: chsd ldrs: 7th & rdn st: wknd over 2f out: t.o) | 2½.13 |
| 4874 | Linpac Express **(64)** *(CWCElsey)* 9-4 LDettori (1) (chsd ldrs: 6th & wkng st: t.o) | 14 |
| 9325 | Notable Exception **(60)** (Jt-Fav) *(JWHills)* 9-0 DHolland (17) (lw: rdn ½-wy: no rspnse: t.o) | 15 |
| 11313 | Sparkling Vision **(45)** (bl) *(MrsGRReveley)* 7-13 JLowe (2) (swtg: chsd ldrs tl rdn & wknd ½-wy: p.u ent st) | 0 |

**6/1** Notable Exception, Storm Drum, **7/1** Bartolomeo (USA), Mustahil (IRE), **8/1** Shanti Flyer (IRE), **9/1** Alternation (FR), Snow Board, **10/1** Linpac Express, **11/1** Simply George, **12/1** Sparkling Vision, In No Doubt, **14/1** Siolfor (USA), **16/1** MISS PIN UP, Barton Pride (IRE), **20/1** Ellafitzetty (IRE), **50/1** Laughton Lady. CSF £549.91, CT £6,739.52. Tote £27.30: £4.40 £15.30 £4.40 £2.30 (£840.60). Mr E. Baldwin (NEWMARKET) bred by Brook Bloodstock P L C. 16 Rn

3m 4.9 (6.4)
SF–39/21/29/23/6/13

T/Plpt: £409.50 (6.05 Tckts). IM

## 961–PONTEFRACT (L-H)

### Monday, June 8th [Good]

Going Allowance: 5f-6f: 0.10 sec (G); Rest: minus 0.20 sec (F)   Wind: almost nil   Vis: mod

Stalls: low

**1287**   JUNE MILE STKS (Mdn 3-Y.O) £2385.00 (£660.00: £315.00)   1m 4y   2-45 (2-47)

| | | |
|---|---|---|
| 9894 | Calpella *(JARToller)* 8-9 MRoberts (6) (lw: trckd ldr: led over 2f out: hld on wl fnl f) | —1 |
| | Whirl *(JRFanshawe)* 8-9 WRSwinburn (7) (lengthy: scope: bit bkwd: stdy hdwy ½-wy: ev ch fnl f: nt qckn nr fin) | 1.2 |
| | Brambleberry *(MrsSJSmith)* 8-7 ‡7JMarshall (1) (w'like: bit bkwd: dwlt: hdwy ½-wy: ev ch over 1f out: one pce) | 4.3 |
| 10124 | Magnetic Point (USA) **(64)** *(AAScott)* 8-9 JFortune (8) (lw: unruly s: hld up: hdwy ½-wy: chal over 2f out: edgd lft & wknd 1f out) | ½.4 |
| 835 | Be My Habitat *(NAGraham)* 9-0 JQuinn (2) (effrt 3f out: outpcd 2f out: r.o wl nr fin) | ½.5 |
| 9383 | Ivana (IRE) (bl) (Fav) *(WJarvis)* 8-9 BRaymond (4) (trckd ldrs gng wl: hdwy & ev ch over 1f out: rdn & fnd nil) | ½.6 |
| | Master Copy (IRE) (v) *(CBBBooth)* 9-0 GOldroyd (5) (led tl hdd over 2f out: sn btn) | 12.7 |
| | Well Ahead *(MJohnston)* 8-9 DMcKeown (3) (leggy: scope: sn pushed along & a bhd) | 8.8 |
| 10555 | Alto (bl) *(JGFitzGerald)* 9-0 KFallon (9) (prom 5f) | 9 |
| | Gaveko (USA) (bl) *(JGFitzGerald)* 9-0 TLucas (10) (rangy: scope: bit bkwd: prom to ½-wy: sn rdn & wknd) | 10 |

**11/8** Ivana (IRE), **5/2** CALPELLA, **6/1** Whirl, **7/1** Magnetic Point (USA), **25/1** Well Ahead, Alto, Gaveko (USA), **33/1** Be My Habitat, **50/1** Ors. CSF £16.63, Tote £3.90: £1.10 £2.20 £9.70 (£9.30). Mr Saeed Manana (NEWMARKET) bred by Newmarket Thoroughbred Breeders P L C. 10 Rn

1m 45.5 (3.9)
SF–13/10/-/-/-/-

**1288**   DEWSBURY (S) STKS   £2363.20 (£655.20: £313.60)   1¼m 6y   3-15 (3-17)

| | | |
|---|---|---|
| 1184* | Cold Shower (IRE) **(54)** (Fav) *(JAGlover)* 3–8-5 JFortune (4) (lw: trckd ldrs: led wl over 1f out: rdn & r.o wl) | —1 |
| 1142 | Breakdancer (IRE) **(55)** *(MrsJRRamsden)* 3–8-5 MRoberts (1) (hld up & bhd: effrt & swtchd 3f out: r.o wl: too much to do) | 1.2 |
| 11426 | Copper Trader *(KSBridgwater)* 3–7-9 ‡5BDoyle (5) (lw: a chsng ldrs: outpcd 2f out: styd on ins fnl f) | 10.3 |
| 1109 | Paper Craft **(43)** (v) *(MJohnston)* 5–9-11 DMcKeown (13) (led tl hdd wl over 1f out: sn outpcd) | nk.4 |
| 1052 | Little Ivor **(46)** (v) *(DenysSmith)* 3–8-5 KFallon (2) (bhd: effrt 3f out: nvr nr to chal) | 5.5 |
| | Pinecone Peter **(39)** (bl) *(OBrennan)* 5–9-4 ‡7SWilliams (14) (reminders after s: styd on fnl 3f: n.d) | 6.6 |
| 9134 | Between Two Fires **(53)** *(JBerry)* 3–8-7 GCarter (7) (mid div: effrt 4f out: no imp) | 1½.7 |

**1289—1290**

1070 Heart Flutter **(48)** *(ASmith)* 3–8-5 PBurke (8) (lw: effrt 4f out: nvr trbld ldrs) ...... hd.8
1090 Cardea Castle (IRE) **(25)** *(BEllison)* 4–8-13 GHind (6) (a bhd) ........................... 1¹/₂.9
      Dara Melody (IRE) **(60)** *(JGFitzGerald)* 3–8-5 TLucas (3) (hld up & bhd: n.d) ...... s.h.10
1044 Cold Blow **(34)** *(JWharton)* 5–8-13 PRobinson (10) (in tch tl rdn & wknd 3f out) 2¹/₂.11
806⁴ Speedy Beauty *(BHanbury)* 3–8-0 NCarlisle (12) (lw: cl up tl wknd 2f out) ........ 2.12
      Dartington Blake *(JDooler)* 8–9-4 NConnorton (15) (swtg: dwlt: sn rcvrd: wknd
            6f out) ....................................................................... 12.13
951 Premier Venues **(41)** (bl) *(SGNorton)* 4–9-11 KDarley (11) (b: in tch: chsd ldrs
            4f out: rdn & wknd over 2f out) ............................................. 2¹/₂.14

**Evens** COLD SHOWER (IRE), **11/2** Breakdancer (IRE), Speedy Beauty, **9/1** Between Two Fires(op 6/1), **12/1** Dara Melody (IRE), **14/1** Copper Trader(op 8/1), Paper Craft, **16/1** Little Ivor, **25/1** Pinecone Peter, **33/1** Premier Venues, Heart Flutter, Cold Blow, **50/1** Cardea Castle (IRE), **100/1** Dartington Blake. CSF £8.15, Tote £2.10: £1.30 £2.20 £3.00 (£5.30). Claremont Management Services (WORKSOP) bred by Leinster Stud in Ireland. 14 Rn; Bt in 4,400 gns                                                                      2m 12 (3.7)
                                                                      SF—34/32/2/31/1/2

**1289**      BUTTERCROSS H'CAP (0-90) £3655.00 (£1090.00: £520.00: £235.00)
              6f                                                        3-45 (3-48)

1050* Densben **(63)** (Jt-Fav) *(DenysSmith)* 8–8-5 KFallon (3) (lw: bhd: hdwy over 2f
            out: r.o u.p to ld wl ins fnl f) ....................................................... —1
984 Pageboy **(82)** (Jt-Fav) *(PCHaslam)* 3–8-10 ‡5JWeaver (7) (lw: chsd ldrs: led 2f
            out tl wl ins fnl f: r.o) ........................................................... ³/₄.2
1021⁴ Duckington **(72)** *(MHEasterby)* 8–9-0 KDarley (8) (lw: trckd ldrs: nt clr
            run 2f out tl swtchd ins fnl f: r.o) .............................................. 6.3
1154 Mbulwa **(65)** *(SEKettlewell)* 6–8-7 JFortune (2) (chsd ldrs: drvn along ¹/₂-wy:
            btn whn sltly hmpd over 1f out) ............................................... 1¹/₂.4
948 In a Whirl (USA) **(51)** *(DWChapman)* 4–7-7 SWood (6) (w ldr tl wknd over 1f out) 1¹/₂.5
723⁰ Cronk's Courage **(0C)** (v) *(CJNoton)* 6 0 10 MRoberts (5) (led 4f: edgd rt &
            grad wknd) ...................................................................... 5.6
719 Nur (USA) **(76)** *(HThomsonJones)* 3–8-9 RHills (4) (spd to ¹/₂-wy: sn rdn & wknd) 8.7
                  LONG HANDICAP: In a Whirl (USA) 7-3.

**7/2** DENSBEN, Duckington, Pageboy, **9/2** Cronk's Courage, **5/1** Nur (USA), **14/1** In a Whirl (USA), **25/1** Mbulwa. CSF £14.88, CT £39.66. Tote £4.40: £2.30 £2.60 (£8.80). Mrs Janet M. Pike (BISHOP AUCKLAND) bred by D. W. Pike. 7 Rn                                                                      1m 16.8 (2.8)
                                                                      SF—77/49/29/16/–/–

**1290**      PONTEFRACT CUP (H'cap) (0-70) £2490.00 (£690.00: £330.00)
              2m 1f 216y                                                4-15 (4-16)

790⁴ Patroclus **(45)** *(RVoorspuy)* 7–8-7 SDawson (8) (b: bhd: hdwy 4f out: styd on
            wl to ld wl ins fnl f) .......................................................... —1
805² Creeager **(66)** *(JWharton)* 10–9-7 ‡7SWilliams (7) (lw: hld up & bhd: hdwy 6f
            out: chsd ldrs appr st: styd on) ............................................... 1.2
      Mr Taylor **(35)** *(HJCollingridge)* 7–7-4⁽⁴⁾ ‡7CHawksley (2) (a chsng ldrs: outpcd
            3f out: styd on gamely nr fin) ................................................ nk.3
1119* Samain (USA) **(41)** *(JAGlover)* 5–8-3 NCarlisle (3) (lw: hld up & bhd: hdwy
            on bit 5f out: led 1f out: rdn ins fnl f: no ex) .............................. hd.4
1022⁴ Sagaman (GER) **(53)** *(LJCodd)* 6–9-1 MRoberts (9) (b: lw: hdwy ¹/₂-wy: led over
            3f out: qcknd: hdd wl over 1f out: no ex) ..................................... nk.5
1137³ Singing Reply (USA) **(35)** *(DMarks)* 4–7-9 EJohnson (13) (swtg: nvr bttr than
            mid div) ........................................................................ 10.6
987³ Seldom In **(47)** *(JWharton)* 6–8-9 JQuinn (11) (lw: hdwy 7f out: sn prom: rdn &
            btn over 2f out) ............................................................... 6.7
      Isabeau (USA) **(50)** *(KAMorgan)* 5–8-2 DaleGibson (1) (nvr trbld ldrs) ........ nk.8
1125⁵ Vision of Wonder **(31)** *(JSKing)* 8–7-7 DanaMellor (5) (n.d) .................. 1¹/₂.9
1119⁶ Enkindle **(33)** *(BWMurray)* 5–7-9⁽²⁾ AMackay (6) (led 4f: led 7f out tl over 3f out:
            sn wknd) ........................................................................ 10
1119 Jawani (IRE) **(50)** (v) *(DrJDScargill)* 4–8-10 WRSwinburn (4) (chsd ldrs tl wknd
            5f out) ......................................................................... 11
799 Absolutely Right **(52)** *(JWhite)* 4–8-7 ‡5RPrice (14) (led after 4f to 7f out: sn
            wknd) ........................................................................... 12
905 Isobar **(31)** (bl) *(MCChapman)* 6–7-7 SWood (12) (chsd ldrs tl wknd 6f out) .. 13
      Rajanpour (USA) **(52)** (bl) *(RCurtis)* 7–9-0 GBardwell (10) (bit bkwd: chsd ldrs tl
            wknd 6f out: p.u 2f out) ...................................................... 0
            LONG HANDICAP: Mr Taylor 7-6, Vision of Wonder 7-3, Enkindle 7-2, Isobar 7-3.

**3/1** Samain (USA), **5/1** Sagaman (GER), **6/1** Seldom In, **15/2** Jawani (IRE), **8/1** Isabeau(op 12/1), **9/1** PATROCLUS, **10/1** Creeager, **16/1** Mr Taylor, **20/1** Enkindle, **25/1** Vision of Wonder, Rajanpour (USA), Singing Reply (USA), **33/1** Ors. CSF £90.32, CT £1,297.08. Tote £10.40: £3.00 £5.20 £3.10 (£85.20). Miss J. Newell (POLEGATE) bred by Sir Gerald Glover. 14 Rn                                                                      3m 57.7 (5.5)
                                                                      SF—2/15/–/–/–/–

**1291**    YOUNGSTERS STKS (2-Y.O) £2898.00 (£864.00: £412.00: £186.00)    **6f** 4-45 (4-46)

11035 **Little Too Much (IRE)** (Fav) *(GHarwood)* 8-11  MRoberts (7) (lw: a gng wl: led
        wl over 1f out: qcknd: easily) ...................................................... —1
   877* Key to My Heart (IRE) *(DMoffatt)* 9-6  JFortune (2) (lw: led over 4f: no ch w wnr)    6.2
   924* Razaroo (USA) *(JEtherington)* 9-3  TLucas (1) (lw: plld hrd: trckd ldrs: effrt over
        2f out: nt qckn) ....................................................................   3.3
   1120* Formaestre (IRE) *(MHTompkins)* 8-12  PRobinson (4) (lw: chsd ldrs 4f: sn rdn &
        btn) ..................................................................................   8.4
   1071 Free Market *(GMMoore)* 8-11  KFallon (3) (outpcd after 2f: n.d) ................   3.5
   770 Volunteer Point (IRE) *(MrsSABramall)* 8-11  SWood (5) (sn outpcd & bhd) ........   7.6
   968* Maybe Gold *(DWPArbuthnot)* 9-3  WRSwinburn (6) (b.nr hind: lw: w ldrs tl hmpd
        over 2f out: eased fnl 2f) ......................................................... 1½.7

**11/8** LITTLE TOO MUCH (IRE), **7/2** Key to My Heart (IRE), Formaestre (IRE)(5/2—4/1), **9/2** Razaroo (USA), **14/1**
Maybe Gold, **100/1** Volunteer Point (IRE), **150/1** Free Market. CSF £7.02, Tote £2.70: £1.30 £2.00 (£4.50). Mr J.
Garcia-Roady (PULBOROUGH) bred by Bloodstock Management International in Ireland. 7 Rn  1m 17.5 (3.5)
                                                                                SF—39/24/9/–/–/–

**1292**    BATLEY H'CAP (0-70) £2364.00 (£654.00: £312.00)    **1¼m 6y**    5-15 (5-16)
                                (Weights raised 2 lb)
   1150* **I'M Electric (50)** (Fav) *(RCurtis)* 6–9-5 (6x)  NDay (1) (lw: a cl up: led over 1f out:
        r.o u.p) ............................................................................... —1
   8003 Supertop (55) *(PWHarris)* 4–9-10  WRSwinburn (6) (lw: led tl hdd over 1f out:
        r.o) ................................................................................. 1½.2
   Garda's Gold (26) *(RDickin)* 9–7-9(1)  SDawson (4) (in tch: effrt 3f out: styd on wl
        fnl f) ................................................................................ 1½.3
   11226 Faryal (48) *(JLSpearing)* 3–8-4  PRobinson (5) (trckd ldrs: effrt 2f out: r.o nr fin) hd.4
   11523 Boring (USA) (59) *(WStorey)* 3–9-1  MRoberts (3) (b: a.p: effrt over 2f out: wknd
        ins fnl f) ............................................................................. 4.5
   9626 Young Jason (53) *(FHLee)* 9–9-8  RLappin (2) (lw: hld up: effrt 3f out: no imp) .. ¾.6

**6/4** I'M ELECTRIC, **3/1** Supertop, **6/1** Boring (USA), **13/2** Faryal, **8/1** Young Jason, **16/1** Garda's Gold. CSF
£5.95, Tote £2.30: £1.40 £2.00 (£3.80). Mr B. A. McGarrigle (EPSOM) bred by White Lodge Stud Ltd. 6 Rn
                                                                                2m 15 (6.7)
                                                                                SF—18/20/–/–/–/–

T/Plpt: £139.00 (29.3 Tckts).                                                            AA

# PONTEFRACT (L-H)
## Tuesday, June 9th [Good to firm]
Going Allowance: 5f-8f: minus 0.20 sec (F); Rest: nil sec (G)                Wind: almost nil

Stalls: low

**1293**    WHITELANE-PONTEFRACT APP'CE SERIES STKS (Rnd 1) (Mdn 3-Y.O) £2322.00
        (£642.00: £306.00)    **6f**                                2-45 (2-48)

   7644 **Saddlehome (USA) (76)** *(RMWhitaker)* 8-7  AGarth (7) (mde all: wnt clr over 2f
        out: unchal) ......................................................................... —1
   Double Shift *(RDickin)* 8-2  PTurner (2) (neat: str: chsd ldrs: rdn & hdwy 2f out:
        kpt on: no ch w wnr) ................................................................   8.2
   10062 Swinging Tich (Fav) *(BAMcMahon)* 8-2  SSanders (4) (lw: prom: rdn & outpcd
        over 2f out: no imp fnl f) ..........................................................   5.3
   11455 Arjjil *(MHTompkins)* 8-2 ‡§MGodsafe (6) (bhd: effrt ½-wy: kpt on same pce) ..... 2½.4
   11444 Virginia Cottage (46) (bl) *(BAMcMahon)* 8-2  JBramhill (3) (chsd wnr: wknd wl
        over 1f out) ......................................................................... 2½.5
   Liberty Glen *(BEllison)* 8-2  GParkin (1) (w'like: dwlt: a in rr) ..................... nk.6
   Over Sharp (56) *(JWhite)* 8-2  CHawksley (5) (s.s: sme hdwy ½-wy: sn btn) .... 2½.7

**5/4** Swinging Tich, **9/4** SADDLEHOME (USA), **9/1** Arjjil, **11/1** Double Shift(op 6/1), **12/1** Virginia Cottage, **25/1**
Liberty Glen, **33/1** Over Sharp. CSF £21.72, Tote £2.90: £1.50 £4.40 (£31.50). Hyde Sporting Promotions/
Saddlehome Farm (WETHERBY) bred by J. A. Haverhals in USA. 7 Rn             1m 16.2 (2.2)
                                                                                SF—49/12/–/–/–/–

**1294**    GROVE (S) H'CAP (3 & 4-Y.O) (0-60) £2578.80 (£716.80: £344.40)
        **1m 4y**                                                  3-15 (3-19)

   11723 **Crown Reserve (35)** *(MJRyan)* 4–8-4 ‡3DBiggs (20) (lw: a.p: rdn to ld appr fnl f:
        hung lft: hld on wl) ................................................................. —1

1146 Tahitian **(50)** (bl) *(MrsJRRamsden)* 3–8–11 KDarley (14) (mid div: effrt over 3f out: styd on wl u.p fnl f) .................................................. 1½.**2**

1070 Bobbie Bold **(37)** *(RO'Leary)* 4–8–9 MBirch (9) (led: rdn over 2f out: hdd appr fnl f: sltly hmpd & no ex nr fin) ........................................ ½.**3**

1089² Chance Report **(38)** *(FHLee)* 4–8–10 RCochrane (19) (swtg: a.p: rdn wl over 2f out: nt clr run over 1f out: kpt on same pce fnl f) ............. ½.**4**

1153⁵ Richmond (IRE) **(56)** (bl) *(SGNorton)* 4–9–7 ‡7OPears (11) (b: hdwy 3f out: rdn wl over 1f out: nt qckn ins fnl f) .......................... 1.**5**

1172 Miss Magenta (IRE) **(33)** *(RThompson)* 4–8–5 AMunro (8) (mid div: effrt over 2f out: kpt on u.p ins fnl f) ................................. s.h.**6**

1034 Gemdoubleyou **(27)** *(FJordan)* 4–7–6 ‡7CHawksley (5) (s.s: hdwy 3f out: styd on: nvr nrr) ...................................................... 2.**7**

1029 Brush Wolf (USA) **(40)** *(JMBradley)* 3–7–10 ‡5ATucker (2) (n.d) .......... 3.**8**

1052³ Dots Dee **(35)** *(JMBradley)* 3–7–10(1) AMackay (10) (lw: effrt & sme hdwy over 2f out: n.d) .......................................................... ¾.**9**

1150 Friendlypersuasion (IRE) **(40)** *(RHollinshead)* 4–8–12 WRyan (7) (prom tl wknd over 2f out) ............................................................ nk.**10**

1001⁴ Akura (IRE) **(52)** *(MJohnston)* 3–8–13 DMcKeown (21) (chsd ldrs: rdn 3f out: wknd 2f out) ........................................................ hd.**11**

1089 Emerald Ears **(51)** *(EWeymes)* 3–8–12 LDettori (22) (effrt & hdwy 3f out: wknd over 1f out) ....................................................... ½.**12**

1089 Station Express (IRE) **(34)** *(BEllison)* 4–8–1(4) ‡5JWeaver (12) (nvr nr ldrs) .. s.h.**13**

1145³ Lord Leitrim (IRE) **(49)** (Fav) *(NACallaghan)* 3–8–10 BRaymond (3) (lw: rdn over 3f out: nvr nr ldrs) .................................................. 2½.**14**

1041 Vital Voltage (IRE) **(47)** *(MWEllerby)* 3–8–8 SMorris (6) (effrt on outside appr st: sn btn) ................................................................ ¾.**15**

1087 Debjanjo **(37)** *(JRJenkins)* 4–8–9 GDuffield (15) (mid div: rdn along ½-wy: sn btn) ........................................................................ 2½.**16**

806 Magnetic Prince **(37)** *(CDlum)* 0 7 12 RFox (10) (bhd: rdn & btn ½-wy) ..... hd.**17**

913 Broad Appeal **(46)** *(WJPearce)* 4–8–11 ‡7PTurner (18) (mid div: effrt 3f out: hmpd & wknd wl over 1f out) ................................. 2½.**18**

1052 King Optimist **(41)** *(ASmith)* 3–7–11 ‡5SMaloney (4) (bhd: stumbled 4f out: sn btn) ................................................................. ½.**19**

1040 Tender Monarch (IRE) **(35)** *(PJBevan)* 3–7–10 JLowe (17) (prom to ½-wy) ... s.h.**20**

567 Syke Lane **(43)** *(RMWhitaker)* 3–8–4 ACulhane (16) (chsd ldrs: chal 2f out: sn hmpd & wknd qckly) ................................................. 2.**21**

1142 So Beguiling (USA) **(47)** *(MrsALMKing)* 3–8–8 JQuinn (1) (t.o) ............ 22

**4/1** Lord Leitrim (IRE)(op 10/1), **6/1** Richmond (IRE), **8/1** Chance Report, Akura (IRE), **9/1** Tahitian, **10/1** Bobbie Bold, Station Express (IRE), **12/1** CROWN RESERVE, **14/1** Debjanjo, **16/1** King Optimist, Miss Magenta (IRE), Dots Dee, **20/1** Syke Lane, Friendlypersuasion (IRE), So Beguiling (USA), **25/1** Emerald Ears, Brush Wolf (USA), Gemdoubleyou, **33/1** Ors. CSF £125.05, CT £1,063.18. Tote £15.50: £3.30 £3.10 £4.90 £2.00 (£92.90). Mr F. A. J. Cosgrove (NEWMARKET) bred by M. F. Kentish. 22 Rn; No bid                1m 45.7 (4.1)
SF—28/30/26/25/33/16

**1295**  PONTEFRACT PARK H'CAP (0-100) £3622.50 (£1080.00: £515.00: £232.50)
1¼m 6y
3-45 (3-46)

422★ **Mr Confusion (IRE) (77)** *(SGNorton)* 4–8–9 ‡7OPears (1) (lw: a.p: smooth hdwy to ld appr fnl f: shkn up & r.o wl) .................................. —**1**

1181² Busted Rock **(85)** (Fav) *(MrsLPiggott)* 7–9–10 LPiggott (2) (lw: hld up in tch: hdwy appr st: ev ch 1f out: nt qckn nr fin) ................... ¾.**2**

1035² Trial Times (USA) **(75)** *(WAO'Gorman)* 3–8–1 AMunro (3) (chsd ldrs: effrt 3f out: kpt on one pce fnl f) .......................................... 2½.**3**

713⁵ Katy's Lad **(73)** *(BAMcMahon)* 5–8–12 RCochrane (8) (led 4f: cl up: led wl over 3f out: hdd & wknd appr fnl f) ................................. 3.**4**

1110³ Able Lassie **(70)** *(MrsGRReveley)* 4–8–9 JLowe (4) (lw: chsd ldrs: outpcd 5f out: hdwy 3f out: nt qckn appr fnl f) ............................ hd.**5**

829★ Dawn Success **(64)** *(DWChapman)* 6–8–3 SWood (5) (hdwy appr st: sn rdn & no imp) ...................................................... 1½.**6**

1181⁶ Polonez Prima **(83)** *(JEBanks)* 5–9–3 ‡5LNewton (6) (swtg: hld up & bhd: outpcd over 3f out: n.d) ..................................................... 10.**7**

747 Highbrook (USA) **(75)** *(MHTompkins)* 4–9–0 PRobinson (9) (plld hrd: chsd ldrs tl hmpd & wknd 3f out) ........................................... 7.8

1063⁵ St Patrick's Day **(63)** *(CEBrittain)* 4–7–11 ‡5BDoyle (3) (swtg: plld hrd: led after 4f: hdd & wknd qckly wl over 3f out: t.o) ........................... 9

**9/4** Busted Rock, **6/1** Able Lassie, MR CONFUSION (IRE), **7/1** Katy's Lad, **8/1** St Patrick's Day, **17/2** Trial Times (USA), **10/1** Dawn Success, **20/1** Ors. CSF £18.21, CT £101.40. Tote £8.10: £2.20 £1.40 £1.80 (£9.50). Mr R. Fenwick-Gibson (BARNSLEY) bred by D. P. O'Brien in Ireland. 9 Rn             2m 10.6 (2.3)
SF—52/65/37/42/38/29

## 1296

JUVENILE AUCTION STKS (I) (Mdn 2-Y.O) £2469.00 (£684.00: £327.00)
6f
4-15 (4-16)

| | | |
|---|---|---|
| 682³ | **Royal Folly (IRE)** *(CWCElsey)* 7-5⁽¹⁾ ‡⁵NKennedy (9) (chsd ldrs: rdn over 2f out: led 1f out: edgd lft: kpt on u.p) | —1 |
| 568⁶ | Peaceful Air *(EWeymes)* 7-13 JQuinn (12) (in tch: effrt over 2f out: kpt on ins fnl f) | 1½.2 |
| 1092 | Don't Be Saki (IRE) *(JEtherington)* 7-13 JLowe (11) (in tch: rdn 2f out: styd on ins fnl f) | 2.3 |
| 968² | Waterlord (IRE) *(CGCox)* 8-2 AMunro (5) (lw: mde most tl hdd & no ex 1f out) | nk.4 |
| 924³ | Canny Lad (Fav) *(JGFitzGerald)* 8-0 KDarley (1) (w ldr gng wl: rdn over 1f out: wknd) | 2.5 |
| | Sweet Romeo *(MJohnston)* 8-0 RPElliott (8) (w'like: scope: bit bkwd: hmpd after s: bhd tl hdwy over 2f out: n.m.r: fin wl) | s.h.6 |
| 1140⁴ | Alice Bay *(DHaydnJones)* 7-6 ‡³JFanning (7) (lw: hmpd after 1f: hdwy 3f out: no imp over 1f out) | ½.7 |
| 947⁴ | Pinkerton's Silver *(MHEasterby)* 7-11 ‡⁵SMaloney (13) (chsd ldrs over 3f) | 3.8 |
| 361⁴ | Irish Roots (IRE) *(CTinkler)* 8-9 MBirch (4) (bhd: hdwy u.p wl over 1f out: wknd ins fnl f) | 1.9 |
| 514 | Strephon (IRE) *(MHTompkins)* 8-7 PRobinson (2) (chsd ldrs tl rdn & btn ½-wy) | 1½.10 |
| 968 | Miss Bridge (IRE) *(MBell)* 7-9 AMackay (6) (sn outpcd) | nk.11 |
| 1046 | Moonshine Dancer *(MrsGRReveley)* 8-12 JFortune (10) (a bhd) | 3.12 |
| 769 | Canazei *(DonEnricoIncisa)* 7-9 JakiHuston (3) (a outpcd) | nk.13 |

**6/5** Canny Lad, **11/2** ROYAL FOLLY (IRE), **6/1** Waterlord (IRE), **8/1** Irish Roots (IRE), **10/1** Don't Be Saki (IRE), **16/1** Alice Bay, **20/1** Miss Bridge (IRE), Peaceful Air, Strephon (IRE), Pinkerton's Silver, **33/1** Sweet Romeo, Moonshine Dancer, **100/1** Canazei. CSF £10.20, Tote £6.70: £2.20 £6.40 £3.60 (£155.90). Mr Richard Berenson (MALTON) bred by Liam Ward in Ireland. 13 Rn
1m 18 (4)

## 1297

E.B.F. THORNE STKS (Mdn 2-Y.O) £2782.50 (£770.00: £367.50)  **5f**
4-45 (4-45)

| | | |
|---|---|---|
| 907 | **Lowrianna (IRE)** *(DHaydnJones)* 8-9 RCochrane (5) (bhd: effrt ½-wy: styd on wl u.p to ld ins fnl f) | —1 |
| 1071³ | Indian Secret (IRE) *(BEWilkinson)* 8-11 ‡³JFanning (8) (lw: w ldrs: carried rt wl over 1f out: nt qckn nr fin) | 1.2 |
| 803³ | Press the Bell (Fav) *(JBerry)* 9-0 JCarroll (1) (lw: sn led: hung bdly rt 2f out: hdd & wknd u.p ins fnl f) | 1.3 |
| | Valere Knight (IRE) *(CGCox)* 9-0 AMunro (4) (w'like: a chsng ldrs: effrt 2f out: r.o ins fnl f) | 1.4 |
| 770³ | Sharro *(PAKelleway)* 9-0 PRobinson (7) (led early: chsd ldrs tl rdn & no imp fnl f) | ¾.5 |
| 568 | April Point (IRE) *(RHollinshead)* 8-9 WRyan (6) (in tch tl wknd wl over 1f out) | 1.6 |
| | Yfool *(JRFanshawe)* 8-9 GDuffield (2) (lt-f: nvr wnt pce) | 3.7 |
| 1046 | Emmandee *(MWEasterby)* 9-0 TLucas (3) (broke wl: sn outpcd: bdly hmpd over 2f out: nt rcvr) | hd.8 |

**4/9** Press the Bell, **7/1** Yfool, **10/1** Indian Secret (IRE), Sharro, **14/1** Valere Knight (IRE), Emmandee, **16/1** LOWRIANNA (IRE), **33/1** April Point (IRE). CSF £145.26, Tote £15.60: £2.60 £2.20 £1.10 (£91.50). Mr Richard Bruce Morris (PONTYPRIDD) bred by R. Percival and John Kent in Ireland. 8 Rn
65.5 sec (4)
SF—15/13/12/8/5/–

## 1298

IRON BRIDGE H'CAP (3-Y.O) (0-70) £2805.00 (£780.00: £375.00)
1½m 8y
5-15 (5-16)

| | | |
|---|---|---|
| 1041 | **Brier Creek (USA) (70)** (Fav) *(JHMGosden)* 9-7 RCochrane (12) (lw: hld up & bhd: nt clr run over 2f out: r.o strly to ld wl ins fnl f) | —1 |
| 1041 | Admirals Secret (USA) **(58)** *(CFWall)* 8-9 NDay (4) (lw: hdwy over 3f out: led appr fnl f: hung lft: hdd nr fin) | ½.2 |
| 1041 | Bentico **(53)** *(MAJarvis)* 8-4 AMunro (13) (lw: a in tch: effrt over 2f out: nt qckn ins fnl f) | 2.3 |
| 804 | Very Evident (IRE) **(63)** *(BWHills)* 9-0 DHolland (11) (lw: chsd ldrs: rdn & wknd wl over 1f out) | 6.4 |
| 910⁵ | Indian Territory **(64)** *(DHaydnJones)* 9-1 WRyan (8) (hdwy over 3f out: rdn & styd on same pce fnl 2f) | hd.5 |
| 972 | Pie Hatch (IRE) **(42)** *(SirMarkPrescott)* 7-7 JQuinn (10) (mid div: outpcd & rdn along over 3f out: styd on wl ins fnl f) | s.h.6 |
| 1052⁴ | Elsa **(42)** *(RJHolder)* 7-7 JLowe (9) (chsd clr ldr: led 4f out tl hdd & wknd appr fnl f) | nk.7 |
| | Mystery Lad (IRE) **(62)** (bl) *(NACallaghan)* 8-13 GDuffield (3) (stdd s: hdwy over 3f out: rdn & btn 2f out) | 1½.8 |

1188* Moor Lodge (USA) **(69)** *(MHTompkins)* 9-6 (5x) PRobinson (2) (hld up & bhd: hdwy on outside 2f out: sn btn) .......................................... nk.9

448 Rowandene (IRE) **(49)** *(MHEasterby)* 7-9 ‡5SMaloney (7) (chsd ldrs tl wknd over 2f out) .......................................... 8.10

1088² Sahara Shield **(70)** *(AAScott)* 9-7 BRaymond (5) (lw: hdwy whn nt clr run 3f out: sn btn) .......................................... 11

1131 Kentucky Chicken (USA) **(42)** *(MissLCSiddall)* 7-7 EJohnson (1) (led tl hdd & wknd 4f out: t.o) .......................................... 12

1041³ Don't Forsake Me **(60)** *(DMorley)* 8-11 LDettori (6) (in tch tl wknd qckly 6f out: p.u 2f out) .......................................... 0

LONG HANDICAP: Pie Hatch (IRE) 7-0, Kentucky Chicken (USA) 7-3.

**3/1** BRIER CREEK (USA), **5/1** Moor Lodge (USA), Admirals Secret (USA), **11/2** Bentico, **7/1** Don't Forsake Me, **10/1** Very Evident (IRE), **14/1** Sahara Shield, **16/1** Indian Territory, **20/1** Mystery Lad (IRE), **25/1** Rowandene (IRE), Elsa, **50/1** Pie Hatch (IRE), **100/1** Kentucky Chicken (USA) 7-3. CSF £17.90, CT £74.07. Tote £4.30: £1.80 £2.30 £2.70 (£19.10). Sheikh Mohammed (NEWMARKET) bred by Allen E Paulson in USA. 13 Rn　2m 38.5 (4)
SF—43/30/21/19/19/–

**1299**　　JUVENILE AUCTION STKS (II) (Mdn 2-Y.O) £2469.00 (£684.00: £327.00)
　　　　　**6f**　　　　　　　　　　　　　　　　　　　　　　　　　　　　　　　　　5-45 (5-47)

1149 **Atherton Green (IRE)** *(JAGlover)* 8-4 DMcKeown (8) (in tch: hdwy & nt clr run appr fnl f: swtchd & styd on strly to ld cl home) .................. —1

1112⁶ Prime Painter *(RFFisher)* 8-4 JLowe (12) (lw: a.p: chal wl over 1f out: led ins fnl f tl ct cl home) .......................................... nk.2

1112² Hot Off the Press (Fav) *(RMWhitaker)* 8-0 PBurke (13) (lw: hdwy on outside ½-wy: ev ch 1f out: nt qckn nr fin) .......................................... 1.3

924 Newinsky *(CTinkler)* 8-3 GDuffield (7) (a.p: rdn to ld appr fnl f: sn hdd & nt qckn).. s.h.4

Buzz-D-Babe *(BEllison)* 7-11 †3JFanning (4) (leggy: bit bkwd: sn outpcd & drvn along: gd hdwy over 1f out: nt clr run: fin wl) .................. ⁹/4.5

1202 Wentbridge Lad (IRE) (bl) *(BAMcMahon)* 8-0 KDarley (6) (lw: s.i.s: hmpd s: sn drvn along: gd hdwy whn nt clr run thrght fnl f: unlucky) .. 1¹/2.6

1019³ Ann Hill (IRE) *(RHollinshead)* 7-3⁽¹⁾ ‡7AGarth (3) (chsd ldrs: rdn 2f out: no ex ins fnl f) .......................................... 1.7

Cyprus Creek *(NTinkler)* 8-3⁽¹⁾ ABacon (11) (w'like: leggy: sn outpcd & wl bhd: styd on fnl 2f) .......................................... 1¹/2.8

Kafioca (IRE) *(MHTompkins)* 8-0⁽³⁾ PRobinson (2) (neat: scope: chsd ldrs: effrt & nt clr run appr fnl f: nt rcvr) .......................................... ³/4.9

Danger Baby *(BobJones)* 8-5 VSmith (9) (leggy: unf: outpcd ¹/2-wy: nd after) ¹/2.10

Benzoe (IRE) *(MWEasterby)* 8-5⁽¹⁾ TLucas (1) (w'like: scope: lw: led tl hdd appr fnl f: wknd) .......................................... hd.11

Blakes Beau *(MHEasterby)* 8-7 MBirch (5) (w'like: bit bkwd: unruly stalls: spd over 3f) .......................................... 12

Sudden Spin *(JBerry)* 8-10 JCarroll (10) (w'like: leggy: scope: wl outpcd fr ¹/2-wy) 13

**3/1** Hot Off the Press, **6/1** Wentbridge Lad (IRE), **7/1** Kafioca (IRE), Ann Hill (IRE), Buzz-B-Babe, **9/1** ATHERTON GREEN (IRE), Sudden Spin, Prime Painter, **16/1** Newinsky, Benzoe (IRE), **20/1** Blakes Beau, Danger Baby, **33/1** Cyprus Creek (IRE). CSF £86.34, Tote £15.80: £5.40 £2.70 £1.70 (£100.80). Atherton and Green (WORKSOP) bred by Limestone Stud in Ireland. 13 Rn　　　　　　　　　　　　　1m 19.7 (5.7)

T/Plpt: £164.40 (26.5 Tckts).　　　　　　　　　　　　　　　　　　　　　　0'R

**967—SALISBURY (R-H)**

**Tuesday, June 9th [Good to firm]**

Going Allowance: 5f: minus 0.45 sec; Rest: minus 0.30 sec (F)　　　　　Wind: nil

Stalls: high

**1300**　　E.B.F. RUBBING HOUSE STKS (Mdn 2-Y.O.F) £2678.40 (£742.40: £355.20)
　　　　　**5f**　　　　　　　　　　　　　　　　　　　　　　　　　　　　　　　　2-30 (2-31)

1057² **Hamsah (IRE)** (Jt-Fav) *(DRCElsworth)* 8-11 WCarson (6) (w ldr: led over 2f out: comf) .......................................... —1

1164² Musical Prospect (USA) *(RHannon)* 8-11 MRoberts (9) (a.p & rdn along: chsd wnr fnl f: no imp) .......................................... 3.2

907 Avril Etoile *(LJHolt)* 8-4 ‡7CAvery (3) (a.p: r.o ins fnl f) .......................................... 1.3

White Shadow (IRE) (Jt-Fav) *(RCharlton)* 8-11 PatEddery (11) (unf: hdwy 2f out: styd on fnl f) .......................................... 2.4

Chatterberry *(LJHolt)* 8-11 AMcGlone (2) (no hdwy fnl 2f) .......................................... 2.5

Marwell Mitzi *(WGRWightman)* 8-11 JWilliams (5) (b.hind: w'like: nvr nr to chal) ³/4.6

Jarena (IRE) *(GLewis)* 8-11 BRouse (10) (cmpt: stdy hdwy fnl 2f: r.o) .............. ¾.**7**
Fancied *(HCandy)* 8-11 CRutter (8) (lengthy: unf: prom over 2f) ...................... ¾.**8**
650⁶ Hawaii Star (IRE) *(GLewis)* 8-11 PaulEddery (7) (led over 2f) ..................... ¾.**9**
703 Don't Tell Dick *(DRLaing)* 8-11 TyroneWilliams (1) (a wl bhd: t.o) .................. 12.**10**

**7/4** HAMSAH (IRE), White Shadow (IRE), **3/1** Musical Prospect (USA), **9/1** Fancied(12/1—8/1), **16/1** Hawaii Star (IRE), **33/1** Jarena (IRE), **50/1** Ors. CSF £7.73, Tote £2.50: £1.30 £1.50 £11.10 (£2.90). Sheikh Ahmed Al Maktoum (WHITSBURY) bred by Sheikh Ahmed bin Rashid al Maktoum in Ireland. 10 Rn　　60.56 sec (0.56)
SF—41/29/18/17/9/6

**1301**　　CITY BOWL H'CAP (F & M) (0-90) £3720.00 (£1110.00: £530.00: £240.00)
　　　　　1½m
　　　　　　　　　　　　　　　　　　　　　　　　　　　　　　　3-00 (3-02)

387 **Lobinda (78)** *(JLDunlop)* 3–8-3 MRoberts (3) (hdwy 3f out: str run fnl f: led last stride) ....................................................... —**1**
1220* Crystal Cross (USA) **(78)** *(Fav) (IABalding)* 3–8-0 (5x) ‡3SO'Gorman (8) (hdwy 3f out: led nr fin: hdd post) ........................................ s.h.**2**
964² Broom Isle **(55)** *(MrsAKnight)* 4–7-7(3) ‡3FNorton (11) (2nd tl led over 3f out: sn clr: hdd cl home) ....................................... ¾.**3**
726⁶ Seal Indigo (IRE) **(87)** *(RHannon)* 4–10-0 PatEddery (5) (hdwy 3f out: nt qckn) .................................................................. 5.**4**
205⁴ Shar Emblem **(52)** *(SDow)* 4–7-7 DaleGibson (9) (no hdwy fnl 3f) ...................... ¾.**5**
1083² Blushing Belle **(62)** (bl) *(PFICole)* 4–8-3 TQuinn (10) (swtg: prom tl wknd 3f out) 6.**6**
1044³ Miss Witch **(53)** *(HCandy)* 4–7-1 ‡7AntoinetteArmes (1) (led tl wknd over 3f out) 3.**7**
815 Itqan (IRE) **(87)** *(BWHills)* 4–10-0 WCarson (4) (nvr plcd to chal) ................... s.h.**8**
Miss Foxtrot **(74)** *(JLDunlop)* 4–9-1 WRSwinburn (6) (a bhd) ......................... 3½.**9**
832 Celia Brady **(62)** *(HCandy)* 4–8-3 CRutter (4) (plld hrd: lost pl 7f out: t.o fnl 4f) 5.**10**

**13/8** Crystal Cross (USA), **6/1** Broom Isle, **7/1** Seal Indigo (IRE), **8/1** Itqan (IRE), **9/1** Miss Witch, **10/1** Blushing Belle, **12/1** LOBINDA, **14/1** Miss Foxtrot, **16/1** Celia Brady, **20/1** Shar Emblem. CSF £31.08, CT £124.44. Tote £10.20: £3.30 £1.30 £1.90 (£13.90). Hesmonds Stud (ARUNDEL) bred by Hesmonds Stud Ltd. 10 Rn
2m 33.23 (0.63)
SF—47/43/34/59/22/20

**1302**　　BISHOPSTONE GRADUATION STKS (3-Y.O) £2984.00 (£824.00: £392.00)
　　　　　1¾m
　　　　　　　　　　　　　　　　　　　　　　　　　　　　　　　3-30 (3-33)

1026* **Not in Doubt (USA)** *(HCandy)* 9-1 CRutter (2) (lw: hld up: led wl over 1f out: r.o wl) ...................................................................... —**1**
873* Faugeron **(80)** *(Fav) (GWragg)* 9-1 WRSwinburn (1) (2nd tl led over 2f out: hdd wl over 1f out) ................................................. 3½.**2**
1068⁴ Lemon's Mill (USA) **(82)** *(JHMGosden)* 8-10 PatEddery (led tl over 2f out) ...... 3½.**3**

**Evens** Faugeron, **7/4** Lemon's Mill (USA), **4/1** NOT IN DOUBT (USA)(op 5/2). CSF £7.45, Tote £4.60 (£1.90). Mrs David Blackburn (WANTAGE) bred by Gallagher's Stud in USA. 3 Rn　　3m 0.40 (2.20)
SF—37/30/18

**1303**　　ROTHMANS ROYALS NORTH SOUTH CHALLENGE SERIES H'CAP (0-90) £3720.00
　　　　　(£1110.00: £530.00: £240.00)　　**6f 212y**　　　　　　　4-00 (4-02)
　　　　　　　　　　　　　　　　　(Weights raised 5 lb)

1133 **Superoo (71)** *(JSutcliffe)* 6–9-0 WRSwinburn (11) (hdwy over 2f out: led over 1f out: hrd rdn: r.o) ................................................ —**1**
1174* Sugemar **(59)** *(JARToller)* 6–8-2 (7x) MRoberts (5) (a.p: ev ch 1f out: r.o) ........ nk.**2**
976* Piquant **(80)** *(Jt-Fav) (LordHuntingdon)* 5–9-4 ‡5DHarrison (4) (lw: chsd ldr: ev ch over 1f out: nt qckn) .......................................... 1.**3**
1032 Beatle Song **(61)** *(RJHodges)* 4–8-4 PaulEddery (1) (led tl over 1f out: r.o one pce) ........................................................................... s.h.**4**
936 Mahsul (IRE) **(55)** *(CJBenstead)* 4–7-12 WCarson (7) (lw: hdwy over 2f out: r.o ins fnl f) ....................................................... s.h.**5**
1061 Absonal **(79)** *(RHannon)* 5–9-8 PatEddery (6) (hdwy over 2f out: nt qckn fnl f) .. 1.**6**
1114³ La Bamba **(80)** *(GAPritchard-Gordon)* 6–9-9 WHood (12) (hdwy over 4f out: nrst fin) ............................................................... 2½.**7**
1174 Annabelle Royale **(80)** *(MrsNMacauley)* 6–9-9 JWilliams (2) (swtg: prom 4f) ..... ½.**8**
809³ Lady Lacey **(55)** (v) *(GBBalding)* 5–7-12 DaleGibson (8) (prom 4f) .................... 1.**9**
1028⁵ Bertie Wooster **(81)** *(RJHolder)* 9–9-3 ‡7SDrowne (9) (stumbled s: a bhd) ........ 2.**10**
1061 Takenhall **(61)** *(MJFetherston-Godley)* 7–8-4 NAdams (10) (hmpd over 4f out: a bhd) ................................................................... 6.**11**
1133² Kimberley Park **(71)** *(Jt-Fav) (DWPArbuthnot)* 4–9-0 TQuinn (3) (mid div tl wknd qckly 3f out: t.o) ..................................... 25.**12**

11/2 Kimberley Park, Piquant, **13/2** La Bamba, **7/1** Sugemar, **8/1** SUPEROO, **9/1** Takenhall(op 6/1), **10/1** Mahsul (IRE), Absonal, **12/1** Lady Lacey, **20/1** Bertie Wooster, **25/1** Ors. CSF £56.31, CT £299.36. Tote £10.70: £2.80 £2.50 £2.10 (£48.60). Mrs P. A. Garner (EPSOM) bred by Irish Thoroughbred Holdings Ltd. 12 Rn
1m 26.55 (0.85)
SF—55/42/55/40/33/54/47

## 1304　　　LAVERSTOCK STKS (I) (Mdn 3-Y-O) £2304.40 (£638.40: £305.20)　　**1m** 4-30 (4-36)

| | | |
|---|---|---|
| | **Tissisat (USA)** (IABalding) 9-0 PatEddery (6) (w'like: scope: a.p: led over 2f out: comf) | —1 |
| 833⁴ | Top Song (Fav) (RHannon) 8-9 MRoberts (3) (lw: led over 4f: r.o one pce) | 3½.2 |
| | Crystado (FR) (DRCElsworth) 9-0 JWilliams (4) (b: w ldr: led over 3f out tl over 2f out) | 1.3 |
| 511 | Southwold Air (JLDunlop) 9-0 WCarson (1) (a abt same pl) | 5.4 |
| | Headless Heights (PMitchell) 9-0 TQuinn (9) (b.nr fore: w'like: bit bkwd: hdwy 3f out: wknd over 1f out) | 6.5 |
| 1086⁵ | Bells of Longwick (57) (DRLaing) 8-9 TyroneWilliams (5) (no hdwy fnl 2f) | 2½.6 |
| 1029⁴ | Eiras Mood (RDickin) 8-9 PaulEddery (7) (prom tl rdn & wknd over 3f out) | 1.7 |
| | Spinayab (EAWheeler) 8-9 SWhitworth (10) (a bhd) | 3½.8 |
| | Nonanno (AJChamberlain) 9-0 GBaxter (8) (bit bkwd: prom 4f: t.o) | 12.9 |
| 938 | Rowan Empire (MMadgwick) 8-9 PD'Arcy (11) (b: lt-f: a bhd: t.o) | 2½.10 |

6/4 Top Song, **5/2** Crystado (FR), **4/1** TISSISAT (USA)(op 7/4), **10/1** Southwold Air, **12/1** Eiras Mood(10/1—16/1), **20/1** Bells of Longwick, **33/1** Headless Heights, **50/1** Ors. CSF £10.08, Tote £4.00: £1.90 £1.20 £1.30 (£4.90). The Queen (KINGSCLERE) bred by The Queen in USA. 10 Rn
1m 40.64 (1.34)
SF—44/28/30/15/–/–

## 1305　　　SWANAGE H'CAP (0-80) £2364.00 (£654.00: £312.00)　　**5f**　　5-00 (5-03)

| | | |
|---|---|---|
| 945³ | **Fangin (75)** (WGMTurner) 3-9-3 ‡³TSprake (1) (mde all: r.o wl) | —1 |
| 1176⁶ | Iron King (68) (JLSpearing) 6-9-7 NHowe (8) (hdwy 2f out: chsd wnr fnl f: r.o) | 2.2 |
| 1167³ | Divine Pet (62) (Fav) (WGRWightman) 7-9-1 WNewnes (10) (lw: outpcd: gd hdwy fnl 2f: fin wl) | 2½.3 |
| 909 | Unveiled (64) (RJHodges) 4-9-3 MRoberts (9) (nvr nrr) | nk.4 |
| | Ayr Raider (66) (WRMuir) 5-9-5 SWhitworth (3) (bit bkwd: nrst fin) | 1½.5 |
| 1138³ | Miss Precocious (43) (v) (DShaw) 4-7-7⁽³⁾ ‡³FNorton (6) (no hdwy fnl 2f) | hd.6 |
| 1199³ | Ashtina (68) (RJHodges) 7-9-7 WCarson (7) (lw: chsd wnr tl wknd 1f out) | 1½.7 |
| 1111⁴ | Dawes of Nelson (41) (MJBolton) 7-7-8 NCarlisle (5) (nvr nr to chal) | ¾.8 |
| 1167★ | Darussalam (67) (RLee) 5-9-6 (7x) PatEddery (2) (a bhd) | ¾.9 |
| 801 | Spectacle Jim (55) (bl) (JO'Donoghue) 3-8-0 NAdams (11) (prom 3f) | 1½.10 |
| 1167 | Gone Savage (72) (GBBalding) 4-9-11 JWilliams (4) (prom tl wknd qckly over 1f out) | 1.11 |

LONG HANDICAP: Miss Precocious 7-5.

3/1 Divine Pet(op 5/1), **7/2** Darussalam, **5/1** Ashtina, **15/2** FANGIN, **10/1** Gone Savage, **14/1** Iron King, Miss Precocious, Dawes of Nelson, **16/1** Unveiled, **25/1** Ayr Raider, **33/1** Spectacle Jim. CSF £92.76, CT £347.68. Tote £9.20: £2.30 £5.70 £1.40 (£79.90). Mr Simon Swift (SHERBORNE) bred by Melbury Park Stud. 11 Rn
59.78 sec (equals best: U.22)
SF—62/58/38/39/35/8

## 1306　　　LAVERSTOCK STKS (II) (Mdn 3-Y-O) £2304.40 (£638.40: £305.20)　　**1m** 5-30 (5-31)

| | | |
|---|---|---|
| 944³ | **Zawaahy (USA)** (Jt-Fav) (AAScott) 8-9 WRSwinburn (8) (a.p: led wl over 1f out: v.easily) | —1 |
| 989 | Selaginella (MRChannon) 8-9 MHills (5) (w ldr: led over 3f out tl over 2f out: r.o one pce) | 6.2 |
| 833² | Will of Steel (Jt-Fav) (HCandy) 9-0 CRutter (4) (a.p: led over 2f out tl wl over 1f out) | s.h.3 |
| 699 | Christian Flight (IRE) (RHannon) 8-6 ‡³RPerham (6) (no hdwy fnl 3f) | 7.4 |
| 1173 | Flash of Straw (IRE) (GLewis) 9-0 RaymondBerry (9) (nvr nr to chal) | ¾.5 |
| 1148⁴ | Silky Siren (EAWheeler) 8-9 SWhitworth (4) (nvr nr ldrs) | ¾.6 |
| 833 | Sirmoor (IRE) (64) (RHannon) 9-0 SRaymont (7) (bhd fnl 3f) | s.h.7 |
| | Basha (USA) (JLDunlop) 8-9 WCarson (1) (b.hind: leggy: unf: scope: bhd fnl 3f) | 5.8 |
| 1086⁶ | Jorrocks (47) (MDixon) 9-0 AClark (11) (hdwy 4f out: wknd over 2f out) | ¾.9 |
| | Guesstimation (USA) (JHMGosden) 9-0 PatEddery (2) (cmpt: bkwd: dwlt: a bhd) | 2½.10 |
| 894 | Hinton Harry (IRE) (SMellor) 9-0 DanaMellor (10) (led tl wknd qckly over 3f out) | 2.11 |

9/4 Will of Steel, ZAWAAHY (USA), **7/2** Guesstimation (USA)(op 7/4), **11/2** Basha (USA), **20/1** Silky Siren, **25/1** Flash of Straw (IRE), Sirmoor (IRE), Christian Flight (IRE), Selaginella, **66/1** Ors. CSF £50.34, Tote £1.30 £3.20 £1.50 (£44.40). Maktoum Al Maktoum (NEWMARKET) bred by Barronstwn St, Swett'ham St & J. P. McManus in USA. 11 Rn
1m 42.25 (2.95)
SF—14/–/–/–/–/–/–

T/Plpt: £75.90 (60.55 Tckts).　　　　　　　　　　　　　　　　　　　　　　　Hn

1184—**BEVERLEY (R-H)**
**Wednesday, June 10th [Firm]**
Going Allowance: minus 0.35 sec per fur (F)                    Wind: fresh half bhd

Stalls: high

**1307**   EUROPEAN BUSINESS AND MANAGEMENT (S) STKS (2-Y.O) £2402.40 (£666.40: £319.20)   **5f**
2-00 (2-02)

1118³ **Coconut Johnny** (bl) (Fav) (GMMoore) 8-11 KFallon (5) (lw: mde virtually all: drvn clr 1f out: r.o) .................................................. —1
1121³ Dead Calm (v) (CTinkler) 8-11 MBirch (3) (lw: wnt lft s: sn w wnr: rdn 2f out: kpt on sme pce) ................................................ 1½.2
1071 Bluebella (MrsPABarker) 8-6 GHind (6) (outpcd after wl over 1f: styd on appr fnl f: nt rch ldrs) .......................................... 1.3
1140 Zinjaal (IRE) (BHanbury) 8-11 WRSwinburn (4) (lw: trckd ldrs: rdn over 1f out: wnt rt: sn wknd: eased whn no ch) ................ 3½.4
574 Never in Touch (MBrittain) 8-6 JLowe (7) (nvr in tch: sn wl outpcd & drvn along) ............................................................ ½.5
402⁵ Samanthas Joy (TFairhurst) 8-3 ‡³JFanning (2) (unruly s: outpcd after 2f: sn bhd) ................................................... 6.6

**4/5** COCONUT JOHNNY, **9/4** Dead Calm, **6/1** Zinjaal (IRE), **14/1** Never in Touch, **16/1** Samanthas Joy, **33/1** Bluebella. CSF £3.12, Tote £1.70: £1.10 £1.60 (£1.70). Crestmart Ltd (MIDDLEHAM) bred by A. C. Birkle. 6 Rn;
No bid                                                                63.4 sec (1.9)
SF—24/18/9/–/–/–

**1308**   UNIVERSITY OF HUMBERSIDE H'CAP (3-Y.O) (0-90) £3752.50 (£1120.00: £535.00: £242.50)   **1m 1f 207y**
2-30 (2-31)

878* **Milanese (74)** (DMorley) 9-0 MBirch (10) (mde all: qcknd over 2f out: r.o wl) .... —1
883 Reel of Tulloch (IRE) **(64)** (PCHaslam) 8-4 DMcKeown (1) (hld up: gd hdwy on ins over 2f out: n.m.r: swtchd & r.o wl nr fin) ............ 1.2
732⁴ Al Haal (USA) **(72)** (PTWallwyn) 8-12 WCarson (9) (lw: a chsng ldr: rdn over 2f out: r.o one pce fnl f) ............................. ½.3
1049² Pyare Square **(74)** (bl) (IABalding) 8-11 ‡³SO'Gorman (4) (lw: hld up: effrt on outside 2f out: sn rdn: kpt on: nvr nr to chal) ..... 2.4
999⁴ Roly Wallace **(63)** (bl) (KTIvory) 8-3 GBardwell (3) (jnd ldrs over 4f out: ev ch & rdn 2f out: one pce) ........................... nk.5
1195² Nicely Thanks (USA) **(66)** (Fav) (TDBarron) 8-6 AlexGreaves (5) (lw: hld up: hdwy 5f out: rdn & nt clr run over 1f out: nvr able to chal) ... 1.6
341 Nocatchim **(65)** (BWHills) 8-5 DHolland (8) (lw: chsd ldrs: rdn over 2f out: wknd over 1f out) ............................. 1½.7
983 Hadaad (USA) **(81)** (AAScott) 9-7 WRSwinburn (6) (trckd ldrs: effrt 2f out: grad wknd) ....................................... ½.8
1068⁵ Al Ramis (IRE) **(73)** (CEBrittain) 8-13 MRoberts (7) (plld hrd: hdwy on ins to jn ldrs: wknd 2f out) ...................... 1½.9

**7/2** Nicely Thanks (USA), **4/1** Hadaad (USA), **9/2** Al Ramis (IRE), **6/1** Al Haal (USA), **7/1** Nocatchim, **8/1** Pyare Square, **9/1** MILANESE, **16/1** Ors. CSF £119.32, CT £848.32. Tote £11.10: £3.00 £5.50 £2.00 (£82.70). Sir William McAlpine (NEWMARKET) bred by Mrs William McAlpine. 9 Rn        2m 5.5 (3.5)
SF—30/18/25/20/11/12

**1309**   ELTHERINGTON H'CAP (0-70) £3080.00 (£920.00: £440.00: £200.00)   **7f 100y**
3-00 (3-01)

1185* **Kateb (IRE) (66)** (Fav) (RWArmstrong) 3-9-10 (5x) WCarson (3) (lw: s.i.s: bhd: hdwy on outside over 2f out: r.o wl to ld wl ins fnl f) ............ —1
1159* Thewaari (USA) **(61)** (AAScott) 3-9-5 (5x) WRSwinburn (11) (swtg: trckd ldrs: led just ins fnl f: no ex nr fin) ....................... nk.2
1122 Spanish Express **(49)** (RBoss) 3-8-7 MTebbutt (8) (effrt 3f out: styd on fnl f: nt rch ldrs) ................................... 2.3
1122 Creego **(45)** (JAGlover) 3-8-3 DHolland (6) (chsd ldrs: led over 1f out tl jst ins fnl f) ................................................. 1.4
1122² Super Summit **(58)** (JPearce) 3-8-11 ‡⁵RPrice (7) (lw: chsd ldrs tl rdn & outpcd over 2f out: kpt on: nvr able to chal) .......... hd.5
1052 Treasure Beach **(42)** (MBrittain) 3-8-0 JLowe (14) (sn bhd: hdwy over 2f out: kpt on: nvr nr to chal) ........................ ½.6
1172 Harlequin Girl **(39)** (bl) (KTIvory) 4-8-7 GBardwell (13) (chsd ldrs: one pce fnl 2f) ................................................ s.h.7

1157 Royal Girl **(52)** *(MissSEHall)* 5–9–6  BRaymond (1) (lw: sn bhd: effrt on outside
  3f out: styd on one pce) .................................................................................... ¹/₂.8
  Allegramente **(60)** *(RO'Leary)* 3–9–4  MBirch (12) (hmpd & bhd after 2f: kpt on
  fnl 2f) ........................................................................................................................ nk.9
896⁶ Master Hyde (USA) **(55)** (bl) *(PMitchell)* 3–8–8 ‡5JWeaver (9) (swtg: led tl hdd &
  wknd wl over 1f out) .......................................................................................... 3¹/₂.10
1012 Young Musician (IRE) **(62)** *(JGFitzGerald)* 3–9–6  KFallon (4) (chsd ldrs tl wknd
  2f out) ...................................................................................................................... 1¹/₂.11
1075 Intrepid Fort **(52)** *(BWMurray)* 3–8–10  AClark (10) (nvr nr to chal) ............ 1¹/₂.12
  Caveat Vendor **(49)** *(PCHaslam)* 4–9–3  DMcKeown (5) (hld up & plld hrd: a bhd) 13
997 Bellatrix **(57)** *(CEBrittain)* 4–9–11  MRoberts (2) (chsd ldrs tl lost pl over 2f out) ... 14

4/1 KATEB (IRE), 5/1 Thewaari (USA), 6/1 Super Summit, 7/1 Master Hyde (USA), Royal Girl, 9/1 Creego,
Bellatrix, 14/1 Young Musician (IRE), 16/1 Spanish Express, 20/1 Harlequin Girl, Caveat Vendor, 25/1
Allegramente, 33/1 Ors. CSF £24.18, CT £271.88. Tote £4.10: £1.70 £1.80 £3.20 (£4.10). Mr Hamdan
Al-Maktoum (NEWMARKET) bred by A. Tarry in Ireland. 14 Rn                    1m 32.1 (1.9)
                                                                               SF—43/37/19/12/19/6

**1310**     GELDER & KITCHEN CENTENARY SPRINT H'CAP (0-70) £2774.40 (£768.40: £367.20)
             **5f**                                                      3-30 (3-32)

(Weights raised 6 lb)
1020 **Don't Run Me Over (44)** *(BCMorgan)* 3–8–0⁽¹⁾  MRoberts (10) (led after 1f: r.o
  wl appr fnl f) ............................................................................................................. —1
1235² Morpick **(52)** (v) *(JPLeigh)* 5–8–9 ‡7StephenDavies (1) (lw: a chsng ldrs: rdn 2f
  out: kpt on fnl f) ...................................................................................................... 2.2
980 Drum Sergeant **(60)** (bl) *(JParkes)* 5–9–10  AlexGreaves (12) (lw: trckd ldrs: effrt
  over 1f out: unable qckn) .......................................................................................... nk.3
1111 Johanna Thyme **(40)** *(RBastiman)* 5–8–4  JQuinn (11) (styd on appr fnl f: nt rch
  ldrs) ........................................................................................................................ 1¹/₂.4
1271 Jive Music **(35)** *(NBycroft)* 6–7–8⁽³⁾ ‡5SMaloney (8) (led 1f: chsd ldrs rdn 2f out:
  kpt on same pce) ...................................................................................................... hd.5
1162³ Spring High **(50)** (bl) *(KTIvory)* 5–9–0  GBardwell (7) (chsd ldrs tl wknd over 1f
  out) ........................................................................................................................... nk.6
1050 Here Comes a Star **(51)** *(JMCarr)* 3–9–5  SMorris (2) (nvr rchd ldrs) ............ ¹/₂.7
1278 Minizen Music (IRE) **(37)** *(MBrittain)* 4–8–1  JLowe (7) (nvr plcd to chal) ............ hd.8
1111 Crail Harbour **(54)** (bl) *(PCHaslam)* 6–9–4  DMcKeown (9) (sn bhd: effrt & n.m.r
  2f out: no imp) .......................................................................................................... nk.9
1177* Yes **(49)** (Fav) *(DTThom)* 4–8–6 ‡7PBowe (8) (lw: sn bhd: effrt ¹/₂-wy: n.d) ...... nk.10
1154‡ Sammy Slew (USA) **(66)** (bl) *(SGNorton)* 3–9–1 ‡7OPears (4) (effrt ¹/₂-wy: hrd rdn
  & edgd lft over 1f out: sn wknd) ................................................................................ 2.11
1157² Miss Brightside **(31)** *(ASmith)* 4–7–2 ‡7CHawksley (3) (lw: b.nr fore: sn outpcd) 1.12

4/1 Yes, 11/2 Sammy Slew (USA), 15/2 Crail Harbour, 9/1 Spring High, Drum Sergeant, Johanna Thyme, 10/1
Morpick, Miss Brightside, 12/1 DON'T RUN ME OVER, 14/1 Minizen Music (IRE), 16/1 Ors. CSF £115.13, CT
£1,033.26. Tote £13.30: £3.20 £2.20 £3.90 (£91.80). Mr G. Whitaker (BURTON-ON-TRENT). 12 Rn
                                                                               63.6 sec (2.1)
                                                                               SF—7/8/22/–/–/–

**1311**     'WIN WITH THE TOTE' H'CAP (0-70) £2880.50 (£798.00: £381.50)
             **1m 3f 216y**                                             4-00 (4-01)

(Weights raised 1 lb)
1190 **Sarsta Grai (50)** *(MHEasterby)* 4–8–8 ‡5SMaloney (1) (lw: effrt 5f out: led over 1f
  out: jst hld on) ......................................................................................................... —1
1087⁶ Naseer (USA) **(59)** (Fav) *(NACallaghan)* 5–8–6  MRoberts (6) (trckd ldrs: led 2f
  out: sn hdd: nt qckn nr fin) .................................................................................... s.h.2
1034⁴ Drinks Party (IRE) **(34)** *(JWharton)* 4–7–11  WCarson (8) (lw: effrt 4f out: kpt on
  one pce u.p fnl 2f: nvr able to chal) .......................................................................... 3.3
  Trojan Lancer **(61)** *(DrJDScargill)* 6–9–10  WRyan (2) (hld up & bhd: hdwy fnl 3f:
  nrst fin) ..................................................................................................................... 1¹/₂.4
1274 Talish **(45)** *(TDBarron)* 4–8–1 ‡7VHalliday (9) (plld hrd: trckd ldrs tl wknd over 2f
  out) ........................................................................................................................... 6.5
761⁵ Floating Line **(59)** *(PWigham)* 4–9–8  MWigham (5) (lw: led tl over 2f out: wknd
  over 1f out) .............................................................................................................. 1.6
974 Reklaw **(35)** *(MDHammond)* 5–7–12  JQuinn (4) (lw: a in rr) ................................ 5.7
  Iwan **(55)** (v) *(KAMorgan)* 4–9–4  DMcKeown (7) (chsd ldrs tl rdn & outpcd 3f
  out: sn bhd) ............................................................................................................. 1.8
1002² Grey Commander **(43)** *(MBrittain)* 4–8–6  JLowe (3) (sn w ldr: lost pl over 2f out:
  sn bhd) .................................................................................................................... 3.9

5/2 Naseer (USA), 3/1 Drinks Party (IRE), 13/2 Trojan Lancer, 8/1 SARSTA GRAI, 9/1 Floating Line, Grey
Commander, 11/1 Reklaw, 14/1 Talish, 20/1 Iwan. CSF £27.21, CT £68.09. Tote £7.70: £1.60 £1.70 £1.50
(£11.20). Mr T. K. Kindon (MALTON) bred by P. F. and I. Mummery. 9 Rn                    2m 33.6 (2)
                                                                               SF—32/29/14/38/3/22

**1312**      POLYGON QUALITY MANAGEMENT STKS (Mdn) £2186.80 (£604.80: £288.40)
              **7f 100y**                                              4-30 (4-32)

10296 **Kalko** *(CEBrittain)* 3-8-11 MRoberts (7) (chsd ldrs tl outpcd over 2f out: styd on
              wl u.p fnl f: led nr fin) ........................................... —1
8654 Music in My Life (IRE) **(65)** (Fav) *(WJarvis)* 3-8-6 WCarson (5) (lw: led: clr over
              2f out: wknd ins fnl f: jst ct) ..................................... nk.2
8993 Traders Dream **(69)** *(TThomsonJones)* 3-8-11 SWhitworth (3) (lw: a chsng
              ldrs: kpt on u.p fnl 2f: nt qckn ins fnl f) ...................... ½.3
11892 Fairford *(JGFitzGerald)* 3-8-11 KFallon (4) (lw: chsd ldrs: effrt 3f out: kpt on u.p:
              hung rt: wknd ins fnl f) ........................................... 2½.4
         Bandoline *(BWHills)* 3-8-6 DHolland (6) (chsd ldrs: effrt over 2f out: grad wknd) 1.5
         Giddy Heights (IRE) *(JPLeigh)* 3-7-13 ‡7StephenDavies (8) (leggy: unf: sn bhd:
              sme hdwy over 2f out: nvr nr ldrs) ............................. 2½.6
9464 Whitrigg Lad *(WWHaigh)* 3-8-11 DMcKeown (1) (gd hdwy on outside 3f out: sn
              ev ch: rdn & wknd 2f out) ........................................ 5.7
         Aurora Lad *(MrsSJSmith)* 5-9-0 ‡7JMarshall (9) (bit bkwd: s.s: a bhd) .............. 12.8

**7/4** Music in My Life (IRE), **11/4** Traders Dream, **9/2** KALKO, **7/1** Fairford, Bandoline, **16/1** Giddy Heights (IRE),
**33/1** Ors. CSF £12.62, Tote £5.10: £2.00 £1.30 £1.10 (£5.00). The Dowager Lady Beaverbrook
bred by Dayspring Co Ltd. 8 Rn                                        1m 33.1 (2.9)
                                                                     SF—15/9/12/4/–/–

**1313**      NEW UNIVERSITY STKS (Mdn 3-Y.O) £2441.60 (£677.60: £324.80)
              **1m 3f 216y**                                            5-00 (5-03)

         **Sheriffmuir** *(LMCumani)* 9-0 LDettori (6) (str: rangy: scope: bit bkwd: chsd
              ldrs: styd on wl to ld over 1f out: sn clr) ...................... —1
7373 Zamaan Ya Zamaan (IRE) *(MAJarvis)* 9-0 GCrealock (1) (chsd ldrs: pushed
              along 5f out: styd on same pce fnl 2f) ......................... 4.2
10795 Betelgeuse (Fav) *(HRACecil)* 8-9 WRyan (11) (trckd ldrs: rdn over 2f out: r.o
              same pce) .......................................................... 1½.3
6804 Lady Dundee (USA) *(MrsJCecil)* 8-9 AClark (9) (lw: led 4f: led over 3f out tl hdd
              & wknd over 1f out) ............................................... 2.4
11263 Tour Leader (NZ) *(TDBarron)* 9-0 AlexGreaves (10) (hld up: stdy hdwy over 3f
              out: nvr rchd ldrs) ................................................. 3.5
11826 Hazaaf (USA) *(AAScott)* 9-0 BRaymond (7) (lw: rr div: effrt over 4f out: kpt on:
              nvr able to chal) ................................................... hd.6
     835 Believe it *(CEBrittain)* 9-0 MRoberts (2) (chsd ldr: led 8f out tl over 3f out: sn
              wknd & eased) ..................................................... 12.7
         Pot Hunting *(WJarvis)* 9-0 DHolland (4) (w'like: scope: rn green: sn pushed
              along & wl bhd: sme hdwy 2f out: r.d) .......................... 3½.8
    1147 Perfect Light **(56)** *(MrsSJSmith)* 8-7 ‡7JMarshall (5) (unruly in stalls: plld hrd: a
              in rr) ................................................................ 5.9
    1280 Court Rise (USA) *(RWArmstrong)* 9-0 BCrossley (3) (lw: in tch: rdn & lost pl 5f
              out: sn bhd) ........................................................ 1.10

**11/4** Betelgeuse, **100/30** SHERIFFMUIR(op 11/8), **9/2** Lady Dundee (USA), **15/2** Pot Hunting, **10/1** Zamaan Ya
Zamaan (IRE), Hazaaf (USA), Believe it, **16/1** Tour Leader (NZ), **25/1** Ors. CSF £34.06, Tote £2.70: £1.10 £2.00
£1.60 (£10.80). Sheikh Mohammed (NEWMARKET) bred by Stetchworth Park Stud Ltd. 10 Rn  2m 32.8 (1.2)
                                                                     SF—46/38/30/26/25/24

T/Plpt: £64.10 (55.25 Tckts).                                                         WG

## 988—KEMPTON (R-H)
### Wednesday, June 10th [Good]
Going Allowance: minus 0.05 sec per fur (G)                        Wind: almost nil

Stalls: low

**1314**      SILK & FRAZIER CLAIMING STKS    £2700.00 (£750.00: £360.00)   **6f**   6-35 (6-37)

     980 **Breezy Day (77)** *(BAMcMahon)* 6-8-10 TQuinn (2) (lw: a.p: led over 1f out: rdn
              out) ................................................................. —1
9706 Regal Racer **(84)** (Fav) *(DRCElsworth)* 3-8-11 SCauthen (4) (swtg: chsd ldr:
              led over 2f out tl over 1f out: ev ch fnl f: r.o) ................ nk.2
966* Massiba (IRE) **(77)** *(BHanbury)* 3-8-11 WRSwinburn (11) (lw: hdwy over 2f out:
              hrd rdn over 1f out: one pce) .................................... 3½.3
     992 Harry's Coming **(56)** *(RJHodges)* 3-8-10 RCochrane (7) (a.p: rdn 3f out: one
              pce) ................................................................. 3.4

9675 My Czech Mate (53) (RHannon) 3–8-4 AMcGlone (3) (outpcd: hdwy over 1f out: r.o) ........................................................................... 2¹/₂.5
9622 Yonge Tender (56) (bl) (CNWilliams) 5–8-10 JCurant (1) (s.s: hdwy fnl 2f: r.o) .. 2.6
10643 Blue Topaze (RJHolder) 4–9-0 ADicks (6) (swtg: prom over 2f) ...................... 1¹/₂.7
11043 Walk in the Park (83) (RSimpson) 3–7-12 ‡⁵ATucker (12) (a.p: ev ch 2f out: wknd over 1f out) ............................................................................. 3¹/₂.8
Dorking Lad (59) (MHTompkins) 10–8-7 ‡⁵CHodgson (10) (swtg: no hdwy fnl 2f) .......................................................................................... 1¹/₂.9
7792 Lord High Admiral (CAN) (73) (RHannon) 4–9-0 ‡3RPerham (8) (lw: s.s: hdwy 3f out: wknd 2f out) ..................................................................... 2.10
1160★ Liffey River (USA) (51) (MrsLPiggott) 4–8-13 LPiggott (9) (b: lw: spd 4f) ......... nk.11
1104 Fabled Orator (46) (PHowling) 7–8-12 TyroneWilliams (15) (b.nr hind: lw: led over 3f) ................................................................................. hd.12
10913 Ednego Bay (IRE) (v) (MMcCormack) 4–8-11 JReid (5) (lw: spd over 3f) ......... ¹/₂.13
945 Greetland Rock (44) (PHowling) 4–8-13 JWilliams (13) (swtg: a bhd) ............. 8.14
Calibairn (DJSCosgrove) 4–8-11 PaulEddery (14) (a bhd) ......................... 8.15

4/1 Regal Racer(3/1—9/2), 5/1 BREEZY DAY, Lord High Admiral (CAN), Walk in the Park (IRE)(5/1—9/1), Massiba (IRE), 20/1 Harry's Coming, Yonge Tender, Liffey River (USA), Dorking Lad, 33/1 Blue Topaze, My Czech Mate, 50/1 Ors. CSF £23.86, Tote £8.80: £2.70 £1.80 £2.20 (£16.60). Mrs J. McMahon (TAMWORTH) bred by John I. O'Byrne. 15 Rn; Massiba (IRE) clmd M Heaton-Ellis £21,053 1m 13.37 (2.07)
SF—49/49/35/22/6/4

**1315** FAIRCLOUGH STKS (Mdn 3-Y.O.F) £2595.00 (£720.00: £345.00)
7f (J.C) 7-05 (7-08)

393 **Star Goddess (USA)** (MRChannon) 8-11 BRouse (11) (4th st: led over 1f out: rdn out) ............................................................................... —1
Goodniteout (IRE) (89) (DRCElsworth) 8-11 SCauthen (12) (3rd st: hrd rdn over 1f out: r.o) ........................................................................ 2.2
Laundry Maid (78) (HCandy) 8-11 CRutter (14) (led over 5f: unable qckn) ....... nk.3
9895 Raven Runner (Fav) (IABalding) 8-11 RCochrane (7) (hdwy wl over 1f out: one pce fnl f) ................................................................... 1¹/₂.4
9386 Belated (HThomsonJones) 8-11 RHills (2) (6th st: one pce fnl 2f) ................... 2.5
989 Agnes Flemming (USA) (PWHarris) 8-11 PaulEddery (6) (n.m.r on ins over 2f out: hdwy over 1f out: r.o) ............................................... nk.6
Batchworth Bound (EAWheeler) 8-6 ‡⁵DHarrison (3) (neat: bit bkwd: nvr nr to chal) ...................................................................................... s.h.7
Miss Cresta (HCandy) 8-11 WNewnes (9) (hdwy over 1f out: r.o) ................... 1¹/₂.8
Alyafill (USA) (BHanbury) 8-11 WRSwinburn (10) (unf: nvr nrr) .................... 1.9
Acara (CJames) 8-11 JWilliams (1) (leggy: scope: bhd fnl 2f) .................... s.h.10
9926 Cashmiriana (IRE) (75) (MissHCKnight) 8-11 SWhitworth (16) (hdwy 5f out: 5th st: wknd 2f out) ................................................................ 2¹/₂.11
Gladeer (IRE) (WCarter) 8-6 ‡⁵NGwilliams (5) (lw: w ldr: 2nd st: wknd over 2f out) . 1.12
Nick-Ela-Noo (IRE) (RHannon) 8-8 ‡3RPerham (8) (scope: a bhd) .................. 2.13
Magic Penny (CACyzer) 8-11 TQuinn (15) (wl grwn: bit bkwd: bhd fnl 2f) ......... 6.14
Executive Flare (DSasse) 8-11 PD'Arcy (13) (a bhd) .......................... 3¹/₂.15

3/1 Raven Runner (USA), 7/2 Goodniteout (IRE), 8/1 STAR GODDESS (USA)(tchd 12/1), 10/1 Alyafill (USA)(op 6/1), Miss Cresta(8/1—12/1), 11/1 Cashmiriana (IRE), 12/1 Belated, Laundry Maid(8/1—14/1), Magic Penny(8/1—14/1), Nick-Ela-Noo (IRE)(8/1—14/1), 20/1 Executive Flare(op 8/1), Gladeer (IRE), 33/1 Ors. CSF £37.05, Tote £12.90: £3.30 £1.40 £4.50 (£27.60). Mr K. Higson (UPPER LAMBOURN) bred by Mrs. Jackie Ward Ramos in USA. 15 Rn 1m 27.33 (3.13)
SF—45/39/38/33/27/26

**1316** STRUTT & PARKER H'CAP (3-Y.O) (0-90) £2820.00 (£840.00: £400.00: £180.00)
1³/₄m 7-35 (7-36)

9794 **Mootawel (USA)** (73) (HThomsonJones) 8-9 RHills (2) (swtg: 4th st: led over 1f out: r.o wl) ............................................................... —1
6874 Hidden Light (IRE) (76) (MAJarvis) 8-12 AMunro (6) (lw: hdwy 5f out: 2nd st: led wl over 1f out: sn hdd: unable qckn) ................................ 2¹/₂.2
1241 A a Bamba (60) (NACallaghan) 7-5(1) ‡⁵DHarrison (3) (lw: 6th st: rdn over 1f out: one pce) .......................................................... hd.3
1041 Rolling the Bones (USA) (66) (JRFanshawe) 8-2 GCarter (5) (lw: 5th st: rdn 3f out: one pce) ......................................................... ³/₄.4
8484 Aremef (USA) (85) (MrsJCecil) 9-7 PaulEddery (4) (lw: led over 12f) .............. 10.5
8815 Dolly Madison (IRE) (65) (BWHills) 8-1 WCarson (1) (chsd ldr over 9f: 3rd st: wknd wl over 1f out) ............................................... 3¹/₂.6

11/4 Hidden Light (IRE), 3/1 Aremef (USA), 9/2 Dolly Madison (IRE), MOOTAWEL (USA), 8/1 A a Bamba, 9/1 Rolling the Bones (USA). CSF £15.65, Tote £5.40: £2.00 £1.60 (£8.60). Mr Hamdan Al-Maktoum (NEWMARKET) bred by Gallagher Stud. 6 Rn 3m 6.35 (9.75)

## 1317

GOULDENS OLYMPIC RIDERS INVITATION H'CAP (Amateurs) (0-80) £2200.50 (£618.00: £301.50) **1m 1f** 8-05 (8-08)

962⁵ **Shining Jewel (63)** *(MrsLPiggott)* 5-11-8 VirginiaLeng (8) (lw: 3rd st: rdn fnl f: led nr fin) ............................................................ —1
592 Causley **(69)** *(BAMcMahon)* 7-12-0 NickSkelton (10) (w ldr: led 6f out: hrd rdn fnl f: hdd nr fin) ................................................. nk.2
987 Arrastra **(62)** *(IABalding)* 4-11-7 JaneHolderness-Roddam (6) (lw: 5th st: rdn fnl f: r.o) ............................................. 1½.3
1005 Armashocker **(48)** *(DSasse)* 4-10-7 LornaClarke (4) (swtg: hdwy fnl 2f: r.o) ...... 4.4
1109² Bengal Tiger (IRE) **(54)** (bl) (Fav) *(JAkehurst)* 4-10-13 JohnWhitaker (5) (led 3f: 2nd st: wknd over 1f out) ................................ 1.5
905 Jarras **(48)** (bl) *(CASmith)* 7-10-7 KateMeacham (1) (6th st: no hdwy fnl 3f) ..... ½.6
912 Always Ready **(50)** *(RLee)* 6-10-9⁽²⁾ JoeTuri (7) (b: nvr nrr) .......................... 1.7
832 Gibbot **(48)** *(PHowling)* 7-10-7 MaryThomson (3) (s.s: a bhd) .......................... 8.8
1087 Shrewd Girl (USA) **(58)** *(BWHills)* 4-11-3 EmileFaurie (9) (bhd fnl 3f) ............. 1.9
866³ Jurran **(59)** *(HThomsonJones)* 7-11-4 MichaelWhitaker (2) (racd wd: bhd fnl 6f) 2.10
1130⁵ Freaky Deaky **(54)** *(NACallaghan)* 5-10-13 RichardWalker (11) (4th st: wknd over 2f out) ....................................... ½.11

LONG HANDICAP: Jarras 10-1, Always Ready 9-10, Gibbot 9-6.

**3/1** Bengal Tiger (IRE)(op 2/1), **4/1** Causley(5/2—9/2), **9/2** SHINING JEWEL, **13/2** Jurran, **9/1** Arrastra(8/1—12/1), **10/1** Always Ready, **12/1** Shrewd Girl (USA)(op 8/1), **14/1** Freaky Deaky(op 7/1), **33/1** Ors. CSF £21.58, CT £137.36. Tote £6.70: £2.20 £2.00 £2.70 (£16.40). Mr D. W. Rolt (NEWMARKET) bred by H. Ward. 11 Rn
1m 57.50 (7.50)
SF—17/22/10/–/–/–

## 1318

KIER H'CAP (0-80) £3340.00 (£1000.00: £480.00: £220.00) **1½m** 8-35 (8-36)
(Weights raised 1 lb)

1147³ **Good for a Loan (60)** *(RLee)* 5-8-10 PatEddery (5) (6th st: swtchd rt 2f out: led over 1f out: drvn out) ............................... —1
1044 Sharp Top **(46)** *(MJRyan)* 4-7-10 GBardwell (1) (3rd st: led over 2f out tl over 1f out: r.o) ........................................... ½.2
831⁶ Mahrajan **(63)** *(CJBenstead)* 8-8-13 TQuinn (6) (hdwy 3f out: rdn over 1f out: unable qckn) ......................................... 3.3
1016★ Taylors Prince **(62)** *(HJCollingridge)* 5-8-12 JQuinn (11) (lw: hdwy 5f out: 5th st: nt clr run & lost pl over 2f out: one pce) .......................... 3.4
1147 Rare Detail (IRE) **(74)** *(MrsLPiggott)* 4-9-10 LPiggott (4) (2nd st: led 3f out tl over 2f out: wknd wl over 1f out) .......................... ¾.5
1041 Liability Order **(67)** *(RBoss)* 3-7-10 ‡5DHarrison (2) (hdwy over 1f out: nvr nrr) nk.6
431 Statajack (IRE) **(72)** (bl) *(DRCElsworth)* 4-9-8 SCauthen (10) (swtg: 4th st: wknd 2f out) .................................... 1.7
926★ El Volador **(66)** *(RJO'Sullivan)* 5-9-2 RCochrane (3) (hdwy 3f out: rdn 2f out: sn wknd) ................................................. 2.8
1137⁶ Puff Puff **(53)** *(MissBSanders)* 6-8-5 DaleGibson (7) (s.s: a bhd) .................. 2.9
Himlaj (USA) **(53)** *(SMellor)* 7-8-3 DanaMellor (12) (bit bkwd: bhd fnl 3f) ........ 4.10
831 Run Free **(48)** *(PatMitchell)* 7-9-6⁽⁵⁾ ‡3DBiggs (9) (bhd fnl 6f) ...................... 1½.11
1163★ Snow Blizzard **(50)** (Fav) *(SDow)* 4-8-0 (4x) WCarson (8) (led 9f) ................... ½.12

LONG HANDICAP: Run Free 6-12.

**7/2** Snow Blizzard, **5/1** Mahrajan, El Volador, **11/2** GOOD FOR A LOAN, **9/1** Statajack (IRE), **11/1** Taylors Prince(7/1—12/1), **12/1** Rare Detail (IRE)(op 8/1), Sharp Top, **14/1** Liability Order, **16/1** Puff Puff, **50/1** Ors. CSF £63.46, CT £319.98. Tote £5.30: £1.80 £3.70 £2.10 (£32.80). Racing Investments (PRESTEIGNE) bred by Mrs William McAlpine. 12 Rn
2m 37.61 (7.41)
SF—16/1/12/5/15/–

## 1319

RICHARD ELLIS STKS (Mdn 3-Y-O) £2721.00 (£756.00: £363.00) **1¼m (J.C)** 9-05 (9-09)

1207² **Milzig (USA) (92)** (Fav) *(DRCElsworth)* 9-0 TQuinn (10) (5th st: led over 2f out: r.o wl) .............................................. —1
Fieldridge *(CRNelson)* 9-0 JReid (3) (2nd st: ev ch fnl 2f: r.o) .................... ½.2
Ajzem (USA) *(MRStoute)* 9-0 WRSwinburn (4) (scope: lw: rdn & lost pl over 4f out: rallied over 1f out: r.o wl ins fnl f) ....................... nk.3
Guilty Secret (IRE) *(PWChapple-Hyam)* 8-9 PaulEddery (14) (lw: 4th st: ev ch ins fnl f: r.o) .................................... s.h.4
Amoruccio (USA) *(GHarwood)* 9-0 RCochrane (11) (w'like: scope: hdwy over 2f out: shkn up wl over 1f out: nt qckn) ............................. 3.5
1033³ Pippin Park (USA) *(HCandy)* 8-9 CRutter (5) (3rd st: one pce fnl 2f) ............... nk.6
989⁶ Rosina Mae *(LordHuntingdon)* 8-9 AMunro (6) (rdn & hdwy 2f out: nvr nrr) ..... nk.7
Bustinetta *(JRFanshawe)* 8-2 ‡7NVarley (8) (unf: nvr nr to chal) ................ 2½.8
1012³ Reflecting (IRE) *(JHMGosden)* 9-0 PatEddery (16) (led over 7f) ...................... 1.9

546³ Allmosa *(TJNaughton)* 8-9 GCarter (9) (swtg: nvr nrr) .................................... 1.10
Maradonna (USA) *(LMCumani)* 9-0 LDettori (1) (w'like: scope: bit bkwd: prom
    7f) .......................................................................................................... ³/₄.11
Lycian Moon *(JLDunlop)* 8-9 WNewnes (7) (unf: 6th st: wknd over 2f out) ..... 15.12
Aldavera *(MDixon)* 9-0 DaleGibson (12) (unf: scope: a bhd) ............................ ³/₄.13
Red-Michelle *(EAWheeler)* 8-4 ‡5DHarrison (2) (w'like: prom 5f) ...................... 2.14
Jovial Man (IRE) *(SMellor)* 9-0 JWilliams (15) (cmpt: bit bkwd: a bhd) ............. 15
1122 Triple Trouble *(48)* *(HJCollingridge)* 9-0 JQuinn (13) (swtg: a bhd: t.o) ............ 16

**100/30** MILZIG (USA)(5/1—3/1), **9/2** Pippin Park (USA)(6/1—4/1), **6/1** Reflecting (IRE), **7/1** Guilty Secret
(IRE)(4/1—8/1), Rosina Mae, **15/2** Fieldridge(7/1—14/1), **10/1** Amoruccio (USA)(op 3/1), Ajzem (USA)(6/1—
12/1), **14/1** Maradonna (USA), **20/1** Bustinetta, **25/1** Lycian Moon, **33/1** Allmosa, **50/1** Ors. CSF £29.94, Tote
£3.90: £1.80 £2.50 £4.60 (£15.90). Mrs J. E. Ohlsson (WHITSBURY) bred by E. W. Thomas & Partners. 16 Rn
2m 7.45 (5.45)
SF—40/39/38/32/31/25

T/Trio: Race 5: £96.80 (14.2 Tckts). T/Plpt: £232.50 (15.7 Tckts).                          AK

1263—**SOUTHWELL (L-H)** Fibresand
**Wednesday, June 10th [Standard]**
Going Allowance: minus 0.05 sec per fur (FS)                    Wind: mod half against

Stalls: 5f-6f high, remainder low
**1320**    SHOPPACHECK H'CAP (3-Y-O) (0-70) £2363.20 (£655.20: £313.60)
      **1m (AWT)**                                              2-15 (2-17)

1004★ **Coastal Express** *(67)* (Fav) *(EWeymes)* 9-7 LDettori (3) (mde all: clr 2f out:
    easily) ................................................................................................... —1
1000 Grubby *(16)* *(RHollinshead)* 7-6 †7AGarth (1) (a p: 3rd st: kpt on one pce fnl f) ,, 4.2
1185⁴ Spray of Orchids *(49)* *(JEtherington)* 8-3 PRobinson (15) (hld up: hdwy ent st:
    nrst fin) .................................................................................................. 1¹/₂.3
1004 High Success *(52)* (bl) *(WAO'Gorman)* 8-1⁽⁴⁾ ‡5EmmaO'Gorman (6) (hld up: r.o
    appr fnl f: nvr plcd to chal) ...................................................................... ¹/₂.4
1152 Leonadis Polk *(60)* *(WJPearce)* 9-0 DNicholls (8) (hld up: hdwy 2f out: nt rch
    ldrs) ...................................................................................................... s.h.5
1172 Kate Royale *(53)* (bl) *(GCBravery)* 8-7 MHills (5) (chsd ldrs: 6th & rdn st: no imp
    fnl 2f) ................................................................................................... 1¹/₂.6
833 Trainee (USA) *(53)* *(WJHaggas)* 8-7 NDay (16) (sme hdwy fnl 2f: nvr nrr) ...... 1¹/₂.7
1004 Grand Fellow (IRE) *(57)* (bl) *(JDBethell)* 8-11 AMunro (14) (hdwy & 4th st: wknd
    over 2f out) ........................................................................................... 5.8
1004 Roxy Music (IRE) *(55)* *(GAPritchard-Gordon)* 8-9 GDuffield (7) (chsd ldrs 5f: sn
    wknd: t.o) .............................................................................................. 6.9
678⁵ Nest *(60)* *(LordHuntingdon)* 8-9 ‡5DHarrison (4) (swtg: wnt 2nd ¹/₂-wy: wknd 2f
    out: t.o) ............................................................................................... hd.10
1004³ Sie Amato (IRE) *(55)* *(CaptJWilson)* 8-9 GCarter (9) (lw: prom: 5th st: sn rdn &
    wknd: t.o) ............................................................................................. nk.11
904⁵ Mill Burn *(51)* *(ICampbell)* 8-2 ‡3DBiggs (10) (a bhd: t.o) ............................... 1.12
912 Daily Sport Girl *(55)* *(PABlockley)* 8-2 †7GParkin (13) (bit bkwd: a bhd: t.o) ..... 4.13
348 Rostands Hero (IRE) *(50)* *(HJCollingridge)* 8-4 NHowe (2) (b: bit bkwd: s.s: a
    outpcd: t.o) ........................................................................................... nk.14
1043⁴ Specialist Dream (IRE) *(52)* *(LJCrood)* 8-6⁽⁴⁾ VSmith (11) (a bhd: t.o) ............. 6.15
604 Molten Copper (IRE) *(64)* *(MWEasterby)* 9-4 TLucas (12) (a bhd: t.o) ........... hd.16

**100/30** COASTAL EXPRESS(5/1—3/1), **6/1** Nest(7/2—13/2), Sie Amato (IRE), **10/1** Mill Burn, **12/1** Spray of
Orchids, Trainee (USA)(op 5/1), **14/1** Roxy Music (IRE), Leonadis Polk, High Success, **16/1** Kate Royale, **20/1**
Grand Fellow (IRE), **25/1** Molten Copper (IRE), Daily Sport Girl, **33/1** Ors. CSF £93.91, CT £1,072.66. Tote
£4.20: £1.20 £5.80 £1.70 £2.90 (£57.50). Mrs R. L. Heaton (MIDDLEHAM) bred by Bechmann Stud. 16 Rn
1m 43.8 (4.5)
SF—34/-/2/-/10/-

**1321**    BASS LEISURE SIA (S) STKS (2-Y-O) £2441.60 (£677.60: £324.80)
      **6f (AWT)**                                              2-45 (2-47)

**Time's Arrow (IRE)** *(GCBravery)* 8-11 MHills (9) (w'like: hld up: rapid hdwy 2f
    out: str run to ld ins fnl f) ........................................................................... —1
1264² Pretzel (IRE) (v) *(NTinkler)* 8-11 LDettori (3) (led tl hdd & outpcd ins fnl f) ......... 4.2
1191⁵ Plum First (bl) *(NBycroft)* 8-11 SWhitworth (4) (lw: chsd ldr: ev ch 1f out: sn rdn
    & btn) .................................................................................................... 2¹/₂.3
1121★ A Bridge Too Far (IRE) (Fav) *(WJPearce)* 8-11 DNicholls (1) (prom: hrd rdn 2f
    out: one pce) ........................................................................................... 1¹/₂.4
1171 Golden Klair *(CJHill)* 8-6 TyroneWilliams (14) (hdwy ent st: nt rch ldrs) ........... 2¹/₂.5

1121⁴ Nellie's Gamble (bl) (APStringer) 8-6 JFortune (16) (lw: in tch: effrt 2f out: kpt on one pce) .................. hd.6
1140* Toff Sundae (GLewis) 9-2 PaulEddery (12) (nvr plcd to chal) .................. 1½.7
882² Clangold (JBerry) 8-6 GCarter (13) (chsd ldrs: rdn 2f out: nvr nr to chal) .......... ¾.8
1178 Rose Flyer (IRE) (MCChapman) 8-6 NAdams (11) (nvr trbld ldrs) .................. 3.9
889 Jersey Bob (IRE) (JSWainwright) 8-11 WNewnes (5) (m.n.s) .................. 2½.10
Longlife (IRE) (MHTompkins) 8-11 PRobinson (6) (neat: bkwd: m.n.s) .................. 2.11
Jocks Joker (CaptJWilson) 8-11 GDuffield (10) (w'like: leggy: bkwd: chsd ldrs 4f) .................. 1.12
561 Rythmic Rascal (MBrittain) 8-11 AMunro (7) (a bhd) .................. 3.13
Knayton Lodger (MWEasterby) 8-6 TLucas (15) (scope: bkwd: s.s: a bhd) 1½.14
Snug Surprise (JSWainwright) 8-6 AMackay (8) (w'like: scope: bit bkwd: outpcd: t.o) .................. 3.15

3/1 A Bridge Too Far (IRE)(op 5/1), 9/2 Plum First(6/1—4/1), 11/2 Clangold(4/1—6/1), 8/1 Toff Sundae(op 5/1), Pretzel (IRE), 9/1 Longlife (IRE), 10/1 TIME'S ARROW (IRE)(6/1—12/1), 16/1 Golden Klair, 20/1 Knayton Lodger(op 10/1), Jersey Bob (IRE), Jocks Joker, 25/1 Rythmic Rascal, Nellie's Gamble, Snug Surprise, 33/1 Rose Flyer (IRE). CSF £88.26, Tote £34.40: £7.50 £2.00 £1.60 (£219.30). Mr G. C. Bravery (NEWMARKET) bred by Mrs M. Lowry in Ireland. 15 Rn; Bt in 6,500 gns
1m 16.7 (3.3)
SF—25/9/–/–/–/–

---

### 1322

GALA CLUBS STKS (Mdn 2-Y.O) £2422.00 (£672.00: £322.00)
6f (AWT)

3-15 (3-19)

Zilfi (USA) (PFICole) 9-0 AMunro (11) (lt-f: a chsng ldrs: rdn along 2f out: r.o strly to ld nr fin) .................. —1
971³ Stormy Heights (JRJenkins) 8-9 GBaxter (3) (led: rdn clr ins fnl f: ct cl home) ½.2
1071² Nutty Brown (Fav) (SGNorton) 9-0 NConnorton (4) (lw: a.p: ev ch 1f out: no ex ins fnl f) .................. 2½.3
769 Don't Jump (IRE) (MHTompkins) 8-9 PRobinson (3) (lw: bhd & outpcd tl r.o appr fnl f) .................. 3.4
Green Sword (WAO'Gorman) 8-9 ‡5EmmaO'Gorman (2) (w'like: bkwd: chsd ldrs: kpt on one pce fnl 2f) .................. 1½.5
795 Apollo de Oriente (JSWainwright) 9-0 WNewnes (8) (prom 4f) .................. 2½.6
Desert Laughter (IRE) (RHollinshead) 9-0 PaulEddery (5) (w'like: leggy: bit bkwd: s.s: sme hdwy fnl 2f: nvr nrr) .................. ½.7
470 Lucayan Treasure (JBerry) 9-0 GCarter (1) (outpcd) .................. ½.8
1171 Big Gem (MCChapman) 8-7 ‡7SWilliams (4) (chsd ldrs: over 3f: t.o) .................. 6.9
Noble Measure (IRE) (SirMarkPrescott) 9-0 GDuffield (9) (lt-f: sltly dipped: a bhd: t.o) .................. 8.10

4/1 Nutty Brown(op 5/2), 5/1 ZILFI (USA)(op 3/1), Lucayan Treasure(4/1—6/1), 6/1 Noble Measure (IRE)(op 7/2), 8/1 Stormy Heights, Don't Jump (IRE)(op 14/1), 10/1 Green Sword(op 5/1), 12/1 Desert Laughter (IRE)(16/1—20/1), 33/1 Apollo de Oriente, 50/1 Big Gem. CSF £38.52, Tote £3.90: £1.60 £3.20 £1.20 (£23.20). Mr Fahd Salman (WHATCOMBE) bred by Newgate Stud Farm Inc in USA. 10 Rn  1m 17.1 (3.7)
SF—20/13/12/–/–/–

---

### 1323

NOTTINGHAMSHIRE COAL STKS (Mdn) £2284.80 (£632.80: £302.40)
7f (AWT)

3-45 (3-49)

1005² Turtle Beach (74) (AAScott) 3-9-0 JFortune (12) (lw: a.p: 2nd st: hrd rdn appr fnl f: led post) .................. —1
Hubbers Favourite (MrsNMacauley) 4-9-5 NDay (10) (led: hrd rdn fnl f: ct last stride) .................. s.h.2
727² Lady Roxanne (Fav) (LordHuntingdon) 3-8-4 ‡5DHarrison (14) (a.p: 4th st: ev ch ins fnl f: r.o) .................. hd.3
1148² Missy-S (IRE) (50) (GAPritchard-Gordon) 3-8-9 GCarter (8) (hdwy & 5th st: kpt on ins fnl f) .................. 1½.4
1173⁴ Whitehall (IRE) (CRNelson) 3-9-0 MHills (15) (prom: 3rd st: wknd over 1f out) ... 5.5
Swell Time (IRE) (bl) (CNAllen) 4-8-12 ‡7GForster (3) (b.hind: hdwy 2f out: kpt on ins fnl f) .................. ¾.6
919 Lunagraphe (USA) (BobJones) 4-9-5 VSmith (5) (swtg: chsd ldrs: 6th & rdn st: sn btn) .................. 2½.7
Quantity Surveyor (SirMarkPrescott) 3-9-0 GDuffield (2) (leggy: nvr nr to chal) 1½.8
Drop a Curtsey (JDBethell) 3-8-9 AMunro (4) (lt-f: unf: s.s: nvr rchd ldrs) .......... 6.9
Hiram B Birdbath (JAGlover) 6-9-3 ‡7SWilliams (9) (bit bkwd: outpcd) .................. 2.10
Tina's Game (APStringer) 4-9-2 ‡3FNorton (7) (bkwd: a bhd) .................. 2½.11
594 Mint Addition (54) (KOCunningham-Brown) 3-8-6 ‡3DBiggs (6) (m.n.s) .......... 2½.12
1268⁶ Arighi Boy (JEBanks) 3-8-7 ‡7JSwinnerton (11) (bit bkwd: a bhd) .................. 2.13
353 Millefiori (KSBridgwater) 3-8-9 NAdams (4) (lost pl 3f out: t.o) .................. 5.14
Kay Largo (IRE) (50/1) Withdrawn (ref to ent stalls) : not under orders

**5/4** Lady Roxanne(op 2/1), **11/4** TURTLE BEACH(2/1—100/30), **10/1** Quantity Surveyor(op 5/1), Missy-S (IRE)(7/1—11/1), **14/1** Whitehall (IRE)(op 5/1), **33/1** Drop a Curtsey, Hiram B Birdbath, Mint Addition, **50/1** Ors. CSF £116.65, Tote £3.10: £1.50 £6.80 £1.50 (£81.00). Mrs P. D. Rossdale (NEWMARKET) bred by Mrs P. D. Rossdale. 14 Rn
1m 30.9 (4.3)
SF—30/34/18/18/8/4

## 1324
THORNTONS H'CAP (0-70) £2324.00 (£644.00: £308.00)  1½m (AWT) 4-15 (4-15)

| | | | |
|---|---|---|---|
| 575 | **Atlantic Way (35)** *(CJHill)* 4-7-7 NAdams (hld up: 7th st: hdwy on ins to ld over 1f out: hrd rdn: all out) | —1 |
| 1150⁴ | Mizyan (IRE) **(59)** *(Fav)* *(JEBanks)* 4-8-12 ‡⁵LNewton (6) (lw: hdwy 5f out: 3rd st: ev ch ins fnl f: r.o) | ½.2 |
| 1132⁴ | Modesto (USA) **(70)** *(KOCunningham-Brown)* 4-9-11 ‡³DBiggs (3) (b: lw: led tl hdd appr fnl f: rdn & no ex nr fin) | 2½.3 |
| 905² | Mr Wishing Well **(53)** *(RJRWilliams)* 6-8-11 GCarter (5) (lw: hld up: gd hdwy & 4th st: rdn 2f out: one pce) | 1½.4 |
| 1037³ | Tanoda **(46)** *(MBrittain)* 6-8-4 AMunro (7) (chsd ldr: 2nd st: wknd 2f out) | 8.5 |
| | Everso Irish **(58)** *(MHTompkins)* 3-8-0⁽³⁾ PRobinson (2) (b.nr fore: chsd ldrs: 6th & rdn st: sn btn) | 2.6 |
| 895 | Midday Show (USA) **(60)** *(JRJenkins)* 5-9-4 GBaxter (8) (b.hind: a bhd: 8th st) | 1½.7 |
| 1184 | Shining Wood **(43)** *(JSWainwright)* 4-8-1 AMackay (1) (prom tl 5th & wkng st) | 1½.8 |

LONG HANDICAP: Atlantic Way 6-13.

**4/1** Mizyan (IRE)(op 5/2), **9/2** Tanoda, **5/1** Modesto (USA), Mr Wishing Well, **11/2** Everso Irish, **7/1** Midday Show (USA)(14/1—16/1), **8/1** ATLANTIC WAY, **16/1** Shining Wood. CSF £37.49, CT £160.95. Tote £16.40: £2.70 £1.70 £3.00 (£54.70). Mr C. John Hill (BARNSTAPLE) bred by Mrs M. L. Parry and P. M. Steele-Mortimer. 8 Rn
2m 40.1 (5.9)
SF—14/32/40/23/–/–

## 1325
GALA CLUBS SIA H'CAP (0-70) £2147.60 (£593.60: £282.80)  5f (AWT) 4-45 (4-45)
(Weights raised 1 lb)

| | | | |
|---|---|---|---|
| 1235⁴ | **Arc Lamp (47)** *(JAGlover)* 6-8-11 JFortune (8) (lw: chsd ldrs: effrt over 1f out: rdn to ld wl ins fnl f) | —1 |
| 1278 | The Shanahan Bay **(52)** (v) *(MrsNMacauley)* 7-8-9 ‡⁷SWilliams (7) (b: lw: s.i.s: hdwy wl over 1f out: hrd rdn fnl f: fin fast) | ¾.2 |
| 1263³ | Sobering Thoughts **(38)** (bl) *(DWChapman)* 6-8-2 SWood (5) (a.p: led ½-wy tl ct nr fin) | ¾.3 |
| 587 | Drummer's Dream (IRE) **(43)** *(MrsNMacauley)* 4-8-7 PRobinson (4) (led to ½-wy: no ex fnl f) | ¾.4 |
| 1263⁶ | Hinari Video **(60)** *(MJohnston)* 7-9-10 RPElliott (2) (spd 3f) | 5.5 |
| 1266⁶ | Strip Cartoon (IRE) **(49)** (bl) *(SRBowring)* 4-8-6 ‡⁷MHarris (6) (lw: w ldrs to ½-wy) | ½.6 |
| 1030 | Royal Bear **(29)** *(JMBradley)* 10-7-7 NAdams (9) (outpcd) | 6.7 |
| 349⁴ | Barbezieux **(30)** (bl) *(TJNaughton)* 5-7-8 DaleGibson (3) (b: outpcd) | 2½.8 |
| 1050 | Lets Go Sabo **(47)** *(DWChapman)* 4-8-11 GBaxter (1) (outpcd fnl 2f) | 9 |

LONG HANDICAP: Royal Bear 7-3.

**3/1** Sobering Thoughts, **5/1** ARC LAMP, **6/1** Strip Cartoon (IRE), **13/2** Barbezieux(5/1—8/1), **15/2** Hinari Video(9/2—8/1), **9/1** Drummer's Dream (IRE)(op 6/1), **12/1** The Shanahan Bay, **16/1** Lets Go Sabo, **20/1** Royal Bear. CSF £51.48, CT £172.26. Tote £3.90: £1.80 £2.50 £1.10 (£21.10). Mr B. Bruce (WORKSOP) bred by H. J. Joel. 9 Rn
60.6 sec (2.6)
SF—40/35/25/27/24/4

T/Plpt: £50.00 (39.55 Tckts).
IM

## 1108—HAMILTON (R-H)
### Wednesday, June 10th [Firm]
Going Allowance: St: minus 0.40 sec; Rnd: minus 0.25 sec (F)  Wind: almost nil

Stalls: low

## 1326
LANGS SUPREME SCOTCH WHISKY H'CAP (0-80) £2807.00 (£777.00: £371.00)
5f 4y  7-00 (7-03)

| | | | |
|---|---|---|---|
| 1187⁶ | **Prince Belfort (67)** *(MPNaughton)* 4-9-9 ‡⁵JWeaver (5) (lw: trckd ldrs: led wl over 1f out: rdn & r.o) | —1 |
| 1054⁶ | Nevada Mix **(44)** *(MissLAPerratt)* (1) (lw: swtchd & effrt ½-wy: sn ev ch: nt qckn ins fnl f) | 2.2 |
| 1271⁵ | Lombard Ocean **(64)** *(MO'Neill)* 3-8-12 ‡⁵SMaloney (4) (lw: led over 3f: kpt on) | s.h.3 |
| 1111* | Diet **(66)** (v) *(Fav)* *(MissLAPerratt)* 6-9-6 ‡⁷RHavlin (2) (lw: cl up 3f out: sn rdn & outpcd) | 2½.4 |
| | Okaku **(37)** *(DBurchell)* 5-7-7⁽⁵⁾ ‡⁵NKennedy (3) (outpcd & bhd fr ½-wy) | 10.5 |

LONG HANDICAP: Okaku 7-0.

**10/11** Diet, **5/2** PRINCE BELFORT, **6/1** Lombard Ocean, **8/1** Nevada Mix(4/1—11/1), **20/1** Okaku. CSF £17.71, Tote £3.80: £1.30 £1.90 (£10.70). Mrs Carole Sykes (RICHMOND) bred by Concorde Bloodstock Agency Ltd. 5 Rn
59.4 sec (1.1)
SF—47/20/26/24/–/

## 1327
HAMILTON ADVERTISER STKS (Mdn 2-Y-O) £2385.00 (£660.00: £315.00)
6f 5y
7-30 (7-34)

1161² **Captain le Saux (IRE)** (Fav) *(MBell)* 9-0 MHills (9) (lw: a.p: rdn to ld ins fnl: r.o wl) ......................................................................................................................... —1

1112³ Principal Player (USA) *(WBentley)* 9-0 MBirch (2) (led: hrd rdn & wandered 1f out: sn hdd & btn) .................................................................................. 2.2

975⁵ Umbubuzi (USA) *(FHLee)* 9-0 MRoberts (4) (chsd ldrs: rdn whn n.m.r: appr fnl f: no ex) .............................................................................................. 2¹/₂.3

Storm Venture (IRE) *(WJPearce)* 9-0 DNicholls (5) (w'like: lengthy: scope: chsd ldrs: kpt on one pce fnl 2f) ................................................................ ¹/₂.4

Milngavie (IRE) *(MJohnston)* 9-0 DMcKeown (3) (cmpt: scope: bit bkwd: prom over 4f) ........................................................................................... 6.5

Lofty Deed (USA) *(SirMarkPrescott)* 9-0 GDuffield (1) (w'like: bit bkwd: s.s: wl bhd tl sme late hdwy) ..................................................................... 7.6

828 White Creek (IRE) *(JBerry)* 9-0 JCarroll (3) (disp ld 4f: sn wknd) .................. ³/₄.7

Grumpy's Grain (IRE) *(MissLAPerratt)* 8-11 ‡³JFanning (7) (w'like: scope: bit bkwd: sn pushed along: lost tch fr ¹/₂-wy) .................................................. 3.8

1071 Selvole (v) *(MissLAPerratt)* 8-9 BRaymond (8) (w ldrs 4f: sn rdn & fnd nil) ....... 1¹/₂.9

**5/6** CAPTAIN LE SAUX (IRE), **3/1** Principal Player (USA), **7/1** Umbubuzi (USA), **10/1** Lofty Deed (USA)(8/1—12/1), **14/1** Grumpy's Grain (IRE)(op 8/1), **20/1** Milngavie (IRE), White Creek (IRE), **25/1** Storm Venture (IRE), **50/1** Selvole. CSF £4.14, Tote £2.20: £1.20 £1.70 £2.20 (£3.40). Mr P. A. Philipps (NEWMARKET) bred by Swettenham Stud in Ireland. 9 Rn
1m 11.6 (1.6)
SF—20/12/2/–/–/–

## 1328
FIT-THE-BEST EVEREST H'CAP (3-Y-O) (0-70) £2259.00 (£624.00: £297.00)
6f 5y
8-00 (8-01)
(Weights raised 9 lb)

1271* **Educated Pet (56)** (Fav) *(MJohnston)* 9-2 (7x) DMcKeown (5) (lw: hld up: qcknd to ld ins fnl f: r.o wl) ................................................................. —1

1155² Coolaba Prince (IRE) **(55)** *(FHLee)* 9-4 MRoberts (4) (trckd ldrs: hdwy on ins over 1f out: r.o wl: edgd rt nr fin) ..................................................... nk.2

1155³ Legitim **(35)** *(JMJefferson)* 7-6⁽²⁾ ‡³JFanning (1) (led: hdd & hung rt over 2f out: btn whn hmpd appr fnl f: fin 4th, 4l: plcd 3rd) .............................. 3

1155⁶ Manuleader **(56)** (bl) *(WJPearce)* 9-2 DNicholls (3) (led 2f out: hrd rdn appr fnl f: sn hdd: nt qckn: fin 3rd, ¹/₂l: disq: plcd 4th) ............................... 4

1146 Dandy Desire **(61)** *(BCMorgan)* 9-7 GDuffield (6) (lw: a.p: effrt over 2f out: wknd over 1f out) ................................................................................. 5.5

904 Palacegate King **(55)** *(JBerry)* 9-1 JCarroll (3) (lw: cl up 3f: sn wknd) ............... 8.6

*Stewards Enquiry: Nicholls suspended 19-22/6/92 (careless riding). Manuleader disq. (interference to Legitim fnl f).*

**13/8** EDUCATED PET, **11/4** Coolaba Prince (IRE), **7/2** Legitim, **7/1** Palacegate King, **8/1** Dandy Desire, **16/1** Manuleader. CSF £6.55, Tote £2.20: £1.50 £1.50 (£2.30). Mr Billy Morgan (MIDDLEHAM) bred by Highfield Stud Ltd. 6 Rn
1m 11.8 (1.8)
SF—18/16/–/–/–/–

## 1329
TENNENTS H'CAP (0-80) £3003.00 (£833.00: £399.00) **1m 65y** 8-30 (8-32)
(Weights raised 16 lb)

1114 **Silver Haze (58)** *(WAStephenson)* 8-9-10 MBirch (4) (hld up: smooth hdwy to ld over 1f out: hrd rdn: edgd lft & styd on) ............................................. —1

1153 Manulife **(67)** *(WJPearce)* 3-9-8 DNicholls (6) (hld up: hdwy 3f out: edgd rt appr fnl f: sn ev ch: r.o) .......................................................................... nk.2

1018 Mofador (GER) **(53)** *(FHLee)* 8-9-0 ‡⁵NKennedy (2) (lw: cl up: led over 4f out: edgd lft & hdd 1f out: hmpd whn btn jst ins fnl f) ......................... 2¹/₂.3

Rapid Mover **(29)** *(TCraig)* 5–7-9⁽²⁾ PBurke (1) (bit bkwd: led over 4f: ev ch tl wknd over 1f out) ..................................................................................... 1¹/₂.4

1184⁶ Honey Boy Simba **(37)** (v) *(MO'Neill)* 6–7-10 ‡⁷DarrenMoffatt (5) (lw: bhd: hrd rdn 3f out: styd on: no imp) ........................................................... 2.5

1126 Marian Evans **(35)** *(TCraig)* 5–7-12 ‡³JFanning (3) (chsd ldrs tl wknd 4f out) .... 15.6

LONG HANDICAP: Rapid Mover 7-1.

*Stewards Enquiry: Nicholls suspended 23-26/6/92 (excessive use of whip).*

**85/40** Mofador (GER), **9/4** Manulife, **5/2** Honey Boy Simba, **7/1** SILVER HAZE(6/1—10/1), **20/1** Rapid Mover, **25/1** Marian Evans. CSF £21.78, Tote £5.80: £2.20 £2.20 (£11.80). Mr P. Piller (BISHOP AUCKLAND) bred by Ryan Jarvis. 6 Rn
1m 47.7 (4.4)
SF—14/11/–/–/–/–

**1330**  SAINTS & SINNERS STKS (Mdn 3-Y.O) £2072.00 (£572.00: £272.00)
1m 3f 16y                                                                        9-00 (9-00)

804⁵ **Sovereign Page (USA)** (Fav) (BHanbury) 9-0 BRaymond (3) (lw: mde all: styd
      on wl fnl f) ............................................................................................... —1
1158³ Baher (USA) (bl) (NACallaghan) 9-0 GDuffield (2) (lw: trckd ldrs: chal 4f out: nt
      qckn u.p fnl 2f) .......................................................................................... ³/₄.2
1079² Maji (70) (DMorley) 8-9 MRoberts (4) (lw: a.p: effrt 4f out: rdn & one pce fr over
      2f out) ......................................................................................................... 1.3
1088⁵ Storm Gayle (IRE) (MJohnston) 8-9 DMcKeown (1) (hld up: effrt 4f out: no imp) 10.4

**11/10** SOVEREIGN PAGE (USA), **6/4** Maji, **6/1** Storm Gayle (IRE)(tchd 10/1), **13/2** Baher (USA). CSF £7.37, Tote
£2.80 (£9.00). Mrs J. M. Beeby (NEWMARKET) bred by T. Holland Martin in USA. 4 Rn      2m 22.2 (3.2)
                                                                                          SF—41/39/32/12

**1331**  SPORTING CLUB OF MEXICO STKS (Amateurs) £2427.00 (£672.00: £321.00)
1¹/₂m 17y                                                                        9-30 (9-31)

1248 **Shadideen (USA)** (67) (MissLAPerratt) 4-10-9 ‡⁵MissLPerratt (5) (lw: hld up:
      hdwy appr st: effrt 4f out: led over 1f out: r.o) ...................................... —1
      Silver Hello (45) (MissLAPerratt) 6-11-0 ‡⁵MrMLightbody (7) (a.p: rdn to ld 2f
      out: sn hdd & nt qckn) ............................................................................. 2¹/₂.2
718 Moving Out (79) (Fav) (SirMarkPrescott) 4-12-1 MrsEMellor (4) (lw: led 8f out:
      qcknd 5f out: hdd 2f out: kpt on) ............................................................ nk.3
1184⁵ Not Yet (35) (EWeymes) 8-11-10 ‡⁵MrJWeymes (1) (sn wl bhd: effrt 5f out: nvr
      nrr) ............................................................................................................. 8.4
      Gay Ruffian (45) (DBurchell) 6-11-0 ‡⁵MrNMiles (6) (cl up: rdn 4f out: sn
      outpcd) ....................................................................................................... 5.5
      Hello Georgie (bl) (TCraig) 0 10 0 ‡⁵MrAMcPheroon (2) (lod 1f: rdn & loot toh
      over 5f out) ................................................................................................ 6.6

**1/2** Moving Out, **11/2** SHADIDEEN (USA)(4/1—6/1), **6/1** Not Yet(tchd 10/1), **8/1** Gay Ruffian(op 5/1), **12/1**
Silver Hello, **66/1** Hello Georgie. CSF £52.29, Tote £6.10: £2.50 2.10 (£11.50). Miss L. A. Perratt (AYR) bred by
Marystead Farm in USA. 6 Rn                                                        2m 38.5 (6.5)
                                                                                          SF—28/28/42/22/1/—

T/Plpt: £503.30 (4.5 Tckts).                                                              AA

# HAMILTON (R-H)
## Thursday, June 11th [Firm]
Going Allowance: St: minus 0.40 sec; Rnd: minus 0.25 sec (F)        Wind: almost nil

Stalls: low

**1332**  ALMADA CLAIMING STKS (Mdn 2-Y.O) £1932.00 (£532.00: £252.00)
5f 4y                                                                            2-25 (2-26)

759⁴ **Dailysportdutch** (PAKelleway) 8-6 PRobinson (3) (hld up: hdwy 2f out:
      squeezed thro to ld appr fnl f: r.o wl) .................................................... —1
759⁵ First Option (Fav) (MHEasterby) 8-12 MBirch (2) (lw: trckd ldrs: effrt 2f out:
      hung rt: chal over 1f out: r.o) .................................................................. 1.2
889 My Godson (WJPearce) 8-7 LCharnock (6) (a chsng ldrs: ev ch 2f out: hung lft
      appr fnl f: nt qckn) .................................................................................... 3¹/₂.3
439 Duchess de Belfort (JBerry) 8-7 JCarroll (1) (led: edgd rt most of wy: hdd over
      1f out: no ex) ............................................................................................. 1.4
1056 Lucky Owl (PMonteith) 7-13 ‡⁷RHavlin (5) (bhd: effrt ¹/₂-wy: no imp) ................ 6.5
1127⁴ Sea-Ayr (IRE) (MissLAPerratt) 8-0 ‡³JFanning (7) (lw: chsd ldrs over 3f: sn
      wknd) .......................................................................................................... 2¹/₂.6
769 Dazzling Baby (MDods) 8-2 JLowe (4) (cl up 3f: sn wknd) ................................. 8.7

**Evens** First Option, **7/2** My Godson, **5/1** Duchess de Belfort(3/1—6/1), **6/1** DAILYSPORTDUTCH(op 3/1), **20/1**
Sea-Ayr (IRE), **25/1** Lucky Owl, **66/1** Dazzling Baby. CSF £11.99, Tote £4.20: £2.00 1.80 (£2.20). Roldvale
Limited (NEWMARKET) bred by C. F. Buckton. 7 Rn                                     60.1 sec (1.8)
                                                                                          SF—18/20/1/—/—/—

**1333**  STONEFIELD (S) STKS (3 & 4-Y.O) £2206.40 (£610.40: £291.20)        6f 5y 3-00 (3-02)

1272² **Murray's Mazda (IRE)** (66) (JBerry) 3–8-8 GDuffield (1) (lw: hld up: n.m.r &
      hdwy to ld over 1f out: r.o) ....................................................................... —1
1040* Our Rita (63) (Fav) (PAKelleway) 3–8-10 PRobinson (6) (a.p: hdwy & ev ch over
      1f out: nt qckn) .......................................................................................... 2.2

1326³ Lombard Ocean **(64)** *(MO'Neill)* 3–8-10 ‡⁵SMaloney (5) (lw: led tl hdd 1f out: no ex) .................................................................................................. ½.3

594 Cashtal Queen **(50)** *(JBerry)* 3–8-10 JCarroll (3) (b: prom: hdwy & ev ch 2f out: btn whn sltly hmpd 1f out) .............................. 4.4

1145 Agwa *(BHanbury)* 3–8-8 BRaymond (2) (cl up tl wknd over 4f) ............... nk.5

1130 Francis Ann **(49)** *(MissLAPerratt)* 4–9-2 ‡³JFanning (4) (w ldrs over 4f) ............... 4.6

**4/5** Our Rita(tchd 5/4), **4/1** Lombard Ocean(3/1—5/1), **9/2** MURRAY'S MAZDA (IRE), **14/1** Cashtal Queen(op 6/1), **16/1** Agwa(12/1—20/1), **20/1** Francis Ann(op 7/1). CSF £8.19, Tote £4.90: £1.30 £1.50 (£2.40). Mr Murray Grubb (COCKERHAM) bred by Patrick Kennedy in Ireland. 6 Rn; No bid  1m 11.7 (1.7)
SF–12/6/4/–/–/–

**1334** HIGH PARK MEDIAN AUCTION STKS (Mdn 3-Y.O) £2072.00 (£572.00: £272.00)
1m 65y  3-30 (3-32)

869³ **Wellington Rock (USA) (Fav)** *(JARToller)* 8-8 PRobinson (4) (lw: hld up & bhd: smooth hdwy to ld 1f out: sn qcknd clr) ............................... —1

1182³ Blue Sea *(MAJarvis)* 9-0 BRaymond (5) (lw: chsd ldrs: outpcd 2f out: styd on ins fnl f) .................................................................................. 3.2

1049³ Canaan Lane **(72)** *(AHarrison)* 8-5 KFallon (2) (trckd ldrs: led & qcknd wl over 2f out: hdd 1f out: sn btn) ............................................ ¾.3

Cumbrian Classic *(LLungo)* 8-8 MBirch (1) (led tl hdd wl over 2f out: sn btn) ... 12.4

1109 Ebony Isle **(40)** *(PMonteith)* 7-8⁽¹⁾ ‡⁷RHavlin (3) (chsd ldrs tl wknd over 2f out) .. 3.5

**8/11** WELLINGTON ROCK (USA), **7/4** Blue Sea, **6/1** Canaan Lane(op 4/1), **66/1** Ebony Isle, **100/1** Cumbrian Classic. CSF £2.32, Tote £1.70: £1.40 £1.10 (£1.70). Duke of Devonshire (NEWMARKET) bred by Runnymede Farm Incorporated in USA. 5 Rn  1m 47.3 (4)
SF–34/31/20/–/–

**1335** P & O CONTAINERS SCOTLAND H'CAP (3-Y.O) (0-80) £3003.00 (£833.00: £392.00)
1m 1f 36y  4-00 (4-00)

(Weights raised 2 lb)

1025⁴ **Drummer Hicks (59) (Fav)** *(EWeymes)* 8-2 DMcKeown (1) (lw: mde all: rdn & qckncd over 2f out: r.o wl) ...................................... —1

970⁵ Khazar (USA) **(61)** *(SirMarkPrescott)* 8-4 GDuffield (3) (lw: hld up: effrt over 2f out: hrd rdn & r.o wl towards fin) ............................ s.h.2

921⁴ Eid (USA) **(78)** (bl) *(DMorley)* 9-7 MBirch (4) (plld hrd: trckd wnr: effrt 3f out: wknd over 1f out) ............................................... 7.3

1126⁵ Bee Dee Ell (USA) **(51)** *(MissLAPerratt)* 7-5⁽¹⁾ ‡³JFanning (2) (prom tl wknd wl over 1f out) ................................................... 1½.4

1109 Brilliant Disguise **(58)** *(PMonteith)* 7-8⁽⁸⁾ ‡⁷RHavlin (5) (chsd ldr tl wknd over 2f out) ...................................................... 4.5

LONG HANDICAP: Bee Dee Ell (USA) 7-5, Brilliant Disguise 7-0.

**10/11** DRUMMER HICKS(tchd 6/4), **5/2** Eid (USA), **4/1** Khazar (USA), **16/1** Bee Dee Ell (USA)(op 10/1), **66/1** Brilliant Disguise. CSF £4.56, Tote £2.40: £1.10 £2.70 (£5.30). Mrs N. Napier (MIDDLEHAM) bred by Mrs N. Napier. 5 Rn  1m 57.4 (3.1)
SF–8/9/5/–/–

**1336** EXTEL FINANCIAL SYSTEMS H'CAP (3-Y.O) (0-70) £2880.50 (£798.00: £381.50)
1m 3f 16y  4-30 (4-33)

(Weights raised 1 lb)

1152⁵ **Sir Norman Holt (IRE) (52)** *(FHLee)* 8-5 DMcKeown (1) (lw: cl up: led over 4f out: hld on wl fnl 2f) ...................................... —1

1131⁶ Glowing Devil **(56)** *(TDBarron)* 8-9 AlexGreaves (8) (sn cl up: chal 4f out: kpt on wl towards fin) ........................................... ½.2

1129⁶ Anguish (IRE) **(51)** *(NACallaghan)* 8-4 JLowe (4) (hld up & bhd: hdwy on ins 4f out: ev ch 2f out: no ex cl home) ................. hd.3

915✳ Philgun **(63)** *(CWCElsey)* 8-11 ‡⁵SMaloney (5) (in tch: effrt 4f out: stumbled over 2f out: styd on wl) ................................. 1.4

1052⁶ Fair Flyer (IRE) **(52)** *(PMonteith)* 7-12 ‡⁷RHavlin (3) (chsd ldrs: effrt 3f out: nt qckn fnl 2f) ...................................... 3.5

1252 Batabanoo **(68) (Fav)** *(MrsGRReveley)* 9-7 MBirch (6) (lw: hld up: hdwy on outside 4f out: hrd rdn 2f out: sn btn) ............ nk.6

Great Max (IRE) **(63)** *(SirMarkPrescott)* 9-2 GDuffield (2) (prom tl drvn along & lost pl appr st: hdwy 4f out: wknd over 2f out) ............ 10.7

1128³ Shakela (USA) **(50)** *(BHanbury)* 8-0 ‡³JFanning (7) (led tl hdd over 4f out: sn wl bhd) ...................................................... 30.8

**11/8** Batabanoo, **4/1** Philgun, **6/1** Great Max (IRE), **7/1** SIR NORMAN HOLT (IRE), **9/1** Fair Flyer (IRE), **12/1** Glowing Devil, **16/1** Shakela (USA)(10/1—20/1), **20/1** Anguish (IRE)(op 12/1). CSF £73.44, CT £1,442.79. Tote £21.50: £3.10 £2.50 £5.80 (£162.10). Mr D. Holt (WILMSLOW) bred by Ovidstown Investments Ltd in Ireland. 8 Rn  2m 21.5 (2.5)
SF–39/42/36/41/22/44

## 1337

CLYDE H'CAP (0-70) £2304.40 (£638.40: £305.20)　　1m 5f 9y　　5-05 (5-07)

1274* **Luks Akura (35)** (v) *(MJohnston)* 4–7–0 (4x) ‡⁷MBaird (3) (s.s: hdwy to ld after 3f: clr fnl 3f: easily) ............... —1

1108³ Racing Raskal (36) (Fav) *(CaptJWilson)* 5–7–8 JLowe (5) (lw: a chsng ldrs: rdn 4f out: btn 3f out) ............... 12.2

805 Hamilton Lady (IRE) (38) *(DMoffatt)* 4–7–3 ‡⁷DarrenMoffatt (2) (bhd & rdn 4f out: styd on & no imp) ............... 2¹/₂.3

1248 Must Be Magical (USA) (38) *(FHLee)* 4–7–5⁽²⁾ ‡⁵NKennedy (1) (led 3f: chsd ldrs tl wknd 4f out) ............... 8.4

Affair of Honour (IRE) (68) *(JJO'Neill)* 4–9–5 ‡⁷ADobbin (4) (lw: outpcd & bhd appr st: n.d after) ............... 10.5

LONG HANDICAP: Luks Akura 7-6.

**6/4** Racing Raskal, **7/2** LUKS AKURA, Affair of Honour (IRE), **9/2** Hamilton Lady (IRE), **50/1** Must Be Magical (USA). CSF £8.23, Tote £5.30: £2.30 1.50 (£3.30). Luks Ind Co (UK) Ltd (MIDDLEHAM) bred by Hesmonds Stud Ltd. 5 Rn　　　2m 46.4 (0.5 under best; 0.7)

SF—12/–/–/–/–

T/Plpt: £126.00 (17.3 Tckts).　　　AA

## 1026—CHEPSTOW (L-H)

## Thursday, June 11th [Good to firm]

Going Allowance: 5f-6f: minus 0.30 (F); Rest: minus 0.70 sec (H)　　　Wind: mod across

Stalls: high

## 1338

ORSINO H'CAP (Amateurs) (0-70) £1982.00 (£552.00: £266.00)　　7f 16y　6-30 (6-34)

(Weights raised 2 lb)

1032 **La Belle Vie (64)** *(RJBaker)* 6–12–0 MrRFarrant (9) (hld up: hdwy 2f out: led wl ins fnl f: r.o wl) ............... —1

1054³ Bill Moon (47) *(PJFeilden)* 6–10–11 MissJFeilden (3) (a.p: led 1f out tl wl ins fnl f) ............... 3.2

1054⁵ Profit a Prendre (50) *(DAWilson)* 8–11–0 MissJAllison (22) (b: chsd ldr: ev ch 1f out: one pce) ............... 2.3

448 Johnston's Express (IRE) (36) *(EJAlston)* 4–9–11 ‡³MrRWilkinson (20) (bit bkwd: hdwy fnl 2f: r.o) ............... ³/₄.4

1138* Martinosky (60) *(WGRWightman)* 6–11–7 ‡³MissMClark (11) (a.p: stumbled 2f out: one pce) ............... s.h.5

Navaresque (50) *(RJHodges)* 7–10–9 ‡⁵MrTPiper (6) (bkwd: hld up: hdwy over 2f out: one pce fnl f) ............... ³/₄.6

1174⁵ Susanna's Secret (51) (bl) (Fav) *(WCarter)* 5–11–1 MissYHaynes (16) (led 6f) . nk.7

948 Now Boarding (33) *(RJHodges)* 5–9–11 MrsSHembrow (2) (nvr nr to chal) ....... 3.8

594³ Orchard Bay (53) *(DRTucker)* 3–10–2 ‡⁵MissSRowe (17) (lw: n.d) ............... 1¹/₂.9

515 Erris Express (52) *(JSMoore)* 7–10–13 ‡³MissDPomeroy (21) (s.s: hdwy over 3f out: wknd fnl f) ............... 1¹/₂.10

1143² Spanish Whisper (35) *(JRBostock)* 5–9–13 MrsLPearce (13) (lw: nvr trbld ldrs) . 1.11

1105 Corrin Hill (64) *(BWHills)* 5–12–0 MissEJohnsonHoughton (18) (b: n.d) ........... 3.12

949 Dazla (31) *(RRowe)* 5–9–4 ‡⁵MrsCDunwoody (8) (n.d) ............... 2.13

949 Do the Business (IRE) (45) (bl) *(CNAllen)* 3–9–8 ‡⁵MrVLukaniuk (1) (bhd fnl 2f) 1¹/₂.14

1064⁶ Tachyon Park (50) *(PHowling)* 10–10–9⁽¹²⁾ ‡⁵MrKWhiting (14) (spd over 4f) ... 2¹/₂.15

891 Young India (44) *(DBurchell)* 5–10–5 ‡³MrNMiles (10) (b: hind: prom over 4f) nk.16

Kalamoss (47) *(NRMitchell)* 3–10–1 MrsRVickery (19) (m.n.s) ............... hd.17

1085 Shapely Deb (46) (bl) *(DRLaing)* 3–9–9⁽³⁾ ‡⁵MrGHope (5) (m.n.s) ............... ³/₄.18

More Larks (IRE) (47) *(MBJames)* 4–10–11 MissLWallace (7) (bit bkwd: t.o) .. 10.19

Sporting Wednesday (34) *(JSMoore)* 7–9–7⁽¹⁾ ‡⁵MissACallandar (4) (t.o) ....... 12.20

*Stewards Enquiry: Haynes suspended 20-23/6/92 (careless riding).*

**100/30** Susanna's Secret(9/2—11/4), **11/2** Profit a Prendre, **6/1** Spanish Whisper, **9/1** Bill Moon(6/1—10/1), **10/1** LA BELLE VIE, **11/1** Martinosky(7/1—12/1), **12/1** Corrin Hill(6/1—14/1), Johnston's Express (IRE), **20/1** Young India, Orchard Bay, **25/1** Navaresque, **33/1** Tachyon Park, **50/1** Do the Business (IRE), Sporting Wednesday, Erris Express, Now Boarding, **66/1** Ors. CSF £88.41, CT £500.27. Tote £14.30: £3.10 £1.80 £1.30 £6.80 (£56.70). Mr Robin Lawson (TIVERTON) bred by Mrs S. O'Riordan. 20 Rn　　1m 22 (1.5)

SF—46/20/17/–/21/7

## 1339

TARMAC CONSTRUCTION H'CAP (0-70) £2390.00 (£665.00: £320.00)
1m 14y　　　7-00 (7-06)

277 **Royal Dartmouth (USA) (46)** *(BRMillman)* 7–8–6 JWilliams (9) (b: hld up: hdwy wl over 1f out: r.o to ld nr fin) ............... —1

1255⁵ Taunting (IRE) (57) *(MBlanshard)* 4–9–3 RCochrane (15) (hdwy 2f out: fin wl) . nk.2

580 Lord's Final (35) *(CRBarwell)* 5–7–9 NCarlisle (14) (led over 6f: r.o wl) ............ nk.3

| 1032[2] | Charmed Knave (51) (DRLaing) 7–8-11 TyroneWilliams (12) (lw: a.p: led over 1f out: hdd cl home) | hd.4 |
| 1267 | Revoke (USA) (44) (CJHill) 5–8-4 DHolland (7) (hdwy over 2f out: nt qckn fnl f) | 2.5 |
| 1284[3] | Please Please Me (IRE) (36) (KOCunningham-Brown) 4–7-7[2] ‡3FNorton (8) (hdwy over 1f out: nvr nrr) | hd.6 |
| 592 | Aldahe (47) (BRMillman) 7–8-7 AMackay (23) (led over 6f) | s.h.7 |
| 936 | Lucky Noire (63) (GHarwood) 4–9-2 ‡7GayeHarwood (16) (nvr nr to chal) | hd.8 |
| 832 | Rosietoes (USA) (51) (LGCottrell) 4–8-11 TRogers (18) (prom 6f) | hd.9 |
| | Fast Operative (39) (KOCunningham-Brown) 5–7-10 ‡3DBiggs (5) (bit bkwd: swtg: m.n.s) | 1.10 |
| 1032[3] | Persian Dynasty (44) (Fav) (JMBradley) 8–8-4 NAdams (22) (lw: chsd ldrs: n.m.r 2f out: wknd fnl f) | 2.11 |
| | Hightown-Princess (IRE) (47) (JSMoore) 4–8-7 AClark (20) (bkwd: s.s: n.d) | nk.12 |
| 967 | Scarlet Princess (42) (RJHodges) 4–8-2 MRoberts (14) (w ldrs 6f) | 2.13 |
| 592[6] | Tartar's Bow (57) (RJHolder) 5–8-10 ‡7SDrowne (11) (prom over 5f) | nk.14 |
| | Impressive Lad (35) (RRowe) 6–7-9 JQuinn (13) (n.d) | ½.15 |
| 1143 | Rag Time Belle (35) (MWEckley) 6–7-9[2] GeeArmytage (19) (bhd fnl 2f) | 2.16 |
| 1106 | Asterix (64) (JMBradley) 4–9-10 WNewnes (1) (prom over 5f) | 2.17 |
| 888[3] | Prime Mover (60) (DBurchell) 4–9-1 ‡5KRutter (3) (b.off hind: bhd fnl 2f) | ½.18 |
| 1278[6] | Nazare Blue (42) (MrsBarbaraWaring) 5–8-2[1] NHowe (2) (m.n.s) | ½.19 |
| 1235[6] | Nuclear Express (56) (RLee) 5–9-2 GBaxter (6) (m.n.s) | 4.20 |
| 1261 | King of Mileen (46) (DShaw) 6–8-6[1] JReid (17) (b: virtually p.u 1f out: fin lame) | 30.21 |

*Stewards Enquiry: J. Williams suspended 20-23/6/92 (excessive use of whip).*

3/1 Persian Dynasty, 5/1 Charmed Knave, 7/1 Revoke (USA)(12/1—16/1), 8/1 Prime Mover, 9/1 Please Please Me (IRE)(8/1—12/1), 14/1 Scarlet Princess, 16/1 Taunting (IRE), Tartar's Bow, Rosietoes (USA), ROYAL DARTMOUTH (USA), 20/1 Lucky Noire, Nazare Blue, 25/1 Nuclear Express, Aldahe, Rag Time Belle, 33/1 Asterix, King of Mileen, 50/1 Fast Operative, 66/1 Ors. CSF £242.57, CT £13,797.36. Tote £16.10: £4.10 £3.30 £16.10 £1.30 (£90.90). Axminster Carpets Limited (CULLOMPTON) bred by Craig B. Singer in USA. 21 Rn

1m 33.4 (0.9)

## 1340

GARDEN FESTIVAL CLAIMING STKS (3-Y.O) £1548.00 (£428.00: £204.00)
5f 16y

7-30 (7-33)

| 559 | **Echo-Logical (94)** (Fav) (JBerry) 9-7 PatEddery (2) (a gng wl: led over 2f out: v.easily) | —1 |
| 1006[6] | Shocking Times (59) (RSimpson) 7-8[1] ‡5ATucker (6) (swtg: rdn 3f out: hdwy over 1f out: no ch w wnr) | 5.2 |
| 1162 | Savalaro (53) (JFfitch-Heyes) 7-12 AMackay (4) (lw: w ldrs: one pce fnl 2f) | 2.3 |
| 899[6] | Beveled Edge (BPalling) 8-3[1] JWilliams (8) (lw: dwlt: nrst fin) | 1.4 |
| 1276 | Rivet (59) (bl) (MBlanshard) 8-5 JReid (7) (outpcd) | 2½.5 |
| 1138 | Belthorn (39) (JJBridger) 8-0 TyroneWilliams (3) (bit bkwd: led over 2f: wknd over 1f out) | 2.6 |
| 1040 | Spareathought (CNAllen) 7-12 GBardwell (5) (outpcd: t.o) | 6.7 |

40/95 ECHO-LOGICAL, 5/1 Savalaro, 10/1 Shocking Times, 12/1 Rivet, 25/1 Beveled Edge, 50/1 Spareathought, 66/1 Belthorn. CSF £5.16, Tote £1.50: £1.20 £2.40 (£5.10). The Liverpool Daily Post and Echo Ltd (COCKERHAM) bred by Mrs M. J. Dandy. 7 Rn

58 sec (1)

SF—57/10/6/7/–/–

## 1341

WORTHINGTON BEST BITTER H'CAP (0-70) £2337.50 (£650.00: £312.50)
1¼m 36y

8-00 (8-03)

| | **Muizenberg (62)** (JACEdwards) 5–9-9 ‡5DHarrison (7) (lw: hld up: hdwy over 3f out: led 2f out: comf) | —1 |
| 1106 | Tiger Claw (USA) (54) (RJHodges) 6–9-6 RCochrane (6) (lw: hld up: hdwy over 2f out: r.o ins fnl f) | 3½.2 |
| 1146 | Systematic (59) (RHannon) 3–8-12 MRoberts (16) (7th st: hdwy 4f out: ev ch 2f out: one pce) | ½.3 |
| 810 | Eleckydo (49) (RJHodges) 3–7-13 ‡3FNorton (4) (lw: hdwy over 2f out: r.o ins fnl f) | ½.4 |
| 1179 | St Athans Lad (45) (bl) (RCurtis) 4–8-11 GBardwell (15) (bit bkwd: chsd ldr: led over 5f out to 2f: sn btn) | 2.5 |
| 1008[2] | Premier Dance (44) (DHaydnJones) 5–8-10 AMunro (8) (8th st: hdwy on ins over 3f out: one pce fnl 3f) | nk.6 |
| 1125[3] | Famous Beauty (49) (RHollinshead) 5–8-8 ‡7DCarson (5) (dwlt: nrst fin) | nk.7 |
| 1143 | Give Me Hope (IRE) (37) (GHYardley) 4–8-3 JQuinn (14) (lw: 5th st: ev ch over 2f out: wknd over 1f out) | 2.8 |
| 831 | Merry Marigold (52) (JDRoberts) 6–9-4 JWilliams (9) (lw: nvr nr rdrs) | ½.9 |
| 999* | Spectacular Dawn (67) (Fav) (JLDunlop) 3–9-6 PatEddery (1) (rdn & nt clr run 3f out: hdwy 2f out: eased whn btn fnl f) | 2½.10 |
| 997 | Head Turner (39) (CPWildman) 4–8-5 CRutter (12) (bit bkwd: 6th st: wknd 3f out) | 1½.11 |

831 Hills of Hoy **(52)** *(KCBailey)* 6–9–4 JReid (9) (lw: 4th st: wknd over 2f out) ..... 1¹/₂.**12**
1041 Borram (IRE) **(58)** *(DNicholson)* 3–8–11 AClark (13) (a bhd) .............................. 4.**13**
    Emrys **(44)** *(DBurchell)* 9–8–5 ‡⁵KRutter (8) (bkwd: 3rd st: wknd 2f out) ........... 3.**14**
1087 Sam the Man **(43)** *(JFitch-Heyes)* 5–8–9 AMackay (3) (lw: a bhd: t.o) ........... 15.**15**
809 Beija Flor **(60)** *(FJordan)* 5–9–12 WNewnes (10) (led over 4f: 2nd st: wknd 4f
    out: t.o) ................................................................................................ **16**

**5/2** Spectacular Dawn, **6/1** Tiger Claw (USA), **13/2** Premier Dance, **8/1** Hills of Hoy, Merry Marigold(11/1—7/1),
**17/2** Famous Beauty(5/1—9/1), **11/1** Systematic(7/1—12/1), **20/1** MUIZENBERG, **40/1** Eleckydo, St Athans
Lad, **50/1** Ors. CSF £119.03, CT £1,254.14. Tote £20.40: £2.80 £1.90 £3.10 £9.20 (£161.50). Mr D. A. Davies
(ROSS-ON-WYE) bred by Tally Ho Stud Co Ltd. 16 Rn           2m 6.6 (2.3)
                                           SF—18/8/–/–/–/–

---

**1342**      E.B.F. OLIVIA STKS (Mdn 2-Y.O.F) £2920.20 (£812.20: £390.60)    **6f 16y** 8-30 (8-37)

**Bright Generation (IRE)** *(PFICole)* 8–11 AMunro (5) (lt-f: swvd rt s: hdwy 3f out:
    led 1f out: r.o wl) ....................................................................................... —**1**
    Latest Flame (IRE) *(MRChannon)* 8–11 PatEddery (16) (leggy: scope: led 5f: no
    ch w wnr) ................................................................................................ 6.**2**
    Toledo Queen **(Fav)** *(PWChapple-Hyam)* 8–11 JReid (4) (neat: lt-f: s.s:
    hdwy over 3f out: rdn over 1f out: one pce) ....................... 1.**3**
    Creative Flair (USA) *(PFICole)* 8–11 TQuinn (13) (unf: scope: bkwd: a.p: rdn
    over 3f out: r.o ins fnl f) ............................................................ hd.**4**
1149³ Fleur Power (IRE) *(BPalling)* 8-4 ‡⁷StephenDavies (7) (lw: no hdwy fnl 2f) ........ ¹/₂.**5**
    Fairylike (CAN) *(PFICole)* 8–11 CRutter (14) (w'like: bhd: rdn over 3f out: nvr nr
    to chal) ................................................................................................ 3.**6**
1161 Ascom Pager Too *(PHowling)* 8–11 JQuinn (1) (b.hind: no hdwy fnl 2f) .............. 3.**7**
907 Anifera *(R.IHodges)* 8-8 ‡³TSprake (10) (nvr trbld ldrs) ...................... s.h.**8**
    Polly Leach *(BRMillman)* 8–11 AMackay (15) (w'like: bkwd: prom 4f) ........... s.h.**9**
1279⁵ Is She Quick *(MrsJCDawe)* 8–11 JWilliams (6) (swtg: n.d) ...................... 3¹/₂.**10**
    Gloddaeth Isa *(JBerry)* 8–11 NCarlisle (11) (w'like: bkwd: prom 4f) ............ nk.**11**
    Gold Tassel *(RHannon)* 8–11 MRoberts (8) (lt-f: m.n.s) ...................... ¹/₂.**12**
    Blue Sombrero (IRE) *(RJHolder)* 8–11 NAdams (3) (w'like: bit bkwd: s.s: a bhd) nk.**13**
    Jafetica *(DRLaing)* 8–11 TyroneWilliams (17) (lt-f: b: swtg: w ldrs 4f) ......... 6.**14**
    Shropshire Blue *(RDickin)* 8–11 RCochrane (12) (unf: bkwd: m.n.s) ............ 2.**15**
    Dynavour House *(MWEckley)* 8–11 GeeArmytage (2) (leggy: lt-f: bkwd: s.s: a
    bhd: t.o) ................................................................................................ **16**
        852 Sedgy's Sister (25/1) Withdrawn (lame at s) : not under orders

**5/4** Toledo Queen (IRE)(tchd 2/1), **7/2** BRIGHT GENERATION (IRE)(5/1—3/1), **8/1** Latest Flame (IRE)(op 4/1),
**9/1** Gold Tassel, **12/1** Creative Flair (USA)(7/1—14/1), **16/1** Gloddaeth Isa, **20/1** Fleur Power (IRE), Fairylike
(CAN), **33/1** Is She Quick, **40/1** Jafetica, **66/1** Ors. CSF £29.90, Tote £5.00: £1.60 £2.40 £1.70 (£16.10). Mr
Fahd Salman (WHATCOMBE) bred by Newgate Stud Co in Ireland. 16 Rn      1m 10.3 (1.3)
                                     SF—35/17/13/12/–/–

---

**1343**      GOOD NIGHT H'CAP (0-70) £1786.00 (£496.00: £238.00)    **6f 16y**    9-00 (9-06)

967 Kirriemuir **(31)** *(KOCunningham-Brown)* 4–7–7 NCarlisle (13) (dwlt: hdwy 2f
    out: str run to ld last strides) ..................................................... —**1**
1160² Idir Linn (IRE) **(39)** (bl) **(Fav)** *(DJGMurray-Smith)* 4–8–1 CRutter (14) (lw: a.p:
    rdn over 2f out: led ins fnl f: ct last strides) ......................... hd.**2**
1278⁵ Queen's Tickle **(53)** (bl) *(APJarvis)* 3–8–6 SWhitworth (8) (b.nr hind: led over 5f:
    nt qckn) ................................................................................................ 1¹/₂.**3**
738 Proud Brigadier (IRE) **(51)** *(WCarter)* 4–8–13 RCochrane (2) (lw: hdwy over 2f
    out: ev ch over 1f out: nt qckn) ............................................. 1¹/₂.**4**
245² Inswinger **(33)** *(WGRWightman)* 6–7–7 GBardwell (16) (bit bkwd: chsd ldrs: rdn
    over 3f out: edgd rt over 1f out: r.o ins fnl f) ....................... 2.**5**
941 Old Comrades **(54)** *(LGCottrell)* 5–9–2 TRogers (6) (lw: swtg: rdn & hdwy 2f out:
    one pce fnl f) ........................................................................... s.h.**6**
1084 My Ruby Ring **(43)** *(DRLaing)* 5–8–5 TyroneWilliams (9) (b: b.hind: prom: rdn
    over 2f out: wknd over 1f out) ................................................ 2.**7**
    Amethystine (USA) **(64)** *(RJHodges)* 6–9–9 ‡³TSprake (12) (bkwd: prom 4f) ..... nk.**8**
1160⁶ Fay Eden (IRE) **(51)** *(RJHodges)* 4–8–6 JWilliams (11) (lw: a bhd) .......... s.h.**9**
1167 Luna Bid **(65)** *(MBlanshard)* 9–9–13 JReid (15) (bhd: hdwy whn hmpd over 1f
    out: nt rcvr) ........................................................................... 1¹/₂.**10**
1160⁵ Domiana **(34)** *(MBlanshard)* 4–7–10 JQuinn (5) (a bhd) ...................... 2.**11**
967⁶ Wessex Milord **(33)** *(JABennett)* 7–7–2⁽²⁾ ‡⁷ClaireBalding (3) (b: a bhd) ..... nk.**12**
1193 Prepare (IRE) **(44)** *(RJHolder)* 4–8–6 JWilliams (11) (lw: a bhd) ............ s.h.**13**
    Nikki Dow **(34)** *(PHowling)* 6–7–7⁽¹⁾ ‡³FNorton (7) (b: bkwd: a bhd) .......... 2¹/₂.**14**
735 Miss Bell Ringer **(42)** *(CJHill)* 4–8–1 ‡³DBiggs (1) (swvd lft s: a in rr: t.o) ......... 15.**15**
                    LONG HANDICAP: Wessex Milord 7-6.

**15/8** Idir Linn (IRE), **7/1** Inswinger, **8/1** Old Comrades, My Ruby Ring, Luna Bid, **12/1** Fay Eden (IRE), **14/1** Proud Brigadier (IRE), Queen's Tickle, Prepare (IRE), **20/1** Amethystine (USA), Domiana, **33/1** Miss Bell Ringer, **50/1** KIRRIEMUIR & Ors. CSF £138.25, CT £1,356.53. Tote £81.20: £12.00 £1.60 £4.40 (£1,265.50). Mr R. N. Short (STOCKBRIDGE) bred by Dr W. J. Heffernan. 15 Rn

          1m 9.9 (0.9)
SF—25/32/32/32/6/16

T/Plpt: £244.10 (10.65 Tckts).

          KH

## 1164—NEWBURY (L-H)

### Thursday, June 11th [Good to firm]

Going Allowance: St: minus 0.20 sec; Rnd: nil sec per fur (F)        Wind: nil

Stalls: 3rd & 4th low, remainder high

### 1344

CORK GULLY APP'CE H'CAP (0-90) £3318.75 (£990.00: £343.13 each)
1m (st)                        2-00 (2-02)

| | | |
|---|---|---|
| 1106⁴ | **Camden's Ransom (USA) (66)** (Fav) (DRCElsworth) 5-8-9 ‡³RossBerry (3) (led over 4f: led ins fnl f: r.o wl) | —1 |
| 1195³ | Aardvark (67) (RMWhitaker) 6-8-13 GParkin (5) (swtg: a.p: rdn over 2f out: led over 1f out tl ins fnl f) | 1¹/₂.2 |
| 983 | Strong Suit (IRE) (90) (RHannon) 3-9-11 MarkDenaro (1) (lw: hdwy 2f out: ev ch 1f out: nt qckn) | hd.3 |
| 1106 | Mulciber (72) (GHarwood) 4-9-4 PHoughton (7) (a.p: led 3f out tl over 1f out: one pce) | d.h.3 |
| 1018³ | Charming Gift (52) (RJRWilliams) 5-7-12 GMitchell (2) (hdwy 2f out: one pce fnl f) | 1¹/₂.5 |
| 1058 | Shot Stopper (64) (MJHeaton-Ellis) 4-8-7 ‡³RuthCoulter (4) (lw: nvr nr to chal) | 3¹/₂.6 |
| | Keep Your Word (59) (GBBalding) 6-8-5⁽¹⁾ TraceyPurseglove (8) (prom 6f) | 5.7 |
| 1201 | Foolish Touch (61) (v) (WJMusson) 10-8-7 PBowe (6) (b: lw: hdwy 3f out: hrd rdn 2f out: sn wknd) | 2.8 |

**7/2** CAMDEN'S RANSOM (USA), **9/2** Foolish Touch, Charming Gift, **5/1** Aardvark, **7/1** Strong Suit, **10/1** Shot Stopper, **14/1** Ors. CSF £18.86, CT R, A & SS £47.78, CR A & M £89.56. Tote £4.50: £1.70 £1.20 SS £1.00 M £1.80 (£8.40). Mr Bob Cullen (WHITSBURY) bred by Dr and Mrs Chris Elia and Phil Needham in USA. 8 Rn

          1m 39.90 (2.90)
SF—28/27/38/28/6/4

### 1345

GEORGE SMITH MEMORIAL H'CAP (3-Y-O) (0-100) £5253.50 (£1568.00: £749.00: £339.50)   **6f 8y**              2-35 (2-37)

| | | |
|---|---|---|
| 851⁵ | Sunday's Hill (99) (MBlanshard) 9-7 JReid (10) (lw: a.p: led ins fnl f: drvn out) | —1 |
| 1157 | Thrie-Na-Helah (IRE) (73) (v) (RMWhitaker) 7-9 DaleGibson (6) (w ldrs: ev ch fnl f: r.o) | nk.2 |
| 870 | Windpower (IRE) (85) (JBerry) 8-7 GCarter (4) (lw: hdwy over 2f out: led over 1f out tl ins fnl f) | hd.3 |
| 1117³ | Truthful Image (73) (bl) (MJRyan) 7-9 GBardwell (9) (swtchd rt wl over 1f out: hdwy fnl f: nvr nrr) | s.h.4 |
| 935* | Milagro (87) (Fav) (RHannon) 8-9 MRoberts (2) (led over 4f out tl over 1f out) | 3¹/₂.5 |
| 941 | Jigsaw Boy (78) (RJHolder) 8-0 NAdams (7) (lw: no hdwy fnl 2f) | 3.6 |
| 1060 | Bold Memory (99) (DRCElsworth) 9-7 SCauthen (5) (b.hind: swtg: led over 1f: wknd 2f out) | 3.7 |
| | Spell of the Yukon (USA) (79) (IABalding) 7-12 ‡³SO'Gorman (8) (a bhd) | 5.8 |
| 2277⁴ | Trove (89) (bl) (MrsNMacauley) 8-11 LDettori (1) (outpcd) | 6.9 |

**3/1** Milagro, **4/1** Bold Memory, **6/1** Windpower (IRE)(op 9/1), **7/1** Trove, **9/1** Thrie-Na-Helah (IRE), **10/1** Truthful Image, Jigsaw Boy, **12/1** SUNDAY'S HILL, **14/1** Spell of the Yukon (USA). CSF £99.20, CT £643.78. Tote £16.30: £2.90 £2.20 £2.00 (£37.90). Mr Stanley Hinton (UPPER LAMBOURN) bred by R. A. and J. H. Popely. 9 Rn

          1m 12.83 (1.03)
SF—62/35/46/33/33/12

### 1346

COOPERS & LYBRAND SUMMER H'CAP (3-Y-O) (0-90) £6810.00 (£2040.00: £980.00: £450.00)   **1¹/₂m 5y**          3-10 (3-12)

(Weights raised 5 lb)

| | | |
|---|---|---|
| 848³ | Inchcailloch (IRE) (85) (Fav) (RCharlton) 9-7 PatEddery (1) (lw: mde all: r.o wl) | —1 |
| 693⁶ | Sadler's Way (75) (GLewis) 8-11 PaulEddery (3) (4th st: rdn over 3f out: chsd wnr fnl f: no imp) | 1¹/₂.2 |
| 1027 | Jupiter Moon (73) (CEBrittain) 8-9 AMunro (2) (lw: 2nd st: ev ch 2f out: r.o one pce) | ³/₄.3 |
| | Valseur (USA) (75) (MrsJCecil) 8-11 JReid (7) (lw: 6th st: one pce fnl 2f) | 1¹/₂.4 |

1068 Judge and Jury **(65)** (bl) *(MJFetherston-Godley)* 7-10 ‡5DHarrison (6) (hdwy on
ins 3f out: wknd over 1f out) ............................................... ³/₄.**5**
816 Stani (USA) **(82)** *(BHanbury)* 9-4 WRSwinburn (8) (lw: 3rd st: wknd 2f out) ....... 6.**6**
511 Regal Lover (IRE) **(70)** *(MBell)* 8-6 MHills (4) (5th st: wknd over 3f out) ........... sh.**7**
848² Poinciana **(72)** *(RHannon)* 8-8 MRoberts (5) (a bhd: hrd rdn 3f out: no rspnse) hd.**8**

**11/4** INCHCAILLOCH (IRE), **3/1** Poinciana, **5/1** Stani (USA), **6/1** Valseur (USA), **9/1** Judge and Jury, Sadler's
Way, **16/1** Regal Lover (IRE), **20/1** Jupiter Moon. CSF £24.20, CT £365.92. Tote £2.70: £1.40 £2.00 £5.70
(£10.40). Sir Philip Oppenheimer (BECKHAMPTON) bred by Hascombe and Valiant Studs in Ireland. 8 Rn
2m 33.68 (3.98)
SF—67/54/50/49/32/52

---

**1347** BALLYMACOLL STUD STKS (listed race) (3-Y.O.F) £10965.00 (£3270.00: £1560.00:
£705.00)  1¼m 6y
3-45 (3-47)

1101a⁵ **Feminine Wiles (IRE) (105)** *(PWChapple-Hyam)* 8-9 PaulEddery (7) (lw: 2nd
st: led over 2f out: all out) ................................................... —**1**
710² Yildiz *(BWHills)* 8-9 MHills (1) (lw: led 3f: 3rd st: rallied over 1f out: ev ch ins fnl f:
r.o) ............................................................................................ s.h.**2**
850² Jezebel Monroe (USA) **(97)** *(RCharlton)* 8-9 WRSwinburn (3) (4th st: ev ch over
1f out: nt qckn) ....................................................................... 1½.**3**
1180★ Bineyah (IRE) (Fav) *(MRStoute)* 8-9 PatEddery (6) (led after 3f tl over 2f out) ..... 4.**4**
553 Gong *(PTWalwyn)* 8-9 RCochrane (2) (5th st: wknd over 2f out) .................. 3½.**5**
Solar Star (USA) **(108)** *(MBell)* 8-9 AMunro (4) (7th st: a bhd) ........................ nk.**6**
1101a Cottonwood *(LordHuntingdon)* 8-9 LDettori (5) (6th st: a bhd) ...................... hd.**7**

**9/4** Bineyah (IRE), **11/4** Jezebel Monroe (USA), **9/2** FEMININE WILES (IRE), **6/1** Solar Star (USA)(op 12/1), **8/1**
Yildiz, **9/1** Cottonwood, **33/1** Gong. CSF £34.53, Tote £5.80: £2.90 £2.80 (£21.60). Mr R. E. Sangster
(MARLBOROUGH) bred by Barronstown Bloodstock Ltd in Ireland. 7 Rn
2m 6.54 (3.54)
SF—60/59/56/48/46/45/44

---

**1348** KINGSCLERE STKS (2-Y.O) £5162.50 (£1540.00: £735.00: £332.50)
6f 8y
4-20 (4-22)

**Perfect Halo (USA)** *(PFICole)* 8-7 TQuinn (2) (leggy: scope: hdwy u.p: stdy
hdwy 2f out: led ins fnl f: pushed out) ................................. —**1**
Redenham (USA) *(RHannon)* 8-7 JReid (6) (unf: scope: led: edgd lft & hdd ins
fnl f) ........................................................................................ 1½.**2**
1056★ White Crown (USA) *(BHanbury)* 8-11 WRSwinburn (7) (swtg: a.p: r.o one pce
fnl 2f) ..................................................................................... 2½.**3**
Manila Bay (USA) (Fav) *(MBell)* 8-7 AMunro (4) (leggy: a.p: rdn 2f out: nt qckn) 3.**4**
Bagalino (USA) *(RCharlton)* 8-7 PatEddery (8) (w'like: scope: hld up: effrt over
2f out: sn btn) ........................................................................ 3½.**5**
Eleusis (FR) *(PWChapple-Hyam)* 8-7 PaulEddery (5) (str: scope: bkwd: no
hdwy fnl 2f) .............................................................................. 1½.**6**
Ribbold *(CEBrittain)* 8-7 MRoberts (3) (unf: scope: prom 3f: wknd qckly) ........... 4.**7**
Shiro *(RJRWilliams)* 8-9 RCochrane (1) (w'like: bit bkwd: wl bhd fnl 3f) .......... 3½.**8**

**15/8** Manila Bay (USA), **9/2** PERFECT HALO (USA), **5/1** White Crown (USA), **7/1** Bagalino (USA), Redenham
(USA), **8/1** Eleusis (FR), **12/1** Ribbold, **16/1** Shiro. CSF £33.40, Tote £6.40: £1.90 £2.50 £1.80 (£24.80). Mr
Fahd Salman (WHATCOMBE) bred by Echo Valley Horse Farm Inc in USA. 8 Rn
1m 12.70 (0.90)
SF—51/45/39/23/9/3

---

**1349** E.B.F. KENNETT STKS (Mdn 2-Y.O.C & G) £3817.50 (£1140.00: £545.00: £247.50)
6f 8y
4-55 (4-57)

**Chaddleworth (IRE)** (Fav) *(PWChapple-Hyam)* 9-0 JReid (5) (lengthy: lw: a
gng wl: led over 1f out: comf) ............................................. —**1**
Needle Gun (IRE) *(CEBrittain)* 9-0 SCauthen (3) (leggy: chsd ldr: rdn over 1f
out: r.o: no ch w wnr) ......................................................... 3½.**2**
828 Finavon *(IABalding)* 9-0 RCochrane (1) (led over 4f) ..................................... ³/₄.**3**
Contract Court (USA) *(CACyzer)* 9-0 TQuinn (4) (w'like: bkwd: no hdwy fnl 2f) .. 8.**4**
Baulking Towers *(MMcCormack)* 9-0 WNewnes (2) (wl grwn: prom over 3f) .... 15.**5**
Rusty Raja *(RHannon)* 9-0 WRSwinburn (7) (wl grwn: bit bkwd: nvr nr to chal) .. 8.**6**
Colonial Heights (IRE) *(RHannon)* 9-0 PatEddery (6) (unf: scope: lw: dwlt:
hdwy 4f out: wknd over 2f out) .............................................. 3.**7**

**4/6** CHADDLEWORTH (IRE), **5/1** Needle Gun (IRE)(4/1—6/1), **13/2** Colonial Heights (IRE), **9/1** Finavon(op 5/1),
**10/1** Rusty Raja(op 5/1), **20/1** Ors. CSF £4.87, Tote £1.70: £1.40 £2.40 (£4.50). Mr R. E. Sangster
(MARLBOROUGH) bred by Barronstown Bloodstock Ltd in Ireland. 7 Rn
1m 13.53 (1.73)
SF—41/27/24/–/–/–

T/Trio: Race 2: £127.70 (6.3 Tckts). T/Jkpt: £52,213.70 (1.2 Tckts). T/Plpt: £350.30 (19.1 Tckts).      Hn

839a—**LEOPARDSTOWN (L-H)**

**Monday, June 1st [Good]**

Going Allowance: St: minus 0.40 sec; Rest: minus 0.15 sec (F)

**1350a**     CARA BALLYOGAN STKS (Gp 3)    £13668.00   **5f**

| | | |
|---|---|---|
| 819* | **FREDDIE LLOYD (USA)** *(NACallaghan)* 3-8-8 JReid (mde all: clr fr ½-wy) ....... | —1 |
| 1096a² | Maledetto (IRE) *(Ireland)* 3-8-8 CRoche (bhd: rdn ½-wy: hdwy 2f out: r.o u.p ins fnl f) | 1.2 |
| | Flowing (USA) (Fav) *(Ireland)* 4-9-5 MJKinane (in tch: chsd ldr: no imp fr wl over 1f out: kpt on) | hd.3 |
| 1096a⁴ | Title Roll (IRE) *(Ireland)* 4-9-5 SCraine (bhd: hdwy ½-wy: no imp fr over 1f out: styd on) | 4½.4 |
| | Clandolly (IRE) *(Ireland)* 4-9-0 DVSmith (prom: rdn 2f out: wknd over 1f out) .... | 3.5 |
| 656⁴ | Food of Love *(Ireland)* 4-9-0 PShanahan (in tch: rdn after ½-wy: no imp wl over 1f out) | 3½.6 |
| | Bradawn Breever (IRE) (bl) *(Ireland)* 3-9-5 RJGriffiths (gd early spd: mid div ½-wy: sn no imp) | hd.7 |
| | Jambo Jambo (IRE) (bl) *(Ireland)* 4-9-0 RHughes (in tch: rdn ½-wy: no imp) .... | 3.8 |

**7/4** Flowing (USA), **3/1** Maledetto (IRE), **5/1** Title Roll (IRE), **6/1** FREDDIE LLOYD (USA), **7/1** Food of Love, **10/1** Bradawn Breever (IRE), **20/1** Jambo Jambo (IRE), **25/1** Clandolly (IRE). Tote £7.10: £1.60 £1.50 £1.30 (£11.70). Mr Michael Hill (NEWMARKET) bred by Jerry M.Cutrona Snr in USA. 8 Rn     58 sec (U.1)

SF–74/70/80/62/45/31

**1351a**     COMPAQ GLENCAIRN STKS (listed race)    £7850.00   **1m 1f**

| | | |
|---|---|---|
| | **Approach The Bench (IRE)** *(Ireland)* 4-8-12 JReid ............................................. | —1 |
| | Committed Dancer (USA) *(Ireland)* 3-9-3 MJKinane ...................................... | ¾.2 |
| 954a | Dowland (IRE) *(Ireland)* 4-9-2 PVGilson .................................................... | ½.3 |
| | Kooyonga (IRE) *(Ireland)* 4-9-7 WJO'Connor (btn further 1¾/4l) ..................... | 5 |

Tote £7.50: £2.10 £2.90 £5.50 (£41.90). Mr J.E.Mulhern (J.E.Mulhern,IRELAND) bred by Swettenham Stud in Ireland. 8 Rn     1m 52.9 (2.4)

SF–42/45/42

**CHANTILLY (R-H)**

**Thursday, June 4th [Soft]**

Going Allowance: minus 0.30 sec per fur (F)

**1352a**     PRIX DU GROS-CHENE (Gp 2) (C & F) £25800.00   **5f**

| | | |
|---|---|---|
| 656* | **Monde Bleu** (Fav) *(France)* 4-9-2 DBoeuf (s.s: hdwy to ld 1f out: r.o wl: comf) . | —1 |
| | Showbrook (IRE) *(France)* 3-8-13 CBlack (mid div: effrt on ins wl over 1f out: gd late hdwy: r.o) | 1.2 |
| | Wedding of the Sea (USA) *(France)* 3-8-3 MdeSmyter (broke wl: led 4f: faltered nr fin) | 1.3 |
| | Irish Shoal (USA) *(France)* 4-8-13 CAsmussen (a cl up: one pce fnl f) .............. | 2.4 |
| 284a* | Rayon Bleu (FR) *(France)* 5-8-13 MBoutin (hld up: effrt fr 2f out: r.o wl) ......... | 3.5 |
| | Regal Scintilla (bl) *(France)* 3-8-6 GGuignard (hld up: sme late hdwy) ............. | ¾.6 |
| | La Pitie (USA) *(France)* 3-8-3 PBruneau (prom: ev ch 2f out: sn wknd) .............. | 1.7 |
| | Ski Chief (USA) *(France)* 4-9-2 SCauthen (s.i.s: a outpcd) ................................ | nk.8 |
| | Maratha (USA) *(France)* 3-8-3 ODoleuze (m.n.s) ............................................. | 6.9 |
| | Another Charger (IRE) *(France)* 3-8-6 NJeanpierre (n.d) ................................. | hd.10 |

**19/10** MONDE BLEU, **5/2** Ski Chief (USA), **21/4** Showbrook (IRE), **6/1** Maratha (USA), **17/2** Wedding of the Sea (USA), **10/1** Irish Shoal (USA), **19/1** Rayon Bleu (FR), **20/1** Regal Scintilla, **22/1** La Pitie (USA), **41/1** Another Charger (IRE). Tote 2.90f: 1.30f 2.00f 2.00f (15.20f). Mr D.Wildenstein (A.Fabre,FRANCE) bred by Dayton Ltd. 10 Rn     59.1 sec (U.6)

SF–84/77/63/65/53/43

1095a—**CURRAGH (R-H)**

**Saturday, June 6th [Good to soft]**

Going Allowance: 5f-7f: 0.20 sec (G); Rest: 0.40 sec per fur (Y)

**1353a**     OAKS TRIAL (listed race) (3-Y.O.F) £7738.00   **1m 3f**

| | | |
|---|---|---|
| | **Misako Togo (USA)** *(Ireland)* 3-9-3 MJKinane .............................................. | —1 |
| | Pollys Glow (IRE) *(Ireland)* 3-8-12 KJManning ............................................. | 1½.2 |
| | Gorgeous Dancer (IRE) *(Ireland)* 3-8-12 WJSupple ...................................... | ¾.3 |

Tote £5.90: £2.50 £5.40 £3.70 (£42.10). Mr Allen E.Paulson (D.K.Weld,IRELAND) bred by Allen E.Paulson in USA. 8 Rn     2m 29.8 (13.5)

SF–12/–/–

## 1354a    GALLINULE STKS (Gp 2) (3-Y.O.C & F) £21495.00   1¼m

| | |
|---|---|
| 953a³ **Brief Truce (USA)** (Fav) *(Ireland)* 3–8–11 MJKinane (prom: pushed along st: chal to ld wl over 1f out: kpt on wl) | —1 |
| 840a² Firing Line (IRE) (bl) *(Ireland)* 3–8–11 SCraine (led: hdd & no ex u.p wl over 1f out: kpt on) | 1.2 |
| Nordic Brief (IRE) *(Ireland)* 3–8–11 WJSupple (hld up: hdwy 4f out: no imp 2f out: styd on) | 3.3 |
| Mining Tycoon (IRE) *(Ireland)* 3–8–11 KJManning (prom: rdn & chal st: no ex u.p fr 2f out: wknd ins fnl f) | 6.4 |
| Home Counties (IRE) (bl) *(Ireland)* 3–8–11 JPMurtagh (s.i.s: bhd: rdn bef st: no imp fr 2f out) | 1½.5 |
| Hereafter (USA) (bl) *(Ireland)* 3–8–11 DHogan (mid div: rdn st: n.d) | 7.6 |

1/2 BRIEF TRUCE (USA), 4/1 Firing Line (IRE), 6/1 Nordic Brief (IRE), 9/1 Mining Tycoon (IRE), 12/1 Home Counties (IRE), 20/1 Hereafter (USA). Tote £1.20: £1.20 £1.80 (£2.60). Moyglare Stud Farms Ltd (D.K.Weld,IRELAND) bred by Moyglare Stud Farm Ltd in USA. 6 Rn    2m 9 (6)
SF—77/75/69/57/54/40

## BELMONT PARK (L-H)
### Saturday, June 6th [Good]

## 1355a    BELMONT STKS (Grade 1) (3-Y.O.C & F) £267379.00   1½m (dirt)

| | |
|---|---|
| **A P Indy (USA)** *(America)* 3–9–0 EDelahoussaye | —1 |
| 722★ MY MEMOIRS *(RHannon)* 3–9–0 JBailey | ¾.2 |
| Pine Bluff (USA) *(America)* 3–9–0 CMcCarron | nk.3 |

Tote 4.20 (1-2) 3.80 11.60 (1-2-3) 3.00 6.60 4.20 (Exacta (2 dol) 73.20). Mr T.Tsurumaki (N.Drysdale,AMERICA) bred by W.S.Farish & W.J.Kilroy in USA. 11 Rn    2m 26.1

## 1352a—CHANTILLY (R-H)
### Sunday, June 7th [Good]
Going Allowance: 0.05 sec per fur (G)

## 1356a    PRIX DU JOCKEY-CLUB LANCIA (Gp 1) (3-Y.O.C & F) £257998.00   1½m

| | |
|---|---|
| 1094a³ **Polytain (FR)** *(France)* 3–9–2 LDettori (hld up: hdwy st: chal & led wl over 1f out: styd on wl) | —1 |
| Marignan (USA) (Jt-Fav) *(France)* 3–9–2 DBoeuf (hld up: gd hdwy fr 2f out: swvd & str run on outside fnl f: r.o wl) | 1½.2 |
| 959a² Contested Bid (USA) *(France)* 3–9–2 PatEddery (hld up: chal st: kpt on wl fnl f) | ¾.3 |
| 959a★ Johann Quatz (FR) *(France)* 3–9–2 FHead (a cl up: n.m.r & sltly hmpd 2f out: chal 1f out: one pce) | ¾.4 |
| 843a⁵ Modhish (IRE) *(France)* 3–9–2 MJKinane (a.p: chal on ins & led 2f out: hdd wl over 1f out: one pce ins fnl f) | 2.5 |
| 1015★ BINKHALDOUN (USA) *(HThomsonJones)* 3–9–2 RHills (mid div: chal on outside 2f out: swtchd & one pce fnl f) | nose.6 |
| 959a³ Apple Tree (FR) *(France)* 3–9–2 TJarnet (unruly bef s: a cl up on ins: chal & one pce fr 2f out) | 2½.7 |
| 843a★ Adieu Au Roi (IRE) *(France)* 3–9–2 MBoutin (unruly s: hld up in rr: gd hdwy u.p st: nvr nrr) | nk.8 |
| Dajraan (IRE) *(France)* 3–9–2 SCauthen (cl up: chal & one pce st: grad wknd) | s.h.9 |
| 837a² Paix Blanche (FR) (Jt-Fav) *(France)* 3–8–13 ALequeux (mid div: n.m.r 3f out: nvr nrr) | nk.10 |
| 959a⁴ Silver Kite (USA) *(France)* 3–9–2 SGuillot (mid div: one pce st: n.d) | 2.11 |
| 711² JAPE (USA) *(PFICole)* 3–9–2 AMunro (led to 2f out: one pce & grad wknd fnl f) | ½.12 |
| 843a² Glanville (USA) *(France)* 3–9–2 WMongil (effrt st: nvr nrr) | ½.13 |
| Jamshid (JPN) *(France)* MdeSmyter (n.d) | 3.14 |
| 1094a★ Break Bread (USA) *(France)* 3–9–2 CAsmussen (hld up: one pce st: nvr nrr) | nk.15 |
| 843a³ Prince Polino (USA) *(France)* ELegrix (prom tl st: wknd & t.o fnl 2f) | 20.16 |
| 635a★ Grand Plaisir (IRE) *(France)* 3–9–2 GGuignard (prom tl rdn & wknd st: t.o: fin lame) | dist.17 |

4/1 Paix Blanche (FR), Marignan (USA), 5/1 Apple Tree (FR), 21/4 Johann Quatz (FR), 35/4 Modhish (IRE), Dajraan (IRE), 9/1 Break Bread (USA), 10/1 Grand Plaisir (FR), 14/1 Contested Bid (USA), Jape (USA), 16/1 Adieu Au Roi (IRE), 27/1 Prince Polino (USA), 33/1 Glanville (USA), 37/1 POLYTAIN (FR), 40/1 Binkhaldoun (USA), 48/1 Silver Kite (USA), 52/1 Jamshid (JPN). Tote 37.50f: 8.20f 3.40f 4.60f (314.90f). Mrs B.Houillion (A.Spanu,FRANCE) bred by SNC Lagardere Elevage in France. 17 Rn    2m 30.3 (2.3)
SF—85/80/78/74/73/68/67

### 1357a

PRIX DE SANDRINGHAM (Gp 3) (3-Y.O.F) £20640.00    **1m**

|  | **Marble Maiden** *(France)* 3–8–11  SCauthen | —1 |
| 958a[2] | Hydro Calido *(USA) (France)* 3–8–11  FHead | nk.2 |
| 380a[2] | Royale Bobbe *(FR) (France)* 3–8–11  CLeScrill | 1.3 |

Tote 3.90f: 1.40f 1.10f (SF: 9.90f). Sheikh Mohammed (A.Fabre,FRANCE) bred by Sheikh Mohammed bin Rashid al Maktoum. 5 Rn
1m 39.5 (2.8)
SF—61/60/57

### 1101a—SAN SIRO  (R-H)
#### Sunday, June 7th [Heavy]

### 1358a

TROFEO CINO DEL DUCA (listed race)    £20930.00    **1½m**

|  | **Erdelistan (FR)** *(Italy)* 5–8–11  JHeloury | —1 |
| 929 | HALF A TICK *(USA) (PFlCole)* 4–8–11  TQuinn | 1.2 |
|  | Tarvisio *(Italy)* 5–8–11  SDettori | 1¾.3 |
| 929 | HAILSHAM *(CAN) (CEBrittain)* 4–8–11  MRoberts (btn further 7¾l) | 6 |

Tote 22L: 17L 22L (70L). Lady M.Stable (L.d'Auria,ITALY) bred by Aga Khan in France. 7 Rn    2m 35.1

### 1359a

PREMIO EMILIO TURATI (Gp 2)    £41860.00    **1m**

|  | **Misil (USA)** *(Italy)* 4–9–3  GDettori | —1 |
| 842a[5] | Judge Decision *(FR) (France)* 3–8–7  WRSwinburn | 7.2 |
| 956a★ | SIKESTON *(USA) (CEBrittain)* 6–9–3  MRoberts | nose.3 |

Tote 46L: 14L 12L 12L (65L). Scuderia Laghi (V.Caruso,ITALY) bred by G.Watts Humphrey in USA. 8 Rn
1m 40.8

### 1012—DONCASTER  (L-H)
#### Friday, June 12th [Good to firm]
Going Allowance: minus 0.40 sec per fur (F)    Wind: slt bhd

Stalls: high

### 1360

HOLMFIRTH STKS (2-Y.O) £1478.00 (£408.00: £194.00)    **5f**    6-45 (6-46)

|  | **In Case (USA)** (Fav) *(RCharlton)* 8-11 PatEddery (3) (w'like: str: bkwd: a.p: jnd ldr 1f out: shkn up to ld last stride) | —1 |
| 859[4] | My Bonus *(DJSCosgrove)* 8-8 ‡5DHarrison (2) (chsd ldrs: led over 1f out: ct post) | s.h.2 |
| 817 | Isotonic *(GMMoore)* 9-2 KFallon (4) (swtg: prom: rdn 2f out: r.o one pce) | 4.3 |
| 877[4] | Daaniera (IRE) (bl) *(JBerry)* 9-4 JCarroll (1) (lw: racd alone centre: led: drifted lft & hdd over 1f out: sn btn) | 3.4 |
|  | La Madrigal *(JWharton)* 8-6 MBirch (5) (bkwd: spd stands' side 3f) | 1.5 |
| 1118[4] | Bold County *(MJohnston)* 8-13 DMcKeown (6) (swtg: s.s: a bhd & outpcd) | 1.6 |

**6/4** IN CASE (USA)(op 4/5), **2/1** Daaniera (IRE), **8/1** My Bonus, **10/1** Bold County, La Madrigal, **20/1** Isotonic. CSF £11.56, Tote £2.30: £1.20 £1.80 £1.70 £1.80 (£4.90). Mr K. Abdulla (BECKHAMPTON) bred by Overbrook Farm, Eaton & Tally Ho Farms in USA. 6 Rn
59.26 sec (0.56)
SF—46/42/34/24/8/11

### 1361

EASTSIDE MAGAZINE H'CAP (0-80) £1744.00 (£484.00: £232.00)    7-15 (7-15)
**2m 110y**

| 1022[3] | **Farsi (78)** (bl) (Fav) *(RHollinshead)* 4-9-12 WRyan (4) (hld up: stdy hdwy 6f out: 3rd st: led wl over 1f out: sn clr) | —1 |
| 1125 | Sonic Signal (47) (v) *(MJHaynes)* 6-7-7[3] ‡3FNorton (3) (lw: wnt 2nd ½-wy: led 5f out tl ins fnl f: kpt on: no ch w wnr) | 3.2 |
| 1125[6] | Caroles Clown (44) *(MJHaynes)* 6-7-0 ‡7DToole (6) (hld up: hdwy 4f out: styd on ins fnl f: nvr nr) | ¾.3 |
| 987[4] | Magsood (56) (bl) *(SMellor)* 7-8-5 DanaMellor (5) (lw: hld up: 6th st: styd on one pce fnl 2f) | 1½.4 |
| 1108 | Megan's Flight (50) (v) *(THCaldwell)* 7-7-8 ‡5NKennedy (1) (prom: 2nd & rdn st: wknd over 2f out) | 20.5 |
| 990 | Green Lane (USA) (77) *(IABalding)* 4-9-4 ‡7DGriffiths (7) (lw: prom tl 5th & wkng st: t.o) | 10.6 |
|  | Ibn Sina (USA) (50) *(RO'Leary)* 5-7-13 LCharnock (2) (bit bkwd: led tl hdd 5f out: 4th & wkng st: t.o) | 3½.7 |
| 1190★ | Cost Effective (44) (v) *(MBrittain)* 5-7-7 (4x) JLowe (8) (prom tl wknd over 4f out: t.o) | 2.8 |

LONG HANDICAP: Sonic Signal 7-3, Caroles Clown 6-8, Cost Effective 6-9.

**13/8** FARSI, **7/2** Green Lane (USA), **5/1** Cost Effective, **13/2** Sonic Signal, **10/1** Magsood, **12/1** Caroles Clown, **33/1** Ors. CSF £11.65, CT £82.18. Tote £2.70: £1.30 £1.70 £2.40 (£7.20). Mr J. F. Bower (UPPER LONGDON) bred by Lord Howard de Walden. 8 Rn　　　　　3m 34.44 (1.63 under best; 5.44)

---

### 1362　WHITBY CLAIMING STKS　£1632.00 (£452.00: £216.00)　1¹/₂m　7-45 (7-45)

| | | |
|---|---|---|
| 951⁵ | **Kirby Opportunity (56)** *(JPearce)* 4–8-7 ‡⁵RPrice (7) (chsd ldrs: 3rd st: led over 2f out: sn clr) | —1 |
| 1083³ | Maryland Willie *(NACallaghan)* 5–9-2 PatEddery (8) (b: led 7f out tl over 2f out: sn rdn: one pce) | 8.2 |
| 1234⁴ | Feeling Foolish (IRE) **(54)** (bl) *(TFairhurst)* 3–7-11 ‡³JFanning (5) (lw: hld up: 4th st: rdn 3f out: one pce) | 2.3 |
| 1255* | Firefighter **(70)** (Fav) *(RHollinshead)* 3–8-10 WRyan (1) (lw: hld up: hdwy & 6th st: rdn 2f out: no imp) | 2.4 |
| 1125 | Angelica Park **(46)** *(JWharton)* 6–8-8 ‡⁷SWilliams (9) (hld up: effrt over 2f out: no imp) | 7.5 |
| 902 | Taurian Princess *(ANLee)* 3–7-1 ‡⁷CHawksley (4) (lw: s.s: sn rcvrd: 5th st: wknd 3f out) | 4.6 |
| | Custardorcream *(RonaldThompson)* 5–9-4 LCharnock (6) (bit bkwd: led 5f: wknd over 3f out) | 3.7 |
| 1070 | Tauzio (IRE) *(JMackie)* 4–9-9 MBirch (2) (bit bkwd: prom over 8f: sn lost tch: t.o) | 6.8 |
| 1016⁶ | Foursingh **(41)** (bl) *(CBBBooth)* 4–9-2 ACulhane (3) (lw: chsd ldrs: 2nd st: wknd over 3f out: t.o) | 15.9 |

**7/4** Firefighter(op Evens), **11/4** Maryland Willie, **9/2** KIRBY OPPORTUNITY, **9/1** Feeling Foolish (IRE), **10/1** Angelica Park, **33/1** Foursingh, Taurian Princess, **50/1** Ors. CSF £15.53, Tote £6.40: £1.80 £1.70 £1.30 (£6.60). Mr Peter Bradley (NEWMARKET) bred by Highfield Stud Ltd. 9 Rn　　2m 32.18 (1.58)
SF—29/22/–/8/–/–

---

### 1363　YORKSHIRE TELEVISION H'CAP (3-Y.O.F) (0-90) £2532.00 (£702.00: £336.00)
### 1m (rnd)　　8-15 (8-16)

(Weights raised 4 lb)

| | | |
|---|---|---|
| 401⁴ | Olette **(73)** *(GWragg)* 8-12 MHills (3) (made all: hrd rdn fnl f: all out) | —1 |
| 1146² | Elanmatina (IRE) **(74)** (Fav) *(CFWall)* 8-13 NDay (5) (lw: hld up: 4th st: effrt u.p 2f out: unable qckn ins fnl f) | 2.2 |
| 970 | Greetland Folly **(82)** (v) *(RMWhitaker)* 9-7 ACulhane (1) (lw: s.i.s: hld up: 7th st: gd hdwy 2f out: rdn & nt qckn fnl f) | nk.3 |
| 970 | Wild Strawberry **(77)** *(JMPEustace)* 9-2 MTebbutt (7) (prom: 2nd st: shkn up over 2f out: one pce) | 3.4 |
| 1115* | Round the River **(70)** *(WWHaigh)* 8-9 DMcKeown (2) (prom: 3rd st: rdn 2f out: n.m.r ins fnl f: nt rcvr) | 1¹/₂.5 |
| 1055 | Ferrovia **(54)** *(JWWatts)* 7-7 JLowe (4) (swtg: hld up: 6th st: effrt 3f out: wknd ins fnl f) | hd.6 |
| | El Rabab (USA) **(71)** *(HThomsonJones)* 8-10 RHills (6) (hld up: 5th st: reminders 3f out: no imp) | 6.7 |

LONG HANDICAP: Ferrovia 7-6.

**5/2** Elanmatina (IRE), **7/2** OLETTE, **4/1** El Rabab (USA), Round by the River, **9/1** Ferrovia, **10/1** Wild Strawberry, **16/1** Greetland Folly. CSF £12.30, Tote £3.70: £1.90 £1.70 (£5.40). Sir Philip Oppenheimer (NEWMARKET) bred by P. D. and Mrs Player. 7 Rn　　1m 37.21 (0.91)
SF—36/31/38/24/12/–

---

### 1364　ST JOHN AMBULANCE STKS (Mdn 3-Y.O) £1562.00 (£432.00: £206.00)
### 5f　　8-45 (8-45)

| | | |
|---|---|---|
| | **Western Approach (USA)** (Fav) *(JHMGosden)* 8-9 PatEddery (6) (lw: led after 2f: clr appr fnl f: v.easily) | —1 |
| 1183² | Nagida *(JARToller)* 8-9 WNewnes (7) (a.p: rdn wl over 1f out: one pce) | 3¹/₂.2 |
| | Katie-a (IRE) *(RMWhitaker)* 8-9 ACulhane (3) (bit bkwd: chsd ldrs: r.o one pce fnl 2f) | 3¹/₂.3 |
| 428 | Jaromic **(52)** *(PFTulk)* 9-0 WRyan (5) (bit bkwd: led 2f: hrd rdn ins fnl f: sn btn) | 1¹/₂.4 |
| 669 | Our John **(48)** (v) *(RonaldThompson)* 9-0 LCharnock (4) (lw: outpcd) | 2.5 |
| 1075 | The Dream Maker (IRE) **(44)** *(MrsNMacauley)* 8-9 NCarlisle (1) (lw: prom 3f) | 1¹/₂.6 |
| 1000⁴ | Sharp as You Like **(47)** (v) *(JEtherington)* 9-0 JLowe (2) (spd on outside 3f: t.o) | 8.7 |

**8/11** WESTERN APPROACH (USA)(1/2—4/5), **2/1** Nagida, **8/1** Katie-a (IRE), **25/1** Sharp as You Like, **33/1** The Dream Maker (IRE), Jaromic, **50/1** Our John. CSF £2.54, Tote £1.60: £1.30 £1.40 (£1.70). Mr K. Abdulla (NEWMARKET) bred by Juddmonte Farms Incorporated in USA. 7 Rn　　58.33 sec (U.37)
SF—62/48/34/33/25/14

**1365**     PENNINE H'CAP (0-80) £1646.00 (£456.00: £218.00)     7f        9-15 (9-18)

1243⁴ **Quiet Victory (44)** (bl) *(MissLCSiddall)* 5-8-2 ‡3FNorton (8) (a.p: led over 2f out: hld on gamely) ............................................. —1
1278² Mu-Arrik **(50)** (bl) (Jt-Fav) *(DAWilson)* 4-8-11 GCarter (13) (lw: a.p: hrd rdn fnl f: r.o) ............................................. ½.2
1303² Sugemar **(57)** (Jt-Fav) *(JARToller)* 6-9-4 (5x) WNewnes (11) (lw: hdwy 2f out: hrd rdn & r.o fnl f) ............................................. nk.3
887⁵ Wild Prospect **(66)** *(CTinkler)* 4-9-13 MBirch (10) (lw: led tl over 2f out: hrd rdn appr fnl f: kpt on) ............................................. 1½.4
1157⁴ Claudia Miss **(61)** *(WWHaigh)* 5-9-8 ACulhane (7) (lw: chsd ldrs over 5f) .......... 2.5
1247 Glenstal Princess **(63)** *(RHollinshead)* 5-9-10 PatEddery (6) (hdwy ½-wy: effrt u.p over 1f out: nt pce to chal) ............................................. s.h.6
1325* Arc Lamp **(52)** *(JAGlover)* 6-8-13 (5x) JFortune (1) (prom tl rdn & wknd wl over 1f out) ............................................. 2.7
1254⁵ The Can Can Man **(67)** *(MJohnston)* 5-10-0 DMcKeown (4) (lw: prom: rdn over 2f out: sn btn) ............................................. nk.8
449 Too Eager **(57)** (bl) *(MWEasterby)* 6-9-4 TLucas (9) (bhd: rdn over 2f out: no imp) ............................................. 3½.9
158 Pilar **(47)** *(MrsNMacauley)* 4-8-8 NCarlisle (5) (bit bkwd: bhd fnl 3f) ............. 1½.10
1160 Stelby **(58)** *(OBrennan)* 8-8-12 ‡7SWilliams (3) (spd 4f) ............................................. 2½.11
1157³ Creselly **(64)** *(JGFitzGerald)* 5-9-11 KFallon (2) (lw: prom tl hrd rdn & wknd over 2f out) ............................................. 1½.12

**7/2** Sugemar, Mu-Arrik, **6/1** The Can Can Man, **8/1** Creselly, **17/2** Glenstal Princess, **9/1** Arc Lamp, **10/1** QUIET VICTORY, Wild Prospect, **12/1** Claudia Miss, **20/1** Stelby, Too Eager, **25/1** Pilar. CSF £45.74, CT £141.29. Tote £13.60: £3.00 £1.80 £1.60 (£26.30). Mr J. E. Wilson (TADCASTER) bred by Anne E. Thompson. 12 Rn
1m 25.47 (2.07)

T/Trio: Race 6: £43.80 (18.6 Tckts). T/Plpt: £37.30 (62.55 Tckts).                    IM

1257—**GOODWOOD (R-H)**

**Friday, June 12th [Good to firm]**
Going Allowance: minus 0.20 sec per fur (F)                    Wind: mod bhd

Stalls: low

**1366**     BBC SOUTH TODAY H'CAP (Amateurs) (0-70) £2302.50 (£640.00: £307.50)
**1m 1f**                    6-40 (6-45)

1063 **Albert (44)** *(DAWilson)* 5-10-1 MissJAllison (2) (hdwy 2f out: led ins fnl f: easily) —1
232 Brown Carpet **(31)** (bl) *(CAHorgan)* 5-8-11(1) ‡5MissDPomeroy (19) (7th st: hdwy 3f out: led over 1f out tl ins fnl f: unable qckn) ........... 4.2
942* Blockade (USA) **(67)** *(MBell)* 3-10-7 ‡5MrsGBell (5) (led after 2f tl over 1f out: one pce) ............................................. hd.3
1267⁶ Night Transaction **(44)** *(AHide)* 5-9-10 ‡5MissLHide (20) (4th st: ev ch over 1f out: one pce) ............................................. hd.4
1270² Overpower **(61)** (Fav) *(MHTompkins)* 8-10-13 ‡5MrGOxley (7) (hdwy over 1f out: r.o ins fnl f) ............................................. 1.5
1143 Quinta Royale **(50)** *(WGMTurner)* 5-10-2 ‡5MrsJGault (9) (9th st: one pce fnl 2f) 1½.6
1143* Thundering **(33)** *(AWJones)* 7-9-4(1) ‡5MissIDWJones (16) (rdn 3f out: nvr nrr) .. hd.7
1009* Brilliant **(64)** *(JPearce)* 4-11-7 MrsLPearce (10) (hdwy 2f out: r.o one pce) ..... 1½.8
994⁵ Rio Trusky **(45)** *(MDIUsher)* 3-8-13 ‡5MrsAUsher (12) (led 2f: 2nd st: wknd 2f out) ............................................. 5.9
1175 Stinger **(67)** *(CRNelson)* 3-10-12 MissJWinter (3) (5th st: wknd 2f out) ........ 2½.10
997⁶ Moving Force **(40)** *(EAWheeler)* 5-9-6 ‡5MrGLewis (8) (lw: 6th st: wknd over 2f out) ............................................. s.h.11
1213⁴ Lindeman **(48)** *(SDow)* 3-9-2 ‡5MrTCuff (4) (3rd st: wknd 2f out) .................... s.h.12
Rose Cut (USA) **(51)** *(DJSCosgrove)* 5-10-3 ‡5MrsDCamp-Simpson (13) (bhd fnl 3f) ............................................. ½.13
448 Tapestry Dancer **(40)** *(MJHaynes)* 4-9-11 MissYHaynes (11) (a bhd) ............. 2.14
1084 Saysana **(32)** *(AMoore)* 5-8-12(3) ‡5MrKGoble (17) (s.s: a bhd) ................. 8.15
1085 Red Jack (IRE) **(60)** *(JAkehurst)* 3-10-0 ‡5MissSFrancome (14) (rdn along: bhd fnl 4f) ............................................. 16
Lady Bunting **(40)** *(RVoorspuy)* 5-9-6 ‡5MrPClose (1) (bhd fnl 4f) .................... 17
1163 Excelsis **(52)** *(JRJenkins)* 6-10-4 ‡5MrsARutherford (6) (prom 5f) .................... 18
1076⁶ Mayles Lass **(47)** *(JJBridger)* 3-9-1(6) ‡5MissMBridger (18) (bhd fnl 4f: t.o) ......... 19
1009 Sporting Weekend (FR) **(64)** *(DSasse)* 5-11-2(13) ‡5MrCRanson (15) (s.s: hdwy 5f out: 8th st: hmpd, tried to p.u & uns rdr wl over 1f out) ....... 0
LONG HANDICAP: Saysana 8-13, Mayles Lass 8-11.
*Stewards Enquiry: Lewis suspended 21-24/6/92 (careless riding).*

7/2 Overpower, 13/2 Blockade (USA), 7/1 Moving Force, 15/2 Thundering, 8/1 ALBERT, Brilliant, 10/1 Lindeman, 14/1 Quinta Royale, 20/1 Brown Carpet, 25/1 Night Transaction, 33/1 Tapestry Dancer, Lady Bunting, Stinger, Excelsis, Red Jack (IRE), Sporting Weekend (FR), 50/1 Rose Cut (USA), 66/1 Ors. CSF £143.71, CT £1,008.48. Tote £10.30 : £2.30 £17.50 £1.90 £5.20 (£942.80). Mr T. S. M. S. Riley-Smith (EPSOM) bred by T. M. Saud. 20 Rn
1m 55.36 (4.66)
SF—18/–/11/–/13/–

---

**1367**    BBC RADIO SURREY CLAIMING STKS (3-Y.O) £1882.50 (£520.00: £247.50)
1½m                      7-05 (7-10)

972⁴ **Dare to Dream (IRE)** (53) (GLewis) 8-8 PaulEddery (4) (3rd st: hrd rdn & led over 1f out: r.o) .................................................. —1
1242³ White Wedding (70) (Fav) (PFICole) 8-4 TQuinn (1) (b: 4th st: hrd rdn & led 3f out: hdd over 1f out: unable qckn) ........................................ 2.2
1158⁴ Afore Jane (GHarwood) 8-4 AClark (5) (led 4f: led 6f out to 3f out: hrd rdn & wknd over 1f out) ................................................... 4.3
908 Sports View (49) (RJHolder) 8-6 MRoberts (3) (5th st: rdn over 2f out: sn wknd) 2.4
1324⁶ Everso Irish (58) (v) (MHTompkins) 8-10 PRobinson (2) (b: led 8f out to 6f out: 2nd st: wknd wl over 1f out) ............................................ ½.5

13/8 White Wedding, 9/4 DARE TO DREAM (IRE), 4/1 Sports View, 7/1 Afore Jane, 12/1 Everso Irish. CSF £5.93, Tote £3.10: £1.40 £1.60 (£2.70). Mrs Shirley Robins (EPSOM) bred by Bhima Breeding Partnership in Ireland. 5 Rn
2m 37.68 (5.98)
SF—10/2/–/–/–

---

**1368**    BBC RADIO SOLENT H'CAP (0-80) £1935.00 (£535.00: £255.00)    **6f**    7-35 (7-37)
(Weights raised 1 lb)

1167² **Rainbow Fleet** (53) (Fav) (DMarks) 4-8-9 JReid (3) (hld up: rdn & led wl over 1f out: r.o wl) ..................................................... —1
1278⁴ Coppermill Lad (47) (LJHolt) 9-8-3 MRoberts (6) (outpcd: gd hdwy 2f out: ev ch ins fnl f: r.o) ................................................... 1.2
1219⁴ Pop to Stans (77) (JPearce) 3-9-10 WCarson (2) (lw: rdn & no hdwy fnl 2f) ...... 4.3
1159 Grey Charmer (IRE) (64) (bl) (CJames) 3-8-11 TQuinn (4) (led 5f out tl wl over 1f out: one pce) ................................................ s.h.4
1013 Greatest of All (IRE) (38) (RHannon) 4-7-8 GBardwell (1) (led 1f: hrd rdn over 2f out: wknd wl over 1f out) ............................................ 2½.5
808³ Neither Nor (73) (RJHolder) 3-9-6 JWilliams (5) (rdn over 2f out: sn wknd) ....... 6.6

9/4 RAINBOW FLEET, 5/2 Pop to Stans, 4/1 Coppermill Lad, 9/2 Neither Nor, 9/1 Grey Charmer (IRE), 20/1 Greatest of All (IRE). CSF £10.80, Tote £2.80: £2.00 £1.80 (£4.80). Mr R. J. F. Brothers (UPPER LAMBOURN) bred by Colin G. R. Booth. 6 Rn
1m 11.17 (0.77)
SF—55/45/50/36/9/11

---

**1369**    UNIVERSITY OF SUSSEX CLAIMING STKS    £2075.00 (£575.00: £275.00)
7f                          8-05 (8-06)

1212⁶ **Across the Bay** (73) (v) (SDow) 5–8-13 TQuinn (4) (4th st: led wl over 1f out: rdn & r.o wl wn) ............................................... —1
1030 Sea Cloud (USA) (41) (MBlanshard) 3–7-8 JQuinn (5) (led over 5f: hrd rdn: unable qckn ins fnl f) ........................................... 2½.2
705⁶ Soleil Dancer (IRE) (90) (Fav) (NTinkler) 4–9-2 WCarson (2) (lw: 3rd st: one pce fnl 2f) ................................................... 2½.3
783 Christian Warrior (74) (RHannon) 3–8-3 MRoberts (3) (6th st: rdn over 2f out: r.o one pce) ................................................. 1.4
1201 Just a Step (83) (MMcCormack) 6–9-2 JReid (1) (2nd st: wkng whn n.m.r over 2f out) .................................................... 8.5
One Dollar More (BGubby) 4–8-11 NAdams (7) (5th st: hrd rdn over 3f out: bhd fnl 2f) ..................................................... 2.6

13/8 Soleil Dancer (IRE), 9/4 Just a Step, 7/2 ACROSS THE BAY, 5/1 Christian Warrior, 50/1 Ors. CSF £67.24, Tote £4.30: £1.80 £6.20 (£44.20). Mr J. A. Redmond (EPSOM) bred by Patrick McGrath and Liam Slattery. 6 Rn
1m 25.87 (1.17)
SF—60/33/47/31/20/9

---

**1370**    E.B.F. BBC RADIO SUSSEX STKS (Mdn 2-Y.O) £2950.00 (£880.00: £420.00: £190.00)
6f                          8-35 (8-37)

1135³ **Port Lucaya** (RHannon) 9-0 WCarson (4) (lw: chsd ldr: led over 2f out: rdn out) —1
933³ Cissbury Ring (Fav) (LadyHerries) 9-0 MRoberts (1) (a.p: rdn over 2f out: unable qckn fnl f) .......................................... 1½.2
City Rocket (PJMakin) 9-0 TQuinn (5) (w'like: scope: bit bkwd: s.s: swtchd rt & hdwy over 2f out: one pce) ................................. 3½.3

1103² Soleil Rayon (IRE) *(MMcCormack)* 9-0 JReid (2) (lw: led over 3f: wknd fnl f) ...... 2.4
1202 Pondering *(SDow)* 9-0 PaulEddery (6) (prom 4f) .................................................... 2.5
476 Gabhadera *(BGubby)* 8-9 NAdams (3) (s.s: a wl bhd) ...................................... 10.6

**9/4** Cissbury Ring, **5/2** Soleil Rayon (IRE)(op 6/4), **3/1** PORT LUCAYA, **7/2** City Rocket, **20/1** Pondering, **50/1** Gabhadera. CSF £9.77, Tote £4.00: £2.00 £1.70 (£4.70). Mr Edward St George (MARLBOROUGH) bred by Cheveley Park Stud Ltd. 6 Rn
                                                              1m 12.54 (2.14)
                                                             SF—33/27/13/5/–/–

**1371**    BBC RADIO KENT H'CAP (3-Y.O) (0-80) £2232.50 (£620.00: £297.50)
         1¼m                                  9-05 (9-11)

(Weights raised 2 lb)
1041 **Tempelhof (IRE) (58)** *(JWHills)* 8-1 DHolland (10) (lw: mde all: drvn out) .......... —1
1070³ Highland Battle (USA) **(60)** (Fav) *(IABalding)* 8-3 MRoberts (1) (7th st: hdwy
          over 2f out: ev ch 1f out: r.o) ......................................................... 1.2
930 Severine (USA) **(61)** *(JLDunlop)* 8-4 TQuinn (2) (5th st: r.o one pce fnl 2f: fin
          4th, s.h: plcd 3rd) ......................................................................... 3
910³ Sky Train (IRE) **(65)** *(JLDunlop)* 8-8 AMunro (12) (swtg: bmpd over 2f out: n.m.r
          over 1f out: rallied: r.o in fin 5th, ¾l: plcd 4th) ............................... 4
1175² Majal (IRE) **(78)** *(BHanbury)* 9-7 JReid (5) (s.i.s: gd hdwy 2f out: ev ch over 1f
          out: one pce: fin 6th, nk: plcd 5th) ............................................... 5
1041 Cappahoosh (IRE) **(55)** *(HJCollingridge)* 7-12 JQuinn (11) (2nd st: one pce fnl
          2f) ................................................................................................ nk.7
972² Hester Stanhope **(65)** *(PWHarris)* 8-8 PaulEddery (9) (8th st: no hdwy fnl 3f) .. 2½.8
972 Athar (IRE) **(59)** *(PTWalwyn)* 8-2 WCarson (7) (4th st: wknd 2f out) ................. 6.9
999² Nectar Collector **(70)** *(CFWall)* 8-13 AMcGlone (4) (dwlt: hdwy 9f out: 3rd st:
          wknd over 2f out) ......................................................................... nk.10
621 Nomadic Rose **(62)** *(BWHills)* 8-5 KTsui (3) (a bhd) ........................................ 6.11
972⁶ Vivitz (IRE) **(58)** (v) *(GBBalding)* 8-1 NAdams (13) (bhd fnl 4f: p.u ins fnl f: lame) ... 0
1146³ Deevee **(50)** *(CJBenstead)* 7-7 TyroneWilliams (8) (hdwy & hung rt 2f out: ev ch
          1f out: one pce: fin 3rd, 2½l: disq: plcd last) ............................... 0
LONG HANDICAP: Deevee 7-5.

*Stewards Enquiry: Deevee disq. (interference to Sky Train (IRE) 2f out).*

**9/2** Highland Battle (USA), **5/1** Majal (IRE), **6/1** Hester Stanhope, Sky Train (IRE), **7/1** Severine (USA), **9/1** Nectar Collector, TEMPELHOF (IRE)(12/1—8/1), Deevee, **11/1** Vivitz (IRE), **16/1** Athar (IRE), Cappahoosh (IRE), **33/1** Nomadic Rose. CSF £49.58, CT £285.07. Tote £15.90: £3.50 £2.00 £2.40 (£26.50). Mr R. E. Sangster (LAMBOURN) bred by J. Hamilton in Ireland. 12 Rn
                                                  2m 9.76 (4.76)
                                               SF—19/19/14/16/28

T/Trio: Race 6: £118.50 (13.3 Tckts). T/Plpt: £200.40 (16.5 Tckts).            LMc

1320— **SOUTHWELL (L-H)** Fibresand
**Friday, June 12th [Standard]**
Going Allowance: 0.05 sec per fur (SL)                     Wind: almost nil

Stalls: high

**1372**    'BLOODY LANE' H'CAP (0-70) £2422.00 (£672.00: £322.00)
         1½m (AWT)                               2-30 (2-30)

(Weights raised 8 lb)
1265* **Five to Seven (USA) (75)** *(SGNorton)* 3–9-6 (6x) ‡⁷SWilliams (2) (mde all: wnt
          clr 7f out: drvn out: unchal) ......................................................... —1
777* La Reine Rouge (IRE) **(48)** (Fav) *(PJMakin)* 4–8-13 ‡³TSprake (7) (hdwy 7f out:
          chsd wnr appr st: sn hrd rdn & no imp) ....................................... 12.2
1248 Cheeky Pot **(52)** (v) *(DenysSmith)* 4–9-6 NConnorton (4) (bhd: reminders 7f
          out: hdwy 4f out: styd on same pce fnl 2f) ................................. 15.3
905⁶ Sweet Bubbles (IRE) **(52)** *(CACyzer)* 4–8-13 ‡⁷TMcLaughlin (8) (prom tl lost pl
          8f out: sme hdwy u.p over 4f out: sn btn) ................................... 3.4
1150 Make Me Proud (IRE) **(56)** *(RWArmstrong)* 3–8-8 BCrossley (9) (sn bhd &
          pushed along: sme hdwy 6f out: sn wknd) ................................. 10.5
761 Crimson Cloud (IRE) **(46)** *(NTinkler)* 4–9-0 DNicholls (5) (chsd wnr to ½-wy: sn
          pushed along & wknd) ................................................................. 4.6
1179⁶ Thunder Bug (USA) **(44)** *(APJames)* 4–8-12 JLowe (1) (chsd ldrs: drvn along &
          wknd 5f out) ................................................................................. hd.7
1147⁶ Walking Saint **(40)** *(GraemeRoe)* 5–8-8 MHills (10) (prom: chsd wnr ½-wy tl
          wknd appr st) ............................................................................... ½.8
1267 Shaieef (IRE) **(56)** *(RJRWilliams)* 4–9-10 RHills (6) (a bhd: t.o fr ½-wy) ........... 25.9

**2/1** La Reine Rouge (IRE)(op 3/1), **4/1** FIVE TO SEVEN (USA)(op 2/1), **9/2** Sweet Bubbles (IRE), **9/1** Crimson Cloud (IRE), **10/1** Thunder Bug (USA), **12/1** Make Me Proud (IRE)(op 20/1), **14/1** Cheeky Pot, **16/1** Walking Saint, **25/1** Shaieef (IRE). CSF £11.69, CT £89.42. Tote £4.50: £1.60 £1.40 £2.70 (£4.80). The Five to Seven Partnership (BARNSLEY) bred by William A. Marquard in USA. 9 Rn
2m 41 (6.8)
SF–44/13/–/–/–/–

---

**1373**      WATERLOO CLAIMING STKS (2-Y.O) £2265.20 (£627.20: £299.60)
                  5f (AWT)                                            3-00 (3-01)

| | | |
|---|---|---|
| 1191[3] | **Classic Storm** (Fav) *(JBerry)* 8-9 GCarter (1) (w ldrs: rdn over 2f out: styd on to ld nr fin) | —1 |
| 1307[6] | Samanthas Joy *(TFairhurst)* 8-1 PBurke (2) (w ldrs: led over 1f out tl ct cl home) | nk.2 |
| 1036[6] | Another Kingdom *(JWharton)* 8-5 ‡3DBiggs (4) (chsd ldrs: rdn along ½-wy: styd on ins fnl f) | 2.3 |
| 924 | Jasmin Isle *(MissGayKelleway)* 8-7 AMackay (3) (w ldrs tl wknd wl over 1f out) | 7.4 |
| 772 | Tee-Emm *(PHowling)* 8-9 BCrossley (6) (slt ld over 3f: sn rdn & wknd) | 2½.5 |
| | Merryhill Kerry (IRE) *(JLHarris)* 8-2 JLowe (7) (a outpcd) | 4.6 |
| | He Nose You Know (IRE) *(CNAllen)* 8-12 MHills (5) (s.i.s: nvr wnt pce) | nk.7 |

*Stewards Enquiry: Burke suspended 21-24/6/92 (improper use of whip).*

**10/11** CLASSIC STORM(4/6—5/4), **100/30** Another Kingdom(6/1—3/1), **5/1** He Nose You Know (IRE)(op 5/2), **13/2** Jasmin Isle(op 12/1), **14/1** Samanthas Joy(12/1—20/1), **20/1** Merryhill Kerry (IRE), **33/1** Tee-Emm. CSF £13.69. Tote £2.00: £1.40 £7.50 (£6.10). Mr D. J. Ayres (COCKERHAM) bred by Concorde Breeding and Racing International P'Ship. 7 Rn
61.4 sec (3.4)
SF–32/23/19/–/–/–

---

**1374**      OAG WARM HOMES STKS (Mdn 3 Y.O) £2266.20 (£627.20: £299.60)
                  1m 3f (AWT)                                      3-30 (3-31)

| | | |
|---|---|---|
| 911[5] | **Themeda** *(CRNelson)* 8-9 JLowe (3) (led 2f: led 6f out: r.o strly fnl 2f) | —1 |
| 835 | Noel (IRE) **(60)** *(GAPritchard-Gordon)* 9-0 GCarter (7) (trckd ldrs gng wl: effrt & ev ch appr st: nt pce of wnr fnl 2f) | 5.2 |
| | Pippas Song (Fav) *(GWragg)* 8-9 RHills (1) (dwlt: trckd ldrs: effrt & pushed along 6f out: wknd 2f out) | 3½.3 |
| 1005[3] | Iron Baron (IRE) **(64)** *(RHollinshead)* 8-7 ‡7EHusband (6) (bhd: hdwy over 5f out: wknd over 2f out) | 5.4 |
| 1268[3] | Captain Marmalade **(63)** *(DTThom)* 9-0 NConnorton (5) (rn wd bnd after 1f: chsd ldrs tl wknd 5f out) | s.h.5 |
| 878[5] | By Arrangement (IRE) **(69)** *(RGuest)* 8-9 WWoods (2) (led after 2f tl hdd & wknd 6f out) | 12.6 |
| | Sir Vidar (IRE) *(MBell)* 9-0 MHills (4) (a bhd: lost tch ½-wy) | 12.7 |

**9/4** Pippas Song, **7/2** THEMEDA, **9/2** Sir Vidar (IRE), **7/1** Captain Marmalade(5/1—9/1), **9/1** Iron Baron (IRE)(op 6/1), **10/1** By Arrangement (IRE)(12/1—8/1), **12/1** Noel (IRE). CSF £35.30, Tote £4.40: £2.90 £5.60 (£18.60). Miss D. A. Colvile (UPPER LAMBOURN) bred by P. D. and Mrs Player. 7 Rn
2m 29.8 (8.3)
SF–18/13/1/–/–/–

---

**1375**      JOHN SMITH'S BITTER AUCTION STKS (Mdn 2-Y.O) £2480.80 (£688.80: £330.40)
                  6f (AWT)                                           4-00 (4-03)

| | | |
|---|---|---|
| 1092[2] | **Daytona Beach (IRE)** (Fav) *(RHollinshead)* 8-11 NConnorton (6) (mde all: sddle slipped & hung rt appr st: kpt on u.p fnl f) | —1 |
| 682[5] | Colfax Starlight *(BSRothwell)* 8-1 SWood (1) (unruly stalls: a chsng ldrs: rdn & styd on same pce fnl 2f) | 2½.2 |
| | Dontbetalking (IRE) *(JWharton)* 7-12 ‡3DBiggs (7) (hdwy ½-wy: rdn 2f out: nt qckn u.p fnl f) | nk.3 |
| 859 | Spanish Thread *(GAPritchard-Gordon)* 8-2 RHills (9) (s.i.s: sn rcvrd to jn wnr: rdn 2f out: wknd appr fnl f) | 1½.4 |
| | Carnbrea Snip *(MBell)* 8-2 MHills (3) (chsd ldrs tl rdn & wknd wl over 1f out) | s.h.5 |
| 1036[5] | Mister Blake *(WAO'Gorman)* 8-2 ‡5EmmaO'Gorman (2) (effrt appr st: nvr able to rch ldrs) | 7.6 |
| | Domes of Silence *(JBerry)* 8-6 GCarter (4) (chsd ldrs over 3f: sn lost pl) | 6.7 |
| | Raggerty (IRE) *(JBerry)* 8-10 PBurke (8) (nvr wnt pce) | 1½.8 |
| 1307[5] | Never in Touch (bl) *(MBrittain)* 8-0 JLowe (3) (hmpd after 1f: sn bhd) | 1½.9 |

**9/4** DAYTONA BEACH (IRE)(6/4—5/2), **7/2** Mister Blake(2/1—4/1), **5/1** Carnbrea Snip, **8/1** Colfax Starlight(op 16/1), **10/1** Domes of Silence, **12/1** Raggerty (IRE), **16/1** Spanish Thread, **25/1** Ors. CSF £18.07, Tote £2.90: £1.50 £1.90 £3.10 (£16.30). Mr P. D. Savill (UPPER LONGDON) bred by Miss H. Dean in Ireland. 9 Rn
1m 18.9 (5.5)

### 1376

AGINCOURT H'CAP (0-70) £2382.80 (£660.80: £316.40)　　1m (AWT)　　4-30 (4-33)

| | | |
|---|---|---|
| 1090[6] | **Tyrian Purple (IRE) (48)** *(RHollinshead)* 4-8-8 ‡[7]MHumphries (2) (mde all: pushed clr over 1f out: readily) | —1 |
| 1267[2] | Buddy's Friend (IRE) **(52)** (Fav) *(RJRWilliams)* 4-9-5 MHills (3) (a.p: rdn 2f out: nt pce of wnr appr fnl f) | 4.2 |
| 1266 | Eliza Wooding (37) *(CJHill)* 4-8-1 ‡[3]DBiggs (9) (hdwy u.p over 2f out: styd on: nvr nrr) | ½.3 |
| 1267[4] | China Sky (45) *(CNAllen)* 4-8-12 GCarter (4) (chsd ldrs: rdn over 2f out: wknd over 1f out) | 1.4 |
| 1267[3] | Sareen Express (IRE) (48) *(MrsJCDawe)* 4-8-10 ‡[5]ATucker (10) (prom: hrd rdn appr st: one pce fnl 2f) | 8.5 |
| 1172 | Golden Beau (29) *(AHarrison)* 10-7-10 AMackay (13) (bhd tl sme late hdwy) | 2.6 |
| 1114[6] | Tara's Delight (61) *(WAO'Gorman)* 5-9-9 ‡[5]EmmaO'Gorman (8) (dwlt: sn prom: c wd st: sn wknd) | 2.7 |
| 1266 | Watermill Girl (47) *(DTThom)* 4-8-4 NConnorton (6) (a in rr) | 3.8 |
| 572 | Colonel Fairfax (34) *(JWWatts)* 4-8-1 JLowe (7) (w ldr tl rdn & wknd over 2f out) | 4.9 |
| 1070 | Lady Ghislaine (FR) (32) *(ASReid)* 5-7-6 ‡[7]PMcCabe (5) (prom 3f: sn lost pl) | 8.10 |
| 1267 | Edgewise (29) *(DMorris)* 9-7-3[3] ‡[7]TWilson (11) (a bhd) | 12.11 |
| 1106 | Ackers Wood (37) *(KRBurke)* 4-8-4 AShoults (12) (bhd fr ½-wy) | 12 |

LONG HANDICAP: Edgewise 7-6.

**3/1** Buddy's Friend (IRE)(op 2/1), **9/2** Eliza Wooding(op 8/1), **8/1** TYRIAN PURPLE (IRE), Sareen Express (IRE), China Sky, **9/1** Tara's Delight(op 6/1), **10/1** Colonel Fairfax, **16/1** Ackers Wood, **18/1** Edgewise(op 50/1), **20/1** Golden Beau, **33/1** Ors. CSF £29.79, CT £1,100.09. Tote £12.00; £2.60 £1.90 £1.80 (£10.60). Rykneld Thoroughbred Co Ltd (UPPER LONGDON) bred by Niels Schibbye in Ireland. 12 Rn 1m 44.4 (5.1)
SF—23/22/2/10/–/–

### 1377

HASTINGS APP'CE H'CAP (0-70) £2226.00 (£616.00: £294.00)　　7f (AWT)　　5-05 (5-06)

| | | |
|---|---|---|
| 1267★ | **Sandmoor Denim (47)** (Jt-Fav) *(SRBowring)* 5-8-8 (6x) MHarris (5) (hld up & bhd: smooth hdwy appr st: rdn over 1f out: r.o to ld post) | —1 |
| 1075 | Lift Boy (USA) **(44)** *(DenysSmith)* 3-7-4 ‡[5]CTeague (4) (led: rdn wl over 1f out: ct last stride) | s.h.2 |
| 587 | Mushy Boff (51) (Jt-Fav) *(CJHill)* 4-8-12 PBowe (9) (chsd ldrs: kpt sltly wd & lost pl appr st: styd on strly ins fnl f) | nk.3 |
| 1266[2] | Wellsy Lad (USA) **(60)** *(DWChapman)* 5-9-7 SWilliams (2) (hdwy over 2f out: styd on wl fnl f) | s.h.4 |
| 1258 | Sergeant Meryll (35) *(PHowling)* 8-7-5 ‡[5]KateMason (7) (w ldr: rdn over 2f out: wknd ins fnl f) | 1½.5 |
| 774 | Beechwood Cottage (57) *(ABailey)* 9-8-13 ‡[5]WHollick (3) (s.s: wl bhd tl styd on wl fnl 2f) | 4.6 |
| 1243 | Daisy Grey (49) (bl) *(ASReid)* 4-8-10 PMcCabe (6) (chsd ldrs over 4f: sn btn) | 10.7 |
| 918 | Saladan Knight (67) *(JGFitzGerald)* 7-9-9 ‡[5]MHunt (1) (eyeshield: chsd ldrs to st: wknd qckly) | 15.8 |

**3/1** SANDMOOR DENIM(op 2/1), Mushy Boff(5/1—11/4), **7/2** Wellsy Lad (USA)(op 9/4), **8/1** Saladan Knight, **9/1** Daisy Grey, **16/1** Sergeant Meryll, Lift Boy (USA), **20/1** Beechwood Cottage. CSF £38.85, CT £128.24. Tote £3.30: £1.40 £2.80 £1.10 (£46.80). Mr E. H. Lunness (EDWINSTOWE) bred by Rathasker Stud. 8 Rn 1m 31.6 (5)
SF—24/5/26/34/–/9

T/Plpt: £21.00 (71.75 Tckts).　　　　　　　　　　　　　　　　　　　　　　　　　　　　O'R

### 1057—SANDOWN (R-H)

## Friday, June 12th [Good to firm, Good patches]

Going Allowance: St: minus 0.20 sec; Rnd: minus 0.10 sec (F)　　　　　Wind: nil

Stalls: high

### 1378

ORLEANS AUCTION STKS (Mdn 2-Y.O) £3008.00 (£838.00: £404.00)　　5f 6y　　2-15 (2-22)

| | | |
|---|---|---|
| 645[2] | **Aradanza** (Fav) *(MRChannon)* 8-1 WCarson (12) (mde all: rdn & r.o wl fnl f) | —1 |
| 968 | Our Shadee (USA) *(KTIvory)* 8-0 GBardwell (10) (chsd wnr: ev ch 1f out: nt qckn) | 2½.2 |
| 1039[3] | Soldiers Bay *(LordHuntingdon)* 8-2 AMunro (2) (a.p: r.o ins fnl f) | ½.3 |
| 933[6] | Heart of Spain *(PJMakin)* 8-8 WRSwinburn (7) (hdwy & rdn over 2f out: styd on one pce) | 2½.4 |
| | Buffalo River *(MHTompkins)* 8-3 PRobinson (3) (w'like: bit bkwd: nrst fin) | 3½.5 |

1208 Petite Vino *(JJBridger)* 7-9 NAdams (5) (lw: no hdwy fnl 2f) ............................... nk.6
Maribella *(PFICole)* 7-4(2) ‡7JDSmith (4) (scope: bit bkwd: no hdwy fnl 2f) ......... ¾.7
Recit D'Argent *(CJames)* 8-0 AMcGlone (9) (unf: bit bkwd: spd 3f) ................... 3½.8
Glen Miller *(JWPayne)* 8-7(7) BRaymond (13) (str: bit bkwd: s.s: nvr nrr) .......... ½.9
Pennine Lad (IRE) *(BGubby)* 8-0 NCarlisle (8) (leggy: s.s: nrst fin) ................. s.h.10
339² Auntie Ginger *(PButler)* 7-9 AProud (1) (lw: racd alone stands' side: prom over
2f) ................................................................................................. 1½.11
1135 Right Will Prevail *(GLewis)* 9-2 BRouse (6) (a bhd) ..................................... 2½.12
Sharp Imp *(JSutcliffe)* 8-0 CRutter (11) (w'like: a bhd) ................................ 1½.13

**4/5** ARADANZA(op 5/4), **9/2** Heart of Spain, **8/1** Soldiers Bay(op 5/1), **12/1** Glen Miller(op 5/1), **14/1** Auntie
Ginger(10/1—16/1), **25/1** Sharp Imp, Right Will Prevail, **33/1** Buffalo River, Maribella, **50/1** Ors. CSF £42.32,
Tote £1.70: £1.10 £12.00 £1.70 (£45.80). Mrs P. Lewis (UPPER LAMBOURN) bred by Mrs P. Lewis. 13 Rn
61.15 sec (1.65)
SF—34/23/23/19/–/–

**1379**     KIDSONS IMPEY TROPHY (H'cap) (0-90) £3655.00 (£1090.00: £520.00: £235.00)
**7f 16y**                                                                                2-50 (2-54)

1174 **Jaldi (IRE) (56)** *(Fav)* *(JSutcliffe)* 4-8-11 MRoberts (9) (lw: mde virtually all:
pushed out) ............................................................................................. —1
1167 Highland Magic (IRE) **(63)** *(MJFetherston-Godley)* 4-9-4 WRSwinburn (1)
(b.off hind: 6th st: hdwy 2f out: edgd rt: r.o) .......................................... ½.2
1193⁵ Veloce (IRE) **(55)** *(MO'Neill)* 4-8-10 JFortune (5) (5th st: r.o one pce fnl 2f) .... 1½.3
925★ Hopeful Bid (IRE) **(76)** *(RHannon)* 3-9-7 BRaymond (7) (lw: 2nd st: ev ch 2f out:
one pce) ............................................................................................... 2.4
1062⁴ Louisville Belle (IRE) **(59)** *(MDIUsher)* 3-8-4 CRutter (3) (b.nr hind: hdwy over
2f out: wknd over 1f out) ......................................................................... ½.5
1110² Pimsboy **(55)** (v) *(P4Blockley)* 5-8-10 AClark (2) (4th st: ev ch 2f out: wkng whn
hmpd over 1f out) ................................................................................... 1½.6
Arabat **(60)** *(MPNaughton)* 5-9-1 AMunro (4) (a bhd) ...................................... 6.7
1177³ Kaths Choice **(39)** *(HJCollingridge)* 4-7-1 ‡7CHawksley (8) (swtg: s.s: a bhd) . s.h.8
1107 Gemini Bay **(79)** (bl) *(RVoorspuy)* 3-9-10 SDawson (6) (3rd st: wknd over 3f
out: t.o) ................................................................................................ 12.9

**15/8** JALDI (IRE), **7/2** Hopeful Bid (IRE), **8/1** Veloce (IRE), **9/1** Louisville Belle (IRE), Highland Magic (IRE), **10/1**
Kaths Choice(12/1—8/1), Pimsboy, **14/1** Arabat(10/1—16/1), **33/1** Gemini Bay. CSF £17.69, CT £99.98. Tote
£2.60: £1.50 £2.30 £1.90 (£21.00). Mr Albert Finney (EPSOM) bred by Albert Finney in Ireland. 9 Rn
1m 30.21 (3.21)
SF—38/43/30/35/16/17

**1380**     MORE LANE CLAIMING STKS     £2693.00 (£748.00: £359.00)     **5f 6y**     3-20 (3-25)

1154² **Finjan (89)** *(MPNaughton)* 5-8-9 MRoberts (5) (a.p: led ins fnl f: r.o wl) .......... —1
1350a⁶ Food of Love **(106)** (bl) *(Fav)* *(JBerry)* 4-8-9 TQuinn (6) (led tl ins fnl f) .......... 1½.2
1199⁴ Love Returned **(83)** *(WJarvis)* 5-8-9 MTebbutt (1) (hld up: ev ch 1f out: wknd nr
fin) ...................................................................................................... hd.3
1167 Thornfield Boy **(75)** *(RJHolder)* 6-8-2 NAdams (4) (prom 3f) ........................... 3.4
1138² Gabibti (IRE) **(60)** *(BGubby)* 4-8-1 JQuinn (3) (swtg: bhd fnl 2f) ..................... ½.5
1064★ Tango Time (4/1) Withdrawn (lame at s) : not under orders

**4/5** Food of Love, **3/1** FINJAN, Love Returned, **16/1** Gabibti (IRE), **33/1** Thornfield Boy. CSF £5.86, Tote £4.30:
£1.30 £1.10 (£2.00). Mrs R. Olivier (RICHMOND) bred by Swettenham Stud. 5 Rn     59.97 sec (0.47)
SF—65/59/58/39/36

**1381**     ALLIED DUNBAR H'CAP (0-95) £3436.00 (£1033.00: £499.00: £232.00)
**1¾m**                                                                              3-50 (3-53)

861⁴ **Gay Glint (82)** *(NAGraham)* 5-9-7 SCauthen (6) (lw: 6th st: led wl over 1f out:
drvn out) .............................................................................................. —1
1163² Prosequendo (USA) **(64)** *(MDixon)* 5-8-3 DaleGibson (12) (hdwy 3f out: ev ch
over 1f out: r.o) ...................................................................................... 1½.2
1065★ Wick Pound **(54)** (bl) *(Fav)* *(JABOld)* 6-7-7 RFox (3) (swtg: 4th st: nt clr run over
2f out & over 1f out: nt rcvr) .................................................................... 3.3
Manzoor Sayadan (USA) **(68)** *(RSimpson)* 4-8-7 SWhitworth (11) (5th st: r.o
one pce fnl 2f) ....................................................................................... ¾.4
937 Marine Society **(72)** *(PTWalwyn)* 4-8-11 AMunro (7) (lw: 7th st: n.m.r 2f out: r.o
one pce) ............................................................................................... s.h.5
1147⁴ Caspian Beluga **(54)** *(MrsAKnight)* 4-7-7 GBardwell (9) (swtg: 2nd st: wknd
over 1f out) ........................................................................................... 1½.6
1169 High Beacon **(80)** (bl) *(KCBailey)* 5-9-5 JReid (4) (led 4f: 3rd st: wknd over 1f
out) ...................................................................................................... ¾.7

| | | |
|---|---|---|
| 937[4] | Empire Blue **(68)** *(PFICole)* 9-8-7 TQuinn (13) (b: swtg: nvr nr to chal) | hd.8 |
| | Paris of Troy **(67)** *(NATwiston-Davies)* 4-8-6 JWilliams (2) (led after 4f tl wknd wl over 1f out) | ¹/₂.9 |
| | Trifolio **(89)** *(NJHenderson)* 5-10-0 BRouse (5) (bhd fnl 3f) | nk.10 |
| 1169³ | Intricacy **(60)** *(CCElsey)* 4-7-13 JQuinn (8) (a bhd) | 2¹/₂.11 |
| 1147* | Moonlight Quest **(80)** *(BHanbury)* 4-9-5 (5x) WRSwinburn (10) (swtg: s.s: a bhd) | nk.12 |
| 1065 | Tsunami **(68)** *(CEBrittain)* 4-8-7 MRoberts (1) (bhd fnl 6f) | ³/₄.13 |

LONG HANDICAP: Wick Pound 7-3, Caspian Beluga 7-6.

**9/4** Wick Pound, **5/1** GAY GLINT, Moonlight Quest, **7/1** Prosequendo (USA), **8/1** Paris of Troy, **12/1** Tsunami, **14/1** Empire Blue, Intricacy, Caspian Beluga, Marine Society, **20/1** High Beacon, **25/1** Manzoor Sayadan (USA), **33/1** Trifolio. CSF £41.29, CT £96.03. Tote £5.90: £2.10 £1.90 £1.70 (£24.80). Mr Paul G. Jacobs (NEWMARKET) bred by Ballymacoll Stud Farm Ltd. 13 Rn
3m 0.89 (0.74 under best; 6.19)
SF—31/10/—/6/9/—

---

**1382**  GODFREY MERRITT AMISS GROUP H'CAP (3-Y.O) (0-90) £3640.75 (£1096.00: £530.50: £247.75)   **1m 1f**   4-25 (4-27)

(Weights raised 7 lb)

| | | |
|---|---|---|
| 1105⁴ | **Baluga (76)** *(GHarwood)* 9-0 AClark (3) (lw: mde all: all out) | —1 |
| 695 | Lady of Sardinia (BEL) **(70)** *(JWPayne)* 8-8 AMunro (2) (3rd st: ev ch fnl f: r.o) | 1.2 |
| 930 | Googly **(58)** *(WGRWightman)* 7-10 GBardwell (7) (lw: 6th st: ev ch over 1f out: r.o one pce) | 1¹/₂.3 |
| 925⁵ | Elwazir (USA) **(68)** *(PTWalwyn)* 8-6 WCarson (4) (2nd st: ev ch over 1f out: nt qckn) | hd.4 |
| 1005* | Shirley's Train (USA) **(78)** (Fav) *(LordHuntingdon)* 9-2 SCauthen (8) (lw: 4th st: hmpd wl over 1f out: r.o ins fnl f) | s.h.5 |
| 695 | Holiday Island **(73)** *(CEBrittain)* 8-11 MRoberts (9) (nvr nr to chal) | ³/₄.6 |
| 1078⁴ | Miss Doody **(63)** (v) *(MRChannon)* 8-1 PaulEddery (10) (hdwy 2f out: one pce fnl f) | hd.7 |
| 1025 | Red Kite **(65)** *(MBell)* 8-3 JQuinn (1) (lw: 7th st: hdwy 2f out: wknd fnl f) | ³/₄.8 |
| 653 | Walking on Water **(80)** *(RFJohnsonHoughton)* 8-4 JReid (6) (lw: a bhd) | hd.9 |
| 1153³ | Mashakel (USA) **(83)** *(BHanbury)* 9-7 WRSwinburn (5) (b: lw: 5th st: wknd over 2f out: t.o) | 8.10 |

**7/4** Shirley's Train (USA), **13/2** Mashakel (USA), **7/1** Lady of Sardinia (BEL), **15/2** BALUGA, **8/1** Elwazir (USA), **9/1** Holiday Island, **11/1** Googly, **12/1** Red Kite, Miss Doody, **20/1** Walking on Water. CSF £56.56, CT £532.54. Tote £7.90: £2.40 £2.30 £2.40 (£22.60). Mr J. C. Thompson (PULBOROUGH) bred by K. J. and Mrs Buchanan. 10 Rn
1m 54.52 (3.12)
SF—40/31/14/23/32/12

---

**1383**  JUNE STKS (Mdn 3-Y.O) £2924.00 (£814.00: £392.00)   **1¹/₄m 7y**   5-00 (5-02)

| | | |
|---|---|---|
| 481 | **Host (IRE)** *(CEBrittain)* 9-0 MRoberts (7) (mde all: all out) | —1 |
| | Laughsome *(JHMGosden)* 8-9 SCauthen (2) (w'like: scope: bit bkwd: 4th st: hrd rdn fnl 2f: r.o wl ins fnl f) | hd.2 |
| 1069 | Lady Buchan (Fav) *(MrsJCecil)* 8-9 JReid (6) (2nd st: ev ch over 1f out: wknd fnl f) | 3.3 |
| 804² | Unforgiving Minute *(PWHarris)* 9-0 PaulEddery (4) (3rd st: wknd over 2f out) | 2¹/₂.4 |
| | Dawn Flight *(LadyHerries)* 9-0 JWilliams (3) (wl grwn: 5th st: wknd 3f out) | 4.5 |
| | Lifford (USA) *(MRStoute)* 8-7 ‡7KPattinson (1) (w'like: scope: s.s: a last: t.o) | 12.6 |

**15/8** Lady Buchan, **2/1** Unforgiving Minute, **4/1** Laughsome, **6/1** HOST (IRE)(8/1—10/1), **16/1** Lifford (USA), **25/1** Dawn Flight. CSF £27.04, Tote £9.20: £3.30 £1.80 (£11.50). The Dowager Lady Beaverbrook (NEWMARKET) bred by Barronstown Stud in Ireland. 6 Rn
2m 8.51 (4.21)
SF—48/42/36/36/28/—

T/Trio: Race 4: £31.10 (26 Tckts). T/Jkpt: Not won; £2,424.90 to Sandown 13/6/92. T/Plpt: £106.30 (55.65 Tckts).
Hn

---

## SANDOWN (R-H)
### Saturday, June 13th [Firm]

Going Allowance: minus 0.20 sec per fur (F)   Wind: almost nil

Stalls: high

---

**1384**  E.B.F. SURVEYORS STKS (Mdn 2-Y.O.F) £2777.00 (£772.00: £371.00)   **5f 6y**   2-20 (2-24)

| | | |
|---|---|---|
| | **Greenlet (IRE)** (Fav) *(MRStoute)* 8-11 WRyan (6) (scope: dwlt: hdwy over 2f out: led over 1f out: comf) | —1 |

Magication *(CEBrittain)* 8-6 ‡5BDoyle (5) (unf: scope: bit bkwd: s.s: rdn thrght: hdwy over 1f out: r.o wl ins fnl f) ........................................ 2.2
Bangles *(LordHuntingdon)* 8-11 MRoberts (3) (leggy: unf: led over 3f: unable qckn) ........................................ nk.3
665⁵ Girl Next Door *(NAGraham)* 8-11 JQuinn (4) (lw: a.p: hrd rdn 1f out: one pce) ... 5.4
584⁵ Perfect Passion *(JJBridger)* 8-11 PRobinson (9) (swtg: a.p: rdn over 1f out: one pce) ........................................ s.h.5
1259 Lady of Shadows *(SDow)* 8-11 WNewnes (8) (prom 3f) ........................................ 2¹/₂.6
Chummy's Idea (IRE) *(JSutcliffe)* 8-6 ‡5DHarrison (2) (cmpt: bit bkwd: a bhd) .... 2.7
1103 Mouchez le Nez (IRE) *(JAkehurst)* 8-11 DHolland (7) (a bhd) ........................................ 2.8
Dragonmist (IRE) *(GLewis)* 8-11 BRouse (1) (leggy: bit bkwd: s.s: a wl bhd) ... 1¹/₂.9

**11/8** GREENLET (IRE), **13/8** Bangles, **15/2** Girl Next Door(5/1—10/1), **14/1** Dragonmist (IRE)(10/1—16/1), **20/1** Magication, Perfect Passion, **33/1** Ors. CSF £25.52, Tote £2.40: £1.20 £3.30 £1.30 (£25.10). Sheikh Mohammed (NEWMARKET) bred by Sheikh Mohammed bin Rashid al Maktoum in Ireland. 9 Rn
61.10 sec (1.60)
SF—45/32/36/16/15/5

## 1385
VALUATION CLAIMING STKS (3-Y.O) £2798.00 (£778.00: £374.00)
1¹/₄m 7y　　　　　　　　　　　　　　　　　2-55 (2-58)

1123⁶ Misty View (67) *(MAJarvis)* 8-4 WRyan (5) (6th st: hrd rdn over 1f out: led ins fnl f: r.o wl) ........................................ —1
1213★ Plan Ahead (68) (Fav) *(GLewis)* 8-11 ‡5DHarrison (1) (lw: gd hdwy 3f out: led 2f out tl ins fnl f: unable qckn) ........................................ ³/₄.2
1257² King of Normandy (IRE) (70) *(RHannon)* 8-5 MRoberts (2) (lw: led 8f: rdn: r.o) .. 1.3
1150 Cool Society (USA) (67) *(CRNelson)* 8-7 DHolland (3) (3rd st: hrd rdn over 1f out: r.o) ........................................ s.h.4
1172⁵ Slanderinthestrand (IRE) (44) *(MJHaynes)* 8-7 BRouse (7) (dwlt: 4th st: hrd rdn over 2f out: wknd over 1f out) ........................................ 10.5
1175 Ideal Candidate (50) *(CACyzer)* 8-0 ‡7TMcLaughlin (6) (rdn over 4f out: 5th st: wknd over 1f out) ........................................ hd.6
1085 Lord Belmonte (IRE) (35) (bl) *(CACyzer)* 8-1 JQuinn (4) (2nd st: wknd over 2f out) ........................................ 12.7

**7/4** Plan Ahead, **3/1** MISTY VIEW, **100/30** King of Normandy (IRE), **5/1** Cool Society (USA), **33/1** Ors. CSF £8.01, Tote £4.20: £1.80 £1.70 (£3.20). Mr K. G. Powter (NEWMARKET) bred by W. L. Caley. 7 Rn　2m 9.12 (4.82)
SF—22/13/19/20/–/–

## 1386
BAKER LORENZ SUMMER APP'CE H'CAP (3-Y.O) (0-90) £3117.50 (£935.00: £450.00:
£207.50)　5f 6y　　　　　　　　　　　　3-25 (3-26)

1238★ Optical (IRE) (74) *(MPNaughton)* 8-12 CMunday (6) (hdwy over 1f out: led wl ins fnl f: r.o wl) ........................................ —1
1328★ Educated Pet (63) (Fav) *(MJohnston)* 7-8 (7x) ‡7MBaird (5) (lw: hld up: led 1f out tl wl ins fnl f: unable qckn) ........................................ 1.2
1204³ Bodari (72) *(DAWilson)* 8-10 JTate (2) (led 2f: ev ch ins fnl f: one pce) ........... s.h.3
1204² Inherent Magic (IRE) (77) *(MMcCormack)* 8-11 ‡4JHunter (3) (w ldr: led 3f out to 1f out: ev ch ins fnl f: one pce) ........................................ nk.4
1204 Memsahb (83) *(JBerry)* 9-0 ‡7SGiles (4) (prom 3f) ........................................ 3¹/₂.5
1117² Super Rocky (78) *(RBastiman)* 8-13 ‡3HBastiman (1) (prom over 3f) ........................................ 1.6
*Stewards Enquiry: Obj. to Educated Pet by Hunter overruled.*

**100/30** Educated Pet, **7/2** Bodari, Inherent Magic (IRE), **4/1** OPTICAL (IRE), **5/1** Super Rocky, **7/1** Memsahb(op 12/1). CSF £16.98, Tote £4.20: £1.80 £2.10 (£3.70). Mrs H. H. Wane (RICHMOND) bred by Oliver Murphy in Ireland. 6 Rn　60.63 sec (1.13)
SF—56/34/49/49/38/33

## 1387
BAKER LORENZ SILVER GAVEL H'CAP (0-100) £7181.00 (£2168.00: £1054.00:
£497.00)　1¹/₄m 7y (Weights raised 9 lb)　　3-55 (3-58)

816⁵ Zalon (IRE) (90) (Fav) *(JHMGosden)* 3-9-3 DHolland (3) (mde all: hrd rdn 2f out: r.o wl) ........................................ —1
1147⁵ Rising Tempo (IRE) (59) *(CACyzer)* 4-7-13 JQuinn (7) (5th st: hrd rdn over 1f out: unable qckn) ........................................ 3¹/₂.2
1132★ Mahfil (67) *(RAkehurst)* 4-8-4 ‡3FNorton (5) (2nd st: hrd rdn 2f out: one pce) .. hd.3
993² Knock Knock (84) *(IABalding)* 7-9-7 ‡3SO'Gorman (1) (4th st: one pce fnl 2f) . 1¹/₂.4
1008★ Scottish Bambi (74) *(RHannon)* 4-9-0 PRobinson (6) (3rd st: one pce fnl 3f) .... ³/₄.5
1061⁶ Croupier (84) *(CEBrittain)* 5-9-10 MRoberts (2) (6th st: no hdwy fnl 3f) .......... 1¹/₂.6
1203⁶ Northern Conqueror (IRE) (70) *(TJNaughton)* 4-8-5 ‡5DHarrison (4) (a bhd) ..... 8.7

**13/8** ZALON (IRE), **5/1** Mahfil(op 11/4), **13/2** Rising Tempo (IRE), Croupier, **8/1** Knock Knock, **9/1** Scottish Bambi, **10/1** Northern Conqueror (IRE). CSF £11.42, Tote £2.50: £1.90 £3.20 (£11.40). Sheikh Mohammed (NEWMARKET) bred by Mrs A. Whitehead in Ireland. 7 Rn　2m 10.30 (6)
SF—23/–/2/16/7/14

**1388**   BAKER LORENZ H'CAP (0-90) £3322.25 (£998.00: £481.50: £223.25)
**1m 14y**                                                              4-30 (4-33)

1106* **Akkazao (IRE) (75)** (Fav) *(WCarter)* 4-8-11 ‡⁵NGwilliams (6) (mde all: drvn out) —1
  692 Santi Sana **(67)** (bl) *(LadyHerries)* 4-8-8 WRyan (2) (2nd st: ev ch fnl 3f: r.o) ... hd.2
1153* Gilderdale **(87)** *(JWHills)* 10-9-9 ‡⁵DHarrison (3) (hdwy & edgd rt over 1f out: r.o
      ins fnl f) ........................................................................ 1.3
  912³ Abso **(68)** *(RHannon)* 4-8-9 RHills (1) (lw: 5th st: edgd rt over 1f out: r.o one
      pce) ........................................................................ 1½.4
1047 Self Expression **(86)** *(IABalding)* 4-9-13 MRoberts (5) (3rd st: one pce fnl 2f) 2½.5
      Diaco **(70)** *(MAJarvis)* 7-8-11 PRobinson (4) (6th st: rdn over 1f out: one pce) .. 2.6
  931 Altermeera **(69)** *(MrsBarbaraWaring)* 4-8-10 NHowe (8) (lw: 4th st: wknd over
      2f out) ........................................................................ hd.7
1111⁶ Languedoc **(67)** *(MPNaughton)* 5-8-8 DHolland (7) (lw: s.s: a bhd) ............... ½.8

11/4 AKKAZAO (IRE), 3/1 Gilderdale, 5/1 Self Expression, 6/1 Abso, 8/1 Santi Sana, 11/1 Languedoc, 12/1
Diaco, 16/1 Altermeera. CSF £22.64, CT £62.93. Tote £3.40: £1.70 £2.10 £1.50 (£12.80). Mr Ernie Penfold
(EPSOM) bred by Red House Stud in Ireland. 8 Rn                                        1m 41.08 (1.88)
                                                                          SF–45/41/53/34/44/22


**1389**   BAKER LORENZ STKS (Mdn 3-Y.O) £2672.00 (£742.00: £356.00)
**7f 16y**                                                              5-05 (5-08)

      **Our Occasion** *(RHannon)* 9-0 MRoberts (1) (lw: 5th st: rdn over 2f out: str run
      ins fnl f: led last strides) ........................................................ —1
1105³ Red Archer **(66)** (bl) *(PJMakin)* 9-0 WNewnes (4) (3rd st: led on bit over 1f out:
      rdn fnl f: hdd last strides) ........................................................ nk.2
  899² Sharptino (Fav) *(RAkehurst)* 9-0 DHolland (2) (lw: led 6f out tl over 1f out:
      unable qckn) ........................................................................ 6.3
1173⁵ Little Park **(64)** *(GAPritchard-Gordon)* 8-2 ‡⁷PTurner (3) (4th st: wknd over 2f
      out) ........................................................................ 5.4
1323⁵ Whitehall (IRE) *(CRNelson)* 8-9 ‡⁵DHarrison (5) (lw: led 1f: 2nd st: wknd 2f out) . 8.5

11/8 Sharptino, 9/4 OUR OCCASION, 7/2 Red Archer, 10/1 Whitehall (IRE)(op 6/1), 14/1 Little Park(op 8/1). CSF
£9.57, Tote £2.90: £1.20 £2.00 (£6.30). Simon Ellis Ltd (MARLBOROUGH) bred by Grange Thoroughbreds. 5
Rn                                                                          1m 29.14 (2.14)
                                                                          SF–47/46/28/1/–


**1390**   HANOVER SQUARE H'CAP (0-70) £3113.00 (£868.00: £419.00)
**1m 3f 91y**                                                              5-40 (5-43)
                            (Weights raised 8 lb)

1005 **Father Hayes (USA) (57)** (Jt-Fav) *(WJPearce)* 4-9-9 DNicholls (9) (3rd st:
      qcknd & led 3f out: drvn out) ........................................................ —1
  987⁵ Smiling Chief (IRE) **(51)** *(CACyzer)* 4-9-3 ‡⁷TMcLaughlin (4) (2nd st: chsd wnr
      fnl 3f: hrd rdn over 1f out: unable qckn) ........................................ 2½.2
1087 Bronze Runner **(38)** (bl) *(EAWheeler)* 8-8-1 ‡³FNorton (8) (hdwy over 1f out: r.o
      ins fnl f) ........................................................................ ½.3
1150 Scenic Dancer **(58)** (v) *(AHide)* 4-9-10 WNewnes (5) (lw: 4th st: rdn over 1f out:
      r.o) ........................................................................ 1½.4
1044 Easy Purchase **(56)** *(RJHolder)* 5-9-1 ‡⁷SDrowne (13) (lw: nvr nr to chal) ....... 3½.5
  530 The Yomper (FR) **(35)** *(RCurtis)* 10-7-8 ‡⁷CHawksley (6) (swtg: led over 8f) ...... 2.6
1037⁴ Pleasure Ahead **(35)** *(MDixon)* 5-7-10 ‡⁵NGwilliams (2) (nvr nrr) .................... 1½.7
1037³ Master Line **(42)** *(HCandy)* 11-8-1 ‡⁷SDrake (10) (5th st: wknd over 2f out) .... s.h.8
      Hallow Fair **(39)** *(CAHorgan)* 7-8-5 JQuinn (7) (b.hind: a bhd) .......................... 8.9
1083⁴ Thin Red Line **(50)** (v) *(JRJenkins)* 8-9-2 MRoberts (3) (lw: bhd fnl 5f) ............ 5.10
1258² Devil's Soul **(55)** (bl) *(RAkehurst)* 4-9-7 DHolland (12) (s.s: hdwy over 4f out:
      6th st: wknd 2f out) ........................................................................ 2.11
1147² Shadow Bird **(58)** (Jt-Fav) *(GAPritchard-Gordon)* 5-9-5 ‡⁵DHarrison (14) (b.nr
      hind: dwlt: bhd fnl 3f) ........................................................................ nk.12

4/1 FATHER HAYES (USA), Shadow Bird, 7/1 Devil's Soul, Thin Red Line, 15/2 Scenic Dancer, 9/1 Smiling Chief
(IRE), Pleasure Ahead, 10/1 Bronze Runner, 12/1 Easy Purchase, 14/1 Master Line, 20/1 Hallow Fair, 33/1 The
Yomper (FR). CSF £39.46, CT £319.16. Tote £5.30: £1.90 £4.10 £4.70 (£38.90). Mr R. J. Pearce
(HAMBLETON) bred by William Floyd in USA. 12 Rn                              2m 25.21 (3.51)
                                                                          SF–51/33/23/43/27/2

T/Trio: Race 7: £158.50 (12.7 Tckts). T/Jkpt: £3,855.90 (1.4 Tckts). T/Plpt: £39.90 (186.8 Tckts).     AK

811—**YORK (L-H)**
**Friday, June 12th [Firm]**
Going Allowance: St: nil sec; Rest: minus 0.20 sec per fur (F)　　　　Wind: almost nil
Stalls: high

**1391**　ROTHMANS ROYALS NORTH SOUTH CHALLENGE SERIES (H'cap) (3-Y.O) (0-90)
　　　　£6108.00 (£1824.00: £872.00: £396.00)　**6f 214y**　　　2-10 (2-13)

1086* **Owner's Dream (USA)** (73) *(BHanbury)* 8-10 WRyan (2) (lw: mde virtually all:
　　　　r.o wl fnl f) ........................................................................... —1
　576⁶ **Waders Dream (IRE)** (72) *(JEBanks)* 8-9 RCochrane (8) (a cl up: disp ld over 2f
　　　　out: nt qckn nr fin) .................................................................. nk.2
　983⁴ **Cool Luke (IRE)** (78) *(GMMoore)* 9-1 KFallon (6) (a chsng ldrs: rdn over 2f out:
　　　　kpt on wl) ............................................................................. 2.3
1075* **First Gold** (60) (bl) *(Jt-Fav) (JWharton)* 7-8 ‡³JFanning (7) (lw: pushed along
　　　　after 3f: hdwy 2f out: nvr able to chal) ..................................... ¾.4
1206³ **Euro Festival** (84) *(MissLCSiddall)* 9-7 PatEddery (1) (a chsng ldrs: n.m.r 2f
　　　　out: r.o one pce) .................................................................... 2.5
1193³ **Straw Thatch** (74) *(MJohnston)* 8-11 DMcKeown (9) (lw: swtg: æffrt ½-wy: sn
　　　　hrd drvn & no imp) ................................................................. 1½.6
　963* **Express Gift** (67) *(MrsGRReveley)* 7-11 ‡⁷DarrenMoffatt (4) (lw: outpcd
　　　　& bhd ½-wy: styd on: n.d) ...................................................... hd.7
1173³ **Jato** (74) (bl) *(WJHaggas)* 8-6 ‡⁵JWeaver (3) (lw: nvr wnt pce) ........ 2½.8
　　　　1236⁴ Salda (7/1) Withdrawn : not under orders — Rule 4 applies

5/1 Express Gift, First Gold, **6/1** Waders Dream (IRE), **13/2** Straw Thatch, Cool Luke (IRE), **7/1** Euro Festival, **9/1**
OWNER'S DREAM (USA), **12/1** Jato. CSF £16.31, CT £218.76, Toto £12.40: £3.10 £2.60 £1.70 (£24.80). Mr B.
Hanbury (NEWMARKET) bred by Rogers Trust in USA. 8 Rn　　　　1m 23.60 (1.20)
　　　　　　　　　　　　　　　　　　　　　　　　　　　SF—57/55/55/32/53/38

**1392**　WILLIAM STONES H'CAP (0-100) £5796.00 (£1728.00: £824.00: £372.00)
　　　　**5f**　　　　　　　　　　　　　　　　　　　2-40 (2-41)

1187² **Martina** (61) *(Jt-Fav) (JWharton)* 4—7-12 ‡³JFanning (3) (disp ld tl led 2f out:
　　　　hdd ins fnl f: rallied to ld cl home) ........................................... —1
　686 **Lucedeo** (81) *(JLSpearing)* 8-9-7 LDettori (7) (in tch: hdwy 2f out: led ins fnl f:
　　　　no ex cl home) ....................................................................... nk.2
1199 **Absolution** (81) *(MPNaughton)* 8-9-2 ‡⁵JWeaver (5) (lw: in tch: hdwy ½-wy: ev
　　　　ch over 1f out: nt qckn nr fin) .................................................. hd.3
1247⁵ **Gondo** (77) *(EJAlston)* 5-9-3 KFallon (6) (lw: bhd: hdwy 2f out: r.o) ...... ½.4
1212⁴ **Gorinsky (IRE)** (76) (bl) *(JBerry)* 4-9-2 JCarroll (2) (disp ld 3f: kpt on same pce) ½.5
1053* **Tongue Tied** (70) *(Jt-Fav) (JWharton)* 4-8-10 WRyan (9) (lw: a chsng ldrs: shkn
　　　　up 2f out: kpt on same pce) .................................................... hd.6
1199 **Heaven-Liegh-Grey** (88) *(MJohnston)* 4-10-0 DMcKeown (1) (lw: disp ld 3f: sn
　　　　wknd) .................................................................................... 3½.7
　559³ **My Sovereign (USA)** (76) *(JRFanshawe)* 3-8-8 GDuffield (4) (lw: a outpcd &
　　　　bhd) ...................................................................................... 2½.8
1138⁶ **Tauber** (65) *(PatMitchell)* 8-8-2 ‡³SO'Gorman (8) (chsd ldrs tl wknd 1f out) ...... 1.9

9/2 MARTINA, Tongue Tied, **11/2** Gorinsky (IRE), My Sovereign (USA), **15/2** Absolution, Gondo, **10/1** Lucedeo,
**12/1** Ors. CSF £42.65, CT £297.05. Tote £4.50: £1.70 £2.70 £2.50 (£23.80). Mr M. J. Yarrow (MELTON
MOWBRAY) bred by M. J. Yarrow. 9 Rn　　　　　　　　　　　　　　59.17 sec (1.67)
　　　　　　　　　　　　　　　　　　　　　　　　　　　SF—50/72/66/65/62/55

**1393**　INNOVATIVE MARKETING SPRINT (H'cap) (0-110) £11062.50 (£3300.00: £1575.00:
　　　　£712.50)　**6f**　　　　　　　　　　　　　3-10 (3-11)

1247² **Dominuet** (80) *(JLSpearing)* 7-8-8 GHind (12) (hdwy ½-wy: swtchd appr fnl f:
　　　　r.o wl to ld nr fin) ................................................................... —1
　819² **Macrobian** (93) *(MHEasterby)* 8-9-2 ‡⁵SMaloney (10) (lw: led: rdn over
　　　　1f out: r.o wl: jst ct) ............................................................... s.h.2
　980² **Beau Venture (USA)** (84) *(FHLee)* 4-8-12 PatEddery (11) (trckd ldrs: effrt over
　　　　1f out: sn ev int fnl f) ............................................................. 1½.3
　712³ **Colossus** (73) *(CEBrittain)* 4-8-1 GCrealock (9) (lw: in tch: effrt over 2f out: wnt
　　　　rt: r.o) .................................................................................. 1.4
1167⁵ **Fascination Waltz** (73) *(DShaw)* 5-7-10 ‡⁵NKennedy (8) (a chsng ldrs: hdwy u.p
　　　　2f out: nt qckn fnl f) ............................................................... 1.5
1014⁶ **Corn Futures** (78) (v) *(JPLeigh)* 4-8-6 DMcKeown (7) (outpcd ½-wy: hdwy
　　　　whn hmpd wl over 1f out: nrst fin) ............................................ nk.6

1212³ Love Legend (90) *(DWPArbuthnot)* 7-8-13 ‡⁵RPrice (4) (hdwy ½-wy: chal 2f
out: kpt on one pce) .......................................................................... 1.7

1134⁴ Cumbrian Waltzer (100) (Jt-Fav) *(MHEasterby)* 7-10-0 MBirch (1) (a chsng
ldrs: effrt 2f out: nt qckn) ................................................................. hd.8

1107⁴ Petraco (IRE) (78) (bl) *(LJCodd)* 4-8-3 ‡³FNorton (2) (lw: cl up tl wknd over 1f
out) ................................................................................................... ³⁄4.9

992³ Seneca Reef (IRE) (86) *(IABalding)* 4-9-0 RCochrane (5) (lw: chsd ldrs tl wknd
over 1f out) ....................................................................................... 1½.10

1014³ Resolute Bay (84) (v) *(RMWhitaker)* 6-8-12 ACulhane (6) (lw: sn drvn along:
n.d) .................................................................................................. 1½.11

813 Amron (84) *(JBerry)* 5-8-12 JCarroll (3) (lw: outpcd & bhd after 2f) ............ 7.12

5/1 Macrobian, Cumbrian Waltzer, 7/1 Resolute Bay, Beau Venture (USA), 8/1 Seneca Reef (IRE), Petraco (IRE),
9/1 Love Legend, 10/1 Fascination Waltz, DOMINUET, 12/1 Colossus, 16/1 Amron, 33/1 Corn Futures. CSF
£57.81, CT £349.49. Tote £16.10: £4.10 £1.60 £2.20 (£44.00). Mrs Robert Heathcote (ALCESTER) bred by
Heathavon Stables Ltd. 12 Rn 　　　　　　　　　　　　　　　　　　　　　　　　　　　1m 11.59 (1.39)
SF—66/73/63/48/39/48

**1394** 　　SHEPHERD CONSTRUCTION APP'CE H'CAP (0-95) £5162.50 (£1540.00: £735.00:
£332.50) 　**1m 3f 195y** 　　　　　　　　　　　　　　　　　　　　　3-40 (3-47)

1090* **Azureus (IRE) (69)** *(MrsGRReveley)* 4-9-0 ‡³DarrenMoffatt (5) (lw: hdwy 6f out:
led over 3f out: qcknd clr: wknd nr fin) ................................................. —1

1003* Northern Kingdom (USA) (71) (Fav) *(SGNorton)* 3-8-0 ‡³OPears (6) (lw: plld
hrd: prom tl lost pl ent st: hdwy 3f out: styd on wl nr fin) ...... ³⁄4.2

1126* Eden's Close (76) (v) *(MHTompkins)* 3-7-11 ‡¹¹SMulvey (3) (hld up: effrt & bdly
hmpd wl over 3f out: swtchd & r.o nr fin) ........................... nk.3

1065⁴ Belafonte (63) *(RJHolder)* 5-8-8 ‡³SDrowne (7) (a chsng ldrs: effrt over 3f out:
styd on) ............................................................................................. s.h.4

1211 Express Account (68) *(RJRWilliams)* 5-8-5 ‡¹¹GMitchell (9) (trckd ldrs: outpcd
3f out: hdwy 2f out: styd on one pce appr fnl f) ................... hd.5

Rosgill (69) *(PMitchell)* 6-9-3 JWeaver (4) (hld up: nt clr run ent st: hdwy 2f out:
n.m.r nr fin) ..................................................................................... 2.6

964⁶ Eire Leath-Sceal (58) *(MBrittain)* 5-8-1 ‡⁵JMarshall (10) (led tl hdd 7f out: ev ch tl
wknd wl over 2f out) ........................................................................ 4.7

1016⁵ Checkpoint Charlie (63) *(JMPEustace)* 7-8-11 AntoinetteArmes (11) (lw: dwlt:
plld hrd: hdwy to ld 7f out: hdd over 3f out: sn wknd) ......... 7.8

467⁶ Hillzah (USA) (80) *(RBastiman)* 4-9-11 ‡³HBastiman (1) (dwlt: plld hrd: a bhd) ...... 9

916* Young George (61) *(MDods)* 5-8-9 RPrice (12) (prom to st: sn rdn & wknd) ...... 10

974 Mardessa (9/1) Withdrawn (jockey not qualified to ride) : not under orders

4/1 Northern Kingdom (USA), 9/2 Eden's Close, 6/1 Express Account, 7/1 Belafonte, 8/1 AZUREUS (IRE), 9/1
Checkpoint Charlie, 10/1 Young George, Eire Leath-Sceal, 11/1 Rosgill, 20/1 Hillzah (USA). CSF £37.43, CT
£148.12. Tote £9.30: £2.60 £1.70 £1.50 (£16.20). Mr J. C. Murdoch (SALTBURN) bred by Ballygoran Stud in
Ireland. 10 Rn 　　　　　　　　　　　　　　　　　　　　　　　　　　　　　　　2m 30.21 (3.21)
SF—44/28/24/29/30/38

**1395** 　　MERCHANT ADVENTURERS MEDIAN AUCTION STKS (Mdn 3-Y-O) £4113.00 (£1224.00:
£582.00: £261.00) 　**1m 5f 194y** 　　　　　　　　　　　　　　4-10 (4-11)

1165³ **Newton Point (58)** (Jt-Fav) *(GAPritchard-Gordon)* 9-0 GDuffield (1) (sn led:
just hld on) ...................................................................................... —1

487³ Free Transfer (IRE) (60) *(PFTulk)* 9-0 WRyan (3) (hld up: effrt 2f out: r.o wl: jst
failed) ............................................................................................... s.h.2

868 Kojiki *(LMCumani)* 9-0 LDettori (5) (led early: chsd ldrs: drvn along 6f out: r.o
one pce) .......................................................................................... 3½.3

1139² Prince Mercury (66) (bl) *(JLDunlop)* 9-0 PatEddery (4) (sn trckng ldr: drvn
along 3f out: grad wknd) ................................................................ 2.4

1033⁴ Diamond Wedding (USA) (Jt-Fav) *(NAGraham)* 8-9 RCochrane (2) (prom: effrt
ent st: wknd over 2f out) ................................................................ 5.5

9/4 Diamond Wedding (USA), NEWTON POINT, 5/2 Prince Mercury, 13/2 Kojiki, 16/1 Free Transfer (IRE). CSF
£23.53, Tote £4.10: £1.80 £3.50 (£16.50). Mr A. M. Ennever (NEWMARKET) bred by Stetchworth Park Stud Ltd.
5 Rn 　　　　　　　　　　　　　　　　　　　　　　　　　　　　　　　　　　　2m 57.33 (3.73)
SF—35/34/27/23/8

**1396** 　　UNIVERSITY OF YORK TURF CLUB GRADUATION STKS (2-Y.O.F) £4269.00 (£1272.00:
£606.00: £273.00) 　**6f** 　　　　　　　　　　　　　　　　　　　4-40 (4-40)

1056² **Ten to Six** (Fav) *(EWeymes)* 8-8 WNewnes (1) (lw: trckd ldrs: led wl over 1f out:
r.o wl) ............................................................................................... —1

Where's the Dance *(CEBrittain)* 8-5 GCrealock (5) (cmpt: scope: hld up: effrt 2f
out: r.o wl nr fin) ............................................................................. ³⁄4.2

1186⁵ Petite Epaulette *(WJarvis)* 9-1 RCochrane (4) (lw: trckd ldr: led over 2f out tl wl over 1f out: nt qckn wl ins fnl f) ........................................ nk.3

Nemea (USA) *(JRFanshawe)* 8-5 GDuffield (6) (rangy: scope: s.i.s: sn trckng ldrs: outpcd 2f out: no imp after) ........................................ 5.4

770⁵ Tarnside Rosal *(JEtherington)* 9-1 TLucas (3) (plld hrd: trckd ldrs over 3f: sn btn) ........................................ 1½.5

1233* Charity Express (IRE) *(JBerry)* 9-1 JCarroll (7) (lw: unruly in stalls: led tl hdd over 2f out: sn wknd) ........................................ 8.6

**5/2** TEN TO SIX, **11/4** Petite Epaulette, **100/30** Nemea (USA), **9/2** Charity Express (IRE), **6/1** Where's the Dance, **10/1** Tarnside Rosal. CSF £16.84, Tote £3.00: £1.50 £3.70 (£18.50). Mrs V. Moorey (MIDDLEHAM) bred by I. W. T. and Mrs Loftus. 6 Rn
1m 14.43 (4.23)
SF—10/4/13/–/–/–

T/Trio: Race 3: £90.10 (24.8 Tckts). T/Plpt: £197.10 (51.2 Tckts). AA

# YORK (L-H)
## Saturday, June 13th [Firm]
Going Allowance: St: minus 0.25 sec; Rest: minus 0.40 sec (F)          Wind: almost nil

Stalls: high

**1397**  E.B.F. TIMEFORM CHARITY DAY STKS (Mdn 2-Y.O) £4503.00 (£1344.00: £642.00: £291.00)  **6f**
2-15 (2-18)

**Lindon Lime (USA)** *(Fav)* *(PFICole)* 9-0 AMunro (2) (rangy: scope: mde virtually all: rn green fr ½-wy: shkn up 2f out: r.o wl nr fin) .. —1

Marillette (USA) *(JHMGosden)* 8-9 WRSwinburn (4) (neat: unf: lw: v.unruly gng to s: trckd wnr: disp ld ½-wy: eased whn hld nr fin) 1½.2

Blue Laws (IRE) *(JGFitzGerald)* 9-0 TLucas (1) (w'like: scope: bit bkwd: outpcd ½-wy: kpt on fnl f) ........................................ 7.3

Best Appearance (IRE) *(JGFitzGerald)* 9-0 KFallon (3) (cmpt: bit bkwd: s.i.s: rn v.green: nvr wnt pce: wl bhd fr ½-wy) ........................................ 12.4

**8/11** LINDON LIME (USA), **6/4** Marillette (USA), **16/1** Ors. CSF £2.12, Tote £1.90 (£1.40). Mr Fahd Salman (WHATCOMBE) bred by Lucy G. Bassett in USA. 4 Rn
1m 13.12 (2.92)
SF—12/1/–/–

**1398**  CADOGAN STKS (Mdn 3-Y.O) £6400.00 (£1900.00: £900.00: £400.00)  **7f 202y**
2-45 (2-45)

**Kristianstad** *(Fav)* *(MrsJCecil)* 9-0 PaulEddery (2) (lw: hld up: effrt 3f out: led wl ins fnl f) ........................................ —1

919² Agincourt Song (USA) **(73)** *(JLDunlop)* 9-0 WCarson (5) (led: r.o u.p fnl 2f: hdd & nt qckn nr fin) ........................................ ½.2

So Smug (USA) *(JHMGosden)* 8-9 RCochrane (1) (lw: s.s: hld up: stdy hdwy over 2f out: ev ch ins fnl f: r.o) ........................................ nk.3

1252² Ajo (IRE) **(84)** *(MRStoute)* 9-0 LDettori (3) (trckd ldrs: disp ld 3f: rdn & wknd over 1f out) ........................................ 1½.4

**6/4** KRISTIANSTAD, **9/4** Ajo (IRE), **9/2** So Smug (USA), **5/1** Agincourt Song (USA). CSF £7.41, Tote £2.00 (£4.80). Sheikh Mohammed (NEWMARKET) bred by Sheikh Mohammed bin Rashid al Maktoum. 4 Rn
1m 37.82 (1.82)
SF—25/23/17/17

**1399**  QUEEN MOTHER'S CUP (Stks) (Ladies)  £10601.25 (£3210.00: £1567.50: £746.25)  **1m 3f 195y**
3-15 (3-17)

1169* **Sea Goddess (87)** *(WJarvis)* 4-10-7 MrsLPearce (8) (lw: mde all: styd on wl fnl 2f) ........................................ —1

1168⁵ Safa **(92)** *(AAScott)* 4-10-2 MissTBracegirdle (7) (lw: hld up: gng wl: wnt 2nd over 3f out: effrt over 1f out: kpt on) ........................................ 1.2

623² Hierarch (USA) *(LordHuntingdon)* 3-9-5 HRHThePrincessRoyal (5) (lw: hld up & bhd: gd hdwy over 1f out: r.o strly towards fin) ........................................ 1½.3

855³ Hebridean *(Fav)* *(HCandy)* 5-10-2 ‡⁵MrsCDunwoody (10) (lw: chsd ldrs: drvn along 3f out: sn wknd) ........................................ 3½.4

1009⁴ Elaine Tully (IRE) **(77)** *(MJHeaton-Ellis)* 4-10-0 ‡‡MissFHaynes (4) (lw: bhd tl kpt on fnl 3f: nvr nr to chal) ........................................ 4.5

850⁶ Good Reference (IRE) **(89)** *(MBell)* 3-9-2 ‡⁵MrsGBell (2) (lw: b.nr fore: sn chsng ldrs: lost pl over 3f out) ........................................ 6.6

431 Widyan (USA) **(95)** *(PFICole)* 4-10-12 MissMClark (6) (bhd: effrt ent st: sn wknd) ........................................ s.h.7

1250* Jack Button (IRE) **(71)** (bl) *(BobJones)* 3-9-8 MissDianaJones (1) (chsd ldrs tl lost pl over 3f out) ........................................... 2¹/₂.8

1137³ The Karaoke King **(68)** *(RHannon)* 3-9-0 ‡⁵MrsJBoggis (9) (chsd ldrs to st: sn lost pl) ............................................................. 1¹/₂.9

1194⁴ Master's Crown (USA) *(MCChapman)* 4-10-2 ‡⁵MissAYardley (3) (swtg: bhd whn sddle slipped & uns rdr over 3f out) ...................... 0

**7/4** Hebridean, **7/2** SEA GODDESS, **6/1** Safa, **8/1** Hierarch (USA), **17/2** Good Reference (IRE), **9/1** Widyan (USA), **12/1** Elaine Tully (IRE), **20/1** Jack Button (IRE), **25/1** The Karaoke King, **100/1** Master's Crown (USA). CSF £24.09, Tote £3.50: £1.40 £2.20 £2.10 (£12.40). Lord Howard de Walden (NEWMARKET) bred by Seend Stud. 10 Rn 2m 28.49 (1.49)
SF—58/51/37/41/31/7

---

**1400** WILLIAM HILL GOLDEN SPURS TROPHY (H'cap) (3-Y.O) (0-110) £24552.75 (£7347.00: £3523.50: £1611.75) **6f** 3-45 (3-49)

(Weights raised 9 lb)

1134 **Orthorhombus (96)** (bl) *(GLewis)* 9-2 PaulEddery (1) (lw: w ldrs: led over 1f out: r.o wl u.p) ................................... —1

870² Double Blue **(89)** (Fav) *(MJohnston)* 8-9 DMcKeown (5) (lw: mde most: rdn & nt qckn ins fnl f) ...................... nk.2

870⁶ Heather Bank **(94)** *(JBerry)* 9-0 JCarroll (3) (a chsng ldrs: rdn over 2f out: kpt on wl fnl f) ................................ 1¹/₂.3

1224a² Flute (USA) **(88)** *(CEBrittain)* 8-8 WRSwinburn (11) (lw: s.i.s: bhd tl hdwy ¹/₂-wy: styd on wl fnl f) ......... ¹/₂.4

870³ Master Planner **(92)** *(CACyzer)* 8-12 KFallon (9) (a chsng ldrs: effrt & ev ch 2f out: unable qckn) ............ hd.5

870* Splice **(93)** *(JRFanshawe)* 8-6 ‡⁷NVarley (4) (lw: trckd ldrs: effrt 2f out: wknd wl ins fnl f) ......................... 3.6

673 Master of Passion **(101)** *(JMPEustace)* 9-7 LPiggott (2) (chsd ldrs: rdn over 2f out: sn btn) ........................ 3¹/₂.7

607⁶ Phyliel (USA) **(83)** *(MRStoute)* 8-3 AMunro (7) (in rr fr ¹/₂-wy) ..................... 3.8

1187* Branston Abby (IRE) **(92)** *(JWharton)* 8-12 (7x) MBirch (6) (lw: reard up s: bhd: sme hdwy ¹/₂-wy: sn lost pl) ............ 4.9

1042⁴ Parisien Singer **(85)** *(IABalding)* 8-5 RCochrane (10) (chsd ldrs tl wknd over 2f out) ..................................... 3.10

792* Ghalyoon (USA) **(84)** *(PTWalwyn)* 8-4 WCarson (8) (b.off hind: chsd ldrs: rdn ¹/₂-wy: sn bhd & eased) ............. 7.11

**3/1** Double Blue, **6/1** Splice, **7/1** Master Planner, Ghalyoon (USA), **15/2** ORTHORHOMBUS, **8/1** Branston Abby (IRE), Phyliel (USA), **11/1** Heather Bank, Flute (USA), **25/1** Ors. CSF £29.57, CT £228.22. Tote £6.40: £2.30 £1.40 £2.60 (£10.30). Mr M. J. E. Thornhill (EPSOM) bred by Cliveden Stud. 11 Rn 1m 10.05 (U.15)
SF—75/67/66/58/61/43

---

**1401** DANIEL PRENN ROYAL YORKSHIRE STKS (listed race) (3-Y.O) £11355.00 (£3390.00: £1620.00: £735.00) **1¹/₄m 85y** 4-15 (4-17)

601⁵ **Bobzao (IRE) (98)** *(WCarter)* 8-11 AMunro (1) (lw: chsd ldrs: rdn to ld wl over 1f out: r.o strly fnl f) ......................... —1

823* Polish Blue (USA) **(103)** (Fav) *(MRStoute)* 9-0 WRSwinburn (4) (lw: effrt over 3f out: ev ch & rdn 2f out: nt qckn fnl f) ...... 3.2

991* Torrey Canyon (USA) **(116)** *(RCharlton)* 9-4 RCochrane (3) (lw: hld up: effrt & reminders over 3f out: hrd rdn & ev ch wl over 1f out: wknd) 5.3

944* Boloardo **(86)** *(CEBrittain)* 8-11 MBirch (5) (lw: chsd ldrs: disp ld 5f out tl rdn & wknd 2f out) ............................ nk.4

655 Artic Tracker (USA) **(105)** *(CRNelson)* 9-0 JReid (2) (led tl hdd & wknd wl over 1f out) ........................... ¹/₂.5

**5/4** Polish Blue (USA), **13/8** Torrey Canyon (USA), **11/2** Artic Tracker (USA), **16/1** BOBZAO (IRE) & Ors. CSF £34.57, Tote £27.30: £4.40 £1.30 (£16.90). T. G. Mills Limited (EPSOM) bred by Airlie Stud in USA. 5 Rn 2m 6.38 (U1.12)
SF—67/64/58/50/52

---

**1402** CRAWLEY WARREN H'CAP (0-110) £8460.00 (£2520.00: £1200.00: £540.00) **1m 205y** 4-45 (4-46)

1047⁴ **Lucky Guest (90)** (Fav) *(JLDunlop)* 5-9-7 WCarson (3) (lw: hld up: nt clr run 2f out: squeezed thro to ld ins fnl f: jst hld on) ............ —1

Legal View (USA) **(90)** *(LMCumani)* 4-9-7 LDettori (2) (hld up: effrt & swtchd rt wl over 1f out: r.o wl ins fnl f) ................... s.h.2

1061* Pay Homage **(97)** *(IABalding)* 4-10-0 JReid (6) (hld up: stdy hdwy 4f out: ev ch ins fnl f: unable qckn) ..................... 1¹/₂.3

1168[4] Flaming Arrow (97) *(HRACecil)* 4–10-0 WRSwinburn (5) (trckd ldrs: ev ch 2f
out: rdn & nt qckn fnl f) .................................................................. nk.4

479[2] No Submission (USA) (84) *(CRNelson)* 6–9-1 PaulEddery (1) (led tl hdd & no
ex ins fnl f) .................................................................... ¹/2.5

1018 Regent Lad (74) *(MissLCSiddall)* 8–8-5 MBirch (4) (lw: sn trckng ldr: rdn &
wknd over 2f out) ........................................................ 15.6

**11/4 LUCKY GUEST, 3/1** Pay Homage, **9/2** Flaming Arrow, **5/1** No Submission (USA), **13/2** Regent Lad, **7/1**
Legal View (USA). CSF £19.06, Tote £2.90: £1.60 £2.90 (£11.80). Windflower Overseas Holdings Inc
(ARUNDEL) bred by Windflower Overseas. 6 Rn 1m 49.48 (0.48)
SF—46/45/47/46/31/–

---

**1403**    MACMILLAN NURSE APPEAL H'CAP (0-105) £6400.00 (£1900.00: £900.00: £400.00)
**6f 214y**                                                                    5-15 (5-18)

1154* **Ringland (USA) (80)** *(PCHaslam)* 4–9-5 LPiggott (12) (a chsng ldrs: rdn to ld
over 1f out: edgd lft: hld on wl u.p) ...................................... —1

887 Super Benz (75) *(TFairhurst)* 6–8-11 ‡3JFanning (1) (b.off fore: led tl over 1f out:
nt qckn nr fin) ..................................................................... ³/4.2

1203 Rocton North (IRE) (87) *(RHannon)* 4–9-12 BRaymond (6) (sn bhd: gd hdwy
over 1f out: r.o nr fin) .................................................. s.h.3

1133[3] Bold Angel (82) *(MHEasterby)* 5–9-2 ‡5SMaloney (4) (hld up: effrt ¹/2-wy: styd on
wl fnl f) .......................................................................... ¹/2.4

1114* Sharpalto (82) *(MrsGRReveley)* 5–9-7 JLowe (8) (lw: sn bhd & pushed along:
hdwy ¹/2-wy: rdn & nt qckn over 1f out) ........................... nk.5

796[6] State Flyer (62) (v) *(CBBBooth)* 4–7-10(4) ‡5LNewton (2) (s.i.s: hdwy ¹/2-wy: kpt
on wl u.p fnl f) ............................................................... nk.6

1289[3] Duckington (72) (Fav) *(MHEasterby)* 8–8-11 MBirch (13) (trckd ldrs: effrt over
2f out: wknd over 1f out) ............................................... 3.7

941[2] Tender Moment (IRE) (73) *(CEBrittain)* 4–8-12 WRSwinburn (11) (lw: chsd ldrs
tl wknd over 1f out) .................................................... 2¹/2.8

1253[6] Morgannwg (IRE) (80) *(RDickin)* 4–9-5 RCochrane (10) (in tch: effrt ¹/2-wy: no
imp) ............................................................................ nk.9

1157[3] Eternal Flame (66) *(JWHills)* 4–8-2 ‡3RPerham (3) (hld up: effrt & hmpd 3f out: nt
rcvr) ........................................................................... 1¹/2.10

813 Gentle Hero (USA) (89) *(MPNaughton)* 6–9-9 ‡5JWeaver (7) (in tch tl wknd 2f
out) ........................................................................... 1¹/2.11

1247[4] Northern Spark (67) *(CWThornton)* 4–8-6 WCarson (9) (chsd ldrs: lost pl &
edgd lft 3f out: sn bhd) .............................................. ³/4.12

**5/1** Duckington, **13/2** Northern Spark, Sharpalto, **7/1** Morgannwg (IRE), Tender Moment (IRE), **8/1** RINGLAND
(USA), Bold Angel, Eternal Flame, **16/1** Rocton North (IRE), Super Benz, Gentle Hero (USA), **33/1** State Flyer. CSF
£114.19, CT £1,813.98. Tote £8.70: £2.70 £5.20 £3.60 (£181.80). Mr S. A. B. Dinsmore (MIDDLEHAM) bred by
Robinson Farm in USA. 12 Rn 1m 22.83 (0.43)
SF—57/47/61/49/53/27

T/Trio: Race 4: £36.80 (96.2 Tckts). T/Plpt: £72.30 (209.95 Tckts). WG

---

906—**BATH (L-H)**
**Saturday, June 13th [Firm]**
Going Allowance: 5f 11y-5f 161y: minus 0.30; Rest: minus 0.45 (F)                Wind: nil

Stalls: low

**1404**    JUNE (S) STKS    £2810.00 (£785.00: £380.00)    1¹/4m 46y        2-00 (2-05)

896 **High Post (46)** (Jt-Fav) *(DMarks)* 3–8-11 TQuinn (13) (hld up: gd hdwy to ld 2f
out: hdd ins fnl f: led post) ...................................... —1

1338 Now Boarding (33) *(RJHodges)* 5–8-7 ‡7SDrowne (10) (hld up: hdwy over 3f
out: led over 2f out: sn hdd: led ins fnl f: hdd post) .......... s.h.2

City Line *(DRLaing)* 3–8-6 GBardwell (17) (swtg: led tl over 2f out: btn whn n.m.r
ins fnl f) ..................................................................... 2.3

1034 Mystic Panther (40) *(RJHolder)* 4–8-12 ‡7RWaterford (5) (hdwy 3f out: one pce
fnl 2f) ...................................................................... 3¹/2.4

Le Saule D'Or (30) *(APJames)* 5–9-5 AMackay (6) (dwlt: hdwy 2f out: nt rch
ldrs) ........................................................................ 2¹/2.5

776[5] Great Impostor (46) *(RJHodges)* 4–9-2 ‡3DBiggs (11) (5th st: no hdwy fnl 2f) .... 3.6

1143 Just Ready (IRE) (32) *(GAHam)* 4–9-10 ADicks (12) (hdwy on ins whn hmpd 2f
out: nt rcvr) ............................................................. hd.7

114 Romola Nijinsky (Jt-Fav) *(PDEvans)* 4–9-0 DaleGibson (8) (b: prom 6f) ............. 3.8

Little Bang (33) *(KBishop)* 4–9-0 RFox (9) (s.i.s: nvr nrr) ......................... nk.9

1147 Muzo (USA) (65) *(JMBradley)* 5–9-10 JWilliams (19) (nvr nr ldrs) ................. 2.10

Ugly *(RPCHoad)* 6-9-5 MWigham (3) (bit bkwd: s.s: a bhd) ............... ½.**11**
Free Expression *(PLeach)* 7-9-5 SWhitworth (20) (s.s: a bhd) ......... 1½.**12**
Saxon Lad (USA) **(48)** *(GPEnright)* 6-9-10 AClark (18) (4th st: wknd 2f out) . 1½.**13**
1034 Set Up *(DBurchell)* 4-9-5 NAdams (7) (2nd st: wknd over 2f out) ........... 6.**14**
1003⁵ Mittenoski Pet *(TJNaughton)* 3-8-1 GCarter (14) (6th st: wknd over 2f out) .. ½.**15**
Aristocratic Peter (USA) **(30)** (bl) *(DCJermy)* 5-8-12 ‡⁷MJermy (2) (a bhd) ...... 3.**16**
Jamais Bleu **(48)** (bl) *(TJNaughton)* 3-8-1 ‡⁵RPrice (15) (a bhd) ......... hd.**17**
899 On the Rampage (bl) *(RHannon)* 3-8-1 AMcGlone (4) (3rd st: wknd 3f out) .. s.h.**18**
Just Cracker *(PLeach)* 7-9-5 TyroneWilliams (1) (t.o) .................. 12.**19**
Siddington Lodge (IRE) *(AJChamberlain)* 4-9-0 ‡⁵ATucker (16) (bit bkwd: t.o) ... 20

**5/1** HIGH POST, Romola Nijinsky, **8/1** Now Boarding(6/1—11/1), **9/1** Muzo (USA), **10/1** Great Impostor(op 6/1), On the Rampage(op 9/1), **11/1** City Line(7/1—12/1), **14/1** Mittenoski Pet, **16/1** Mystic Panther(op 8/1), **20/1** Saxon Lad (USA), Set Up, **25/1** Jamais Bleu, **33/1** Free Expression, Just Cracker, Le Saule D'Or, Just Ready (IRE), Little Bang, **50/1** Ors. CSF £41.81, Tote £5.60: £2.60 £5.70 £3.30 (£55.90). Mr V. Squeglia (UPPER LAMBOURN) bred by Gaberson Ltd. 20 Rn; Bt in 7,600 gns. Now Boarding clmd B Higham £6,000
2m 9.5 (1.8)
SF—34/29/24/23/25/16

**1405** KELSTON MEDIAN AUCTION STKS (2-Y.O) £2897.50 (£810.00: £392.50)
5f 161y
2-30 (2-31)

**Mr Martini (IRE)** *(CEBrittain)* 8-11 GCrealock (4) (unf: a.p: chal whn hung lft ins
fnl f: led nr fin) ................................................... —**1**
1112* Second Colours (USA) **(Fav)** *(PSFelgate)* 9-2 JWilliams (1) (lw: led tl hdd cl
home) ............................................................... hd.**2**
Conbrio Star *(CGCox)* 8-11 AClark (3) (w'like: scope: hld up: hdwy 3f out: wknd
fnl f) ............................................................... 8.**3**
Yet to Dance *(RJHolder)* 8-6 ADicks (5) (leggy: bhd fnl 2f) ............. 3½.**4**
My Foxy Lady *(DHaydnJones)* 8-6 TyroneWilliams (6) (scope: bhd fnl 3f: t.o) . 20.**5**

**4/6** Second Colours (USA), **7/2** MR MARTINI (IRE)(2/1—4/1), **5/1** My Foxy Lady, **10/1** Yet to Dance, **16/1** Conbrio Star(10/1—20/1). CSF £6.29, Tote £4.00: £2.10 £1.20 (£2.10). Circlechart Ltd (NEWMARKET) bred by Mrs W. Hanson in Ireland. 5 Rn
1m 11.1 (1.8)
SF—27/31/—/—/—

**1406** ELECTRIC H'CAP (0-90) £4776.00 (£1428.00: £684.00: £312.00)
5f 161y
3-05 (3-06)

438 **African Chimes (69)** *(WAO'Gorman)* 5-8-2 ‡⁵EmmaO'Gorman (2) (hld up:
hdwy 2f out: led ins fnl f: r.o wl) .................................... —**1**
1167 Cee-En-Cee **(70)** (bl) **(Fav)** *(MMcCourt)* 8-8-8 TQuinn (3) (lw: a.p: led 2f out tl
ins fnl f) .......................................................... 1½.**2**
1107 Baligay **(79)** *(RJHodges)* 7-9-0 ‡³TSprake (5) (lw: hdwy over 1f out: r.o) ........... 2.**3**
1305² Iron King **(67)** *(JLSpearing)* 6-8-5 GBardwell (1) (dwlt: hdwy over 1f out: nvr nrr) 2.**4**
1263 No Quarter Given **(72)** *(PSFelgate)* 7-8-10 JWilliams (9) (s.i.s: hdwy over 2f
out: wknd over 1f out) .............................................. 2½.**5**
1167⁴ Teanarco (IRE) **(60)** *(RJHolder)* 4-7-12 DaleGibson (6) (prom over 3f) ........ ¾.**6**
596 Sports Post Lady (IRE) **(60)** *(CJHill)* 4-7-12 NAdams (4) (rdn along: led 3f tl
wknd 2f out) ....................................................... 2.**7**
1135⁵ Hard to Figure **(90)** *(RJHodges)* 6-10-0 SWhitworth (8) (lw: w ldrs tl wknd over
1f out) ............................................................. 1½.**8**
1199 Loft Boy **(70)** (bl) *(JDBethell)* 9-8-8 TyroneWilliams (10) (spd over 3f) .......... 2.**9**
1219⁵ Soba Guest (IRE) **(74)** *(JBerry)* 3-8-3 GCarter (7) (led over 2f) ........... 3.**10**

**4/1** Cee-En-Cee(tchd 6/1), **9/2** Iron King, **13/2** Loft Boy, Hard to Figure, **7/1** Soba Guest (IRE), **8/1** Teanarco (IRE)(6/1—9/1), **10/1** AFRICAN CHIMES, Sports Post Lady (IRE)(5/1—12/1), **14/1** Baligay, **16/1** No Quarter Given. CSF £47.20, CT £517.22. Tote £10.40: £2.80 £1.70 £4.60 (£12.40). Mr D. G. Wheatley (NEWMARKET) bred by Noel Cogan. 10 Rn
1m 9.5 (0.2)
SF—50/50/48/31/26/11

**1407** BONUSPRINT H'CAP (0-80) £4175.00 (£1250.00: £600.00: £275.00)
2m 1f 34y
3-40 (3-41)

(Weights raised 17 lb)
1125 **Paper Dance (54)** *(RJHolder)* 4-9-6 JWilliams (3) (swtg: hld up in rr: hdwy 6f
out: led over 3f out: r.o wl) ........................................ —**1**
1179⁵ Nikatino **(47)** *(DrJDScargill)* 6-9-0 TQuinn (8) (hdwy 7f out: 3rd st: ev ch over 1f
out: nt qckn) ...................................................... 3.**2**
790³ Fanlight **(55)** **(Fav)** *(RAkehurst)* 4-9-7 TyroneWilliams (2) (5th st: r.o one pce fnl
3f) ................................................................ 5.**3**
1179² Skisurf **(53)** *(CEBrittain)* 6-9-6 GCrealock (7) (lw: 6th & nt clr run on ins st: plld
out 3f out: one pce fnl 2f) ......................................... s.h.**4**

937[3] Chucklestone **(57)** *(JSKing)* 9-9-10 TRogers (6) (rdn along: chsd ldr: led 10f
out to 8f out: 2nd st: wknd 3f out: t.o) ................................... 25.5
See Now **(50)** *(MrsAKnight)* 7-9-3 NCarlisle (4) (a bhd: t.o) ............................... 1.6
1163[6] Touching Star **(50)** (bl) *(PJHobbs)* 7-9-3 AMcGlone (9) (led 8f out tl over 3f out:
4th & wkng st: t.o) ............................... 15.7
342 Rousillon to Be **(42)** *(MissBSanders)* 5-8-9 DaleGibson (11) (dropped rr 8f out:
t.o) ............................... 3.8
1065 Bravo Star (USA) **(33)** *(PLeach)* 7-7-11 ‡3DBiggs (10) (led 7f: bhd fnl 6f: t.o) ... 10.9

**3/1** Fanlight, **9/2** Chucklestone, **5/1** Skisurf, Nikatino, PAPER DANCE, **7/1** Rousillon to Be, **10/1** Touching
Star(7/1—14/1), **33/1** Bravo Star (USA), **50/1** See Now. CSF £28.86, CT £80.46. Tote £5.50: £1.60 £1.30
£1.70 (£19.30). Mr M. Dallimore (BRISTOL) bred by Michael Kent. 9 Rn     3m 45.1 (1.1)
SF—18/11/13/11/–/–

## 1408

BEDMINSTER CLAIMING STKS (Mdn 3-Y.O) £2582.50 (£720.00: £347.50)
1¼m 46y             4-10 (4-17)

509 **Thunderbird One (USA)** *(CRNelson)* 8-4 NAdams (8) (swtg: 3rd st: led over 1f
out: edgd lft ins fnl f: jst hld on) ............................... —1
1150[6] Forgetful **(56)** (Fav) *(RHannon)* 7-9 NCarlisle (12) (4th st: swtchd rt ins fnl f: r.o
wl) ............................... s.h.2
1069 American Boogie (FR) **(68)** *(CEBrittain)* 8-9 GCrealock (14) (a.p: led over 3f
out: hdd & edgd rt over 1f out: nt qckn ins fnl f) ............................... 1½.3
1079 Baby Wizzard *(IABalding)* 7-11 CRutter (13) (hdwy & 5th st: hrd rdn over 1f out:
r.o one pce) ............................... s.h.4
972 Pride of Britain (CAN) **(46)** *(LGCottrell)* 8-2 RFox (10) (hdwy 3f out: r.o ins fnl f) s.h.5
944 Last Orders (USA) **(47)** *(RHannon)* 7-9 GBardwell (4) (swtg: no hdwy fnl 4f) ...... 7.6
1033 Dizzy Dame *(MRChannon)* 7-13 GCarter (6) (6th st: wknd over 2f out) ........... 3½.7
621 Bella Run **(49)** *(RJHodges)* 7 11[5] ‡3TSprake (0) (prom 6f) ............................... 2.8
810 Benefact (USA) **(43)** (v) *(DWPArbuthnot)* 7-10[1] ‡5RPrice (7) (led over 6f: 2nd st:
wknd over 2f out) ............................... nk.9
Fairspear **(65)** *(LGCottrell)* 8-7 TRogers (1) (a bhd) ............................... 6.10
Andare *(RJHodges)* 8-4 ADicks (5) (str: scope: s.s: a bhd) ............................... 5.11
1029 Fairy Princess (IRE) *(RHollinshead)* 7-13 TyroneWilliams (11) (s.s: a bhd: t.o) 15.12
1123[4] Dave's Lass *(MBurchell)* 7-3[1] ‡7TWilson (2) (s.s: a bhd: t.o) ............................... 8.13
1145 Donald Stuart *(MTate)* 9-0 JWilliams (3) (t.o) ............................... 2.14

**4/1** Forgetful, **9/2** THUNDERBIRD ONE (USA), American Boogie (FR)(3/1—5/1), Dizzy Dame, **6/1** Baby
Wizzard(8/1—10/1), **10/1** Fairspear(6/1—12/1), Pride of Britain (CAN), **14/1** Dave's Lass(20/1—12/1), Last
Orders (USA)(op 8/1), **20/1** Benefact (USA), **33/1** Fairy Princess (IRE), Donald Stuart, Bella Run, **66/1** Andare.
CSF £24.19, Tote £7.00: £2.40 £2.00 £2.20 (£14.00). Mr C. R. Nelson (UPPER LAMBOURN) bred by Winborne
Farm Incorporated in USA. 14 Rn; Forgetful clmd R T Williams £6,854     2m 9.1 (1.4)
SF—31/21/32/19/23/2

## 1409

CHARLCOMBE AUCTION STKS (Mdn 2-Y.O) £2652.50 (£740.00: £357.50)
5f 11y             4-40 (4-48)

1077[2] **Dark Eyed Lady (IRE)** *(DWPArbuthnot)* 7-10[4] ‡5RPrice (10) (w ldr: led over 2f
out: r.o wl) ............................... —1
1039[2] Birchwood Sun *(RHollinshead)* 7-9 ‡7MHumphries (12) (hdwy 2f out: r.o wl ins
fnl f) ............................... ¾.2
1067[5] Rocket to the Moon (IRE) (Fav) *(PWChapple-Hyam)* 8-8 ‡3TSprake (9) (w ldrs:
ev ch over 1f out: r.o) ............................... nk.3
1251[3] Brigadore Gold *(RHannon)* 7-11 AMcGlone (4) (hdwy 2f out: one pce fnl f) ....... 3.4
1208[3] Red Leader (IRE) *(PFICole)* 8-3[1] TQuinn (13) (hdwy 3f out: ev ch wl over 1f
out: one pce) ............................... hd.5
1092[3] The Institute Boy *(KRBurke)* 8-5 AShoults (7) (no hdwy fnl 2f) ............................... 2½.6
1103[3] Credit Squeeze *(RFJohnsonHoughton)* 8-2 SWhitworth (15) (nvr nr to chal) ...... ¾.7
986[5] Infant Protege (USA) *(CEBrittain)* 7-13[2] GCrealock (3) (nvr trbld ldrs) ...... 2½.8
Lorins Gold *(AndrewTurnell)* 7-11 ‡5ATucker (2) (wl grown: bkwd: n.d) ............ 2.9
470 Risky Number *(JSMoore)* 8-2 NAdams (1) (led over 2f) ............................... 1.10
Bohemian Queen *(JLSpearing)* 7-11 AMackay (14) (neat: bkwd: a bhd) ............ 1.11
Melisio *(CPWildman)* 7-11 CRutter (11) (w'like: bkwd: s.s: a bhd) ............... ½.12
791[5] Knyaz *(LGCottrell)* 8-2 RFox (8) (t.o) ............................... 10.13
968[5] Halloria *(WGRWightman)* 7-11 GBardwell (6) (outpcd: t.o) ............................... ¾.14

**6/4** Rocket to the Moon (IRE)(op 9/4), **7/2** Red Leader (IRE)(op 9/4), **6/1** Brigadore Gold, Birchwood Sun, **7/1**
Credit Squeeze(5/1—8/1), **10/1** DARK EYED LADY (IRE), **12/1** The Institute Boy(8/1—20/1), **20/1** Halloria,
Infant Protege (USA), **25/1** Knyaz, **33/1** Lorins Gold, Melisio, **50/1** Ors. CSF £74.90, Tote £14.20: £3.00 £2.60
£1.50 (£27.60). Mrs M. Gutkin (COMPTON) bred by J. Stan Cosgrove in Ireland. 14 Rn     61.5 sec (1)
SF—32/28/40/15/20/12

T/Plpt: £43.10 (87.1 Tckts).             KH

1132—**LINGFIELD (L-H)**

**Saturday, June 13th [Good to firm, Firm back st]**

Going Allowance: minus 0.30 sec per fur (F)                          Wind: almost nil

Stalls: high

**1410**     LURCHER STKS (Mdn 3-Y.O) £1646.00 (£456.00: £218.00)   **6f**      6-30 (6-31)

       **Hardliner (76)** *(CFWall)* 9-0  NDay (1) (hld up: led 2f out: hrd rdn: r.o wl) .......... —1
   12774 Masrur (USA) **(63)** *(RWArmstrong)* 9-0  BCrossley (3) (lw: led 5f out to 3f out:
                     unable qckn) ....................................................................... 3.2
    994 Efra **(69)** (Fav) *(RHannon)* 8-7 ‡7DGibbs (2) (lw: led 1f: led 3f out to 2f out: sn
                     wknd) ............................................................................... 5.3

**4/5** Efra, **15/8** Masrur (USA), **9/2** HARDLINER(op 3/1). CSF £10.69, Tote £3.40 (£2.80). Mr David M. Adams
(NEWMARKET) bred by Miss D. Birkbeck. 3 Rn                              1m 11.04 (2.44)
                                           SF—16/4/–

**1411**     G.S.P. CLAIMING STKS   £1926.00 (£536.00: £258.00)   **7f 140y**     7-00 (7-06)

   12143 **Canadian Capers (69)** (Jt-Fav) *(MRChannon)* 3-8-0  JQuinn (13) (mde all: hrd
                     rdn over 1f out) ................................................................ —1
   1276* Certain Lady **(61)** *(GBlum)* 3-7-11 ‡5DHarrison (7) (a.p: rdn & ev ch over 1f out:
                     r.o) ..................................................................... 1½.2
   11742 Domicksky **(78)** *(MJRyan)* 4-9-7 ‡3DBiggs (9) (lw: hld up: rdn over 1f
                     out: unable qckn) ............................................................ 2½.3
   1159 Mastamist **(39)** (bl) *(RVoorspuy)* 3-7-13 ‡5BDoyle (2) (reminder over 6f out: hrd
                     rdn over 3f out: r.o) ....................................................... 2½.4
   5266 Millsolin (IRE) **(55)** *(ARDavison)* 4-9-1  CandyMorris (16) (b: no hdwy fnl 2f) ..... 1.5
   1085 Confound (IRE) **(35)** *(JJAkehurst)* 3-8-1  DHolland (10) (hrd rdn over 3f out: nvr
                     nr to chal) ................................................................ 1½.6
       Kingsfold Pet *(MJHaynes)* 3-8-8  BRouse (11) (leggy: scope: nvr nrr) ................ 2.7
   9256 Our Eddie **(67)** (v) *(BGubby)* 3-8-6  WNewnes (4) (prom over 5f) ...................... ¾.8
   11452 Girton Degree **(50)** (v) *(SDow)* 3-7-11 ‡3FNorton (5) (spd over 5f) ............... ½.9
       Sovereign Heights *(MRChannon)* 4-8-7 ‡7LMahoney (8) (bit bkwd: a bhd) ...... 3.10
   1182 Otter Bush *(GBlum)* 3-8-6  BCrossley (1) (s.s: a bhd) ............................ 2½.11
    998 Trioming *(APJones)* 6-9-1  NDay (6) (prom 5f: t.o) ...................................... 20.12

**9/4** Domicksky, CANADIAN CAPERS, **9/2** Certain Lady, **9/1** Girton Degree, **10/1** Our Eddie(8/1—12/1), **14/1**
Kingsfold Pet, **20/1** Confound (IRE), Millsolin (IRE), **25/1** Sovereign Heights, **50/1** Otter Bush, Mastamist, **66/1**
Trioming. CSF £12.89, Tote £3.30: £1.60 £1.60 £1.30 (£7.40). Mr Peter Taplin (UPPER LAMBOURN) bred by
Doublet Ltd. 12 Rn                                                    1m 30.59 (2.09)
                                  SF—20/12/28/–/11/–

**1412**     POINTER H'CAP (3-Y.O) (0-90) £2954.00 (£819.00: £392.00)   **7f**     7-30 (7-32)
                      (Weights raised 4 lb)

   1012* **Mizoram (USA) (76)** (Fav) *(HRACecil)* 8-11 ‡7StephenDavies (1) (led over 3f:
                     led over 1f out: rdn out) ................................................. —1
   9854 Hi-Tech Honda (IRE) **(65)** *(CEBrittain)* 8-7  JQuinn (6) (w ldr: led over 3f out tl
                     over 1f out: unable qckn) ................................................ 1½.2
   8013 Mogwai (IRE) **(65)** (bl) *(RFJohnsonHoughton)* 8-7  TQuinn (4) (a.p: hrd rdn
                     over 1f out: one pce) ...................................................... nk.3
   6705 Try Leguard (IRE) **(79)** *(WCarter)* 9-7  WNewnes (5) (lw: s.s: nvr nr to chal) ....... 7.4
    992 Sandcastle City **(75)** *(RHannon)* 9-3  AMcGlone (2) (prom over 4f) ................ nk.5
   1206 Vanborough Lad **(72)** *(MJHaynes)* 8-11 ‡3DBiggs (3) (racd alone: bhd fnl 4f) .. 2½.6

**6/5** MIZORAM (USA), **11/2** Mogwai (IRE), **6/1** Hi-Tech Honda (IRE), Vanborough Lad, Try Leguard (IRE), **14/1**
Sandcastle City. CSF £8.02, Tote £2.30: £1.30 £2.30 (£5.60). Sheikh Mohammed (NEWMARKET) bred by
Bedford Farms, Skymarc Farm in USA. 6 Rn                               1m 23.09 (1.79)
                            SF—38/29/28/21/16/2

**1413**     SPRINGER H'CAP (0-80) £2012.40 (£556.40: £265.20)   **1¼m**     8-00 (8-01)

   10875 **Chatham Island (59)** *(CEBrittain)* 4-8-4 ‡5BDoyle (4) (lw: mde all: hrd rdn 1f
                     out: r.o wl) ............................................................... —1
   10813 Prince Hannibal **(78)** (Fav) *(JLDunlop)* 5-10-0  TQuinn (1) (5th st: chsd wnr over
                     1f out: r.o) ............................................................... ¾.2
   4176 Long Furlong **(58)** *(RAkehurst)* 4-8-8  BRouse (3) (lw: 3rd st: one pce fnl 2f) .. 2½.3
    422 Dancing Sensation (USA) **(45)** *(JWharton)* 5-7-9  JQuinn (2) (4th st: one pce fnl
                     2f) ........................................................................ 2½.4

1203* Vanroy **(69)** (v) *(JRJenkins)* 8-9-5  SWhitworth (5) (6th st: a bhd) ............... 3¹/₂.**5**
     Island Blade (IRE) **(58)** *(RAkehurst)* 3-7-6[1] ‡³FNorton (6) (s.s: hdwy 9f out: 2nd
         st: wknd wl over 1f out) ............................................ ³/₄.**6**

**11/4** Prince Hannibal, **7/2** Long Furlong, CHATHAM ISLAND, **4/1** Vanroy, Island Blade (IRE)(op 8/1), **10/1**
Dancing Sensation (USA). CSF £13.66, Tote £4.50: £2.20 £1.90 (£6.90). Mr B. H. Voak (NEWMARKET) bred by
G. C. Hughes. 6 Rn                                            2m 7.48 (4.48)
                                                     SF—15/37/12/–/11/–

## 1414
MOTT MACDONALD STKS (3-Y.O) £2259.00 (£624.00: £297.00)
1m 3f 106y                                     8-30 (8-32)

1079* **Rainridge** (v) *(JLDunlop)* 8-11  AMcGlone (1) (swtg: mde all: qcknd over 4f out:
         r.o wl) ............................................ —**1**
1207* Scrutineer (USA) **(90)** (Fav) *(JHMGosden)* 8-11  DHolland (2) (lw: chsd wnr: hrd
         rdn ins fnl f: r.o) ............................ 1.**2**
1227a⁵ Hero's Light (USA) **(85)** *(PFICole)* 9-5  TQuinn (3) (lw: s.s: 3rd st: hrd rdn over 1f
         out: unable qckn) ........................ 2¹/₂.**3**

**4/6** Scrutineer (USA), **7/4** RAINRIDGE, **6/1** Hero's Light (USA)(4/1—13/2). CSF £3.22, Tote £2.60 (£1.30). Mr
P. G. Goulandris (ARUNDEL) bred by Hesmonds Stud Ltd. 3 Rn          2m 28.40 (6.40)

## 1415
RETRIEVER H'CAP (0-70) £1779.50 (£492.80: £235.40)   **5f**         9-00 (9-02)
(Weights raised 1 lb)

1262³ **Shades of Jade (41)** *(JJBridger)* 4-8-4  SWhitworth (2) (mde all: clr over 3f out:
         r.o wl) ............................................ —**1**
1144² So Superb **(69)** (Fav) *(JLDunlop)* 3-9-10  TQuinn (11) (lw: hdwy over 2f out:
         chsd wnr over 1f out no imp) ........ 3¹/₂.**2**
1162² Catalani **(51)** *(TJNaughton)* 7–9-0  DHolland (3) (b: a.p: one pce fnl 2f) ...... 2.**3**
1084⁵ Three Lucky (IRE) **(39)** *(MDIUsher)* 4–7-13 ‡³DBiggs (6) (hdwy 2f out: one pce)  1.**4**
1144⁵ Bishopstone Bill **(42)** *(SMellor)* 3–7-11  DanaMellor (9) (nvr nr to chal) ........... 1¹/₂.**5**
1199 Joe Sugden **(59)** (v) *(PHowling)* 8–9-8  NCarlisle (5) (prom 3f) ..................... nk.**6**
897 L'Ete (IRE) **(55)** *(PMitchell)* 4–8-11 ‡⁷DCripps (8) (lw: swtchd lft 3f out: mid div
         whn hmpd over 1f out) .................... 2¹/₂.**7**
1162 Battling Bella (USA) **(58)** (bl) *(JSutcliffe)* 3-8-13  BRouse (1) (swtg: prom 3f:
         wkng whn hmpd over 1f out) .......... 2.**8**
     Tyrone Turbo (USA) **(47)** *(JAkehurst)* 3–8-2  AMcGlone (10) (swtg: a bhd: sddle
         slipped) ........................................ 1¹/₂.**9**
1325 Barbezieux **(38)** (bl) *(TJNaughton)* 4-8-1  JQuinn (7) (a bhd) .................... 1.**10**
1162 Very Good **(45)** (bl) *(PHowling)* 3–7-11 ‡³FNorton (4) (swtg: spd 3f) .............. 3.**11**

**13/8** So Superb, **3/1** Catalani, **15/2** L'Ete (IRE), **8/1** Tyrone Turbo (USA), **9/1** Barbezieux, **10/1** Joe Sugden,
Battling Bella (USA)(8/1—14/1), **14/1** Three Lucky (IRE)(op 11/1), **16/1** SHADES OF JADE, **25/1** Bishopstone Bill,
**40/1** Very Good. CSF £45.06, CT £102.73. Tote £15.80: £3.40 £1.50 £1.60 (£28.20). Mr W. Wood (LIPHOOK)
bred by W. A. Wood. 11 Rn                                        57.60 sec (0.60)
                                                  SF—48/54/36/17/9/33

T/Plpt: £103.90 (15.45 Tckts).                                            AK

## 1281—NOTTINGHAM (L-H)
### Saturday, June 13th [Good to firm]
Going Allowance: minus 0.10 sec per fur (F)                         Wind: slt across

Stalls: low

## 1416
YOUNGSTERS (S) STKS (2-Y.O) £1632.00 (£452.00: £216.00)   **5f 13y**     6-15 (6-17)

     **Regent's Lady** *(CJames)* 8-6  GBaxter (3) (lt-f: mde all: rdn & r.o wl fnl f) .......... —**1**
     Meadmore Magic *(JLHarris)* 8-6  JWilliams (5) (unf: bkwd: in tch: hdwy 2f out:
         no ex ins fnl f) ............................ 3¹/₂.**2**
1140⁵ Over the Dec *(BAMcMahon)* 8-6  JFortune (2) (dwlt: hdwy over 2f out: rdn & no
         ex over 1f out) ............................ 4.**3**
574 Westmead Nick *(JBerry)* 8-11  GCarter (4) (lw: chsd ldrs tl wknd over 1f out) .. 2¹/₂.**4**
1151⁵ Sharisa (Fav) *(JBerry)* 8-6  KFallon (1) (plld hrd: w wnr 3f) .................... 2.**5**

**5/2** Sharisa(op 6/4), **11/4** REGENT'S LADY(3/1—9/2), **7/2** Westmead Nick(op 2/1), **4/1** Over the Dec, **6/1**
Meadmore Magic(tchd 14/1). CSF £16.25, Tote £3.60: £1.90 £1.70 (£11.60). Mr C. James (NEWBURY) bred by
Mrs J. Saville. 5 Rn; Bt in 3,800 gns                                   61.66 sec (2.9)
                                                  SF—24/10/–/–/–

**1417**     NOTTINGHAM EVENING POST H'CAP (3-Y.O) (0-70) £1730.00 (£480.00: £230.00)
6f 15y
6-45 (6-48)

1146 **Hob Green (50)** *(MrsJRRamsden)* 8-4 GBaxter (9) (hdwy to ld 2f out: shkn up & sn clr: unchal) ......................................... —1
Honey Heather (IRE) **(56)** *(CFWall)* 8-10 BRaymond (2) (bit bkwd: in tch: chsd wnr over 1f out: no imp) ........................... 2½.2
1219² Night Asset **(64)** (bl) *(GLewis)* 9-4 PaulEddery (11) (hdwy 2f out: r.o fnl f: nt trble ldrs) ........................................... 1½.3
1277⁶ Peerage Prince **(61)** (bl) *(PatMitchell)* 8-12 ‡³SO'Gorman (7) (lw: stumbled s: led over 3f out to 2f out: no ex) ........... ¾.4
*1263* Sara Anne (IRE) **(59)** *(LJCodd)* 8-13 LDettori (1) (lw: chsd ldrs: rdn 2f out: sn btn) ................................................ 3.5
1075 Young Valentine **(67)** *(RMWhitaker)* 9-7 ACulhane (8) (lw: prom 4f) ................ nk.6
1277 Nigals Friend **(63)** *(DHaydnJones)* 9-3 JWilliams (4) (dwlt: sn prom: ev ch over 2f out: sn btn) .................................. 1½.7
Coat of Dreams **(56)** *(RBastiman)* 8-10 DMcKeown (3) (swtg: spd 3f) .......... 3½.8
1338 Do the Business (IRE) **(45)** (bl) *(CNAllen)* 7-13 WAAntongeorgi (5) (dwlt: a outpcd) ............................................. 2½.9
997 Saifan **(66)** *(DMorris)* 9-6 MTebbutt (10) (swtg: a bhd) ................................ ½.10
582 Stormbuster **(55)** *(PSFelgate)* 8-4 ‡⁵CHodgson (6) (led over 2f: sn wknd) ..... 1½.11
1155⁵ Music Dancer **(60)** *(JBerry)* 9-0 GCarter (12) (dwlt: a in rr) ...................... 3.12

**7/4** Night Asset, **6/1** Saifan, **13/2** Music Dancer, **9/1** Sara Anne (IRE), **10/1** Young Valentine, **12/1** Peerage Prince, **14/1** Nigals Friend(op 8/1), Stormbuster, **16/1** HOB GREEN, Honey Heather (IRE)(op 10/1), **20/1** Ors. CSF£221.73, CT£612.52. Tote £23.80: £4.60 £5.00 £1.30 (£232.50). Mrs A. E. Sigsworth (THIRSK) bred by L. C. and Mrs A. E. Sigsworth. 12 Rn                                                      1m 13.7 (2.7)
SF—24/20/22/13/2/9

**1418**     B.B.C. RADIO NOTTINGHAM GRADUATION STKS (3-Y.O) £2322.00 (£642.00: £306.00)
6f 15y
7-15 (7-20)

1183★ **Toussaud (USA)** (Fav) *(JHMGosden)* 9-2 PaulEddery (4) (hld up: led on bit 2f out: cleverly) ...................................... —1
Storm Dove (USA) **(88)** *(RCharlton)* 9-2 LDettori (3) (led 4f: rdn & r.o) ......... ½.2
1166⁶ Alsaarm (USA) **(94)** *(JLDunlop)* 9-7 WCarson (5) (lw: w ldr over 4f: one pce) ..... 5.3
966⁶ Lord Lambson **(60)** *(RMWhitaker)* 9-0 ACulhane (6) (lw: spd 4f) .................... 6.4
984⁵ Lifetime Fame **(78)** *(JWPayne)* 9-7 RCochrane (1) (lw: dwlt: swtchd rt after 2f: sn rdn & btn) .................................... 5.5
Merryhill Madam **(71)** *(JLHarris)* 8-9 JWilliams (7) (reard s: a bhd) ............... 1½.6
966 Stamshaw *(BAMcMahon)* 8-9 JFortune (1) (sn bhd) .......................................... 5.7

**Evens** TOUSSAUD (USA)(op 13/8), **11/4** Alsaarm (USA), **4/1** Storm Dove (USA), **7/1** Lifetime Fame, **20/1** Merryhill Madam, **50/1** Lord Lambson, **100/1** Stamshaw. CSF £5.58. Tote £2.60: £1.60 £2.30 (£3.50). Mr K. Abdulla (NEWMARKET) bred by Juddmonte Farms Incorporated in USA. 7 Rn            1m 12.7 (1.7)
SF—56/54/39/8/–/–

**1419**     MANN EGERTON TOYOTA H'CAP (0-70) £1926.00 (£536.00: £258.00)
1¾m 15y
7-45 (7-46)

1256³ **Beau Quest (60)** *(RMWhitaker)* 5-9-4 ACulhane (12) (hdwy & 3rd st: led over 1f out: rdn & swished tail: r.o) .................. —1
1125² White River **(37)** (v) *(DHaydnJones)* 6-7-9 TyroneWilliams (15) (hld up: hdwy & 4th st: led over 2f out to 1f out: kpt on) .... 1½.2
1290⁴ Samain (USA) **(41)** (Fav) *(JAGlover)* 5-7-13 GCarter (9) (hdwy & 6th st: ev ch over 2f out: one pce) ........................ 2½.3
1108★ Sea Paddy **(52)** *(RBastiman)* 4-8-3 ‡⁷HBastiman (2) (bhd: gd hdwy over 3f out: one pce appr fnl f) ........................ 2½.4
1169⁵ Naseem Elbarr (USA) **(65)** *(ACStewart)* 4-9-9 MRoberts (5) (lw: chsd ldrs: 5th st: n.m.r 3f out: plld out 2f out: sn rdn & btn) .... 2.5
1163⁵ Poppy Charm **(35)** *(RCurtis)* 5-7-7 DaleGibson (6) (led 2f: led ent st: hdd over 2f out: sn btn) ............................. s.h.6
426 Smilingatstrangers **(45)** (v) *(MrsBarbaraWaring)* 4-8-3⁽⁵⁾ NHowe (8) (lost pl 6f out: r.o fnl 2f) ................................ s.h.7
1119³ Merton Mill **(59)** *(DMorley)* 5-9-3 BRaymond (7) (lost pl 6f out: n.d after) ......... 3.8
1125⁴ Pondered Bid **(40)** (bl) *(PatMitchell)* 8-7-9⁽²⁾ ‡³SO'Gorman (1) (bhd: rdn 3f out: nvr able to chal) ..................... s.h.9
1125 Access Cruise (USA) **(48)** *(BAMcMahon)* 5-8-6 JFortune (14) (lw: led after 2f: hdd & 2nd st: wknd over 2f out) ............ 1½.10
1190⁶ Newark Antiquefair **(37)** *(BCMorgan)* 4-7-6⁽²⁾ ‡³JFanning (11) (chsd ldrs: 8th st: wknd 2f out) ......................... hd.11
1125 Kanooz (IRE) **(42)** (bl) *(SMellor)* 4-8-0 CRutter (4) (nvr nr to chal) .................. ½.12

NOTTINGHAM, June 13, 1992

Commanche Sioux (IRE) **(55)** *(KAMorgan)* 4–8-13 DMcKeown (3) (a bhd) ....... 6.13
1125 Doolar (USA) **(52)** *(PTDalton)* 5–8-10 JLowe (10) (prom tl 7th & wkng st) ........ 3.14
LONG HANDICAP: Poppy Charm 7-1, Newark Antiquefair 6-11.

**2/1** Samain (USA)(op 3/1), **4/1** Naseem Elbarr (USA), **6/1** Merton Mill(op 4/1), **8/1** Sea Paddy, **9/1** BEAU QUEST(op 6/1), White River, **11/1** Access Cruise (USA), **12/1** Pondered Bid, **20/1** Commanche Sioux (IRE), **33/1** Poppy Charm, **50/1** Ors. CSF £84.99, CT £208.21. Tote £9.70: £2.20 £2.60 £1.30 (£26.80). Mr G. A. Farndon (WETHERBY) bred by Barrettstown Stud Farms Ltd. 14 Rn                                    3m 3.9 (5.4)
SF—36/10/9/8/24/–

**1420** LONG EATON MEDIAN AUCTION STKS (3-Y.O) £2322.00 (£642.00: £306.00)
1m 1f 213y                                                                                    8-15 (8-21)

1069⁴ **Legal Embrace (CAN)** (Fav) *(JRFanshawe)* 8-6 GCarter (4) (chsd ldr: led wl over 1f out: comf) .............................................................................................. —1
1175³ Viva Darling **(69)** *(BAMcMahon)* 8-11 BRaymond (5) (lw: hld up: 4th st: rdn over 2f out: ev ch wl over 1f out: no imp ins fnl f) ....................................... 1.2
Briggs Lad (IRE) **(74)** *(WJarvis)* 8-11 MTebbutt (1) (plld hrd: 3rd st: rdn & kpt on fnl f) ............................................................................................ 2½.3
1189³ Knight Pawn *(JPLeigh)* 8-11 DMcKeown (3) (set slow pce: qcknd 3f out: hdd wl over 1f out: one pce) ........................................................................ 1½.4
1122⁵ Gallant Jack (IRE) **(64)** *(DHaydnJones)* 8-11 PaulEddery (2) (stdd s: last st: effrt 3f out: no imp appr fnl f) ................................................................ 3.5

**8/11** LEGAL EMBRACE (CAN), **4/1** Viva Darling, **11/2** Briggs Lad (IRE), **9/1** Gallant Jack (IRE), **11/1** Knight Pawn. CSF £3.98, Tote £1.80: £1.30 £1.50 (£2.70). Mrs Jacqueline Slaytor (NEWMARKET) bred by John H. Slaytor in Canada. 5 Rn                                                                           2m 13.6 (11.1)

**1421** 'FAMILY NIGHT OUT' H'CAP (0-70) £1856.00 (£516.00: £248.00)
1m 54y                                                                                         8-45 (8-51)

763 **Deputy Tim (44)** *(RBastiman)* 9–8-3 DMcKeown (14) (a.p: 4th st: plld out over 1f out: led ins fnl f: rdn out) ........................................................ —1
1018⁶ Habeta (USA) **(69)** *(JWWatts)* 6–9-7 ‡7EHusband (15) (a.p: 3rd st: led 2f out tl ins fnl f: r.o) ............................................................................ 1.2
1376⁵ Sareen Express (IRE) **(40)** *(MrsJCDawe)* 4–7-10 ‡3JFanning (7) (bhd: hdwy over 3f out: r.o wl fnl f) ............................................................... hd.3
696 Cartel **(57)** (Fav) *(JLHarris)* 5–9-2 LDettori (4) (lw: led 1f: 2nd st: led over 3f out to 2f out: sn rdn: no imp fnl f) ................................................. 1½.4
1089⁴ Falcons Dawn **(53)** (bl) *(MO'Neill)* 5–8-12 JFortune (2) (lw: led after 1f tl over 3f out: kpt on) ................................................................... ½.5
1172² Jolizal **(38)** (v) *(DMorris)* 4–7-11 JLowe (1) (chsd ldrs: 8th st: one pce fnl 2f) .. 1½.6
1044 Casilla **(34)** *(HCandy)* 4–7-0 ‡7AntoineArmes (8) (lw: sme late hdwy: n.d) ..... hd.7
1203 Jokist **(64)** *(WJarvis)* 9–9-9 MTebbutt (16) (nvr plcd to chal) ..................... nk.8
1284 Serlby Connection **(45)** *(SRBowring)* 7–8-4 GBaxter (3) (b: bit bkwd: bhd tl r.o fnl 2f) ................................................................................... ¾.9
494² Golden Torque **(68)** *(RBastiman)* 5–9-6 ‡7HBastiman (11) (bit bkwd: stdd & lost pl after 1f: n.d after) .......................................................... 2.10
77 Les Amis **(45)** *(MJRyan)* 5–8-4 GCarter (10) (hdwy 4f out: ev ch over 2f out: sn wknd) ....................................................................................... 1.11
1075⁶ North Flyer **(52)** *(BAMcMahon)* 3–7-7⁽7⁾ ‡7SSanders (12) (chsd ldrs: 5th st: wknd 2f out) ......................................................................... 2½.12
1146 Dominant Serenade **(58)** (bl) *(PWHarris)* 3–8-6 PaulEddery (13) (hdwy & 7th st: wknd 3f out) ....................................................................... 1½.13
112⁵ Petticoat Power **(56)** *(MrsBarbaraWaring)* 6–9-1 NHowe (9) (b: 6th st: wkng whn hmpd 3f out) ..................................................................... 2½.14
1243 Preamble **(48)** *(MrsJRRamsden)* 3–7-10 DaleGibson (5) (lw: bhd fnl 4f) ......... 2½.15
Evening Dress **(49)** *(TThomsonJones)* 3–7-11⁽2⁾ CRutter (6) (bit bkwd: hdwy & 9th st: wknd over 3f out) .................................................... 16

**5/1** Cartel(op 12/1), **7/1** Habeta (USA), **8/1** Golden Torque, **17/2** Falcons Dawn, **9/1** Jolizal, Jokist(op 5/1), **10/1** North Flyer, Sareen Express (IRE), **12/1** Petticoat Power, **14/1** Dominant Serenade, **16/1** Les Amis, Preamble, **20/1** Serlby Connection, Evening Dress, **25/1** DEPUTY TIM, **33/1** Casilla. CSF £185.33, CT £1,732.45. Tote £24.30: £4.10 £2.90 £2.00 £1.70 (£511.50). Mrs P. Bastiman (WETHERBY) bred by P. Trant. 16 Rn
1m 44.3 (4.7)
SF—7/22/-/11/5/–

T/Plpt: £141.60 (11.75 Tckts).                                                                          Dk

1139—**WOLVERHAMPTON (L-H)**
**Saturday, June 13th [Good to firm, Rnd Firm]**
Going Allowance: minus 0.15 sec per fur (F)    Wind: almost nil

Stalls: high

**1422**    DAWLEY STKS (Mdn 2-Y.O.F) £1035.00 (£285.00: £135.00)    **5f**    6-20 (6-23)

986⁶ **Aberlady** *(MAJarvis)* 8-6 ‡⁵KRutter (1) (lw: chsd ldrs: led 1f out: jst hld on) ......... —1
721⁵ Margaret's Gift *(JBerry)* 8-11 JCarroll (6) (lw: led 3f: rallied ins fnl f: jst failed) .... ¹/₂.2
1251⁵ Manor Adventure (Jt-Fav) *(BAMcMahon)* 8-11 AMunro (2) (lw: s.i.s: sn prom:
    led 2f out to 1f out: one pce) ...................................... 1¹/₂.3
1120³ Cloudy Reef *(RHollinshead)* 8-4 ‡⁷AGarth (8) (lw: hdwy appr fnl f: nvr able to
    chal) ........................................ 3.4
1208 Rich Midas (IRE) *(GLewis)* 8-4 ‡⁷BRussell (4) (b.hind: spd over 3f) .................. 2¹/₂.5
1120² Breakfast Boogie (Jt-Fav) *(JRFanshawe)* 8-11 GDuffield (7) (nvr gng pce of ldrs) ³/₄.6
584⁴ Miss Whittingham (IRE) *(JBerry)* 8-11 MHills (5) (in tch: rdn wl over 1f out: sn
    btn) .................................... 3¹/₂.7
986 Last Typhoon *(EHOwenjun)* 8-6 ‡⁵NKennedy (3) (outpcd) .................. 5.8

**9/4** Breakfast Boogie, Manor Adventure, **5/1** Margaret's Gift, **9/1** Rich Midas (IRE), **12/1** ABERLADY, Cloudy
Reef(op 7/1), **14/1** Miss Whittingham (IRE), **33/1** Last Typhoon. CSF £63.41, Tote £13.70: £2.60 £2.60 £1.50
(£95.10). Mr M. Sinclair (NEWMARKET) bred by Farmers Hill and Fitzroy Studs. 8 Rn    60.1 sec (2.8)
SF—21/24/18/–/–/–

**1423**    FEATHERSTONE (S) H'CAP (3, 4 & 5-Y.O) (0-60) £1297.50 (£360.00: £172.50)
1³/₄m 134y    6-50 (6-52)

1008⁶ **Little Big (38)** *(CDBroad)* 5–8-1 ‡⁵RPrice (8) (hld up: hdwy 3f out: styd on to ld cl
    home) ...................................... —1
    Noncommital (37) *(JMackie)* 5–8-5 AClark (5) (bit bkwd: hld up: hdwy 3f out:
    led wl ins fnl f tl ct cl home) ................................ nk.2
875 Juris Prudence (IRE) (47) *(BAMcMahon)* 4–8-10 ‡⁵KRutter (9) (a.p: 5th st: r.o
    one pce fnl 2f) ................................ 5.3
1163³ Mamalama (38) *(LJHolt)* 4–8-6 AMunro (12) (a.p: 2nd st: led 3f out: sn hdd:
    rallied appr fnl f: nvr ex) ................................ 1¹/₂.4
1239² Carrolls Marc (IRE) (54) *(PJFeilden)* 4–9-8 JCarroll (6) (swtg: hld up: styd on fnl
    2f: nvr nrr) ................................ 2.5
1145 Shafayif (51) *(BHanbury)* 3–8-0 NAdams (1) (hdwy 8f out: 4th st: led over 2f out
    tl wl ins fnl f: sn rdn & btn) ................................ ¹/₂.6
1257 In the Spotlight (IRE) (48) (bl) *(RCurtis)* 4–8-11 ‡⁵ATucker (10) (nvr plcd to chal) ³/₄.7
166 Lifetimes Ambition (45) *(TCasey)* 4–8-13 PBurke (13) (b: bkwd: chsd ldrs: effrt
    3f out: no imp) ................................ 1¹/₂.8
169 Noble Fellow (42) (bl) *(JPSmith)* 5–8-10 MHills (11) (chsd ldrs: 7th st: wknd 3f
    out: t.o) ................................ 8.9
805 Enfant du Paradis (IRE) (Fav) *(PDEvans)* 4–8-8 GDuffield (7) (led tl hdd & wknd
    3f out: t.o) ................................ 1¹/₂.10
    Dancing Tudor (51) *(THCaldwell)* 4–9-0 ‡⁵NKennedy (4) (bit bkwd: prom: 3rd
    st: wknd over 2f out: t.o) ................................ hd.11
1280⁶ The Jones Boy (FR) (60) *(GHJones)* 5–9-7 ‡⁷DMeredith (2) (hdwy ¹/₂-wy: 6th st:
    wknd 3f out: t.o) ................................ 5.12
593 Shadowland (48) *(MJCharles)* 4–8-9 ‡⁷AGarth (14) (lw: a bhd: t.o) ......... 20.13
    *Stewards Enquiry: Clark suspended 22-25/6/92 (excessive use of whip).*

**3/1** Enfant du Paradis (IRE), **7/2** Carrolls Marc (IRE)(3/1—5/1), Mamalama, **9/1** Shafayif, **12/1** Lifetimes
Ambition(op 7/1), **14/1** LITTLE BIG, **16/1** Juris Prudence (IRE), **20/1** Ors. CSF £232.80, CT £3,984.79. Tote
£19.00: £3.60 £10.10 £3.40 (£467.10). Mrs A. J. Broad (WESTBURY-ON-SEVERN) bred by Miss B.
Galway-Greer. 13 Rn; Bt in 3,400 gns    3m 10.3 (4.3)
SF—23/26/21/14/26/3

**1424**    E.B.F. ALDERSLEY STKS (Mdn 2-Y.O.C & G) £2040.00 (£565.00: £270.00)
7f    7-20 (7-23)

933 **Regal Aura (IRE)** *(GHarwood)* 9-0 AClark (5) (mde all: hrd rdn fnl f: hld on
    gamely) ...................................... —1
    Prevene (IRE) (Fav) *(PFICole)* 9-0 AMunro (7) (w'like: str: hld up: 6th st:
    reminders 2f out: rapid hdwy fnl f: fin fast) ...................... nk.2
    Antester (IRE) *(PWChapple-Hyam)* 9-0 WRyan (8) (w'like: hld up:
    7th st: rdn & hdwy over 2f out: ev ch fnl f: r.o) ................ hd.3
    Almansour (USA) *(HRACecil)* 9-0 WRyan (8) (w'like: chsd wnr: 2nd st: ev ch ins
    fnl: unable qckn) ................................ nk.4

    Bristol Fashion *(MBell)* 9-0 MHills (1) (scope: bit bkwd: prom: 3rd st: hrd rdn &
          ev ch 1f out: one pce) .......................................................... 1½.**5**
    Share a Moment (CAN) *(RHollinshead)* 9-0 JCarroll (4) (cmpt: bkwd: nvr nr ldrs) 6.**6**
1039 Junction Twentytwo *(CDBroad)* 9-0 RHills (10) (s.s: hdwy & 5th st: wknd 2f out) 2½.**7**
 828 Mad Mytton *(ABailey)* 9-0 AMackay (9) (prom: 4th st: wknd over 2f out) ....... hd.**8**
    Rare Occurance *(MJCharles)* 9-0 GDuffield (6) (lengthy: w'like: bkwd: s.s: a
          bhd: t.o) ............................................................................ 6.**9**
 907 Both Barrels *(RJHolder)* 9-0 NAdams (3) (sn bhd: t.o fnl 3f) ............ dist.**10**

**7/4** Prevene (IRE), **3/1** Almansour (USA), **4/1** Antester (IRE)(op 2/1), **5/1** REGAL AURA (IRE), **8/1** Mad Mytton,
**16/1** Bristol Fashion(op 8/1), **20/1** Share a Moment (CAN), **33/1** Rare Occurance, **50/1** Junction Twentytwo,
**66/1** Both Barrels. CSF £14.61, Tote £9.70: £1.80 £1.90 £1.40 (£21.10). Skytraders Racing (PULBOROUGH)
bred by Upstream Ltd in Ireland. 10 Rn                                 1m 27.9 (3.6)
                                                  SF—30/29/28/27/22/4

---

**1425**     PATTINGHAM MEDIAN AUCTION GRADUATION STKS (3-Y.O.F) £1108.50 (£306.00:
          £145.50)   **1m 200y**                               7-50 (7-53)

 989 **Miss Haggis** *(RBoss)* 8-11 JReid (2) (lw: wnt 2nd 7f out: led 2f out: rdn out) ..... —**1**
1182⁵ Tafsir *(HThomsonJones)* 8-11 RHills (1) (3rd st: styd on u.p wl ins fnl f: nt rch
          wnr) .................................................................................. 2½.**2**
1078² Hissma (88) (Fav) *(HRACecil)* 9-4 WRyan (4) (led to 2f out: sn hrd rdn & btn) 3½.**3**
    Vellandrucha *(JABennett)* 8-11 JCarroll (3) (swtg: bit bkwd & bhd: 4th
          st: effrt u.p 2f out: no imp) .............................................. 6.**4**

**1/3** Hissma, **11/2** MISS HAGGIS(3/1—6/1), Tafsir(4/1—13/2), **66/1** Vellandrucha. CSF £25.11, Tote £4.10
(£3.70). Mr P. Asquith (NEWMARKET) bred by Cheveley Park Stud Ltd. 4 Rn         1m 55.4 (6.9)

---

**1426**     DAISY BANK H'CAP (3-Y.O) (0-80) £1329.00 (£369.00: £177.00)
          **1m 200y**                                   8-20 (8-23)

                           (Weights raised 4 lb)
1025 **Timurid (FR) (60)** *(JLDunlop)* 8-8 JReid (4) (swtg: chsd ldrs: 4th st: led over 1f
          out: r.o strly) ..................................................................... —**1**
1158⁵ Weeheby (USA) (67) *(AAScott)* 9-1 WRSwinburn (1) (lw: 5th st: rdn over 2f out:
          styd on ins fnl f) .............................................................. 1½.**2**
1146⁶ Eastleigh (65) *(RHollinshead)* 8-13 WRyan (8) (swtg: hld up: 6th st: kpt on wl
          ins fnl f: nvr nrr) ............................................................. 4.**3**
 728 Witches Coven (49) *(MBell)* 7-6 ‡⁵NKennedy (6) (prom: 2nd st: rdn 2f out: one
          pce) .................................................................................. 2.**4**
1146⁴ Toss the Dice (60) (Fav) *(MAJarvis)* 8-8 AMunro (5) (led after 2f tl over 1f out:
          wknd ins fnl f) ................................................................ nk.**5**
1122 Kingchip Boy (50) *(MJRyan)* 7-12 AMackay (2) (lw: led 2f: 3rd st: rdn & wknd wl
          over 1f out) .................................................................... 10.**6**
1148⁶ Spot the Dove (58) *(RJPrice)* 8-2 ‡³TSprake (7) (a bhd: t.o) ............... ½.**7**
 994³ Morsun (73) *(DMorley)* 9-0 ‡⁷EBentley (3) (lw: a bhd: t.o) ................... 1½.**8**

**9/4** Toss the Dice, **5/1** TIMURID (FR), Morsun(op 3/1), Weeheby (USA)(4/1—6/1), **6/1** Witches Coven(op 10/1),
**7/1** Eastleigh, **12/1** Kingchip Boy(8/1—14/1), **25/1** Spot the Dove. CSF £28.73, CT £160.43. Tote £6.20: £2.20
£2.30 £1.50 (£12.30). Mr Cyril Humphris (ARUNDEL) bred by Cyril Humphris in France. 8 Rn  1m 52.9 (4.4)
                                            SF—8/10/–/–/–/–

---

**1427**     CHAPEL ASH H'CAP (0-70) £1182.00 (£327.00: £156.00)   **5f**      8-50 (8-52)

1262* **The Noble Oak (IRE) (61)** (bl) (Jt-Fav) *(MMcCormack)* 4-9-8 JReid (2) (lw:
          a.p: led 2f out: rdn out) ................................................... —**1**
1282 Last Straw (37) *(AWJones)* 4-7-5 ‡⁷ClaireBalding (3) (chsd ldrs: swtchd rt over
          1f out: fin fast) ................................................................ hd.**2**
 876 Simmie's Special (67) *(RHollinshead)* 4-9-7 ‡⁷SWynne (4) (led 3f: rdn & no ex
          ins fnl f) ........................................................................... 2.**3**
1278³ Klairover (46) (Jt-Fav) *(CJHill)* 5-8-7 NAdams (5) (hdwy appr fnl f: nvr plcd to
          chal) .................................................................................. 2.**4**
1282* Rednet (60) (Jt-Fav) *(PDEvans)* 5-9-7 (7x) AMunro (8) (b: chsd ldrs stands'
          side: nvr able to chal) ..................................................... ½.**5**
1138 Banbury Flyer (58) *(MrsALMKing)* 4-9-5 RHills (5) (spd over 3f) ............... 1½.**6**
1030 Starchy Cove (42) *(BRCambidge)* 5-7-12 ‡⁵RPrice (9) (spd stands' side 3f) ..... nk.**7**
1162⁵ Rays Mead (47) *(LJHolt)* 4-8-1 ‡⁷CAvery (10) (swtg: outpcd) ............... nk.**8**
*1263* R a Express (41) *(BAMcMahon)* 7-8-2⁽³⁾ GDuffield (1) (spd on outside 3f) ... ¾.**9**
    Dreamtime Echo (39) *(JBalding)* 4-8-0 PBurke (6) (bkwd: a bhd & outpcd) ... ¾.**10**

**4/1** Klairover, Rednet, THE NOBLE OAK (IRE), **5/1** Banbury Flyer, **9/1** Starchy Cove(6/1—10/1), **10/1** Last Straw, Rays Mead, **14/1** Simmie's Special, **16/1** R a Express, **40/1** Dreamtime Echo. CSF £40.08, CT £467.39. Tote £5.40: £1.90 £2.30 £3.40 (£32.70). Mr M. McCormack (WANTAGE) bred by Rosemount Stud in Ireland. 10 Rn

59.3 sec (2)
SF—53/21/43/21/33/25

T/Plpt: £1,317.70 (1 Tckts).
IM

1076—**BRIGHTON (L-H)**
## Monday, June 15th [Firm]
Going Allowance: minus 0.30 sec per fur (F)
Wind: almost nil

Stalls: low

**1428**  SUSSEX CRICKETER (HOVE) H'CAP (3-Y.O) (0-70) £2441.60 (£677.60: £324.80)
6f 209y
2-00 (2-01)

| | | | |
|---|---|---|---|
| 1159⁴ | **Court Minstrel (54)** *(LJHolt)* 8-6⁽¹⁾ JReid (6) (5th st: led over 2f out: r.o wl) | | —1 |
| 1122 | Chatino **(61)** *(CEBrittain)* 8-13 TQuinn (7) (hdwy over 2f out: chsd wnr over 1f out: r.o) | | 3.2 |
| 1261 | Lady Sabo **(69)** *(GLewis)* 9-7 PaulEddery (4) (4th st: one pce fnl 3f) | | 4.3 |
| 1309 | Master Hyde (USA) **(55)** (bl) *(PMitchell)* 8-7 MRoberts (3) (2nd st: ev ch over 2f out: wknd over 1f out) | | ¾.4 |
| | Cap Camarat (CAN) **(53)** *(PFICole)* 7-12 ‡⁷JDSmith (1) (3rd st: rdn & swtchd rt over 1f out: one pce) | | ¾.5 |
| 1147 | Kentucky Starlet (USA) **(56)** (bl) *(RHannon)* 8-8 WCarson (11) (nvr nr to chal) | | 4.6 |
| 1159⁶ | Day of History (IRE) **(44)** *(CACyzer)* 7-7⁽¹⁾ ‡³FNorton (9) (nvr nrr) | | ½.7 |
| 1040⁴ | Palacegate Gold (IRE) **(60)** *(RJHodges)* 8-12 RCochrane (10) (a bhd) | | 3.8 |
| 1145 | Nominee Prince **(43)** *(RGuest)* 7-9 JQuinn (5) (6th st: wknd over 3f out) | | s.h.9 |
| 1159² | Countercheck (IRE) **(55)** (Fav) *(CFWall)* 8-7 NDay (2) (led over 4f) | | 1½.10 |
| 1257 | Cushty **(41)** (bl) *(JELong)* 7-7 NAdams (8) (a bhd) | | 2½.11 |

LONG HANDICAP: Cushty 7-1.

**5/2** Countercheck (IRE), **4/1** COURT MINSTREL, **15/2** Kentucky Starlet (USA), **8/1** Lady Sabo, **10/1** Master Hyde (USA), **12/1** Chatino, Palacegate Gold (IRE)(op 7/1), Day of History (IRE)(op 7/1), **14/1** Cap Camarat (CAN)(op 8/1), **33/1** Nominee Prince, **66/1** Cushty. CSF £44.46, CT £329.31. Tote £4.40: £2.00 £4.30 £2.70 (£118.80). Mr G. W. Knight (BASINGSTOKE) bred by Keith Freeman. 11 Rn

1m 21.2 (1.2)
SF—42/40/36/20/9/7

**1429**  MOULSECOOMB CLAIMING STKS (2-Y.O) £2284.80 (£632.80: £302.40)
5f 213y
2-30 (2-38)

| | | | |
|---|---|---|---|
| 1149⁴ | **Break My Heart** (Fav) *(PFICole)* 8-12 AMunro (7) (lw: 4th st: led over 1f out: hrd rdn: r.o wl) | | —1 |
| 1161 | Lochore *(RIngram)* 8-3 ‡⁵NGwilliams (5) (hrd rdn & hdwy over 1f out: r.o wl ins fnl f) | | 1.2 |
| 1178* | Burishki (bl) *(GAPritchard-Gordon)* 8-3 GCarter (9) (6th st: hrd rdn over 1f out: r.o) | | ¾.3 |
| 581 | Gypsy Legend *(WGMTurner)* 7-13 ‡³TSprake (4) (2nd st: led over 2f out tl over 1f out: unable qckn) | | 1.4 |
| | Karinska *(SirMarkPrescott)* 8-5 GDuffield (1) (leggy: scope: s.s: hdwy over 1f out: r.o) | | nk.5 |
| 1038 | Touch N' Glow *(RHannon)* 8-7 SRaymont (8) (s.s: hdwy over 1f out: nvr nrr) | | ½.6 |
| 907 | Morning News (IRE) *(MHTompkins)* 8-9 PRobinson (6) (5th st: one pce fnl 2f) | | hd.7 |
| 1077⁶ | Victorian Star *(PButler)* 8-0 AProud (3) (led over 3f) | | 10.8 |
| 782 | Freebyjove *(PButler)* 8-0 TyroneWilliams (2) (3rd st: wknd 3f out) | | 8.9 |

**13/8** BREAK MY HEART(tchd 11/4), **3/1** Karinska, **5/1** Lochore(4/1—8/1), Burishki(4/1—6/1), **14/1** Morning News (IRE)(op 5/1), Touch N' Glow(op 5/1), **16/1** Gypsy Legend, **66/1** Ors. CSF £10.11, Tote £2.90: £1.30 £1.40 £1.70 (£5.30). Mr Fahd Salman (WHATCOMBE) bred by Newgate Stud Co. 9 Rn

1m 11 (2.6)
SF—10/—/—/—/—/—

**1430**  COSMOPOLITAN HOTEL (BRIGHTON) H'CAP (0-70) £2363.20 (£655.20: £313.60)
1m 3f 196y
3-00 (3-06)

(Weights raised 11 lb)

| | | | |
|---|---|---|---|
| 1087* | **Top Royal (66)** (Fav) *(JLDunlop)* 3-9-5 WCarson (10) (lw: rdn over 4f out: 2nd st: led 2f out: comf) | | —1 |
| 1087³ | Serious Time **(46)** *(SirMarkPrescott)* 4-9-1 GDuffield (6) (a.p: led over 4f out to 2f out: unable qckn) | | 3.2 |
| 1341² | Tiger Claw (USA) **(54)** *(RJHodges)* 6-9-9 RCochrane (8) (hdwy 4f out: 6th st: one pce fnl 2f) | | 3½.3 |

```
1292³  Garda's Gold (25) (RDickin) 9-7-8 SDawson (7) (4th st: wknd over 2f out) ........ 8.4
1318   Puff Puff (55) (MissBSanders) 6-9-10 WNewnes (9) (lw: nvr nr to chal) .......... ³/4.5
 942³  Dominant Force (69) (RHannon) 3-9-8 MRoberts (1) (5th st: wknd over 2f out) 1¹/2.6
       Tring Park (40) (RCurtis) 6-8-9 GBardwell (5) (a bhd) ...................................... 10.7
1110⁵  Lucky Barnes (33) (v) (PABlockley) 5-8-2 AMackay (2) (bhd fnl 4f) .............. s.h.8
1081⁴  Fitness Fanatic (38) (JTGifford) 4-8-7 JQuinn (4) (led over 5f out tl over 4f out:
       3rd st: wknd 3f out) .................................................................... 3¹/2.9
1257   Casniktony (41) (bl) (AMoore) 3-7-8 NAdams (3) (led over 6f) ...................... 15.10
```

**11/8** TOP ROYAL, **7/2** Tiger Claw (USA), **11/2** Serious Time, **7/1** Garda's Gold, **10/1** Puff Puff, **12/1** Dominant
Force(op 8/1), **14/1** Fitness Fanatic, **66/1** Ors. CSF £9.49, CT £20.40. Tote £2.50: £1.20 £1.90 £1.30 (£7.60).
Mr Aubrey Ison (ARUNDEL) bred by Miss G. Abbey. 10 Rn                           2m 30.1 (3.1)
                                                                            SF—38/28/29/–/12/7

## 1431
BRIGHTON MILE CHALLENGE TROPHY (H'cap) (0-90) £3687.50 (£1100.00: £525.00:
£237.50)  **7f 214y**                                                         3-30 (3-32)
                          (Weights raised 1 lb)

```
1104*  Talent (USA) (77) (v) (LordHuntingdon) 4-9-10 AMunro (5) (mde all: rdn
       out) .............................................................................................. —1
1104⁴  Durneltor (65) (RHannon) 4-8-12 MRoberts (1) (3rd st: rdn & ev ch 2f out:
       unable qckn) ................................................................................ 3.2
1201⁴  Helios (71) (RSimpson) 4-9-4 WRyan (2) (lw: 5th st: rdn over 2f out: one pce) 1¹/2.3
1266³  Ain'tlifelikethat (51) (bl) (TJNaughton) 5-7-12 GCarter (4) (b: 4th st: wknd over
       1f out) .......................................................................................... 3¹/2.4
       Trattoria (USA) (70) (JSutcliffe) 3-8-6 BRouse (3) (2nd st: wknd over 2f out) ... 15.5
```

**2/1** TALENT (USA), **9/4** Ain'tlifelikethat(op 4/1), **100/30** Helios, **7/2** Durneltor, **25/1** Trattoria (USA). CSF £8.82,
Tote £2.90: £1.50 £2.10 (£3.80). The Queen (WEST ILSLEY) bred by The Queen in USA. 5 Rn  1m 34.4 (2.2)
                                                                                 SF—41/20/21/–

## 1432
HOVE STKS (Mdn 3-Y.O.F) £1932.00 (£532.00: £252.00)  **7f 214y**               4-00 (4-01)

```
 699³  Rose Elegance (WRMuir) 8-11 SWhitworth (5) (lw: 3rd st: led 2f out: drvn out) . —1
1209⁵  Donia (USA) (PFICole) 8-11 AMunro (1) (5th st: hrd rdn over 1f out: r.o ins fnl f) nk.2
 922⁴  Queen Caroline (USA) (HRACecil) 8-11 WRyan (4) (lw: 4th st: hrd rdn over 1f
       out: unable qckn) ......................................................................... 1¹/2.3
 934⁶  Miss Bluebird (IRE) (98) (Fav) (PAKelleway) 8-11 MRoberts (3) (b.hind: led 6f:
       one pce) ........................................................................................ ¹/2.4
1306²  Selaginella (MRChannon) 8-11 TQuinn (6) (2nd st: wknd over 2f out) ............. 10.5
 393   Cee Beat (v) (EAWheeler) 8-11 TRogers (2) (virtually ref to r: a t.o) .................. dist.6
```

**7/4** Miss Bluebird (IRE)(5/4—2/1), **9/4** ROSE ELEGANCE(2/1—3/1), **7/2** Queen Caroline (USA)(3/1—9/2), **7/1**
Donia (USA), **11/1** Selaginella(op 7/1), **100/1** Cee Beat. CSF £15.73, Tote £3.80: £1.70 £2.80 (£19.10). Mr A. N.
Miller (LAMBOURN) bred by E. A. Badger. 6 Rn                                    1m 35.3 (3.1)
                                                                          SF—15/14/9/7/–/–

## 1433
BEVENDEAN STKS (Mdn 3-Y.O) £1932.00 (£532.00: £252.00)  **6f 209y**            4-30 (4-31)

```
1218   Courageous Knight (73) (RHannon) 9-0 WCarson (1) (led 3f: 2nd st: led 1f
       out: rdn out) ................................................................................. —1
1293²  Double Shift (RDickin) 8-9 TQuinn (2) (led 4f out to 1f out: r.o) ........................ ³/4.2
1086³  La Kermesse (USA) (65) (Fav) (JHMGosden) 8-9 JWilliams (6) (3rd st: rdn over
       2f out: unable qckn) ...................................................................... 5.3
 925   Tom's Apache (54) (WRWilliams) 8-7 †⁷CMunday (4) (dwlt: 5th st: nvr nr to chal) ³/4.4
       Sea-Deer (LJHolt) 9-0 JReid (5) (w'like: bkwd: 6th st: a bhd) ........................... nk.5
       Blue Drifter (IRE) (JSutcliffe) 9-0 BRouse (3) (w'like: bkwd: 4th st: wknd over 2f
       out) .............................................................................................. 2¹/2.6
```

**5/4** La Kermesse (USA), **13/8** COURAGEOUS KNIGHT, **5/1** Double Shift, **10/1** Sea-Deer, **33/1** Blue Drifter (IRE),
**66/1** Tom's Apache. CSF £9.45, Tote £2.50: £1.60 £1.80 (£4.70). Mr T. E. Bucknall (MARLBOROUGH) bred by
C. A. Blackwell. 6 Rn                                                           1m 23.1 (3.1)
                                                                          SF—22/15/–/–/–/–

## 1434
LEVY BOARD APP'CE H'CAP (0-70) £2206.40 (£610.40: £291.20)
**6f 209y**                                                                   5-00 (5-01)
                          (Weights raised 1 lb)
```
 344   Norfolkiev (FR) (57) (MMoubarak) 6-9-7 CHawksley (7) (lw: 2nd st: led 2f out:
       pushed out) ................................................................................. —1
 913   Chloes Diamond (IRE) (45) (JLSpearing) 4-8-9 EHusband (2) (3rd st: rdn over
       1f out: r.o) ..................................................................................... ¹/2.2
 515   Faynaz (50) (v) (WRMuir) 6-9-0 KimMcDonnell (4) (led 5f: unable qckn) .......... 2.3
```

1174⁴ Kawwas **(44)** *(WHolden)* 7-8-8 BRussell (9) (4th st: rdn over 2f out: one pce) .. ¹/₂.4
1032 Green's Stubbs **(33)** *(ABarrow)* 5-7-11 SSanders (5) (5th st: hrd rdn over 2f
    out: one pce) ............................................................................... 2.5
1032⁴ Juvenara **(43)** (Fav) *(CJHill)* 6-8-7 PBowe (8) (nvr nr to chal) ......................... 1¹/₂.6
1172⁴ Kelly's Kite **(30)** *(HJCollingridge)* 4-7-8 TWilson (10) (dwlt: nvr nrr) ................. ¹/₂.7
1261 Liu Liu San (IRE) **(36)** *(PButler)* 4-7-9 ‡5DToole (3) (s.s: a bhd) ........................ 8.8
1314 Greetland Rock **(44)** *(PHowling)* 4-8-8 DebbieBiggs (1) (6th st: wknd over 2f out) 4.9
1093 Tara's Girl **(60)** (v) *(PABlockley)* 5-9-10 GParkin (6) (dwlt: a wl bhd) ............. 20.10

**2/1** Juvenara, **7/2** Kawwas, **11/2** NORFOLKIEV (FR)(op 3/1), **6/1** Faynaz(op 4/1), **7/1** Tara's Girl(tchd 20/1), **16/1** Chloes Diamond (IRE), Kelly's Kite, Green's Stubbs, **33/1** Greetland Rock, **50/1** Liu Liu San (IRE). CSF £77.58, CT £498.58. Tote £6.30: £1.90 £2.50 £2.80 (£36.60). Ecurie Fustok (NEWMARKET) bred by Pierre de Gaste and Pierre Camus Denais in France. 10 Rn                    1m 22.8 (2.8)
                                                                          SF—33/19/18/10/–

T/Plpt: £41.50 (72.35 Tckts).                                                        AK

1126—**EDINBURGH (R-H)**

## Monday, June 15th [Firm, Good to firm patches]

Going Allowance: minus 0.35 sec per fur (F)                    Wind: slt half against

Stalls: centre

**1435**   E.B.F. WILLOWBRAE STKS (Mdn 2-Y.O) £2414.40 (£678.40: £331.20)
           5f                                                            2-15 (2-20)

917² **Make it Happen (IRE)** (Fav) *(JBerry)* 9-0 JCarroll (2) (lw: slt ld to ¹/₂-wy: a cl up:
        r.o u.p tl ld post) ..................................................................... —1
     Petered Out *(TDBarron)* 9-0 AlexGreaves (8) (neat: w ldrs: led ¹/₂-wy: jst ct) ... s.h.2
     Don't Tell Jean *(NBycroft)* 8-9 SWood (4) (cmpt: str: bit bkwd: a wl ldrs: shkn up
        over 1f out: no ex nr fin) ............................................................. ¹/₂.3
1233³ Meconopsis *(TFairhurst)* 8-6 ‡3JFanning (1) (s.i.s: sn w ldrs tl wknd ins fnl f) ...... 1.4
     Cambus Bay *(WTKemp)* 8-9 JLowe (3) (unf: bit bkwd: s.s: a wl bhd) .............. 20.5

**4/11** MAKE IT HAPPEN (IRE), **11/4** Meconopsis(op 13/8), **16/1** Don't Tell Jean(op 10/1), Petered Out(op 6/1), **66/1** Cambus Bay. CSF £6.50, Tote £1.40: £1.10 £6.90 (£5.00). Mr Robert Aird (COCKERHAM) bred by A. F. O'Callaghan in Ireland. 5 Rn                                                    62.9 sec (5.2)

**1436**   JOPPA CLAIMING STKS   £2081.50 (£584.00: £284.50)   5f   2-45 (2-51)

1212 **Plain Fact (80)** *(AHarrison)* 7-9-6 KFallon (9) (s.s: sn pushed along: hdwy over
        1f out: led & qcknd ins fnl f) ........................................................ —1
1114⁵ Best Effort **(48)** *(MPNaughton)* 6-8-9 ‡5JWeaver (1) (lw: hdwy ¹/₂-wy: r.o: nt pce
        of wnr) ................................................................................. 1.2
879⁵ Imperial Bid (FR) *(DenysSmith)* 4-9-3 ‡7CTeague (5) (sn outpcd & bhd: r.o wl fnl
        f) ...................................................................................... 2.3
714 Tino Tere **(93)** (bl) *(JBerry)* 3-8-12 JCarroll (3) (led: clr after 2f: wknd &
        hdd ins fnl f) ......................................................................... 1¹/₂.4
1235 Brisas **(47)** (bl) *(TFairhurst)* 5-8-13 ‡3JFanning (2) (lw: a chsng ldrs: rdn & nt
        qckn fnl 2f) .......................................................................... 1¹/₂.5
1045⁴ Midnight Lass **(40)** (v) *(WJPearce)* 4-7-12 ‡5SMaloney (4) (sn drvn along: nvr
        trbld ldrs) ........................................................................... 1¹/₂.6
1006⁵ Lawnswood Prince (IRE) **(63)** *(JLSpearing)* 3-8-5 DMcKeown (8) (chsd ldrs
        over 3f) .............................................................................. 1¹/₂.7
1271 Castle Cary **(22)** *(TCraig)* 6-8-9 LCharnock (7) (spd 3f: sn wknd) ................... 2¹/₂.8

**6/5** Tino Tere, **2/1** PLAIN FACT, **8/1** Imperial Bid (FR), **12/1** Best Effort, **20/1** Brisas, Lawnswood Prince (IRE), **33/1** Ors. CSF £22.49, Tote £3.30: £1.60 £2.50 £2.20 (£9.50). Mrs B. Ramsden (MIDDLEHAM) bred by Clanville Lodge Stud. 8 Rn                                              60.1 sec (2.4)
                                                                          SF—23/8/8/–/–/–

**1437**   MILLERHILL H'CAP (0-80) £2200.50 (£618.00: £301.50)   1m 7f 16y   3-15 (3-20)

1241³ **Fen Princess (IRE) (40)** *(PCHaslam)* 4-8-3 ‡5JWeaver (6) (trckd ldrs: led over
        3f out: sn clr) ....................................................................... —1
1119 Sexy Mover **(26)** *(WStorey)* 5-7-8 SWood (4) (lw: bhd tl styd on wl fnl 2f: no ch
        w wnr) ................................................................................ 6.2
     Attadale **(60)** *(LLungo)* 4-10-0 DNicholls (5) (in tch: hdwy to chase wnr 2f out:
        no imp) ............................................................................... 1.3
1239⁴ J P Morgan **(44)** (v) *(MPNaughton)* 4-8-12 KFallon (7) (led 3f: chsd ldrs: led
        appr st: hdd over 3f out: sn btn) .................................................... 5.4

1108 Alpha Helix (30) (v) (MissLAPerratt) 9–7-9 ‡3JFanning (2) (bhd: sme hdwy appr st: n.d) ............................................................................. 5.5

1337* Luks Akura (41) (v) (MJohnston) 4–8-2 (4x) ‡7MBaird (1) (lw: racd wd: led after 5f tl hdd appr st: sn wknd) ........................... 1½.6

1329⁶ Marian Evans (35) (TCraig) 5–8-3 LCharnock (3) (wl bhd fnl 5f) ...................... dist.7

**4/7** Luks Akura, **5/1** FEN PRINCESS (IRE), **7/1** Attadale, **10/1** Alpha Helix, **12/1** J P Morgan(op 8/1), **14/1** Sexy Mover, **50/1** Marian Evans. CSF £57.41, Tote £4.00: £2.10 £5.70 (£114.30). Mr S. A. B. Dinsmore (MIDDLEHAM) bred by Ballymacoll Stud Farm Ltd in Ireland. 7 Rn            3m 17.7 (7.2)

## 1438
TRANENT H'CAP (3-Y.O) (0-70) £2263.50 (£636.00: £310.50)
**1m 3f 32y**                                        3-45 (3-45)

(Weights raised 7 lb)

1188² **Reach for Glory (57)** (RMWhitaker) 9-5 ACulhane (1) (a.p: effrt 3f out: led ins fnl f) ................................................................. —1

1188⁴ Stingray City (USA) (55) (v) (JEtherington) 4-8-12 ‡5JWeaver (8) (led 2f: cl up: led wl over 3f out tl ins fnl f: kpt on) ............... ½.2

1298⁶ Pie Hatch (IRE) (35) (SirMarkPrescott) 7-11 JLowe (4) (shkn up to ld after 2f: hdd wl over 3f out: one pce) .................. 2.3

1288² Breakdancer (IRE) (56) (Fav) (MrsJRRamsden) 9-4 DMcKeown (5) (hld up & bhd: hdwy ent st: swtchd wl over 1f out: nt qckn) ............. 3½.4

Hot Tip (45) (BEllison) 8-4 ‡3JFanning (2) (effrt ent st: styd on: no imp) 2.5

Shayna Maidel (45) (MBell) 8-7 MHills (3) (lw: prom: hdwy to trck ldrs appr st: rdn & btn 3f out) ....................................... 5.6

1122³ The Dandy Don (57) (v) (DenysSmith) 9-5 KFallon (6) (lw: hld up: effrt appr st: rdn & no imp) ............................ 2½.7

457 Mr News (IRE) (59) (WJPearce) 9-7 DNicholls (7) (trckd ldrs tl grad wknd fnl 4f) 2.8

**9/4** Breakdancer (IRE), **3/1** Shayna Maidel, **6/1** Stingray City (USA), **7/1** The Dandy Don (IRE), REACH FOR GLORY, Pie Hatch (IRE), **14/1** Mr News (IRE), **33/1** Hot Tip. CSF £44.49, CT £277.50. Tote £6.00: £1.60 £1.90 £2.20 (£21.10). Mr R. M. Whitaker (WETHERBY) bred by Ridgecourt Stud. 8 Rn            2m 25.8 (6.1)
SF—5/-/-/-/-/-

## 1439
LEITH CLAIMING STKS (Mdn) £2081.50 (£584.00: £284.50)    **7f 15y**    4-15 (4-16)

1130⁴ **Rose Gem (IRE) (54)** (Fav) (PCHaslam) 3–7-9 DaleGibson (6) (mde all: shkn up 2f out: r.o wl) ........................... —1

Northern Graduate (USA) (54) (MrsGRReveley) 3–8-3(1) MHills (5) (s.i.s: hld up & bhd: r.o fnl 3f: too much to do) ........... 2½.2

1184 Miss Parkes (43) (JBerry) 3–8-3 JCarroll (4) (lw: in tch: hdwy wl over 3f out: one pce appr fnl f) ............................. ¾.3

1294 Syke Lane (43) (RMWhitaker) 3–7-4 ‡3JFanning (2) (a chsng ldrs: rdn 3f out: one pce) .................................... 3.4

1270 Perspicacity (39) (MDods) 5–8-11 JLowe (1) (bhd tl sme late hdwy) .......... 2.5

950 Charlie Love (WStorey) 3–7-12 LCharnock (7) (swtg: in tch: effrt ent st: grad wknd) .................................. 2½.6

1271⁶ Minsk (22) (TCraig) 6–8-3 PBurke (3) (cl up tl wknd over 2f out) .............. 1½.7

**10/11** ROSE GEM (IRE)(4/5—11/8), **3/1** Northern Graduate (USA)(op 6/4), **11/2** Syke Lane, **8/1** Miss Parkes(op 3/1), **12/1** Minsk, **14/1** Charlie Love, **25/1** Perspicacity. CSF £4.50, Tote £1.80: £1.30 £1.80 (£2.90). Mrs M. E. F. Haslam (MIDDLEHAM) bred by F. Feeney in Ireland. 7 Rn            1m 27.6 (1.4)
SF—24/24/22/—/1/15

## 1440
LEVY BOARD H'CAP (3-Y.O) (0-70) £2295.00 (£645.00: £315.00)
**7f 15y**                                        4-45 (4-49)

(Weights raised 1 lb)

1159³ **Bear With Me (IRE) (59)** (Fav) (MBell) 9-7 MHills (2) (led after 2f: kpt on wl fnl 2f) ........................................ —1

749 Denim Blue (55) (CWThornton) 9-3 DMcKeown (5) (lw: cl up: hmpd appr st: styd on u.p fnl f) ......................... 2.2

1001³ Crimson Consort (IRE) (31) (v) (DonEnricoIncisa) 7-0 ‡7ClaireBalding (11) (a chsng ldrs: n.m.r 2f out: styd on nr fin) .......... s.h.3

1281³ Hot Punch (49) (PCalver) 8-4 ‡7CAdamson (9) (led 2f: chsd ldrs: one pce appr fnl f) .............................. 1½.4

1246 Oyston's Life (46) (JBerry) 8-8 JCarroll (7) (bhd: hdwy 3f out: styd on wl) ...... d.h.4

1157 Ten High (IRE) (40) (BEllison) 8-2 JLowe (6) (lw: bhd & rdn ent st: styd on: nrst fin) ........................... 1½.6

749 Aegaen Lady (53) (JEtherington) 8-10 ‡5JWeaver (4) (chsd ldrs: ev ch & rdn over 2f out: grad wknd) .................. 2.7

1243⁶ Kick on Majestic (IRE) (43) (bl) (NBycroft) 8-5 SWood (10) (effrt ent st: n.d) .... ¾.8

Blunham Express (52) (TFairhurst) 8-11 ‡3JFanning (8) (chsd ldrs tl wknd 3f out) ......................................... 2½.9

1075 Chester Belle **(38)** *(PCHaslam)* 8-0 DaleGibson (3) (in tch tl wknd 2f out: eased
    ins fnl f) ............................................................ ³/₄.**10**
    Canbrack (IRE) **(59)** *(WAStephenson)* 9-7 KFallon (1) (dwlt: a bhd) ................ **1.11**
        LONG HANDICAP: Crimson Consort (IRE) 7-6.

**5/2** BEAR WITH ME (IRE), **9/2** Crimson Consort (IRE), **7/1** Kick on Majestic (IRE), **8/1** Chester Belle(op 5/1), **9/1** Aegaen Lady(12/1—8/1), **10/1** Hot Punch(op 6/1), **14/1** Denim Blue(op 8/1), Ten High (IRE), **16/1** Canbrack (IRE), **20/1** Blunham Express(op 12/1), **25/1** Oyston's Life. CSF £33.41, CT £137.44. Tote £2.70: £1.10 £2.80 £1.90 (£19.90). Mrs T. Stopford-Sackville (NEWMARKET) bred by Tsarina Stud in Ireland. 11 Rn
                                                      1m 28.3 (2.1)
                                                 SF—39/29/—/10/14/3

---

## 1441     COCKENSIE H'CAP (0-70) £2295.00 (£645.00: £315.00)   **1m 16y**   5-15 (5-19)

1270⁵ **Routing (52)** *(MDHammond)* 4–8-11 JCarroll (2) (lw: hld up: gd hdwy over 2f
    out: led over 1f out: r.o wl) ...................................... —**1**
1270³ Lawnswood Junior **(50)** (Fav) *(JLSpearing)* 5–8-9 DMcKeown (6) (in tch: effrt 3f
    out: styd on u.p fnl f) .............................................. **4.2**
1335⁴ Bee Dee Ell (USA) **(48)** *(MissLAPerratt)* 3–7-7 ‡³JFanning (10) (mid div: hdwy 2f
    out: styd on nr fin) .............................................. 1¹/₂.**3**
1270⁴ Stand At Ease **(34)** *(WStorey)* 7–7-7 SWood (9) (bhd tl styd on fnl 3f: nvr nrr)   s.h.**4**
1129⁴ Leave it to Lib **(55)** *(PCalver)* 5–9-0 DaleGibson (11) (lw: w ldrs: led wl over 3f
    out tl hdd over 1f out: sn btn) ................................. ³/₄.**5**
1329⁴ Rapid Mover **(38)** *(TCraig)* 5–7-11⁽⁴⁾ PBurke (4) (bhd tl styd on fnl 2f) ................ **2.6**
1129★ Blue Grit **(41)** (bl) *(MDods)* 6–8-0 LCharnock (3) (s.i.s: hdwy appr st: one pce
    fnl f) ................................................................. s.h.**7**
1109 Saint Bene't (IRE) **(43)** (bl) *(PCHaslam)* 4–7-11 ‡⁵SMaloney (4) (trckd ldrs: effrt
    3f out: sn btn) ........................................................ **2.8**
419 Rostovol **(37)** (v) *(DRFranks)* 7–7-10 JLowe (5) (b: a bhd) .......................... **4.9**
    Jane's Brave Boy **(34)** *(TCraig)* 10–7-0 ‡⁷DarrenMoffatt (7) (cl up to st: sn bhd) **10.10**
1114⁴ Canaan Valley **(69)** *(JGFitzGerald)* 4–10-0 KFallon (12) (lw: unruly in stalls: led
    tl hdd wl over 3f out: sn wknd & eased) ......................... s.h.**11**
        LONG HANDICAP: Stand At Ease 7-6, Rapid Mover 6-8, Jane's Brave Boy 6-9.

**3/1** Lawnswood Junior, **4/1** Leave it to Lib, **9/2** Blue Grit, **11/2** Canaan Valley(op 7/2), **12/1** Stand At Ease, **14/1** Rapid Mover, ROUTING, Bee Dee Ell (USA)(10/1—16/1), **16/1** Saint Bene't (IRE), **33/1** Rostovol, **50/1** Jane's Brave Boy. CSF £51.92, CT £555.84. Tote £10.50: £2.80 £1.90 (£15.40). Mrs M. A. Doohan (MIDDLEHAM) bred by Fonthill Stud. 11 Rn
                                         1m 40.1 (1.5)
                                      SF—32/18/–/–/15/–

T/Plpt: £110.00 (16.8 Tckts).                                AA

---

## 799—WINDSOR (Fig.8)

### Monday, June 15th [Good]

Going Allowance: minus 0.25 sec per fur (F)                           Wind: nil

Stalls: high

## 1442     PANMURE GORDON (S) STKS (2-Y.O) £1884.00 (£524.00: £252.00)
        **5f 217y**                                     6-35 (6-38)

1149⁶ **True Story (IRE)** (Fav) *(RHannon)* 8-8 ‡³RPerham (15) (hdwy over 2f out: led
    over 1f out: all out) .............................................. —**1**
1036 Homemaker *(RJHolder)* 8-6 JWilliams (20) (hdwy 2f out: ev ch fnl f: r.o) .......... hd.**2**
928 Mighty Miss Magpie (IRE) *(MRChannon)* 8-1 ‡⁵BDoyle (17) (hdwy 2f out: r.o ins
    fnl f) ................................................................ 3¹/₂.**3**
1264⁴ Madam Cyn's Risk (di) *(NACallaghan)* 8-6 PatEddery (13) (gd hdwy 2f out: hrd
    rdn over 1f out: one pce fnl f) ................................. **2.4**
1202⁶ All Promises *(PButler)* 8-6 TyroneWilliams (9) (w ldrs: led 2f out tl over 1f out) ... **2.5**
928 Wealthywoo *(JSMoore)* 8-6 BRouse (5) (a.p: one pce fnl 2f) ................... 1¹/₂.**6**
    Tropical Tia (IRE) *(RVoorspuy)* 8-6 CRutter (19) (b.hind: a.p: ev ch over 1f out:
    wknd ins fnl f) ...................................................... hd.**7**
1178³ Heroic Deed (v) *(MHTompkins)* 8-11 PRobinson (11) (lw: nvr nr to chal) ............. **2.8**
1208 Water Diviner (bl) *(RFJohnsonHoughton)* 8-11 KDarley (22) (nvr trbld ldrs) ..... hd.**9**
    Stroika (IRE) *(CJames)* 8-6 WNewnes (7) (w'like: bit bkwd: n.d) ...................... **2.10**
733 Run on Rebel (IRE) (bl) *(PFICole)* 8-11 TQuinn (21) (w ldrs: led 3f out to 2f out:
    wkng whn hmpd over 1f out) ..................................... nk.**11**
928 Jaybee-Jay *(MJHaynes)* 8-11 RCochrane (10) (prom 3f) ..................... s.h.**12**
703 Buckski Echo *(TMJones)* 8-6 ‡⁵KRutter (24) (lw: n.d) ......................... 2¹/₂.**13**
1077 School of Science *(RPCHoad)* 8-4 ‡⁷PTurner (12) (prom over 3f) ................. 1¹/₂.**14**
1202⁵ Awesome Risk *(GLewis)* 8-6 PaulEddery (16) (lw: prom over 3f) ............... **2.15**
1120 Princess of Alar *(BPalling)* 8-6 RHills (4) (bit bkwd: m.n.s) ......................... s.h.**16**

584⁶ Sterling Princess *(JRJenkins)* 8-6 SWhitworth (2) (swtg: led 3f: sn wknd) ........ ¾.17
588 Total Truth *(JWhite)* 7-13 ‡7CAvery (18) (prom 3f) ................................................. 2.18
1171⁵ Secret Tale *(GBlum)* 8-6 JQuinn (1) (m.n.s) ....................................................... 1.19
1121 Kill the Plague (USA) (bl) *(APJones)* 8-11 NAdams (23) (swtg: a bhd) .............. ½.20
1161 Mac Tomb *(KOCunningham-Brown)* 8-8 ‡3DBiggs (6) (m.n.s) .......................... ¾.21
1121 Krayyan Dawn (bl) *(RVoorspuy)* 8-11 SDawson (14) (a bhd) ............................ 2.22
Tax Avoidance (IRE) *(SDow)* 7-13 ‡7MJermy (8) (str: bkwd: a bhd) ............ nk.23

2/1 TRUE STORY (IRE), 7/1 Mighty Miss Magpie (IRE)(op 4/1), 15/2 Awesome Risk(7/2—8/1), 8/1 Madam
Cyn's Risk(5/1—10/1), 9/1 Homemaker(op 6/1), 10/1 Heroic Deed(op 6/1), 14/1 All Promises, 16/1 Run on
Rebel (IRE)(7/1—20/1), 20/1 Water Diviner, Jaybee-Jay, Total Truth, 25/1 Stroika (IRE), Wealthywoo, 33/1
Krayyan Dawn, Princess of Alar, 50/1 Ors. CSF £21.80, Tote £3.70: £1.80 £3.10 £2.40 (£17.40). Mr Guy Hart
(MARLBOROUGH) bred by Cecil Harris Bloodstock Ltd in Ireland. 23 Rn; No bid
           1m 12.7 (2.2)
           SF—20/19/–/–/–/–

**1443**   TIME MAGAZINE GRADUATION STKS (2-Y-O) £1861.00 (£516.00: £247.00)
      5f 10y                         7-00 (7-04)

1186⁶ Area Girl *(SirMarkPrescott)* 8-13 GDuffield (1) (mde all: all out) ...................... —1
1196³ Night Melody (IRE) *(Fav)* *(RHannon)* 9-7 KDarley (3) (a.p: ev ch fnl 2f: hrd rdn:
        r.o) ............................................................................................................ nk.2
1196⁴ Final Frontier (IRE) *(RAkehurst)* 8-11 WCarson (7) (lw: a.p: rdn over 1f out: nt
        qckn) .......................................................................................................... 5.3
907⁴ Beaver Brook *(RHannon)* 8-11 BRaymond (8) (nvr nrr) ...................................... hd.4
Florac (IRE) *(MJHeaton-Ellis)* 8-6 WNewnes (6) (neat: spd 3f) ......................... 2.5
1103 Coy Boy (IRE) *(GLewis)* 8-11 PaulEddery (5) (nvr nr to chal) ............................ 3.6
Bonita Bee *(LJHolt)* 8-6 JReid (9) (w'like: scope: bit bkwd: dwlt: nvr trbld ldrs) nk.7
446 Soleil D'Or (bl) *(MMcCormack)* 8-11 SCauthen (2) (prom tl hrd rdn & wknd 2f
        out) ............................................................................................................ 4.8
Take the Mick *(EAWheeler)* 8-6 ‡5DHarrison (10) (w'like: s.s: a wl bhd) ............. 3.9
Fiveofive (IRE) *(NACallaghan)* 8-6 PatEddery (4) (leggy: outpcd: t.o) ............... 1.10

9/4 Night Melody (IRE), 5/2 Final Frontier (IRE)(7/4—11/4), 7/2 AREA GIRL, 8/1 Beaver Brook(6/1—10/1), 10/1
Fiveofive(op 4/1), 14/1 Soleil D'Or, 20/1 Bonita Bee, Florac, 25/1 Take the Mick, 33/1 Coy Boy (IRE).
CSF £12.07, Tote £5.90: £1.60 £1.50 £1.40 (£7.00). Mr W. E. Sturt (NEWMARKET) bred by Edmond and
Richard Kent. 10 Rn                               60.4 sec (1.4)
           SF—46/36/33/23/22/9/2

**1444**   DATASERV H'CAP (3-Y-O) (0-100) £3655.00 (£1090.00: £520.00: £235.00)
      1¹/₄m 7y                         7-30 (7-31)
        (Weights raised 1 lb)
628³ Alhamad (89) *(Fav)* *(HRACecil)* 9-7 PatEddery (1) (swtg: led after 3f: qcknd
        over 1f out: easily) ...................................................................................... —1
1218 Shrewd Partner (IRE) (80) *(DRCElsworth)* 8-12 SCauthen (4) (4th st: ev ch 2f
        out: hrd rdn: r.o one pce) .......................................................................... 2¹/₂.2
1218⁵ Grog (IRE) (71) *(MRChannon)* 7-12 ‡5DHarper (2) (led 3f: 2nd st: once pce fnl 2f) 1¹/₂.3
963 Billy Blazer (76) *(MHTompkins)* 8-8 KDarley (3) (5th st: hdwy 4f out: wknd over
        2f out) ........................................................................................................ 2.4
804 Busman (IRE) (75) *(MajorWRHern)* 8-7 WCarson (3) (3rd st: wknd 2f out: eased
        whn btn) ...................................................................................................... 2.5

13/8 ALHAMAD, 7/2 Busman (IRE), 4/1 Billy Blazer(op 5/2), 5/1 Grog (IRE), 6/1 Shrewd Partner (IRE). CSF
£10.19, Tote £2.20: £1.30 £2.10 (£5.10). Prince A. A. Faisal (NEWMARKET) bred by Nawara Stud Co Ltd. 5 Rn
                              2m 6.3 (3.3)
           SF—49/35/18/24/19

**1445**   TILDA RICE H'CAP (0-90) £2700.00 (£750.00: £360.00)   **5f 217y**     8-00 (8-02)

992² Paddy Chalk (76) *(Jt-Fav)* *(LJHolt)* 6-9-0 JReid (11) (b: a.p: led ins fnl f: all out) —1
Running Glimpse (IRE) (64) *(MissBSanders)* 4-7-13 ‡3FNorton (14) (led 5f:
        rallied ins fnl f) ........................................................................................ s.h.2
Superbrave (71) *(WJarvis)* 4-8-9 MTebbutt (6) (gd hdwy over 1f out: r.o ins fnl f) s.h.3
1282⁴ Young Shadowfax (55) *(CNAllen)* 5-7-7 GBardwell (8) (b.nr hind: hdwy fnl 2f:
        nvr nrr) ...................................................................................................... s.h.4
1305⁴ Unveiled (64) *(RJHodges)* 4-8-2 MRoberts (13) (gd hdwy 2f out: hrd rdn over
        1f out: r.o) .................................................................................................. hd.5
1278★ Bernstein Bette (67) *(Jt-Fav)* *(PSFelgate)* 6-8-5 WRyan (15) (nrst fin) ............ 1¹/₂.6
1167 Everglades (IRE) (68) *(RCharlton)* 4-8-6 RCochrane (16) (hdwy fnl f: r.o) ........ hd.7
1247⁶ Macfarlane (73) *(MJFetherston-Godley)* 4-8-11 PatEddery (4) (lw: w ldr: led 1f
        out tl wknd ins fnl f) .................................................................................. ¾.8
1303⁴ Beatle Song (61) *(RJHodges)* 4-7-13 JQuinn (12) (nvr nr to chal) .................... 1.9
970² Holetown (85) *(RHannon)* 3-9-0 WCarson (7) (prom 3f) ................................... 8.10

579 Clifton Charlie (USA) **(92)** *(MRChannon)* 4–10-2 TQuinn (2) (n.d) ................. 2¹/₂.11
550 Rhythmic Dancer **(77)** *(JLSpearing)* 4–9-1 JWilliams (5) (prom 4f) ................. ³/₄.12
909* Leigh Crofter **(70)** (bl) *(RJHolder)* 3–7-13 NAdams (1) (lw: m.n.s) ............. 5.13
906* Desert Dagger **(80)** *(MajorWRHern)* 3–8-9 SCauthen (3) (lw: spd 3f) ............. 1.14
1177⁵ Caromish (USA) **(72)** *(MDIUsher)* 5–8-10 MWigham (10) (swtg: prom 3f) ........ 8.15
1415 L'Ete (IRE) **(59)** *(PMitchell)* 4–7-6⁽⁴⁾ ‡⁵DHarrison (9) (reard & fell s) ........................ 0

**11/2** Bernstein Bette, PADDY CHALK, **6/1** Desert Dagger(tchd 9/1), **8/1** Unveiled, **9/1** Macfarlane, **10/1** Holetown, **11/1** Leigh Crofter, **12/1** Beatle Song, Caromish (USA), Running Glimpse (IRE), **16/1** Everglades (IRE), Young Shadowfax, **25/1** L'Ete (IRE), Superbrave, **33/1** Ors. CSF £68.55, CT £1,418.69. Tote £7.00: £1.80 £4.00 £6.00 £3.40 (£83.50). Mrs R. G. Wellman (BASINGSTOKE) bred by Countess of Durham. 16 Rn
1m 11.2 (0.7)
SF—56/40/49/32/25/37

**1446**
TAITTINGER CHAMPAGNE H'CAP (3-Y.O) (0-70) £2616.00 (£726.00: £348.00)
1m 3f 135y
8-30 (8-33)

(Weights raised 6 lb)
1165⁴ **Ivor's Flutter (62)** (Fav) *(DRCElsworth)* 9-5 JWilliams (2) (hdwy 3f out: led wl
over 1f out: easily) ...................................................... —1
1163 Heavenly Waters **(51)** *(RFJohnsonHoughton)* 8-8 RHills (10) (b.hind: hdwy
over 2f out: hrd rdn over 1f out: r.o) ....................................... 4.2
972⁵ Affirmed's Destiny (USA) **(50)** *(JLDunlop)* 8-7 WCarson (5) (3rd st: r.o one pce
fnl 2f) ............................................................... 2.3
1260 Dancing Years (USA) **(58)** *(MRChannon)* 9-1 BRouse (6) (nvr nr) ..................... 1.4
1041⁵ Dubitable **(58)** *(HCandy)* 9-1 CRutter (3) (6th st: ev ch 2f out: one pce) .......... 1.5
1311² Naseer (USA) **(59)** *(NACallaghan)* 9-2 PatEddery (12) (unruly s: 2nd st: led
over 2f out tl wknd wl over 1f out) ........................................ 2.6
799 Express Signmaker (IRE) **(49)** *(JWhite)* 8-1 ‡⁵RPrice (14) (no hdwy fnl 3f) ...... hd.7
1257³ Cavo Greco (USA) **(61)** *(PFICole)* 9-4 TQuinn (11) (4th st: wknd over 2f out) .... nk.8
1260 Formal Invitation (IRE) **(62)** *(GLewis)* 9-5 PaulEddery (4) (b: hdwy 3f out: hrd
rdn & wknd 2f out) ..................................................... hd.9
1220⁵ Russian Vision **(64)** *(AAScott)* 9-7 BRaymond (8) (lw: prom 6f) ..................... 2.10
806* Fly for Gold (IRE) **(58)** *(DWPArbuthnot)* 9-1 MRoberts (13) (n.d) ...................... hd.11
1260³ Erlemo **(50)** (bl) *(CJBenstead)* 8-7 TyroneWilliams (9) (led tl wknd over 2f out) nk.12
788 Striking Image (IRE) **(63)** *(RHannon)* 9-6 JReid (7) (5th st: wknd 3f out) ........... 2.13
1105⁵ Kathy Fair (IRE) **(45)** *(RJBaker)* 8-2 RFox (4) (t.o fnl 4f) .............................. 14

**11/4** IVOR'S FLUTTER(tchd 5/1), **7/2** Naseer (USA), **9/2** Fly for Gold (IRE), **11/2** Affirmed's Destiny (USA), **11/1** Dubitable, **12/1** Cavo Greco (USA)(op 8/1), Russian Vision(op 8/1), **14/1** Erlemo, Formal Invitation (IRE), **20/1** Striking Image (IRE), Dancing Years (USA), Heavenly Waters, **33/1** Ors. CSF £59.40, Tote £4.70: £1.60 £12.10 £22.00 (£240.30). Mr W. I. M. Perry (WHITSBURY) bred by W. I. M. Perry. 14 Rn
2m 26.9 (4.4)
SF—37/18/13/19/17/14

**1447**
PAVILION GRADUATION STKS (3-Y.O.C & G) £1861.00 (£516.00: £247.00)
1¹/₄m 7y
9-00 (9-03)

**Welsh Mill (IRE)** *(LordHuntingdon)* 8-11 MRoberts (1) (h.d.w: 4th st: led over
1f out: r.o wl) ......................................................... —1
1210² Big Easy (IRE) **(92)** (Jt-Fav) *(MrsJCecil)* 8-11 PaulEddery (11) (2nd st: led over
4f out tl over 2f out: rallied fnl f: r.o) ...................................... ¹/₂.2
Bilateral (USA) **(100)** *(HRACecil)* 9-7 PatEddery (2) (lw: 3rd st: led over
2f out tl over 1f out) .................................................... 4.3
427 Quadrireme *(MajorWRHern)* 8-11 WCarson (9) (bit bkwd: led tl over 4f out:
eased whn btn over 1f out) .............................................. 2¹/₂.4
Jumaira Shark (CAN) *(JHMGosden)* 8-11 SCauthen (5) (w'like: scope: bkwd:
7th st: nrst fin) ......................................................... ³/₄.5
1245⁶ Mahairy (USA) *(AAScott)* 8-11 BRaymond (4) (8th st: nvr nr to chal) ................. 3¹/₂.6
857 Master of the Rock *(PJMakin)* 8-11 TQuinn (7) (nvr nr ldrs) ............................ ¹/₂.7
1182 Muktaar (USA) *(JRFanshawe)* 8-11 WRSwinburn (3) (6th st: wknd 3f out) .......... 1.8
Debt Swap (USA) *(JHMGosden)* 8-11 RCochrane (10) (wl grwn: b.nr hind:
dwlt: a bhd) ........................................................... 5.9
Hang Ten *(LMCumani)* 8-11 LDettori (6) (gd sort: 5th st: wknd over 3f out) ..... ³/₄.10
Three and a Half *(MissLBower)* 8-11 AClark (8) (str: bkwd: dwlt: a t.o) ........ dist.11

**2/1** Bilateral (USA), Big Easy (IRE), **6/1** Hang Ten(10/1—5/1), **7/1** WELSH MILL (IRE), **10/1** Jumaira Shark (CAN), **12/1** Muktaar (USA), **33/1** Quadrireme, Debt Swap (USA), **50/1** Mahairy (USA), **66/1** Ors. CSF £20.75, Tote £8.70: £1.70 £1.30 £1.40 (£9.80). Lord Weinstock (WEST ILSLEY) bred by Ballymacoll Stud Farm Ltd in Ireland. 11 Rn
2m 7.1 (4.1)
SF—31/30/32/17/15/8

T/Plpt: £21.80 (130.9 Tckts).
Hn

874—**THIRSK (L-H)**
**Tuesday, June 16th [Firm]**
Going Allowance: minus 0.30 sec per fur (F)                    Wind: fresh against

Stalls: high

**1448**    BBC RADIO YORK LATEST NEWS, GREATEST MUSIC (S) STKS (2-Y.O) £2304.40
       (£638.40: £305.20)    **6f**                              2-15 (2-16)

1321³ Plum First (bl) *(NBycroft)* 8-11 SWhitworth (2) (lw: mde all: wandered u.p over
       1f out: drvn out) ..................................................................... —1
882⁶ Annie Rose (bl) *(TDBarron)* 7-13 ‡⁷VHalliday (9) (a chsng ldrs: styd on u.p nr fin) 1¹/₂.2
1007⁴ Workingforpeanuts (IRE) *(CASmith)* 8-6 AProud (1) (mid div: effrt ¹/₂-wy:
       swtchd & r.o wl fnl f) ........................................................... ¹/₂.3
1233⁴ Summers Dream *(BRichmond)* 8-6 KFallon (11) (swtg: hmpd after s: in tch:
       shkn up ¹/₂-wy: styd on) ..................................................... 1¹/₂.4
     Arctic Guest (IRE) *(MJohnston)* 8-6 DMcKeown (4) (lengthy: scope: s.i.s:
       hmpd over 1f out: styd on wl nr fin) .................................... s.h.5
1240 Charlies Reward *(WLBarker)* 8-11 LCharnock (6) (effrt ¹/₂-wy: sn chsng ldrs &
       hrd drvn: nt qckn ins fnl f) ................................................. s.h.6
     Girl At the Gate *(MBell)* 8-6 DHolland (7) (b.hind: leggy: unf: mid div: hdwy
       ¹/₂-wy: rdn & one pce appr fnl f) ........................................... nk.7
1151⁶ Sunshine in Ramsey *(TFairhurst)* 8-3 ‡³JFanning (10) (hmpd after s: n.m.r
       ¹/₂-wy: nvr able to chal) ...................................................... ¹/₂.8
1151³ Fanfan (IRE) (bl) (Fav) *(MHEasterby)* 8-6 KDarley (8) (lw: chsd wnr: rdn whn
       hmpd over 1f out: sn wknd) ................................................ s.h.9
1321 Knavton Lodger (bl) *(MWEasterby)* 8-6 TLucas (13) (drvn along ¹/₂-wy: nvr nr to
       chal) .............................................................................. s.h.10
1127² Oscars Quest *(JBerry)* 8-11 JCarroll (3) (lw: wnt rt after s: chsd ldrs tl wknd over
       1f out) ............................................................................ 1.11
396 Great Mashhor *(JSWainwright)* 8-11 AMackay (12) (a bhd) ................. 7.12
1151 Archipellago Girl *(BBeasley)* 8-1 ‡⁵SMaloney (5) (a outpcd & bhd) ....... 5.13

**11/4** Fanfan (IRE)(2/1—3/1), **6/1** Oscars Quest, **7/1** PLUM FIRST, Workingforpeanuts (IRE)(op 12/1), **9/1** Annie
Rose, **10/1** Girl At the Gate(op 9/2), **11/1** Arctic Guest (IRE), Sunshine in Ramsey(op 7/1), **12/1** Knavton Lodger,
Summers Dream, **25/1** Ors. CSF £66.87, Tote £7.90: £1.90 £2.60 £2.60 (£28.10). Mrs Dyanne Benjamin
(BRANDSBY) bred by Limestone Stud. 13 Rn; No bid                         1m 14.8 (4.6)

**1449**    BBC RADIO YORK H'CAP (0-80) £2703.00 (£748.00: £357.00)    **1m**    2-50 (2-59)

1108 **Persuasius (IRE) (50)** (bl) *(BBeasley)* 4–8-4 JCarroll (3) (mde all: styd on u.p
       fnl 2f) ............................................................................. —1
1175 Waseela (IRE) (63) (Jt-Fav) *(AAScott)* 3–8-7 JFortune (4) (chsd ldrs: hdwy over
       2f out: nt qckn ins fnl f) ..................................................... 2.2
1193 Gant Bleu (FR) (44) *(RMWhitaker)* 5–7-12 DaleGibson (6) (stdd s: hld up: hdwy
       ent st: edgd lft fnl 2f: nvr able to chal) ................................ 2¹/₂.3
1248⁵ Flying Down to Rio (IRE) (53) (Jt-Fav) *(MPNaughton)* 4–8-2 ‡⁵DHarrison (1) (lw:
       outpcd & bhd: hdwy over 1f out: r.o) .................................... 1¹/₂.4
1294² Tahitian (49) *(MrsJRRamsden)* 3–7-7 SWood (8) (lw: outpcd & bhd tl styd on
       fnl 3f) ............................................................................ hd.5
1329³ Mofador (GER) (53) *(FHLee)* 8–8-7 RLappin (2) (lw: trckd ldr: effrt & ch over 2f
       out: wknd over 1f out) ........................................................ 1¹/₂.6
1114 My Nominee (62) *(SEKettlewell)* 4–9-2 SWebster (7) (in tch to st) ......... 4.7
1154³ Mca Below the Line (64) *(BBeasley)* 4–9-4 LCharnock (5) (effrt ent st: sn rdn &
       n.d) ................................................................................ 2¹/₂.8
542 Victoria Road (IRE) (74) *(MHEasterby)* 4–9-9 ‡⁵SMaloney (9) (lw: hld up: lost tch
       appr st) ........................................................................... 10.9

LONG HANDICAP: Tahitian 7-6.

**9/2** Waseela (IRE), Flying Down to Rio (IRE), **5/1** Tahitian, **6/1** Mofador (GER), Mca Below the Line, **9/1** Victoria
Road (IRE), **10/1** Gant Bleu (FR), **12/1** PERSUASIUS (IRE), **20/1** My Nominee. CSF £58.73, CT £627.20. Tote
£22.00: £3.60 £2.00 £2.10 (£152.80). Mr J. Silfverling (HAMBLETON) bred by W. Polly in Ireland. 9 Rn
                                                                          1m 37.4 (1.4)
                                                              SF—33/30/13/12/2/11

**1450**    ALIVE DAIRY PRODUCTS MEDIAN AUCTION STKS (Mdn 2-Y.O) £2265.20 (£627.20:
       £299.60)    **5f**                                            3-25 (3-27)

1251⁶ **Bold Seven (IRE)** *(FHLee)* 8-5 RLappin (7) (chsd ldrs: styd on u.p to ld cl
       home) ............................................................................. —1

1092⁶ Arkendale Diamond (USA) *(BBeasley)* 8-7  LCharnock (4) (lw: cl up: led over 2f out: hrd drvn fnl f: nt qckn nr fin) ................................... nk.2

924 Hawaymyson (IRE) *(JHJohnson)* 8-10  KFallon (8) (w ldrs: hdwy u.p 2f out: nt clr run 1f out: swtchd & r.o) ................................... 1¹/₂.3

807² Two Times Twelve (IRE) (Fav) *(JBerry)* 8-10  JCarroll (3) (w ldrs: chal over 2f out: rdn & btn 1f out) ................................... ³/₄.4

751⁴ Riston Lady (IRE) *(BSRothwell)* 8-2  JFortune (6) (lw: trckd ldrs: effrt 2f out: nvr able to chal) ................................... ¹/₂.5

568⁴ Pride's Desire *(TDBarron)* 8-2  AlexGreaves (2) (trckd ldrs: effrt & hung lft over 1f out: sn btn) ................................... 2¹/₂.6

1191⁶ Cizard (IRE) *(AWPotts)* 8-2  AProud (1) (led over 3f: sn wknd) ................................... 3¹/₂.7

1291⁶ Volunteer Point (IRE) *(MrsSABramall)* 8-7  SWood (5) (lw: a outpcd & bhd) ................................... 3.8

**6/4** Two Times Twelve (IRE), **3/1** BOLD SEVEN (IRE), **11/2** Pride's Desire, **7/1** Riston Lady (IRE), Arkendale Diamond (USA), **25/1** Hawaymyson (IRE), **33/1** Ors. CSF £22.06, Tote £3.20: £1.30 £1.70 £3.60 (£13.30). Mr F. H. Lee (WILMSLOW) bred by Airlie Stud in Ireland. 8 Rn
59.6 sec (1.9)
SF—23/24/21/18/8/–

---

**1451**   'FIRST FOR SPORT'-BBC RADIO YORK H'CAP (0-80) £2726.80 (£754.80: £360.40)
6f
4-00 (4-00)

(Weights raised 7 lb)

668 **Sully's Choice (USA)** (48) (bl) *(DWChapman)* 11-8-5  SWood (2) (mde all: hld on wl fnl f) ................................... —1

992 Pretonic (63) (Fav) *(MJohnston)* 8-10  DMcKeown (4) (lw: hld up: nt clr run & swtchd 1f out: rdn & hung lft: edgd rt & nt qckn nr fin) ................................... 1.2

1263⁴ Waverley Star (46) (bl) *(SGNorton)* 7-8-3  LCharnock (6) (lw: chsd wnr: hrd drvn 2f out tl wknd nr fin) ................................... s.h.3

1167 Hawa Layaam (IRE) (73) (v) *(AAScott)* 3-9-8  JFortune (5) (chsd ldrs: rdn 2f out: r.o one pce) ................................... 2.4

1266 Verdant Boy (56) *(MPNaughton)* 9-8-8 ‡5DHarrison (1) (lw: prom tl wknd over 1f out) ................................... 6.5

Make Or Mar (67) *(BEllison)* 8-9-10  KDarley (3) (spd over 3f: sn rdn & wknd) ................................... 5.6

**5/2** Pretonic, **11/4** Hawa Layaam (IRE), **7/2** Waverley Star, **9/2** SULLY'S CHOICE (USA), **8/1** Verdant Boy, **20/1** Make or Mar. CSF £15.06, Tote £5.00: £2.20 £1.70 (£6.50). Mr Walter Nelson (YORK) bred by E. W. & J. K. Thomas & Partners in USA. 6 Rn
1m 12.4 (2.2)
SF—11/22/4/15/–/–

---

**1452**   BBC RADIO YORK FM STEREO INFORMATION H'CAP (0-90) £2703.00 (£748.00: £357.00)   1¹/₂m
4-35 (4-35)

(Weights raised 18 lb)

921² **Persian Fantasy** (73) (Fav) *(JLDunlop)* 3-9-10  GDuffield (2) (lw: sn pushed along: hdwy u.p ent st: styd on to ld ins fnl f) ................................... —1

1184⁴ First Bid (44) *(RMWhitaker)* 5-8-10  ACulhane (1) (outpcd ¹/₂-wy: hdwy appr st: disp ld over 2f out tl ins fnl f: no ex) ................................... 1¹/₂.2

1195⁵ Sinclair Lad (IRE) (53) *(RHollinshead)* 4-9-5  DHolland (4) (bhd: hdwy 4f out: disp ld over 2f out: wknd & eased ins fnl f) ................................... 6.3

1437⁶ Luks Akura (43) (v) *(MJohnston)* 4-8-9 (6x)  DMcKeown (5) (led tl hdd over 2f out: sn btn) ................................... 3¹/₄.4

1190 Quip (31) *(MPNaughton)* 7-7-6⁽²⁾ ‡5DHarrison (3) (lw: chsd ldr: jnd ldr 7f out tl btn ent st) ................................... 2¹/₂.5

1248 Mahaasin (37) *(LJCodd)* 4-7-10 ‡7DarrenMoffatt (6) (chsd ldrs tl wknd & stumbled bdly ent st: wl bhd after) ................................... 25.6

**2/1** PERSIAN FANTASY, **3/1** Luks Akura, **4/1** Sinclair Lad (IRE), **6/1** First Bid, **8/1** Quip, **12/1** Mahaasin. CSF £12.75, Tote £2.30: £1.60 £2.20 (£4.00). Windflower Overseas Holdings Inc (ARUNDEL) bred by Windflower Overseas. 6 Rn
2m 32.4 (2.4)
SF—50/33/30/13/–/–

---

**1453**   'I LISTEN TO YOUR HEART'-BBC RADIO YORK GRADUATION STKS   £3066.80 (£741.20)   1¹/₂m
5-10 (5-10)

**Duke of Paducah (USA)** (108) (Fav) *(GHarwood)* 5-9-12  GDuffield (2) (lw: trckd ldr: led appr st: sn clr: canter) ................................... —1

1157 Fiction (60) *(MPNaughton)* 3-7-12 ‡5DHarrison (1) (led: hung rt & hdd appr st: sn wl btn) ................................... 30.2

**1/33** DUKE OF PADUCAH (USA), **25/1** Fiction. Tote £1.10. Mr J. Garcia-Roady (PULBOROUGH) bred by Hill 'n Dale Farm in USA. 2 Rn
2m 40.2 (10.2)

T/Plpt: £243.90 (9.1 Tckts).
AA

# ROYAL ASCOT (R-H)
## Tuesday, June 16th [Good to firm]
Going Allowance: minus 0.20 sec per fur (F)　　　　　　　　Wind: mod half bhd

Stalls: centre

**1454**　　QUEEN ANNE STKS (Gp 2)　£54972.00 (£20517.60: £9808.80: £4221.60)
　　　　　**1m (st)**　　　　　　　　　　　　　　　　　　　　　2-30 (2-31)

849² **Lahib (USA)** (Fav) *(JLDunlop)* 4-9-2 WCarson (5) (lw: a.p: rdn over 2f out: led
　　　nr fin) ...................................................................................... —1

　　Second Set (IRE) *(LMCumani)* 4-9-8 LDettori (1) (bit bkwd: a.p: n.m.r over 2f
　　　out: led ins fnl f: hrd rdn: hdd nr fin) ........................................ hd.2

1359a³ Sikeston (USA) *(CEBrittain)* 6-9-8 MRoberts (7) (lw: w ldr: led over 3f out tl ins
　　　fnl f: r.o) ................................................................................. ½.3

1231a³ Exit To Nowhere (USA) *(FBoutin,France)* 4-9-2 FHead (3) (lw: hld up: hmpd on
　　　ins over 1f out: str run ins fnl f: r.o wl) ...................................... s.h.4

1351a★ Approach The Bench (IRE) *(JEMulhern,Ireland)* 4-9-2 JReid (8) (lw: hdwy 2f
　　　out: hrd rdn over 1f out: unable qckn) ......................................... 3.5

849³ Rudimentary (USA) *(HRACecil)* 4-9-5 PatEddery (2) (a.p: nt clr run over 2f out:
　　　hmpd over 1f out: nt rcvr) ......................................................... 1½.6

378a³ Goofalik (USA) *(JEHammond,France)* 5-9-5 SCauthen (6) (hdwy 2f out: wknd
　　　1f out) ...................................................................................... 2½.7

954a³ Star of Gdansk (USA) (bl) *(JSBolger,Ireland)* 4-9-2 CRoche (9) (a.p: hrd rdn &
　　　edgd lft over 1f out: sn wknd) .................................................... s.h.8

1058³ Lovealoch (IRE) *(MBell)* 4-8-13 MHills (4) (lw: led over 4f: wknd over 2f out: bhd
　　　whn hmpd over 1f out) ................................................................ 10.9

**100/30** LAHIB (USA), **4/1** Second Set (IRE), **5/1** Exit to Nowhere (USA), **11/2** Rudimentary (USA), **15/2** Goofalik
(USA), **11/1** Star of Gdansk (USA), **20/1** Sikeston (USA), Approach the Bench (IRE), **25/1** Lovealoch (IRE). CSF
£14.90, Tote £3.80: £1.50 £1.50 £4.20 (£5.50). Mr Hamdan Al-Maktoum (ARUNDEL) bred by Hamdan Bin
Rashid Al Maktoum in USA. 9 Rn　　　　　　　　　　　　　　　　　1m 38.64 (U.76)
　　　　　　　　　　　　　　　　　　　　　　　　　　SF—90/95/93/86/77/75

**1455**　　PRINCE OF WALES'S STKS (Gp 2)　£58536.00 (£21883.80: £10491.90: £4548.30)
　　　　　**1¼m**　　　　　　　　　　　　　　　　　　　　　　3-05 (3-06)

557⁴ **Perpendicular** *(HRACecil)* 4-9-3 WRyan (10) (lw: hdwy over 2f out: hrd rdn fnl
　　　f: r.o: fin 2nd, 1½l: awrdd r) ...................................................... —1

1066³ Young Buster (IRE) (bl) *(GWragg)* 4-9-3 WRSwinburn (11) (3rd st: led wl over 1f
　　　out: hdd & hmpd ins fnl f: nt rcvr: fin 3rd, hd: plcd 2nd) .............. 2

1351a⁵ Kooyonga (IRE) *(MKauntze,Ireland)* 4-9-4 WJO'Connor (6) (lw: hdwy 2f out: sn
　　　rdn: led & edgd rt fnl f: r.o wl: fin 1st: disq: plcd 3rd) ................. 3

1205³ Terimon *(CEBrittain)* 6-9-7 MRoberts (5) (hdwy over 3f out: 5th st: rdn over 1f
　　　out: r.o) ................................................................................... 1½.4

1230a² Lucky Lindy (IRE) *(RHannon)* 3-8-5 MJKinane (8) (4th st: one pce fnl 2f) ...... 1½.5

1066★ Opera House (Fav) *(MRStoute)* 4-9-5 SCauthen (1) (rdn over 2f out: nvr nr to
　　　chal) ........................................................................................ 1½.6

849 Desert Sun *(HRACecil)* 4-9-3 PatEddery (4) (lw: nvr nrr) .......................... nk.7

1198 Thourios *(GHarwood)* 3-8-5 AClark (9) (led over 8f) ............................... 2.8

557 Gussy Marlowe *(CEBrittain)* 4-9-0 LDettori (3) (2nd st: wknd wl over 1f out) ... 2½.9

1232a⁴ Karinga Bay *(GLewis)* 5-9-3 BRouse (2) (bhd fnl 3f) ............................... hd.10

1231a⁵ Tel Quel (FR) *(AFabre,France)* 4-9-7 WCarson (7) (lw: 6th st: wknd over 2f out) s.h.11

*Stewards Enquiry: Kooyonga (IRE) disq. (interference to Young Buster (IRE) ins fnl f). O'Connor suspended
25-30/6/92 (careless riding & excessive use of whip).*

**5/2** Opera House, **6/1** Terimon, Lucky Lindy (IRE), **7/1** Tel Quel (FR), **9/1** Young Buster (IRE), Kooyonga (IRE),
**10/1** Desert Sun, **20/1** PERPENDICULAR, **25/1** Gussy Marlowe, Thourios, **40/1** Karinga Bay. CSF £162.40, Tote
£23.50: £4.80 £2.70 £2.90 (£119.50). Lord Howard of Walden (NEWMARKET) bred by Lord Howard de
Walden. 11 Rn　　　　　　　　　　　　　　　　　　　　　2m 4.13 (U.17)
　　　　　　　　　　　　　　　　　　　　　　　　　　SF—86/82/81/82/63/74

**1456**　　ST JAMES'S PALACE STKS (Gp 1) (3-Y.O.C & F) £118188.00 (£44010.40: £20955.20:
　　　　　£8926.40)　**1m (rnd)**　　　　　　　　　　　　　3-45 (3-46)

1354a★ **Brief Truce (USA)** (bl) *(DKWeld,Ireland)* 9-0 MJKinane (2) (gd sort: lw: 5th st:
　　　hrd rdn over 1f out: led last stride) ............................................ —1

1197★ Zaahi (USA) *(HThomsonJones)* 9-0 RHills (4) (lw: led: hrd rdn over 1f out: hdd
　　　last stride) .............................................................................. s.h.2

953a² Ezzoud (IRE) (v) *(MRStoute)* 9-0 PatEddery (5) (lw: 3rd st: rdn over 2f out:
　　　unable qckn) ............................................................................ 1½.3

1198 Rodrigo de Triano (USA) *(PWChapple-Hyam)* 9-0 LPiggott (7) (plld out 2f out: hdwy over 1f out: r.o) .................................................................................... s.h.4
741a Arazi (USA) *(Fav)* *(FBoutin,France)* 9-0 SCauthen (1) (w'like: 6th st: rdn over 2f out: nvr nr to chal) .................................................. ¾.5
991³ Casteddu *(JWPayne)* 9-0 AMunro (6) (lw: 4th st: one pce fnl 2f) ................. 3.6
655 River Falls *(RHannon)* 9-0 BRaymond (8) (lw: plld hrd: bhd fnl 2f) ............. 4.7
1229a Beldi (USA) *(CEBrittain)* 9-0 MRoberts (3) (2nd st: wknd over 2f out) ........... 8.8

**10/11** Arazi (USA), **4/1** Rodrigo de Triano (USA), **6/1** Ezzoud (IRE), **8/1** Zaahi (USA), **20/1** Casteddu, **25/1** BRIEF TRUCE (USA), **40/1** River Falls, **100/1** Beldi (USA). CSF £174.49, Tote £19.80: £3.00 £1.80 £1.10 (£66.50). Moyglare Stud Farms Ltd (IRELAND) bred by Moyglare Stud Farm Ltd in USA. 8 Rn     1m 39.32 (U.28)
SF—80/79/74/73/71/62

**1457**   COVENTRY STKS (Gp 3) (2-Y.O) £25731.00 (£9586.05: £4568.03: £1949.92)
6f                                                            4-20 (4-21)

1023* **Petardia** (Jt-Fav) *(GWragg)* 8-13 WRSwinburn (1) (lw: hld up: led over 1f out: all out) .................................................................. —1
1161* So Factual (USA) *(GHarwood)* 8-13 PatEddery (4) (lw: hdwy over 1f out: ev ch ins fnl f: r.o wl) ................................................................ s.h.2
611* Pips Pride *(RHannon)* 8-13 WCarson (2) (a.p: hrd rdn over 1f out: unable qckn) 2.3
828* Ardkinglass *(HRACecil)* 8-13 JReid (12) (a.p: led 2f out tl over 1f out: one pce) .................................................... nk.4
1017* Geisway (CAN) *(RHannon)* 8-13 MJKinane (6) (a.p: hrd rdn over 1f out: one pce) .................................................................. ½.5
933² Canaska Star *(PAKelleway)* 8-13 PRobinson (11) (lw: led 4f) ................... 7.6
952a Tahdeed (USA) (Jt-Fav) *(JSBolger,Ireland)* 8-13 CRoche (5) (w'like: leggy: lw: prom 3f) ...................................................... 1½.7
1161³ Friendly Brave (USA) *(WCarter)* 8-13 TQuinn (10) (spd 4f) .................. 4.8
1039⁴ Walnut Burl (IRE) *(LJHolt)* 8-13 AMcGlone (9) (a bhd) ................... 3½.9
988* New Capricorn (USA) *(MAJarvis)* 8-13 BRaymond (8) (lw: spd over 3f) ......... nk.10
1171³ Persian Revival (FR) *(BAMcMahon)* 8-13 LDettori (7) (outpcd) ......... ½.11
1249² Shebl (USA) *(MRStoute)* 8-13 SCauthen (3) (a bhd) ................... 2.12

**5/1** PETARDIA, Tahdeed (USA), Ardkinglass, **11/2** So Factual (USA), **7/1** Shebl (USA), **8/1** Geisway (CAN)(op 7/1), **40/1** Friendly Brave (USA), Canaska Star, **66/1** New Capricorn (USA), **100/1** Walnut Burl (IRE). CSF £28.71, Tote £5.60: £1.70 £2.20 £1.50 (£14.10). Mollers Racing (NEWMARKET) bred by Highfield Stud Ltd and The Glen Andred Stud. 12 Rn     1m 13.95 (0.35)
SF—68/67/59/58/56/28

**1458**   KING EDWARD VII STKS (Gp 2) (3-Y.O.C & G) £67473.00 (£25309.65: £12204.83: £5367.52)  1½m                                        4-55 (4-55)

711⁴ **Beyton (USA)** *(RHannon)* 8-8 MJKinane (6) (4th st: led wl over 1f out: r.o wl) ... —1
927* Jeune *(GWragg)* 8-8 WRSwinburn (11) (lw: 5th st: nt clr run on ins over 1f out: r.o wl ins fnl f) ......................................................... 2.2
1198⁶ Alflora (IRE) *(CEBrittain)* 8-8 TQuinn (9) (lw: 3rd st: hrd rdn over 1f out: r.o) ¾.3
1168* Sonus (IRE) *(JHMGosden)* 8-8 RCochrane (3) (lw: hdwy over 1f out: r.o) ......... 3.4
1080* Alphard *(HRACecil)* 8-8 MRoberts (2) (lw: hdwy over 1f out: r.o) .......... ¾.5
781³ Bonny Scot (IRE) *(LMCumani)* 8-8 LDettori (5) (lw: led over 2f: 2nd st: wknd over 1f out) ..................................................... 2.6
741a Thyer (USA) (bl) *(JSBolger,Ireland)* 8-8 CRoche (8) (rdn & hdwy over 2f out: wknd 1f out) .................................................. ½.7
1141* Peto *(Fav)* *(HRACecil)* 8-8 SCauthen (1) (led over 9f out tl wl over 1f out: sn wknd) .......................................................... ½.8
Colorific *(BWHills)* 8-8 PatEddery (7) (bit bkwd: a bhd) ................... 2.9
732* Sun Seeker (IRE) *(MRStoute)* 8-8 JReid (10) (lw: 6th st: wknd 2f out) .......... s.h.10
1015³ Surf *(MrsJCecil)* 8-8 PaulEddery (2) (a bhd) .......................... 12.11
655 Badie (USA) *(JLDunlop)* 8-8 WCarson (4) (bhd fnl 4f) ................. 2½.12

**7/4** Peto, **9/2** Jeune, **7/1** Sonus (IRE), **12/1** Sun Seeker (IRE), Alphard, Badie (USA), BEYTON (USA), **14/1** Bonny Scot (IRE), **16/1** Alflora (IRE), **20/1** Colorific, Thyer (USA), **33/1** Surf. CSF £62.45, Tote £32.40: £5.90 £1.60 £3.70 (£36.90). Mr D. F. Cock (MARLBOROUGH) bred by Side Hill Stud & Floors Farming in USA. 12 Rn     2m 29.41 (U.09)
SF—71/67/65/59/57/53

**1459**   ASCOT STKS (H'cap) (0-115) £18227.00 (£5456.00: £2618.00: £1199.00)
2½m                                                            5-30 (5-31)
(Weights raised 10 lb)

990⁴ **Gondolier (86)** *(Fav)* *(HRACecil)* 4-9-9 PatEddery (3) (lw: led after 2f: rdn out) . —1
937⁵ Requested **(70)** *(RAkehurst)* 5-8-9 AMunro (15) (hdwy 4f out: 3rd st: rdn over 2f out: unable qckn) ...................................... 2½.2
1022⁶ Crystal Spirit **(83)** *(IABalding)* 5–9-8 JReid (17) (lw: led 2f: 2nd st: hrd rdn over 1f out: one pce) ........................................ 2.3

| | | |
|---|---|---|
| 1022² | Good Hand (USA) **(85)** *(JWWatts)* 6–9-10  NConnorton (21) (hdwy over 2f out: r.o) | hd.4 |
| 362 | Cabochon **(71)** *(DMorley)* 5–8-10  WCarson (7) (gd hdwy 4f out: r.o) | 1½.5 |
| 937⁶ | Tamarpour (USA) **(74)** *(MCPipe)* 5–8-13  MRoberts (9) (b: hdwy fnl 3f: nvr nrr) | 4.6 |
| 1047⁴ | Line Drummer (USA) **(77)** *(PAKelleway)* 4–9-0  PRobinson (20) (b: 5th st: wknd over 2f out) | 8.7 |
| 990 | Brandon Prince (IRE) **(78)** (bl) *(IABalding)* 4–9-1  RCochrane (16) (lw: hdwy 5f out: wknd over 2f out) | 1½.8 |
| 990⁶ | Bardolph (USA) **(81)** *(PFICole)* 5–9-6  TQuinn (4) (b.off hind: rdn 5f out: 6th st: wknd over 2f out) | 2½.9 |
| 1290² | Creeager **(66)** *(JWharton)* 10–8-5  JQuinn (12) (lw: a mid div) | 10.10 |
| 1065² | Mull House **(60)** *(FJO'Mahony)* 5–7-13  RFox (14) (lw: a mid div) | 2.11 |
| | Battle on **(70)** *(JSBolger,Ireland)* 5–8-9  CRoche (5) (bit bkwd: 4th st: wknd over 2f out) | ½.12 |
| | Engelaab (USA) *(MAO'Toole,Ireland)* 4–8-9  MJKinane (19) (lw: a mid div) | nk.13 |
| 1169 | Classic Statement **(54)** *(RLee)* 6–7-0  ‡⁷CHawksley (2) (a mid div) | 6.14 |
| 1301⁵ | Shar Emblem **(59)** *(SDow)* 4–7-7(3) ‡³FNorton (13) (prom over 14f) | ¾.15 |
| 1256 | Coleridge **(68)** *(DShaw)* 4–8-5  GCarter (10) (a bhd) | hd.16 |
| 675★ | Aswamedh **(62)** *(PJHobbs)* 4–7-13  NAdams (14) (a bhd) | 10.17 |
| 1022★ | Aahsaylad **(78)** *(FHLee)* 6–8-12 ‡⁵NKennedy (6) (lw: bhd fnl 4f) | 6.18 |
| 771★ | Row Ree **(66)** *(PJHobbs)* 4–8-3  JWilliams (1) (prom 15f) | 2.19 |
| 718 | Go South **(72)** (bl) *(JRJenkins)* 8–8-11  LDettori (11) (lw: hrd rdn 6f out: a bhd) | nk.20 |
| 1290★ | Patroclus **(55)** *(RVoorspuy)* 7–7-8(1) (3x) SDawson (8) (b: a bhd) | nk.21 |

LONG HANDICAP: Classic Statement 7-3, Shar Emblem 7-3, Patroclus 7-1.

**7/1** GONDOLIER, **9/1** Requested, **10/1** Crystal Spirit, Go South, Tamarpour (USA), **11/1** Bardolph (USA), **12/1** Mull House, Brandon Prince (IRE), Good Hand (USA), **14/1** Line Drummer (USA), Cabochon, Row Ree, Aahsaylad, **20/1** Battle on, Engelaab, Creeager, **25/1** Coleridge, Patroclus, **33/1** Aswamedh, **66/1** Ors. CSF £67.39, CI £595.86. Tote £5.00. £1.00. £2.50. £2.00. £3.70. (£26.30). Lord Howard de Walden (NEWMARKET) bred by Lord Howard de Walden. 21 Rn

4m 20.39 (4.39)

SF—25/18/19/20/4/3

T/Trio: Race 1: £48.60 (55.3 Tckts), Race 2: £1,015.30 (3 Tckts), Race 4: £43.00 (82.2 Tckts), Race 5: £89.10 (44.3 Tckts) and Race 6: £120.30 (52 Tckts). T/Jkpt: Not won; £24,684.00 to Royal Ascot 17/6/92. T/Plpt: £849.30 (52.8 Tckts). AK

## ROYAL ASCOT  (R-H)

### Wednesday, June 17th [Good to firm]

Going Allowance: minus 0.30 sec per fur (F)

Wind: fresh half bhd

Stalls: centre 1st, 2nd & 4th

**1460**  JERSEY STKS (Gp 3) (3-Y.O) £40466.40 (£15095.87: £7210.44: £3096.29)
7f

2-30 (2-33)

| | | |
|---|---|---|
| 982★ | Prince Ferdinand **(117)** *(MMcCormack)* 9-1  JReid (8) (lw: hld up: hdwy over 2f out: led ins fnl f: all out) | —1 |
| 991² | Pursuit of Love **(117)** *(HRACecil)* 9-1  MJKinane (10) (lw: a.p: led over 1f out tl ins fnl f: rallied cl home) | ½.2 |
| | Fair Cop (USA) *(PFICole)* 9-1  AMunro (11) (b.off hind: a.p: ev ch over 1f out: unable qckn) | 1½.3 |
| 840a⁴ | Reported (IRE) *(VictorBowens,Ireland)* 8-10  WJO'Connor (4) (leggy: scope: a.p: led over 2f out tl over 1f out: kpt on) | 1.4 |
| 1058² | Cloud of Dust **(104)** *(JLDunlop)* 8-7  TQuinn (2) (swtg: s.s: hdwy u.p over 2f out: nvr nrr) | 3.5 |
| 1354a³ | Nordic Brief (IRE) (bl) *(JSBolger,Ireland)* 8-10  CRoche (3) (w'like: scope: swtg: led over 4f: wknd over 1f out) | hd.6 |
| 958a⁵ | Euphonic (USA) (Fav) *(AFabre,France)* 8-7  PatEddery (5) (w'like: scope: prom: rdn 2f out: sn btn) | nk.7 |
| 1043★ | Pater Noster (USA) *(MrsJCecil)* 8-10  PaulEddery (7) (nvr nrr) | nk.8 |
| 862⁵ | King Olaf (IRE) **(105)** *(PWChapple-Hyam)* 8-10  LPiggott (3) (hdwy over 3f out: wknd over 2f out) | 5.9 |
| 1197 | Mizaaya **(100)** *(MRStoute)* 8-10  WRSwinburn (9) (lw: nvr nr to chal) | 2.10 |
| 1197² | Misterioso **(102)** *(DRCElsworth)* 8-12  CAsmussen (6) (swtg: outpcd) | 1½.11 |
| 1031★ | Hamas (IRE) **(104)** *(PTWalwyn)* 8-10  WCarson (12) (in tch: effrt 3f out: no rspnse) | 3½.12 |

**100/30** Euphonic (USA), **6/1** PRINCE FERDINAND, Pursuit of Love, **9/1** Hamas (IRE), Fair Cop (USA), **10/1** King Olaf (IRE), **11/1** Pater Noster (USA), Misterioso, **12/1** Cloud of Dust, **16/1** Mizaaya, **25/1** Nordic Brief (IRE), **40/1** Reported (IRE). CSF £38.14, Tote £5.90: £2.30 £1.90 £2.90 (£10.60). Miss J. Winch (WANTAGE) bred by Greensward Racing Ltd. 12 Rn

1m 25.94 (0.26 under best; U.56)

SF—78/76/71/63/51/53

**1461** QUEEN MARY STKS (Gp 3) (2-Y.O.F) £23976.00 (£8913.30: £4231.65: £1789.05)
5f
3-05 (3-08)

1067★ Lyric Fantasy (IRE) (Fav) (RHannon) 8-8 MRoberts (10) (lw: mde all: clr 2f out: impressive) ...... —1
1038★ Mystic Goddess (USA) (MRStoute) 8-8 PatEddery (11) (lw: hdwy 2f out: r.o fnl f: no ch w wnr) ...... 5.2
645★ Toocando (IRE) (CNAllen) 8-8 RCochrane (2) (chsd ldrs: kpt on u.p ins fnl f) . 1½.3
811★ Marina Park (MJohnston) 8-8 DMcKeown (12) (lw: hdwy ½-wy: rdn 2f out: one pce) ...... 2½.4
709★ Lucky Parkes (JBerry) 8-8 JCarroll (4) (chsd ldrs: no hdwy fnl 2f) ...... ½.5
721★ Holly Golightly (RHannon) 8-8 JReid (13) (chsd ldrs: rdn 2f out: one pce) ...... s.h.6
961★ Star Family Friend (IRE) (MHTompkins) 8-8 PRobinson (7) (chsd ldrs: no hdwy fnl 2f) ...... s.h.7
1342³ Toledo Queen (IRE) (PWChapple-Hyam) 8-8 PaulEddery (3) (lw: nvr nrr) ...... 1½.8
709⁴ Moodiesburn (IRE) (ABailey) 8-8 AMackay (9) (spd 3f) ...... 1.9
1067 Carranita (IRE) (BPalling) 8-8 JWilliams (6) (a bhd) ...... 2.10
1300★ Hamsah (IRE) (DRCElsworth) 8-8 SCauthen (5) (prom to ½-wy: sn lost tch) 3½.11
1208² Belle Soiree (SDow) 8-8 TQuinn (9) (a bhd: t.o) ...... 8.12
1164★ Amirati (USA) (AAScott) 8-8 WRSwinburn (8) (lw: outpcd: t.o) ...... 3.13

11/8 LYRIC FANTASY (IRE), 7/1 Hamsah (IRE), 15/2 Mystic Goddess (USA), 8/1 Amirati (USA)(op 5/1), 10/1 Toocando (IRE), 12/1 Lucky Parkes, 14/1 Star Family Friend (IRE), 16/1 Holly Golightly, 20/1 Toledo Queen (IRE), 33/1 Carranita (IRE), Marina Park, 100/1 Ors. CSF £11.80, Tote £2.30: £1.50 £2.10 £2.70 (£7.80). Lord Carnarvon (MARLBOROUGH) bred by Minch Bloodstock in Ireland. 13 Rn
59.72 sec (0.53 under 2y best; U.78)
SF—80/60/54/44/42/41/40

**1462** CORONATION STKS (Gp 1) (3-Y.O.F) £107886.00 (£40153.80: £19101.90: £8118.30)
1m (rnd)
3-45 (3-48)

1097a★ Marling (IRE) (Fav) (GWragg) 9-0 WRSwinburn (7) (hld up: 6th st: qcknd to ld wl over 1f out: rdn out) ...... —1
958a★ Culture Vulture (USA) (PFICole) 9-0 TQuinn (3) (hld up & bhd: 5th st: chsd wnr appr fnl f: unable qckn) ...... ¾.2
1058⁵ Katakana (USA) (MRStoute) 9-0 SCauthen (6) (lw: plld hrd: 3rd st: n.m.r appr fnl f: sn btn) ...... 6.3
845a⁴ Wiedniu (USA) (LordHuntingdon) 9-0 MRoberts (1) (led tl hdd over 1f out) ...... s.h.4
958a⁴ Absurde (FR) (FBoutin,France) 9-0 FHead (4) (swtg: hld up: 4th st: effrt 2f out: sn rdn: wknd over 1f out) ...... s.h.5
1148★ Mahasin (USA) (JLDunlop) 9-0 WCarson (5) (lw: plld hrd: chsd ldr: 2nd st: wkng whn hmpd over 1f out: t.o) ...... 12.6
631 Soiree (IRE) (BWHills) 9-0 DHolland (2) (a in rr: lost tch & 7th st: t.o) ...... 10.7

8/11 MARLING (IRE), 9/2 Culture Vulture (USA), 9/1 Mahasin (USA), Absurde (FR)(op 6/1), 14/1 Wiedniu (USA), 16/1 Katakana (USA), 33/1 Soiree (IRE). CSF £4.30, Tote £1.80: £1.30 £1.70 (£2.00). Mr E. J. Loder (NEWMARKET) bred by E. J. Loder in Ireland. 7 Rn
1m 39.01 (U.59)
SF—73/71/53/52/51/15

**1463** ROYAL HUNT CUP (H'cap) (0-115) £36267.10 (£10916.80: £5283.40: £2466.70)
1m (st)
4-20 (4-29)
(Weights raised 3 lb)

Colour Sergeant (78) (LordHuntingdon) 4-7-8 ‡⁵DHarrison (11) (chsd ldrs: led 2f out: rdn out) ...... —1
824 Gymcrak Premiere (92) (MHEasterby) 4-8-13 GCarter (4) (lw: hdwy 2f out: str chal fnl f: r.o) ...... nk.2
824³ Dorset Duke (86) (bl) (GWragg) 5-8-7 MHills (1) (hld up: hdwy over 2f out: r.o wl ins fnl f) ...... 1.3
610² High Low (USA) (90) (Jt-Fav) (WJHaggas) 4-8-11 PatEddery (3) (led stands' side 6f: rdn & r.o fnl f) ...... 2.4
936³ Cru Exceptionnel (72) (PJMakin) 4-7-7 DaleGibson (8) (a.p: ev ch over 1f out: no ex fnl f) ...... hd.5
1254★ Marine Diver (74) (BRMillman) 6-7-9 (7x) AMackay (29) (racd far side: hdwy 2f out: nvr nrr) ...... 3.6
1061⁴ Field of Honour (83) (LMCumani) 4-8-4 LDettori (10) (hld up: styd on appr fnl f: nvr nrr) ...... hd.7
1201⁵ Parliament Piece (98) (v) (RMWhitaker) 6-9-5 WRSwinburn (18) (lw: chsd ldrs far side: led over 1f out: sn rdn & wknd) ...... hd.8
1254 Knight of Mercy (100) (RHannon) 6-9-7 BRaymond (32) (racd far side: hld up: gd hdwy 2f out: one pce fnl f) ...... nk.9
1201★ Go Executive (94) (CEBrittain) 4-9-1 (7x) GCrealock (2) (swtg: prom stands' side tl wknd appr fnl f) ...... 1½.10
1257★ Pelorus (85) (DRCElsworth) 7-7-13 (5x) ‡⁷JHunter (14) (lw: led far side over 5f) hd.11

824 Mudaffar (IRE) **(89)** *(RWArmstrong)* 4–8–10 LPiggott (21) (lw: m.n.s) ............ nk.12
1351a² Committed Dancer (USA) *(DKWeld,Ireland)* 5–9–10 MJKinane (9) (lw: chsd ldrs
    stands' side over 6f) ............................................... hd.13
1201⁶ Cape Pigeon (USA) **(80)** *(LGCottrell)* 7–8–1 (5x) AMunro (31) (lw: hdwy 2f out:
    wknd appr fnl f) ............................................... ½.14
1303⁶ Absonal **(81)** *(RHannon)* 5–8–2 WCarson (5) (nvr plcd to chal) ...................... nk.15
1061³ Daswaki (CAN) **(84)** *(RHannon)* 4–8–5 BRouse (27) (swtg: prom far side 6f) .... 1.16
824 Heart of Darkness **(98)** (bl) *(IABalding)* 4–9–5 RCochrane (23) (m.n.s) ............ 1.17
712² Arany **(91)** *(MHTompkins)* 5–8–12 PRobinson (26) (m.n.s) ......................... 2½.18
Ballykett Prince (IRE) (bl) *(JSBolger,Ireland)* 4–9–7 CRoche (6) (lw: prom
    stands' side over 5f) ............................................... nk.19
1200³ Double Echo (IRE) **(72)** *(JDBethell)* 4–7–7 TyroneWilliams (28) (prom far side:
    led over 2f out: sn hdd & btn) ............................................... 1½.20
824 Band on the Run **(98)** *(BAMcMahon)* 5–9–5 TQuinn (22) (lw: nvr nr to chal) .... ½.21
976² Eclipsing (IRE) **(78)** *(RCharlton)* 4–7–13 PaulEddery (17) (lw: m.n.s) ............ 1.22
1133 Wild and Loose **(86)** *(DRCElsworth)* 4–8–7 CAsmussen (16) (m.n.s) ............ 1.23
1402³ Pay Homage **(98)** *(IABalding)* 4–9–5 (7x) JReid (12) (s.s: a bhd) ................ 1.24
824 High Premium **(85)** *(MrsJRRamsden)* 4–8–6 KDarley (25) (racd far side: prom tl
    wknd 2f out) ............................................... 1½.25
931⁶ Roseate Lodge **(77)** *(RWArmstrong)* 6–7–12 BCrossley (20) (lw: m.n.s) ...... s.h.26
1303² Superoo **(79)** *(JSutcliffe)* 6–7–9 (5x) ‡5ATucker (15) (m.n.s) ................... nk.27
824 Berlin Wall (IRE) **(79)** *(PWChapple-Hyam)* 4–7–11 ‡3FNorton (7) (prom stands'
    side over 4f) ............................................... 2.28
1153² Tell No Lies **(84)** (Jt-Fav) *(MHEasterby)* 5–8–5 MRoberts (19) (lw: m.n.s) ...... 1.29
976⁴ King of Chance (IRE) **(81)** *(MrsJRRamsden)* 4–8–2 DHolland (13) (m.n.s) ........ 5.30
1380⁴ Thornfield Boy **(80)** *(RJHolder)* 6–8–1 NAdams (24) (m.n.s) ...................... ½.31
    LONG HANDICAP: Double Echo (IRE) 7-6.

11/1 High Low (USA), Tell No Lies, 12/1 High Premium, Cru Exceptionnel, Field of Honour, 14/1 Band on the Run,
Cape Pigeon (USA), 16/1 Eclipsing (IRE), Absonal, 18/1 Mudaffar (IRE), Superoo, 20/1 Wild and Loose, Heart of
Darkness, COLOUR SERGEANT, Daswaki (CAN), 25/1 Parliament Piece, King of Chance (IRE), Pay Homage,
Committed Dancer (USA), 28/1 Go Executive, 33/1 Gymcrak Premiere, Arany, Ballykett Prince (IRE), Berlin Wall
(IRE), Dorset Duke, Knight of Mercy, Marine Diver, Double Echo (IRE), Pelorus, 66/1 Thornfield
Boy. CSF £525.97, CT £17,414.67. Tote £45.50: £9.00 £13.10 £9.70 £1.90 (£390.40). The Queen (WEST
ILSLEY) bred by The Queen. 31 Rn
           1m 38.07 (0.10 under best; U1.33)
            SF—64/82/73/71/52/45/53

**1464**   QUEEN'S VASE (Gp 3) (3-Y.O) £35037.00 (£13014.60: £6169.80: £2598.60)
    **2m 45y**                  4-55 (5-00)

940* **Landowner (IRE) (81)** *(JHMGosden)* 8–11 RCochrane (2) (hld up: gd hdwy
    over 2f out: qcknd to ld wl over 1f out: sn clr) ...................... —1
848* Belgran (USA) **(93)** *(HRACecil)* 8–11 PatEddery (4) (lw: hld up: stdy hdwy 6f
    out: hrd rdn over 2f out: r.o) ............................................... 6.2
1074* Goldsmiths' Hall **(98)** (Fav) *(GWragg)* 8–11 SCauthen (10) (hld up: 6th st: hrd
    rdn over 1f out: kpt on) ............................................... ¾.3
Currency Basket (IRE) *(PO'Leary,Ireland)* 8–11 MJKinane (11) (gd sort: hld up
    & bhd: hdwy over 2f out: hrd rdn: r.o) ............................... nk.4
1260² Teddy's Play (USA) **(72)** *(JWHills)* 8–11 RHills (7) (lw: chsd ldrs: 5th st: one pce
    fnl 2f) ............................................... 4.5
812* Ambiguously Regal (USA) *(MrsJCecil)* 8–11 PaulEddery (5) (led tl hdd & wknd
    wl over 1f out) ............................................... 2½.6
Appealing Bubbles (IRE) (bl) *(JSBolger,Ireland)* 8–11 CRoche (3) (w'like:
    scope: chsd ldr: sn rdn along: 2nd st: wkng whn bmpd
    over 2f out) ............................................... 8.7
1198 Paradise Navy *(CEBrittain)* 8–11 TQuinn (6) (lw: prom: 3rd st: wknd wl over 1f
    out) ............................................... s.h.8
1207³ Idoni *(CEBrittain)* 8–11 MRoberts (1) (lw: chsd ldrs: 4th st: sn wknd: t.o) ........... 6.9
823⁴ Iywaan (IRE) *(PTWalwyn)* 8–11 WCarson (8) (lw: bhd fnl 4f: t.o) .................... 1.10
1026² Eightandahalf (IRE) **(83)** *(PWChapple-Hyam)* 8–11 JReid (9) (dwlt: a bhd: t.o) 15.11

3/1 Goldsmiths' Hall, 100/30 Belgran (USA), 6/1 Iywaan (IRE), Ambiguously Regal (USA), 8/1 LANDOWNER
(IRE), 12/1 Idoni, 16/1 Appealing Bubbles (IRE), 25/1 Currency Basket (IRE), Eightandahalf (IRE), Paradise Navy,
66/1 Teddy's Play (USA). CSF £31.61, Tote £9.70: £2.20 £1.60 £1.40 (£17.10). Sheikh Mohammed
(NEWMARKET) bred by Sheikh Mohammed bin Rashid al Maktoum in Ireland. 11 Rn
           3m 25.29 (0.86 under best; U1.21)
            SF—61/55/54/53/49/46/38

**1465**   BESSBOROUGH H'CAP (0-115) £18656.00 (£5588.00: £2684.00: £1232.00)
    **1½m**                 5-30 (5-35)

1194² **Spinning (98)** *(IABalding)* 5–9–3 RCochrane (8) (hld up: hdwy over 2f out:
    hung rt & led ins fnl f: r.o) ............................................... —1

1211 Regent's Folly (IRE) **(90)** *(WJarvis)* 4–8-9 TQuinn (19) (hld up: gd hdwy 2f out: no ex nr fin) ............................................................. ¾.2
726* Matador (USA) **(95)** *(RCharlton)* 5–9-0 PatEddery (16) (b.off hind: lw: a.p: 3rd st: led over 1f out tl ins fnl f) .................................. ¾.3
1211⁴ Kansk **(90)** (Jt-Fav) *(JHMGosden)* 4–8-9 SCauthen (14) (stdy hdwy ½-wy: 5th st: one pce fnl f) ...................................... 1.4
608³ Shambo **(107)** *(CEBrittain)* 5–9-12 MRoberts (10) (lw: hdwy over 2f out: fin wl) nk.5
815 Kiveton Kabooz **(81)** *(LMCumani)* 4–8-0⁽¹⁾ PRobinson (20) (chsd ldrs: 7th st: one pce fnl 2f) ........................................ s.h.6
1137* Pharly Story **(93)** *(MCPipe)* 4–8-12 LPiggott (4) (lw: prom: led 4f out tl appr fnl f: rdn & no ex fnl f) .......................... ¾.7
1211 Libk **(90)** *(HThomsonJones)* 4–8-9 RHills (12) (lw: a.p: 2nd st: wknd wl over 1f out) ........................................... 7.8
Dreams End **(87)** *(GWragg)* 4–8-6 MHills (3) (hdwy over 5f out: 4th st: wknd 2f out) ............................................ 1½.9
815² Rinja (USA) **(85)** *(DWPArbuthnot)* 5–8-4 JLowe (9) (b.hind: m.n.s) ............ ¾.10
1200* Hashar (IRE) **(94)** (Jt-Fav) *(DRCElsworth)* 4–8-13 CAsmussen (17) (chsd ldrs 8f) ......................................... hd.11
1059⁴ Hateel **(109)** *(PTWalwyn)* 6–10-0 WCarson (1) (nvr nrr) ............... 10.12
1137² Ambassador Royale **(79)** *(PFICole)* 4–7-12 AMunro (13) (nvr nr ldrs) .... hd.13
1211 Kimbers (IRE) **(98)** *(CRNelson)* 4–9-3 JReid (15) (lw: a bhd) ........................ nk.14
240 Gaelic Myth (USA) *(TStack,Ireland)* 5–9-11 SCraine (11) (m.n.s) ............ ½.15
1181* Gulf Sailor (IRE) **(84)** (Jt-Fav) *(MRStoute)* 4–8-3 DHolland (7) (lw: chsd ldrs: 6th st: sn wknd) ........................................ 5.16
1059⁶ Jaffa Line **(104)** *(DRCElsworth)* 4–9-9 WRSwinburn (2) (a bhd) ............ ½.17
1168 Duc de Berry (USA) **(96)** *(GHarwood)* 4–9-1 AClark (6) (lw: s.i.s: a bhd) .... 2½.18
1301⁴ Seal Indigo (IRE) **(87)** *(RHannon)* 4–8-6 MJKinane (5) (lw: chsd ldrs 8f) ......... ¾.19
993⁶ Arabian Bold (IRE) **(82)** *(WJHaggas)* 4–8-1 JQuinn (18) (led 8f: wknd qckly: t.o) 25.20

**8/1** Gulf Sailor (IRE), Kansk, Hashar (IRE), **9/1** Matador (USA)(12/1—8/1), Rinja (USA), **10/1** Libk, **11/1** Dreams End, **12/1** Pharly Story, Hateel, **14/1** Ambassador Royale (IRE), Kiveton Kabooz, **16/1** Shambo, Regent's Folly (IRE), **25/1** Kimbers (IRE), SPINNING, Arabian Bold (IRE), Seal Indigo (IRE), **33/1** Ors. CSF £357.87, CT £3,493.97. Tote £42.80: £7.30 £9.60 £1.70 £3.70 (£725.20). Mr Paul Mellon (KINGSCLERE) bred by Paul Mellon. 20 Rn ........................................ 2m 27.82 (U1.68)
SF—84/74/77/70/86/59/69

T/Trio: Race 1: £37.80 (103.4 Tckts), Race 2: £32.50 (95.7 Tckts), Race 4: £7,818.60 (1.1 Tckts), Race 5: £5.10 (633.3 Tckts) and Race 6: £5,255.00 (1 Tckt). T/Jkpt: Not won; £53,718.90 to Royal Ascot 18/6/92. T/Plpt: £92.40 (498.5 Tckts). IM

# ROYAL ASCOT  (R-H)
## Thursday, June 18th [Good to firm]
Going Allowance: minus 0.25 sec per fur (F)  Wind: mod half bhd

Stalls: centre

**1466**  KING GEORGE V H'CAP (3-Y.O) (0-100) £18227.00 (£5456.00: £2618.00: £1199.00) 1½m
2-30 (2-35)

1141² Source of Light **(87)** *(RCharlton)* 8-10 PatEddery (17) (hld up: gd hdwy to ld 1f out: edgd rt: r.o) .......................... —1
1175* Wild Fire **(80)** (Jt-Fav) *(GWragg)* 8-3 MRoberts (1) (hdwy 7f out: 2nd st: led over 2f out to 1f out: one pce) ............... 2½.2
1225a* Inner City (IRE) **(98)** *(LMCumani)* 9-7 LDettori (11) (lw: hld up: gd hdwy over 2f out: rdn & hld whn hmpd ins fnl f) ......... ¾.3
1025³ Bayaireg (USA) **(85)** *(AAScott)* 8-8 WRSwinburn (13) (hld up: hdwy 5f out: 5th st: one pce fnl 2f) ......................... 2.4
1068² Kinglow (USA) **(85)** *(MrsJCecil)* 8-8 PaulEddery (9) (lost pl after 4f: styd on again fnl 2f) ......................... 2.5
1165⁵ Trumpet **(74)** *(LordHuntingdon)* 7-11 AMunro (3) (mid div: rdn 3f out: kpt on ins fnl f) ............................... ½.6
1245⁵ Turgenev (IRE) **(89)** *(JHMGosden)* 8-12 SCauthen (7) (s.i.s: bhd: styd on fnl 2f: nvr nrr) .......................... s.h.7
1152⁵ Glide Path (USA) **(83)** (Jt-Fav) *(JWHills)* 8-6 MHills (12) (lw: prom: 4th st: rdn & wknd wl over 1f out) ................ 1½.8
1068³ Flight Lieutenant (USA) **(89)** *(PMitchell)* 8-12 LPiggott (18) (lw: chsd ldrs: 6th st: sn rdn & btn) ...................... ¾.9
1394³ Eden's Close **(77)** (v) *(MHTompkins)* 8-0⁽¹⁾ PRobinson (16) (lw: a mid div) .. s.h.10
788² Folia **(87)** *(HRACecil)* 8-10 MJKinane (20) (lw: a in rr) ................. ¾.11
816 Bold Stroke **(91)** *(JLDunlop)* 9-0 WCarson (10) (led to 2f: wknd qckly) ............ 3.12
1220² Major's Law (IRE) **(80)** *(CEBrittain)* 8-3 GDuffield (14) (a bhd) ................. ¾.13

1011² Simply-H (IRE) **(82)** *(MBell)* 8-5 JReid (8) (lw: prom: 3rd st: wknd 2f out: t.o) . 10.14
1346³ Jupiter Moon **(73)** *(CEBrittain)* 7-10 JQuinn (15) (lw: prom over 9f: sn wknd: t.o) 7.15
1082* Simonov **(82)** *(GHarwood)* 8-5 AClark (2) (chsd ldr over 8f: sn wknd: t.o) ..... s.h.16
1280* Sayh **(90)** *(MAJarvis)* 8-13 BRaymond (5) (t.o) ................................................ 1¹/₂.17
1156* Best Gun **(75)** *(CWCElsey)* 7-12 NCarlisle (6) (a bhd: t.o) ............................ hd.18
1346² Sadler's Way **(75)** *(GLewis)* 7-7 ‡5DHarrison (19) (a bhd: t.o) ........................ 25.19

**8/1** Glide Path (USA), Wild Fire, **10/1** Turgenev (IRE), **11/1** Bayaireg (USA), **11/1** SOURCE OF LIGHT, Inner City (IRE), **14/1** Folia, Sayh, Simonov, Sadler's Way, Trumpet, **16/1** Simply-H (IRE), Eden's Close, Kinglow (USA), **20/1** Bold Stroke, **33/1** Ors. CSF £92.67, CT £1,059.79. Tote £12.00: £2.70 £2.10 £2.50 £2.80 (£48.50). Mr K. Abdulla (BECKHAMPTON) bred by Juddmonte Farms. 19 Rn     2m 29.56 (0.06)
SF—65/53/69/52/48/36

---

**1467**     CORK AND ORRERY STKS (Gp 3)    £40265.40 (£15018.82: £7171.91: £3077.87)
      6f                                                3-05 (3-18)

827* Shalford (IRE) **(120)** (Fav) *(RHannon)* 4-9-4 MRoberts (16) (lw: mde virtually
           all centre: clr wl over 1f out) ........................................ —1
827³ Amigo Menor **(108)** (bl) *(DJGMurray-Smith)* 6-9-0 CRutter (18) (lw: hld up:
           prom: hrd rdn over 1f out: no imp) ............................... 5.2
991⁵ Spanish Storm (IRE) **(100)** *(SPCWoods)* 3-8-2 WWoods (9) (disp ld stands'
           side: r.o wl fnl f) ................................................... 1.3
1134³ Fylde Flyer **(109)** *(JBerry)* 3-8-2 JCarroll (3) (lw: led stands' side: rdn fnl f: one
           pce) ................................................................... s.h.4
827⁶ Montendre **(104)** *(MMcCormack)* 5-8-10 JReid (1) (hdwy 2f out: nvr nr to chal) ¹/₂.5
1097a Bezelle *(CCollins,Ireland)* 3-8-2 PShanahan (6) (nvr nrr) ............................ 3.6
1134² Central City **(108)** *(RHannon)* 3-7-13 WCarson (14) (chsd ldrs: effrt u.p wl over
           1f out: sn btn) ...................................................... nk.7
1060³ Medaille D'Or **(107)** (v) *(JWPayne)* 4-8-10 AMunro (12) (lw: prom: rdn 2f out:
           sn outpcd) .......................................................... 1¹/₂.8
1096a* Street Rebel (CAN) *(NMeade,Ireland)* 4-9-0 RHughes (5) (nvr gng pce of ldrs) hd.9
879³ Sir Harry Hardman **(100)** (v) *(FHLee)* 4-8-10 PaulEddery (10) (spd over 3f) .. 1¹/₂.10
1136³ Beware of Agents **(95)** *(MJohnston)* 3-8-2 DMcKeown (15) (racd far side: a
           outpcd) ............................................................... nk.11
982³ Wilde Rufo **(105)** (v) *(PAKelleway)* 3-8-2 PRobinson (7) (lw: sn pushed along: a
           outpcd) ............................................................... ³/₄.12
Festive Cheer (IRE) *(TStack,Ireland)* 3-8-2 MHills (8) (lw: outpcd) .................. 1.13
982⁵ Colway Bold **(104)** *(JWWatts)* 3-8-2 GDuffield (11) (bhd fnl 2f) ................. 1¹/₂.14
1350a² Maledetto (IRE) *(JSBolger,Ireland)* 3-8-2 DHolland (17) (str: effrt over 2f out:
           no imp) ............................................................... 2¹/₂.15
1253 Sizzling Saga (IRE) **(108)** *(JBerry)* 4-8-10 LPiggott (4) (spd to ¹/₂-wy: sn wknd:
           t.o) ................................................................... 6.16
1253⁵ Appledorn **(85)** *(BAMcMahon)* 5-8-7 LDettori (13) (outpcd: t.o) ................. 17

**3/1** SHALFORD (IRE), **100/30** Central City, **12/1** Maledetto (IRE), Fylde Flyer, Bezelle, Street Rebel (CAN), **14/1** Amigo Menor, Medaille D'Or, **16/1** Festive Cheer (IRE), **20/1** Montendre, **25/1** Sizzling Saga (IRE), Colway Bold, Wilde Rufo, **33/1** Beware of Agents, Sir Harry Hardman, **50/1** Spanish Storm (IRE), **100/1** Appledorn. CSF £41.22, Tote £4.30: £2.00 £4.80 £12.30 (£23.60). Mr D. F. Cock (MARLBOROUGH) bred by D. M. Dick in Ireland. 17 Rn     1m 12.53 (0.13 under best; U1.07)
SF—96/72/56/55/61/46

---

**1468**     GOLD CUP (Gp 1)    £108549.00 (£40315.45: £19107.73: £8042.82)
      2¹/₂m                                            3-45 (3-52)

1059* Drum Taps (USA) (Fav) *(LordHuntingdon)* 6-9-2 LDettori (3) (lw: chsd ldrs:
           3rd st: led wl over 1f out: hrd rdn: r.o wl) ............................ —1
1059² Arcadian Heights *(GWragg)* 4-9-0 WRSwinburn (2) (lw: hld up: 4th st: hrd rdn
           over 1f out: r.o) ..................................................... 2.2
1099a⁴ Turgeon (USA) *(JEPease,France)* 4-9-2 SCauthen (1) (lw: hld up: 5th st: rdn
           over 2f out: styd on) ................................................ 3.3
855* Endoli (USA) *(CEBrittain)* 5-9-2 MRoberts (6) (chsd ldrs: 2nd st: led 2f out: sn
           hdd & btn) ........................................................... 1.4
1099a³ Mardonius (bl) *(AFabre,France)* 6-9-2 PatEddery (4) (lw: hld up: 6th st: rdn 2f
           out: no imp) .......................................................... 8.5
1059³ Tyrone Bridge (bl) *(MCPipe)* 6-9-2 PShanahan (5) (led: sn clr: wknd & hdd 2f
           out) ................................................................... 2¹/₂.6

**7/4** DRUM TAPS (USA), **4/1** Endoli (USA), **5/1** Turgeon (USA), **11/2** Arcadian Heights, **9/1** Mardonius, **10/1** Tyrone Bridge. CSF £10.18, Tote £2.60: £1.60 £1.70 (£4.10). Mr Yoshio Asakawa (WEST ILSLEY) bred by William Powell and Bates Newton in USA. 6 Rn     4m 18.29 (2.29)
SF—29/25/24/23/15/12

**1469**　　NORFOLK STKS (Gp 3) (2-Y.O) £22707.00 (£8426.85: £3988.43: £1672.72)
　　　　　**5f**　　　　　　　　　　　　　　　　　　　　　　4-20 (4-25)

859* Niche (RHannon) 8-8 LPiggott (5) (lw: w ldrs: led over 1f out: rdn out) .............. —1
971* Silver Wizard (USA) (Fav) (GLewis) 8-13 PaulEddery (4) (prom: rdn ½-wy: r.o
　　　　　wl ins fnl f) ......................................................................................... hd.2
907* Darbonne (USA) (GHarwood) 8-13 SCauthen (3) (swrvd s: sn outpcd: rdn &
　　　　　hdwy over 1f out: fin wl) .......................................................... 1½.3
943* Elle Shaped (IRE) (RHannon) 8-13 MRoberts (9) (led tl over 1f out: one pce) .... 1.4
1017² Kamaatera (IRE) (AAScott) 8-13 WRSwinburn (1) (lw: r.o ins fnl f: nvr nrr) ...... hd.5
1135* Kahellan (FR) (LMCumani) 8-13 LDettori (7) (lw: chsd ldrs: rdn 2f out: nvr able
　　　　　to chal) ............................................................................................. 2.6
817² Sabre Rattler (JBerry) 8-13 JCarroll (2) (lw: gd spd over 3f) ............................. 3.7
1135² Windrush Boy (MMcCormack) 8-13 JReid (8) (chsd ldrs over 3f) ................ 1½.8
1196² Ihtiraz (HThomsonJones) 8-13 RHills (6) (lw: outpcd) ............................... 3½.9

**5/4** Silver Wizard (USA), **6/1** Kahellan (FR), **7/1** Ihtiraz, **15/2** Darbonne (USA), **9/1** NICHE(12/1—8/1), **10/1**
Kamaatera (IRE), **16/1** Elle Shaped (IRE), **20/1** Sabre Rattler, **40/1** Windrush Boy. CSF £19.65, Tote £6.00:
£1.40 £1.10 £2.20 (£4.40). Lord Carnarvon (MARLBOROUGH) bred by Highclere Stud. 9 Rn
　　　　　　　　　　　　　　　　　　　　　　　　　　　　　61.48 sec (0.98)
　　　　　　　　　　　　　　　　　　　　　　　　　　SF—49/53/47/43/42/34

**1470**　　RIBBLESDALE STKS (Gp 2) (3-Y.O.F) £58833.00 (£21997.65: £10548.83: £4575.52)
　　　　　**1½m**　　　　　　　　　　　　　　　　　　　　　　4-55 (4-57)

1101a² Armarama (Fav) (CEBrittain) 8-8 MRoberts (7) (lw: mde all: clr over 1f out: r.o
　　　　　strly) ................................................................................................. —1
934² Niodini (USA) (v) (MRStoute) 8-8 SCauthen (9) (hld up: 6th st: hdwy over 1f out:
　　　　　r.o fnl f: no ch w wnr) .............................................................. 2.2
1180² Blushing Storm (USA) (JRFanshawe) 8-8 WRSwinburn (8) (hdwy over 4f out:
　　　　　3rd st: one pce fnl 2f) ................................................................ 4.3
1124* Delve (IRE) (JLDunlop) 8-8 WCarson (10) (chsd wnr: 2nd st: hrd drvn & wknd
　　　　　over 1f out) ....................................................................................... 3.4
1319⁴ Guilty Secret (IRE) (PWChapple-Hyam) 8-8 PaulEddery (5) (lw: chsd ldrs: 5th
　　　　　st: rdn & btn over 1f out) ........................................................ 1½.5
　　　Arrikala (IRE) (JSBolger,Ireland) 8-8 WJO'Connor (3) (str: dwlt: hld up in rr: effrt
　　　　　over 2f out: no imp) ................................................................... ¾.6
1217³ Pearl Angel (MissBSanders) 8-8 LPiggott (4) (lw: stdd s: effrt 4f out: rdn ent st:
　　　　　sn btn) ............................................................................................. 5.7
1217⁶ Fawaayid (USA) (JSBolger,Ireland) 8-8 CRoche (6) (lw: chsd ldrs: 6th & rdn st:
　　　　　sn bhd) ............................................................................................. 7.8

**5/2** ARMARAMA, **4/1** Delve (IRE), **9/2** Niodini (USA)(op 3/1), **7/1** Pearl Angel, Fawaayid (USA), **9/1** Guilty Secret
(IRE), **20/1** Arrikala (IRE), **25/1** Blushing Storm (USA). CSF £12.71, Tote £3.50: £1.40 £1.40 £3.20 (£4.00). Mr
C. T. Olley (NEWMARKET) bred by Someries Stud. 8 Rn　　　　　　　　　2m 29.87 (0.37)
　　　　　　　　　　　　　　　　　　　　　　　　　　SF—60/56/48/42/39/37

**1471**　　CHESHAM STKS (listed race) (2-Y.O) £16082.00 (£4796.00: £2288.00: £1034.00)
　　　　　**6f**　　　　　　　　　　　　　　　　　　　　　　5-30 (5-31)

1249* Humam (IRE) (Fav) (HThomsonJones) 8-12 RHills (2) (lw: a.p: rdn over 1f out:
　　　　　led ins fnl f: r.o gamely) ............................................................ —1
611³ Lord President (USA) (PFICole) 8-12 AMunro (1) (led tl hdd ins fnl f: rdn &
　　　　　unable qckn nr fin) ........................................................................ 1.2
995* Nuryandra (GWragg) 8-7 WRSwinburn (7) (a.p: rdn 2f out: one pce) .............. 3½.3
　　　Aljazzaf (CEBrittain) 8-12 MRoberts (4) (w'like: scope: lw: hld up: rdn 2f out: r.o
　　　　　one pce) ........................................................................................... s.h.4
　　　Great Diplomat (IRE) (PJProndorgast,Ireland) 8-12 PatEddery (6) (str: scope:
　　　　　hld up: outpcd 2f out: sn bhd) ................................................... 5.5
1186* Jervia (JWWatts) 8-11 SCauthen (5) (lw: hld up: rdn 2f out: no rspnse) .......... 1½.6

**2/1** HUMAM (IRE), **3/1** Lord President (USA), **7/2** Nuryandra(op 2/1), **13/2** Jervia(10/1—6/1), **7/1** Great
Diplomat (IRE), **12/1** Aljazzaf. CSF £8.14, Tote £3.00: £1.90 £3.30 (£6.00). Mr Hamdan Al-Maktoum
(NEWMARKET) bred by Dene Investments N.V. in Ireland. 6 Rn　　　　　1m 14.26 (0.66)
　　　　　　　　　　　　　　　　　　　　　　　　　　SF—55/51/36/40/20/13

T/Trio: Race 1: £113.60 (34.1 Tckts), Race 2: £650.30 (6 Tckts), Race 4: £6.40 (505.6 Tckts) and Race 5:
£36.70 (68.1 Tckts). T/Jkpt: £7,951.90 (0.65 Tckts). £37,644.86 to Royal Ascot 19/6/92. T/Plpt: £33.00
(1,282.8 Tckts).　　　　　　　　　　　　　　　　　　　　　　　　　　　　　　IM

# ROYAL ASCOT (R-H)
## Friday, June 19th [Good to firm]
Going Allowance: minus 0.10 sec per fur (F)

Wind: str across

Stalls: centre

**1472**    WINDSOR CASTLE STKS (2-Y.O) £15790.00 (£4720.00: £2260.00: £1030.00)
     5f

2-30 (2-32)

1192³ **Satank (USA)** *(JWWatts)* 8-13 PatEddery (7) (lw: mde all: hrd rdn over 1f out: r.o wl) ........................................................ —1

645³ Surprise Offer *(RHannon)* 8-13 MJKinane (8) (lw: a.p: hrd rdn over 1f out: ev ch ins fnl f: unable qckn) ............................................ ¾.2

1240* Colyan (IRE) (Fav) *(MRStoute)* 9-6 WRSwinburn (5) (hrd rdn & hdwy over 1f out: r.o wl ins fnl f) ............................................ ½.3

1067² Hazy Kay (IRE) *(PAKelleway)* 8-8 PRobinson (3) (hrd rdn over 2f out: hdwy over 1f out: r.o one pce) ....................................... 3.4

1370³ City Rocket *(PJMakin)* 8-13 TQuinn (1) (outpcd: hdwy fnl f: r.o) ........ s.h.5

1215³ Sheila's Secret (IRE) *(WCarter)* 9-1 RCochrane (4) (lw: w wnr: hrd rdn over 1f out: wknd fnl f) ....................................... 3½.6

1259³ Comanche Companion *(TJNaughton)* 8-8 DHolland (10) (a bhd) .............. ¾.7

1405* Mr Martini (IRE) *(CEBrittain)* 9-6 MRoberts (9) (a bhd) .................. 2½.8

1186² Magic Pearl *(EJAlston)* 8-8 LPiggott (6) (s.s: outpcd) .............. d.h.8

952⁵ Sober Lad (IRE) *(JBerry)* 9-6 JCarroll (2) (hdwy 2f out: wknd over 1f out) ..... 2½.10

**5/2** Colyan (IRE), **4/1** Hazy Kay (IRE), **5/1** Satank (USA), **9/1** Sober Lad (IRE), **12/1** City Rocket, Magic Pearl, **16/1** Comanche Companion, **20/1** Mr Martini (IRE), **25/1** Sheila's Secret (IRE). CSF £38.97, Tote £9.20. £2.00 £1.90 £1.90 (£10.60). Mr R. E. Sangster (RICHMOND) bred by Bud Boschert's Stables, Inc in USA. 10 Rn
       61.82 sec (1.32)
       SF—63/60/65/41/45/33

**1473**    HARDWICKE STKS (Gp 2)    £56125.20 (£20867.16: £9908.58: £4191.06)
     1½m

3-05 (3-05)

1205² **Rock Hopper** (Fav) *(MRStoute)* 5–8-12 PatEddery (2) (lw: 3rd st: rdn over 2f out: led wl ins fnl f: all out) ........................................ —1

1205 Sapience *(DRCElsworth)* 6-8-12 RCochrane (5) (lw: 2nd st: led 2f out tl wl ins fnl f: r.o wl) .................................................. s.h.2

1059⁵ Luchiroverte (IRE) *(CEBrittain)* 4-8-9 MRoberts (1) (lw: 4th st: rdn & hmpd 2f out: unable qckn) ........................................... 3½.3

954a⁴ Runyon (IRE) *(TStack,Ireland)* 4-8-9 MKinane (3) (5th st: edgd lft 2f out: one pce) ................................................... ½.4

1205 Mellaby (USA) *(MRStoute)* 4-8-9 BRaymond (4) (led 10f: wknd 2f out) ....... 2.5

**8/15** ROCK HOPPER, **4/1** Sapience, **7/1** Luchiroverte (IRE), **10/1** Runyon (IRE), **50/1** Mellaby (USA). CSF £2.95, Tote £1.50: £1.20 £1.80 (£2.00). Maktoum Al Maktoum (NEWMARKET) bred by Gainsborough Stud Management Ltd. 5 Rn
       2m 29.19 (U.31)
       SF—89/88/78/77/73

**1474**    WOKINGHAM H'CAP (0-115) £36927.50 (£11120.00: £5385.00: £2517.50)
     6f

3-45 (3-50)

(Weights raised 1 lb)

1247³ **Red Rosein (80)** *(CaptJWilson)* 6–8-1 GCarter (29) (b.off hind: hdwy over 1f out: hrd rdn & led wl ins fnl f: r.o wl) ............................ —1

1400² Double Blue (89) (Fav) *(MJohnston)* 3–8-2 MRoberts (28) (lw: led tl wl ins fnl f: r.o) ......................................................... ¾.2

935⁴ Kayvee (93) *(GHarwood)* 3–8-6 AClark (21) (a.p: ev ch over 1f out: r.o) .......... hd.3

813⁴ Lochsong (80) *(IABalding)* 4–8-1 WCarson (17) (lw: a.p: hrd rdn over 1f out: unable qckn) ........................................... 1.4

935² So Rhythmical (74) *(GHEden)* 8–7-4⁽¹⁾ ‡§BDoyle (24) (b.off hind: swtg: a.p: hrd rdn 2f out: ev ch over 1f out: one pce fnl f) ......................... nk.5

1199 Sylvan Breeze (84) *(PMitchell)* 4–8-5 SWhitworth (23) (hld up: rdn over 2f out: one pce fnl f) ................................................... ½.6

1345³ Windpower (IRE) (85) *(JBerry)* 3–7-12 NCarlisle (22) (lw: a.p: rdn over 2f out: one pce) .............................................. 1½.7

1199 Terrhars (IRE) (103) *(RHannon)* 4-9-7 ‡³RPerham (26) (hrd rdn & no hdwy fnl 2f) ¾.8

1134² Bold Lez (100) *(MJHaynes)* 5–9-7 SCauthen (12) (a.p: rdn over 2f out: one pce) ............................................. 1½.9

1133 Baysham (USA) (83) (bl) *(BRMillman)* 6–8-4 DHolland (15) (lw: a.p: hrd rdn over 1f out: eased whn btn ins fnl f) ....................... 1.10

853² Consigliere **(86)** *(RCharlton)* 4–8-7 PatEddery (1) (a.p: hrd rdn wl over 1f out: eased whn btn ins fnl f) ........................ ¾.11
1107⁶ Grand Prix **(84)** *(DRCElsworth)* 7–8-5 LDettori (20) (hrd rdn & hdwy over 1f out: nvr nrr) ........................ hd.12
236⁵ Tbab (IRE) **(95)** *(CEBrittain)* 4–9-2 WRSwinburn (4) (bkwd: a.p: hrd rdn over 1f out: eased whn btn ins fnl f) ........................ hd.13
1400⁵ Master Planner **(92)** *(CACyzer)* 3–8-5 PRobinson (16) (lw: prom 4f) ........................ ¾.14
1014⁵ Profilic **(79)** *(CaptJWilson)* 7–8-0 RHills (19) (lw: s.s: nvr nrr) ........................ hd.15
1303 Bertie Wooster **(84)** *(RJHolder)* 9–8-5 NAdams (25) (nvr nrr) ........................ nk.16
1303 Annabelle Royale **(80)** *(MrsNMacauley)* 6–8-1 BCrossley (13) (outpcd) ........................ hd.17
1201 Nordic Brave **(77)** *(MBrittain)* 6–7-12 (7x) TyroneWilliams (14) (spd 4f) ........................ 2.18
853² Prenonamoss **(87)** *(DWPArbuthnot)* 4–8-8 TQuinn (2) (b.hind: bhd fnl 2f) ........................ ½.19
1212 Green Dollar **(90)** *(EAWheeler)* 9–8-6 ‡5DHarrison (6) (lw: a bhd) ........................ ½.20
1212² Letsbeonestaboutit **(92)** (bl) *(MrsNMacauley)* 6–8-6 ‡7SWilliams (7) (prom 4f) ........................ ¾.21
813 Panikin **(91)** *(JWharton)* 4–8-12 JWilliams (8) (bhd fnl 3f) ........................ nk.22
1201³ Bold Habit **(88)** *(BBeasley)* 7–8-9 RCochrane (5) (lw: a bhd) ........................ s.h.23
Ciseaux (USA) **(92)** *(DKWeld,Ireland)* 3–8-5 MJKinane (11) (w'like: leggy: outpcd) ........................ 1½.24
825 The Old Chapel **(95)** *(BAMcMahon)* 3–8-8 BRaymond (3) (bhd fnl 3f) ........................ 1½.25
1167 Aughfad **(84)** (v) *(TCasey)* 6–8-5 (7x) JReid (30) (bhd fnl 2f) ........................ 1½.26
Bit of a Lark **(95)** *(RHollinshead)* 4–9-2 PaulEddery (9) (bkwd: prom 3f) ........................ 4.27
1253³ Stack Rock **(101)** *(EJAlston)* 5–9-8 KFallon (18) (lw: bhd fnl 2f) ........................ 28
1167 Pharoah's Dancer **(77)** *(EAWheeler)* 5–7-12 JQuinn (10) (bhd fnl 3f) ........................ 29

**6/1** Double Blue(tchd 11/1), **7/1** Consigliere, **8/1** Lochsong, **12/1** Bold Lez, **14/1** Ciseaux (USA), Stack Rock, Bold Habit, **16/1** Prenonamoss, **20/1** Green Dollar, So Rhythmical, Tbab (IRE), **25/1** Sylvan Breeze, Grand Prix, Letsbeonestaboutit, Panikin, Windpower (IRE), **33/1** Pharoah's Dancer, Kayvee, Bertie Wooster, RED ROSEIN, Terrhars (IRE), Profilic, Master Planner, Aughfad, Baysham (USA), **50/1** Ors. CSF £210.51, CT £5,969.67. Tote £65.10: £12.10 £1.30 £8.10 £1.80 (£136.80). Exors of the late Mr J. S. Gittins (PRESTON) bred by Lodge Park Stud. 29 Rn ........................ 1m 14.14 (0.54)
SF—64/62/65/56/44/57

---

**1475**  KING'S STAND STKS (Gp 2)  £59368.20 (£22110.31: £10530.16: £4488.33)
5f  4-20 (4-21)

Sheikh Albadou (Jt-Fav) *(AAScott)* 4–9-3 WRSwinburn (1) (b.hind: hld up: led over 1f out: r.o wl) ........................ —1
827² Mr Brooks *(RHannon)* 5–9-3 LPiggott (2) (lw: hrd rdn & hdwy over 1f out: r.o ins fnl f) ........................ ½.2
1060⁴ Elbio *(PJMakin)* 5–9-3 LDettori (7) (lw: hld up: swtchd rt 2f out: ev ch ins fnl f: r.o) ........................ nk.3
437³ Wolfhound (USA) *(JHMGosden)* 3–8-10 SCauthen (6) (lw: hrd rdn over 1f out: hdwy fnl f: r.o wl) ........................ hd.4
1107⁵ El Yasaf (IRE) *(MCPipe)* 4–9-3 JWilliams (9) (a.p: ev ch ins fnl f: unable qckn) .. ½.5
1350a³ Flowing (USA) *(DKWeld,Ireland)* 4–9-0 MJKinane (3) (a.p: ev ch over 1f out: one pce) ........................ hd.6
1352a* Monde Bleu (Jt-Fav) *(AFabre,France)* 4–9-3 PatEddery (10) (lw: a.p: ev ch ins fnl f: one pce) ........................ s.h.7
656² Paris House *(JBerry)* 3–8-10 JCarroll (4) (lw: led 3f out tl over 1f out: sn wknd) . 5.8
1060² Blyton Lad *(BBeasley)* 6–9-3 SWebster (5) (lw: hmpd 4f out: a bhd) ........................ 5.9
740a Another Episode (IRE) *(JBerry)* 3–8-10 GCarter (8) (led 2f) ........................ 12.10

**7/2** SHEIKH ALBADOU, Monde Bleu, **9/2** Elbio, **6/1** Paris House, **15/2** Mr Brooks, **11/1** Wolfhound (USA), **12/1** Flowing (USA), **16/1** Blyton Lad, **50/1** Another Episode (IRE), **100/1** El Yasaf (IRE). CSF £26.58, Tote £3.50: £1.70 £1.80 £1.80 (£20.10). Mr Hilal Salem (NEWMARKET) bred by Highclere Stud Ltd. 10 Rn ........................ 60.50 sec (equals standard)
SF—93/91/90/82/87/83

---

**1476**  BRITANNIA H'CAP (3-Y.O.C & G) (0-110) £18656.00 (£5588.00: £2684.00: £1232.00)
1m (st)  4-55 (5-02)

1206* Efharisto **(79)** *(CEBrittain)* 8-0 MRoberts (2) (a.p: hrd rdn over 1f out: led last strides) ........................ —1
680² Bold Boss **(79)** *(RHanbury)* 8-0(1) PRobinson (4) (hdwy ovor 2f out: led over 1f out tl ins fnl f: r.o wl) ........................ nk.2
983* Sharpitor (IRE) **(98)** *(WJarvis)* 9-5 JReid (5) (lw: hdwy 2f out: hrd rdn & led ins fnl f: hdd last strides) ........................ s.h.3
931 Trooping (IRE) **(81)** *(GHarwood)* 8-2(1) AClark (1) (lw: led over 6f: unable qckn) 4.4
816 Mutabahi (CAN) **(88)** *(RWArmstrong)* 8-9 WCarson (6) (lw: hdwy over 2f out: one pce) ........................ hd.5
1105* Grand Vitesse (IRE) **(80)** *(RHannon)* 8-1 GCarter (3) (lw: a.p: hrd rdn over 1f out: one pce) ........................ s.h.6
1182* Little Bean **(81)** *(GWragg)* 8-2 MHills (15) (lw: hdwy over 2f out: hrd rdn over 1f out: one pce) ........................ 5.7

1166⁵ Shati (IRE) **(95)** *(HThomsonJones)* 9-2  RHills (14) (prom 5f) ....................... ³/₄.8
858* Philidor **(88)** *(JMPEustace)* 8-9  RCochrane (10) (lw: prom over 6f) .................... 2.9
1218⁶ Set Table (USA) **(85)** *(JHMGosden)* 8-6  BRaymond (16) (nvr nr to chal) ...... 2¹/₂.10
558* Irek **(91)** (Jt-Fav) *(LordHuntingdon)* 8-12  SCauthen (18) (lw: spd over 6f) ...... s.h.11
1035⁶ Bid for Six (USA) **(85)** *(RHannon)* 8-3 ‡³RPerham (19) (nvr nrr) ...................... ³/₄.12
704³ Amaze **(100)** *(LadyHerries)* 9-7  PaulEddery (7) (b: lw: rdn over 2f out: nvr nrr) 1¹/₂.13
1168 Deserve **(92)** *(HRACecil)* 8-13  WRyan (8) (prom 6f) .................................. nk.14
1136² Mougins (IRE) **(97)** *(DRCElsworth)* 9-4  TQuinn (22) (hdwy over 2f out: wknd
         over 1f out) ...................................................................................... hd.15
1218* Marabella Star (USA) **(97)** *(HRACecil)* 8-11 ‡7StephenDavies (21) (lw: spd over
         6f) ................................................................................................... 7.16
647⁴ Taylor Quigley (USA) **(99)** (bl) *(CNAllen)* 8-13 ‡7GForster (20) (prom 5f) ...... 2¹/₂.17
1133 Rocky Waters (USA) **(85)** *(GLewis)* 8-6  BRouse (17) (prom 5f) .................. 1¹/₂.18
1246² Trafalgar Boy (USA) **(88)** *(JEtherington)* 8-9  LDettori (13) (lw: gd spd over 5f) 2¹/₂.19
1047² Asaasy **(97)** *(MRStoute)* 9-4  PatEddery (12) (a bhd) ................................ ¹/₂.20
816* Ecliptic (IRE) **(87)** (Jt-Fav) *(PWChapple-Hyam)* 8-8  DHolland (9) (b.hind: lw:
         bhd fnl 3f) ...................................................................................... 2¹/₂.21
783⁴ Usaidit **(72)** *(WCarter)* 7-7  JQuinn (11) (lw: bhd fnl 2f) ............................ 4.22
1206⁵ Merlins Wish (USA) **(86)** *(RHannon)* 8-7  MJKinane (23) (a bhd) .................. 6.23
                                   LONG HANDICAP: Usaidit 7-5.

**6/1** Ecliptic (IRE), Irek, **8/1** Philidor(op 12/1), **10/1** Sharpitor (IRE), **11/1** Asaasy (USA), **12/1** Little Bean, **14/1**
Grand Vitesse (IRE), Mougins (IRE), Merlins Wish (USA), EFHARISTO, **16/1** Marabella Star (USA), **20/1** Trafalgar
Boy (USA), Deserve, **25/1** Trooping (IRE), Set Table (USA), **33/1** Rocky Waters (USA), Mutabahi (CAN), Bid for
Six (USA), Amaze, **40/1** Ors. CSF £440.90, CT £5,193.86. Tote £21.90: £4.00 £7.10 £2.30 £12.20 (£195.00).
The Dowager Lady Beaverbrook (NEWMARKET) bred by Barrettstown Stud Farms Ltd. 23 Rn  1m 39.96 (0.56)
                                                                                         SF—65/64/82/53/59/50

**1477**    QUEEN ALEXANDRA STKS    £15530.00 (£4640.00: £2220.00: £1010.00)
            2³/₄m 34y                                                        5-30 (5-32)

981* **Romany Rye (100)** *(GWragg)* 4-9-2  WRSwinburn (8) (2nd st: led over 1f out:
         drvn out) ........................................................................................ —1
1459* Gondolier **(86)** *(HRACecil)* 4-9-5  PatEddery (2) (chsd ldr: led over 7f out tl over
         1f out: hrd rdn & ev ch ins fnl f: r.o) ...................................................... nk.2
Great Marquess (bl) (Fav) *(JEPease,France)* 5–9-7  SCauthen (6) (3rd st: hrd
         rdn over 2f out: sn wknd) ................................................................... 15.3
Muir Station (USA) **(97)** (bl) *(JSBolger,Ireland)* 4-8-12  CRoche (9) (hdwy 12f
         out: rdn over 6f out: wknd 4f out) ........................................................ 7.4
1290³ Mr Taylor **(30)** *(HJCollingridge)* 7–9-0  VSmith (4) (nvr nrr) ...................... 15.5
981⁴ Haitham **(91)** *(RAkehurst)* 5–9-7  LPiggott (7) (led over 14f: wknd 4f out) ........ 1¹/₂.6
760 Clifton Hampden **(66)** *(LadyHerries)* 4–8-5  WRyan (1) (hdwy 12f out: wknd
         4f out) ............................................................................................. hd.7
1280⁴ Ptolemy (FR) *(MissCKnight)* 5–8-7  JReid (5) (a bhd: t.o) ............................. 20.8
1423* Little Big **(38)** *(CDBroad)* 5–9-0  MHills (3) (a bhd: t.o) ........................... 9

**11/4** Great Marquess, **3/1** ROMANY RYE, **7/2** Gondolier, **4/1** Muir Station (USA), **8/1** Haitham(op 14/1), **33/1**
Ptolemy (FR), **50/1** Clifton Hampden, **66/1** Little Big, **100/1** Mr Taylor. CSF £12.72, Tote £3.30: £1.30 £1.30
£1.80 (£5.00). Sir Philip Oppenheimer (NEWMARKET) bred by Hascombe and Valiant Studs. 9 Rn
                                                                                   4m 54.15 (7.15)
                                                                                 SF—9/11/–/–/–/–

T/Trio: Race 1: £38.80 (76.3 Tckts), Race 3: £10,137.20 (1 Tckt), Race 4: £26.10 (117.3 Tckts), Race 5:
£378.10 (16.1 Tckts) and Race 6: £4.40 (712.2 Tckts). T/Jkpt: Not won; £70,628.21 to Ascot 20/6/92. T/Plpt:
£72.70 (512.35 Tckts).                                                                        AK

1070—**RIPON  (R-H)**
**Wednesday, June 17th [Firm]**
Going Allowance: St: minus 0.70 sec; Rnd: minus 0.50 sec (H)              Wind: almost nil

Stalls: low
**1478**    JOSHUA TETLEY 'ASCOT IN THE DALES' STKS (Mdn 3-Y.O) £2595.00 (£720.00:
            £345.00)  1¹/₄m                                                  2-15 (2-18)

864⁶ **Halley (USA)** (Jt-Fav) *(HRACecil)* 8-7 ‡7StephenDavies (6) (cl up: led 4f out:
         pushed along & r.o wl: eased ins fnl f) ................................................... —1
Impeccable Charm (USA) (Jt-Fav) *(JHMGosden)* 8-9  GDuffield (1) (unf: scope:
         s.i.s: rdn & sn cl up: outpcd ent st: hdwy u.p 3f out: no ch w
         wnr) ................................................................................................ 1.2
Shardra *(MJCamacho)* 8-9  NConnorton (4) (leggy: unf: hld up: hdwy over 3f
         out: nvr nr to chal) ........................................................................... 10.3

Kalaflo *(PCalver)* 8-9 NCarlisle (5) (lengthy: dwlt: hld up: effrt 3f out: n.d) ........ 3½.4
10494 Olliver Duckett *(PCalver)* 9-0 WNewnes (3) (led tl hdd 4f out: wandered u.p over
2f out: sn wknd) ........................................................................................... 12.5
Mary Macblain **(51)** *(JLHarris)* 8-9 KFallon (2) (a bhd: hung bdly lft fnl 3f) .......... 6.6

**13/8** Impeccable Charm (USA)(op Evens), HALLEY (USA), **11/2** Olliver Duckett, **14/1** Shardra, **20/1** Kalaflo, **33/1** Mary Macblain. CSF £4.15, Tote £2.20: £1.20 £1.30 (£2.10). Sheikh Mohammed (NEWMARKET) bred by Crescent Farm in USA. 6 Rn
2m 5.1 (1.6)
SF—27/27/7/–/–/–

## 1479

DISHFORTH (S) STKS (2-Y-O) £2343.60 (£649.60: £310.80)   **6f**   2-50 (2-51)

3656 **Blue Radiance** *(TFairhurst)* 8-3 ‡3JFanning (8) (lw: w ldr: led over 2f out: styd on
wl) ..................................................................................................... —1
1151★ Trevorsninepoints *(NTinkler)* 8-6 GDuffield (4) (lw: led: hung rt: hdd over 2f out:
kpt on one pce) ................................................................................ 3.2
11705 Midarida (IRE) (Fav) *(RJRWilliams)* 8-6 WRyan (9) (a chsng ldrs: outpcd over 2f
out: no imp after) ............................................................................. 2½.3
1249 Weaver George (IRE) *(MHEasterby)* 8-6 ‡5SMaloney (6) (chsd ldrs: rdn ½-wy:
no imp) ............................................................................................. ½.4
Forthemoment *(PCalver)* 8-6 NCarlisle (2) (cmpt: s.i.s: hdwy ½-wy: nvr plcd to
chal) ................................................................................................. nk.5
12643 Niteowlady (bl) *(SGNorton)* 8-6 JFortune (1) (chsd ldrs 4f: sn btn) ................ 2½.6
1321 Jersey Bob (IRE) *(JSWainwright)* 8-11 PBurke (5) (in tch over 3f: sn btn) .......... ½.7
Colmar *(RBastiman)* 8-6 KFallon (7) (leggy: bit bkwd: sn wl bhd: stdy hdwy
½-wy: n.d) ....................................................................................... 1½.8
Our Paul *(BWMurray)* 8-11 ACulhane (3) (neat: unf: s.i.s: sn t.o) ..................... 25.9

**7/4** Midarida (IRE), **3/1** Weaver George (IRE)(4/1—5/2), **4/1** Trevorsninepoints, **6/1** Colmar(op 10/1), **7/1** Niteowlady, **12/1** BLUE RADIANCE, **16/1** Forthemoment(op 10/1), **25/1** Our Paul, **33/1** Jersey Bob (IRE). CSF £60.82, Tote £14.90: £2.00 £1.70 £1.70 (£37.20). Mr J. G. Brearley (MIDDLEHAM) bred by J. G. and Mrs J. M. Brearley. 9 Rn; No bid
1m 12.7 (1)

## 1480

TETLEY BITTER H'CAP (0-100) £7245.00 (£2160.00: £1030.00: £465.00)
**1m**
3-25 (3-26)

1193★ **Major Mouse (74)** *(WWHaigh)* 4—8-3 ACulhane (1) (hld up & bhd: effrt 3f out:
str run fnl f to ld cl home) ................................................................ —1
1021 Yousefia (USA) **(84)** *(MRStoute)* 3—8-3(1) MrsNMacauley (4) (led tl hdd over 4f out:
led over 1f out: no ex cl home) ...................................................... hd.2
3872 Big Leap (IRE) **(89)** (Fav) *(MMoubarak)* 3—8-8 GDuffield (3) (lw: hld up: effrt
over 3f out: hdwy over 1f out: nvr able to chal) .............................. 2.3
10476 Star Connection **(66)** *(RMWhitaker)* 4—7-6 ‡3JFanning (6) (cl up: led over 4f out:
tl over 1f out: no ex) ....................................................................... nk.4
10615 St Ninian **(99)** *(MHEasterby)* 6—10-0 WRyan (7) (lw: trckd ldrs: effrt 3f out: one
pce appr fnl f) ................................................................................ s.h.5
12035 Brown Fairy (USA) **(69)** *(MrsNMacauley)* 4—7-9(3) ‡3DBiggs (2) (hld up: effrt over
3f out: no imp) ............................................................................... 1.6
10182 Genair (FR) **(64)** *(MrsGRReveley)* 7—7-0 ‡7DarrenMoffatt (5) (chsd ldrs: rdn 4f
out: btn wl over 2f out) .................................................................. 1.7
LONG HANDICAP: Genair (FR) 7-3.

**5/2** Big Leap (IRE), **11/4** St Ninian, **6/1** Genair (FR), **13/2** MAJOR MOUSE, **15/2** Star Connection(5/1—8/1), **8/1** Yousefia (USA), **10/1** Brown Fairy (USA). CSF £49.11, Tote £8.90: £3.30 £3.00 (£25.00). Mr N. Barber (MALTON) bred by Mrs V. Haigh. 7 Rn
1m 37.8 (0.1)
SF—27/26/25/8/43/7

## 1481

BEAUMONTS INSURANCE DERBY H'CAP (Ladies) (0-70) £2574.00 (£714.00: £342.00)
1½m 60y
4-00 (4-00)

(Weights raised 11 lb)
1163 **Cathos (FR) (52)** *(DAWilson)* 7—11-7 MissJAllison (5) (b: hdwy appr st: led wl
over 4f out: qcknd clr: styd on wl) ................................................... —1
13362 Glowing Devil **(56)** *(TDBarron)* 3—10-10 MissIDWJones (8) (led 2f: chsd ldrs:
outpcd over 3f out: styd on wl fnl f) ............................................... 1½.2
1248 Marandisa **(41)** *(MPNaughton)* 5—10-10 MissPRobson (2) (hdwy appr st: styd
on fnl 3f: nt pce to chal) ................................................................ 3½.3
12482 Lots of Luck **(51)** (Fav) *(JPearce)* 9—11-6 MissTPearce (3) (trckd ldrs: chal ent st:
outpcd over 3f out: no imp after) .................................................... ¾.4
1311★ Sarsta Grai **(51)** *(MHEasterby)* 4—11-6 (6x) MrsSEasterby (6) (lw: chsd ldrs tl
outpcd over 3f out: n.d after) .......................................................... ½.5
1106 Champenoise **(50)** *(MBell)* 4—11-2 ‡3MrsLLawson (4) (swtg: hdwy 4f out: c wd:
no imp) ........................................................................................... 2.6

1184 **Ghylldale (38)** (v) *(RBastiman)* 4–10-4 ‡³MissLRevell (7) (swtg: led after 2f tl over 4f out: wknd 3f out) .......... ½.7

*1372* Thunder Bug (USA) **(42)** *(APJames)* 4–10-11 MissHMcCaull (1) (hld up & bhd: hdwy 8f out: c wd st: sn outpcd) .......... 12.8

951 Media Star **(28)** *(TKersey)* 7–9-8⁽³⁾ ‡³MissJMiddleton (9) (b: rn wd st: a bhd) ...... nk.9

**6/4** Lots of Luck, **7/2** Sarsta Grai, **5/1** Glowing Devil, **8/1** CATHOS (FR), **10/1** Ghylldale, **16/1** Champenoise, **20/1** Thunder Bug (USA), Marandisa, **33/1** Media Star. CSF £44.42, CT £703.14. Tote £8.90: £1.90 £1.40 £5.80 (£12.90). Mr D. A. Wilson (EPSOM) bred by M. Olivier Nicol in France. 9 Rn　　2m 40 (6)
SF—15/1/–/–/–/–

---

**1482** RUSHLEVEL CONSTRUCTION H'CAP (0-80) £2265.20 (£627.20: £299.60)
1½m 60y　　　　　　　　4-35 (4-40)

829 **Rousitto (68)** *(RHollinshead)* 4–10-0 WRyan (6) (hld up: hdwy 4f out: slt ld over 1f out: shkn up & r.o) .......... —1

267⁵ Demokos (FR) **(40)** *(APStringer)* 7–7-9 ‡⁵SMaloney (4) (swtg: a.p: led over 3f out tl over 1f out: kpt on wl) .......... ½.2

1048² Inan (USA) **(71)** (Fav) *(JLDunlop)* 3–9-2 GDuffield (1) (dwlt: hdwy gng wl 4f out: rdn 3f out: styd on one pce fnl f) .......... 1.3

1073⁴ Bold Elect **(63)** *(PWigham)* 4–9-9 MWigham (7) (lw: s.i.s: hld up & bhd: styd on fnl 3f: nrst fin) .......... ½.4

1237★ West Stow **(73)** *(MRStoute)* 3–8-13 ‡⁵JJones (3) (cl up tl outpcd 3f out) ...... 12.5

1252⁶ Miss Hyde (USA) **(59)** (v) *(JAGlover)* 3–8-4 JFortune (8) (led tl hdd over 3f out: sn btn) .......... 3½.6

1108 Lord Advocate **(37)** *(MPNaughton)* 4–7-6 ‡⁵BDoyle (5) (a bhd) .......... ½.7

1311⁵ Talish **(40)** *(TDBarron)* 4–7-11 ‡³JFanning (2) (cl up tl wknd over 3f out) .......... 10.8

**2/1** Inan (USA), **11/4** West Stow(7/4—3/1), **11/2** Miss Hyde (USA), **15/2** Talish(12/1—7/1), **9/1** ROUSITTO(8/1—12/1), **12/1** Bold Elect, **14/1** Ors. CSF £103.85, CT £318.06. Tote £11.80: £2.00 £2.60 £1.20 (£58.90). Mrs G. E. Maloney (UPPER LONGDON) bred by White Lodge Stud Ltd. 8 Rn　　2m 35.2 (1.2)
SF—42/8/27/33/–/–

---

**1483** JOSHUA TETLEY H'CAP (0-80) £2924.00 (£872.00: £416.00: £188.00)
5f　　　　　　　　5-10 (5-14)

1305★ **Fangio (81)** (Fav) *(WGMTurner)* 3–9-5 (6x) ‡³TSprake (4) (lw: mde all: r.o wl fnl 2f) .......... —1

1436★ Plain Fact **(86)** *(AHarrison)* 7–9-13 (6x) ‡⁷SWilliams (1) (a.p: effrt 2f out: nt qckn ins fnl f) .......... 1½.2

1187⁴ Real Stunner **(70)** *(MPNaughton)* 5–9-4 KFallon (5) (lw: s.i.s: hdwy & swtchd over 1f out: r.o) .......... 1½.3

1427³ Simmie's Special **(67)** *(RHollinshead)* 4–9-1 WRyan (3) (chsd wnr: effrt ½-wy: btn appr fnl f) .......... nk.4

1235³ Catherines Well **(69)** *(MWEasterby)* 9–9-3 TLucas (6) (lw: a chsng ldrs: nt qckn fnl 2f) .......... s.h.5

1282² Lincstone Boy (IRE) **(55)** (bl) *(BBeasley)* 4–8-3⁽¹⁰⁾ SWebster (2) (sn pushed along: bhd fr ½-wy) .......... 5.6

1199 Sir Tasker **(73)** *(JLHarris)* 4–9-2 ‡⁵SMaloney (7) (lw: spd 3f: sn wknd) .......... 3½.7

**15/8** FANGIO, **11/2** Catherines Well, **6/1** Lincstone Boy (IRE), **7/1** Plain Fact, Real Stunner, **15/2** Simmie's Special, **9/1** Sir Tasker. CSF £13.66, Tote £2.50: £1.70 £3.60 (£6.40). Mr Simon Swift (SHERBORNE) bred by Melbury Park Stud. 7 Rn　　57.7 sec (0.3 under best; U.9)
SF—53/55/40/36/37/3

---

**1484** ACC STKS (Mdn) £2284.40 (£632.80: £302.40)　　**6f**　　5-40 (5-41)

1309 **Royal Girl (56)** *(MissSEHall)* 5–9-2 NConnorton (11) (in tch: hdwy 2f out: led ins fnl f: r.o wl) .......... —1

1055³ Patience Please *(MHEasterby)* 3–8-3 ‡⁵SMaloney (10) (chsd ldr: led wl over 1f out tl ins fnl f: r.o) .......... 1½.2

428⁶ Mufid (USA) (Fav) *(MajorWRHern)* 3–8-13 WRyan (3) (lw: bhd: hdwy u.p ½-wy: styd on) .......... 6.3

Cottage Gallery (IRE) *(WAStephenson)* 4–9-2 SWebster (2) (chsd ldrs: rdn & no hdwy fnl 2f) .......... ¾.4

1418⁴ Lord Lambson **(60)** *(RMWhitaker)* 3–8-13 ACulhane (8) (hdwy ½-wy: shkn up over 1f out: no imp) .......... 4.5

750³ Canon Kyle (IRE) **(68)** (v) *(MHEasterby)* 3–8-13 TLucas (6) (lw: trckd ldrs: effrt 2f out: grad lost pl) .......... 1.6

Caherea School *(RO'Leary)* 3–8-8 LCharnock (1) (bit bkwd: swtg: sn outpcd & bhd) .......... 4.7

Lightning Decision *(JPSmith)* 4–9-0 ‡⁷SWynne (12) (leggy: spd 4f) .......... 1.8

Miss Grosse Nez (IRE) **(55)** *(CWThornton)* 3–8-8 NCarlisle (9) (a outpcd & bhd) nk.9

Dublin Dream *(MBrittain)* 3–8–8 PSedgwick (5) (led over 4f: wknd qckly) .......... **1**.10
765 On the Hop (IRE) *(APStringer)* 3–8–5 ‡³JFanning (4) (wnt rt after s: sn wl bhd) . **5**.11
Joie de Patina *(SGNorton)* 3–8–8 JFortune (7) (unf: bit bkwd: rn green,
　　　　　　　　　　wandered, stumbled bdly & uns rdr after 1f) ............................ **0**

**6/4** Mufid (USA), **5/1** Patience Please(op 3/1), **11/2** Canon Kyle (IRE)(9/1—5/1), **7/1** ROYAL GIRL, **12/1** Lord
Lambson, **14/1** Joie de Patina, **16/1** Miss Grosse Nez (IRE), **50/1** Cottage Gallery (IRE), On the Hop (IRE),
Caherea School, Dublin Dream, **66/1** Lightning Decision. CSF £37.28, Tote £10.20: £2.60 £1.70 £1.70
(£18.20). Miss S. E. Hall (MIDDLEHAM) bred by John and Mrs McNamara. 12 Rn　　　　1m 10.4 (U1.3)
　　　　　　　　　　　　　　　　　　　　　　　　　　　　　　　　　　　SF—44/25/11/11/–/–/

T/Plpt: £111.20 (30.45 Tckts).　　　　　　　　　　　　　　　　　　　　　　　　　AA

# RIPON (R-H)

## Thursday, June 18th [Firm]

Going Allowance: minus 0.20 sec per fur (F)　　　　　　　Wind: fresh half against

Stalls: low

**1485**　　　E.B.F. SAPPER STKS (Mdn 2-Y.O) £2616.00 (£726.00: £348.00)　　**6f**　　2-15 (2-19)

**Majestic Hawk (USA)** (Fav) *(MMoubarak)* 9-0 TQuinn (1) (w'like: str: scope:
　　　　　mde virtually all: shkn up & edgd rt ins fnl f: jst hld on) ........ —**1**
1249 Wufud (USA) *(JLDunlop)* 9-0 RCochrane (10) (chsd ldrs: drvn along 2f out: r.o
　　　　　wl nr fin) .................................................................. s.h.**2**
1249 Hawl (USA) *(AAScott)* 9-0 GHind (9) (lw: in tch: shkn up 2f out: styd on fnl f) ... **3**.3
1023³ Chiltern Hundreds (USA) *(Mrs.ICecil)* 9-0 BCrossley (8) (lw: w wnr: effrt over 1f
　　　　　out: grad wknd) ..................................................... ³/₄.4
1171⁴ Hadeer's Dance *(RWArmstrong)* 9-0 CNutter (3) (lw: hld up: stdy hdwy 2f out:
　　　　　r.o fin) .............................................................. 2¹/₂.5
Royal Diva *(MissSEHall)* 8-9 SWebster (6) (leggy: scope: s.i.s: outpcd: kpt on
　　　　　fnl f) ................................................................ 1¹/₂.6
Careless Son *(MissSEHall)* 9-0 NConnorton (2) (cmpt: bit bkwd: w ldrs: outpcd
　　　　　& lost pl ¹/₂-wy: kpt on nr fin) ..................................... 1¹/₂.7
Atlantic Sunset (IRE) *(MWEasterby)* 9-0 KDarley (4) (w'like: leggy: bit bkwd: sn
　　　　　trckng ldrs: wknd over 1f out) ...................................... hd.8
Pineto *(JBerry)* 9-0 GCarter (5) (str: bit bkwd: sn bhd & rdn along) ............... 12.9
Yardley Court *(BBeasley)* 9-0 LCharnock (7) (leggy: sn w ldrs: edgd rt & lost pl
　　　　　¹/₂-wy: sn bhd) ...................................................... **10**

**8/11** MAJESTIC HAWK (USA), **7/2** Wufud (USA), **9/1** Hawl (USA)(op 6/1), **11/1** Chiltern Hundreds (USA)(op
7/1), Hadeer's Dance(op 7/1), **12/1** Pineto(op 8/1), **20/1** Atlantic Sunset (IRE), **33/1** Careless Son, **50/1** Royal
Diva, **66/1** Yardley Court. CSF £4.25, Tote £1.80: £1.10 £1.10 £3.20 (£2.80). Ecurie Fustok (NEWMARKET) bred
by Buckram Oak Farm in USA. 10 Rn　　　　　　　　　　　　　　　　　　1m 15.2 (3.5)
　　　　　　　　　　　　　　　　　　　　　　　　　　　　　　　　SF—6/5/–/–/–/–

**1486**　　　WINDHILL (S) H'CAP (3-Y.O) (0-60) £2578.80 (£716.80: £344.40)　　**1m**　2-50 (2-53)
　　　　　　　　　　　　　　(Weights raised 5 lb)

1294 Akura (IRE) (52) *(MJohnston)* 9-4 RPElliott (15) (trckd ldrs: led 2f out: sn clr) ... —**1**
1052⁵ The Dominant Gene (35) *(JRJenkins)* 8-1 EJohnson (1) (a chsng ldrs: kpt on
　　　　　u.p fnl 2f: no ch w wnr) ............................................. **4**.2
1089⁵ Mummys Rocket (32) *(MO'Neill)* 7-12 SWood (16) (chsd ldrs: styd on same
　　　　　pce fnl 2f) .......................................................... ¹/₂.3
1276³ Have a Nightcap (49) (bl) *(MAJarvis)* 9-1 GCrealock (7) (a chsng ldrs: led 4f out
　　　　　to 2f out: one pce) ................................................. hd.4
1195 Stoproveritate (51) *(SGNorton)* 8-10 ‡⁷OPears (9) (trckd ldrs: effrt 3f out: kpt on:
　　　　　nvr nr to chal) ...................................................... **2**.5
1070 Dancing Wild (40) *(MrsGRReveley)* 8-6 JLowe (2) (plld hrd: w ldrs: disp ld 4f
　　　　　out to 2f out: grad wknd) ........................................... ¹/₂.6
1154 Dame Helene (USA) (37) *(PCHaslam)* 7-10 ‡⁷NicolaHowarth (10) (hld up & bhd:
　　　　　hdwy 2f out: styd on nr fin) ......................................... **2**.7
1294 Vital Voltage (IRE) (47) *(MWEllerby)* 8-13 SMorris (13) (s.i.s: bhd tl kpt on fnl 2f) 1¹/₂.8
1276⁵ Medbourne (IRE) (40) *(JLHarris)* 8-6 GCarter (11) (lost pl after 2f: sme hdwy 2f
　　　　　out: n.d) ............................................................ ¹/₂.9
1277 Katie's Dream (IRE) (51) (Fav) *(PSFelgate)* 9-3 TQuinn (12) (b: chsd ldrs: effrt
　　　　　over 3f out: wknd over 2f out) ...................................... 1¹/₂.10
520 Jester's Gem (40) *(BWMurray)* 8-3 ‡³JFanning (5) (lw: led 2f: chsd ldrs tl lost pl
　　　　　3f out) .............................................................. **1**.11
1052 Lingdale Lass (55) *(MrsGRReveley)* 9-0 ‡⁷SCopp (3) (lw: in tch tl lost pl 3f out) 6.12

1276 Missal (IRE) **(38)** (bl) *(PatMitchell)* 7-11 ‡⁷RTurner (6) (plld hrd: led after 2f tl 4f
out: sn wknd) .......................................................... 1½.**13**
1288⁵ Little Ivor **(46)** (v) *(DenysSmith)* 8-12 KFallon (8) (lw: nvr nr ldrs) ................. s.h.**14**
949 Miss Movie World **(44)** *(NBycroft)* 8-10 LCharnock (14) (hld up: a bhd) ............. **15**
1172 Placid Lady **(34)** *(WCarter)* 7-9 ‡⁵NGwilliams (4) (lw: dwlt: sn chsng ldrs: rn
wd appr st: sn lost pl) ........................................... **16**

**7/2** Katie's Dream (IRE)(3/1—9/2), **5/1** Stoproveritate, **7/1** Have a Nightcap, **8/1** AKURA (IRE), Dancing Wild,
The Dominant Gene, **11/1** Medbourne (IRE), **12/1** Miss Movie World, Little Ivor, Mummys Rocket, **16/1** Placid
Lady (IRE), **20/1** Vital Voltage (IRE), Lingdale Lass, Dame Helene (USA), **25/1** Jester's Gem, **33/1** Missal (IRE).
CSF £75.35, CT £734.94. Tote £12.40: £2.90 £2.60 £2.10 £1.80 (£45.80). Mr Billy Morgan (MIDDLEHAM) bred
by J. Mamakos in Ireland. 16 Rn; No bid                                                    1m 41.3 (3.6)
SF—26/–/–/8/–/–

**1487**   NORMAN WELLS MEMORIAL CHALLENGE TROPHY (H'cap) (0-100) £5433.75
          (£1620.00: £772.50: £348.75)   **6f**                          3-25 (3-27)

*(Weights raised 1 lb)*
1271³ **Filicaia (59)** *(DonEnricoIncisa)* 6–7-11⁽¹⁾ ‡⁷ClaireBalding (1) (lw: s.i.s: sn bhd:
swtchd outside over 1f out: r.o strly to ld ins fnl f) ................. —**1**
1212★ Poets Cove **(84)** (Jt-Fav) *(MMcCormack)* 4–9-5 RCochrane (5) (hld up:
smooth hdwy to ld 2f out: rdn & nt qckn ins fnl f) ................. 1½.**2**
1235★ Furiella **(73)** *(PCHaslam)* 4–8-8 KDarley (6) (chsd ldrs: effrt & ev ch over 1f out) 3½.**3**
1247★ Crystal Jack (FR) **(81)** (Jt-Fav) *(FHLee)* 4–8-11 ‡⁵NKennedy (3) (lw: w ldrs: rdn
2f out: sn wknd) ................................................ 2½.**4**
1403 Gentle Hero (USA) **(89)** *(MPNaughton)* 6–9-10 GHind (2) (lw: led to ½-wy: sn
rdn & wl outpcd: kpt on fnl f) .............................. s.h.**5**
1293★ Saddlehome (USA) **(76)** *(RMWhitaker)* 3–7-10 ‡⁷AGarth (7) (chsd ldrs: led
½-wy: hdd 2f out: sn lost pl & bhd) ...................... 10.**6**
879 Langtonian **(84)** *(JBerry)* 5–0-11 GCarter (1) (w ldrs tl rdn & lost pl over 2f out:
sn bhd) ............................................................ 3.**7**
LONG HANDICAP: Filicaia 6-13.

**3/1** Crystal Jack (FR), Poets Cove, **4/1** Saddlehome (USA), **9/2** Furiella, **12/1** Langtonian, FILICAIA, **14/1** Gentle
Hero (USA). CSF £43.34, Tote £8.20: £2.00 £1.80 (£14.10). Don Enrico Incisa (COVERHAM) bred by Rathduff
Stud. 7 Rn                                                                      1m 12.7 (1)
SF—29/55/30/36/22/–

**1488**   PRICE WATERHOUSE H'CAP (0-80) £3080.00 (£920.00: £440.00: £200.00)
          **1¼m**                                                        4-00 (4-01)

*(Weights raised 8 lb)*
1248 **Halston Prince (60)** *(MrsJRRamsden)* 5–9-9 GBaxter (3) (lw: mde all: drvn out
fnl f) ................................................................ —**1**
1195⁴ Who's Tef (IRE) **(60)** *(MHEasterby)* 4–9-4 ‡⁵SMaloney (5) (lw: trckd ldrs: effrt
over 2f out: styd on fnl f: nt rch wnr) ...................... 1½.**2**
1153⁴ Tarda **(52)** *(MrsGRReveley)* 5–9-1 JLowe (7) (hld up & bhd: effrt over 2f out:
n.m.r: r.o fnl f) ................................................ nk.**3**
1336³ Anguish (IRE) **(51)** *(NACallaghan)* 3–8-2 GCarter (2) (sn chsng ldrs: effrt &
outpcd over 2f out: kpt on fnl f) .......................... 2.**4**
1284⁴ Sanawi **(53)** *(PDEvans)* 5–8-13 ‡³FNorton (6) (sn chsng ldrs: outpcd & lost pl
over 2f out: styd on ins fnl f) .............................. hd.**5**
1308² Reel of Tulloch (IRE) **(64)** (Fav) *(PCHaslam)* 3–9-1 KDarley (4) (lw: hld up: effrt
& drvn along over 3f out: no imp) ........................ nk.**6**
1245 Kiveton Tycoon (IRE) **(73)** (bl) *(JAGlover)* 3–9-3 ‡⁷SWilliams (8) (lw: hld up: effrt
over 3f out: sn lost pl: swtchd outside ins fnl f: n.d) ...... 3.**7**
1072 Pride of Pendle **(53)** *(PCalver)* 3–8-4 DaleGibson (1) (chsd ldrs: drvn along
over 2f out: lost pl over 2f out) .......................... 1½.**8**

**3/1** Reel of Tulloch (IRE), **100/30** Tarda, **11/2** Who's Tef (IRE), **13/2** Anguish (IRE), **7/1** HALSTON PRINCE, **8/1**
Kiveton Tycoon (IRE), **10/1** Sanawi, **20/1** Pride of Pendle(op 10/1). CSF £40.76, CT £136.47. Tote £7.60: £3.10
£2.10 £2.00 (£18.10). Mr K. E. Wheldon (THIRSK) bred by Dr R. Brennan. 8 Rn     2m 9.8 (6.3)
SF—26/18/14/–/7/8

**1489**   GRANTLEY STKS (Mdn 2-Y.O) £2284.80 (£632.80: £302.40)   **5f**      4-35 (4-36)

619³ **Make Mine a Double** *(MissSEHall)* 9-0 NConnorton (5) (chsd ldrs: effrt 2f out:
r.o to ld ins fnl f) ............................................ —**1**
1259 Mysterious Ways (FR) (Fav) *(MrsJCecil)* 9-0 BCrossley (4) (led: hdd & no ex ins
fnl f) ............................................................ ½.**2**
Dancing Domino *(MHEasterby)* 9-0 KDarley (6) (w'like: bit bkwd: sn chsng ldrs:
kpt on fnl 2f) ................................................ 3.**3**
I Do Care *(JBerry)* 9-0 GCarter (1) (cmpt: scope: bit bkwd: w ldrs tl rdn & wknd
over 1f out) .................................................. 1½.**4**

874[4] Caldervale *(ABailey)* 9-0 AMackay (2) (dwlt: hld up & bhd: stdy hdwy 2f out:
n.m.r ins fnl f: fin strly) ............................................................... 1½.5

1112 El Guapo *(TFairhurst)* 8-11 ‡³JFanning (3) (chsd ldrs: rdn ½-wy: wknd 2f out) . nk.6

Mansooree (USA) *(AAScott)* 9-0 GHind (8) (str: cmpt: bit bkwd: sn chsng ldrs &
drvn along: wknd 2f out) ............................................................ nk.7

Hynes Torpedo *(BBeasley)* 9-0 LCharnock (7) (small: cmpt: s.i.s: a bhd) ........ 15.8

*Stewards Enquiry: Trainer & rdr of Caldervale each fined £600 under Rule 151 (failure to run horse on its merits).*

2/1 Mysterious Ways (FR)(5/4—9/4), 7/2 MAKE MINE A DOUBLE, 4/1 Mansooree (USA)(op 7/4), 5/1 I Do
Care(op 3/1), 9/1 Caldervale, 12/1 Dancing Domino(op 6/1), 20/1 Hynes Torpedo, 33/1 El Guapo. CSF £10.74,
Tote £5.30: £1.90 £1.10 £2.10 (£5.80). Mr I. V. Matthews (MIDDLEHAM) bred by Nidd Park Stud. 8 Rn
61.9 sec (3.3)
SF—14/12/–/–/–/–

**1490**  HOB GREEN APP'CE STKS (Mdn) £2265.20 (£627.20: £299.60)
1½m 60y                                                   5-10 (5-11)

**Anchorage (IRE)** (Fav) *(HRACecil)* 3–7-13 StephenDavies (7) (lw: hld up:
smooth hdwy over 2f out: qcknd to ld ins fnl f: readily) ........ —1

1330² Baher (USA) (70) (bl) *(NACallaghan)* 3–7-13 ‡⁵JTate (3) (lw: led to 7f out: led
over 2f out: rdn & edgd lft over 1f out: no ch w wnr) .......... 1½.2

1180⁵ Iota *(MrsJCecil)* 3–7-13 PTurner (6) (plld hrd early: trckd ldrs: effrt 2f out: one
pce whn swtchd rt over 1f out) .................................. 1½.3

1313² Zamaan Ya Zamaan (IRE) *(MAJarvis)* 3–8-4 KRutter (4) (chsd ldrs: drvn along
over 3f out: sn lost pl) .......................................... 15.4

687 Noble Vienna (USA) (46) *(RHollinshead)* 3–7-13 ‡⁵JDennis (1) (lw: trckd ldr: led
7f out tl over 2f out: sn wknd) ................................. hd.5

Tathir (CAN) *(DMorley)* 4–9-0 ‡⁵EBentley (8) (leggy: b: b.hind: bhd fnl 3f) ...... 15.6

Star Catch *(WCarter)* 3–8-4 NGwilliams (5) (leggy: unf: a bhd: t.o fnl 3f) ...... 25.7

Prefabricate (FR) (32) *(JLHarris)* 6–9-0 ‡⁵MHarris (2) (prom 7f: sn t.o) ........... dist.8

8/11 ANCHORAGE (IRE), 9/2 Zamaan Ya Zamaan (IRE), 11/2 Baher (USA), 7/1 Iota, 14/1 Tathir (CAN), 25/1
Noble Vienna (USA), Star Catch, 100/1 Prefabricate (FR). CSF £5.62, Tote £1.60: £1.10 £1.70 £1.50 (£3.90).
Sheikh Mohammed (NEWMARKET) bred by Cotswold Stud and London Thoroughbred Services. 8 Rn
2m 36.9 (2.9)
SF—32/29/26/1/–/–

**1491**  LEVY BOARD H'CAP (3-Y.O) (0-70) £3184.00 (£952.00: £456.00: £208.00)
2m                                                       5-40 (5-42)
(Weights raised 7 lb)

1195 Thakawah (63) *(RWArmstrong)* 9-7 BCrossley (4) (bhd: hdwy & prom ½-wy:
led over 3f out: drvn along & styd on wl) ...................... —1

1188 Kadari (56) *(AHarrison)* 9-0 KFallon (10) (lw: hld up: hdwy & prom 6f out: hrd
drvn & kpt on fnl 4f: no ch w wnr) ............................ 8.2

1190 Escadaro (USA) (39) (bl) *(SGNorton)* 7-4 ‡⁷CHawksley (7) (chsd ldrs: drvn
along ½-wy: one pce fnl 4f) ..................................... 1.3

1188³ Pharlander (IRE) (45) (bl) *(MHEasterby)* 7-12 ‡⁵SMaloney (9) (led tl hdd 10f out:
chsd ldrs: kpt on same pce u.p fnl 3f) ......................... nk.4

1188 Desert Mist (35) (bl) *(SirMarkPrescott)* 8-7 LCharnock (8) (sn w ldr: led 10f out tl
over 3f out: wandered & nt r.o) ................................ 1½.5

1286* Miss Pin Up (49) (Fav) *(PatMitchell)* 8-4 (4x) ‡³DBiggs (1) (lw: trckd ldrs: effrt
over 4f out: no imp) ............................................. ¾.6

1316³ A a Bamba (56) *(NACallaghan)* 8-7 ‡⁷JTate (5) (dwlt s: hld up: hdwy over 4f out:
rdn & wknd over 2f out) ........................................ 5.7

810 Elgin (41) *(ABailey)* 7-13 AMackay (6) (plld hrd early: prom tl lost pl 7f out) ..... nk.8

1234³ Mr Elk (37) *(MrsGRReveley)* 8-1⁽¹⁾ RHills (3) (a bhd: reminders ½-wy) ......... 7.9

1048* Tricycle (IRE) (46) *(JWWatts)* 8-4 JLowe (2) (lw: trckd ldrs tl rdn & lost pl over 3f
out: sn bhd) ...................................................... 1.10

11/10 Miss Pin Up, 5/1 Tricycle (IRE), 11/2 A a Bamba, 10/1 Pharlander (IRE), 12/1 Mr Elk, 14/1 THAKAWAH,
Kadari, 16/1 Escadaro (USA), 20/1 Desert Mist, 25/1 Elgin. CSF £172.18, CT £2,859.76. Tote £23.30: £4.10
£3.60 £9.10 (£67.20). Mr Hamdan Al-Maktoum (NEWMARKET) bred by Shadwell Estate Company Limited. 10
Rn
3m 28.5 (3.5)
SF—40/25/–/7/–/10

T/Plpt: £48.20 (54.65 Tckts).                                                                   WG

955a— **SAINT-CLOUD** (L-H)

**Monday, June 8th [Heavy]**

Going Allowance: 0.80 sec per fur (S)

**1492a**  PRIX DE ROYAUMONT (Gp 3) (3-Y.O.F) £20640.00   1½m

379a² **Berceau (USA)** *(France)* 3-9-2 PatEddery ........................................... —1

837a³ Triple Tiara (USA) *(France)* 3-9-2 SCauthen .......................................... ¾.2

Shamawna (IRE) *(France)* 3-9-2 WMongil ............................................ 1½.3
Tote 9.90f: 4.20f 1.90f (12.30f). Mr K.Abdulla (A.Fabre,FRANCE) bred by Rhydian Morgan Jones in USA. 7 Rn
2m 42.3 (12)
SF—78/76/73

**1493a**　　PRIX DE LA JONCHERE (Gp 3) (3-Y.O.C & G) £20640.00　**1m**

842⁶ Take Risks (FR) *(France)* 3-8-11 MBoutin .......................................... —1
655 Steinbeck (USA) *(France)* 3-9-1 SCauthen ......................................... 1.2
1094a² Standiford (USA) *(France)* 3-8-11 PatEddery ..................................... s.h.3
Tote 3.90f: 1.60f 1.20f 1.30f (10.10f). Mr D.Tsui (J.Lesbordes,FRANCE) bred by Haras de Manneville in France.
8 Rn
1m 47.7 (9.1)
SF—58/58/54

1352a—**CHANTILLY (R-H)**

**Tuesday, June 9th [Good]**

Going Allowance: minus 0.10 sec per fur (F)

**1494a**　　PRIX DU CHEMIN DE FER DU NORD (Gp 3)　£20640.00　**1m**

As Que To (FR) (bl) *(France)* 4-8-11 DBoeuf ............................................ —1
838a³ Star Of Cozzene (USA) *(France)* 4-9-1 FHead ................................... 1½.2
Hello Pink (FR) *(France)* 4-8-11 ABadel ................................................ s.h.3
Tote 6.40f: 1.60f 1.30f (SF: 15.50f). Mr E.Zorbibe (E.Lellouche,FRANCE) bred by Olivier Nicol in France. 6 Rn
1m 38.8 (2.1)
SF—55/53/49

**TIPPERARY (L-H)**

**Thursday, June 11th [Good to soft]**

**1495a**　　KENTZ CORPORATION CONCORDE STKS (Gp 3)　£10748.00　**7f**

Rami (USA) (bl) *(Ireland)* 5-9-7 MJKinane (hld up: hdwy over 2f out: chal over
1f out: led wl ins fnl f: r.o) ....................................................... —1
Poolesta (IRE) (Fav) *(Ireland)* 3-8-6 JPMurtagh (prom: chal 2f out: jnd ldrs over
1f out: rdn, hdd & no ex wl ins fnl f: kpt on) ........................... ¾.2
Malvernico (IRE) *(Ireland)* 4-9-7 CRoche (chsd ldr: rdn & jnd ldr over 1f out: kpt
on) ................................................................................. ½.3
1463 ARANY (MHTompkins) 5-9-7 CHodgson (prom tl nt clr run over 1f out: swtchd
& r.o ins fnl f) .................................................................. 1.4
1350a Bradawn Breever (IRE) (bl) *(Ireland)* 3-9-7 RJGriffiths (led tl hdd over 1f out: sn
wknd) ............................................................................. 1½.5
Albona (bl) *(Ireland)* 4-9-4 DavidEddery (in rr tl sme hdwy fnl 2f: n.d) ........... ¾.6
Them Times (IRE) (bl) *(Ireland)* 3-8-6 PVGilson (hld up: sme hdwy over 2f out:
sn bhn) ........................................................................... 5.7
1097a Caurselle (IRE) *(Ireland)* 3-8-6 KJManning (n.d: bhd fnl 2f) ................... 8.8

7/4 Poolesta (IRE), 5/2 RAMI (USA), 5/1 Malvernico (IRE), Arany, 8/1 Caurselle (IRE), 14/1 Bradawn Breever
(IRE), 20/1 Albona, 25/1 Them Times (IRE). Tote £3.30: £1.50 £1.40 £1.70 (£4.40). Mr Hamdan Al-Maktoum
(D.K.Weld,IRELAND) bred by Clovelly Farms in USA. 8 Rn
1m 34.4

1223a—**CAPANNELLE (R-H)**

**Friday, June 12th [Heavy]**

**1496a**　　CRITERIUM DI ROMA (Gp 3) (2-Y.O) £27907.00　**6f**

Future Storm (USA) *(Italy)* 2-8-8 VMezzatesta (fin 2nd, ¾l: awrdd r) ............... —1
1223a★ Mister Naif (USA) *(Italy)* 2-8-11 FJovine (fin 1st: disq: plcd 2nd) ........... 2
Rossi Ernesto (ITY) *(Italy)* 2-8-11 ALuongo (fin 4th, ¾l: plcd 3rd) ............... 3
Secrage (USA) *(Italy)* 2-8-8 BJovine (fin 5th, 6½l: plcd 4th) ..................... 4
1103★ FUTURBALLA (JLDunlop) 2-8-11 LPiggott (fin 3rd, 3½l: disq: plcd 5th) .......... 5
*Stewards Enquiry: Mister Naif (USA) disq. (interference to Future Storm (USA) ins fnl f). Futurballa disq. (interference
to Secrage (USA)).*

Tote 46L: 21L 20L 34L (68L). A.J.B.Stable (A.Renzoni,ITALY) bred by Overbrook Farm in USA. 6 Rn  1m 12.5

380a—**EVRY (R-H)**

**Saturday, June 13th [Good]**

Going Allowance: minus 0.25 sec per fur (F)

**1497a**　　GRAND PRIX D'EVRY (Gp 2)　£36120.00　**1½m**

743a² Pistolet Bleu (IRE) (Jt-Fav) *(France)* 4-8-9 DBoeuf (hld up: 6th st: hdwy wl
over 1f out: led ins fnl f: easily) ........................................... —1

743a[5] Art Bleu (bl) (Jt-Fav) *(France)* 5–8–10[(1)] CAubert (trckd ldr: 2nd st: led 2f out tl ins fnl f: r.o) ............................................................. ¹/₂.2

1231a Magic Night (FR) *(France)* 4–8–13 ABadel (last st: hdwy over 1f out: fin fast: nrst fin) ....................................................................... 1¹/₂.3

955a[6] Toulon *(France)* 4–9–2 PatEddery (s.s: hdwy & 3rd st: effrt over 1f out: kpt on one pce) .................................................................. 1¹/₂.4

743a[4] Fortune's Wheel (IRE) *(France)* 4–8–13 MBoutin (mid div: 5th st: effrt over 1f out: unable qckn) ............................................... 5.5

641a* Fabulous Hostess (USA) *(France)* 4–8–6 GGuignard (7th st: effrt wl over 1f out: sn btn) ......................................................... ¹/₂.6

Sagace's Choice (USA) *(France)* 4–8–6 DRegnard (mid div: 4th st: one pce: wknd fnl f) .................................................................. ³/₄.7

Exploration (USA) (bl) *(France)* 5–8–9 GToupel (led tl hdd 2f out: sn wknd) ....... 4.8

**6/10** PISTOLET BLEU (IRE), Art Bleu (bl) (Jt-Fav) *(France)* 5–8–10[(1)], **11/4** Fabulous Hostess (USA), **9/2** Toulon, Exploration (USA), **23/4** Magic Night (FR), **11/1** Fortune's Wheel (IRE), **29/1** Sagace's Choice (USA). Tote 1.60f: 1.10f 2.30f 1.20f (29.40f). Mr D.Wildenstein (E.Lellouche,FRANCE) bred by Dayton Ltd. in Ireland. 8 Rn
2m 29.81 (0.21)
SF–63/62/63/63/50/42

## 1356a—CHANTILLY (R-H)
### Sunday, June 14th [Good]
Going Allowance: minus 0.10 sec per fur (F)

**1498a**  PRIX DE DIANE HERMES (Gp 1) (3-Y.O.F) £144479.00  1¹/₄m 110y

1098a[2] Jolypha (USA) *(France)* 3–9–2 PatEddery (a cl up: 4th st: led 2f out: r.o wl) ...... —1

1098a Sheba Dancer (FR) *(France)* 3–9–2 ELegrix (bhd early: last st: hdwy on outside 3f out: r.o wl ins fnl f) ............................................. 1.2

1098a[3] Verveine (USA) *(France)* 3–9–2 DBoeuf (hld up: 11th st: hdwy fr 2f out: nrst fin) s.h.3

958a[3] Guislaine (FR) *(France)* 3–9–2 CAsmussen (mid div: 8th st: hdwy 2f out: r.o fnl f) 1¹/₂.4

1098a* Rosefinch (USA) *(France)* 3–9–2 SCauthen (2nd st: ev ch 2f out: kpt on one pce fnl f) ................................................................... s.nk.5

845a[3] Urban Sea (USA) *(France)* 3–9–2 MBoutin (7th st: n.m.r 2f out: gd late hdwy: nrst fin) ................................................................. ¹/₂.6

1098a[4] Trishyde (USA) (Fav) *(France)* 3–9–2 FHead (trckd ldrs: 5th st: effrt 2f out: nt clr run: unable qckn fnl f) ............................................ 3.7

1098a[6] Good to Dance (IRE) *(France)* 3–9–2 TJarnet (in rr: 10th st: unable qckn: n.d) .. ¹/₂.8

934* OUMALDAAYA (USA) *(JLDunlop)* 3–9–2 WCarson (led tl hdd 2f out: sn wknd) nose.9

Decided Air (IRE) *(France)* 3–9–2 WRSwinburn (9th st: n.d) ................... 10.10

African Peace (USA) *(France)* 3–9–2 SGuillot (6th st: sn wknd) ............... 11

837a* Garendare *(France)* 3–9–2 WMongil (trckd ldrs: 3rd st: sn wknd) ........... 12

**9/4** Trishyde (USA), **36/10** JOLYPHA (USA), **4/1** Guislaine (FR), **19/4** Rosefinch (USA), Decided Air (IRE), African Peace (USA), **21/4** Garendare, Verveine (USA), **10/1** Oumaldaaya (USA), **17/1** Good to Dance (IRE), **24/1** Urban Sea (USA), **29/1** Sheba Dancer (FR). Tote 4.60f: 1.70f 6.10f 2.20f (88.70f). Mr K.Abdulla (A.Fabre,FRANCE) bred by Juddmonte Farms Inc. in USA. 12 Rn
2m 9.5 (0.8)
SF–84/82/81/78/77/76/70

**1499a**  PRIX DU LYS (Gp 3) (3-Y.O.C & G) £20640.00  1¹/₂m

Songlines (FR) *(France)* 3–8–9 OBenoist ............................................. —1

Non Partisan (USA) *(France)* 3–8–9 PatEddery .................................. 1.2

Mendocino (USA) *(France)* 3–8–9 FHead .......................................... s.h.3

Tote 4.60f: 1.90f 1.60f (SF: 11.90f). Sir R.McAlpine (E.Bartholomew,FRANCE) bred by Sir R.McAlpine in France.
5 Rn
2m 33.6 (5.6)
SF–27/26/25

## 859—NEWMARKET (R-H) July Course
### Friday, June 19th [Good]
Going Allowance: minus 0.05 sec per fur (G)  Wind: mod half bhd

Stalls: high

**1500**  CLICQUOT ROSE APP'CE H'CAP (0-85) £3132.00 (£936.00: £448.00: £204.00)
7f  6-45 (6-46)

(Weights raised 6 lb)

482 **Native Idol (USA) (77)** *(JRFanshawe)* 3–9–1 ‡[7]NVarley (7) (trckd ldrs: led ins fnl f: rdn out) ........................................................... —1

1201 Dream Carrier (IRE) **(65)** (bl) *(RHannon)* 4–8–12 ‡[7]DO'Neill (10) (lw: chsd ldrs: rdn 2f out: r.o fnl f) ............................................. 1.2

**1501—1502**

698 Tajigrey (48) *(RCurtis)* 3–7-3 ‡⁴CHawksley (2) (dwlt: rdn 3f out: r.o wl appr fnl f) .......... s.h.3
1303 Takenhall (61) *(MJFetherston-Godley)* 7–9-1 MichaelDenaro (3) (lw: in tch:
lost pl 3f out: r.o appr fnl f) ........................................................ nk.4
1258* Skipper to Bilge (69) *(MAJarvis)* 5–9-9 KRutter (9) (lw: led over 4f: btn appr fnl f) 1¹⁄₂.5
Mel's Rose (70) *(DrJDScargill)* 7–9-6 ‡⁴BLane (1) (prom: ev ch 2f out: r.o one
pce) ................................................................ nk.6
1411⁵ Millsolin (IRE) (55) *(ARDavison)* 4–8-2 ‡⁷RRussell (4) (prom: led over 2f out tl
hdd & wknd ins fnl f) ........................................................ ¹⁄₂.7
1379⁶ Pimsboy (55) (bl) *(PABlockley)* 5–8-2 ‡⁷GParkin (5) (a.p: ev ch over 1f out: sn
wknd) ........................................................ ³⁄₄.8
1391² Waders Dream (IRE) (72) (Fav) *(JEBanks)* 3–9-3 LNewton (6) (lw: hld up: hdwy
over 2f out: ev ch over 1f out: sn rdn & wknd) ...................... 4.9
1136⁶ Executive Spirit (74) *(DSasse)* 3–8-12 ‡⁷DDunnachie (8) (prom over 3f: t.o) ... 10.10
LONG HANDICAP: Tajigrey 7-2.
*Stewards Enquiry: Newton suspended 28-29/6/92 (excessive use of whip).*

**5/4** Waders Dream (IRE), **9/2** Skipper to Bilge, **11/2** Takenhall, **11/1** Pimsboy, **12/1** Millsolin (IRE)(op 8/1),
Dream Carrier (IRE), NATIVE IDOL (USA), **14/1** Mel's Rose, **20/1** Executive Spirit, **50/1** Tajigrey. CSF £132.07,
CT £6,131.84. Tote £13.40: £2.80 £3.90 £10.40 (£125.00). Mr David Thompson (NEWMARKET) bred by
Cheveley Park Stud in USA. 10 Rn
1m 27.06 (2.66)
SF—56/50/26/51/54/50

**1501**    ST PETERSBURG H'CAP (0-90) £3817.50 (£1140.00: £545.00: £247.50)
1¹⁄₂m
7-15 (7-17)

1298* **Brier Creek (USA)** (75) (Fav) *(JHMGosden)* 3–8-10 (5x) RCochrane (6) (lw:
hld up: gd hdwy over 2f out: led ins fnl f: rdn out) ................. —1
1153⁶ Bescaby Boy (61) *(JWharton)* 6–8-11 JWilliams (10) (hld up: hdwy 3f out: r.o fnl
f) ........................................................ 1¹⁄₂.2
1452⁴ Luks Akura (44) (v) *(MJohnston)* 4–7-1⁽¹⁾ (5x) ‡⁷CHawksley (5) (led tl wknd &
hdd ins fnl f) ........................................................ 3.3
1211 Kaytak (FR) (70) *(JRJenkins)* 5–9-6 PatEddery (9) (hld up: hdwy 3f out: one
pce appr fnl f) ........................................................ 1.4
1318² Sharp Top (48) *(MJRyan)* 4–7-9⁽²⁾ ‡³DBiggs (2) (chsd ldrs 8f) ................... 2¹⁄₂.5
1381 Paris of Troy (67) *(NATwiston-Davies)* 4–9-3 GCarter (8) (chsd ldrs over 9f) .... 15.6
1150² High Savannah (66) *(MAJarvis)* 4–8-11 ‡⁵RRutter (3) (chsd ldrs 6f) ............ 1¹⁄₂.7
1147 Briggsmaid (56) *(JMPEustace)* 4–8-6 MTebbutt (7) (swtg: bhd fnl 4f) .............. nk.8
1211 Latour (64) *(CEBrittain)* 4–9-0 MRoberts (4) (effrt ¹⁄₂-wy: nvr trbld ldrs) ....... ¹⁄₂.9
1088* Mr Flood (USA) (89) *(MrsJCecil)* 3–9-10 PaulEddery (1) (lw: chsd ldrs 7f) ....... 5.10
LONG HANDICAP: Luks Akura 7-6.

**10/11** BRIER CREEK (USA)(op 6/4), **6/1** Sharp Top, **7/1** Kaytak (FR), Mr Flood (USA), **9/1** High Savannah, **10/1**
Latour, **12/1** Paris of Troy, Bescaby Boy, Luks Akura(op 8/1), **20/1** Briggsmaid. CSF £15.65, CT £102.30. Tote
£2.20: £1.10 £2.60 £2.70 (£13.60). Sheikh Mohammed (NEWMARKET) bred by Allen E Paulson in USA. 10 Rn
2m 33.70 (5)
SF—40/38/8/39/7/1

**1502**    NICOLE PONSARDIN STKS (Mdn 2-Y.O) £3817.50 (£1140.00: £545.00: £247.50)
6f
7-45 (7-49)

1249³ **Woodenville (USA)** (Fav) *(LMCumani)* 9-0 LDettori (6) (led tl ins fnl f: rdn to ld
wl ins fnl f) ........................................................ —1
Covered Wagon (USA) *(JHMGosden)* 9-0 PatEddery (10) (scope: bit bkwd: w
wnr: led ins fnl f: sn hld & nt qckn) ........................................ ³⁄₄.2
Chain Dance *(MRStoute)* 8-9 WRSwinburn (8) (unf: scope: hdwy over 1f out:
fin wl) ........................................................ 2.3
Timothy Casey *(NCWright)* 9-0 GDuffield (13) (str: scope: bkwd: prom: one
pce appr fnl f) ........................................................ 1¹⁄₂.4
Miss Fayruz (IRE) *(MrsLPiggott)* 8-9 JWilliams (4) (unf: b.hind: chsd ldrs over
3f) ........................................................ 3¹⁄₂.5
Lagen *(CEBrittain)* 8-11 ‡³RonHillis (11) (w'like: scope: bkwd: in tch: rdn 2f out:
sn btn) ........................................................ 1.6
Blue Blazer *(BHanbury)* 9-0 AShoults (7) (leggy: scope: bit bkwd: in tch over 3f) 1¹⁄₂.7
Keltic Danseuse (IRE) *(MrsLPiggott)* 8-2 ‡⁷GMilligan (12) (lt-f: prom over 3f: btn
whn hung lft fnl f) ........................................................ 1¹⁄₂.8
Prairie Grove *(RHannon)* 8-9 BRaymond (2) (leggy: scope: dwlt: bhd fnl 3f) ... s.h.9
Honour and Glory *(BobJones)* 9-0 VSmith (3) (lengthy: bit bkwd: dwlt: wl bhd tl
sme late hdwy) ........................................................ nk.10
Divine Rain *(JWPayne)* 9-0 RCochrane (9) (w'like: leggy: bit bkwd: dwlt:
outpcd) ........................................................ 2¹⁄₂.11
Keating (AUS) *(MrsJCecil)* 9-0 PaulEddery (1) (scope: bkwd: spd 3f: t.o) ....... 15.12

Cuddly Date *(DTThom)* 8-4 ‡⁵EmmaO'Gorman (5) (scope: bit bkwd: s.i.s: rdn & rn green ½-wy: t.o) ............................................ **13**

4/5 WOODENVILLE (USA)(op 5/4), 4/1 Timothy Casey, 7/1 Covered Wagon (USA), 8/1 Chain Dance(6/1—9/1), 14/1 Keating (AUS), 16/1 Prairie Grove, 33/1 Divine Rain, Lagen, Miss Fayruz (IRE), Keltic Danseuse (IRE), 40/1 Honour and Glory, Blue Blazer, 50/1 Cuddly Date. CSF £8.16, Tote £2.00: £1.10 £1.70 £2.80 (£4.30). Mr Richard L. Duchossois (NEWMARKET) bred by L. Clay Camp & Wylie Tuttle in USA. 13 Rn  1m 15.17 (3.67)
SF—20/17/4/3/–/–

## 1503
YELLOW LABEL CLAIMING STKS (3-Y.O) £3184.00 (£952.00: £456.00: £208.00)
1m
8-15 (8-19)

1214⁴ **First Century (IRE) (79)** *(PFICole)* 9-0 TQuinn (9) (w ldrs: led 3f out tl over 1f out: rallied to ld ins fnl f) ......................................... —1
1308 Al Ramis (IRE) **(73)** (Fav) *(CEBrittain)* 8-8 MRoberts (10) (a.p: led over 1f out tl ins fnl f: r.o) ......................................... nk.2
1374⁶ By Arrangement (IRE) **(69)** *(RGuest)* 7-13 WCarson (7) (prom: outpcd 3f out: kpt on appr fnl f) ......................................... 3½.3
1895⁵ A Nymph Too Far (IRE) **(50)** *(DrJDSCargill)* 7-13 DHolland (4) (b.hind: chsd ldrs: rdn over 2f out: kpt on same pce) ......................................... 2.4
1374⁵ Captain Marmalade **(63)** *(DTThom)* 9-0 SWebster (6) (dwlt: r.o fnl 2f: nrst fin) ... 4.5
1320 Roxy Music (IRE) **(68)** *(GAPritchard-Gordon)* 8-0 ‡⁵DHarrison (12) (hdwy 4f out: wknd over 1f out) ......................................... s.h.6
1281⁶ Mansber (IRE) **(55)** *(PatMitchell)* 8-11 ‡³DBiggs (8) (chsd ldrs 4f) ......................................... 1½.7
1145★ Norman Warrior *(DMorris)* 8-7 ‡⁷StephenDavies (11) (bhd: rdn 4f out: nvr rchd ldrs) ......................................... nk.8
857 Rose Edge *(JWHills)* 9-0 RHills (5) (led 5f: sn wknd: t.o) ......................................... 10.9
1158 After the Fire *(ANLee)* 8-4 JQuinn (3) (t: a bhd: t.o) ......................................... 2.10
1276 Swan Star **(37)** *(GBlum)* 8-3 RFox (2) (s.i.s: hdwy 5f out: wknd 3f out: t.o) ..... s.h.11
1070 Legend Dulac (IRE) (8/1) Withdrawn (bolted bef s) : not under orders — Rule 4 applies

9/4 Al Ramis (IRE)(7/4—3/1), 3/1 FIRST CENTURY (IRE), 5/1 Norman Warrior, 8/1 By Arrangement (IRE), 12/1 A Nymph Too Far (IRE), 14/1 Roxy Music (IRE), 16/1 Captain Marmalade, 25/1 Mansber (IRE), Rose Edge, 33/1 Ors. CSF £8.99, Tote £3.80: £1.80 £1.30 £1.90 (£3.60). Lord Donoughmore (WHATCOMBE) bred by Limestone Stud in Ireland. 11 Rn
1m 40.81 (3.11)
SF—47/40/20/14/17/2

## 1504
LE PRIX DE LA GRANDE DAME H'CAP (0-90) £5299.00 (£1582.00: £756.00: £343.00)
1m
8-45 (8-47)

1366³ **Blockade (USA) (67)** *(MBell)* 3-8-3 MHills (2) (t: mde all: rdn out) ......................................... —1
Northern Rainbow **(74)** *(PFICole)* 4-9-6 TQuinn (4) (lw: a.p: chsd wnr fr ½-wy: no imp fnl f) ......................................... 1.2
1246★ Combative (IRE) **(83)** (v) (Fav) *(JHMGosden)* 3-9-5 PatEddery (1) (chsd ldrs: rdn over 1f out) ......................................... 2.3
1303⁵ Mahsul (IRE) **(55)** *(CJBenstead)* 4-8-1 GDuffield (11) (hdwy over 1f out: nrst fin) 1.4
1061 Wesaam (USA) **(90)** (bl) *(MajorWRHern)* 3-9-12 WCarson (7) (chsd ldrs: bmpd 2f out: kpt one pce) ......................................... 1½.5
1402⁶ Regent Lad **(74)** *(MissLCSiddall)* 2-9-6 MRoberts (3) (lw: r.o u.p fnl 2f: nvr able to chal) ......................................... ½.6
1133 Candle King (IRE) **(53)** (bl) *(MJFetherston-Godley)* 4-7-8 ‡⁵DHarrison (13) (hdwy 3f out: wknd wl over 1f out) ......................................... 1½.7
1212 Princess Tara **(76)** *(GLewis)* 4-9-8 PaulEddery (6) (chsd ldrs: rdn & hung rt 2f out: r.o) ......................................... 1.8
1339² Taunting (IRE) **(57)** *(MBlanshard)* 4-8-3 JQuinn (8) (lw: nvr nr to chal) ......................................... 10.9
Sistadari **(70)** *(LMCumani)* 4-9-2 LDettori (12) (bhd fnl 4f) ......................................... 1.10
1261 Rise Up Singing **(74)** *(WJMusson)* 4-9-6 RCochrane (5) (chsd: a bhd) ......................................... ¾.11
1308 Hadaad (USA) **(81)** *(AAScott)* 3-9-3 WRSwinburn (10) (spd 4f: sn wknd) ...... 1½.12
1376⁴ China Sky **(47)** *(CNAllen)* 4-7-7 GBardwell (9) (plld hrd: prom 5f) ......................................... s.h.13
LONG HANDICAP: China Sky 7-3.

3/1 Combative (IRE)(op 7/4), 9/2 Princess Tara, 5/1 BLOCKADE (USA), 7/1 Mahsul (IRE), 8/1 Wesaam (USA)(tchd 12/1), 9/1 Hadaad (USA), 10/1 Taunting (IRE), 12/1 Sistadari(op 8/1), 14/1 Rise Up Singing, Regent Lad, 16/1 Northern Rainbow, China Sky, 25/1 Candle King. CSF £83.86, CT £270.49. Tote £8.00: £2.40 £8.30 £2.20 (£153.20). Mr A. M. Warrender (NEWMARKET) bred by Patricia C. Warrender in USA. 13 Rn
1m 39.44 (1.74)
SF—57/71/64/43/63/55

## 1505
WIDOW STKS (Mdn 3-Y.O) £4045.00 (£1210.00: £580.00: £265.00)
1¼m
9-15 (9-19)

835² **Dress Sense (IRE)** (Fav) *(LMCumani)* 9-0 LDettori (4) (chsd ldrs: rdn over 1f out: qcknd to ld ins fnl f) ......................................... —1

United Kingdom (USA) *(HRACecil)* 8-9 SCauthen (3) (lt-f: unf: a.p: qcknd to ld over 1f out: hdd & no ex ins fnl f) ............................................. 1.2

710³ Iftakhaar (USA) *(MajorWRHern)* 9-0 WCarson (7) (lw: led over 8f: sn outpcd) . 1¹/₂.3

Anna of Saxony *(JHMGosden)* 8-9 RCochrane (5) (unf: scope: s.i.s: stdy hdwy over 1f out: nrst fin) ............................................................. ¹/₂.4

Al Karnak (IRE) *(MMoubarak)* 8-7 ‡⁷StephenDavies (12) (scope: bit bkwd: chsd ldrs: kpt on one pce fnl 2f) ......................................................... nk.5

Resplendent *(NCWright)* 8-9 GDuffield (15) (prom over 7f) ................................ 2.6

Jade Mistress *(AHide)* 8-9 JWilliams (11) (lengthy: bit bkwd: hld up: nvr plcd to chal) ................................................................................ 4.7

Savash (USA) *(MMoubarak)* 9-0 TQuinn (1) (lw: hdwy over 2f out: wknd over 1f out) ................................................................................... 1.8

Wild Applause (IRE) *(JHMGosden)* 8-9 PatEddery (2) (w'like: leggy: hld up: stdy hdwy 4f out: eased whn btn appr fnl f) ...................................... 3.9

370 Port in a Storm *(WJarvis)* 9-0 WRSwinburn (10) (lw: plld hrd: chsd ldr 8f) ...... s.h.10

Maligned (IRE) *(JRFanshawe)* 8-9 GCarter (13) (w'like: bit bkwd: nvr nr to chal) 1.11

1175 Socks and Shares (66) *(PWHarris)* 9-0 PaulEddery (14) (prom over 7f) ........ 2¹/₂.12

1176³ Alcoy (IRE) (68) *(PAKelleway)* 9-0 PRobinson (8) (t: lw: chsd ldrs tl rdn & wknd over 2f out) ............................................................... 3.13

1182 Princess Evita (FR) *(RGuest)* 8-2 ‡⁷SEiffert (9) (a bhd: t.o) ........................... 12.14

Old Fox (FR) *(DSasse)* 9-0 WRyan (6) (leggy: a bhd: t.o) .............................. 6.15

**7/4** DRESS SENSE (IRE), **4/1** Iftakhaar (USA)(op 7/1), **5/1** United Kingdom (USA)(op 9/4), Savash (USA)(op 8/1), **7/1** Wild Applause (IRE)(4/1—8/1), **20/1** Resplendent, Alcoy (IRE), Anna of Saxony, **25/1** Port in a Storm, **33/1** Socks and Shares, Al Karnak (IRE), Maligned (IRE), **40/1** Old Fox (FR), **50/1** Ors. CSF £12.15, Tote £2.90: £1.40 £2.00 £1.80 (£4.20). Sheikh Mohammed (NEWMARKET) bred by Mrs R. B. Kennard in Ireland. 15 Rn
2m 8.94 (6.34)
SF—32/25/27/21/18/16

T/Plpt: £116.00 (21.6 Tokto).     Dk

# AYR (L-H)

## Friday, June 19th [Firm, Good to firm patches]

Going Allowance: minus 0.20 sec per fur (F)     Wind: almost nil

Stalls: low

**1506**    CUNNING PARK STKS (Mdn 2-Y.O.F) £2148.00 (£603.00: £294.00)    **5f**   2-15 (2-16)

795⁵ Juliet Bravo (Jt-Fav) *(BBeasley)* 8-11 LCharnock (5) (lw: led after 1f: hld on wl fnl f) ................................................................................ —1

1233² Moving Image (IRE) *(MBell)* 8-11 GBaxter (4) (b.off hind: lw: a.p: hdwy ¹/₂-wy: ev ch ins fnl f: kpt on) ...................................................... ¹/₂.2

Minshaar *(BHanbury)* 8-11 GHind (3) (neat: unf: bit bkwd: s.i.s: hdwy ¹/₂-wy: sn chsng wnr: no ex fnl f) ................................................... 1¹/₂.3

1296² Peaceful Air *(EWeymes)* 8-11 ACulhane (2) (outpcd after 2f: styd on fnl f: nvr able to chal) ..................................................................... nk.4

1208⁵ Bergliot (Jt-Fav) *(JBerry)* 8-8 ‡³JFanning (1) (led 1f: cl up tl outpcd ¹/₂-wy: sn wknd) ................................................................................ 10.5

**5/2** Bergliot, JULIET BRAVO, **4/1** Peaceful Air, **6/1** Moving Image (IRE)(op 3/1), **8/1** Minshaar. CSF £13.68, Tote £4.30: £2.10 £1.80 (£7.90). Mrs Jan Hopper (HAMBLETON) bred by Lady Juliet de Chair. 5 Rn
60.33 sec (2.33)
SF—31/29/23/22/–

**1507**    DALMILLING (S) STKS (3-Y.O) £2232.00 (£627.00: £306.00)    **1m**   2-50 (2-55)

Cobblers Hill (56) *(JWhite)* 9-0 DaleGibson (5) (b: chsd ldrs: rdn ent st: hdwy to ld wl over 1f out: kpt on gamely) ............................................... —1

1309 Allegramente (60) (Fav) *(RO'Leary)* 8-9 LCharnock (4) (lw: trckd ldrs gng wl: smooth hdwy to disp ld over 2f out: hrd rdn: no ex nr fin) . nk.2

1145 Hataal (IRE) (39) *(JBalding)* 8-4 GHind (6) (outpcd & bhd tl r.o.u.p fnl 2f: nrst fin) 1¹/₂.3

1276² Throw Away Line (46) *(JEtherington)* 8-4 NConnorton (1) (chsd ldrs: rdn whn nt clr run & swtchd over 1f out: styd on one pce) ............ nk.4

223⁵ Meltonby (64) *(NTinkler)* 8-12 ‡³FNorton (2) (lw: led tl hdd wl over 1f out: grad wknd) ............................................................................... 2¹/₂.5

1334⁵ Ebony Isle (39) *(PMonteith)* 8-1 ‡³JFanning (3) (unruly s: outpcd appr st: wl bhd after) ............................................................................... 15.6

**15/8** Allegramente, **5/2** COBBLERS HILL, **3/1** Meltonby(op 2/1), **6/1** Throw Away Line(op 4/1), **11/1** Hataal (IRE), **100/1** Ebony Isle. CSF £7.27, Tote £4.90: £2.20 £1.50 (£12.60). Mr G. J. Green (WENDOVER) bred by B. C. Allen. 6 Rn; No bid
1m 41.14 (3.94)
SF—17/11/2/–/–/–

**1508** KIDSONS IMPEY TROPHY (H'cap) (0-90) £2872.00 (£856.00: £408.00: £184.00)
7f
3-25 (3-26)

1284 **Sir Arthur Hobbs (56)** (FHLee) 5–7-11 ‡5NKennedy (5) (effrt 3f out: qcknd to ld
1f out: r.o) ...................... —1
1345² Thrie-Na-Helah (IRE) **(70)** (v) (Fav) (RMWhitaker) 3–8-7 AColhane (1) (lw: chsd
ldrs: rdn to ld over 2f out: hdd 1f out: one pce) ................. 2¹/₂.2
1254 Tusky **(82)** (MJCamacho) 4–10-0 SMorris (3) (lw: effrt ent st: styd on: nvr able
to chal) ....................... 1¹/₂.3
1365⁴ Wild Prospect **(66)** (CTinkler) 4–8-12 LCharnock (6) (led tl hdd over 2f out:
wknd over 1f out) ....................... 1¹/₂.4
1403⁶ State Flyer **(58)** (v) (CBBBooth) 4–8-4 NConnorton (2) (lw: hld up: effrt over 2f
out: hrd rdn & no imp) ....................... nk.5
872⁶ Never so Sure **(77)** (ABailey) 4–9-9 AMackay (4) (nvr plcd to chal) ......... 3.6
1403² Super Benz **(75)** (TFairhurst) 6–9-4 ‡3JFanning (7) (b.off fore: w ldrs: rdn 3f out:
wknd 2f out) ....................... 5.7

**5/2** Thrie-Na-Helah (IRE), **4/1** Super Benz, **9/2** Wild Prospect, **7/1** SIR ARTHUR HOBBS, **10/1** State Flyer(op
6/1), Never so Sure, **14/1** Tusky. CSF £21.45, Tote £9.40: £3.00 £2.00 (£17.50). Mr John Hardman
(WILMSLOW) bred by A. Tarry. 7 Rn                                  1m 24.97 (0.71 under best; 0.97)
SF—47/49/65/44/35/45

**1509** B.E.N. H'CAP (0-90) £2671.00 (£808.00: £394.00: £187.00)   **1¹/₄m**
4-00 (4-01)

1394* **Azureus (IRE) (71)** (Fav) (MrsGRReveley) 4–9-7 ‡7DarrenMoffatt (4) (lw: trckd
ldrs: led wl over 1f out: sn qknd clr) ....................... —1
1248³ Buckingham Band (USA) **(44)** (bl) (FHLee) 4–7-10 ‡5NKennedy (5) (lw: bhd:
effrt over 2f out: r.o wl nr fin) ....................... 1¹/₂.2
931² Execution Only (IRE) **(65)** (v) (JWWatts) 4–9-8 GHind (1) (trckd ldrs: effrt over 2f
out: r.o one pce fnl f) ....................... ¹/₂.3
777³ Princess Roxanne **(53)** (ABailey) 5–8-10 AMackay (3) (led tl hdd wl over 1f out:
grad lost pl) ....................... 2.4
1331* Shadideen (USA) **(67)** (MissLAPerratt) 4–9-7 (5x) ‡3JFanning (2) (lw: cl up tl rdn
& wknd over 1f out) ....................... 2¹/₂.5

**Evens** AZUREUS (IRE), **4/1** Execution Only (IRE), **5/1** Buckingham Band (USA), **8/1** Princess Roxanne, **9/1**
Shadideen (USA). CSF £5.71, Tote £2.00: £1.20 £2.20 (£7.80). Mr J. C. Murdoch (SALTBURN) bred by
Ballygoran Stud in Ireland. 5 Rn                                  2m 8.99 (3.69)
SF—50/22/47/31/37

**1510** SNODGRASS MEDIAN AUCTION STKS (Mdn 3-Y.O) £2445.00 (£600.00)
1m 5f 13y
4-35 (4-35)

1074² **Suez Canal (IRE) (74)** (Fav) (PWChapple-Hyam) 8-11 ‡3FNorton (2) (lw: mde
all: v.easily) ....................... —1
Double Sherry (RMWhitaker) 8-9 AColhane (1) (leggy: unf: a chsng wnr: rdn
over 2f out: no imp) ....................... ¹/₂.2

**1/5** SUEZ CANAL (IRE), **4/1** Double Sherry. Tote £1.30. Mr R. E. Sangster (MARLBOROUGH) bred by
Swettenham Stud in Ireland. 2 Rn                                  2m 55.08 (8.88)

**1511** ROZELLE H'CAP (0-90) £2570.00 (£720.00: £350.00)   **5f**
5-10 (5-10)

1393³ **Beau Venture (USA) (84)** (Fav) (FHLee) 4–9-7 ‡5NKennedy (1) (lw: trckd ldrs:
effrt over 1f out: qcknd to ld cl home: cleverly) ................. —1
1392* Martina **(70)** (JWharton) 4–8-9 (7x) ‡3FNorton (2) (lw: led: qcknd 2f out: r.o: no
ex nr fin) ....................... ¹/₂.2
676 Consulate **(65)** (JBalding) 6–8-7 GHind (3) (bhd: effrt 2f out: styd on wl nr fin) .. 3.3
1053⁶ Barrys Gamble **(81)** (bl) (TFairhurst) 6–9-6 ‡3JFanning (5) (sn chsng ldrs: hrd
drvn 2f out: r.o one pce) ....................... nk.4
1392⁵ Gorinsky (IRE) **(76)** (bl) (JBerry) 4–9-4 LCharnock (4) (lw: chsd ldrs tl outpcd
appr fnl f) ....................... 3.5

**6/4** BEAU VENTURE (USA), **7/2** Martina, Gorinsky (IRE), **6/1** Barrys Gamble, **14/1** Consulate(op 7/1). CSF £6.23,
Tote £3.10: £1.50 £1.90 (£4.20). Mrs A. L. Stacey (WILMSLOW) bred by Mrs C. Oliver Iselin III in USA. 5 Rn
59.17 sec (1.17)
SF—64/50/36/48/34

T/Plpt: £104.50 (10.35 Tckts).                                                               AA

# AYR (L-H)
## Saturday, June 20th [Firm]
Going Allowance: 5f-8f: minus 0.20 sec; Rest: minus 0.40 sec (F)　　　　Wind: slt against

Stalls: low

**1512**　　　GREENWELL MONTAGU APP'CE H'CAP (0-70) £2190.00 (£615.00: £300.00)
　　　　　6f　　　　　　　　　　　　　　　　　　　　　　　　　　　　　　　2-15 (2-17)

269² **Nordan Raider (37)** (Fav) *(MJCamacho)* 4–7-13 JMarshall (2) (lw: w ldr: led 2f
　　　　　out: sn qcknd clr) .................................................... —1
1271 Chateau Nord (49) *(JBerry)* 3–7-12 ‡5PRoberts (1) (a chsng ldrs: styd on u.p fnl
　　　　　2f: no ch w wnr) .................................................... 3½.2
1310 Yes (54) *(DTThom)* 4–9-2 PBowe (4) (a chsng ldrs: effrt over 2f out: nvr able to
　　　　　chal) .................................................... 1½.3
1326⁴ Diet (66) (v) *(MissLAPerratt)* 6–10-0 RHavlin (6) (led 4f: sn rdn & btn) ............... 6.4
794⁶ B Grade (39) *(JBalding)* 7–8-1 ClaireBalding (7) (s.i.s: nvr trbld ldrs) ............... nk.5
1326² Nevada Mix (44) *(MissLAPerratt)* 8–8-6 DCarson (5) (lw: s.i.s: n.d) ............... 1½.6

**9/4** NORDAN RAIDER, **100/30** Diet, **7/2** Nevada Mix, **7/1** Yes, **8/1** B Grade, **14/1** Chateau Nord(op 8/1). CSF
£23.90, Tote £3.00: £1.80 £4.70 (£14.80). Miss J. A. Camacho (MALTON) bred by B. Nordan. 6 Rn
　　　　　　　　　　　　　　　　　　　　　　　　　　　　　1m 12.46 (2.06)
　　　　　　　　　　　　　　　　　　　　　　　　　　　　　SF—20/5/17/5/–/–

**1513**　　　BELLEISLE MEDIAN AUCTION STKS (2-Y-O) £2263.50 (£636.00: £310.50)
　　　　　5f　　　　　　　　　　　　　　　　　　　　　　　　　　　　　　　2-45 (2-47)

1240³ **Shadow Jury** *(JSWainwright)* 9-4 GBaxter (2) (lw: disp ld tl led 2f out: hdd & no
　　　　　ex ins fnl f: fin 2nd, 2l: awrdd r) .................................................... —1
1443★ Area Girl (Fav) *(SirMarkPrescott)* 8-13 GDuffield (4) (lw: disp ld: rdn 2f out: nt
　　　　　qckn fnl f: fin 3rd, s.h: plcd 2nd) .................................................... 2
　　　Scored Again *(RMWhitaker)* 8-11 ACulhane (5) (w'like: leggy: dwlt: hdwy &
　　　　　prom ½-wy: nt qckn fnl f: fin 4th, 2l: plcd 3rd) .................................................... 3
1196⁵ Two Moves in Front (IRE) *(JBerry)* 9-1 JCarroll (1) (disp ld 3f: btn whn hmpd
　　　　　over 1f out: fin 5th, 4l: plcd 4th) .................................................... 4
877² Finmental (IRE) *(ABailey)* 9-1 AMackay (3) (chsd ldrs: nt clr run & swtchd 1f out:
　　　　　led fnl f: r.o: fin 1st: disq: plcd last) .................................................... 0
*Stewards Enquiry: Finmental disq.(interference to Two Moves in Front). Mackay suspended 29/6-2/7/92 (careless
riding).*

**10/11** Area Girl, **7/4** Finmental (IRE)(Evens—6/4), **9/2** Scored Again(10/1—4/1), **20/1** SHADOW JURY(op 8/1),
**25/1** Two Moves in Front (IRE)(op 8/1). CSF £39.13, Tote £9.30: £2.50 £1.60 (£4.70). Mr J. H. Pickard
(MALTON) bred by J. S. Bell. 5 Rn　　　　　　　　　　　　　　　　　　　　60.53 sec (2.53)
　　　　　　　　　　　　　　　　　　　　　　　　　　　　　SF—25/19/9/–/30

**1514**　　　REDBURN H'CAP (3-Y-O) (0-70) £2514.00 (£704.00: £342.00)　**5f**　　3-15 (3-28)

1386² **Educated Pet (65)** (Fav) *(MJohnston)* 9-5 DMcKeown (2) (effrt ½-wy: led over
　　　　　1f out: r.o wl) .................................................... —1
1333★ Murray's Mazda (IRE) (67) *(JBerry)* 9-7 JCarroll (1) (lw: bhd: hdwy 2f out: ch
　　　　　over 1f out: r.o) .................................................... 2.2
1075⁵ Joyful Thought (47) (bl) *(MrsJRRamsden)* 8-1⁽²⁾ KDarley (5) (unruly gng to s:
　　　　　mde most tl hdd over 1f out: no ex) .................................................... 2.3
1282 Miss Siham (IRE) (52) *(JBalding)* 7-13 ‡7ClaireBalding (4) (chsd ldrs: ev ch wl
　　　　　over 1f out: nt qckn) .................................................... hd.4
1155 Hemsworth Lad (IRE) (64) *(PCalver)* 9-4 KDuffield (3) (cl up to ½-wy: sn wknd) 3.5

**5/4** EDUCATED PET, **100/30** Joyful Thought(op 2/1), **7/2** Murray's Mazda (IRE), **8/1** Miss Siham
(IRE)(12/1—20/1), **9/1** Hemsworth Lad (IRE)(op 4/1). CSF £5.68, Tote £2.40: £1.40 £1.90 (£2.60). Mr Billy
Morgan (MIDDLEHAM) bred by Highfield Stud Ltd. 5 Rn　　　　　　　　　59.96 sec (1.96)
　　　　　　　　　　　　　　　　　　　　　　　　　　　　　SF—46/40/12/9/16

**1515**　　　E.B.F.ROMAN WARRIOR SHIELD (Stks) (Mdn 2-Y-O) £2853.00 (£864.00: £422.00:
　　　　　£201.00)　**7f**　　　　　　　　　　　　　　　　　　　　　3-45 (3-57)

1296⁶ **Sweet Romeo** *(MJohnston)* 9-0 DMcKeown (4) (lw: disp ld tl led wl over 1f out:
　　　　　rdn & r.o wl) .................................................... —1
1249⁵ Harpoon Louie (USA) (Fav) *(MHEasterby)* 9-0 KDarley (10) (a.p: effrt over 2f
　　　　　out: hrd rdn & r.o wl) .................................................... nk.2
924 Fort Vally *(BWMurray)* 8-9 GBaxter (9) (plld hrd: trckd ldrs: effrt over 2f out: r.o) 1½.3
924 Lancaster Pilot *(RMWhitaker)* 9-0 ACulhane (3) (lw: disp ld over 5f: r.o one pce) 1½.4

1299² Prime Painter *(RFFisher)* 9-0 JLowe (12) (mid div & drvn along 3f out: styd on: no imp) .................................................................................................. nk.5
571 Ttyfran *(FHLee)* 9-0 RLappin (9) (hld up & bhd: hdwy over 2f out: nvr nr to chal) ½.6
720 Calcutta Flyer (IRE) *(PWChapple-Hyam)* 8-11 ‡³TSprake (6) (in tch: effrt 3f out: no imp) ....................................................................................................... hd.7
1332⁵ Lucky Owl *(PMonteith)* 8-2 ‡⁷RHavlin (7) (nvr trbld ldrs) ........................... 3½.8
Lawnswood Quay *(JBerry)* 9-0 JCarroll (1) (neat: lw: chsd ldrs 4f: sn lost pl) .. 1½.9
Rushalong *(RDEWoodhouse)* 8-7 ‡⁷JMarshall (2) (cmpt: bit bkwd: in tch to ½-wy) ................................................................................................................. ½.10
1327⁶ Lofty Deed (USA) *(SirMarkPrescott)* 9-0 GDuffield (11) (s.i.s: nvr wnt pce) .... 1½.11
1450 Volunteer Point (IRE) *(MrsSABramall)* 9-0 AMackay (8) (a bhd) ........................ ½.12

**Evens** Harpoon Louie (USA), **7/2** SWEET ROMEO, **13/2** Calcutta Flyer (IRE)(10/1—6/1), **8/1** Prime Painter, **14/1** Fort Vally, **16/1** Lofty Deed (USA), **20/1** Lancaster Pilot, Lawnswood Quay, **50/1** Ttyfran, Volunteer Point (IRE), **66/1** Lucky Owl, **100/1** Rushalong. CSF £7.36, Tote £6.20: £1.70 £1.50 £4.00 (£6.30). The Fairyhouse 1992 Partnership (MIDDLEHAM) bred by Somerhall Bloodstock Ltd. 12 Rn          1m 27.34 (3.34)
SF—29/28/18/18/17/15

---

**1516**   McMASTER STORES SCOTTISH H'CAP (3-Y.O) (0-90) £2762.00 (£836.00: £408.00: £194.00)   **1m**                                                                4-20 (4-28)

599 **Legendary (IRE) (65)** *(PWChapple-Hyam)* 7-11⁽³⁾ ‡³TSprake (1) (trckd ldrs: effrt over 2f out: swvd rt over 1f out: r.o wl to ld cl home) .... —1
1382 Red Kite **(63)** *(MBell)* 7-12 AMackay (5) (lw: set slow pce: qcknd over 1f out: r.o wl: jst ct) ...................................................................................................... ¾.2
1062³ Battle Colours (IRE) **(86)** *(SirMarkPrescott)* 7-7 GDuffield (3) (hld up: effrt 3f out: hdwy whn hmpd over 1f out: r.o wl) ................................................... nk.3
1312² Music in My Life (IRE) **(65)** (Fav) *(WJarvis)* 8-0 KDarley (6) (a.p: effrt 3f out: ch over 1f out: r.o one pce) .......................................................................... 1½.4
1391 Salda **(70)** *(RMWhitaker)* 8-5 ACulhane (4) (w ldr: effrt 3f out: wknd over 1f out) ½.5
1153 Tancred Grange **(70)** *(MissSEHall)* 8-5 JCarroll (4) (b.off hind: hld up: effrt ent st: sn rdn & no imp) ..................................................................................... 1½.6
883 North Esk (USA) **(81)** *(JWWatts)* 9-2 JLowe (2) (lw: hld up & bhd: nvr nr to chal) ¾.7

**11/4** Music in My Life (IRE), **3/1** Battle Colours (IRE), **9/2** Salda(tchd 3/1), **5/1** Red Kite(tchd 8/1), **7/1** Tancred Grange, **9/1** LEGENDARY (IRE), **16/1** North Esk (USA)(op 7/1). CSF £48.27, Tote £8.50: £3.20 £2.40 (£27.50). Mr R. E. Sangster (MARLBOROUGH) bred by Swettenham Stud in Ireland. 7 Rn          1m 41.03 (3.83)
SF—2/1/23/-/-/-

---

**1517**   LONGHILL CLAIMING STKS (Mdn 3-Y.O) £2232.00 (£627.00: £306.00) **1¼m**                                                                               4-50 (4-58)

1438⁴ **Breakdancer (IRE) (58)** *(MrsJRRamsden)* 8-5 GBaxter (3) (b.off fore: cl up: led ½-wy: qcknd ent st: r.o wl) ................................................................ —1
1109³ Miliyel *(PMonteith)* 7-7 ‡⁷RHavlin (2) (lw: hld up: effrt over 2f out: r.o: nt pce to chal) ......................................................................................................... 1½.2
1287 Master Copy (IRE) *(CBBooth)* 8-7 GOldroyd (1) (set slow pce to ½-wy: sn bhd: hdwy over 1f out: shkn up & r.o wl) ......................................................... ¾.3
1033⁶ Kaytura (Fav) *(MHTompkins)* 8-6 GDuffield (4) (hld up: effrt over 3f out: r.o one pce) ...................................................................................................... 2½.4
1441³ Bee Dee Ell (USA) **(46)** *(MissLAPerratt)* 8-9 JCarroll (5) (plld hrd: cl up tl outpcd fnl 2f) .......................................................................................................... 4.5

**8/11** Kaytura, **2/1** BREAKDANCER (IRE), **11/2** Miliyel(8/1—5/1), **9/1** Bee Dee Ell (USA), **25/1** Master Copy (IRE). CSF £12.54, Tote £3.40: £1.40 £1.60 (£5.40). Mr R. C. Moody (THIRSK) bred by Sheikh Mohammed bin Rashid al Maktoum in Ireland. 5 Rn, plld hrd: chsd J.Thom £8,600          2m 16.87 (11.57)

---

**1518**   DOONFOOT H'CAP (0-80) £2710.00 (£760.00: £370.00)   **1m 5f 13y**          5-20 (5-26)

1419★ **Beau Quest (65)** (Jt-Fav) *(RMWhitaker)* 5-9-9 ACulhane (5) (hdwy ent st: led over 1f out: r.o) ............................................................................ —1
1152⁴ Stapleton (IRE) **(73)** (Jt-Fav) *(JWWatts)* 3-9-1 GDuffield (9) (hld up: hdwy over 3f out: ev ch wl over 1f out: styd on wl towards fin) ............... ½.2
1269⁴ Cov Tel Lady **(65)** *(MHTompkins)* 3-8-7 AMackay (3) (lw: in tch: hdwy appr st: ev ch 2f out: nt pce towards fin) ................................................................. ½.3
675³ Bay Tern (USA) **(43)** *(MHEasterby)* 6-8-1 JLowe (6) (led after 2f tl hdd over 1f out: one pce) .......................................................................................... ½.4
761 Deb's Ball **(55)** *(DMoffatt)* 6-8-13 JCarroll (4) (hld up & bhd: swtchd & gd hdwy over 2f out: ev ch ins fnl f: wknd towards fin) ......................................... nk.5
1188⁵ Arctic Splendour (USA) **(58)** *(PWChapple-Hyam)* 3-7-11⁽³⁾ ‡³TSprake (7) (b.off hind: prom: effrt 3f out: wknd 2f out) .................................................. 12.6

1336★ Sír Norman Holt (IRE) **(57)** *(FHLee)* 3–7-13 RLappin (2) (lw: led 2f: cl up tl wknd
wl over 1f out) ............................................................................................ **4.7**
  533 Take One **(47)** *(RRLamb)* 6–7-12 ‡⁷RHavlin (8) (lw: cl up tl wknd wl over 2f out) 1½.8
14375 Alpha Helix **(37)** (v) *(MissLAPerratt)* 9–7-2⁽²⁾ ‡⁷ClaireBalding (10) (a wl bhd) ....... 2.9
     Hthaal (USA) **(68)** *(LLungo)* 4–9-12 DMcKeown (1) (bit bkwd: a bhd) .............. 1.10
LONG HANDICAP: Alpha Helix 7-2.

**7/2** BEAU QUEST, Stapleton (IRE), **9/2** Cov Tel Lady, **5/1** Sir Norman Holt (IRE), **11/2** Arctic Splendour
(USA)(4/1—6/1), **8/1** Deb's Ball, **10/1** Bay Tern (USA), **20/1** Hthaal (USA), **33/1** Take One, **50/1** Alpha Helix. CSF
£16.40, CT £52.95. Tote £4.70: £1.90 £1.90 £2.10 (£10.40). Mr G. A. Farndon (WETHERBY) bred by
Barrettstown Stud Farms Ltd. 10 Rn      2m 46.53 (.12 under best: 0.33)
SF—54/45/36/29/40/–

T/Plpt: £208.70 (12.35 Tckts).                                       AA

## 1151–**REDCAR (L-H)**

### Friday, June 19th [Firm]

Going Allowance: minus 0.10 sec per fur (F)                  Wind: str half against

Stalls: high

**1519**     NEWTON CLAIMING STKS    £2265.20 (£627.20: £299.60)    **1¼m**    2-10 (2-10)

  8094 Rose Glen **(59)** *(ABailey)* 6–8-10 ‡⁵ATucker (5) (lw: in tch: effrt 3f out: styd on
u.p to ld wl ins fnl f) ..................................................................................... —1
1288★ Cold Shower (IRE) **(55)** *(JAGlover)* 3–8-7 JFortune (2) (lw: a.p: rdn wl over 2f
out: n.m.r over 1f out: styd on wl nr fin) ..................................................... 1½.2
11423 Winged Whisper (USA) **(66)** (Fav) *(CWThornton)* 3–8-7 DMcKeown (7) (b: bhd:
hld up: hdwy on outside 3f out: hung lft fnl 2f: r o) ................................... s.h.3
11094 Cool Parade (USA) **(50)** (bl) *(GMMoore)* 4–8-11 ‡⁷OPears (4) (trckd ldrs: chal
over 2f out: no ex ins fnl f) ........................................................................ s.h.4
12692 Henbury Hall (IRE) **(65)** *(MrsGRReveley)* 4–9-8 KDarley (11) (cl up: led 4f out:
edgd lft: hdd wl ins fnl f) ............................................................................. ¾.5
  1288 Premier Venues **(41)** (bl) *(SGNorton)* 4–8-10 ‡⁵SMaloney (8) (b: s.i.s: bhd tl
hdwy 4f out: sn rdn: no imp fnl 2f) .............................................................. 6.6
     Calachuchi **(69)** *(MJCamacho)* 5–9-5 JLowe (9) (t: mid div: effrt over 3f out: sn
wknd) ......................................................................................................... 1½.7
  1070 Mypeto *(PCalver)* 3–8-6 WNewnes (10) (effrt 4f out: nvr trbld ldrs) ............... s.h.8
     Super Charge (bl) *(MWEllerby)* 3–8-6 PBurke (6) (led tl hdd 4f out: sn btn) .......... 9
  11564 Blushing Gold (bl) *(MrsJJordan)* 3–8-0 ‡⁷PAllinson (1) (chsd ldrs tl wknd 4f out) . 10
     Gaynor's Boy (IRE) *(TKersey)* 3–8-10 AProud (3) (b: bit bkwd: a bhd) ............... 11

**100/30** Winged Whisper (USA), **7/2** Cold Shower (IRE), **4/1** ROSE GLEN, **5/1** Calachuchi, **6/1** Henbury Hall (IRE),
**10/1** Cool Parade (USA), **25/1** Premier Venues, **33/1** Mypeto, **50/1** Ors. CSF £17.33, Tote £3.90: £1.30 £1.20
£1.50 (£9.30). Mr D. G. Furlong (TARPORLEY) bred by R. G. Bonson. 11 Rn; Winged Whisper (USA) clmd K R
Tomlinson £7,011                               2m 8.3 (5.8)
SF—28/22/21/24/33/9

**1520**     NRS H'CAP (0-70) £2402.40 (£666.40: £319.20)    **1m 3f**    2-40 (2-45)

13352 Khazar (USA) **(61)** (Fav) *(SirMarkPrescott)* 3–8-5 GDuffield (4) (lw: hld up: stdy
hdwy on outside over 3f out: led & edgd lft 1f out: hld on wl) —1
14523 Sinclair Lad (IRE) **(53)** *(RHollinshead)* 4–8-11 KDarley (4) (hld up: hdwy over 2f
out: hung lft u.p: r.o) ................................................................................... ¾.2
12955 Able Lassie **(70)** *(MrsGRReveley)* 4–9-9 ‡⁵SMaloney (8) (hld up: hdwy on
outside over 2f out: kpt on wl u.p ins fnl f) .................................................. nk.3
11843 Be the Best **(40)** *(MPNaughton)* 4–7-12 AMunro (11) (chsd ldrs: effrt 3f out:
n.m.r fnl 2f: r.o nr fin) ................................................................................. s.h.4
  1125 Doctor's Remedy **(35)** (bl) *(MrsJJordan)* 6–7-0 ‡⁷KimMcDonnell (12) (cl up: led
over 3f out wl over 1f out: kpt on) .............................................................. 1½.5
  1150 Sharquin **(36)** *(MBrittain)* 5–7-8 JLowe (3) (b: bhd: chsd ldrs: rdn over 3f out:
wknd appr fnl f) ......................................................................................... ¾.6
11956 Statia (IRE) **(35)** *(DonEnricoIncisa)* 4–7-7 JakiHouston (6) (b: led tl hdd over 3f
out: kpt on same pce) ................................................................................ hd.7
  1394 Checkpoint Charlie **(63)** *(JMPEustace)* 7–9-7 MTebbutt (2) (lw: s.i.s: hld up &
bhd: effrt over 3f out: no imp) .................................................................... 1.8
  9656 Escape Talk **(37)** *(JDooler)* 5–7-2⁽²⁾ ‡⁷AGarth (10) (chsd ldrs tl rdn & wknd 2f
out: sn wknd) ............................................................................................ s.h.9
14045 Le Saule D'Or **(35)** *(APJames)* 5–7-0 ‡⁷CHawksley (9) (chsd ldrs: chal over 3f
out: sn wknd) ............................................................................................ 5.10
  829 Bold Ambition **(64)** *(TKersey)* 5–9-8 AProud (1) (b: lw: prom tl wknd over 3f out) hd.11
  1157 Grey Realm **(37)** *(REBarr)* 4–7-9 PBurke (5) (a in rr) .............................................. 12

LONG HANDICAP: Doctor's Remedy 7-0, Statia (IRE) 7-4, Escape Talk 6-6, Le Saule D'Or 7-2.

**2/1 KHAZAR (USA), 13/2** Checkpoint Charlie, Be the Best, Able Lassie, **7/1** Sinclair Lad (IRE), **10/1** Le Saule D'Or, Sharquin, **16/1** Statia (IRE), **20/1** Bold Ambition, Doctor's Remedy, **50/1** Ors. CSF £16.21, CT £72.58. Tote £2.40: £1.80 £2.20 £2.30 (£7.90). Mr Saeed Manana (NEWMARKET) bred by Kentucky Select Bloodstock I in USA. 12 Rn
2m 20.5 (4.8)
SF—32/36/47/21/6/12

## 1521

BROTTON SEAFOODS CLAIMING STKS    £2709.00 (£749.00: £357.00)
2m 4y
3-10 (3-10)

312³ **Broctune Grey (59)** *(MrsGRReveley)* 8-8-9 KDarley (5) (hld up: stdy hdwy 6f out: rdn over 3f out: styd on to ld ins fnl f) ............................ —1

1179 **Briggscare (67)** *(WJarvis)* 6-9-0 MTebbutt (4) (b: lw: a chsng ldrs: rdn to ld over 1f out: edgd lft: hdd & no ex ins fnl f) ................................ 2¹/₂.2

1239⁶ **Dari Sound (IRE) (47)** *(JGFitzGerald)* 4-9-0 TLucas (2) (hld up in tch: outpcd 4f out: styd on wl u.p fnl 2f) ................................ 2.3

1381 **Empire Blue (68)** *(Fav)* *(PFICole)* 9-9-0 CRutter (6) (b: hld up & bhd: effrt 4f out: no imp fnl 2f) ................................ hd.4

1362² **Maryland Willie** *(NACallaghan)* 5-8-2 ‡7JTate (7) (b: chsd ldr: led 4f out: sn qcknd clr: hdd & wknd over 1f out) ................................ s.h.5

76 **Adjaristan (52)** *(RSimpson)* 5-8-7 ‡5ATucker (3) (b: hind: led tl hdd 4f out: sn wknd) ................................ 4.6

1361 **Ibn Sina (USA) (50)** (bl) *(RO'Leary)* 5-8-8 MBirch (1) (a bhd) ................................ 20.7

**7/4** Empire Blue, **100/30** BROCTUNE GREY(op 2/1), **4/1** Briggscare, **5/1** Maryland Willie, **12/1** Dari Sound (IRE), **20/1** Ors. CSF £15.80, Tote £3.20: £1.60 £2.20 (£11.30). Mr D. Playforth (SALTBURN) bred by G. Reed. 7 Rn
3m 32.1 (7.1)
SF—8/10/7/6/—/—

## 1522

SUTER H'CAP (0-90) £3752.50 (£1120.00: £535.00: £242.50)    **5f**    3-40 (3-42)
(Weights raised 20 lb)

1281² **Cranfield Comet (60)** *(Fav)* *(JBerry)* 3-8-11 GDuffield (4) (squeezed out s: sn bhd: gd hdwy to ld over 1f out: r.o wl) ................................ —1

1310 **Here Comes a Star (51)** *(JMCarr)* 4-8-9 WNewnes (1) (lw: hdwy & n.m.r over 1f out: swtchd & styd on wl nr fin) ................................ 1.2

1365 **Arc Lamp (54)** *(JAGlover)* 6-8-12 (7x) JFortune (6) (dwlt: sn trckng ldrs gng wl: n.m.r over 1f out: r.o wl ins fnl f) ................................ hd.3

764 **Rock Opera (IRE) (57)** *(MPNaughton)* 4-9-1 JakiHouston (9) (bit bkwd: w ldrs: rdn over 1f out: edgd lft & nt qckn nr fin) ................................ 1¹/₂.4

876⁶ **Samsolom (66)** *(JBalding)* 4-9-10 KDarley (5) (chsd ldrs: rdn wl over 1f out: unable qckn ins fnl f) ................................ 2.5

1162⁶ **Lady's Mantle (USA) (42)** *(RBastiman)* 8-7-9 ‡5SMaloney (8) (swtg: w ldrs tl wknd appr fnl f) ................................ ³/₄.6

1045³ **Lord Magester (FR) (47)** *(MrsGRReveley)* 5-8-12 JLowe (3) (nvr trbld ldrs) ................................ ³/₄.7

918 **North of Watford (47)** *(MPNaughton)* 7-8-5 AMunro (10) (lw: w ldrs tl wknd over 1f out) ................................ hd.8

1310⁵ **Jive Music (35)** *(NBycroft)* 6-7-0 ‡7CHawksley (2) (b.off fore: chsd ldrs over 3f) . 1.9

1436⁵ **Brisas (47)** (bl) *(TFairhurst)* 5-8-5 PBurke (7) (lw: chsd ldrs 3f: sn lost pl) ....... ³/₄.10
LONG HANDICAP: Jive Music 7-1.

**4/1** CRANFIELD COMET, **5/1** North of Watford, **11/2** Lady's Mantle (USA), **6/1** Arc Lamp, Samsolom, **8/1** Lord Magester (FR), **12/1** Here Comes a Star(op 8/1), **16/1** Brisas, Jive Music, **20/1** Rock Opera (IRE). CSF £44.72, CT £257.66. Tote £2.90: £2.00 £2.70 £2.80 (£65.10). Cranfield Industries Limited (COCKERHAM) bred by J. R. C. and Mrs Wren. 10 Rn
59.4 sec (2.7)
SF—33/27/29/26/27/—

## 1523

INGS MEDIAN AUCTION STKS (3-Y.O) £2186.80 (£604.80: £288.40)    **7f**    4-10 (4-10)

**Mrs Fisher (IRE) (90)** *(SirMarkPrescott)* 9-7 GDuffield (3) (lw: trckd ldrs: rdn to ld 1f out: r.o wl) ................................ —1

1244* **Fusion (USA) (74)** *(PFICole)* 9-2 AMunro (1) (cl up: outpcd & rdn over 2f out: kpt on fnl f) ................................ 2.2

1236* **Boursin (IRE) (88)** *(Fav)* *(PCalver)* 9-7 WNewnes (2) (lw: led: rdn over 1f out: sn hdd & no ex) ................................ 1.3

**8/11** Boursin (IRE), **3/1** Fusion (USA), **100/30** MRS FISHER (IRE). CSF £9.70. Tote £4.40 (£4.90). Mr G. D. Waters (NEWMARKET) bred by G. D. Waters in Ireland. 3 Rn
1m 26.6 (4.4)
SF—31/20/22

## 1524

GRINDALE STKS (Mdn 2-Y.O) £2265.20 (£627.20: £299.60)    **6f**    4-40 (4-41)

1056⁵ **Mhemeanles** *(MHEasterby)* 9-0 MBirch (5) (lw: hdwy over 2f out: led over 1f out: r.o strly) ................................ —1

1259 Raging Thunder (Fav) *(GLewis)* 9-0 KDarley (4) (chsd ldrs: swtchd ins wl over 1f out: sn squeezed thro to chal: kpt on same pce) ............ 3.2
1056 Paajib (IRE) *(CTinkler)* 9-0 TLucas (3) (b.hind: a in tch: effrt & ev ch 1f out: nt qckn nr fin) ............ hd.3
1327² Principal Player (USA) *(WBentley)* 9-0 AMunro (2) (lw: mde most: bmpd & hdd over 1f out: unable qckn) ............ 3.4
1240⁶ Eightofus *(GMMoore)* 9-0 DMcKeown (6) (lw: bhd: hdwy over 2f out: n.d) ...... 2¹/₂.5
793³ Tanagome (USA) (bl) *(SGNorton)* 9-0 JFortune (7) (chsd ldrs: bdly hmpd wl over 1f out: nt rcvr) ............ 3¹/₂.6
Gussie Fink-Nottle (IRE) *(TDBarron)* 9-0 AlexGreaves (1) (w'like: scope: w ldrs tl wknd over 1f out) ............ 1.7
Simply a Star (IRE) *(MWEasterby)* 9-0 JLowe (9) (leggy: unf: s.s: rn green: nvr wnt pce) ............ 6.8
751⁵ General Brooks (IRE) *(JBerry)* 9-0 GDuffield (8) (w ldrs: rdn ¹/₂-way: hmpd wl over 1f out: sn bhd) ............ ¹/₂.9

**5/2** Raging Thunder, **7/2** Principal Player (USA)(op 7/4), **4/1** MHEMEANLES, **7/1** General Brooks (IRE), **8/1** Gussie Fink-Nottle (IRE)(12/1—11/2), Tanagome (USA), **12/1** Paajib (IRE), **16/1** Simply a Star (IRE), **33/1** Eightofus. CSF £14.51, Tote £5.30: £1.80 £1.50 £4.10 (£8.30). Mr Les Ford (MALTON) bred by Miss J. Chaplin. 9 Rn　　　　　1m 13.6 (4.3)

## 1525　　　　LEVY BOARD STKS　　£2562.00 (£707.00: £736.00)　　**6f**　　　5-15 (5-15)

1380* **Finjan (87)** (Fav) *(MPNaughton)* 5-9-10 AMunro (4) (lw: a.p: led over 1f out: readily) ............ —1
1393⁶ Corn Futures **(78)** (v) *(JPLeigh)* 4–8-12 DMcKeown (3) (trckd ldrs: effrt 2f out: ev ch 1f out: nt qckn) ............ 1.2
851³ Threepence **(95)** *(JBerry)* 3–8-13 GDuffield (2) (led: hung lft over 2f out: hdd over 1f out: no ex) ............ nk.3
1368³ Pop to Stans **(75)** *(JPearce)* 3–8-11 ‡SRPrice (1) (lw: stumbled s: jnd ldr after wl over 1f: rdn & wknd over 2f out) ............ 10.4

**7/4** FINJAN, **2/1** Threepence, **5/2** Corn Futures, **9/1** Pop to Stans. CSF £5.86, Tote £2.00 (£6.90). Mrs R. Olivier (RICHMOND) bred by Swettenham Stud. 4 Rn　　　　　1m 11.8 (2.1)
　　　　　SF—48/32/32/–

T/Plpt: £103.00 (17.05 Tckts).　　　　　0'R

# REDCAR (L-H)
## Saturday, June 20th [Firm]
Going Allowance: 5f-7f: minus 0.30 sec; Rest: minus 0.45 sec (F)　　　Wind: almost nil

Stalls: high

## 1526　　　　LIVERTON (S) STKS (2-Y.O) £2422.00 (£672.00: £322.00)　　**7f**　　　1-45 (1-51)

770 **Kentucky Dreams** *(JBerry)* 8-11 GCarter (9) (trckd ldrs: led over 1f out: sn clr: comf) ............ —1
1149 Kiss in the Dark *(MrsGRReveley)* 8-6 KFallon (20) (swtg: a chsng ldrs: ev ch 2f out: nt qckn fnl f) ............ 2¹/₂.2
588 Surprise Partner *(MJohnston)* 8-11 RPElliott (15) (hdwy ¹/₂-wy: styd on appr fnl f) ............ 1¹/₂.3
Comtec's Legend *(JFBottomley)* 8-11 ‡NKennedy (19) (lt-f: unf: a bhd tl styd on wl fnl 2f) ............ 1.4
1151⁴ Bella Bambola (IRE) *(SGNorton)* 8-6 LCharnock (13) (lw: w ldrs: rdn & wknd over 1f out) ............ hd.5
1448² Annie Rose (bl) *(TDBarron)* 7-13 ‡7VHalliday (1) (led tl hdd over 1f out: sn wknd) 1¹/₂.6
1299³ Hot Off the Press (Jt-Fav) *(RMWhitaker)* 8-11 DaleGibson (17) (lw: chsd ldrs: drvn along ¹/₂-way: edgd lft & no imp) ............ hd.7
Merry Mermaid *(JFBottomley)* 8-6 PBurke (2) (lengthy: unf: s.s: bhd tl hdwy ¹/₂-wy: kpt on fnl f) ............ 1¹/₂.8
782 Stay Great *(WCarter)* 8-6 ‡5NGwilliams (3) (swtg: chsd ldrs: rdn ¹/₂-wy: sn wknd) 2¹/₂.9
759 Jarabosky *(MWEllerby)* 8-11 SMorris (8) (w ldrs tl wknd over 2f out) ............ 3.10
Loch Mere *(CTinkler)* 8-6 TLucas (5) (small: neat: s.s: bhd tl sme late hdwy) .. hd.11
1121² Yeveed (IRE) (Jt-Fav) *(MHEasterby)* 8-6 MBirch (12) (lw: in tch: hrd rdn ¹/₂-wy: sn wknd) ............ s.h.12
877 Our Price *(GMMoore)* 8-11 JQuinn (18) (in tch: drvn along ¹/₂-wy) ............ 2¹/₂.13
665 Apollo's Sister *(MrsJJordan)* 8-6 WNewnes (11) (unf: unruly & uns rdr bef s: nvr nr ldrs) ............ 1.14
1151 Private Liner *(RonaldThompson)* 8-11 NConnorton (7) (lw: w ldrs tl rdn & wknd 2f out) ............ nk.15

| | | | |
|---|---|---|---|
| 1149 | Heavenly Body *(JWWatts)* 8-6 WRyan (6) (in tch 4f: sn wknd) | 1.16 |
| 1375 | Never in Touch *(MBrittain)* 8-6 PSedgwick (16) (bhd fnl 2f) | 3¹/₂.17 |
| 1448 | Sunshine in Ramsey *(TFairhurst)* 8-3 ‡³JFanning (10) (w ldrs tl wknd over 2f out) | hd.18 |
| 1023⁵ | Shotley Again *(NBycroft)* 8-11 SWebster (14) (chsd ldrs 4f: sn lost pl) | nk.19 |
| 568 | Lady Lawn *(JMCarr)* 8-6 SWood (4) (bhd fnl 3f) | 3.20 |

**9/4** Hot Off the Press(op 7/2), Yeveed (IRE), **10/1** Bella Bambola (IRE), Annie Rose, **12/1** Heavenly Body(op 7/1), **14/1** Kiss in the Dark, KENTUCKY DREAMS, Private Liner, **16/1** Stay Great, Sunshine in Ramsey, Surprise Partner, **20/1** Our Price, Loch Mere, Shotley Again, Comtec's Legend, **25/1** Merry Mermaid, Never in Touch, **33/1** Ors. CSF £218.97, Tote £28.70: £5.90 £4.80 £14.00 (£749.70). Mrs J. M. Bradford-Nutter (COCKERHAM) bred by Ravenstonedale Fold and Bloodstock. 20 Rn; Bt in 4,200 gns

1m 25.6 (3.4)
SF—15/2/2/–/–/–

## 1527

DAILY MIRROR BELLE H'CAP (Ladies) (0-75) £3101.00 (£861.00: £413.00)
1m
(Weights raised 2 lb)
2-20 (2-23)

| | | | |
|---|---|---|---|
| 1366⁴ | **Night Transaction (44)** *(AHide)* 5–10-2 ‡³MissLHide (7) (lw: hdwy ¹/₂-wy: r.o wl to ld over 1f out: sn clr) | —1 |
| 1284 | Major Ivor **(58)** *(MrsGRReveley)* 7–11-5 MissMJuster (13) (lw: hld up & bhd: hdwy over 2f out: edgd lft & styd on fnl f: no ch w wnr) | 3¹/₂.2 |
| 1248 | No Comebacks **(47)** *(EJAlston)* 4–10-1⁽⁵⁾ ‡⁷MissSBarclay (12) (s.s: bhd tl styd on wl fnl 2f) | ³/₄.3 |
| 1309² | Thewaari (USA) **(64)** (Fav) *(AAScott)* 3–10-12 ‡³MissTBracegirdle (2) (lw: hld up: gd hdwy to ld over 2f out: hdd & wknd over 1f out) | 2¹/₂.4 |
| 662⁵ | Eriny (USA) **(67)** *(SGNorton)* 3–11-4 MrsJCrossley (14) (hdwy & prom ¹/₂-wy: nt qckn fnl 2f) | nk.5 |
| 1294⁴ | Chance Report **(38)** *(FHLee)* 4–9-10 ‡³MissDPomeroy (9) (b.hind: bhd tl styd on fnl 2f) | ³/₄.6 |
| 1243⁵ | Hizeem **(28)** *(MPNaughton)* 6–8-10 ‡⁷MissABycroft (5) (lw: hdwy & prom ¹/₂-wy: one pce fnl 2f) | ³/₄.7 |
| 1338 | Spanish Whisper **(34)** *(JRBostock)* 5–9-9 MrsLPearce (8) (chsd ldrs tl wknd 2f out) | 2¹/₂.8 |
| 1195 | Top Scale **(40)** (v) *(WWHaigh)* 5–9-9 MissIDWJones (10) (in tch: effrt ¹/₂-wy: kpt on fnl 2f: nvr nr to chal) | 1.9 |
| 1488² | Who's Tef (IRE) **(60)** *(MHEasterby)* 4–11-4 ‡³MrsSEasterby (6) (lw: chsd ldrs tl wknd over 2f out) | 4.10 |
| 1150 | Fair Dare **(41)** *(CBBBooth)* 4–9-9⁽⁵⁾ ‡⁷MissCKing (15) (lw: sn bhd) | 1.11 |
| 1338³ | Profit a Prendre **(49)** *(DAWilson)* 8–10-10 MissJAllison (1) (b: lw: chsd ldrs: led over 3f out: hdd & wknd over 2f out) | 2.12 |
| 1337⁴ | Must Be Magical (USA) **(28)** *(FHLee)* 4–8-10 ‡⁷MissCBurgess (4) (chsd ldrs tl lost pl over 3f out) | hd.13 |
| 1441 | Saint Bene't (IRE) **(43)** (bl) *(PCHaslam)* 4–10-4 MissABillot (11) (led tl over 3f out: sn wknd) | s.h.14 |
| 1284⁶ | King's Shilling (USA) **(51)** *(MrsSOliver)* 5–10-12 MissJWinter (3) (chsd ldrs tl lost pl over 3f out: sn bhd) | 15.15 |

**7/2** Thewaari (USA), **5/1** Profit a Prendre, **7/1** Spanish Whisper, Who's Tef (IRE), **8/1** NIGHT TRANSACTION, **10/1** Major Ivor(8/1—12/1), **12/1** King's Shilling (USA), **14/1** Eriny (USA), Top Scale, Chance Report, **20/1** Saint Bene't (IRE), **25/1** Hizeem, **33/1** Ors. CSF £82.43, CT £2,275.77. Tote £9.20: £3.40 £2.90 £10.90 (£24.40). Mr Anthony Hide (NEWMARKET) bred by Alan Gibson. 15 Rn

1m 36.9 (1.9)
SF—33/36/16/19/24/–

## 1528

RONALDSHAY H'CAP (3-Y.O) (0-70) £3202.80 (£890.80: £428.40)
1m 1f
(Weights raised 4 lb)
2-50 (2-51)

| | | | |
|---|---|---|---|
| 1426★ | **Timurid (FR) (66)** *(JLDunlop)* 9-7 WRyan (2) (lw: hld up: stdy hdwy 3f out: led jst ins fnl f: r.o wl) | —1 |
| 1142 | Marowins **(50)** *(EJAlston)* 8-5 KFallon (11) (sn bhd & drvn along: gd hdwy on outside over 2f out: hung lft: styd on wl fnl f) | 1¹/₂.2 |
| 1072★ | Talented Ting (IRE) **(63)** *(PCHaslam)* 9-1 ‡³JFanning (1) (lw: a chsng ldrs: rdn over 3f out: r.o one pce appr fnl f) | 1¹/₂.3 |
| 1175⁴ | Mindomica **(65)** *(MBell)* 9-6 MTebbutt (5) (trckd ldrs: effrt over 2f out: kpt on same pce) | 2¹/₂.4 |
| 1146★ | Elizabethan Air **(54)** *(ANLee)* 8-9 JQuinn (13) (swtg: hld up: effrt 3f out: hmpd 2f out: styd on fnl f) | ³/₄.5 |
| 972³ | Freephone (CAN) **(55)** (bl) *(JWHills)* 8-10 WNewnes (7) (lw: swtg: led after 2f: hdd & wknd jst ins fnl f) | 2.6 |
| 1072³ | Essayeffsee **(56)** (bl) *(MHEasterby)* 8-11 MBirch (6) (b.hind: led 2f: disp ld over 3f out tl wknd 2f out) | ³/₄.7 |
| 1154⁶ | Chantry Bellini **(56)** *(CWThornton)* 8-11 GHind (10) (sn bhd: hdwy 2f out: styd on nr fin) | 2¹/₂.8 |
| 457 | Tees Gazette Girl **(47)** *(MrsGRReveley)* 8-2 DaleGibson (9) (lw: sn wl bhd: sme late hdwy) | 3.9 |

1287⁴ Magnetic Point (USA) **(64)** *(AAScott)* 9-5 JFortune (8) (lw: chsd ldrs tl wknd 3f out) ............................................................................. nk.10

Kayartis **(40)** *(MrsGRReveley)* 7-2 ‡7DarrenMoffatt (4) (chsd ldrs tl lost pl over 5f out) ....................................................................... 1.11

798 Floral Bouquet **(44)** *(MJCamacho)* 7-13 LCharnock (16) (chsd ldrs: rdn over 3f out: sn lost pl) ................................................ s.h.12

Head for the Stars (IRE) **(63)** *(APStringer)* 8-13 ‡5SMaloney (12) (bit bkwd: hld up & a bhd) .......................................................... nk.13

1210 Caithness Rock **(60)** *(MAJarvis)* 9-1 TLucas (17) (chsd ldrs tl wknd over 3f out) 1¹⁄₂.14

1122 Boon Hill **(47)** *(MWEllerby)* 8-2 SMorris (15) (bhd whn stumbled ent st) ....... 3.15

1189⁴ Qualitair Memory (IRE) **(47)** *(JFBottomley)* 8-2 GCarter (3) (s.s: a in rr) ......... 2.16

1453² Fiction **(60)** *(MPNaughton)* 9-1 JakiHouston (14) (a bhd) ................................. 12.17

**9/2** Freephone (CAN), **5/1** TIMURID (FR), **11/2** Elizabethan Air, **8/1** Mindomica, Talented Ting (IRE), **10/1** Magnetic Point (USA), Caithness Rock, Essayeffsee, **14/1** Chantry Bellini, **16/1** Kayartis, **25/1** Head for the Stars (IRE), Marowins, Qualitair Memory (IRE), **33/1** Ors. CSF £121.46, CT £937.00. Tote £6.00: £1.90 £3.30 £3.40 £2.00 (£198.70). Mr Cyril Humphris (ARUNDEL) bred by Cyril Humphris in France. 17 Rn
1m 51.8 (2.8)
SF—5/–/–/–/–/–

---

**1529** ROTHMANS ROYALS NORTH SOUTH CHALLENGE SERIES H'CAP (0-80) £2950.00 (£880.00: £420.00: £190.00) **7f** 3-25 (3-27)

1261 **Affordable (63)** *(WCarter)* 4-8-8 ‡5NGwilliams (2) (lw: chsd ldrs: rdn over 2f out: r.o to ld ins fnl f) ........................................................................ —1

1365³ Mu-Arrik **(54)** (bl) *(DAWilson)* 4-8-4 GCarter (3) (lw: s.i.s: hdwy ¹⁄₂-wy: r.o u.p fnl f) ....................................................................................... nk.2

1379 Arabat **(55)** (v) *(MPNaughton)* 5-8-5 NConnorton (5) (lw: sn w ldr: led over 2f out tl hdd & no ex ins fnl f) ................................................ ³⁄₄.3

615⁶ Chain Shot **(49)** *(MHEasterby)* 7-7-8 ‡5SMaloney (1) (lw: prom tl outpcd & lost pl ¹⁄₂-wy: hdwy over 1f out: styd on nr fin) .......................... ¹⁄₂.4

1403 Northern Spark **(63)** *(CWThornton)* 4-8-13 MBirch (4) (prom tl lost pl ¹⁄₂-wy: hdwy u.p over 1f out: kpt on wl nr fin) ........................... 1.5

1303 La Bamba **(78)** (Fav) *(GAPritchard-Gordon)* 6-10-0 WHood (6) (dwlt s: hld up: hdwy over 2f out: ev ch over 1f out: wknd jst ins fnl f) ......... ³⁄₄.6

1365 The Can Can Man **(64)** *(MJohnston)* 5-9-0 RPElliott (7) (led tl over 2f out: wknd over 1f out) ....................................................... ³⁄₄.7

**100/30** La Bamba, **7/2** Mu-Arrik, **9/2** AFFORDABLE, **11/2** Chain Shot(7/1—9/2), **6/1** Northern Spark, **13/2** The Can Can Man, **12/1** Arabat(tchd 20/1). CSF £19.28, Tote £6.30: £3.00 £2.00 (£14.10). Miss Maha Kalaji (EPSOM) bred by Pinfold Stud and Farms Ltd. 7 Rn
1m 23.7 (1.5)
SF—40/35/34/21/37/50

---

**1530** UGTHORPE H'CAP (0-70) £2363.20 (£655.20: £313.60) **1m 5f 135y** 3-55 (3-56)

1108² **Brodessa (64)** *(MrsGRReveley)* 6-9-10 MBirch (1) (lw: trckd ldrs: n.m.r on over 2f out: hrd rdn & styd on to ld ins fnl f: all out) ............ —1

1179★ Greenwich Bambi **(57)** *(WCarter)* 4-9-2 ‡5NGwilliams (8) (lw: effrt u.p over 3f out: led wl over 1f out: styd on ins fnl f) ......................... s.h.2

1395★ Newton Point **(70)** (Fav) *(GAPritchard-Gordon)* 3-8-13 GCarter (3) (lw: a chsng ldrs: effrt over 3f out: r.o same pce fnl 2f) .................... 3¹⁄₂.3

1452⁵ Quip **(33)** *(MPNaughton)* 7-7-7 JakiHouston (6) (lw: led tl wl over 1f out: one pce) .......................................................................... ¹⁄₂.4

1274 Grouse-N-Heather **(57)** *(MrsGRReveley)* 3-8-0 DaleGibson (11) (hld up & bhd: effrt u.p over 3f out: styd on fnl 2f: nt rch ldrs) .............. hd.5

598 Grove Serendipity (IRE) **(61)** (v) *(AHide)* 4-9-7 WRyan (4) (trckd ldrs: effrt 3f out: grad wknd) ....................................................... 2¹⁄₂.6

1520⁵ Doctor's Remedy **(33)** (bl) *(MrsJJordan)* 6-7-0 ‡7KimMcDonnell (2) (chsd ldrs tl outpcd fnl 3f) .................................................... 3.7

1481 Thunder Bug (USA) **(42)** *(APJames)* 4-8-11 ‡5RPrice (7) (chsd ldrs tl wknd over 2f out) ..................................................... nk.8

1290 Enkindle **(34)** *(BWMurray)* 5-7-5⁽¹⁾ ‡3JFanning (9) (chsd ldrs tl wknd over 2f out) 2¹⁄₂.9

1248 Ben's Beauty **(41)** *(MrsSOliver)* 4-7-8⁽⁸⁾ ‡7HHumphries (5) (a bhd: reminders 5f out) ...................................................................... 10

Mighty Glow **(46)** (bl) *(JHJohnson)* 8-8-6 JFortune (10) (bhd fnl 5f: t.o) ............ 11

LONG HANDICAP: Quip 7-3, Doctor's Remedy 7-2, Enkindle 7-0, Ben's Beauty 6-6.

**9/4** Newton Point, **3/1** BRODESSA, **9/2** Greenwich Bambi, **8/1** Grove Serendipity (IRE), Grouse-N-Heather, **20/1** Mighty Glow, Thunder Bug (USA), Quip, Doctor's Remedy, **25/1** Ben's Beauty, **33/1** Enkindle. CSF £16.60, CT £33.05. Tote £3.30: £1.80 £2.30 £1.30 (£7.50). Mr R. W. S. Jevon (SALTBURN) bred by B. Fairs. 11 Rn
2m 54.6 (0.1 under best; 3.6)
SF—14/1/–/–/–/–

**1531**    STAITHES AUCTION STKS (Mdn 2-Y.O) £2856.00 (£791.00: £378.00)
5f                                                          4-30 (4-32)

1378  **Maribella** (PFlCole) 7-10 ‡7JDSmith (8) (chsd ldrs: edgd lft over 1f out: styd on
           wl to ld nr fin) .................................................................. —1
 877  Nominator (Fav) (RHollinshead) 8-10 WRyan (6) (w ldrs: edgd bdly lft & led
           over 1f out: no ex nr fin) .................................................. 1¹/₂.2
1299  Benzoe (IRE) (MWEasterby) 8-9 TLucas (9) (w ldrs: hung bdly lft 2f out: kpt on
           fnl f) ........................................................................... 1¹/₂.3
 793⁴  Creagmhor (JBerry) 8-7 GCarter (2) (lw: w ldrs: rdn & swvd rt over 1f out: sn
           wknd) ......................................................................... 3¹/₂.4
1208  Gorodenka Boy (MrsJJordan) 8-1 ‡7PAllinson (1) (s.i.s: hdwy to ld over 3f out:
           hdd & sltly hmpd over 1f out: sn wknd) ............................. hd.5
      Chicago (IRE) (CTinkler) 8-10 MBirch (3) (unf: scope: w ldrs: hung bdly rt &
           wknd over 1f out) ......................................................... 1¹/₂.6
      Missed the Boat (IRE) (TDBarron) 8-9 AlexGreaves (11) (leggy: scope: bit
           bkwd: in tch: edgd lft: hmpd & wknd over 1f out) ................ 1.7
      Honeymoon Dawn (RMWhitaker) 8-0 DaleGibson (4) (leggy: unf: s.i.s: nvr wnt
           pce) ........................................................................... 1¹/₂.8
      Colonel Future (JWWatts) 8-7 NConnorton (10) (w'like: str: bit bkwd: rn green
           & sn outpcd) ................................................................ hd.9
1023⁴  Pressure Off (JHJohnson) 9-0 JFortune (5) (lw: unruly stalls: hung bdly lft & sn
           wl outpcd) ................................................................... 6.10
*Stewards Enquiry: Obj. to Maribella & Nominator by Mrs J Jordan overruled.*

**7/2** Nominator, **4/1** Benzoe (IRE)(9/2—3/1), **9/2** Creagmhor, **11/2** MARIBELLA, **6/1** Chicago (IRE)(8/1—10/1),
**10/1** Colonel Future(op 6/1), **12/1** Missed the Boat (IRE)(op 8/1), Pressure Off, **16/1** Honeymoon Dawn, **25/1**
Gorodenka Boy. CSF £25.09, Tote £5.60: £2.20 £1.60 £2.00 (£6.50). Mr George Johnson (WHATCOMBE) bred
by G. Johnson. 10 Rn                                                                    58.8 sec (2.1)
                                                                                       SF—10/18/11/—/—/—

**1532**    FORTY ACRE STKS (Mdn 3-Y.O) £1932.00 (£532.00: £252.00)   1m   5-00 (5-09)

1183³  **Alkarif** (USA) (70) (AAScott) 9-0 JFortune (6) (lw: mde all: clr over 2f out: hung
           lft & drvn out fnl f) ........................................................ —1
1182⁴  Galactic Miss (Fav) (JLDunlop) 8-9 GCarter (4) (lw: trckd ldrs: effrt & outpcd
           over 2f out: styd on fnl f) .............................................. 3¹/₂.2
      Be My Everything (IRE) (RHollinshead) 8-9 WRyan (2) (hdwy to jn ldrs ¹/₂-wy:
           effrt over 2f out: kpt on same pce) ................................... 2.3
      Jumaira Star (USA) (JHMGosden) 9-0 GHind (8) (w'like: str: trckd ldrs: hung
           bdly lft over 2f out: sn wknd & eased) ............................... 7.4
      Zaire (v) (JWWatts) 9-0 NConnorton (7) (neat: sn chsng ldrs: drvn along ¹/₂-wy:
           wknd over 2f out) .......................................................... 1.5
      Not Gordons (JHJohnson) 9-0 SMorris (1) (bit bkwd: chsd ldrs tl lost pl 3f out:
           sn bhd) ....................................................................... 15.6
      George Henry (TDBarron) 9-0 AlexGreaves (3) (str: bkwd: wl outpcd fr ¹/₂-wy) 12.7
      Followmegirls (MrsALMKing) 8-9 JQuinn (5) (leggy: bit bkwd: chsd ldrs tl wknd
           over 3f out: sn bhd) ...................................................... 7.8
      Pips Promise (JMJefferson) 8-7 ‡7MHunt (9) (leggy: bit bkwd: a in rr) ...... 5.9

**10/11** Galactic Miss(op 6/4), **3/1** Jumaira Star (USA)(op 13/8), **5/1** ALKARIF (USA), **8/1** Zaire, **14/1** Be My
Everything (IRE), **25/1** George Henry, **50/1** Ors. CSF £10.02, Tote £6.50: £1.70 £1.10 £1.70 (£4.10). Mr
Hamdan Al-Maktoum (NEWMARKET) bred by Lillie F. Webb in USA. 9 Rn          1m 35.9 (0.9)
                                                                          SF—33/17/11/—/—/—

T/Plpt: £1,467.10 (2.6 Tckts).                                                          WG

607—**ASCOT** (R-H)
**Saturday, June 20th [Good]**
Going Allowance: minus 0.10 sec per fur (F)                       Wind: mod half bhd

Stalls: 2nd, 5th & 6th high, remainder centre

**1533**    RITZ CLUB FERN HILL H'CAP (3-Y.O.F) (0-110) £11745.00 (£3150.00: £1680.00:
£765.00)   1m (st)                                           2-00 (2-01)

(Weights raised 5 lb)
1287*  **Calpella** (75) (JARToller) 8-6 MRoberts (11) (a.p: ev ch whn hmpd & swtchd
           over 1f out: r.o whn: fin 2nd, ¹/₂l: awrdd r) ......................... —1
1216³  Nashville Blues (IRE) (80) (JWHills) 8-11 MHills (10) (lw: a.p: hung lft & led wl
           over 1f out: all out: fin 1st: disq: plcd 2nd) ........................ 2
1379⁵  Louisville Belle (IRE) (65) (MDIUsher) 7-5(3) ‡5DHarrison (5) (lw: hdwy over 2f
           out: swtchd rt over 1f out: r.o) ........................................ 5.3

1306* **Zawaahy (USA) (78)** (Fav) *(AAScott)* 8-9 WRSwinburn (2) (a.p: hrd rdn over 2f out: r.o one pce) ................................................................ 3¹/₂.4
1209* **Hugging (79)** *(MMcCormack)* 8-10 JReid (7) (swtg: a.p: one pce fnl 2f) ........... ¹/₂.5
  938 **Change the Will (67)** *(MDIUsher)* 7-12 CRutter (1) (lw: nvr nrr) ........................ 2¹/₂.6
1214* **Clare Kerry Lass (80)** *(JRFanshawe)* 8-11 PaulEddery (9) (lw: no hdwy fnl 2f) . hd.7
1189* **Forest Dew (USA) (74)** *(MHTompkins)* 8-5 PRobinson (6) (lw: nvr nr to chal) . s.h.8
  938* **Jade Vale (83)** *(JWHills)* 9-0 RHills (13) (prom over 5f) ................................. ³/₄.9
       **Castilian Queen (USA) (81)** *(JHMGosden)* 8-12 DHolland (3) (led: hdd & bdly hmpd wl over 1f out) .................................................... 1.10
1166 **She's Pleased (USA) (83)** *(LMCumani)* 9-0 LDettori (4) (a bhd) ..................... 3¹/₂.11
      **Alto Jane (90)** *(GHarwood)* 9-7 RCochrane (12) (bhd fnl 3f) ........................... 1.12
1062² **Rafah (77)** *(BHanbury)* 8-8 BRaymond (8) (lw: prom 4f) ............................... 1¹/₂.13
             LONG HANDICAP: Louisville Belle (IRE) 7-2.
*Stewards Enquiry: Nashville Blues disq. (interference to Calpella). Hills suspended 29/6-2/7/92 (careless riding).*

**5/1** Zawaahy (USA), **7/1** Nashville Blues (IRE), **15/2** Rafah, CALPELLA, **8/1** Castilian Queen (USA), **10/1** Jade Vale, Clare Kerry Lass, She's Pleased, **12/1** Forest Dew (USA), **14/1** Hugging, **20/1** Alto Jane, **33/1** Change the Will, **40/1** Louisville Belle (IRE). CSF £52.40, CT £1,765.12. Tote £7.60: £2.40 £3.00 £10.90 (£28.70). Mr Saeed Manana (NEWMARKET) bred by Newmarket Thoroughbred Breeders P L C. 13 Rn
                                        1m 40.42 (1.02)
                               SF—63/70/33/40/39/19

---

## 1534

HAAGEN DAZS H'CAP (0-100) £10598.00 (£3164.00: £1512.00: £686.00)
**2m 45y**                                               2-30 (2-41)

(Weights raised 5 lb)

1026⁴ **For Mog (USA) (76)** *(CEBrittain)* 3–8-4 MRoberts (7) (lw: hrd rdn over 3f out: hdwy over 2f out: led over 1f out: r.o wl) ............................. —1
1361⁶ Green Lane (USA) **(75)** *(IABalding)* 4–9-8 JReid (10) (lw: a.p: st: hrd rdn over 1f out: nt qckn) ................................................... 4.2
1459 Line Drummer (USA) **(77)** *(PAKelleway)* 4–9-10 PRobinson (1) (b. lw. led 5f out tl over 1f out) ................................................... 2¹/₂.3
1381⁴ Manzoor Sayadan (USA) **(68)** *(RSimpson)* 4–9-1 SWhitworth (2) (5th st: hrd rdn 2f out: one pce) ............................................... 5.4
         Princess Moodyshoe **(67)** *(MCPipe)* 4–9-0 DHolland (9) (nr in rr: rdn 5f out: styd on fnl 2f) ................................................ 2¹/₂.5
1190 Beldale Star **(55)** *(RAkehurst)* 9–8-2 TyroneWilliams (8) (b: 2nd st: wknd 2f out) 1¹/₂.6
1361⁴ Magsood **(54)** (bl) *(SMellor)* 7–8-1 DanaMellor (4) (lw: 3rd st: wknd over 2f out) 1¹/₂.7
1211 Barrish **(72)** (Fav) *(RAkehurst)* 6–9-5 WCarson (5) (swtg: plld hrd: prom tl wknd & 6th st: t.o) ...................................... 30.8
1290 Rajanpour (USA) **(50)** (bl) *(RCurtis)* 7–7-11 GBardwell (3) (lw: a bhd: t.o) ........ hd.9
         Abbotsham **(47)** *(WRWilliams)* 7–7-8(1) NAdams (6) (led tl wknd qckly 5f out: t.o) ........................................ 10.10
              LONG HANDICAP: Abbotsham 6-5.

**100/30** Barrish, **5/1** Manzoor Sayadan (USA), Line Drummer (USA), **11/2** Princess Moodyshoe, FOR MOG (USA), **9/1** Green Lane (USA), **10/1** Beldale Star, **20/1** Magsood, **25/1** Rajanpour (USA), **100/1** Abbotsham. CSF £48.11, CT £237.48. Tote £6.30: £1.60 £2.10 £2.10 (£21.20). Mr Luciano Gaucci (NEWMARKET) bred by Joseph Allen in USA. 10 Rn
                                        3m 31.27 (4.77)
                               SF—26/40/39/25/21/8

---

## 1535

GRAND MET H'CAP (3-Y.O) (0-115) £17859.50 (£5336.00: £2553.00: £1161.50)
**5f**                                               3-00 (3-13)

(Weights raised 6 lb)

1117* **Taufan Blu (IRE) (89)** (bl) *(MJohnston)* 8-7 MRoberts (15) (lw: gd hdwy over 1f out: r.o to ld last strides) ................................. —1
1204⁶ Cradle Days **(78)** *(RHannon)* 7-10 NAdams (10) (a.p: led over 1f out tl fnl strides) ................................................... nk.2
  656 Miss Nosey Parker (IRE) **(100)** *(RHannon)* 9-1 ‡3RPerham (8) (a.p: ev ch over 1f out: nt qckn) ................................... 2¹/₂.3
1386* Optical (IRE) **(79)** (Fav) *(MPNaughton)* 7-6 ‡5DHarrison (11) (lw: hdwy fnl f: nvr nrr) .............................................. 1¹/₂.4
1386³ Bodari **(75)** *(DAWilson)* 7-7 GBardwell (12) (a.p: nt qckn fnl f) ..................... s.h.5
 982⁶ Bunty Boo **(84)** *(BAMcMahon)* 8-2 WCarson (3) (led over 3f) ........................ nk.6
1204⁵ Wild Honour (IRE) **(85)** (v) *(WRMuir)* 8-3 AMunro (16) (lw: outpcd: nrst fin) ...... 1¹/₂.7
1204* Allthruthenight (IRE) **(87)** *(LJHolt)* 8-5(1) JReid (1) (swtg: no hdwy fnl 2f) ....... s.h.8
 714* Cindora (IRE) **(93)** *(MHTompkins)* 8-11 PRobinson (14) (lw: nvr nr to chal) ...... s.h.9
1352⁶ Regal Scintilla **(103)** *(JEHammond, France)* 9-7 SCauthen (2) (n.d) ................... 3.10
1364² Nagida **(77)** *(JARToller)* 7-9 NCarlisle (13) (prom over 5f) .......................... s.h.11
 834⁴ Mamma's Too **(99)** *(JBerry)* 9-3 LPiggott (4) (lw: prom 3f) ............................ nk.12
1345 Bold Memory **(96)** *(DRCElsworth)* 9-0 PatEddery (6) (b.hind: a wl bhd) ........ 1¹/₂.13
         Nifty Fifty (IRE) **(96)** *(JBerry)* 9-0 TQuinn (7) (chsd ldr 3f) ........................... ¹/₂.14
 860² Myasha (USA) **(78)** *(MrsLPiggott)* 7-7(3) ‡3FNorton (5) (a bhd) ...................... 2¹/₂.15

1204⁴ Absolutely Nuts **(82)** *(BAMcMahon)* 8-0 TyroneWilliams (9) (lw: a bhd: hmpd
over 2f out) ............................................................................................................. 1¹/₂.**16**
    LONG HANDICAP: Bodari 7-5, Myasha (USA) 7-4.

**6/1** Optical (IRE), **13/2** TAUFAN BLU (IRE), **7/1** Miss Nosey Parker (IRE), **8/1** Allthruthenight (IRE), Cindora (IRE),
**11/1** Wild Honour (IRE), **12/1** Bunty Boo, Bold Memory, **14/1** Mamma's Too, **16/1** Regal Scintilla, Absolutely
Nuts, Cradle Days, Bodari, **20/1** Nagida, Nifty Fifty (IRE), **25/1** Myasha (USA). CSF £100.07, CT £698.82. Tote
£8.90: £2.30 £4.60 £1.50 £2.00 (£151.90). Hambleton Lodge Equine Premix Ltd (MIDDLEHAM) bred by Mrs S.
O'Riordan in Ireland. 16 Rn                              61.19 sec (0.69)
                                            SF—69/57/66/37/37/45

**1536**      SOUTHERN COMFORT GRADUATION STKS (2-Y.O) £10325.00 (£3080.00: £1470.00:
                £665.00)   **6f**                                      3-35 (3-41)

1283² **High Tycoon (IRE)** (Fav) *(MrsJCecil)* 8-12 LDettori (8) (w ldrs: led over 2f out:
v.easily) ............................................................................................... —**1**
    L'Aigle D'Or (USA) *(GLewis)* 8-12 PaulEddery (2) (w'like: scope: hdwy 2f out:
r.o ins fnl) ............................................................................................. 3.**2**
    Norfolk Hero *(DJGMurray-Smith)* 8-12 JReid (1) (wl grwn: bit bkwd: a.p: r.o one
pce fnl f) ............................................................................................ s.h.**3**
    Tajdid (IRE) *(HThomsonJones)* 8-12 RHills (3) (str: outpcd: styd on fnl f) ........... 7.**4**
    Pamar *(CEBrittain)* 8-12 MRoberts (6) (str: scope: nvr nr to chal) ..................... 2.**5**
1259⁵ Play Hever Golf *(TJNaughton)* 8-12 PatEddery (7) (led over 3f) ..................... 2¹/₂.**6**
1378² Our Shadee (USA) *(KTIvory)* 8-12 GBardwell (5) (lw: bhd fnl 2f) ..................... 10.**7**
650* Rain Splash *(RHannon)* 8-13 WCarson (4) (bhd fnl 3f) ..................... 2¹/₂.**8**

**5/2** HIGH TYCOON (IRE), **11/4** Tajdid (IRE)(2/1—100/30), **3/1** Rain Splash, **11/2** Pamar, **10/1** Play Hever Golf,
**16/1** L'Aigle D'Or (USA)(8/1—20/1), **20/1** Our Shadee (USA), **33/1** Norfolk Hero. CSF £35.49, Tote £3.10:
£1.40 £2.50 £3.70 (£32.40). Mr R. N. Tikkoo (NEWMARKET) bred by Rowanstown Stud in Ireland. 8 Rn
                                      1m 15.81 (2.21)
                                     SF—42/30/29/1/–/–

**1537**      CHURCHILL STKS (3-Y.O) £8996.00 (£2678.00: £1274.00: £572.00)
               **1¹/₂m**                                       4-10 (4-11)

1225a² **Profusion (97)** (Fav) *(PFICole)* 8-11 AMunro (1) (4th st: hdwy on ins over 1f
out: qcknd to ld ins fnl f) ................................................................. —**1**
1319* Milzig (USA) **(90)** *(DRCElsworth)* 8-11 SCauthen (4) (3rd st: rdn 2f out: ev ch ins
fnl f: r.o) ............................................................................................ 2.**2**
1198 Lobilio (USA) **(83)** *(CEBrittain)* 8-11 MRoberts (3) (lw: led tl ins fnl f) ............ 1¹/₂.**3**
1399³ Hierarch (USA) *(LordHuntingdon)* 8-11 WRSwinburn (2) (lw: 2nd st: ev ch 2f
out: wknd ins fnl f) ............................................................................ ³/₄.**4**

**11/10** PROFUSION, **3/1** Hierarch (USA), **9/2** Lobilio (USA)(op 3/1), **5/1** Milzig (USA). CSF £5.84, Tote £2.00
(£3.40). Mr Fahd Salman (WHATCOMBE) bred by Dr F. Krief. 4 Rn            2m 32.62 (3.12)
                                     SF—54/50/47/45

**1538**      E.B.F. HALIFAX STKS (Mdn 2-Y.O.F) £7310.00 (£2180.00: £1040.00: £470.00)
               **6f**                                         4-40 (4-41)

    **Sumoto** (Fav) *(GWragg)* 8-11 WRSwinburn (1) (w'like: scope: lw: hld up: led
over 1f out: comf) ............................................................................. —**1**
    Sayyedati *(CEBrittain)* 8-11 MRoberts (2) (w'like: scope: lw: a.p: ev ch 1f out:
r.o) ...................................................................................................... 2.**2**
    Zenith *(IABalding)* 8-11 JReid (7) (w'like: scope: a.p: led over 2f out tl over 1f
out: wknd ins fnl f) ............................................................................ 8.**3**
    Kennedys Prima *(AAScott)* 8-11 BRaymond (6) (w'like: scope: bit bkwd: no
hdwy fnl 2f) ....................................................................................... 3¹/₂.**4**
    Lakab (USA) *(HThomsonJones)* 8-11 RHills (4) (scope: dwlt: hdwy over 3f out:
wknd over 1f out) ............................................................................... s.h.**5**
    Baydon Belle (USA) *(GLewis)* 8-11 PaulEddery (3) (leggy: prom 4f) ..................... 3.**6**
    Blazing Soul (IRE) *(PAKelleway)* 8-11 PRobinson (5) (leggy: lw: led over 3f) ... s.h.**7**
    Early Song *(PTWalwyn)* 8-11 PatEddery (8) (w'like: scope: bit bkwd: outpcd: a
bhd) ..................................................................................................... ³/₄.**8**

**10/11** SUMOTO, **5/1** Lakab (USA)(3/1—6/1), **6/1** Sayyedati(op 4/1), Zenith, **7/1** Early Song, **20/1** Kennedys
Prima, **25/1** Baydon Belle (USA), **33/1** Blazing Soul (IRE). CSF £7.42, Tote £2.10: £1.20 £2.00 £1.90 (£5.40). Sir
Philip Oppenheimer (NEWMARKET) bred by Hascombe and Valiant Studs. 8 Rn        1m 14.82 (1.22)
                                       SF—61/53/21/7/6/–

**1539**      TOTE SEVENTH RACE H'CAP (0-100) £7375.00 (£2200.00: £1050.00: £475.00)
               **1¹/₄m**                                       5-10 (5-11)

    **Charlo (90)** *(JHMGosden)* 4–9-9 SCauthen (6) (3rd st: led wl over 1f out: comf) —**1**

1200² Fire Top **(93)** (Fav) *(RAkehurst)* 7-9-12 PatEddery (5) (led tl wl over 1f out: r.o) .... 5.2
1081² Abingdon Flyer (IRE) **(72)** (bl) *(RHannon)* 4-8-5 JReid (7) (4th st: r.o one pce fnl
2f) .................................................................................................................. 2.3
360² Starlight Flyer **(95)** (bl) *(MMoubarak)* 5-10-0 LDettori (2) (2nd st: ev ch 2f out:
sn wknd) ....................................................................................................... 5.4
Jungle Dancer (IRE) **(87)** *(MRStoute)* 4-9-6 PD'Arcy (4) (outpcd & wl bhd:
hdwy & 5th st: one pce) .................................................................... 7.5
Diamond Cut (FR) **(71)** *(MCPipe)* 4-8-4 MRoberts (1) (rdn along: prom tl wknd
& 6th st) ......................................................................................................... 6.6
1203³ Jimlil **(79)** *(BPalling)* 4-8-12 RHills (3) (a bhd: 7th st) ........................................ 10.7

**11/4** Fire Top, **4/1** Starlight Flyer(3/1—9/2), **5/1** Diamond Cut (FR), CHARLO, **6/1** Jimlil, **7/1** Abingdon Flyer
(IRE), **16/1** Jungle Dancer (IRE). CSF £17.87, Tote £4.70: £2.80 1.50 (£6.90). Sheikh Mohammed
(NEWMARKET) bred by D. J. and Mrs Deer. 7 Rn                                                              2m 5.93 (1.63)
                                                                                                 SF—83/76/51/64/42/14

T/Trio: Race 1: £618.80 (3 Tckts), Race 2: £51.30 (30.5 Tckts) and Race 3: £179.10 (20.3 Tckts). T/Jkpt:
£10,906.90 (8.3 Tckts). T/Plpt: £179.60 (124.3 Tckts).                                                              Hn

---

## 1410—**LINGFIELD (L-H)**

## **Saturday, June 20th [Turf Good to firm, Firm back st, AWT Standard]**
Going Allowance: AWT: minus 0.45 sec (FS); Turf: minus 0.20 sec (F)

Stalls: high                                                                         Wind: mod half against

**1540**   SOO BIRTHDAY APP'CE STKS (Mdn 3-Y.O) £1618.00 (£448.00: £214.00)
        **1m (AWT)**                                                                        6-00 (6-02)

1323⁴ Missy-S (IRE) **(50)** *(GAPritchard-Gordon)* 8-9 DHarrison (5) (lw: hdwy over 2f
out: led ins fnl f: r.o wl) ........................................................................ —1
1213 Lamore Ritorna **(54)** *(KOCunningham-Brown)* 8-9 FNorton (3) (lw: led 6f out:
qcknd 2f out: hdd ins fnl f: unable qckn) ............................................ 2.2
526 Forest Law (USA) **(75)** (Fav) *(PFICole)* 9-0 SO'Gorman (7) (b.nr hind: a.p: hrd
rdn over 1f out: one pce) ....................................................................... 3¹/₂.3
1411 Girton Degree **(49)** (v) *(SDow)* 8-9 MJerry (2) (lw: led 2f: one pce fnl 3f) ....... 2.4
804 Prove It's Gold *(TMJones)* 8-9 KRutter (4) (nvr nr to chal) ................................. 6.5
1315 Magic Penny *(CACyzer)* 8-6 ‡³TMcLaughlin (6) (prom over 6f) ......................... hd.6
1183⁵ Millyrous (IRE) *(RGuest)* 8-4 ‡⁵SEiffert (1) (bhd fnl 4f) .................................... 3¹/₂.7
True Contender *(CACyzer)* 8-9 RPerham (8) (str: bit bkwd: a bhd) ...................... 2¹/₂.8

**10/11** Forest Law (USA)(6/4—7/4), **11/4** MISSY-S (IRE), **5/1** Lamore Ritorna, **9/1** True Contender, **10/1** Girton
Degree, **12/1** Magic Penny(op 7/1), **14/1** Millyrous (IRE), **25/1** Prove It's Gold. CSF £18.58, Tote £3.10: £1.30
1.80 1.10 (£13.60). Mrs Stephanie Goodman (NEWMARKET) bred by A. F. O'Callaghan in Ireland. 8 Rn
                                                                                                 1m 38.49 (1.79)
                                                                                                 SF—17/11/5/–/–/–

**1541**   E.B.F. SAFFRON STKS (Mdn 2-Y.O) £2385.00 (£660.00: £315.00)
                                                           **5f**     6-30 (6-32)

Maroof (USA) *(RWArmstrong)* 9-0 WCarson (2) (cmpt: bit bkwd: led over 3f
out: pushed out) ........................................................................................ —1
933 Young Ern *(SDow)* 9-0 BRouse (3) (hld up: hrd rdn over 1f out: ev ch ins fnl f:
unable qckn) ............................................................................................... 1.2
595 Pirates Gold (IRE) *(MJHeaton-Ellis)* 8-9 ‡⁵DHarrison (4) (lw: hdwy 2f out: unable
qckn fnl f) ................................................................................................... 1¹/₂.3
933⁴ Simply Finesse (Fav) *(RAkehurst)* 8-11 ‡³RPerham (1) (a.p: ev ch 2f out: wknd
fnl f) ............................................................................................................. 4.4
1300 Hawaii Star (IRE) *(GLewis)* 8-9 PaulEddery (10) (nvr nr to chal) ..................... s.h.5
803⁶ Will's Legacy *(WCarter)* 8-11 ‡³FNorton (9) (lw: s.s: a bhd) ............................. 3.6
1170 Generally *(PatMitchell)* 8-6 ‡³SO'Gorman (5) (a bhd) ...................................... ³/₄.7
Frasers Hill (IRE) *(PFICole)* 8-9 TQuinn (8) (b.nr hind: leggy: led over 1f: wknd
over 2f out) .................................................................................................. 2.8
1208⁴ Stardust Express *(MJohnston)* 9-0 BRaymond (7) (bhd fnl 2f) ........................ 2¹/₂.9
*Stewards Enquiry: Obj. to Maroof (USA) by Rouse overruled.*

**5/2** Simply Finesse, **7/2** Stardust Express(4/1—6/1), **4/1** MAROOF (USA)(3/1—5/1), **6/1** Frasers Hill (IRE)(op
2/1), **7/1** Will's Legacy, **11/1** Hawaii Star (IRE)(8/1—12/1), **14/1** Young Ern, Pirates Gold (IRE), **33/1** Generally.
CSF £52.15, Tote £5.00: £1.90 4.60 3.00 (£88.40). Mr Hamdan Al-Maktoum (NEWMARKET) bred by
Shadwell Frm Inc. & Shadwell Estate Co. Ltd in USA. 9 Rn                                           59.82 sec (2.82)
                                                                                                 SF—24/20/9/–/–/–

**1542**  IPC WOMEN'S MAGAZINES GROUP H'CAP (0-70) £1856.80 (£514.80: £246.40)
1¼m
7-00 (7-03)

| | | | |
|---|---|---|---|
| 1341 | **Spectacular Dawn (65)** *(JLDunlop)* 3–9-0  WCarson (3): (led over 4f: 2nd st: led wl over 1f out: r.o wl) | —1 |
| 1032 | Neptune's Pet **(64)** *(GLewis)* 4–9-11  DHolland (8): (lw: led over 5f out tl wl over 1f out: unable qckn) | 3½.2 |
| 1195★ | Sarah-Clare **(58)** (Fav) *(RAkehurst)* 4–9-2 ‡³RPerham (2): (3rd st: hrd rdn over 2f out: one pce) | 1½.3 |
| 1323⁶ | Swell Time (IRE) **(32)** *(CNAllen)* 4–7-7  GBardwell (4): (b.hind: 4th st: hrd rdn over 2f out: one pce) | hd.4 |
| 192⁶ | Dutch Czarina **(43)** *(MissBSanders)* 4–8-1 ‡³FNorton (1): (lw: 5th st: rdn over 2f out: r.o ins fnl f) | s.h.5 |
| 774 | Sciacca **(34)** *(CWeedon)* 5–7-9⁽²⁾ SDawson (5): (lw: s.s: nvr nr to chal) | 3½.6 |
| | Bwana Kali **(32)** (bl) *(JABennett)* 10–7-0 ‡⁷CHawksley (7): (b: 6th st: a bhd) | 12.7 |
| 182³ | Telegraphic **(56)** *(MBell)* 3–8-5  TQuinn (9): (lw: bhd fnl 6f) | 15.8 |
| 1323 | Mint Addition **(45)** *(KOCunningham-Brown)* 3–7-8  NCarlisle (6): (a bhd) | 1.9 |

LONG HANDICAP: Swell Time (IRE) 7-5, Sciacca 7-5, Bwana Kali 7-5.

**11/8** Sarah-Clare, **9/4** SPECTACULAR DAWN, **6/1** Neptune's Pet, **8/1** Telegraphic(op 5/1), **10/1** Swell Time (IRE), **14/1** Dutch Czarina(op 8/1), **20/1** Mint Addition, **33/1** Ors. CSF £16.56, CT £22.89. Tote £3.30: £1.40 £1.70 £1.50 (£11.30). Mr Peter S. Winfield (ARUNDEL) bred by Peter Winfield. 9 Rn     2m 7.63 (4.63)
SF—34/38/26/2/9/–

**1543**  HONEYWOOD H'CAP (0-80) £2186.80 (£604.80: £288.40)
1½m (AWT)
7-30 (7-31)

| | | | |
|---|---|---|---|
| 1081★ | **Monarda (70)** *(PFICole)* 5–10-0  TQuinn (1): (a.p: led 2f out: r.o wl) | —1 |
| 1324⁴ | Mr Wishing Well **(51)** *(RJRWilliams)* 6–8-9  DHolland (7): (lw: hdwy over 5f out: hrd rdn over 1f out: unable qckn) | 1½.2 |
| 340 | Springs Welcome **(68)** *(CACyzer)* 6 9 5 ‡⁷TMcLaughlin (4): (rdn thrght: hdwy over 2f out: r.o ins fnl f) | 1½.3 |
| 1341 | Merry Marigold **(50)** *(JDRoberts)* 6–8-8  TLang (2): (b: hdwy 6f out: led over 2f out: sn hdd: one pce) | nk.4 |
| 1372⁴ | Sweet Bubbles (IRE) **(48)** *(CACyzer)* 4–8-6  AMorris (8): (lw: a.p: one pce fnl 3f) | 2½.5 |
| 993⁵ | Tiger Shoot **(55)** (Fav) *(DJSCosgrove)* 5–8-13  AShoults (3): (led over 9f) | 2.6 |
| | Native Magic **(64)** *(RWArmstrong)* 6–9-8  BCrossley (6): (lw: a bhd) | 3½.7 |
| 331⁵ | Sparkler Gebe **(49)** *(RJO'Sullivan)* 6–8-7  PaulEddery (5): (prom 9f) | 5.8 |
| 1376 | Watermill Girl **(36)** *(DTThom)* 4–7-1⁽¹⁾ ‡⁷CHawksley (9): (a bhd) | 3.9 |

LONG HANDICAP: Watermill Girl 7-2.

**11/4** Tiger Shoot, **7/2** Mr Wishing Well, **4/1** MONARDA, **11/2** Merry Marigold, **13/2** Springs Welcome, **8/1** Sweet Bubbles (IRE), **10/1** Sparkler Gebe, **12/1** Native Magic, **40/1** Watermill Girl. CSF £19.31, CT £85.82. Tote £4.10: £1.70 £1.30 £2.70 (£6.70). Mr Fahd Salman (WHATCOMBE) bred by Newgate Stud Ltd. 9 Rn     2m 29.76 (0.36)
SF—56/34/41/29/22/25

**1544**  CHOICEST H'CAP (Amateurs) (0-70) £1660.00 (£460.00: £220.00)
1m (AWT)
8-00 (8-03)

| | | | |
|---|---|---|---|
| 1203⁴ | **Usa Dollar (65)** (bl) *(BGubby)* 5–11-9 ‡⁵MrPDaw (3): (hdwy over 1f out: rdn fnl f: led last stride) | —1 |
| 1143³ | Times Are Hard **(40)** *(CASmith)* 8–9-12 ‡⁵MrNMiles (7): (a.p: hrd rdn over 1f out: led nr fin: hdd last stride) | s.h.2 |
| 1338² | Bill Moon **(47)** (Fav) *(PJFeilden)* 6–10-10  MissJFeilden (11): (lw: a.p: hrd rdn over 1f out: r.o wl ins fnl f) | s.h.3 |
| 1145 | Up the Punjab **(65)** *(SDow)* 3–10-13 ‡⁵MrTCuff (6): (a.p: led over 3f out tl hdd nr fin) | hd.4 |
| 1404★ | High Post **(53)** *(DMarks)* 3–10-6  MissKMarks (8): (led over 4f: wknd 2f out) | 5.5 |
| 1377⁶ | Beechwood Cottage **(54)** (bl) *(ABailey)* 9–11-3  MissDianaJones (8): (lw: prom over 5f) | 1½.6 |
| 1319 | Allmosa **(65)** *(TJNaughton)* 3–10-13 ‡⁵MrsJNaughton (1): (b: nvr nr to chal) | 2½.7 |
| 1278 | Verro (USA) **(34)** (bl) *(JABennett)* 5–9-11 ‡⁵MissAPurdy (10): (lw: prom 5f) | 2.8 |
| 333 | Sockem **(38)** *(CNWilliams)* 5–10-1  MrsJCrossley (4): (lw: bhd fnl 3f) | 4.9 |
| | Priok **(35)** *(WGRWightman)* 9–9-7 ‡⁵MissLHide (9): (bit bkwd: a bhd) | 1.10 |
| | One Magic Moment (IRE) **(60)** *(CACyzer)* 4–11-4 ‡⁵MrsMCornelius (12): (bhd fnl 4f) | 2.11 |
| | More Ice **(42)** *(CWeedon)* 6–10-0⁽⁷⁾ ‡⁵MrRDyer (2): (a wl bhd) | 10.12 |

LONG HANDICAP: Verro (USA) 9-11.

**6/4** Bill Moon, **5/1** High Post, Up the Punjab, **7/1** USA DOLLAR, **8/1** Beechwood Cottage, **10/1** Times Are Hard(8/1—12/1), **14/1** Allmosa, **16/1** Sockem, **20/1** Verro (USA)(op 12/1), **33/1** Priok, One Magic Moment (IRE), **50/1** More Ice. CSF £74.27, CT £149.57. Tote £9.80: £2.40 £2.40 £1.10 (£22.40). Brian Gubby Ltd (BAGSHOT) bred by Brian Gubby Ltd. 12 Rn     1m 38.83 (2.13)
SF—51/25/36/38/16/22

**1545**　　SUMMER H'CAP (0-90) £2660.00 (£735.00: £350.00)　**5f**　　8-30 (8-32)
(Weights raised 18 lb)

1415* **Shades of Jade (52)** (Fav) *(JJBridger)* 4–8-12 TQuinn (1) (mde all: drvn out) ... —1
1338[5] Martinosky **(60)** *(WGRWightman)* 6–9-6 PaulEddery (3) (rdn over 3f out: chsd
wnr over 2f out: r.o wl) ............................................................. hd.2
1392 Tauber **(63)** *(PatMitchell)* 8–9-6 ‡[3]SO'Gorman (4) (outpcd: swtchd lft & hdwy 2f
out: unable qckn) ....................................................................... 4.3
1445[2] Running Glimpse (IRE) **(64)** *(MissBSanders)* 4–9-7 ‡[3]FNorton (2) (bhd fnl 2f) . 2[1]/2.4

**13/8** SHADES OF JADE, **5/2** Tauber, **11/4** Martinosky, **3/1** Running Glimpse (IRE). CSF £6.41, Tote £2.60
(£4.50). Mr W. Wood (LIPHOOK) bred by W. A. Wood. 4 Rn　　　　　58.75 sec (1.75)
SF–43/50/34/25

T/Plpt: £43.40 (37.1 Tckts).　　　　　　　　　　　　　　　　　　　　　　　　　　　AK

---

1372—**SOUTHWELL** (L-H) Fibresand
**Saturday, June 20th [Standard]**
Going Allowance: minus 0.10 sec per fur (FS)　　　　　　　　　　　Wind: slt across

Stalls: high

**1546**　　PORTLAND AND MANSFIELD BRICK STKS (Mdn) £1276.50 (£354.00: £169.50)
**1³/₄m (AWT)**　　　　　　　　　　　　　　　　　　　　　6-35 (6-41)

1430[2] **Serious Time (52)** *(SirMarkPrescott)* 4–9-0 CNutter (9) (a.p: led 3f out: sn clr:
rdn over 1f out: jst hld on) ................................................................ —1
291 Milly Black (IRE) **(44)** *(JLHarris)* 4–8-4 ‡[5]SMaloney (13) (hdwy & 5th st: wnt 2nd
over 1f out: wkd & r.o ins fnl f) ............................................................ s.h.2
974 Stradbroke **(30)** *(MBJames)* 5–9-0 AProud (12) (hdwy 7f out. 3rd st. one pce fnl
2f) ...................................................................................... 20.3
1190[3] Domain **(53)** (bl) *(RJWeaver)* 4–8-9 ‡[5]RPrice (10) (lw: led: rdn 6f out: hdd
3f out: 2nd st: wknd 2f out) ............................................................ s.h.4
1399 Master's Crown (USA) *(MCChapman)* 4–8-7 ‡[7]SWilliams (3) (swtg: s.i.s: hdwy
8f out: 4th st: wknd 2f out) ................................................................ 2.5
Cheap Metal (bl) *(RIngram)* 7–9-0 PBurke (14) (prom tl rdn & wknd 6f out) .. 20.6
1317[4] Armashocker **(48)** *(DSasse)* 4–8-9 ‡[5]EmmaO'Gorman (1) (nvr nrr) ............ 3.7
Duchess of Savoy (IRE) *(JEBanks)* 4–8-2 ‡[7]JSwinnerton (4) (b: nvr nr ldrs) ...... ³/₄.8
Lorica D'Or *(PFTulk)* 5–8-7 ‡[7]TWilson (7) (bkwd: a bhd: t.o) ........................ 10.9
Nip *(ASReid)* 4–8-2 ‡[7]PMcCabe (2) (prom tl 6th & wkng st: t.o) .................... 2.10
1009 Attic Wit (FR) *(RJHolder)* 6–9-0 NAdams (5) (a bhd: t.o) .......................... 15.11
Dry Gin *(MCChapman)* 9–9-0 KFallon (8) (prom 6f: t.o) .............................. 2[1]/2.12
1312 Aurora Lad *(MrsSJSmith)* 5–8-7 ‡[7]GParkin (6) (swtg: a bhd: t.o) ................ 15.13

**7/4** Domain, **5/2** SERIOUS TIME, **8/1** Master's Crown (USA), **10/1** Duchess of Savoy (IRE), **12/1** Armashocker,
**16/1** Milly Black (IRE), **20/1** Lorica D'Or, Dry Gin, Aurora Lad, **25/1** Attic Wit (FR), **33/1** Stradbroke, Nip, **40/1**
Cheap Metal. CSF £40.31, Tote £3.10: £1.70 £2.50 £8.60 (£7.80). Mr G. Moore (NEWMARKET) bred by W. D. J.
Ropner. 13 Rn　　　　　　　　　　　　　　　　　　　　　　　　　　　　　3m 7.2 (7.9)
SF–7/–/–/–/–/–

**1547**　　PORTLAND AND MANSFIELD ASPHALT (S) STKS (2-Y.O) £1287.00 (£357.00: £171.00)
**5f (AWT)**　　　　　　　　　　　　　　　　　　　　　　　7-05 (7-10)

1264* **Matthew David** *(MBrittain)* 8-9 ‡[5]SMaloney (1) (a.p: led over 1f out: r.o wl) —1
1321[2] Pretzel (IRE) (v) *(NTinkler)* 8-11 WRyan (10) (lw: led over 3f: nt qckn fnl f) ......... 2.2
286 Brave Bidder *(BGubby)* 8-6 JQuinn (2) (a.p: ev ch over 1f out: nt qckn) ......... hd.3
1373[3] Another Kingdom *(JWharton)* 8-8 ‡[3]DBiggs (6) (a.p: ev ch over 1f out: one pce) ¹/₂.4
Jordywrath *(ICampbell)* 8-11 MTebbutt (12) (leggy: lt-f: hld up: hdwy fnl f: nvr
plcd to chal) ............................................................................. 2.5
1322 Big Gem *(MCChapman)* 8-4 ‡[7]SWilliams (4) (nvr nr to chal) ........................ 2[1]/2.6
1332[3] My Godson (bl) *(BBeasley)* 8-11 LCharnock (14) (prom over 3f) .................. 1.7
1373[2] Samanthas Joy (Fav) *(TFairhurst)* 8-3 ‡[3]JFanning (9) (spd 3f) ................... ¹/₂.8
1373[5] Tee-Emm *(PHowling)* 8-11 CNutter (7) (a bhd) .......................................... 1.9
561 Grand Game (v) *(DHaydnJones)* 8-11 TyroneWilliams (5) (hrd rdn over 2f out:
no rspnse) .............................................................................. 1[1]/2.10
Hajaan *(BBeasley)* 8-6 PBurke (8) (leggy: bkwd: s.s: t.o) .......................... 10.11
1332 Dazzling Baby *(MDods)* 8-6 KFallon (13) (wnt lft s: outpcd: t.o) ................ 30.12
1127[3] Betrayed Withdrawn (crashed thro paddock rails) : not under orders

**9/4** Samanthas Joy, **7/2** Pretzel (IRE), **5/1** My Godson, MATTHEW DAVID, **6/1** Another Kingdom, **12/1**
Jordywrath, **14/1** Hajaan, **16/1** Grand Game, **25/1** Tee-Emm, **33/1** Ors. CSF £24.27, Tote £5.40: £1.80 £1.40
£7.80 (£8.70). M. D. M. Racing (Thoroughbreds) Limited (WARTHILL) bred by MDM Racing (Thoroughbreds)
Ltd. 12 Rn; Sold I Booth 5,000 gns　　　　　　　　　　　　　　　　　　62.8 sec (4.8)

**1548**    BARFIELD BUSINESS CENTRE NEWARK H'CAP (3-Y-O) (0-70) £1255.50 (£348.00: £166.50)    **1m 3f (AWT)**        7-35 (7-36)

(Weights raised 4 lb)

| | | |
|---|---|---|
| 1180 | **Shakinski (51)** *(MJRyan)* 8-3 ‡³DBiggs (4) (s.i.s: hdwy & 6th st: edgd lft ins fnl f: rdn to ld cl home) | —1 |
| 1320³ | Spray of Orchids **(49)** *(JEtherington)* 8-4 KDarley (10) (hdwy 5f out: 4th st: led over 1f out: hdd nr fin) | 1.2 |
| 1123⁵ | Holy Wanderer (USA) **(52)** *(DWPArbuthnot)* 8-2 ‡⁵RPrice (7) (lw: hld up & bhd: gd hdwy 5f out: led 3f out: hdd over 1f out: one pce) | 2.3 |
| 1320⁴ | High Success **(50)** (Fav) *(WAO'Gorman)* 8-0⁽²⁾ ‡⁵EmmaO'Gorman (5) (lw: hdwy & c wd over 2f out: nvr nr to chal) | 10.4 |
| 1052* | Gay Ming **(41)** *(RHollinshead)* 7-3⁽²⁾ ‡⁷AGarth (6) (nvr nr ldrs) | 8.5 |
| 1287 | Alto **(47)** (bl) *(JGFitzGerald)* 8-2 JQuinn (9) (eyeshield: hdwy 7f out: wknd 4f out) | 6.6 |
| 1276⁴ | Bernie Silvers **(49)** *(MCChapman)* 8-4 KFallon (11) (prom 7f) | 1½.7 |
| 1123 | Istanbullu **(48)** *(MBell)* 8-3 MHills (2) (led 8f: 2nd st: wknd over 2f out) | 2.8 |
| 734 | Monorose **(58)** *(DHaydnJones)* 8-13 TyroneWilliams (1) (prom: rdn 6f out: 3rd st: wknd 2f out) | 7.9 |
| 649 | Nobby Barnes **(66)** *(RWArmstrong)* 9-7 JHo (3) (5th st: wknd 2f out) | 3.10 |
| 1320 | Molten Copper (IRE) **(57)** (bl) *(MWEasterby)* 8-12 TLucas (8) (w ldr tl wknd 5f out: t.o) | 25.11 |

**4/1** High Success, **9/2** Spray of Orchids, Holy Wanderer (USA), **6/1** Gay Ming, **8/1** Istanbullu, **12/1** Bernie Silvers, Molten Copper (IRE), Nobby Barnes, **14/1** Monorose, **16/1** SHAKINSKI & Ors. CSF £83.41, CT £354.13. Tote £15.60: £3.60 £1.80 £1.70 (£91.40). Mr N. H. Tampkins (NEWMARKET) bred by Miss K. Rausing. 11 Rn

2m 26 (4.5)

SF—33/32/26/4/–/–

**1549**    NATIONAL PLANT AND TRANSPORT PLC STKS (Mdn 2-Y-O) £1203.00 (£333.00: £159.00)    **7f (AWT)**        8-05 (8-07)

| | | |
|---|---|---|
| 1251 | **Mohican Brave (IRE)** *(JGFitzGerald)* 9-0 KFallon (12) (eyeshield: plld hrd: 3rd st: led over 1f out: hung rt ins fnl f: r.o) | —1 |
| | Noyan (Fav) *(MBell)* 9-0 MHills (7) (w'like: scope: s.i.s: hdwy 4f out: rdn to ld 2f out: sn hdd: hmpd ins fnl f: r.o) | 1½.2 |
| 1322³ | Nutty Brown *(SGNorton)* 9-0 KDarley (1) (5th st: nt clr run on ins 2f out: swtchd rt over 1f out: r.o ins fnl f) | 1.3 |
| 1112 | Doc Spot *(CaptJWilson)* 8-11 ‡³DBiggs (8) (7th st: r.o fnl f: nrst fin) | 8.4 |
| 1017⁵ | Sophie's Boy *(MHEasterby)* 9-0 MBirch (4) (led 5f) | nk.5 |
| 968 | Daring King (v) *(DSasse)* 9-0 DaleGibson (9) (plld hrd: 6th st: wknd 2f out) | ½.6 |
| 1375² | Colfax Starlight *(BSRothwell)* 8-9 SWood (10) (2nd st: wknd 2f out) | 1.7 |
| | Turfmans Vision *(RHollinshead)* 9-0 WRyan (11) (lt-f: s.s: a bhd) | 1½.8 |
| | Benevolent *(SirMarkPrescott)* 9-0 GDuffield (3) (w'like: bit bkwd: bhd fnl 4f) | ½.9 |
| | Travelling Lad *(BBeasley)* 9-0 LCharnock (2) (lt-f: s.i.s: a bhd) | nk.10 |
| 1378 | Pennine Lad (IRE) *(BGubby)* 9-0 NAdams (6) (dwlt: a bhd) | 2½.11 |
| | Calenick Lass *(JGFitzGerald)* 8-9 GBardwell (5) (leggy: unf: t.o) | 20.12 |

**7/4** Noyan, **11/4** Benevolent, **4/1** Nutty Brown, **7/1** Sophie's Boy, **9/1** Colfax Starlight, **16/1** Turfmans Vision, MOHICAN BRAVE (IRE), **20/1** Pennine Lad (IRE), Travelling Lad, Calenick Lass, **25/1** Daring King, **33/1** Doc Spot. CSF £48.40, Tote £16.20: £3.90 £1.80 £1.20 (£53.90). Mr J. Dick (MALTON) bred by Airlie Stud in Ireland. 12 Rn

1m 30.6 (4)

SF—29/24/21/–/–/–

**1550**    PORTLAND AND FIBRESAND H'CAP (0-70) £1318.50 (£366.00: £175.50)    **7f (AWT)**        8-35 (8-40)

(Weights raised 4 lb)

| | | |
|---|---|---|
| 1376* | **Tyrian Purple (IRE) (56)** *(RHollinshead)* 4-8-12 ‡⁷MHumphries (8) (2nd st: led over 2f out: jst hld on) | —1 |
| 1266* | Hawaii Storm (FR) **(48)** *(MissAJWhitfield)* 4-8-11 DaleGibson (6) (lw: 8th st: hdwy 2f out: rdn & edgd lft over 1f out: r.o ins fnl f) | s.h.2 |
| 1377⁴ | Wellsy Lad (USA) **(61)** *(DWChapman)* 5-9-10 SWood (5) (5th st: rdn over 1f out: one pce) | 4.3 |
| 1377* | Sandmoor Denim **(49)** *(SRBowring)* 5-8-5 ‡⁷MHarris (12) (hld up: hdwy fnl 2f: r.o) | ¾.4 |
| 1411 | Our Eddie **(63)** (bl) *(BGubby)* 3-9-3 KFallon (14) (hdwy over 1f out: r.o ins fnl f) | nk.5 |
| 1364⁶ | The Dream Maker (IRE) **(42)** *(MrsNMacauley)* 3-7-10 LCharnock (4) (led over 4f: r.o one pce fnl 2f) | 1½.6 |
| 1323 | Lunagraphe (USA) **(36)** *(BobJones)* 4-7-13 JQuinn (2) (7th st: no hdwy fnl 2f) | s.h.7 |
| 1032 | Quinzii Martin **(57)** (v) *(DHaydnJones)* 4-9-6 TyroneWilliams (3) (4th st: wknd 2f out) | s.h.8 |
| 1267⁵ | Qualitair Rhythm (IRE) **(50)** *(ICampbell)* 4-8-13 MTebbutt (15) (hld up & bhd: stdy hdwy fnl 2f: nvr plcd to chal) | s.h.9 |
| 1377⁵ | Sergeant Meryll **(35)** *(PHowling)* 8-7-9 ‡³DBiggs (16) (bhd fnl 2f) | nk.10 |

963 Lowlands Boy **(56)** *(TFairhurst)* 3-8-7 ‡³JFanning (5) (3rd st: wknd 2f out) ....... 1.11
775⁴ A Little Precious **(58)** *(Fav) (JRBostock)* 6-9-7 GDuffield (9) (a bhd) ............... hd.12
1376³ Eliza Wooding **(37)** *(CJHill)* 4-8-0 NAdams (11) (a bhd) .................................. ½.13
　　　Vague Nancy (IRE) **(38)** *(CJHill)* 4-8-1 AProud (1) (bit bkwd: dwlt: a bhd) ........ 5.14
　　　Where's Ruth (IRE) **(65)** *(MWEasterby)* 3-9-5 TLucas (10) (bit bkwd: a bhd: t.o) 7.15
1323² Hubbers Favourite **(54)** *(MrsNMacauley)* 4-8-10 ‡⁷SWilliams (13) (lw: chsd ldrs
　　　tl 6th & wkng st: t.o) .................................................................................... 1.16

**3/1** A Little Precious(op 6/1), **11/2** Sandmoor Denim, **7/1** Hubbers Favourite, **8/1** TYRIAN PURPLE (IRE), **10/1** Hawaii Storm (FR), **11/1** Wellsy Lad (USA), Eliza Wooding, Quinzii Martin, **12/1** Qualitair Rhythm (IRE)(op 8/1), **14/1** Lowlands Boy, **16/1** Sergeant Meryll, **20/1** Where's Ruth (IRE), **25/1** Vague Nancy (IRE), **33/1** Ors. CSF £86.05, CT £821.83. Tote £8.90: £2.20 £2.40 £2.60 £1.50 (£33.80). Rykneld Thoroughbred Co Ltd (UPPER LONGDON) bred by Niels Schibbye in Ireland. 16 Rn　　　　　　　　　　　　1m 29.6 (3)
　　　　　　　　　　　　　　　　　　　　　　　　　　　　　　　　SF—42/40/41/20/31/5

**1551**　　PORTLAND COLLEGE AND MANSFIELD SAND H'CAP (0-70) £1297.50 (£360.00:
　　　　　£172.50)　　　6f **(AWT)**　　　　　　　　　　　　　　　9-05 (9-09)

1325⁶ **Strip Cartoon (IRE) (46)** (bl) *(SRBowring)* 4-8-3 ‡⁷MHarris (9) (led 4f out: clr 2f
　　　out: rdn out) ............................................................................................ —1
496 Swinging Lady **(54)** *(WWHaigh)* 4-8-13 ‡⁵SMaloney (10) (b.hind: 5th st: r.o one
　　　pce fnl 2f) ................................................................................................. 3.2
1451³ Waverley Star **(47)** (bl) *(SGNorton)* 7-8-11 LCharnock (1) (3rd st: r.o one pce
　　　fnl 2f) ....................................................................................................... nk.3
1325³ Sobering Thoughts **(41)** (bl) *(DWChapman)* 6-8-5 SWood (12) (6th & c wd st:
　　　rdn over 1f out: r.o) ................................................................................... nk.4
1325² The Shanahan Bay **(54)** (v) *(Jt-Fav) (MrsNMacauley)* 7-8-11 ‡⁷SWilliams (2) (b:
　　　7th st: hdwy whn nt clr run over 1f out: swtchd lft: one pce) ³/₄.5
1377³ Mushy Boff **(52)** *(CJHill)* 4-9-2 NAdams (4) (lw: hld up: hdwy over 1f out: r.o) ... 1.6
209⁶ Supor Hoightо **(60)** (bl) *(MissA IWhitfield)* 4-9-10 DaleGibson (11) (nvr nr to chal) 2.7
1271 King Victor (IRE) **(45)** (bl) *(RO'Leary)* 4-8-9 MBirch (6) (4th & c wd st: eased
　　　whn btn fnl f) ............................................................................................. hd.8
1263 Serious Hurry **(33)** *(SirMarkPrescott)* 4-9-9 GDuffield (3) (bhd fnl 2f) ................. 2.9
1487³ Furiella **(64)** *(Jt-Fav) (PCHaslam)* 4-10-0 DMcKeown (13) (s.s: a bhd) ............. 1.10
1310 Minizen Music (IRE) **(34)** *(MBrittain)* 4-7-12 TyroneWilliams (4) (led 2f: 2nd st:
　　　wknd 2f out) ............................................................................................... 2¹/₂.11
752 Damaaz (IRE) **(32)** *(JSWainwright)* 4-7-7³ ‡³JFanning (8) (a bhd) ...................... ¹/₂.12
1338 More Larks **(48)** (bl) *(MBJames)* 4-8-12 AProud (14) (swvd rt s: t.o) ..... 10.13
　　　　　　　　　　LONG HANDICAP: Damaaz (IRE) 7-1.

**4/1** The Shanahan Bay, Furiella(op 5/2), **13/2** Waverley Star, **7/1** Sobering Thoughts, Mushy Boff, **9/1** STRIP CARTOON (IRE)(8/1—12/1), **10/1** Swinging Lady, **12/1** Super Heights, **14/1** Serious Hurry, Minizen Music (IRE), **16/1** King Victor (IRE), **20/1** Damaaz (IRE), **33/1** More Larks. CSF £94.61, CT £585.14. Tote £10.40: £2.30 £3.30 £1.90 (£42.20). Mrs Irene Pryce (EDWINSTOWE) bred by John Kelly in Ireland. 13 Rn
　　　　　　　　　　　　　　　　　　　　　　　　　　　　　　　1m 15.9 (2.5)
　　　　　　　　　　　　　　　　　　　　　　　　　　　　　SF—27/25/22/15/18/19

T/Plpt: £153.80 (10.8 Tckts).　　　　　　　　　　　　　　　　　　　　　　KH

1006—**WARWICK (L-H)**
**Saturday, June 20th [Firm]**
Going Allowance: 5f: minus 0.20 sec; Rest: minus 0.40 sec (F)　　　Wind: slt against

Stalls: low

**1552**　　HENLEY IN ARDEN H'CAP (0-70) £2324.00 (£644.00: £308.00)　　5f　　6-15 (6-21)

1427 Rays Mead **(45)** *(LJHolt)* 4-8-4⁽¹⁾ WNewnes (3) (b: swtg: a.p: led 2f out: clr 1f
　　　out: hld on) ................................................................................................ —1
1282⁶ Petitesse **(47)** *(GBlum)* 4-8-6 RFox (5) (chsd ldrs: effrt over 1f out: r.o wl ins fnl
　　　f) .............................................................................................................. ³/₄.2
1406⁴ Iron King **(69)** (v) *(JLSpearing)* 6-9-7 ‡⁷EHusband (6) (hdwy ¹/₂-wy: rdn over 1f
　　　out: kpt on) ............................................................................................... hd.3
1305⁵ Ayr Raider **(64)** (bl) *(WRMuir)* 5-9-9 SWhitworth (11) (reard & lost ground s:
　　　hdwy 2f out: hrd rdn & r.o fnl f) ................................................................ 2.4
1271² Supreme Desire **(44)** *(ASmith)* 4-8-3⁽⁸⁾ SWebster (15) (hdwy over 1f out: hrd
　　　rdn & r.o fnl f) ........................................................................................... ¹/₂.5
1278 Tippling (USA) **(34)** *(PBurgoyne)* 5-7-0 ‡⁷AntoinetteArmes (16) (r.o appr fnl f:
　　　nvr nrr) ..................................................................................................... 2.6
1338 Tachyon Park **(38)** (v) *(PHowling)* 10-7-6 ‡⁵BDoyle (1) (chsd ldrs: no hdwy appr
　　　fnl f) ......................................................................................................... ³/₄.7
1162 Ever so Artistic **(38)** *(PHowling)* 5-7-11 CRutter (12) (spd over 3f) .................... ¹/₂.8

1138[5] Hitchin a Ride **(58)** (bl) *(MPMuggeridge)* 5–9–3 RCochrane (14) (chsd ldrs 3f) .... s.h.**9**
1415[3] Catalani **(51)** (Fav) *(TJNaughton)* 7–8–10 AMunro (8) (b: spd 3f) .................... hd.**10**
　　Cal's Boy **(41)** (bl) *(JPSmith)* 3–7–7 RStreet (2) (bkwd: outpcd) .................... nk.**11**
1364[4] Jaromic **(52)** *(PFTulk)* 3–7–11 ‡[7]MichaelBradley (13) (chsd ldrs: rdn & wknd 2f
　　out) .................................................................................... 3¹/₂.**12**
*1325* Royal Bear **(40)** *(JMBradley)* 10–7–8[(6)] ‡[5]ATucker (7) (bhd: rdn ¹/₂-wy: no
　　rspnse) ............................................................................... 1¹/₂.**13**
1415 Tyrone Turbo (USA) **(47)** *(JAkehurst)* 3–7–8 ‡[5]NKennedy (10) (b.hind: led 3f:
　　wknd qckly) .......................................................................... 1¹/₂.**14**
1138[4] Bridle Talk (IRE) **(50)** *(MMcCormack)* 3–8–2[(1)] AClark (9) (lw: reluctant to r: a
　　t.o) .................................................................................... 20.**15**
LONG HANDICAP: Tippling (USA) 7-4, Cal's Boy 7-5, Royal Bear 6-12.

**5/1** Catalani, **11/2** Iron King, **6/1** Ayr Raider, Supreme Desire, Petitesse, **10/1** Tyrone Turbo (USA)(8/1—12/1),
**11/1** Hitchin a Ride, **14/1** Bridle Talk (IRE), **20/1** Jaromic, RAYS MEAD, **25/1** Tachyon Park, **33/1** Cal's Boy,
Tippling (USA), Ever so Artistic, **50/1** Royal Bear. CSF £125.74, CT £696.44. Tote £22.00: £4.40 £2.40 £1.90
(£63.30). Miss D. M. Green (BASINGSTOKE) bred by Miss D. M. Green. 15 Rn　　59.6 sec (1.6)
SF—38/37/51/45/23/–

**1553**　　HAMPTON GRADUATION STKS (2-Y.O.F) £2145.00 (£595.00: £285.00)
　　　　6f　　　　　　　　　　　　　　　　　　　　　　　　　　6-45 (6-50)

1259 **Mrs West (USA)** (Fav) *(JLDunlop)* 8-11 PatEddery (4) (hld up: wnt 2nd st: rdn
　　appr fnl f: r.o to ld wl ins fnl f) ................................................. —**1**
1186 Laurel Delight *(JBerry)* 9-4 RCochrane (1) (lw: led: shkn up over 1f out: hdd wl
　　ins fnl f) ............................................................................. 2.**2**
　　Ballon *(CEBrittain)* 8-11 MRoberts (3) (wl grwn: bit bkwd: chsd ldrs: sn pushed
　　along: 3rd st: outpcd appr fnl f) ................................................. 4.**3**
　　Oriental Princess *(MrsSOliver)* 8-7[(3)] ‡[7]EHusband (2) (lt-f: s.v.s: a bhd: 4th & t.o
　　st) ..................................................................................... 12.**4**

**5/6** MRS WEST (USA), **3/1** Laurel Delight(op 2/1), Ballon, **33/1** Oriental Princess. CSF £3.41, Tote £2.00
(£2.10). Mr S. Khaled (ARUNDEL) bred by Palides Investments in USA. 4 Rn　　1m 14.9 (2.9)

**1554**　　ASHORNE (S) STKS (2-Y.O) £1046.40 (£290.40: £139.20)　　6f　　7-15 (7-19)

1233[6] **Simply Amiss** *(SirMarkPrescott)* 8-6 MRoberts (9) (prom tl outpcd ¹/₂-wy:
　　hdwy 2f out: led appr fnl f: sn clr: easily) .................................... —**1**
1409 Risky Number *(JSMoore)* 8-6 ‡[5]ATucker (1) (chsd ldrs: 4th st: ev ch 1f out: one
　　pce) ................................................................................... 3.**2**
1299 Kafioca (IRE) (Fav) *(MHTompkins)* 8-6 PRobinson (2) (chsd ldrs: 5th st: effrt 2f
　　out: kpt on u.p fnl f) .............................................................. 3.**3**
1140[3] Grey Runner *(BPalling)* 7-13 ‡[7]StephenDavies (2) (led tl hdd & wknd appr fnl f) 1¹/₂.**4**
*1264* Miss Fitness *(DrJDScargill)* 8-6 AMunro (10) (bhd: rdn 2f out: nvr nr to chal) .... 3.**5**
1384[6] Lady of Shadows *(SDow)* 8-6 WNewnes (7) (hdwy 2f out: sn rdn: nt rch ldrs) . 3¹/₂.**6**
*1264* I'Ll Risk it *(JBerry)* 8-7[(1)] RCochrane (1) (lw: dwlt: sn rcvrd: 2nd st: wknd wl over
　　1f out) ................................................................................ 3.**7**
1007 Clare's Boy *(JMBradley)* 8-4 ‡[7]MichaelBradley (6) (lt-f: bkwd: prom tl 6th &
　　wkng st: t.o) ......................................................................... 10.**8**
791 Mdm Racer (IRE) *(JBerry)* 8-11 JReid (5) (w ldr: 3rd & rn wd ent st: sn bhd & t.o) 6.**9**

**5/4** Kafioca (IRE), **7/2** SIMPLY AMISS, **13/2** Grey Runner(5/1—8/1), Lady of Shadows, **9/1** Mdm Racer (IRE),
**12/1** Risky Number, **14/1** Miss Fitness(10/1—16/1), **20/1** I'Ll Risk it, **33/1** Clare's Boy. CSF £42.24, Tote £4.70:
£1.30 £4.00 £1.60 (£82.60). Mr Neil Greig (NEWMARKET) bred by Somerhall Bloodstock Ltd. 9 Rn; Bt in 6,200
gns　　　　　　　　　　　　　　　　　　　　　　　　　　　　　　　1m 14.9 (2.9)

**1555**　　KNIGHTWAY PROMOTIONS H'CAP (0-85) £2856.00 (£791.00: £378.00)
　　　　1¹/₄m 169y　　　　　　　　　　　　　　　　　　　　　　7-45 (7-46)

1387[4] **Knock Knock (83)** (Fav) *(IABalding)* 7–10-0 RCochrane (5) (hld up & bhd: 4th
　　st: qcknd to ld ins fnl f: readily) ................................................ —**1**
993 Dovale **(66)** *(WJarvis)* 4–8-11 JReid (3) (lw: chsd ldr: 3rd st: swtchd & led 1f out:
　　sn hdd: unable qckn: nr fin) ...................................................... 1.**2**
1284* Sooty Tern **(51)** *(JMBradley)* 5–7–10 CRutter (4) (led to 1f out: rdn & no ex ins
　　fnl f) .................................................................................. ³/₄.**3**
1371[4] Sky Train (IRE) **(67)** *(JLDunlop)* 3–7–12[(2)] AMunro (1) (hld up: 5th st: effrt &
　　n.m.r over 1f out: rdn & r.o nr fin) .............................................. hd.**4**
1180[4] Whisper's Shadow **(75)** *(MHTompkins)* 3–8–6 PRobinson (6) (bit bkwd: a.p:
　　wnt 2nd st: hrd rdn & wknd appr fnl f) ........................................ 3.**5**
　　Gesnera **(54)** *(KWhite)* 4–7–13 RFox (2) (bkwd: a bhd: 6th st: t.o) ............... 12.**6**

**7/4** KNOCK KNOCK, **5/2** Sooty Tern, **4/1** Sky Train (IRE), **9/2** Whisper's Shadow, **8/1** Dovale(6/1—10/1), **50/1**
Gesnera. CSF £14.52, Tote £2.60: £1.70 £2.60 (£7.70). Mr G. M. Smart (KINGSCLERE) bred by Lodge Park
Stud. 6 Rn　　　　　　　　　　　　　　　　　　　　　　　　　2m 17.6 (4.1)
SF—29/10/–/–/–/–

**1556**   WARWICK OAKS STKS (3-Y.O.F) £3557.50 (£1060.00: £505.00: £227.50)
1¹/₂m 115y                                                        8-15 (8-16)

1101a³ **Up Anchor (IRE) (104)** *(Fav) (PFICole)* 8-13 AMunro (3) (lw: hld up: 2nd st: led
over 1f out: rdn out) ............................................................ —1
1073★ Truben (USA) **(86)** *(HRACecil)* 8-13 PatEddery (2) (lw: chsd ldr: led 4f out tl
over 1f out: rallied gamely u.p nr fin) ................................... ³/₄.2
922★ Spikenard *(PTWalwyn)* 8-13 RCochrane (1) (lw: hld up: 4th st: hdwy 2f out: hrd
rdn & r.o wl fnl f) .................................................................. nk.3
818³ Nina's Chocolates (USA) *(CEBrittain)* 8-10 MRoberts (4) (lw: led 8f: 3rd st:
eased whn btn appr fnl f) ................................................... 12.4

**8/13** UP ANCHOR (IRE)(4/6—4/9), **2/1** Truben (USA), **10/1** Nina's Chocolates (USA)(5/1—11/1), **20/1**
Spikenard. CSF £2.14, Tote £1.60 (£1.60). Mr Fahd Salman (WHATCOMBE) bred by Universal Stables in Ireland.
4 Rn                                                                 2m 39.3 (1.8)
SF—31/29/28/1

**1557**   FERNDALE H'CAP (3-Y.O) (0-80) £2363.20 (£655.20: £313.60)   7f   8-45 (8-45)
(Weights raised 8 lb)

1166³ **Morocco (IRE) (69)** *(Fav) (RCharlton)* 9-7 PatEddery (1) (lw: chsd ldr: 2nd st:
led over 1f out: rdn out) ...................................................... —1
1062 Douraj (IRE) **(60)** *(CEBrittain)* 8-12 MRoberts (2) (lw: led tl hdd over 1f out:
rallied u.p: no ex nr fin) ........................................................ 1.2
1157⁵ Ustka **(66)** *(MRStoute)* 9-4 RCochrane (3) (b.hind: hld up: 5th st: hdwy 2f out:
nt rch ldrs) ............................................................................ 3.3
1277⁵ Sudanor (IRE) **(65)** *(MJHeaton-Ellis)* 9-3 JReid (4) (chsd ldrs: 3rd st: rdn 2f out:
one pce) ................................................................................ 1.4
1304⁶ Bells of Longwick **(56)** *(DRLaing)* 8-1 ‡⁷PBowe (5) (b.hind: swtg: chsd ldrs: 4th
st: wknd wl over 1f out) ....................................................... 8.5

**11/0** MOROCCO (IRE), **6/2** Ustka, **4/1** Sudanor (IRE). **15/2** Douraj (IRE)(5/1—8/1), **25/1** Bells of Longwick. CSF
£9.67, Tote £2.10: £1.30 £3.00 (£6.00). Mr Martin Myers (BECKHAMPTON) bred by Nikita Investments in
Ireland. 5 Rn                                                       1m 24.9 (0.7)
SF—54/42/39/35

T/Plpt: £49.30 (31.55 Tckts).                                       IM

## 1435—**EDINBURGH (R-H)**

### Monday, June 22nd [Firm]

Going Allowance: minus 0.45 sec per fur (F)                         Wind: almost nil

Stalls: 1st & 2nd centre, remainder high

**1558**   ISLE OF MAY STKS (Mdn 3-Y.O) £2169.00 (£609.00: £297.00)   5f   2-15 (2-15)

1238³ **High Principles (54)** *(JBerry)* 9-0 JCarroll (1) (mde all: hung rt 2f out: r.o) ........ —1
1364³ Katie-a (IRE) *(Fav) (RMWhitaker)* 8-9 ACulhane (4) (lw: plld hrd: w wnr: sltly
hmpd wl over 1f out: rdn & no imp after) ........................... 2¹/₂.2
1436 Lawnswood Prince (IRE) **(63)** *(JLSpearing)* 9-0 KDarley (2) (lw: prom: effrt
¹/₂-wy: rdn & no imp) ........................................................... 2.3
218⁴ Colour Solutions *(TDBarron)* 8-2 ‡⁷VHalliday (3) (chsd ldrs 3f: sn btn) ........ 2.4

**8/11** Katie-a (IRE)(op 5/4), **2/1** HIGH PRINCIPLES(6/4—9/4), **9/2** Colour Solutions, **12/1** Lawnswood Prince
(IRE)(op 4/1). CSF £4.05, Tote £2.60 (£1.40). Heathavon Stables Limited (COCKERHAM) bred by Heathavon
Stables Ltd. 4 Rn                                                   59.5 sec (1.8)
SF—19/4/1/–

**1559**   CRAIGLEITH CLAIMING STKS (2-Y.O) £2050.00 (£575.00: £280.00)   5f   2-45 (2-46)

1373★ **Classic Storm** *(Fav) (JBerry)* 8-9 JCarroll (7) (mde most: shkn up over 1f out:
r.o) ........................................................................................ —1
1332² First Option *(MHEasterby)* 8-12 KDarley (1) (lw: w wnr: effrt over 1f out: nt qckn) 2¹/₂.2
1240⁵ Bright Gem *(TFairhurst)* 8-6 ‡³JFanning (6) (sn w ldrs: rdn 2f out: one pce) ..... 1¹/₂.3
1233 Not Earsay *(EWeymes)* 7-6 ‡⁷MHumphries (5) (lw: bhd tl styd on wl fnl f) ........ 2¹/₂.4
1435² Petered Out *(TDBarron)* 8-7 ‡⁷VHalliday (2) (chsd ldrs: sn pushed along: no imp
fr ¹/₂-wy) ................................................................................ ¹/₂.5
1321⁶ Nellie's Gamble (bl) *(APStringer)* 7-8 ‡⁵SMaloney (4) (s.i.s: n.d) ...................... 1¹/₂.6
1435⁵ Cambus Bay *(WTKemp)* 8-3 JLowe (3) (sn outpcd & wl bhd) ......................... 20.7

**Evens** CLASSIC STORM, **9/4** First Option(3/1—2/1), **7/1** Petered Out(op 3/1), **12/1** Bright Gem(op 6/1), **50/1**
Not Earsay, Nellie's Gamble, **100/1** Cambus Bay. CSF £3.16, Tote £1.80: £1.40 £1.30 (£3.20). Mr D. J. Ayres
(COCKERHAM) bred by Concorde Breeding and Racing International P'Ship. 7 Rn; Classic Storm clmd
R.Berenson £9,270                                                   59.2 sec (1.5)
SF—20/13/1/–/–/–

**1560**     YVONNE MURRAY M.B.E. H'CAP (0-80) £2221.50 (£624.00: £304.50)
             **1m 7f 16y**
                                                                    3-15 (3-16)
                              (Weights raised 13 lb)

12743 **Sapphirine (60)** *(RMWhitaker)* 5–9–10 ACulhane (6) (a cl up: led over 2f out: r.o
               u.p) ..................................................................................... —1
1437* **Fen Princess (IRE) (44)** (Fav) *(PCHaslam)* 4–8–8 (4x) DMcKeown (2) (hld up:
               lost pl appr st: effrt over 3f out: hrd rdn & r.o wl nr fin) ....... hd.2
1119  My Desire (60) *(MrsGRReveley)* 4–9–5 ‡5SMaloney (5) (lw: hld up: hdwy appr st:
               ev ch 2f out: nt qckn ins fnl f) .................................................. ½.3
1381  Intricacy (59) *(CCElsey)* 4–9–9 JLowe (4) (trckd ldrs: effrt 3f out: one pce) ...... 3½.4
      Lyphard's Song (IRE) (37) *(NAGraham)* 4–8–1(2) KDarley (3) (swtg: led tl hdd
               over 2f out: r.o one pce) ........................................................ nk.5
13623 Feeling Foolish (IRE) (52) (bl) *(TFairhurst)* 3–7–9 ‡3JFanning (1) (b.off hind: lw:
               bhd: effrt ent st: sn btn) ............................................................. 30.6

**11/10** Fen Princess (IRE), **11/2** SAPPHIRINE, My Desire, **6/1** Intricacy, **15/2** Feeling Foolish (IRE), **16/1**
Lyphard's Song (IRE). CSF £11.41, Tote £3.40: £2.10 £2.50 (£3.20). Mr Frazer Hines (WETHERBY) bred by E. J.
Loder in Ireland. 6 Rn                                                            3m 20.8 (10.3)

**1561**     HADDINGTON MEDIAN AUCTION STKS (Mdn 3-Y.O) £2445.00 (£600.00)
             **1m 3f 32y**
                                                                    3-45 (3-46)

14203 **Briggs Lad (IRE) (68)** (Fav) *(WJarvis)* 9-0 MTebbutt (2) (lw: mde all: shkn up
               over 1f out: qcknd: comf) ........................................................... —1
13343 Canaan Lane (69) *(AHarrison)* 9-0 KFallon (1) (lw: chsd wnr: effrt u.p over 2f
               out: nt qckn appr fnl f) ............................................................. 3½.2

**4/7** BRIGGS LAD (IRE), **6/4** Canaan Lane. Tote £1.50. Mr F. W. Briggs (NEWMARKET) bred by Topazio Est Vaduz
in Ireland. 2 Rn                                                                  2m 27 (7.3)

**1562**     LINLITHGOW CLAIMING STKS (Mdn) £2242.50 (£630.00: £307.50)
             **1m 16y**
                                                                    4-15 (4-16)

1075  **Spanish Performer (50)** *(TFairhurst)* 3–7–10 ‡3JFanning (4) (lw: bhd: hdwy 2f
               out: qcknd to ld wl ins fnl f) .................................................... —1
14392 Northern Graduate (USA) (53) (Fav) *(MrsGRReveley)* 3–8–4 KDarley (2) (chsd
               ldrs: ev ch 1f out: hrd rdn & r.o one pce) ................................ 1.2
14374 J P Morgan (44) (v) *(MPNaughton)* 4–9–0 KFallon (7) (s.i.s: sn rcvrd & led: hdd
               & no ex wl ins fnl f) ................................................................... hd.3
14393 Miss Parkes (43) *(JBerry)* 3–8–4 JCarroll (5) (lw: bhd: effrt over 2f out: styd on
               one pce fnl f) ............................................................................. 2.4
14395 Perspicacity (39) *(MDods)* 5–8–7 JLowe (3) (bhd: hdwy on outside over 3f out:
               ev ch 2f out: wknd 1f out) ......................................................... 2.5
14865 Stoproveritate (51) *(SGNorton)* 3–7–6 ‡7DarrenMoffatt (1) (lw: chsd ldrs: effrt 2f
               out: no rspnse) ......................................................................... 1½.6
14416 Rapid Mover (23) *(TCraig)* 5–8–10 NConnorton (6) (led early: chsd ldr tl wknd
               fnl 2f) ........................................................................................ 2.7
9496  Never Late (56) *(MHEasterby)* 3–7–10 ‡5SMaloney (8) (chsd ldrs: effrt 2f out: nt
               run on) ...................................................................................... 3½.8

**11/10** Northern Graduate (USA)(4/5—11/8), **4/1** Never Late, **15/2** Perspicacity, **8/1** SPANISH PERFORMER,
Stoproveritate(op 5/1), **10/1** Miss Parkes, **14/1** J P Morgan, **50/1** Rapid Mover. CSF £17.27, Tote £11.30: £2.30
£1.30 £2.20 (£9.40). Mr B. Harland (MIDDLEHAM) bred by S. F. Strong. 8 Rn               1m 42.4 (3.8)

**1563**     FIRTH OF FORTH H'CAP (3-Y.O) (0-70) £2221.50 (£624.00: £304.50)
             **7f 15y**
                                                                    4-45 (4-46)
                              (Weights raised 7 lb)

1320* **Coastal Express (62)** (Fav) *(EWeymes)* 9-6 WNewnes (2) (a.p: led 2f out: hld
               on gamely) .............................................................................. —1
14404 Oyston's Life (46) *(JBerry)* 8-4 JCarroll (1) (in tch: hdwy to chal over 1f out: r.o) hd.2
14402 Denim Blue (55) *(CWThornton)* 8-13 DMcKeown (4) (lw: lost pl appr st: effrt &
               n.m.r over 2f out: r.o wl nr fin) ............................................... ½.3
11852 Thornton Gate (55) *(MHEasterby)* 8-13 MBirch (6) (led tl hdd 2f out: hrd rdn &
               kpt on one pce) ......................................................................... nk.4
9943  Dragon Spirit (63) (bl) *(SPCWoods)* 9-7 WWoods (3) (lw: chsd ldrs: hdwy u.p
               over 1f out: btn whn hmpd wl ins fnl f) .................................... 2½.5
13365 Fair Flyer (IRE) (51) (v) *(PMonteith)* 8-9 NConnorton (5) (cl up tl grad wknd fnl
               2f) .............................................................................................. 1½.6

**4/5** COASTAL EXPRESS, **9/2** Thornton Gate, **6/1** Denim Blue, **15/2** Dragon Spirit(5/1—8/1), **10/1** Oyston's
Life(8/1—12/1), **14/1** Fair Flyer (IRE). CSF £8.91, Tote £1.60: £1.10 £4.00 (£18.60). Mrs R. L. Heaton
(MIDDLEHAM) bred by Bechmann Stud. 6 Rn                                           1m 27.7 (1.5)
                                                          SF—36/19/26/25/25/8

**1564**    LEVY BOARD APP'CE H'CAP (0-70) £2169.00 (£609.00: £297.00)
7f 15y
5-15 (5-17)

913[3] **Valley of Time (FR) (38)** (Fav) *(TCraig)* 4–8-4 DarrenMoffatt (4) (mde all: r.o wl fnl 2f) .................................... —1

1449[3] **Gant Bleu (FR) (44)** *(RMWhitaker)* 5–8-10 GParkin (3) (lw: trckd wnr after 3f: effrt 1f out: nt qckn nr fin) .................... ½.2

1343 **Wessex Milord (29)** *(JABennett)* 7–7-9 JMarshall (5) (b: chsd ldrs: outpcd ent st: n.d fin) .................... 7.3

1512[3] **Yes (54)** *(DTThom)* 4–9-6 PBowe (2) (chsd ldrs: rdn 3f out: no imp) .................... ¾.4

**Stairway to Heaven (IRE) (62)** (bl) *(TDBarron)* 4–10-0 VHalliday (1) (bit bkwd: s.i.s: effrt ent st: n.d) .................... ¾.5

**Baton Boy (27)** *(SGNorton)* 11–7-7 MHumphries (7) (bit bkwd: a bhd) .................... 1.6

615 **Say You Will (31)** (v) *(MPNaughton)* 8–7-11 DCarson (6) (prom tl outpcd ent st: n.d after) .................... ¾.7

LONG HANDICAP: Baton Boy 7-0.

**11/8** VALLEY OF TIME (FR), **4/1** Gant Bleu (FR), **5/1** Yes, **8/1** Say You Will, **10/1** Wessex Milord, **14/1** Stairway to Heaven (IRE)(op 7/1), **16/1** Baton Boy. CSF £6.85, Tote £2.30: £2.20 1.60 (£3.20). Mr James Glass (DUNBAR) bred by M. Fustok in France. 7 Rn
1m 26.8 (0.6)
SF—34/38/2/25/31/–

T/Plpt: £6.90 (206.15 Tckts).    AA

---

1416—**NOTTINGHAM (L-H)**

**Monday, June 22nd [Good to firm, Firm patches]**

Going Allowance: nil sec per fur (F)     Wind: almost nil

Stalls: high

**1565**    YOURS MAGAZINE CLAIMING STKS (3-Y.O) £2402.40 (£666.40: £319.20)
1m 1f 213y
2-00 (2-03)

1142[4] **Handy Lass** *(JWharton)* 7-11 JQuinn (2) (mde all: rdn clr appr fnl f) .................... —1

355 **Expansionist** *(SPCWoods)* 8-4 MHills (1) (lw: in tch: 6th st: chsd wnr fnl f: no imp) .................... 4.2

1123[3] **Silver Samurai (62)** *(RHollinshead)* 8-9 WRyan (6) (chsd ldrs: 4th st: ev ch over 3f out: no ex fnl 2f) .................... 1½.3

1382 **Mashakel (USA) (82)** (Fav) *(BHanbury)* 9-7 BRaymond (8) (b: swtg: hld up: 7th st: effrt over 2f out: kept on one pce) .................... 1.4

1156[3] **Sakbah (USA)** *(JRFanshawe)* 8-0(3) GCarter (4) (prom: 3rd st: one pce fnl 2f) . 2½.5

1070★ **Ace Girl (54)** *(SRBowring)* 7-13 ‡3FNorton (7) (chsd wnr: 2nd st: wknd 3f out) ... 6.6

**New Years Eve** *(PJMakin)* 8-6 ‡3TSprake (7) (leggy: lt-f: a bhd) .................... 2.7

**Izitallworthit** *(JMackie)* 8-4 GHind (10) (unf: bkwd: s.i.s: effrt 5f out: wknd over 2f out) .................... 1½.8

1268 **Aislabie Airborne** *(MrsNMacauley)* 8-5 SWhitworth (5) (5th st: wknd 3f out) ....... 7.9

1276 **My Boy Buster** *(CJHill)* 8-2 NAdams (3) (a bhd) .................... 2.10

**7/4** Mashakel (USA), **4/1** Ace Girl(3/1—9/2), **9/2** Silver Samurai, **6/1** HANDY LASS, **7/1** Sakbah (USA)(op 9/2), **10/1** New Years Eve, **20/1** My Boy Buster, **25/1** Izitallworthit, **33/1** Ors. CSF £142.63, Tote £4.50: £1.20 £36.60 £1.60 (£75.80). Mr J. Rose (MELTON MOWBRAY) bred by John Rose. 10 Rn
2m 8.8 (6.3)
SF—20/19/21/31/5/–

**1566**    SHADWELL STUD APP'CE SERIES H'CAP (0-70) £2532.00 (£702.00: £336.00)
1¾m 15y
2-30 (2-30)

1361[3] **Caroles Clown (40)** *(MJHaynes)* 6–8-1 ‡7DToole (7) (chsd ldrs: 5th st: rdn to ld wl over 1f out: pushed clr fnl f) .................... —1

1419 **Pondered Bid (37)** (bl) *(PatMitchell)* 8–8-5 RPerham (5) (b: chsd ldrs: rdn & 3rd st: styd on fnl f) .................... 10.2

1179[3] **Sweet Request (43)** (bl) *(JRBostock)* 4–8-8 ‡3CHawksley (2) (lw: chsd ldr tl led 5f out: hdd wl over 1f out: one pce) .................... hd.3

**War Beat (53)** *(PJBevan)* 4–9-7 BDoyle (1) (bit bkwd: bhd: rdn 3f out: styd on: nrst fin) .................... 2½.4

**Ryewater Dream (57)** *(RJHodges)* 4–9-11 TSprake (4) (swtg: bkwd: led 9f: 2nd st: wknd over 1f out) .................... hd.5

1419[4] **Sea Paddy (52)** *(RBastiman)* 4–9-3 ‡3HBastiman (9) (swtg: chsd ldrs: 4th st: rdn & btn 3f out) .................... 5.6

1390 **Master Line (40)** *(HCandy)* 11–8-1 ‡7SDrake (6) (swtg: in tch 9f) .................... ½.7

1341 **Famous Beauty (48)** *(RHollinshead)* 5–8-9 ‡7JDennis (11) (dwlt: rdn over 4f out: a bhd) .................... 4.8

| | | |
|---|---|---|
| 1237² | Playful Juliet (CAN) **(40)** *(BRCambidge)* 4–8-8 RPrice (10) (a bhd) | ¾.9 |
| 1248★ | Forelino (USA) **(66)** (Fav) *(JLDunlop)* 3–8-10 ‡7KateAhern (8) (hld up: wnt poor 6th st: sn btn) | 1½.10 |
| 501 | Lord Future (IRE) **(35)** *(AWPotts)* 4–8-3 OPears (3) (b.hind: bhd fnl 6f: t.o) | 30.11 |

**9/4** Forelino (USA), **4/1** Sea Paddy, **13/2** Famous Beauty, **7/1** Sweet Request, **8/1** Pondered Bid, **14/1** CAROLES CLOWN(op 8/1), **16/1** Master Line, **20/1** Playful Juliet (CAN), Lord Future (IRE), **25/1** Ryewater Dream, **33/1** War Beat. CSF £107.97, CT £773.78. Tote £12.50: £2.20 £1.90 £2.20 (£41.30). Mr M. J. Haynes (EPSOM) bred by P. F. and I. Mummery. 11 Rn
                                                 3m 5.2 (6.7)
                                            SF—20/4/6/14/17/–

## 1567     POST OFFICE STKS (Mdn 3-Y.O) £2265.20 (£627.20: £299.60)     2m 9y    3-00 (3-02)

| | | |
|---|---|---|
| 1156² | **Cantanta (70)** (bl) *(RCharlton)* 8-9 RCochrane (3) (lw: a.p: 3rd st: led 2f out: pushed out) | —1 |
| 1313³ | Betelgeuse *(HRACecil)* 8-9 WRyan (2) (led 1f: chsd ldr: 2nd st: led 4f out to 2f out: one pce) | 2½.2 |
| | Bandao *(JMackie)* 9-0 GHind (8) (w'like: bkwd: bhd: hdwy ½-wy: 5th st: kpt on fnl 3f) | 10.3 |
| 1286 | Ellafitzetty (IRE) **(54)** (bl) *(RFJohnsonHoughton)* 8-9 MRoberts (5) (swtg: hdwy & poor 6th st: r.o fnl 2f) | ¾.4 |
| 1374³ | Pippas Song *(GWragg)* 8-6 ‡3FNorton (9) (bhd: 7th st: sn rdn & no imp) | 5.5 |
| 1024² | King's Treasure (USA) **(79)** (Fav) *(IABalding)* 9-0 JReid (6) (lw: chsd ldrs: 4th & rdn st: sn btn) | 2½.6 |
| | Ghostly Glow *(CCElsey)* 9-0 TRogers (1) (bit bkwd: bhd fr ½-wy) | 10.7 |
| 625 | Kajaani (IRE) **(74)** (bl) *(PFICole)* 9-0 TQuinn (7) (swtg: led after 1f to 4f out: sn rdn & wknd) | ½.8 |
| 1313 | Pot Hunting *(WJarvis)* 9-0 WCarson (11) (prom: rdn ½-wy: sn lost tch) | ½.9 |
| 1265 | Royal Opera Star *(JRBosley)* 9-0 GeeArmytage (10) (swtg: t.o fnl 10f) | 30.10 |
| 1313 | Perfect Light **(54)** *(MrsSJSmith)* 9-0 SWhitworth (4) (chsd ldrs 8f: t.o) | nk.11 |

**7/4** King's Treasure (USA), **7/2** Betelgeuse, **11/2** CANTANTA, **7/1** Kajaani (IRE)(op 4/1), **8/1** Pippas Song, **12/1** Pot Hunting, **25/1** Ellafitzetty (IRE), Perfect Light, **33/1** Bandao, **50/1** Ors. CSF £23.91, Tote £5.20: £1.70 £1.30 £12.20 (£10.50). Mr K. Abdulla (BECKHAMPTON) bred by Juddmonte Farms. 11 Rn
                                                 3m 32.4 (8)
                                            SF—15/12/7/1/–/–

## 1568     RECLINERS UNLIMITED H'CAP (3-Y.O) (0-70) £2598.40 (£722.40: £347.20)     1m 1f 213y    3-30 (3-30)
                                 (Weights raised 4 lb)

| | | |
|---|---|---|
| 1336 | **Great Max (IRE) (60)** *(SirMarkPrescott)* 9-1 GDuffield (3) (in rr tl hdwy 3f out: rdn to ld ins fnl f) | —1 |
| 1519² | Cold Shower (IRE) **(60)** *(JAGlover)* 8-8 ‡7SWilliams (1) (hld up: 5th st: ev ch over 1f out: rdn & r.o ins fnl f) | 1½.2 |
| 848⁵ | Leap in the Dark (IRE) **(66)** (Fav) *(JLDunlop)* 9-7 WCarson (8) (prom: 3rd st: led over 2f out: hdd & no ex ins fnl f) | 2½.3 |
| 1175⁶ | Roca Murada (IRE) **(49)** *(MJRyan)* 8-1 ‡3DBiggs (2) (6th st: ev ch over 1f out: sn rdn & wknd) | 8.4 |
| 1298 | Kentucky Chicken (USA) **(38)** (bl) *(MissLCSiddall)* 7-7 EJohnson (5) (lw: sn prom: 2nd st: wknd 3f out) | ¾.5 |
| 1417 | Do the Business (IRE) **(41)** (bl) *(CNAllen)* 7-10 WAAntongeorgi (6) (led: qcknd over 4f out: hdd over 2f out: wknd appr fnl f) | 5.6 |
| 858 | Royal Print (IRE) **(55)** *(WRMuir)* 8-10 SWhitworth (7) (swtg: chsd ldrs: 4th st: wknd over 2f out) | 1½.7 |
| 1294 | Magnetic Prince **(40)** *(GBlum)* 7-2⁽²⁾ ‡7CHawksley (4) (bhd: 7th st: effrt 4f out: sn btn) | 12.8 |

LONG HANDICAP: Kentucky Chicken (USA) 7-5, Magnetic Prince 7-0.

**4/7** Leap in the Dark (IRE), **4/1** Cold Shower (IRE), **6/1** Roca Murada (IRE), **10/1** Royal Print (IRE)(op 6/1), **14/1** GREAT MAX (IRE), **33/1** Ors. CSF £67.55, CT £77.13. Tote £12.30: £1.90 £1.30 £1.10 (£8.30). Sir Mark Prescott (NEWMARKET) bred by J. B. Clarke in Ireland. 8 Rn
                                                 2m 8.8 (6.3)
                                            SF—38/28/36/–/–/–

## 1569     STANNAH LIFTS MEDIAN AUCTION GRADUATION STKS (2-Y.O.C & G) £2912.40 (£806.40: £385.20)     6f 15y    4-00 (4-00)

| | | |
|---|---|---|
| 581² | **Tioman Island** (Fav) *(PFICole)* 8-11 TQuinn (2) (prom: led over 2f out: rdn out) | —1 |
| 988 | Special Risk (IRE) *(MBell)* 8-11 MHills (6) (hld up: plld out over 2f out: ev ch 1f out: unable qckn ins fnl f) | 1½.2 |
| 1249⁴ | Savings Bank *(GAPritchard-Gordon)* 8-11 GCarter (5) (lw: trckd ldrs: ev ch 1f out: unable qckn) | ¾.3 |
| 968⁴ | Bold Acre (bl) *(DRLaing)* 8-11 RCochrane (4) (swtg: dwlt: sn chsng ldrs: no imp fnl 2f) | 2.4 |

Pure Madness (USA) *(DrJDScargill)* 8-11 AMunro (1) (leggy: w'like: swrvd lft s: spd over 3f) .......... 10.5

*1373* He Nose You Know (IRE) (v) *(CNAllen)* 8-11 MRoberts (3) (led over 3f: sn bhd) 10.6

**4/9** TIOMAN ISLAND, **4/1** Savings Bank, **14/1** Special Risk (IRE)(op 7/1), **16/1** Pure Madness (USA), Bold Acre(op 7/1), **25/1** He Nose You Know (IRE). CSF £6.93, Tote £1.40: £1.10 £2.80 (£6.00). H. H. Sultan Ahmad Shah (WHATCOMBE) bred by Whitsbury Manor Stud. 6 Rn                     1m 14.9 (3.9)
SF—19/13/10/2/–/–

---

**1570**  YOURS MAGAZINE 'FOR THE YOUNG AT HEART' H'CAP (0-70) £2618.00 (£728.00: £350.00)  **6f 15y**                                       4-30 (4-34)

(Weights raised 2 lb)

1314⁴ Harry's Coming (58) *(RJHodges)* 8-9-10 RCochrane (8) (hld up: hdwy to ld ins fnl f: readily) .......... —1

1310² Morpick (53) (v) (Jt-Fav) *(JPLeigh)* 5-8-12 ‡⁷StephenDavies (17) (a.p: ev ch 1f out: one pce) .......... 2¹/₂.2

1278 Ganeshaya (44) (bl) *(MFBarraclough)* 3-8-2 NCarlisle (19) (led tl hdd & wknd ins fnl f) .......... 2.3

1427⁶ Banbury Flyer (55) *(MrsALMKing)* 4-9-7 MRoberts (11) (chsd ldrs: rdn 2f out: kpt on fnl f) .......... 1.4

1282 Vendredi Treize (33) *(SRBowring)* 9-7-13 NAdams (14) (b: chsd ldrs: no imp fnl 2f) .......... hd.5

1365* Quiet Victory (49) (bl) *(MissLCSiddall)* 5-8-12 ‡³FNorton (15) (bhd: r.o appr fnl f: nrst fin) .......... 1.6

1309⁴ Creego (43) *(JAGlover)* 3-8-1 DHolland (12) (prom 4f) .......... nk.7

1193 Flashy's Son (48) *(MDHammond)* 4-9-0 BRaymond (7) (b.off hind: nvr nrr) ..... ¹/₂.8

1415⁵ Bishopstone Bill (37) *(SMellor)* 3-7-9 DanaMellor (18) (in tch: no imp appr fnl f) 1¹/₂.9

1310⁴ Johanna Thyme (38) (Jt-Fav) *(RBastiman)* 5-8-4 JQuinn (16) (bhd tl r.o appr fnl f) .......... 1.10

1160³ Dickens Lane (53) *(RJHodges)* 5-9-2 ‡³TSprake (1) (lw: in tch: rdn 2f out: no imp) .......... ¹/₂.11

C Sharp (48) *(WRMuir)* 5-9-0 SWhitworth (3) (swtg: bkwd: dwlt: n.d) ............ 1¹/₂.12

1343 My Ruby Ring (41) *(DRLaing)* 5-8-0 ‡⁷KimMcDonnell (9) (b: swtg: w ldrs over 3f) ¹/₂.13

1271 Foxes Diamond (36) *(BEllison)* 4-8-2 GHind (13) (chsd ldrs tl wknd 2f out) ..... ¹/₂.14

1427 Dreamtime Echo (35) *(JBalding)* 4-7-8 ‡⁷ClaireBalding (5) (nvr nr to chal) ....... 2.15

1314 Fabled Orator (46) (bl) *(PHowling)* 7-8-12 WRyan (10) (b.nr hind: gd spd over 3f) .......... 2.16

*1551* Minizen Music (IRE) (34) *(MBrittain)* 4-8-0 GBardwell (6) (spd 3f) ............. ³/₄.17

1177⁴ Cumbrian Cavalier (51) *(JRBostock)* 3-8-2 ‡⁷JTate (4) (dwlt: a bhd) ............. 1¹/₂.18

Sally Saad (45) *(DJSCosgrove)* 4-8-11 AShoults (2) (bkwd: t.o) .......... 19

**11/2** Johanna Thyme, Morpick, **6/1** Quiet Victory, **7/1** Creego, **8/1** HARRY'S COMING, **10/1** Banbury Flyer, **12/1** My Ruby Ring, **14/1** Minizen Music (IRE), Fabled Orator, **16/1** Cumbrian Cavalier(op 8/1), Dickens Lane, **20/1** Ganeshaya, Foxes Diamond, Bishopstone Bill, **25/1** Dreamtime Echo, Flashy's Son, **33/1** Ors. CSF £53.71, CT £812.61. Tote £7.40: £1.50 £1.50 £3.50 £2.30 (£39.00). Mrs D. A. Wetherall (SOMERTON) bred by T. E. Herring. 19 Rn                     1m 13.6 (2.6)
SF—58/36/18/33/10/19

---

**1571**  'SENIOR CITIZENS' AUCTION STKS (Mdn 2-Y.O) £1932.00 (£532.00: £252.00)  **6f 15y**                                       5-00 (5-02)

1092⁴ For the Present *(TDBarron)* 8-8 AlexGreaves (12) (a.p: ev ch fnl f: rdn to ld post) .......... —1

847 Quick Silver Boy *(DBurchell)* 8-5 MHills (8) (dwlt: sn chsng ldrs: rdn & edgd lft over 1f out: led ins fnl f: hdd post) .......... s.h.2

Anniversaire (Jt-Fav) *(BobJones)* 8-10 VSmith (13) (w'like: scope: led: edgd lft & hdd ins fnl f) .......... s.h.3

Look Who's Here (IRE) *(BAMcMahon)* 8-7 JFortune (6) (w'like: bit bkwd: prom: one pce appr fnl f) .......... 3.4

1299⁵ Buzz-B-Babe *(BEllison)* 8-6 MRoberts (10) (swtg: wnt lft s: in tch: rdn 2f out: one pce) .......... nk.5

1251 Park Dance *(WJarvis)* 8-8 BRaymond (4) (prom: nt qckn appr fnl f) .......... 3.6

1103 Stevie's Wonder (IRE) *(WCarter)* 9-0 RCochrane (11) (a bhd) .......... 1¹/₂.7

1409² Birchwood Sun (Jt-Fav) *(RHollinshead)* 8-8 WRyan (1) (in tch: no imp fnl 2f) .. s.h.8

1251 Nancy (IRE) *(CWCElsey)* 7-10 ‡⁵NKennedy (2) (n.d) .......... s.h.9

1161 Galactic Fury *(BStevens)* 8-6 AMcGlone (3) (s.s: a bhd) .......... 1¹/₂.10

1170⁴ Red Ballet *(MrsNMacauley)* 8-3 NCarlisle (9) (swtg: dwlt: a bhd) .......... nk.11

791 Duchess Dianne (IRE) *(RJHolder)* 8-1 NAdams (5) (chsd ldrs: rdn ¹/₂-wy: sn wknd) .......... 1¹/₂.12

1342 Ascom Pager Too *(PHowling)* 8-5 JQuinn (7) (w ldr over 2f: sn bhd) .......... 2¹/₂.13

**5/2** Birchwood Sun, Anniversaire(op 4/1), **6/1** Buzz-B-Babe(op 4/1), **7/1** Park Dance(op 7/2), **8/1** Red Ballet, **9/1** FOR THE PRESENT(op 6/1), **11/1** Duchess Dianne (IRE), **12/1** Nancy (IRE), Stevie's Wonder (IRE), **25/1** Look Who's Here (IRE), Quick Silver Boy, Ascom Pager Too, **33/1** Galactic Fury. CSF £204.56, Tote £16.80: £3.90 £3.90 £2.30 (£311.30). Mrs J. Hazell (THIRSK) bred by R. Barber. 13 Rn                 1m 14.6 (3.6)
SF—22/18/22/7/5/-

T/Plpt: £82.10 (36.45 Tckts).                                                          Dk

1442—**WINDSOR   (Fig.8)**

## Monday, June 22nd [Good to firm, Good home st]
Going Allowance: minus 0.30 sec per fur (F)                          Wind: almost nil

Stalls: high

**1572**      CHISWICK (S) H'CAP (3 & 4-Y.O) (0-60) £1746.00 (£486.00: £234.00)
            1¼m 7y                                          6-35 (6-38)
                        (Weights raised 1 lb)

| | | |
|---|---|---|
| 1385⁶ | **Ideal Candidate (44)** *(CACyzer)* 3–8-9 GCarter (9) (gd hdwy 3f out: led over 1f out: rdn out) | —1 |
| 1404⁶ | Great Impostor (33) (bl) *(RJHodges)* 4–8-10 RCochrane (7) (gd hdwy 2f out: r.o wl ins fnl f) | ¾.2 |
| 1034 | Trendy Auctioneer (IRE) (34) (bl) *(MCPipe)* 4–8-11 RHills (25) (lw: 5th st: hrd rdn 2f out: r.o) | ½.3 |
| 809 | Chew it Over (IRE) (47) *(CASmith)* 4-9-10 MWigham (21) (3rd st: one pce fnl 2f) | 2¹/₂.4 |
| 1385⁵ | Slanderinthestrand (IRE) (44) (v) (Fav) *(MJHaynes)* 3–8-9 BRouse (3) (hdwy 5f out: 6th st: ev ch 2f out: one pce) | 1.5 |
| 1423⁴ | Mamalama (38) *(LJHolt)* 4–9-1 JReid (15) (hdwy 2f out: nvr nrr) | 2¹/₂.6 |
| 1452⁶ | Mahaasin (37) *(I.JCodd)* 4–9-0 LDettori (2) (4th st: hrd rdn 2f out: wknd over 1f out) | hd.7 |
| 1341 | Head Turner (32) *(CPWildman)* 4–8-9 CRutter (19) (rdn over 2f out: nvr nr to chal) | ½.8 |
| 1258³ | Betalongabill (50) (bl) *(MMadgwick)* 3–9-1 JQuinn (1) (7th st: no hdwy fnl 3f) | 1¹/₂.9 |
| 1172 | Foreign Assignment (IRE) (42) (bl) *(JWhite)* 4–9-5 DaleGibson (14) (lw: s.i.s: hdwy fnl 2f: nvr nrr) | ¾.10 |
| 1294 | Lord Leitrim (IRE) (50) *(NACallaghan)* 3–9-1 PatEddery (23) (lw: led over 8f) | nk.11 |
| 1294* | Crown Reserve (41) *(MJRyan)* 4–9-1 ‡3DBiggs (20) (nvr trbld ldrs) | 5.12 |
| 1213⁶ | Dollar Wine (IRE) (55) (bl) *(RHannon)* 3–9-6 SRaymont (22) (lw: 8th st: wknd over 3f out) | 1¹/₂.13 |
| 891 | Lady Baraka (IRE) (41) *(MissGayKelleway)* 4–8-11 ‡7MSimpson (4) (n.d) | hd.14 |
| 1143 | Primera Ballerina (44) *(JRBosley)* 4–9-2 ‡5NGwilliams (12) (swtg: nvr nr ldrs) | nk.15 |
| 1214 | Smudgemupum (51) *(MissBSanders)* 3–9-2 BCrossley (5) (chsd ldr 7f) | 1¹/₂.16 |
| 912 | Lamastre (52) *(RJHodges)* 3–9-0 ‡3RPerham (24) (a mid div) | nk.17 |
| 1404 | Just Ready (IRE) (32) *(GAHam)* 4–8-9 ADicks (10) (a bhd) | ¾.18 |
| 778 | In the Print (47) *(MrsBarbaraWaring)* 4–9-10 NHowe (17) (bhd fnl 3f) | ½.19 |
| 529 | Marpatann (IRE) (48) *(ASReid)* 3–8-13 TRogers (11) (s.s: a bhd) | nk.20 |
| 525³ | Internal Affair (44) *(JPearce)* 4–9-7 WCarson (13) (mid div 6f) | 5.21 |
| | Kahhal (IRE) (35) *(MrsAKnight)* 4–8-9 ‡3FNorton (8) (a bhd) | 2¹/₂.22 |
| 1214 | Tulapet (48) *(SDow)* 3–8-13 GDuffield (6) (mid div 6f) | nk.23 |
| 799 | Daunt Not (47) *(JWhite)* 4–9-5 ‡5ATucker (18) (b: prom 5f: 9th & wkng st) | 1¹/₂.24 |
| 776 | Hanjessdan (40) *(DHaydnJones)* 4–9-3 TyroneWilliams (16) (prom 4f: t.o) | 25 |

**13/2** Slanderinthestrand (IRE)(14/1—6/1), **7/1** Internal Affair, **8/1** Lord Leitrim (IRE), **9/1** Crown Reserve(op 6/1), Daunt Not(op 5/1), **10/1** Great Impostor, Dollar Wine (IRE)(op 5/1), Head Turner, **12/1** Betalongabill(op 6/1), Mahaasin(op 8/1), **16/1** Tulapet, Trendy Auctioneer (IRE), Lady Baraka (IRE)(op 10/1), Mamalama(op 10/1), **20/1** Foreign Assignment (IRE), IDEAL CANDIDATE, Marpatann (IRE), Chew it Over (IRE)(op 12/1), **25/1** Kahhal (IRE), Smudgemupum, **33/1** Ors. CSF £227.95, CT £3,043.69. Tote £59.20: £11.30 £2.70 £4.90 £4.40 (£230.70). Mr R. M. Cyzer (HORSHAM) bred by Lt-Col and Mrs D. Coker. 25 Rn; Bt in 3,800 gns  2m 7.6 (4.6)
SF—19/18/18/26/9/10

**1573**      E.B.F. MARBLE ARCH STKS (Mdn 2-Y.O) £1891.80 (£524.80: £251.40)
            5f 10y                                          7-00 (7-03)

| | | |
|---|---|---|
| 555² | **Joyofracing** (Fav) *(WAO'Gorman)* 9-0 PatEddery (11) (lw: mde virtually all: easily) | —1 |
| | True Precision *(JDBethell)* 8-9 BRaymond (9) (b.nr hind: neat: a.p: chsd wnr fnl 2f: r.o) | ¹/₂.2 |
| | Allez Bianco *(RJHolder)* 8-9 DHolland (6) (unf: bit bkwd: hdwy 3f out: one pce fnl 2f) | 6.3 |
| 856⁴ | Pair of Jacks (IRE) *(WRMuir)* 9-0 SWhitworth (7) (a.p: rdn 2f out: one pce) | nk.4 |
| | Special One *(JWHills)* 8-9 RHills (10) (cmpt: bkwd: s.s: hdwy fnl 2f: nvr nr to chal) | 5.5 |

Prince Manki *(RHannon)* 8-11 ‡³RPerham (4) (unf: prom 3f) ............................ 2½.6
1378 Sharp Imp *(JSutcliffe)* 9-0 BRouse (3) (b.off hind: prom over 2f) ...................... 1.7
Warm Spell *(LordHuntingdon)* 9-0 LDettori (1) (str: bkwd: outpcd) ............... s.h.8
1196 Hillsdown Boy (IRE) *(SDow)* 9-0 GDuffield (2) (lw: bhd fnl 2f) ...................... s.h.9
1442 Tax Avoidance (IRE) *(SDow)* 8-9 GCarter (8) (a bhd) ............................... 1.10
Rostand (IRE) *(LJHolt)* 9-0 JReid (5) (leggy: bit bkwd: s.i.s: outpcd) .............. nk.11

**2/7** JOYOFRACING, **7/1** Warm Spell, **8/1** Pair of Jacks (IRE)(op 5/1), **20/1** Rostand (IRE)(op 12/1), **33/1** Prince
Manki, Hillsdown Boy (IRE), Sharp Imp, Allez Bianco, Special One, True Precision, **100/1** Tax Avoidance (IRE).
CSF £12.46, Tote £1.40: £1.00 £9.50 9.60 (£32.70). Mr N. S. Yong (NEWMARKET) bred by The Duke of
Marlborough. 11 Rn     60.8 sec (1.8)
SF—34/27/3/7/–/–

---

**1574**    PRINCESS MARY OBOLENSKY UNDERWOOD & KENNETH DIACRE MEMORIAL H'CAP
      (3-Y.O) (0-70) £1716.00 (£476.00: £228.00)    **1m 3f 135y**     7-30 (7-31)

12983 **Bentico (56)** *(MAJarvis)* 8-8 PatEddery (11) (mde all: clr wl over 1f out: r.o) ...... —1
13712 Highland Battle (USA) **(63)** *(IABalding)* 9-1 RCochrane (9) (6th st: rdn 4f out:
      styd on) .................................................................. 1.2
1446* Ivor's Flutter **(69)** (Fav) *(DRCElsworth)* 9-7 (7x) SCauthen (8) (7th st: hrd rdn &
      hdwy over 1f out: r.o) ................................................. ½.3
12755 Storm Dust **(69)** *(JRFanshawe)* 9-7 GCarter (6) (9th st: rdn & hdwy 2f out: r.o
      ins fnl f) ................................................................... hd.4
12104 Maestroso (IRE) **(66)** (bl) *(RFJohnsonHoughton)* 9-4 JReid (7) (2nd st: one
      pce fnl 3f) ............................................................. 3½.5
1428 Day of History (IRE) **(44)** *(CACyzer)* 7-7(11) ‡³FNorton (3) (4th st: wknd over 1f
      out) ....................................................................... 2.6
1260 My Senor **(43)** *(MMadgwick)* 7-9 JQuinn (10) (5th st: no hdwy fnl 3f) ........ 2.7
1382 Miss Doody **(62)** (v) *(MRChannon)* 9-0 RHills (2) (8th st: nvr nr to chal) ......... 1.8
1298⁵ Indian Territory **(62)** *(DHaydnJones)* 9-0 TyroneWilliams (12) (lw: 3rd st: hrd
      rdn & wknd over 2f out) .............................................. 1.9
1245 Suzie Sue (IRE) **(61)** *(DWPArbuthnot)* 8-13 DHolland (4) (b.hind: s.s: a bhd) s.h.10
296 Amalfi **(50)** *(JPearce)* 8-2 DaleGibson (13) (lw: s.s: a bhd) .................... 3.11
940⁵ Sybaritic Sam (IRE) **(60)** *(NACallaghan)* 8-12 BRaymond (1) (a bhd: b.to) ....... 10.12
1298 Mystery Lad (IRE) **(59)** (bl) *(NACallaghan)* 8-11 GDuffield (5) (b: s.s: a bhd: t.o) 7.13

**Evens** Ivor's Flutter(6/4—10/11), **4/1** BENTICO, **9/2** Highland Battle (USA), **12/1** Maestroso (IRE), Sybaritic Sam
(IRE), **14/1** Storm Dust(8/1—16/1), **20/1** Miss Doody, **33/1** Mystery Lad (IRE), **50/1** Ors. CSF £22.24, CT
£28.11. Tote £5.20: £1.80 £1.60 £1.30 (£15.90). Mr Mark Christofi (NEWMARKET) bred by Britton House Stud.
13 Rn     2m 27.6 (5.1)
SF—8/13/18/17/7/–

---

**1575**    PALL MALL STKS (2-Y.O) £1722.40 (£476.40: £227.20)    **5f 10y**     8-00 (8-01)

1208* **Sharp Prod (USA)** (Fav) *(LordHuntingdon)* 9-2 SCauthen (3) (led over 3f: led
      ins fnl f: rdn out) ...................................................... —1
13602 My Bonus *(DJSCosgrove)* 8-6 ‡⁵DHarrison (2) (chsd wnr: led over 1f out tl ins fnl
      f: r.o) ..................................................................... ¾.2
Penang Star (IRE) *(WAO'Gorman)* 8-6 ‡⁵EmmaO'Gorman (1) (w'like: scope: lw:
      a in rr) ................................................................... 2½.3

**8/13** SHARP PROD (USA), **7/4** My Bonus, **11/1** Penang Star (IRE)(5/1—14/1). CSF £1.88, Tote £1.50 (£1.20).
The Queen (WEST ILSLEY) bred by D. O. B. Syndicate in USA. 3 Rn     61.8 sec (2.8)
SF—16/3/–

---

**1576**    HEATHROW H'CAP (3-Y.O) (0-90) £2574.00 (£714.00: £342.00)
      **5f 217y**     8-30 (8-31)

13143 **Massiba (IRE) (78)** *(MJHeaton-Ellis)* 8-13 BRaymond (4) (lw: mde all: clr over
      1f out: comf) ........................................................... —1
445 Ponsardin **(86)** *(SirMarkPrescott)* 9-7 GDuffield (6) (a.p: chsd wnr over 1f out:
      no imp) ................................................................... 5.2
12382 Treasure Time (IRE) **(58)** *(JWhite)* 7-7 DaleGibson (9) (lw: chsd wnr: rdn 2f out:
      unable qckn) ............................................................ 1.3
13454 Truthful Image **(74)** (bl) *(MJRyan)* 8-9 GCarter (10) (hrd rdn & hdwy 2f out: one
      pce) ...................................................................... ½.4
1204 Walking Possession **(79)** *(RBoss)* 9-0 PatEddery (8) (lw: rdn 3f out: hdwy over
      1f out: r.o) .............................................................. hd.5
1219 Noble Power (IRE) **(78)** *(BPalling)* 8-13 RCochrane (1) (a mid div) ............... 1½.6
12193 Uccello **(76)** (Fav) *(LJHolt)* 8-11 JReid (2) (no hdwy fnl 2f) .................... 7.7
997 Crimson Blade **(61)** *(PWHarris)* 7-7(3) ‡³FNorton (7) (s.s: a bhd) ............. s.h.8
14172 Peerage Prince **(68)** *(PatMitchell)* 7-9(4) ‡³SO'Gorman (3) (lw: prom 3f) ........... 1½.9
1345 Trove **(86)** *(MrsNMacauley)* 9-7 NDay (1) (hdwy 3f out: wknd 2f out) .............. 1.10

1412⁵ Sandcastle City **(71)** *(RHannon)* 8-6 WCarson (5) (rdn 4f out: wknd 2f out) .. s.h.**11**
LONG HANDICAP: Treasure Time (IRE) 7-3, Crimson Blade 7-1.

**7/2** Uccello, **5/1** Truthful Image, **11/2** MASSIBA (IRE), **6/1** Ponsardin, Sandcastle City(8/1—5/1), **7/1** Walking Possession, **8/1** Treasure Time (IRE)(6/1—10/1), **12/1** Trove, **14/1** Peerage Prince, **16/1** Noble Power (IRE), **33/1** Crimson Blade. CSF £39.14, CT £250.16. Tote £8.30: £2.80 £2.00 £3.10 (£26.10). Mr F. J. Sainsbury (WROUGHTON) bred by Gainsborough Stud Management Ltd in Ireland. 11 Rn               1m 11.3 (0.8)
SF—47/35/3/17/21/14

**1577**   KNIGHTSBRIDGE STKS (3-Y.O) £1891.80 (£524.80: £251.40)   1¼m 7y 9-00 (9-04)

1447⁵ **Jumaira Shark (CAN)** *(JHMGosden)* 8-12 SCauthen (17) (5th st: led over 1f out: comf) ...............................................................................................................................—1
  679³ Kaisar (GER) **(80)** *(HRACecil)* 8-11 ‡7StephenDavies (16) (swtg: led over 6f: led over 2f out tl over 1f out: unable qckn) .............................. 1½.2
  440 Hideyoshi (USA) **(Fav)** *(DRCElsworth)* 8-12 WCarson (10) (8th st: hdwy 3f out: r.o ch 2f out: r.o one pce) ....................................................... nk.3
1182² Wrets *(MRStoute)* 8-12 PatEddery (15) (lw: 3rd st: led over 3f out tl over 2f out: one pce) .......................................................................... 2½.4
1425★ Miss Haggis *(RBoss)* 8-13 JReid (9) (4th st: ev ch 2f out: one pce) ................... 1.5
1275 Dajitus *(MJHeaton-Ellis)* 8-12 DHolland (4) (b: lw: 7th st: no hdwy fnl 3f) ......... 3½.6
1115² Rienroe (IRE) *(NAGraham)* 8-7 RCochrane (5) (9th st: hdwy 3f out: wknd wl over 1f out) ............................................................................................... 1.7
  Swan Heights *(JRFanshawe)* 8-7 GDuffield (6) (unf: scope: 2nd st: wknd over 2f out) .................................................................................................. nk.8
  Blue Flag (USA) *(LordHuntingdon)* 8-12 LDettori (14) (str: scope: nvr nrr) ........ ½.9
1313⁶ Hazaaf (USA) *(AAScott)* 8-12 BRaymond (7) (lw: lost pl 7f out: styd on fnl 2f) . ½.10
1287⁵ Be My Habitat *(NAGraham)* 8-12 JQuinn (3) (lw: a bhd) ................................ 1.11
  393 Killshandra (IRE) *(MrsBarbaraWaring)* 8-7 NHowe (1) (6th st: wknd 3f out) ...... ½.12
1319 Jovial Man (IRE) *(SMellor)* 8-12 MWigham (13) (bit bkwd: a bhd) ..................... ½.13
  674⁵ Gerish (IRE) *(JPearce)* 8-7 DaleGibson (11) (lw: a bhd) .................................. 1.14
1319 Red-Michelle *(EAWheeler)* 8-2 ‡5DHarrison (8) (a bhd) ............................... 3½.15
  693⁴ General Dixie (USA) (25/1) Withdrawn (ref to ent stalls) : not under orders

**6/4** Hideyoshi (USA), **2/1** JUMAIRA SHARK (CAN), **7/2** Wrets, **9/1** Kaisar (GER)(7/1—16/1), **12/1** Miss Haggis(8/1—14/1), **25/1** Rienroe (IRE), Be My Habitat, **33/1** Hazaaf (USA), Swan Heights, Blue Flag (USA), **66/1** Ors. CSF £22.37, Tote £3.90: £1.60 £2.80 £1.20 (£24.30). Sheikh Ahmed Al Maktoum (NEWMARKET) bred by Richard R. Kennedy in Canada. 15 Rn               2m 6.3 (3.3)
SF—35/31/31/26/25/17

T/Plpt: £83.10 (26.65 Tckts).                                      LMc

## 1422—WOLVERHAMPTON (L-H)

### Monday, June 22nd [St Good to firm, Rnd Firm]
Going Allowance: St: nil sec; Rnd: minus 0.20 sec per fur (F)        Wind: almost nil

Stalls: high

**1578**   E.B.F. DR ABERNETHY STKS (Mdn 2-Y.O.F) £1917.50 (£530.00: £252.50)
            **7f**                                                        6-40 (6-44)

1120⁴ Hawayah (IRE) *(BHanbury)* 8-11 WRSwinburn (6) (lw: mde all: clr ½-wy: unchal) —1
  548⁶ Full Exposure *(WJarvis)* 8-11 PRobinson (7) (swtg: chsd ldrs: 5th st: rdn 2f out: kpt on fnl f: no ch w wnr) ................................................................ 3½.2
1443 Fiveofive (IRE) *(NACallaghan)* 8-11 PaulEddery (5) (lw: chsd ldrs: 3rd st: kpt on one pce over 1f out) ........................................................................... 2.3
  Domovoy *(CEBrittain)* 8-6 ‡5BDoyle (3) (w'like: scope: bkwd: s.i.s.: 6th st: styd on fnl 2f: nvr nrr) ........................................................................... hd.4
1342⁴ Creative Flair (USA) **(Fav)** *(PFICole)* 8-11 TQuinn (4) (chsd wnr: 2nd st: rdn & wknd 2f out) ............................................................................... 5.5
  Noteability *(JBerry)* 8-8 ‡3TSprake (1) (w'like: str: bkwd: chsd ldrs: 4th st: wknd over 2f out) ........................................................................... 10.6
  Hokey Pokey (FR) *(DSasse)* 8-11 AMunro (2) (b: leggy: unf: swtg: a bhd: t.o) . 10.7

**Evens** Creative Flair (USA), **100/30** HAWAYAH (IRE), **7/1** Full Exposure, **12/1** Domovoy(op 4/1), **16/1** Noteability(op 7/1), **33/1** Ors. CSF £21.81, Tote £3.70: £1.90 £2.80 (£9.10). Mr Muttar Salem (NEWMARKET) bred by Gainsborough Stud Management Ltd in Ireland. 7 Rn               1m 27.9 (3.6)
SF—22/11/5/—/—/—

**1579**   HOPEFUL (S) STKS (2-Y.O) £1245.00 (£345.00: £165.00)   **5f**   7-10 (7-12)

1077★ **Not so Generous (IRE)** *(WGMTurner)* 8-7 ‡3TSprake (3) (swtg: a.p: led ½-wy: edgd rt 1f out: r.o wl) .......................................................................—1

1178⁶ Nut Bush (bl) *(NACallaghan)* 8-11 MRoberts (9) (s.i.s: hdwy 2f out: rdn over 1f out: one pce) ............................................................ 2½.2

1191² Ban Ri (IRE) (Fav) *(MHTompkins)* 8-6 PRobinson (10) (a.p: ev ch over 1f out: unable qckn) ............................................................ 1.3

Screech *(CJames)* 8-6 GBaxter (5) (scope: bit bkwd: chsd ldrs on outside: effrt over 1f out: nt pce to chal) ............................ s.h.4

Palacegate Prince *(JBerry)* 8-11 AMunro (4) (w'like: lw: dwlt: hdwy appr fnl f: nrst fin) ............................................................ 2½.5

1342 Gloddaeth Isa *(JBerry)* 8-6 NCarlisle (2) (gd spd over 3f) .............................. 1½.6

1140⁶ Spanish Tower *(RJHolder)* 8-11 NAdams (1) (lw: prom: ev ch over 1f out: wknd ins fnl f) ............................................................ 2.7

1443 Soleil D'Or (bl) *(MMcCormack)* 8-11 TQuinn (6) (led to ½-wy: wknd over 1f out) 2½.8

Balustrade Boy (IRE) *(BStevens)* 8-11 AMcGlone (4) (lt-f: outpcd) .................. nk.9

Ok Guv (bl) *(JBalding)* 8-11 GHind (8) (w'like: bkwd: outpcd: t.o) .................. 20.10

**7/4** Ban Ri (IRE), **4/1** NOT SO GENEROUS (IRE), **7/1** Nut Bush, **8/1** Palacegate Prince, Gloddaeth Isa(7/1—14/1), **10/1** Soleil D'Or(12/1—8/1), **11/1** Spanish Tower(7/1—12/1), **20/1** Screech, **33/1** Balustrade Boy (IRE), **50/1** Ok Guv. CSF £29.81, Tote £5.10: £1.80 £1.40 £1.10 (£10.30). Mr E. Goody (SHERBORNE) bred by P. J. Foley in Ireland. 10 Rn; Bt in 3,000 gns
61 sec (3.7)
SF—19/13/14/3/–/–

**1580**  JOSEPH SUNLIGHT CUP (H'cap) (0-80) £1213.50 (£336.00: £160.50)
1³/₄m 134y
7-40 (7-41)

1260⁴ Three Wells (78) (Fav) *(JLDunlop)* 3-9-1 MRoberts (7) (lw: hld up: 4th st: led 2f out: comf) ............................................................ —1

1419² White River (41) (v) *(DHaydnJones)* 6-7-10⁽¹⁾ AMackay (3) (lost pl ½-wy: gd hdwy 2f out: fin wl) ............................................................ ¾.2

1381⁵ Marine Society (72) *(PTWalwyn)* 4-9-13 AMunro (6) (led after 1f to 2f out: kpt on u.p ins fnl f) ............................................................ 1.3

1179⁴ Lookingforarainbow (IRE) (60) *(BobJones)* 4-9-1 VSmith (4) (led 1f: 6th & lost pl st: rallied 3f out: rdn & hung rt over 1f out: sn btn) ........ 10.4

1423 Enfant du Paradis (IRE) *(PDEvans)* 4-7-2⁽²⁾ ‡7CHawksley (8) (hdwy & 5th st: rdn 2f out: sn btn) ............................................................ 1½.5

1190 Nipotina (41) *(RHollinshead)* 6-7-3⁽³⁾ ‡7AGarth (5) (chsd ldrs: 3rd st: wknd over 2f out:) ............................................................ 3.6

234 Kayfaat (USA) (68) *(MCPipe)* 4-9-9 WRSwinburn (1) (chsd ldrs 9f: hrd rdn & wknd 3f out) ............................................................ 5.7

1481 Media Star (42) *(TKersey)* 7-7-6⁽⁴⁾ ‡5NKennedy (10) (b: lw: hld up: rapid hdwy ½-wy: 2nd st: wknd 3f out) ............................................ ¾.8

My Chiara (61) (v) *(PJBevan)* 6-9-2 PaulEddery (2) (lw: a bhd: rdn 3f out: no rspnse) ............................................................ 5.9

LONG HANDICAP: Enfant du Paradis (IRE) 7-6, Media Star 6-8.

**7/4** THREE WELLS, **6/1** Lookingforarainbow (IRE)(5/1—4/1), **7/1** My Chiara, White River, **8/1** Kayfaat (USA), **9/1** Marine Society, **14/1** Nipotina, **16/1** Enfant du Paradis (IRE), **66/1** Media Star. CSF £12.84, CT £71.98. Tote £1.90: £1.10 £1.50 £2.10 (£5.10). Mr P. G. Goulandris (ARUNDEL) bred by Hesmonds Stud Ltd. 9 Rn
3m 14.7 (8.7)

**1581**  SPRINGFIELD H'CAP (3-Y.O) (0-70) £1371.00 (£381.00: £183.00)  7f  8-10 (8-14)
(Weights raised 7 lb)

946² **Daaris (USA) (63)** *(DMorley)* 9-7 WRyan (6) (2nd st: led over 3f out: hrd rdn & hld on gamely) ............................................................ —1

1417² Honey Heather (IRE) (58) (Jt-Fav) *(CFWall)* 9-2 WRSwinburn (4) (prom: 3rd st: hrd rdn & ev ch over 1f out: r.o) ...................................... ¾.2

1245 Venture Fourth (55) *(EJAlston)* 8-13 GBaxter (7) (lw: s.i.s: bhd: hdwy 3f out: styd on ins fnl f) ............................................................ 2½.3

735 Kindred Cameo (55) *(GLewis)* 8-13 PaulEddery (3) (prom: 4th st: one pce fnl 2f) ............................................................ 8.4

1369² Sea Cloud (USA) (50) (Jt-Fav) *(MBlanshard)* 8-8 TQuinn (5) (led tl over 3f out: sn hrd rdn & btn) ............................................................ 1.5

697 Libra Legend (USA) (61) *(CEBrittain)* 9-5 MRoberts (8) (lw: chsd ldrs: 5th st: hrd rdn over 2f out: sn btn) ............................................ 1.6

911 Gunmaker (48) *(RJHolder)* 8-6 NAdams (2) (nvr nr ldrs) ............................ 1½.7

332 Lady of Letters (41) *(TThomsonJones)* 7-13 AMackay (10) (6th & rdn st: sn bhd) ............................................................ 1½.8

1281⁴ Double Lark (56) (bl) *(RHollinshead)* 9-0 AMunro (9) (lw: s.s: a bhd) .......... 2.9

**7/2** Honey Heather (IRE), Sea Cloud (USA), **9/2** DAARIS (USA), **6/1** Libra Legend (USA), **9/1** Double Lark, **10/1** Kindred Cameo(12/1—8/1), **25/1** Lady of Letters, **33/1** Ors. CSF £17.52, CT £325.59. Tote £4.40: £1.60 £1.60 £12.90 (£5.10). Mr Hamdan Al-Maktoum (NEWMARKET) bred by Don Dick in USA. 9 Rn
1m 27.1 (2.8)
SF—44/37/26/2/–/–

## 1582

HIGHGATE CLAIMING STKS    £1213.50 (£336.00: £160.50)    1½m 70y 8-40 (8-41)

1419 **Access Cruise (USA) (46)** *(BAMcMahon)* 5-9-5 TQuinn (3) (hld up & bhd: 4th st: hdwy 3f out: styd on strly to ld nr fin) ............................. —1

1362* Kirby Opportunity **(62)** *(Fav)* *(JPearce)* 4-8-9 ‡⁵RPrice (7) (wnt 2nd st: led over 3f out: rdn & hung rt fnl f: ct cl home) ............................. nk.2

1423 Dancing Tudor **(48)** *(THCaldwell)* 4-8-9 ‡⁵NKennedy (2) (chsd ldr: led 7f out tl over 3f out: hrd rdn over 1f out: one pce) ............................. 7.3

626 Capital Bond (IRE) **(62)** *(RJHolder)* 4-8-12 ‡⁷SDrowne (4) (lw: chsd ldrs: 3rd st: rdn over 2f out: sn btn) ............................. ½.4

1280 Cool Apollo (NZ) *(JCMcConnochie)* 5-9-7 MRoberts (1) (bit bkwd: led over 5f: wknd qckly & 5th st: t.o) ............................. dist.5

8/15 Kirby Opportunity, 9/2 ACCESS CRUISE (USA), Capital Bond (IRE), 14/1 Cool Apollo (NZ), 33/1 Dancing Tudor. CSF £7.23, Tote £4.10: £2.00 £1.00 (£3.00). Mr M. Hines-Randle (TAMWORTH) bred by Jerry Wheeler in USA. 5 Rn; Kirby Opportunity clmd P Leach £8,001            2m 39.6 (7.9)

## 1583

MORGAN H'CAP (0-70) £1203.00 (£333.00: £72.00 each)    5f    9-10 (9-13)

1522³ **Arc Lamp (48)** *(Jt-Fav)* *(JAGlover)* 6-8-7 JFortune (13) (a.p: rdn to ld 1f out: edgd lft: r.o) ............................. —1

Samson-Agonistes **(69)** *(BAMcMahon)* 6-9-7 ‡⁷SSanders (1) (led: sn clr: edgd rt & hdd 1f out: one pce) ............................. 1½.2

1415² So Superb **(70)** (bl) *(Jt-Fav)* *(JLDunlop)* 3-9-8 TQuinn (12) (a.p: rdn wl over 1f out: swtchd rt & r.o fnl f) ............................. 1.3

1427² Last Straw **(40)** *(AWJones)* 4-7-6 ‡⁷ClaireBalding (7) (chsd ldrs: kpt on wl ins fnl f) ............................. d.h.4

1154⁵ Ballad Dancer **(55)** *(EJAlston)* 7-9-0 GBaxter (11) (s.s: outpcd tl r.o ins fnl f) ... hd.5

1325⁴ Drummer's Dream (IRE) **(41)** (v) *(MrsNMacauley)* 4-8-0 PRobinson (3) (chsd ldrs over 3f) ............................. 1½.6

1552⁵ Supreme Desire **(43)** *(ASmith)* 4-8-2(7) SWebster (5) (lw: s.s: nvr nrr) ............................. ½.7

615 Hinari Hi Fi **(43)** *(PDEvans)* 7-7-9 ‡⁷HayleyWilliams (9) (nvr gng pce of ldrs) ..... ½.8

1238⁶ Cheshire Annie (IRE) **(56)** *(WCarter)* 3-8-8 PaulEddery (10) (outpcd) ............................. 2½.9

1310* Don't Run Me Over **(51)** *(BCMorgan)* 3-8-8 MRoberts (8) (outpcd) ............................. ¾.10

1427⁵ Rednet **(56)** *(PDEvans)* 5-9-1 AMunro (6) (b: dwlt: a bhd) ............................. 1.11

596 Barbara's Cutie **(43)** *(MBlanshard)* 4-8-2 NAdams (4) (swtg: spd 3f) ............................. 1½.12

1552 Cal's Boy **(44)** (bl) *(JPSmith)* 3-7-10(3) AMackay (2) (outpcd) ............................. 4.13

LONG HANDICAP: Cal's Boy 7-5.

4/1 ARC LAMP, So Superb, 11/2 Don't Run Me Over, 8/1 Last Straw, Rednet, 9/1 Cheshire Annie (IRE), 11/1 Drummer's Dream (IRE), Supreme Desire(op 7/1), 12/1 Ballad Dancer, 16/1 Samson-Agonistes, 33/1 Barbara's Cutie, Hinari Hi Fi, 66/1 Cal's Boy. CSF £61.74, CT AL, SA & SS £127.35, AL, SA & LS £228.96. Tote £5.00: £2.00 £4.30 SS £0.90 LS £1.20 (£73.20). Mr B. Bruce (WORKSOP) bred by H. J. Joel. 13 Rn   59.7 sec (2.4)          SF—45/53/50/20/41/21

T/Plpt: £8.10 (139.30 Tckts).                                IM

## 1428—BRIGHTON (L-H)

### Tuesday, June 23rd [Firm]

Going Allowance: minus 0.40 sec per fur (F)                Wind: almost nil

Stalls: low

## 1584

E.B.F. EASTBOURNE STKS (Mdn 2-Y.O) £2325.90 (£642.40: £305.70)
5f 213y             2-00 (2-01)

1202² **Crusade (IRE)** *(Fav)* *(RHannon)* 9-0 JReid (1) (lw: mde all: clr over 1f out: v.easily) ............................. —1

1135⁵ Le Couteau *(DWPArbuthnot)* 9-0 WCarson (2) (3rd st: lost pl 3f out: r.o one pce fnl f) ............................. 7.2

1273⁶ Wishing Cap (USA) *(SirMarkPrescott)* 9-0 GDuffield (3) (2nd st: wknd 2f out) .. hd.3

1/5 CRUSADE (IRE), 11/2 Le Couteau(3/1—6/1), 9/1 Wishing Cap (USA)(op 5/1). CSF £1.73, Tote £1.20 (£1.40). Kennet Valley Thoroughbreds Ltd (MARLBOROUGH) bred by David Barry in Ireland. 3 Rn   1m 9.2 (0.8)                           SF—36/8/7

## 1585

LEWES STKS (Mdn) £1932.00 (£532.00: £252.00)    1m 1f 209y    2-30 (2-31)

1209³ **Avice Caro (USA)** *(Fav)* *(JHMGosden)* 3-8-5(1) PatEddery (3) (2nd st: led over 2f out: comf) ............................. —1

944⁵ Dexter Chief *(IABalding)* 3-8-9 RCochrane (2) (lw: rdn 5f out: 3rd st: chsd wnr wl over 1f out: no imp) ............................. 5.2

**1586—1589**

1312³ Traders Dream **(69)** *(TThomsonJones)* 3–8-9 SWhitworth (4) (b: lw: led over 7f) 8.3
663² Docket (USA) *(BHanbury)* 4–8-9 ‡⁷VBray (1) (s.s: 4th st: a bhd) ..................... 6.4

**1/3** AVICE CARO (USA), **11/2** Dexter Chief(op 7/2), **6/1** Traders Dream, **14/1** Docket (USA). CSF £2.70, Tote £1.40 (£1.80). Sheikh Mohammed (NEWMARKET) bred by Darley Stud Management Co Ltd in USA. 4 Rn
1m 59.6 (1.6)
SF—35/29/13/1

---

**1586** MONTPELIER (S) STKS (2-Y.O) £2180.40 (£582.40: £277.20) **6f 209y** 3-00 (3-01)

1442² **Homemaker** *(RJHolder)* 8-6 NAdams (2) (6th st: led over 1f out: hrd rdn: r.o wl) —1
1149 Ombre Darme (IRE) (bl) *(JWPayne)* 8-11 AMunro (6) (lw: 4th st: hrd rdn over 1f
out: r.o) ............................................................. 2.2
1442³ Mighty Miss Magpie (IRE) *(MRChannon)* 8-6 PatEddery (1) (led over 5f: unable
qckn) ................................................................. 1.3
1429⁴ Gypsy Legend *(WGMTurner)* 8-3 ‡³TSprake (5) (5th st: r.o one pce fnl 2f) ........ ½.4
1448⁵ Arctic Guest (IRE) (Fav) *(MJohnston)* 8-6 DMcKeown (3) (3rd st: hrd rdn over 1f
out: one pce) ........................................................ nk.5
1307⁴ Zinjaal (IRE) *(BHanbury)* 8-4 ‡⁷VBray (4) (lw: plld hrd: 2nd st: wknd over 2f out) 25.6

**4/5** Arctic Guest (IRE)(op 5/4), **2/1** HOMEMAKER(7/4—11/4), **7/2** Mighty Miss Magpie (IRE)(tchd 6/1), **20/1** Gypsy Legend(op 7/1), **25/1** Ombre Darme (IRE), **50/1** Zinjaal (IRE). CSF £33.68, Tote £3.40: £1.20 £3.30 (£18.00). Mr R. J. Glenn (BRISTOL) bred by Richard Castle. 6 Rn; No bid
1m 23.7 (3.7)

---

**1587** OPERATIC SOCIETY CHALLENGE CUP (H'cap) (0-90) £3557.50 (£1060.00: £505.00: £227.50) **1m 3f 196y** 3-30 (3-32)

**Pharamineux (71)** *(RAkehurst)* 6–9-13 TQuinn (1) (lw: 3rd st: led over 1f out:
rdn out) .............................................................. —1
1430★ Top Royal **(70)** (Fav) *(JLDunlop)* 3–8-11 (4x) WCarson (3) (led over 1¼f: led rdn
ins fnl f: r.o wl) ...................................................... s.h.2
1318 El Volador **(66)** *(RJO'Sullivan)* 5–9-8 RCochrane (7) (6th st: one pce fnl 2f) ..... 5.3
1286 Simply George **(62)** *(RBoss)* 3–8-3 GDuffield (5) (5th st: hrd rdn over 1f out: sn
wknd) ................................................................ 2.4
1430³ Tiger Claw (USA) **(54)** *(RJHodges)* 6–8-3 ‡⁷SDrowne (6) (4th st: wknd over 2f
out) ................................................................. 4.5
1387 Northern Conqueror (IRE) **(63)** *(TJNaughton)* 4–9-5 PatEddery (4) (2nd st:
wknd over 2f out) .................................................... ½.6

**8/13** Top Royal, **5/1** El Volador, **8/1** Tiger Claw (USA)(op 5/1), **9/1** PHARAMINEUX(op 6/1), Northern Conqueror (IRE)(op 6/1), **14/1** Simply George. CSF £15.28, Tote £10.20: £3.80 £1.10 (£4.40). Mr Nicholas Roteman (EPSOM) bred by J. L. C. Pearce. 6 Rn
2m 29.8 (2.8)
SF—37/20/21/–/–/–

---

**1588** PALACE H'CAP (0-70) £2265.20 (£627.20: £299.60) **6f 209y** 4-00 (4-04)

1243² **Hamadryad (IRE) (66)** *(WCarter)* 4–9-7 ‡⁵NGwilliams (8) (b.off fore: lw: hdwy 2f
out: led over 1f out: r.o wl) ........................................... —1
1431² Durneltor **(65)** *(RHannon)* 4–9-11 PatEddery (2) (3rd st: ev ch fnl f: r.o) ........... ½.2
1343⁶ Old Comrades **(52)** *(LGCottrell)* 5–8-12 TRogers (1) (b.nr hind: n.m.r over 2f
out: hrd rdn & hdwy over 1f out: r.o) ................................... 2.3
1339 Aldahe **(45)** *(BRMillman)* 7–8-5 TQuinn (7) (5th st: nt clr run over 1f out: unable
qckn) ................................................................ ½.4
1344³ Faynaz **(50)** (v) *(WRMuir)* 6–8-10 SWhitworth (4) (2nd st: led over 3f out tl over
1f out: sn wknd) ..................................................... 3½.5
1343 Prepare (IRE) **(41)** *(RJHolder)* 4–8-1 NAdams (6) (nvr nr to chal) ................... 2.6
1445⁵ Unveiled **(62)** (Fav) *(RJHodges)* 4–9-8 WCarson (10) (6th st: wknd 3f out) ....... ½.7
1212 Surrey Racing **(68)** *(GLewis)* 4–10-0 PaulEddery (9) (4th st: wknd 2f out) ....... 2.8
1032 Foo Foo **(33)** *(DMarks)* 4–7-7 EJohnson (5) (a bhd) ............................ 6.9
1159 Royal Circus **(45)** (bl) *(PWHarris)* 3–7-7⁽³⁾ ‡³FNorton (3) (led over 3f) ............. ½.10
LONG HANDICAP: Foo Foo (IRE) 7-1, Royal Circus 6-13.

**3/1** Unveiled, **4/1** Durneltor, Aldahe, **5/1** HAMADRYAD (IRE)(6/1—4/1), **7/1** Old Comrades, Surrey Racing(op 4/1), **8/1** Faynaz(op 5/1), **25/1** Prepare (IRE), **50/1** Ors. CSF £25.55, CT £131.36. Tote £7.20: £1.90 £1.90 £1.50 (£12.40). Miss Maha Kalaji (EPSOM) bred by P. Myerscough in Ireland. 10 Rn
1m 21.3 (1.3)
SF—45/47/28/19/13/–

---

**1589** LEVY BOARD H'CAP (0-70) £2856.00 (£791.00: £378.00) **7f 214y** 4-30 (4-32)

964 **Indian Slave (IRE) (47)** *(RGuest)* 4–8-8 PatEddery (11) (lw: 2nd st: led over 3f
out: hrd rdn over 1f out: r.o wl) ....................................... —1
1388⁴ Abso **(67)** *(RHannon)* 4–10-0 JReid (9) (hdwy & hung lft over 1f out: r.o ins fnl f) 2.2

13394 Charmed Knave **(53)** *(DRLaing)* 7–9–0 TyroneWilliams (6) (3rd st: chsd wnr over 2f out tl unable qckn) ............................................ 2½.3
13093 Spanish Express **(48)** (Fav) *(RBoss)* 3–7–13 WCarson (12) (4th st: one pce fnl 2f) ............................................................ 2½.4
14282 Chatino **(61)** *(CEBrittain)* 3–8–12 TQuinn (8) (lw: hdwy & n.m.r over 1f out: one pce) ............................................................ s.h.5
13386 Navaresque **(49)** *(RJHodges)* 7–8–10 RCochrane (10) (6th st: no hdwy fnl 3f) 3½.6
14412 Lawnswood Junior **(50)** *(JLSpearing)* 5–8–11 KDarley (4) (5th st: wknd wl over 1f out) ............................................................ 1.7
   Dodgy **(57)** (v) *(SDow)* 5–9–4 GDuffield (3) (led over 4f: wknd 2f out) ............ 2½.8
   728 Chinaman **(53)** *(WGRWightman)* 3–8–4 WNewnes (2) (hrd rdn over 2f out: a bhd) 2.9
13396 Please Please Me (IRE) **(35)** *(KOCunningham-Brown)* 4–7–7[1] ‡3FNorton (1) (a bhd) ............................................................ hd.10
12842 Grey Illusions **(42)** *(LJHolt)* 4–8–3 NAdams (7) (a bhd) ............................ 4.11

**11/4** Spanish Express(tchd 6/1), **5/1** Abso, **11/2** Lawnswood Junior, **6/1** Chatino, **13/2** Navaresque, **7/1** Charmed Knave, **9/1** INDIAN SLAVE (IRE)(6/1—10/1), **14/1** Please Please Me (IRE)(8/1—16/1), **16/1** Grey Illusions(op 8/1), Dodgy, **33/1** Chinaman. CSF £54.59, CT £316.64. Tote £11.90: £2.60 £2.30 £3.60 (£58.80). Mr R. Axford (NEWMARKET) bred by Ivan W. Allan in Ireland. 11 Rn    1m 33.4 (1.2)
SF—28/42/20/–/9/–

---

**1590**   MARINE H'CAP (0-70) £2167.20 (£599.20: £285.60)   **5f 213y**   5-00 (5-02)
(Weights raised 2 lb)

10842 Shikari's Son **(54)** *(JWhite)* 5–9–10 GDuffield (1) (5th st: hrd rdn over 1f out: led ins fnl f: r.o wl) ............................................................ —1
   624 Restore **(53)** (bl) *(RVoorspuy)* 9–9–9 SDawson (5) (4th st: ev ch ins fnl f: unable qckn) ............................................................ 1½.2
13434 Proud Brigadier (IRE) **(49)** (Fav) *(WCarter)* 4–9–5 RCochrane (8) (3rd st: led over 1f out tl ins fnl f: one pce) ............................................................ 1½.3
1054 Count Me Out **(37)** (bl) *(JPearce)* 7–8–2 ‡5RPrice (2) (s.s: 6th st: nvr nr to chal) 3½.4
   113 Oratel Flyer **(29)** (v) *(RThompson)* 5–7–13 AMackay (3) (led over 4f) ............ 3.5
1343★ Kirriemuir **(36)** *(KOCunningham-Brown)* 4–8–6 NCarlisle (9) (a bhd) ............ 3.6
1415 Barbezieux **(35)** *(TJNaughton)* 5–8–5 WNewnes (6) (a bhd) ............................ ¾.7
1206 Mexican Dancer **(55)** (bl) *(RJHolder)* 3–9–3 NAdams (4) (2nd st: wknd over 2f out) ............................................................ 2.8
   My Ducats (IRE) **(30)** *(TCasey)* 4–7–11 ‡3FNorton (10) (s.s: a wl bhd) ............ 12.9

**9/4** Proud Brigadier (IRE), **3/1** SHIKARI'S SON, **7/1** Kirriemuir, **13/2** Restore(8/1—10/1), **7/1** Mexican Dancer(9/2—8/1), **11/1** Count Me Out, **12/1** Oratel Flyer, **16/1** Barbezieux, **33/1** My Ducats (IRE). CSF £22.53, CT £48.15. Tote £4.70: £1.30 £2.80 £1.10 (£22.90). Mr Alan Spargo (WENDOVER) bred by W. H. Joyce. 9 Rn    1m 9.4 (1.2)
SF—42/35/25/–/–/–

T/Plpt: £29.30 (85.85 Tckts).   AK

---

1344—**NEWBURY (L-H)**
## Tuesday, June 23rd [Good to firm]
Going Allowance: minus 0.10 sec per fur (F)   Wind: nil

Stalls: 1st & 3rd centre, remainder low

**1591**   MID-SUMMER STKS (Mdn 2-Y.O.F) £3288.00 (£984.00: £472.00: £216.00)
**6f 8y**   6-30 (6-36)

**Na-Ayim (IRE)** *(AAScott)* 8-11 WCarson (8) (b.off hind: w'like: scope: hdwy over 2f out: rdn fnl f: led last stride) ............................ —1
13004 White Shadow (IRE) (Fav) *(RCharlton)* 8-11 PatEddery (1) (led tl fnl stride) ...... s.h.2
   Cape Weaver *(JHMGosden)* 8-11 SCauthen (14) (scope: hld up: bit bkwd: hdwy 2f out: nt qckn ins fnl f) ............................ 3½.3
   Action Night *(MMoubarak)* 8-11 LDettori (9) (neat: bkwd: w ldrs over 4f) ............ 1.4
12792 Moon Watch *(JRFanshawe)* 8-11 WRSwinburn (12) (a.p: no hdwy fnl 2f) ...... nk.5
13422 Latest Flame (IRE) *(MRChannon)* 8-11 TQuinn (7) (b.off hind: dwlt: hdwy 3f out: one pce fnl 2f) ............................ 4.6
   Ballet *(LordHuntingdon)* 8-11 AMunro (3) (unf: spd 4f) ............................ s.h.7
   Mimique (GER) *(CEBrittain)* 8-6 ‡5BDoyle (6) (w ldrs: rdn & unbalanced over 2f out: nt rcvr) ............................ 6.8
   Honorary Guest *(DJGMurray-Smith)* 8-11 CRutter (11) (w'like: scope: dwlt: nvr nr to chal) ............................ s.h.9
   Exhibit Air (IRE) *(RHannon)* 8-8 ‡3RPerham (10) (str: scope: bit bkwd: outpcd) hd.10
   Arewenearlythere (IRE) *(MBlanshard)* 8-11 JReid (2) (unf: bkwd: outpcd) ........ 2.11
   973 Easy Touch (bl) *(MDIUsher)* 8-11 GBardwell (13) (rdn: a bhd) ............................ 4.12

Arawa *(DMarks)* 8-11 AMcGlone (15) (leggy: unf: bit bkwd: s.s: a bhd) ......... 2½.**13**
1164⁵ Tartouka *(GLewis)* 8-11 PaulEddery (5) (prom 4f) ..................................... 1.**14**
Sparky's Song *(JWHills)* 8-11 MHills (4) (neat: outpcd) ..................................... 2.**15**

**7/4** White Shadow (IRE), **9/2** Moon Watch, **5/1** Latest Flame (IRE), **10/1** NA-AYIM (IRE)(tchd 7/2), Cape Weaver(4/1—12/1), Ballet(7/1—12/1), **20/1** Tartouka, Action Night, **25/1** Mimique (GER), Exhibit Air (IRE), **33/1** Sparky's Song, Arewenearlythere (IRE), **50/1** Ors. CSF £27.20, Tote £12.90: £3.70 £1.80 £3.00 (£22.40). Mr Hamdan Al-Maktoum (NEWMARKET) bred by Lyonstown Stud and Swettenham Stud in Ireland. 15 Rn
1m 13.92 (2.12)
SF—43/42/28/12/11/–

**1592** NEWBURY TRADE STANDS H'CAP (3-Y.O) (0-100) £3655.00 (£1090.00: £520.00: £235.00) **1m 5f 61y** 7-00 (7-05)

(Weights raised 6 lb)
1139* **Garden District (70)** (Fav) *(RCharlton)* 8-7 PatEddery (4) (mde all: clr over 2f out: unchal) ............................................................................................................ —**1**
1346⁵ Judge and Jury **(64)** (bl) *(MJFetherston-Godley)* 8-1 MRoberts (3) (4th st: hrd rdn & chsd wnr 3f out: faltered over 1f out) ................................ 12.**2**
599 Arctic Circle (IRE) **(60)** *(MissAJWhitfield)* 7-11 DaleGibson (2) (3rd st: rdn 4f out: no rspnse) ............................................................... 1½.**3**
1301* Lobinda **(84)** *(JLDunlop)* 9-7 WCarson (1) (lw: plld hrd: 2nd st: wknd 3f out: sddle slipped) ................................................................ nk.**4**

**6/4** GARDEN DISTRICT(op Evens), **13/8** Lobinda, **100/30** Judge and Jury, **20/1** Arctic Circle (IRE). CSF £5.87, Tote £2.10 (£2.60). Mr K. Abdulla (BECKHAMPTON) bred by Sir Gordon Brunton. 4 Rn 2m 50.99 (5.29)
SF—27/–/–/13

**1593** KINGSTON SMITH H'CAP (0-90) £3460.00 (£1030.00: £490.00: £220.00) **5f 34y** 7-30 (7-32)

1535² **Cradle Days (78)** (Fav) *(RHannon)* 3-9-8 MRoberts (3) (lw: a.p: led ins fnl f: r.o wl) ................................................................ —**1**
1392⁶ Tongue Tied **(69)** *(JWharton)* 4-9-6 WCarson (4) (law: led tl ins fnl f: nt qckn) ..... 3.**2**
1310⁶ Spring High **(46)** (bl) *(KTIvory)* 5-7-11 GBardwell (2) (same pl most of wy: one pce fnl 2f) ............................................ 1½.**3**
1415⁴ Three Lucky (IRE) **(46)** *(MDIUsher)* 4-7-6⁽⁴⁾ ‡5DHarrison (6) (no hdwy fnl 2f) ...... 5.**4**
1345 Spell of the Yukon (USA) **(77)** *(IABalding)* 3–9-7 JReid (1) (wl bhd fnl 2f) ............ 7.**5**
LONG HANDICAP: Three Lucky (IRE) 7-1.

**5/4** CRADLE DAYS, **2/1** Tongue Tied, **6/1** Spring High, **7/1** Spell of the Yukon (USA), **16/1** Three Lucky (IRE). CSF £3.98, Tote £2.00: £1.30 £1.50 (£1.70). Mr T. A. Johnsey (MARLBOROUGH) bred by T. A. Johnsey. 5 Rn
62.25 sec (1.55)
SF—67/53/24/–/–

**1594** WIMPEY HOBBS H'CAP (3-Y.O.F) (0-100) £3590.00 (£1070.00: £510.00: £230.00) **1¼m 6y** 8-00 (8-02)

(Weights raised 13 lb)
1128* **Only Royale (IRE) (76)** (Fav) *(LMCumani)* 9-7 LDettori (5) (lw: 4th st: led wl over 1f out: pushed out) ............................................ —**1**
1105² Wassl This Then (IRE) **(67)** *(DWPArbuthnot)* 8-12 TQuinn (7) (lw: 3rd st: ev ch over 1f out: r.o) ............................................ 1½.**2**
293⁶ Elegant Touch **(75)** *(MMoubarak)* 9-6 PatEddery (2) (6th st: rdn & hdwy 3f out: one pce fnl 2f) ............................................ 5.**3**
1025 Brave the Wind **(61)** *(IABalding)* 8-3‡³SO'Gorman (3) (led tl wknd wl over 1f out) 1.**4**
1363⁴ Wild Strawberry **(74)** *(JMPEustace)* 9-5 JReid (6) (2nd st: wknd 2f out) ............. 1.**5**
1152 Teslemi (USA) **(70)** *(BHanbury)* 9-1 WRSwinburn (1) (lw: 5th st: hrd rdn & wknd over 3f out: t.o) ............................................ 20.**6**

**9/4** ONLY ROYALE (IRE), **5/2** Wassl This Then (IRE), **4/1** Elegant Touch, **15/2** Teslemi (USA)(12/1—7/1), **8/1** Brave the Wind, **9/1** Wild Strawberry. CSF £7.90, Tote £3.00: £2.00 £1.80 (£2.70). Mr G. Sainaghi (NEWMARKET) bred by Barronstown Stud in Ireland. 6 Rn 2m 8.48 (5.48)
SF—42/30/28/9/23/–

**1595** WILDHERN STKS (2-Y.O.C & G) £3655.00 (£1090.00: £520.00: £235.00) **7f 64y (rnd)** 8-30 (8-31)

1348² **Redenham (USA)** (Fav) *(RHannon)* 8-11 JReid (3) (lw: a gng wl: 2nd st: qcknd & led wl over 1f out: easily) ............................................ —**1**
Suivez *(CEBrittain)* 8-8 LDettori (2) (gd sort: bit bkwd: led tl wl over 1f out: r.o: no ch w wnr) ............................................ 5.**2**
Greystoke *(LordHuntingdon)* 8-8 WRSwinburn (1) (lengthy: scope: 4th st: r.o one pce fnl 2f) ............................................ 4.**3**

1202* Iommelli (IRE) *(PAKelleway)* 9-1 MRoberts (4) (lw: 5th st: rdn & hdwy over 3f
out: wknd 2f out) ............................................................................................... 3.4
　　Bonar Bridge (USA) *(RHannon)* 8-8 PatEddery (5) (scope: bit bkwd: 3rd st:
wknd 3f out) ........................................................................................................ 4.5

**2/5** REDENHAM (USA), **4/1** Iommelli (IRE), **7/1** Greystoke, **12/1** Suivez(8/1—14/1), **20/1** Bonar Bridge (USA).
CSF £6.00, Tote £1.50: £1.10 £2.70 (£5.50). Mr B. E. Nielsen (MARLBOROUGH) bred by Dr J. Fred Miller III in
USA. 5 Rn　　　　　　　　　　　　　　　　　　　　　　　　　　　　　　1m 30.67 (3.37)
　　　　　　　　　　　　　　　　　　　　　　　　　　　　　　　　　SF—35/17/5/3/–

**1596**　　210 FM AVEBURY STKS　£3687.50 (£1100.00: £525.00: £237.50)
　　　　　　**1m 7y (rnd)**　　　　　　　　　　　　　　　　　　9-00 (9-02)

1136* **Hazaam (USA)** (Fav) *(MRStoute)* 3–8-12 SCauthen (3) (lw: 6th st: hdwy over 2f
out: led over 1f out: r.o wl) ............................................................................... —1
1398* Kristianstad **(87)** *(MrsJCecil)* 3–9-0 PaulEddery (4) (lw: 3rd st: led wl over 1f
out: sn hdd: r.o wl) ............................................................................................ ¾.2
1058⁶ Ships Lantern **(95)** *(CFWall)* 3–8-3 NCarlisle (7) (4th st: ev ch 2f out: r.o one
pce) ...................................................................................................................... 5.3
704 Berseto (USA) **(90)** *(HRACecil)* 3–8-8 PatEddery (2) (lw: led tl wknd wl over 1f
out) ....................................................................................................................... 5.4
　　Cheveley Dancer (USA) *(AWDenson)* 4–9-4 WNewnes (5) (swtg: 2nd st: wknd
over 2f out) ......................................................................................................... ¾.5
1280 Tinkosumtin *(PBurgoyne)* 6–8-8 TQuinn (6) (7th st: a bhd) ........................ 5.6
　　Lord Alfie *(RJHodges)* 3–8-2 ‡TSprake (1) (5th st: wknd 3f out) .................. 1.7

**4/6** HAZAAM (USA), **4/1** Kristianstad(3/1—5/1), **5/1** Berseto, **15/2** Ships Lantern, **33/1** Lord Alfie, **50/1**
Cheveley Dancer (USA), **100/1** Tinkosumtin. CSF £3.84, Tote £1.50: £1.30 £1.60 (£2.10). Sheikh Mohammed
(NEWMARKET) bred by Darley Stud Management Co Ltd in USA. 7 Rn　　　　1m 37.27 (1.27)
　　　　　　　　　　　　　　　　　　　　　　　　　　　　　SF—67/67/41/31/39/14

T/Plpt: £8.70 (346.1 Tckts).　　　　　　　　　　　　　　　　　　　　　　　Hn

**1170—YARMOUTH (L-H)**

**Tuesday, June 23rd [Good to firm]**
Going Allowance: minus 0.40 sec per fur (F)　　　　　　　　Wind: mod across

Stalls: 6th & 7th low, remainder high

**1597**　　TOTE PLACE ONLY STKS (Mdn 3-Y.O) £2364.00 (£654.00: £312.00)
　　　　　　**1m 3y**　　　　　　　　　　　　　　　　　　　2-15 (2-18)

440⁴ **Coniston Water (USA)** (Fav) *(JHMGosden)* 9-0 SCauthen (6) (still bit bkwd: w
ldr: led over 2f out: shkn up & r.o fnl f) ............................................................ —1
1383³ Lady Buchan *(MrsJCecil)* 8-9 BRaymond (2) (hld up: hdwy 2f out: ev ch 1f out:
r.o) ........................................................................................................................ ½.2
　　Lap of Luxury *(WJarvis)* 8-9 NDay (8) (leggy: unf: chsd ldrs: kpt on fnl f) .... 1½.3
481⁵ Lake Dominion **(75)** *(PWHarris)* 9-0 MRoberts (4) (led over 5f: one pce) ........ 1½.4
　　Bold Steve *(LMCumani)* 9-0 LDettori (3) (unf: scope: pushed along ½-wy: n.d) 7.5
　　Dancing Boat *(AAScott)* 9-0 WRSwinburn (5) (cmpt: str: bkwd: bhd fnl 3f) .... 2.6
833 Lord Neptune **(65)** *(MAJarvis)* 9-0 GCrealock (1) (hdwy 4f out: wknd 2f out) .. s.h.7
　　1173² Laura (6/1) Withdrawn (lame at s) : not under orders

**1/4** CONISTON WATER (USA), **7/2** Lady Buchan, **6/1** Dancing Boat, **10/1** Bold Steve, **12/1** Lake Dominion, **14/1**
Lap of Luxury, **20/1** Lord Neptune. CSF £3.07, Tote £1.20: £1.40 £1.60 (£1.90). Sheikh Mohammed
(NEWMARKET) bred by Ralph C. Wilson Jnr. 7 Rn　　　　　　　　　　　1m 37.3 (2)
　　　　　　　　　　　　　　　　　　　　　　　　　　　　　SF—22/15/10/10/–/–

**1598**　　LEVY BOARD CLAIMING STKS　£3002.00 (£896.00: £428.00: £194.00)
　　　　　　**7f 3y**　　　　　　　　　　　　　　　　　　　2-45 (2-50)

1503² **Al Ramis (IRE) (70)** (Fav) *(CEBrittain)* 3–8-4 MRoberts (5) (chsd ldrs: rdn 2f
out: r.o wl to ld wl ins fnl f) ............................................................................... —1
1411³ Domicksky **(77)** *(MJRyan)* 4–9-1 ‡³DBiggs (1) (hld up: plld out 2f out: led over 1f
out: hdd & no ex ins fnl f) .................................................................................. 1.2
1426 Morsun **(67)** *(DMorley)* 3–8-9 WRSwinburn (7) (lw: hdwy over 1f out: r.o wl ins
fnl f) ..................................................................................................................... ½.3
997 Coral Flutter **(44)** (bl) *(JWPayne)* 5–8-4 JQuinn (2) (swtg: prom: led 2f out tl
over 1f out: one pce) .......................................................................................... ¾.4
127 Chaff **(34)** *(DMorris)* 5–8-5 ‡⁷StephenDavies (3) (wl bhd tl sme hdwy appr fnl f) . 7.5
1411² Certain Lady **(67)** *(GBlum)* 3–7-6 ‡⁵DHarrison (8) (prom over 4f) ...................... nk.6
1281⁵ Loose Zeus (USA) **(52)** *(CFWall)* 3–8-4(1) NDay (6) (led 5f) ................................. 1.7

1034 Blazing Pearl **(21)** *(JLHarris)* 4–8–4  DHolland (4) (bhd fnl 2f) ........................ 1½.**8**
1146 Sasparella **(70)** *(WJarvis)* 3–7-11 ‡⁷GMilligan (9) (dwlt: sn prom: rdn & wknd 2f
out) ............................................ d.h.**8**
1314⁶ Yonge Tender **(56)** (bl) *(CNWilliams)* 5–8-10  JCurant (11) (prom over 4f) ......... 7.**10**
Aspirant *(SirMarkPrescott)* 4–8-9  CNutter (10) (s.i.s: sn chsng ldrs: wknd 3f
out) ........................................... 1½.**11**
*1376* Edgewise **(17)** *(DMorris)* 9–8-11  MBirch (12) (sn bhd) ........................... ½.**12**
1040 Princess Annie **(41)** *(GBlum)* 3–7-3⁽¹⁾ ‡⁷CHawksley (13) (t.o fnl 2f) ...................... 13

**9/4** AL RAMIS (IRE), **7/2** Certain Lady(op 9/4), **4/1** Domicksky, **8/1** Morsun, **10/1** Yonge Tender(8/1—12/1),
Sasparella, **14/1** Loose Zeus (USA), **20/1** Aspirant, **33/1** Ors. CSF £11.75, Tote £2.80: £1.30 £1.90 £1.90
(£4.60). Mr Mohamed Obaida (NEWMARKET) bred by Mrs W. J. Taylor & Impshire T'breds Plc in Ireland. 13 Rn
1m 23.6 (0.8)
SF—36/44/36/29/9/–

---

**1599**       TOTE CREDIT H'CAP (0-90) £3590.00 (£1070.00: £510.00: £230.00)
            **7f 3y**                                    3-15 (3-17)

1275⁶ **Sebosan (72)** (bl) *(SPCWoods)* 3–8-9  WWoods (2) (lw: prom: led over 2f out:
drvn out) ....................................... —**1**
1474 Annabelle Royale **(75)** *(MrsNMacauley)* 6–9-7  LDettori (3) (a.p: led 3f out: sn
hdd: rdn & r.o fnl f) ............................ 1½.**2**
1295³ Trial Times (USA) **(75)** *(WAO'Gorman)* 3–8-7 ‡⁵EmmaO'Gorman (6) (led 4f: sn
rdn & kpt on) ................................... 2½.**3**
1434★ Norfolkiev (FR) **(57)** *(Fav)* *(MMoubarak)* 6–7-10 ‡⁷CHawksley (5) (lw: dwlt: a
chsng ldrs: no imp fnl 2f) ........................ hd.**4**
1338 Susanna's Secret **(49)** *(WCarter)* 5–7-9  JLowe (4) (lw: squeezed out s: plld hrd:
chsd ldrs over 4f) .............................. 2½.**5**
1254⁴ Langtry Lady **(82)** *(M.IRyan)* 6–10-0  MRoberts (1) (bhd: effrt 2f out: sn no imp) . 1.**6**
1309 Bellatrix **(53)** *(CEBrittain)* 4–7-13  GCrealock (7) (prom over 3f: t.o) ............. 10.**7**

**5/2** Norfolkiev (FR), **7/2** Annabelle Royale, **9/2** Langtry Lady, **5/1** Susanna's Secret, **11/2** Trial Times (USA),
**10/1** SEBOSAN, **16/1** Bellatrix. CSF £42.21, Tote £13.80: £5.60 £2.10 (£27.90). High Point Bloodstock Ltd
(NEWMARKET) bred by J. Smith. 7 Rn
1m 23.2 (0.4)
SF—47/54/32/20/11/41

---

**1600**       E.B.F. STKS (Mdn 2-Y.O.F) £2280.00 (£630.00: £300.00)   **7f 3y**   3-45 (3-46)

**Shamisen** *(CEBrittain)* 8-11  MRoberts (2) (unf: scope: a.p: rdn over 1f out: r.o
to ld wl ins fnl f) ................................ —**1**
Self Assured (IRE) *(Fav)* *(HRACecil)* 8-11  WRyan (4) (narrow: unf: led tl rdn &
hdd wl ins fnl f) ................................ hd.**2**
Cashell *(MRStoute)* 8-11  SCauthen (3) (cmpt: bit bkwd: chsd ldrs: nt qckn fnl
2f) ............................................ 8.**3**
Midnight Mischief *(MJRyan)* 8-11  PRobinson (1) (leggy: unf: s.i.s: a t.o) ......... 20.**4**
Tower of Ivory (IRE) *(WAO'Gorman)* 8-6 ‡⁵EmmaO'Gorman (5) (neat: disp ld 4f:
sn t.o) ......................................... 1.**5**

**Evens** Self Assured (IRE), **9/4** Cashell, **3/1** SHAMISEN(5/2—4/1), **16/1** Midnight Mischief(op 8/1), **25/1** Tower
of Ivory (IRE). CSF £6.52, Tote £3.80: £1.90 £1.60 (£4.20). Mr Saeed Manana (NEWMARKET) bred by Floors
Farming & London Thoroughbred Services Ltd. 5 Rn
1m 24.8 (2)
SF—25/24/–/–/–

---

**1601**       BET WITH THE TOTE (S) STKS (2-Y.O) £2186.80 (£604.80: £288.40)
            **5f 43y**                                    4-15 (4-16)

1479² **Trevorsninepoints** *(Jt-Fav)* *(NTinkler)* 8-11  MBirch (8) (mde all: pushed clr
appr fnl f) ..................................... —**1**
*1373⁴* Jasmin Isle *(MissGayKelleway)* 8-6  MRoberts (3) (hdwy over 2f out: rdn & chsd
wnr appr fnl f: no imp) .......................... 4.**2**
*1264⁵* Russet Way *(MrsNMacauley)* 8-6  NDay (6) (w wnr 3f: one pce) ................. 1.**3**
1416² Meadmore Magic *(Jt-Fav)* *(JLHarris)* 8-6  DHolland (2) (b.off hind: dwlt: chsd
ldrs: one pce fnl 2f) ............................. 5.**4**
1442 Sterling Princess *(JRJenkins)* 8-6  WRyan (7) (in tch over 2f) .................. ¾.**5**
1442 Secret Tale *(GBlum)* 8-6  JQuinn (5) (a bhd) .................................. ½.**6**
*1264* Get Daily Sport *(PAKelleway)* 8-6  PRobinson (1) (bhd fnl 2f) ................. 1.**7**
1541 Generally *(PatMitchell)* 8-1 ‡⁵DHarrison (4) (in tch over 2f) ................... ¾.**8**

**7/4** Meadmore Magic, TREVORSNINEPOINTS, **6/1** Jasmin Isle, **8/1** Russet Way(10/1—16/1), **12/1** Generally,
**33/1** Ors. CSF £11.93, Tote £2.30: £1.50 £1.30 £1.60 (£7.10). Captain F. M. E. Jacobsen (MALTON) bred by
Peter Thomas. 8 Rn; Sold T S Child 5,500 gns
61.9 sec (1.6)
SF—25/4/–/–/–/–

**1602**    TOTE DUAL FORECAST H'CAP (3-Y.O) (0-70) £2448.00 (£678.00: £324.00)
1¾m 17y
4-45 (4-46)

| | | |
|---|---|---|
| 802 | **Anar (IRE) (45)** (WCarter) 7-3[1] ‡7CHawksley (1) (prom: 3rd st: rdn to ld ins fnl f) | —1 |
| 1316⁴ | Rolling the Bones (USA) (66) (JRFanshawe) 9-3 GCarter (3) (chsd ldrs: 5th st: led 2f out: hdd, rdn & edgd rt ins fnl f) | hd.2 |
| 1260⁵ | Last Conquest (IRE) (65) (Jt-Fav) (PFICole) 8-9 ‡7JDSmith (2) (lw: hdwy & 4th st: rdn & hung lft over 3f out: r.o fnl f) | 3.3 |
| 1188⁶ | Bashamah (IRE) (55) (CEBrittain) 8-6 MRoberts (5) (last st: r.o fnl 2f: nvr able to chal) | 2.4 |
| 1330³ | Maji (70) (DMorley) 9-7 MBirch (6) (prom: 2nd st: led over 2f out: sn hdd & edgd lft) | ½.5 |
| 1126² | Restless Minstrel (USA) (66) (Jt-Fav) (LMCumani) 9-3 LDettori (7) (led over 11f: sn btn) | 7.6 |
| 566 | Petty Cash (52) (DrJDScargill) 8-3 JQuinn (4) (6th st: a bhd: t.o) | 15.7 |

*Stewards Enquiry: Carter suspended 2-5/7/92 (careless riding).*

**11/4** Last Conquest (IRE), Restless Minstrel (USA), **7/2** Rolling the Bones (USA)(op 6/1), Maji, **10/1** Bashamah (IRE), **25/1** ANAR (IRE) & Ors. CSF £101.49, Tote £23.90: £4.70 1.50 (£34.50). Miss Maha Kalaji (EPSOM) bred by Cyril Humphris in Ireland. 7 Rn     3m 3.3 (5.3)

**1603**    TOTE PLACEPOT H'CAP (0-80) £2924.00 (£872.00: £416.00: £188.00)
1¼m 21y
5-15 (5-17)

| | | |
|---|---|---|
| 1413* | **Chatham Island (61)** (Fav) (CEBrittain) 4–9-7 MRoberts (5) (mde all: rdn out) | ..—1 |
| 1308* | Milanese (79) (DMorley) 3–9-13 MBirch (3) (chsd wnr: 2nd st: ev ch over 3f out tl unable qckn fnl f) | 1½.2 |
| 1317* | Shining Jewel (64) (MrsLPiggott) 5–9-3 ‡7GMilligan (1) (lw: 4th st: plld out over 1f out: r.o ins fnl f) | 1½.3 |
| 1309* | Kateb (IRE) (71) (RWArmstrong) 3–9-5 BRaymond (4) (chsd ldrs: 3rd st: rdn over 2f out: wknd fnl f) | 3.4 |
| 1181³ | Rival Bid (USA) (60) (MAJarvis) 4–9-6 WRyan (2) (s.i.s: last st: rdn 3f out: a bhd) | 6.5 |

**2/1** CHATHAM ISLAND, **5/2** Kateb (IRE), **5/1** Ors. CSF £10.92, Tote £2.00: £1.40 2.50 (£7.60). Mr B. H. Voak (NEWMARKET) bred by G. C. Hughes. 5 Rn     2m 7.9 (3.5)

SF—32/35/22/18/7

T/Plpt: £249.20 (11.55 Tckts).     Dk

## 709—CHESTER (L-H)

### Wednesday, June 24th [Good to firm]

Going Allowance: minus 0.20 sec per fur (F)     Wind: slt half against

Stalls: low

**1604**    TARVIN CLAIMING STKS    £4207.50 (£1260.00: £605.00: £277.50)
1¼m 75y
6-30 (6-30)

| | | |
|---|---|---|
| 1519* | **Rose Glen (59)** (Fav) (ABailey) 6–8-2 ‡5ATucker (6) (s.i.s: hdwy ½-wy: led over 2f out: sn clr: eased nr fin) | —1 |
| 1490⁵ | Noble Vienna (USA) (46) (RHollinshead) 3–8-2 WRyan (1) (hld up: hdwy 4f out: 3rd st: r.o u.p fnl f: nrst fin) | ½.2 |
| 1408* | Thunderbird One (USA) (CRNelson) 3–8-0 NAdams (3) (lw: hld up: hdwy 4f out: 2nd st: rdn 1f out: one pce) | ¾.3 |
| 1255 | Neltegrity (58) (THCaldwell) 3–8-1 ‡5NKennedy (4) (lw: chsd ldrs: 4th st: wknd wl over 1f out) | 12.4 |
| 913 | Brown as a Berry (IRE) (30) (WStorey) 4–8-10 SWebster (5) (chsd ldrs: 6th & rdn st: sn btn) | 3.5 |
| 1048⁶ | Northern Emperor (IRE) (41) (MHEasterby) 3–7-7 ‡5SMaloney (2) (prom: led 5f out tl over 2f out: 5th & wkng st) | 3.6 |
| | Bradmore's Vision (LJBarratt) 6–8-7 ‡3FNorton (7) (b: bit bkwd: led after 1f to 5f out: wknd 3f out: 7th & t.o st) | 20.7 |

**4/6** ROSE GLEN, **5/2** Thunderbird One (USA), **15/2** Neltegrity, **12/1** Noble Vienna (USA), **25/1** Northern Emperor (IRE), **50/1** Ors. CSF £9.36, Tote £1.60: £1.20 3.10 (£5.20). Mr D. G. Furlong (TARPORLEY) bred by R. G. Bonson. 7 Rn     2m 12.55 (2.55)

SF—43/42/38/15/18/—

**1605**    MIRA SHOWERS GRADUATION STKS (2-Y.O) £4207.50 (£1260.00: £605.00: £277.50)
7f 2y
7-00 (7-01)

| | | |
|---|---|---|
| 1397* | **Lindon Lime (USA)** (Fav) (PFICole) 9-4 AMunro (1) (lw: hld up: wnt 2nd st: led wl over 1f out: r.o strly) | —1 |

**1606—1608**

1424* Regal Aura (IRE) *(GHarwood)* 9-4 JCarroll (2) (lw: hld up: 3rd st: effrt over 1f
out: no ex ins fnl f) ............................................................. 5.2

Civil Law (IRE) *(RHollinshead)* 8-11 WRyan (5) (w'like: bkwd: s.s: hdwy 3f out:
5th st: styd on strly ins fnl f) ........................................... hd.3

1424 Mad Mytton *(ABailey)* 8-11 AMackay (4) (led tl hdd & wknd wl over 1f out) ...... 10.4

720⁶ Cardinal Dogwood (USA) *(MBrittain)* 8-11 GDuffield (3) (bit bkwd: sn pushed
along: outpcd ½-wy: 6th & t.o st) ..................................... 2¹/₂.5

877⁵ Panic Button (IRE) *(MHEasterby)* 8-6 MBirch (6) (chsd ldrs: reminders ½-wy:
4th st: wknd over 1f out) .................................................... 1.6

**10/11** LINDON LIME (USA), **7/2** Regal Aura (IRE), **4/1** Panic Button (IRE), **14/1** Mad Mytton, **16/1** Civil Law (IRE),
**25/1** Cardinal Dogwood (USA). CSF £4.33, Tote £1.80: £1.30 £2.40 (£2.60). Mr Fahd Salman (WHATCOMBE)
bred by Lucy G. Bassett in USA. 6 Rn
1m 28.50 (2.30)
SF–49/34/26/–/–/–

**1606** CORBETT BOOKMAKERS TROPHY (H'cap) (0-100) £5608.00 (£1684.00: £812.00:
£376.00) 1m 7f 195y 7-30 (7-30)

(Weights raised 16 lb)

1241* **Our Aisling (70)** (Fav) *(SGNorton)* 4–9-0 ‡⁷OPears (2) (lw: a.p: led ent st: styd
on strly) ............................................................................ —1

1301³ Broom Isle **(58)** *(MrsAKnight)* 4–8-6 ‡³FNorton (1) (lw: led tl hdd & 2nd st: styd
on one pce) ......................................................................... 2.2

1341* Muizenberg **(69)** *(JACEdwards)* 5–9-6 WRyan (6) (lw: stdd s: plld hrd: hdwy
over 5f out: 3rd & rdn st: kpt on one pce) ................................. ½.3

1241² Northants **(50)** *(WStorey)* 6–8-1 BCrossley (4) (b: outpcd & lost pl 6f out: rallied
& 4th st: styd on ins fnl f) ...................................................... nk.4

1459 Go South **(72)** (bl) *(JRJenkins)* 8–9-9 GBaxter (5) (hld up: hdwy 7f out: outpcd
over 3f out: 5th & btn st) ....................................................... 3.5

1256⁶ Shoofe (USA) **(73)** *(DMorley)* 4 9-10 MBirch (3) (chsd ldr 12f: lost pl: 6th st) .. s.h.6

**9/4** OUR AISLING, **4/1** Northants, **5/1** Muizenberg, Go South, **13/2** Broom Isle, **8/1** Shoofe (USA). CSF £14.55,
Tote £2.60: £1.60 £2.70 (£9.80). Mr A. K. Smeaton (BARNSLEY) bred by A. K. Smeaton. 6 Rn
3m 33.86 (8.86)

**1607** GMS INDUSTRIAL FASTENERS H'CAP (0-100) £4919.00 (£1472.00: £706.00: £323.00)
5f 16y 8-00 (8-01)

1487⁴ **Crystal Jack (FR) (81)** (Fav) *(FHLee)* 4–8-10 BRaymond (4) (chsd ldrs:
swtchd outside over 1f out: str burst to ld ins fnl f) .............. —1

1199 Touch of White **(80)** *(JEBanks)* 6–8-9 AMunro (8) (chsd ldrs: ev ch whn n.m.r 1f
out: r.o wl nr fin) ................................................................. 1¹/₂.2

1365⁶ Glenstal Princess **(67)** *(RHollinshead)* 5–7-3(3) ‡⁷AGarth (2) (s.i.s: outpcd tl gd
hdwy appr fnl f: fin wl) ......................................................... ½.3

819 Amber Mill **(85)** *(JBerry)* 4–9-0 JCarroll (7) (lw: a.p: led 1f out: sn hdd: unable
qckn fnl f) .......................................................................... s.h.4

1305 Ashtina **(67)** *(RJHodges)* 7–7-7 ‡³FNorton (1) (lw: led to 1f out: rdn & no ex fnl f) s.h.5

1157 Debsy Do (USA) **(76)** *(SGNorton)* 3–7-7(5) ‡⁵SMaloney (3) (lw: dwlt: sn chsng
ldrs: rdn over 1f out: one pce) ................................................ 2.6

1392 Heaven-Liegh-Grey **(85)** *(MJohnston)* 4–9-0 DMcKeown (6) (lw: disp ld over
3f: ev ch 1f out: wknd fnl f) ................................................... ½.7

1199* Viceroy **(99)** (bl) *(BBeasley)* 5–10-0 GDuffield (5) (lw: outpcd: a bhd) ............... ¾.8

LONG HANDICAP: Glenstal Princess 7-4, Debsy Do (USA) 7-5.

**7/2** CRYSTAL JACK (FR), **4/1** Viceroy, Ashtina, **13/2** Touch of White, **15/2** Amber Mill, **8/1** Heaven-Liegh-Grey,
**9/1** Debsy Do (USA), **14/1** Glenstal Princess. CSF £24.08, CT £253.82. Tote £3.30: £1.50 £1.70 £2.90
(£17.70). Mrs B. Facchino (WILMSLOW) bred by Daniel Fernandez and Paul Vuillard in France. 8 Rn
61.25 sec (0.65)
SF–63/56/34/58/36/28

**1608** MIRA SHOWERS H'CAP (3-Y.O) (0-100) £4191.00 (£1248.00: £594.00: £267.00)
7f 122y 8-30 (8-30)

1010* **Hand on Heart (IRE) (61)** *(WJHaggas)* 7-3 ‡⁷SallyRadford-Howes (6) (chsd
ldrs: 3rd st: led 1f out: hld on gamely) ................................. —1

1062⁶ By Hand **(75)** *(WJHaggas)* 8-10 NDay (5) (a.p: 2nd st: slt ld over 1f out: sn hdd:
hrd rdn & r.o fnl f) ............................................................... nk.2

1516³ Battle Colours (IRE) **(86)** (Fav) *(SirMarkPrescott)* 9-7 GDuffield (1) (lw: chsd
ldrs: drvn along ½-wy: 4th st: swtchd ins over 1f out: r.o) ....... 1¹/₂.3

1159⁵ Sir Oliver (IRE) **(68)** *(RJHodges)* 8-0 ‡³FNorton (4) (lw: hld up & bhd: 6th st:
hdwy over 1f out: unable qckn fnl f) ...................................... nk.4

1246 Castlerea Lad **(81)** *(RHollinshead)* 9-2 WRyan (2) (hld up: 5th st: effrt appr fnl f:
no imp) ............................................................................. 1.5

1508² Thrie-Na-Helah (IRE) **(75)** (v) *(RMWhitaker)* 8-10 AColhane (3) (lw: led tl hdd
over 1f out: one pce) ..................................................... nk.6

**9/4** Battle Colours (IRE), **3/1** By Hand, **7/2** Thrie-Na-Helah (IRE), **7/1** HAND ON HEART (IRE) & Ors. CSF £26.73,
Tote £7.50: £2.50 £1.80 (£7.70). Mrs M. M. Haggas (NEWMARKET) bred by Kellsboro House Stud in Ireland. 6
Rn                                                               1m 35.76 (3.06)
SF—7/27/33/11/26/19

**1609**     GATEWAY TO WALES HOTEL STKS (Mdn 2-Y.O.F) £3418.00 (£1024.00: £492.00:
£226.00)     **5f 16y**                                          9-00 (9-00)

1322² **Stormy Heights** (Fav) *(JRJenkins)* 8-11 GBaxter (4) (a.p: hrd rdn over 1f out:
r.o to ld ins fnl f: sn clr) ..........................................  —1
1450⁵ Riston Lady (IRE) (bl) *(BSRothwell)* 8-11 DHolland (1) (lw: led: qcknd clr over 1f
out: rdn, wknd & hdd ins fnl f) ................................... 3.2
1422 Miss Whittingham (IRE) *(JBerry)* 8-11 JCarroll (2) (bhd: r.o appr fnl f: nvr nrr) . 1½.3
1422⁴ Cloudy Reef *(RHollinshead)* 8-4 ‡7AGarth (3) (chsd ldrs: rdn over 1f out: one
pce) ........................................................... 1½.4
Goodbye Millie *(SGNorton)* 8-11 JFortune (5) (scope: bkwd: s.s: hdwy ½-wy:
outpcd ent st: sn bhd) .......................................... 1½.5

**6/4** STORMY HEIGHTS, **7/2** Cloudy Reef, **4/1** Goodbye Millie, **5/1** Riston Lady (IRE), **15/2** Miss Whittingham
(IRE). CSF £8.39, Tote £2.10: £1.40 £2.10 (£4.90). Miss Elizabeth Colver (ROYSTON) bred by Miss E. Colver. 5
Rn                                                               63.22 sec (2.62)
SF—25/13/7/–/–

T/Plpt: £21.70 (208.2 Tckts).                                         IM

1314—**KEMPTON  (R-H)**
**Wednesday, June 24th [Good to firm]**
Going Allowance: minus 0.35 sec per fur (F)                        Wind: nil

Stalls: high

**1610**     BARBECUE STKS (Mdn 2-Y.O) £2511.00 (£696.00: £333.00)    **6f**    6-40 (6-46)

1443⁶ **Coy Boy (IRE)** *(GLewis)* 9-0 PaulEddery (14) (a.p: led 1f out: all out) ............  —1
Fret (USA) (Fav) *(PFICole)* 9-0 TQuinn (4) (leggy: scope: a.p: rdn over 3f out:
r.o wl ins fnl f) ................................................ nk.2
345³ Iron Merchant (IRE) *(RAkehurst)* 9-0 LDettori (12) (lw: led 5f: r.o) ............ hd.3
Able Choice (IRE) *(RWArmstrong)* 9-0 PatEddery (3) (wl grwn: a.p: ev ch over
1f out: nt qckn) ................................................ 5.4
Premium *(WJHaggas)* 9-0 MHills (7) (unf: scope: nvr nr to chal) ............. 3.5
Hallplace *(MRChannon)* 9-0 RHills (9) (wl grwn: nvr nrr) .................. 3.6
Lake Princess (IRE) *(SDow)* 8-9 WNewnes (13) (leggy: nrst fin) .............. 1½.7
Akenside *(DRCElsworth)* 9-0 SCauthen (10) (str: bit bkwd: a mid div) .......... hd.8
1378⁶ Petite Vino *(JJBridger)* 8-9 SWhitworth (8) (spd over 3f) ................. 3½.9
1384 Chummy's Idea (IRE) *(JSutcliffe)* 8-9 BRouse (6) (a bhd) ................. 3.10
1443 Take the Mick *(EAWheeler)* 8-9 ‡5DHarrison (5) (a bhd) ................. 2½.11
1405³ Conbrio Star *(CGCox)* 8-11 ‡3TSprake (2) (prom 3f: t.o) .................. 12
Dark and Stormy *(MDixon)* 9-0 DaleGibson (11) (leggy: s.s: p.u 4f out) ........... 0

**8/13** Fret (USA), **6/1** Iron Merchant (IRE), **15/2** Akenside(op 16/1), **12/1** Premium(6/1—14/1), **16/1** Able Choice
(IRE), **20/1** COY BOY (IRE), **25/1** Hallplace, **33/1** Chummy's Idea (IRE), **50/1** Ors. CSF £31.85, Tote £18.00:
£2.40 £1.30 £1.50 (£15.10). Mr Nigel H. Morris (EPSOM) bred by Leo Collins in Ireland. 13 Rn
1m 11.91 (0.61)
SF—46/45/44/24/12/–

**1611**     FUNFAIR GRADUATION STKS (3-Y.O.F) £3236.00 (£968.00: £464.00: £212.00)
**1m (J.C)**                                                    7-10 (7-12)

630⁵ **Party Cited (USA) (91)** *(DRCElsworth)* 8-8 JWilliams (6) (3rd st: led over 2f out:
r.o wl) ...................................................... —1
Pelargonia *(RCharlton)* 8-8 MHills (10) (lw: hmpd over 4f out: hdwy over 2f out:
ev ch ins fnl f: r.o) ............................................ ¾.2
818⁴ Enaya **(99)** *(RWArmstrong)* 9-0 WCarson (8) (led over 4f out tl over 2f out: r.o
one pce) ..................................................... 4.3
1398³ So Smug (USA) (Fav) *(JHMGosden)* 8-8 RCochrane (14) (hmpd over 4f out:
6th st: r.o: nt rch ldrs) ......................................... 2½.4
1287² Whirl *(JRFanshawe)* 8-8 WRSwinburn (12) (hdwy over 2f out: eased whn btn
over 1f out) .................................................. s.h.5

1432★ Rose Elegance *(WRMuir)* 8-7 ‡⁷KimMcDonnell (9) (swtg: nvr nrr) ...................... ¹/₂.**6**
    Shimmer *(LordHuntingdon)* 8-8 MRoberts (1) (w'like: scope: hdwy fnl 2f: r.o) 2¹/₂.**7**
289★ Brightness *(MMoubarak)* 9-0 LDettori (7) (lw: 2nd st: wknd over 1f out) .......... nk.**8**
989² Queen Warrior *(PTWalwyn)* 8-8 PatEddery (4) (a bhd) .................................... 1¹/₂.**9**
1315★ Star Goddess (USA) **(84)** *(MRChannon)* 9-0 BRouse (3) (4th st: wknd over 1f
    out) .................................................................................. 1¹/₂.**10**
    Unification (IRE) *(RAkehurst)* 8-8 TQuinn (14) (lw: grwn: s.s: a bhd) .................. 4.**11**
1315 Batchworth Bound *(EAWheeler)* 8-3 ‡⁵DHarrison (11) (bhd fnl 4f) ................ ¹/₂.**12**
787⁶ Sally Fast *(BPalling)* 8-1 ‡⁷StephenDavies (13) (lw: 5th st: wknd over 2f out) .... 5.**13**
1306 Basha (USA) *(JLDunlop)* 8-8 SCauthen (2) (b.hind: swtg: a wl bhd: t.o) ......... 15.**14**
1315 Miss Cresta **(70)** *(HCandy)* 8-8 WNewnes (15) (swtg: led over 3f: faltered over
    4f out: t.o) .......................................................................... 20.**15**

**5/2** So Smug (USA), **11/2** Queen Warrior(8/1—5/1), Star Goddess (USA), **13/2** Enaya, PARTY CITED (USA), **8/1**
Whirl, **9/1** Brightness, **14/1** Shimmer(op 7/1), **16/1** Miss Cresta, **20/1** Rose Elegance, **25/1** Basha (USA),
Pelargonia, **33/1** Ors. CSF £154.17, Tote £9.20: £2.60 £8.50 £1.90 (£303.30). Mr Raymond Tooth
(WHITSBURY) bred by Rogers Trust in USA. 15 Rn
                                                      1m 36.96 (0.36)
                                                  SF—47/45/39/25/24/21

---

**1612**    TAYLOR WALKER H'CAP (0-80) £3080.00 (£920.00: £440.00: £200.00)
        1¹/₂m                                     7-40 (7-41)

905★ **Discord (70)** (Fav) *(LordHuntingdon)* 6–10-0 MRoberts (3) (hdwy & 5th st: led
    over 1f out: r.o wl) ................................................................ —**1**
831 Western Dynasty **(65)** *(MJRyan)* 6–9-9 LDettori (9) (4th st: ev ch over 1f out: r.o) 1¹/₂.**2**
1381⁶ Caspian Beluga **(52)** *(MrsAKnight)* 4–8-10 JQuinn (4) (led tl over 2f out: led wl
    over 1f out: sn hdd: r.o) .......................................................... 2¹/₂.**3**
1318★ Good for a Loan **(67)** *(RLee)* 5–9-11 PatEddery (12) (lw: 3rd st: ev ch over 1f
    out: nt qckn) ......................................................................... ¹/₂.**4**
1318 Statajack (IRE) **(69)** (bl) *(DRCElsworth)* 4–9-13 TQuinn (5) (swtg: 2nd st: led
    over 2f out tl wknd wl over 1f out) ............................................ 7.**5**
1394⁶ Rosgill **(69)** *(PMitchell)* 6–9-13 SCauthen (2) (b.off fore: bhd tl hdwy over 2f out:
    nvr nr to chal) ...................................................................... 10.**6**
1390⁴ Scenic Dancer **(58)** *(AHide)* 4–9-2 WNewnes (6) (lw: s.s: nvr nrr) ................ ¹/₂.**7**
    Bee Beat **(62)** (bl) *(EAWheeler)* 4–9-1 ‡⁵DHarrison (7) (lw: nvr trbld ldrs) ....... 2¹/₂.**8**
1390² Smiling Chief (IRE) **(54)** *(CACyzer)* 4–8-5 ‡⁷TMcLaughlin (13) (lw: prom tl wknd
    & 6th st) ............................................................................. s.h.**9**
1257 Predestine **(55)** *(MMadgwick)* 7–8-13 PaulEddery (11) (b: lw: bhd fnl 4f) ...... 8.**10**
    Fighting Brave **(67)** (bl) *(NAGraham)* 5–9-11 RCochrane (10) (swtg: bhd fnl 4f) 2¹/₂.**11**
    Finaldream (IRE) **(67)** *(AWDenson)* 4–9-11 JWilliams (1) (bit bkwd: a bhd: t.o) 8.**12**
    Snickersnee **(70)** *(MDixon)* 4–10-0 DaleGibson (8) (lw: t.o fnl 6f) ................... 25.**13**

**9/4** DISCORD, **7/1** Good for a Loan(op 9/2), Western Dynasty(5/1—8/1), **8/1** Scenic Dancer, Rosgill, **10/1**
Caspian Beluga, Smiling Chief (IRE), **11/1** Statajack (IRE), **16/1** Predestine, **25/1** Bee Beat, **33/1** Ors. CSF
£18.01, CT £119.67. Tote £3.10: £1.80 £3.50 £2.40 (£14.80). Mr Yoshio Asakawa (WEST ILSLEY) bred by
Knockaney Stud. 13 Rn
                                                     2m 32.14 (1.94)
                                                  SF—52/44/26/38/26/6

---

**1613**    LBC NEWSTALK 97.3 FM GALA STKS (listed race) £8893.75 (£2650.00: £1262.50:
        £568.75)   1¹/₄m (J.C)                           8-10 (8-10)

1197⁵ **Mohican Girl (102)** *(JRFanshawe)* 4–9-5 MRoberts (3) (lw: 3rd st: led over 2f
    out: drvn out) ....................................................................... —**1**
1168² Fair Average **(106)** *(HCandy)* 4–9-7 WNewnes (2) (2nd st: ev ch over 1f out: r.o) 1¹/₂.**2**
1401⁵ Artic Tracker (USA) **(105)** *(CRNelson)* 3–8-9 SCauthen (5) (lw: 5th st: hrd rdn
    over 1f out: r.o one pce) ........................................................ 1¹/₂.**3**
929² Jura **(106)** (Fav) *(HRACecil)* 4–9-7 PatEddery (1) (lw: 4th st: hrd rdn 2f out: one
    pce) .................................................................................... ¹/₂.**4**
1197³ Pfalz **(103)** *(MRStoute)* 4–9-5 WRSwinburn (4) (lw: led tl wknd over 2f out) ....... ¹/₂.**5**
855 Fly Away Soon (USA) **(109)** *(PFICole)* 4–9-10 TQuinn (6) (6th st: hdwy over 2f
    out: wknd over 1f out) ............................................................ 5.**6**

**11/10** Jura, **100/30** Fair Average, **5/1** MOHICAN GIRL, **13/2** Pfalz(9/2—7/1), **8/1** Artic Tracker (USA)(op 12/1),
**12/1** Fly Away Soon (USA)(op 8/1). CSF £21.45, Tote £6.60: £2.10 £2.60 (£22.80). Mr A. R. G. Cane
(NEWMARKET) bred by R. H. Cowell. 6 Rn
                                                     2m 3.11 (1.11)
                                                  SF—59/58/43/54/51/46

---

**1614**    '1812' OVERTURE H'CAP (0-80) £3236.00 (£968.00: £464.00: £212.00)
        6f                                            8-40 (8-42)

1545³ **Tauber (63)** *(PatMitchell)* 8–8-11 ‡³SO'Gorman (3) (a.p: led 2f out: r.o wl) ......... —**1**

| | | | |
|---|---|---|---|
| 1201 | How's Yer Father **(77)** *(RJHodges)* 6–9-11 ‡³TSprake (11) (rdn over 2f out: hdwy over 1f out: ev ch ins fnl f: r.o) | ³/₄.2 |
| 992 | Zeboim **(66)** (v) *(WRMuir)* 6–8-10 ‡⁷KimMcDonnell (1) (a.p: r.o ins fnl f) | ½.3 |
| 1445⁴ | Young Shadowfax **(55)** *(CNAllen)* 5–8-6 GBardwell (2) (b.nr hind: hdwy 2f out: r.o ins fnl f) | ³/₄.4 |
| 1570 | My Ruby Ring **(43)** *(DRLaing)* 5–7-8⁽¹⁾ TyroneWilliams (6) (b: swtg: a.p: hrd rdn fnl 2f: nt qckn) | s.h.5 |
| 1393⁵ | Fascination Waltz **(71)** *(DShaw)* 5–9-8 GCarter (8) (a.p: no hdwy fnl 2f) | ½.6 |
| 1247 | Garth **(75)** (v) *(PJMakin)* 4–9-12 LDettori (13) (hdwy over 2f out: hrd rdn & ev ch over 1f out: nt qckn) | ½.7 |
| 909⁵ | Respectable Jones **(68)** (Jt-Fav) *(GBBalding)* 6–9-5 JWilliams (17) (lw: hdwy on ins 2f out: nt rch ldrs) | 2.8 |
| 1062 | Sea Prodigy **(57)** *(MBlanshard)* 3–8-0 JQuinn (12) (led over 1f: wknd over 1f out) | hd.9 |
| 1368⁴ | Grey Charmer (IRE) **(60)** *(CJames)* 3–8-3 TQuinn (9) (lw: nvr nrr) | 1.10 |
| 821 | Panchellita (USA) **(74)** *(JSutcliffe)* 3–9-3 BRouse (7) (lw: nrst fin) | s.h.11 |
| 1091⁴ | Pipe Opener **(58)** *(JLSpearing)* 4–8-9 GHind (15) (outpcd) | 3½.12 |
| 1278 | Everset (FR) **(61)** (Jt-Fav) *(WJMusson)* 4–8-12 RCochrane (14) (spd over 3f) | ½.13 |
| 1212 | Judgement Call **(62)** *(PHowling)* 5–8-13 WNewnes (5) (spd over 3f) | 3.14 |
| | Almasa **(65)** *(DMorris)* 4–8-9 ‡⁷StephenDavies (16) (outpcd) | ½.15 |
| 42 | Tylers Wood **(50)** *(SDow)* 7–8-1 PaulEddery (4) (led over 4f out tl wknd 2f out) | s.h.16 |

LONG HANDICAP: My Ruby Ring 7-6.

*1305* Spectacle Jim (25/1) Withdrawn (broke loose in stabling area) : not under orders
Stewards Enquiry: Bardwell suspended 3-6/7/92 (excessive of the whip).

**11/2** Everset (FR)(10/1—5/1), Respectable Jones, **7/1** Fascination Waltz(6/1—9/1), Garth, **8/1** How's Yer Father, **9/1** Young Shadowfax, **10/1** Pipe Opener, **12/1** Sea Prodigy, **16/1** Grey Charmer (IRE), Judgement Call, Almasa, TAUBER, **20/1** Panchellita (USA), My Ruby Ring, Zeboim, **50/1** Tylers Wood. CSF £136.44, CT £2,376.63. Tote £23.60: £4.20 £2.10 £3.70 £1.60 (£64.70). Mrs Catherine Reed (NEWMARKET) bred by Ivor Carroll. 16 Rn                                                                       1m 11.98 (0.68)
SF—41/52/35/28/14/41/43

---

**1615** FIREWORKS H'CAP (0-80) £3288.00 (£984.00: £472.00: £216.00)
7f (rnd)                                                                              9-10 (9-11)

| | | | |
|---|---|---|---|
| 1434⁴ | Kawwas **(44)** *(WHolden)* 7–7-8 TyroneWilliams (4) (7th st: hdwy over 2f out: led over 1f out: r.o wl) | —1 |
| 1379² | Highland Magic (IRE) **(66)** *(MJFetherston-Godley)* 4–8-11 ‡⁵DHarrison (2) (b.off hind: 9th st: hdwy fnl 2f: nvr nrr) | ³/₄.2 |
| 1261 | Dance on Sixpence **(64)** *(HJCollingridge)* 4–9-0 JQuinn (6) (5th st: ev ch over 1f out: nt qckn) | 2.3 |
| 1380⁵ | Gabibti (IRE) **(60)** *(BGubby)* 4–8-10 LDettori (7) (swtg: 4th st: rdn over 2f out: one pce) | hd.4 |
| 1338* | La Belle Vie **(71)** *(RJBaker)* 6–9-7 GCarter (3) (8th st: nrst fin) | nk.5 |
| 1261⁴ | Tea Dust (IRE) **(65)** (Fav) *(PJMakin)* 4–9-1 TQuinn (1) (3rd st: ev ch fnl 1f out: wknd fnl f) | 1.6 |
| 1261⁶ | Cheveux Mitchell **(77)** (v) *(MRChannon)* 5–9-13 RHills (8) (lw: led over 4f) | 1½.7 |
| 1150 | Melodic Habit **(43)** *(MrsAKnight)* 5–7-7 DaleGibson (5) (lw: 2nd st: led over 2f out tl wknd over 1f out) | 2½.8 |
| 1266 | On Y Va (USA) **(63)** *(RJRWilliams)* 5–8-6 ‡⁷GMitchell (9) (lw: 6th st: wknd 2f out) | 1½.9 |

LONG HANDICAP: Melodic Habit 6-12.

**100/30** Tea Dust (IRE), **4/1** Highland Magic (IRE)(op 5/2), **9/2** Cheveux Mitchell, **6/1** La Belle Vie, KAWWAS(op 10/1), **7/1** Gabibti (IRE), **10/1** Dance on Sixpence, **14/1** On Y Va (USA), **50/1** Melodic Habit. CSF £29.21, CT £217.88. Tote £9.40: £1.90 £1.60 £3.10 (£26.70). Whitting Commodities Ltd (NEWMARKET) bred by Michael Smurfit. 9 Rn                                                                      1m 25.83 (1.83)
SF—15/30/27/22/32/23

T/Trio: Race 5: £453.00 (4 Tckts). T/Plpt: £245.80 (20.2 Tckts).                    Hn

---

**1269—CARLISLE (R-H)**

## Wednesday, June 24th [Hard]

Going Allowance: 5f-7f: minus 0.40 sec; Rest: minus 0.55 sec (H)        Wind: slt across

Stalls: high

**1616** E.B.F. SILLOTH STKS (Mdn 2-Y.O) £2477.80 (£685.80: £327.40)    5f    2-15 (2-18)

| | | | |
|---|---|---|---|
| 581⁶ | Trentesimo (IRE) *(JBerry)* 9-0 JCarroll (3) (lw: disp ld tl led 2f out: rdn & r.o wl) | —1 |
| | Dahliz (IRE) (Fav) *(HThomsonJones)* 9-0 NCarlisle (1) (neat: bit bkwd: sn outpcd & bhd: styd on u.p fnl 2f: nrst fin) | 1½.2 |
| 1435³ | Don't Tell Jean *(NBycroft)* 8-9 SWood (4) (disp ld 3f: r.o one pce) | ½.3 |
| 1056 | Sounds Risky *(GMMoore)* 8-9 KFallon (2) (spd to ½-wy: sn bhd) | 25.4 |

**4/6** Dahliz (IRE), **5/2** TRENTESIMO (IRE)(2/1—3/1), **5/1** Don't Tell Jean(op 3/1), **25/1** Sounds Risky. CSF £4.43, Tote £4.10 (£2.00). Mr B. R. Allen (COCKERHAM) bred by E. O'Leary in Ireland. 4 Rn      61.7 sec (1.5)
SF—30/24/17/–

---

**1617**    CASTLE CARROCK H'CAP (0-70) £2226.00 (£616.00: £294.00)
       **5f 207y**                              2-45 (2-48)

| | | |
|---|---|---|
| 1157 | **Granny Mc (54)** *(EJAlston)* 5-9-2 KFallon (8) (lw: hdwy ½-wy: r.o fnl f to ld nr fin) | —1 |
| 1522 | Brisas **(47)** (bl) *(TFairhurst)* 5-8-6 ‡3JFanning (1) (lw: cl up: led 2f out: nt qckn nr fin) | hd.2 |
| 1451² | Pretonic **(63)** (Fav) *(MJohnston)* 4-9-11 DMcKeown (5) (lw: bhd: plld outside & effrt ½-wy: rdr lost whip over 1f out: styd on ins fnl f) | ½.3 |
| 1130 | Dreams Eyes **(34)** *(RBastiman)* 4-7-7⁽³⁾ ‡3FNorton (6) (bhd: hdwy u.p ½-wy: kpt on: one pce ins fnl f) | nk.4 |
| 1421 | North Flyer **(50)** *(BAMcMahon)* 4-7-11⁽⁶⁾ ‡7SSanders (3) (hdwy 2f out: styd on fnl f: n.m.r nr fin) | ½.5 |
| *1551* | King Victor (IRE) **(43)** (bl) *(RO'Leary)* 4-8-5 MBirch (7) (lw: w ldrs: disp ld 2f out: sn hdd & grad wknd) | 2½.6 |
| 419 | Our Amber **(31)** *(DWChapman)* 5-7-7 SWood (4) (chsd ldrs: outpcd ½-wy: n.d after) | 4.7 |
| 1570 | Foxes Diamond **(36)** (v) *(BEllison)* 4-7-12 NCarlisle (9) (lw: led 4f: sn wknd) | ½.8 |
| | Come on My Girl (IRE) **(55)** *(TAKCuthbert)* 4-9-3 JCarroll (2) (racd wd: lost tch fr ½-wy) | 12.9 |

LONG HANDICAP: Dreams Eyes 7-6, Our Amber 7-5.

**2/1** Pretonic, **9/2** GRANNY MC, **6/1** Dreams Eyes, **9/1** North Flyer(op 6/1), Our Amber, **10/1** King Victor (IRE), **14/1** Foxes Diamond, Brisas(10/1—16/1), **20/1** Come on My Girl (IRE). CSF £54.02, CT £145.74. Tote £4.80: £2.60 £2.90 £1.10 (£28.80). Mrs S. Y. Alston (PRESTON) bred by Macbiehill Estates Ltd. 9 Rn   1m 13.4 (1.1)
CF   32/21/38/6/7/5

---

**1618**    TENNENTS CLAIMING STKS    £2324.00 (£644.00: £308.00)    **5f 207y**    3-15 (3-15)

| | | |
|---|---|---|
| 825 | **Love Jazz (USA) (89)** *(TDBarron)* 3-9-0 KDarley (5) (lw: trckd ldrs: smooth hdwy to ld 2f out: r.o) | —1 |
| 1314★ | Breezy Day **(77)** (Fav) *(BAMcMahon)* 6-8-9 BRaymond (4) (lw: stumbled s: chsd ldrs: disp ld 2f out: nt qckn fnl f) | 1.2 |
| 1436³ | Imperial Bid (FR) *(DenysSmith)* 4-8-13 ‡7CTeague (1) (effrt ½-wy: edgd rt: styd on nr fin) | nk.3 |
| 1512⁶ | Nevada Mix **(44)** *(MissLAPerratt)* 8-8-7 ‡3JFanning (6) (chsd ldr tl wknd over 1f out) | 4.4 |
| 1451⁶ | Make Or Mar **(67)** *(BEllison)* 8-8-3 JLowe (2) (led 4f: sn rdn & btn) | 2.5 |
| 1514² | Murray's Mazda (IRE) **(67)** *(JBerry)* 3-8-6 JCarroll (3) (lw: s.s: hdwy ½-wy: rdn & no imp appr fnl f) | ¾.6 |

**9/4** Breezy Day, **5/2** Murray's Mazda (IRE), **3/1** LOVE JAZZ (USA), **6/1** Imperial Bid (FR)(op 4/1), **16/1** Nevada Mix(op 10/1), **25/1** Make Or Mar. CSF £9.28, Tote £4.20: £1.90 £1.70 (£6.80). Mr P. D. Savill (THIRSK) bred by Marian Conrad and Jim Herbener in USA. 6 Rn   1m 13.4 (1.1)
SF—30/21/24/–/–/–

---

**1619**    TENNENT'S LAGER CARLISLE BELL (H'cap) (0-85) £3054.20 (£846.20: £404.60)
       **7f 214y**                              3-45 (3-47)

| | | |
|---|---|---|
| 1270★ | **Spanish Verdict (63)** (Fav) *(DenysSmith)* 5-9-8 DHolland (4) (trckd ldr: slt ld 2f out: r.o) | —1 |
| 1317² | Causley **(69)** *(BAMcMahon)* 7-10-0 BRaymond (3) (lw: led tl hdd 2f out: kpt on u.p) | 1½.2 |
| 1366⁵ | Overpower **(64)** *(MHTompkins)* 8-9-9 PRobinson (1) (a chsng ldrs: effrt over 2f out: edgd rt & styd on) | s.h.3 |
| 1441⁴ | Stand At Ease **(34)** *(WStorey)* 7-7-7 SWood (2) (sn outpcd & bhd: n.d) | 15.4 |
| 1480 | Genair (FR) **(60)** *(MrsGRReveley)* 7-9-5 KFallon (5) (lw: p.u after 1f: lame) | 0 |

LONG HANDICAP: Stand At Ease 7-6.

**2/1** SPANISH VERDICT, **3/1** Genair (FR), **100/30** Overpower, **7/2** Causley, **16/1** Stand At Ease. CSF £8.48, Tote £2.30: £1.50 £2.00 (£4.00). Cox & Allen (Kendal) Ltd (BISHOP AUCKLAND) bred by Hyde Stud. 5 Rn   1m 38.3 (U.4)
SF—48/49/43/–

---

**1620**    HEADS NOOK STKS (Mdn 3-Y.O.F) £2069.20 (£571.20: £271.60)
       **6f 206y**                              4-15 (4-16)

| | | |
|---|---|---|
| 1449² | **Waseela (IRE) (63)** (Fav) *(AAScott)* 8-11 JFortune (3) (lw: trckd ldrs: led on bit over 2f out: qcknd: easily) | —1 |

1315 Alyafill (USA) *(BHanbury)* 8-11 BRaymond (2) (lw: w ldr: led over 3f out tl over 2f
out: kpt on: no ch w wnr) ............................................ 2¹/₂.2
1440 Blunham Express **(52)** *(TFairhurst)* 8-8 ‡³JFanning (4) (s.i.s: sn prom: effrt over
2f out: one pce) ............................................ 4.3
1040 Cledeschamps *(MWEllerby)* 8-11 SMorris (1) (led tl hdd over 3f out) ............ 1¹/₂.4

**8/11** WASEELA (IRE), **6/5** Alyafill (USA), **20/1** Blunham Express(op 12/1), **100/1** Cledeschamps. CSF £1.88,
Tote £1.80 (£1.30). Sheikh Ahmed Al Maktoum (NEWMARKET) bred by Sheikh Ahmed bin Rashid al Maktoum in
Ireland. 4 Rn                                              1m 27.5 (2.3)
                                                          SF—21/13/–/–

**1621**       WETHERAL CLAIMING STKS    £2175.00 (£600.00: £285.00)
               1³/₄m 32y                                   4-45 (4-46)

1521* **Broctune Grey (59)** (Fav) *(MrsGRReveley)* 8-8-12 KDarley (3) (lw: pushed
along ¹/₂-wy: wnt 2nd 4f out: led wl over 1f out: sn clr) ........ —1
11845 Banana Cufflinks (USA) **(37)** (v) *(MHTompkins)* 6-8-11 PRobinson (4) (lw: led:
qcknd clr 4f out: hdd wl over 1f out: sn btn) ................ 3.2
14235 Carrolls Marc (IRE) **(52)** *(PJFeilden)* 4-8-4 ‡JFanning (2) (lw: trckd ldr tl outpcd
4f out: sn rdn & btn) ...................................... 12.3
13373 Hamilton Lady (IRE) **(36)** *(DMoffatt)* 4-7-11 ‡⁷DarrenMoffatt (1) (lw: outpcd 4f
out: sn bhd) ............................................. 1¹/₂.4

**10/11** BROCTUNE GREY, **7/4** Carrolls Marc (IRE), **7/1** Banana Cufflinks (USA)(4/1—8/1), **12/1** Hamilton Lady
(IRE)(op 8/1). CSF £6.22, Tote £1.90 (£2.60). Mr D. Playforth (SALTBURN) bred by G. Reed. 4 Rn
                                                          3m 3.5 (6.5)

**1622**       BURGH BARONY RACES COMMEMORATION CUP (H'cap) (Amateurs) (0-70) £2284.80
               (£632.80: £302.40)    1¹/₂m                  5-15 (5-17)

                            (Weights raised 13 lb)
964 **Carlingford (USA) (47)** *(MPNaughton)* 6-11-8 ‡⁴MrRGreen (5) (lw: mde all: sn
wl clr: unchal) ........................................... —1
12484 Sunset Reins Free **(37)** (Fav) *(EJAlston)* 7-10-12 ‡⁴MrRWilkinson (3) (lw: hld
up: effrt 5f out: styd on: too much to do) ................... 7.2
1366 Thundering **(31)** *(AWJones)* 7-10-10 MissIDWJones (2) (hld up: effrt appr st:
nvr able to chal) ......................................... 1¹/₂.3
13314 Not Yet **(37)** *(EWeymes)* 8-10-12 ‡⁴MrJWeymes (6) (lw: led chsng group: effrt
appr st: no imp) ......................................... hd.4
362 Merchant of Venice **(49)** *(MHTompkins)* 4-11-10 ‡⁴MrMJenkins (4) (lw: sn
outpcd & bhd) ........................................... 20.5
Roucellist Bay **(35)** *(VThompson)* 4-11-0 MrSLyons (1) (sn outpcd & wl bhd) . 20.6

**5/2** Sunset Reins Free, **11/4** Not Yet, **3/1** Thundering, **9/2** CARLINGFORD (USA), **7/1** Merchant of
Venice(5/1—8/1), **50/1** Roucellist Bay. CSF £15.26, Tote £5.40: £2.10 £2.40 (£9.20). Mrs H. H. Wane
(RICHMOND) bred by Hugh G. King, III in USA. 6 Rn                  2m 34.9 (5.4)

T/Plpt: £38.70 (46.1 Tckts).                                      AA

# CARLISLE (R-H)
## Thursday, June 25th [Hard]
Going Allowance: 5f-7f: minus 0.40 sec; Rest: minus 0.50 sec (H)        Wind: fresh across

Stalls: high

**1623**   CUMREW (S) STKS (2-Y-O) £2343.60 (£649.60: £310.80)    **6f 206y**   2-15 (2-16)

1448 **Fanfan (IRE)** (bl) (Fav) *(MHEasterby)* 8-6 KDarley (3) (mde all: clr 3f out: comf) —1
14794 Weaver George (IRE) *(MHEasterby)* 8-11 MBirch (2) (sn chsng wnr: effrt 3f out:
nt pce to chal) ........................................... 2¹/₂.2
11785 Suitability (IRE) (v) *(PCHaslam)* 8-6 DMcKeown (6) (plld hrd: hld up: effrt 3f out:
no imp) ................................................. 8.3
1448 Knayton Lodger (bl) *(MWEasterby)* 8-6 TLucas (7) (chsd ldrs: effrt 3f out: rdn &
no imp) ................................................. ¹/₂.4
1526 Sunshine in Ramsey *(TFairhurst)* 8-3 ‡JFanning (4) (lw: bhd: sme hdwy u.p
over 2f out: n.d) ......................................... 3¹/₂.5
1526 Jarabosky *(MWEllerby)* 8-11 SMorris (5) (cl up tl ducked lft & lost pl after 2f: sn
bhd) ................................................... 4.6
*1375* Raggerty (IRE) *(JBerry)* 8-11 JCarroll (1) (lw: s.i.s: hdwy ¹/₂-wy: sn rdn & btn) . 10.7

**7/4** FANFAN (IRE)(5/2—13/8), **5/2** Suitability (IRE), **7/2** Weaver George (IRE), **10/1** Knayton Lodger, **12/1**
Raggerty (IRE)(op 8/1), **16/1** Sunshine in Ramsey(op 10/1), **33/1** Jarabosky. CSF £7.87, Tote £2.90: £1.90
£2.00 (£4.90). Mr P. D. Savill (MALTON) bred by Peter Savill in Ireland. 7 Rn; No bid          1m 28.1 (2.9)
                                                          SF—6/3/–/–/–/–

**1624**    BBC RADIO CUMBRIA CLAIMING STKS (F & M) £2343.60 (£649.60: £310.80)
6f 206y
2-45 (2-48)

1154 **Laurel Queen (IRE) (58)** *(JBerry)* 4–9-0 JCarroll (1) (lw: cl up: led over 2f out: rdn ins fnl f: r.o) ............................................................................ —1
1562* Spanish Performer **(50)** *(TFairhurst)* 3–7-9 ‡3JFanning (2) (lw: s.i.s: hdwy 2f out: r.o wl nr fin) ............................................................................ hd.2
1130 Ravecino **(41)** *(JSHaldane)* 3–7-6(1) ‡5NKennedy (6) (lw: led tl hdd over 2f out: one pce) ............................................................................ 8.3
1363³ Greetland Folly **(83)** (v) *(Fav) (RMWhitaker)* 3–8-8 ACulhane (4) (lw: hmpd after s: sn chsng ldrs: c wd & effrt ent st: sn rdn & btn) ............... 1.4
1115⁴ Ty High (IRE) **(77)** *(TDBarron)* 4–8-9 AlexGreaves (8) (nvr nr to chal) .............. 6.5
1001 Will-O-Bay *(RHollinshead)* 4–8-3 KDarley (3) (chsd ldr tl rdn & wknd over 2f out) nk.6
1294 Gemdoubleyou **(25)** (bl) *(FJordan)* 4–8-7 DMcKeown (5) (chsd ldrs: effrt 3f out: sn rdn & wknd) ............................................................................ 1¹⁄₂7

**4/7** Greetland Folly, **4/1** Spanish Performer, **6/1** LAUREL QUEEN (IRE), **20/1** Ty High (IRE), **33/1** Ravecino, **50/1** Gemdoubleyou, **66/1** Will-O-Bay. CSF £26.61, Tote £4.70: £1.70 £1.70 (£3.80). Laurel Queen (Limited (COCKERHAM) bred by E. Lonergan in Ireland. 7 Rn
1m 26.5 (1.3)
SF—39/19/—/5/—/–

**1625**    NORWEB 'SMART HEAT' H'CAP (3-Y.O) (0-70) £2128.00 (£588.00: £280.00)
5f
3-15 (3-17)
(Weights raised 2 lb)

1512² **Chateau Nord (49)** *(JBerry)* 8-5 JCarroll (7) (lw: hld up: swtchd & effrt over 1f out: led ins fnl f: rdn & r.o) ............................................................................ —1
1155* Invigilate **(54)** (Jt-Fav) *(MPNaughton)* 8-10 NConnorton (3) (lw: cl up: led over 1f out tl ins fnl f) ............................................................................ 1¹⁄₂2
1377² Lift Boy (USA) **(44)** *(DenysSmith)* 7-7 ‡7CTeague (8) (a chsng ldrs: styd on one pce fnl 2f) ............................................................................ 0.3
1514* Educated Pet **(72)** (Jt-Fav) *(MJohnston)* 10-0 (7x) DMcKeown (9) (lw: chsd ldrs: nt clr run 2f out: kpt on ins fnl f) ............................................... nk.4
1130 Melody Anne **(38)** *(JSHaldane)* 8-8 LCharnock (5) (b.hind: disp ld tl hdd over 1f out: grad wknd) ............................................................................ 2¹⁄₂5
949 Kalar **(44)** *(DWChapman)* 8-0 SWood (4) (disp ld tl hdd over 1f out: sn rdn & btn) ............................................................................ 1.6
1155⁴ Capital Idea (IRE) **(55)** (v) *(RonaldThompson)* 8-6 ‡5NKennedy (6) (s.i.s: a outpcd & bhd) ............................................................................ 2.7
1440 Chester Belle **(38)** (v) *(PCHaslam)* 7-5 ‡3JFanning (2) (cl up over 3f) ............... s.h.8
1293⁵ Virginia Cottage **(46)** *(BAMcMahon)* 8-2 JFortune (1) (sn outpcd & wl bhd) ....... 8.9

**100/30** Invigilate, Educated Pet, **9/2** Capital Idea (IRE), **6/1** CHATEAU NORD, Lift Boy (USA), **20/1** Chester Belle, Virginia Cottage, **33/1** Kalar, **50/1** Melody Anne. CSF £22.78, CT £95.02. Tote £5.30: £1.40 £1.40 £1.90 (£6.00). The Melville Stewart Partnership (COCKERHAM) bred by Hillfields Stud. 9 Rn
60.4 sec (0.2)
SF—47/46/17/51/7/9

**1626**    UCB FILMS CUMBERLAND PLATE (H'cap) (3-Y.O) (0-85) £3318.75 (£990.00: £472.50: £213.75)   1¹⁄₂m
3-45 (3-47)

1220⁴ **Mujid (IRE) (61)** *(Fav) (HThomsonJones)* 8-7 RHills (3) (lw: a.p: effrt 4f out: styd on u.p to ld ins fnl f) ............................................................................ —1
1438² Stingray City (USA) **(55)** (v) *(JEtherington)* 8-1 KDarley (5) (led 2f: led 5f out: qcknd clr: hdd & no ex ins fnl f) ............................................... 2.2
1420² Viva Darling **(69)** *(BAMcMahon)* 9-1 JFortune (4) (effrt 4f out: sn rdn & styd on: nvr able to chal) ............................................................................ 5.3
1335⁵ Eid (USA) **(75)** *(DMorley)* 9-7 MBirch (2) (lw: hld up: effrt over 3f out: sn rdn & no imp) ............................................................................ 2¹⁄₂4
1438* Reach for Glory **(62)** *(RMWhitaker)* 8-8 (5x) ACulhane (6) (lw: outpcd 5f out: rdn & no imp after) ............................................................................ 5.5
1276 Amber Glow (IRE) **(47)** *(LJCodd)* 7-7 JLowe (1) (led after 2f to 5f out: wknd over 3f out) ............................................................................ 8.6
LONG HANDICAP: Amber Glow (IRE) 7-0.

**11/8** MUJID (IRE), **7/2** Viva Darling, **4/1** Stingray City (USA), **11/2** Reach for Glory, **9/1** Eid (USA), **66/1** Amber Glow (IRE). CSF £6.84, Tote £2.00: £1.50 £2.10 (£3.10). Mr Hamdan Al-Maktoum (NEWMARKET) bred by Shadwell Estate Company Limited in Ireland. 6 Rn
2m 31.9 (2.4)
SF—9/—/3/4/—/–

**1627**    RAYOPHANE H'CAP (3-Y.O) (0-70) £2422.00 (£672.00: £322.00)
7f 214y
4-15 (4-18)
(Weights raised 6 lb)

1155 **Great Lord (IRE) (59)** *(JWWatts)* 9-7 PRobinson (6) (lw: trckd ldrs: qcknd to ld ins fnl f: r.o wl) ............................................................................ —1

| | | |
|---|---|---|
| 366 | Phil-Man **(46)** *(TFairhurst)* 8-5 ‡³JFanning (12) (cl up: led over 1f out tl ins fnl f: r.o) | 2¹/₂.**2** |
| 1320² | Grubby **(45)** *(RHollinshead)* 8-0 ‡⁷AGarth (10) (led: edgd lft over 2f out: hdd over 1f out: one pce) | 1¹/₂.**3** |
| 1185 | Barmbrack **(44)** *(RMWhitaker)* 8-6 ACulhane (11) (lw: mid div: styd on fnl 3f: nvr able to chal) | nk.**4** |
| 1320 | Specialist Dream (IRE) **(47)** *(LJCodd)* 8-9 JLowe (5) (a cl up: one pce fnl 2f) | nk.**5** |
| 34⁵ | Bold Melody **(48)** *(PCHaslam)* 8-10 DMcKeown (8) (swtchd & effrt over 2f out: styd on: nvr nrr) | ¹/₂.**6** |
| 1277³ | Ripsnorter (IRE) **(58)** (Fav) *(SirMarkPrescott)* 9-6 GDuffield (7) (lw: s.i.s: drvn along & bhd: hdwy 2f out: nrst fin) | 1¹/₂.**7** |
| 1312 | Whitrigg Lad **(52)** *(WWHaigh)* 9-0 SWebster (1) (bhd: effrt ent st: n.d) | 1¹/₂.**8** |
| 745 | Doughman **(49)** (v) *(JEtherington)* 8-11 NConnorton (4) (lw: nvr bttr than mid div) | ¹/₂.**9** |
| 1417 | Coat of Dreams **(54)** *(RBastiman)* 9-2 KFallon (3) (prom: rdn 3f out: hmpd & sn lost pl) | 1¹/₂.**10** |
| 1440 | Kick on Majestic (IRE) **(43)** *(NBycroft)* 8-5 SWood (9) (bhd: effrt & swtchd 3f out: n.d) | 2.**11** |
| 1486 | Vital Voltage (IRE) **(40)** (bl) *(MWEllerby)* 8-2 SMorris (2) (lw: hdwy on outside appr st: sn rdn & btn) | 1¹/₂.**12** |

**13/8** Ripsnorter (IRE), **7/1** GREAT LORD (IRE), Grubby(op 4/1), **10/1** Coat of Dreams, **11/1** Kick on Majestic (IRE), **12/1** Vital Voltage (IRE), **14/1** Phil-Man, **16/1** Bold Melody, **20/1** Doughman, **25/1** Specialist Dream (IRE), Barmbrack, **33/1** Whitrigg Lad. CSF £86.57, CT £641.86. Tote £6.40: £2.10 £5.00 £2.40 (£118.50). Sheikh Mohammed (RICHMOND) bred by Farmleigh Partners in Ireland. 12 Rn     1m 39.5 (0.8)
                                                   SF—35/11/1/6/8/7

---

**1628**    CARLISLE RACE CLUB MEDIAN AUCTION STKS (3-Y.O) £2346.40 (£565.60)
         **7f 214y**                                       4-45 (4-46)

| | | |
|---|---|---|
| 1334* | **Wellington Rock** (USA) (Fav) *(JARToller)* 9-4 PRobinson (2) (lw: mde all: v.easily) | —**1** |
| 1272³ | Tellgas *(WStorey)* 8-11 SWebster (1) (a chsng wnr: reminders ¹/₂-wy: no imp) | 8.**2** |

**1/12** WELLINGTON ROCK (USA)(op 1/8), **8/1** Tellgas(op 4/1). Tote £1.10. Duke of Devonshire (NEWMARKET) bred by Runnymede Farm Incorporated in USA. 2 Rn     1m 43.3 (4.6)

---

**1629**    LEVY BOARD H'CAP (0-70) £2427.00 (£672.00: £321.00)    **6f 206y**    5-15 (5-16)
                                       (Weights raised 8 lb)

| | | |
|---|---|---|
| 1564² | **Gant Bleu** (FR) **(44)** *(RMWhitaker)* 5–9-2 ACulhane (4) (lw: hld up: nt clr run 2f out: qcknd to ld ins fnl f: r.o) | —**1** |
| 1449* | Persuasius (IRE) **(55)** (bl) *(BBeasley)* 4–9-13 (5x) LCharnock (6) (led: hrd drvn over 1f out: hdd ins fnl f: no ex) | 2¹/₂.**2** |
| 1294³ | Bobbie Bold **(38)** *(RO'Leary)* 4-8-10 MBirch (5) (lw: a chsng ldrs: effrt over 2f out: one pce) | 1¹/₂.**3** |
| 1441* | Routing **(57)** (Fav) *(MDHammond)* 4–10-1 (5x) JCarroll (2) (lw: hld up: effrt & ch over 1f out: nt run on) | 4.**4** |
| | Zinger **(46)** *(TFairhurst)* 4–9-1 ‡³JFanning (1) (prom tl outpcd appr fnl f) | 10.**5** |
| 1341 | Beija Flor **(50)** (bl) *(FJordan)* 5–9-8 DMcKeown (3) (outpcd & bhd from ¹/₂-wy) | 30.**6** |

**9/4** Routing, **5/2** Persuasius, **7/2** GANT BLEU (FR), **4/1** Bobbie Bold, **20/1** Zinger. 6 Ors. CSF £11.81, Tote £3.60: £1.30 £1.90 £1.90 (£5.90). Mr E. C. Alton (WETHERBY) bred by Souren Vanian in France. 6 Rn    1m 26.8 (1.6)
                                                 SF—36/39/17/24/–/–

T/Plpt: £20.30 (119.2 Tckts).                                     AA

---

## 1300—SALISBURY (R-H)

### Wednesday, June 24th [Firm]

Going Allowance: St: minus 0.20 sec; Rnd: minus 0.45 sec (F)        Wind: nil

Stalls: high    Flag start: 4th race

**1630**    E.B.F. SOUTHAMPTON STKS (Mdn 2-Y.O.C & G) £2807.00 (£777.00: £371.00)
         **6f 212y**                                       2-00 (2-01)

| | | |
|---|---|---|
| | **Known Approach** (USA) (Fav) *(PFICole)* 9-0 TQuinn (1) (w'like: chsd ldr: led 4f out: rdn out) | —**1** |
| | Woodhaunter (USA) *(JHMGosden)* 9-0 SCauthen (6) (gd sort: scope: s.s: rdn 3f out: hdwy 2f out: r.o one pce fnl f) | 2.**2** |
| 1297⁵ | Sharro *(PAKelleway)* 9-0 MRoberts (5) (led 3f: wknd wl over 1f out) | 6.**3** |
| | Poly Vision (IRE) *(MRChannon)* 9-0 PatEddery (2) (unf: a.p: hrd rdn over 2f out: wknd over 1f out) | s.h.**4** |

847 Rockover *(RHannon)* 9-0 SRaymont (3) (rdn 4f out: sn bhd) ............................ nk.**5**
1259 Remembrance Day (IRE) *(RHannon)* 9-0 JReid (4) (lw: prom 4f) ......................... 6.**6**

**8/11** KNOWN APPROACH (USA), **2/1** Woodhaunter (USA), **15/2** Sharro, **14/1** Poly Vision (IRE)(op 8/1), **16/1** Ors. CSF £2.91, Tote £2.00: £1.20 £1.70 (£2.50). Mr Christopher Heath (WHATCOMBE) bred by Anthony Warrender in USA. 6 Rn
1m 28.39 (2.69)
SF—38/32/14/13/12/–

## 1631

ALDERHOLT SPRINT H'CAP (0-100) £5775.00 (£1725.00: £825.00: £375.00)
6f
2-30 (2-32)

1474[3] **Kayvee (89)** (Fav) *(GHarwood)* 3-9-1 MRoberts (10) (lw: mde virtually all: clr 2f out: comf) ......................................................... —**1**
1393★ Dominuet **(84)** *(JLSpearing)* 7-9-4 GHind (4) (hdwy 2f out: chsd wnr over 1f out: no imp) ............................................. 4.**2**
1107 Masnun (USA) **(87)** *(RJO'Sullivan)* 7-9-4 ‡3DBiggs (9) (a.p: rdn over 3f out: r.o one pce fnl f) ...................................... 1½.**3**
1445 Clifton Charlie (USA) **(92)** *(MRChannon)* 4-9-12 TQuinn (5) (swtg: a.p: rdn 4f out: one pce fnl 2f) ................................. ½.**4**
1314[2] Regal Racer **(86)** *(DRCElsworth)* 3-8-12 SCauthen (11) (swtg: prom 4f) ......... 3½.**5**
1406[3] Baligay **(78)** *(RJHodges)* 7-8-12 PatEddery (6) (lw: no hdwy fnl 2f) .................. 2.**6**
1212 Duplicity (IRE) **(93)** *(LJHolt)* 4-9-13 JReid (3) (nvr nrr) ................................... 3.**7**
Paley Prince (USA) **(94)** *(MDIUsher)* 6-10-0 MWigham (2) (sn bhd) .................. 5.**8**
559 Isdar (USA) **(86)** *(HThomsonJones)* 3-8-12 RHills (8) (lw: sn rdn along: a bhd) 2½.**9**
1393 Seneca Reef (IRE) **(84)** *(IABalding)* 4-9-4 RCochrane (7) (spd over 3f) .............. ½.**10**

**Evens** KAYVEE(op 7/4), **6/1** Regal Racer, **7/1** Baligay, Masnun (USA), **10/1** Isdar (USA), **11/1** Dominuet, Duplicity (IRE), **12/1** Seneca Reef (IRE), **25/1** Paley Prince (USA), **33/1** Clifton Charlie (USA). CSF £14.24, CT £58.30. Tote £2.40: £1.20 £2.30 £2.80 (£8.10). Mr J. H. Richmond-Watson (PULBOROUGH) bred by Normanhy Stud Ltd. 10 Rn
1m 12.66 (0.36)
SF—70/57/51/37/29/21

## 1632

GIBBS MEW BIBURY CUP (H'cap) (3-Y.O) (0-90) £4425.00 (£1320.00: £630.00: £285.00)   1½m
(Weights raised 3 lb)
3-00 (3-01)

1158★ **Lyphantastic (USA) (79)** (Fav) *(MRStoute)* 9-3 MRoberts (5) (lw: mde virtually all: rdn over 3f out: r.o wl) ............................................. —**1**
1371[3] Severine (USA) **(61)** *(JLDunlop)* 7-13 WCarson (6) (hld up: lost pl 7f out: rallied 3f out: r.o ins fnl f) ......................................... 3½.**2**
1308[4] Pyare Square **(73)** (bl) *(IABalding)* 8-11 JReid (3) (lw: hld up: rdn & hdwy 3f out: ev ch over 1f out: one pce) ................................ s.h.**3**
1374★ Themeda **(72)** *(CRNelson)* 8-10 SCauthen (7) (bhd tl styd on fnl 2f: n.d) ......... 1½.**4**
1220 Sastago (USA) **(83)** *(JHMGosden)* 9-7 PatEddery (1) (prom: rdn over 3f out: wknd over 1f out) .................................................. 6.**5**
Delta Foxtrot (USA) **(69)** *(DWPArbuthnot)* 8-7 TQuinn (4) (h.d.w: bit bkwd: prom: rdn over 4f out: wknd 3f out) ................................... 6.**6**
1446 Erlemo **(55)** (bl) *(CJBenstead)* 7-7 TyroneWilliams (2) (lw: rdn 4f out: sn bhd) . hd.**7**
LONG HANDICAP: Erlemo 7-2.

**11/4** LYPHANTASTIC (USA)(op 11/8), **3/1** Sastago (USA)(tchd 5/1), Severine (USA), Delta Foxtrot (USA)(tchd 5/1), **6/1** Pyare Square, Themeda(op 4/1), **25/1** Erlemo. CSF £11.19, Tote £3.20: £1.80 £1.70 (£3.70). Miss Sandra H. Payson (NEWMARKET) bred by Sandra Payson in USA. 7 Rn
2m 32.52 (U.08)
SF—50/25/36/32/31/7

## 1633

HAMPSHIRE STKS   £3427.50 (£1020.00: £485.00: £217.50)   1¾m   3-30 (3-33)

1176★ **Rain Rider** (Fav) *(JLDunlop)* 3-8-8 WCarson (3) (lw: hld up: led 2f out: r.o wl) .. —**1**
687★ Glaisdale (IRE) **(86)** *(HRACecil)* 3-8-8 SCauthen (4) (lw: led 3f: led over 2f out: sn hdd: r.o) ........................................... ¾.**2**
1302★ Not in Doubt (USA) **(90)** *(HCandy)* 3-8-8 SRutter (1) (lw: hld up & bhd: rdn & hdwy 3f out: nt qckn fnl f) ................................. 1.**3**
Almanot *(RCurtis)* 5-9-1 WNewnes (2) (lengthy: unf: lw: plld hrd: led after 3f tl over 2f out: sn btn & eased) ................................. 20.**4**

**6/4** RAIN RIDER, **7/4** Not in Doubt (USA), **2/1** Glaisdale (IRE)(6/4—9/4), **50/1** Almanot. CSF £4.70, Tote £2.30 (£2.10). Mrs E. M. H. Ogden White (ARUNDEL) bred by Ash Hill Stud. 4 Rn   3m 11.5 (hand) (13.3)

## 1634

HERBERT AND GWEN BLAGRAVE MEMORIAL H'CAP (3-Y.O) (0-100) £4142.50 (£1240.00: £595.00: £272.50)   1m 1f 209y   4-00 (4-03)

1382★ **Baluga (81)** (Fav) *(GHarwood)* 8-12 MRoberts (1) (lw: mde all: rdn over 2f out: r.o wl) ........................................................ —**1**
1319[2] Fieldridge **(90)** *(CRNelson)* 9-7 JReid (7) (hld up: rdn over 3f out: plld out over 2f out: ev ch over 1f out: r.o nr fin) .................... ½.**2**

1382 Walking on Water **(77)** (bl) *(RFJohnsonHoughton)* 8-8 RCochrane (6) (hdwy on ins & n.m.r 4f out: r.o one pce fnl 2f) .............................. 3.3

1399[6] Good Reference (IRE) **(89)** *(MBell)* 9-6 MHills (4) (b: chsd wnr: ev ch 2f out: one pce) .......................................................................... 1.4

1444[2] Shrewd Partner (IRE) **(80)** *(DRCElsworth)* 8-11 SCauthen (5) (no hdwy fnl 3f) .. ¾.5

1207[5] Rebel Call **(84)** *(RHannon)* 9-1 PatEddery (2) (plld hrd: bhd fnl 3f) ................. 3½.6

671 Sword Master **(81)** *(BobJones)* 8-12 WCarson (3) (prom 7f) ....................... 2½.7

**5/2** BALUGA, **11/4** Fieldridge, **4/1** Shrewd Partner (IRE), **13/2** Rebel Call, **7/1** Good Reference (IRE)(op 4/1), **9/1** Sword Master(12/1—8/1), **11/1** Walking on Water(8/1—12/1). CSF £9.92, Tote £2.90: £2.00 £1.80 (£4.10). Mr J. C. Thompson (PULBOROUGH) bred by K. J. and Mrs Buchanan. 7 Rn 2m 7.19 (2.49)
SF—28/36/17/27/16/13

**1635** E.B.F. WEYHILL STKS (Mdn 2-Y.O-F) £2611.20 (£723.20: £345.60) **5f** 4-30 (4-35)

1300[5] **Chatterberry** (Jt-Fav) *(LJHolt)* 8-11 JReid (3) (lw: mde all: clr over 1f out: comf) —1

Sophisticated Air *(IABalding)* 8-11 RCochrane (8) (unf: scope: hdwy 2f out: chsd wnr over 1f out: r.o) ......................................................... 2½.2

Catherineofaragon *(WGRWightman)* 8-11 JWilliams (6) (wl grwn: s.s: gd hdwy fnl f: r.o) ............................................................................ 2.3

1164[4] Brockton Dancer (Jt-Fav) *(RHannon)* 8-11 PatEddery (5) (lw: rdn over 2f out: hdwy over 1f out: eased whn btn wl ins fnl f) ...................... 1½.4

Villavina *(SDow)* 8-11 MRoberts (2) (unf: dwlt: sn rcvrd: no hdwy fnl 2f) ......... 1½.5

Patong Beach *(JWHills)* 8-11 MHills (9) (str: no hdwy fnl 2f) ............................ hd.6

Hariti (IRE) *(DRCElsworth)* 8-11 SCauthen (7) (scope: s.s: nvr nrr) ............... 2.7

Champagne Grandy *(MRChannon)* 8-11 RHills (10) (leggy: unf: prom 3f) ........ ¾.8

791 De Chine *(JSMoore)* 8-8 ‡3DBiggs (1) (prom over 2f) ............................ nk.9

807 Kind of Cute *(CCElsey)* 8-11 TRogers (4) (lw: prom over 2f) ..................... s.h.10
*Yours by Right (33/1) Withdrawn (ref to ent stalls) : not under orders*

**2/1** CHATTERBERRY, Brockton Dancer, **5/1** Hariti (IRE)(4/1—6/1), **13/2** Sophisticated Air, **10/1** Champagne Grandy, Patong Beach, **12/1** Villavina(8/1—14/1), **33/1** Ors. CSF £16.87, Tote £3.40: £1.50 £2.00 £3.50 (£7.30). Mr David Hicks (BASINGSTOKE) bred by D. A. and Mrs Hicks. 10 Rn 61.83 sec (1.83)
SF—40/30/22/16/10/9

**1636** DOWNTON H'CAP (3-Y.O) (0-80) £3314.00 (£992.00: £476.00: £218.00) **6f 212y** 5-00 (5-01)

1304[4] **Southwold Air (66)** *(JLDunlop)* 8-7 WCarson (7) (lw: a.p: hrd rdn to ld last strides) ......................................................................................... —1

1062 Super Serenade **(72)** (Fav) *(GBBalding)* 8-13 JWilliams (1) (swtg: led over 4f out: rdn clr 2f out: ct last strides) ......................................................... hd.2

Call the Bureau **(75)** *(MJHeaton-Ellis)* 9-2 JReid (3) (b: a.p: hrd rdn & one pce fnl 2f) ................................................................................................ 3½.3

938 Mariette Larkin **(66)** *(GBBalding)* 8-4 ‡3SO'Gorman (8) (hld up & plld hrd: hdwy on ins 2f out: nt rch ldrs) ................................................................... ¾.4

898[4] Sovereign Rock (IRE) **(73)** *(RHannon)* 9-0 MRoberts (4) (bhd: rdn 4f out: nvr nr to chal) ....................................................................................... 1½.5

1319 Triple Trouble **(53)** *(HJCollingridge)* 7-8[1] JQuinn (2) (dwlt: rdn & hdwy 3f out: wknd wl over 1f out) ..................................................................... hd.6

1400 Parisien Singer **(70)** *(IABalding)* 9-7 RCochrane (5) (dr.nr hind: lw: a bhd) ...... 7.7

1379 Gemini Bay **(70)** (bl) *(RVoorspuy)* 8-11 SDawson (6) (led over 2f: sn hrd rdn: wknd over 2f out) ............................................................................ 2.8
LONG HANDICAP: Triple Trouble 7-3.

**5/2** Super Serenade, **11/4** Sovereign Rock (IRE), **7/2** SOUTHWOLD AIR, **6/1** Parisien Singer, **8/1** Mariette Larkin, **10/1** Call the Bureau, **12/1** Gemini Bay, **33/1** Triple Trouble. CSF £13.00, CT £74.74. Tote £3.80: £1.80 £1.20 £1.80 (£5.10). Lady Cohen (ARUNDEL) bred by M. E. Wates. 8 Rn 1m 27.91 (2.21)
SF—39/44/33/18/23/2

T/Plpt: £47.10 (68.7 Tckts). KH

# SALISBURY (R-H)
## Thursday, June 25th [Firm]
Going Allowance: St: minus 0.20 sec; Rnd: 0.45 sec per fur (F) Wind: nil

Stalls: high

**1637** NOEL CANNON MEMORIAL TROPHY (H'cap) (0-90) £4386.00 (£1308.00: £624.00: £282.00) **1m** 2-00 (2-01)
(Weights raised 6 lb)

1504[4] **Mahsul (IRE) (55)** *(CJBenstead)* 4-8-1 WCarson (6) (hld up: hdwy to ld over 2f out: qcknd clr: eased wl ins fnl f) ............................................... —1

1304* Tissisat (USA) **(82)** *(Fav) (IABalding)* 3-9-4 JReid (5) (lw: hld up: rdn over 2f out:
　　　　r.o ins fnl f) ................................................................ 1½.**2**
936⁶ Aitch N'Bee **(74)** *(LadyHerries)* 9-9-6 LDettori (4) (rdn & hdwy over 1f out: r.o) s.h.**3**
1388³ Akkazao (IRE) **(78)** *(WCarter)* 4-9-5 ‡⁵NGwilliams (3) (led over 5f: one pce) ...... ¾.**4**
1284　Quietly Impressive (IRE) **(53)** (bl) *(MBell)* 4-7-13 JQuinn (7) (lw: no hdwy fnl 2f)　4.**5**
1344⁴ Camden's Ransom (USA) **(69)** *(DRCElsworth)* 5-9-1 JWilliams (8) (swtg: prom
　　　　over 6f) ................................................................ 2½.**6**
　　　Co-Chin (IRE) **(84)** *(GLewis)* 3-9-6 PaulEddery (2) (hdwy over 3f out: wknd 2f
　　　　out) ................................................................ 6.**7**
　　　Northern Trial (USA) **(72)** *(CRNelson)* 4-9-1 ‡3FNorton (1) (prom 5f) ............... nk.**8**

**5/4** Tissisat (USA), **9/2** Camden's Ransom (USA), Akkazao (IRE)(op 3/1), **6/1** MAHSUL (IRE), **10/1** Aitch
N'Bee(op 5/1), **14/1** Quietly Impressive (IRE), **16/1** Northern Trial (USA)(op 10/1), **33/1** Co-Chin (IRE). CSF
£13.98, CT £69.91. Tote £6.60: £1.50 £1.20 £2.80 (£5.40). Mr Hamdan Al-Maktoum (EPSOM) bred by
Derrinstown Stud Ltd in Ireland. 8 Rn　　　　　　　　　　　　　　　　1m 41.46 (2.16)
　　　　　　　　　　　　　　　　　　　　　　　　　SF—31/43/44/41/9/17

**1638**　TATTERSALLS AUCTION SERIES STKS (Qualifier) (Mdn 2-Y.O) £2807.00 (£777.00:
　　　　£371.00)　**5f**　　　　　　　　　　　　　　　　　　　　2-30 (2-34)

928　**Caps Ninety-Two (IRE) (82)** *(DrJDScargill)* 8-3 JQuinn (1) (hdwy 2f out: hrd rdn to
　　　　ld wl ins fnl f: r.o) ................................................................ —**1**
807　Kensworth Lady *(MBlanshard)* 8-2 CRutter (4) (w ldrs: led over 2f out: edgd lft
　　　　over 1f out: hrd rdn & hdd wl ins fnl f) ................................... nk.**2**
　　　Spicy Affair *(DrJDScargill)* 8-4 DHolland (2) (w'like: bit bkwd: hdwy 2f out: one
　　　　pce fnl f) ................................................................ 4.**3**
791³ Heber Spring (IRE) *(Fav) (RHannon)* 8-8 MRoberts (6) (led over 2f: one pce)　1½.**4**
　　　Cherubini *(JRFanshawe)* 8-8 LDettori (7) (leggy: s.i.s: nvr nrr) .................. ¾.**5**
　　　Steppin High *(LordHuntingdon)* 8-11 AMunro (3) (w'like: bit bkwd: nvr nr to
　　　　chal) ................................................................ s h **6**
　　　After the Last *(RHannon)* 8-3 ‡3RPerham (5) (neat: bit bkwd: nrst fin) ......... nk.**7**
971⁴ Gaynor Goodman (IRE) *(JSMoore)* 8-1(1) PaulEddery (5) (prom: rdn over 2f
　　　　out: wknd wl over 1f out) ................................................ 3.**8**
　　　Grand Baie *(SDow)* 8-5 TQuinn (8) (w'like: w ldrs 3f) ................. 1½.**9**

**6/4** Heber Spring (IRE)(tchd 5/2), **9/4** Steppin High, **7/2** Cherubini, **8/1** Kensworth Lady(5/1—10/1), **14/1**
Gaynor Goodman (IRE)(op 7/1), **20/1** Spicy Affair(6/1—16/1), **33/1** CAPS NINETY-TWO
(IRE) & Ors. CSF £259.39, Tote £36.50: £5.10 £1.50 £4.70 (£192.80). Mr A. C. Edwards (NEWMARKET) bred
by Irish National Stud Co Ltd in Ireland. 9 Rn　　　　　　　　　　　　　61.70 sec (1.70)
　　　　　　　　　　　　　　　　　　　　　　　　　SF—35/33/19/15/14/16

**1639**　VEUVE CLICQUOT CHAMPAGNE STKS (2-Y.O) £11960.00 (£3360.00: £1640.00)
　　　　**6f**　　　　　　　　　　　　　　　　　　　　　　　　3-00 (3-01)

1348* **Perfect Halo (USA)** *(Fav) (PFICole)* 9-7 AMunro (1) (lw: mde virtually all: hrd
　　　　rdn over 1f out: r.o wl) ................................................ —**1**
1291* Little Too Much (IRE) *(GHarwood)* 9-3 MRoberts (4) (lw: chsd wnr over 3f out:
　　　　ev ch whn rdn & edgd lft ins fnl f: nt qckn) ......................... 1.**2**
1370* Port Lucaya *(RHannon)* 9-3 WCarson (5) (lw: chsd wnr over 2f: wknd over 2f
　　　　out) ................................................................ 6.**3**

**8/11** PERFECT HALO (USA), **7/4** Little Too Much (IRE), **5/1** Port Lucaya. CSF £2.28, Tote £1.70 (£1.50). Mr Fahd
Salman (WHATCOMBE) bred by Echo Valley Horse Farm Inc in USA. 3 Rn　　　1m 14.21 (1.91)
　　　　　　　　　　　　　　　　　　　　　　　　　SF—45/37/13

**1640**　CARNARVON CHALLENGE CUP (H'cap) (Amateurs) (0-70) £3444.00 (£1032.00:
　　　　£496.00: £228.00)　**1½m**　　　　　　　　　　　　　　3-30 (3-32)

1044⁶ **Marchman (48)** *(JSKing)* 7-11-0 MrsLPearce (1) (led over 4f out: r.o wl) —**1**
1481* Cathos (FR) **(57)** *(Fav) (DAWilson)* 7-11-9 (5x) MissJAllison (17) (b.hind: swtg:
　　　　hld up & plld hrd: stdy hdwy 4f out: ev ch 2f out: one pce) . 7.**2**
　　　Back to Form **(31)** *(WGMTurner)* 7-9-6(1) ‡⁵MrsCPrice (7) (plld hrd: lost pl 5f
　　　　out: styd on fnl 2f) ................................................ 4.**3**
1065⁵ Run High **(55)** *(PMitchell)* 7-9-6 MrRTeal (13) (b.hind: swtg: bhd tl hdwy 3f
　　　　out: one pce fnl f) ................................................ ¾.**4**
1317³ Arrastra **(62)** *(IABalding)* 4-12-0 MissCBalding (14) (hdwy 5f out: ev ch 2f out:
　　　　sn wknd) ................................................................ 5.**5**
　　　Flying Ziad (CAN) **(34)** *(RCurtis)* 9-9-9(1) ‡⁵MrGBrown (11) (lw: prom tl wknd
　　　　over 2f out) ................................................................ 1½.**6**
761　Thimbalina **(40)** *(DAWilson)* 6-10-6 MissLHide (12) (swtg: prom tl wknd over 2f
　　　　out) ................................................................ 1½.**7**
1239³ Quiet Riot **(42)** *(JWhite)* 10-10-3 ‡⁵MrMMannish (3) (lw: nvr nrr) .................. ½.**8**
　　　Algaihabane (USA) **(37)** (bl) *(PJHobbs)* 6-10-3 MrsSHobbs (5) (led over 7f) .. 3½.**9**
1143⁶ Talaton Flyer **(27)** *(PJHobbs)* 6-9-2 ‡MrGLewis (15) (b: prom 6f) ................. 5.**10**

Spirit Sam **(27)** *(PJFeilden)* 7-9-2 ‡⁵MrSRees (18) (swtg: prom: rn wd bnd 6f
out: wknd 3f out) ......................................................... d.h.10
1248 First Exhibition **(27)** *(MrsAKnight)* 5-9-7 MrDSalter (10) (b.off fore: b.nr hind: a
bhd) ............................................................ nk.12
Coxann **(35)** *(JCMcConnochie)* 6-9-10 ‡⁵MrETolhurst (6) (lw: a bhd) .............. 2.13
1318 Himlaj (USA) **(49)** *(SMellor)* 7-11-1 MrsEMellor (19) (a bhd) .................... 1.14
Nice Picture (IRE) **(43)** *(RChampion)* 4-10-9 MrGJohnsonHoughton (2)
(b.hind: bhd fnl 4f) ................................................ hd.15
1407 Bravo Star (USA) **(44)** *(PLeach)* 7-10-5⁽¹⁷⁾ ‡⁵MissAStaddon (4) (a bhd) ........... 2.16
1317 Gibbot **(45)** *(PHowling)* 7-10-6⁽¹²⁾ ‡⁵MrSWhiting (8) (s.s: a bhd) .............. 1½.17
1163 Singing Detective **(27)** *(RCurtis)* 5-9-2 ‡⁵MissEMills (16) (bhd fnl 6f) .......... 2.18
1160 Yeoman Bound **(33)** *(KTIvory)* 4-9-13⁽⁶⁾ MrDMarshall (9) (b.hind: a bhd) ....... ¾.19
LONG HANDICAP: Talaton Flyer 9-6, Spirit Sam 9-4, First Exhibition 9-5, Singing Detective 9-5,
Yeoman Bound 9-2.

**5/2** Cathos (FR), **5/1** MARCHMAN(4/1—6/1), Arrastra, **11/2** Run High, **7/1** Talaton Flyer(10/1—6/1), **15/2**
Thimbalina, **16/1** Algaihabane (USA), Himlaj (USA), Flying Ziad (CAN), **20/1** Quiet Riot, Coxann, **33/1** Bravo Star
(USA), Back to Form, Nice Picture (IRE), Singing Detective, First Exhibition, Spirit Sam, **50/1** Ors. CSF £20.13, CT
£395.57. Tote £6.80: £1.90 £1.60 £7.30 £1.90 (£10.10). Mrs P. M. King (SWINDON) bred by Lord Edwin
McAlpine. 19 Rn                                                      2m 35.61 (3.01)
SF—44/39/–/27/24/–

---

**1641**   TISBURY MEDIAN AUCTION GRADUATION STKS (3-Y-O) £3132.00 (£936.00: £448.00:
£204.00)   **6f 212y**                                             4-00 (4-02)

1209² Lady Debra Darley *(RHannon)* 8-6 MRoberts (6) (rdn 4f out: led ins fnl f: r.o wl) —1
385⁶ Rose Indien (FR) **(101)** (Fav) *(MMoubarak)* 9-1 LDettori (3) (lw: led: hrd rdn
over 1f out: hdd & nt qckn ins fnl f) ................................. 2½.2
1209⁶ Flying Wind *(JSutcliffe)* 8-6 BRouse (7) (lw: nvr nrr) .................... 6.3
High Baccarat **(54)** *(CCElsey)* 8-11 TQuinn (1) (w ldr over 3f) ................ s.h.4
862⁶ Simple Sound (IRE) **(49)** *(MAJarvis)* 9-2 GCrealock (4) (rdn over 3f out: sn bhd) .... 4.5
1304 Spinayab **(66)** 9-1 Withdrawn (broke out of stalls) : not under orders

**4/5** Rose Indien (FR), **11/8** LADY DEBRA DARLEY, **12/1** Simple Sound (IRE)(op 8/1), **33/1** Flying Wind, **50/1**
High Baccarat. CSF £2.72, Tote £2.30: £1.30 £1.20 (£1.50). Mrs M. R. T. Rimell (MARLBOROUGH) bred by R.
P. Williams. 5 Rn                                                   1m 26.56 (0.86)
SF—58/59/32/36/29

---

**1642**   MARTIN CLAIMING H'CAP (3-Y-O) (0-70) £3101.00 (£861.00: £413.00)
**1m**                                                             4-30 (4-32)
(Weights raised 3 lb)

1308⁵ Roly Wallace **(61)** (bl) *(KTIvory)* 9-1 GBardwell (16) (b.hind: plld out 2f out: str
run fnl f: led cl home) .................................................. —1
1411⁴ Mastamist **(42)** (bl) *(RVoorspuy)* 7-10 NAdams (9) (gd hdwy over 1f out: ev ch
ins fnl f: r.o) ....................................................... nk.2
787 Spanish Glory **(52)** (bl) *(IABalding)* 8-6 AMunro (17) (a.p: led over 1f out: hdd nr
fin) ............................................................... s.h.3
1426⁶ Kingchip Boy **(44)** *(MJRyan)* 7-9 ‡³DBiggs (12) (hdwy wl over 1f out: r.o ins fnl f) 2.4
1040 Red Ink **(54)** *(JSutcliffe)* 8-8 MRoberts (8) (led over 3f: nt qckn fnl 2f) ............. nk.5
408 Rockbourne **(55)** *(DRCEllsworth)* 8-9 WCarson (1) (hdwy 2f out: ev ch over 1f
out: wknd fnl f) ..................................................... 3.6
1503⁴ A Nymph Too Far (IRE) **(50)** *(DrJDScargill)* 8-4 DHolland (13) (nrst fin) .......... ½.7
1248⁶ Abeloni **(57)** *(AAScott)* 8-11 BRaymond (7) (swtg: w ldrs: ev ch 2f out: sn wknd) s.h.8
969³ Super Beauty **(58)** *(GBBalding)* 8-12 JWilliams (14) (nvr nrr) .................. 2.9
1257 Laughing Falcon **(52)** (bl) *(JLDunlop)* 8-6 LDettori (5) (prom 6f) ............... 2.10
1105⁶ Tadora (IRE) **(53)** *(CJBenstead)* 8-7 TyroneWilliams (11) (hdwy over 2f out:
wknd over 1f out) ................................................... hd.11
1486* Akura (IRE) **(50)** (Fav) *(MJohnston)* 8-4 RPElliott (4) (led over 4f out tl wknd
over 1f out) ........................................................ 1½.12
1408 Bella Run **(42)** *(RJHodges)* 7-7⁽³⁾ ‡³FNorton (10) (a bhd) .................... 2.13
801 Sea Crusader **(53)** *(MBlanshard)* 8-7 JReid (3) (prom over 5f) .............. ¾.14
1145⁶ Fine as Fivepence **(42)** *(MrsAKnight)* 7-5⁽³⁾ ‡⁵DHarrison (6) (prom 5f) .......... 1.15
1277 Boogie Bopper (IRE) **(67)** (bl) *(MBell)* 9-7 TQuinn (2) (b.hind: reminder after s:
sn prom: wknd 2f out) ............................................... 1.16
1314⁵ My Czech Mate **(56)** *(RHannon)* 8-10 AMcGlone (15) (a bhd) ................. 1.17
LONG HANDICAP: Bella Run 7-6, Fine as Fivepence 7-6.

**15/8** Akura (IRE), **6/1** Red Ink(op 12/1), **8/1** Spanish Glory(12/1—14/1), **10/1** My Czech Mate(op 6/1), **12/1**
Mastamist(op 8/1), A Nymph Too Far (IRE), Laughing Falcon(op 6/1), Super Beauty, **14/1** Boogie Bopper (IRE),
Abeloni(op 6/1), Rockbourne, **20/1** ROLY WALLACE, **25/1** Ors. CSF £1,914.31. Ors. CSF
£243.37, CT £1,914.31. Tote £40.50: £5.60 £3.10 £3.20 £2.70 (£152.80). Mr K. T. Ivory (RADLETT) bred by
Wallace Farms (Stud) Ltd. 17 Rn                                     1m 41.66 (2.36)
SF—42/22/31/14/26/18

**1643** ALINGTON H'CAP (3-Y.O) (0-75) £3845.25 (£1152.00: £553.50: £254.25)
1m 1f 209y                                                                5-00 (5-03)

(Weights raised 1 lb)

1385* Misty View (67) (MAJarvis) 9-1 WRyan (6) (hld up & bhd: hdwy over 2f out:
                           swtchd rt 1f out: hrd rdn to ld last stride) ............................... —1
14443 Grog (IRE) (71) (MRChannon) 9-0 ‡5BDoyle (2) (led: rdn over 2f out: edgd lft 1f
                           out: hdd last stride) ............................................................... s.h.2
13414 Eleckydo (48) (RJHodges) 7-7(1) ‡3FNorton (13) (swtg: prom: rdn over 4f out:
                           ev ch over 1f out: nt qckn) ................................................... 1½.3
13854 Cool Society (USA) (67) (CRNestead) 9-1 NAdams (12) (a.p: jnd ldr 3f out: one
                           pce fnl f) ........................................................................... 2.4
1371 Deevee (50) (CJBenstead) 7-12 TyroneWilliams (8) (swtg: hdwy 5f out: hrd rdn
                           over 2f out: ev ch over 1f out: one pce) ........................ 2½.5
1252 Le Baron Perche (FR) (70) (CJames) 9-4 GBaxter (4) (swtg: a.p: eased whn btn
                           ins fnl f) ............................................................................... ¾.6
1277 Court Circular (71) (LordHuntingdon) 9-5 AMunro (3) (lw: prom over 6f) ......... ¾.7
14262 Weeheby (USA) (70) (bl) (Fav) (AAScott) 9-4 BRaymond (11) (lw: hdwy 5f out:
                           wknd 3f out) ......................................................................... 1½.8
4934 Dune River (73) (SirMarkPrescott) 9-7 MRoberts (9) (stumbled & lost pl
                           bnd 6f out: rallied over 3f out: wknd 3f out) ....................... s.n.9
1158 Royal Glint (60) (IABalding) 8-8 JReid (7) (a bhd) ................................... s.h.10
788 Arsaad (63) (PTWalwyn) 8-11 WCarson (5) (a bhd: t.o fnl 3f) ............... 15.11
       Grecian Belle (52) (DAWilson) 8-0 DHolland (1) (swtg: bhd fnl 5f: t.o fnl 3f) ... 12.12

100/30 Weeheby (USA), 7/2 MISTY VIEW, 5/1 Dune River(6/1—8/1), 15/2 Grog (IRE)(12/1—7/1), 9/1 Court
Circular(4/1—10/1), Arsaad (USA)(6/1—10/1), 10/1 Cool Society (USA), 11/1 Deevee(8/1—12/1), 14/1
Eleckydo, 20/1 Le Baron Perche (FR), Royal Glint, 25/1 Grecian Belle. CSF £30.92, CT £317.29. Tote £4.90:
£1.70 £2.10 £2.90 (£25.20). Mr K. G. Powter (NEWMARKET) bred by W. L. Caley. 12 Rn     2m 7.58 (2.88)
                                                                              SF   27/25/1/19/—/15

T/Plpt: £594.10 (6.7 Tckts).                                                                            KH

## LYON (L-H)
### Monday, June 15th [Good]

**1644a** GRAND PRIX DE LYON (listed race)   £23736.00   1m 3f

      Oumnaz (FR) (France) 3-8-4 NJeanpierre ........................................................... —1
955a3 Lights Out (FR) (France) 6—9-10 WMongil ................................................... ½.2
      Past Master (USA) (France) 4—9-10 TJarnet ..................................................... 2.3
11694 BE A HONEY (NAGraham) 4—9-0 FHead (btn further 16¾al) ...................... 9
Tote 13.70f: 2.00f 1.60f 1.80f (17.60f). Ecurie Belles Provinces (X.Betron,FRANCE) bred by R.L.Jolibois in
France. 9 Rn                                                                               2m 13

## DORTMUND (R-H)
### Sunday, June 21st [Good]

**1645a** GROSSER PREIS DER DORTMUNDER WIRTSCHAFT (Gp 3)   £26408.00   1m 1f

      Iron Fighter (GER) (Germany) 3-8-3 ARiding ..................................................... —1
551 ENHARMONIC (USA) (LordHuntingdon) 5-9-0 WRyan ..................................... 2.2
      The Tender Track (USA) (France) 5—9-0 WMongil ............................................ 1¼.3
13992 SAFA (AAScott) 4—8-7 BRaymond (btn more than further 4l) .......................... 11
Tote 71DM: 30DM 39DM 78DM (SF: 945DM). Mr V.Storckmann (H.Steinmetz,GERMANY) bred by W.Scholtes in
Germany. 14 Rn                                                                             1m 47

### 1358a—SAN SIRO (R-H)
### Sunday, June 21st [Soft]

**1646a** GRAN PREMIO DI MILANO (Gp 1)   £116279.00   1½m

1221a* MASHAALLAH (USA) (JHMGosden) 4-9-6 SCauthen ..................................... —1
1205⁶ Saganeca (USA) (France) 4-9-3 TJarnet ......................................................... ¾.2
956a3 Lara's Idea (Italy) 4-9-3 VMezzatesta ......................................................... 1½.3
1205⁵ Always Friendly (HCandy) 4-9-3 AMunro ....................................................... nk.4
1205 SNURGE (PFICole) 5-9-6 TQuinn .................................................................. nk.5
1226a4 MARCUS THORPE (USA) (PAKelleway) 4-9-6 PRobinson (btn further 4l) ........... 7
Tote 49L: 19L 37L 25L (314L). Sheikh Ahmed Al Maktoum (NEWMARKET) bred by W.S.Farish, W.T.Carter &
E.J.Hudson Jnr in USA. 10 Rn                                                                2m 31.5

## FREUDENAU (R-H) Austria
### Sunday, June 21st [Good]

**1647a**   OSTERREICHISCHES DERBY (3-Y.O.C & F) £16533.00   1½m

      **Rubico (USA)** *(Germany)* 3-9-0 OSchick ................................................ —1
      Wiofino (GER) *(Germany)* 3-9-0 HPLudewig ............................... 9.2
  1298² ADMIRALS SECRET (USA) *(CFWall)* 3-9-0 NDay ........................... 5.3
Tote (10 Sch stake) 26Sch: 22Sch 24sch 26Sch (68Sch). Stall Sternental (H.A.Blume,GERMANY) bred by
Elmendorf Farm in USA. 16 Rn                                                                  2m 36.8

---

1404—**BATH (L-H)**
### Friday, June 26th [Hard]
Going Allowance: minus 0.45 sec per fur (H)                                          Wind: nil

Stalls: low

**1648**   GRITTLETON STKS (Mdn 3-Y.O.F) £1730.00 (£480.00: £230.00)
    1¼m 46y                                                          6-30 (6-31)

  1124² **Ardisia (USA)** (86) (Fav) *(PFICole)* 8-11 AMunro (4) (mde all: shkn up over 1f
      out: r.o wl) ......................................................................... —1
  1082⁴ Choppy Choppy (USA) (74) *(BWHills)* 8-11 DHolland (3) (3rd st: hrd rdn & ev
      ch over 1f out: eased whn btn ins fnl f) ................................. 6.2
    La Joya (IRE) *(GHarwood)* 8-11 AClark (1) (wl grwn: bit bkwd: dwlt: 2nd st: rdn
      & wknd 3f out) .................................................................... 15.3
    Priceless Pet *(JJBridger)* 8-11 SWhitworth (2) (bit bkwd: lost tch 6f out: last &
      t.o st) .............................................................................. dist.4

2/7 ARDISIA (USA)(tchd 1/2), **11/2** Choppy Choppy (USA)(7/2—6/1), **17/2** La Joya (IRE)(9/2—9/1), **100/1**
Priceless Pet. CSF £2.04, Tote £1.40 (£1.50). Mr Fahd Salman (WHATCOMBE) bred by Newgate Stud Farm
Incorporated in USA. 4 Rn                                                          2m 9 (1.3)
                                       SF—39/27/–/–

**1649**   MID-SUMMER CLAIMING STKS (3-Y.O) £1660.00 (£460.00: £220.00)
    5f 161y                                                          7-00 (7-01)

  1428³ **Lady Sabo** (69) (Fav) *(GLewis)* 8-6 PaulEddery (2) (chsd ldr: hrd rdn over 1f
      out: led ins fnl f: cleverly) ..................................................... —1
  1338 Orchard Bay (49) *(DRTucker)* 8-5 NAdams (1) (hld up: rdn over 2f out: r.o ins fnl
      f) .................................................................................... ¾.2
  1340⁶ Belthorn (40) *(JJBridger)* 8-5⁽¹⁾ SWhitworth (3) (led: hrd rdn over 1f out: hdd ins
      fnl f) ............................................................................... 2½.3

1/4 LADY SABO, **4/1** Orchard Bay, **12/1** Belthorn. CSF £1.59, Tote £1.20 (£1.10). Cronk Thoroughbred Racing
Ltd (EPSOM) bred by Cheveley Park Stud Ltd. 3 Rn                                    1m 12.1 (2.8)

**1650**   CHARLES SAUNDERS H'CAP (3-Y.O) (0-80) £2756.00 (£766.00: £368.00)
    1m 5y                                                          7-30 (7-33)

                         (Weights raised 5 lb)
  1160⁴ **Emaura** (54) *(KOCunningham-Brown)* 8-1 DHolland (7) (mde all: rdn over 1f
      out: r.o wl) ......................................................................... —1
  1286 Mustahil (IRE) (65) *(RJHodges)* 8-12 PaulEddery (4) (lw: w ldr: 3rd st: ev ch ins
      fnl f: r.o) ........................................................................... nk.2
  1523² Fusion (USA) (74) (Fav) *(PFICole)* 9-7 AMunro (2) (5th st: hdwy over 2f out: ev
      ch over 1f out: nt qckn) ...................................................... 1½.3
  896 Marvelous Molly (64) *(IABalding)* 8-8 ¼³SO'Gorman (1) (hld up & plld hrd: 4th st:
      one pce fnl 2f) .................................................................... 4.4
  1389² Red Archer (70) (bl) *(PJMakin)* 9-3 WNewnes (8) (swtg: hld up & bhd: 7th st: no
      hdwy fnl 2f) ....................................................................... 1½.5
  1219 Duty Sergeant (IRE) (54) *(MPMuggeridge)* 8-1 TyroneWilliams (3) (6th & rdn st:
      no hdwy) ........................................................................... ¾.6
  1433⁴ Tom's Apache (54) *(WRWilliams)* 8-1 NAdams (5) (swtg: plld hrd: last st: a bhd) 3.7
  1214⁵ Red Sombrero (65) *(LGCottrell)* 8-12 TRogers (6) (2nd st: wknd 2f out) ............ 4.8

7/4 Fusion (USA), **9/4** Red Archer(3/1—2/1), **9/1** Red Sombrero(op 5/1), **10/1** Mustahil (IRE)(8/1—12/1),
Marvelous Molly(op 6/1), **16/1** Duty Sergeant (IRE)(op 10/1), **20/1** EMAURA. CSF
£167.34, CT £476.77. Tote £19.70: £2.80 £2.60 £1.20 (£130.30). Mr D. Bass (STOCKBRIDGE) bred by Mrs P.
J. Van Straubenzee and C. J. R. Trotter. 8 Rn                                    1m 40 (0.7)
                                     SF—22/32/36/11/15/–

**1651**      HAMSWELL H'CAP (0-80) £2154.00 (£594.00: £282.00)     **5f 11y**     8-00 (8-01)

12622 **Fivesevenfiveo (66)** (Fav) *(RJHodges)* 4–10-0 PaulEddery (3) (chsd ldr: hrd rdn fnl f: led last stride) .................................................. —1
1282   Saint Systems **(44)** *(CJHill)* 6–8-6 TyroneWilliams (1) (hrd rdn & hung rt over 2f out: one pce) .............................................. s.h.2
*1325*5 Hinari Video **(48)** *(MJohnston)* 7–8-10 RPElliott (2) (pushed along: led: hrd rdn over 1f out: hdd last stride) .............................. 3.3

**11/8** FIVESEVENFIVEO, **13/8** Saint Systems, **9/4** Hinari Video. CSF £3.66, Tote £2.00 (£2.30). Mr George W. Baker (SOMERTON) bred by Roger C. Denton. 3 Rn      61.9 sec (1.4)
SF—41/18/10

**1652**      SWAINSWICK STKS (Mdn 2-Y.O) £1520.00 (£420.00: £200.00)     **5f 11y**     8-30 (8-34)

12733 **Tahasun (IRE)** *(HThomsonJones)* 9-0 RHills (6) (lw: plld out & hdwy over 2f out: led over 1f out: edgd lft ins fnl f: r.o wl) ..................... —1
    Bellsabanging *(DRLaing)* 9-0 TyroneWilliams (2) (unf: led: edgd rt 2f out: hdd & bmpd over 1f out: btn whn n.m.r ins fnl f) ................ 2¹/₂.2
383²   Conspicuous (IRE) (Fav) *(PFICole)* 9-0 AMunro (4) (b: w ldr: n.m.r over 2f out: r.o ins fnl f) .......................................... ³/₄.3
    Leave a Kiss *(IABalding)* 8-6 ‡3SO'Gorman (3) (small: cmpt: a.p: r.o one pce fnl f) ........................................................... 1.4
1300   Jarena (IRE) *(GLewis)* 8-9 PaulEddery (7) (prom over 3f) ........................ 2.5
7016   Nikki Noo Noo *(CJHill)* 8-9 NAdams (5) (a bhd) ................................. 1.6
    Mad March Hare *(DRTucker)* 8-9 ‡5RPrice (1) (neat: s.s: a to) .............. 15.7

**8/11** Conspicuous (IRE), **9/2** TAHASUN (IRE)(op 3/1), **6/1** Jarena (IRE), **12/1** Bellsabanging(8/1—14/1), **14/1** Leave a Kiss(op 8/1), Nikki Noo Noo(8/1—16/1), **40/1** Mad March Hare. CSF £45.67, Tote £4.80: £2.50 £3.00 (£26.40). Mr Hamdan Al-Maktoum (NEWMARKET) bred by Shadwell Estate Company Limited in Ireland. 7 Rn      62.4 sec (1.9)
SF—17/7/4/–/–/–

**1653**      CLIFTON H'CAP (0-80) £2337.50 (£650.00: £312.50)     **2m 1f 34y**     9-00 (9-01)

14075 **Chucklestone (54)** *(JSKing)* 9–8-5 PaulEddery (2) (mde all: rdn 4f out: r.o) ...... —1
1459   Mull House **(60)** *(FJO'Mahony)* 5–8-4 ‡7TMcLaughlin (5) (lw: hld up: wnt 2nd st: hrd rdn & ev ch 2f out: one pce) ..................... 3.2
15342 Green Lane (USA) **(75)** (Fav) *(IABalding)* 4–9-9 ‡3SO'Gorman (4) (lw: hld up: 3rd st: hrd rdn & wknd 2f out) ..................... 8.3
*1372*   Walking Saint **(43)** *(GraemeRoe)* 5–7-8(1) TyroneWilliams (1) (hld up: last & rdn st: wknd over 2f out) .............................. 20.4
                     LONG HANDICAP: Walking Saint 7-5.

**4/5** Green Lane (USA), **5/2** Mull House, **3/1** CHUCKLESTONE, **33/1** Walking Saint. CSF £9.85, Tote £3.10 (£3.90). Mr Mark O'Connor (SWINDON) bred by R. B. Stokes. 4 Rn      3m 49.5 (5.5)
T/Plpt: £214.20 (5.4 Tckts).                                    KH

## 1366—GOODWOOD (R-H)

### Friday, June 26th [Good to firm]

Going Allowance: minus 0.20 sec per fur (F)               Wind: almost nil

Stalls: low

**1654**      TAKE 7 APP'CE H'CAP (0-70) £1917.50 (£530.00: £252.50)     **5f**     6-45 (6-47)

13682 **Coppermill Lad (48)** *(LJHolt)* 9–8-2 ‡8CAvery (6) (s.s: wl bhd 3f: gd hdwy over 1f out: led wl ins fnl f: rdn out) ...................... —1
1282   Lucy Dancer (IRE) **(54)** (v) *(CGCox)* 4–8-11 ‡5JHunter (3) (led: hrd rdn over 1f out: hdd wl ins fnl f) .................................. 1.2
15524 Ayr Raider **(64)** (bl) (Fav) *(WRMuir)* 5–9-4 ‡8KimMcDonnell (2) (a.p: ev ch 2f out: r.o one pce) ....................................... hd.3
1500   Millsolin (IRE) **(55)** *(ARDavison)* 4–8-12 ‡5PBowe (1) (a.p: ev ch 2f out: one pce fnl f) ........................................................ nk.4
13056 Miss Precocious **(38)** (v) *(DShaw)* 4–8-0 BDoyle (5) (lw: s.s: gd hdwy over 3f out: wknd fnl f) .............................................. 3¹/₂.5

**6/4** Ayr Raider, **7/2** COPPERMILL LAD, **4/1** Miss Precocious(3/1—9/2), Lucy Dancer (IRE), **12/1** Millsolin (IRE)(op 8/1). CSF £15.47, Tote £2.80: £1.60 £1.60 (£5.20). Mr L. J. Holt (BASINGSTOKE) bred by Miss J. Samuel. 5 Rn      59.11 sec (1.51)
SF—41/48/52/44/16

**1655**  FSI CLAIMING STKS (3-Y.O) £1970.00 (£545.00: £260.00)  1½m  7-15 (7-19)

1408⁴  Baby Wizzard *(IABalding)* 8-0 CRutter (5) (6th st: hdwy 3f out: led ins fnl f: all
out) ............................................................................................................ —1

1255⁴  Saif Al Adil (IRE) **(58)** *(BHanbury)* 7-12 ‡⁵DHarrison (4) (lw: led 2f: 2nd st: led 3f
out tl over 1f out: r.o wl) ........................................................................ s.h.2

1367³  Afore Jane **(50)** *(GHarwood)* 8-1 ‡⁵JJones (1) (4th st: rdn 2f out: r.o w ins fnl f)  nk.3

1385³  King of Normandy (IRE) **(69)** (Fav) *(RHannon)* 8-9 MRoberts (2) (3rd st: hrd rdn
3f out: led over 1f out tl ins fnl f: one pce) ...................................... 2½.4

1165⁵  Lyn's Return (IRE) **(62)** *(RSimpson)* 8-6‡⁵ATucker (6) (lw: hdwy 4f out: 5th st: ev
ch over 2f out: wknd wl over 1f out) ...................................................... 8.5

1446  Cavo Greco (USA) **(61)** *(PFlCole)* 8-7 TQuinn (3) (led after 2f to 3f out: wknd 2f
out) ........................................................................................................ ½.6

*Stewards Enquiry: Rutter suspended 5-8/7/92 (excessive use of whip).*

**11/8** King of Normandy (IRE), **5/2** Lyn's Return (IRE), **11/2** BABY WIZZARD(8/1—5/1), **7/1** Saif Al Adil (IRE)(op
4/1), **10/1** Afore Jane, **12/1** Cavo Greco (USA)(op 7/1). CSF £37.00, Tote £7.20: £2.60 £2.20 (£35.70). Mr
David Myers (KINGSCLERE) bred by D. Myers. 6 Rn  2m 39.88 (8.18)

**1656**  LASMO NORTH SEA H'CAP (0-90) £3590.00 (£1070.00: £510.00: £230.00)
1m 1f  7-40 (7-45)

1210⁵  Alessandrina (USA) **(74)** *(MRStoute)* 3-8-8 WCarson (4) (2nd st: led 2f out:
rdn out) .............................................................................................. —1

1366★  Albert **(52)** *(DAWilson)* 5-7-11 GCarter (1) (4th & rdn st: chsd wnr fnl 2f: unable
qckn fnl f) ........................................................................................... 2½.2

1388²  Santi Sana **(69)** (bl) (Fav) *(LadyHerries)* 4-9-0 MRoberts (5) (b.off hind: plld
hrd: led 7f: nt r.o) ................................................................................... 3.3

1431³  Helios **(71)** *(RSimpson)* 4-9-2 JReid (2) (lw: 3rd st: wknd over 1f out) .......... 1½.4

**7/4** Santi Sana, **2/1** ALESSANDRINA (USA), Albert, **8/1** Helios(op 5/1). CSF £6.21, Tote £3.20 (£3.40). Mr
Malcolm Parrish (NEWMARKET) bred by Calumet Farm in USA. 4 Rn  1m 56.23 (5.53)

**1657**  GOODWOOD GOLF CLUB CENTENARY AUCTION (S) STKS (2-Y.O) £2075.00 (£575.00:
£275.00)  6f  8-10 (8-11)

1409  Hallorina *(WGRWightman)* 8-0 GBardwell (4) (lw: mde virtually all: rdn out) ...... —1

1429³  Burishki (bl) *(GAPritchard-Gordon)* 7-13 ‡⁵DHarrison (1) (hld up: hrd rdn 1f out:
r.o ins fnl f) ....................................................................................... ¾.2

928⁴  Kingsdown Cavalier (Fav) *(RHannon)* 8-6 BRouse (5) (a.p: ev ch over 1f out:
unable qckn) ........................................................................................ 1½.3

*1321*  Toff Sundae *(GLewis)* 8-9 JReid (3) (lw: hld up: nt clr run over 2f out: hrd rdn
over 1f out: one pce) ........................................................................ 2.4

1370⁵  Pondering *(SDow)* 8-5 TQuinn (7) (s.i.s: hdwy 3f out: ev ch over 1f out: wknd fnl
f) ................................................................................................... 1½.5

Arctic Agnes (USA) *(RAkehurst)* 8-0 GCarter (2) (unf: bit bkwd: prom 4f) .......... ¾.6

**6/4** Kingsdown Cavalier, **3/1** Pondering, **5/1** Toff Sundae, Burishki, **8/1** Arctic Agnes (USA), **20/1** HALLORINA.
CSF £100.91, Tote £20.60: £4.40 £1.90 (£36.10). Mrs J. A. Thomson (UPHAM) bred by W. G. R. Wightman and
Mrs J. A. Thomson. 6 Rn; No bid  1m 13.39 (2.99)
SF–2/–/–/–/–/–

**1658**  E.B.F. GOODWOOD METALCRAFT STKS (Mdn 2-Y.O) £2898.00 (£864.00: £299.00 each)
6f  8-40 (8-41)

1259⁴  Polar Storm (IRE) (Fav) *(LadyHerries)* 8-9 GCarter (6) (lw: chsd ldr: led over 1f
out: all out) .......................................................................................... —1

Ventiquattrofogli (IRE) *(JLDunlop)* 9-0 JReid (3) (w'like: scope: bit bkwd: hld
up: shkn up over 1f out: ev ch fnl f: r.o wl) ...................................... hd.2

1103⁶  Embankment (IRE) *(RHannon)* 9-0 MRoberts (4) (led over 4f: hrd rdn: r.o) ...... hd.3

Abbey's Gal *(IABalding)* 8-9 RCochrane (5) (unf: scope: s.i.s: hdwy 3f out: hrd
rdn & ev ch fnl f: r.o) ........................................................................... d.h.3

Empire Pool *(LordHuntingdon)* 8-9 ‡⁵DHarrison (1) (leggy: unf: s.i.s: outpcd) .... 8.5

If it Suits *(RAkehurst)* 9-0 TQuinn (2) (str: bhd fnl 3f: t.o) .................................. 25.6

**6/4** POLAR STORM (IRE), **5/2** Ventiquattrofogli (IRE), **11/4** Embankment (IRE)(2/1—7/2), **8/1** Abbey's
Gal(6/1—10/1), **10/1** Empire Pool(op 6/1), **12/1** If it Suits. CSF £6.18, Tote £3.30: £1.80 £2.00 (£4.40). Dexam
International Limited (LITTLEHAMPTON) bred by Pegasus Securities Leasing (Pty) Ltd. in Ireland. 6 Rn
1m 12.53 (2.13)
SF–29/33/32/27/–/–

**1659**  WEALD AND DOWNLAND MUSEUM H'CAP (3-Y.O) (0-80) £2092.50 (£580.00: £277.50)
1m  (Weights raised 3 lb)  9-10 (9-11)

1428★  Court Minstrel **(60)** *(LJHolt)* 8-5 (7x) JReid (2) (4th st: nt clr run over 2f out: led
ins fnl f: drvn out) ................................................................................... —1

1246³ Common Council (76) *(GAPritchard-Gordon)* 9-7 GCarter (1) (swtg: 2nd st: led over 2f out tl ins fnl f: r.o) .................................. ¹/₂.2
1389★ Our Occasion (72) (Fav) *(RHannon)* 9-3 MRoberts (4) (plld hrd: 3rd & rdn st: faltered over 1f out: ev ch ins fnl f: r.o) .................................. ¹/₂.3
1382⁴ Elwazir (USA) (68) *(PTWalwyn)* 8-13 WCarson (3) (lw: led over 5f) .................................. 8.4

**13/8** Our Occasion, **7/4** COURT MINSTREL(5/2—7/2), **7/2** Elwazir (USA), **9/2** Common Council(op 5/2). CSF £8.68, Tote £3.50 (£5.10). Mr G. W. Knight (BASINGSTOKE) bred by Keith Freeman. 4 Rn　1m 40.41 (2.81)
SF—25/39/33/5

T/Plpt: £1,045.60 (2.6 Tckts).　　　　　　　　　　　　　　　　　　　　　　　　LMc

## 1360—**DONCASTER (L-H)**
### Friday, June 26th [Firm, Good to firm fnl 5f]
Going Allowance: St: minus 0.15 sec; Rnd: minus 0.30 sec (F)　　　Wind: almost nil

Stalls: high

**1660**　　MARGARET AUCTION STKS (Mdn 2-Y.O) £2070.00 (£570.00: £270.00)
　　　　　7f　　　　　　　　　　　　　　　　　　　　　2-15 (2-17)

1485⁵ **Hadeer's Dance** (Fav) *(RWArmstrong)* 9-0 LPiggott (8) (bhd: hdwy on outside over 2f out: led over 1f out: rdn clr: eased nr fin) .................. —1
1170² Sweet Disorder (IRE) *(GAPritchard-Gordon)* 8-9 WRyan (4) (hld up: effrt & hdwy over 2f out: kpt on u.p fnl f) .................................. 1¹/₂.2
1296³ Don't Be Saki (IRE) *(JEtherington)* 8-9 JLowe (2) (chsd ldrs: rdn to ld 2f out: sn hdd: kpt on same pce) .................................. s.h.3
　682 Duplicate *(MHEasterby)* 9-0 MBirch (1) (bit bkwd: a.p: chal 2f out: edgd lft u.p & rio ex fnl f) .................................. 2.4
1299⁶ Wentbridge Lad (IRE) (bl) *(BAMcMahon)* 9-0 KDarley (7) (lw: in tch: effrt over 2f out: no imp fnl f) .................................. 1¹/₂.5
1279 Persian Fountain (IRE) *(BSRothwell)* 8-9 JFortune (9) (lw: rdn along 3f out: nt pce to chal) .................................. 2.6
287⁴ Master Sinclair (IRE) *(RHollinshead)* 9-0 WCarson (13) (lw: in tch tl grad wknd fnl 2f) .................................. ¹/₂.7
　446 Legal Dancer *(RJRWilliams)* 9-0 RCochrane (14) (hld up: effrt on ins 2f out: n.d) .................................. nk.8
1299⁴ Newinsky (v) *(CTinkler)* 8-9 TLucas (3) (w ldrs tl rdn & wknd 2f out) .................................. 2¹/₂.9
　*1321* Rose Flyer (IRE) *(MCChapman)* 8-9 SWebster (6) (bit bkwd: disp ld: hung lft virtually thrght: wknd u.p 2f out) .................................. s.h.10
1296 Moonshine Dancer *(MrsGRReveley)* 9-0 KFallon (5) (lw: nvr trbld ldrs) .......... hd.11
　　Flashella (IRE) *(TFairhurst)* 8-6 ‡3JFanning (10) (small: lt-f: bit bkwd: mde most 5f: edgd lft & sn btn) .................................. ¹/₂.12
1299 Danger Baby *(BobJones)* 9-0 VSmith (11) (bit bkwd: rdn along & wl outpcd fr ¹/₂-wy) .................................. 1¹/₂.13
1149 Crab 'n Lobster (IRE) *(MrsJRRamsden)* 8-9 GBaxter (12) (sme hdwy 3f out: sn rdn & wknd) .................................. ¹/₂.14

**7/4** HADEER'S DANCE(op 3/1), **5/1** Sweet Disorder(op 3/1), **6/1** Wentbridge Lad (IRE), **7/1** Don't Be Saki (IRE), **8/1** Master Sinclair (IRE), **10/1** Newinsky, **14/1** Legal Dancer, **16/1** Crab 'n Lobster (IRE), Duplicate, **20/1** Danger Baby, **25/1** Moonshine Dancer, **33/1** Ors. CSF £12.31, Tote £3.00: £1.60 £1.70 £2.30 (£5.40). Mr Khalifa Dasmal (NEWMARKET) bred by Stetchworth Park Stud Ltd. 14 Rn　1m 26.89 (3.49)
SF—32/22/21/20/15/4

**1661**　　A. F. BUDGE STKS (Ladies) (Mdn) £2070.00 (£570.00: £270.00)　　7f　　2-45 (2-47)

1484² **Patience Please** *(MHEasterby)* 3-9-13 ‡5MrsSEasterby (1) (hdwy over 2f out: led wl ins fnl f: r.o) .................................. —1
　715⁴ Mainly Me (77) *(PTWalwyn)* 3-9-13 ‡5MissRNugent (3) (jnd ldrs on bit ¹/₂-wy: sn led: hdd wl ins fnl f: r.o) .................................. hd.2
　　Ergon *(DJSCosgrove)* 3-9-13 ‡5MrsDCamp-Simpson (8) (bit bkwd: mde most tl hdd over 2f out: wknd over 1f out) .................................. 6.3
1055² Isle of Innisfree (USA) (74) (bl) (Fav) *(HRACecil)* 3-10-9 MissJAllison (9) (w ldrs: rdn 3f out: hung lft & sn btn) .................................. 2¹/₄.4
1312⁴ Fairford *(JGFitzGerald)* 3-10-4 ‡5MrsRSpence (10) (lw: w ldrs tl grad wknd fnl 2f) 7.5
1293⁶ Liberty Glen *(BEllison)* 3-9-13 ‡5MrsCKing (7) (swtg: swvd rt after s: cl up to ¹/₂-wy: sn lost pl) .................................. 1¹/₂.6
1248 The Metropole (IRE) (45) *(AWPotts)* 3-10-4 ‡5MissSJudge (11) (b.hind: bit bkwd: chsd ldrs 4f) .................................. 1.7
　　Mahzooz (72) *(MMoubarak)* 3-10-4 ‡5MissIFoustok (5) (bkwd: nvr nr to chal) . 1¹/₂.8
1137 One of the Lads *(BRCambidge)* 10-10-13 ‡5MrsHNoonan (4) (bit bkwd: bhd fr ¹/₂-wy) .................................. 7.9

1137 Wild Persian (IRE) **(42)** (bl) *(PatMitchell)* 3–9–13 ‡⁵MissLGlayzer (6) (swtg: prom
early: outpcd fr ¹/₂-wy) ...................................................... 8.10
Dont Embarrass Me *(TKersey)* 3–10–4 ‡⁵MissJMiddleton (2) (w'like: bkwd: s.i.s:
a in rr) ...................................................... 3¹/₂.11

**2/1** Isle of Innisfree (USA)(op Evens), **5/2** PATIENCE PLEASE, **4/1** Mainly Me(3/1—9/2), **6/1** Fairford(op 4/1),
**8/1** Mahzooz, **50/1** Liberty Glen, Ergon, Wild Persian (IRE), **100/1** Ors. CSF £12.05, Tote £3.20: £1.20 £1.40
£20.20 (£6.00). Mr I. Bray (MALTON) bred by Pitts Farm Stud. 11 Rn                    1m 27.51 (4.11)
SF—36/35/17/19/–/–

## 1662

STONES BEST BITTER H'CAP (0-100) £5120.00 (£1520.00: £720.00: £320.00)
1¹/₄m 60y                                                            3-15 (3-16)

11814 **Arak (USA) (68)** (Jt-Fav) *(RWArmstrong)* 4–8–1 WCarson (4) (lw: mde all: r.o
gamely fnl 3f) ...................................................... —1
1402* Lucky Guest **(94)** (Jt-Fav) *(JLDunlop)* 5–9–13 LPiggott (2) (lw: hld up: swtchd
outside & chal appr fnl f: nt qckn nr fin) ............................ 1¹/₂.2
1465* Spinning **(98)** *(IABalding)* 5–10–3 (5x) RCochrane (3) (trckd wnr: effrt 3f out:
edgd lft & no rspnse) ...................................................... 5.3
15093 Execution Only (IRE) **(65)** (v) *(JWWatts)* 4–7–12 JLowe (1) (lw: bhd: drvn along
4f out: no imp) ...................................................... 6.4

**2/1** ARAK (USA), Lucky Guest, **9/4** Spinning, **6/1** Execution Only (IRE). CSF £6.06, Tote £2.90 (£2.70). Mr
Hamdan Al-Maktoum (NEWMARKET) bred by Mill Ridge Farm Ltd. in USA. 4 Rn           2m 6.90 (U.10)
SF—58/81/75/30

## 1663

BASS DEVELOPMENTS LIMITED 10TH ANNIVERSARY H'CAP (3-Y.O.F) £2415.00
(£665.00: £315.00)   7f                                            3-50 (3-52)

(Weights raised 6 lb)

15274 **Thewaari (USA) (64)** (Fav) *(AAScott)* 9–7 WRSwinburn (1) (lw: hld up: gd hwdy
to ld ins fnl f: rdn out) ...................................................... —1
1185 Gold Belt (IRE) **(50)** *(RHollinshead)* 8–7 WRyan (9) (swtg: hld up: swtchd ins 2f
out: sn ev ch: hung lft: r.o wl fnl f) ...................................................... ¹/₂.2
5226 Battuta **(52)** *(REarnshaw)* 8–9 KFallon (7) (chsd ldrs: drvn along 3f out: kpt on wl
fnl f) ...................................................... nk.3
1284 Breeze Away **(57)** *(RMWhitaker)* 9–0 ACulhane (8) (lw: a cl up: chal & slt ld over
1f out: sn hdd & wknd) ...................................................... 3.4
14866 Dancing Wild **(40)** *(MrsGRReveley)* 7–4 ‡⁷DarrenMoffatt (2) (swtg: plld hrd early:
w ldrs tl wknd fnl f) ...................................................... s.h.5
10104 Horizontale **(47)** *(CEBrittain)* 8–4⁽¹⁾ MBirch (11) (lw: a.p: rdn to chal 2f out: wknd
fnl f: btn & eased nr fin) ...................................................... 2.6
*1265* Safari Park **(40)** *(BSRothwell)* 7–11 JQuinn (5) (w ldrs over 4f: no ex) ............ 2¹/₂.7
15074 Throw Away Line **(46)** *(JEtherington)* 8–3 NConnorton (6) (chsd ldrs: rdn & btn
wl over 1f out) ...................................................... nk.8
13206 Kate Royale **(48)** (bl) *(GCBravery)* 8–5 AMackay (3) (trckd ldrs: chal 3f out: sn
lost pl) ...................................................... 1¹/₂.9
1072 My Jersey Pearl (IRE) **(46)** *(DonEnricoIncisa)* 7–10 ‡⁷ClaireBalding (12) (s.i.s: a
in rr) ...................................................... 2.10
13433 Queen's Tickle **(53)** *(APJarvis)* 8–10 WCarson (4) (b.nr hind: lw: mde most tl
rdn & wknd over 1f out: eased whn btn) ...................................................... ¹/₂.11
*1267* Super-Sub **(51)** *(GFleming)* 8–1 ‡⁷OPears (10) (bhd fr ¹/₂-wy) ...................... 1¹/₂.12

**85/40** THEWAARI (USA), **5/1** Queen's Tickle, Horizontale, **8/1** Breeze Away, **9/1** Throw Away Line, **10/1** Dancing
Wild, **12/1** Kate Royale, **16/1** My Jersey Pearl (IRE), Gold Belt (IRE), **20/1** Battuta, **25/1** Super-Sub, **50/1** Safari
Park. CSF £34.97, CT £521.19. Tote £2.80: £1.60 £4.00 £9.10 (£25.90). Mr Saeed Suhail (NEWMARKET) bred
by John Franks in USA. 12 Rn                                            1m 25.91 (2.51)
SF—53/37/38/34/9/17

## 1664

HOME FIRE STKS (2-Y.O) £3840.00 (£1140.00: £540.00: £240.00)   6f   4-25 (4-25)

11922 **Saint Express** *(RMWhitaker)* 8–11 ACulhane (1) (lw: wnt rt s: a.p: rdn 2f out: led
jst ins fnl f: drvn out) ...................................................... —1
11863 Willshe Gan *(DenysSmith)* 8–6 KFallon (5) (lw: led: rdn over 1f out: sn hdd:
rallied wl nr fin) ...................................................... ¹/₂.2
1513 Finmental (IRE) (Fav) *(ABailey)* 8–11 AMackay (3) (a.p: hung lft u.p 2f out: nt
qckn ins fnl f) ...................................................... ¹/₂.3
1299 Ann Hill (IRE) *(RHollinshead)* 8–6 WRyan (4) (swtg: in tch: rdn along ¹/₂-wy: no
imp) ...................................................... 3.4
1192 Norstano *(MHEasterby)* 8–11 MBirch (2) (sltly hmpd after s: in tch tl wknd 2f out) 3.5

**7/4** Finmental (IRE), **15/8** SAINT EXPRESS, **5/2** Willshe Gan, **14/1** Norstano, **33/1** Ann Hill (IRE). CSF £6.46, Tote
£2.80: £1.50 £1.50 (£2.70). Mr M. G. St Quinton (WETHERBY) bred by R. M. Whitaker. 5 Rn   1m 13.73 (2.73)
SF—25/18/21/4/–

**1665**　　BRITISH COAL H'CAP (0-90) £3200.00 (£950.00: £450.00: £200.00)
　　　　　　1¹/₂m　　　　　　　　　　　　　　　　　　　　　　5-00 (5-01)

1501* **Brier Creek (USA) (81)** (Fav) *(JHMGosden)* 3–8–7 (4x) RCochrane (1) (lw:
　　　　mde all: rdn & kpt on strly fnl 2f) .................................................. —1
1318⁴ Taylors Prince (62) *(HJCollingridge)* 5–8–3 JQuinn (2) (trckd wnr: chal over 2f
　　　　out: one pce fnl f) ................................................................ 2.2
　　　　Secret Society (86) *(MJCamacho)* 5–9–13 NConnorton (3) (bkwd: hld up:
　　　　smooth hdwy over 3f out: grad lost pl fnl 2f) ......................... 3.3
1252³ Bigwheel Bill (IRE) (77) *(JWWatts)* 3–8–3 JLowe (4) (trckd wnr tl wknd 3f out) . 10.4

**4/7** BRIER CREEK (USA), **5/1** Taylors Prince, Bigwheel Bill (IRE), **8/1** Secret Society. CSF £3.50, Tote £1.50
(£1.60). Sheikh Mohammed (NEWMARKET) bred by Allen E Paulson in USA. 4 Rn　　2m 31.92 (1.32)
　　　　　　　　　　　　　　　　　　　　　　　　　　　　　　　　　　SF—44/36/54/10

**1666**　　SPINAL INJURIES ASSOCIATION GRADUATION STKS (3-Y.O) £2560.00 (£760.00:
　　　　　　£360.00: £160.00)　　1¹/₂m　　　　　　　　　　　　5-30 (5-30)

1313* Sheriffmuir (84) (Fav) *(LMCumani)* 9–4 JQuinn (1) (lw: trckd ldr: led on bit over
　　　　2f out: shkn up to go clr appr fnl f: eased) ............................. —1
1316⁵ Aremef (USA) (84) *(MrsJCecil)* 9–4 WRSwinburn (2) (led tl hdd over 2f out: no
　　　　ch w wnr) ........................................................................... 3.2
881* Awol *(HRACecil)* 8–13 WRyan (3) (trckd ldrs: effrt 3f out: nt pce to chal) ......... 2¹/₂.3
395² Desert Force (IRE) (83) (bl) *(MMoubarak)* 8–11 GBaxter (4) (lw: bhd: hdwy 4f
　　　　out: drvn along & wknd 3f out) ............................................... 8.4

**5/6** SHERIFFMUIR, **7/2** Awol, **4/1** Desert Force (IRE), **5/1** Aremef (USA). CSF £5.04, Tote £1.60 (£3.60). Sheikh
Mohammed (NEWMARKET) bred by Stetchworth Park Stud Ltd. 4 Rn　　2m 29.95 (1.66 under best; U.65)
　　　　　　　　　　　　　　　　　　　　　　　　　　　　　　　　　　SF—74/68/58/40

T/Plpt: £89.30 (30.5 Tckts).　　　　　　　　　　　　　　　　　　　　　　　　Q'R

# DONCASTER (L-H)
## Saturday, June 27th [Firm, Good to firm fnl 5f]
Going Allowance: minus 0.25 sec per fur (F)　　　　　　　　　　　　Wind: nil

Stalls: high

**1667**　　LEVY BOARD APP'CE H'CAP (3-Y.O) (0-70) £1305.60 (£361.60: £172.80)
　　　　　　1³/₄m 132y　　　　　　　　　　　　　　　　　　　　　6-15 (6-16)

1491⁶ **Miss Pin Up (53)** *(PatMitchell)* 8–4 DBiggs (3) (s.s: hld up: hdwy 3f out: led over
　　　　1f out: drvn out) ................................................................. —1
1298 Elsa (42) *(RJHolder)* 7–3 ‡4CHawksley (1) (led: rdn 3f out: hdd over 1f out: kpt
　　　　on same pce) ...................................................................... 2¹/₂.2
1491* Thakawah (74) (Fav) *(RWArmstrong)* 9–11 SWilliams (4) (trckd ldr: effrt & ev ch
　　　　over 3f out: sn drvn along: wknd 1f out: eased whn btn) ..... 2.3
1034 Elsharh (IRE) (42) *(JAGlover)* 7–3 ‡4ClaireBalding (2) (prom tl wknd 5f out: n.d
　　　　after) ................................................................................ 15.4
　　　　　　LONG HANDICAP: Elsa 7-4, Elsharh (IRE) 7-3.

**1/2** Thakawah, **11/4** MISS PIN UP, **9/1** Elsa, **33/1** Elsharh (IRE). CSF £17.08, Tote £2.90 (£6.80). Mr E. Baldwin
(NEWMARKET) bred by Brook Bloodstock P L C. 4 Rn　　　　　　　　3m 12.34 (8.74)

**1668**　　E.B.F. LONSDALE STKS (Mdn 2-Y.O.F) £3054.00 (£912.00: £436.00: £198.00)
　　　　　　6f　　　　　　　　　　　　　　　　　　　　　　　　　6-45 (6-46)

　　　　Dalalah *(HThomsonJones)* 8–11 RHills (1) (small: lt-f: cl up: led 2f out: hrd rdn
　　　　fnl f: jst hld on) .................................................................... —1
1384² Magication *(CEBrittain)* 8–11 MRoberts (5) (lw: disp ld tl hdd 2f out: styd on wl
　　　　u.p fnl f: jst failed) ............................................................... s.h.2
1283⁴ Jade Runner *(MrsNMacauley)* 8–11 NDay (6) (disp ld 4f: drvn along & nt pce to
　　　　chal ins fnl f) ...................................................................... 7.3
　　　　Contrac Countess (IRE) *(BSRothwell)* 8–11 JQuinn (2) (cmpt: bit bkwd: cl up tl
　　　　rdn & wknd appr fnl f) ........................................................... 3¹/₂.4
　　　　Dayflower (USA) (Fav) *(HRACecil)* 8–11 WRyan (4) (lengthy: scope: ref to leave
　　　　stalls: t.n.p) ......................................................................... 0

**8/11** Dayflower (USA), **5/2** Magication, **5/1** DALALAH, **11/1** Jade Runner, **66/1** Contrac Countess (IRE). CSF
£16.69, Tote £6.40: £2.60 £1.20 (£6.00). Mr Hamdan Al-Maktoum (NEWMARKET) bred by Shadwell Estate
Company Limited. 5 Rn　　　　　　　　　　　　　　　　　　　　　1m 14.26 (3.26)
　　　　　　　　　　　　　　　　　　　　　　　　　　　　　　　　　　SF—2/1/–/–/–

**1669** TETLEY BITTER H'CAP (3-Y.O) (0-85) £2364.00 (£654.00: £312.00) 5f 7-15 (7-17)
(Weights raised 5 lb)

1117⁴ Ned's Bonanza (73) (MDods) 9-3 JLowe (2) (chsd ldrs: hrd drvn wl over 1f out: edgd lft: styd on strly to ld nr fin) ............ —1
1412² Hi-Tech Honda (IRE) (67) (Fav) (CEBrittain) 8-11 MRoberts (7) (sn drvn along: hdwy & swtchd 2f out: styd on strly ins fnl f) ............ hd.2
1386⁶ Super Rocky (77) (RBastiman) 9-0 ‡7HBastiman (3) (dwlt: sn rcvrd: led after 1f: clr over 1f out: ct nr fin) ............ hd.3
Miss Vaxette (69) (JLSpearing) 8-13 GHind (6) (sn pushed along: hdwy 2f out: nt pce to chal) ............ 2¹/₂.4
949 My Abbey (71) (EJAlston) 9-1 KFallon (5) (cl up to ¹/₂-wy: sn lost pl) ............ 3.5
1484 Dublin Dream (50) (MBrittain) 7-8⁽¹⁾ JQuinn (4) (led 1f: prom tl wknd over 1f out) 3¹/₂.6
1238⁴ Baladee Pet (53) (MrsVAAconley) 7-11 LCharnock (8) (sn pushed along: bdly hmpd 2f out: nt rcvr) ............ 3.7

LONG HANDICAP: Dublin Dream 7-0.
*582 Creche (7/1) Withdrawn (unruly in stalls) : not under orders — Rule 4 applies*

9/4 Hi-Tech Honda (IRE), 9/2 Super Rocky, 11/2 NED'S BONANZA, 7/1 My Abbey, Baladee Pet, 9/1 Miss Vaxette(tchd 14/1), 25/1 Dublin Dream. CSF £14.50, CT £38.67. Tote £6.40: £2.20 1.80 (£5.30). Mr Ned Jones (DARLINGTON) bred by D. W. McHarg. 7 Rn 59.80 sec (1.10)
SF—56/49/51/40/30/–

**1670** BENTLEY (S) STKS (2-Y.O) £1660.00 (£460.00: £220.00) 6f 7-45 (7-48)

**Silent Expression** (DMorris) 8-6 MTebbutt (2) (lengthy: scope: a gng wl: led on bit 2f out: sn clr: impressive) ............ —1
1524⁵ Eightofus (GMMoore) 8-11 DMcKeown (11) (chsd ldrs: drvn along ¹/₂-wy: styd on fnl f: no ch w wnr) ............ 10.2
Good Image (Fav) (APJarvis) 8-11 PaulEddery (5) (leggy: scope: mid div: rdn along wl over 2f out: swtchd & kpt on fnl f) ............ ¹/₂.3
1307³ Bluebella (MrsPABarker) 8-6 GHind (10) (w ldr tl infn 2f out: styd on one pce) ... 1.4
1046 Beat the Bagman (IRE) (BBeasley) 8-4 ‡7SWilliams (7) (s.i.s: hld up: stdy hdwy 2f out: nt clr run over 1f out: r.o wl towards fin) ............ 1.5
*1321 Rythmic Rascal (MBrittain) 8-6 ‡5SMaloney (6) (prom: rdn over 2f out: no ex ins fnl f)* ............ d.h.5
1409 Bohemian Queen (JLSpearing) 8-6 KDarley (9) (nvr trbld ldrs) ............ s.h.7
Bay Rum (BBeasley) 8-6 LCharnock (13) (lengthy: scope: bkwd: s.s: hdwy over 1f out: n.d) ............ ¹/₂.8
1554 Mdm Racer (IRE) (JBerry) 8-11 JCarroll (12) (led tl hdd 2f out: grad wknd) ............ ¹/₂.9
*1547 Hajaan (BBeasley) 8-6 PBurke (4) (dwlt: sn rcvrd: in tch over 3f)* ............ 1.10
*1373⁶ Merryhill Kerry (IRE) (JLHarris) 8-6 MRoberts (8) (spd to ¹/₂-wy: sn btn)* ............ 8.11
Monastic Flight (IRE) (BSRothwell) 8-11 JQuinn (1) (unf: s.i.s: hdwy after 2f: wknd 2f out) ............ nk.12
924 Beckswhite Abbey (BBeasley) 8-6 JLowe (3) (a bhd: t.o) ............ 10.13

3/1 Good Image, 4/1 Eightofus, Bluebella, 7/1 SILENT EXPRESSION(op 4/1), 8/1 Merryhill Kerry (IRE), 10/1 Beat the Bagman (IRE), 12/1 Bohemian Queen, 14/1 Bay Rum, 20/1 Monastic Flight (IRE), 25/1 Ors. CSF £38.63, Tote £9.50: £3.20 1.80 1.90 (£22.30). Mrs Rosalie Hawes (NEWMARKET) bred by J. B. H. Stevens. 13 Rn; Bt in 7,000 gns 1m 12.81 (1.81)
SF—26/–/–/–/–/–

**1671** SOUTH YORKSHIRE STAYERS H'CAP (0-70) £1970.00 (£545.00: £260.00) 2m 110y 8-15 (8-15)

1419 **Merton Mill** (57) (bl) (DMorley) 5–9-8 PaulEddery (3) (hld up: smooth hdwy over 3f out: jnd ldrs on bit 2f out: led 1f out: hrd hld) ............ —1
1361 Cost Effective (36) (MBrittain) 5–8-1⁽²⁾ KDarley (2) (trckd ldr: led 4f out: hrd rdn over 2f out: hdd 1f out: kpt on: no ch w wnr) ............ 1¹/₂.2
1407² Nikatino (51) (Fav) (DrJDScargill) 6–9-2 JQuinn (8) (hld up: gd hdwy to chal 3f out: sn rdn: nt qckn ins fnl f) ............ 1.3
1241⁵ Rexy Boy (28) (WLBarker) 5–7-7 LCharnock (6) (bhd: effrt & pushed along 5f out: hung lft u.p 3f out: nt pce of ldrs) ............ 6.4
1190⁴ Topcliffe (39) (v) (MrsVAAconley) 5–8-4 DMcKeown (4) (prom: nt clr run 4f out to 2f out: r.o ins fnl f) ............ hd.5
1290 Isobar (28) (MCChapman) 6–7-7 SWood (9) (chsd ldrs tl wknd 4f out) ............ 1.6
1566² Pondered Bid (37) (bl) (PatMitchell) 8–8-2 GDuffield (5) (led: hdd 4f out: grad wknd) ............ 5.7

LONG HANDICAP: Isobar 7-3.

7/4 Nikatino, 3/1 MERTON MILL, 5/1 Pondered Bid, 6/1 Cost Effective, 7/1 Topcliffe, 11/1 Rexy Boy, 25/1 Isobar. CSF £19.83, CT £36.19. Tote £4.00: £2.30 2.30 (£11.80). Lord Clinton (NEWMARKET) bred by Greenland Park Stud. 7 Rn 3m 38.34 (9.34)

**1672**     CORPORATION STKS (Mdn 3 & 4-Y.O) £1758.00 (£488.00: £234.00)
1¼m 60y            8-45 (8-45)

    **Imperial Ballet (IRE)** (Fav) *(HRACecil)* 3–8-9 WRyan (4) (s.s: led after 1f: rdn &
wnt clr fnl 2f: easily) ............................................................. —1
1227a⁴ Big Blue **(92)** *(CEBrittain)* 3–8-9 MRoberts (2) (led 1f: trckd wnr: effrt 3f out:
hung lft 2f out: sn wl outpcd) .................................................. 10.2
    1532⁵ Zaire (v) *(JWWatts)* 3–8-9 GDuffield (5) (chsd ldrs: effrt 4f out: wknd over 2f out) 2½.3
    Kanvass *(JRFanshawe)* 3–8-9 NDay (1) (leggy: scope: bhd: effrt on outside 3f
out: sn rdn & btn) ............................................................ hd.4

**11/10** IMPERIAL BALLET (IRE)(4/6—5/4), **5/4** Big Blue(2/1—11/10), **15/2** Kanvass, **16/1** Zaire(op 10/1). CSF
£2.75, Tote £2.10: (£1.50). Mr R. E. Sangster (NEWMARKET) bred by Swettenham Stud in Ireland. 4 Rn
                     2m 9.71 (2.71)
                     SF–43/23/18/17

---

**1673**     GEORGE WOOLSTON H'CAP (0-70) £2197.50 (£610.00: £292.50)
1m (rnd)            9-15 (9-17)

    1344⁵ **Charming Gift (50)** (Fav) *(RJRWilliams)* 5–8-8 KDarley (8) (in tch: pushed
along 3f out: styd on to ld wl ins fnl f) ..................................... —1
    1175 Buzzards Bellbuoy **(60)** *(HJCollingridge)* 3–8-8 JQuinn (6) (led after 1f: rdn
over 2f out: hdd & nt qckn wl ins fnl f) ...................................... ¾.2
    1550⁴ Sandmoor Denim **(50)** *(SRBowring)* 5–8-8 SWebster (1) (hdwy over 3f out: kpt
on u.p fnl 2f) .............................................................. 1½.3
    1557² Douraj (IRE) **(63)** *(CEBrittain)* 3–8-11 MRoberts (5) (chsd ldrs: effrt 3f out: nt clr
run over 1f out: swtchd & styd on u.p nr fin) .............................. ½.4
    1376 Colonel Fairfax **(36)** *(JWWatts)* 4–7-5⁽¹⁾ ‡3JFanning (16) (chsd ldrs: rdn & edgd
lft 3f out: nt qckn fnl 2f) .................................................. 1.6
    1421* Deputy Tim **(47)** *(RBastiman)* 9–8-5 DMcKeown (11) (chsd ldrs: effrt over 3f
out: hung lft over 2f out: no ex appr fnl f) ............................... 2.6
    1421⁴ Cartel **(56)** *(JLHarris)* 5–9-0 PaulEddery (14) (prom tl rdn & nt qckn 2f out:
eased whn btn ins fnl f) .................................................. 3.7
    1284 Parr (IRE) **(51)** *(JMackie)* 4–8-9 GHind (3) (hdwy over 2f out: n.d) ................. 1.8
    1421² Habeta (USA) **(70)** *(JWWatts)* 6–10-0 GDuffield (13) (effrt 4f out: nt rch ldrs) ... 1½.9
    1663 Queen's Tickle **(53)** *(APJarvis)* 3–7-10 ‡5SMaloney (12) (hdwy 3f out: nt rch
ldrs) ..................................................................... ½.10
    1527⁶ Chance Report **(40)** *(FHLee)* 4–7-9⁽³⁾ ‡3DBiggs (7) (in tch: effrt whn bdly hmpd
over 2f out: nt rcvr) ..................................................... 1½.11
    1520 Bold Ambition **(50)** *(TKersey)* 5–8-8 KFallon (15) (bhd tl sme late hdwy) ........ nk.12
    1195 Futures Gift (IRE) **(55)** *(AWPotts)* 3–8-3 AProud (4) (a in rr) .................... hd.13
    1122 Premier Major (IRE) **(48)** *(BBeasley)* 3–7-10 LCharnock (17) (a bhd) ............. 2.14
    Sky Cat **(52)** *(CTinkler)* 3–8-10 MBirch (10) (led 1f: cl up tl n.m.r & wknd 3f out) 3.15
    1309⁶ Treasure Beach **(45)** *(MBrittain)* 3–7-7 JLowe (2) (s.i.s: a bhd) ............... 1½.16
    1185 Noble Cause (IRE) **(54)** *(REarnshaw)* 3–8-2 JCarroll (9) (prom tl wknd qckly 3f
out) ...................................................................... nk.17

LONG HANDICAP: Colonel Fairfax 7-5, Treasure Beach 7-2.

**5/1** CHARMING GIFT, **11/2** Douraj (IRE), **7/1** Sandmoor Denim, Deputy Tim, **8/1** Habeta (USA)(op 9/2), Parr
(IRE)(op 5/2), **10/1** Cartel, **14/1** Futures Gift (IRE), **16/1** Chance Report, Queen's Tickle, **20/1** Buzzards Bellbuoy,
**25/1** Noble Cause (IRE), Sky Cat, Colonel Fairfax, **33/1** Premier Major (IRE), Treasure Beach, **50/1** Bold Ambition.
CSF £95.34, CT £569.80. Tote £7.00: £1.80 £3.40 £1.10 (£77.00). Mr Colin G. R. Booth (NEWMARKET) bred by
R. P. Ryan. 17 Rn                                  1m 38.28 (1.98)
                     SF–34/32/27/28/5/13

T/Trio: Race 7: £377.70 (3.1 Tckts). T/Plpt: £139.30 (20.5 Tckts).           O'R

---

1540—**LINGFIELD (L-H)**

### Friday, June 26th [Turf Good to firm, Firm back st; AWT Standard]

Going Allowance: Turf: minus 0.30 sec (F); AWT: minus 0.40 sec (FS)     Wind: almost nil

Stalls: high, 4th race centre

**1674**     PIEBALD STKS (Mdn 3 & 4-Y.O) £2324.00 (£644.00: £308.00)     1m 1f    2-40 (2-43)

    1268⁴ **Prince of Darkness (IRE)** (Fav) *(SirMarkPrescott)* 3–8-10 GDuffield (5) (swtg:
dwlt: hdwy over 5f out: 3rd st: led 3f out: comf) ......................... —1
    1128² Indian Style (IRE) **(55)** *(RGuest)* 3–8-0 ‡5DHarrison (3) (led 6f: unable qckn) ... 2½.2
    1306 Guesstimation (USA) *(JHMGosden)* 3–8-10 DHolland (4) (bit bkwd: 2nd & rn
wd st: hrd rdn over 1f out: eased whn btn ins fnl f) ..................... 8.3

1411 Sovereign Heights *(MRChannon)* 4–9-0 ‡7LMahoney (2) (4th st: hrd rdn over 2f
out: one pce) .................................................................................. ¾.4
13045 Headless Heights *(PMitchell)* 3–8-10 TQuinn (8) (lw: dwlt: nvr nr to chal) ......... s.h.5
*1266*5 Persian Bud (IRE) *(39) (JRBosley)* 4–9-2 ‡9NGwilliams (1) (b: 5th st: hrd rdn
over 2f out: one pce) ........................................................................ hd.6
Carpentier (USA) *(MJHaynes)* 3–8-10 BRouse (7) (leggy: a bhd) ...................... 6.7
Helleborus *(SDow)* 4–9-2 WNewnes (6) (plld hrd: rn wd bnd over 7f out: 6th st:
wknd over 3f out) .......................................................................... 7.8

**Evens** PRINCE OF DARKNESS (IRE), **4/1** Headless Heights, **5/1** Indian Style (IRE), **11/2** Guesstimation (USA),
Carpentier (USA)(7/2—6/1), **25/1** Helleborus, **40/1** Ors. CSF £6.59, Tote £2.40: £1.10 £1.70 £1.90 (£2.90). Pin
Oak Stable (NEWMARKET) bred by Whitechurch Stud in Ireland. 8 Rn          1m 55.33 (6.03)

---

## 1675

ROAN (S) STKS (2-Y.O) £2343.60 (£649.60: £310.80)          7f          3-10 (3-14)

11784 **Strike-a-Pose** (Fav) *(CNWilliams)* 8-6 TQuinn (12) (led 1f: led over 2f out: comf)  —1
B B Glen *(DMorris)* 8-6 WNewnes (7) (unf: bit bkwd: s.s: gd hdwy over 1f out:
r.o) ............................................................................................... 4.2
*1321* Longlife (IRE) *(MHTompkins)* 8-4 ‡7SMulvey (13) (lw: gd hdwy over 1f out: r.o
one pce) ....................................................................................... 4.3
15862 Mighty Miss Magpie (IRE) *(MRChannon)* 8-1 ‡5BDoyle (3) (a.p: rdn over 3f out:
one pce) ................................................................................... 2½.4
1442 Jaybee-Jay *(MJHaynes)* 8-11 BRouse (14) (nvr nr to chal) ......................... 1½.5
581 Moonstruck Bard *(SPCWoods)* 8-11 WWoods (4) (swtg: hdwy over 2f out:
wknd 1f out) ................................................................................ 2½.6
1442 Water Diviner (bl) *(RFJohnsonHoughton)* 8-11 DHolland (8) (prom over 4f) ...... 1.7
1515 Lofty Deed (USA) (bl) *(SirMarkPrescott)* 8-11 GDuffield (11) (swtg: led 6f out tl
over 2f out: sn wknd) ..................................................................... nk.8
1342 Apifera *(RJHodges)* 8-6 PaulEddery (10) (swtg: bhd fnl 2f) ...................... 2.9
Rachelly *(ARDavison)* 8-6 CandyMorris (4) (neat: bkwd: a bhd) .................... 3.10
1170 Persian Traveller (IRE) *(CNAllen)* 8-11 GBardwell (2) (prom over 4f) ......... 2½.11
1442 Mac Tomb *(KOCunningham-Brown)* 8-11 KTsui (9) (swtg: a bhd) ................. 12.12

**7/4** STRIKE-A-POSE, **7/2** Mighty Miss Magpie (IRE), **4/1** Moonstruck Bard(5/1—12/1), **5/1** Persian Traveller
(IRE)(14/1—9/2), **10/1** Apifera(op 5/1), **12/1** Lofty Deed (USA)(op 5/1), **14/1** Water Diviner, B B Glen, **33/1** Ors.
CSF £28.64, Tote £2.90: £1.50 £7.70 £7.50 (£330.60). Mr David J. Chapman (NEWMARKET) bred by Mrs R. D.
Peacock. 12 Rn; No bid                                                              1m 23.50 (2.20)
SF—27/15/1/–/–/–

---

## 1676

SUNDERLANDS H'CAP (3-Y.O) (0-80) £2499.20 (£691.20: £329.60)
6f (AWT)                                                           3-45 (3-46)

(Weights raised 10 lb)

*1263*★ **Palacegate Racing** (70) (Fav) *(JBerry)* 9-7 GCarter (3) (a.p: led over 2f out: rdn
out) ............................................................................................... —1
1219 Jucea (65) *(DWPArbuthnot)* 9-2 TQuinn (4) (lw: a.p: led over 3f out tl over 2f
out: ev ch over 1f out: unable qckn) ............................................... 1½.2
7926 Ben Bluff (52) *(LGCottrell)* 7-12 ‡5DHarrison (2) (lw: outpcd: nvr nrr) ......... 5.3
472 In the Game (IRE) (61) *(MissAJWhitfield)* 8-12 NAdams (1) (led over 2f) ...... 5.4

**6/4** PALACEGATE RACING(op Evens), **9/4** Jucea, **5/2** Ben Bluff, **6/1** In the Game (IRE). CSF £5.12, Tote £2.10
(£2.70). Palacegate Corporation Ltd (COCKERHAM) bred by D. Rabey. 4 Rn          1m 12.40 (1.80)
SF—23/12/–/–

---

## 1677

BAY H'CAP (0-90) £2782.50 (£770.00: £367.50)          7f 140y          4-15 (4-16)

(Weights raised 4 lb)

12106 **Ler Cru (IRE)** (64) *(CEBrittain)* 3–8-6 GDuffield (5) (lw: chsd ldr: led over 1f out:
rdn out) ....................................................................................... —1
1261★ Premier Prince (58) *(LGCottrell)* 6–8-10 TRogers (1) (lw: a.p: hrd rdn over 2f
out: unable qckn) ......................................................................... 2½.2
13443 Mulciber (72) (bl) (Fav) *(GHarwood)* 4–9-10 TQuinn (2) (led 6f: hrd rdn: one
pce) ............................................................................................ 1½.3
1343 Amethystine (USA) (62) *(RJHodges)* 6–8-7 ‡7SDrowne (7) (a.p: hrd rdn over 2f
out: one pce) ............................................................................... hd.4
1404 Saxon Lad (USA) (45) (v) *(GPEnright)* 6–7-11 GBardwell (8) (bhd fnl 4f) ....... 6.5
1598 Yonge Tender (56) (bl) *(CNWilliams)* 5–8-1 ‡7AntoinetteArmes (6) (bhd fnl 4f) 1½.6
8956 Glassblower (68) *(RAkehurst)* 5–9-6 GCarter (4) (a bhd) ........................ 15.7

**2/1** Mulciber, **3/1** Premier Prince, LER CRU (IRE)(7/2—5/1), **6/1** Yonge Tender(tchd 10/1), **8/1** Amethystine
(USA)(6/1—9/1), **10/1** Glassblower(7/1—11/1), **50/1** Saxon Lad (USA). CSF £12.49, CT £19.91. Tote £5.30:
£2.20 £2.20 (£10.10). Mrs C. E. Brittain (NEWMARKET) bred by Peter Kelly in Ireland. 7 Rn  1m 30.40 (1.90)
SF—29/25/34/16/–/–

**1678**  SKEWBALD STKS (Mdn 3-Y.O) £1932.00 (£532.00: £252.00)    7f (AWT)  4-45 (4-46)

6345 **Badawiah (74)** (Fav) *(WAO'Gorman)* 8-9 GCarter (1) (b: lw: hld up: led on bit
   ins fnl f: comf) ............................................................................... —1
13895 Whitehall (IRE) **(63)** *(CRNelson)* 9-0 GBardwell (4) (lw: a:p: rdn over 3f out: ev
   ch ins fnl f: r.o) ........................................................................... nk.2
 1320 Grand Fellow (IRE) **(51)** (bl) *(JDBethell)* 8-11 ‡3DBiggs (6) (a.p: led over 2f out tl
   ins fnl f: unable qckn) ................................................................... 4.3
14336 Blue Drifter (IRE) *(JSutcliffe)* 9-0 BRouse (3) (a.p: rdn over 2f out: one pce) ... 2½.4
  804 Highland Flame *(ANLee)* 8-9 ‡5DHarrison (2) (nvr nr to chal) ....................... nk.5
14325 Selaginella **(68)** *(MRChannon)* 8-9 TQuinn (5) (lw: led over 4f) ....................... 3.6
 1323 Quantity Surveyor *(SirMarkPrescott)* 9-0 GDuffield (7) (lw: bhd fnl 3f) ............. 2½.7

**4/11** BADAWIAH, **8/1** Selaginella(op 3/1), **11/1** Blue Drifter (IRE)(14/1—8/1), **12/1** Whitehall (IRE)(op 7/1),
Quantity Surveyor(op 6/1), **33/1** Ors. CSF £5.73, Tote £1.40: £1.10 £6.70 (£6.30). Mr S. Fustok (NEWMARKET)
bred by Ahmed M. Foustok. 7 Rn                                            1m 25.28 (1.28)
                                                        SF—34/38/23/18/12/3

**1679**  GREY H'CAP (3-Y.O) (0-70) £2265.20 (£627.20: £299.60)    1½m (AWT) 5-20 (5-21)
                              (Weights raised 10 lb)
14085 **Pride of Britain (CAN) (46)** *(LGCottrell)* 8-2 ‡5DHarrison (7) (lw: a:p: led over 3f
   out: hrd rdn over 1f out: r.o wl) ..................................................... —1
14264 Witches Coven **(50)** *(MBell)* 8-4 ‡7PTurner (6) (swtg: chsd ldr: led 4f out tl over 3f
   out: ev ch over 1f out: unable qckn) ............................................... 4.2
1572★ Ideal Candidate **(49)** *(CACyzer)* 8-10 (5x) GCarter (1) (a.p: rdn over 2f out: one
   pce) ............................................................................................ 4.3
 9153 Perforate **(60)** (bl) *(SirMarkPrescott)* 9-7 GDuffield (5) (b.hind: hld up: hrd
   rdn over 1f out: one pce) .............................................................. 2½.4
12503 Millador **(50)** *(MHTompkins)* 8-4 ‡7SMulvey (3) (nvr nr to chal) ..................... ½.5
 1408 Benefact (USA) **(42)** *(DWPArbuthnot)* 8-3 GBardwell (2) (led 8f) ...................... 10.6
14464 Dancing Years (USA) **(58)** (v) *(MRChannon)* 9-5 BRouse (4) (a bhd) ............... 1½.7
14884 Anguish (IRE) **(53)** *(NACallaghan)* 8-7 ‡7JTate (8) (a bhd) ............................ 2½.8

**11/4** Perforate, **7/2** PRIDE OF BRITAIN (CAN), **9/2** Dancing Years (USA), **5/1** Ideal Candidate(6/1—4/1), **6/1**
Witches Coven, Anguish (IRE)(7/2—13/2), **25/1** Ors. CSF £23.71, CT £94.29. Tote £4.00: £1.50 £1.50 £2.00
(£7.30). Pride of Britain Limited (CULLOMPTON) bred by Blue Spruce Farm in Canada. 8 Rn  2m 29.63 (0.23)
                                                        SF—38/32/30/35/17/–

**1680**  LEVY BOARD APP'CE H'CAP (0-70) £2226.00 (£616.00: £294.00)
       1¼m                                                            5-55 (5-56)
                              (Weights raised 1 lb)
15425 **Dutch Czarina (43)** *(MissBSanders)* 4-8-11 AntoinetteArmes (1) (lw: mde all:
   rdn out) ...................................................................................... —1
11062 Marzocco **(56)** *(JFfitch-Heyes)* 4-9-10 DBiggs (2) (lw: 3rd st: rdn over 2f out: ev
   ch ins fnl f: r.o) ........................................................................... hd.2
14042 Now Boarding **(39)** *(RJHodges)* 5-8-7 SDrowne (3) (2nd st: ev ch ins fnl f:
   unable qckn) ............................................................................... 1.3
13852 Plan Ahead **(68)** (Fav) *(GLewis)* 3-9-5 ‡5DRussell (4) (4th st: rdn over 2f out: r.o
   one pce) ..................................................................................... 2.4

**Evens** Plan Ahead(11/8—8/11), **15/8** Marzocco, **5/1** Now Boarding(op 3/1), **10/1** DUTCH CZARINA(7/1—12/
1). CSF £26.12, Tote £10.50 (£8.70). Mr Leonard Fuller (EPSOM) bred by L. Fuller. 4 Rn  2m 15.55 (12.55)
T/Plpt: £42.70 (54.5 Tckts).                                                         AK

## LINGFIELD (L-H)
### Saturday, June 27th [Turf Good to firm, Firm back st, AWT Standard]
Going Allowance: Turf: minus 0.40 sec (F); AWT: minus 0.50 sec (FS)    Wind: almost nil

Stalls: high

**1681**  JAKSBRIDGE APP'CE GRADUATION STKS (3-Y.O) £1330.20 (£367.20: £174.60)
       7f (AWT)                                                      6-00 (6-02)

12183 **Confronter (77)** (bl) (Fav) *(PFICole)* 9-4 JDSmith (1) (swtg: w ldr: led over 3f
   out: unchal) ............................................................................... —1
 1476 Taylor Quigley (USA) **(94)** (bl) *(CNAllen)* 9-4 PBowe (4) (hld up: rdn over 2f out:
   chsd wnr fnl f: no imp) ................................................................ 5.2

*1540²* Lamore Ritorna **(50)** *(KOCunningham-Brown)* 8-6 JHunter (3) (swtg: led over
3f: wknd fnl f) ........................................................................................ 5.3
　　　 Hullo Mary Doll *(RIngram)* 8-1 ‡⁵RossBerry (5) (leggy: bit bkwd: s.s: a wl bhd) 10.4
1315 Executive Flare *(DSasse)* 8-1 ‡⁵SMulvey (2) (s.s: a wl bhd: t.o) ...................... 15.5

**10/11** CONFRONTER, **11/10** Taylor Quigley (USA), **11/1** Lamore Ritorna(8/1—12/1), **50/1** Ors. CSF £2.23, Tote
£2.10: £1.10 £1.20 (£1.50). Mr Yahya Nasib (WHATCOMBE) bred by Hamilton Bloodstock (UK) Ltd. 5 Rn
1m 23.37 (0.53 under best; U.63)
SF—60/45/18/–/–

---

**1682**　　LYDD CLAIMING STKS　　£1720.80 (£478.80: £230.40)　　**1m (AWT)**　　6-30 (6-32)

*1376* Tara's Delight **(59)** *(WAO'Gorman)* 5-8-3 ‡⁵EmmaO'Gorman (8) (b.hind: s.s:
hdwy 5f out: led over 3f out: clr over 1f out: all out) ....................... —1
*1550* Hubbers Favourite **(49)** *(MrsNMacauley)* 4-8-5 MHills (2) (lw: led over 4f:
bmpd on ins 3f out: r.o wl ins fnl f) ................................................ s.h.2
　　　 Pearl Ransom *(WGRWightman)* 5-8-3 GBardwell (5) (rdn thrght: lost pl 5f out:
rallied over 1f out: r.o wl ins fnl f) ................................................. hd.3
　　　 Harcliff *(DJSCosgrove)* 3-9-0 AShoults (9) (b.hind: leggy: lt-f: s.s: hdwy 5f out:
lost pl 3f out: rallied over 1f out: r.o) ............................................ 1½.4
*1087²* Dazzle the Crowd (IRE) **(62)** (Fav) *(CACyzer)* 4-9-5 GCarter (6) (lw: rdn thrght:
hdwy over 2f out: r.o one pce) .......................................................... 2.5
*1323* Drop a Curtsey *(JDBethell)* 3-7-10 RStreet (3) (s.s: nvr nr to chal) ............... ¾.6
*1366* Tapestry Dancer **(32)** *(MJHaynes)* 4-8-8 BRaymond (4) (bhd fnl 5f) ................. hd.7
　　　 Modern Art (IRE) *(RAkehurst)* 4-8-9 ‡³RPerham (1) (prom over 4f) ................. 1½.8
*1544* One Magic Moment (IRE) **(53)** *(CACyzer)* 4-8-7 ‡⁷TMcLaughlin (7) (a.p: bmpd
3f out: wknd over 1f out) .................................................................... 1.9
*Stewards Enquiry: Obj. to Tara's Delight by Hills overruled.*

**6/4** Dazzle the Crowd (IRE), **5/2** TARA'S DELIGHT, **11/2** Hubbers Favourite, **7/1** Modern Art (IRE)(4/1—8/1),
**10/1** Harcliff, **16/1** One Magic Moment (IRE), Tapestry Dancer, **50/1** Ors. CSF £16.48, Tote £3.30: £1.30 £2.00
£5.00 (£7.30). Maclaine Racing (NEWMARKET) bred by Burton Agnes Stud Co Ltd. 9 Rn　　1m 39.21 (2.51)

---

**1683**　　MANSTON STKS (Mdn 3-Y-O) £1242.00 (£342.00: £162.00)　　**6f**　　7-00 (7-11)

*1315⁴* **Raven Runner (USA)** (Fav) *(IABalding)* 8-9 JReid (4) (mde all: hrd rdn 1f out:
r.o wl) ................................................................................................. —1
*1389³* Sharptino *(RAkehurst)* 8-11 ‡³RPerham (1) (lw: hld up: rdn over 2f out: hung rt
over 1f out: unable qckn) ................................................................. 7.2
　　　 Wandering Stranger **(78)** *(PJMakin)* 8-6 ‡³TSprake (2) (bit bkwd: w wnr: rdn
over 2f out: wknd fnl f) .................................................................... 1½.3
*1244³* Gizlaan (USA) *(BHanbury)* 8-9 BRaymond (5) (swtg: a.p: one pce fnl 2f) ........... 2.4
*1183⁶* Under the Bridge *(PWHarris)* 9-0 SWhitworth (6) (outpcd: nvr nr to chal) ........ 4.5
*1433⁵* Sea-Deer *(LJHolt)* 9-0 MHills (3) (bit bkwd: hdwy 2f out: wknd over 1f out) ..... ¾.6
*1183⁴* Emigrator (bl) *(GBlum)* 9-0 AShoults (9) (prom 4f) .................................. 2½.7
　　　 Bridge Street Boy *(DJGMurray-Smith)* 9-0 GCarter (7) (cmpt: bhd fnl 4f) ........ 5.8
*1276* Fisianna (50/1) Withdrawn (ref to ent stalls) : not under orders

**5/6** RAVEN RUNNER (USA), **11/2** Wandering Stranger, **6/1** Sharptino(op 5/2), **8/1** Gizlaan (USA)(tchd 14/1), **9/1**
Bridge Street Boy(8/1—20/1), **10/1** Sea-Deer(op 5/1), **33/1** Emigrator, **50/1** Under the Bridge. CSF £6.71, Tote
£2.20: £1.30 £1.90 £1.30 (£3.90). Mrs Ronald K. Kirk (KINGSCLERE) bred by Ronald K. Kirk in USA. 8 Rn
1m 10.05 (1.45)
SF—18/–/–/–/–/–

---

**1684**　　CAVALIER H'CAP (F & M) (0-90) £2490.00 (£690.00: £330.00)　　**7f**　　7-30 (7-34)

*1418²* **Storm Dove (USA) (88)** (Fav) *(RCharlton)* 3-9-11 MHills (4) (hld up: led over 2f
out: rdn over 1f out: easily) ............................................................... —1
*821⁵* La Dama Bonita (USA) **(83)** *(DWPArbuthnot)* 3-9-6 JReid (1) (lw: hld up: rdn
over 2f out: chsd wnr over 1f out: no imp) ...................................... 3½.2
*1545⁴* Running Glimpse (IRE) **(65)** *(MissBSanders)* 4-8-11 DaleGibson (5) (a.p: rdn
over 2f out: one pce) ........................................................................ 2.3
*1201* Caroles Express **(77)** *(RAkehurst)* 4-9-6 ‡³RPerham (2) (lw: led over 4f: one
pce) ................................................................................................... s.h.4
*1615⁴* Gabibti (IRE) **(60)** *(BGubby)* 4-8-6 GCarter (3) (swtg: spd over 4f) ................. 7.5

**4/5** STORM DOVE (USA), **4/1** La Dama Bonita (USA), **6/1** Gabibti (IRE), Caroles Express(4/1—7/1), **11/1**
Running Glimpse (IRE)(7/1—12/1). CSF £4.36, Tote £1.70: £1.40 £2.00 (£2.30). Mr K. Abdulla
(BECKHAMPTON) bred by Juddmonte Farms Inc in USA. 5 Rn
1m 21.69 (0.39)
SF—63/51/38/46/18

**1685**      BARRACUDA H'CAP (0-80) £1562.00 (£432.00: £206.00)      **6f (AWT)**      8-00 (8-01)

15086 **Never so Sure (76)** (Jt-Fav) *(ABailey)* 4-9-7 ‡7PBowe (3) (a.p: led over 1f out:
  rdn out) ................................................................................................ —1
13432 Idir Linn (IRE) **(44)** (v) *(DJGMurray-Smith)* 4-7-10 CRutter (11) (hdwy
  over 3f out: hrd rdn over 1f out: unable qckn) ................................ 4.2
15515 The Shanahan Bay **(54)** (v) *(MrsNMacauley)* 7-8-13 ‡3TSprake (1) (b: led over 4f:
  one pce) ............................................................................................ 1½.3
16144 Young Shadowfax **(56)** (Jt-Fav) *(CNAllen)* 5-8-11 ‡7GForster (2) (b.nr hind: a.p:
  hrd rdn over 1f out: one pce) ........................................................ s.h.4
1500 Executive Spirit **(69)** *(DSasse)* 3-8-13 GCarter (4) (hdwy over 1f out: nvr nrr) ... ½.5
12125 Invocation **(76)** *(AMoore)* 5-9-11 ‡3RPerham (10) (b.nr hind: nvr nr to chal) ...... ¾.6
830 Erik Odin **(46)** *(MrsLPiggott)* 5-7-5 ‡7GMilligan 7 (b: b.hind: prom over 4f) ... 2½.7
1266 Gallery Artist (IRE) **(63)** *(RGuest)* 4-9-1 JReid (5) (lw: prom over 3f) ................ 3.8
13435 Inswinger **(41)** (bl) *(WGRWightman)* 6-7-7 GBardwell (6) (bhd fnl 2f) .............. 2.9
10006 Cellito (IRE) **(57)** (bl) *(WAO'Gorman)* 3-7-12(2) ‡3EmmaO'Gorman (8) (lw: a
  bhd) ............................................................................................ 1½.10
15906 Kirriemuir **(43)** *(KOCunningham-Brown)* 4-7-9(2) SDawson (12) (a bhd) ......... hd.11
1551 Super Heights **(59)** *(MissAJWhitfield)* 4-8-11 DaleGibson (9) (lw: rdn thrght: a
  bhd) ............................................................................................ s.h.12
  LONG HANDICAP: Kirriemuir 7-2.

**5/1** Idir Linn (IRE), Young Shadowfax, NEVER SO SURE(op 8/1), **6/1** The Shanahan Bay, **13/2** Invocation, **10/1**
Inswinger(8/1—12/1), **12/1** Super Heights, Cellito (IRE), **14/1** Gallery Artist (IRE), Kirriemuir, **16/1** Erik
Odin, **20/1** Executive Spirit. CSF £29.94, CT £144.69. Tote £11.10: £3.30 £1.80 £2.40 (£30.30). Mrs M.
O'Donnell (TARPORLEY) bred by Mrs P. A. Clark. 12 Rn      1m 10.87 (0.27)
  SF—41/–/1/–/–/–

**1686**      CRUMPET H'CAP (0-80) £1618.00 (£448.00: £214.00)      **1m 3f 106y**      8-30 (8-31)
  (Weights raised 5 lb)

13826 **Holiday Island (72)** (Fav) *(CEBrittain)* 3-9-1 MHills (7) (2nd st: led over 2f out:
  hrd rdn over 1f out: r.o wl) ............................................................ —1
1190 Sandro **(56)** *(JRFanshawe)* 3-7-13 GBardwell (2) (led 9f: hrd rdn over 1f out:
  unable qckn) .................................................................................... 2½.2
1612 Smiling Chief (IRE) **(54)** *(CACyzer)* 4-8-11 JReid (4) (lw: 3rd st: hrd rdn over 1f
  out: one pce) .................................................................................. 1.3
14305 Puff Puff **(52)** *(MissBSanders)* 6-8-9 GCarter (6) (dwlt: 5th st: rdn over 2f out:
  one pce) ............................................................................................ 1½.4
14136 Island Blade (IRE) **(52)** *(RAkehurst)* 3-7-9 SDawson (5) (6th st: wknd over 1f out) 8.5
  Miss Sarahsue **(36)** *(JELong)* 6-7-7 RStreet (3) (swtg: hdwy over 6f out: wknd
  4f out) ............................................................................................ 8.6
  Every One a Gem **(67)** *(MDixon)* 5-9-10 DaleGibson (1) (bit bkwd: 4th st: wknd
  over 3f out) ...................................................................................... 15.7
  LONG HANDICAP: Miss Sarahsue 6-6.

**2/1** HOLIDAY ISLAND(op 3/1), **100/30** Puff Puff, **4/1** Smiling Chief (IRE), **5/1** Every One a Gem(8/1—10/1), **6/1**
Island Blade (IRE)(op 7/2), **13/2** Sandro(op 7/2), **50/1** Miss Sarahsue. CSF £15.39, Tote £2.90: £2.10 £3.10
(£10.60). Mr C. E. Brittain (NEWMARKET) bred by L. H. J. Ward. 7 Rn      2m 29.15 (7.15)
T/Plpt: £18.40 (92.45 Tckts).      AK

## 1114—**NEWCASTLE (L-H)**

### Friday, June 26th [Good to firm]

Going Allowance: St: nil sec (G); Rnd: minus 0.30 sec per fur (F)      Wind: slt half bhd

Stalls: high

**1687**      TYNE TEES TELEVISION NORTHERN LIFE APP'CE H'CAP (0-75) £3028.00 (£904.00:
  £432.00: £196.00)      **1¼m 32y**      5-45 (5-46)
  (Weights raised 3 lb)

713 **Jazilah (FR) (57)** (Fav) *(MrsGRReveley)* 4-9-0 NNorton (8) (swtg: mde all: drvn
  along over 2f out: styd on strly u.p fnl f) .................................... —1
15092 Buckingham Band (USA) **(44)** (bl) *(FHLee)* 4-8-1 TSprake (1) (hld up: hdwy on
  ins 3f out: hrd rdn & styd on fnl f: no ch w wnr) ........................ 3½.2
1329* Silver Haze **(60)** *(WAStephenson)* 8-9-3 JFanning (7) (trckd ldrs: effrt 2f out: r.o
  one pce fnl f) .................................................................................. ½.3
8915 Queens Tour **(37)** *(MBrittain)* 7-7-8(1) SMaloney (3) (b: lw: chsd ldrs: effrt 3f
  out: kpt on u.p: no imp) ................................................................ ¾.4
12956 Dawn Success **(61)** *(DWChapman)* 6-9-4 SWilliams (6) (lw: trckd wnr: effrt 2f
  out: wknd ins fnl f) ........................................................................ hd.5

965[5] Touch Above **(59)** *(TDBarron)* 6-9-2 VHalliday (4) (swtg: bhd: hdwy on outside over 2f out: nvr able to chal) .................................................. 1¹/₂.**6**

1421 Golden Torque **(67)** *(RBastiman)* 5-9-10 HBastiman (5) (lw: hdwy on outside appr st: rdn & lost pl over 2f out) ...................................... 12.**7**

875 Into the Future **(36)** *(APStringer)* 5-7-7 CHawksley (2) (lw: sn drvn along: sme hdwy appr st: sn lost pl) .............................................. 8.**8**

LONG HANDICAP: Queens Tour 7-5, Into the Future 6-9.

**6/4** JAZILAH (FR), **6/1** Touch Above(op 4/1), Buckingham Band (USA), Golden Torque(op 7/2), **13/2** Dawn Success, **7/1** Silver Haze, **20/1** Queens Tour, **50/1** Into the Future. CSF £10.49, CT £43.60. Tote £2.80: £1.30 £2.10 £1.30 (£6.10). Mr S. Aitken (SALTBURN) bred by Derrinstown Stud Ltd in France. 8 Rn   2m 9.88 (3.18)
SF—38/18/33/8/31/26

**1688** NORTHERN ROCK GOSFORTH PARK CUP (H'cap) (0-110) £11452.50 (£3420.00: £1635.00: £742.50)   **5f**   6-15 (6-20)

1607 **Viceroy (99)** (v) *(BBeasley)* 5-9-7 ‡7SWilliams (9) (trckd ldrs: led 2f out: r.o u.p fnl f) ........................................................................ —**1**

1393 Cumbrian Waltzer **(98)** *(MHEasterby)* 7-9-13 MBirch (6) (hdwy ¹/₂-wy: hrd rdn & ev ch fnl f: r.o) .......................................................... s.h.**2**

980[5] Eager Deva **(92)** *(RHollinshead)* 5-9-0 ‡7SWynne (12) (hld up: smooth hdwy & nt clr run over 1f out: r.o ins fnl f) .......................... 3¹/₂.**3**

1475[5] El Yasaf (IRE) **(83)** (Fav) *(MCPipe)* 4-8-9 ‡3FNorton (4) (lw: w ldrs: drvn along ¹/₂-wy: kpt on same pce) ........................................ hd.**4**

1380[3] Love Returned **(82)** *(WJarvis)* 5-8-11 MTebbutt (10) (lw: hld up: swtchd outside ¹/₂-wy: nt qckn over 1f out) ............................ 3¹/₂.**5**

1392[2] Lucedeo **(83)** *(JLSpearing)* 8-8-12 DMcKeown (11) (hld up: effrt 2f out: wknd 1f out) ................................................................ ¹/₂.**6**

1607 Heaven-Liegh-Grey **(85)** (bl) *(MJohnson)* 4-9-0 KDarley (7) (lw: led 3f: sn wknd) ¹/₂.**7**

1511[4] Barrys Gamble **(81)** (bl) *(TFairhurst)* 6-8-7 ‡3JFanning (5) (s.i.s: bhd: effrt u.p ¹/₂-wy: n.d) ........................................................ ¹/₂.**8**

1406⋆ African Chimes **(76)** (bl) *(WAO'Gorman)* 5-8-0 ‡5EmmaO'Gorman (8) (trckd ldrs tl wknd 2f out) ............................................ 1¹/₂.**9**

1199 Never in the Red **(91)** *(JBerry)* 4-9-6 JCarroll (3) (lw: chsd ldrs to ¹/₂-wy: sn bhd) 8.**10**

1483⋆ Fangio **(88)** *(WGMTurner)* 3-8-7 (7x) ‡3TSprake (1) (lw: chsd ldrs: drvn along ¹/₂-wy: sn wknd) ...................................................... 1.**11**

1392[4] Gondo **(77)** *(EJAlston)* 5-8-6 KFallon (2) (lw: rdn & bhd fr ¹/₂-wy) ............ 2¹/₂.**12**

**2/1** El Yasaf (IRE), **7/1** Lucedeo, African Chimes(10/1—12/1), **8/1** Fangio, Cumbrian Waltzer, **10/1** Gondo, **14/1** Eager Deva, Love Returned, **16/1** Never in the Red, **20/1** Barrys Gamble, VICEROY, **25/1** Heaven-Liegh-Grey. CSF £158.23, CT £2,108.75. Tote £43.00: £9.50 £2.00 £4.10 (£145.10). Mr Franco Gamma (HAMBLETON) bred by Jeremy Green and Sons. 12 Rn   61.53 sec (3.13)
SF—45/50/23/17/5/4

**1689** ANGERTON STKS (Mdn 2-Y.O) £3882.50 (£1160.00: £555.00: £252.50)   **6f**   6-45 (6-47)

1273[2] **So so** *(TDBarron)* 8-9 AlexGreaves (4) (trckd ldrs: led 2f out: r.o u.p fnl f) .......... —**1**

1151 Lettermore *(RMWhitaker)* 8-9 ACulhane (6) (lw: chsd ldrs: ev ch & rdn 1f out: edgd lft & styd on) ...................................................... 1¹/₂.**2**

Panther (IRE) *(CWCElsey)* 9-0 KDarley (3) (w'like: s.i.s: bhd: hdwy on outside 2f out: ev ch 1f out: carried lft & nt qckn) ...................... nk.**3**

The Premier Expres *(BBeasley)* 9-0 LCharnock (1) (w'like: str: bit bkwd: s.s: rn green: hdwy & wnt rt over 1f out: styd on wl) .............. 1.**4**

874[3] Garnock Valley (Fav) *(JBerry)* 9-0 JCarroll (2) (lw: w ldrs: led over 3f out to 2f out: wknd over 1f out) ............................................ 6.**5**

1279 Desirable Miss *(MBrittain)* 8-4 ‡5SMaloney (8) (led tl over 3f out: wkng whn bdly hmpd over 1f out) ................................................ 7.**6**

Tri My Way (IRE) *(RRLamb)* 8-9 PBurke (7) (leggy: unf: s.i.s: sn chsng ldrs: wknd 2f out) ............................................................ hd.**7**

Daves Chance *(TFairhurst)* 8-11 ‡3JFanning (5) (w'like: leggy: sn drvn along & wl outpcd) .......................................................... 3¹/₂.**8**

**8/13** Garnock Valley, **3/1** SO SO, **9/1** Panther (IRE), **11/1** The Premier Expres(op 7/1), **12/1** Daves Chance, **25/1** Lettermore, Tri My Way (IRE), **50/1** Desirable Miss. CSF £57.72, Tote £3.80: £1.30 £3.20 £1.50 (£46.70). Mr Geoffrey Martin (THIRSK) bred by Mrs S. C. Barron. 8 Rn   1m 17.68 (6.18)

**1690** BRANDLING STKS (2-Y.O) £3785.00 (£1130.00: £540.00: £245.00)   **7f**   7-15 (7-20)

1457[4] **Ardkinglass** (Fav) *(HRACecil)* 8-11 PatEddery (4) (lw: mde all: qcknd over 1f out: unchal) ........................................................ —**1**

Persian Brave (IRE) *(MBell)* 8-6 MHills (1) (w'like: scope: s.i.s: hdwy ½-wy: r.o
fnl f: no ch w wnr) ............................................ 3.2

266⁶ Exodus (IRE) *(MHEasterby)* 8-6 KDarley (6) (trckd ldrs tl outpcd fnl 2f) ............ 7.3

1291³ Razaroo (USA) *(JEtherington)* 8-11 TLucas (3) (swtg: chsd ldrs: rdn 2f out: sn
wknd) ........................................................ 3¹/₂.4

Admission (IRE) *(MHEasterby)* 8-6 MBirch (2) (wl grwn: scope: bit bkwd: sn
trckng ldrs: lost pl over 2f out) ...................................... 7.5

Royal Rebeka *(MBrittain)* 7-10 ‡5SMaloney (5) (leggy: unf: bit bkwd: chsd ldrs to
½-wy: sn rdn & wl bhd) ............................... dist.6

**1/4 ARDKINGLASS, 4/1** Persian Brave (IRE), **14/1** Razaroo (USA)(op 8/1), **25/1** Admission (IRE), **33/1** Exodus
(IRE), **66/1** Royal Rebeka. CSF £1.94, Tote £1.30: £1.10 £1.80 (£1.90). Sir David Wills (NEWMARKET) bred by
Sir H. D. H. Wills. 6 Rn                                                                                    1m 28.97 (4.67)
SF—26/12/–/–/–/–

## 1691

DATAFORM (U.K.) H'CAP (0-80) £7700.00 (£2300.00: £1100.00: £500.00)
1¹/₂m 93y                                                                        7-45 (7-47)

1044* **Daisy Girl (59)** *(JMackie)* 6-8-9 PatEddery (2) (lw: hld up: hdwy to ld over 2f
out: drvn out) .......................................... —1

1241⁴ Latvian (66) *(RAllan)* 5-9-2 SWebster (3) (lw: chsd ldrs: effrt over 2f out: hrd rdn
& kpt on fnl f) ....................................... 1¹/₂.2

1482² Demokos (FR) (43) *(APStringer)* 7-7-7 DaleGibson (5) (chsd ldrs: rdn 3f out:
r.o one pce) ........................................... 2¹/₂.3

1311⁴ Trojan Lancer (61) *(DrJDScargill)* 6-8-11 WRyan (1) (lw: bhd tl styd on fnl 2f) 1¹/₂.4

*1324*⁵ Tanoda (49) *(MBrittain)* 6-7-8 ‡5SMaloney (8) (lw: chsd ldrs: led over 4f out tl
over 2f out: grad wknd) ................................... 2¹/₂.5

1501³ Luks Akura (48) (v) *(MJohnston)* 4-7-5 ‡7CHawksley (6) (led 1f: chsd ldr tl lost pl
over 2f out) ........................................... 7.6

1256⁴ I Perceive (70) *(FHLee)* 5-9-6 DMcKeown (7) (lw:lt: hld up: smooth hdwy appr
st: rdn & fnd nil 2f out) ................................. ½.7

1047³ Westholme (USA) (78) (Fav) *(MHEasterby)* 4-10-0 MBirch (10) (hld up: lost pl
appr st: n.d after) ...................................... 5.8

1390* Father Hayes (USA) (66) *(BBeasley)* 4-9-2 NDay (9) (trckd ldrs: drvn along
appr st: sn wknd & bhd) .................................... 30.9

1518 Take One (50) (bl) *(RRLamb)* 6-7-7⁽³⁾ ‡7RHavlin (4) (led after 1f tl over 4f out: hrd
rdn & sn wl bhd) ....................................... ½.10

LONG HANDICAP: Demokos (FR) 7-4.

**11/4** Westholme (USA), **3/1** DAISY GIRL, **9/2** Father Hayes (USA), **7/1** Trojan Lancer, I Perceive, **9/1** Latvian,
**12/1** Demokos (FR), Luks Akura, **20/1** Tanoda, **50/1** Take One. CSF £30.09, CT £271.88. Tote £4.30: £1.70
£2.20 £2.80 (£19.50). Mr S. Taberner (CHURCH BROUGHTON) bred by S. Taberner. 10 Rn
2m 38.26 (0.14 under best: U.24)
SF—60/64/38/53/31/14

## 1692

DOBSON PEACOCK H'CAP (0-100) £7180.00 (£2140.00: £1020.00: £460.00)
1m                                                                                8-15 (8-20)

(Weights raised 9 lb)

1303³ **Piquant (80)** *(LordHuntingdon)* 5-9-8 PatEddery (1) (lw: mde all: drvn along 2f
out: r.o strly) ........................................ —1

1218 Showgi (USA) (85) *(JRFanshawe)* 3-9-3 WRSwinburn (2) (lw: chsd ldrs: drvn
along 3f out: hrd rdn, swtchd & styd on wl ins fnl f) ........... hd.2

1504* Blockade (USA) (72) (Fav) *(MBell)* 3-8-4 (5x) MHills (3) (t: swtg: trckd ldr gng
wl: effrt & ev ch 2f out: nt qckn fnl f) ...................... 1.3

1393 Resolute Bay (82) *(RMWhitaker)* 6-9-10 ACulhane (7) (lw: hld up: gd hdwy on
outside over 2f out: kpt on u.p: nvr nr to chal) ............. 2¹/₄.4

492 Martini Executive (65) (bl) *(BBeasley)* 4-8-7 LCharnock (5) (chsd ldrs: gd hdwy
on ins over 2f out: wknd jst ins fnl f) ...................... nk.5

1393 Petraco (IRE) (76) *(LJCodd)* 4-9-4 JCarroll (6) (effrt over 2f out: sn rdn & wknd) 6.6

1193² American Hero (74) *(CTinkler)* 4-9-2 MBirch (4) (chsd ldrs tl rdn & wknd over 2f
out: sn bhd) ............................................. 15.7

**7/4** Blockade (USA), **11/4** PIQUANT(7/4—3/1), **4/1** Showgi (USA), **11/2** American Hero, **10/1** Resolute Bay,
**16/1** Petraco (IRE)(op 10/1), **20/1** Martini Executive. CSF £13.84, Tote £3.20: £2.00 £2.50 (£5.00). The Queen
(WEST ILSLEY) bred by The Queen. 7 Rn                                                      1m 41.44 (2.44)
SF—36/30/14/26/8/1

## 1693

WILLIAM EDWIN NEESHAM GRADUATION STKS   £4560.00 (£1260.00: £600.00)
1¹/₄m 32y                                                                         8-45 (8-46)

1444* **Alhamad (89)** (Fav) *(HRACecil)* 3-8-11 PatEddery (2) (lw: led after 1f: pushed
clr over 1f out: comf) ................................. —1

1141³ Kasikci (82) *(RHollinshead)* 3–8-6 WRyan (3) (effrt over 2f out: sn rdn: styd on ins fnl f) ............................................................................ 7.2

Cumbrian Challenge (IRE) (88) *(MHEasterby)* 3–9-0 MBirch (1) (bit bkwd: plld hrd & led 1f: effrt over 2f out: wknd nr fin) ........................ 1½.3

**1/7** ALHAMAD, **11/2** Cumbrian Challenge (IRE), **14/1** Kasikci. CSF £2.56, Tote £1.20 (£2.60). Prince A. A. Faisal (NEWMARKET) bred by Nawara Stud Co Ltd. 3 Rn
2m 8.36 (1.66)
SF—50/31/36

T/Plpt: £271.20 (8 Tckts). WG

# NEWCASTLE (L-H)
## Saturday, June 27th [Good to firm]
Going Allowance: St: minus 0.15 sec; Rnd: minus 0.25 sec (F)      Wind: almost nil

Stalls: high

**1694**   DURHAM CLAIMING STKS (2-Y.O) £8155.00 (£2440.00: £1170.00: £535.00)
6f
2-15 (2-16)

1327* **Captain le Saux (IRE)** (Fav) *(MBell)* 8-9 WRSwinburn (8) (lw: trckd ldrs: nt clr run 2f out: qcknd to ld ins fnl f) ............................... —1

1375* Daytona Beach (IRE) *(RHollinshead)* 8-4 KDarley (7) (lw: mde most tl hdd ins fnl f: kpt on) ............................................................. 2.2

1513* Shadow Jury *(JSWainwright)* 8-9 GBaxter (6) (lw: w ldrs: rdn over 1f out: r.o one pce) .......................................................................... hd.3

1240² Grand Dancer (IRE) *(RJRWilliams)* 8-5 RCochrane (2) (chsd ldrs: hdwy & ev ch over 1f out: no ex wl ins fnl f) ........................................ nk.4

1450* Bold Seven (IRE) *(FHLee)* 8-11(1) RLappin (4) (chsd ldrs over 4f) ......... 8.5

751* Contract Elite (IRE) *(CWThornton)* 8-8 GDuffield (3) (lw: cl up to ½-wy: sn rdn & btn) ...................................................................................... 10.6

1291⁵ Free Market *(GMMoore)* 7-13 JLowe (4) (spd to ½-wy: sn rdn & wknd) ......... 1½.7

**Evens** CAPTAIN LE SAUX (IRE), **5/1** Shadow Jury, **6/1** Daytona Beach (IRE), **17/2** Grand Dancer (IRE), **9/1** Contract Elite (IRE), **10/1** Bold Seven (IRE), **50/1** Free Market. CSF £7.11, Tote £2.00: £1.40 £2.00 (£4.10). Mr P. A. Philipps (NEWMARKET) bred by Swettenham Stud in Ireland. 7 Rn; Captain le Saux (IRE) clmd W McGuire £40,200
1m 13.58 (2.08)
SF—35/22/26/21/–/–

**1695**   EARSDON STKS   £3730.00 (£1030.00: £490.00)   1m
2-45 (2-46)

1285² **Lead the Dance (101)** *(HRACecil)* 3–8-12 WRyan (2) (lw: trckd ldr: led over 1f out: styd on) ...................................................................... —1

808² Ernestan (100) (Fav) *(MHEasterby)* 3–8-12 MBirch (1) (hld up: effrt 3f out: wandered u.p: r.o towards fin) ............................................ 1.2

1168⁶ Badawi (USA) (95) *(JHMGosden)* 4–9-3 RCochrane (3) (led: qcknd 3f out: hdd over 1f out: no ex) ...................................................... 2.3

**6/4** Ernestan, **13/8** LEAD THE DANCE, **9/4** Badawi (USA). CSF £3.98, Tote £1.80 (£1.70). Sheikh Mohammed (NEWMARKET) bred by Sheikh Mohammed bin Rashid al Maktoum. 3 Rn
1m 41.90 (2.90)
SF—24/21/20

**1696**   JOURNAL 'GOOD MORNING' H'CAP (0-110) £7180.00 (£2140.00: £1020.00: £460.00)
7f
3-15 (3-17)

1445³ **Superbrave (72)** *(WJarvis)* 6–8-3 JCarroll (8) (lw: hld up: swtchd & effrt 2f out: str run to ld cl home) ..................................................... —1

1474 Nordic Brave (73) *(MBrittain)* 6–8-4 KDarley (2) (lw: w ldr: led over 2f out: r.o u.p: jst ct) .......................................................................... ½.2

1403 Duckington (69) *(MHEasterby)* 8–7-9 ‡⁵SMaloney (7) (lw: trckd ldrs: hdwy to chal ins fnl f: no ex towards fin) ........................................ ¾.3

1403⁵ Sharpalto (82) *(MrsGRReveley)* 5–8-13 JLowe (10) (lw: hld up: hdwy over 2f out: rdn appr fnl f: nvr able to chal) ........................... 5.4

1504² Northern Rainbow (78) *(PFICole)* 4–8-6 ‡³JFanning (9) (chsd ldrs: effrt over 2f out: r.o one pce) ................................................ 4.5

1463 Parliament Piece (97) *(RMWhitaker)* 6–10-0 WRSwinburn (5) (in tch: effrt over 2f out: no imp) .............................................................. hd.6

1474 Letsbeonestaboutit (89) (bl) *(MrsNMacauley)* 6–9-6 DMcKeown (3) (led tl hdd over 2f out: grad wknd) ..................................................... 3½.7

1403³ Rocton North (IRE) (89) (Fav) *(RHannon)* 4–9-6 RCochrane (6) (nvr gng wl: a bhd) ............................................................................. 2.8

1508³ Tusky **(82)** (v) *(MJCamacho)* 4–8-13 SMorris (4) (trckd ldrs: effrt over 2f out: sn btn) ............................................................................................................ 5.9

1488* Halston Prince **(66)** *(MrsJRRamsden)* 5–7-6 ‡⁵DHarrison (1) (lw: cl up 4f: sn rdn & wknd) ............................................................................................... 12.10

**2/1** Rocton North (IRE), **6/1** Northern Rainbow, **13/2** Sharpalto, **7/1** SUPERBRAVE, Duckington, Parliament Piece, **8/1** Halston Prince, **16/1** Tusky, Nordic Brave, **25/1** Letsbeonestaboutit. CSF £100.36, CT £749.03. Tote £9.90: £2.50 £5.70 £2.10 (£53.80). Mr Willie W. Robertson (NEWMARKET) bred by Woodditton Stud Ltd. 10 Rn
1m 24.88 (0.58)
SF—64/63/52/55/36/57

---

**1697**     NEWCASTLE BROWN ALE NORTHUMBERLAND PLATE (H'cap)   £42159.00
(£15681.00: £7590.50: £3177.50: £1338.75: £603.25)   **2m 19y**   3-50 (3-51)

(Weights raised 8 lb)

861² **Witness Box (USA) (95)** *(JHMGosden)* 5–9-9 GDuffield (9) (lw: a cl up: effrt over 2f out: edgd lft 1f out: led wl ins fnl f: jst hld on) ..................... —1

1459⁵ Cabochon **(72)** *(DMorley)* 5–8-0(1) PaulEddery (2) (lw: hld up: hdwy 2f out: swtchd 1f out: r.o wl: jst failed) ........................................ s.h.2

990² Satin Lover **(89)** (Jt-Fav) *(NTinkler)* 4–9-3 RCochrane (8) (lw: a cl up: rdn over 2f out: slt ld ins fnl f: sn hdd: r.o) ........................................ ½.3

1059 Hawait Al Barr **(96)** *(MRStoute)* 4–9-10 WRSwinburn (5) (b.off hind: led: qcknd 3f out: hdd ins fnl f: no ex) .................................... 1½.4

1256* Highflying **(79)** *(GMMoore)* 6–8-7 (3x) KFallon (12) (lw: hdwy 5f out: hrd rdn & edgd lft wl over 1f out: styd on) ............................... ¾.5

1534³ Line Drummer (USA) **(77)** *(PAKelleway)* 4–8-2 ‡³JFanning (11) (b: a chsng ldrs: one pce fnl 3f) ............................................. ¾.6

1211² Quick Ransom **(77)** *(MJohnston)* 4–8-5 DMcKeown (1) (hld up & bhd: styd on fnl 3f: nvr able to chal) ........................... ¾.7

1459² Requested **(70)** (Jt-Fav) *(RAkehurst)* 5–7-9 ‡³FNorton (10) (trckd ldrs: effrt appr st: wknd wl over 1f out) ........................ ¾.8

1361² Farsi **(81)** (bl) *(RHollinshead)* 4–8-9 (3x) WRyan (4) (prom: pushed along appr st: hdwy u.p 2f out: sn btn) .......................... ¾.9

1518* Beau Quest **(66)** *(RMWhitaker)* 5–7-8 (6x) DaleGibson (6) (lw: hld up: hdwy 7f out: no imp) .......................... 3½.10

990³ Star Player **(87)** *(RJBaker)* 6–8-10 ‡⁵DHarrison (3) (a in rr) ...................... 8.11

552 Mrs Barton (IRE) **(67)** *(BWHills)* 4–7-9 JLowe (7) (sn drvn along: lost tch over st) .......................................... 2½.12

1459 Aahsaylad **(78)** *(FHLee)* 6–8-1 ‡⁵NKennedy (13) (a last: rdn & lost tch 5f out: t.o) 13

Stewards Enquiry: Obj. to Witness Box (USA) by Eddery overruled.

**5/1** Satin Lover, Requested, **6/1** WITNESS BOX (USA), **13/2** Hawait Al Barr, **7/1** Highflying, **8/1** Cabochon, **11/1** Farsi, **14/1** Aahsaylad, Star Player, Beau Quest, **16/1** Quick Ransom, **20/1** Ors. CSF £52.40, CT £238.75. Tote £6.90: £2.40 £3.50 £1.90 (£54.20). Sheikh Mohammed (NEWMARKET) bred by Hill 'N' Dale Farms and Gainesway Farm in USA. 13 Rn
3m 25.48 (U.02)
SF—69/45/61/66/48/42

---

**1698**     WYNYARD CLASSIC NORTHUMBERLAND SPRINT TROPHY (H'cap) (3-Y.O) (0-115)
£11257.50 (£3360.00: £1605.00: £727.50)   **6f**   4-20 (4-30)

(Weights raised 5 lb)

884² **Big Hand (IRE) (73)** *(JWWatts)* 7–7 JLowe (7) (mde all: r.o wl fnl f) .................. —1

870⁵ Venture Capitalist **(82)** *(RHannon)* 8-2 NCarlisle (6) (lw: a chsng ldrs: hdwy over 1f out: nt pce to chal) ........................ 3½.2

1535⁴ Taufan Blu (IRE) **(95)** (bl) *(DMcKeown)* 9-1 DMcKeown (2) (reminders after 1f: bhd tl hrd rdn & hdwy 2f out: nrst fin) ............. 1½.3

1576² Ponsardin **(86)** (bl) *(SirMarkPrescott)* 8-6 GDuffield (5) (cl up tl wknd appr fnl f) 1.4

1400³ Heather Bank **(94)** *(JBerry)* 9-0 JCarroll (3) (chsd ldrs tl rdn & btn over 1f out) . ¾.5

1246⁴ Devon Dancer **(78)** (v) *(MHEasterby)* 7-7(5) ‡⁵SMaloney (4) (swtg: bhd: effrt over 2f out: nt clr run ins fnl f: n.d) ................... nk.6

1400* Orthorhombus **(101)** (bl) *(GLewis)* 9-7 PaulEddery (1) (lw: chsd ldrs over 4f: sn rdn & wknd) ........................... 5.7

LONG HANDICAP: Big Hand (IRE) 7-5, Devon Dancer 7-4.

**9/4** Taufan Blu (IRE), **100/30** Orthorhombus, **4/1** Heather Bank, **5/1** Ponsardin, **9/1** BIG HAND (IRE), Venture Capitalist, **12/1** Devon Dancer. CSF £74.12, Tote £9.30: £3.00 £3.40 (£27.70). Mrs M. M. Haggas (RICHMOND) bred by Holborn Trust Co in Ireland. 7 Rn
1m 12.72 (1.22)
SF—37/32/39/26/31/9

---

**1699**     E.B.F. HEXHAM STKS (Mdn 2-Y.O) £3622.50 (£1080.00: £515.00: £232.50)
**5f**   4-50 (4-56)

**Mistertopogigo (IRE)** *(BBeasley)* 9-0 DNicholls (8) (str: scope: bit bkwd: in tch: effrt 2f out: shkn up to ld wl ins fnl f) ........................ —1

10714 The Sharp Bidder (IRE) *(RHollinshead)* 9-0 PaulEddery (9) (lw: trckd ldrs: led over 1f out & qcknd: hdd wl ins fnl f: no ex) .............. 1¹/₂.2
14503 Hawaymyson (IRE) *(JHJohnson)* 9-0 KFallon (3) (hdwy 2f out: styd on: nrst fin) 4.3
12973 Press the Bell *(JBerry)* 9-0 JCarroll (10) (led tl hdd over 1f out: no ex) ............ 1¹/₂.4
First Slice *(JBerry)* 8-9 GDuffield (4) (leggy: lt-f: s.i.s: outpcd & bhd tl styd on fnl 2f) ................ 1¹/₂.5
1524 Gussie Fink-Nottle (IRE) *(TDBarron)* 9-0 AlexGreaves (5) (cl up tl grad wknd fnl 2f) ................ ¹/₂.6
14893 Dancing Domino (Fav) *(MHEasterby)* 9-0 KDarley (7) (in tch: hung lft ¹/₂-wy: no imp) ................ s.h.7
Doc Cottrill *(MrsJRRamsden)* 9-0 GBaxter (6) (w'like: leggy: s.i.s: bhd tl sme late hdwy) ................ 1¹/₂.8
12972 Indian Secret (IRE) *(BEWilkinson)* 8-11 ‡³JFanning (1) (chsd ldrs tl wknd over 1f out) ................ 4.9
720 Cracker Jack (bl) *(TFairhurst)* 9-0 SWebster (2) (sn outpcd & bhd) .............. 10.10

3/1 Dancing Domino, 4/1 Press the Bell, Indian Secret (IRE), 6/1 MISTERTOPOGIGO (IRE), Doc Cottrill, The Sharp Bidder (IRE), 8/1 Hawaymyson (IRE), 17/2 Gussie Fink-Nottle (IRE), 12/1 First Slice, 33/1 Cracker Jack. CSF £46.00, Tote £16.60: £3.50 £2.00 £2.20 (£100.40). Mr Giovanni Alessi (HAMBLETON) bred by Tullamaine Castle Stud in Ireland. 10 Rn
61.24 sec (2.84)
SF—22/33/22/6/–/–/–

**1700**     ROTHBURY H'CAP (3-Y.O) (0-80) £3850.00 (£1150.00: £550.00: £250.00)
1¹/₄m 32y                                                         5-20 (5-25)

(Weights raised 9 lb)

1335★ **Drummer Hicks (63)** *(Fav)* *(EWeymes)* 9-4 WRSwinburn (1) (lw: trckd ldrs: led 2f out qcknd: comf) ................ —1
14495 Tahitian (49) (bl) *(MrsJRRamsden)* 8-4 GBaxter (5) (hld up: effrt 3f out: styd on: nt pce of wnr) ................ 3¹/₂.2
13086 Nicely Thanks (USA) (66) *(TDBarron)* 9-7 AlexGreaves (8) (lw: hld up & bhd: effrt whn n.m.r 3f out: styd on: nrst fin) ................ 2¹/₂.3
Tales of Wisdom (62) *(SirMarkPrescott)* 9-3 GDuffield (4) (chsd ldrs: pushed along appr st: one pce fnl 2f) ................ hd.4
10702 Charioteer (62) *(PCHaslam)* 9-3 DMcKeown (2) (lw: bhd: effrt ent st: styd on u.p: n.d) ................ 3.5
1025 Dramatic Pass (IRE) (53) (bl) *(MrsGRReveley)* 8-8 KDarley (9) (cl up: rdn ent st: wknd over 2f out) ................ 2.6
13364 Philgun (64) *(CWCElsey)* 9-0 ‡⁵SMaloney (11) (led tl hdd 2f out: sn btn) .......... nk.7
1190 Haut-Brion (IRE) (54) *(WStorey)* 8-9 SWebster (3) (bhd tl styd on u.p fnl 2f: nrst fin) ................ 1¹/₂.8
12984 Very Evident (IRE) (61) *(BWHills)* 9-2 PaulEddery (6) (chsd ldrs to st: sn wknd) 10.9
12525 Doyce (63) *(JEtherington)* 9-4 NConnorton (7) (prom to st: sn bhd) ................ 10
15284 Mindomica (63) *(MBell)* 9-4 MTebbutt (10) (in tch to st: sn wknd) ................ 11
*Stewards Enquiry: Webster suspended 6-9/7/92 (excessive use of whip).*

4/1 DRUMMER HICKS, 9/2 Very Evident (IRE), 13/2 Tahitian, 7/1 Charioteer, 8/1 Nicely Thanks (USA), Philgun, Mindomica, Dramatic Pass (IRE), 11/1 Tales of Wisdom, 12/1 Doyce, 33/1 Haut-Brion (IRE). CSF £30.37, CT £188.92. Tote £4.60: £2.30 £2.90 £3.00 (£23.30). Mrs N. Napier (MIDDLEHAM) bred by Mrs N. Napier. 11 Rn
2m 9.89 (3.19)
SF—47/26/38/33/27/14

T/Trio: Race 4: £120.10 (18.9 Tckts). T/Plpt: £1,775.90 (5.05 Tckts).                AA

1500—**NEWMARKET (L-H)** July Course
**Friday, June 26th [Good to firm]**
Going Allowance: minus 0.30 sec per fur (F)                              Wind: nil

Stalls: high

**1701**     CHAMPAGNE POMMERY STKS (Mdn 2-Y.O.C & G) £3655.00 (£1090.00: £520.00: £235.00)     **6f**                                    2-00 (2-01)

**Wharf (USA)** *(Fav)* *(HRACecil)* 9-0 PatEddery (1) (unf: scope: a.p: led over 1f out: pushed out) ................ —1
Right Win (IRE) *(RHannon)* 9-0 MRoberts (4) (leggy: led over 4f out: eased whn btn ins fnl f) ................ 3¹/₂.2
Jallaaf (USA) *(LMCumani)* 9-0 LDettori (8) (leggy: scope: prom: rdn 2f out: sn outpcd) ................ 12.3
Najaran (USA) *(MRStoute)* 9-0 JReid (6) (cmpt: str: bit bkwd: in tch: no imp fnl 2f) ................ ¹/₂.4

Generic (FR) *(RWArmstrong)* 9-0 BCrossley (3) (rangy: scope: bit bkwd: chsd ldrs: outpcd over 2f out: kpt on fnl f) ................................ ³/4.5
1489 Mansooree (USA) *(AAScott)* 9-0 WRSwinburn (7) (w ldr tl wknd 2f out) ............ ³/4.6
1489⁵ Caldervale *(ABailey)* 9-0 BRaymond (2) (lw: n.d) ................................ hd.7
Scorcher (IRE) *(CEBrittain)* 9-0 SCauthen (5) (unf: bit bkwd: pushed along ¹/2-wy: sn bhd) ................................ 8.8

**1/2** WHARF (USA), **9/2** Right Win (IRE), **8/1** Najaran (USA)(op 5/1), **20/1** Jallaaf (USA), Mansooree (USA), Caldervale, **25/1** Scorcher (IRE), **33/1** Generic (FR). CSF £3.47, Tote £1.40: £1.10 £1.80 £1.90 (£4.20). Mr K. Abdulla (NEWMARKET) bred by Juddmonte Farms Inc in USA. 8 Rn
1m 12.25 (0.75)
SF—49/35/–/–/–/–

---

**1702** MARSHALL OF CAMBRIDGE H'CAP (3-Y.O) (0-90) £3557.50 (£1060.00: £505.00: £227.50) 5f
2-30 (2-31)

1535⁵ **Bodari (73)** *(DAWilson)* 8-8 MRoberts (3) (mde all: rdn out) ................ —1
1386⁴ Inherent Magic (IRE) **(77)** *(MMcCormack)* 8-12 AClark (5) (lw: hld up: hdwy appr fnl f: nt rch wnr) ................ 1.2
1113⁴ Hot Lavender (CAN) **(69)** *(CFWall)* 8-4 AMunro (2) (swtg: w wnr tl rdn & no ex appr fnl f) ................ hd.3
1535 Wild Honour (IRE) **(85)** *(WRMuir)* 9-6 SWhitworth (6) (chsd ldrs: rdn over 1f out: one pce) ................ s.h.4
1535 Allthruthenight (IRE) **(86)** *(LJHolt)* 9-7 JReid (1) (chsd ldrs: rdn & no ex appr fnl f) ................ ³/4.5
1522* Cranfield Comet **(70)** *(JBerry)* 8-5⁽²⁾ (8x) PatEddery (4) (lw: dwlt: hdwy 2f out: sn rdn & no imp) ................ 1¹/2.6

**11/4** Cranfield Comet, **3/1** BODARI, **5/1** Wild Honour (IRE), Inherent Magic (IRE), **11/2** Allthruthenight (IRE), **10/1** Hot Lavender (CAN). CSF £15.96, Tote £3.60: £2.20 £1.80 (£9.00). Mr R. J. Thomas (EPSOM) bred by Robert J. Thomas. 6 Rn
59.40 coo (0.10)
SF—56/56/47/62/60/38

---

**1703** TARTAN INTERNATIONAL H'CAP (0-105) £5744.00 (£1712.00: £816.00: £368.00) 1¹/4m
3-00 (3-04)

1203² **Barford Lad (79)** *(JRFanshawe)* 5–8-10 LDettori (6) (swtg: trckd ldrs: plld out over 1f out: led 1f out: edgd rt & rdn out) ................ —1
1124³ Anne Bonny **(86)** *(JRFanshawe)* 3–8-5⁽¹⁾ PatEddery (4) (lw: chsd ldr tl led over 1f out: sn hdd & no ex) ................ ³/4.2
1132⁶ Green Medina (IRE) **(68)** (bl) *(MBell)* 4–7-13 RHills (5) (led tl hdd & no ex appr fnl f) ................ 6.3
1200⁶ Andrath **(82)** (Fav) *(CEBrittain)* 4–8-13 MRoberts (3) (chsd ldrs: rdn & btn wl over 1f out: eased fnl f: t.o) ................ 20.4
1060 Line Engaged (USA) **(94)** *(PTWalwyn)* 4–9-11 AMunro (2) (chsd ldrs tl wknd qckly over 2f out: t.o) ................ 6.5
1169 Shahdjat (IRE) **(94)** *(KCBailey)* 4–9-11 JReid (1) (a wl bhd: t.o) ................ 8.6

**7/4** Andrath (IRE), **9/4** Anne Bonny, **4/1** BARFORD LAD, **13/2** Green Medina (IRE)(7/1—10/1), **16/1** Shahdjat (IRE), **33/1** Line Engaged (USA). CSF £12.34, Tote £4.50: £2.00 £1.40 (£6.00). Mrs Christine Handscombe (NEWMARKET) bred by W. L. Caley. 6 Rn
2m 3.45 (0.85)
SF—58/51/33/7/7/–

---

**1704** EASTERN ELECTRICITY STKS (Mdn 3-Y.O) £3817.50 (£1140.00: £545.00: £247.50) 1¹/2m
3-35 (3-41)

857⁶ *Spring (JLDunlop)* 8-9 BRaymond (7) (lw: hld up: hdwy over 3f out: led 1f out: pushed out) ................ —1
Grand Master (IRE) **(106)** *(PFICole)* 9-0 AMunro (1) (lw: a.p: led wl over 1f out: sn hdd: r.o) ................ 2¹/2.2
1069⁵ Alum Bay (Fav) *(HRACecil)* 9-0 PatEddery (6) (chsd ldr tl led 7f out: hdd wl over 1f out: eased whn btn wl ins fnl f) ................ 15.3
Chatterer (USA) *(GHarwood)* 9-0 SCauthen (4) (tall: scope: wl bhd tl stdy hdwy fnl 3f) ................ 4.4
Christmas Cactus *(JHMGosden)* 8-9 GHind (5) (w'like: unf: bit bkwd: a bhd) .... 6.5
1464 Paradise Navy *(CEBrittain)* 9-0 MRoberts (3) (lw: led tl hdd & hmpd 7f out: ev ch 4f out: sn wknd) ................ 6.6
857 Folkboat *(BWHills)* 8-9 JReid (2) (in tch tl wknd 4f out) ................ 6.7

**13/8** Alum Bay, **3/1** Grand Master (IRE), **7/2** SPRING, **10/1** Paradise Navy, **12/1** Chatterer (USA)(op 6/1), **20/1** Christmas Cactus, **25/1** Folkboat. CSF £13.21, Tote £3.80: £2.10 £2.20 (£6.10). Lord Halifax (ARUNDEL) bred by Lord Halifax. 7 Rn
2m 30.90 (1.10 under bst: 2.20)
SF—37/37/7/–/–/–

**1705**  EDEN PARK CLAIMING STKS (3 & 4-Y.O) £2560.00 (£760.00: £360.00: £160.00)
        1¼m                                                    4-05 (4-15)

785³ **Bowden Boy (IRE) (67)** (bl) (Fav) *(NACallaghan)* 4–9-0 PatEddery (16) (hld
        up: hdwy to ld ins fnl f: drvn out) ......................................... —1
     Nothing Doing (IRE) *(WJHaggas)* 3–8-0 RHills (10) (w'like: unf: bit bkwd: hld
        up: hdwy wl over 1f out: ev ch ins fnl f: no ex) ..................... 3.2
932  Big Pat (50) *(JPearce)* 3–8-0 PRobinson (15) (chsd ldrs: r.o wl ins fnl f) ......... 1½.3
1503³ By Arrangement (IRE) (65) *(RGuest)* 3–7-11 DaleGibson (2) (a.p: led over 1f
        out tl ins fnl f: one pce) ............................................... s.h.4
1317⁵ Bengal Tiger (54) (bl) *(JAkehurst)* 4–9-2 BRaymond (5) (lw: prom: ev ch
        over 1f out: sn btn) ..................................................... 1½.5
1505  Alcoy (IRE) (69) *(PAKelleway)* 3–8-1(1) GHind (12) (t: led tl hdd & one pce appr
        fnl f) .................................................................... 2½.6
1165  Chief of Staff (80) *(PFICole)* 3–9-2 AMunro (4) (hld up: hdwy 4f out: ev ch over
        1f out: wknd fnl f) ....................................................... ½.7
799⁵  Majed (IRE) (71) *(NACallaghan)* 4–9-6 MRoberts (6) (hdwy 3f out: nvr able to
        chal) ..................................................................... 2.8
868  Bit on the Side (IRE) *(WJMusson)* 3–8-3 JHBrown (17) (bit bkwd: nvr nr to chal) 6.9
     Carrantuohill (IRE) *(SPCWoods)* 3–7-11 BCrossley (13) (prom tl wknd wl over
        1f out) ................................................................... 2.10
1142  Evening Stables *(JWharton)* 3–7-13 CRutter (14) (in tch: rdn 4f out: sn btn) .. 1½.11
1411  Otter Bush *(GBlum)* 3–8-0 AShoults (9) (sn bhd) ........................... nk.12
1311  Iwan (52) (v) *(KAMorgan)* 4–8-12 NDay (7) (n.d) ............................ ½.13
1568⁵ Kentucky Chicken (USA) (36) (bl) *(MissLCSiddall)* 3–8-3 AMcGlone (3) (lw:
        n.d) ...................................................................... 2½.14
     Rahif *(MrsGRReveley)* 4–10-0 SCauthen (11) (bit bkwd: prom: ev ch 2f out: sn
        wknd) ..................................................................... 4.15
     Cream of the Crop (IRE) *(JWharton)* 4–9-10 JWilliams (1) (bhd fr ½-wy) ....... 4.16
1033  Sugar Loaf (IRE) (bl) *(NAGraham)* 3–8-6(1) JReid (8) (s.i.s: a.t.o) ........... 10.17

**9/2** BOWDEN BOY (IRE), **5/1** Chief of Staff, Rahif, **6/1** Majed (IRE), **13/2** By Arrangement (IRE), **15/2** Alcoy (IRE),
**12/1** Bengal Tiger (IRE), **16/1** Cream of the Crop (IRE), **25/1** Big Pat, **33/1** Ors. CSF £140.39, Tote £5.30: £2.00
£6.10 £4.40 (£112.90). Mr T. A. Foreman (NEWMARKET) bred by Lord Dundas in Ireland. 17 Rn; Majed (IRE)
clmd K Reveley £10,000                                                      2m 6.20 (3.60)
                                                                    SF—34/14/11/7/23/5

**1706**  ROBERT WALTERS TAX RECRUITMENT H'CAP (0-90) £3850.00 (£1150.00: £550.00:
        £250.00)   7f                                                    4-35 (4-42)
                              (Weights raised 2 lb)
1379★ **Jaldi (IRE) (61)** (Fav) *(JSutcliffe)* 4–8-2 MRoberts (6) (lw: a.p: led wl over 1f out:
        rdn out) .................................................................. —1
618²  Sahel (IRE) (80) *(JHMGosden)* 4–9-7 SCauthen (3) (lw: in tch: hdwy 3f out: rdn
        & ev ch over 1f out: no ex fnl f) ......................................... 1½.2
1206⁴ Tate Dancer (IRE) (80) *(RWArmstrong)* 3–8-12 PRobinson (7) (swtg: prom: led
        4f out tl wl over 1f out: one pce) ........................................ 4.3
1500⁴ Takenhall (58) *(MJFetherston-Godley)* 7–7-13 CRutter (4) (lw: bhd tl r.o fnl 2f:
        nvr able to chal) ......................................................... ½.4
1247  Final Shot (72) *(MHEasterby)* 5–8-13 GHind (9) (hdwy 3f out: one pce appr fnl f) 1½.5
1344  Foolish Touch (57) *(WJMusson)* 10–7-12 DaleGibson (8) (b: swtg: bhd: rdn 2f
        out: kpt on: nt rch ldrs) ................................................. ¾.6
813  Choir Practice (83) *(WJHaggas)* 5–9-10 NDay (10) (lw: swtg: dwlt: nvr trbld ldrs) hd.7
1379⁴ Hopeful Bid (IRE) (75) *(RHannon)* 3–8-7 BRaymond (2) (chsd ldrs tl wknd 2f out) 2.8
1387⁶ Croupier (90) *(CEBrittain)* 5–9-7 GCrealock (1) (swtg: prom over 5f) ......... 1½.9
1504⁶ Regent Lad (70) *(MissLCSiddall)* 8–8-11 PatEddery (12) (chsd ldrs: swtchd rt
        ½-wy: no imp fnl 2f) ...................................................... s.h.10
1500★ Native Idol (USA) (77) *(JRFanshawe)* 3–8-2 ‡⁷NVarley (5) (lw: in tch tl hmpd
        ½-wy: nt rcvr) ............................................................ nk.11
     Wing Park (82) *(GAPritchard-Gordon)* 8–9-9 JReid (11) (b: bit bkwd: led 3f:
        hmpd & sn t.o) ............................................................ 12

**2/1** JALDI (IRE), **9/2** Sahel (IRE), **6/1** Hopeful Bid (IRE), **8/1** Takenhall, **9/1** Native Idol (USA), **10/1** Regent Lad,
**12/1** Tate Dancer (IRE), Croupier, **20/1** Choir Practice, Foolish Touch, **25/1** Final Shot, **33/1** Wing Park. CSF
£12.00, CT £85.08. Tote £3.10: £1.30 £2.40 £3.80 (£6.30). Mr Albert Finney (EPSOM) bred by Albert Finney in
Ireland. 12 Rn                                                              1m 24.77 (0.37)
                                                                    SF—51/65/44/29/38/21

**1707**  BRITISH OLYMPIC APPEAL STKS (F & M) £4308.00 (£1284.00: £612.00: £276.00)
        6f                                                              5-10 (5-10)

1364★ **Western Approach (USA) (94)** (Fav) *(JHMGosden)* 3–8-10 PatEddery (3)
        (mde all: shkn up appr fnl f: comf) ....................................... —1

1467 Appledorn **(85)** *(BAMcMahon)* 5–9–6 JReid (5) (hdwy 3f out: ev ch over 1f out:
　　　　sn rdn & unable qckn) ............................................................. 4.2
11345 High Sevens **(95)** *(HCandy)* 3–8–12 CRutter (1) (hdwy 2f out: one pce appr fnl f) 1.3
14006 Splice **(92)** *(JRFanshawe)* 3–8–12 MRoberts (6) (sn pushed along: nvr trbld ldrs) 6.4
14833 Real Stunner **(70)** *(MPNaughton)* 5–9–4 GHind (4) (chsd wnr over 3f) ............ 1½.5
15252 Corn Futures **(76)** (v) *(JPLeigh)* 4–9–1 SCauthen (7) (lw: n.d) ...................... 6.6
11155 Share Holder *(MissGayKelleway)* 4–9–1 GayKelleway (2) (b.hind: spd over 2f) .. 2.7

**4/6** WESTERN APPROACH (85), **11/4** Splice, **5/1** High Sevens, **16/1** Corn Futures, **25/1** Real Stunner, **40/1**
Appledorn, **100/1** Share Holder. CSF £21.25, Tote £1.80: £1.10 £6.00 (£30.20). Mr K. Abdulla (NEWMARKET)
bred by Juddmonte Farms Incorporated in USA. 7 Rn　　　　　　　　1m 12.89 (1.39)
　　　　　　　　　　　　　　　　　　　　　　　　　　　　　　　SF—32/26/14/–/–/–

T/Trio: Race 6: £22.60 (43.8 Tckts). T/Jkpt: Not won; £1,129.15 to Newmarket 27/6/92. T/Plpt: £139.80 (30.1
Tckts).　　　　　　　　　　　　　　　　　　　　　　　　　　　　　　　Dk

## NEWMARKET (L-H) July Course
## Saturday, June 27th [Good to firm]
Going Allowance: minus 0.10 sec per fur (F)　　　　　　　　　　Wind: nil

Stalls: 3rd & 7th high, remainder low

**1708**　　KINGS HEAD, DULLINGHAM CLAIMING STKS (3-Y.O) £4012.50 (£1200.00: £575.00:
　　　　　£262.50)　**1m**　　　　　　　　　　　　　　　　　2-00 (2-01)

12132 **Wave Hill (90)** (Fav) *(HRACecil)* 9–10 PatEddery (2) (lw: hld up in tch: rdn to ld
　　　　　ins fnl f: drvn out) ............................................................. —1
　　　Kertale (IRE) **(60)** *(RBoss)* 8–6 LDettori (3) (a.p. led 2f out tl ins fnl f: r.o) .......... ½.2
　　604 Lonesome Train (USA) **(54)** (v) *(JHMGosden)* 9–2 WCarson (4) (a.p: led over 2f
　　　　　out to 2f out: one pce) ....................................................... 5.3
14083 American Boogie (FR) **(63)** *(CEBrittain)* 8–12 MRoberts (1) (led tl over 2f out:
　　　　　one pce) ................................................................... 2.4
13894 Little Park **(56)** *(GAPritchard-Gordon)* 8–2 ‡7PTurner (6) (hld up: rdn 3f out: no
　　　　　hdwy) ..................................................................... 3.5
12345 Soft Note (IRE) **(MBell)** 8–5 ‡7RAdams (7) (b.hind: nvr nr to chal) ................ ¾.6
　1503 Mansber (IRE) **(55)** *(PatMitchell)* 8–12 BRaymond (8) (in rr whn rdn 3f out: sn
　　　　　btn) ....................................................................... ¾.7
　1214 Wayward Son **(GLewis)** 8–12 JQuinn (9) (in tch tl over 2f out) ................... nk.8
　　　Vicky's Mark **(JMPEustace)** 8–7 PRobinson (3) (neat: scope: dwlt: a bhd) ...... 1½.9

**1/2** WAVE HILL, **7/2** American Boogie (FR), **16/1** Lonesome Train (USA)(op 10/1), **33/1** Little Park, Mansber
(IRE), **40/1** Ors. CSF £20.12, Tote £1.60: £1.10 £3.30 £2.60 (£18.20). Mrs H. G. Cambanis (NEWMARKET) bred
by Stilvi Compania Financiera S A. 9 Rn; Wave Hill clmd J.Whelan £16,950
　　　　　　　　　　　　　　　　　　　　　　　　　　　　　SF—46/26/21/11/–/–

**1709**　　SLIP ANCHOR STKS (Mdn 2-Y.O) £3655.00 (£1090.00: £520.00: £235.00)
　　　　　**7f**　　　　　　　　　　　　　　　　　　　　　2-30 (2-30)

14242 **Prevene (IRE)** *(PFICole)* 9–0 LDettori (1) (a in tch: led over 2f out: rdn over 1f
　　　　　out: r.o wl) ................................................................ —1
　　　Double Bass (USA) (Fav) *(HRACecil)* 9–0 PatEddery (5) (gd sort: scope: led tl
　　　　　over 2f out: unable qckn fnl f) ............................................. 1½.2
　1457 Friendly Brave (USA) *(WCarter)* 8–9 ‡5NGwilliams (2) (lw: a in tch: styd on one
　　　　　pce fnl 2f) ................................................................. 1½.3
　　　Safir (USA) *(JLDunlop)* 9–0 WCarson (3) (w'like: unf: hdwy 4f out: n.m.r 2f out:
　　　　　sn btn) .................................................................... 6.4
15026 Lagen *(CEBrittain)* 8–11 ‡3RonHillis (7) (bhd fr ½-wy) ....................... 3½.5
　　　Range Rider (IRE) *(CEBrittain)* 9–0 MRoberts (4) (cmpt: bkwd: w ldr: ev ch over
　　　　　2f out: sn wknd) .......................................................... 1½.6
　　　October Brew (USA) *(GLewis)* 9–0 BRaymond (6) (scope: sn outpcd: bhd fr
　　　　　½-wy) ..................................................................... ¾.7

**8/11** Double Bass (USA), **5/2** PREVENE (IRE), **8/1** Safir (USA), **11/1** Friendly Brave (USA), **12/1** Range Rider
(IRE)(op 6/1), **25/1** October Brew (USA), **33/1** Lagen. CSF £4.85, Tote £3.90: £1.70 £1.20 (£2.40). Mr Fahd
Salman (WHATCOMBE) bred by Swettenham Stud and Partners in Ireland. 7 Rn　　1m 26.27 (1.87)
　　　　　　　　　　　　　　　　　　　　　　　　　　　　　SF—61/56/46/33/19/17

**1710**　　BANSTEAD FRED ARCHER STKS (listed race) £10770.00 (£3210.00: £1530.00:
　　　　　£690.00)　**1½m**　　　　　　　　　　　　　　　　3-05 (3-05)

　　**Jahafil (105)** *(MajorWRHern)* 4–9–1 WCarson (5) (mde all: pushed out) ............ —1

1465⁵ Shambo **(107)** *(CEBrittain)* 5–8–11 MRoberts (6) (lw: hdwy 4f out: ev ch 1f out: hrd rdn & unable qckn) .................... 3.2

1168³ Tetradonna (IRE) *(RHannon)* 4–8–6 LDettori (3) (plld hrd early: trckd ldr: rdn & ev ch over 1f out: one pce) .................... 1½.3

1455 Desert Sun **(114)** *(HRACecil)* 4–8–11 PatEddery (4) (in tch: n.m.r 2f out: rdn & fnd nil appr fnl f) .................... 1½.4

648⁶ Surrealist (IRE) **(110)** *(BWHills)* 4–9–1 JReid (1) (lw: prom: rdn 3f out: wknd appr fnl f) .................... ¾.5

1194★ Torchon **(103)** (Fav) *(GWragg)* 4–9–1 MHills (2) (lw: bhd: rdn wl over 2f out: sn btn) .................... 3.6

**2/1** Torchon, **100/30** Shambo, **7/2** Desert Sun, **5/1** Surrealist (IRE), **10/1** JAHAFIL & Ors. CSF £39.68, Tote £10.90: £3.50 £2.20 (£22.20). Mr Hamdan Al-Maktoum (LAMBOURN) bred by Hesmonds Stud Ltd. 6 Rn
2m 30.84 (0.06 under best; 2.14)
SF—68/58/50/52/54/48

**1711** VAN GEEST CRITERION STKS (Gp 3) £17164.00 (£6382.20: £3031.10: £1282.70)
7f
3-35 (3-35)

1418★ **Toussaud** (USA) **(86)** *(JHMGosden)* 3–8–4 PatEddery (2) (qcknd thro gap to ld appr fnl f: sn clr: rdn out) .................... —1

1460★ Prince Ferdinand **(117)** (Fav) *(MMcCormack)* 3–8–12 JReid (1) (lw: hld up in rr: plld out 2f out: rdn & r.o fnl f: fin wl) .................... ¾.2

1456⁶ Casteddu **(109)** *(JWPayne)* 3–8–7 WCarson (4) (lw: hld up: rdn 3f out: hdwy 2f out: r.o fnl f) .................... nk.3

1463 Band on the Run **(98)** *(BAMcMahon)* 5–9–2 PRobinson (3) (lw: a in tch: kpt on fnl 2f) .................... 1.4

1467 Wilde Rufo **(105)** *(PAKelleway)* 3–8–7 MRoberts (6) (trckd ldr: led over 2f out tl appr fnl f: sn wknd) .................... 4.5

1456 River Falls **(114)** *(RHannon)* 3–9–1 BRaymond (5) (lw: led tl over 2f out: sn wknd) .................... 4.6

444 Forest Tiger (USA) *(MMoubarak)* 3–8–7 LDettori (7) (plld hrd early: prom to 2f out: sn wknd) .................... ¾.7

**11/10** Prince Ferdinand, **7/2** Casteddu, **9/2** Forest Tiger (USA), **7/1** TOUSSAUD (USA), **14/1** River Falls, **16/1** Wilde Rufo, **20/1** Band on the Run(op 8/1). CSF £15.21, Tote £7.00: £2.70 £1.50 (£5.30). Mr K. Abdulla (NEWMARKET) bred by Juddmonte Farms Incorporated in USA. 7 Rn
1m 24.80 (0.40)
SF—74/80/74/80/59/55

**1712** HASCOMBE STUD H'CAP (3-Y.O) (0-100) £4425.00 (£1320.00: £630.00: £285.00)
1m
4-05 (4-07)

**Speaker's House** (USA) **(91)** *(PFICole)* 9-6 PatEddery (2) (hld up last: hdwy wl over 2f out: led ins fnl f: rdn out) .................... —1

1516² Red Kite **(64)** *(MBell)* 7-7 JQuinn (4) (lw: a.p: w ldr ½-wy: led over 2f out tl ins fnl f: r.o) .................... 1½.2

Main Bid (IRE) **(92)** *(MMoubarak)* 9-7 LDettori (1) (a.p: outpcd 2f out: rdn & r.o ins fnl f) .................... hd.3

1476⁵ Mutabahi (CAN) **(88)** *(RWArmstrong)* 9-3 WCarson (5) (in tch: rdn 3f out: one pce fnl 2f) .................... 3½.4

1173★ Robingo (IRE) **(79)** (Fav) *(CEBrittain)* 8-8 MRoberts (6) (lw: led after 1f tl over 2f out: wknd over 1f out) .................... ½.5

1166⁴ Basilica **(69)** *(CEBrittain)* 7-7 ‡5BDoyle (3) (led 1f: prom tl rdn & btn over 2f out) .................... 1.6

Hidden Laughter (USA) **(86)** *(BWHills)* 9-1 MHills (7) (swtg: prom over 5f) .................... 4.7

**11/4** Robingo (IRE), **3/1** Mutabahi (CAN)(9/4—7/2), **4/1** Red Kite, **5/1** SPEAKER'S HOUSE (USA), **7/1** Main Bid (IRE), **14/1** Hidden Laughter (USA), **16/1** Basilica. CSF £23.22, Tote £6.10: £2.20 £2.10 (£12.10). Mr M. Arbib (WHATCOMBE) bred by Wakefield Farm in USA. 7 Rn
1m 40.89 (3.19)
SF—46/14/41/26/15/–

**1713** EWAR STUD FARM STKS (2-Y.O.F) £8893.75 (£2650.00: £1262.50: £568.75)
6f
4-35 (4-35)

**Ivanka** (IRE) *(CEBrittain)* 8-8 MRoberts (4) (scope: squeezed out s: last tl hdwy 2f out: led over 1f out: r.o wl) .................... —1

1384★ Greenlet (IRE) (Fav) *(MRStoute)* 8-8 PatEddery (2) (hld up: hdwy 2f out: ev ch 1f out: unable qckn ins fnl f) .................... 1½.2

1461⁶ Holly Golightly *(RHannon)* 8-11 JReid (5) (w ldrs: ev ch over 1f out: rdn & r.o one pce) .................... nk.3

1396³ Petite Epaulette *(WJarvis)* 8-8 WCarson (1) (led tl over 1f out: sn wknd) .................... 5.4

Les Etoiles (IRE) *(MMoubarak)* 8-8 LDettori (3) (unf: prom 4f: wknd qckly) .................... 20.5

8/13 Greenlet (IRE), **3/1** IVANKA (IRE), **13/2** Holly Golightly(3/1—7/1), **10/1** Les Etoiles (IRE)(6/1—12/1), **12/1** Petite Epaulette(op 6/1). CSF £5.46, Tote £4.70: £2.00 £1.10 (£2.70). Mr Ali Saeed (NEWMARKET) bred by Stackallan Stud in Ireland. 5 Rn
1m 14.41 (2.91)
SF—24/18/20/–/–

**1714**  NEWMARKET DAY CENTRE APP'CE STKS (Mdn) £2820.00 (£840.00: £400.00: £180.00)
1¾m 175y
5-10 (5-13)

1316² **Hidden Light (IRE) (78)** (Fav) *(MAJarvis)* 3–8-4 KRutter (4) (a.p: led over 3f out: hrd rdn over 1f out: r.o) ................................ —1
Santarem (USA) *(WJHaggas)* 4–9-2 RonHillis (8) (bit bkwd: hld up: grad hdwy fr 6f out: disp ld over 2f out to 1f out: one pce) ............. 2½.2
1220⁶ Bar Billiards (73) (bl) *(RFJohnsonHoughton)* 3–8-4 BDoyle (5) (led 2f: hdwy 4f out: styd on u.p fnl 2f) ................................ 4.3
1423³ Juris Prudence (IRE) (47) *(BAMcMahon)* 4–8-13 ‡3SSanders (3) (chsd ldrs: no hdwy fnl 4f) ............................ 2½.4
Flying Speed (USA) *(MCPipe)* 4–9-7 StephenDavies (2) (lw: a.p: led 5f out tl over 3f out: one pce) ................................ 6.5
1490² Baher (USA) (76) (bl) *(NACallaghan)* 3–8-4 JTate (7) (lw: led after 2f to 5f out: wknd qckly 3f out) .................... dist.6
Bootikin *(CWCElsey)* 4–9-2 NGwilliams (1) (in tch to ½-wy: sn t.o) .............. ½.7
Spring Play (bl) *(JAkehurst)* 8–9-4 ‡3DDunnachie (6) (a bhd: t.o fnl 8f) ............. dist.8

**6/4** HIDDEN LIGHT (IRE), **3/1** Baher (USA), **11/2** Flying Speed (USA), **13/2** Bar Billiards, **10/1** Santarem (USA), **12/1** Juris Prudence (IRE), **20/1** Bootikin, **40/1** Spring Play. CSF £2.50: £1.40 £2.20 £1.80 (£10.10). Lord Harrington (NEWMARKET) bred by Lord Harrington in Ireland. 8 Rn
3m 11.63 (5.63)
SF—19/28/12/18/20/–

T/Jkpt: Not won; £4,708.35 to Sandown 3/7/92. T/Plpt: £47.60 (160.5 Tckts).
RC

---

1338—**CHEPSTOW  (L-H)**
**Saturday, June 27th [Good to firm]**
Going Allowance: minus 0.30 sec per fur (F)                           Wind: nil

Stalls: high

**1715**  E.B.F. WOODPECKER STKS (Mdn 2-Y.O) £2464.50 (£682.00: £325.50)
6f 16y
2-20 (2-22)

**Alderney Prince (USA)** (Fav) *(PFICole)* 9-0 CRutter (4) (w'like: mde all: shkn up over 1f out: comf) ................................ —1
1135 Kintwyn (v) *(DRLaing)* 9-0 TyroneWilliams (2) (lw: swtg: a.p: jnd wnr 2f out: rdn appr 1f out: one pce) ................................ 1½.2
Hotel California (IRE) *(JWHills)* 8-9 BRouse (3) (lt-f: unf: prom tl outpcd 2f out: r.o u.p towards fin) ................................ s.h.3
1424 Junction Twentytwo *(CDBroad)* 9-0 MWigham (1) (bhd: rdn along ½-wy: kpt on ins fnl f) ................................ 1.4

**1/2** ALDERNEY PRINCE (USA), **9/4** Hotel California (IRE), **11/1** Kintwyn, **25/1** Junction Twentytwo. CSF £5.32, Tote £1.50 (£2.30). Mr Fahd Salman (WHATCOMBE) bred by Newgate Stud Farm Inc in USA. 4 Rn
1m 11.7 (2.7)
SF—10/4/–/–

**1716**  ROTHMANS ROYALS NORTH SOUTH CHALLENGE SERIES H'CAP (0-80) £3590.00 (£1070.00: £510.00: £230.00)   1m 14y
2-50 (2-52)

1376² **Buddy's Friend (IRE) (51)** *(RJRWilliams)* 4–8-10 AClark (9) (lw: a.p: led 2f out: rdn out) ................................ —1
1555³ Sooty Tern (51) (Fav) *(JMBradley)* 5–8-10 NAdams (4) (w ldrs: ev ch 2f out: unable qckn fnl f) ................................ 3.2
1339³ Lord's Final (37) *(CRBarwell)* 5–7-10 AMackay (8) (swtg: led to 2f out: kpt on one pce) ................................ 2½.3
1339 Lucky Noire (61) *(GHarwood)* 4–8-13 ‡7GayeHarwood (6) (lw: a.p: hmpd & swtchd lft 3f out: r.o one pce appr fnl f) ................................ 1½.4
1203 Valiant Words (63) (bl) *(RAkehurst)* 5–9-8 BRouse (5) (lw: hld up: effrt u.p 2f out: nvr nr to chal) ................................ 2.5
1421³ Sareen Express (IRE) (41) *(MrsJCDawe)* 4–7-9 ‡5ATucker (2) (swtg: in rr: rdn over 2f out: no imp) ................................ 4.6
1339⁵ Revoke (USA) (42) *(CJHill)* 5–7-12 ‡3DBiggs (7) (swtg: chsd ldrs: rdn wl over 2f out: eased whn btn fnl f) ................................ 1.7

1500² Dream Carrier (IRE) **(66)** (bl) *(RHannon)* 4–9–4 ‡7DO'Neill (1) (lw: w ldrs: swvd lft 3f out: rdn & wknd over 1f out) ...................................... 1¹/₂.**8**
 1343 Fay Eden (IRE) **(48)** *(RJHodges)* 4–8–4 ‡3TSprake (3) (bhd: rdn along ¹/₂-wy: no imp) ...................................... nk.**9**

**3/1** Sooty Tern, **5/1** Valiant Words, **11/2** BUDDY'S FRIEND (IRE), **7/1** Revoke (USA)(op 7/2), Dream Carrier (IRE)(op 4/1), Lord's Final, **10/1** Sareen Express (IRE)(5/1—11/1), Lucky Noire, **20/1** Fay Eden (IRE). CSF £21.39, CT £106.73. Tote £4.30: £1.30 £1.10 £3.10 (£6.00). Mr Colin G. R. Booth (NEWMARKET) bred by John and Mrs McNamara in Ireland. 9 Rn       1m 33.3 (0.8)
                                                  SF—48/39/17/29/32/–

---

**1717**      CHAFFINCH STKS (3-Y.O) £2984.00 (£824.00: £392.00)    **5f 16y**      3-20 (3-21)

1340★ **Echo-Logical (94)** (Fav) *(JBerry)* 9–4  GCarter (1) (lw: a.p: led over 1f out: sn clr: eased nr fin) ...................................... —**1**
 1314 Walk in the Park **(78)** *(RSimpson)* 8-8 ‡5ATucker (2) (lw: s.i.s: hld up: gd hdwy fnl f: fin fast) ...................................... ¹/₂.**2**
 1117 Vailmont (USA) **(97)** *(IABalding)* 8-10 ‡3SO'Gorman (3) (swtg: led tl over 1f out: rdn & outpcd fnl f) ...................................... 3¹/₂.**3**

**Evens** ECHO-LOGICAL(op 6/4), **6/5** Vailmont (USA)(op 4/6), **7/1** Walk in the Park(4/1—8/1). CSF £5.31, Tote £1.70 (£2.80). The Liverpool Daily Post and Echo Ltd (COCKERHAM) bred by Mrs M. J. Dandy. 3 Rn
                                                    58.6 sec (1.6)
                                                   SF—42/30/18

---

**1718**      MEDALLION ENERGY SAVING HOMES H'CAP (0-70) £2532.00 (£702.00: £336.00)    **7f 16y**          3-55 (3-58)

1445 **Beatle Song (60)** *(RJHodges)* 4–9-7 ‡3TSprake (12) (lw: a.p: led over 1f out: r.o strly) ...................................... —**1**
1589³ Charmed Knave **(53)** (Fav) *(DRLaing)* 7–9-3  TyroneWilliams (3) (lw: a chsng ldrs: led 2f out: sn hdd: rdn & no ex nr fin) ...................................... 1¹/₂.**2**
1339 Asterix **(59)** (v) *(JMBradley)* 4–9-9  JWilliams (2) (hld up: hdwy 2f out: r.o wl ins fnl f) ...................................... ¹/₂.**3**
*1267* Reina **(33)** (bl) *(JDBethell)* 4–7–4 ‡7KateDovey (1) (b.nr fore: prom: rdn over 1f out: unable qckn) ...................................... 2.**4**
1366 Moving Force **(40)** *(EAWheeler)* 5–8-4⁽²⁾ SWhitworth (7) (lw: chsd ldrs: effrt over 1f out: nvr able to chal) ...................................... 1¹/₂.**5**
1339 Rosietoes (USA) **(49)** *(LGCottrell)* 4–8-13  TRogers (8) (lw: prom: no hdwy fnl 2f) 1.**6**
1430 Lucky Barnes **(31)** (bl) *(FJYardley)* 5–7–9 AMackay (6) (led to 2f out: sn hrd rdn & btn) ...................................... ³/₄.**7**
          Spanish Love **(35)** *(CGCox)* 6–7–8 ‡5ATucker (11) (bkwd: m.n.s) ...................................... 3.**8**
1369⁴ Christian Warrior **(68)** *(RHannon)* 3–9-9 BRouse (9) (prom: rdn 3f out: sn wknd) ¹/₂.**9**
1434⁶ Juvenara **(41)** *(CJHill)* 6–8-5 NAdams (10) (a bhd) ...................................... 2.**10**
1193⁶ Sly Prospect (USA) **(64)** *(KWhite)* 4–9-7 ‡7AGarth (5) (a bhd) ...................................... ³/₄.**11**
          Latin Mass **(34)** *(ABarrow)* 4–7-12 RFox (4) (bhd most of wy: t.o) ...................................... 15.**12**

**3/1** Charmed Knave(tchd 9/2), **5/1** BEATLE SONG, **13/2** Juvenara(3/1—7/1), **7/1** Moving Force, Christian Warrior, **9/1** Asterix, **10/1** Rosietoes (USA), Spanish Love, **14/1** Sly Prospect (USA), **20/1** Lucky Barnes, **33/1** Reina, **40/1** Latin Mass. CSF £20.20, CT £124.73. Tote £6.20: £2.10 £1.50 £2.60 (£7.40). Miss R. Dobson (SOMERTON) bred by Littleton Stud. 12 Rn       1m 22.4 (1.9)
                                                  SF—47/38/42/3/12/18

---

**1719**      SWALLOW H'CAP (0-70) £2490.00 (£690.00: £330.00)    **2¹/₄m 33y**      4-25 (4-28)

1260⁶ **Winter Lightning (48)** *(PTWalwyn)* 3–7-12 RFox (6) (hld up in tch: 5th st: led ins fnl f: jst hld on) ...................................... —**1**
1419 Smilingatstrangers **(40)** *(MrsBarbaraWaring)* 4–8-10 NHowe (2) (hld up: mid div: gd hdwy over 1f out: str run fnl f: jst failed) ...................................... hd.**2**
1234² Natral Exchange (IRE) **(51)** (v) *(JWHills)* 3–8-1 TyroneWilliams (1) (chsd ldr tl led 10f out: rdn & hld ins fnl f) ...................................... 1¹/₂.**3**
1290 Vision of Wonder **(26)** *(JSKing)* 8–7-11 AMackay (5) (hdwy 9f out: 3rd st: rdn over 3f out: kpt on one pce) ...................................... 2¹/₂.**4**
1459 Patroclus **(50)** (Fav) *(RVoorspuy)* 7–9-7 SDawson (9) (swtg: hld up & bhd: styd on fnl 2f: nvr nrr) ...................................... 2¹/₂.**5**
1521⁶ Adjaristan **(52)** *(RSimpson)* 5–9-4 ‡5ATucker (4) (led 8f: 2nd st: wknd over 1f out) ...................................... 2.**6**
1361² Sonic Signal **(48)** (v) *(MJHaynes)* 6–8-12 ‡7DToole (10) (hld up: 6th st: nvr nr ldrs) ...................................... 1¹/₂.**7**
          Sifton's Pride (CAN) **(54)** *(GHarwood)* 4–9-10 AClark (7) (bkwd: chsd ldrs 12f: grad wknd: t.o) ...................................... 8.**8**

1190[5] Lidanzia **(38)** *(RJHolder)* 4-8-8 JWilliams (8) (chsd ldrs: 4th st: wknd 3f out: p.u
    & dismntd ins fnl f: lame) ...................................................................... 0

**7/2** Patroclus, **5/1** Lidanzia(tchd 10/1), Natral Exchange (IRE), **6/1** Sonic Signal, **7/1** Sifton's Pride
(CAN)(3/1—8/1), **10/1** Vision of Wonder, **14/1** WINTER LIGHTNING, **16/1** Smilingatstrangers(op 8/1), **20/1**
Adjaristan. CSF £166.55, CT £1,041.58. Tote £22.70: £5.00 £4.80 £1.40 (£254.70). Mrs R. B. Kennard
(LAMBOURN) bred by Mrs R. B. Kennard. 9 Rn        No time taken

**1720**     STARLING STKS (Mdn 3-Y.O) £2532.00 (£702.00: £336.00)     1½m 23y   5-00 (5-02)

864[4] **Rajai (IRE) (78)** (bl) (Fav) *(JLDunlop)* 9-0 AClark (1) (swtg: lost pl ½-way: 7th &
    rdn st: gd hdwy to ld over 2f out: sn clr) ............................. —1
1466 Sadler's Way **(73)** *(GLewis)* 9-0 BRouse (6) (swtg: led tl hdd over 2f out: kpt on
    one pce) ............................................................................ 4.2
1383[5] Dawn Flight *(LadyHerries)* 9-0 JWilliams (2) (bit bkwd: hld up: hdwy & 4th st: r.o
    one pce fnl 2f) ..................................................................... ¾.3
1420[5] Gallant Jack (IRE) **(64)** *(DHaydnJones)* 9-0 MWigham (4) (swtg: trckd ldrs:
    outpcd & 6th st: btn whn hmpd 2f out) ................................ 2½.4
    Oribi *(PFICole)* 8-9 CRutter (7) (b: b.nr hind: rangy: bit bkwd: s.i.s: sn chsng
    ldrs: 5th st: rn green: sn btn) ............................................ s.h.5
1404[3] City Line *(DRLaing)* 9-0 TyroneWilliams (3) (swtg: prom: 3rd st: rdn over 3f out:
    sn btn) .............................................................................. 5.6
512[6] Cryptic Clue (USA) *(MJHeaton-Ellis)* 9-0 NAdams (5) (bit bkwd: chsd ldrs: wnt
    2nd st: rdn & hdwy 3f out: sn wknd) ................................... s.h.7

**2/1** RAJAI (IRE), **3/1** Sadler's Way, **4/1** Oribi(2/1—11/2), **6/1** Dawn Flight, **10/1** Cryptic Clue (USA)(op 6/1),
**14/1** Gallant Jack (IRE), **20/1** City Line. CSF £8.02, Tote £2.40: £1.60 £1.30 (£2.80). Mr Hamdan Al-Maktoum
(ARUNDEL) bred by Kilcarn Stud in Ireland. 7 Rn     2m 34.4 (3.1)
       SF—33/25/23/18/12/7

**1721**     EXTRA LEVY H'CAP (0-70) £3027.50 (£840.00: £402.50)     1¼m 36y   5-30 (5-34)
                 (Weights raised 1 lb)

1063[2] **Samurai Gold (USA) (48)** (v) *(PTWalwyn)* 4-8-12 AMackay (8) (a.p: 3rd st: led
    2f out: hrd rdn: all out) ....................................................... —1
50 Pusey Street Boy **(39)** *(JRBosley)* 5-8-3 AClark (1) (swtg: hld up & bhd: gd
    hdwy 2f out: fin fast) .......................................................... hd.2
1341[6] Premier Dance **(42)** *(DHaydnJones)* 5-8-6 TyroneWilliams (10) (swtg: a.p: 4th
    st: jnd wnr over 1f out: rdn & nt qckn nr fin) ..................... 1½.3
1292[2] Supertop **(58)** *(PWHarris)* 4-9-3 ‡5ATucker (7) (hld up: hdwy 3f out: kpt on ins
    fnl f) ................................................................................ 1.4
    Lexus (IRE) **(48)** *(RJRWilliams)* 4-8-12 JWilliams (11) (swtg: bit bkwd: prom:
    5th st: rdn over 1f out: one pce) ........................................ 2.5
726 Clear Light **(60)** *(CASmith)* 5-9-10 MWigham (4) (hld up: effrt ent st: nt trble
    ldrs) ................................................................................. ¾.6
1550 Eliza Wooding **(37)** *(CJHill)* 4-8-1 NAdams (3) (s.i.s: nvr plcd to chal) ............... 1.7
1413[3] Long Furlong **(55)** (Fav) *(RAkehurst)* 4-9-5 BRouse (9) (hld up: hdwy & 6th st:
    swtchd rt & wknd over 2f out) ............................................ 2½.8
1339 Tartar's Bow **(52)** *(RJHolder)* 5-8-9 ‡7SDrowne (5) (in tch over 7f: sn wknd: t.o)   6.9
1434[5] Green's Stubbs **(30)** *(ABarrow)* 5-7-8 RFox (6) (chsd ldr: 2nd st: wknd over 2f
    out: t.o) ............................................................................ s.h.10
1404 Free Expression **(31)** *(PLeach)* 7-7-9 EJohnson (2) (bit bkwd: led: clr ½-way:
    wknd & hdd 2f out: t.o) ....................................................... 2.11

**2/1** Long Furlong, **7/2** SAMURAI GOLD (USA), **11/2** Premier Dance, Supertop, **14/1** Lexus (IRE), Eliza
Wooding(op 5/1), **16/1** Clear Light, **20/1** Tartar's Bow, Green's Stubbs, **33/1** Pusey Street Boy, **50/1** Free
Expression. CSF £89.09, CT £574.83. Tote £3.70: £1.30 £6.50 £2.20 (£304.50). Mr I. Karageorgis
(LAMBOURN) bred by Regal Oak Farm in USA. 11 Rn     2m 8.5 (4.2)
       SF—26/16/16/25/16/26

T/Plpt: £39.70 (64.5 Tckts).          IM

## 1552—WARWICK (L-H)

### Saturday, June 27th [Firm]

Going Allowance: minus 0.40 sec per fur (F)          Wind: nil

Stalls: low
**1722**     ROYAL SHOW STKS (Mdn 3-Y.O) £1380.00 (£380.00: £180.00)
      1½m 115y                 6-30 (6-31)

    **Storm Crossing (USA)** (Fav) *(GHarwood)* 9-0 PatEddery (3) (h.d.w: hld up:
    3rd st: led wl over 1f out: easily) .......................................... —1

902³ Receptionist *(HRACecil)* 8-9 AMcGlone (4) (led over 10f: no ch w wnr) .............. 3.2
1158² Desert Peace (IRE) *(PFICole)* 9-0 TQuinn (2) (2nd st: ev ch 2f out: one pce) .... ³/₄.3
　　Sea Plane *(MajorWRHern)* 9-0 WCarson (1) (nt grwn: pushed along 4f out: last
　　　　st: sn bhd) .................................................................. 3.4

**Evens** STORM CROSSING (USA)(tchd 13/8), **7/4** Desert Peace (IRE), **6/1** Ors. CSF £6.54, Tote £2.50 (£4.30).
Mr K. Abdulla (PULBOROUGH) bred by Juddmonte Farms Incorporated in USA. 4 Rn　　2m 40.3 (2.8)
　　　　　　　　　　　　　　　　　　　　　　　　　　　　　　　　SF—22/11/14/8


**1723**　　WARWICK VASE STKS (3-Y-O) £4470.00 (£1080.00)　　1¹/₄m 169y　　7-00 (7-01)

1505* **Dress Sense (IRE)** (Fav) *(LMCumani)* 9-0 LDettori (2) (lw: 2nd tl led over 1f out:
　　　　r.o wl) ...................................................................... —1
14473 Bilateral (USA) **(100)** *(HRACecil)* 8-10 PatEddery (1) (set slow pce tl qcknd 3f
　　　　out: hdd over 1f out: r.o) .............................................. ³/₄.2

**4/7** DRESS SENSE (IRE), **6/4** Bilateral (USA)(4/5—7/4). Tote £1.50. Sheikh Mohammed (NEWMARKET) bred by
Mrs R. B. Kennard in Ireland. 2 Rn　　　　　　　　　　　　　　　　　　　　　2m 31.4 (17.9)


**1724**　　BRITISH TIMKEN H'CAP (3-Y.O) (0-80) £2206.40 (£610.40: £291.20)
　　　　1m　　　　　　　　　　　　　　　　　　　　　　　　　　　　7-30 (7-32)
　　　　　　　　　　　　　(Weights raised 6 lb)
1532* **Alkarif (USA) (70)** (Fav) *(AAScott)* 9-3 WCarson (1) (mde all: rdn over 1f out:
　　　　r.o wl) ...................................................................... —1
1557* Morocco (IRE) **(74)** *(RCharlton)* 9-7 PatEddery (3) (wnt 2nd st: hrd rdn & ev ch
　　　　over 1f out: nt qckn ins fnl f) ........................................ 2¹/₂.2
1642 A Nymph Too Far (IRE) **(52)** *(DrJDScargill)* 7-10 ‡3FNorton (2) (chsd wnr tl 3rd
　　　　st: wknd wl over 1f out) ............................................... 10.3

**10/11** ALKARIF (USA), **5/4** Morocco (IRE)(op 8/11), **8/1** A Nymph Too Far (IRE)(4/1—9/1). CSF £2.25, Tote
£1.70 (£1.20). Mr Hamdan Al-Maktoum (NEWMARKET) bred by Lillie F. Webb in USA. 3 Rn　　1m 37.2 (0.2)
　　　　　　　　　　　　　　　　　　　　　　　　　　　　　　　　SF—52/48/–


**1725**　　STONELEIGH (S) STKS (3 & 4-Y.O) £1674.00 (£464.00: £222.00)　　7f　　8-00 (8-02)

510⁶ **Rock Song (IRE) (52)** *(PFICole)* 3-8-11 TQuinn (2) (hld up: 5th st: led wl over
　　　　1f out: sn clr: r.o wl) ................................................... —1
　868 Honey Vision **(48)** (bl) *(GHEden)* 3-8-6 JWilliams (5) (bhd tl gd hdwy over 1f
　　　　out: r.o) ................................................................... 3.2
1449 Mca Below the Line **(63)** (bl) (Fav) *(BBeasley)* 4-9-13 JFortune (1) (rdn along 4f
　　　　out: 7th st: r.o one pce fnl 2f) ....................................... 2¹/₂.3
1540⁴ Girton Degree **(47)** (v) *(SDow)* 3-8-6 LDettori (10) (6th st: one pce fnl 2f) ........ hd.4
15075 Meltonby **(58)** *(NTinkler)* 3-8-13 WNewnes (9) (b.hind: 2nd st: wknd over 1f out) 2.5
1627 Doughman **(49)** (bl) *(JEtherington)* 3-8-11 PatEddery (7) (nvr nr to chal) ....... 1¹/₂.6
　366 Bold Mood **(52)** *(JBerry)* 3-8-4 ‡7PRoberts (6) (lw: led over 5f) ................. 1¹/₂.7
1184 Kind Style (IRE) **(26)** *(RHollinshead)* 4-8-13 ‡7EHusband (3) (hdwy 5f out: 3rd
　　　　st: wknd 2f out) .......................................................... 4.8
1243 Savanga (USA) **(37)** (v) *(MMcCormack)* 4-9-13 AClark (8) (a bhd) ................. 5.9
　　Qualitair Reality *(MFBarraclough)* 4-8-12 ‡3FNorton (4) (swtg: bhd fnl 2f) ...... ³/₄.10
1142 Peggy Mainwaring **(46)** (bl) *(RJHolder)* 3-8-6 NAdams (11) (hdwy over 3f out:
　　　　4th st: wknd 2f out) ..................................................... s.h.11

**11/4** Mca Below the Line, **3/1** Meltonby, **11/2** ROCK SONG (IRE), **6/1** Girton Degree, **10/1** Savanga (USA), **11/1**
Bold Mood, Doughman(op 7/1), Peggy Mainwaring(op 7/1), **14/1** Honey Vision, **20/1** Kind Style (IRE), **50/1**
Qualitair Reality. CSF £75.63, Tote £6.70: £2.30 £3.50 £2.20 (£30.00). Mr Stephen Crown (WHATCOMBE) bred
by Airlie Stud in Ireland. 11 Rn; Bt in 5,000 gns　　　　　　　　　　　　　　1m 26.3 (2.1)
　　　　　　　　　　　　　　　　　　　　　　　　　　　　　SF—23/9/22/–/–/–


**1726**　　EAST MIDLANDS ELECTRICITY H'CAP (0-90) £2709.00 (£749.00: £357.00)
　　　　1³/₄m 194y　　　　　　　　　　　　　　　　　　　　　　　8-30 (8-30)
　　　　　　　　　　　　　　　　　　(Weights raised 10 lb)
1606² **Broom Isle (58)** *(MrsAKnight)* 4-9-2 ‡3FNorton (1) (lw: mde all: rdn clr wl over 1f
　　　　out: r.o wl) ............................................................... —1
13944 Belafonte **(63)** (Fav) *(RJHolder)* 5-9-5 ‡5ATucker (3) (lw: hld up: rdn over 4f out:
　　　　2nd st: one pce fnl 2f) .................................................. 7.2
1543⁴ Merry Marigold **(47)** *(JDRoberts)* 6-8-8 JWilliams (2) (b: b.hind: racd wd: rdn 4f
　　　　out: last st: one pce fnl 2f) ............................................ nk.3

**11/10** Belafonte, **7/4** BROOM ISLE, **3/1** Merry Marigold. CSF £3.76, Tote £2.60 (£1.80). Mr Vivian Guy
(CULLOMPTON) bred by Lord Bolton. 3 Rn　　　　　　　　　　　　　　　　　3m 18.7 (9.7)

**1727**     LEAMINGTON PROMS H'CAP (0-80) £2186.80 (£604.80: £288.40)     **5f**   9-00 (9-00)
(Weights raised 6 lb)

15832 **Samson-Agonistes (69)** (Fav) (BAMcMahon) 6-9-9 TQuinn (6) (lw: mde all: rdn out) ............................................................................................... —1

1583* Arc Lamp (62) (JAGlover) 6–9–2 (7x) JFortune (1) (lw: w wnr: hrd rdn & ev ch wl over 1f out: nt qckn) ......................................................... 1½.2

1552* Rays Mead (50) (LJHolt) 4–8–4(1) WNewnes (5) (a.p: hrd rdn over 1f out: r.o one pce) ......................................................................................... ¾.3

15522 Petitesse (49) (GBlum) 4–8-3 RFox (4) (a.p: rdn over 1f out: one pce) .............. ¾.4

15523 Iron King (70) (JLSpearing) 6–9-3 ‡7EHusband (2) (dwlt: hdwy over 1f out: nt rch ldrs) ........................................................................................... 1.5

1282 Fair Enchantress (57) (bl) (JABennett) 4–8-6 ‡5ATucker (3) (outpcd) ................. 3.6

**2/1** SAMSON-AGONISTES, **5/2** Petitesse, **4/1** Iron King, **5/1** Rays Mead, **7/1** Arc Lamp, **12/1** Fair Enchantress(op 8/1). CSF £15.23, Tote £2.90: £1.80 £2.70 (£12.90). Mr J. B. Wilcox (TAMWORTH) bred by D. W. Pike. 6 Rn                                                                                                 58.9 sec (0.9)
SF—51/38/23/19/29/6

T/Plpt: £112.80 (9.25 Tckts).                                                                                                        KH

---

1326—**HAMILTON (R-H)**
**Monday, June 29th [Firm]**
Going Allowance: minus 0.40 sec per fur (F)                                          Wind: almost nil

Stalls: low

**1728**     GLASGOW AUCTION STKS (Mdn 2-Y.O) £1492.00 (£412.00: £196.00)
**5f 4y**                                                                                      6-45 (6-47)

11512 **Field of Vision (IRE)** (bl) (MJohnston) 8-6 DMcKeown (3) (mde all: r.o wl) ....... —1

12086 Gangleader (Fav) (SPCWoods) 8-7 WWoods (2) (lw: chsd ldrs: effrt 2f out: styd on: nvr able to chal) .................................................................. 2½.2

10925 Club Verge (IRE) (EJAlston) 8-3(1) KFallon (5) (lw: wnt rt s: nvr trbld ldrs) ........... 5.3

1531 Missed the Boat (IRE) (v) (TDBarron) 8-4 AlexGreaves (1) (cl up: rdn ½-wy: sn outpcd) ................................................................................... hd.4

15314 Creagmhor (13/2) Withdrawn (lame at s) : not under orders

**85/40** Gangleader, **9/4** FIELD OF VISION (IRE), Club Verge (IRE), **4/1** Missed the Boat (IRE). CSF £7.07, Tote £2.50: £2.10 (£3.30). Mr R. W. Huggins (MIDDLEHAM) bred by Sean Collins in Ireland. 4 Rn   59.4 sec (1.1)
SF—30/21/–/–

**1729**     WETHERBY'S SPRINT H'CAP (0-70) £1753.20 (£485.20: £231.60)
**5f 4y**                                                                                      7-15 (7-16)
(Weights raised 5 lb)

15222 **Here Comes a Star (52)** (JMCarr) 4–9-7 SMorris (7) (hld up: hdwy 2f out: led ins fnl f: edgd lft & r.o) .................................................................. —1

1522 North of Watford (44) (MPNaughton) 7–8-13 DMcKeown (3) (mde most tl hdd ins fnl f: kpt on) ..................................................................... ½.2

1625* Chateau Nord (57) (Fav) (JBerry) 3–9-5 (7x) JCarroll (6) (lw: chsd ldrs: chal 2f out: nt qckn fnl f) ................................................................ 1½.3

15905 Oratel Flyer (29) (v) (RThompson) 5–7-12 PBurke (4) (w ldrs: rdn over 2f out: btn whn n.m.r appr fnl f) ....................................................... 1.4

15835 Ballad Dancer (55) (EJAlston) 7–9-10 KFallon (8) (lw: in tch & drvn along: styd on fnl f: nvr able to chal) ................................................... ¾.5

14844 Cottage Gallery (IRE) (38) (WAStephenson) 4–8-4 ‡3JFanning (5) (cl up tl rdn & btn appr fnl f) ................................................................. 1½.6

12714 The Right Time (45) (bl) (JParkes) 7–8-9 ‡5SMaloney (1) (s.i.s: nvr trbld ldrs) .... 3.7

668 Uppance (30) (DWChapman) 4–7-13 SWood (2) (sn outpcd) ............................ ½.8

1617 Come on My Girl (IRE) (55) (TAKCuthbert) 4–9-10 SWebster (9) (prom 3f) ......... 3½.9

**3/1** Chateau Nord, **7/2** The Right Time, **5/1** HERE COMES A STAR, **11/2** Ballad Dancer, **6/1** Cottage Gallery (IRE), **7/1** North of Watford(op 4/1), **11/1** Oratel Flyer, **33/1** Uppance, **50/1** Come on My Girl (IRE). CSF £37.13, CT £112.27. Tote £5.90: £1.30 £1.80 £1.40 (£16.00). Mrs June Goodridge (MALTON) bred by A. and M. Scarfe. 9 Rn                                                                                                                 59.5 sec (1.2)
SF—43/33/33/8/31/5

**1730**     MITCHELL LIBRARY CLAIMING STKS (3-Y.O) £1562.00 (£432.00: £206.00)
**1m 1f 36y**                                                                                 7-45 (7-46)

1642 **Akura (IRE) (61)** (MJohnston) 8-1 RPElliott (2) (mde all: clr 2f out: easily) ......... —1

15636 Fair Flyer (IRE) **(51)** *(PMonteith)* 8-2 ‡3JFanning (1) (lw: chsd wnr most of wy: rdn & no imp fnl 3f) ............................................................................ 12.2

1507★ Cobblers Hill **(59)** (Fav) *(JWhite)* 8-7 DaleGibson (3) (lw: chsd ldrs: outpcd 4f out: sn rdn & btn) ........................................................................ 8.3

Solstice *(MrsGRReveley)* 8-9 KDarley (4) (cmpt: dwlt: hdwy appr st: sn outpcd & bhd) .......................................................................................... 1½.4

**4/5** Cobblers Hill(5/4—8/11), **9/4** AKURA (IRE)(op 6/4), **11/2** Fair Flyer (IRE), **8/1** Solstice(6/1—10/1). CSF £11.76, Tote £2.90 (£10.10). Mr Billy Morgan (MIDDLEHAM) bred by J. Mamakos in Ireland. 4 Rn 1m 57.3 (3)

## 1731
WARBURG SECURITIES H'CAP (0-70) £2427.00 (£672.00: £321.00)
**1m 65y**
                              8-15 (8-17)

1051★ **Sweet Mignonette (47)** (Fav) *(MrsGRReveley)* 4-8-10 KDarley (2) (bhd: hdwy 4f out: led over 1f out: r.o) ............................................................ —1

16925 Martini Executive **(65)** (bl) *(BBeasley)* 4-10-0 DNicholls (3) (lw: bhd: rdn 4f out: hdwy 2f out: r.o) ................................................................ 2.2

1527 Hizeem **(30)** *(MPNaughton)* 6-7-7 JakiHouston (8) (outpcd & bhd: hdwy & wnt lft over 2f out: r.o) ................................................................ 1½.3

1564★ Valley of Time (FR) **(38)** *(TCraig)* 4-9-11 PBurke (5) (in tch: hdwy & ev ch 2f out: one pce appr fnl f) ........................................................ 1.4

12884 Paper Craft **(50)** (v) *(MJohnston)* 5-8-13 DMcKeown (6) (chsd ldrs tl outpcd over 2f out: styd on nr fin) .................................................. nk.5

10515 Tempering **(51)** *(DWChapman)* 6-9-0 SWood (10) (lw: cl up: rdn over 3f out: one pce) .......................................................................... s.h.6

1482 Talish **(36)** (v) *(TDBarron)* 4-7-10 ‡3JFanning (7) (lw: led tl hdd over 2f out: grad wknd) ................................................................................ ½.7

1441 Blue Grit **(40)** (bl) *(MDods)* 6-7-12 ‡5SMaloney (1) (pushed along: sn chsng ldrs: led over 2f out tl over 1f out: wknd) .................................. 1½.8

15632 Oyston's Life **(46)** *(JBerry)* 3-7-13 LCharnock (9) (hld up: effrt & swtchd over 2f out: sn rdn & no imp) ................................................ s.h.9

Musket Shot **(43)** *(VThompson)* 4-8-6 KFallon (4) (outpcd ent st: t.o) ................ 10
LONG HANDICAP: Hizeem 7-4.

**7/4** SWEET MIGNONETTE, **4/1** Valley of Time (FR), **9/2** Martini Executive, **13/2** Oyston's Life, **11/1** Blue Grit, **14/1** Hizeem, **16/1** Talish, Tempering, **20/1** Paper Craft, **33/1** Musket Shot. CSF £10.29, CT £79.58. Tote £3.00: £1.20 £1.90 £3.60 (£6.90). Mr M. J. Ogden (SALTBURN) bred by Countess of Durham. 10 Rn 1m 46.1 (2.8)
SF−6/18/−/−/−/−

## 1732
BURRELL COLLECTION STKS (Mdn 3-Y.O) £1450.00 (£400.00: £190.00)
**6f 5y**
                              8-45 (8-47)

15763 **Treasure Time (IRE) (54)** (Fav) *(JWhite)* 8-9 DaleGibson (5) (lw: mde most: pushed out) ........................................................................ —1

15624 Miss Parkes **(48)** *(JBerry)* 8-9 JCarroll (3) (lw: outpcd tl hdwy 2f out: no imp) .... 7.2

15175 Bee Dee Ell (USA) **(47)** *(MissLAPerratt)* 8-11 ‡3JFanning (1) (sn drvn along & lost tch: sme hdwy 2f out: n.d) .................................. 3.3

Fort Derry (IRE) *(EJAlston)* 9-0 KFallon (2) (lengthy: str: s.i.s: outpcd & bhd tl sme late hdwy) .............................................................. 2.4

13344 Cumbrian Classic *(LLungo)* 9-0 DMcKeown (4) (disp ld to ½-wy: sn rdn & wknd) 5.5

**1/2** TREASURE TIME (IRE)(op 1/3), **9/2** Miss Parkes, Fort Derry (IRE), **12/1** Bee Dee Ell (USA), **20/1** Cumbrian Classic. CSF £3.46, Tote £1.40: £1.10 £1.70 (£1.80). Mrs Rita Bates (WENDOVER) bred by Mrs D. Davison in Ireland. 5 Rn 1m 11 (1)
SF−27/−/−/−/−

## 1733
SCOTTISH EXHIBITION CENTRE H'CAP (0-70) £1784.00 (£494.00: £236.00)
**1½m 17y**
                              9-15 (9-20)

1622★ **Carlingford (USA) (51)** (Fav) *(MPNaughton)* 6-9-3 (4x) KFallon (3) (lw: chsd ldr: led 2f out: rdn & r.o) ................................................ —1

16916 Luks Akura **(46)** (v) *(MJohnston)* 4-8-5 ‡7HBastiman (1) (lw: led tl hdd 2f out: r.o one pce) ............................................................ 2½.2

1562 Rapid Mover **(31)** (bl) *(TCraig)* 5-7-11(2) PBurke (8) (a chsng ldrs: effrt 4f out: one pce fnl 2f) ................................................ ¾.3

15095 Shadideen (USA) **(62)** *(MissLAPerratt)* 4-9-11 ‡3JFanning (6) (lw: hdwy ent st: sn rdn & nvr able to chal) .............................. ¾.4

Danza Heights **(37)** *(MrsGRReveley)* 6-8-3 JLowe (4) (sn trckng ldrs: effrt 3f out: sn ev ch & rdn: wknd over 1f out) ............................ ½.5

15196 Premier Venues **(40)** *(SGNorton)* 4-8-1 ‡5SMaloney (2) (b: bhd: hdwy 4f out: rdn & btn over 2f out) ........................................ 2½.6

12395 Lisalee (IRE) **(35)** (bl) *(JParkes)* 4-8-1 LCharnock (9) (nvr wnt pce) ................ 8.7

1518 Alpha Helix **(27)** (v) *(MissLAPerratt)* 9-7-7 DaleGibson (5) (a bhd) ................ 15.8

16226 Roucellist Bay **(35)** *(VThompson)* 4-8-1 SWood (7) (prom to st: sn rdn & wknd) .. 9
LONG HANDICAP: Alpha Helix 7-6.

## 1734—1736

**7/4** CARLINGFORD (USA), **5/2** Danza Heights, **5/1** Shadideen (USA)(tchd 8/1), **13/2** Luks Akura, **7/1** Premier Venues, **16/1** Alpha Helix, **25/1** Rapid Mover, **66/1** Lisalee (IRE), **100/1** Roucellist Bay. CSF £13.40, CT £196.26. Tote £2.70: £1.70 £1.50 £3.60 (£8.30). Mrs H. H. Wane (RICHMOND) bred by Hugh G. King, III in USA. 9 Rn
2m 34.5 (2.5)
SF—30/13/3/29/6/–

T/Plpt: £40.20 (35.3 Tckts). AA

### 1287—PONTEFRACT (L-H)
**Monday, June 29th [Firm]**
Going Allowance: 5f-6f: minus 0.15 sec; Rest: minus 0.30 sec (F)     Wind: slt half against

Stalls: low

**1734**    E.B.F. WRAGBY STKS (Mdn 2-Y.O.F) £2611.00 (£721.00: £343.00)    **5f** 2-15 (2-16)

|  | |
|---|---|
| **Alasib** (Fav) *(MMoubarak)* 8-11 LDettori (4) (lengthy: scope: trckd ldrs gng wl: led on bit over 1f out: pushed out: comf) | —1 |
| 1422² Margaret's Gift *(JBerry)* 8-11 JCarroll (3) (led: hrd drvn 2f out: hdd over 1f out: no ch w wnr) | 1.2 |
| 1375⁴ Spanish Thread *(GAPritchard-Gordon)* 8-11 RCochrane (1) (a chsng ldrs: rdn & nt qckn fnl 2f) | 2¹/₂.3 |
| 1506³ Minshaar *(BHanbury)* 8-11 BRaymond (5) (w'like: bit bkwd: hld up: trckd ldrs: effrt ¹/₂-wy: kpt on same pce) | 3.4 |
| Sandmoor Satin *(MHEasterby)* 8-11 MBirch (2) (b.hind: dwlt: a outpcd: bhd fnl 2f) | 15.5 |

**11/10** ALASIB, **2/1** Margaret's Gift, **9/2** Minshaar, **12/1** Sandmoor Satin(op 8/1), **20/1** Spanish Thread. CSF £3.61, Tote £1.80: £1.10 £1.50 (£1.90). Ecurie Fustok (NEWMARKET) bred by Ahmed M. Foustok. 5 Rn
63.6 sec (2.1)
SF—40/36/26/14/–

**1735**    SMEATON (S) H'CAP (3-Y.O) (0-60) £2304.40 (£638.40: £305.20)
**1¹/₂m 8y**    2-45 (2-45)
(Weights raised 12 lb)

| | |
|---|---|
| 1438³ **Pie Hatch (IRE) (36)** (Fav) *(SirMarkPrescott)* 8-9 GDuffield (6) (chsd ldr: led over 4f out: drvn clr appr st: styd on: rdn out) | —1 |
| 1548⁵ Gay Ming **(39)** *(RHollinshead)* 8-5 ‡7AGarth (3) (hld up: hdwy to chase wnr 2f out: edgd rt & r.o u.p fnl f) | 2¹/₂.2 |
| 1423⁶ Shafayif **(48)** *(BHanbury)* 9-7 BRaymond (2) (lw: plld hrd: trckd ldrs: effrt over 2f out: sn wknd) | 20.3 |
| Phargold (IRE) **(42)** *(PCHaslam)* 9-1 DMcKeown (1) (led tl over 4f out: sn lost pl) | 8.4 |
| 1288 Heart Flutter **(41)** (bl) *(ASmith)* 9-0 PBurke (4) (trckd ldrs tl rdn & lost pl 4f out) | 2.5 |
| 1486 Dame Helene (USA) **(33)** *(PCHaslam)* 8-3 ‡3JFanning (5) (hld up & bhd: lost tch 5f out) | 10.6 |

**6/4** PIE HATCH (IRE), **3/1** Shafayif, **4/1** Gay Ming, **9/2** Dame Helene (USA), **14/1** Phargold (IRE), **25/1** Heart Flutter. CSF £7.62, Tote £2.30: £1.40 £1.80 (£3.70). Miss Elizabeth Aldous (NEWMARKET) bred by Newtownbarry House Stud in Ireland. 6 Rn; Bt in 3,800 gns
2m 37.6 (3.1)
SF—28/19/–/–/–

**1736**    MID-SUMMER H'CAP (0-100) £3622.50 (£1080.00: £515.00: £232.50)
**6f**    3-15 (3-16)

| | |
|---|---|
| 1289⋆ Densben **(67)** *(DenysSmith)* 8–8-3 KFallon (6) (hdwy over 2f out: led over 1f out: sn clr) | —1 |
| 1474 Green Dollar **(91)** *(EAWheeler)* 9–9-10 ‡3FNorton (4) (lw: sn bhd: hdwy over 1f out: r.o ins fnl f: no ch w wnr) | 2¹/₂.2 |
| 1289² Pageboy **(84)** *(PCHaslam)* 3–8-12 LPiggott (1) (lw: led tl hdd over 1f out: kpt on same pce u.p) | 2.3 |
| 1607³ Glenstal Princess **(61)** *(RHollinshead)* 5–7-4 ‡7AGarth (3) (swtg: chsd ldrs: rdn & outpcd over 2f out: kpt on fnl f) | ¹/₂.4 |
| 1310³ Drum Sergeant **(62)** (bl) *(JParkes)* 5–7-7⁽²⁾ ‡5SMaloney (2) (lw: sn w ldrs: r.o same pce over 1f out) | 1¹/₂.5 |
| 1474 Windpower (IRE) **(84)** (Fav) *(JBerry)* 3–8-12 JCarroll (5) (lw: hld up: hdwy on ins over 2f out: nt clr run & nt rcvr) | ³/₄.6 |
| 1617³ Pretonic **(64)** *(MJohnston)* 4–8-0 RPElliott (7) (racd wd: chsd ldrs tl lost pl over 2f out) | 1.7 |

**11/4** Windpower (IRE), **7/2** DENSBEN, **5/1** Pageboy, Glenstal Princess, **7/1** Pretonic, **8/1** Green Dollar, **11/1** Drum Sergeant. CSF £27.40, Tote £5.30: £3.50 £3.50 (£39.00). Mrs Janet M. Pike (BISHOP AUCKLAND) bred by D. W. Pike. 7 Rn
1m 16.2 (2.2)
SF—27/38/18/–/–/7

## 1737
JULY MILE STKS (Mdn 3-Y.O) £2427.00 (£672.00: £321.00)  **1m 4y**  3-45 (3-48)

| | | | |
|---|---|---|---|
| 1476⁴ | **Trooping (IRE) (81)** (Fav) *(GHarwood)* 9-0 AClark (1) (lw: mde virtually all: drvn clr 3f out: hrd rdn & styd on) | | —1 |
| 387 | Shakreen (USA) **(69)** *(MrsLPiggott)* 8-9 LPiggott (6) (wnt 2nd ½-wy: kpt on u.p fnl 2f: no ch w wnr) | | 3.2 |
| 1319 | Reflecting (IRE) *(JHMGosden)* 9-0 RCochrane (7) (hdwy 3f out: r.o fnl f) | | s.h.3 |
| | Waaza (USA) *(AAScott)* 9-0 BRaymond (5) (w'like: s.i.s: bhd tl styd on over 1f out: r.o nr fin) | | ¾.4 |
| | Negative Pledge (USA) *(JHMGosden)* 8-9 GHind (4) (leggy: scope: s.s: sn bhd: sme hdwy over 1f out: nvr nr ldrs) | | 10.5 |
| 618 | Primo Pageant *(MJCamacho)* 9-0 NConnorton (2) (bit bkwd: reminders & lost pl ½-wy: sn bhd) | | 2.6 |
| 1154 | Rasco **(49)** *(JEtherington)* 9-0 LDettori (3) (w wnr 4f: sn wknd) | | 15.7 |

**8/13** TROOPING (IRE), **4/1** Reflecting (IRE), **7/1** Shakreen (USA), **10/1** Waaza (USA), **16/1** Negative Pledge (USA)(op 10/1), **20/1** Primo Pageant, **40/1** Rasco. CSF £5.74, Tote £1.60: £1.20 £2.20 (£4.00). Mr Nigel Grandfield (PULBOROUGH) bred by James M. Egan in Ireland. 7 Rn
1m 43.7 (2.1)
SF—33/19/23/21/–/–

## 1738
SPINDRIFTER SPRINT STKS (2-Y.O) £2690.00 (£800.00: £380.00: £170.00)
**6f**
4-15 (4-15)

| | | | |
|---|---|---|---|
| 1531² | **Nominator** (Fav) *(RHollinshead)* 8-11 LDettori (3) (mde all: clr over 2f out: v.easily) | | —1 |
| 1515⁴ | Lancaster Pilot *(RMWhitaker)* 8-11 ACulhane (4) (w ldr 3f: edgd rt over 1f out: no ch w wnr) | | 7.2 |
| 1299★ | Atherton Green (IRE) *(JAGlover)* 9-3 DMcKeown (4) (lw: trckd ldrs: effrt & hung lft 2f out: kpt on same pce) | | nk.3 |
| 1489★ | Make Mine a Double *(MissSEHall)* 9-3 NConnorton (2) (lw: trckd ldrs: effrt & n.m.r 2f out: swtchd ins 1f out: sn wknd & eased) | | 12.4 |

**6/4** NOMINATOR(op 9/4), **9/4** Make Mine a Double, **3/1** Lancaster Pilot, **5/1** Atherton Green (IRE). CSF £5.93, Tote £2.60 (£3.80). Mr J. D. Graham (UPPER LONGDON) bred by Auldyn Stud Ltd. 4 Rn
1m 17.9 (3.9)
SF—1/–/–/–/

## 1739
HOUGHTON H'CAP (0-70) £2490.00 (£690.00: £330.00)  **1¼m 6y**  4-45 (4-46)

| | | | |
|---|---|---|---|
| 1687★ | **Jazilah (FR) (57)** (Fav) *(MrsGRReveley)* 4-9-10 MBirch (7) (lw: swtg: mde virtually all: drvn clr over 1f out: rdn out) | | —1 |
| 1527 | Top Scale **(36)** (v) *(WWHaigh)* 6-8-3 NConnorton (3) (hld up gng wl: hdwy over 2f out: edgd lft: r.o u.p: nt rch wnr) | | 1½.2 |
| 1488⁶ | Reel of Tulloch (IRE) **(64)** *(PCHaslam)* 3-9-5 LPiggott (2) (lw: hld up & bhd: gd hdwy 3f out: r.o u.p fnl f: nt rch ldrs) | | 2.3 |
| 965³ | Rapid Lad **(30)** *(JLSpearing)* 14-7-11 JLowe (13) (hld up: gd hdwy & n.m.r over 1f out: kpt on fnl f) | | hd.4 |
| 1520 | Escape Talk **(26)** *(JDooler)* 5-7-7 NCarlisle (15) (chsd ldrs: rdn 3f out: one pce) | | 3.5 |
| 1390³ | Bronze Runner **(40)** (bl) *(EAWheeler)* 8-8-4 ‡³FNorton (10) (lw: chsd ldrs: effrt u.p over 2f out: wknd over 1f out) | | 1.6 |
| 1482⁶ | Miss Hyde (USA) **(55)** (v) *(JAGlover)* 3-8-10 JFortune (1) (lw: chsd ldrs: rdn 3f out: sn wknd) | | ½.7 |
| 1376⁶ | Golden Beau **(29)** *(AHarrison)* 10-7-3(¹) ‡⁷AGarth (8) (swtg: nvr nr to chal) | | 2.8 |
| 1520 | Statia (IRE) **(32)** *(DonEnricoIncisa)* 4-7-6 ‡⁷DarrenMoffatt (4) (b: sn bhd: hdwy over 1f out: n.d) | | ¾.9 |
| 1298 | Sahara Shield **(65)** *(AAScott)* 3-9-6 BRaymond (11) (b.nr fore: lw: chsd ldrs: edgd lft & wknd over 1f out) | | 1.10 |
| 1242⁵ | Humour (IRE) **(63)** *(CFWall)* 3-9-4 NDay (12) (effrt on outside 5f out: wknd over 2f out) | | ½.11 |
| 1568² | Cold Shower (IRE) **(61)** *(JAGlover)* 3-8-9 ‡⁷SWilliams (14) (trckd ldrs: rdn 2f out: hung lft & sn wknd) | | 1.12 |
| 1519⁴ | Cool Parade (USA) **(58)** (bl) *(GMMoore)* 4-9-4 ‡⁷OPears (6) (a in rr) | | 3.13 |
| 1452² | First Bid **(47)** *(RMWhitaker)* 5-9-0 ACulhane (5) (lw: bhd & drvn along 6f out: n.d) | | 1½.14 |
| 1582³ | Dancing Tudor **(48)** *(THCaldwell)* 4-9-1 GDuffield (9) (plld hrd: w wnr tl wknd qckly over 4f out: sn bhd) | | 15.15 |

LONG HANDICAP: Escape Talk 7-1.

**Evens** JAZILAH (FR), **8/1** Cold Shower (IRE), **9/1** Reel of Tulloch (IRE), **10/1** First Bid, **12/1** Bronze Runner, Sahara Shield, **16/1** Humour (IRE), Miss Hyde (USA), Cool Parade (USA), Top Scale, **20/1** Rapid Lad, **25/1** Statia (IRE), **33/1** Ors. CSF £20.83, CT £108.07. Tote £2.20: £1.40 £6.10 £2.50 (£29.70). Mr S. Aitken (SALTBURN) bred by Derrinstown Stud Ltd. in France. 15 Rn
2m 11.6 (3.3)
SF—47/23/35/12/–/11

**1740**　　LEVY BOARD H'CAP (F & M) (0-75) £2511.00 (£696.00: £333.00)
　　　　　1½m 8y

　　　　　　　　　　　　　　　　　　　　　　　　　　　　　　5-15 (5-15)

1419³ **Samain (USA) (43)** *(JAGlover)* 5–8-1 NCarlisle (5) (s.s: sn rcvrd: effrt over 2f
　　　　　out: led ins fnl f: r.o u.p)　　　　　　　　　　　　　　　　　—1

1242² **Oak Apple (USA) (62)** *(Fav) (BHanbury)* 3–8-5 BRaymond (7) (lw: trckd ldrs:
　　　　　plld hrd: rdn to ld wl over 1f out: hdd & nt qckn ins fnl f) ... nk.2

1518⁵ **Deb's Ball (55)** *(DMoffatt)* 6–8-6 ‡7DarrenMoffatt (6) (bhd ½-wy: hdwy over 2f
　　　　　out: r.o fnl f)　　　　　　　　　　　　　　　　　　　　1½.3

1566 **Famous Beauty (48)** *(RHollinshead)* 5–7-13 ‡7DCarson (4) (lw: trckd ldrs: kpt
　　　　　on fnl 2f)　　　　　　　　　　　　　　　　　　　　　½.4

1390 **Shadow Bird (55)** *(GAPritchard-Gordon)* 5–8-10 ‡3FNorton (1) (lw: trckd ldrs:
　　　　　effrt & n.m.r over 1f out: sn wknd)　　　　　　　　　　　8.5

1520³ **Able Lassie (70)** *(MrsGRReveley)* 4–10-0 GDuffield (2) (set slow pce to ½-wy:
　　　　　hdd wl over 1f out: sn wknd)　　　　　　　　　　　　　6.6

1560＊ **Sapphirine (66)** *(RMWhitaker)* 5–9-10 (6x) ACulhane (3) (lw: trckd ldrs: effrt
　　　　　over 2f out: wknd over 1f out)　　　　　　　　　　　　2.7

**7/2** Oak Apple (USA), **4/1** Deb's Ball, Able Lassie, **9/2** SAMAIN (USA), **5/1** Shadow Bird, **7/1** Sapphirine, **12/1** Famous Beauty. CSF £19.83, Tote £5.30: £2.60 £2.40 (£10.10). Countrywide Classics Limited (WORKSOP) bred by Stephen D. Peskoff in USA. 7 Rn　　　　　　　　　2m 41.8 (7.3)

T/Plpt: £33.10 (84 Tckts).　　　　　　　　　　　　　　　　　　　　WG

---

1572-**WINDSOR (Fig.8)**

**Monday, June 29th [Good to firm, Good home st]**

Going Allowance: minus 0.30 sec per fur (F)　　　　　　　　　　Wind: nil

Stalls: high

**1741**　　DUNHILL LIGHTS (S) H'CAP (3 & 4-Y.O) (0-60) £1814.00 (£504.00: £242.00)
　　　　　1m 67y

　　　　　　　　　　　　　　　　　　　　　　　　　　　　　　6-35 (6-37)

580 **Mardior (30)** (bl) *(WGRWightman)* 4–7-12 GCarter (19) (mde virtually all: drvn
　　　　　out)　　　　　　　　　　　　　　　　　　　　　　　—1

1276⁶ **Broughton's Tango (IRE) (42)** (bl) *(WJMusson)* 3–8-0 JQuinn (4) (b: 4th st: ev
　　　　　ch whn swvd bdly lft ins fnl f)　　　　　　　　　　　　1.2

1278 **Flying Promise (39)** *(RABennett)* 4–8-7 WNewnes (3) (swtg: 2nd st: ev ch 1f
　　　　　out: hrd rdn & nt qckn)　　　　　　　　　　　　　　　½.3

1294⁶ **Miss Magenta (IRE) (31)** *(RThompson)* 4–7-6 ‡7CHawksley (13) (swtg: hdwy fnl
　　　　　3f: nvr nrr)　　　　　　　　　　　　　　　　　　　nk.4

1446 **Kathy Fair (IRE) (40)** *(RJBaker)* 3–7-12 RFox (1) (swtg: nrst fin)　　　　2.5

1705⁵ **Bengal Tiger (IRE) (54)** (bl) *(Fav) (JAkehurst)* 4–9-8 DHolland (5) (swtg: 8th st:
　　　　　　　＊　one pce fnl 3f)　　　　　　　　　　　　　　　½.6

1589 **Please Please Me (IRE) (34)** *(KOCunningham-Brown)* 4–7-11 ‡5RPrice (10) (gd
　　　　　hdwy & hrd rdn 2f out: wknd fnl f)　　　　　　　　　　2½.7

1309 **Harlequin Girl (37)** *(KTIvory)* 4–8-5 GBardwell (17) (7th st: hrd rdn 3f out: wknd
　　　　　over 1f out)　　　　　　　　　　　　　　　　　　　1.8

806 **Odoen (USA) (42)** (v) *(MRChannon)* 3–7-9 ‡5BDoyle (15) (nvr nr to chal)　　3½.9

1159 **Bo Knows Best (IRE) (41)** *(JSutcliffe)* 3–7-13 BCrossley (11) (n.d)　　2½.10

Aragon Court (38) *(JPearce)* 4–8-3⁽⁴⁾ ‡3RPerham (14) (swtg: n.d)　　2.11

1265⁶ **Catel Ring (IRE) (40)** *(ICampbell)* 3–7-12 AMcGlone (1) (b.hind: 5th whn
　　　　　slipped bdly ent st: nt rcvr)　　　　　　　　　　　　　2½.12

1572 **Lord Leitrim (IRE) (50)** *(NACallaghan)* 3–8-8 TQuinn (6) (lw: hrd rdn 3f out: no
　　　　　rspnse)　　　　　　　　　　　　　　　　　　　　　¾.13

1572 **Lamastre (52)** *(RJHodges)* 3–8-7 ‡3TSprake (16) (n.d)　　　　　　　1½.14

1486⁴ **Have a Nightcap (49)** (bl) *(MAJarvis)* 3–8-7 WCarson (2) (swtg: a bhd)　　2½.15

1404 **Romola Nijinsky (60)** *(PDEvans)* 4–10-0 MRoberts (9) (lw: 5th st: wknd 4f out) ½.16

1385 **Lord Belmonte (IRE) (40)** *(CACyzer)* 3–7-9⁽⁵⁾ ‡3BBiggs (8) (swtg: 3rd st: rdn &
　　　　　wknd 4f out)　　　　　　　　　　　　　　　　　　½.17

1343 **Domiana (31)** *(MBlanshard)* 4–7-13 AMunro (18) (swtg: n.d)　　　　1.18

1590 **My Ducats (IRE) (32)** *(TCasey)* 4–7-9⁽²⁾ ‡5NGwilliams (7) (s.s: a bhd: t.o) 12.19

**11/4** Bengal Tiger (IRE), **5/1** Broughton's Tango (IRE)(7/1—9/2), **11/2** Have a Nightcap, **8/1** Romola Nijinsky(6/1—10/1), **9/1** Lord Leitrim (IRE)(6/1—10/1), **10/1** Catel Ring (IRE)(op 6/1), Please Please Me (IRE)(12/1—8/1), **14/1** Harlequin Girl, Odoen (USA)(op 7/1), **16/1** Miss Magenta (IRE)(op 8/1), **20/1** Bo Knows Best (IRE), Domiana, MARDIOR, Kathy Fair (IRE), Lamastre, **33/1** Ors. CSF £126.51, CT £3,107.69. Tote £65.60: £9.70 £2.30 £5.90 £1.80 (£136.50). Mrs J. A. Thomson (UPHAM) bred by W. G. R. Wightman and Mrs J. A. Thomson. 19 Rn; No bid　　　　　　　　　　　　　1m 44.4 (2.8)

SF—6/5/10/–/–/16

**1742** CALOR GAS STKS (2-Y.O.F) £1970.00 (£545.00: £260.00) 5f 217y 7-00 (7-02)

1502³ **Chain Dance** (Fav) *(MRStoute)* 8-8 WRSwinburn (2) (hld up: led ins fnl f: all out) .................................................................................................. —1
Glowing Jade *(MRChannon)* 8-8 PatEddery (7) (unf: scope: bit bkwd: led: edgd lft over 1f out: hrd rdn: hdd ins fnl f: r.o wl) .............. s.h.2
Russia With Love *(JDBethell)* 8-8 AMunro (1) (w'like: bit bkwd: w ldrs: ev ch over 1f out: nt qckn) .................................................. 6.3
1057⁶ Agil's Pet *(JSutcliffe)* 8-8 BRouse (6) (no hdwy fnl 2f) ............................ 10.4
1396⁶ Charity Express (IRE) *(JBerry)* 8-13 GCarter (3) (w ldrs 4f) ..................... 2.5
Petiole *(WRMuir)* 8-8 SWhitworth (5) (w'like: bit bkwd: bhd fnl 3f) ............ 3½.6

**30/100** CHAIN DANCE(op 1/2), **3/1** Glowing Jade, **16/1** Charity Express (IRE)(op 8/1), **40/1** Ors. CSF £1.78,
Tote £1.40: £1.10 £1.70 (£1.70). Mr J. M. Greetham (NEWMARKET) bred by J. M. Greetham. 6 Rn
1m 12.7 (2.2)
SF—14/13/–/–/–/–

**1743** COLGATE-PALMOLIVE H'CAP (0-80) £2057.50 (£570.00: £272.50)
1m 3f 135y 7-30 (7-31)
(Weights raised 2 lb)

1163 Incola (39) *(HCandy)* 6-7-0 ‡⁷AntoinetteArmes (5) (lw: hdwy on ins 4f out: led over 1f out: r.o wl) ................................................. —1
1574* Bentico (61) (Fav) *(MAJarvis)* 3-8-0 (5x) WCarson (8) (led 3f: 2nd st: led over 4f out tl over 1f out: r.o) .................................... ½.2
1539³ Abingdon Flyer (IRE) (70) (bl) *(RHannon)* 4-9-10 JReid (2) (swtg: 6th st: ev ch over 1f out: nt qckn) ........................................ 3½.3
1543⁶ Tiger Shoot (53) *(DJSCosgrove)* 5-8-7 AShoults (6) (swtg: 4th st: one pce fnl 2f) ................................................................. 3½.4
1318³ Mahrajan (65) *(CJBenstead)* 8-9-5 TQuinn (4) (hdwy 3f out: rdn & wknd over 1f out) ................................................................. 2.5
598⁵ Horizon (IRE) (62) *(TThomsonJones)* 4-9-2 SWhitworth (3) (3rd st: wknd 2f out) 2.6
1542³ Sarah-Clare (57) *(RAkehurst)* 4-8-8 ‡³RPerham (1) (hdwy & 5th st: wknd over 2f out) ................................................................. 1.7
1519³ Winged Whisper (USA) (61) *(CASmith)* 3-8-0 MRoberts (7) (b.off hind: lw: led after 3f: rn wd st: hdd & wknd over 1f out) ............... 10.8
LONG HANDICAP: Incola 7-4.

**11/8** Bentico, **9/2** Mahrajan, **7/1** Abingdon Flyer (IRE)(6/1—9/1), Winged Whisper (USA), Tiger Shoot, **8/1**
Sarah-Clare(9/2—9/1), **16/1** INCOLA, **25/1** Horizon (IRE). CSF £38.06, CT £164.43. Tote £18.20: £2.70 £1.30
£1.50 (£23.40). Mrs David Blackburn (WANTAGE) bred by Mrs D. Blackburn. 8 Rn
2m 25.9 (3.4)
SF—3/16/33/9/17/10

**1744** EXTEL FINANCIAL SYSTEMS STKS (2-Y.O) £2005.00 (£555.00: £265.00)
5f 10y 8-00 (8-01)

971¹² **Fortune Cay (IRE)** (Fav) *(RHannon)* 9-3 PatEddery (3) (mde all: drvn out) ...... —1
1472⁶ Sheila's Secret (IRE) (bl) *(WCarter)* 8-12 JReid (2) (a.p: r.o ins fnl f) ............... 7.2
1202 Tuscan Dawn *(JBerry)* 9-3 GCarter (1) (w wnr: hrd rdn 2f out: wknd fnl f) ....... 2½.3
1443 Bonita Bee *(LJHolt)* 8-6 MRoberts (9) (s.s: gd hdwy fnl 2f: nvr nrr) ................ 5.4
Magirika (IRE) *(MMoubarak)* 8-11 LDettori (7) (neat: bit bkwd: prom tl hrd rdn & wknd 2f out) ................................................ ½.5
1547³ Brave Bidder *(BGubby)* 8-1 ‡⁵DHarrison (5) (no hdwy fnl 2f) ......................... 2½.6
Felt Lucky (IRE) *(MRChannon)* 8-11 TQuinn (4) (w'like: bkwd: dwlt: a bhd) ..... nk.7
Lincoln Imp (USA) *(AMoore)* 8-11 BRouse (6) (str: bit bkwd: a bhd) .................. 6.8
Barniemeboy *(RABennett)* 8-11 WNewnes (8) (leggy: s.s: a bhd: t.o) .................. 15.9

**4/9** FORTUNE CAY (IRE)(op 4/6), **4/1** Sheila's Secret (IRE)(5/2—6/1), **9/1** Magirika (IRE)(5/1—10/1), **12/1**
Tuscan Dawn(7/1—14/1), **25/1** Bonita Bee, **66/1** Ors. CSF £2.81, Tote £1.50: £1.20 £1.40 £2.20 (£2.00). Mr
Edward St George (MARLBOROUGH) bred by W. J. Byrne in Ireland. 9 Rn
59.7 sec (0.7)
SF—59/26/21/–/–/–

**1745** TRAVIS PERKINS H'CAP (3-Y.O) (0-80) £1952.50 (£540.00: £257.50)
5f 217y 8-30 (8-33)

649 **Arabellajill** (80) *(RHannon)* 9-4 ‡³RPerham (4) (a.p: led wl over 1f out: pushed out) ....................................................................... —1
1345⁶ Jigsaw Boy (75) *(RJHolder)* 9-2 JWilliams (2) (lw: hdwy 2f out: r.o ins fnl f) ....... 2.2
1277 Paradise Forum (66) *(CAHorgan)* 8-7 AMunro (8) (swtg: a.p: hrd rdn over 1f out: nt qckn) ................................................................ hd.3
1702⁶ Cranfield Comet (64) *(JBerry)* 8-5 GCarter (3) (chsd ldr: ev ch 2f out: one pce) 1.4
1428 Palacegate Gold (IRE) (55) *(RJHodges)* 7-10 JQuinn (7) (reluctant to ent stalls: prom 4f) ................................................................. ½.5
1418⁵ Lifetime Fame (78) (bl) (Jt-Fav) *(JWPayne)* 9-5 RCochrane (5) (swtg: led over 4f) ................................................................. 3.6

Sizzling Affair **(59)** *(TCasey)* 7-11(1) ‡³TSprake (9) (bhd fnl 4f) .................... 2.7
1410² Masrur (USA) **(66)** (Jt-Fav) *(RWArmstrong)* 8-7 WCarson (6) (lw: stumbled s: a
bhd) .................................................................................................... 8.8

**100/30** Masrur (USA), Lifetime Fame, **4/1** Jigsaw Boy(3/1—9/2), **9/2** Cranfield Comet(op 3/1), **8/1** Palacegate
Gold (IRE), **9/1** ARABELLAJILL(op 6/1), **20/1** Paradise Forum, **50/1** Sizzling Affair. CSF £40.53, CT £628.84.
Tote £10.90: £2.50 £1.70 £4.60 (£17.50). Mrs J. Cash (MARLBOROUGH) bred by Mrs J. Cash. 8 Rn
1m 11.7 (1.2)
SF—44/34/24/18/7/18

### 1746
PIPER CHAMPAGNE AND RAFFLES NIGHTCLUB GRADUATION STKS (3-Y.O) £1907.20
(£529.20: £253.60)   **1¹/₄m 7y**                               9-00 (9-01)

1447² **Big Easy (IRE) (87)** (bl) **(Fav)** *(MrsJCecil)* 9-0 PaulEddery (8) (mde all: comf) .. —1
1319 Bustinetta *(JRFanshawe)* 8-9 WRSwinburn (5) (2nd st: hrd rdn over 2f out: no
imp) ................................................................................................ 3¹/₂.2
1505⁵ Al Karnak (IRE) *(MMoubarak)* 9-0 LDettori (3) (5th st: rdn 3f out: one pce) ......... ¹/₂.3
440 Pompion (USA) *(JHMGosden)* 9-0 WCarson (4) (b.nr fore: 3rd st: one pce fnl
3f) ........................................................................................................ 1.4
Etiquette *(LordHuntingdon)* 8-9 AMunro (6) (w'like: scope: s.s: 6th st: hdwy 2f
out: nvr nr to chal) .......................................................................... 1¹/₂.5
1447 Debt Swap (USA) *(JHMGosden)* 9-0 RCochrane (2) (b.nr hind: hdwy 3f out:
one pce fnl 2f) .................................................................................... 2.6
Friendly House (IRE) *(MAJarvis)* 9-0 GCrealock (1) (w'like: scope: lw: a bhd: t.o) 12.7
1476 Amaze **(97)** *(LadyHerries)* 9-10 JReid (7) (b: 4th st: wknd 3f out: t.o) ................. 15.8

**13/8** BIG EASY (IRE), **9/4** Al Karnak (IRE)(tchd 7/2), **5/1** Amaze(op 5/2), **11/2** Bustinetta(5/1—10/1), **9/1**
Etiquette, **33/1** Pompion (USA), Debt Swap (USA), **50/1** Friendly House (IRE). CSF £10.95, Tote £2.50: £1.30
£1.70 £1.40 (£11.40). Mr James H. Stone (NEWMARKET) bred by Airlie Stud in Ireland. 8 Rn   2m 5.9 (2.9)
SF—41/29/33/31/23/24

T/Plpt: £40.40 (67.3 Tckts).                                                                      Hn

## 1578—**WOLVERHAMPTON (L-H)**
### Monday, June 29th [Hard 11f-14f, Firm 5f-11f, Good to firm remainder]
Going Allowance: St: minus 0.20 sec; Rnd: minus 0.35 sec (F)                **Wind: almost nil**

Stalls: high

### 1747
LEVY BOARD H'CAP (0-70) £2406.00 (£666.00: £318.00)   **1m 200y**   2-00 (2-03)

1542² **Neptune's Pet (65)** *(GLewis)* 4-10-0 JReid (8) (mde all: clr over 2f out: unchal) —1
1284 Irish Groom **(35)** (bl) *(JPSmith)* 5-7-12 NAdams (7) (swtg: hdwy 3f out: hrd rdn
& one pce fnl 2f) .............................................................................. 4.2
1488⁵ Sanawi **(52)** *(PDEvans)* 5-9-1 AMunro (9) (s.s: hdwy fnl 2f: fin wl) .................. s.h.3
1527³ No Comebacks **(44)** **(Fav)** *(EJAlston)* 4-8-7 GBaxter (2) (prom: 4th st: no hdwy
fnl 3f) ................................................................................................ 5.4
1421 Les Amis **(42)** *(MJRyan)* 5-8-5 GCarter (4) (hdwy ent st: rdn 3f out: one pce) 2¹/₂.5
Fern Heights **(59)** *(CDBroad)* 5-9-8 JWilliams (11) (bit bkwd: s.s: hdwy ent st:
nt rch ldrs) ........................................................................................ 3.6
1338 Dazla **(34)** *(RRowe)* 5-7-4(4) ‡⁷CHawksley (6) (s.i.s: sme late hdwy: n.d) ......... ¹/₂.7
1195 Marjons Boy **(30)** *(CDBroad)* 5-7-7 NCarlisle (13) (nvr plcd to chal) ............... nk.8
Harry's Lady (IRE) **(48)** *(TThomsonJones)* 4-8-11 SWhitworth (10) (b: bit
bkwd: chsd wnr: 2nd st: rdn & wknd over 2f out) .................................... ¹/₂.9
358 Shamshom Al Arab (IRE) **(42)** (bl) *(WCarter)* 4-8-0 ‡⁵NGwilliams (1) (bit bkwd:
unruly st: dwlt: a bhd) ..................................................................... 3.10
1504 Taunting (IRE) **(57)** *(MBlanshard)* 4-9-6 MRoberts (3) (chsd ldrs: 6th & rdn st:
wknd 3f out) .................................................................................... 3.11
1339 Hightown-Princess (IRE) **(45)** *(JSMoore)* 4-8-3 ‡⁵ATucker (5) (swtg: prom: 5th
st: wknd over 3f out) ........................................................................ 2¹/₂.12
1542⁴ Swell Time (IRE) **(30)** (bl) *(CNAllen)* 4-7-7 GBardwell (14) (b.hind: swtg: prom:
3rd st: wknd over 3f out) ................................................................... 2¹/₂.13
1018 Sally Fay (IRE) **(49)** *(TKersey)* 4-8-12 JQuinn (12) (b: chsd ldrs: 7th & wkng st:
t.o) ................................................................................................. 10.14

LONG HANDICAP: Dazla 7-5.

**4/1** No Comebacks(5/1—6/1), **5/1** NEPTUNE'S PET, **11/2** Sanawi, **13/2** Taunting (IRE), **8/1** Les Amis, **10/1**
Swell Time (IRE)(op 6/1), **12/1** Marjons Boy(op 8/1), **14/1** Hightown-Princess (IRE)(op 8/1), **16/1** Shamshom Al
Arab (IRE)(op 10/1), **20/1** Irish Groom, **25/1** Harry's Lady (IRE), **33/1** Sally Fay (IRE), **66/1** Ors. CSF £87.70, CT
£518.28. Tote £6.00: £2.40 £5.50 £2.30 (£148.60). K. B. Symonds and Partners (EPSOM) bred by D. G. Mason.
14 Rn                                                                                          1m 50.5 (2)
SF—37/-/11/-/-/-

**1748** LATECOMERS STKS (Mdn 2-Y.O.F) £2206.40 (£610.40: £291.20) 7f 2-30 (2-35)

13972 **Marillette (USA)** *(Fav)* *(JHMGosden)* 8-11 PatEddery (3) (3rd st: led over 1f out: eased nr fin) .................................................................................. —1

Foolish Heart (IRE) *(NAGraham)* 8-11 MRoberts (6) (unf: scope: lw: 5th st: hdwy on ins to ld 3f out: hdd over 1f out: one pce) ........................... 2.2

9864 Heathyards Gem *(RHollinshead)* 8-11 WRyan (5) (prom: 4th st: kpt on one pce fnl 3f) ............................................................................................................ 7.3

968 General Chase *(RJHolder)* 8-11 JWilliams (2) (chsd ldr: 2nd st: rdn & wknd 2f out) ................................................................................................................. nk.4

1279 Galejade *(DHaydnJones)* 8-11 JReid (1) (led 4f: wknd qckly 2f out) .......... 1½.5

1279 Petite Louie *(WCarter)* 8-6 ‡5NGwilliams (4) (bit bkwd: a bhd: 6th st: rdn 2f out: no imp) ..................................................................................................... s.h.6

**1/6** MARILLETTE (USA)(op 1/3), **11/1** Heathyards Gem(6/1—12/1), Galejade(6/1—12/1), **20/1** Foolish Heart (IRE)(op 8/1), **100/1** Ors. CSF £4.15, Tote £1.10: £1.10 £3.10 (£3.60). Sheikh Mohammed (NEWMARKET) bred by Robert Clay & Rogers Trust in USA. 6 Rn 1m 26 (0.2 under 2y best: 1.7)
SF—35/29/8/7/2/–

**1749** 'GO ALL WEATHER' (S) STKS (2-Y.O) £2343.60 (£649.60: £310.80) 7f 3-00 (3-03)

15264 **Comtec's Legend** *(JFBottomley)* 8-1 ‡5NKennedy (8) (hld up: swtchd rt & hdwy appr fnl f: str run to ld wl ins fnl f) ............................................... —1

14483 Workingforpeanuts (IRE) *(CASmith)* 8-6 JReid (9) (hld up: 6th st: hrd rdn 2f out: r.o strly nr fin) ..................................................................................... nk.2

15864 Gypsy Legend *(WGMTurner)* 8-3 ‡3TSprake (7) (4th st: hrd rdn & ev ch appr fnl f: unable qckn) ........................................................................................... 1½.3

15542 Risky Number *(JSMoore)* 8-6 ‡5ATucker (10) (led: rdn over 2f out: hdd wl ins fnl f) ............................................................................................................................ 1.4

1586★ Homemaker *(Fav)* *(RJHolder)* 8-11 NAdams (3) (dwlt: hdwy & 5th st: effrt 2f out: nvr able to chal) ..................................................................................................... 1½.5

15792 Nut Bush (bl) *(NACallaghan)* 8-11 PatEddery (5) (3rd st: rdn over 2f out: ev ch appr fnl f: eased whn btn) ....................................................................................... 2.6

1549 Calenick Lass *(DHaydnJones)* 8-6 TyroneWilliams (1) (chsd ldr: 2nd st: wknd over 2f out) .............................................................................................................. 1.7

645 My Ballyboy *(ABailey)* 8-4 ‡7PBowe (11) (a bhd) ................................... ¾.8

1342 Dynavour House *(MWEckley)* 8-6 JWilliams (2) (bhd fr ½-wy: t.o) ........ dist.9

Mr Wellright *(APJames)* 8-11 SDawson (4) (lt-f: unf: s.s: a bhd: t.o) ...... dist.10

759 The Rover's *(RonaldThompson)* 8-11 WRyan (6) (t.o fr ½-wy) .................. s.h.11

**11/4** Homemaker, **4/1** Nut Bush, Workingforpeanuts (IRE), **13/2** COMTEC'S LEGEND(op 4/1), **7/1** My Ballyboy(op 4/1), Risky Number, **8/1** Gypsy Legend(6/1—9/1), **25/1** Mr Wellright, **50/1** Ors. CSF £32.63, Tote £6.80: £1.90 £1.50 £2.30 (£10.10). Mr P. Bottomley (MALTON) bred by Qualitair Stud Ltd. 11 Rn; No bid 1m 28.1 (3.8)

**1750** BOSCOBEL OAK H'CAP (3-Y.O.F) (0-70) £2382.80 (£660.80: £316.40)
1m 3-30 (3-31)

15775 **Miss Haggis (73)** *(Fav)* *(RBoss)* 9-10 PatEddery (7) (lw: hld up: gd hdwy 3f out: led appr fnl f: qcknd clr) ......................................................................... —1

10416 Edgeaway (64) *(JWHills)* 9-1 WNewnes (3) (lw: 6th st: hdwy 3f out: kpt on appr fnl f: no ch w wnr) .......................................................................................... 1½.2

1676 Good as Gold (IRE) (53) *(JLSpearing)* 8-4 MRoberts (8) (hld up: swtchd rt & hdwy over 2f out: nvr nrr) ............................................................................. 2½.3

11483 Sharp Dance (50) *(BSmart)* 8-1 NAdams (1) (plld hrd: 7th st: lost pl over 3f out: styd on fnl f) ........................................................................................................... nk.4

8844 Manbaa (IRE) (55) *(HThomsonJones)* 8-6 RHills (9) (chsd ldrs: 4th st: hrd drvn 2f out: one pce) ................................................................................................... nk.5

Kay Beeyou (IRE) (62) *(TThomsonJones)* 8-13 SWhitworth (4) (b: bit bkwd: led 5f: outpcd fnl 2f) ........................................................................................... 1½.6

5465 My Grain (47) *(RHollinshead)* 7-5(5) ‡7MHumphries (2) (5th st: rdn over 2f out: sn wknd) ............................................................................................................. 1.7

14386 Shayna Maidel (43) *(MBell)* 7-8 JQuinn (5) (2nd st: led 3f out: hdd & rdn appr fnl f: sn btn) ................................................................................................................. 4.8

10704 Slumber Thyme (IRE) (48) *(JGFitzGerald)* 7-13 GCarter (6) (3rd st: wknd over 2f out) .................................................................................................................... 2.9

LONG HANDICAP: My Grain 7-0.

**3/1** MISS HAGGIS, **7/2** Manbaa (IRE), **11/2** Edgeaway, **6/1** Slumber Thyme (IRE), **12/1** Shayna Maidel, Sharp Dance, **14/1** Good as Gold (IRE), **20/1** Kay Beeyou (IRE), **33/1** My Grain. CSF £16.80, CT £144.08. Tote £2.40: £1.30 £1.60 £1.40 (£8.30). Mr P. Asquith (NEWMARKET) bred by Cheveley Park Stud Ltd. 9 Rn 1m 40.7 (3.4)
SF—17/3/–/–/–/–

## 1751
TRYSULL GRADUATION STKS (3-Y.O) £2346.40 (£565.60)　**1½m 70y**　4-00 (4-00)

1490* **Anchorage (IRE)** (Fav) *(HRACecil)* 8-6　PatEddery (1) (mde all: drew clr fnl 3f: canter) ................................................ —1

1693² Kasikci **(82)** *(RHollinshead)* 8-11　WRyan (2) (chsd wnr: 2nd s: lost tch 3f out: t.o) ......................................................... dist.2

**1/9** ANCHORAGE (IRE), **7/1** Kasikci. Tote £1.10. Sheikh Mohammed (NEWMARKET) bred by Cotswold Stud & London T'bred Services in Ireland. 2 Rn　　　　　　　　　　　　　2m 39.1 (7.4)

## 1752
PERTON CLAIMING STKS　£2226.00 (£616.00: £294.00)　**5f**　4-30 (4-32)

1483² **Plain Fact (88)** (Fav) *(AHarrison)* 7-9-10　WRSwinburn (8) (lw: hdwy ½-wy: swtchd to ld ins fnl f: r.o) ............................... —1

Metal Boys **(83)** *(RHollinshead)* 5-9-2　WRyan (3) (bit bkwd: a w ldrs: led ins fnl f: r.o) .................................................. 1½.2

1427* **The Noble Oak (IRE) (65)** (bl) *(MMcCormack)* 4-8-10　JReid (6) (a.p: led ½-wy tl ins fnl f) .................................................... 2.3

1436⁴ Tino Tere **(86)** *(JBerry)* 3–8-13　PatEddery (4) (lw: stumbled s: hld up: hdwy 2f out: sn rdn: nt pce to chal) .................... 2½.4

1263 Lady of the Fen **(48)** (bl) *(MrsNMacauley)* 4-8-3　MRoberts (7) (lw: led over 2f: kpt on one pce appr fnl f) .......................... ½.5

1162 Pine Glen Pepper **(32)** *(JAkehurst)* 4-8-5　JWilliams (5) (dwlt: nvr rchd ldrs) ...... ¾.6

1583 Hinari Hi Fi **(43)** *(PDEvans)* 7-7-10　‡7HayleyWilliams (9) (outpcd) ................... 3.7

1583 Barbara's Cutie **(43)** *(MBlanshard)* 4-8-2　NAdams (2) (dwlt: a bhd) ................. hd.8

1427 R a Express **(37)** *(BAMcMahon)* 7–8-1　‡7SSanders (1) (w ldrs: rdn ½-wy: wknd wl over 1f out) ........................................ ¾.9

**7/4** PLAIN FACT, **5/2** Tino Tere(2/1—3/1), **100/30** The Noble Oak (IRE), **10/1** Metal Boys(op 5/1), **11/1** Lady of the Fen, **50/1** Urs. CSF £7.10, Tote £2.60: £1.60 £2.40 £1.20 (£12.60). Mrs B. Ramsden (MIDDLEHAM) bred by Clanville Lodge Stud. 9 Rn; Plain Fact clmd J Hills £13,751　　　　　　　58.7 sec (1.4)

SF—62/48/34/27/15/14

## 1753
SUET H'CAP (3-Y.O) (0-70) £2186.80 (£604.80: £288.40)　**5f**　5-00 (5-02)

1557⁵ **Bells of Longwick (51)** *(DRLaing)* 9-2　TyroneWilliams (7) (b.hind: a.p: hrd rdn over 1f out: led ins fnl f: sn clr) ..................... —1

1276 Tommy Tempest **(47)** *(KRBurke)* 8-12　AShoults (3) (a.p: led 2f out tl ins fnl f: one pce) ............................................... 3½.2

1558* High Principles **(61)** (Fav) *(JBerry)* 9-5 (7x)　‡7PRoberts (1) (a.p: r.o one pce fnl f) 1.3

1552 Bridle Talk (IRE) **(47)** *(MMcCormack)* 8-12　JReid (9) (lw: led 3f: rdn & outpcd ins fnl f) ................................................... nk.4

1583 Cheshire Annie (IRE) **(56)** *(WCarter)* 9-7　JQuinn (4) (lw: spd over 3f) .............. 2.5

1514⁴ Miss Siham (IRE) **(50)** *(JBalding)* 8-8　‡7ClaireBalding (10) (nvr nr to chal) ....... s.h.6

1625 Virginia Cottage **(46)** (bl) *(BAMcMahon)* 8-4　‡7JBramhill (8) (a bhd & outpcd) ... ½.7

994⁴ Camino a Ronda **(44)** *(PatMitchell)* 8-4　‡5DHarrison (2) (b.hind: prom 3f) .......... 3.8

1625 Capital Idea (IRE) **(55)** (bl) *(RonaldThompson)* 9-6　WRyan (3) (outpcd) ............ 2½.9

Bella Bettina **(50)** *(JSMoore)* 8-10　‡5ATucker (6) (b: s.s: sn hrd rdn: a outpcd) nk.10

**7/2** High Principles(op 2/1), **4/1** Cheshire Annie (IRE), Capital Idea (IRE)(tchd 6/1), **5/1** Tommy Tempest(20/1—4/1), **15/2** Miss Siham (IRE), **10/1** Bridle Talk (IRE), **11/1** BELLS OF LONGWICK, **25/1** Virginia Cottage, **33/1** Camino a Ronda, **50/1** Bella Bettina. CSF £59.95, CT £212.68. Tote £16.50: £2.30 £1.70 £2.00 (£44.10). Mrs Marion Wickham (LAMBOURN) bred by Mrs Wickham. 10 Rn　　　　　　　59.3 sec (2)

SF—42/24/27/19/20/6

T/Plpt: £26.40 (69.6 Tckts).　　　　　　　　　　　　　　　　　　　　　　IM

## 1715— CHEPSTOW (L-H)
### Tuesday, June 30th [Good to firm, Firm patches]
Going Allowance: St: minus 0.50 sec (H); Rnd: minus 0.20 sec (F)　　　Wind: almost nil

Stalls: high

## 1754
BREAM CLAIMING STKS (2-Y.O) £2322.00 (£642.00: £306.00)　**6f 16y**　2-00 (2-03)

1559* **Classic Storm** (Fav) *(JBerry)* 8-4　JCarroll (3) (lw: mde all: rdn over 1f out: r.o wl) ................................................... —1

1405² Second Colours (USA) *(PSFelgate)* 8-10　KDarley (1) (lw: swvd lft s: swtchd rt & hdwy 4f out: rdn & ev ch over 1f out: r.o) ....... 1½.2

1202⁴ Calisar *(WGMTurner)* 8-1　‡3TSprake (5) (lw: a.p: hrd rdn & ev ch over 1f out: nt qckn) ....................................................... hd.3

Page 623

1007 Floodlight (IRE) *(RJHolder)* 7-7 NAdams (2) (rdn over 3f out: nvr nr to chal) ... 1½.**4**
1610⁶ Hallplace *(MRChannon)* 8-4 TQuinn (4) (rdn & no hdwy fnl 3f) ......................... hd.**5**
1121⁵ Hawke Bay *(DHaydnJones)* 8-1 TyroneWilliams (6) (lw: w wnr: hrd rdn over 2f
out: sn wknd: t:o) ............................................................. 8.**6**

**11/8** CLASSIC STORM, **2/1** Second Colours (USA), **4/1** Calisar, **7/1** Hallplace, **40/1** Ors. CSF £4.41, Tote £2.20:
£1.40 £1.30 (£2.00). Mr D. J. Ayres (COCKERHAM) bred by Concorde Breeding and Racing International P'Ship.
6 Rn                                                                        1m 11.6 (2.6)

---

**1755** MIDDLE LODGE H'CAP (0-100) £4844.00 (£1442.00: £686.00: £308.00)
**7f 16y**                                                                 2-30 (2-31)

1463 **Cape Pigeon (USA) (84)** *(LGCottrell)* 7-10-0 DHolland (4) (lw: w ldr: rdn &
edgd lft 2f out: led 1f out: hdd ins fnl f: led last stride) ......... —**1**
1706* Jaldi (IRE) **(66)** (Fav) *(JSutcliffe)* 4-8-10 (5x) MRoberts (2) (swtg: hld up: rdn 2f
out: led ins fnl f: hdd last stride) ............................. s.h.**2**
1650² Mustahil (IRE) **(65)** (bl) *(RJHodges)* 3-7-11 ‡3TSprake (5) (led 6f: rallied ins fnl f) ¾.**3**
1431* Talent (USA) **(83)** (v) *(LordHuntingdon)* 4-9-13 AMunro (1) (swtg: prom: rdn &
n.m.r 2f out: one pce) ......................................... 2.**4**
1614² How's Yer Father **(77)** *(RJHodges)* 6-9-2 RCochrane (3) (lw: hld up: rdn 2f out:
one pce) ...................................................... 1.**5**

**10/11** Jaldi (IRE), **7/2** Talent (USA), **13/2** How's Yer Father, **7/1** CAPE PIGEON (USA), **12/1** Mustahil (IRE). CSF
£13.14, Tote £6.70: £3.10 £1.40 (£6.60). Mr E. J. S. Gadsden (CULLOMPTON) bred by Ashwood
Thoroughbreds, Inc. in USA. 5 Rn                                            1m 20.5 (equals standard)
SF—62/43/28/52/43

---

**1756** NPI CELEBRATION H'CAP (0-70) £2343.00 (£648.00: £309.00)   **7f 16y**   3-00 (3-02)
(Weights raised 5 lb)

774 **Zinbaq (37)** *(CJBenstead)* 6-8-3 TyroneWilliams (3) (lw: hld up & bhd: swtchd
rt over 3f out: hdwy to ld nr fin) ............................... —**1**
1406⁶ Teanarco (IRE) **(58)** *(RJHolder)* 4-9-10 AMunro (5) (a.p: rdn 2f out: ev ch ins fnl
f: r.o) ........................................................ ½.**2**
1527 Profit a Prendre **(48)** *(DAWilson)* 8-8-9 ‡5DHarrison (2) (b: a.p: led over 1f out tl
nr fin) ........................................................ nk.**3**
1588⁴ Aldahe **(45)** (Fav) *(BRMillman)* 7-8-11 MRoberts (6) (led over 5f: r.o) ............ hd.**4**
1589⁶ Navaresque **(49)** *(RJHodges)* 7-9-1 RCochrane (1) (lw: hld up: hdwy 3f out:
hrd rdn 2f out: sn wknd) ....................................... 6.**5**
Castle Maid **(44)** *(RJHodges)* 5-8-7 ‡3TSprake (4) (bkwd: bhd: rdn over 3f out:
t.o fnl 2f) ..................................................... 15.**6**

**11/10** Aldahe, **4/1** Navaresque, **6/1** Profit a Prendre, **13/2** Teanarco (IRE), **11/1** ZINBAQ(8/1—12/1), **33/1** Castle
Maid. CSF £63.68, Tote £13.30: £4.80 £1.80 (£30.80). Mrs R. W. S. Baker (EPSOM) bred by Michael Doyle. 6
Rn                                                                         1m 21.3 (0.8)
SF—24/43/27/28/14/–

---

**1757** LION'S LODGE H'CAP (0-100) £5026.00 (£1498.00: £714.00: £322.00)
**5f 16y**                                                                 3-30 (3-32)

1474 **Bit of a Lark (92)** *(RHollinshead)* 4-9-5 ‡7SWynne (8) (w ldr: led 3f out: pushed
out) .......................................................... —**1**
1445* Paddy Chalk **(78)** (Fav) *(LJHolt)* 6-8-12 JReid (1) (b: hdwy 2f out: ev ch ins fnl f:
r.o) .......................................................... nk.**2**
1651* Fivesevenfiveo **(74)** *(RJHodges)* 4-8-8 (8x) RCochrane (2) (lw: a.p: hrd rdn &
ev ch over 1f out: nt qckn fnl f) ............................... 1.**3**
1511² Martina **(70)** *(JWharton)* 4-8-4 JWilliams (3) (lw: no hdwy fnl 2f) ................ 3.**4**
1631⁴ Clifton Charlie (USA) **(88)** *(MRChannon)* 4-9-8 TQuinn (4) (swtg: hdwy over 1f
out: nvr nrr) ................................................. s.h.**5**
1625⁴ Educated Pet **(73)** *(MJohnston)* 3-8-0 JLowe (7) (lw: nvr trbld ldrs) ............ 1.**6**
1631 Paley Prince (USA) **(94)** *(MDIUsher)* 6–10-0 MWigham (5) (bit bkwd: s.i.s: a bhd) 2.**7**
1545* Shades of Jade **(63)** *(JJBridger)* 4-7-6(4) ‡5DHarrison (6) (led 2f: wknd 2f out) ... 4.**8**
LONG HANDICAP: Shades of Jade 7-3.

**100/30** Paddy Chalk(9/2—3/1), **7/2** Martina, **6/1** Fivesevenfiveo(5/1—15/2), Educated Pet, Clifton Charlie
(USA)(9/2—7/1), **8/1** Shades of Jade, **20/1** BIT OF A LARK, **25/1** Paley Prince (USA). CSF £74.99, CT £362.79.
Tote £13.80: £3.20 £1.50 £2.00 (£63.50). Mr R. E. Mason (UPPER LONGDON) bred by Auldyn Stud Ltd. 8 Rn
58 sec (1)
SF—35/27/19/3/20/–

---

**1758** NPI CELEBRATION STKS (Mdn 3-Y.O) £2427.00 (£672.00: £321.00)
**1¼m 36y**                                                                4-00 (4-02)

**Her Honour** *(LordHuntingdon)* 8-9 AMunro (4) (w'like: leggy: 4th st: hdwy 2f
out: led ins fnl f: r.o wl) ..................................... —**1**

1334² Blue Sea *(MAJarvis)* 9-0 BRaymond (2) (2nd st: led over 1f out: sn hdd: r.o) ..... 1.2
1069³ Free Mover (IRE) (Fav) *(NAGraham)* 9-0 RCochrane (5) (3rd st: rdn over 2f out:
    swtchd rt over 1f out: styd on nr fin) ....................................... 1.3
1319⁶ Pippin Park (USA) *(HCandy)* 8-9 CRutter (3) (led over 8f: wknd ins fnl f) ............. 1.4
1319 Lycian Moon *(JLDunlop)* 8-9 TQuinn (1) (lw: hld up & bhd: last st: t.o fnl 2f) ..... 12.5

**1/2** Free Mover (IRE)(op Evens), **9/2** Blue Sea(op 5/2), **5/1** Pippin Park (USA), **10/1** HER HONOUR(4/1—11/1),
**20/1** Lycian Moon. CSF £46.59, Tote £7.30: £2.00 £1.80 (£7.10). Mr Jocelyn Hambro (WEST ILSLEY) bred by
Waverton Farm (Stow). 5 Rn
                                             2m 9.3 (5)
                                        SF—25/28/26/19/–

---

**1759**   SUMMER (S) STKS (3 & 4-Y.O) £2226.00 (£616.00: £294.00)
       1¼m 36y                                          4-30 (4-34)

1255⁶ **Misty Goddess (IRE)** (51) (Jt-Fav) *(MAJarvis)* 4-9-2 ‡5RRutter (10) (hld up: 6th
    st: hdwy to ld over 2f out: pushed out) ....................................... —1
1574 Miss Doody (62) (v) (Jt-Fav) *(MRChannon)* 3-8-9 RCochrane (5) (4th st: ev ch
    whn jinked rt 1f out: wknd rt rdn & r.o) ..................................... nk.2
1404⁴ Mystic Panther (38) *(RJHolder)* 4-9-7 MRoberts (6) (hld up & bhd: rdn & hdwy
    3f out: r.o ins fnl f) ........................................................ 2½.3
1301⁶ Blushing Belle (59) (bl) *(PFICole)* 4-9-7 TQuinn (12) (5th st: r.o one pce fnl 2f) ½.4
1317 Shrewd Girl (USA) (57) *(BWHills)* 4-9-2 DHolland (8) (led: brght centre ent st:
    hdd over 2f out: wknd over 1f out) ......................................... 7.5
*1548* Monorose (58) (v) *(DHaydnJones)* 3-8-4 TyroneWilliams (9) (wnt 2nd st: wknd
    2f out) ..................................................................... 1.6
1408 Fairspear (60) *(LGCottrell)* 3-8-9 TRogers (13) (bit bkwd: prom 6f) ................ 3½.7
1598 Aspirant *(SirMarkPrescott)* 4-9-7 CNutter (1) (bit bkwd: s.s: hld up & plld hrd:
    nvr nrr) ................................................................... s.h.8
1085⁴ Simon Ellis (IRE) (43) *(DRLaing)* 3-8-2 ‡7KimMcDonnell (4) (b.hind: prom 6f) . 2½.9
    Tresilian Owl *(RJHodges)* 4-9-4 ‡3TSprake (14) (w'like: bit bkwd: s.s: a bhd) 2½.10
412 Suemax (IRE) *(RJHodges)* 4-9-2 ADicks (7) (bkwd: bhd fnl 5f) ....................... 4.11
1572 In the Print (47) *(MrsBarbaraWaring)* 4-9-7 NHowe (2) (t: 3rd st: wknd 3f out) 2½.12
1572 Hanjessdan (40) *(DHaydnJones)* 4-9-7 JWilliams (11) (t.o) ........................... 10.13
1572 Kahhal (IRE) (35) *(MrsAKnight)* 4-8-11 ‡5DHarrison (3) (t.o) ......................... 2.14

**3/1** MISTY GODDESS (IRE)(5/2—4/1), Miss Doody, **4/1** Blushing Belle, **8/1** Shrewd Girl (USA)(op 4/1), **11/1**
Mystic Panther(5/1—12/1), **14/1** Fairspear(op 8/1), **16/1** Aspirant, Simon Ellis (IRE), Monorose, **20/1** Tresilian
Owl, **33/1** Hanjessdan, In the Print, Suemax (IRE), **50/1** Kahhal (IRE). CSF £12.69, Tote £5.10: £1.60 £2.10
£2.10 (£10.50). Mr J. R. Good (NEWMARKET) bred by A. P. Tierney in Ireland. 14 Rn; Bt in 10,000 gns
                                        2m 9.2 (4.9)
                                     SF—33/25/32/31/12/–

---

**1760**   LEVY BOARD SEVENTH RACE H'CAP (0-70) £2343.00 (£648.00: £309.00)
       1¼m 36y                                          5-00 (5-01)

    **Bighayir** (55) (bl) (Fav) *(MCPipe)* 5-9-8 MRoberts (6) (a gng wl: 6th st: led over
    2f out: easily) ............................................................. —1
1317⁶ Jarras (42) (bl) *(CASmith)* 7-8-9 JReid (8) (hld up: last st: hdwy 3f out: chsd wnr
    over 1f out: no imp) ....................................................... 3½.2
1339 Impressive Lad (30) *(RRowe)* 6-7-6 ‡5DHarrison (4) (lw: 7th st: hdwy to ld 3f out:
    sn hdd: one pce) .......................................................... 3.3
1290 Absolutely Right (50) *(JWhite)* 4-9-3 JWilliams (7) (lw: s.s: 8th st: hdwy 4f out:
    wknd over 2f out) ......................................................... 2½.4
    Casienne (IRE) (42) *(RJHolder)* 4-8-9 NAdams (5) (bit bkwd: hdwy & 5th st:
    wknd over 2f out) ......................................................... ½.5
1404 Muzo (USA) (50) *(JMBradley)* 5-8-12 ‡5ATucker (9) (plld hrd: 2nd st: led over 3f
    out: sn hdd & wknd) ...................................................... 4.6
1301 Miss Witch (50) *(HCandy)* 4-9-3 CRutter (2) (prom: led over 4f out tl over 3f out:
    sn wknd) .................................................................. 2½.7
1481⁶ Champenoise (49) (bl) *(MBell)* 4-9-2 JCarroll (3) (lw: hld up: 4th st: wknd over
    3f out: t.o) ................................................................ 12.8
1566⁵ Ryewater Dream (57) *(RJHodges)* 4-9-10 RCochrane (1) (swtg: led over 5f:
    3rd & rdn st: wknd over 3f out: t.o) ......................................... 2.9

**2/1** BIGHAYIR, **7/2** Miss Witch, Absolutely Right, **8/1** Champenoise, **10/1** Ryewater Dream(op 7/1), **14/1**
Casienne (IRE), **20/1** Jarras, Impressive Lad, **40/1** Muzo (USA). CSF £34.95, CT £571.20. Tote £3.10: £1.40
£2.80 £2.10 (£20.20). Mr A. J. Lomas (WELLINGTON) bred by Red House Stud. 9 Rn
                                        2m 9 (4.7)
                                     SF—41/21/–/18/9/4

T/Plpt: £199.70 (16.40 Tckts).                                        KH

## 1158—FOLKESTONE (R-H)

### Tuesday, June 30th [St Course Firm, Rnd Hard]
Going Allowance: St: minus 0.20 sec (F); Rnd: minus 0.45 sec (H)          Wind: almost nil

Stalls: low

**1761**  LESLIE AMES MEMORIAL H'CAP (3-Y-O) (0-70) £2226.00 (£616.00: £294.00)
**6f 189y**                   (Weights raised 1 lb)                         1-45 (1-46)

15983 **Morsun (67)** (bl) *(DMorley)* 9-7 PaulEddery (5) (hld up: led over 2f out: clr over
          1f out: easily) ..................................................................................... —1
1428   Countercheck (IRE) **(55)** *(CFWall)* 8-9 NDay (3) (lw: 3rd st: hrd rdn over 1f out:
          unable qckn) ......................................................................................... 4.2
1572   Tulapet **(48)** (v) *(SDow)* 8-2 PRobinson (4) (lw: led over 4f: 2nd st: one pce fnl
          2f) ........................................................................................................ ½.3
15583  Lawnswood Prince (IRE) **(57)** *(JLSpearing)* 8-11 WNewnes (6) (lw: s.s: 6th st:
          nvr nr to chal) ...................................................................................... 1½.4
1440*  Bear With Me **(65)** (Fav) *(MBell)* 9-5 PatEddery (1) (b.nr hind: rdn 3f out:
          4th st: eased whn btn over 1f out) ....................................................... 5.5
1614   Sea Prodigy **(57)** *(MBlanshard)* 8-11 JQuinn (2) (lw: 5th st: a bhd) .............. nk.6

**5/6** Bear With Me (IRE), **7/2** MORSUN(5/2—4/1), **9/2** Countercheck (IRE), **9/1** Sea Prodigy, **25/1** Lawnswood
Prince (IRE), **40/1** Tulapet. CSF £17.43, Tote £3.60: £1.50 £2.10 (£9.60). Mr John B. Sunley (NEWMARKET)
bred by Sunley Stud. 6 Rn                                                     1m 23 (1.4)
                                                                      SF—39/15/6/10/3/–

**1762**  E.B.F. ROMNEY MARSH SYNDICATE STKS (Mdn 2-Y-O) £2324.00 (£644.00: £308.00)
**6f**                                                                       2-15 (2-16)

15412 **Young Ern** *(SDow)* 9-0 BRouse (7) (hld up: led wl over 1f out: r.o wl) ........ —1
14433  Final Frontier (IRE) *(RAkehurst)* 8-11 ‡3RPerham (8) (lw: a.p: led over 2f out tl wl
          over 1f out: unable qckn) ...................................................................... 4.2
14094  Brigadore Gold *(RHannon)* 8-2 ‡7DGibbs (5) (led over 3f: ev ch wl over 1f out:
          one pce) ................................................................................................. 2.3
15242  Raging Thunder *(GLewis)* 9-0 PaulEddery (6) (lw: dwlt: hdwy over 1f out: nvr
          nrr) ........................................................................................................ ¾.4
15025  Miss Fayruz (IRE) *(MrsLPiggott)* 8-9 LPiggott (4) (b.hind: nvr nr to chal) ...... 1.5
15692  Special Risk (IRE) (Fav) *(MBell)* 9-0 PatEddery (3) (rdn & no hdwy fnl 3f) ........ 2½.6
15415  Hawaii Star (IRE) *(GLewis)* 8-9 GCarter (2) (spd over 3f) ............................. 6.7
         Princess Nebia *(BJMcMath)* 8-9 RHills (1) (unf: bit bkwd: a bhd) ................. 4.8

**7/4** Special Risk (IRE), **7/2** Raging Thunder(op 2/1), **9/2** YOUNG ERN(6/1—4/1), **13/2** Final Frontier
(IRE)(9/2—7/1), **15/2** Miss Fayruz (IRE)(9/2—8/1), **25/1** Brigadore Gold, Hawaii Star (IRE), **33/1** Princess
Nebia. CSF £29.79, Tote £5.90: £1.30 £1.80 £1.20 (£41.80). Mr M. F. Kentish (EPSOM) bred by M. F. Kentish. 8
Rn                                                                           1m 12.4 (1.7)
                                                                      SF—42/23/6/15/6/1

**1763**  GODFREY EVANS STKS    £2238.00 (£618.00: £294.00)    6f        2-45 (2-47)

14324 **Miss Bluebird (IRE) (82)** (bl) *(PAKelleway)* 3-8-6(2) PatEddery (2) (b.hind:
          mde all: hrd rdn over 1f out: r.o wl) ........................................................ —1
14746  Sylvan Breeze **(84)** (Fav) *(PMitchell)* 4-9-3 SWhitworth (5) (chsd wnr fnl 4f: hrd
          rdn & wandered over 1f out: unable qckn) ............................................. 6.2
13155  Belated *(HThomsonJones)* 3-8-4 RHills (3) (lw: a.p: one pce fnl 2f) .............. 1½.3
16784  Blue Drifter (IRE) *(JSutcliffe)* 3-8-9 BRouse (4) (a wl bhd) .......................... 15.4
1707   Share Holder (bl) *(MissGayKelleway)* 4-8-5 ‡7AntoinetteArmes (1) (b.hind: bhd
          fnl 3f) ..................................................................................................... s.h.5

**Evens** Sylvan Breeze, **7/4** MISS BLUEBIRD (IRE), **5/1** Belated(7/2—11/2), **16/1** Blue Drifter (IRE)(op 10/1), **50/1**
Share Holder. CSF £3.76, Tote £2.60: £1.50 £1.30 (£2.00). Mr P. A. Kelleway (NEWMARKET) bred by
Collinstown Stud Farm Ltd in Ireland. 5 Rn                                    1m 11.9 (1.2)
                                                                      SF—44/31/12/–/–

**1764**  BRIDGE (S) STKS (2-Y-O) £2284.80 (£632.80: £302.40)    5f    3-15 (3-18)

9735  **Zany Zanna (IRE)** *(GAPritchard-Gordon)* 8-6 PRobinson (10) (a.p: hrd rdn &
          led over 1f out: r.o wl) .......................................................................... —1
15736  Prince Manki *(RHannon)* 8-8 ‡3RPerham (5) (hdwy over 2f out: nt clr run over 1f
          out: swtcd rt & r.o) ................................................................................ 1½.2
15794  Screech (Fav) *(CJames)* 8-6 PatEddery (6) (lw: led over 2f: ev ch 1f out: unable
          qckn) ...................................................................................................... 1½.3
1638   Gaynor Goodman (IRE) *(JSMoore)* 8-1 ‡5RPrice (3) (lw: a.p: one pce fnl 2f) .... 2½.4
1202   No Extras (IRE) (bl) *(JSutcliffe)* 8-11 BRouse (11) (s.s: hdwy over 2f out: one
          pce) ........................................................................................................ hd.5

*1547* Tee-Emm *(PHowling)* 8-11 BCrossley (2) (a.p: led over 2f out tl over 1f out: sn wknd) .................................................. 2¹/₂.**6**
1442⁵ All Promises *(PButler)* 8-6 JQuinn (7) (spd over 2f) ...................................... 3.**7**
1140 Genesis Four (bl) *(JRJenkins)* 8-11 SWhitworth (1) (lw: a bhd) ...................... 3.**8**
1429 Victorian Star *(PButler)* 7-13 ‡⁷DToole (9) (a bhd) ..................................... 1¹/₂.**9**
1442 Tropical Tia (IRE) *(RVoorspuy)* 8-6 SDawson (4) (b.hind: a bhd) ............... 15.**10**

**5/2** Screech, **100/30** ZANY ZANNA (IRE), **11/2** No Extras (IRE)(7/2—6/1), Gaynor Goodman (IRE)(4/1—6/1), **13/2** All Promises(10/1—16/1), Prince Manki(5/2—7/1), **25/1** Tropical Tia (IRE), **33/1** Genesis Four, Tee-Emm, **50/1** Victorian Star. CSF £24.28, Tote £4.40: £1.40 £2.30 £1.50 (£9.00). Mr Giles W. Pritchard-Gordon (NEWMARKET) bred by Limestone Stud in Ireland. 10 Rn; No bid          60.9 sec (2.1)
SF—30/26/18/3/12/2

**1765**  LEVY BOARD H'CAP (0-70) £2343.00 (£648.00: £309.00)  **1m 7f 92y** 3-45 (3-47)
(Weights raised 5 lb)
1592★ **Garden District (74)** (Fav) *(RCharlton)* 3-10-0 (4x) PatEddery (1) (lw: led 13f out: rdn over 5f out: qcknd 2f out: eased in fnl f) ............... —**1**
1459 Shar Emblem **(50)** *(SDow)* 4-9-8 LPiggott (2) (lost pl 7f out: 3rd st: rallied over 1f out: one pce) .................................. 2¹/₂.**2**
1566★ Caroles Clown **(40)** *(MJHaynes)* 6-8-5 ‡⁷DToole (3) (led over 2f: 2nd st: one pce fnl 2f) .......................................... nk.**3**

**2/7** GARDEN DISTRICT, **9/2** Caroles Clown(3/1—5/1), **8/1** Shar Emblem(op 4/1). CSF £2.53, Tote £1.30 (£1.70). Mr K. Abdulla (BECKHAMPTON) bred by Sir Gordon Brunton. 3 Rn          3m 23.5 (4.5)

**1766**  DISK MAKER CHALLENGE CUP (H'cap) (0-70) £2322.00 (£642.00: £306.00)
**1¹/₂m**          4-15 (4-15)
1318 **Snow Blizzard (50)** (Fav) *(SDow)* 4-8-8 LPiggott (1) (lw: led 11f out: clr over 1f out: comf) ........................................ —**1**
1640 Thimbalina **(40)** *(DAWilson)* 6—7-12 GCarter (5) (b: 4th st: hrd rdn over 1f out: unable qckn) ...................................... 5.**2**
1220 Dordogne **(57)** *(RAkehurst)* 3-7-11 ‡³FNorton (6) (lw: led 1f: 3rd st: hrd rdn over 1f out: one pce) .................................... 1¹/₂.**3**
*1543*★ Monarda **(70)** *(PFICole)* 5-9-7 ‡⁷JDSmith (3) (lw: 2nd & ev ch whn rn wd st: one pce fnl 2f) ....................................... 1¹/₂.**4**
1446 Formal Invitation (IRE) **(60)** *(GLewis)* 3-8-3 PaulEddery (2) (b: 5th st: bhd fnl 2f) 8.**5**
Rabbit's Foot **(35)** *(RJO'Sullivan)* 4-7-7 JQuinn (4) (bit bkwd: a bhd: t.o fnl 5f) 30.**6**

**15/8** SNOW BLIZZARD, **9/4** Monarda, **9/2** Thimbalina(6/1—7/2), **7/1** Formal Invitation (IRE), **10/1** Dordogne(7/1—12/1), **20/1** Rabbit's Foot. CSF £9.69, Tote £2.30: £1.40 £3.20 (£5.20). Mr M. F. Kentish (EPSOM) bred by M. F. Kentish. 6 Rn          2m 33.3 (0.6 under best; U.2)
SF—42/22/18/39/5/–

**1767**  FRIENDS OF FOLKESTONE H'CAP (Amateurs) (0-70) £2265.20 (£627.20: £299.60)
**1m 1f 149y**          4-45 (4-46)
(Weights raised 15 lb)
1481⁴ **Lots of Luck (49)** *(JPearce)* 9-12-0 MrsLPearce (3) (5th st: rdn over 1f out: led ins fnl f: r.o wl) ...................................... —**1**
*1540*★ Missy-S (IRE) **(52)** (Fav) *(GAPritchard-Gordon)* 3-11-1 ‡⁴MrPPritchard-Gordon (7) (lw: 3rd st: rdn over 1f out: unable qckn) ..................... 4.**2**
1034⁵ Broughton Blues (IRE) **(34)** (bl) *(WJMusson)* 4-10-9 ‡⁴MrsJMusson (5) (b: 4th st: one pce fnl 2f) .................................. nk.**3**
1371 Athar (IRE) **(52)** *(PTWalwyn)* 3-11-5 MissJWinter (6) (lw: 2nd st: led 1f out tl ins fnl f: one pce) ...................................... 1.**4**
1366 Rio Trusky **(40)** *(MDIUsher)* 3-10-3 ‡⁴MrsAUsher (4) (swtg: led: clr 8f out: hdd 1f out: sn wknd) ......................................... 2¹/₂.**5**
1640 Spirit Sam **(24)** *(PJFeilden)* 7–9-13 ‡⁴MrSRees (2) (6th st: a bhd) .................. 7.**6**
494 Buzzards Crest **(33)** *(BobJones)* 7–10-8 ‡⁴MissDianaJones (1) (a bhd: t.o) ...... 25.**7**

**6/4** Missy-S (IRE)(tchd 5/2), **13/8** LOTS OF LUCK, **6/1** Broughton Blues (IRE)(op 4/1), **7/1** Athar (IRE)(5/1—10/1), **10/1** Buzzards Crest, **25/1** Rio Trusky, **50/1** Spirit Sam. CSF £4.63, Tote £2.50: £1.70 £1.30 (£2.10). Burton Park Country Club (NEWMARKET) bred by Mrs C. M. Allan. 7 Rn          2m 3.5 (5.8)

T/Plpt: £51.90 (35.35 Tckts).          AK

1196—**EPSOM (L-H)**
**Wednesday, July 1st [Good]**
Going Allowance: 0.20 sec per fur (G)          Wind: slt half against

Stalls: 2nd & 4th high, remainder low

**1768**  EPSOM AND EWELL H'CAP (0-90) £3655.00 (£1090.00: £520.00: £235.00)
**1¹/₂m 10y**          6-30 (6-35)
1387³ **Mahfil (68)** *(RAkehurst)* 4-9-2 TQuinn (5) (4th st: led over 2f out: rdn out) ......... —**1**

1211 Loki (IRE) **(73)** *(GLewis)* 4–9–2 ‡⁵DHarrison (4) (chsd ldr: led over 5f out tl over 2f out: unable qckn) ........................................................ 3.2

1301² Crystal Cross (USA) **(83)** (Fav) *(IABalding)* 3–8–13 ‡⁵ATucker (1) (3rd st: hrd rdn over 2f out: one pce) ........................................................ ¾.3

1381 High Beacon **(77)** (bl) *(KCBailey)* 5–9–8 ‡³RPerham (2) (led over 6f: 2nd st: wknd 2f out) ........................................................ 7.4

**5/4** Crystal Cross (USA), **7/4** MAHFIL(op 11/10), **6/1** High Beacon, **7/1** Loki (IRE). CSF £10.37, Tote £2.40 (£4.60). Mr G. S. Beccle (EPSOM) bred by Derrinstown Stud Ltd. 4 Rn
2m 42.72 (7.72)
SF–49/43/38/33

## 1769

TATTENHAM AUCTION STKS (Mdn 2-Y.O) £2343.00 (£648.00: £309.00)
6f
7-00 (7-02)

928⁵ **Glowing Dancer** *(JRJenkins)* 8-9 RCochrane (1) (lw: led over 3f: hrd rdn over 1f out: led last strides) ........................................................ —1

1573³ Allez Bianco *(RJHolder)* 8-0 DHolland (4) (lw: 3rd st: led ins fnl f: hrd rdn & hdd last strides) ........................................................ nk.2

1457 Walnut Burl (IRE) *(LJHolt)* 8-9 JReid (2) (4th st: led over 2f out tl ins fnl f: unable qckn) ........................................................ ¾.3

Racing Telegraph (Fav) *(JPearce)* 8-6(1) (leggy: plld hrd: 6th st: hdwy over 1f out: r.o) ........................................................ ½.4

968⁶ Christian Spirit *(RHannon)* 8-0 ‡⁵DHarrison (5) (swtg: 5th st: hrd rdn over 2f out: one pce) ........................................................ 4.5

1573 Sharp Imp *(JSutcliffe)* 8-5 BRouse (3) (2nd st: wknd 2f out) ........................................................ 15.6

**2/1** Racing Telegraph, **100/30** Allez Bianco(2/1—7/2), **7/2** Walnut Burl (IRE)(op 2/1), **9/2** GLOWING DANCER, **8/1** Christian Spirit(op 4/1), **33/1** Sharp Imp. CSF £18.02, Tote £5.30: £2.60 £1.60 (£8.20). Mr A. Escudero (ROYSTON) bred by John David Abell. 6 Rn
1m 13.85 (5.85)
SF–2/–/–/–/–

## 1770

LBC NEWSTALK 97.3 FM STKS (Mdn 3-Y.O) £2831.50 (£784.00: £374.50)
1¼m 18y
7-35 (7-39)

1573³ Hideyoshi (USA) (Fav) *(DRCElsworth)* 9-0 WCarson (2) (2nd st: led over 2f out: rdn out) ........................................................ —1

Let's Get Lost *(WJHaggas)* 9-0 MRoberts (6) (lw: 3rd & styd far side st: led 3f out tl over 2f out: rdn & r.o) ........................................................ 1½.2

1411 Kingsfold Pet *(MJHaynes)* 9-0 BRouse (7) (led 7f: eased whn btn over 2f out) . 10.3

1505 Maligned (IRE) *(JRFanshawe)* 8-9 GCarter (3) (5th st: wknd over 2f out) ........................................................ ½.4

Corinthian God (IRE) *(DAWilson)* 9-0 DHolland (4) (bkwd: hrd rdn over 5f out: 4th st: wknd over 3f out: t.o) ........................................................ 20.5

1478² Impeccable Charm (USA) *(JHMGosden)* 8-9 PatEddery (5) (s.s: a wl bhd: 6th & styd far side st: t.o) ........................................................ 2.6

Twice as Much *(DAWilson)* 8-9 WNewnes (1) (str: bit bkwd: s.s: a wl bhd: styd far side st: t.o) ........................................................ 7

**8/11** HIDEYOSHI (USA), **7/2** Impeccable Charm (USA)(5/2—4/1), Let's Get Lost(op 2/1), **20/1** Maligned (IRE), **25/1** Kingsfold Pet, **66/1** Ors. CSF £3.71, Tote £1.80: £1.30 £1.90 (£2.80). Mr Yoshiki Akazawa (WHITSBURY) bred by Bertram and Mrs R. Firestone in USA. 7 Rn
2m 12.19 (7.69)
SF–43/40/20/14/–/–

## 1771

W.S. ATKINS H'CAP (0-90) £3557.50 (£1060.00: £505.00: £227.50)
6f 8-05 (8-10)

1684³ **Running Glimpse (IRE) (65)** *(MissBSanders)* 4–8-6 MRoberts (3) (2nd st: led over 3f out: rdn out) ........................................................ —1

7⁵⁵ Assignment **(74)** *(JFitch-Heyes)* 6–9-1 TQuinn (7) (5th st: hrd rdn over 1f out: unable qckn) ........................................................ 3½.2

1212 Gallant Hope **(57)** (bl) *(LGCottrell)* 10–7-12 RFox (6) (lw: 6th st: hdwy fnl f: r.o) ½.3

1474 Aughfad **(83)** (v) *(TCasey)* 6–9-10 JReid (4) (lw: led over 2f: one pce) . 2.4

1607⁵ Ashtina **(67)** (Fav) *(RJHodges)* 7–8-8 RCochrane (1) (lw: 3rd st: hrd rdn over 1f out: one pce) ........................................................ 1.5

1474★ Red Rosein **(87)** *(CaptJWilson)* 6–10-0 GCarter (1) (b.off hind: s.s: nvr nr to chal) 2.6

1614 Tylers Wood **(55)** *(SDow)* 7–7-7(3) ‡³FNorton (5) (4th st: wknd fnl f) ........................................................ hd.7

LONG HANDICAP: Tylers Wood 7-5.

**11/4** Ashtina, **7/2** Red Rosein, Aughfad, **4/1** RUNNING GLIMPSE (IRE), **6/1** Gallant Hope, **12/1** Assignment, **25/1** Tylers Wood. CSF £41.97, Tote £4.70: £2.00 £4.20 (£37.00). Copyforce Ltd (EPSOM) bred by B. W. Hills and Mrs V. Shaw in Ireland. 7 Rn
1m 11.26 (3.26)
SF–51/46/27/45/25/37

## 1772

BURGH HEATH CLAIMING STKS (3-Y.O) £2322.00 (£642.00: £306.00)
1m 114y
8-40 (8-41)

1341³ **Systematic (58)** *(RHannon)* 8-13 MRoberts (4) (5th st: led ins fnl f: rdn out) ..... —1

1503* First Century (IRE) **(77)** *(Fav)* *(PFlCole)* 9-0　TQuinn (5) (2nd st: led over 2f out tl ins fnl f: r.o) ..................................... ¾.**2**

1655⁵ Lyn's Return (IRE) **(62)** *(RSimpson)* 8-7 ‡⁵ATucker (2) (lw: 3rd & styd far side st: led 3f out tl over 2f out: rdn & r.o) .................. 1½.**3**

*1544*⁴ Up the Punjab **(59)** *(SDow)* 8-1　WCarson (7) (led over 5f: unable qckn) ........... 1½.**4**

1581⁴ Kindred Cameo **(55)** *(GLewis)* 7-9 ‡⁵DHarrison (3) (lw: hdwy over 3f out: one pce fnl 2f) ........................................ 1½.**5**

1366 Lindeman **(47)** *(SDow)* 8-8　JReid (6) (lw: 6th st: wknd over 1f out) ............... 4.**6**

1572⁵ Slanderinthestrand (IRE) **(44)** (v) *(MJHaynes)* 8-6　BRouse (8) (styd far side st: a bhd) .................................................. 4.**7**

*1550*⁵ Our Eddie **(63)** (bl) *(BGubby)* 8-8　NAdams (1) (b.nr hind: lw: styd far side st: a bhd) ...................................................... ½.**8**

1528⁶ Freephone (CAN) **(53)** (bl) *(JWHills)* 8-11　WNewnes (9) (lw: 4th st: wknd 3f out: t.o) ..................................................... 20.**9**

**6/4** First Century (IRE)(op Evens), **4/1** Up the Punjab, **7/1** SYSTEMATIC, **15/2** Lyn's Return (IRE), Freephone (CAN), **16/1** Slanderinthestrand (IRE), Our Eddie, **20/1** Lindeman, **25/1** Kindred Cameo. CSF £17.17, Tote £6.50: £2.00 £1.40 £2.30 (£7.00). Mrs F. Cooney and Mrs A. Turner (MARLBOROUGH) bred by A. L. Robinson. 9 Rn; First Century (IRE) clmd B R Millman £13,258　　　　　　　　　　　1m 48.09 (7.09)
SF—18/17/7/–/–/–

**1773**　LANGLEY VALE H'CAP (0-90) £3720.00 (£1110.00: £530.00: £240.00)
　　　　7f　　　　　　　　　　　　　　　　　　　　　　　　9-10 (9-12)

1476 **Rocky Waters (USA) (83)** *(GLewis)* 3-8-13　BRouse (6) (mde all: r.o wl) ........... —**1**

1339* Royal Dartmouth (USA) **(55)** *(BRMillman)* 7-7-7　NCarlisle (7) (b: hdwy 2f out: r.o wl ins fnl f) ............................................... s.h.**2**

1588² Durneltor **(65)** *(Fav)* *(RHannon)* 4-8-3　MRoberts (1) (5th st: rdn over 2f out: unable qckn) ...................................... 4.**3**

1261⁵ Belfort Ruler **(64)** *(BGubby)* 5-8-2　NAdams (8) (4th st: ev ch over 2f out: wknd over 1f out) ........................................... 1.**4**

1474 Prenonamoss **(84)** *(DWPArbuthnot)* 4-9-8　JReid (11) (b.hind: 6th st: one pce fnl 3f) .................................................. ½.**5**

1684⁴ Caroles Express **(77)** *(RAkehurst)* 4-8-12 ‡³RPerham (4) (2nd st: wknd 2f out) nk.**6**

1599⁴ Norfolkiev (FR) **(63)** *(MMoubarak)* 6-8-1　DHolland (2) (lw: 3rd st: eased whn btn fnl f) ............................................ 7

1529² Mu-Arrik **(58)** *(DAWilson)* 4-7-7⁽³⁾ ‡³FNorton (9) (a bhd) ............................ 8

1406² Cee-En-Cee **(73)** (bl) *(MMcCourt)* 8-8-11　TQuinn (5) (bhd fnl 3f) .................. 9

1412⁴ Try Leguard (IRE) **(77)** *(WCarter)* 3-8-7　GCarter (10) (lw: a bhd) ................ 10

1369* Across the Bay **(78)** (v) *(SDow)* 5-9-2　WCarson (12) (a bhd) ....................... 11
LONG HANDICAP: Royal Dartmouth (USA) 7-3.

**7/2** Durneltor, **5/1** Across the Bay, Caroles Express, **6/1** Mu-Arrik, **7/1** Prenonamoss, **8/1** Norfolkiev (FR), **9/1** Cee-En-Cee, **10/1** Try Leguard (IRE), **11/1** ROCKY WATERS (USA), **16/1** Ors. CSF £162.49, CT £688.79. Tote £18.00: £3.20 £4.00 £1.70 (£168.20). Mr K. Higson (EPSOM) bred by Dan C. Pitts in USA. 11 Rn
1m 24.8 (hand) (4.3)<br>SF—55/34/32/29/47/39

T/Trio: Race 6: £419.40 (5 Tckts). T/Plpt: £221.70 (14.65 Tckts).　　　　　　　　　　AK

## 1721—**WARWICK (L-H)**

### Wednesday, July 1st [Good, Good to soft patches]

Going Allowance: 5f-6f: 0.30 sec; Rest: minus 0.05 sec per fur (G)　　Wind: mod against

Stalls: low

**1774**　WARWICK FESTIVAL STKS (Mdn 3-Y.O.C & G) £1932.00 (£532.00: £252.00)
　　　　7f　　　　　　　　　　　　　　　　　　　　　　　　2-30 (2-34)

1745 **Masrur (USA) (66)** *(RWArmstrong)* 9-0　WCarson (4) (lw: racd wd: led 3f: 2nd & c stands' side st: led over 1f out: r.o wl) ................ —**1**

1636² Super Serenade **(72)** *(Fav)* *(GBBalding)* 9-0　JWilliams (3) (led 4f out: hdd & hung rt over 1f out: hrd rdn: nt qckn) ............... 2.**2**

Quarrington Hill *(KSBridgwater)* 8-7 ‡⁷TArrand (1) (leggy: unf: bit bkwd: s.s: lost tch 4f out: last st: t.o) ..................... dist.**3**

**4/11** Super Serenade, **5/2** MASRUR (USA)(op 11/8), **25/1** Quarrington Hill. CSF £3.61, Tote £2.70 (£1.30). Mr Hamdan Al-Maktoum (NEWMARKET) bred by Universal Stables in USA. 3 Rn　　1m 32.4 (8.2)

**1775**　NATTRASS GILES CLAIMING STKS (2-Y.O) £2206.40 (£610.40: £291.20)
　　　　6f　　　　　　　　　　　　　　　　　　　　　　　　3-00 (3-04)

1161 **Bourbon Jack** *(Fav)* *(JWPayne)* 8-13　AMunro (3) (3rd st: led wl over 1f out: rdn out) ..................................................... —**1**

Page 629

709⁶ Bird Hunter *(NACallaghan)* 9-2 WCarson (1) (pushed along: led 4f out: hdd wl
    over 1f out: one pce) ............................................................................................ 4.2
1442⁶ Wealthywoo *(JSMoore)* 7-8 NCarlisle (2) (led 2f: 2nd st: ev ch 2f out: wknd over
    1f out) ............................................................................................................ 5.3

**11/10** BOURBON JACK(Evens—6/4), **6/5** Bird Hunter(op 4/5), **7/1** Wealthywoo. CSF £2.51, Tote £2.10 (£1.40).
Mr Ettore Landi (NEWMARKET) bred by Whitsbury Manor Stud. 3 Rn        1m 18.4 (6.4)
SF—7/–/–

**1776**    KIDSONS IMPEY TROPHY (H'cap) (0-80) £3041.00 (£908.00: £434.00: £197.00)
       **6f**                                                        3-30 (3-35)

1614 **Respectable Jones (68)** *(GBBalding)* 6-10-0 JWilliams (9) (hld up: 6th st:
    hdwy over 1f out: r.o to ld nr fin) .............................................................. —1
1570★ Harry's Coming (65) **(Fav)** *(RJHodges)* 8-9-8 (7x) ‡³TSprake (8) (last st: hdwy
    2f out: led wl ins fnl f: hdd cl home) ............................................................ ½.2
1614⁵ My Ruby Ring (41) *(DRLaing)* 5-8-1 TyroneWilliams (7) (b.hind: 4th & rdn st: ev
    ch over 1f out: nt qckn fnl f) ..................................................................... ¾.3
1570³ Ganeshaya (44) (bl) *(MFBarraclough)* 3-7-11 NCarlisle (5) (lw: led tl wl ins fnl f) s.h.4
1445 Everglades (IRE) (68) *(RCharlton)* 4-10-0 RCochrane (2) (5th st: wknd over 1f
    out) ............................................................................................................ 4.5
1570⁴ Banbury Flyer (55) *(MrsALMKing)* 4-9-1 AMunro (1) (2nd st: ev ch over 1f out:
    wknd qckly) ................................................................................................ 2.6
1111⁵ Glenfield Greta (64) *(PSFelgate)* 4-9-7 ‡³FNorton (3) (7th st: no hdwy) ............ hd.7
1216⁶ Forest Fairy (71) *(RBoss)* 3-9-5 ‡⁵DHarrison (4) (3rd st: wknd 2f out) ............. 1.8
1333⁴ Cashtal Queen (50) *(JBerry)* 3-8-3 GCarter (6) (lw: 8th st: a bhd: t.o) ............. 8.9

**3/1** Harry's Coming, **13/2** Forest Fairy, Everglades (IRE), **7/1** Banbury Flyer, **8/1** My Ruby Ring, **10/1** Ganeshaya,
Glenfield Greta, RESPECTABLE JONES, **12/1** Cashtal Queen. CSF £35.84, CT £215.25. Tote £11.60: £2.00
£1.50 £3.60 (£10.30). Mrs Ernest Weinstein (DORCHESTER) bred by E. and Mrs Weinstein. 9 Rn  1m 17 (5)
SF—50/42/18/13/28/7

**1777**    LEVY BOARD CLAIMING STKS (3-Y.O) £2406.00 (£666.00: £318.00)
       **2m 20y**                                                  4-00 (4-02)

1567⁴ **Ellafitzetty (IRE) (54)** (bl) *(RFJohnsonHoughton)* 8-0 AMunro (9) (a.p: rdn to
    ld 3f out: wl clr over 1f out: unchal) ........................................................... —1
1286⁴ Alternation (FR) (53) (bl) **(Fav)** *(PFICole)* 8-6 TQuinn (7) (led 13f: 3rd st: one
    pce) ............................................................................................................ 12.2
1172 Rich Pickings (36) *(CACyzer)* 7-13 ‡⁷TMcLaughlin (5) (hld up: stdy hdwy 6f out:
    wnt 2nd st: no ch w wnr) .......................................................................... 1½.3
1567 Ghostly Glow (v) *(CCElsey)* 8-13 TRogers (8) (chsd ldr tl 4th & wkng st) ............ 7.4
804 Scultore (USA) (62) *(MRChannon)* 8-13 WNewnes (2) (poor 7th st: a in rr) ...... 10.5
1446 Express Signmaker (IRE) (47) *(JWhite)* 8-12 DaleGibson (4) (prom: rdn 9f out:
    wknd 5f out: poor 6th st) ......................................................................... ½.6
1572 Marpatann (IRE) (48) *(ASReid)* 8-1 ‡⁷PMcCabe (4) (poor 5th st: a bhd) ......... ¾.7
1294 So Beguiling (USA) (39) *(MrsALMKing)* 7-13 ‡³FNorton (6) (t.o fnl 8f) ............. dist.8

**7/4** Alternation (FR), **9/4** ELLAFITZETTY (IRE), **4/1** Scultore (USA), **8/1** Express Signmaker (IRE), **14/1** Rich
Pickings, So Beguiling (USA), **33/1** Ghostly Glow, **40/1** Marpatann (IRE). CSF £6.49, Tote £2.90: £1.10 £1.10
£2.00 (£2.20). Mr A. P. Hamilton (DIDCOT) bred by T. J. Monaghan in Ireland. 8 Rn   3m 40.9 (14.9)

**1778**    ROTHMANS ROYALS NORTH SOUTH CHALLENGE SERIES H'CAP (3-Y.O) (0-80)
       £2976.00 (£888.00: £424.00: £192.00)    **1m**             4-30 (4-33)
       (Weights raised 9 lb)

1724★ **Alkarif (USA) (75)** **(Fav)** *(AAScott)* 9-12 (5x) WCarson (3) (mde all: sn clr: rdn
    over 1f out: r.o wl) ..................................................................................... —1
1146 Ghurrah (IRE) (60) *(CJBenstead)* 8-11 JWilliams (4) (sn wl bhd: last st: rapid
    hdwy over 1f out: ev ch ins fnl f: r.o) ......................................................... ½.2
1750² Edgeaway (64) *(JWHills)* 9-1 WNewnes (1) (chsd wnr: 2nd st: ev ch over 1f out:
    one pce) .................................................................................................... 3.3
1426³ Eastleigh (64) *(RHollinshead)* 9-1 WRyan (2) (3rd st: rdn & wknd over 1f out) ... 7.4

**11/10** ALKARIF (USA), **100/30** Edgeaway, Eastleigh, **8/1** Ghurrah (IRE)(5/1—10/1). CSF £7.45, Tote £1.60
(£4.60). Mr Hamdan Al-Maktoum (NEWMARKET) bred by Lillie F. Webb in USA. 4 Rn    1m 41 (4)
SF—46/29/24/3

**1779**    E.B.F. ROYAL STKS (Mdn 2-Y.O) £2320.00 (£640.00: £304.00)    **5f**    5-00 (5-01)

*1375⁵* Carnbrea Snip *(MBell)* 8-9 TQuinn (2) (lw: mde all: rdn over 1f out: edtgd lft: r.o
    wl) ............................................................................................................ —1
1283³ The Fed (Fav) *(RMWhitaker)* 9-0 ACulhane (4) (chsd wnr: r.o one pce fnl 2f) ..... 3.2
1489⁴ I Do Care *(JBerry)* 9-0 GCarter (3) (rdn over 2f out: one pce) ............................ 8.3
1279³ Cinders Girl *(JMPEustace)* 8-9 GDuffield (1) (lw: hld up: hrd rdn over 2f out: sn
    wl bhd) ..................................................................................................... 15.4

**5/4** The Fed, **2/1** Cinders Girl, **4/1** I Do Care, **11/2** CARNBREA SNIP. CSF £12.45, Tote £10.60 (£7.20). Mrs S. M. Crompton (NEWMARKET) bred by Mrs J. R. Hine and Miss J. Bunting. 4 Rn 62.5 sec (4.5)
SF—35/18/-/-/

**1780** STONELEIGH APP'CE STKS (Mdn 3-Y.O) *(1m)* 5-30 - **Abandoned**—Insufficient entries

T/Plpt: £662.60 (3.35 Tckts). KH

## 1233—CATTERICK (L-H)

### Wednesday, July 1st [Good to firm]

Going Allowance: minus 0.05 sec per fur (F) Wind: fresh half against

Stalls: low

**1781** COTHERSTONE STKS (Mdn 3-Y.O.) £1257.00 (£303.00) **5f 212y** 6-30 (6-32)

1625³ **Lift Boy (USA) (44)** (Fav) *(DenysSmith)* 9-0 KFallon (1) (mde all: qcknd over 2f out: easily) .................................................................. —1
Blyostka (USA) **(52)** *(GAPritchard-Gordon)* 8-9 WHood (2) (a chsng wnr: hung rt over 2f out: no imp) ................................................. 10.2

**4/11** LIFT BOY (USA)(op 4/7), **9/4** Blyostka (USA)(op 5/4). Tote £1.30. Mr J. A. Bianchi (BISHOP AUCKLAND) bred by Paul and Arnold Bryant in USA. 2 Rn 1m 14.4 (3.9)
SF—16/-

**1782** PALACEGATE RACING (S) STKS (2-Y.O) £1161.00 (£321.00: £153.00) **5f** 7-00 (7-04)

*1547* **My Godson** (bl) *(BBeasley)* 8-11 LCharnock (1) (cl up: led ¹/₂-wy: qcknd clr 1f out) ........................................................................... —1
1670⁴ Bluebella *(MrsPABarker)* 8-6 KDarley (6) (disp ld to ¹/₂-wy: r.o one pce) ......... 3¹/₂.2
1579⁵ Palacegate Prince (Fav) *(JBerry)* 8-11 JCarroll (8) (a chsng ldrs: rdn ¹/₂-wy: styd on: nvr able to chal) .................................................. 3.3
*1321* Jocks Joker *(CaptJWilson)* 8-11 JLowe (5) (s.i.s: hdwy ¹/₂-wy: nvr nr to chal) .... 1.4
Poppet Plume *(GMMoore)* 8-6 KFallon (4) (cmpt: bit bkwd: rn green & sn bhd: styd on fnl 2f: n.d) .............................................. hd.5
920 Dunnington *(MWEasterby)* 8-6 TLucas (2) (in tch: effrt ¹/₂-wy: no imp) ................ 2.6
1526 Lady Lawn *(JMCarr)* 8-6 SMorris (3) (lw: in tch: nt clr run ¹/₂-wy: sn rdn & btn) .. 1.7
*1547* Betrayed *(PCHaslam)* 8-3 ‡³JFanning (7) (disp ld to ¹/₂-wy: sn wknd) ................ 3.8

**11/10** Palacegate Prince, **2/1** Poppet Plume(9/4—6/4), **17/2** Bluebella, **10/1** MY GODSON, **12/1** Betrayed(op 7/1), **20/1** Dunnington, Jocks Joker, **100/1** Lady Lawn. CSF £81.41, Tote £16.60: £2.20 £1.20 £1.20 (£30.00). Mrs M. J. Russell (HAMBLETON) bred by Mrs M. Russell. 8 Rn; No bid 61.3 sec (3.8)
SF—18/-/-/-/-/-/

**1783** NORTHERN ECHO H'CAP (3-Y.O) (0-70) £1688.00 (£468.00: £224.00) **1¹/₂m 44y** 7-30 (7-31)
(Weights raised 16 lb)

1528 **Kayartis (36)** *(MrsGRReveley)* 8-3 JLowe (2) (lw: pushed along & hdwy 6f out: sn chsng ldrs: styd on u.p fnl f to ld nr fin) ........................... —1
1195 Bilberry **(47)** (Jt-Fav) *(CWCElsey)* 9-0 LCharnock (3) (lw: led: rdn 3f out: r.o: jst ct) ...................................................................... s.h.2
1486 Little Ivor **(42)** *(DenysSmith)* 8-2 ‡⁷CTeague (1) (lw: chsd ldrs tl outpcd 5f out: sn lost pl: hdwy 2f out: nt qckn ins fnl f) ............................ 1¹/₂.3
1528 Chantry Bellini **(51)** *(CWThornton)* 9-4 DMcKeown (6) (lw: chsd ldrs: outpcd ent st: styd on u.p) ............................................. nk.4
1517³ Master Copy (IRE) **(50)** *(CBBBooth)* 9-3 GOldroyd (6) (lw: prom: hdwy to chal 5f out: rdn & edgd lft 2f out: wknd over 1f out) ......... 6.5
1438 Mr News (IRE) **(54)** (bl) *(BBeasley)* 9-7 DNicholls (4) (lw: hld up: hdwy ent st: sn rdn & no imp) .................................................. 8.6
*Stewards Enquiry: Lowe suspended 10-13/7/92 (excessive use of whip).*

**3/1** Master Copy (IRE), Bilberry(op 5/1), **100/30** Chantry Bellini, **9/2** Mr News (IRE), **6/1** KAYARTIS, **12/1** Little Ivor. CSF £22.62, Tote £6.20: £2.10 £1.80 (£15.10). Mrs J. M. Allen (SALTBURN) bred by R. R. Evans Bloodstock Ltd. 6 Rn 2m 42.2 (8.2)
SF—1/12/-/12/-/-/

**1784** AYSGARTH CLAIMING STKS £1192.50 (£330.00: £157.50) **1¹/₂m 44y** 8-00 (8-00)

1530⁵ **Grouse-N-Heather (57)** (Fav) *(MrsGRReveley)* 3-7-13 ‡³JFanning (4) (hld up: effrt over 2f out: qcknd to ld wl ins fnl f) ................................. —1

1482 **Lord Advocate (33)** (v) *(MPNaughton)* 4–8-10 ‡⁵JWeaver (1) (chsd ldrs: led & qcknd 5f out: hdd & no ex wl ins fnl f) ............................ 1½.2

Souson (IRE) *(MWEasterby)* 4–8-13 TLucas (2) (lw: hld up: hdwy appr st: rdn over 1f out: styd on) ............................ hd.3

1152⁶ Salu (56) *(JEtherington)* 3–8-0 KDarley (7) (in tch: outpcd 4f out: styd on fnl 2f) 3½.4

1519 Calachuchi (65) *(MJCamacho)* 5–9-2 NConnorton (5) (t: lw: trckd ldrs: effrt over 2f out: btn appr fnl f) ............................ 1.5

1089 Chiparopai (IRE) (39) *(WStorey)* 4–8-6 SWebster (6) (cl up tl outpcd over 4f out: sn bhd: styd on again nr fin) ............................ 1.6

773⁵ John Shaw (USA) (67) *(JSWainwright)* 4–9-4 PBurke (3) (led tl hdd 5f out: btn whn eased ins fnl f) ............................ 3.7

**7/4** GROUSE-N-HEATHER, **11/4** Calachuchi(op 7/4), **5/1** Souson (IRE), Salu, **9/1** John Shaw (USA), **20/1** Ors. CSF £28.32, Tote £3.10: £2.20 £3.90 (£18.10). Mr Robbie Cameron (SALTBURN) bred by R. A. Cameron. 7 Rn
2m 39.5 (5.5)
SF—24/32/34/14/28/16

## 1785

HAMBLETON THOROUGHBREDS H'CAP (3-Y.O) (0-70) £1562.00 (£432.00: £206.00)
5f 212y
8-30 (8-32)

1625² **Invigilate (54)** (Fav) *(MPNaughton)* 8-2 ‡⁵JWeaver (2) (trckd ldrs on ins: led on bit appr fnl f: v.cheekily) ............................ —1

1583 Don't Run Me Over (51) *(BCMorgan)* 8-4 DMcKeown (4) (lw: led after 1f tl appr fnl f: r.o: no ch w wnr) ............................ ½.2

1625⁶ Kalar (44) *(DWChapman)* 7-11 SWood (1) (led 1f: hung rt appr st: nt qckn appr fnl f) ............................ 6.3

1440 Aegaen Lady (49) *(JEtherington)* 8-2 JLowe (3) (lw: chsd ldrs: carried wd appr st: sn rdn & btn) ............................ 2.4

1236⁵ Brambles Way (59) *(WLBarker)* 8-12 KDarley (5) (chsd ldrs: carried wd appr st: sn btn) ............................ 2½.5

901 Barnsview (44) (bl) *(MWEllerby)* 7-11 PBurke (7) (spd 4f) ............................ 7.6

**4/6** INVIGILATE, **11/2** Don't Run Me Over, **6/1** Brambles Way(op 4/1), **7/1** Aegaen Lady, **20/1** Kalar, **33/1** Barnsview. CSF £4.54, Tote £1.60: £1.10 £2.60 (£2.70). Mrs H. H. Wane (RICHMOND) bred by Bechmann Stud. 6 Rn
1m 14 (3.5)
SF—12/12/–/–/–/–

## 1786

STAINDROP STKS (Mdn) £1108.50 (£306.00: £145.50) 7f
9-00 (9-01)

1433³ **La Kermesse (USA) (63)** (Fav) *(JHMGosden)* 3–8-8 JCarroll (4) (sn trckng ldrs: led over 1f out: r.o) ............................ —1

1122 April Shadow (50) *(CWThornton)* 3–8-8 DMcKeown (6) (hld up & bhd: effrt over 2f out: r.o: nrst fin) ............................ 1.2

489⁵ Crept Out (IRE) (63) *(MissSEHall)* 3–8-13 NConnorton (3) (in tch: hdwy over 2f out: kpt on: nvr able to chal) ............................ ¾.3

1484⁶ Canon Kyle (IRE) (66) *(MHEasterby)* 3–8-13 MBirch (1) (led tl over 1f out: one pce) ............................ s.h.4

1269³ Reilton *(JParkes)* 5–9-2 ‡⁵JWeaver (2) (chsd ldrs: rdn & no hdwy fr wl over 2f out) ............................ 1½.5

1328⁴ Manuleader (56) (bl) *(BBeasley)* 3–8-13 DNicholls (7) (w ldr: rdn ent st: nt r.o) .. 4.6

1484 Miss Grosse Nez (IRE) (51) *(CWThornton)* 3–8-5 ‡³JFanning (5) (nvr trbld ldrs) 3½.7

**9/4** LA KERMESSE (USA)(op 6/4), **3/1** Manuleader, Crept Out (IRE), **6/1** Canon Kyle (IRE), **12/1** Reilton, **16/1** April Shadow, **33/1** Miss Grosse Nez (IRE). CSF £29.18, Tote £2.80: £1.60 £4.80 (£16.30). Sheikh Mohammed (NEWMARKET) bred by Swettenham Stud in USA. 7 Rn
1m 26.4 (3.2)
SF—41/38/41/40/43/23

T/Plpt: £46.70 (22.35 Tckts).
AA

## CATTERICK (L-H)
### Thursday, July 2nd [Good to firm]

Going Allowance: 5f: minus 0.40 sec; Rest: minus 0.20 sec (F)    Wind: fresh across

Stalls: low

## 1787

WETHERBY RACING BUREAU H'CAP (0-70) £2476.80 (£634.80: £326.40)
5f
2-30 (2-34)

1522⁴ **Rock Opera (IRE) (55)** (Fav) *(MPNaughton)* 4–8-7 ‡⁵JWeaver (1) (hdwy ½-wy: rdn to ld wl ins fnl f) ............................ —1

1551 Serious Hurry (56) (bl) *(SirMarkPrescott)* 4–8-13 GDuffield (6) (lw: led tl hdd & no ex wl ins fnl f) ............................ nk.2

**1788—1790**

14835 Catherines Well **(67)** *(MWEasterby)* 9–9-10 TLucas (4) (lw: a chsng ldrs: kpt on
one pce fnl f) .................................................................... 2.3
1729* Here Comes a Star **(59)** *(JMCarr)* 4–9-2 (7x) SMorris (3) (effrt ½-wy: sn rdn & no
imp) .................................................................... ½.4
10505 Jovial Kate (USA) **(44)** *(BEllison)* 5–8-1 NCarlisle (2) (chsd ldrs tl rdn & btn over
1f out) .................................................................... 3.5
1570 Dreamtime Echo **(37)** *(JBalding)* 4–7-1(1) ‡7ClaireBalding (5) (lw: sn outpcd &
bhd) .................................................................... 7.6
16693 Super Rocky **(77)** (bl) *(RBastiman)* 3–9-7 ‡7HBastiman (7) (b: lw: w ldr to ½-wy:
wknd qckly & eased: fin lame) .................................................................... 1½.7
LONG HANDICAP: Dreamtime Echo 7-6.

**15/8** ROCK OPERA (IRE), **7/2** Super Rocky, **9/2** Catherines Well, **11/2** Here Comes a Star, **9/1** Jovial Kate (USA),
**12/1** Serious Hurry, **50/1** Dreamtime Echo. CSF £20.09, Tote £2.80: £1.90 £2.70 (£9.20). Mr Philip Davies
(RICHMOND) bred by B. R. and Mrs Firestone in Ireland. 7 Rn
58.2 sec (0.7)
SF–39/44/47/37/10/–

**1788** LAUREL RACING CLUB CLAIMING STKS (2-Y.O) £2147.60 (£593.60: £282.80)
5f 212y
3-00 (3-01)

15843 **Wishing Cap (USA)** (Fav) *(SirMarkPrescott)* 8-2 GDuffield (6) (lw: trckd ldrs: slt
ld over 1f out: all out) .................................................................... —1
14486 Charlies Reward *(WLBarker)* 7-12 LCharnock (7) (chsd ldr: chal over 1f out: hrd
rdn & kpt on) .................................................................... hd.2
1524 General Brooks (IRE) (v) *(JBerry)* 8-8 JCarroll (1) (led tl hdd over 1f out) ...... 2½.3
9473 Boldville Bash (IRE) *(TDBarron)* 8-12 KDarley (5) (nvr plcd to chal) ...... 2½.4
15594 Not Earsay *(EWeymes)* 7-5(1) ‡3JFanning (4) (lw: in tch: effrt ent st: no imp) ...... 3.5
Sean's Delight *(JMCarr)* 8-3 SMorris (5) (neat: unf: s.s: outpcd & bhd tl sme late
hdwy) .................................................................... 1½.6
Laurel King *(JBerry)* 8-12 LDettori (2) (cmpt: str: scope: bit bkwd: outpcd & bhd
after 1f: n.d after) .................................................................... 1.7

**13/8** WISHING CAP (USA), **11/4** Boldville Bash (IRE), **5/1** Laurel King, **6/1** General Brooks (IRE), **12/1** Charlies
Reward(op 8/1), **14/1** Not Earsay, **20/1** Sean's Delight. CSF £18.59, Tote £2.70: £1.30 £3.90 £3.00 (£13.30). Pinnacle
Racing Stable (NEWMARKET) bred by Michael Cahan & Dr Geroulis in USA. 7 Rn; Charlies Reward clmd Laurel
Leisure Ltd. £3,000
1m 13.7 (3.2)

**1789** 'GROUP 1 RACING' H'CAP (0-70) £2511.80 (£694.80: £331.40)
1m 7f 177y
3-30 (3-34)

(Weights raised 6 lb)
16714 **Rexy Boy (28)** *(WLBarker)* 5–7-13 LCharnock (7) (mde all: kpt on wl fnl 2f) ...... —1
11902 King William **(32)** (Fav) *(JLSpearing)* 7–8-3 JLowe (1) (hld up: hdwy appr st: rdn
to chal ins fnl f: nt qckn nr fin) .................................................................... 1.2
13372 Racing Raskal **(36)** *(CaptJWilson)* 5–8-7 JCarroll (2) (a chsng ldrs: outpcd ent
st: swtchd & styd on appr fnl f) .................................................................... 3½.3
15805 Enfant du Paradis (IRE) *(PDEvans)* 4–8-8 LDettori (4) (a chsng ldrs: ev ch ent st:
sn rdn & grad wknd) .................................................................... 1.4
15664 War Beat **(53)** *(PJBevan)* 4–9-5 ‡5BDoyle (5) (cl up tl outpcd wl over 2f out) ...... 6.5
1733 Lisalee (IRE) **(35)** (bl) *(JParkes)* 4–8-6 NConnorton (3) (lw: in tch: rdn 5f out: no
imp) .................................................................... 4.6
14372 Sexy Mover **(26)** *(WStorey)* 5–7-11 SWood (8) (lost pl 6f out: n.d after) ...... 3.7

**6/4** King William, **5/2** Sexy Mover, **11/2** REXY BOY, War Beat, Enfant du Paradis (IRE), **66/1**
Lisalee (IRE). CSF £26.07, CT £47.12. Tote £9.40: £2.90 £1.70 (£7.30). Mr Jack Collins (RICHMOND) bred by
Brickfield Bloodstock Agency Ltd. 7 Rn
3m 30.6 (9.6)

**1790** TATTERSALLS AUCTION SERIES STKS (Qualifier) (Mdn 2-Y.O) £2872.00 (£856.00:
£408.00: £184.00) 5f 212y
4-00 (4-01)

12514 **Spring Sunrise** *(MBlanshard)* 7-11 ‡FNorton (5) (trckd ldrs: led & qcknd ent st:
comf) .................................................................... —1
6824 Hi Nod *(MJCamacho)* 8-6 NConnorton (6) (lw: a.p: effrt over 2f out: r.o: nt pce
of wnr) .................................................................... ½.2
14896 El Guapo *(TFairhurst)* 8-3 ‡3JFanning (1) (hdwy & n.m.r 2f out: styd on: no imp) 2½.3
1251 Sweetings Scampy (IRE) (Fav) *(MHEasterby)* 8-4 MBirch (4) (cl up: edgd lft
over 2f out: grad wknd) .................................................................... 6.4
1531 Colonel Future *(JWWatts)* 8-7 GDuffield (2) (led tl hdd ent st: btn whn sltly
hmpd over 2f out) .................................................................... 2½.5

**11/8** Sweetings Scampy (IRE), **2/1** SPRING SUNRISE, **4/1** Hi Nod, **15/2** Colonel Future, **25/1** El Guapo. CSF
£9.39, Tote £2.50: £1.20 £1.80 (£4.20). Mr R. J. Campbell (UPPER LAMBOURN) bred by Littleton Stud. 5 Rn
1m 13.5 (3)

**1791**    GYMCRAK THOROUGHBRED RACING COMPANY H'CAP (3-Y.O) (0-80) £2646.20
        (£733.20: £350.60)    **7f**                          4-30 (4-32)

(Weights raised 1 lb)

| | | |
|---|---|---|
| 1451⁴ | **Hawa Layaam (IRE) (71)** (v) (Fav) *(AAScott)* 9-1 LDettori (7) (lw: sn led: hld on wl u.p fnl f) | —1 |
| 1050⁶ | Most Surprising (IRE) **(52)** *(RMWhitaker)* 7-10 PBurke (5) (a chsng ldrs: ev ch over 1f out: kpt on) | nk.2 |
| 1607⁶ | Debsy Do (USA) **(69)** *(SGNorton)* 8-6⁷OPears (4) (s.i.s: sn rcvrd & chsd ldrs: nt qckn appr fnl f) | 5.3 |
| 1507² | Allegramente **(53)** *(RO'Leary)* 7-11 LCharnock (2) (lw: a in tch: kpt on fnl 2f: nvr plcd to chal) | ¼.4 |
| 1363⁶ | Ferrovia **(50)** (bl) *(JWWatts)* 7-8 GBardwell (8) (s.i.s: sn drvn along & hdwy: one pce fnl 2f) | hd.5 |
| | Gymcrak Tycoon **(77)** *(MHEasterby)* 9-7 MBirch (11) (lw: in tch: nt qckn fnl 2f) | hd.6 |
| 1624² | Spanish Performer **(55)** *(TFairhurst)* 7-10 (5x) ‡3JFanning (3) (lw: dwlt: wl bhd tl r.o wl fnl 2f) | ¾.7 |
| 1252 | Najeb (USA) **(75)** *(BHanbury)* 9-5 AMullis (10) (swtg: sn pushed along: n.d) | 2½.8 |
| 1246 | Military Expert **(68)** *(CaptJWilson)* 8-12 JLowe (9) (led early: chsd ldrs to st: sn wknd) | 5.9 |
| | All Earz (IRE) **(61)** *(REarnshaw)* 8-5(5) ACulhane (1) (bhd: hmpd & lost tch appr st: n.d after) | 2.10 |
| 1075 | Pitch Black (IRE) **(58)** *(MWEasterby)* 7-9 ‡JMarshall (6) (in tch to st: grad wknd) | 1.11 |

**7/2** HAWA LAYAAM (IRE), **6/1** Ferrovia, **13/2** Allegramente, **7/1** Spanish Performer, **8/1** Debsy Do (USA), **9/1** Most Surprising (IRE), Gymcrak Tycoon(op 6/1), **12/1** Pitch Black (IRE), **16/1** All Earz (IRE), Najeb (USA), **20/1** Military Expert. CSF £31.94, CT £214.51. Tote £3.90: £1.80 £2.40 £1.50 (£12.50). Mr Juma Humaid (NEWMARKET) bred by Ballydoyle Stud in Ireland. 11 Rn       1m 25.3 (2.1)
                                                   SF–48/28/23/12/8/34

**1792**    M.D.M. RACING TERRIFIC TYRNIPPY STKS (Mdn 3-Y.O.F) £2245.60 (£621.60: £296.80)
     **1½m 44y**                                5-00 (5-02)

| | | |
|---|---|---|
| 1312⁵ | **Bandoline (57)** *(BWHills)* 8-11 DHolland (3) (gd hdwy 5f out: rdn to ld 1f out: r.o) | —1 |
| | Mystic Memory *(SirMarkPrescott)* 8-11 GDuffield (2) (bhd tl hdwy 5f out: outpcd ent st: styd on & ev ch over 1f out: kpt on) | 1½.2 |
| 553⁵ | Marabou (USA) (Fav) *(LMCumani)* 8-11 LDettori (4) (hld up: hdwy 5f out: led over 2f out: sn rdn: hdd 1f out: sn btn) | 1.3 |
| 1242⁶ | Clear Sound *(GWragg)* 8-8 ‡3FNorton (1) (lw: dwlt: sn rcvrd: led appr st: hdd over 2f out: sn btn) | 1.4 |
| 1486 | Medbourne (IRE) **(37)** *(JLHarris)* 8-6 ‡5SMaloney (6) (lw: outpcd 6f out: a bhd) | 7.5 |
| 1478⁶ | Mary Macblain **(51)** *(JLHarris)* 8-11 MBirch (5) (led tl hdd appr st: sn wknd) | 20.6 |
| | Sulaah Rose *(MrsJJordan)* 8-11 ACulhane (7) (cl up tl outpcd 7f out: sn bhd: t.o) | 7 |

**1/3** Marabou (USA)(op 1/2), **9/2** Mystic Memory, **10/1** Clear Sound, **12/1** Bandoline(op 7/1), **66/1** Mary Macblain, **200/1** Sulaah Rose, **300/1** Medbourne (IRE). CSF £58.01, Tote £10.10: £2.60 £1.90 (£9.90). Sheikh Mohammed (LAMBOURN) bred by Sheikh Mohammed bjn Rashid al Maktoum. 7 Rn     2m 37.5 (3.5)
                                                   SF–38/35/33/6/–/–

**1793**    LEVY BOARD H'CAP (0-70) £2490.00 (£690.00: £330.00)    **7f**      5-30 (5-35)

| | | |
|---|---|---|
| 1441⁵ | **Leave it to Lib (53)** *(PCalver)* 5-8-6 ‡7JTate (12) (lw: trckd ldrs: led ins fnl f: r.o) | —1 |
| 1243★ | Euroblake **(68)** *(TDBarron)* 5-10-0 AlexGreaves (10) (swtg: s.i.s: hdwy ent st: r.o: nrst fin) | 2.2 |
| 1529⁴ | Chain Shot **(48)** (bl) *(MHEasterby)* 7-8-3 ‡5SMaloney (5) (led tl hdd ins fnl f: no ex) | nk.3 |
| 1508⁴ | Wild Prospect **(65)** (Fav) *(CTinkler)* 4-9-11 MBirch (4) (lw: chsd ldrs: effrt over 2f out: nt qckn) | 3½.4 |
| 1294 | Broad Appeal **(40)** (bl) *(BBeasley)* 4-7-7 ‡7AGarth (14) (dwlt: bhd tl r.o wl fnl f) | 1½.5 |
| 1629★ | Gant Bleu (FR) **(48)** *(RMWhitaker)* 5-8-8 (5x) ACulhane (6) (lw: hld up: effrt on outside 2f out: nvr able to chal) | ¾.6 |
| 1274⁶ | Wsom (IRE) **(43)** *(JMCarr)* 4-8-3 SMorris (8) (mid div: effrt over 2f out: no imp) | ½.7 |
| 1570⁶ | Quiet Victory **(49)** (bl) *(MissLCSiddall)* 5-8-6 ‡3FNorton (3) (lw: sn drvn along: nvr bttr than mid div) | 1½.8 |
| | Gott's Desire **(47)** *(RBastiman)* 6-8-0 ‡7HBastiman (9) (chsd ldrs tl wknd wl over 1f out) | 1.9 |
| 1235³ | Angel Train (IRE) **(37)** (bl) *(JParkes)* 4-7-11 LCharnock (1) (outpcd & bhd after 2f: n.d) | ½.10 |
| 1529³ | Arabat **(55)** (bl) *(MPNaughton)* 5-9-1 NConnorton (13) (prom to st) | 1½.11 |
| | Gleneliane (IRE) **(40)** *(JLHarris)* 4-8-0 DHolland (11) (sn bhd) | 10.12 |

1434² Chloes Diamond (IRE) **(48)** *(JLSpearing)* 4-8-8 JLowe (7) (hmpd & rn v.wd 4f
out: wl bhd after) ........................................ nk.13
*1617²* Brisas (11/1) Withdrawn (ref to ent stalls) : not under orders — Rule 4 applies

**4/1** Wild Prospect, **5/1** Gant Bleu (FR), **7/1** Euroblake, **8/1** Chloes Diamond (IRE), Quiet Victory, Arabat, **10/1**
LEAVE IT TO LIB, Chain Shot, **14/1** Wsom (IRE), **16/1** Gott's Desire, **20/1** Angel Train (IRE), **25/1** Broad Appeal,
**33/1** Gleneliane (IRE). CSF £71.15, CT £580.02. Tote £9.70: £2.70 £3.00 £5.40 (£52.90). Mrs C. Calver
(RIPON) bred by S. Emmet. 13 Rn
1m 25.2 (2)
SF—41/57/31/42/5/18

T/Plpt: £302.00 (7.9 Tckts).
AA

## 1597—**YARMOUTH (L-H)**
### Wednesday, July 1st [Firm]
Going Allowance: minus 0.20 sec per fur (F)
Wind: mod across

Stalls: high

**1794** LEVY BOARD CLAIMING H'CAP (I) (0-60) £2448.00 (£678.00: £324.00)
1m 3y
2-15 (2-18)

(Weights raised 4 lb)

1642⁴ **Kingchip Boy (44)** (Jt-Fav) *(MJRyan)* 3-8-4 ‡³DBiggs (4) (hdwy over 2f out: sn
rdn & wandered: wnt rt & led nr fin) ............................... —1
*1544³* Bill Moon **(49)** (Jt-Fav) *(PJFeilden)* 6-9-0 ‡⁷StephenDavies (2) (hld up: gd hdwy
appr fnl f: bmpd nr fin: fin wl) ............................... hd.2
210 Pickles **(47)** *(PCHaslam)* 4-9-5 LPiggott (7) (led: rdn over 1f out: edgd lft & ct nr
fin) ............................... hd.3
1747³ Sanawi **(52)** *(PDEvans)* 5-9-10 LDettori (1) (lw: a.p: rdn & no ex appr fnl f) ..... 3¹/₂.4
1504 Candle King (IRE) **(49)** (hl) (Jt-Fav) *(MJFetherston-Godley)* 4-9-7 MRoberts (9)
(lw: dwlt: nvr trbld ldrs) ............................... 1¹/₂.5
1598⁵ Chaff **(35)** *(DMorris)* 5-8-7(1) MTebbutt (5) (prom over 6f) ............................... hd.6
*1001* Lady Risk Me **(33)** *(JRBostock)* 3-7-3 ‡⁷CHawksley (6) (swtg: bhd: rdn 3f out:
nvr able to chal) ............................... 1¹/₂.7
1598⁴ Coral Flutter **(44)** (bl) (Jt-Fav) *(JWPayne)* 5-9-2 JQuinn (3) (hld up: effrt 3f out:
sn no imp) ............................... ³/₄.8
1503⁶ Roxy Music (IRE) **(54)** (bl) *(GAPritchard-Gordon)* 3-9-3 WRSwinburn (8) (lw:
sn chsng ldrs: wknd 2f out) ............................... 2¹/₂.9

**9/2** Candle King (IRE), Bill Moon, Coral Flutter, KINGCHIP BOY(7/1—4/1), **6/1** Sanawi, **10/1** Roxy Music (IRE),
**12/1** Pickles(op 8/1), **16/1** Chaff, **50/1** Lady Risk Me. CSF £22.40, CT £197.71. Tote £5.40: £1.80 £1.40 £1.70
(£12.90). Four Jays Racing Partnership (NEWMARKET) bred by R. M. Scott. 9 Rn
1m 40.1 (4.8)

**1795** FASTOLFF (S) STKS (3 & 4-Y.O) £2324.00 (£644.00: £308.00)
7f 3y
2-45 (2-49)

1243³ **Inseyab (58)** (Jt-Fav) *(PCHaslam)* 4-8-13 LPiggott (10) (chsd ldrs: led wl over
2f out: clr appr fnl f: easily) ............................... —1
1588 Surrey Racing **(68)** (Jt-Fav) *(GLewis)* 4-9-4 PaulEddery (8) (chsd ldrs: rdn 2f
out: kpt on fnl f) ............................... 4.2
1581⁶ Libra Legend (USA) **(61)** *(CEBrittain)* 3-8-5 MRoberts (5) (led 2f: ev ch over 2f
out: one pce) ............................... ¹/₂.3
*1548* Bernie Silvers **(46)** *(MCChapman)* 3-8-5 RHills (9) (hld up: rdn over 1f out: kpt
on one pce) ............................... 1¹/₂.4
1741 Have a Nightcap **(50)** *(MAJarvis)* 3-8-6(1) BRaymond (1) (chsd ldrs: no hdwy
fnl 2f) ............................... 4.5
1649² Orchard Bay **(49)** *(DRTucker)* 3-8-5 NAdams (3) (prom: ev ch over 2f out: sn
rdn & btn) ............................... nk.6
1708² Kertale (IRE) **(60)** *(RBoss)* 3-8-5 LDettori (2) (lw: chsd ldrs 4f) ............................... 1.7
1572 Internal Affair **(44)** *(JPearce)* 4-8-8 ‡⁵RPrice (7) (dwlt: nvr trbld ldrs) ............... hd.8
1040 Pink'n Black (IRE) **(60)** *(GBlum)* 3-8-5 JQuinn (6) (led after 2f tl hdd wl over 2f
out: sn wknd) ............................... 5.9
1284 Classic Exhibit **(47)** *(SPCWoods)* 3-8-5 WWoods (4) (swtg: dwlt: rdn 3f out: nvr
rchd ldrs) ............................... 8.10

**5/2** INSEYAB, Surrey Racing, **3/1** Kertale (IRE), **15/2** Libra Legend (USA), **20/1** Pink'n Black (IRE), **25/1** Orchard
Bay, Internal Affair, **33/1** Ors. CSF £8.58, Tote £3.70: £1.50 £1.80 £1.80 (£5.80). Mrs P. Haslam (MIDDLEHAM)
bred by Gainsborough Stud Management Ltd. 10 Rn; Bt in 4,250 gns
1m 26 (3.2)
SF—19/12/-/-/-/-

**1796** E.B.F. MARITIME MUSEUM STKS (Mdn 2-Y.O) £2196.00 (£606.00: £288.00)
7f 3y
3-15 (3-15)

**Fitzcarraldo (USA)** (Fav) *(LMCumani)* 9-0 LDettori (4) (gd sort: lw: mde all:
qcknd 2f out: pushed out) ............................... —1

Beneficial *(GWragg)* 9-0 WRSwinburn (3) (w'like: scope: trckd ldr: pushed along over 2f out: kpt on wl) ............................................................... 1½.2
Indian Flash (IRE) *(RGuest)* 8-9 LPiggott (1) (unf: scope: bit bkwd: in tch: rdn ½-wy: nt trble ldrs) ................................................................... 6.3
Behaanis (USA) *(AAScott)* 9-0 BRaymond (5) (rangy: scope: plld hrd: trckd ldrs: no imp fnl 2f) ................................................................. hd.4

**4/6** FITZCARRALDO (USA)(op Evens), **7/4** Beneficial, **13/2** Behaanis (USA)(4/1—7/1), **16/1** Indian Flash (IRE). CSF £2.36, Tote £1.60 (£1.70). Sheikh Mohammed (NEWMARKET) bred by Gerald W. Leigh in USA. 4 Rn
1m 26.7 (3.9)
SF—20/15/–/–

## 1797

LEVY BOARD CLAIMING H'CAP (II) (0-60) £2448.00 (£678.00: £324.00)
1m 3y
3-45 (3-51)

1434 **Kelly's Kite (28)** *(HJCollingridge)* 4–7-11 JQuinn (4) (prom: led 2f out: pushed out) ................................................................................................... —1
1544² Times Are Hard (37) *(CASmith)* 8–8-6 BRaymond (1) (chsd ldrs: ev ch over 1f out: unable qckn) ........................................................................ 2½.2
1527² Major Ivor (59) (Fav) *(MrsGRReveley)* 7–10-0 MRoberts (5) (bhd: hdwy 2f out: r.o ins fnl f) ................................................................................... hd.3
912 Tendresse (IRE) (35) *(DRTucker)* 4–8-4 NAdams (3) (hdwy ½-wy: ev ch over 1f out: sn rdn & nt qckn) ....................................................... 2½.4
1439* Rose Gem (IRE) (54) *(PCHaslam)* 3–9-0 LPiggott (8) (b: prom: led 3f out to 2f out: wknd over 1f out) ............................................................. 2½.5
1589 Grey Illusions (42) (bl) *(LJHolt)* 4–8-11 LDettori (7) (s.s: nvr rchd ldrs) ............ 1½.6
1598 Edgewise (26) *(DMorris)* 9–7-2(2) ‡7CHawksley (9) (a bhd) ........................ 6.7
1570 Creego (43) *(JAGlover)* 3–8-3 JFortune (6) (lw: stdd s: rdn ½-wy: a bhd) ....... 1½.8
1284 Roger Rabbit (FR) (44) (bl) *(RBoss)* 3–8-1 ‡3DBiggs (2) (led 5f: sn wknd) ....... 3.9
LONG HANDICAP: Edgewise 7-0.

**11/4** Major Ivor, **7/2** Rose Gem (IRE), **7/1** Roger Rabbit (FR), **15/2** Creego, **8/1** Grey Illusions(6/1—9/1), Times Are Hard, Tendresse (IRE), **12/1** KELLY'S KITE, **33/1** Edgewise. CSF £92.86, CT £309.33. Tote £13.10: £2.00 £2.20 £1.50 (£43.60). Mr H. J. Collingridge (NEWMARKET) bred by H. J. Collingridge. 9 Rn  1m 38.5 (3.2)
SF—11/12/33/1/3/–

## 1798

STURDEE STKS (Amateurs) (Mdn) £2072.00 (£572.00: £272.00)
1m 3f 101y
4-15 (4-17)

1399 **The Karaoke King (68)** *(RHannon)* 3–10-6 ‡5MrsJBoggis (1) (lw: prom: 3rd st: led on bit ins fnl f: pushed out) .................................................................. —1
1546⁵ Master's Crown (USA) *(MCChapman)* 4–11-4 ‡5MrMChapman (4) (led tl over 2f out: ev ch 1f out: r.o) ............................................................................ 2.2
1366 Rose Cut (USA) (45) (bl) *(DJSCosgrove)* 5–11-4 ‡5MrsDCamp-Simpson (3) (chsd ldrs: 4th st: hung rt & r.o appr fnl f) .................................. 2½.3
1425² Tafsir (Fav) *(HThomsonJones)* 3–10-1 ‡5MrGHaine (9) (hld up: 6th st: hdwy to ld over 2f out: hdd & btn ins fnl f: eased nr fin) ........................ s.h.4
1577 Gerish (IRE) *(JPearce)* 3–10-6 MrsLPearce (5) (chsd ldrs: 5th st: rdn 3f out: one pce) ............................................................................................... 8.5
1568⁶ Do the Business (IRE) (41) *(CNAllen)* 3–10-6 ‡5MrVLukaniuk (5) (lw: s.i.s: a bhd) 3.6
1323 Hiram B Birdbath (bl) *(JAGlover)* 6–11-5(1) ‡5MrSAstaire (7) (a bhd) .................. 3.7
615 Breezy Sailor (25) *(RThompson)* 6–11-4 ‡5MissHCarrington (6) (b: plld hrd: prom: 2nd st: wknd qckly: t.o) ................................................... dist.8
Stewards Enquiry: Haine fined £100 under Rule 151 (ii) (failure to ensure best possible placing).

**4/5** Tafsir(op 1/2), **11/4** THE KARAOKE KING, **7/1** Gerish (IRE)(tchd 16/1), **16/1** Do the Business (IRE)(op 10/1), Hiram B Birdbath, **33/1** Master's Crown (USA), **66/1** Ors. CSF £59.16, Tote £4.10: £1.30 £2.50 £3.10 (£27.30). Mr P. F. Boggis (MARLBOROUGH) bred by Stud-On-The-Chart. 8 Rn  2m 31.4 (7.4)
SF—23/31/26/8/–/–

## 1799

SOUTH WALSHAM H'CAP (0-80) £2872.00 (£856.00: £408.00: £184.00)
1m 3y
4-45 (4-47)

1603³ **Shining Jewel (64)** (Fav) *(MrsLPiggott)* 5–8-13 LPiggott (7) (hld up: hdwy 2f out: led ins fnl f: pushed out) ................................................... —1
1626⁴ Eid (USA) (75) (v) *(DMorley)* 3–9-1 MRoberts (5) (a.p: outpcd 2f out: ev ch ins fnl f: r.o) ................................................................................. ½.2
1421 Jokist (63) *(WJarvis)* 9–8-12 MTebbutt (4) (hld up: hdwy to ld over 1f out: hdd & no ex ins fnl f) ............................................................................... ¾.3
1295 Polonez Prima (76) *(JEBanks)* 5–9-11 NDay (1) (chsd ldrs: ev ch over 1f out: one pce) ............................................................................................. ¾.4
Cradle of Love (USA) (79) *(JWHills)* 4–10-0 RHills (6) (hdwy 3f out: ev ch over 1f out: sn btn) ...................................................................... 1½.5

16034 Kateb (IRE) **(71)** *(RWArmstrong)* 3-8-11 BRaymond (9) (hld up: rdn & no imp fnl 2f) ............................................................ 3/4.**6**
1504 Sistadari **(65)** *(LMCumani)* 4-9-0 LDettori (2) (lw: led over 6f) ......................... 31/2.**7**
1503 Norman Warrior **(60)** *(DMorris)* 3-8-0 JQuinn (8) (nvr trbld ldrs) .................... 31/2.**8**
*3*55 Barkston Singer **(60)** *(JLHarris)* 5-8-9 PaulEddery (3) (lw: chsd ldrs: rdn 4f out: sn btn) ................................................................ 11/2.**9**

**5/2** SHINING JEWEL, **5/1** Jokist(4/1—6/1), **11/2** Polonez Prima, **6/1** Kateb (IRE)(4/1—7/1), **7/1** Eid (USA), **8/1** Sistadari, **16/1** Norman Warrior, **25/1** Cradle of Love (USA), **33/1** Barkston Singer. CSF £17.94, CT £69.31. Tote £3.60: £1.50 £1.60 £2.00 (£7.40). Mr D. W. Rolt (NEWMARKET) bred by H. Ward. 9 Rn   1m 38.7 (3.4)
                                                             SF—24/24/19/30/28/9

**1800**    ORMESBY H'CAP (0-70) £2406.00 (£666.00: £318.00)   13/4m 17y   5-15 (5-16)
                                  (Weights raised 11 lb)

11192 Farmer's Pet **(66)** (Fav) *(GAPritchard-Gordon)* 3-9-9 LDettori (6) (mde all: qcknd clr 2f out: unchal) ....................................... —**1**
15015 Sharp Top **(51)** *(MJRyan)* 4-9-6 ‡3DBiggs (1) (prom tl lost pl 8f out: chsd wnr fnl 2f: no imp) ............................................... 7.**2**
14466 Naseer (USA) **(61)** *(NACallaghan)* 3-8-11 ‡7JTate (3) (reard s: bhd: 6th st: rdn & kpt on fnl 2f) ............................................... 11/2.**3**
1367★ Dare to Dream (IRE) **(61)** *(GLewis)* 3-9-4 PaulEddery (8) (prom: 2nd st: rdn 3f out: sn btn) ................................................ s.h.**4**
1501 Briggsmaid **(52)** *(JMPEustace)* 4-9-10 MTebbutt (2) (hdwy, 3rd & rn wd st: wknd 2f out) ...................................................... 2.**5**
15663 Sweet Request **(43)** *(JRBostock)* 4-9-1 LPiggott (7) (lw: pushed along 1/2-wy: sn wl bhd) ................................................ 8.**6**
16024 Bashamah (IRE) **(55)** (bl) *(CEBrittain)* 3-8-12 MRoberts (5) (chsd ldr tl 4th st: rdn 3f out: sn wknd) ........................................ 1/2.**7**
1313 Court Hise (USA) **(54)** *(RWArmstrong)* 3-8-11 RCrossley (4) (5th st: sn wl bhd) 12.**8**

**7/4** FARMER'S PET(op 3/1), **5/1** Dare to Dream (IRE), **13/2** Bashamah (IRE)(9/1—6/1), **15/2** Sharp Top, **8/1** Briggsmaid, **9/1** Naseer (USA)(op 6/1), **11/1** Sweet Request(7/1—12/1), **33/1** Court Rise (USA). CSF £13.52, CT £76.53. Tote £2.80: £1.30 £2.00 £4.00 (£12.50). Mr D. R. Midwood (NEWMARKET) bred by Normanby Stud Ltd. 8 Rn                                     3m 6.3 (8.3)

**1801**    JELLICOE STKS (Mdn 2-Y.O)  *(6f 3y)*  5-45 - **Abandoned**—Insufficient entries

T/Plpt: £57.50 (57.95 Tckts).                                            Dk

# YARMOUTH (L-H)
## Thursday, July 2nd [Good to firm]
Going Allowance: minus 0.30 sec per fur (F)                              Wind: mod half bhd

Stalls: high

**1802**    HIGH STEWARD CLAIMING STKS  £2108.40 (£582.40: £277.20)
           13/4m 17y                                        2-20 (2-20)

1621★ Broctune Grey **(64)** (Fav) *(MrsGRReveley)* 8-8-13 MRoberts (4) (chsd ldrs: wnt 2nd 1/2-wy: led over 2f out: rdn & r.o appr fnl f) ............. —**1**
15212 Briggscare **(67)** *(WJarvis)* 6-9-6 MTebbutt (1) (b: hld up: hdwy & 3rd st: chal on bit over 1f out: rdn & fnd nil fnl f) ....................... 3/4.**2**
13625 Angelica Park **(46)** (bl) *(JWharton)* 8-8-6 JQuinn (2) (led tl over 2f out: one pce) 8.**3**
     Last of Mohicans *(CWeedon)* 4-8-6 GBaxter (5) (bit bkwd: chsd ldrs tl 4th, rdn & btn st) ................................................ 15.**4**
1239 Sailor Boy **(43)** *(ASReid)* 6-8-4 BCrossley (3) (chsd ldr to 1/2-wy: last st: sn t.o) 25.**5**

**4/9** BROCTUNE GREY(4/7—4/6), **5/2** Briggscare, **10/1** Angelica Park(op 5/1), **33/1** Sailor Boy, **66/1** Last of Mohicans. CSF £1.95, Tote £1.60: £1.20 £1.30 (£1.70). Mr D. Playforth (SALTBURN) bred by G. Reed. 5 Rn
                                                 3m 5.8 (7.8)

**1803**    FRED ARMSTRONG APP'CE H'CAP (3-Y.O) (0-70) £2049.60 (£565.60: £268.80)
           6f 3y                                          2-50 (2-54)

1581★ Daaris (USA) **(70)** (Fav) *(DMorley)* 9-8 (7x) EBentley (2) (prom: led over 2f out: edgd lft & hdd over 1f out: rallied to ld nr fin) ...................... —**1**
1219 Indian Endeavour **(69)** *(RGuest)* 9-7 SEiffert (4) (led over 3f: led over 1f out tl ct nr fin) ................................................ hd.**2**
14284 Master Hyde (USA) **(53)** (v) *(PMitchell)* 8-0[(1)] ‡5DCripps (1) (chsd ldrs: rdn & lost pl over 2f out: r.o fnl f) ........................... 11/2.**3**

1570 Cumbrian Cavalier **(51)** *(JRBostock)* 8-3 GMilligan (3) (reard s: a wl bhd) ........ 25.4
1000⁵ Forza Azzurri (IRE) **(65)** (bl) *(MrsNMacauley)* 9-3 MHarris (5) (uns rdr s) ................ 0

**13/8** DAARIS (USA), **5/2** Indian Endeavour, **11/2** Forza Azzurri (IRE), **13/2** Master Hyde (USA)(9/2—7/1), **10/1** Cumbrian Cavalier. CSF £5.34, Tote £2.30: £1.20 £1.60 (£3.40). Mr Hamdan Al-Maktoum (NEWMARKET) bred by Don Dick in USA. 5 Rn
1m 12.6 (2)
SF—32/30/3/–/–

---

**1804**　　　DENNIS SAWYER, WESTMINSTER AGENT, (S) STKS (2-Y-O) £2245.60 (£621.60:
　　　　　　£296.80)　　**6f 3y**　　　　　　　　　　　　　　3-20 (3-24)

1161⁵ **Skullcap** (Fav) *(DMorley)* 8-11 WRSwinburn (6) (hdwy after 2f: led over 2f out:
　　　　rdn clr ins fnl f) ....................................................... —1
1375⁶ Mister Blake (bl) *(WAO'Gorman)* 8-8 ‡³EmmaO'Gorman (1) (swvd lft s: a.p: ev
　　　　ch over 1f out: no ex) .................................................... 2¹/₂.2
1547⁵ Jordywrath *(ICampbell)* 8-11 MTebbutt (2) (chsd ldrs tl lost pl over 2f out: r.o fnl
　　　　f) .................................................................... 4.3
561⁶ Abilene *(JARToller)* 8-6 DaleGibson (7) (s.s: hdwy over 2f out: edgd lft over 1f
　　　　out: sn btn) ........................................................... 1¹/₂.4
1448⁴ Summers Dream *(BRichmond)* 8-6 MRoberts (4) (led over 3f) ..................... 2¹/₂.5
1601⁶ Secret Tale *(GBlum)* 8-6 JQuinn (5) (in tch over 3f) ............................ 25.6
1657² Burishki (7/2) Withdrawn (reard & uns rdr in stalls) : not under orders — Rule 4 applies

**13/8** SKULLCAP, **3/1** Jordywrath, **7/1** Abilene(6/1—10/1), **10/1** Summers Dream(6/1—14/1), **16/1** Mister Blake(op 6/1), **50/1** Secret Tale. CSF £14.42, Tote £1.90: £1.20 £4.50 (£7.50). Mr Christopher Spence (NEWMARKET) bred by Chieveley Manor Enterprises. 6 Rn; Sold G Wiltshire 5,750 gns
1m 13 (2.4)
SF—13/–/–/–/–/–

---

**1805**　　　WESTMINSTER-MOTOR TAXI INSURANCE STKS　　£3330.00 (£990.00: £470.00:
　　　　　　£210.00)　　**7f 3y**　　　　　　　　　　　　　　3-50 (3-53)

1599² **Annabelle Royale (75)** *(MrsNMacauley)* 6-9-9 MRoberts (1) (lw: chsd ldrs: sn
　　　　pushed along: ev ch 2f out: led 1f out: rdn & r.o v.gamely) . —1
　　　Desert Splendour **(73)** *(CEBrittain)* 4-9-9 WRSwinburn (4) (lw: hdwy 4f out: led
　　　　2f out to 1f out: unable qckn) ........................................ nk.2
1042³ Mathaayl (USA) **(83)** (bl) *(HThomsonJones)* 3–8–6 RHills (3) (led 5f: sn btn) .... 10.3
　　　Mesaafi (IRE) **(104)** (Fav) *(MajorWRHern)* 3–8-10 SCauthen (2) (lw: plld hrd:
　　　　prom to ¹/₂-wy: wknd qckly: t.o) ...................................... 25.4

**5/4** Mesaafi (IRE)(4/6—11/8), **13/8** ANNABELLE ROYALE, **7/1** Desert Splendour, **8/1** Mathaayl (USA)(op 4/1). CSF £9.63, Tote £2.10 (£7.00). Mr P. W. Saunders (MELTON MOWBRAY) bred by Stud-On-The-Chart. 4 Rn
1m 24.2 (1.4)
SF—57/56/9/–

---

**1806**　　　LEVY BOARD H'CAP (F & M) (0-70) £2807.00 (£777.00: £371.00)
　　　　　　**7f 3y**　　　　　　　　　　　　　　　　　　4-20 (4-23)

1794 **Coral Flutter (44)** (bl) *(JWPayne)* 5–8-7 JQuinn (2) (mde all: sn clr: rdn & hld
　　　　on wl fnl f) ............................................................ —1
1403 Eternal Flame **(64)** *(JWHills)* 4–9-13 RHills (5) (chsd wnr: ev ch 1f out: no ex) ... 3.2
1599 Bellatrix **(53)** *(CEBrittain)* 4-9-2 MRoberts (4) (chsd ldrs: rdn 3f out: r.o appr fnl
　　　　f) .................................................................... 3¹/₂.3
796 Millfit (USA) **(66)** *(BHanbury)* 3-9-0 ‡⁷VBray (1) (hld up: no imp fnl 3f) ............... ³/₄.4
1503 Swan Star **(41)** (v) *(GBlum)* 3-7-5⁽³⁾ ‡⁵DHarrison (4) (dwlt: bhd fnl 3f: t.o) ........ 20.5
1663★ Thewaari (USA) **(69)** *(AAScott)* 3-9-10 (5x) WRSwinburn (3) (lw: hld up:
　　　　rdn ¹/₂-wy: eased whn btn appr fnl f: t.o) ............................ 2¹/₂.6
　　　　LONG HANDICAP: Swan Star 7-6.

**13/8** Thewaari (USA), **5/2** Eternal Flame, **6/1** Millfit (USA), **8/1** Bellatrix, CORAL FLUTTER(op 9/2), **50/1** Swan Star. CSF £24.78, Tote £5.50: £2.10 £1.60 (£8.30). Mrs J. W. Payne (NEWMARKET) bred by Lady Juliet de Chair. 6 Rn
1m 24.7 (1.9)
SF—33/44/22/18/–/–

---

**1807**　　　TAXINEWS STKS (Mdn) £2284.80 (£632.80: £302.40)　　**1m 3y**　　4-50 (4-51)

　　　**Riviera Vista** (Fav) *(GWragg)* 3–8-10 RHills (4) (lw: trckd ldr: led on bit wl over
　　　　1f out: easily) ........................................................ —1
1597⁵ Bold Steve *(LMCumani)* 3–8-10 JFortune (1) (lw: led after 2f tl wl over 1f out: rdn
　　　　& no ch w wnr) ....................................................... 2.2
698³ Wafi (USA) *(BHanbury)* 3–8-10 WRSwinburn (3) (hld up: rdn over 2f out: no
　　　　imp) ................................................................. 3¹/₂.3
699 Winnie Reckless *(CEBrittain)* 3–8-5 MRoberts (2) (led 2f: wl bhd fnl 3f: t.o) ...... 25.4

**1/3** RIVIERA VISTA(1/2—4/7), **5/1** Wafi (USA)(op 2/1), Bold Steve, **25/1** Winnie Reckless. CSF £2.58, Tote £1.50 (£3.10). Mr J. L. C. Pearce (NEWMARKET) bred by J. L. C. Pearce. 4 Rn
1m 37.6 (2.3)
SF—25/19/11/–

**1808**      HICKLING H'CAP (0-90) £3180.00 (£880.00: £420.00)      1¼m 21y      5-20 (5-21)

   1662★ **Arak (USA) (73)** *(RWArmstrong)* 4–9-0 (5x) SCauthen (2) (mde all: rdn & hld
             on wl fnl f) ..................................................................... —1
   1295² Busted Rock **(87)** (Fav) *(MrsLPiggott)* 7–10-0 LPiggott (3) (hld up: 3rd st: chal
             1f out: unable qckn nr fin) ................................................ ½.2
   1603★ Chatham Island **(66)** *(CEBrittain)* 4–8-7 (5x) MRoberts (1) (lw: sn pushed
             along: 2nd st: rdn 3f out: no ex appr fnl f) ................... ¾.3

**11/8** Busted Rock, **7/4** ARAK (USA), **15/8** Chatham Island. CSF £4.26, Tote £2.40 (£4.60). Mr Hamdan
Al-Maktoum (NEWMARKET) bred by Mill Ridge Farm Ltd. in USA. 3 Rn        2m 5.8 (1.4)
                                                    SF—56/69/46

T/Plpt: £40.80 (54.35 Tckts).                                                             Dk

## 1584—**BRIGHTON (L-H)**

## Thursday, July 2nd [Firm]

Going Allowance: minus 0.30 sec per fur (F)                    Wind: mod half bhd

Stalls: low

**1809**      WOODINGDEAN STKS (Mdn 2-Y.O) £1932.00 (£532.00: £252.00)
           **6f 209y**                                                2-10 (2-12)

   1485² Wufud (USA) (Fav) *(JLDunlop)* 9-0 WCarson (4) (3rd st: led over 2f out: rdn
             out) ............................................................................... —1
   1424⁴ Almansour (USA) *(HRACecil)* 9-0 PatEddery (1) (lw: 4th st: ev ch ins fnl f:
             unable qckn) ................................................................. 1.2
         Impair (USA) (hl) *(PFICole)* 9-0 AMunro (5) (leggy: lw: 5th st: hrd rdn over 1f
             out: r.o) ....................................................................... s.h.3
   1170 Pickupadailysport *(MissGayKelleway)* 9-0 JReid (3) (led over 2f: ev ch over 2f
             out: sn wknd) ............................................................... 8.4
   1591 Easy Touch (bl) *(MDIUsher)* 8-9 TQuinn (2) (swtg: led over 4f out tl over 2f out:
             sn wknd) ....................................................................... 6.5

**10/11** WUFUD (USA), **6/5** Almansour (USA), **10/1** Impair (USA)(op 5/1), **100/1** Ors. CSF £2.21, Tote £2.00:
£1.40 £1.10 (£1.20). Mr Hamdan Al-Maktoum (ARUNDEL) bred by Mrs Lois Wagers Beattie in USA. 5 Rn
                                                             1m 22.5 (2.5)
                                                          SF—31/28/27/3/–

**1810**      KINGSTON (S) H'CAP (0-60) £2343.60 (£649.60: £310.80)      1m 3f 196y      2-40 (2-45)
                                (Weights raised 5 lb)

        **Dr Zeva (25)** *(MDixon)* 6–7-7 ‡⁵ATucker (4) (lw: 5th st: led over 1f out: comf) .... —1
   1621² Banana Cufflinks (USA) **(37)** (v) (Fav) *(MHTompkins)* 6–8-10 PRobinson (3)
             (led over 10f: unable qckn) ........................................... 2.2
     409 Romanian (IRE) **(48)** *(ARDavison)* 4–9-7 PatEddery (6) (lw: lost pl 6f out: hrd
             rdn over 4f out: 6th st: rallied over 1f out: r.o) ................. 1½.3
   1491⁵ Desert Mist **(38)** (bl) *(SirMarkPrescott)* 3–7-9⁽⁴⁾ ‡³DBiggs (5) (swtg: 2nd st: one
             pce fnl 2f) .................................................................... ¾.4
   1257⁵ Molly Splash **(51)** *(CACyzer)* 5–9-10 TQuinn (9) (hdwy 5f out: 4th st: rdn over 2f
             out: one pce) ............................................................... 2½.5
   1572 Head Turner **(32)** *(CPWildman)* 4–8-5 AMunro (11) (hrd rdn & no hdwy fnl 3f) .. 7.6
   1411⁶ Confound (IRE) **(40)** *(JAkehurst)* 3–8-7 TyroneWilliams (1) (3rd st: wknd over
             2f out) ........................................................................... ¾.7
   1572⁶ Mamalama **(38)** JReid (8) (a mid div) ................................................... 1½.8
   1404 Little Bang **(30)** *(KBishop)* 4–8-3 RFox (2) (lw: nvr nrr) ........................... 1.9
     773 Solid Steel (IRE) **(45)** *(AMoore)* 4–9-4 CandyMorris (14) (bhd fnl 3f) ............ 3½.10
   1572 Primera Ballerina **(44)** *(JRBosley)* 4–8-12 ‡⁵NGwilliams (12) (bhd fnl 7f) ...... hd.11
   1640 Quiet Riot **(42)** *(JWhite)* 10–9-1 JWilliams (7) (b: s.s: bhd fnl 4f) ............... 4.12
   1686⁶ Miss Sarahsue **(21)** *(JELong)* 6–7-8 NAdams (10) (swtg: a bhd) ............ 1½.13
   1087 San Roque **(24)** (v) *(SWoodman)* 7–7-11 SDawson (13) (prom 6f) ................. 15.14

**3/1** Banana Cufflinks (USA)(5/2—9/2), **9/2** Mamalama, Quiet Riot, Romanian (IRE), Molly Splash, **9/1** Head
Turner(5/1—10/1), **12/1** Desert Mist(7/1—14/1), **14/1** Little Bang(10/1—16/1), **20/1** Confound (IRE), DR
ZEVA, Solid Steel (IRE), **33/1** Ors. CSF £81.51, CT £445.90. Tote £17.00: £4.30 £2.20 £2.60 (£42.10). Mr G. R.
Butterfield (EPSOM) bred by Major-Gen Sir George Burns. 14 Rn; No bid         2m 31.2 (4.2)
                                                       SF—1/14/22/–/18/–

**1811**      JOE BLANKS MEMORIAL CHALLENGE CUP (H'cap) (0-70) £2950.00 (£880.00: £420.00:
           £190.00)    **7f 214y**                                                3-10 (3-14)

   1588³ Old Comrades **(52)** *(LGCottrell)* 5–8-12 TRogers (2) (3rd st: rdn over 3f out:
             led ins fnl f: r.o wl) ....................................................... —1

1589* Indian Slave (IRE) **(52)** (Fav) *(RGuest)* 4–8–12 (5x) PatEddery (3) (lw: led tl ins fnl f: r.o) .................................................. ¾.2

1388[6] Diaco **(68)** *(MAJarvis)* 7–10–0 AMunro (1) (6th st: hdwy 2f out: r.o one pce) ... 1½.3

1636* Southwold Air **(71)** *(JLDunlop)* 3–9–8 (5x) WCarson (6) (lw: 4th st: rdn over 3f out: r.o ins fnl f) .................................................. hd.4

1552 Hitchin a Ride **(55)** *(MPMuggeridge)* 5–8–12 ‡3DBiggs (5) (2nd st: wknd over 2f out) .................................................. 8.5

1674[6] Persian Bud (IRE) **(39)** *(JRBosley)* 4–7–8 ‡5NGwilliams (4) (5th st: wknd 3f out) s.h.6

**6/4** Indian Slave (IRE), **3/1** Southwold Air, **7/2** Diaco, OLD COMRADES, **25/1** Hitchin a Ride, **50/1** Persian Bud (IRE). CSF £9.09, Tote £4.70: £2.20 1.40 (£3.90). Mr John Boswell (CULLOMPTON) bred by Corral's Farm and Stud. 6 Rn
1m 33.7 (1.5)
SF–39/37/48/41/7/–

---

**1812**   PEVENSEY H'CAP (3-Y.O) (0–70) £2147.60 (£593.60: £282.80)
1m 1f 209y
3–40 (3-42)

(Weights raised 4 lb)

1555[4] **Sky Train (IRE) (65)** (Fav) *(JLDunlop)* 9-7 AMunro (5) (lw: 3rd st: led 1f out: comf) .................................................. —1

1650[6] Duty Sergeant (IRE) **(54)** (bl) *(MPMuggeridge)* 8-7 ‡3DBiggs (2) (led 5f out to 1f out: unable qckn) .................................................. 4.2

1505 Princess Evita (FR) **(47)** *(RGuest)* 8-3 PRobinson (4) (lost pl over 4f out: 5th st: one pce fnl 3f) .................................................. 7.3

1517* Breakdancer (IRE) **(58)** *(WRMuir)* 9-0 SWhitworth (3) (b: 2nd st: wknd 2f out) ... 5.4

1540[5] Prove It's Gold **(44)** *(TMJones)* 8-0 NAdams (1) (led 5f: 4th st: wknd over 3f out) 10.5

**10/11** SKY TRAIN (IRE), **11/8** Breakdancer (IRE), **9/1** Duty Sergeant (IRE)(5/1—10/1), **33/1** Princess Evita (FR), **50/1** Prove It's Gold. CSF £8.03, Tote £1.80: £1.10 2.10 (£4.50). Lord Chelsea (ARUNDEL) bred by Lord Chelsea in Ireland. 5 Rn
2m 1.7 (3.7)
SF—40/18/–/–/–

---

**1813**   ROCK GARDENS CLAIMING STKS   £2128.00 (£588.00: £280.00)
6f 209y
4–10 (4-13)

997 **Monte Bre (40)** *(RAkehurst)* 6–9-3 AMunro (8) (lw: 3rd st: led 2f out: comf) ...... —1

1340[2] Shocking Times **(58)** *(RSimpson)* 3–7–11 ‡5ATucker (2) (4th st: hrd rdn 2f out: unable qckn) .................................................. 5.2

1589 Dodgy **(57)** (v) (Fav) *(SDow)* 5–9-5 TQuinn (1) (2nd st: ev ch over 1f out: one pce) .................................................. 1½.3

298 Great Hall **(54)** *(PDCundell)* 3–8–9 JWilliams (4) (6th st: r.o one pce fnl 2f) ...... 1½.4

1339 Nazare Blue **(38)** *(MrsBarbaraWaring)* 5–9-3 NHowe (3) (b: lw: 5th st: one pce fnl 3f) .................................................. ¾.5

1581[5] Sea Cloud (USA) **(51)** *(MBlanshard)* 3–8–6(1) JReid (5) (led 5f) .................................................. ¾.6

1597 Lord Neptune **(65)** (bl) *(MAJarvis)* 5–9-0 GCrealock (6) (lw: a bhd) .................................................. 4.7

1366 Lady Bunting **(37)** *(RVoorspuy)* 5–8–12 SDawson (7) (a bhd) .................................................. 6.8

**5/2** Dodgy, **7/2** Lord Neptune, **4/1** Shocking Times, **9/2** Sea Cloud (USA), **8/1** MONTE BRE(op 9/2), **10/1** Great Hall, **12/1** Lady Bunting, **25/1** Nazare Blue. CSF £38.83, Tote £7.30: £2.90 1.30 1.40 (£12.00). Mr G. S. Beccle (EPSOM) bred by Dieter Hofemeier. 8 Rn
1m 21.8 (1.6)
SF—44/4/20/4/9/–

---

**1814**   PRESTON PARK H'CAP (0–70) £2128.00 (£588.00: £280.00)   5f 213y   4-40 (4-41)

1590* **Shikari's Son (61)** *(JWhite)* 5–9-8 (7x) PRobinson (3) (5th st: led ins fnl f: r.o wl) —1

1545[2] Martinosky **(62)** (Fav) *(WGRWightman)* 6–9-9 JWilliams (4) (3rd st: ev ch ins fnl f: r.o) .................................................. nk.2

1445 Caromish (USA) **(67)** *(MDIUsher)* 5–10-0 MWigham (5) (b.off hind: led tl ins fnl f: unable qckn) .................................................. 2½.3

1590[2] Restore **(53)** (bl) *(RVoorspuy)* 9–9-0 SDawson (2) (lw: 6th st: one pce fnl 2f) ..... 2.4

1614 Judgement Call **(62)** *(PHowling)* 5–9-9 JReid (6) (lw: 4th st: one pce fnl 2f) ...... ½.5

1593[4] Three Lucky (IRE) **(37)** *(MDIUsher)* 4–7–9(1) ‡3DBiggs (1) (lw: 2nd st: eased whn btn over 1f out) .................................................. 8.6

**15/8** Martinosky, **7/2** Restore, SHIKARI'S SON, **9/2** Caromish (USA), **6/1** Three Lucky (IRE), **8/1** Judgement Call(6/1—9/1). CSF £11.06, Tote £5.40: £2.00 1.90 (£4.90). Mr Alan Spargo (WENDOVER) bred by W. H. Joyce. 6 Rn
1m 9.4 (1)
SF—52/52/47/25/32/–

T/Plpt: £8.60 (256.95 Tckts).

AK

1230a—**LONGCHAMP (R-H)**
**Monday, June 22nd [Good to soft]**
Going Allowance: 0.40 sec per fur (S)

**1815a**          PRIX BERTEUX (Gp 3) (3-Y.O) £20640.00     **1m 7f (Grande)**

**Djais (FR)** *(France)* 3–8-8 CBlack ....................................................... —1
642a In-Quarto (bl) *(France)* 3–8-8 DBoeuf .............................................. hd.2
Hot Favourite (FR) *(France)* 3–8-6[1] ELegrix ........................................ hd.3
Tote 10.80f: 2.60f 1.60f 2.70f (22.60f). Mr A-R Chalk (J.Pease,FRANCE) bred by Horse France in France. 8 Rn
3m 22 (9.7)
SF—57/56/53

1353a—**CURRAGH (R-H)**
**Saturday, June 27th [Good]**
Going Allowance: 5f-8f: minus 0.10 sec; Rest: minus 0.35 sec (F)

**1816a**          IRISH INDEPENDENT NEWSPAPERS PRETTY POLLY STKS (Gp 2) (F & M) £24533.00
1¼m

1097a² **Market Booster (USA)** *(Ireland)* 3–8-6 MJKinane (cl up: trckd ldrs st: wnt 2nd
wl over 1f out: rdn to ld wl ins fnl f: r.o) ................................. —1
1232a³ RUBY TIGER (Fav) *(PFICole)* 5–9-9 TQuinn (prom: led over 4f out: hdd & no ex
wl ins fnl f) .................................................................................. 1.2
1097a⁰ Khanata (USA) *(Ireland)* 3–8-6 JPMurtagh (towards rr ½-wy: chsd ldrs ent st:
no ex wl out: kpt on wl) .............................................................. 1.3
Via Borghese (USA) *(Ireland)* 3–8-6 PVGilson (mid div: hdwy bef st: no ex wl
over 1f out) ................................................................................ 5.4
Equal Eloquence (USA) *(Ireland)* 3–8-6 RHughes (towards rr: hdwy & chsd ldrs
st: no imp fr wl over 1f out) ......................................................... 2½.5
343² CRYSTAL PATH (FR) *(MMoubarak)* 4–9-6 DHolland (in tch: hdwy 5f out: rdn
over 2f out: sn no imp) ................................................................ 2½.6
1455 GUSSY MARLOWE *(CEBrittain)* 4–9-6 WNewnes (sn led: hdd over 4f out: ev ch
st: wknd wl over 1f out) ............................................................... 4½.7
Aqua Lily *(Ireland)* 4–9-6 PShanahan (in rr ½-wy: rdn & sn wknd st) .......... 12.8

**6/4** Ruby Tiger, **9/4** MARKET BOOSTER (USA), **6/1** Khanata (USA), **13/2** Via Borghese (USA), **8/1** Crystal Path
(FR), **10/1** Gussy Marlowe, **16/1** Equal Eloquence (USA), **66/1** Aqua Lily. Tote £2.40: £1.10 £1.20 £1.70
(£2.30). Moyglare Stud Farms Ltd. (D.K.Weld,IRELAND) bred by Moyglare Stud Farms Ltd. in USA. 8 Rn
2m 0.6 (1.5 under best; U2.4)
SF—76/91/72/62/57/66/57

**CURRAGH (R-H)**
**Sunday, June 28th [Good]**
Going Allowance: 5f-8f: minus 0.20 sec; Rest: minus 0.45 sec (F)

**1817a**          SEA WORLD INTERNATIONAL STKS (Gp 2)     £24533.00     **1m**

1454³ **SIKESTON (USA)** *(CEBrittain)* 6–10-0 MRoberts (gd early spd: mid div ½-wy:
chsd ldrs st: chal wl over 1f out: led 1f out: r.o) ........................... —1
557 SURE SHARP (USA) *(BWHills)* 5–9-5 DHolland (sn led: hdd & no ex u.p over 1f
out: kpt on) ................................................................................ 2.2
1495a* Rami (USA) (bl) *(Ireland)* 5–9-5 MJKinane (in rr: hdwy over 2f out: kpt on wl fnl f) hd.3
953a⁶ Portico (USA) *(Ireland)* 3–8-7 WRSwinburn (prom: ch over 2f out: disp ld wl
over 1f out: led over 1f out: hdd & no ex fnl f) .............................. ½.4
1097a³ Tarwiya (IRE) (Fav) *(Ireland)* 3–8-6[2] JPMurtagh (towards rr: hdwy, swtchd lft &
chal wl over 1f out: rdn & no ex fnl f) ......................................... 1½.5
1197⁴ FLASHFOOT *(IABalding)* 4–9-5 RCochrane (in tch: cl up st: ev ch fr 2f out: no
ex over 1f out: kpt on) ................................................................. 1½.6
1454⁵ Approach The Bench (IRE) *(Ireland)* 4–9-5 PatEddery (towards rr: hdwy to
chase ldrs 2f out: rdn & no imp over 1f out: kpt on) ............. ½.7
1100a FLYING BRAVE *(JLDunlop)* 4–9-9 JReid (prom early: ev ch st: no ex & wknd wl
over 1f out) ................................................................................ nk.8
1495a³ Malvernico (IRE) *(Ireland)* 4–9-5 CRoche (rr st: effrt over 2f out: no imp over 1f
out) ........................................................................................... nk.9

5/2 Tarwiya (IRE), **3/1** SIKESTON (USA), 5/1 Rami (USA), 6/1 Portico (USA), 9/1 Flashfoot, Approach The Bench (IRE), **12/1** Sure Sharp (USA), 14/1 Malvernico (IRE), **20/1** Flying Brave. Tote £3.70: £2.00 £3.60 £2.40 (£22.10). Mr Luciano Gaucci (NEWMARKET) bred by John R.Gaines, H.Rodes Hart & William Simon in USA. 9 Rn
1m 37 (equals standard)
SF—90/75/74/60/54/62

## 1818a
JOHN ROARTY MEMORIAL RAILWAY STKS (Gp 3) (2-Y.O) £14720.00 **6f**

Ivory Frontier (IRE) (Fav) *(Ireland)* 2–8–10 CRoche (led: hdd jst ins fnl f: rallied u.p to ld towards fin: r.o) ............................................................. —1
Shahik (USA) *(Ireland)* 2–8–10 RJGriffiths (prom: chal 2f out: led jst ins fnl l: no ex & hdd towards fin) ......... hd.2
Tropical *(Ireland)* 2–8–7 MJKinane (trckd wnr on ins: n.m.r wl over 1f out: swtchd 1f out: kpt on: nt rch ldrs) ......... 1½.3
Staviski *(Ireland)* 2–8–10 KJManning (towards rr ½-wy: rdn 2f out: no ex over 1f out: kpt on) ......... 3.4
Libran Wood (IRE) *(Ireland)* 2–8–10 JReid (n.d fr ½-wy) ......... 5½.5
Coral Sound (IRE) *(Ireland)* 2–8–7 RHughes (cl up early: ev ch over 2f out: sn rdn: wknd wl over 1f out) ......... 1½.6

11/10 IVORY FRONTIER (IRE), 6/4 Tropical, 6/1 Shahik (USA), 10/1 Coral Sound (IRE), 16/1 Libran Wood (IRE), 25/1 Staviski. Tote £2.30: £1.80 £2.50 (£8.70). Mr Peter J.P.Gleeson (J.S.Bolger,IRELAND) bred by Natasi Ltd. in Ireland. 6 Rn
1m 13.7 (3.1)
SF—10/9/–/–/–/–

## 1819a
BUDWEISER IRISH DERBY (Gp 1) (3-Y.O.C & F) £331308.00 **1½m**

1198² St Jovite (USA) *(Ireland)* 3–9–0 CRoche (prom: led over 5f out: rdn clr & r.o strly fr 3f out: unchal: impressive) ......... 1
1198* DR DEVIOUS (IRE) (Fav) *(PWChapple-Hyam)* 3–9–0 JReid (in tch: hdwy & wnt 2nd over 4f out: chsd wnr st: sn rdn: no imp 2f out: kpt on) 12.2
1356a³ Contested Bid (USA) *(France)* 3–9–0 PatEddery (in tch: wnt 4th 5f out: 3rd & rdn st: no imp fr 2f out: kpt on) ......... 1.3
Dive for Cover (USA) *(France)* 3–9–0 DHolland (hdwy fr 5f out: 4th & rdn st: no imp fr 2f out) ......... 3.4
1456³ EZZOUD (IRE) *(MRStoute)* 3–9–0 WRSwinburn (towards rr: hdwy st: wnt 6th wl over 1f out: kpt on) ......... ¾.5
1356a² Marignan (USA) *(France)* 3–9–0 DBoeuf (towards rr: hdwy & 7th 4f out: n.d fr wl over 1f out: kpt on) ......... nk.6
1095a* Ormsby (IRE) *(Ireland)* 3–9–0 MJKinane (bhd: 9th st: hdwy on ins over 2f out: kpt on: n.d) ......... 5.7
1401⁴ BOLOARDO *(CEBrittain)* 3–9–0 MRoberts (in tch: 5th st: sn wknd & n.d fnl 2f) . 10.8
1464* LANDOWNER (IRE) *(JHMGosden)* 3–9–0 RCochrane (in tch early: 8th & hmpd 4f out: n.d st) ......... s.h.9
1354a⁴ Mining Tycoon (IRE) *(Ireland)* 3–9–0 KJManning (in tch: 3rd ½-wy: 6th & u.p 4f out: sn lost pl) ......... 4½.10
1464 Appealing Bubbles (IRE) (bl) *(Ireland)* 3–9–0 CEverard (sn led: rdn after 4f: hdd over 5f out: wknd qckly & sn bhd) ......... 6.11

4/5 Dr Devious (IRE), 7/2 ST JOVITE (USA), 7/1 Landowner (IRE), 10/1 Ezzoud (IRE), 11/1 Marignan (USA), Contested Bid (USA), 20/1 Ormsby (IRE), 66/1 Dive for Cover (USA), Boloardo, 100/1 Mining Tycoon (IRE), 200/1 Appealing Bubbles (IRE). Tote £4.20: £1.70 £1.30 £2.10 (£3.40). Mrs Virginia Kraft Payson (J.S.Bolger,IRELAND) bred by Virginia Kraft Payson in USA. 11 Rn 2m 26.6 (unofficial) (2 under best; U3.7)
SF—95/71/69/63/61/60/50

## 1820a
P.V. DOYLE MEMORIAL SCURRY PREMIER H'CAP £14019.00 **6f 63y**

Gentle Step (IRE) *(Ireland)* 3–8–3 MRoberts ......... —1
1474² DOUBLE BLUE *(MJohnston)* 3–8–11 DMcKeown ......... 1.2
Simply Amber (IRE) *(Ireland)* 4–8–13 PatEddery ......... 1½.3
Tote £75.40: £8.20 £1.50 £2.30 £1.80 (£86.90). Mr David F.Jefferson (T.Stack,IRELAND) bred by T.J.Rooney in Ireland. 17 Rn
1m 15.6 (1.1)
SF—23/17/30

## 1821a
ANHEUSER BUSCH CURRAGH CUP (Stks) (listed race) £14720.00 **1¾m**

1470⁶ Arrikala (IRE) *(Ireland)* 3–8–7 CRoche ......... —1
1226a⁵ PARTING MOMENT (USA) *(IABalding)* 5–9–8 JReid ......... ½.2
Sleet Skier *(Ireland)* 5–9–13 MJKinane ......... 3.3
1465 HATEEL *(PTWalwyn)* 6–9–8 RJGriffiths (btn further 9½l) ......... 5
826⁵ FURTHER FLIGHT *(BWHills)* 6–10–0 MHills (btn 22l by wnr) ......... 6

Tote £20.40: £3.60 £4.00. Mr D.H.W.Dobson (J.S.Bolger,IRELAND) bred by Miss K.Rausing & Mrs S.M.Rogers in Ireland. 7 Rn
2m 55.4 (equals best; U.6)
SF—50/64/63/35/39

### 1815a—LONGCHAMP (R-H)
**Saturday, June 27th [Good]**
Going Allowance: nil sec per fur (G)

**1822a**  PRIX DE LA PORTE MAILLOT (Gp 3)  £20640.00  **7f (Nouvelle)**

| | | |
|---|---|---|
| 1285★ | **DILUM (USA)** (PFICole) 3-8-8 AMunro | —1 |
| 842a³ | Lion Cavern (USA) (France) 3-9-0 SCauthen | 4.2 |
| | BOG TROTTER (USA) (WJHaggas) 4-9-2 LPiggott | ¹/₂.3 |

Tote 11.10f: 2.70f 1.20f 2.80f (10.20f). Mr Fahd Salmon (WHATCOMBE) bred by Ron Con Ltd. in USA. 8 Rn
1m 20.4 (0.4)
SF—88/82/82

### LONGCHAMP (R-H)
**Sunday, June 28th [Good]**
Going Allowance: minus 0.25 sec per fur (F)

**1823a**  GRAND PRIX DE PARIS LOUIS VUITTON (Gp 1) (3-Y.O.C & F) £154799.00  **1¹/₄m (Grande)**

| | | |
|---|---|---|
| 537a★ | **Homme de Loi (IRE)** (France) 3-9-2 TJarnet (a cl up: 3rd st: chal 2f out to ld wl over 1f out: hung rt 1f out: r.o wl nr fin) | —1 |
| 1230a★ | Kitwood (USA) (France) 3-9-2 SCauthen (hld up: 7th st: gd hdwy fr wl over 1f out: r.o ins fnl f: one pce cl home) | ³/₄.2 |
| 1498a⁴ | Guislaine (FR) (France) 3-8-13 CAsmussen (in tch: 6th st: chal & hmpd 1f out: fin wl: unlucky) | ¹/₂.3 |
| 1356a⁴ | Adieu Au Roi (IRE) (France) 3-9-2 MBoutin (hld up & bhd: last st: hdwy fr wl over 1f out: fin wl) | 1.4 |
| 1498a³ | Verveine (USA) (France) 3-8-13 WMongil (hld up early: 9th st: nt clr run & bdly hmpd 2f out: r.o wl fnl f) | s.nk.5 |
| | Olanthe (USA) (bl) (France) 3-9-2 SGuillot (led tl wl over 1f out: grad wknd) | ¹/₂.6 |
| 1198 | POLLEN COUNT (USA) (JHMGosden) 3-9-2 WCarson (prom & 2nd st: grad wknd wl over 1f out) | ¹/₂.7 |
| 1356a⁴ | Johann Quatz (FR) (bl) (Fav) (France) 3-9-2 FHead (swtg: plld hrd early: 5th st: effrt wl over 1f out: sn btn) | s.h.8 |
| | Vasarelli (IRE) (Italy) 3-9-2 AMunro (8th st: effrt 2f out: n.d) | 1¹/₂.9 |
| 957a⁴ | ALHIJAZ (JLDunlop) 3-9-2 LPiggott (mid div: 4th st: effrt 2f out: sn rdn & btn) | ¹/₂.10 |

2/1 Johann Quatz (FR), 5/2 Pollen Count (USA), Olanthe (USA), Kitwood (USA), 11/2 Homme de Loi (IRE), 13/2 Verveine (USA), 27/4 Guislaine (FR), 10/1 Alhijaz, 18/1 Adieu Au Roi (IRE), 29/1 Vasarelli (IRE). Tote 4.70f: 1.70f 1.50f 2.00f (7.30f). Mr Paul de Moussac (A.Fabre,FRANCE) bred by Mrs E.Mulhern in Ireland. 10 Rn
2m 3.9 (0.7)
SF—70/68/64/65/61/63/62

**1824a**  PRIX DE MALLERET (Gp 2) (3-Y.O.F) £30960.00  **1¹/₂m (Grande)**

| | | |
|---|---|---|
| 1498a | **Trishyde (USA)** (France) 3-8-9 FHead (last early: 5th st: gd hdwy fr 2f out: led cl home) | —1 |
| 1098a⁵ | Trampoli (USA) (France) 3-8-9 TJarnet (cl up: 3rd st: led wl over 1f out: outpcd & hdd cl home) | ¹/₂.2 |
| | Afaladja (IRE) (Fav) (France) 3-8-9 WMongil (in tch & 4th st: effrt 2f out: r.o one pce) | 4.3 |
| | Halesia (USA) (France) 3-8-9 ELegrix (a.p: led st tl wl over 1f out: one pce towards fin) | nk.4 |
| | Dancing Fan (USA) (France) 3-8-9 GMosse (led tl hdd st: wknd qckly) | 2.5 |
| 1492a★ | Berceau (USA) (France) 3-8-9 SCauthen (a bhd: m.n.s) | 2.6 |

6/4 Afaladja (IRE), 5/2 TRISHYDE (USA), 15/4 Berceau (USA), 24/4 Trampoli (USA), 33/4 Dancing Fan (USA), 9/1 Halesia (USA). Tote 3.50f: 2.10f 2.60f (SF: 19.50f). Mr S.Niarchos (F.Boutin,FRANCE) bred by Flaxman Holdings Ltd. in USA. 6 Rn
2m 28.6 (U1.4)
SF—79/78/70/69/65/61

### HAMBURG (R-H)
**Sunday, June 28th [Good]**

**1825a**  IDEE HANSA-PREIS (Gp 2)  £49296.00  **1m 3f**

| | | |
|---|---|---|
| 1232a² | **Lomitas** (Germany) 4-9-8 ABoschert | —1 |

1229a CAPTAIN HORATIUS (IRE) *(JLDunlop)* 3–8-3 WRyan ........................................ 4.2
　　　Capwell *(Germany)* 3–7-12 ABest ................................................................... 3.3
Tote 15DM: 12DM 14DM (SF: 48DM). Gestut Fahrhof (A.Wohler,GERMANY) bred by Gestut Fahrhof. 6 Rn
　　　　　　　　　　　　　　　　　　　　　　　　　　　　　　　　　　　　2m 18.8

## 1646a—SAN SIRO (R-H)
### Sunday, June 28th [Good]

### 1826a
PREMIO NICO CASTELLINI (listed race)　£20930.00　1¼m

1358a² **HALF A TICK (USA)** *(PFICole)* 4–9-1 TQuinn .......................................... —1
　　　Sheer Precocity *(Italy)* 5–9-1 SLandi ............................................................. 2.2
　　　Taff's Acre (IRE) *(Italy)* 3–8-7 JCarroll ........................................................... 2.3
Tote 45L: 18L 40L 15L (537L). Mr C.J.Wates (WHATCOMBE) bred by Robert Masterson in USA. 13 Rn　2m 2.7

### 1827a
PREMIO VITTORIO CRESPI (listed race) (2-Y.O.F) £20930.00　6f

1067³ **ANCESTRAL DANCER** *(MBell)* 2–8-9 JCarroll .......................................... —1
1496a⁴ Secrage *(Italy)* 2–8-11 VMezzatesta ......................................................... 2.2
1279* JUST SPECULATION (IRE) *(PFICole)* 2–8-9 TQuinn ................................... 1¾.3
Tote 20L: 11L 13L 11L (60L). Innlaw Racing (NEWMARKET) bred by Hillfields Stud. 8 Rn　1m 9.5

## 1245—HAYDOCK (L-H)
### Thursday, July 2nd [Firm]
Going Allowance: St: minus 0.40 sec; Rnd: minus 0.20 sec (F)　　　Wind: fresh half bhd

Stalls: high

### 1828
ROBERT BOWETT (LEEDS) FOR SAAB H'CAP (0-90) £2322.00 (£642.00: £306.00)
5f　　　　　　　　　　　　　　　　　　　　　　　　　　　　　6-35 (6-36)

1688⁶ Lucedeo (83) *(JLSpearing)* 8–9-10 DMcKeown (3) (dwlt: bhd: gd hdwy appr
　　　fnl f: r.o strly to ld last stride) ..................................................................... —1
　1688 Gondo (77) (v) *(EJAlston)* 5–9-4 KFallon (4) (a.p: led ½-wy tl ct post) ......... s.h.2
1707⁵ Real Stunner (69) (Fav) *(MPNaughton)* 5–8-5 ‡5JWeaver (5) (a.p: swtchd to
　　　chal 2f out: rdn & nt qckn fnl f) ..................................................................... 2½.3
1483⁴ Simmie's Special (65) *(RHollinshead)* 4–8-6 WRyan (2) (led to ½-wy: rdn over
　　　1f out: one pce) ........................................................................................... 1.4
1607⁴ Amber Mill (85) *(JBerry)* 4–9-12 JCarroll (1) (lw: chsd ldrs: rdn 2f out: sn btn) 1½.5
**5/2** Real Stunner, **100/30** Amber Mill, **7/2** Gondo, **4/1** LUCEDEO, **6/1** Simmie's Special. CSF £15.88, Tote £4.20:
£2.20 £1.50 (£7.00). Non-Stop Promotions & Marketing Ltd (ALCESTER) bred by J. Dillon. 5 Rn
　　　　　　　　　　　　　　　　　　　　　　　　　　　　　　　　59.10 sec (0.10)
　　　　　　　　　　　　　　　　　　　　　　　　　　　　　　　　SF—68/61/38/35/49

### 1829
SAAB MANCHESTER CLAIMING STKS　£1590.00 (£440.00: £210.00)
6f　　　　　　　　　　　　　　　　　　　　　　　　　　　　　7-05 (7-06)

1467 **Sizzling Saga (IRE) (102)** *(JBerry)* 4–9-13 JCarroll (4) (lw: mde all: clr ½-wy:
　　　unchal) ........................................................................................................ —1
1618² Breezy Day (77) (Fav) *(BAMcMahon)* 6–8-12 TQuinn (2) (lw: chsd wnr thrght:
　　　pushed along 3f out: no imp) ....................................................................... 7.2
1696 Letsbeonestaboutit (89) (bl) *(MrsNMacauley)* 6–9-5 DMcKeown (5) (dwlt: bhd
　　　& rdn along after 2f: kpt on appr fnl f: nvr nrr) ............................................. 2.3
1618* Love Jazz (USA) (89) *(TDBarron)* 3–9-4 KDarley (1) (lw: prom: rdn 2f out: sn
　　　btn) ............................................................................................................. hd.4
　　　Gemini Fire (82) *(MPNaughton)* 8–9-4 ‡5JWeaver (6) (bit bkwd: s.s: hdwy 2f out:
　　　nvr nr to chal) ............................................................................................. 3½.5
1487 Langtonian (77) *(JBerry)* 3–8-12 NCarlisle (3) (spd 4f) ................................. hd.6
1380 Tango Time (87) *(NTinkler)* 4–9-4 RCochrane (7) (sn bhd & pushed along: t.o
　　　fnl 2f) ......................................................................................................... 10.7
**11/4** Breezy Day, **7/2** SIZZLING SAGA (IRE), **4/1** Tango Time, Love Jazz (USA), **5/1** Letsbeonestaboutit, **16/1**
Gemini Fire, **33/1** Langtonian. CSF £12.92, Tote £4.70: £1.70 £2.30 (£11.50). Mr J. David Abell (COCKERHAM)
bred by Ballygoran Stud in Ireland. 7 Rn　　　　　　　　　　　1m 10.72 (0.13 under best; U.98)
　　　　　　　　　　　　　　　　　　　　　　　　　　　　　　　　SF—85/42/41/39/25/18

**1830**　　ANDERSON MOTORS OF STOCKPORT STKS (Mdn 3-Y.O.F) £1876.40 (£520.40:
　　　　　£249.20)　　**1¼m 120y**　　　　　　　　　　　　　　　　　　7-35 (7-36)

　　　**Cutleaf** *(WJarvis)* 8-11 JCarroll (5) (gd sort: bit bkwd: hld up: 3rd st: shkn up to
　　　　　ld wl over 1f out: styd on strly) ............................................. —1
　　　Shahaamh (IRE) *(HThomsonJones)* 8-11 RHills (1) (lengthy: scope: bit bkwd:
　　　　　chsd ldr: 2nd st: ev ch fnl f: unable qckn) ........................ 1½.2
　　1383² Laughsome **(Fav)** *(JHMGosden)* 8-11 PatEddery (4) (led tl appr fnl f: sn hrd
　　　　　rdn: squeezed 1f out: one pce) ....................................... 1½.3
　　　Farah *(HThomsonJones)* 8-11 NCarlisle (3) (w'like: leggy: chsd ldrs tl lost pl &
　　　　　5th st: t.o fnl 2f) ......................................................... 20.4
　　　Tajfehn (USA) *(BHanbury)* 8-11 WRyan (2) (w'like: str: bkwd: s.i.s: a bhd &
　　　　　struggling: effrt 4th st: t.o fnl 2f) ................................... 20.5

**2/5** Laughsome(op 4/5), **7/2** Shahaamh (IRE), **11/1** CUTLEAF(op 6/1), **20/1** Tajfehn (USA), **33/1** Farah. CSF
£42.25, Tote £6.20: £1.50 £1.60 (£13.10). Lord Howard de Walden (NEWMARKET) bred by Lord Howard de
Walden. 5 Rn　　　　　　　　　　　　　　　　　　　　　　　　　　2m 14.69 (2.99)
　　　　　　　　　　　　　　　　　　　　　　　　　　　　　　　SF—46/43/40/−/−


**1831**　　SAAB GREAT BRITAIN JULY TROPHY (Stks) (listed race) (3-Y.O.C & G) £9500.00
　　　　　(£2625.00: £1250.00)　　**1m 3f 200y**　　　　　　　　　8-05 (8-07)

　　1458⁵ **Alphard (106)** *(HRACecil)* 8-10 WRyan (3) (mde all: rdn over 1f out: r.o strly) ... —1
　　1401★ Bobzao (IRE) **(105)** *(WCarter)* 9-1 AMunro (2) (lw: plld hrd: chsd wnr: 2nd st:
　　　　　effrt over 2f out: rdn appr fnl f: unable qckn) ...................... 2½.2
　　1466★ Source of Light **(95)** **(Fav)** *(RCharlton)* 8-10 PatEddery (1) (lw: plld hrd: hld up:
　　　　　3rd st: effrt u.p 2f out: no imp: eased whn btn fnl f) ............... 8.3

**11/8** Source of Light(Evens—6/4), **13/8** ALPHARD, **3/1** Bobzao (IRE)(4/1—5/2). CSF £5.21, Tote £2.60
(£2.50). Mr D. K. Harris (NEWMARKET) bred by Brook Bloodstock P L C. 3 Rn　　2m 30.95 (2.95)
　　　　　　　　　　　　　　　　　　　　　　　　　　　　　　　SF—42/42/21


**1832**　　MAYFIELD GARAGE OF LIVERPOOL STKS (Mdn 2-Y.O) £1646.00 (£456.00: £218.00)
　　　　　**6f**　　　　　　　　　　　　　　　　　　　　　　　　8-35 (8-37)

　　1457 **Persian Revival (FR)** *(BAMcMahon)* 9-0 TQuinn (1) (lw: led after 1f: drew clr
　　　　　appr fnl f: unchal) ......................................................... —1
　　1327⁴ Storm Venture (IRE) **(Fav)** *(BBeasley)* 9-0 DNicholls (4) (hdwy u.p over 2f out:
　　　　　nvr nr to chal) .............................................................. 6.2
　　　Flashman *(FHLee)* 9-0 PatEddery (3) (gd sort: bit bkwd: dwlt: drvn to jn wnr
　　　　　½-wy: rdn 2f out: sn btn) ................................................ 5.3
　　1578⁶ Noteability *(JBerry)* 8-9 JCarroll (2) (still bkwd: led 1f: wknd wl over 2f out) ..... 1½.4
　　　Grey Pride *(JBerry)* 9-0 NCarlisle (5) (w'like: scope: outpcd: a bhd) ............... 1½.5

**13/8** Storm Venture (IRE), **2/1** Flashman, **100/30** PERSIAN REVIVAL (FR), **10/1** Noteability, **14/1** Grey Pride.
CSF £8.69, Tote £3.50: £1.90 £1.30 (£3.30). Mr Michael Sturgess (TAMWORTH) bred by Myrina Holdings Inc in
France. 5 Rn　　　　　　　　　　　　　　　　　　　　　　　　1m 12.83 (1.13)
　　　　　　　　　　　　　　　　　　　　　　　　　　　　　　　SF—30/6/−/−/−


**1833**　　SAAB TOTAL SERVICE H'CAP (0-90) £2364.00 (£654.00: £312.00)
　　　　　**7f 30y**　　　　　　　　　　　　　　　　　　　　　9-00 (9-00)
　　　　　　　　　　　(Weights raised 3 lb)
　　1588★ **Hamadryad (IRE) (71)** *(WCarter)* 4-8-8 (5x) ‡⁵NGwilliams (2) (b.off fore: lw:
　　　　　dwlt: hdwy & 2nd st: led 2f out: rdn out) .............................. —1
　　1193⁴ Kummel King **(64)** *(EJAlston)* 4-8-6 KFallon (5) (led 5f: hrd rdn & kpt on: no ch
　　　　　w wnr) ........................................................................ 2.2
　　1379³ Veloce (IRE) **(55)** *(MO'Neill)* 4-7-8 ‡³JFanning (4) (lw: a.p: 3rd st: rdn 2f out: one
　　　　　pce) ........................................................................... 2½.3
　　1508★ Sir Arthur Hobbs **(64)** **(Fav)** *(FHLee)* 5-8-1 ‡⁵NKennedy (1) (lw: hld up: 4th st:
　　　　　effrt wl over 1f out: no imp) ............................................ ¾.4
　　1692⁴ Resolute Bay **(82)** *(RMWhitaker)* 6-9-10 ACulhane (3) (lw: hld up: 5th st: effrt
　　　　　over 2f out: nvr able to chal) ........................................... nk.5

**9/4** Sir Arthur Hobbs, **7/2** Resolute Bay, HAMADRYAD (IRE), Veloce (IRE), **6/1** Kummel King. CSF £20.20, Tote
£3.80: £1.60 £2.70 (£12.40). Miss Maha Kalaji (EPSOM) bred by P. Myerscough in Ireland. 5 Rn
　　　　　　　　　　　　　　　　　　　　　　　　　　　　1m 29.60 (2.30)
　　　　　　　　　　　　　　　　　　　　　　　　　　　SF—38/30/10/15/37

T/Plpt: £538.80 (5.4 Tckts).　　　　　　　　　　　　　　　　　　　　　IM

## HAYDOCK (L-H)
### Friday, July 3rd [Good to soft]
Going Allowance: St: minus 0.10 sec; Rnd: 0.30 sec per fur (G)   Wind: almost nil   Vis: mod

Stalls: high

**1834**   FRED ARCHER H'CAP (3-Y.O) (0-90) £3002.00 (£896.00: £428.00: £194.00)
**2m 45y**                                                     2-15 (2-15)

(Weights raised 15 lb)
1399 **Jack Button (IRE) (71)** *(BobJones)* 9-7  NDay (2) (led 2f: 2nd st: jnd ldr wl over
1f out: led ins fnl f: r.o) ................................................ —**1**
1765★ Garden District **(73)** (Fav) *(RCharlton)* 9-9 (3x) WRyan (4) (led after 2f: rdn over
1f out: hdd & no ex fnl f) ........................................ ¹/₂.**2**
1602³ Last Conquest (IRE) **(65)** *(PFICole)* 9-1  CRutter (3) (lw: hld up: 3rd st: swtchd rt
2f out: kpt on same pce) ..................•............ 2.**3**
1491 Tricycle (IRE) **(44)** *(JWWatts)* 7-8  RFox (1) (lw: bhd: 4th st: rdn 3f out: sn t.o) .. 30.**4**

**4/5** Garden District, **7/2** JACK BUTTON (IRE), Last Conquest (IRE), **12/1** Tricycle (IRE). CSF £6.41, Tote £4.50
(£2.10). A. and B. Racing (NEWMARKET) bred by Empress Syndicate in Ireland. 4 Rn       3m 40.03 (12.83)
SF—27/28/18/–

**1835**   PETER WALKER BREWERY CLAIMING STKS (2-Y.O) £2206.40 (£610.40: £291.20)
**6f**                                                          2-45 (2-46)

1554★ **Simply Amiss** (Fav) *(SirMarkPrescott)* 8-1  GDuffield (5) (mde all: clr 2f out:
v.easily) .................................................... —**1**
1616★ Trentesimo (IRE) *(JBerry)* 8-10  JCarroll (1) (chsd ldrs: rdn over 1f out: kpt on:
no ch w wnr) ................................................ 4.**2**
1409⁶ The Institute Boy *(KRBurke)* 8-9  AShoults (3) (lw: chsd wnr: rdn over 1f out: one
pce) ...................................................... 2¹/₂.**3**
650⁴ Hairraising *(NACallaghan)* 8-1  WCarson (2) (nvr nr to chal) .................. 2¹/₂.**4**
1660 Master Sinclair (IRE) *(RHollinshead)* 8-4  WRyan (6) (lw: swvd s: sn chsng ldrs:
wknd wl over 1f out) ......................................... 2.**5**
1524 Simply a Star (IRE) *(MWEasterby)* 8-4  KDarley (4) (lw: lost tch ¹/₂-wy: sn rdn: no
imp) ...................................................... 3.**6**

**7/4** SIMPLY AMISS(op 3/1), **3/1** Hairraising(op 2/1), **7/2** Trentesimo (IRE), **7/1** Master Sinclair (IRE), **8/1** The
Institute Boy, **16/1** Simply a Star (IRE). CSF £7.92, Tote £2.90: £1.60 1.60 (£3.40). Mr Neil Greig
(NEWMARKET) bred by Somerhall Bloodstock Ltd. 6 Rn       1m 14.83 (3.13)
SF—13/6/–/–/–/–

**1836**   JOHNNY OSBORNE H'CAP (0-90) £3546.00 (£981.00: £468.00)
**1m 3f 200y**                                                 3-20 (3-20)

(Weights raised 5 lb)
1482³ **Inan (USA) (72)** *(JLDunlop)* 3–8-5  WCarson (4) (lw: mde all: hrd drvn over 1f
out: hld on gamely) .......................................... —**1**
1211⁴ Opera Ghost **(78)** (Fav) *(PWHarris)* 6–9-10  WRyan (1) (lw: chsd wnr: 2nd st: ev
ch & rdn over 1f out: unable qckn) .............................. nk.**2**
1394 Mardessa **(60)** *(FHLee)* 4–8-6  RLappin (2) (lw: hld up: 3rd st: effrt & ev ch 2f out:
rdn & btn appr fnl f) ......................................... 2¹/₂.**3**

**6/5** Opera Ghost, **2/1** INAN (USA), **3/1** Mardessa(op 2/1). CSF £4.14, Tote £2.00 (£1.30). Mr Hamdan
Al-Maktoum (ARUNDEL) bred by Clovelly Farms in USA. 3 Rn       2m 44.07 (16.07)

**1837**   KNIGHTON GROUP H'CAP (0-90) £2976.00 (£888.00: £424.00: £192.00)
**6f**                                                         3-55 (3-56)

(Weights raised 1 lb)
1576★ **Massiba (IRE) (82)** (Fav) *(MJHeaton-Ellis)* 3–9-1 (4x) GDuffield (4) (mde all: clr
over 1f out: easily) .......................................... —**1**
1631² Dominuet **(84)** *(JLSpearing)* 7–9-10  GHind (2) (hdwy 2f out: chsd wnr appr fnl f:
no imp) .................................................... 2¹/₂.**2**
1736⁴ Glenstal Princess **(61)** *(RHollinshead)* 5–8-1  WCarson (3) (chsd ldrs: kpt on
u.p ins fnl f: nt pce to chal) .................................. 2.**3**
1474 Prolific **(77)** *(CaptJWilson)* 7–9-3  WRyan (5) (hld up: effrt over 1f out: nvr nr to
chal) ..................................................... nk.**4**
1451★ Sully's Choice (USA) **(53)** (bl) *(DWChapman)* 11–7-7  SWood (1) (w wnr 2f: rdn
2f out: sn btn) .............................................. 7.**5**
LONG HANDICAP: Sully's Choice (USA) 7-6.

**1838—1840**

**5/4** MASSIBA (IRE), **7/2** Dominuet, **11/2** Profilic, Glenstal Princess, **9/1** Sully's Choice (USA). CSF £5.43, Tote £2.10: £1.50 £2.50 (£3.40). Mr F. J. Sainsbury (WROUGHTON) bred by Gainsborough Stud Management Ltd in Ireland. 5 Rn
1m 12.73 (1.03)
SF—69/68/37/52/–

---

## 1838
FRANK WOOTTON (S) STKS (2-Y.O) £2167.20 (£599.20: £285.60)    **5f**   4-25 (4-26)

|     |     |     |
| --- | --- | --- |
| 889 | **Our Mica** (bl) *(JBerry)* 8-11 JCarroll (5) (mde all: clr over 1f out: rdn out) .......... | —1 |
| 1307² | Dead Calm (Fav) *(CTinkler)* 8-11 GDuffield (2) (chsd ldrs: outpcd & rdn over 2f out: r.o fnl f: nt rch wnr) ............................ | 1¹/₂.2 |
| 1296 | Canazei (v) *(DonEnricoIncisa)* 8-6 JakiHouston (1) (bhd: rdn ¹/₂-wy: styd on fnl f) ................................. | 2¹/₂.3 |
| 1547² | Pretzel (IRE) (v) *(NTinkler)* 8-11 KDarley (3) (spd over 3f) ............................... | 1¹/₂.4 |
|     | Flash of Joy *(CDBroad)* 8-1 ‡⁵ATucker (4) (s.s: a outpcd: t.o) ........................... | 15.5 |

**5/4** Dead Calm, **9/4** Pretzel (IRE), **3/1** OUR MICA, **16/1** Ors. CSF £6.99, Tote £3.80: £1.70 £1.10 (£2.90). Mr Mike Dodds (COCKERHAM) bred by Aspley Bloodstock. 5 Rn; No bid
62.99 sec (3.99)

---

## 1839
STEVE DONOGHUE STKS (Mdn 3-Y.O) £2385.00 (£660.00: £315.00)
**1m 30y**
4-55 (4-55)

|     |     |     |
| --- | --- | --- |
| 693 | **Majjra** (USA) *(JHMGosden)* 9-0 GDuffield (4) (2nd st: jnd ldr over 2f out: led ins fnl f: all out) .................... | —1 |
| 1398² | Agincourt Song (USA) **(85)** (Fav) *(JLDunlop)* 9-0 WCarson (5) (led tl ins fnl f: hrd rdn & rallied cl home) ................................. | hd.2 |
| 1329² | Manulife **(68)** *(BBeasley)* 9-0 DNicholls (3) (3rd st: rdn over 1f out: one pce) ..... | 5.3 |
| 1532³ | Be My Everything (IRE) *(NHollinshead)* 8-9 WRyan (1) (hld up: 5th st: effrt 3f out: wknd over 1f out) .................... | hd.4 |
|     | Hot Prospect *(JEtherington)* 8-9 NDay (2) (hld up: 4th st: drvn along 3f out: no imp) .................... | 3¹/₂.5 |

**2/7** Agincourt Song (USA), **11/2** MAJJRA (USA)(op 3/1), **10/1** Manulife, Be My Everything (IRE), **33/1** Hot Prospect. CSF £7.68, Tote £4.80: £1.40 £1.10 (£2.30). Sheikh Mohammed (NEWMARKET) bred by Hermitage Farm & Kennelot Stables Ltd in USA. 5 Rn
1m 47.70 (7.30)
SF—26/25/10/4/–

T/Plpt: £115.90 (31.9 Tckts).
IM

---

# HAYDOCK (L-H)
## Saturday, July 4th [Good becoming Good to soft]
Going Allowance: St: nil sec; Rnd: 0.15 sec per fur (G)      Wind: mod across

Stalls: high

## 1840
JUDDMONTE CLAIMING STKS (Qualifier)   £2637.00 (£732.00: £351.00)
**1¹/₄m 120y**
2-00 (2-01)

|     |     |     |
| --- | --- | --- |
| 565 | **Eagle Feather** (IRE) **(65)** (Fav) *(JLDunlop)* 4–9-1 JReid (1) (a.p: 2nd st: led wl over 1f out: drew clr nr fin) .................... | —1 |
| 1501² | Bescaby Boy **(64)** *(JWharton)* 6–9-0 ‡⁷SWilliams (6) (hld up: 4th st: ev ch 1f out: no ex fnl f) .................... | 2¹/₂.2 |
| 1619³ | Overpower **(64)** *(MHTompkins)* 8–8-12 PRobinson (5) (lw: hld up: 5th st: stdy hdwy fnl 2f: rdn & one pce fnl f) .................... | ¹/₂.3 |
| 1329⁵ | Honey Boy Simba **(33)** (v) *(MO'Neill)* 6–8-9 JFortune (9) (hld up: 5th st: rdn 3f out: one pce) .................... | 6.4 |
| 1519⁵ | Henbury Hall (IRE) **(63)** *(MrsGRReveley)* 4–8-13 LDettori (8) (lw: prom: 3rd st: rdn over 1f out: sn btn) .................... | 3¹/₂.5 |
| 1544⁶ | Beechwood Cottage **(38)** (bl) *(ABailey)* 9–8-2 ‡⁷WHollick (7) (b.hind: lw: s.i.s: 7th st: a bhd) .................... | 1¹/₂.6 |
| 1509⁴ | Princess Roxanne **(52)** (bl) *(ABailey)* 5–7-13 ‡⁷DWright (3) (lw: led tl hdd & wknd wl over 1f out) .................... | ³/₄.7 |
| 1255 | Wheels of Weetman **(30)** *(MissSJWilton)* 5–8-10 GDuffield (2) (hld up: a bhd: 8th st: rdn 3f out: t.o) .................... | 25.8 |

**3/1** EAGLE FEATHER (IRE), **7/2** Overpower, **9/2** Bescaby Boy, **5/1** Henbury Hall (IRE), **11/2** Princess Roxanne, **20/1** Honey Boy Simba, **25/1** Beechwood Cottage, **50/1** Wheels of Weetman. CSF £14.72, Tote £3.80: £1.60 £1.30 £1.50 (£9.30). Mr J. L. Dunlop (ARUNDEL) bred by Rathbeale Stud in Ireland. 8 Rn
2m 17.46 (5.76)
SF—59/53/50/35/32/18

**1841**     EDWARD SYMMONS & PARTNERS H'CAP (0-90) £3574.00 (£1072.00: £516.00:
             £238.00)    1¼m 120y                                    2-35 (2-36)
                              (Weights raised 5 lb)
1705* **Bowden Boy (IRE) (65)** (bl) (Jt-Fav) *(NACallaghan)* 4–8–11  PatEddery (2) (a.p:
             2nd st: led 2f out: hrd rdn fnl f: hld on) ...........................  —1
1371* Tempelhof (IRE) **(63)** (Jt-Fav) *(JWHills)* 3–7–6 ‡5DHarrison (1) (lw: led to 2f out:
             sn rdn & outpcd: swtchd rt: styd on fnl f) .......................  ½.2
1509* Azureus (IRE) **(78)** *(MrsGRReveley)* 4–9–3 ‡7DarrenMoffatt (3) (lw: hld up: 3rd &
             c stands' side st: rdn 2f out: edgd lft fnl f: r.o) ...............  1½.3
1295⁴ Katy's Lad **(71)** *(BAMcMahon)* 5–9–3 JReid (6) (hld up: 4th st: effrt & ev ch 2f
             out: kpt on ins fnl f) ..............................................  1½.4
1604* Rose Glen **(62)** *(ABailey)* 6–8–1 ‡7OPears (4) (bhd: 5th st: effrt over 2f out: rdn &
             btn appr fnl f) ......................................................  2.5

**5/2** Tempelhof (IRE), BOWDEN BOY (IRE), **4/1** Rose Glen, **9/2** Katy's Lad, **5/1** Azureus (IRE). CSF £8.65, Tote
£2.70: £1.50 £1.90 (£3.90). Mr T. A. Foreman (NEWMARKET) bred by Lord Dundas in Ireland. 5 Rn
                                                                          2m 22.22 (10.52)
                                                                          SF—7/–/9/6/–

**1842**     OLD NEWTON CUP (H'cap) (0-115) £20387.50 (£6100.00: £2925.00: £1337.50)
             1m 3f 200y                                             3-10 (3-11)
1465³ **Matador (USA) (96)** (Fav) *(RCharlton)* 5–9–2  PatEddery (5) (lw: led 1f: 3rd st:
             led 3f out: sn hdd: led over 1f out: all out) ...................  —1
1697 Quick Ransom **(77)** *(MJohnston)* 4–7–8 ‡3JFanning (2) (lw: hld up: 7th st: hdwy
             u.p 3f out: r.o strly nr fin) ........................................  nk.2
1665³ Secret Society **(85)** *(MJCamacho)* 5–8–5  NConnorton (1) (lw: a.p: 5th st: rdn wl
             over 1f out: styd on ins fnl f) .....................................  ¾.3
1211* Castoret **(75)** *(JWHills)* 6–7–4 ‡5DHarrison (7) (hld up: 6th st: led over 2f out tl
             over 1f out: hrd rdn & no ex fnl f) ................................  1.4
343 Percy's Girl (IRE) **(97)** *(GWragg)* 4–9–0 ‡3FNorton (6) (bit bkwd: hld up & bhd:
             8th st: gd hdwy 3f out: ev ch: rdn & unable qckn fnl f) ......  s.h.5
1465 Pharly Story **(92)** *(MCPipe)* 4–8–12 LDettori (8) (lost pl ½-wy: hdwy 2f out: nvr
             able to chal) .........................................................  1½.6
644a⁴ Per Quod (USA) **(108)** *(BHanbury)* 7–10–0 WRyan (10) (b: bit bkwd: led after 1f
             to 3f out: grad wknd) .................................................  4.7
1710² Shambo **(107)** *(CEBrittain)* 5–9–3 LPiggott (4) (lw: hld up: hdwy & 4th st: rdn &
             wknd 2f out) .........................................................  1½.8
1634² Fieldridge **(92)** *(CRNelson)* 3–7–13 DHolland (3) (lw: prom: 2nd st: ev ch 3f out:
             sn rdn & wknd: t.o) ..................................................  10.9

**11/4** MATADOR (USA), **4/1** Quick Ransom, **11/2** Castoret, Shambo, **8/1** Pharly Story, Fieldridge(op 5/1), **10/1**
Secret Society, Per Quod (USA), **16/1** Percy's Girl (IRE). CSF £14.49, CSF £90.66. Tote £3.50: £1.80 £2.00 £2.90
(£11.10). Mr K. Abdulla (BECKHAMPTON) bred by Flaxman Holdings Limited in USA. 9 Rn   2m 34.18 (6.18)
                                                                          SF—58/35/44/27/50/45

**1843**     LANCASHIRE OAKS STKS (Gp 3) (F & M) £20580.00 (£7704.00: £3702.00: £1614.00)
             1m 3f 200y                                             3-45 (3-49)
1470² **Niodini (USA) (106)** (v) *(MRStoute)* 3–8–4  PaulEddery (7) (a.p: 2nd st: led over
             2f out: qcknd clr: rdn & hld on gamely) .........................  —1
1470* Armarama *(CEBrittain)* 3–8–9 LPiggott (9) (prom: 4th st: rdn 2f out: str run fnl f:
             no ex nr fin) .........................................................  1½.2
1470³ Blushing Storm (USA) *(JRFanshawe)* 3–8–4 GDuffield (8) (lw: wl bhd tl styd on
             fnl 2f) ................................................................  1½.3
707² Shirley Valentine (Fav) *(HRACecil)* 3–8–4 PatEddery (3) (chsd ldrs: 6th st: rdn 3f
             out: styd on one pce) ...............................................  1½.4
11a⁵ Sought Out (IRE) *(JEHammond,France)* 4–9–6 CAsmussen (1) (a.p: 3rd st: rdn
             wl over 1f out: one pce) .............................................  s.h.5
1211 Fragrant Hill **(100)** (bl) *(IABalding)* 4–9–3 LDettori (10) (lw: s.i.s: hld up & bhd:
             hdwy 3f out: hrd rdn over 1f out: nvr able to chal) ...........  3½.6
850³ Mystery Play (IRE) **(104)** *(BWHills)* 3–8–4 DHolland (6) (lw: hdwy ½-wy: 5th st:
             wknd 2f out) .........................................................  2½.7
1399* Sea Goddess **(95)** *(WJarvis)* 4–9–3 JReid (2) (lw: led tl hdd over 2f out: sn rdn &
             btn: t.o) ..............................................................  15.8
1347³ Jezebel Monroe (USA) **(97)** *(RCharlton)* 3–8–4 SRaymont (5) (lw: a bhd: t.o) ...  2.9
1470⁴ Delve (IRE) **(92)** *(JLDunlop)* 3–8–4 WRyan (4) (a in rr: t.o fnl 2f) .............  5.10
929³ Gai Bulga **(103)** *(GWragg)* 4–9–3 PRobinson (11) (lw: chsd ldrs 7f: sn lost tch:
             t.o) ...................................................................  10.11

**3/1** Shirley Valentine(op 6/1), **7/2** Armarama, **6/1** Sought Out (IRE), **7/1** NIODINI (USA), **9/1** Sea Goddess, **10/1**
Gai Bulga, Mystery Play (IRE), Jezebel Monroe (USA), **16/1** Ors. CSF £32.55, Tote £7.80: £2.10 £1.90 £4.50
(£10.40). Sheikh Mohammed (NEWMARKET) bred by Triple C Thorostock in USA. 11 Rn   2m 32.66 (4.66)
                                                                          SF—62/64/56/53/68/58

**1844**    COCK OF THE NORTH STKS (listed race) (2-Y.O) £7310.00 (£2180.00: £1040.00: £470.00)   **6f**

4-20 (4-20)

1019* **Son Pardo** *(RHannon)* 8-12 JReid (5) (lw: w ldrs: led over 1f out tl ins fnl f: rallied u.p to ld nr fin) ...................................................................... —1

1472³ Colyan (IRE) (Fav) *(MRStoute)* 8-12 PatEddery (2) (lw: hld up: gd hdwy to ld ins fnl f: edgd lft: hrd rdn & ct cl home) ........................................... hd.2

1192⁶ Glowing Value (IRE) *(JBerry)* 8-12 CAsmussen (3) (lw: a.p: swtchd & ev ch over 1f out: unable qckn) ..................................................... 3½.3

1291² Key to My Heart *(DMoffatt)* 8-12 JFortune (4) (lw: led tl over 1f out: rdn & outpcd fnl f) .................................................................. 8.4

**4/6** Colyan (IRE), **5/2** SON PARDO, **7/1** Key to My Heart (IRE), **11/1** Glowing Value (IRE). CSF £4.45, Tote £3.00 (£1.50). N.T.C. (Racing) Limited (MARLBOROUGH) bred by R. T. and Mrs Watson. 4 Rn   1m 13.93 (2.23)
SF—54/53/41/9

**1845**    E.B.F. JULY STKS (Mdn 2-Y.O.F) £2807.00 (£777.00: £371.00)   **6f**   4-55 (4-55)

**Love of Silver** (USA) (Fav) *(CEBrittain)* 8-11 LPiggott (3) (w'like: leggy: lw: hld up: led over 1f out: r.o strly) ......................................... —1

1609⁵ Goodbye Millie *(SGNorton)* 8-11 JFortune (2) (bit bkwd: led tl over 1f out: kpt on one pce) ......................................................... 2½.2

1297 Yfool *(JRFanshawe)* 8-11 GDuffield (1) (hld up: effrt & ev ch 2f out: rdn & wknd appr fnl f) ............................................................ 1½.3

**4/6** LOVE OF SILVER (USA), **3/1** Yfool, **7/2** Goodbye Millie. CSF £2.86, Tote £1.50 (£1.90). Mr Ali Saeed (NEWMARKET) bred by Brylynn Farm in USA. 3 Rn   1m 15.87 (4.17)
SF—13/3/–

**1846**    SHADWELL STUD APP'CE SERIES H'CAP (0-90) £3622.50 (£1080.00: £515.00: £232.50)   **1m 30y**

5-30 (5-32)

(Weights raised 1 lb)

1391 **Express Gift (64)** *(MrsGRReveley)* 3–7-7 ‡³DarrenMoffatt (5) (lw: a.p: 2nd st: led over 1f out: r.o wl) ...................................... —1

1254² Sagebrush Roller **(77)** (Fav) *(JWWatts)* 4–9-4 DHarrison (6) (lw: hld up & bhd: 6th st: hdwy 2f out: r.o strly nr fin) ............................. ½.2

1619² Causley **(69)** *(BAMcMahon)* 7–8-5 ‡⁵SSanders (7) (led: rdn 2f out: hdd over 1f out: kpt on u.p) ......................................... 1.3

1833⁴ Sir Arthur Hobbs **(64)** *(FHLee)* 5–8-5 NKennedy (3) (lw: hld up: 3rd st: n.m.r over 1f out: rdn & wknd fnl f) ..................................... 6.4

1388⁵ Self Expression **(83)** *(IABalding)* 4–9-3 ‡⁷DGriffiths (1) (lw: hld up: 5th st: hdwy on ins 3f out: rdn & wknd appr fnl f) .......................... 1½.5

1270⁶ Lombard Ships **(55)** *(MO'Neill)* 5–7-10 SMaloney (4) (lw: prom: 4th st: rdn 2f out: sn btn) ...................................................... d.h.5

**9/4** Sagebrush Roller, **100/30** EXPRESS GIFT, **7/2** Causley, **11/2** Sir Arthur Hobbs, **8/1** Self Expression, **11/1** Lombard Ships. CSF £10.54, Tote £4.20: £1.80 £1.70 (£4.60). Mr H. Young (SALTBURN) bred by H. Young. 6 Rn   1m 45.72 (5.32)
SF—17/40/24/6/13/–

T/Trio: Race 3: £32.40 (72.75 Tckts). T/Plpt: £100.40 (42.4 Tckts).     IM

1546—**SOUTHWELL (L-H)** Fibresand

**Friday, July 3rd [Standard]**

Going Allowance: minus 0.30 sec per fur (FS)        Wind: almost nil

Stalls: high

**1847**    EAST MIDLANDS ELECTRICITY PLC H'CAP (0-70) £2598.40 (£722.40: £347.20)   **1m (AWT)**

2-30 (2-36)

1673³ **Sandmoor Denim (48)** *(SRBowring)* 5–8-7 SWebster (14) (trckd ldrs: effrt 2f out: r.o wl u.p to ld nr fin) ........................................ —1

1550² Hawaii Storm (FR) **(55)** *(MissAJWhitfield)* 4–9-0 DaleGibson (9) (hdwy ½-wy: led over 1f out: nt qckn nr fin) ................................ ¾.2

1712² Red Kite **(64)** (Fav) *(MBell)* 3–8-7 ‡⁷PTurner (1) (lw: chsd ldrs: hmpd over 5f out: one pce) ................................................ 5.3

572 No Decision **(47)** *(MWEasterby)* 5–8-6 TLucas (8) (bhd tl r.o fnl 2f) ................... 3.4

1323* Turtle Beach **(70)** *(AAScott)* 3–9-6 JFortune (5) (lw: led 2f: hmpd over 5f out: led over 2f out tl hdd & wknd over 1f out) ....................... 2.5

*1546* Armashocker **(44)** *(DSasse)* 4–8–3[(1)] GBaxter (10) (s.i.s: sn wl bhd: styd on fnl 2f: nt rch ldrs) ............................................................................................... 1.6

*1550* Quinzii Martin **(56)** *(DHaydnJones)* 4–9–1 TyroneWilliams (4) (chsd ldrs tl wknd over 2f out) ............................................................................................... 1½.7

*1682*[2] Hubbers Favourite **(49)** *(MrsNMacauley)* 4–8–8 RHills (12) (led 6f out tl over 2f out: sn wknd & hmpd) ............................................................................................... 1½.8

Rupples **(41)** *(MCChapman)* 5–7–7[(7)] ‡[7]CHawksley (3) (chsd ldrs bhd: sme hdwy 2f out: n.d) ............................................................................................... 3½.9

*1284* Top One **(60)** *(CJHill)* 7–9–5 NAdams (7) (chsd ldrs tl lost pl 3f out) ............ 5.10

*1441* Canaan Valley **(66)** (bl) *(JGFitzGerald)* 4–9–11 KFallon (2) (eyeshield: unruly s: chsd ldrs tl lost pl 3f out) ............................................................................. ¾.11

Mart Lagache (FR) **(35)** *(DWChapman)* 4–7–1 ‡[7]DarrenMoffatt (13) (lw: sn wl bhd) ............................................................................................... 6.12

L'Amour Precieux **(56)** *(MWEasterby)* 3–8–6 LCharnock (6) (prom over 4f: bhd fnl 2f) ............................................................................................... 1.13

*1528* Boon Hill **(46)** *(MWEllerby)* 3–7–10[(3)] PBurke (11) (chsd ldrs tl lost pl 3f out: sn bhd) ............................................................................................... 3.14

LONG HANDICAP: Rupples 7-3, Boon Hill 7-1.

**100/30** Red Kite, **13/2** Hawaii Storm (FR), **7/1** Hubbers Favourite, SANDMOOR DENIM, **10/1** Turtle Beach, **12/1** Quinzii Martin, No Decision, Canaan Valley, **16/1** Top One, **20/1** L'Amour Precieux, **33/1** Armashocker, Mart Lagache (FR), Rupples, **50/1** Boon Hill. CSF £45.61, CT £161.62. Tote £7.70: £2.30 £3.00 £1.90 (£19.80). Mr E. H. Lunness (EDWINSTOWE) bred by Rathasker Stud. 14 Rn

SF—26/31/9/–/7/–

# 1848

SILVER BIRCH CLAIMING STKS (2-Y.O) £2480.80 (£688.80: £330.40)
**7f (AWT)**

3-00 (3-15)

*1448* **Girl At the Gate** *(MBell)* 8-1 RHills (13) (b.hind: trckd ldrs: led over 2f out: sn clr) ............... —1

*1623*★ Fantan (IRE) (bl) (Fav) *(MHEasterby)* 8-8 TLucas (5) (a chsng ldrs: kpt on fnl 2f: no ch w wnr) ............................................................................................... 6.2

*1442* Awesome Risk *(GLewis)* 7-7 DaleGibson (6) (chsd ldrs: rdn 3f out: one pce) .. 1½.3

Fayre Find *(MHTompkins)* 7-11[(5)] ‡[7]SMulvey (4) (s.i.s: sn wl bhd: styd on fnl 2f) ` 7.4

*1547*★ Matthew David *(MBrittain)* 8-6 ‡[5]SMaloney (10) (lw: sn led: hdd over 2f out: wknd over 1f out) ............................................................................................... 1.5

*1264*[6] Peak Fitness *(JAGlover)* 8-4 JFortune (8) (chsd ldrs: rdn over 3f out: no imp) ... 1.6

*1547*[6] Big Gem *(MCChapman)* 8-5[(1)] SWebster (1) (led early: chsd ldrs tl wknd over 2f out) ............................................................................................... 1½.7

*1296* Alice Bay *(DHaydnJones)* 7-13 TyroneWilliams (12) (swtg: chsd ldrs tl lost pl 3f out) ............................................................................................... hd.8

*588* Ukam's Lady *(RHannon)* 7-13 AMcGlone (3) (chsd ldrs: sn drvn along: lost pl 3f out) ............................................................................................... 3.9

*1670* Bay Rum *(BBeasley)* 7-8[(1)] LCharnock (11) (sn wl bhd) ....................................... nk.10

*1299* Cyprus Creek (IRE) *(NTinkler)* 7-13[(4)] AFByParkin (7) (s.i.s: a wl bhd) ............... nk.11

Glowing Path *(CJHill)* 8-12 NAdams (9) (leggy: s.s: a in rr) ................................... 2.12

*701* Dorazine (20/1) Withdrawn (broke out of stalls) : not under orders

**11/4** Fanfan (IRE)(9/4—4/1), **7/2** Matthew David, **7/1** Ukam's Lady(op 4/1), **8/1** GIRL AT THE GATE, **17/2** Bay Rum(12/1—7/1), **10/1** Cyprus Creek (IRE), **11/1** Fayre Find, **12/1** Awesome Risk(op 8/1), **14/1** Alice Bay, **20/1** Glowing Path, **25/1** Peak Fitness, **33/1** Big Gem. CSF £30.22, Tote £7.40: £2.30 £2.10 £2.50 (£16.10). Mr John G. Morley (NEWMARKET) bred by Ruckmans Farm. 12 Rn

1m 29.1 (2.5)

SF—18/7/–/–/–/–

# 1849

POWERMAX STKS (I) (Mdn 3-Y.O) £2186.80 (£604.80: £288.40)
**7f (AWT)**

3-30 (3-38)

*1678* **Quantity Surveyor** *(SirMarkPrescott)* 9-0 CNutter (9) (lw: chsd ldrs: sn drvn along: styd on fnl f: led wl ins fnl f) ........................................................ —1

*1627*[3] Grubby **(46)** (Fav) *(RHollinshead)* 8-2 ‡[7]AGarth (7) (led: nt qckn cl home) .......... 2.2

Take by Storm (IRE) *(GMMoore)* 9-0 WNewnes (4) (lengthy: unf: s.i.s: wl bhd: stdy hdwy over 2f out: r.o wl nr fin) ............................................... 3.3

*1661*[5] Fairford (bl) *(JGFitzGerald)* 9-0 KFallon (8) (eyeshield: chsd ldrs: ev ch 2f out: wknd 1f out) ............................................................................................... 1½.4

*1503* Legend Dulac (IRE) *(JLHarris)* 9-0 GBaxter (3) (plld hrd: trckd ldrs: ev ch over 2f out: wknd over 1f out) ................................................................................ s.h.5

*1312*[6] Giddy Heights (IRE) *(JPLeigh)* 8-2 ‡[7]StephenDavies (1) (chsd ldrs tl wknd over 1f out) ............................................................................................... 6.6

Trevveethan (IRE) *(JBalding)* 8-7 ‡[7]ClaireBalding (6) (swtg: sn wl bhd) .............. 7.7

Oriental Song *(KSBridgwater)* 8-8[(6)] ‡[7]SWilliams (2) (rangy: bit bkwd: s.i.s: sn chsng ldrs: lost pl 3f out) ............................................................. 5.8

Wave to Me *(NTinkler)* 9-0 LCharnock (5) (wl grwn: bkwd: s.s: rn green: a wl bhd) ............................................................................................... 20.9

**3/1** Grubby, **9/2** Fairford(op 2/1), **5/1** Giddy Heights (IRE), Legend Dulac (IRE)(op 12/1), **8/1** QUANTITY SURVEYOR, Wave to Me(op 5/1), **10/1** Take by Storm (IRE), **20/1** Oriental Song, **33/1** Trevveethan (IRE). CSF £30.21, Tote £8.50: £2.60 £1.10 £3.90 (£7.30). Lady Fairhaven (NEWMARKET) bred by Lord Fairhaven. 9 Rn
1m 28.8 (2.2)
SF—35/17/20/15/14/–

**1850**     PROVIDENT MUTUAL H'CAP (3-Y.O) (0-70) £2363.20 (£655.20: £313.60)
1½m (AWT)                                                                                    4-00 (4-03)
(Weights raised 7 lb)

1548³ Holy Wanderer (USA) (54) (DWPArbuthnot) 8-10 ‡⁵RPrice (11) (b.hind: hld up
gng wl: smooth hdwy 4f out: led wl over 1f out: easily) ....... —1
1362⁴ Firefighter (60) (Fav) (RHollinshead) 9-7 RHills (2) (sn drvn along: wnt prom 6f
out: styd on u.p fnl 2f: no ch w wnr) ..................................... 5.2
1679² Witches Coven (50) (MBell) 8-4 ‡PTurner (4) (sn trckng ldrs: led over 4f out tl
over 1f out: one pce) ........................................................ 4.3
1548⁶ Alto (44) (JGFitzGerald) 8-5(1) KFallon (9) (eyeshield: sn chsng ldrs: one pce
fnl 2f) ........................................................................... 1½.4
1739 Miss Hyde (USA) (55) (v) (JAGlover) 9-2 JFortune (8) (sn w ldr: led 10f out tl
over 4f out: wknd over 2f out) ............................................. 12.5
1246 Chill Wind (50) (NBycroft) 8-11 SWebster (1) (prom tl lost pl 5f out) ............... 1½.6
1286 Linpac Express (59) (bl) (CWCElsey) 9-6 NNewnes (7) (lw: hld up: wnt prom 8f
out: rdn & lost pl over 3f out) ............................................ 2.7
921⁶ Sweet Noble (IRE) (55) (JGFitzGerald) 8-9 ‡⁷MHunt (10) (eyeshield: bhd & drvn
along ½-wy) .................................................................... nk.8
1275⁴ Speedo Movement (60) (BAMcMahon) 9-0 ‡⁷SSanders (12) (s.i.s: sn prom: lost
pl 5f out) ...................................................................... 2½.9
806 Major Risk (52) (bl) (PAKelleway) 8-13 AMcGlone (3) (a in rr) ...................... 1½.10
1655² Saif Al Adil (IRE) (58) (BHanbury) 9-5 GBaxter (5) (lw: chsd ldrs: rdn & lost pl
over 4f out: sn bhd) .......................................................... 10.11
1519 Super Charge (38) (bl) (MWEllerby) 7-13 PBurke (6) (led 2f: chsd ldrs: rdn 5f
out: sn wknd: bhd) ........................................................... 15.12

**5/2** Firefighter, **7/2** Witches Coven, **7/1** Sweet Noble (IRE), HOLY WANDERER (USA), **8/1** Saif Al Adil (IRE), **12/1** Speedo Movement(op 7/1), **14/1** Miss Hyde (USA), Super Charge, Chill Wind, **25/1** Alto, **33/1** Linpac Express. CSF £26.68, CT £71.64. Tote £8.80: £1.90 £1.90 £1.10 (£11.10). Mr Michael Pescod (COMPTON) bred by Parrish Hill Farm et. al. in USA. 12 Rn
2m 38.8 (4.6)
SF—14/15/–/–/–/–

**1851**     E.B.F. SYCAMORE STKS (Mdn 2-Y.O) £2245.60 (£621.60: £296.80)
5f (AWT)                                                                                    4-30 (4-32)

1601⁴ Meadmore Magic (JLHarris) 8-9 GBaxter (5) (mde all: edgd lft 1f out: drvn out)  —1
Dream a Bit (JGFitzGerald) 8-9 KFallon (8) (w'like: leggy: scope: hdwy ½-wy:
ev ch ins fnl f: r.o) ......................................................... 1.2
1531³ Benzoe (IRE) (Fav) (MWEasterby) 9-0 TLucas (4) (w wnr: rdn over 1f out:
unable qckn) ................................................................... 1.3
1120 Sure Risk (RHannon) 8-9 AMcGlone (2) (chsd ldrs: rdn ½-wy: kpt on) .............. 1½.4
1360⁵ La Madrigal (JWharton) 8-9 WNewnes (3) (chsd ldrs: outpcd ½-wy: kpt on fnl f) 1.5
1660 Rose Flyer (IRE) (MCChapman) 8-9 SWebster (9) (hung lft thrght: nvr nr ldrs) .. 5.6
1616⁴ Sounds Risky (GMMoore) 8-4 ‡⁵JWeaver (6) (chsd ldrs tl lost pl ½-wy) ............. 1.7
1609³ Miss Whittingham (IRE) (JBerry) 8-9 RHills (11) (outpcd fr ½-wy) ................... 2.8
Comet Whirlpool (IRE) (BBeasley) 9-0 LCharnock (1) (w'like: str: scope: nvr
wnt pce) ........................................................................ 6.9
1559⁵ Petered Out (TDBarron) 9-0 DaleGibson (10) (sn bhd & drvn along) ............... 8.10
231 Badenoch Burner (NTinkler) 8-9 ‡⁵SMaloney (7) (b: s.i.s: sn prom: hung bdly lft
½-wy: sn lost pl & bhd) ..................................................... 7.11

**6/4** Benzoe (IRE)(op 9/4), **4/1** Sure Risk, **8/1** Petered Out(6/1—9/1), La Madrigal, **10/1** Miss Whittingham (IRE)(op 5/1), **14/1** MEADMORE MAGIC, Dream a Bit, **16/1** Comet Whirlpool (IRE), **25/1** Ors. CSF £172.08, Tote £11.30: £2.10 £4.50 £1.70 (£252.70). Mr M. Holmes (MELTON MOWBRAY) bred by White Lodge Farm Stud. 11 Rn
61.3 sec (3.3)

**1852**     POWERMAX STKS (II) (Mdn 3-Y.O) £2167.20 (£599.20: £285.60)
7f (AWT)                                                                                    5-00 (5-05)

1678² Whitehall (IRE) (63) (Jt-Fav) (CRNelson) 9-0 NAdams (2) (lw: mde virtually all:
drvn clr over 2f out: jst hld on) ........................................... —1
1268² Nellie Dean (62) (Jt-Fav) (JARToller) 8-9 DaleGibson (4) (trckd ldrs tl drn &
outpcd over 2f out: styd on fnl f: nt rch wnr) ......................... ½.2
1617⁵ North Flyer (45) (BAMcMahon) 8-7 ‡⁷SSanders (3) (plld hrd: sn disp ld: rdn &
outpcd over 2f out: kpt on fnl f) .......................................... s.h.3
1540 Millyrous (IRE) (RGuest) 8-9 WNewnes (6) (sn bhd: kpt on fnl 2f: nt rch ldrs) .... ¾.4

1486　Miss Movie World **(38)** *(NBycroft)* 8-9　SWebster (1) (sn bhd: some hdwy 2f out:
n.d) ................................................................................................ 3¹/₂.5
944　June's Lear Fan (CAN) *(PAKelleway)* 9-0　KFallon (7) (chsd ldrs tl grad wknd fnl
2f) ................................................................................................ s.h.6
Faustnluce Lady *(GAHam)* 8-9　ADicks (9) (bit bkwd: unruly s: s.s: sn bhd) ....... ¹/₂.7
1505　Old Fox (FR) *(DSasse)* 9-0　GBaxter (8) (sn chsng ldrs: wknd over 2f out: eased
whn no ch) ................................................................................... 7.8
797³　Milton Rooms (IRE) **(56)** (bl) *(CBBBooth)* 9-0　GOldroyd (5) (lw: s.i.s: a in rr) ... nk.9

**9/4** WHITEHALL (IRE)(2/1—3/1), Nellie Dean(op 11/8), **9/2** North Flyer, **14/1** Millyrous (IRE), **16/1** June's Lear
Fan (CAN), Milton Rooms (IRE), **20/1** Old Fox (FR), Faustnluce Lady, **33/1** Miss Movie World. CSF £6.97, Tote
£3.70: £1.40 1.20 1.70 (£3.10). Mr John W. Mitchell (UPPER LAMBOURN) bred by Grange Farm (Barnby
Moor) Ltd in Ireland. 9 Rn
1m 30.2 (3.6)
SF—14/7/4/4/–/–

**1853**　　ASH APP'CE H'CAP (0-70) £2167.20 (£599.20: £285.60)　　**5f (AWT)**　　5-30 (5-32)

1522⁶　**Lady's Mantle (USA) (42)** *(RBastiman)* 8-8-1⁽³⁾　‡⁴HBastiman (3) (mde all: r.o
u.p fnl f) ..................................................................................... —1
1685³　The Shanahan Bay **(54)** (v) *(MrsNMacauley)* 7-9-3　TSprake (5) (b: trckd ldrs:
chal 1f out: rdn & nt qckn) ......................................................... ³/₄.2
1310　Miss Brightside **(35)** *(ASmith)* 4-7-8　‡⁴CHawksley (4) (chsd ldrs: hrd rdn ¹/₂-wy:
kpt on same pce) ........................................................................ 2¹/₂.3
1570²　Morpick **(53)** (v) *(JPLeigh)* 5-9-2　KRutter (8) (chsd ldrs: outpcd & lost pl ¹/₂-wy:
hdwy over 1f out: styd on) ........................................................... s.h.4
1617　Our Amber **(30)** *(DWChapman)* 5-7-3　‡⁴DarrenMoffatt (2) (s.i.s: sn in tch: kpt on
fnl 2f) ......................................................................................... s.h.5
1727²　Arc Lamp **(58)** *(JAGlover)* 6-9-7 (7x)　SWilliams (6) (b.hind: in tch: drvn along
¹/₂-wy: nvr able to chal) ................................................................ 2.6
1522　Jive Music **(32)** (bl) *(NBycroft)* 6-7-9　SMaloney (1) (w ldrs tl wknd over 1f out) . ¹/₂.7
1651³　Hinari Video **(57)** (Fav) *(MJohnston)* 7-9-6　LNewton (7) (outpcd: drvn along
¹/₂-wy: n:d) ................................................................................. 3.8
1618⁵　Make Or Mar **(62)** *(BEllison)* 8-9-11　OPears (9) (s.i.s: a bhd) ......................... 10.9
LONG HANDICAP: Our Amber 7-6.

**13/8** Hinari Video(op 5/1), **3/1** Morpick(9/4—100/30), **9/2** Arc Lamp(op 3/1), **6/1** The Shanahan Bay, **8/1**
LADY'S MANTLE (USA), **14/1** Miss Brightside, Jive Music, **16/1** Make Or Mar, **25/1** Our Amber. CSF £55.94, CT
£623.31. Tote £10.30: £3.00 £2.00 £5.20 (£24.10). Mr I. B. Barker (WETHERBY) bred by Newchance Farm and
Marshall A. Raff in USA. 9 Rn
59.4 sec (1.4)
SF—29/42/9/30/2/26

T/Plpt: £13.50 (127.65 Tckts).
WG

**1307—BEVERLEY (R-H)**

**Friday, July 3rd [Good becoming Good to soft]**
Going Allowance: 1st & 2nd races: 0.10 sec (G); Rest: 0.50 sec (Y)　　Wind: fresh bhd

Stalls: high

**1854**　　BOOTHFERRY PARK STKS (Mdn 2-Y.O) £1548.00 (£428.00: £204.00)
**5f**　　6-45 (6-48)

**Classic Story (USA)** (Fav) *(MMoubarak)* 9-0　LDettori (5) (str: scope: s.i.s: sn
trckng ldrs: led on bit wl over 1f out: pushed out) ............... —1
1616²　Dahliz (IRE) *(HThomsonJones)* 9-0　NCarlisle (4) (lw: w ldr: led ¹/₂-wy tl wl over
1f out: r.o) ................................................................................. 1¹/₂.2
1701⁶　Mansooree (USA) *(AAScott)* 9-0　BRaymond (7) (led to ¹/₂-wy: rdn & btn over 1f
out) ........................................................................................... 3.3
924　Kingston Brown *(JBerry)* 9-0　MBirch (1) (chsd ldrs 3f: sn outpcd) .................. 3.4
Humber's Supreme (IRE) *(BSRothwell)* 8-9　NConnorton (2) (small: neat: unf:
dwlt: a outpcd & wl bhd) ............................................................ 10.5

**4/6** CLASSIC STORY (USA), **3/1** Dahliz (IRE), **4/1** Mansooree (USA), **12/1** Kingston Brown, **20/1** Humber's
Supreme (IRE). CSF £3.36, Tote £1.70: £1.10 £1.30 (£1.70). Ecurie Fustok (NEWMARKET) bred by Buckram
Oak Farm in USA. 5 Rn
64.7 sec (3.2)
SF—46/40/28/16/–

**1855**　　POCKLINGTON (S) H'CAP (3-Y.O) (0-60) £1632.00 (£452.00: £216.00)
**1m 1f 207y**　　7-10 (7-12)

(Weights raised 4 lb)
1705³　Big Pat **(50)** (Fav) *(JPearce)* 9-2　‡⁵RPrice (4) (hdwy 6f out: led 2f out: edgd rt &
styd on wl) ................................................................................ —1

1528 Qualitair Memory (IRE) **(41)** *(JFBottomley)* 8-12 PBurke (5) (chsd ldr: led over 3f out tl hdd 2f out: one pce) ................................................. 5.**2**
15073 Hataal (IRE) **(44)** *(JBalding)* 9-1 GHind (2) (lw: bhd: hdwy appr st: rdn & n.d) .. 12.**3**
1627 Vital Voltage (IRE) **(40)** *(MWEllerby)* 8-11 SMorris (3) (chsd ldrs tl outpcd wl over 2f out) ................................................. 1¹/₂.**4**
1486 Jester's Gem **(35)** *(BWMurray)* 8-6 KDarley (6) (led tl hdd over 3f out: sn wknd) 8.**5**
1294 Tender Monarch (IRE) **(28)** *(PJBevan)* 7-13 NCarlisle (1) (chsd ldrs to st: sn rdn & btn) ................................................. 2¹/₂.**6**

**4/5** BIG PAT, **4/1** Qualitair Memory (IRE), **9/2** Hataal (IRE), **13/2** Vital Voltage (IRE), **14/1** Jester's Gem, **20/1** Tender Monarch (IRE). CSF £4.78, CT £9.00. Tote £1.90: £1.20 £1.90 (£2.90). Burton Park Country Club (NEWMARKET) bred by Mrs P. J. Lewis. 6 Rn; Bt in 5,400 gns
2m 11.8 (9.8)
SF—14/-/-/-/-/-

**1856** WM JACKSON & SON H'CAP (3-Y.O) (0-100) £3905.00 (£1080.00: £515.00)
1m 100y
7-35 (7-35)

15045 **Wesaam (USA) (87)** *(MajorWRHern)* 9-7 WCarson (1) (mde all: pushed along 2f out: r.o: comf) ................................................. —**1**
1412★ Mizoram (USA) **(82)** *(HRACecil)* 8-9 ‡7StephenDavies (2) (chsd wnr: chal over 3f out: edgd rt & r.o one pce appr fnl f) .................. 3.**2**
13984 Ajo (IRE) **(83)** *(MRStoute)* 9-3 MBirch (3) (chsd ldrs tl outpcd fnl 3f) ................ 20.**3**

**11/8** Mizoram (USA), WESAAM (USA), **4/1** Ajo (IRE). CSF £3.17, Tote £2.30 (£1.30). Mr Hamdan Al-Maktoum (LAMBOURN) bred by R.Smiser West, Gerald Robins & Timothy Sams in USA. 3 Rn
1m 50.9 (8.2)
SF—47/26/-

**1857** NORWOOD MEDIAN AUCTION STKS (Mdn 3-Y.O) £1478.00 (£408.00: £194.00)
1m 3f 216y
8-05 (8-06)

**Arfey (IRE)** *(TThomsonJones)* 8-7 WCarson (3) (b: led: qcknd ent st: r.o wl) .... —**1**
1567 Kajaani (IRE) **(74)** *(PFICole)* 9-0 TQuinn (2) (hld up & bhd: swtchd stands' side over 2f out: r.o wl) ................................................. 1.**2**
14903 Iota **(70)** (Fav) *(MrsJCecil)* 8-9 PaulEddery (4) (trckd ldrs: ev ch over 2f out: hrd rdn & r.o one pce) ................................................. 2.**3**
14784 Kalaflo *(PCalver)* 8-2 NCarlisle (1) (w ldr tl wknd over 3f out) ................................................. dist.**4**

**Evens** Iota, **9/4** Kajaani (IRE), **3/1** ARFEY (IRE), **16/1** Kalaflo. CSF £9.29, Tote £4.20 (£3.70). Mr Hamdan Al-Maktoum (UPPER LAMBOURN) bred by Gay O'Callaghan in Ireland. 4 Rn
2m 45.7 (14.1)
SF—12/17/8/-

**1858** JACKSONS CATERING STKS (2-Y.O) £2343.00 (£648.00: £309.00)
7f 100y
8-35 (8-36)

1496a5 **Futurballa** (Fav) *(JLDunlop)* 9-1 WCarson (2) (hld up: swtchd centre over 2f out: sn led: v.easily) ................................................. —**1**
Red Cent *(JEtherington)* 8-8 TLucas (1) (w'like: scope: bit bkwd: cl up: disp ld over 2f out: no ch w wnr) ................................................. 2.**2**
1056 Yorkshire Rock *(MHEasterby)* 8-11 MBirch (3) (led tl hdd over 2f out: sn wknd) 12.**3**

**1/7** FUTURBALLA, **7/1** Yorkshire Rock, **20/1** Red Cent. CSF £2.69, Tote £1.10 (£2.30). Gerecon Italia (ARUNDEL) bred by J. L. Woolford. 3 Rn
1m 41.5 (11.3)

**1859** CRAVEN PARK H'CAP (0-80) £2703.00 (£748.00: £357.00) **1m 1f 207y** 9-05 (9-08)
(Weights raised 1 lb)

1542★ **Spectacular Dawn (72)** (Jt-Fav) *(JLDunlop)* 3-9-7 WCarson (3) (lw: mde all: shkn up 2f out: r.o wl) ................................................. —**1**
1248 Smoke **(39)** *(JParkes)* 6-7-13 NCarlisle (4) (lw: hld up: hdwy over 2f out: nt qckn ins fnl f) ................................................. 3.**2**
1527 Who's Tef (IRE) **(62)** *(MHEasterby)* 4-9-3 ‡5SMaloney (1) (lw: hld up: stdy hdwy to chal 2f out: nt qckn fnl f) ................................................. ¹/₂.**3**
1365 Stelby **(52)** *(OBrennan)* 8-8-12 JFortune (6) (s.i.s: hld up & bhd: smooth hdwy to chal wl over 1f out: rdn & nt qckn) ................................................. ¹/₂.**4**
16876 Touch Above **(59)** *(TDBarron)* 6-9-5 AlexGreaves (7) (cl up tl outpcd ins fnl f) nk.**5**
15943 Elegant Touch **(75)** (Jt-Fav) *(MMoubarak)* 3-9-10 LDettori (5) (trckd wnr: effrt 2f out: one pce) ................................................. s.h.**6**

**9/4** SPECTACULAR DAWN, Elegant Touch, **4/1** Smoke, **11/2** Touch Above, **6/1** Who's Tef (IRE), **20/1** Stelby. CSF £11.21, CT £43.00. Tote £3.20: £1.80 £1.60 (£9.10). Mr Peter S. Winfield (ARUNDEL) bred by Peter Winfield. 6 Rn
2m 12.9 (10.9)
SF—48/20/37/31/37/41

T/Plpt: £62.40 (19.6 Tckts).
AA

## BEVERLEY (R-H)
### Saturday, July 4th [Soft]
Going Allowance: St: 0.20 sec (G); Rnd: 0.50 sec per fur (Y)          Wind: fresh across

Stalls: high

**1860**          LAIR GATE (S) STKS (2-Y.O) £2128.00 (£588.00: £280.00)          **7f 100y**      1-55 (2-01)

1660⁵ **Wentbridge Lad (IRE)** (bl) (BAMcMahon) 8-11 KFallon (6) (lw: sn outpcd & wl
          bhd: c wd st: hdwy over 1f out: r.o wl to ld cl home) ............ —1
1623² Weaver George (IRE) (Jt-Fav) (MHEasterby) 8-11 MBirch (7) (chsd ldrs: c wd
          st: led 2f out tl hdd & no ex cl home) ............................... 2.2
 1549⁴ Doc Spot (CaptJWilson) 8-11 JLowe (3) (outpcd appr st: c wd: ev ch ins fnl f: nt
          qckn nr fin) ............................................................... hd.3
 1670 Bohemian Queen (JLSpearing) 8-6 GHind (4) (bhd: effrt ent st: styd on) ........ 1¹/₂.4
 1321⁴ A Bridge Too Far (IRE) (BBeasley) 8-13 LCharnock (1) (lw: led tl hdd 2f out:
          wknd appr fnl f) ......................................................... 12.5
 1526* Kentucky Dreams (Jt-Fav) (JBerry) 9-4 JCarroll (2) (lw: cl up: chal ent st: wknd
          wl over 1f out) .......................................................... 8.6
 1623⁴ Knayton Lodger (bl) (MWEasterby) 8-6 TLucas (5) (lw: cl up tl wknd 2f out) ..... nk.7

2/1 Weaver George (IRE), Kentucky Dreams, 5/2 WENTBRIDGE LAD (IRE), 8/1 A Bridge Too Far (IRE), 14/1 Doc
Spot, 20/1 Knayton Lodger, 25/1 Bohemian Queen. CSF £8.26, Tote £4.20: £1.80 £2.00 (£8.00). Mr G.
Charlesworth (TAMWORTH) bred by Peter Doyle in Ireland. 7 Rn; No bid; Kentucky Dreams clmd C Harrison
£5,751                                                                          1m 39.4 (9.2)
                                                                                SF—14/8/7/–/–/–

**1861**          WALKINGTON HAYRIDE H'CAP (3-Y.O) (0-90) £3557.50 (£1060.00: £505.00: £227.50)
          **5f**                                                         2-30 (2-32)
                              (Weights raised 1 lb)
1386⁵ Memsahb (79) (JBerry) 9-7 JCarroll (4) (a cl up: led ins fnl f: r.o) ............ —1
1757⁶ Educated Pet (73) (Jt-Fav) (MJohnston) 9-1 DMcKeown (2) (hld up: led &
          qcknd 2f out: hdd ins fnl f: kpt on) ................................... ¹/₂.2
1669⁴ Miss Vaxette (67) (JLSpearing) 8-9 GHind (3) (a chsng ldrs: effrt ¹/₂-wy: nvr able
          to chal) ................................................................... 2¹/₂.3
 1535 Absolutely Nuts (78) (Jt-Fav) (BAMcMahon) 9-2 MBirch (1) (lw: led 3f: sn btn) .. 4.4

9/4 Absolutely Nuts, Educated Pet, 5/2 Miss Vaxette, 3/1 MEMSAHB. CSF £9.56, Tote £4.00 (£4.80). The
Sussex Stud Limited (COCKERHAM) bred by The Sussex Stud. 4 Rn                    64.5 sec (3)
                                                                                SF—67/59/43/38

**1862**          MILLERS MILE STKS (Mdn) £3460.00 (£1030.00: £490.00: £220.00)
          **1m 100y**                                                    3-00 (3-00)

1319³ Ajzem (USA) (Fav) (MRStoute) 3-8-11 MBirch (4) (b: lw: mde most: styd on
          u.p fnl f) ................................................................ —1
1304³ Crystado (FR) (DRCElsworth) 3-8-11 JWilliams (5) (plld hrd: trckd ldrs: disp ld
          1f out: hung lft: no ex nr fin) ......................................... ³/₄.2
1055⁶ Vanart (WWHaigh) 3-8-11 DMcKeown (2) (lw: plld hrd: trckd ldrs tl wknd over 2f
          out) ...................................................................... 8.3
 1786⁵ Reilton (JParkes) 5-9-1 ‡5JWeaver (1) (cl up tl wknd over 2f out) ............. 3¹/₂.4

4/6 AJZEM (USA), 7/4 Crystado (FR), 13/2 Vanart, 16/1 Reilton. CSF £2.36, Tote £1.60 (£1.40). Maktoum Al
Maktoum (NEWMARKET) bred by Gainsborough Farm Incorporated in USA. 4 Rn        1m 50.9 (8.2)
                                                                                SF—37/35/11/4

**1863**          SURFACHEM H'CAP (Ladies) (0-70) £2382.80 (£660.80: £316.40)
          **1m 100y**                                                    3-30 (3-36)
                              (Weights raised 7 lb)
 1366 **Brilliant (60)** (JPearce) 4-11-0 MrsLPearce (4) (lw: hld up: hdwy stands' side
          over 2f out: led appr fnl f: r.o) ....................................... —1
          Bidweaya (USA) (36) (JLEyre) 5-8-11 ‡7MissMCarson (6) (cl up: led 4f out tl
          appr fnl f: kpt on) ...................................................... 2.2
 1488 Pride of Pendle (46) (PCalver) 3-9-5 MrsAFarrell (8) (lw: led 2f: a cl up: ev ch &
          rdn over 1f out: kpt on) ................................................. s.h.3
 1620* Waseela (IRE) (65) (Fav) (AAScott) 3-10-5 ‡5MissTBracegirdle (10) (a.p: ev ch
          over 1f out: kpt on one pce) ........................................... ³/₄.4
 1527* Night Transaction (51) (AHide) 5-10-0 ‡5MissLHide (1) (lw: hld up: swtchd
          stands' side & hdwy over 2f out: nt qckn fnl f) ..................... ¹/₂.5
          Night Club (GER) (34) (bl) (JPSmith) 8-8-9 ‡7MrsCDunwoody (5) (swtg: chsd
          ldrs: ev ch 2f out: r.o one pce) ....................................... ³/₄.6

1562³ J P Morgan **(44)** (v) *(MPNaughton)* 4–9-12 MissPRobson (7) (lw: outpcd & bhd
ent st: styd on fnl f) .................................................................... ³/4.**7**
1661 The Metropole (IRE) **(45)** *(AWPotts)* 3–8-11 ‡⁷MissSJudge (9) (b.nr hind: bhd:
hdwy stands' side 2f out: sn btn) ......................................... 6.**8**
829 Doctor Roy **(60)** *(NBycroft)* 4–10-7 ‡⁷MissABycroft (3) (dwlt: hdwy to ld after 2f:
hdd 4f out: wknd 3f out) ...................................................... 6.**9**
1289⁴ Mbulwa **(56)** *(SEKettlewell)* 6–10-5 ‡⁵MrsDKettlewell (11) (chsd ldrs to st: sn
wknd) ...................................................................................... 2.**10**

**11/4** Waseela (IRE), **3/1** Night Transaction, **7/2** BRILLIANT, **5/1** J P Morgan, **12/1** Mbulwa(op 7/1), **16/1** Doctor
Roy, **20/1** Pride of Pendle, **25/1** The Metropole (IRE), **33/1** Ors. CSF £85.22, CT £1,812.23. Tote £4.00: £1.80
£8.50 £3.10 (£429.30). Mr Arthur Old (NEWMARKET) bred by Stanley Estate and Stud Co. 10 Rn
1m 52.6 (9.9)
SF—42/5/12/24/17/–

**1864**     GOOLE H'CAP (0-70) £2343.60 (£649.60: £310.80)    **1m 3f 216y**    4-00 (4-01)
(Weights raised 3 lb)

1482⁴ **Bold Elect (63)** *(PWigham)* 4–9-10 MWigham (3) (hld up: hdwy ent st: r.o u.p to
ld ins fnl f) ............................................................................... —**1**
1739 First Bid **(47)** *(RMWhitaker)* 5–8-8 ACulhane (6) (trckd ldr: led & qcknd over 2f
out: hdd ins fnl f: kpt on) ...................................................... 1¹/2.**2**
1195 Athene Noctua **(34)** *(BAMcMahon)* 7–7-2⁽²⁾ ‡⁷CHawksley (2) (lw: a cl up: led
over 3f out tl over 2f out: r.o one pce) ................................... 2.**3**
1311 Grey Commander **(40)** *(MBrittain)* 4–8-1 JLowe (4) (lw: cl up: led 9f out tl over 3f
out: one pce) .......................................................................... 8.**4**
1242⁴ Top Table **(68)** (Fav) *(MRStoute)* 3–9-2 MBirch (5) (lw: led tl hdd 9f out: ev ch tl
outpcd fnl 3f) ......................................................................... 4.**5**
Janeswood (IRE) **(32)** *(JParkes)* 4–7-7 LCharnock (7) (nvr trbld ldrs) ............. 4.**6**
Alamshah (IRE) **(66)** *(JAGlover)* 4–8-10 ‡⁷SWilliams (1) (hld up: lost pl appr st:
n.d after) ................................................................................ I.**7**
LONG HANDICAP: Athene Noctua 7-6.

**6/4** Top Table, **7/2** Grey Commander, **4/1** BOLD ELECT, **5/1** First Bid, **6/1** Athene Noctua(op 14/1), **20/1** Ors.
CSF £23.84, Tote £6.00: £2.70 £2.80 (£15.50). Mrs J. L. Wigham (MALTON) bred by Home Stud Ltd. 7 Rn
2m 44.1 (12.5)
SF—45/26/2/–/–/–

**1865**     WOOD LANE STKS (Mdn 3-Y.O) £1932.00 (£532.00: £252.00)    **5f**    4-30 (4-32)

1558² **Katie-a (IRE) (50)** (Fav) *(RMWhitaker)* 8–9 ACulhane (8) (lw: hld up: effrt over 1f
out: r.o wl to ld wl ins fnl f) ................................................... —**1**
1238⁵ Auction King (IRE) **(61)** *(ASmith)* 9–0 SWebster (7) (lw: racd alone far side: led &
sn clr: hung lft: hdd & no ex wl ins fnl f) ................................ 1¹/2.**2**
*1268* Admirals Realm *(BAMcMahon)* 9-0 MBirch (2) (led stands' side over 3f: one
pce) ........................................................................................ 3¹/2.**3**
1669 Baladee Pet **(53)** *(MrsVAAconley)* 9-0 KFallon (6) (unruly s: a chsng ldrs: rdn 2f
out: sn btn) ............................................................................. 3.**4**
1484 Joie de Patina *(SGNorton)* 8-9 BCrossley (5) (outpcd & bhd tl sme late hdwy) .. 3.**5**
Tip it In *(ASmith)* 9-0 JLowe (3) (s.s: a bhd) ............................. ³/4.**6**
Stylish Dutch *(MWEasterby)* 8-9 TLucas (1) (in tch to ¹/2-wy) ........................... nk.**7**

**13/8** KATIE-A (IRE), **5/2** Auction King (IRE), **4/1** Baladee Pet, **10/1** Joie de Patina, **12/1** Stylish Dutch, **14/1** Ors.
CSF £6.12, Tote £1.90: £1.50 £1.80 (£1.60). Mr D. J. Soley (WETHERBY) bred by Stephen Stanhope in Ireland. 7
Rn
66 sec (4.5)
SF—25/24/10/–/–/–

**1866**     WESTWOOD H'CAP (0-80) £2750.60 (£761.60: £363.80)    **2m 35y**    5-00 (5-02)

1560³ **My Desire (61)** *(MrsGRReveley)* 4–8-12 JLowe (2) (lw: hdwy ¹/2-wy: led 3f out:
sn wl clr) ................................................................................. —**1**
1331³ Moving Out **(77)** (Fav) *(SirMarkPrescott)* 4–10-0 MBirch (5) (lw: cl up: led 4f out
to 3f out: one pce) ................................................................. 12.**2**
1667³ Thakawah **(73)** *(RWArmstrong)* 3–8-7 BCrossley (7) (trckd ldrs: effrt & ev ch
over 3f out: sn rdn & btn) ....................................................... 5.**3**
1733² Luks Akura **(45)** (v) *(MJohnston)* 4–7-3 ‡⁷CHawksley (4) (led tl hdd 4f out: sn
outpcd) ................................................................................... 2.**4**
1671⁶ Isobar **(42)** *(MCChapman)* 6–7-7 SWood (4) (sn pushed along: n.d) ................. 3.**5**
1671² Cost Effective **(42)** *(MBrittain)* 5–7-7 LCharnock (6) (sn pushed along: a bhd) . 12.**6**
1671⁵ Topcliffe **(45)** (bl) *(MrsVAAconley)* 5–7-10⁽³⁾ PBurke (8) (lw: lost tch ¹/2-wy: sn
t.o) ......................................................................................... 25.**7**
LONG HANDICAP: Isobar 6-3, Cost Effective 7-1, Topcliffe 7-2.

**11/8** Moving Out(5/2—5/4), **7/2** Thakawah, **4/1** MY DESIRE, **7/1** Cost Effective, Luks Akura, **17/2** Topcliffe, **25/1** Isobar. CSF £10.51, CT £20.07. Tote £4.60: £2.50 £1.60 (£5.00). Mrs M. A. Spensley (SALTBURN) bred by W. G. Barker. 7 Rn　　　　　　　　　　　　　　　　　　　　　　　　　　　　3m 46.8 (16.1)

SF—17/21/–/–/–/–

T/Plpt: £668.30 (3.7 Tckts).　　　　　　　　　　　　　　　　　　　　　　　　　AA

## 1378—SANDOWN (R-H)

### Friday, July 3rd [Good becoming Good to soft]
Going Allowance: 1st-4th: 0.20 sec (G); Rest: 0.50 sec (Y)　　　　　Wind: almost nil

Stalls: low

**1867**　　SHA TIN STKS (Mdn 2-Y.O.F) £2532.00 (£702.00: £336.00)　　**7f 16y**　　2-00 (2-05)

**East Liberty (USA)** *(IABalding)* 8-11 RCochrane (7) (w'like: scope: lw: 2nd st: rdn over 2f out: led over 1f out: r.o wl) ................................. —1
1396² Where's the Dance *(Fav) (CEBrittain)* 8-11 MRoberts (3) (led over 5f: unable qckn) ................................................................ 1½.2
852⁵ Actinella (USA) *(RHannon)* 8-11 PatEddery (9) (5th st: rdn 3f out: r.o one pce) .. 2.3
　　Olympic Run *(JLDunlop)* 8-11 LDettori (10) (w'like: scope: bit bkwd: rdn & hdwy over 2f out: r.o one pce) ........................................ 1½.4
　　Beyond the Limit *(LadyHerries)* 8-11 JWilliams (11) (unf: scope: s.s: nvr nr to chal) .............................................................. 4.5
1384 Dragonmist (IRE) *(GLewis)* 8-11 BRouse (5) (3rd st: wknd over 2f out) ........ 4.6
　　Tresaria (IRE) *(PHowling)* 8-11 DHolland (12) (leggy: bit bkwd: hdwy over 3f out: wknd over 2f out) ............................................ hd.7
　　Half a Dozen (USA) *(AAScott)* 8-11 WRSwinburn (4) (b.off hind: w'like: scope: bhd fnl 2f) ...................................................... 2.8
　　Dutch Debutante *(MissBSanders)* 8-11 JReid (2) (w'like: bit bkwd: 4th st: wknd over 2f out) .......................................................... ½.9
1342 Polly Leach *(BRMillman)* 8-11 AMackay (8) (hdwy 5f out: 6th st: wknd over 3f out) .................................................................. 1½.10
　　Don't Forget Marie (IRE) *(RHannon)* 8-8 ‡³RPerham (1) (unf: bit bkwd: s.s: a bhd) ............................................................... 3½.11
　　*Bonny Princess (33/1) Withdrawn (ref to ent stalls) : not under orders*

**9/4** Where's the Dance, **9/2** Actinella (USA)(op 2/1), **5/1** Half a Dozen (USA)(op 3/1), **6/1** EAST LIBERTY (USA), Olympic Run(op 7/2), **20/1** Don't Forget Marie (IRE), **25/1** Beyond the Limit, **33/1** Ors. CSF £17.95, Tote £10.90: £2.60 £1.30 £1.80 (£11.50). Mr Paul Mellon (KINGSCLERE) bred by Rokeby Farms in USA. 11 Rn

1m 35.03 (8.03)

**1868**　　WHARF DRAGON STKS (listed race) (2-Y.O) £6872.50 (£2080.00: £1015.00: £482.50)　　**5f 6y**　　2-35 (2-40)

1461⁴ **Marina Park** *(MJohnston)* 8-10 DMcKeown (5) (mde virtually all: rdn out) ........ —1
1573* Joyofracing *(Fav) (WAO'Gorman)* 8-12 PatEddery (2) (lw: hld up: ev ch 1f out: unable qckn) .............................................. 2.2
514* Zuno Warrior *(GLewis)* 8-12 PaulEddery (6) (hld up: rdn over 2f out: one pce) 1½.3
1573² True Precision *(JDBethell)* 8-7 AMunro (1) (a.p: hrd rdn over 1f out: one pce) . nk.4
1259⁵ Marchwell Lad *(MRChannon)* 8-12 MRoberts (3) (nvr nr to chal) ................ 1½.5
1161⁶ Platinum Venture *(SPCWoods)* 8-12 WWoods (4) (spd over 2f) ................ 12.6

**7/4** Joyofracing(5/4—5/2), **5/2** MARINA PARK, **100/30** Marchwell Lad, **7/1** True Precision(op 9/2), **8/1** Zuno Warrior, **33/1** Platinum Venture. CSF £7.18, Tote £3.40: £1.90 £1.70 (£3.20). Laharna Ltd (MIDDLEHAM) bred by Laharna Ltd. 6 Rn

62.77 sec (3.27)

SF—50/44/38/32/31/–

**1869**　　ROYAL HONG KONG JOCKEY CLUB TROPHY (H'cap) (0-115) £50770.00 (£15310.00: £7430.00: £3490.00)　　**1¼m 7y**　　3-10 (3-17)

1539² **Fire Top (91)** *(RAkehurst)* 7–8-9 TQuinn (18) (led 6f out: drvn out) ................ —1
1539* Charlo **(94)** *(Fav) (JHMGosden)* 4–8-12 (4x) SCauthen (15) (lw: 3rd st: hrd rdn over 1f out: r.o wl) ........................................... ½.2
1476³ Sharpitor (IRE) **(98)** *(WJarvis)* 3–8-5 JReid (1) (10th st: hdwy & hmpd over 2f out: r.o wl ins fnl f) .................................... hd.3
1637⁶ Camden's Ransom (USA) **(80)** *(DRCElsworth)* 5–7-7(5) ‡⁵BDoyle (12) (14th st: gd hdwy over 1f out: r.o wl) ................................. 2½.4
1061 Steerforth (IRE) **(97)** *(ACStewart)* 4–9-1 MRoberts (17) (rdn 6f out: hmpd & lost pl over 4f out: 12th st: rallied over 1f out: r.o) .................... nk.5

713[6] Green's Ferneley (IRE) **(87)** *(RCharlton)* 4-8-5 PatEddery (7) (6th st: rdn over
3f out: unable qckn) ............................................................................ 1½.**6**
854[3] Montpelier Boy **(80)** *(LordHuntingdon)* 4-7-12 AMunro (22) (mid div whn
snatched up 7f out: 18th st: gd hdwy over 1f out: r.o) ........ ¾.**7**
1388[3] Gilderdale **(86)** *(JWHills)* 10-7-13 (4x) ‡5DHarrison (16) (11th st: hmpd over 2f
out: nvr nr to chal) ............................................................................ ¾.**8**
1463 Pelorus **(86)** *(DRCEIsworth)* 7-7-11[(2)] (4x) ‡7JHunter (2) (s.i.s: 16th st: hdwy
over 1f out: r.o one pce) .................................................................... ½.**9**
1229a Courtline Jester **(86)** *(MAJarvis)* 3-7-7 JQuinn (19) (mid div whn hmpd & lost pl
over 6f out: 17th st: nvr nrr) ......................................................... 1½.**10**
1402[5] No Submission (USA) **(84)** *(CRNelson)* 6-8-2 DHolland (10) (led 4f: 2nd st:
wknd over 1f out) ............................................................................. 1½.**11**
1210★ Royal Seaton **(90)** *(BRMillman)* 3-7-8[(3)] (4x) ‡3DBiggs (8) (s.s: 13th st: hrd rdn
over 2f out: nvr nrr) ......................................................................... 1½.**12**
Lifewatch Vision *(DKWeld,Ireland)* 5-9-12 MJKinane (13) (lw: lost pl over 7f out:
19th st: nvr nrr) ................................................................................ ½.**13**
1463[2] Gymcrak Premiere **(92)** (v) *(MHEasterby)* 4-8-10 MBirch (6) (8th st: wknd wl
over 1f out) ....................................................................................... 10.**14**
1068[2] In the Picture (IRE) **(86)** *(RHannon)* 3-7-7 NCarlisle (21) (swtg: 20th st: a bhd) 1½.**15**
815★ Linpac West **(101)** *(CWCElsey)* 6-9-5 BRaymond (4) (lw: 5th st: wknd over 2f
out) ................................................................................................... **16**
927 Viardot (IRE) **(94)** *(MRStoute)* 3-8-1 PRobinson (3) (rdn thrght: mid div whn
hmpd over 6f out: 15th st) ................................................................ **17**
1463[6] Marine Diver **(75)** *(BRMillman)* 6-7-7 (4x) AMackay (11) (9th st: wknd over 2f
out) ................................................................................................... **18**
1035[3] Congress (IRE) **(86)** *(MRStoute)* 3-7-7 JLowe (20) (7th st: wknd over 2f out) ..... 19
1047★ Rose Alto **(87)** *(JRFanshawe)* 4-8-5[(1)] LDettori (5) (4th st: wknd over 2f out) ...... 20
LONG HANDICAP: Camden's Ransom (USA) 6-12, Courtline Jester 7-3, Congress (IRE) 7-4.

**11/4** Charlo, **10/1** Gymcrak Premiere, Sharpituo (IRE), Royal Seaton, **11/1** Green's Ferneley (IRE), **12/1**
Montpelier Boy, Viardot (IRE), **14/1** FIRE TOP, Steerforth (IRE), **16/1** In the Picture (IRE), Congress (IRE),
Courtline Jester, **20/1** Linpac West, **25/1** Lifewatch Vision, Gilderdale, **33/1** No Submission (USA), Pelorus,
Marine Diver, Rose Alto, **50/1** Camden's Ransom (USA). CSF £51.66, CT £397.65. Tote £16.20: £2.60 £1.90
£2.60 £12.20 (£24.90). Mrs A. Valentine (EPSOM) bred by R. F. Johnson Houghton. 20 Rn   2m 9.17 (4.87)
SF—66/68/60/43/64/51

**1870**   CAPITAL CITYBUS TROPHY (H'cap) (3-Y-O) (0-95) £7262.50 (£2200.00: £1075.00:
£512.50)   **7f 16y**                                                          3-45 (3-51)

1206[2] **Noble Pet (79)** *(PJMakin)* 8-9 TQuinn (4) (gd hdwy 2f out: hrd rdn fnl f: led nr
fin) ..................................................................................................... —**1**
1684★ Storm Dove (USA) **(94)** (Fav) *(RCharlton)* 9-10 (6x) PatEddery (8) (4th st: led 1f
out: hrd rdn: hdd nr fin) ................................................................... ¾.**2**
1391[5] Euro Festival **(82)** *(MissLCSiddall)* 8-12 RCochrane (7) (hdwy over 2f out: led
over 1f out: sn hdd: hrd rdn: r.o) .................................................... ¾.**3**
1474 Master Planner **(91)** *(CACyzer)* 9-0 ‡7TMcLaughlin (12) (2nd st: rdn & led over 2f
out: hdd over 1f out: one pce) ......................................................... 5.**4**
1323[3] Lady Roxanne **(84)** *(LordHuntingdon)* 7-13 ‡5DHarrison (9) (nvr nr to chal) ........ 5.**5**
1637 Co-Chin (IRE) **(84)** *(GLewis)* 9-0 PaulEddery (1) (nvr nrr) ........................... 1½.**6**
1706[3] Tate Dancer (IRE) **(80)** *(RWArmstrong)* 8-10 JHo (13) (led over 4f) .................. 3½.**7**
1631[5] Regal Racer **(86)** *(DRCEIsworth)* 9-2 SCauthen (6) (6th st: wknd over 2f out) ... ½.**8**
1599★ Sebosan **(78)** (bl) *(SPCWoods)* 8-8 (6x) WWoods (3) (bhd fnl 3f) ..................... 5.**9**
1035 Spanish Miner (USA) **(87)** *(AAScott)* 9-3 BRaymond (5) (a bhd) .................... 1½.**10**
1476 Merlins Wish (USA) **(84)** *(RHannon)* 9-0 MJKinane (2) (bhd fnl 3f) .................. hd.**11**
1480[2] Yousefia (USA) **(87)** (v) *(MRStoute)* 9-3 WRSwinburn (10) (lw: 3rd st: eased
whn btn wl over 1f out) ..................................................................... 1½.**12**
1636[6] Triple Trouble **(63)** *(HJCollingridge)* 7-7 JQuinn (14) (5th st: wknd 3f out) ....... 7.**13**
1677★ Ler Cru (IRE) **(70)** *(CEBrittain)* 8-0 (6x) MRoberts (11) (lw: bhd fnl 4f) .............. ½.**14**
LONG HANDICAP: Triple Trouble 6-6.

**11/4** Storm Dove (USA), **11/2** Ler Cru (IRE), **9/1** Yousefia (USA), **10/1** NOBLE PET, **11/1** Sebosan, Merlins Wish
(USA), **14/1** Euro Festival, Lady Roxanne, Regal Racer, **16/1** Master Planner, **25/1** Spanish Miner (USA), Tate
Dancer (IRE), **40/1** Co-Chin (IRE), **100/1** Triple Trouble. CSF £33.36, CT £352.58. Tote £8.30: £2.30 £1.40
£4.00 (£9.20). Mr A. W. Schiff (MARLBOROUGH) bred by A. W. Schiff. 14 Rn     1m 30.71 (3.71)
SF—60/73/59/46/16/26

**1871**   SINO GROUP TROPHY (H'cap) (3-Y-O) (0-100) £6872.50 (£2080.00: £1015.00:
£482.50)   **5f 6y**                                                          4-15 (4-21)

(Weights raised 11 lb)
1702★ **Bodari (78)** *(DAWilson)* 8-11 (5x) ‡5DHarrison (8) (led 3f out: hrd rdn fnl f: r.o wl)   —**1**
1702[2] Inherent Magic (IRE) **(77)** *(MMcCormack)* 9-1 AClark (2) (rdn & hdwy over 2f
out: hrd rdn & ev ch ins fnl f: r.o) ................................................... hd.**2**

1702³ Hot Lavender (CAN) **(69)** *(CFWall)* 8-7 AMunro (5) (a.p: hrd rdn over 1f out: r.o
ins fnl f) ............................................................................ nk.3
1785★ Invigilate **(59)** *(MPNaughton)* 7-8 (5x) ‡³JFanning (1) (gd hdwy over 1f out: nt clr
run 1f out: hmpd ins fnl f: nt rcvr) ............................ ¹/₂.4
1649★ Lady Sabo **(73)** *(GLewis)* 8-11 (5x) PaulEddery (3) (rdn & hdwy over 2f out: r.o
ins fnl f) ............................................................................ ³/₄.5
1669² Hi-Tech Honda (IRE) **(67)** *(Fav)* *(CEBrittain)* 8-5 MRoberts (7) (led 2f: wknd
over 1f out) ...................................................................... 4.6
1669★ Ned's Bonanza **(78)** *(MDods)* 9-2 (5x) JLowe (6) (spd over 3f) .......................... 3.7
1702⁴ Wild Honour (IRE) **(83)** *(WRMuir)* 9-7 SWhitworth (4) (bhd fnl 2f) ...................... ³/₄.8

**7/2** Hi-Tech Honda (IRE), **9/2** Invigilate, **5/1** Inherent Magic (IRE), **11/2** Wild Honour (IRE), **13/2** BODARI, **15/2**
Hot Lavender (CAN), **11/1** Ned's Bonanza(8/1—12/1), **12/1** Lady Sabo. CSF £35.20, CT £223.38. Tote £8.20:
£2.70 £2.00 £2.40 (£19.20). Mr R. J. Thomas (EPSOM) bred by Robert J. Thomas. 8 Rn   63.74 sec (4.24)
SF—62/65/56/41/55/33

**1872**　　YEAR OF THE MONKEY CLAIMING STKS (3-Y.O) £2819.00 (£784.00: £377.00)
　　　　　**1m 3f 91y**　　　　　　　　　　　　　　　　　　　　　　　　　　4-50 (4-53)

1680⁴ **Plan Ahead (68)** *(GLewis)* 7-9 ‡⁵DHarrison (8) (hdwy over 2f out: led wl over 1f
out: r.o wl) ...................................................................... —1
1079⁶ Asian Punter (IRE) **(60)** *(AHide)* 8-5 TQuinn (14) (hdwy 3f out: ev ch over 1f out:
unable qckn) ................................................................... 1¹/₂.2
1466⁶ Trumpet **(72)** *(Fav)* *(LordHuntingdon)* 8-11 MRoberts (5) (rdn 5f out: 5th st: one
pce fnl f) ........................................................................ 1¹/₂.3
1298 Moor Lodge (USA) **(69)** *(MHTompkins)* 8-7 PRobinson (1) (hdwy 3f out: r.o
one pce fnl 2f) ................................................................ 1¹/₂.4
Drought (IRE) *(MRStoute)* 7-9 ‡³FNorton (12) (leggy: lt-f: gd hdwy over 1f out:
r.o) ................................................................................. s.h.5
1565⁴ Mashakel (USA) **(82)** *(BHanbury)* 8-3 MHills (9) (b: hdwy over 2f out: wknd fnl f) 3.6
1655⁴ King of Normandy (IRE) **(70)** *(RHannon)* 8-4⁽¹⁾ MJKinane (7) (nvr nrr) .................. 2.7
1705² Nothing Doing (IRE) **(83)** *(WJMusson)* 8-3 JHBrown (2) (b: nvr nrr) .................... 2¹/₄.8
1383⁶ Lifford (USA) *(MRStoute)* 8-5 PatEddery (2) (nvr nrr) ........................................ 4.9
1642 Laughing Falcon **(52)** (v) *(JLDunlop)* 7-12 JLowe (10) (2nd st: wknd over 2f
out) ............................................................................... 1¹/₂.10
1068⁶ Bel Baraka (IRE) **(65)** *(DRCElsworth)* 8-5 JWilliams (11) (led 10f) ..................... nk.11
1642 Super Beauty **(58)** *(GBBalding)* 7-8 JQuinn (6) (6th st: wknd over 2f out) ...... 10.12
1643⁴ Cool Society (USA) **(67)** *(CRNelson)* 7-13 DHolland (4) (3rd st: wknd over 2f
out) ............................................................................... 15.13
1176⁴ Temple Knight *(CACyzer)* 8-6 ‡⁷TMcLaughlin (13) (4th st: wkng whn hmpd &
uns rdr over 2f out) ...................................................... 0

**3/1** Trumpet, **7/1** Moor Lodge (USA), PLAN AHEAD, **9/1** Mashakel (USA), **10/1** Nothing Doing (IRE), King of
Normandy (IRE), **12/1** Cool Society (USA), Drought (IRE), Asian Punter (IRE), Super Beauty, **16/1** Bel Baraka
(IRE), Lifford (USA), **25/1** Laughing Falcon, **33/1** Temple Knight. CSF £83.59, Tote £6.30: £1.50 £5.50 £1.90
(£150.40). Planflow (Leasing) Ltd (EPSOM) bred by R. F. and Mrs Knipe. 14 Rn; Trumpet clmd J O'Shea
£18,875, Mashakel (USA) clmd S Bullard £10,552　　　　　　　　　2m 31.93 (10.23)
SF—36/43/46/39/26/28

T/Trio: Race 3: £50.70 (60.8 Tckts) and Race 4: £32.60 (49.1 Tckts). T/Jkpt: Not won; £7,497.45 to Sandown
4/7/92. T/Plpt: £22.80 (393.1 Tckts).　　　　　　　　　　　　　　　　　　　　　　　　　　　　AK

# SANDOWN (R-H)
## Saturday, July 4th [Soft]
Going Allowance: St: 0.40 sec; Rnd: 0.60 sec per fur (Y)　　　　　　　Wind: slt against

Stalls: low

**1873**　　E.B.F. INDEPENDENCE STKS (Mdn 2-Y.O.C & G) £2427.00 (£672.00: £321.00)
　　　　　**7f 16y**　　　　　　　　　　　　　　　　　　　　　　　　　　　　　　2-15 (2-17)

**Scottish Peak (IRE)** *(LordHuntingdon)* 9-0 WRSwinburn (8) (w'like: scope:
4th st: led over 1f out: comf) ....................................... —1
Darecliff (USA) *(RHannon)* 9-0 MRoberts (9) (w'like: scope: hmpd 5f out: rdn
over 3f out: r.o ins fnl f) ............................................... 7.2
1595⁵ Bonar Bridge (USA) *(RHannon)* 9-0 MJKinane (4) (led 4f: hmpd 2f out: r.o one
pce: fin 4th, s.h: plcd 3rd) ........................................... 3
1709³ Friendly Brave (USA) *(Fav)* *(WCarter)* 8-9 ‡⁵NGwilliams (5) (2nd st: led 3f out:
swvd lft 2f out: sn hdd: nt qckn: fin 3rd, s.h: plcd 4th) ......... 4
Festin *(JLDunlop)* 9-0 WCarson (6) (neat: 6th st: hrd rdn over 1f out: eased whn
btn ins fnl f) ................................................................... 8.5

1630⁴ Poly Vision (IRE) *(MRChannon)* 9-0 RHills (2) (swtg: 5th st: wknd 3f out) ........ 1¹/₂.6
1259 Koa *(MJHeaton-Ellis)* 9-0 RCochrane (3) (b: lw: 3rd st: wknd 2f out) ................. hd.7
      Mr Copyforce *(MissBSanders)* 9-0 MHills (1) (scope: bkwd: s.s: a wl bhd) ........ 3.8

**11/4** Friendly Brave (USA), **3/1** SCOTTISH PEAK (IRE), **7/2** Darecliff (USA), **5/1** Festin, **14/1** Bonar Bridge (USA),
**20/1** Poly Vision (IRE), **33/1** Ors. CSF £12.23, Tote £3.30: £1.40 £1.70 £2.60 (£5.80). Lord Weinstock (WEST
ILSLEY) bred by Ballymacoll Stud Farm Ltd in Ireland. 8 Rn                                    1m 35.03 (8.03)
                                                                        SF—43/22/20/16/–/–

**1874**        ANNIVERSARY H'CAP (0-100) £4943.75 (£1490.00: £722.50: £338.75)
                **2m 78y**                                                 2-50 (2-53)

1459 **Brandon Prince (IRE) (76)** (bl) *(IABalding)* 4-9-0 RCochrane (8) (5th st: led 2f
                out: hrd rdn over 1f out: r.o) ................................................ —1
      Majestic Image **(70)** *(LordHuntingdon)* 6-8-8 AMunro (6) (hdwy over 2f out:
                hrd rdn over 1f out: r.o) ....................................................... 2.2
1534⁴ Manzoor Sayadan (USA) **(66)** *(RSimpson)* 4-8-4 SWhitworth (4) (lw: hdwy
                over 2f out: hrd rdn over 1f out: unable qckn) ........................ 5.3
1539⁵ Jungle Dancer (IRE) **(83)** (v) *(MRStoute)* 4-9-7 PD'Arcy (9) (swtg: 3rd st: n.m.r
                on ins over 1f out: r.o one pce) .......................................... 1¹/₂.4
1316* Mootawel (USA) **(78)** (Fav) *(HThomsonJones)* 3–7-13 RHills (10) (lw: 6th st:
                n.m.r 3f out: wknd 2f out) .................................................. 3¹/₂.5
1256² Prince Sobur **(61)** *(MBlanshard)* 6-7-13 JQuinn (5) (2nd st: wknd 2f out) ...... 1¹/₂.6
      First Victory **(90)** *(RHannon)* 6-10-0 MJKinane (11) (led over 14f) .................. 1¹/₂.7
1534⁶ Beldale Star **(56)** *(RAkehurst)* 9-7-8⁽¹⁾ TyroneWilliams (1) (b: 4th st: wknd over
                2f out) ................................................................................ 3¹/₂.8
1606⁵ Go South **(68)** (bl) *(JRJenkins)* 8–8-6 MRoberts (7) (a bhd: hrd rdn 6f out: t.o
                whn reluctant to r over 3f out) ................................................... 9
                                LONG HANDICAP: Beldale Star 7-4.

**7/2** Mootawel (USA), **4/1** Go South(11/2—7/2), **9/2** BRANDON PRINCE (IRE)(3/1—5/1), **5/1** Majestic Image,
Prince Sobur, **16/1** Manzoor Sayadan (USA), **20/1** Beldale Star, First Victory, **25/1** Jungle Dancer (IRE). CSF
£24.57, CT £292.65. Tote £6.30: £1.90 £2.10 £3.20 (£19.70). Mr R. P. B. Michaelson (KINGSCLERE) bred by
Sheikh Mohammed bin Rashid al Maktoum in Ireland. 9 Rn                                        3m 47.20 (17.20)
                                                                        SF—26/18/9/24/–/–

**1875**        STARS AND STRIPES SPRINT STKS (listed race)    £10406.25 (£3150.00: £1537.50:
                **5f 6y**       £731.25)                                    3-25 (3-28)

1467 **Medaille D'Or (109)** (v) *(JWPayne)* 4-9-3 AMunro (7) (lw: hdwy over 1f out: hrd
                rdn fnl f: led last strides) ....................................................... —1
1474 Tbab (IRE) **(94)** *(CEBrittain)* 4-9-3 WRSwinburn (6) (a.p: led over 2f out: hrd rdn
                ins fnl f: hdd last strides) ..................................................... hd.2
1474 Bold Lez **(101)** *(MJHaynes)* 5-9-3 SCauthen (2) (lw: hmpd 3f out: hdwy fnl f: r.o
                wl) ..................................................................................... 2¹/₂.3
1467 Sir Harry Hardman **(100)** (v) *(FHLee)* 4-9-3 BRaymond (8) (swtg: hld up: rdn
                over 2f out: unable qckn) ....................................................... ¹/₂.4
1535³ Miss Nosey Parker (IRE) **(100)** (Fav) *(RHannon)* 3–8-6 MRoberts (4) (lw: led 3f
                out tl over 2f out: one pce) ................................................... 1¹/₂.5
1474 Terrhars (IRE) **(101)** *(RHannon)* 4-9-3 RPerham (9) (spd over 3f) ................. 1¹/₂.6
1467³ Spanish Storm (IRE) **(104)** *(SPCWoods)* 3-8-11 WWoods (5) (lw: led 2f: wknd
                over 1f out) ........................................................................ hd.7
1199² Farfelu **(97)** (bl) *(WRMuir)* 5-9-3 SWhitworth (3) (bhd fnl 2f) ....................... 4.8

**6/4** Miss Nosey Parker (IRE), **5/1** Bold Lez, **6/1** MEDAILLE D'OR, Tbab (IRE), **7/1** Spanish Storm (IRE)(op 9/2),
**9/1** Farfelu(12/1—8/1), **10/1** Terrhars (IRE), **16/1** Sir Harry Hardman. CSF £40.16, Tote £7.60: £2.10 £2.10
£1.70 (£34.00). Mr J. G. K. Borrett (NEWMARKET) bred by Mrs N. V. Fox. 8 Rn           62.55 sec (3.05)
                                                                        SF—82/81/71/69/52/57

**1876**        CORAL-ECLIPSE STKS (Gp 1)    £152356.00 (£57021.80: £27390.90: £11931.30)
                **1¹/₄m 7y**                                               4-10 (4-14)

1455³ Kooyonga (IRE) (Fav) *(MKauntze,Ireland)* 4-9-4 WJO'Connor (6) (lw: 11th st:
                hdwy 2f out: led over 1f out: rdn out) ...................................... —1
1455⁶ Opera House *(MRStoute)* 4-9-7 SCauthen (7) (lw: 3rd st: led wl over 1f out: sn
                hdd: unable qckn) ............................................................... 1¹/₂.2
1473² Sapience *(DRCElsworth)* 6-9-7 RCochrane (9) (lw: 12th st: hdwy over 2f out:
                hrd rdn fnl f: r.o) ................................................................ 1¹/₂.3
341² Free Flyer (IRE) *(MMoubarak)* 3–8-10 RHills (13) (lw: 9th st: hdwy 3f out: hrd
                rdn over 2f out: one pce) ...................................................... ¹/₂.4
1198⁵ Twist and Turn *(HRACecil)* 3–8-10 MJKinane (4) (4th st: ev ch over 1f out: one
                pce) ................................................................................ nk.5

1231a★ Zoman (USA) *(PFlCole)* 5-9-7 AMunro (5) (7th st: hdwy 2f out: r.o one pce) ... hd.**6**
 1473★ Rock Hopper (v) *(MRStoute)* 5-9-7 WRSwinburn (10) (lw: 6th st: rdn over 2f
   out: nvr nr to chal) ................................................................................ 1½.**7**
1231a² Arcangues (USA) *(AFabre,France)* 4-9-7 TJarnet (8) (2nd st: led 3f out tl wl
   over 1f out: sn wknd) .......................................................................... nk.**8**
 1455⁴ Terimon *(CEBrittain)* 6-9-7 MRoberts (3) (racd wd: hdwy over 4f out: 10th & c
   stands' side st: wknd 2f out) ............................................................... 5.**9**
 1455² Young Buster (IRE) (bl) *(GWragg)* 4-9-7 MHills (12) (lw: hdwy 8f out: 8th st:
   wknd 3f out) ........................................................................................ 12.**10**
 1473⁵ Mellaby (USA) *(MRStoute)* 4-9-7 BRaymond (2) (led 7f) .............................. 15.**11**
 1358a⁶ Hailsham (CAN) *(CEBrittain)* 4-9-7 WCarson (11) (5th st: wknd 3f out) ...... 15.**12**

**7/2** KOOYONGA (IRE), **5/1** Arcangues (USA), **11/2** Zoman (USA), **8/1** Opera House, Rock Hopper, Twist and
Turn, **9/1** Terimon(12/1—8/1), **14/1** Sapience, Young Buster (IRE), **33/1** Free Flyer (IRE), **66/1** Hailsham (CAN),
**200/1** Mellaby (USA). CSF £28.41, Tote £4.10: £1.90 £2.60 £4.50 (£27.10). Mr M. Haga (IRELAND) bred by
Ovidstown Bloodstock Ltd in Ireland. 12 Rn                                    2m 10.83 (6.53)
                                                                              SF—99/99/96/84/83/93/90

---

**1877**    FOURTH OF JULY H'CAP (0-115) £10455.00 (£3165.00: £1545.00: £735.00)
            **1m 14y**                                                         4-45 (4-48)

 1539⁴ **Starlight Flyer (90)** (bl) (Fav) *(MMoubarak)* 5-9-4 WRSwinburn (11) (mde all:
   drvn out) ............................................................................................... —**1**
 1463 Mudaffar (IRE) **(87)** *(RWArmstrong)* 4-9-1 SCauthen (9) (dwlt: hdwy wl over 1f
   out: r.o fnl f) ........................................................................................ 2½.**2**
 1463 Eclipsing (IRE) **(75)** *(RCharlton)* 4-8-3 MHills (6) (6th st: chsd wnr over 2f out tl
   ins fnl f: unable qckn) ......................................................................... 3½.**3**
 1344³ Strong Suit (IRE) **(90)** *(RHannon)* 3-8-9 MJKinane (2) (lost pl over 4f out: hung
   lft 3f out: one pce fnl 2f) ..................................................................... 2½.**4**
 1463 Pay Homage **(96)** *(IABalding)* 4-9-10 RCochrane (4) (hdwy 3f out: one pce fnl
   2f) ......................................................................................................... 3.**5**
 667 Sabotage (FR) **(91)** *(MRStoute)* 6-9-0 ‡5JJones (3) (b.hind: 4th st: wknd over 1f
   out) ....................................................................................................... 1½.**6**
 1463 Daswaki (CAN) **(84)** *(RHannon)* 4-8-12 BRouse (1) (hdwy over 2f out: wknd wl
   over 1f out) .......................................................................................... 6.**7**
 1463⁵ Cru Exceptionnel **(75)** *(PJMakin)* 4-8-3 MRoberts (10) (3rd st: rdn over 2f out:
   wknd over 1f out) ................................................................................. ¾.**8**
 1656⁴ Helios **(75)** *(RSimpson)* 4-7-12 ‡5ATucker (5) (s.s: a bhd) ........................... 1.**9**
 1399 Widyan (USA) **(89)** (bl) *(PFlCole)* 4-9-3 AMunro (7) (lw: 2nd st: wknd over 3f
   out) ....................................................................................................... 5.**10**
 1598★ Al Ramis (IRE) **(84)** *(CEBrittain)* 3-8-3 JQuinn (8) (lw: 5th st: wknd 3f out) ....... 4.**11**
                LONG HANDICAP: Cru Exceptionnel 8-0, Helios 7-10, Al Ramis 7-5.

**11/4** STARLIGHT FLYER, **4/1** Cru Exceptionnel, **5/1** Mudaffar (IRE), **9/1** Daswaki (CAN), **10/1** Eclipsing (IRE),
**11/1** Pay Homage, **12/1** Strong Suit (IRE)(op 7/1), **20/1** Al Ramis (IRE), **25/1** Ors. CSF £15.44, CT £104.02. Tote
£3.10: £1.50 £1.70 £2.80 (£5.90). Ecurie Fustok (NEWMARKET) bred by Buckram Thoroughbred Enterprises
Inc. 11 Rn                                                                    1m 45.18 (5.98)
                                                                              SF—86/75/52/50/56/41

---

**1878**    VICTORIA AMATEUR TURF CLUB H'CAP (0-90) £3163.00 (£949.00: £457.00: £211.00)
            **5f 6y**                                                          5-20 (5-24)

 1305 **Gone Savage (70)** *(GBBalding)* 4-8-9 SCauthen (8) (mde all: rdn out) ............. —**1**
 1564⁴ Yes **(54)** *(DTThom)* 4-7-0 ‡7KimMcDonnell (3) (lw: hdwy over 1f out: r.o ins fnl f) 1½.**2**
 1212 Olifantsfontein **(77)** *(RSimpson)* 4-8-11 ‡5ATucker (4) (a.p: hrd rdn over 1f out:
   r.o) ....................................................................................................... s.h.**3**
 1445 Macfarlane **(72)** *(MJFetherston-Godley)* 4-8-11 WRSwinburn (5) (hld up: rdn
   over 1f out: unable qckn) .................................................................... 3½.**4**
 1614⁶ Fascination Waltz **(69)** *(DShaw)* 5-8-8 AMunro (6) (lw: hdwy over 2f out: one
   pce) ...................................................................................................... ¾.**5**
 1326★ Prince Belfort **(72)** *(MPNaughton)* 4-8-11 MRoberts (2) (prom over 3f) ............ 1½.**6**
 1305 Dawes of Nelson **(54)** *(MJBolton)* 7-7-7 JQuinn (1) (bhd fnl 2f) ..................... ¾.**7**
 1474 Baysham (USA) **(81)** (bl) (Fav) *(BRMillman)* 6-9-6 WCarson (7) (hdwy 2f out:
   eased wn btn ins fnl f) ......................................................................... 2.**8**
 1757⁵ Clifton Charlie (USA) **(89)** *(MRChannon)* 4-10-0 RHills (9) (bhd fnl 2f) ............... 3.**9**
                LONG HANDICAP: Yes 7-4, Dawes of Nelson 6-7.

**4/1** Baysham (USA), **9/2** Macfarlane, **11/2** Olifantsfontein(4/1—6/1), Prince Belfort, **7/1** GONE SAVAGE, **10/1**
Fascination Waltz, Clifton Charlie (USA), **12/1** Yes, **16/1** Dawes of Nelson. CSF £73.00, CT £443.84. Tote £9.60:
£2.20 £3.20 £2.10 (£67.70). Mr Rex L. Mead (DORCHESTER) bred by Mrs C. F. Van Straubenzee and R. Mead. 9
Rn                                                                            63.64 sec (4.14)
                                                                              SF—52/23/47/33/27/24

**1879**　SPINAL INJURIES ASSOCIATION H'CAP (0-90) £3215.00 (£965.00: £465.00: £215.00)
　　　　　1m 3f 91y　　　　　　　　　　　　　　　　　　　　　　　　　5-50 (5-55)

1555² Dovale (67) *(WJarvis)* 4–8–5 AMunro (8) (2nd st: led over 2f out: r.o wl) ............ —1
*1543*³ Springs Welcome (60) *(CACyzer)* 6–7–12 MRoberts (2) (3rd st: hrd rdn over 1f
　　　　　　　out: r.o wl ins fnl f) ........................................................... nk.2
1640² Cathos (FR) (57) *(DAWilson)* 7–7–9 RFox (7) (6th st: hdwy over 1f out: r.o) .... 2¹/₂.3
1501⁴ Kaytak (FR) (70) (Fav) *(JRJenkins)* 5–8–8 MJKinane (3) (5th st: rdn over 2f out:
　　　　　　　r.o one pce) ............................................................... 1.4
1465 Duc de Berry (USA) (90) *(GHarwood)* 4–10–0 SCauthen (1) (led 9f: one pce) .. nk.5
　　　Hajaim (IRE) (88) *(CEBrittain)* 4–9–12 WRSwinburn (4) (4th st: hrd rdn over 1f
　　　　　　　out: one pce) .............................................................. hd.6

2/1 Kaytak (FR)(6/4—9/4), 4/1 Springs Welcome(op 6/1), Hajaim (IRE), 6/1 Duc de Berry (USA)(tchd 10/1),
13/2 DOVALE(op 7/2), 8/1 Cathos (FR). CSF £29.17, CT £187.88. Tote £5.00: £2.30 £2.70 (£18.00). Mrs E. G.
Lambton (NEWMARKET) bred by Lord Bristol. 6 Rn　　　　　　　　　　　　　　2m 34.58 (12.88)
　　　　　　　　　　　　　　　　　　　　　　　　　　　　　　　　　　　SF—30/22/14/25/44/41

T/Trio: Race 4: £176.80 (19.2 Tckts) and Race 5: £36.20 (55.6 Tckts). T/Jkpt: £10,375.40 (0.2 Tckts);
£11,216.68 to Newmarket 7/7/92. T/Plpt: £600.40 (25.05 Tckts).　　　　　　　　　　　　AK

**1648—BATH (L-H)**

## Saturday, July 4th [Good to firm]

Going Allowance: 5f 11y-5f 161y: nil (G); Rest: minus 0.15 sec (F)　　　Wind: mod across

Stalls: low

**1880**　WESTON AUCTION STKS (Mdn 2-Y.O) £1590.00 (£440.00: £210.00)
　　　　　5f 161y　　　　　　　　　　　　　　　　　　　　　　　　　2-20 (2-21)

　　　Sharp Gazelle *(BSmart)* 7-13 DaleGibson (3) (leggy: bit bkwd: hdwy 2f out:
　　　　　　　swtchd rt ins fnl f: r.o wl to ld cl home) ............................... —1
1409⁵ Red Leader (IRE) (Fav) *(PFICole)* 8-4 TQuinn (5) (lw: led 3f out: rdn fnl f: hdd nr
　　　　　　　fin) ........................................................................ nk.2
　　　Kismetim *(GLewis)* 8-8 AClark (1) (unf: scope: dwlt: sn rdn along: hdwy 2f out:
　　　　　　　r.o ins fnl f) ............................................................. 1.3
973⁶ Superensis *(WRMuir)* 8-1 ‡³TSprake (6) (w ldrs tl wknd over 1f out) ............ 4.4
　　　Brigante Di Cielo *(RHannon)* 8-4 AMcGlone (4) (str: scope: bkwd: bhd fnl 2f) .... 6.5
1251 Hills Raceaid (IRE) *(JBerry)* 7-13 NAdams (2) (led over 2f: wknd over 2f out) ... 7.6

7/4 Red Leader (IRE), 3/1 Kismetim(9/4—7/2), 15/2 Brigante Di Cielo(5/2—8/1), 8/1 SHARP GAZELLE(16/1—
7/1), Superensis, 17/2 Hills Raceaid (IRE)(4/1—9/1). CSF £20.15, Tote £11.30: £1.80 £1.70 (£18.60). Mr M.
Pattimore (LAMBOURN) bred by Aston Park Stud. 6 Rn　　　　　　　　　　　　　　1m 13 (3.7)
　　　　　　　　　　　　　　　　　　　　　　　　　　　　　　　　　　　SF—11/15/15/–/–/–

**1881**　SOUTHMEAD STKS (Mdn 3-Y.O) £1576.00 (£436.00: £208.00)
　　　　　1m 3f 144y　　　　　　　　　　　　　　　　　　　　　　　2-50 (2-53)

1704² Grand Master (IRE) (100) (Fav) *(PFICole)* 9-0 TQuinn (4) (2nd st: led over 2f
　　　　　　　out: sn rdn clr) ........................................................... —1
1447⁴ Quadrireme (75) *(MajorWRHern)* 9-0 AClark (1) (led 9f: one pce) ............... 4.2
　910 Whatcomesnaturally (USA) *(JWHills)* 8-9 SDawson (3) (rdn 4f out: 3rd & wkng
　　　　　　　st) ....................................................................... 12.3
1577 Killshandra (IRE) *(MrsBarbaraWaring)* 8-9 NHowe (2) (lost tch 4f out: poor last
　　　　　　　st) ....................................................................... 4.4

2/9 GRAND MASTER (IRE)(2/7—2/11), 5/1 Quadrireme(op 5/2), 11/1 Whatcomesnaturally (USA), 33/1
Killshandra (IRE). CSF £1.87, Tote £1.30 (£1.40). Mr Fahd Salman (WHATCOMBE) bred by Hullin Co N V in
Ireland. 4 Rn　　　　　　　　　　　　　　　　　　　　　　　　　　　　2m 30.2 (3.5)
　　　　　　　　　　　　　　　　　　　　　　　　　　　　　　　　　　　SF—49/41/12/4

**1882**　KENNETH ROBERTSON H'CAP (3-Y.O) (0-90) £2693.00 (£748.00: £359.00)
　　　　　1m 5f 22y　　　　　　　　　　　　　　　　　　　　　　　3-20 (3-22)

　　　　　　　　　　　　　　(Weights raised 5 lb)
1220³ Yenoora (IRE) (60) *(PFICole)* 8-3 TQuinn (4) (b.nr hind: chsd ldr: 2nd st: hrd
　　　　　　　rdn wl over 1f out: led ins fnl f: all out) .............................. —1
1574² Highland Battle (USA) (66) (Jt-Fav) *(IABalding)* 8-6 ‡SO'Gorman (1) (led tl hdd
　　　　　　　ins fnl f: r.o) ........................................................... ¹/₂.2
1720* Rajai (IRE) (78) (bl) (Jt-Fav) *(JLDunlop)* 9-7 AClark (5) (wnt 3rd st: hrd rdn over
　　　　　　　2f out: swtchd rt over 1f out: hung lft: nt run on) .................... 1¹/₂.3
1446² Heavenly Waters (53) *(RFJohnsonHoughton)* 7-3 ‡⁷AntoinetteArmes (6)
　　　　　　　(b.hind: wl bhd 7f out: 6th st: hdwy 3f out: nt rch ldrs) ........ 6.4

1592² Judge and Jury (64) (bl) (MJFetherston-Godley) 8-7 NAdams (3) (lw: rdn 7f out: poor 5th st: t.o) ............................................................ 15.5
1260⁵ Mr Poppleton (61) (DWPArbuthnot) 7-13 ‡⁵RPrice (2) (b.hind: prom: rdn 4f out: 4th & wkng st: t.o) ............................................................ 10.6

**11/4** Highland Battle (USA), Rajai, (IRE), **7/2** Heavenly Waters(tchd 11/2), **6/1** YENOORA (IRE), **15/2** Mr Poppleton, **10/1** Judge and Jury. CSF £20.93, Tote £7.00: £2.80 £1.90 (£10.70). Mr Reg Hester (WHATCOMBE) bred by Binfield Manor Farms Ltd in Ireland. 6 Rn
2m 52.1 (4.4)
SF—26/28/40/–/–/–

---

**1883**　　ST JOHNS AMBULANCE CADET GOLDEN JUBILEE H'CAP (3-Y.O) (0-90) £2609.00
　　　　　　(£724.00: £347.00)　　**5f 161y**
3-50 (4-00)

(Weights raised 11 lb)

1576⁴ **Truthful Image (72)** (bl) (MJRyan) 9-2 ‡³DBiggs (1) (hld up: led wl over 1f out: r.o wl) ............................................................ —1
966³ Sure Lord (IRE) (70) (WRMuir) 9-3 AClark (5) (a.p: r.o ins fnl f: nt trble wnr) .... 2¹/₂.2
1576 Uccello (74) (LJHolt) 9-7 AMcGlone (3) (b.nr fore: lw: led over 1f: sltly hmpd 2f out: r.o one pce) ............................................................ 2¹/₂.3
1583³ So Superb (70) (bl) (JLDunlop) 9-3 TQuinn (4) (led over 4f out: wandered over 2f out: hrd rdn & hdd wl over 1f out: sn btn) .................... nk.4
1745⁴ Cranfield Comet (65) (bl) (JBerry) 8-12 NAdams (6) (w ldrs tl c wd over 3f out: t.o fnl 2f) ............................................................ 20.5

*Stewards Enquiry: Quinn fined £250 under Rule 151 (ii) (failure to ensure best possible placing)*

**5/4** So Superb(tchd 2/1), **4/1** TRUTHFUL IMAGE, **9/2** Cranfield Comet(op 3/1), **5/1** Uccello, **6/1** Sure Lord (IRE). CSF £23.14, Tote £5.10: £1.80 £2.20 (£12.50). Mrs Margaret Baxter (NEWMARKET) bred by A. Bromley. 5 Rn
1m 13.2 (3.9)
SF—24/15/9/4/–

---

**1884**　　TYSOE CLAIMING STKS (2-Y.O) £1884.00 (£524.00: £252.00)　　**5f 11y**　4-20 (4-24)

1513² **Area Girl** (Fav) (SirMarkPrescott) 8-7 TQuinn (4) (mde all: clr 2f out: unchal) .... —1
1754² Second Colours (USA) (v) (PSFelgate) 9-0 KDarley (1) (pushed along: chsd wnr fnl 3f: no imp fnl 2f) ............................................................ 5.2
1638⁴ Heber Spring (IRE) (bl) (RHannon) 8-4 ‡⁷MarkDenaro (2) (prom: hung lft & wknd qckly 2f out) ............................................................ 8.3
1332⁴ Duchess de Belfort (JBerry) 8-4 AClark (3) (wl bhd fnl 2f) .................... 7.4

**4/6** AREA GIRL(tchd 11/10), **3/1** Second Colours (USA)(op 6/4), **5/1** Heber Spring (IRE)(op 5/2), **15/2** Duchess de Belfort. CSF £3.12, Tote £1.70 (£2.00). Mr W. E. Sturt (NEWMARKET) bred by Edmond and Richard Kent. 4 Rn
63.1 sec (2.6)
SF—41/28/–/–

---

**1885**　　BATH EVENING CHRONICLE H'CAP (3 & 4-Y.O) (0-70) £1996.00 (£556.00: £268.00)
　　　　　　**1m 5y**
4-50 (4-51)

1500³ **Tajigrey (48)** (RCurtis) 3-7-9 ‡⁵BDoyle (2) (3rd st: led 2f out: hrd rdn & edgd rt ins fnl f: r.o) ............................................................ —1
1716⁶ Sareen Express (IRE) (40) (MrsJCDawe) 4-7-10⁽¹⁾ ‡⁵RPrice (5) (hdwy & 5th st: ev ch whn carried rt ins fnl f: r.o) ............................................................ hd.2
1650* Emaura (60) (KOCunningham-Brown) 3-8-9 ‡³DBiggs (9) (led 6f: sn wknd) ....... 7.3
1659⁴ Elwazir (USA) (66) (PTWalwyn) 3-9-4 TQuinn (10) (4th st: btn whn n.m.r on ins wl over 1f out) ............................................................ ¹/₂.4
1642³ Spanish Glory (56) (v) (IABalding) 3-8-5 ‡³SO'Gorman (11) (2nd st: wknd 2f out) 2.5
1589² Abso (67) (Fav) (RHannon) 4-10-0 KDarley (7) (lw: nvr trbld ldrs) .................... ¹/₂.6
1425⁴ Vellandrucha (52) (JABennett) 3-8-4 AMcGlone (6) (6th st: no hdwy) ............. ³/₄.7
1252 Quiet Miss (60) (MrsAKnight) 3-8-7 ‡⁵RPrice (8) (rdn & hung rt over 2f out: a bhd) ............................................................ ¹/₂.8
1421 Casilla (32) (HCandy) 4-7-0 ‡⁷AntoinetteArmes (4) (carried rt over 2f out: a bhd) 3¹/₂.9
1143 Glen Finnan (32) (MPMuggeridge) 4-7-7 NAdams (3) (a bhd) ............................ 4.10

LONG HANDICAP: Casilla 7-6.

*Stewards Enquiry: Obj. to Tajigrey by Quinn overruled.*

**7/2** Abso(3/1—9/2), **9/2** Spanish Glory(op 5/2), **6/1** Emaura(4/1—13/2), **7/1** Elwazir (USA)(op 4/1), Casilla(20/1—6/1), **8/1** TAJIGREY(op 5/1), Sareen Express (IRE)(op 4/1), **12/1** Quiet Miss, **14/1** Glen Finnan, **16/1** Vellandrucha. CSF £65.94, CT £378.81. Tote £11.10: £3.00 £2.20 £1.80 (£28.30). Albury Racing Limited (EPSOM) bred by Macbiehill Estates Ltd. 10 Rn
1m 41.3 (2)
SF—33/33/25/32/13/34

T/Plpt: £94.00 (23.6 Tckts).
KH

1565—**NOTTINGHAM  (L-H)**
**Saturday, July 4th [Good becoming Good to soft]**
Going Allowance: 0.40 sec per fur (Y)                                    Wind: slt across

Stalls: high

**1886**   'PRETTY WOMAN' CLAIMING STKS (2-Y.O) £1506.00 (£416.00: £198.00)
5f 13y                                                                   6-15 (6-16)

1300 **Fancied** (Fav) *(HCandy)* 8-7  CRutter (5) (lw: chsd ldrs: led wl over 1f out: sn clr:
      easily) ................................................................... —1
1579★ Not so Generous (IRE) *(WGMTurner)* 8-0 ‡3TSprake (6) (lw: led: edgd lft after 2f:
      hdd & no ex wl over 1f out) ...................................... 7.2
595 Sefio *(JBerry)* 8-8  JCarroll (4) (bhd: hdwy appr fnl f: swtchd & r.o ins fnl f) ....... hd.3
1601² Jasmin Isle *(MissGayKelleway)* 8-0 ‡3FNorton (3) (w ldr: ev ch wl over 1f out: sn
      rdn & no ex) ........................................................... nk.4
1307★ Coconut Johnny (bl) *(GMMoore)* 8-11 ‡5JWeaver (1) (prom: rdn 2f out: sn btn) . 7.5
1416★ Regent's Lady *(CJames)* 8-7  SWhitworth (2) (spd 3f) ....................................... 3¹/₂.6

**11/4** FANCIED, **100/30** Coconut Johnny, **7/2** Not so Generous (IRE)(op 7/4), **9/2** Regent's Lady, **6/1** Jasmin
Isle(8/1—9/2), **20/1** Sefio. CSF £11.50, Tote £3.80: £2.20 £2.50 (£6.90). Mr H. R. Mould (WANTAGE) bred by
Grange Stud (UK). 6 Rn                                                              64.1 sec (5.4)
                                                                        SF—25/-/-/-/-/-/-

**1887**   E.B.F. EXECUTIVE STAND STKS (Mdn 2-Y.O) £1826.00 (£506.00: £242.00)
6f 15y                                                                   6-45 (6-47)

**Pizza Connection** (Fav) *(JLDunlop)* 9-0  WRyan (5) (str: scope: bit bkwd: hld
      up: hdwy to ld wl over 1f out: shkn up & r.o) ........................ —1
1575³ Penang Star (IRE) *(WAO'Gorman)* 8-11 ‡3EmmaO'Gorman (3) (chsd ldrs: shkn
      up over 2f out: ev ch over 1f out: one pce) ............................ 2.2
Crystal Key *(CEBrittain)* 8-9  GCrealock (6) (leggy: lt-f: led over 4f: sn rdn & no
      ex) ..................................................................... 2¹/₂.3
We Are Doomed *(JRFanshawe)* 9-0  GDuffield (7) (cmpt: bit bkwd: w ldr over 3f) 7.4
1378 Glen Miller *(JWPayne)* 9-0  MTebbutt (4) (prom over 3f) ...................................... s.h.5
Palacegate Sunset *(JBerry)* 9-0  JCarroll (1) (leggy: outpcd) ........................ nk.6
1660 Legal Dancer *(RJRWilliams)* 9-0  RCochrane (2) (prom 4f: wknd qckly) .......... 6.7

**7/4** PIZZA CONNECTION(tchd 3/1), **7/2** Penang Star (IRE), **11/2** Palacegate Sunset(op 5/2), **7/1** We Are
Doomed, **8/1** Crystal Key(op 5/1), **12/1** Legal Dancer, **16/1** Glen Miller. CSF £7.72, Tote £3.70: £2.10 £2.40
(£5.10). Gerecon Italia (ARUNDEL) bred by Mrs M. de Jong. 7 Rn                      1m 17.8 (6.8)
                                                                        SF—12/1/-/-/-/-/-

**1888**   LEGAL HELPLINE LEDGER H'CAP (0-80) £2092.50 (£580.00: £277.50)
6f 15y                                                                   7-15 (7-18)

(Weights raised 2 lb)
1339 **Scarlet Princess (41)** *(RJHodges)* 4-7-9 ‡3FNorton (6) (lw: hdwy 2f out: rdn to
      ld ins fnl f) ............................................................ —1
1654³ Ayr Raider (64) (bl) *(WRMuir)* 5-9-7  SWhitworth (9) (prom: led over 3f out tl hdd
      & nt qckn ins fnl f) ...................................................... 1.2
1445⁶ Bernstein Bette (67) (Fav) *(PSFelgate)* 6-9-10  WRyan (1) (hld up & bhd: hdwy
      fnl f: nrst fin) ......................................................... 5.3
1084⁶ Farmer Jock (59) *(MrsNMacauley)* 10-9-2  BRaymond (8) (chsd ldrs: n.m.r
      over 1f out: sn btn) .................................................... hd.4
668 Long Lane Lady (48) *(JMackie)* 6-8-5  GHind (7) (led over 2f: wknd appr fnl f) 1¹/₂.5
1040⁵ Double Feature (IRE) (62) *(MrsJRRamsden)* 3-8-7 ‡5JWeaver (2) (bhd: effrt
      over 1f out: no imp) ..................................................... 3.6
1651² Saint Systems (45) *(CJHill)* 6-8-2  PaulEddery (3) (chsd ldrs 4f) ........................ 1.7
1551★ Strip Cartoon (IRE) (56) (bl) *(SRBowring)* 4-8-6 ‡7MHarris (4) (lw: gd spd centre
      over 3f) ................................................................ 4.8
1614 Everset (FR) (57) *(WJMusson)* 4-9-0  RCochrane (5) (dwlt: a bhd: t.o) ............ 15.9

**7/2** Bernstein Bette(3/1—9/2), **9/2** Ayr Raider, **13/2** Saint Systems(7/2—7/1), **7/1** Strip Cartoon (IRE), Double
Feature (IRE)(9/2—8/1), **9/1** Long Lane Lady(12/1—7/1), **10/1** SCARLET PRINCESS(7/1—11/1), **12/1** Farmer
Jock(op 8/1), **14/1** Everset (FR). CSF £48.78, CT £170.33. Tote £9.60: £1.90 £1.90 £2.10 (£26.90). Mr D. J. F.
Phillips (SOMERTON) bred by D. J. F. Phillips. 9 Rn                                 1m 15.9 (4.9)
                                                                        SF—31/53/36/27/10/-/

**1889** TRENT FM H'CAP (0-70) £1716.00 (£476.00: £228.00) **1m 54y** 7-45 (7-47)
(Weights raised 5 lb)
1627 **Ripsnorter (IRE) (57)** (Fav) *(SirMarkPrescott)* 3–9-0 GDuffield (6) (trckd ldrs tl 5th st: rdn 2f out: led ins fnl f: rdn out) .................................... —1
1550* Tyrian Purple (IRE) (50) *(RHollinshead)* 4–8-9 ‡7MHumphries (4) (lw: led over 7f: r.o) ............................................................. 2½.2
1673 Cartel (54) *(JLHarris)* 5–9-6 PaulEddery (5) (lw: chsd ldr: ev ch over 2f out: one pce appr fnl f) ........................................ 8.3
15645 Stairway to Heaven (IRE) (58) (bl) *(TDBarron)* 4–9-10 AlexGreaves (1) (chsd ldrs: 3rd st: rdn 2f out: sn btn) ........................ 1.4
1520 Le Saule D'Or (30) *(APJames)* 5–7-3(2) ‡7CHawksley (3) (s.s: sn rdn along: hdwy: 4th & c wd st: wknd over 2f out) .......... 1½.5
1239 Emma Victoria (35) *(TKersey)* 4–8-1 JLowe (2) (b: lw: chsd ldrs tl 6th & btn st) 10.6

**13/8** RIPSNORTER (IRE), **9/4** Tyrian Purple (IRE)(op 5/4), **9/2** Cartel, **8/1** Le Saule D'Or(op 16/1), **9/1** Stairway to Heaven (IRE), **66/1** Emma Victoria. CSF £5.31, Tote £2.60: £1.30 £2.00 (£2.90). Mr B. Haggas (NEWMARKET) bred by Barronstown Bloodstock Ltd in Ireland. 6 Rn 1m 48.6 (9)
SF—13/-/-/-/-/-

**1890** CENTRAL PARK AND PRIORY CARAVAN H'CAP (3-Y.O) (0-70) £1828.00 (£508.00: £244.00) **1m 1f 213y** 8-15 (8-18)
(Weights raised 3 lb)
1568* **Great Max (IRE) (65)** (Jt-Fav) *(SirMarkPrescott)* 9-5 GDuffield (8) (lw: plld hrd: 6th st: rdn to ld 1f out: r.o wl) ....................... —1
Affa (53) *(TThomsonJones)* 8-7 SWhitworth (3) (b: lw: a.p: 4th st: led over 1f out: sn hdd & no ex) .......................... 1½.2
1371 Cappahoosh (IRE) (53) *(HJCollingridge)* 8-7 JQuinn (9) (led over 8f: kpt on) . 3½.3
972 Wakil (IRE) (47) *(CJBenstead)* 8-1 WCarson (14) (lw: prom: 3rd st: no ex fnl 2f) ¼.4
12924 Faryal (48) *(JLSpearing)* 8-2 GHind (11) (prom: 2nd st: ev ch 3f out: wknd 2f out) ................................................. 8.5
1643 Arsaad (USA) (v) *(PTWalwyn)* 8-8 RCochrane (16) (hld up: hdwy 4f out: no imp fnl 2f) ............................................... 4.6
1700² Tudor Da Samba (62) *(JRFanshawe)* 9-2 DHolland (4) (nvr nr to chal) ............ 3½.7
1700² Tahitian (50) (bl) *(MrsJRRamsden)* 8-4 MRoberts (2) (lw: hld up: hmpd 6f out: nvr rchd ldrs) .......................... 2.8
13095 Super Summit (56) *(JPearce)* 8-5 ‡5RPrice (12) (dwlt: nvr trbld ldrs) ............. 1½.9
940 Classical Charmer (52) *(BRMillman)* 8-6 JWilliams (5) (effrt & 10th st: no hdwy fnl 3f) ..................................... 1.10
18124 Breakdancer (IRE) (60) *(WRMuir)* 9-0 CRutter (6) (lw: hdwy 4f out: wknd 2f out)2½.11
17126 Basilica (67) *(CEBrittain)* 9-2 ‡5BDoyle (15) (plld hrd: chsd ldrs: 8th st: sn rdn & btn) .............................. 6.12
509 Clifton Chase (61) (Jt-Fav) *(MAJarvis)* 9-1 BRaymond (1) (bhd fnl 4f) ............. nk.13
16042 Noble Vienna (USA) (60) *(RHollinshead)* 9-0 WRyan (17) (hld up: hdwy, 9th & c wd st: sn wknd) .................... hd.14
1528 Head for the Stars (IRE) (57) *(APStringer)* 8-11 KFallon (7) (a bhd) ............. 1.15
1371 Hester Stanhope (60) *(PWHarris)* 9-0 PaulEddery (13) (lw: 7th st: sn wknd) .... 3.16
14862 The Dominant Gene (40) *(JRJenkins)* 7-8(1) EJohnson (10) (stdd & lost pl after 2f: sn t.o: no ch after) .............. 6.17
LONG HANDICAP: The Dominant Gene 7-4.

**9/2** Clifton Chase(op 20/1), GREAT MAX (IRE), **6/1** Tahitian(op 4/1), **8/1** Super Summit(op 5/1), Cappahoosh (IRE)(10/1—5/1), **11/1** Noble Vienna (USA)(op 7/1), **14/1** Faryal(op 7/1), Wakil (IRE), The Dominant Gene, Hester Stanhope(op 8/1), Basilica, **16/1** Classical Charmer, Arsaad (USA), **20/1** Breakdancer (IRE), Tudor Da Samba, **33/1** Ors. CSF £140.31, CT £1,108.56. Tote £6.20: £2.80 £7.20 £1.50 £3.50 (£397.30). Sir Mark Prescott (NEWMARKET) bred by J. B. Clarke in Ireland. 17 Rn 2m 12.4 (9.9)
SF—46/31/24/17/2/–

**1891** EAST MIDLANDS RACING CLUB STKS (Mdn 3-Y.O) £1380.00 (£380.00: £180.00) **1¾m 15y** 8-45 (8-47)
1720² **Sadler's Way (73)** *(GLewis)* 9-0 PaulEddery (5) (trckd ldrs: 4th st: rdn to ld wl over 2f out: jst hld on) ........................ —1
Puritan (CAN) *(GHarwood)* 9-0 WCarson (4) (w'like: scope: in tch: 5th st: hdwy 2f out: rdn fnl f: nt rch wnr) .............. nk.2
979² Seekin Cash (USA) (Fav) *(JWWatts)* 9-0 MRoberts (6) (led after 2f: rdn 4f out: hdd wl over 2f out: one pce) ............ 4.3
14904 Zamaan Ya Zamaan (IRE) *(MAJarvis)* 9-0 BRaymond (3) (prom: rdn 6f out: 4th st: wknd 3f out) ................... 10.4
1265² Alderbrook *(MrsJCecil)* 9-0 GDuffield (1) (led 2f: 2nd st: ev ch over 2f out: sn btn) ...................... 2½.5

*1003*⁴ In the Money (IRE) **(70)** *(RHollinshead)* 9-0 WRyan (7) (in tch tl 6th & bhd st: sn
t.o) .......................................................................................................... **25.6**
1705⁶ Alcoy (IRE) **(60)** *(PAKelleway)* 9-0 GayKelleway (2) (t: a bhd: t.o fnl 4f) ............ **30.7**

**5/4** Seekin Cash (USA), **3/1** Puritan (CAN)(2/1—7/2), **5/1** SADLER'S WAY(op 3/1), **7/1** Zamaan Ya Zamaan
(IRE), **10/1** Alderbrook, **12/1** In the Money (IRE), **20/1** Alcoy (IRE). CSF £20.24, Tote £5.60: £2.50 £2.10
(£9.80). Mr A. J. Richards (EPSOM) bred by Mareco Ltd. 7 Rn 3m 12 (13.5)
SF—21/20/12/–/–/–

T/Plpt: £82.40 (19.9 Tckts). Dk

## 1558—EDINBURGH (R-H)
### Monday, July 6th [Good to firm]
Going Allowance: minus 0.30 sec per fur (F) Wind: almost nil

Stalls: high

**1892** RAMBLING RIVER H'CAP (Amateurs) (0-70) £2038.00 (£568.00: £274.00)
5f 2-15 (2-16)

(Weights raised 12 lb)

1436² **Best Effort (52)** *(Fav)* *(MPNaughton)* 6–11-7 MissPRobson (3) (lw: a cl up: effrt
appr fnl f: r.o to ld last strides) .......................................................... —**1**
1729 The Right Time **(45)** (bl) *(JParkes)* 7–11-0 MrsAFarrell (4) (cl up: disp ld ½-wy:
led appr fnl f: hdd & no ex cl home) ..................................... hd.**2**
*1853* Jive Music **(32)** (bl) *(NBycroft)* 6–9-10 ‡5MissABycroft (2) (racd stands' side: led
tl hdd appr fnl f: styd on) ............................................................ ½.**3**
1729³ Chateau Nord **(55)** *(JBerry)* 3–11-4 MrDParker (1) (lw: chsd ldrs: ev ch 2f out:
sn rdn & outpcd) ........................................................................... 3½.**4**

**6/4** BEST EFFORT, **13/8** Chateau Nord, **11/2** The Right Time, **6/1** Jive Music. CSF £8.00, Tote £2.10 (£2.70). Mr
Raymond Miquel (RICHMOND) bred by Aldershawe Stud Farm. 4 Rn 60.5 sec (2.8)
SF—49/41/21/29

**1893** HOLYROOD CLAIMING STKS (Mdn 3-Y-O) £2066.00 (£576.00: £278.00)
1m 7f 16y 2-45 (2-46)

1574 **Mystery Lad (IRE) (53)** (bl) *(NACallaghan)* 8-2 JCarroll (2) (b: prom: hdwy to ld
8f out: styd on u.p fnl 2f) ........................................................... —**1**
1517³ Miliyel **(51)** *(PMonteith)* 7-10 ‡5SMaloney (3) (s.i.s: hld up: jnd ldrs ½-wy: chal 2f
out: sn rdn: nt qckn fnl f) ............................................................ 1.**2**
1491 Mr Elk **(37)** (bl) *(MrsGRReveley)* 8-5 MBirch (4) (led & set mod pce: hdd 8f out:
prom tl rdn & wknd 3f out) ........................................................ 7.**3**
1491³ Escadaro (USA) **(39)** (bl) *(SGNorton)* 8-0 ‡7OPears (1) (chsd ldrs tl lost pl appr
st: n.d after) ................................................................................. 1½.**4**
1478³ Shardra *(MJCamacho)* 8-2 NConnorton (5) (prom: ev ch ent st: sn rdn & wknd) dist.**5**
1567³ Bandao **(Fav)** *(JMackie)* 8-11 GHind (6) (lw: jnd ldrs after 2f: lost pl ½-wy: sn
rdn: t.o whn virtually p.u ent st) .............................................. dist.**6**

**13/8** Bandao, **3/1** Miliyel, **4/1** MYSTERY LAD (IRE)(3/1—9/2), **8/1** Escadaro (USA), **10/1** Mr Elk.
CSF £14.80, Tote £9.60: £2.50 £1.90 (£12.00). Gallagher Properties Ltd (NEWMARKET) bred by Hamwood
Stud in Ireland. 6 Rn 3m 20.4 (9.9)

**1894** WATSONIANS F.C. H'CAP (0-80) £2304.00 (£644.00: £312.00)
1½m 31y 3-15 (3-17)

(Weights raised 13 lb)

1733✱ **Carlingford (USA) (57)** *(Fav)* *(MPNaughton)* 6–9-4 (5x) KFallon (4) (a.p:
carried wd ent st: sn led: hdd 2f out: rdn & ld appr fnl f: edgd rt:
kpt on) ........................................................................................ —**1**
1622⁴ Not Yet **(44)** *(EWeymes)* 8–8-0(7) ‡5JWeaver (5) (in tch: led 2f out: carried rt &
hdd appr fnl f: styd on) ............................................................... 1.**2**
1482⁵ West Stow **(70)** *(MRStoute)* 3–9-4 MBirch (8) (a chsng ldrs: ev ch whn hmpd
appr fnl f: swtchd rt: styd on wl nr fin) ................................... nk.**3**
*1372*³ Cheeky Pot **(45)** (v) *(DenysSmith)* 4–8-6 NConnorton (9) (prom: rdn ½-wy:
styd on fnl 2f: no imp) ................................................................. 3½.**4**
1691³ Demokos (FR) **(43)** *(APStringer)* 7–7-13 ‡5SMaloney (2) (chsd ldrs: carried wd
ent st: ev ch 3f out: one pce) ..................................................... hd.**5**
1528 Caithness Rock **(53)** *(MAJarvis)* 3–8-1 JLowe (7) (led: rn wd ent st: sn hdd &
btn) ............................................................................................... 3.**6**
1733³ Rapid Mover **(32)** (bl) *(TCraig)* 5–7-0 ‡7DarrenMoffatt (3) (led: effrt ent st: styd
on: n.d) ........................................................................................ 2.**7**
1800³ Naseer (USA) **(61)** *(NACallaghan)* 3–8-9 JCarroll (6) (a bhd) ........................ 15.**8**

1518 Hthaal (USA) **(63)** *(LLungo)* 4–9-10 DNicholls (1) (in tch to ½-wy: btn whn eased ent st: sn wl bhd) ...................................................... 15.9
LONG HANDICAP: Rapid Mover 7-4.
*Stewards Enquiry: Obj. to Carlingford (USA) & Not Yet by Birch overruled.*

**9/4** CARLINGFORD (USA), **5/2** Demokos (FR), **11/2** Naseer (USA), **7/1** West Stow, **11/1** Not Yet(op 7/1), **12/1** Caithness Rock(op 7/1), **14/1** Rapid Mover, **25/1** Ors. CSF £24.82, CT £134.38. Tote £3.50: £2.00 £1.80 £1.70 (£32.00). Mrs H. H. Wane (RICHMOND) bred by Hugh G. King, III in USA. 9 Rn          2m 35.5 (3)
SF–38/18/35/16/8/4

---

**1895**     E.B.F. EVEREST STKS (Mdn 2-Y.O) £2192.00 (£612.00: £296.00)     **5f**     3-45 (3-56)

1699⁴ **Press the Bell** **(Fav)** *(JBerry)* 9-0 JCarroll (2) (mde all: rdn & r.o fnl f) ............... —1
1699⁶ Gussie Fink-Nottle (IRE) *(TDBarron)* 9-0 AlexGreaves (1) (in tch: hdwy to chal 2f out: styd on) ........................................................ ¾.2
First Play *(JBerry)* 8-9 MBirch (5) (neat: cl up: ev ch 2f out: rdn & nt qckn appr fnl f) ................................................................. 2.3
1112 Sensabo *(MissLAPerratt)* 8-4 ‡5JWeaver (4) (w ldrs: rdn ½-wy: wknd wl over 1f out) ................................................................. 3.4
1734³ Spanish Thread *(GAPritchard-Gordon)* 8-9 KFallon (3) (prom: rdn 2f out: sn wknd) ................................................................ 2½.5

**Evens** PRESS THE BELL, **9/4** Spanish Thread(op 6/4), **3/1** Gussie Fink-Nottle (IRE), **10/1** First Play, **33/1** Sensabo. CSF £4.65, Tote £2.40: £1.40 £1.70 (£3.90). Mr Sydney Mason (COCKERHAM) bred by Sydney Mason. 5 Rn          60.2 sec (2.5)
CF £0/17/4/—/—

---

**1896**     CRAIGMILLAR (S) STKS     £2136.00 (£596.00: £288.00)     **7f 15y**     4-15 (4-22)

1725³ **Mca Below the Line (60)** (bl) **(Fav)** *(BBeasley)* 4–9-0 DNicholls (5) (chsd ldrs: rdn to ld ent fnl f: all out) ................................. —1
1731 Talish **(36)** (v) *(TDBarron)* 4–9-0 AlexGreaves (2) (a.p: led over 2f out: hdd ent fnl f: sn rallied & styd on) ........................... hd.2
1732² Miss Parkes **(48)** *(JBerry)* 3–7-10 LCharnock (8) (chsd ldrs: rdn 2f out: styd on same pce ins fnl f) ........................................ 1½.3
1486³ Mummys Rocket **(32)** (bl) *(MO'Neill)* 3–7-10 SWood (9) (hld up & bhd: hdwy 3f out: styd on fnl f: nrst fin) ................................... ½.4
1624³ Ravecino **(40)** *(JSHaldane)* 3–7-10 ‡5SMaloney (4) (cl up: lft in ld ent st: hdd over 2f out: grad wknd) .................................... 1.5
1729 Come on My Girl (IRE) **(51)** *(TAKCuthbert)* 4–8-9 GHind (7) (in tch tl wknd wl over 2f out) ............................................... 2½.6
1732⁵ Cumbrian Classic *(LLungo)* 3–8-4⁽³⁾ KFallon (1) (s.i.s: a bhd) ............ 5.7
980 Goodbye Mr Marks (IRE) **(62)** *(NBycroft)* 4–8-9 JCarroll (3) (led tl rrn wd ent st: sn bhd) ................................................................. 8.8
Bluefaulds *(TCraig)* 3–8-2⁽¹⁾ NConnorton (6) (a in rr) ...................... 9

**6/4** MCA BELOW THE LINE, **2/1** Miss Parkes, **8/1** Talish, **11/1** Goodbye Mr Marks (IRE)(op 7/1), **12/1** Ravecino(op 8/1), Mummys Rocket, **16/1** Come on My Girl (IRE), **50/1** Cumbrian Classic, **100/1** Bluefaulds. CSF £13.38, Tote £1.90: £1.20 £3.30 £1.30 (£21.90). Mike Clynes Associates Ltd (HAMBLETON) bred by T. Barratt. 9 Rn; Sold D W Barker 5,000 gns          1m 28.5 (2.3)
SF–34/33/10/8/5/10

---

**1897**     WALLYFORD AUCTION STKS (Mdn 2-Y.O) £2122.00 (£592.00: £286.00)
**7f 15y**          4-45 (4-49)

1506⁴ **Peaceful Air** *(EWeymes)* 7-13 ‡5JWeaver (3) (a chsng ldrs: led appr fnl f: sn clr: comf) ................................................................. —1
1515⁵ Prime Painter *(RFFisher)* 8-9 JLowe (5) (led tl hdd appr fnl f: nt qckn) ........... 4.2
1689⁴ The Premier Expres *(BBeasley)* 8-12 DNicholls (9) (a.p: ev ch 2f out: sn rdn & no ex) ............................................................... nk.3
1112 Ho-Joe (IRE) *(AHarrison)* 8-6 ‡5SMaloney (7) (bhd: styd on fnl 2f: nvr nr to chal) 1½.4
1660² Sweet Disorder (IRE) **(Fav)** *(GAPritchard-Gordon)* 8-3 KFallon (4) (hdwy & nt clr run 2f out: one pce) ..................................... s.h.5
1297 Emmandee *(MWEasterby)* 8-7 TLucas (1) (cl up: rdn & hung lft 2f out: sn btn) .. 6.6
Grand as Owt *(DenysSmith)* 8-11 NConnorton (2) (hdwy 3f out: rdn, n.m.r & swtchd over 2f out: sn btn) ............................. 1.7
Laurel Etoile *(JBerry)* 8-6 JCarroll (8) (s.i.s: effrt ent st: sn btn) ........................ 4.8
German Legend *(RRLamb)* 8-2 ‡7RHavlin (6) (in tch to st: sn wknd) ............... 3½.9

**Evens** Sweet Disorder (IRE)(op 6/4), **4/1** The Premier Expres, **9/2** PEACEFUL AIR, **11/2** Prime Painter, **20/1** Emmandee, Laurel Etoile, **33/1** Ho-Joe (IRE), **50/1** Grand as Owt, **100/1** German Legend. CSF £27.90, Tote £5.70: £1.30 £2.40 £1.90 (£19.60). Mr T. A. Scothern (MIDDLEHAM) bred by Theakston Stud. 9 Rn
1m 28.8 (2.6)
SF—14/12/14/3/–/–

**1898**   DUNBAR H'CAP (0-70) £2301.00 (£636.00: £303.00)   **1m 7f 16y**   5-15 (5-15)

| | | |
|---|---|---|
| 1560² | **Fen Princess (IRE)** (46) (Fav) (PCHaslam) 4–8-7 ‡5JWeaver (9) (trckd ldrs: led over 2f out: styd on wl) | —1 |
| 1437³ | Attadale (60) (LLungo) 4–9-12 DNicholls (5) (leggy: unf: hld up in tch: hdwy & bdly hmpd wl over 2f out: styd on wl fnl f) | 4.2 |
| 1372⁶ | Crimson Cloud (IRE) (46) (NTinkler) 4-8-12 LCharnock (6) (neat: bkwd: led: hdd ent st: kpt on same pce fnl 2f) | 1.3 |
| 1733 | Alpha Helix (27) (v) (MissLAPerratt) 9–7-7 SWood (4) (bhd: styd on fnl 2f: nrst fin) | hd.4 |
| 1730² | Fair Flyer (IRE) (49) (PMonteith) 3–7-8(1) ‡5SMaloney (3) (neat: cl up: led ent st: hdd over 2f out: no ex) | s.h.5 |
| 1423² | Noncommital (42) (JMackie) 5–8-8 GHind (1) (prom: rdn ent st: sn wknd) | 15.6 |
| 1733⁴ | Shadideen (USA) (62) (MissLAPerratt) 4–9-7 ‡7RHavlin (2) (chsd ldrs: wknd 3f out) | ½.7 |
| 369 | Sioux Perfick (46) (CWThornton) 3–7-10 JLowe (8) (wl bhd fr ½-wy) | 7.8 |
| | Kir (IRE) (60) (v) (DRFranks) 4–9-12 KFallon (7) (in tch: rdn ½-wy: bhd st) | 6.9 |
| | LONG HANDICAP: Alpha Helix 7-6. | |

**10/11** FEN PRINCESS (IRE), **11/4** Attadale, **15/2** Noncommital, **9/1** Shadideen (USA), **16/1** Fair Flyer (IRE), **20/1** Crimson Cloud (IRE), Kir (IRE), **50/1** Ors. CSF £4.01, CT £24.94. Tote £1.90: £1.10 £1.20 £7.50 (£5.30). Mr S. A. B. Dinsmore (MIDDLEHAM) bred by Ballymacoll Stud Farm Ltd in Ireland. 9 Rn
3m 15.4 (4.9)
SF—9/24/9/–/–/–

T/Plpt: £67.50 (22.2 Tckts).
GB

## 1275—LEICESTER (R-H)

### Monday, July 6th [Good]

Going Allowance: minus 0.10 sec per fur (F)                 Wind: mod half against

Stalls: high

**1899**   ANSELLS STKS (Mdn 2-Y-O) £2559.20 (£711.20: £341.60)   **7f 9y**   2-00 (2-05)

| | | |
|---|---|---|
| 1610² | **Fret (USA)** (Fav) (PFICole) 9-0 AMunro (8) (led 4f out: rdn over 1f out: r.o wl) | —1 |
| 1630² | Woodhaunter (USA) (JHMGosden) 9-0 SCauthen (10) (lw: a.p: r.o one pce fnl 2f) | 4.2 |
| 1502 | Blue Blazer (BHanbury) 9-0 GDuffield (14) (a.p: rdn 2f out: one pce) | nk.3 |
| 1424⁶ | Share a Moment (CAN) (RHollinshead) 9-0 KDarley (5) (a.p: one pce fnl 2f) | 1½.4 |
| 1538⁴ | Kennedys Prima (AAScott) 8-9 RBaymond (1) (w ldrs over 5f) | 2½.5 |
| 703⁴ | Jonsalan (WCarter) 9-0 JReid (13) (nvr nrr) | nk.6 |
| | Clear Honey (USA) (BHanbury) 8-9 WRSwinburn (2) (leggy: lt-f: hld up: rdn over 1f out: eased whn btn fnl f) | 2.7 |
| | Farafashion (MRLeach) 9-0 RFox (7) (w'like: bkwd: nvr nr to chal) | 2.8 |
| | Gypsy Crystal (USA) (RMWhitaker) 8-9 AculHane (6) (scope: bit bkwd: bhd fnl 2f) | 1½.9 |
| 383 | Coppot Tel (IRE) (CEBrittain) 9-0 MRoberts (15) (prom 5f) | ¾.10 |
| | Daring Past (RBoss) 9-0 MTebbutt (11) (w'like: leggy: dwlt: a bhd) | ½.11 |
| | Side Bar (MJRyan) 9-0 PRobinson (4) (leggy: lt-f: bit bkwd: a bhd) | 2½.12 |
| | Kaloochi (RHannon) 9-0 WCarson (12) (neat: s.s: a bhd) | ¾.13 |
| 1571 | Stevie's Wonder (IRE) (WCarter) 8-9 ‡5NGwilliams (9) (bit bkwd: a bhd: t.o) | 10.14 |
| 595 | Ambivalentattitude (MDIUsher) 9-0 MWigham (3) (led 3f: sn lost pl: t.o) | 4.15 |

**1/2** FRET (USA), **7/2** Woodhaunter (USA)(op 2/1), **14/1** Jonsalan, Kennedys Prima(8/1—16/1), **25/1** Kaloochi, Clear Honey (USA)(op 8/1), **33/1** Blue Blazer, Coppot Tel (IRE), **50/1** Daring Past, Stevie's Wonder (IRE), Gypsy Crystal (USA), Share a Moment (CAN), **66/1** Side Bar, Farafashion, **100/1** Ambivalentattitude. CSF £3.11, Tote £1.50: £1.20 £1.30 £4.20 (£1.30). Mr Fahd Salman (WHATCOMBE) bred by Gainesway Thoroughbred Limited in USA. 15 Rn
1m 26.9 (4.6)
SF—20/8/7/2/–/–

**1900**   SUTTON (S) STKS (2-Y-O) £2226.00 (£616.00: £294.00)   **5f 218y**   2-30 (2-33)

| | | |
|---|---|---|
| 1573 | **Warm Spell** (LordHuntingdon) 8-11 LDettori (4) (lw: a.p: led stands' side over 2f out: hrd rdn: led last stride) | —1 |
| 1251 | Guv'nors Gift (MHTompkins) 8-6 PRobinson (5) (lw: a.p: led over 1f out: ct last stride) | s.h.2 |

1526  Merry Mermaid (Fav) *(JFBottomley)* 8-6  PBurke (11) (s.s: hdwy over 2f out: nt
          qckn fnl f) ................................................................................................. 2.3
*1321*  Clangold *(JBerry)* 8-6  GCarter (1) (prom stands' side: r.o one pce fnl 2f) .......... ¾.4
  988  Shades of Croft *(MDIUsher)* 8-11  MWigham (9) (no hdwy fnl 2f) ...................... 2.5
  476  Risk a Little *(MJHeaton-Ellis)* 8-6  MRoberts (3) (bit bkwd: led stands' side over
          3f: no ex) ................................................................................................ ½.6
1586⁵  Arctic Guest (IRE) *(MJohnston)* 8-6  DMcKeown (10) (prom 4f) ...................... ¾.7
1579  Balustrade Boy (IRE) *(BStevens)* 8-11  AMcGlone (2) (a bhd) .......................... 3.8
1554⁴  Grey Runner *(BPalling)* 8-6  WRyan (6) (led over 4f: wknd qckly: t.o) .............. 12.9
         Dream Princess *(JFBottomley)* 8-1 ‡⁵NKennedy (7) (neat: bkwd: s.s: a bhd: t.o) nk.10
1670⁵  Rythmic Rascal *(MBrittain)* 8-11  KDarley (8) (prom 4f: t.o) ......................... 1½.11

**7/2** Merry Mermaid(5/1—3/1), **4/1** WARM SPELL(op 5/2), **5/1** Risk a Little, **6/1** Clangold(op 4/1), **7/1** Arctic
Guest (IRE)(4/1—8/1), **8/1** Guv'nors Gift, **10/1** Grey Runner, **25/1** Rythmic Rascal, **33/1** Ors. CSF £33.18, Tote
£4.70: £2.10 £2.30 £1.90 (£22.70). Lord Carnarvon (WEST ILSLEY) bred by R. H. Cowell and Mrs R. B. Collie.
11 Rn; Sold R Simpson 4,500 gns                                                                    1m 15.4 (5.4)

---

**1901**    NUFFIELD ORTHOTICS APPEAL H'CAP (3-Y.O) (0-80) £3340.00 (£1000.00: £480.00:
            £220.00)  **1m 1f 218y**                                                    3-00 (3-01)

                                  (Weights raised 5 lb)
1318⁶  **Liability Order (65)** *(RBoss)* 8-11  PatEddery (8) (3rd st: led over 2f out: hrd rdn
          over 1f out: all out) ...................................................................................... —1
1363  El Rabab (USA) **(67)** *(HThomsonJones)* 8-13  RHills (11) (6th st: hdwy 3f out:
          rdn 2f out: styd on ins fnl f) ........................................................................ 1.2
1528²  Marowins **(53)** *(EJAlston)* 7-10 ‡³FNorton (9) (gd hdwy over 3f out: rdn 2f out: nt
          qckn fnl f) ................................................................................................. 1½.3
1577  Be My Habitat **(63)** (Fav) *(NAGraham)* 8-9  JQuinn (4) (lw: hld up: hdwy on ins 3f
          out: one pce fnl 2f) ..................................................................................... 5.4
1585²  Dexter Chief **(75)** (v) *(IABalding)* 9-7  SCauthen (2) (lw: led over 7f: wknd over 1f
          out) .......................................................................................................... 2.5
  674³  Irish Honey (IRE) **(54)** *(BHanbury)* 8-0⁽¹⁾  MRoberts (12) (2nd st: wknd 3f out) ...... 7.6
  788  Silken Words (USA) **(70)** *(WRMuir)* 9-2  SWhitworth (7) (lw: 5th st: rdn 4f out:
          wknd over 2f out) ....................................................................................... ¾.7
1308³  Al Haal (USA) **(71)** *(PTWalwyn)* 9-3  WCarson (1) (lw: sn bhd) .................... 3.8
1052  Double the Stakes (USA) **(52)** *(FHLee)* 7-7⁽⁵⁾ ‡⁵NKennedy (6) (plld hrd: hdwy &
          4th st: wknd over 3f out: t.o) ........................................................................ 20.9
  832  Andy Jack **(64)** *(MJHeaton-Ellis)* 8-10  MHills (10) (lw: a bhd: t.o fnl 3f) ........ 10.10
                      LONG HANDICAP: Double the Stakes (USA) 7-3.

**4/1** Be My Habitat, **9/2** Al Haal (USA), **5/1** LIABILITY ORDER, **11/2** Marowins, **6/1** El Rabab (USA), **7/1** Dexter
Chief, **12/1** Irish Honey (IRE), **16/1** Andy Jack, Double the Stakes (USA), **25/1** Silken Words (USA). N. J. Dent. 10 Rn
CT £157.11. Tote £5.90: £1.50 £3.10 £1.90 (£13.50). Madagans Plc (NEWMARKET) bred by N. J. Dent.
                                                                                          2m 7.7 (5)
                                                                                  SF—37/37/17/20/28/—

---

**1902**    TATTERSALLS AUCTION SERIES STKS (Qualifier) (Mdn 2-Y.O) £3262.00 (£976.00:
            £468.00: £214.00)  **5f 218y**                                              3-30 (3-32)

1699²  **The Sharp Bidder (IRE)** *(RHollinshead)* 8-5  PaulEddery (15) (a.p: led ins fnl f:
          rdn out) ..................................................................................................... —1
         Heavenly Risk *(RHannon)* 8-6⁽¹⁾  PatEddery (5) (w'like: leggy: bit bkwd: dwlt:
          hdwy & nt clr run 2f out: r.o ins fnl f) .............................................................. ¾.2
         Snowy River (FR) *(DrJDScargill)* 8-8  RCochrane (9) (w'like: leggy: bit bkwd:
          a.p: led over 2f out ins fnl f: r.o) ..................................................................... s.h.3
1378³  Soldiers Bay (Fav) *(LordHuntingdon)* 8-7  AMunro (8) (prom: rdn over 2f out: r.o
          ins fnl f) .................................................................................................... ¾.4
1689³  Panther (IRE) *(CWCElsey)* 8-7  KDarley (10) (w ldrs: ev ch 2f out: one pce) ..... 2½.5
         Viv's Pet *(AHide)* 8-4  JWilliams (3) (lt-f: bit bkwd: hdwy over 1f out: nvr nr to
          chal) ......................................................................................................... 3.6
         Andrula Mou *(RBoss)* 8-2  DHolland (1) (w'like: bkwd: s.s: nrst fin) ................ ¾.7
1409  Lorins Gold *(AndrewTurnell)* 8-1 ‡⁵ATucker (14) (bit bkwd: prom: ev ch 2f out:
          wknd qckly) ............................................................................................... s.h.8
1409  Infant Protege (USA) *(CEBrittain)* 8-0  RHills (2) (lw: prom over 3f) ................ 3.9
         Charrua *(JRFanshawe)* 8-5  GDuffield (16) (scope: bit bkwd: n.d) ................... ½.10
         Boisterous *(WRMuir)* 8-11  SCauthen (4) (wl grwn: bkwd: prom over 3f) ........ nk.11
         Altruistic (IRE) *(CFWall)* 8-4  MRoberts (13) (small: lt-f: n.d) ........................ s.h.12
  968  Daisy James (IRE) *(JMPEustace)* 8-1  JQuinn (4) (bhd fnl 2f) ......................... 1.13
1296  Strephon (IRE) *(MHTompkins)* 8-8  PRobinson (11) (bhd fnl 2f: t.o) ................. 6.14
  928  Trepidation (IRE) *(MJFetherston-Godley)* 8-2 ‡⁵DHarrison (6) (bhd fnl 3f: t.o) ... 2½.15
1178²  Poco Pierna (IRE) *(WCarter)* 7-12 ‡⁵NGwilliams (12) (led over 3f: wknd qckly:
          t.o) ........................................................................................................... 3½.16

**6/5** Soldiers Bay, **4/1** THE SHARP BIDDER (IRE), **13/2** Panther (IRE), **10/1** Charrua(7/1—14/1), **11/1** Heavenly Risk(8/1—12/1), **14/1** Snowy River (FR), **16/1** Altruistic (IRE), **20/1** Boisterous, **25/1** Poco Pierna (IRE), Infant Protege (USA), **33/1** Daisy James (IRE), Andrula Mou, Strephon (IRE), **50/1** Ors. CSF £48.86, Tote £5.10: £1.80 £2.80 £5.10 (£15.80). Mrs Robert Heathcote (UPPER LONGDON) bred by J. O'Connell in Ireland. 16 Rn
1m 14 (4)

## 1903
MADAGANS CLAIMING STKS (3-Y.O) £2441.60 (£677.60: £324.80)
1m 8y
4-00 (4-02)

1708[4] **American Boogie (FR) (59)** *(CEBrittain)* 8-11 MRoberts (10) (hld up: hdwy 2f out: hung lft ins fnl f: str run to ld nr fin) ................................. —1

1772[3] Lyn's Return (IRE) **(60)** *(RSimpson)* 8-6 ‡[5]ATucker (5) (a.p: hrd rdn & ev ch whn hung lft ins fnl f: r.o) ......................... ¹/₂.2

*129* Dancing Beau (IRE) **(78)** (Fav) *(MrsLPiggott)* 8-9 LPiggott (1) (bit bkwd: a.p: led over 2f out to 1f out: r.o) ......................... s.h.3

1565[6] Ace Girl **(54)** *(SRBowring)* 8-0 JQuinn (4) (led over 5f: led over 1f out tl hdd nr fin) ............................. 1.4

Cheeka *(MRLeach)* 8-6 RFox (2) (wl grwn: bit bkwd: swvd lft s: wl bhd tl gd hdwy over 1f out: wl) ........................ 3.5

1568 Royal Print (IRE) **(48)** (bl) *(WRMuir)* 8-11 SWhitworth (3) (lw: prom: rdn & ev ch over 2f out: wknd over 1f out) ................. 7.6

1276 Tamasha **(54)** *(CJHill)* 8-3 NAdams (7) (nvr trbld ldrs) ........................ 3.7

1708[3] Lonesome Train (USA) **(63)** (v) *(JHMGosden)* 8-11 WCarson (13) (prom 6f) ..... 3.8

Arrogant Daughter *(JWPayne)* 7-13 AMunro (11) (bkwd: s.s: n.d) ................ 2¹/₂.9

1583 Cal's Boy **(37)** *(JPSmith)* 8-11 JReid (8) (prom 5f: t.o) ......................... 8.10

*195*★ Lord Naskra (USA) *(WAO'Gorman)* 8-6 ‡[3]EmmaO'Gorman (9) (bit bkwd: t.o) ... 7.11

1627[2] Phil-Man **(48)** *(TFairhurst)* 8-3 ‡[3]JFanning (14) (chsd ldrs tl rdn & wknd over 2f out: t.o) .............................. 2.12

*1001* Qualitair Idol **(40)** (v) *(JFBottomley)* 8-1 PBurke (12) (prom 5f: t.o) ............... 2¹/₂.13

Bella's Match **(42)** *(BPalling)* 7-13 RHills (6) (still unf: a bhd: t.o fnl 2f) ............ 15.14

**5/2** Dancing Beau (IRE)(tchd 4/1), **9/2** Lyn's Return (IRE), **5/1** Lonesome Train (USA), AMERICAN BOOGIE (FR), **6/1** Lord Naskra (USA)(op 4/1), **10/1** Ace Girl, **14/1** Arrogant Daughter, Phil-Man, **20/1** Tamasha, Royal Print (IRE), **33/1** Cheeka, **40/1** Qualitair Idol, Bella's Match, **50/1** Cal's Boy. CSF £29.40, Tote £5.60: £2.90 £1.90 £1.40 (£10.20). Mr A. J. Richards (NEWMARKET) bred by Horses Aktiengesellschaft in France. 14 Rn
1m 39.9 (4.9)
SF—11/4/6/–/–/–

## 1904
MANNY BERNSTEIN BOOKMAKERS H'CAP (0-70) £2758.00 (£763.00: £364.00)
5f 2y
4-30 (4-31)

1729[2] **North of Watford (44)** (Fav) *(MPNaughton)* 7-8-12 MRoberts (3) (hld up: r.o to ld wl ins fnl f) ......................... —1

1282[3] Fighter Squadron **(51)** (v) *(JAGlover)* 4-8-6 ‡[7]SWilliams (2) (lw: hld up: hrd rdn over 2f out: hdwy over 1f out: r.o) ......................... 1.2

1787[2] Serious Hurry **(56)** (bl) *(SirMarkPrescott)* 4-9-10 GDuffield (6) (lw: racd alone far side: led over 1f out: hrd rdn: hdd wl ins fnl f) ............ nk.3

1785[2] Don't Run Me Over **(51)** *(BCMorgan)* 3-8-13 DMcKeown (4) (lw: led over 3f: one pce fnl f) ........................ 1¹/₂.4

1570 Minizen Music (IRE) **(31)** *(MBrittain)* 4-7-13 AMunro (8) (prom over 3f) ............. 6.5

1654[2] Lucy Dancer (IRE) **(54)** (v) *(CGCox)* 4-8-5 AClark (1) (rdn over 2f out: sn bhd) .. 2.6

1590 Barbezieux **(32)** (bl) *(TJNaughton)* 5-8-0(2) GCarter (9) (bhd fnl 2f) ......... ¹/₂.7

1282[5] Hotfoot Hannah (IRE) **(45)** *(PSFelgate)* 4-8-10 ‡[3]JFanning (5) (b: dwlt: rdn over 2f out: a bhd) ......................... 3¹/₂.8

**11/4** NORTH OF WATFORD, **4/1** Fighter Squadron, **9/2** Serious Hurry, **11/2** Don't Run Me Over, Lucy Dancer (IRE)(8/1—5/1), **8/1** Hotfoot Hannah (IRE), **11/1** Minizen Music (IRE), **16/1** Barbezieux. CSF £14.19, CT £44.43. Tote £3.20: £1.90 £1.70 £1.70 (£9.80). Mrs H. H. Wane (RICHMOND) bred by M. G. Masterson. 8 Rn
60.9 sec (2.2)
SF—44/34/51/34/–/11

## 1905
SCRAPTOFT H'CAP (0-70) £3199.00 (£889.00: £427.00)
7f 9y
5-00 (5-02)

534[6] **Doulab's Image (66)** *(JAGlover)* 5-9-4 ‡[7]SWilliams (8) (gd hdwy over 1f out: str run to ld ins fnl f: r.o) ......................... —1

1756[3] Profit a Prendre **(48)** *(DAWilson)* 8-8-2 ‡[5]DHarrison (12) (b: lw: s.s: hdwy over 2f out: str run ins fnl f: fin wl) ......................... nk.2

1568[4] Roca Murada (IRE) **(47)** *(MJRyan)* 3-7-9(3) ‡[3]DBiggs (15) (hld up: gd hdwy 2f out: r.o ins fnl f) ......................... ¹/₂.3

1338[4] Johnston's Express (IRE) **(35)** *(EJAlston)* 4-7-8 JQuinn (13) (a.p: led 2f out tl wl ins fnl f) ......................... 1.4

1716 Revoke (USA) **(40)** *(CJHill)* 5–7-8 ‡5NKennedy (19) (hdwy 2f out: ev ch 1f out: one pce) .................... hd.**5**
13282 Coolaba Prince (IRE) **(57)** (v) *(Fav)* *(FHLee)* 3–8-8 MRoberts (3) (a.p: no hdwy fnl 2f) .................... 5.**6**
17945 Candle King (IRE) **(49)** (bl) *(MJFetherston-Godley)* 4–8-8 AMunro (2) (nvr nr to chal) .................... 1½.7
1741 Harlequin Girl **(37)** *(KTIvory)* 4–7-7 ‡3FNorton (9) (prom 5f) .................... ½.**8**
1146 Bold Setko (IRE) **(61)** *(JMPEustace)* 3–8-12 RCochrane (11) (prom 5f) .......... hd.**9**
15995 Susanna's Secret **(47)** *(WCarter)* 5–8-1 ‡5NGwilliams (18) (lw: prom: rdn & wknd 2f out) .................... 2.**10**
1642 My Czech Mate **(53)** *(RHannon)* 3–8-4 RHills (14) (lw: prom 5f) .................... 4.**11**
15705 Vendredi Treize **(42)** *(SRBowring)* 9–7-8(8) ‡7MHumphries (7) (b: prom over 4f) nk.**12**
1343 Miss Bell Ringer **(39)** *(CJHill)* 4–7-12 NAdams (17) (n.d) .................... s.h.**13**
16776 Yonge Tender **(50)** (bl) *(CNWilliams)* 5–8-9 JCurant (10) (n.d) .................... hd.**14**
1718 Sly Prospect (USA) **(60)** (bl) *(KWhite)* 4–8-12 ‡7AGarth (5) (prom: led 3f out to 2f out: sn wknd) .................... ¾.**15**
*1550* Sergeant Meryll **(35)** *(PHowling)* 8–7-8 DaleGibson (1) (s.s: a bhd) .................... 1.**16**
Two Birds **(63)** *(CAHorgan)* 3–9-0 AClark (16) (bit bkwd: t.o) .................... 5.**17**
11153 Yazaly (USA) **(69)** (v) *(AAScott)* 3–9-6 WRSwinburn (4) (led 4f: sn hrd rdn: eased whn btn over 1f out: t.o) .................... 2½.**18**
LONG HANDICAP: Vendredi Treize 7-3.

**7/2** Coolaba Prince (IRE)(op 7/1), **7/1** Profit a Prendre, Roca Murada (IRE), **15/2** Bold Setko (IRE)(12/1—14/1), **9/1** Revoke (USA), Susanna's Secret(7/1—12/1), **10/1** Yazaly (USA), Johnston's Express (IRE)(8/1—12/1), **14/1** Yonge Tender(10/1—16/1), Candle King (IRE)(8/1—16/1), **16/1** DOULAB'S IMAGE, **20/1** My Czech Mate, Vendredi Treize, **33/1** Ors. CSF £124.62, CT £797.70. Tote £34.40: £9.10 £1.60 £2.70 £2.40 (£104.50). Claremont Management Services (WORKSOP) bred by Hadi Al Tajir. 18 Rn      1m 26.4 (4.1)
    SF—32/15/6/2/1/–

T/Plpt: £85.10 (21.15 Tckts).                                                 KH

1478—**RIPON (R-H)**
## Monday, July 6th [Good]
Going Allowance: minus 0.20 sec per fur (F)                 Wind: slt across

Stalls: low

**1906**     SKELLGATE STKS (Mdn) £1730.00 (£480.00: £230.00)   **1m 1f**     7-00 (7-02)

16722 Big Blue **(90)** *(CEBrittain)* 3–8-10 MRoberts (2) (led after 2f: rdn over 3f out: kpt on gamely) .................... —**1**
North Russia (CAN) *(JHMGosden)* 3–8-10 RCochrane (11) (w'like: in tch: hdwy 3f out: rdn to chal appr fnl f: rn green: nt qckn nr fin) .......... 1.**2**
8182 Resounding Success (IRE) *(Fav)* *(BWHills)* 3–8-5 DHolland (4) (led 2f: chsd wnr: rdn & ev ch over 2f out: no ex fnl f) .................... 2½.**3**
17374 Waaza (USA) *(AAScott)* 3–8-10 JFortune (5) (lw: chsd ldrs: rdn & ev ch over 2f out: wknd fnl f) .................... 5.**4**
Moon Risk *(RMWhitaker)* 3–8-5 ACulhane (9) (bhd: stdy hdwy over 2f out: nvr plcd to chal) .................... 1½.**5**
14204 Knight Pawn *(JPLeigh)* 3–8-10 DMcKeown (3) (hdwy 3f out: nvr rchd ldrs) .... 1½.**6**
Only a Rose *(CWThornton)* 3–8-5 MBirch (6) (leggy: bhd tl hdwy u.p 2f out: styd on same pce) .................... s.h.**7**
1440 Canbrack (IRE) **(54)** *(WAStephenson)* 3–8-10 GBaxter (7) (chsd ldrs tl wknd over 2f out: eased whn btn) .................... 4.**8**
Ima Red Neck (USA) *(JHMGosden)* 3–8-10 WRyan (12) (str: cmpt: bit bkwd: sltly hmpd after s: a bhd) .................... nk.**9**
Indian Heather (IRE) (bl) *(JParkes)* 4–9-1 RLappin (1) (lengthy: unf: mid div tl lost pl over 3f out: sn wl bhd) .................... 20.**10**

**2/1** Resounding Success (IRE), **9/4** BIG BLUE, **4/1** Waaza (USA), **7/1** North Russia (CAN), **20/1** Knight Pawn, Ima Red Neck (USA)(op 8/1), **25/1** Moon Risk, **33/1** Only a Rose, **50/1** Ors. CSF £17.23, Tote £2.60: £1.30 £1.60 £1.30 (£7.90). Mrs Celia Miller (NEWMARKET) bred by M. McCalmont. 10 Rn   1m 54.1 (3.9)
    SF—10/7/–/–/–/–

**1907**     ST MARYGATE (S) STKS (3-Y.O) £1458.60 (£404.60: £193.80)   **1¼m**   7-25 (7-32)

17592 Miss Doody **(59)** (v) *(Fav)* *(MRChannon)* 8-9 RCochrane (9) (s.i.s: sn bhd & pushed along: hdwy on ins 3f out: led 1f out: rdn out) ........ —**1**
7976 Speedy Sioux **(57)** *(CWThornton)* 8-9 MRoberts (11) (chsd ldr: led over 2f out: sn rdn: hdd 1f out: no ex) .................... 2.**2**
*1374*4 Iron Baron (IRE) **(64)** *(RHollinshead)* 9-0 WRyan (7) (hld up: stdy hdwy 3f out: edgd lft & kpt on same pce appr fnl f) .................... 3½.**3**

**1908—1910**

1725⁵ Meltonby **(52)** *(NTinkler)* 8-9 GBaxter (5) (lw: stdy hdwy 3f out: kpt on: nvr nr to
chal) ........................................................................................... 1½.4

1735³ Shafayif **(48)** *(BHanbury)* 8-2 ‡⁷VBray (6) (led: clr over 4f out: hung lft & hdd over
2f out: sn btn) ............................................................................. 4.5

1783⁶ Mr News (IRE) **(54)** *(BBeasley)* 9-0 JFortune (13) (lw: in tch: grad lost pl wl over
2f out) ........................................................................................ 1.6

1335⁵ Brilliant Disguise **(42)** *(PMonteith)* 8-9 GDuffield (3) (sme hdwy over 2f out: n.d) nk.7

1620⁴ Cledeschamps *(MWEllerby)* 8-9 SMorris (10) (chsd ldrs tl wknd over 2f out) .. 1½.8

1627 Whitrigg Lad **(48)** *(WWHaigh)* 9-0 DMcKeown (14) (swtg: in tch: hung lft fnl 4f:
btn 3f out) .................................................................................. 2.9

1725 Bold Mood **(45)** *(JBerry)* 9-0 GCarter (8) (lw: effrt over 3f out: sn btn) ............. 7.10

1532 George Henry *(TDBarron)* 8-7 ‡⁷VHalliday (4) (bit bkwd: a bhd: rn wd ent st) .. 3.11
Dick Whittington **(51)** *(CTinkler)* 9-0 MBirch (1) (lw: hdwy to chase ldrs appr st:
sn lost pl) ................................................................................... 2.12

1661 Dont Embarrass Me *(TKersey)* 9-0 DHolland (12) (b: bit bkwd: a bhd) ............. 3.13

**11/10** MISS DOODY, **13/2** Iron Baron (IRE), **7/1** Meltonby, **8/1** Speedy Sioux, **10/1** Whitrigg Lad, **12/1** Mr News
(IRE), **14/1** Shafayif, **16/1** Brilliant Disguise, **20/1** Bold Mood, **25/1** Dick Whittington, George Henry, **33/1** Dont
Embarrass Me, **50/1** Cledeschamps. CSF £11.85, Tote £2.20: £1.20 £2.70 £2.10 (£9.80). Mr Vincent Herridge
(UPPER LAMBOURN) bred by G. Herridge. 13 Rn; Bt in 5,400 gns                     2m 7.3 (3.8)
SF—37/33/31/23/8/18

---

**1908**   NATIONAL MEDICAL AGENCY H'CAP (0-90) £2768.00 (£824.00: £392.00: £176.00)
**6f**                                                                          7-50 (7-56)

1771⁶ **Red Rosein (87)** *(CaptJWilson)* 6–10-0 GCarter (2) (b.off hind: in tch: smooth
hdwy 2f out: led ins fnl f: eased nr fin) ...................................... —1

1487* Filicaia **(65)** *(DonEnricoIncisa)* 6–7-13 ‡⁷ClaireBalding (5) (lw: s.i.s: bhd tl hdwy
on outside 2f out: styd on fnl f: nt qckn nr fin) ......................... 2.2

*1551* Furiella **(71)** *(PCHaslam)* 4–8-7 ‡⁵JWeaver (1) (chsd ldr: led wl over 1f out: hdd
ins fnl f: no ex) ......................................................................... 1½.3

1529⁵ Northern Spark **(62)** (Fav) *(CWThornton)* 4–8-3 MRoberts (4) (chsd ldrs: drvn
along ½-wy: kpt on fnl f) ........................................................... hd.4

1706⁵ Final Shot **(68)** *(MHEasterby)* 5–8-9 MBirch (6) (prom tl hrd rdn & lost pl ½-wy:
sn btn) ..................................................................................... 2.5

1333³ Lombard Ocean **(64)** *(MO'Neill)* 3–7-12 JQuinn (3) (led tl hdd & wknd wl over 1f
out) .......................................................................................... 3.6

398 Toshiba Comet **(78)** (bl) *(BBeasley)* 5–9-5 DNicholls (7) (prom on outside 4f) .. ¾.7

**11/4** Northern Spark, **4/1** Final Shot, **11/2** Furiella, RED ROSEIN, **6/1** Filicaia, **10/1** Lombard Ocean, **11/1** Toshiba
Comet. CSF £32.65, Tote £5.90: £2.60 £2.20 (£19.20). Exors of the late Mr J. S. Gittins (PRESTON) bred by
Lodge Park Stud. 7 Rn                                                            1m 12.3 (0.6)
SF—78/41/48/38/36/13

---

**1909**   SINGER & FRIEDLANDER H'CAP (3-Y.O) (0-70) £2051.40 (£570.40: £274.20)
**1½m 60y**     (Weights raised 7 lb)                                            8-20 (8-21)

1700⁴ Tales of Wisdom **(60)** *(SirMarkPrescott)* 9-6 AMunro (2) (lw: trckd ldrs: rdn to
ld 2f out: kpt on wl fnl f) .......................................................... —1

1446 Russian Vision **(61)** *(AAScott)* 9-7 JFortune (9) (led 1f: a.p: rdn to chal wl over 1f
out: no ex nr fin) ....................................................................... 1½.2

798⁴ Thor Power (IRE) **(48)** *(DTThom)* 8-8 RCochrane (1) (bhd: hdwy over 3f out:
swtchd ins & styd on u.p fnl f) .................................................. 1.3

1700 Haut-Brion (IRE) **(48)** *(WStorey)* 8-7 LCharnock (3) (in tch: hdwy & ev ch over 1f
out: nt qckn ins fnl f) ................................................................ ¾.4

1783² Bilberry **(47)** *(CWCElsey)* 8-7 LCharnock (5) (led after 1f: drvn along 3f out: hdd
2f out: styd on one pce) .............................................................. 1½.5

1446³ Affirmed's Destiny (USA) **(51)** (Fav) *(JLDunlop)* 8-11 MRoberts (4) (hld up:
hdwy on outside to chal over 2f out: sn rdn: wknd over 1f out) 2.6

1700⁵ Charioteer **(60)** *(PCHaslam)* 9-1 ‡⁵JWeaver (8) (chsd ldrs: rdn & ev ch over 3f
out: wknd 2f out) ...................................................................... 7.7
Capital Lad **(38)** *(MAvison)* 7-12 JLowe (6) (stdd s: a bhd) ........................... 12.8

1150 David's Own **(47)** *(SMellor)* 8-7 DanaMellor (7) (a in rr: lost tch fnl 5f) ............. 15.9

**9/4** Affirmed's Destiny (USA), **11/4** TALES OF WISDOM, **5/1** Charioteer, Bilberry, **11/1** Thor Power (IRE), **12/1**
Russian Vision, **14/1** Haut-Brion (IRE), **25/1** David's Own, **33/1** Capital Lad. CSF £32.57, CT £292.30. Tote
£4.10: £1.70 £2.80 £2.30 (£17.90). Mr Fahd Salman (NEWMARKET) bred by Newgate Stud Co. 9 Rn
2m 39.6 (5.6)
SF—26/24/9/4/3/3

---

**1910**   E.B.F. ST AGNESGATE STKS (Mdn 2-Y.O) £1548.00 (£428.00: £204.00)
**6f**                                                                          8-50 (8-52)

1610⁵ **Premium** (Fav) *(WJHaggas)* 9-0 MRoberts (3) (lw: s.i.s: drvn & hdwy ½-wy:
squeezed thro: led ins fnl f: edgd lft cl home) ............................ —1

15156 Ttyfran *(FHLee)* 9-0 DMcKeown (5) (w ldrs: rdn wl over 1f out: kpt on fnl f) ....... 3/4.2
　Rhett's Choice *(JBerry)* 8-9 GCarter (6) (leggy: scope: bit bkwd: a.p: rdn & slt ld
　　1f out: sn hdd: no ex nr fin) ............................................ 1/2.3
13844 Girl Next Door *(NAGraham)* 8-9 JQuinn (1) (led tl hdd 1f out: no ex) .................. 2.4
　Queen of the Quorn *(GMMoore)* 8-9 RCochrane (8) (w'like: unf: bit bkwd: s.i.s:
　　hdwy appr fnl f: kpt on nr fin) ........................................ 21/2.5
16993 Hawaymyson (IRE) *(JHJohnson)* 8-9 ‡5JWeaver (7) (in tch: rdn over 2f out:
　　wknd appr fnl f) ..................................................... 1/2.6
　Musical Phone *(JPLeigh)* 9-0 KFallon (4) (leggy: scope: s.s: hdwy to chase ldrs
　　1/2-wy: edgd rt & wknd fnl f) ........................................ 2.7
　Challenger Row (IRE) *(CWThornton)* 9-0 MBirch (9) (b.hind: w'like: leggy:
　　scope: in tch 4f) .................................................... 1.8
　Fairy Wish *(CWThornton)* 9-0 GDuffield (2) (cmpt: unf: bit bkwd: s.s: a outpcd) 10.9

**5/6** PREMIUM, **4/1** Hawaymyson (IRE)(3/1—9/2), **9/1** Girl Next Door(op 6/1), **11/1** Rhett's
Choice(6/1—12/1), **16/1** Queen of the Quorn(op 10/1), **20/1** Challenger Row (IRE), **33/1** Ors. CSF £8.54, Tote
£1.80: £1.10 £1.80 £2.30 (£6.00). Kennet Valley Thoroughbreds Ltd (NEWMARKET) bred by Mrs N.
Cunliffe-Lister. 9 Rn 　　　　　　　　　　　　　　　　　　　1m 13.3 (1.6)
　　　　　　　　　　　　　　　　　　　　　　SF—44/41/34/26/16/14

**1911** KIRKGATE H'CAP (0-70) £1702.00 (£472.00: £226.00) **1m** 9-20 (9-28)

*1372* **Shaieef (IRE) (50)** *(RJRWilliams)* 4–8-10 RCochrane (13) (bhd: hdwy on ins wl
　　over 2f out: led jst ins fnl f: r.o wl) ................................. —1
17312 Martini Executive **(63)** (bl) *(BBeasley)* 4–9-9 DNicholls (10) (lw: trckd ldrs gng
　　wl: rdn to ld over 1f out: sn hdd: kpt on) ........................... 11/2.2
1673 Habeta (USA) **(68)** *(JWWatts)* 6–10-0 GDuffield (6) (lw: hdwy 3f out: nt clr run
　　over 1f out: swtchd & kpt on fnl f) .................................. s.h.3
16294 Routing **(57)** *(MDHammond)* 4–9-3 DMcKeown (5) (hld up & bhd: hmpd over
　　2f out: swtchd & styd on strly fnl f) ................................. 21/2.4
1528 Magnetic Point (USA) **(59)** *(AAScott)* 3–8-6 JFortune (11) (led: clr over 3f out:
　　hung lft & hdd over 1f out) .......................................... hd.5
1673 Futures Gift (IRE) **(52)** *(AWPotts)* 3–8-0 ‡3DBiggs (9) (swtg: hdwy over 3f out:
　　kpt on: nvr able to chal) ............................................ 3/4.6
16873 Silver Haze **(59)** *(WAStephenson)* 8–9-5 MBirch (3) (hld up: hdwy & nt clr run
　　over 2f out: n.d) .................................................... 1/2.7
14496 Mofador (GER) **(50)** *(FHLee)* 8–8-10 RLappin (8) (lw: chsd ldr tl rdn & wknd 2f
　　out) ................................................................. 11/2.8
1255 Lightning Spark **(42)** *(MAvison)* 3–7-7 JLowe (2) (lw: sme hdwy over 3f out: n.d) hd.9
17943 Pickles **(47)** (Fav) *(PCHaslam)* 4–8-2 ‡5JWeaver (1) (lw: hdwy on outside over 3f
　　out: sn ev ch: wknd u.p fnl f) ....................................... 1/2.10
*1320*5 Leonadis Polk **(55)** *(JHJohnson)* 3–8-6 KFallon (4) (prom tl wknd over 2f out) . 4.11
　Yeoman Bid **(39)** (bl) *(JDooler)* 5–7-10 ‡3JFanning (3) (chsd ldrs tl wknd 3f out:
　　sn lost tch) ......................................................... 25.12
　Graceland Lady (IRE) **(37)** *(MrsSMAustin)* 4–7-11 PBurke (12) (bit bkwd:
　　unruly s: sn bhd: lost tch fnl 3f) .................................... 11/2.13
　　　　　　　LONG HANDICAP: Lightning Spark 7-5.

**4/1** Pickles, **5/1** Martini Executive, **6/1** Silver Haze, **7/1** Habeta (USA), **8/1** Routing, **10/1** Mofador (GER),
Magnetic Point (USA), **12/1** Futures Gift (IRE), **14/1** Leonadis Polk, **20/1** Lightning Spark, **33/1** SHAIEEF (IRE),
**50/1** Ors. CSF £173.51, CT £1,184.73. Tote £25.10: £5.40 £1.80 £2.30 (£145.30). Mr Terry Minahan
(NEWMARKET) bred by H. H. Aga Khan in Ireland. 13 Rn 　　　　　　1m 40.1 (2.4)
　　　　　　　　　　　　　　　　　　　　SF—36/44/48/29/21/9

T/Plpt: £47.80 (51 Tckts). 　　　　　　　　　　　　　　　　　　　O'R

1741—**WINDSOR (Fig.8)**
**Monday, July 6th [Good]**
Going Allowance: minus 0.05 sec per fur (G) 　　　　　　　　Wind: nil

Stalls: high

**1912** MAIDENHEAD APP'CE (S) H'CAP (3-Y.O) (0-60) £1544.40 (£428.40: £205.20)
**5f 217y** 6-35 (6-37)

1572 **Smudgemupum (44)** *(MissBSanders)* 8-9 MJermy (3) (hdwy 2f out: hrd rdn
　　over 1f out: led ins fnl f: r.o wl) ................................... —1
12772 Kipini **(49)** (Jt-Fav) *(WJMusson)* 9-0 PBowe (10) (swtg: a.p: hrd rdn & ev ch 1f
　　out: r.o) ............................................................. 3/4.2
1642 Sea Crusader **(51)** (bl) *(MBlanshard)* 9-2 JHunter (8) (swtg: led tl ins fnl f) ........ 2.3

1085⁵ Rocky Bay **(43)** *(DHaydnJones)* 8-3 ‡⁵SianWilliams (18) (lw: a.p: r.o one pce fnl
　　　　　2f) ........................................................................................................ ³/₄.**4**
1572 Dollar Wine (IRE) **(50)** (v) *(RHannon)* 8-10 ‡⁵WendyJones (11) (nvr nrr) ...... 1¹/₂.**5**
1146 Aragona **(49)** (bl) *(PDCundell)* 9-0 DGibbs (5) (nrst fin) ....................................... nk.**6**
1642 Bella Run **(35)** *(RJHodges)* 8-0 SDrowne (7) (lw: no hdwy fnl 2f) ....................... nk.**7**
1278 Red Verona **(42)** (Jt-Fav) *(EAWheeler)* 8-7 BThomas (13) (nvr nr to chal) ........ nk.**8**
1741 Lamastre **(44)** *(RJHodges)* 8-4 ‡⁵RWaterfield (6) (nvr trbld ldrs) ..................... 1¹/₂.**9**
1486 Missal (IRE) **(36)** (bl) *(PatMitchell)* 7-10⁽⁴⁾ ‡⁵RTurner (15) (lw: n.d) .................. ³/₄.**10**
1040 Tagetes **(56)** (bl) *(JPearce)* 9-7 FArrowsmith (16) (spd 4f) ............................ 1¹/₂.**11**
734 Little Nod **(54)** *(JWhite)* 9-5 TWilson (14) (lw: n.d) ......................................... 1¹/₂.**12**
1679⁶ Benefact (USA) **(42)** (bl) *(DWPArbuthnot)* 8-7 DDunnachie (12) (n.d) .............. ¹/₂.**13**
1214 Excelled (IRE) **(42)** *(BGubby)* 8-7 CAvery (3) (prom over 3f) ............................. s.h.**14**
1753 Camino a Ronda **(44)** *(PatMitchell)* 8-9 GMilligan (17) (lw: spd over 3f) ......... s.h.**15**
939 Pearly Wine **(52)** (v) *(GBBalding)* 9-3 TraceyPurseglove (4) (prom over 2f: t.o) 15.**16**
1753 Bella Bettina **(50)** (bl) *(JSMoore)* 8-10 ‡⁵DO'Neill (9) (b: t.o) ........................... s.h.**17**

**9/2** Red Verona(8/1—3/1), Kipini, **7/1** Dollar Wine (IRE)(op 4/1), **8/1** Rocky Bay, **9/1** Benefact (USA)(op 5/1),
**10/1** Aragona(7/1—12/1), **12/1** Little Nod(op 7/1), **14/1** Lamastre(op 8/1), Sea Crusader, Pearly White(op 8/1),
Tagetes(op 8/1), **16/1** SMUDGEMUPUM, **33/1** Ors. CSF £84.71, CT £960.29. Tote £40.60: £6.30 1.80 £4.10
£2.30 (£133.90). Mr Mark L. Champion (EPSOM) bred by P. Cook. 17 Rn; No bid
　　　　　　　　　　　　　　　　　　　　　　　　　　　　　　　　　1m 14.5 (4)
　　　　　　　　　　　　　　　　　　　　　　　　　　　　　　　SF—9/11/5/–/–/–

---

**1913**　　E.B.F. DATCHET STKS (Mdn 2-Y.O) £1968.80 (£546.80: £262.40)
　　　　　　**5f 10y**　　　　　　　　　　　　　　　　　　　　　　　　　**7-00 (7-04)**

1469⁵ **Kamaatera (IRE)** (Fav) *(AAScott)* 9-0 WRSwinburn (1) (lw: chsd ldr: led over 1f
　　　　　out: hrd drvn & edgd rt: r.o) ..................................................... —**1**
1450⁴ Two Times Twelve (IRE) (bl) *(JBerry)* 9-0 MHills (3) (lw: led over 3f: r.o one pce) 2¹/₂.**2**
1541⁴ Simply Finesse *(RAkehurst)* 9-0 TQuinn (12) (hdwy over 1f out: r.o ins fnl f) ... 3¹/₂.**3**
Princely Favour (IRE) *(RHannon)* 9-0 PatEddery (8) (scope: bit bkwd: a.p: rdn
　　　　　over 2f out: nt qckn) ............................................................................. 4.**4**
1591⁴ Action Night *(MMoubarak)* 8-9 LDettori (11) (no hdwy fnl 2f) ......................... nk.**5**
Kyrenia Game *(PMitchell)* 8-6 ‡³SO'Gorman (2) (lt-f: s.s: nrst fin) .................. 3¹/₂.**6**
Star Minstrel (IRE) *(MMcCormack)* 9-0 JReid (9) (unf: bit bkwd: nvr nr to chal) ... 1.**7**
1573⁴ Pair of Jacks (IRE) *(WRMuir)* 9-0 SWhitworth (15) (lw: nvr nrr) ..................... ³/₄.**8**
1742⁴ Agil's Pet *(JSutcliffe)* 8-9 BRouse (4) (nvr nr ldrs) ........................................ 1.**9**
Tequila Twist (IRE) *(AAScott)* 8-9 BRaymond (5) (w'like: prom 3f) ................... ¹/₂.**10**
Dents du Midi (USA) *(RWArmstrong)* 8-9 BCrossley (2) (neat: n.d) ................. 5.**11**
Mr Butch *(MRChannon)* 9-0 PaulEddery (6) (scope: n.d) ................................... 2¹/₂.**12**
1349⁶ Rusty Raja *(RHannon)* 9-0 KDarley (10) (a bhd) ........................................... 3¹/₂.**13**
Out of Hours *(DrJDScargill)* 8-9 JWilliams (14) (w'like: bkwd: s.s: a bhd) ....... nk.**14**

**8/11** KAMAATERA (IRE)(1/2—4/5), **3/1** Action Night(5/2—4/1), **4/1** Princely Favour (IRE)(op 6/1), **20/1** Two
Times Twelve (IRE), **33/1** Rusty Raja, Simply Finesse, Star Minstrel (IRE), Tequila Twist (IRE), Out of Hours, Mr
Butch, **50/1** Ors. CSF £18.92, Tote £1.70: £1.20 £2.30 £3.60 (£10.00). Maktoum Al Maktoum (NEWMARKET)
bred by Mrs R. B. Kennard in Ireland. 14 Rn
　　　　　　　　　　　　　　　　　　　　　　　　　　　　　　61.1 sec (2.1)
　　　　　　　　　　　　　　　　　　　　　　　　　　　　　SF—53/43/29/13/7/1

---

**1914**　　TRIPLEPRINT H'CAP (3-Y.O) (0-80) £2679.00 (£744.00: £357.00)
　　　　　　**1m 3f 135y**　　　　　　　　　　　　　　　　　　　　　　**7-30 (7-31)**

700⁶ **Citiqueen (IRE) (70)** *(HRACecil)* 8-12 SCauthen (2) (lw: 3rd st: led over 1f out:
　　　　　drvn out) ........................................................................................... —**1**
1346 Regal Lover (IRE) **(68)** *(MBell)* 8-10 MHills (1) (lw: led tl over 1f out: r.o) ......... 1.**2**
1679³ Ideal Candidate **(51)** *(CACyzer)* 7-7 NAdams (5) (hdwy fnl 3f: nvr nrr) ........... 1¹/₂.**3**
1330* Sovereign Page (USA) **(79)** *(BHanbury)* 9-7 BRaymond (3) (lw: 2nd st: ev ch
　　　　　over 1f out: one pce) ....................................................................... ¹/₂.**4**
1643³ Eleckydo **(51)** *(RJHodges)* 7-7 DaleGibson (12) (nvr nrr) .............................. 10.**5**
1447⁶ Mahairy (USA) **(70)** *(AAScott)* 8-12 WRSwinburn (6) (lw: 6th st: no hdwy) ......... 1.**6**
1679 Dancing Years (USA) **(58)** *(MRChannon)* 7-9 ‡⁵BDoyle (10) (nrst fin) ............... 2.**7**
1346⁴ Valseur (USA) **(75)** *(MrsJCecil)* 9-3 PaulEddery (8) (lw: 5th st: rdn 4f out:
　　　　　sn wknd) .............................................................................................. nk.**8**
1574 Suzie Sue (IRE) **(59)** *(DWPArbuthnot)* 8-1 KDarley (9) (b.hind: lw: nvr nr to chal) 2¹/₂.**9**
1505 Socks and Shares **(66)** *(PWHarris)* 8-8 WNewnes (7) (lw: n.d) ...................... 2.**10**
1634³ Walking on Water **(75)** (bl) *(RFJohnsonHoughton)* 9-3 JReid (11) (lw: dwlt: a
　　　　　bhd: hmpd over 6f out) ........................................................................ 4.**11**
1430⁶ Dominant Force **(64)** *(RHannon)* 8-3 1³RPerham (4) (n.d) ............................. 2¹/₂.**12**
1447 Master of the Rock **(70)** *(PJMakin)* 8-12 TQuinn (13) (4th st: wknd 4f out) ....... 7.**13**
　　　　　　LONG HANDICAP: Ideal Candidate 7-6, Eleckydo 7-4.

**7/4** Valseur (USA), **5/1** Mahairy (USA)(op 10/1), **7/1** CITIQUEEN (IRE)(5/1—8/1), **8/1** Sovereign Page (USA)(6/1—9/1), **11/1** Master of the Rock(8/1—12/1), **12/1** Walking on Water(op 8/1), **14/1** Eleckydo, Dominant Force, **16/1** Dancing Years (USA), Ideal Candidate, **20/1** Regal Lover (IRE), **33/1** Ors. CSF £126.21, CT £1,973.52. Tote £5.10: £1.40 £6.00 £3.20 (£148.80). Mr Ivan Allan (NEWMARKET) bred by Ivan W. Allan in Ireland. 13 Rn                                                      2m 28 (5.5)
SF—37/33/13/40/–/9

---

**1915**   J O HAMBRO STKS (2-Y.O) £2302.50 (£640.00: £307.50)   **5f 217y**   8-00 (8-02)

| | | |
|---|---|---|
| 1639³ | **Port Lucaya** (Fav) *(RHannon)* 9-4 WCarson (12) (lw: a:p: hrd rdn over 3f: ev ch fnl f: carried lft: r.o: fin 2nd, hd: awrdd r) | —1 |
| 1610³ | Iron Merchant (IRE) *(RAkehurst)* 8-11 TQuinn (13) (lw: a:p: led & edgd lft ins fnl f: all out: fin 1st: disq: plcd 2nd) | 2 |
| 1694⁴ | Grand Dancer (IRE) (bl) *(RJRWilliams)* 8-6 MHills (6) (led tl ins fnl f: btn whn bmpd) | 5.3 |
| | Garp (FR) *(MRStoute)* 8-11 PatEddery (9) (unf: scope: s.s: gd hdwy fnl 2f: nvr nrr) | 3¹/₂.4 |
| 1744 | Lincoln Imp (USA) *(AMoore)* 8-11 BRouse (8) (no hdwy fnl 2f) | hd.5 |
| 1259 | Newbury Coat *(MMcCormack)* 8-11 WNewnes (7) (chsd ldr over 4f) | 4.6 |
| 1591 | Arawa *(DMarks)* 8-6 AMcGlone (11) (s.s: nrst fin) | hd.7 |
| | Wolf Power (IRE) *(TThomsonJones)* 8-11 KDarley (4) (str: scope: dwlt: hdwy 4f out: wknd 3f out) | ³/₄.8 |
| | Sea Baron *(MBlanshard)* 8-11 JReid (10) (str: scope: s.s: a bhd) | ¹/₂.9 |
| 1259⁶ | Without a Flag (USA) *(CACyzer)* 8-11 WRSwinburn (1) (outpcd) | 1¹/₂.10 |
| 803 | Monet Order *(JRJenkins)* 8-6 SWhitworth (5) (t.o) | 10.11 |

*Stewards Enquiry: Iron Merchant (IRE) disq. (interference to Port Lucaya ins fnl f).*

**7/4** PORT LUCAYA, **9/4** Garp (FR)(3/1—7/4), **3/1** Iron Merchant (IRE)(5/2—4/1), **10/1** Sea Baron(op 9/2), **12/1** Grand Dancer (IRE)(op 8/1), **16/1** Newbury Coat, **33/1** Ors. CSF £7.85, Tote £2.70: £1.20 £1.40 £1.40 (£3.30). Mr Edward St George (MARLBOROUGH) bred by Cheveley Park Stud Ltd. 11 Rn          1m 13.3 (2.8)
SF—41/35/9/–/–/–

---

**1916**   NATIONAL ASSOCIATION OF BOYS' CLUBS H'CAP (0-90) £2700.80 (£748.80: £358.40)
**1m 67y**   8-30 (8-31)

(Weights raised 8 lb)

| | | |
|---|---|---|
| 1476² | **Bold Boss (86)** (Fav) *(BHanbury)* 3-9-10 LPiggott (5) (lw: 2nd st: led 2f out tl over 1f out: hrd rdn to ld last strides: all out) | —1 |
| 1504³ | Combative (IRE) (83) (v) *(JHMGosden)* 3-9-7 PatEddery (4) (lw: 4th st: rdn 4f out: led over 1f out tl fnl strides) | hd.2 |
| 930 | Thinking Twice (USA) (71) *(PWHarris)* 3-8-9 PaulEddery (10) (3rd st: ev ch over 1f out: r.o one pce) | 2.3 |
| 1413⁵ | Vanroy (68) (v) *(JRJenkins)* 8-9-1 SWhitworth (8) (5th st: r.o one pce fnl 2f) | nk.4 |
| 1611 | Brightness (76) *(MMoubarak)* 3-9-0 LDettori (9) (led to 2f out) | 3.5 |
| 1266 | Tickham Vixen (IRE) (47) *(JDBethell)* 8-11 TyroneWilliams (3) (nvr nr to chal) | 1¹/₂.6 |
| 1303 | Lady Lacey (53) (v) *(GBBalding)* 5-8-0 DaleGibson (7) (nvr trbld ldrs) | 2.7 |
| 1716⁴ | Lucky Noire (59) *(GHarwood)* 4-7-13 ‡⁷GayeHarwood (2) (lw: hdwy 3f out: wknd over 1f out) | 1¹/₂.8 |
| 634 | Karen Louise (70) *(MissHCKnight)* 3-8-8 JReid (6) (7th st: hdwy 3f out: wknd 2f out) | 8.9 |
| 1476 | Bid for Six (USA) (82) *(RHannon)* 3-9-6 WCarson (4) (6th st: wknd 3f out) | 6.10 |

**9/4** BOLD BOSS, **3/1** Combative (IRE), **5/1** Brightness, **8/1** Bid for Six (USA), **10/1** Lady Lacey, Lucky Noire, Thinking Twice (USA), **12/1** Vanroy, **33/1** Karen Louise, **50/1** Tickham Vixen (IRE). CSF £9.65, CT £52.95. Tote £3.00: £1.60 £1.30 £4.00 (£3.80). Mr O. Zawawi (NEWMARKET) bred by Dr O. Zawawi. 10 Rn   1m 44.4 (2.8)
SF—62/58/40/45/35/10

---

**1917**   STAINES STKS   £2285.00 (£635.00: £305.00)   **1¹/₄m 7y**   9-00 (9-02)

| | | |
|---|---|---|
| 1611✳ | **Party Cited (USA) (91)** *(DRCElsworth)* 3-8-9 JWilliams (9) (7th st: led wl over 1f out: drvn clr) | —1 |
| 1402⁴ | Flaming Arrow (97) *(HRACecil)* 4-9-4 WRSwinburn (1) (4th st: ev ch over 1f out: nt qckn) | 3¹/₂.2 |
| 1347² | Yildiz (Fav) *(BWHills)* 3-8-2 MHills (11) (led 4f: 2nd st: led 3f out tl wl over 1f out) | 2.3 |
| 1674⁵ | Headless Heights *(PMitchell)* 3-8-7 TQuinn (13) (lw: 5th st: wknd 2f out) | 8.4 |
| 1596⁵ | Cheveley Dancer (USA) *(AWDenson)* 4-9-4 WNewnes (10) (swtg: led after 4f to 3f out) | ¹/₂.5 |
| 1447 | Hang Ten *(LMCumani)* 3-8-7 LDettori (8) (lw: wl bhd tl r.o fnl 2f) | 3¹/₂.6 |
| 1306⁶ | Silky Siren *(EAWheeler)* 3-8-5⁽³⁾ SWhitworth (12) (8th st: no hdwy fnl 3f) | 3.7 |
| 1705 | Bit on the Side (IRE) *(WJMusson)* 3-7-9 ‡⁷PBowe (5) (nvr nr to chal) | ³/₄.8 |
| 1720 | Cryptic Clue (USA) *(MJHeaton-Ellis)* 3-8-7 AMcGlone (4) (b: lw: 3rd st: wknd over 2f out) | ¹/₂.9 |

| | | |
|---|---|---|
| 1612 | Finaldream (IRE) **(64)** *(AWDenson)* 4-8-13 BRouse (3) (n.d) | $^{1}/_{2}$.**10** |
| | Forge *(PDCundell)* 4-9-4 TRogers (6) (b.off fore: lw: n.d) | 2.**11** |
| 1577 | Jovial Man (IRE) *(SMellor)* 3-8-7 JReid (15) (n.d) | 1$^{1}/_{2}$.**12** |
| 1596⁶ | Tinkosumtin *(PBurgoyne)* 6-8-13 MWigham (7) (n.d) | $^{3}/_{4}$.**13** |
| | Firebird Lad *(RCurtis)* 4-8-13 ‡⁵ATucker (14) (n.d) | 1$^{1}/_{2}$.**14** |
| 1280 | Gabesia *(HJCollingridge)* 4-8-6 ‡⁷CHawksley (2) (6th st: wknd 4f out: t.o) | 8.**15** |

**11/8** Yildiz, **7/4** Flaming Arrow, **4/1** PARTY CITED (USA)(5/2—9/2), **10/1** Hang Ten, **25/1** Cheveley Dancer (USA), **40/1** Silky Siren, **50/1** Headless Heights, **66/1** Ors. CSF £11.39, Tote £5.70: £1.90 £1.10 £1.40 (£6.40). Mr Raymond Tooth (WHITSBURY) bred by Rogers Trust in USA. 15 Rn
2m 6.8 (3.8)
SF—52/54/34/23/33/15

T/Plpt: £17.60 (148 Tckts).                                         Hn

## 1734—**PONTEFRACT (L-H)**

### Tuesday, July 7th [Good to firm, Good fnl 3f]
Going Allowance: 5f-6f: 0.10 sec (G); Rest: minus 0.20 sec (F)
Wind: almost nil

Vis: 6th & 7th races fair

Stalls: low

---

**1918**  WHITELANE-PONTEFRACT APP'CE SERIES STKS (Rnd 2) (Mdn 3-Y.O) £2385.00
      (£660.00: £315.00)  **6f**                                2-20 (2-41)

| | | |
|---|---|---|
| 1532 | **Followmegirls** *(MrsALMKing)* 8-2 AGarth (3) (chsd ldrs: n.m.r & swtchd outside 1f out: r.o wl to ld wl ins fnl f) | —**1** |
| 1433² | Double Shift (Fav) *(RDickin)* 8-2 PTurner (10) (lw: w ldr: rdn over 2f out: led over 1f out tl hdd wl ins fnl f) | 2$^{1}/_{2}$.**2** |
| 727 | Call to the Bar (IRE) *(CGCox)* 8-2 JHunter (4) (led tl over 1f out: r.o one pce) | 1$^{1}/_{2}$.**3** |
| 1661³ | Ergon *(DJSCosgrove)* 8-2 MSimpson (9) (lw: chsd ldrs: outpcd $^{1}/_{2}$-wy: kpt on fnl 2f) | 1$^{1}/_{2}$.**4** |
| 1753 | Virginia Cottage **(41)** *(BAMcMahon)* 8-2 JBramhill (11) (chsd ldrs: rdn $^{1}/_{2}$-wy: wnt lft wl over 1f out: styd on fnl f) | $^{3}/_{4}$.**5** |
| 1683⁴ | Gizlaan (USA) *(BHanbury)* 8-2 VBray (8) (s.s: bhd tl kpt on fnl 2f) | 3.**6** |
| 1661⁶ | Liberty Glen *(BEllison)* 8-2 OPears (6) (chsd ldrs: rdn & wkng whn hmpd wl over 1f out) | $^{3}/_{4}$.**7** |
| 1852³ | North Flyer **(47)** *(BAMcMahon)* 8-7 SSanders (7) (lw: chsd ldrs: rdn $^{1}/_{2}$-wy: sn lost pl) | $^{3}/_{4}$.**8** |
| 1581 | Double Lark **(53)** *(RHollinshead)* 8-2 ‡⁵JDennis (1) (lw: s.s: a in rr) | 3.**9** |
| 1865⁵ | Joie de Patina *(SGNorton)* 8-2 CHawksley (5) (s.i.s: a wl bhd) | 10.**10** |
| 863³ | O'Donnell's Folly **(60)** *(ABailey)* 8-2 ‡⁵DWright (2) (v.unruly, collapsed & died in stalls: Withdrawn under Starter's orders: all stakes refunded) | 0 |

*Stewards Enquiry: Obj. to Followmegirls by Simpson overruled.*

**13/8** Double Shift, **9/2** O'Donnell's Folly, **6/1** Ergon, **7/1** Gizlaan (USA), **17/2** North Flyer, **12/1** Double Lark, **33/1** Call to the Bar (IRE), Virginia Cottage, Joie de Patina, **50/1** Liberty Glen, **100/1** FOLLOWMEGIRLS. CSF £231.97, Tote £72.10: £12.90 £1.30 £7.10 (£77.20). Mr J. Martin (STRATFORD-ON-AVON) bred by Haddon Stud. 11 Rn
1m 18.4 (4.4)
SF—12/2/1/–/–/–

---

**1919**  TANSHELF STKS (Mdn 3-Y.O) £2427.00 (£672.00: £321.00)  **1$^{1}/_{2}$m 8y**  2-50 (3-06)

| | | |
|---|---|---|
| 1180³ | **Funoon (IRE)** (Fav) *(MRStoute)* 8-9 BRaymond (5) (lw: mde virtually all: qcknd clr 3f out: canter) | —**1** |
| 1746 | Friendly House (IRE) *(MAJarvis)* 8-9 ‡⁵KRutter (2) (sn pushed along: chsd wnr fnl 2f) | 10.**2** |
| 1287 | Gaveko (USA) *(JGFitzGerald)* 9-0 KFallon (1) (effrt & n.m.r over 3f out: rdn & wknd over 1f out) | 10.**3** |
| | Kickcashtal *(BAMcMahon)* 9-0 DMcKeown (4) (rangy: swtg: chsd ldrs tl wknd 2f out) | 12.**4** |
| 448⁵ | Galley Gossip **(56)** *(RBrotherton)* 9-0 JWilliams (3) (pld v.hrd: sn disp ld: rn wd bnd 7f out: rdn & wknd over 3f out: sn bhd) | dist.**5** |

**1/11** FUNOON (IRE), **14/1** Friendly House (IRE)(op 9/1), **25/1** Galley Gossip, **33/1** Ors. CSF £2.33, Tote £1.10: £1.10 £2.20 (£2.40). Maktoum Al Maktoum (NEWMARKET) bred by Lyonstown Stud in Ireland. 5 Rn
2m 42.6 (8.1)

---

**1920**  KING RICHARD III H'CAP (0-90) £3054.00 (£912.00: £436.00: £198.00)
      **5f**                                                3-20 (3-28)

| | | |
|---|---|---|
| 1752² | **Metal Boys (83)** *(RHollinshead)* 5-9-4 ‡⁷SWynne (5) (trckd ldrs: qcknd to ld over 1f out: hld on wl) | —**1** |

1736⁵ Drum Sergeant (60) (bl) *(JParkes)* 5–8-2 NCarlisle (4) (trckd ldrs: effrt & n.m.r over 1f out: r.o ins fnl f) ............................... 1.2

Ballasecret (74) *(RDickin)* 4–8-9 ‡7PTurner (9) (bit bkwd: w ldrs: led 2f out: sn hdd: kpt on fnl f) ............................... ¾.3

1392 My Sovereign (USA) (74) *(JRFanshawe)* 3–8-10 GCarter (7) (lw: sn outpcd: hdwy ½-wy: styd on wl u.p over 1f out: n.m.r & one pce ins fnl f) ............................... hd.4

1511³ Consulate (63) *(JBalding)* 6–8-5 KDarley (8) (lw: sn outpcd: hdwy 2f out: styd on wl fnl f) ............................... 1½.5

813 Adwick Park (86) *(TDBarron)* 4–10-0 AlexGreaves (10) (sn bhd: stdy hdwy over 1f out: styd on strly nr fin) ............................... 1½.6

1727* Samson-Agonistes (73) (Fav) *(BAMcMahon)* 6–9-1 DMcKeown (2) (lw: sn w ldrs: rdn, n.m.r & wknd over 1f out) ............................... 1½.7

669⁶ Cromer's Express (59) *(MissLCSiddall)* 3–7-2(1) ‡7DarrenMoffatt (6) (a in rr: swtchd rt ½-wy) ............................... 1½.8

1676* Palacegate Racing (75) *(JBerry)* 3–8-11 JCarroll (1) (lw: led to 2f out: wkng whn bdly hmpd jst ins fnl f) ............................... ½.9

1776⁶ Banbury Flyer (54) *(MrsALMKing)* 4–7-7(2) ‡3FNorton (3) (w ldrs: wkng whn bdly hmpd jst ins fnl f) ............................... ½.10

**13/8** Samson-Agonistes, **5/1** METAL BOYS, **7/1** My Sovereign (USA), **8/1** Palacegate Racing, Consulate, Banbury Flyer, **10/1** Drum Sergeant, **25/1** Cromer's Express, Adwick Park, **33/1** Ballasecret. CSF £49.56, CT £1,357.93. Tote £6.10: £2.20 £2.80 £7.10 (£14.70). North Staffs Racing Club (UPPER LONGDON) bred by Patrick Walshe. 10 Rn
64 sec (2.5)
SF–64/44/50/48/37/54

## 1921

NYQUIST H'CAP (0-80) £3817.00 (£1140.00: £545.00: £247.50)  **1m 4y** 3-50 (3-54)
(Weights raised 3 lb)

1846³ **Causley (69)** (Jt-Fav) *(BAMcMahon)* 7–9-10 DMcKeown (6) (lw: mde all: clr 2f out: drvn along & styd on gamely) ............................... —1

1090⁵ Golden Chip (IRE) (64) *(APStringer)* 4–9-0 ‡5SMaloney (3) (a chsng ldrs: effrt over 2f out: kpt on: no imp) ............................... 3.2

1627* Great Lord (IRE) (66) (Jt-Fav) *(JWWatts)* 3–8-12 BRaymond (2) (lw: hld up: hdwy 3f out: rdn over 1f out: hung lft: kpt on nr fin) ............................... s.h.3

1634 Sword Master (74) *(BobJones)* 3–9-6 GCarter (1) (lw: sn bhd: drvn along ½-wy: kpt on fnl 2f) ............................... 3½.4

1718 Spanish Love (42) *(CGCox)* 6–7-4(4) ‡7CHawksley (7) (chsd wnr tl wknd over 2f out) ............................... 3½.5

1563⁵ Dragon Spirit (61) (bl) *(SPCWoods)* 3–8-7 WWoods (5) (lw: chsd ldrs: rdn 3f out: sn lost pl) ............................... 7.6

1157 Penny Orchid (IRE) (75) *(BBeasley)* 3–9-7 DNicholls (4) (effrt 5f out: wknd over 3f out: eased whn no ch) ............................... 7.7
LONG HANDICAP: Spanish Love 7-0.

**5/2** CAUSLEY, Great Lord (IRE), **5/1** Sword Master, **6/1** Golden Chip (IRE), **7/1** Dragon Spirit, **12/1** Penny Orchid (IRE), **50/1** Spanish Love. CSF £15.70, Tote £3.00: £1.40 £2.40 (£6.40). Mr Henry Pearce (TAMWORTH) bred by L. M. Shepherd. 7 Rn
1m 45.1 (3.5)
SF–34/15/12/9/–/–

## 1922

BRADLEY H'CAP (0-70) £2679.00 (£744.00: £357.00)  **1¼m 6y** 4-20 (4-25)

593 **Westfield Moves (IRE) (52)** *(HJCollingridge)* 4–8-13 VSmith (17) (hdwy over 3f out: led ins fnl f: r.o) ............................... —1

1687 Golden Torque (64) *(RBastiman)* 5–9-4 ‡7HBastiman (10) (lw: hld up & bhd: gd hdwy & nt clr rn 3f out: r.o wl u.p fnl f: nt rch wnr) ............................... 1.2

1311⁶ Floating Line (57) *(PWigham)* 4–9-4 ACulhane (11) (a chsng ldrs: kpt on same pce fnl f) ............................... ¾.3

1687⁴ Queens Tour (34) *(MBrittain)* 7–7-9 JLowe (12) (hdwy 4f out: led over 2f out tl ins fnl f: one pce) ............................... nk.4

1430⁴ Garda's Gold (33) *(RDickin)* 9–7-1(1) ‡7DarrenMoffatt (4) (lw: s.i.s: bhd: hdwy on outside over 3f out: kpt on: nvr able to chal) ............................... 1½.5

1520² Sinclair Lad (IRE) (54) (Fav) *(RHollinshead)* 4–9-1 WRyan (18) (lw: trckd ldrs: effrt over 2f out: wknd over 1f out) ............................... 5.6

1274 Cornhill Melody (33) *(JLSpearing)* 4–7-8(1) AMackay (7) (styd on fnl 2f: nvr nr to chal) ............................... ¾.7

1585⁴ Docket (USA) (57) *(BHanbury)* 4–9-4 DMcKeown (2) (chsd ldrs tl wknd 2f out) ............................... s.h.8

1501 High Savannah (65) *(MAJarvis)* 4–9-12 BRaymond (19) (chsd ldrs tl wknd wl over 1f out) ............................... hd.9

Red Jam Jar (40) *(JMackie)* 7–8-1 GCarter (1) (bit bkwd: swtg: chsd ldrs tl lost pl 2f out) ............................... hd.10

1063⁶ Swift Silver (50) *(WJMusson)* 5–8-11 JHBrown (9) (b: hld up & bhd: stdy hdwy 2f out: fin strly: nvr plcd to chal) ............................... 1½.11

1438[5] Hot Tip **(44)** *(BEllison)* 3–7-8[(1)] NCarlisle (3) (swtg: hld up: stdy hdwy 5f out: n.m.r & wknd over 1f out) ............................................. hd.**12**

1691[4] Trojan Lancer **(60)** *(DrJDScargill)* 6–9-0 ‡7BLane (15) (lw: hld up & bhd: stdy hdwy over 1f out: nvr plcd to chal) ...................... s.h.**13**

713 Admiralty Way **(51)** *(RBrotherton)* 6–8-12 JWilliams (16) (swtg: chsd ldrs tl lost pl 3f out) ........................................................ nk.**14**

1527 Spanish Whisper **(35)** *(JRBostock)* 5–7-3[(3)] ‡7CHawksley (14) (mde most tl hdd & wknd over 2f out) .................................. 1½.**15**

1673 Parr (IRE) **(48)** *(JMackie)* 4–8-9 KFallon (5) (lw: chsd ldrs: drvn along ½-way: lost pl 3f out) .............................................. 3½.**16**

1784 John Shaw (USA) **(67)** *(JSWainright)* 4–10-0 PBurke (6) (n.d) .................... 4.**17**

1213 First Heiress (IRE) **(57)** (v) *(MRStoute)* 3–8-7 MBirch (13) (w ldrs tl wknd over 2f out: t.o) ........................................ **18**

1777 So Beguiling (USA) **(46)** *(MrsALMKing)* 3–7-7[(3)] ‡3FNorton (8) (swtg: w ldrs tl lost pl over 4f out: t.o) ................................ **19**

LONG HANDICAP: Garda's Gold 6-13, Cornhill Melody 7-2, So Beguiling (USA) 7-3.
*Stewards Enquiry: Brown fined £300 under Rule 151 (failure to run horse on its merits).*

**5/1** Sinclair Lad (IRE)(6/1—8/1), **11/2** Floating Line, **7/1** Swift Silver, **9/1** Trojan Lancer, **10/1** First Heiress (IRE)(8/1—12/1), **12/1** WESTFIELD MOVES (IRE), High Savannah, Golden Torque, Docket (USA)(op 8/1), Queens Tour, **14/1** Parr (IRE), **16/1** Garda's Gold, **20/1** Hot Tip, **25/1** Spanish Whisper, Admiralty Way, **33/1** Red Jam Jar, Cornhill Melody, **50/1** Ors. CSF £145.84, CT £822.08. Tote £10.70: £2.20 £4.90 £2.80 £2.40 (£114.20). Mr H. J. Collingridge (NEWMARKET) bred by Eugene Matthews in Ireland. 19 Rn   2m 11.8 (3.5)
SF—44/47/45/21/10/28

---

**1923**  MONKHILL AUCTION STKS (Mdn 2-Y.O) £2427.00 (£672.00: £321.00)
6f                                                        4-55 (4-56)

1327[5] **Milngavie (IRE)** (Jt-Fav) *(MJohnston)* 9 0 DMcKeown (10) (lw: chsd ldrs: r.o strly to ld wl ins fnl f) ........................... —**1**

*1549* Colfax Starlight *(BSRothwell)* 8-9 JFortune (2) (led: clr over 1f out: rdn & no ex nr fin) ............................................. ¾.**2**

1638[5] Cherubini (Jt-Fav) *(JRFanshawe)* 9-0 GCarter (3) (lw: sn wl outpcd: hdwy over 1f out: styd on nr fin) ................... 2½.**3**

Daily Sport's Gift *(JBerry)* 9-0 JCarroll (6) (lengthy: unf: s.i.s: outpcd: hdwy over 1f out: kpt on) ............................ ¾.**4**

1297[4] Valere Knight (IRE) *(CGCox)* 9-0 JBramhill (8) (lw: trckd ldrs tl wknd 2f out) ... 2½.**5**

Oxrib *(CTinkler)* 9-0 TLucas (5) (w'like: bit bkwd: s.s: hdwy on outside ½-way: rn green & wknd 1f out) ................... 2½.**6**

1660 Newinsky (v) *(CTinkler)* 9-0 BRaymond (9) (w ldrs 4f: sn lost pl) .............. 2½.**7**

1690[5] Admission (IRE) *(MHEasterby)* 9-0 MBirch (1) (sn outpcd) ................ 4.**8**

1531 Honeymoon Dawn *(RMWhitaker)* 8-9 ACulhane (7) (trckd ldrs tl wknd 2f out) .................................................. 1½.**9**

**3/1** MILNGAVIE (IRE), Cherubini, **7/2** Valere Knight (IRE), **7/1** Newinsky, **14/1** Daily Sport's Gift(op 7/1), Colfax Starlight, Admission (IRE)(op 8/1), **16/1** Honeymoon Dawn, **33/1** Oxrib. CSF £37.34, Tote £4.30: £1.40 £3.00 £1.40 (£36.00). Mr A. S. Robertson (MIDDLEHAM) bred by D. Oldrey and D. P. Aykroyd in Ireland. 9 Rn
1m 19.5 (5.5)
SF—2/–/–/–/–/–

---

**1924**  LEVY BOARD H'CAP (0-70) £2807.00 (£777.00: £371.00)   6f        5-25 (5-26)
(Weights raised 2 lb)

1731 **Blue Grit (40)** *(MDods)* 6–8-6 KFallon (4) (lw: trckd ldrs: led over 1f out: drvn clr: eased nr fin) ........................... —**1**

1508[5] State Flyer **(58)** (v) *(CBBBooth)* 4–9-3 ‡7GForster (4) (lw: s.s: gd hdwy on outside over 2f out: edgd lft u.p: kpt on: no ch w wnr) ........ 1.**2**

*1550* A Little Precious **(58)** (Fav) *(JRBostock)* 6–9-10 BRaymond (5) (hld up: hdwy on ins 2f out: nt clr rn: r.o ins fnl f) .......... 2.**3**

1570 Johanna Thyme **(36)** *(RBastiman)* 5–7-13 ‡3FNorton (7) (lw: a chsng ldrs: styd on one pce fnl 2f) ................... nk.**4**

794 Chaplins Club (USA) **(45)** (bl) *(DWChapman)* 12–8-11 KDarley (9) (sn wl outpcd: hdwy over 3f out: styd on wl) ....... 2½.**5**

1583[3] Last Straw **(40)** *(AWJones)* 4–8-6 NCarlisle (3) (lw: chsd ldrs: wkng whn n.m.r 1f out) ........................... 1½.**6**

1793[3] Chain Shot **(48)** (bl) *(MHEasterby)* 7–9-0 MBirch (1) (lw: w ldr: led over 2f out: hdd & wknd over 1f out) ...... 1.**7**

1328[5] Dandy Desire **(55)** *(BCMorgan)* 3–9-0 DMcKeown (8) (chsd ldrs over 3f: sn wknd) ............................ 2½.**8**

541 Kabera **(28)** *(DWChapman)* 4–7-8 SWood (2) (led: hung rt & hdd over 2f out: sn lost pl) ............................ 5.**9**

**9/4** A Little Precious, **4/1** Last Straw, **9/2** Chain Shot, **6/1** State Flyer, Johanna Thyme, **11/1** Dandy Desire, **12/1** Chaplins Club (USA), **14/1** BLUE GRIT, **66/1** Kabera. CSF £90.05, CT £240.10. Tote £21.10: £3.10 £1.90 £1.50 (£48.80). Mr C. Michael Wilson (DARLINGTON) bred by Collinstown Stud Farm Ltd. 9 Rn        1m 17.6 (3.6)
SF—32/39/38/12/14/3

T/Plpt: £143.40 (20.15 Tckts).                                                                        WG

1701—**NEWMARKET (R-H)** July Course

**Tuesday, July 7th [Good]**

Going Allowance: minus 0.20 sec per fur (F)                               Wind: slt bhd

Stalls: low

**1925**     PLANTATION STKS (Mdn 2-Y.O) £4386.00 (£1308.00: £624.00: £282.00)
            **7f**                                                    2-00 (2-02)

1471² **Lord President (USA)** *(Fav)* *(PFICole)* 9-0 AMunro (6) (lw: mde all: shkn up
        appr fnl f: r.o wl) ............................................................ —1
      Lacotte (IRE) *(JHMGosden)* 9-0 SCauthen (1) (gd sort: bkwd: a chsng ldrs: effrt
        2f out: r.o) .................................................................. 5.2
      Persiansky (IRE) *(BHanbury)* 9-0 WRSwinburn (4) (cmpt: scope: hld up & bhd:
        hdwy over 2f out: nt qckn fnl f) ............................................. 4.3
      Cristal Flite *(RHannon)* 8-9 WCarson (2) (w'like: scope: b.nr hind: dwlt: pushed
        along & hdwy ½-wy: nt qckn appr fnl f) ...................................... ¾.4
      Declassified (USA) *(LMCumani)* 9-0 LDettori (5) (str: scope: bkwd: hld up:
        swtchd & effrt 2f out: edgd lft & nvr nr to chal) ......................... 2½.5
      Mukhamedov *(HRACecil)* 9-0 PatEddery (3) (wl grwn: bkwd: s.i.s: sn trckng
        ldrs: pushed along 3f out: wknd 2f out: eased) ............................. 5.6
      Rusty Reel *(CEBrittain)* 9-0 MRoberts (3) (w'like: scope: lw: spd over 3f: sn
        bhd) ........................................................................ nk.7

**5/4** LORD PRESIDENT (USA)(6/4—Evens), **7/4** Mukhamedov(Evens—9/4), **4/1** Lacotte (IRE), **25/1** Declassified (USA)(op 8/1), **33/1** Cristal Flite, **50/1** Ors. CSF £6.29, Tote £2.20: £1.30 £2.60 (£4.40). Mr Fahd Salman (WHATCOMBE) bred by H.J.Boone Jnr, H.Boone III, S.A.Boone etc in USA. 7 Rn    1m 26.61 (2.21)
SF—46/31/19/12/9/–

**1926**     FAIRVIEW NEW HOMES H'CAP (3-Y.O) (0-110) £7765.00 (£2320.00: £1110.00:
            £505.00)   **6f**                                          2-35 (2-38)

1870⁴ **Master Planner (91)** *(CACyzer)* 8-7 TQuinn (6) (lw: a.p: led over 1f out: hung
        lft: r.o) .................................................................... —1
  673* Night Manoeuvres (105) *(HCandy)* 8-7 WNewnes (13) (lw: sn outpcd & bhd:
        hdwy 2f out: r.o wl) ........................................................ 2.2
1400⁴ Flute (USA) (88) *(Fav)* *(CEBrittain)* 8-4 MRoberts (10) (lw: s.i.s: sn rcvrd to
        chase ldrs: nt qckn fnl f) .................................................. 1.3
1345⁵ Milagro (87) *(RHannon)* 8-3 WCarson (2) (mde most tl hdd over 1f out: kpt on
        same pace) ................................................................ ¾.4
1467⁴ Fylde Flyer (105) *(JBerry)* 9-7 LPiggott (9) (disp ld over 4f: sn rdn & btn) ......... 2.5
  678⁴ Don't Smile (80) *(MHTompkins)* 7-5⁽³⁾ ‡$DHarrison (7) (sn drvn along: hdwy 2f
        out: nvr nr to chal) ........................................................ 1.6
1219* Hazm (USA) (90) *(HThomsonJones)* 8-6 RHills (12) (w ldrs tl wknd appr fnl f) . nk.7
1400  Master of Passion (97) *(JMPEustace)* 8-13 RCochrane (3) (disp ld 4f: grad
        wknd) ...................................................................... ¾.8
1345* Sunday's Hill (102) *(MBlanshard)* 9-4 JReid (5) (w trbld ldrs) .................. ½.9
1608⁵ Castlerea Lad (79) *(RHollinshead)* 7-9 JQuinn (4) (chsd ldrs over 4f) ......... ½.10
1533  Jade Vale (78) *(JWHills)* 7-8 SDawson (11) (nvr wnt pce) .................... ¾.11
1596⁴ Berseto (84) *(HRACecil)* 8-0 AMcGlone (8) (s.i.s: drvn along thrght & a
        bhd) ........................................................................ 2.12
  381a Sylvan Sabre (IRE) (94) *(PMitchell)* 8-10 WRSwinburn (1) (unruly s: dwlt: a
        bhd) ....................................................................... 3½.13
                LONG HANDICAP: Don't Smile 7-3.

**5/1** Flute (USA), **6/1** Night Manoeuvres, **7/1** Berseto (USA), Fylde Flyer, **9/1** MASTER PLANNER, **10/1** Hazm (USA), Milagro, **14/1** Don't Smile, Sunday's Hill, **16/1** Jade Vale, **20/1** Master of Passion, Castlerea Lad, **33/1** Sylvan Sabre (IRE). CSF £55.36, CT £272.63. Tote £10.70: £3.40 £1.10 £1.70 (£26.40). Mr R. M. Cyzer (HORSHAM) bred by C. A. Cyzer. 13 Rn                                    1m 12.51 (1.01)
SF—49/55/34/30/40/6

**1927**     HILLSDOWN CHERRY HINTON STKS (Gp 3) (2-Y.O.F) £19305.00 (£7169.00: £3397.00:
            £1429.00)   **6f**                                         3-05 (3-06)

1538² **Sayyedati** *(Fav)* *(CEBrittain)* 8-9 MRoberts (7) (lw: stdd s: qcknd to ld 2f out:
        rdn out) .................................................................... —1

1461³ Toocando (IRE) *(CNAllen)* 8-9 RCochrane (4) (s.i.s: hld up: hdwy 2f out: hrd rdn & r.o wl fnl f) ............................................ ¹/₂.2
1461² Mystic Goddess (USA) *(MRStoute)* 8-9 PatEddery (2) (lw: cl up: led over 3f out to 2f out: hrd rdn & r.o) ................................ s.h.3
1469* Niche *(RHannon)* 9-0 LPiggott (6) (lw: trckd ldrs: disp ld over 2f out: rdn & nt qckn appr fnl f) .......................... 2¹/₂.4
1171* Spark (IRE) *(CWCElsey)* 8-9 LDettori (5) (a.p: drvn along ¹/₂-wy: no imp) .......... 5.5
1461 Amirati (USA) *(AAScott)* 8-9 WRSwinburn (3) (spd over 3f: sn wknd) ................. 6.6
1215* Anonymous (99) *(CEBrittain)* 8-9 SCauthen (1) (led over 2f: sn outpcd & bhd) 12.7

**6/4** SAYYEDATI, **2/1** Mystic Goddess, **5/1** Niche(3/1—11/2), **10/1** Amirati (USA), Toocando (IRE)(7/1—12/1), **33/1** Anonymous, **100/1** Spark (IRE). CSF £14.76, Tote £2.70: £1.60 £3.10 (£11.40). Mr Mohamed Obaida (NEWMARKET) bred by Gainsborough Stud Management Ltd. 7 Rn   1m 12.86 (1.36)
SF—44/42/41/36/11/-

---

**1928**    H & K COMMISSIONS H'CAP (3-Y.O.F) (0-110) £11647.50 (£3480.00: £1665.00: £757.50)   7f
3-35 (3-36)

1750² **Miss Haggis (79)** (Jt-Fav) *(RBoss)* 8-9 (6x) PatEddery (7) (lw: hld up: smooth hdwy over 2f out: led appr fnl f: rdn & r.o) .................................... —1
1523³ Mrs Fisher (IRE) (90) *(SirMarkPrescott)* 9-6 GDuffield (3) (chsd ldrs: rdn & ev ch 2f out: r.o) ............................ 1¹/₂.2
1641* Lady Debra Darley (77) (Jt-Fav) *(RHannon)* 8-7 MRoberts (1) (lw: a cl up centre: hrd rdn appr fnl f: nt qckn nr fin) .......................... hd.3
1533 Castilian Queen (USA) (79) *(JHMGosden)* 8-9 (5³) RCochrane (6) (hld up & bhd: hdwy 2f out: r.o) .......................... s.h.4
1533³ Louisville Belle (IRE) (66) *(MDIUsher)* 7-5³ ‡5DHarrison (4) (a.p: n.m.r over 1f out: kpt on one pce) ............................ 1¹/₂.5
1363² Elanmatina (IRE) (76) *(CFWall)* 8-6 NDay (5) (chsd ldrs: outpcd whn sltly hmpd over 2f out: stya on fnl f) .......................... 2¹/₄.6
1641² Rose Indien (FR) (90) *(MMoubarak)* 9-6 LDettori (8) (w ldrs tl wknd ins fnl f) ...... 2.7
1611³ Enaya (90) *(RWArmstrong)* 9-6 WCarson (1) (lw: cl up: led over 2f out tl appr fnl f: no ex) .......................... ¹/₂.8
1678* Badawiah (74) *(WAO'Gorman)* 8-4 AMunro (12) (b: hld up: effrt over 2f out: n.d) 3¹/₂.9
1363* Olette (79) *(GWragg)* 8-9 WRSwinburn (14) (racd centre: led tl hdd over 2f out: edgd lft & sn wknd) .......................... hd.10
1216 Swallowcliffe (91) *(PTWalwyn)* 9-7 JReid (9) (hld up: effrt & wnt lft 3f out: sn btn) 5.11
1124⁴ Mount Helena (84) *(HRACecil)* 9-0 SCauthen (10) (lw: chsd ldrs tl wknd 2f out) 1¹/₂.12
631 Nimble Deer (75) *(NCWright)* 8-0 ‡5BDoyle (2) (led far side over 4f: sn wknd) 1¹/₂.13
1597² Lady Buchan (79) *(MrsJCecil)* 8-9 PaulEddery (13) (racd centre: effrt ¹/₂-wy: sn btn) .......................... 12.14
LONG HANDICAP: Louisville Belle (IRE) 7-6.

**13/2** Lady Debra Darley, MISS HAGGIS, **7/1** Mount Helena(10/1—6/1), Rose Indien (FR), **9/1** Castilian Queen (USA), **10/1** Mrs Fisher (IRE), Olette, **12/1** Badawiah, **14/1** Enaya, Elanmatina (IRE), Lady Buchan, Louisville Belle (IRE), **33/1** Ors. CSF £63.25, CT £398.31. Tote £6.80: £2.70 £2.10 £1.50 (£20.40). Mr P. Asquith (NEWMARKET) bred by Cheveley Park Stud Ltd. 14 Rn   1m 26.15 (1.75)
SF—48/50/40/41/18/25

---

**1929**    PRINCESS OF WALES'S STKS (Gp 2)   £40746.00 (£15156.80: £7203.40: £3053.80)
1¹/₂m
4-10 (4-11)

1205* **Saddlers' Hall (IRE)** (Fav) *(MRStoute)* 4-9-5 PatEddery (2) (lw: trckd ldr: led over 1f out: pushed along & r.o wl) ........................... —1
1473³ Luchiroverte (IRE) *(CEBrittain)* 4-9-0 MRoberts (1) (lw: led tl hdd over 1f out: kpt on wl) .......................... 3.2
1646a* Mashaallah (USA) *(JHMGosden)* 4-9-5 SCauthen (3) (a chsng ldrs: rdn over 4f out: kpt on wl) .......................... ¹/₂.3
1646a⁴ Always Friendly *(HCandy)* 4-8-11 AMunro (4) (s.i.s: drvn along 4f out: a last) .... 3.4

**4/7** SADDLERS' HALL (IRE), **4/1** Mashaallah (USA), **13/2** Always Friendly, **10/1** Luchiroverte (IRE). CSF £5.23, Tote £1.50 (£3.20). Lord Weinstock (NEWMARKET) bred by Ballymacoll Stud Farm Ltd. in Ireland. 4 Rn   2m 31.01 (2.31)
SF—58/47/51/37

---

**1930**    CHESTERFIELD H'CAP (0-100) £5900.00 (£1760.00: £840.00: £380.00)
1m
4-45 (4-47)

1706² **Sahel (IRE) (85)** *(JHMGosden)* 4-9-5 SCauthen (11) (hld up: hdwy 2f out: led ins fnl f: r.o wl) .......................... —1
1799⁴ Polonez Prima (76) (Fav) *(JEBanks)* 5-8-5 ‡5LNewton (2) (lw: chsd ldrs: rdn to ld over 1f out: sn hdd: kpt on) .......................... 1¹/₂.2

626* Little Rousillon **(65)** *(ACStewart)* 4–7-13 MRoberts (7) (in tch: drvn along over 2f out: r.o wl nr fin) ........................................ nk.3

1795* Inseyab **(63)** *(PCHaslam)* 4–7-8 (5x) ‡³JFanning (10) (chsd ldrs: rdn & ev ch over 1f out: r.o one pce) ........................................ 1.4

*1544** Usa Dollar **(60)** (bl) *(BGubby)* 5–7-8(1) JQuinn (5) (hdwy ½-wy: sn rdn: chsd ldrs 2f out: nt qckn) ........................................ 2.5

1463 Absonal **(77)** *(RHannon)* 5–8-11 PatEddery (4) (hld up & bhd: effrt over 2f out: styd on) ........................................ s.h.6

1463 Heart of Darkness **(94)** (bl) *(IABalding)* 4–10-0 JReid (12) (lw: hld up & bhd: hdwy 3f out: nt qckn fnl f) ........................................ s.h.7

1504 Rise Up Singing **(70)** (bl) *(WJMusson)* 4–8-4 TQuinn (3) (led: hrd rdn 2f out: hdd appr fnl f: wknd nr fin) ........................................ ½.8

1365³ Sugemar **(62)** *(JARToller)* 6–7-10(1) WCarson (8) (in tch: pushed along ½-wy: wknd 2f out) ........................................ 6.9

Elegant Friend **(74)** *(MHTompkins)* 4–8-8 PRobinson (9) (a bhd) ........................................ 1½.10

392 State Dancer (USA) **(88)** *(MMoubarak)* 5–9-8 LDettori (1) (chsd ldrs tl rdn & wknd over 2f out) ........................................ 2½.11

1061 *Venus Observed **(92)** *(HCandy)* 4–9-5 ‡7AntoinetteArmes (6) (chsd ldrs: chal & rdn 3f out: sn wknd) ........................................ 8.12

LONG HANDICAP: Usa Dollar 7-4.

**9/2** Polonez Prima(6/1—4/1), **5/1** SAHEL (IRE)(7/1—9/2), **8/1** Little Rousillon, **9/1** Sugemar, State Dancer (USA), **10/1** Inseyab, Venus Observed, Absonal, Heart of Darkness, **12/1** Usa Dollar, **14/1** Rise Up Singing, **33/1** Elegant Friend. CSF £26.08, CT £162.93. Tote £4.40: £1.80 £2.30 £2.10 (£6.80). Sheikh Mohammed (NEWMARKET) bred by Oldtown Stud in Ireland. 12 Rn

1m 39.62 (1.92)
SF—52/33/26/18/12/28

**1931** SOHAM H'CAP (0-90) £4935.00 (£1470.00: £700.00: £315.00)  **5f**  5-15 (5-16)

1771⁴ Aughfad **(83)** (v) *(TCasey)* 6–9-7 JReid (9) (cl up centre: effrt 2f out: r.o strly fnl f to ld nr fin) ........................................ —1

1406⁵ No Quarter Given **(70)** *(PSFelgate)* 7–8-8 TQuinn (6) (sn led centre: led over 1f out: r.o wl to ld cl home: jst ct) ........................................ nk.2

1837² Dominuet **(85)** (Jt-Fav) *(JLSpearing)* 7–9-9 GHind (8) (lw: s.i.s: hdwy centre ½-wy: ev ch ins fnl f: r.o) ........................................ hd.3

1736³ Pageboy **(84)** (bl) *(PCHaslam)* 3–9-2 LPiggott (2) (racd far side: led: hrd rdn fnl f: ct cl home) ........................................ ½.4

1247 Pallium (IRE) **(73)** *(MPNaughton)* 4–8-6 ‡5JWeaver (3) (a chsng ldrs far side: hrd rdn over 1f out: kpt on) ........................................ hd.5

1607² Touch of White **(81)** (bl) *(JEBanks)* 6–9-5 RCochrane (1) (trckd ldrs far side: effrt over 1f out: hrd rdn & nt qckn) ........................................ 2.6

1763² Sylvan Breeze **(84)** *(PMitchell)* 4–9-8 SWhitworth (4) (effrt ½-wy: rdn & no imp) 2½.7

1593² Tongue Tied **(69)** (Jt-Fav) *(JWharton)* 4–8-7 WCarson (5) (spd centre 3f: sn wknd) ........................................ 10.8

1757 Paley Prince (USA) **(90)** *(MDIUsher)* 6–10-0 SCauthen (7) (outpcd & bhd fr ½-wy) ........................................ 2½.9

**4/1** Tongue Tied, Dominuet, **5/1** Touch of White, **13/2** Pageboy, **8/1** AUGHFAD, **10/1** No Quarter Given, Pallium (IRE), **12/1** Sylvan Breeze(op 8/1), **20/1** Paley Prince (USA). CSF £71.46, Tote £9.20: £2.70 £2.10 £2.10 (£63.50). Mr M. Mac Carthy (UPPER LAMBOURN) bred by M. Mac Carthy. 9 Rn

59.69 sec (0.69)
SF—73/59/73/64/53/58

T/Trio: Race 2: £27.80 (42.7 Tckts) and race 3: £22.10 (63.8 Tckts). T/Jkpt: £15,233.10 (0.85 Tckts); £3,087.79 to Newmarket 8/7/92. T/Plpt: £30.00 (314.1 Tckts).
AA

# NEWMARKET (R-H) July Course
## Wednesday, July 8th [Good]
Going Allowance: nil sec per fur (G)                    Wind: almost nil

Stalls: low

**1932** ELLESMERE (S) STKS (2-Y.O) £3817.50 (£1140.00: £545.00: £247.50)  **7f**

2-00 (2-02)

Wynona (IRE) *(GCBravery)* 8-12 WRSwinburn (8) (lt-f: unf: hld up: swtchd outside & hdwy 2f out: led 1f out: r.o strly) ........................................ —1

1775² Bird Hunter *(NACallaghan)* 8-6 ‡7JTate (5) (mde most tl 1f out: hrd rdn & unable qckn fnl f) ........................................ 3½.2

1675* Strike-a-Pose (Jt-Fav) *(CNWilliams)* 8-8 JQuinn (6) (plld hrd: a.p: rdn & kpt on ins fnl f) ........................................ ½.3

1638 After the Last (Jt-Fav) *(RHannon)* 8-13 WCarson (4) (lw: w ldr: rdn & no ex fnl f) ½.4

1442 Heroic Deed *(MHTompkins)* 8-13 PRobinson (9) (hld up: hdwy 2f out: nt rch ldrs) .................... 2¹/₂.**5**
1749* Comtec's Legend *(JFBottomley)* 8-3 ‡⁵NKennedy (2) (mid div: rdn 2f out: styd on: nt pce to chal) .................... 3.**6**
　　　Home Affair *(DTThom)* 8-12 LDettori (3) (neat: dwlt: sn rcvrd: rdn & wknd fnl 2f) nk.**7**
1591 Arewenearlythere (IRE) *(MBlanshard)* 8-8 WRyan (1) (chsd ldrs: rdn 3f out: sn btn) .................... 5.**8**
　928 Miss Ribbons *(PatMitchell)* 8-9 ‡³DBiggs (10) (rdn along ¹/₂-wy: nvr plcd to chal) 1.**9**
1754⁵ Hallplace *(MRChannon)* 9-7 PatEddery (12) (lw: chsd ldrs 5f: sn lost pl) ........ 1¹/₂.**10**
1630³ Sharro *(PAKelleway)* 9-7 MRoberts (7) (chsd ldrs over 4f: sn rdn & wknd: t.o) . 5.**11**
1571 Galactic Fury *(BStevens)* 8-13 AMcGlone (11) (bhd fr ¹/₂-wy: t.o) .................... ³/₄.**12**

**5/2** After the Last(op 5/1), Strike-a-Pose, **6/1** WYNONA (IRE)(7/2—13/2), **13/2** Bird Hunter(op 4/1), **8/1** Sharro(6/1—9/1), Hallplace, **10/1** Comtec's Legend, **20/1** Arewenearlythere (IRE), Heroic Deed, Home Affair, **33/1** Ors. CSF £47.35, Tote £8.90: £2.00 £2.10 £1.80 (£35.40). Mrs M. Wyn Griffith (NEWMARKET) bred by Rathduff Stud in Ireland. 12 Rn; Bt in 8,500 gns; Bird Hunter clmd R Mous £10,000
SF—35/18/18/21/13/–

**1933**　　　MORE O'FERRALL PLC STKS (Mdn 3-Y.O) £4581.00 (£1368.00: £654.00: £297.00)
　　　　　　**1¹/₄m**　　　　　　　　　　　　　　　　　　　2-35 (2-40)

1505² **United Kingdom (USA)** (Fav) *(HRACecil)* 8-9 SCauthen (8) (lw: a.p: led over 1f out: v.easily) .................... —**1**
　531² Garden of Heaven (USA) *(CEBrittain)* 9-0 MRoberts (3) (a.p: led 2f out tl appr fnl f: sn outpcd) .................... 3.**2**
　433⁶ Blessington (USA) *(JHMGosden)* 9-0 WCarson (2) (a.p: ev ch 2f out: one pce fnl f) .................... 2¹/₂.**3**
　　　Larrikin (USA) *(LordHuntingdon)* 8-9 WRSwinburn (7) (leggy: scope: s.i.s: stdy hdwy fnl 3f: nrst fin) .................... 4.**4**
1505⁶ Resplendent *(NCWright)* 8-9 GDuffield (6) (lw: led to 2f out: sn rdn & btn) ........ 2.**5**
1505 Wild Applause (IRE) *(JHMGosden)* 8-9 LDettori (5) (b.nr hind: s.i.s: styd on ins fnl f: nvr nrr) .................... 1¹/₂.**6**
1672⁴ Kanvass *(JRFanshawe)* 9-0 GCarter (1) (chsd ldrs: rdn over 3f out: grad wknd) ¹/₂.**7**
　　　Green Flower *(MRStoute)* 8-9 PatEddery (11) (neat: hld up in rr: sme hdwy appr fnl f: nvr nrr) .................... ¹/₂.**8**
　　　Jahangir (IRE) *(BHanbury)* 9-0 BRaymond (4) (w'like: scope: prom tl grad wknd fnl 3f) .................... ¹/₂.**9**
1505 Jade Mistress *(AHide)* 8-9 WRyan (9) (chsd ldrs 7f: sn outpcd) .................... hd.**10**
1516⁴ Music in My Life (IRE) (63) *(WJarvis)* 8-9 LPiggott (10) (hld up: a.p: rdn 3f out: sn wknd & t.o) .................... 25.**11**

**Evens** UNITED KINGDOM (USA), **3/1** Blessington (USA), **7/1** Garden of Heaven (USA)(6/1—10/1), **14/1** Larrikin (USA)(8/1—16/1), **16/1** Green Flower (USA)(op 6/1), Wild Applause (IRE), Resplendent, **33/1** Music in My Life (IRE), **50/1** Ors. CSF £8.77, Tote 2.10: £1.20 £1.80 £1.70 (£4.50). Sheikh Mohammed (NEWMARKET) bred by Darley Stud Management Company Ltd in USA. 11 Rn
2m 7.66 (5.06)
SF—45/44/39/26/22/19

**1934**　　　H.E. LIMITED DUKE OF CAMBRIDGE H'CAP (3-Y.O) (0-115) £15400.00 (£4600.00: £2200.00: £1000.00)　**1¹/₄m**　　　　　　　　　3-10 (3-13)

1080² **Duke of Eurolink (87)** *(LMCumani)* 7-13³ ‡⁵JWeaver (11) (chsd ldrs: led over 2f out: pushed clr fnl f) .................... —**1**
1466 Bold Stroke (88) *(JLDunlop)* 8-5 WCarson (10) (lw: plld hrd: a.p: kpt on u.p fnl f: no ch w wnr) .................... 2¹/₂.**2**
1029* Scandalmonger (USA) (79) *(BWHills)* 7-5² ‡⁵DHarrison (1) (lw: s.s: stdy hdwy 4f out: effrt & ch 2f out: one pce fnl f) .................... ³/₄.**3**
1466⁴ Bayaireg (USA) (85) *(AAScott)* 8-2 JFortune (6) (stdd s: hdwy on ins 3f out: n.m.r over 1f out: one pce) .................... 1¹/₂.**4**
1577* Jumaira Shark (CAN) (84) (Fav) *(JHMGosden)* 8-1 PaulEddery (2) (hld up: hdwy & ev ch over 2f out: unable qckn) .................... 3.**5**
1643² Grog (IRE) (79) *(MRChannon)* 7-5³ ‡⁵BDoyle (7) (chsd ldr: led over 3f out tl over 2f out: sn btn) .................... ¹/₂.**6**
1466 Sayh (87) *(MAJarvis)* 8-4 LDettori (3) (led tl over 3f out: sn rdn & wknd) .......... 4.**7**
　789* Green Lane (IRE) (88) *(RCharlton)* 8-5² PatEddery (9) (chsd ldrs: rdn along over 2f out: sn outpcd) .................... 3¹/₂.**8**
1703² Anne Bonny (88) *(JRFanshawe)* 8-5 GDuffield (8) (lw: hld up: plld hrd: effrt over 3f out: no imp) .................... 1.**9**
1533* Calpella (83) *(JARToller)* 8-0 MRoberts (4) (lw: hld up: hdwy on outside 3f out: sn rdn & btn) .................... 1¹/₂.**10**
1197 Fair Crack (IRE) (104) *(RHannon)* 9-7 BRaymond (5) (a in rr: no imp) .......... 1¹/₂.**11**
LONG HANDICAP: Grog (IRE) 7-4.

**1935—1937**

**15/8** Jumaira Shark (CAN), **11/2** Calpella, Bayaireg (USA), **15/2** Green Lane (IRE), **10/1** Anne Bonny, Scandalmonger (USA), **12/1** Bold Stroke, Sayh, **16/1** DUKE OF EUROLINK, **25/1** Grog (IRE), **33/1** Fair Crack (IRE). CSF £175.54, CT £1,835.71. Tote £17.60: £4.00 £3.10 £3.10 (£122.60). Eurolink Computer Services Ltd (NEWMARKET) bred by A. G. Antoniades. 11 Rn                                                                                           2m 7 (4.40)
SF—41/42/26/34/27/16

---

**1935**  FALMOUTH STKS (Gp 2) (F & M) £33390.00 (£12429.50: £5914.75: £2515.75)
        1m                                                                                    3-40 (3-44)

1816a **Gussy Marlowe** *(CEBrittain)* 4–9-1 MRoberts (7) (lw: a.p: led appr fnl f: pushed
        clr & edgd lft fnl f: r.o) ....................................................... —1
1454 Lovealoch (IRE) *(MBell)* 4–9-1 MHills (5) (hld up: outpcd 3f out: gd hdwy fnl 2f:
        no ch w wnr) ....................................................... 3½.2
1462⁴ Wiedniu (USA) *(Jt-Fav) (LordHuntingdon)* 3–8-6 LPiggott (1) (lw: hld up:
        smooth hdwy to ld over 2f out: hrd rdn & hdd appr fnl f) .... ¾.3
845a Twafeaj (USA) *(BHanbury)* 3–8-6 WRSwinburn (2) (hld up & bhd: gd hdwy on
        outside 2f out: no ex fnl f) ....................................................... nk.4
1460 Misterioso (v) *(DRCElsworth)* 3–8-6 WCarson (4) (lw: prom tl rdn & wknd appr
        fnl f) ....................................................... 4.5
1596³ Ships Lantern *(CFWall)* 3–8-6 NCarlisle (3) (plld hrd: chsd ldrs tl wknd over 2f
        out) ....................................................... 3½.6
1462³ Katakana (USA) *(Jt-Fav) (MRStoute)* 3–8-6 PatEddery (6) (led tl hdd & wknd
        over 2f out) ....................................................... 4.7

**5/2** Katakana (USA), Wiedniu (USA), **11/2** Twafeaj (USA), Lovealoch (IRE), **7/1** GUSSY MARLOWE, **8/1** Misterioso, **25/1** Ships Lantern. CSF £40.71, Tote £10.20: £3.10 £3.10 (£21.00). Mrs John Van Geest (NEWMARKET) bred by Mrs John Van Geest. 7 Rn                                                              1m 40.24 (2.54)
SF—63/52/41/40/28/17

---

**1936**  JULY STKS (Gp 3) (2-Y.O.C & G) £13674.00 (£5075.20: £2402.60: £1008.20)
        6f                                                                                    4-10 (4-11)

1701* **Wharf (USA)** *(Fav) (HRACecil)* 8-10 PatEddery (3) (lw: a.p: led 1f out: hrd rdn:
        all out) ....................................................... —1
1457⁶ Canaska Star *(PAKelleway)* 8-10 SCauthen (6) (hld up: hdwy wl over 1f out: str
        chal fnl f: jst hld) ....................................................... nk.2
1457³ Pips Pride *(RHannon)* 8-10 WCarson (2) (lw: mde most to 1f out: rdn & no ex fnl
        f) ....................................................... 3½.3
1485* Majestic Hawk (USA) *(MMoubarak)* 8-10 LDettori (5) (lw: hld up: hdwy to chal
        over 2f out: sn rdn: nt qckn) ....................................................... 1.4
1744* Fortune Cay (IRE) *(RHannon)* 8-10 WRSwinburn (1) (disp ld: ev ch 1f out:
        unable qckn) ....................................................... hd.5
1471⁴ Aljazzaf *(CEBrittain)* 8-10 MRoberts (4) (unruly s: prom 3f: sn outpcd) ............. 7.6

**4/6** WHARF (USA), **4/1** Pips Pride(op 9/4), **8/1** Fortune Cay (IRE)(6/1—9/1), **9/1** Majestic Hawk (USA)(op 6/1), **11/1** Aljazzaf, **66/1** Canaska Star. CSF £22.65, Tote £1.70: £1.30 £6.10 (£28.10). Mr K. Abdulla (NEWMARKET) bred by Juddmonte Farms Inc in USA. 6 Rn                                                              1m 13.49 (1.99)
SF—56/55/41/37/36/8

---

**1937**  PRINCESS STKS (Mdn 2-Y.O.F) £4503.00 (£1344.00: £642.00: £291.00)
        6f                                                                                    4-45 (4-46)

        **Lake Pleasant (IRE)** *(RHannon)* 8-11 BRaymond (6) (neat: scope: a.p: rdn
        appr fnl f: str run fnl f to ld cl home) ....................................................... —1
1591³ Cape Weaver *(Fav) (JHMGosden)* 8-11 SCauthen (3) (b.off hind: plld hrd: mde
        most tl ct cl home) ....................................................... ½.2
        Magique Rond Point (USA) *(HRACecil)* 8-11 PatEddery (9) (w'like: scope: disp
        ld: ev ch tl no ex nr fin) ....................................................... ½.3
        Rapid Repeat (IRE) *(MrsJCecil)* 8-11 PaulEddery (10) (w'like: lw: s.i.s:
        hdwy ½-wy: one pce ins fnl f) ....................................................... 2½.4
1300² Musical Prospect (USA) *(RHannon)* 8-11 MRoberts (1) (lw: chsd ldrs: rdn over
        1f out: one pce) ....................................................... 2½.5
        Westering *(WJarvis)* 8-11 PRobinson (2) (neat: bkwd: hld up & bhd: styd on fnl
        2f: nvr nrr) ....................................................... 4.6
        Cosmic Star *(SPCWoods)* 8-11 WWoods (12) (str: cmpt: bkwd: outpcd) ........... 4.7
        Arjuzah (IRE) *(JHMGosden)* 8-11 WCarson (7) (w'like: scope: bkwd: prom tl
        wknd wl over 1f out) ....................................................... 2.8
        First Affair *(MRStoute)* 8-11 WRSwinburn (5) (b.off hind: cmpt: scope: a in rr) . nk.9
        Aalu (IRE) *(CEBrittain)* 8-11 LDettori (8) (w'like: spd 4f: sn lost tch: t.o) ........... 5.10

**1938—1940**

7/2 Cape Weaver, **4/1** Arjuzah (IRE)(tchd 6/1), **5/1** Musical Prospect (USA), **11/2** Magique Rond Point (USA)(op 7/2), **6/1** Rapid Repeat (IRE)(12/1—14/1), **8/1** LAKE PLEASANT (IRE)(op 4/1), **12/1** First Affair, **20/1** Aalu (IRE), **33/1** Ors. CSF £34.14, Tote £12.80: £2.70 £1.70 £2.10 (£16.70). A. F. Budge (Equine) Limited (MARLBOROUGH) bred by Sir Stanley Grinstead in Ireland. 10 Rn 1m 15.16 (3.66)
SF—24/22/20/10/–/–

| **1938** | REG DAY MEMORIAL TROPHY (H'cap) (0-100) £4464.00 (£1332.00: £636.00: £288.00) 2m 24y | 5-15 (5-20) |
|---|---|---|

1465⁴ **Kansk (90)** (Fav) *(JHMGosden)* 4-9-4 SCauthen (4) (hld up: shkn up to ld ins fnl f: r.o wl) ..... —1

1653² **Mull House (68)** *(FJO'Mahony)* 5-7-5⁽³⁾ ‡5DHarrison (1) (a.p: led over 2f out tl ins fnl f) ..... 1½.2

1697 **Farsi (81)** (bl) *(RHollinshead)* 4-8-9 WRyan (5) (b.nr fore: hld up: rdn over 2f out: styd on fnl f) ..... hd.3

1073 **Magic Secret (68)** *(PCHaslam)* 4-7-10 EJohnson (3) (bhd: effrt 4f out: nt rch ldrs) ..... 4.4

724⁶ **Close Friend (IRE) (100)** *(BWHills)* 4-10-0 PatEddery (8) (hld up: effrt over 4f out: rdn & no imp) ..... 6.5

1866² **Moving Out (77)** *(SirMarkPrescott)* 4-8-5 MHills (7) (led tl over 2f out: sn rdn & wknd) ..... 3.6

605 **Shentit (FR) (73)** *(JLDunlop)* 4-8-1 PRobinson (2) (lw: bhd & rdn 5f out: no imp) 5.7

1606* **Our Aisling (76)** *(SGNorton)* 4-7-11⁽¹⁾ ‡7OPears (6) (plld hrd: hld up: rdn 4f out: sn btn) ..... ½.8

1381* **Gay Glint (88)** *(NAGraham)* 5-9-2 WRSwinburn (9) (lw: jnd ldr 6f out: rdn & wknd 2f out) ..... 1.9

LONG HANDICAP: Mull House 7-2.

**2/1** KANSK, **5/1** Our Aisling, **13/2** Gay Glint(op 4/1), Farsi, **9/1** Moving Out, Mull House(op 16/1), **10/1** Close Friend (IRE), **14/1** Shentit (FR), **20/1** Magic Secret. CSF £10.00, CT £01.20, Tote £2.30: £1.50 £2.60 £2.40 (£21.60). Sheikh Mohammed (NEWMARKET) bred by Sheikh Mohammed bin Rashid al Maktoum. 9 Rn 3m 30.81 (7.81)
SF—26/–/14/–/19/–

T/Trio: Race 3: £1,888.30 (1 Tckt). T/Jkpt: Not won; £5,910.29 to Newmarket 9/7/92. T/Plpt: £539.20 (17.25 Tckts). IM

# NEWMARKET (R-H) July Course
## Thursday, July 9th [Good]
Going Allowance: minus 0.05 sec per fur (G)                                    Wind: almost nil

Stalls: low

| **1939** | CHILD & CO. SUPERLATIVE STKS (listed race) (2-Y.O) £8975.00 (£2675.00: £1275.00: £575.00) 7f | 2-00 (2-01) |
|---|---|---|

1690* **Ardkinglass** *(HRACecil)* 9-0 PatEddery (6) (cl up: slt ld over 2f out: shkn up appr fnl f: r.o wl) ..... —1

1348³ **White Crown (USA)** *(BHanbury)* 8-11 WRSwinburn (1) (sn trckng ldrs: effrt 2f out: r.o u.p) ..... 2½.2

1471* **Humam (IRE)** (Fav) *(HThomsonJones)* 9-2 RHills (2) (lw: trckd ldrs: outpcd 2f out: hrd rdn & kpt on) ..... ¾.3

1457⁵ **Geisway (CAN)** *(RHannon)* 8-11 WCarson (3) (lw: in tch: pushed along 3f out: r.o fnl f) ..... ¾.4

1600* **Shamisen** *(CEBrittain)* 8-6 MRoberts (5) (led tl hdd over 2f out: wknd over 1f out) ..... 6.5

1595⁴ **Iommelli (IRE)** *(PAKelleway)* 8-11 LDettori (4) (lw: in tch tl outpcd over 2f out) ..... 3.6

1502⁷ **Timothy Casey** *(NCWright)* 8-11 SCauthen (7) (hld up: effrt over 2f out: n.d) ..... ½.7

**6/5** Humam (IRE), **7/2** ARDKINGLASS(5/2—4/1), **5/1** Geisway (CAN)(op 11/4), **13/2** Shamisen, **12/1** Timothy Casey(8/1—14/1), **20/1** White Crown (USA), **66/1** Iommelli (IRE). CSF £49.75, Tote £4.90: £2.10 £4.00 (£92.80). Sir David Wills (NEWMARKET) bred by Sir H. D. H. Wills. 7 Rn 1m 26.07 (1.67)
SF—70/59/62/55/32/28

| **1940** | BAHRAIN TROPHY (Stks) (listed race) (3-Y.O) £9688.00 (£2884.00: £1372.00: £616.00) 1³⁄₄m 175y | 2-35 (2-37) |
|---|---|---|

1633* **Rain Rider** (Jt-Fav) *(JLDunlop)* 8-10 WCarson (5) (lw: trckd ldrs: effrt over 2f out: r.o to ld wl ins fnl f) ..... —1

1458⁶ **Bonny Scot (IRE) (104)** (Jt-Fav) *(LMCumani)* 9-1 LDettori (1) (lw: cl up: led & qcknd over 2f out: hrd rdn, hdd & no ex nr fin) ..... ½.2

1665* **Brier Creek (USA) (90)** *(JHMGosden)* 8-10 RCochrane (4) (led tl hdd over 2f out: sn outpcd) ..... 15.3

1534* For Mog (USA) **(84)** *(CEBrittain)* 8-10 MRoberts (3) (cl up tl wknd over 2f out) 3½.4
1395² Free Transfer (IRE) **(69)** *(PFTulk)* 8-10 JReid (2) (lost tch fnl 4f) ...................... 12.5
1464³ Goldsmiths' Hall **(98)** *(GWragg)* 8-10 SCauthen (6) (swvd sltly s: sddle slipped
　　　 & uns rdr) ...................................................................................................... 0

**9/4** Bonny Scot (IRE), RAIN RIDER, **100/30** Goldsmiths' Hall(2/1—7/2), **13/2** Brier Creek (USA), **8/1** For Mog (USA), **50/1** Free Transfer (IRE). CSF £7.29, Tote £2.90: £1.80 £1.90 (£4.60). Mrs E. M. H. Ogden White (ARUNDEL) bred by Ash Hill Stud. 6 Rn　　　　　　　　　　　　　　　　　　3m 12.72 (6.72)
　　　　　　　　　　　　　　　　　　　　　　　　　　　　　　　　　SF—22/26/6/2/–

**1941**　　TNT AVIATION H'CAP (3-Y.O) (0-110) £9625.00 (£2125.00 each: £625.00)
　　　　　1m　　　　　　　　　　　　　　　　　　　　　　　　　3-05 (3-08)
　　　　　　　　　　　　　(Weights raised 10 lb)
　1476 **Little Bean (79)** (Jt-Fav) *(GWragg)* 8-6 RCochrane (9) (lw: hld up: hdwy 2f out:
　　　　　str run fnl f to ld cl home) ..................................................................... —1
　1480³ Big Leap (IRE) **(89)** *(MMoubarak)* 9-2 LDettori (6) (hld up: stdy hdwy to ld over
　　　　　1f out: r.o u.p: no ex cl home) ................................................................. nk.2
　1476* Efharisto **(87)** (Jt-Fav) *(CEBrittain)* 9-0 MRoberts (8) (a cl up: chal over 1f out:
　　　　　r.o) .............................................................................................................. d.h.2
　　942 Lord Vivienne (IRE) **(72)** *(PFICole)* 7-10 ‡³FNorton (2) (w ldrs: led 4f out to 3f
　　　　　out: kpt on one pce) ..................................................................................... 3½.4
　1628* Wellington Rock (USA) **(80)** *(JARToller)* 8-7 PatEddery (5) (lw: hld up & bhd:
　　　　　hdwy 3f out: rdn 2f out: r.o) ..................................................................... 1½.5
　1599³ Trial Times (USA) **(73)** *(WAO'Gorman)* 7-11 ‡³EmmaO'Gorman (10) (w ldrs: slt
　　　　　ld 3f out tl hdd & wknd over 1f out) ......................................................... s.h.6
　1476⁶ Grand Vitesse (IRE) **(80)** *(RHannon)* 8-7 JReid (11) (hld up: effrt 3f out: no imp) 1½.7
　1476 Shati (IRE) **(92)** *(HThomsonJones)* 9-5 RHills (7) (in tch tl outpcd over 3f out: no
　　　　　imp after) .................................................................................................. nk.8
　　585² Majboor (IRE) **(94)** *(PTWalwyn)* 9-7 WCarson (4) (prom: drvn along 3f out:
　　　　　wknd 2f out) .............................................................................................. 1½.9
　1692² Showgi (USA) **(88)** *(JRFanshawe)* 9-1 WRSwinburn (3) (lw: chsd ldrs 6f) ......... 8.10
　1166* Risk Master **(81)** *(CAHorgan)* 8-8 AMcGlone (1) (led tl hdd 4f out: sn wknd) . 2½.11

**4/1** Efharisto, LITTLE BEAN, **6/1** Wellington Rock (USA), **8/1** Big Leap (IRE), **9/1** Showgi (USA), **10/1** Risk Master, **12/1** Lord Vivienne (IRE), **20/1** Ors. CSF w BL £16.78, w E £9.74, CT w BL & E £60.04, w E & LB £53.45. Tote £4.70: £1.60 £2.40 BL £1.70 E (w BL £7.10, w E £3.40). Sir Philip Oppenheimer (NEWMARKET) bred by Hascombe and Valiant Studs. 11 Rn　　　　　　　1m 39.67 (1.97)
　　　　　　　　　　　　　　　　　　　　　　　　　　　　　SF—56/65/66/35/41/30

**1942**　　JULY CUP (Gp 1)　　£92619.50 (£34200.50: £16350.25: £6613.75: £2556.88:
　　　　　£934.12)　**6f**　　　　　　　　　　　　　　　　　　　3-40 (3-42)
　1475² **Mr Brooks** *(RHannon)* 5-9-6 LPiggott (6) (lw: hld up: gd hdwy over 1f out:
　　　　　edgd lft: r.o to ld wl ins fnl f) ................................................................... —1
　1460² Pursuit of Love *(HRACecil)* 3-8-13 PatEddery (4) (lw: trckd ldrs: nt clr run &
　　　　　swtchd rt over 1f out: swtchd lft 1f out: r.o wl) ........................................ hd.2
　1475* Sheikh Albadou (Fav) *(AAScott)* 4-9-6 WRSwinburn (7) (b.hind: lw: cl up: led &
　　　　　qcknd wl over 1f out: hdd wl ins fnl f: r.o) ............................................... nk.3
　1475³ Elbio *(PJMakin)* 5-9-6 LDettori (5) (lw: trckd ldrs: n.m.r over 1f out: r.o) ......... 1½.4
　1475 Paris House *(JBerry)* 3-8-13 JCarroll (8) (s.i.s: sn trckng ldrs: led wl over 1f out:
　　　　　sn hdd & btn) .............................................................................................. 6.5
　1475⁴ Wolfhound (USA) *(JHMGosden)* 3-8-13 SCauthen (8) (lw: prom: shkn up 2f
　　　　　out: nt qckn) .............................................................................................. 1½.6
　1467* Shalford (IRE) *(RHannon)* 4-9-6 MRoberts (1) (slt ld over 4f: sn btn) ............. 3.7
　1875² Tbab (IRE) *(CEBrittain)* 4-9-6 BRaymond (3) (swtg: w ldrs 4f: sn rdn & btn) .... d.h.7

**15/8** Sheikh Albadou, **9/4** Shalford (IRE), **5/1** Wolfhound (USA), **13/2** Pursuit of Love, **9/1** Elbio, **16/1** MR BROOKS, **33/1** Paris House, **50/1** Tbab (IRE). CSF £103.41, Tote £12.40: £1.70 £1.40 £1.40 (£31.50). Mr Paul Green (MARLBOROUGH) bred by Mrs J. R. Rossdale. 8 Rn　　　　　　　　　1m 11.80 (0.30)
　　　　　　　　　　　　　　　　　　　　　　　　　　　　　SF—94/86/92/86/55/49

**1943**　　LADBROKE BUNBURY H'CAP (0-115) £21525.00 (£6450.00: £3100.00: £1425.00)
　　　　　**7f**　　　　　　　　　　　　　　　　　　　　　　　4-10 (4-14)
　1474 **Consigliere (85)** *(RCharlton)* 4-9-1 PaulEddery (5) (b: trckd ldrs: led over 2f
　　　　　out & qcknd: hrd rdn & jst hld on) .......................................................... —1
　　692 Ashdren **(79)** *(AHarrison)* 5–8-9 WRSwinburn (9) (hdwy over 2f out: r.o wl fnl f) hd.2
　1463 Knight of Mercy **(98)** *(RHannon)* 6-10-0 BRaymond (2) (in tch: hdwy 3f out: sn
　　　　　chsng ldrs: kpt on wl fnl f) ........................................................................ nk.3
　1463 Superoo **(74)** *(JSutcliffe)* 6-8-4 WNewnes (7) (lw: hld up & bhd: hdwy 3f out: r.o
　　　　　wl nr fin) .................................................................................................... s.h.4

1696\* Superbrave **(77)** *(WJarvis)* 6–8–7 JCarroll (13) (lw: bhd: nt clr run 3f out: hdwy
over 1f out: r.o wl) ............................................................................. 2.5

1712[4] Mutabahi (CAN) **(87)** *(RWArmstrong)* 3–8–9 WCarson (3) (outpcd & bhd tl
hdwy 3f out: nrst fin) ............................................................. nk.6

1463 Field of Honour **(81)** *(LMCumani)* 4–8–11 LDettori (12) (hld up: effrt over 2f out:
r.o one pce fnl f) ........................................................................... 1½.7

1771\* Running Glimpse (IRE) **(69)** *(MissBSanders)* 4–9–7 ‡[3]FNorton (20) (lw: w
ldrs centre: nt qckn appr fnl f) ................................................. s.h.8

1201 Deprecator (USA) **(91)** *(JHMGosden)* 4–9–7 RCochrane (19) (b.hind: swtg:
hdwy stands' side 2f out: r.o) ................................................... 1½.9

653[3] Sir Boudle (IRE) **(85)** *(CRNelson)* 3–8–7 JReid (14) (bhd tl styd on wl fnl 2f) .. 1½.10

1615 Cheveux Mitchell **(75)** (v) *(MRChannon)* 5–8–5 RHills (1) (swtg: led tl hdd over
2f out: sn outpcd) ...................................................................... nk.11

1529\* Affordable **(65)** *(WCarter)* 4–7–9 JQuinn (16) (chsd ldrs centre: hrd rdn 2f out:
grad wknd) ................................................................................. nk.12

1133[4] Mango Manila **(88)** *(CAHorgan)* 7–9–4 SCauthen (8) (b: hld up & bhd: effrt 2f
out: nvr rchd ldrs) ..................................................................... nk.13

1391\* Owner's Dream (USA) **(78)** *(BHanbury)* 3–7–9 ‡[5]DHarrison (18) (swtg: cl up
centre over 5f) .......................................................................... ¾.14

1403\* Ringland (USA) **(84)** *(PCHaslam)* 4–9–0 LPiggott (10) (prom early: bhd fr ½-wy) ½.15

1696[2] Nordic Brave **(76)** *(MBrittain)* 6–8–6 AMunro (4) (chsd ldrs far side over 4f) .. 1½.16

1463[4] High Low (USA) **(90)** *(WJHaggas)* 4–9–6 PatEddery (6) (cl up far side over 4f) ½.17

1463 Go Executive **(92)** *(CEBrittain)* 4–9–3 ‡[5]BDoyle (15) (chsd ldrs centre over 4f) 1½.18

1487[5] Gentle Hero **(85)** *(MPNaughton)* 6–8–10 ‡[5]JWeaver (17) (prom centre
over 4f) ..................................................................................... hd.19

1805[2] Desert Splendour **(73)** (Fav) *(CEBrittain)* 4–8–3 MRoberts (11) (lw: w ldr centre
4f: sn rdn & wknd) ..................................................................... 1½.20

**7/1** Desert Splendour(9/1—6/1), **8/1** High Low (USA), **9/1** Superbrave, **10/1** Field of Honour, CONSIGLIERE,
**11/1** Mango Manila, Superoo, **12/1** Ringland (USA), **14/1** Gentle Hero (USA), Deprecator (USA), **16/1** Owner's
Dream (USA), Knight of Mercy, **20/1** Running Glimpse (IRE), Mutabahi (CAN), Sir Boudle (IRE), **25/1** Nordic
Brave, Go Executive, **33/1** Ors. CSF £270.66, CT £4,668.65. Tote £12.50: £2.90 £5.30 £5.40 £4.30 (£192.30).
Mr Terry Ellis (BECKHAMPTON) bred by E. Aldridge. 20 Rn
                                                1m 26.02 (1.62)
SF−71/64/82/57/54/55

---

**1944**    E.B.F. FULBOURN STKS (Mdn 2-Y.O.C & G) £4347.00 (£1296.00: £618.00: £279.00)
           **6f**                                                     4-45 (4-46)

1701[2] **Right Win (IRE)** (Fav) *(RHannon)* 9–0 MRoberts (5) (lw: mde all: qcknd 2f out:
easily) ........................................................................................ −1

Wathik (USA) *(HThomsonJones)* 9–0 RHills (4) (gd sort: bit bkwd: a chsng ldrs:
kpt on fnl 2f: no chn w wnr) ...................................................... 3.2

Devilry *(GLewis)* 9–0 PaulEddery (1) (gd sort: lw: w ldrs tl outpcd wl over 2f out) 4.3

Bezique (USA) *(JHMGosden)* 9–0 SCauthen (6) (cmpt: bkwd: a chsng ldrs:
shkn up 2f out: nt qckn) ............................................................ hd.4

1502 Divine Rain *(JWPayne)* 9–0 RCochrane (2) (sn outpcd & wl bhd: hdwy 2f out:
eased fnl f) ................................................................................ 5.5

968 Venture Prints *(RChampion)* 9–0 JReid (3) (prom tl outpcd fnl 2f) ................. ½.6

**4/9** RIGHT WIN (IRE), **5/1** Bezique (USA), **11/2** Wathik (USA)(op 5/2), **12/1** Devilry, **40/1** Divine Rain, **100/1**
Venture Prints. CSF £3.46, Tote £1.50: £1.20 £1.90 (£2.90). Mr Conal Kavanagh (MARLBOROUGH) bred by
Ovidstown Investments Ltd in Ireland. 6 Rn
                                             1m 15.70 (4.20)
SF−10/−/−/−/−/

T/Trio: Race 3: £23.20 (80.9 Tckts) and Race 4: any 2 fr 1st 3 w any £35.60 (88.3 Tckts). T/Jkpt: Not won;
£12,042.09 to York 10/7/92. T/Plpt: £193.80 (60.05 Tckts).                        AA

---

1880—**BATH (L-H)**

**Wednesday, July 8th [Firm]**

Going Allowance: 5f-5f 161y: minus 0.30 (F); Rest: minus 0.50 (H)       Wind: almost nil

Stalls: low

**1945**    SALTFORD APP'CE H'CAP (0-70) £2192.00 (£612.00: £296.00)
           **1¼m 46y**                                            2-15 (2-16)

(Weights raised 2 lb)

1680[3] **Now Boarding (39)** *(RJHodges)* SDrowne (8) (chsd ldr: 2nd st: led 2f
out: edgd lft over 1f out & ins fnl f: r.o) ................................... −1

1572[3] Trendy Auctioneer (IRE) **(37)** (bl) (Fav) *(MCPipe)* 4–8–12 SWynne (1) (hdwy on
ins 7f out: 3rd st: ev ch fnl f: r.o) ............................................. hd.2

1341 Emrys **(37)** *(DBurchell)* 9–8–12 SMulvey (5) (led over 8f: btn whn n.m.r wl ins fnl f) ...................................................................................................... 1¹/₂.**3**

1341 Hills of Hoy **(47)** *(KCBailey)* 6–9–5 ‡³SBusfield (2) (lw: hld up: 4th st: no hdwy fnl 3f) ...................................................................................................... 8.**4**

1739⁶ Bronze Runner **(40)** (bl) *(EAWheeler)* 8–9–1 GMilligan (6) (hdwy 7f out: 5th & wkng st) ...................................................................................................... 3.**5**

891 At Peace **(51)** *(JWhite)* 6–9–12⁽²⁾ TThompson (7) (b: 6th st: a bhd) .................. s.h.**6**

1682 *Tapestry Dancer **(35)** (MJHaynes)* 4–8–10 DToole (4) (last st: t.o fnl 3f) ........ 30.**7**

**3/1** Trendy Auctioneer (IRE), **100/30** NOW BOARDING, **7/2** Hills of Hoy, **4/1** Bronze Runner, **7/1** At Peace(5/1—8/1), **14/1** Tapestry Dancer, **16/1** Emrys. CSF £13.21, CT £123.67. Tote £3.50: £1.80 £1.80 (£6.70). Miss M. E. Gibbon (SOMERTON) bred by Heytesbury Stud. 7 Rn
2m 11 (3.3)
SF—17/14/11/2/–/–

**1946**     E.B.F. EVERSHOT STKS (Mdn 2-Y.O) £2929.50 (£812.00: £388.50)
        **5f 161y**
2-50 (2-53)

1658² **Ventiquattrofogli (IRE)** (Fav) *(JLDunlop)* 9-0 JReid (3) (a.p: led over 1f out: hrd rdn fnl f: r.o) ...................................................................................... —**1**

1652³ Conspicuous (IRE) *(PFICole)* 9-0 AMunro (2) (a.p: rdn & ev ch fnl f: r.o) .......... hd.**2**

1635² Sophisticated Air *(IABalding)* 8-9 RCochrane (1) (s.i.s: hdwy on ins 3f out: r.o one pce fnl 2f) .......................................................................................... 6.**3**

Fairy Story (IRE) *(JWHills)* 8-9 RHills (6) (unf: scope: bkwd: plld out over 1f out: r.o fnl f: nvr nrr) ............................................................................................ ³/₄.**4**

1652² Bellsabanging *(DRLaing)* 9-0 TyroneWilliams (7) (led over 4f: hrd rdn & wknd fnl f) ...................................................................................................... 1¹/₂.**5**

Sian Wyn *(JBerry)* 8-9 JCarroll (5) (leggy: unf: lw: prom: rdn over 3f out: wknd over 2f out) ............................................................................................ 7.**6**

Kildee Lad *(APJones)* 9-0 NAdams (8) (str: cmpt: bit bkwd: dwlt: rdn & hdwy over 3f out: wknd 1f out) ........................................................................ 1¹/₂.**7**

555 Perigord (IRE) *(WRMuir)* 9-0 SWhitworth (9) (lw: prom: hrd rdn & edgd rt over 2f out: wknd wl over 1f out) .................................................................. 1.**8**

1283 Go Orange *(JLSpearing)* 8-9 NHowe (4) (dwlt: a bhd: t.o) ................................ 5.**9**

1610 Conbrio Star *(CGCox)* 9-0 AClark (10) (bhd fnl 2f: t.o) .............................. 2¹/₂.**10**

**13/8** VENTIQUATTROFOGLI (IRE), **5/2** Sophisticated Air(2/1—3/1), **7/2** Conspicuous (IRE), **7/1** Bellsabanging, **11/1** Fairy Story (IRE)(10/1—16/1), **16/1** Sian Wyn(op 8/1), **33/1** Perigord (IRE), **50/1** Conbrio Star, Kildee Lad, **66/1** Go Orange. CSF £8.11, Tote £2.20: £1.10 £1.40 £1.30 (£5.80). Gerecon Italia (ARUNDEL) bred by Kiltinan Farms Inc in Ireland. 10 Rn
1m 10.6 (1.3)
SF—40/39/10/7/6/–

**1947**     BE HOPEFUL H'CAP (0-80) £3673.00 (£1099.00: £527.00: £241.00)
        **1m 5y**
3-25 (3-27)

1747★ **Neptune's Pet (71)** (Fav) *(GLewis)* 4-10-0 (6x) JReid (2) (hld up: 7th st: hdwy 3f out: rdn to ld wl ins fnl f) .................................................. —**1**

1681★ *Confronter **(77)** (PFICole)* 3-9-11 TQuinn (9) (swtg: hld up: 8th st: hdwy 3f out: led over 1f out: hdd wl ins fnl f) .................................................. nk.**2**

1756⁴ Aldahe **(44)** *(BRMillman)* 7-8-1 DaleGibson (3) (2nd st: ev ch 2f out: one pce) .. 6.**3**

931 Lord Oberon (IRE) **(67)** *(RJO'Sullivan)* 4-9-10 AMunro (1) (9th st: hdwy fnl 2f: nvr nrr) ...................................................................................................... 1.**4**

1721 Green's Stubbs **(36)** (v) *(ABarrow)* 5-7-7 NAdams (4) (swtg: led over 6f out tl wknd over 1f out) .................................................................................. 4.**5**

1755³ Mustahil (IRE) **(70)** *(RJHodges)* 3-9-1 ‡³TSprake (8) (swtg: 6th st: wknd 2f out) . 4.**6**

1677³ Mulciber **(71)** (bl) *(GHarwood)* 4-10-0 AClark (6) (prom: 4th & rdn st: wknd 3f out) ...................................................................................................... 5.**7**

Ballymac Girl **(60)** *(CTNash)* 4-9-3 WNewnes (7) (b: s.s: last st: a in rr) .......... hd.**8**

1718² Charmed Knave **(55)** *(DRLaing)* 7-8-12 TyroneWilliams (10) (lw: 5th st: wknd 2f out) ...................................................................................................... 1.**9**

1885³ Emaura **(60)** *(KOCunningham-Brown)* 3-8-8 DHolland (5) (led over 1f: 3rd & rdn st: wknd over 2f out) .......................................................... 1¹/₂.**10**

LONG HANDICAP: Green's Stubbs 6-8.

**4/1** NEPTUNE'S PET, **9/2** Confronter, **13/2** Lord Oberon (IRE), Aldahe(op 4/1), **7/1** Mustahil (IRE), **8/1** Charmed Knave, **9/1** Mulciber, **12/1** Emaura(op 8/1), **50/1** Ors. CSF £19.55, CT £87.99. Tote £4.20: £1.60 £1.90 £2.10 (£5.00). K. B. Symonds and Partners (EPSOM) bred by D. G. Mason. 10 Rn   1m 38.9 (0.1 under best; U.4)
SF—60/56/14/34/–/–

**1948**     LIMPLEY STOKE STKS (Mdn 3-Y.O.F) £2178.00 (£608.00: £294.00)
        **1¹/₄m 46y**
3-55 (3-58)

689⁵ **Cunning** (Fav) *(LMCumani)* 8-11 RCochrane (2) (hld up: 4th st: led wl over 1f out: sn clr: eased ins fnl f) .................................................. —**1**

| | | |
|---|---|---|
| 1319 | Rosina Mae *(LordHuntingdon)* 8-11 AMunro (6) (rdn over 2f out: styd on fnl f: no ch w wnr) | 2½.2 |
| 1594² | Wassl This Then (IRE) **(72)** *(DWPArbuthnot)* 8-11 TQuinn (4) (led over 2f: 2nd st: led 3f out tl wl over 1f out: one pce) | 1.3 |
| 1408² | Forgetful **(56)** *(DBurchell)* 8-6 ‡⁵RPrice (5) (3rd st: wknd wl over 1f out) | 6.4 |
| 1648² | Choppy Choppy (USA) **(74)** *(BWHills)* 8-11 DHolland (1) (led 8f out to 3f out: sn wknd: t.o.) | 15.5 |
| | Alto Princess *(APJones)* 8-11 NAdams (3) (leggy: unf: bkwd: swtg: s.s: last st: rdn 3f out: t.o fnl 2f) | hd.6 |

**11/8** CUNNING, **3/1** Wassl This Then (IRE), **4/1** Rosina Mae(op 9/4), **5/1** Choppy Choppy (USA), **14/1** Forgetful, **66/1** Alto Princess. CSF £6.91, Tote £1.90: £1.10 £2.80 (£6.20). Fittocks Stud Limited (NEWMARKET) bred by R. G. Stokes. 6 Rn
2m 7.6 (U.1)
SF—48/43/41/24/–/–

---

### 1949
LEVY BOARD CLAIMING STKS    £3125.50 (£868.00: £416.50)
1¼m 46y
4-25 (4-27)

| | | |
|---|---|---|
| 1714⁵ | **Flying Speed (USA)** *(MCPipe)* 4-9-9 GBaxter (7) (lw: hld up: hdwy 2f out: led & edgd lft ins fnl f: r.o wl) | —1 |
| 1534⁵ | Princess Moodyshoe **(65)** *(MCPipe)* 4-8-12 DHolland (2) (5th st: ev ch whn n.m.r ins fnl f: r.o wl) | 2½.2 |
| 1257⁶ | Edge of Darkness **(63)** *(JWHills)* 3-8-3 RHills (8) (3rd st: led wl over 1f out tl ins fnl f: one pce) | 1½.3 |
| 1766⁵ | Formal Invitation (IRE) **(60)** *(GLewis)* 3-8-10 BRouse (9) (b: swtg: hdwy over 3f out: one pce fnl 2f) | 2.4 |
| 1741 | Please Please Me (IRE) **(31)** *(KOCunningham-Brown)* 4-8-8 TQuinn (12) (6th st: no hdwy fnl 2f) | 4.5 |
| 1760 | Ryewater Dream **(56)** *(RJHodges)* 4-8-6 ‡³TSprake (11) (led 6f: led over 3f out tl over 1f out: on wknd) | s,h.6 |
| 1686 | Every One a Gem **(64)** *(MDixon)* 5-8-13 DaleGibson (6) (nvr trbld ldrs) | ½.7 |
| *1682* | Modern Art (IRE) *(RAkehurst)* 4-9-0 ‡³RPerham (3) (prom: led over 4f out tl over 3f out: wknd over 2f out) | 2.8 |
| | Rustyside *(CTNash)* 5-9-0 SWhitworth (5) (a bhd) | 2.9 |
| 1574⁶ | Day of History (IRE) **(42)** *(CACyzer)* 3-8-8 WNewnes (4) (a bhd) | 1.10 |
| 1465 | Ambassador Royale (IRE) **(76)** (Fav) *(PFICole)* 4-9-10 AMunro (13) (rdn & 4th st: wknd 3f out) | 4.11 |
| 1582⁴ | Capital Bond (IRE) **(56)** *(RJHolder)* 4-9-2 JWilliams (10) (a bhd) | nk.12 |
| | Shecangosah *(RJHodges)* 3-7-11 NAdams (1) (w'like: dwlt: sn rcvrd: wknd over 4f out: t.o) | 13 |

*Stewards Enquiry: Obj. to Flying Speed (USA) by Holland overruled.*

**Evens** Ambassador Royale (IRE)(op 7/4), **11/2** Princess Moodyshoe, **13/2** Edge of Darkness(9/2—7/1), **11/1** FLYING SPEED (USA)(5/1—12/1), **14/1** Every One a Gem, Capital Bond (IRE), Formal Invitation (IRE)(op 7/1), **20/1** Ryewater Dream, Modern Art (IRE), **25/1** Please Please Me (IRE), **33/1** Day of History (IRE), **50/1** Shecangosah, **66/1** Rustyside. CSF £68.61, Tote £17.10: £2.60 £1.60 £1.80 (£20.40). Mr F. Barr (WELLINGTON) bred by Buckram Oak Farm in USA. 13 Rn
2m 8.5 (0.8)
SF—51/35/23/26/16/11

---

### 1950
BROCKHAM H'CAP (3-Y.O) (0-70) £2232.50 (£620.00: £297.50)
(Weights raised 6 lb)
5f 11y 5-00 (5-01)

| | | |
|---|---|---|
| 1753★ | **Bells of Longwick (58)** *(DRLaing)* 9-5 (7x) TyroneWilliams (6) (w ldr: led over 1f out: drvn out) | —1 |
| 1732★ | Treasure Time (IRE) **(63)** *(JWhite)* 9-10 (7x) DaleGibson (2) (led over 3f: hrd rdn & nt qckn fnl f) | 1½.2 |
| 1753³ | High Principles **(60)** (Fav) *(JBerry)* 9-7 JCarroll (5) (a.p: rdn over 2f out: r.o ins fnl f) | s.h.3 |
| 734 | Sizzling Rose **(40)** *(WCarter)* 7-8 ‡⁷CHawksley (3) (no hdwy fnl 2f) | 2.4 |
| 1570 | Bishopstone Bill **(33)** *(SMellor)* 7-8 DanaMellor (1) (rdn & lost pl over 3f out: n.d) | ¾.5 |

**13/8** High Principles, **2/1** BELLS OF LONGWICK(op 5/4), **3/1** Treasure Time (IRE), **9/1** Bishopstone Bill, **16/1** Sizzling Rose. CSF £7.93, Tote £2.60: £1.80 £1.90 (£5.00). Mrs Marion Wickham (LAMBOURN) bred by Mrs Wickham. 5 Rn
62.7 sec (2.2)
SF—31/30/26/–/–

---

### 1951
HAMILTON H'CAP (0-80) £3020.00 (£905.00: £435.00: £200.00)
2m 1f 34y
5-30 (5-31)

| | | |
|---|---|---|
| 1653★ | **Chucklestone (57)** *(JSKing)* 9-8-10 TQuinn (5) (lw: led: rdn 6f out: clr 3f out: r.o wl) | —1 |
| 1671★ | Merton Mill **(62)** (bl) (Fav) *(DMorley)* 5-9-1 RHills (8) (lw: hld up: hdwy & 4th st: hrd rdn & chsd wnr over 2f out: nt qckn fnl f) | 1.2 |

Page 687

1407* Paper Dance **(61)** *(RJHolder)* 4–9-0 JWilliams (3) (lw: hld up & bhd: hdwy & 5th st: styd on fnl 2f) .................................................. 3.3
1810³ Romanian (IRE) **(48)** *(ARDavison)* 4–8-1 AMunro (1) (3rd st: no hdwy fnl 3f) ... 3¹/₂.4
1653³ Green Lane (USA) **(75)** *(IABalding)* 4–10-0 RCochrane (9) (lw: 2nd st: rdn & wknd over 2f out) .................................................. 5.5
1534 Magsood **(52)** (bl) *(SMellor)* 7–8-5 DanaMellor (7) (prom tl wknd qckly 4f out: t.o) .................................................. dist.6
1430 Fitness Fanatic **(40)** *(JTGifford)* 4–7-7 DaleGibson (4) (hld up & plld hrd: 6th & wkng st: t.o fnl 2f) .................................................. 3¹/₂.7
Easter Lee **(48)** *(RJHodges)* 12–7-12 ‡³TSprake (6) (dropped rr 8f out: sn t.o) dist.8
LONG HANDICAP: Fitness Fanatic 7-2.

**13/8** Merton Mill, **3/1** Paper Dance, **4/1** Green Lane (USA), **5/1** CHUCKLESTONE, **14/1** Romanian (IRE)(10/1—16/1), **16/1** Magsood, **25/1** Fitness Fanatic, **66/1** Easter Lee. CSF £13.32, CT £26.01. Tote £5.40: £2.10 £1.50 £1.50 (£6.10). Mr Mark O'Connor (SWINDON) bred by R. B. Stokes. 8 Rn
3m 44 (equals standard)
SF—11/15/11/–/16/–

T/Plpt: £23.00 (125.5 Tckts).          KH

## 1610—**KEMPTON (R-H)**
### Wednesday, July 8th [Good]
Going Allowance: St: 0.15 sec; Rest: minus 0.05 sec per fur (G)        Wind: nil

Stalls: low

**1952**    LBC NEWSTALK 97.3 FM CLAIMING STKS    £3132.00 (£936.00: £448.00: £204.00)
     6f                                               6-30 (6-31)

853 **A Prayer for Wings (94)** (Fav) *(JSutcliffe)* 8–8-12 MRoberts (8) (b: dwlt: hdwy over 2f out: led over 1f out: rdn out) ...................................... —1
1717² Walk in the Park **(80)** *(RSimpson)* 3–7-9 ‡⁵ATucker (1) (lw: hmpd on ins 4f out: swtchd rt over 3f out: hdwy 2f out: unable qckn fnl f) ......... 1¹/₂.2
1829³ Letsbeonestaboutit **(86)** *(MrsNMacauley)* 6–8-12 LDettori (5) (a.p: led over 2f out tl over 1f out: one pce) .................................................. ³/₄.3
1116² Easy Line **(89)** *(PJFeilden)* 9–8-10 WCarson (6) (b: lw: hld up: rdn over 1f out: one pce) .................................................. s.h.4
*1682*³ Pearl Ransom *(WGRWightman)* 5–8-0 GBardwell (4) (lw: outpcd) .................. 8.5
1343 Luna Bid **(63)** *(MBlanshard)* 9–8-10 JReid (7) (lw: hdwy over 2f out: wknd over 1f out) .................................................. ¹/₂.6
1761³ Tulapet **(42)** (v) *(SDow)* 3–7-7 ‡³FNorton (3) (lw: spd 3f) .................. 1¹/₂.7
1718 Christian Warrior **(64)** (bl) *(RHannon)* 3–8-2 AMcGlone (2) (lw: led over 3f) ...... 7.8

**13/8** A PRAYER FOR WINGS(3/1—6/4), **2/1** Easy Line, **11/2** Walk in the Park(4/1—6/1), **13/2** Letsbeonestaboutit(4/1—7/1), **12/1** Luna Bid(8/1—14/1), **33/1** Christian Warrior, Pearl Ransom, **50/1** Tulapet. CSF £10.57, Tote £2.80: £1.30 £1.40 £2.00 (£6.40). Mr S. Powell (EPSOM) bred by Dr Peter C. Yorke. 8 Rn
1m 13.99 (2.69)
SF—62/39/53/50/8/16

**1953**    FUTURES AND OPTIONS STKS (Mdn 3-Y.O) £2616.00 (£726.00: £348.00)
     1¹/₂m                                                7-00 (7-03)

1505⁴ **Anna of Saxony** (Fav) *(JHMGosden)* 8-9 SCauthen (4) (hld up: 3rd st: qcknd & led over 2f out: clr over 1f out: v.easily) ...................................... —1
1347⁵ Gong *(PTWalwyn)* 8-9 PatEddery (3) (led over 1f: 2nd st: led 3f out tl over 2f out: unable qckn) .................................................. 3.2
1505³ Iftakhaar (USA) *(MajorWRHern)* 9-0 WCarson (1) (lw: led over 10f out to 3f out: one pce) .................................................. 2.3
623 Shesadelight *(JLDunlop)* 8-9 LDettori (2) (rdn & hdwy over 4f out: 5th st: one pce fnl 3f) .................................................. 5.4
1577 Swan Heights *(JRFanshawe)* 8-9 GCarter (6) (lw: 6th st: no hdwy fnl 3f) ......... 2¹/₂.5
1746⁵ Debt Swap (USA) *(JHMGosden)* 9-0 PaulEddery (7) (b.nr hind: lw: a bhd) ...... 10.6
Oozlem (IRE) *(CAHorgan)* 9-0 AMcGlone (9) (a bhd) .................. s.h.7
Belle Isis (USA) *(LordHuntingdon)* 8-9 WRSwinburn (8) (w'like: scope: 4th st: wknd 3f out) .................................................. 10.8
1158⁶ River Hawk *(RFJohnsonHoughton)* 9-0 JReid (5) (bhd fnl 7f: t.o) ............ 7.9

**8/13** ANNA OF SAXONY(Evens—4/7), **3/1** Iftakhaar (USA), **11/2** Gong(7/2—6/1), **12/1** Belle Isis (USA), **33/1** Shesadelight, Swan Heights, Debt Swap (USA), **66/1** River Hawk, **100/1** Oozlem (IRE). CSF £5.04, Tote £1.80: £1.10 £1.70 £1.20 (£3.80). Sheikh Mohammed (NEWMARKET) bred by Sheikh Mohammed bin Rashid al Maktoum. 9 Rn
2m 36.66 (6.46)
SF—25/19/20/5/–/–/

## 1954
CASNA GROUP CLEANING SERVICES H'CAP (0-90) £3002.00 (£896.00: £428.00: £194.00)   **1m (rnd)**   7-30 (7-31)
(Weights raised 5 lb)

| | | |
|---|---|---|
| 401 | **Redisham (74)** *(JHMGosden)* 3–8-11 SCauthen (5) (lw: 2nd st: hrd rdn 2f out: led 1f out: r.o wl) | —1 |
| 1344 | Keep Your Word **(55)** *(GBBalding)* 6–8-1 NAdams (4) (4th st: nt clr run on ins over 1f out: swtchd lft ins fnl f: r.o) | 1¹⁄₂.2 |
| 1637⁴ | Akkazao (IRE) **(78)** *(WCarter)* 4–9-5 ‡5NGwilliams (7) (lw: led 7f: unable qckn) | s.h.3 |
| 1772★ | Systematic **(63)** *(RHannon)* 3–8-0 (5x) MRoberts (1) (3rd st: rdn over 2f out: one pce) | 1¹⁄₂.4 |
| 1773² | Royal Dartmouth (USA) **(51)** *(Fav) (BRMillman)* 7–7-11 NCarlisle (3) (b: lw: plld hrd: 5th st: one pce fnl 3f) | 2¹⁄₂.5 |
| 1312★ | Kalko **(70)** *(CEBrittain)* 3–8-7 TQuinn (2) (lw: 6th st: no hdwy fnl 3f) | 2¹⁄₂.6 |
| 1706⁴ | Takenhall **(59)** *(MJFetherston-Godley)* 7–8-5(1) PatEddery (6) (lw: bhd fnl 5f) .... | 5.7 |

**5/2** Royal Dartmouth (USA), **7/2** Takenhall, **4/1** Systematic, **11/2** Akkazao (IRE), **8/1** Keep Your Word, **9/1** REDISHAM & Ors. CSF £68.01, Tote £11.70: £3.00 £3.00 (£51.70). Sheikh Mohammed (NEWMARKET) bred by Kirtlington Stud Ltd. 7 Rn
1m 42 (4.80)
SF—19/4/21/–/–/–

## 1955
ECONOMIST H'CAP (3-Y.O) (0-90) £4857.50 (£1460.00: £705.00: £327.50)
**1¹⁄₄m (J.C)**   8-00 (8-03)
(Weights raised 4 lb)

| | | |
|---|---|---|
| 1414² | **Scrutineer (USA) (84)** *(Fav) (JHMGosden)* 9-7 SCauthen (6) (lw: mde all: hrd rdn 2f out: r.o wl) | —1 |
| 1533⁴ | Zawaahy (USA) **(76)** *(AAScott)* 8-13 WRSwinburn (1) (hdwy 2f out: r.o wl ins fnl f) | 1.2 |
| 1634⁵ | Shrewd Partner (IRE) **(79)** *(DRCElsworth)* 9-2 TQuinn (2) (2nd st: rdn over 2f out: unable qckn) | 1¹⁄₂.3 |
| 1382³ | Googly **(58)** *(WGHWightman)* 7-9 QDardwell (10) (lw: rdn 6f out: nt clr run over 2f out: str run fnl f: fin wl) | 3.4 |
| 1778² | Ghurrah (IRE) **(60)** *(CJBenstead)* 7-11 WCarson (7) (bhd whn hmpd over 1f out: gd hdwy fnl f: r.o wl) | 2¹⁄₂.5 |
| 1686★ | Holiday Island **(76)** *(CEBrittain)* 8-13 MRoberts (5) (hdwy over 2f out: wknd wl over 1f out) | ¹⁄₂.6 |
| 1382³ | Lady of Sardinia (BEL) **(73)** *(JWPayne)* 8-0 AMunro (3) (6th st: wknd over 2f out) | s.h.7 |
| 1280⁵ | Cosmic Future **(72)** *(SPCWoods)* 8-9 WWoods (12) (nvr nr to chal) | s.h.8 |
| 1214 | Aedean **(63)** *(CAHorgan)* 8-0 AMcGlone (11) (lw: nvr nrr) | 3¹⁄₂.9 |
| 330 | Mathal (USA) **(63)** *(MRStoute)* 7-11 ‡3FNorton (4) (4th st: wknd over 2f out) | 2¹⁄₂.10 |
| 1478★ | Halley (USA) **(75)** *(HRACecil)* 8-2 WRyan (8) (lw: 3rd st: wknd 2f out) | ³⁄₄.11 |
| 1666² | Aremef (USA) **(84)** *(MrsJCecil)* 9-7 PaulEddery (9) (rdn 6f out: 5th st: wknd 3f out) | ³⁄₄.12 |

**9/2** SCRUTINEER (USA), **5/1** Lady of Sardinia (BEL), **11/2** Halley (USA), **6/1** Zawaahy (USA), **15/2** Aremef (USA)(14/1—7/1), Ghurrah (IRE), **10/1** Mathal (USA)(8/1—12/1), Holiday Island, **14/1** Shrewd Partner (IRE), Googly, **25/1** Cosmic Future, **33/1** Aedean. CSF £31.36, CT £330.09. Tote £6.00: £2.30 £2.00 £3.40 (£19.70). Sheikh Mohammed (NEWMARKET) bred by Luella M. Jensen & Kennelot Stables in USA. 12 Rn
2m 6.14 (4.14)
SF—61/51/51/24/21/36

## 1956
GRE PROPERTIES STKS (Mdn 3-Y.O.F) £2856.00 (£791.00: £378.00)
**1m (J.C)**   8-30 (8-33)

| | | |
|---|---|---|
| 1315⁶ | **Agnes Flemming (USA) (70)** *(PWHarris)* 8-11 PaulEddery (4) (led 7f: hrd rdn: led last stride) | —1 |
| 1611² | Pelargonia **(Fav)** *(RCharlton)* 8-11 PatEddery (8) (lw: 3rd st: led 1f out: hrd drvn: hdd last stride) | s.h.2 |
| | Walimu (IRE) *(CFWall)* 8-11 NDay (7) (w'like: scope: 6th st: rdn over 2f out: r.o one pce) | 3.3 |
| | Mere Chants *(DRCElsworth)* 8-11 WCarson (9) (s.s: hdwy 6f out: 2nd st: hrd rdn over 1f out: one pce) | s.h.4 |
| | Maritime Lady (USA) *(MRStoute)* 8-11 WRSwinburn (6) (4th st: one pce fnl 2f) .. | 2.5 |
| | First Fling (IRE) *(RCharlton)* 8-11 SRaymont (1) (unf: scope: hdwy over 2f out: one pce) | ¹⁄₂.6 |
| 989 | Mist of the Marsh (USA) *(JHMGosden)* 8-11 SCauthen (3) (a bhd) | 8.7 |
| | Vanuatu (IRE) *(TThomsonJones)* 8-11 SWhitworth (2) (unf: bhd fnl 5f) | 2.8 |
| | Bracing (IRE) *(GHarwood)* 8-11 AClark (5) (wl grwn: s.s: hdwy over 4f out: 5th st: wknd 3f out) | 10.9 |

**1/4** Pelargonia(op 1/2), **6/1** Maritime Lady (USA)(op 10/1), **16/1** Mere Chants, Bracing (IRE), Mist of the Marsh (USA), **25/1** Walimu (IRE), **33/1** AGNES FLEMMING (USA), **50/1** Ors. CSF £43.10, Tote £37.50: 3.60 £1.10 £5.10 (£9.10). Mrs P. W. Harris (BERKHAMSTED) bred by Pendley Farm in USA. 9 Rn   1m 41.18 (4.58)
SF—22/21/12/11/5/3

## 1957

E.B.F. BULL & BEAR STKS (Mdn 2-Y.O.F) £2658.00 (£738.00: £354.00)
6f                                           9-00 (9-04)

| | | |
|---|---|---|
| 1591[2] | White Shadow (IRE) (Fav) (RCharlton) 8-11 PatEddery (5) (swtg: a.p: hrd rdn over 1f out: led ins fnl f: r.o wl) | —1 |
| 1164[3] | Simply Sooty (BRMillman) 8-11 GBaxter (4) (led tl ins fnl f: r.o) | ¾.2 |
| 1635[3] | Catherineofaragon (WGRWightman) 8-11 JWilliams (1) (a.p: rdn over 1f out: r.o wl ins fnl f) | s.h.3 |
| 733 | Newington Butts (IRE) (RAkehurst) 8-11 AMunro (8) (a.p: one pce fnl 2f) | 8.4 |
| 1342 | Jafetica (DRLaing) 8-11 BRouse (12) (a.p: rdn over 2f out: one pce) | hd.5 |
| 1610 | Lake Princess (IRE) (SDow) 8-11 TQuinn (14) (outpcd: hdwy fnl 2f: nvr nrr) | 1½.6 |
| | Heretical Miss (RHannon) 8-8 ‡3RPerham (10) (lt-f: prom 4f) | nk.7 |
| 973 | Manon Lescaut (APJarvis) 8-11 PaulEddery (9) (outpcd: nvr nrr) | hd.8 |
| | Nahlati (IRE) (CEBrittain) 8-11 SCauthen (6) (cmpt: spd 4f) | s.h.9 |
| | Crystal Stone (TThomsonJones) 8-11 SWhitworth (2) (unf: scope: outpcd) | s.h.10 |
| | Bright Wales (MMcCormack) 8-11 JReid (11) (cmpt: a bhd) | 1½.11 |
| | Lidoma (IRE) (JLDunlop) 8-11 WCarson (13) (leggy: scope: a bhd) | 1½.12 |
| | So Saucy (CEBrittain) 8-11 MRoberts (3) (leggy: s.s: a bhd) | 3.13 |
| 1610 | Petite Vino (JJBridger) 8-11 NAdams (7) (lw: bhd fnl 3f) | 1½.14 |

2/5 WHITE SHADOW (IRE)(1/2—1/3), 8/1 Simply Sooty, 10/1 So Saucy, 11/1 Catherineofaragon, 12/1 Nahlati (IRE)(8/1—14/1), Lidoma (IRE), 25/1 Lake Princess (IRE), 33/1 Jafetica, Manon Lescaut, Bright Wales, 50/1 Ors. CSF £6.00, Tote £1.60: £1.10 £1.80 £2.20 (£4.70). Mr K. Abdulla (BECKHAMPTON) bred by Juddmonte Farms in Ireland. 14 Rn
1m 15.57 (4.27)
SF—29/26/25/–/–/–

T/Plpt: £92.80 (38.4 Tckts).                                             AK

## 1519—REDCAR (L-H)

### Wednesday, July 8th [Good]

Going Allowance: minus 0.25 sec per fur (F)                  Wind: almost nil

Stalls: high

## 1958

JULIE KRONE STKS (Mdn) £1590.00 (£440.00: £210.00)    **1m 3f**       6-40 (6-41)

| | | |
|---|---|---|
| 1746[3] | Al Karnak (IRE) (Fav) (MMoubarak) 3–8-9 JulieKrone (3) (a gng wl: wnt 2nd appr st: led over 3f out: sn clr) | —1 |
| 1287 | Well Ahead (MJohnston) 3–8-4 DMcKeown (1) (cl up to st: sn drvn along: kpt on one pce: no ch w wnr) | 20.2 |
| 1705 | Rahif (MrsGRReveley) 4–9-7 KDarley (2) (s.i.s: hld up: effrt 4f out: one pce u.p fnl 2f) | 3½.3 |
| 1490[6] | Tathir (CAN) (DMorley) 4–9-7 MBirch (4) (b: b.hind: led tl hdd over 3f out: wknd qckly: eased whn btn) | 25.4 |

2/11 AL KARNAK (IRE), 9/1 Rahif, 16/1 Tathir (CAN), 20/1 Well Ahead. CSF £3.75, Tote £1.10 (£3.70). Ecurie Fustok (NEWMARKET) bred by A. T. Robinson in Ireland. 4 Rn
2m 19.5 (3.8)
SF—30/–/–/–

## 1959

LISA CROPP CLAIMING STKS (2-Y.O) £1688.00 (£468.00: £224.00)    7f   7-10 (7-14)

| | | |
|---|---|---|
| 1788[4] | Boldville Bash (IRE) (TDBarron) 8-11 KDarley (9) (a.p: chal wl over 1f out: led ins fnl f: hld on wl) | —1 |
| 1429[6] | Touch N' Glow (JLSpearing) 8-1 JLowe (13) (trckd ldrs: chal wl over 1f out: nt qckn nr fin) | nk.2 |
| 1526[2] | Kiss in the Dark (MrsGRReveley) 8-3 KFallon (12) (effrt & outpcd over 2f out: styd on strly u.p fnl f) | 1½.3 |
| 1429[5] | Karinska (Fav) (SirMarkPrescott) 8-3 GDuffield (5) (a.p: led 2f out: sn rdn: hdd & no ex ins fnl f) | ½.4 |
| 1429 | Morning News (IRE) (MHTompkins) 8-7 JulieKrone (10) (a.p: effrt & n.m.r 2f out: wknd fnl f) | 8.5 |
| 1479 | Jersey Bob (IRE) (JSWainwright) 8-3 PBurke (3) (led tl hdd & wknd 2f out) | 3.6 |
| 1689[2] | Lettermore (RMWhitaker) 8-1 ACulhane (7) (effrt 3f out: hung lft & no hdwy fnl 2f) | 1½.7 |
| 1321 | Snug Surprise (JSWainwright) 8-1 AMackay (4) (prom over 4f) | ½.8 |
| 1479[5] | Forthemoment (PCalver) 7-11 ‡3JFanning (6) (chsd ldrs: hung lft & wknd over 2f out) | 1.9 |
| 1835[6] | Simply a Star (IRE) (MWEasterby) 8-9 TLucas (11) (effrt over 2f out: nvr rchd ldrs: wknd fnl f) | hd.10 |
| | Sainted Sue (JSHaldane) 8-2 LCharnock (2) (unf: prom to ½-wy: sn lost pl) | 3.11 |
| 1848 | Cyprus Creek (IRE) (v) (NTinkler) 8-6 SusanneBerneklint (1) (bhd fr ½-wy) | s.h.12 |
| | Sevinch (MWEasterby) 7-9 ‡7JMarshall (8) (lengthy: scope: stumbled s: rdr lost irons: a last) | 12.13 |

**1960—1961**

**5/2** Karinska, **9/2** BOLDVILLE BASH (IRE), **11/2** Lettermore, **7/1** Touch N' Glow, **8/1** Kiss in the Dark, **10/1** Forthemoment, **11/1** Morning News (IRE), **25/1** Simply a Star (IRE), Cyprus Creek (IRE), **33/1** Sevinch, **50/1** Ors. CSF £33.28, Tote £5.70: £1.40 £2.30 £1.80 (£24.20). Mr P. D. Savill (THIRSK) bred by Louis A. Walshe in Ireland. 13 Rn; Touch N'Glow clmd Full Circle Thoroughbreds £5,010　　　　　　　　　　　　　1m 25 (2.8)
SF—29/18/15/13/–/–

**1960**　　FAIRFIELD INDUSTRIES INTERNATIONAL CHALLENGE CUP (H'cap) (0-80) £3002.00
　　　　　(£896.00: £428.00: £194.00)　**1¼m**　　　　　　　7-40 (7-41)

1520★ Khazar (USA) **(64)** *(SirMarkPrescott)* 3-9-0 GDuffield (9) (a wl plcd: led 3f out: hrd rdn 2f out: hld on wl) .............................................................................. —1
1528★ Timurid (FR) **(73)** *(JLDunlop)* 3-9-9 MBirch (7) (a.p: rdn 3f out: kpt on strly fnl f) ½.2
1731★ Sweet Mignonette **(52)** (Fav) *(MrsGRReveley)* 4-8-13 (5x) KDarley (8) (chsd ldrs: effrt over 3f out: styd on u.p ins fnl f) .................................. ½.3
1449⁴ Flying Down to Rio (IRE) **(52)** *(MPNaughton)* 4-8-13 JulieKrone (4) (a.p: sltly outpcd 3f out: nt clr run & swtchd wl over 1f out: edgd lft & r.o wl) 1½.4
1516⁶ Tancred Grange **(66)** *(MSSEHall)* 3-9-2 NConnorton (5) (b.off hind: plld hrd early: in tch: rdn over 3f out: wknd over 1f out) ................................. 4.5
　　　　Explosive Speed **(58)** *(MDHammond)* 4-9-5 DMcKeown (1) (hld up: styd on fnl 3f: nvr nrr) ................................................................................. s.h.6
1687⁵ Dawn Success **(60)** (bl) *(DWChapman)* 6-9-7 SWood (2) (set stdy pce: qcknd appr st: hdd 3f out: sn wknd) ...................................................... 1½.7
1516 North Esk (USA) **(78)** *(JWWatts)* 3-10-0 JLowe (6) (stdd s: hld up: effrt over 3f out: no imp) ................................................................................. 2.8
1791 Spanish Performer **(51)** *(TFairhurst)* 3-7-12 ‡3JFanning (3) (a bhd) .................. 10.9

**11/4** Sweet Mignonette, **7/2** Timurid (FR), **6/1** Tancred Grange(10/1—12/1), KHAZAR (USA), **8/1** Flying Down to Rio (IRE), Dawn Success, **12/1** North Esk (USA), **16/1** Spanish Performer, **20/1** Explosive Speed (USA). CSF £25.64, CT £63.93. Tote £5.80: £1.90 £1.50 £1.30 (£6.10). Mr Saeed Manana (NEWMARKET) bred by Kentucky Select Bloodstock I in USA. 9 Rn　　　　　　　　　　　　　　　　　2m 10.1 (7.6)

**1961**　　REDCAR MOTOR MART H'CAP (0-70) £1674.00 (£464.00: £222.00)　**7f** 8-10 (8-13)

1793⁶ Gant Bleu (FR) **(50)** *(RMWhitaker)* 5-8-10 JulieKrone (16) (a.p: led on bit 2f out: pushed out) ................................................................................. —1
1570 Flashy's Son **(45)** *(MDHammond)* 4-8-5 GDuffield (5) (in tch: hdwy to chal over 1f out: nt qckn nr fin) ............................................................. 1.2
1905⁴ Johnston's Express (IRE) **(35)** *(EJAlston)* 4-7-9 JQuinn (2) (hdwy on outside over 2f out: sn ev ch: unable qckn ins fnl f) ........................ nk.3
1365⁵ Claudia Miss **(59)** *(WWHaigh)* 5-9-5 DMcKeown (4) (mid div: hdwy & ev ch wl over 1f out: no ex nr fin) ....................................................... 3.4
1793 Quiet Victory **(49)** (bl) *(MissLCSiddall)* 5-8-4 ‡5SMaloney (8) (cl up: sn pushed along: chal 3f out: wandered u.p: wknd fnl f) .................... 1½.5
1484★ Royal Girl **(63)** *(MissSEHall)* 5-9-9 NConnorton (11) (effrt & hdwy 3f out: kpt on fnl f) ................................................................................................. hd.6
1663³ Battuta **(54)** *(REarnshaw)* 3-8-6 KFallon (7) (effrt & hdwy over 2f out: no ex u.p fnl f) ...................................................................................................... hd.7
1731³ Hizeem **(33)** *(MPNaughton)* 6-7-7 JakiHouston (6) (rdn & sme hdwy 3f out: hung lft: kpt on same pce) ................................................................. s.h.8
1731 Oyston's Life **(48)** *(JBerry)* 3-8-0 JoannaMorgan (12) (in tch tl rdn & wknd fnl 2f) ....................................................................................................... 1½.9
1793 Arabat **(55)** (bl) *(MPNaughton)* 5-9-1 SusanneBerneklint (15) (led tl hdd & wknd 2f out) ...................................................................................... ¾.10
1793² Euroblake **(68)** (Fav) *(TDBarron)* 5-10-0 AlexGreaves (18) (s.i.s: nvr nr ldrs) . nk.11
1522 Lord Magester (FR) **(51)** *(MrsGRReveley)* 5-8-11 JLowe (3) (in tch on outside 4f) .......................................................................................................... 3.12
　　　　Imhotep **(50)** *(MrsGRReveley)* 5-8-10 LCharnock (17) (prom to ½-wy: lost pl 2f out) ................................................................................................ 1½.13
1550 Lowlands Boy **(53)** *(TFairhurst)* 3-8-2 ‡3JFanning (10) (prom 4f) ................... 1½.14
1673 Sky Cat **(49)** *(CTinkler)* 8-8-9 KDarley (13) (rdn along & bhd fnl 3f) ............... 1.15
1786² April Shadow **(50)** *(CWThornton)* 3-8-2 ACulhane (9) (effrt ½-wy: sn btn) ...... ½.16
1449 Victoria Road (IRE) **(67)** *(MHEasterby)* 4-9-13 MBirch (14) (a bhd: t.o) ............. 17
LONG HANDICAP: Hizeem 7-1.

**11/2** Euroblake, **7/1** Royal Girl, **9/1** Johnston's Express (IRE), GANT BLEU (FR), **10/1** Claudia Miss, **12/1** Arabat, Quiet Victory, April Shadow, **14/1** Lord Magester (FR), Battuta, **16/1** Flashy's Son, Victoria Road (IRE), **20/1** Oyston's Life, **25/1** Ors. CSF £128.04, CT £1,193.67. Tote £8.80: £2.40 £3.80 £2.10 £2.10 (£1,022.40). Mr E. C. Alton (WETHERBY) bred by Souren Vanian in France. 17 Rn　　　　　　　　1m 24.8 (2.6)
SF—31/23/12/27/7/25

**1962**  MIDDLESBROUGH FOOTBALL CLUB APP'CE H'CAP (3-Y.O) (0-70) £1618.00 (£448.00: £214.00)  **1m 3f**  8-40 (8-41)
(Weights raised 2 lb)

1528 **Tees Gazette Girl (41)** *(MrsGRReveley)* 7-3 ‡5ClaireBalding (3) (wl bhd: stdy hdwy 4f out: styd on wl to ld wl ins fnl f) ............................. —1

17833 Little Ivor **(42)** *(DenysSmith)* 7-2‡7CTeague (7) (chsd ldrs: chal & led u.p over 2f out: hdd wl ins fnl f: no ex) ............................. 2½.2

17834 Chantry Bellini **(51)** *(CWThornton)* 7-11 ‡7KSked (4) (sn wl bhd: hdwy & swtchd outside over 3f out: styd on fnl f) ............................. 6.3

16025 Maji **(68)** (Fav) *(DMorley)* 9-4‡3EBentley (1) (chsd clr ldr: led over 2f out: sn disp ld: wknd fnl f: eased nr fin) ............................. nk.4

1486 Lingdale Lass **(53)** *(MrsGRReveley)* 7-13(1) ‡7SCopp (5) (bhd: hdwy u.p over 3f out: hung lft & no imp fnl 2f) ............................. 7.5

Sing Another **(42)** *(MrsGRReveley)* 7-9 DarrenMoffatt (6) (plld hrd: led & sn wl clr: hdd over 2f out: wandered & wknd qckly) ............................. 15.6

375 Rap Up Fast (USA) **(49)** *(CWThornton)* 8-2 JMarshall (2) (in tch tl wknd over 3f out) ............................. 8.7

*Stewards Enquiry: Bentley fined £130 under Rule 151 (ii) (failure to ensure best possible placing).*

**6/4** Maji, **9/2** Little Ivor, **6/1** Sing Another, Chantry Bellini, **10/1** TEES GAZETTE GIRL, **11/1** Lingdale Lass, **20/1** Rap Up Fast (USA). CSF £47.31, Tote £14.00: £2.50 £2.30 (£26.50). North Eastern Evening Gazette Limited (SALTBURN) bred by Floors Farming. 7 Rn                    2m 23.1 (7.4)

**1963**  SUSANNE BERNEKLINT STKS (Mdn 2-Y.O) £1520.00 (£420.00: £200.00)  **5f**  9-10 (9-11)

Cockerham Ranger *(JBerry)* 9-0 JulieKrone (1) (unf: racd wd: a.p: edgd lft 2f out: sn led: r.o strly) ............................. —1

15133 Scored Again (Fav) *(RMWhitaker)* 9-0 ACulhane (3) (sltly hmpd st: trckd ldrs: effrt 2f out: kpt on u.p fnl f) ............................. 1½.2

1071 Bold Philip *(BBeasley)* 8-7 ‡7SWilliams (5) (sn pushed along: hdwy over 1f out: styd on wl) ............................. ¾.3

14502 Arkendale Diamond (USA) *(BBeasley)* 9-0 DNicholls (2) (led tl hdd wl over 1f out: kpt on same pce) ............................. 1½.4

17284 Missed the Boat (IRE) *(TDBarron)* 9-0 AlexGreaves (4) (w ldr: pushed along ½-wy: hdd wl over 2f out: kpt on one pce) ............................. ½.5

**10/11** Scored Again(op 1/2), **3/1** COCKERHAM RANGER(4/1—9/2), **7/2** Arkendale Diamond (USA), **20/1** Missed the Boat (IRE), **33/1** Bold Philip. CSF £5.74, Tote £2.70: £1.40 £1.40 (£2.70). Mr Alan Berry (COCKERHAM) bred by Ravenstonedale Fold and Bloodstock. 5 Rn                    62 sec (5.3)

T/Plpt: £140.30 (10.7 Tckts).                                                                 WG

# REDCAR (L-H)

## Thursday, July 9th [Good to soft]

Going Allowance: 0.15 sec per fur (G)                                          Wind: nil

Stalls: high

**1964**  JOLLY SAILOR (S) H'CAP (0-60) £2970.80 (£828.80: £400.40)  **7f**  2-10 (2-19)

19245 **Chaplins Club (USA) (45)** *(DWChapman)* 12–9-3 KDarley (6) (swtchd rt s: hdwy over 2f out: edgd rt: r.o u.p to ld nr fin) ............................. —1

1034 Lime Street Lil **(25)** *(DAWilson)* 4–7-8‡3JFanning (9) (a chsng ldr: led over 1f out tl nr fin) ............................. ¾.2

15933 Spring High **(44)** (bl) *(KTIvory)* 5–8-9 ‡7CScally (16) (b: chsd ldrs: nt qckn over 1f out) ............................. ¾.3

16293 Bobbie Bold **(37)** *(RO'Leary)* 4–8-9 KFallon (27) (hdwy ½-wy: sltly hmpd over 1f out: styd on nr fin) ............................. ¾.4

14394 Syke Lane **(38)** *(RMWhitaker)* 3–8-2 ACulhane (17) (a.p: r.o one pce fnl 2f) ............................. 2.5

1243 Cool Enough **(41)** *(MrsJRRamsden)* 11–8-13 MHills (5) (hld up: hdwy over 2f out: styd on fnl f) ............................. hd.6

16046 Northern Emperor (IRE) **(35)** *(MHEasterby)* 3–7-8(1) ‡5SMaloney (4) (led & sn clr: hdd over 1f out: sn wknd) ............................. nk.7

17935 Broad Appeal **(40)** (bl) *(BBeasley)* 4–8-5 ‡7PTurner (19) (styd on appr fnl f: nt rch ldrs) ............................. nk.8

763 Enchanted Flyer **(30)** (bl) *(TWDonnelly)* 3–8-4 NConnorton (15) (sn bhd: hdwy & hrd rdn fnl 2f: nt rch ldrs) ............................. nk.9

Joseph's Wine (IRE) **(40)** *(RBastiman)* 3–8-4 DMcKeown (24) (bit bkwd: hdwy fnl 2f: nrst fin) ............................. ¾.10

15625 Perspicacity **(39)** *(MDods)* 5–8-11 JLowe (10) (nvr rchd ldrs) ............................. ¾.11

16045 Brown as a Berry (IRE) **(30)** *(WStorey)* 4–8-2 BCrossley (12) (bhd tl hdwy fnl 2f) nk.12

1673 Chance Report (36) *(FHLee)* 4–8-8 RLappin (8) (chsd ldr tl wknd over 2f out) ³/₄.13
    Final Bout (28) *(MrsGRReveley)* 4–7-7 ‡⁷DarrenMoffatt (23) (lw: sme hdwy 2f
    out: n.d) ................................................................. ¹/₂.14
1590⁴ Count Me Out (34) *(JPearce)* 7–8-1 ‡⁵RPrice (18) (nvr bttr than mid div) ........ ³/₄.15
1840⁶ Beechwood Cottage (38) (bl) *(ABailey)* 9–8-10 KTsui (11) (lw: chsd ldrs tl rdn &
    wknd 2f out) ................................................................. hd.16
1793 Angel Train (IRE) (37) (bl) *(JParkes)* 4–8-9 LCharnock (3) (chsd ldrs tl wknd
    ¹/₂-wy) ................................................................. ¹/₂.17
1896² Talish (36) (v) (Fav) *(TDBarron)* 4–8-8 AlexGreaves (22) (bhd fnl 3f) .............. 1¹/₂.18
1145 Angel's Wing (34) *(RMWhitaker)* 3–7-7⁽²⁾ ‡⁵NKennedy (28) (n.d) ................. nk.19
1786 Miss Grosse Nez (IRE) (51) (bl) *(CWThornton)* 3–8-8 ‡⁷KSked (26) (a bhd) ...... ³/₄.20
1855⁴ Vital Voltage (IRE) (36) *(MWEllerby)* 3–8-0⁽¹⁾ SMorris (20) (a bhd) .................. 8.21
*1847* L'Amour Precieux (56) *(MWEasterby)* 3–9-6 TLucas (2) (bhd fnl 3f) .................. 8.22
1798 Breezy Sailor (25) (bl) *(RThompson)* 6–7-11 PBurke (14) (t: t.o) ....................... 23
    Honey Snugfit (54) *(MWEasterby)* 3–8-11 ‡⁷JMarshall (7) (bit bkwd: chsd ldrs tl
    lost pl ¹/₂-wy: t.o) ................................................................. 24
    *1055 Scottish Ruby (14/1) Withdrawn (burst out of stalls) : not under orders*

**9/2** Talish, **9/1** Bobbie Bold, Broad Appeal, **11/1** Cool Enough, Chance Report, **12/1** Beechwood Cottage, Count Me Out, Perspicacity, CHAPLINS CLUB (USA), **14/1** Spring High, **16/1** Syke Lane, **20/1** Enchanted Player, Lime Street Lil, Northern Emperor (IRE), Brown as a Berry (IRE), **25/1** Angel Train (IRE), Final Bout, Vital Voltage (IRE), **50/1** Ors. CSF £220.08, CT £3,078.24. Tote £18.40: £3.50 £6.80 £2.00 £2.90 (Wnr or 2nd w any £5.00). Mr P. D. Savill (YORK) bred by Flying I Ranch in USA. 24 Rn; No bid
                                   1m 27 (4.8)
                              SF–47/32/35/33/20/30

---

**1965**    EVENING GAZETTE STKS (2-Y.O) £3132.00 (£936.00: £448.00: £204.00)
       7f                                                    2-45 (2-45)

1690² Persian Brave (IRE) (Fav) *(MDoll)* 8 11 MHills (6) (lw: mde all: qcknd ¹/₂-wy: r.o
    wl u.p fnl f) ................................................................. — 1
1569⋆ Tioman Island *(PFICole)* 9–4 TQuinn (5) (trckd ldrs: chal over 1f out: sn rdn: nt
    qckn nr fin) ................................................................. hd.2
1524⋆ Mhemeanles *(MHEasterby)* 9–2 MBirch (1) (trckd ldrs: ev ch over 1f out: rdn &
    unable qckn) ................................................................. 2¹/₂.3
1664² Willshe Gan *(DenysSmith)* 8-11 KFallon (4) (lw: trckd ldrs: sltly outpcd ¹/₂-wy:
    styd on u.p fnl 2f: nvr able to chal) ................................................................. 1.4
1571⁵ Buzz-B-Babe *(BEllison)* 8-11 DMcKeown (2) (trckd ldrs tl wl outpcd ¹/₂-wy: sn
    bhd) ................................................................. 8.5
    Red Fan (IRE) *(JWWatts)* 8-11 NConnorton (3) (w'like: str: scope: bit bkwd:
    prom tl outpcd ¹/₂-wy: sn bhd) ................................................................. 1¹/₂.6

**4/5** PERSIAN BRAVE (IRE)(5/4—8/11), **11/4** Tioman Island(op 7/4), **7/1** Willshe Gan, **10/1** Red Fan (IRE)(8/1—12/1), **12/1** Mhemeanles, **33/1** Buzz-B-Babe. CSF £3.47, Tote £1.80: £1.40 £1.60 £1.20. Persian Partnership (NEWMARKET) bred by Roncon Ltd. in Ireland. 6 Rn
                                1m 27.9 (5.7)
                              SF–27/33/23/15/–/–

---

**1966**    RED CROSS H'CAP (0-80) £2679.20 (£741.20: £353.60)    **1m 1f**    3-15 (3-16)

1292⁶ Young Jason (49) *(FHLee)* 9–8-5 ‡⁵NKennedy (4) (dwlt: bhd: hdwy over 2f out:
    swtchd outside over 1f out: led ins fnl f) ................................................................. — 1
    Jubran (USA) (65) *(MPNaughton)* 6–9-12 JakiHouston (2) (trckd ldrs: led over
    1f out: hdd & nt qckn ins fnl f) ................................................................. ¹/₂.2
1911² Martini Executive (63) (bl) *(BBeasley)* 4–9-10 LCharnock (3) (hld up: hdwy over
    2f out: ev ch over 1f out: one pce) ................................................................. 2¹/₂.3
1488³ Tarda (55) *(MrsGRReveley)* 5–9-2 KDarley (6) (lw: hld up: effrt 3f out: rdn &
    wknd over 1f out) ................................................................. 2¹/₂.4
1703³ Green Medina (IRE) (64) (bl) *(MBell)* 4–9-11 MHills (7) (led: rdn over 2f out: hdd
    & wknd over 1f out) ................................................................. 1¹/₂.5
1619⁴ Stand At Ease (33) *(WStorey)* 7–7-5⁽¹⁾ ‡³JFanning (1) (effrt & hrd rdn over 3f out:
    nvr rchd ldrs) ................................................................. 3.6
1739² Top Scale (36) (v) (Fav) *(WWHaigh)* 6–7-11 JLowe (5) (lw: chsd ldrs: brought
    wd st: rdn & wknd 2f out) ................................................................. ¹/₂.7

**11/4** Top Scale, **3/1** Tarda, **4/1** Martini Executive, **9/2** Green Medina (IRE), **12/1** YOUNG JASON, **20/1** Stand At Ease, **33/1** Jubran (USA). CSF £190.65, Tote £9.10: £2.00 £3.30 (£73.40). Mrs Gillian Lee (WILMSLOW) bred by Mrs R. B. Kennard. 7 Rn
                                1m 55.8 (6.8)
                              SF–10/29/19/3/7/–

---

**1967**    SEA PIGEON H'CAP (0-90) £2782.50 (£770.00: £367.50)    **1³/₄m 19y**    3-50 (3-51)
                (Weights raised 7 lb)

1800⋆ **Farmer's Pet (70)** (Fav) *(GAPritchard-Gordon)* 3–8-9 (4x) GCarter (6) (racd
    wd: mde all: drvn clr over 3f out: styd on strly) ................................................................. — 1

1580* Three Wells **(85)** *(JLDunlop)* 3–9–10 TQuinn (2) (lw: hld up: hdwy on outside to chal wnr over 2f out: wnt bdly lft: kpt on) ............................ 2¹/₂.2

1530* Brodessa **(70)** *(MrsGRReveley)* 6–9–10 MBirch (5) (trckd ldrs: effrt 3f out: hung lft u.p: one pce) ............................ 8.3

1864* Bold Elect **(67)** *(PWigham)* 4–9–7 (4x) KFallon (8) (chsd ldrs: hrd rdn to 3f out: wandered & kpt on same pce) ............................ 1¹/₂.4

Silk Degrees **(41)** *(WStorey)* 6–7–6[1] ‡³JFanning (7) (hld up: sme hdwy 4f out: wknd over 2f out) ............................ 1¹/₂.5

Count My Blessings **(54)** *(JLEyre)* 7–8–8 MHills (3) (b: trckd wnr tl wknd over 3f out) ............................ 6.6

1740 Sapphirine **(62)** *(RMWhitaker)* 5–9–2 ACulhane (4) (sn drvn along: wl bhd fnl 3f) 20.7

7/4 FARMER'S PET(op 11/10), **3/1** Three Wells, **9/2** Brodessa, **5/1** Bold Elect, **12/1** Sapphirine, **33/1** Silk Degrees, **50/1** Count My Blessings. CSF £6.73, CT £14.49. Tote £2.20: £1.30 £1.80 (£3.50). Mr D. R. Midwood (NEWMARKET) bred by Normanby Stud Ltd. 7 Rn
3m 6.2 (8.6)
SF—30/40/24/18/–/–

**1968**  ST JOHN AMBULANCE H'CAP (0-80) £2869.60 (£795.60: £380.80)
1m 3f
4-20 (4-20)

1864² **First Bid (47)** (Fav) *(RMWhitaker)* 5–7–11 ‡JFanning (5) (trckd ldrs: led over 2f out: r.o wl u.p fnl f) ............................ —1

1394 Hillzah (USA) **(74)** *(RBastiman)* 4–9–13 MHills (2) (hld up: hdwy to disp ld over 2f out: nt qckn ins fnl f) ............................ ³/₄.2

1530 Doctor's Remedy **(40)** *(MrsJJordan)* 6–7–0 ‡⁷KimMcDonnell (6) (trckd ldrs: one pce fnl 2f) ............................ 2¹/₂.3

1530⁴ Quip **(40)** *(MPNaughton)* 7–7–7 JakiHouston (4) (led tl over 2f out: kpt on fnl f) nk.4

1747 Marjons Boy **(41)** (bl) *(CDBroad)* 5–8–7[1] NCarlisle (3) (hdwy & prom 3f out: one pce) ............................ s.h.5

1394 Young George **(60)** *(MDods)* 5–8–13 KFallon (7) (lw: dwlt: hdwy & n.m.r over 2f out: sn rdn: one pce) ............................ s.h.6

1181 Barbary Reef (IRE) **(48)** *(GHEden)* 4–8–1 GCarter (1) (hld up: hdwy & n.m.r over 2f out: sn rdn: kpt on same pce) ............................ hd.7

LONG HANDICAP: Doctor's Remedy 6-11, Quip 6-10, Marjons Boy 6-11.

11/4 FIRST BID, **100/30** Barbary Reef (IRE), **4/1** Young George, **5/1** Hillzah (USA)(8/1—9/2), **11/1** Quip, **16/1** Marjons Boy, **20/1** Doctor's Remedy. CSF £14.25, Tote £3.00: £1.80 £2.20 (£9.40). Thomlinson's (WETHERBY) bred by R. M. Whitaker. 7 Rn
2m 24.6 (8.9)
SF—11/39/–/–/–/17

**1969**  E.B.F. MERMAID STKS (Mdn 2-Y.O.F) £2322.00 (£642.00: £306.00)
5f 4-55 (4-57)

1506² **Moving Image (IRE)** (Fav) *(MBell)* 8–11 MHills (1) (b.hind: trckd ldr: led over 1f out: rdn & r.o wl nr fin) ............................ —1

650 Sea Exhibition (IRE) *(MBlanshard)* 8–11 GCarter (6) (led: hdd over 1f out: kpt on) ............................ 1¹/₂.2

886³ Palm Chat *(LMCumani)* 8–11 JFortune (4) (chsd ldrs: rdn 2f out: wknd 1f out) 1¹/₂.3

My Cherrywell *(MrsVAAconley)* 8–11 KFallon (5) (lt-f: unf: prom tl outpcd ¹/₂-wy: kpt on u.p fnl f) ............................ ³/₄.4

769 Sweet Poppy *(JSWainwright)* 8–11 LCharnock (3) (prom tl outpcd ¹/₂-wy: sn bhd) 6.5

Bajan Affair *(MissLCSiddall)* 8–11 DMcKeown (2) (unf: scope: swvd lft s: rn green: in tch tl wknd 2f out) ............................ 3.6

13/8 MOVING IMAGE (IRE), **2/1** Palm Chat(op 5/4), **11/4** Sea Exhibition (IRE), **16/1** Bajan Affair, **20/1** Sweet Poppy, **33/1** My Cherrywell. CSF £6.20, Tote £2.10: £1.50 £2.30 (£4.90). Cheveley Park Stud (NEWMARKET) bred by Patrick J. Power in Ireland. 6 Rn
60.9 sec (4.2)
SF—28/22/16/13/–/–

T/Plpt: £727.80 (3.05 Tckts).
WG

**1754—CHEPSTOW (L-H)**
## Thursday, July 9th [Good to firm]
Going Allowance: minus 0.20 sec per fur (F)
Wind: almost nil

Stalls: high

**1970**  LYSAGHT H'CAP (Amateurs) (0-70) £1842.00 (£512.00: £246.00)
2¹/₄m 33y
6-30 (6-34)

(Weights raised 20 lb)

40⁴ **Glenstal Priory (44)** *(PFICole)* 5–11-3 ‡⁵MissMClark (4) (a.p: 4th st: led over 2f out: r.o wl) ............................ —1

1789² King William **(32)** (Fav) *(JLSpearing)* 7-10-5 ‡5MissTSpearing (2) (bhd tl gd hdwy over 4f out: ev ch 2f out: nt qckn fnl f) ...................... 2½.**2**

1459 Classic Statement **(49)** *(RLee)* 6-11-8 ‡5MrsCLee (12) (b: lw: plld hrd: a.p: 3rd st: led over 3f out tl over 2f out: one pce) ...................... 2.**3**

1765³ Caroles Clown **(47)** *(MJHaynes)* 6-11-11 MissYHaynes (3) (hld up: 8th st: r.o one pce fnl 2f) ...................... s.h.**4**

1640³ Back to Form **(30)** *(WGMTurner)* 7-10-3 ‡5MrsCPrice (3) (hdwy & 7th st: one pce fnl 3f) ...................... 3.**5**

1640 Algaihabane (USA) **(35)** (bl) *(PJHobbs)* 6-10-8 ‡5MrsSHobbs (10) (hdwy over 3f out: nvr nr to chal) ...................... 1.**6**

1477⁵ Mr Taylor **(37)** *(HJCollingridge)* 7-10-10 ‡5MrPClose (8) (lw: nvr trbld ldrs) ........ 8.**7**

1719⁴ Vision of Wonder **(25)** *(JSKing)* 8-10-3 MrsLPearce (5) (bhd tl hdwy 4f out: n.d) ¾.**8**

790 Lady Westgate **(25)** *(GBBalding)* 8-9-12 ‡5MrsCSmallman (11) (lw: bhd tl hdwy 4f out: wknd over 1f out) ...................... 2½.**9**

1143 Just for Kicks **(25)** *(JJO'Neill)* 6-10-3 MrPCraggs (1) (lw: n.d) ...................... 1.**10**

1765² Shar Emblem **(50)** *(SDow)* 4-11-9 ‡5MrTCuff (14) (prom 12f) ...................... nk.**11**

1290⁶ Singing Reply (USA) **(32)** *(DMarks)* 4-10-10 MissKMarks (9) (b: b.hind: plld hrd: led 3f: led 9f out tl wknd over 3f out) ...................... 2.**12**

103 Cold Marble (USA) **(43)** *(DRTucker)* 7-11-2 ‡5MissSRowe (15) (bit bkwd: a bhd)3½.**13**

1640 Coxann **(30)** *(JCMcConnochie)* 6-10-3 ‡5MrETolhurst (18) (lw: hdwy & 6th st: wknd over 3f out) ...................... 2½.**14**

1009 Sonalto **(40)** *(DLWilliams)* 6-10-13 ‡5MissVHaigh (16) (a bhd: t.o) ...................... 6.**15**

1430 Tring Park **(35)** *(RCurtis)* 6-10-8 ‡5MrGBrown (13) (led after 3f: hdd 9f out: 2nd st: wknd qckly 4f out: t.o) ...................... 3.**16**

1423 Lifetimes Ambition **(40)** *(TCasey)* 4-10-13 ‡5MissEFolkes (6) (b: prom: 9th & wkng st: t.o) ...................... 1½.**17**

1661 One of the Lads **(40)** *(BRCambidge)* 10-10-13 ‡5MrsHNoonan (17) (plld hrd: chsd ldrs 9f: t.o) ...................... 15.**18**

**4/1** King William, **11/2** Mr Taylor, Vision of Wonder(op 7/2), **10/1** Caroles Clown, **12/1** GI FNSTAL PRIORY(op 8/1), Singing Reply (USA)(20/1—25/1), **14/1** Lady Westgate, Shar Emblem(op 8/1), **16/1** Classic Statement(op 10/1), **20/1** Just for Kicks, Back to Form, Algaihabane (USA), **25/1** Lifetimes Ambition, **33/1** Tring Park, **50/1** Coxann, **66/1** Ors. CSF £53.96, CT £711.31. Tote £9.90: £2.10 £1.70 £3.50 £2.20 (£27.10). Norman Hill Plant Hire Ltd (WHATCOMBE) bred by Swettenham Stud. 18 Rn 4m 6.9

---

**1971** RIVER WYE H'CAP (0-70) £2302.50 (£640.00: £307.50) 1¼m 36y 7-00 (7-03)

1760★ **Bighayir (61)** (bl) *(MCPipe)* 5-9-10 (6x) MRoberts (8) (s.i.s: hdwy 3f out: led over 1f out: edgd lft: r.o wl) ...................... —**1**

1301 Celia Brady **(56)** *(HCandy)* 4-9-5 CRutter (5) (hdwy on ins over 2f out: rdn & r.o ins fnl f) ...................... 1½.**2**

1165⁶ Kandy Secret (USA) **(60)** *(RHannon)* 3-8-9 ‡3RPerham (7) (hdwy 3f out: ev ch over 1f out: nt qckn) ...................... ½.**3**

1721² Pusey Street Boy **(42)** *(JRBosley)* 5-8-5 AClark (12) (hdwy fnl 2f: r.o) ...................... 2½.**4**

1566 Forelino (USA) **(62)** *(JLDunlop)* 3-9-0 LDettori (2) (5th st: no hdwy fnl 3f) ...................... 3½.**5**

1388 Altermeera **(65)** *(MrsBarbaraWaring)* 4-10-0 NHowe (9) (nvr nr to chal) ...................... nk.**6**

1444⁵ Busman (IRE) **(68)** *(MajorWRHern)* 3-9-6 WCarson (11) (hdwy on ins 4f out: rdn to ld over 2f out: hdd over 1f out: eased whn btn) ...................... ½.**7**

1122 Sirtelimar (IRE) **(61)** *(BobJones)* 3-8-13 VSmith (16) (lw: 4th st: ev ch over 2f out: wknd wl over 1f out) ...................... nk.**8**

1760² Jarras **(42)** (bl) *(CASmith)* 7-8-5 JWilliams (4) (hdwy 4f out: wknd 2f out) ...................... hd.**9**

1341⁵ St Athans Lad **(40)** *(RCurtis)* 7-8-3 GBardwell (1) (dwlt: sn rcvrd: led over 8f out tl wknd over 2f out) ...................... 3.**10**

1760⁵ Muzo (USA) **(50)** *(JMBradley)* 5-8-8 ‡5ATucker (3) (7th st: wknd 3f out) ...................... 4.**11**

1572² Great Impostor **(38)** (bl) *(RJHodges)* 4-7-12(1) ‡3TSprake (13) (9th st: bhd fnl 3f) 3.**12**

1102⁵ Distant Memory **(60)** *(JWHills)* 3-8-12 RHills (1) (2nd st: wknd 3f out) ...................... s.h.**13**

1653⁴ Walking Saint **(38)** *(GraemeRoe)* 5-8-1 TyroneWilliams (15) (b.hind: 6th st: wknd over 3f out) ...................... 1½.**14**

1720⁴ Gallant Jack (IRE) **(64)** *(DHaydnJones)* 3-9-2 PaulEddery (14) (lw: led over 1f: 3rd st: wknd over 2f out) ...................... ½.**15**

Old Speckled Hen **(41)** *(TCasey)* 4-8-4 AMunro (6) (8th st: wknd over 3f out) . 1.**16**

**13/8** BIGHAYIR, **5/1** Busman (IRE), **7/1** Pusey Street Boy(5/1—15/2), Forelino (USA), **12/1** Sirtelimar (IRE)(op 8/1), Jarras(8/1—14/1), **16/1** Great Impostor(12/1—20/1), **20/1** Distant Memory, Celia Brady, Gallant Jack (IRE), **25/1** Kandy Secret (USA), **33/1** Altermeera, Muzo (USA), Old Speckled Hen, St Athans Lad, **50/1** Walking Saint. CSF £35.86, CT £621.53. Tote £2.70: £1.30 £6.10 £7.20 £2.00 (£56.70). Mr A. J. Lomas (WELLINGTON) bred by Red House Stud. 16 Rn 2m 9.6 (5.3)

SF—37/29/18/9/11/24

**1972**    WELSH BREWERS PREMIER STKS   £14117.50 (£4240.00: £2045.00: £947.50)
     1½m 23y          7-30 (7-31)

1198³ **Silver Wisp (USA) (120)** (Fav) *(GLewis)* 3-8-7 PaulEddery (1) (chsd ldr: 2nd
     st: shkn up to ld over 1f out: readily) ............................ —1
1710⋆ Jahafil **(113)** *(MajorWRHern)* 4-9-11 WCarson (2) (set slow pce: qcknd 7f out:
     hdd over 1f out: nt qckn) ............................ 1½.2
1537⋆ Profusion **(97)** *(PFICole)* 3-8-10 AMunro (3) (b.nr hind: hld up: 4th st: r.o one
     pce fnl 2f) ............................ 2.3
1710⁶ Torchon **(103)** *(GWragg)* 4-9-11 RHills (5) (lw: hld up: last st: hdwy on ins 3f
     out: wknd wl over 1f out) ............................ 8.4
1800⁴ Dare to Dream (IRE) **(61)** *(GLewis)* 3-8-7 BRouse (4) (3rd st: bhd fnl 3f: t.o) ... 25.5

**4/7** SILVER WISP (USA), **7/2** Jahafil, **13/2** Profusion, **10/1** Torchon, **66/1** Dare to Dream (IRE). CSF £2.90, Tote
£1.50: £1.10 £1.50 (£2.00). Mrs Shirley Robins (EPSOM) bred by Buckram Oak Farm in USA. 5 Rn
                                            2m 47.6 (16.3)

**1973**    MAPLE MEDIAN AUCTION GRADUATION STKS (2-Y.O) £1590.00 (£440.00: £210.00)
     5f 16y          8-00 (8-02)

1699⋆ **Mistertopogigo (IRE)** *(BBeasley)* 9-4 DNicholls (1) (lw: led 4f out: hung rt fnl
     2f: r.o) ............................ —1
1744³ Tuscan Dawn *(JBerry)* 9-4 JCarroll (5) (led 1f: w wnr: n.m.r ins fnl f: r.o) ...... nk.2
1573⁵ Special One *(JWHills)* 8-6 RHills (2) (swvd lft s: outpcd tl hdwy over 1f out: nvr
     nrr) ............................ 2½.3
1734⋆ Alasib (Fav) *(MMoubarak)* 8-13 LDettori (3) (chsd ldrs: hrd rdn 2f out: no
     rspnse) ............................ nk.4
1715² Kintwyn (v) *(DRLaing)* 8-11 TyroneWilliams (6) (rdn 3f out: sn bhd) ............ 8.5

**8/11** Alasib, **9/4** MISTERTOPOGIGO (IRE), **7/1** Tuscan Dawn, **14/1** Special One, **33/1** Kintwyn. CSF £14.83, Tote
£2.90: £1.40 £1.70 (£8.30). Mr Giovanni Alessi (HAMBLETON) bred by Tullamaine Castle Stud in Ireland. 5 Rn
                                           59.6 secs (2.6)
                                       SF—32/31/9/15/–

**1974**    FLEUR DE LYS STKS (Mdn 3-Y.O.F) £1660.00 (£460.00: £220.00)
     7f 16y          8-30 (8-34)

1315³ **Laundry Maid (78)** *(HCandy)* 8-11 CRutter (6) (mde all: rdn out) ............ —1
434⁵ Shalabia *(MMoubarak)* 8-11 LDettori (2) (b: b.hind: hld up: ev ch over 1f out:
     rdn & nt qckn fnl f) ............................ 1.2
1216⁵ Petite Sonnerie **(81)** (Fav) *(GLewis)* 8-11 PaulEddery (7) (hld up: hdwy 3f out:
     ev ch 2f out: sn hrd rdn: one pce) ............................ 2½.3
1304² Top Song **(68)** *(RHannon)* 8-11 MRoberts (4) (w ldr tl rdn & wknd 2f out) ...... 6.4
1852 Faustnluce Lady *(GAHam)* 8-11 ADicks (3) (bit bkwd: no hdwy fnl 2f) ......... 3½.5
1611 Sally Fast *(BPalling)* 8-11 JWilliams (9) (a bhd) ............................ 1½.6
1641 Spinayab *(EAWheeler)* 8-11 SWhitworth (8) (rdn 3f out: sn bhd: t.o) ............ 8.7
     Tinkers Fairy *(DTThom)* 8-11 CDwyer (5) (leggy: unf: bit bkwd: dwlt: bhd most
     of wy: t.o) ............................ 5.8
     Blue Is True (IRE) *(LJBarratt)* 8-11 RHills (1) (w ldrs 4f: t.o) ............ 8.9

**15/8** Petite Sonnerie, **3/1** Top Song, **7/2** LAUNDRY MAID, **4/1** Shalabia(op 5/2), **33/1** Blue Is True (IRE), **100/1**
Ors. CSF £15.63, Tote £4.70: £1.30 £1.60 £1.30 (£7.50). Mr C. J. R. Trotter (WANTAGE) bred by C. J. R. Trotter.
9 Rn                                               1m 22.7 (2.2)
                                       SF—43/40/32/14/3/–

**1975**    ALVESTON STKS (Mdn) £1688.00 (£468.00: £224.00)    1m 14y      9-00 (9-04)

850⁵ **Petal Girl** (Fav) *(RHannon)* 3-8-7 MRoberts (4) (swtg: hdwy 2f out: hrd rdn to ld
     ins fnl f: r.o) ............................ —1
1505 Savash (USA) **(80)** *(MMoubarak)* 3-8-12 LDettori (1) (hld up: hdwy over 2f out:
     led over 1f out tl ins fnl f: hrd rdn: r.o) ............................ hd.2
1611 Batchworth Bound *(EAWheeler)* 3-8-7 SWhitworth (5) (a.p: led 2f out tl over 1f
     out: sn wknd) ............................ 10.3
1650 Tom's Apache **(50)** (v) *(WRWilliams)* 3-8-7 ‡⁵ATucker (9) (led over 4f: wknd wl
     over 1f out) ............................ 1.4
     Bright Sea (USA) **(42)** *(WRWilliams)* 4-9-7 NHowe (8) (prom: led over 3f out to
     2f out: wknd qckly) ............................ 1.5
     Joshua John (IRE) *(BRMillman)* 3-8-12 JWilliams (7) (leggy: unf: b.nr hind: a
     bhd: t.o) ............................ 15.6
     Salinger *(JWHills)* 4-9-7 RHills (6) (w ldrs over 4f: t.o) ............ 1½.7
     Alrayed (USA) *(MajorWRHern)* 4-9-7 WCarson (3) (sn bhd: t.o fnl 4f) ............ 12.8
1674 Helleborus *(SDow)* 4-9-2 PaulEddery (2) (t.o fnl 4f) ............ 30.9

**10/11** PETAL GIRL, **9/4** Savash (USA), **7/2** Alrayed (USA)(4/1—11/2), **12/1** Salinger(tchd 25/1), **66/1** Ors. CSF £3.50, Tote £2.00: £1.30 £1.50 £2.80 (£2.80). Mr John L. Moore (MARLBOROUGH) bred by John L. Moore. 9 Rn
1m 35.6 (3.1)
SF—22/26/–/–/–/–

T/Plpt: £12.60 (195.10 Tckts).
KH

1886—**NOTTINGHAM (L-H)**
**Thursday, July 9th [Good, Good to firm patches]**
Going Allowance: St: 0.10 sec; Rnd: minus 0.05 sec per fur (G)

Stalls: low　　　　　　　　Wind: slt across　Vis: 3rd-6th mod

**1976**　VICHYSOISE CLAIMING STKS　£2559.20 (£711.20: £341.60)
1m 1f 213y　　　　　　　　　　2-20 (2-24)

| | | |
|---|---|---|
| 1565[3] | Silver Samurai (60) (RHollinshead) 3-8-8 WRyan (2) (plld out & hdwy over 2f out: led over 1f out: sn pushed clr) | —1 |
| 1255[3] | Light Hand (69) (Fav) (MHTompkins) 6-9-2 PRobinson (6) (hld up: 9th st: n.m.r 2f out: rdn & r.o fnl f: nt trble wnr) | 3½.2 |
| 1257[4] | Shoehorn (60) (MCPipe) 5-9-0 AClark (18) (chsd ldrs: 6th st: rdn & r.o fnl f) .. | 1½.3 |
| 1768[2] | Loki (IRE) (73) (GLewis) 4-9-7 ‡3DBiggs (14) (a.p: 4th st: one pce fnl 2f) | 1½.4 |
| 1637 | Northern Trial (USA) (68) (CRNelson) 4-9-3 NAdams (9) (led 2f: 2nd st: led 3f out tl hdd & wknd over 1f out) | 1½.5 |
| 1903[2] | Lyn's Return (IRE) (60) (RSimpson) 3-8-8 ‡5ATucker (13) (lw: a.p: 3rd st: ev ch 3f out: wknd appr fnl f) | 1½.6 |
| 1797 | Roger Rabbit (FR) (46) (RRoss) 3-8-6[2] MTebbutt (1) (nvr nrr) | 2.7 |
| 1565[2] | Expansionist (57) (SPCWoods) 3-8-8 WWoods (19) (lw: blkd: hdwy over 3f out: one pce appr fnl f) | 1½.8 |
| 1810[5] | Molly Splash (51) (CACyzer) 5-8-13 GDuffield (15) (chsd ldrs: 8th st: one pce fnl 2f) | 2½.9 |
| 1783[5] | Master Copy (IRE) (50) (v) (CBBBooth) 3-8-9 GOldroyd (5) (n.d) | ¾.10 |
| 1598 | Blazing Pearl (21) (v) (JLHarris) 4-8-2 ‡7GForster (7) (chsd ldrs 6f) | ½.11 |
| 1792[5] | Medbourne (IRE) (37) (JLHarris) 3-8-0 DHolland (4) (led after 2f tl hdd & wknd 3f out) | 2½.12 |
| 1797 | Edgewise (17) (DMorris) 9-8-11 ‡7StephenDavies (8) (swtg: a bhd) | 2½.13 |
| 962 | Randybay (JMackie) 7-9-10 GBaxter (16) (b: dwlt: a bhd) | 1½.14 |
| 1565 | Izitallworthit (JMackie) 3-8-6 GHind (12) (a bhd) | ½.15 |
| 1813[4] | Great Hall (54) (PDCundell) 3-8-5 JWilliams (21) (chsd ldrs 5f) | 1.16 |
| 1798[3] | Rose Cut (USA) (45) (bl) (DJSCosgrove) 5-9-5 AShoults (10) (7th st: sn rdn: wknd 3f out) | 1.17 |
| | L'Acquesiana (27) (DShaw) 4-8-5 ‡7SWilliams (17) (b: in tch 6f) | 5.18 |
| 530 | Always Alex (35) (PDEvans) 5-8-7 ‡5LNewton (11) (a bhd) | 5.19 |
| | Arcadian Princess (MissAJWhitfield) 3-8-6 DaleGibson (3) (b.nr fore: prom 5f) | 1.20 |
| 1150 | Littledale (USA) (33) (h&b) (DJGMurray-Smith) 6-9-0 CRutter (20) (dwlt: gd hdwy after 3f: 5th st: wknd qckly 3f out) | 2½.21 |

*Stewards Enquiry: Obj. to Silver Samurai by Robinson overruled.*

**2/1** Light Hand, **5/1** Shoehorn(8/1—12/1), **6/1** Loki (IRE)(op 4/1), **7/1** Lyn's Return (IRE)(op 4/1), **10/1** Expansionist(op 5/1), **12/1** SILVER SAMURAI(op 6/1), **14/1** Molly Splash(op 8/1), **16/1** Littledale (USA), Northern Trial (USA)(op 10/1), Roger Rabbit (FR), **20/1** Great Hall, **25/1** Master Copy (IRE), **33/1** L'Acquesiana, Izitallworthit, Rose Cut (USA), Edgewise, Medbourne (IRE), **50/1** Ors. CSF £39.09, Tote £9.70: £2.20 £4.00 £3.10 (£12.40). Mrs B. Facchino (UPPER LONGDON) bred by Elisha Holdings. 21 Rn　2m 7.4 (4.9)
SF—40/41/36/40/33/21

**1977**　SALMON MAYONNAISE H'CAP (3-Y.O) (0-70) £2539.60 (£705.60: £338.80)
1¾m 15y　　　　　　　　　　2-55 (2-58)

| | | |
|---|---|---|
| 1667* | Miss Pin Up (55) (Fav) (PatMitchell) 8-7 ‡3DBiggs (5) (hld up: hdwy & 5th st: led over 2f out: sn clr: rdn out) | —1 |
| 1735[2] | Gay Ming (41) (RHollinshead) 7-3[2] ‡7AGarth (2) (swtg: hld up: hdwy 3f out: r.o fnl f: nt rch wnr) | ¾.2 |
| 1286[2] | Laughton Lady (42) (MrsNMacauley) 7-11 NAdams (13) (hld up & bhd: hdwy 4f out: rdn & no ex appr fnl f) | 6.3 |
| 1491[2] | Kadari (53) (AHarrison) 8-8 WRyan (15) (prom: 3rd st: one pce fnl 3f) | 3½.4 |
| 1679[4] | Perforate (57) (bl) (SirMarkPrescott) 8-12 GDuffield (7) (b.hind: led 3f: 2nd st: wknd 2f out) | 4.5 |
| 1777[3] | Rich Pickings (38) (CACyzer) 7-7 GBardwell (4) (lw: hdwy & 9th st: kpt on appr fnl f: nvr able to chal) | 3½.6 |
| 1602* | Anar (IRE) (48) (WCarter) 7-10 ‡7CHawksley (6) (swtg: in tch: no hdwy fnl 3f) ... | ½.7 |

| | | |
|---|---|---|
| 1705 | Kentucky Chicken (USA) **(39)** (bl) *(MissLCSiddall)* 7-8[1] EJohnson (16) (led after 3f: hdd & wknd over 2f out) | 3.8 |
| 1777[2] | Alternation (FR) **(53)** (bl) *(PFICole)* 8-8 CRutter (12) (hdwy 8f out: 4th st: wknd 3f out) | 4.9 |
| 1592[3] | Arctic Circle (IRE) **(58)** *(MissAJWhitfield)* 8-13 DaleGibson (1) (lw: nvr trbld ldrs) | 2½.10 |
| 1577 | Hazaaf (USA) **(65)** *(AAScott)* 9-6 DHolland (11) (chsd ldrs: 6th st: wknd 3f out) | ¾.11 |
| 1565 | Aislabie Airborne **(46)** *(MrsNMacauley)* 7-12[3] ‡³TSprake (8) (8th st: sn rdn & btn) | s.h.12 |
| 1234* | Full Sight (IRE) **(56)** *(MHTompkins)* 8-11 PRobinson (9) (7th st: sn wknd) | 1½.13 |
| 940* | Chipper **(62)** *(RBoss)* 9-3 MTebbutt (10) (lw: in tch: wkng whn virtually p.u fnl f: fin lame) | 15.14 |
| 1374 | Sir Vidar (IRE) **(66)** (v) *(MBell)* 9-7 AClark (3) (t.o fnl 8f) | 25.15 |
| 1265[4] | Field of Dreams **(50)** *(CFWall)* 8-5 NDay (14) (t.o fnl 4f) | 12.16 |

LONG HANDICAP: Rich Pickings 7-5, Kentucky Chicken (USA) 6-13.

**4/1** MISS PIN UP(tchd 6/1), **5/1** Full Sight (IRE)(op 5/2), **7/1** Chipper, Anar (IRE), **15/2** Gay Ming, **8/1** Perforate, **11/1** Kadari(8/1—12/1), **12/1** Hazaaf (USA), Rich Pickings(op 8/1), **14/1** Alternation (FR)(op 8/1), **16/1** Laughton Lady, **20/1** Sir Vidar (IRE), **25/1** Field of Dreams, Arctic Circle (IRE), **33/1** Ors. CSF £36.32, CT £424.40. Tote £5.50: £1.70 £1.20 £2.90 £2.00 (£22.20). Mr E. Baldwin (NEWMARKET) bred by Brook Bloodstock P L C. 16 Rn                                                                  3m 4.5 (6)
                                                                                   SF—26/6/2/6/2/–

---

**1978**        GREEN SALAD (S) H'CAP (0-60) £2774.80 (£772.80: £372.40)        **6f 15y**  3-25 (3-34)

| | | |
|---|---|---|
| 1663[4] | **Breeze Away (54)** (Jt-Fav) *(RMWhitaker)* 3-9-6 DaleGibson (6) (a.p: led over 1f out: edgd rt & r.o u.p) | —1 |
| 1853[3] | Miss Brightside **(35)** *(ASmith)* 4-8-1 ‡7CHawksley (1) (lw: led over 4f: no ex fnl f) | 1½.2 |
| 1167 | Cash a Million (FR) **(46)** *(PDCundell)* 4-9-5 TRogers (3) (prom: ev ch 2f out: kpt on one pce) | nk.3 |
| 1793 | Gleneliane (IRE) **(40)** (bl) *(JLHarris)* 4-8-6 ‡7GForster (2) (lw: racd far side: hld up: rdn & kpt on fnl 2f) | 1.4 |
| 1718[4] | Reina **(31)** (bl) *(JDBethell)* 4-8-4 SDawson (24) (led stands' side: no ch appr fnl f) | 1½.5 |
| 1752[6] | Pine Glen Pepper **(32)** *(JAkehurst)* 4-8-5 JWilliams (16) (lw: hdwy over 1f out: nvr able to chal) | hd.6 |
| 1905 | Vendredi Treize **(30)** *(SRBowring)* 9-8-3 NAdams (5) (b: a.p: ev ch 2f out: wknd fnl f) | 1½.7 |
| 1813[5] | Nazare Blue **(38)** (v) *(MrsBarbaraWaring)* 5-8-11 NHowe (12) (swtchd far side & r.o fnl 2f: nvr able to chal) | hd.8 |
| 1314 | Dorking Lad **(55)** *(MHTompkins)* 10-10-0 PRobinson (18) (r.o fnl 2f: nvr rchd ldrs) | hd.9 |
| 1708 | Wayward Son **(49)** *(GLewis)* 3-8-12 ‡3DBiggs (26) (bhd: hdwy 2f out: nvr rchd ldrs) | ¾.10 |
| 1570 | Dickens Lane **(49)** *(RJHodges)* 5-9-5 ‡3RPerham (11) (lw: chsd ldrs: no ch fnl 2f) | hd.11 |
| 1583[6] | Drummer's Dream (IRE) **(39)** (v) *(MrsNMacauley)* 4-8-12 NDay (9) (led centre 4f: sn wknd) | s.h.12 |
| 1654[5] | Miss Precocious **(35)** (v) *(DShaw)* 4-8-3 ‡5ATucker (20) (s.s: n.d) | 2.13 |
| 1741 | Domiana **(31)** *(MBlanshard)* 4-8-4 GBaxter (17) (n.d) | ¾.14 |
| 1904 | Barbezieux **(30)** *(TJNaughton)* 5-8-3 GBardwell (22) (b: n.d) | 2.15 |
| 1752 | Hinari Hi Fi **(46)** *(PDEvans)* 7-8-8 ‡5LNewton (23) (prom stands' side tl wknd over 2f out) | 1½.16 |
| 1417 | Stormbuster **(51)** *(PSFelgate)* 3-9-3 WRyan (19) (prom stands' side over 3f: sn wknd) | hd.17 |
| 1795 | Classic Exhibit **(47)** (bl) *(SPCWoods)* 3-8-8 WWoods (21) (n.d) | ½.18 |
| 1795[3] | Libra Legend **(56)** *(CEBrittain)* 3-9-8 DHolland (15) (prom stands' side over 3f) | s.h.19 |
| 1617[4] | Dreams Eyes **(35)** (Jt-Fav) *(RBastiman)* 4-8-1[2] ‡7HBastiman (14) (b.hind: s.i.s: nt rcvr) | ½.20 |
| 1364[5] | Our John **(48)** (v) *(RonaldThompson)* 3-9-0 AProud (10) (lw: n.d) | 1½.21 |
| 1552[6] | Tippling (USA) **(31)** *(PBurgoyne)* 5-7-11 ‡7AntoinetteArmes (13) (t.o) | 8.22 |
| 1759 | In the Print **(37)** (v) *(MrsBarbaraWaring)* 4-8-10 CRutter (8) (t.o) | 2½.23 |
| | 1904 Minizen Music (IRE) (14/1) Withdrawn (bolted bef s) : not under orders | |

**8/1** BREEZE AWAY, Dreams Eyes, **9/1** Pine Glen Pepper, **10/1** Libra Legend (USA)(op 6/1), Vendredi Treize, **11/1** Nazare Blue, **12/1** Reina, Hinari Hi Fi, **14/1** Miss Precocious, Miss Brightside, **16/1** Dorking Lad, Dickens Lane, **20/1** Tippling (USA), Cash a Million (FR), Our John, Stormbuster, Gleneliane (IRE), Drummer's Dream (IRE), **25/1** Ors. CSF £114.71, CT £1,996.19. Tote £13.70: £3.80 £2.50 £3.60 £6.90 (£43.60). Mr G. F. Pemberton (WETHERBY) bred by F. C. T. Wilson. 23 Rn; No bid                                        1m 16.2 (5.2)
                                                                                   SF—14/–/6/–/–/–

**1979**    SUMMER PUDDING MEDIAN AUCTION STKS (2-Y.O) £2461.20 (£683.20: £327.60)
        5f 13y                                     4-00 (4-01)

1868[2] Joyofracing (Fav) (WAO'Gorman) 9-0 DHolland (5) [trckd ldr: shkn up to ld
               over 1f out: eased nr fin] ............ **—1**
1575[2] My Bonus (DJSCosgrove) 8-9 WRyan (1) [led over 3f: rdn & no ex fnl f] ........ 1½.**2**
1360[3] Isotonic (GMMoore) 8-13 NAdams (3) [chsd ldrs: sn rdn: no imp fnl 2f] ............ 4.**3**
      Gweek (IRE) (PAKelleway) 8-6 PRobinson (4) [cmpt: chsd ldrs 3f] ............ 2½.**4**
      Stapleford Lass (SPCWoods) 8-6 WWoods (6) [neat: lt-f: sn wl bhd] ............. 1½.**5**
1283* Tom Piper (JBerry) 9-0 GDuffield (2) [chsd ldrs over 2f: sn rdn & wknd] ............ 3.**6**

**4/6** JOYOFRACING, **4/1** Tom Piper(op 5/2), My Bonus, **16/1** Gweek (IRE)(op 6/1), Isotonic(op 5/1), **33/1**
Stapleford Lass. CSF £3.90, Tote £1.80: £1.10 £1.80 (£1.70). Mr N. S. Yong (NEWMARKET) bred by The Duke
of Marlborough. 6 Rn                                           61.8 sec (3.1)
                                                SF—48/37/25/8/2/–

**1980**    STRAWBERRIES AND CREAM STKS (F & M) £2600.40 (£719.40: £343.20)
        1¾m 15y                                      4-30 (4-31)

1556[3] Spikenard (PTWalwyn) 3-8-6 PRobinson (3) [mde all: rdn 2f out: hld on wl nr
                 fin] ............ **—1**
1751* Anchorage (IRE) (Fav) (HRACecil) 3-8-6 WRyan (1) [stdd & propped s: hdwy &
                 2nd st: ev ch 2f out: sn rdn: unable qckn nr fin] ................ s.h.**2**
1286 Shanti Flyer (IRE) (47) (SPCWoods) 3-8-3 WWoods (2) [lw: chsd wnr tl rdn &
                 3rd st: sn bhd] ............ 20.**3**

**1/4** Anchorage (IRE), **3/1** SPIKENARD, **40/1** Shanti Flyer (IRE). CSF £4.05, Tote £2.80 (£1.10). Lord Howard de
Walden (LAMBOURN) bred by Lord Howard de Walden. 3 Rn                 3m 11.8 (13.3)

**1981**    AGRANACUC APP'CE STKS (Mdn 3 Y.O) £1922.00 (£532.00: £252.00)
        1m 54y                                      5-00 (5-01)

1643 Weeheby (USA) (67) (AAScott) 9-0 JTate (3) [sn led: rdn & hld on wl fnl f] ....... **—1**
      Much Sought After (DMorley) 9-0 EBentley (1) [b.hind: hld up: 2nd st: ev ch 2f
                 out: r.o u.p ins fnl f] ................ ¾.**2**
4415 Retender (USA) (Fav) (LMCumani) 8-9 ‡JCHarris (2) [led early: 3rd st: ev ch 3f
                 out tl nt qckn ins fnl f] ............ s.h.**3**

**4/6** Retender (USA), **9/4** WEEHEBY (USA), **4/1** Much Sought After. CSF £8.02, Tote £2.70 (£2.00). Maktoum Al
Maktoum (NEWMARKET) bred by Courtney & Congleton in USA. 3 Rn            1m 48.4 (8.8)
T/Plpt: £411.10 (5.4 Tckts).                                                 Dk

## 1822a—LONGCHAMP (R-H)
### Wednesday, July 1st [Soft]
Going Allowance: 0.30 sec per fur (G)

**1982a**    PRIX DU BOIS (Gp 3) (2-Y.O) £20640.00   5f

    **Glorieux Dancer (FR)** (France) 2-8-9 MBoutin ..................................................... **—1**
    Showgum (FR) (France) 2-8-7 AJunk ................................................................. 2½.**2**
    Pantagruel (FR) (bl) (France) 2-8-9 ELegrix .......................................................... 2.**3**
Tote 2.00f: 1.10f 1.30f (SF: 4.50f). Mr W.Wolf (R.Collet,FRANCE) bred by L. Romanet, W. Wolf & H. Bensoussen
in France. 4 Rn                                                  59.8 sec (2.8)
                                                SF—69/57/51

## 1497a—EVRY (R-H)
### Thursday, July 2nd [Soft]
Going Allowance: nil sec per fur (G)

**1983a**    PRIX DE RIS-ORANGIS (Gp 3)    £20640.00   6f

1352a[3] **Wedding of the Sea (USA)** (France) 3-8-6 TJarnet ........................................... **—1**
1467 CENTRAL CITY (RHannon) 3-8-6 BRaymond ....................................... 1½.**2**
    Silicon Bavaria (FR) (France) 5-9-1 MBoutin .......................................... 1½.**3**
1467[2] AMIGO MENOR (bl) (DJGMurray-Smith) 6-9-4 CRutter (btn further 4l) ................. **8**
Tote 2.10f: 1.20f 3.40f 2.10f (19.80f). Sheikh Mohammed (A. Fabre,FRANCE) bred by Darley Stud Management
Co Ltd. in USA. 9 Rn                                           1m 10.69 (0.69)
                                                SF—78/72/75

1492a—**SAINT-CLOUD (L-H)**

**Sunday, July 5th [Soft]**

Going Allowance: minus 0.05 sec per fur (G)

**1984a**     GRAND PRIX DE SAINT-CLOUD (Gp 1) (C & F) £154799.00   1½m

1497a★ **Pistolet Bleu (IRE)** *(France)* 4-9-8 DBoeuf (mid div: gd hdwy wl over 2f out: led 2f out: sn clr: easily) .................................................. —1

1497a³ Magic Night (FR) *(France)* 4-9-5 ABadel (hld up in rr: hdwy 2f out: ev ch wl over 1f out: kpt on one pce: no ch w wnr) ................................ 5.2

1205⁴ Subotica (FR) (Fav) *(France)* 4-9-5 TJarnet (trckd ldrs: hdwy 2f out: hrd rdn & one pce fnl f) ............................................................. 2½.3

1646a² Saganeca (USA) *(France)* 4-9-5 GMosse (hld up: hdwy 2f out: sn hrd rdn & one pce) ............................................................. 3.4

    Danae de Brule (FR) (bl) *(France)* 5-9-5 RLaplanche (a.p: led 4f out tl hdd 2f out: sn btn) .......................................................... 10.5

1497a² Art Bleu (bl) *(France)* 5-9-8 CAubert (mid div st: n.d) ........................ 2.6

    L'Oiseau Bleu Roi (USA) *(France)* 5-9-8 PBruneau (led to 4f out: wknd qckly) .. 8.7

**Evens** Subotica (FR), **14/10** Art Bleu, L'Oiseau Bleu Roi (USA), PISTOLET BLEU (IRE), **13/4** Magic Night (FR), **37/4** Saganeca (USA), **22/1** Danae de Brule (FR). Tote 2.40f: 1.60f 2.00f (SF: 11.10f). Mr D.Wildenstein (E.Lellouche,FRANCE) bred by Dayton Ltd. in Ireland. 7 Rn    2m 30.3 (equals standard)
SF—102/89/87/78/58/57/41

1826a—**SAN SIRO (R-H)**

**Saturday, July 4th [Heavy]**

**1985a**     PREMIO GINO MANTOVANI (listed race) (2-Y.O) £20930.00   7f 110y

1827a★ **ANCESTRAL DANCER** *(MBell)* 2-8-9 WNewnes ................................. —1

1827a³ JUST SPECULATION (IRE) *(PFICole)* 2-8-7 GBaxter ............................ 2¼.2

    Zaira da Cesena (USA) *(Italy)* 2-8-8(1) SSoto ....................................... 1.3

Tote 17L: 12L 13L 14L (21L). Innlaw Racing (NEWMARKET) bred by Hillfields Stud. 8 Rn    1m 35.5

1774—**WARWICK (L-H)**

**Friday, July 10th [Good to firm]**

Going Allowance: minus 0.05 sec per fur (G)        Wind: almost nil

Stalls: low

**1986**     TRICITY BENDIX APP'CE CLAIMING STKS (3-Y.O)   £2069.20 (£571.20: £271.60)
1m                                             2-30 (2-31)

1705 **Chief of Staff (75)** *(PFICole)* 8-6 ‡³JDSmith (6) (hld up & bhd: 4th st: gd hdwy 2f out: led ins fnl f: r.o) ......................................... —1

1604⁴ Neltegrity **(56)** (v) *(THCaldwell)* 8-8 ‡³EHusband (3) (lw: led: clr 5f out: wknd & hdd ins fnl f) ............................................. 2.2

1839⁵ Hot Prospect *(JEtherington)* 8-4 KRutter (4) (hdwy 4f out: 3rd st: wknd over 1f out) ................................................................. 7.3

1903³ Dancing Beau (IRE) **(78)** (Fav) *(MrsLPiggott)* 8-4 ‡⁷WAldwinckle (2) (chsd ldr: 2nd st: wknd over 1f out) ......................................... 1.4

1681⁴ Hullo Mary Doll *(RIngram)* 8-1 ‡³RossBerry (5) (prom 4f: last & wkng st) ............ 2.5

1005⁵ Up All Night *(JWHills)* 8-1 ‡³AntoinetteArmes (1) (swvd lft s: squeezed out on ins & uns rdr after 1f) ........................................... 0

**13/8** Dancing Beau (IRE), **5/2** CHIEF OF STAFF, **4/1** Up All Night, **9/1** Neltegrity(op 5/1), **12/1** Hot Prospect(op 8/1), **40/1** Hullo Mary Doll. CSF £19.70, Tote £2.70: £1.40 £2.90 (£11.30). Mr Fahd Salman (WHATCOMBE) bred by Lord Halifax. 6 Rn    1m 41 (4)
SF—26/22/–/–/–/–

**1987**     TRICITY BENDIX H'CAP (0-80) £3255.10 (£971.80: £464.40: £210.70)
5f                                                 3-00 (3-02)

(Weights raised 7 lb)

    **Jess Rebec (49)** *(LGCottrell)* 4-8-4 NCarlisle (1) (lw: outpcd & in rr: rdn & gd hdwy over 1f out: str run to ld wl ins fnl f) ............................. —1

1727³ Rays Mead **(49)** (Jt-Fav) *(LJHolt)* 4-8-4 WNewnes (4) (w ldrs: ev ch ins fnl f: r.o) 1.2

1757 Shades of Jade **(55)** *(JJBridger)* 4-8-10 SWhitworth (9) (led tl wl ins fnl f) ....... s.h.3

1305 Darussalam **(69)** *(RLee)* 5-9-10 RCochrane (8) (lw: gd hdwy fnl f: fin wl) .......... ½.4

1776³ My Ruby Ring **(41)** *(DRLaing)* 5–7-3 ‡⁷KimMcDonnell (2) (b: a.p: r.o one pce fnl
f) .................................................................................................................... hd.5
1727⁵ Iron King **(69)** (v) *(JLSpearing)* 6–9-10 NHowe (3) (hdwy fnl f: nt rch ldrs) .......... 2.6
1753² Tommy Tempest **(47)** (Jt-Fav) *(KRBurke)* 3–7-10 JQuinn (5) (no hdwy fnl 2f) .. hd.7
1522⁵ Samsolom **(63)** (Jt-Fav) *(JBalding)* 4–9-4 AClark (7) (lw: prom over 3f) ............ ³/₄.8
1725⁵ Lady of the Fen **(48)** *(MrsNMacauley)* 4–8-0 ‡³FNorton (6) (bhd fnl 2f: t.o) ...... 30.9

**5/1** Tommy Tempest, Rays Mead, Samsolom, **11/2** Darussalam, **6/1** Iron King, **13/2** Shades of Jade, **15/2** My
Ruby Ring, **14/1** Lady of the Fen, **16/1** JESS REBEC(op 10/1). CSF £86.70, CT £527.02. Tote £18.90: £3.00
£1.40 £2.90 (£54.50). Mr Byron J. Stokes (CULLOMPTON) bred by K. J. Mercer. 9 Rn    59.8 sec (1.8)
SF—49/45/50/62/26/53

**1988**     SYD MERCER MEMORIAL TROPHY (H'cap) (0-80) £2929.50 (£812.00: £388.50)
     2¹/₄m 214y                         3-30 (3-32)
(Weights raised 1 lb)

1719² **Smilingatstrangers (42)** (v) *(MrsBarbaraWaring)* 4–7-1 ‡⁷CHawksley (8) (hld
up: rdn along 4f out: 7th st: hdwy to ld over 1f out: r.o) ....... —1
1407⁴ Skisurf **(52)** *(CEBrittain)* 6–8-4 GCrealock (5) (hld up: stdy hdwy 5f out: 6th st:
ev ch over 1f out: r.o) .......................................................... ³/₄.2
1606⁶ Shoofe (USA) **(72)** *(DMorley)* 4–9-10 WRyan (1) (a.p: 5th st: ev ch over 1f out:
one pce) ................................................................................. 3¹/₂.3
1560⁵ Lyphard's Song (IRE) **(44)** *(NAGraham)* 4–7-7⁽³⁾ ‡³FNorton (9) (a.p: 3rd st: led
2f out tl over 1f out: no ex) ...................................................... ³/₄.4
1874 Go South **(68)** (bl) *(JRJenkins)* 8–9-6 JFortune (4) (hdwy 5f out: wknd wl over
1f out) ................................................................................... ¹/₂.5
1697 Mrs Barton (IRE) **(64)** (Fav) *(BWHills)* 4–9-2 DHolland (6) (chsd ldr: pushed
along 10f out: 2nd st: ev ch 2f out: wknd over 1f out) ....... 1¹/₂.6
1290 Seldom In **(47)** *(JWharton)* 6–7-13 JQuinn (3) (hdwy 5f out: 4th st: wknd 2f out:
t.o) ...................................................................................... 15.7
1361⁵ Megan's Flight **(44)** (v) *(THCaldwell)* 7–7-3⁽¹⁾ ‡⁷AGarth (10) (led tl wknd 2f out:
t.o) ........................................................................................ 5.8
1640 First Exhibition **(43)** *(MrsAKnight)* 5–7-9⁽²⁾ NCarlisle (7) (rdn 6f out: a bhd: t.o fnl
4f) ........................................................................................... 7.9
1640 Nice Picture (IRE) **(46)** *(RChampion)* 4–7-7⁽⁵⁾ ‡⁵BDoyle (2) (rdn 7f out: a bhd: t.o
fnl 4f) ................................................................................... 10.10
LONG HANDICAP: Lyphard's Song (IRE) 6-13, First Exhibition 6-4, Nice Picture (IRE) 7-6.

**7/2** Mrs Barton (IRE)(11/2—3/1), **9/2** Skisurf(3/1—5/1), SMILINGATSTRANGERS(op 3/1), **11/2** Shoofe (USA),
**6/1** Go South, Seldom In, **33/1** Lyphard's Song (IRE), **40/1** Megan's Flight, **50/1** First Exhibition, **66/1** Nice
Picture (IRE). CSF £22.19, CT £98.04. Tote £5.20: £2.00 £1.90 £2.10 (£9.50). Mr Harry Chisman
(CHIPPENHAM) bred by T. McCarthy. 10 Rn      4m 14.9 (10.9)

**1989**     MOLLINGTON (S) NURSERY     £2324.00 (£644.00: £308.00)    **6f**      4-00 (4-03)
(Weights raised 17 lb)

1547⁴ **Another Kingdom** *(JWharton)* 9-2 JWilliams (1) (lw: hdwy on ins & 4th st: hrd
rdn to ld ins fnl f: r.o wl) ...................................................... —1
928⁶ Be Polite (IRE) (Fav) *(MBell)* 9-7 RHills (4) (3rd st: led over 1f out tl hdd & nt qckn
ins fnl f) ............................................................................... 2.2
1749⁴ Risky Number *(JSMoore)* 8-12 ‡⁵ATucker (5) (5th st: hdwy over 1f out: hrd rdn &
ev ch ins fnl f: nt qckn) ........................................................ s.h.3
1121 Walid's Princess (IRE) (bl) *(JWharton)* 8-7 JQuinn (2) (rdn & bhd: last st: hdwy
over 1f out: nt clr run ins fnl f: r.o) ........................................ 1.4
1749⁶ Nut Bush *(NACallaghan)* 9-7 WRyan (6) (chsd ldr: 2nd & rdn st: led wl over 1f
out: sn hdd: eased whn btn wl ins fnl f) ................................ 4.5
1749³ Gypsy Legend (bl) *(WGMTurner)* 8-9 NWewnes (3) (swtg: led over 4f) ......... 2¹/₂.6

**7/4** Be Polite (IRE), **7/2** Gypsy Legend, Risky Number, **6/1** ANOTHER KINGDOM(op 3/1), Walid's Princess (IRE),
**8/1** Nut Bush(5/1—9/1). CSF £17.35, Tote £8.10: £2.40 £1.40 (£7.30). Mr W. Wharton (MELTON MOWBRAY)
bred by A. B. Barraclough. 6 Rn; Bt in 3,800 gns      1m 16.3 (4.3)
SF—10/7/–/–/–/–

**1990**     HALOGEN STKS (Mdn 3-Y.O) £2635.50 (£728.00: £346.50)    **1³/₄m 194y**    4-30 (4-32)

1464⁵ **Teddy's Play (USA) (80)** (Fav) *(JWHills)* 9-0 RHills (3) (lw: mde all: clr 2f out:
unchal) ................................................................................ —1
1704⁵ Christmas Cactus *(JHMGosden)* 9-0 RCochrane (1) (hld up: wnt 2nd 6f out:
rdn & one pce fnl 2f) ............................................................ 6.2
864⁵ Alizari (USA) (bl) *(GHarwood)* 9-0 AClark (2) (chsd wnr tl rdn 6f out: last & btn st) 4.3

**4/11** TEDDY'S PLAY (USA)(4/6—2/7), **5/2** Alizari (USA)(6/4—3/1), **8/1** Christmas Cactus(5/1—10/1). CSF
£3.18, Tote £1.60 (£2.20). Mr Christopher Wright (LAMBOURN) bred by Allan Mactier & Theatrical Syndicate in
USA. 3 Rn      3m 16 (7)
SF—23/12/13

**1991** WARWICK AUCTION STKS (Mdn 2-Y.O) £2284.80 (£632.80: £302.40)
5f
5-00 (5-04)

| | |
|---|---|
| 1443⁵ **Florac (IRE)** *(MJHeaton-Ellis)* 8-5⁽¹⁾ WNewnes (3) (b.hind: lw: a:p: hrd rdn over 1f out: r.o to ld nr fin) | —1 |
| The Bethanian *(WRMuir)* 8-6 SWhitworth (6) (leggy: led tl ct cl home) | ½.2 |
| 1880² Red Leader (IRE) (Fav) *(PFICole)* 8-6 AClark (1) (a.p: rdn 2f out: hrd rdn & ev ch ins fnl f: nt qckn) | ¾.3 |
| Troon *(MrsLPiggott)* 8-8 JWilliams (8) (b: b.hind: unf: dwlt: hdwy over 1f out: fin wl) | nk.4 |
| 1164 Sui Generis (IRE) *(CGCox)* 7-9 ‡⁵ATucker (4) (chsd ldrs: r.o one pce fnl 2f) | nk.5 |
| 255⁵ Critical Mass *(JBerry)* 8-10 RCochrane (5) (outpcd tl hdwy over 1f out: n.d) | 2.6 |
| 1378 Recit D'Argent *(CJames)* 8-5 JQuinn (7) (prom 3f) | 4.7 |
| Senor L'Amour *(AndrewTurnell)* 8-5 RHills (2) (str: scope: bkwd: dwlt: a in rr: t.o) | 10.8 |

2/1 Red Leader (IRE), 9/4 FLORAC (IRE), 7/2 The Bethanian(5/2—4/1), 6/1 Critical Mass(4/1—7/1), 12/1 Troon(op 5/1), 16/1 Recit D'Argent, 33/1 Ors. CSF £10.64, Tote £3.80: £1.50 £1.60 £1.20 (£9.30). Lady Scott (WROUGHTON) bred by Mrs P. L. Yong in Ireland. 8 Rn
61 sec (3)
SF—26/25/22/23/9/16

T/Plpt: £71.60 (25.05 Tckts).
KH

---

1604—**CHESTER (L-H)**
**Friday, July 10th [Good]**
Going Allowance: minus 0.20 sec per fur (F)
Wind: almost nil

Stalls: low

**1992** WATERGATE APP'CE H'CAP (0-70) £3174.50 (£882.00: £423.50)
7f 122y
6-30 (6-33)

(Weights raised 1 lb)

| | |
|---|---|
| **Kinlacey (51)** *(BAMcMahon)* 5–8-12 SSanders (13) (bit bkwd: chsd ldrs: 2nd st: led wl ins fnl f: sn clr) | —1 |
| 1889² Tyrian Purple (IRE) (50) *(RHollinshead)* 4–8-11 MHumphries (12) (led 5f out tl hdd wl ins fnl f) | 3.2 |
| 1747⁴ No Comebacks (44) *(EJAlston)* 4–8-5 GMitchell (15) (hdwy & 6th st: kpt on over 1f out: nt rch ldrs) | 5.3 |
| 1729⁵ Ballad Dancer (55) *(EJAlston)* 7–8-11 ‡⁵SKnott (9) (bhd: hdwy over 2f out: nrst fin) | nk.4 |
| 28³ Cee-Jay-Ay (63) *(JBerry)* 5–9-10 SHaworth (3) (bkwd: sn bhd & outpcd: gd hdwy over 1f out: fin wl) | 2.5 |
| 213 Green's Cassatt (USA) (50) *(WMBrisbourne)* 4–8-11 DCarson (5) (swtg: hdwy fnl 2f: nt rch ldrs) | s.h.6 |
| Crofter's Cline (50) *(ABailey)* 8–8-6 ‡⁵WHollick (14) (bkwd: chsd ldrs tl 3rd & wkng st) | nk.7 |
| 1608* Hand on Heart (IRE) (64) *(WJHaggas)* 3–9-2 SallyRadford-Howes (16) (hdwy ½-wy: 4th & rdn st: sn btn) | 3¼.8 |
| 1833³ Veloce (IRE) (55) (bl) (Fav) *(MO'Neill)* 4–9-2 AGarth (2) (hdwy 3f out: hrd rdn & 5th st: sn btn) | s.h.9 |
| 1718 Lucky Barnes (37) (bl) *(FJYardley)* 5–7-7⁽⁵⁾ ‡⁵JDennis (8) (prom over 4f) | hd.10 |
| 1527 Must Be Magical (USA) (32) (bl) *(FHLee)* 4–7-7 DWright (6) (a in rr) | nk.11 |
| 1627 Kick on Majestic (IRE) (41) (bl) *(NBycroft)* 3–7-7 TWilson (10) (m.n.s) | ½.12 |
| 1417⁵ Sara Anne (IRE) (55) *(WMBrisbourne)* 3–8-7 DDunnachie (7) (prom 4f) | ½.13 |
| Sequestrator (39) *(PDEvans)* 9–7-9⁽⁷⁾ ‡⁵HayleyWilliams (11) (chsd ldrs over 4f: sn lost tch: t.o) | 14 |
| 914² Malcesine (IRE) (57) *(CaptJWilson)* 3–8-4 ‡⁵AnnaLaw (17) (t.o) | 15 |
| 1627 Coat of Dreams (51) *(RBastiman)* 3–8-3⁽¹⁾ HBastiman (1) (swtg: led over 2f: wknd over 3f out: t.o) | 16 |
| 1245 Blimpers Disco (39) *(EHOwenjun)* 3–7-13⁽¹⁾ JMarshall (4) (a bhd: t.o) | 17 |
| 857 Baharlilys (55) *(NCWright)* 3–8-2 ‡⁵ADaly (18) (s.s: a bhd: t.o) | 18 |

LONG HANDICAP: Lucky Barnes 7-3, Must Be Magical (USA) 6-12, Kick on Majestic (IRE) 7-4, Sequestrator 6-10.

7/2 Veloce (IRE), 6/1 Tyrian Purple (IRE), Hand on Heart (IRE), 7/1 Cee-Jay-Ay, 9/1 Ballad Dancer, 12/1 No Comebacks(op 8/1), 16/1 Coat of Dreams, Malcesine (IRE), 20/1 Sara Anne (IRE), KINLACEY, Kick on Majestic (IRE), 25/1 Baharlilys, 33/1 Blimpers Disco, Crofter's Cline, 50/1 Ors. CSF £125.64, CT £1,383.69. Tote £53.70: £8.70 £2.00 £3.10 £2.40 (£130.80). Mr Michael G. T. Stokes (TAMWORTH) bred by J. E. Sainsbury and Mrs P. E. White. 18 Rn
1m 35.28 (2.58)
SF—36/26/5/10/17/3

**1993**　　ALICE HAWTHORN STKS (Mdn 2-Y.O.F) £3870.00 (£1070.00: £510.00)
　　　　　**5f 16y**　　　　　　　　　　　　　　　　　　　　　7-00 (7-01)

1609² **Riston Lady (IRE)** *(BSRothwell)* 8-11　DHolland (3) (w ldr: led ent st: qcknd clr
　　　　　　　　over 1f out: rdn out nr fin) ..................................... —1
1384³ Bangles (Fav) *(LordHuntingdon)* 8-11　MRoberts (2) (swtg: led: hrd drvn ½-wy:
　　　　　　　　hdd ent st: sn rdn: kpt on nr fin) ......................................... 1½.2
　　　　 Sicily Oak *(DMcCain)* 8-11　GBardwell (1) (leggy: scope: bit bkwd: s.s: a bhd &
　　　　　　　　outpcd) ......................................................................... 7.3

**1/5** Bangles(op 1/8), **5/1** RISTON LADY (IRE), **16/1** Sicily Oak. CSF £6.27, Tote £4.10 (£1.30). Mrs G. M. Z.
Spink (CATWICK) bred by D. Cordell-Lavarack in Ireland. 3 Rn　　　　　　　　63.55 sec (2.95)
　　　　　　　　　　　　　　　　　　　　　　　　　　　　　　　SF—18/8/–

**1994**　　RED DEER H'CAP (3-Y.O) (0-100) £5442.50 (£1640.00: £795.00: £372.50)
　　　　　**5f 16y**　　　　　　　　　　　　　　　　　　　　　7-30 (7-32)

1535⁶ **Bunty Boo (82)** *(BAMcMahon)* 8-9　TQuinn (1) (mde virtually all: hrd rdn fnl f:
　　　　　　　　hld on gamely) ................................................................ —1
　　　　 Artistic Reef **(92)** *(GHEden)* 9-5　PatEddery (3) (lw: disp ld: rdn over 1f out: r.o) hd.2
　 1219 Sharling **(72)** *(JHMGosden)* 7-13　AMcGlone (5) (faltered after 1f: sn rcvrd:
　　　　　　　　chsd ldrs: rdn & no ex fnl f) ............................................... 2.3
1717* Echo-Logical **(94)** (Fav) *(JBerry)* 9-7　JCarroll (7) (lw: a.p: rdn to chal over 1f out:
　　　　　　　　unable qckn ins fnl f) ....................................................... 1.4
1871³ Hot Lavender (CAN) **(70)** *(CFWall)* 7-11⁽¹⁾　AMunro (6) (chsd ldrs: sltly hmpd
　　　　　　　　½-wy: kpt on u.p fnl f) ..................................................... 2½.5
　　　　 Miss Shadowfax **(67)** *(CNAllen)* 7-8　GBardwell (2) (bit bkwd: outpcd & sn bhd) 7.6
　 1289 Nur (USA) **(71)** *(HThomsonJones)* 7-12　NCarlisle (4) (lw: sn rdn along: a
　　　　　　　　outpcd) ........................................................................ 3½.7

**9/4** Echo-Logical, **100/30** BUNTY BOO, **7/2** Hot Lavender (CAN), **6/1** Sharling, Artistic Reef, **14/1** Nur (USA),
**25/1** Miss Shadowfax. CSF £21.49, Tote £4.30: £2.00 £2.50 (£13.10). Mrs R. C. Mayall (TAMWORTH) bred by
Mrs J. McMahon. 7 Rn　　　　　　　　　　　　　　　　　　　　62.07 sec (1.47)
　　　　　　　　　　　　　　　　　　　　　　　　　SF—45/54/27/45/11/–

**1995**　　CARDINAL PUFF GRADUATION STKS (2-Y.O) £4370.00 (£1310.00: £630.00: £290.00)
　　　　　**7f 2y**　　　　　　　　　　　　　　　　　　　　　8-00 (8-04)

1748* **Marillette (USA)** (Jt-Fav) *(JHMGosden)* 8-13　PatEddery (5) (lw: hld up: hdwy
　　　　　　　　3f out: led over 1f out: r.o) ............................................... —1
1630* Known Approach (USA) (Jt-Fav) *(PFICole)* 9-4　TQuinn (1) (lw: prom: hrd drvn
　　　　　　　　2f out: kpt on ins fnl f: nvr nrr) .......................................... 1.2
　 828⁴ Totally Unique (USA) *(MBell)* 8-11　MHills (6) (led ½-wy tl over 1f out: kpt on one
　　　　　　　　pce) ............................................................................ 1½.3
1605³ Civil Law (IRE) *(RHollinshead)* 8-11　WRyan (2) (bhd & outpcd tl styd on appr fnl
　　　　　　　　f: nt rch ldrs) ................................................................. 3.4
1536⁵ Pamar *(CEBrittain)* 8-11　MRoberts (4) (bit bkwd: led to ½-wy: wknd 2f out:
　　　　　　　　eased whn btn) ............................................................. 10.5
　　　　　1728³ Club Verge (IRE) (40/1) Withdrawn (lame at s) : not under orders

**7/4** MARILLETTE (USA), Known Approach (USA), **11/2** Civil Law (IRE), **6/1** Pamar, **7/1** Totally Unique (USA)(op
12/1). CSF £5.25, Tote £2.50: £1.70 £1.70 (£2.50). Sheikh Mohammed (NEWMARKET) bred by Robert Clay &
Rogers Trust in USA. 5 Rn　　　　　　　　　　　　　　　　　1m 28.94 (2.74)
　　　　　　　　　　　　　　　　　　　　　　　　　SF—37/39/27/18/–

**1996**　　GRENADIER H'CAP (0-90) £3704.00 (£1112.00: £536.00: £248.00)
　　　　　**1½m 66y**　　　　　　　　　　　　(Weights raised 6 lb)　　　8-30 (8-32)

1841⁵ **Rose Glen (62)** *(ABailey)* 6-8-4　‡⁵ATucker (4) (hld up: hdwy over 2f out: 2nd st:
　　　　　　　　rdn to ld wl ins fnl f) ....................................................... —1
1606³ Muizenberg **(70)** *(JACEdwards)* 5-9-3　WRyan (2) (lw: stdd s: hld up & bhd:
　　　　　　　　hdwy & 4th st: ev ch ins fnl f: r.o) ...................................... hd.2
1274² Mingus (USA) **(56)** *(MrsJRRamsden)* 5-8-3　MRoberts (6) (dwlt: sn chsng ldrs:
　　　　　　　　led 2f out tl wl ins fnl f) ................................................... 1.3
1556² Truben (USA) **(86)** (Fav) *(HRACecil)* 3-9-6　PatEddery (1) (b.nr hind: hld up:
　　　　　　　　effrt & pushed along 3f out: 6th & btn ent st) ...................... 8.4
　 940³ Cultured **(79)** *(MRStoute)* 3-8-13　RCochrane (5) (lw: chsd ldrs: 5th & rdn st: sn
　　　　　　　　btn) ............................................................................ 5.5
1465 Arabian Bold (IRE) **(77)** *(WJHaggas)* 4-9-10　MHills (7) (lw: led to 2f out: 3rd &
　　　　　　　　wkng st) ...................................................................... 3½.6
　　　　 Alicante **(47)** *(FJYardley)* 5-7-8⁽¹⁾　JQuinn (3) (bkwd: lost pl over 4f out: 7th & t.o
　　　　　　　　st) .............................................................................. 6.7
　　　　　　　　　LONG HANDICAP: Alicante 7-5.

**15/8** Truben (USA), **3/1** Mingus (USA), **7/2** Cultured, **6/1** ROSE GLEN, **8/1** Muizenberg, **12/1** Arabian Bold (IRE), **50/1** Alicante. CSF £46.32, Tote £6.40: £2.70 £3.00 (£27.30). Mr D. G. Furlong (TARPORLEY) bred by R. G. Bonson. 7 Rn                                                        2m 41.92 (5.32)
SF—13/25/9/10/–/–

## 1997
HENRY GEE STKS (Mdn 3-Y.O) £3817.50 (£1140.00: £545.00: £247.50)
**1¼m 75y**                                                 9-00 (9-02)

1245² **Greek Gold (IRE)** (Fav) *(MRStoute)* 9-0 PatEddery (6) (led after 2f: qcknd clr ent fnl f: easily) .................................................................................................. —1
1770² Let's Get Lost *(WJHaggas)* 9-0 MRoberts (1) (b.nr fore: b.hind: led 2f: 3rd st: one pce fnl f) ......................................................................................... 5.2
1395⁵ Diamond Wedding (USA) **(70)** *(NAGraham)* 8-9 TQuinn (4) (chsd wnr most of wy: 2nd st: outpcd appr fnl f) ...................................................................... 1.3
1287³ Brambleberry *(MrsSJSmith)* 8-7 ‡7JMarshall (3) (bit bkwd: chsd ldrs: 4th & rdn st: no imp) ............................................................................................... 2.4
Tomashenko *(JMackie)* 9-0 JQuinn (5) (wl grwn: bkwd: s.v.s: hdwy 5f out: effrt over 2f out: 5th & rdn st: sn btn) .................................................... 15.5
Law Faculty (IRE) *(GAHam)* 9-0 JCarroll (2) (w'like: bit bkwd: s.s: bhd & rdn ½-wy: 6th & t.o st) ..................................................................................... 20.6

**5/4** GREEK GOLD (IRE), **11/8** Let's Get Lost, **8/1** Diamond Wedding (USA), **12/1** Brambleberry, **20/1** Tomashenko, **25/1** Law Faculty (IRE). CSF £3.31, Tote £2.30: £1.60 £1.50 (£1.70). Lord Weinstock (NEWMARKET) bred by Ballymacoll Stud Farm Ltd in Ireland. 6 Rn               2m 15.43 (5.43)
SF—26/16/9/3/–/–

T/Trio: Race 1: any 2 fr 1st 3 w any £14.30 (77.1 Tckts). T/Plpt: £749.40 (7.25 Tckts).        IM

# CHESTER (L-H)
## Saturday, July 11th [Good to soft]
Going Allowance: 0.30 sec per fur (Y)                            Wind: slt bhd   Vis: mod

Stalls: low    Flag start: 4th race

## 1998
ECCLESTON GRADUATION STKS (2-Y.O) £5812.50 (£1740.00: £835.00: £382.50)
**6f 18y**                                                 2-20 (2-21)

1868³ **Zuno Warrior** (Fav) *(GLewis)* 9-3 PaulEddery (2) (s.i.s: rdn along thrght: kpt on to ld last stride) .................................................................................. —1
1738* Nominator *(RHollinshead)* 9-3 BRaymond (3) (a.p: led over 1f out: ct post) .... s.h.2
1664³ Finmental (IRE) *(ABailey)* 9-3 AMackay (1) (led tl over 1f out: rdn & wknd fnl f) . 6.3
659 Onewithwhitepaw *(ABailey)* 8-11 GCarter (4) (bit bkwd: chsd ldrs over 3f: sn rdn & outpcd) ..................................................................................... 25.4

**10/11** ZUNO WARRIOR, **5/2** Nominator, **11/4** Finmental (IRE), **25/1** Onewithwhitepaw. CSF £3.48, Tote £1.90 (£1.80). Mr Vic Fatah (EPSOM) bred by Stowell Hill Ltd. 4 Rn               1m 18.96 (5.66)
SF—26/25/1/–

## 1999
ALDFORD CLAIMING STKS £3492.50 (£1040.00: £495.00: £222.50)
**5f 16y**                                                 2-50 (2-54)

594 **Ever so Lonely (55)** (bl) *(ABailey)* 3-7-0 ‡7DWright (3) (broke smartly: mde all: rdn clr fnl f) .................................................................................................. —1
1829 Tango Time **(84)** *(NTinkler)* 4-8-5 KDarley (4) (wl bhd & outpcd tl r.o ins fnl f) . 10.2
1752³ The Noble Oak (IRE) **(65)** (bl) *(MMcCormack)* 4-8-4 PaulEddery (1) (chsd wnr: rdn over 1f out: wknd fnl f) .......................................................................... 1½.3
1475 Another Episode (IRE) **(104)** (Fav) *(JBerry)* 3-8-13 JCarroll (5) (lw: half reard & lost ground s: sn pushed along: rdn & btn appr fnl f) ........ nk.4
1752 R a Express **(37)** *(BAMcMahon)* 7-8-4 GCarter (2) (sn outpcd: a bhd) ............... 5.5

**6/5** Another Episode (IRE)(8/11—5/4), **9/4** The Noble Oak (IRE), **4/1** Tango Time, **10/1** R a Express, **20/1** EVER SO LONELY. CSF £81.59, Tote £17.50: £3.10 £1.90 (£36.10). Mr A. Bailey (TARPORLEY) bred by L. J. Barratt. 5 Rn                                          64.05 sec (3.45)
SF—33/12/5/13/–

## 2000
CHESHIRE YEOMANRY H'CAP (3-Y.O) (0-100) £7304.00 (£2192.00: £1056.00: £488.00)    **7f 122y**                                        3-20 (3-27)

1778⁴ **Eastleigh (63)** *(RHollinshead)* 7-3⁽²⁾ ‡7AGarth (7) (led 4f out: hld on gamely nr fin) ............................................................................................................... —1
1608² By Hand **(77)** (Jt-Fav) *(WJHaggas)* 8-10 JCarroll (8) (b.off fore: chsd ldrs: 2nd st: styd on u.p ins fnl f) ................................................................................ ¾.2

1659² Common Council (77) (Jt-Fav) *(GAPritchard-Gordon)* 8-10 GCarter (4) (bhd: hdwy 4f out: 3rd st: kpt on one pce appr fnl f) .................. 2¹/₂.3
1829⁴ Love Jazz (USA) (88) *(TDBarron)* 9-7 KDarley (6) (lw: bhd: hdwy ¹/₂-wy: 4th & rdn st: no imp) ........................................ 6.4
1712⁵ Robingo (IRE) (77) *(CEBrittain)* 8-10 PaulEddery (6) (lw: s.s: a bhd: 6th st: t.o) 15.5
1870 Yousefia (USA) (85) *(MRStoute)* 9-4 BRaymond (1) (chsd ldr 3f: wknd & 5th st: t.o) ........................................ 1¹/₂.6
1669⁵ My Abbey (68) *(EJAlston)* 8-1 PBurke (3) (swtg: led over 3f: wknd qckly: 7th & t.o st) ........................................ 30.7

3/1 By Hand, Common Council, 5/1 Yousefia (USA), 11/2 Robingo (IRE), 6/1 Love Jazz (USA), 10/1 EASTLEIGH, 12/1 My Abbey. CSF £37.18, CT £101.74. Tote £12.00: £2.90 £2.00 (£17.00). Mr J. E. Bigg (UPPER LONGDON) bred by Hever Castle Stud. 7 Rn
1m 38.82 (6.12)
SF—18/37/29/22/–/–

**2001**    CHESTER SUMMER H'CAP (0-90) £5725.00 (£1720.00: £830.00: £385.00)
2¹/₄m 117y       3-50 (3-51)

1580 **My Chiara (56)** *(PJBevan)* 6–7-12 BCrossley (6) (hld up: stdy hdwy to ld 3f out: sn clr: unchal) ........................................ —1
1834* Jack Button (IRE) (75) (v) (Fav) *(BobJones)* 3–7-12 AMackay (1) (hld up: hdwy 6f out: 2nd st: styd on one pce) ........................................ 6.2
1697 Star Player (84) *(RJBaker)* 6–9-12 PaulEddery (7) (lw: hld up: hdwy 4f out: 3rd st: no imp) ........................................ 7.3
1459⁴ Good Hand (USA) (86) *(JWWatts)* 6–10-0 BRaymond (5) (mde most over 13f: wknd & poor 5th st) ........................................ 20.4
1726× Broom Isle (64) *(MrsAKnight)* 4–8-1 ‡⁵NKennedy (3) (prom over 14f out: 6th & t.o st) ........................................ 7.5
Dollar Seeker (USA) (60) *(ARailey)* 8–8-2⁽³⁾ GCarter (2) (b: bit bkwd: chsd ldrs: led 5f out: rdn & hdd 3f out: 4th & btn st) ........................................ dist.6
1970 Sonalto (53) (bl) *(DLWilliams)* 6–7-9⁽²⁾ PBurke (4) (w ldr tl wknd 6f out: 7th & t.o st) ........................................ dist.7

LONG HANDICAP: Sonalto 6-10.

2/1 Jack Button (IRE), 7/2 Good Hand (USA), Star Player, 5/1 Broom Isle, 8/1 MY CHIARA(op 12/1), 20/1 Dollar Seeker (USA), 50/1 Sonalto. CSF £22.93, Tote £9.40: £2.80 £1.90 (£10.70). Mr A. Eaton (UTTOXETER) bred by Henry Cecil Bloodstock Ltd. 7 Rn
4m 18.5 (hand) (19.5)

**2002**    E.B.F. RETAIL ADVERTISING SERVICES STKS (Mdn 2-Y.O) £4077.50 (£1220.00: £585.00: £267.50)   7f 2y       4-20 (4-25)

1017³ **Icy South (USA)** (Fav) *(JHMGosden)* 9-0 PaulEddery (4) (b.nr fore: swtg: mde all: rdn & r.o wl fnl f) ........................................ —1
1424⁵ Bristol Fashion *(MBell)* 9-0 ACulham (10) (lw: hld up: hdwy & 4th st: ev ch fnl f: unable qckn) ........................................ 1¹/₂.2
595⁵ Pistol (IRE) *(PFICole)* 9-0 BCrossley (11) (chsd ldrs: 3rd st: r.o one pce fnl f) .... 2.3
1549 Turfmans Vision *(RHollinshead)* 8-7 ‡⁷AGarth (3) (hld up: hdwy fnl 2f: nt rch ldrs) 5.4
1910² Ttyfran *(FHLee)* 8-9 ‡⁵NKennedy (2) (prom: 5th & rdn st: wknd 1f out) ........ nk.5
1701 Caldervale *(ABailey)* 9-0 AMackay (8) (prom: 2nd & rdn st: wknd over 1f out) .. 1.6
1515 Lawnswood Quay *(JBerry)* 9-0 JCarroll (5) (bit bkwd: a bhd) ........................ 5.7
Glorious Island *(RFJohnsonHoughton)* 9-0 BRaymond (7) (w'like: bkwd: s.s: a wl bhd) ........................................ 4.8
1553³ Ballon *(CEBrittain)* 8-6 ‡³RonHillis (6) (a in rr) ........................................ 3.9
1569³ Savings Bank *(GAPritchard-Gordon)* 9-0 GCarter (9) (lw: chsd ldrs: 6th & wkng st) ........................................ s.h.10
Target Line *(DMcCain)* 8-7 ‡⁷SWilliams (1) (lengthy: bkwd: s.s: a bhd: t.o) .... dist.11

13/8 ICY SOUTH (USA)(op Evens), 5/1 Savings Bank, 13/2 Ttyfran, 7/1 Bristol Fashion, 8/1 Pistol (IRE), 11/1 Ballon, 14/1 Glorious Island(op 8/1), Lawnswood Quay, 20/1 Caldervale, 33/1 Turfmans Vision, 40/1 Target Line. CSF £13.74, Tote £2.80: £1.50 £2.40 £2.70 (£8.20). Mr Saeed Manana (NEWMARKET) bred by Robin Scully in USA. 11 Rn
1m 31.49 (5.29)
SF—52/47/41/19/20/22

**2003**    CITY WALL H'CAP (0-100) £5959.00 (£1792.00: £866.00: £403.00)
6f 18y       4-50 (4-56)
(Weights raised 1 lb)

1685* **Never so Sure (80)** (bl) *(ABailey)* 4–8-5 ‡⁷DWright (5) (bhd: hdwy on outside 2f out: led ins fnl f: r.o wl) ........................................ —1
1736⁶ Windpower (IRE) (84) *(JBerry)* 3–8-9 JCarroll (9) (lw: a.p: led over 1f out tl ins fnl f) ........................................ 2.2
1837³ Glenstal Princess (64) *(RHollinshead)* 5–7-3⁽³⁾ ‡⁷AGarth (2) (hld up: hdwy 2f out: fin wl) ........................................ ¹/₂.3

1837⁴ Profilic **(75)** *(CaptJWilson)* 7–8-2 ‡⁵KRutter (10) (b.nr hind: lw: hld up: gd hdwy appr fnl f: fin wl) ............................................... 1¹/₂.**4**

1736² Green Dollar **(92)** *(EAWheeler)* 9–9-3 ‡⁷SWilliams (12) (chsd ldrs: rdn wl over 1f out: one pce) ...................................... 2¹/₂.**5**

1607★ Crystal Jack (FR) **(86)** *(Fav)* *(FHLee)* 4–9-4 BRaymond (3) (a.p: hrd rdn appr fnl f: one pce) ...................................... 1¹/₂.**6**

1474⁵ So Rhythmical **(75)** *(GHEden)* 8–8-7 AMackay (8) (b.off hind: chsd ldrs: rdn wl over 1f out: sn btn) .............................. ³/₄.**7**

1828² Gondo **(78)** *(EJAlston)* 5–8-5 ‡⁵NKennedy (7) (hmpd & snatched up after 1f: nt rcvr) ......................................... ³/₄.**8**

1289⁶ Cronk's Courage **(80)** (v) *(EJAlston)* 6–8-12 BCrossley (11) (led tl hdd & wknd appr fnl f) ...................................... nk.**9**

1393 Love Legend **(88)** *(DWPArbuthnot)* 7–9-6 PaulEddery (4) (chsd ldrs over 4f) 3¹/₂.**10**

1908★ Red Rosein **(94)** *(CaptJWilson)* 6–9-12 (7x) GCarter (1) (b.off hind: lw: in tch: hdwy 2f out: wknd qckly appr fnl f) ............... 1¹/₂.**11**

1707² Appledorn **(88)** (bl) *(BAMcMahon)* 5–9-6 AClane (6) (prom tl wknd u.p ent st) 4.**12**

LONG HANDICAP: Glenstal Princess 7-5.

**7/2** Crystal Jack (FR), **9/2** NEVER SO SURE, **7/1** So Rhythmical, **15/2** Red Rosein, **9/1** Love Legend, Gondo, **10/1** Glenstal Princess, **11/1** Windpower (IRE), Green Dollar(8/1—12/1), **12/1** Appledorn(op 8/1), **16/1** Ors. CSF £352.59, CT £437.42. Tote £5.80: £2.00 £3.10 £2.70 (£72.50). Mrs M. O'Donnell (TARPORLEY) bred by Mrs P. A. Clark. 12 Rn      1m 17.38 (4.08)

         SF—45/41/19/26/31/26

T/Trio: Race 6: £317.00 (6.3 Tckts). T/Plpt: £567.30 (12.4 Tckts).     IM

---

1674—**LINGFIELD (L-H)**

**Friday, July 10th [Turf Good, Good to firm back st, AWT Standard]**

Going Allowance: Turf: nil (G); AWT: minus 0.30 sec per fur (FS)     Wind: almost nil

Stalls: high

**2004**    NPI STKS (Mdn 3 & 4-Y.O.F) £2147.60 (£593.60: £282.80)

      1¹/₂m (AWT)                         2-15 (2-16)

1567⁵ **Pippas Song** (v) *(GWragg)* 3–8-9 NDay (4) (chsd ldr: led over 2f out: hrd rdn over 1f out: r.o wl) ............................. —**1**

1313⁴ Lady Dundee (USA) **(65)** *(MrsJCecil)* 3–8-9 PaulEddery (5) (led over 9f: ev ch over 1f out: unable qckn) ......................... 2¹/₂.**2**

1792² Mystic Memory *(Fav)* *(SirMarkPrescott)* 3–8-9 GDuffield (3) (hld up: rdn over 4f out: ev ch over 2f out: one pce) ............. nk.**3**

1682⁶ Drop a Curtsey *(JDBethell)* 3–8-6 ‡³DBiggs (2) (bhd fnl 4f) ........................ 10.**4**

1540 True Contender *(CACyzer)* 3–8-9 AMorris (1) (rdn & hdwy 8f out: wknd over 4f out: t.o whn p.u over 1f out: dead) ...................... 0

**1/2** Mystic Memory(4/6—4/9), **9/4** Lady Dundee (USA)(7/4—3/1), **9/1** PIPPAS SONG(op 5/1), **33/1** Drop a Curtsey, **66/1** True Contender. CSF £27.35, Tote £5.80: £1.40 £1.50 (£7.50). Sir Philip Oppenheimer (NEWMARKET) bred by Hascombe and Valiant Studs. 5 Rn     2m 31.72 (2.32)

         SF—36/31/30/7/–

**2005**    CHARTERHOUSE (S) STKS (2-Y.O) £2520.00 (£700.00: £336.00)    **5f**    2-45 (3-05)

1764★ **Zany Zanna (IRE)** *(Fav)* *(GAPritchard-Gordon)* 8–11 GDuffield (15) (a.p: led over 1f out: hrd rdn & r.o wl) ....................... —**1**

1652⁶ Nikki Noo Noo *(CJHill)* 8–6 NAdams (17) (a.p: hrd rdn over 2f out: ev ch over 1f out: unable qckn) .............................. 2.**2**

1764 Tropical Tia (IRE) *(RVoorspuy)* 8–6 SDawson (12) (swtchd lft & hdwy wl over 1f out: hrd rdn: r.o one pce) ...................... ³/₄.**3**

1782★ My Godson (bl) *(BBeasley)* 9–2 LCharnock (2) (a.p: hrd rdn & ev ch over 1f out: one pce) ................................. ¹/₂.**4**

1764⁴ Gaynor Goodman (IRE) (bl) *(JSMoore)* 8–6 BRouse (10) (lw: led over 3f: hrd rdn: one pce) ........................................ hd.**5**

882 Petite Lass *(WCarter)* 8–6 ‡⁵NGwilliams (9) (b.off hind: lw: a.p: one pce fnl 2f) .... 4.**6**

Hy Wilma *(RJHodges)* 8-3 ‡³TSprake (5) (leggy: nvr nr to chal) ....................... 1¹/₂.**7**

1838⁵ Flash of Joy *(CDBroad)* 8-6 CRutter (18) (a mid div) ............................ 1¹/₂.**8**

Downlands Aris *(TJNaughton)* 8-1 ‡⁵DHarrison (16) (neat: bit bkwd: nvr nrr) ...... 5.**9**

1754⁶ Hawke Bay *(DHaydnJones)* 8-11 TyroneWilliams (6) (mid div whn hmpd over 2f out: n.d after) ........................................ 6.**10**

Keamari *(BForsey)* 8-1 ‡⁵RPrice (3) (neat: bit bkwd: outpcd) ................... ¹/₂.**11**

1554⁶ Lady of Shadows *(SDow)* 7-13 ‡⁷MJermy (11) (outpcd) ........................... 1.**12**

1657⁶ Arctic Agnes (USA) *(RAkehurst)* 8-3 ‡³DBiggs (1) (b.nr fore: bhd whn hmpd over
2f out) ...................................................................................................... ³/₄.**13**

*1375* Domes of Silence *(JBerry)* 8-11 BCrossley (7) (lw: a bhd) ................................... **14**

Joyful Escapade *(MrsNMacauley)* 8-6 NDay (4) (neat: bit bkwd: s.s: a bhd) ....... **15**

1764³ Screech *(CJames)* 8-6 GBaxter (8) (hmpd 3f out: mid dlv whn stumbled & fell
over 2f out) ............................................................................................................ 0

*1762 Hawaii Star (IRE) (6/1) Withdrawn (broke out of stalls) : not under orders*

**6/4** ZANY ZANNA (IRE), **5/2** Nikki Noo Noo, **6/1** Screech, **8/1** Gaynor Goodman (IRE), **12/1** My Godson, Petite
Lass, **20/1** Arctic Agnes (USA), Lady of Shadows, **25/1** Downlands Aris, Domes of Silence, **33/1** Ors. CSF
£6.50, Tote £2.80: £1.70 £1.90 £24.70 (£4.90). Mr Giles W. Pritchard-Gordon (NEWMARKET) bred by
Limestone Stud in Ireland. 16 Rn; Bt in 4,600 gns
60.19 sec (3.19)
SF—33/20/17/25/14/–

## 2006
JARDINE INSURANCE BROKERS H'CAP (3-Y.O) (0-80) £3174.50 (£882.00: £423.50)
**7f**
3-20 (3-35)

(Weights raised 6 lb)

1642 **Tadora (IRE) (48)** *(CJBenstead)* 7-11 TyroneWilliams (7) (w ldr: led over 2f
out: rdn out) ..........................................................................................................—**1**

1761² Morsun **(77)** (bl) *(DMorley)* 9-12 (5x) PaulEddery (5) (lw: hdwy over 1f out: hrd
rdn & ev ch ins fnl f: unable qckn) ................................................ 1.**2**

1159 Mabonne **(58)** *(JLDunlop)* 8-7 BRouse (6) (hld up: hrd rdn & ev ch over 1f out:
one pce) .................................................................................. 3.**3**

1659* Court Minstrel **(62)** (Fav) *(LJHolt)* 8-11 GDuffield (3) (hld up: rdn over 3f out:
one pce) ................................................................................ ³/₄.**4**

*1676*³ Ben Bluff **(52)** *(LGCottrell)* 7-10 ‡⁵DHarrison (1) (led over 4f) .......................... 6.**5**

1745³ Paradise Forum **(66)** *(CAHorgan)* 9-1 DaleGibson (2) (lw: hld up: rdn over 2f
out: sn wknd) ......................................................................... 3.**6**

**11/10** Court Minstrel(7/4 Evono), **5/2** Morsun(7/4—3/1), **9/2** Ben Bluff, **9/1** Paradise Forum(op 5/1), **12/1**
Mabonne(op 6/1), **16/1** TADORA (IRE)(op 10/1). CSF £51.89, Tote £15.80: £2.20 £1.40 (£15.70). Mr R. Lamb
(EPSOM) bred by John Noonan in Ireland. 6 Rn
1m 25.08 (3.78)
SF—26/52/24/–/3

## 2007
AEGON EQUESTRIAN H'CAP (3-Y.O) (0-70) £2245.60 (£621.60: £296.80)
**1½m (AWT)**
3-50 (3-59)

(Weights raised 7 lb)

1914³ **Ideal Candidate (50)** *(CACyzer)* 8-8 ‡³DBiggs (7) (a.p: led 2f out: rdn out) ........ —**1**

*1679*² Pride of Britain (CAN) **(54)** (Fav) *(LGCottrell)* 8-10 ‡⁵DHarrison (6) (lw: hdwy 5f
out: chsd wnr over 1f out: r.o) ................................................ 2.**2**

1735² Pie Hatch (IRE) **(41)** *(SirMarkPrescott)* 8-2 (5x) GDuffield (2) (led 10f: unable
qckn) ......................................................................................
4.**3**

*1544* Allmosa **(60)** *(TJNaughton)* 9-7 PaulEddery (3) (b: chsd ldr over 9f) ................... 2.**4**

*1850*² Holy Wanderer (USA) **(59)** *(DWPArbuthnot)* 9-1 (5x) ‡⁵RPrice (5) (plld hrd: no
hdwy fnl 3f) ..........................................................................
4.**5**

1663 Kate Royale **(44)** (bl) *(GCBravery)* 8-5 AMackay (4) (bhd fnl 4f) ......................... 6.**6**

1705 Otter Bush **(47)** *(GBlum)* 8-8 AShoults (1) (bhd fnl 8f: t.o) .............................. 20.**7**

**9/4** Pride of Britain (CAN), **5/2** Holy Wanderer (USA), **4/1** Pie Hatch (IRE)(op 5/2), **5/1** IDEAL CANDIDATE, **13/2**
Allmosa(8/1—10/1), **20/1** Kate Royale, **50/1** Otter Bush. CSF £16.19, Tote £5.50: £2.80 £1.50 (£7.50). Mr R.
M. Cyzer (HORSHAM) bred by Lt-Col and Mrs D. Coker. 7 Rn
2m 33.93 (4.53)
SF—13/11/–/6/–/–

## 2008
ORIGIN TECHNOLOGY IN BUSINESS CLAIMING STKS (2-Y.O) £2343.60 (£649.60:
£310.80)    **6f (AWT)**
4-20 (4-26)

*1321** **Time's Arrow (IRE)** (Fav) *(GCBravery)* 9-7 NDay (6) (b.off hind: lw: chsd ldr:
led over 2f out: pushed out) ................................................... —**1**

1804² Mister Blake (bl) *(WAO'Gorman)* 8-11 ‡³EmmaO'Gorman (1) (a.p: chsd wnr
over 1f out: r.o) ....................................................................... 2.**2**

*1848*³ Awesome Risk *(GLewis)* 8-1 ‡DBiggs (12) (b.off hind: lw: hdwy over 2f out:
unable qckn) ..........................................................................
6.**3**

1804 Burishki (bl) *(GAPritchard-Gordon)* 8-2 ‡⁵DHarrison (9) (s.i.s: rdn thrght: hdwy
over 3f out: one pce fnl 2f) ..................................................... ½.**4**

1409 Melisio *(CPWildman)* 8-12 CRutter (2) (lw: nvr nr to chal) ......................... 1½.**5**

1670⁵ Beat the Bagman (IRE) *(BBeasley)* 8-8 LCharnock (10) (prom 3f) .................. hd.**6**

1835² Trentesimo (IRE) *(JBerry)* 9-7 GDuffield (5) (led over 3f) ............................ 2.**7**

1657⁵ Pondering *(SDow)* 8-13 PaulEddery (3) (lw: outpcd) ................................... 5.**8**

1744⁶ Brave Bidder *(BGubby)* 7-13 ‡⁷CAvery (13) (prom over 3f) ......................... s.h.**9**

1370⁶ Gabhadera *(BGubby)* 8-6 SDawson (4) (s.s: a wl bhd) ................................. 8.**10**

*1321*⁵ Golden Klair *(CJHill)* 8-11 NAdams (7) (b: a bhd) ..................................... 5.**11**

*1549*⁶ Daring King (v) *(DSasse)* 9-2 DaleGibson (11) (a bhd: t.o) ........................ 20.**12**

**13/8** TIME'S ARROW (IRE), **4/1** Mister Blake, Burishki, **11/2** Trentesimo (IRE), **6/1** Beat the Bagman (IRE)(8/1—10/1), **12/1** Awesome Risk(8/1—14/1), **14/1** Pondering, **20/1** Brave Bidder, Golden Klair, **25/1** Daring King, **33/1** Ors. CSF £10.43, Tote £3.20: £1.80 £1.70 £2.60 (£10.70). Mr Richard J. Gray (NEWMARKET) bred by Mrs M. Lowry in Ireland. 12 Rn; Beat the Bagman (IRE) clmd J R Duffy £6,153
1m 11.65 (.14 under 2y best; 1.05)
SF—50/32/–/–/1/–

**2009**　　　　AL AMEAD H'CAP (0-80) £2880.00 (£800.00: £384.00)　　**6f**　　　4-50 (4-55)
(Weights raised 2 lb)

| | | |
|---|---|---|
| 8975 | **Fay's Song (IRE) (72)** (Jt-Fav) *(RAkehurst)* 4-9-1 ‡7LCarter (10) (lw: hld up: nt clr run over 1f out: swtchd lft: led wl ins fnl f: r.o wl) | —1 |
| 1614★ | Tauber (67) (Jt-Fav) *(PatMitchell)* 8-9-0 ‡3SO'Gorman (8) (a.p: led ins fnl f: sn hdd: unable qckn) | 2½.2 |
| 17712 | Assignment (74) *(JFfitch-Heyes)* 4-9-6 10 PaulEddery (11) (lw: a.p: led 3f out tl ins fnl f: one pce) | 1.3 |
| 17762 | Harry's Coming (65) (Jt-Fav) *(RJHodges)* 8-8-12 ‡3TSprake (4) (hld up: hrd rdn over 1f out: one pce) | 2½.4 |
| 18144 | Restore (54) (bl) *(RVoorspuy)* 9-8-4 SDawson (7) (lw: outpcd: hdwy 2f out: one pce) | 2½.5 |
| 12613 | Quick Steel (55) (bl) *(TPMcGovern)* 4-8-0 ‡5DHarrison (2) (s.s: nvr nrr) | 1½.6 |
| 1614 | Panchellita (USA) (70) *(JSutcliffe)* 3-8-13 BRouse (6) (lw: nvr nr to chal) | 2.7 |
| 1614 | Almasa (62) (v) *(DMorris)* 4-8-5 ‡7StephenDavies (1) (outpcd) | 1½.8 |
| 1406 | Sports Post Lady (IRE) (57) *(CJHill)* 4-8-7 NAdams (3) (lw: led 3f) | nk.9 |
| 14103 | Efra (66) (bl) *(RHannon)* 3-8-9 GDuffield (5) (spd 3f) | 15.10 |

**7/2** FAY'S SONG (IRE), Tauber, Harry's Coming, **9/2** Assignment, **11/1** Quick Steel, **12/1** Efra, Sports Post Lady (IRE)(8/1—14/1), **16/1** Ors. CSF £16.65, CT £53.50. Tote £5.90: £1.90 £1.80 £1.60 (£11.90). Mr S. Harper (EPSOM) bred by E. O'Leary in Ireland. 10 Rn
1m 11.41 (2.81)
SF—45/34/40/18/–/–

T/Plpt: £339.50 (9.95 Tckts).　　　　　　　　　　　　　　　　　　　　　　　　AK

# LINGFIELD (L-H)

## Saturday, July 11th [Turf Good, Good to firm back st, AWT Standard]
Going Allowance: Turf: minus 0.10 (F); AWT: minus 0.55 sec (FS)　　Wind: mod half bhd

Stalls: 2nd race centre, remainder high

**2010**　　BET WITH THE TOTE NURSERY　£8090.00 (£2420.00: £1160.00: £530.00)
6f　　　　　　　　　　　　　　　　　　　2-10 (2-13)
(Weights raised 6 lb)

| | | |
|---|---|---|
| 1575★ | **Sharp Prod (USA)** (Fav) *(LordHuntingdon)* 9-2 PatEddery (6) (a.p: led over 2f out: hrd rdn over 1f out: r.o wl) | —1 |
| 859 | Simmering *(GWragg)* 8-7 RHills (15) (lw: hdwy over 2f out: hrd rdn over 1f out: ev ch ins fnl f: unable qckn) | 1½.2 |
| 1472 | Mr Martini (IRE) (bl) *(CEBrittain)* 8-11 GCrealock (10) (a.p: led 3f out tl over 2f out: ev ch over 1f out: one pce) | 2.3 |
| 975★ | King Paris (IRE) *(MBell)* 9-2 MHills (13) (lw: rdn & hdwy over 1f out: r.o one pce) | 3.4 |
| 1775★ | Bourbon Jack *(JWPayne)* 9-0 WRyan (11) (a.p: nvr nr to chal) | ¾.5 |
| 1915 | Without a Flag (USA) *(CACyzer)* 7-10 ‡5ATucker (8) (lw: rdn over 2f out: nvr nr to chal) | 6.6 |
| 14434 | Beaver Brook *(RHannon)* 8-6 DaleGibson (5) (nvr nrr) | hd.7 |
| 9735 | Chinnery (IRE) *(JMPEustace)* 8-13 ‡7StephenDavies (12) (prom over 4f) | hd.8 |
| 3673 | George Roper *(MRChannon)* 8-6 GHind (9) (a mid div) | hd.9 |
| 17622 | Final Frontier (IRE) *(RAkehurst)* 8-4 ‡3DBiggs (7) (lw: a bhd) | 2½.10 |
| 1472 | Sober Lad (IRE) (bl) *(JBerry)* 9-7 NDay (14) (led 3f) | 1.11 |
| 1149★ | Tee Gee Jay *(CNWilliams)* 7-11 ‡7JTate (3) (b.hind: a bhd) | 2.12 |
| 1670★ | Silent Expression *(DMorris)* 8-9 MTebbutt (2) (bhd fnl 2f) | 8.13 |
| 1036★ | Nicki-J (IRE) *(RHannon)* 8-8 ‡3RPerham (4) (a wl bhd: t.o) | 20.14 |

**100/30** SHARP PROD (USA)(5/1—3/1), **9/2** King Paris (IRE), **13/2** Silent Expression, **8/1** Simmering, Bourbon Jack, **10/1** Sober Lad (IRE)(5/1—3/1), **11/2** Mr Martini (IRE)(op 8/1), **12/1** Nicki-J (IRE), **16/1** Final Frontier (IRE)(op 10/1), **20/1** Beaver Brook, **25/1** Chinnery (IRE), **33/1** Ors. CSF £28.82, CT £259.99. Tote £2.70: £1.40 £3.20 £5.50 (£36.10). The Queen (WEST ILSLEY) bred by The Queen in USA. 14 Rn
1m 10.23 (1.63)
SF—58/43/39/32/27/–

**2011**　　CALOR SILVER TROPHY (Stks) (listed race)　£11160.00 (£3330.00: £1590.00: £720.00)　　**7f 140y**　　　　　　　　　　　2-40 (2-42)

| | | |
|---|---|---|
| 1455 | **Thourios (110)** (bl) *(GHarwood)* 3-8-7 MHills (5) (lw: mde all: all out) | —1 |
| 1711★ | Toussaud (USA) (110) (Fav) *(JHMGosden)* 3-8-9 PatEddery (1) (a.p: hrd rdn & ev ch fnl f: r.o wl) | s.h.2 |

1711³ Casteddu (110) *(JWPayne)* 3–8-7 RHills (2) (hld up: hrd rdn over 1f out: unable qckn) .................................................................................. 7.3
1822a³ Bog Trotter (USA) (118) *(WJHaggas)* 4–9-9 NDay (4) (b.nr fore: lw: chsd wnr over 5f) ...................................................................... 2¹/₂.4
1711 Forest Tiger (USA) *(MMoubarak)* 3–8-7 JWeaver (3) (plld hrd: a bhd) ............ 12.5
1198 Ninja Dancer (USA) (100) *(MrsJCecil)* 3–8-7 WRyan (6) (lw: a bhd: t.o) ............ 15.6

**2/1** Toussaud (USA), **5/2** Casteddu, **7/2** THOURIOS, **4/1** Bog Trotter (USA)(tchd 6/1), **10/1** Forest Tiger (USA), **16/1** Ninja Dancer (USA). CSF £11.11, Tote £4.70: £2.40 £1.80 (£5.30). Mr Athos Christodoulou (PULBOROUGH) bred by A. Christodoulou. 6 Rn
1m 28.46 (U.04)
SF—82/83/60/68/16/–

---

**2012**  KRUG CHAMPAGNE H'CAP (0-90) £3752.50 (£1120.00: £535.00: £242.50)
1¹/₄m
3-10 (3-14)

565 **Vallance (61)** *(PWHarris)* 4–8-13 GHind (2) (2nd st: led 2f out: hrd rdn & edgd lft wl over 1f out: r.o wl) .................................................. —1
1387² Rising Tempo (IRE) (60) *(CACyzer)* 4–8-12 WRyan (7) (hdwy over 2f out: hrd rdn over 1f out: r.o one pce) ...................................... 3¹/₂.2
1466 Simonov (79) *(GHarwood)* 3–9-6 PatEddery (1) (lw: led 8f: hmpd wl over 1f out: one pce) ............................................................. nk.3
1387⁵ Scottish Bambi (73) *(RHannon)* 4–9-11 RHills (6) (lw: 4th st: hrd rdn over 1f out: one pce) ............................................................. 2.4
1612 Scenic Dancer (55) (v) *(AHide)* 4–8-7 WWoods (8) (5th st: hrd rdn over 1f out: one pce) ............................................................. 1.5
1666⁴ Desert Force (IRE) (77) *(MMoubarak)* 3–8-13 ‡⁵JWeaver (10) (lw: nvr nr to chal) 3.6
Texan Tycoon (72) *(RAkehurst)* 4–9-10 NDay (3) (b.nr hind: nvr nrr) ............ 1¹/₂.7
1680² Marzocco (58) *(JFfitch-Heyes)* 4–8-10 MHills (5) (lw: hmpd 7f out: no hdwy fnl 3f) .................................................................................. 8.8
746⁵ Jathaab (IRE) (77) *(MRStoute)* 3–8-13 ‡JJones (11) (bhd fnl 4f) ............ 2¹/₂.9
1716⁵ Valiant Words (60) (Fav) *(RAkehurst)* 5–8-9 ‡³RPerham (4) (3rd st: wknd over 2f out) ................................................................................ hd.10
1841★ Bowden Boy (IRE) (69) (bl) *(NACallaghan)* 4–9-0 ‡JTate (9) (hdwy over 5f out: 6th st: wknd over 2f out) ...................................... 2¹/₂.11

**7/2** Valiant Words, **9/2** Simonov, **5/1** Rising Tempo (IRE), **6/1** Bowden Boy (IRE), **8/1** Desert Force (IRE), **12/1** Jathaab (IRE), Marzocco, Scenic Dancer, Scottish Bambi, **25/1** VALLANCE, **33/1** Texan Tycoon. CSF £135.51, CT £617.98. Tote £56.80: £10.80 £1.90 £1.80 (£208.90). Mrs P. W. Harris (BERKHAMSTED) bred by Pendley Farm. 11 Rn
2m 9.07 (6.07)
SF–28/20/27/28/8/8

---

**2013**  LADBROKE ALL WEATHER H'CAP (0-85) £8025.00 (£2400.00: £1150.00: £525.00)
7f (AWT)
3-40 (3-46)

1773 **Norfolkiev (FR) (61)** *(MMoubarak)* 6–8-2 ‡⁵JWeaver (8) (led over 2f: led over 2f out: r.o wl) .................................................. —1
1930⁵ Usa Dollar (68) (bl) *(BGubby)* 5–9-0 WRyan (2) (hdwy over 2f out: r.o wl ins fnl f) ³/₄.2
1870 Ler Cru (IRE) (70) (bl) *(CEBrittain)* 3–8-8 GCrealock (7) (lw: hdwy over 2f out: r.o) .................................................................................. 3.3
1608³ Battle Colours (IRE) (80) *(SirMarkPrescott)* 3–9-4 CNutter (4) (a.p: hrd rdn over 1f out: one pce) ............................................................. s.h.4
1677² Premier Prince (59) *(LGCottrell)* 6–8-5 NCarlisle (9) (lw: hdwy fnl 2f: r.o) ........ s.h.5
432 Appealing Times (USA) (82) *(WAO'Gorman)* 3–9-3 ‡³EmmaO'Gorman (16) (w ldr: led over 4f out tl over 2f out: one pce) ...................... s.h.6
1706 Choir Practice (79) *(JHaggas)* 3–9-10 NDay (10) (nvr nr to chal) ...................... 2.7
1685⁶ Invocation (74) *(AMoore)* 5–9-3 ‡³DBiggs (6) (b.nr hind: lw: prom over 5f) ...... 2¹/₂.8
1773⁵ Prenonamoss (82) *(DWPArbuthnot)* 4–9-9 ‡⁵RPrice (11) (b.hind: nvr nrr) ........ 1¹/₂.9
1615² Highland Magic (IRE) (67) (Fav) *(MJFetherston-Godley)* 4–8-13 PatEddery (12) (a mid div) .................................................... 2¹/₂.10
1718★ Beatle Song (63) *(RJHodges)* 4–8-9 MHills (5) (prom over 4f) ...................... ¹/₂.11
1799³ Jokist (63) *(WJarvis)* 9–8-9 MTebbutt (14) (a bhd) .................................... 2.12
Amadeus Aes (71) (v) *(DMorris)* 3–8-2 ‡⁷StephenDavies (3) (prom over 5f) ........... nk.13
411 Kissavos (63) (v) *(CCElsey)* 6–8-9 TRogers (13) (b.hind: lw: a bhd) .............. 2¹/₂.14
1685⁵ Executive Spirit (67) *(DSasse)* 3–8-2 ‡³RPerham (15) (lw: a bhd) .................. 2¹/₂.15
1813★ Monte Bre (60) *(RAkehurst)* 6–8-6 RHills (1) (eyeshield: lw: prom 4f) .............. 15.16

**9/2** Highland Magic (IRE)(6/1—4/1), **11/2** Battle Colours (IRE), **9/1** Beatle Song, **10/1** Monte Bre, Premier Prince, **11/1** Usa Dollar, **12/1** Jokist, Prenonamoss, Ler Cru (IRE), Invocation, **14/1** Choir Practice, NORFOLKIEV (FR), **20/1** Ors. CSF £150.92, CT £1,721.28. Tote £19.10: £3.20 £3.00 £4.30 £1.60 (£217.60). Ecurie Fustok (NEWMARKET) bred by Pierre de Gaste and Pierre Camus Denais in France. 16 Rn
1m 23.22 (0.15 under best: U.78)
SF—42/52/37/46/32/43

**2014**  SEEBOARD CLAIMING H'CAP (0-70) £2857.60 (£793.60: £380.80)
1m 3f 106y                                    4-10 (4-17)

2007* **Ideal Candidate (57)** *(CACyzer)* 3–8-9 (7x) ‡3DBiggs (7) (6th st: led 1f out: r.o
wl) .................................................................... —1
1810* Dr Zeva (32) *(Fav)* *(MDixon)* 6–7-8 ‡5ATucker (3) (2nd st: led over 2f out to 1f
out: unable qckn) ............................................. 2½.2
1366² Brown Carpet (31) (bl) *(CAHorgan)* 5–7-12 NCarlisle (8) (hdwy over 2f out: r.o
one pce) ............................................................. 3.3
1682⁵ Dazzle the Crowd (IRE) (57) *(CACyzer)* 4–9-10 WRyan (11) (rdn thrght: hdwy 2f
out: r.o one pce) ................................................ ½.4
1655³ Afore Jane (57) *(GHarwood)* 3–8-7 ‡5JJones (1) (led over 3f: 5th st: one pce fnl
3f) ...................................................................... hd.5
1655* Baby Wizzard (54) *(IABalding)* 3–8-9 MHills (9) (3rd st: one pce fnl 3f) ......... s.h.6
1542⁶ Sciacca (28) *(CWeedon)* 5–7-9 EJohnson (14) (led over 6f out tl over 2f out: sn
wknd) ................................................................. 3.7
1907* Miss Doody (65) (v) *(MRChannon)* 3–9-6 (7x) PatEddery (15) (nvr nr to chal) .. nk.8
The Oil Baron (40) *(RPCHoad)* 6–8-7(2) NDay (12) (bhd fnl 6f) .......................... 5.9
597⁵ Oco Royal (68) (bl) *(JFfitch-Heyes)* 3–9-6 ‡3RPerham (4) (4th st: wknd over 2f
out) .................................................................... 6.10
1971 Great Impostor (37) (bl) *(RJHodges)* 4–8-4 GHind (13) (bhd fnl 2f) ................ 2.11
1810 Mamalama (35) *(LJHolt)* 4–8-2 DaleGibson (16) (a bhd) ............................ 10.12
Eastern Whisper (USA) (61) *(AMoore)* 5–10-0 CandyMorris (6) (led 8f out tl
over 6f out: sn wknd) ......................................... 12.13

**5/1** Dr Zeva, **11/2** Miss Doody, **6/1** Baby Wizzard, IDEAL CANDIDATE(5/1—8/1), **13/2** Dazzle the Crowd (IRE),
**8/1** Afore Jane, Mamalama(op 12/1), **10/1** Great Impostor, Brown Carpet, **33/1** Ors. CSF £34.87, CT £268.50.
Tote £8.20: £2.60 £2.10 £5.00 (£31.30). Mr R. M. Cyzer (HORSHAM) bred by Lt-Col and Mrs D. Coker. 13 Rn;
Ideal Candidate clmd T Naughton £12,501                                2m 30.27 (8.27)

**2015**  CHAMPAGNE JACQUART STKS (Mdn 3-Y.O) £2245.60 (£621.60: £296.80)
6f                                            4-40 (4-50)

1535 **Nagida (75)** *(Fav)* *(JARToller)* 8-9 RHills (7) (a.p: led 3f out: rdn out) ............... —1
1683⁵ Under the Bridge *(PWHarris)* 8-9 ‡5ATucker (10) (a.p: bmpd on ins over 1f out:
unable qckn) .................................................... 2.2
925⁴ Nbaat (USA) *(CJBenstead)* 9-0 DBiggs (9) (a.p: ev ch 2f out: bmpd over 1f out:
one pce) ........................................................... 2½.3
1683⁶ Sea-Deer *(LJHolt)* 9-0 MHills (4) (lw: hdwy over 1f out: nvr nrr) ...................... 2.4
399³ Black Coral (IRE) *(CFWall)* 8-9 NCarlisle (11) (a.p: ev ch 2f out: one pce) 1½.5
Face the Future *(PWHarris)* 9-0 GHind (5) (w'like: bit bkwd: nvr nr to chal) ..... 2.6
1803 Forza Azzurri (IRE) (65) (bl) *(MrsNMacauley)* 9-0 NDay (6) (led 3f) .............. 3.7
Miss Oasis *(PJMakin)* 8-9 PatEddery (8) (bit bkwd: outpcd) ........................... 7.8
Clean Gate *(PDCundell)* 9-0 TRogers (3) (unf: bit bkwd: outpcd) ..................... 1.9
Admiral Albert (IRE) (60) *(RAkehurst)* 8-11 ‡3RPerham (2) (a bhd) ................. 3.10
1086 Ballycastle Mary (IRE) *(TJNaughton)* 8-9 WRyan (12) (swvd lft s: a bhd) ...... 12.11

**6/4** NAGIDA, **3/1** Nbaat (USA), **7/2** Miss Oasis, **8/1** Black Coral (IRE), **16/1** Under the Bridge(op 10/1), **20/1**
Sea-Deer, **25/1** Forza Azzurri (IRE), Face the Future, **33/1** Ors. CSF £25.81, Tote £2.50: £1.20 £3.70 £1.50
(£24.60). Mr J. A. R. Toller (NEWMARKET) bred by Mrs John Trotter. 11 Rn        1m 11.73 (3.13)
SF—21/13/8/–/–/–

**2016**  HOLIDAY CLUB PONTIN'S GRADUATION STKS    £2924.00 (£872.00: £416.00:
£188.00)  6f                                  5-10 (5-14)

1763* **Miss Bluebird (IRE) (89)** (bl) *(Fav)* *(PAKelleway)* 3–8-12 PatEddery (4)
(b.hind: chsd ldr: hrd rdn over 3f out: led ins fnl f: r.o) —1
1931 Sylvan Breeze (82) (v) *(PMitchell)* 4–9-3 MHills (5) (led: hrd rdn over 1f out: hdd
ins fnl f: unable qckn) ........................................ 2.2
1418³ Alsaarm (USA) (90) *(JLDunlop)* 3–9-3 WRyan (1) (lw: a.p: rdn over 4f out: one
pce) ................................................................... 5.3
Born to Be *(SDow)* 3–8-12 NDay (2) (bhd fnl 2f) .......................................... 8.4
1641⁵ Simple Sound (IRE) (70) (bl) *(MAJarvis)* 3–9-3 GCrealock (3) (a wl bhd) ........... 4.5

**6/5** MISS BLUEBIRD (IRE), **11/4** Alsaarm (USA), **7/2** Born to Be, **7/1** Sylvan Breeze, **25/1** Simple Sound (IRE).
CSF £8.66, Tote £1.90: £1.40 £2.40 (£5.60). Mr P. A. Kelleway (NEWMARKET) bred by Collinstown Stud Farm
Ltd. in Ireland. 5 Rn                                          1m 10.41 (1.81)
SF—50/47/27/–/–

T/Plpt: £112.00 (46.25 Tckts).

AK

1391—**YORK (L-H)**
**Friday, July 10th [Good to soft]**
Going Allowance: 0.20 sec per fur (G)

Wind: almost nil

Stalls: high

**2017**      BLACK DUCK STKS (2-Y.O) £6192.00 (£1712.00: £816.00)   **6f**      2-00 (2-01)

654³ **Splendent (USA)** (Fav) (PFICole) 8-11 AMunro (2) (lw: trckd ldr: led over 2f
    out: r.o wl nr fin) ....................................................... —1
1541* **Maroof (USA)** (RWArmstrong) 9-0 WCarson (1) (lw: chsd ldrs: outpcd over 2f
    out: gd hdwy to disp ld ins fnl f: no ex nr fin) ..................... ½.2
1584* **Crusade (IRE)** (RHannon) 9-0 JReid (3) (lw: led tl hdd over 2f out: wknd over 1f
    out) ............................................................................... 5.3

**4/6** SPLENDENT (USA), **11/4** Maroof (USA), **9/2** Crusade (IRE). CSF £2.44, Tote £1.50 (£1.20). Mr Fahd Salman
(WHATCOMBE) bred by Derry Meeting Farm et. al. in USA. 3 Rn      1m 13.74 (3.54)
SF—50/51/31

**2018**      RALPH COUNTRY HOMES H'CAP (3-Y.O) (0-90) £7505.00 (£2240.00: £1070.00:
    £485.00)  **1m 205y**      2-35 (2-35)

1700* **Drummer Hicks (70)** (EWeymes) 8-3 DMcKeown (2) (lw: mde all: qcknd over
    2f out: r.o wl) ............................................................... —1
1637² **Tissisat (USA) (83)** (IABalding) 9-2 JReid (3) (a.p: effrt over 2f out: r.o nr fin) .. 1½.2
546* **Ma Bella Luna (74)** (JLDunlop) 8-7 MRoberts (8) (lw: trckd ldrs: effrt & ch over
    2f out: nt qckn ins fnl f) ............................................... 1.3
1846* **Express Gift (64)** (Fav) (MrsGRReveley) 7-11 WCarson (7) (lw: mid div: effrt
    over 3f out: kpt on one pce) ...................................... 1½.4
1577⁴ **Wrets (77)** (MRStoute) 8-10 PatEddery (5) (lw: cl up: effrt & ch over 2f out:
    eased ins fnl f) ............................................................. 1½.5
1693³ **Cumbrian Challenge (IRE) (88)** (MHEasterby) 9-7 MBirch (9) (hld up & bhd:
    hdwy over 3f out: nvr rchd ldrs) ................................ 1.6
878² **Remany (73)** (JRFanshawe) 8-6 GCarter (1) (trckd ldrs tl wknd over 2f out) ....... 8.7
1642* **Roly Wallace (66)** (bl) (KTIvory) 7-13 GBardwell (6) (lw: bhd: effrt 4f out: n.d) .... 3.8
1216⁴ **Rocality (79)** (RHannon) 8-12 SCauthen (4) (swtg: a bhd: eased fnl 3f) ............... 6.9

**11/4** Express Gift, **11/2** Wrets, DRUMMER HICKS, Tissisat (USA), **15/2** Ma Bella Luna, **9/1** Remany, **12/1**
Cumbrian Challenge (IRE), Rocality, **16/1** Roly Wallace. CSF £32.85, CT £205.68. Tote £5.80: £1.80 £1.60
£1.80 (£12.10). Mrs N. Napier (MIDDLEHAM) bred by Mrs N. Napier. 9 Rn      1m 53.85 (4.85)
SF—43/51/39/24/32/39

**2019**      A. F. BUDGE H'CAP (0-110) £9084.00 (£2712.00: £1296.00: £588.00)
    **5f**      3-10 (3-12)

1511* **Beau Venture (USA) (87)** (FHLee) 4-8-8 ‡5NKennedy (3) (hld up: effrt over 2f
    out: qcknd to ld ins fnl f) ........................................... —1
1688 **Never in the Red (89)** (v) (JBerry) 4-9-1 JCarroll (2) (mde most tl hdd & no ex
    ins fnl f) ........................................................................ 3.2
1757⁴ **Martina (70)** (JWharton) 4-7-7 ‡3JFanning (8) (lw: a in tch: hdwy u.p 2f out: styd
    on wl) ........................................................................... ¾.3
1247 **Playful Poet (72)** (MHEasterby) 5-7-7(5) ‡5SMaloney (5) (disp ld over 3f: grad
    wknd) ........................................................................... ½.4
1688² **Cumbrian Waltzer (100)** (Fav) (MHEasterby) 7-9-12 MBirch (9) (swtg: outpcd tl
    styd on wl appr fnl f) .................................................... 1.5
1474 **Grand Prix (83)** (DRCElsworth) 7-8-9(1) SCauthen (7) (swtg: nvr nr to chal) ...... ¾.6
1920³ **Ballasecret (74)** (RDickin) 4-8-0 WCarson (1) (spd 3f) ................................ s.h.7
    **Sahara Star (106)** (MRStoute) 3-9-12 PatEddery (4) (b: effrt ½-wy: nvr trbld ldrs) 3.8
1393² **Absolution (82)** (MPNaughton) 8-8-3 ‡5JWeaver (6) (lw: outpcd ½-wy: n.d after) 1.9
1688³ **Eager Deva (91)** (RHollinshead) 5-9-3 LPiggott (10) (lw: dwlt: a outpcd & wl
    bhd) ............................................................................. 5.10

LONG HANDICAP: Playful Poet 7-6.

**9/2** Cumbrian Waltzer, **11/2** BEAU VENTURE (USA), Sahara Star, Absolution, **7/1** Eager Deva, **9/1** Martina,
Ballasecret, **10/1** Grand Prix, **12/1** Playful Poet, **16/1** Never in the Red. CSF £77.14, CT £709.79. Tote £6.50:
£2.60 £4.60 £4.00 (£69.00). Mrs A. L. Stacey (WILMSLOW) bred by Mrs C. Oliver Iselin III in USA. 10 Rn
    59.73 sec (2.23)
SF—70/65/40/38/67/47

**2020**  OLWAY SLATE (H'cap) (3-Y-O) (0-100) £7700.00 (£2300.00: £1100.00: £500.00)
1m 3f 195y
3-40 (3-41)

1466 **Folia (82)** *(HRACecil)* 8-11 SCauthen (1) (lw: trckd ldrs: swtchd over 3f out: led wl over 2f out: hrd rdn fnl f: r.o wl) ..... —1

1466⁵ Kinglow (USA) **(82)** (bl) *(MrsJCecil)* 8-11 JReid (7) (lw: hld up & bhd: gd hdwy 3f out: disp ld 1f out: nt qckn nr fin) ..... hd.2

1420★ Legal Embrace (CAN) **(78)** *(JRFanshawe)* 8-7 GCarter (2) (a.p: chal over 3f out: one pce fnl 2f) ..... 10.3

1394² Northern Kingdom (USA) **(73)** *(SGNorton)* 8-2 KDarley (4) (lw: outpcd & bhd 6f out: styd on fnl 2f: nrst fin) ..... 3½.4

1466 Eden's Close **(75)** (v) *(MHTompkins)* 8-4 PRobinson (6) (cl up tl wknd wl over 2f out) ..... 3.5

1346★ Inchcailloch (IRE) **(86)** (Fav) *(RCharlton)* 9-1 PatEddery (3) (swtg: led tl hdd wl over 2f out: sn btn) ..... 12.6

1739³ Reel of Tulloch (IRE) **(64)** *(PCHaslam)* 7-0 ‡7DarrenMoffatt (8) (effrt ent st: n.d) 1½.7

1466 Jupiter Moon **(70)** *(CEBrittain)* 7-13 MRoberts (9) (lw: prom tl wknd over 3f out) nk.8

**13/8** Inchcailloch (IRE), **3/1** FOLIA(4/1—9/2), **11/2** Kinglow (USA), **8/1** Legal Embrace (CAN), **17/2** Jupiter Moon, **11/1** Eden's Close, **12/1** Northern Kingdom (USA), **16/1** Reel of Tulloch (IRE). CSF £19.63, CT £111.98. Tote £5.20: £1.70 £2.00 £2.90 (£16.70). Sheikh Mohammed (NEWMARKET) bred by Sheikh Mohammed bin Rashid al Maktoum. 8 Rn
2m 33.40 (6.40)
SF—57/56/32/20/16/3

**2021**  MONKS CROSS STKS £5692.00 (£1696.00: £808.00: £364.00)
7f 202y
4-10 (4-10)

1197 **Susurration (USA) (111)** (Jt-Fav) *(JHMGosden)* 5-9-5 WRSwinburn (3) (lw: chsd ldrs: pushed along ½-wy: led wl over 1f out: r.o wl) ..... —1

1460 Hamas (IRE) **(102)** *(PTWalwyn)* 3-8-9 WCarson (6) (hld up: pushed thro wl over 2f out: ev ch appr fnl f: r.o) ..... 1½.2

1695★ Lead the Dance **(102)** *(HRACecil)* 3-8-6 PatEddery (1) (lw: a.p: nt clr run 2f out: hdwy & ev ch ins fnl f: sddle slipped & eased nr fin) ..... 1.3

1253★ Norton Challenger **(108)** (v) *(MHEasterby)* 5-9-7 MBirch (5) (hld up: hdwy 4f out: ev ch 2f out: nt qckn & nt qckn) ..... ¾.4

1480⁵ St Ninian **(99)** *(MHEasterby)* 6-9-4 LPiggott (2) (led tl hdd wl over 1f out: sn btn) 2½.5

1596² Kristianstad **(100)** (Jt-Fav) *(MrsJCecil)* 3-8-9 SCauthen (4) (lw: chsd ldrs: btn whn hmpd wl over 2f out: sn wl bhd) ..... 20.6

**9/4** Kristianstad, SUSURRATION (USA), **100/30** Lead the Dance, **11/2** Hamas (IRE), **13/2** Norton Challenger, **14/1** St Ninian. CSF £14.48, Tote £3.00: £1.60 £2.70 (£10.30). Pin Oak Stable (NEWMARKET) bred by Pin Oak Farm in USA. 6 Rn
1m 38.73 (2.73)
SF—88/73/67/80/69/–

**2022**  PETERGATE MEDIAN AUCTION STKS (3-Y-O) £4560.00 (£1260.00: £600.00)
1m 205y
4-40 (4-41)

1712★ **Speaker's House (USA) (98)** *(PFICole)* 9-5 TQuinn (2) (lw: hld up: qcknd to ld ins fnl f: comf) ..... —1

Seattle Rhyme (USA) **(120)** (Fav) *(DRCElsworth)* 9-5 SCauthen (3) (h.d.w: cl up: led ent st: shkn up 1f out: nt qckn & hdd ins fnl f) ..... 1½.2

1126⁶ Invisible Armour *(PCHaslam)* 8-7 EJohnson (1) (led tl hdd ent st: sn rdn: wl outpcd fnl 3f) ..... 15.3

**1/2** Seattle Rhyme (USA)(op 1/3), **15/8** SPEAKER'S HOUSE (USA), **50/1** Invisible Armour. CSF £2.91, Tote £2.80 (£1.10). Mr M. Arbib (WHATCOMBE) bred by Wakefield Farm in USA. 3 Rn
1m 53.77 (4.77)
SF—60/55/–

**2023**  LEVY BOARD H'CAP (0-95) £7570.00 (£2260.00: £1080.00: £490.00)
1m 3f 195y
5-10 (5-11)

(Weights raised 1 lb)

1842² **Quick Ransom (77)** (Fav) *(MJohnston)* 4–9-0 DMcKeown (4) (lw: a cl up: led 3f out: rdn & r.o wl) ..... —1

1465 Seal Indigo (IRE) **(80)** *(RHannon)* 4-9-3 JReid (2) (lw: hld up: hdwy 3f out: ev ch 1f out: one pce) ..... 1½.2

681 Farat (USA) **(75)** *(JLDunlop)* 4-8-12 PatEddery (1) (swtg: led 1f: trckd ldrs: outpcd over 3f out & sn bhd: styd on nr fin) ..... 7.3

1073² Lord Hastie (USA) **(80)** *(SGNorton)* 4-9-3 MRoberts (6) (lw: led after 1f to 3f out: wknd fnl 2f) ..... s.h.4

1256 Uluru (IRE) **(87)** *(MrsJRRamsden)* 4-9-10 KDarley (3) (bit bkwd: trckd ldrs: hdwy ent st: lost pl fnl 3f) ..... 7.5

1808² Busted Rock **(87)** *(MrsLPiggott)* 7–9-10 LPiggott (5) (lw: hld up & bhd: effrt 4f out: n.d) .......................................................................................... 1½.**6**

**6/4** QUICK RANSOM, **4/1** Busted Rock(3/1 — 9/2), **9/2** Lord Hastie (USA), **11/2** Seal Indigo (IRE), **9/1** Farat (USA), **12/1** Uluru (IRE)(op 8/1). CSF £9.26, Tote £2.60: £1.60 £2.50 (£7.50). Mr J. S. Morrison (MIDDLEHAM) bred by Benham Stud. 6 Rn
2m 35.42 (8.42)
SF—40/40/21/25/18/15

T/Trio: Race 2: £29.40 (32 Tckts), Race 3: £267.00 (5.1 Tckts), Race 4: £50.50 (22.1 Tckts). T/Jkpt: £15,774.00 (1 Tckt). T/Plpt: £648.80 (12.8 Tckts).
AA

# YORK (L-H)
## Saturday, July 11th [Good becoming Good to soft]
Going Allowance: 5f-8f: 0.10 (G); Rest: 0.20 sec per fur (G)  Wind: fresh half bhd

Stalls: high

**2024**  JERVAULX MEDIAN AUCTION STKS (Mdn 2-Y.O) £5205.00 (£1560.00: £750.00: £345.00)  **6f**  2-00 (2-02)

**Urry Urry Urry** *(MJCamacho)* 8-5 NConnorton (19) (leggy: scope: a chsng ldrs: effrt & rn green over 1f out: r.o wl to ld ins fnl f) ........... —**1**
1742² Glowing Jade (Fav) *(MRChannon)* 8-2 WCarson (18) (lw: trckd ldrs: led over 3f out: rdn & nt qckn ins fnl f) .................................................... 1½.**2**
First Veil *(DRCElsworth)* 8-9 SCauthen (2) (w'like: lw: hmpd s: sn trckng ldrs: disp ld over 2f out tl wknd over 1f out) ................................ 3.**3**
Silverlocks *(MissSEHall)* 8-5 SWebster (14) (leggy: bit bkwd: sn bhd: gd hdwy over 1f out. hung lft: qtyd on wl nr fin) ................................ nk.**4**
1668⁴ Magication *(CEBrittain)* 8-2 MRoberts (17) (lw: a chsng ldrs: effrt 2f out: rdn & r.o one pce) ..................................................... ½.**5**
Olivadi (IRE) *(LMCumani)* 9-0 LDettori (16) (w'like: chsd ldrs tl wknd over 1f out) 2.**6**
1605⁵ Cardinal Dogwood (USA) (bl) *(MBrittain)* 8-7 AMunro (4) (led over 2f: wknd over 1f out) ..................................................... ½.**7**
Hoy-Liegh-Rag *(MJohnston)* 8-10 DMcKeown (3) (lengthy: scope: bit bkwd: sltly hmpd s: hdwy ½-wy: kpt on: nvr able to chal) ........ 3½.**8**
Silver Groom (IRE) *(APJarvis)* 8-7 JReid (9) (w'like: bit bkwd: chsd ldrs tl wknd over 2f out) ................................................... ½.**9**
Milbank Challenger *(MHEasterby)* 8-7 MBirch (5) (unf: bit bkwd: swvd rt s: sn in tch: wandered u.p ½-wy: grad lost pl) .......................... 1.**10**
Astrac Trio (USA) *(SGNorton)* 9-0 JQuinn (12) (rangy: scope: mid div & rdn ½-wy: n.d) ..................................................... 3½.**11**
Hyde's Happy Hour *(NTinkler)* 9-0 DNicholls (13) (wl grwn: unf: bit bkwd: nvr bttr than mid div) ................................................ hd.**12**
Shomberg (IRE) *(PCalver)* 8-10 WNewnes (1) (rangy: scope: bit bkwd: hmpd s: sme hdwy 2f out: nvr nr ldrs) ................................ nk.**13**
1327³ Umbubuzi (USA) *(FHLee)* 8-7 RLappin (11) (lw: chsd ldrs over 3f: sn wknd) .... 1.**14**
Muraadi Ana (IRE) *(AAScott)* 8-7 JFortune (6) (unf: scope: bdly hmpd s: a bhd) 1½.**15**
Scoffera *(NTinkler)* 8-2 LCharnock (20) (w'like: str: bkwd: sme hdwy ½-wy: sn lost pl) ..................................................... 2½.**16**
975⁴ Northern Bluff *(JWWatts)* 8-10 DHolland (10) (lw: chsd ldrs to ½-wy: sn wknd) nk.**17**
1515 Rushalong *(RDEWoodhouse)* 8-3 ‡⁷JMarshall (15) (a outpcd) ..................... ½.**18**
1699 Doc Cottrill *(MrsJRRamsden)* 8-10 KFallon (8) (unruly s: reard up & bdly hmpd s: a bhd) ..................................................... 2.**19**
Smart Teacher (USA) *(PWHarris)* 8-10 RCochrane (7) (unf: swvd lft s: sddle slipped & uns rdr sn after) .......................................... 0

**2/1** Glowing Jade, **5/1** First Veil, **11/2** Magication, **8/1** Olivadi (IRE), **12/1** Northern Bluff, Muraadi Ana (IRE), Umbubuzi (USA), **14/1** Silver Groom (IRE), Doc Cottrill, **16/1** Astrac Trio (USA), Milbank Challenger, URRY URRY URRY, **20/1** Smart Teacher (USA), Shomberg (IRE), **25/1** Hoy-Liegh-Rag, Cardinal Dogwood (USA), Silverlocks, **33/1** Ors. CSF £56.20, Tote £42.50: £7.00 £1.70 £4.20 (£64.10). Lady Matthews (MALTON) bred by Lady Matthews. 20 Rn
1m 12.78 (2.58)
SF—51/42/37/32/27/31

**2025**  FRIARGATE GRADUATION STKS (2-Y.O) £5390.00 (£1610.00: £770.00: £350.00)  **6f 214y**  2-35 (2-36)

1457 **New Capricorn** (USA) *(MAJarvis)* 9-0 RCochrane (4) (trckd ldr: effrt over 2f out: r.o wl u.p fnl f: led post) ..................................... —**1**
1502* Woodenville (USA) (Fav) *(LMCumani)* 9-0 LDettori (3) (lw: led: drvn along: qcknd over 2f out: r.o: jst ct) ....................................... s.h.**2**

1715* Alderney Prince (USA) *(PFlCole)* 9-0 AMunro (2) (trckd ldrs: effrt 3f out: sn
outpcd: kpt on u.p) ...................................................................................... 4.3
     Irish Dominion *(MissSEHall)* 8-11 NConnorton (1) (w'like: cmpt: dwlt: rn green:
hdwy & prom over 2f out: wknd over 1f out) ...................................... nk.4

**21/20** Woodenville (USA), **5/2** Alderney Prince (USA), **3/1** NEW CAPRICORN (USA), **14/1** Irish Dominion. CSF
£6.27, Tote £4.40 (£2.80). Mr Kamal Bhatia (NEWMARKET) bred by Stonereath Farms Inc in USA. 4 Rn
1m 27.74 (5.34)
SF—31/30/18/14

---

**2026**      JOHN SMITH'S BITTER H'CAP (0-90) £6004.00 (£1792.00: £856.00: £388.00)
         **7f 202y**                           3-10 (3-11)

(Weights raised 12 lb)

1921² **Golden Chip (IRE) (64)** *(APStringer)* 4-9-1 ‡⁵SMaloney (5) (chsd ldr: led over
3f out: jst hld on) ................................................................................ —1
   1863 Doctor Roy **(56)** *(NBycroft)* 4-8-12 AMunro (3) (b.off hind: outpcd over 3f out:
n.m.r & swtchd outside over 1f out: styd on wl) .............................. s.h.2
   *1847\** Sandmoor Denim **(50)** *(SRBowring)* 5-8-6 JQuinn (3) (trckd ldrs: effrt over 3f
out: chal over 1f out: nt qckn ins fnl f) ........................................... 1.3
    482 Shujan (USA) **(77)** *(RWArmstrong)* 3-9-10 WCarson (1) (hmpd & lost pl after 1f:
drvn along 5f out: styd on fnl 2f) ..................................................... 7.4
  1255 Stylish Gent **(55)** (bl) *(NTinkler)* 5-8-11 LCharnock (4) (trckd ldrs: rdn & n.m.r
over 2f out: sn wknd) ................................................................. 2¹/₂.5
  1716* Buddy's Friend (IRE) **(58)** (Fav) *(RJRWilliams)* 4-9-0 RCochrane (6) (lw: hld up
& plld hrd: effrt over 2f out: sn wknd) ........................................ 8.6
  1696 Halston Prince **(66)** *(MrsJRRamsden)* 5-9-8 JReid (7) (lw: led tl hdd over 3f out:
sn lost pl: t.o) ............................................................................. 7

**5/2** Buddy's Friend (IRE), **7/2** Shujan (USA), **4/1** Sandmoor Denim, **5/1** GOLDEN CHIP (IRE), **8/1** Halston Prince,
**16/1** Ors. CSF £59.20, Tote £6.10. £2.60 £4.10 (£49.20). Mr A. H. Jackson (THIRSK) bred by C. and J. Sandys
and Barbara McCourt in Ireland. 7 Rn
1m 39.87 (3.87)
SF—55/51/42/39/18/–

---

**2027**      FOSTER'S SILVER CUP (Stks) (listed race) £9218.75 (£2750.00: £1312.50: £593.75)
         **1m 7f 195y**                          3-40 (3-42)

1468⁶ **Tyrone Bridge (104)** *(MCPipe)* 6-9-6 MRoberts (1) (chsd ldr: led over 2f out:
sn hrd drvn: styd on strly fnl f) ..................................................... —1
1821a⁵ Hateel **(107)** *(PTWalwyn)* 6-9-6 WCarson (5) (lw: hld up & bhd: hdwy on bit 5f
out: chal over 1f out: rdn & wknd ins fnl f) ..................................... 4.2
1821a² Parting Moment (USA) **(102)** *(IABalding)* 5-9-8 RCochrane (3) (lw: hld up: effrt
5f out: rdn & styd on one pce fnl f) ................................................ 7.3
  1477⁶ Haitham **(91)** *(RAkehurst)* 5-9-3 JReid (6) (hld up: hdwy 5f out: one pce fnl 3f) . 2.4
  1879² Springs Welcome **(62)** *(CACyzer)* 4-8-12 DMcKeown (2) (chsd ldr: led 4f out tl
over 2f out: grad wknd) ............................................................... 1¹/₂.5
  1644a Be a Honey **(90)** *(NAGraham)* 4-8-12 LDettori (4) (trckd ldrs tl wknd over 3f out) 20.6
  1477² Gondolier **(94)** (Fav) *(HRACecil)* 4-9-3 SCauthen (2) (lw: led: drvn along over
4f out: sn hdd: wknd qckly 3f out: eased) ..................................... 30.7

**11/8** Gondolier, **7/2** Hateel, **4/1** TYRONE BRIDGE, **5/1** Parting Moment (USA), **14/1** Haitham, **20/1** Be a Honey,
**100/1** Springs Welcome. CSF £17.12, Tote £5.30: £2.10 £2.20 (£8.50). Mr Paul Green (WELLINGTON) bred by
Swettenham Stud. 7 Rn
3m 31.54 (11.54)
SF—23/19/14/7/–/–

---

**2028**      JOHN SMITH'S MAGNET CUP (H'cap) (0-115) £38457.00 (£11556.00: £5578.00:
         £2589.00)    **1¹/₄m 85y**                 4-15 (4-24)

1295* **Mr Confusion (IRE) (83)** *(SGNorton)* 4-8-3 ‡⁷Pears (14) (lw: a.p: led over 1f
out: rdn & edgd lft ins fnl f: fin 1st: disq: reinstated) .................... —1
  1463 Tell No Lies **(86)** *(MHEasterby)* 5-8-13 MBirch (10) (hld up & bhd: hdwy over 3f
out: hmpd & styd on wl nr fin) ...................................................... 1.2
  1869⁵ Steerforth (IRE) **(97)** *(ACStewart)* 4-9-10 MRoberts (6) (lw: led over 3f out:
styng on whn sltly hmpd ins fnl f) ................................................ 1.3
  1691 Westholme (USA) **(78)** *(MHEasterby)* 4-8-0 ‡⁵SMaloney (1) (effrt 5f out: styd on
same pce fnl 2f: nvr rchd ldrs) ..................................................... 7.4
  1465 Hashar (IRE) **(94)** *(DRCElsworth)* 4-9-7 JFortune (18) (lw: bhd tl styd on wl fnl
3f: hung lft u.p: nt rch ldrs) ......................................................... 3.5
1495a⁴ Arany **(93)** *(MHTompkins)* 5-9-6 JReid (12) (hld up: smooth hdwy over 3f out:
wknd 2f out) ................................................................................ 6.6
  1555* Knock Knock **(83)** *(IABalding)* 7-8-10 RCochrane (17) (hld up & bhd: styd on
fnl 3f: nt rch ldrs) ....................................................................... 3¹/₂.7
  1466² Wild Fire **(79)** *(GWragg)* 3-7-6 ‡³FNorton (8) (prom: ev ch 3f out: rdn & wknd 2f
out) ............................................................................................ ¹/₂.8

1869 Gymcrak Premiere **(92)** *(MHEasterby)* 4–9-5 DMcKeown (15) (hld up & bhd: hdwy 4f out: wknd over 2f out) .................................... nk.9
657 Corcina **(78)** *(MBell)* 4–7-12 ‡7PTurner (5) (b.off fore: w ldrs: led over 5f out tl over 3f out: sn wknd) ................................ nk.10
1476 Irek **(92)** *(LordHuntingdon)* 3–8-8[(1)] SCauthen (2) (lw: sn pushed along: hdwy & prom over 5f out: wknd over 2f out) .......................... 1½.11
1703[4] Andrath (IRE) **(82)** *(CEBrittain)* 4–8-9 AMunro (19) (in tch: hrd drvn 5f out: wknd over 2f out) ................................... 1½.12
1799[5] Cradle of Love (USA) **(79)** *(JWHills)* 4–8-6 WNewnes (3) (sn bhd) .................. 5.13
1662[2] Lucky Guest **(94)** *(JLDunlop)* 5–9-7 WCarson (4) (lw: hld up & plld hrd early: hmpd 7f out: hdwy 4f out: wknd over 2f out: eased) ........ hd.14
1402[2] Legal View (USA) **(93)** *(Fav)* *(LMCumani)* 4–9-6 LDettori (16) (lw: in tch: hrd drvn over 3f out: no rspnse) ............................ 5.15
1869 No Submission (USA) **(83)** *(CRNelson)* 6–8-10 DHolland (13) (led 1f: chsd ldrs tl lost pl over 3f out) ............................... 2.16
1746★ Big Easy (IRE) **(87)** (bl) *(MrsJCecil)* 3–7-12 ‡5DHarrison (7) (led after 1f tl over 5f out: rdn & wknd 4f out) ........................... 3½.17

**Subsequent Stewards Enquiry: Mr Confusion originally disqualified (carelsss riding). After a meeting of the Jockey Club Disciplinary Committee on July 16th, the decision was reversed. All bets settled on Tell No Lies.**

**4/1** Legal View (USA), **6/1** Steerforth (IRE) (op 4/1), **7/1** Irek, Wild Fire, **8/1** Mr Confusion (IRE), **10/1** Lucky Guest, **12/1** Hashar (IRE), Big Easy (IRE), **14/1** Westholme (USA), **16/1** TELL NO LIES, **20/1** Gymcrak Premiere, Arany, Knock Knock, **25/1** Andrath (IRE), **33/1** No Submission (USA), Corcina, **50/1** Cradl of Love (USA), CSF £107.77, CT £778.64. Tote £20.40: £3.80 £2.60 £2.20 £7.10 (£110.00). Mr R. Fenwick-Gibson (BARNSLEY) bred by D. P. O'Brien in Ireland. 17 Rn
2m 12.06 (4.56)
SF—64/72/82/44/59/46

**2029**    WFRSTER'S GREEN LABEL BEST H'CAP (3-Y.O) (0-90) £6004.00 (£1792.00: £856.00: £388.00)    **6f**    4-45 (4-57)

1391[4] **First Gold (60)** (bl) *(JWharton)* 7-8 JQuinn (11) (hdwy ½-wy: r.o wl u.p to ld wl ins fnl f) ................................................ —1
1698[6] Devon Dancer **(73)** (v) *(MHEasterby)* 8-7 MBirch (9) (w ldrs: styd on u.p fnl f) ... 1.2
1187[5] Arctic Appeal (IRE) **(87)** *(JBerry)* 9-7 DMcKeown (10) (led stands' side: rdn over 1f out: no ex nr fin) .......................... s.h.3
1871[4] Invigilate **(62)** *(Fav)* *(MPNaughton)* 7-5[(2)] ‡5DHarrison (7) (lw: hld up: hdwy ½-wy: n.m.r & styd on same pce fnl f) ................. nk.4
1487[6] Saddlehome (USA) **(76)** *(RMWhitaker)* 8-10 MRoberts (3) (lw: led far side: rdn over 1f out: kpt on same pce) ................. hd.5
1698[2] Venture Capitalist **(84)** *(RHannon)* 9-4 JReid (5) (lw: sn bhd: hdwy u.p over 2f out: kpt on wl fnl f) ................................ nk.6
1870[3] Euro Festival **(85)** *(MissLCSiddall)* 9-5 RCochrane (2) (lw: hld up & bhd: hdwy u.p 2f out: styd on nr fin) ........................ 1.7
1661[2] Patience Please **(75)** *(MHEasterby)* 8-4 ‡5SMaloney (12) (chsd ldrs: rdn ½-wy: wknd wl over 1f out) ........................ 7.8
1926[6] Don't Smile **(73)** *(MHTompkins)* 8-7 LDettori (6) (in tch w to ½-wy: eased whn no ch) ....................................... 2.9
1865[2] Auction King (IRE) **(60)** *(ASmith)* 7-1 ‡7CHawksley (4) (s.i.s: a in rr) .............. nk.10
1684[2] La Dama Bonita (USA) **(84)** *(DWPArbuthnot)* 9-4 WCarson (5) (a bhd) .............. nk.11
1523[3] Boursin (IRE) **(85)** *(PCalver)* 9-5 WNewnes (8) (lw: w ldrs: rdn ½-wy: edgd lft: sn wknd) ......................................... ¾.12

**11/4** Invigilate, **6/1** Venture Capitalist, Don't Smile, **8/1** La Dama Bonita (USA), **9/1** FIRST GOLD, Euro Festival, **10/1** Saddlehome (USA), Patience Please, **12/1** Boursin (IRE), **14/1** Devon Dancer, **16/1** Arctic Appeal (IRE), **25/1** Auction King (IRE). CSF £120.19, CT £1,822.51. Tote £14.50: £3.20 £6.60 £5.60 (£200.80). Mr J. L. Ashby (MELTON MOWBRAY) bred by Messinger Stud Ltd. 12 Rn
1m 13.45 (3.25)
SF—27/36/49/18/36/43

**2030**    FISHERGATE NURSERY    £5526.50 (£1652.00: £791.00: £360.50)    **5f** 5-15 (5-21)
(Weights raised 3 lb)

1851★ **Meadmore Magic** *(JLHarris)* 7-7[(3)] ‡3FNorton (6) (mde virtually all: edgd lft u.p jst ins fnl f: r.o wl) ......................... —1
1469 Sabre Rattler *(JBerry)* 9-7 RCochrane (1) (lw: w wnnr: rdn ½-wy: sltly hmpd ins fnl f: kpt on wl) ......................... ½.2
1694[5] Bold Seven (IRE) *(FHLee)* 8-0 RLappin (2) (sn outpcd: hdwy u.p over 1f out: styd on strly nr fin) .................... hd.3
1448★ Plum First (bl) *(NBycroft)* 7-8 SWood (4) (sn chsng ldrs: kpt on wl fnl f) ............ ½.4
1360★ In Case (USA) *(Fav)* *(RCharlton)* 8-11 LDettori (5) (lw: trckd ldrs: effrt over 1f out: styd on same pce u.p) ................. 2.5
1571★ For the Present *(TDBarron)* 8-8 AlexGreaves (8) (s.i.s: bhd: sme hdwy ½-wy: nvr nr to chal) ............................ 4.6

1240⁴ Super Seve (IRE) *(JBerry)* 9-1  DMcKeown (3) (w ldrs tl wknd 2f out) .............. 2¹/₂.7
1506★ Juliet Bravo *(BBeasley)* 8-3  LCharnock (7) (w ldrs 3f: sn wknd) ..................... 4.8
1251★ Nicky Mygirl *(MBrittain)* 7-11  JQuinn (9) (prom early: wl outpcd fr ¹/₂-wy) .......... 4.9
*Stewards Enquiry: Obj. to Meadmore Magic by Cochrane overruled.*

**7/4** In Case (USA), **3/1** Sabre Rattler, **8/1** Juliet Bravo, **9/1** For the Present, **10/1** Super Seve (IRE), MEADMORE
MAGIC, Plum First, **11/1** Ors. CSF £41.03, CT £321.61. Tote £12.20: £2.40 £1.60 £2.60 (£23.20). Mr M.
Holmes (MELTON MOWBRAY) bred by White Lodge Farm Stud. 9 Rn        60.30 sec (2.80)
SF—33/59/37/29/38/19

T/Trio: Race 5: £941.40 (4.2 Tckts). T/Jkpt: Not won; £3,502.90 to Sandown 16/7/92. T/Plpt: £5,033.10 (3.2
Tckts).     WG

---

## 1630—SALISBURY (R-H)

### Saturday, July 11th [Good to soft, Soft patches]

Going Allowance: 0.10 sec per fur (G)         Wind: mod against

Stalls: low

**2031**    MYROBELLA STKS (Mdn 2-Y.O) £2092.50 (£580.00: £277.50)    **5f**    2-00 (2-03)

856³ **Ansellman** *(MJHaynes)* 9-0  NHowe (7) (a.p: led over 2f out: hung rt fnl f: all out)   —1
1913⁴ Princely Favour (IRE) *(RHannon)* 9-0  SRaymont (8) (a.p: ev ch fnl f: r.o) ......... nk.2
Clear Look (Fav) *(PFICole)* 8-9  TQuinn (5) (leggy: scope: a.p: hrd rdn & ev ch
over 1f out: btn whn hmpd wl ins fnl f) .................................. 2.3
703⁵ Chili Heights *(GBBalding)* 9-0  JWilliams (5) (hdwy over 2f out: r.o one pce fnl f) nk.4
1146⁶ Bodandere *(MJFetherston-Godley)* 8-6  ‡3SO'Gorman (2) (hdwy over 2f out: nt
rch ldrs) ....................................................... 3¹/₂.5
1635 Champagne Grandy *(MRChannon)* 8-9  ‡7LMahoney (13) (nvr nrr) ............. 1¹/₂.6
1762³ Brigadore Gold *(RHannon)* 8-9  TyroneWilliams (11) (prom over 3f) ............. 1¹/₂.7
1541³ Pirates Gold (IRE) *(MJHeaton-Ellis)* 9-0  AMcGlone (14) (prom over 3f) ......... ¹/₂.8
Imafifer (IRE) *(WRMuir)* 9-0  SWhitworth (4) (w'like: bit bkwd: a bhd) ......... 2.9
July Bride *(MJHaynes)* 8-9  BRouse (1) (lt-f: unf: s.s: a bhd) ............... ³/₄.10
Fanfold (IRE) *(AWDenson)* 8-9  NAdams (9) (leggy: bit bkwd: a bhd) ....... nk.11
Step on it *(CPWildman)* 8-9  CRutter (12) (unf: bit bkwd: rdn over 2f out: a bhd) d.h.11
Tayish *(TThomsonJones)* 9-0  AClark (3) (w'like: bit bkwd: s.i.s: a bhd) ......... nk.13
1300⁶ Marwell Mitzi *(WGRWightman)* 8-9  GBardwell (6) (b.hind: led over 2f: wknd
qckly over 1f out) .......................................... 3.14

**4/7** Clear Look(2/1—1/2), **10/1** Princely Favour (IRE)(7/1—12/1), ANSELLMAN(op 5/1), **12/1** Pirates Gold
(IRE)(6/1—14/1), Tayish(op 5/1), **14/1** Brigadore Gold(op 8/1), **16/1** Step on it, Chili Heights, **20/1** July Bride,
**25/1** Marwell Mitzi, **33/1** Champagne Grandy, **50/1** Ors. CSF £105.05, Tote £10.90: £2.50 £2.90 £1.40
(£29.30). Ansells of Watford (EPSOM) bred by W. L. Caley. 14 Rn       63.12 sec (3.12)
SF—48/47/34/38/16/6

**2032**    OWEN TUDOR H'CAP (0-70) £2784.00 (£774.00: £372.00)    **6f**    2-30 (2-34)

1314 **Blue Topaze** (56) *(RJHolder)* 4-9-0  JWilliams (19) (gd hdwy over 1f out: led ins
fnl f: drvn out) ............................................. —1
1905² Profit a Prendre (48) (Jt-Fav) *(DAWilson)* 8-8-6  BRouse (11) (b: lw: hdwy &
hung lft over 1f out: r.o wl ins fnl f) ........................... nk.2
1814★ Shikari's Son (63) *(JWhite)* 5-9-7  TQuinn (20) (hdwy over 1f out: ev ch ins fnl f:
r.o) ....................................................... ¹/₂.3
1773 Mu-Arrik (54) *(DAWilson)* 4-8-5  ‡7SharonMillard (18) (b.nr fore: a.p: ev ch over
1f out: nt qckn fnl f) ....................................... 2¹/₂.4
1952⁶ Luna Bid (63) *(MBlanshard)* 9-9-7  CRutter (2) (hdwy & edgd rt over 1f out: r.o) nk.5
Maria Cappuccini (50) *(KOCunningham-Brown)* 4-8-8  AMcGlone (17) (prom:
ev ch over 1f out: wknd fnl f) ............................... 2.6
1576 Sandcastle City (67) (bl) *(RHannon)* 3-8-11  ‡7MarkDenaro (8) (prom: n.m.r
over 1f out: wknd fnl f) ..................................... ¹/₂.7
1463 Thornfield Boy (70) *(RJHolder)* 6-9-7  ‡7SDrowne (14) (led tl wknd ins fnl f) ...... s.h.8
1654★ Coppermill Lad (51) (Jt-Fav) *(LJHolt)* 9-8-2  ‡7CAvery (3) (late hdwy: nrst fin) ...... s.h.9
1677⁴ Amethystine (USA) (60) *(RJHodges)* 6-9-1  ‡3TSprake (7) (prom: ev ch over 1f
out: wknd fnl f) ............................................ 1.10
1654⁴ Millsolin (IRE) (53) *(ARDavison)* 4-8-4  ‡7BRussell (4) (prom over 4f) ......... 3¹/₂.11
John O'Dreams (45) *(MrsJCDawe)* 7-8-3  RFox (10) (swtchd rt over 1f out: stdy
hdwy fnl f: nrst fin) ........................................ ¹/₂.12
1636⁴ Mariette Larkin (63) *(GBBalding)* 3-8-11  ‡3SO'Gorman (12) (n.d) ............. ¹/₂.13
1305³ Divine Pet (62) *(WGRWightman)* 7-9-6  GBardwell (15) (bhd fnl 2f) ........... 3.14
1614 Pipe Opener (54) *(JLSpearing)* 4-8-12  NHowe (5) (n.d) ...................... 2¹/₂.15
1570 C Sharp (46) *(WRMuir)* 5-8-4  SWhitworth (9) (prom over 3f) ............... d.h.15

1773⁴ Belfort Ruler **(62)** *(BGubby)* 5–9-6 AClark (13) (prom: btn whn hmpd over 1f out) .................................................................................................................. s.h.**17**
1133⁶ Darakah **(58)** *(CJHill)* 5–9-2 NAdams (16) (a bhd) ................................. 1¹/₂.**18**
1084⁴ Cronk's Quality **(44)** *(DCJermy)* 9–8-2 TyroneWilliams (6) (bhd fnl 2f: t.o) ....... 6.**19**

**9/2** Profit a Prendre(tchd 7/1), Coppermill Lad(6/1—4/1), **8/1** Shikari's Son(op 5/1), Sandcastle City, **9/1** Divine Pet, **11/1** Darakah, **12/1** Luna Bid, Cronk's Quality(op 8/1), **14/1** Millsolin (IRE), BLUE TOPAZE, **16/1** Mu-Arrik, **20/1** Mariette Larkin, Maria Cappuccini, Amethystine (USA), C Sharp, **25/1** Ors. CSF £79.87, CT £516.23. Tote £23.70: £4.90 £1.30 £1.70 £6.00 (£88.50). Mr M. S. Saunders (BRISTOL) bred by Ahmed M. Foustok. 19 Rn
1m 16.54 (4.24)
SF—27/18/31/5/20/–

## 2033

FELSTEAD H'CAP (Amateurs) (0-70) £2805.00 (£780.00: £375.00)
**1m 1f 209y**      3-00 (3-04)

1766² **Thimbalina (38)** *(DAWilson)* 6–9-0 ‡³MissLHide (9) (stdy hdwy 5f out: r.o to ld wl ins fnl f) ......................................................................................................... —**1**
1587⁵ Tiger Claw (USA) **(50)** *(RJHodges)* 6–10-1 MrsJHembrow (4) (hdwy 5f out: led ins fnl f: sn hdd: r.o) ........................................................................................ ¹/₂.**2**
708 Sean's Scholar (USA) **(49)** *(CNAllen)* 5–9-11 ‡³MissRLowes (14) (mid div: rdn 5f out: hdwy over 1f out: r.o wl) ........................................................................ hd.**3**
1150 Super Morning **(49)** *(GBBalding)* 6–9-11 ‡³MrDSalter (1) (hld up: hdwy 4f out: ev ch over 2f out: r.o one pce) ...................................................................... ¹/₂.**4**
1767* Lots of Luck **(54)** (Fav) *(JPearce)* 9–10-5 MrsLPearce (2) (a.p: led over 3f out tl wknd ins fnl f) ......................................................................................................... 1.**5**
*1543*² Mr Wishing Well **(54)** *(RJRWilliams)* 6–10-5 MrsJCrossley (11) (b.nr hind: wl bhd 7f: gd hdwy over 1f out: r.o) ........................................................................ nk.**6**
1798* The Karaoke King **(68)** *(RHannon)* 3–10-5 ‡³MrsJBoggis (3) (hdwy 4f out: wknd wl over 1f out) ............................................................................................... 5.**7**
1747⁶ Fern Heights **(56)** *(CDBroad)* 5–10-4 ‡³MissCJakoway (10) (rlwlt: sn prom: ev ch over 2f out: wknd wl over 1f out) ................................................................ 3.**8**
1879³ Cathos (FR) **(56)** *(DAWilson)* 7–10-7 MrsEMellor (5) (b: dwlt: nvr nr ldrs) ....... d.h.**8**
1125 Polistatic **(37)** *(CAHorgan)* 5–8-13 ‡³MissDPomeroy (12) (nvr trbld ldrs) ......... ¹/₂.**10**
1767³ Broughton Blues (IRE) **(35)** (bl) *(WJMusson)* 4–9-0 MissJFeilden (16) (b: chsd ldrs 5f) ................................................................................................................. 1.**11**
1721* Samurai Gold (USA) **(52)** (v) *(PTWalwyn)* 4–10-0 ‡³MissTBracegirdle (13) (a bhd) .......................................................................................................................... s.h.**12**
1656² Albert **(52)** *(DAWilson)* 5–10-3 MissJAllison (7) (nvr nrr) ................................ 1¹/₂.**13**
*1544*⁵ High Post **(50)** *(DMarks)* 3–9-4 MissKMarks (15) (prom 7f) ........................... 2.**14**
1743⁶ Horizon (IRE) **(59)** (bl) *(TThomsonJones)* 4–10-7 ‡³MrGHaine (8) (led after 2f tl over 3f out: sn wknd) .................................................................................. nk.**15**
Littleton Lullaby **(35)** *(MMadgwick)* 7–8-11 ‡³MissDAlbion (18) (prom 6f: t.o) .... 8.**16**
1743³ Abingdon Flyer (IRE) **(70)** *(RHannon)* 4–11-4 ‡³MrRHannon (17) (led 2f: wknd 2f out: eased whn btn fnl f) ............................................................................... 3.**17**
1640 Gibbot **(58)** *(PHowling)* 7–10-6⁽²³⁾ ‡³MrSWhiting (5) (s.s: t.o fnl 3f) ............... 15.**18**
LONG HANDICAP: Broughton Blues (IRE) 8-13, Gibbot 8-12.

**11/4** Lots of Luck, **11/2** Cathos (FR), THIMBALINA(16/1—5/1), **7/1** Albert, **8/1** Samurai Gold (USA), The Karaoke King(op 4/1), **10/1** Mr Wishing Well, **12/1** Abingdon Flyer (IRE)(op 8/1), **14/1** Horizon (IRE), High Post, Tiger Claw (USA), **20/1** Sean's Scholar (USA), Super Morning, Broughton Blues (IRE), **33/1** Ors. CSF £89.45, CT £1,387.18. Tote £8.50: £1.60 £3.40 £4.00 £3.30 (£224.40). Mr T. S. M. S. Riley-Smith (EPSOM) bred by James W. H. Hartley. 18 Rn
2m 13.72 (9.02)
SF—20/34/29/28/34/33

## 2034

QUEENPOT STKS (I) (Mdn 2-Y.O) £2075.00 (£575.00: £275.00)
**6f 212y**      3-30 (3-34)

**Woodchat (USA)** *(PFICole)* 9-0 TQuinn (6) (unf: scope: led over 4f out: hrd rdn fnl f: r.o wl) .......................................................................................................... —**1**
Blush Rambler (USA) *(MRStoute)* 9-0 PD'Arcy (4) (w'like: a.p: ev ch fnl f: nt qckn cl home) .................................................................................................... 2.**2**
Semillon *(GHarwood)* 9-0 AClark (13) (unf: scope: bit bkwd: swtchd rt & hdwy 3f out: ev ch 2f out: hrd rdn & one pce) ................................................... 7.**3**
Southern Memories (IRE) *(RHannon)* 9-0 SRaymont (1) (unf: scope: bit bkwd: chsd ldr: r.o one pce fnl 2f) ................................................................................. 2¹/₂.**4**
1202 Aberdeen Heather *(DRCEIsworth)* 9-0 JWilliams (10) (prom 5f) ...................... 2.**5**
Top Pet (IRE) *(RHannon)* 9-0 AMcGlone (2) (leggy: bit bkwd: plld hrd: led over 2f: wknd over 2f out) ....................................................................................... 5.**6**
1536² L'Aigle D'Or (USA) (Fav) *(GLewis)* 9-0 BRouse (14) (lw: prom over 4f) ............ 2¹/₂.**7**
1149 Secret Formula *(GBBalding)* 9-0 CRutter (7) (n.d) ............................................. 1¹/₂.**8**
1635 De Chine *(JSMoore)* 8-9 SWhitworth (11) (nvr nr ldrs) ....................................... 4.**9**
Romalito *(MBlanshard)* 9-0 NHowe (12) (cmpt: bit bkwd: dwlt: a bhd) ............. nk.**10**

El Grando *(KOCunningham-Brown)* 9-0 GBardwell (8) (unf: dwlt: a bhd) ......... **4.11**
Yellow Rattle *(MajorWRHern)* 8-9 BProcter (3) (unf: scope: n.d) ................... nk.**12**
907 Alaska Bay *(RJHolder)* 9-0 ADicks (9) (n.d) ....................................................... 1/2.**13**
1867 Bonny Princess *(JDBethell)* 8-9 TyroneWilliams (5) (unf: spd 3f: t.o) ........... 7.**14**

**6/4** L'Aigle D'Or (USA)(tchd 5/2), **3/1** Blush Rambler (USA), WOODCHAT (USA)(op 2/1), **6/1** Semillon(op 8/1), **12/1** Top Pet (IRE)(8/1—14/1), **16/1** Southern Memories (IRE)(op 10/1), Aberdeen Heather, Yellow Rattle, **40/1** Ors. CSF £14.15, Tote £3.70: £2.10 £1.50 £2.00 (£9.30). Mr Fahd Salman (WHATCOMBE) bred by Oak Crest Farm in USA. 14 Rn                                                                                      1m 30.49 (4.79)
SF−38/32/11/3/−/−

**2035**          FAIR TRIAL H'CAP (0-90) £2950.00 (£880.00: £420.00: £190.00)    **1m**  4-00 (4-03)
(Weights raised 4 lb)

1634★ **Baluga (85)** *(GHarwood)* 3−9-10 AClark (8) (mde all: hrd rdn over 1f out: all out) −**1**
833³ Express Service **(78)** *(PJMakin)* 3-9-0 ‡³TSprake (4) (hdwy 3f out: ev ch fnl f: r.o) ......................................................................................... hd.**2**
1916 Lady Lacey **(53)** (v) *(GBBalding)* 5−7-12 ‡³SO'Gorman (3) (chsd wnr: ev ch over 1f out: one pce fnl f) ................................................................ 3¹/₂.**3**
1637³ Aitch N'Bee **(75)** *(LadyHerries)* 9−9-9 JWilliams (7) (hld up: hdwy over 2f out: nt clr run & swtchd rt over 1f out: nt qckn ins fnl f) ................ 1¹/₂.**4**
1433★ Courageous Knight **(76)** *(RHannon)* 3−9-1 SWhitworth (2) (nvr nrr) ................... 2.**5**
1637★ Mahsul (IRE) **(61)** (Fav) *(CJBenstead)* 4−8-9 TQuinn (1) (hld up: hdwy over 2f out: wknd ins fnl f) ........................................................ 6.**6**
515 Spring to the Top **(56)** *(JWPayne)* 5−8-4 AMcGlone (5) (prom tl wknd wl over 1f out) ....................................................................................... 3¹/₂.**7**
1261 Lucknam Dreamer **(70)** *(MrsBarbaraWaring)* 4−9-4 NHowe (6) (prom tl wknd qckly fnl f) ...................................................................... 5.**8**
*Stewards Enquiry: Clark suspended 20-23/7/92 (excessive use of whip).*

**9/4** Mahsul (IRE), **100/30** Express Service(6/1−3/1), **5/1** Aitch N'Bee, **6/1** BALUGA(op 7/2), **8/1** Courageous Knight(11/2−9/1), Spring to the Top(6/1−10/1), **9/1** Lady Lacey, **20/1** Lucknam Dreamer. CSF £26.16, CT £166.93. Tote £5.20: £1.90 £1.60 £2.20 (£19.00). Mr J. C. Thompson (PULBOROUGH) bred by K. J. and Mrs Buchanan. 8 Rn                                                                               1m 45.09 (5.79)
SF−35/24/−/17/3/−

**2036**          CRESTED LARK H'CAP (0-70) £2742.00 (£762.00: £366.00)    **1¹/₂m**  4-30 (4-32)

1612³ **Caspian Beluga (52)** *(MrsAKnight)* 4−8-13 SWhitworth (14) (mde all: clr 8f out: hrd rdn 3f out: r.o wl) ............................................................. −**1**
1643⁶ Le Baron Perche (FR) **(66)** *(CJames)* 3−9-0 BRouse (6) (hdwy over 3f out: hrd rdn over 1f out: r.o ins fnl f) ................................................... 2.**2**
*1324*★ Atlantic Way **(35)** *(CJHill)* 4−7-10 NAdams (17) (hdwy 6f out: jnd wnr over 2f out: sn hrd rdn: one pce) ..................................................... 3¹/₂.**3**
505 Rocquaine Bay **(37)** *(MJBolton)* 5−7-7⁽²⁾ ‡⁵BDoyle (10) (hdwy 3f out: styd on fnl f) ................................................................................................. 1/2.**4**
Holly Brown **(45)** *(PJHobbs)* 9−8-3 ‡³TSprake (18) (prom: eased whn btn over 1f out) ............................................................................................. 3.**5**
1577⁶ Dajitus **(67)** *(MJHeaton-Ellis)* 3−9-1 TyroneWilliams (12) (prom: hrd rdn over 2f out: sn wknd) .................................................................... 3.**6**
627★ Matching Green **(72)** (Fav) *(GBBalding)* 3−9-6 JWilliams (9) (nvr plcd to chal) . hd.**7**
1770⁵ Corinthian God (IRE) **(45)** *(DAWilson)* 3−7-7 DanaMellor (3) (nvr trbld ldrs) ...... 1/2.**8**
1760⁵ Casienne (IRE) **(39)** *(RJHolder)* 4−8-0 RFox (15) (prom over 9f: eased whn btn fnl f) ................................................................................................ 1/2.**9**
1390⁵ Easy Purchase **(55)** *(RJHolder)* 5−8-9 ‡⁷SDrowne (1) (hld up & bhd: hdwy 4f out: wknd over 2f out) ............................................................... 2.**10**
Ross Graham **(65)** *(MrsBarbaraWaring)* 4−9-12 NHowe (2) (plld hrd: chsd ldrs tl rdn & wknd 3f out) ...................................................... 1¹/₂.**11**
1747 Hightown-Princess (IRE) **(40)** *(JSMoore)* 4−7-12⁽²⁾ ‡³SO'Gorman (13) (t.o) ...... 8.**12**
1721⁶ Clear Light **(56)** *(CASmith)* 5−9-3 MWigham (20) (prom over 8f: t.o) ................ 7.**13**
1390 Hallow Fair **(37)** *(CAHorgan)* 7−7-12⁽¹⁾ AMcGlone (7) (t.o) ............................... 8.**14**
*1544* Priok **(35)** *(WGRWightman)* 9−7-10 GBardwell (11) (bhd fnl 4f: t.o) ................. 1/2.**15**
Erin's Town **(43)** *(WCarter)* 6−7-13 ‡⁵NGwilliams (16) (chsd wnr 8f: t.o) ........ 3¹/₂.**16**
Woodlands Crown **(34)** *(DCTucker)* 9−7-2⁽²⁾ ‡⁷GMilligan (19) (virtually p.u 4f out) **17**
LONG HANDICAP: Woodlands Crown 7-1.

**9/2** Matching Green, **5/1** CASPIAN BELUGA, Easy Purchase(op 12/1), **6/1** Atlantic Way(4/1−13/2), **7/1** Le Baron Perche (FR)(5/1−10/1), **9/1** Clear Light, **10/1** Dajitus, **12/1** Casienne (IRE), **16/1** Ross Graham, Hallow Fair, Rocquaine Bay, **20/1** Priok, Erin's Town, Woodlands Crown, **25/1** Ors. CSF £44.83, CT £211.17. Tote £5.80: £1.50 £3.00 £1.20 £6.80 (£48.10). Mr L. J. Hawkings (CULLOMPTON) bred by Wretham Stud. 17 Rn
2m 40.21 (7.61)
SF−35/32/7/3/7/13

**2037**　　QUEENPOT STKS (II) (Mdn 2-Y.O) £2057.50 (£570.00: £272.50)
　　　　　　**6f 212y**　　　　　　　　　　　　　　　　　　　　5-00 (5-04)

1370[2] **Cissbury Ring** (Fav) *(LadyHerries)* 9-0 JWilliams (3) (lw: a.p: led over 3f out: sn
　　　　　clr & hung rt: r.o wl) ..................................................................... —1
15694 Bold Acre *(DRLaing)* 9-0 TyroneWilliams (5) (a.p: chsd wnr fnl 3f: no imp) ...... 10.2
　　　　　Delta Downs *(RHannon)* 8-9 SRaymont (9) (leggy: unf: hdwy fnl 2f: r.o) .......... nk.3
13493 Finavon *(IABalding)* 8-11 ‡3SO'Gorman (7) (a.p: one pce fnl 3f) ...................... nk.4
1342 Blue Sombrero (IRE) *(RJHolder)* 8-9 RFox (8) (nvr nrr) ........................... 4.5
　　　　　Play With Me (IRE) *(JLDunlop)* 8-9 AMcGlone (6) (cmpt: wl bhd 4f: sme hdwy
　　　　　fnl 2f) ............................................................................. 6.6
1549 Pennine Lad (IRE) *(BGubby)* 9-0 NAdams (11) (nvr nr ldrs) ..................... s.h.7
13495 Baulking Towers *(MMcCormack)* 9-0 TQuinn (2) (chsd ldrs over 4f) ............ 1½.8
12964 Waterlord (IRE) *(CGCox)* 9-0 NHowe (4) (led over 3f: wknd qckly) ............... 2.9
　　　　　Pyramis Prince (IRE) *(MRChannon)* 9-0 LornaVincent (1) (unf: bit bkwd: dwlt: a
　　　　　bhd: t.o) ......................................................................... 20.10
1744 Barniemeboy *(RABennett)* 9-0 BRouse (10) (a bhd: t.o) ..................... 8.11
　　　　　*Nomination Gold (50/1) Withdrawn (ref to enter stalls) : not under orders*

2/1 CISSBURY RING(3/1—6/4), 5/2 Delta Downs(tchd 4/1), 3/1 Finavon(2/1—4/1), 5/1 Play With Me
(IRE)(3/1—6/1), 11/1 Baulking Towers(7/1—14/1), 14/1 Waterlord (IRE), 16/1 Bold Acre, 25/1 Blue Sombrero
(IRE), Pyramis Prince (IRE), 33/1 Pennine Lad (IRE), 50/1 Barniemeboy. CSF £36.39, Tote £2.50: £1.10 £3.40
£1.70 (£19.80). Lavinia Duchess of Norfolk (LITTLEHAMPTON) bred by Lavinia Duchess of Norfolk. 11 Rn
　　　　　　　　　　　　　　　　　　　　　　　　　　　　　　　　1m 30.02 (4.32)
　　　　　　　　　　　　　　　　　　　　　　　　　　　　　　　　SF—46/16/10/11/–/–

T/Plpt: £2,134.70 (1.4 Tckts).　　　　　　　　　　　　　　　　　　　　　　　KH

---

1847— **SOUTHWELL (L-H)** Fibresand

### Saturday, July 11th [Standard]
Going Allowance: minus 0.30 sec per fur (FS)　　　　　　　　　Wind: almost nil

Stalls: low

**2038**　　BUTTERFLY STKS (Mdn 2-Y.O) £1035.00 (£285.00: £135.00)　　**7f (AWT)** 6-30 (6-33)

17482 **Foolish Heart (IRE)** (Fav) *(NAGraham)* 8-9 MRoberts (7) (trckd ldrs: led over 2f
　　　　　out: r.o: comf) ...................................................................... —1
10386 Trundley Wood *(GAPritchard-Gordon)* 8-4 ‡5DHarrison (9) (hdwy appr st: ev ch
　　　　　whn edgd lft over 1f out: nt qckn) ............................................... 3.2
15246 Tanagome (USA) (v) *(SGNorton)* 9-0 KTsui (3) (lw: sn outpcd & wl bhd: r.o fnl
　　　　　2f) .................................................................................. 7.3
17903 El Guapo *(TFairhurst)* 8-11 ‡3JFanning (1) (lw: trckd ldrs: effrt ent st: one pce) 1½.4
1549 Travelling Lad *(BBeasley)* 9-0 DNicholls (6) (s.i.s: hdwy over 2f out: nvr trbld
　　　　　ldrs) ............................................................................... 2.5
　　　　　Society Gown (USA) *(TDBarron)* 9-0 KDarley (5) (w'like: scope: bit bkwd: nvr
　　　　　plcd to chal) ....................................................................... 5.6
15782 Full Exposure *(WJarvis)* 8-9 AMunro (4) (led tl hdd over 2f out: sn wknd) ...... 2.7
1056 Hallmote *(JGFitzGerald)* 9-0 KFallon (8) (lw: chsd ldrs: sn pushed along: wknd
　　　　　over 2f out) ..................................................................... 1½.8
　　　　　River Fire (IRE) *(JBerry)* 8-9 JFortune (2) (neat: bit bkwd: sn outpcd & wl bhd) . 6.9

10/11 FOOLISH HEART (IRE)(5/4—4/5), 5/1 Full Exposure, 9/1 Trundley Wood, Travelling Lad(6/1—10/1),
14/1 Tanagome (USA), 16/1 Society Gown (USA)(op 8/1), River Fire (IRE)(op 10/1), El Guapo, 25/1 Hallmote.
CSF £9.63, Tote £2.20: £1.40 £2.10 £2.20 (£8.80). Mr Richard Berenson (NEWMARKET) bred by Gerry
Canavan in Ireland. 9 Rn　　　　　　　　　　　　　　　　　　　　　　　　1m 28.4 (1.8)
　　　　　　　　　　　　　　　　　　　　　　　　　　　　　　　　SF—36/22/11/3/–/–

**2039**　　EMPEROR (S) STKS (2-Y.O) £1213.50 (£336.00: £160.50)　　**7f (AWT)**　7-00 (7-07)

　　　　　**Allegrissima** *(JBerry)* 8-6 JFortune (6) (neat: unf: lw: a cl up: hrd rdn to ld ins fnl
　　　　　f) ................................................................................... —1
19005 Shades of Croft *(MDIUsher)* 8-11 MRoberts (4) (lw: led tl hdd ins fnl f: no ex) 2½.2
　　　　　Carnea *(JGFitzGerald)* 8-6 KFallon (7) (leggy: unf: dwlt: sn rcvrd & chsd ldrs:
　　　　　one pce fnl 2f) .................................................................... 6.3
18605 A Bridge Too Far (IRE) (Fav) *(BBeasley)* 8-12(1) DNicholls (1) (sn outpcd & bhd:
　　　　　hdwy & c wd st: no imp) ........................................................... 5.4
286 Egg *(TDBarron)* 8-11 KDarley (3) (chsd ldrs to st: grad wknd) .................. 1.5
1479 Colmar *(RBastiman)* 8-6 DMcKeown (2) (hld up: effrt over 2f out: n.d) ....... 3.6
1526 Apollo's Sister *(MrsJJordan)* 8-3 ‡3JFanning (5) (bolted gng to s: prom over 4f:
　　　　　sn wknd) .......................................................................... 5.7

**3/1** A Bridge Too Far (IRE)(tchd 9/2), **7/2** ALLEGRISSIMA, Shades of Croft, **4/1** Egg(op 5/2), **11/2** Colmar, **12/1** Carnea(7/1—14/1), **20/1** Apollo's Sister. CSF £15.65, Tote £3.30: £2.10 £2.10 (£8.00). Mr P. E. T. Chandler (COCKERHAM) bred by G. C. Hughes. 7 Rn; Bt in 3,600 gns
1m 30 (3.4)
SF—10/7/–/–/–/

**2040**    CHINESE H'CAP (0-70) £1245.00 (£345.00: £165.00)    **6f (AWT)**    7-30 (7-35)

| | | | |
|---|---|---|---|
| 1682 | **One Magic Moment (IRE) (37)** (CACyzer) 4–8-7 KFallon (4) (a cl up: led over 1f out: all out) | —1 |
| 1888 | **Strip Cartoon (IRE) (55)** (bl) (SRBowring) 4–9-11 MRoberts (6) (lw: led tl hdd over 1f out: kpt on wl) | nk.2 |
| 1847 | **Quinzii Martin (53)** (DHaydnJones) 4–9-9 JQuinn (10) (lw: hld up & bhd: hdwy 2f out: r.o nr fin) | hd.3 |
| 1904² | **Fighter Squadron (56)** (v) (JAGlover) 3–9-5 JFortune (5) (trckd ldrs: hmpd appr st: swtchd & hdwy over 2f out: hrd rdn: r.o) | ¾.4 |
| 1787⁵ | **Jovial Kate (USA) (55)** (BEllison) 5–9-11 AMunro (2) (a chsng ldrs: nt qckn fnl 2f) | 2.5 |
| 1685² | **Idir Linn (IRE) (46)** (v) (DJGMurray-Smith) 4–9-2 CRutter (14) (lw: effrt appr st: styd on: nt pce to chal) | 1½.6 |
| 1793 | **Gott's Desire (45)** (RBastiman) 6–9-11 DMcKeown (1) (hdwy whn hmpd over 1f out: n.d) | 2.7 |
| 1551² | **Swinging Lady (55)** (WWHaigh) 4–9-8 ‡3FNorton (13) (b.hind: hdwy 2f out: nvr nr to chal) | hd.8 |
| 1786⁶ | **Manuleader (56)** (v) (BBeasley) 3–9-5 DNicholls (12) (prom to st) | ½.9 |
| 1853⁵ | **Our Amber (28)** (DWChapman) 5–7-12 SWood (11) (sn in tch: rdn & btn 2f out) | hd.10 |
| 63 | **Henry Will (40)** (TFairhurst) 8–8-7 ‡3JFanning (3) (nvr trbld ldrs) | ½.11 |
| 890 | **Speedy Classic (USA) (61)** (CTinkler) 3–9-10 KTsui (7) (drvn along & chsd ldrs tl wknd 2f out) | ¾.12 |
| 1682⋆ | **Tara's Delight (58)** (WAO'Gorman) 5–9-11 ‡3EmmaO'Gorman (9) (b.hind: s.s: hdwy ent st: n.d) | s.h.13 |
| 140⁶ | **State Governor (58)** (DWChapman) 4–9-7 ‡7MHarris (8) (cl up 4f: wknd qckly) | 6.14 |

**4/1** Fighter Squadron(op 6/1), **7/1** Strip Cartoon (IRE), Idir Linn (IRE), **9/1** ONE MAGIC MOMENT (IRE), **10/1** Tara's Delight, Jovial Kate (USA), **11/1** Swinging Lady(8/1—12/1), Gott's Desire, **16/1** Manuleader, **16/1** Speedy Classic (USA), Quinzii Martin, **20/1** Our Amber, State Governor, **25/1** Henry Will. CSF £65.34, CT £911.28. Tote £10.10: £3.20 £2.70 £3.70 (£73.90). Mr R. M. Cyzer (HORSHAM) bred by Bishop's Down Farm in Ireland. 14 Rn
1m 15.4 (2)
SF—17/34/31/24/22/7

**2041**    EAST MIDLANDS ELECTRICITY PLC H'CAP (3-Y.O) (0-70) £1234.50 (£342.00: £163.50)    **1m (AWT)**    8-00 (8-03)

| | | | |
|---|---|---|---|
| 1527⁵ | **Eriny (USA) (67)** (SGNorton) 8-13 ‡7OPears (2) (a.p: led 2f out: r.o u.p) | —1 |
| 1741 | **Lord Leitrim (IRE) (44)** (NACallaghan) 7-8 ‡3JFanning (8) (trckd ldrs: ev ch over 1f out: r.o) | ½.2 |
| 1767² | **Missy-S (IRE) (53)** (Fav) (GAPritchard-Gordon) 8-1 ‡5DHarrison (4) (hdwy 4f out: styd on wl: nrst fin) | 2½.3 |
| 1320 | **Sie Amato (IRE) (53)** (CaptJWilson) 8-6 JFortune (3) (cl up: led over 3f out tl hdd 2f out: one pce) | 3.4 |
| 1548 | **Nobby Barnes (61)** (RWArmstrong) 9-0 JHo (13) (lw: styd on fnl 3f: nvr nrr) | ¾.5 |
| 1678⁵ | **Highland Flame (47)** (ANLee) 7-7 ‡7CHawksley (12) (sn pushed along: sme hdwy 2f out: nvr rchd ldrs) | 3.6 |
| 1890 | **Basilica (60)** (CEBrittain) 8-13 MRoberts (6) (sn outpcd & bhd: styd on wl fnl 2f) | ½.7 |
| 1550⁶ | **The Dream Maker (IRE) (40)** (MrsNMacauley) 7-6 LCharnock (9) (lw: led over 1f: cl up tl wknd over 2f out) | ½.8 |
| 762⁶ | **Dancing Pet (43)** (WWHaigh) 7-7(1) ‡3FNorton (1) (b.hind: lw: hdwy ent st: one pce fnl 2f) | 1½.9 |
| 1849 | **Trevveethan (IRE) (43)** (JBalding) 7-3(3) ‡7ClaireBalding (11) (swtg: outpcd & bhd tl sme late hdwy) | 6.10 |
| 369 | **Ballyranter (62)** (HJCollingridge) 9-1 JQuinn (7) (n.d) | 1½.11 |
| 1418⁶ | **Merryhill Madam (68)** (JLHarris) 9-7 DHolland (5) (chsd ldrs tl wknd over 2f out) | 3.12 |
| 1550 | **Where's Ruth (IRE) (62)** (bl) (MWEasterby) 9-1 TLucas (10) (led over 6f out to 3f out: sn lost pl) | 5.13 |

LONG HANDICAP: The Dream Maker (IRE) 7-6, Trevveethan (IRE) 6-13.

**7/2** Missy-S (IRE), **4/1** ERINY (USA), **6/1** Basilica(op 4/1), **9/1** Sie Amato (IRE), **10/1** Highland Flame, **12/1** Lord Leitrim (IRE)(op 8/1), Merryhill Madam, **14/1** The Dream Maker (IRE), Nobby Barnes, **16/1** Ballyranter, Dancing Pet, **20/1** Where's Ruth (IRE), **50/1** Trevveethan (IRE). CSF £47.77, CT £170.56. Tote £4.80: £1.60 £2.90 £1.90 (£59.50). Mr R. W. Cousins (BARNSLEY) bred by Arthur I. Appleton in USA. 13 Rn
1m 41.6 (2.3)
SF—28/7/5/–/–/–

**2042**    NATIONAL PLANT AND TRANSPORT H'CAP (0-70) £1245.00 (£345.00: £165.00)
       **1³/₄m (AWT)**                                     8-30 (8-32)

1125 **Moot Point (USA) (57)** (bl) *(JRJenkins)* 4-9-7 SWhitworth (10) (in tch: led over
       1f out: hrd rdn & r.o) ..................................................... —1
 790 Intrepid Lass **(42)** *(HCandy)* 5-8-6 CRutter (11) (in tch: hdwy u.p appr st: styd
       on: nt pce of wnr) ..................................................... 1¹/₂.2
1560⁴ Intricacy **(64)** *(CCElsey)* 4-9-9 ‡5DHarrison (1) (lw: sn bhd: hdwy over 2f out: r.o
       wl nr fin) ..................................................... 2.3
1893⁴ Escadaro (USA) **(45)** (v) *(SGNorton)* 3-7-1⁽¹⁾ ‡7CHawksley (3) (dwlt: drvn along
       & bhd tl gd hdwy 7f out: sn chsng ldrs: one pce fnl 2f) ...... 2.4
1419 Commanche Sioux (IRE) **(51)** (v) *(KAMorgan)* 4-8-8 ‡7SWilliams (9) (hdwy 8f
       out: led 6f out tl hdd & wknd over 1f out) ..................... 3.5
1798 Hiram B Birdbath **(35)** (bl) (Fav) *(JAGlover)* 6-7-10 ‡3FNorton (5) (lw: prom tl
       outpcd appr st: hdwy u.p over 2f out: no imp) ................ 2¹/₂.6
1521³ Dari Sound (IRE) **(52)** *(JGFitzGerald)* 4-9-2 KFallon (7) (lw: prom tl rdn & wknd
       ent st) ..................................................... 1¹/₂.7
*1543*⁵ Sweet Bubbles (IRE) **(47)** *(CACyzer)* 4-8-11 DMcKeown (12) (led tl hdd 9f out:
       drvn along appr st: no imp after) ........................... d.h.7
1864⁴ Grey Commander **(38)** (v) *(MBrittain)* 4-8-2 KDarley (8) (chsd ldrs: rdn 5f out:
       wknd ent st) ..................................................... ¹/₂.9
*1546*² Milly Black (IRE) **(45)** *(JLHarris)* 4-8-9 DHolland (4) (cl up: led 9f out to 6f out:
       wknd appr st) ..................................................... 8.10
*1543* Native Magic **(63)** *(RWArmstrong)* 6-9-13 MRoberts (2) (bhd: hdwy 8f out:
       wknd 5f out: sn eased) ..................................................... 11
     Banker Mason (USA) **(35)** *(WLBarker)* 6-7-13 AProud (6) (t.o fnl 6f) ............... 12
             LONG HANDICAP: Escadaro (USA) 7-2.

**9/£** Hiram B Birdbath, **6/1** Sweet Bubbles (IRE), **15/2** Milly Black (IRE), **8/1** Native Magic, Intrepid Lass, Grey
Commander, **9/1** Dari Sound (IRE), **12/1** Commanche Sioux (IRE), MOOT POINT (USA), **20/1** Escadaro
(USA), **40/1** Banker Mason (USA). CSF £95.63, CT £827.85. Tote £18.40: £5.50 £3.20 £2.50 (£73.70). Mr A.
Escudero (ROYSTON) bred by Nydrie Stud in USA. 12 Rn             3m 4.9 (5.6)
                                                          SF—9/–/4/–/–/–

**2043**    SKIPPER STKS (Mdn 3-Y.O) £1035.00 (£285.00: £135.00)    **1¹/₂m (AWT)** 9-00 (9-01)

     **Upper House** (v) (Fav) *(GWragg)* 9-0 MRoberts (1) (lw: chsd ldrs: pushed
       along 7f out: styd on to ld appr fnl f: sn clr) ................. —1
1555⁵ Whisper's Shadow **(73)** *(MHTompkins)* 8-9 KDarley (7) (trckd ldrs: led 3f out:
       sn hrd drvn: hdd over 1f out: no ex) ........................... 4.2
1316⁶ Dolly Madison (IRE) **(61)** *(BWHills)* 8-9 DHolland (4) (hld up: hdwy to disp ld 8f
       out: ev ch tl outpcd fnl 2f) ..................................... 6.3
*1852*⁶ June's Lear Fan (CAN) *(PAKelleway)* 9-0 KFallon (5) (mde most tl hdd 3f out:
       wknd 2f out) ..................................................... 2.4
1737⁵ Negative Pledge (USA) *(JHMGosden)* 8-4 ‡5DHarrison (6) (b.hind: bhd: rdn 5f
       out: n.d) ..................................................... 12.5
1737⁶ Primo Pageant *(MJCamacho)* 9-0 NConnorton (3) (prom tl rdn & wknd 4f out) .. 3.6
1532 Pips Promise *(JMJefferson)* 9-0 JFortune (8) (chsd ldrs to ¹/₂-wy: sn bhd) ....... 25.7

**6/4** UPPER HOUSE, **3/1** Whisper's Shadow(7/4—100/30), **9/2** Negative Pledge (USA), **11/2** Dolly Madison
(IRE), **14/1** June's Lear Fan (CAN), **16/1** Primo Pageant, **33/1** Pips Promise. CSF £6.24, Tote £2.70: £1.50
£1.90 (£3.80). Sir Philip Oppenheimer (NEWMARKET) bred by Hascombe and Valiant Studs. 7 Rn   2m 38 (3.8)
                                                         SF—26/13/1/2/–/–

T/Plpt: £179.30 (10.9 Tckts).                                                            AA

## 1892—EDINBURGH (R-H)

### Monday, July 13th [Good to firm]
Going Allowance: St: nil sec (G); Rnd: minus 0.30 sec per fur (F)        Wind: fresh against
Stalls: high

**2044**    E.B.F. BRIDGE OF STEEL STKS (Mdn 2-Y.O) £2248.00 (£628.00: £304.00)
       **5f**                                             2-15 (2-17)

     **Grinnell** *(DenysSmith)* 9-0 KFallon (6) (w'like: scope: bit bkwd: s.i.s: outpcd:
       hdwy over 1f out: r.o wl to ld nr fin) ........................... —1
1699⁵ First Slice (Fav) *(JBerry)* 8-9 JCarroll (2) (lw: chsd ldrs: rdn to disp ld wl ins fnl f:
       kpt on) ..................................................... ¹/₂.2
1485 Atlantic Sunset (IRE) (v) *(MWEasterby)* 9-0 KDarley (4) (chsd ldrs: rdn & edgd
       lft over 1f out: led ins fnl f: hdd & no ex nr fin) ............. ¹/₂.3

1569⁵ Pure Madness (USA) *(DrJDScargill)* 9-0 GDuffield (1) (lw: mde most tl hdd ins fnl f: no ex) .......................................................... nk.4
1327 Selvole (v) *(MissLAPerratt)* 8-6 ‡³JFanning (5) (prom: effrt 2f out: btn 1f out) ... 3¹/₂.5
1120⁶ Magic Orb *(JLSpearing)* 8-9 DMcKeown (3) (lw: cl up: outpcd whn hmpd over 1f out: sn wknd) ....................................................... 1¹/₂.6

**Evens** First Slice, **5/2** Atlantic Sunset (IRE), **9/2** Pure Madness (USA), **7/1** Magic Orb, **25/1** GRINNELL, **33/1** Selvole. CSF £50.61, Tote £10.90: £5.90 £2.00 (£9.40). Mr David McCune (BISHOP AUCKLAND) bred by J. F. Buchanan. 6 Rn
62.2 sec (4.5)
SF—10/3/6/5/–/–

---

**2045** NEWBATTLE (S) H'CAP (0-60) £2346.00 (£656.00: £318.00)
1m 7f 16y
2-45 (2-46)

(Weights raised 5 lb)
1810⁴ **Desert Mist (38)** (bl) *(SirMarkPrescott)* 3-8-0⁽²⁾ GDuffield (10) (lw: trckd ldrs: led appr st: sn qcknd clr: drvn out) .......................... —1
1898⁴ Alpha Helix **(23)** (v) *(MissLAPerratt)* 9-7-12 ‡³JFanning (7) (hdwy appr st: styd on u.p: no imp fnl 2f) ........................................ 5.2
1108 Brusque (USA) **(28)** *(DonEnricoIncisa)* 8-7-13 ‡⁷ClaireBalding (11) (bhd tl styd on wl fnl 3f: hung rt: nrst fin) ..................... hd.3
1898★ Fen Princess (IRE) **(51)** (Fav) *(PCHaslam)* 4-9-10 (5x) ‡⁵JWeaver (2) (lw: a.p: effrt ent st: one pce appr fnl f) ................. 3¹/₂.4
1789³ Racing Raskal **(35)** *(CaptJWilson)* 5-8-13 JCarroll (4) (hdwy ¹/₂-wy: sn prom: one pce fnl 3f) ........................................... 10.5
1784⁶ Chiaropai (IRE) **(39)** (v) *(WStorey)* 4-9-3 SWebster (8) (in tch: effrt 6f out: hrd rdn & no imp) ........................................ 2¹/₂.6
1907 Brilliant Disguise **(42)** *(PMonteith)* 3-7-13 ‡⁵SMaloney (3) (nvr bttr than mid div) 12.7
1968⁴ Quip **(29)** *(MPNaughton)* 7-8-7 JakiHouston (6) (led tl hdd 9f out: wknd 6f out) 4.8
1530 Enkindle **(26)** (bl) *(BWMurray)* 5-8-4 LCharnock (1) (lw: cl up: led 8f out tl appr st: wkng whn hmpd ent st: eased) ................ 8.9
1687 Into the Future **(24)** (v) *(APStringer)* 5-8-2 JFortune (5) (hdwy 9f out: sn prom: wknd ent st) ............................................ 10.10
1893³ Mr Elk **(37)** (bl) *(MrsGRReveley)* 3-7-13 DaleGibson (9) (prom to ¹/₂-wy: sn bhd) ............................................................... ³/₄.11

**6/4** Fen Princess (IRE), **6/1** Quip, Racing Raskal, **9/1** DESERT MIST, **10/1** Alpha Helix, **14/1** Chiaropai (IRE), **16/1** Brusque (USA), Enkindle, Mr Elk, **25/1** Brilliant Disguise, **33/1** Into the Future. CSF £85.68, CT £1,284.87. Tote £8.10: £2.40 £3.60 £5.00 (£40.40). Mrs C. R. Philipson (NEWMARKET) bred by Mrs C. R. Philipson. 11 Rn; Sold David McCune 3,700 gns
3m 16.5 (6)

---

**2046** LE GARCON D'OR H'CAP (0-70) £2192.00 (£612.00: £296.00) **5f** 3-15 (3-19)
(Weights raised 7 lb)
1892★ **Best Effort (59)** *(MPNaughton)* 6-9-6 (7x) ‡⁵JWeaver (3) (hld up: effrt & n.m.r ¹/₂-wy: qcknd to ld ins fnl f) .................. —1
1892² The Right Time **(43)** (bl) *(JParkes)* 7-8-9 JFortune (1) (sn drvn along: hdwy ¹/₂-wy: led appr fnl f: sn hdd & nt qckn) ...... 2¹/₂.2
1904³ Serious Hurry **(58)** (Fav) *(SirMarkPrescott)* 4-9-10 GDuffield (6) (lw: cl up: led ¹/₂-wy tl appr fnl f: nt qckn) ............. 1¹/₂.3
1781★ Lift Boy (USA) **(45)** *(DenysSmith)* 3-8-5 KFallon (5) (a cl up: hrd rdn over 1f out: one pce) ........................................ 2.4
1892³ Jive Music **(30)** (bl) *(NBycroft)* 6-7-7 ‡³JFanning (2) (led to ¹/₂-wy: wknd appr fnl f) ............................................... 1¹/₂.5

**6/4** Serious Hurry, **4/1** BEST EFFORT, The Right Time, **5/1** Jive Music, **13/2** Lift Boy (USA)(5/1—8/1). CSF £17.53, Tote £4.70: £3.00 £1.60 (£6.40). Mr Raymond Miquel (RICHMOND) bred by Aldershawe Stud Farm. 5 Rn
60.6 sec (2.9)
SF—48/27/36/9/–

---

**2047** GEORGE BOYD H'CAP (0-80) £2640.00 (£740.00: £360.00) **1m 3f 32y** 3-45 (3-46)
1894★ **Carlingford (USA) (60)** (Fav) *(MPNaughton)* 6-8-5 (5x) ‡⁵JWeaver (1) (mde all: hld on gamely fnl f) ........................ —1
1841³ Azureus (IRE) **(78)** *(MrsGRReveley)* 4-9-7 ‡⁷DarrenMoffatt (4) (lw: trckd wnr: chal over 1f out: nt qckn nr fin) ............ hd.2
1691² Latvian **(69)** *(RAllan)* 5-9-5 SWebster (3) (lw: trckd ldrs 7f out: effrt over 2f out: nt r.o fnl f) ................................... 1¹/₂.3
1894² Not Yet **(44)** *(EWeymes)* 8-7-5⁽¹⁾ ‡³JFanning (2) (hld up: hdwy on ins & ev ch over 1f out: nt r.o) .............................. 1¹/₂.4
LONG HANDICAP: Not Yet 7-1.

**13/8** CARLINGFORD (USA), **2/1** Azureus (IRE), **3/1** Latvian, **11/2** Not Yet. CSF £5.05, Tote £2.50 (£3.20). Mrs H. H. Wane (RICHMOND) bred by Hugh G. King, III in USA. 4 Rn
2m 25.9 (6.2)

---

### 2048

DUNBAR CLAIMING STKS   £2374.00 (£664.00: £322.00)   **1m 16y**   4-15 (4-18)

| | | |
|---|---|---|
| 1624* | **Laurel Queen (IRE) (58)** *(JBerry)* 4–9-5 JCarroll (7) (lw: mde all: r.o u.p fnl f) ... | —1 |
| 1863 | Mbulwa **(52)** *(SEKettlewell)* 6–8-10 JFortune (1) (b: a cl up: chal ins fnl f: hrd rdn & r.o) | ½.2 |
| 1930⁴ | Inseyab **(60)** (Fav) *(PCHaslam)* 4–9-5 DMcKeown (4) (s.i.s: hdwy ent st: rdn 2f out: r.o one pce) | 2.3 |
| 1966⁶ | Stand At Ease **(32)** *(WStorey)* 7–8-8 SWebster (8) (styd on fnl 2f: nrst fin) | 3½.4 |
| 1732³ | Bee Dee Ell (USA) **(47)** (v) *(MissLAPerratt)* 3–8-11 DaleGibson (3) (lw: in tch: rdn 3f out: no imp) | 1½.5 |
| 1960 | Spanish Performer **(51)** *(TFairhurst)* 3–8-1 ‡³JFanning (2) (lw: sn trckng ldrs: effrt over 2f out: sn btn) | ¾.6 |
| 1863 | J P Morgan **(42)** (v) *(MPNaughton)* 4–8-9 ‡⁵JWeaver (5) (lw: nvr wnt pce) | 2½.7 |
| 1896⁶ | Come on My Girl (IRE) **(48)** *(TAKCuthbert)* 4–8-7 LCharnock (6) (chsd ldrs to st: sn wknd) | 4.8 |

**5/6** Inseyab, **3/1** LAUREL QUEEN (IRE)(op 2/1), **8/1** Mbulwa, **10/1** Spanish Performer, **11/1** J P Morgan, **12/1** Come on My Girl (IRE), **25/1** Bee Dee Ell (USA), **66/1** Stand At Ease. CSF £25.76, Tote £3.40: £1.20 £2.60 £1.40 (£54.60). Laurel (Leisure) Limited (COCKERHAM) bred by E. Lonergan in Ireland. 8 Rn
1m 40.2 (1.6)
SF—45/34/37/15/13/1

---

### 2049

PRESTONPANS MEDIAN AUCTION STKS (Mdn 2-Y.O) £2360.00 (£660.00: £320.00)
**7f 15y**   4-45 (4-47)

| | | |
|---|---|---|
| 1515² | **Harpoon Louie (USA)** (Fav) *(MIICasterby)* 0 1 KDarley (3) (lw: cl up: carried wd appr st: sn rcvrd: hrd rdn fnl f: led nr fin) | —1 |
| 1897⁴ | Ho-Joe (IRE) *(AHarrison)* 8-7 ‡⁵SMaloney (4) (b.off hind: lw: prom: led wl over 2f out: r.o u.p: jst ct) | ½.2 |
| 1660 | Moonshine Dancer *(MrsGRReveley)* 8-12 DaleGibson (6) (lw: effrt ent st: styd on fnl f: nrst fin) | 3½.3 |
| | Royal Meadow (IRE) *(JBerry)* 9-1 JCarroll (2) (w'like: s.i.s: hdwy over 2f out: nvr rchd ldrs) | nk.4 |
| 1515³ | Fort Vally *(BWMurray)* 8-7 DMcKeown (7) (led tl rn v.wd & lost pl appr st: hdwy 3f out: hmpd over 1f out: no imp) | 1.5 |
| 1851² | Dream a Bit *(JGFitzGerald)* 8-7 KFallon (1) (hdwy ent st: rdn & hung lft over 1f out: sn btn) | hd.6 |
| 1689 | Tri My Way (IRE) *(RRLamb)* 7-11 ‡⁷RHavlin (5) (cl up: lft in ld appr st: hdd wl over 2f out: sn btn) | 3.7 |

**4/6** HARPOON LOUIE (USA), **5/1** Dream a Bit, **11/2** Fort Vally, **8/1** Ho-Joe (IRE), **10/1** Royal Meadow (IRE)(op 5/1), **33/1** Moonshine Dancer, **66/1** Tri My Way (IRE). CSF £6.78, Tote £1.50: £1.30 £2.60 (£6.40). Mr P. D. Savill (MALTON) bred by John Franks in USA. 7 Rn
1m 30.2 (4)

---

### 2050

WATSONIANS F.C. H'CAP (3-Y.O) (0-70) £2427.00 (£672.00: £321.00)
**7f 15y**   5-15 (5-16)

(Weights raised 3 lb)

| | | |
|---|---|---|
| 1797⁵ | **Rose Gem (IRE) (51)** *(PCHaslam)* 8-7 DaleGibson (5) (lw: mde all: qcknd clr 3f out: r.o wl) | —1 |
| 1903 | Phil-Man **(48)** *(TFairhurst)* 8-1 ‡³JFanning (2) (hdwy ent st: styd on: no imp) | 3½.2 |
| 1440³ | Crimson Consort (IRE) **(38)** (v) *(DonEnricoIncisa)* 7-1(1) ‡⁷ClaireBalding (1) (lw: bhd: rn sltly wd st: styd on fnl 2f: nvr able to chal) | 1½.3 |
| 1761⁴ | Lawnswood Prince (IRE) **(52)** *(JLSpearing)* 8-8 DMcKeown (4) (bhd tl styd on u.p fnl 2f) | 3.4 |
| 1663⁵ | Dancing Wild **(37)** *(MrsGRReveley)* 7-0 ‡⁷DarrenMoffatt (7) (lw: plld hrd: cl up: effrt 2f out: grad wknd) | s.h.5 |
| 1563* | Coastal Express **(65)** (Fav) *(EWeymes)* 9-2 ‡⁵JWeaver (3) (lw: chsd ldrs: hmpd appr st: rdn over 2f out: sn btn) | 3.6 |
| 82⁵ | Dark Midnight (IRE) **(62)** *(RRLamb)* 8-11 ‡⁷RHavlin (6) (chsd ldrs tl stumbled bdly appr st: sn lost pl) | 30.7 |
| | LONG HANDICAP: Crimson Consort (IRE) 7-3. | |

**5/4** Coastal Express, **4/1** ROSE GEM (IRE), **15/2** Crimson Consort (IRE), Dancing Wild, **10/1** Phil-Man, Lawnswood Prince (IRE), **33/1** Dark Midnight (IRE). CSF £34.77, Tote £4.30: £2.30 £7.90 (£20.50). Mrs M. E. F. Haslam (MIDDLEHAM) bred by F. Feeney in Ireland. 7 Rn
1m 27.6 (1.4)
SF—40/23/4/16/–/14

T/Plpt: £236.10 (8.25 Tckts).
AA

1912—**WINDSOR (Fig.8)**
**Monday, July 13th [Good]**
Going Allowance: 5f-6f: minus 0.20 sec (F); Rest: nil sec (G)          Wind: slt half bhd

Stalls: high

**2051**     SPUR (S) STKS (3 & 4-Y.O) £1657.80 (£460.80: £221.40)     1¼m 7y     6-30 (6-32)

| | | | |
|---|---|---|---|
| 354 | **Shaffaaf (USA) (55)** *(PDEvans)* 4–8-9 BRaymond (3) (4th st: led wl ins fnl f: r.o wl) | | —1 |
| 1741[6] | Bengal Tiger (IRE) **(53)** (bl) *(JAkehurst)* 4–9-0 PatEddery (19) (led: hrd rdn over 2f out: hdd wl ins fnl f) | | nk.2 |
| 1855★ | Big Pat **(58)** (Fav) *(JPearce)* 3–7-12 ‡5RPrice (20) (hmpd 6f out: 7th st: hrd rdn 2f out: r.o ins fnl f) | | ¾.3 |
| 1759 | Fairspear **(54)** (v) *(LGCottrell)* 3–7-12 GBardwell (2) (2nd st: ev ch 2f out: hrd rdn: one pce) | | ½.4 |
| 799 | Count Robert (USA) *(MrsJSPerrin)* 4–8-9 SDawson (22) (lw: gd hdwy fnl 2f: nvr nrr) | | s.h.5 |
| 1572[4] | Chew it Over (IRE) **(47)** *(CASmith)* 4–8-9 MWigham (7) (gd late hdwy: nrst fin) | | ½.6 |
| *1678[6]* | Selaginella **(67)** *(MRChannon)* 3–7-7[5] ‡5BDoyle (23) (lw: 5th st: one pce fnl 2f) | | 1½.7 |
| | Rapid Rosie **(30)** *(DRLaing)* 4–8-4 TyroneWilliams (1) (nvr nr to chal) | | 2½.8 |
| | Umbria *(CJames)* 3–7-2[2] ‡7CHawksley (5) (8th st: wknd 2f out) | | nk.9 |
| 1772[5] | Kindred Cameo **(50)** *(GLewis)* 3–7-5[3] ‡5DHarrison (6) (n.d) | | 7.10 |
| *1320* | Daily Sport Girl **(51)** *(FJYardley)* 3–7-10[1] ‡3SO'Gorman (16) (3rd st: wknd 3f out) | | 1.11 |
| 1976 | L'Acquesiana **(27)** *(DShaw)* 4–8-4 AMackay (21) (b: lw: n.d) | | s.h.12 |
| 1759 | Tresilian Owl *(RJHodges)* 4–8-6 ‡3TSprake (4) (n.d) | | nk.13 |
| | Soft Verges *(WCarter)* 4–7 13 ‡5NGwilliams (13) (bit bkwd: n.d) | | s.h.14 |
| 1872 | Super Beauty **(51)** *(GBBalding)* 3–7-8[1] JQuinn (15) (n.d) | | ¾.15 |
| | Birling Ashes **(30)** *(JRJenkins)* 4–8-9 SWhitworth (18) (bit bkwd: n.d) | | 1.16 |
| 1949 | Shecangosah *(RJHodges)* 3–7-7 RStreet (8) (6th st: wknd 3f out) | | 12.17 |
| 1705 | Carrantuohill (IRE) **(52)** *(SPCWoods)* 3–7-12[5] BCrossley (11) (9th st: wknd 4f out) | | 8.18 |
| 1026 | St Piran's Lass **(41)** *(RJHolder)* 3–7-8[1] RFox (14) (n.d) | | ¾.19 |
| 1369[6] | One Dollar More **(55)** *(BGubby)* 4–8-2 ‡7CAvery (10) (bhd fnl 4f) | | 2.20 |
| 1447 | Three and a Half (v) *(MissLBower)* 3–7-13[1] AMcGlone (9) (a bhd) | | 12.21 |
| *191* | Easy Delta **(46)** *(MDixon)* 3–7-8[6] ‡5ATucker (17) (bit bkwd: a bhd) | | 1.22 |

*1338 Kalamoss (33/1) Withdrawn (rdr inj. at Wolverhampton - no suitable replacement) : not under orders*

**9/4** Big Pat, **4/1** Bengal Tiger (IRE), **7/1** Super Beauty(tchd 12/1), SHAFFAAF (USA)(op 14/1), **10/1** Selaginella(op 6/1), Kindred Cameo(op 6/1), Carrantuohill (IRE), **12/1** Chew it Over (IRE), Umbria(op 8/1), **14/1** Fairspear(op 8/1), **25/1** Soft Verges, One Dollar More, **33/1** Ors. CSF £38.93, Tote £12.60: £3.30 £2.10 £1.70 (£39.20). Mr R. Cave (WELSHPOOL) bred by Maverick Productions & Derry Meeting Farm in USA. 22 Rn; Bt in 3,200 gns; Umbria clmd P Stone £6,000          2m 9.5 (6.5)
SF—30/34/16/15/25/24

**2052**     WINDSOR AUCTION STKS (Mdn 2-Y.O) £1632.00 (£452.00: £216.00)
5f 10y          6-55 (7-00)

| | | | |
|---|---|---|---|
| | **Millyant** *(RGuest)* 8-8 MRoberts (1) (w'like: chsd ldr: led wl over 1f out: easily) | | —1 |
| 1913[2] | Two Times Twelve (IRE) (bl) *(JBerry)* 8-6[1] PatEddery (2) (lw: led over 3f: hrd rdn: no ch w wnr) | | 2.2 |
| 1038[3] | Bichette (Fav) *(RHannon)* 8-3 AMcGlone (8) (outpcd: hdwy over 1f out: edgd lft & r.o fnl f) | | 2.3 |
| 1744 | Felt Lucky (IRE) *(MRChannon)* 8-6 BRouse (5) (a.p: one pce fnl 2f) | | 2.4 |
| 1638[6] | Steppin High *(LordHuntingdon)* 8-6[1] LDettori (7) (lw: outpcd: nrst fin) | | ½.5 |
| 1913 | Tequila Twist (IRE) *(AAScott)* 8-6 BRaymond (4) (prom 3f) | | 8.6 |
| 1906[6] | Risk a Little *(MJHeaton-Ellis)* 8-0 RHills (6) (a bhd) | | ¾.7 |
| 1502 | Cuddly Date *(DTThom)* 8-0 JQuinn (3) (spd 3f) | | ½.8 |
| 1902 | Trepidation (IRE) (bl) *(MJFetherston-Godley)* 8-7 WRyan (9) (a bhd: t.o) | | 10.9 |

**Evens** Bichette, **13/8** Two Times Twelve (IRE), **8/1** MILLYANT, **14/1** Steppin High, Tequila Twist (IRE)(op 6/1), **33/1** Felt Lucky (IRE), **66/1** Ors. CSF £21.15, Tote £8.40: £2.00 £1.10 £1.20 (£5.60). Bradmill Ltd (NEWMARKET) bred by Jim and Mrs Strange. 9 Rn          61.1 sec (2.1)
SF—32/22/11/6/9/–

**2053**     TOUCHE ROSS H'CAP (3-Y.O) (0-70) £2215.00 (£615.00: £295.00)
5f 217y          7-20 (7-28)

*(Weights raised 2 lb)*

| | | | |
|---|---|---|---|
| *1268[5]* | **Ingenuity (52)** *(LordHuntingdon)* 8-5 MRoberts (5) (w ldrs: led 3f out: r.o wl) | | —1 |

1912² Kipini (49) *(WJMusson)* 8-2 JHBrown (7) (swtg: hdwy 3f out: chsd wnr & hrd rdn over 1f out: no imp) .......................................................... 3¹/₂.2
1614 Grey Charmer (IRE) (56) *(CJames)* 8-9 RCochrane (3) (hdwy fnl 2f: nvr nrr) ...... 2.3
 621 Chance to Dream (56) *(RHannon)* 8-9 SRaymont (13) (lw: hdwy 2f out: nrst fin) 2.4
1725★ Rock Song (IRE) (57) *(Fav)* *(PFICole)* 8-10 TQuinn (9) (lw: hdwy fnl 2f: nt rch ldrs) ...................................................................................... nk.5
1445 Leigh Crofter (68) (bl) *(RJHolder)* 9-0 ‡7SDrowne (14) (lw: spd over 4f) ...... 1¹/₂.6
1912 Red Verona (44) (bl) *(EAWheeler)* 7-6⁽²⁾ ‡5DHarrison (16) (swtg: led after 1f to 3f out) ............................................................................................ 2.7
1763⁴ Blue Drifter (58) *(JSutcliffe)* 8-11 BRouse (17) (nvr nr to chal) ...................... 1.8
1576 Peerage Prince (59) *(PatMitchell)* 8-9 ‡3SO'Gorman (2) (no hdwy fnl 2f) ......... 2¹/₂.9
1650 Red Sombrero (61) (v) *(LGCottrell)* 9-0 TRogers (8) (lw: prom 4f) ............... hd.10
1912★ Smudgemupum (44) *(MissBSanders)* 7-11 GBardwell (11) (n.d) ...................... 2.11
      Wilco (55) *(AndrewTurnell)* 8-8 PatEddery (4) (bit bkwd: spd over 3f) ............. ¹/₂.12
1905 Two Birds (63) *(CAHorgan)* 9-2 AMcGlone (1) (s.s: a bhd) .......................... ¹/₂.13
1306⁵ Flash of Straw (IRE) (60) *(GLewis)* 8-13 RaymondBerry (12) (lw: bhd fnl 3f) . 1¹/₂.14
1558⁴ Colour Solutions (47) *(TDBarron)* 8-0 TyroneWilliams (18) (led 1f: wknd 3f out) 3.15
1576 Crimson Blade (52) *(PWHarris)* 8-5 JQuinn (6) (n.d) ..................................... hd.16
1678³ Grand Fellow (62) (bl) *(JDBethell)* 9-1 DBiggs (15) (a bhd: t.o) ...................... 7.17
1813² Shocking Times (12/1) Withdrawn (ref to ent stalls) : not under orders — Rule 4 applies

**4/1** Rock Song (IRE)(tchd 6/1), **7/1** Smudgemupum(op 4/1), INGENUITY(5/1—8/1), **8/1** Kipini(op 5/1), Wilco, **9/1** Grey Charmer (IRE)(12/1—8/1), **12/1** Red Verona(op 8/1), Leigh Crofter, **14/1** Grand Fellow (IRE), Red Sombrero(op 8/1), **16/1** Colour Solutions, Blue Drifter (IRE), **20/1** Peerage Prince, **25/1** Chance to Dream, **33/1** Ors. CSF £59.62, CT £416.61. Tote £8.10: £1.60 £2.10 £2.80 £5.70 (£24.60). The Queen (WEST ILSLEY) bred by The Queen. 17 Rn
                                    1m 12.1 (1.6)
                                    SF—35/18/17/9/9/7

**2054**    AGE NO H'CAP (0-00) £2663.00 (£708.00: £339.00)      1m 3f 135y      7-50 (7-56)
                                (Weights raised 4 lb)

1743⁵ **Mahrajan (62)** *(CJBenstead)* 8-9-0 TQuinn (7) (hdwy over 2f out: led over 1f out: r.o wl) .................................................................................... —1
1840² Bescaby Boy (65) *(JWharton)* 8-9 JWilliams (2) (6th st: ev ch over 1f out: r.o) 3.2
1872★ Plan Ahead (68) (Jt-Fav) *(GLewis)* 3-8-2 ‡5DHarrison (10) (lw: stdy hdwy over 2f out: ev ch 1f out: nt qckn) ..................................................... 2¹/₂.3
1313⁵ Tour Leader (NZ) (68) (Jt-Fav) *(TDBarron)* 3-8-7 MRoberts (8) (lw: mid div: hrd rdn over 2f out: styd on one pce) ............................................... 1.4
1726² Belafonte (62) *(RJHolder)* 5-9-0 PatEddery (11) (led tl wknd over 1f out) ......... nk.5
1482★ Rousitto (72) *(RHollinshead)* 4-9-10 WRyan (6) (lw: nvr nrr) .............................. ³/₄.6
1909² Russian Vision (61) (bl) *(AAScott)* 3-8-0 RHills (3) (2nd st: ev ch 2f out: sn wknd) ...................................................................................... ¹/₂.7
1612 Bee Beat (60) (bl) *(EAWheeler)* 4-8-12 RCochrane (5) (dwlt: 7th st: wknd over 1f out) ................................................................................ ¹/₂.8
1890² Affa (55) *(TThomsonJones)* 4-8-11 NAdams (1) (b: 5th st: wknd over 2f out) ...... 7.9
      Hymne D'Amour (USA) (51) *(MissHCKnight)* 4-8-3⁽¹⁾ SWhitworth (12) (3rd st: wknd over 2f out) ................................................................... 3.10
      Someone Brave (48) *(BobJones)* 4-8-0 JQuinn (9) (swtg: 4th st: wknd 3f out: t.o) .................................................................................... 15.11
1612 Snickersnee (66) *(MDixon)* 4-9-4 AClark (4) (lw: bhd fnl 6f: t.o) ..................... 8.12

**9/2** Tour Leader (NZ), Plan Ahead, **5/1** Belafonte(6/1—4/1), **7/1** MAHRAJAN, **8/1** Rousitto, Russian Vision, **9/1** Affa, Bescaby Boy, **16/1** Someone Brave, **20/1** Bee Beat, **33/1** Snickersnee, **50/1** Hymne D'Amour (USA). CSF £64.33, CT £290.53. Tote £8.40: £2.80 £2.00 £1.60 (£36.70). Mrs F. A. Harris (EPSOM) bred by David and Mrs Shirley. 12 Rn
                                    2m 30 (7.5)
                                    SF—25/22/2/5/11/19

**2055**    FIAT MOTOR SALES NIMBLE STKS (2-Y.O.F) £2856.00 (£791.00: £378.00)    5f 217y      8-20 (8-22)

1461 **Carranita (IRE)** *(BPalling)* 8-9 ‡7StephenDavies (3) (a.p: led 2f out: r.o wl) ......... —1
1658³ Abbey's Gal (Fav) *(IABalding)* 8-8 RCochrane (12) (led 4f: ev ch ins fnl f: r.o) ... ³/₄.2
1668★ Dalalah *(HThomsonJones)* 8-13 RHills (5) (a.p: nt qckn fnl f) ............................... 3.3
1536 Rain Splash *(RHannon)* 8-10 ‡3RPerham (1) (lw: nrst fin) .............................. 2¹/₂.4
      Rock the Boat *(RHannon)* 8-8 MRoberts (9) (w'like: s.s: rdn thrght: sn prom: no hdwy fnl 2f) ............................................................................... 1¹/₂.5
1779★ Carnbrea Snip *(MBell)* 8-13 MHills (7) (spd 4f) ............................................. 1.6
1578⁵ Creative Flair (USA) *(PFICole)* 8-8 TQuinn (2) (a bhd) ................................... 3¹/₂.7
1609★ Stormy Heights *(JRJenkins)* 8-13 LDettori (10) (swtg: prom tl hrd rdn & wknd 2f out) ...................................................................................... 3¹/₂.8
1541 Frasers Hill (IRE) *(PFICole)* 8-8 CRutter (6) (a bhd) ...................................... ¹/₂.9
1297⁶ Lowrianna (IRE) *(DHaydnJones)* 8-13 PatEddery (11) (spd over 3f: t.o) ........... 8.10
1915 Monet Order *(JRJenkins)* 8-8 SWhitworth (4) (lw: a bhd: t.o) ............................ 4.11

**15/8** Abbey's Gal(tchd 3/1), **9/4** Rock the Boat(op 5/4), **7/1** Dalalah(9/2—9/1), **9/1** Lowrianna (IRE)(12/1—8/1), Carnbrea Snip(8/1—12/1), **10/1** CARRANITA (IRE)(tchd 16/1), Rain Splash, **16/1** Stormy Heights, **20/1** Creative Flair (USA), **40/1** Frasers Hill (IRE), **50/1** Monet Order. CSF £30.63, Tote £21.60: £4.60 £1.80 £2.20 (£38.20). Lamb Lane Associates (COWBRIDGE) bred by Mrs Anita Quinn in Ireland. 11 Rn    1m 11.1 (0.6)
SF—59/55/48/35/27/28

**2056**    CARR, KITCAT AND AITKEN GRADUATION STKS (3-Y.O) £1799.40 (£498.40: £238.20)
1¼m 7y
8-50 (8-53)

1672* **Imperial Ballet (IRE)** (Fav) (HRACecil) 9-8 PatEddery (1) (lw: 2nd st: led 3f out: v.easily) .................................................................................................... —1
1722³ Desert Peace (IRE) (PFICole) 9-0 TQuinn (4) (lw: 4th st: styd on fnl 2f: no ch w wnr) ......................................................................................................... 6.2
1275* Clurican (IRE) (77) (DNicholson) 9-8 JWilliams (2) (swtg: led to 3f out: r.o one pce) ........................................................................................................... hd.3
814⁵ Super Sarena (IRE) (102) (RSimpson) 8-9 WRyan (3) (3rd st: wknd 2f out) ...... 8.4
Woodcock Wendy (MJBolton) 8-9 CRutter (5) (unf: s.s: a last: t.o fnl 5f) ........ dist.5

**1/4** IMPERIAL BALLET (IRE), **8/1** Desert Peace (IRE), Super Sarena (IRE)(op 5/1), **20/1** Clurican (IRE), **50/1** Woodcock Wendy. CSF £2.81, Tote £1.20: £1.10 £2.40 (£2.20). Mr R. E. Sangster (NEWMARKET) bred by Swettenham Stud in Ireland. 5 Rn    2m 8.1 (5.1)
SF—57/37/44/15/–

T/Plpt: £30.10 (90.8 Tckts).    Hn

1747—**WOLVERHAMPTON (L-H)**

**Monday, July 13th [Good to soft]**

Going Allowance: St: 0.30 sec (Y); Rnd: 0.20 sec per fur (G)    Wind: nil

Stalls: high

**2057**    WHITMORE REANS APP'CE H'CAP (3-Y.O) (0-70) £2511.00 (£696.00: £333.00)
1½m 70y
2-00 (2-05)

(Weights raised 1 lb)

1626³ Viva Darling (67) (Jt-Fav) (BAMcMahon) 9-7 SSanders (9) (lw: wnt 3rd st: led over 3f out: ran on nr fin) ...................................................................... —1
1750 Shayna Maidel (39) (MBell) 7-7 MHumphries (1) (lw: 6th st: hdwy over 2f out: ev ch fnl f: r.o) ...................................................................................... hd.2
804 Wilkins (52) (JRFanshawe) 8-6 NVarley (2) (led to 8f out: 4th st: rallied 2f out: kpt on) ................................................................................................ ¾.3
1518³ Cov Tel Lady (67) (MHTompkins) 9-2 ‡⁵SMulvey (6) (lw: led 8f out tl over 3f out: sn rdn & btn) .................................................................. 2½.4
1139³ Elite Reg (50) (PFICole) 8-4 JDSmith (8) (hld up: c wd & styd on fnl 2f: nvr nrr) d.h.4
1052 Cherry Bob (44) (CWThornton) 7-7⁽⁵⁾ ‡⁵KSked (4) (hld up & bhd: effrt over 3f out: nvr nr to chal) ......................................................................... ¾.6
1270 Sea Lord (39) (KWHogg) 7-7 AGarth (10) (chsd ldrs: 5th st: wknd 3f out) .......... 2.7
1142⁵ Tina Meena Lisa (42) (EHOwenjun) 7-10 CHawksley (7) (prom: 2nd st: wknd over 3f out) ................................................................................. 8.8
1041 Brotherlyaffection (49) (RHollinshead) 7-12⁽²⁾ ‡⁵CarlLlewellyn (3) (a bhd: t.o) ... 10.9
810² Child Star (FR) (46) (DMarks) 8-0 AntoinetteArmes (5) (uns rdr after s) ............. 0
LONG HANDICAP: Shayna Maidel 7-4, Cherry Bob 7-6, Sea Lord 7-4.

**4/1** Cov Tel Lady, VIVA DARLING, **5/1** Child Star (FR), **8/1** Elite Reg, **9/1** Wilkins, Tina Meena Lisa, **12/1** Shayna Maidel, **14/1** Cherry Bob, **16/1** Brotherlyaffection, **20/1** Sea Lord. CSF £43.48, CT £362.54. Tote £4.00: £1.30 £5.40 £4.90 (£132.00). Mr Anthony Laurence Macias (TAMWORTH) bred by Elisha Holdings. 10 Rn
2m 48.5 (16.8)

**2058**    WORFIELD (S) STKS (2-Y.O) £2574.00 (£714.00: £342.00)    7f    2-30 (2-39)

1675 Water Diviner (bl) (RFJohnsonHoughton) 8-11 DHolland (10) (led 1f: 2nd st: led 3f out: clr fnl f) ........................................................................ —1
1675² B B Glen (DMorris) 8-6 MTebbutt (4) (swtg: chsd ldrs: 5th st: styd on ins fnl f) ... 3.2
543⁶ Mrs Dawson (DrJDScargill) 8-6 JQuinn (5) (7th st: styd on fnl 2f: nvr able to chal) .......................................................................................... nk.3
1860* Wentbridge Lad (IRE) (BAMcMahon) 9-1 TQuinn (12) (s.i.s: hdwy over 2f out: nvr nrr) ...................................................................................... 2.4
1754⁴ Floodlight (IRE) (RJHolder) 8-6 NAdams (14) (hdwy 3f out: nt rch ldrs) ............ 1½.5
1442 Stroika (IRE) (Jt-Fav) (CJames) 8-6 MRoberts (7) (prom: 6th st: hrd rdn over 2f out: no imp) ....................................................................................... ¾.6
1749² Workingforpeanuts (IRE) (Jt-Fav) (CASmith) 8-6 JReid (11) (lw: s.s: nvr nr ldrs) 3.7
1860⁴ Bohemian Queen (JLSpearing) 8-6 GHind (3) (nvr nr to chal) ......................... 1.8

*1848*⁴ Fayre Find *(MHTompkins)* 8-6 PRobinson (13) (m.n.s) ..................................... nk.**9**
1121⁶ Lady Argent (IRE) *(APJarvis)* 8-6 SWhitworth (2) (a in rr) ........................... 1½.**10**
1442 Princess of Alar *(BPalling)* 7-13 ‡7StephenDavies (8) (lw: prom: 4th st: wknd
     over 2f out) ................................................................ 8.**11**
1749 My Ballyboy (bl) *(ABailey)* 8-11 PatEddery (6) (led after 1f out to 3f out: wknd
     qckly) .......................................................................... 2½.**12**
1675⁵ Jaybee-Jay *(MJHaynes)* 8-11 TyroneWilliams (1) (prom: 3rd st: wknd 3f out: t.o) **13**
1749 Dynavour House *(MWEckley)* 8-6 JWilliams (9) (a bhd: t.o) ........................... **14**

**7/2** Stroika (IRE)(op 8/1), Workingforpeanuts (IRE), **5/1** B B Glen(op 3/1), **11/2** Wentbridge Lad (IRE), **15/2** My Ballyboy(4/1—8/1), **10/1** Fayre Find(op 6/1), **14/1** Bohemian Queen(8/1—16/1), **16/1** Floodlight (IRE)(12/1—20/1), WATER DIVINER(op 8/1), **25/1** Mrs Dawson, Jaybee-Jay, **33/1** Lady Argent (IRE), Princess of Alar, **50/1** Dynavour House. CSF £94.00, Tote £38.20: £12.90 £3.10 £11.50 (£99.50). Mr R. F. Johnson Houghton (DIDCOT) bred by N. E. and Mrs Poole. 14 Rn; No bid
                                          1m 30.6 (6.3)
                                          SF—23/9/8/11/–/–

## 2059

WIN WITH THE TOTE H'CAP (0-70) £2637.00 (£732.00: £351.00)
**1³/₄m 134y**                               3-00 (3-09)

1740⁴ **Famous Beauty (44)** *(RHollinshead)* 5–8-0 ‡7DCarson (7) (hld up & bhd: hdwy
     & 5th st: led over 3f out: styd on strly) ............................. —**1**
1874⁶ Prince Sobur **(59)** *(MBlanshard)* 6–9-8 JReid (13) (chsd ldrs: effrt 3f out: rdn &
     r.o fnl f) ....................................................................... 1½.**2**
1800⁵ Briggsmaid **(50)** *(JMPEustace)* 4–8-13 MTebbutt (4) (hdwy 6f out: 7th st: ev ch
     appr fnl f: r.o one pce) ................................................. 2.**3**
1419⁵ Naseem Elbarr (USA) **(64)** (Fav) *(ACStewart)* 4–9-13 MRoberts (11) (lw: a.p:
     2nd st: led 4f out: sn hdd: eased whn btn ins fnl f) ............ 3.**4**
1580² White River **(44)** *(DHaydnJones)* 6–8-7 TyroneWilliams (2) (hld up: hdwy 6f
     out: 6th st: hrd rdn over 2f out: eased whn btn) ............... 12.**5**
1789⁵ War Beat **(49)** *(PJBevan)* 4–8-12 JQuinn (9) (lw: hdwy 8f out: 3rd st: wknd over
     2f out) ......................................................................... 1.**6**
1311³ Drinks Party (IRE) **(34)** *(JWharton)* 4–7-6 ‡5NKennedy (14) (lw: in tch tl wknd
     over 2f out) .................................................................. s.h.**7**
1759⁴ Blushing Belle **(55)** *(PFICole)* 4–9-4 TQuinn (5) (prom 10f) ........................ 8.**8**
1686³ Smiling Chief (IRE) **(51)** *(CACyzer)* 4–9-0 LDettori (1) (hdwy ent st: rdn 3f out:
     eased whn btn) ............................................................. ½.**9**
1582* Access Cruise (USA) **(52)** *(BAMcMahon)* 5–8-8 ‡7SSanders (12) (half reard s:
     wnt prom after 3f: 8th & wkng st) .................................. 2.**10**
1555⁶ Gesnera **(46)** *(KWhite)* 4–8-2 ‡7AGarth (8) (hdwy ½-wy: 4th st: wknd 3f out) . 1½.**11**
1802³ Angelica Park **(46)** *(JWharton)* 6–8-9 JWilliams (10) (swtg: led 10f out to 4f out:
     wknd qckly) .................................................................. 1½.**12**
*46* Vinstan **(47)** *(CASmith)* 6–8-10 MWigham (6) (bit bkwd: led over 4f: sn lost tch) 7.**13**
     Q-Eight (IRE) **(59)** *(APJarvis)* 4–9-8 SWhitworth (3) (bkwd: a bhd: t.o) ............ 12.**14**

**5/1** Naseem Elbarr (USA)(6/1—4/1), **6/1** Prince Sobur, White River, **10/1** FAMOUS BEAUTY, Drinks Party (IRE), Access Cruise (USA), **12/1** Blushing Belle, Smiling Chief (IRE)(op 8/1), Angelica Park, **14/1** Briggsmaid, War Beat, **25/1** Q-Eight (IRE), **50/1** Gesnera, **66/1** Vinstan. CSF £61.11, CT £762.66. Tote £11.50: £3.10 £2.80 £3.50 (£25.10). Mr J. E. Bigg (UPPER LONGDON) bred by Etablissement Equine Investments. 14 Rn
                                           3m 16.4 (10.4)
                                          SF—11/30/17/25/–/–

## 2060

ROTHMANS ROYALS NORTH SOUTH CHALLENGE SERIES H'CAP (0-80) £3184.00
(£952.00: £456.00: £208.00)   **7f**               3-30 (3-38)

1905* **Doulab's Image (71)** (bl) *(JAGlover)* 5–8-13 (5x) ‡7SWilliams (1) (hld up: 6th st:
     shkn up to ld 1f out: sn clr) .......................................... —**1**
1656³ Santi Sana **(67)** (bl) (Fav) *(LadyHerries)* 4–9-2 MRoberts (2) (b.off hind: led 6f:
     rdn & no ex fnl f) .......................................................... 3½.**2**
1614 Garth **(73)** (v) *(PJMakin)* 4–9-8 LDettori (9) (hld up & bhd: hdwy & nt clr run appr
     fnl f: rdn & r.o nr fin) .................................................... ¾.**3**
1773 Across the Bay **(76)** (v) *(SDow)* 5–9-11 TQuinn (7) (chsd ldr: 2nd st: rdn over 2f
     out: one pce) ................................................................ 1.**4**
1756⁵ Navaresque **(45)** *(RJHodges)* 7–7-8 JQuinn (4) (lw: prom: 4th st: rdn & wknd fnl
     f) ................................................................................. 2½.**5**
1718³ Asterix **(60)** (v) *(JMBradley)* 4–8-9 PatEddery (8) (chsd ldrs: 3rd st: rdn 3f out:
     wknd wl over 1f out) ...................................................... 3½.**6**
     Urshi-Jade **(44)** *(KWhite)* 4–7-7 NAdams (6) (bkwd: s.i.s: hdwy & 5th st: rdn 3f
     out: sn btn) .................................................................. s.h.**7**
1474 Bertie Wooster **(79)** *(RJHolder)* 9–10-0 JWilliams (5) (lw: s.s: effrt over 3f out:
     no imp) ........................................................................ ½.**8**
1306³ Will of Steel **(73)** *(HCandy)* 3–9-0 CRutter (3) (s.s: a bhd) ........................... 4.**9**
               LONG HANDICAP: Urshi-Jade 6-12.

3/1 Santi Sana, 9/2 DOULAB'S IMAGE, 11/2 Asterix, 6/1 Will of Steel, 13/2 Across the Bay, 8/1 Garth, 12/1 Navaresque(op 8/1), Bertie Wooster(16/1 – 10/1), 66/1 Urshi-Jade. CSF £17.09, CT £93.13. Tote £6.50: £2.00 £1.60 £1.40 (£9.80). Claremont Management Services (WORKSOP) bred by Hadi Al Tajir. 9 Rn  1m 29 (4.7)
SF—49/41/45/45/6/10

### 2061　　JULY CLAIMING STKS　£2469.00 (£684.00: £327.00)　5f　　　4-00 (4-05)

| | | |
|---|---|---|
| 1535 | **Mamma's Too (94)** *(Fav) (JBerry)* 3-8-13  PatEddery (5) (lw: a.p: rdn wl over 1f out: r.o to ld last stride) | —1 |
| 1999³ | The Noble Oak (IRE) **(65)** (bl) *(MMcCormack)* 4-8-6  JReid (1) (chsd ldr: led 1f out: rdn clr: ct last stride) | s.h.2 |
| 1339 | Nuclear Express **(52)** *(RLee)* 5-7-13 ‡7SDrowne (7) (lw: hdwy over 1f out: rdn & kpt on ins fnl f) | 1¹/₂.3 |
| 1999* | Ever so Lonely **(55)** (bl) *(ABailey)* 3-7-2 ‡7DWright (2) (led 4f: no ex ins fnl f) | 1¹/₂.4 |
| 1411 | Trioming **(40)** *(APJones)* 6-8-6  NAdams (3) (a.p: rdn over 1f out: one pce) | ¹/₂.5 |
| 1920* | Metal Boys **(82)** *(RHollinshead)* 5-9-2  WRyan (4) (lw: prom: ev ch over 1f out: one pce) | 1.6 |
| | Black Boy (IRE) *(JAGlover)* 3-8-3 ‡3FNorton (13) (w'like: bit bkwd: s.i.s: hdwy ¹/₂-wy: nvr able to chal) | ¹/₂.7 |
| 1757³ | Fivesevenfiveo **(74)** *(RJHodges)* 4-9-5  PaulEddery (8) (lw: chsd ldrs: rdn 2f out: sn btn) | ¹/₂.8 |
| 1417 | Nigals Friend **(60)** (v) *(DHaydnJones)* 3-8-4  JWilliams (14) (outpcd) | 2.9 |
| 785⁶ | Litmore Dancer **(55)** *(JMBradley)* 4-7-8 ‡7MichaelBradley (9) (outpcd) | 1.10 |
| 1741 | Lord Belmonte (IRE) **(32)** (bl) *(CACyzer)* 3-8-0  DBiggs (11) (outpcd: t.o) | 10.11 |
| 1552 | Royal Bear **(25)** *(JMBradley)* 10-8-6  TQuinn (10) (outpcd: t.o) | 2¹/₂.12 |
| 1683 | Bridge Street Boy *(DJGMurray-Smith)* 3-8-0  CRutter (6) (outpcd: t.o) | 2¹/₂.13 |

3/1 MAMMA'S TOO(op 2/1), 4/1 Ever so Lonely, Metal Boys, 8/1 The Noble Oak (IRE), 9/1 Fivesevenfiveo, 11/1 Nuclear Express(op 33/1), 16/1 Nigals Friend, 33/1 Litmore Dancer, 50/1 Trioming, Black Boy (IRE), 66/1 Bridge Street Boy, Lord Belmonte (IRE), 100/1 Royal Bear. CSF £23.26, Tote £3.40: £1.60 £2.20 £2.10 (£8.80). Mr J. K. Brown (COCKERHAM) bred by R. Brewis. 13 Rn　　60.7 sec (3.4)
SF—61/53/40/23/39/45

### 2062　　WESTON STKS (Mdn 3-Y-O) £2070.00 (£570.00: £270.00)　1m　　4-30 (4-33)

| | | |
|---|---|---|
| 857 | **Second Call** *(HCandy)* 8-9  CRutter (4) (lw: 5th st: hrd rdn 2f out: styd on to ld nr fin) | —1 |
| 1839⁴ | Be My Everything (IRE) *(RHollinshead)* 8-9  WRyan (8) (hld up: hdwy 4f out: led 2f out: edgd rt appr fnl f: hdd nr fin) | nk.2 |
| 1597⁴ | Lake Dominion **(75)** *(PWHarris)* 9-0  PaulEddery (7) (2nd st: led over 3f out to 2f out: kpt on u.p ins fnl f) | 1¹/₂.3 |
| | Hameem (IRE) *(AAScott)* 9-0  WRSwinburn (6) (gd sort: bit bkwd: chsd ldrs: 4th st: wknd over 1f out: eased whn btn) | 15.4 |
| | Always Lynsey (IRE) *(MissLCSiddall)* 8-9  TQuinn (1) (w'like: leggy: scope: bit bkwd: prom: 3rd st: wknd over 2f out) | 12.5 |
| 1732⁴ | Fort Derry (IRE) *(EJAlston)* 8-7 ‡7SKnott (3) (s.i.s: 6th st: wknd over 3f out) | ¹/₂.6 |
| 1807² | Bold Steve **(Fav)** *(LMCumani)* 9-0  LDettori (2) (lw: led tl hdd over 3f out: eased whn btn appr fnl f) | s.h.7 |
| | Dreams to Wotan *(MJWilkinson)* 9-0  NAdams (5) (str: scope: bkwd: s.s: a bhd: t.o) | 20.8 |

5/2 Bold Steve, 3/1 Lake Dominion, 7/2 SECOND CALL, 4/1 Hameem (IRE)(op 2/1), 9/1 Be My Everything (IRE), 33/1 Fort Derry (IRE), 50/1 Ors. CSF £30.07, Tote £5.60: £1.20 £1.90 £1.30 (£35.60). Mr C. J. R. Trotter (WANTAGE) bred by C. J. R. Trotter. 8 Rn　　1m 44 (6.7)
SF—19/18/18/–/–/–

### 2063　　LEVY BOARD SEVENTH RACE H'CAP (3-Y-O) (0-70) £2343.00 (£648.00: £309.00)　5f　　　5-00 (5-03)

(Weights raised 3 lb)

| | | |
|---|---|---|
| 1825⁵ | **Miss Movie World (40)** *(NBycroft)* 7-5⁽²⁾ ‡5NKennedy (2) (hld up: sn rdn along: hdwy 2f out: led wl ins fnl f: sn clr) | —1 |
| 1776⁴ | Ganeshaya **(43)** (bl) *(MFBarraclough)* 7-10 ‡3FNorton (3) (lw: led: sn clr: wknd & hdd wl ins fnl f) | 2¹/₂.2 |
| 1785³ | Kalar **(39)** *(DWChapman)* 7-9  SWood (1) (hdwy ¹/₂-wy: r.o one pce appr fnl f) | 3.3 |
| 1912³ | Sea Crusader **(51)** (bl) *(MBlanshard)* 8-7  WRyan (5) (chsd ldr over 3f: sn rdn & wknd) | 1¹/₂.4 |
| 1865* | Katie-a (IRE) **(58)** **(Fav)** *(RMWhitaker)* 9-0  ACulhane (7) (dwlt: outpcd) | 6.5 |
| 1145 | Bassetlaw Belle **(37)** *(SRBowring)* 7-7  NAdams (6) (s.s: outpcd) | 1.6 |
| 1676² | Jucea **(65)** *(DWPArbuthnot)* 9-7  TQuinn (4) (lw: chsd ldrs 3f: sn wknd) | 4.7 |

LONG HANDICAP: Bassetlaw Belle 7-5.

BEVERLEY, July 13, 1992

**2064–2066**

2/1 Katie-a (IRE), **5/2** Ganeshaya, **9/2** Jucea(3/1—5/1), **8/1** Sea Crusader(op 5/1), Kalar(op 5/1), **10/1** MISS MOVIE WORLD(7/1—12/1), **33/1** Bassetlaw Belle. CSF £33.36, Tote £22.90: £10.30 £1.50 (£30.30). Mr Stephen Johnson (BRANDSBY) bred by J. Williams. 7 Rn

61.1 sec (3.8)
SF—31/26/13/19/2/–

T/Plpt: £398.10 (7.75 Tckts).                                                                                                IM

## 1854—BEVERLEY (R-H)
### Monday, July 13th [Good to soft]
Going Allowance: St: 0.50 sec (Y); Rnd: 0.20 sec per fur (G)                          Wind: nil

Stalls: high

**2064**    POCKLINGTON MEDIAN AUCTION STKS (3-Y.O) £1492.00 (£412.00: £196.00)
1m 3f 216y                                                                6-35 (6-35)

1574⁴ **Storm Dust (70)** (Fav) *(JRFanshawe)* 8-11 GCarter (3) (lw: trckd ldrs: effrt on ins over 2f out: hrd rdn to ld wl ins fnl f: all out) .................. —1
1857★ Arfey (IRE) **(65)** *(TThomsonJones)* 9-1 WCarson (4) (b: led: rdn over 1f out: r.o wl nr fin) ........................................................... hd.2
Tudor Island *(CEBrittain)* 8-11 AMunro (1) (lw: chsd ldr: disp ld 5f out: rdn & hung rt over 2f out: one pce) ................................ 2¹/₂.3
1798⁴ Tafsir (63) *(HThomsonJones)* 8-6 NCarlisle (2) (effrt & pushed along over 3f out: edgd lft over 1f out: one pce) ..................... 4.4
1906 Only a Rose *(CWThornton)* 8-6 MBirch (5) (effrt & drvn along over 3f out: no imp) ............................................................... 2¹/₂.5

**6/4** STORM DUST(11/10—Evens), **7/4** Arfey (IRE), **4/1** Tafsir(6/1—13/2), **12/1** Tudor Island, **16/1** Only a Rose. CSF £4.30, Tote £2.40: £1.10 £1.50 (£2.20). Mr John R. Sims (NEWMARKET) bred by Stanley Stud. 5 Rn
2m 42.6 (11)
SF—11/14/5/–/–

**2065**    I. J. BLAKEY HAULAGE H'CAP (0-90) £2872.00 (£856.00: £408.00: £184.00)
1m 1f 207y                                                                7-05 (7-09)
(Weights raised 3 lb)

1922³ **Floating Line (57)** *(PWigham)* 4-8-5 GCarter (5) (trckd ldrs: effrt 3f out: rdn to ld over 1f out: r.o wl) ................................... —1
1739★ Jazilah (FR) **(64)** *(MrsGRReveley)* 4-8-12 KDarley (1) (swtg: trckd ldr: led over 3f out: nt qckn fnl f) ................................... ³/₄.2
1859⁵ Touch Above (58) *(TDBarron)* 6-8-6 AlexGreaves (3) (hld up: effrt over 2f out: styd on same pce: nvr able to chal) ................. 1¹/₂.3
1859² Smoke (45) *(JParkes)* 6-7-7 NCarlisle (2) (hld up: effrt 3f out: r.o one pce) .... 2¹/₂.4
1808★ Arak (USA) **(76)** (Fav) *(RWArmstrong)* 4-9-10 WCarson (4) (lw: led tl over 3f out: wknd over 1f out) ............................................ nk.5
1603² Milanese (80) *(DMorley)* 3-9-3 MBirch (6) (lw: trckd ldrs tl wknd 2f out: sn lost pl) ..................................................................... 10.6
LONG HANDICAP: Smoke 7-2.

**9/4** Arak (USA), **3/1** Jazilah (FR), **9/2** Milanese, **11/2** FLOATING LINE, **8/1** Touch Above, **9/1** Smoke. CSF £20.31, Tote £8.40: £2.60 £1.60 (£16.60). Mrs J. L. Wigham (MALTON) bred by R. Kalman. 6 Rn
2m 8.2 (6.2)
SF—49/54/45/27/57/30

**2066**    LADIES DAY H'CAP (Amateurs) (0-80) £1970.00 (£545.00: £260.00)
1m 100y                                                                  7-35 (7-36)

1863³ **Pride of Pendle (47)** *(PCalver)* 3-9-7 MrsAFarrell (8) (chsd ldrs: led over 2f out: clr 1f out: jst hld on) ....................................... —1
1863★ **Brilliant (65)** (Fav) *(JPearce)* 4-11-6 MrsLPearce (6) (hld up: sltly hmpd 4f out: gd hdwy 2f out: edgd lft: styd on wl u.p: jst failed) ............ nk.2
1622³ Thundering (35) *(AWJones)* 7-9-4⁽⁴⁾ MissIDWJones (4) (chsd ldrs: one pce fnl 2f) ............................................................... 5.3
1018 Breezed Well (59) *(CNAllen)* 6-10-7 ‡7MissRLowes (2) (trckd ldrs: carried wd 4f out: styd on fnl 2f: nvr rchd ldrs) ......................... 1.4
Al Badeto (32) *(JNorton)* 5-9-1⁽¹⁾ MissPRobson (3) (chsd ldrs: one pce fnl 3f) . ¹/₂.5
1725⁶ Doughman (45) *(JNorton)* 3-8-12 ‡7MissMCarson (1) (s.s: sn bhd: hrd rdn & kpt on fnl 2f) ........................................................ nk.6
1661⁶ Mainly Me (75) *(PTWalwyn)* 3-11-0 ‡7MissRNugent (5) (plld hrd: sddle slipped: hdwy & prom 2f out: sn wknd) ............................. 1.7
1794² Bill Moon (53) *(PJFeilden)* 6-10-8 MissJFeilden (10) (led: clr 5f out: hdd over 2f out: sn wknd) ........................................... 10.8

Page 729

1911 Yeoman Bid **(40)** *(JDooler)* 5–9-2[1] ‡7MrDWilcox (7) (s.s: a in rr) .................... 10.9
1661 Mahzooz **(70)** *(MMoubarak)* 3–10-9‡7MissIFustok (9) (chsd ldrs tl lost pl over 4f
                    out: sn wl bhd) .................................................. 30.10
                    LONG HANDICAP: Al Badeto 8-3.
          *Stewards Enquiry: Miss M Carson suspended 22-25/7/92 (excessive use of whip).*

**2/1** Brilliant, **7/2** Thundering, **4/1** Bill Moon, **7/1** Mainly Me, **8/1** PRIDE OF PENDLE, **14/1** Breezed Well, **20/1**
Mahzooz, **25/1** Doughman, **33/1** Yeoman Bid, **50/1** Al Badeto. CSF £23.57, CT £62.23. Tote £10.90: £1.70
£1.50 £1.60 (£11.80). Mr W. B. Imison (RIPON) bred by James Simpson. 10 Rn          1m 51.6 (8.9)

---

**2067**    EAST YORKSHIRE GLAZING CLAIMING STKS (2-Y.O) £2820.00 (£840.00: £400.00:
            £180.00)   **5f**                                          8-05 (8-06)

1754* **Classic Storm** (Jt-Fav) *(JBerry)* 8-9 JCarroll (4) (lw: chsd ldr: led over 1f out:
                    hld on wl) ...................................................... —1
15593 Bright Gem *(TFairhurst)* 7-13 ‡3JFanning (2) (chsd ldrs: effrt ½-wy: kpt on same
                    pce u.p fnl f) ................................................. 1½.2
1191* Purchased by Phone (IRE) (Jt-Fav) *(JSWainwright)* 8-3 AMunro (6) (led: edgd
                    lft & hdd over 1f out: edgd rt u.p & wknd jst ins fnl f) ...... 2½.3
17825 Poppet Plume *(GMMoore)* 8-3 WCarson (3) (lw: outpcd ½-wy: kpt on fnl
                    f) ............................................................. nk.4
          Minster Man (IRE) *(BSRothwell)* 8-9 DHolland (1) (cmpt: bit bkwd: swvd lft s: sn
                    wl bhd: hdwy over 1f out: edgd rt & styd on wl) ............... s.h.5
16943 Shadow Jury *(JSWainwright)* 9-0 PBurke (5) (unruly in stalls: s.i.s: chsd ldrs:
                    styng on whn bdly hmpd ins fnl f: nt rcvr) ................... 2½.6

**2/1** CLASSIC STORM, Purchased by Phone (IRE), **11/4** Shadow Jury, **15/2** Poppet Plume, **14/1** Bright Gem,
**25/1** Minster Man (IRE). CSF £23.36, Tote £3.20: £1.90 £3.50 (£19.20). Mr D. J. Ayres (COCKERHAM) bred by
Concorde Breeding and Racing International P'Ship. 6 Rn; Shadow Jury clmd D Walker £15,750  66.5 sec (5)
                                                              SF—45/29/23/22/27/22

---

**2068**    BIRTHRIGHT AUCTION STKS (2-Y.O) £2127.50 (£590.00: £282.50)
            **7f 100y**                                              8-35 (8-35)

16606 **Persian Fountain (IRE)** *(BSRothwell)* 7-12 SWood (1) (sn bhd: hdwy on
                    outside over 2f out: styd on u.p to ld wl ins fnl f) ......... —1
*1549*6 Mohican Brave (IRE) *(JGFitzGerald)* 8-7 KDarley (2) (lw: trckd ldrs: hmpd 3f out
                    & 2f out: hdwy to ld 1f out: sn hdd & nt qckn) .............. 3½.2
18736 Poly Vision (IRE) *(MRChannon)* 8-2 DHolland (5) (trckd ldrs: outpcd over 3f
                    out: edgd rt & styd on wl) .................................. hd.3
1515* Sweet Romeo *(MJohnston)* 8-11 DMcKeown (4) (lw: sn trckng ldr: ev ch & rdn
                    over 1f out: kpt on same pce) .............................. hd.4
12023 No Reservations (IRE) (Fav) *(RFJohnsonHoughton)* 8-5 AMunro (6) (led: rdn 2f
                    out: hdd & wknd 1f out) ..................................... 2.5
1660* Hadeer's Dance *(RWArmstrong)* 8-12 WCarson (7) (chsd ldrs: rdn & edgd lft
                    u.p over 2f out: sn wknd) .................................. 7.6
          Wild Expression *(CTinkler)* 8-6 MBirch (3) (lengthy: scope: bkwd: s.i.s: a bhd) 15.7

**9/4** No Reservations (IRE), **5/2** Sweet Romeo, **3/1** Hadeer's Dance, **6/1** Mohican Brave (IRE), **14/1** Poly Vision
(IRE), **16/1** PERSIAN FOUNTAIN (IRE)(op 33/1), **25/1** Wild Expression. CSF £95.19, Tote £25.00: £4.00 £3.00
(£56.10). Mr A. N. Barrett (CATWICK) bred by Killarkin Stud in Ireland. 7 Rn          1m 37.2 (7)
                                                              SF—2/–/–/–/–

---

**2069**    HULL H'CAP (3-Y.O) (0-80) £2726.80 (£754.80: £360.40)   **1m 3f 216y**  9-05 (9-05)
                    (Weights raised 2 lb)
12502 **Eurotwist (66)** (Fav) *(TDBarron)* 8-10 AlexGreaves (5) (lw: trckd ldrs gng wl:
                    hdwy on ins to ld over 2f out: rdn & r.o wl fnl f) ........... —1
19094 Haut-Brion (IRE) **(52)** *(WStorey)* 7-7[3] ‡3JFanning (1) (chsd ldr: hrd drvn over 4f
                    out: one pce fnl 2f) ......................................... 5.2
17844 Salu **(56)** *(JEtherington)* 8-0 KDarley (4) (led tl over 2f out: kpt on same pce) .. 4.3
1914 Walking on Water **(75)** (bl) *(RFJohnsonHoughton)* 9-5 GCarter (3) (stdd s: effrt
                    5f out: n.d) ................................................ 5.4
941 Jairzinho (USA) **(77)** *(MRChannon)* 9-7 LornaVincent (2) (prom tl lost pl over 3f
                    out: sn bhd) ............................................... 25.5
                    LONG HANDICAP: Haut-Brion (IRE) 7-6.

**11/10** EUROTWIST, **4/1** Walking on Water, **5/1** Haut-Brion (IRE), **7/1** Ors. CSF £6.32, Tote £1.80: £1.50 £1.60
(£4.00). Mr W. G. Swiers (THIRSK) bred by Waresley Park Stud Ltd. 5 Rn          2m 42.9 (11.3)
                                                              SF—7/–/–/–/–

T/Plpt: £162.40 (12.2 Tckts).                                               WG

## BEVERLEY (R-H)
### Tuesday, July 14th [Good to soft]
Going Allowance: nil sec per fur (G)                                    Wind: almost nil

Stalls: high

**2070**  LEVY BOARD STKS (3-Y.O.F) £3395.00 (£1010.00: £480.00: £215.00)
1m 1f 207y                                                                2-00 (2-00)

1648* Ardisia (USA) (86) (Fav) (PFICole) 9-1 MRoberts (3) (mde all: r.o strly fnl 2f) .... —1
19774 Kadari (53) (AHarrison) 9-1 BRaymond (4) (lw: a.p: effrt over 2f out: styd on: no ch w wnr) ........................................................................ 7.2
1830* Cutleaf (WJarvis) 9-1 JCarroll (1) (lw: s.i.s: sn rcvd: chal ent st: rdn & btn 2f out) 5.3
1911 Lightning Spark (40) (MAvison) 8-11 MBirch (2) (hld up: effrt ent st: rdn & no imp) ...................................................................................... nk.4

10/11 ARDISIA (USA), 11/10 Cutleaf, 20/1 Kadari, 50/1 Lightning Spark. CSF £10.38, Tote £1.70 (£3.90). Mr Fahd Salman (WHATCOMBE) bred by Newgate Stud Farm Incorporated in USA. 4 Rn      2m 7.3 (5.3)
SF—48/34/24/19

**2071**  ELECTROLUX H'CAP (0-80) £2846.00 (£848.00: £404.00: £182.00)
2m 35y                                                                     2-30 (2-31)

1866* My Desire (67) (MrsGRReveley) 4-9-4 JLowe (5) (lw: trckd ldrs: effrt whn nt clr run 3f out: hdwy over 1f out: r.o to ld cl home) .................. —1
1740* Samain (USA) (48) (JAGlover) 9-6 NCarlisle (4) (hld up: stdy hdwy 3f out: led 1f out: r.o: jst ct) ...................................................... nk.2
16972 Cabochon (77) (Fav) (DMorley) 5-10-0 PaulEddery (1) (lw: hld up: hdwy 5f out: rdn to ld over 1f out: sn hdd. kpt on same pce) ................ ¾.3
18982 Attadale (61) (LLungo) 4-8-12(1) DNicholls (3) (chsd ldrs: led over 2f out tl hdd & wknd appr fnl f) ............................................ 7.4
1894 Hthaal (USA) (63) (LLungo) 4-9-0 KFallon (2) (led tl hdd over 2f out: sn btn) ... 15.5

13/8 Cabochon, 2/1 MY DESIRE, 4/1 Samain (USA), 6/1 Attadale, 33/1 Hthaal (USA). CSF £9.15, Tote £2.60: £1.30 £1.80 (£3.80). Mrs M. A. Spensley (SALTBURN) bred by W. G. Barker. 5 Rn      3m 42.8 (12.1)

**2072**  SHARP CLAIMING STKS (3-Y.O) £2898.00 (£864.00: £412.00: £186.00)
7f 100y                                                                    3-00 (3-00)

13635 Round by the River (67) (Fav) (WWHaigh) 8-5 GDuffield (2) (dwlt: sn pushed along: hdwy ent st: rdn to ld jst fnl f) ............................ —1
19034 Ace Girl (55) (SRBowring) 7-5(1) ‡3FNorton (7) (led: clr over 2f out: hdd jst fnl f: no ex) ................................................... 1½.2
18496 Giddy Heights (IRE) (JPLeigh) 7-13 MRoberts (1) (lw: sn pushed along: hdwy ent st: edgd rt & one pce fnl 2f) ................................ 4.3
18494 Fairford (63) (JGFitzGerald) 8-4 KFallon (4) (sn drvn along: nvr trbld ldrs) .... 6.4
1901 Double the Stakes (USA) (43) (FHLee) 7-8 ‡5NKennedy (5) (swtg: w ldr tl wknd 3f out) ........................................................... 10.5
1907 Bold Mood (45) (JBerry) 8-4 JCarroll (6) (lw: chsd ldrs tl rdn & wknd over 3f out) 5.6

13/8 ROUND BY THE RIVER, 15/8 Ace Girl, 5/1 Fairford, 8/1 Double the Stakes (USA), 12/1 Giddy Heights (IRE), 20/1 Bold Mood. CSF £4.95, Tote £2.30: £1.90 £1.60 (£2.40). Mr W. W. Haigh (MALTON) bred by Norton Court Stud Farm Ltd. 6 Rn      1m 35.2 (5)
SF—16/–/–/–/–/–

**2073**  COMET H'CAP (0-90) £4503.00 (£1344.00: £642.00: £291.00)   5f   3-30 (3-32)
(Weights raised 1 lb)

853 Misdemeanours Girl (IRE) (62) (MRChannon) 4-7-12 ‡5BDoyle (6) (lw: chsd ldrs: styd on to ld wl ins fnl f) ....................................... —1
20194 Playful Poet (66) (Fav) (MHEasterby) 5-8-2 ‡5SMaloney (3) (b.off hind: led tl hdd wl ins fnl f) ..................................................... 1½.2
19314 Pageboy (82) (bl) (PCHaslam) 3-9-3 KDarley (4) (sn pushed along: hdwy 2f out: r.o nr fin) .................................................. 1.3
19202 Drum Sergeant (59) (bl) (JParkes) 5-8-0 NCarlisle (8) (sltly hmpd ½-wy: hdwy over 1f out: styd on) ........................................ ½.4
19242 State Flyer (64) (v) (CBBBooth) 4-7-12(6) ‡7GForster (7) (dwlt: bhd tl styd on wl fnl f) ............................................................... nk.5
Seamere (83) (bl) (BRCambidge) 9-9-10 JLowe (5) (bit bkwd: rn wl over 4f) ... ½.6
18284 Simmie's Special (62) (RHollinshead) 4-8-3 PaulEddery (1) (lw: cl up 3f: grad wknd) ............................................................. hd.7
18295 Gemini Fire (82) (MPNaughton) 8-9-4 ‡5JWeaver (10) (s.i.s: n.d) .............. 2.8

1908 Toshiba Comet **(78)** (bl) *(BBeasley)* 5–9-5 DNicholls (9) (nvr wnt pce) ........... 2½.**9**
1861* Memsahb **(82)** *(JBerry)* 3–9-3 JCarroll (2) (lw: spd 3f: sn wknd) ............... d.h.**9**

**7/2** Playful Poet, **9/2** Pageboy, **7/1** Memsahb, Drum Sergeant, **15/2** MISDEMEANOURS GIRL (IRE), **8/1** Gemini
Fire, **12/1** Simmie's Special, **14/1** State Flyer, **16/1** Ors. CSF £31.06, CT £119.35. Tote £8.90: £2.40 £1.90
£2.00 (£29.80). Mr M. G. Michaels (UPPER LAMBOURN) bred by A. F. O'Callaghan in Ireland. 10 Rn
63.6 sec (2.1)
SF—42/40/51/32/29/53

### 2074
SONY AUCTION STKS (Mdn 2-Y-O) £3002.00 (£896.00: £428.00: £194.00)
5f
4-00 (4-02)

1734² **Margaret's Gift** *(JBerry)* 8-0 JCarroll (1) (chsd ldrs: led over 1f out: styd on u.p) —**1**
Chevrotain *(JWWatts)* 8-8 GDuffield (7) (gd sort: scope: bit bkwd: dwlt: outpcd
& bhd tl hdwy & swtchd 2f out: r.o wl) ............... 1½.**2**
1902 Andrula Mou *(RBoss)* 8-0 MRoberts (3) (a chsng ldrs: hdwy u.p 2f out: nt qckn
ins fnl f) ............... 1½.**3**
1571³ Anniversaire (Fav) *(BobJones)* 8-5 NDay (10) (lw: chsd ldrs: outpcd after 2f:
hdwy over 1f out: styd on one pce) ............... 1½.**4**
1296⁵ Canny Lad *(JGFitzGerald)* 8-1 KDarley (5) (lw: led tl hdd over 1f out: grad wknd) 1½.**5**
1902⁶ Viv's Pet *(AHide)* 8-3 JWilliams (9) (mid div: stdy hdwy over 1f out: nvr nr to
chal) ............... nk.**6**
*1851* Comet Whirlpool (IRE) *(BBeasley)* 8-9 LCharnock (6) (w ldrs tl ½-wy: grad wknd) 4.**7**
1668⁴ Contrac Countess (IRE) *(BSRothwell)* 7-6 ‡³FNorton (2) (s.i.s: n.d) ............... nk.**8**
*1322⁶* Apollo de Oriente *(JSWainwright)* 8-4 PBurke (8) (w ldrs tl wknd over 1f out) ..... 2.**9**
Ring Tom (IRE) *(MWEasterby)* 8-4⁽²⁾ TLucas (4) (lengthy: bit bkwd: stumbled s:
a bhd) ............... 1.**10**

**5/4** Anniversaire, **6/1** Andrula Mou, **13/2** MARGARET'S GIFT, Chevrotain, **7/1** Canny Lad, **10/1** Viv's Pet(op 6/1),
**20/1** Ring Tom (IRE), Contrac Countess (IRE), **33/1** Ors. CSF £46.19, Tote £6.00: £1.70 £1.80 £1.50 (£10.40).
Mrs T. G. Holdcroft (COCKERHAM) bred by John L. Moore. 10 Rn
63.9 sec (2.4)
SF—38/40/26/25/15/16

### 2075
HOOVER H'CAP (3-Y-O) (0-80) £2976.00 (£888.00: £424.00: £192.00)
1m 100y
4-30 (4-31)
(Weights raised 3 lb)

1890³ **Cappahoosh (IRE) (51)** (Fav) *(HJCollingridge)* 8-2 MRoberts (5) (lw: mde all:
hld on wl fnl f) —**1**
1791⁴ Allegramente **(52)** *(RO'Leary)* 8-3 MBirch (2) (trckd ldrs gng wl: hdwy to chal
ins fnl f: nt qckn) ............... ¾.**2**
*1679* Anguish (IRE) **(51)** *(NACallaghan)* 7-13 ‡³FNorton (9) (mid div: hdwy whn n.m.r
& swtchd ins fnl f: nrst fin) ............... 3.**3**
1417⁶ Young Valentine **(64)** *(RMWhitaker)* 9-1 ACulhane (4) (plld hrd: hld up & bhd:
hdwy 2f out: wknd 1f out) ............... ¾.**4**
1906 Canbrack (IRE) **(54)** *(WAStephenson)* 8-5 JLowe (1) (lw: chsd ldrs: ev ch over
2f out: hung rt & wknd ent fnl f) ............... ½.**5**
1839³ Manulife **(68)** *(BBeasley)* 9-5 DNicholls (6) (hld up & bhd: sme hdwy whn hmpd
over 1f out: n.d) ............... 1½.**6**
1791 Najeb (USA) **(70)** *(BHanbury)* 9-7 BRaymond (8) (chsd ldr tl wknd 2f out) ...... 5.**7**
1563³ Denim Blue **(56)** *(CWThornton)* 8-7 GDuffield (7) (cl up: rdn ent st: wknd over 1f
out) ............... 5.**8**
1484 Caherea School **(42)** *(RO'Leary)* 7-7 LCharnock (3) (s.i.s: n.d) ............... 12.**9**
LONG HANDICAP: Caherea School 7-5.

**15/8** CAPPAHOOSH (IRE), **4/1** Denim Blue, **6/1** Manulife, **13/2** Allegramente, **9/1** Anguish (IRE), **11/1** Young
Valentine, **12/1** Najeb (USA), **20/1** Canbrack (IRE), **33/1** Caherea School. CSF £13.71, CT £79.59. Tote £2.40:
£1.40 £2.20 £2.30 (£8.40). Mrs P. A. L. Butler (NEWMARKET) bred by Lodge Park Stud in Ireland. 9 Rn
1m 49.2 (6.5)

### 2076
TOSHIBA NURSERY £3184.00 (£952.00: £456.00: £208.00) **7f 100y** 5-00 (5-01)

1249⁶ **Argyle Cavalier (IRE)** *(FHLee)* 7-4⁽²⁾ ‡⁵NKennedy (2) (hld up & bhd: hdwy on
outside 2f out: led appr fnl f: r.o) —**1**
889* Amerigue *(MissSEHall)* 7-7 NCarlisle (5) (hdwy ½-wy: n.m.r over 1f out: styd on
wl nr fin) ............... 1½.**2**
1605² Regal Aura (IRE) *(GHarwood)* 9-7 MRoberts (1) (lw: chsd ldrs: rdn to chal 2f
out: no ex ins fnl f) ............... s.h.**3**
1959* Boldville Bash (IRE) (Fav) *(TDBarron)* 7-7 (7x) ‡³JFanning (7) (plld hrd: cl up: led
over 2f out tl over 1f out: sn btn) ............... 2.**4**
1738³ Atherton Green (IRE) *(JAGlover)* 8-11 MBirch (6) (sn outpcd & bhd: hdwy 2f
out: n.d) ............... 2½.**5**

1694⁶ Contract Elite (IRE) *(CWThornton)* 8-7 GDuffield (3) (lw: chsd ldr tl rdn & btn wl
over 1f out) ...................................................... 3¹/₂.6
1660³ Don't Be Saki (IRE) *(JEtherington)* 8-1 JLowe (4) (chsd ldrs tl wknd fnl 2f) ......... 5.7
*1549³* Nutty Brown *(SGNorton)* 8-4 NConnorton (8) (led tl hdd over 2f out: sn btn) ... 10.8
LONG HANDICAP: Argyle Cavalier (IRE) 7-6.

**15/8** Boldville Bash (IRE), **9/2** Regal Aura (IRE), **11/2** ARGYLE CAVALIER (IRE)(op 3/1), **15/2** Nutty Brown, **8/1**
Don't Be Saki (IRE), **10/1** Amerigue, **12/1** Ors. CSF £50.87, CT £241.71. Tote £6.70: £1.80 £2.50 £2.10
(£25.70). E. H. Jones (Paints) Ltd (WILMSLOW) bred by Oldtown Bloodstock Holdings Ltd in Ireland. 8 Rn
1m 34.9 (4.7)
SF—5/3/30/–/6/–

T/Plpt: £41.00 (79.4 Tckts).        AA

---

## 1761—FOLKESTONE (R-H)
### Tuesday, July 14th [Good to firm]
Going Allowance: minus 0.10 sec per fur (F)        Wind: almost nil

Stalls: low

### 2077    LEAS H'CAP (0-70) £2532.00 (£702.00: £336.00)    1m 1f 149y    1-45 (1-48)

1747 **Shamshom Al Arab (IRE) (35)** *(WCarter)* 4-7-9 DBiggs (14) (hdwy & nt clr run
wl over 1f out: swtchd lft: led wl ins fnl f: rdn out) ................ —1
1721 Long Furlong **(52)** *(Fav)* *(RAkehurst)* 4-8-9 ‡³RPerham (6) (hdwy over 1f out:
led ins fnl f: sn hdd: unable qckn) ......................................... ½.2
606⁶ Amazon Express **(54)** *(CEBrittain)* 3-8-3(¹) TQuinn (12) (mid div whn nt clr run
3f out & over 1f out: hdwy fnl f: r.o) ...................................... ³/₄.3
1574 Sybaritic Sam (IRE) **(56)** *(NACallaghan)* 3-8-5 GOarter (5) (hdwy over 1f out: r.o) 1.4
1643⁵ Deevee **(47)** *(CJBenstead)* 3-7-10 TyroneWilliams (2) (hdwy 3f out: 5th st: rdn
over 1f out: one pce) ........................................................ 2.5
1724³ A Nymph Too Far (IRE) **(46)** *(DrJDScargill)* 3-7-2 ‡⁷CHawksley (13) (4th st: one
pce fnl 2f) .................................................................. ³/₄.6
1041⁴ Murasil (USA) **(68)** *(MajorWRHern)* 3-9-3 WCarson (10) (lw: led: hrd rdn over 1f
out: hdd ins fnl f: eased whn btn) ......................................... 1.7
1760³ Impressive Lad **(33)** *(RRowe)* 6-7-7 JQuinn (4) (lw: 6th st: wknd over 1f out) .... 2.8
1674² Indian Style (IRE) **(55)** *(RGuest)* 3-7-13 ‡⁵DHarrison (9) (2nd st: wknd over 1f
out) ......................................................................... 1.9
1718⁵ Moving Force **(37)** *(EAWheeler)* 5-7-11 AMackay (8) (swtg: dwlt: a bhd) ......... 2.10
1917 Finaldream (IRE) **(64)** *(AWDenson)* 4-9-10 BRouse (3) (a bhd) ..................... 2.11
1763⁵ Share Holder **(48)** *(MissGayKelleway)* 4-8-8 RCochrane (1) (b.hind: bhd fnl 2f) 1.12
1750⁴ Sharp Dance **(49)** *(BSmart)* 3-7-12 DaleGibson (11) (swtg: 3rd st: wknd over 1f
out) ......................................................................... 3.13
1813 Lady Bunting **(37)** *(RVoorspuy)* 5-7-11 SDawson (7) (a bhd) ..................... 12.14
LONG HANDICAP: Impressive Lad 7-4.

**3/1** Long Furlong(tchd 9/2), **5/1** Murasil (USA), **6/1** Sybaritic Sam (IRE), **8/1** Deevee, **9/1** Sharp Dance(op 5/1),
**11/1** A Nymph Too Far (IRE), **12/1** Impressive Lad, Indian Style (IRE)(op 8/1), **14/1** Moving Force(op 7/1),
SHAMSHOM AL ARAB (IRE), **16/1** Amazon Express, **33/1** Ors. CSF £55.41, CT £642.62. Tote £53.70: £7.80
£1.20 £6.90 (£175.30). Miss Maha Kalaji (EPSOM) bred by Des De Vere Hunt in Ireland. 14 Rn   2m 3.7 (6)
SF—11/24/16/16/3/–

### 2078    SHELWING MEDIAN AUCTION STKS (Mdn 3-Y.O) £2070.00 (£570.00: £270.00)
      1m 1f 149y       2-15 (2-18)

Blazon of Troy *(TThomsonJones)* 9-0 TQuinn (6) (2nd st: hrd rdn over 1f out:
led ins fnl f: r.o wl) ....................................................... —1
*1265³* King's Guest (IRE) **(56)** *(GAPritchard-Gordon)* 9-0 AMcGlone (1) (lw: led tl ins
fnl f: unable qckn) .......................................................... 2.2
1079⁴ Continuity *(Fav)* *(GHarwood)* 8-9 AClark (4) (hdwy over 3f out: 3rd st: one pce
fnl 2f) ...................................................................... 5.3
1650⁴ Marvelous Molly **(62)** *(IABalding)* 8-9 RCochrane (4) (hdwy over 3f out: rdn
over 2f out: 4th st: wknd over 1f out) ..................................... 5.4
1585³ Traders Dream **(67)** *(TThomsonJones)* 9-0 SWhitworth (7) (s.s: 5th st: wknd
over 1f out) ................................................................. 6.5
524⁵ Blackpatch Hill **(64)** *(JLDunlop)* 9-0 WCarson (2) (b: 6th st: a bhd) .............. 8.6
1010 Red Mirage (IRE) **(58)** *(MMcCormack)* 8-9 RStreet (5) (lw: bhd fnl 5f) .......... 15.7

**13/8** Continuity, **4/1** Blackpatch Hill(op 2/1), **9/2** Marvelous Molly(7/2—11/2), Traders Dream, **9/1** King's Guest
(IRE), **20/1** Red Mirage (IRE), **25/1** BLAZON OF TROY. CSF £187.66, Tote £19.70: £5.10 £4.80 (£75.60). Mr T.
Thomson Jones (UPPER LAMBOURN) bred by Seend Stud. 7 Rn    2m 3.3 (5.6)
SF—34/30/15/5/–/–

## 2079

WINDFALL H'CAP (3-Y.O.F) (0-70) £2448.00 (£678.00: £324.00)
6f 189y                                                                    2-45 (2-48)

14286 **Kentucky Starlet (USA) (52)** *(RHannon)* 8-3 WCarson (2) (mde virtually all: hrd rdn over 1f out: r.o wl) ...................... —1

12465 May Hills Legacy (IRE) **(70)** *(DWPArbuthnot)* 9-7 TQuinn (6) (4th st: hrd rdn over 1f out: unable qckn) ...................... 2.2

17252 Honey Vision **(47)** (bl) *(GHEden)* 7-12 DaleGibson (1) (hrd rdn & hdwy over 1f out: one pce) ...................... 3.3

15285 Elizabethan Air **(53)** *(ANLee)* 8-4 JQuinn (5) (5th st: hrd rdn over 1f out: one pce) ...................... ¾.4

17372 Shakreen (USA) **(69)** *(MrsLPiggott)* 9-6 RCochrane (4) (s.s: hdwy over 1f out: nvr nrr) ...................... 5.5

16636 Horizontale **(45)** (bl) *(CEBrittain)* 7-10 GBardwell (3) (nvr nr to chal) ...................... 1½.6

10853 Walkonthemoon **(54)** *(MMcCormack)* 8-5 AClark (7) (lw: 3rd st: wknd over 1f out) ...................... 5.7

16413 Flying Wind **(60)** (bl) *(JSutcliffe)* 8-11 BRouse (8) (6th st: wknd 2f out) ...................... hd.8

1643 Royal Glint **(52)** (bl) *(IABalding)* 8-3 GCarter (10) (b: a bhd) ...................... hd.9

17506 Kay Beeyou (IRE) **(58)** *(TThomsonJones)* 8-9 SWhitworth (11) (b: 2nd st: wknd over 1f out) ...................... 2½.10

1952 Tulapet **(46)** (v) *(SDow)* 7-11 DBiggs (9) (lw: prom over 4f) ...................... ½.11

**7/2** Shakreen (USA), **5/1** Elizabethan Air, **6/1** Flying Wind, **15/2** Honey Vision, **8/1** Horizontale, **9/1** Kay Beeyou (IRE), **10/1** KENTUCKY STARLET (USA), **11/1** Walkonthemoon, May Hills Legacy (IRE), **25/1** Ors. CSF £102.57, CT £787.26. Tote £7.60: £2.50 £2.90 £3.30 (£190.50). Mr W. F. Hawkings (MARLBOROUGH) bred by Indian Creek in USA. 11 Rn
1m 25.4 (3.8)
SF—22/34/2/6/7/–

## 2080

LONDON FRIENDS (S) STKS (2-Y.O) £2469.00 (£684.00: £327.00)   6f   3-15 (3-18)

19002 **Guv'nors Gift** (Fav) *(MHTompkins)* 8-6 PRobinson (2) (hld up: led wl over 1f out: r.o wl) ...................... —1

17645 No Extras (IRE) *(JSutcliffe)* 8-11 BRouse (4) (swtg: hmpd s: hdwy & squeezed thro over 2f out: ev ch over 1f out: unable qckn) ...................... 4.2

1902 Infant Protege (USA) *(CEBrittain)* 8-6 AMcGlone (8) (a.p: led 2f out tl wl over 1f out: one pce) ...................... 1½.3

18094 Pickupadailysport *(MissGayKelleway)* 8-11 RCochrane (6) (jinked s: nvr nr to chal) ...................... 5.4

17753 Wealthywoo (bl) *(JSMoore)* 8-6 TQuinn (7) (lw: led 4f) ...................... 2.5

19004 Clangold *(JBerry)* 8-6 GCarter (3) (outpcd) ...................... ¾.6

16756 Moonstruck Bard (bl) *(SPCWoods)* 8-11 WWoods (1) (racd alone: bhd fnl 3f) ...................... 6.7

17695 Christian Spirit (bl) *(RHannon)* 8-11 WCarson (9) (lw: w ldr tl wknd & bmpd over 2f out: t.o) ...................... 20.8

**13/8** GUV'NORS GIFT, **9/2** No Extras (IRE), **5/1** Christian Spirit, **15/2** Clangold(4/1—8/1), **8/1** Pickupadailysport(tchd 16/1), Moonstruck Bard(op 5/1), **12/1** Wealthywoo(op 8/1), **16/1** Infant Protege (USA)(op 10/1). CSF £9.59, Tote £2.60: £1.20 £1.60 £3.30 (£9.90). The Tompkins Team (NEWMARKET) bred by Stud-On-The-Chart. 8 Rn; Bt in 3,500 gns
1m 15.8 (5.1)

## 2081

BARRETT NURSERY   £2406.00 (£666.00: £318.00)   5f   3-45 (3-47)
(Weights raised 6 lb)

1291 **Maybe Gold** *(DWPArbuthnot)* 8-11 TQuinn (3) (b.nr hind: dwlt: hdwy 2f out: led over 1f out: rdn out) ...................... —1

1601★ Trevorsninepoints *(MJRyan)* 8-9 PRobinson (7) (led over 3f: unable qckn) ...................... 2.2

8116 Defenceless *(RHannon)* 8-13 BRouse (2) (a.p: rdn over 1f out: one pce) ...................... ½.3

17425 Charity Express (IRE) *(JBerry)* 9-6 GCarter (1) (outpcd: hdwy fnl f: r.o) ...................... s.h.4

18804 Superensis (bl) *(WRMuir)* 8-9 SWhitworth (6) (a.p: ev ch over 1f out: wknd fnl f) ...................... 2½.5

16382 Kensworth Lady *(MBlanshard)* 9-7 RCochrane (4) (hld up: shkn up over 1f out: nvr nr to chal) ...................... hd.6

1728★ Field of Vision (IRE) (bl) (Fav) *(MJohnston)* 8-13 DMcKeown (5) (spd over 2f) ...................... 3.7

**7/4** Field of Vision (IRE), **11/4** Trevorsninepoints, **11/2** Defenceless, **9/1** MAYBE GOLD(op 4/1), Charity Express (IRE), **10/1** Superensis(op 6/1), **12/1** Kensworth Lady(op 6/1). CSF £32.26, Tote £8.00: £4.50 £1.40 (£16.70). Mr George S. Thompson (COMPTON) bred by P. F. Boggis. 7 Rn
61.5 sec (2.7)
SF—33/23/25/31/10/21

## 2082

WHITE HOUSE STKS (Mdn 3-Y.O) £2070.00 (£570.00: £270.00)   5f   4-15 (4-16)

1138 **Temple Fortune (USA) (66)** (Fav) *(RHannon)* 8-9 WCarson (1) (racd stands' side: hld up: led over 1f out: hrd rdn & r.o wl) ...................... —1

1315 Cashmiriana (IRE) **(69)** *(MissHCKnight)* 8-9 SWhitworth (3) (chsd ldr: hrd rdn over 1f out: r.o one pce) ...................... 3.2

1552 Jaromic **(47)** *(PFTulk)* 9-0 RCochrane (4) (lw: led over 3f: unable qckn) ......... hd.3
1649³ Belthorn **(39)** *(JJBridger)* 8-9 TyroneWilliams (2) (racd stands' side: bhd fnl 2f) 15.4
1115⁶ Al-Dahlawia (IRE) **(45)** *(GAPritchard-Gordon)* 8-9 GCarter (5) (b.hind: a bhd) .. 10.5

**8/11** TEMPLE FORTUNE (USA), **2/1** Cashmiriana (IRE), **12/1** Jaromic(op 7/1), **14/1** Belthorn(op 8/1), **25/1** Al-Dahlawia (IRE). CSF £2.44, Tote £1.40: £1.10 £1.30 (£1.90). Mr L. H. J. Ward (MARLBOROUGH) bred by Dr E. W. Thomas in USA. 5 Rn                                       61 sec (2.2)
SF—41/29/33/–/–

---

**2083**      ST LOYES COLLEGE H'CAP (0-70) £2574.00 (£714.00: £342.00)
             **2m 93y**                                                     4-45 (4-47)

1530³ **Newton Point (70)** (bl) (Jt-Fav) *(GAPritchard-Gordon)* 3-8-11 RCochrane (1)
            (a.p: qcknd & led over 4f out: clr over 3f out: comf) ............. —1
1395⁴ Prince Mercury **(66)** *(JLDunlop)* 3-8-7 WCarson (4) (lw: hdwy 3f out: 4th st: rdn
            over 1f out: r.o) .............................................. 2.2
 507 Podrida **(48)** *(RJO'Sullivan)* 6-8-1⁽¹⁾ ‡⁵KRutter (6) (hdwy 2f out: r.o) ........ hd.3
1686⁴ Puff Puff **(50)** *(MissBSanders)* 6-8-8 GCarter (12) (hdwy over 4f out:
            2nd st: wknd 1f out) ......................................... 5.4
 530⁵ Scent of Battle **(38)** *(MJHaynes)* 4-7-3 ‡⁷DToole (9) (lw: 6th st: no hdwy fnl 2f) s.h.5
 790 Trojan Envoy **(35)** *(WCarter)* 4-7-7 NAdams (8) (led 12f: 3rd st: wknd 2f out) .... 6.6
 708 Dutyful **(48)** *(MJHaynes)* 6-8-6 DBiggs (10) (nvr nr to chal) ............... 10.7
1874 Beldale Star **(51)** *(RAkehurst)* 9-8-6 ‡³RPerham (3) (b: 5th st: wknd 2f out) ........ 8.8
1640⁶ Flying Ziad (CAN) **(35)** *(RCurtis)* 9-7-7 GBardwell (2) (lw: prom over 12f) ....... ¹/₂.9
1137⁴ Peace King **(70)** *(GHarwood)* 6-10-0 MPerrett (11) (lw: hrd rdn 9f out: bhd fnl
            7f) ......................................................... 10.10
 612⁵ Spring Forward **(37)** (v) *(REPeacock)* 8-7-9⁽²⁾ TyroneWilliams (7) (a bhd) ....... 10.11
1747 Dazla **(38)** *(RRowe)* 5-7-3⁽³⁾ ‡⁷CHawksley (5) (lw: s.s: a bhd) ............. 10.12
            LONG HANDICAP. Trojan Envoy 7-2, Flying Ziad (CAN) 7-3, Spring Forward 7-5, Dazla 7-0.

**4/1** Puff Puff, NEWTON POINT, **6/1** Prince Mercury, **8/1** Scent of Battle, Beldale Star(op 5/1), **9/1** Dutyful, **10/1** Peace King(op 5/1), Spring Forward, **12/1** Flying Ziad (CAN), Trojan Envoy, **33/1** Podrida, **40/1** Dazla. CSF £27.86, CT £652.14. Tote £4.60: £1.70 £2.50 £7.10 (£10.10). Mr A. M. Ennever (NEWMARKET) bred by Stetchworth Park Stud Ltd. 12 Rn                                        3m 40.7 (8.2)

T/Plpt: £1,900.90 (1.3 Tckts).                                               AK

---

1899—**LEICESTER (R-H)**

**Tuesday, July 14th [Good]**

Going Allowance: 0.10 sec per fur (G)                                  Wind: nil

Stalls: centre

**2084**      BLABY (S) STKS (3-Y.O) £1557.00 (£432.00: £207.00)   **1m 8y**   6-30 (6-32)

1849⁵ **Legend Dulac (IRE) (46)** *(JLHarris)* 8-11 PRobinson (11) (led tl hdd 3f out: led
            2f out: rdn clr fnl f) ......................................... —1
 738 Sure Shot Norman **(54)** *(JSutcliffe)* 8-11 TQuinn (14) (a.p: led 3f out: sn hdd:
            rdn & one pce fnl f) .......................................... 3¹/₂.2
1705⁴ By Arrangement (IRE) **(55)** (Fav) *(RGuest)* 8-6 DaleGibson (5) (bhd & outpcd tl
            r.o u.p appr fnl f) ........................................... hd.3
1907 Dick Whittington **(51)** *(CTinkler)* 8-11 MTebbutt (4) (hdwy over 2f out: kpt on ins
            fnl f: nvr nrr) ................................................ nk.4
1907⁴ Meltonby **(52)** *(NTinkler)* 8-11 LDettori (13) (hdwy over 3f out: rdn & no ex fnl f) 1¹/₂.5
1070 Any Dream Would Do *(CWThornton)* 8-6 DMcKeown (1) (b.hind: lw: nvr plcd to
            chal) ........................................................ ¹/₂.6
1404 On the Rampage **(49)** *(PMitchell)* 8-3 ‡³SO'Gorman (9) (nvr nr ldrs) ........... hd.7
1772 Freephone (CAN) **(51)** *(JWHills)* 8-11 SWhitworth (8) (lw: chsd ldrs tl wknd
            qckly wl over 1f out) ......................................... 8.8
1323 Arighi Boy *(JEBanks)* 8-11 JQuinn (3) (bit bkwd: a bhd) .................. 1¹/₂.9
1795 Kertale (IRE) **(54)** *(RBoss)* 8-11 JCarroll (2) (chsd ldrs 5f) ............. 2¹/₂.10
1918 Double Lark **(53)** *(RHollinshead)* 8-4 ‡⁷AGarth (15) (prom over 5f) .......... 1¹/₂.11
1145 Cheren Boy *(BForsey)* 8-11 NHowe (12) (prom tl wknd qckly over 2f out: t.o) 12.12
      Jody's Gamble *(KRBurke)* 8-11 JFortune (6) (w'like: leggy: bit bkwd: p.u after
            2f: lame) ..................................................... 0

**7/2** By Arrangement (IRE), **5/1** Kertale (IRE), **6/1** Freephone (CAN)(op 7/2), **7/1** Any Dream Would Do, Meltonby, **9/1** Sure Shot Norman, **10/1** LEGEND DULAC (IRE)(12/1—8/1), **16/1** Double Lark, **25/1** Jody's Gamble, **33/1** Arighi Boy, **50/1** Ors. CSF £84.95, Tote £17.00: £3.80 £2.10 £1.70 (£79.50). Mr B. McAllister (MELTON MOWBRAY) bred by Chippenham Lodge Stud in Ireland. 13 Rn; No bid        1m 40.9 (5.9)
SF—20/9/3/7/2/–

## 2085

RADIO LEICESTER NURSERY £2022.50 (£560.00: £267.50) **5f 2y** 7-00 (7-02)
(Weights raised 13 lb)

| | | |
|---|---|---|
| 1979² | **My Bonus** (DJSCosgrove) 9-2 ‡⁵DHarrison (4) (b.hind: hld up: hdwy over 2f out: led over 1f out: r.o wl) | —1 |
| 1191⁴ | Costa Verde (KWHogg) 9-3 WRyan (2) (chsd ldrs: rdn over 1f out: kpt on ins fnl f) | ¾.2 |
| 1609⁴ | Cloudy Reef (RHollinshead) 7-12 ‡⁷AGarth (5) (a.p: led ½-wy to over 1f out: rallied u.p ins fnl f) | hd.3 |
| 439 | The Wend (DTThom) 8-1 JQuinn (7) (swtg: chsd ldrs: no hdwy fnl 2f) | 3.4 |
| 1291⁴ | Formaestre (IRE) (MHTompkins) 9-4 PRobinson (3) (led to ½-wy: sn rdn & btn) | 1.5 |
| 1851⁴ | Sure Risk (Fav) (RHannon) 8-0 MRoberts (1) (spd to ½-wy: rdn & hung rt over 1f out: sn btn) | 3.6 |
| 1838* | Our Mica (bl) (JBerry) 8-7 JCarroll (6) (sn prom: rdn along ½-wy: grad wknd) | 1½.7 |

**9/4** Sure Risk, 3/1 MY BONUS, 11/2 Formaestre (IRE), Costa Verde, Our Mica(4/1—6/1), 12/1 Cloudy Reef(op 7/1), 33/1 The Wend. CSF £17.86, Tote £3.40: £1.80 £2.20 (£8.30). Crazy Horse Bloodstock (NEWMARKET) bred by Edmond and Richard Kent. 7 Rn
61.9 sec (3.2)
SF—48/46/26/17/30/–

## 2086

UPPINGHAM H'CAP (0-80) £2553.00 (£708.00: £339.00) **1m 3f 183y** 7-30 (7-40)

| | | |
|---|---|---|
| 1274⁴ | **Kinoko** (40) (KWHogg) 4-7-3 ‡⁷AGarth (2) (hld up & bhd: hdwy 3f out: led appr fnl f: r.o wl) | —1 |
| 1611² | Western Dynasty (68) (MJRyan) 6-9-10 LDettori (8) (a.p: 2nd st: ev ch 2f out: rallied ins fnl f) | 1½.2 |
| 1740⁵ | Shadow Bird (52) (GAPritchard-Gordon) 5-8-8 WRSwinburn (5) (hld up: 6th st: gd hdwy to ld over 2f out: hdd jst ins fnl f: one pce) | ¾.3 |
| 766 | Mysterious Maid (USA) (56) (JPearce) 5-8-7 ‡⁵RPrice (6) (bit bkwd: hld up: hdwy 3f out: styd on strly ins fnl f) | nk.4 |
| 1691⁵ | Tanoda (48) (MBrittain) 6-8-4 PRobinson (4) (hld up & bhd: hdwy over 2f out: nvr nr to chal) | 3.5 |
| 1864³ | Athene Noctua (40) (BAMcMahon) 7-7-3⁽³⁾ ‡⁷CHawksley (1) (prom: 3rd st: rdn & wknd over 2f out) | 8.6 |
| 1881² | Quadrireme (75) (MajorWRHern) 3-9-4 AClark (7) (led tl hdd & wknd over 2f out) | ½.7 |
| 1799 | Barkston Singer (52) (JLHarris) 5-8-3 ‡⁵JWeaver (9) (chsd ldrs: 4th st: wknd over 3f out) | 3.8 |
| 1901⁴ | Be My Habitat (63) (NAGraham) 3-8-6 RCochrane (3) (chsd ldrs: 5th st: wkng st: t.o fnl 2f) | 30.9 |

LONG HANDICAP: Athene Noctua 7-1.

**2/1** Western Dynasty(5/2—3/1), 4/1 Quadrireme(3/1—5/1), 5/1 Shadow Bird, 9/1 Tanoda, 10/1 Be My Habitat(op 6/1), Mysterious Maid (USA)(op 6/1), 12/1 Athene Noctua, 20/1 KINOKO, 25/1 Barkston Singer. CSF £56.29, CT £217.40. Tote £14.90: £2.40 £1.50 £1.70 (£58.10). Mr Anthony White (ISLE OF MAN) bred by Auldyn Stud Ltd. 9 Rn
2m 35.8 (7)
SF—17/49/31/29/20/–

## 2087

APPLEBY CLAIMING STKS £1702.00 (£472.00: £226.00)
**1m 3f 183y** 8-00 (8-06)

| | | |
|---|---|---|
| 1971* | **Bighayir** (65) (bl) (MCPipe) 5-9-10 MRoberts (7) (hld up: hdwy 3f out: sn hrd rdn: led ins fnl f: cleverly) | —1 |
| 1976* | Silver Samurai (60) (RHollinshead) 3-8-7 WRyan (10) (s.s: hld up & bhd: gd hdwy over 3f out: r.o wl nr fin) | hd.2 |
| 1565* | Handy Lass (JWharton) 3-8-1 JQuinn (4) (a.p: 3rd st: led 3f out tl ins fnl f: sn btn) | 3.3 |
| 1872⁴ | Moor Lodge (USA) (69) (MHTompkins) 3-8-12 PRobinson (11) (hld up: styd on fnl 2f: nvr nr) | 1½.4 |
| 1850 | Major Risk (52) (bl) (PAKelleway) 3-8-2 DHolland (3) (led 8f: rdn & wknd over 2f out) | 10.5 |
| 1640 | Himlaj (USA) (44) (SMellor) 7-9-3 DanaMellor (1) (chsd ldrs: 5th st: wknd over 2f out) | 3½.6 |
| 1872 | Lifford (USA) (MRStoute) 3-8-11 WRSwinburn (9) (lw: chsd ldrs: 4th st: ev ch over 2f out: sn rdn & wknd: eased whn btn) | 1½.7 |
| 1265⁵ | Stratford Lady (44) (bl) (JAGlover) 3-7-12 DBiggs (8) (lw: chsd ldrs: 6th st: wknd over 2f out) | 1.8 |
| | Dancer's Leap (IRE) (JEBanks) 4-8-9 ‡⁷JSwinnerton (5) (lengthy: str: bkwd: s.i.s: a bhd) | 3.9 |
| 326 | My Turn Next (30) (KWHogg) 4-8-8 ‡⁷EHusband (2) (bkwd: chsd ldr: 2nd st: led 4f out to 3f out: sn wknd) | 2.10 |
| 806 | Salmon Dancer (IRE) (34) (MFBarraclough) 3-8-5 AClark (6) (a bhd: t.o) | 20.11 |

**13/8** BIGHAYIR, **3/1** Handy Lass, **5/1** Silver Samurai, Moor Lodge (USA)(op 3/1), **12/1** Lifford (USA), **25/1** Salmon Dancer (IRE), **33/1** Major Risk, Himlaj (USA), Dancer's Leap (IRE), **50/1** Ors. CSF £10.17, Tote £2.80: £1.70 £1.30 £1.70 (£4.00). Mr A. J. Lomas (WELLINGTON) bred by Red House Stud. 11 Rn; Handy Lass clmd R Hale £7,001       2m 36.7 (7.9)
SF—43/25/13/21/–/–

## 2088

CARDINAL WOLSEY H'CAP (3-Y.O) (0-70) £2180.00 (£605.00: £290.00)
**7f 9y**                                    8-30 (8-34)

| | |
|---|---|
| 1905³ | **Roca Murada (IRE) (44)** (Fav) *(MJRyan)* 7-9 DBiggs (6) (hld up: jnd ldr 2f out: led ins fnl f: r.o) ............ —1 |
| 1636⁵ | Sovereign Rock (IRE) **(70)** *(RHannon)* 9-7 LDettori (9) (a.p: led 2f out tl wl ins fnl f) ............ ¹/₂.2 |
| 1589⁴ | Spanish Express **(46)** *(RBoss)* 7-6 ‡⁵NKennedy (5) (lw: chsd ldrs: rdn over 1f out: r.o one pce) ............ 3¹/₂.3 |
| 1663² | Gold Belt (IRE) **(53)** *(RHollinshead)* 8-4 WRyan (11) (s.i.s: bhd: hdwy over 2f out: kpt on ins fnl f: nvr nrr) ............ 3¹/₂.4 |
| 1581³ | Venture Fourth **(52)** *(EJAlston)* 8-3 KFallon (1) (hld up: hdwy ¹/₂-wy: wknd over 1f out) ............ 2¹/₂.5 |
| 1761⁶ | Sea Prodigy **(56)** *(MBlanshard)* 8-7⁽³⁾ RCochrane (10) (chsd ldrs: effrt u.p 2f out: no imp) ............ 2¹/₂.6 |
| 1581² | Honey Heather (IRE) **(59)** *(CFWall)* 8-10 WRSwinburn (2) (lw: chsd ldr over 4f: wknd over 1f out) ............ ³/₄.7 |
| 1919⁵ | Galley Gossip **(56)** *(RBrotherton)* 8-7 JWilliams (7) (a in rr) ............ 1¹/₂.8 |
| 2006★ | Tadora (IRE) **(54)** *(CJBenstead)* 8-5 (6x) TyroneWilliams (8) (prom tl wknd over 2f out) ............ 4.9 |
| 1903⁶ | Royal Print (IRE) **(48)** (bl) *(WRMuir)* 7-13 JQuinn (4) (lw: led 5f: sn wknd) ..... 2¹/₂.10 |

**5/2** ROCA MURADA (IRE), **5/1** Honey Heather (IRE), **10/1** Spanish Express, **7/1** Tadora (IRE), **8/1** Gold Belt (IRE)(op 5/1), Sovereign Rock (IRE), **12/1** Venture Fourth(op 8/1), **16/1** Sea Prodigy, **20/1** Royal Print (IRE), **50/1** Galley Gossip. CSF £20.43, CT £103.51. Tote 3.80: £1.70 £2.50 £1.80 (£14.70). Mr Tim Corby (NEWMARKET) bred by John Houghton in Ireland. 10 Rn      1m 26.2 (3.9)
SF—33/57/17/18/9/5

## 2089

GLEBE STKS (Mdn 3-Y.O) £1646.00 (£456.00: £218.00)    **1m 3f 183y**     9-00 (9-01)

| | |
|---|---|
| 1758³ | **Free Mover (IRE)** *(NAGraham)* 9-0 MRoberts (6) (lw: a.p: 3rd st: led over 1f out: qcknd fnl f: comf) ............ —1 |
| 1577 | Blue Flag (USA) *(LordHuntingdon)* 9-0 LDettori (3) (lw: s.s: bhd: 6th st: gd hdwy over 2f out: r.o ins fnl f) ............ 2.2 |
| 1722² | Receptionist *(HRACecil)* 8-9 WRyan (7) (chsd 3f: 4th st: hrd rdn 2f out: kpt on) ... ¹/₂.3 |
| 1720³ | Dawn Flight *(LadyHerries)* 9-0 JWilliams (4) (lw: chsd ldrs: 5th st: ev ch fr 3f out: unable qckn fnl f) ............ nk.4 |
| *1850* | Speedo Movement **(60)** *(BAMcMahon)* 8-2 ‡⁷SSanders (1) (s.s: 7th st: effrt 3f out: styd on fr over 1f out: nvr able to chal) ............ 2.5 |
| 1319⁵ | Amoruccio (USA) (Fav) *(GHarwood)* 9-0 RCochrane (2) (lw: led after 3f: rdn over 2f out: hdd over 1f out: sn btn) ............ ³/₄.6 |
| 1341 | Borram (IRE) **(50)** *(DNicholson)* 9-0 AClark (5) (chsd ldrs: 2nd st: wknd over 3f out: t.o) ............ 30.7 |

**15/8** Amoruccio (USA)(op Evens), **5/2** FREE MOVER (IRE)(9/4—7/2), **4/1** Blue Flag (USA)(11/4—9/2), **7/1** Receptionist, **8/1** Dawn Flight, **50/1** Speedo Movement, **66/1** Borram (IRE). CSF £11.71, Tote £3.90: £1.90 £2.40 £2.40 (£8.90). Chesa Racing (NEWMARKET) bred by Lord Rotherwick in Ireland. 7 Rn     2m 39.3 (10.5)
SF—7/3/–/1/–/–

T/Plpt: £59.00 (38.55 Tckts).               IM

## 739a—MAISONS-LAFFITTE (L-H)
### Tuesday, July 7th [Heavy]
Going Allowance: 0.50 sec per fur (Y)

## 2090a

PRIX MESSIDOR (Gp 3)    £20640.00    **1m**

| | |
|---|---|
| 1493a★ | **Take Risks (FR)** *(France)* 3–8-11 MBoutin ............ —1 |
| 1231a | Metal Storm (FR) *(France)* 4–9-2 TJarnet ............ nk.2 |
| 1816a⁶ | CRYSTAL PATH (FR) *(MMoubarak)* 4–8-13 DHolland ............ nose.3 |

Tote 6.90f: 2.00f 2.10f 4.10f (18.70f). Mr D.Tsui (J.Lesbordes,FRANCE) bred by Haras de Manneville in France. 8 Rn      1m 41 (5.7)
SF—73/76/72

1983a—**EVRY (R-H)**

**Thursday, July 9th [Good to soft]**

Going Allowance: nil sec per fur (G)

### 2091a

PRIX CHLOE (Gp 3) (3-Y.O.F) £20640.00    **1m 1f**

|  | **Formidable Flight** (bl) *(France)* 3–8–9 ELegrix .................................................... | —1 |
| 1217⁴ | SARATOGA SOURCE (USA) *(IABalding)* 3–8–9 CBlack .......................................... | 1.2 |
|  | Faribole (IRE) *(France)* 3–8–9 OBenoist ......................................................... | s.nk.3 |

Tote 2.90f: 1.50f 2.90f 3.80f (22.70f). Ecurie I.M.Fares (P.Bary,FRANCE) bred by Fares Stables Ltd. 10 Rn
1m 52.5 (2.2)
SF—62/59/58

1495a—**TIPPERARY (L-H)**

**Thursday, July 9th [Good]**

### 2092a

COOLMORE DANEHILL TIPPERARY SPRINT (listed race)    £8063.00    **5f**

| 1475⁶ | **Flowing (USA)** *(Ireland)* 4–9–7 MJKinane ...................................................... | —1 |
| 1467 | Maledetto (IRE) *(Ireland)* 3–8–10 KJManning ................................................... | 3.2 |
| 1495a⁵ | Bradawn Breever (IRE) (bl) *(Ireland)* 3–9–8 RJGriffiths ................................... | hd.3 |

Tote £1.60: £1.10 £1.40 £1.20 (£3.80). Mrs J.Maxwell Moran (D.K.Weld,IRELAND) bred by Tommy Stack in USA. 8 Rn
57.2 sec

1816a—**CURRAGH (R-H)**

**Saturday, July 11th [Good to soft]**

Going Allowance: nil sec per fur (G)

### 2093a

SHERNAZAR E.B.F. CURRAGH STKS (Gp 3) (2-Y.O) £13435.00    **5f**

| 1818a³ | **Tropical** (Fav) *(Ireland)* 2–8–7 MJKinane (cl up: led over 1f out: rdn clr & wandered fnl f) ..................................................... | —1 |
|  | Bint Albadou (IRE) *(Ireland)* 2–8–7 CRoche (s.i.s: outpcd & wl bhd ½-wy: r.o wl fr over 1f out) .................................................... | 2½.2 |
| 1818a² | Shahik (USA) *(Ireland)* 2–8–10 RJGriffiths (chsd ldrs: kpt on wl fnl f: no imp) ..... | hd.3 |
|  | Pinch The Devil (IRE) *(Ireland)* 2–8–10 RHughes (led tl hdd over 1f out: no ex) | 1½.4 |
| 1472★ | SATANK (USA) *(JWWatts)* 2–8–10 GDuffield (chsd ldr to ½-wy: rdn over 1f out: sn btn) .................................................................. | 2.5 |
|  | Gate Lodge (IRE) *(Ireland)* 2–8–7 WJO'Connor (bhd tl sme hdwy over 1f out: nvr able to chal) ............................................... | hd.6 |
|  | L'Ecrivain (IRE) *(Ireland)* 2–8–7 SCraine (spd 3f: sn btn) .................................. | ½.7 |
| 952a³ | Hideout (USA) *(Ireland)* 2–8–8⁽¹⁾ JPMurtagh (prom to ½-wy: sn wknd) ............... | 7.8 |

9/4 TROPICAL, 7/2 Satank (USA), Shahik (USA), **9/2** Gate Lodge (IRE), **9/1** Bint Albadou (IRE), **14/1** Hideout (USA), **25/1** L'Ecrivain (IRE), **33/1** Pinch The Devil (IRE). Tote £2.60: £1.30 £2.50 £1.40 (£14.00). The Sussex Stud Ltd. (D.K.Weld,IRELAND) bred by The Sussex Stud Ltd. 8 Rn
60.8 sec (2.3)
SF—47/37/39/33/25/16

### 2094a

KILDANGAN STUD IRISH OAKS (Gp 1) (3-Y.O.F) £113084.00    **1½m**

| 1217★ | **USER FRIENDLY** (Fav) *(CEBrittain)* 3–9–0 GDuffield (a.p: led appr st: styd on wl u.p) ................................................................. | —1 |
| 1816a★ | Market Booster (USA) *(Ireland)* 3–9–0 MJKinane (in tch: chsd wnr over 2f out: ev ch over 1f out: kpt on: no ex nr fin) ................................ | nk.2 |
| 1821a★ | Arrikala (IRE) *(Ireland)* 3–9–0 KJManning (bhd tl hdwy on ins 3f out: nt clr run fr over 1f out: snatched up ins fnl f: r.o) ........................ | ½.3 |
| 1347⁴ | BINEYAH (IRE) *(MRStoute)* 3–9–0 WRSwinburn (mid div: styd on one pce fnl 2f) | 2½.4 |
| 1816a³ | Khanata (USA) *(Ireland)* 3–9–0 JPMurtagh (mid div: sme hdwy over 2f out: sn rdn & btn) ..................................................... | 10.5 |
| 1843² | ARMARAMA *(CEBrittain)* 3–9–0 PRobinson (chsd ldr tl lost pl over 3f out: btn st) | 4½.6 |
|  | Ebony and Ivory (IRE) *(Ireland)* 3–9–0 RJGriffiths (n.d) ................................... | 1½.7 |
| 1356a | Paix Blanche (FR) *(France)* 3–9–0 DBoeuf (prom 2f: bhd & btn appr st) ............. | 7.8 |
| 1101a★ | Ivyanna (IRE) (bl) *(France)* 3–9–0 CRoche (led tl hdd appr st: wknd qckly) ........ | 5.9 |

8/11 USER FRIENDLY, 9/2 Market Booster (USA), **11/2** Ivyanna (IRE), **10/1** Khanata (USA), **14/1** Armarama, **25/1** Bineyah (IRE), Paix Blanche (FR), Arrikala (IRE), **100/1** Ebony and Ivory (IRE). Tote £1.50: £1.20 £1.90 £6.20 (£3.60). Mr W.J.Gredley (NEWMARKET) bred by Stetchworth Park Stud Ltd. 9 Rn
2m 33.7 (3.4)
SF—66/65/64/59/39/30

## 1982a—LONGCHAMP (R-H)
### Sunday, July 12th [Soft]
Going Allowance: 0.35 sec per fur (Y)

**2095a**          LA COUPE (Gp 3)    £20640.00    1¼m 110y (Grande)

| | | |
|---|---|---|
| 1066² | **Wiorno** *(France)* 4-9-2 TJarnet | —1 |
| 1473⁴ | Runyon (IRE) *(Ireland)* 4-8-11 CAsmussen | ½.2 |
| 955⁴ | Deja (USA) *(France)* 4-8-11 ODoleuze (fin 4th, 2½l: plcd 3rd) | 3 |
| 1221a² | Glity (USA) *(France)* 4-8-11 ELegrix (fin 3rd, 5l: disq: plcd 4th) | 4 |
| 1613² | FAIR AVERAGE *(HCandy)* 4-8-7 WNewnes | 2.5 |

*Stewards Enquiry: Glity (USA) disq. (interference to Deja (USA) ins fnl f).*
Tote 2.70f: 1.70f 2.60f (SF: 9.50f). Mrs A.Plesch (A.Fabre,FRANCE) bred by Mayday Investments Ltd. 7 Rn          2m 15.2 (5.6)
SF—83/77/62/67/54

**2096a**          PRIX HUBERT DE CHAUDENAY (Gp 2) (3-Y.O) £30960.00          1m 7f (Moyenne)

| | | |
|---|---|---|
| 1356a | **Dajraan (IRE)** (Jt-Fav) *(France)* 3-8-8 TJarnet (trckd ldr: 4th st: hdwy 2f out: led ins fnl f: r.o wl: all out) | —1 |
| 1815a² | In-Quarto (bl) *(France)* 3-8-11 DBoeuf (mid div: 3rd st: hdwy to ld wl over 1f out: hdd ins fnl f: kpt on wl) | ½.2 |
| 1815a★ | Djais (FR) *(France)* 3-8-11 CBlack (cl up: 2nd st: ev ch over 1f out: r.o wl ins fnl f) | s.h.3 |
| 1815a³ | Hot Favourite (FR) *(France)* 3-8-8 CAsmussen (led tl hdwy wl over 1f out: kpt on one pce) | ¾.4 |
| | Montello (bl) *(France)* 3-8-11 FHead (6th st: hdwy over 2f out: sn one pce) | 1½.5 |
| 1819a | LANDOWNER (IRE) (Jt-Fav) *(JHMGosden)* 3-8-11 RCochrane (mid div: 5th st: effrt over 2f out: nvr able to chal) | nk.6 |
| 1647a★ | Rubico (USA) (bl) *(Germany)* 3-9-2 OSchick (a in rr: ti.U) | 3 7 |
| | Crisol *(Germany)* 3-8-6 ALequeux (last st: n.d) | 1½.8 |

**8/10** Landowner (IRE), DAJRAAN (IRE), **13/4** In-Quarto, **21/4** Hot Favourite (FR), **6/1** Montello, **13/2** Rubico (USA), **9/1** Djais (FR), **24/1** Crisol. Tote 1.80f: 1.20f 1.30f 1.40f (7.70f). Sheikh Mohammed (A.Fabre,FRANCE) bred by Stackallen Stud in Ireland. 8 Rn          3m 20.6 (8.6)
SF—61/63/62/58/59/58/60


## HOPPEGARTEN (R-H) Germany
### Sunday, July 12th [Good]

**2097a**          BERLIN-BRANDENBURG TROPHY DER LANDESBANK BERLIN (Gp 3) £77465.00
1m

| | | |
|---|---|---|
| 1100a² | **Irish Stew (GER)** (bl) *(Germany)* 4-9-7 AStarke | —1 |
| 1817a | FLYING BRAVE (bl) *(JLDunlop)* 4-9-7 JReid | ½.2 |
| 1645a² | ENHARMONIC (USA) *(LordHuntingdon)* 5-9-7 WRyan | 3.3 |

Tote 80DM: 27DM 37DM (SF: 598DM). Gestut Smienderhan (H.Blume,GERMANY) bred by Gestut Schlenderhan in Germany. 6 Rn          1m 36.6


## 2038—SOUTHWELL (L-H) Fibresand
### Wednesday, July 15th [Standard]
Going Allowance: minus 0.25 sec per fur (FS)                    Wind: almost nil

Stalls: low

**2098**          MAYFAIR (S) STKS (2-Y.O) £2385.00 (£660.00: £315.00)          6f (AWT)     2-15 (2-16)

| | | |
|---|---|---|
| 1782³ | **Palacegate Prince** (Fav) *(JBerry)* 8-11 JCarroll (8) (lw: led after 2f: rdn over 1f out: drew clr fnl f) | —1 |
| 1526 | Private Liner *(RonaldThompson)* 8-11 JLowe (1 i) (a.p: ev ch appr fnl f: rdn & hng lft: one pce) | 5.2 |
| 1851 | Sounds Risky (bl) *(GMMoore)* 8-6 WNewnes (6) (led 2f: rdn 2f out: kpt on ins fnl f) | 1½.3 |
| 1804⁵ | Summers Dream *(BRichmond)* 8-6 KFallon (9) (hdwy ½-wy: kpt on one pce fnl 2f) | nk.4 |
| 1959⁵ | Morning News (IRE) *(MHTompkins)* 8-4 ‡⁷MGodsafe (1) (sme hdwy fnl 2f: nvr nrr) | ¾.5 |
| 1900 | Grey Runner *(BPalling)* 8-6 AMunro (10) (mid div: effrt u.p over 2f out: no imp) | 6.6 |
| | Jasilu *(MWEasterby)* 8-8⁽²⁾ CDwyer (4) (wl grwn: bkwd: s.s: a bhd) | 2½.7 |

1860 Knayton Lodger (bl) *(MWEasterby)* 8-6 TLucas (7) (hmpd sn after s: hdwy
½-wy: rdn & btn wl over 1f out) .................... ¾.8
Bold Treasure (IRE) *(MrsNMacauley)* 9-6 NDay (2) (w'like: leggy: bkwd: a bhd) 4.9
1670 Hajaan *(BBeasley)* 8-6 PBurke (5) (spd 4f) .................... hd.10
1554 Clare's Boy *(JMBradley)* 8-11 NAdams (3) (chsd ldrs to ½-wy: rdn & rn v.green:
sn bhd & t.o) .................... 10.11

**5/2** PALACEGATE PRINCE(7/2—9/4), **4/1** Morning News (IRE)(11/4—9/2), **8/1** Grey Runner, **10/1** Bold
Treasure (IRE)(op 5/1), **12/1** Private Liner, Summers Dream, Sounds Risky, Jasilu(op 5/1), **25/1** Knayton
Lodger, Hajaan, **33/1** Clare's Boy. CSF £27.39, Tote £2.70: £1.30 £3.10 £4.20 (£18.20). Palacegate
Corporation Ltd (COCKERHAM) bred by D. B. Lamplough. 11 Rn; Bt in 3,600 gns
1m 16.3 (2.9)
SF—9/–/–/–/–

---

## 2099

BATTERSEA H'CAP (0-80) £2364.00 (£654.00: £312.00)    **6f (AWT)**    2-45 (2-46)
(Weights raised 3 lb)

2040 **Swinging Lady (55)** *(WWHaigh)* 4-8-6 ‡³FNorton (1) (b.hind: mde all: clr over
1f out: r.o) .................... —1
2040⁵ Jovial Kate (USA) **(55)** *(BEllison)* 5-8-9 AMunro (2) (swtg: chsd ldrs: rdn along
½-wy: styd on ins fnl f) .................... 2½.2
2040⁴ Fighter Squadron **(56)** (v) *(JAGlover)* 3-8-3 JFortune (6) (lw: a.p: rdn over 1f
out: one pce) .................... nk.3
1870 Tate Dancer (IRE) **(77)** (Fav) *(RWArmstrong)* 3-9-10 MRoberts (9) (swtg: prom:
hrd rdn 2f out: one pce) .................... 1.4
1550³ Wellsy Lad (USA) **(61)** *(DWChapman)* 5-9-1 SWood (3) (prom tl rdn & wknd
appr fnl f) .................... 1½.5
1847 Hubbers Favourite **(50)** *(MrsNMacauley)* 4-8-4⁽²⁾ NDay (4) (lw: nvr nr to chal) .. 2.6
1978⁴ Gleneliane (IRE) **(39)** *(JLHarris)* 4-7-8 JQuinn (7) (nvr nr ldrs) .................... hd.7
1920 Palacegate Racing **(75)** *(JBerry)* 3-9-8 JCarroll (10) (b.nr hind: chsd ldrs: rdn
over 2f out: sn btn) .................... 1½.8
1903 Lord Naskra (USA) **(71)** *(WAO'Gorman)* 3–9–1 ‡³EmmaO'Gorman (5) (s.i.s: a bhd) 4.9
2040* One Magic Moment (IRE) **(44)** *(CACyzer)* 4-7-12 (7x) DBiggs (8) (prom tl hrd
drvn & wknd 2f out) .................... 2.10
LONG HANDICAP: Gleneliane (IRE) 7-2.

**4/1** Tate Dancer (IRE), **9/2** Fighter Squadron(op 3/1), **5/1** One Magic Moment (IRE), **9/1** Wellsy Lad (USA),
Palacegate Racing(op 5/1), Gleneliane (IRE)(op 6/1), **11/1** SWINGING LADY(16/1—10/1), **12/1** Jovial Kate
(USA), **16/1** Hubbers Favourite(op 10/1), **20/1** Lord Naskra (USA)(op 8/1). CSF £112.05, CT £602.39. Tote
£11.30: £3.10 £2.80 £1.10 (£29.90). Mrs P. A. Valentine (MALTON) bred by Brian Mills. 10 Rn  1m 14.8 (1.4)
SF—34/27/20/37/22/3

---

## 2100

CHELSEA CLAIMING STKS (3-Y.O) £2343.00 (£648.00: £309.00)
**1½m (AWT)**    3-15 (3-16)

1604³ **Thunderbird One (USA)** *(CRNelson)* 9-0 NAdams (6) (lw: hld up, hdwy & 3rd
st: led 2f out: rdn out) .................... —1
1850² Firefighter **(64)** (Fav) *(RHollinshead)* 9-6 WRyan (3) (hld up: hdwy 5f out: 4th st:
hrd rdn appr fnl f: r.o) .................... nk.2
1679⁵ Millador **(47)** *(MHTompkins)* 8-3 ‡⁷MGodsafe (9) (a.p: 2nd st: ev ch 2f out: wknd
fnl f) .................... 10.3
1276 Tanana **(50)** *(JGFitzGerald)* 8-8 KFallon (2) (led to 2f out: sn rdn & wknd) ...... 2½.4
Ste-Jen (IRE) *(GMMoore)* 9-3 WNewnes (4) (w'like: bkwd: s.i.s: bhd: hdwy ent
st: nt rch ldrs) .................... 5.5
1719* Winter Lightning **(51)** *(DJWintle)* 8-11 MRoberts (7) (chsd ldrs: lost pl 7f out:
effrt & 5th st: sn rdn & btn) .................... 3.6
1294 Dots Dee **(33)** *(JMBradley)* 8-2 AMunro (4) (chsd ldrs 8f: sn lost tch: t.o) .................... 7.7
2057 Sea Lord **(36)** *(KWHogg)* 8-6 ‡⁷AGarth (1) (prom tl 6th & wkng st: t.o) .................... 15.8
1705 Evening Stables *(JWharton)* 8-6 JQuinn (8) (lw: a in rr: t.o) .................... 20.9

**Evens** Firefighter, **9/2** Winter Lightning, **7/1** THUNDERBIRD ONE (USA)(op 9/2), **11/1** Millador, **12/1** Ste-Jen
(IRE), **16/1** Dots Dee, Tanana, **33/1** Ors. CSF £13.61, Tote £6.50: £2.20 £1.10 £2.40 (£4.90). Mr C. R. Nelson
(UPPER LAMBOURN) bred by Winborne Farm Incorporated in USA. 9 Rn; Thunderbird One (USA) clmd P Darling
£7,757
2m 39.7 (5.5)
SF—15/20/–/–/–/–

---

## 2101

ARMCHAIR CLUB H'CAP (0-70) £2448.00 (£678.00: £324.00)
**1½m (AWT)**    3-45 (3-46)

1324² **Mizyan (IRE) (62)** *(JEBanks)* 4-9-6 NDay (2) (lw: a.p: 2nd st: chal over 1f out:
rdn to ld wl ins fnl f) .................... —1
1894⁴ Cheeky Pot **(43)** (v) *(DenysSmith)* 4-8-1 JLowe (12) (lw: led: hrd rdn 2f out: hdd
wl ins fnl f) .................... 2.2

1747 Swell Time (IRE) **(37)** *(CNAllen)* 4–7–6[(2)] ‡3FNorton (13) (b.hind: bhd: styd on fnl 2f: nrst fin) ............................................................................................................. 4.3

20275 Springs Welcome **(69)** *(CACyzer)* 6–9–13 AMunro (9) (s.i.s: hld up & bhd: hdwy 4f out: styd on one pce) ................................................................................ 1½.4

2086★ Kinoko **(45)** *(KWHogg)* 4–7–10 (5x) ‡7AGarth (8) (hld up & bhd: gd hdwy & 5th st: rdn & wknd fnl f) ................................................................................. hd.5

1390 Pleasure Ahead **(48)** *(MDixon)* 5–8–6 DaleGibson (10) (bhd: effrt & 7th st: nt trble ldrs) ............................................................................................................. 6.6

18476 Armashocker **(41)** *(DSasse)* 4–7–13 DBiggs (5) (nvr plcd to chal) ....................... 5.7

17842 Lord Advocate **(44)** (v) (Fav) *(MPNaughton)* 4–8–2 MRoberts (1) (rdn & lost pl ½-wy: 6th & btn st) .................................................................................. 2.8

The Liquidiser **(52)** *(RHollinshead)* 5–8–10 WRyan (11) (swtg: bkwd: hdwy ½-wy: 4th st: wknd over 2f out) ....................................... nk.9

19224 Queens Tour **(35)** *(MBrittain)* 7–7–7 JQuinn (3) (chsd ldrs 6f: sn lost tch) ......... 2.10

1971 Muzo (USA) **(43)** (v) *(JMBradley)* 5–8–1 NAdams (7) (chsd ldrs: 3rd & rdn st: sn lost pl) ...................................................................................... 1½.11

1419 Kanooz (IRE) **(37)** (bl) *(SMellor)* 4–7–9 DanaMellor (6) (effrt ½-wy: sn rdn & wknd) ........................................................................................... 1.12

Anderson Rose **(35)** *(DJWintle)* 4–7–7 RStreet (4) (b: a bhd) ....................... nk.13

LONG HANDICAP: Swell Time (IRE) 7-2, Kinoko 7-12, Queens Tour 7-6, Anderson Rose 6-13.

**11/4** Lord Advocate, **4/1** MIZYAN (IRE), **9/2** Springs Welcome, **9/1** Kinoko(op 6/1), **12/1** Cheeky Pot, **14/1** Pleasure Ahead(op 8/1), Queens Tour, **20/1** Armashocker, **25/1** Swell Time (IRE), **33/1** Muzo (USA), Kanooz (IRE), The Liquidiser, **50/1** Anderson Rose. CSF £44.67, CT £950.85. Tote £4.50: £2.20 £2.50 £3.80 (£16.20). Mr E. Carter (NEWMARKET) bred by S. Niarchos in Ireland. 13 Rn

2m 37.7 (3.5)
SF—41/18/1/33/1/–

---

**2102**     BLACKFRIARS STKS (Mdn 2-Y.O) £2427.00 (£672.00: £321.00)
       **7f (AWT)**

4-15 (4-17)

15492 **Noyan** (Fav) *(MBell)* 9-0 MHills (9) (swtg: s.i.s: sn prom: 2nd st: led 2f out: r.o wl) ................................................................................................................... —1

Soloman Springs (USA) *(SGNorton)* 9-0 JQuinn (1) (leggy: bit bkwd: bhd: hdwy & 6th st: styd on strly fnl f) ....................................................... 2½.2

Dhahran *(PFICole)* 9-0 AMunro (6) (w'like: scope: bit bkwd: a.p: 4th st: sn rdn & outpcd: styd on ins fnl f) ......................................................... 4.3

Heart Broken *(JGFitzGerald)* 8-9 KFallon (7) (cmpt: bkwd: led over 4f out to 2f out: wknd ins fnl f) .................................................................... 2.4

Manx Monarch *(RHollinshead)* 8-9 WRyan (2) (lt-f: bit bkwd: dwlt: styd on fnl 2f: nvr nrr) ................................................................................................. 4.5

18972 Prime Painter *(RFFisher)* 9-0 JLowe (5) (prom: hmpd after 2f: 5th st: wknd 2f out) ............................................................................................................... 1.6

1046 Pine Ridge Lad (IRE) *(BBeasley)* 9-0 DNicholls (8) (hdwy 4f out: 3rd st: slipped & eased wl over 1f out) ................................................ 1½.7

La Bonita (IRE) *(JBerry)* 8-9 JCarroll (3) (w'like: bkwd: led over 2f: hmpd ½-wy: sn bhd: t.o) ................................................................................... 15.8

Saga Blue *(BobJones)* 8-9 NDay (4) (dipped: lt-f: bkwd: a bhd) ....................... 15.9

**11/10** NOYAN(tchd 7/4), **3/1** Dhahran(op 6/4), **6/1** Prime Painter, **9/1** Kinoko(op 6/1), Pine Ridge Lad (IRE), **16/1** Heart Broken, **25/1** Ors. CSF £25.89, Tote £2.10: £1.30 £3.20 £1.70 (£14.20). Mr Yucel Birol (NEWMARKET) bred by Oakgrove Stud. 9 Rn

1m 29.7 (3.1)
SF—27/19/7/–/–/–

---

**2103**     BDO BINDER HAMLYN H'CAP (0-70) £2406.00 (£666.00: £318.00)
       **1m (AWT)**

4-45 (4-45)

(Weights raised 4 lb)

18472 **Hawaii Storm (FR) (58)** (Jt-Fav) *(MissAJWhitfield)* 4–9–10 NAdams (1) (hdwy ½-wy: rdn to chal & hung lft 1f out: led nr fin) ....................... —1

18474 No Decision **(47)** (bl) *(MWEasterby)* 5–8–13 TLucas (2) (led: rdn over 1f out: ct cl home) .................................................................................................... ½.2

2041★ Eriny (USA) **(72)** (Jt-Fav) *(SGNorton)* 3–9–8 (5x) ‡7OPears (4) (lw: hld up: 6th st: rdn & wknd appr fnl f) ........................................................... 5.3

1550 Lunagraphe (USA) **(33)** *(BobJones)* 4–7–13 JQuinn (5) (chsd ldrs: rdn over 3f out: 5th & btn st) ....................................................................... 7.4

17972 Times Are Hard **(42)** *(CASmith)* 8–8–8 AMunro (6) (lw: prom & rdn st: sn lost tch) 5.5

2040 State Governor **(58)** *(DWChapman)* 4–9–10 SWood (3) (lost pl 4f out: 6th & btn st: t.o) ............................................................................................................... 8.6

**5/2** Eriny (USA), HAWAII STORM (FR), **4/1** No Decision(tchd 6/1), **9/2** Times Are Hard, **11/1** Lunagraphe (USA), **14/1** State Governor. CSF £11.66, Tote £3.60: £2.20 £2.00 (£10.80). Mr Andreas Sofroniou (LAMBOURN) bred by Horse France in France. 6 Rn

1m 42.3 (3)
SF—35/23/17/–/–/–

**2104**     LEVY BOARD STKS (Mdn 3-Y.O.F) £2196.00 (£606.00: £288.00)
           **7f (AWT)**                                                                    5-15 (5-16)

1849² **Grubby (46)** (Fav) *(RHollinshead)* 8-4 ‡⁷AGarth (2) (mde all: r.o wl) ............ —1
2041 Merryhill Madam **(68)** (v) *(JLHarris)* 8-11 JCarroll (5) (chsd wnr thrght: 2nd st:
           rdn over 2f out: one pce) ...................................................... 2.2
1903 Arrogant Daughter *(JWPayne)* 8-11 AMunro (1) (lw: sn bhd & pushed along:
           5th st: rdn 2f out: kpt on ins fnl f) ........................................ 5.3
     Mummy's Brew *(BBeasley)* 8-11 PBurke (4) (leggy: lt-f: s.i.s: 4th st: rdn & btn
           appr fnl f) ................................................................. 6.4
1852⁴ Millyrous (IRE) **(54)** *(RGuest)* 8-11 WNewnes (n.d) .................................. 7.5
1681 Executive Flare (20/1) Withdrawn (inj. whn colliding w paddock rails) : not under orders

**13/8** GRUBBY(5/2—6/4), **3/1** Merryhill Madam, Millyrous (IRE), **5/1** Arrogant Daughter, **14/1** Mummy's Brew.
CSF £6.52, Tote £2.50: £1.10 £1.50 (£2.90). Mrs A. Mutch (UPPER LONGDON) bred by Mrs O. R. Mutch. 5 Rn
                                                                                         1m 31 (4.4)

T/Plpt: £19.20 (132.05 Tckts).                                                                  IM

**1794—YARMOUTH (L-H)**

## Wednesday, July 15th [Good]
Going Allowance: St: 0.20 sec; Rnd: nil sec per fur (G)                        Wind: slt against

Stalls: low

**2105**     BATCHELDER H'CAP (0-70) £2259.00 (£624.00: £297.00)     **6f 3y**     6-30 (6-37)

1964³ **Spring High (44)** (bl) *(KTIvory)* 5–8-11 GBardwell (9) (lw: mde all: rdn fnl f: jst
           hld on) ................................................................... —1
1964² Lime Street Lil **(29)** *(DAWilson)* 4–7-3⁽³⁾ ‡⁷CHawksley (7) (chsd ldrs: ev ch ins fnl
           f) ........................................................................ nk.2
1878² Yes **(55)** (Fav) *(DTThom)* 4–9-8 BRaymond (8) (hdwy over 2f out: r.o ins fnl f) 2½.3
1888⁴ Farmer Jock **(56)** *(MrsNMacauley)* 10–9-9 GKing (4) (plld hrd: chsd ldrs: rdn
           over 1f out: kpt on same pce) ............................................... hd.4
1978 Dorking Lad **(55)** *(MHTompkins)* 10–9-8 RCochrane (1) (r.o fnl 2f: nvr able to
           chal) ..................................................................... d.h.4
1803⁴ Cumbrian Cavalier **(46)** *(JRBostock)* 3–8-6⁽¹⁾ LDettori (3) (bhd: effrt 2f out: no
           imp) ..................................................................... 3½.6
1803² Indian Endeavour **(68)** *(RGuest)* 3–10-0 LPiggott (6) (w ldrs over 4f) ................ 3.7
108⁶ Savinien (IRE) **(45)** *(PJFeilden)* 3–8-5 NDay (4) (a bhd) ........................... 1½.8
1727⁴ Petitesse **(48)** *(GBlum)* 4–9-1 RFox (3) (plld hrd: gd spd over 3f) ................... 1.9
                      LONG HANDICAP: Lime Street Lil 7-6.

**7/2** Yes, **5/1** Lime Street Lil, Indian Endeavour, **7/1** SPRING HIGH, Petitesse, **8/1** Farmer Jock, **10/1** Dorking Lad,
**14/1** Cumbrian Cavalier, **66/1** Savinien (IRE). CSF £36.23, CT £115.84. Tote £13.00: £2.80 £1.40 £1.40
(£19.60). Mr K. T. Ivory (RADLETT) bred by Mrs P. A. Brown. 9 Rn                          1m 14.8 (4.2)
                                                                           SF—37/14/37/37/36/6

**2106**     HARRISON (S) STKS (2-Y.O) £1548.00 (£428.00: £204.00)     **7f 3y**     7-00 (7-01)

1762⁵ **Miss Fayruz (IRE)** (Fav) *(MrsLPiggott)* 8-8⁽²⁾ LPiggott (3) (lw: set steady pce:
           qcknd 2f out: cleverly) .................................................... —1
1675 Lofty Deed (USA) *(SirMarkPrescott)* 8-11 MRoberts (4) (lw: trckd ldrs: ev ch fnl
           f: unable qckn nr fin) ..................................................... ½.2
     April Double (IRE) *(MHTompkins)* 8-6 PRobinson (1) (leggy: trckd wnr: outpcd
           2f out: r.o again ins fnl f) ............................................... 2½.3
1554⁵ Miss Fitness *(DrJDScargill)* 8-6 LDettori (2) (stdd s: hdwy 2f out: ev ch over 1f
           out: wknd fnl f) .......................................................... 1.4
1887 Legal Dancer *(RJRWilliams)* 8-11 RCochrane (5) (hld up: rdn 2f out: a bhd) .... nk.5

**5/4** MISS FAYRUZ (IRE), **9/4** April Double (IRE)(4/1—2/1), **11/2** Legal Dancer(7/2—6/1), **11/1** Ors. CSF
£11.52, Tote £2.00: £1.10 £2.20 (£4.40). Mr K. Philipp (NEWMARKET) bred by Owen Bourke in Ireland. 5 Rn; Bt
in 3,000 gns                                                                             1m 30.6 (7.8)

**2107**     APPLEGATE H'CAP (3-Y.O.F) (0-70) £2322.00 (£642.00: £306.00)
           **1m 3y**                                                                      7-30 (7-31)
                              (Weights raised 5 lb)

1863⁴ **Waseela (IRE) (65)** (Jt-Fav) *(AAScott)* 9-7 JFortune (3) (lw: trckd ldr: rdn to ld
           2f out: r.o wl) ........................................................... —1
1761⁵ Bear With Me (IRE) **(65)** *(MBell)* 9-7 MHills (1) (lw: b.nr hind: led 6f: kpt on) .... 2½.2
1992 Hand on Heart (IRE) **(64)** *(WJHaggas)* 9-6 NDay (2) (chsd ldrs: rdn over 1f out:
           r.o) ...................................................................... ½.3
1806⁴ Millfit (USA) **(64)** *(BHanbury)* 9-6 BRaymond (5) (plld hrd: chsd ldrs: one pce fnl
           2f) ....................................................................... 1½.4

1786* La Kermesse (USA) (63) (Jt-Fav) (JHMGosden) 9-5 RCochrane (4) (plld hrd & bhd: hdwy 3f out: wknd ins fnl f) .......................................... hd.5

3/1 La Kermesse (USA), WASEELA (IRE), **7/2** Hand on Heart (IRE), **4/1** Bear With Me (IRE), **9/2** Millfit (USA). CSF £13.48, Tote £4.50: £2.20 £2.30 (£7.30). Sheikh Ahmed Al Maktoum (NEWMARKET) bred by Sheikh Ahmed bin Rashid al Maktoum in Ireland. 5 Rn
1m 41.8 (6.5)
SF—34/26/23/18/16

## 2108 RIVER BURE STKS (Mdn 2-Y.O) £2259.00 (£624.00: £297.00)  6f 3y  8-00 (8-05)

1283 **Tajdif (USA)** (DMorley) 9-0 MHills (2) (trckd ldrs: qcknd to ld over 1f out: comf) —1
Royal Flex (USA) (MrsLPiggott) 8-9 LPiggott (1) (tall: unf: sn prom: led wl over 1f out: sn hdd & no ex) .................... 4.2
1701³ Jallaaf (USA) (Fav) (LMCumani) 9-0 LDettori (4) (chsd ldrs: rdn 2f out: kpt on same pce) .................................... 3.3
1668³ Jade Runner (MrsNMacauley) 8-9 MRoberts (7) (prom: hung rt ½-wy: one pce fnl 2f) .................................... ½.4
18875 Glen Miller (JWPayne) 9-0 RCochrane (6) (led 1f: one pce fnl 2f) ................ ½.5
1932 Home Affair (DTThom) 8-9 BRaymond (5) (led after 1f tl wl over 1f out) ...... s.h.6
Ume River (IRE) (MHTompkins) 9-0 PRobinson (8) (w'like: scope: bit bkwd: s.i.s: a bhd) .................................... 8.7
1899 Side Bar (MJRyan) 9-0 MTebbutt (3) (lw: a bhd) ................................ hd.8
1571 Red Ballet (MrsNMacauley) 8-9 NDay (9) (s.s: a bhd: t.o) .................... 12.9

**4/7** Jallaaf (USA), **5/1** Jade Runner(8/1—7/2), **7/1** Royal Flex (USA)(op 7/2), **14/1** Home Affair, **20/1** Red Ballet, TAJDIF (USA)(op 8/1), **25/1** Ume River (IRE), Glen Miller, **40/1** Side Bar. CSF £139.09, Tote £22.10: £3.70 £1.70 £1.10 (£54.80). Mr Hamdan Al-Maktoum (NEWMARKET) bred by Miss Barbara Hunter in Ireland. 9 Rn
1m 14.5 (3.9)
SF—46/25/18/11/14/8

## 2109 COURTHOUSE CLAIMING STKS £2427.00 (£672.00: £321.00)  1¾m 17y  8-30 (8-31)

18725 **Drought (IRE)** (Fav) (MRStoute) 3-8-5 LDettori (2) (chsd ldrs: 3rd & sn c wd st: led over 2f out: pushed out) .................................... —1
1543 Sparkler Gebe (49) (bl) (RJO'Sullivan) 6-8-13 RCochrane (4) (in tch: 5th st: rdn & r.o appr fnl f) .................................... 3½.2
1800² Sharp Top (51) (MJRyan) 4-9-6 PRobinson (1) (lw: led tl hdd over 2f out: kpt on) .................................... 1.3
1802² Briggscare (67) (WJarvis) 6-9-11 MTebbutt (5) (b: chsd ldrs: 4th st: one pce fnl 2f) .................................... 1½.4
1976 Roger Rabbit (FR) (40) (RBoss) 8-8-0 MRoberts (3) (lw: hld up & bhd: poor 6th st: kpt on fnl 2f) .................................... 1½.5
1980³ Shanti Flyer (IRE) (47) (SPCWoods) 3-8-3 WWoods (7) (lw: chsd ldr: 2nd st: wknd over 3f out) .................................... 10.6
1404 Ugly (RPCHoad) 6-9-5 MWigham (6) (sn pushed along: in tch tl last st: sn t.o) 15.7

**7/4** DROUGHT (IRE)(op Evens), **9/4** Briggscare(3/1—7/2), **4/1** Sharp Top, **13/2** Roger Rabbit (FR), **16/1** Shanti Flyer (IRE), Sparkler Gebe, **50/1** Ugly. CSF £24.07, Tote £2.40: £1.40 £3.60 (£21.70). Mr J. M. Greetham (NEWMARKET) bred by J. M. Greetham in Ireland. 7 Rn
3m 7 (9)

## 2110 HORNING H'CAP (0-70) £2259.00 (£624.00: £133.50 each)  1¼m 21y  9-00 (9-02)

2012 **Bowden Boy (IRE) (69)** (bl) (NACallaghan) 4-10-0 MRoberts (4) (lw: plld hrd: a.p: 2nd st: led over 4f out to 2f out: rallied to ld 1f out) ....... —1
1665² Taylors Prince (63) (HJCollingridge) 5-9-1 ‡7CHawksley (7) (chsd ldrs: 4th st: led 2f out to 1f out: sn btn) .................................... 1.2
18815 Rive-Jumelle (IRE) (65) (MBell) 4-9-10 MHills (3) (lw: in tch: 5th st: kpt on fnl 2f: nt rch ldrs) .................................... 1½.3
1890 Clifton Chase (55) (MAJarvis) 3-8-3 GCrealock (5) (hld up: 6th st: r.o fnl 2f: nvr able to chal) .................................... d.h.3
19685 Marjons Boy (34) (bl) (CDBroad) 5-7-0 ‡7DWright (1) (reluctant to r: sn wl bhd: last st: c wd st: n.d) .................................... 8.5
Rashita (35) (GHEden) 5-7-8(1) GKing (6) (led tl hdd & wknd over 4f out) ........ 10.6
1799* Shining Jewel (67) (Fav) (MrsLPiggott) 5-9-12 LPiggott (2) (prom: 3rd st: ev ch 2f out: sn btn: eased fnl f) .................................... hd.7
LONG HANDICAP: Marjons Boy 7-0, Rashita 6-12.

**9/4** Shining Jewel(3/1—2/1), **100/30** Rive-Jumelle (IRE), **4/1** Taylors Prince, **9/2** BOWDEN BOY (IRE)(3/1—5/1), **15/2** Clifton Chase, **12/1** Marjons Boy, **50/1** Rashita. CSF £21.02, Tote £5.60: 3.00 £2.10 (£11.50). Mr T. A. Foreman (NEWMARKET) bred by Lord Dundas in Ireland. 7 Rn
2m 10.8 (6.4)
SF—50/42/41/20/–/–

T/Plpt: £72.70 (22.3 Tckts).
Dk

1781—**CATTERICK (L-H)**
**Wednesday, July 15th [Good]**
Going Allowance: minus 0.30 sec per fur (F)

Wind: almost nil

Stalls: low

**2111**     'A' ONE APP'CE CLAIMING STKS     £2259.00 (£624.00: £297.00)
**1m 5f 175y**                                                              2-30 (2-31)

1784* **Grouse-N-Heather (60)** (Fav) (MrsGRReveley) 3–8-2 JFanning (1) (lw: trckd
    ldrs: effrt ent st: led 1f out: comf) ............................................ —1
1893* Mystery Lad (IRE) **(53)** (bl) (NACallaghan) 3–7-13 ‡3JTate (3) (b: lw: led: qcknd
    clr 4f out: hdd 1f out: no ch w wnr) ................................. 2.2
1520⁴ Be the Best **(40)** (MPNaughton) 4–8-13 JWeaver (5) (a chsng ldrs: wnt 2nd 7f
    out: outpcd 4f out: no imp after) ..................................... 10.3
1580 Media Star **(25)** (TKersey) 7–8-12 ‡3MHarris (2) (outpcd 5f out: n.d) ...... 1½.4
1977 Full Sight (IRE) **(56)** (v) (MHTompkins) 3–8-3 ‡3SMulvey (4) (bhd: effrt 5f out: sn
    rdn & no imp) .......................................................... 1½.5

**4/7** GROUSE-N-HEATHER, **5/1** Mystery Lad (IRE), **11/2** Be the Best, **9/1** Full Sight (IRE), **66/1** Media Star. CSF
£3.54, Tote £1.60: £1.10 £1.40 (£2.30). Mr Robbie Cameron (SALTBURN) bred by R. A. Cameron. 5 Rn
3m 3 (7.8)

**2112**     HUDDERSFIELD (S) STKS (2-Y.O) £2364.00 (£654.00: £312.00)     **7f**     3-00 (3-05)

1790² **Hi Nod** (Fav) (MJCamacho) 8-11 NConnorton (2) (swtg: trckd ldrs: led wl over
    1f out: rdn & r.o) ..................................................... —1
1554³ Kafioca (IRE) (MHTompkins) 8-6 PRobinson (8) (lw: a chsng ldrs: styd on u.p
    fnl 2f: nvr able to chal) ............................................... 3½.2
1848 Bay Rum (bl) (BBeasley) 8-6 LCharnock (10) (cl up: led over 2f out tl wl over 1f
    out: one pce) ......................................................... 2½.3
Mughal Princess (IRE) (MrsJRRamsden) 8-6 DMcKeown (9) (neat: scope:
    s.i.s: outpcd appr st: styd on appr fnl f) ........................... ¾.4
1860³ Doc Spot (CaptJWilson) 8-11 GDuffield (4) (swtg: chsd ldrs: drvn along 4f out:
    no imp) ............................................................... nk.5
1848² Fanfan (IRE) (bl) (MHEasterby) 8-11 KDarley (3) (led tl hdd over 2f out: sn btn) . 8.6
1788⁶ Sean's Delight (JMCarr) 8-6 SMorris (7) (lw: nvr wnt pce) .................. hd.7
Rose of Man (JBerry) 8-6 GCarter (5) (str: scope: bit bkwd: a rr div) ........... 1½.8
1959 Sevinch (MWEasterby) 7-13 ‡7JMarshall (6) (sn outpcd & bhd) ............... 2.9
1959² Touch N' Glow (NTinkler) 8-6 MBirch (1) (lw: reluctant to go to s: ref to r: t.n.p) 0

**5/2** HI NOD, **3/1** Fanfan (IRE), **4/1** Touch N' Glow, **9/2** Kafioca (IRE), **10/1** Doc Spot, **20/1** Bay Rum, Mughal
Princess (IRE), **25/1** Rose of Man, **33/1** Sean's Delight, **50/1** Sevinch. CSF £13.74, Tote £3.70: £1.70 £1.50
£6.00 (£7.40). Mr Brian Nordan (MALTON) bred by B. Nordan. 10 Rn; Bt in 4,400 gns     1m 26.3 (3.1)
SF—19/3/–/–/–/–

**2113**     TETLEY BITTER H'CAP (0-90) £3172.50 (£945.00: £450.00: £202.50)
**1½m 44y**                                                              3-30 (3-30)

(Weights raised 4 lb)
1295 **Highbrook (USA) (68)** (MHTompkins) 4–9-9 PRobinson (6) (lw: a gng wl: bhd
    tl hdwy on bit to ld 1f out: easily) ................................. —1
1996³ Mingus (USA) **(56)** (MrsJRRamsden) 5–8-11 DMcKeown (3) (hld up: effrt & nt
    clr run 2f out: hdwy appr fnl f: no ch w wnr) .................... 2.2
1968* First Bid **(50)** (RMWhitaker) 5–8-2 (3x) ‡3JFanning (4) (chsd ldrs: rdn to ld over
    1f out: sn hdd & one pce) .......................................... s.h.3
2047* Carlingford (USA) **(58)** (Fav) (MPNaughton) 6–8-8 (3x) ‡5JWeaver (2) (disp ld tl
    led 6f out: hdd over 1f out: sn btn) ............................... 10.4
1841⁴ Katy's Lad **(69)** (BAMcMahon) 5–9-10 TQuinn (1) (lw: disp ld tl hdd 6f out: ev ch
    tl outpcd fnl 2f) ..................................................... s.h.5
1242* Kirsten **(78)** (WJarvis) 3–9-1 ‡5StephenDavies (5) (chsd ldrs: pushed along 4f
    out: wknd 2f out) .................................................... 10.6

**2/1** Carlingford (USA), **3/1** Kirsten, **4/1** Mingus (USA), **11/2** Katy's Lad, **7/1** HIGHBROOK (USA), **9/1** First Bid.
CSF £32.38, Tote £5.40: £3.20 £2.50 (£9.70). Mr Nick Cook (NEWMARKET) bred by Larry Stewart in USA. 6 Rn
2m 36.4 (2.4)
SF—49/33/23/9/24/–

**2114**     LEYBURN STKS (Mdn 3-Y.O) £2259.00 (£624.00: £297.00)     **7f**     4-00 (4-06)

1643 **Dune River (68)** (SirMarkPrescott) 9-0 GDuffield (3) (lw: mde most: hld on
    gamely fnl f) ......................................................... —1

1086⁴ Silica (USA) **(62)** *(JHMGosden)* 8-9　DHolland (5) (w wnr: rdn over 1f: r.o wl) ... s.h.2
1956⁵ Maritime Lady (USA) (Fav) *(MRStoute)* 8-9　WRSwinburn (2) (trckd ldrs: effrt
　　　　over 2f out: hrd rdn & nt qckn fnl f) ........................................ 2.3
　1418 Stamshaw *(BAMcMahon)* 8-2　‡⁷JBramhill (1) (reluctant to enter stalls: prom tl
　　　　outpcd wl over 2f out) ............................................................ 10.4
　　　Sparkling Skies *(EWeymes)* 8-9　DMcKeown (4) (neat: bit bkwd: nvr wnt pce) .... 6.5

**1/2** Maritime Lady (USA), **11/4** DUNE RIVER, **15/2** Silica (USA), **66/1** Ors. CSF £18.07, Tote £3.80: £1.10 £2.00
(£7.50). Mr P. G. Goulandris (NEWMARKET) bred by Hesmonds Stud Ltd. 5 Rn　　　　1m 26.8 (3.6)
　　　　　　　　　　　　　　　　　　　　　　　　　　　　　　　　　SF—15/9/3/–/–

## 2115　　JOSHUA TETLEY H'CAP (0-70) £2364.00 (£654.00: £312.00)　**5f**　　4-30 (4-32)

1787³ **Catherines Well (65)** *(MWEasterby)* 9–9-13　KDarley (5) (b: lw: trckd ldrs: led 1f
　　　　out: comf) ......................................................................... —1
1924⁶ Last Straw **(40)** *(AWJones)* 4–7-9　‡⁷ClaireBalding (6) (lw: a cl up: chal ins fnl f: nt
　　　　pce of wnr) ...................................................................... 1¹/₂.2
1787＊ Rock Opera (IRE) **(59)** (Fav) *(MPNaughton)* 4–9-2　‡⁵JWeaver (2) (lw: bhd: hdwy
　　　　u.p 2f out: edgd lft fnl f: nrst fin) ..................................... 1.3
1729⁶ Cottage Gallery (IRE) **(36)** *(WASimpson)* 4–7-7⁽¹⁾　‡⁵SMaloney (4) (w ldr: led
　　　　2f out to 1f out: nt qckn) .................................................. ³/₄.4
　*1551*⁴ Sobering Thoughts **(40)** (bl) *(DWChapman)* 6–7-13　‡³JFanning (3) (led 3f: drvn
　　　　along & grad wknd) .......................................................... 2.5
1514⁵ Hemsworth Lad (IRE) **(61)** *(PCalver)* 3–9-3　ACulhane (7) (lw: sn drvn along: nvr
　　　　trbld ldrs) ....................................................................... 5.6
　1865 Stylish Dutch **(46)** *(MWEasterby)* 3–7-9　‡⁷JMarshall (1) (cl up 3f: sn wknd) ........ 6.7

**11/8** Rock Opera (IRE), **11/2** CATHERINES WELL, **6/1** Cottage Gallery (IRE), Last Straw, Sobering Thoughts,
**10/1** Hemsworth Lad (IRE), **25/1** Stylish Dutch. CSF £33.83, Tote £4.30: £1.90 £2.20 (£10.40). Mr Robert Cox
(SHERIFF HUTTON) bred by R. J. Powell. 7 Rn　　　　　　　　　　　　　58.9 sec (1.4)
　　　　　　　　　　　　　　　　　　　　　　　　　　　　　　　　SF—55/17/34/8/6/–

## 2116　　DEWSBURY STKS (Mdn) £2469.00 (£684.00: £327.00)　**1¹/₂m 44y**　　5-00 (5-00)

　789 **Dime Bag** *(BWHills)* 3–8-3　KTsui (1) (trckd ldrs: n.m.r 2f out: pushed thro to ld
　　　　1f out: r.o u.p) .................................................................. —1
　529³ Wand (IRE) (Fav) *(HRACecil)* 3–8-3　AMcGlone (4) (lw: a cl up: chal over 2f out:
　　　　sltly hmpd & nt qckn fnl f) ................................................. 3¹/₂.2
　　　Super Blues *(TDBarron)* 5–9-2　AlexGreaves (7) (w'like: str: bhd: hdwy 6f out:
　　　　styd on wl nr fin) .............................................................. ³/₄.3
1933 Green Flower (USA) *(MRStoute)* 3–8-3　TQuinn (2) (lw: led: qcknd ent st: edgd
　　　　rt 2f out: hdd 1f out: sn btn) ............................................. 2.4
　　　Nijmegen *(JGFitzGerald)* 4–9-7　KDarley (6) (lw: chsd ldrs: effrt over 2f out: no
　　　　imp) ................................................................................ 2¹/₂.5
　　　Tilden Park *(PJBevan)* 6–9-2　NConnorton (5) (w'like: bhd: hdwy 6f out: one
　　　　pce fnl 3f) ........................................................................ 2¹/₂.6
1976 Randybay *(JMackie)* 7–9-7　MBirch (3) (b: hdwy & in tch 7f out: outpcd 4f out:
　　　　n.d after) .......................................................................... 3.7

**6/4** Wand (IRE), **11/4** Green Flower (USA), **9/2** DIME BAG, Nijmegen, **33/1** Super Blues, **66/1** Randybay, **100/1**
Tilden Park. CSF £10.66, Tote £4.80: £1.60 £1.40 (£3.20). K. Al-Said (LAMBOURN) bred by Charlton Down
Stud. 7 Rn　　　　　　　　　　　　　　　　　　　　　　　　　　2m 39.8 (5.8)

## 2117　　LEVY BOARD H'CAP (F & M) (0-80) £2846.00 (£848.00: £404.00: £182.00)
　　　　**5f 212y**　　　　　　　　　　　　　　　　　　　　　　　　5-30 (5-31)

1829² **Breezy Day (77)** (Fav) *(BAMcMahon)* 6–10-0　TQuinn (3) (lw: mde all: clr 1f out:
　　　　eased nr fin) ...................................................................... —1
1608⁶ Thrie-Na-Helah (IRE) **(73)** *(RMWhitaker)* 3–9-3　ACulhane (2) (lw: cl up tl outpcd
　　　　& lost pl ¹/₂-wy: styd on u.p fnl 2f: no ch w wnr) .................... ¹/₂.2
　1562 Never Late **(55)** (v) *(MHEasterby)* 3–7-8⁽⁶⁾　‡⁵SMaloney (4) (lw: w wnr: hrd rdn &
　　　　btn over 1f out) ................................................................ 1¹/₂.3
1828³ Real Stunner **(67)** *(MPNaughton)* 5–9-1　‡³JFanning (1) (lw: cl up tl outpcd
　　　　¹/₂-wy: btn after) ............................................................... 12.4

**5/4** BREEZY DAY, **3/1** Real Stunner, Thrie-Na-Helah (IRE), **7/1** Never Late. CSF £4.77, Tote £2.20 (£2.50). Mrs J.
McMahon (TAMWORTH) bred by John I. O'Byrne. 4 Rn　　　　　　　　　1m 13.5 (3)
　　　　　　　　　　　　　　　　　　　　　　　　　　　　　　　SF—19/6/–/–

T/Plpt: £192.20 (13.55 Tckts).　　　　　　　　　　　　　　　　　　　　　AA

# CATTERICK (L-H)
## Thursday, July 16th [Good to firm]
Going Allowance: minus 0.15 sec per fur (F)

Wind: slt against

Stalls: low

### 2118
WOOD HOUSE AUCTION STKS (Mdn 2-Y.O) £2301.00 (£636.00: £303.00)
7f

2-30 (2-32)

| 1409 | **Credit Squeeze** (RFJohnsonHoughton) 8-9 RHills (4) (lw: chsd ldrs: rdn to ld over 1f out: hung lft: styd on wl) | —1 |
| | Mr Cube (IRE) (Fav) (PFICole) 9-0 TQuinn (8) (str: cmpt: sn chsng ldrs: led 4f out tl over 1f out: unable qckn) | 4.2 |
| 1378⁵ | Buffalo River (MHTompkins) 8-11 NDay (5) (lw: outpcd & hrd drvn ent st: styd on fnl f: nt rch ldrs) | 2.3 |
| 2038⁴ | El Guapo (TFairhurst) 8-3 ‡³JFanning (6) (lw: a chsng ldrs: effrt over 2f out: one pce) | 1.4 |
| 1897 | Laurel Etoile (JBerry) 8-6 GCarter (1) (led over 1f: chsd ldrs tl lost pl ½-wy) | 7.5 |
| 1171⁶ | Five Clubs (IRE) (DTThom) 8-0 JLowe (3) (led over 5f out to 4f out: wknd 3f out) | 4.6 |
| 1790⁵ | Colonel Future (JWWatts) 8-7 NConnorton (2) (chsd ldrs tl lost pl 4f out) | 1½.7 |
| 1046 | Covent Garden Girl (MWEasterby) 8-3⁽¹⁾ TLucas (7) (s.i.s: a in rr) | 6.8 |

2/1 Mr Cube (IRE), 9/4 Buffalo River, 3/1 CREDIT SQUEEZE, 9/1 Five Clubs (IRE), 14/1 El Guapo, 16/1 Colonel Future, 20/1 Laurel Etoile, 33/1 Covent Garden Girl. CSF £9.45, Tote £4.30: £1.40 £1.10 £1.10 (£5.50). Mr R. C. Naylor (DIDCOT) bred by Home Stud Ltd. 8 Rn
1m 26.3 (3.1)
SF—32/25/16/5/–/–

### 2119
LEEDS CLAIMING STKS (3-Y.O) £2259.00 (£624.00: £297.00)

5f 212y

3-00 (3-03)

| 1786³ | **Crept Out (IRE)** (64) (Jt-Fav) (MissSEHall) 8-4 NConnorton (3) (b.nr hind: hdwy over 2f out: hung lft u.p: styd on to ld wl ins fnl f) | —1 |
| 1829⁶ | Langtonian (75) (bl) (Jt-Fav) (JBerry) 8-11 NCarlisle (4) (lw: led & sn clr: rdn over 1f out: wknd wl ins fnl f) | 1½.2 |
| | Nordoora (IRE) (JLHarris) 7-8⁽³⁾ ‡⁵SMaloney (5) (leggy: s.i.s: hdwy ½-wy: ev ch ins fnl f: kpt on) | s.h.3 |
| | Ivors Princess (MrsGRReveley) 7-11 ‡³JFanning (1) (effrt u.p over 2f out: styd on: nvr rchd ldrs) | 1½.4 |
| 34⁴ | Miss Narnia (46) (MDods) 7-10 JLowe (6) (chsd ldr tl wknd over 2f out) | 3.5 |
| 1776 | Cashtal Queen (44) (JBerry) 7-7 ‡⁷PRoberts (2) (b: s.i.s: a in rr) | ¾.6 |
| | Scorton (IRE) (50/1) Withdrawn (unruly s & ref to ent stalls) : not under orders | |

15/8 CREPT OUT (IRE), Langtonian, 5/1 Ivors Princess, 6/1 Cashtal Queen, 12/1 Nordoora (IRE), 25/1 Miss Narnia. CSF £5.57, Tote £2.90: £1.30 £1.30 (£2.60). Mr W. G. Barker (MIDDLEHAM) bred by J. Kennedy in Ireland. 6 Rn
1m 13.6 (3.1)
SF—10/11/–/–/–/–

### 2120
COLBORN H'CAP (0-70) £2807.00 (£777.00: £371.00)
(Weights raised 3 lb)

1m 7f 177y

3-30 (3-32)

| 1789 | **Sexy Mover** (31) (WStorey) 5–7-6⁽²⁾ ‡³JFanning (2) (chsd ldrs: drvn along 7f out: styd on to ld over 1f out: hld on wl) | —1 |
| 1882⁴ | Heavenly Waters (50) (Fav) (RFJohnsonHoughton) 3–7-12 RHills (6) (b.nr hind: hld up: hdwy over 3f out: swtchd over 1f out: styd on wl: nt rch wnr) | nk.2 |
| 2042 | Dari Sound (IRE) (52) (JGFitzGerald) 4–9-2 KFallon (8) (lw: chsd ldrs: drvn along 7f out: one pce fnl 2f) | 5.3 |
| 1909³ | Thor Power (IRE) (48) (DTThom) 3–7-10 JLowe (9) (bhd & reminders 6f out: styd on fnl 2f: nt rch ldrs) | 1½.4 |
| 1419 | Newark Antiquefair (33) (BCMorgan) 4–7-6⁽⁴⁾ ‡⁵NKennedy (11) (chsd ldrs tl outpcd 4f out: kpt on appr fnl f) | nk.5 |
| 1789* | Rexy Boy (30) (WLBarker) 5–7-8 NCarlisle (7) (mde most tl over 1f out: wknd) | nk.6 |
| 1606⁴ | Northants (50) (WStorey) 6–9-0 BCrossley (10) (b: lw: sn bhd & pushed along: bhd tl sme hdwy 2f out: n.d) | 5.7 |
| 1518⁴ | Bay Tern (USA) (44) (MHEasterby) 6–8-3 ‡⁵SMaloney (5) (jnd ldr 10f out: disp ld tl wknd over 2f out) | 2½.8 |
| 1784³ | Souson (IRE) (60) (MWEasterby) 4–9-10 TLucas (1) (hld up & bhd: rapid hdwy 5f out: shkn up & wknd over 2f out) | ¾.9 |
| 232 | Un Souverain (29) (WBentley) 4–7-7 SWood (3) (chsd ldrs tl lost pl over 4f out: sn bhd) | 4.10 |

LONG HANDICAP: Sexy Mover 7-1, Newark Antiquefair 7-1, Un Souverain 7-5.

**3/1** Heavenly Waters, **9/2** Northants, **6/1** Bay Tern (USA), **7/1** Souson (IRE), **8/1** Thor Power (IRE), Rexy Boy, **10/1** Dari Sound (IRE), **25/1** SEXY MOVER, **33/1** Newark Antiquefair, **50/1** Un Souverain. CSF £87.26, CT £693.12. Tote £30.10: £4.80 £1.40 £2.30 (£59.80). Mr Alan Crook (CONSETT) bred by J. M. O'Connor. 10 Rn
3m 28.2 (7.2)

---

**2121**  TUNSTALL STKS (2-Y.O) £2660.40 (£734.40: £349.20)  **5f 212y**  4-05 (4-06)

1443[2]  **Night Melody (IRE)** *(RHannon)* 9-7  MHills (1) (lw: hld up: smooth hdwy ½-wy: shkn up to ld jst ins fnl f: r.o wl: eased nr fin) ...................... —1

1844[3]  Glowing Value (IRE) *(JBerry)* 9-4  GCarter (2) (b: chsd ldr: sn drvn along: rdn over 2f out: slt ld over 1f out: sn hdd: nt qckn) .................. 2.2

1946[2]  Conspicuous (IRE) (Fav) *(PFICole)* 8-11  TQuinn (3) (led: rdn over 1f out: sn hdd & btn) ........................................................ 1½.3

**8/11** Conspicuous (IRE), **11/4** NIGHT MELODY (IRE), **100/30** Glowing Value (IRE). CSF £8.65, Tote £3.60 (£5.10). Mr P. D. Savill (MARLBOROUGH) bred by Leo Collins in Ireland. 3 Rn
1m 12.2 (1.7)
SF—56/45/32

---

**2122**  GROVE STKS (Mdn 3-Y.O) £2196.00 (£606.00: £288.00)  **1m 7f 177y**  4-40 (4-41)

1714[3]  **Bar Billiards (72)** (bl) (Fav) *(RFJohnsonHoughton)* 9-0  TQuinn (1) (lw: chsd ldr: drvn along 5f out: hrd rdn over 3f out: led over 1f out: all out) ........ —1

1719[3]  Natral Exchange (IRE) (51) (v) *(JWHills)* 9-0  RHills (3) (lw: led tl over 1f out: one pce) ................................................................ 3.2

1481[2]  Glowing Devil (59) *(TDBarron)* 9-0  AlexGreaves (4) (trckd ldrs tl bdly outpcd over 4f out: sn lost tch) .............................. 20.3

Rampal (IRE) (v) *(GWragg)* 9-0  MHills (2) (w'like: lengthy: bit bkwd: hung violently lft thrght: soon lost tch ½-wy: nt keen) .............. 30.4

**11/10** BAR BILLIARDS, **3/1** Rampal (IRE), Glowing Devil, **7/1** Natral Exchange (IRE). CSF £7.30, Tote £1.90 (£4.40). Mrs E. W. Richards (DIDCOT) bred by Ewar Stud Farms. 4 Rn
3m 28.3 (7.3)

---

**2123**  CATARACTONIUM H'CAP (0-70) £2905.00 (£805.00: £385.00)  **7f**  5-10 (5-19)

1793*  **Leave it to Lib (60)** *(PCalver)* 5–8-11 ‡7JTate (8) (lw: in tch: r.o u.p on outside to ld over 1f out: drvn out) ........................................ —1

1792[6]  Mary Macblain (46) *(JLHarris)* 3–7-6[4] ‡5NKennedy (10) (b.nr hind: chsd ldrs: rdn & hung bdly lft fnl 2f: styd on nr fin) ................ 1½.2

1785[5]  Brambles Way (56) (v) *(WLBarker)* 3–8-7  AProud (1) (swtg: chsd ldrs: effrt & swtchd rt 1f out: kpt on u.p) ................................ 1½.3

1793[4]  Wild Prospect (63) *(CTinkler)* 4–9-7  MBirch (4) (led after 1f: rdn 2f out: sn hdd: kpt on same pce) ........................................ s.h.4

767  Watch Me Go (IRE) (54) *(BobJones)* 3–8-5  NDay (3) (lw: sn outpcd & bhd: gd hdwy over 1f out: r.o strly nr fin) ............................ nk.5

1853[4]  Morpick (53) *(JPLeigh)* 5–8-11  TQuinn (7) (sn prom: effrt 2f out: styd on same pce fnl f) ................................................ ½.6

1564  Say You Will (35) (v) *(MPNaughton)* 8–7-7  JakiHouston (11) (swtg: led 1f: chsd ldrs tl lost pl ½-wy: kpt on again fnl f) .................. hd.7

1961  Euroblake (70) (Fav) *(TDBarron)* 5–9-7 ‡7SWilliams (2) (swtg: hld up & bhd: hdwy 2f out: sltly hmpd 1f out: nvr rchd ldrs) ............ 1½.8

1673[5]  Colonel Fairfax (35) *(JWWatts)* 4–7-7  JLowe (5) (chsd ldr tl wknd over 1f out) .. ½.9

1978  Minizen Music (IRE) (41) *(MBrittain)* 4–7-8[6] ‡5SMaloney (9) (lw: chsd ldrs tl lost pl over 1f out) .................................... s.h.10

2040  Henry Will (43) *(TFairhurst)* 8–7-12 ‡3JFanning (6) (w ldrs tl rdn & wknd wl over 1f out) ............................................ 1.11

LONG HANDICAP: Mary Macblain 7-0, Say You Will 6-13, Colonel Fairfax 7-5, Minizen Music (IRE) 7-3.
*1847* Canaan Valley (20/1) Withdrawn (unruly s & ref to ent stalls) : not under orders

**3/1** Euroblake, **5/1** Wild Prospect, LEAVE IT TO LIB, **15/2** Watch Me Go (IRE), **17/2** Colonel Fairfax, **9/1** Morpick, **12/1** Brambles Way, **20/1** Henry Will, Minizen Music (IRE), **25/1** Say You Will, **33/1** Mary Macblain. CSF £117.84, CT £1,677.09. Tote £5.80: £2.30 £7.20 £2.70 (£350.20). Mrs C. Calver (RIPON) bred by S. Emmet. 11 Rn
1m 25.4 (2.2)
SF—49/25/35/48/31/35

T/Plpt: £308.30 (7.2 Tckts).

WG

1867—**SANDOWN (R-H)**

**Wednesday, July 15th [Good]**

Going Allowance: St: nil sec; Rnd: 0.05 sec per fur (G)　　　Wind: nil

Stalls: high

**2124**　E.B.F. SUPERSLOANE STKS (Mdn 2-Y.O) £2735.00 (£760.00: £365.00)
　　　**5f 6y**　　　　　　　　　　　　　　　　　　　　　　6-25 (6-28)

　　　　　**Realities (USA)** *(GHarwood)* 9-0　JReid (9) (w'like: scope: w ldr: led on bit over
　　　　　2f out: comf) ..................................................................................... —1
17694 Racing Telegraph *(JPearce)* 8-9 ‡5RPrice (7) (lw: outpcd: hdwy over 1f out: r.o)　3.2
　1915 Iron Merchant (IRE) *(Fav)* *(RAkehurst)* 9-0　PatEddery (3) (lw: a.p: rdn over 2f
　　　　　out: unable qckn: fin 4th, 1½l: plcd 3rd) .................................................. 3
18803 Kismetim *(GLewis)* 9-0　PaulEddery (1) (prom over 2f: fin 5th, 5l: plcd 4th) ......... 4
　　　　　**Delay No More** *(PMitchell)* 9-0　SCauthen (6) (leggy: bit bkwd: bhd fnl 2f: fin 6th,
　　　　　3½l: plcd 5th) ................................................................................... 5
17646 Tee-Emm *(PHowling)* 9-0　BCrossley (8) (led over 2f) ..................................... ½.7
18973 The Premier Expres *(BBeasley)* 8-7 ‡7SWilliams (2) (s.s: a bhd) ...................... 6.8
　　　　　**Easy Access (IRE)** *(RHannon)* 8-11 ‡3RPerham (5) (b.off hind: leggy: outpcd:
　　　　　rapid hdwy 1f out: r.o: fin 3rd, nk: disq: plcd last) ..................................... 0
*Stewards Enquiry: Obj. to Easy Access (IRE) by Clerk of the Scales sustained. Perham fined £130 (failure to weigh
in).*

**10/11** Iron Merchant (IRE)(5/4—4/6), **3/1** REALITIES (USA)(6/4—7/2), **6/1** Racing Telegraph, **7/1** Kismetim,
**16/1** Easy Access (IRE), **20/1** The Premier Expres, Delay No More, **66/1** Tee-Emm. CSF £20.76, Tote £4.60:
£1.60 £1.60 £1.10 (£14.80). Mr Simon Karmel (PULBOROUGH) bred by Kathleen Crompton & Russell B. Jones
Jnr in USA. 8 Rn　　　　　　　　　　　　　　　　　　　　　　　62.35 sec (2.85)
　　　　　　　　　　　　　　　　　　　　　　　　　　　　　　SF—43/26/27/24/4/–

**2125**　HARPERS & QUEEN H'CAP (0-70) £3197.00 (£892.00: £431.00)
　　　　　**1m 14y**　　　　　　　　　　　　　　　　　　　　6-55 (7-01)

　1794★ **Kingchip Boy (48)** *(MJRyan)* 3-7-11 ‡5ATucker (11) (hdwy over 1f out: led nr
　　　　　fin: r.o wl) ...................................................................................... —1
18856 Abso (65) *(RHannon)* 4-10-0　JReid (1) (hdwy 2f out: led wl ins fnl f: sn hdd:
　　　　　unable qckn) .................................................................................. 1½.2
　　　　　Swift Romance (IRE) (63) *(BRMillman)* 4-9-12　JWilliams (10) (b.hind: hdwy
　　　　　over 1f out: r.o wl ins fnl f) ................................................................ 1.3
17163 Lord's Final (35) *(CRBarwell)* 5-7-7 ‡5DHarrison (5) (swtg: hrd rdn & hdwy over
　　　　　1f out: r.o) ...................................................................................... s.h.4
18852 Sareen Express (IRE) (44) *(MrsJCDawe)* 4-8-2 ‡5RPrice (9) (swtg: hdwy over 1f
　　　　　out: nvr nrr) ..................................................................................... 1½.5
17434 Tiger Shoot (51) (v) *(DJSCosgrove)* 5-9-0　WRSwinburn (14) (swtg: led over 6f:
　　　　　led ins fnl f: sn hdd: one pce) ............................................................. s.h.6
　1572 Betalongabill (48) (bl) *(MMadgwick)* 3-7-9 ‡7CAvery (20) (6th st: one pce fnl 2f) 1½.7
　1756★ Zinbaq (40) *(CJBenstead)* 6-8-3　TyroneWilliams (6) (lw: nvr nr to chal) .......... hd.8
　1674★ Prince of Darkness (IRE) (72) *(Fav)* *(RAkehurst)* 3-9-12　GDuffield (2)
　　　　　(swtg: 4th st: led over 1f out tl ins fnl f: sn wknd) ..................................... ½.9
　1339 Fast Operative (37) *(KOCunningham-Brown)* 5-8-0　NCarlisle (17) (prom 6f) .. 1½.10
15574 Sudanor (IRE) (62) *(MJHeaton-Ellis)* 3-9-2　PatEddery (7) (2nd st: wknd over 1f
　　　　　out) ............................................................................................. 2½.11
15876 Northern Conqueror (IRE) (59) *(TJNaughton)* 4-9-8　PaulEddery (16) (swtg: a
　　　　　mid div) ........................................................................................ hd.12
　1791 All Earz (IRE) (54) *(REarnshaw)* 3-8-8　AMackay (13) (swtg: a mid div) .......... nk.13
　1747 Harry's Lady (IRE) (43) *(TThomsonJones)* 4-8-6　SWhitworth (4) (b: 3rd st:
　　　　　wknd over 2f out) ............................................................................ nk.14
　6046 Tiffany's Case (IRE) (51) *(CAHorgan)* 3-8-5　RHills (19) (a bhd) ................... ¾.15
　1421 Petticoat Power (53) (v) *(MrsBarbaraWaring)* 6-9-2　NHowe (18) (b: rdn thrght:
　　　　　a bhd) .......................................................................................... hd.16
　1041 Chummy's Child (IRE) (55) *(JSutcliffe)* 3-8-9　BRouse (12) (lw: a bhd) ........... 2.17
　1284 Lazy Rhythm (USA) (51) *(RAkehurst)* 6-8-11 ‡3FNorton (15) (lw: a bhd) .......... 2.18
　1905 Sergeant Meryll (35) *(PHowling)* 8-7-5 ‡7KateMason (8) (s.s: hdwy over 4f out:
　　　　　5th st: wknd over 2f out) ................................................................... 1½.19

**4/1** Prince of Darkness (IRE), **11/2** Tiger Shoot, **6/1** Lazy Rhythm (USA), **9/1** Sudanor (IRE), **11/1** Sareen Express
(IRE), **14/1** Zinbaq, KINGCHIP BOY, Lord's Final, All Earz (IRE), **16/1** Northern Conqueror (IRE), Tiffany's Case
(IRE), **20/1** Chummy's Child (IRE), Betalongabill, **25/1** Swift Romance (IRE), Abso, Petticoat Power, **33/1** Ors.
CSF £256.64, CT £6,139.53. Tote £16.80: £2.70 £3.80 £6.80 £2.50 (£222.60). Four Jays Racing Partnership
(NEWMARKET) bred by R. M. Scott. 19 Rn　　　　　　　　　　　　　　　1m 44.49 (5.29)
　　　　　　　　　　　　　　　　　　　　　　　　　　　　　　SF—10/35/31/–/11

**2126**  YELLOWGLEN H'CAP (0-90) £2929.00 (£877.00: £421.00: £193.00)
7f 16y                                                                 7-25 (7-29)

2029 **Euro Festival (85)** *(MissLCSiddall)* 3-9-9 ‡⁵DHarrison (1) (lw: s.s: hdwy 2f out:
led over 1f out: comf) ...................................................... —1
1716 Dream Carrier (IRE) **(64)** (Jt-Fav) *(RHannon)* 4-9-1 PatEddery (6) (hdwy over 1f
out: r.o) ................................................................................. 6.2
1943 Owner's Dream (USA) **(78)** *(BHanbury)* 3-9-7 WRyan (12) (led over 2f: 2nd st:
led over 3f out tl over 2f out: unable qckn) ............... 1¹/₂.3
1615 On Y Va (USA) **(59)** *(RJRWilliams)* 5-8-10 DHolland (7) (b.off hind: 6th st: one
pce fnl 2f) ............................................................................ 2¹/₂.4
1246 Act of Union (IRE) **(71)** *(BBeasley)* 3-9-0 LCharnock (9) (lw: 3rd st: led over 2f
out tl over 1f out: sn wknd) .......................................... 2.5
1615³ Dance on Sixpence **(62)** (Jt-Fav) *(HJCollingridge)* 4-8-13 JQuinn (10) (no
hdwy fnl 3f) ......................................................................... 3¹/₂.6
1773⁶ Caroles Express **(74)** *(RAkehurst)* 4-9-4 ‡⁷LCarter (4) (4th st: wknd over 2f out) s.h.7
1773 Try Leguard (IRE) **(75)** *(WCarter)* 3-9-4 GDuffield (11) (lw: s.s: nvr nrr) ........... 1¹/₂.8
1641⁴ High Baccarat **(73)** *(CCElsey)* 3-7-11 JLowe (8) (lw: bhd fnl 5f) .................... 1.9
1529⁶ La Bamba **(76)** *(GAPritchard-Gordon)* 6-9-13 WHood (2) (s.s: a bhd) ............. 4.10
1035⁵ Ahbab (IRE) **(80)** *(PTWalwyn)* 3-9-9 WCarson (5) (5th st: wknd 3f out) ............. 2.11
1883³ Uccello **(72)** *(LJHolt)* 3-9-1 JReid (3) (hdwy 5f out: led over 4f out tl over 3f out:
wknd over 2f out) ........................................................... 3¹/₂.12

**11/2** Dream Carrier (IRE), Dance on Sixpence, **7/1** La Bamba, **8/1** Owner's Dream (USA), On Y
Va (USA), **10/1** EURO FESTIVAL, Caroles Express, High Baccarat, **11/1** Act of Union (IRE), **12/1** Try Leguard
(IRE), **14/1** Uccello. CSF £63.18, CT £433.35. Tote £11.00: £3.10 £2.80 £2.90 (£31.60). Mr Christopher Price
(TADCASTER) bred by H. Alexander and R. E. Sangster. 12 Rn          1m 30.53 (3.53)
SF—61/35/36/17/15/3

**2127**  LBC NEWSTALK 97.3 FM MIKE DICKIN H CAP (0-90) £2951.75 (£884.00: £424.50:
£194.75) 5f 6y                                                        7-55 (8-00)

1878³ **Olifantsfontein (78)** *(RSimpson)* 4-9-2 WRyan (8) (a.p: hrd rdn over 1f out: led
nr fin) .................................................................................. —1
1878★ Gone Savage **(76)** (Fav) *(GBBalding)* 4-9-0 SCauthen (12) (b.hind: led: rdn fnl
f: hdd nr fin) ....................................................................... s.h.2
1474 Bold Habit **(88)** *(BBeasley)* 7-9-5 ‡⁷SWilliams (9) (lw: hld up: rdn over 1f out: r.o
wl ins fnl f) ......................................................................... ¹/₂.3
1752★ Plain Fact **(90)** *(JWHills)* 7-10-0 GDuffield (11) (swtg: a.p: rdn over 1f out: r.o) hd.4
1631³ Masnun (USA) **(86)** *(RJO'Sullivan)* 7-9-10 DBiggs (5) (hdwy over 2f out: nt clr
run wl over 1f out: r.o ins fnl f) ....................................... 1.5
1757² Paddy Chalk **(80)** *(LJHolt)* 6-9-4 JReid (7) (b: hdwy over 1f out: r.o) .............. nk.6
1931 Paley Prince **(89)** *(MDIUsher)* 6-9-13 WRSwinburn (10) (lw: no hdwy fnl 2f) 2.7
Cantoris **(88)** *(RJRWilliams)* 6-9-12 DHolland (1) (prom 3f) ............................. 1¹/₂.8
1771⁵ Ashtina **(65)** *(RJHodges)* 7-8-3 JQuinn (4) (spd over 3f) ............................. 1.9
1931⁵ Pallium (IRE) **(73)** *(MPNaughton)* 4-8-6 ‡SJWeaver (3) (swtg: a bhd) ............. ³/₄.10
1952³ Letsbeonestaboutit **(83)** *(MrsNMacauley)* 6-9-7 DMcKeown (2) (a bhd) ........... ¹/₂.11
2032 John O'Dreams **(55)** (v) *(MrsJCDawe)* 7-7-7 AMackay (6) (a bhd) .................. 3.12
LONG HANDICAP: John O'Dreams 6-11.

**9/4** Gone Savage(3/1—2/1), **9/2** Bold Habit, **15/2** Plain Fact, **8/1** OLIFANTSFONTEIN, **10/1** Paddy Chalk, **12/1**
Pallium (IRE), **14/1** Masnun (USA), **16/1** Letsbeonestaboutit, Cantoris, Ashtina, **20/1** Paley Prince (USA), **100/1**
John O'Dreams. CSF £24.69, CT £84.90. Tote £9.90: £2.50 £1.60 £2.40 (£9.20). Mr Trevor Painting (FOXHILL)
bred by Whitsbury Manor Stud. 12 Rn          61.30 sec (1.80)
SF—66/63/66/74/66/59

**2128**  BON CHIC, BON GENRE CLAIMING STKS (3-Y.O) £2630.00 (£730.00: £350.00)
1¹/₄m 7y                                                              8-25 (8-30)

1971³ **Kandy Secret (USA) (60)** (v) *(RHannon)* 8-7 PatEddery (4) (swtg: hrd rdn over
3f out: hdwy over 1f out: led nr fin) ................................ —1
1911⁵ Magnetic Point (USA) **(59)** *(AAScott)* 8-2 AMunro (1) (5th st: led wl over 1f out:
hrd rdn ins fnl f: hdd nr fin) ........................................... nk.2
1870 Regal Racer **(82)** (Fav) *(DRCEIsworth)* 8-7 WCarson (6) (swtg: chsd ldr 5f: 4th
st: rdn 2f out: rallied over 1f out: swtchd fnl f: r.o wl) hd.3
1872 Nothing Doing (IRE) *(WJMusson)* 8-5 JReid (5) (lw: 2nd st: led over 2f out tl wl
over 1f out: unable qckn) ................................................ 6.4
694 Beam Me Up Scotty (IRE) **(54)** *(PMitchell)* 8-3 NCarlisle (7) (6th st: one pce fnl
3f) .......................................................................................... 3¹/₂.5
932 Princess of Orange **(58)** *(CCElsey)* 7-9 JQuinn (8) (swtg: led over 7f) ............. ¹/₂.6
1682⁴ Harcliff *(DJSCosgrove)* 8-10 AShoults (9) (b.hind: dwlt: bhd fnl 6f) .................. 20.7

1977 Kentucky Chicken (USA) **(30)** (bl) *(MissLCSiddall)* 7-9 ‡5DHarrison (3) (lw:
hdwy over 4f out: 3rd st: wknd over 2f out) ......................... 2.8
1770 Twice as Much *(DAWilson)* 7-9 JLowe (2) (lw: s.i.s: a bhd) .................................... 5.9
*Stewards Enquiry: Eddery suspended 24-28/7/92 (excessive use of whip).*

**5/2** Regal Racer(7/4—3/1), **3/1** KANDY SECRET (USA)(7/2—9/4), **4/1** Nothing Doing (IRE), **6/1** Harcliff(10/1—
11/2), **9/1** Princess of Orange, Magnetic Point (USA), **20/1** Beam Me Up Scotty (IRE), **33/1** Ors. CSF £27.80,
Tote £3.70: £1.80 £2.10 £1.50 (£15.30). Mr C. S. Chiles (MARLBOROUGH) bred by John P. Costelloe &
Camelot Thoroughbreds in USA. 9 Rn
2m 11.44 (7.14)
SF—27/21/25/11/2/–

**2129** OKAY YAH H'CAP (0-100) £3301.00 (£988.00: £474.00: £217.00)
**1³/₄m** 8-55 (8-58)

1874⁴ **Jungle Dancer (IRE) (82)** *(MRStoute)* 4-9-2 DHolland (1) (4th st: rdn over 3f
out: led last strides) ......................................................... —1
1874³ Manzoor Sayadan (USA) **(66)** *(RSimpson)* 4-7-9 ‡5ATucker (8) (5th st: led over
1f out: hrd rdn: hdd last strides) ..................................... nk.2
1256⁵ Castle Courageous **(92)** (Fav) *(LadyHerries)* 5-9-12 WRyan (7) (6th st: rdn
over 2f out: r.o ins fnl f: fin 4th, nk: plcd 3rd) ...................... 3
2042³ Intricacy **(59)** *(CCElsey)* 4-7-7 JLowe (2) (rdn over 3f out: nvr nr to chal: fin 5th,
2¹/₂l: plcd 4th) ................................................................. 4
1381² Prosequendo (USA) **(68)** *(MDixon)* 5-8-2 DaleGibson (9) (rdn over 3f out: nvr
nrr: fin 6th, s.h: plcd 5th) .................................................. 5
1132⁵ Retouch **(93)** *(PFICole)* 6-9-13 PatEddery (5) (lw: led 13f out tl over 1f out: 4th
& wkng whn snatched up ins fnl f) .............................. 1¹/₂.7
1580³ Marine Society **(74)** *(PTWalwyn)* 4-8-8 AMunro (3) (lw: 2nd st: led over 2f out tl
over 1f out: sn wknd) .................................................... hd.8
1399⁴ Hebridean **(94)** *(HCandy)* 5-10-0 CRutter (4) (lw: led 1f: 3rd st: sqeezed thro
ins fnl f: r.o: fin 3rd, 2l: disq: plcd last) ............................... 0
LONG HANDICAP: Intricacy 7-4.
*Stewards Enquiry: Hebridean disq. (interference to Retouch). Obj. to Jungle Dancer by Tucker overruled. Rutter
suspended 24-27/7/92 (careless riding).*

**11/4** Castle Courageous, **4/1** Hebridean(op 5/2), **9/2** Prosequendo (USA), **6/1** Retouch, **7/1** Manzoor Sayadan
(USA), JUNGLE DANCER (IRE), **10/1** Marine Society, **20/1** Intricacy. CSF £50.13, CT £152.11. Tote £8.10:
£2.00 £1.80 £1.90 (£22.90). Lord White of Hull (NEWMARKET) bred by Barronstown Stud in Ireland. 8 Rn
3m 5.09 (10.39)
SF—5/–/12/10/–/–

T/Trio: Race 2: £1,975.30 (1.1 Tckts). T/Plpt: £86.40 (66.85 Tckts). AK

# SANDOWN (R-H)
## Thursday, July 16th [Good]
Going Allowance: nil sec per fur (G) Wind: nil

Stalls: high

**2130** E.B.F. RAYNES PARK STKS (Mdn 2-Y.O.C & G) £2819.00 (£784.00: £377.00)
**7f 16y** 2-15 (2-22)

1709² **Double Bass (USA)** (Fav) *(HRACecil)* 9-0 SCauthen (5) (lw: chsd ldr: led over
4f out: drvn out) ............................................................. —1
Carelaman *(JLDunlop)* 9-0 JReid (6) (w'like: scope: 6th st: shkn up over 1f out:
r.o wl ins fnl f: bttr for r) ................................................ ¹/₂.2
La Chance *(CEBrittain)* 9-0 MRoberts (1) (gd sort: hdwy over 1f out: r.o ins fnl f:
bttr for r) .................................................................... ¹/₂.3
1658⁵ Empire Pool *(LordHuntingdon)* 9-0 WRSwinburn (8) (lw: 3rd st: hrd rdn over 1f
out: r.o) ..................................................................... s.h.4
1873³ Bonar Bridge (USA) *(RHannon)* 9-0 RCochrane (3) (4th st: wknd over 1f out) ... 5.5
1902² Heavenly Risk *(RHannon)* 9-0 PatEddery (4) (led over 2f: 2nd st: ev ch wl over
1f out: sn wknd) .......................................................... s.h.6
1349⁴ Contract Court (USA) *(CACyzer)* 9-0 AMunro (2) (5th st: wknd over 1f out) ...... nk.7
1485³ Hawl (USA) *(AAScott)* 9-0 WCarson (7) (swtg: a bhd) ........................... 2.8

**2/5** DOUBLE BASS (USA), **9/1** Hawl (USA)(tchd 6/1), **10/1** Heavenly Risk(op 9/2), **16/1** La Chance(op 5/1), **20/1**
Bonar Bridge (USA), Carelaman, **33/1** Empire Pool, **100/1** Contract Court (USA). CSF £8.55, Tote £1.40: £1.10
£3.30 £2.40 (£10.60). Sheikh Mohammed (NEWMARKET) bred by Robert Hill,Gregg Hill & George Strawbridge
in USA. 8 Rn
1m 32.14 (5.14)
SF—23/21/19/18/3/2

## 2131

FOX WARREN H'CAP (3-Y.O) (0-80) £3254.00 (£977.00: £471.00: £218.00)
**5f 6y** 　　　　　　　　　　　　　　　　　2-45 (2-49)
(Weights raised 2 lb)

| | | |
|---|---|---|
| 2029[4] | **Invigilate (60)** (Fav) *(MPNaughton)* 8-8 MRoberts (4) (lw: a.p: rdn over 1f out: led nr fin) | —1 |
| 1753[5] | Cheshire Annie (IRE) **(53)** *(WCarter)* 8-1 JQuinn (5) (led 1f: led over 2f out: hrd rdn fnl f: hdd nr fin) | nk.2 |
| 1683[3] | Wandering Stranger **(73)** *(PJMakin)* 9-7 WRSwinburn (3) (lw: hdwy over 1f out: r.o) | 2.3 |
| 1593[5] | Spell of the Yukon (USA) **(72)** *(IABalding)* 9-6 JReid (1) (led 4f out tl over 2f out: unable qckn) | 1½.4 |
| 2053 | Smudgemupum **(45)** *(MissBSanders)* 7-0 ‡7CHawksley (2) (no hdwy fnl 2f) | ½.5 |
| 1263 | Justamanda **(59)** *(WHolden)* 8-7 SDawson (6) (a bhd) | 3½.6 |
| 1920 | Cromer's Express **(58)** (v) *(MissLCSiddall)* 8-1 ‡5DHarrison (7) (swtg: s.s: a bhd) | 2½.7 |

LONG HANDICAP: Smudgemupum 7-6.

**10/11** INVIGILATE, **7/1** Wandering Stranger, **8/1** Cheshire Annie (IRE), Smudgemupum, **10/1** Spell of the Yukon (USA), **12/1** Cromer's Express, **20/1** Justamanda. CSF £7.72, Tote £1.50: £1.40 £3.40 (£6.80). Mrs H. H. Wane (RICHMOND) bred by Bechmann Stud. 7 Rn 　　　　　　　　　62.23 sec (2.73)
SF—39/31/43/36/–/14

## 2132

MILCARS STKS (2-Y.O.F) £6775.00 (£2050.00: £1000.00: £475.00)
**7f 16y** 　　　　　　　　　　　　　　　　　3-20 (3-22)

| | | |
|---|---|---|
| 1342★ | **Bright Generation (IRE)** *(PFICole)* 9-1 AMunro (3) (4th st: led wl over 1f out: easily) | —1 |
| 1471[3] | Nuryandra (Fav) *(GWragg)* 9-1 WRSwinburn (5) (swtg: 3rd st: ev ch over 2f out: unable qckn) | 7.2 |
| 1867★ | East Liberty (USA) *(IABalding)* 0 1 RCochrane (4) (lw: 2nd st: led over 2f out to wl over 1f out: one pce) | s h.3 |
| 1867[2] | Where's the Dance *(CEBrittain)* 8-11 MRoberts (1) (led over 4f) | 12.4 |

**5/4** Nuryandra, **5/2** BRIGHT GENERATION (IRE), **4/1** East Liberty (USA)(3/1—9/2), **5/1** Where's the Dance. CSF £5.76, Tote £3.00 (£2.00). Mr Fahd Salman (WHATCOMBE) bred by Newgate Stud Co in Ireland. 4 Rn
1m 31.47 (4.47)
SF—34/13/12/–

## 2133

HEATHROW STKS (Mdn) £2714.00 (£754.00: £362.00) **1m 14y** 　3-55 (3-58)

| | | |
|---|---|---|
| 1933[2] | **Garden of Heaven (USA)** (Fav) *(CEBrittain)* 3-8-13 MRoberts (2) (lw: mde all: rdn over 1f out: r.o) | —1 |
| | Move a Minute (USA) *(DRCElsworth)* 3-8-13 RCochrane (4) (w'like: scope: bit bkwd: 4th st: rdn over 1f out: r.o wl ins fnl f) | s.h.2 |
| | Gunner's Daughter *(HCandy)* 3-8-8 CRutter (1) (b.hind: w'like: scope: 2nd st: hrd rdn 2f out: unable qckn) | 3½.3 |
| 1933 | Jahangir (IRE) *(BHanbury)* 3-8-13 BRaymond (5) (3rd st: wkng whn n.m.r on ins over 1f out) | 3.4 |
| 833[6] | Heavyweight (IRE) *(CAHorgan)* 3-8-13 AMcGlone (6) (5th st: wknd over 3f out) | 15.5 |
| | 1974[4] Top Song (10/1) Withdrawn (lame at s) : not under orders | |

**1/2** GARDEN OF HEAVEN (USA), **3/1** Gunner's Daughter, **6/1** Move a Minute (USA), **20/1** Jahangir (IRE), **33/1** Heavyweight (IRE). CSF £4.10, Tote £1.40: £1.10 £1.90 (£1.90). Mr Luciano Gaucci (NEWMARKET) bred by Edward A. Seltzer in USA. 5 Rn 　　　　　　　　　　1m 44.96 (5.76)
SF—13/12/–/–/–

## 2134

NORMAN HILL H'CAP (3-Y.O) (0-100) £3601.75 (£1084.00: £524.50: £244.75)
**1¾m** 　　　　　　　　　　　　　　　　　4-25 (4-27)

| | | |
|---|---|---|
| 1977★ | **Miss Pin Up (60)** *(PatMitchell)* 7-9(1) (4x) DBiggs (6) (5th st: led ins fnl f: pushed out) | —1 |
| 1666[3] | Awol **(75)** (Fav) *(HRACecil)* 8-10 PatEddery (5) (lw: led over 5f: 2nd st: led over 1f out tl ins fnl f: unable qckn) | 2½.2 |
| 1587[2] | Top Royal **(74)** *(JLDunlop)* 8-9 WCarson (3) (chsd ldr: led over 8f out tl over 1f out: one pce) | 1½.3 |
| 1466 | Turgenev (IRE) **(86)** *(JHMGosden)* 9-7 SCauthen (1) (swtg: hrd rdn 3f out: hdwy over 1f out: r.o) | 2.4 |
| 1632[4] | Themeda **(72)** *(CRNelson)* 8-7 JReid (2) (nvr nr to chal) | ¾.5 |
| 1567[6] | King's Treasure (USA) **(75)** *(IABalding)* 8-10 RCochrane (4) (lw: 4th st: wknd wl over 1f out) | 1½.6 |
| 1602[2] | Rolling the Bones (USA) **(69)** *(JRFanshawe)* 8-4 AMunro (7) (3rd st: wknd over 2f out) | 1½.7 |
| | Castillet **(85)** *(GHarwood)* 9-6 AClark (8) (6th st: n.m.r over 2f out: sn wknd) | 5.8 |

**5/2** Awol(3/1—2/1), **3/1** Turgenev (IRE), **5/1** MISS PIN UP, **6/1** Themeda, Top Royal, **10/1** King's Treasure (USA), Rolling the Bones (USA), **16/1** Castillet. CSF £18.25, CT £72.23. Tote £5.10: £1.70 £1.50 £1.70 (£8.30). Mr E. Baldwin (NEWMARKET) bred by Brook Bloodstock P L C. 8 Rn                                3m 3.95 (9.25)

**2135**        WELLINGTON APP'CE H'CAP (0-70) £2756.00 (£766.00: £368.00)
             1¼m 7y                                                          5-00 (5-02)

1743 **Sarah-Clare (54)** (Jt-Fav) (RAkehurst) 4–8-10 ‡7LCarter (7) (swtg: 4th st: led
             over 2f out: all out) ............................................................ —1
1922 Swift Silver **(50)** (WJMusson) 5–8-6 ‡7PBowe (2) (5th st: rdn over 1f out: r.o wl
             ins fnl f) ...................................................................... hd.2
2033★ Thimbalina **(42)** (Jt-Fav) (DAWilson) 6–7-12 (4x) ‡7SharonMillard (8) (s.i.s:
             hdwy 2f out: r.o) ............................................................ 2.3
1971⁶ Altermeera **(65)** (MrsBarbaraWaring) 4–9-10 ‡4GParkin (6) (rdn & hdwy over 2f
             out: r.o one pce) ........................................................... hd.4
1914 Dominant Force **(64)** (bl) (RHannon) 3–8-10 ‡7DGibbs (1) (2nd st: ev ch over 2f
             out: wknd wl over 1f out) ................................................. 10.5
1945² Trendy Auctioneer (IRE) **(37)** (bl) (Jt-Fav) (MCPipe) 4–7-10 ‡4NVarley (9) (nvr nr
             to chal) ...................................................................... 1.6
       Smartie Lee **(59)** (PFICole) 5–9-8 TMcLaughlin (4) (swtg: 6th st: wknd over 2f
             out) .......................................................................... 1.7
1390⁶ The Yomper (FR) **(33)** (RCurtis) 10–7-10 CHawksley (5) (swtg: led over 7f) ....... 7.8
1945⁴ Hills of Hoy **(47)** (bl) (KCBailey) 6–8-10 CMunday (3) (swtg: 3rd st: wknd 3f out) 12.9

**7/2** Trendy Auctioneer (IRE), Thimbalina, SARAH-CLARE(5/2—4/1), **5/1** Swift Silver(4/1—6/1), **8/1** Altermeera(op 12/1), **12/1** Hills of Hoy, **16/1** The Yomper (FR), Smartie Lee, **33/1** Dominant Force. CSF £20.08, CT £59.07. Tote £3.80: £1.60 £2.30 £1.60 (£15.10). Miss Clare Coyne (EPSOM) bred by M. F. Kentish. 9 Rn
                                                                            2m 9.66 (5.36)
                                                            SF—42/37/25/50/16/–

T/Jkpt: £264.10 (21.45 Tckts). T/Plpt: £10.20 (583.09 Tckts).
                                                                            AK

## 1970–CHEPSTOW (L-H)
### Thursday, July 16th [Good]
Going Allowance: St: 0.05 sec per fur; Rnd: nil sec per fur (G)        *Flag start: 4th race*

Stalls: high                                                Wind: almost nil

**2136**        ALDERNEY APP'CE STKS    £1646.00 (£456.00: £218.00)    1½m 23y    6-30 (6-31)

       **Michelozzo (USA)** (RHannon) 6–9-5 ‡5MarkDenaro (7) (swtg: wnt 2nd st: led 1f
             out: pushed out) ........................................................... —1
1577² Kaisar (GER) **(84)** (Fav) (HRACecil) 3–8-12 StephenDavies (1) (led: hrd rdn &
             hdd 1f out: nt qckn) ....................................................... 3.2
1613⁶ Fly Away Soon (USA) **(102)** (PFICole) 4–9-7 ‡3JDSmith (4) (last st: hdwy 3f out:
             hrd rdn 2f out: one pce) .................................................. 4.3
 773 Tel E Thon (PJJones) 5–9-3 ‡7AWhelan (6) (no hdwy fnl 3f) ...................... 5.4
1477 Ptolemy (FR) (MissHCKnight) 5–9-2 ‡3AGarth (2) (chsd ldr: 3rd st: rdn over 3f
             out: wknd wl over 1f out) ................................................. 1.5
       New Halen (APJames) 11–9-2 ‡3GForster (3) (lw: dwlt: 5th & rdn st: t.o fnl 3f) .. 20.6

**Evens** Kaisar (GER)(op 13/8), **7/4** Fly Away Soon (USA)(5/4—15/8), **5/1** MICHELOZZO (USA), **25/1** Ptolemy (FR), **150/1** Tel E Thon, **200/1** New Halen. CSF £9.71, Tote £4.40: £2.20 £1.10 (£3.60). Mr Edward St George (MARLBOROUGH) bred by Charles Rowe in USA. 6 Rn
                                                                            2m 38.4 (7.1)
                                                            SF—34/21/22/8/5/–

**2137**        MUMBLES STKS (Mdn 3-Y.O) £1702.00 (£472.00: £226.00)    1¼m 36y    7-00 (7-03)

1906² **North Russia (CAN)** (Fav) (JHMGosden) 9-0 SCauthen (9) (chsd ldr: 2nd st:
             led over 3f out: edgd lft over 2f out: pushed out) ....................... —1
1620² Alyafill (USA) (BHanbury) 8-9 BRaymond (2) (5th st: hrd rdn 3f out: r.o fnl f: nt
             trble wnr) ................................................................... 1.2
 857 Garachico (USA) (bl) (GHarwood) 9-0 MRoberts (8) (plld hrd: led over 6f out:
             swtchd rt over 2f out: one pce) .......................................... 3.3
 387 Constructivist (IRE) **(70)** (BWHills) 9-0 DHolland (3) (3rd st: hrd rdn over 3f out:
             wknd over 2f out) .......................................................... nk.4
1275 Anditisitis (USA) (DWPArbuthnot) 8-9 ‡5RPrice (11) (6th st: no hdwy fnl 3f) ......... 4.5
 481 Private Practice (MJHeaton-Ellis) 8-9 WNewnes (6) (leggy: unf: bit bkwd: dwlt:
             nvr nr ldrs) ................................................................ 8.6
1770³ Kingsfold Pet (MJHaynes) 9-0 BRouse (12) (hld up: 4th st: wknd over 2f out) . 2½.7

Corpus *(RJHodges)* 8-11 ‡³TSprake (4) (leggy: bit bkwd: hld up: 7th & wkng st) ³/₄.8
1974⁵ Faustnluce Lady *(WGRWightman)* 8-9 ADicks (5) (a bhd: t.o fnl 4f) .................... 12.9
Siberian Swing *(JDRoberts)* 8-9 TLang (7) (t.o fnl 4f) ...................................... 25.10
Jarretts Wilshegar *(CLPopham)* 8-11 ‡³RPerham (1) (w'like: t.o fnl 5f) ................. 11

8/11 NORTH RUSSIA (CAN)(tchd 2/5), 9/2 Garachico (USA)(7/1—8/1), 9/1 Constructivist (IRE)(14/1—8/1),
14/1 Anditisitis (USA)(7/1—16/1), Alyafill (USA), 16/1 Kingsfold Pet, 20/1 Private Practice, 66/1 Ors. CSF
£11.14, Tote £1.80: £1.30 £2.00 £1.50 (£4.80). Sheikh Mohammed (NEWMARKET) bred by Windfields Farm in
Canada. 11 Rn    2m 9.4 (5.1)
SF—49/42/41/40/27/11

**2138** TRAFALGAR HOUSE CONSTUCTION (REGIONS) NURSERY £2856.00 (£791.00:
£378.00) **6f 16y**    7-30 (7-33)
(Weights raised 9 lb)

1657* **Hallorina** *(WGRWightman)* 8-0 GBardwell (2) (mde all: hrd rdn 2f out: r.o wl) .... —1
1442* True Story (IRE) (Fav) *(RHannon)* 8-9 MRoberts (7) (w ldrs: ev ch whn edgd lft
2f out: nt qckn) .................................................. 2.2
1584² Le Couteau *(DWPArbuthnot)* 8-8 JReid (5) (lw: a.p: r.o one pce fnl 2f) .............. 1.3
1754³ Calisar *(WGMTurner)* 8-11 ‡³TSprake (6) (lw: prom: wknd fnl f) .................... 3¹/₂.4
1790* Spring Sunrise *(MBlanshard)* 8-5 ‡³FNorton (3) (prom over 4f) .................... ¹/₂.5
1835* Simply Amiss *(SirMarkPrescott)* 9-7 GDuffield (4) (hdwy 4f out: wknd 2f out) .... 4.6
1571 Duchess Dianne (IRE) (bl) *(RJHolder)* 8-1 NAdams (1) (bhd fnl 2f) ............... 5.7

15/8 True Story (IRE)(op 3/1—tchd 7/4), 7/2 Simply Amiss(2/1—9/2), 9/2 Spring Sunrise, 8/1 HALLORIN
A(6/1—9/1), 9/1 Le Couteau, 10/1 Duchess Dianne (IRE)(8/1—16/1), 14/1 Calisar. CSF £22.01, Tote £7.80:
£3.20 £2.00 (£11.30). Mrs J. A. Thomson (UPHAM) bred by W. G. R. Wightman and Mrs J. A. Thomson. 7 Rn
1m 13.6 (4.6)
SF—2/3/–/–/–/–

**2139** 3IR GORDON RICHARDS GRADUATION STKS (3-Y.O) £2562.00 (£618.00)
**2m 49y**    8-00 (8-01)

1633² **Glaisdale (IRE) (90)** (Fav) *(HRACecil)* 9-4 SCauthen (2) (led 3f: rdn to ld over
3f out: edgd rt over 2f out: r.o wl) .................................... —1
1714* Hidden Light (IRE) **(79)** *(MAJarvis)* 8-6 ‡⁵KRutter (1) (led after 3f: hdd over 3f
out: hrd rdn & edgd rt 2f out: no ex fnl f) ........................... 3¹/₂.2

1/2 GLAISDALE (IRE), 7/4 Hidden Light (IRE). Tote £1.50. Sheikh Mohammed (NEWMARKET) bred by Ron Con
Ltd in Ireland. 2 Rn    3m 42.2 (flag) (14.4)

**2140** UNIVERSITY AND LITERARY CLUB STKS (F & M) £1900.00 (£525.00: £250.00)
**7f 16y**    8-30 (8-32)

1928² **Mrs Fisher (IRE) (90)** (Fav) *(SirMarkPrescott)* 3-8-13 GDuffield (2) (mde
virtually all: clr over 1f out: v.easily) .............................. —1
1533⁵ Hugging **(77)** *(MMcCormack)* 3-8-10 JReid (1) (swtg: chsd wnr fnl 3f: no imp) 2¹/₂.2
1918* Followmegirls *(MrsALMKing)* 3-8-0 ‡⁷AGarth (3) (swtg: prom tl rdn & wknd 2f
out) .................................................................. 10.3
1315 Acara (IRE) *(CJames)* 3-8-7 JWilliams (4) (plld hrd: w wnr tl wknd qckly over 3f
out: t.o) ............................................................. 7.4

2/5 MRS FISHER (IRE), 3/1 Hugging, 20/1 Ors. CSF £1.82, Tote £1.40 (£1.50). Mr G. D. Waters (NEWMARKET)
bred by G. D. Waters in Ireland. 4 Rn    1m 25.2 (4.7)
SF—28/17/–

**2141** LUNDY ISLAND H'CAP (0-70) £1730.00 (£480.00: £230.00)    **6f 16y**    9-00 (9-06)

1814² **Martinosky (63)** (Fav) *(WGRWightman)* 6-9-8 JWilliams (4) (lw: hld up: rdn to
ld wl ins fnl f: r.o) ................................................. —1
1888² Ayr Raider **(67)** (bl) *(WRMuir)* 5-9-12 SWhitworth (13) (a.p: r.o wl ins fnl f) ........ ¹/₂.2
1888* Scarlet Princess **(47)** *(RJHodges)* 4-8-3 ‡³FNorton (15) (hdwy over 2f out: led
over 1f out tl wl ins fnl f) ......................................... nk.3
1685 Kirriemuir **(36)** *(KOCunningham-Brown)* 4-7-9(1) SDawson (14) (b.nr hind: gd
hdwy fnl f: fin wl) ................................................... 1¹/₂.4
1590³ Proud Brigadier (IRE) **(48)** *(WCarter)* 4-8-7 JReid (10) (hdwy over 2f out: ev ch
over 1f out: one pce) ............................................... hd.5
1752 Barbara's Cutie **(39)** *(MBlanshard)* 4-7-12(1) DHolland (6) (led 3f out tl over 1f
out) ................................................................. 3.6
1947⁵ Green's Stubbs **(34)** (v) *(ABarrow)* 5-7-7 NAdams (7) (swtg: w ldrs: ev ch over
1f out: wknd fnl f) .................................................. ³/₄.7
1278 Goody Four Shoes **(45)** *(DRTucker)* 4-7-13(2) ‡⁵RPrice (11) (late hdwy: nrst fin) ³/₄.8
1340⁴ Beveled Edge **(54)** *(BPalling)* 3-8-2 ‡⁵StephenDavies (8) (swtg: prom 4f) ......... nk.9
1916⁶ Tickham Vixen (IRE) **(47)** *(JDBethell)* 4-8-6 TyroneWilliams (3) (bhd most of
wy) ................................................................. 1¹/₂.10

1978 Domiana **(39)** (bl) *(MBlanshard)* 4–7-7[5] ‡[5]BDoyle (1) (prom 3f) ..................... d.h.**10**
1718 Juvenara **(40)** *(CJHill)* 6–7-6[2] ‡[7]AGarth (12) (prom 4f) ................................. 2.**12**
1542 Bwana Kali **(34)** (bl) *(JABennett)* 10–7-7 GBardwell (5) (b: sn wl bhd) .......... 1½.**13**
*1685* Super Heights **(58)** (bl) *(MissAJWhitfield)* 4–8-12 ‡[5]ATucker (9) (a bhd) ............. 1.**14**
1162 Miramede **(42)** *(RJHodges)* 4–7-12[6] ‡[3]TSprake (2) (led 3f: sn wknd) ............ 3.**15**
LONG HANDICAP: Green's Stubbs 6-10, Domiana 7-0, Bwana Kali 6-12.

**5/2** MARTINOSKY(op 6/1), **6/1** Ayr Raider, Proud Brigadier (IRE), **13/2** Juvenara(6/1—4/1), **9/1** Scarlet Princess(op 6/1), **14/1** Beveled Edge, Kirriemuir, **20/1** Green's Stubbs, Goody Four Shoes(op 10/1), **25/1** Tickham Vixen (IRE), Miramede, Super Heights, **33/1** Domiana, **50/1** Barbara's Cutie, **66/1** Bwana Kali. CSF £16.86, CT £108.94. Tote £3.40: £1.70 £2.30 £3.00 (£8.90). Mr D. B. Clark (UPHAM) bred by David B. Clark. 15 Rn                                                                               1m 12.4 (3.4)
                                                                               SF–46/48/24/10/21/–

T/Plpt: £9.40 (231.9 Tckts).                                                                               KH

---

## 1728—HAMILTON (R-H)
### Thursday, July 16th [Good to firm]
Going Allowance: minus 0.35 sec per fur (F)                                    Wind: slt across

Stalls: low

**2142**   GLENGOYNE SINGLE HIGHLAND MALT SCOTCH WHISKY H'CAP (3-Y.O) (0-70)
£2611.20 (£723.20: £345.60)   **1m 3f 16y**                              2-05 (2-06)
(Weights raised 2 lb)
1914[2] **Regal Lover (IRE) (68)** *(MBell)* 9-7 MHills (6) (chsd ldrs: rdn to ld appr fnl f: r.o)   —**1**
919[3] Hanley's Hands (IRE) **(58)** (Fav) *(MHTompkins)* 8-11 PRobinson (1) (lw: hld up: effrt 4f out: edgd rt: styd on to chal ins fnl f: nt qckn nr fin) ¾.**2**
1286 Bartolomeo (USA) **(45)** *(MrsJRRamsden)* 7-12 AMackay (7) (cl up: led 7f out tl appr fnl f: no ex) 2½.**3**
1962★ Tees Gazette Girl **(41)** *(MrsGRReveley)* 7-1 ‡[7]ClaireBalding (4) (bhd: drvn along 4f out: styd on wl: nr fin) 1½.**4**
1438 The Dandy Don (IRE) **(52)** *(DenysSmith)* 8-5 JCarroll (3) (lw: in tch: effrt 4f out: no imp) 10.**5**
1735[4] Phargold **(40)** *(PCHaslam)* 7-7 LCharnock (5) (led 4f: cl up tl wknd 2f out) 8.**6**
1855[2] Qualitair Memory (IRE) **(41)** *(JFBottomley)* 7-8 PBurke (2) (lw: chsd ldrs tl outpcd over 3f out: sn btn) 3½.**7**
LONG HANDICAP: Phargold (IRE) 7-6.

**Evens** Hanley's Hands (IRE), **11/4** REGAL LOVER (IRE), **13/2** Tees Gazette Girl, **14/1** Bartolomeo (USA), Qualitair Memory (IRE), **16/1** The Dandy Don (IRE), **33/1** Phargold (IRE). CSF £5.59, Tote £2.80: £1.10 £1.20 (£1.70). Mr A. A. Bridgewater (NEWMARKET) bred by Mrs P. Grubb in Ireland. 7 Rn          2m 21.2 (2.2)
                                                                               SF–48/36/18/4/2/–

**2143**   WESTWOOD AUCTION GRADUATION STKS (2-Y.O) £2280.00 (£630.00: £300.00)
**5f 4y**                                                                      2-35 (2-36)

1513[4] **Two Moves in Front (IRE)** *(JBerry)* 9-4 DMcKeown (3) (lw: disp ld 3f: sn rdn & outpcd: styd on agn to ld ins fnl f) —**1**
1973[2] Tuscan Dawn (Fav) *(JBerry)* 9-4 JCarroll (1) (lw: disp ld tl led 2f out: sn hrd drvn: hdd & no ex ins fnl f) 1.**2**
1638★ Caps Ninety-Two (IRE) *(DrJDSCargill)* 8-8 ‡[5]JWeaver (2) (lw: a chsng ldrs: hdwy u.p over 1f out: nvr nr to chal) 2.**3**
2045[5] Selvole (v) *(MissLAPerratt)* 7-10 ‡[7]RHavlin (4) (chsd ldrs: hung lft over 1f out: sn btn) 3.**4**

**2/5** Tuscan Dawn, **3/1** Caps Ninety-Two (IRE), **10/1** TWO MOVES IN FRONT (IRE)(8/1—12/1), **40/1** Selvole. CSF £14.30, Tote £5.60 (£2.00). Mr Robert Aird (COCKERHAM) bred by Newlands House Stud in Ireland. 4 Rn          59.5 sec (1.2)
                                                                               SF–45/41/23/–

**2144**   PENROSE HILL H'CAP (0-70) £2454.40 (£678.40: £323.20)   **6f 5y**   3-05 (3-08)
(Weights raised 2 lb)
1961[2] **Flashy's Son (45)** (Fav) *(MDHammond)* 4–8-8 ‡[5]JWeaver (2) (b.off hind: a w ldr: r.o u.p fnl f to ld post) —**1**
1617★ Granny Mc **(56)** *(EJAlston)* 5–9-10 PRobinson (4) (led: rdn fnl f: jst ct) .......... s.h.**2**
1878 Dawes of Nelson **(41)** *(MJBolton)* 7–8-9 AMackay (1) (lw: trckd ldrs: effrt ½-wy: nt pce to chal) 1½.**3**
*Stewards Enquiry: Obj. to Flashy's Son by Robinson overruled.*

**11/8** FLASHY'S SON, **2/1** Granny Mc(op 5/4), **5/2** Dawes of Nelson. CSF £3.73, Tote £1.80 (£1.80). Lee Construction (Newcastle) Ltd (MIDDLEHAM) bred by Brian A. Shovelton (North Wales) Ltd. 3 Rn
1m 11.4 (1.4)<br>SF—24/39/19

---

**2145**     BURNBANK CLAIMING STKS (2-Y.O) £2385.00 (£660.00: £315.00)
               **6f 5y**                                                 3-40 (3-47)

1884[2] **Second Colours (USA)** (Fav) *(PSFelgate)* 8-8 KDarley (1) (mde all: shkn up over 1f out: r.o: eased nr fin) ................................. —1

1923[4] Daily Sport's Gift *(JBerry)* 8-4 JCarroll (3) (lw: a chsng wnr: rdn to chal over 1f out: nt qckn) ................................. 2$\frac{1}{2}$.2

Anne's Bay (IRE) *(DMoffatt)* 7-5 ‡7DarrenMoffatt (2) (neat: bit bkwd: uns rdr & bolted bef s: outpcd & bhd after 1f) ................................. 30.3

**1/3** SECOND COLOURS (USA)(tchd 4/7), **5/2** Daily Sport's Gift(6/4—3/1), **20/1** Anne's Bay (IRE)(op 6/1). CSF £1.49, Tote £1.40 (£1.40). Mr P. D. Savill (MELTON MOWBRAY) bred by Dinnaken Farm in USA. 3 Rn
1m 12.4 (2.4)<br>SF—4/—/—

---

**2146**     RUTHERGLEN MEDIAN AUCTION STKS (Mdn 3-Y.O) £2238.00 (£618.00: £294.00)
               **1m 65y**                                                4-10 (4-17)

1562[2] **Northern Graduate (USA) (53)** (Fav) *(MrsGRReveley)* 8-2 KDarley (2) (lw: disp ld tl led over 2f out: styd on wl) ................................. —1

1505 Port in a Storm *(WJarvis)* 8-11 JCarroll (1) (disp ld tl hdd over 2f out: edgd lft & nt qckn) ................................. 8.2

1903 Qualitair Idol **(48)** *(JFBottomley)* 7-11 PBurke (3) (lw: chsd ldrs: effrt 4f out: no imp) ................................. 3$\frac{1}{2}$.3

009 Shadaylou (IRE) **(18)** *(MissLAPerratt)* 7-10 †7RHavlin (5) (chsd ldrs: hdwy 4f out: sn rdn & btn) ................................. $\frac{3}{4}$.4

*Valkyrie Reef (14/1) Withdrawn (ref to ent stalls) : not under orders — Rule 4 applies*

**11/10** NORTHERN GRADUATE (USA)(6/4—Evens), **6/4** Port in a Storm(Evens—13/8), **7/1** Qualitair Idol(6/1—10/1), **25/1** Shadaylou (IRE). CSF £2.71, Tote £2.10: £3.00 (£1.20). Mr P. D. Savill (SALTBURN) bred by Ann Trimble & Donald T. Johnson in USA. 4 Rn
1m 45.7 (2.4)<br>SF—10/—/—/—

---

**2147**     GLASGOW FAIR APP'CE H'CAP (3 & 4-Y.O) (0-70) £2406.00 (£666.00: £318.00)
               **1m 1f 36y**                                            4-45 (4-45)

                               (Weights raised 3 lb)

1528[3] **Talented Ting (IRE) (63)** *(PCHaslam)* 3-8-12 ‡5NicolaHowarth (5) (a cl up: led 3f out: rdn & styd on wl) ................................. —1

1840[5] Henbury Hall (IRE) **(60)** *(MrsGRReveley)* 4-9-4 ‡5SCopp (3) (lw: led tl hdd 3f out: ev ch tl wknd nr fin) ................................. 1$\frac{1}{2}$.2

1336[6] Batabanoo **(68)** *(MrsGRReveley)* 3-9-8 SWynne (1) (lw: chsd ldrs: effrt 3f out: one pce) ................................. 5.3

1964 Broad Appeal **(38)** (bl) *(BBeasley)* 4-8-1 DCarson (6) (lt-f: a.p: effrt over 3f out: no imp) ................................. $\frac{3}{4}$.4

1855[3] Hataal (IRE) **(39)** *(JBalding)* 3-7-7 ClaireBalding (4) (lw: bhd: effrt 4f out: n.d) ................................. 2$\frac{1}{2}$.5

1533 Forest Dew (USA) **(70)** (Fav) *(MHTompkins)* 3-9-5 ‡5SMulvey (2) (lw: bhd: rdn over 3f out: n.d) ................................. $\frac{3}{4}$.6

**2/1** Forest Dew (USA), **3/1** Batabanoo, **4/1** TALENTED TING (IRE)(3/1—9/2), **7/1** Broad Appeal, **8/1** Henbury Hall (IRE)(op 4/1), **10/1** Hataal (IRE). CSF £29.06, Tote £3.00: £2.60 £6.30 (£14.80). Mr Martin Wickens (MIDDLEHAM) bred by R. A. Keogh in Ireland. 6 Rn
1m 59.4 (5.1)

T/Plpt: £303.20 (3.1 Tckts).                                                            AA

---

## HAMILTON (R-H)
### Friday, July 17th [Good to firm]
Going Allowance: St: minus 0.50; Rest: minus 0.30 sec per fur (F)       Wind: almost nil

Stalls: low

**2148**     GINESTRI ICE CREAM H'CAP (0-70) £2406.00 (£666.00: £318.00)
               **1$\frac{1}{2}$m 17y**                                                6-45 (6-48)

1735[5] **Danza Heights (37)** (Fav) *(MrsGRReveley)* 6-8-0 JLowe (4) (lw: trckd ldrs: led & qcknd over 3f out: sn clr: easily) ................................. —1

206⁴ Carol's Pet (IRE) **(47)** *(MJohnston)* 4–8-5 ‡⁵JWeaver (1) (a cl up: led 4f out: sn hdd & one pce) ............................................ **4.2**

1621⁴ Hamilton Lady (IRE) **(33)** *(DMoffatt)* 4–7-10 AMackay (5) (lw: led 2f: chsd ldrs: rdn over 3f out: : no imp) ............................................ ³/₄.3

1893² Miliyel **(51)** *(PMonteith)* 3–8-2 LCharnock (3) (hld up: hdwy 4f out: rdn 2f out: sn btn) ............................................ ¹/₂.4

1968⁶ Young George **(60)** *(MDods)* 5–9-9 KFallon (2) (a.p: wnt 2nd 3f out: sn hrd rdn & no imp) ............................................ s.h.5

1740³ Deb's Ball **(65)** *(DMoffatt)* 6–9-7 ‡⁷DarrenMoffatt (7) (lw: dwlt: bhd tl styd on fnl 2f) ............................................ nk.6

New Beginning **(42)** *(JSHaldane)* 9–8-5 KDarley (6) (b: led after 2f tl hdd 4f out: eased wl over 2f out: t.o) ............................................ **7**

6/4 DANZA HEIGHTS, 3/1 Young George, 7/1 Carol's Pet (IRE)(8/1—5/1), Miliyel, 12/1 Deb's Ball(op 8/1), 14/1 Hamilton Lady, (IRE), 66/1 New Beginning. CSF £10.46, Tote £2.50: £1.60 £2.90 (£13.50). Mrs M. Williams (SALTBURN) bred by The Champagne Syndicate. 7 Rn                     2m 36.4 (4.4)
SF—6/–/–/–

**2149** CLYDE CLAIMING STKS £2259.00 (£624.00: £297.00)   **1m 3f 16y**   7-15 (7-16)

1740⁶ **Able Lassie (68)** (Fav) *(MrsGRReveley)* 4–8-11 ‡³JFanning (3) (lw: trckd ldr: slt ld 3f out: shkn up over 1f out: sn clr & eased) ............................................ —1

2101 Lord Advocate **(43)** (v) *(MPNaughton)* 4–8-7 ‡⁵JWeaver (1) (led tl hdd 3f out: kpt on u.p: no ch w wnr fnl f) ............................................ 2.2

Supreme Court **(38)** *(MDods)* 5–8-10 KFallon (2) (outpcd & lost tch 7f out: n.d after) ............................................ dist.3

2/11 ABLE LASSIE, 5/1 Lord Advocate, 33/1 Supreme Court. CSF £1.33, Tote £1.20 (£1.10). Mr Robbie Cameron (SALTBURN) bred by R. A. Cameron. 3 Rn                     2m 23.6 (4.6)
SF—18/10/–

**2150** SUNDAY MAIL H'CAP (0-80) £2454.40 (£678.40: £323.20)   **1m 65y**   7-45 (7-46)

1619* **Spanish Verdict (67)** (Fav) *(DenysSmith)* 5–9-13 KFallon (4) (lw: in tch: effrt 3f out: r.o u.p to ld wl ins fnl f) ............................................ —1

1966⁴ Tarda **(55)** *(MrsGRReveley)* 5–9-1 KDarley (2) (trckd ldrs: chal 3f out: sn hrd drvn & one pce) ............................................ 1¹/₂.2

1960⁴ Flying Down to Rio (IRE) **(52)** *(MPNaughton)* 4–8-7 ‡⁵JWeaver (1) (swtg: cl up: led 4f out: rdn over 2f out: hdd & no ex wl ins fnl f) ............................................ nk.3

1911 Silver Haze **(59)** *(WAStephenson)* 8–9-5 MBirch (3) (lw: hld up: effrt 4f out: sn hrd rdn & btn) ............................................ 20.4

1129 Master Plan (FR) **(35)** *(MissLAPerratt)* 6–7-6⁽²⁾ ‡³JFanning (5) (led tl hdd 4f out: sn wknd) ............................................ 6.5

LONG HANDICAP: Master Plan (FR) 6-11.

7/4 SPANISH VERDICT, 9/4 Flying Down to Rio (IRE), 7/2 Tarda, 4/1 Silver Haze, 33/1 Master Plan (FR). CSF £7.75, Tote £2.50: £1.50 £2.00 (£3.40). Cox & Allen (Kendal) Ltd (BISHOP AUCKLAND) bred by Hyde Stud. 5 Rn
1m 45 (1.7)
SF—51/34/25/–

**2151** CAROUSEL SNOWBALL (S) STKS (3-Y.O) £2280.00 (£630.00: £300.00)   **6f 5y**   8-15 (8-16)

1978 **Our John (48)** *(RonaldThompson)* 8–7 AMackay (3) (trckd ldrs: rdn to ld ins fnl f: r.o wl) ............................................ —1

1753⁶ Miss Siham (IRE) **(47)** *(JBalding)* 8-2 ‡⁷ClaireBalding (5) (lw: led tl hdd ins fnl f: sn btn) ............................................ 3¹/₂.2

1753 Capital Idea (IRE) **(51)** (v) *(RonaldThompson)* 9-0 JLowe (2) (cl up tl outpcd over 1f out: styd on nr fin) ............................................ 1¹/₂.3

1618⁶ Murray's Mazda (IRE) **(68)** (Fav) *(JBerry)* 9-0 JCarroll (6) (lw: plld hrd trckd ldrs: effrt 2f out: nt r.o fnl f) ............................................ 1.4

1962⁵ Lingdale Lass **(52)** (bl) *(MrsGRReveley)* 8-9 MBirch (4) (hld up & bhd: effrt ¹/₂-wy: sn hrd rdn & btn) ............................................ 7.5

1625⁵ Melody Anne **(34)** *(JSHaldane)* 8-2 LCharnock (1) (b.hind: spd 4f: sn wknd) ............................................ 6.6

4/7 Murray's Mazda (IRE), 5/2 Lingdale Lass, 8/1 Capital Idea (IRE)(op 4/1), 9/1 Miss Siham (IRE), 16/1 Melody Anne, 20/1 OUR JOHN. CSF £153.18, Tote £11.10: £3.60 £2.30 (£106.20). Haggswood Partnerships (DONCASTER) bred by Burley Lodge Stud and Mrs S. Kumaramangalam. 6 Rn; No bid
1m 11.1 (1.1)
SF—9/–/–

**2152** JOE PUNTER NURSERY £2454.40 (£678.40: £323.20)   **5f 4y**   8-45 (8-45)
(Weights raised 11 lb)

2145* **Second Colours (USA)** *(PSFelgate)* 10-0 (7x) KDarley (1) (lw: sn disp ld: led ¹/₂-wy: r.o wl fnl f) ............................................ —1

1989[2] Be Polite (IRE) (Fav) (MBell) 7-13 ‡5JWeaver (4) (a chng ldrs: hdwy u.p over 1f out: r.o) .......................................................................................... 1.2
1435* Make it Happen (IRE) (bl) (JBerry) 9-6 JCarroll (2) (disp ld to ½-wy: hrd rdn appr fnl f: kpt on) ........................................................................... ¾.3
1541 Stardust Express (MJohnston) 8-10 RPElliott (3) (trckd ldrs: hdwy 2f out: wknd appr fnl f) ........................................................................................ 4.4

**5/6** Be Polite (IRE)(5/4—4/5), **9/4** Make it Happen (IRE), **4/1** SECOND COLOURS (USA), **8/1** Stardust Express. CSF £8.00, Tote £5.00 (£3.90). Mr P. D. Savill (MELTON MOWBRAY) bred by Dinnaken Farm in USA. 4 Rn
59.8 sec (1.5)
SF—34/1/19/–

**2153**   TRABROUN H'CAP (0-70) £2196.00 (£606.00: £288.00)   **5f 4y**   9-15 (9-16)

2144[3] **Dawes of Nelson (41)** (MJBolton) 7-7-13 JLowe (1) (lw: mde all: qcknd 1f out: comf) ...................................................................................... —1
1787[4] Here Comes a Star (56) (Jt-Fav) (JMCarr) 4-9-0 SMorris (4) (trckd ldrs: hdwy & ev ch over 1f out: rdn & nt qckn) ................................................. 1½.2
1853 Hinari Video (46) (MJohnston) 7-8-4 RPElliott (2) (lw: a chsng ldrs: hrd drvn 2f out: nt qckn) ....................................................................................... 2½.3
1878[6] Prince Belfort (70) (Jt-Fav) (MPNaughton) 4-9-9 ‡5JWeaver (5) (lw: chsd ldrs: rdn 2f out: grad wknd) ....................................................................... 2½.4
1892[4] Chateau Nord (56) (JBerry) 3-8-9 JCarroll (3) (prom tl outpcd fnl 2f) ............... 3.5

**11/4** Prince Belfort, Here Comes a Star, **7/2** Chateau Nord, DAWES OF NELSON, **9/2** Hinari Video. CSF £12.97, Tote £4.50: £2.10 £1.20 (£4.70). Mr A. R. M. Galbraith (SHREWTON) bred by D. Cornwall. 5 Rn 58.4 sec (0.1)
SF—35/44/24/33/7

T/Plpt: £914.50 (1.7 Tckts).   AA

2038—**SOUTHWELL (L-H)** Fibresand

**Friday, July 17th [Standard]**

Going Allowance: 5f: minus 0.30; Rest: minus 0.15 sec per fur (FS)   Wind: slt half bhd

Stalls: high

**2154**   EMPEROR H'CAP (0-70) £2175.00 (£600.00: £285.00)   **5f (AWT)**   2-10 (2-10)

1978 **Drummer's Dream (IRE) (39)** (v) (MrsNMacauley) 4-8-12 PRobinson (2) (chsd ldrs: rdn wl over 1f out: styd on to ld cl home) ........... —1
2105* Spring High (62) (bl) (KTIvory) 5-10-0 (7x) ‡7CScally (3) (a cl up: led appr fnl f tl hdd nr fin) ........................................................................................ s.h.2
2061[5] Trioming (40) (Fav) (APJones) 6-8-13 NAdams (1) (mde most tl hdd & wknd appr fnl f) ............................................................................................... 4.3
2040 Our Amber (28) (DWChapman) 5-8-1 SWood (4) (w ldr: sn drvn along: wknd wl over 1f out) ...................................................................................... 5.4

**7/4** Trioming, **5/2** DRUMMER'S DREAM (IRE), Spring High(op Evens), **7/1** Our Amber. CSF £7.89, Tote £3.20 (£3.10). Mrs Gail Orbell (MELTON MOWBRAY) bred by Sean Gorman in Ireland. 4 Rn 59.7 sec (1.7)
SF—34/49/18/–

**2155**   SKIPPER (S) STKS (3 & 4-Y.O) £2553.00 (£708.00: £339.00)   **1½m (AWT)**   2-40 (2-41)

1907[3] **Iron Baron (IRE) (65)** (RHollinshead) 3-8-10[(1)] SPerks (2) (lw: hld up in tch: smooth hdwy 2f out: led & hung lft over 1f out: sn clr) ................ —1
1759[6] Monorose (51) (v) (DHaydnJones) 3-8-4 TyroneWilliams (4) (chsd ldrs: hrd drvn to ld 3f out: hdd & sltly hmpd over 1f out: no ch w wnr) ..... 3.2
1777[4] Ghostly Glow (52) (v) (CCElsey) 3-8-9 TRogers (1) (led 2f: prom: hrd rdn & outpcd 3f out: kpt on fnl f) ......................................................... 1½.3
2042 Milly Black (IRE) (45) (JLHarris) 4-8-13 ‡3FNorton (5) (bhd: outpcd 7f out: styd on u.p fnl 2f) ............................................................................ 3.4
1288[3] Copper Trader (46) (KSBridgwater) 3-8-4 NAdams (6) (lw: plld hrd: a.p: w ldr 6f out tl wknd wl over 2f out) ....................................................... 4.5
1885[4] Elwazir (USA) (64) (Fav) (DMarks) 3-8-9 PRobinson (7) (led after 2f tl wknd 3f out) ............................................................................................... 12.6
Light-of-the-Loch (AWPotts) 4-9-2 AProud (3) (a bhd: lost tch 7f out) ............... 10.7
*Stewards Enquiry: Obj. to Iron Baron (IRE) by Williams overruled.*

**2/1** Elwazir (USA)(op 5/4), **100/30** IRON BARON (IRE), **9/2** Copper Trader(5/1—8/1), Milly Black (IRE), **10/1** Monorose, **16/1** Ghostly Glow, **20/1** Light-of-the-Loch. CSF £30.25, Tote £4.10: £1.80 £5.70 (£17.50). Mrs B. Facchino (UPPER LONGDON) bred by Mrs D. Jackson in Ireland. 7 Rn; No bid 2m 40.9 (6.7)
SF—11/–/1/–/–/–

**2156** MELFIN U.K. LIMITED H'CAP (3-Y.O) (0-70) £2448.00 (£678.00: £324.00)
1½m (AWT) 3-15 (3-15)
(Weights raised 2 lb)

2007³ Pie Hatch (IRE) (45) (SirMarkPrescott) 8-0⁽³⁾ GDuffield (3) (lw: chsd ldr: led
over 3f out: clr wl over 1f out: styd on wl) ............................ —1
2014* Ideal Candidate (55) (Fav) (TJNaughton) 8-5 (5x) ‡⁵DHarrison (6) (bhd: pushed
along 6f out: hdwy over 3f out: kpt on fnl 2f: nt rch wnr) ...... 2.2
1548² Spray of Orchids (53) (JEtherington) 8-8 PRobinson (1) (in tch tl lost pl over 6f
out: hdwy u.p 3f out: kpt on) ........................................... 2¹/₂.3
1971 Gallant Jack (IRE) (64) (v) (DHaydnJones) 9-5 TyroneWilliams (5) (lw: a.p: w
wnr over 3f out: wknd wl over 1f out) ................................ 4.4
1372⁵ Make Me Proud (IRE) (48) (bl) (RWArmstrong) 8-3 BCrossley (2) (led tl hdd &
wknd qckly over 3f out) .................................................... 15.5
1371 Nectar Collector (65) (CFWall) 9-6 NDay (4) (sme hdwy u.p over 3f out: sn
wknd) ............................................................................ s.h.6
533⁶ Tolls Choice (IRE) (66) (MWEasterby) 9-7 TLucas (7) (plld hrd early: bhd fnl 5f) 30.7

5/4 Ideal Candidate(tchd 2/1), 100/30 PIE HATCH (IRE)(9/4—7/2), 5/1 Spray of Orchids(op 3/1), 13/2 Nectar
Collector, 10/1 Tolls Choice (IRE)(op 6/1), 12/1 Gallant Jack (IRE)(op 6/1), 14/1 Make Me Proud (IRE). CSF
£8.20, Tote £3.50: £2.60 £1.10 (£4.50). Miss Elizabeth Aldous (NEWMARKET) bred by Newtownbarry House
Stud in Ireland. 7 Rn
2m 38.4 (4.2)
SF—26/25/23/26/–/–

**2157** TATTERSALLS AUCTION SERIES STKS (Qualifier) (Mdn 2-Y.O) £2454.40 (£678.40:
£323.20) 6f (AWT) 3-50 (3-51)

1887² Penang Star (IRE) (Fav) (WAO'Gorman) 8-8 ‡³EmmaO'Gorman (3) (lw: hdwy
¹/₂-wy: led 2f out: r.o wl) ................................................. —1
Abergele (JGFitzGerald) 8-13 GDuffield (4) (lengthy: scope: led 1f out:
sn rdn & kpt on same pce fnl f) ....................................... 2¹/₂.2
1923² Colfax Starlight (BSRothwell) 8-0 SWood (1) (reard stalls & s.s: led after 1f tl
hdd 2f out: wknd over 1f out) .......................................... 4.3
1675 Persian Traveller (IRE) (CNAllen) 7-12 ‡7GForster (2) (rdn & outpcd fr ¹/₂-wy) ..... 2.4
1886³ Sefio (JBerry) 8-8 GCarter (5) (prom tl rdn & wknd 2f out) ...................... 6.5

6/4 PENANG STAR (IRE)(op 10/11), 5/2 Colfax Starlight, 100/30 Abergele, 7/1 Sefio(op 7/2), 16/1 Persian
Traveller (IRE). CSF £6.39, Tote £2.20: £1.20 £2.10 (£5.60). Mr N. S. Yong (NEWMARKET) bred by B. Kennedy
in Ireland. 5 Rn
1m 15.8 (2.4)
SF—28/23/–/–/–

**2158** SHOOSMITH & HARRISON CLAIMING STKS (2-Y.O) £2217.00 (£612.00: £291.00)
7f (AWT) 4-20 (4-20)

1989* Another Kingdom (JWharton) 8-6 JQuinn (3) (led 1f: chsd ldr: led 2f out: sn clr) —1
1788* Wishing Cap (USA) (Fav) (SirMarkPrescott) 8-11 GDuffield (2) (lw: hld up: drvn
along over 2f out: styd on fnl f: no ch w wnr) .................... 3.2
1788 Laurel King (bl) (JBerry) 9-3 GCarter (1) (s.s: led after 1f tl hdd 2f out: sn rdn &
btn) ............................................................................. 2¹/₂.3
1900 Dream Princess (JFBottomley) 7-12 PBurke (4) (prom tl wknd u.p 2f out) ......... 4.4

Evens Wishing Cap (USA)(tchd 6/4), 7/4 ANOTHER KINGDOM(op 11/10), 3/1 Laurel King, 33/1 Dream
Princess. CSF £3.96, Tote £2.70 (£1.70). Mr W. Wharton (MELTON MOWBRAY) bred by A. B. Barraclough. 4 Rn
1m 30.7 (4.1)
SF—15/11/9/–

**2159** RED ADMIRAL H'CAP (0-70) £2406.00 (£666.00: £318.00) 7f (AWT) 4-55 (4-56)

2103* Hawaii Storm (FR) (63) (MissAJWhitfield) 4-10-0 (5x) ‡⁵ATucker (5) (lw: hdwy
appr st: rdn to ld over 1f out: kpt on) .............................. —1
2026³ Sandmoor Denim (54) (Jt-Fav) (SRBowring) 5-9-3 ‡7MHarris (3) (lw: s.s: hdwy
3f out: ev ch appr fnl f: unable qckn) ............................... 1.2
2063* Miss Movie World (43) (NBycroft) 3-8-1 (5x) ‡5NKennedy (2) (hdwy 3f out: rdn
2f out: swtchd outside & styd on wl nr fin) ........................ ³/₄.3
2099 Gleneliane (IRE) (36) (bl) (JLHarris) 4-7-13⁽²⁾ ‡7GForster (6) (chsd ldrs tl rdn &
unable qckn fnl 2f) ........................................................ 2.4
2040³ Quinzii Martin (53) (v) (Jt-Fav) (DHaydnJones) 4-9-9 TyroneWilliams (7) (chsd
ldrs: chal 2f out: wknd appr fnl f) .................................... 1¹/₂.5
1978⁵ Reina (31) (bl) (JDBethell) 4-8-1 SDawson (4) (cl up: led ¹/₂-wy tl hdd &wknd
over 1f out) ................................................................. 3.6
1598⁶ Certain Lady (54) (GBlum) 3-8-12 ‡5DHarrison (8) (cl up tl wknd 2f out) ............ 3.7
2040 Tara's Delight (58) (WAO'Gorman) 5-9-11 ‡³EmmaO'Gorman (9) (s.i.s: hdwy
on outside 4f out: wknd 2f out) ....................................... s.h.8
1847 Top One (51) (CJHill) 7-9-7 NAdams (1) (led to ¹/₂-wy: wknd over 2f out) .......... 7.9

3/1 Quinzii Martin(op 9/2), Sandmoor Denim, 7/1 HAWAII STORM (FR), **9/1** Top One(op 6/1), Miss Movie World, **11/1** Tara's Delight(8/1—12/1), **12/1** Ors. CSF £26.15, CT £171.88. Tote £9.80: £2.60 £1.80 £3.20 (£10.30). Mr Andreas Sofroniou (LAMBOURN) bred by Horse France in France. 9 Rn

1m 29.7 (3.1)

SF—52/37/19/7/28/–

T/Plpt: £51.20 (20.5 Tckts). O'R

---

1448 — **THIRSK (L-H)**
**Friday, July 17th [Good to firm]**
Going Allowance: St: minus 0.40; Rest; minus 0.20 sec per fur (F)      Wind: fresh half bhd

Stalls: high

**2160**      LEVY BOARD APP'CE H'CAP (0-70) £2595.00 (£720.00: £345.00)      **1m**  2-15 (2-18)

1911* **Shaieef (IRE) (54)** *(RJRWilliams)* 4–8-8 (4x) ‡[7]GMitchell (1) (s.i.s: hld up & bhd: hdwy & pushed along over 2f out: r.o wl to ld wl ins fnl f) .... —**1**
1992[2] Tyrian Purple (IRE) **(54)** (Fav) *(RHollinshead)* 4–9-1 MHumphries (3) (lw: led: nt qckn ins fnl f) ............................................................ 1½.**2**
891[4] Errema **(46)** *(CTinkler)* 7–8-7 JMarshall (9) (sn bhd: gd hdwy over 2f out: r.o one pce fnl f) .................................... 1½.**3**
1992[4] Ballad Dancer **(53)** *(EJAlston)* 7–8-7 ‡[7]SKnott (5) (hdwy on outside over 2f out: ev ch over 1f out: kpt on same pace) ................... hd.**4**
1440[4] Hot Punch **(49)** *(PCalver)* 3–7-9 ‡[7]CAdamson (2) (chsd ldrs tl outpcd 2f out: kpt on same pce) ............................. 4.**5**
1889[4] Stairway to Heaven (IRE) **(55)** (bl) *(TDBarron)* 4–9-2 SWynne (7) (sn bhd: sme hdwy 2f out: n.d) ................................. nk.**6**
1981* Weeheby (USA) **(71)** *(AAScott)* 5–9-10 (4x) JTate (6) (hdwy to chase ldrs 5f out: rdn & wknd 2f out) ............................... 1.**7**
1344[2] Aardvark **(67)** *(RMWhitaker)* 6–10-0 GParkin (11) (lw: chsd ldrs: ev ch whn rdn 2f out: edgd rt & sn wknd) ................ hd.**8**
1862[4] Reilton **(57)** *(JParkes)* 5–9-4 PBowe (8) (nvr nr to chal) ............................... 1.**9**
1964 Talish **(37)** (v) *(TDBarron)* 4–7-12[4] VHalliday (4) (chsd ldr: ev ch tl rdn & wknd 2f out) ......................... 4.**10**
1889[5] Le Saule D'Or **(32)** *(APJames)* 5–7-7 DWright (10) (s.s: a wl bhd) ................. 6.**11**
LONG HANDICAP: Le Saule D'Or 7-0.

7/2 Tyrian Purple (IRE), **4/1** SHAIEEF (IRE), **5/1** Aardvark, 7/1 Weeheby (USA), **15/2** Talish, 8/1 Stairway to Heaven (IRE), **16/1** Ballad Dancer, Errema, Hot Punch, **20/1** Le Saule D'Or, **25/1** Reilton. CSF £17.74, CT £186.39. Tote £5.50: £1.50 £1.60 £7.60 (£11.30). Mr Terry Minahan (NEWMARKET) bred by H. H. Aga Khan in Ireland. 11 Rn

1m 38.7 (2.7)

SF—29/31/18/17/–/13

**2161**      WESTOW STKS (2-Y.O) £2914.60 (£805.60: £383.80)      **5f**      2-45 (2-47)

2121* **Night Melody (IRE)** *(RHannon)* 9-3 KDarley (4) (lw: trckd ldrs: squeezed thro on ins just ins fnl f: r.o wl to ld last strides) ............................. —**1**
1461[5] Lucky Parkes (Fav) *(JBerry)* 8-12 JCarroll (5) (led: hung lft thrght: rdn & edgd lft 1f out: jst ct) ....................................................... nk.**2**
1998[2] Nominator *(RHollinshead)* 9-3 WRyan (2) (lw: trckd ldrs: ev ch over 1f out: kpt on same pce) ........................................... 4.**3**
Primula Bairn *(MrsJRRamsden)* 8-6 MBirch (3) (rangy: unf: bit bkwd: unruly s: dwlt: chsd ldrs: drvn along ½-wy: outpcd 1f out) ............. 1½.**4**
1854* Classic Story (USA) *(MMoubarak)* 8-12 ‡[5]JWeaver (1) (lw: unruly in stalls: w ldr: ev ch over 1f out: wknd jst ins fnl f) .................... 1½.**5**

6/5 Lucky Parkes, 5/2 Classic Story (USA), **3/1** NIGHT MELODY (IRE), **10/1** Nominator, **25/1** Primula Bairn. CSF £6.85, Tote £5.20: £2.00 £1.30 (£3.00). Mr P. D. Savill (MARLBOROUGH) bred by Leo Collins in Ireland. 5 Rn

58 sec (0.3)

SF—57/51/40/23/23

**2162**      NESS (S) STKS (3-Y.O) £2469.00 (£684.00: £327.00)      **1m**      3-20 (3-23)

2084[6] **Any Dream Would Do** *(CWThornton)* 8-9 GHind (3) (hdwy & prom ½-wy: led over 1f out: rdn clr) ............................... —**1**
1964 Angel's Wing **(32)** *(RMWhitaker)* 8-9 ACulhane (7) (hld up: hdwy over 2f out: styd on u.p fnl f: no ch w wnr) ................ 6.**2**
1663 Throw Away Line **(42)** *(REBarr)* 8-9 SWebster (5) (a chsng ldrs: styd on one pce u.p fnl 2f) ........................................ hd.**3**
1907 Cledeschamps *(MWEllerby)* 8-9 SMorris (9) (chsd ldrs tl wknd 2f out) ............... 4.**4**
490 Noggings (IRE) **(63)** (Fav) *(NTinkler)* 9-0 MBirch (1) (lw: w ldrs: led 4f out: shkn up over 2f out: sn hdd & fnd nil) ........................ 7.**5**

1750 Slumber Thyme (IRE) (42) *(JGFitzGerald)* 8-9 KFallon (8) (sn drvn along: hdwy
   over 2f out: kpt on same pce) .............................................. ¹/₂.6
1964 Miss Grosse Nez (IRE) (47) *(CWThornton)* 8-6 ‡3JFanning (11) (b.hind: hld up
   & bhd: sme hdwy 2f out: n.d) .............................................. 3¹/₂.7
   Nashoon (IRE) (63) *(MissLCSiddall)* 8-9 ‡5SMaloney (6) (lw: plld hrd: trckd ldrs:
   rdn over 2f out: nt r.o) .............................................. 8.8
1890 Head for the Stars (IRE) (50) *(APStringer)* 8-9 JFortune (10) (chsd ldrs tl lost pl
   3f out) .............................................. ³/₄.9
2075 Caherea School (40) *(RO'Leary)* 8-9 NConnorton (4) (led to 4f out: sn lost pl) 10.10

**15/8** Noggings (IRE)(op 3/1), **4/1** ANY DREAM WOULD DO, **9/2** Throw Away Line(op 3/1), **6/1** Slumber Thyme (IRE), **9/1** Head for the Stars (IRE), **10/1** Nashoon (IRE), **16/1** Miss Grosse Nez (IRE), Angel's Wing, **25/1** Caherea School, **33/1** Cledeschamps. CSF £59.99, Tote £4.80: £1.80 £10.40 £2.00 (£107.00). Mr Guy Reed (MIDDLEHAM) bred by C. A. Blackwell. 10 Rn; No bid
1m 39.3 (3.3)
SF—21/3/2/—/—/—

---

### 2163
THIRSK LICENSED TRADERS H'CAP (0-80) £3047.60 (£843.60: £402.80)
6f
(Weights raised 5 lb)
3-55 (4-01)

1888⁶ **Double Feature (IRE) (58)** *(MrsJRRamsden)* 3–8-9 MBirch (4) (chsd ldrs: styd
   on wl appr fnl f: led ins fnl f: drvn out) .............................................. —1
   Parfait Amour (73) *(RMWhitaker)* 3–9-3 ‡7SWynne (8) (trckd ldrs: hung lft fr
   ¹/₂-wy: nt clr run & swtchd over 1f out: styd on ins fnl f) ..... nk.2
1837⁵ Sully's Choice (USA) (51) (bl) *(DWChapman)* 3-8-9 DWilliams (5) (lw: led:
   rdn over 1f out: hdd & no ex ins fnl f) .............................................. 1¹/₂.3
1406 Soba Guest (IRE) (72) *(JBerry)* 3-9-9 JCarroll (6) (lw: hld up: effrt ¹/₂-wy: styd
   on u.p fnl f) .............................................. ¹/₂.4
1451⁵ Verdant Boy (53) *(MPNaughton)* 9–8-10 JakiHouston (3) (lw: sn chsng ldrs &
   drvn along: rdn & edgd lft over 1f out: kpt on wl) .............................................. nk.5
1793 Brisas (48) (bl) *(TFairhurst)* 5–8-2 ‡3JFanning (2) (w ldr tl rdn & wknd jst Ins fnl f) nk.6
1987 Samsolom (63) *(JBalding)* 4–9-6 GHind (1) (lw: trckd ldrs: ev ch 2f out: wknd
   over 1f out) .............................................. 4.7
1736 Pretonic (62) (Fav) *(MJohnston)* 4–9-5 TWilliams (7) (lw: s.i.s: hdwy & swtchd
   outside over 1f out: nvr rchd ldrs) .............................................. ¹/₂.8
   *Stewards Enquiry: Maloney suspended 26-27/7/92 (misuse of the whip).*

**7/2** Pretonic, **4/1** Brisas, **11/2** Sully's Choice (USA), **6/1** Samsolom, Soba Guest (IRE), **7/1** DOUBLE FEATURE (IRE), **12/1** Parfait Amour, **14/1** Verdant Boy. CSF £71.21, CT £443.61. Tote £8.50: £2.10 £2.90 £1.60 (£65.00). Mr K. E. Wheldon (THIRSK) bred by A. Shaw in Ireland. 8 Rn
1m 11.1 (0.9)
SF—29/36/16/34/20/11

---

### 2164
WESTHORPE STKS (Mdn 3-Y.O) £2301.00 (£636.00: £303.00)
6f
4-25 (4-27)

1763³ **Belated** *(HThomsonJones)* 8-9 RHills (4) (trckd ldr: led wl over 1f out: edgd
   bdly lft: sn clr) .............................................. —1
1786⁴ Canon Kyle (IRE) (64) (bl) *(MHEasterby)* 9-0 MBirch (6) (reminders early: led:
   hrd rdn over 2f out: hdd over 1f out: no ch w wnr) .............................................. 8.2
1975³ Batchworth Bound *(EAWheeler)* 8-9 SWhitworth (2) (a chsng ldrs: rdn & nt
   qckn fnl 2f) .............................................. 2.3
   J'Arrive *(JPearce)* 8-4 ‡5RPrice (5) (unf: s.i.s: bhd tl kpt on fnl 2f) .............................................. 5.4
1883⁴ So Superb (68) (bl) (Fav) *(JLDunlop)* 9-0 JCarroll (3) (sn bhd & pushed along:
   hdwy over 2f out: nt r.o) .............................................. ³/₄.5
1865⁶ Tip it In *(ASmith)* 9-0 SWebster (1) (sn outpcd) .............................................. 3¹/₂.6
1309 Young Musician (IRE) (58) (bl) *(JGFitzGerald)* 9-0 NConnorton (7) (dwlt: sn
   chsng ldrs: rdn & lost pl over 2f out) .............................................. 6.7

**11/8** So Superb, **9/4** BELATED, **5/1** Batchworth Bound, **13/2** Canon Kyle (IRE), **14/1** Young Musician (IRE), **16/1** J'Arrive, **33/1** Tip it In. CSF £16.40, Tote £3.30: £1.70 £2.40 (£7.80). Mrs H. T. Jones (NEWMARKET) bred by Mrs H. T. Jones. 7 Rn
1m 11.4 (1.2)
SF—23/—/—/—/—/—

---

### 2165
STOKESLEY STKS (Mdn 3-Y.O) £2364.00 (£654.00: £312.00)
7f
5-00 (5-01)

1778³ **Edgeaway (65)** (v) (Fav) *(JWHills)* 8-9 RHills (1) (mde all: rdn clr over 1f out) .... —1
2029 Auction King (60) *(ASmith)* 9-0 SWebster (4) (effrt over 3f out: sn hrd drvn:
   kpt on: no imp) .............................................. 2¹/₂.2
1862³ Vanart *(WWHaigh)* 9-0 ACulhane (3) (rn in snatches: jnd ldrs 4f out: rdn & wknd
   over 1f out: eased) .............................................. 10.3
   Mondova (IRE) *(FHLee)* 8-9 RLappin (2) (w'like: scope: bit bkwd: chsd wnr tl rn
   green & lost pl over 3f out) .............................................. 6.4

**4/9** EDGEAWAY, **7/2** Vanart, **9/1** Auction King (IRE), **10/1** Mondova (IRE). CSF £4.43, Tote £1.40 (£3.10). The Thoroughbred Exchange (LAMBOURN) bred by L. K. McCreery. 4 Rn
1m 26 (2.7)
SF—33/30/—/—/—/—

**2166**    HUTTON WANDESLEY H'CAP (0-80) £3021.00 (£836.00: £399.00)
     1½m                                     5-30 (5-30)
                       (Weights raised 11 lb)

1922² **Golden Torque (64)** (Fav) *(RBastiman)* 5–9-3 ‡7HBastiman (2) (lw: hld up: effrt
            over 3f out: led 1f out: r.o u.p) ......................................... —1
2113² Mingus (USA) **(56)** *(MrsJRRamsden)* 5–9-2 MBirch (4) (lw: trckd ldr: led over 2f
            out: rdn over 1f out: hung lft: nt qckn nr fin) ...................... ½.2
 67⁴ Duggan **(56)** *(RJRWilliams)* 5–9-2 RHills (3) (chsd ldrs: effrt 3f out: rdn over 1f
            out: one pce) ........................................................... 7.3
2045 Quip **(33)** *(MPNaughton)* 7-7-7 JakiHouston (1) (led tl over 2f out: sn wknd) .... 4.4
                 LONG HANDICAP: Quip 7-3.

**Evens** GOLDEN TORQUE, **7/4** Mingus (USA), **11/2** Duggan(4/1—6/1), **12/1** Quip(10/1—8/1). CSF £3.00, Tote
£1.90 (£1.70). Mr Trevor J. Smith (WETHERBY) bred by H. F. Craig Harvey. 4 Rn      2m 33.8 (3.8)
                                                   SF—41/39/25/–

T/Plpt: £54.90 (42 Tckts).                                                WG

## 1591—**NEWBURY (L-H)**

### Friday, July 17th [Good, Good to soft back st]
Going Allowance: 0.65 sec per fur (Y)                         Wind: slt half against

Stalls: centre

**2167**    E.B.F. ECCHINSWELL STKS (Mdn 2-Y.O) £3850.00 (£1150.00: £550.00: £250.00)
     6f 8y                                        2-00 (2-05)

1536³ **Norfolk Hero** (Fav) *(DJGMurray-Smith)* 9-0 JReid (10) (a.p: rdn over 1f out: led
            ins fnl f: r.o wl) ....................................................... —1
1658³ Embankment (IRE) *(RHannon)* 9-0 MRoberts (7) (led 4f: unable qckn) .............. ??
     Shamam (USA) *(PTWalwyn)* 9-0 WCarson (15) (leggy: hdwy over 3f out: hrd
            rdn wl over 1f out: r.o) ................................................ ¾.3
1915 Sea Baron *(MBlanshard)* 9-0 LDettori (3) (lw: a.p: hrd rdn over 1f out: r.o) ...... ½.4
     Regalsett *(RHannon)* 8-11 ‡3RPerham (2) (unf: scope: bit bkwd: hrd rdn 2f out:
            hdwy over 1f out: r.o wl ins fnl f) ................................... ½.5
     Daily Sport Don *(RHannon)* 9-0 PatEddery (6) (wl grwn: bit bkwd: w ldr: led 2f
            out: edgd rt 1f out: hdd ins fnl f: one pce) ........................ hd.6
1915⁵ Lincoln Imp (USA) *(AMoore)* 9-0 BRouse (5) (nvr nr to chal) ........................ 6.7
     Frivolous Air *(IABalding)* 8-9 RCochrane (4) (unf: s.s: nvr nrr) ..................... s.h.8
     Highland Host *(JLDunlop)* 9-0 WRSwinburn (12) (unf: bit bkwd: s.s: nvr nrr) .. 1½.9
1902 Boisterous *(WRMuir)* 9-0 AMunro (8) (bhd fnl 3f) ................................... 6.10
 995⁶ Inonder *(MDIUsher)* 8-9 JWilliams (1) (b.off hind: a bhd) ......................... s.h.11
1370⁴ Soleil Rayon (IRE) *(MMcCormack)* 9-0 LPiggott (11) (lw: a bhd) .................. 1½.12
     Cursory Glance (IRE) *(AAScott)* 8-9 BRaymond (14) (str: bkwd: a bhd) .......... 7.13
     Resist the Force (USA) *(CACyzer)* 9-0 TQuinn (9) (wl grwn: bit bkwd: prom over
            3f) ...................................................................... 2.14

**2/1** NORFOLK HERO, **5/2** Embankment (IRE), **7/1** Shamam (USA), **10/1** Resist the Force (USA)(op 16/1), **12/1**
Soleil Rayon (IRE), Cursory Glance (IRE), Frivolous Air(op 8/1), **14/1** Daily Sport Don(op 7/1), **20/1** Highland
Host, Sea Baron, **33/1** Ors. CSF £7.99, Tote £3.10: £1.50 £1.40 £2.30 (£4.10). Lady D. M. Watts (UPPER
LAMBOURN) bred by Lady McAlpine. 14 Rn                                  1m 20.07 (8.27)
                                                   SF—12/4/1/–/–/–

**2168**    WATERMILL STKS (Mdn 3-Y.O) £3200.00 (£950.00: £450.00: £200.00)
     1¼m 6y                                       2-35 (2-48)

 707 **Tafrah (IRE)** *(MajorWRHern)* 8-9 WCarson (1) (2nd st: led on bit over 3f out:
            easily) ................................................................... —1
1746² Bustinetta (Fav) *(JRFanshawe)* 8-9 WRSwinburn (7) (5th st: hrd rdn wl over 1f
            out: unable qckn) ...................................................... 1½.2
     Billy Bunter *(HCandy)* 9-0 CRutter (4) (w'like: scope: 6th st: 4th whn hmpd on
            ins over 1f out: r.o wl ins fnl f) ..................................... ¾.3
     Bird Watcher *(MajorWRHern)* 9-0 BProcter (6) (wl grwn: bit bkwd: led 1f: 3rd st:
            hrd rdn & edgd lft over 1f out: one pce) ............................ hd.4
     Fortune Star (IRE) *(JLDunlop)* 9-0 JReid (2) (w'like: bit bkwd: shkn up & hdwy
            over 1f out: r.o wl ins fnl f) ......................................... s.h.5
1953 Oozlem (IRE) *(CAHorgan)* 9-0 AMcGlone (9) (rdn over 3f out: nvr nr to chal) .... 5.6
     California Dreamin *(DWPArbuthnot)* 8-9 TQuinn (8) (unf: scope: unruly s: s.s:
            led 9f out tlover 3f out: wknd) ...................................... 7.7
     Fathom Five (IRE) *(IABalding)* 8-9 RCochrane (3) (unf: scope: s.s: 4th st: wknd
            over 2f out) ............................................................. ¾.8
        *Leonardo (50/1) Withdrawn (bolted gng to s) : not under orders*

**11/10** Bustinetta(op 4/6), **5/1** TAFRAH (IRE), **6/1** Fathom Five (IRE), **13/2** California Dreamin, **15/2** Fortune Star (IRE)(op 5/1), **14/1** Billy Bunter, **25/1** Bird Watcher, **50/1** Oozlem (IRE). CSF £10.63, Tote £5.30: £1.40 £1.10 £2.60 (£4.20). Mr Hamdan Al-Maktoum (LAMBOURN) bred by Ballydoyle Stud in Ireland. 8 Rn

2m 15.77 (12.77)

SF—32/29/32/31/30/20

## 2169

HACKWOOD STKS (listed race) £10878.00 (£3264.00: £1572.00: £726.00)
6f 8y        3-10 (3-18)

| | |
|---|---|
| 1467⁵ **Montendre (104)** *(MMcCormack)* 5–9-3 JReid (12) (swtg: gd hdwy over 1f out: led ins fnl f: r.o wl) | —1 |
| 465⁴ Notley **(110)** *(RHannon)* 5–9-3 WCarson (10) (lw: hdwy over 3f out: led over 1f out tl ins fnl f: unable qckn) | ¾.2 |
| 1757★ Bit of a Lark **(97)** *(RHollinshead)* 4–9-0 LDettori (6) (hdwy 2f out: ev ch ins fnl f: one pce) | 2.3 |
| 1698³ Taufan Blu (IRE) **(95)** (bl) *(MJohnston)* 3–8-3 DMcKeown (7) (lw: s.s: hdwy over 1f out: r.o ins fnl f) | 1½.4 |
| 1698 Orthorhombus **(101)** (bl) *(GLewis)* 3–8-8 PaulEddery (13) (swtg: hld up: led 3f out tl over 2f out: one pce) | nk.5 |
| 1983a² Central City **(106)** (Fav) *(RHannon)* 3–8-6 PatEddery (8) (a.p: led over 2f out tl over 1f out: ev ch ins fnl f: one pce) | ½.6 |
| 1983a Amigo Menor **(105)** (bl) *(DJGMurray-Smith)* 6–9-7 CRutter (11) (lw: nvr nr to chal) | 1½.7 |
| 1875★ Medaille D'Or **(109)** (v) *(JWPayne)* 4–9-3 AMunro (9) (no hdwy fnl 2f) | 1½.8 |
| 1926★ Master Planner **(89)** *(CACyzer)* 3–8-8 TQuinn (1) (lw: prom 4f) | 4.9 |
| Bletchley Park (IRE) **(105)** *(AAScott)* 3–8-11 BRaymond (5) (prom 4f) | 3¼.10 |
| 1926 Sunday's Hill **(102)** *(MBlanshard)* 3–8-8 RCochrane (2) (prom over 3f) | 3½.11 |
| 1829★ Sizzling Saga (IRE) **(106)** *(JBerry)* 4–9-3 LPiggott (4) (led 3f) | 4.12 |
| 1875 Spanish Storm (IRE) **(104)** *(SPCWoods)* 3–8-8 WWoods (3) (outpcd) | 13 |

**3/1** Central City, **6/1** MONTENDRE, **7/1** Sizzling Saga (IRE), Notley, **15/2** Medaille D'Or, **8/1** Taufan Blu (IRE), **10/1** Orthorhombus, Amigo Menor, **14/1** Master Planner, **16/1** Spanish Storm (IRE), **20/1** Sunday's Hill, Bit of a Lark, **25/1** Bletchley Park (IRE). CSF £48.13, Tote £8.10: £2.50 £2.90 £5.30 (£21.10). Mr David Mort (WANTAGE) bred by A. B. Phipps. 13 Rn

1m 17.20 (5.40)

SF—73/70/62/45/49/45/54

## 2170

BIRKDALE GROUP H'CAP (3-Y.O.F) (0-100) £3850.00 (£1150.00: £550.00: £250.00)
1¹⁄₄m 6y        3-45 (3-48)

(Weights raised 6 lb)

| | |
|---|---|
| 1594★ **Only Royale (IRE) (85)** (Fav) *(LMCumani)* 9-7 LDettori (2) (lw: 4th st: plld out over 1f out: led wl ins fnl f: r.o wl) | —1 |
| 1955⁴ Googly **(58)** *(WGRWightman)* 7-8 GBardwell (1) (lw: hmpd on ins 8f out: 5th st: hrd rdn & led ins fnl f: sn hdd: unable qckn) | 1½.2 |
| 7873 Dazzling Fire (IRE) **(71)** *(BWHills)* 8-7 DHolland (3) (2nd st: ev ch ins fnl f: one pce) | 2½.3 |
| 1997³ Diamond Wedding (USA) **(70)** *(NAGraham)* 8-6 MRoberts (6) (lw: led 9f out tl ins fnl f: one pce) | ½.4 |
| 1216² Muhit (USA) **(75)** *(PTWalwyn)* 8-11 WCarson (5) (lw: led 1f: 3rd st: hrd rdn over 1f out: wknd fnl f) | 6.5 |
| 1594⁴ Brave the Wind **(57)** *(IABalding)* 7-7 RFox (4) (s.s: 6th st: wknd 2f out) | 8.6 |

**7/4** ONLY ROYALE (IRE), **4/1** Googly, **9/2** Muhit (USA), **5/1** Brave the Wind, **9/1** Dazzling Fire (IRE), **10/1** Diamond Wedding (USA). CSF £8.40, Tote £2.50: £1.70 £1.90 (£4.90). Mr G. Sainaghi (NEWMARKET) bred by Barronstown Stud in Ireland. 6 Rn

2m 13.74 (10.74)

SF—65/35/43/41/34

## 2171

CHATTIS HILL STKS (Mdn 2-Y.O.F) £3673.00 (£1099.00: £527.00: £241.00)
5f 34y        4-20 (4-22)

| | |
|---|---|
| 811³ **Poker Chip** (Fav) *(IABalding)* 8-11 RCochrane (4) (lw: w ldr: led 2f out: all out) | —1 |
| 1635⁴ Brockton Dancer *(RHannon)* 8-11 MRoberts (7) (hld up: rdn over 1f out: fin wl) | hd.2 |
| 1652⁵ Jarena (IRE) *(GLewis)* 8-11 PaulEddery (5) (lw: hld up: rdn over 1f out: ev ch ins fnl f: r.o) | nk.3 |
| Saraswati *(PJMakin)* 8-11 WRSwinburn (8) (unf: s.s: hdwy over 1f out: r.o) | 2¹⁄₄.4 |
| 1957² Simply Sooty *(BRMillman)* 8-11 JWilliams (9) (a.p: ev ch 2f out: wknd fnl f) | 4.5 |
| 1384⁵ Perfect Passion *(JJBridger)* 8-11 LDettori (10) (nvr nr to chal) | 4.6 |
| Petonellajill *(RHannon)* 8-8 ‡³RPerham (8) (w'like: s.s: a bhd) | nk.7 |
| Dotty's Walker (FR) *(CACyzer)* 8-11 TQuinn (2) (wl grwn: bkwd: prom over 3f) | nk.8 |
| Kimbolton Korker *(AAScott)* 8-11 BRaymond (6) (b.hind: neat: led 3f) | 2¹⁄₄.9 |
| Barassie *(PMitchell)* 8-11 MHills (1) (unf: s.s: a bhd) | 15.10 |

**8/13** POKER CHIP, **7/2** Simply Sooty(4/1—11/2), **9/1** Brockton Dancer(op 5/1), **14/1** Saraswati(op 8/1), Kimbolton Korker(op 6/1), **20/1** Petonellajill, **25/1** Jarena (IRE), **33/1** Ors. CSF £7.90, Tote £1.50: £1.10 £1.40 £4.50 (£4.80). Mr J. C. Smith (KINGSCLERE) bred by Littleton Stud. 10 Rn

66.53 sec (5.83)
SF—45/44/43/33/17/1

**2172**    WHITE HORSE H'CAP (0-90) £3557.50 (£1060.00: £505.00: £227.50)
**2m**                                                                            4-50 (4-51)

1938² **Mull House (60)** (Fav) (FJO'Mahony) 5–8-0 WCarson (1) (3rd st: hrd rdn over
1f out: led ins fnl f: drvn out) ............................................... —1

2059² Prince Sobur **(59)** (MBlanshard) 6–7-13 MRoberts (9) (lw: 5th st: led 1f out tl ins
fnl f: unable qckn) ............................................................... 1.2

1988² Skisurf **(57)** (CEBrittain) 6–7-6(4) ‡5BDoyle (5) (hdwy 2f out: hrd rdn over 1f out:
r.o ins fnl f) ....................................................................... ½.3

1459 Bardolph (USA) **(79)** (PFICole) 5–9-5 TQuinn (8) (b.off hind: 4th st: led over 1f
out: sn hdd: one pce) ......................................................... 4.4

1988⁵ Go South **(66)** (bl) (JRJenkins) 8–8-6 NCarlisle (7) (lw: nvr nr to chal) ............. 1½.5

1768⁴ High Beacon **(70)** (KCBailey) 5–8-7 ‡3RPerham (4) (led over 14f) .............. 2½.6

1567⁺ Cantana **(76)** (bl) (RCharlton) 3–8-0 PaulEddery (2) (6th st: no hdwy fnl 2f) .... nk.7

1703⁶ Shahdjat (IRE) **(84)** (KCBailey) 4–9-10 MPerrett (3) (lw: 2nd st: ev ch 2f out:
wknd over 1f out) .............................................................. 2½.8

1874 First Victory **(88)** (RHannon) 6–10-0 PatEddery (6) (hdwy on ins over 3f out: nt
clr run over 2f out: sn wknd) ............................................... nk.9

LONG HANDICAP: Skisurf 7-6.

**100/30** MULL HOUSE, **9/2** Prince Sobur, **5/1** Bardolph (USA), **11/2** Cantana(4/1—6/1), First Victory, **13/2** Skisurf, **8/1** Go South, **20/1** High Beacon, **25/1** Shahdjat (IRE). CSF £18.55, CT £86.17. Tote £4.00: £1.70 £1.30 £2.30 (£5.40). Mr M. Lowry (LINGFIELD) bred by D. J. and Mrs Deer. 9 Rn

3m 40.89 (14.19)
SF—48/46/38/61/46/44/36

**2173**    LEVY BOARD H'CAP (0-90) £4347.00 (£1296.00: £618.00: £279.00)
**1m (st)**                                                                        5-20 (5-22)

1877³ **Eclipsing (IRE) (75)** (RCharlton) 4–9-4 PatEddery (1) (lw: a gng wl: led ins fnl f:
comf) ............................................................................... —1

1954² Keep Your Word **(55)** (Fav) (GBBalding) 6–7-12 AMunro (5) (chsd ldr: led over
1f out tl ins fnl f: unable qckn) ........................................... 2.2

364⁺ Mossy Rose **(60)** (LordHuntingdon) 6–8-3 MRoberts (2) (lw: hld up: hrd rdn
over 1f out: one pce) ........................................................ 4.3

1930⁶ Absonal **(77)** (RHannon) 5–9-6 RCochrane (4) (lw: hld up: rdn over 1f out: one
pce) ............................................................................... ½.4

1412⁶ Vanborough Lad **(70)** (MJHaynes) 3–8-5 JWilliams (6) (rdn 3f out: bhd fnl 2f) 2½.5

1869 Gilderdale **(84)** (JWHills) 10–9-13 MHills (3) (lw: led over 6f) ...................... ½.6

**2/1** Keep Your Word, **5/2** ECLIPSING (IRE), **9/2** Mossy Rose, **5/1** Absonal, **6/1** Gilderdale(op 4/1), **10/1** Vanborough Lad. CSF £8.22, Tote £2.90: £1.50 £2.10 (£3.10). Mr Jeremy Tree (BECKHAMPTON) bred by S. Niarchos in Ireland. 6 Rn

1m 46.92 (9.92)
SF—33/7/–/15/–/12

T/Trio: Race 3: £281.20 (6.1 Tckts). T/Jkpt: Not won; £1,206.30 to Newbury 18/7/92. T/Plpt: £26.50 (212 Tckts).                                                                        AK

# NEWBURY (L-H)

## Saturday, July 18th [Good to soft]

Going Allowance: 0.35 sec per fur (G)                            Wind: almost nil

Stalls: 1st, 5th & 7th, remainder centre

**2174**    ARLINGTON INTERNATIONAL RACECOURSE STKS    £4575.00 each (£1000.00:
£450.00)   **1¼m 6y**                                                          1-30 (1-31)

954a⁵ **Adam Smith (109)** (Fav) (LMCumani) 4–9-0 LDettori (2) (lw: 4th st: hrd rdn fnl f:
led cl home: all out) ......................................................... —1

1458 Peto **(103)** (HRACecil) 3–8-5(1) PatEddery (4) (2nd tl led over 2f out: hdd nr fin:
r.o) ................................................................................ —1

1842⁵ Percy's Girl (IRE) **(97)** (GWragg) 4–8-9 WRSwinburn (3) (led tl over 2f out: r.o
one pce) ......................................................................... 2½.3

1383⁺ Host (IRE) **(90)** (CEBrittain) 3–8-4 MRoberts (1) (3rd st: wknd over 1f out) ....... 15.4

**11/10** ADAM SMITH, **13/8** PETO, **5/1** Percy's Girl (IRE), **12/1** Host (IRE)(op 8/1). CSF £1.58 AS & P, £1.84 P & AS, Tote £1.10 AS, £1.20 P (£1.70). Adam Smith: Lord White of Hull (NEWMARKET) bred by London Thoroughbred Services Ltd. Peto: Sheikh Mohammed (NEWMARKET) bred by P. T. Tellwright. 4 Rn

2m 11.46 (8.46)
SF—50/41/40/5

## 2175

MTOTO DONNINGTON CASTLE STKS (2-Y.O.C & G) £8629.00 (£2572.00: £1226.00: £553.00)   **7f (st)**   2-00 (2-03)

1939² **White Crown (USA)** *(BHanbury)* 8-12 WRSwinburn (3) (mde all: r.o wl) ........... —1
1939⁴ Geisway (CAN) *(RHannon)* 8-12 PatEddery (5) (w wnr over 5f: r.o one pce) ...... 4.2
1709★ Prevene (IRE) *(PFICole)* (Fav) 8-12 TQuinn (2) (hld up: ev ch 2f out: r.o one
pce) ................................................................................................ hd.3
1762★ Young Ern *(SDow)* 8-12 LPiggott (4) (hld up: hdwy over 1f out: r.o one pce) .... s.h.4
Ericolin (IRE) *(CEBrittain)* 8-8 MRoberts (6) (w'like: scope: prom over 4f) ......... 6.5
383⁶ Grand Applause (IRE) *(RSimpson)* 8-8 ATucker (1) (prom 4f: t.o) .................... 10.6

7/4 Prevene (IRE), 5/2 WHITE CROWN (USA), 3/1 Geisway (CAN), 6/1 Young Ern, 8/1 Ericolin (IRE)(4/1—9/1), 50/1 Grand Applause (IRE). CSF £10.31, Tote £2.90: £2.00 £2.20 (£5.70). Mr Saeed Suhail (NEWMARKET) bred by David Mowat & Fawn Leap Farm in USA. 6 Rn   1m 30.18 (5.68)
SF—52/40/39/38/14/–

## 2176

NEWBURY SALES SUPER SPRINT TROPHY (Stks) (2-Y.O) £59232.00 (£22008.00: £10634.00: £4430.00: £1845.00: £811.00)   **5f 34y**   2-30 (2-32)

1461★ **Lyric Fantasy (IRE)** (Fav) *(RHannon)* 8-11 MRoberts (11) (led after 1f: easily) .. —1
1378⁸ Aradanza *(MRChannon)* 8-5 PatEddery (9) (hdwy over 1f out: r.o ins fnl f) ........ 6.2
2031¹² Princely Favour (IRE) *(RHannon)* 8-4 BRouse (10) (hdwy over 1f out: r.o ins fnl
f) ........................................................................................................ hd.3
1979★ Joyofracing *(WAO'Gorman)* 9-1 DHolland (6) (gd spd 4f) ............................ ¾.4
1472² Surprise Offer *(RHannon)* 8-6 JReid (8) (led 1f: wknd over 1f out) ................. 3.5
1664★ Saint Express *(RMWhitaker)* 8-10 AColhane (4) (prom tl hrd rdn & wknd over 1f
out) ..................................................................................................... 4.6
1991★ Florac (IRE) *(MJHeaton-Ellis)* 8-2 AMcGlone (7) (nvr nr to chal) .................... hd.7
1991⁶ Critical Mass *(JBerry)* 8-8 TQuinn (5) (a bhd) ........................................... 3¹/₂.8
1915³ Grand Dancer (IRE) (bl) *(RJRWilliams)* 8-0 JQuinn (3) (wl bhd fnl 2f) ............... 2.9
803★ Risk Me's Girl *(RHannon)* 7-13 GCarter (1) (bhd fnl 2f) ................................ 1¹/₂.10
Lady Honda (IRE) *(CEBrittain)* 8-6 GCrealock (2) (s.s: a t.o) ........................... 10.11

2/5 LYRIC FANTASY (IRE), 9/1 Risk Me's Girl, Aradanza, 10/1 Surprise Offer, 12/1 Joyofracing, 20/1 Saint Express, 33/1 Florac (IRE), 50/1 Lady Honda (IRE), Grand Dancer (IRE), 66/1 Critical Mass. CSF £5.66, Tote £1.60: £1.10 £1.40 £6.80 (£4.50). Lord Carnarvon (MARLBOROUGH) bred by Minch Bloodstock in Ireland. 11 Rn   63.22 sec (2.52)
SF—82/46/44/52/31/19

## 2177

NEWBURY ROSE BOWL STKS (listed race) (2-Y.O) £9150.00 (£2525.00: £1200.00)   **6f 8y**   3-05 (3-06)

1469² **Silver Wizard (USA)** (Fav) *(GLewis)* 8-11 PaulEddery (1) (mde all: pushed out) —1
1915★ Port Lucaya *(RHannon)* 8-11 JReid (2) (chsd wnr: hrd rdn & ev ch ins fnl f: r.o) hd.2
1536★ High Tycoon (IRE) *(MrsJCecil)* 9-2 LPiggott (3) (rdn along: hdwy 3f out: hrd rdn
& wknd over 1f out) ............................................................................... 8.3

4/6 SILVER WIZARD (USA), 6/4 High Tycoon (IRE), 14/1 Port Lucaya. CSF £5.24, Tote £1.60: (£3.10). Mrs Shirley Robins (EPSOM) bred by Bounding Basque Breeding Syndicate in USA. 3 Rn   1m 16.25 (4.45)
SF—50/49/22

## 2178

JULY H'CAP (3-Y.O) (0-100) £5900.00 (£1760.00: £840.00: £380.00)   **1m 5f 61y**   3-40 (3-42)

1980★ **Spikenard (86)** *(PTWalwyn)* 9-3 TQuinn (4) (5th st: led 2f out: drvn out) ........... —1
1768³ Crystal Cross (USA) (80) *(IABalding)* 8-11 JReid (6) (6th st: ev ch over 1f out:
r.o) ..................................................................................................... ¾.2
1792★ Bandoline (67) *(BWHills)* 7-12 DHolland (8) (bhd tl hdwy over 2f out: r.o one
pce) ..................................................................................................... 6.3
1633³ Not in Doubt (USA) (90) *(HCandy)* 9-7 CRutter (7) (hdwy 4f out: one pce fnl 2f) ¾.4
1743² Bentico (64) (Fav) *(MAJarvis)* 7-9 JQuinn (5) (led to 2f out) ......................... 2.5
1643 Court Circular (66) (v) *(LordHuntingdon)* 7-6 ‡⁵DHarrison (1) (4th st: rdn over 4f
out: sn wknd) ...................................................................................... 10.6
566★ Kaiser Wilhelm (80) *(HRACecil)* 8-11 AMcGlone (3) (2nd st: wknd 3f out) ......... 1.7
1466 Simply-H (IRE) (80) *(MBell)* 8-4 ‡⁷PTurner (9) (3rd st: wknd 3f out) .................. 3.8
Alqairawaan (82) *(JLDunlop)* 8-4 WRSwinburn (2) (a bhd: t.o fnl 5f) ................. 5.9

7/2 Bentico(5/1—3/1), 4/1 Kaiser Wilhelm(3/1—9/2), 9/2 Crystal Cross (USA), 6/1 Bandoline, Not in Doubt (USA), 8/1 SPIKENARD, Simply-H (IRE), 9/1 Court Circular, 14/1 Alqairawaan. CSF £44.64, CT £219.29. Tote £9.10: £2.20 £1.80 £2.60 (£14.80). Lord Howard de Walden (LAMBOURN) bred by Lord Howard de Walden. 9 Rn   2m 54.36 (8.66)
SF—62/45/20/41/11/–

## 2179

SHRIVENHAM H'CAP (0-100) £3785.00 (£1130.00: £540.00: £245.00)
5f 34y

4-10 (4-12)

1931★ **Aughfad (86)** (v) *(TCasey)* 6–9-0 JReid (4) (a.p: led wl over 1f out: comf) .......... —1
1952² Walk in the Park **(81)** *(RSimpson)* 3–7-13 ‡⁵ATucker (7) (gd hdwy 2f out: nt qckn
fnl f) ...................................................................................... 2.2
1875⁶ Terrhars (IRE) **(100)** *(RHannon)* 4–10-0 AMcGlone (8) (hdwy 2f out: rdn over 1f
out: nt qckn) ........................................................................ 1½.3
1487² Poets Cove **(86)** (Fav) *(MMcCormack)* 4–9-0 WRSwinburn (5) (hdwy over 2f
out: n.m.r over 1f out: one pce) .................................... 2½.4
1828★ Lucedeo **(85)** *(JLSpearing)* 8–8-13 JWilliams (6) (hdwy 2f out: nvr nr to chal) .. hd.5
2019 Eager Deva **(90)** *(RHollinshead)* 5–9-4 LPiggott (3) (prom over 3f) ................. s.h.6
1931⁶ Touch of White **(78)** *(JEBanks)* 6–8-6 PaulEddery (2) (led over 3f) ................. 5.7
1199 Miami Banker **(69)** (bl) *(PHowling)* 6–7-11 JQuinn (1) (chsd ldr over 3f: wknd
qckly) .................................................................................... 7.8

**3/1** Poets Cove, **4/1** AUGHFAD, **5/1** Walk in the Park, **13/2** Touch of White, Terrhars (IRE), **7/1** Eager Deva,
Lucedeo, **14/1** Miami Banker. CSF £23.46, CT £117.13. Tote £5.60: £1.80 £1.50 £2.00 (£15.30). Mr M. Mac
Carthy (UPPER LAMBOURN) bred by M. Mac Carthy. 8 Rn                       64.57 sec (3.87)
SF—58/35/58/34/32/36

## 2180

LEVY BOARD H'CAP (0-90) £4503.00 (£1344.00: £642.00: £291.00)
1½m 5y

4-40 (4-45)

(Weights raised 2 lb)

1836² **Opera Ghost (79)** (Fav) *(PWHarris)* 6–9-7 WRSwinburn (6) (4th st: led wl over
1f out: all out) ........................................................................ —1
2023² Seal Indigo (IRE) **(82)** *(RHannon)* 4–9-10 JReid (1) (hdwy over 2f out: ev ch fnl f:
r.o) ........................................................................................ nk.2
1842⁴ Castoret **(76)** *(JWHills)* 6–8-13 ‡³DHarrison (9) (hdwy over 2f out: ev ch 1f out: nt
qckn) ...................................................................................... 1,3
2012² Rising Tempo (IRE) **(60)** *(CACyzer)* 4–8-2 JQuinn (5) (6th st: ev ch over 1f out:
wknd fnl f) .............................................................................. 3½.4
513 Army of Stars **(82)** *(CEBrittain)* 7–9-10 GCrealock (7) (3rd st: led over 2f out tl
wknd wl over 1f out) .............................................................. 8.5
1016 Sultan's Son **(70)** *(JohnRUpson)* 6–8-12 BRouse (2) (5th st: wknd 3f out) ......... 7.6
1211³ Roberty Lea **(69)** *(TFairhurst)* 4–8-8 ‡³JFanning (4) (led tl wknd over 2f out) ..... nk.7
1879★ Dovale **(70)** *(WJarvis)* 4–8-12 LPiggott (3) (2nd st: wknd 3f out) .................. 10.8

**7/2** OPERA GHOST, **4/1** Dovale, **5/1** Castoret, Seal Indigo (IRE), **11/2** Rising Tempo (IRE), Roberty Lea, **10/1**
Army of Stars, **33/1** Sultan's Son. CSF £20.40, CT £79.49. Tote £3.80: £1.50 £2.00 £1.90 (£9.90). Mrs P. W.
Harris (BERKHAMSTED) bred by Pendley Farm. 8 Rn                       2m 37.16 (7.46)
SF—74/76/63/45/51/25

T/Trio: Race 3: £47.90 (37 Tckts). T/Jkpt: £623.10 (5.55 Tckts). T/Plpt: £34.20 (215.95 Tckts).          Hn

1925—**NEWMARKET (R-H)** July Course
### Friday, July 17th [Good]
Going Allowance: minus 0.10 sec per fur (F)                       Wind: fresh half bhd

Stalls: high

## 2181

KING'S GAP STKS (3-Y.O) £4503.00 (£1344.00: £642.00: £291.00)
1½m

6-30 (6-31)

1704★ **Spring** *(JLDunlop)* 8–11 WCarson (2) (lw: hld up: stdy hdwy over 3f out: led 2f
out: r.o wl) ............................................................................ —1
1693★ Alhamad **(99)** *(HRACecil)* 9-5 PatEddery (1) (lw: hld up: hdwy over 2f out: styd
on ins fnl f: no ch w wnr) ........................................................ 2.2
1940 Goldsmiths' Hall **(98)** *(GWragg)* 9-5 SCauthen (4) (lw: led & sn clr: rdn & hdd 2f
out: kpt on one pce) .............................................................. ¾.3
1666² Sheriffmuir **(94)** (Fav) *(LMCumani)* 9-5 LDettori (5) (chsd ldrs: effrt u.p & hung
lft over 1f out: nvr able to chal) ............................................ ½.4
509 Back Billy (IRE) *(CEBrittain)* 8-7 PRobinson (3) (prom tl wknd qckly over 3f out) 5.5
781 L'Hermine **(90)** *(HCandy)* 8-12 WNewnes (6) (chsd ldr 8f: sn rdn & lost tch: t.o) 15.6

**6/4** Sheriffmuir(5/4—2/1), **2/1** SPRING, **7/2** Goldsmiths' Hall, **6/1** Alhamad, **33/1** L'Hermine, **66/1** Back Billy
(IRE). CSF £13.12, Tote £2.50: £1.60 £2.50 (£6.50). Lord Halifax (ARUNDEL) bred by Lord Halifax. 6 Rn
2m 30.72 (0.12 under best; 2.02)
SF—65/69/67/66/44/19

**2182**   TRAVIS PERKINS H'CAP (F & M) (0-90) £3850.00 (£1150.00: £550.00: £250.00)
1¼m                                                                     7-00 (7-01)

(Weights raised 2 lb)

1955⁵ **Ghurrah (IRE) (61)** (Jt-Fav) *(CJBenstead)* 3–8–0 WCarson (6) (lw: a.p: led 2f
out: hrd drvn fnl f: hld on gamely) .................................... —1

1643* Misty View **(71)** (Jt-Fav) *(MAJarvis)* 3–8–10 WRyan (3) (a.p: jnd wnr appr fnl f:
hrd rdn & r.o) ........................................................ nk.2

2033³ Sean's Scholar (USA) **(49)** *(CNAllen)* 5–7–12 WAAntongeorgi (1) (led to 2f out:
rdn & no ex nr fin) ................................................... ½.3

1210³ Valley of Fire **(85)** *(JRFanshawe)* 3–9–10 SCauthen (4) (lw: hld up: hdwy 3f out:
rdn over 1f out: unable qckn) ........................................ 1.4

2110³ Rive-Jumelle (IRE) **(65)** (Jt-Fav) *(MBell)* 4–8–7 ‡⁷PTurner (5) (chsd ldrs: effrt & ev
ch 3f out: sn rdn & btn) ............................................. 4.5

1976² Light Hand **(69)** (v) *(MHTompkins)* 6–9–4 PRobinson (2) (hld up & bhd: hdwy 2f
out: sn rdn: no imp) ................................................. ½.6

4/1 GHURRAH (IRE), Misty View(op 5/2), Rive-Jumelle (IRE), **9/2** Valley of Fire, **11/2** Ors. CSF £17.87, Tote
£5.10: £2.10 £2.10 (£8.70). Mr Hamdan Al-Maktoum (EPSOM) bred by Shadwell Estate Company in Ireland. 6
Rn                                                                   2m 9.30 (6.70)
SF—9/18/5/29/4/14

**2183**   KIDSONS IMPEY TROPHY (H'cap) (0-90) £3720.00 (£1110.00: £530.00: £240.00)
7f                                                                     7-30 (7-32)

1930² **Polonez Prima (75)** (Fav) *(JEBanks)* 5–9–0 NDay (7) (hld up: hdwy 3f out: led
appr fnl f: pushed clr) .............................................. —1

1474 Panikin **(89)** *(JWharton)* 4–9–7 ‡⁷SWilliams (6) (lw: chsd ldr: ev ch appr fnl f: one
pce) ................................................................. 2½.2

1598² Domicksky **(75)** *(MJRyan)* 4–9–0 DBiggs (5) (stdd s: hdwy 2f out: rdn & r.o wl
ins fnl f) ........................................................... ½.3

1685⁴ Young Shadowfax **(55)** *(CNAllen)* 5–7–8 GBardwell (1) (b.nr hind: chsd ldrs:
rdn 2f out: kpt on) .................................................. 1.4

1877⁴ Strong Suit (IRE) **(88)** *(RHannon)* 3–9–6 JReid (3) (hld up & bhd: effrt 2f out: nt
rch ldrs) ........................................................... ¾.5

1961* Gant Bleu (FR) **(56)** *(RMWhitaker)* 5–7–9 (6x) DaleGibson (2) (lw: led: qcknd clr
3f out: wknd & hdd over 1f out) ..................................... 4.6

1403 Tender Moment (IRE) **(71)** *(CEBrittain)* 4–8–10 MRoberts (4) (hld up: hdwy over
2f out: eased whn btn fnl f) ......................................... ½.7

1805* Annabelle Royale **(77)** *(MrsNMacauley)* 6–9–2 LDettori (8) (hld up in tch: rdn 3f
out: sn btn) ........................................................ 1½.8

7/4 POLONEZ PRIMA, **6/1** Annabelle Royale, Domicksky, Strong Suit (IRE), **7/1** Gant Bleu (FR), **15/2** Tender
Moment (IRE), **9/1** Panikin, **14/1** Young Shadowfax. CSF £17.87, CT £74.18. Tote £3.00: £1.50 £2.10 £2.00
(£13.00). Mr B. J. Butterworth (NEWMARKET) bred by D. M. Dick. 8 Rn              1m 26.45 (2.05)
SF—59/58/49/26/50/13

**2184**   ANTEC INTERNATIONAL H'CAP (0-80) £3882.50 (£1160.00: £555.00: £252.50)
1m                                                                     8-00 (8-02)

1673² **Buzzards Bellbuoy (63)** *(HJCollingridge)* 3–8–8 JQuinn (9) (mde all far side:
qcknd clr over 2f out: hld on) ....................................... —1

1706⁶ Foolish Touch **(54)** *(WJMusson)* 10–8–7 PatEddery (10) (b: hld up & bhd: rapid
hdwy over 1f out: unable qckn nr fin) ................................ hd.2

1956* Agnes Flemming (USA) **(75)** *(PWHarris)* 3–9–6 (5x) PaulEddery (2) (chsd ldrs
far side: rdn 3f out: r.o wl ins fnl f) ............................... s.h.3

1760 Champenoise **(44)** *(MBell)* 4–7–11 DBiggs (3) (hdwy over 3f out: styd on u.p fnl
f) .................................................................. 1.4

1930³ Little Rousillon **(65)** *(ACStewart)* 4–9–4 MRoberts (5) (prom far side: rdn
along over 2f out: one pce) .......................................... nk.5

2066⁴ Breezed Well **(59)** *(CNAllen)* 6–8–12 WAAntongeorgi (1) (chsd ldrs far side: rdn
& no hdwy fnl 2f) ................................................... 1.6

1923 Queer: of Dreams **(43)** *(DrJDScargill)* 4–7–7⁽³⁾ ‡³FNorton (8) (mid div: rdn 3f out:
no imp) ............................................................. 8.7

1659³ Our Occasion **(72)** *(RHannon)* 3–9–3 JReid (7) (lw: s.s: a in rr) ............... hd.8

1930 Elegant Friend **(74)** *(MHTompkins)* 4–9–13 PRobinson (4) (chsd ldrs over 5f: sn
btn) ............................................................... 1.9

1594⁵ Wild Strawberry **(72)** *(JMPEustace)* 3–9–3 MTebbutt (6) (chsd ldrs far side over
4f) ................................................................ 5.10

1811³ Diaco **(68)** *(MAJarvis)* 7–9–7 AMunro (11) (a in rr: t.o) .................... 8.11

1463 Roseate Lodge **(71)** *(RWArmstrong)* 6–9–10 LPiggott (13) (racd stands' side: a
bhd: t.o) .......................................................... 2½.12

2035[6] Mahsul (IRE) **(61)** *(CJBenstead)* 4–9-0 WCarson (12) (dwlt: racd stands' side: t.o fnl 3f) ............................................................................................ hd.**13**
1916[5] Brightness **(76)** *(MMoubarak)* 3–9-7 LDettori (14) (led stands' side over 5f: sn wknd: t.o) .................................................................................... 10.**14**
LONG HANDICAP: Queen of Dreams 7-6.

**15/8** Little Rousillon, **13/2** Mahsul (IRE), **7/1** Roseate Lodge, **8/1** Our Occasion, Diaco, **9/1** Foolish Touch, **12/1** BUZZARDS BELLBUOY, Brightness, **14/1** Agnes Flemming (USA), Champenoise, **16/1** Wild Strawberry, **20/1** Breezed Well, Elegant Friend, **33/1** Queen of Dreams. CSF £120.11, CT £1,435.42. Tote £17.80: £3.50 £3.00 £4.00 (£39.50). Mr N. H. Gardner (NEWMARKET) bred by N. H. Gardner. 14 Rn    1m 39.73 (2.03)
SF—52/50/62/36/56/49

## 2185
VIDEOFAX STKS (Mdn 2-Y.O.F)    £3752.50 (£1120.00: £535.00: £242.50)
7f
8-30 (8-31)

1668 **Dayflower (USA)** (Fav) *(HRACecil)* 8-11 SCauthen (2) (lw: dwlt: sn prom: shkn up to ld ins fnl f: r.o strly) ............................................................ —**1**
Reine de Neige *(AAScott)* 8-11 WRSwinburn (8) (cmpt: scope: bit bkwd: a.p: led over 2f out tl ins fnl f: eased whn btn) ...................................... 2.**2**
Sehailah *(MrsLPiggott)* 8-11 LPiggott (1) (w'like: unf: s.i.s: hdwy 3f out: styd on ins fnl f: nvr nrr) ............................................................ 3.**3**
Darshay (FR) *(RHannon)* 8-11 MRoberts (9) (lt-f: leggy: lost pl over 2f out: styd on again ins fnl f) ............................................................ 1.**4**
Marros Mill *(MBell)* 8-11 MHills (6) (cmpt: bhd: sme hdwy fnl 2f: nvr nr to chal) 2½.**5**
1867[3] Actinella (USA) *(RHannon)* 8-11 PatEddery (10) (led tl hdd over 2f out: eased whn btn fnl f) ............................................................ 1.**6**
Pure Misk *(BHanbury)* 8-11 BRaymond (5) (neat: lw: dwlt: effrt after 2f: wknd over 2f out) ............................................................ 1½.**7**
Madam Caprice *(RGuest)* 8-11 LDettori (4) (neat: bit bkwd: chsd ldrs 5f) ......... nk.**8**
1999 Gypsy Crystal (USA) *(RMWhitaker)* 8-11 DaleGibson (7) (a bhd: t.o) ............ 5.**9**
More Than Love *(PAKelleway)* 8-11 DHolland (3) (cmpt: bkwd: chsd ldrs 4f: sn wknd: t.o) ............................................................ 1½.**10**

**4/5** DAYFLOWER (USA), **9/2** Reine de Neige(5/2—5/1), **5/1** Actinella (USA)(op 8/1), **10/1** Darshay (FR)(8/1—12/1), **16/1** Sehailah, Pure Misk, **25/1** Marros Mill, **40/1** Ors. CSF £5.31, Tote £2.10: £1.20 £1.80 £2.00 (£3.50). Sheikh Mohammed (NEWMARKET) bred by W Lazy T Ltd in USA. 10 Rn    1m 26.87 (2.47)
SF—48/42/33/30/22/19

## 2186
WAVERTREE STKS (Mdn 3-Y.O) £3655.00 (£1090.00: £520.00: £235.00)
1m
9-00 (9-01)

1862[2] **Crystado (FR)** (Fav) *(DRCElsworth)* 9-0 JWilliams (2) (hld up: hdwy 3f out: led ent fnl f: sn clr) ............................................................ —**1**
1737[3] Reflecting (IRE) **(74)** *(JHMGosden)* 9-0 PatEddery (5) (a.p: led over 2f out tl over 1f out: kpt on nr fin) ............................................................ 3½.**2**
Many a Quest (USA) *(LMCumani)* 9-0 LDettori (3) (gd sort: lw: a.p: led over 1f out: sn hdd: one pce) ............................................................ ¾.**3**
1981[2] Much Sought After *(DMorley)* 9-0 MRoberts (4) (b.hind: hdwy 3f out: ev ch appr fnl f: eased) ............................................................ 5.**4**
Night Gown *(MissGayKelleway)* 8-9 DHolland (6) (w'like: leggy: led over 5f: sn wknd) ............................................................ 8.**5**
Questing (USA) *(JHMGosden)* 9-0 SCauthen (8) (bkwd: s.i.s: a in rr) ................. 3.**6**
1447 Muktaar (USA) *(JRFanshawe)* 9-0 WRSwinburn (7) (chsd ldrs: rdn 3f out: sn wknd) ............................................................ nk.**7**
Top Sire *(JHMGosden)* 9-0 MHills (1) (cmpt: bkwd: t.o fr ½-wy) ..................... 20.**8**

**2/1** CRYSTADO (FR)(5/2—3/1), **7/2** Reflecting (IRE), **9/2** Much Sought After(10/1—12/1), Many a Quest (USA)(op 9/4), **13/2** Questing (USA)(op 4/1), **16/1** Muktaar (USA), **20/1** Top Sire, **50/1** Night Gown. CSF £9.34, Tote £3.50: £1.40 £1.50 £1.70 (£5.50). Mr A. Foustok (WHITSBURY) bred by Ahmad Fustok in France. 8 Rn    1m 41.74 (4.04)
SF—27/16/14/–/–/–

T/Trio: Race 4: £215.90 (7.2 Tckts). T/Plpt: £261.90 (14.8 Tckts).    IM

# NEWMARKET (R-H) July Course
## Saturday, July 18th [Good]
Going Allowance: minus 0.10 sec per fur (F)    Wind: slt half bhd

Stalls: centre

## 2187
RISBY CLAIMING STKS (3-Y.O) £2872.00 (£856.00: £408.00: £184.00)
1m
2-15 (2-18)

2084[3] **By Arrangement (IRE) (56)** *(RGuest)* 7-1[(1)] ‡7CHawksley (5) (chsd ldrs: led ins fnl f: pushed out) ............................................................ —**1**

2029 **Don't Smile (71)** (Fav) *(MHTompkins)* 8-1 PRobinson (7) (lw: hld up & bhd: gd hdwy 2f out: rdn & r.o fnl f) ........................................... 2¹/₂.2

Relatively Risky *(JWharton)* 7-9 NAdams (9) (a.p: led over 3f out tl hdd & wknd ins fnl f) ........................................... 3.3

2018 **Roly Wallace (62)** (bl) *(KTIvory)* 8-0 GBardwell (8) (hld up: hdwy over 2f out: hrd rdn & nt rch ldrs) ........................................... 4.4

1903 **Lonesome Train (USA) (54)** (bl) *(JHMGosden)* 7-12 WCarson (1) (in tch: outpcd ¹/₂-wy: kpt on ins fnl f) ........................................... ¹/₂.5

1872 **Bel Baraka (IRE) (61)** *(DRCEllsworth)* 8-4 JWilliams (6) (led tl hdd over 3f out: wknd appr fnl f) ........................................... 3¹/₂.6

*2013* Executive Spirit (67) *(DSasse)* 9-0 GDuffield (4) (a bhd) ........................................... 3¹/₂.7

2032 **Sandcastle City (64)** *(RHannon)* 8-4 MHills (2) (a bhd) ........................................... hd.8

**11/4** Don't Smile, **9/2** Roly Wallace, Bel Baraka (IRE)(op 7/1), BY ARRANGEMENT (IRE), **7/1** Lonesome Train (USA), **9/1** Sandcastle City(op 6/1), **16/1** Executive Spirit, **33/1** Relatively Risky. CSF £16.00, Tote £6.00: £1.50 £1.50 £4.80 (£7.60). Mr C. J. Mills (NEWMARKET) bred by Graigueshoneen Stud in Ireland. 8 Rn
1m 40.51 (2.81)
SF—19/25/10/3/–/–

## 2188

INVESCO M.I.M. H'CAP (0-90) £4092.00 (£1221.00: £583.00: £264.00)
6f
2-45 (2-46)

1928 **Rose Indien (FR) (87)** *(MMoubarak)* 3-9-5 LDettori (11) (a.p: led 2f out: clr fnl f) **—1**

1952⁴ **Easy Line (87)** *(PJFeilden)* 9-9-11 BRaymond (7) (b: hdwy appr fnl f: rdn & r.o ins fnl f) ........................................... 2.2

1745★ **Arabellajill (87)** *(RHannon)* 3-9-2‡³RPerham (4) (in tch: nt clr run over 1f out: r.o strly ins fnl f) ........................................... ¹/₂.3

1406 **Hard to Figure (90)** *(RJHodges)* 6-9-7‡⁷SDrowne (5) (s.s: hdwy after 2f: r.o ins fnl f) ........................................... nk.4

1877 **Helios (68)** *(RSimpson)* 4-8-6 GBardwell (3) (led to ¹/₂-wy: one pce appr fnl f) .. 1.5

1745² **Jigsaw Boy (76)** *(RJHolder)* 3-8-8 SCauthen (8) (lw: prom: rdn & carried rt over 1f out: one pce) ........................................... ¹/₂.6

1987⁴ **Darussalam (70)** *(RLee)* 5-8-8 WAAntongeorgi (10) (chsd ldrs: rdn over 1f out: one pce) ........................................... hd.7

1878 **Clifton Charlie (USA) (86)** (bl) *(MRChannon)* 4-9-10 WCarson (9) (lw: chsd ldrs: rdn ¹/₂-wy: sn btn) ........................................... 1¹/₂.8

1870⁶ **Co-Chin (IRE) (79)** *(GLewis)* 3-8-11 AClark (12) (lw: stdd s: effrt over 2f out: no imp) ........................................... ¹/₂.9

1928⁴ **Castilian Queen (USA) (80)** (Fav) *(JHMGosden)* 3-8-12 RCochrane (2) (hld up: hdwy 2f out: bdly hmpd ent fnl f: nt rcvr) ........................................... s.h.10

1576⁵ **Walking Possession (77)** (bl) *(RBoss)* 3-8-9 PRobinson (13) (s.i.s: sn rcvrd: led ¹/₂-wy to 2f out: wknd fnl f) ........................................... 2¹/₂.11

1920⁴ **My Sovereign (USA) (74)** (v) *(JRFanshawe)* 3-8-6 GDuffield (5) (hdwy ¹/₂-wy: wknd wl over 1f out) ........................................... nk.12

2009² **Tauber (69)** *(PatMitchell)* 8-8-4‡³SO'Gorman (6) (mid div: bmpd over 1f out: sn btn & eased: t.o) ........................................... 15.13

**5/2** Castilian Queen (USA), **7/1** ROSE INDIEN (FR), **9/1** Arabellajill, Darussalam, **10/1** My Sovereign (USA), **11/1** Jigsaw Boy, **12/1** Tauber, **14/1** Clifton Charlie (USA), Hard to Figure, **16/1** Easy Line, Co-Chin (IRE), **20/1** Walking Possession, **25/1** Helios. CSF £99.54, CT £923.93. Tote £6.60: £2.70 £4.20 £2.20 (£39.60). Ecurie Fustok (NEWMARKET) bred by Francois Geffroy in France. 13 Rn
1m 13.19 (1.69)
SF—59/57/46/50/31/31/30

## 2189

CHEMIST BROKERS STKS £4056.25 (£1210.00: £577.50: £261.25)
1¹/₄m
3-15 (3-17)

1229a³ **Masad (IRE)** (Fav) *(LMCumani)* 3-9-0 LDettori (5) (hld up gng wl: swtchd lft over 1f out: qcknd to ld ins fnl f: impressive) ........................................... **—1**

500³ **Tik Fa (USA) (100)** *(BHanbury)* 3-9-0 BRaymond (6) (a.p: led appr fnl f: sn hdd: rallied nr fin) ........................................... 2¹/₂.2

1933★ **United Kingdom (USA) *(HRACecil)* 3-8-9 SCauthen (3) (lw: hld up: led over 1f out: edgd rt: hdd ins fnl f: sn btn) ........................................... ³/₄.3

1928 **Enaya (84)** *(RWArmstrong)* 3-8-9 RCochrane (4) (hld up & bhd: styd on fnl 2f: nvr able to chal) ........................................... 3¹/₂.4

1458 **Badie (USA) (102)** *(JLDunlop)* 3-9-0 WCarson (2) (led after 2f: shkn up 2f out: sn hdd: eased whn btn) ........................................... 6.5

1917⁵ **Cheveley Dancer (USA)** *(AWDenson)* 4-9-10 MHills (1) (swtg: chsd ldr 7f: sn rdn & outpcd: t.o) ........................................... 10.6

**11/8** MASAD (IRE), **6/4** United Kingdom (USA)(op Evens), **7/1** Badie (USA)(op 4/1), **8/1** Tik Fa (USA), **20/1** Enaya, **80/1** Cheveley Dancer (USA). CSF £11.27, Tote £2.30: £1.50 £2.60 (£7.70). Mrs G. Zanocchio (NEWMARKET) bred by Azienda Agricola San Jore in Ireland. 6 Rn
2m 8.15 (5.55)
SF—34/29/22/15/8/–

**2190** PRIMULA STKS (Mdn 2-Y.O) £3817.50 (£1140.00: £545.00: £247.50)
6f
3-45 (3-46)

**Normanton Park** *(RHannon)* 9-0 BRaymond (5) (w'like: mde all: rdn out fnl f) ... —**1**
Royal Roller (IRE) *(CNAllen)* 8-7 ‡7GForster (1) (cmpt: bkwd: hld up: hdwy
½-wy: sn ev ch: r.o one pce fnl f) .................................................. 2.**2**
1610⁴ Able Choice (IRE) *(Fav)* *(RWArmstrong)* 9-0 PatEddery (2) (a.p: drifted rt over
1f out: rdn & no ex fnl f) .......................................................... ½.**3**
Henequin (USA) *(JHMGosden)* 8-9 SCauthen (7) (neat: hld up: hdwy & ev ch
over 1f out: unable qckn) .......................................................... 2.**4**
Ikhtisas (USA) *(BHanbury)* 8-9 WCarson (3) (w'like: leggy: hld up: hmpd over
1f out: swtchd rt: nt rcvr) ........................................................ 2½.**5**
Early to Rise *(CACyzer)* 9-0 DBiggs (4) (str: w'like: bkwd: s.s: effrt & rn green
½-wy: no imp) ...................................................................... 8.**6**
2031 Fanfold (IRE) *(AWDenson)* 8-9 MHills (6) (spd 4f: sn rdn & wknd) .................. 1.**7**

**10/11** Able Choice (IRE)(op 6/4), **4/1** NORMANTON PARK(op 9/4), **5/1** Ikhtisas (USA), **11/2** Henequin (USA),
**20/1** Royal Roller (IRE), Early to Rise, **33/1** Fanfold (IRE). CSF £58.03, Tote £5.60: £2.80 £5.10 (£56.40). A. F.
Budge (Equine) Limited (MARLBOROUGH) bred by Bishop Wilton Stud. 7 Rn
1m 14.49 (2.99)
SF—28/13/18/5/–/–

**2191** FOOD BROKERS TROPHY (H'cap) (3-Y.O) (0-115) £20062.50 (£6000.00: £2875.00:
£1312.50) 1m
4-15 (4-17)

(Weights raised 12 lb)
1941² **Big Leap (IRE) (93)** *(MMoubarak)* 9-7 LDettori (13) (hld up: hdwy 3f out: nt clr
run appr fnl f: str run to ld last stride) ..................................... —**1**
1708⋆ Wave Hill (82) *(RHannon)* 8-7 ‡3RPerham (10) (lw: led to ½-wy: led 1f out tl ct
last stride) ......................................................................... s.h.**2**
2028 Irek (88) *(LordHuntingdon)* 9-2 SCauthen (11) (lw: a.p: ev ch over 1f out: rallied
u.p nr fin) ........................................................................... hd.**3**
1807⋆ Riviera Vista (87) *(Fav)* *(GWragg)* 9-1 MRoberts (1) (a.p: ev ch 1f out: unable
qckn) ................................................................................ nk.**4**
1928⋆ Miss Haggis (85) *(RBoss)* 8-13 PatEddery (2) (bhd: hdwy over 2f out: rdn & ev
ch ins fnl f: unable qckn) ......................................................... 1½.**5**
1943⁶ Mutabahi (CAN) (86) *(RWArmstrong)* 9-0 WCarson (5) (hld up: gd hdwy appr
fnl f: rdn & no ex ins fnl f) ....................................................... nk.**6**
1476 Philidor (85) *(JMPEustace)* 8-13 RCochrane (4) (lw: prom: rdn over 2f out: one
pce appr fnl f) ...................................................................... 4.**7**
1634⁴ Good Reference (IRE) (86) *(MBell)* 9-0 PRobinson (9) (prom tl wknd over 1f
out) ................................................................................. hd.**8**
2126⋆ Euro Festival (85) *(MissLCSiddall)* 8-13 DMcKeown (8) (hld up: effrt & veered rt
2f out: no imp) ..................................................................... 3½.**9**
2013³ Ler Cru (IRE) (72) (bl) *(CEBrittain)* 7-9 ‡5BDoyle (12) (chsd ldrs: led ½-wy to 1f
out: wknd fnl f) .................................................................... nk.**10**
1476 Trafalgar Boy (USA) (84) *(JEtherington)* 8-12 BRaymond (6) (lw: in tch: rdn
½-wy: sn btn) ...................................................................... 1½.**11**
1533 Nashville Blues (IRE) (87) *(JWHills)* 9-1 MHills (7) (hld up: effrt over 2f out: wknd
fnl f) ................................................................................ 1½.**12**
1218 The Power of One (79) *(RSimpson)* 8-7 GDuffield (3) (chsd ldrs 6f: sn outpcd) 1½.**13**
LONG HANDICAP: Ler Cru (IRE) 7-11.

**11/4** Riviera Vista, **5/1** Euro Festival, **6/1** Miss Haggis, **7/1** Nashville Blues (IRE)(op 12/1), **8/1** Philidor, **17/2** BIG
LEAP (IRE), **10/1** Mutabahi (CAN), **14/1** Irek, Wave Hill, **20/1** Trafalgar Boy (USA), **33/1** Ors. CSF £113.75, CT
£1,497.37. Tote £10.30: £2.90 £4.70 £4.20 (£106.90). Ecurie Fustok (NEWMARKET) bred by The Mount Coote
Partnership in Ireland. 13 Rn
1m 40.37 (2.67)
SF—55/40/48/46/38/38

**2192** FOOD BROKERS-FISHERMAN'S FRIEND H'CAP (3-Y.O) (0-90) £3877.50 (£1155.00:
£550.00: £247.50) 5f
4-45 (4-46)

1861² **Educated Pet (75)** *(MJohnston)* 8-10 DMcKeown (4) (a.p: rdn 1f out: r.o strly to
ld post) ............................................................................. —**1**
1593⋆ Cradle Days (86) *(Fav)* *(RHannon)* 9-7 WCarson (2) (lw: led ½-wy: hrd drvn fnl
f: ct cl home) ...................................................................... s.h.**2**
1871² Inherent Magic (IRE) (78) *(MMcCormack)* 8-13 AClark (1) (w ldrs: ev ch 1f out:
unable qckn nr fin) ................................................................ 1½.**3**
1776 Forest Fairy (66) *(RBoss)* 8-1 MRoberts (3) (hmpd s: chsd ldrs 3f) ............... 3½.**4**
939⁶ Walstead (IRE) (68) *(DAWilson)* 8-3 GDuffield (6) (sn outpcd) .................... 3½.**5**
1669 Creche (73) (bl) *(MrsNMacauley)* 8-8 NDay (5) (led to ½-wy: wknd wl over 1f
out) ................................................................................. 1½.**6**

**15/8** Cradle Days, **3/1** Inherent Magic (IRE), **9/2** EDUCATED PET, **11/2** Forest Fairy, **8/1** Creche(tchd 12/1), **14/1** Walstead (IRE). CSF £12.60, Tote £4.70: £1.60 £1.60 (£4.80). Mr Billy Morgan (MIDDLEHAM) bred by Highfield Stud Ltd. 6 Rn
60.05 sec (1.05)
SF—65/75/61/35/22/21

### 2193    LIMEKILN NURSERY    £3915.00 (£1170.00: £560.00: £255.00)    7f    5-15 (5-16)

| | | | |
|---|---|---|---|
| 2010⁴ | **King Paris (IRE)** *(MBell)* 8-10 MHills (7) (hdwy ½-wy: led ins fnl f: r.o wl) | | —1 |
| 2010³ | Mr Martini (IRE) (bl) *(CEBrittain)* 8-8 MRoberts (6) (lw: led tl hdd ins fnl f: rallied u.p nr fin) | | 1.2 |
| 1995* | Marillette (USA) (Fav) *(JHMGosden)* 9-7 SCauthen (1) (dwlt: hdwy 2f out: rdn & nt qckn fnl f) | | 2½.3 |
| 2010 | Chinnery (IRE) *(JMPEustace)* 8-7 RCochrane (3) (lw: hld up & bhd: hdwy wl over 1f out: nvr nr to chal) | | 3½.4 |
| 1161⁴ | Cashable *(JRJenkins)* 8-7 SWhitworth (5) (w ldr tl wknd 2f out) | | 1½.5 |
| 1170* | Walsham Witch *(MHTompkins)* 8-4 PRobinson (8) (chsd ldrs: rdn 2f out: eased whn btn fnl f) | | 1½.6 |
| 1854³ | Mansooree (USA) *(AAScott)* 7-10 GKing (4) (w ldrs: ev ch 3f out: sn hrd rdn & wknd) | | 5.7 |

**6/4** Marillette (USA), **4/1** KING PARIS (IRE), **5/1** Mr Martini (IRE), **11/2** Walsham Witch, **15/2** Mansooree (USA), **14/1** Chinnery (IRE), **16/1** Cashable. CSF £22.60, CT £38.28. Tote £5.00: £2.70 £2.80 (£9.90). Mrs Pauline Karpidas (NEWMARKET) bred by Mrs P. Karpidas in Ireland. 7 Rn
1m 26.59 (2.19)
SF—53/48/52/27/22/14

T/Trio: Race 5: £343.20 (8.8 Tckts). T/Plpt: £545.30 (15.6 Tckts).
IM

## 2004—LINGFIELD (L-H)

### Saturday, July 18th [Turf Good to firm, AWT Standard]

Going Allowance: Turf: minus 0.40 sec (F); AWT: minus 0.70 sec (FS)    Wind: slt half bhd

Stalls: 5th centre, remainder high

### 2194    ARUNDEL APP'CE STKS    £1393.20 (£385.20: £183.60)    7f (AWT)    6-00 (6-00)

| | | | |
|---|---|---|---|
| 1947² | **Confronter (80)** (Fav) *(PFICole)* 3-9-3 ‡³JDSmith (3) (w ldr: led ins fnl f: pushed out) | | —1 |
| 1698⁴ | Ponsardin (86) *(SirMarkPrescott)* 3-9-6 DBiggs (2) (led: hrd rdn over 1f out: hdd ins fnl f: r.o) | | ¾.2 |
| 1535 | Myasha (USA) (66) *(MrsLPiggott)* 3-9-3 ‡³GMilligan (4) (eyeshield: b.hind: hld up: wknd 2f out) | | 15.3 |
| | Hibiscus Ivy (AUS) *(DJSCosgrove)* 4-8-9 ‡³PBowe (1) (bhd fnl 4f: t.o) | | 15.4 |

**8/11** CONFRONTER, **11/8** Ponsardin, **10/1** Myasha (USA)(op 6/1), **100/1** Hibiscus Ivy (AUS). CSF £2.04, Tote £1.70 (£1.40). Mr Yahya Nasib (WHATCOMBE) bred by Hamilton Bloodstock (UK) Ltd. 4 Rn
1m 22.99 (0.23 under best; U1.01)
SF—55/56/8/–

### 2195    WORTH (S) STKS (2-Y.O) £1287.00 (£357.00: £171.00)    6f    6-25 (6-28)

| | | | |
|---|---|---|---|
| 2008³ | **Awesome Risk** *(GLewis)* 8-6 DBiggs (10) (b.off hind: a.p: rdn over 4f out: led ins fnl f: drvn out) | | —1 |
| 1886⁴ | Jasmin Isle *(MissGayKelleway)* 8-6 DHolland (11) (led: hrd rdn over 1f out: hdd ins fnl f: r.o) | | ¾.2 |
| 1913 | Mr Butch *(MRChannon)* 8-11 TQuinn (6) (hdwy over 2f out: hrd rdn over 1f out: unable qckn) | | 5.3 |
| 2034 | De Chine *(JSMoore)* 7-13 ‡⁷CHawksley (4) (hdwy 2f out: r.o one pce) | | 2½.4 |
| 2005 | Arctic Agnes (USA) *(RAkehurst)* 8-3 ‡³RPerham (8) (b.nr fore: a.p: one pce fnl 2f) | | 1½.5 |
| 1946 | Conbrio Star (bl) *(CGCox)* 8-11 GBardwell (12) (lw: w ldr 4f) | | nk.6 |
| 2005² | Nikki Noo Noo (Fav) *(CJHill)* 8-6 NAdams (2) (nvr nr to chal) | | 3½.7 |
| 1429 | Freebyjove *(PButler)* 8-6 RFox (9) (nvr nrr) | | 1½.8 |
| 1848 | Ukam's Lady (v) *(RHannon)* 8-6 AMcGlone (13) (a mid div) | | hd.9 |
| 1900 | Balustrade Boy (IRE) *(BStevens)* 8-11 MTebbutt (7) (a bhd) | | 1½.10 |
| 928 | Southampton *(GBBalding)* 8-11 JWilliams (5) (a bhd) | | s.h.11 |
| 1442 | Buckski Echo *(TMJones)* 8-4 ‡⁷JDSmith (3) (prom over 3f) | | 6.12 |
| 595 | Persian Noble *(CJHill)* 8-11 TRogers (1) (lw: a bhd) | | 12.13 |

**7/2** Nikki Noo Noo, **4/1** Jasmin Isle, AWESOME RISK(3/1—5/1), **6/1** De Chine, **8/1** Mr Butch, **9/1** Ukam's Lady, **14/1** Southampton, **16/1** Arctic Agnes (USA), **20/1** Balustrade Boy (IRE), **25/1** Persian Noble, **33/1** Ors. CSF £20.48, Tote £4.90: £1.90 £1.70 £2.50 (£8.30). Roldvale Limited (EPSOM) bred by Roldvale Ltd. 13 Rn; No bid
1m 10.58 (1.98)
SF—4/1/–

**2196** CHARTERHOUSE STKS (Mdn 3-Y.O) £1330.20 (£367.20: £174.60)
7f (AWT)                                                        6-50 (6-53)

1774² **Super Serenade (74)** (GBBalding) 9-0 MRoberts (3) (lw: hld up: led over 1f
out: pushed out) ............................................................... —1
2041⁵ Nobby Barnes (59) (RWArmstrong) 9-0 JHo (5) (hld up: rdn over 1f out: r.o ins
fnl f) ........................................................................ 1½.2
1611 Queen Warrior (Fav) (PTWalwyn) 8-9 DHolland (2) (chsd ldr: hrd rdn 3f out: led
over 2f out tl over 1f out: edgd lft: unable qckn) ............... 1½.3
1681³ Lamore Ritorna (50) (KOCunningham-Brown) 8-9 TQuinn (1) (hld up: one pce
fnl 2f) ...................................................................... 2½.4
248² Easy Does it (53) (v) (MrsAKnight) 8-9 SWhitworth (4) (led over 4f: 3rd & wkng
whn hmpd on ins 1f out) .............................................. 4.5

**4/6** Queen Warrior, **13/8** SUPER SERENADE, **16/1** Nobby Barnes(op 10/1), **33/1** Ors. CSF £18.11, Tote £2.50:
£1.20 £3.00 (£9.40). Mr Jack Maxwell (DORCHESTER) bred by J. Maxwell. 5 Rn    1m 24 (equals standard)
SF—37/32/22/14/2

**2197** PULBOROUGH H'CAP (3-Y.O) (0-80) £1900.00 (£525.00: £250.00)
2m (AWT)                                                        7-20 (7-21)

1882* **Yenoora (IRE) (63)** (Fav) (PFICole) 9-3 TQuinn (5) (b.hind: swtg: led 1f: led
over 7f out: clr over 2f out: eased ins fnl f) ..................... —1
1977⁵ Perforate (57) (bl) (SirMarkPrescott) 9-11 GDuffield (3) (b.hind: led 15f out tl
over 7f out: r.o one pce) .............................................. 3.2
2014⁵ Afore Jane (55) (GHarwood) 8-4 ‡5JJones (1) (b.hind: hld up: chsd wnr 6f out:
one pce) ................................................................... nk.3
2020 Jupiter Moon (67) (bl) (CFBrittain) 9-7 MRoberts (2) (lw: rdn thrght: hdwy 9f
out: wknd 6f out: t.o) ................................................... 25.4
1872 Temple Knight (55) (CACyzer) 8-9 DBiggs (4) (bhd fnl 7f: t.o) ............... 25.5

**Evens** YENOORA (IRE), **4/1** Jupiter Moon(3/1—9/2), Perforate, **13/2** Afore Jane, **10/1** Temple Knight(op 5/1).
CSF £5.23, Tote £2.00: £1.30 £1.90 (£3.40). Mr Reg Hester (WHATCOMBE) bred by Binfield Manor Farms Ltd in
Ireland. 5 Rn                                                3m 21.48 (1.22 under best; U1.52)
SF—6/3/–/–/–

**2198** RICE AGRICULTURAL H'CAP (0-70) £1856.00 (£516.00: £248.00)
7f 140y                                                        7-50 (7-53)

(Weights raised 4 lb)
1916 **Lucky Noire (55)** (Fav) (GHarwood) 4-9-9 AClark (18) (lw: rdn & hdwy over 2f
out: led ins fnl f: edgd lft: r.o wl) .................................. —1
2125 Fast Operative (37) (KOCunningham-Brown) 5-8-5 RFox (19) (led over 2f: led
over 3f out tl ins fnl f: unable qckn) ............................... 1½.2
1727⁶ Fair Enchantress (54) (JABennett) 4-9-8 DHolland (14) (a.p: ev ch ins fnl f: one
pce) ......................................................................... nk.3
1813³ Dodgy (53) (v) (SDow) 5-9-7 TQuinn (17) (a.p: hrd rdn over 1f out: one pce) ... 2.4
2051 L'Acquesiana (58) (v) (DShaw) 4-7-9 RStreet (12) (b: rdn over 2f out: hdwy
over 1f out: r.o) ........................................................... 2.5
1885* Tajigrey (53) (RCurtis) 3-8-6 ‡7CHawksley (4) (hdwy over 1f out: r.o) ......... 1.6
2006³ Mabonne (55) (JLDunlop) 3-9-1 AMunro (1) (lw: hdwy over 2f out: nvr nr to
chal) ........................................................................ 1.7
1160 Beljinski (31) (BJMcMath) 4-7-6(1) ‡7JDSmith (20) (prom over 5f) ............. 1.8
2032 Darakah (56) (CJHill) 5-9-10 NAdams (15) (nvr nrr) ..................... s.h.9
1905 Harlequin Girl (33) (bl) (KTIvory) 4-8-1 GBardwell (7) (led 5f out tl over 3f out: sn
wknd) ...................................................................... s.h.10
1917 Tinkosumtin (22) (PBurgoyne) 6-8-11 TRogers (16) (a mid div) ............. 3½.11
1797⁶ Grey Illusions (36) (bl) (LJHolt) 4-8-4 AMcGlone (3) (swtg: nvr nrr) .......... ¾.12
1261² Pigalle Wonder (50) (RJO'Sullivan) 4-9-4 DBiggs (9) (prom 5f) ............. 2.13
1306 Hinton Harry (IRE) (43) (SMellor) 3-8-3 DanaMellor (11) (nvr nrr) ........... 4.14
1806³ Bellatrix (49) (CEBrittain) 4-9-3 MRoberts (13) (lw: prom over 5f: eased whn
btn over 1f out) ........................................................... nk.15
1885 Quiet Miss (55) (MrsAKnight) 3-9-1 SWhitworth (5) (bhd fnl 3f) ............. s.h.16
1797* Kelly's Kite (33) (HJCollingridge) 4-8-1 JQuinn (6) (bhd fnl 2f) ............. nk.17
2105² Lime Street Lil (28) (DAWilson) 4-7-5 ‡5DHarrison (8) (prom 5f) ............ 1½.18

**5/1** LUCKY NOIRE, **6/1** Pigalle Wonder, **7/1** Lime Street Lil, **15/2** Darakah, **8/1** Kelly's Kite, Dodgy, **10/1** Bellatrix,
Mabonne(12/1—8/1), **12/1** Tajigrey(8/1—14/1), **16/1** Fair Enchantress, Fast Operative, **20/1** Quiet Miss, **25/1**
Grey Illusions, **33/1** Ors. CSF £80.65, CT £1,107.14. Tote £7.30: £2.40 £6.80 £4.70 £1.80 (£61.30). Mrs Carol
Harrison (PULBOROUGH) bred by T. J. G. Read. 18 Rn                          1m 30.36 (1.86)
SF—36/13/29/22/–/–

**2199**　　SEVENOAKS H'CAP (0-70) £1456.20 (£403.20: £192.60)　**5f**　　8-20 (8-21)
(Weights raised 6 lb)

20326 **Maria Cappuccini (48)** (KOCunningham-Brown) 4-9-2 DHolland (10) (lw: gd hdwy over 1f out: led ins fnl f: r.o wl) .................................... —1

1138 Ski Captain (51) (PHowling) 8-9-5 DBiggs (9) (lw: chsd ldr: ev ch ins fnl f: unable qckn) ......................................... 1.2

19873 Shades of Jade (56) (Fav) (JJBridger) 4-9-10 SWhitworth (8) (led tl ins fnl f: one pce) ..................................... ½.3

1030 Frimley Parkson (34) (v) (PHowling) 8-8-2 JQuinn (6) (hdwy over 1f out: one pce) ........................................ 2.4

1771 Tylers Wood (47) (SDow) 7-9-1 TQuinn (3) (spd over 3f) ............... 3½.5

1978 Barbezieux (29) (bl) (TJNaughton) 5-7-6(4) ‡5DHarrison (1) (b: nvr nr to chal) .... 1.6

19046 Lucy Dancer (IRE) (53) (CGCox) 4-9-0 ‡7JHunter (5) (a.p: hrd rdn over 2f out: wkng whn hmpd over 1f out) ........................ 1½.7

17294 Oratel Flyer (27) (RThompson) 5-7-9 RFox (4) (bhd fnl 2f) .............. 4.8

2009 Sports Post Lady (IRE) (54) (CJHill) 4-9-8 NAdams (2) (bhd fnl 2f) ........... 3.9

2/1 Shades of Jade, 100/30 MARIA CAPPUCCINI, 6/1 Lucy Dancer (IRE), 13/2 Oratel Flyer, 8/1 Ski Captain(5/1—9/1), 11/1 Sports Post Lady (IRE), 12/1 Tylers Wood(op 8/1), 16/1 Frimley Parkson, 25/1 Barbezieux. CSF £28.57, CT £61.09. Tote £4.90: £1.70 £2.90 £1.10 (£13.80). Mr D. Bass (STOCKBRIDGE) bred by Laharna Ltd. 9 Rn　　　　57.72 sec (0.72)
SF—48/47/50/20/19/–

T/Plpt: £27.80 (25.4 Tckts).　　　　　　　　　　　　　　　　　　　　　AK

1906-**RIPON (R-H)**

**Saturday, July 18th [Good]**

Going Allowance: St: minus 0.40 sec; Rnd: minus 0.10 sec (F)　　　Wind: slt half bhd

Stalls: low

**2200**　　TRYTON FOODS YORKSHIRE PUDDING STKS (Mdn 3-Y.O) £2427.20 (£674.20: £323.60)
**1¼m**　　　　　　　　　　　　　　　　　　　　　　2-35 (2-40)

1933 **Kanvass** (JRFanshawe) 8-7 ‡7NVarley (5) (chsd ldrs: led 3f out: edgd lft over 1f out: sn clr) ........................... —1

19974 Brambleberry (MrsSJSmith) 8-7 ‡7JMarshall (1) (chsd ldrs: led over 3f out: sn hdd: r.o one pce appr fnl f) ................. 5.2

Shadanza (IRE) (APStringer) 9-0 TLucas (7) (leggy: s.i.s: sn wl bhd: hdwy over 2f out: r.o wl nr fin) ........................... 1½.3

7374 Portree (Fav) (HRACecil) 8-9 WRyan (6) (w ldr: led 4f out: sn hdd: wknd 2f out) nk.4

1906 Ima Red Neck (USA) (JHMGosden) 9-0 NCarlisle (9) (sn bhd: hdwy 4f out: kpt on wl fnl 2f) ...................................... 1½.5

19975 Tomashenko (JMackie) 9-0 GHind (4) (bit bkwd: sn bhd: sme hdwy 2f out: n.d) 10.6

19064 Waaza (USA) (AAScott) 9-0 JFortune (3) (dwlt s: chsd ldrs: drvn along & rn wd st: wandered & lost pl over 2f out) ............ 10.7

18563 Ajo (IRE) (80) (MRStoute) 8-11 ‡3FNorton (3) (led: sddle slipped: hdd 4f out: sn lost pl & eased) ........................ 8.8

Precious Henry (BEWilkinson) 8-9 ‡5SMaloney (8) (w'like: bkwd: s.s: a wl bhd) 15.9

5/4 Portree(Evens—6/4), 7/2 Ajo (IRE), 11/2 Waaza (USA), 12/1 Ima Red Neck (USA), KANVASS, 16/1 Brambleberry, 25/1 Tomashenko, 50/1 Ors. CSF £146.67, Tote £16.50: £2.70 £1.70 £8.40 (£61.10). Sheikh Mohammed (NEWMARKET) bred by Sheikh Mohammed bin Rashid al Maktoum. 9 Rn　　2m 8.6 (5.1)
SF—32/22/26/20/22/2

**2201**　　HENRY BUTCHER (S) STKS　£2092.50 (£580.00: £277.50)　**6f**　　3-05 (3-07)

19616 **Royal Girl (61)** (Fav) (MissSEHall) 5-9-2 NConnorton (1) (hdwy to ld over 2f out: pushed clr: comf) ................. —1

2009 Almasa (58) (DMorris) 4-8-11 ‡5JWeaver (3) (chsd ldrs: styd on u.p fnl 2f: no ch w wnr) .................................. 4.2

1583 Supreme Desire (40) (ASmith) 4-8-11 SWebster (10) (sn w ldrs: hrd rdn over 2f out: kpt on same pce) .............. 2.3

1853 Make Or Mar (57) (BEllison) 8-8-9 ‡7OPears (2) (led tl wknd over 1f out) .... hd.4

18885 Long Lane Lady (45) (JMackie) 6-9-2 GHind (6) (chsd ldrs tl wknd over 2f out) 1½.5

1685 Gallery Artist (IRE) (58) (RGuest) 4-9-4 ‡3FNorton (7) (chsd ldrs: hrd rdn ½-wy: sn wknd) ................................ 3½.6

19992 Tango Time (80) (NTinkler) 4-9-7 DNicholls (9) (hdwy & ev ch over 2f out: sn rdn & wknd) .............................. 2.7

20462 The Right Time (45) (bl) (JParkes) 7-9-7 JFortune (8) (lw: s.i.s: hdwy & prom ½-wy: sn rdn: wknd over 1f out) ............ 1½.8

1020 Glencroft **(60)** (bl) *(DWChapman)* 8-9-7 SWood (4) (t: reard s: a bhd) .............. 8.9
1961 Lord Magester (FR) **(48)** *(MrsGRReveley)* 5-9-2 WRyan (5) (sn outpcd & bhd) 15.**10**

**6/5** ROYAL GIRL **(66)** Tango Time, **8/1** Almasa, The Right Time, **12/1** Lord Magester (FR), Gallery Artist (IRE), **14/1** Glencroft, **16/1** Supreme Desire, **25/1** Long Lane Lady, **40/1** Make Or Mar. CSF £11.97, Tote £2.50: £1.60 £2.10 £3.40 (£9.40). Miss S. E. Hall (MIDDLEHAM) bred by John and Mrs McNamara. 10 Rn; No bid
1m 12.3 (0.6)
SF—42/23/15/12/13/1

## 2202　BELL-RINGER H'CAP (0-100) £5952.00 (£1776.00: £848.00: £384.00)
1¹/₄m　　　　　　　　　　　　　　　　　　　3-35 (3-37)
(Weights raised 2 lb)

2012* **Vallance (67)** *(PWHarris)* 4-8-3 JFortune (7) (lw: chsd ldr: drvn along 3f out: r.o wl u.p to ld nr fin) ................................ —1
1914⁴ Sovereign Page (USA) **(79)** (Jt-Fav) *(BHanbury)* 3-8-5 WRyan (3) (led: clr 7f out: rdn over 1f out: jst ct) ........................ nk.2
2028² Tell No Lies **(88)** (Jt-Fav) *(MHEasterby)* 5-9-10 TLucas (1) (hld up & bhd: hdwy over 3f out: nt rch ldrs) ................ 4.3
1911⁴ Routing **(60)** *(MDHammond)* 4-7-7(3) ‡3FNorton (6) (hld up: effrt over 3f out: kpt on same pce) .................... 2.4
1859³ Who's Tef (IRE) **(63)** *(MHEasterby)* 4-7-8(1) ‡5SMaloney (2) (trckd ldrs: effrt 3f out: edgd rt & grad wknd) ............ 6.5
296* Daru (USA) **(84)** (v) *(JHMGosden)* 3-8-10 GHind (5) (s.i.s: sn pushed along: outpcd 4f out: n.d after) ........................ s.h.6
1859⁶ Elegant Touch **(78)** *(MMoubarak)* 3-7-13(5) ‡5JWeaver (8) (chsd ldrs tl lost pl 3f out) ........................ 3.7
1618³ Imperial Bid (FR) **(88)** *(DenysSmith)* 4-9-3 ‡7CTeague (4) (hld up & bhd: rdn over 3f out: n.d) ................ 4.8

**100/30** Sovereign Page (USA)(9/£　3/1), Tell No Lies(op 9/4), **6/1** Elegant Touch, Daru (USA), **13/2** VALLANCE, **8/1** Routing(op 12/1), Who's Tef (IRE), **25/1** Imperial Bid (FR). CSF £20.45, CT £76.21 Tote £8.00: £2.10 £1.60 £1.50 (£26.30). Mrs P. W. Harris (BERKHAMSTED) bred by Pendley Farm. 8 Rn　2m 6.7 (3.2)
SF—47/48/59/24/13/28

## 2203　GOLDEN GRAIN H'CAP (0-80) £2950.00 (£880.00: £420.00: £190.00)
6f　　　　　　　　　　　　　　　　　　　　4-05 (4-06)

32 **Miss Aragon (46)** *(MissLCSiddall)* 4-7-7(3) ‡3FNorton (2) (trckd ldrs: led over 2f out: r.o wl fnl f) ........................ —1
1908⁵ Final Shot **(65)** *(MHEasterby)* 5-8-10 ‡5SMaloney (3) (a chsng ldrs: r.o fnl f) ... 1¹/₂.2
2003 Cronk's Courage **(78)** (v) *(EJAlston)* 6-10-0 DNicholls (6) (led tl over 2f out: wknd over 1f out) ........................ 5.3
1908² Filicaia **(66)** (Fav) *(DonEnricoIncisa)* 6-8-9 ‡7ClaireBalding (1) (sn outpcd: hdwy over 2f out: rdn over 1f out: kpt on same pce) .......... ³/₄.4
2032⁵ Luna Bid **(61)** *(MBlanshard)* 9-8-11 WRyan (5) (trckd ldrs: hung rt thrght: effrt 2f out: sn wknd) ........................ 2.5
1908⁴ Northern Spark **(60)** (bl) *(CWThornton)* 4-8-10 GHind (4) (lw: chsd ldrs: rdn ¹/₂-wy: sn wknd & bhd) ........................ 12.6
LONG HANDICAP: Miss Aragon 7-4.

**5/2** Filicaia, **100/30** Luna Bid, **4/1** Northern Spark, **9/2** Final Shot, **7/1** Cronk's Courage, **16/1** MISS ARAGON. CSF £72.83, Tote £18.60: £3.60 £2.40 (£32.70). Mr T. Charlesworth (TADCASTER) bred by J. A. Griffiths. 6 Rn
1m 12.2 (0.5)
SF—21/32/30/8/2/–

## 2204　TRIMOCO VEHICLE LEASING H'CAP (0-70) £2540.60 (£706.60: £339.80)
1¹/₂m 60y　　　　　　　　　　　　　　　4-35 (4-37)

1967⁴ **Bold Elect (66)** *(PWigham)* 4-10-0 MWigham (3) (lw: bhd: gd hdwy 4f out: led over 2f out: drvn out) ........................ —1
1800⁶ Sweet Request **(39)** (bl) *(JRBostock)* 4-7-12 ‡3FNorton (12) (dwlt s: bhd: hdwy 4f out: edgd lft u.p over 1f out: kpt on nr fin) ........................ ³/₄.2
1394 Eire Leath-Sceal **(56)** *(MBrittain)* 5-8-13 ‡5SMaloney (8) (lw: chsd ldrs: ev ch tl rdn & outpcd over 1f out) ........................ 7.3
1739 Statia (IRE) **(31)** *(DonEnricoIncisa)* 4-7-7 JakiHouston (10) (sn bhd: hdwy & edgd bdly lft over 2f out: nt rch ldrs) ........................ 5.4
1922 Red Jam Jar **(33)** *(JMackie)* 7-7-9 LCharnock (5) (b: chsd ldrs: led 4f out tl over 2f out: wknd) ........................ 6.5
2069* Eurotwist **(70)** (Fav) *(TDBarron)* 3-9-1 (4x) ‡5JWeaver (7) (lw: hld up & bhd: gd hdwy whn bdly hmpd over 3f out: nt rcvr) ........................ 7.6
1922 John Shaw (USA) **(55)** *(JSWainwright)* 4-9-3 PBurke (9) (rr div & reminders 8f out: n.d) ........................ nk.7
1976 Edgewise **(31)** *(DMorris)* 9-7-7 SWood (2) (chsd ldrs tl lost pl 4f out) ................ 8.8

2033 Horizon (IRE) **(53)** (bl) *(TThomsonJones)* 4–9-1 DNicholls (1) (chsd ldrs tl lost
pl over 3f out) ..................................................................................... 2.9

1567 Perfect Light **(51)** *(MrsSJSmith)* 3–7-8⁽⁵⁾ ‡7JMarshall (11) (plld hrd: led: rn wd 4f
out: sn hdd & wknd) ............................................................................ 2.10

One for the Boys **(42)** *(CaptJWilson)* 5–8-4 TLucas (4) (b: bit bkwd: sn chsng
ldrs: wknd 4f out) ................................................................................ 6.11

1292⁵ Boring (USA) **(57)** *(WStorey)* 3–8-7 SWebster (6) (b: s.i.s: a in rr) .............. s.h.12

1894⁵ Demokos (FR) **(41)** *(APStringer)* 7–8-3 JFortune (13) (chsd ldrs tl wknd over 3f
out: sn bhd) ........................................................................................ 15.13

LONG HANDICAP: Statia (IRE) 7-3, Edgewise 6-7.

2/1 Eurotwist, 5/1 Demokos (FR), 8/1 Boring (USA), 17/2 Sweet Request, Horizon (IRE), 9/1 BOLD ELECT, 11/1
Eire Leath-Sceal, 14/1 Red Jam Jar, 25/1 Statia (IRE), 33/1 Perfect Light, One for the Boys, 50/1 Ors. CSF
£76.33, CT £774.38. Tote £11.80: £3.40 £2.80 £3.20 (£62.90). Mrs J. L. Wigham (MALTON) bred by Home
Stud Ltd. 13 Rn                                                                                                      2m 39 (5)
SF—52/20/20/–/–/–

## 2205

E.B.F. BRADFORD STKS (Mdn 2-Y.O) £2465.00 (£685.00: £329.00)     **6f**     5-05 (5-08)

**Storiths (IRE)** *(JWWatts)* 9-0 NConnorton (3) (w'like: leggy: chsd ldrs:
squeezed thro to ld jst ins fnl f: edgd rt & sn clr) ................... —1

1899⁵ Kennedys Prima (Fav) *(AAScott)* 8-9 JFortune (16) (led far side: rdn over 1f out:
r.o) ...................................................................................................... 3.2

Classic Image (IRE) *(MMoubarak)* 8-9 ‡5JWeaver (2) (lengthy: unf: scope: led
stands' side: edgd rt 1f out: sn hdd & kpt on same pce) ... hd.3

2024 Milbank Challenger *(MHEasterby)* 8-9 ‡5SMaloney (7) (chsd ldr stands' side tl
rdn & wknd over 1f out) ....................................................................... 6.4

1273 Bardia *(DonEnricoIncisa)* 8-9 JakiHouston (4) (bit bkwd: hdwy 2f out: kpt on nr
fin) ....................................................................................................... 2.5

2024 Muraadi Ana (IRE) *(AAScott)* 9-0 NCarlisle (1) (chsd ldr stands' side tl wknd
over 2f out) ....................................................................................... ¹/₂.6

1699 Indian Secret *(BEWilkinson)* 9-0 DNicholls (13) (chsd ldrs stands' side tl wknd
2f out) ................................................................................................ 1¹/₂.7

1910 Challenger Row (IRE) *(CWThornton)* 9-0 RPElliott (15) (b.hind: nvr rchd ldrs) .. ¹/₂.8

Court Pianist (IRE) *(CWCElsey)* 9-0 SWebster (17) (cmpt: nvr nr to chal) ........ 1.9

1616³ Don't Tell Jean *(NBycroft)* 8-9 SWood (14) (unruly paddock: chsd ldrs tl wknd
over 2f out) ....................................................................................... ¹/₂.10

1689⁶ Desirable Miss (bl) *(MBrittain)* 8-9 PSedgwick (12) (chsd ldrs far side: wnt bdly
lft u.p ¹/₂-wy: sn lost pl) ....................................................................... ³/₄.11

2024 Rushalong *(RDEWoodhouse)* 9-0 TLucas (6) (sn outpcd) ............................. hd.12

1782² Bluebella *(MrsPABarker)* 8-2 ‡7JTate (9) (prom over 3f: sn lost pl) ............... 1¹/₂.13

1779³ I Do Care *(JBerry)* 9-0 BCrossley (5) (in tch to ¹/₂-wy: sn wknd) .................. ¹/₂.14

1969⁶ Bajan Affair *(MissLCSiddall)* 8-2 ‡7OPears (11) (unruly paddock: s.i.s: sme
hdwy ¹/₂-wy: sn wknd) .......................................................................... ¹/₂.15

Song in Your Heart *(AHarrison)* 8-9 ‡5LNewton (8) (leggy: scope: bit bkwd: s.s:
a bhd) ................................................................................................ 10.16

Codden Lad *(NTinkler)* 9-0 LCharnock (10) (cmpt: bit bkwd: s.s: a wl bhd) . 1¹/₂.17

5/2 Kennedys Prima, 11/4 Classic Image (IRE)(op 6/5), 7/1 STORITHS (IRE), 8/1 I Do Care(op 12/1), 12/1 Don't
Tell Jean, Indian Secret (IRE), 14/1 Milbank Challenger, Muraadi Ana (IRE), 20/1 Challenger Row (IRE), 25/1
Bluebella, 33/1 Codden Lad, Court Pianist (IRE), Song in Your Heart, Desirable Miss, 50/1 Ors. CSF £25.03, Tote
£11.10: £2.60 £1.90 £2.40 (£17.10). Mrs M. Irwin (RICHMOND) bred by J. F. O'Malley in Ireland. 17 Rn
1m 12.6 (0.9)
SF—34/17/16/–/–/–

T/Plpt: £2,719.10 (2 Tckts).                                                                                          WG

## 2057—**WOLVERHAMPTON (L-H)**

### Saturday, July 18th [Good to firm, Good fnl 8f]

Going Allowance: 5f: minus 0.10 sec (F); Rnd: nil sec per fur (G)                          Wind: mod bhd

Stalls: high

## 2206

PLYVINE H'CAP (0-70) £1203.00 (£333.00: £159.00)     **5f**     6-15 (6-15)
(Weights raised 1 lb)

1904 **Hotfoot Hannah (IRE) (43)** *(PSFelgate)* 4–8-10 WRyan (4) (hdwy 2f out: rdn to
ld wl ins fnl f: r.o) .............................................................................. —1

1950★ Bells of Longwick **(62)** *(DRLaing)* 3–9-10 TyroneWilliams (6) (a.p: led 2f out:
hrd rdn & hdd wl ins fnl f) ................................................................. 1.2

1987² Rays Mead **(50)** (Fav) *(LJHolt)* 4–9-3 WNewnes (2) (a.p: hrd rdn & ev ch over 1f
out: nt qckn ins fnl f) ......................................................................... 1¹/₂.3

WOLVERHAMPTON, July 18, 1992    2207 – 2209

1865³ Admirals Realm (52) *(BAMcMahon)* 3–8–7 ‡7SSanders (5) (lw: dwlt: hdwy 3f out: hrd rdn over 1f out: r.o one pce) ............................ ¹⁄₂.4
  221 Lonely Lass (44) *(AWJones)* 6–8–4 ‡7DWright (1) (chsd ldrs tl wknd fnl f) ........... 5.5
1908⁶ Lombard Ocean (58) *(MO'Neill)* 3–9–6 BRaymond (3) (s.i.s: a bhd) ............ 2.6
  Le Chic (55) *(DWChapman)* 6–9–1 ‡7SWilliams (7) (led 3f) ........................... 4.7
1992 Sara Anne (IRE) (52) *(WMBrisbourne)* 3–9–0 LDettori (8) (bhd fnl 2f) ............ 1¹⁄₂.8

**5/2** Rays Mead, **11/4** Bells of Longwick, **5/1** HOTFOOT HANNAH (IRE), **7/1** Lombard Ocean, **12/1** Sara Anne (IRE)(op 8/1), **14/1** Ors. CSF £17.64, CT £37.01. Tote £5.80: £1.60 £1.90 £1.50 (£9.40). Mr John S. Martin (MELTON MOWBRAY) bred by James Hender in Ireland. 8 Rn
60.1 sec (2.8)
SF–30/40/27/15/–/–

**2207**    MR SIZZLE (S) STKS (2-Y.O) £1318.50 (£366.00: £175.50)    **5f**    6-45 (6-46)

1734⁴ **Minshaar** (Fav) *(BHanbury)* 8-6 BRaymond (8) (a.p: led over 2f out: clr whn hung lft ins fnl f: easily) .................................. —1
1838² Dead Calm *(CTinkler)* 8-11 LDettori (4) (lw: hld up: hdwy over 2f out: chsd wnr over 1f out: no imp) ............................ 3.2
1788³ General Brooks (IRE) (v) *(JBerry)* 8-11 GCarter (2) (led over 2f: one pce) ........... 5.3
2005 Keamari *(BForsey)* 8-1 ‡5RPrice (3) (pushed along: no hdwy fnl 2f) ............ 1¹⁄₂.4
2052 Risk a Little *(MJHeaton-Ellis)* 8-6 WRyan (6) (no hdwy fnl 2f) .................... 3.5
1416³ Over the Dec *(BAMcMahon)* 7-13 ‡7JBramhill (7) (lw: prom tl hrd rdn & wknd wl over 1f over) ................................. 1.6
1140 Bell Lad (IRE) *(CASmith)* 8-11 AProud (5) (prom over 2f) ....................... 6.7
  Monet Monet Monet *(WCarter)* 8-1 ‡5NGwilliams (9) (leggy: lt-f: s.s: a t.o) ....... 8.8
  Chapel Mere *(DMcCain)* 8-6 WNewnes (1) (leggy: bkwd: s.s: sn t.o) ............ 7.9

**6/4** MINSHAAR, **7/2** Dead Calm, General Brooks (IRE), **9/1** Risk a Little(op 5/1), **16/1** Over the Dec(op 8/1), **20/1** Monot Monet Monet(op 8/1), **50/1** Ors. CSF £6.53, Tote £2.90: £1.10 £1.20 £1.60 (£2.70). Mr Saeed Suhail (NEWMARKET) bred by Gainsborough Stud Management Ltd. 9 Rn. Sold Mrs P Joynes 5,600 gns
60.7 sec (0.4)
SF–14/7/–/–/–

**2208**    RACE CLUB INTERNATIONAL STKS (Mdn 2-Y.O.C & G) £1308.00 (£363.00: £174.00)    **7f**    7-15 (7-17)

1457 **Shebl (USA)** (Fav) *(MRStoute)* 9-0 PatEddery (8) (3rd st: led 2f out: comf) ........ —1
1809² Almansour (USA) *(HRACecil)* 9-0 WRyan (4) (led 5f: r.o one pce) ............... 2.2
1873⁵ Festin *(JLDunlop)* 9-0 WCarson (3) (6th st: hdwy 3f out: one pce fnl 2f) ......... 5.3
  Mr Geneaology (USA) *(JLSpearing)* 9-0 GHind (6) (unf: scope: s.s: last st: hdwy over 1f out: nrst fin) .............. nk.4
  Dusty Point (IRE) *(BHanbury)* 9-0 TyroneWilliams (9) (str: scope: bkwd: s.i.s: pushed along & sn rcvrd: 4th st: wknd 2f out) ......... 2.5
  The Gold Souk (IRE) *(JLDunlop)* 9-0 GCarter (7) (leggy: dwlt: 7th st: a bhd) ...... 3.6
  United Colours *(LMCumani)* 9-0 LDettori (2) (w'like: scope: bkwd: 5th st: wknd 3f out) ........................ 1.7
1796⁴ Behaanis (USA) *(AAScott)* 9-0 WNewnes (1) (8th st: a bhd) ................. ³⁄₄.8
1925³ Persiansky (IRE) *(BHanbury)* 9-0 BRaymond (5) (bolted bef s: chsd ldr: 2nd st: wknd 3f out: t.o) ............... 30.9

**4/7** SHEBL (USA)(tchd Evens), **11/2** Almansour (USA), **6/1** Festin, **11/1** Persiansky (IRE)(6/1—12/1), **12/1** United Colours(op 7/1), **33/1** The Gold Souk (IRE), **40/1** Behaanis (USA), **50/1** Mr Geneaology (USA), **66/1** Dusty Point (IRE). CSF £4.53, Tote £1.70: £1.40 £1.00 £2.10 (£2.40). Sheikh Ahmed Al Maktoum (NEWMARKET) bred by G. M. Breeding Farms Inc in USA. 9 Rn
1m 24.2 (3.9)
SF–42/39/21/20/14/2

**2209**    NEW INNS CLAIMING STKS    £1329.00 (£369.00: £177.00)    **7f**    7-45 (7-47)

1795² **Surrey Racing** (63) *(GLewis)* 4–8-8 BRouse (10) (3rd st: led wl over 2f out: r.o wl) ........................... —1
1776 Glenfield Greta (60) *(PSFelgate)* 4–8-3 ‡3FNorton (12) (swtchd rt & hdwy over 2f out: hung lft & r.o fnl f) .......... nk.2
1199 Slip-a-Snip (66) *(GBBalding)* 5–7-13 ‡5RPrice (11) (6th st: ev ch over 1f out: nt qckn fnl f) .................. 2.3
  596 Whippet (72) *(JABennett)* 8–8-9 GHind (5) (5th st: r.o one pce fnl 2f) ......... ¹⁄₂.4
1725 Kind Style (IRE) (26) *(RHollinshead)* 4–8-7 WRyan (6) (hdwy over 2f out: nvr nr to chal) ............ 1¹⁄₂.5
1369⁵ Just a Step (80) (Fav) *(MMcCormack)* 6–8-13 JReid (2) (2nd st: wknd over 1f out) ............ 1.6
1978 Nazare Blue (36) (v) *(MrsBarbaraWaring)* 5–8-8 NHowe (8) (b: hld up: no hdwy fnl 2f) .................. hd.7
1974⁶ Sally Fast (58) *(BPalling)* 3–7-6 ‡7ADaly (9) (dwlt: a bhd: t.o) ............ 10.8
1774³ Quarrington Hill (KSBridgwater)* 3–8-3 AProud (3) (4th st: wknd over 3f out: t.o) 6.9

Page 775

Son of Pearl (IRE) *(OBrennan)* 4-8-7 WNewnes (6) (bkwd: a bhd: t.o) .......... s.h.**10**
1759 Kahhal (IRE) **(23)** (bl) *(MrsAKnight)* 4-8-0 ‡3TSprake (1) (led over 4f: wknd over
2f out: t.o) .................................................................. 10.**11**

*Stewards Enquiry: Norton suspended 27-28/7/92 (excessive use of whip).*

**6/4** Just a Step, **3/1** SURREY RACING, **6/1** Glenfield Greta, **12/1** Slip-a-Snip(op 7/1), **16/1** Sally Fast, Whippet, Nazare Blue, **33/1** Kind Style (IRE), Son of Pearl (IRE), **50/1** Ors. CSF £19.30, Tote £3.60: £1.50 £1.60 £2.10 (£9.00). Mr K. Higson (EPSOM) bred by W. R. Swinburn. 11 Rn
1m 27.4 (3.1)
SF—48/42/32/40/33/36

---

**2210**     EYTON HALL H'CAP (0-70) £1413.00 (£393.00: £189.00)     **1m**     8-15 (8-17)

1747[2] **Irish Groom (35)** (bl) *(JPSmith)* 5-7-4 ‡7AGarth (2) (7th st: hdwy 2f out: rdn to ld
wl ins fnl f) ................................................................... —**1**
1741[4] Miss Magenta (IRE) **(35)** *(RThompson)* 4-7-4(4) ‡7NicolaHowarth (15) (dwlt: gd
hdwy over 2f out: led over 1f out tl wl ins fnl f) ..................... hd.**2**
1947[4] Lord Oberon (IRE) **(66)** *(RJO'Sullivan)* 4-10-0 JReid (13) (hdwy fnl 2f: r.o) ...... ½.**3**
1846[5] Lombard Ships **(50)** *(MO'Neill)* 5-8-12 BRaymond (18) (hdwy 2f out: r.o ins fnl
f) ........................................................................... 2½.**4**
1992★ Kinlacey **(60)** (Fav) *(BAMcMahon)* 5-9-8 WCarson (12) (6th st: ev ch 2f out:
eased whn btn ins fnl f) .................................................... 2.**5**
1859[4] Stelby **(51)** *(OBrennan)* 8-8-13 WNewnes (14) (bhd tl hdwy fnl 2f: nvr nrr) ...... ¾.**6**
2125[5] Sareen Express (IRE) **(44)** *(MrsJCDawe)* 4-8-1 ‡5RPrice (5) (4th st: led wl over
2f out tl over 1f out) ........................................................ s.h.**7**
1922 Admiralty Way **(43)** *(RBrotherton)* 6-8-5 TyroneWilliams (4) (4th st: ev ch over
2f out tl wknd over 1f out) .................................................. 1.**8**
2035[3] Lady Lacey **(53)** (v) *(GBBalding)* 5-8-8 ‡7TraceyPurseglove (7) (lw: dwlt: hdwy
& 7th st: wknd 2f out) ...................................................... nk.**9**
Remwood Girl **(35)** *(KSBridgwater)* 6-7-11 NCarlisle (8) (bkwd: nvr nr ldrs) ... 2.**10**
Rockridge **(43)** *(KSBridgwater)* 5-8-5 NHowe (17) (n.d) ............................... ½.**11**
Miss Sarajane **(48)** *(RHollinshead)* 8-8-10 WRyan (19) (bkwd: n.d) .................. 6.**12**
Norfolk Thatch **(38)** *(KSBridgwater)* 6-8-0 AProud (9) (chsd ldr: 2nd st: wknd 3f
out) ........................................................................ 3.**13**
1992[6] Green's Cassatt (USA) **(47)** *(WMBrisbourne)* 4-8-2 ‡7DCarson (8) (lw: 5th st:
wknd over 3f out) .......................................................... nk.**14**
1992 Blimpers Disco **(42)** (bl) *(EHOwenjun)* 3-7-3 ‡7DWright (11) (t.o) .................. 15.**15**
1889[3] Cartel **(52)** *(JLHarris)* 5-9-0 LDettori (16) (led over 4f: wknd qckly: t.o) .......... 15.**16**

**5/2** Kinlacey(2/1—3/1), **5/1** Lord Oberon (IRE)(tchd 14/1), **15/2** Cartel, **8/1** IRISH GROOM(tchd 14/1), **9/1** Sareen Express (IRE), **10/1** Lady Lacey, **16/1** Stelby, Lombard Ships, Miss Sarajane, **20/1** Green's Cassatt (USA), Miss Magenta (IRE), Norfolk Thatch, **25/1** Remwood Girl, **50/1** Ors. CSF £144.83, CT £808.34. Tote £8.20: £1.80 £3.10 £2.30 £3.40 (£151.50). Mr J. T. Stimpson (RUGELEY) bred by Mrs G. Doyle. 16 Rn
1m 41.2 (3.9)
SF—18/17/53/29/33/22

---

**2211**     PATTISON HUGHES H'CAP (3-Y.O) (0-70) £1318.50 (£366.00: £175.50)
1¾m 134y     8-45 (8-46)

(Weights raised 4 lb)
2057 **Child Star (FR) (46)** *(DMarks)* 8-5 SDawson (4) (mde all: clr 4f out: rdn over 1f
out: jst hld on) ............................................................. —**1**
1977[2] Gay Ming **(45)** (Fav) *(RHollinshead)* 7-11 ‡7AGarth (9) (hld up & bhd: hdwy 3f
out: edgd lft & r.o ins fnl f) ............................................... hd.**2**
1977[3] Laughton Lady **(42)** *(MrsNMacauley)* 7-12 ‡3FNorton (5) (6th st: r.o one pce fnl
2f) ......................................................................... 5.**3**
1766[3] Dordogne **(54)** *(RAkehurst)* 8-13 JReid (6) (chsd wnr: 2nd st: hrd rdn & one pce
fnl 2f) ..................................................................... nk.**4**
1574 Indian Territory **(59)** *(DHaydnJones)* 9-4 TyroneWilliams (3) (bhd tl gd hdwy 6f
out: 3rd st: wknd 2f out) .................................................. nk.**5**
1962[3] Chantry Bellini **(49)** *(CWThornton)* 8-8 NCarlisle (1) (b.hind: nvr trbld ldrs) ........ 4.**6**
1901 Silken Words (USA) **(62)** *(WRMuir)* 9-7 LDettori (7) (nvr nr ldrs) .................... 2½.**7**
1949[4] Formal Invitation (IRE) **(60)** *(GLewis)* 9-5 BRouse (10) (a bhd) ....................... 5.**8**
1997[6] Law Faculty (IRE) **(57)** *(GAHam)* 9-2 ADicks (8) (5th st: hrd rdn & wknd 3f out) . 4.**9**
1881[4] Killshandra (IRE) **(48)** *(MrsBarbaraWaring)* 8-7 NHowe (2) (4th st: wknd 3f out:
t.o) ....................................................................... 8.**10**

**9/4** Gay Ming, **9/2** CHILD STAR (FR), **6/1** Dordogne, **13/2** Laughton Lady, **7/1** Chantry Bellini, **11/1** Formal Invitation (IRE), **12/1** Silken Words (USA), **16/1** Indian Territory, **40/1** Ors. CSF £14.10, CT £57.58. Tote £4.80: £1.70 £1.70 £2.00 (£5.20). Mr P. J. Pearson (UPPER LAMBOURN) bred by Sheikh Mohammed bin Rashid al Maktoum in France. 10 Rn
3m 17.8 (11.8)
T/Plpt: £22.70 (75.8 Tckts).
KH

## 1506—AYR (L-H)
**Saturday, July 18th [Good]**
Going Allowance: St: minus 0.15 sec (F); Rnd: 0.05 sec per fur (G)　　Wind: str half against

Stalls: high

### 2212
E.B.F. MILLPORT STKS (Mdn 2-Y.O) £2427.00 (£672.00: £321.00)　　7f　2-20 (2-24)

1424[3] **Antester (IRE)** (Fav) *(PWChapple-Hyam)* 9-0 RHills (5) (led tl hdd wl over 1f
out: led ins fnl f: styd on wl) ..............................................　—1
Mondragon *(MrsGRReveley)* 9-0 KDarley (1) (leggy: unf: a.p: rn green to
½-wy: hdwy to ld over 1f out: hdd ins fnl f: no ex) ..............　½.2
2002[6] Caldervale *(ABailey)* 9-0 AMackay (3) (hld up: hdwy 2f out: r.o) ...............　s.h.3
1327 Grumpy's Grain (IRE) *(MissLAPerratt)* 9-0 JCarroll (2) (cl up tl outpcd fnl 2f) .... 12.4

2/5 ANTESTER (IRE)(1/2—1/3), 100/30 Mondragon(2/1—7/2), 7/1 Caldervale, 66/1 Grumpy's Grain (IRE).
CSF £2.07, Tote £1.20: (£1.70). Mr Luciano Gaucci (MARLBOROUGH) bred by Hadi Al Tajir in Ireland. 4 Rn
1m 28.83 (4.83)
SF—33/31/30/–

### 2213
HIGHSPEED PRODUCTION H'CAP (0-80) £2801.00 (£848.00: £414.00: £197.00)
**7f**　　　　　　　　　　　　　　　　　　2-50 (2-56)

(Weights raised 1 lb)

1911 **Pickles (47)** *(PCHaslam)* 4-8-5 KDarley (1) (mde all: qcknd over 2f out: r.o wl) 　—1
1391[6] Straw Thatch (73) (Fav) *(MJohnston)* 3-9-10 JLowe (4) (lw: hld up: hdwy over
2f out: nt pce of wnr) ..........................................　3½.2
1846[4] Sir Arthur Hobbs (63) *(FHLee)* 5-9-2 ‡5NKennedy (2) (lw: plld hrd: effrt over 2f
out: rdn & no imp: sddle slipped) ..........................　3.3
2048[5] Bee Dee Ell (USA) (50) (v) *(MissLAPerratt)* 3-7-8[3] ‡7RHavlin (3) (bolted gng to
s: plld hrd: w wnr tl wknd over 2f out) ....................　7.4

15/8 Straw Thatch, 2/1 Sir Arthur Hobbs, 9/4 PICKLES, 16/1 Bee Dee Ell (USA)(op 8/1). CSF £6.06, Tote £3.10
(£5.50). Hambleton Thoroughbreds Plc (MIDDLEHAM) bred by Lord Vestey. 4 Rn　　1m 27.82 (3.82)
SF—39/47/27/–

### 2214
TOTE BOOKMAKERS SPRINT TROPHY (H'cap) (0-110) £11745.00 (£3510.00: £1680.00:
£765.00)　**6f**　　　　　　　　　　　　　　3-20 (3-26)

1698★ **Big Hand (IRE) (84)** *(JWWatts)* 3-8-6 JLowe (5) (mde most: kpt on wl u.p fnl f) 　—1
1736★ Densben (76) *(DenysSmith)* 8-8-4 KFallon (10) (trckd ldrs: hdwy to disp ld
appr fnl f: nt qckn nr fin) ........................................　½.2
2003★ Never so Sure (88) (bl) (Fav) *(ABailey)* 4-9-2 AMackay (7) (hld up: hdwy ½-wy:
hrd rdn fnl f) ..............................................　2½.3
1920[6] Adwick Park (84) *(TDBarron)* 4-8-12 AlexGreaves (8) (bhd: hdwy 2f out: rdn &
nvr able to chal) .......................................　1½.4
2019[5] Cumbrian Waltzer (98) *(MHEasterby)* 7-9-12 MBirch (4) (lw: chsd ldrs: hrd rdn
over 1f out: one pce) .......................................　1.5
2003[4] Profilic (75) *(CaptJWilson)* 7-8-3 KDarley (3) (outpcd & bhd ½-wy: sme late
hdwy) ..................................................　2.6
1908[3] Furiella (69) *(PCHaslam)* 4-7-11 DaleGibson (2) (lw: in tch: hdwy 2f out: sn hrd
drvn & wknd) ..............................................　1.7
1512[4] Diet (68) (bl) *(MissLAPerratt)* 6-7-5[3] ‡5NKennedy (9) (lt-f: disp ld tl wknd fnl 2f) nk.8
879[4] Tamim (USA) (99) *(HThomsonJones)* 3-9-7 RHills (1) (lw: cl up 4f: sn rdn &
wknd) ...................................................　1½.9
LONG HANDICAP: Diet 7-6.

7/2 Never so Sure, 9/2 Cumbrian Waltzer, 11/2 Adwick Park, 13/2 BIG HAND (IRE), 15/2 Profilic, 8/1 Densben,
12/1 Furiella, 14/1 Tamim (USA), 20/1 Diet. CSF £49.21, CT £183.13. Tote £3.70: £1.50 £3.20 £2.40 (£15.00).
Mrs M. M. Haggas (RICHMOND) bred by Holborn Trust Co in Ireland. 9 Rn　　1m 11.47 (1.07)
SF—53/49/51/41/51/20

### 2215
RUSSIAN WINTER TROPHY (H'cap) (0-90) £2723.00 (£824.00: £402.00: £191.00)
**5f**　　　　　　　　　　　　　　　　　　3-50 (3-56)

2019 **Absolution (79)** (Fav) *(MPNaughton)* 8-9-3 KFallon (4) (chsd ldrs: qcknd to ld
wl ins fnl f) ..............................................　—1
2019[2] Never in the Red (90) (v) *(JBerry)* 4-10-0 JCarroll (2) (lw: cl up: led wl over 1f
out: hrd rdn, wandered & nt qckn ins fnl f) ...............　1½.2
996[5] Sigama (USA) (80) *(FHLee)* 6-8-13 ‡5NKennedy (3) (lw: led over 3f: wknd ins fnl
f) .......................................................　2½.3
1920[5] Consulate (63) *(JBalding)* 6-8-1[1] KDarley (1) (chsd ldrs: effrt 2f out: sn btn) .... 3.4

**7/4** ABSOLUTION, **2/1** Never in the Red, **11/4** Consulate, **11/2** Sigama (USA). CSF £5.39, Tote £2.40 (£2.50). Mr
M. F. Hyman (RICHMOND) bred by Newsells Park Stud. 4 Rn                        59.21 sec (1.21)
                                                                              SF—64/69/44/20

**2216**     CAMPBELTOWN CLAIMING STKS (3 & 4-Y.O) £2262.00 (£632.00: £306.00)
             7f                                                               4-20 (4-22)

2048* **Laurel Queen (IRE) (58)** (Fav) *(JBerry)* 4–8-13 JCarroll (4) (lw: reard s: sn
             rcvrd & chsd ldrs: led appr fnl f: r.o gamely) ..................... —1
20483 Inseyab **(61)** *(PCHaslam)* 4–8-11 KDarley (2) (a cl up: chal over 1f out: hrd rdn
             & r.o) .................................................................. hd.2
749² Princess Maxine (IRE) **(50)** *(MissLAPerratt)* 3–7-13 DaleGibson (1) (lw: led:
             hung rt appr st: hdd over 1f out: no ex) ........................... 3½.3
17314 Valley of Time (FR) **(44)** *(TCraig)* 4–8-4 ‡7DarrenMoffatt (3) (chsd ldr tl outpcd fnl
             3f) ....................................................................... 7.4

**6/4** LAUREL QUEEN (IRE), **13/8** Inseyab, **5/2** Princess Maxine (IRE), **14/1** Valley of Time (FR). CSF £4.30, Tote
£2.40 (£1.50). Laurel (Leisure) Limited (COCKERHAM) bred by E. Lonergan. 4 Rn      1m 28.37 (4.37)
                                                                              SF—39/36/13/–

**2217**     SOUTH WEST SAAB H'CAP (0-70) £2318.00 (£648.00: £314.00)
             1m 5f 13y                                                        4-50 (4-52)

19384 **Magic Secret (66)** (Fav) *(PCHaslam)* 4–9-12 KDarley (4) (a cl up: led over 3f
             out: hld on wl fnl f) ..................................................... —1
1898 Shadideen (USA) **(57)** *(MissLAPerratt)* 4–9-3 JCarroll (5) (lw: trckd ldrs: swtchd
             over 2f out: chalappr fnl f: nt qckn nr fin) ........................ 1.2
1687² Buckingham Band (USA) **(44)** (bl) *(FHLee)* 4–7-13 ‡5NKennedy (6) (lw: effrt 7f
             out: sn drvn along & chsng ldrs: styd on: no imp) ................. 3.3
467 Grey Power **(66)** *(MrsGRReveley)* 5–9-12 MBirch (7) (trckd ldrs after 5f: rdn ent
             st: grad wknd fnl 2f) .................................................... 10.4
76 Touching Times **(55)** *(TCraig)* 4–8-8 ‡7DarrenMoffatt (3) (bhd tl sme late hdwy) . 5.5
Palm House **(38)** *(GRichards)* 7–7-10 AMackay (2) (bit bkwd: chsd ldrs to st: sn
             wknd) ...................................................................... ¾.6
15076 Ebony Isle **(46)** *(MissLAPerratt)* 3–7-7 JLowe (2) (led tl hdd & wknd over 3f out) 25.7
                                                      LONG HANDICAP: Ebony Isle 6-12.

**13/8** MAGIC SECRET, **9/4** Buckingham Band (USA), **4/1** Shadideen (USA), **8/1** Grey Power, **25/1** Touching
Times, **33/1** Palm House, **50/1** Ebony Isle. CSF £7.70, Tote £2.00: £1.70 £1.90 (£7.40). Hambleton
Thoroughbreds Plc (MIDDLEHAM) bred by Gainsborough Stud Management Ltd. 7 Rn    2m 54.96 (8.76)
                                                                              SF—31/20/–/3/–/–

T/Plpt: £87.50 (18.9 Tckts).                                                   AA

# AYR (L-H)
## Monday, July 20th [Good]
Going Allowance: St: minus 0.20; Rnd: minus 0.10 sec per fur (F)              Wind: almost nil

Stalls: high

**2218**     DAILY RECORD CLAIMING STKS (Mdn 3 & 4-Y.O) £2284.50 (£642.00: £313.50)
             1m                                                               2-15 (2-18)

2216³ **Princess Maxine (IRE) (50)** (Fav) *(MissLAPerratt)* 3–8-9 DaleGibson (2) (trckd
             ldrs: slt ld over 1f out: all out) ......................................... —1
1958³ Rahif *(MrsGRReveley)* 4–9-8 LPiggott (6) (led tl hdd over 1f out: rallied u.p: nt
             qckn nr fin) ................................................................ hd.2
17595 Shrewd Girl (USA) **(53)** *(BWHills)* 4–8-10 KDarley (4) (a.p: effrt & ch 2f out: one
             pce) ........................................................................ 5.3
2048 J P Morgan **(42)** (v) *(MPNaughton)* 4–9-3 JReid (1) (sn outpcd & bhd: c wd:
             styd on fnl 2f: n.d) ....................................................... 2.4
1896³ Miss Parkes **(48)** (bl) *(JBerry)* 3–8-6 JCarroll (3) (lw: s.i.s: sn prom: wknd over
             2f out) ..................................................................... 6.5
1992 Must Be Magical (USA) **(23)** (v) *(FHLee)* 4–8-11 ‡5NKennedy (5) (lw: cl up tl rdn
             & wknd over 2f out) ...................................................... 7.6

**5/2** PRINCESS MAXINE (IRE), **3/1** Shrewd Girl (USA), **100/30** Rahif, **5/1** Miss Parkes, **9/1** J P Morgan, **40/1** Must
Be Magical (USA). CSF £9.80, Tote £3.00: £1.50 £1.80 (£5.30). Mr J. Fox (AYR) bred by Ronnie Boland in
Ireland. 6 Rn                                                                  1m 40.56 (3.36)
                                                                              SF—31/43/15/16/–/–

**2219** ROTHMANS ROYALS NORTH SOUTH CHALLENGE SERIES (H'cap) (0-90) £4279.50
(£1296.00: £633.00: £301.50) **1m**　　　　　　　　2-45 (2-47)

(Weights raised 14 lb)

2026* **Golden Chip (IRE) (68)** *(APStringer)* 4-9-3 ‡5SMaloney (10) (lw: mde all: qcknd over 2f out: hld on wl fnl f) .................... —1

796² Forever Diamonds (59) *(MHEasterby)* 5-8-13 KDarley (5) (lw: hld up: effrt ent st: hdwy over 1f out: r.o u.p) .................... hd.2

2026² Doctor Roy (60) (Fav) *(NBycroft)* 4-9-0 WCarson (8) (lw: chsd ldrs: drvn along 3f out: styd on: nt pce to chal) .................... 3¹/₂.3

1966³ Martini Executive (66) (bl) *(BBeasley)* 4-9-6 DNicholls (9) (hld up & bhd: effrt over 2f out: styd on nr fin) .................... 2.4

1911³ Habeta (USA) (70) *(JWWatts)* 6-9-10 PatEddery (2) (lw: trckd wnr: effrt over 2f out: one pce) .................... s.h.5

1966* Young Jason (54) *(FHLee)* 9-8-3 ‡5NKennedy (7) (lw: hld up & bhd: effrt ent st: nrst fin) .................... s.h.6

1992⁵ Cee-Jay-Ay (60) *(JBerry)* 5-9-0 JCarroll (1) (chsd ldrs tl outpcd fnl 2f) .................... s.h.7

1110⁶ Thisonesforalice (51) *(AHarrison)* 4-8-2 ‡3JFanning (3) (cl up tl wknd over 2f out) .................... 1¹/₂.8

2147⁶ Forest Dew (USA) (70) *(MHTompkins)* 3-9-2 RHills (6) (lw: in tch: rdn 3f out: grad wknd) .................... 4.9

**7/2** Doctor Roy, **9/2** Habeta (USA), **13/2** Cee-Jay-Ay, **7/1** Young Jason, Martini Executive, **15/2** Forever Diamonds, **8/1** GOLDEN CHIP (IRE), **12/1** Forest Dew (USA), **25/1** Thisonesforalice. CSF £58.16, CT £222.73. Tote £9.10: £2.60 £2.10 £1.40 (£17.00). Mr A. H. Jackson (THIRSK) bred by C. and J. Sandys and Barbara McCourt in Ireland. 9 Rn　　　　　　　　1m 40.56 (3.36)
SF—41/36/26/26/29/7

**2220** TENNENTS SCOTTISH CLASSIC (Stks) (Gp 3) £15030.00 (£5622.75: £2698.88: £1173.37) **1¹/₄m**　　　　　　　　3-15 (3-18)

1869³ **Sharpitor (IRE) (105)** (v) *(WJarvis)* 3-8-6 JReid (3) (trckd ldrs: stdy hdwy over 1f out: rdn to ld wl ins fnl f) .................... —1

1458³ Alflora (IRE) (111) *(CEBrittain)* 3-8-6 MRoberts (2) (lw: cl up: slt ld 2f out: hrd rdn & r.o: nt qckn nr fin) .................... nk.2

1466³ Inner City (IRE) (101) *(LMCumani)* 3-8-6 LDettori (1) (lw: hld up & bhd: hdwy 2f out: edgd lft: r.o wl) .................... nk.3

557 Ile de Chypre (108) *(GHarwood)* 7-9-9 MHills (6) (b.hind: qcknd ent st: hdd 2f out: rdn & grad wknd) .................... 3¹/₂.4

El Prado (IRE) (Fav) *(MVO'Brien,Ireland)* 3-8-6 LPiggott (5) (outpcd & lost pl appr st: hdwy u.p 2f out: no imp) .................... 2.5

1817a⁶ Flashfoot (107) *(IABalding)* 4-9-2 RCochrane (7) (s.i.s: hld up & bhd: effrt over 3f out: rdn & n.d) .................... 6.6

1401² Polish Blue (USA) (103) *(MRStoute)* 3-8-6 PatEddery (4) (lw: prom tl outpcd wl over 2f out) .................... 15.7

**9/4** El Prado (IRE), **5/2** Inner City (IRE), **9/2** SHARPITOR (IRE), **11/2** Alflora (IRE), **6/1** Polish Blue (USA), **14/1** Flashfoot, **20/1** Ile de Chypre. CSF £27.52, Tote £6.80: £1.20 £3.50 (£30.10). Mr Henry Lopes (NEWMARKET) bred by Dr J. J. Ryan in Ireland. 7 Rn　　　　　　　　2m 6.03 (1.15 under best; U.73)
SF—75/74/73/83/62/60

**2221** GARRY OWEN CUP (Nursery) £3387.50 (£1025.00: £500.00: £237.50)
**5f**　　　　　　　　3-45 (3-48)

1998³ **Finmental (IRE)** *(ABailey)* 9-2 ‡5ATucker (7) (lw: bhd: hdwy 2f out: led ins fnl f: r.o wl) .................... —1

2030³ Bold Seven (IRE) *(FHLee)* 8-0 ‡5NKennedy (6) (s.i.s: hdwy 2f out: r.o nr fin) .... 2¹/₂.2

2152⁴ Stardust Express *(MJohnston)* 7-12 JLowe (3) (led tl hdd ins fnl f: no ex u.p) .. s.h.3

2067⁴ Bright Gem *(TFairhurst)* 7-6(2) ‡3JFanning (2) (trckd ldrs: effrt over 1f out: nt qckn) .................... 3¹/₂.4

2152* Second Colours (USA) *(PSFelgate)* 8-10 (5x) KDarley (5) (cl up: drvn along ¹/₂-wy: grad wknd) .................... s.h.5

1963* Cockerham Ranger *(JBerry)* 8-12 JCarroll (4) (cl up over 3f: sn rdn & btn) .... 8.6

1973* Mistertopogigo (IRE) (Fav) *(BBeasley)* 9-3 DNicholls (1) (plld hrd: cl up tl rdn & fnd nil over 1f out) .................... 2¹/₂.7

LONG HANDICAP: Bright Gem 7-4.

**9/4** Mistertopogigo (IRE), **3/1** Second Colours (USA), **5/1** Cockerham Ranger, Bold Seven (IRE), **6/1** FINMENTAL (IRE), **7/1** Bright Gem, **33/1** Stardust Express. CSF £33.81, Tote £7.20: £2.60 £2.80 (£24.70). Mrs M. O'Donnell (TARPORLEY) bred by E. Lonergan in Ireland. 7 Rn
59.37 sec (1.37)
SF—55/39/26/6/23/–

---

**2222**    TENNENT TROPHY (H'cap) (0-110) £6970.00 (£2110.00: £1030.00: £490.00)
     **1m 7f**                               4-15 (4-17)

(Weights raised 19 lb)

| | | |
|---|---|---|
| 2023³ | **Farat (USA) (72)** (Fav) *(JLDunlop)* 4–8–11 MRoberts (1) (b: lw: trckd ldrs: nt clr run & swtchd 2f out: r.o strly fnl f to ld nr fin) | —1 |
| 1697 | **Aahsaylad (75)** (v) *(FHLee)* 6–9–0 DMcKeown (3) (in tch: hdwy to ld 2f out: clr 1f out: hrd rdn & no ex cl home) | hd.2 |
| 1301 | **Itqan (IRE) (85)** *(BWHills)* 4–9–10 WCarson (6) (hld up: hdwy 3f out: rdn 2f out: hung rt: sn btn) | 8.3 |
| 2071⁴ | **Attadale (60)** *(LLungo)* 4–7–10 ‡³JFanning (2) (lw: led 2f: cl up tl outpcd appr fnl f) | 1½.4 |
| 1691* | **Daisy Girl (67)** *(JMackie)* 6–8–6 PatEddery (4) (trckd ldrs: n.m.r 2f out: sn rdn & btn) | 3.5 |
| 2001⁶ | **Dollar Seeker (USA) (55)** (bl) *(ABailey)* 8–7–8⁽¹⁾ AMackay (5) (led after 2f tl hdd 2f out: sn wknd) | 15.6 |

**15/8** FARAT (USA), **3/1** Daisy Girl, **9/2** Itqan (IRE), **5/1** Aahsaylad, **15/2** Attadale, **25/1** Dollar Seeker (USA). CSF £10.45, Tote £2.70: £1.70 £2.40 (£8.10). Lady Swaythling (ARUNDEL) bred by Dick Lossen and Partners in USA. 6 Rn
3m 14.14 (1.64)
SF—65/67/61/31/35/8

---

**2223**    E.B.F. TAM O'SHANTER STKS (Mdn 2-Y.O) £2253.00 (£633.00: £309.00)
     **6f**                                   4-45 (4-47)

| | | |
|---|---|---|
| 1854² | **Dahliz (IRE)** (Fav) *(HThomsonJones)* 9-0 RHills (2) (led tl hdd over 1f out: rallied to ld nr fin) | —1 |
| 1689⁵ | **Garnock Valley** *(JBerry)* 9-0 JCarroll (5) (sn chsng ldrs: led over 1f out: hrd rdn & r.o: jst ct) | hd.2 |
| 1915 | **Wolf Power (IRE)** *(TThomsonJones)* 9-0 KDarley (1) (lw: w ldrs: disp ld 2f out: rdn & nt qckn ins fnl f) | nk.3 |
| 1348⁶ | **Eleusis (FR)** *(PWChapple-Hyam)* 9-0 JReid (7) (a chsng ldrs: kpt on wl nr fin) | 1½.4 |
| 1332⁶ | **Sea-Ayr (IRE)** *(MissLAPerratt)* 8-6 ‡³JFanning (6) (s.i.s: hdwy ½-wy: rdn & no imp appr fnl f) | 4.5 |
| | **Peacefull Reply (USA)** *(FHLee)* 9-0 MRoberts (3) (cmpt: wnt lft s: hung lft thrght: chsd ldrs 4f) | 12.6 |
| 1998⁴ | **Onewithwhitepaw** (bl) *(ABailey)* 9-0 AMackay (4) (lw: bmpd s: prom tl rdn & wknd over 3f out) | 1½.7 |

**13/8** DAHLIZ (IRE), **3/1** Eleusis (FR)(op 2/1), **4/1** Garnock Valley, **5/1** Wolf Power (IRE), **11/1** Peacefull Reply (USA), **25/1** Onewithwhitepaw, **33/1** Sea-Ayr (IRE). CSF £8.30, Tote £2.50: £1.80 £3.00 (£5.40). Mr Hamdan Al-Maktoum (NEWMARKET) bred by Shadwell Estate Company Limited in Ireland. 7 Rn    1m 12.61 (2.21)
SF—32/31/30/24/–/–

---

**2224**    DAILY RECORD H'CAP (0-75) £3355.00 (£1015.00: £495.00: £235.00)
     **5f**                                   5-15 (5-18)

| | | |
|---|---|---|
| 2073² | **Playful Poet (69)** *(MHEasterby)* 5–9–6 ‡⁵SMaloney (1) (b.hind: lw: mde all: all out) | —1 |
| 2215⁴ | **Consulate (62)** *(JBalding)* 6–9–4 KDarley (2) (hld up: hdwy 2f out: ev ch 1f out: r.o nr fin) | nk.2 |
| 2153³ | **Hinari Video (46)** *(MJohnston)* 7–8–2 DMcKeown (4) (a chsng ldrs: kpt on wl fnl f) | ½.3 |
| 2163⁶ | **Brisas (48)** (bl) *(TFairhurst)* 5–8–1 ‡³JFanning (6) (lw: cl up tl rdn & btn over 1f out) | 3½.4 |
| 1904* | **North of Watford (50)** (Fav) *(MPNaughton)* 7–8–6 MRoberts (3) (lw: sn drvn along: bhd fr ½-wy) | 3.5 |

**8/11** North of Watford(op 5/4), **7/2** PLAYFUL POET(op 2/1), **11/2** Hinari Video, **9/1** Brisas, **10/1** Consulate. CSF £27.78, Tote £4.00: £2.30 £2.30 (£13.80). Mr Peter C. Bourke (MALTON) bred by Rosemount Stud. 5 Rn
59.45 sec (1.45)
SF—57/54/36/21/14

T/Plpt: £504.30 (9.25 Tckts).                                             AA

## 1945—BATH (L-H)
### Monday, July 20th [Good to soft]
Going Allowance: 5f 11y-5f 161y: minus 0.10 sec; Rest: nil sec (G)  Wind: slt across

Stalls: low  Vis: 1st & 2nd poor

**2225**  BATH AUCTION STKS (Mdn 2-Y.O) £2343.00 (£648.00: £309.00)
5f 161y  2-00 (2-03)

| | | |
|---|---|---|
| 2031⁴ | **Chili Heights** (Fav) *(GBBalding)* 8-7 JWilliams (2) (a.p: led ins fnl f: r.o wl) | —1 |
| 2037 | Waterlord (IRE) *(CGCox)* 8-6 NHowe (7) (led tl ins fnl f: r.o) | ³/₄.2 |
| 1635 | Kind of Cute *(CCElsey)* 8-4⁽¹⁾ TQuinn (4) (hdwy wl over 1f out: r.o ins fnl f) | 2¹/₂.3 |
| 1769² | Allez Bianco *(RJHolder)* 8-2 DHolland (8) (a.p: r.o one pce fnl 2f) | s.h.4 |
| 2167⁶ | Daily Sport Don *(RHannon)* 8-6 AMcGlone (5) (w ldr tl wknd fnl f) | 5.5 |
| 886⁵ | Rahon (IRE) *(PWChapple-Hyam)* 8-8 PaulEddery (6) (chsd ldrs: eased whn btn ins fnl f) | 1.6 |
| 847⁶ | Body Language *(IABalding)* 8-4 AMunro (1) (chsd ldrs 3f) | 4.7 |
| 1652 | Mad March Hare *(DRTucker)* 8-5 NAdams (3) (bit bkwd: a bhd) | 3¹/₂.8 |
| 1899 | Ambivalentattitude *(MDIUsher)* 8-6 CRutter (9) (a bhd) | nk.9 |
| 968 | World Express (IRE) *(BRMillman)* 8-7 WNewnes (10) (a bhd) | 3.10 |

**15/8** CHILI HEIGHTS, **100/30** Daily Sport Don(2/1—4/1), **4/1** Allez Bianco, **9/2** Body Language, **8/1** Rahon (IRE)(6/1—9/1), **16/1** Kind of Cute(op 8/1), Waterlord (IRE)(op 10/1), **33/1** World Express (IRE), **50/1** Ors. CSF £30.90, Tote £3.30: £1.60 £2.10 £3.60 (£21.70). Mr B. T. Attenborough (DORCHESTER) bred by J. Crofts. 10 Rn  No time taken

**2226**  TAXINEWS H'CAP (0-90) £3301.00 (£908.00: £474.00: £217.00)
1m 5f 22y  2-30 (2-31)

| | | |
|---|---|---|
| 1766⁴ | **Monarda** (67) *(PFICole)* 5-8-7 AMunro (6) (hld up: 3rd st: led over 2f out: r.o wl) | —1 |
| 1951³ | Paper Dance (61) *(RJHolder)* 4-8-1 DHolland (1) (led over 9f out to 6f out: 2nd st: hrd rdn over 2f out: one pce) | 2¹/₂.2 |
| 1399⁵ | Elaine Tully (IRE) (77) *(MJHeaton-Ellis)* 4-9-3 WNewnes (5) (4th & rdn st: styd on fnl 2f) | s.h.3 |
| 1879⁵ | Duc de Berry (USA) (88) *(GHarwood)* 4-10-0 SCauthen (3) (lw: led over 3f: led 6f out tl over 2f out: sn btn) | 10.4 |
| | Taffy Jones (53) *(MMcCormack)* 13-7-7 RStreet (4) (bkwd: rdn & dropped rr 8f out: last & t.o st) | 20.5 |
| | Mountain Retreat (70) *(GAHam)* 6-8-10 JWilliams (2) (bkwd: hld up & plld hrd: poor 5th st: t.o fnl 3f) | 4.6 |
| | | LONG HANDICAP: Taffy Jones 5-5. |

**15/8** MONARDA, **11/4** Duc de Berry (USA), **7/2** Paper Dance, Elaine Tully (IRE), **16/1** Mountain Retreat(op 10/1), **66/1** Taffy Jones. CSF £8.44, Tote £2.60: £1.50 £1.90 (£3.90). Mr Fahd Salman (WHATCOMBE) bred by Newgate Stud Ltd. 6 Rn  2m 51.9 (4.2)
SF—51/40/55/46/–/–

**2227**  TOTE COMPUTER H'CAP (0-90) £4659.00 (£1392.00: £666.00: £303.00)
5f 161y  3-00 (3-02)

(Weights raised 1 lb)

| | | |
|---|---|---|
| 2032★ | **Blue Topaze** (59) *(RJHolder)* 4-8-8 JWilliams (3) (in rr & rdn over 3f out: gd hdwy over 2f out: led over 1f out: r.o wl) | —1 |
| 2073★ | Misdemeanours Girl (IRE) (69) *(MRChannon)* 4-8-13 (7x) ‡⁵BDoyle (5) (hdwy over 1f out: r.o ins fnl f) | 3¹/₂.2 |
| 2127 | John O'Dreams (44) *(MrsJCDawe)* 7-7-7 RFox (6) (a.p: led over 2f out tl over 1f out) | 2¹/₂.3 |
| 2015⁶ | Nagida (75) *(JARToller)* 3-9-4 WRSwinburn (7) (swtg: a.p: ev ch over 1f out) | ¹/₂.4 |
| 2053⁶ | Leigh Crofter (68) (bl) *(RJHolder)* 3-8-4 ‡⁷SDrowne (8) (no hdwy fnl 2f) | hd.5 |
| 1588 | Unveiled (64) *(RJHodges)* 4-8-10 ‡⁸TSprake (10) (bhd & rdn 3f out: nvr nrr) | 1¹/₂.6 |
| 1631⁶ | Baligay (75) *(RJHodges)* 7-9-10 SCauthen (2) (prom over 3f) | 1¹/₂.7 |
| 1883★ | Truthful Image (78) (bl) *(MJRyan)* 3-9-7 DBiggs (9) (prom 4f) | 2¹/₂.8 |
| 2009³ | Assignment (74) *(JFitch-Heyes)* 6-9-9 TQuinn (4) (led over 3f: wknd over 1f out) | nk.9 |
| 1773 | Cee-En-Cee (72) (bl) *(MMcCourt)* 8-9-2 ‡⁵DHarrison (1) (lw: bhd fnl 3f) | 2.10 |
| 2013⁶ | Appealing Times (USA) (73) *(WAO'Gorman)* 3-8-13 ‡³EmmaO'Gorman (11) (prom 3f: t.o) | 10.11 |
| | | LONG HANDICAP: John O'Dreams 7-6. |

**3/1** BLUE TOPAZE, **5/1** Nagida(4/1—6/1), **7/1** Misdemeanours Girl (IRE), Baligay, **15/2** Cee-En-Cee, **9/1** Truthful Image, **10/1** Appealing Times (USA), **11/1** Assignment(8/1—12/1), **12/1** Unveiled, Leigh Crofter, **50/1** John O'Dreams. CSF £23.79, CT £811.32. Tote £3.90: £1.90 £2.50 £9.90 (£14.10). Mr M. S. Saunders (BRISTOL) bred by Ahmed M. Foustok. 11 Rn
1m 11.1 (1.8)
SF—48/42/12/35/20/6

## 2228
STAPLETON STKS (Mdn 3-Y.O) £2442.50 (£680.00: £327.50)
1m 3f 144y
3-30 (3-32)

1891² **Puritan (CAN)** (Fav) (GHarwood) 9-0 SCauthen (5) (lw: w ldr: 2nd st: led 1f out:
readily) ..................................................................................... —1
1722⁴ Sea Plane (MajorWRHern) 9-0 AMunro (3) (4th st: styd on fnl 2f) .................. 1½.2
1882² Highland Battle (USA) (68) (IABalding) 8-11 ‡³SO'Gorman (1) (led tl hdd & nt
qckn 1f out) .................................................................................. ½.3
1953⁵ Swan Heights (JRFanshawe) 8-9 WRSwinburn (8) (rdn & 3rd st: wknd & rdn
over 1f out) ................................................................................. 12.4
2014 Oco Royal (65) (JFfitch-Heyes) 9-0 DBiggs (4) (6th st: hdwy 3f out: wknd 2f
out) ........................................................................................... 6.5
633⁵ Post Impressionist (IRE) (68) (BWHills) 8-9 DHolland (6) (rdn & lost pl 8f out:
poor 7th st) .................................................................................. 4.6
1304 Eiras Mood (RDickin) 8-9 TQuinn (2) (hld up & bhd: hdwy 5f out: 5th st: wknd
over 2f out) ................................................................................. 1½.7
2051 Kalamoss (42) (NRMitchell) 8-9 NAdams (7) (poor last st: a bhd) .................. s.h.8

**4/6** PURITAN (CAN)(op Evens), **7/2** Highland Battle (USA), **8/1** Post Impressionist (IRE), **9/1** Swan Heights(6/1—10/1), **14/1** Sea Plane(op 7/1), **33/1** Oco Royal, Eiras Mood, **50/1** Kalamoss. CSF £10.81, Tote £1.80 £1.10 £1.40 £1.30 (£6.20). Sheikh Mohammed (PULBOROUGH) bred by Angus Glen Farm Ltd in Canada.
8 Rn
2m 33.2 (6.5)
SF—35/32/28/2/–/–

## 2229
ST JOHN AMBULANCE BRIGADE STKS (Mdn 3-Y.O) £2693.00 (£748.00: £359.00)
5f 11y
4-00 (4-06)

434³ **Sunley Silks** (Fav) (MRChannon) 8-9 PaulEddery (5) (a.p: hrd rdn over 2f out:
led ins fnl f: r.o) ............................................................................. —1
2082⁴ Belthorn (39) (JJBridger) 8-9 SWhitworth (2) (led 3f: ev ch fnl f: r.o) ............. ¾.2
1753⁴ Bridle Talk (IRE) (46) (MMcCormack) 8-9 CRutter (4) (a.p: ev ch 1f out: nt qckn) ½.3
Mister Jolson (RJHodges) 8-11 ‡³TSprake (6) (b.off hind: a.p: ev ch 1f out) ...... s.h.4
1918² Double Shift (RDickin) 8-9 TQuinn (7) (hdwy 2f out: r.o one pce fnl f) ........... hd.5
2053 Red Verona (39) (EAWheeler) 8-9 JWilliams (11) (swtg: s.s: hdwy 2f out: nt rch
ldrs) .......................................................................................... 1½.6
1918³ Call to the Bar (IRE) (CGCox) 8-7 ‡⁷JHunter (10) (w ldrs: led 2f out: rdn & swvd lft
over 1f out: hdd ins fnl f) .................................................................. 1.7
Queen Canute (IRE) (FHLee) 8-9 DHolland (1) (leggy: bit bkwd: s.i.s: bhd fnl 2f:
t.o) ............................................................................................ 8.8
2015 Clean Gate (PDCundell) 9-0 TRogers (12) (a bhd: t.o) ............................... nk.9
96 Laggard's Quest (CDBroad) 9-0 NAdams (9) (prom over 2f: t.o) .................... 25.10
Elhasna (USA) (3/1) Withdrawn (ref to ent stalls) : not under orders  — Rule 4 applies

**15/8** SUNLEY SILKS(11/10—2/1), **5/1** Queen Canute (IRE)(7/2—6/1), Double Shift, **8/1** Call to the Bar (IRE)(tchd 14/1), **14/1** Bridle Talk (IRE), **33/1** Belthorn, Mister Jolson, Clean Gate, **50/1** Ors. CSF £33.34, Tote £2.50: £1.20 £3.70 £2.30 (£25.60). Sunley Holdings Plc (UPPER LAMBOURN) bred by Sunley Stud. 10 Rn
63.3 sec (2.8)
SF—29/26/24/25/22/16

## 2230
WESTMINSTER-MOTOR TAXI INSURANCE H'CAP (3-Y.O) (0-80) £3353.00 (£1004.00:
£482.00: £221.00) 1m 5y
4-30 (4-35)

(Weights raised 1 lb)
1692³ **Blockade (USA) (73)** (MBell) 9-2 SCauthen (3) (t: mde virtually all: rdn over 2f
out: r.o wl) .................................................................................. —1
1947⁶ Mustahil (IRE) (66) (RJHodges) 8-6 ‡³TSprake (4) (chsd wnr: 2nd st: ev ch fnl f) nk.2
1941⁴ Lord Vivienne (IRE) (71) (PFICole) 9-0 TQuinn (7) (3rd st: rdn over 2f out:
wknd ins fnl f) ............................................................................. 3½.3
1916³ Thinking Twice (USA) (70) (PWHarris) 8-13 PaulEddery (6) (4th st: hrd rdn 3f
out: r.o one pce fnl 2f) ..................................................................... ½.4
1812² Duty Sergeant (IRE) (52) (bl) (MPMuggeridge) 7-9 DBiggs (1) (last st: nvr nrr) . ¾.5
1146 Singers Image (62) (v) (GBBalding) 8-5⁽¹⁾ JWilliams (9) (lw: hdwy & 6th st:
wknd over 2f out) ......................................................................... ¾.6
511⁴ Maple Bay (IRE) (72) (PJMakin) 9-1 WRSwinburn (2) (5th st: rdn 3f out: eased
whn btn ins fnl f) ......................................................................... ¾.7

1516* Legendary (IRE) **(68)** *(PWChapple-Hyam)* 8-11 DHolland (8) (nvr gng wl: rn wd & 7th st: eased whn btn 2f out) ............................................. 30.8

**11/4** Lord Vivienne (IRE), **100/30** BLOCKADE (USA)(3/1—9/2), **4/1** Thinking Twice (USA)(5/1—100/30), **11/2** Maple Bay (IRE)(8/1—4/1), **6/1** Legendary (IRE)(op 3/1), **9/1** Mustahil (IRE), **14/1** Duty Sergeant (IRE), **25/1** Singers Image. CSF £30.64, CT £85.51. Tote £3.80: £1.30 £3.00 £1.60 (£12.70). Mr A. M. Warrender (NEWMARKET) bred by Patricia C. Warrender in USA. 8 Rn 1m 42.4 (3.1)
SF—56/45/42/39/19/27

## 2231
LEVY BOARD SEVENTH RACE STKS £2820.00 (£840.00: £400.00: £180.00)
**1m 5f 22y** 5-00 (5-01)

780⁴ **Miss Plum (85)** *(HRACecil)* 3-8-1 WRyan (4) (mde all: clr over 2f out: r.o wl) .... —1
1510* Suez Canal (IRE) **(74)** (bl) *(PWChapple-Hyam)* 3-8-6 DHolland (2) (chsd wnr over 9f out: 2nd st: rdn 3f out: one pce) ............................................. 12.2
1881³ Grand Master **(100)** (Fav) *(PFICole)* 3-8-6 AMunro (3) (hld up & 3rd: rdn & chsd wnr fnl 3f: no imp) ............................................. 1½.3
1919⁴ Funoon (IRE) *(MRStoute)* 3-8-1 PaulEddery (5) (w ldr tl stdd over 9f out: 4th & rdn st: one pce fnl 3f) ............................................. ½.4
Muscadine *(AJChamberlain)* 5-9-0⁽³⁾ LornaVincent (1) (a bhd: t.o & last st) .... dist.5

**8/11** Grand Master (IRE), **9/4** MISS PLUM, **6/1** Funoon (IRE)(op 7/2), **15/2** Suez Canal (IRE)(4/1—8/1), **66/1** Muscadine. CSF £16.20, Tote £3.00: £1.90 £1.70 (£6.90). Mr Edward St George (NEWMARKET) bred by E. G. P. St George. 5 Rn 2m 53.2 (5.5)
32/13/10/4/–

T/Plpt: £18.10 (161.5 Tckts). KH

## 1970- NOTTINGHAM (L-H)

### Monday, July 20th [Good to soft]

Going Allowance: St: 0.20 (G) sec; Rnd: 0.60 sec per fur (Y)        Wind: almost nil

Stalls: high        Vis: 5th & 6th poor, 4th mod

## 2232
OFF SPINNER CLAIMING STKS (2-Y.O) £1684.20 (£466.20: £222.60)
**6f 15y** 6-15 (6-17)

1531* **Maribella** (Fav) *(PFICole)* 8-3 TQuinn (4) (chsd ldrs: shkn up to ld over 1f out: sn clr) ............................................. —1
928 Sabo's Express *(RHannon)* 8-5 ‡³RPerham (3) (bit bkwd: dwlt: sn chsng ldrs on outside: rdn wl over 1f out: kpt on) ............................................. 6.2
Evergreen Tango *(JWharton)* 8-5⁽¹⁾ WNewnes (6) (leggy: lt-f: bit bkwd: outpcd & bhd tl r.o appr fnl f: nrst fin) ............................................. nk.3
2005 Domes of Silence *(JBerry)* 8-2 PRobinson (8) (led tl hdd & wknd over 1f out) . 1½.4
1887⁶ Palacegate Sunset *(JBerry)* 8-4 GCarter (7) (spd over 4f) ............................................. nk.5
1835⁵ Master Sinclair (IRE) *(RHollinshead)* 7-11 ‡⁷AGarth (5) (prom tl rdn & wknd appr fnl f) ............................................. ½.6
1835³ The Institute Boy *(KRBurke)* 8-8 RCochrane (2) (prom over 2f: eased whn btn fnl f) ............................................. 2.7
Goan Girl *(PSFelgate)* 7-13 JQuinn (1) (small: bkwd: s.s: outpcd: t.o) ............................................. 20.8

**4/9** MARIBELLA(8/11—2/5), **13/2** The Institute Boy, **9/1** Sabo's Express(5/1—10/1), **14/1** Palacegate Sunset, **16/1** Evergreen Tango(op 8/1), **20/1** Master Sinclair (IRE), **33/1** Ors. CSF £5.41, Tote £1.30: £1.00 £2.90 £3.50 (£5.20). Mr George Johnson (WHATCOMBE) bred by G. Johnson. 8 Rn 1m 16.1 (5.1)
SF—11/–/–/–/–/–

## 2233
E.B.F. SAM AND ARTHUR STAPLES STKS (Mdn 2-Y.O) £2126.40 (£590.40: £283.20)
**6f 15y** 6-45 (6-47)

1348 **Shiro** *(RJRWilliams)* 9-0 RCochrane (7) (s.s: swtchd stands' side ½-wy: hdwy 2f out: led ins fnl f: r.o) ............................................. —1
Tropical Waters (USA) *(MMoubarak)* 8-4 ‡⁵JWeaver (12) (lt-f: hld up & prom: led over 1f out tl ins fnl f: unable qckn nr fin) ............................................. ½.2
1135⁴ Bold Face (IRE) *(RFJohnsonHoughton)* 9-0 PRobinson (14) (led 2f: rdn over 1f out: one pce) ............................................. 7.3
1910 Musical Phone *(JPLeigh)* 9-0 NConnorton (5) (a.p: led 4f out tl over 1f out: wknd fnl f) ............................................. ¾.4
Saxon Magic *(JABennett)* 8-9 JQuinn (13) (w'like: bit bkwd: s.i.s: bhd tl r.o u.p ins fnl f) ............................................. 1.5
Smarginato (IRE) (Fav) *(JLDunlop)* 9-0 PatEddery (10) (unf: scope: bkwd: hdwy over 2f out: rdn appr fnl f: sn btn) ............................................. 5.6

Unfinishedbusiness *(TJNaughton)* 8-11 ‡³RPerham (11) (leggy: lt-f: dwlt: sn
  chsng ldrs: wknd 2f out) ................................................. nk.7

1715³ Hotel California (IRE) *(JWHills)* 8-9 WRSwinburn (1) (w ldrs: rdn 2f out: sn btn) . 5.8
Melodic Drive *(PSFelgate)* 9-0 KFallon (3) (wl grwn: bkwd: s.s: a bhd) .............. 2.9
Amillionmemories *(MrsBarbaraWaring)* 9-0 NHowe (4) (w'like: bkwd: spd on
  outside over 4f) ......................................................... 1.10
Legal Risk *(DHaydnJones)* 8-9 TyroneWilliams (6) (lt-f: m.n.s) ................... s.h.11

2024 Smart Teacher (USA) *(PWHarris)* 9-0 JFortune (9) (outpcd) ............ 1½.12
1913 Star Minstrel (IRE) *(MMcCormack)* 9-0 WNewnes (8) (lw: m.n.s) ............ ¾.13
Palacegate Touch *(JBerry)* 9-0 GCarter (2) (lt-f: bit bkwd: s.s: a bhd) ......... 3½.14

**11/4** Smarginato (IRE) (op 5/4), **9/2** Tropical Waters (USA) (op 3/1), **5/1** Bold Face (IRE) (4/1—6/1), **8/1** SHIRO,
**9/1** Hotel California (IRE) (op 6/1), **10/1** Palacegate Touch (op 6/1), **12/1** Melodic Drive, Star Minstrel (IRE), **14/1**
Smart Teacher (USA), **20/1** Legal Risk, **33/1** Ors. CSF £43.50, Tote £17.60: £4.90 £2.40 £2.00 (£174.80). Mr
Saeed Manana (NEWMARKET) bred by Sheikh Mohammed bin Rashid al Maktoum. 14 Rn   1m 15.3 (4.3)
                                                SF—38/26/8/5/–/–

---

**2234**    RICHMOND AND BARRETT APP'CE (S) STKS  £1772.00 (£492.00: £236.00)
        6f 15y                                      7-20 (7-20)

1920 **Samson-Agonistes (73)** *(BAMcMahon)* 6-9-7 SSanders (2) (chsd ldr: led
    over 1f out: r.o wl) ...................................................... —1
1615 Melodic Habit (34) *(MrsAKnight)* 5-9-2 SWynne (6) (lw: led tl hdd appr fnl f: kpt
    on u.p) ................................................................ ¾.2
2163 Pretonic (62) (Jt-Fav) *(MJohnston)* 4-9-2 MHumphries (10) (hdwy 2f out: r.o wl
    ins fnl f) .............................................................. ½.3
2061³ Nuclear Express (52) (Jt-Fav) *(RLee)* 5-9-7 SDrowne (9) (hdwy appr fnl f: r.o
    ins fnl f: nvr nrr) ..................................................... 1½.4
1314 Ednego Bay (IRE) (bl) *(MMcCormack)* 4-9-0 EHusband (5) (chsd ldrs: rdn wl
    over 1f out: one pce) .................................................. ½.5
1978² Miss Brightside (37) *(ASmith)* 4-8-9 CHawksley (7) (bhd & rdn over 2f out: nvr
    plcd to chal) ......................................................... 8.6
2201⁴ Make Or Mar (57) *(BEllison)* 8-9-2 GParkin (4) (hdwy u.p over 2f out: nvr nr to
    chal) ................................................................. ½.7
Upthorpe Girl *(APJarvis)* 3-8-3 DCarson (8) (w'like: rangy: bkwd: outpcd & a
    bhd) ................................................................. hd.8
2084 Double Lark (50) *(RHollinshead)* 3-8-8 PBowe (3) (outpcd: a bhd: t.o) .......... 6.9
1883⁵ Cranfield Comet (63) *(JBerry)* 3-9-1 SHaworth (1) (led over 3f: sn wknd: t.o) .. 4.10

**4/1** Pretonic, Nuclear Express (3/1—5/1), **11/2** SAMSON-AGONISTES (op 7/2), **6/1** Miss Brightside (12/1—11/
2), Ednego Bay (IRE) (op 6/1), **10/1** Cranfield Comet, Upthorpe Girl (8/1—16/1), **12/1** Make Or Mar, **20/1** Ors. CSF
£90.77, Tote £4.60: £2.00 £3.20 £2.10 (£46.90). Mr J. B. Wilcox (TAMWORTH) bred by D. W. Pike. 10 Rn; No
bid                                                 1m 15.5 (4.5)
                                            SF—41/33/31/30/21/–

---

**2235**    ARTHUR CARR CUP (H'cap) (0-70) £1872.20 (£519.20: £248.60)
        1¾m 15y                                      7-50 (7-51)

(Weights raised 5 lb)

**My Swan Song (33)** *(JPSmith)* 7-7-3⁽²⁾ ‡⁷AGarth (6) (hld up: 7th st: styd on to ld
    ins fnl f) .............................................................. —1
1530² Greenwich Bambi (61) (Fav) *(WCarter)* 4-9-5 ‡⁵NGwilliams (3) (chsd ldrs: 5th
    st: led over 2f out: sn hdd: ev ch fnl f: unable qckn) ........... 2.2
1580⁴ Lookingforararainbow (IRE) (58) *(BobJones)* 4-8-9 JQuinn (8) (lw: hld up: hdwy
    on bit to ld wl over 1f out: hdd & no ex fnl f) ................. 1½.3
1972⁵ Dare to Dream (IRE) (60) *(GLewis)* 3-8-9 PaulEddery (10) (chsd ldrs: 3rd st: led
    3f out: sn hdd: rdn & btn appr fnl f) ............................. 3½.4
1947 Ballymac Girl (53) *(CTNash)* 4-9-2 WNewnes (7) (b: hld up & bhd: effrt over 2f
    out: styd on) ......................................................... ½.5
1671 Pondered Bid (37) (bl) *(PatMitchell)* 8-8-0⁽¹⁾ GCarter (4) (b: chsd ldrs: 4th st: ev
    ch 2f out: sn wknd) ................................................. 6.6
1988 Megan's Flight (38) *(THCaldwell)* 7-7-8 ‡⁷MHumphries (5) (wnt 6th st: wknd
    over 2f out) ......................................................... 1½.7
1970 Lifetimes Ambition (35) *(TCasey)* 4-7-12 PBurke (9) (b: led: sn clr: hdd 4f out:
    sn rdn & btn) ....................................................... 2½.8
2059 Q-Eight (IRE) (59) *(APJarvis)* 4-9-8 WRSwinburn (2) (still bkwd: a bhd: t.o) .... 10.9
2059 Access Cruise (USA) (52) *(BAMcMahon)* 5-9-1 JFortune (1) (chsd ldrs: 2nd st:
    led 4f out to 3f out: wknd qckly: t.o) ........................... 7.10

**11/4** Greenwich Bambi, **7/2** Dare to Dream (IRE), **4/1** Lookingforararainbow (IRE) (op 5/2), **6/1** Pondered Bid (op
7/2), **8/1** Access Cruise (USA), **14/1** Q-Eight (IRE), Lifetimes Ambition, **20/1** Megan's Flight, Ballymac Girl, **50/1**
MY SWAN SONG. CSF £173.66, CT £641.39. Tote £33.00: £4.30 £2.30 £1.70 (£343.20). Mr Brian McGowan
(RUGELEY) bred by Mrs M. Hemphill. 10 Rn                                3m 16.6 (18.1)

**2236**  GEORGE AND JOHN DUNN STKS (Mdn 3-Y.O) £1518.00 (£418.00: £198.00)
1m 54y                                                              8-20 (8-21)

1956² **Pelargonia** (Fav) *(RCharlton)* 8-9 PatEddery (1) (lw: hld up gng wl: 3rd st: led
                          appr fnl f: wnt clr) .................................................. —1
2062⁴ Hameem (IRE) *(AAScott)* 9-0 WRSwinburn (5) (lw: chsd ldr: 2nd st: led 2f out tl
                          appr fnl f: eased whn btn) ............................................ 4.2
1432³ Queen Caroline (USA) *(HRACecil)* 8-9 WRyan (6) (led to 2f out: kpt on one pce
                          fnl f) ................................................................. 2¹/₂.3
        Spring Saint *(MJHeaton-Ellis)* 9-0 WNewnes (3) (b: bit bkwd: hld up & bhd: 6th
                          st: kpt on appr fnl f: nvr nrr) ....................................... 2¹/₂.4
835  Apollo Red *(PWHarris)* 9-0 PaulEddery (2) (hld up: 6th st: rdn over 2f out: sn
                          outpcd) ............................................................... s.h.5
1956  Mist of the Marsh (USA) *(JHMGosden)* 8-9 RCochrane (4) (dwlt: sn chsng ldrs:
                          4th st: rdn & btn over 2f out) ........................................ 5.6

**4/9** PELARGONIA, **5/1** Queen Caroline (USA)(op 5/2), **7/1** Hameem (IRE), **20/1** Ors. CSF £4.19, Tote £1.20:
£1.10 £3.10 (£2.30). Mr Christopher Heath (BECKHAMPTON) bred by Cheveley Park Stud Ltd. 6 Rn
                                                                            1m 47.6 (8)
                                                            SF—47/40/27/24/23/3

**2237**  COUNTY CRICKET H'CAP (3-Y.O) (0-70) £1856.80 (£514.80: £246.40)
1m 54y                                                              8-50 (8-50)
                          (Weights raised 8 lb)
2084∗ **Legend Dulac (IRE)** (52) (Fav) *(JLHarris)* 8-12 (6x) PRobinson (1) (mde all:
                          hrd rdn fnl f: hld on gamely) ......................................... —1
1986² Neltegrity (58) (v) *(THCaldwell)* 8-11 ‡⁷EHusband (5) (chsd wnr: 2nd st: ev ch
                          over 1f out: unable qckn) ............................................. 2.2
1743  Winged Whisper (USA) (60) *(CASmith)* 9-6 MWigham (8) (b.off hind: s.s: bhd tl
                          styd on fnl 2f: nvr nrr) ............................................... 2.3
1663  Safari Park (35) *(BSRothwell)* 7-9 JQuinn (6) (prom: 3rd st: ev ch over 2f out: sn
                          btn) .................................................................. 4.4
1308  Nocatchim (61) *(BWHills)* 9-7 DHolland (2) (swtg: chsd ldrs: 5th st: rdn over 3f
                          out: no imp) ......................................................... s.h.5
2088  Galley Gossip (52) *(RBrotherton)* 8-5 ‡⁷PBowe (3) (hld up & bhd: 6th st: outpcd
                          3f out: sn t.o) ...................................................... 7.6
1918  North Flyer (47) *(BAMcMahon)* 8-0 ‡⁷SSanders (7) (chsd ldrs: 4th st: wknd over
                          3f out: t.o) ......................................................... 4.7

**7/4** LEGEND DULAC (IRE), **9/2** Neltegrity(op 3/1), Nocatchim, **13/2** North Flyer(op 10/1), Winged Whisper
(USA), **14/1** Safari Park, **16/1** Galley Gossip. CSF £9.33, CT £35.29. Tote £2.40: £1.90 £2.50 (£3.40). Mr B.
McAllister (MELTON MOWBRAY) bred by Chippenham Lodge Stud in Ireland. 7 Rn      1m 48.5 (8.9)
                                                            SF—36/29/32/—/—/—

T/Plpt: £10.10 (122.9 Tckts).                                                        IM

2051—**WINDSOR (Fig.8)**
**Monday, July 20th [Good becoming Good to soft]**
Going Allowance: 0.20 sec per fur (G)                  Wind: almost nil   Vis: 4th poor

Stalls: high

**2238**  MAUREEN MITCHELL MEMORIAL (S) STKS (2-Y.O) £1531.80 (£424.80: £203.40)
5f 217y                                                            6-20 (6-21)

2005  **Hy Wilma** *(RJHodges)* 8-3 ‡³TSprake (7) (hld up: nt clr run over 2f out: swtchd
                          lft: led over 1f out: rdn out) ........................................ —1
1913⁶ Kyrenia Game (Fav) *(PMitchell)* 8-3 ‡³SO'Gorman (9) (a.p: ev ch over 1f out:
                          unable qckn) ......................................................... 2.2
2195⁴ De Chine *(JSMoore)* 8-6 SWhitworth (8) (w ldr: led 2f out tl over 1f out: one pce)  5.3
1171  Lady Relko *(RVoorspuy)* 8-6 SDawson (11) (lw: a.p: hrd rdn over 2f out: one
                          pce) ................................................................. 3¹/₂.4
1140² Admiral Frobisher (USA) (bl) *(CFWall)* 8-11 NDay (10) (led 4f) ................. 3¹/₂.5
1601⁵ Sterling Princess *(JRJenkins)* 8-6 CRutter (2) (spd 4f) ........................ 6.6
2005⁵ Gaynor Goodman (IRE) (bl) *(JSMoore)* 8-6 DBiggs (6) (bhd fnl 2f) ............... 3.7
1675  Apifera *(RJHodges)* 8-3 ‡³FNorton (1) (swtg: a bhd) ............................. 4.8
        Lookatmyfoot *(JSutcliffe)* 8-6 BRouse (3) (leggy: lt-f: bit bkwd: a bhd) ....... 5.9

**2/1** Kyrenia Game(op 4/1), **5/2** Admiral Frobisher (USA)(6/4—11/4), **5/1** De Chine(4/1—6/1), **6/1** Lady Relko,
**10/1** Gaynor Goodman (IRE)(op 4/1), HY WILMA(op 5/1), **14/1** Lookatmyfoot(op 7/1), **16/1** Apifera(op 8/1),
**33/1** Sterling Princess. CSF £31.46, Tote £13.30: £3.90 £1.40 £2.30 (£17.70). Mr R. J. Hodges (SOMERTON)
bred by W. H. F. Carson. 9 Rn; Bt in 2,900 gns                              1m 14.8 (4.3)
                                                            SF—27/19/2/—/—/—

**2239**  MACMILLAN NURSE APPEAL STKS (Mdn 3-Y.O) £1531.80 (£424.80: £203.40)
1¼m 7y                                                  6-45 (6-47)

**Vratislav (USA)** *(JHMGosden)* 9-0  SCauthen (1) (unf: scope: bit bkwd: 2nd st: led over 3f out: hrd rdn: r.o wl) ...................................................... —1
1917⁶ Hang Ten **(Fav)** *(LMCumani)* 9-0  LDettori (4) (lw: 3rd st: ev ch over 2f out: unable qckn) ............................................................................ 10.2
699² Jade Green *(PJMakin)* 8-6 ‡³TSprake (2) (b.hind: 4th st: ev ch wl over 1f out: one pce) ..................................................................................... 1.3
Alif (IRE) *(JLDunlop)* 9-0  AMunro (5) (w'like: bkwd: 6th st: wknd over 2f out) ..... 7.4
Sir Joey (USA) *(RJHolder)* 9-0  JWilliams (6) (w'like: bit bkwd: 5th st: wknd over 2f out) ............................................................................................... 4.5
Alton Belle *(PHowling)* 8-9  JMurray (7) (a bhd) .................................................. 4.6
1069 Snappy's Boy Josh *(PJFeilden)* 9-0  CRutter (2) (plld hrd: led over 6f) ............ 10.7

**4/5** Hang Ten(op 6/4), **3/1** Jade Green, **9/2** VRATISLAV (USA)(op 5/4), **7/1** Alif (IRE)(3/1—8/1), **40/1** Sir Joey (USA), **66/1** Ors. CSF £8.49, Tote £3.40: £1.80 £1.10 (£3.50). Sheikh Mohammed (NEWMARKET) bred by Darley Stud Management Co Ltd in USA. 7 Rn                                      2m 9.1 (6.1)
SF—59/39/29/23/15/2

**2240**  CANCER RELIEF MACMILLAN FUND CLAIMING STKS    £1582.20 (£439.20: £210.60)
1m 67y                                                  7-10 (7-12)

2196⁴ **Lamore Ritorna (50)** *(KOCunningham-Brown)* 3–8-0  DBiggs (6) (led over 5f out: rdn out) ........................................................................................ —1
1916⁴ Vanroy (67) (v) *(JRJenkins)* 8–9-5  SWhitworth (10) (hdwy over 3f out: hrd rdn over 1f out: ev ch ins fnl f: r.o) ............................................... ½.2
1741 Aragon Court (32) *(JPearce)* 4–8-3 ‡⁵RPrice (12) (6th st: one pce fnl 2f) .......... 2¹/₂.3
2013 Kissavos (51) *(CCElsey)* 6–8-9  TRogers (5) (b.off hind: hdwy over 2f out: hrd rdn over 1f out: one pce) ......................................................... s.h.4
2051⁵ Count Robert (USA) *(MissJacquelineSDoyle)* 5  SDawson (11) (hld up: swtchd lft over 2f out: nvr nr to chal) ................................................. 3¹/₂.5
1986 Up All Night (64) *(JWHills)* 3–7-10 ‡⁵DHarrison (1) (no hdwy fnl 3f) ................... ¾.6
1773³ Durneltor (64) (bl) (Fav) *(RHannon)* 4–9-2  AMcGlone (2) (4th st: wknd over 1f out) ........................................................................................... 3.7
351 Anatroccolo (41) *(RABennett)* 5–8-0 ‡³FNorton (8) (nvr nrr) ................................. 2.8
Bounder Rowe *(JFfitch-Heyes)* 5–8-7  LDettori (3) (3rd st: wknd over 2f out) ... 2.9
Salar's Spirit *(WGMTurner)* 6–8-4 ‡³TSprake (7) (5th st: wknd over 2f out) ....... 2.10
2079 Royal Glint (52) *(IABalding)* 3–7-10 ‡³SO'Gorman (9) (a bhd) ........................... ¾.11
1741³ Flying Promise (39) *(RABennett)* 4–8-9  AMunro (4) (led over 2f: 2nd st: wknd 4f out) ............................................................................................ 10.12

*Stewards Enquiry: Trainer & rdr of Count Robert each fined £325 under Rule 151 (failure to run horse on its merits).*

**11/10** Durneltor, **3/1** Vanroy(op 2/1), **9/2** Up All Night, **10/1** Count Robert (USA), **16/1** Flying Promise, Kissavos(op 8/1), **20/1** LAMORE RITORNA, **25/1** Royal Glint, Anatroccolo, **33/1** Bounder Rowe, **50/1** Ors. CSF £81.27, Tote £14.40: £2.20 £1.40 £8.60 (£33.00). Mr D. Bass (STOCKBRIDGE) bred by A. A. Papotto and D. B. Seear. 12 Rn                                                          1m 47.3 (5.7)
SF—24/41/17/22/13/–

**2241**  POLO RALPH LAUREN H'CAP (0-80) £1549.50 each (£321.00)
1m 3f 135y           (Weights raised 6 lb)              7-40 (7-41)

1948³ **Wassl This Then (IRE) (70)** *(DWPArbuthnot)* 3–9-1 ‡⁵RPrice (5) (4th st: hrd rdn over 1f out: jnd ldr nr fin) ...................................................... —1
1743* Incola (41) **(Fav)** *(HCandy)* 6–8-3  CRutter (3) (2nd st: led 3f out: all out) ........... —1
2033 Polistatic (34) *(CAHorgan)* 5–7-10  DaleGibson (2) (3rd st: ev ch wl over 1f out: unable qckn) ................................................................................... 2.3
2054* Mahrajan (67) *(CJBenstead)* 8–10-1 (5x)  BRaymond (4) (5th st: ev ch over 1f out: one pce) ................................................................................ 1¹/₂.4
2036 Easy Purchase (52) *(RJHolder)* 5–9-0  JWilliams (1) (5th st: a bhd) ..................... 2.5
2033 Littleton Lullaby (34) *(MMadgwick)* 7–7-10(3)  SDawson (6) (led over 8f) ........... 15.6
LONG HANDICAP: Littleton Lullaby 7-4.

**7/4** INCOLA, **3/1** Mahrajan(op 7/4), **9/2** Polistatic(op 3/1), **5/1** Easy Purchase, **11/2** WASSL THIS THEN (IRE)(op 7/2), **33/1** Littleton Lullaby. CSF £7.58 WTT & I, £5.50 I & WTT, Tote £1.40 I £2.40 WTT: £1.70 £1.70 (£6.30). Wassl This Then (IRE): Mrs Josephine Carter (COMPTON) bred by Delmare Syndicate Number Two in Ireland. Incola: Mrs David Blackburn (WANTAGE) bred by Mrs D. Blackburn. 6 Rn          2m 42.3 (19.8)

**2242**  CHEVELEY PARK STUD NURSERY    £1952.50 (£540.00: £257.50)
5f 217y                                                  8-10 (8-12)

1409* **Dark Eyed Lady (IRE)** *(DWPArbuthnot)* 8-7  TQuinn (2) (mde virtually all: qcknd over 2f out: wandered: eased nr fin) .......................... —1

1887* Pizza Connection (Fav) *(JLDunlop)* 8-10  SCauthen (7) (hld up: chsd wnr fnl 2f: hrd rdn: r.o) ............................................................... 1.2
1969* Moving Image (IRE) *(MBell)* 8-5  MHills (6) (a.p: one pce fnl 2f) ............ 5.3
2031 Brigadore Gold *(RHannon)* 7-3(3) ‡7AWhelan (5) (prom over 3f out) ........ 1½.4
1273* Cliburnel News (IRE) *(MHTompkins)* 9-0 ‡7SMulvey (4) (outpcd) .......... ¾.5
1910⁴ Girl Next Door *(NAGraham)* 7-7(2) ‡3FNorton (1) (prom over 3f) .......... 10.6

LONG HANDICAP: Brigadore Gold 7-5.

**4/5** Pizza Connection(4/6—Evens), **9/2** Moving Image (IRE), **6/1** Brigadore Gold(8/1—5/1), **8/1** Girl Next Door(op 5/1), **10/1** DARK EYED LADY (IRE)(op 5/1), **16/1** Cliburnel News (IRE). CSF £18.37, Tote £5.50: £2.10 £1.20 (£3.20). Mrs M. Gutkin (COMPTON) bred by J. Stan Cosgrove in Ireland. 6 Rn        1m 17 (6.5)

## 2243
ROBERT HOLDEN LTD H'CAP  *(1m 67y)*  8-40 - **Abandoned**—torrential rain & darkness

T/Plpt: £31.20 (78.75 Tckts).                                                                                    AK

## 2044—**EDINBURGH (R-H)**
## Tuesday, July 21st [Good to firm]
Going Allowance: nil sec per fur (G)                                                Wind: slt against

Stalls: high

## 2244
MUSSELBURGH LINKS APP'CE STKS   £2158.50 (£606.00: £295.50)
1½m 31y                                                                   2-00 (2-00)

2047⁰ **Latvian (69)** (hl) *(RAllan)* 5-9-4  JWeaver (2) (lw: mde most: wandered u.p fnl 2f: kpt on) ......................................................... —1
2020⁴ Northern Kingdom (USA) **(71)** (v) (Fav) *(SGNorton)* 3-8-6  OPears (5) (trckd wnr: chal over 2f out: hung lft & rt: nt r.o) ........................ 3½.2
2116³ Super Blues *(TDBarron)* 5-8-10  SWilliams (3) (lw: hld up & bhd: hdwy 2f out: nvr plcd to chal) .................................................. 5.3
2217 Ebony Isle (37) (bl) *(MissLAPerratt)* 3-7-9 ‡3RHavlin (4) (trckd ldrs tl lost pl ent st) .............................................................. 20.4

**11/10** Northern Kingdom (USA), **6/4** LATVIAN, **7/2** Super Blues, **66/1** Ebony Isle. CSF £3.48, Tote £3.10 (£1.70). Mr J. P. Seymour (CORNHILL-ON-TWEED) bred by Fittocks Stud Ltd. 4 Rn      2m 38.5 (6)
SF—44/25/19/–

## 2245
VOGRIE PARK (S) H'CAP (3 & 4-Y.O) (0-60) £2232.00 (£627.00: £306.00)
5f                                                                          2-30 (2-31)
(Weights raised 1 lb)

1162 **Galaxy Express (37)** *(GHEden)* 4-9-2  GDuffield (7) (b: trckd ldrs: nt clr run & swtchd over 1f out: r.o to ld cl home) ........................ —1
2063³ Kalar (39) *(DWChapman)* 3-8-13  SWood (8) (lw: disp ld tl led over 1f out: ct cl home) .................................................. s.h.2
2115⁴ Cottage Gallery (IRE) **(35)** (Fav) *(WAStephenson)* 4-9-0  BRaymond (6) (disp ld tl hdd appr fnl f: nt qckn) ...................................... 2.3
2201³ Supreme Desire (40) *(ASmith)* 4-9-5  SWebster (1) (chsd ldrs: rdn & kpt on one pce appr fnl f) ................................................ ½.4
1987 Tommy Tempest (48) *(KRBurke)* 3-9-8  JFortune (3) (chsd ldrs tl rdn & btn over 1f out) ....................................................... 2.5
2048 Come on My Girl (IRE) (45) (bl) *(TAKCuthbert)* 4-9-5 ‡5JWeaver (4) (s.s: hdwy over 1f out: nvr rchd ldrs) .................................... 1½.6
2119⁵ Miss Narnia (46) (bl) *(MDods)* 3-8-13 ‡7OPears (5) (dwlt: n.d) .......... 5.7

**5/2** Cottage Gallery (IRE), **7/2** Supreme Desire, **5/1** Tommy Tempest, Kalar, **7/1** GALAXY EXPRESS(op 9/2), **10/1** Miss Narnia, **14/1** Come on My Girl (IRE). CSF £37.16, CT £99.48. Tote £8.10: £3.00 £3.30 (£11.90). Mr M. F. Eden (NEWMARKET) bred by D. Lowe. 7 Rn; No bid      61.1 sec (3.4)
SF—34/30/23/26/21/12

## 2246
GULLANE H'CAP (0-70) £2369.60 (£665.60: £324.80)    **1m 7f 16y**   3-00 (3-00)
(Weights raised 13 lb)

2045² **Alpha Helix (23)** (v) *(MissLAPerratt)* 9-7-8 ‡3JFanning (6) (a.p: led over 2f out: r.o u.p) ................................................ —1
2059³ Briggsmaid (50) *(JMPEustace)* 4-9-10  MTebbutt (2) (hld up: hdwy appr st: chal over 2f out: nt qckn fnl f) ...................................... 2.2
2057² Shayna Maidel (37) *(MBell)* 3-7-7(1) ‡3FNorton (3) (lw: in tch: hdwy & ev ch 2f out: rdn & one pce) .......................................... 1½.3
2045³ Brusque (USA) (28) *(DonEnricoIncisa)* 8-7-9 ‡7ClaireBalding (1) (chsd ldrs tl lost pl appr st: hdwy 2f out: hung rt: styd on) ................ 1½.4

2148* Danza Heights **(41)** (Fav) *(MrsGRReveley)* 6-9-1 (4x) JLowe (5) (lw: dwlt: sn trckng ldrs: led appr st: hdd over 2f out: rdn & fnd nil) ..... 1½.5
1731 Musket Shot **(38)** (bl) *(VThompson)* 4-8-12 JFortune (4) (led tl hdd appr st: wknd qckly) ...................................................................... dist.6

**4/7** Danza Heights, **100/30** Shayna Maidel, **8/1** Briggsmaid, **12/1** ALPHA HELIX, **14/1** Brusque (USA), **66/1** Musket Shot. CSF £83.08, Tote £6.60: £2.10 £2.10 (£51.30). Mr J. W. M. M. Richard (AYR) bred by Mrs S. M. Rogers. 6 Rn                                                                                    3m 21.5 (11)

## 2247
BRAIDS CLAIMING STKS (2-Y.O) **£2211.00** (£621.00: £303.00)                    **7f 15y**  3-30 (3-32)

2039* **Allegrissima** *(JBerry)* 8-6 JCarroll (1) (mde all: rdn & r.o wl fnl f) ...................... —1
1515 Lucky Owl *(MissLAPerratt)* 7-9-1 ‡³JFanning (2) (chsd ldrs: hdwy & ev ch 1f out: nt qckn) ........................................................................................ 2.2
782³ Take Your Partner (IRE) (Jt-Fav) *(MJohnston)* 8-0 JLowe (5) (in tch: hdwy u.p 2f out: nvr able to chal) ........................................................................ ¾.3
2038⁶ Society Gown (USA) (Jt-Fav) *(TDBarron)* 8-8 KDarley (3) (chsd wnr: rdn ent st: one pce) ........................................................................................ nk.4
1897 German Legend *(RRLamb)* 8-8 ‡⁷RHavlin (4) (a last) ........................................ 10.5

**7/4** Take Your Partner (IRE)(op 3/1), Society Gown (USA)(5/2—6/4), **5/2** ALLEGRISSIMA(op 4/6), **10/1** Lucky Owl(op 16/1), **25/1** German Legend. CSF £20.67, Tote £2.20: £2.00 £2.70 (£11.10). Mr P. E. T. Chandler (COCKERHAM) bred by G. C. Hughes. 5 Rn                                                          1m 30.7 (4.5)
                                                                                    SF—25/8/11/18/–

## 2248
E.B.F. ROYAL MUSSELBURGH STKS (Mdn 2-Y.O.F) **£2392.00** (£672.00: £328.00)             **7f 15y**  4-00 (4-02)

1899 **Clear Honey (USA)** (Fav) *(BHanbury)* 8-11 BRaymond (5) (mde all: clr over 1f out: styd on wl) .................................................................... —1
859⁶ Dowreyna *(MRStoute)* 8-11 GDuffield (3) (lost pl after 1f: hdwy 2f out: r.o wl nr fin) .............................................................................. 1.2
Drumdonna (IRE) *(JBerry)* 8-11 JCarroll (2) (cmpt: bit bkwd: a chsng ldrs: r.o one pce fnl 2f) ................................................................. 5.3
Free Dancer *(RAllan)* 8-11 SWebster (6) (w'like: bit bkwd: s.s: sn prom: nt qckn fnl 2f) ...................................................................... 2¼.4
1957 Crystal Stone *(TThomsonJones)* 8-11 DMcKeown (1) (lw: cl up tl lost pl & rn sltly wd st: n.d after) ........................................................ nk.5
1946 Go Orange (bl) *(JLSpearing)* 8-11 KDarley (4) (cl up tl rn v.wd st: sn t.o: sddle slipped & p.u 1f out) ........................................................ 0

**5/4** CLEAR HONEY (USA), **6/4** Dowreyna(5/4—2/1), **5/1** Drumdonna (IRE)(6/1—4/1), **10/1** Crystal Stone(op 5/1), **33/1** Free Dancer, **100/1** Go Orange. CSF £3.48, Tote £2.00: £1.60 £1.60 (£1.90). Mr Nasser Abdullah (NEWMARKET) bred by James A.Philpott Jnr & Robert Trussell Jnr in USA. 6 Rn                 1m 29.7 (3.5)
                                                                                    SF—47/34/29/21/20

## 2249
MUIRFIELD H'CAP (0-70) **£2481.60** (£697.60: £340.80)                            **1m 16y**  4-30 (4-32)

1863² **Bidweaya (USA) (37)** *(JLEyre)* 5-7-12 ‡⁷OPears (2) (lw: trckd ldrs: led wl over 2f out: sn rdn clr) ................................................... —1
2142⁵ The Dandy Don (IRE) **(52)** *(DenysSmith)* 3-8-12 KFallon (4) (effrt over 3f out: styd on: no imp) ................................................ 3.2
1890 Super Summit **(54)** (Fav) *(JPearce)* 3-9-0 KDarley (3) (squeezed out after 1f: bhd tl hdwy on outside over 2f out: nvr able to chal) .... nk.3
Dust D'Throne (USA) **(37)** *(MissLCSiddall)* 4-8-2 ‡³FNorton (1) (cl up: chal over 3f out: one pce fnl 2f) ......................................... ¾.4
1918⁶ Gizlaan (USA) **(58)** *(BHanbury)* 3-9-4 BRaymond (7) (led tl hdd wl over 2f out: sn outpcd) .................................................. s.h.5
2075⁶ Manulife **(68)** *(BBeasley)* 3-9-7 ‡⁷SWilliams (6) (lw: hld up & bhd: effrt ent st: no rspnse) ................................................. 7.6
2154⁴ Our Amber **(25)** *(DWChapman)* 5-7-7 SWood (5) (chsd ldrs tl outpcd fnl 3f) ... nk.7
2146⁴ Shadaylou (IRE) **(48)** *(MissLAPerratt)* 3-8-5 ‡³JFanning (8) (hld up: effrt over 3f out: n.d) ...................................................... 7.8

**3/1** Super Summit, **7/2** BIDWEAYA (USA), **9/2** The Dandy Don (IRE), **5/1** Manulife, **7/1** Gizlaan (USA), **10/1** Dust D'Throne (USA), **20/1** Our Amber, **25/1** Shadaylou (IRE). CSF £17.81, CT £45.74. Tote £4.30: £1.40 £1.80 £1.30 (£7.80). Mr Jeff Slaney (DEWSBURY) bred by W. and R. Barnett Ltd. in USA. 8 Rn            1m 41.8 (3.2)
                                                                                    SF—36/41/42/28/43/25

## 2250
LUFTNESS H'CAP (0-70) **£2343.00** (£648.00: £309.00)                            **1m 3f 32y**  5-00 (5-00)
(Weights raised 9 lb)

1960⁶ **Explosive Speed (USA) (53)** *(MDHammond)* 4-9-9 DMcKeown (3) (led 2f: chsd ldr: led over 2f out: sn hdd: hrd rdn to ld ins fnl f) ....... —1

21422 Hanley's Hands (IRE) **(58)** (Fav) *(MHTompkins)* 3–9–3 PRobinson (5) (lw: trckd ldrs: hdwy to ld 2f out: sn rdn: hdd & no ex ins fnl f) ........... ³/₄.**2**

Kenyatta (USA) **(65)** *(DenysSmith)* 3–9–10 KFallon (1) (hld up: shkn up over 3f out: r.o nr fin) ...................................................................... 1¹/₂.**3**

19076 Mr News (IRE) **(48)** (bl) *(BBeasley)* 3–8–7 LCharnock (2) (lw: led after 2f tl over 2f out: sn btn) ......................................................................... 6.**4**

**8/11** Hanley's Hands (IRE), **11/8** EXPLOSIVE SPEED (USA), **16/1** Kenyatta (USA), **33/1** Mr News (IRE). CSF £2.63, Tote £3.00 (£1.40). Wetherby Racing Bureau Plc (MIDDLEHAM) bred by Buckram Oak Farm in USA. 4 Rn

2m 26 (6.3)

SF—46/38/42/13

T/Plpt: £89.50 (23.1 Tckts). AA

## 2077—FOLKESTONE (R-H)

## Tuesday, July 21st [Soft becoming Good to soft]

Going Allowance: St: minus 0.15 sec (F); Rnd: 0.10 sec per fur (G) Wind: slt half bhd

Stalls: low

**2251** COOMES (S) H'CAP (I) (3, 4 & 5-Y.O) (0-60) £2448.00 (£678.00: £324.00)
1m 1f 149y 1-45 (1-47)

20753 **Anguish (IRE) (51)** (Fav) *(NACallaghan)* 3–9–2 PatEddery (3) (hdwy 3f out: 6th st: hrd rdn & led over 1f out: r.o wl) ...................................... —**1**

2077 Moving Force **(37)** *(EAWheeler)* 5–8–12 SWhitworth (7) (lost pl over 2f out: rallied fnl f: r.o) ........................................................................... 2.**2**

1741* Mardior **(33)** *(WGRWightman)* 4–8–8 JWilliams (2) (hdwy over 1f out: r.o one poo) ........................................................................................... ¹/₂.**3**

1721 Eliza Wooding **(35)** *(CJHill)* 4–8–10 NAdams (8) (s.s: rdn 5f out: hdwy on ins over 2f out: 5th st: nt clr run over 1f out: r.o) ...................... ³/₄.**4**

1992 Lucky Barnes **(29)** (bl) *(FJYardley)* 5–8–4⁽¹⁾ TQuinn (9) (chsd ldr over 6f: 4th st: hrd rdn over 1f out: one pce) .............................................. 2¹/₂.**5**

20512 Bengal Tiger (IRE) **(53)** (bl) *(JAkehurst)* 4–10–0 LDettori (1) (2nd st: led 2f out tl over 1f out: sn wknd) .................................................... 3¹/₂.**6**

2051 Rapid Rosie **(30)** *(DRLaing)* 4–8–5 TyroneWilliams (5) (swtg: rdn 3f out: 3rd st: wknd over 1f out) ............................................................. 10.**7**

Kisu Kali **(53)** *(JFfitch-Heyes)* 5–9–9 ‡5DHarrison (4) (lw: bhd fnl 3f) ................ 8.**8**

1978 Libra Legend (USA) **(53)** *(CEBrittain)* 3–9–4 MRoberts (6) (lw: led: clr 7f out: hdd 2f out: wknd qckly) .................................................. 2.**9**

**5/2** ANGUISH (IRE), **3/1** Bengal Tiger (IRE), **5/1** Libra Legend (USA), Mardior, **8/1** Eliza Wooding(op 9/2), **11/1** Moving Force(op 7/1), **12/1** Rapid Rosie(op 8/1), **25/1** Ors. CSF £28.34, CT £117.99. Tote £3.40: £1.60 £2.90 £1.70 (£33.90). Mrs J. Callaghan (NEWMARKET) bred by Barronstown Bloodstock Ltd in Ireland. 9 Rn; Bt in 3,900 gns

2m 8.4 (10.7)

**2252** MARGATE STKS (Mdn) £2070.00 (£570.00: £270.00) **1m 1f 149y** 2-15 (2-15)

18392 **Agincourt Song (USA) (81)** (Fav) *(JLDunlop)* 3–8–11 PatEddery (4) (lw: mde all: comf) ........................................................................................ —**1**

1922 High Savannah **(62)** *(MAJarvis)* 4–9–2 RCochrane (2) (lw: 3rd st: chsd wnr fnl 2f: hrd rdn: no imp) ................................................................. 1¹/₂.**2**

16483 La Joya (IRE) **(GHarwood)** 3–8–6 TQuinn (5) (2nd st: wknd over 1f out) ............ 10.**3**

Lily Moreton *(MJHeaton-Ellis)* 3–8–6 JReid (6) (scope: bit bkwd: 4th st: no hdwy fnl 2f) ............................................................................ 2¹/₂.**4**

1033 Mayaasa (USA) **(77)** *(RWArmstrong)* 3–8–6 MRoberts (3) (hrd rdn 3f out: 5th st: no hdwy fnl 2f) ...................................................................... s.h.**5**

16743 Guesstimation (USA) *(JPearce)* 3–8–6 ‡5RPrice (1) (6th st: a bhd: t.o) ............... 30.**6**

**4/9** AGINCOURT SONG (USA)(tchd 4/6), **9/2** High Savannah, **11/2** Mayaasa (USA)(op 7/2), **10/1** La Joya (IRE), **33/1** Ors. CSF £3.31, Tote £1.50: £1.10 £2.40 (£2.60). Lord Chelsea (ARUNDEL) bred by Viscount Chelsea in USA. 6 Rn

2m 6.5 (8.8)

**2253** COOMES (S) H'CAP (II) (3, 4 & 5-Y.O) (0-60) £2448.00 (£678.00: £324.00)
1m 1f 149y 2-45 (2-48)

1976 **Molly Splash (49)** *(CACyzer)* 5–9–11 GCarter (3) (hdwy over 2f out: 4th st: led 1f out: r.o wl) .......................................................................... —**1**

2014 Sciacca **(24)** *(CWeedon)* 5–8–0 SDawson (10) (lw: gd hdwy over 2f out: led over 1f out: sn hdd: nt qckn) .................................................... ³/₄.**2**

21016 Pleasure Ahead **(33)** *(MDixon)* 5–8–9 DaleGibson (6) (hrd rdn & hdwy over 1f out: r.o) .......................................................................... 7.**3**

2051 Daily Sport Girl **(50)** *(FJYardley)* 3–9-2 JQuinn (5) (lw: 3rd st: ev ch over 1f out:
    wknd fnl f) ........................................................................................ 1½.4
1810 Confound (IRE) **(36)** *(JAkehurst)* 3–8-2 TyroneWilliams (12) (led 2f: led 3f out tl
    over 1f out: sn wknd) .......................................... 4.5
1643 Grecian Belle **(42)** *(DAWilson)* 3–8-8 WNewnes (7) (swtg: hdwy over 1f out: nvr
    nrr) ........................................................................................ 1½.6
1759³ Mystic Panther **(52)** *(RJHolder)* 4–10-0 MRoberts (4) (nvr nr to chal) ............. s.h.7
    Play the Blues **(27)** *(RGFrost)* 5–8-3 AMunro (1) (a mid div) ................... s.h.8
1949⁵ Please Please Me (IRE) **(31)** (bl) *(KOCunningham-Brown)* 4–8-7 TQuinn (14)
    (5th st: wknd over 1f out) .................................. 3.9
*2101* Muzo (USA) **(43)** (v) *(JMBradley)* 5–9-5 JWilliams (11) (swtg: led over 7f out to
    3f out: 2nd st: wknd 2f out) .................... 2½.10
1720⁶ City Line **(42)** (Fav) *(DRLaing)* 3–8-8 PatEddery (13) (6th st: wknd 2f out) ........ 6.11
2015 Ballycastle Mary (IRE) **(42)** *(TJNaughton)* 3–8-8 PaulEddery (8) (lw: a bhd) ..... 7.12
2083 Dazla **(28)** *(RRowe)* 5–7-13 ‡5DHarrison (9) (reluctant to r: a bhd) ................... 7.13

**3/1** City Line, **5/1** Please Please Me (IRE), Pleasure Ahead, Mystic Panther(op 3/1), **13/2** MOLLY SPLASH, **15/2** Sciacca(12/1—7/1), **12/1** Confound (IRE), **16/1** Dazla, Play the Blues, Muzo (USA), **20/1** Grecian Belle, Ballycastle Mary (IRE), **25/1** Daily Sport Girl. CSF £58.01, CT £254.57. Tote £9.40: £2.60 £2.60 £1.90 (£38.40). Mr R. M. Cyzer (HORSHAM) bred by S. Wingfield Digby. 13 Rn; No bid                    2m 6.9 (9.2)

## 2254

COOMES MORNING SERVICE H'CAP (0-70) £2406.00 (£666.00: £318.00)
   **6f 189y**                                                                3-15 (3-18)

2032² **Profit a Prendre (50)** (Fav) *(DAWilson)* 8–9-5 MRoberts (14) (b: bmpd over 2f
    out: 3rd st: led ins fnl f: rdn out) ............................................... —1
*1267* Barlogan **(50)** *(CFWall)* 4–9-5 RCochrane (6) (a.p: led over 3f out tl ins fnl f: r.o
    wl) ................................................................ s.h.2
1921⁵ Spanish Love **(32)** *(CGCox)* 6–7-10(1) ‡8ATucker (2) (hdwy 3f out: 2nd st: hrd
    rdn over 1f out: unable qckn) ............................ 2.3
1756² Teanarco (IRE) **(59)** *(RJHolder)* 4–10-0 AMunro (9) (led over 3f: 4th st: hrd rdn
    over 1f out: one pce) .......................................... 1½.4
1905 Miss Bell Ringer **(35)** *(CJHill)* 4–8-4 NAdams (13) (hdwy 3f out: 6th st: r.o one
    pce fnl 2f) ................................................. ½.5
1950⁵ Bishopstone Bill **(31)** *(SMellor)* 3–7-7 DanaMellor (8) (bmpd over 2f out: 5th st:
    one pce fnl 2f) ............................................ 1½.6
2032⁴ Mu-Arrik **(52)** *(DAWilson)* 4–9-0 ‡7SharonMillard (11) (b: no hdwy fnl 2f) ........ s.h.7
1978⁶ Pine Glen Pepper **(31)** (bl) *(JAkehurst)* 4–8-0 DHolland (4) (lw: nvr nrr) .......... s.h.8
1811★ Old Comrades **(56)** *(LGCottrell)* 5–9-11 TRogers (12) (b.nr hind: nvr nr to chal) hd.9
1952⁵ Pearl Ransom **(50)** *(WGRWightman)* 5–9-5 JWilliams (15) (lw: a bhd) ............ 8.10
2050⁴ Lawnswood Prince (IRE) **(52)** *(JLSpearing)* 3–9-0 WNewnes (10) (lw: bhd fnl 3f) 3.11
1975⁵ Bright Sea (USA) **(42)** *(WRWilliams)* 4–8-11 NHowe (7) (lw: a bhd) .............. 1.12
    LONG HANDICAP: Bishopstone Bill 7-5.

**9/4** PROFIT A PRENDRE, **5/1** Old Comrades, **7/1** Teanarco (IRE), Miss Bell Ringer(op 12/1), **8/1** Mu-Arrik(op 9/2), Pearl Ransom, **10/1** Barlogan, Spanish Love, **14/1** Pine Glen Pepper, **20/1** Ors. CSF £26.88, CT £180.74. Tote £2.50: £1.10 £5.90 £3.50 (£25.50). Mr Peter Thorne (EPSOM) bred by Exors of the late Miss E. B. Rigden. 12 Rn                                                        1m 26.9 (5.3)
                                 SF—36/34/5/32/6/–

## 2255

COOMES H'CAP (0-80) £3028.00 (£904.00: £432.00: £196.00)    **1½m**    3-45 (3-46)

1163⁴ **Bold Resolution (IRE) (51)** *(CACyzer)* 4–8-9 GCarter (5) (rdn 3f out: 4th st: led
    ins fnl f: r.o wl) ................................................. —1
2109³ Sharp Top **(51)** *(MJRyan)* 4–8-9 DBiggs (9) (a.p: led over 2f out tl ins fnl f:
    unable qckn) ................................................. 1½.2
2077★ Shamshom Al Arab (IRE) **(39)** *(WCarter)* 4–7-4 (4x) ‡7CHawksley (2) (lw: 6th st:
    hdwy over 1f out: r.o) ......................................... hd.3
    Antico Nativo (IRE) **(55)** *(SDow)* 4–8-13 TQuinn (1) (3rd st: hrd rdn over 1f out:
    one pce) ................................................. 1.4
1859★ Spectacular Dawn **(79)** *(JLDunlop)* 3–9-11 JReid (3) (lw: led over 9f: 2nd
    st: wknd over 1f out) ......................................... 2½.5
2054 Bee Beat **(60)** (bl) *(EAWheeler)* 4–9-4 WNewnes (4) (lw: nvr nr to chal) .......... 2½.6
*1324* Midday Show (USA) **(56)** (bl) *(JRJenkins)* 5–9-0 LDettori (8) (rdn over 3f out:
    5th st: wknd 2f out) ......................................... 12.7
2054 Snickersnee **(66)** *(MDixon)* 4–9-10 DaleGibson (6) (lw: a bhd) ....................... 12.8
1976⁴ Loki (IRE) **(70)** *(GLewis)* 4–9-9 ‡5DHarrison (10) (lw: bhd fnl 4f: sddle slipped) s.h.9

**5/2** Spectacular Dawn, **100/30** Sharp Top, **9/2** Shamshom Al Arab (IRE)(op 3/1), BOLD RESOLUTION (IRE), **6/1** Loki (IRE), **14/1** Midday Show (USA), Antico Nativo (IRE)(op 7/1), **25/1** Bee Beat, **33/1** Snickersnee. CSF £19.87, CT £66.58. Tote £6.90: £1.60 £1.20 £1.90 (£9.10). Mr R. M. Cyzer (HORSHAM) bred by G. O'Brien in Ireland. 9 Rn                                                        2m 41.6 (8.1)
                              SF—26/21/1/22/29/17

**2256**    E.B.F. COOMES STKS (Mdn 2-Y.O) £2406.00 (£666.00: £318.00)    5f    4-15 (4-16)

1208 **Second Chance (IRE)** *(PMitchell)* 9-0 PatEddery (2) (lw: mde virtually all: hrd
rdn over 1f out: r.o wl) ........................................................ —1
1536[6] **Play Hever Golf (Fav)** *(TJNaughton)* 9-0 GCarter (4) (a.p: ev ch ins fnl f: unable
qckn) ........................................................................ 2.2
1946 Kildee Lad *(APJones)* 9-0 NAdams (6) (lw: hld up: rdn over 3f out: one pce) .. 3½.3
1937 Aalu (IRE) *(CEBrittain)* 8-9 MRoberts (7) (w wnr: ev ch whn hung rt over 2f out:
one pce) .................................................................... s.h.4
1946[5] Bellsabanging *(DRLaing)* 9-0 TyroneWilliams (8) (hld up: hrd rdn over 1f out:
one pce) .................................................................... 1.5
Recipdico Mist (IRE) *(TJNaughton)* 8-4 ‡[5]DHarrison (5) (unf: s.s: a bhd) ......... 2½.6

**7/4** Play Hever Golf, **2/1** Bellsabanging(5/2—3/1), **4/1** Aalu (IRE), SECOND CHANCE (IRE), **25/1** Ors. CSF
£11.48, Tote £4.90: £2.30 £1.40 (£5.60). Down and Outs Racing (EPSOM) bred by Michael G. O'Brien in Ireland.
6 Rn                                                  60.9 sec (2.1)
SF—43/35/21/15/16/–

**2257**    COOMES NURSERY   £2660.00 (£735.00: £350.00)    5f    4-45 (4-46)

2080[5] **Wealthywoo** (bl) *(JSMoore)* 7-8[(1)] JQuinn (2) (lw: led over 3f: hrd rdn: led nr fin)   —1
1422* **Aberlady (Fav)** *(MAJarvis)* 8-11 ‡[5]KRutter (5) (hld up: led over 1f out: hrd rdn:
hdd nr fin) ................................................................. nk.2
1969[2] Sea Exhibition (IRE) *(MBlanshard)* 9-0 GCarter (4) (w wnr: ev ch ins fnl f: r.o) ... ½.3
1171[2] Mr Nevermind (IRE) *(GLewis)* 9-7 BRouse (3) (swvd rt s: a bhd) ........................ 6.4
LONG HANDICAP: Wealthywoo 7-0.

**8/11** Aberlady(op 5/4), **5/2** Sea Exhibition (IRE), **4/1** Mr Nevermind (IRE)(op 2/1), **8/1** WEALTHYWOO(4/1—10/
1). CSF £14.87, Tote £7.20 (£5.60). Mr G. A. Bosley (ANDOVER) bred by G. A. Bosley and T. H. Clarkin. 4 Rn
61.7 sec (2.9)
SF—7/23/24/13

**2258**    COOMES SENIOR CITIZENS STKS (3-Y.O)   *(6f 189y)*   5-15 - **Abandoned**—
Insufficient entries

T/Plpt: £33.90 (99.65 Tckts).                                                   AK

1958—**REDCAR (L-H)**
## Wednesday, July 22nd [Good to firm]
Going Allowance: minus 0.20 sec per fur (F)                                Wind: almost nil

Stalls: high

**2259**    ANIMAL HEALTH TRUST (S) STKS (2-Y.O) £2511.00 (£696.00: £333.00)
7f                                                6-30 (6-31)

1900 **Arctic Guest (IRE)** *(MJohnston)* 8-6 DMcKeown (1) (hdwy ½-wy: sn prom: led
& edgd rt appr fnl f: kpt on) ......................................... —1
1900[3] Merry Mermaid *(JFBottomley)* 8-6 PBurke (4) (lw: w ldr: rdn over 2f out: n.m.r
over 1f out: hung u.p & unable qckn ins fnl f) ................... 1½.2
2112* Hi Nod (Fav) *(MJCamacho)* 8-11 NConnorton (6) (lw: led: rdn & edgd lft over 2f
out: hdd appr fnl f: hmpd & snatched up nr fin) ................. 2.3
2112 Sevinch *(MWEasterby)* 7-13 ‡[7]JMarshall (3) (chsd ldrs tl edgd lft & wknd 3f out) 10.4
2098 Jasilu *(MWEasterby)* 8-6 TLucas (2) (prom early: hung lft & wl outpcd fr ½-wy) hd.5
2112 Touch N' Glow *(NTinkler)* 8-6 MBirch (5) (virtually ref to r: a wl t.o) ................ 30.6

**4/9** Hi Nod(op 4/6), **4/1** Merry Mermaid, **5/1** Touch N' Glow, **12/1** ARCTIC GUEST (IRE)(6/1—14/1), **50/1** Ors.
CSF £54.82, Tote £16.50: 4.30 £2.00 (£49.10). The Fairyhouse 1992 Partnership (MIDDLEHAM) bred by
Swettenham Stud in Ireland. 6 Rn; No bid                                   1m 25.6 (3.4)
SF—20/15/14/–/–/–

**2260**    NORTHERN UPHOLSTERY FURNITURE GROUP H'CAP (0-80) £3200.00 (£950.00:
£450.00: £200.00)   **1m 1f**                                  7-00 (7-00)

1968[3] **Doctor's Remedy (36)** *(MrsJJordan)* 6-7-0 ‡[7]KimMcDonnell (1) (hld up: stdy
hdwy on outside over 3f out: led over 1f out: edgd lft: r.o) .. —1
1954* Redisham (79) *(JHMGosden)* 8-9 PaulEddery (2) (lw: chsd ldr: led 3f out:
hung lft: hdd over 1f out: kpt on nr fin) ......................... ¾.2
2065[2] Jazilah (FR) (64) (Fav) *(MrsGRReveley)* 4-9-7 MBirch (5) (chsd ldrs: rdn & ev
ch over 2f out: r.o ins fnl f) ........................................ 1.3

1700 Mindomica **(60)** *(MBell)* 3–8–8 MHills (3) (hld up: hdwy on bit 3f out: sn ev ch: led briefly over 1f out: unable qckn) ...................................... **1.4**
1692 American Hero **(71)** *(CTinkler)* 4–9–9 ‡5SMaloney (4) (led: qcknd appr st: hdd 3f out: sn btn & eased) ...................................... **25.5**
LONG HANDICAP: Doctor's Remedy 7-1.

**11/8** Jazilah (FR), **5/2** Redisham, **7/2** Mindomica, **8/1** American Hero, **14/1** DOCTOR'S REMEDY. CSF £44.16, Tote £11.00: £2.80 £1.20 (£9.70). Mr J. O. Addison (LAMBOURN) bred by Miss R. Jeffreys. 5 Rn
1m 52.7 (3.7)
SF—–/29/20/4/–

## 2261
A.F. BUDGE H'CAP (0-70) £3200.00 (£950.00: £450.00: £200.00)
**2m 4y**    7-30 (7-31)

1802* **Broctune Grey (64)** *(MrsGRReveley)* 8–9–13 KDarley (4) (lw: hld up: gd hdwy over 3f out: led 2f out: sn clr: drvn out) ...................................... **—1**
2120* Sexy Mover **(31)** *(Fav)* *(WStorey)* 5–7–5(1) (5x) ‡3JFanning (5) (chsd ldrs: effrt 4f out: chal 3f out: no ex w wnr) ...................................... **3½.2**
21206 Rexy Boy **(30)** *(WLBarker)* 5–7–7 JLowe (6) (led: rdn over 3f out: hdd & no ex 2f out) ...................................... **nk.3**
288 Arctic Oats **(46)** *(WWHaigh)* 7–8–9 DMcKeown (3) (chsd ldr: rdn 3f out: grad wknd fnl 2f) ...................................... **¾.4**
683 Dodger Dickins **(37)** *(RHollinshead)* 5–7–7 ‡7AGarth (1) (bhd: pushed along 7f out: styd on fnl 3f: nrst fin) ...................................... **¾.5**
19884 Lyphard's Song (IRE) **(40)** *(NAGraham)* 4–8–3 JQuinn (2) (swtg: trckd ldrs tl rdn & wknd over 3f out) ...................................... **30.6**
LONG HANDICAP: Sexy Mover 7-5.

**11/4** Sexy Mover, **3/1** BROCTUNE GREY, **7/2** Lyphard's Song (IRE), **11/2** Dodger Dickins, **8/1** Rexy Boy, **9/1** Arctic Oats. CSF £10.77, Tote £3.20: £1.50 1.80 (£4.50). Mr D. Playforth (SALTBURN) bred by G. Reed. 6 Rn
3m 29.6 (4.6)
SF—35/–/–/–/–/

## 2262
TARMAC H'CAP (0-90) £3200.00 (£950.00: £450.00: £200.00)    **6f**    8-00 (8-00)
(Weights raised 5 lb)

22142 **Densben (76)** *(Fav)* *(DenysSmith)* 8–9–7 KFallon (4) (lw: hld up: gd hdwy to ld jst ins fnl f: drvn out) ...................................... **—1**
2214 Diet **(64)** (bl) *(MissLAPerratt)* 6–8–4 ‡5NKennedy (3) (led: rdn 2f out: hdd jst ins fnl f: unable qckn) ...................................... **1½.2**
22146 Profilic **(75)** *(CaptJWilson)* 7–9–6 WRyan (2) (chsd ldrs: edgd lft over 1f out: sn outpcd) ...................................... **3.3**
20004 Love Jazz (USA) **(85)** *(TDBarron)* 3–9–10 KDarley (1) (lw: prom tl grad wknd over 1f out) ...................................... **5.4**

**4/6** DENSBEN, **3/1** Profilic, **5/1** Love Jazz (USA), **15/2** Diet. CSF £5.45, Tote £1.50 (£3.80). Mrs Janet M. Pike (BISHOP AUCKLAND) bred by D. W. Pike. 4 Rn
1m 10.7 (1.4)
SF—55/32/36/20

## 2263
POLYPIPE STKS (Mdn) £2070.00 (£570.00: £270.00)    **1m**    8-30 (8-34)

**Nile Delta (IRE)** *(Fav)* *(HRACecil)* 3–8–13 WRyan (3) (str: w'like: bit bkwd: a.p: rdn to ld appr fnl f: drvn out) ...................................... **—1**
11736 Cachou (USA) **(69)** *(JHMGosden)* 3–8–8 PaulEddery (1) (chsd ldrs: rdn & ev ch 2f out: kpt on u.p fnl f) ...................................... **nk.2**
19584 Tathir (CAN) *(DMorley)* 4–9–7 MBirch (2) (b: b.hind: led: rdn 2f out: hdd appr fnl f: no ex) ...................................... **1½.3**
1673 Premier Major (IRE) **(42)** *(BBeasley)* 3–9–0(1) DNicholls (4) (hld up in tch tl grad lost pl fnl 2f) ...................................... **8.4**
Mini Fete (FR) *(JParkes)* 3–8–8 JFortune (5) (unf: bit bkwd: rn green & sn pushed along: outpcd over 3f out: sn bhd) ...................................... **1½.5**

**4/6** NILE DELTA (IRE), **13/8** Cachou (USA), **12/1** Tathir (CAN), **40/1** Premier Major (IRE), **50/1** Mini Fete (FR). CSF £2.04, Tote £1.70: £1.10 £1.10 (£1.40). Mrs H. G. Cambanis (NEWMARKET) bred by Stilvi Compania Financiera S A in Ireland. 5 Rn
1m 40 (5)

## 2264
D.F.S. AUCTION STKS (Mdn 2-Y.O) £2070.00 (£570.00: £270.00)    **5f**    9-00 (9-02)

19103 **Rhett's Choice** *(Fav)* *(JBerry)* 7-8 ‡3JFanning (8) (lw: s.s: sn rdn: hdwy over 1f out: swtchd ins & styd on strly to ld nr fin) ...................................... **—1**
21024 Heart Broken *(JGFitzGerald)* 8-6 KFallon (3) (lw: hdwy ½-wy: rdn to ld & edgd rt ins fnl f: hdd nr fin) ...................................... **1.2**
19912 The Bethanian *(WRMuir)* 7-13 JQuinn (2) (b.hind: led: rdn over 1f out: hung lft & hdd ins fnl f: no ex) ...................................... **¾.3**

2207² **Dead Calm** *(CTinkler)* 7-8 ‡⁵SMaloney (7) (prom: rdn & ev ch whn nt clr run ins
　　　　　fnl f: nt rcvr) ........................................................................ 1¹/₂.4
1969⁵ Sweet Poppy *(JSWainwright)* 7-8 LCharnock (6) (nvr trbld ldrs) .............. 3¹/₂.5
1963⁴ Arkendale Diamond (USA) (bl) *(BBeasley)* 8-4 ‡⁷SWilliams (1) (rdn & hung bdly
　　　　　rt fnl 2f: sn wknd) ....................................................................... 2.6
1251 Sky Wish *(MissSEHall)* 8-0(1) KDarley (5) (sn wl bhd: sme hdwy fnl f) .............. 1¹/₂.7
1531⁶ Chicago (IRE) *(CTinkler)* 8-8 MBirch (4) (bhd fr ¹/₂-wy) .............. 3.8

**15/8 RHETT'S CHOICE, 9/4** The Bethanian, **6/1** Heart Broken, **8/1** Sky Wish, **10/1** Dead Calm, **12/1** Chicago
(IRE), **14/1** Arkendale Diamond (USA), **50/1** Sweet Poppy. CSF £12.74, Tote £2.90: £1.10 £2.10 (£11.30). Mrs
J. M. Bradford-Nutter (COCKERHAM) bred by J. R. C. and Mrs Wren. 8 Rn　　　　58.6 sec (1.9)
　　　　　　　　　　　　　　　　　　　　　　　　　　　　　　　SF—22/30/20/9/–/–

T/Plpt: £77.70 (18.5 Tckts).　　　　　　　　　　　　　　　　　　　　　　　　　　　O'R

## 2124—SANDOWN (R-H)

### Wednesday, July 22nd [Good, Good to soft patches]

Going Allowance: 0.25 sec per fur (G)　　　　　　　　　　　　　　Wind: almost nil

Stalls: low

**2265**　　BROOKLANDS CLAIMING STKS (3-Y.O) £2630.00 (£730.00: £350.00)
　　　　　**5f 6y**　　　　　　　　　　　　　　　　　　　　　　　6-20 (6-23)

2179² **Walk In the Park (81)** (Fav) *(RSimpson)* 7-10 ‡⁵ATucker (1) (rdn over 3f out: nt
　　　　　clr run over 1f out: rapid hdwy to ld ins fnl f: easily) .............. —1
1999⁴ Another Episode (IRE) **(96)** *(JBerry)* 9-0 JCarroll (5) (lw: led: clr 3f out: hdd ins
　　　　　fnl f: unable qckn) ....................................................................... 3.2
2131⁴ Spell of the Yukon (USA) **(72)** *(IABalding)* 8-9 JReid (3) (rdn over 2f out: nvr nr
　　　　　to chal) ...................................................................................... 6.3
1708 Mansber (IRE) **(54)** (bl) *(PatMitchell)* 7-13 ‡⁵DHarrison (4) (swtg: rdn & no hdwy
　　　　　fnl 2f) ...................................................................................... ¹/₂.4
Little Saboteur **(76)** (bl) *(PJMakin)* 7-11 AMunro (2) (chsd ldr over 3f) .............. 4.5

**11/10 WALK IN THE PARK, 11/4** Another Episode (IRE), **9/2** Little Saboteur, **6/1** Spell of the Yukon
(USA)(4/1—8/1), **33/1** Mansber (IRE). CSF £4.28, Tote £2.10: £1.10 £1.70 (£2.70). Mr M. J. Lewin (FOXHILL)
bred by Rodney Meredith. 5 Rn　　　　　　　　　　　　　　　　　　63.14 sec (3.64)
　　　　　　　　　　　　　　　　　　　　　　　　　　　　　　　SF—34/40/11/–/–

**2266**　　RACING SCHOOLS APP'CE H'CAP (3-Y.O) (0-70) £2532.00 (£702.00: £336.00)
　　　　　**1m 14y**　　　　　　　　　　　　　　　　　　　　　　6-50 (6-55)

1428⁵ **Cap Camarat (CAN) (50)** *(PFICole)* 8-2 DBiggs (12) (swtg: 6th st: led 1f out:
　　　　　rdn out) ..................................................................................... —1
1947 Emaura **(56)** *(KOCunningham-Brown)* 8-2 ‡⁶MBressington (10) (led 7f: unable
　　　　　qckn) ........................................................................................ 3¹/₂.2
2128² Magnetic Point (USA) **(58)** *(AAScott)* 8-10 JTate (3) (swtg: 4th st: ev ch 1f out:
　　　　　one pce) .................................................................................... s.h.3
2041³ Missy-S (IRE) **(53)** *(GAPritchard-Gordon)* 8-5 DHarrison (8) (lw: rdn over 3f out:
　　　　　nt clr run over 1f out: hdwy fnl f: r.o) ............................ 2¹/₂.4
1954⁴ Systematic **(62)** (Fav) *(RHannon)* 8-8 ‡⁶MarkDenaro (4) (nvr nr to chal) .............. nk.5
Mr Tate (IRE) **(60)** *(RAkehurst)* 8-9 ‡³LCarter (7) (w'like: 5th st: one pce fnl 2f) . hd.6
1767⁵ Rio Trusky **(42)** *(MDIUsher)* 7-8(1) ATucker (1) (3rd st: wknd over 1f out) .............. ³/₄.7
1917⁴ Headless Heights **(65)** *(PMitchell)* 9-3 JWeaver (2) (lw: s.s: nvr nrr) .............. 2.8
1142 Wrycrest **(50)** *(RCharlton)* 7-10 ‡⁶RhonaGent (5) (a bhd) .............. 1¹/₂.9
1956⁴ Mere Chants **(69)** *(DRCElsworth)* 9-1 ‡⁶RossBerry (9) (hdwy on ins whn hmpd
　　　　　2f out & over 1f out: nt rcvr) ........................................... nk.10
2078⁴ Marvelous Molly **(62)** *(IABalding)* 8-8 ‡⁶DGriffiths (6) (2nd st: wknd wl over 1f
　　　　　out) .......................................................................................... 8.11
2079 Tulapet **(46)** *(SDow)* 7-9 ‡³AMartinez (11) (lw: a bhd) ........................ 10.12
　　　　　　　　LONG HANDICAP: Rio Trusky 7-2.

**3/1 Systematic, 9/2** Magnetic Point (USA), **6/1** Missy-S (IRE)(op 7/2), **7/1** Headless Heights, **15/2** CAP
CAMARAT (CAN), **8/1** Mere Chants, **12/1** Mr Tate (IRE)(op 8/1), Emaura, **20/1** Wrycrest, Marvelous Molly, Rio
Trusky, **33/1** Tulapet. CSF £87.82, CT £417.95. Tote £8.60: £2.30 £4.50 £1.80 (£71.50). Mr Fahd Salman
(WHATCOMBE) bred by Donald Phillip and Reid Esplin in Canada. 12 Rn　　　1m 44.62 (5.42)
　　　　　　　　　　　　　　　　　　　　　　　　　　　　　　SF—37/26/33/20/22/22

**2267**　　FAREBROTHER H'CAP (0-80) £2921.00 (£878.00: £424.00: £197.00)
　　　　　**1³/₄m**　　　　　　　　　　　　　　　　　　　　　　7-20 (7-22)

2129⁴ **Intricacy (56)** *(CCElsey)* 4-8-11 MRoberts (1) (2nd st: led over 3f out: r.o wl) ... —1

2083⁵ Scent of Battle **(41)** *(MJHaynes)* 4–7-10(3) WCarson (5) (lw: led 4f: 3rd st: hrd rdn over 1f out: unable qckn) .......... 2¹/₂.2

2083* Newton Point **(72)** (bl) *(Fav) (GAPritchard-Gordon)* 3–8-13 (4x) RCochrane (10) (plld hrd: 6th st: n.m.r over 2f out: hdwy fnl f: r.o) ...... 1¹/₂.3

2071² Samain (USA) **(48)** *(JAGlover)* 5–8-3 NCarlisle (4) (lw: rdn over 3f out: hdwy over 1f out: r.o) ...... s.h.4

1521⁴ Empire Blue **(65)** *(PFICole)* 9–9-6 TQuinn (8) (b: nvr nr to chal) .......... ¹/₂.5

2129² Manzoor Sayadan (USA) **(66)** *(RSimpson)* 4–9-2 ‡5ATucker (9) (5th st: one pce fnl 3f) .......... nk.6

2235⁶ Pondered Bid **(40)** (bl) *(PatMitchell)* 8–7-9(2) DBiggs (3) (b: nvr nrr) .......... 3.7

1879⁴ Kaytak (FR) **(68)** *(JRJenkins)* 5–9-9 PatEddery (2) (nvr nrr) .......... nk.8

2083⁴ Puff Puff **(50)** *(MissBSanders)* 6–8-5 GCarter (11) (4th st: wknd 2f out) .......... 1¹/₂.9

Mount Nelson **(69)** *(DWPArbuthnot)* 6–9-10 JReid (7) (b: b.nr hind: bit bkwd: led 10f out tl over 3f out: sn wknd) .......... 2.10

2033 Cathos (FR) **(55)** *(DAWilson)* 7–8-10 BRouse (6) (b: a bhd) .......... 1¹/₂.11

LONG HANDICAP: Pondered Bid 7-5.

**4/1** Newton Point, **5/1** Manzoor Sayadan (USA), Samain (USA), **11/2** Kaytak (FR), **7/1** Empire Blue, **8/1** INTRICACY, **9/1** Scent of Battle, **10/1** Cathos (FR), Puff Puff, **25/1** Pondered Bid, **33/1** Mount Nelson. CSF £75.27, CT £307.89. Tote £9.50: £2.40 £3.80 £2.10 (£58.00). Mr Richard Berenson (LAMBOURN) bred by Lavinia Duchess of Norfolk. 11 Rn                                              3m 7.88 (13.18)

---

**2268**  SURREY RACING H'CAP (0-100) £3171.00 (£948.00: £454.00: £207.00)
7f 16y                                                                                    7-50 (7-51)

2126² **Dream Carrier (IRE) (65)** (Jt-Fav) *(RHannon)* 4–8-5(1) PatEddery (2) (lw: 5th st: led 2f out: rdn out) .......... —1

2060⁴ Across the Bay **(76)** (v) *(SDow)* 5–9-2 TQuinn (7) (3rd st: ev ch wl over 1f out: unable qckn) .......... 3¹/₂.2

2191 Euro Festival **(90)** (Jt-Fav) *(MissLCSiddall)* 3–9-4 (5x) ‡5DHarrison (5) (lw: hdwy wl over 1f out: one pce) .......... ¹/₂.3

1755* Cape Pigeon (USA) **(88)** *(LGCottrell)* 7–10-0 AMunro (1) (lw: 2nd st: led 3f out to 2f out: one pce) .......... 2.4

832 Prince of the Sea (IRE) **(84)** *(DWPArbuthnot)* 4–9-10 BProcter (3) (b: 6th st: nvr nr to chal) .......... 3¹/₂.5

1870 Spanish Miner (USA) **(82)** (bl) *(AAScott)* 3–9-1 WRSwinburn (6) (lw: led 4f) ..... 10.6

1926 Sylvan Sabre (IRE) **(89)** *(PMitchell)* 3–9-8 MRoberts (4) (4th st: wknd over 2f out) .. 7.7

**9/4** Euro Festival(5/2—6/4), DREAM CARRIER (IRE), **9/2** Cape Pigeon (USA), **7/1** Spanish Miner (USA)(op 12/1), **9/1** Across the Bay, **12/1** Sylvan Sabre (IRE), **33/1** Prince of the Sea (IRE). CSF £19.70, Tote £2.50: £1.70 £3.20 (£10.70). Mrs J. Reglar (MARLBOROUGH) bred by Mellon Stud in Ireland. 7 Rn            1m 31.14 (4.14)
SF—55/55/55/59/44/5

---

**2269**  TRAVIS PERKINS STKS (Mdn 2-Y.O) £2840.00 (£790.00: £380.00)
7f 16y                                                                                   8-20 (8-24)

1925⁶ **Mukhamedov** *(HRACecil)* 9-0 PatEddery (8) (lw: 3rd st: led ins fnl f: rdn out) .... —1

1469 Ihtiraz (Fav) *(HThomsonJones)* 9-0 RHills (5) (swtg: 5th st: led over 1f out tl ins fnl f: unable qckn) .......... 1¹/₂.2

470 Anaheim (IRE) *(RHannon)* 9-0 JReid (1) (led over 5f: one pce) .......... 4.3

1342 Gold Tassel *(RHannon)* 8-6 ‡3RPerham (9) (dwlt: 6th st: rdn over 2f out: one pce) .......... 3¹/₂.4

1709⁶ Range Rider (IRE) *(CEBrittain)* 9-0 MRoberts (10) (no hdwy fnl 2f) .......... 1¹/₂.5

Seren Quest *(AWDenson)* 8-9 WNewnes (2) (unf: led bkwd: s.s: nvr nrr) .......... 1¹/₂.6

1595³ Greystoke *(LordHuntingdon)* 9-0 WRSwinburn (6) (4th st: wknd over 2f out) .......... 4.7

Juliasdarkinvader *(AMoore)* 9-0 CandyMorris (7) (w'like: bkwd: 2nd st: wknd over 2f out) .......... 1.8

2167 Boisterous *(WRMuir)* 9-0 AMunro (4) (lw: a bhd) .......... 7.9

1610 Dark and Stormy *(MDixon)* 8-9 ‡5ATucker (3) (dwlt: a bhd) .......... 10

**6/5** Ihtiraz(6/4—Evens), **11/4** Greystoke, **7/2** MUKHAMEDOV(7/4—4/1), **10/1** Range Rider (IRE), **12/1** Anaheim (IRE)(14/1—8/1), **20/1** Gold Tassel, **50/1** Boisterous, **66/1** Ors. CSF £8.10, Tote £4.60: £1.60 £1.20 £2.10 (£3.70). Mr David St. George (NEWMARKET) bred by Side Hill Stud and The Duke of Roxburghe's Stud. 10 Rn            1m 32.23 (5.23)
SF—48/43/31/15/15/5

---

**2270**  LBC NEWSTALK 97.3 FM STKS (Mdn 3-Y.O.F) £2777.00 (£772.00: £371.00)
1¹/₄m 7y                                                                                 8-50 (8-57)

1953² **Gong** *(PTWalwyn)* 8-11 PatEddery (6) (mde all: qcknd wl over 1f out: pushed out) .......... —1

1315² Goodniteout (IRE) **(80)** *(DRCElsworth)* 8-11 WCarson (5) (lw: 2nd st: rdn over 3f out: no imp) .......... 2¹/₂.2

1843³ Blushing Storm (USA) (Fav) *(JRFanshawe)* 8-11 WRSwinburn (1) (3rd st: rdn over 2f out: one pce) .................................... ¹/₂.3
1611 Shimmer *(LordHuntingdon)* 8-11 JReid (3) (4th st: rdn over 2f out: wknd over 1f out) ............................................................ 8.4
1830² Shahaamh (IRE) *(HThomsonJones)* 8-11 RHills (2) (5th st: rdn over 2f out: wknd over 1f out) ...................................... 7.5
2128 Twice as Much *(DAWilson)* 8-11 WNewnes (4) (lw: 6th st: a bhd: t.o) ................ 25.6

**8/13** Blushing Storm (USA)(tchd Evens), **4/1** Goodniteout (IRE), **13/2** Shahaamh (IRE), **9/1** GONG(op 5/1), **10/1** Shimmer, **100/1** Twice as Much. CSF £40.90, Tote £8.40: £2.30 £1.70 (£10.40). Mr A. D. G. Oldrey (LAMBOURN) bred by Seend Stud. 6 Rn　　　　　　　　　　2m 10.62 (6.32)
SF—59/54/52/36/22/–

T/Trio: Race 3: £224.30 (8.1 Tckts). T/Plpt: £124.10 (37.65 Tckts).　　　　　　　AK

## 1660—DONCASTER (L-H)
### Wednesday, July 22nd [Good]
Going Allowance: minus 0.15 sec per fur (F)　　　　　　　Wind: almost nil

Stalls: high

**2271**　STAR SUPPORTS SUNDAY RACING STKS (2-Y.O) £3483.00 (£963.00: £459.00)
　　　　**5f**　　　　　　　　　　　　　　　　　　　　2-30 (2-31)

2161★ Night Melody (IRE) (Fav) *(RHannon)* 9-7 KDarley (3) (hld up: stdy hdwy to ld ins fnl f: comf) .............................................. —1
2161³ Nominator *(RHollinshead)* 9-4 WRSwinburn (2) (lw: cl up: led over 1f out tl ins fnl f: nt pce of wnr) ........................................ 1.2
1004⁴ Area Girl *(SirMarkPrescott)* 9-2 GDuffield (1) (led tl hdd over 1f out: sn btn) ....... 5.3

**4/7** NIGHT MELODY (IRE), **5/2** Area Girl, **6/1** Nominator. CSF £3.33, Tote £1.40 (£2.60). Mr P. D. Savill (MARLBOROUGH) bred by Leo Collins in Ireland. 3 Rn　　　　　60.70 sec (2)
SF—51/44/22

**2272**　DONCASTER EXHIBITION CENTRE SUNDAY RACING (S) STKS (3 & 4-Y.O) £2385.00
　　　　(£660.00: £315.00)　**1¹/₂m**　　　　　　　　　3-00 (3-01)

2155★ **Iron Baron** (IRE) (57) (Fav) *(RHollinshead)* 3-8-13 SPerks (5) (a gng wl: led on bit wl over 1f out: shkn up & qcknd clr) ............................ —1
2128 Kentucky Chicken (USA) (30) (bl) *(MissLCSiddall)* 3-8-4 DMcKeown (7) (w ldr: led ent st: hdd wl over 1f out: no ch w wnr) ........................ 10.2
1294 King Optimist (37) *(ASmith)* 3-8-9 SWebster (1) (chsd ldrs: outpcd 5f out: styd on fnl f: no imp) .................................. s.h.3
　　Whitwell Hill *(MrsVAAconley)* 3-8-5⁽¹⁾ KFallon (4) (leggy: unf: dwlt: sn prom: outpcd 4f out: n.d after) .......................... 6.4
1739 Dancing Tudor (40) (v) *(THCaldwell)* 4-9-4 ‡³JFanning (2) (led tl hdd ent st: wknd over 3f out) ........................................ 4.5
1864⁶ Janeswood (IRE) (28) *(JParkes)* 4-9-2 LCharnock (3) (prom tl rdn & wknd 4f out) ................................................... s.h.6
1906 Indian Heather (IRE) *(JParkes)* 4-8-11 ‡⁵OPears (6) (b: effrt u.p 4f out: n.d) ..... 12.7

**1/3** IRON BARON (IRE), **10/1** King Optimist, **12/1** Dancing Tudor(op 8/1), Whitwell Hill, **14/1** Kentucky Chicken (USA), **20/1** Janeswood (IRE), **25/1** Indian Heather (IRE). CSF £6.21, Tote £1.40: £1.30 £3.00 (£5.30). Mrs B. Facchino (UPPER LONGDON) bred by Mrs D. Jackson in Ireland. 7 Rn; No bid　　2m 36.86 (6.26)
SF—18/–/–/–/–/–

**2273**　WARDS SHEFFIELD BEST BITTER H'CAP (0-80) £3465.00 (£1035.00: £495.00:
　　　　£225.00)　**1¹/₄m 60y**　　　　　　　　　　3-30 (3-33)
　　　　　　　　　　(Weights raised 10 lb)

1922⁶ **Sinclair Lad** (IRE) (53) *(RHollinshead)* 4-8-13 KDarley (7) (hld up & bhd: stdy hdwy 3f out: r.o u.p to ld wl ins fnl f) ............................ —1
　　Top Villain (33) *(BSRothwell)* 6-7-7 JQuinn (2) (prom tl lost pl appr st: hdwy 3f out: n.m.r & styd on wl fnl f) .............................. 1¹/₂.2
2166² Mingus (USA) (57) *(MrsJRRamsden)* 5-9-3 MBirch (6) (swtg: trckd ldrs: hung lft fnl 3f: led appr fnl f: hrd rdn & no ex nr fin) .................. s.h.3
1721⁴ Supertop (57) *(PWHarris)* 4-9-3 WRSwinburn (4) (lw: hld up: hdwy over 3f out: rdn & one pce appr fnl f) ........................ 2.4
1673 Bold Ambition (44) *(TKersey)* 5-8-4 AProud (3) (bhd: effrt over 3f out: one pce fnl 2f) ............................................... nk.5
1520⁶ Sharquin (34) *(MBrittain)* 5-7-8⁽¹⁾ JLowe (1) (lw: led 2f: chsd ldrs: led over 3f out tl over 1f out: wknd) .................................. 2.6

1836³ Mardessa **(59)** *(FHLee)* 4–9-5 RLappin (5) (dwlt: hdwy whn nt clr run 3f out: sn rdn & no imp) .................................................. 6.7

1836* Inan (USA) **(74)** (Fav) *(JLDunlop)* 3–9-10 WCarson (9) (lw: hdwy & prom appr st: wandered 3f out: sn wknd) .......................... 2½.8

2026⁵ Stylish Gent **(51)** (bl) *(NTinkler)* 5–8-11 LCharnock (8) (led after 2f tl ovr 3f out: sn lost pl) ............................................. 12.9

LONG HANDICAP: Top Villain 7-4.

**3/1** Inan (USA), **7/2** Mingus (USA), **4/1** Supertop, **5/1** Mardessa, **15/2** SINCLAIR LAD (IRE), **12/1** Sharquin, **14/1** Top Villain, **20/1** Stylish Gent, **33/1** Bold Ambition. CSF £90.19, CT £391.34. Tote £9.30: £2.30 £3.70 £1.60 (£127.50). Sinclair Developments Limited (UPPER LONGDON) bred by John Burns in Ireland. 9 Rn
2m 10.41 (3.41)
SF—50/27/50/46/32/18

**2274**    TATTERSALLS AUCTION SERIES STKS (Qualifier) (Mdn 2-Y.O) £3262.00 (£976.00: £468.00: £214.00)  **6f**                      4-00 (4-04)

2130⁶ **Heavenly Risk** *(RHannon)* 8-5 PatEddery (1) (lw: trckd ldrs: led wl over 1f out: rdn & r.o wl) .............................. —1

2024⁴ Silverlocks *(MissSEHall)* 8-7 NConnorton (7) (a chsng ldrs: effrt 2f out: styd on: nt pce of wnr) .................................. 2½.2

1571⁴ Look Who's Here (IRE) *(BAMcMahon)* 8-7 WCarson (3) (lw: a chsng ldrs: nt qckn fnl f) ...................................... 1½.3

2124² Racing Telegraph (Fav) *(JPearce)* 8-0 ‡5RPrice (14) (led tl hdd wl over 1f out: nt qckn) .............................. 2½.4

2049⁵ Fort Vally *(BWMurray)* 8-3 DMcKeown (6) (a in tch centre: kpt on one pce fnl 2f) 2½.5

1991⁴ Troon *(MrsLPiggott)* 8-11 JWilliams (5) (b.hind: racd centre: in tch: styd on fnl 2f) .................................. 3.6

1790⁴ Sweetings Scampy (IRE) *(MHEasterby)* 8-4 MBirch (4) (mid div: sme hdwy 2f out: n.d) ................................ 1½.7

*1375³* Dontbetalking (IRE) *(JWharton)* 7-12 ‡3JFanning (13) (lw: hld up: swtchd & sme hdwy 2f out: nvr nr to chal) ............... 1½.8

1571 Birchwood Sun *(RHollinshead)* 8-1 ‡7MHumphries (2) (prom 4f) ................... hd.9

7015 Folly Vision (IRE) *(RHannon)* 8-9 KDarley (12) (cl up 4f: sn lost pl) ............. s.h.10

2024 Scoffera *(NTinkler)* 8-3 LCharnock (10) (bit bkwd: bhd: sme hdwy ½-wy: sn wknd) .......................... 2.11

1923⁶ Oxrib *(CTinkler)* 8-6 TLucas (11) (dwlt: a bhd) .......................... ½.12

Fergus Garber *(JMCarr)* 8-7 SMorris (9) (cmpt: bkwd: a bhd) ............ nk.13

677⁵ Glow of Hope *(EJAlston)* 8-3 MHills (8) (hld up & plld hrd: nvr nr to chal) ...... s.h.14

**11/8** Racing Telegraph, **4/1** Silverlocks, **9/2** HEAVENLY RISK, **9/1** Troon, **10/1** Look Who's Here (IRE), **12/1** Birchwood Sun, **16/1** Folly Vision (IRE), Dontbetalking (IRE), Fort Vally, Sweetings Scampy (IRE), **20/1** Glow of Hope, **33/1** Ors. CSF £25.87, Tote £5.20: £1.60 £2.10 £2.30 (£10.00). Roldvale Limited (MARLBOROUGH) bred by J. D. Hurd. 14 Rn
1m 13.38 (2.38)
SF—25/17/11/–/–/–

**2275**    TUBORG H'CAP (3-Y.O.F) (0-80) £3494.25 (£1044.00: £499.50: £227.25)  **7f**                     4-30 (4-31)

1928³ **Lady Debra Darley (78)** (Fav) *(RHannon)* 9-6 PatEddery (2) (lw: trckd ldrs: rdn wl over 1f out: rdn & hld on wl) .............................. —1

1277* Fen Dance (IRE) **(79)** *(PJMakin)* 9-7 WRSwinburn (3) (lw: trckd ldrs: effrt 2f out: r.o wl) .................................... ¾.2

2062² Be My Everything (IRE) **(63)** *(RHollinshead)* 8-5 KDarley (5) (swtg: hld up: hdwy 2f out: r.o wl fnl f) .............................. 1½.3

2029² Devon Dancer **(75)** (v) *(MHEasterby)* 9-3 MBirch (4) (led over 5f: put head in air: sn btn) .............................. 5.4

1961 Battuta **(52)** *(REarnshaw)* 7-8(1) AMackay (1) (prom over 4f) ............... nk.5

2117² Thrie-Na-Helah (IRE) **(73)** (v) *(RMWhitaker)* 9-1 ACulhane (7) (hld up: effrt over 2f out: sn btn) .............................. 2½.6

1281 Baie Petite **(56)** *(AWJones)* 7-7⁽⁵⁾ ‡5NKennedy (6) (cl up 4f: sn lost pl) ............ 15.7

LONG HANDICAP: Baie Petite 7-0.

**11/10** LADY DEBRA DARLEY, **3/1** Fen Dance (IRE), **5/1** Be My Everything (IRE), Devon Dancer, **8/1** Thrie-Na-Helah (IRE), **16/1** Battuta, **50/1** Baie Petite. CSF £5.45, Tote £2.10: £1.40 £2.10 (£3.30). Mrs M. R. T. Rimell (MARLBOROUGH) bred by R. P. Williams. 7 Rn
1m 26.59 (3.19)
SF—43/42/21/18/–/7

**2276**    'COME RACING NEXT SUNDAY' H'CAP (0-90) £3201.75 (£954.00: £454.50: £204.75)  **1m (rnd)**                5-00 (5-01)

2146* **Northern Graduate (USA) (60)** *(MrsGRReveley)* 3–8-5 (7x) KDarley (2) (w ldr: led over 3f out: hung rt: r.o) .............................. —1

Chequers (IRE) **(74)** *(RJRWilliams)* 3–9-5ˉ MHills (6) (hld up: hdwy 3f out: ev ch 1f out: nt qckn) .......... 1.2

2035² Express Service **(81)** (Fav) *(PJMakin)* 3–9-12 WRSwinburn (4) (lw: hld up: effrt whn hmpd over 2f out: lost pl: r.o ins fnl f) ......... nk.3

2184 Queen of Dreams **(40)** *(DrJDScargill)* 4–7-7 JQuinn (3) (hld up: hdwy whn n.m.r over 2f out: swtchd ins: nt qckn fnl f) ......... 1¹/₂.4

1564³ Wessex Milord **(40)** *(JABennett)* 7–7-0 ‡⁷ClaireBalding (5) (b: set stdy pce tl hdd over 3f out: sn wknd) ......... 10.5

LONG HANDICAP: Queen of Dreams 7-6, Wessex Milord 6-7.

**10/11** Express Service, **2/1** NORTHERN GRADUATE (USA)(6/4—9/4), **11/2** Chequers (IRE), **17/2** Queen of Dreams, **40/1** Wessex Milord. CSF £11.85, Tote £2.50: £1.40 £1.80 (£13.10). Mr P. D. Savill (SALTBURN) bred by Ann Trimble & Donald T. Johnson in USA. 5 Rn
1m 41.04 (4.74)
SF—2/13/19/–/–

T/Plpt: £47.10 (89.45 Tckts). AA

# DONCASTER (L-H)
## Thursday, July 23rd [Good]
Going Allowance: minus 0.20 sec per fur (F) Wind: slt half against

Stalls: high

**2277** DONCASTER STALLHOLDERS AUCTION STKS (Mdn 2-Y.O) £1758.00 (£488.00: £234.00) **7f** 6-20 (6-29)

2074² **Chevrotain** (Fav) *(JWWatts)* 9-0 WRyan (16) (lw: chsd ldrs: effrt over 1f out: edgd lft: r.o wl to ld ins fnl f) ......... —1

Drandonhurst *(IABalding)* 9-0 WCarson (2) (w'like: swvd lft s: sn chsng ldrs: led over 1f out: hdd & nt qckn nr fin) ......... nk.2

1630⁵ Rockover *(RHannon)* 9-0 PatEddery (14) (led: rdn & hung lft 2f out: sn hdd: r.o one pce) ......... 5.3

2102 Pine Ridge Lad (IRE) *(BBeasley)* 9-0 DNicholls (12) (in tch: styd on u.p fnl f) ... hd.4

1923³ Cherubini *(JRFanshawe)* 9-0 NCarlisle (9) (lw: trckd ldrs tl outpcd over 1f out) 1¹/₂.5

1965⁵ Buzz-B-Babe *(BEllison)* 9-0 JFortune (1) (chsd ldrs tl wknd 2f out) ......... nk.6

Burning Cost *(GAPritchard-Gordon)* 8-9 NDay (7) (w'like: scope: sn bhd: hdwy over 2f out: nvr nr to chal) ......... 1¹/₂.7

1571² Quick Silver Boy *(DBurchell)* 9-0 CRutter (5) (a chsng ldrs: rdn & one pce fnl 2f) nk.8

Cure the King (IRE) *(SGNorton)* 8-9 ‡⁵OPears (13) (wl grwn: b.hind: rn green & bhd: stdy hdwy ¹/₂-wy: eased whn no ch over 1f out) ......... 3.9

2076 Don't Be Saki (IRE) *(JEtherington)* 8-9 JLowe (10) (w ldrs tl wknd over 2f out) . 5.10

1296 Irish Roots (IRE) *(CTinkler)* 9-0 MBirch (4) (chsd ldrs tl lost pl over 2f out) ......... 4.11

2024 Hyde's Happy Hour *(NTinkler)* 9-0 ABacon (8) (nvr wnt pce) ......... 1¹/₂.12

Certain Way (IRE) *(CTinkler)* 9-0 TLucas (5) (cmpt: str: sn bhd) ......... 1.13

Granderise (IRE) *(NTinkler)* 9-0 LCharnock (3) (s.s: a bhd) ......... 1¹/₂.14

1959 Snug Surprise *(JSWainwright)* 8-2 ‡⁷JMarshall (15) (bhd & hung bdly lft ¹/₂-wy: n.d) ......... 5.15

Bold Reality *(JSWainwright)* 9-0 SPerks (17) (b: w'like: s.s: a in rr) ......... 1.16

Aviator's Dream *(50/1)* Withdrawn (unruly & ref to ent stalls) : not under orders

**Evens** CHEVROTAIN(4/6—5/4), **11/2** Rockover, **8/1** Cherubini, **14/1** Pine Ridge Lad (IRE), Quick Silver Boy, **16/1** Brandonhurst(op 5/1), Cure the King (IRE)(op 10/1), **20/1** Don't Be Saki (IRE), **25/1** Burning Cost, Buzz-B-Babe, **50/1** Ors. CSF £17.47, Tote £1.90: £1.30 £2.30 £2.20 (£10.50). Sheikh Mohammed (RICHMOND) bred by Grange Stud (UK). 16 Rn
1m 27.55 (4.15)
SF—17/16/1/–/–/–

**2278** DONCASTER CORN EXCHANGE H'CAP (0-80) £2427.00 (£672.00: £321.00) **2m 110y** 6-50 (6-54)

1988★ **Smilingatstrangers (46)** (v) (Fav) *(MrsBarbaraWaring)* 4–7-12 JLowe (2) (lw: trckd ldrs tl rdn along 6f out: hdwy to ld over 2f out: r.o wl u.p ins fnl f) ......... —1

2042² Intrepid Lass **(44)** *(HCandy)* 5–7-10 CRutter (7) (chsd ldrs: led over 3f out: hdd & nt qckn fnl f) ......... 2.2

1988³ Shoofe (USA) **(72)** *(DMorley)* 4–9-10 WRyan (5) (hld up & bhd: stdy hdwy 7f out: effrt over 3f out: styd on same pce fnl 2f) ......... 2¹/₂.3

1970⁴ Caroles Clown **(46)** *(MJHaynes)* 6–7-5 ‡⁷DToole (3) (chsd ldrs tl lost pl 6f out: styd on one pce u.p fnl 3f) ......... 1.4

1967⁶ Count My Blessings **(48)** *(JLEyre)* 7–8-0 NCarlisle (1) (b: led to 12f out: rdn & lost pl over 3f out) ......... 7.5

1970³ Classic Statement **(49)** *(RLee)* 6–8-1 WCarson (8) (in tch: effrt & rdn over 4f out: lost pl 3f out) ......... 1.6

1132 Access Ski **(76)** *(RBoss)* 5–10-0 NDay (4) (lw: led 12f out tl over 3f out: sn wknd)   3½.7
1938 Shentit (FR) **(70)** *(JLDunlop)* 4–9-8 GDuffield (6) (a bhd: pushed along 12f out:
            n.d) ............................................................................................................. 7.8

**11/4** SMILINGATSTRANGERS, **4/1** Shoofe (USA), **11/2** Classic Statement, **6/1** Shentit (FR), Intrepid Lass, **7/1** Caroles Clown, **14/1** Access Ski, **20/1** Count My Blessings. CSF £18.02, CT £58.22. Tote £3.40: £1.70 £1.70 £1.70 (£8.10). Mr Harry Chisman (CHIPPENHAM) bred by T. McCarthy. 8 Rn            3m 36.74 (7.74)

## 2279

WARDS THORNE BEST BITTER H'CAP (3-Y.O) (0-80) £2343.00 (£648.00: £309.00)
**5f**                                                                                    7-20 (7-25)
                        (Weights raised 3 lb)

2063² **Ganeshaya (45)** (bl) *(MFBarraclough)* 7-7 NCarlisle (1) (lw: chsd ldrs: led
            ½-wy: drvn out fnl f) ...................................................................... —1
2082* Temple Fortune (USA) **(71)** *(RHannon)* 9-5 (5x) PatEddery (7) (lw: trckd ldrs:
            effrt & n.m.r 2f out: r.o u.p fnl f: nt rch wnr) ............................. ½.2
1861³ Miss Vaxette **(65)** *(JLSpearing)* 8-13 MRoberts (4) (w ldrs: nt qckn fnl f) ........... 2.3
2245² Kalar **(45)** *(DWChapman)* 7-7 SWood (5) (lw: led to ½-wy: sn rdn: wknd over 1f
            out) ........................................................................................................ 3.4
2192⁶ Creche **(73)** (bl) *(MrsNMacauley)* 9-7 NDay (6) (lw: s.i.s: a bhd) ........................ 2.5
1994⁵ Hot Lavender (CAN) **(68)** *(CFWall)* 9-2 LDettori (2) (w ldrs tl rdn & wknd
            over 1f out) .................................................................................... 1½.6
            LONG HANDICAP: Ganeshaya 7-5, Kalar 7-1.

**11/4** Hot Lavender (CAN), **3/1** Miss Vaxette, Temple Fortune (USA), **9/2** GANESHAYA, **8/1** Creche, **14/1** Kalar. CSF £17.10, Tote £6.00: £2.40 £1.80 (£12.60). Abbots Salford Caravan Park (CLAVERDON) bred by Campbell Stud. 6 Rn                                                                           60.43 sec (1.73)
                                                                                   SF—24/48/34/2/22/11

## 2280

'DAZZLING DONCASTER MARKETS' H'CAP (0-90) £3080.00 (£920.00: £440.00:
£200.00)   **6f**                                                                 7-50 (7-51)

2073⁵ **State Flyer (61)** (v) *(CBBBooth)* 4–7-12⁽¹⁾ ‡7GForster (2) (lw: s.i.s: hdwy ½-wy:
            hrd rdn to ld over 1f out: kpt on) ................................................. —1
1987⁶ Iron King **(67)** *(JLSpearing)* 6–8-11 MRoberts (1) (lw: s.i.s: effrt & hrd rdn over
            1f out: styd on ins fnl f) ................................................................ ¾.2
2040² Strip Cartoon (IRE) **(53)** (bl) *(SRBowring)* 4–7-11 JQuinn (5) (w ldr: led over 2f
            out tl over 1f out: styd on nr fnl) ................................................. nk.3
2029⁶ Venture Capitalist **(84)** *(RHannon)* 3–9-8 PatEddery (7) (lw: hmpd after
            100y: smooth hdwy ½-wy: rdn over 1f out: kpt on same pce) ...... 1½.4
1272* Boy Martin **(72)** *(MJohnston)* 3–8-10 DMcKeown (6) (sn chsng ldrs: effrt over 1f
            out: nvr able to chal) .................................................................... ¾.5
2163³ Sully's Choice (USA) **(51)** (bl) *(DWChapman)* 11–7-9 SWood (4) (lw: led to
            ½-wy: wknd over 1f out) .................................................................. 5.6
2073 Gemini Fire **(82)** *(MPNaughton)* 8–9-7 ‡5JWeaver (3) (trckd ldrs tl wknd qckly
            over 2f out: sn bhd) ...................................................................... 15.7

**13/8** Venture Capitalist(11/4—6/4), **6/1** Iron King, Strip Cartoon (IRE), **7/1** Sully's Choice (USA), Gemini Fire, **8/1** STATE FLYER, **17/2** Boy Martin. CSF £48.36, Tote £10.30: £3.10 £2.80 (£19.90). Mrs Pam Flowers (FLAXTON) bred by Mrs Pam Flowers. 7 Rn                                                                    1m 13.24 (2.24)
                                                                                   SF—15/25/10/29/14/–

## 2281

WEMBLEY STKS (Amateurs)   £1688.00 (£468.00: £224.00)
**1¼m 60y**                                                                      8-20 (8-26)

1842⁶ **Pharly Story (91)** (Fav) *(MCPipe)* 4–10-1 MrsLPearce (1) (trckd ldrs: smooth
            hdwy 3f out: r.o wl) ......................................................................... —1
1917² Flaming Arrow **(95)** *(HRACecil)* 4–10-1 MissJAllison (7) (lw: trckd ldrs: led &
            qcknd 3f out: r.o) ............................................................................ ¾.2
2066³ Thundering **(31)** *(AWJones)* 7–10-1 MissIDWJones (6) (in tch: styd on one pce
            u.p fnl 3f: no ch w 1st 2) .............................................................. 15.3
1739⁵ Escape Talk **(20)** *(JDooler)* 5–9-10 MrsAFarrell (11) (bhd tl styd on u.p fnl 3f) 3½.4
912 Texan Clamour (FR) **(52)** *(JSMoore)* 4–9-12 ‡3MrsSMoore (2) (b.off hind: chsd
            ldrs: no imp fnl 3f) ........................................................................ nk.5
1063⁴ Captain My Captain (IRE) **(50)** *(RBrotherton)* 4–9-12 ‡3MissVHill (10) (plld hrd:
            trckd ldrs tl lost pl 3f out) ........................................................... 3½.6
1863 The Metropole (IRE) **(40)** *(AWPotts)* 3–9-2 ‡3MissSJudge (4) (b.off hind: kpt on
            fnl 3f: n.d) ..................................................................................... ½.7
My Lindianne *(JDooler)* 5–9-7 ‡3MrDWilcox (3) (unruly s: s.s: hdwy 8f out: lost pl
            over 3f out) ...................................................................................... 10.8
1484 Lightning Decision *(JPSmith)* 4–10-0⁽²⁾ ‡3MissSSharratt (9) (plld hrd: trckd ldrs
            tl lost pl 4f out) ............................................................................. ¾.9
Oh so Handy *(RCurtis)* 4–9-12 ‡3MrGBrown (5) (led tl over 3f out: sn lost pl) .. nk.10
Comme Ci Comme Ca *(BEllison)* 6–10-1⁽³⁾ ‡3MrSBrown (8) (b: dwlt: a bhd) ..... 8.11
Stormy's Mad *(GFleming)* 8–10-3⁽⁵⁾ ‡3MrDRobinson (12) (b: wl bhd fnl 3f) ..... 15.12

**10/11** PHARLY STORY, **6/5** Flaming Arrow, **16/1** Thundering, **66/1** Captain My Captain (IRE), **100/1** Comme Ci Comme Ca, Lightning Decision, The Metropole (IRE), Escape Talk, Oh so Handy, Stormy's Mad, Texan Clamour (FR), **200/1** My Lindianne. CSF £2.02, Tote £2.40: £1.20 £1.20 £1.50 (£1.40). Mr A. J. Lomas (WELLINGTON) bred by Deepwood Farm Stud. 12 Rn                                                      2m 12.34 (5.34)
SF—42/40/10/–/–/–

---

**2282**   'COME TO DONCASTER MARKETS' GRADUATION STKS (3-Y.O) £2406.00 (£666.00: £318.00)   **7f**                                                        8-50 (8-53)

      **Freewheel (USA)** (Fav) (LMCumani) 9-0 LDettori (2) (trckd ldr: effrt over 2f out:
              led ins fnl f: drvn out) ....................................................................... —1
1941  Majboor (IRE) **(92)** (PTWalwyn) 9-2 WCarson (1) (lw: led: qcknd over 2f out: no
              ex ins fnl f) ............................................................................ ¾.2
      Last Exit **(85)** (WJarvis) 9-0 MRoberts (4) (hld up & plld hrd: effrt over 2f out: no
              imp) ....................................................................................... 2½.3

**10/11** FREEWHEEL (USA), **2/1** Majboor (IRE)(3/1—7/4), **7/2** Last Exit. CSF £2.78, Tote £1.60 (£1.70). Mr W. S. Farish III (NEWMARKET) bred by W.S.Farish, E.J.Hudson & E.J.Hudson, Jr. in USA. 3 Rn      1m 26.87 (3.47)
SF—27/27/17

T/Plpt: £37.00 (79.95 Tckts).                                                                                  WG

---

## 2105—**YARMOUTH (L-H)**

### Wednesday, July 22nd [Good]

Going Allowance: minus 0.25 sec per fur (F)                                        Wind: slt across

Stalls: high

**2283**   SCRATBY H'CAP (0-70) £2532.00 (£702.00: £336.00)   **7f 3y**         2-15 (2-19)
                          (Weights raised 2 lb)

      **Queen of Shannon (IRE) (63)** (DMorris) 4-9-10 MTebbutt (4) (swtg: chsd ldrs:
              led over 1f out: rdn out) .................................................................. —1
1930  Sugemar **(59)** (Fav) (JARToller) 6-9-6 MRoberts (5) (sn pushed along: prom:
              ev ch over 1f out: unable qckn) ..................................................... 2.2
2126⁴ On Y Va (USA) **(59)** (RJRWilliams) 5–9–6 RCochrane (3) (hdwy 4f out: rdn & kpt
              on fnl f) ................................................................................... 1½.3
1806* Coral Flutter **(50)** (bl) (JWPayne) 5–8–4 ‡7BLane (1) (led centre: rdn to ld over 2f
              out: hdd & wknd over 1f out) ......................................................... 2½.4
731   Ushba (FR) **(58)** (CGCox) 4-9-5 WNewnes (6) (racd alone: stands' side: led
              over 4f: sn rdn & btn) ................................................................. 3½.5
2105⁴ Dorking Lad **(53)** (MHTompkins) 10–9–0 PRobinson (2) (dwlt: rdn over 3f out: a bhd) 1½.6

**2/1** Sugemar, **11/4** On Y Va (USA), **5/1** Dorking Lad, **11/2** Coral Flutter, **10/1** QUEEN OF SHANNON (IRE), **16/1** Ushba (FR)(op 10/1). CSF £27.38, Tote £12.90: £2.50 £1.70 (£17.70). The Killoughery Family (NEWMARKET) bred by George Killoughery in Ireland. 6 Rn                                                    1m 25.4 (2.6)
SF—44/34/29/5/9/2

---

**2284**   ELIZABETH SIMPSON (S) STKS (2-Y.O) £2448.00 (£678.00: £324.00)
           **7f 3y**                                                                    2-45 (2-47)

2108  **Red Ballet** (bl) (MrsNMacauley) 8-6 MRoberts (8) (mde all: rdn & hld on wl fnl f) —1
2058² B B Glen (Fav) (DMorris) 8-6 WNewnes (4) (lw: stdd s: hdwy over 2f out: r.o fnl f) 1½.2
1932⁵ Heroic Deed (MHTompkins) 8-11 PRobinson (7) (lw: hld up: hdwy 3f out: rdn &
              no ex appr fnl f) ......................................................................... ¾.3
1804⁴ Abilene (JARToller) 8-6 DaleGibson (1) (prom: rdn 3f out: no ex appr fnl f) ...... nk.4
1670³ Good Image (APJarvis) 8-11 PaulEddery (2) (chsd ldrs: rdn over 2f out: one
              pce) ...................................................................................... 5.5
      My Miss Molly (IRE) (MissGayKelleway) 8-6 WAAntongeorgi (6) (b.hind: leggy:
              lt-f: a bhd) ............................................................................... 2.6
1479³ Midarida (IRE) (RJRWilliams) 8-7⁽¹⁾ RCochrane (3) (prom 5f) ........................ 1½.7
1804⁶ Secret Tale (GBlum) 8-6 AShoults (5) (a bhd: t.o) ...................................... 25.8

**100/30** B B Glen, **7/2** Midarida (IRE), Heroic Deed, **4/1** Good Image, **9/1** RED BALLET, **14/1** Abilene, **33/1** Ors. CSF £24.53, Tote £6.50: £1.40 £1.70 £1.30 (£12.60). Mr Donald Cooper (MELTON MOWBRAY) bred by Collin Stud. 8 Rn; No bid                                                                    1m 28.3 (5.5)

---

**2285**   J. MEDLER LTD AUCTION STKS (Mdn 2-Y.O) £3080.00 (£920.00: £440.00: £200.00)
           **7f 3y**                                                                    3-15 (3-18)

973²  **Hung Parliament** (Fav) (BWHills) 8-0 DHolland (5) (a.p: led ins fnl f: rdn & jst
              hld on) ..................................................................................... —1
1902³ Snowy River (FR) (DrJDScargill) 9-1 RCochrane (4) (dwlt: hdwy over 3f out: led
              2f out tl ins fnl f: rallied & jst failed) ................................................ s.h.2

2068³ Poly Vision (IRE) *(MRChannon)* 8-3 TQuinn (12) (swtg: wnt lft s: a:p: led over 2f
out: sn hdd: no ex fnl f) .................................................. 2½.3
1571 Nancy (IRE) *(CWCElsey)* 7-9 ‡³FNorton (6) (lw: hdwy over 2f out: r.o wl fnl f) .. s.h.4
1899 Daring Past *(RBoss)* 8-7 MRoberts (7) (bhd: rdn 3f out: kpt on fnl 2f) .......... 1.5
1957 Manon Lescaut *(APJarvis)* 8-8 PaulEddery (8) (chsd ldrs: rdn ½-w: sn btn) ..... 4.6
2108⁶ Home Affair *(DTThom)* 7-12 DBiggs (11) (wnt lft s: stumbled after 1f: prom tl
wknd over 1f out) ........................................................ 4.7
574 Shynon *(MHTompkins)* 7-12(1) ‡⁷SMulvey (3) (swtg: n.d) ...................... s.h.8
2118³ Buffalo River *(MHTompkins)* 8-13 PRobinson (1) (spd 5f) ................... 6.9
2008² Mister Blake (bl) *(WAO'Gorman)* 8-2 ‡³EmmaO'Gorman (2) (led over 4f: sn
wknd) ................................................................... 2½.10
Rousilla *(KTIvory)* 8-9 GBardwell (10) (unf: scope: s.s: a bhd) ............... 1.11
Distant Spring (IRE) *(GAPritchard-Gordon)* 8-13 WHood (9) (unf: s.s: a bhd) .. 7.12

5/2 HUNG PARLIAMENT, 5/1 Snowy River (FR), 6/1 Poly Vision (IRE)(op 4/1), 7/1 Mister Blake, 9/1 Home
Affair(16/1—8/1), 11/1 Nancy (IRE), 12/1 Buffalo River(op 8/1), 14/1 Daring Past(op 8/1), 20/1 Manon
Lescaut, 33/1 Ors. CSF £14.52, Tote £2.70: £1.80 £1.90 £2.70 (£5.20). Mr W. J. Gredley (LAMBOURN) bred by
Mrs P. A. Clark. 12 Rn                                                   1m 27.9 (5.1)

## 2286
BEAUCHAMP STKS (Mdn 2-Y.O) £2301.00 (£636.00: £303.00)   **6f 3y**   3-45 (3-47)

Ibraz (USA) (Jt-Fav) *(HThomsonJones)* 9-0 RHills (1) (leggy: scope: dwlt:
hdwy 2f out: led ins fnl f: rdn out) ...................................... —1
Fortensky (USA) (Jt-Fav) *(LMCumani)* 9-0 LDettori (6) (w'like: scope: chsd
ldrs: led over 1f out tl ins fnl f: unable qckn) .......................... ½.2
1925 Rusty Reel *(CEBrittain)* 9-0 MRoberts (2) (led over 4f: n.m.r & nt qckn ins fnl f) 1½.3
1578³ Fiveofive (IRE) *(NACallaghan)* 8-9 WRyan (7) (dwlt: bhd: swtchd lft & hdwy over
1f out: r.o wl fnl f) ..................................................... nk.4
2024 Silver Groom (IRE) *(APJarvis)* 9-0 PaulEddery (3) (prom 4f: sn wknd) ......... 8.5
Romeo Oscar *(BWHills)* 9-0 DHolland (5) (lt-f: unf: w ldr 4f: sn rdn & wknd) ... 3.6
Bold Star *(AAScott)* 9-0 BRaymond (4) (unf: scope: bkwd: bhd fnl 3f) ......... 3½.7

7/4 Fortensky (USA), IBRAZ (USA), 10/1 Romeo Oscar, Bold Star(op 9/2), Fiveofive (IRE), 11/1 Rusty Reel, 25/1
Silver Groom (IRE). CSF £4.95, Tote £2.60: £2.00 £1.20 (£2.40). Mr Hamdan Al-Maktoum (NEWMARKET) bred
by Holtsinger Inc in USA. 7 Rn                                           1m 14.7 (4.1)

## 2287
LYDIA EVA STKS (Mdn) £2343.00 (£648.00: £309.00)   **1¾m 17y**   4-15 (4-16)

1567² Betelgeuse (74) *(HRACecil)* 3–8-3(1) WRyan (6) (mde all: rdn clr over 3f out:
unchal) ................................................................... —1
Hunting Ground *(GHarwood)* 4–9-7 MPerrett (5) (chsd ldrs: pushed along 10f
out: sn lost pl: poor 5th st: r.o fnl 2f) ................................. 10.2
2056² Desert Peace (IRE) *(PFICole)* 3–8-7 TQuinn (3) (lw: in tch: pushed along
8f out: 3rd st: rdn over 3f out: one pce) ................................. s.h.3
1714² Santarem (USA) *(WJHaggas)* 4–9-2 NDay (4) (b: bit bkwd: chsd ldrs: rdn 3f out: one pce) 6.4
1953⁶ Debt Swap (USA) *(JHMGosden)* 3–8-7 RCochrane (1) (b.nr hind: hld up: 4th st:
effrt 4f out: wknd qckly 2f out) ......................................... 10.5
1239 Yorkshire Fisher (IRE) *(MissGayKelleway)* 4–9-0 ‡⁷MSimpson (2) (b: chsd ldr 6f:
sn t.o: last st) .......................................................... dist.6

9/4 Desert Peace (IRE)(3/1—2/1), 11/4 Santarem (USA), 100/30 BETELGEUSE, 7/1 Hunting Ground(op 4/1),
10/1 Debt Swap (USA)(op 5/1), 66/1 Yorkshire Fisher (IRE). CSF £20.98, Tote £2.60: £1.60 £3.10 (£8.40). Mr
D. K. Harris (NEWMARKET) bred by Brook Bloodstock P L C. 6 Rn            3m 3.7 (6.7)

## 2288
CAISTER H'CAP (0-90) £3523.50 (£1053.00: £504.00: £229.50)   **1¼m 21y**   4-45 (4-45)

2113* Highbrook (USA) (73) *(MHTompkins)* 4–9-1 (5x) PRobinson (6) (hld up:
5th st: qcknd to ld over 1f out: sn clr) .................................. —1
1642 Boogie Bopper (IRE) (64) *(MBell)* 3–7-7(1) ‡³FNorton (2) (bhd: rdn 2f out: r.o wl
fnl f: nt rch wnr) ....................................................... 3.2
829 Kinematic (USA) (86) *(JHMGosden)* 4–10-0 PaulEddery (3) (lw: 2nd & pushed
along st: ev ch 2f out: unable qckn) ..................................... ¾.3
2023⁶ Busted Rock (86) *(MrsLPiggott)* 7–10-0 LPiggott (1) (lw: hld up: 4th st: effrt &
n.m.r.w wl over 1f out: no ex fnl f) ..................................... ½.4
2110* Bowden Boy (IRE) (72) (bl) *(NACallaghan)* 4–9-0 (5x) WRyan (5) (sn led & clr:
hdd 2f out: n.m.r & sn btn) .............................................. 6.5
1955⁶ Holiday Island (74) *(CEBrittain)* 3–8-6 MRoberts (4) (swtg: prom: 3rd st: rdn
over 3f out: wknd 2f out) ................................................ 2½.6

Evens HIGHBROOK (USA), 9/2 Busted Rock, 5/1 Bowden Boy (IRE), 6/1 Holiday Island(op 4/1), 8/1 Kinematic
(USA), 16/1 Boogie Bopper (IRE). CSF £14.66, Tote £2.30: £1.10 £3.50 (£21.10). Mr Nick Cook (NEWMARKET)
bred by Larry Stewart in USA. 6 Rn                                       2m 7.9 (3.5)
SF—41/13/46/45/17/4

**2289**    LEVY BOARD H'CAP (0-80) £3028.00 (£904.00: £432.00: £196.00)
      1m 3y                                 5-15 (5-17)

(Weights raised 6 lb)

2160* Shaieef (IRE) (56) (Fav) (RJRWilliams) 4–8-13 RCochrane (2) (hld up: hdwy over 2f out: led ins fnl f: r.o wl) ............ —1

2088* Roca Murada (IRE) (53) (MJRyan) 3–8-2 (5x) DBiggs (5) (lw: stdd s: hdwy 3f out: led over 1f out tl ins fnl f: unable qckn) ... 2.2

1863⁵ Night Transaction (50) (AHide) 5–8-0 ‡7NVarley (4) (hdwy 4f out: led 2f out: sn hdd & btn) ............ 4.3

2110 Shining Jewel (67) (MrsLPiggott) 5–9-10 LPiggott (7) (lw: chsd ldrs: rdn 2f out: kpt on fnl f) ............ s.h.4

1954⁶ Kalko (68) (CEBrittain) 3–9-3 MRoberts (3) (lw: prom: one pce fnl 2f) ............ 3½.5

2077 Share Holder (48) (MissGayKelleway) 4–7-12 ‡7CHawksley (1) (b.hind: led after 2f to 2f out: sn btn) ............ 2.6

1794⁶ Chaff (36) (DMorris) 5–7-7 GBardwell (6) (led 2f: bhd fnl 2f) ............ 7.7

LONG HANDICAP: Chaff 7-4.

**11/10** SHAIEEF (IRE), **7/2** Shining Jewel, **4/1** Roca Murada (IRE), **5/1** Night Transaction, **9/1** Kalko(op 5/1), **25/1** Chaff, **33/1** Share Holder. CSF £6.55, Tote £2.10: £1.10 £3.30 (£3.90). Mr Terry Minahan (NEWMARKET) bred by H. H. Aga Khan in Ireland. 7 Rn      1m 39.2 (3.9)
                                                    SF–11/–/–/–/–/–

T/Plpt: £27.60 (106.1 Tckts).                                         Dk

# YARMOUTH (L-H)

## Thursday, July 23rd [Good to firm]

Going Allowance: St; 0.10 sec; Rest: minus 0.10 sec per fur (F)      Wind: fresh against

Stalls: 5th & 6th low, remainder high

**2290**    NORTH WALSHAM H'CAP (0-70) £2856.00 (£791.00: £378.00)    **6f 3y**    2-20 (2-22)

2203⁵ Luna Bid (61) (MBlanshard) 9–10-0 RCochrane (14) (lw: hld up: squeezed thro over 1f out: qcknd to ld ins fnl f) ............ —1

2105⁴ Farmer Jock (56) (MrsNMacauley) 10–9-9 MRoberts (3) (trckd ldrs: ev ch 1f out: no ex ins fnl f) ............ 1½.2

1992 Coat of Dreams (45) (bl) (RBastiman) 3–8-6 MHills (13) (lw: led tl hdd & no ex ins fnl f) ............ 1.3

2201⁵ Almasa (58) (DMorris) 4–9-6 ‡5StephenDavies (10) (chsd ldrs: effrt & nt clr run 2f out: n.m.r 1f out: nt rcvr) ............ 2.4

1964 Count Me Out (30) (bl) (JPearce) 7–7-11 DaleGibson (1) (prom: ev ch 2f out: one pce) ............ s.h.5

1905 Yonge Tender (46) (bl) (CNWilliams) 5–8-13 JCurant (4) (reard s: wl bhd tl plld out & r.o wl appr fnl f) ............ 1½.6

2141 Goody Four Shoes (43) (DRTucker) 4–8-5 ‡5RPrice (7) (chsd ldrs 4f: sn rdn & btn) ............ hd.7

1924³ A Little Precious (57) (Fav) (JRBostock) 6–9-10 WRSwinburn (6) (lw: chsd ldrs: no hdwy fnl 2f) ............ s.h.8

1978 Dickens Lane (47) (bl) (RJHodges) 5–9-0 WCarson (8) (chsd ldrs: wkng whn hmpd & snatched up appr fnl f: nt rcvr) ............ hd.9

2105³ Yes (55) (DTThom) 4–9-8 LPiggott (5) (prom tl wknd appr fnl f) ............ 2.10

2053² Kipini (51) (WJMusson) 3–8-12 LDettori (2) (swtg: chsd ldrs over 3f) ............ 1.11

2198 Harlequin Girl (33) (bl) (KTIvory) 4–8-0 GBardwell (9) (dwlt: sn prom: wknd 2f out) ............ 2.12

1964 Breezy Sailor (26) (v) (RThompson) 6–7-7 DanaMellor (12) (b: lw: gd spd over 3f: sn wknd) ............ 5.13

LONG HANDICAP: Breezy Sailor 6-10.

**5/1** A Little Precious(4/1—6/1), **11/2** Dickens Lane(4/1—6/1), **7/1** Kipini, Yes, Farmer Jock, **8/1** LUNA BID, **10/1** Coat of Dreams, **11/1** Yonge Tender, **12/1** Harlequin Girl(8/1—14/1), **14/1** Goody Four Shoes(op 7/1), **16/1** Almasa(op 10/1), **20/1** Count Me Out, **50/1** Breezy Sailor. CSF £60.31, CT £525.42. Tote £12.50: £2.30 £2.80 £4.00 (£43.90). Mr M. Blanshard (UPPER LAMBOURN) bred by Pinfold Stud and Farms Ltd. 13 Rn
                                                 1m 14.7 (4.1)
                                                 SF–44/33/12/16/–/4

**2291**    GOLDEN MILE (S) H'CAP (3 & 4-Y.O) (0-60) £2679.00 (£744.00: £357.00)
      1m 3y                                   2-50 (2-57)

(Weights raised 5 lb)

2184⁴ Champenoise (44) (MBell) 4–9-8 MHills (11) (chsd ldrs stands' side: rdn to ld ins fnl f) ............ —1

1741⁵ Kathy Fair (IRE) **(38)** *(RJBaker)* 3–8–8 RFox (2) (swtg: prom far side: led over 1f out tl hdd & no ex ins fnl f) .......................................... ½.2

2210² Miss Magenta (IRE) **(31)** **(Fav)** *(RThompson)* 4–8–9 MRoberts (16) (hld up: hdwy 3f out: kpt on fnl f) ........................................... ½.3

1741² Broughton's Tango (IRE) **(43)** (bl) *(WJMusson)* 3–8–13 LDettori (5) (prom stands' side: one pce appr fnl f) ............................... 2½.4

1797⁴ Tendresse (IRE) **(33)** *(DRTucker)* 4–8–11 GBardwell (6) (swtg: dwlt: sn prom: one pce fnl 3f) .................................. hd.5

*1543* Watermill Girl **(32)** *(DTThom)* 4–8–10 WRSwinburn (8) (prom far side: led over 3f out tl over 1f out: sn btn) .......................... 2.6

2240³ Aragon Court **(32)** *(JPearce)* 4–8–5 ‡⁵RPrice (7) (hld up: stdy hdwy fnl 2f: gng on fin) ............................................ s.h.7

*2041²* Lord Leitrim (IRE) **(44)** *(NACallaghan)* 3–9–0 WCarson (17) (lw: prom stands' side: ev ch over 2f out: one pce) .................... s.h.8

1964 Joseph's Wine (IRE) **(38)** *(RBastiman)* 3–8–8 RHills (18) (lw: dwlt: sn chsng ldrs: no hdwy fnl 2f) ................................... 3.9

2125 All Earz (IRE) **(54)** *(REarnshaw)* 3–9–10 LPiggott (3) (lw: led far side over 4f) ... 5.10

1964⁴ Bobbie Bold **(37)** (bl) *(RO'Leary)* 4–9–1 MBirch (15) (swtg: prom: led stands' side over 3f out: hdd 2f out: sn btn) ...................... 1½.11

2060 Urshi-Jade **(35)** *(KWhite)* 4–8–13 VSmith (19) (lw: nvr trbld ldrs) ............ 1.12

1978 Wayward Son **(47)** *(GLewis)* 3–9–3 PaulEddery (4) (prom far side 4f) ........ 2½.13

*2159⁴* Gleneliane (IRE) **(39)** (bl) *(JLHarris)* 4–8–10 ‡⁷GForster (20) (led stands' side over 4f) ................................................ ½.14

2198 Lime Street Lil **(28)** *(DAWilson)* 4–8–6 GCarter (13) (chsd ldrs: rdn over 3f out: sn btn) ..................................... 2.15

1745⁵ Palacegate Gold (IRE) **(52)** (bl) *(RJHodges)* 3–9–8 RCochrane (9) (prom stands' side 4f) .................................... 4.16

1978 Dreams Eyes **(34)** (bl) *(RBastiman)* 4–8–5⁽¹⁾ ‡⁷HBastiman (1) (b: b.hind: hdwy to ld far side over 3f out: sn hdd & wknd) ............. 4.17

2051 Carrantuohill (IRE) **(47)** (bl) *(SPCWoods)* 3–9–3 WWoods (14) (prom stands' side over 4f) ............................... 1½.18

1145 Albany Spark **(36)** (bl) *(GHEden)* 3–8–6 DaleGibson (12) (s.s: a wl bhd) ........ 10.19

**7/2** Miss Magenta (IRE)(tchd 7/1), **13/2** Broughton's Tango (IRE)(9/2—7/1), **7/1** CHAMPENOISE, Lord Leitrim (IRE), **15/2** Bobbie Bold, **8/1** Lime Street Lil, **9/1** Aragon Court, **14/1** Tendresse (IRE), Gleneliane (IRE), **16/1** Carrantuohill (IRE), All Earz (IRE), **20/1** Dreams Eyes, **25/1** Joseph's Wine (IRE), Kathy Fair (IRE), **33/1** Ors. CSF £166.02, CT £668.18. Tote £9.60: £1.90 £6.10 £1.50 £2.00 (£246.70). Mrs Daphne Kilgour (NEWMARKET) bred by Hyde Stud. 19 Rn; No bid

1m 41.9 (6.6)
SF—21/5/4/–/–/–

---

**2292**   E.B.F. SCROBY SANDS STKS (Mdn 2-Y.O.F) £2322.00 (£642.00: £306.00)
7f 3y

3-20 (3-24)

Informatrice (USA) **(Fav)** *(HRACecil)* 8–11 SCauthen (2) (tall: scope: stdd s: hld up: hdwy on bit to ld ins fnl f: canter) ............................ —1

Russia Pobeda (USA) *(MrsLPiggott)* 8–11 LPiggott (3) (b.nr hind: leggy: scope: led tl rdn & no ex ins fnl f: no ch w wnr) ...................... 1.2

1502 Keltic Danseuse (IRE) *(MrsLPiggott)* 8–4 ‡⁷GMilligan (5) (chsd ldrs: rdn & edgd lft over 1f out: no imp) ............................. 2½.3

1937 First Affair *(MRStoute)* 8–11 WRSwinburn (1) (b.off hind: a:p: ev ch 2f out: no ex appr fnl f) ................................ 2.4

Soul Dream (USA) *(MrsJCecil)* 8–11 PaulEddery (6) (w'like: lt-f: chsd ldrs: pushed along ½-wy: sn wknd) ..................... 6.5

1887³ Crystal Key *(CEBrittain)* 8–11 MRoberts (4) (prom 4f: sn wknd) ............ 10.6

**4/7** INFORMATRICE (USA), **9/2** Crystal Key, **9/1** Soul Dream (USA), **10/1** Russia Pobeda (USA), First Affair(op 6/1), **25/1** Keltic Danseuse (IRE). CSF £7.45, Tote £1.50: £1.10 £3.50 (£6.60). Sheikh Mohammed (NEWMARKET) bred by Maylands Stud Ltd in USA. 6 Rn

1m 29.1 (6.3)
SF—13/10/–/–/–/–

---

**2293**   ACLE STKS (Mdn 3-Y.O) £2364.00 (£654.00: £312.00)   7f 3y

3-50 (3-52)

*2013* Amadeus Aes **(79)** (v) *(DMorris)* 9–0 RCochrane (3) (mde all: clr ½-wy: unchal) —1

822⁶ Turret Gates *(JARToller)* 9–0 MRoberts (9) (w wnr: outpcd ½-wy: rdn & kpt on fnl f) ........................................ 5.2

1981³ Retender (USA) **(Fav)** *(LMCumani)* 9–0 LDettori (7) (prom: rdn & one pce fnl 2f) hd.3

1532⁴ Jumaira Star (USA) *(JHMGosden)* 9–0 SCauthen (1) (bit bkwd: bhd tl r.o fnl 2f) . 4.4

Mashaaer (USA) *(RWArmstrong)* 9–0 WCarson (5) (chsd ldrs: rdn 3f out: fnd nil) hd.5

Romance (IRE) *(MJHeaton-Ellis)* 8–9 MHills (8) (unf: scope: nvr nr to chal) ........ 6.6

Art Critic (IRE) *(MJHeaton-Ellis)* 9–0 PaulEddery (4) (bit bkwd: a bhd) ............ 1½.7

Groovey Dancer *(BJMcMath)* 9–0 JQuinn (2) (leggy: chsd ldrs 4f) ................... 10.8

1974 Tinkers Fairy *(DTThom)* 8–9 CDwyer (6) (swtg: spd 3f: sn bhd: t.o) ................. 25.9

**6/4** Retender (USA)(tchd 5/2), **9/4** Mashaaer (USA), **7/2** Jumaira Star (USA)(9/4—4/1), **10/1** Turret Gates(8/1—12/1), **11/1** AMADEUS AES(16/1—10/1), **33/1** Romance (IRE), **50/1** Ors. CSF £102.35, Tote £10.80: £1.10 £2.60 £1.40 (£28.20). Mr John Peters (NEWMARKET) bred by J. A. Peters. 9 Rn  1m 27.8 (5)
SF—35/20/19/7/1/–

**2294**　　　CITY OF NORWICH CLAIMING STKS　　£2846.00 (£848.00: £404.00: £182.00)
　　　　　　　1m 3f 101y　　　　　　　　　　　　　　　　　　　　　　　　4-20 (4-20)

| | | |
|---|---|---|
| 2111² | **Mystery Lad (IRE) (53)** (bl) *(NACallaghan)* 3–8-5 MRoberts (2) (b: chsd ldrs: 3rd st: led wl over 1f out: pushed clr) | —1 |
| 2149* | **Able Lassie (68)** (Fav) *(MrsGRReveley)* 4–9-9 LPiggott (4) (hld up: 5th st: shkn up 4f out: led 2f out: sn hdd & btn: eased ins fnl f) | 7.2 |
| 2007⁶ | Kate Royale **(39)** *(GCBravery)* 3–7-10 JQuinn (3) (in tch: 4th st: one pce fnl 3f) | 1¹/₂.3 |
| 1810² | Banana Cufflinks (USA) **(43)** (v) *(MHTompkins)* 6–9-0 PRobinson (1) (lw: led & qcknd out: sn hdd & wknd 2f out) | 1¹/₂.4 |
| 1949 | Every One a Gem **(57)** *(MDixon)* 5–9-2 DaleGibson (5) (dwlt: last st: nvr trbld ldrs) | 2¹/₂.5 |
| 2204 | Edgewise **(17)** *(DMorris)* 9–8-7 ‡⁵StephenDavies (6) (chsd ldrs: 2nd & rn wd st: sn btn) | ¹/₂.6 |

**8/13** Able Lassie, **4/1** MYSTERY LAD (IRE), **13/2** Every One a Gem, **7/1** Banana Cufflinks (USA)(10/1—6/1), **20/1** Kate Royale, **33/1** Edgewise. CSF £6.90, Tote £4.60: £1.40 £1.30 (£3.10). Gallagher Properties Ltd (NEWMARKET) bred by Hamwood Stud in Ireland. 6 Rn　　　　2m 27.7 (3.7)
SF—43/47/17/32/29/17

**2295**　　　BELTON H'CAP (0-90) £3172.50 (£945.00: £450.00: £202.50)
　　　　　　　1³/₄m 17y　　　　　　　　　　　　　　　　　　　　　　　　4-50 (4-51)

| | | |
|---|---|---|
| 2172² | **Prince Sobur (59)** (Fav) *(MBlanshard)* 6–8-13 RCochrane (5) (lw: chsd ldr: 2nd st: rdn to ld 2f out: r.o) | —1 |
| 2042 | Native Magic **(70)** (bl) *(RWArmstrong)* 6–9-10 LPiggott (4) (lw: led tl hdd 2f out: rdn & kpt on) | 2¹/₂.2 |
| 1621³ | Carrolls Marc (IRE) **(50)** *(PJFeilden)* 4–8-4 MRoberts (2) (b.hind: dwlt: 5th st: r.o fnl 3f: nvr able to chal) | 7.3 |
| 2129⁵ | Prosequendo (USA) **(68)** *(MDixon)* 5–9-8 DaleGibson (1) (hld up: 4th st: rdn over 3f out: sn btn) | 1¹/₂.4 |
| 2043² | Whisper's Shadow **(73)** *(MHTompkins)* 3–8-13 PRobinson (6) (swtg: bhd: last st: effrt over 2f out: no imp) | ¹/₂.5 |
| 1951² | Merton Mill **(65)** (bl) *(DMorley)* 5–9-5 PaulEddery (3) (b: lw: chsd ldrs: poor 3rd st: wknd over 3f out) | 7.6 |

**7/4** PRINCE SOBUR, **7/2** Merton Mill, **9/2** Carrolls Marc (IRE), **5/1** Prosequendo (USA), **10/1** Whisper's Shadow(op 6/1), **12/1** Native Magic. CSF £18.02, Tote £3.00: £2.00 £2.60 (£9.10). Mr C. R. Buttery (UPPER LAMBOURN) bred by Crimbourne Stud. 6 Rn　　　　3m 4.9 (6.9)
SF—30/36/2/17/7/–

T/Plpt: £47.80 (58.9 Tckts).　　　　　　　　　　　　　　　　　　　　　　　　　　　　Dk

# YARMOUTH (L-H)

## Friday, July 24th [Good to firm]

Going Allowance: minus 0.20 sec per fur (F)　　　　　　　　　　　　Wind: mod half bhd

Stalls: centre

**2296**　　　STAR H'CAP (3-Y.O) (0-70) £2532.00 (£702.00: £336.00)　　**1m 3f 101y**　2-10 (2-11)

| | | |
|---|---|---|
| 1933⁵ | **Resplendent (70)** *(NCWright)* 9-7 WRyan (3) (a gng wl: 5th st: chal on bit appr fnl f: shkn up to ld ins fnl f) | —1 |
| 1909* | Tales of Wisdom **(65)** (Fav) *(SirMarkPrescott)* 9-2 AMunro (7) (chsd ldrs: 3rd st: led over 2f out: hdd & no ex ins fnl f) | 2.2 |
| 1890 | Tudor Da Samba **(57)** *(JRFanshawe)* 8-8 GCarter (2) (swtg: bhd: 7th & pushed along st: ev ch 2f out: sn rdn & no ex) | 3.3 |
| 869⁵ | Wheeler's Wonder (IRE) **(50)** *(NCWright)* 7-10 ‡⁵BDoyle (1) (chsd ldrs: 6th st: rdn & kpt on appr fnl f) | 1.4 |
| 1812³ | Princess Evita (FR) **(42)** *(RGuest)* 7-0 ‡⁷CHawksley (5) (prom: 4th st: rdn over 3f out: kpt on same pce) | s.h.5 |
| 1977 | Aislabie Airborne **(42)** *(MrsNMacauley)* 7-7 NAdams (6) (led 2f: led ent st: hdd & wknd qckly over 2f out) | 25.6 |
| 1408⁶ | Last Orders (USA) **(47)** (bl) *(PMitchell)* 7-9 ‡³SO'Gorman (8) (dwlt: a bhd: t.o) | 15.7 |
| 1602 | Petty Cash **(42)** *(DrJDScargill)* 7-7 GBardwell (4) (swtg: led after 2f: hdd & wknd ent st: t.o) | 25.8 |

LONG HANDICAP: Princess Evita (FR) 7-5, Aislabie Airborne 7-1.

**4/5** Tales of Wisdom, **4/1** RESPLENDENT, **6/1** Wheeler's Wonder (IRE), **12/1** Princess Evita (FR), Tudor Da Samba, **33/1** Last Orders (USA), **40/1** Ors. CSF £7.16, CT £28.14. Tote £5.10: £1.40 £1.10 £2.20 (£2.90). Mr W. J. Gredley (NEWMARKET) bred by Stetchworth Park Stud Ltd. 8 Rn
2m 28.4 (4.4)
SF—40/31/17/3/–/–

### 2297

HAZELHURST (S) STKS (3-Y.O) £2301.00 (£636.00: £303.00)
1¼m 21y
2-40 (2-42)

2187* **By Arrangement (IRE) (55)** (Fav) *(RGuest)* 7-13 ‡⁷CHawksley (7) (dwlt: last, pushed along & c wd st: led appr fnl f: rdn out) .......... —1

2051 Selaginella **(62)** *(MRChannon)* 8-1 ‡⁵BDoyle (4) (led tl hdd appr fnl f: rdn & wknd ins fnl f) ................. 1½.2

2051³ Big Pat **(58)** *(JPearce)* 8-6 ‡⁵RPrice (2) (chsd ldrs: 4th st: rdn & one pce appr fnl 2f) .................. s.h.3

1976 Expansionist **(57)** *(SPCWoods)* 8-11 WWoods (8) (lw: chsd ldrs: 6th & carried wd st: rdn 3f out: kpt on one pce) .......... nk.4

2125 Chummy's Child (IRE) **(55)** *(JSutcliffe)* 8-11 AMunro (5) (lw: chsd ldrs tl 7th st: n.d after) .................. 3.5

1142 Rumbelow **(50)** *(JRJenkins)* 8-11 WRyan (6) (prom: 2nd st: wknd 3f out) .......... 8.6

5675 Speed Oil **(52)** *(RBastiman)* 8-4 ‡⁷HBastiman (3) (dwlt: effrt & 5th st: nt clr run: no imp fnl 3f) .................. 1½.7

2084 On the Rampage **(49)** *(PMitchell)* 8-3 ‡³SO'Gorman (1) (chsd ldrs: 3rd st: wknd 3f out) .................. 1.8

**7/4** BY ARRANGEMENT (IRE)(Evens—2/1), **5/2** Big Pat, **5/1** Expansionist(7/2—6/1), **11/2** Selaginella, **14/1** Chummy's Child (IRE), **20/1** Ors. CSF £11.59, Tote £2.10: £1.30 £1.50 £1.10 (£5.60). Mr C. J. Mills (NEWMARKET) bred by Graigueshoneen Stud in Ireland. 8 Rn; No bid
2m 10.5 (6.1)
SF—4/3/7/11/5/–

### 2298

FURZEDOWN STKS (Mdn) £2532.00 (£702.00: £336.00)  1¼m 21y   3-10 (3-11)

835 **Million in Mind (IRE)** *(MrsJCecil)* 3–8-9 WNewnes (7) (lw: a.p: 2nd st: led 1f out: pushed out) .................. —1

1704³ Alum Bay (Fav) *(HRACecil)* 3–8-9 WRyan (8) (lw: hdwy to ld after 2f: hdd 1f out: rdn & r.o) .................. ¾.2

1611⁵ Whirl *(JRFanshawe)* 3-8-4 GCarter (5) (chsd ldrs: 4th st: one pce fnl 2f) .......... 4.3

1830³ Laughsome *(JHMGosden)* 3–8-4 MHills (4) (trckd ldrs: 5th st: rdn 3f out: sn btn: eased fnl f) .................. 3.4

Melody Mountain (IRE) *(CEBrittain)* 3–8-4 GCrealock (6) (leggy: unf: chsd ldrs: 3rd st: no imp fnl 3f) .................. 1.5

Anna Comnena (IRE) *(LMCumani)* 3–8-0(1) ‡⁵JWeaver (1) (lengthy: scope: bit bkwd: hmpd & bhd after 2f: effrt over 2f out: r.o) .......... 1½.6

Charmed Life *(HRACecil)* 3–8-9 AMcGlone (2) (unf: bit bkwd: led tl hdd, stumbled & lost pl after 2f: 6th st: no hdwy) .......... 4.7

Place Mat *(DrJDScargill)* 3–8-4 JQuinn (3) (unf: b.hind: bdly hmpd & lost pl after 2f: btn after) .................. ½.8

**Evens** Alum Bay(op 7/4), **100/30** Whirl, **4/1** Laughsome(5/2—9/2), **10/1** Anna Comnena (IRE)(op 4/1), Charmed Life(8/1—12/1), **14/1** MILLION IN MIND (IRE), **20/1** Melody Mountain (IRE), **50/1** Place Mat. CSF £29.82, Tote £7.10: £1.50 £1.20 £1.20 (£23.20). The Million in Mind Partnership (NEWMARKET) bred by William Farish in Ireland. 8 Rn
2m 11.4 (7)
SF—5/3/–/–/–/–

### 2299

CARLTON NURSERY   £3231.00 (£891.00: £423.00)   6f 3y   3-40 (3-42)

1056⁴ **Expo Mondial (IRE)** (Fav) *(JMPEustace)* 9-7 MTebbutt (3) (trckd ldr: qcknd to ld appr fnl f: sn pushed clr) .................. —1

1769* Glowing Dancer *(JRJenkins)* 9-7 WRyan (2) (led tl hdd & no ex appr fnl f) .......... 2.2

2085⁴ The Wend *(DTThom)* 8-4 JQuinn (1) (swtg: plld hrd: chsd ldrs: ev ch 2f out: one pce) .................. 1.3

**Evens** EXPO MONDIAL (IRE), **5/4** Glowing Dancer(tchd 4/5), **5/1** The Wend. CSF £2.53, Tote £1.80 (£1.60). Mr Yat Fai Hung (NEWMARKET) bred by Barronstown Bloodstock Ltd in Ireland. 3 Rn
1m 14.3 (3.7)
SF—9/1/–

### 2300

BURLINGTON STKS (Mdn 3-Y.O) £2217.00 (£612.00: £291.00)   6f 3y   4-10 (4-11)

**Scala Milano** *(KTIvory)* 8-9 GBardwell (2) (lw: plld hrd: mde all: rdn out) .......... —1

1113³ Rock Band (IRE) **(67)** *(LMCumani)* 8-9 ‡JWeaver (1) (lw: swvd lft s: hld up: rdn over 2f out: r.o fnl f) .................. 1½.2

2015⁵ Black Coral (IRE) **(68)** (Fav) *(CFWall)* 8-9 AMunro (3) (chsd wnr: rdn over 2f out: one pce fnl f) .................. ½.3

**11/10** Black Coral (IRE), **6/5** Rock Band (IRE), **4/1** SCALA MILANO. CSF £8.36, Tote £4.10 (£2.50). Mr P. J. C. Simmonite (RADLETT) bred by P. J. C. Simmonite. 3 Rn
1m 12 (1.4)
SF—43/37/35

### 2301
AVENUE H'CAP (0-70) £2820.00 (£840.00: £400.00: £180.00)     **5f 43y**     4-45 (4-46)

2199² **Ski Captain** (51) (Fav) *(PHowling)* 8–8-13 WNewnes (1) (lw: mde all: rdn out) .. —1
21543 Trioming **(40)** *(APJones)* 6–8-2 NAdams (5) (lw: outpcd tl r.o wl appr fnl f: nt rch wnr) ........................................................................................ 1¹/₂.2
21416 Barbara's Cutie **(38)** *(MBlanshard)* 4–8-0 JQuinn (3) (prom: chsd wnr over 2f out tl no ex ins fnl f) ...................................................... 1.3
14836 Lincstone Boy (IRE) **(47)** (bl) *(SRBowring)* 4–8-9 SWebster (2) (lw: trckd wnr: rdn over 2f out: sn wknd) ........................................ 1.4
236 Maid Welcome **(66)**(bl)*(MrsNMacauley)* 5–10-0 AMunro (4) (spd to ¹/₂-wy: sn bhd)4.5
21056 Cumbrian Cavalier **(47)** (bl) *(JRBostock)* 3–8-4⁽²⁾ WRyan (6) (a bhd) .......... 2¹/₂.6

**85/40** SKI CAPTAIN, **3/1** Trioming, **100/30** Maid Welcome, **7/1** Lincstone Boy (IRE)(op 4/1), **15/2** Barbara's Cutie(14/1—7/1), **12/1** Cumbrian Cavalier(op 8/1). CSF £8.42, Tote £2.10: £1.40 £2.70 (£3.90). Mr B. P. Dickson (GUILDFORD) bred by Miss Sandra Hitchcock. 6 Rn
61.7 sec (1.4)
SF—51/34/28/33/36/2

T/Plpt: £131.30 (16.9 Tckts).
Dk

## 1809—**BRIGHTON (L-H)**
### Thursday, July 23rd [Good to firm]
Going Allowance: minus 0.40 sec per fur (F)
Wind: slt half bhd

Stalls: low

### 2302
CHIPPENDALE APP'CE STKS (Mdn) £2070.00 (£570.00: £270.00)
1m 3f 196y     2-00 (2-07)

15396 **Diamond Cut (FR)** (66) (Fav) *(MCPipe)* 4–9-7 EHusband (1) (lw: 3rd st: led 3f out: clr 2f out: easily) .......................................... —1
20564 Super Sarena (IRE) **(102)** *(RSimpson)* 3–8-4 DGibbs (7) (4th st: chsd wnr fnl 2f: no imp) ........................................................................ 5.2
17704 Maligned (IRE) *(JRFanshawe)* 3–8-4 NVarley (4) (5th st: one pce fnl 3f) ........ 10.3
2077 Indian Style (IRE) **(55)** *(RGuest)* 3–8-4 CHawksley (2) (lw: led 9f) ................ 3.4
1574 My Senor **(39)** *(MMadgwick)* 3–8-9 CAvery (6) (6th st: no hdwy fnl 3f) .............. 2.5
19705 Back to Form **(29)** *(WGMTurner)* 7–9-7 TMcLaughlin (3) (lw: 2nd st: wknd over 2f out) .................................................................. 7.6
1810 Miss Sarahsue **(20)** *(JELong)* 6–9-2 LeesaLong (5) (bhd fnl 7f) ................ 12.7
1949 Rustyside *(CTNash)* 5–9-2 SDrowne (8) (bhd fnl 6f) .................................... hd.8

**Evens** DIAMOND CUT (FR)(tchd 6/4), **5/2** Super Sarena (IRE), **13/2** Maligned (IRE), **8/1** Indian Style (IRE)(op 5/1), **14/1** My Senor(op 7/1), **20/1** Back to Form, **100/1** Ors. CSF £3.92, Tote £2.20: £1.10 £1.70 £2.10 (£3.10). Mr F. Barr (WELLINGTON) bred by Jean,Andre & Eric Laborde & Claude Duval in France. 8 Rn   2m 30.5 (3.5)
SF—24/–/–/–/–/–

### 2303
RAGGETTS (S) STKS (3-Y.O) £2469.00 (£684.00: £327.00)     **6f 209y**     2-30 (2-35)

2159 **Certain Lady** (67) *(GBlum)* 8-4 ‡⁵DHarrison (1) (lw: hdwy on ins over 2f out: swtchd over1f out: hrd rdn to ld ins fnl f: r.o wl) ......................... —1
12146 Coniston Lake (IRE) **(59)** *(GLewis)* 9-0 BRouse (13) (lw: 3rd st: led wl over 1f out tl ins fnl f: unable qckn) .................................... 1.2
2053 Red Sombrero **(61)** *(LGCottrell)* 9-0 AMunro (10) (lw: hdwy 2f out: r.o) .......... 1¹/₂.3
1759 Simon Ellis (IRE) **(43)** (v) *(DRLaing)* 9-0 TyroneWilliams (4) (lw: hdwy over 1f out: r.o) ........................................................ 2.4
19502 Treasure Time (IRE) **(63)** *(JWhite)* 8-9 NAdams (6) (lw: led over 5f) ............... nk.5
1852★ Whitehall (IRE) **(64)** *(CRNelson)* 9-0 JReid (11) (lw: 4th st: wknd wl over 1f out) 5.6
21316 Rock Song (IRE) **(57)** (Fav) *(PFICole)* 9-0 TQuinn (12) (lw: no hdwy fnl 3f) ........ 3.7
2079 Justamanda **(59)** *(WHolden)* 8-9 SDawson (5) (nvr nrr) .................................... ¹/₂.8
2079 Walkonthemoon **(54)** *(MMcCormack)* 8-9 WNewnes (3) (lw: 5th st: eased whn btn over 1f out) ............................................... nk.9
21315 Smudgemupum **(48)** *(MissBSanders)* 8-7 ‡⁷CHawksley (9) (6th st: wknd over 2f out) ........................................................ 1¹/₂.10
2051 Shecangosah *(RJHodges)* 8-9 DHolland (2) (bhd fnl 4f) ......................... 1¹/₂.11
Julia Sabina **(50)** *(CCElsey)* 8-9 TRogers (8) (2nd st: wknd wl over 2f out) ..... 8.12
2053 Shocking Times (12/1) Withdrawn (uns rdr & ref to ent stalls) : not under orders — Rule 4 applies

**11/4** Rock Song (IRE), **7/2** Treasure Time (IRE), **11/2** Coniston Lake (IRE)(8/1—5/1), Whitehall (IRE), **6/1** CERTAIN LADY, **12/1** Justamanda, **14/1** Walkonthemoon, **16/1** Red Sombrero, **20/1** Smudgemupum, **33/1** Simon Ellis (IRE), **50/1** Ors. CSF £36.60, Tote £7.10: £1.90 £2.20 £3.50 (£25.10). Mrs Bridget Blum (NEWMARKET) bred by Dunchurch Lodge Stud. 12 Rn; No bid
1m 22.1 (2.1)
SF—17/24/19/13/7/–

**2304**   BRIGHTON SUMMER CHALLENGE CUP (H'cap) (0-90) £4503.00 (£1344.00: £642.00: £291.00)   **6f 209y**
3-00 (3-02)

(Weights raised 7 lb)

| | | |
|---|---|---|
| 1943 | **Cheveux Mitchell (73)** (v) (Jt-Fav) (MRChannon) 5-9-6 TQuinn (5) (3rd st: hrd rdn over 1f out: led last strides) | —1 |
| 2013* | Norfolkiev (FR) (63) (Jt-Fav) (MMoubarak) 6-8-5 ‡5JWeaver (3) (lw: 2nd st: led over 2f out: hrd rdn: hdd last strides) | hd.2 |
| 21885 | Helios (68) (RSimpson) 4-9-1 JReid (2) (4th st: hrd rdn over 1f out: r.o wl) | hd.3 |
| 1833* | Hamadryad (IRE) (77) (WCarter) 4-9-5 ‡5NGwilliams (1) (s.s: rdn thrght: 6th st: hrd rdn over 2f out: r.o one pce) | 1½.4 |
| 15885 | Faynaz (48) (v) (WRMuir) 6-7-2 ‡7KimMcDonnell (6) (lw: led over 4f: one pce) | 1.5 |
| 2013 | Monte Bre (60) (RAkehurst) 6-8-7 AMunro (4) (lw: 5th st: one pce fnl 2f) | 2½.6 |

**5/2** Norfolkiev (FR), CHEVEUX MITCHELL(tchd 4/1), **9/2** Hamadryad (IRE)(3/1—5/1), **5/1** Helios, **10/1** Monte Bre(8/1—12/1), **12/1** Faynaz. CSF £8.39, Tote £3.90: £2.00 £2.50 (£3.70). Chitty Ltd (UPPER LAMBOURN) bred by Colby Bloodstock. 6 Rn
1m 21.5 (1.5)
SF—41/25/34

**2305**   FITZHERBERT H'CAP (0-70) £2427.00 (£672.00: £321.00)   **1m 1f 209y**   3-30 (3-31)

| | | |
|---|---|---|
| 20125 | **Scenic Dancer (51)** (v) (AHide) 4-9-5 WNewnes (11) (lw: gd hdwy over 1f out: hrd rdn: led nr fin) | —1 |
| 20364 | Rocquaine Bay (36) (MJBolton) 5-8-4(1) JWilliams (5) (gd hdwy over 1f out: led ins fnl f: hdd nr fin) | nk.2 |
| 20332 | Tiger Claw (USA) (51) (RJHodges) 6-9-5 DHolland (9) (5th st: hrd rdn over 1f out: ev ch ins fnl f: edgd lft & unable qckn) | 2½.3 |
| 20772 | Long Furlong (52) (Fav) (RAkehurst) 4-9-3 ‡3RPerham (4) (lw: 2nd st: led over 1f out tl ins fnl f: 4th & wkng whn bdly hmpd wl ins fnl f) | 2½.4 |
| 2012 | Marzocco (54) (bl) (JFfitch-Heyes) 4-9-3 ‡5DHarrison (1) (led over 8f) | 2½.5 |
| 1885 | Casilla (27) (HCandy) 4-7-9 SDawson (10) (lw: 3rd st: hrd rdn over 2f out: wknd over 1f out) | 2.6 |
| | Sixofus (IRE) (53) (WGMTurner) 4-9-4 ‡3TSprake (8) (4th st: wknd over 1f out) | 1.7 |
| 2033 | Albert (50) (DAWilson) 5-9-4 BRouse (7) (lw: a bhd) | 1½.8 |
| 1812* | Sky Train (IRE) (70) (JLDunlop) 3-10-0 AMunro (3) (6th st: wknd over 2f out) | s.h.9 |
| 1872 | Cool Society (USA) (60) (CRNelson) 3-9-4 JReid (6) (lw: bhd fnl 3f) | s.h.10 |
| 20144 | Dazzle the Crowd (IRE) (55) (CACyzer) 4-9-9 TQuinn (2) (lw: a bhd) | 7.11 |

**3/1** Long Furlong, **9/2** Tiger Claw (USA), **5/1** Sky Train (IRE)(4/1—6/1), Dazzle the Crowd (IRE), **15/2** Cool Society (USA)(6/1—9/1), **8/1** Marzocco, **10/1** SCENIC DANCER, **12/1** Albert, **14/1** Rocquaine Bay, **20/1** Sixofus (IRE). CSF £135.64, CT £668.79. Tote £12.90: £2.40 £3.30 £1.70 (£182.70). Mr A. S. Helaissi (NEWMARKET) bred by Alan Gibson. 11 Rn
2m 0.9 (2.9)
SF—36/20/30/22/17/–

**2306**   BEAU BRUMMEL CLAIMING STKS (Mdn 2-Y.O) £2343.00 (£648.00: £309.00)   **5f 213y**
4-00 (4-02)

| | | |
|---|---|---|
| 1635 | **Yours by Right** (WGMTurner) 8-3 ‡3TSprake (10) (str: 2nd st: led over 2f out: hrd rdn over 1f out: comf) | —1 |
| 20815 | Superensis (bl) (WRMuir) 9-0 SWhitworth (3) (lw: led over 3f: no imp) | 5.2 |
| 1170 | Scenic Reef (IRE) (JMPEustace) 8-7 TQuinn (9) (lw: hdwy over 2f out: hrd rdn over 1f out: one pce) | 1.3 |
| 1957 | Petite Vino (bl) (JJBridger) 8-5 NAdams (2) (hdwy over 2f out: one pce) | 3½.4 |
| 21244 | Kismetim (Fav) (GLewis) 9-0 BRouse (5) (5th st: one pce fnl 3f) | 2.5 |
| 2005 | Lady of Shadows (v) (SDow) 8-6 WNewnes (8) (6th st: wknd over 2f out) | 2½.6 |
| 20985 | Morning News (IRE) (v) (MHTompkins) 8-2 ‡7SMulvey (6) (4th st: wknd over 2f out) | 1.7 |
| 1140 | Steven's Dream (IRE) (JWhite) 8-0 ‡7CAvery (11) (lw: a bhd) | 1.8 |
| 21023 | Dhahran (PFICole) 9-2 AMunro (1) (lw: 3rd st: wknd over 2f out: wknd) | 2.9 |
| 1675 | Mac Tomb (KOCunningham-Brown) 8-9 TRogers (7) (a bhd) | ½.10 |
| | Montana D'Or (RCurtis) 8-1 ‡5NGwilliams (4) (neat: bkwd: a bhd) | s.h.11 |

**11/8** Kismetim, **7/4** Dhahran, **5/1** Scenic Reef (IRE)(4/1—7/1), **12/1** Morning News (IRE)(7/1—14/1), **14/1** Superensis(op 7/1), **16/1** Steven's Dream (IRE)(op 10/1), **20/1** YOURS BY RIGHT, **50/1** Ors. CSF £242.71, Tote £35.60: £3.70 £3.20 £1.70 (£421.90). Mr John Turner (SHERBORNE) bred by R. J. Turner. 11 Rn
1m 9.6 (1.2)
SF—17/8/–/–/–/–

**2307**　　BLACKMANTLE H'CAP (0-70) £2427.00 (£672.00: £321.00)　　**5f 213y**　4-30 (4-31)

20323 **Shikari's Son (64)** (Fav) *(JWhite)* 5-9-13 TQuinn (3) (4th st: bmpd over 1f out: led ins fnl f: r.o wl) ...................................................................... —1

2032 Divine Pet **(60)** *(WGRWightman)* 7-9-9 JWilliams (4) (lw: outpcd: gd hdwy over 1f out: r.o wl ins fnl f) ................................................................ ³/₄.2

19875 My Ruby Ring **(41)** *(DRLaing)* 5-8-4 TyroneWilliams (11) (b: b.hind: 2nd st: led over 1f out tl ins fnl f: unable qckn) ............................................ 2.3

2032 Amethystine (USA) **(58)** *(RJHodges)* 6-9-0 ‡7SDrowne (8) (hdwy & n.m.r over 1f out: one pce) ............................................................................ nk.4

20095 Restore **(51)** (bl) *(RVoorspuy)* 9-9-0 SDawson (5) (lw: hdwy over 1f out: r.o) .... 1.5

20533 Grey Charmer (IRE) **(56)** (bl) *(CJames)* 3–8-13 JReid (6) (nvr nr to chal) ........... ¹/₂.6

1338 Erris Express **(49)** *(JSMoore)* 7-8-5 ‡7DGibbs (10) (hdwy over 2f out: one pce) 1¹/₂.7

*119* Fontaine Lady **(40)** *(TThomsonJones)* 5-8-3 SWhitworth (1) (5th st: wknd over 1f out) ..................................................................................................... 2.8

2199★ Maria Cappuccini **(55)** *(KOCunningham-Brown)* 4-9-4 (7x) DHolland (8) (lw: 6th st: wknd 2f out) ...................................................................... nk.9

18143 Caromish (USA) **(65)** *(MDIUsher)* 5-10-0 MWigham (7) (3rd st: ev ch whn bmpd over 1f out: sn wknd) ................................................ nk.10

2053 Sea Crusader **(50)** (bl) *(MBlanshard)* 3–8-7 WNewnes (9) (swtg: led over 4f) 2¹/₂.11

2053 Flash of Straw (IRE) **(60)** *(GLewis)* 3–9-3 RaymondBerry (2) (lw: a bhd) .......... 5.12

**5/2** SHIKARI'S SON, **7/2** Divine Pet, **4/1** Maria Cappuccini, **7/1** Grey Charmer (IRE), **10/1** Restore, My Ruby Ring(op 6/1), **12/1** Caromish (USA)(op 8/1), **16/1** Amethystine (USA)(op 10/1), **20/1** Sea Crusader, **25/1** Erris Express, Fontaine Lady, **33/1** Flash of Straw (IRE). CSF £12.43, CT £74.33. Tote £3.30: £1.50 £2.10 £1.40 (£8.30). Mr Alan Spargo (WENDOVER) bred by W. H. Joyce. 12 Rn　　　　　　　1m 9.1 (0.7)
SF—51/44/17/26/22/19

T/Plpt: £390.80 (9 Tckts).　　　　　　　　　　　　　　　　　　　　　　　　　　AK

---

**2142**—**HAMILTON (R-H)**
**Thursday, July 23rd [Firm]**
Going Allowance: 5f-6f: minus 0.50 (H): Rest: nil sec per fur (G)　　　Wind: str bhd

Stalls: low

**2308**　TILLIETUDLEUM MEDIAN AUCTION GRADUATION STKS (2-Y.O) £2322.00 (£642.00: £306.00)　**5f 4y**　　　　　　　　　　　　2-10 (2-11)

13606 **Bold County** *(MJohnston)* 9-2 RPElliott (1) (trckd ldrs: led appr fnl f: sn qcknd clr: eased nr fin: comf) .................................................. —1

22233 Wolf Power (IRE) (Fav) *(TThomsonJones)* 8-11 KDarley (2) (chsd ldrs: effrt 2f out: ev ch tl nt qckn fnl f) .......................................... 4.2

2031 Tayish *(TThomsonJones)* 8-11 DMcKeown (3) (led: rdn 2f out: hdd appr fnl f: sn edgd rt & wknd) .......................................... 2¹/₂.3

**1/4** Wolf Power (IRE), **5/1** BOLD COUNTY, **6/1** Tayish. CSF £6.75, Tote £2.80 (£1.20). The Fairyhouse 1992 Partnership (MIDDLEHAM) bred by Someries Stud. 3 Rn　　　　　　　59.1 sec (0.8)
SF—36/19/9

**2309**　LEE CLAIMING STKS (2-Y.O) £2343.00 (£648.00: £309.00)　**6f 5y**　2-40 (2-41)

2098★ **Palacegate Prince** (Fav) *(JBerry)* 8-10 JCarroll (3) (mde all: drvn clr appr fnl f: styd on wl) ................................................................... —1

20443 Atlantic Sunset (IRE) *(MWEasterby)* 8-8 KDarley (1) (trckd ldr gng wl: effrt & ev ch wl over 1f out: nt qckn) .......................................... 5.2

21453 Anne's Bay (IRE) *(DMoffatt)* 7-8 ‡7DarrenMoffatt (2) (w ldr: rdn ¹/₂-wy: ev ch 2f out: sn wknd) ...................................................... 8.3

**8/13** PALACEGATE PRINCE, **11/8** Atlantic Sunset (IRE), **33/1** Anne's Bay (IRE). CSF £1.69, Tote £1.50 (£1.20). Palacegate Corporation Ltd (COCKERHAM) bred by D. B. Lamplough. 3 Rn　　　　1m 12.3 (2.3)

**2310**　ARTHUR BALDING H'CAP (3-Y.O) (0-70) £2499.20 (£691.20: £329.60)　**6f 5y**　　　　　　　　　　　　　　　　　　　3-10 (3-12)

(Weights raised 4 lb)

19503 **High Principles (60)** (Jt-Fav) *(JBerry)* 9-7 JCarroll (1) (led after 1f: clr & edgd rt fr ¹/₂-wy: drvn out) ................................................... —1

2151★ Our John **(50)** (Jt-Fav) *(RonaldThompson)* 8-11 (7x) AMackay (4) (hdwy u.p 2f out: ev ch ins fnl f: styd on) .................................. 1.2

21512 Miss Siham (IRE) **(47)** *(JBalding)* 8-1 ‡7ClaireBalding (2) (led 1f: chsd wnr: ev ch ent fnl f: nt qckn) ............................................. 1¹/₂.3

*2159*3 Miss Movie World **(45)** (Jt-Fav) *(NBycroft)* 8-1 (7x) NKennedy (3) (bhd & outpcd ¹/₂-wy: styd on fnl f: nrst fin) .................................. ¹/₂.4

9/4 Miss Movie World, Our John, HIGH PRINCIPLES, **6/1** Miss Siham (IRE). CSF £6.81, Tote £3.40 (£2.50).
Heathavon Stables Limited (COCKERHAM) bred by Heathavon Stables Ltd. 4 Rn
1m 10.3 (0.3)
SF—41/27/11/9

### 2311
COREHOUSE CLAIMING STKS (Mdn 3-Y.O) £2511.00 (£696.00: £333.00)
**1m 65y**
3-40 (3-46)

16276 **Bold Melody (49)** (Jt-Fav) *(PCHaslam)* 8-1[1] KDarley (6) (a trckng ldrs: led
over 3f out: pushed clr 2f out: comf) .................................. —1
16203 Blunham Express (48) *(TFairhurst)* 7-13 ‡3JFanning (4) (a chsng ldrs: rdn 2f
out: styd on: no ch w wnr) ........................................... 6.2
21475 Hataal (IRE) (39) *(JBalding)* 7-5 ‡7ClaireBalding (8) (s.i.s: bhd tl styd on fnl 2f:
nrst fin) ........................................................... 1½.3
22134 Bee Dee Ell (USA) (47) *(MissLAPerratt)* 8-2 ‡5NKennedy (2) (prom: effrt over 2f
out: one pce) ..................................................... 3.4
17304 Solstice *(MrsGRReveley)* 8-9 GDuffield (1) (led tl hdd over 3f out: wknd 2f out) . 1.5
21194 Ivors Princess (Jt-Fav) *(MrsGRReveley)* 8-3 DMcKeown (7) (chsd ldrs tl rdn &
wknd over 2f out) ................................................. s.h.6
Montrave (99) *(PMonteith)* 9-0 JCarroll (9) (w'like: bkwd: sn in tch: rdn & wknd
over 3f out: sn wl bhd) .......................................... 15.7
*Shut Up (33/1) Withdrawn (ref to ent stalls) : not under orders*

9/4 Ivors Princess, **BOLD MELODY**, **9/2** Blunham Express, **15/2** Hataal (IRE), Bee Dee Ell (USA), **20/1** Ors. CSF
£11.86, Tote £2.20: £1.90 £2.60 (£8.50). Mrs P. Haslam (MIDDLEHAM) bred by Deepwood Farm Stud. 7 Rn
1m 47.1 (3.8)
SF—30/10/-/-/-/-

### 2312
CRAIGNETHAN H'CAP (0-70) £2633.60 (£729.60: £348.80)   **1m 3f 16y**   4-10 (4-11)
(Weights raised 1 lb)

1840 **Princess Roxanne (50)** (bl) *(ABailey)* 5-9-1 AMackay (4) (hld up: hdwy to ld 3f
out: sn qcknd clr: drvn out) ...................................... —1
1890★ Great Max (IRE) (70) (Fav) *(SirMarkPrescott)* 3-9-10 GDuffield (2) (cl up: rdn &
sltly outpcd over 2f out: styd on to chal ins fnl f: nt qckn nr fin) ½.2
20223 Invisible Armour (47) *(PCHaslam)* 3-8-1 EJohnson (3) (prom tl rdn & outpcd
over 2f out: styd on again fnl f) ................................. 3.3
20642 Arfey (IRE) (65) *(TThomsonJones)* 3-9-5 KDarley (1) (b: led & set mod pce:
hdd 3f out: wknd wl over 1f out) ................................ 7.4

4/5 Great Max (IRE), **6/4** Arfey (IRE), **5/1** PRINCESS ROXANNE, **10/1** Invisible Armour. CSF £10.12, Tote £8.00
(£3.60). Mrs M. O'Donnell (TARPORLEY) bred by Mrs C. Van C. Anthony. 4 Rn
2m 25.2 (6.2)
SF—39/47/18/22

### 2313
KIRKTON H'CAP (0-70) £2427.00 (£672.00: £321.00)   **1m 5f 9y**   4-40 (4-40)
(Weights raised 5 lb)

22462 **Briggsmaid (50)** *(JMPEustace)* 4-9-3 MTebbutt (1) (hld up: jnd ldrs gng wl 3f
out: rdn ins fnl f to ld cl home) ................................ —1
22172 Shadideen (USA) (57) (Fav) *(MissLAPerratt)* 4-9-10 JCarroll (2) (hld up: hdwy
ent st: rdn to ld 3f out: hdd & no ex u.p nr fin) ............... 1½.2
21482 Carol's Pet (IRE) (47) *(MJohnston)* 4-9-0 RPElliott (3) (chsd ldr: led 4f out to 3f
out: one pce fnl 2f) ............................................ 3½.3
21483 Hamilton Lady (IRE) (33) *(DMoffatt)* 4-8-0 AMackay (4) (led tl hdd 4f out: wknd
over 2f out) ................................................... 5.4

13/8 Shadideen (USA), **9/4** BRIGGSMAID, **3/1** Carol's Pet (IRE)(5/2—4/1), **6/1** Hamilton Lady (IRE). CSF £5.84,
Tote £2.80 (£3.30). Mr F. W. Briggs (NEWMARKET) bred by John L. Moore. 4 Rn
2m 51.4 (5.7)
SF—46/50/33/9

T/Plpt: Not won; £1,532.20 to Ayr 24/7/92.
GB

## OSTEND  (R-H) Belgium
## Sunday, July 12th [Good]

### 2314a
PRIX ALBERT VAN LOO (3-Y.O) £5124.00   **1m 3f**

Les Arts (FR) *(France)* 3-8-9 AHeylen ........................... —1
Philroso (BEL) *(Belgium)* 3-8-9 MHendryckx .................... ½.2
Karagourpoulos *(Belgium)* 3-8-7 RVindevogel ................... ¾.3
1466 FLIGHT LIEUTENANT (USA) *(PMitchell)* 3-8-7 LPiggott (btn further ¾'al) ...... 5
Tote 74f: 19f 24f 30f. Mr J. de Cock (J-M. Capitte,FRANCE) bred by Baron David de Rothschild in France. 9 Rn
2m 23.4

## NAPLES (R-H)
### Sunday, July 12th [Good]

**2315a**    PREMIO LIBERO PERLINI (listed race)  £20930.00  1¼m

844a³ **Guado d'Annibale (IRE)** *(Italy)* 3–8-0 JacquelineFreda ................................. —1
1646a MARCUS THORPE (USA) *(PAKelleway)* 4–8-10 FJovine ................................. s.nk.2
1226a² Kohinoor (IRE) *(Italy)* 4–8-10 DZarroli ................................. 1.3
Tote 79L: 18L 15L 14L (224L). Aterno Stud (A.Renzoni,ITALY) bred by Aterno Stud in Ireland. 10 Rn  2m 0.3

---

1984a—**SAINT-CLOUD (L-H)**
### Tuesday, July 14th [Good]
Going Allowance: nil sec per fur (G)

**2316a**    PRIX EUGENE ADAM (Gp 2) (3-Y.O) £41280.00  1¼m

1823a **POLLEN COUNT (USA)** *(JHMGosden)* 3–8-11 SCauthen (mde all: qcknd 2f
out: rdn ins fnl f: drvn out) ................................. —1
1198 GREAT PALM (USA) (Fav) *(PFlCole)* 3–8-11 AMunro (a.p: 2nd st: rdn & ev ch 1f
out: r.o) ................................. ½.2
Fast Cure (USA) *(France)* 3–8-11 ELegrix (6th st: hdwy wl over 1f out: sn ev ch:
r.o) ................................. hd.3
1499a² Non Partisan (USA) *(France)* 3–8-11 PatEddery (trckd ldrs: 3rd st: rdn wl over 1f
out: kpt on one pce) ................................. ¾.4
1356a Break Bread (USA) *(France)* 3–8-11 CAsmussen (4th st: effrt wl over 1f out: one
pce) ................................. 2½.5
1499a⁰ Mendooino (USA) *(France)* 3–8-11 FHead (7th st: outpcd 2f out: r.o ins fnl f) ...... 1.6
Moskovskaya (USA) *(France)* 3–8-8 TJarnet (5th ot: rdn & one pce 2f out) ...... ½.7
635a⁴ Dadarissime (FR) *(France)* 3–8-11 RBriard (a bhd) ................................. 1½.8
1831¹² BOBZAO (IRE) *(WCarter)* 3–8-11 LPiggott (nvr able to chal) ................................. ¾.9
1356a Glanville (USA) (bl) *(France)* 3–8-11 GMosse (a bhd) ................................. 10
2/1 Great Palm (USA), 7/2 Break Bread (USA), 15/4 Non Partisan (USA), 9/1 Mendocino (USA), Moskovskaya
(USA), 11/1 Fast Cure (USA), 12/1 POLLEN COUNT (USA), 18/1 Bobzao (IRE), 20/1 Ors. Tote 13.10f: 3.40f
1.90f 3.30f (17.70f). Sheikh Mohammed (NEWMARKET) bred by Muckler Stables Inc. in USA. 10 Rn
2m 5.6 (1.6)
SF—81/80/79/77/72/70

---

## SAINT-CLOUD (L-H)
### Friday, July 17th [Good]
Going Allowance: nil sec per fur (G)

**2317a**    PRIX MONADE  £6192.00  1m

**Acteur Francais (USA)** *(France)* 4–8-7 TJarnet ................................. —1
Booming (FR) *(France)* 4–8-7 MBoutin ................................. 1.2
Masskana (IRE) *(France)* 4–8-8 OPoirier ................................. nk.3
Tote 1.60f: 1.10f 1.30f 1.40f (4.40f). Mr P. de Moussac (A.Fabre,FRANCE) bred by Marylands Stud in USA. 9 Rn
1m 41.2 (2.6)
SF—54/51/51

---

1350a—**LEOPARDSTOWN (L-H)**
### Saturday, July 18th [Good]
Going Allowance: nil sec per fur (G)

**2318a**    BALLYCORUS STKS (listed race)  £8061.00  7f

**Pre-Eminent** (bl) *(Ireland)* 5–9-11 MJKinane ................................. —1
1495a² Poolesta (IRE) *(Ireland)* 3–8-9(3) JPMurtagh ................................. 1½.2
429 Miznah (IRE) *(Ireland)* 3–9-2 CRoche ................................. 1½.3
1347⁶ SOLAR STAR (USA) *(MBell)* 3–8-6 AMunro (btn further 8¾l) ................................. 6
Tote £4.80: £1.50 £1.30 £1.60 (£5.00). Dr Michael Smurfit (D.K.Weld,IRELAND) bred by Dunderry Stud. 8 Rn
1m 29.4 (4.4)
SF—45/24/26

---

2091a—**EVRY (R-H)**
### Saturday, July 18th [Good]
Going Allowance: minus 0.20 sec per fur (F)

**2319a**    PRIX MINERVE (Gp 3) (3-Y.O.F) £20640.00  1½m

**Linnga (IRE)** *(France)* 3–8-9 GGuignard ................................. —1

1498a[6] Urban Sea (USA) *(France)* 3-8-9 MBoutin ................................................................... nk.2
1498a Decided Air (IRE) *(France)* 3-8-9 CAsmussen ............................................................ nk.3
Tote 2.10f: 1.40f 1.80f (8.40f). H.H.Aga Khan (A. de Royer-Dupre,FRANCE) bred by H.H.Aga Khan in Ireland. 7
Rn                                                                                                                        2m 30.72 (1.12)
                                                                                                                            SF—60/59/58

## 2090a—MAISONS-LAFFITTE (L-H)

### Sunday, July 19th [Good to soft]
Going Allowance: minus 0.35 sec per fur (F)

**2320a**   PRIX ROBERT PAPIN (Gp 2) (2-Y.O.C & F) £36120.00   **5f 110y**

Didyme (USA) *(Fav) (France)* 2-8-11 GMosse (5th tl hdwy wl over 1f out: led 1f
out: r.o wl) ............................................................................................................... —1
Creaking Board *(France)* 2-8-9 ELegrix (trckd ldr: led 2f out to 1f out: hrd rdn:
kpt on) ................................................................................................................... nk.2
Rouquette *(France)* 2-8-9 ABadel (a in tch: hdwy wl over 1f out: one pce fnl f) 2¹⁄₂.3
Grand Vefour (USA) *(France)* 2-8-11 ESaint-Martin (hdwy wl over 1f out: one
pce) ....................................................................................................................... s.nk.4
1982a* Glorieux Dancer (FR) *(France)* 2-8-11 MBoutin (led tl wl over 2f out: sn wknd) . ¹⁄₂.5
Miss Kadrou (FR) *(France)* 2-8-9 GDubroeucq (a outpcd & bhd) ...................... ¹⁄₂.6
Berinsfield (bl) *(France)* 2-8-11 SCauthen (trckd ldr: led briefly wl over 2f out:
wknd qckly) .......................................................................................................... 2¹⁄₂.7

Evens DIDYME (USA), 9/4 Berinsfield, 5/1 Creaking Board, 15/2 Glorieux Dancer (FR), 11/1 Rouquette, 18/1
Miss Kadrou (FR), 25/1 Grand Vefour (USA). Tote 2.00f: 1.60f 2.40f (SF: 6.00f). Mr J. Wertheimer (Mrs C.
Head,FRANCE) bred by Wertheimer & Frere in USA. 7 Rn                                                          64.5 sec (U.7)
                                                                                                                            SF—73/67/57/58/26/52/44

## TURIN (R-H)

### Sunday, July 19th [Good]

**2321a**   PREMIO F I A BREEDERS CUP (listed race) (2-Y.O) £20930.00   **7f 110y**

1985a* ANCESTRAL DANCER *(MBell)* 2-9-0 MHills ................................................................ —1
1985a[3] Zaira da Cesena (USA) *(Italy)* 2-8-8 GDettori ................................................ 2¹⁄₄.2
Darubena (ITY) *(Italy)* 2-8-8 WCarson ............................................................... ³⁄₄.3
Tote 14L: 11L 16L 16L (47L). Innlaw Racing (NEWMARKET) bred by Hillfields Stud. 10 Rn      1m 32.6

**2322a**   PREMIO ROYAL MARES (Gp 3) (F) £27907.00   **1m**

Mountain Ash *(Italy)* 3-8-5(1) MHills ................................................................... —1
1460[5] CLOUD OF DUST *(JLDunlop)* 3-8-4 TQuinn .............................................. ³⁄₄.2
Polish Style (USA) *(France)* 3-8-4 WCarson .................................................... 2.3
Tote 195L: 32L 19L 15L (1,072L). Scuderia Azzurra (B.Agriformi,ITALY) bred by Clanville Lodge Stud. 17 Rn
                                                                                                                            1m 34.2

**2323a**   ST LEGER ITALIANO (Gp 3) (3-Y.O) £32558.00   **1³⁄₄m 110y**

1356a JAPE (USA) *(PFICole)* 3-9-2 AMunro .......................................................... —1
979* SILVERNESIAN (USA) *(JLDunlop)* 3-9-2 WCarson ........................................ 3¹⁄₂.2
1940[4] FOR MOG (USA) *(CEBrittain)* 3-9-2 MRoberts ......................................... 3.3
Tote 16L: 10L 10L 10L (24L). Mr Fahd Salman (WHATCOMBE) bred by Kinderhill Select Bloodstock in USA. 7 Rn
                                                                                                                            3m 11

## 1616—CARLISLE (R-H)

### Friday, July 24th [Firm, Good to firm patches]
Going Allowance: minus 0.40 sec per fur (F)                                       Wind: mod half against

Stalls: high

**2324**   CUMBRIA TOURIST BOARD STKS (Mdn 3-Y.O) £2217.00 (£612.00: £291.00)
                **6f 206y**                                                                          2-20 (2-21)

2164[2] Canon Kyle (IRE) (64) *(MHEasterby)* 9-0 MBirch (3) (chsd ldr: 2nd st: led over
1f out: pushed out) ................................................................................................ —1
1761[2] Countercheck (IRE) (54) *(Fav) (CFWall)* 9-0 DMcKeown (2) (lw: led: shkn up
over 2f out: hdd over 1f out: r.o one pce) ........................................................... 2¹⁄₂.2
2104[4] Mummy's Brew *(BBeasley)* 8-9 LCharnock (1) (s.i.s: 3rd & rdn st: sn lost tch) . 20.3

4/5 Countercheck (IRE), 5/4 CANON KYLE (IRE), 9/1 Mummy's Brew. CSF £2.54, Tote £2.00 (£1.20). Lady
Murless (MALTON) bred by Lady Murless in Ireland. 3 Rn                                    1m 26.4 (1.2)
                                                                                                                            SF—40/32/–

**2325**   GRAHAM (COMMERCIALS) LTD H'CAP (0-70) £2668.60 (£739.60: £353.80)
5f 207y
2-50 (2-52)

1961³ **Johnston's Express (IRE)** (37) *(EJAlston)* 4-8-1 PRobinson (2) (bhd: hdwy 2f
out: ev ch whn hmpd ins fnl f: checked nr fin: fin 2nd, 1l:
awrdd r) .................................................................................... —1

1924* Blue Grit (46) *(MDods)* 6-8-10 KFallon (5) (swtg: bhd: hdwy 2f out: rdn & edgd
rt: led wl ins fnl f: fin 1st: disq: plcd 2nd) ............................... 2

2234³ Pretonic (62) *(MJohnston)* 4-9-12 DMcKeown (4) (a:p: led wl over 1f out tl wl
ins fnl f) ................................................................................ nk.3

2003³ Glenstal Princess (61) *(RHollinshead)* 5-9-4 ‡7AGarth (7) (lw: hdwy over 2f out:
rdn & kpt on fnl f: nt pce to chal) ........................................... 2.4

2203* Miss Aragon (47) (Fav) *(MissLCSiddall)* 4-8-6 (7x) ‡5OPears (8) (lw: a:p: led
over 2f out tl over 1f out: sn outpcd) ..................................... 3¹/₂.5

1964 Northern Emperor (IRE) (41) *(MHEasterby)* 3-7-8⁽⁶⁾ ‡5SMaloney (3) (spd over
4f: sn hrd rdn & wknd) .......................................................... s.h.6

2032 Pipe Opener (50) *(JLSpearing)* 4-9-9 GDuffield (1) (nvr nr to chal) ............... 2.7

1904* Don't Run Me Over (50) *(BCMorgan)* 3-8-8 JCarroll (10) (led tl over 2f out: sn
rdn & wknd) .......................................................................... 3¹/₂.8

1978 Hinari Hi Fi (37) *(PDEvans)* 7-7-12 ‡3JFanning (9) (chsd ldrs over 4f) ........... 3.9

2245⁶ Come on My Girl (IRE) (45) *(TAKCuthbert)* 4-8-9 LCharnock (6) (chsd ldrs 4f:
sn outpcd: t.o) ...................................................................... 7.10

LONG HANDICAP: Northern Emperor (IRE) 7-5.
*Stewards Enquiry: Obj. to Blue Grit by Robinson sustained. Fallon suspended 2-5/8/92 (careless riding).*

**9/4** Miss Aragon, **5/1** JOHNSTON'S EXPRESS (IRE), Glenstal Princess, **11/2** Blue Grit, **7/1** Don't Run Me Over,
**17/2** Pretonic, **12/1** Hinari Hi Fi, **14/1** Northern Emperor (IRE), **20/1** Pipe Opener, **25/1** Come on My Girl (IRE).
CSF £32.48, CT £215.09. Tote £7.20: £2.10 £2.10 £2.60 (£15.10). Mr Frank McKevitt (PRESTON) bred by
Collinstown Stud Farm Ltd in Ireland. 10 Rn                                      1m 13.3 (1)
SF—15/28/39/23/–/–

**2326**   SCANIA CUMBRIA DISTRIBUTORS CHAMPION APP'CE H'CAP (0-70) £2735.80
(£758.80: £363.40)   7f 214y
3-20 (3-21)

1960⁵ **Tancred Grange** (61) *(MissSEHall)* 3-8-7 ‡5OPears (9) (b.off hind: led 3f: 3rd st:
led over 2f out: rdn & r.o gamely) ........................................... —1

2205⁵ Who's Tef (IRE) (62) *(MHEasterby)* 4-9-7 SMaloney (5) (chsd ldrs: 2nd st:
outpcd over 2f out: rallied fnl f: r.o) ...................................... 1¹/₂.2

1992³ No Comebacks (42) *(EJAlston)* 4-7-8 ‡7GMitchell (6) (stumbled & lost pl 5f out:
gd hdwy 2f out: styd on ins fnl f) ........................................... nk.3

1966 Top Scale (36) (v) (Jt-Fav) *(WWHaigh)* 6-7-9 NKennedy (3) (a:p: 3rd st: rdn &
outpcd over 2f out: kpt on u.p appr fnl f) ................................ ¹/₂.4

2147² Henbury Hall (IRE) (60) *(MrsGRReveley)* 4-9-0 ‡5DarrenMoffatt (8) (led
after 3f tl over 2f out: wknd fnl f) .......................................... 1¹/₂.5

1794³ Sanawi (52) *(PDEvans)* 5-8-6 ‡5LNewton (1) (5th st: rdn over 2f out: nvr able to
chal) ..................................................................................... nk.6

2147⁴ Broad Appeal (38) (bl) *(BBeasley)* 4-7-6 ‡5AGarth (2) (6th st: effrt over 2f out: no
imp) ....................................................................................... 5.7

1964 Brown as a Berry (IRE) (34) *(WStorey)* 4-7-7 JFanning (4) (lw: a bhd) ............ 2¹/₂.8

LONG HANDICAP: Brown as a Berry (IRE) 7-1.

**3/1** Top Scale, Henbury Hall (IRE), **11/2** TANCRED GRANGE, **6/1** Sanawi, No Comebacks, **13/2** Who's Tef (IRE),
**10/1** Broad Appeal, **20/1** Brown as a Berry (IRE). CSF £38.75, CT £204.38. Tote £7.20: £1.90 £1.10 £1.80
(£11.40). Mr W. G. Barker (MIDDLEHAM) bred by Brickfield Bloodstock Agency Ltd. 8 Rn      1m 39.4 (0.7)
SF—34/43/15/14/28/19

**2327**   SCANIA TRUCKS CLAIMING STKS (3-Y.O) £2217.00 (£612.00: £291.00)
6f 206y
3-50 (3-50)

489³ **Jefferson Davis (IRE)** (69) (Fav) *(BBeasley)* 9-3 DNicholls (2) (mde all: clr
over 1f out: rdn out) .............................................................. —1

2119* Crept Out (IRE) (64) *(MissSEHall)* 9-0 NConnorton (3) (chsd ldrs: 4th st: styd
on u.p appr fnl f: nvr nrr) ...................................................... 2¹/₂.2

1961 Oyston's Life (46) *(JBerry)* 9-0 JCarroll (4) (lw: prom: 3rd st: rdn over 2f out:
unable qckn) ......................................................................... ³/₄.3

2162⁴ Cledeschamps (MWEllerby) 8-0 SMorris (1) (chsd wnr: 2nd st: rdn 2f out: sn
btn) ....................................................................................... 4.4

1961 Lowlands Boy (49) *(TFairhurst)* 8-11 ‡3JFanning (4) (outpcd & bhd: 5th st: t.o fnl
2f) ......................................................................................... 5.5

**8/11** JEFFERSON DAVIS (IRE)(op 11/10), **7/4** Crept Out (IRE), **5/1** Oyston's Life, **16/1** Lowlands Boy, **20/1**
Cledeschamps. CSF £2.73, Tote £1.80: £1.40 £1.10 (£1.80). The Confederacy (HAMBLETON) bred by Rose
O'Reilly in Ireland. 5 Rn                                               1m 27.3 (2.1)
SF—29/18/16/–/–

**2328**   CHAS KENDALL AUCTION STKS (2-Y.O) £2556.60 (£707.60: £337.80)
5f 207y
4-25 (4-26)

1946* **Ventiquattrofogli (IRE)** *(JLDunlop)* 9-4 GDuffield (4) (lw: a.p: rdn to chal over 1f out: qcknd to ld nr fin) .................... —1

2271² Nominator (Fav) *(RHollinshead)* 9-4 KDarley (1) (lw: led after 2f: hrd rdn & ct wl ins fnl f) .................... ½.2

2074* Margaret's Gift *(JBerry)* 8-13 JCarroll (2) (lw: swtg: hld up: rdn 2f out: nt pce to chal) .................... 1½.3

1670² Eightofus *(GMMoore)* 8-11 DMcKeown (3) (led 2f: lost tch sn after ½-wy: t.o) . 15.4

6/5 Nominator, 5/4 VENTIQUATTROFOGLI (IRE), 4/1 Margaret's Gift, 33/1 Eightofus. CSF £3.15, Tote £2.20 (£1.50). Gerecon Italia (ARUNDEL) bred by Kiltinan Farms Inc in Ireland. 4 Rn
1m 13.6 (1.3)
SF—30/28/17/–

**2329**   MARKS & SPENCER H'CAP (0-80) £2887.20 (£799.20: £381.60)   1½m 5-00 (5-01)
(Weights raised 6 lb)

1452* **Persian Fantasy (79)** (Fav) *(JLDunlop)* 3-9-10 GDuffield (4) (lw: hld up: 3rd st: effrt 2f out: hrd rdn to ld wl ins fnl f) .................... —1

1866⁴ Luks Akura (45) (v) *(MJohnston)* 4–7–9 ‡7MBaird (1) (lw: led & sn clr: hdd wl ins fnl f: rallied cl home) .................... nk.2

2166³ Duggan (56) *(RJRWilliams)* 5–8–13 DMcKeown (3) (lw: chsd ldr: rdn along 4f out: 2nd st: wknd 2f out) .................... 7.3

1518² Stapleton (IRE) (76) (bl) *(JWWatts)* 3–9-7 PRobinson (2) (lw: hld up & bhd: 4th st: rdn wl over 1f out: no rspnse) .................... 6.4

7/4 PERSIAN FANTASY, 9/4 Stapleton (IRE), Duggan, 7/1 Luks Akura. CSF £10.62, Tote £2.50 (£7.60). Windflower Overseas Holdings Inc (ARUNDEL) bred by Windflower Overseas. 4 Rn
2m 30.3 (1.2 under best; 0.8)
SF—54/24/28/24

T/Plpt: £268.30 (5.2 Tckts).
IM

## 1918—PONTEFRACT (L-H)

### Friday, July 24th [Good to firm]

Going Allowance: minus 0.20 sec per fur (F)
Wind: slt half bhd

Stalls: low

**2330**   PORTER'S LODGE CLAIMING STKS (2-Y.O) £2259.00 (£624.00: £297.00)
5f
6-45 (6-46)

2008 **Trentesimo (IRE)** *(JBerry)* 8-11 GCarter (1) (mde all: r.o wl u.p over 1f out: sn clr) .................... —1

2085³ Cloudy Reef *(RHollinshead)* 7-8 ‡7AGarth (2) (sn chsng wnr: effrt & rdn over 1f out: kpt on same pce) .................... 3.2

1479* Blue Radiance (Fav) *(TFairhurst)* 8-6 ACulhane (3) (chsd ldrs: rdn & outpcd ½-wy: kpt on one pce) .................... 1½.3

1835⁴ Hairraising (bl) *(NACallaghan)* 7-8 ‡7JTate (4) (sn chsng ldrs: effrt ½-wy: nvr able to chal) .................... 1½.4

2005³ Tropical Tia (IRE) *(RVoorspuy)* 8-0 SDawson (5) (plld hrd: effrt on outside over 2f out: edgd lft & sn wknd) .................... 8.5

2/1 Blue Radiance, 11/4 TRENTESIMO (IRE), 3/1 Cloudy Reef, 5/1 Hairraising, 10/1 Tropical Tia (IRE). CSF £10.43, Tote £3.00: £1.60 £2.10 (£5.00). Mr B. R. Allen (COCKERHAM) bred by E. O'Leary in Ireland. 5 Rn
63.6 sec (2.1)
SF—35/6/12/–/–

**2331**   MILL DAM MEDIAN AUCTION STKS (Mdn 3-Y.O) £2280.00 (£630.00: £300.00)
1¼m 6y
7-10 (7-12)

**Last Embrace (IRE)** *(LordHuntingdon)* 8-9 WRSwinburn (3) (hdwy to jn ldr 4f out: rdn to ld wl over 1f out: drvn clr) .................... —1

1857³ Iota (63) (Fav) *(MrsJCecil)* 8-9 MRoberts (1) (led: hrd rdn over 1f out: wknd ins fnl f) .................... 12.2

Secret Treaty (IRE) *(PWChapple-Hyam)* 8-9 PaulEddery (2) (rangy: unf: sn trckng ldr: effrt over 3f out: one pce) .................... 6.3

Soul Trader *(BWHills)* 8-6 DLee (4) (chsd ldr: drvn along 6f out: lost pl 4f out) ... 8.4

1933 Jade Mistress *(AHide)* 8-9 JWilliams (5) (sn pushed along: lost pl 4f out: sn wl bhd) .................... 25.5

7/4 Iota, 3/1 LAST EMBRACE (IRE), 4/1 Secret Treaty (IRE)(op 7/4), 9/2 Jade Mistress, 10/1 Soul Trader. CSF £8.06, Tote £3.70: £1.70 £1.40 (£2.90). Mr E. J. Loder (WEST ILSLEY) bred by E. J. Loder in Ireland. 5 Rn
2m 9.9 (1.6)
SF—59/35/23/4/–

**2332**    TETLEY BITTER H'CAP (0-90) £3590.00 (£1070.00: £510.00: £230.00)
      1¼m 6y                                        7-35 (7-37)

(Weights raised 6 lb)

2273* **Sinclair Lad (IRE) (59)** (Fav) *(RHollinshead)* 4–9-0 (6x) WRSwinburn (1) (lw: hld up gng wl: smooth hdwy to ld jst ins fnl f: sn clr) .................. —1

2204³ **Eire Leath-Sceal (56)** *(MBrittain)* 5–8-11 MRoberts (2) (lw: led: sn hrd drvn: hdd over 2f out: led over 1f out: sn hdd & no ch w wnr) .................. 3¹/₂.2

1960 **North Esk (USA) (74)** *(JWWatts)* 3–9-5 JLowe (5) (swtg: hld up: effrt over 2f out tl nt clr run over 1f out: nvr nr to chal) ........................ ¾.3

1968 **Barbary Reef (IRE) (46)** *(GHEden)* 4–9-10 GCarter (4) (jnd ldr 6f out: led over 2f out tl hdd & wknd over 1f out) ...................... 1¹/₂.4

1073 **Chiefs Babu (69)** *(RO'Leary)* 4–9-10 MBirch (3) (prom tl rdn & lost pl over 3f out: sn wl bhd & eased) ...................... dist.5

**6/4** SINCLAIR LAD (IRE), **11/4** Eire Leath-Sceal, **4/1** Barbary Reef (IRE), **13/2** Chiefs Babu, **8/1** North Esk (USA). CSF £5.73, Tote £2.30: £1.40 £1.60 (£2.10). Sinclair Developments Limited (UPPER LONGDON) bred by John Burns in Ireland. 5 Rn                                 2m 11.9 (3.6)
                                                   SF—44/34/40/19/–

---

**2333**    ST JOHN AMBULANCE H'CAP (0-70) £2385.00 (£660.00: £315.00)    **5f**   8-05 (8-05)

2099³ **Fighter Squadron (53)** (bl) *(JAGlover)* 3–8-4 ‡⁷SWilliams (5) (hdwy 2f out: hung bdly lft: styd on to ld nr fin) ...................... —1

2115² **Last Straw (37)** *(AWJones)* 4–7-7 ‡⁷ClaireBalding (6) (w ldr: led over 2f out tl cl home) ...................... nk.2

2073 **Simmie's Special (62)** *(RHollinshead)* 4–9-4 ‡⁷SWynne (2) (led tl over 2f out: ev ch 1f out: kpt on same pce) ...................... 1¹/₂.3

2199 **Oratel Flyer (30)** (v) *(HThompson)* 5–7-7 JLowe (3) (sn outpcd: hdwy over 1f out: nvr nr to chal) ...................... 1¹/₂.4

325 **Spanish Realm (45)** *(MBrittain)* 5–8-8 GDuffield (4) (b.hind: chsd ldr: sn drvn along: wknd over 1f out) ...................... 5

2224⁵ **North of Watford (50)** (Fav) *(MPNaughton)* 7–8-13 MRoberts (7) (trckd ldrs: rdn & wandered over 1f out: sn lost pl) ...................... 1¹/₂.6

     **Kabcast (63)** (bl) *(DWChapman)* 7–9-12 SWood (1) (hdwy on ins & prom 2f out: wknd over 1f out) ...................... 4.7

LONG HANDICAP: Oratel Flyer 7-4.

**9/4** North of Watford, **7/2** FIGHTER SQUADRON, **4/1** Last Straw, **5/1** Simmie's Special, **8/1** Oratel Flyer, **12/1** Kabcast, **20/1** Spanish Realm. CSF £16.53, Tote £3.50: £2.30 £1.90 (£5.00). Claremont Management Services (WORKSOP) bred by Coxland Stud. 7 Rn                              63.3 sec (1.8)
                                                   SF—34/22/41/10/17/16

---

**2334**    YORKSHIRE TELEVISION H'CAP (3-Y.O) (0-70) £2763.00 (£768.00: £369.00)
      1¹/₂m 8y                                       8-35 (8-36)

(Weights raised 3 lb)

1574⁵ **Maestroso (IRE) (64)** *(RFJohnsonHoughton)* 9-4 MRoberts (2) (lw: hdwy over 3f out: led over 1f out: styd on wl u.p) ...................... —1

1977 **Hazaaf (USA) (60)** *(AAScott)* 9-0 WRSwinburn (1) (trckd ldrs: effrt & rdn over 2f out: r.o one pce: fin 3rd, 1¹/₂l: plcd 2nd) ...................... 2

908 **Mr Ziegfeld (USA) (67)** *(SirMarkPrescott)* 9-7 GDuffield (8) (hld up & plld hrd: bhd: hdwy over 2f out: nvr nr to chal: fin 4th, 6l: plcd 3rd) .......... 3

    **Aide Memoire (IRE) (50)** *(CBBBooth)* 8-4⁽²⁾ ACulhane (4) (bhd: sme hdwy 2f out: n.d: fin 5th, 1¹/₂l: plcd 4th) ...................... 4

1901⁶ **Irish Honey (IRE) (47)** *(BHanbury)* 8-1 BCrossley (10) (lw: chsd ldrs: sn rdn along: one pce fnl 3f) ...................... 1¹/₂.6

1850 **Sweet Noble (IRE) (55)** *(JGFitzGerald)* 8-9 MBirch (9) (w ldrs tl wknd over 2f out) ...................... 12.7

1700⁶ **Dramatic Pass (IRE) (48)** *(MrsGRReveley)* 8-2 JLowe (3) (sn bhd & drvn along) 7.8

1089 **Fait Accompli (FR) (46)** *(JJO'Neill)* 8-0 SWood (6) (led tl over 3f out: wknd over 2f out) ...................... s.h.9

1686² **Sandro (54)** *(JRFanshawe)* 8-8 GCarter (9) (chsd ldrs: rdn & hmpd over 3f out: sn lost pl) ...................... 4.10

2070² **Kadari (52)** (v) *(AHarrison)* 8-6 PaulEddery (7) (hmpd & led over 3f out: hdd over 1f out: one pce: fin 2nd, 2¹/₂l: disq: plcd last) ................. 0

*Stewards Enquiry: Kadari disq. (interference to Sandro over 3f out).Eddery suspended 3-9/8/92 (careless riding).*

**11/4** Kadari(op 5/1), **7/2** MAESTROSO (IRE), **9/2** Sandro, **6/1** Dramatic Pass (IRE), Mr Ziegfeld (USA), **10/1** Irish Honey (IRE), **11/1** Hazaaf (USA), **12/1** Sweet Noble (IRE), **25/1** Ors. CSF £40.99, CT £210.79. Tote £4.30: £1.40 £2.50 £2.60 (£5.10). Mrs Trisha Dunbar (DIDCOT) bred by P. Larkin in Ireland. 10 Rn           2m 37.5 (3)
                                                   SF—50/33/38/33/13/7

**2335**  E.B.F. GLASSHOUGHTON STKS (Mdn 2-Y.O.C & G) £2301.00 (£636.00: £303.00)
6f
9-05 (9-07)

1915⁴ Garp (FR) (Fav) (MRStoute) 9-0 WRSwinburn (6) (trckd ldrs: effrt & rdn 2f out: led jst ins fnl f: sn hdd: led post) ........ —1

2024 Hoy-Liegh-Rag (MJohnston) 9-0 MRoberts (5) (lw: trckd ldr: led ins fnl f: hrd rdn & r.o: ct post) ......... hd.2

Fyfield Flyer (IRE) (PWChapple-Hyam) 9-0 PaulEddery (3) (s.i.s: sn trckng ldrs: rn green & edgd rt over 1f out: kpt on) .............. 4.3

1397⁴ Best Appearance (IRE) (JGFitzgerald) 9-0 MBirch (4) (bit bkwd: s.i.s: bhd: gd hdwy over 1f out: r.o: nt rch ldrs) ........ 2.4

See Us There (IRE) (JBerry) 9-0 GCarter (1) (cmpt: bit bkwd: trckd ldrs: pushed along ½-wy: wknd over 1f out) .............. 5.5

1744⁵ Magirika (IRE) (MMoubarak) 9-0 GDuffield (2) (led to 2f out: sn wknd) .............. 3.6

**5/6** GARP (FR), **7/2** Fyfield Flyer (IRE), **9/2** Hoy-Liegh-Rag, **7/1** Magirika (IRE), **12/1** See Us There (IRE)(op 8/1), **20/1** Best Appearance (IRE). CSF £5.47, Tote £2.00: £1.30 £2.30 (£3.70). Mr Khalifa Sultan (NEWMARKET) bred by Patrick Barbe & Hubert Honore in France. 6 Rn
1m 16.8 (2.8)
SF—20/19/3/–/–/–

T/Plpt: £26.50 (77.3 Tckts).
WG

**Friday, July 24th [Good]**
Going Allowance: St: 0.15 sec (G); Rnd: minus 0.10 sec per fur (F)     Wind: almost nil

Stalls: centre

**2336**  CRANBOURNE CHASE STKS (Mdn 3-Y.O) £10052.00 (£2996.00: £1428.00: £644.00)
1¼m
2-00 (2-04)

Fast Manouvre (FR) (MMoubarak) 9-0 TQuinn (4) (b: 4th st: led over 1f out: rdn out) ......... —1

Kasmayo (JHMGosden) 9-0 WCarson (5) (6th w: hdwy over 1f out: r.o) ......... 2½.2

1537³ Lobilio (USA) (90) (CEBrittain) 9-0 MRoberts (3) (lw: led over 8f: unable qckn) ..... hd.3

1245³ Triennium (USA) (LMCumani) 9-0 LDettori (2) (swtg: rdn over 4f out: 5th st: one pce fnl 2f) ......... 7.4

1537⁴ Hierarch (USA) (LordHuntingdon) 9-0 WRSwinburn (6) (lw: 2nd st: hrd rdn over 1f out: eased whn btn fnl f) ........ 2.5

1933³ Blessington (USA) (v) (JHMGosden) 9-0 SCauthen (7) (3rd st: hrd rdn over 2f out: sn wknd) .............. 8.6

2168 Leonardo (PRHedger) 9-4⁽⁴⁾ EMcKinley (1) (leggy: lt-f: s.s: a bhd: t.o fnl 3f) .... dist.7

**9/4** Blessington (USA), **4/1** Lobilio (USA), **9/2** Hierarch (USA), **9/2** Triennium (USA)(op 3/1), **13/2** FAST MANOUVRE (FR), **10/1** Kasmayo, **50/1** Leonardo. CSF £55.84, Tote £2.40: £3.50 £2.70 (£42.80). Ecurie Fustok (NEWMARKET) bred by Buckram Thoroughbred Enterprises in France. 7 Rn
2m 6.33 (2.03)
SF—70/65/64/50/46/30

**2337**  PALAN H'CAP (0-100) £10598.00 (£3164.00: £1512.00: £686.00)  6f  2-30 (2-37)

2060 **Bertie Wooster (79)** (RJHolder) 9-8-11 LDettori (6) (hdwy over 1f out: led ins fnl f: r.o wl) ......... —1

1943 Running Glimpse (IRE) (73) (MissBSanders) 4-8-5 MRoberts (11) (a.p: led over 1f out tl ins fnl f: unable qckn) .............. 1½.2

1943 Nordic Brave (75) (MBrittain) 6-8-7 JLowe (12) (a.p: ev ch over 1f out: one pce) .. hd.3

1943 Sir Boudle (IRE) (83) (CRNelson) 3-8-9 DHolland (10) (hdwy over 1f out: r.o) . nk.4

1837★ Massiba (IRE) (90) (Fav) (MJHeaton-Ellis) 3-9-2 BRaymond (5) (lw: led over 4f: one pce) .............. 2.5

1871⁵ Lady Sabo (70) (GLewis) 3-7-5 ‡⁵DHarrison (1) (lw: nvr nr to chal) .............. nk.6

1692⁶ Petraco (IRE) (74) (LJCodd) 4-8-6 NCarlisle (7) (a.p: one pce fnl 2f) .............. ½.7

2013 Choir Practice (79) (WJHaggas) 5-8-11 NDay (2) (swtg: outpcd) .............. 1½.8

2169³ Bit of a Lark (96) (RHollinshead) 4-10-0 PaulEddery (4) (bhd fnl 2f) .............. 3½.9

2127⁴ Plain Fact (90) (JWHills) 7-9-8 WRSwinburn (8) (hld up: hrd rdn over 2f out: eased whn btn over 1f out) .............. 2.10

2203² Final Shot (65) (MHEasterby) 5-7-8 ‡³FNorton (9) (swtg: a bhd) .............. 5.11

1400 Ghalyoon (USA) (11/1) Withdrawn (lame): not under orders

**7/2** Massiba (IRE), **9/2** Final Shot, **13/2** Running Glimpse (IRE), **7/1** Bit of a Lark, **10/1** Petraco (IRE), Sir Boudle (IRE), Choir Practice, **11/1** Plain Fact, **14/1** Lady Sabo, **16/1** BERTIE WOOSTER & Ors. CSF £107.63, CT £1,546.18. Tote £17.70: £3.90 £2.10 £4.70 (£75.20). Miss Amanda J. Rawding (BRISTOL) bred by Mrs J. A. Rawding. 11 Rn
1m 16.06 (2.46)
SF—66/54/55/56/55/29

**2338**　VIRGINIA WATER STKS (Mdn 2-Y.O.F) £9688.00 (£2884.00: £1372.00: £616.00)
6f　　　　　　　　　　　　　　　　　　　　　　　　　　　3-00 (3-03)

**Dancing Bloom (IRE)** (Fav) *(MRStoute)* 8-11 WRSwinburn (3) (unf: scope:
　　　　mde all: comf) ...................................................................... —1
City Times (IRE) *(BAMcMahon)* 8-11 TQuinn (1) (unf: hld up: rdn over 1f out:
　　　　r.o) ...................................................................................... 4.2
Magic Street *(MMoubarak)* 8-11 LDettori (5) (w'like: scope: hld up: rdn over 1f
　　　　out: unable qckn) .............................................................. hd.3
Mataris *(PTWalwyn)* 8-11 RCochrane (2) (w'like: bit bkwd: hdwy over 1f out: r.o) nk.4
Thawakib (IRE) *(JLDunlop)* 8-11 WCarson (7) (w'like: scope: bit bkwd: prom 4f) 6.5
Dittisham (USA) *(RHannon)* 8-11 MRoberts (6) (w'like: scope: spd 4f) .......... 5.6
Lys (IRE) *(CEBrittain)* 8-11 SCauthen (4) (neat: spd over 3f) ...................... 8.7

**13/8** DANCING BLOOM (IRE)(5/2—6/4), **2/1** Thawakib (IRE)(2/1—5/4), **9/2** Dittisham (USA)(3/1—5/1), **10/1**
Magic Street(8/1—12/1), **16/1** Ors. CSF £23.07, Tote £2.80: £2.00 £3.20 (£21.60). Lord Weinstock
(NEWMARKET) bred by Ballymacoll Stud Farm Ltd in Ireland. 7 Rn
　　　　　　　　　　　　　　　　　　　　　　　　　　　　　　　1m 16.97 (3.37)
　　　　　　　　　　　　　　　　　　　　　　　　　　　　　SF—48/32/31/30/6/–

---

**2339**　BROWN JACK H'CAP (0-110) £11160.00 (£3330.00: £1590.00: £720.00)
2m 45y　　　　　　　　　　　　　　　　　　　　　　　　　3-30 (3-31)
　　　　　　　　　　(Weights raised 1 lb)

1938 **Gay Glint (85)** *(NAGraham)* 5-9-0 MRoberts (3) (lw: 3rd st: led 1f out: rdn out) . —1
1697 Requested **(74)** *(RAkehurst)* 5-8-3 TQuinn (2) (2nd st: led 2f out to 1f out:
　　　　unable qckn) .................................................................. 1½.2
1874▲ Brandon Prince (IRE) **(82)** (bl) *(IABalding)* 4-8-11 RCochrane (10) (5th st: r.o
　　　　one pce fnl 2f) ................................................................. 2½.3
990▲ Aude la Belle (FR) **(75)** *(MrsAKnight)* 4-8-1 J²Norton (7) (swtg: hdwy over 3f
　　　　out: 6th st: r.o one pce fnl 2f) ....................................... 1.4
1938▲ Kansk **(95)** *(JHMGosden)* 4-9-10 SCauthen (4) (led over 14f) ................ 1½.5
2071³ Cabochon **(77)** *(DMorley)* 5-8-6 WCarson (1) (nvr nr to chal) ................... 1.6
2129▲ Jungle Dancer (IRE) **(85)** (v) *(MRStoute)* 4-9-0 DHolland (5) (swtg: nvr nrr) ½.7
2071▲ My Desire **(70)** *(MrsGRReveley)* 4-7-13 (3x) JLowe (11) (lw: bhd fnl 5f) .......... 7.8
1874² Majestic Image **(72)** (Fav) *(LordHuntingdon)* 6-7-10 ‡⁵DHarrison (8) (lw: a bhd) 3½.9
2001³ Star Player **(82)** *(RJBaker)* 6-8-11 LDettori (6) (lw: 4th st: wknd wl over 1f out) hd.10
2217▲ Magic Secret **(69)** *(PCHaslam)* 4-7-12 (3x) DaleGibson (9) (prom 12f) .......... 8.11

**11/4** Majestic Image, **11/2** Cabochon, **7/1** Brandon Prince (IRE), My Desire, Kansk, **15/2** Requested, **10/1** Star
Player, **12/1** Aude la Belle (FR), Jungle Dancer (IRE), **16/1** GAY GLINT & Ors. CSF £126.55, CT £851.18. Tote
£17.80: £4.20 £2.50 £2.90 (£68.70). Mr Paul G. Jacobs (NEWMARKET) bred by Ballymacoll Stud Farm Ltd. 11
Rn　　　　　　　　　　　　　　　　　　　　　　　　　　3m 28.54 (2.04)
　　　　　　　　　　　　　　　　　　　　　　　　　　　SF—64/51/56/45/66/47

---

**2340**　E.B.F. SANDWICH STKS (Mdn 2-Y.O.) £9688.00 (£2884.00: £1372.00: £616.00)
7f　　　　　　　　　　　　　　　　　　　　　　　　　　　4-05 (4-07)

817⁴ **Salatin (USA)** *(PTWalwyn)* 9-0 WCarson (1) (lw: a.p: led 3f out: comf) .......... —1
2034² Blush Rambler (USA) (Fav) *(MRStoute)* 9-0 SCauthen (4) (plld hrd: hrd rdn over
　　　　1f out: unable qckn) .......................................................... 1½.2
1873² Darecliff (USA) *(RHannon)* 9-0 MRoberts (3) (lw: led 4f: one pce) ......... nk.3
Visto Si Stampi (IRE) *(JLDunlop)* 9-0 TQuinn (2) (gd sort: hld up: rdn over 1f
　　　　out: eased whn btn ins 1f) ................................................ 4.4

**4/7** Blush Rambler (USA), **3/1** SALATIN (USA), **13/2** Darecliff (USA)(9/2—7/1), **12/1** Visto Si Stampi (IRE)(op
7/1). Tote £3.90 (£1.80). Mr Hamdan Al-Maktoum (LAMBOURN) bred by Flaxman Holdings Ltd in USA. 4 Rn
　　　　　　　　　　　　　　　　　　　　　　　　　　　　　1m 30.67 (4.17)
　　　　　　　　　　　　　　　　　　　　　　　　　　　　SF—53/48/47/35

---

**2341**　CHESTER APP'CE H'CAP (0-100) £3406.50 (£1017.00: £486.00: £220.50)
1m (rnd)　　　　　　　　　　　　　　　　　　　　　　　4-35 (4-37)

1930 **State Dancer (USA) (83)** *(MMoubarak)* 5-9-2 StephenDavies (10) (4th st: led
　　　　over 1f out: all out) ............................................................. —1
1692▲ Piquant **(84)** (Fav) *(LordHuntingdon)* 5-9-0 ‡³DHarrison (6) (led 1f: 3rd st: ev ch
　　　　fnl f: r.o wl) ...................................................................... s.h.2
1877⁶ Sabotage (FR) **(88)** *(MRStoute)* 6-9-4 ‡³JJones (8) (lw: led 7f out tl over 1f out:
　　　　unable qckn: fin 4th, ½l: plcd 3rd) .................................. 3
1877⁵ Pay Homage **(95)** *(IABalding)* 4-9-4 ‡¹⁰DGriffiths (3) (hdwy on ins 2f out: hmpd
　　　　over 1f out: nt rcvr: fin 5th, 1½l: plcd 4th) ...................... 4
1869⁴ Camden's Ransom(USA) **(75)** *(DRCElsworth)* 5-8-2 ‡⁶JHunter (2) (nvr nr to chal) 1½.6
1954³ Akkazao (IRE) **(78)** *(WCarter)* 4-8-8 ‡³NGwilliams (1) (5th st: one pce fnl 2f) ... 1½.7
1254³ Two Left Feet **(94)** *(SirMarkPrescott)* 5-9-13 KRutter (4) (lw: nvr nrr) .............. s.h.8

1218[4] Haroldon (IRE) **(84)** *(BPalling)* 3–8-9  FNorton (7) (swtg: 2nd st: wknd wl over 1f out) ............................................................................................................. 2.9
Alnasric Pete (USA) **(62)** *(DAWilson)* 6–6-13[(2)] ‡[10]SharonMillard (5) (b: a bhd) 10.10
1611[6] Rose Elegance **(75)** *(WRMuir)* 3–7-11 ‡[3]KimMcDonnell (9) (6th st: rdn & hung rt over 1f out: edgd lft: r.o: fin 3rd, 2l: disq: plcd last) ......................... 0
LONG HANDICAP: Alnasric Pete (USA) 7-4.
*Stewards Enquiry: Rose Elegance disq. (interference to Pay Homage over 1f out).*

**4/1** Piquant, **9/2** STATE DANCER (USA), Camden's Ransom (USA), **8/1** Rose Elegance, Akkazao (IRE), **9/1** Haroldon (IRE), Two Left Feet, **10/1** Pay Homage, **16/1** Sabotage (FR), **33/1** Alnasric Pete (USA). CSF £21.32, CT £238.48. Tote £5.50: £2.00 £1.70 £3.50 (£9.90). Ecurie Fustok (NEWMARKET) bred by Blue Grass Breeders Inc., et al. in USA. 10 Rn
1m 41.94 (2.34)
SF—55/52/29/48/43/22

**2342**    BALMORAL NURSERY    £6790.00 (£2020.00: £960.00: £430.00)    **6f**  5-10 (5-11)
(Weights raised 1 lb)

2068[5] **No Reservations (IRE)** *(RFJohnsonHoughton)* 8-0 ‡[5]DHarrison (1) (mde all: drvn out) ......................................................................................................... —1
1998★ Zuno Warrior **(Fav)** *(GLewis)* 9-7  PaulEddery (3) (lw: a.p: hrd rdn over 1f out: r.o wl ins fnl f) ............................................................................... nk.2
2031★ Ansellman *(MJHaynes)* 9-7  SCauthen (4) (lw: chsd wnr: ev ch over 1f out: unable qckn) ................................................................................. 2¹/₂.3
2055[4] Rain Splash *(RHannon)* 9-3  MRoberts (2) (lw: hld up: hrd rdn over 1f out: wknd fnl f) ........................................................................................... 5.4
1880★ Sharp Gazelle *(BSmart)* 8-2  DaleGibson (5) (hdwy over 2f out: wknd over 1f out) ........................................................................................ ¹/₂.5

**2/1** Zuno Warrior, **11/4** NO RESERVATIONS (IRE), **7/2** Rain Splash, **9/2** Ansellman, **10/1** Sharp Gazelle(8/1—12/1). CSF £8.08, Tote £3.50: £1.40 £1.50 (£3.40). C. W. Sumner and Jim Short (DIDCOT) bred by R. Entenmann in Ireland. 5 Rn
1m 17.34 (3.74)
SF—30/50/40/16/–

T/Trio: Races 2 & 4: £168.10 (8.3 Tckts), £256.80 (7.2 Tckts) T/Jkpt: Not won; £2,256.90 to Ascot 25/7/92. T/Plpt: £9,390.80 (0.65 Tckts); £4,441.62 to Ascot 25/7/92.
AK

# ASCOT (R-H)
## Saturday, July 25th [Good to firm]
Going Allowance: St: 0.10 sec (G); Rnd: minus 0.10 sec per fur (F)          Wind: almost nil

Stalls: 2nd & 4th centre, remainder high

**2343**    WITTELSBACH DIAMOND STKS (Ladies)    £6368.00 (£1904.00: £912.00: £416.00)
    **1m (rnd)**                                2-00 (2-02)

1695[3] **Badawi (USA) (92)** *(JHMGosden)* 4-9-11  MrsLPearce (1) (swtg: 4th st: led over 2f out: sn clr: r.o wl) ................................................................. —1
2194★ Confronter **(80)** *(PFICole)* 3–9-8  MissMClark (6) (lw: 3rd st: chsd wnr fnl 2f: no imp) ................................................................................... 3¹/₂.2
1460[4] Reported (IRE) *(MJHeaton-Ellis)* 3–9-5 ‡[3]MissFHaynes (8) (lw: hdwy & 6th st: one pce fnl 2f) ........................................................................ 1¹/₂.3
2021[3] Lead the Dance **(103)** *(HRACecil)* 3–9-8  MissLStopford-Sackville (10) (plld hrd in rr: swtchd outside over 2f out: gd hdwy over 1f out: nt rch ldrs) ..... 6.4
2307 Caromish (USA) **(65)** *(MDIUsher)* 5–9-11  MrsAUsher (7) (led 3f out tl over 2f out: sn wknd) ............................................................................... 8.5
1463 Berlin Wall (IRE) **(75)** *(PWChapple-Hyam)* 4–9-13 ‡[3]MrsJChapple-Hyam (2) (swtg: led 5f: 2nd st: wknd over 2f out) .............................................. 5.6
1677[5] Saxon Lad (USA) **(40)** *(GPEnright)* 6–9-13 ‡[3]MrsMEnright (5) (lw: 5th st: wknd over 2f out) ........................................................................... 2¹/₂.7
1772[4] Up the Punjab **(53)** *(AMoore)* 3–9-0 ‡3MrsJMoore (3) (bhd fnl 4f) ....... 1¹/₂.8
Take it in Cash *(RDickin)* 3–8-11 ‡[3]MissSDuckett (9) (lw: a bhd) .......... ³/₄.9
2110[5] Marjons Boy **(27)** (bl) *(CDBroad)* 5–9-13 ‡[3]MissSJakeway (4) (lw: dwlt: a bhd) nk.10

**11/8** Lead the Dance, **9/4** Reported (IRE), **100/30** BADAWI (USA), **10/1** Confronter, **25/1** Berlin Wall (IRE), **50/1** Caromish (USA), **100/1** Up the Punjab, **200/1** Ors. CSF £31.87, Tote £4.60: £1.30 £1.60 £1.30 (£15.00). Sheikh Mohammed (NEWMARKET) bred by Mill Ridge Farm Ltd in USA. 10 Rn
1m 42.11 (2.51)
SF—61/47/39/24/3/–

**2344**    PRINCESS MARGARET STKS (Gp 3) (2-Y.O.F) £19170.00 (£7071.00: £3310.50: £1348.50)    **6f**                                2-35 (2-36)

1868★ **Marina Park** *(MJohnston)* 8-11  DMcKeown (4) (lw: mde virtually all: r.o wl) ....... —1

```
2024³  First Veil (DRCElsworth) 8-8 WCarson (3) (dwlt: hdwy 2f out: hrd rdn over 1f
              out: r.o) ........................................................................................ 1¹/₂.2
1937*  Lake Pleasant (IRE) (RHannon) 8-8 BRaymond (6) (w ldrs: rdn over 1f out: nt
              qckn) .............................................................................................. 1¹/₂.3
2024*  Urry Urry Urry (MJCamacho) 8-8 NConnorton (5) (lw: w ldrs 4f) .......................... 2.4
1713*  Ivanka (IRE) (Fav) (CEBrittain) 8-8 SCauthen (2) (spd 4f) .................................. 5.5
2055*  Carranita (IRE) (BPalling) 8-8 PaulEddery (1) (lw: spd over 3f) ............................. 7.6
```

**7/4** Ivanka (IRE), **100/30** MARINA PARK, **5/1** Urry Urry Urry, **11/2** Lake Pleasant (IRE), **7/1** First Veil, **12/1** Carranita (IRE). CSF £22.59, Tote £4.40: £2.00 £2.80 (£16.90). Laharna Ltd (MIDDLEHAM) bred by Laharna Ltd. 6 Rn       1m 16.01 (2.41)
                                      SF—61/52/46/38/18/–

---

**2345**    KING GEORGE VI & QUEEN ELIZABETH DIAMOND STKS (Gp 1)    £261216.00
         (£97172.80: £46186.40: £19584.80)    1¹/₂m             3-20 (3-21)

```
1819a* St Jovite (USA) (Fav) (JSBolger,Ireland) 3-8-9 SCraine (2) (lw: mde all: qcknd
              clr over 2f out: r.o wl) ............................................................................. —1
1929*  Saddlers' Hall (IRE) (MRStoute) 4-9-7 WCarson (1) (lw: 4th st: styd on fnl 2f: nt
              rch wnr) ......................................................................................................... 6.2
1876²  Opera House (MRStoute) 4-9-7 SCauthen (3) (2nd st: hrd rdn over 2f out: no
              imp) ............................................................................................................. ¹/₂.3
1876³  Sapience (DRCElsworth) 6-9-7 RCochrane (7) (lw: chsd wnr 7f: 3rd st: r.o one
              pce) ............................................................................................................. ¹/₂.4
1876   Rock Hopper (MRStoute) 5-9-7 WRSwinburn (6) (lw: 7th st: hdwy 2f out: nvr nr
              to chal) ......................................................................................................... hd.5
1870   Terimon (CEBrittain) 6-9-7 MRoberts (4) (a bhd: last st) ................................... 8.6
1972*  Silver Wisp (USA) (QLowis) 3-8-9 PaulEddery (5) (lw: 6th st: no ch after) ......... ³/₄.7
1458²  Jeune (GWragg) 3-8-9 MHills (8) (lw: l.idwy 4f oul: 5th & wkng st) ..................... ³/₄.8
```

**4/5** ST JOVITE (USA), **7/2** Saddlers' Hall (IRE)(5/2—4/1), **8/1** Silver Wisp (USA), **10/1** Jeune, **14/1** Opera House, **16/1** Sapience, **22/1** Rock Hopper, **33/1** Terimon. CSF £4.21, Tote £2.10: £1.50 £1.80 £2.10 (£3.80). Mrs Virginia Kraft Payson (IRELAND) bred by Virginia Kraft Payson in USA. 8 Rn     2m 30.85 (1.35)
                                      SF—70/70/69/68/67/51

---

**2346**    E.B.F. GRANVILLE STKS (Mdn 2-Y.O.C & G) £10770.00 (£3210.00: £1530.00: £690.00)
         6f                                             4-00 (4-02)

```
       Rapid Success (USA) (DRCElsworth) 9-0 RCochrane (7) (unf: scope: dwlt:
              hdwy 2f out: led ins fnl f: pushed out) ...................................................... —1
       Abtaal (Fav) (HThomsonJones) 9-0 RHills (6) (gd sort: a.p: led wl over 1f out tl
              ins fnl f) ...................................................................................................... nk.2
       Gran Senorum (USA) (PFICole) 9-0 AMunro (2) (w'like: scope: led over 2f: styd
              on fnl f) ...................................................................................................... 3¹/₂.3
       My Patriarch (JLDunlop) 9-0 LDettori (8) (w'like: scope: bit bkwd: nvr nrr) ........ ¹/₂.4
       Eastern Memories (IRE) (RHannon) 9-0 MRoberts (3) (unf: bit bkwd: led over 3f
              out tl over 2f out) ..................................................................................... 1¹/₂.5
       Anaxagoras (AAScott) 9-0 BRaymond (4) (w'like: bit bkwd: no hdwy fnl 2f) ...... 2¹/₂.6
       Mawayed (USA) (PTWalwyn) 9-0 WCarson (1) (cmpt: bit bkwd: swvd lft s: prom
              4f) ................................................................................................................ 4.7
       Red Admiral (PCHaslam) 9-0 DMcKeown (5) (w'like: scope: w ldrs: led over 2f
              out tl wknd qckly wl over 1f out) ............................................................... nk.8
```

**5/6** Abtaal, **9/2** Mawayed (USA), **8/1** Eastern Memories (IRE), Gran Senorum (USA)(op 3/1), **10/1** RAPID SUCCESS (USA)(tchd 16/1), **16/1** My Patriarch, **25/1** Red Admiral, **33/1** Anaxagoras. CSF £18.46, Tote £8.60: £1.80 £1.30 £2.40 (£10.80). Mr Yoshiki Akazawa (WHITSBURY) bred by Meadow Grove Farm in USA. 8 Rn     1m 16.58 (2.98)
                                      SF—52/51/37/35/29/19

---

**2347**    SANDRINGHAM H'CAP (0-110) £11257.50 (£3360.00: £1605.00: £727.50)
         1¹/₄m                                          4-30 (4-32)

```
2028   Knock Knock (85) (IABalding) 7-9-0 LDettori (12) (lw: hdwy 2f out: qcknd to ld
              ins fnl f) ...................................................................................................... —1
1465   Gulf Sailor (IRE) (82) (MRStoute) 4-8-11 WRSwinburn (11) (5th st: ev ch fnl f:
              r.o) ............................................................................................................ ³/₄.2
1869   Montpelier Boy (78) (LordHuntingdon) 4-8-7 AMunro (10) (4th st: led over 1f
              out tl ins fnl f) ............................................................................................ nk.3
1465   Dreams End (83) (GWragg) 4-8-12 MHills (6) (hdwy 3f out: ev ch 1f out: no
              qckn) ....................................................................................................... s.h.4
1808³  Chatham Island (67) (CEBrittain) 4-7-5(3) ‡5BDoyle (4) (lw: led tl over 1f out: r.o) 1¹/₂.5
1413²  Prince Hannibal (78) (JLDunlop) 5-8-7 RCochrane (8) (nvr nrr) ........................ 2.6
```

1063 Danzarin (IRE) **(76)** *(RHannon)* 4–8-5 BRaymond (7) (swtg: nrst fin) .................. 4.7
1869 Courtline Jester **(84)** (bl) *(MAJarvis)* 3–8-3 PaulEddery (4) (lw: 3rd st: wknd 2f out) .............................................................. 3½.8
Sharp Dream **(64)** *(BSmart)* 4–7-7 DaleGibson (3) (bhd fnl 5f) .......................... nk.9
1916* Bold Boss **(90)** *(BHanbury)* 3–8-9 LPiggott (5) (2nd st: wknd 2f out) ............. nk.10
1869⁶ Green's Ferneley (IRE) **(85)** (bl) *(RCharlton)* 4–9-0 WCarson (1) (b: 6th st: wknd over 2f out) ............................ 1½.11
1869² Charlo **(99)** (Fav) *(JHMGosden)* 4–10-0 SCauthen (2) (bhd fnl 5f) .................. hd.12

4/1 Charlo(3/1—9/2), 11/2 Green's Ferneley (IRE), Montpelier Boy, 7/1 Bold Boss, Gulf Sailor (IRE), Dreams End, 14/1 Prince Hannibal, 16/1 Courtline Jester(op 10/1), Chatham Island, 25/1 KNOCK KNOCK, 33/1 Ors. CSF £169.27, CT £1,001.66. Tote £22.90: £5.20 £2.70 £2.00 (£109.70). Mr G. M. Smart (KINGSCLERE) bred by Lodge Park Stud. 12 Rn
2m 6.41 (2.11)
SF—69/64/59/63/39/51

### 2348
CROCKER BULTEEL H'CAP (0-110) £10770.00 (£3210.00: £1530.00: £690.00)
1m (st)
5-00 (5-09)

1463* **Colour Sergeant (85)** *(LordHuntingdon)* 4–9-3 WRSwinburn (6) (hld up: led over 1f out: rdn out) ....................... —1
2191² Wave Hill **(85)** *(RHannon)* 3–8-9 WCarson (3) (lw: a.p: ev ch fnl f: r.o) ............. 1½.2
2183³ Domicksky **(74)** *(MJRyan)* 4–8-6 RCochrane (8) (swtg: hdwy over 1f out: r.o ins fnl f) ......................................... 1.3
1930* Sahel (IRE) **(90)** (Fav) *(JHMGosden)* 4–9-8 SCauthen (9) (lw: hld up: nt clr run fnl 2f: r.o nr fin) ...................... hd.4
1877* Starlight Flyer **(96)** (bl) *(MMoubarak)* 5–10-0 LDettori (7) (hld up: ev ch over 1f out: wknd fnl f) ...................... ¾.5
1943 Desert Splendour **(73)** *(CEBrittain)* 4–8-5 MHills (5) (led 2f out tl wknd over 1f out) ........................................ d.h.5
1943 High Low (USA) **(88)** *(WJHaggas)* 4–9-6 LPiggott (2) (w ldr tl wknd 2f out) ......... 7.7
2304* Cheveux Mitchell **(78)**(v) *(MRChannon)* 5–8-10 (5x) RHills (4) (led tl wknd 2f out)1½.8
2035* Baluga **(89)** (v) *(GHarwood)* 4–8-13 AClark (1) (lw: prom 5f) ......................... 5.9

100/30 Sahel (IRE), 9/2 COLOUR SERGEANT, 13/2 Wave Hill, 15/2 Starlight Flyer, 8/1 High Low (USA), Baluga, 10/1 Domicksky, Desert Splendour(8/1—12/1), 16/1 Cheveux Mitchell(12/1—20/1). CSF £29.93, CT £246.40. Tote £3.80: £1.50 £1.70 £2.30 (£10.60). The Queen (WEST ILSLEY) bred by The Queen. 9 Rn
1m 41.75 (2.35)
SF—79/66/60/75/79/56

### 2349
BLACKNEST H'CAP (0-100) £7375.00 (£2200.00: £1050.00: £475.00)
1½m
5-30 (5-39)

1465 **Libk (88)** *(HThomsonJones)* 4–9-5 RHills (7) (lw: hdwy & 5th st: led & qcknd clr over 2f out: r.o wl) ................... —1
2134⁴ Turgenev (IRE) **(85)** (Fav) *(JHMGosden)* 3–8-4 RCochrane (1) (lw: 3rd st: chsd wnr fnl 2f: hrd rdn: r.o) ................. 1½.2
1879⁶ Hajaim (IRE) **(86)** *(CEBrittain)* 4–9-3 SCauthen (2) (lw: hld up in rr: hdwy & hmpd over 2f out: r.o wl) ............... ½.3
1934 Green Lane (IRE) **(80)** *(RCharlton)* 3–7-13 WCarson (3) (lw: nvr nr to chal) ....... 7.4
431⁶ Grand Hawk (USA) **(79)** *(MMoubarak)* 4–8-10 LDettori (5) (6th st: wknd 2f out) . 4.5
1534 Barrish **(72)** *(RAkehurst)* 6–8-3(1) AClark (4) (swtg: 4th st: wknd over 2f out) ...... 7.6
1938⁵ Close Friend (IRE) **(97)** (bl) *(BWHills)* 4–10-0 MHills (8) (led tl wknd over 2f out) 2½.7
1465 Kimbers (IRE) **(92)** *(CRNelson)* 4–9-9 WRSwinburn (6) (lw: 2nd st: wknd over 2f out) ................................... 2½.8
Dante's View (USA) **(90)** *(PRHedger)* 4–9-7 MPerrett (9) (prom 7f) .................. 1½.9

100/30 Turgenev (IRE), 7/2 Grand Hawk (USA), 4/1 Green Lane (IRE), 15/2 LIBK, 8/1 Hajaim (IRE), 9/1 Barrish, 10/1 Close Friend (IRE), 16/1 Kimbers (IRE), 33/1 Dante's View (USA). CSF £30.70, CT £187.51. Tote £7.60: £2.10 £1.80 £2.60 (£19.80). Mr Hamdan Al-Maktoum (NEWMARKET) bred by Derrinstown Stud Ltd. 9 Rn
2m 31.64 (2.14)
SF—72/54/66/34/37/16

T/Trio: Race 5: £249.10 (21.3 Tckts). T/Jkpt: Not won; £11,487.15 to Goodwood 28/7/92. T/Plpt: £136.40 (212.55 Tckts).
Hn

## 2212—AYR (L-H)

### Friday, July 24th [Good]

Going Allowance: St: nil (G); Rnd: minus 0.20 sec per fur (F)
Wind: almost nil

Stalls: high

### 2350
AYRSHIRE LEADER STKS (Mdn 2-Y.O.F) £1467.00 (£412.00: £201.00)
6f
6-45 (6-47)

1969³ **Palm Chat** *(LMCumani)* 8-11 JFortune (4) (lw: mde most: drvn along over 1f out: r.o: pushed out cl home) ............................... —1

Runrig (IRE) *(MissLAPerratt)* 8-8 ‡³JFanning (6) (neat: bit bkwd: dwlt: hdwy
½-wy: rn green appr fnl f: r.o wl nr fin) ............................... ½.2
Cherhill (IRE) (Fav) *(PWChapple-Hyam)* 8-11 SWhitworth (2) (lengthy: unf:
dwlt: sn rcvrd & trckd ldrs: effrt 2f out: nt qckn) .................. 6.3
Apache Squaw *(CWThornton)* 8-11 GHind (3) (neat: leggy: lw: chsd ldrs over
4f: sn outpcd) .................................................... nk.4
2044² First Slice *(JBerry)* 8-11 JCarroll (5) (disp ld over 2f out: sn drvn along: grad
wknd) ............................................................. 5.5
2049 Tri My Way (IRE) *(RRLamb)* 8-4 ‡⁷RHavlin (1) (spd over 3f: sn wknd) ............... 1½.6

**6/5** Cherhill (IRE), **9/4** PALM CHAT, **6/1** First Slice, **10/1** Apache Squaw(7/1—11/1), **20/1** Runrig (IRE), **50/1** Tri
My Way (IRE). CSF £29.66, Tote £3.30: £2.30 1.20 (£6.70). Sheikh Mohammed (NEWMARKET) bred by
Sheikh Mohammed bin Rashid al Maktoum. 6 Rn　　　　　　　　　1m 14.02 (3.62)
　　　　　　　　　　　　　　　　　　　　　　　　　　　　　　　　　SF—25/20/–/–/–/

**2351**　　AYRSHIRE POST CHATLINE CLAIMING STKS　　£1523.00 (£428.00: £209.00)
　　　　　**1m**　　　　　　　　　　　　　　　　　　　　　　　7-15 (7-19)

2216* **Laurel Queen (IRE) (58)** (Fav) *(JBerry)* 4–8-12 JCarroll (2) (lw: trckd ldrs: led
over 2f out: hld on wl fnl f) ....................................... —1
2218* Princess Maxine (IRE) (50) *(MissLAPerratt)* 3–7-12 ‡³JFanning (6) (lw: hld up:
stdy hdwy 3f out: chal ins fnl f: nt qckn nr fin) ................... ¾.2
1961⁴ Claudia Miss **(58)** *(WWHaigh)* 5–8-3 ‡⁵SMaloney (3) (trckd ldrs: hdwy & ev ch 2f
out: rdn & nt qckn) ................................................ 2.3
1961 Imhotep **(45)** *(MrsGRReveley)* 5–8-3 ‡⁷DarrenMoffatt (1) (wnt rt s: led & sn clr:
hdd over 2f out: edgd rt & one pce) ................................ 1½.4
2149³ Supreme Court **(38)** (bl) *(MDods)* 5–8-3 ‡⁵NKennedy (5) (chsd ldr tl rdn &
outpcd over 3f out) ................................................ 12.5
Clair Soleil (USA) *(DanysSmith)* 5–8-6 KFallon (4) (cmpt: str: bit bkwd: sn
outpcd & bhd: n.d) ................................................ 1½.6

**10/11** LAUREL QUEEN (IRE), **3/1** Princess Maxine (IRE), Claudia Miss, **25/1** Clair Soleil (USA), **33/1** Imhotep,
**100/1** Supreme Court. CSF £3.84, Tote £2.00: £1.10 £2.00 (£2.70). Laurel (Leisure) Limited (COCKERHAM)
bred by E. Lonergan in Ireland. 6 Rn　　　　　　　　　　　　　1m 40.76 (3.56)
　　　　　　　　　　　　　　　　　　　　　　　　　　　　　　　　　SF—20/4/3/–/–/–

**2352**　　HOURSTONS LADIES NIGHT H'CAP (0-80) £1891.70 (£531.20: £259.10)
　　　　　**7f**　　　　　　　　　　　　　　　　　　　　　　　7-45 (7-49)

2219* **Golden Chip (IRE) (71)** *(APStringer)* 4–9-1 (3x) ‡⁵SMaloney (4) (lw: mde all:
rdn 2f out: kpt on wl) ............................................. —1
2213* Pickles **(50)** (Fav) *(PCHaslam)* 4–7-13 (3x) KDarley (2) (s.i.s: sn chsng wnr:
chal over 2f out: no ex ins fnl f) ................................. 1.2
2150⁴ Spanish Verdict **(70)** *(DenysSmith)* 5–9-5 (3x) KFallon (3) (lw: hld up: effrt 3f
out: styd on fnl f: nrst fin) ...................................... 2.3
2160⁴ Ballad Dancer **(53)** *(EJAlston)* 7–8-2 PRobinson (1) (lw: effrt ½-wy: styd on: nt
pce to chal) ...................................................... nk.4
1365 Creselly **(60)** *(JGFitzGerald)* 5–8-4 ‡⁵JWeaver (6) (chsd ldrs: rdn 3f out: one pce) ¾.5
2163⁵ Verdant Boy **(53)** *(MPNaughton)* 9–8-2 JakiHouston (5) (bhd: effrt over 3f out:
nvr able to chal) ................................................. 1.6
1200 Spanish Grandee (USA) **(77)** *(PWChapple-Hyam)* 4–9-12 SWhitworth (7) (b.off
hind: w ldrs tl rdn & wknd 2f out: eased fnl f) .................... 8.7

**5/2** Pickles, **7/2** GOLDEN CHIP (IRE), **5/1** Spanish Verdict, **6/1** Ballad Dancer, **7/1** Creselly, **10/1** Spanish
Grandee (USA), **11/1** Verdant Boy. CSF £11.81, Tote £3.80: £2.20 1.70 (£3.40). Mr A. H. Jackson (THIRSK)
bred by C. and J. Sandys and Barbara McCourt in Ireland. 7 Rn　　　　1m 27.18 (3.18)
　　　　　　　　　　　　　　　　　　　　　　　　　　　　　SF—53/34/48/30/30/25

**2353**　　KILMARNOCK STANDARD PRETTY WOMAN H'CAP (3-Y.O) (0-80) £1636.80 (£459.80:
　　　　　£224.40)　　**7f**　　　　　　　　　　　　　　　　　　8-15 (8-16)

2050* **Rose Gem (IRE) (56)** (Fav) *(PCHaslam)* 8-4 (5x) KDarley (2) (mde all: shkn up
& r.o strly fnl 2f) ................................................ —1
2213² Straw Thatch **(73)** *(MJohnston)* 9-7 DMcKeown (3) (lw: trckd wnr: effrt over 2f
out: nt qckn appr fnl f) .......................................... 3.2
2163⁴ Soba Guest (IRE) **(72)** *(JBerry)* 8-13 ‡⁷SHaworth (1) (lw: trckd ldrs: effrt 3f out:
outpcd fnl 2f) .................................................... 7.3

**8/11** ROSE GEM (IRE), **5/2** Straw Thatch, **3/1** Soba Guest (IRE). CSF £2.73, Tote £1.40 (£1.50). Mrs M. E. F.
Haslam (MIDDLEHAM) bred by F. Feeney in Ireland. 3 Rn　　　　　　1m 27.59 (3.59)
　　　　　　　　　　　　　　　　　　　　　　　　　　　　　　　　　SF—36/44/22

**2354**  WEST SOUND RADIO LADYKILLER (S) STKS  £1516.00 (£426.00: £208.00)
1¼m
8-45 (8-47)

1089 **Kagram Queen** (53) *(MrsGRReveley)* 4–8-13 KDarley (2) (lw: hld up & bhd: hdwy 3f out: led ins fnl f: r.o u.p) ..................... —1

2312★ Princess Roxanne (50) (bl) *(ABailey)* 5–9-6 AMackay (4) (lw: trckd ldrs: led over 2f out: sn hrd rdn: hdd & nt qckn ins fnl f) ..................... 1.2

2160 Reilton (57) *(JParkes)* 5–8-8 ‡5OPears (6) (hld up & bhd: hdwy on outside over 2f out: edgd lft & nt qckn fnl f) ..................... 1.3

2111³ Be the Best (40) *(MPNaughton)* 4–8-8 ‡5JWeaver (1) (led tl hdd 5f out: ev ch tl outpcd ins fnl f) ..................... s.h.4

1907² Speedy Sioux (56) (Fav) *(CWThornton)* 3–7-9 ‡3JFanning (3) (lw: hld up: effrt 3f out: styd on: nt pce to chal) ..................... 1.5

327⁴ Simply Candy (IRE) (48) *(APStringer)* 4–8-3 ‡5SMaloney (8) (plld hrd: sn cl up: led 5f out tl over 2f out: sn wknd) ..................... 10.6

1964 Perspicacity (37) *(MDods)* 5–8-3 ‡5NKennedy (5) (plld hrd: prom to st: sn outpcd) ..................... 10.7

**6/4** Speedy Sioux, **5/2** Princess Roxanne, **5/1** KAGRAM QUEEN, **8/1** Reilton, **10/1** Be the Best, **14/1** Simply Candy (IRE), **33/1** Perspicacity. CSF £17.16, Tote £7.10: £2.90 £2.30 (£8.40). Mrs E. A. Kettlewell (SALTBURN) bred by E. W. and E. A. Kettlewell. 7 Rn; No bid
2m 11.72 (6.42)
SF—15/20/6/5/–/–

**2355**  CARRICK GAZETTE H'CAP (3-Y.O) (0-70) £1736.90 (£488.40: £238.70)
1¼m
9-15 (9-18)

2147★ **Talented Ting (IRE)** (63) (Fav) *(PCHaslam)* 8-9 ‡5JWeaver (1) (lw: hld up: hdwy over 2f out: nt clr run & swtchd over 1f out: led wl ins fnl f) . —1

2041⁴ Sie Amato (IRE) (49) *(CaptJWilson)* 7-11 ‡3JFanning (7) (lw: chsd ldrs: led wl over 1f out: nt qckn nr fin) ..................... ³/₄.2

1976 Master Copy (IRE) (48) (bl) *(CBBBooth)* 7-8(¹) ‡5SMaloney (3) (a.p: led & qcknd over 2f out: hdd over 1f out: no ex) ..................... 3.3

1901³ Marowins (53) *(EJAlston)* 8-4 KFallon (2) (bhd tl hdwy 3f out: nt pce to chal) . 2¹/₂.4

1921⁴ Sword Master (70) (v) *(BobJones)* 9-7 NDay (8) (lw: bhd: effrt 3f out: wandered u.p: styd on nr fin) ..................... ¹/₂.5

1921³ Great Lord (IRE) (66) *(JWWatts)* 9-3 PRobinson (6) (hld up: effrt over 3f out: no rspnse) ..................... 1¹/₂.6

2142³ Bartolomeo (USA) (45) *(MrsJRRamsden)* 7-10 AMackay (5) (sn cl up: qcknd to ld over 3f out: hdd over 2f out: sn btn) ..................... s.h.7

1850⁶ Chill Wind (42) *(NBycroft)* 7-7 LCharnock (4) (chsd ldrs: rdn ent st: sn btn) ..................... 8.8

1175 Kelimutu (52) *(CFWall)* 8-3 JCarroll (9) (led tl hdd over 3f out: wknd qckly) ..................... 20.9

**9/4** TALENTED TING (IRE), **9/2** Sword Master, sword Lord (IRE), **11/2** Marowins, **7/1** Bartolomeo (USA), **10/1** Kelimutu, **16/1** Master Copy (IRE), **25/1** Ors. CSF £45.83, CT £654.78. Tote £3.20: £1.40 £4.60 £4.30 (£34.10). Mr Martin Wickens (MIDDLEHAM) bred by R. A. Keogh in Ireland. 9 Rn
2m 7.45 (2.15)
SF—53/39/30/32/47/38

T/Plpt: £110.30 (41.85 Tckts). AA

## AYR (L-H)
## Saturday, July 25th [Good, Good to soft patches]
Going Allowance: nil sec per fur (G)  Wind: fresh half against

Stalls: high

**2356**  E.B.F. CAMBUSDOON STKS (Mdn 2-Y.O.C & G) £2459.20 (£691.20: £337.60)
7f
2-10 (2-14)

1899² **Woodhaunter (USA)** *(JHMGosden)* 9-0 GHind (1) (lw: mde all: shkn up 2f out: r.o wl) ..................... —1

1348⁴ Manila Bay (USA) (Fav) *(MBell)* 9-0 KDarley (7) (lw: trckd ldrs: chal over 2f out: nt qckn fnl f) ..................... 4.2

1897 Grand as Owt *(DenysSmith)* 8-11 ‡3JFanning (5) (trckd ldrs tl rn v.wd ent st: gd hdwy & hung lft 2f out: sn ev ch: no ex fnl f) ..................... 1.3

1515 Calcutta Flyer (IRE) *(PWChapple-Hyam)* 9-0 MTebbutt (6) (lw: in tch: effrt 3f out: no imp) ..................... 6.4

2049⁴ Royal Meadow (IRE) *(JBerry)* 9-0 JCarroll (2) (chsd ldrs tl wknd over 2f out) ..................... 7.5

Blakes Reach *(RRLamb)* 8-7 ‡7RHavlin (4) (small: str: bkwd: bhd: hdwy ent st: sn rdn & btn) ..................... 4.6

**4/11** Manila Bay (USA), **5/2** WOODHAUNTER (USA), **14/1** Royal Meadow (IRE)(op 6/1), **25/1** Calcutta Flyer (IRE), **33/1** Grand as Owt, **100/1** Blakes Reach. CSF £3.80, Tote £3.70: £1.10 £1.10 (£1.40). Sheikh Mohammed (NEWMARKET) bred by Deer Lawn Farm in USA. 6 Rn
1m 30.34 (6.34)
SF—5/–/–/–/–/–

**2357**　SCOTS WHA'HAE H'CAP (Amateurs) (0-80) £2295.00 (£645.00: £315.00)
1¼m 192y　　　　　　　　　　　　　　　　　　　　2-40 (2-44)

(Weights raised 6 lb)

2135² **Swift Silver (53)** (Fav) *(WJMusson)* 5-10-13 MrsJMusson (6) (b: lw: chsd clr
　　　ldrs: led over 1f out: styd on) ............................................ —1
2149² Lord Advocate (43) (v) *(MPNaughton)* 4-10-3 MissPRobson (8) (disp ld tl led
　　　after 3f: sn clr: hdd over 1f out: kpt on wl) ...................... 1½.2
1767 Buzzards Crest (33) *(BobJones)* 7-9-7 MissDianaJones (10) (lw: effrt appr st:
　　　styd on fnl f: no imp) ..................................................... 5.3
2086³ Shadow Bird (53) *(GAPritchard-Gordon)* 5-10-13 MrPPritchardGordon (4) (lw:
　　　hdwy appr st: sn chsng ldrs: one pce fnl 2f) ...................... nk.4
2355⁴ Marowins (53) *(EJAlston)* 3-10-2 MrRWilkinson (5) (lw: hdwy 4f out: one pce
　　　fnl 2f) ............................................................................... 4.5
2217³ Buckingham Band (USA) (44) (v) *(FHLee)* 4-10-4 MrsGRees (9) (lw: outpcd tl
　　　styd on nr fin) ................................................................. nk.6
1967 Sapphirine (61) *(RMWhitaker)* 5-11-7 MrFHines (3) (nvr wnt pce) ............... 1.7
1970 Just for Kicks (33) *(JJO'Neill)* 6-9-7 MrsNCraggs (2) (hdwy appr st: sn rdn & btn) 5.8
2050 Dark Midnight (IRE) (56) *(RRLamb)* 3-10-5 MissSLamb (7) (disp ld 3f: wknd ent
　　　st: sn bhd: t.o) ................................................................. 9
LONG HANDICAP: Just for Kicks 8-11.

**9/4** SWIFT SILVER, **7/2** Shadow Bird, **9/2** Buckingham Band, **7/1** Lord Advocate, **8/1** Marowins, **12/1**
Buzzards Crest, **20/1** Sapphirine, **50/1** Ors. CSF £16.26, CT £131.30. Tote £2.60: £1.40 £2.60 £2.10 (£7.10).
The Hon Mr John Corbett (NEWMARKET) bred by Dr O. Zawawi. 9 Rn　　2m 24.46 (10.76)
　　　　　　　　　　　　　　　　　　　　　　　　　　　　　　SF—19/6/–/5/–/–

**2358**　DAILY STAR H'CAP (0-90) £2697.00 (£816.00: £398.00: £189.00)
1m 5f 13y　　　　　　　　　　　　　　　　　　　　3-10 (3-13)

(Weights raised 17 lb)

2313★ **Briggsmaid (54)** (Fav) *(JMPEustace)* 4-9-1 (4x) MTebbutt (3) (hld up: smooth
　　　hdwy appr st: led over 1f out: r.o) ..................................... —1
2313³ Carol's Pet (IRE) (46) *(MJohnston)* 4-8-2 ‡5JWeaver (2) (lw: led & sn clr: hdd
　　　over 1f out: kpt on same pce) .......................................... 5.2
2217⁴ Grey Power (63) *(MrsGRReveley)* 5-9-10 KDarley (1) (lw: chsd ldr: pushed
　　　along appr st: r.o one pce) ............................................... 10.3
Fairgroundprincess (42) *(FHLee)* 4-8-3 RLappin (4) (bit bkwd: sn outpcd: n.d) 7.4

**5/4** BRIGGSMAID, **5/2** Grey Power, **3/1** Carol's Pet (IRE), **6/1** Fairgroundprincess(op 10/1). CSF £5.08, Tote
£1.60 (£1.90). Mr F. W. Briggs (NEWMARKET) bred by John L. Moore. 4 Rn　　2m 55.58 (9.38)
　　　　　　　　　　　　　　　　　　　　　　　　　　　　　　SF—7/–/–/–

**2359**　STAR FORM CLAIMING STKS　£2169.00 (£609.00: £297.00)　**5f**　3-40 (3-41)

1994⁴ **Echo-Logical (92)** (Fav) *(JBerry)* 3-9-7 JCarroll (2) (chsd ldrs: led wl over 1f
　　　out: pushed out) ............................................................. —1
2352⁴ Ballad Dancer (52) *(EJAlston)* 7-8-9 ‡5JWeaver (4) (lw: outpcd tl hdwy 2f out:
　　　r.o wl nr fin) ................................................................... ¾.2
2061⁴ Ever so Lonely (66) (bl) *(ABailey)* 3-7-13 ‡7DWright (3) (led & sn clr: hdd wl over
　　　1f out: wknd) .................................................................. 6.3
2119² Langtonian (70) (bl) *(JBerry)* 3-9-0 NCarlisle (1) (chsd ldrs over 3f: sn wknd) .. ¾.4

**2/5** ECHO-LOGICAL, **4/1** Ever so Lonely, **13/2** Langtonian, **11/1** Ballad Dancer. CSF £4.87, Tote £1.10 (£6.80).
The Liverpool Daily Post and Echo Ltd (COCKERHAM) bred by Mrs M. J. Dandy. 4 Rn; Echo-Logical clmd P Savill
£15,000　　　　　　　　　　　　　　　　　　　　　　　　　59.93 sec (1.93)
　　　　　　　　　　　　　　　　　　　　　　　　　　　　　　SF—68/43/9/21

**2360**　SCOTTISH RACING CLUB NURSERY　£2369.60 (£665.60: £324.80)
6f　　　　　　　　　　　　　　　　　　　　　　4-15 (4-18)

2024 **Umbubuzi (USA)** *(FHLee)* 8-4 RLappin (4) (lw: chsd ldrs tl outpcd ½-wy: styd
　　　on u.p to ld ins fnl f) ...................................................... —1
2030⁴ Plum First (bl) *(NBycroft)* 8-2 ‡5SMaloney (3) (led & sn clr: hdd & no ex ins fnl f) 3.2
1897★ Peaceful Air *(EWeymes)* 8-11 ‡5JWeaver (6) (chsd ldr: rdn 2f out: r.o one pce) 1½.3
2143★ Two Moves in Front (IRE) *(JBerry)* 9-7 JCarroll (5) (chsd ldrs: outpcd over 2f
　　　out: no imp after) ........................................................... 2.4
2223⁵ Sea-Ayr (IRE) *(MissLAPerratt)* 7-7⁽³⁾ ‡3JFanning (7) (lw: hld up: effrt & swtchd 2f
　　　out: nvr able to chal) ...................................................... ¾.5
2076⁶ Contract Elite (IRE) *(CWThornton)* 8-9 GHind (2) (lw: in tch: rdn ½-wy: n.d after) ½.6
2212³ Caldervale (Fav) *(ABailey)* 8-12 AMackay (1) (lw: sn drvn along: sme hdwy over
　　　2f out: sn btn) ................................................................. 5.7
LONG HANDICAP: Sea-Ayr (IRE) 6-12.

**11/4** Caldervale, **7/2** Peaceful Air, **5/1** Plum First, Two Moves in Front (IRE), **6/1** UMBUBUZI (USA), **10/1** Contract Elite (IRE), **16/1** Sea-Ayr (IRE). CSF £31.81, Tote £9.40: £2.10 £2.40 (£19.70). Semi-Chem Bargain Centres (WILMSLOW) bred by Glencrest Farm in USA. 7 Rn

1m 13.79 (3.39)
SF—22/8/11/13/–/–

### 2361
AILSA CRAIG H'CAP (3-Y.O) (0-70) £2347.20 (£659.20: £321.60)    **6f**    4-45 (4-49)

(Weights raised 7 lb)

| | |
|---|---|
| 1905⁶ **Coolaba Prince (IRE) (57)** *(FHLee)* 9-4 RLappin (5) (chsd ldrs: styd on wl fnl f to ld nr fin) | —1 |
| 2310⁴ Miss Movie World (47) *(Fav) (NBycroft)* 8-3 ‡⁵SMaloney (4) (cl up: led 2f out: rdn ins fnl f: wandered & jst ct) | nk.2 |
| 2088 Honey Heather (IRE) (58) *(CFWall)* 9-5 NCarlisle (3) (lw: a.p: effrt over 2f out: kpt on nr fin) | 1½.3 |
| 2310* High Principles (67) *(JBerry)* 10-0 (7x) JCarroll (6) (led 4f: sn rdn & grad wknd) | 4.4 |
| 1924 Dandy Desire (51) *(BCMorgan)* 8-9 ‡³JFanning (1) (lw: bhd: hdwy ½-wy: sn rdn & no imp) | 3.5 |
| 2162 Nashoon (IRE) (53) (bl) *(MissLCSiddall)* 9-0 GHind (2) (t: dwlt: hdwy to chase ldrs after 2f: wknd ½-wy) | 15.6 |

**7/4** Miss Movie World, **3/1** COOLABA PRINCE (IRE), **4/1** High Principles, **9/2** Honey Heather (IRE), **12/1** Dandy Desire, **25/1** Nashoon (IRE). CSF £8.22, Tote £3.40: £1.70 £1.40 (£4.00). Mr P. J. Cosgrove bred by Lodge Park Stud in Ireland. 6 Rn

1m 13.17 (2.77)
SF—48/32/42/35/4/–

T/Plpt: £21.70 (87.90 Tckts).      AA

---

## 2098 — SOUTHWELL (L-H) Fibresand

### Saturday, July 25th [Standard]

Going Allowance: minus 0.20 sec per fur (FS)      Wind: slt across

Stalls: high

### 2362
GIN STKS (Mdn 3-Y.O) £1161.00 (£321.00: £153.00)    **1m (AWT)**    6-30 (6-31)

| | |
|---|---|
| 1849³ **Take by Storm (IRE)** *(Fav) (GMMoore)* 9-0 WNewnes (4) (lw: s.i.s: smooth hdwy over 4f out: sn trckng ldrs: led over 1f out: comf) | —1 |
| 2078² King's Guest (IRE) (62) *(GAPritchard-Gordon)* 9-0 AMcGlone (1) (led: shkn up over 2f out: hdd over 1f out: unable qckn) | 3.2 |
| 2041 Ballyranter (57) *(HJCollingridge)* 9-0 JQuinn (2) (sn outpcd: gd hdwy over 3f out: styd on same pce fnl 2f) | 3.3 |
| 2015 Forza Azzurri (IRE) (55) (bl) *(MrsNMacauley)* 8-9 ‡⁵SWilliams (8) (chsd ldrs: chal appr st: sn hrd rdn: wknd appr fnl f) | 6.4 |
| 822 Klingon (IRE) (67) *(RHollinshead)* 9-0 SPerks (6) (sn bhd: sme hdwy over 2f out: n.d) | 2.5 |
| Heavy Rock (IRE) *(RFMarvin)* 8-6 ‡³RonHillis (3) (unf: bit bkwd: a bhd: lost tch over 3f out) | 12.6 |
| 1849 Wave to Me *(NTinkler)* 9-0 LCharnock (5) (s.i.s: sn cl up: wknd qckly over 3f out) | dist.7 |

**5/6** TAKE BY STORM (IRE), **3/1** King's Guest (IRE), **7/1** Klingon (IRE)(op 4/1), Ballyranter(8/1—14/1), **16/1** Forza Azzurri (IRE), **20/1** Wave to Me, **33/1** Heavy Rock (IRE). CSF £3.97, Tote £2.00: £1.40 £1.80 (£3.00). Miss V. Foster (MIDDLEHAM) bred by Abbeville Stud in Ireland. 7 Rn

1m 43.4 (4.1)
SF—14/5/–/–/–

### 2363
SHERRY (S) STKS (2-Y.O) £1234.50 (£342.00: £163.50)    **6f (AWT)**    7-00 (7-02)

| | |
|---|---|
| 1804³ **Jordywrath** *(ICampbell)* 8-11 MTebbutt (4) (lw: a.p: gng wl: led on bit over 1f out: sn clr: hrd hld) | —1 |
| 2098³ Sounds Risky (bl) *(GMMoore)* 8-11 WNewnes (9) (led: rdn over 2f out: hdd over 1f out: no ch w wnr) | 6.2 |
| 2039² Shades of Croft *(Fav) (MDIUsher)* 8-11 MRoberts (10) (lw: a.p: effrt appr st: wknd appr fnl f) | 3.3 |
| 2039⁵ Egg *(TDBarron)* 8-11 AlexGreaves (6) (lw: sn bhd: drvn along wl over 2f out: styd on strly u.p fnl f) | s.h.4 |
| 1416⁴ Westmead Nick *(JBerry)* 8-4 ‡⁷PRoberts (3) (lw: chsd ldrs: rdn ½-wy: wknd over 1f out) | s.h.5 |
| 2098⁴ Summers Dream (v) *(BRichmond)* 8-6 AMcGlone (8) (sn mid div & rdn along: nvr able to chal) | 3½.6 |
| 1092 Hasta la Vista *(MWEasterby)* 8-11 TLucas (2) (bhd: effrt over 2f out: styd on: nrst fin) | 2.7 |

Burble (bl) *(DWChapman)* 8-6 JQuinn (1) (cmpt: bit bkwd: s.s: hdwy 3f out: wknd over 1f out) .......................... 2.8

1848 Big Gem *(MCChapman)* 8-6 ‡⁵SWilliams (7) (a bhd) ........................... 12.9

2009² Private Liner (bl) *(RonaldThompson)* 8-11 JLowe (11) (unruly s: s.i.s: hdwy to chase ldrs ½-wy: hung bdly lft & sn wknd) ........................ 6.10

1554 I'Ll Risk it *(JBerry)* 8-6 SWhitworth (5) (in tch to ½-wy: sn lost pl: t.o) ................. 11

2/1 Shades of Croft, **100/30** JORDYWRATH, **15/2** Hasta la Vista(op 4/1), **8/1** Private Liner, **17/2** Egg(14/1—8/1), **10/1** Sounds Risky, **14/1** Summers Dream, Westmead Nick, **20/1** I'Ll Risk it, **33/1** Ors. CSF £34.84, Tote £4.50: £1.90 £2.90 £1.50 (£26.30). Ms K. Valentini (NEWMARKET) bred by Mrs R. E. Smith. 11 Rn; Bt in 6,800 gns
1m 16.6 (3.2)
SF—9/–/–/–/–/–

---

## 2364

'FIBRESAND' STKS (Mdn 2-Y.O.C & G) £1161.00 (£321.00: £153.00)
**7f (AWT)**                                                           7-30 (7-32)

2157² **Abergele** *(JGFitzGerald)* 9-0 KFallon (1) (lw: mde all: rdn over 2f out: hld on wl nr fin) .......................... —1

2102² Soloman Springs (USA) (Jt-Fav) *(SGNorton)* 9-0 KDarley (4) (lw: a.p: rdn over 2f out: sltly outpcd over 1f out: kpt on wl u.p nr fin) ...... nk.2

Hula Bay (USA) *(MBell)* 9-0 JQuinn (2) (scope: bit bkwd: dwlt: rdn along 4f out: nvr able to chal) ............................ 8.3

Just You Dare (IRE) (Jt-Fav) *(SirMarkPrescott)* 9-0 MRoberts (3) (leggy: scope: plld hrd early: cl up: effrt appr st: wknd over 1f out) .......... s.h.4

**13/8** Just You Dare (IRE), Soloman Springs (USA)(11/4—3/1), **100/30** ABERGELE, **7/1** Hula Bay (USA)(op 7/2). CSF £8.68, Tote £3.60 (£3.00), A. F. Budge (Equine) Limited (MALTON) bred by Mrs D. O. Joly. 4 Rn
1m 29.5 (2.9)
SF—35/34/10/9

---

## 2365

'FOLKS THAT LIVE ON THE HILL' H'CAP (0-70) £1234.50 (£342.00: £163.50)
**5f (AWT)**                                                           8-00 (8-05)

(Weights raised 3 lb)

1685 **Inswinger (38)** *(WGRWightman)* 6-8-9 GBardwell (6) (mde all: rdn & kpt on wl fnl f) .......................... —1

2115⁵ Sobering Thoughts **(41)** (bl) *(DWChapman)* 6-8-7 ‡⁵SWilliams (8) (lw: chsd ldrs: rdn & styd on fnl f) .......................... ¾.2

2301⁴ Lincstone Boy (IRE) **(47)** (bl) *(SRBowring)* 4-9-4 SWebster (4) (wnt lft s: sn prom: rdn 2f out: unable qckn fnl f) ......................... 1½.3

2041 The Dream Maker (IRE) **(38)** *(MrsNMacauley)* 3-8-4 JQuinn (2) (a.p: rdn & kpt on same pce fnl f) .......................... ½.4

2151³ Capital Idea (IRE) **(50)** *(RonaldThompson)* 3-9-2 JLowe (5) (sn outpcd & drvn along: hdwy appr fnl f: nrst fin) .......................... 2½.5

1076⁵ Fourofus **(58)** *(RBoss)* 3-9-10 MRoberts (1) (in tch: effrt on outside over 2f out: sn rdn & no imp) .......................... nk.6

2154* Drummer's Dream (IRE) **(40)** (v) (Fav) *(MrsNMacauley)* 4-8-11 AMcGlone (9) (chsd ldrs: rdn & outpcd 2f out: sn lost pl) .......................... hd.7

1814⁶ Three Lucky (IRE) **(33)** *(MDIUsher)* 4-8-4 DaleGibson (3) (swtg: sltly hmpd s: a in rr) .......................... 6.8

**3/1** Drummer's Dream (IRE), **100/30** Sobering Thoughts, **4/1** Fourofus, **8/1** INSWINGER(op 5/1), **9/1** The Dream Maker (IRE), **10/1** Lincstone Boy (IRE), **12/1** Three Lucky (IRE), **14/1** Capital Idea (IRE)(op 8/1). CSF £31.92, CT £242.16. Tote £7.00: £1.90 £1.50 £2.10 (£14.40). Mr W. G. R. Wightman (UPHAM) bred by W. G. R. Wightman and Mrs J. A. Thomson. 8 Rn
60.7 sec (2.7)
SF—21/16/21/5/7/14

---

## 2366

NATIONAL PLANT & TRANSPORT H'CAP (0-70) £1255.50 (£348.00: £166.50)
**7f (AWT)**                                                           8-30 (8-39)

2040⁶ **Idir Linn (IRE) (44)** (v) *(DJGMurray-Smith)* 4-8-11 MRoberts (7) (in tch: rdn over 2f out: styd on to ld last strides) .......................... —1

2159² Sandmoor Denim **(57)** (Fav) *(SRBowring)* 5-9-10 SWebster (1) (bhd: hdwy 3f out: nt clr run & swtchd 2f out: led jst ins fnl f: ct nr fin) ..... nk.2

2219 Cee-Jay-Ay **(60)** *(JBerry)* 5-9-13 AlexGreaves (3) (hdwy on outside over 2f out: ev ch 1f out: unable qckn nr fin) .......................... s.h.3

2103² No Decision **(52)** (bl) *(MWEasterby)* 5-9-5 TLucas (8) (dwlt: sn prom: led 2f out: hdd jst ins fnl f: r.o u.p) .......................... 2.4

2099⁵ Wellsy Lad (USA) **(60)** *(DWChapman)* 5-9-8 ‡⁵SWilliams (4) (led after 1f II hdd 2f out: wknd fnl f) .......................... 6.5

302 Gallery Note (IRE) **(54)** *(BWHills)* 3-9-0 DaleGibson (9) (hdwy u.p to chase ldrs appr st: wknd wl over 1f out) .......................... 1½.6

2099² Jovial Kate (USA) (56) (BEllison) 5–9-9 JFortune (10) (s.i.s: hdwy on outside appr st: sn hrd rdn: btn over 1f out) ..................... 2¹/2.7

Silver Concord (48) (GMMoore) 4–9-1 WNewnes (6) (prom to st: sn lost pl) ...... 2.8

2050³ Crimson Consort (IRE) (40) (DonEnricoIncisa) 3–7-7 ‡⁷ClaireBalding (5) (a bhd) .. ¹/2.9

1785⁴ Aegaen Lady (54) (JEtherington) 3–9-0 KDarley (11) (dwlt: sn chsng ldrs: wknd wl over 1f out) ...................................... 6.10

2032 C Sharp (42) (bl) (WRMuir) 5–8-9 SWhitworth (2) (swtg: led 1f: chsd ldrs tl wknd over 2f out) ..................................... 1¹/2.11

9/4 Sandmoor Denim, 11/4 No Decision(tchd 11/2), 9/2 IDIR LINN (IRE), 9/1 Cee-Jay-Ay, Jovial Kate (USA)(op 6/1), 11/1 Wellsy Lad (USA)(6/1—12/1), 16/1 Aegaen Lady, Gallery Note (op 10/1), Crimson Consort (IRE)(12/1—20/1), 33/1 Ors. CSF £15.48, CT £83.36. Tote £5.50: £1.70 £1.50 £2.40 (£9.10). Exors of the late Frank Glennon (UPPER LAMBOURN) bred by Frank Glennon in Ireland. 11 Rn        1m 29.4 (2.8)
SF–34/46/48/34/19/6

## 2367 GAS WARM HOMES H'CAP (0-70) £1255.50 (£348.00: £166.50) 1¹/2m (AWT)

9-00 (9-03)

(Weights raised 3 lb)

2042 **Grey Commander** (34) (MBrittain) 4–8-1 KDarley (6) (mid div: hdwy appr st: rdn to chal 1f out: kpt on wl nr fin) ..................... —1

2004* Pippas Song (69) (v) (GWragg) 3–9-10 MRoberts (7) (lw: a chsng ldrs: led 2f out: disp ld 1f out: r.o) .............................. nk.2

2101³ Swell Time (IRE) (30) (CNAllen) 4–7-11 GBardwell (8) (b.hind: bhd: lost tch over 6f out: hdwy appr st: styd on strly u.p appr fnl f) ....... 3¹/2.3

1798² Master's Crown (USA) (MCChapman) 4–9-0 KFallon (10) (prom: jnd ldrs 6f out: rdn & unable qckn fnl 2f) ............................... 2¹/2.4

2007⁵ Holy Wanderer (USA) (64) (DWPArbuthnot) 3–9-0 ‡⁵RPrice (5) (dwlt: hdwy to trck ldrs 6f out: rdn over 2f out: sn wknd) ............... 7.5

2054 Affa (53) (TThomsonJones) 3–8-8 SWhitworth (2) (chsd ldrs: effrt 3f out: wknd wl over 1f out: sddle slipped) ...................... 1¹/2.6

2036 Erin's Town (36) (WCarter) 6–8-3 DaleGibson (1) (wl bhd tl styd on wl u.p fnl 3f) nk.7

2033⁶ Mr Wishing Well (51) (RJRWilliams) 6–9-4 JQuinn (9) (b.hind: hld up: smooth hdwy 5f out: effrt & ev ch 3f out: wknd qckly 2f out) ........... 2.8

2101² Cheeky Pot (43) (v) (DenysSmith) 4–8-10 JLowe (3) (led after 3f tl hdd & wknd 2f out) ....................................... 9

2042⁵ Commanche Sioux (IRE) (48) (v) (Fav) (KAMorgan) 4–8-10 ‡⁵SWilliams (12) (in tch: effrt 7f out: sn rdn & wknd qckly) ................... 10

2142 Qualitair Memory (IRE) (39) (v) (JFBottomley) 3–7-8⁽¹⁾ PBurke (11) (led tl faltered & hdd after 3f: prom & sn drvn along: wknd qckly appr st: t.o) .................................... 11

LONG HANDICAP: Qualitair Memory (IRE) 7-6.

9/4 Commanche Sioux (IRE), 5/1 Mr Wishing Well(op 8/1), 11/2 Pippas Song(4/1—6/1), 7/1 Swell Time (IRE), 15/2 Holy Wanderer (USA)(5/1—8/1), 12/1 Affa(8/1—14/1), 14/1 Master's Crown (USA), 16/1 GREY COMMANDER, 20/1 Qualitair Memory (IRE), 25/1 Erin's Town. CSF £102.76, CT £634.70. Tote £11.80: £2.50 £1.90 £2.20 (£24.90). Mr R. A. Bromby (WARTHILL) bred by Northgate Lodge Stud Ltd. 11 Rn
2m 39.7 (5.5)
SF–8/30/–/8/–/–

T/Plpt: £73.30 (22.7 Tckts).                                                                          O'R

## 1986—WARWICK (L-H)
### Saturday, July 25th [Good]
Going Allowance: minus 0.30 sec per fur (F)                              Wind: slt bhd

Stalls: low

## 2368 STRATFORD FESTIVAL STKS (Mdn 2-Y.O.F) £1380.00 (£380.00: £180.00) 5f

6-15 (6-17)

2171³ **Jarena (IRE)** (Fav) (GLewis) 8-11 PaulEddery (3) (led over 3f out: clr wl over 1f out: pushed out) ............................ —1

1913⁵ Action Night (MMoubarak) 8-11 AMunro (5) (a.p: hrd rdn 2f out: one pce) ........ 3.2

Falsoola (MRStoute) 8-6 ‡⁵JJones (9) (small: a.p: shkn up over 1f out: r.o one pce) ......................................... hd.3

1880⁶ Hills Raceaid (IRE) (bl) (JBerry) 8-11 NAdams (1) (chsd ldrs: no hdwy fnl 2f) ..... 2.4

Merch Fach (IRE) (JDRoberts) 8-11 JWilliams (8) (lengthy: bit bkwd: s.s: nvr nrr) 6.5

1851 Miss Whittingham (IRE) (bl) (JBerry) 8-11 GCarter (6) (led over 1f: wknd 2f out) 1.6

1342 Shropshire Blue (RDickin) 8-11 SDawson (7) (bhd fnl 2f: t.o) ................... 7.7

It Bites (IRE) (APJames) 8-6 ‡⁵RPrice (4) (leggy: unf: bkwd: s.s: a in rr: t.o) ....... ³/4.8

**11/10** JARENA (IRE), **11/8** Falsoola(4/6—13/8), **7/2** Action Night, **20/1** Miss Whittingham (IRE), **33/1** It Bites (IRE), Hills Raceaid (IRE), **50/1** Ors. CSF £6.13, Tote £2.30: £1.20 £1.30 £1.40 (£4.60). Miss V. McNeill (EPSOM) bred by Rannfields Stud Farm in Ireland. 8 Rn
59.6 sec (1.6)
SF—35/23/37/14/–/–

**2369**   MITCHELLS & BUTLERS SALES H'CAP (0-90) £3523.50 (£1053.00: £504.00: £229.50)
7f
6-45 (6-49)

| | | |
|---|---|---|
| 2060* | **Doulab's Image (78)** (bl) (Jt-Fav) *(JAGlover)* 5–9-3 ‡3FNorton (3) (hld up: hdwy on ins 4f out: 3rd st: led over 1f out: r.o wl) | —1 |
| 1921* | Causley **(74)** *(BAMcMahon)* 7–9-2 DMcKeown(10) (lw: led over 5f: r.o one pce)1¹/₂.2 | |
| 2159* | Hawaii Storm (FR) **(51)** *(MissAJWhitfield)* 4–7-7 NAdams (2) (8th st: gd hdwy on ins over 1f out: r.o) | 2.3 |
| 2060² | Santi Sana **(67)** (Jt-Fav) *(LadyHerries)* 4–8-9 PaulEddery (8) (b.off hind: 5th & rdn st: r.o one pce fnl 2f) | nk.4 |
| 1888³ | Bernstein Bette **(65)** *(PSFelgate)* 6–8-7 JWilliams (4) (6th st: hdwy over 1f out: nt trble ldrs) | .6 |
| 1833⁵ | Resolute Bay **(78)** (bl) *(RMWhitaker)* 6–9-6 ACulhane (1) (lw: 2nd st: wknd over 1f out) | 1¹/₂.6 |
| 2003 | Love Legend **(86)** *(DWPArbuthnot)* 7–10-0 AMunro (6) (b: 4th st: wknd 2f out) s.h.7 | |
| 1500 | Pimsboy **(57)** *(FJYardley)* 5–7-10⁽⁵⁾ ‡3SO'Gorman (7) (7th st: a bhd) | 4.8 |
| 1901 | Andy Jack **(59)** *(MJHeaton-Ellis)* 3–7-8⁽¹⁾ TyroneWilliams (9) (b: chsd ldr over 3f: wknd rapidly & last st: t.o) | 25.9 |

LONG HANDICAP: Hawaii Storm (FR) 6-12.

**9/2** Santi Sana, DOULAB'S IMAGE, **5/1** Causley, **11/2** Bernstein Bette, **6/1** Resolute Bay, **13/2** Hawaii Storm (FR), **10/1** Love Legend(8/1—12/1), **20/1** Pimsboy, **50/1** Andy Jack. CSF £24.30, CT £127.84. Tote £5.50: £2.20 £2.00 £1.00 (£9.60). Claremont Management Services (WORKSOP) bred by Hadi Al Tajir. 9 Rn
1m 25.2 (1)
CF   57/51/22/37/34/42

**2370**   CARLING BLACK LABEL STKS (Mdn 3-Y.O) £1380.00 (£380.00: £180.00)
1¹/₂m 115y
7-15 (7-18)

| | | |
|---|---|---|
| 1906³ | **Resounding Success (IRE)** (Fav) *(BWHills)* 8-9 DHolland (5) (hld up: hdwy & 3rd st: r.o to ld last strides) | —1 |
| 700 | Landed Gentry (USA) **(63)** *(PWChapple-Hyam)* 9-0 PaulEddery (7) (led: rdn 3f out: hdd last strides) | s.h.2 |
| 2137⁵ | Anditisitis (USA) *(DWPArbuthnot)* 9-0 AMunro (3) (chsd ldr: rdn 5f out: 2nd st: one pce fnl 2f) | 4.3 |
| 2089⁵ | Speedo Movement **(60)** *(BAMcMahon)* 8-9 BRaymond (2) (hld up: 4th st: no hdwy fnl 2f) | 5.4 |
| 1948⁶ | Alto Princess *(APJones)* 8-9 NAdams (4) (rdn 6f out: last & wkng st) | 15.5 |

2137 Siberian Swing (100/1) Withdrawn (ref to ent stalls) : not under orders

**4/11** RESOUNDING SUCCESS (IRE)(op 4/7), **8/1** Anditisitis (USA)(op 9/2), Landed Gentry (USA)(op 9/2), **9/1** Speedo Movement, **100/1** Alto Princess. CSF £3.44, Tote £1.40: £1.10 £1.50 (£2.40). Mr R. E. Sangster (LAMBOURN) bred by Mrs T. V. Ryan in Ireland. 5 Rn
2m 43.5 (6)

**2371**   BREW XI NURSERY   £2469.00 (£684.00: £327.00)   **5f**
7-45 (7-46)
(Weights raised 9 lb)

| | | |
|---|---|---|
| 2207* | Minshaar *(KSBridgwater)* 8-10 BRaymond (4) (hdwy on ins over 2f out: led over 1f out: comf) | —1 |
| 1993* | Riston Lady (IRE) *(BSRothwell)* 8-10 DHolland (5) (lw: a.p: chsd wnr over 1f out: no imp) | 3.2 |
| 1886* | Fancied (Fav) *(HCandy)* 9-4 SDawson (3) (lw: bhd tl hdwy over 1f out: r.o ins fnl f) | 1¹/₂.3 |
| 2256* | Second Chance (IRE) *(PMitchell)* 9-3 (7x) PaulEddery (6) (lw: prom over 3f) ... nk.4 | |
| 2081* | Maybe Gold *(DWPArbuthnot)* 9-7 AMunro (2) (b.nr hind: rdn over 2f out: btn whn hmpd ins fnl f) | 2.5 |
| 1553² | Laurel Delight *(JBerry)* 9-0 GCarter (1) (led over 3f) | 3¹/₂.6 |

**2/1** Fancied, **9/2** Laurel Delight, Maybe Gold, **5/1** Second Chance (IRE), **13/2** Riston Lady (IRE)(op 4/1), **15/2** MINSHAAR. CSF £45.86, Tote £8.10: £2.10 £2.00 (£12.20). Mr R. S. Brookhouse (LAPWORTH) bred by Gainsborough Stud Management Ltd. 6 Rn
59.7 sec (1.7)
SF—32/20/22/20/16/–

**2372**   WATERSIDE (S) STKS (3 & 4-Y.O) £1632.00 (£452.00: £216.00)
1¹/₄m 169y
8-15 (8-18)

| | | |
|---|---|---|
| 1759* | **Misty Goddess (IRE) (60)** (Fav) *(MAJarvis)* 4–8-13 ‡5KRutter (8) (hdwy over 3f out: 2nd st: led over 1f out: cleverly) | —1 |

2128⁶ Princess of Orange **(50)** *(CCElsey)* 3-8-2 DHolland (7) (led over 6f out tl over 1f
out: r.o) ........................................................................................ ¹/₂.2

1948⁴ Forgetful **(56)** *(DBurchell)* 3-8-4⁽²⁾ DMcKeown (4) (4th st: rdn over 1f out: r.o
ins fnl f) ........................................................................................ s.h.3

1810 Primera Ballerina **(37)** (v) *(JRBosley)* 4-8-8 ‡⁵NGWilliams (1) (prom: hrd rdn 4f
out: 5th & wkng st) ........................................................................ 7.4

2218³ Shrewd Girl (USA) **(53)** *(BWHills)* 4-8-13 AMunro (2) (lw: 3rd st: ev ch 2f out: sn
wknd) ............................................................................................. 2.5

1642 Fine as Fivepence **(34)** *(MrsAKnight)* 3-7-13 ‡³FNorton (12) (poor 6th st: t.o) .. 12.6
Market Trader *(MFBarraclough)* 3-7-9 ‡⁷CHawksley (3) (bkwd: t.o fnl 5f) ........... 15.7

1810⁶ Head Turner **(28)** *(CPWildman)* 4-8-13 PaulEddery (6) (led over 5f: wknd 4f
out: t.o) ......................................................................................... nk.8

Red Kay Tu *(FJordan)* 3-8-7 NAdams (9) (bit bkwd: s.s: a t.o) .......................... dist.9

**4/5** MISTY GODDESS (IRE)(4/7—6/4), **100/30** Forgetful, **5/1** Princess of Orange, **6/1** Shrewd Girl (USA)(op 4/1), **33/1** Fine as Fivepence, Head Turner, **50/1** Primera Ballerina, Red Kay Tu, **100/1** Market Trader. CSF £5.66, Tote £2.30: £1.40 £1.50 £1.10 (£7.40). Mr J. R. Good (NEWMARKET) bred by A. P. Tierney in Ireland. 9 Rn; bt in 7,200 gns
2m 18.4 (4.9)
SF—17/5/6/—/—/—

### 2373

MARY ARDEN H'CAP (0-80) £2978.50 (£826.00: £395.50)    1³/₄m 194y 8-45 (8-47)

1518⁶ **Arctic Splendour (USA) (55)** *(PWChapple-Hyam)* 3-7-6⁽²⁾ ‡³FNorton (3) (b.off
hind: hld up: 5th & rdn st: led ins fnl f: r.o wl) ........................................ —1

1789⁴ Enfant du Paradis (IRE) *(PDEvans)* 4-7-3⁽³⁾ ‡⁷AGarth (1) (swtg: hld up: stdy
hdwy 5f out: 2nd st: led over 1f out tl ins fnl f) ........................................ 1.2

1726³ Merry Marigold **(49)** *(JDRoberts)* 6-8-4⁽³⁾ JWilliams (9) (b: hdwy over 4f out:
6th st: rdn wl over 1f out: r.o ins fnl f) .................................................. 1.3

1938⁶ Moving Out **(73)** *(SirMarkPrescott)* 4-10-0 AMunro (11) (lw: led tl hdd over 1f
out: r.o one pce) ............................................................................ 1¹/₂.4

1714⁴ Juris Prudence (IRE) **(47)** *(BAMcMahon)* 4-7-9 ‡⁷SSanders (5) (lw: 7th st: no
hdwy fnl 2f) .................................................................................. 4.5

1719 Sonic Signal **(44)** (v) *(MJHaynes)* 6-7-13 NAdams (6) (nvr nrr) ...................... 5.6

1988⁶ Mrs Barton (IRE) **(63)** *(BWHills)* 4-9-4 DHolland (7) (lw: prom: hrd rdn 4f out:
4th st: wknd 2f out) ......................................................................... 10.7

2136⁵ Ptolemy (FR) **(50)** (bl) *(MissHCKnight)* 5-8-5 BRaymond (4) (prom: hrd
rdn 4f out: 3rd st: wknd 2f out) .......................................................... 3¹/₂.8

2110⁶ Rashita **(38)** *(GHEden)* 5-7-7 GKing (8) (swtg: prom tl wknd qckly 7f out: t.o fnl
3f) ............................................................................................... 15.9

1914 Socks and Shares **(60)** *(PWHarris)* 3-8-0⁽¹⁾ GCarter (10) (t.o fnl 4f) ................... 2.10

1037 Tophard **(38)** (bl) *(RLee)* 6-7-0 ‡⁷CHawksley (2) (b: t.o fnl 6f) ....................... 8.11

LONG HANDICAP: Enfant du Paradis (IRE) 7-4, Rashita 6-8, Tophard 7-3.

**100/30** Ptolemy (FR), **7/2** Mrs Barton (IRE)(9/4—4/1), Moving Out, **7/1** Juris Prudence, **9/1** ARCTIC SPLENDOUR (USA)(6/1—10/1), Merry Marigold, **10/1** Sonic Signal, **12/1** Socks and Shares, **16/1** Enfant du Paradis (IRE)(12/1—20/1), **50/1** Ors. CSF £129.97, CT £1,219.73. Tote £10.70: £2.10 £3.10 £2.80 (£37.60). Mr R. E. Sangster (MARLBOROUGH) bred by Swettenham Stud in USA. 11 Rn
3m 11 (2)
SF—13/9/23/45/8/7

T/Plpt: £45.00 (47.3 Tckts).                                                                                          KH

### 1687—NEWCASTLE (L-H)

**Saturday, July 25th [St course Good to firm, Rnd Firm]**

Going Allowance: St: 0.10 sec (G); Rnd: minus 0.25 sec per fur (F)    Wind: fresh half against

Stalls: high

### 2374

COUPLAND CLAIMING STKS (2-Y.O) £2259.00 (£624.00: £297.00)    7f    2-15 (2-16)

Hot Storm *(MJCamacho)* 7-9 LCharnock (2) (cmpt: bit bkwd: s.s: n.m.r 2f out:
squeezed thro & led over 1f out: drvn clr) ........................................... —1

1902 Daisy James (IRE) *(JMPEustace)* 8-2⁽³⁾ GDuffield (5) (stdd s: trckd ldrs: effrt &
n.m.r 2f out: styd on fnl f: no ch w wnr) ............................................... 5.2

2010 George Roper *(MRChannon)* 8-8 WRyan (4) (trckd ldrs: effrt 2f out: r.o one
pce) ........................................................................................... 1¹/₂.3

1442⁴ Madam Cyn's Risk *(NACallaghan)* 7-8⁽¹⁾ PBurke (6) (led tl over 1f out: one pce) 2.4

1959³ Kiss in the Dark *(MrsGRReveley)* 8-1 JLowe (7) (swtg: w ldr: drvn along ¹/₂-wy:
hung lft: wkng whn hmpd 2f out) ......................................................... 3.5

2076² Amerigue (Fav) *(MissSEHall)* 8-4 ‡⁵NKennedy (3) (bhd: effrt & pushed along
¹/₂-wy: wknd over 1f out) .................................................................... 2¹/₂.6

2112 Rose of Man *(JBerry)* 7-6⁽²⁾ ‡⁷PRoberts (4) (racd wd: w ldrs tl wknd qckly 2f out:
sn bhd) ........................................................................................ 8.7

**2/1** Amerigue, **5/2** George Roper, **4/1** Kiss in the Dark, **7/1** Madam Cyn's Risk, **8/1** HOT STORM(op 5/1), **20/1** Ors. CSF £107.27, Tote £8.10: £3.90 £3.80 (£62.60). G. B. Turnbull Ltd (MALTON) bred by G. B. Turnbull Ltd. 7 Rn 1m 28.63 (4.33)
SF—27/19/20/–/–/–

---

## 2375 NORHAM STKS (2-Y.O) £3752.50 (£1120.00: £535.00: £242.50)  7f   2-50 (2-50)

1965★ **Persian Brave (IRE)** (Fav) *(MBell)* 9-2 GDuffield (2) (lw: mde all: shkn up & r.o strly fnl f) ..... —1
1809⁶ Wufud (USA) *(JLDunlop)* 9-2 WRyan (3) (lw: trckd wnr: effrt over 2f out: ev ch over 1f out: kpt on wl u.p) ..... 1½.2
2024 Cardinal Dogwood (USA) *(MBrittain)* 8-11 JLowe (4) (trckd ldrs: outpcd ½-wy: kpt on fnl f) ..... 7.3
2038⁵ Travelling Lad *(BBeasley)* 8-11 LCharnock (1) (hld up: bdly outpcd ½-wy: sn bhd) 20.4

**4/6** PERSIAN BRAVE (IRE), **11/8** Wufud (USA), **25/1** Cardinal Dogwood (USA), **66/1** Travelling Lad. CSF £1.81, Tote £1.60 (£1.20). Persian Partnership (NEWMARKET) bred by Roncon Ltd in Ireland. 4 Rn 1m 28.38 (4.08)
SF—51/46/20/–

---

## 2376 RAMBLING RIVER H'CAP (0-105) £7375.00 (£2200.00: £1050.00: £475.00)
5f   3-35 (3-38)

1688★ **Viceroy (102)** (v) *(BBeasley)* 5-9-9 ‡SWilliams (7) (trckd ldr: effrt over 1f out: r.o wl to ld wl ins fnl f) ..... —1
2215³ Sigama (USA) (78) *(FHLee)* 6-7-13 ‡⁵NKennedy (5) (lw: led: clr ½-wy: rdn over 1f out: wknd nr fin) ..... 1½.2
2215² Never in the Red (90) (bl) *(JBerry)* 4-9-2 JFortune (10) (s.i.s: hdwy on ins over 1f out: edgd lft u.p: styd on wl) ..... ¾.3
Allinson's Mate (IRE) (78) *(TDBarron)* 4-8-4 AlexGreaves (8) (bhd: effrt & n.m.r over 1f out: styd on strly nr fin) ..... 1.4
2215★ Absolution (82) (Jt-Fav) *(MPNaughton)* 8-8-8 KFallon (9) (lw: chsd ldrs: effrt & carried lft 1f out: kpt on same pce) ..... s.h.5
2214⁵ Cumbrian Waltzer (96) (Jt-Fav) *(MHEasterby)* 7-9-8 MBirch (3) (in tch: effrt u.p 2f out: kpt on: nvr nr to chal) ..... 1½.6
2192★ Educated Pet (78) *(MJohnston)* 3-7-13 JLowe (6) (chsd ldrs: effrt ½-wy: no imp) ..... 2½.7
2404 Lucedeo (84) *(JLSpearing)* 8-8-10 GDuffield (1) (s.i.s: nvr nr ldrs) ..... ¾.8
2404 Paley Prince (USA) (85) *(MDIUsher)* 6-8-11 MWigham (2) (b: nvr nr to chal) .. 2½.9
2179⁶ Eager Deva (88) *(RHollinshead)* 5-9-0 WRyan (4) (lw: a in rr) ..... ½.10

**5/1** Cumbrian Waltzer, Absolution, **6/1** Never in the Red, Educated Pet, **8/1** Eager Deva, **17/2** VICEROY, **9/1** Lucedeo, **12/1** Sigama (USA), **14/1** Paley Prince (USA), **25/1** Allinson's Mate (IRE). CSF £87.89, CT £584.37. Tote £13.20: £3.60 £3.30 £1.90 (£77.60). Mr Franco Gamma (HAMBLETON) bred by Jeremy Green and Sons. 10 Rn 59.99 sec (1.59)
SF—87/57/71/55/58/66

---

## 2377 BOTHAL STKS (Mdn 3-Y.O) £2070.00 (£570.00: £270.00)  2m 19y   4-05 (4-07)

2120² **Heavenly Waters (50)** *(RFJohnsonHoughton)* 8-9 WRyan (2) (b.hind: hld up: wnt 2nd 6f out: effrt 2f out: led jst ins fnl f: sn clr) ..... —1
1891³ Seekin Cash (USA) (73) (Fav) *(JWWatts)* 9-0 JLowe (1) (lw: led 8f out: drvn over 2f out: rdn & hung lft 1f out: sn hdd & nt qckn) ..... 2.2
1532⁶ Not Gordons *(JHJohnson)* 9-0 JFortune (3) (led to 8f out: drvn along 4f out: sn bhd) ..... dist.3

**2/5** Seekin Cash (USA), **2/1** HEAVENLY WATERS, **40/1** Not Gordons. CSF £3.05, Tote £2.70 (£1.20). Mr R. Crutchley (DIDCOT) bred by R. E. Crutchley. 3 Rn 3m 41.65 (16.15)

---

## 2378 1993 GREAT NORTH BRITISH TRANSPLANT GAMES H'CAP (0-80) £3840.00 (£1140.00: £540.00: £240.00)  1¼m 32y   4-35 (4-38)

2048² **Mbulwa (52)** *(SEKettlewell)* 6-8-4 JFortune (1) (unruly s: chsd ldrs: rdn & hung lft 2f out: led ins fnl f: all out) ..... —1
2028 Corcina (72) *(MBell)* 4-9-10 GDuffield (2) (b.off fore: led: kpt on wl u.p fnl 2f: hdd & nt qckn ins fnl f) ..... ½.2
1840★ Eagle Feather (IRE) (65) (Fav) *(JLDunlop)* 4-9-3 WRyan (4) (hld up: effrt over 3f out: hung lft: styd on nr fin) ..... nk.3
1966² Jubran (USA) (68) *(MPNaughton)* 6-9-6 KFallon (6) (lw: chsd ldrs: drvn along 4f out: one pce fnl 2f) ..... 2½.4
2273⁶ Sharquin (45) *(MBrittain)* 5-7-6⁽⁴⁾ ‡⁵NKennedy (3) (rn in snatches: effrt over 3f out: nvr nr to chal) ..... 3½.5

2065⁶ Milanese **(78)** *(DMorley)* 3-9-6 MBirch (5) (lw: trckd ldrs: rdn & hung lft over 2f
out: sn lost pl & eased) ................................................ 25.6
LONG HANDICAP: Sharquin 6-13.

**7/4** Eagle Feather (IRE), **7/2** Jubran (USA), **9/2** Milanese, Corcina, **10/1** MBULWA, **20/1** Sharquin. CSF £46.46,
Tote £13.20: £3.70 £1.80 (£31.70). Northumbria Leisure Ltd (MIDDLEHAM) bred by Hascombe and Valiant
Studs. 6 Rn
2m 8.87 (2.17)
SF—43/62/54/52/17/–

## 2379

JACKIE MILBURN MEMORIAL APP'CE H'CAP (0-70) £2448.00 (£678.00: £324.00)
**1m 1f 9y**
5-05 (5-06)

(Weights raised 7 lb)

2150² **Tarda (52)** (Fav) *(MrsGRReveley)* 5-8-12 ‡⁵ClaireBalding (5) (hld up: stdy hdwy
2f out: r.o wl to ld nr fin) ................................................ —1
2066★ Pride of Pendle **(50)** *(PCalver)* 3-8-3 ‡³JTate (8) (chsd ldr: led over 1f out tl nr fin:
r.o) ................................................ nk.2
2048⁴ Stand At Ease **(35)** *(WStorey)* 7-7-9⁽⁵⁾ ‡⁵JMarshall (1) (trckd ldrs: effrt & n.m.r
over 1f out: r.o one pce) ................................................ 1¹⁄₂.3
1961 Sky Cat **(44)** (v) *(CTinkler)* 8–8-9 LNewton (2) (lw: led tl over 1f out: sn wknd) 2¹⁄₂.4
883 Matts Boy **(59)** *(MissSEHall)* 4–9-10 OPears (9) (b.hind: effrt 3f out: kpt on: nvr
nr to chal) ................................................ 3¹⁄₂.5
2150³ Flying Down to Rio (IRE) **(52)** *(MPNaughton)* 4–9-0 ‡³CMunday (7) (trckd ldrs tl
outpcd fnl 2f) ................................................ 1¹⁄₂.6
2210⁶ Stelby **(50)** *(OBrennan)* 8–8-8 ‡⁷RAdams (6) (nvr nr ldrs) ................................................ 5.7
1962² Little Ivor **(42)** *(DenysSmith)* 3–7-5 ‡⁷CTeague (4) (stumbled s: a in rr) ................................................ 1¹⁄₂.8
2162³ *Throw Away Line Withdrawn (no suitable jockey available) : not under orders*

**7/2** TARDA, **4/1** Pride of Pendle, **9/2** Flying Down to Rio (IRE), **5/1** Matts Boy(tchd 10/1), **8/1** Little Ivor, **9/1**
Stelby, **14/1** Ors. CSF £16.22, CT £149.10. Tote £3.20: £1.50 £1.80 £3.30 (£5.30). Mrs Dorothy Horner
(SALTBURN) bred by Countess of Durham. 8 Rn
1m 56.58 (4.28)

## 2380

DILSTON H'CAP (3-Y.O) (0-100) £2794.00 (£832.00: £396.00: £178.00)
**1m**
5-35 (5-37)

2013⁴ **Battle Colours (IRE) (85)** *(SirMarkPrescott)* 9-2 GDuffield (5) (lw: trckd ldr: rdn
to ld over 1f out: jst hld on) ................................................ —1
2018⁶ Cumbrian Challenge (IRE) **(85)** *(MHEasterby)* 9-2 MBirch (2) (trckd ldrs: n.m.r
2f out: swtchd & r.o wl u.p ins fnl f: jst failed) ................................................ hd.2
1723² Bilateral (USA) **(90)** (Fav) *(HRACecil)* 9-7 WRyan (4) (led tl over 1f out: r.o one
pce u.p) ................................................ 2¹⁄₂.3
2006² Morsun **(78)** (bl) *(DMorley)* 8-4 ‡⁵OPears (3) (hld up: effrt 2f out: kpt on: nvr able
to chal) ................................................ nk.4
609 Killy **(87)** *(FHLee)* 8-13 ‡⁵NKennedy (1) (hld up: effrt 2f out: edgd rt u.p: wknd
over 1f out) ................................................ 3.5

**11/10** Bilateral (USA), **4/1** Morsun, **9/2** BATTLE COLOURS (IRE), **5/1** Cumbrian Challenge (IRE), **12/1** Killy. CSF
£22.49, Tote £4.70: £2.00 £1.70 (£10.30). Mr Garth Insoll (NEWMARKET) bred by Stackallan Stud in Ireland. 5
Rn
1m 42.58 (3.58)
SF—18/17/14/–/–

T/Plpt: £2,278.90 (0.2 Tckts); £2,463.78 to Newcastle 27/7/92.
WG

# NEWCASTLE (L-H)

## Monday, July 27th [St course Good to firm, Rnd Firm]

Going Allowance: St: 0.30 (G); Rnd: minus 0.10 sec per fur (F)      Wind: fresh against

Stalls: high

## 2381

E.B.F. FEDERATION BREWERY PALE ALE STKS (Mdn 2-Y.O) £2343.00 (£648.00:
£309.00)  **6f**
2-13 (2-16)

**Azhar** (Fav) *(MRStoute)* 9-0 SCauthen (1) (lw: w'like: trckd ldr: led wl over 1f
out: easily) ................................................ —1
Ashover *(TDBarron)* 9-0 AlexGreaves (2) (cmpt: bit bkwd: trckd ldrs: effrt over
2f out: no ch w wnr) ................................................ 1¹⁄₂.2
1549⁵ Sophie's Boy *(MHEasterby)* 9-0 MBirch (4) (b.nr hind: set slow pce: hung lft
most of wy: hdd wl over 1f out: sn btn) ................................................ 6.3
*Beanshoot (13/2) Withdrawn (lame at s) : not under orders*

**1/7** AZHAR, **6/1** Sophie's Boy, **16/1** Ashover. CSF £2.61, Tote £1.10 (£2.90). Sheikh Ahmed Al Maktoum
(NEWMARKET) bred by Snailwell Stud Co Ltd. 3 Rn
1m 21 (9.50)

## 2382

FEDERATION BREWERY SPECIAL ALE H'CAP (3-Y.O) (0-100) £7115.00 (£2120.00: £1010.00: £455.00) **7f**        2-45 (2-45)

(Weights raised 12 lb)

2126[5] **Act of Union (IRE) (69)** *(BBeasley)* 8-12 LCharnock (3) (lw: disp ld tl led ½-wy: edgd rt over 1f out: kpt on u.p fnl f) ..................... —1

2126[3] **Owner's Dream (USA) (77)** (Fav) *(BHanbury)* 9-6 WRyan (4) (lw: disp ld to ½-wy: sn outpcd: swtchd & styd on wl fnl f) ..................... nk.2

2163[2] **Parfait Amour (76)** *(RMWhitaker)* 9-5 LPiggott (2) (hld up: effrt 3f out: rdn & no imp fnl 2f) ..................... 3½.3

2000[2] **By Hand (78)** *(WJHaggas)* 9-7 NDay (1) (chsd ldrs: effrt 3f out: rdn & one pce) 1½.4

**7/4** Owner's Dream (USA), **2/1** Parfait Amour, **4/1** By Hand, **5/1** ACT OF UNION (IRE). CSF £12.57, Tote £6.70 (£7.30). Mr Derek Atkinson (HAMBLETON) bred by E. J. Loder in Ireland. 4 Rn      1m 32.27 (7.97)
SF—9/16/5/2

## 2383

FEDERATION BREWERY L.C.L. PILS LAGER BEESWING STKS (Gp 3) £16435.00 (£6093.50: £2879.25: £1202.25) **7f**        3-15 (3-21)

2011[3] **Casteddu (110)** (bl) *(JWPayne)* 3-8-7 RCochrane (7) (hld up & bhd: smooth hdwy to ld wl over 1f out: sn qcknd clr) ..................... —1

1817a[2] **Sure Sharp (USA) (111)** *(BWHills)* 5-9-6 SCauthen (6) (lw: chsd ldrs: outpcd over 2f out: r.o fnl f: no ch w wnr) ..................... 5.2

2011[2] **Toussaud (110)** (Fav) *(JHMGosden)* 3-8-10 PaulEddery (4) (lw: hld up: stdy hdwy to chal 2f out: sn rdn & no ex) ..................... hd.3

2021[2] **Hamas (IRE) (102)** *(PTWalwyn)* 3-8-9 WCarson (5) (cl up: led 3f out tl wl over 1f out: sn rdn & btn) ..................... ¾.4

1817a[4] **Portico (USA)** *(MVO'Brien, Ireland)* 3-8-10 LPiggott (1) (hld up: hdwy & ch 2f out: sn rdn & btn) ..................... 7.5

1467 **Colway Bold (102)** *(JWWatts)* 3-8-10 WRyan (3) (lw: led 4f: sn wknd) ..................... 2½.6

1926[3] **Flute (USA) (88)** *(CEBrittain)* 3-8-4 MBirch (2) (w ldrs tl wknd wl over 1f out) ..................... 4.7

**Evens** Toussaud (USA), **5/1** CASTEDDU, **6/1** Hamas (IRE), Sure Sharp (USA), **8/1** Portico (USA), **20/1** Flute (USA), **33/1** Colway Bold. CSF £31.11, Tote £6.50: £2.50 £3.00 (£13.60). Mr Ettore Landi (NEWMARKET) bred by Mrs A. E. Sigsworth. 7 Rn      1m 27.26 (2.96)
SF—80/78/67/62/44/36

## 2384

MARTINI BIANCO SUMMER H'CAP (3-Y.O) (0-70) £3080.00 (£920.00: £440.00: £200.00) **1m**        3-45 (3-47)

2107★ **Waseela (IRE) (70)** (Fav) *(AAScott)* 9-7 SCauthen (1) (mde all: shkn up over 1f out: sn clr: eased nr fin) ..................... —1

2147[3] **Batabanoo (66)** *(MrsGRReveley)* 9-3 RCochrane (5) (hld up & bhd: effrt whn nt clr run & swtchd over 1f out: r.o wl nr fin) ..................... 1.2

1847[3] **Red Kite (67)** *(MBell)* 9-4 MHills (6) (a w ldrs: effrt 2f out: r.o one pce) ..................... s.h.3

2123[5] **Watch Me Go (IRE) (53)** *(BobJones)* 8-4 NDay (4) (hld up & bhd: effrt 3f out: styd on nr fin) ..................... 1.4

1961 **April Shadow (55)** *(CWThornton)* 8-6 DMcKeown (2) (plld hrd: in tch: effrt 3f out: nt pce to chal) ..................... ¾.5

2050[2] **Phil-Man (46)** *(TFairhurst)* 7-8 ‡JFanning (7) (chsd ldrs: rdn & one pce fnl 2f) 1½.6

1528 **Essayeffsee (54)** (bl) *(MHEasterby)* 8-5 MBirch (8) (b.hind: lw: broke wl: stdd: effrt 3f out: nvr nrr) ..................... 5.7

1627[4] **Barmbrack (46)** *(RMWhitaker)* 7-11[2] WCarson (4) (cl up tl rdn & wknd 2f out) ¾.8

**3/1** WASEELA (IRE), **7/2** Watch Me Go (IRE), Red Kite, **7/1** Batabanoo, **10/1** Essayeffsee, Phil-Man, Barmbrack, **16/1** April Shadow. CSF £22.06, CT £68.38. Tote £3.50: £1.10 £1.80 £1.60 (£11.60). Sheikh Ahmed Al Maktoum (NEWMARKET) bred by Sheikh Ahmed bin Rashid al Maktoum in Ireland. 8 Rn      1m 42.96 (3.96)
SF—35/29/29/13/13/–

## 2385

FEDERATION BREWERY HIGH LEVEL BROWN ALE STKS (Mdn) £2070.00 (£570.00: £270.00) **1m 1f 9y**        4-15 (4-16)

2018[5] **Wrets (76)** *(MRStoute)* 3-8-12 SCauthen (3) (trckd ldrs: chal 3f out: styd on u.p to ld wl ins fnl f) ..................... —1

1611[4] **So Smug (USA) (81)** (Fav) *(JHMGosden)* 3-8-7 RCochrane (4) (lw: led: shkn up over 2f out: no ex wl ins fnl f) ..................... ½.2

2116[5] **Nijmegen** *(JGFitzGerald)* 4-9-7 KFallon (1) (sn outpcd & bhd: styd on fnl 2f: n.d) 10.3

1577 **Rienroe (IRE)** *(NAGraham)* 3-8-7 DMcKeown (2) (lw: trckd ldrs tl rdn & btn 2f out) ..................... 1½.4

**4/6** So Smug (USA), **6/4** WRETS, **16/1** Rienroe (IRE), **20/1** Nijmegen. CSF £2.82, Tote £2.60 (£1.30). Mrs Denis Haynes (NEWMARKET) bred by Wretham Stud. 4 Rn      1m 55.50 (3.20)
SF—37/30/14/–

**2386** FEDERATION BREWERY MEDALLION LAGER H'CAP (3-Y.O) (0-80) £3882.50 (£1160.00: £555.00: £252.50) **1½m 93y** 4-45 (4-45)

1914* **Citiqueen (IRE)** (77) (Fav) (HRACecil) 9-7 SCauthen (3) (lw: hld up: hdwy appr st: led on bit appr fnl f: easily) ............................................. —1

2142⁶ Regal Lover (IRE) (73) (MBell) 9-3 MHills (4) (lw: w ldr: disp ld 3f out: nt qckn fnl f) ................................................................................... 1½.2

1864⁵ Top Table (64) (MRStoute) 8-8 PaulEddery (1) (lw: mde most tl hdd over 1f out: r.o one pce) ......................................................................... hd.3

2113⁶ Kirsten (74) (WJarvis) 9-4 JCarroll (2) (lw: hdwy & prom: forced wd st: sn rdn & btn) ............................................................................. 10.4

**5/6** CITIQUEEN (IRE), **7/2** Regal Lover (IRE), **4/1** Top Table, **6/1** Kirsten. CSF £3.94, Tote £1.70 (£2.00). Mr Ivan Allan (NEWMARKET) bred by Ivan W. Allan in Ireland. 4 Rn 2m 41.89 (3.39)
SF—61/54/44/34

**2387** FEDERATION BREWERY 'THE TASTE OF TYNESIDE' NURSERY £3525.00 (£1050.00: £500.00: £225.00) **6f** 5-15 (5-16)

1396⁵ **Tarnside Rosal** (JEtherington) 8-4 JCarroll (4) (hld up: qcknd to ld ins fnl f: sn clr) ...................................................................................... —1

1694* Captain le Saux (IRE) (Fav) (MBell) 9-10 MHills (5) (chsd ldrs: pushed along over 2f out: swtchd & ev ch appr fnl f: r.o one pce) ............. 5.2

2030 Juliet Bravo (BBeasley) 8-9 LCharnock (2) (lw: disp ld tl led ½-wy: hdd & no ex ins fnl f) .......................................................................... nk.3

1965⁴ Willshe Gan (DenysSmith) 9-4 KFallon (3) (chsd ldrs: bmpd after 2f: rdn 2f out: nt qckn) ............................................................................ 5.4

1979³ Isotonic (GMMoore) 8-11 DMcKeown (6) (disp ld to ½-wy: btn whn sltly hmpd 1f out) ........................................................................... ½.5

2157⁵ Sefio (bl) (JBerry) 7-6⁽²⁾ ‡³JFanning (1) (chsd ldrs: hung rt after 2f: sn wknd) ... 15.6

**4/6** Captain le Saux (IRE)(op 11/10), **4/1** Willshe Gan, **13/2** Isotonic, **12/1** Juliet Bravo, Sefio, **14/1** TARNSIDE ROSAL. CSF £24.08, Tote £13.90: £2.80 1.10 (£11.40). Mrs Ann Lockhart (MALTON) bred by R. G. Percival. 6 Rn 1m 16.57 (5.07)
SF—24/24/8/–/–/–

T/Plpt: £293.50 (21.95 Tckts). AA

## 2206—WOLVERHAMPTON (L-H)

**Saturday, July 25th [Good]**
Going Allowance: 0.05 sec per fur (G) Wind: almost nil

Stalls: high

**2388** GOOSEBERRY STKS (Mdn 2-Y.O) £2070.00 (£570.00: £270.00) **5f** 1-50 (1-52)

1973³ **Special One** (JWHills) 8-9 DHolland (1) (hmpd s: hdwy u.p 2f out: led wl ins fnl f: comf) ................................................................................ —1

2052² Two Times Twelve (IRE) (bl) (Fav) (JBerry) 9-0 GCarter (7) (lw: led tl hdd wl ins fnl f) .............................................................................. hd.2

1779² The Fed (RMWhitaker) 9-0 ACulhane (3) (lw: prom: hrd rdn appr fnl f: one pce) 4.3

2031⁵ Bodandere (MJFetherston-Godley) 8-9 RPobinson (2) (s.i.s: sn chsng ldrs: wknd over 1f out) ......................................................................... nk.4

Ok Bertie (DMorris) 8-9 ‡⁵StephenDavies (5) (cmpt: bit bkwd: chsd ldrs: rdn wl over 1f out: sn wknd) ....................................................... 2½.5

Musical Times (MrsNMacauley) 8-9 NDay (6) (lt-f: outpcd: a bhd) ...................... nk.6

1832⁵ Grey Pride (JBerry) 9-0 GBardwell (4) (chsd ldrs: stumbled over 1f out: sn btn) nk.7

**2/1** Two Times Twelve (IRE), **4/1** The Fed(op 2/1), SPECIAL ONE, **5/1** Ok Bertie, **6/1** Bodandere(op 5/2), **16/1** Musical Times, **33/1** Grey Pride. CSF £11.82, Tote £4.70: £2.60 1.20 (£4.00). Mrs Christine Shove (LAMBOURN) bred by Christian Marner. 7 Rn 60.9 sec (3.6)
SF—28/32/16/10/–/–

**2389** TAYBERRY (S) STKS (2-Y.O) £2637.00 (£732.00: £351.00) **7f** 2-25 (2-28)

1932³ **Strike-a-Pose** (Fav) (CNWilliams) 8-6 JQuinn (4) (6th st: led wl over 2f out: r.o wl) ................................................................................................. —1

2058 Workingforpeanuts (IRE) (CASmith) 8-1 ‡⁵DHarrison (6) (reard s: bhd tl gd hdwy over 2f out: hrd rdn fnl f: fin wl) ................................... ½.2

2195* Awesome Risk (GLewis) 8-6 DBiggs (10) (swtg: hdwy 3f out: hrd rdn appr fnl f: unable qckn) ................................................................ 2½.3

1989⁶ Gypsy Legend (WGMTurner) 8-3 ‡³TSprake (3) (5th st: styd on one pce fnl 2f) 2½.4

2138 Duchess Dianne (IRE) *(RJHolder)* 8-6 GCarter (11) (hdwy 3f out: rdn & wknd
appr fnl f) ............................................................................... s.h.5
2058* Water Diviner (bl) *(RFJohnsonHoughton)* 8-11 DHolland (8) (led after 2f tl wl
over 2f out: wknd fnl f) ......................................................... ¹/₂.6
2108⁴ Jade Runner *(MrsNMacauley)* 8-6 NDay (5) (lw: prom: 3rd st: wknd 2f out) .. 2¹/₂.7
1675³ Longlife (IRE) *(MHTompkins)* 8-11 PRobinson (9) (lw: chsd ldrs over 4f) ........ 6.8
2195 Southampton (bl) *(GBBalding)* 8-11 JWilliams (13) (nvr nr to chal) ............. ³/₄.9
1932 Arewenearlythere (IRE) *(MBlanshard)* 8-3 ‡³FNorton (2) (4th st: wknd over 2f
out) ............................................................................................. 4.10
1989⁴ Walid's Princess (IRE) (bl) *(JWharton)* 8-6 NAdams (12) (s.s: hdwy on ins 3f
out: hrd rdn & wknd 2f out) ................................................... 2.11
2005 Hawke Bay *(DHaydnJones)* 8-11 TyroneWilliams (7) (a bhd) ..................... s.h.12
968 Border Dream *(WGMTurner)* 8-11 BCrossley (1) (led 2f: 2nd st: wknd 3f out:
t.o) .............................................................................................. 7.13

**2/1** STRIKE-A-POSE, **6/1** Awesome Risk(op 4/1), Jade Runner(8/1—5/1), **13/2** Water Diviner(4/1—7/1), **7/1**
Workingforpeanuts (IRE), **16/1** Longlife (IRE)(op 8/1), Walid's Princess (IRE), **20/1** Duchess Dianne (IRE),
Gypsy Legend, **33/1** Arewenearlythere (IRE), Southampton, Border Dream, **50/1** Hawke Bay. CSF £15.65, Tote
£3.00: £1.70 £2.60 £1.90 (£19.70). Mr David J. Chapman (NEWMARKET) bred by Mrs R. D. Peacock. 13 Rn; Bt
in 3,200 gns                      1m 29.1 (4.8)
SF—26/19/16/5/7/10

---

**2390**      RASPBERRY NURSERY    £2364.00 (£654.00: £312.00)    **5f**     2-55 (2-56)
(Weights raised 4 lb)

2081⁴ **Charity Express (IRE)** *(JBerry)* 9-0 GCarter (3) (a.p: shkn up to ld over 1f out:
r.o strly) ...................................................................................... —1
2085* My Bonus (Fav) *(D.ISCosgrove)* 9-2 ‡⁵DHarrison (1) (b.hind: hld up: hdwy & ev
ch 1f out: unable qckn) ............................................................ 3.2
1886² Not so Generous (IRE) *(WGMTurner)* 7-11 ‡³TSprake (4) (lw: led tl hdd over 1f
out: sn rdn & btn) ...................................................................... 1¹/₂.3
528³ Luckifosome *(PDEvans)* 7-13 JQuinn (2) (bit bkwd: chsd ldrs over 3f: sn
outpcd) ...................................................................................... 6.4

**8/11** My Bonus(5/4—4/6), **7/2** CHARITY EXPRESS (IRE)(2/1—4/1), Not so Generous (IRE)(5/2—4/1), **11/1**
Luckifosome(7/1—12/1). CSF £6.37, Tote £5.50 (£1.70). Express Marie Curie Racing Club (COCKERHAM) bred
by Ennistown Stud in Ireland. 4 Rn                         60.9 sec (3.6)
SF—33/23/–/–

---

**2391**      LOGANBERRY H'CAP (0-80) £2898.00 (£864.00: £412.00: £186.00)
1³/₄m 134y                                      3-25 (3-26)

1882³ **Rajai (IRE) (78)** (bl) *(JLDunlop)* 3–9-5 GCarter (3) (a.p: 3rd st: led 3f out: rdn &
edgd lft appr fnl f: drvn out) .................................................... —1
2059⁵ White River (42) (v) *(DHaydnJones)* 6–7-12 TyroneWilliams (2) (hld up: hdwy
6f out: 6th st: chsd wnr fnl 2f: no imp) ................................... 2¹/₂.2
1988 Seldom In (43) *(JWharton)* 6–7-13 JQuinn (8) (lw: hld up: 7th st: styd on fnl 2f:
nvr nrr) ....................................................................................... 3.3
2129 Marine Society (71) (v) *(PTWalwyn)* 4–9-13 PRobinson (1) (lw: chsd ldrs: 4th
st: rdn & wknd over 1f out) ...................................................... hd.4
2042* Moot Point (USA) (55) (bl) *(JRJenkins)* 4–8-11 SWhitworth (9) (lw: hld up: effrt
& 5th st: hrd rdn & ev ch over 2f out: sn wknd) ...................... 2¹/₂.5
1894³ West Stow (70) (Fav) *(MRStoute)* 3–8-8 ‡³FNorton (5) (led tl hdd & wknd 3f out) 2¹/₂.6
2122² Bar Billiards (70) (bl) *(RFJohnsonHoughton)* 3–8-11 DHolland (7) (w ldr: 2nd
st: rdn over 3f out: eased whn btn fnl 2f: t.o) .......................... 10.7
1971 Walking Saint (37) *(GraemeRoe)* 5–7-0 ‡⁷CHawksley (6) (b.hind: chsd ldrs: rdn
& lost pl ent st: t.o) ................................................................... 15.8
2036 Hallow Fair (37) *(CAHorgan)* 7–7-7 NAdams (4) (b.hind: bit bkwd: s.s: a bhd: t.o) 6.9
LONG HANDICAP: Walking Saint 7-0, Hallow Fair 7-3.

**5/2** West Stow, **5/1** RAJAI (IRE), Moot Point (USA)(op 3/1), **11/2** White River, **7/1** Bar Billiards, Marine Society,
**14/1** Seldom In, **16/1** Hallow Fair, **50/1** Walking Saint. CSF £30.24, CT £327.04. Tote £4.60: £2.10 £1.70 £2.10
(£10.80). Mr Hamdan Al-Maktoum (ARUNDEL) bred by Kilcarn Stud in Ireland. 9 Rn      3m 13.4 (7.4)
SF—38/12/7/34/13/5

---

**2392**      BLACKBERRY CLAIMING STKS (3 & 4-Y.O) £2574.00 (£714.00: £342.00)
1m 200y                                  3-55 (3-57)

2187² **Don't Smile (70)** (Fav) *(MHTompkins)* 3–8-3 PRobinson (6) (dwlt: 7th st: stdy
hdwy to ld ins fnl f) ................................................................... —1
2051* Shaffaaf (USA) (55) *(PDEvans)* 4–8-12 JQuinn (10) (lw: a.p: 4th st: led on bit
over 3f out: hdd ins fnl f: no ex) ............................................... 2.2
2125 Northern Conqueror (IRE) (56) *(TJNaughton)* 4–8-10 GCarter (8) (swtg: hdwy
& 6th st: outpcd 2f out: r.o wl ins fnl f) .................................... hd.3

2057 Tina Meena Lisa **(46)** *(EHOwenjun)* 3–7-9[9] ‡7SSanders (11) (hld up: gd hdwy 3f out: ev ch fnl 2f: unable qckn nr fin) ............................. ³/₄.4

1911⁶ Futures Gift (IRE) **(51)** *(AWPotts)* 3–8-3 DBiggs (1) (lw: bhd tl r.o fnl 2f: nt rch ldrs) ............................. 4.5

1976⁵ Northern Trial (USA) **(61)** *(CRNelson)* 4–8-7 NAdams (12) (a.p: 2nd st: led 4f out tl over 3f out: wknd appr fnl f) ............................. 2¹/₂.6

2061 Litmore Dancer **(51)** *(JMBradley)* 4–7-9 ‡7MichaelBradley (2) (chsd ldrs: 5th st: wknd over 2f out) ............................. ¹/₂.7

1741 Romola Nijinsky **(54)** *(PDEvans)* 4–7-13[2] ‡5RPrice (5) (led 5f: wknd over 2f out: t.o) ............................. 12.8

Northern Nation **(48)** *(WClay)* 4–8-7 JWilliams (9) (bit bkwd: chsd ldrs 5f: sn wknd: t.o) ............................. 7.9

2155⁶ Elwazir (USA) **(60)** *(DMarks)* 3–8-3 SDawson (7) (s.s: a bhd: t.o) ............................. 8.10

1759 Hanjessdan **(25)** *(DHaydnJones)* 4–8-7 TyroneWilliams (3) (prom: 3rd st: rdn & wknd 3f out: t.o) ............................. 6.11

**5/4** DON'T SMILE, **9/2** Shaffaaf (USA)(4/1—6/1), **11/2** Northern Trial (USA)(3/1—6/1), **9/1** Northern Conqueror (IRE)(5/1—10/1), **11/1** Elwazir (USA)(6/1—12/1), **12/1** Futures Gift (IRE)(14/1—18/1), **25/1** Tina Meena Lisa, **33/1** Romola Nijinsky, Litmore Dancer, **40/1** Northern Nation, **100/1** Hanjessdan. CSF £7.11, Tote £1.80: £1.10 £1.80 £3.60 (£4.40). Mr B. Schmidt-Bodner (NEWMARKET) bred by Grange Farm (Barnby Moor) Ltd. 11 Rn
1m 54.5 (6)
SF—6/9/6/–/–/–

**2393**　　STRAWBERRY H'CAP (3-Y.O) (0-80) £3028.00 (£904.00: £432.00: £196.00)
　　　　　**1m**　　　　　　　　　　　　　　　　　　　　　　　　　　　　4-25 (4-26)
　　　　　　　　　　　(Weights raised 6 lb)

2125 **Tiffany's Case (IRE) (48)** *(CAHorgan)* 7-9[1] SDawson (8) (hld up: brought wd over 2f out: styd on to ld wl ins fnl f) ............................. —1

2237³ Winged Whisper (USA) **(60)** *(CASmith)* 8-2 ‡5DHarrison (5) (b.off hind: lw: s.s: gd hdwy 3f out: led 2f out tl wl ins fnl f: rallied nr fin) ............................. nk.2

2066 Mainly Me **(71)** *(PTWalwyn)* 9-4 PRobinson (3) (hdwy & 6th st: rdn & one pce appr fnl f) ............................. 2¹/₂.3

2123² Mary Macblain **(49)** *(JLHarris)* 7-7[1] ‡3FNorton (6) (b.off hind: chsd ldrs: 5th st: wknd appr fnl f) ............................. 5.4

1627⁵ Specialist Dream (IRE) **(47)** *(LJCodd)* 7-8 NAdams (7) (dwlt: sn chsng ldrs: 3rd st: ev ch 2f out: wknd over 1f out) ............................. hd.5

1811⁴ Southwold Air **(71)** *(JLDunlop)* 9-4 GCarter (2) (lw: chsd ldr: 2nd st: wknd wl over 1f out: t.o) ............................. 12.6

2000⋆ Eastleigh **(67)** *(RHollinshead)* 8-7 ‡7AGarth (4) (led: qcknd clr ent st: wknd & hdd 2f out: t.o) ............................. ³/₄.7

1928⁶ Elanmatina (IRE) **(74)** (Fav) *(CFWall)* 9-7 NDay (1) (lw: hld up: 4th st: ev ch whn almost b.d 2f out: nt rcvr) ............................. 7.8

**11/4** Elanmatina (IRE), **5/1** Southwold Air, Specialist Dream (IRE)(op 10/1), **6/1** Winged Whisper (USA), Eastleigh(op 4/1), **7/1** Mainly Me, Mary Macblain(op 4/1), **12/1** TIFFANY'S CASE (IRE). CSF £76.88, CT £501.21. Tote £11.50: £1.60 £1.40 £2.20 (£44.50). Mr John Kelsey-Fry (BILLINGBEAR) bred by Mrs C. L. Weld in Ireland. 8 Rn
1m 43.2 (5.9)
T/Plpt: £374.40 (4.05 Tckts).　　　　　　　　　　　　　　　　　　　　　　IM

# WOLVERHAMPTON (L-H)
## Monday, July 27th [Good]
Going Allowance: St: 0.20 sec; Rnd: 0.05 sec per fur (G)　　　　　Wind: str bhd

Stalls: high

**2394**　　TENNENT'S PILSNER APP'CE CLAIMING STKS　　£1618.00 (£448.00: £214.00)
　　　　　**1m 200y**　　　　　　　　　　　　　　　　　　　　　　6-15 (6-18)

2326⁶ **Sanawl (52)** *(PDEvans)* 5–8-2 ‡5HayleyWilliams (3) (s.i.s: hdwy 3f out: styd on strly to ld cl home) ............................. —1

2392² Shaffaaf (USA) **(55)** *(PDEvans)* 4–9-0 SWynne (9) (lw: a.p: led over 1f out: wknd & ct last stride) ............................. s.h.2

1294 Friendlypersuasion (IRE) **(35)** *(RHollinshead)* 4–8-7 EHusband (12) (a chsng ldrs: led over 2f out tl over 1f out: kpt on one pce) ............................. 5.3

2393² Winged Whisper (USA) **(60)** (Fav) *(CASmith)* 3–8-3 MHumphries (5) (lw: b.off hind: hdwy 2f out: styd on ins fnl f: nvr nrr) ............................. 4.4

2077⁶ A Nymph Too Far (IRE) **(42)** *(DrJDScargill)* 3–7-7 CHawksley (10) (b.hind: hdwy fnl 2f) ............................. 3¹/₂.5

2291 Urshi-Jade **(35)** *(KWhite)* 4–8-5 TWilson (4) (chsd ldrs: rdn 2f out: sn btn) ............................. 2¹/₂.6

1964 Beechwood Cottage **(34)** (bl) *(ABailey)* 9–8-2 ‡5WHollick (7) (nvr plcd to chal) .. 2.7
2210 Norfolk Thatch **(34)** *(KSBridgwater)* 6–8-7 PBowe (8) (a in rr) ........................... ¾.4.8
1992 Sequestrator **(21)** *(PDEvans)* 9–8-7 DWright (13) (led after 1f to 3f out: wknd
    qckly) ................................................................................ 2.9
    Homile *(BAMcMahon)* 4–8-12 JBramhill (4) (bkwd: chsd ldrs 6f: sn lost tch) .. hd.10
2086 Barkston Singer **(44)** *(JLHarris)* 5–8-2 GParkin (2) (led 1f: led 3f out: sn hdd &
    wknd: t:o) ........................................................................... 7.11
2135 Hills of Hoy **(36)** *(KCBailey)* 6–8-7 DGibbs (1) (hmpd after 1f: bhd fnl 3f: t.o) .. 4.12

**9/4** Winged Whisper (USA), **11/4** Shaffaaf (USA), **8/1** SANAWI(op 5/1), **10/1** A Nymph Too Far (IRE), **12/1** Homile, **14/1** Barkston Singer, **20/1** Hills of Hoy, Friendlypersuasion (IRE), Urshi-Jade, **25/1** Norfolk Thatch, Beechwood Cottage, **50/1** Sequestrator. CSF £27.65, Tote £7.50: £3.70 £1.90 £2.30 (£6.70). Mr P. D. Evans (WELSHPOOL) bred by J. Wigan and W. Hastings-Bass. 12 Rn     1m 54.3 (5.8)
                                                   SF—8/19/–/–/–/–/

## 2395
STONES BITTER H'CAP (0-90) £1718.20 (£475.20: £226.60)    **5f**     6-45 (6-47)
(Weights raised 13 lb)

2280² **Iron King (67)** (Jt-Fav) *(JLSpearing)* 6–8-11 ‡7AGarth (5) (rdn sn after s: hdwy
    appr fnl f: led ins fnl f: r.o wl) ................................................. —1
2234* Samson-Agonistes **(73)** *(BAMcMahon)* 6–9-10 TQuinn (7) (lw: led over 3f: hrd
    rdn & hung lft appr fnl f: unable qckn) ...................................... 2.2
1987* Jess Rebec **(53)** (Jt-Fav) *(LGCottrell)* 4–8-4 NCarlisle (8) (hdwy ½-wy: n.m.r &
    squeezed over 1f out: kpt on u.p) .............................................. hd.3
1445 Rhythmic Dancer **(73)** *(JLSpearing)* 4–9-10 GHind (2) (hdwy to ld over 1f out:
    hdd & wknd ins fnl f) ............................................................. 2.4
2127 Pallium (IRE) **(71)** (v) *(MPNaughton)* 4–9-3 ‡5JWeaver (4) (lw: chsd ldrs: rdn
    over 1f out: nt pce to chal) ...................................................... 2.5
£189 Darussalam **(69)** *(RLee)* 5–9-6 WCarson (3) (disp ld over 3f: rdn & btn 1f out) .. 1.6
2188 My Sovereign **(USA) (71)** (v) *(IRFanshawe)* 3–9-3 GCarter (1) (chsd ldrs 3f: sn
    rdn & btn: t:o) ...................................................................... 5.7
    Lonsom Lass **(70)** *(LJBarratt)* 4–9-7 RHills (6) (b: w ldrs 3f: sn outpcd: t.o) ........ 0.8

**7/2** Jess Rebec, IRON KING, **9/2** Darussalam, **5/1** Pallium (IRE)(tchd 9/1), Samson-Agonistes, **9/1** My Sovereign (USA), **25/1** Rhythmic Dancer, **50/1** Lonsom Lass. CSF £19.16, CT £56.76. Tote £3.20: £1.20 £1.50 £1.60 (£7.10). Mr Tom Coleman (ALCESTER) bred by L. Hutch. 8 Rn     60.5 sec (3.2)
                                                   SF—53/58/37/49/34/33

## 2396
BEER BARREL (S) STKS (2-Y.O) £1604.00 (£444.00: £212.00)    **5f**     7-15 (7-20)

588² **Convenient Moment** *(JBerry)* 8-6 GCarter (3) (mde all: rdn & rn green appr fnl
    f: r.o) ................................................................................. —1
2242⁶ Girl Next Door (Fav) *(NAGraham)* 8-6 RCochrane (4) (a.p: ev ch 1f out: unable
    qckn fnl f) ........................................................................... 1½.2
2205 Bluebella *(MrsPABarker)* 8-6 PaulEddery (1) (a.p: rdn over 1f out: one pce) .... 3.3
2207⁶ Over the Dec (bl) *(BAMcMahon)* 8-6 TQuinn (8) (hdwy over 1f out: kpt on ins fnl
    f: nvr nrr) ............................................................................ 3½.4
2080⁶ Clangold (bl) *(JBerry)* 8-6 RHills (5) (chsd ldrs: rdn appr fnl f: nvr able to chal) 2½.5
    Celtic Cherry *(JBalding)* 8-6 GHind (10) (small: bit bkwd: nvr nr to chal) ........... 2,6
786 Purbeck Centenary *(MRChannon)* 8-11 LornaVincent (9) (bit bkwd: spd over
    3f: sn wknd) ........................................................................ 2.7
    Ess-Pee-Cee *(WClay)* 8-1 ‡5RPrice (2) (lt-f: unf: bit bkwd: s.s: outpcd: t.o) .......... 5.8
    Nigels Prospect *(DHaydnJones)* 8-4 ‡7SianWilliams (7) (leggy: lt-f: s.s: a t.o) ... nk.9

**13/8** Girl Next Door, **11/4** CONVENIENT MOMENT(2/1—7/2), **9/2** Bluebella, **9/1** Over the Dec, **10/1** Clangold, **25/1** Purbeck Centenary, **50/1** Ors. CSF £6.96, Tote £4.20: £1.70 £1.50 £1.30 (£3.60). Mr David Fish (COCKERHAM) bred by D. Gill. 9 Rn; Bt in 3,000 gns     61.6 sec (4.3)
                                                   SF—26/20/12/–/–/–

## 2397
HIGHGATE MILD H'CAP (0-70) £1730.00 (£480.00: £230.00)
1⅜m 134y                                             7-45 (7-47)

2057³ **Wilkins (54)** *(JRFanshawe)* 3–8-2 GCarter (11) (a.p: 3rd st: led over 3f out: hrd
    rdn fnl f: styd on) ................................................................. —1
2241³ Polistatic **(34)** *(CAHorgan)* 5–7-11 DaleGibson (2) (gd hdwy 3f out: chsd wnr fnl
    2f: no ex fnl f) ...................................................................... 2.2
2235* My Swan Song **(36)** *(JPSmith)* 7–7-6 (5x) ‡7AGarth (8) (mid div: styd on fnl 2f:
    nvr nrr) .............................................................................. 2.3
1108⁶ Emperor Chang (USA) **(40)** *(RHollinshead)* 5–8-3(3) WRyan (10) (bit bkwd: hld
    up: hdwy over 2f out: nvr nrr) ................................................ 4.4
2059 Gesnera **(40)** *(KWhite)* 4–8-3 NCarlisle (4) (chsd ldrs: 6th st: rdn over 1f out:
    one pce) ............................................................................. nk.5
578² Premier Princess **(38)** *(GAHam)* 6–7-10 ‡5RPrice (7) (bit bkwd: hdwy ½-wy: 5th
    st: wknd wl over 1f out) ......................................................... 8.6

20876 Himlaj (USA) **(44)** *(SMellor)* 7–8-7 DanaMellor (3) (blind nr eye: hld up: hdwy 3f out: wknd appr fnl f) ...................................... ½.7

2373 Tophard **(34)** *(RLee)* 6–7-11 WCarson (9) (b: bhd: effrt u.p 3f out: nt rch ldrs) . 10.8

23732 Enfant du Paradis (IRE) (Fav) *(PDEvans)* 4–7-5 ‡7DWright (12) (sddle slipped: nvr plcd to chal) ..................................... 3½.9

21552 Monorose **(54)** (v) *(DHaydnJones)* 3–8-2(1) RHills (5) (chsd ldrs tl 7th & wkng st) 3.10

2036 Casienne (IRE) **(36)** *(RJHolder)* 4–7-13 RFox (1) (chsd ldrs: 4th st: wknd over 2f out) ..................................... ½.11

Tropical Mist (FR) **(36)** *(GAHam)* 12–7-6(1) ‡7TWilson (14) (a bhd: t.o) ........ 10.12

21726 High Beacon **(65)** (bl) *(KCBailey)* 5–10-0 BRaymond (13) (led after 2f to 10f out: 2nd st: wknd 3f out: t.o) ........................ 2.13

15016 Paris of Troy **(62)** *(NATwiston-Davies)* 4–9-11 SCauthen (6) (led 2f: led 10f out tl over 3f out: sn rdn & wknd: t.o) ............. 20.14

**7/2** Enfant du Paradis (IRE)(op 6/1), **13/2** My Swan Song(4/1—7/1), WILKINS(4/1—7/1), **7/1** Polistatic(5/1—8/1), High Beacon, **8/1** Premier Princess(op 5/1), **9/1** Paris of Troy, **12/1** Monorose, Emperor Chang (USA), **20/1** Casienne (IRE), Tophard, **33/1** Himlaj (USA), Gesnera, **50/1** Tropical Mist (FR). CSF £50.22, CT £288.97. Tote £8.20: £2.60 £2.70 £2.30 (£64.80). Lord Vestey (NEWMARKET) bred by Major J. S. R. Edmunds and J. S. Delahooke. 14 Rn　　　　　　　　　　　　　　　　　　　　　　　　　　3m 12 (6)
SF—35/26/17/20/19/–

---

**2398**　　　E.B.F. TIPSY STKS (Mdn 2-Y.O.C & G) £2092.80 (£580.80: £278.40)　　**7f** 8-15 (8-20)

17962 **Beneficial** (Fav) *(GWragg)* 9-0 MHills (7) (carried wd ent st: gd hdwy 3f out: styd on to ld cl home) .................... —1

20343 Semillon *(GHarwood)* 9-0 AClark (8) (lw: 4th st: led over 2f out: clr fnl f: hrd rdn & ct nr fin) ........................... nk.2

15364 Tajdid (IRE) **(99)** *(HThomsonJones)* 9-0 RHills (11) (lw: wnt 2nd st: ev ch 2f out: r.o one pce) ........................ 5.3

2002 Glorious Island *(RFJohnsonHoughton)* 9-0 TQuinn (9) (led tl hdwy over 2f out: grad wknd) ........................... 2.4

Nu Shan *(MRStoute)* 9-0 SCauthen (4) (cmpt: bkwd: bhd: styd on fnl 2f: nvr nrr) ............................. 2.5

22085 Dusty Point (IRE) *(BHanbury)* 9-0 BRaymond (5) (nvr nr to chal) ........... 2½.6

2208 Behaanis (USA) *(AAScott)* 9-0 JFortune (1) (chsd ldrs: 6th & rn wd ent st: wknd 2f out) ........................ nk.7

18874 We Are Doomed *(JRFanshawe)* 9-0 GCarter (6) (lw: chsd ldrs: 5th st: wknd wl over 2f out) ........................ 2.8

Paper Days *(RJHolder)* 9-0 PaulEddery (3) (lengthy: bkwd: a bhd) .......... ¾.9

17015 Genseric (FR) *(RWArmstrong)* 9-0 WCarson (4) (lw: prom: 3rd st: rdn & wknd over 2f out) ........................ nk.10

22056 Muraadi Ana (IRE) *(AAScott)* 9-0 GKing (1) (mid div: rdn 3f out: sn btn) ......... ½.11

**7/4** BENEFICIAL, **2/1** Tajdid (IRE)(tchd 7/2), **5/1** Semillon, **10/1** Nu Shan (IRE)(op 5/1), **14/1** Genseric (FR), **20/1** Glorious Island, Dusty Point (IRE), **33/1** We Are Doomed, **50/1** Ors. CSF £10.83, Tote £2.90: £1.50 £2.20 £1.40 (£5.30). Sir Robin McAlpine (NEWMARKET) bred by Sir Robin McAlpine. 11 Rn　　　　1m 30.1 (5.8)
SF—19/18/3/–/–/–

---

**2399**　　　BARMAID STKS (Mdn 3-Y.O.F) £1380.00 (£380.00: £180.00)　　**1m**　　8-45 (8-49)

19563 **Walimu** (IRE) (Fav) *(CFWall)* 8-11 SCauthen (4) (lw: wnt 3rd st: hrd rdn 3f out: styd on to ld wl ins fnl f) .................. —1

20795 Shakreen (USA) **(67)** *(MrsLPiggott)* 8-11 RCochrane (2) (lw: led: clr appr fnl f: rdn & hdd wl ins fnl f) ................. 2.2

Raheena (USA) *(JHMGosden)* 8-11 PaulEddery (6) (w'like: scope: bkwd: s.s: 6th st: shkn up 4f out: styd on appr fnl f) .......... 10.3

20884 Gold Belt (IRE) **(51)** *(RHollinshead)* 8-11 WRyan (3) (chsd ldr: 2nd st: ev ch 3f out: sn rdn: wknd appr fnl f) ........... 1½.4

1974 Blue Is True (IRE) *(LJBarratt)* 8-11 RHills (5) (5th st: wknd over 2f out) ............. 8.5

1849 Oriental Song *(KSBridgwater)* 8-6 ‡5SWilliams (1) (bit bkwd: chsd ldrs: 4th st: sn lost tch: t.o) ........................ 15.6

Broadway Ruckus (CAN) *(66/1)* Withdrawn (ref to ent stalls) : not under orders

**6/5** WALIMU (IRE), **9/4** Shakreen (USA), **11/2** Raheena (USA), Gold Belt (IRE), **66/1** Ors. CSF £4.04, Tote £2.00: £1.20 £1.50 (£2.60). Sheikh Ahmed Al Maktoum (NEWMARKET) bred by Sheikh Ahmed bin Rashid al Maktoum in Ireland. 6 Rn　　　　　　　　　　　　　　　　　　　　　　　1m 42.7 (5.4)
SF—22/16/–/–/–/–

T/Plpt: £14.30 (108.75 Tckts).　　　　　　　　　　　　　　　　　　　　　IM

2271─**DONCASTER (L-H)**　　*Off-Course Tote Dividends quoted for all races*
**Sunday, July 26th [Good to firm]**
Going Allowance: St: nil (G); Rnd: minus 0.20 sec per fur (F)　　　Wind: fresh against

Stalls: high

**2400**　　　CORAL 1st SUNDAY RACE (H'cap) (0-110) £10035.20 (£3756.80: £1838.40: £792.00:
　　　　　　£356.00: £181.60)　**7f**　　　　　　　　　　　　　　　　2-05 (2-08)

1253[4]　**Savoyard (99)** (bl) *(MAJarvis)* 4-8-12 WRSwinburn (1) (b: lw: bhd & rdn ½-wy:
　　　　　hdwy 2f out: r.o gamely u.p to ld nr fin) ...............................─1
　2028　Gymcrak Premiere (94) (Fav) *(MHEasterby)* 4-8-7 GCarter (5) (in tch: hdwy
　　　　　over 1f out: led wl ins fnl f: r.o) ...............................s.h.2
2183[2]　Panikin (94) *(JWharton)* 4-8-7 JWilliams (7) (lw: w ldr: led & qcknd clr over 2f
　　　　　out: hdd & no ex wl ins fnl f) ...............................¾.4.3
　1943　Deprecator (USA) (94) *(JHMGosden)* 4-8-7 RCochrane (4) (b.hind: lw: a w
　　　　　ldrs: chal u.p over 1f out: nt qckn) ...............................½.4
　1696　Rocton North (IRE) (94) *(RHannon)* 4-8-7 GDuffield (8) (swtg: drvn along &
　　　　　bhd ½-wy: sme hdwy 2f out: no imp) ...............................5.5
　1943　Go Executive (94) *(CEBrittain)* 4-8-7 MRoberts (6) (lw: cl up over 4f) ...............................½.6
　1474　Stack Rock (98) *(EJAlston)* 5-8-11 LPiggott (3) (led tl hdd over 2f out: wknd
　　　　　over 1f out) ...............................4.7
2021[4]　Norton Challenger (108) (v) *(MHEasterby)* 5-9-7 MBirch (2) (lw: spd over 4f: sn
　　　　　rdn & wknd) ...............................1.8

　　　　LONG HANDICAP: Panikin 8-2, Deprecator (USA) 8-2, Rocton North (IRE) 8-2, Go Executive 8-3.

**27/10** Gymcrak Premiere, **36/10** SAVOYARD, **9/2** Stack Rock, **59/10** Norton Challenger, **61/10** Deprecator
(USA), **97/10** Panikin, **12/1** Go Executive, **123/10** Rocton North (IRE). Tote £4.60: £1.80 £1.10 £2.20 (£10.30).
Lady Butt (NEWMARKET) bred by F. C. T. Wilson. 8 Rn　　　　　　　　1m 25.58 (2.18)
　　　　　　　　　　　　　　　　　　　　　　　　SF─66/00/50/66/41/39

**2401**　　　CHEVELEY PARK STUD H'CAP (0-90) £6736.00 (£2524.00: £1237.00: £535.00:
　　　　　　£242.50: £125.50)　**1¾m 132y**　　　　　　　　　　2-30 (2-32)
　　　　　　　　　　　　(Weights raised 2 lb)

2172＊　**Mull House (68)** (Jt-Fav) *(FJO'Mahony)* 5-8-10 WRSwinburn (8) (lw: a.p: effrt
　　　　　4f out: styd on strly fnl f to ld post) ...............................─1
1697[6]　Line Drummer (USA) (76) *(PAKelleway)* 4-9-4 WCarson (2) (b: chsd ldrs: led 4f
　　　　　out tl over 2f out: r.o & hmpd fnl f: fin 3rd, ¾l: plcd 2nd) ...............................2
2023[4]　Lord Hastie (USA) (78) *(SGNorton)* 4-9-1 ‡5OPears (7) (lw: a.p: slt ld over 2f out:
　　　　　hung lft & ct nr fin: fin 2nd, hd: disq: plcd 3rd) ...............................3
　1922　Trojan Lancer (60) *(DrJDScargill)* 6-8-2[(1)] WRyan (9) (hld up & bhd: hdwy over
　　　　　4f out: kpt on wl fnl f) ...............................nk.4
2180[5]　Army of Stars (78) (Jt-Fav) *(CEBrittain)* 7-9-6 MRoberts (5) (lw: in tch: outpcd 3f
　　　　　out: no imp after) ...............................8.5
1612[4]　Good for a Loan (67) *(RLee)* 5-8-9 LPiggott (10) (lw: hld up & bhd: effrt 4f out:
　　　　　n.d) ...............................5.6
1951[5]　Green Lane (USA) (73) (bl) *(IABalding)* 4-9-1 RCochrane (6) (led after 1f tl after
　　　　　3f: led 8f out to 4f out: sn wknd) ...............................1½.7
　　435　Madagans Grey (82) *(RBoss)* 4-9-10 GDuffield (3) (led 1f: led after 3f to 8f out:
　　　　　cl up tl wknd 3f out) ...............................25.8
　　912　Loudest Whisper (56) (v) *(KSBridgwater)* 4-7-7 ‡5BDoyle (1) (b: swtg: prom tl
　　　　　outpcd appr st: sn bhd) ...............................5.9
1866[5]　Isobar (54) *(MCChapman)* 6-7-7[(3)] ‡3FNorton (4) (chsd ldrs tl rdn & wknd qckly
　　　　　7f out) ...............................3.10

　　　　　　　LONG HANDICAP: Isobar 5-8.
　　　*Stewards Enquiry: Lord Hastie (USA) disq (interference to Line Drummer (USA) ins fnl f).*

**31/10** Army of Stars, **MULL HOUSE**, **36/10** Green Lane (USA), **58/10** Line Drummer (USA), **71/10** Lord Hastie
(USA), **9/1** Good for a Loan, **10/1** Trojan Lancer, **56/1** Madagans Grey, **724/10** Loudest Whisper, **1969/10**
Isobar. Tote £4.10: £1.60 £1.80 £3.30 (£20.50). Mr M. Lowry (LINGFIELD) bred by D. J. and Mrs Deer. 10 Rn
　　　　　　　　　　　　　　　　　　　　　　　　3m 5.97 (2.37)
　　　　　　　　　　　　　　　　　　　　　　　　SF─43/49/47/32/42/26

**2402**　　　MAIL ON SUNDAY TROPHY (Stks)　£12990.00 (£4740.00: £2320.00: £1000.00:
　　　　　　£450.00)　**1¼m 60y**　　　　　　　　　　　　2-55 (2-58)

　1876　**Young Buster (IRE) (117)** *(GWragg)* 4-9-10 MHills (6) (lw: hld up: hdwy on bit
　　　　　to ld ent fnl f: easily) ...............................─1
1876[5]　Twist and Turn (119) (Fav) *(HRACecil)* 3-9-0 WRSwinburn (2) (lw: led: qcknd 4f
　　　　　out: hdd & one pce ins fnl f) ...............................1.2

557 Prince Russanor **(98)** *(JLDunlop)* 4–9-3 WCarson (5) (trckd ldrs: effrt 3f out: sn rdn & no imp) .................................................... 1½.**3**

1229a Spartan Shareef (IRE) **(95)** *(CEBrittain)* 3–8-7 MBirch (3) (bhd: pulled outside & effrt over 2f out: hrd rdn, hung lft & n.d) .................. s.h.**4**

1455⁵ Lucky Lindy (IRE) **(RHannon)** 3–8-12 MRoberts (4) (lw: prom tl rdn over 3f out: no imp after) .................................................... 3.**5**

**2/5** Twist and Turn, **3/1** Lucky Lindy (IRE), **31/10** YOUNG BUSTER (IRE), **583/10** Prince Russanor, **200/1** Spartan Shareef (IRE). Tote £4.10: £1.10 £1.30 (£1.80). Mollers Racing (NEWMARKET) bred by White Lodge Stud Ltd in Ireland. 5 Rn
2m 8.49 (1.49)
SF—74/62/62/51/50

**2403**
TRIPLEPRINT H'CAP (3-Y.O) (0-90) £6620.00 (£2480.00: £1215.00: £525.00: £237.50: £122.50)   **1¼m 60y**
3-20 (3-25)

(Weights raised 4 lb)

21785 **Bentico (63)** *(MAJarvis)* 7-12 JQuinn (8) (sn cl up: led 3f out: sn rdn: jst hld on) —**1**

2018★ Drummer Hicks **(76)** (Fav) *(EWeymes)* 8-11 DMcKeown (7) (lw: a chsng ldrs: effrt over 3f out: snr hrd drvn: styd on wl nr fin) ............ hd.**2**

1444⁴ Billy Blazer **(72)** *(MHTompkins)* 8-7 KDarley (12) (lw: hld up & bhd: gd hdwy over 2f out: hrd rdn fnl f: r.o nr fin) .......................... hd.**3**

1869 Congress (IRE) **(80)** *(MRStoute)* 9-1 SCauthen (3) (led tl hdd 3f out: kpt on: no ex ins fnl f) .................................................... 2½.**4**

1901★ Liability Order **(69)** *(RBoss)* 8-4 MRoberts (6) (hdwy appr st: sn chsng ldrs: hrd rdn 2f out: nt qckn) ........................................ 1.**5**

1960² Timurid (FR) **(76)** *(JLDunlop)* 8-11 WRyan (10) (effrt 4f out: styd on: no imp) . 1½.**6**

2057★ Viva Darling **(71)** *(BAMcMahon)* 7-13 ‡⁷SSanders (4) (prom tl grad wknd fnl 2f) 1½.**7**

1700 Philgun **(58)** *(CWCElsey)* 7-7 JLowe (5) (chsd ldrs tl wknd over 3f out) ........ 15.**8**

Aljernaas **(86)** *(LMCumani)* 9-7 LDettori (2) (bit bkwd: mid div: effrt ent st: sn btn) .................................................... 12.**9**

1213³ Gachette **(65)** *(JSutcliffe)* 7-9 ‡⁵DHarrison (9) (lost tch ½-wy) ...................... nk.**10**

1839★ Majjra (USA) **(82)** *(JHMGosden)* 9-3 GDuffield (1) (lw: chsd ldrs tl rdn & wknd 4f out) nt qckn) .................................................... 30.**11**

21894 Enaya **(84)** *(RWArmstrong)* 9-5 WCarson (11) (bhd & rdn ent st: n.d) .......... 2½.**12**

**26/10** Drummer Hicks, **51/10** Timurid (FR), **69/10** Congress (IRE), **19/2** Gachette, **98/10** Enaya, **113/10** Majjra (USA), **114/10** Liability Order, **12/1** BENTICO, **141/10** Philgun, **149/10** Aljernaas, **225/10** Billy Blazer, **354/10** Viva Darling. Tote £13.00: £2.50 £1.90 £4.70 (£40.70). Mr Mark Christofi (NEWMARKET) bred by Britton House Stud. 12 Rn
2m 8.03 (1.03)
SF—53/65/60/63/50/54

**2404**
VIRGIN ATLANTIC FLYER H'CAP (0-90) £6852.00 (£2568.00: £902.00 each: £247.50: £128.50)   **5f 140y**
3-45 (3-55)

20734 **Drum Sergeant (60)** (bl) (Fav) *(JParkes)* 5-7-12 MRoberts (10) (lw: chsd ldrs: hdwy over 1f out: r.o wl to ld wl ins fnl f) —**1**

2203³ Cronk's Courage **(76)** (v) *(EJAlston)* 6-9-0 LPiggott (11) (led tl hdd & no ex wl ins fnl f) .................................................... 2.**2**

2127 Cantoris **(87)** *(RJRWilliams)* 6-9-11 DHolland (2) (a in tch: hdwy over 1f out: r.o nr fin) .................................................... s.h.**3**

20736 Seamere **(82)** (bl) *(BRCambidge)* 9-9-6 JLowe (12) (lw: trckd ldrs gng wl: hdwy to chal over 1f out: nt qckn nr fin) ...................... d.h.**3**

2163 Samsolom **(61)** *(JBalding)* 4–7-13⁽¹⁾ GHind (9) (a chsng ldrs: kpt on wl u.p fnl f) hd.**5**

2227² Misdemeanours Girl (IRE) **(68)** *(MRChannon)* 4-8-1 ‡⁵BDoyle (14) (lw: bhd: several positions & hmpd after ½-wy: r.o wl nr fin) ................ 1½.**6**

21795 Lucedeo **(84)** *(JLSpearing)* 8-9-8 GDuffield (5) (lw: bhd: nt clr run & swtchd over 1f out: r.o wl) .................................... ½.**7**

18536 Arc Lamp **(62)** *(JAGlover)* 6–7-11 ‡³FNorton (3) (chsd ldrs: nt qckn fnl f) ........ ½.**8**

2127 Paley Prince (USA) **(85)** *(MDIUsher)* 6-9-9 SCauthen (8) (hdwy 2f out: n.m.r: nvr able to chal) .................................... ¾.**9**

2141² Ayr Raider **(69)** (bl) *(WRMuir)* 5–8-7 SWhitworth (6) (reluctant to ent stalls: gd spd 3f: sn rdn & btn) .................................... ¾.**10**

1688 Heaven-Liegh-Grey **(82)** *(MJohnston)* 4–9-6 DMcKeown (15) (cl up to ½-wy: n.m.r & grad wknd) .................................... 2½.**11**

18285 Amber Mill **(82)** *(JBerry)* 4–9-6 JCarroll (4) (spd over 3f) .......................... 1½.**12**

2117★ Breezy Day **(81)** *(BAMcMahon)* 6–9-5 BRaymond (13) (lw: chsd ldrs: n.m.r & outpcd ½-wy: n.d after) .................................... 2½.**13**

1406 Loft Boy **(68)** (bl) *(JDBethell)* 9–8-6 RHills (1) (prom 3f) .......................... 2.**14**

2188 Tauber **(67)** *(PatMitchell)* 8-8-2 ‡³SO'Gorman (7) (w ldrs tl wknd wl over 1f out) 8.**15**

**34/10** DRUM SERGEANT, **13/2** Ayr Raider, **68/10** Cronk's Courage, **7/1** Seamere, **15/2** Misdemeanours Girl (IRE), **88/10** Breezy Day, **148/10** Tauber, **169/10** Loft Boy, **179/10** Cantoris, **218/10** Lucedeo, **23/1** Paley Prince (USA), **255/10** Heaven-Liegh-Grey, **275/10** Amber Mill, **418/10** Samsolom, **84/1** Arc Lamp. Tote £4.40: £2.10 £2.80 C, £2.70 S, £1.30 (£36.40). Mr W. A. Sellers (MALTON) bred by Snarehill Stud Co. 15 Rn   1m 8.61 (1.61)
SF—52/60/70/65/43/39

**2405**   EUROPEAN BREEDERS FUND 1st SUNDAY STKS (Mdn 2-Y.O.F) £4797.20 (£1794.80: £877.40: £377.00: £168.50: £85.10)   **6f**   4-15 (4-21)

1937² **Cape Weaver** (Fav) *(JHMGosden)* 8-11 SCauthen (3) (b.hind: lw: hld up: stdy hdwy to ld 1f out: qcknd: comf) .............................. —1

2055² Abbey's Gal *(IABalding)* 8-11 RCochrane (4) (lw: trckd ldrs gng wl: led 2f out: hdd 1f out: nt pce of wnr) ........................ 2¹/₂.2

2108² Royal Flex (USA) *(MrsLPiggott)* 8-11 LPiggott (11) (b.off hind: lw: led 4f: r.o one pce) .......................................... 3¹/₂.3

2055⁵ Rock the Boat *(RHannon)* 8-11 MRoberts (9) (s.i.s: sn pushed along & chsng ldrs: rdn & one pce fnl 2f) ........................ 3.4

2034 Bonny Princess *(JDBethell)* 8-11 LDettori (2) (hld up: hdwy 2f out: nvr nr to chal) .......................................... 3¹/₂.5

1969⁴ My Cherrywell *(MrsVAAconley)* 8-11 KFallon (1) (chsd ldrs 4f: sn outpcd) ... 5.6

2167 Inonder *(MDIUsher)* 8-11 JWilliams (10) (nvr nr to chal) ................. 3¹/₂.7

1832⁴ Noteability *(JBerry)* 8-11 GCarter (5) (lw: spd over 3f) .................. hd.8

1910⁵ Queen of the Quorn *(GMMoore)* 8-11 DMcKeown (7) (unruly in stalls: dwlt: sn rcvrd: wknd over 2f out) ........................... 5.9

1895³ First Play *(JBerry)* 8-11 JCarroll (2) (b.hind: lw: gd spd over 3f) ......... 3¹/₂.10

2205 Don't Tell Jean (40/1) Withdrawn (unruly & uns rdr twice gng to s) : not under orders

**3/5** CAPE WEAVER, **34/10** Abbey's Gal, **39/10** Rock the Boat, **71/10** Royal Flex (USA), **1202/10** Noteability, **4308/10** Bonny Princess, **48/1** First Play, **827/10** My Cherrywell, **160/1** Queen of the Quorn, **293/1** Inonder. Tote £1.60: £1.10 £1.80 £1.30 (£2.90). Sheikh Mohammed (NEWMARKET) bred by Sheikh Mohammed bin Rashid al Maktoum. 10 Rn                                                                    1m 14.43 (3.43)
                                                                                                                                       SF—29/19/5/–/–/–

**2406**   WEATHERBYS 1st SUNDAY CLAIMING STKS   £5052.40 (£1891.60: £925.80: £399.00: £170.60: £91.70)   **6f**   4-45 (4-49)

1952★ **A Prayer for Wings** (93) (Fav) *(JSutcliffe)* 8-8-13 MRoberts (8) (lw: swtchd lft ¹/₂-wy: shkn up & hdwy over 2f out: qcknd to ld wl ins fnl f: comf) .......................................... —1

2188² Easy Line (89) *(PJFeilden)* 9-8-11 BRaymond (b: lw: in tch: hdwy 2f out: led ins fnl f: sn hdd: r.o) .................... ¹/₂.2

1795 Pink'n Black (IRE) (55) *(GBlum)* 3-7-7⁽³⁾ ‡5DHarrison (7) (chsd ldrs: led wl over 1f out tl ins fnl f: no ex) ........................ 2.3

542 Tigani (73) (bl) *(DWChapman)* 6-8-11 LDettori (5) (bit bkwd: bmpd s: led tl hdd wl over 1f out: kpt on one pce) ........... ³/₄.4

1255² Rambo's Hall *(JAGlover)* 7-9-5 DMcKeown (12) (lw: outpcd tl hdwy 2f out: styd on wl) .......................................... ³/₄.5

2072² Ace Girl (52) *(SRBowring)* 3-7-7 ‡3FNorton (3) (chsd ldrs tl rdn & btn 2f out) ..... 2.6

2280★ State Flyer (60) (v) *(CBBBooth)* 4-8-9 ‡7GForster (4) (lw: bhd: hdwy u.p 2f out: nvr trbld ldrs) ........................... ¹/₂.7

2061⁶ Mamma's Too (86) *(JBerry)* 3-8-10 JCarroll (10) (lw: chsd ldrs 4f: sn rdn & btn) ¹/₂.8

2032 Cronk's Quality (40) *(DCJermy)* 9-8-6 RCochrane (6) (hmpd ¹/₂-wy: nvr trbld ldrs) ......................................... 1¹/₂.9

1004 Premier Envelope (IRE) (53) *(NTinkler)* 3-7-13 LCharnock (2) (hmpd s: sn drvn along & nvr wnt pce) ................. 2¹/₂.10

2061 Black Boy (IRE) *(JAGlover)* 3-8-5 JFortune (11) (s.i.s: n.d) ............... 1.11

1795⁴ Bernie Silvers (46) *(MCChapman)* 3-7-12 JQuinn (1) (swvd rt s: prom to ¹/₂-wy: hung rt & sn bhd: bit slipped) .......... 5.12

**Evens** A PRAYER FOR WINGS, **24/10** Easy Line, **67/10** Mamma's Too, **73/10** Rambo's Hall, **215/10** State Flyer, **27/1** Ace Girl, **342/10** Cronk's Quality, **433/10** Black Boy (IRE), **827/10** Tigani, **838/10** Pink'n Black (IRE), **848/10** Premier Envelope (IRE), **156/1** Bernie Silvers. Tote £2.00: £1.10 £1.80 £9.90 (£3.20). Mr S. Powell (EPSOM) bred by Dr Peter C. Yorke. 12 Rn                                                         1m 13.57 (2.57)
                                                                                                                                       SF—47/43/17/32/37/3

T/Plpt: £54.40 (222.95 Tckts).                                                                                                          AA

## 2194—LINGFIELD (L-H)

### Monday, July 27th [Turf Good, Good to firm back st, AWT Standard]

Going Allowance: Turf: minus 0.10 sec (G); AWT: 0.15 sec (SL)         Wind: mod across

Stalls: centre

**2407**   HORLEY STKS (3-Y.O.F) £3045.60 (£734.40)   **1¹/₄m (AWT)**   2-00 (2-01)

2070★ **Ardlsia** (USA) (86) (Fav) *(PFICole)* 9-0 AMunro (1) (lw: mde all: clr over 3f out: unchal) .................................. —1

2156² Ideal Candidate (57) *(TJNaughton)* 9-0 GCarter (3) (chsd wnr: no imp fnl 4f) .. 20.2

**1/10** ARDISIA (USA), **7/1** Ideal Candidate(op 4/1). Tote £1.10. Mr Fahd Salman (WHATCOMBE) bred by Newgate Stud Farm Incorporated in USA. 2 Rn

2m 11.96 (8.96)
SF—25/–

**2408**    TEENOSO CLAIMING STKS    £2406.00 (£666.00: £318.00)
1¹/₂m (AWT)

2-30 (2-31)

1949² Princess Moodyshoe (62) (Fav) *(MCPipe)* 4–8-12 MRoberts (5) (lw: a.p: led over 2f out: eased ins fnl f) ........................................................ —1

2155³ Ghostly Glow (50) (v) *(CCElsey)* 3–8-1 AMunro (1) (lw: gd hdwy 5f out: hrd rdn 4f out: r.o ins fnl f) ................................................................ ³/₄.2

2059 Smiling Chief (IRE) (54) *(CACyzer)* 4–9-0 ‡7TMcLaughlin (8) (lw: a.p: led over 3f out tl over 2f out: r.o ins fnl f) .................................... hd.3

2007⁴ Allmosa (56) *(TJNaughton)* 3–8-2 GCarter (6) (b: hdwy 5f out: one pce fnl 4f) ... 3.4

1977 Alternation (FR) (58) (bl) *(PFICole)* 3–7-11 DBiggs (7) (a.p: rdn 5f out: one pce) 3¹/₂.5

1731⁶ Tempering (79) *(DWChapman)* 6–9-7 TQuinn (2) (led over 8f) .................... 15.6

2087 Dancer's Leap (IRE) (58) *(JEBanks)* 4–8-4 ‡5JWeaver (4) (lw: prom over 6f) .... 6.7

1777 Marpatann (IRE) (38) *(ASReid)* 3–8-0 NAdams (3) (a bhd: t.o inf 7f) ............. 30.8

**1/2** PRINCESS MOODYSHOE, **7/2** Tempering, **8/1** Alternation (FR)(op 4/1), **10/1** Allmosa(7/1–12/1), **40/1** Ghostly Glow, **50/1** Dancer's Leap (IRE), **66/1** Marpatann (IRE). CSF £22.09, Tote £1.50: £1.10 £2.60 £2.70 (£9.10). Mrs Alison C. Farrant (WELLINGTON) bred by Mrs E. Allwood and Mrs A. C. Farrant. 8 Rn

2m 39.69 (10.29)
SF—13/–/12/–/–/–

**2409**    TATTERSALLS AUCTION SERIES STKS (Qualifier) (Mdn 2-Y.O) £2947.20 (£819.20: £393.60)    7f

3-00 (3-03)

Satin Dancer (Jt-Fav) *(GHarwood)* 8-5 KDarley (2) (unf: scope: a.p: led over 1f out: rdn out) ................................................................................ —1

2037² Bold Acre *(DRLaing)* 8-7 TyroneWilliams (18) (lw: a.p: rdn over 2f out: unable qckn fnl f) .......................................................................... 2¹/₂.2

1748⁴ General Chase *(RJHolder)* 8-0 NAdams (17) (lw: a.p: rdn over 2f out: one pce) ¹/₂.3

Formato Uni (IRE) *(JLDunlop)* 8-11 JReid (16) (leggy: bit bkwd: nt clr run over 2f out: hdwy over 1f out: r.o) ................................................... nk.4

1932 Galactic Fury *(BStevens)* 8-5 MTebbutt (12) (hdwy over 1f out: r.o) ............. ³/₄.5

1591 Exhibit Air (IRE) *(RHannon)* 8-3 MRoberts (1) (led over 3f: led wl over 1f out: sn hdd) .............................................................................. nk.6

2052⁵ Steppin High (Jt-Fav) *(LordHuntingdon)* 8-11 AMunro (11) (hrd rdn & no hdwy fnl 2f) ................................................................................ hd.7

Home From the Hill (IRE) *(MBell)* 8-6 LDettori (13) (leggy: nvr nr to chal) ...... ³/₄.8

645⁶ Marius (IRE) *(BWHills)* 8-6 DHolland (3) (b.hind: no hdwy fnl 2f) ................ 1.9

Misbelief *(JRFanshawe)* 8-2 ‡7NVarley (5) (unf: bit bkwd: nvr nrr) ................. 1.10

Queens Contractor *(MJHeaton-Ellis)* 8-7 WNewnes (9) (w'like: bit bkwd: spd over 5f) ......................................................................... ³/₄.11

Soviet Express *(PFICole)* 8-7 TQuinn (8) (unf: w ldr: led over 3f out tl wl over 1f out: sn wknd) ...................................................................... ¹/₂.12

1573 Hillsdown Boy (IRE) *(SDow)* 8-0 ‡7AMartinez (14) (outpcd) ....................... 2.13

1897⁵ Sweet Disorder (IRE) *(GAPritchard-Gordon)* 8-1 GCarter (7) (hdwy over 3f out: wknd wl over 1f out) ..................................................... 1¹/₂.14

Chiappucci (IRE) *(MAJarvis)* 8-7 GCrealock (19) (w'like: bkwd: a bhd) .......... 1.15

1957⁶ Lake Princess (IRE) *(SDow)* 8-0 JQuinn (6) (a bhd) .................................. 6.16

Supreme Master *(RHannon)* 8-3 ‡3RPerham (15) (str: bkwd: a bhd) .............. 3¹/₂.17

1867 Tresaria (IRE) *(PHowling)* 8-0 GBardwell (10) (a bhd) ............................. 1¹/₂.18

Soojama (IRE) *(RVoorspuy)* 8-8 SDawson (4) (cmpt: bit bkwd: a bhd: t.o) ........ 19

**7/2** Steppin High, SATIN DANCER(op 8/1), **5/1** Formato Uni (IRE)(op 5/2), **6/1** Misbelief(op 12/1), **8/1** Bold Acre(tchd 12/1), Home From the Hill (IRE), Marius (IRE), **9/1** Soviet Express(op 5/1), **10/1** Queens Contractor, Chiappucci (IRE)(op 6/1), **12/1** Sweet Disorder (IRE)(tchd 8/1), **16/1** Exhibit Air (IRE), **25/1** Supreme Master, Lake Princess (IRE), **33/1** Ors. CSF £41.01, Tote £10.80: £3.80 £1.80 £10.30 (£82.10). Mr P. D. Savill (PULBOROUGH) bred by Fonthill Stud. 19 Rn

1m 24.31 (3.01)
SF—35/29/20/30/25/19

**2410**    BEAUTY COUNTER 30th ANNIVERSARY H'CAP (0-90) £3100.80 (£858.80: £410.40)
7f 140y

3-30 (3-30)

(Weights raised 7 lb)

2198⁴ Dodgy (51) (v) *(SDow)* 5–8-0 JQuinn (4) (led tl ins fnl f: hrd rdn: led last stride) —1

2183 Annabelle Royale (75) *(MrsNMacauley)* 6–9-10 LDettori (5) (lw: a.p: rdn over 3f out: led ins fnl f: hdd last stride) ............................................. s.h.2

2210³ Lord Oberon (IRE) (68) (Fav) *(RJO'Sullivan)* 4–9-3 AClark (8) (rdn & hdwy over 1f out: unable qckn) ...................................................... 5.3

2198³ Fair Enchantress (55) *(JABennett)* 4–8-4 DHolland (2) (a.p: rdn over 2f out: wknd over 1f out) ........................................................... 2¹/₂.4

2013⁵ Premier Prince **(59)** *(LGCottrell)* 6–8–8 AMunro (3) (lw: a.p: hrd rdn over 1f out: sn wknd) .................................................................................... 2¹/₂.5

2173⁵ Vanborough Lad **(66)** *(MJHaynes)* 3–8–7 DBiggs (7) (hld up: rdn over 2f out: wknd over 1f out) ....................................................................... 1¹/₂.6

2125² Abso **(67)** *(RHannon)* 4–9–2 JReid (6) (a.p: rdn over 2f out: eased whn btn over 1f out) ..................................................................................... 1¹/₂.7

2073 Toshiba Comet **(75)** (bl) *(BBeasley)* 5–9–10 DNicholls (1) (a bhd) ........... 3¹/₂.8

**7/4** Lord Oberon (IRE)(tchd 4/1), **4/1** Abso(op 5/2), **9/2** Premier Prince, **5/1** Annabelle Royale, **8/1** Fair Enchantress, DODGY, **9/1** Vanborough Lad(op 5/1), **16/1** Toshiba Comet. CSF £48.58, CT £95.89. Tote £6.30: £1.60 £2.10 £1.70 (£12.30). Mr J. A. Redmond (EPSOM) bred by J. A. Redmond. 8 Rn   1m 31.05 (2.55)
SF—36/59/37/16/12/6

**2411**  JOHN ROGERSON MEMORIAL H'CAP (3-Y.O) (0-80) £2811.60 (£777.60: £370.80)
**6f (AWT)**  4-00 (4-03)

2099⁴ **Tate Dancer (IRE) (75)** (Fav) *(RWArmstrong)* 9-6 MRoberts (3) (mde virtually all: rdn out) ...................................................................................... —1

2099 Palacegate Racing **(71)** *(JBerry)* 9-2 GCarter (8) (w wnr: hrd rdn & ev ch over 1f out: unable qckn) ..................................................................... 1¹/₂.2

1500 Waders Dream (IRE) **(76)** (bl) *(JEBanks)* 9-2 ‡5JWeaver (1) (lw: a.p: hrd rdn over 1f out: one pce) ............................................................ 1¹/₂.3

2040 Manuleader **(53)** *(BBeasley)* 7-12 JLowe (4) (hdwy over 3f out: one pce fnl 2f) 1¹/₂.4

1745⁶ Lifetime Fame **(76)** *(JWPayne)* 9-7 AMunro (2) (lw: rdn thrght: nvr nr to chal) .... 4.5

2129⁵ Walstead (IRE) **(63)** *(DAWilson)* 8-8 JWilliams (7) (dwlt: hdwy over 3f out: wknd over 2f out) ....................................................................... 3.6

1928 Badawiah **(74)** *(WAO'Gorman)* 9-5 LDettori (4) (prom over 3f) ...................... hd.7

1803³ Master Hyde (USA) **(55)** (bl) *(PMitchell)* 7-11⁽⁵⁾ ‡3SO'Gorman (5) (bhd fnl 3f) ..... 5.8

2125⁵ Pleasure Quest **(49)** *(DWPArbuthnot)* 7-8⁽¹⁾ JQuinn (6) (bhd fnl 3f) ............. 7.9

**2/1** TATE DANCER (IRE)(op 3/1), **3/1** Waders Dream (IRE), **9/2** Badawiah(4/1—7/1), **6/1** Palacegate Racing, **10/1** Master Hyde (USA), **12/1** Pleasure Quest(op 6/1), Lifetime Fame(op 6/1), **14/1** Walstead (IRE)(op 7/1), **16/1** Manuleader(op 10/1). CSF £15.38, CT £35.06. Tote £3.30: £1.50 £1.20 £1.50 (£7.00). Mrs John Davall (NEWMARKET) bred by Nikita Investments in Ireland. 9 Rn   1m 14.01 (3.41)
SF—56/46/40/16/23/–

**2412**  DORMANSLAND H'CAP (0-80) £2912.40 (£806.40: £385.20)  **2m**  4-30 (4-30)
(Weights raised 1 lb)

1951⋆ Chucklestone **(62)** *(JSKing)* 9–9–4 TQuinn (5) (chsd ldr 11f: 3rd st: hrd rdn over 2f out: led nr fin) ............................................................... —1

1967⋆ Farmer's Pet **(78)** (Fav) *(GAPritchard-Gordon)* 3–9–4 GCarter (10) (lw: led: hrd rdn fnl f: hdd nr fin) ................................................................. ¹/₂.2

2054⁵ Belafonte **(60)** *(RJHolder)* 5–9–2 LDettori (1) (5th st: hrd rdn over 1f out: one pce) ............................................................................................. 2.3

2135 Smartie Lee **(53)** *(PFICole)* 5–8–2 ‡7JDSmith (8) (lw: 4th st: hrd rdn over 2f out: one pce) .................................................................................. 2.4

2109² Sparkler Gebe **(49)** (bl) *(RJO'Sullivan)* 6–8–5 JQuinn (3) (2nd st: wknd over 1f out) ......................................................................................... 2¹/₂.5

2211 Formal Invitation (IRE) **(57)** *(GLewis)* 3–7–6 ‡5DHarrison (7) (b: lw: 6th st: no hdwy fnl 3f) ........................................................................ 3¹/₂.6

2267² Intricacy **(60)** *(CCElsey)* 4–9–2 (4x) MRoberts (11) (bhd fnl 4f) .................. 3¹/₂.7

2083 Dutyful **(43)** *(MJHaynes)* 6–7–13 DBiggs (6) (a bhd) ..................................... 12.8

 Emerald Sunset **(38)** *(ARDavison)* 7–7–8⁽¹⁾ AMackay (2) (bit bkwd: a bhd: t.o) .. 20.9
LONG HANDICAP: Emerald Sunset 7-6.

**5/4** Farmer's Pet(op 2/1), **11/4** CHUCKLESTONE(4/1—9/4), **9/2** Intricacy(op 9/4), **13/2** Belafonte, Sparkler Gebe, **9/1** Formal Invitation (IRE)(12/1—8/1), **12/1** Dutyful(7/1—14/1), **14/1** Smartie Lee(op 8/1), **33/1** Emerald Sunset. CSF £8.10, CT £23.34. Tote £4.10: £1.70 £1.50 £1.70 (£4.40). Mr Mark O'Connor (SWINDON) bred by R. B. Stokes. 9 Rn   3m 30.66 (6.66)
SF—22/21/17/1/1/–

**2413**  LEVY BOARD H'CAP (0-70) £3052.00 (£847.00: £406.00)  **1¹/₄m**  5-00 (5-02)
(Weights raised 9 lb)

1603⁵ **Rival Bid (USA) (55)** (Fav) *(MAJarvis)* 4–9-8 LDettori (5) (dwlt: hdwy over 4f out: 5th st: led over 1f out: pushed out) ........................................... —1

2184⁶ Breezed Well **(57)** *(CNAllen)* 4–9–3 ‡7GForster (1) (hdwy over 2f out: r.o ins fnl f) ³/₄.2

1945⋆ Now Boarding **(41)** *(RJHodges)* 5–8–1 ‡7SDrowne (12) (3rd st: hrd rdn over 1f out: unable qckn) .................................................................... 2¹/₂.3

 May Square (IRE) **(55)** *(MrsAKnight)* 4–9-8 GBardwell (14) (led over 8f: one pce) ........................................................................................ s.h.4

2033 Samurai Gold (USA) **(49)** (v) *(PTWalwyn)* 4–9-2 AMackay (8) (hdwy over 3f out: hrd rdn over 2f out: r.o one pce) ............................................ hd.5

2210 Admiralty Way **(40)** *(RBrotherton)* 6-8-7 TyroneWilliams (6) (hdwy over 2f out: hmpd over 1f out: r.o one pce) ......................................... hd.6
1949 Capital Bond (IRE) **(51)** *(RJHolder)* 4-9-4 JLowe (3) (nvr nr to chal) ................... 2.7
1587⁴ Simply George **(60)** *(RBoss)* 3-9-3 MTebbutt (9) (swtg: 2nd st: wknd over 1f out) 2.8
1037⁶ Rarfy's Dream **(35)** *(JEBanks)* 4-8-2 DBiggs (4) (lw: a mid div) ....................... 4.9
2137 Kingsfold Pet **(57)** *(MJHaynes)* 3-9-0 BRouse (13) (dwlt: nvr nrr) ............... 2¹/₂.10
2043⁴ June's Lear Fan (CAN) **(58)** *(PAKelleway)* 3-9-1 AMcGlone (10) (4th st: wknd 3f out) ................................................................ 1¹/₂.11
2014² Dr Zeva **(32)** *(MDixon)* 6-7-8 ‡⁵ATucker (12) (lw: 6th st: wknd over 2f out:) .. 1.12
2126 High Baccarat **(52)** *(CCElsey)* 3-8-9 TRogers (11) (lw: hdwy 5f out: wknd 4f out) ....................................................................... 10.13
2249⁶ Manulife **(65)** *(BBeasley)* 3-9-8 DNicholls (16) (bhd fnl 7f) ............................ 10.14
Briery Fille **(47)** *(BJMcMath)* 7-9-0 JQuinn (15) (b: bit bkwd: bhd fnl 7f) .......... 8.15
Moreirwen **(31)** *(JO'Donoghue)* 5-7-12 NAdams (7) (s.s: a bhd: t.o fnl 5f) ..... 12.16

**7/2** RIVAL BID (USA), **4/1** Dr Zeva, **5/1** Samurai Gold (USA), **6/1** Breezed Well(7/1—4/1), **8/1** Now Boarding, **9/1** Kingsfold Pet(op 6/1), **14/1** Simply George, **16/1** May Square (IRE), **20/1** Manulife, Capital Bond (IRE), Rarfy's Dream, **25/1** Briery Fille, High Baccarat, Admiralty Way, **33/1** Ors. CSF £26.59, CT £155.78. Tote £4.50: £1.40 £2.40 £1.20 £4.00 (£22.10). Mr David Altham (NEWMARKET) bred by Marvin L. Warner Jnr. in USA. 16 Rn
2m 8.62 (5.62)
SF—42/35/14/34/27/17

T/Plpt: £36.20 (80.53 Tckts). AK

## 2238—WINDSOR (Fig.8)

### Monday, July 27th [Good, Good to firm back st]

Going Allowance: minus 0.30 sec per fur (F)     Wind: slt half bhd

Stalls: high

**2414**     E.B.F. SKY SPORT'S RINGSIDE STKS (Mdn 2-Y-O) £1845.60 (£511.60: £244.80)
**5f 10y**
6-10 (6-13)

1993² **Bangles** *(Fav)* *(LordHuntingdon)* 8-9 MRoberts (7) (mde all: r.o wl) ................ —1
Karukera *(MJHeaton-Ellis)* 8-9 JReid (2) (neat: chsd wnr: ev ch 2f out: no imp) . 4.2
1946⁴ Fairy Story (IRE) **(JWHills)** 8-9 DHolland (1) (wnt lft s: sn prom: r.o ins fnl f) hd.3
847⁵ Geoff's Risk *(GLewis)* 8-9 ‡⁵DHarrison (9) (a.p: one pce fnl 2f) ...................... 2.4
Tony's Mist *(RHannon)* 9-0 SRaymont (8) (lw: nvr nr to chal) .................. ¹/₂.5
1946 Perigord (IRE) *(WRMuir)* 9-0 SWhitworth (3) (spd 3f) .......................... 3¹/₂.6
1944⁶ Venture Prints *(RChampion)* 9-0 JWilliams (4) (a bhd) ..................... 5.7
Sea Strand *(MBlanshard)* 8-9 NHowe (10) (leggy: unf: a wl bhd) .......... 2.8
Grab Sunday Sport *(MissGayKelleway)* 9-0 AMunro (6) (neat: hmpd st: bhd fnl 2f) ....................................................... ³/₄.9

**5/4** BANGLES(op 4/5), **9/4** Fairy Story (IRE)(7/4—11/4), **13/2** Geoff's Risk, **14/1** Grab Sunday Sport(op 5/1), **16/1** Tony's Mist(op 10/1), Sea Strand(op 10/1), Karukera(op 8/1), **33/1** Ors. CSF £20.24, Tote £1.90: £1.10 £3.20 £1.30 (£16.90). Mr J. Rose (WEST ILSLEY) bred by John Rose. 9 Rn
60.1 sec (1.1)
SF—43/27/26/18/21/7

**2415**     CREDIT LYONNAIS LAING H'CAP (0-80) £2595.00 (£720.00: £345.00)
**1¹/₄m 7y**
6-35 (6-39)
(Weights raised 4 lb)

2184 **Mahsul (IRE) (58)** *(CJBenstead)* 4-8-13 JReid (4) (hdwy 3f out: led ins fnl f: r.o wl) ...................................................................... —1
2054 Hymne D'Amour (USA) **(49)** *(MissHCKnight)* 4-8-4 SWhitworth (1) (4th st: hrd rdn & led wl over 1f out: hdd ins fnl f) .................... ³/₄.2
2210 Lady Lacey **(50)** (v) *(GBBalding)* 5-8-5 JWilliams (5) (8th st: nrst fin) ............ 4.3
1971² Celia Brady **(58)** *(HCandy)* 4-8-13 SDawson (9) (5th st: rdn 3f out: one pce) .... 1.4
2128⁴ Nothing Doing (IRE) **(53)** *(WJMusson)* 3-7-12 JQuinn (2) (nvr nr to chal) ........... 3.5
L'Uomo Classics **(69)** *(RRowe)* 5-9-10 MPerrett (8) (6th st: btn whn n.m.r 1f out) ........................................................... 1¹/₂.6
2135 The Yomper (FR) **(40)** *(RCurtis)* 10-7-2⁽²⁾ ‡⁷CHawksley (10) (led to 4f out) ...... 1¹/₂.7
2251* Anguish (IRE) **(56)** *(NACallaghan)* 3-8-1 (5x) MRoberts (11) (3rd st: led 4f out tl wknd wl over 1f out) ........................ 1¹/₂.8
1662⁴ Execution Only (IRE) **(62)** (v) *(JWWatts)* 4-9-3 GDuffield (6) (2nd st: wknd 2f out) ³/₄.9
2135* Sarah-Clare **(58)** *(Fav)* *(RAkehurst)* 4-8-10 ‡³RPerham (3) (s.s: a wl bhd) ...... 3¹/₂.10
Sohail **(47)** *(JWhite)* 9-8-2 NAdams (7) (7th st: wknd 4f out: t.o) ........... 6.11
LONG HANDICAP: The Yomper (FR) 6-11.

**3/1** Sarah-Clare(op 2/1), **4/1** Execution Only (IRE)(tchd 6/1), **9/2** Anguish (IRE), **11/2** Nothing Doing (IRE), **6/1** Celia Brady(op 3/1), **8/1** MAHSUL (IRE), Lady Lacey, **33/1** Ors. CSF £197.09, CT £1,957.92. Tote £7.90: £2.50 £6.90 £2.60 (£202.20). Mr Hamdan Al-Maktoum (EPSOM) bred by Derrinstown Stud Ltd in Ireland. 11 Rn
2m 5.1 (2.1)
SF—48/37/30/36/15/38

**2416**  GEORGE S.HALL LIMITED CLAIMING STKS £1683.00 (£468.00: £225.00)
1¼m 7y
7-00 (7-06)

2240² **Vanroy (67)** (v) *(JRJenkins)* 8-9-12 SWhitworth (7) (hdwy 4f out: led over 2f out: comf) ............................................... —1

2253* Molly Splash **(49)** *(CACyzer)* 5-9-1 DBiggs (12) (7th st: ev ch 2f out: r.o one pce) ............................................... 5.2

2128* Kandy Secret (USA) **(62)** (bl) (Fav) *(RHannon)* 3-8-13 MRoberts (10) (lw: rdn along: mid div tl styd on fnl 3f: nrst fin) ............. ½.3

1371 Nomadic Rose **(55)** *(BWHills)* 3-7-9 DLee (14) (4th st: r.o one pce fnl 2f) . ½.4
Scottish Ball *(SirMarkPrescott)* 3-8-0 GDuffield (16) (unf: lost pl 6f out: rdn & hdwy 3f out: nvr nrr) ............................................... 5.5

1612 Predestine **(51)** *(MMadgwick)* 7-8-11 ‡7CAvery (18) (b: lw: 6th st: no hdwy) .... hd.6

2240 Salar's Spirit *(WGMTurner)* 6-8-7 ‡3TSprake (3) (2nd st: wknd 2f out) .......... ¾.7
Willesdon (USA) **(43)** (v) *(ABarrow)* 8-9-2 NAdams (9) (led tl wknd over 2f out) . 4.8

1172 Allimac Nomis **(45)** *(ICampbell)* 3-8-10 MTebbutt (5) (b: lw: 8th st: no hdwy fnl 3f) ............................................... ½.9

776⁴ Weapon Exhibition **(45)** *(GAHam)* 5-8-7 ADicks (8) (9th st: mid div) ......... 8.10

1421 Evening Dress **(42)** *(ICampbell)* 3-7-11 GBardwell (19) (n.d) ............... 2½.11
Kingfisher Bay *(JWhite)* 7-9-3 VSmith (13) (n.d) ............................ 1.12

580 Striding Edge *(JRJenkins)* 7-9-7 JWilliams (17) (bit bkwd: n.d) ............... ½.13
Tiarum *(GAHam)* 10-8-9 ‡5StephenDavies (11) (3rd st: wknd 4f out) ............ 2.14
Sukey Tawdry **(23)** *(RABennett)* 6-8-9 NHowe (2) (b: bit bkwd) ............... 1.15
Baba's Lady (NZ) *(JRJenkins)* 5-8-3 ‡5DHarrison (4) (bit bkwd: n.d) ........... 7.16
Babarooms Paradise (NZ) *(JRJenkins)* 5-8-10 AMunro (1) (b: n.d) ............. 2.17
Run by Jove (USA) (bl) *(JWhite)* 9-9-5 MPerrett (6) (n.d) .................... ½.18

919 Mash the Tea (IRE) *(HJCollingridge)* 3-8-4 JQuinn (20) (a bhd) ............ 1.19

2015 Admiral Albert (IRE) **(56)** *(RAkehurst)* 3-8-3 ‡3RPerham (15) (lw: 5th st: rdn & wknd 4f out: t.o) ............................................... 25.20

5/2 Kandy Secret (USA), 5/1 VANROY, 6/1 Molly Splash(4/1—7/1), 8/1 Scottish Ball(5/1—14/1), 9/1 Predestine, 10/1 Admiral Albert (IRE), 12/1 Nomadic Rose(7/1—14/1), 14/1 Weapon Exhibition, 20/1 Kingfisher Bay, Run by Jove (USA), 25/1 Allimac Nomis, 33/1 Ors. CSF £34.73, Tote £5.70: £2.20 £2.50 £1.60 (£10.30). Mr Derek Garrad (ROYSTON) bred by S. Taberner. 20 Rn; Allimac Nomis clmd M Spore £10,000, Nomadic Rose clmd G Wiltshire £3,001
2m 6.9 (3.9)
SF—43/22/19/–/–/–

**2417**  G.A.R.RICHARDSON MEMORIAL H'CAP (0-80) £2616.00 (£726.00: £348.00)
1m 67y
7-30 (7-51)

623⁵ **Santana Lady (IRE) (65)** *(MJHeaton-Ellis)* 3-8-5 WNewnes (9) (3rd st: led ins fnl f: r.o wl) ............................................... —1

1716² Sooty Tern **(52)** *(JMBradley)* 5-8-0 NAdams (5) (2nd st: led over 2f out tl ins fnl f) ............................................... ¾.2

2173² Keep Your Word **(57)** (Jt-Fav) *(GBBalding)* 6-8-5 JWilliams (12) (6th st: rdn 2f out: swtchd lft 1f out: nrst fin) ............................................... 1½.3

1949⁶ Rywater Dream **(48)** *(RJHodges)* 4-7-10 DBiggs (1) (led tl over 2f out: r.o one pce) ............................................... s.h.4

1718⁶ Rosietoes (USA) **(48)** *(LGCottrell)* 4-7-8 JLowe (13) (4th st: ev ch over 1f out: hrd rdn: nt qckn) ............................................... ¾.5

2182³ Sean's Scholar (USA) **(49)** *(CNAllen)* 5-7-11 GBardwell (14) (7th st: no hdwy fnl 2f) ............................................... 4.6

2184² Foolish Touch **(56)** *(WJMusson)* 10-8-4 JHBrown (8) (b: wl bhd tl r.o fnl 2f) ...... 2.7

1539 Jimlil **(77)** *(BPalling)* 4-9-6 ‡5StephenDavies (11) (9th st: wknd 2f out) ......... 1.8

2053 Two Birds **(54)** *(CAHorgan)* 3-7-8(1) TyroneWilliams (7) (nvr nr to chal) ......... 4.9

Chica Mia **(55)** *(GAHam)* 8-8-3(4) ADicks (6) (8th st: wknd 3f out) ............... 12.10
Farm Street **(73)** *(TPMcGovern)* 5-9-2 ‡5DHarrison (10) (b: 9th st: nvr nr ldrs) 1½.11

2182* Ghurrah (IRE) **(63)** (Jt-Fav) *(CJBenstead)* 3-8-3 MRoberts (2) (s.s: a wl bhd) nk.12

1974 Spinayab **(56)** *(EAWheeler)* 3-7-10(3) SDawson (4) (t.o fnl 2f) ............... 15.13
LONG HANDICAP: Spinayab 7-2.

2254² Barlogan (5/1) Withdrawn (broke out of stalls, uns rdr & bolted into river) : not under orders

7/2 Ghurrah (IRE), Keep Your Word, 6/1 Foolish Touch, Sean's Scholar (USA), Sooty Tern, Jimlil, 8/1 Rosietoes (USA), 16/1 Rywater Dream, Farm Street, 20/1 SANTANA LADY (IRE), 25/1 Two Birds, Spinayab, 33/1 Chica Mia. CSF £142.73, CT £495.41. Tote £20.10: £4.00 £2.20 £1.70 (£65.20). Mrs Teresa McWilliams (WROUGHTON) bred by Milltown Stud in Ireland. 13 Rn
1m 42.6 (1)
SF—38/31/31/21/17/8

**2418**  STOWELL PARK STUD NURSERY £2022.50 (£560.00: £267.50)
5f 217y
8-00 (8-16)

2081³ **Defenceless** *(RHannon)* 8-6 BRouse (2) (lw: chsd ldrs: led 2f out: edgd lft fnl f: r.o) ............................................... —1

1886[6] Regent's Lady *(CJames)* 7-13 AMcGlone (5) (led 4f: hrd rdn: ev ch ins fnl f: r.o) .... **1**.2
2010 Tee Gee Jay (bl) (Fav) *(CNWilliams)* 8-1 JQuinn (6) (b.hind: hdwy over 1f out:
r.o ins fnl f) ........................................................................................................ 2¹/₂.3
1744[2] Sheila's Secret (IRE) *(WCarter)* 9-7 JReid (9) (nvr nrr) ......................................... **1**.4
1973[5] Kintwyn (v) *(DRLaing)* 8-1 TyroneWilliams (7) (lw: prom tl hrd rdn & wknd over
1f out) ................................................................................................................... nk.5
1913 Pair of Jacks (IRE) *(WRMuir)* 8-8 SWhitworth (4) (lw: no hdwy fnl 2f) ............... **2**.6
2225[2] Waterlord (IRE) *(CGCox)* 8-4 NHowe (8) (hdwy 3f out: wknd over 1f out) ........ s.h.7
1804⋆ Skullcap *(TJNaughton)* 8-11 AMunro (3) (prom 3f) ............................................ **1**.8
1461 Belle Soiree *(SDow)* 8-3 ‡7AMartinez (1) (lw: a last) ......................................... 20.9

**4/1** Tee Gee Jay, **9/2** Pair of Jacks (IRE), **5/1** Skullcap, **6/1** Waterlord (IRE)(op 4/1), **7/1** Belle Soiree,
DEFENCELESS, **8/1** Sheila's Secret (IRE), **12/1** Kintwyn, **14/1** Regent's Lady. CSF £85.72, CT £405.34. Tote
£6.90: £2.20 £3.30 £1.90 (£105.30). Mr N. Ahamad (MARLBOROUGH) bred by Newgate Stud Co. 9 Rn
1m 11.3 (0.8)
SF—40/29/21/37/16/15

### 2419
FAMILY WELFARE ASSOCIATION STKS (Mdn 3-Y.O) £1544.40 (£428.40: £205.20)
5f 217y
8-30 (8-42)

2131[3] **Wandering Stranger (72)** (Fav) *(PJMakin)* 8-9 MRoberts (7) (a.p: squeezed
thro over 1f out: led ins fnl f: r.o) ....................................................................... —1
1883[2] Sure Lord (IRE) (70) *(WRMuir)* 9-0 SWhitworth (5) (w ldrs: led over 2f out tl ins
fnl f: btn whn snatched up cl home) .................................................................... 2.2
2015[3] Nbaat (USA) *(CJBenstead)* 9-0 JWilliams (13) (lw: gd hdwy fnl 2f: nvr nrr) ....... nk.3
2015[4] Sea-Deer *(LJHolt)* 9-0 JReid (8) (hdwy 2f out: r.o ins fnl f) ............................... nk.4
2009 Efra (63) *(RHannon)* 9-0 AMcGlone (2) (lw: led over 3f) .................................... 2¹/₂.5
2140[4] Acara (IRE) *(CJames)* 8-9 JQuinn (4) (nrst fin) .............................................. hd.6
2164[3] Batchworth Bound *(EAWheeler)* 8-4 ‡5DHarrison (6) (nvr nr to chal) ............... 1¹/₂.7
2082[2] Cashmiriana (IRE) (62) *(MissHCKnight)* 8-9 GDuffield (10) (a mid div) ............ 1¹/₂.8
2229 Call to the Bar (IRE) *(CGCox)* 9-0 WNewnes (2) (spd 4f) ............................... ¹/₂.9
2186[5] Night Gown *(MissGayKelleway)* 8-9 AMunro (11) (spd 4f) ............................. 4.10
2265[4] Mansber (IRE) (54) (bl) *(PatMitchell)* 9-0 PBiggs (3) (spd over 3f: t.o) ............. 12.11
1304 Nonanno *(AJChamberlain)* 9-0 NHowe (1) (n.d: t.o) ......................................... 2¹/₂.12

**10/11** WANDERING STRANGER, **6/1** Sure Lord (IRE)(op 11/4), **13/2** Nbaat (USA), **10/1** Cashmiriana (IRE)(op
6/1), **11/1** Night Gown, **12/1** Sea-Deer(op 7/1), **14/1** Efra(op 8/1), **33/1** Batchworth Bound, Call to the Bar (IRE),
**40/1** Ors. CSF £7.49, Tote £2.20: £1.30 £1.70 £2.20 (£4.60). Mr Barrie C. Whitehouse (MARLBOROUGH) bred
by B. Whitehouse. 12 Rn
1m 11.6 (1.1)
SF—37/34/33/32/22/16

T/Plpt: £101.80 (22 Tckts).
Hn

### 2064—**BEVERLEY (R-H)**

## Tuesday, July 28th [Firm]

Going Allowance: St: minus 0.20 sec; Rnd: minus 0.40 sec (F)
Wind: almost nil

Stalls: high

### 2420
LADYGATE (S) H'CAP (0-60) £2805.00 (£780.00: £375.00)
1m 3f 216y 2-15 (2-16)

2281[4] **Escape Talk (21)** *(JDooler)* 5-7-7 GBardwell (2) (lw: bhd: c wd & gd hdwy u.p
ent st: styd on to ld wl ins fnl f) ........................................................................ —1
Turf Dancer (30) *(PCHaslam)* 5-7-9 ‡7NicolaHoward (7) (chsd ldrs: led wl over
2f out tl hdd wl ins fnl f) ..................................................................................... nk.2
1971 Jarras (42) (bl) *(CASmith)* 7-9-0 MHills (13) (bhd: hdwy appr st: sn prom: one
pce fnl f) .............................................................................................................. 4.3
2087 Stratford Lady (42) *(JAGlover)* 3-7-11 ‡5SMaloney (5) (in tch: effrt ent st: one
pce fnl 2f) ............................................................................................................ 3¹/₂.4
2166[4] Quip (28) *(MPNaughton)* 7-8-0 JakiHouston (10) (mid div: effrt appr st: styd
on: no imp) ......................................................................................................... nk.5
2272[6] Janeswood (IRE) (28) (bl) *(JParkes)* 4-8-0 LCharnock (6) (led 2f: cl up tl grad
wknd fnl 2f) ......................................................................................................... 2.6
1574 Amalfi (45) *(JPearce)* 3-8-5 KDarley (4) (nvr bttr than mid div) ...................... 1¹/₂.7
2101 Queens Tour (34) *(MBrittain)* 7-8-6 JLowe (1) (bhd tl sme late hdwy) ............. 5.8
1945[3] Emrys (35) *(DBurchell)* 9-8-0 ‡7SMulvey (11) (chsd ldrs to st) ..................... 1.9
2210 Remwood Girl (32) (Fav) *(KSBridgwater)* 6-8-4 PD'Arcy (8) (led after 2f tl wl
over 2f out: wknd fnl f) ....................................................................................... nk.10
2066[5] Al Badeto (23) *(JNorton)* 5-7-9(2) PBurke (3) (outpcd appr st: n.d after) ......... hd.11
Millie (USA) (56) *(GFleming)* 4-9-9 ‡5OPears (9) (chsd ldr to st) ...................... 3¹/₂.12
2042 Banker Mason (USA) (29) (bl) *(WLBarker)* 6-8-1 AProud (12) (lost tch fnl 4f) ...... 13
LONG HANDICAP: Escape Talk 7-6, Al Badeto 7-6.

**5/1** Remwood Girl(op 3/1), **11/2** ESCAPE TALK(8/1—5/1), **6/1** Jarras, **8/1** Emrys, Queens Tour, **9/1** Quip, **10/1** Amalfi, **12/1** Stratford Lady, **16/1** Al Badeto, **20/1** Millie (USA), Turf Dancer, **33/1** Ors. CSF £92.57, CT £610.17. Tote £6.60: £1.60 £12.70 £2.40 (£72.20). Mrs Sandra C. Dooler (GOOLE) bred by Mrs R. B. Stokes. 13 Rn; No bid                                                                                   2m 34.9 (3.3)

---

**2421**     HUMBERSIDE 1992 H'CAP (0-90) £3418.00 (£1024.00: £492.00: £226.00)
            **7f 100y**                                                               2-45 (2-45)

                              (Weights raised 1 lb)

2160² **Tyrian Purple (IRE) (55)** *(RHollinshead)* 4–8–4 ‡⁷MHumphreys (3) (lw: led tl hdd
            5f out: cl up: styd on to ld ins fnl f) ................................. —1
2352⋆ Golden Chip (IRE) **(74)** *(APStringer)* 4–10–2 (6x) JFortune (4) (lw: led 5f out tl
            ins fnl f: kpt on u.p) ................................................... ½.2
2352⁶ Verdant Boy **(51)** *(MPNaughton)* 9–8–2 ‡⁵JWeaver (1) (a.p: c wd & ev ch 2f out:
            sn hrd rdn & nt qckn) .................................................. 4.3
2326² Who's Tef (IRE) **(59)** (v) *(MHEasterby)* 4–8–10 ‡⁵SMaloney (2) (lw: chsd
            ldrs: chal ent st: hrd rdn & wknd wl over 1f out) ............... 1½.4

**7/4** Who's Tef (IRE), **9/4** TYRIAN PURPLE (IRE), Golden Chip (IRE), **7/1** Verdant Boy. CSF £7.07, Tote £3.00 (£3.60). Rykneld Thoroughbred Co Ltd (UPPER LONGDON) bred by Niels Schibbye in Ireland. 4 Rn
                                                                              1m 32.4 (2.2)
                                                                              SF—12/36/–/–

---

**2422**     DOROTHY LAIRD H'CAP (Ladies) (0-80) £3184.00 (£952.00: £456.00: £208.00)
            **1m 1f 207y**                                                            3-20 (3-21)

2033⁵ Lots of Luck **(53)** *(JPearce)* 9–9–8 MrsLPearce (8) (lw: hld up: effrt over 1f out:
            r.o to ld wl ins fnl f) ................................................... —1
2065⁹ Touch Above **(57)** (Fav) *(TDBarron)* 6–9–12 AlexGreaves (6) (swtg: a.p: led &
            qcknd over 1f out: hrd rdn & hdd wl ins fnl f) ................... ¾.2
2160  Weeheby (USA) **(69)** *(AAScott)* 3–10–0 MissTBracegirdle (4) (led aftcr 1f tl over
            1f out: kpt on one pce) ................................................ 4.3
1996⁵ Cultured **(75)** *(MRStoute)* 3–10–6 MissMJuster (11) (lw: a chsng ldrs: styd on
            one pce fnl 2f) ........................................................... nk.4
2135³ Thimbalina **(45)** *(DAWilson)* 6–8–9 ‡⁵MissLHide (9) (bhd: effrt ent st: styd on:
            nrst fin) ................................................................... hd.5
1846⁵ Self Expression **(80)** *(IABalding)* 4–11–7 MissCBalding (3) (lw: bhd tl styd on wl
            fnl f) ...................................................................... 1½.6
1934⁶ Grog (IRE) **(73)** *(MRChannon)* 3–10–4 LornaVincent (7) (lw: led 1f: cl up tl wknd
            over 1f out) .............................................................. hd.7
2100⋆ Thunderbird One (USA) **(61)** *(DenysSmith)* 3–9–1 ‡⁵MissMCarson (2) (cl up tl
            wknd 2f out) .............................................................. ½.8
1309  Intrepid Fort **(55)** (v) *(BWMurray)* 3–9–0 MrsAFarrell (5) (effrt ent st: sn rdn & no
            imp) ....................................................................... 4.9
2066⁶ Doughman **(55)** *(JNorton)* 3–9–0 MissPRobson (12) (dwlt: n.d) ............... ½.10
1840³ Overpower **(71)** *(MHTompkins)* 8–10–7⁽⁷⁾ ‡⁵MissGOxley (1) (effrt & c wd st: sn
            btn) ....................................................................... 1½.11
2260⁴ Mindomica **(61)** *(MBell)* 3–9–1⁽¹⁾ ‡⁵MrsGBell (10) (dwlt: sme hdwy 5f out: sn
            wknd) ..................................................................... s.h.12

        LONG HANDICAP: Thimbalina 8-11, Intrepid Fort 8-5, Doughman 7-13.

**85/40** Touch Above, **5/1** LOTS OF LUCK, **13/2** Grog (IRE), Thimbalina, **8/1** Cultured, **10/1** Self Expression, **12/1** Overpower(op 8/1), Thunderbird One (USA), **16/1** Weeheby (USA), **20/1** Mindomica, **50/1** Ors. CSF £16.00, CT £150.31. Tote £4.80: £1.60 £1.60 £7.10 (£4.50). Burton Park Country Club (NEWMARKET) bred by Mrs C. M. Allan. 12 Rn                                                                          2m 4.1 (2.1)
                                                                              SF—47/49/43/48/22/59

---

**2423**     NATURAL ROUTE TO EUROPE H'CAP (0-75) £2976.00 (£888.00: £424.00: £192.00)
            **1m 3f 216y**                                                            3-55 (3-58)

2204⁵ **Bold Elect (71)** *(PWigham)* 4–10–0 MWigham (2) (lw: trckd ldrs: led wl over 1f
            out: shkn up & r.o wl) ................................................... —1
2065⁴ Smoke **(40)** (Fav) *(JParkes)* 6–7–11 LCharnock (5) (lw: hld up & bhd: hdwy ent
            st: chsd wnr fnl f: no imp) ............................................. 3½.2
2051⁶ Chew it Over (IRE) **(45)** *(CASmith)* 4–8–2 MHills (4) (led tl hdd wl over 1f out: one
            pce) ....................................................................... 2.3
2378⁵ Sharquin **(36)** *(MBrittain)* 5–7–7 JLowe (1) (cl up: effrt over 2f out: r.o one pce) ½.4
2272⋆ Iron Baron (IRE) **(62)** *(RHollinshead)* 3–8–7 (5x) KDarley (3) (prom: effrt ent st:
            sn rdn & btn) ............................................................ 4.5
2054⁴ Tour Leader (NZ) **(66)** *(TDBarron)* 3–8–11 AlexGreaves (6) (prom tl rdn & btn
            over 2f out) .............................................................. nk.6
                              LONG HANDICAP: Sharquin 7-4.

**9/4** Smoke, **7/2** Iron Baron (IRE), **4/1** Tour Leader (NZ), **9/2** BOLD ELECT, **7/1** Chew it Over (IRE), **12/1** Sharquin. CSF £14.09, Tote £3.70: £2.20 £1.60 (£4.30). Mrs J. L. Wigham (MALTON) bred by Home Stud Ltd. 6 Rn
2m 35.6 (4)
SF—26/–/–/–/–/–

**2424**     'GO RACING IN YORKSHIRE' CLAIMING STKS     £2807.00 (£777.00: £371.00)
5f                                                    4-25 (4-26)

2188 **Walking Possession (73)** (bl) *(RBoss)* 3–8-13 MTebbutt (2) (hld up: effrt 2f
out: styd on fnl f to ld cl home) ........................................ —1
1380² Food of Love **(96)** (Fav) *(JBerry)* 4–9-3 JCarroll (5) (led: rdn ins fnl f: jst ct) ..... hd.2
20616 Metal Boys **(87)** *(RHollinshead)* 5–8-13 ‡7SWynne (3) (lw: a chsng ldrs: effrt 2f
out: nt qckn) .......................................... 3½.3
2201 The Right Time (45) (bl) *(JParkes)* 7–8-3 ‡5OPears (7) (lw: a chsng ldrs: hdwy 2f
out: no ex fnl f) ........................................ hd.4
2099★ Swinging Lady (55) *(WWHaigh)* 4–8-4 ‡5SMaloney (1) (b.hind: racd wd: prom
over 3f) ............................................... 5.5
31 Daley Brioche (47) *(PCHaslam)* 4–9-6 KDarley (4) (sn outpcd & bhd: n.d) ...... 2½.6
85 True Touch *(TDBarron)* 3–8-3 AlexGreaves (6) (spd 3f: sn wknd) ................. hd.7

**5/4** Food of Love, **15/8** Metal Boys, **4/1** WALKING POSSESSION(op 6/1), **14/1** Swinging Lady, **20/1** The Right Time, **33/1** Daley Brioche, **50/1** True Touch. CSF £9.26, Tote £6.70: £2.20 £1.40 (£5.40). Madagans Plc (NEWMARKET) bred by Downclose Stud. 7 Rn
62.7 sec (1.2)
SF—55/58/40/29/10/16

**2425**     HOLDERNESS PONY CLUB AUCTION STKS (Mdn 2-Y-O)  £2782.50 (£770.00: £367.50)
5f                                                    5-00 (5-02)

2052⁴ **Felt Lucky (IRE)** *(MRChannon)* 8-8 SWhitworth (7) (mde all: all out) ................ —1
2264² Heart Broken (Fav) *(JGFitzGerald)* 8-6 MBirch (8) (flw: sn trckng ldr gng wl: effrt
over 1f out: wandered u.p: r.o nr fin) ................ nk.2
2233⁴ Musical Phone *(JPLeigh)* 8-11 NConnorton (11) (a chsng ldrs: rdn & nt qckn fnl
2f) ................................................... 3½.3
Breaking Hearts (IRE) *(APStringer)* 7-9 ‡5SMaloney (3) (unf: dwlt: bhd tl r.o fnl
2f) ................................................... ¾.4
1448 Oscars Quest *(JBerry)* 8-8 JCarroll (9) (chsd ldrs over 3f) ..................... 8.5
1536 Our Shadee (USA) *(KTIvory)* 8-8 GBardwell (5) (nvr wnt pce) ................... 4.6
2067⁵ Minster Man (IRE) *(BSRothwell)* 8-6 MHills (2) (outpcd & bhd fr ½-wy) .......... s.h.7
General Polo (33/1) Withdrawn (bolted gng to s) : not under orders

**13/8** Heart Broken, **5/1** Our Shadee (USA), Musical Phone, **11/2** Minster Man (IRE), FELT LUCKY (IRE), **12/1** Oscars Quest, **25/1** Breaking Hearts (IRE). CSF £14.28, Tote £4.70: £3.10 £1.30 (£4.80). Mr M. Channon (UPPER LAMBOURN) bred by Michael Fennessy in Ireland. 7 Rn
63.6 sec (2.1)
SF—32/29/20/1/–/–

**2426**     E.B.F. MINSTER MOORGATE STKS (Mdn 2-Y-O)  £2880.50 (£798.00: £381.50)
7f 100y                                               5-30 (5-33)

**Qaffal (USA)** *(DMorley)* 9-0 PRobinson (6) (w'like: scope: trckd ldrs: led 1f out:
r.o wl) ................................................. —1
Dee Raft (USA) *(BWHills)* 9-0 MHills (9) (cmpt: scope: hmpd st: a.p: effrt over 1f
out: rdn & r.o nr fin) ................................. s.h.2
2208² Almansour (USA) (Fav) *(HRACecil)* 9-0 AMcGlone (8) (lw: led tl hdd 1f out: kpt
on wl) ................................................. 1½.3
1652⁴ Leave a Kiss *(IABalding)* 8-6 ‡3SO'Gorman (7) (lw: trckd ldrs: effrt & n.m.r 2f out:
nt qckn) ............................................... 2½.4
Native Trio (USA) *(PWHarris)* 9-0 SWhitworth (4) (lt-f: shkn up & hdwy appr st:
styd on wl fnl f) ...................................... hd.5
1899⁴ Share a Moment (CAN) *(RHollinshead)* 9-0 KDarley (10) (lw: hmpd st: bhd: effrt
2f out: nvr able to chal) .............................. 2.6
Beaumont (IRE) *(JPearce)* 9-0 MTebbutt (2) (w'like: unf: in tch: shkn up 2f out:
nt qckn) ............................................... 1.7
1858² Red Cent *(JEtherington)* 9-0 TLucas (3) (cl up tl wknd over 1f out) ................. ¾.8
Bollin Duncan *(MHEasterby)* 9-0 MBirch (5) (w'like: bkwd: hmpd & lost tch after
1f: n.d) ............................................... 8.9
First Reserve *(BSRothwell)* 8-9 ‡5SMaloney (1) (unf: bkwd: bhd & rdn appr st:
n.d) ................................................... 5.10

**5/6** Almansour (USA), **5/1** QAFFAL (USA), **13/2** Dee Raft (USA), **7/1** Share a Moment (CAN), **10/1** Red Cent, **12/1** Leave a Kiss, **14/1** Native Trio (USA), Bollin Duncan, **20/1** Beaumont (IRE), **25/1** First Reserve. CSF £40.00, Tote £6.50: £2.00 £2.00 £1.10 (£26.60). Mr Hamdan Al-Maktoum (NEWMARKET) bred by Cormal Investments Inc in USA. 10 Rn
1m 33.4 (3.2)
SF—7/6/1/–/–/–

T/Plpt: £89.20 (33.25 Tckts).                                          AA

## 2084—LEICESTER (R-H)
### Tuesday, July 28th [Good]
Going Allowance: minus 0.15 sec per fur (F)

Wind: almost nil

Stalls: high

### 2427
COPLOW H'CAP (0-70) £3057.00 (£852.00: £411.00)　**7f 9y**　　6-15 (6-19)

2141⁴ **Kirriemuir (35)** *(KOCunningham-Brown)* 4-7-11 SDawson (8) (a.p: led wl over 1f out: jst hld on) ....................................................... —1

299 Glenscar **(34)** *(JLSpearing)* 6-7-10 RFox (15) (rdn & swtchd rt over 1f out: gd hdwy fnl f: fin wl) ................................................. nk.2

2240⁴ Kissavos **(51)** *(CCElsey)* 6-8-13 TRogers (16) (a.p: r.o one pce fnl 2f) ........... 2½.3

2210 Green's Cassatt (USA) **(42)** *(WMBrisbourne)* 4-8-4 RLappin (20) (lw: hdwy over 2f out: one pce fnl f) ............................... 1½.4

2126⁶ Dance on Sixpence **(60)** (v) (Fav) *(HJCollingridge)* 4-9-8 JQuinn (6) (hld up: stdy hdwy 3f out: rdn over 1f out: one pce) ............... ¾.5

2198² Fast Operative **(39)** *(KOCunningham-Brown)* 5-8-1 DBiggs (4) (prom stands' side 5f) ...................................................... 3.6

1905 Candle King (IRE) **(46)** (bl) *(MJFetherston-Godley)* 4-8-8 AMunro (11) (nvr nr to chal) ................................................. s.h.7

1314 Liffey River (USA) **(51)** *(MrsLPiggott)* 4-8-6 ‡7GMilligan (14) (b: hdwy over 3f out: wknd wl over 1f out) ........................... ¾.8

2198 Tinkosumtin **(38)** *(PBurgoyne)* 6-8-0 AShoults (10) (n.d) ....................... ½.9

1978³ Cash a Million (FR) **(47)** *(PDCundell)* 4-8-9 NHowe (12) (n.d) ................... hd.10

2291⁶ Watermill Girl **(32)** *(DTThom)* 4-7-1 ‡7KimMcDonnell (3) (prom stands' side over 4f) .......................................... 1.11

State of Affairs **(44)** *(CAHorgan)* 5-8-6 DaleGibson (7) (b: bkwd: n.d) ........... nk.12

2060⁶ Asterix **(59)** (v) *(JMBradley)* 4-9-7 ONutter (0) (n.d) ............................ 1.13

1943 Affordable **(64)** *(WCarter)* 4-9-7 ‡5NGwilliams (5) (bhd fnl 2f) ................. 3.14

2125 Harry's Lady (IRE) **(39)** (bl) *(TThomsonJones)* 4-8-1 TyroneWilliams (13) (b: led tl wknd wl over 1f out) ................................. 1½.15

2341 Alnasric Pete (USA) **(57)** *(DAWilson)* 6-9-5 WNewnes (19) (b: n.d) ............ ½.16

1975 Salinger **(53)** *(JWHills)* 4-9-1 RHills (17) (n.d) ............................... 2½.17

Regal Romper (IRE) **(39)** *(MrsSJSmith)* 4-7-8⁽⁷⁾ ‡7JMarshall (18) (bkwd: swtg: w ldr tl wknd over 2f out) ........................... 3½.18

**7/1** Dance on Sixpence, **8/1** Alnasric Pete (USA)(tchd 14/1), Fast Operative, Candle King (IRE), Affordable, **9/1** Asterix(12/1—8/1), **10/1** KIRRIEMUIR, **11/1** Liffey River (USA), Salinger(op 8/1), Kissavos, **16/1** Cash a Million (FR), **20/1** Harry's Lady (IRE), **25/1** Watermill Girl, **33/1** Regal Romper (IRE), State of Affairs, **50/1** Ors. CSF £343.92, CT £6,122.04. Tote £9.60: £1.80 £5.00 £3.10 £3.40 (£247.50). Mr R. N. Short (STOCKBRIDGE) bred by Dr W. J. Heffernan. 18 Rn　　　　　　　　　　1m 25.1 (2.8)
　　　　　　　　　　　　　　　　　　　　　　　　　　SF—25/23/32/18/34/4

### 2428
MOLYNEUX (S) STKS (2-Y.O) £1544.40 (£428.40: £205.20)　**5f 218y**　　6-45 (6-52)

2080² **No Extras (IRE)** *(JSutcliffe)* 8-11 BRouse (6) (a.p: led over 1f out: edgd rt: sn clr: easily) ............................................. —1

2052 Cuddly Date *(DTThom)* 8-6 DBiggs (11) (prom: led over 2f out tl over 1f out: hrd rdn: one pce) ........................................... 5.2

2195³ Mr Butch *(MRChannon)* 8-11 TQuinn (9) (led over 3f: sn lost pl: rallied ins fnl f) ¾.3

2207 Monet Monet Monet *(WCarter)* 8-6 ‡5NGwilliams (13) (a.p: rdn & one pce fnl 2f) nk.4

1838³ Canazei *(DonEnricoIncisa)* 8-6 JakiHouston (12) (no hdwy fnl 2f) ............... 3.5

1959 Forthemoment *(PCalver)* 8-6 DaleGibson (4) (no hdwy fnl 2f) .................... 1½.6

2058 Princess of Alar (bl) *(BPalling)* 8-6 JQuinn (2) (s.i.s: hld up: nvr trbld ldrs) ...... ¾.7

2248 Go Orange (v) *(JLSpearing)* 8-6 NHowe (5) (n.d) ................................ s.h.8

Red Russian **(99)** *(BJMcMath)* 8-4 ‡7CHawksley (1) (leggy: unf: bit bkwd: s.s: a bhd) ......................................... 6.9

2067⁴ Poppet Plume (Fav) *(GMMoore)* 8-6 WNewnes (8) (spd 3f: t.o) ................... 10

2098 Clare's Boy *(JMBradley)* 8-11 CRutter (3) (a bhd: t.o) ............................ 11

Spanish One *(PSFelgate)* 8-6 ‡5ATucker (7) (small: w'like: bkwd: s.s: a t.o) ........ 12

2098 Bold Treasure (IRE) (25/1) Withdrawn (ref to ent stalls) : not under orders

**15/8** Poppet Plume (Fav), **2/1** NO EXTRAS (IRE), **4/1** Mr Butch, **10/1** Forthemoment(op 5/1), **25/1** Canazei, Cuddly Date, **33/1** Ors. CSF £40.33, Tote £3.00: £1.40 £4.40 £2.20 (£25.90). Mr K. Higson (EPSOM) bred by R. J. Cullen in Ireland. 12 Rn; Bt in 5,250 gns　　　　　　　　　1m 13.7 (3.7)
　　　　　　　　　　　　　　　　　　　　　　　　　　SF—5/—/—/—/—

### 2429
RUTLAND H'CAP (3-Y.O) (0-80) £2721.00 (£756.00: £363.00)　**1m 8y**　　7-15 (7-17)
(Weights raised 10 lb)

2393* **Tiffany's Case (IRE) (52)** *(CAHorgan)* 8-3 (5x) RHills (7) (a gng wl: qcknd to ld nr fin: comf) ................................. —1

2125★ Kingchip Boy **(54)** (Fav) *(MJRyan)* 8-0 ‡5ATucker (3) (hld up: hdwy 2f out: led ins fnl f: hdd cl home) ..... 1/2.2

2075★ Cappahoosh (IRE) **(56)** *(HJCollingridge)* 8-7 MRoberts (6) (a.p: led wl over 1f out tl ins fnl f) ..... 2.3

1488 Kiveton Tycoon (IRE) **(70)** *(JAGlover)* 8-7 JFortune (2) (hdwy over 3f out: led over 2f out: hdd & hung rt wl over 1f out) ..... 11/2.4

2062³ Lake Dominion **(70)** (bl) *(PWHarris)* 9-7 WRSwinburn (1) (led over 5f: wknd over 1f out) ..... 11/2.5

2084² Sure Shot Norman **(50)** *(JSutcliffe)* 8-1 PRobinson (5) (chsd ldr over 5f: wknd over 1f out) ..... 11/2.6

Ming Blue **(59)** *(PJMakin)* 8-10 AMunro (8) (bit bkwd: bhd fnl 2f) ..... 1.7

2275³ Be My Everything (IRE) **(66)** *(RHollinshead)* 9-3 WRyan (4) (a bhd) ..... 4.8

Shall We Run **(65)** *(RFJohnsonHoughton)* 9-2 BRaymond (9) (dropped rr over 2f out: t.o) ..... 9

**3/1** Kingchip Boy, **100/30** Sure Shot Norman, **9/2** Cappahoosh (IRE), **6/1** TIFFANY'S CASE (IRE)(op 3/1), **7/1** Be My Everything (IRE), **10/1** Lake Dominion, **12/1** Kiveton Tycoon (IRE), Ming Blue(tchd 8/1), **20/1** Shall We Run. CSF £24.25, CT £83.06. Tote £7.60: £1.90 £1.80 £1.80 (£11.00). Mr John Kelsey-Fry (BILLINGBEAR) Mrs C. L. Weld in Ireland. 9 Rn
1m 39 (4)
SF—11/6/7/16/11/–

---

**2430** ROTHLEY CLAIMING STKS (3-Y.O) £1618.00 (£448.00: £214.00)
1m 1f 218y
7-45 (7-46)

911⁶ **Addicted to Love** *(PJMakin)* 8-6 TQuinn (7) (led 1f: 4th st: led 1f out: r.o wl) ..... —1

20872 Silver Samurai **(70)** *(RHollinshead)* 8-7 WRyan (1) (hld up & bhd: stumbled & 7th st: hdwy over 1f out: r.o ins fnl f) ..... 4.2

1949³ Edge of Darkness **(62)** *(JWHills)* 8-10 RHills (4) (led after 1f tl 1f out: wknd ins fnl f) ..... 3/4.3

2237² Neltegrity **(58)** (v) *(THCaldwell)* 9-0 ‡7EHusband (3) (6th st: hrd rdn over 1f out: r.o one pce) ..... 1.4

2077³ Amazon Express **(54)** *(CEBrittain)* 8-11 MRoberts (8) (lw: 5th st: no hdwy fnl 2f) 21/2.5

1978 Classic Exhibit **(40)** *(SPCWoods)* 8-3 WWoods (6) (plld hrd: 3rd st: hrd rdn over 2f out: wknd over 1f out) ..... nk.6

1955 Lady of Sardinia (BEL) **(70)** (Fav) *(JWPayne)* 8-2 AMunro (2) (plld hrd: 2nd st: wknd over 2f out) ..... 1.7

1663 My Jersey Pearl (IRE) **(40)** *(DonEnricoIncisa)* 7-5 ‡7ClaireBalding (5) (hld up: last st: a in rr: t.o) ..... 7.8

**7/4** Lady of Sardinia (BEL), **85/40** Silver Samurai, **11/2** Amazon Express, **13/2** Edge of Darkness, **11/1** ADDICTED TO LOVE(8/1—12/1), **20/1** Neltegrity, **66/1** Ors. CSF £32.45, Tote £9.90: £2.30 £1.10 £1.60 (£23.50). Mascalls Stud (MARLBOROUGH) bred by Mascalls Stud Farm. 8 Rn
2m 7.4 (4.7)
SF—30/23/24/26/18/9

---

**2431** THISTLETON GAP STKS (Mdn 3-Y.O) £1618.00 (£448.00: £214.00)
1m 3f 183y
8-15 (8-18)

1843⁴ **Shirley Valentine** (Fav) *(HRACecil)* 8-9 WRyan (1) (3rd st: led 2f out: pushed out) ..... —1

2064³ Tudor Island *(CEBrittain)* 9-0 MRoberts (3) (lw: led over 9f: one pce) ..... 31/2.2

2168⁵ Fortune Star (IRE) *(JLDunlop)* 9-0 TQuinn (5) (hld up: 5th st: rdn over 2f out: one pce) ..... 3/4.3

2200² Brambleberry **(75)** *(MrsSJSmith)* 8-7 ‡7JMarshall (8) (chsd ldr: 2nd st: hrd rdn & wknd 2f out) ..... 5.4

2168³ Billy Bunter *(HCandy)* 9-0 CRutter (6) (6th st: hdwy over 3f out: wknd 2f out) ..... 3/4.5

2200⁶ Tomashenko *(JMackie)* 9-0 GHind (7) (hdwy on ins 3f out: wknd wl over 1f out) 11/2.6

1141⁴ My Girl Friday *(WClay)* 8-4 ‡5ATucker (4) (bit bkwd: last st: t.o fnl 3f) ..... 7

1919⁴ Kickcashtal *(BAMcMahon)* 9-0 BRaymond (2) (4th st: wknd qckly over 3f out: sn t.o) ..... 8

**2/5** SHIRLEY VALENTINE, **6/1** Billy Bunter(tchd 4/1), **8/1** Fortune Star (IRE)(11/2—9/1), **11/1** Tudor Island, **33/1** Brambleberry, **66/1** Tomashenko, **200/1** Ors. CSF £5.30, Tote £1.50: £1.10 £1.50 £1.60 (£5.50). Mr K. Abdulla (NEWMARKET) bred by Juddmonte Farms. 8 Rn
2m 33.6 (4.8)
SF—29/27/25/8/13/10

---

**2432** TOM CRIBB STKS (Mdn 3-Y.O) £1646.00 (£456.00: £218.00)
7f 9y
8-45 (8-52)

1916 **Karen Louise (60)** *(MissHCKnight)* 8-9 MRoberts (8) (mde all: qcknd clr wl over 1f out: r.o wl) ..... —1

Climbing High *(IABalding)* 8-9 WRyan (7) (lt-f: unf: hld up: rdn over 1f out: r.o ins fnl f) ..... 3.2

2236² Hameem (IRE) (Fav) *(AAScott)* 9-0 WRSwinburn (4) (lw: chsd wnr: ev ch 2f out: sn hrd rdn: one pce) ..... 3/4.3

2133³ Gunner's Daughter *(HCandy)* 8-9 CRutter (9) (a.p: rdn over 1f out: one pce) .. 1½.4
2125 Sudanor (IRE) **(59)** *(MJHeaton-Ellis)* 9-0 DHolland (3) (prom: rdn over 2f out: wknd over 1f out) ................................................................. 3.5
Spencer's Revenge *(LordHuntingdon)* 9-0 AMunro (1) (w'like: bkwd: dwlt: nvr nrr) ........................................................................................ 3.6
Guiting Girl *(HCandy)* 8-9 SDawson (12) (leggy: bit bkwd: hdwy over 3f out: wknd 2f out) ...................................................................... 1½.7
2015⁶ Face the Future *(PWHarris)* 9-0 PRobinson (11) (bit bkwd: bhd fnl 2f) ............. nk.8
2015² Under the Bridge **(73)** *(PWHarris)* 8-9 ½⁵ATucker (5) (hrd rdn over 2f out: sn bhd) ½.9
1293³ Swinging Tich *(BAMcMahon)* 8-9 TQuinn (6) (a bhd) ...................................... 2.10
Don't Drop Bombs (USA) *(AAScott)* 9-0 BRaymond (2) (bkwd: a bhd: t.o) ......... 11
Wabwom (33/1) Withdrawn (ref to ent stalls) : not under orders

**6/4** Hameem (IRE)(op 5/2), **5/1** Gunner's Daughter, **6/1** Spencer's Revenge(4/1—13/2), **9/1** Climbing High(8/1—12/1), Under the Bridge(8/1—12/1), **16/1** KAREN LOUISE, Swinging Tich, **20/1** Sudanor (IRE), **25/1** Guiting Girl, Don't Drop Bombs (USA), **50/1** Face the Future. CSF £134.89, Tote £12.20: £2.20 £2.30 £1.20 (£62.40). Mr Andrew Shenston (WANTAGE) bred by Pyle Bros Ltd. 11 Rn
1m 24.5 (2.2)
SF—46/37/40/30/26/17

T/Plpt: £49.50 (40.65 Tckts).
KH

---

1654—## GOODWOOD (R-H)
### Tuesday, July 28th [Good, Good to firm patches]
Going Allowance: St: minus 0.15 sec (F); Rest: nil sec per fur (G)       Wind: almost nil

Stalls: low

**2433**  CALIFORNIA H'CAP (3-Y.O) (0-100) £7635.00 (£2280.00: £1090.00: £495.00)
1m                                                                    2.30 (2-35)

2191 Philidor **(81)** (Fav) *(JMPEustace)* 8-7 RCochrane (6) (lw: 5th st: hrd rdn over 1f out: led ins fnl f: r.o wl) ....................................................... —1
1856★ Wesaam (USA) **(93)** *(MajorWRHern)* 9-5 WCarson (8) (lw: 2nd st: led over 3f out tl ins fnl f: unable qckn) .......................................... 1½.2
2035⁵ Courageous Knight **(74)** *(RHannon)* 8-0 AMunro (5) (hrd rdn & hdwy over 1f out: r.o ins fnl f) ............................................................... 1½.3
1941 Grand Vitesse (IRE) **(78)** *(RHannon)* 8-4 MRoberts (9) (led over 4f: one pce) ... ¾.4
934⁵ Juniper Berry (IRE) **(90)** *(PWChapple-Hyam)* 9-2 PaulEddery (2) (hdwy 2f out: hrd rdn wl over 1f out: one pce) ................................... ¾.5
1975² Savash (USA) **(83)** *(MMoubarak)* 8-9 LDettori (3) (lw: 6th st: hrd rdn over 2f out: wknd over 1f out) ............................................... 7.6
2107² Bear With Me (IRE) **(67)** *(MBell)* 7-7 AMackay (4) (b.nr hind: 3rd st: wknd over 1f out) ...................................................................... ¾.7
1856² Mizoram (USA) **(82)** *(HRACecil)* 8-8 SCauthen (7) (lw: 4th st: wknd over 3f out) 15.8
1476 Mougins (IRE) **(95)** *(DRCElsworth)* 9-7 TQuinn (1) (swvd lft & uns rdr s) .............. 0
LONG HANDICAP: Bear With Me (IRE) 7-5.

**4/1** PHILIDOR, **9/2** Grand Vitesse (IRE), **11/2** Wesaam (USA), **13/2** Mizoram (USA), **7/1** Savash (USA), **10/1** Juniper Berry (IRE), **12/1** Mougins (IRE), Bear With Me (IRE), **14/1** Courageous Knight. CSF £23.05, CT £234.70. Tote £4.40: £1.40 £2.00 £3.80 (£11.70). Mr J. C. Smith (NEWMARKET) bred by John A. Jones Morgan. 9 Rn
1m 39.73 (2.13)
SF—61/68/44/46/56/28

**2434**  GORDON STKS (Gp 3) (3-Y.O) £17000.00 (£6362.50: £3056.25: £1331.25)
1½m                                                                   3-10 (3-11)

1940² Bonny Scot (IRE) **(104)** *(LMCumani)* 8-10 LDettori (4) (swtg: 6th st: led ins fnl f: pushed out) ....................................................................... —1
2220² Alflora (IRE) **(111)** *(CEBrittain)* 8-10 MRoberts (3) (2nd st: led 3f out to 2f out: led over 1f out tl ins fnl f: unable qckn) ................................. 2.2
1458★ Beyton (USA) **(114)** *(RHannon)* 9-1 JReid (2) (lw: 4th st: led 2f out tl over 1f out: one pce) ........................................................................ 3½.3
1537² Milzig (USA) **(92)** *(DRCElsworth)* 8-10 TQuinn (6) (3rd st: wknd over 1f out) ...... 4.4
1354a² Firing Line (IRE) (v) (Fav) *(MrTStack)* 8-10 SCraine (5) (leggy: s.s: rdn over 5f out: 5th st: wknd over 2f out) ....................................... 5.5
1831★ Alphard **(106)** *(HRACecil)* 8-10 WRyan (1) (led 9f) ........................................ ¾.6

**11/4** Firing Line (IRE), **100/30** Beyton (USA), **7/2** Alphard(3/1—9/2), **4/1** Alflora (IRE), **6/1** BONNY SCOT (IRE), **40/1** Milzig (USA). CSF £26.25, Tote £6.20: £2.30 £2.40 (£12.70). Lord Weinstock (NEWMARKET) bred by Ballymacoll Stud Farm Ltd in Ireland. 6 Rn
2m 37.21 (5.51)
SF—41/37/35/22/12/10

**2435** WILLIAM HILL STEWARDS' CUP (H'cap) (0-115) £51662.50 (£15550.00: £7525.00: £3512.50) **6f**

3-45 (3-51)

1474[4] Lochsong (82) *(IABalding)* 4-8-0 WCarson (5) (lw: chsd ldr: led over 2f out: rdn out) ........................................................................ —1
1631 Duplicity (IRE) (93) *(LJHolt)* 4-8-11 JReid (9) (hdwy over 1f out: r.o wl ins fnl f) ½.2
1943[a] Consigliere (92) *(RCharlton)* 4-8-10 (7x) PaulEddery (13) (hdwy 2f out: hrd rdn & ev ch over 1f out: r.o) ........................ 1½.3
1698[5] Heather Bank (94) *(JBerry)* 3-8-6 WRyan (4) (a.p: ev ch 1f out: unable qckn) nk.4
2188[4] Hard to Figure (90) *(RJHodges)* 6-8-8 JWilliams (7) (hdwy 2f out: r.o ins fnl f) nk.5
2169 Master Planner (94) *(CACyzer)* 3-8-6 (3x) KFallon (28) (a.p: rdn over 3f out: one pce) .................................................. 2.6
1820a[2] Double Blue (94) (Fav) *(MJohnston)* 3-8-6 MRoberts (21) (lw: a.p: ev ch 2f out: one pce) ........................................ nk.7
1942 Tbab (IRE) (94) *(CEBrittain)* 4-8-12 WRSwinburn (23) (lw: hdwy over 1f out: r.o) hd.8
1926[4] Milagro (87) *(RHannon)* 3-7-13 SRaymont (18) (nvr nr to chal) .................. s.h.9
2003 Appledorn (85) *(BAMcMahon)* 5-8-3 TQuinn (25) (no hdwy fnl 2f) ................ hd.10
1631* Kayvee (97) *(GHarwood)* 3-8-9 AClark (17) (lw: a.p: hrd rdn over 1f out: one pce) .................................................. ½.11
2003[5] Green Dollar (91) *(EAWheeler)* 9-8-9 LPiggott (10) (hld up: rdn over 2f out: one pce) .................................................. hd.12
2169[2] Notley (110) *(RHannon)* 5-9-11 ‡[3]RPerham (26) (spd over 4f) .................. 1.13
1878 Baysham (USA) (83) (bl) *(BRMillman)* 6-7-10[(2)] ‡[5]RPrice (16) (a mid div) .. hd.14
2127[5] Masnun (USA) (87) *(RJO'Sullivan)* 7-8-5 DBiggs (12) (nvr nrr) .................. ½.15
2376* Viceroy (104) (v) *(BBeasley)* 5-9-3 (5x) ‡[5]SWilliams (29) (spd over 4f) ...... hd.16
2169[4] Taufan Blu (IRE) (95) (bl) *(MJohnston)* 3-8-7 DMcKeown (15) (nvr nrr) ...... hd.17
2003 Red Rosein (87) *(CaptJWilson)* 6-8-5 GCarter (27) (b.off hind: nvr nrr) ........ ¾.18
2019* Beau Venture (USA) (92) *(FHLee)* 4-8-5 ‡[5]NKennedy (20) (a mid div) ...... nk.19
2003[6] Crystal Jack (FR) (81) *(FHLee)* 4-7-13 GHind (14) (prom over 4f) .............. ½.20
2019[6] Grand Prix (82) *(DRCElsworth)* 3-8-6 DHolland (8) (outpcd) .................... ½.21
2179[4] Poets Cove (86) *(MMcCormack)* 4-8-4 WNewnes (1) (outpcd) .................. hd.22
2169[5] Orthorhombus (101) (bl) *(GLewis)* 3-8-4 ‡[5]DHarrison (3) (lw: a bhd) .......... s.h.23
2337[2] Bertie Wooster (84) *(RJHolder)* 9-8-2 (5x) RHills (30) (swtg: hdwy 4f out: wknd over 2f out) .................................................. ¾.24
2179* Aughfad (83) (v) *(TCasey)* 6-8-1 GDuffield (4) (lw: led over 3f) .................. ¾.25
1711[5] Wilde Rufo (102) *(PAKelleway)* 3-9-0 BRaymond (2) (a bhd) .................. s.h.26
1875[3] Bold Lez (101) *(MJHaynes)* 5-9-5 SCauthen (22) (bhd fnl 2f) .................. s.h.27
2127 Letsbeonestaboutit (89) *(MrsNMacauley)* 6-8-7 NAdams (6) (prom 4f) ........ hd.28
2188 Clifton Charlie (USA) (88) *(MRChannon)* 4-8-1 ‡[5]BDoyle (24) (bhd fnl 2f) .. ½.29
2214[4] Adwick Park (86) *(TDBarron)* 4-8-4 LDettori (19) (a bhd) .................... 5.30

15/2 Double Blue, 8/1 Kayvee, 10/1 Aughfad(8/1—12/1), LOCHSONG, 12/1 Tbab (IRE), 16/1 Consigliere, Bold Lez, Masnun (USA), Red Rosein, 20/1 Master Planner, Notley, Hard to Figure, Taufan Blu (IRE), Beau Venture (USA), Adwick Park, 25/1 Grand Prix, Orthorhombus, Bertie Wooster, Viceroy, 33/1 Duplicity (IRE), Green Dollar, 40/1 Crystal Jack (FR), 50/1 Milagro, Clifton Charlie (USA), Baysham (USA), Poets Cove, Appledorn, Heather Bank, 66/1 Ors. CSF £279.77, CT £4,724.59. Tote £11.40: £2.50 £8.60 £5.10 £13.40 (£256.80). Mr J. C. Smith (KINGSCLERE) bred by Littleton Stud. 30 Rn
1m 10.86 (0.46)

SF—59/68/61/56/57/47

**2436** OAK TREE STKS (listed race) (F & M) £14620.00 (£4360.00: £2080.00: £940.00) **7f**

4-15 (4-21)

1870[2] Storm Dove (USA) (99) (Fav) *(RCharlton)* 3-8-7 PaulEddery (5) (3rd st: led 2f out: clr over 1f out: r.o wl) .................... —1
2021* Susurration (USA) (111) *(JHMGosden)* 5-9-6 WRSwinburn (1) (4th st: hrd rdn over 1f out: unable qckn) .................... 7.2
2140* Mrs Fisher (IRE) (92) *(SirMarkPrescott)* 3-8-7 GDuffield (2) (2nd st: ev ch 2f out: one pce) .................................. nk.3
429[6] Red Slippers (USA) (106) *(LMCumani)* 3-8-7 LDettori (7) (6th st: rdn over 2f out: n.m.r over 1f out: one pce) .................... 1.4
1462[6] Mahasin (USA) (92) *(JLDunlop)* 3-8-7 WCarson (6) (hdwy over 1f out: nvr nrr) nk.5
2191[5] Miss Haggis (85) *(RBoss)* 3-8-7 TQuinn (3) (nvr nr to chal) .................. 1½.6
1935[5] Splice (92) *(JRFanshawe)* 3-8-7 MRoberts (8) (swtg: nvr nrr) .................. s.h.7
1707[4] Misterioso (104) *(LordHuntingdon)* 3-8-7 AMunro (9) (lw: 5th st: wknd fnl f) .. 1.8
2016* Miss Bluebird (IRE) (89) (bl) *(PAKelleway)* 3-8-7 BRaymond (4) (b.hind: led 5f) 1½.9

5/2 STORM DOVE (USA)(7/2—9/4), 5/1 Red Slippers (USA), Susurration (USA)(7/2—11/2), 11/2 Mahasin (USA), 7/1 Mrs Fisher (IRE), 8/1 Misterioso, 16/1 Splice, 20/1 Miss Haggis, 25/1 Miss Bluebird (IRE). CSF £14.44. Tote £4.00: £1.50 £2.00 £2.00 (£6.80). Mr K. Abdulla (BECKHAMPTON) bred by Juddmonte Farms Inc in USA. 9 Rn
1m 25.67 (0.97)

SF—78/70/56/53/52/47

**2437**　RALPH HUBBARD MEMORIAL NURSERY　£7635.00 (£2280.00: £1090.00: £495.00)
5f　　　　4-45 (4-47)

(Weights raised 9 lb)

2005* **Zany Zanna (IRE)** *(GAPritchard-Gordon)* 7-6 ‡5DHarrison (12) (hdwy over 2f
out: rdn over 1f out: led last stride) ...................... —1

2371² Riston Lady (IRE) *(BSRothwell)* 7-8 ‡3JFanning (11) (a.p: led over 2f out: hrd rdn
ins fnl f: hdd last stride) ...................... s.h.2

2161⁵ Classic Story (USA) *(MMoubarak)* 9-3 LDettori (3) (plld hrd: hdwy wl over 1f
out: r.o) ...................... 2.3

2221* Finmental (IRE) *(ABailey)* 9-8 (6x) ‡5ATucker (10) (lw: hdwy over 1f out: r.o) .... nk.4

2030* Meadmore Magic *(JLHarris)* 8-7 DHolland (2) (lw: a.p: hrd rdn over 1f out:
unable qckn) ...................... 3¹/2.5

2081² Trevorsninepoints *(MJRyan)* 8-0 DBiggs (5) (a.p: one pce fnl 2f) ...................... nk.6

1895* Press the Bell (Fav) *(JBerry)* 7-13 NCarlisle (1) (led over 2f) ...................... 1.7

1658⁴ Polar Storm (IRE) *(LadyHerries)* 8-10 GCarter (7) (prom 2f) ...................... 2.8

2152² Be Polite (IRE) *(MBell)* 7-0 ‡7CHawksley (4) (a bhd) ...................... ¹/2.9

2031 Pirates Gold (IRE) *(MJHeaton-Ellis)* 8-10 WCarson (9) (a bhd) ...................... nk.10

2254 Mr Nevermind (IRE) *(GLewis)* 8-1 ‡5PRice (6) (s.i.s: a bhd) ...................... nk.11

2257³ Sea Exhibition (IRE) *(MBlanshard)* 8-4 MRoberts (8) (prom over 2f) ...................... 2.12

LONG HANDICAP: Be Polite (IRE) 7-6.

**9/2** Press the Bell, **5/1** Polar Storm (IRE), **6/1** Riston Lady (IRE), **7/1** Finmental (IRE), **8/1** ZANY ZANNA (IRE), Classic Story (USA), **10/1** Meadmore Magic, **12/1** Trevorsninepoints, **14/1** Sea Exhibition (IRE), **16/1** Be Polite (IRE), **20/1** Ors. CSF £52.66, CT £362.11. Tote £9.10: £2.20 £2.80 £3.30 (£30.20). Mr Giles W. Pritchard-Gordon (NEWMARKET) bred by Limestone Stud in Ireland. 12 Rn　　58.88 sec (1.28)
SF—38/39/54/58/29/21

**2438**　E.B.F. NEW HAM STKS (Mdn 2-Y.O.F) £6212.00 (£1856.00: £888.00: £404.00)
7f　　　　5-20 (5-21)

1937³ **Magique Rond Point (USA)** (Fav) *(HRACecil)* 8-11 WRyan (14) (3rd st: led ins
fnl f: rdn out) ...................... —1

1538³ Zenith *(IABalding)* 8-11 JReid (4) (lw: 6th st: qcknd: led & edgd rt wl over 1f out:
hdd ins fnl f: unable qckn) ...................... 2.2

Abury (IRE) *(PWChapple-Hyam)* 8-11 PaulEddery (12) (unf: lw: 5th st: hrd rdn
& nt clr run over 1f out: one pce) ...................... 2¹/2.3

Magical Queen (IRE) *(MMoubarak)* 8-11 LDettori (10) (unf: hdwy 2f out: n.m.r
over 1f out: one pce fnl f) ...................... 1¹/2.4

Nicer (IRE) *(BWHills)* 8-11 DHolland (9) (leggy: unf: nvr nr to chal) ...................... 2.5

1957 Nahlati (IRE) *(CEBrittain)* 8-11 SCauthen (11) (led over 5f) ...................... 1¹/2.6

The Strid (IRE) *(JHMGosden)* 8-11 WRSwinburn (8) (str: bit bkwd: shkn up
over 3f out: nvr nrr) ...................... 1¹/2.7

Smart Daisy *(IABalding)* 8-11 RCochrane (3) (scope: hdwy over 2f out: wknd
over 1f out) ...................... s.h.8

1867⁴ Olympic Run *(JLDunlop)* 8-11 WCarson (5) (lw: 2nd st: ev ch over 2f out: wknd
over 1f out) ...................... hd.9

2037³ Delta Downs *(RHannon)* 8-11 BRaymond (2) (4th st: wknd over 1f out) ...................... ³/4.10

1957³ Catherineofaragon *(WGRWightman)* 8-11 JWilliams (1) (bhd fnl 2f) ...................... ³/4.11

1279 Malzeta (IRE) *(MJHeaton-Ellis)* 8-11 MRoberts (6) (a bhd) ...................... hd.12

1867 Don't Forget Marie (IRE) *(RHannon)* 8-11 GCarter (13) (s.s: a bhd) ...................... 3.13

Allesca *(MDIUsher)* 8-11 AMackay (7) (cmpt: bit bkwd: a bhd) ...................... 14

**5/4** MAGIQUE ROND POINT (USA), **5/1** Zenith(4/1—6/1), **6/1** Olympic Run, **9/1** Abury (IRE)(5/1—10/1), **12/1** Magical Queen (IRE)(op 4/1), **14/1** Malzeta (IRE), **16/1** Catherineofaragon, **20/1** Delta Downs, The Strid (IRE), **25/1** Smart Daisy, Nicer (IRE), **33/1** Nahlati (IRE), **50/1** Ors. CSF £8.69, Tote £2.50: £1.60 £2.00 £3.50 (£4.90). Mr Q. Irshid (NEWMARKET) bred by Howell S. Wynne & Larry DeAngelis in USA. 14 Rn　　1m 27.94 (3.24)
SF—49/43/35/30/24/19

T/Trio: Race 3 & 5: £984.30 (7.6 Tckts), £87.70 (25.3 Tckt. T/Jkpt: £13,506.40 (0.1 Tckts), £16,426.75 to Goodwood 29/7/92. T/Plpt: £504.60 (39.8 Tckts).　　AK

## GOODWOOD (R-H)

### Wednesday, July 29th [St course Good, Rnd Good to firm]
Going Allowance: minus 0.20 sec per fur (F)　　　Wind: almost nil

Stalls: low　Flag start: 1st race

**2439**　COUNTRY CLUB HOTELS GOODWOOD H'CAP (0-100) £11160.00 (£3330.00: £1590.00:
£720.00)　2¹/2m　　2-30 (2-32)

2172⁴ **Bardolph (USA)** (76) *(PFICole)* 5-8-10 TQuinn (1) (b.off hind: chsd ldr 14f out:
2nd st: led over 3f out: all out) ...................... —1

| | | | |
|---|---|---|---|
| 1938³ | Farsi **(81)** (bl) *(RHollinshead)* 4–9-1 WRyan (3) (hdwy over 3f out: hrd rdn & ev ch fnl 2f: r.o wl) | | s.h.**2** |
| 2001⁴ | Good Hand (USA) **(84)** *(JWWatts)* 6–9-4 NConnorton (10) (swtg: rdn 12f out: lost pl over 4f out: rallied over 1f out: r.o) | | 5.**3** |
| | Master Foodbroker (IRE) **(82)** *(DRCElsworth)* 4–9-2 JWilliams (6) (b: hdwy over 1f out: r.o ins fnl f) | | 1¹/₂.**4** |
| 2129 | Retouch **(91)** *(PFICole)* 6–9-4 ‡⁷JDSmith (13) (hdwy 10f out: 3rd st: hrd rdn over 2f out: unable qckn) | | nk.**5** |
| 2278 | Access Ski **(76)** *(RBoss)* 5–8-10 NDay (5) (lw: hdwy 5f out: 5th st: wknd over 1f out) | | 7.**6** |
| 2027 | Gondolier **(94)** (Fav) *(HRACecil)* 4–10-0 PatEddery (2) (led over 16f) | | 7.**7** |
| 2027⁴ | Haitham **(89)** *(RAkehurst)* 5–9-9 JReid (8) (a mid div) | | hd.**8** |
| 2001★ | My Chiara **(64)** *(PJBevan)* 6–7-12⁽²⁾ BCrossley (11) (lw: 4th st: wknd 3f out) | | 1¹/₂.**9** |
| 2172³ | Skisurf **(63)** *(CEBrittain)* 6–7-6⁽⁴⁾ ‡⁵BDoyle (9) (6th st: wknd over 3f out) | | 2¹/₂.**10** |
| | Chasmarella **(59)** *(ARDavison)* 7–7-7 EJohnson (4) (lw: chsd ldr 6f: wknd 10f out: t.o) | | 20.**11** |
| 1970 | Mr Taylor **(59)** *(HJCollingridge)* 7–7-7 JQuinn (12) (bhd fnl 6f: t.o) | | s.h.**12** |
| 2172⁵ | Go South **(65)** (bl) *(JRJenkins)* 8–7-13 WCarson (7) (a bhd: t.o) | | 6.**13** |

LONG HANDICAP: Skisurf 7-5, Chasmarella 5-11, Mr Taylor 5-12.
*Stewards Enquiry: Quinn suspended 7-10/8/92 (excessive use of the whip)*

**100/30** Gondolier, **13/2** Haitham, BARDOLPH (USA), **7/1** Good Hand (USA), **9/1** Retouch, Go South(tchd 14/1), Farsi, **10/1** My Chiara, **12/1** Skisurf, **25/1** Master Foodbroker (IRE), **33/1** Access Ski, **66/1** Mr Taylor, **200/1** Chasmarella. CSF £57.12, CT £383.36. Tote £7.90: £2.50 £2.70 £2.80 (£26.60). Sir George Meyrick (WHATCOMBE) bred by McMillin Bros in USA. 13 Rn
4m 14.1 (hand) (U.9)
SF—65/69/67/63/64/49/60

---

| **2440** | SUSSEX STKS (Gp 1) £76700.00 (£28785.00: £13892.50: £6122.50) | |
|---|---|---|
| | **1m** | 3-10 (3-11) |

| | | | |
|---|---|---|---|
| 1462★ | **Marling (IRE)** (Fav) *(GWragg)* 3–8-10 PatEddery (7) (lw: 3rd st: hrd rdn over 1f out: led ins fnl f: r.o wl) | | —**1** |
| 1231a⁶ | Selkirk (USA) *(IABalding)* 4–9-7 RCochrane (4) (lw: 6th st: led over 1f out tl ins fnl f: r.o wl) | | hd.**2** |
| 1454² | Second Set (IRE) *(LMCumani)* 4–9-7 LDettori (5) (4th st: n.m.r over 1f out: r.o ins fnl f) | | ³/₄.**3** |
| 1942³ | Sheikh Albadou (USA) *(AAScott)* 4–9-7 WRSwinburn (1) (b.hind: lw: 7th st: hdwy over 2f out: nt clr run over 1f out: unable qckn) | | 2.**4** |
| 1817a★ | Sikeston (USA) *(CEBrittain)* 6–9-7 MRoberts (2) (5th st: r.o one pce fnl 2f) | | s.h.**5** |
| 1494a² | Star Of Cozzene (USA) *(HRACecil)* 4–9-7 CAsmussen (3) (8th st: hdwy over 1f out: nvr nr to chal) | | 2.**6** |
| 1454⁶ | Rudimentary (USA) *(HRACecil)* 4–9-7 SCauthen (6) (lw: 2nd st: led 2f out tl over 1f out: sn wknd) | | ¹/₂.**7** |
| 2011★ | Thourios (v) *(GHarwood)* 3–8-13 WCarson (8) (lw: led 6f) | | 5.**8** |

**11/10** MARLING (IRE), **7/2** Second Set (IRE)(3/1—9/2), Selkirk (USA), **11/1** Sheikh Albadou, **16/1** Sikeston (USA), **20/1** Thourios, Rudimentary (USA), **33/1** Star of Cozzene (USA). CSF £5.57, Tote £2.10: £1.30 £1.30 £1.60 (£2.80). Mr E. J. Loder (NEWMARKET) bred by E. J. Loder in Ireland. 8 Rn
1m 36.68 (U.92)
SF—86/96/94/88/87/79/77

---

| **2441** | SCOTTISH EQUITABLE RICHMOND STKS (Gp 2) (2-Y.O.C & G) £50460.00 (£18973.00: £9186.50: £4080.50) **6f** | |
|---|---|---|
| | | 3-45 (3-45) |

| | | | |
|---|---|---|---|
| 1844★ | **Son Pardo** *(RHannon)* 8–11 JReid (4) (mde virtually all: hrd rdn fnl f: r.o wl) | | —**1** |
| 1936² | Canaska Star *(PAKelleway)* 8–11 PatEddery (5) (lw: hdwy over 2f out: ev ch ins fnl f: unable qckn) | | 1.**2** |
| 1196★ | Green's Bid *(PFICole)* 8–11 TQuinn (6) (a.p: rdn over 2f out: one pce) | | 1¹/₂.**3** |
| 1469³ | Darbonne (USA) (Fav) *(GHarwood)* 8–11 SCauthen (2) (w wnr: over 1f out: nt r.o) | | 2.**4** |
| 1936³ | Pips Pride *(RHannon)* 8–11 WCarson (3) (plld hrd: nvr nr to chal) | | s.h.**5** |
| 2212★ | Antester (IRE) *(PWChapple-Hyam)* 8–11 PaulEddery (1) (lw: a bhd) | | 1¹/₂.**6** |

**13/8** Darbonne (USA), **5/2** Canaska Star(7/4—11/4), **5/1** Pips Pride, **7/1** SON PARDO, **8/1** Green's Bid, **16/1** Antester (IRE). CSF £23.31, Tote £7.70: £2.50 £1.90 (£10.00). N.T.C. (Racing) Limited (MARLBOROUGH) bred by R. T. and Mrs Watson. 6 Rn
1m 11.26 (0.86)
SF—56/52/46/38/37/31

---

| **2442** | TOTE GOLD TROPHY (H'cap) (0-115) £29990.00 (£9020.00: £4360.00: £2030.00) | |
|---|---|---|
| | **1¹/₂m** | 4-15 (4-20) |
| | (Weights raised 1 lb) | |

| | | | |
|---|---|---|---|
| 1662³ | **Spinning (101)** *(IABalding)* 5–9-10 RCochrane (10) (9th st: hdwy over 2f out: hrd rdn & led ins fnl f: r.o wl) | | —**1** |
| 2180³ | Castoret **(77)** *(JWHills)* 6–7-9 ‡⁵DHarrison (13) (11th st: hdwy 3f out: led 1f out tl ins fnl f) | | ¹/₂.**2** |

1940³ Brier Creek (USA) (92) *(JHMGosden)* 3–8–3 WCarson (8) (13th st: hdwy over 2f
out: r.o ins fnl f) .................................................................................................. ³/₄.3

2180² Seal Indigo (IRE) (83) *(RHannon)* 4–8–6 MRoberts (3) (lw: s.s: 14th st: gd hdwy
over 1f out: fin wl) .............................................................................................. nk.4

2023* Quick Ransom (81) *(MJohnston)* 4–8–4 DMcKeown (7) (4th st: led 3f out to 1f
out: unable qckn) ............................................................................................ 1¹/₂.5

1465⁶ Kiveton Kabooz (82) (Fav) *(LMCumani)* 4–8–5⁽²⁾ LDettori (6) (12th st: hdwy over
2f out: hrd rdn wl over 1f out: r.o one pce) ................................................... nk.6

2288* Highbrook (USA) (80) *(MHTompkins)* 4–8–3 (4x) PRobinson (14) (10th st:
hdwy over 2f out: hrd rdn over 1f out: one pce) ........................................... 3¹/₂.7

1842* Matador (USA) (101) *(RCharlton)* 5–9–10 PatEddery (16) (lw: 7th st: hrd rdn
over 2f out: eased whn btn ins fnl f) ............................................................... 1¹/₂.8

1842³ Secret Society (87) *(MJCamacho)* 5–8–10 NConnorton (4) (6th st: wknd wl
over 1f out) ......................................................................................................... hd.9

1697⁵ Highflying (81) *(GMMoore)* 6–8–4 WNewnes (11) (led 10f out tl over 5f out: led
over 4f out to 3f out: sn wknd) ......................................................................... 3.10

2129³ Castle Courageous (91) *(LadyHerries)* 5–9–0 JReid (15) (led 2f: 5th st: wknd
over 2f out) ......................................................................................................... 5.11

Millionaire's Row (85) *(HRACecil)* 5–8–8 SCauthen (9) (b: 15th st: a bhd) ........ 4.12

2028⁴ Westholme (USA) (77) *(MHEasterby)* 4–7–9⁽¹⁾ ‡⁵SMaloney (12) (lw: led over 5f
out tl over 4f out: 2nd st: wkng whn hmpd on ins over 2f out) 6.13

1958* Al Karnak (IRE) (91) *(MMoubarak)* 3–8–2⁽⁵⁾ TQuinn (5) (8th st: wkng whn hmpd
3f out) ................................................................................................................. 5.14

2349 Kimbers (IRE) (92) (bl) *(CRNelson)* 4–9–1 WRSwinburn (2) (lw: s.s: 16th st: a
bhd) ................................................................................................................... 6.15

1211⁶ Deposki (90) (v) *(MRStoute)* 4–8–10 ‡3FNorton (1) (3rd st: wknd over 2f out) ... 4.16

**6/1** Kiveton Kabooz, **13/2** Highbrook (USA), **8/1** Brier Creek (USA), Secret Society, Al Karnak (IRE)(tchd 12/1),
**10/1** Ceal Indigo (IRE), Matador (USA), **14/1** Quick Ransom, Deposki, SPINNING, **16/1** Millionaire's Row,
Westholme (USA), **20/1** Highflying, Castle Courageous, Castoret, **33/1** Kimbers (IRE). CSF **£240.95**, OT
£2,174.89. Tote £16.20: £2.90 £6.50 £1.80 £2.00 (£181.80). Mr Paul Mellon (KINGSCLERE) bred by Paul
Mellon. 16 Rn                                                                     2m 33.70 (2)
SF—66/36/42/44/39/39

---

**2443**   CHARLTON MILL H'CAP (3-Y.O) (0-100) £5692.00 (£1696.00: £808.00: £364.00)
         **5f**                                                                    4-45 (4-48)

870 **Silca-Cisa** (90) *(MRChannon)* 9-3 PatEddery (3) (a.p: led 1f out: hrd rdn: r.o wl) —1

20295 Saddlehome (USA) (76) *(RMWhitaker)* 8-3 WCarson (5) (a.p: ev ch ins fnl f: r.o) ³/₄.2

1871* Bodari (80) (Fav) *(DAWilson)* 8-7 MRoberts (2) (a.p: led over 1f out: sn hdd: r.o) ¹/₂.3

2265* Walk in the Park (91) *(RSimpson)* 8-13 (8x) ‡⁵ATucker (8) (lw: dwlt: hdwy &
n.m.r over 1f out) .............................................................................................. s.h.4

1702⁵ Allthruthenight (IRE) (85) *(LJHolt)* 8-12 JReid (1) (swtg: hdwy over 1f out: r.o wl
ins fnl f) .............................................................................................................. hd.5

1926 Master of Passion (94) *(JMPEustace)* 9-7 LPiggott (7) (a.p: hrd rdn over 1f out:
one pce) ............................................................................................................ 1¹/₂.6

2280⁵ Boy Martin (72) *(MJohnston)* 7-13 DHolland (6) (lw: nvr nr to chal) ................. s.h.7

1535 Nifty Fifty (IRE) (93) *(JBerry)* 9-6 TQuinn (4) (led over 3f) ...................................... 2.8

**5/2** Bodari, **9/2** Allthruthenight (IRE), SILCA-CISA, **11/2** Saddlehome (USA), **7/1** Master of Passion, **8/1** Walk in
the Park, **10/1** Nifty Fifty (IRE), **14/1** Boy Martin. CSF £28.03, CT £68.71. Tote £6.00: £2.20 £1.70 £1.40
(£14.20). Aldridge Racing Limited (UPPER LAMBOURN) bred by E. Aldridge. 8 Rn        57.77 sec (0.17)
SF—80/63/65/70/68/71/48

---

**2444**   E.B.F. FINDON STKS (Mdn 2-Y.O) £6264.00 (£1872.00: £896.00: £408.00)
         **6f**                                                                    5-20 (5-23)

**Liyakah** (USA) (Fav) *(MajorWRHern)* 8-9 WCarson (10) (leggy: a gng wl: led
over 4f out: easily) .............................................................................................. —1

Carbon Steel (IRE) *(BWHills)* 9-0 DHolland (8) (str: a.p: chsd wnr over 1f out: no
imp) ..................................................................................................................... 2¹/₂.2

2223² Garnock Valley *(JBerry)* 9-0 LPiggott (3) (hdwy over 1f out: r.o ins fnl f) .......... 1¹/₂.3

Lamu Lady (IRE) *(PWChapple-Hyam)* 8-9 PaulEddery (2) (scope: a.p: hrd rdn
over 1f out: one pce) ......................................................................................... ³/₄.4

Bonjour *(JHMGosden)* 9-0 SCauthen (5) (leggy: nvr nr to chal) ............................. ¹/₂.5

Bobbie Dee *(DRCElsworth)* 8-9 JWilliams (7) (w'like: scope: nvr nrr) ..................... 3.6

2124 Easy Access (IRE) *(RHannon)* 9-0 PatEddery (6) (b.off hind: led over 1f: eased
whn btn 1f out) .................................................................................................... ³/₄.7

2205³ Classic Image (IRE) *(MMoubarak)* 9-0 LDettori (9) (spd over 4f) ........................ 2¹/₂.8

On Request (IRE) *(IABalding)* 8-9 RCochrane (4) (unf: s.s: a bhd) ........................ hd.9

Pistols At Dawn (USA) *(RHannon)* 9-0 JReid (1) (unf: scope: a bhd) .................. 2¹/₂.10

Knobbleeneeze *(MRChannon)* 9-0 TQuinn (11) (cmpt: bit bkwd: s.s: a wl bhd) 3¹/₂.11

**15/8** LIYAKAH (USA), **4/1** Carbon Steel (IRE), **9/2** Easy Access (IRE), **8/1** Classic Image (IRE)(5/1—9/1), **10/1** Garnock Valley(op 16/1), **11/1** Bonjour(op 6/1), Lamu Lady (IRE)(op 7/1), **14/1** On Request (IRE), **33/1** Ors. CSF £10.21, Tote £3.30: £1.60 £2.50 £1.70 (£8.70). Mr Hamdan Al-Maktoum (LAMBOURN) bred by Foxfield in USA. 11 Rn
1m 12.04 (1.64)
SF—38/33/27/19/22/5

T/Trio: Races 1: £102.00 (24.4) & Race 4: £668.00 (8.1 Tckts). T/Jkpt: Not won; £26,150.75 to Goodwood 30/7/92. T/Plpt: £174.10 (127.65 Tckts). AK

# GOODWOOD (R-H)
## Thursday, July 30th [Good to firm]
Going Allowance: 2m: minus 0.25 sec; Rest: minus 0.15 sec (F)          Wind: almost nil

Stalls: low

**2445**     LANSON CHAMPAGNE VINTAGE STKS (Gp 3) (2-Y.O) £19030.00 (£7125.25: £3425.13: £1494.62)   **7f**
2-30 (2-31)

2017[2] **Maroof (USA)** *(RWArmstrong)* 8-11 WCarson (5) (lw: 5th st: led 1f out: rdn out) —1
1939[3] Humam (IRE) (Fav) *(HThomsonJones)* 9-0 RHills (1) (lw: 2nd st: led 3f out to 1f out: unable qckn) ................................................................................... 1½.2
2208* Shebl (USA) *(MRStoute)* 8-11 SCauthen (10) (3rd st: hrd rdn over 2f out: r.o one pce) ........................................................................................................ 1.3
2321a* Ancestral Dancer *(MBell)* 8-9 MHills (2) (hdwy over 2f out: hrd rdn over 1f out: r.o one pce) ............................................................................................. nk.4
1639[2] Little Too Much (IRE) *(GHarwood)* 8-11 MRoberts (9) (nt clr run over 1f out: nvr nrr) .............................................................................................................. ½.5
2025[2] Woodenville (USA) *(LMCumani)* 8-11 LDettori (7) (6th st: no hdwy fnl 2f) ........ nk.6
1936[4] Majestic Hawk (USA) *(MMoubarak)* 8-11 WRSwinburn (4) (lw: nvr nr to chal) .. nk.7
2177[2] Port Lucaya *(RHannon)* 8-11 PaulEddery (6) (rdn thrght: nt clr run on ins over 1f out: nvr nrr) .......................................................................................... 2.8
1995[2] Known Approach (USA) *(PFICole)* 8-11 TQuinn (8) (4th st: wknd over 2f out) . 3½.9
1832* Persian Revival (FR) *(BAMcMahon)* 8-11 JReid (3) (led over 4f) .................. 1½.10

**4/1** Humam (IRE), **5/1** Ancestral Dancer(7/1—9/2), **7/1** Little Too Much (IRE), Port Lucaya(op 9/2), **8/1** MAROOF (USA), Majestic Hawk (USA), **10/1** Shebl (USA), Woodenville (USA), **12/1** Known Approach (USA), **25/1** Persian Revival (FR). CSF £36.22, Tote £9.10: £2.40 £1.70 £3.50 (£16.60). Mr Hamdan Al-Maktoum (NEWMARKET) bred by Shadwell Farm Inc & Shadwell Estate Co.Ltd in USA. 10 Rn
1m 25.97 (0.02 under 2y best: 1.27)
SF—62/60/54/51/51/50

**2446**     GOODWOOD CUP (Stks) (Gp 3)    £30204.00 (£11208.20: £5304.10: £2223.70)
**2m**
3-10 (3-11)

1821a[6] **Further Flight (114)** *(BWHills)* 6-9-5 MHills (9) (hdwy 3f out: hrd rdn over 1f out: led last strides) .................................................................................... —1
1697* Witness Box (USA) **(100)** *(JHMGosden)* 5-9-0 SCauthen (2) (2nd st: led 3f out: hrd rdn over 2f out: hdd last strides) ................................................. s.h.2
2096a[6] Landowner (IRE) **(104)** *(JHMGosden)* 3-8-3 WCarson (8) (3rd st: hrd rdn & ev ch over 1f out: unable qckn) .................................................................... 1½.3
1468[2] Arcadian Heights (112) (Jt-Fav) *(GWragg)* 4-9-3 WRSwinburn (10) (lw: rdn over 4f out: gd hdwy over 1f out: r.o wl ins fnl f) ...................................... 3½.4
1929[2] Luchiroverte (IRE) **(111)** (Jt-Fav) *(CEBrittain)* 4-9-0 MRoberts (7) (4th st: hrd rdn over 2f out: wknd fnl f) ..................................................................... 2½.5
Elsurimo (GER) *(BrunoSchuetz,Germany)* 5-9-7 MRimmer (11) (nvr nr to chal) . 2.6
1453* Duke of Paducah (USA) **(108)** *(GHarwood)* 5-9-0 JReid (5) (no hdwy fnl 3f) .... nk.7
2027* Tyrone Bridge (104) *(MCPipe)* 6-9-3 LPiggott (3) (rdn over 6f out: 6th st: wknd over 3f out) ....................................................................................... hd.8
981[3] Le Corsaire (USA) **(100)** *(LMCumani)* 4-9-0 LDettori (6) (bhd fnl 2f) ............... 1½.9
1710[3] Tetradonna (IRE) *(RHannon)* 4-8-11 PaulEddery (4) (led 13f) ......................... 1.10
2027[3] Parting Moment (USA) **(102)** *(IABalding)* 5-9-5 RCochrane (4) (lw: chsd ldr over 14f out til over 7f out: 5th st: wknd 3f out) .......................... 8.11
*Stewards Enquiry: Cauthen suspended 8-11/8/92 (excessive use of whip).*

**9/2** Arcadian Heights, Luchiroverte (IRE), **5/1** Witness Box (USA), Landowner (IRE), **7/1** FURTHER FLIGHT, **10/1** Tyrone Bridge(7/1—11/1), **12/1** Le Corsaire (USA), **16/1** Duke of Paducah (USA), **25/1** Tetradonna (IRE), **33/1** Parting Moment (USA), **50/1** Elsurimo (GER). CSF £37.39, Tote £9.90: £2.80 £2.00 £1.60 (£28.30). Mr S. Wingfield Digby (LAMBOURN) bred by S. Wingfield Digby. 11 Rn
3m 24.04 (1.56 under best: U2.56)
SF—91/85/72/82/76/81

**2447**  SCHWEPPES GOLDEN MILE (H'cap) (0-115) £66235.00 (£19930.00: £9640.00: £4495.00) **1m**  (Weights raised 6 lb)  3-45 (3-50)

1941* **Little Bean (84)** *(GWragg)* 3–8-2 (5x) MHills (8) (15th st: hdwy over 2f out: led over 1f out: r.o wl) .................................................. —1

1877² **Mudaffar (IRE) (87)** *(RWArmstrong)* 4–8-13 LPiggott (16) (17th st: gd hdwy over 1f out: r.o wl ins fnl f) .................................................. 2.2

2183* **Polonez Prima (76)** *(JEBanks)* 5–7-11 ‡5JWeaver (11) (swtg: 12th st: hdwy over 2f out: hrd rdn over 1f out: r.o) .................................................. s.h.3

2341⁶ **Camden's Ransom (USA) (71)** *(DRCElsworth)* 5–7-6(3) ‡5BDoyle (15) (20th st: hrd rdn & hdwy over 1f out: r.o) .................................................. 1½.4

1711⁴ **Band on the Run (98)** *(BAMcMahon)* 5–9-10 TQuinn (21) (lw: 2nd st: hrd rdn over 1f out: unable qckn) .................................................. hd.5

1035* **Magnified (USA) (96)** *(BWHills)* 3–9-0 PaulEddery (10) (mid div whn hmpd 7f out: 16th st: hrd hdwy over 2f out: one pce) .................................................. hd.6

1943⁴ **Superoo (74)** *(JSutcliffe)* 6–8-0 NAdams (7) (rdn whn n.m.r over 1f out: 14th st: hdwy & n.m.r over 1f out: r.o one pce) .................................................. 3.7

1943³ **Knight of Mercy (98)** *(RHannon)* 6–9-10 BRaymond (13) (21st: gd hdwy over 1f out: r.o) .................................................. nk.8

1943 **Field of Honour (81)** *(LMCumani)* 4–8-7 LDettori (14) (6th st: hrd rdn over 1f out: wknd fnl f) .................................................. ½.9

1114² **Jalmusique (93)** *(MHEasterby)* 6–9-5 MBirch (4) (hrd rdn over 2f out: wknd over 1f out) .................................................. 1½.10

1941² **Efharisto (87)** *(Fav)* *(CEBrittain)* 3–8-5 MRoberts (5) (rdn 5f out: 19th st: nvr nrr) nk.12

1869 **Marine Diver (74)** *(BRMillman)* 6–8-0 AMackay (6) (13th st: a mid div) .................................................. 2½.13

1712³ **Main Bid (IRE) (95)** *(MMoubarak)* 3–8-13 WCarson (9) (lw: 18th st: nvr nrr) ..... hd.14

1476 **Set Table (USA) (82)** *(JHMGosden)* 3–8-0 AMcGlone (3) (10th st: a mid div) 1½.15

1460 **Mizaaya (97)** *(MRStoute)* 3–9-1 WRSwinburn (19) (lw: 8th st: hrd rdn over 2f out: nt clr run & eased over 1f out) .................................................. 1½.16

1696⁶ **Parliament Piece (95) (v)** *(RMWhitaker)* 6–9-7 JReid (17) (lw: 7th st: wkng whn bdly hmpd 1f out) .................................................. 1½.17

936* **Saafend (70)** *(JSutcliffe)* 4–7-5 ‡5DHarrison (18) (4th st: wknd over 2f out) .................................................. 3.18

1877 **Daswaki (CAN) (84)** *(RHannon)* 4–8-10 BRouse (12) (11th st: bhd fnl 2f) .................................................. 3½.19

1476 **Ecliptic (IRE) (84)** *(PWChapple-Hyam)* 3–7-13 ‡3FNorton (1) (5th st: wknd over 2f out) .................................................. nk.20

1846² **Sagebrush Roller (77)** *(JWWatts)* 4–8-3 DHolland (20) (3rd st: wknd over 2f out) 8.21

1930 **Heart of Darkness (94) (v)** *(IABalding)* 4–9-6 RCochrane (2) (led over 6f: fin 11th, nk: disq: plcd last) .................................................. 0

*Stewards Enquiry: Heart Of Darkness disq. (interference to Magnified (USA) 7f out). Cochrane suspended 8-11/8/92 (care*

**13/2** Efharisto, **9/1** LITTLE BEAN, **10/1** Mudaffar (IRE), Main Bid (IRE), Polonez Prima, **11/1** Magnified (USA)(8/1—12/1), **12/1** Field of Honour, **14/1** Band on the Run, **16/1** Camden's Ransom (USA), Saafend, **20/1** Jalmusique, Heart of Darkness, Knight of Mercy, **25/1** Ecliptic (IRE), Superoo, Daswaki (CAN), Parliament Piece, Mizaaya, **33/1** Ors. CSF £88.05, CT £838.72. Tote £8.00: £2.00 £2.40 £2.40 £3.70 (£40.00). Sir Philip Oppenheimer (NEWMARKET) bred by Hascombe and Valiant Studs. 21 Rn  1m 38.66 (1.06)
SF—54/59/42/32/63/52

**2448**  KING GEORGE STKS (Gp 3)  £17140.00 (£6363.75: £3014.38: £1266.87)  **5f**  4-15 (4-24)

1350a* **Freddie Lloyd (USA) (109)** *(NACallaghan)* 3–9-0 JReid (12) (mde virtually all: drvn out) .................................................. —1

1475 **Blyton Lad (110)** *(MJCamacho)* 6–9-0 SWebster (5) (hld up: hrd rdn over 2f out: r.o ins fnl f) .................................................. nk.2

1994² **Artistic Reef (92)** *(GHEden)* 3–8-9 AMunro (7) (a.p: hrd rdn over 1f out: r.o ins fnl f) .................................................. s.h.3

1350a⁴ **Title Roll (IRE)** *(TStack,Ireland)* 4–9-2 MRoberts (6) (lw: hdwy over 1f out: r.o wl ins fnl f) .................................................. 1½.4

871² **Harvest Girl (IRE) (101)** *(GAPritchard-Gordon)* 3–8-6 LDettori (9) (hdwy over 1f out: r.o ins fnl f) .................................................. 1.5

1875 **Farfelu (97) (bl)** *(WRMuir)* 5–9-0 SWhitworth (8) (nvr nr to chal) .................................................. 2.6

2169⁶ **Central City (106) (bl)** *(RHannon)* 3–8-6 BRaymond (3) (gd spd over 3f) .................................................. 1½.7

1942⁵ **Paris House (118)** *(Fav)* *(JBerry)* 3–9-3 JCarroll (2) (lw: gd spd over 3f) .................................................. hd.8

1707* **Western Approach (USA) (101)** *(JHMGosden)* 3–8-6 PaulEddery (1) (gd spd over 3f) .................................................. 1.9

1688⁴ **El Yasaf (IRE) (96)** *(MCPipe)* 4–9-0 SCauthen (10) (outpcd) .................................................. 2.10

740a² **Whittingham (IRE) (v)** *(OvidioPessi,Italy)* 3–8-9 WCarson (11) (lw: outpcd) ..... ½.11

**3/1** Paris House, **7/2** Western Approach (USA), **5/1** FREDDIE LLOYD (USA), **6/1** Central City, **9/1** Blyton Lad, **14/1** Title Roll (IRE)(10/1—16/1), **16/1** El Yasaf (IRE), **20/1** Whittingham (IRE), **25/1** Farfelu, Harvest Girl (IRE), **33/1** Artistic Reef. CSF £44.08, Tote £5.00: £1.40 £3.10 £6.40 (£31.30). Mr Michael Hill (NEWMARKET) bred by Jerry M. Cutrona, Snr in USA. 11 Rn  57.88 sec (0.28)
SF—80/79/73/74/60/60

**2449**    CITROEN XM H'CAP (3-Y.O) (0-100) £8090.00 (£2420.00: £1160.00: £530.00)
            7f                                                              4-45 (4-55)
                                   (Weights raised 2 lb)

1773* **Rocky Waters (USA) (88)** (GLewis) 9-5 BRouse (11) (mde all: clr over 1f out:
            rdn out) ...................................................................... —1
1941  Shati (IRE) **(89)** (HThomsonJones) 9-6 RHills (4) (lw: 6th st: hrd rdn over 1f out:
            r.o ins fnl f) ................................................................ 1½.2
1737* Trooping (IRE) **(80)** (GHarwood) 8-11 AClark (13) (nt clr run over 2f out: hdwy
            over 1f out: r.o ins fnl f) .................................................. ¾.3
1707³ High Sevens **(90)** (HCandy) 9-7 CRutter (12) (5th st: hrd rdn over 1f out: r.o ins
            fnl f) ...................................................................... hd.4
2029  La Dama Bonita (USA) **(82)** (DWPArbuthnot) 8-13 TQuinn (15) (hdwy wl over 1f
            out: r.o) ................................................................... nk.5
2196* Super Serenade **(74)** (GBBalding) 8-5 AMunro (7) (hdwy 2f out: hrd rdn over 1f
            out: one pce) .............................................................. 3.6
1806⁶ Thewaari (USA) **(69)** (AAScott) 7-9 ‡5DHarrison (10) (lw: hdwy over 1f out: one
            pce fnl f) ................................................................. 1½.7
1871⁶ Hi-Tech Honda (IRE) **(68)** (CEBrittain) 7-13 MRoberts (1) (hrd rdn & no hdwy fnl
            2f) ........................................................................ ½.8
2275² Fen Dance (IRE) **(79)** (PJMakin) 8-10 WRSwinburn (18) (bhd whn hmpd 3f out:
            nvr nrr) ................................................................... 2½.9
1525³ Threepence **(89)** (JBerry) 9-6 JCarroll (9) (nvr nrr) ........................ 1.10
1624⁴ Greetland Folly **(80)** (RMWhitaker) 8-11 BRaymond (14) (2nd st: wknd over 1f
            out) ...................................................................... 1½.11
1474  The Old Chapel **(89)** (BAMcMahon) 9-6 MHills (2) (nvr nrr) .................. 1.12
      Shaping Up (USA) **(90)** (IABalding) 9-7 JReid (8) (nvr nrr) ................. 1½.13
2079⁴ Kentucky Starlet (USA) **(62)** (RHannon) 7-7 NCarlisle (16) (a bhd) ......... 3½.14
2337⁴ Sir Boudle (IRE) **(83)** (v) (CRNelson) 9-0 SCauthen (5) (bhd fnl 2f) ....... nk.15
658* Claybank (USA) **(90)** (BWHills) 9-7 DHolland (17) (a bhd) .................. 2½.16
2188  Castilian Queen (USA) **(80)** (Fav) (JHMGosden) 8-11 WCarson (6) (3rd st:
            wknd over 2f out) ......................................................... hd.17
2293* Amadeus Aes **(83)** (v) (DMorris) 9-0 (6x) RCochrane (3) (4th st: wknd over 2f
            out) ...................................................................... 1½.18
                    LONG HANDICAP: Kentucky Starlet (USA) 7-4.

**9/2** Castilian Queen (USA), **6/1** Fen Dance (IRE), **9/1** Trooping (IRE), Sir Boudle (IRE), **12/1** ROCKY WATERS
(USA)(op 8/1), **14/1** Amadeus Aes, La Dama Bonita (USA), Shati (IRE), Hi-Tech Honda (IRE), **16/1** Super
Serenade, Thewaari (USA), Claybank (USA), High Sevens, **25/1** Kentucky Starlet (USA), Threepence, Shaping Up
(USA), Greetland Folly, **33/1** The Old Chapel. CSF £157.20, CT £1,453.61. Tote £13.60: £2.70 £6.70 £2.80
£4.30 (£152.60). Mr K. Higson (EPSOM) bred by Dan C. Pitts in USA. 18 Rn          1m 26.70 (2)
                                                                               SF—60/56/45/54/45/28

**2450**    LAVANT NURSERY  £6212.00 (£1856.00: £888.00: £404.00)   **6f**   5-20 (5-21)
                                   (Weights raised 5 lb)

2138* **Hallorina** (WGRWightman) 7-12 GBardwell (8) (mde virtually all: rdn out) .......... —1
1913³ Simply Finesse (RAkehurst) 8-9 SCauthen (3) (a.p: hrd rdn over 1f out: unable
            qckn) ..................................................................... 2.2
2171² Brockton Dancer (Fav) (RHannon) 8-13 MRoberts (2) (b.hind: hdwy 3f out: hrd
            rdn over 1f out: one pce) ................................................. hd.3
2360⁴ Two Moves in Front (IRE) (JBerry) 9-2 ‡5JWeaver (7) (lw: hdwy over 2f out: hrd
            rdn over 1f out: one pce) ................................................. 7.4
1769³ Walnut Burl (IRE) (LJHolt) 8-6 AMunro (5) (nvr nr to chal) ................... 4.5
2167  Soleil Rayon (IRE) (bl) (MMcCormack) 7-12 ‡7AGarth (1) (lw: bhd fnl 3f) ..... 1½.6
2306² Superensis (bl) (WRMuir) 7-11 JQuinn (6) (gd spd over 3f) ................... 1½.7
2008⁴ Burishki (bl) (GAPritchard-Gordon) 7-8 NCarlisle (4) (hdwy over 2f out: wknd
            over 1f out) .............................................................. 15.8

**5/2** Brockton Dancer, **4/1** HALLORINA, **5/1** Simply Finesse, **8/1** Walnut Burl (IRE), Soleil Rayon (IRE), Burishki,
**10/1** Ors. CSF £22.79, CT £53.71. Tote £3.70: £1.40 £1.40 £1.30 (£10.20). Mrs J. A. Thomson (UPHAM) bred
by W. G. R. Wightman and Mrs J. A. Thomson. 8 Rn                                1m 11.91 (1.51)
                                                                               SF—36/39/42/17/–/–

**2451**    LEVY H'CAP (0-90) £6316.00 (£1888.00: £904.00: £412.00)   **1½m**   5-50 (5-59)

2220⁶ **Daru (USA) (77)** (v) (JHMGosden) 3–8-13 SCauthen (6) (gd hdwy over 1f out:
            str run fnl f: led last strides) ........................................... —1
1722* Storm Crossing (USA) **(90)** (GHarwood) 3–9-12 PaulEddery (3) (lw: swtchd rt &
            hdwy over 1f out: ev ch wl ins fnl f: r.o) ................................. ½.2
2086² Western Dynasty **(70)** (MJRyan) 3–9-6 RCochrane (5) (3rd st: led over 1f out:
            hrd rdn: hdd last strides) ................................................. s.h.3
2101⁴ Springs Welcome **(69)** (CACyzer) 6–9-3 DBiggs (12) (rdn over 3f out: gd hdwy
            over 1f out: r.o wl ins fnl f) ............................................ ¾.4

Legion of Honour (73) *(WJarvis)* 4–9–7 AMunro (1) (4th st: hrd rdn & ev ch 1f
out: r.o) .................................................................................................. nk.5
2178 Simply-H (IRE) (79) *(MBell)* 3–9–1 MHills (10) (6th st: ev ch ins fnl f: wknd nr fin) .. nk.6
1768* Mahfil (71) (Fav) *(RAkehurst)* 4–9–5 MRoberts (8) (hdwy over 2f out: one pce fnl
f) ......................................................................................................... 1.7
2128⁵ Beam Me Up Scotty (IRE) (57) *(PMitchell)* 3–7–7 NCarlisle (9) (led over 10f) ...... 3.8
2296* Resplendent (76) *(NCWright)* 3–8–12 (6x) BRaymond (7) (5th st: wknd 2f out) 2¹/₂.9
1656* Alessandrina (USA) (79) *(MRStoute)* 3–9–1 WRSwinburn (4) (2nd st: wknd over
2f out) .............................................................................................. 10.10
2172 Shahdjat (IRE) (79) *(KCBailey)* 4–9–13 MPerrett (11) (lw: bhd fnl 4f) ............... 10.11
LONG HANDICAP: Beam Me Up Scotty (IRE) 6-11.
*1587³ El Volador (8/1) Withdrawn (lame at s) : not under orders — Rule 4 applies*

**11/4** Mahfil, **9/2** Storm Crossing (USA), **6/1** Resplendent, **15/2** Alessandrina (USA), **9/1** Western Dynasty, **12/1**
DARU (USA)(8/1—14/1), **14/1** Simply-H (IRE), Legion of Honour, Springs Welcome, **50/1** Beam Me Up Scotty
(IRE), **66/1** Shahdjat (IRE). CSF £52.33, CT £348.81. Tote £15.00: £3.60 £1.80 £2.30 (£37.60). Sheikh
Mohammed (NEWMARKET) bred by Albert G. Clay & Charlotte Clay Buxton in USA. 11 Rn  2m 38.51 (6.81)
SF—13/25/16/13/16/9

T/Trio: Race 2: £50.60 (50.3 Tckts), Race 3: £123.40 (34.3 Tckts), Race 4: £635.90 (3 Tckts) & Race 5:
£863.70 (3.1 Tckts). T/Jkpt: Not won; £37,337.64 to Goodwood 31/7/92. T/Plpt: £352.10 (67.3 Tckts).  AK

# GOODWOOD (R-H)
## Friday, July 31st [Good to firm, Firm patches]
Going Allowance: 5f: minus 0.25 sec; rest: minus 0.10 sec (F)                    Wind: almost nil

Stalls: low

**2452**    PHILIP CORNES MOLECOMB STKS (Gp 3) (2-Y.O) £20040.00 (£7497.00: £3598.50:
£1564.50)   **5f**                                                    2-30 (2-31)

2052* Millyant *(RGuest)* 8-7 MRoberts (8) (b.hind: chsd ldr: led ins fnl f: pushed out) . —1
1215² Palacegate Episode (IRE) *(JBerry)* 8-7 AMunro (11) (led: hrd rdn ins fnl f: r.o) ....
hdd ins fnl f: r.o) ........................................................................... 1.2
1927⁴ Niche (Fav) *(RHannon)* 8-12 LPiggott (7) (lw: a.p: hrd rdn over 1f out: r.o) ......... 2.3
Preponderance (IRE) *(JGBurns,Ireland)* 8-7 JReid (10) (w'like: carried rt s:
hdwy 3f out: hrd rdn over 1f out: unable qckn) ................................. ³/₄.4
1913* Kamaatera (IRE) *(AAScott)* 8-12 WRSwinburn (5) (hdwy 2f out: hrd rdn over 1f
out: nvr nrr) ................................................................................... ¹/₂.5
1927 Anonymous *(CEBrittain)* 8-7 LDettori (2) (outpcd: nvr nrr) ................................. 2.6
1461 Hamsah (IRE) *(DRCElsworth)* 8-7 WCarson (9) (lw: swvd rt s: hdwy over 2f out:
hrd rdn over 1f out: sn wknd) ........................................................... 2.7
2030² Sabre Rattler (bl) *(JBerry)* 8-12 JCarroll (1) (lw: bhd fnl 2f) .......................... 1¹/₂.8
1713² Greenlet (IRE) *(MRStoute)* 8-7 PatEddery (3) (a bhd) ................................. 2¹/₂.9
2171⁶ Perfect Passion *(JJBridger)* 8-7 SWhitworth (6) (prom 3f) ............................ ¹/₂.10
1868⁵ Marchwell Lad *(MRChannon)* 8-12 TQuinn (4) (bhd fnl 2f) .......................... 3¹/₂.11

**6/4** Niche, **9/2** MILLYANT, **9/1** Greenlet (IRE)(op 6/1), Preponderance (IRE), **12/1** Kamaatera (IRE), Sabre
Rattler, **14/1** Marchwell Lad, Hamsah (IRE), Palacegate Episode (IRE)(20/1—25/1), **33/1** Anonymous, **100/1**
Perfect Passion. CSF £57.52, Tote £6.40: £1.70 £3.90 £1.30 (£81.50). Bradmill Ltd (NEWMARKET) bred by Jim
and Mrs Strange. 11 Rn                                                    57.58 sec (0.02)
SF—68/64/61/53/56/43

**2453**    LESLIE AND GODWIN SPITFIRE H'CAP (3-Y.O) (0-115) £30575.00 (£9200.00:
£4450.00: £2075.00)   **1¼m**                                        3-10 (3-11)

1917* **Party Cited (USA) (101)** *(DRCElsworth)* 9-4 JWilliams (14) (lw: 8th st: led ins
fnl f: r.o wl) .................................................................................... —1
2028 Wild Fire (82) (Jt-Fav) *(GWragg)* 7-13 MRoberts (1) (10th st: gd hdwy 2f out:
hrd rdn ins fnl f: r.o wl) ................................................................... hd.2
2191⁶ Mutabahi (CAN) (85) *(RWArmstrong)* 8-2 WCarson (5) (18th st: hrd rdn & gd
hdwy over 1f out: r.o wl ins fnl f) ..................................................... s.h.3
1869 In the Picture (IRE) (82) *(RHannon)* 7-13 RHills (13) (13th st: hdwy whn nt clr
run on ins over 2f out & over 1f out: r.o wl) ...................................... 1¹/₂.4
1955* Scrutineer (USA) (90) (Jt-Fav) *(JHMGosden)* 8-7 SCauthen (12) (led: hrd rdn
wl over 1f out: hdd ins fnl f: unable qckn) ........................................ nk.5
1831³ Source of Light (95) *(RCharlton)* 8-12 PatEddery (17) (s.s: 17th st: gd hdwy
over 1f out: one pce fnl f) ................................................................ ³/₄.6
1934* Duke of Eurolink (92) *(LMCumani)* 8-9 LDettori (16) (dwlt: hdwy over 4f out: 9th
st: n.m.r over 2f out: swtched lft over 1f out: r.o) .............................. hd.7

1934³ Scandalmonger (USA) **(79)** *(BWHills)* 7-5 ‡⁵DHarrison (11) (15th st: hrd rdn over 2f out: hdwy over 1f out: nvr nrr) .................................. ½.8

King's Loch (IRE) **(102)** *(HRACecil)* 9-5 WRyan (6) (h.d.w: 4th st: rdn over 2f out: wknd over 1f out) ................................................................ hd.9

1997² Let's Get Lost **(77)** *(WJHaggas)* 7-8 JQuinn (15) (b.nr fore: b.off hind: 7th st: wkng whn hmpd over 1f out) ................................................ 2½.10

2018² Tissisat (USA) **(85)** *(IABalding)* 8-2 TQuinn (10) (lw: 3rd st: wknd wl over 1f out) 1.11

1934⁴ Bayaireg (USA) **(84)** *(AAScott)* 8-1 JFortune (8) (5th st: rdn over 2f out: wknd over 1f out) ............................................................ 1.12

2191 The Power of One **(77)** *(RSimpson)* 7-8⁽¹⁾ AMackay (9) (lw: 6th st: wknd over 2f out) ........................................................... 4.13

2182² Misty View **(76)** *(MAJarvis)* 7-0 ‡⁷CHawksley (3) (14th st: a bhd) ............. 1½.14

1928 Swallowcliffe **(83)** *(PTWalwyn)* 8-0 AMunro (4) (11th st: bhd fnl 2f) ......... ½.15

1916 Bid for Six (USA) **(78)** *(RHannon)* 7-9 NAdams (7) (16th st: a bhd) ........... ¾.16

1533 Alto Jane **(84)** *(GHarwood)* 8-1 PaulEddery (2) (12th st: bhd fnl 3f) ......... ¾.17

1613³ Artic Tracker (USA) **(104)** *(CRNelson)* 9-7 WRSwinburn (18) (lw: 2nd st: wknd over 2f out) .................................................................. 7.18

LONG HANDICAP: The Power of One 7-6, Misty View 7-3.

**6/1** Wild Fire, Scrutineer (USA), **7/1** Tissisat (USA), Scandalmonger (USA), Duke of Eurolink, **11/1** Source of Light, **12/1** PARTY CITED (USA), Let's Get Lost, Mutabahi (CAN), **14/1** Bayaireg (USA), **16/1** In the Picture (IRE), **25/1** King's Loch (IRE), **33/1** Ors. CSF £77.19, CT £804.33. Tote £15.80: £2.80 £1.70 £3.20 £3.60 (£97.40). Mr Raymond Tooth (WHITSBURY) bred by Rogers Trust in USA. 18 Rn                     2m 7.54 (2.54)

SF—69/49/51/45/52/55

---

### 2454

SCHRODERS GLORIOUS STKS (listed race)   £25570.00 (£7660.00: £3680.00: £1690.00)   1½m                                                                3-45 (3-47)

2442* **Spinning (101)** *(IABalding)* 5-9-2 RCochrane (3) (lw: 6th st: led over 1f out: pushed out) ............................................................ —1

1972² Jahafil **(113)** (Fav) *(MajorWRHern)* 4-9-7 WCarson (6) (lw: led over 10f: unable qckn) .................................................................. 1½.2

1710⁵ Surrealist (IRE) **(107)** *(BWHills)* 4-9-7 JReid (1) (4th st: rdn over 2f out: one pce) 2.3

2181² Alhamad **(98)** *(HRACecil)* 3-8-4 PatEddery (2) (3rd st: hrd rdn & ev ch over 2f out: one pce) ................................................... 3½.4

2095a⁵ Fair Average **(106)** *(HCandy)* 4-9-2 WNewnes (5) (5th st: wknd over 2f out) .. 2.5

1972⁴ Torchon **(103)** *(GWragg)* 4-9-7 WRSwinburn (4) (lw: 2nd st: wknd 3f out) ....... 12.6

**5/4** Jahafil, **7/2** Alhamad, SPINNING, **10/1** Fair Average, Surrealist (IRE), **14/1** Torchon. CSF £8.13, Tote £4.40: £2.00 £1.10 (£3.00). Mr Paul Mellon (KINGSCLERE) bred by Paul Mellon. 6 Rn                     2m 34.66 (2.96)

SF—60/62/58/34/42/23

---

### 2455

SEEBOARD H'CAP (3-Y.O) (0-110)   £10770.00 (£3210.00: £1530.00: £690.00)   1¾m                                                                4-15 (4-19)

(Weights raised 1 lb)

1834² **Garden District (80)** *(RCharlton)* 8-12 PatEddery (1) (led 8f out: drvn out) ........ —1

1953* Anna of Saxony **(88)** (Fav) *(JHMGosden)* 9-6 SCauthen (3) (swtg: 2nd st: hrd rdn & ev ch fnl 2f: r.o wl) ................................................. hd.2

1967² Three Wells **(89)** *(JLDunlop)* 9-7 WCarson (4) (hdwy on ins over 2f out: n.m.r ins fnl f: r.o) .................................................... 2.3

1302³ Faugeron **(86)** *(GWragg)* 9-4 WRSwinburn (2) (hdwy over 2f out: one pce fnl f) 2.4

2134* Miss Pin Up **(66)** *(PatMitchell)* 7-12 DBiggs (5) (lw: 4th st: rdn over 2f out: one pce) ................................................................ 3.5

2302² Super Serena (IRE) **(88)** *(RSimpson)* 9-6 WRyan (8) (3rd st: wknd over 2f out) .. 2.6

1882⁶ Mr Poppleton **(64)** *(DWPArbuthnot)* 7-5⁽³⁾ ‡⁵DHarrison (7) (lw: 6th st: hrd rdn & no hdwy fnl 2f) ................................................ s.h.7

1556⁴ Nina's Chocolates (USA) **(76)** *(CEBrittain)* 8-8 MRoberts (9) (led 6f) ............... 15.8

2116* Dime Bag **(73)** *(BWHills)* 8-5 DLee (6) (5th st: wknd over 3f out) ................... 1½.9

LONG HANDICAP: Mr Poppleton 7-1.

**10/11** Anna of Saxony, **5/1** GARDEN DISTRICT, **11/2** Miss Pin Up, **10/1** Three Wells, **11/1** Faugeron, **16/1** Dime Bag, **25/1** Nina's Chocolates (USA), **33/1** Ors. CSF £9.65, CT £38.48. Tote £5.20: £1.60 £1.20 £3.00 (£4.10). Mr K. Abdulla (BECKHAMPTON) bred by Sir Gordon Brunton. 9 Rn                     3m 2.70 (3.70)

SF—47/54/51/44/18/36

---

### 2456

E.B.F. SELSEY STKS (Mdn 2-Y.O.C & G)   £6212.00 (£1856.00: £888.00: £404.00)   7f                                                                4-45 (4-50)

**Tenby** (Fav) *(HRACecil)* 9-0 PatEddery (8) (str: 3rd st: rdn to ld over 2f out: clr over 1f out: easily) ................................................. —1

2000³ Pistol (IRE) *(PFICole)* 9-0 TQuinn (11) (4th st: rdn over 2f out: unable qckn) ...... 6.2
　Lt Welsh (USA) *(IABalding)* 9-0 RCochrane (10) (leggy: unf: hdwy on ins over 2f
　out: nt clr run over 1f out: r.o wl: bttr for r) .................................................. 2.3
2034⁵ Aberdeen Heather *(DRCElsworth)* 9-0 JWilliams (4) (lw: hdwy over 1f out: r.o wl
　ins fnl f) ............................................................................................ s.h.4
1873⁴ Friendly Brave (USA) *(WCarter)* 9-0 JCarroll (9) (lw: 2nd st: hrd rdn over 2f out:
　edgd rt wl over 1f out: wknd ins fnl f) .................................................... 1¹/₂.5
2034⁴ Southern Memories (IRE) *(RHannon)* 9-0 MRoberts (5) (led over 4f: 3rd & btn
　whn hmpd on ins wl over 1f out) ............................................................ 1¹/₂.6
2167⁴ Sea Baron *(MBlanshard)* 9-0 LDettori (7) (6th st: wknd wl over 1f out) ............... 2.7
1709⁴ Safir (USA) *(JLDunlop)* 9-0 WCarson (12) (5th st: wknd wl over 1f out) ........... 1¹/₂.8
　654⁶ Never so Lost *(BWHills)* 9-0 DHolland (2) (bhd fnl 2f) ...................................... ³/₄.9
　Mahogany Light (USA) *(GHarwood)* 9-0 SCauthen (1) (str: scope: a bhd) ...... hd.10
　Night Edition *(SDow)* 9-0 WRyan (3) (scope: a bhd) ...................................... s.h.11

**4/6** TENBY(op 11/10), **9/1** Lt Welsh (USA)(op 6/1), Mahogany Light (USA)(op 4/1), Safir (USA), **10/1** Southern
Memories (IRE)(op 6/1), Friendly Brave (USA), **14/1** Pistol (IRE), Never so Lost, **20/1** Sea Baron, **33/1** Ors. CSF
£13.29, Tote £2.00: £1.30 £3.10 £2.50 (£21.50). Mr K. Abdulla (NEWMARKET) bred by Juddmonte Farms. 11
Rn 　　　　　　　　　　　　　　　　　　　　　　　　　　　　　　　　　　　　　1m 26.35 (1.65)
　　　　　　　　　　　　　　　　　　　　　　　　　　　　　　　　　　　　　SF—65/47/41/40/35/30

---

**2457**　CHICHESTER CITY H'CAP (0-100) £7635.00 (£2280.00: £1090.00: £495.00)
　　　　1m 1f 　　　　　　　　　　　　　　　　　　　　　　　　　　　　5-20 (5-20)

1947* Neptune's Pet (75) (Fav) *(GLewis)* 4-8-8 JReid (2) (lw: 3rd st: led over 1f out:
　hung rt: pushed out) ............................................................................. —1
1755⁴ Talent (USA) (82) (v) *(LordHuntingdon)* 4-9-1 AMunro (4) (led over 7f: unable
　qckn) ............................................................................................... 3¹/₂.2
2341⁴ Pay Homage (95) *(IABalding)* 4-10-0 RCochrane (3) (5th st: nt olr run on ins
　over 1f out & ins fnl f: nt rcvr) .............................................................. 2.3
2347 Danzarin (IRE) (76) *(RHannon)* 4-8-9 BRouse (1) (4th st: hrd rdn 3f out: one
　pce) ................................................................................................. ¹/₂.4
1132³ Gueca Solo (81) *(HRACecil)* 4-9-0 WRyan (5) (lw: 2nd st: ev ch over 2f out:
　wknd fnl f) ....................................................................................... 1¹/₂.5

**15/8** NEPTUNE'S PET, **100/30** Pay Homage, **4/1** Talent (USA), Gueca Solo, **9/1** Danzarin (IRE). CSF £8.56, Tote
£2.20: £1.40 £1.60 (£3.20). K. B. Symonds and Partners (EPSOM) bred by D. G. Mason. 5 Rn
　　　　　　　　　　　　　　　　　　　　　　　　　　　　　　　　1m 54.36 (0.15 under best; 3.66)
　　　　　　　　　　　　　　　　　　　　　　　　　　　　　　　　SF—25/21/28/7/7

---

**2458**　CITROEN ZX APP'CE H'CAP (0-90) £6212.00 (£1856.00: £888.00: £404.00)
　　　　7f 　　　　　　　　　　　　　　　　　　　　　　　　　　　　　5-50 (5-51)

2032 **Belfort Ruler (60)** *(BGubby)* 5-7-9 ‡⁴CAvery (7) (5th st: hrd rdn over 1f out: led
　ins fnl f: r.o wl) ................................................................................... —1
2476* Helios (73) *(RSimpson)* 4-8-9 (6x) ‡³ATucker (3) (3rd st: led over 3f out tl ins fnl
　f: r.o wl) ........................................................................................... hd.2
2227* Blue Topaze (65) (Fav) *(RJHolder)* 4-7-11 (6x) ‡⁷SDrowne (10) (hmpd over 5f
　out: hrd rdn & hdwy over 2f out: r.o) ...................................................... 3¹/₂.3
2304⁴ Hamadryad (IRE) (77) *(WCarter)* 4-8-13 ‡³NGwilliams (9) (b.off fore: hrd rdn &
　hdwy 2f out: r.o) ............................................................................... nk.4
　2013 Invocation (72) *(AMoore)* 5-8-11 RPerham (11) (b.nr hind: led over 4f out tl
　over 3f out: wknd fnl f) ........................................................................ 2.5
2127³ Bold Habit (88) *(BBeasley)* 7-9-13 GHusband (2) (lw: nvr nr to chal) ................. 3.6
2476² Profit a Prendre (56) *(DAWilson)* 8-7-2 (6x) ‡⁷SharonMillard (8) (b: 4th st: rdr
　lost iron over 2f out: wknd over 1f out) .................................................. 1¹/₂.7
2268² Across the Bay (74) (v) *(SDow)* 5-8-6 ‡⁷AMartinez (5) (6th st: wknd over 3f out) 2¹/₂.8
1806² Eternal Flame (64) *(JWHills)* 4-8-3 DHarrison (6) (a bhd) .................................. 1.9
2198 Pigalle Wonder (54) *(RJO'Sullivan)* 4-7-3 ‡⁴CHawksley (1) (bhd fnl 3f) .......... 3¹/₂.10
2126 Caroles Express (72) *(RAkehurst)* 4-8-4 ‡⁷LCarter (4) (led over 2f: 2nd st: wknd
　over 3f out) ..................................................................................... 4.11
　　　　　　　LONG HANDICAP: Pigalle Wonder 7-1.

**7/2** Blue Topaze, **4/1** Helios, **6/1** Eternal Flame, Bold Habit, **7/1** Across the Bay, **9/1** Hamadryad (IRE), **10/1** Profit
a Prendre, **12/1** Caroles Express, **20/1** Invocation, **25/1** BELFORT RULER, **33/1** Pigalle Wonder. CSF £116.50,
CT £409.18. Tote £40.30: £5.70 £1.80 £1.90 (£176.30). Brian Gubby Ltd (BAGSHOT) bred by Concorde
Bloodstock Agency Ltd. 11 Rn 　　　　　　　　　　　　　　　　　　　　1m 26.35 (1.65)
　　　　　　　　　　　　　　　　　　　　　　　　　　　　　　　　SF—46/59/36/51/43/50

T/Trio: Races 2 & 4: £272.00 & £15.50 (16.3 & 164.6 Tckts). T/Jkpt: £31,160.00 (1.4 Tckts). T/Plpt: £24.20
(786.05 Tckts). 　　　　　　　　　　　　　　　　　　　　　　　　　　　　　　　　　AK

## GOODWOOD (R-H)

### Saturday, August 1st [Good to firm, Firm patches]
Going Allowance: 5f: minus 0.10 sec; Rest: nil sec per fur (F)                    Wind: nil

Stalls: 1st & 7th centre, remainder high

**2459**     VODAPAGE STKS (Mdn 2-Y.O) £6212.00 (£1856.00: £888.00: £404.00)
             **6f**                                                          2-00 (2-02)

**Forest Wind (USA)** *(Fav) (MMoubarak)* 9-0 LDettori (9) (wl grwn: a gng wl: led
over 3f out: easily) ............................................. —1
Absolute Magic *(WJHaggas)* 9-0 JWilliams (3) (neat: hdwy 2f out: nvr nrr) ...... 10.2
Tajarib (IRE) *(JLDunlop)* 8-9 WCarson (6) (w'like: s.s: gd hdwy fnl 2f: nrst fin) ... 3.3
Show Faith (IRE) *(RHannon)* 9-0 JReid (2) (w'like: scope: led over 2f: one pce
fnl 2f) ............................................................ hd.4
Oare Sparrow *(PTWalwyn)* 8-9 RCochrane (7) (unf: scope: bit bkwd: a.p: one
pce fnl 2f) ..................................................... nk.5
Inderaputeri *(MissGayKelleway)* 8-9 WNewnes (8) (neat: w ldrs over 2f: lost pl:
sme late hdwy) ............................................. ¾.6
Soaking *(BWHills)* 9-0 PatEddery (4) (wl grwn: w ldrs 3f: grad wknd) ............ 2½.7
Call Me Blue *(TJNaughton)* 9-0 GCarter (10) (unf: nvr nr to chal) .................. 1½.8
Glimpse of Heaven *(DRCElsworth)* 8-9 TQuinn (1) (unf: a bhd) ................... nk.9
Game Germaine *(BWHills)* 8-9 DHolland (5) (scope: bit bkwd: a bhd) ............ hd.10

**9/4** FOREST WIND (USA)(7/2—2/1), **7/2** Soaking(2/1—4/1), **6/1** Tajarib (IRE)(4/1—7/1), **7/1** Oare Sparrow(op
4/1), **8/1** Show Faith (IRE)(12/1—7/1), **11/1** Absolute Magic(20/1—10/1), **16/1** Glimpse of Heaven, **33/1** Ors.
CSF £24.06, Tote £3.50: £1.30 £2.40 £1.60 (£21.70). Ecurie Fustok (NEWMARKET) bred by Buckram Oak Farm
in USA. 10 Rn                                                            1m 12.44 (2.04)
                                                                        SF—60/20/3/7/1/-

**2460**     VODAC CHESTERFIELD CUP (H'cap) (0-115) £25765.00 (£7720.00: £3710.00:
             £1705.00)    **1¼m**                                            2-30 (2-34)

                                    (Weights raised 6 lb)
2347* **Knock Knock (88)** *(Fav) (IABalding)* 7-9-0 RCochrane (3) (lw: last st: hdwy 2f
out: r.o to ld last strides) ...................................... —1
2281* Pharly Story (93) *(MCPipe)* 4-9-5 LPiggott (1) (5th st: led over 1f out tl last
strides) ........................................................... s.h.2
1869 Pelorus (80) *(DRCElsworth)* 7-8-6 WCarson (9) (9th st: hdwy 3f out: ev ch over
1f out: nt qckn) ................................................. 1½.3
2173⁶ Gilderdale (83) *(JWHills)* 10-8-9 RHills (6) (8th st: hdwy 2f out: n.m.r ins fnl f) . nk.4
1703* Barford Lad (80) *(JRFanshawe)* 5-8-6 GCarter (4) (2nd st: led over 2f out tl wl
over 1f out) ..................................................... 3.5
2028 Lucky Guest (91) *(JLDunlop)* 5-9-3 LDettori (5) (6th st: nt clr run & wnt rt over 1f
out: nt rcvr) .................................................... ¾.6
2349⁵ Grand Hawk (USA) (77) (bl) *(MMoubarak)* 4-8-0 ‡³FNorton (2) (4th st: ev ch 2f
out: sn wknd) ................................................... 2½.7
1876 Mellaby (USA) (98) (v) *(MRStoute)* 4-9-10 PatEddery (8) (lw: led after 2f out tl
over 2f out: wkng whn hmpd over 1f out) ................... 10.8
1869* Fire Top (94) *(RAkehurst)* 7-9-6 TQuinn (7) (led 2f: 3rd st: wkng whn bdly hmpd
over 1f out) .................................................... ½.9
2028⁵ Hashar (IRE) (90) *(DRCElsworth)* 4-9-2 DHolland (10) (lw: 7th st: hdwy 3f out:
wknd 2f out) ................................................... 4.10
                      *Stewards Enquiry: Norton suspended 10-12/8/92 (careless riding).*

**9/2** KNOCK KNOCK(6/1—4/1), **7/1** Pelorus, Fire Top, **15/2** Lucky Guest, **8/1** Hashar (IRE), Grand Hawk (USA),
**9/1** Gilderdale(6/1—10/1), **11/1** Barford Lad(8/1—12/1), Pharly Story, **12/1** Mellaby (USA). CSF £44.84, CT
£303.45. Tote £3.80: £1.40 £2.20 £2.00 (£16.20). Mr G. M. Smart (KINGSCLERE) bred by Lodge Park Stud. 10
Rn                                                                      2m 8.71 (3.71)
                                                                        SF—63/67/51/53/44/53

**2461**     VODAFONE NASSAU STKS (Gp 2) (F & M) £50980.00 (£19002.75: £9063.88:
             £3878.37)    **1¼m**                                            3-10 (3-13)

1816a² **Ruby Tiger** *(PFICole)* 5-9-1 TQuinn (4) (3rd st: led over 3f out: all out) ............. —1
1217² All At Sea (USA) *(Fav) (HRACecil)* 3-8-6 PatEddery (2) (lw: 5th st: hdwy 3f out:
ev ch fnl f: r.o) ................................................. nk.2
1613* Mohican Girl *(JRFanshawe)* 4-9-1 LDettori (1) (4th st: ev ch over 2f out: r.o one
pce) .............................................................. 3.3
1498a Oumaldaaya (USA) (bl) *(JLDunlop)* 3-8-6 WCarson (6) (led tl over 3f out: one
pce) .............................................................. 3.4
1843⁶ Fragrant Hill (bl) *(IABalding)* 4-9-1 RCochrane (5) (lw: last st: nvr nr to chal) ..... 1.5

1935* Gussy Marlowe *(CEBrittain)* 4-9-4 GCarter (7) (lw: a bhd: 6th st) ...................... 12.6
1843 Gai Bulga *(GWragg)* 4-9-1 RHills (3) (2nd st: wknd 3f out) ................................. 1.7

**8/11** All At Sea (USA), **2/1** RUBY TIGER(6/4—5/2), **12/1** Oumaldaaya (USA), Gussy Marlowe, **25/1** Mohican Girl, **40/1** Fragrant Hill, **50/1** Gai Bulga. CSF £3.71, Tote £3.10: £1.80 £1.20 (£1.80). Mrs Philip Blacker (WHATCOMBE) bred by S. Stanhope and Sheikh M. Alamuddin. 7 Rn                2m 7.78 (2.78)
SF—73/63/66/51/58/37

---

## 2462

VODATA NURSERY   £6836.00 (£2048.00: £984.00: £452.00)   7f   3-45 (3-48)
(Weights raised 2 lb)

2193³ **Marillette (USA)** (Fav) *(JHMGosden)* 9-2 PatEddery (2) (lw: s.s: gd hdwy on
ins over 1f out: qcknd to ld cl home: cleverly) ......................................... —1
2038* Foolish Heart (IRE) *(NAGraham)* 8-1 ‡5JWeaver (11) (5th st: ev ch fnl f: r.o) ...... ½.2
2193⁴ Chinnery (IRE) *(JMPEustace)* 7-6 ‡5NKennedy (12) (4th st: led over 1f out tl nr
fin) ............................................................................................................. nk.3
2167² Embankment (IRE) *(RHannon)* 8-1 GCarter (15) (led: edgd lft over 2f out: hdd
over 1f out) ............................................................................................... 1.4
2010⁵ Bourbon Jack *(JWPayne)* 8-4 RCochrane (7) (hld up: hdwy & hrd rdn 2f out:
one pce) .................................................................................................... 2.5
2038 Full Exposure *(WJarvis)* 7-8 NCarlisle (10) (dwlt: hdwy 2f out: nt qckn fnl f) ...... nk.6
2285⁴ Hung Parliament *(BWHills)* 7-13 DHolland (1) (no hdwy fnl f) ............................. 2.7
2238⁴ Lady Relko *(RVoorspuy)* 7-8(1) SDawson (14) (hdwy & rdn 3f out: wknd over 1f
out) ........................................................................................................ 1½.8
1910* Premium *(WJHaggas)* 7-11 ‡3FNorton (9) (lw: nvr nr to chal) ............................. 1½.9
1900* Warm Spell *(RSimpson)* 7-8 AMackay (4) (lw: a bhd) ....................................... ½.10
2389² Strike-a-Pose *(CNWilliams)* 7-7 NAdams (13) (2nd st: wknd over 2f out) ............ ½.11
2138³ Le Couteau *(DWPArbuthnot)* 7-3(3) ‡7AGarth (6) (bhd fnl 2f) .............................. ½.12
2118² Credit Squeeze *(RFJohnsonHoughton)* 7-13 WCarson (8) (3rd st: wknd over 2f
out) ........................................................................................................ 2.13
2055³ Dalalah *(HThomsonJones)* 8-2 RHills (5) (6th st: wknd over 2f out) ............... ¾.14
2076³ Regal Aura (IRE) *(GHarwood)* 9-7 AClark (3) (7th st: wknd over 2f out) ........ 2½.15
LONG HANDICAP: Lady Relko 6-7, Warm Spell 7-3, Strike-a-Pose 7-1, Le Couteau 7-3.

**4/1** MARILLETTE (USA)(op 7/1), **13/2** Premium, **7/1** Embankment (IRE), **8/1** Credit Squeeze, **9/1** Hung Parliament, **10/1** Dalalah(8/1—12/1), Foolish Heart (IRE), **12/1** Chinnery (IRE)(op 8/1), Warm Spell, **14/1** Strike-a-Pose, Regal Aura (IRE)(12/1—20/1), **16/1** Bourbon Jack, **20/1** Full Exposure, Le Couteau, **66/1** Lady Relko. CSF £43.50, CT £422.85. Tote £5.80: £2.40 £3.50 £2.80 (£28.00). Sheikh Mohammed (NEWMARKET) bred by Robert Clay & Rogers Trust in USA. 15 Rn                1m 28.15 (3.45)
SF—51/34/24/30/27/16

---

## 2463

TURF CLUB CLAIMING STKS   £6056.00 (£1808.00: £864.00: £392.00)
1m                                                                    4-15 (4-17)

2447 **Knight of Mercy (100)** (Fav) *(RHannon)* 6-9-1 JReid (5) (5th st: led over 1f out:
rdn out) ...................................................................................................... —1
2348³ Domicksky (74) *(MJRyan)* 4-8-10 RCochrane (9) (lw: 6th st: hdwy over 2f out:
ev ch over 1f out: nt qckn) ........................................................................ 2½.2
1371⁵ Majal (IRE) (78) *(BHanbury)* 3-8-6 WRyan (6) (2nd st: led 3f out tl over 1f out) .. 1.3
2268⁴ Cape Pigeon (USA) (87) *(LGCottrell)* 7-9-4 PatEddery (3) (lw: 3rd st: wknd 2f
out) ........................................................................................................... 5.4
King Al *(DrJDScargill)* 5-9-7 JWilliams (7) (b: nvr nrr) ........................................ 2.5
1976⁶ Lyn's Return (IRE) (60) *(RSimpson)* 3-8-0 ‡5ATucker (2) (nvr nr to chal) ......... 3½.6
2305⁵ Marzocco (50) (bl) *(JFfitch-Heyes)* 4-8-11 AMackay (1) (led tl wknd 3f out) ........ 8.7
2351* Laurel Queen (IRE) (63) *(JBerry)* 4-8-13 GCarter (4) (4th st: wknd over 2f out) . 7.8

**8/11** KNIGHT OF MERCY, **5/1** Cape Pigeon (USA), Domicksky, **10/1** Majal (IRE)(op 5/1), **11/1** Laurel Queen (IRE), **16/1** King Al, **33/1** Lyn's Return (IRE), **50/1** Marzocco. CSF £5.23, Tote £2.00: £1.20 £1.40 £2.00 (£3.50). Mr M. W. Grant (MARLBOROUGH) bred by C. A. Blackwell. 8 Rn; Domicksky clmd R Simpson £13,650                1m 40.27 (2.67)
SF—60/47/40/37/34/2

---

## 2464

SURPLICE GRADUATION STKS (3-Y.O) £5796.00 (£1728.00: £824.00: £372.00)
1m                                                                    4-45 (4-47)

1711⁶ **River Falls (113)** *(RHannon)* 8-11 JReid (5) (lw: 3rd st: led on bit over 1f out:
rdn & r.o fnl f) ............................................................................................ —1
1229a John Rose (100) *(PAKelleway)* 8-11 GayKelleway (6) (4th st: hrd rdn over 2f
out: r.o ins fnl f) ....................................................................................... 2½.2
2181⁶ L'Hermine (83) *(HCandy)* 8-11 WNewnes (2) (led tl over 2f out) ...................... 1.3
2186* Crystado (FR) *(DRCElsworth)* 9-4 JWilliams (1) (lw: 5th st: one pce fnl 2f) ...... 2.4
2056⁵ Imperial Ballet (IRE) (Fav) *(HRACecil)* 9-4 PatEddery (4) (lw: 2nd st: ev ch 2f
out: sn rdn & wknd) .................................................................................... nk.5
2133² Move a Minute (USA) *(DRCElsworth)* 8-11 RCochrane (3) (last st: a bhd) ......... 6.6

**4/7** Imperial Ballet (IRE), **3/1** RIVER FALLS(op 2/1), **6/1** Move a Minute (USA), **20/1** John Rose(op 12/1), Crystado (FR), **50/1** L'Hermine. CSF £40.15, Tote £3.60: £1.60 £3.00 (£16.20). A. F. Budge (Equine) Limited (MARLBOROUGH) bred by Mrs J. R. Hine and Miss J. Bunting. 6 Rn 1m 40.68 (3.28)
SF–47/39/36/37/36/11

## 2465
TRUNDLE H'CAP (0-85) £5952.00 (£1776.00: £848.00: £384.00) **5f** 5-20 (5-21)

| 2127<sup>6</sup> | **Paddy Chalk (79)** (Fav) (*LJHolt*) 6–9–11 JReid (9) (b: hdwy 2f out: hrd rdn fnl f: led nr fnl f) | —1 |
| 2061 | Fivesevenfiveo **(73)** (*RJHodges*) 4–8–12 ‡⁷SDrowne (3) (a.p: led over 1f out tl nr fin) | s.h.2 |
| 2337 | Petraco (IRE) **(72)** (bl) (*LJCodd*) 4–8–11 ‡⁷WHollick (8) (hdwy 2f out: r.o wl ins fnl f) | hd.3 |
| 2141* | Martinosky **(66)** (*WGRWightman*) 6–8–12 JWilliams (10) (gd hdwy over 1f out: nt qckn ins fnl f) | 2.4 |
| 2032 | Coppermill Lad **(50)** (*LJHolt*) 9–7–3 ‡⁷AGarth (5) (nrst fin) | 1½.5 |
| 1340<sup>3</sup> | Savalaro **(52)** (*JFfitch-Heyes*) 3–7–8<sup>(1)</sup> AMackay (1) (spd over 3f) | 1.6 |
| 2127* | Olifantsfontein **(80)** (bl) (*RSimpson*) 4–9–12 WRyan (6) (led over 3f) | ½.7 |
| 2279<sup>2</sup> | Temple Fortune (USA) **(71)** (*RHannon*) 3–8–13 RCochrane (2) (hrd rdn & hdwy over 1f out: wknd ins fnl f) | s.h.8 |
| 2404 | Amber Mill **(82)** (v) (*JBerry*) 4–10–0 GCarter (7) (lw: prom 3f) | ½.9 |
| 2499<sup>3</sup> | Ski Captain **(56)** (*PHowling*) 8–7–11 ‡⁵NKennedy (4) (lw: spd 2f) | 3.10 |

**9/2** PADDY CHALK, **5/1** Martinosky, **11/2** Temple Fortune (USA), **6/1** Olifantsfontein(op 4/1), **13/2** Ski Captain, **9/1** Petraco (IRE)(12/1—8/1), **12/1** Fivesevenfiveo(8/1—14/1), Coppermill Lad, **16/1** Amber Mill, **33/1** Savalaro. CSF £48.25, CT £413.89. Tote £5.60: £2.10 £3.80 £3.30 (£98.10). Mrs R. G. Wellman (BASINGSTOKE) bred by Countess of Durham. 10 Rn 58.95 sec (1.35)
SF–76/62/60/53/24/25

T/Trio: Race 2: £32.40 (71.9 Tckts), Race 5: £7.30 (253.4. Tckts) & race 7: £206.50 (13.1 Tckts). T/Jkpt: £1,765.40 (1.65 Tckts). T/Plpt: £62.80 (231.55 Tckts). Hn

## 2111—CATTERICK (L-H)

### Wednesday, July 29th [Good to firm]
Going Allowance: 5f: minus 0.45 sec; Rest: minus 0.25 sec (F)   Wind: almost nil

Stalls: low

## 2466
LEVY BOARD APPCE H'CAP (0-70) £2301.00 (£636.00: £303.00) **5f** 2-20 (2-21)

| 2153<sup>4</sup> | **Prince Belfort (68)** (*MPNaughton*) 4–9–7 ‡⁵ADobbin (1) (cl up: led over 1f out: styd on: sddle slipped) | —1 |
| 2115* | Catherines Well **(70)** (Fav) (*MWEasterby*) 9–10–0 JMarshall (3) (lw: trckd ldrs: nt clr run & swtchd over 1f out: r.o wl nr fin) | ½.2 |
| 2333<sup>2</sup> | Last Straw **(41)** (*AWJones*) 4–7–8 ‡⁵ClaireBalding (5) (a chsng ldrs: edgd lft over 1f out: one pce) | 1.3 |
| 2333<sup>3</sup> | Simmie's Special **(60)** (*RHollinshead*) 4–8–13 ‡⁵SWynne (4) (cl up: nt qckn appr fnl f) | 1.4 |
| 2333 | Kabcast **(63)** (bl) (*DWChapman*) 7–9–7 OPears (2) (led tl hdd & wknd appr fnl f) | ¾.5 |
| 2117<sup>3</sup> | Never Late **(49)** (*MHEasterby*) 3–8–2 LNewton (6) (lw: dwlt: nvr trbld ldrs) | 4.6 |
| 2046<sup>5</sup> | Jive Music **(35)** (*NBycroft*) 6–7–7 AGarth (8) (lw: lost tch after 2f) | ½.7 |
| 2291 | Dreams Eyes **(35)** (bl) (*RBastiman*) 4–7–7 CHawksley (7) (b: a bhd) | 2.8 |
| | LONG HANDICAP: Jive Music 6-13, Dreams Eyes 7-5. | |

**2/1** Catherines Well, **3/1** Simmie's Special, **11/2** Last Straw, **8/1** PRINCE BELFORT, **10/1** Never Late(op 6/1), **16/1** Kabcast, **20/1** Dreams Eyes, **33/1** Jive Music. CSF £21.70, CT £73.45. Tote £8.80: £2.30 £1.10 £1.80 (£12.40). Mrs Carole Sykes (RICHMOND) bred by Concorde Bloodstock Agency Ltd. 8 Rn 58.1 sec (0.6)
SF–50/55/17/32/38/7

## 2467
TILTON HOUSE (S) STKS (3, 4 & 5-Y.O) £2217.00 (£612.00: £291.00)
**1m 5f 175y** 2-50 (2-50)

| | **Seraphim (FR)** (*TDBarron*) 3–8–5 AlexGreaves (2) (w'like: leggy: trckd ldr: led 5f out: rdn clr 2f out) | —1 |
| 1481<sup>3</sup> | Marandisa **(40)** (*MPNaughton*) 5–9–0 ‡⁵JWeaver (1) (hdwy 4f out: sn chsng wnr: no imp fnl 2f) | 5.2 |
| 2042<sup>4</sup> | Escadaro (USA) **(39)** (v) (*SGNorton*) 3–8–5 ‡⁵OPears (3) (led tl hdd 5f out: sn outpcd) | hd.3 |
| 2211<sup>6</sup> | Chantry Bellini **(47)** (Fav) (*CWThornton*) 3–8–5 GHind (4) (b.hind: chsd ldrs tl rdn & lost pl after 6f: n.d after) | 10.4 |

**5/4** Chantry Bellini, **9/4** Marandisa, **7/2** Escadaro (USA)(tchd 11/2), **8/1** SERAPHIM (FR)(op 5/1). CSF £22.74, Tote £5.10 (£9.30). Mr Alex Gorrie (THIRSK) bred by Darley Stud Management in France. 4 Rn; No bid
3m 0.1 (4.9)
SF—7/6/–/–

---

**2468**　　ROTHMANS ROYALS NORTH SOUTH CHALLENGE SERIES H'CAP (0-80) £2976.00
　　　　　　(£888.00: £424.00: £192.00)　　**7f**　　　　　　　　3-25 (3-26)
(Weights raised 1 lb)

| | |
|---|---|
| 1811² **Indian Slave (IRE) (54)** (Fav) *(RGuest)* 4–8–2 ‡⁵JWeaver (2) (in tch: qcknd to ld over 1f out: drvn clr) | —1 |
| 1905 Susanna's Secret (45) *(WCarter)* 5–7–5 ‡⁷CHawksley (5) (lw: hdwy ent st: styd on: no ch w wnr) | 6.2 |
| 2249★ Bidweaya (USA) (43) *(JLEyre)* 5–7–10 (6x) JLowe (7) (s.i.s: sn chsng ldrs: rdn over 2f out: r.o one pce) | 2.3 |
| 2123★ Leave it to Lib (66) *(PCalver)* 5–8–12 ‡⁷JTate (10) (lw: led after 1f tl over 1f out: grad wknd) | nk.4 |
| 1833² Kummel King (66) *(EJAlston)* 4–9–5 KFallon (3) (swtg: effrt ent st: styd on: nt pce to chal) | ¹/₂.5 |
| 1896★ Mca Below the Line (60) *(WLBarker)* 4–8–13 SWebster (4) (bhd tl styd on fnl 2f) | 2¹/₂.6 |
| 2040 Gott's Desire (45) *(RBastiman)* 6–7–12 LCharnock (1) (b.hind: lw: cl up early: outpcd 4f out: n.d after) | 2¹/₂.7 |
| 2050⁶ Coastal Express (65) *(EWeymes)* 3–8–11 GDuffield (6) (led 1f: chsd ldrs tl outpcd appr st) | 3¹/₂.8 |
| 1791★ Hawa Layaam (IRE) (78) (v) *(AAScott)* 3–9–10 BRaymond (9) (dwlt: gd hdwy to chal after 3f: wknd 2f out) | s.h.9 |
| Roar on Tour (64) *(MHEasterby)* 3–8–10 MBirch (8) (lost pl after 3f: n.d after) | hd.10 |

**9/2** INDIAN SLAVE (IRE), **5/1** Leave it to Lib, Gott's Desire, **11/2** Bidweaya (USA), **6/1** Hawa Layaam (IRE), **9/1** Kummel King, **10/1** Susanna's Coorot, **14/1** Coastal Express, **16/1** Mca Below the Line, **33/1** Roar on Tour. CSF £43.20, CT £227.84. Tote £6.80: £3.00 £3.60 £4.20 (£19.60). Mr R. Axford (NEWMARKET) bred by Ivan W. Allan in Ireland. 10 Rn
1m 24.4 (1.2)
SF—44/15/14/29/34/20

---

**2469**　　STOCKWELL CLAIMING STKS　£2406.00 (£666.00: £318.00)　**7f**　　4-00 (4-01)

| | |
|---|---|
| 2088³ **Spanish Express (45)** *(RBoss)* 3–8–5 BRaymond (3) (lw: a cl up: led appr st: sn rdn clr: comf) | —1 |
| 2123 Euroblake (69) (Fav) *(TDBarron)* 5–9–6 AlexGreaves (5) (effrt ¹/₂-wy: chsd wnr fnl 2f: no imp) | 2.2 |
| 2123 Say You Will (29) (v) *(MPNaughton)* 8–9–0 JakiHouston (7) (a chsng ldrs: one pce fnl 3f) | 5.3 |
| 1294 Station Express (IRE) (28) *(BEllison)* 4–8–5 ‡⁵JWeaver (4) (a chsng ldrs: effrt appr st: no imp) | ³/₄.4 |
| 2266 Marvelous Molly (bl) *(IABalding)* 3–7–13 AMunro (8) (led tl hdd appr st: sn outpcd) | 2.5 |
| 2209⁴ Whippet (69) *(JABennett)* 8–9–2 GHind (1) (b: outpcd fr ¹/₂-wy) | 2.6 |
| Vandervally *(RMWhitaker)* 3–7–12 PBurke (6) (s.s: nt rcvr) | 2¹/₂.7 |
| 2119⁶ Cashtal Queen (44) *(JBerry)* 3–8–1 JCarroll (2) (b: hld up: rapid hdwy appr st: sn wknd) | 2¹/₂.8 |

**13/8** Euroblake, **3/1** SPANISH EXPRESS(op 9/2), **5/1** Marvelous Molly, **7/1** Whippet, **12/1** Cashtal Queen, **33/1** Station Express (IRE), Say You Will, **50/1** Vandervally. CSF £7.36, Tote £3.50: £1.40 £1.40 £3.10 (£3.60). Mr P. Asquith (NEWMARKET) bred by I. W. T. and Mrs Loftus. 8 Rn
1m 25.9 (2.7)
SF—24/33/13/1/–/–

---

**2470**　　GO RACING IN YORKSHIRE H'CAP (3-Y.O) (0-70) £2978.50 (£826.00: £395.50)
　　　　　　**1m 5f 175y**　　　　　　　　　　4-30 (4-32)
(Weights raised 11 lb)

| | |
|---|---|
| 1783★ **Kayartis (38)** *(MrsGRReveley)* 8-0 JLowe (7) (lw: hld up: hdwy 6f out: rdn to ld over 1f out: edgd lft: styd on) | —1 |
| 1626² Stingray City (USA) (59) (v) *(JEtherington)* 9-7 KDarley (5) (led 4f: chsd ldrs: chal 5f out: hdd over 1f out: kpt on) | nk.2 |
| 2211² Gay Ming (49) *(RHollinshead)* 8-4 ‡⁷AGarth (1) (outpcd 5f out: hdwy 2f out: nvr trbld ldrs) | 2.3 |
| 1977 Anar (IRE) (47) *(WCarter)* 8-2 ‡⁷CHawksley (6) (led after 4f tl hdd ent st: sn rdn & grad wknd) | 3.4 |
| 2069⁴ Haut-Brion (IRE) (47) *(WStorey)* 8-6 ‡³JFanning (2) (prom tl outpcd over 4f out: n.d after) | 6.5 |
| 1708⁶ Soft Note (IRE) (55) *(MBell)* 9-3 AMunro (4) (b.hind: cl up: effrt over 4f out: wknd appr st) | 12.6 |
| 2110³ Clifton Chase (53) (Fav) *(MAJarvis)* 9-1 BRaymond (3) (outpcd & lost tch ¹/₂-wy: rdn & n.d after) | 2¹/₂.7 |

**15/8** Clifton Chase, **4/1** Gay Ming, **9/2** Stingray City (USA), **7/1** KAYARTIS, Anar (IRE), **8/1** Haut-Brion (IRE), **14/1** Soft Note (IRE). CSF £35.49, Tote £5.80: £1.80 £3.60 (£15.40). Mrs J. M. Allen (SALTBURN) bred by R. R. Evans Bloodstock Ltd. 7 Rn                                                                                        3m 2.4 (7.2)

**2471**    'FAMILY DAY' STKS (Mdn 2-Y-O C & G) £2280.00 (£630.00: £300.00)
5f                                                                                                            5-00 (5-02)

| | | |
|---|---|---|
| | **Sea Gazer (IRE)** (Fav) *(TDBarron)* 9-0  KDarley (6) (w'like: mde most: hld on wl fnl f) | —1 |
| 1910[6] | Hawaymyson (IRE) *(JHJohnson)* 8-9 ‡5JWeaver (3) (lw: chsd ldrs: ev ch ins fnl f: kpt on) | ¾.2 |
| 2205[4] | Milbank Challenger *(MHEasterby)* 9-0  MBirch (5) (chsd ldrs: effrt over 1f out: r.o one pce) | ¾.3 |
| 900[3] | Pilgrim Bay (IRE) *(JBerry)* 9-0  JCarroll (1) (lw: w ldrs tl wknd 1f out) | 1½.4 |
| | Hickory Blue *(SGNorton)* 8-9 ‡5OPears (4) (w'like: scope: bit bkwd: dwlt: hdwy over 1f out: nvr nr to chal) | 1½.5 |
| 1670 | Mdm Racer (IRE) *(JBerry)* 9-0  GDuffield (2) (led early: hung rt: w ldrs tl wknd over 1f out) | 1½.6 |

**5/2** SEA GAZER (IRE)(tchd 4/1), **11/4** Hawaymyson (IRE), **4/1** Milbank Challenger, Hickory Blue, **9/2** Pilgrim Bay (IRE), **25/1** Mdm Racer (IRE). CSF £9.75, Tote £5.30: £1.90 £1.70 (£5.70). Mr P. D. Savill (THIRSK) bred by D. Twomey in Ireland. 6 Rn                                                                                       59.2 sec (1.7)
SF—21/13/15/13/2/1

**2472**    LEVY BOARD MEDIAN AUCTION STKS (3-Y-O) £2259.00 (£624.00: £297.00)
7f                                                                                                            5-30 (5-31)

| | | |
|---|---|---|
| 1695[2] | **Ernestan (100)** (Fav) *(MHEasterby)* 9-9  MBirch (2) (chsd ldrs: effrt 2f out: edgd rt: led wl ins fnl f: jst hld on) | —1 |
| 2331[3] | Secret Treaty (IRE) *(PWChapple-Hyam)* 8-1 ‡5JWeaver (3) (lw: chsd ldrs: effrt 2f out: r.o fnl f: jst failed) | s.h.2 |
| 2194[2] | Ponsardin (86) *(SirMarkPrescott)* 9-4  GDuffield (4) (lw: mde most tl hdd & no ex wl ins fnl f) | 1½.3 |
| 2123[3] | Brambles Way (55) (v) *(WLBarker)* 8-6 ‡5OPears (5) (w ldr: disp ld 3f out tl rdn & btn over 1f out) | 2½.4 |
| 2119 | Scorton (IRE) *(MDods)* 8-11  PBurke (1) (stdd s: lost tch fr ½-wy) | dist.5 |

**4/5** ERNESTAN, **5/4** Ponsardin, **12/1** Secret Treaty (IRE), **50/1** Brambles Way, **200/1** Scorton (IRE). CSF £8.85, Tote £1.60: £1.70 £5.70 (£4.30). Mr A. M. Wragg (MALTON) bred by A. M. Wragg. 5 Rn    1m 25.8 (2.6)
SF—29/6/7/–/–

T/Plpt: £1,930.40 (1.15 Tckts).                                                                              AA

## 1768—EPSOM  (L-H)
### Wednesday, July 29th [Good to firm]
Going Allowance: 5f: minus 0.30 sec; Rest: minus 0.40 sec (F)                  Wind: almost nil

Stalls: high

**2473**    LADBROKE APP'CE H'CAP (0-80) £2427.00 (£672.00: £321.00)
1¼m 18y                                                                                                      6-10 (6-16)

| | | |
|---|---|---|
| 2255 | **Loki (IRE) (70)** *(GLewis)* 4-8-13 ‡5BRussell (6) (4th st: led over 1f out: r.o wl) | —1 |
| 829 | Surrey Dancer (68) *(BHanbury)* 4-9-2  DHarrison (5) (6th st: hdwy 1f out: r.o) | 1.2 |
| 2012 | Texan Tycoon (67) *(RAkehurst)* 4-8-10 ‡5TAshley (7) (7th st: ev ch over 1f out: r.o) | hd.3 |
| 31 | My Alibi (IRE) (45) *(SDow)* 4-7-2 ‡5DToole (2) (led tl hdd 2f out: ev ch over 1f out: one pce) | 1½.4 |
| 1949* | Flying Speed (USA) (77) *(MCPipe)* 4-9-8 ‡3KRutter (8) (3rd st: ev ch over 1f out: one pce fnl f) | 1½.5 |
| 2289* | Shaieef (IRE) (64) (Fav) *(RJRWilliams)* 4-8-7 (6x) ‡5GMitchell (1) (prom tl lost pl 5f out: last st: r.o one pce fnl 2f) | nk.6 |
| 2392[3] | Northern Conqueror (IRE) (56) *(TJNaughton)* 4-8-4  NGwilliams (3) (2nd st: led 2f out: sn hdd & wknd) | nk.7 |
| 1520 | Checkpoint Charlie (60) *(JMPEustace)* 7–8-3 ‡5AntoinetteArmes (4) (8th st: nvr nrr) | ½.8 |
| 1996* | Rose Glen (65) *(ABailey)* 6-8-13  ATucker (9) (5th st: hrd rdn over 2f out: wknd over 1f out) | 4.9 |

LONG HANDICAP: My Alibi (IRE) 7-2.

**7/2** Shaieef (IRE)(op 9/4), **5/1** Rose Glen, Flying Speed (USA), **6/1** Surrey Dancer, Checkpoint Charlie(op 10/1), Northern Conqueror (IRE), **13/2** LOKI (IRE), **10/1** Texan Tycoon, **50/1** My Alibi (IRE). CSF £43.58, CT £358.49. Tote £8.70: £2.60 £1.40 £3.30 (£18.10). Mr T. K. Laidlaw (EPSOM) bred by Abbey Lodge Stud in Ireland. 9 Rn
2m 12.90 (8.40)

## 2474
E.B.F. WALTON STKS (Mdn 2-Y.O) £2684.50 (£742.00: £353.50)    **6f**    6-40 (6-44)

1039⁶ **Awestruck** *(WJHaggas)* 9-0 MHills (4) (2nd st: led over 2f out: edgd lft over 1f
  out: r.o) ......................................................................................... —1
1937⁵ Musical Prospect (USA) (Fav) *(RHannon)* 8-9 MRoberts (1) (led: rdn & hdd
  over 2f out: swtchd rt 1f out: r.o) ...................................................... 1½.2
2306⁶ Lady of Shadows (v) *(SDow)* 8-9 WNewnes (2) (3rd st: no hdwy fnl 2f) ....... 6.3
  Petite Jess *(WCarter)* 8-4 ‡⁵NGwilliams (6) (unf: 4th st: rdn over 2f out: one pce) 2.4
2256⁶ Recipdico Mist (IRE) *(TJNaughton)* 8-4 ‡⁵DHarrison (3) (5th st: a bhd) ............ 3½.5
2031 July Bride *(MJHaynes)* 8-9 BRouse (5) (6th st: a bhd) .................................... 12.6

**2/15** Musical Prospect (USA), **12/1** AWESTRUCK(op 6/1), **14/1** Recipdico Mist (IRE)(op 7/1), **20/1** Petite Jess,
**25/1** July Bride, **50/1** Lady of Shadows. CSF £14.13, Tote £10.70: £2.80 £1.10 (£2.50). Mrs David Thompson
(NEWMARKET) bred by Cheveley Park Stud Ltd. 6 Rn                                    1m 9.60 (1.60)
                                                                        SF—40/29/5/–/–/–

## 2475
LONSDALE STKS (Mdn 3-Y.O.F) £2684.50 (£742.00: £353.50)    **7f**    7-10 (7-17)

  **Blue Marine** *(ACStewart)* 8-11 MRoberts (1) (mde all: clr over 2f out: v.easily) .. —1
2114² Silica (USA) **(63)** *(JHMGosden)* 8-11 DHolland (3) (2nd st: hrd rdn over 2f out:
  no imp) ............................................................................................. 8.2
  Dam Certain (IRE) *(AWDenson)* 8-11 WNewnes (4) (w'like: bkwd: 3rd st: a bhd) 7.3
2133 Top Song **(68)** (Fav) *(RHannon)* 8-11 PatEddery (2) (chsd ldr tl lost pl qckly
  over 4f out: poor 4th st: t.o) .............................................................. 25.4

**6/5** Top Song(4/5—5/4), **2/1** Silica (USA), **4/1** BLUE MARINE, **10/1** Dam Certain (IRE). CSF £11.03, Tote £4.30
(£5.90). The Snailwell Stud Company Limited (NEWMARKET) bred by Snailwell Stud Co Ltd. 4 Rn
                                                                        1m 22.21 (1.71)
                                                                        SF—29/8/–/–

## 2476
RING & BRYMER H'CAP (0-80) £3850.00 (£1150.00: £550.00: £250.00)    **7f**    7-40 (7-47)

2304³ **Helios (67)** *(RSimpson)* 4-9-6 JReid (7) (2nd st: led 2f out: rdn out) .................. —1
2254* Profit a Prendre **(56)** *(DAWilson)* 8-8-4 (6x) ‡⁵DHarrison (2) (b: 5th st: r.o one
  pce fnl 2f) ....................................................................................... 3½.2
1954⁵ Royal Dartmouth (USA) **(56)** *(BRMillman)* 7-8-9 JWilliams (3) (lw: 9th st: hdwy
  over 2f out: r.o ins fnl f) .................................................................. ½.3
2125 Zinbaq **(41)** *(CJBenstead)* 6-7-8(¹) DBiggs (6) (lw: 4th st: r.o one pce fnl 2f) ... hd.4
2019 Ballasecret **(72)** *(RDickin)* 4-9-4 ‡⁷DMeredith (9) (led 5f: wknd fnl f) ................. 3.5
1947³ Aldahe **(44)** *(BRMillman)* 7-7-11 AMackay (9) (8th st: nvr nr to chal) ............... 2½.6
2126 Try Leguard (IRE) **(73)** *(WCarter)* 3-9-5 MRoberts (13) (7th st: no hdwy fnl 2f) . ¾.7
1570 Fabled Orator **(41)** *(PHowling)* 7-7-8(¹) JQuinn (11) (b.nr hind: 6th st: rdn over
  2f out: one pce) ............................................................................... 1½.8
1431⁴ Ain'tlifelikethat **(49)** (bl) *(TJNaughton)* 5-8-2 DHolland (12) (s.s: hdwy 3f out:
  wknd 2f out) ................................................................................... 2½.9
  Majestic Melody **(58)** *(WCarter)* 4-8-6 ‡⁵NGwilliams (8) (a bhd) ....................... ½.10
2189⁶ Cheveley Dancer (USA) **(75)** *(AWDenson)* 4-10-0 WNewnes (10) (3rd st: wknd
  over 2f out) ..................................................................................... nk.11
2088² Sovereign Rock (IRE) **(74)** (Fav) *(RHannon)* 3-9-6 PatEddery (4) (a bhd: t.o) 15.12
                              LONG HANDICAP: Zinbaq 7-6.

**9/2** Sovereign Rock (IRE), **5/1** HELIOS, Royal Dartmouth (USA), **13/2** Profit a Prendre, **7/1** Zinbaq, Aldahe(op
9/2), **10/1** Ain'tlifelikethat, **12/1** Cheveley Dancer (USA), Try Leguard (IRE)(op 8/1), **14/1** Ballasecret, **33/1** Ors.
CSF £37.08, CT £159.30. Tote £5.50: £1.90: £2.00 £2.00 (£15.30). Mrs Christine Painting (FOXHILL) bred by
Sunley Stud. 12 Rn                                                     1m 20.56 (0.06)
                                                                        SF—62/32/35/19/34/5

## 2477
LBC NEWSTALK 97.3 FM CLAIMING STKS    £2322.00 (£642.00: £306.00)
1½m 10y                                                                 8-15 (8-22)

1286⁶ **Storm Drum (51)** (bl) *(PJMakin)* 3-8-8 JReid (7) (swtg: 6th st: hdwy on bit 2f
  out: edgd lft over 1f out: led 1f out: sn clr) ...................................... —1
2059 Blushing Belle **(52)** (bl) *(PFICole)* 4-8-11 TQuinn (2) (lw: led 11f: unable qckn) . 6.2
2235⁴ Dare to Dream (IRE) **(60)** *(GLewis)* 3-8-7 ‡⁵ATucker (1) (lw: 5th st: r.o one pce
  fnl 2f) ........................................................................................... 3.3
1850 Saif Al Adil (!RE) **(56)** *(KTIvory)* 3-8-3 ‡⁵DHarrison (3) (2nd st: wknd wl over 1f
  out) ............................................................................................... 4.4
2180⁶ Sultan's Son **(66)** *(JohnRUpson)* 6-8-7 ‡⁵BDoyle (4) (7th st: nvr nr to chal) ..... 1½.5
2087* Bighayir **(74)** (bl) (Fav) *(MCPipe)* 5-9-10 MRoberts (9) (b: hdwy over 6f out: 4th
  st: wknd 2f out) ............................................................................... 2.6

1686⁵ Island Blade (IRE) **(49)** *(RAkehurst)* 3–8-8 PatEddery (5) (lw: 3rd st: wknd over
2f out) ............................................... 2¹/₂.7

2051 Soft Verges *(WCarter)* 4–8-2 ‡⁵NGwilliams (8) (8th st: a bhd) ...................... 4.8

2136⁴ Tel E Thon *(PJJones)* 5–8-5 ‡⁷AWhelan (6) (9th st: a bhd) ..................... 3¹/₂.9

**1/2** Bighayir, **13/2** Blushing Belle, **7/1** Dare to Dream (IRE)(6/1—9/1), **11/1** Sultan's Son(op 7/1), **12/1** Island
Blade (IRE)(op 8/1), **14/1** STORM DRUM, Tel E Thon, **16/1** Saif Al Adil (IRE), **33/1** Soft Verges. CSF £101.66,
Tote £20.20: £4.20 £1.90 £1.40 (£59.00). Mr A. R. C. Hobbs (MARLBOROUGH) bred by Peter McCalmont. 9 Rn
2m 37.43 (2.43)
SF—22/17/7/–/–/–

### 2478
OLYMPIC H'CAP (0-90) £3525.00 (£1050.00: £500.00: £225.00) **5f** 8-45 (8-50)

2376² **Sigama (USA) (78)** (Fav) *(FHLee)* 6–9-6 ‡⁵NKennedy (6) (lw: chsd ldr: led ins
fnl f: r.o) ............................................. —1

2131² Cheshire Annie (IRE) **(55)** *(WCarter)* 3–7-11 JQuinn (5) (swtg: chsd ldrs: ev ch
ins fnl f: r.o) ...................................... nk.2

1552 Catalani **(50)** *(TJNaughton)* 7–7-11 DHolland (8) (b: swtg: hld up: n.m.r over 1f
out: r.o fnl f) ..................................... ¹/₂.3

2046³ Serious Hurry **(57)** (bl) *(SirMarkPrescott)* 4–8-4 MRoberts (1) (hld up: edgd rt
over 1f out: r.o) .................................. nk.4

2016² Sylvan Breeze **(81)** (bl) *(PMitchell)* 4–10-0 MHills (3) (dwlt: rdn over 2f out: one
pce) .................................................. nk.5

2199³ Shades of Jade **(56)** *(JJBridger)* 4–8-3 SWhitworth (2) (led tl ins fnl f: sn wknd) 1¹/₂.6

1771³ Gallant Hope **(57)** (bl) *(LGCottrell)* 10–8-4 NCarlisle (4) (lw: outpcd: nvr nrr) ..... hd.7

**6/4** SIGAMA (USA)(tchd 9/4), **9/2** Serious Hurry, **5/1** Cheshire Annie (IRE), **13/2** Shades of Jade, **15/2** Gallant
Hope(5/1—8/1), Catalani, **10/1** Sylvan Breeze. CSF £9.72, CT £40.74. Tote £2.80: 1.60 £2.60 (£6.50). Mrs
Gillian Lee (WILMSLOW) bred by Welcome Farm in USA. 7 Rn
55.09 sec (0.59)
SF—64/40/38/44/67/36

T/Trio: Race 4: £32.70 (52.3 Tckts). T/Plpt: £314.70 (9.05 Tckts). **SM**

### 2362—SOUTHWELL (L-H) Fibresand
## Wednesday, July 29th [Standard]
Going Allowance: minus 0.25 sec per fur (FS)
Wind: almost nil

Stalls: low
### 2479
HERA STKS (Mdn 3-Y.O) £1150.50 (£318.00: £151.50) **1m (AWT)** 6-15 (6-16)

1971 **Sirtelimar (IRE) (57)** *(BobJones)* 9-0 VSmith (2) (mde all: qcknd clr ent st:
unchal) ............................................... —1

2196² Nobby Barnes **(68)** (Fav) *(RWArmstrong)* 9-0 CKTse (1) (b.hind: a.p: 2nd st:
rdn wl over 1f out: one pce) ..................... 8.2

1244⁸ Kirkby Belle **(49)** *(EWeymes)* 8-9 WRyan (5) (chsd wnr tl 3rd & rdn ent st: sn
btn) .................................................. 8.3

2165⁴ Mondova (IRE) *(FHLee)* 8-9 RLappin (7) (bit bkwd: mid div: pushed along & 4th
st: no imp) ......................................... 4.4

749 Strangersinthenite **(45)** *(JSWainwright)* 9-0 LCharnock (3) (bkwd: bhd: 5th st:
rdn 2f out: no imp) ............................... 4.5

Bee Upstanding (IRE) (bl) *(DrJDScargill)* 8-9 NDay (4) (w'like: lengthy: bkwd:
sn outpcd: a bhd: 6th st: t.o) ................... 12.6

**4/5** Nobby Barnes, **4/1** SIRTELIMAR (IRE), **8/1** Bee Upstanding (IRE)(op 5/1), Kirkby Belle, **14/1** Mondova (IRE),
**16/1** Strangersinthenite. CSF £7.26, Tote £5.10: £1.90 £1.40 (£3.40). Mr D. W. Price (NEWMARKET) bred by
Kilnamoragh Stud in Ireland. 6 Rn
1m 41.3 (2)
SF—40/16/–/–/–/–

### 2480
APOLLO (S) STKS (2-Y.O) £1224.00 (£339.00: £162.00) **7f (AWT)** 6-45 (6-46)

2363³ **Shades of Croft** *(MDIUsher)* 8-12(1) MWigham (1) (mde all: rdn fnl f: hld on
gamely) .............................................. —1

2232⁵ Palacegate Sunset *(JBerry)* 8-11 GCarter (3) (hdwy ¹/₂-wy: 5th st: chsd wnr fnl
2f: hrd rdn: r.o) .................................. ¹/₂.2

1526 Yeveed (IRE) *(MHEasterby)* 8-6 WRyan (6) (outpcd early: 6th st: styd on fnl 2f:
nvr nrr) .............................................. 3.3

1848 Alice Bay *(DHaydnJones)* 8-6 TyroneWilliams (2) (prom: 4th st: rdn 2f out: grad
wknd) ................................................ 4.4

2277⁶ Buzz-B-Babe (Fav) *(BEllison)* 8-11 JFortune (5) (bhd: sn pushed along: sme
late hdwy: nvr nrr) ............................... 2.5

1838⁴ Pretzel (IRE) (v) *(NTinkler)* 8-11 LCharnock (7) (chsd wnr: 2nd st: wknd 2f out:
t.o) ................................................... 10.6

920 Arrochar *(JGFitzGerald)* 8-6 KFallon (4) (prom tl 3rd & wkng st: t.o) ................ 5.7
920 Libby-J *(MWEasterby)* 8-6 TLucas (8) (swtg: s.s: a bhd: t.o) ............................ 2½.8

7/2 Buzz-B-Babe, 4/1 SHADES OF CROFT, 9/2 Pretzel (IRE)(op 3/1), 5/1 Palacegate Sunset(tchd 8/1), 11/2
Yeveed (IRE), 10/1 Libby-J, 16/1 Alice Bay, 25/1 Arrochar. CSF £21.65, Tote £4.20: £1.30 £1.60 £1.70 (£9.80).
Mr M. D. I. Usher (EAST GARSTON) bred by Mrs E. M. Gauvain. 8 Rn; No bid
　　　　　　　　　　　　　　　　　　　　　　　　　　　　　　　　　　　　　1m 30.6 (4)
　　　　　　　　　　　　　　　　　　　　　　　　　　　　　　　　　　　SF—12/9/–/–/–/–

## 2481 THOMPSON & JEWITT INTERNATIONAL H'CAP (0-70) £1203.00 (£333.00: £159.00)
6f (AWT)　　　　　　　　　　　　　　　　　　　　　　　　　　　　7-15 (7-19)

2366 **Jovial Kate (USA)** (56) *(BEllison)* 5-9-13 JFortune (1) (mde all: clr over 1f out:
　　　　r.o) ........................................................................................... —1
2123⁶ Morpick (51) (v) (Fav) *(JPLeigh)* 5-9-3 ‡⁵StephenDavies (3) (a.p: rdn wl over 1f
　　　　out: kpt on: no ch w wnr) ........................................................ 2½.2
2365⁴ The Dream Maker (IRE) (38) *(MrsNMacauley)* 3-8-3 NDay (9) (in tch: kpt on u.p
　　　　wl over 1f out: nrst fin) ............................................................ 4.3
1427 Starchy Cove (39) *(BRCambidge)* 5-8-5 ‡⁵RPrice (11) (hdwy over 2f out: rdn &
　　　　r.o ins fnl f) ....................................................................... s.h.4
2159⁵ Quinzii Martin (53) (v) *(DHaydnJones)* 4-9-5 ‡⁵SWilliams (10) (bhd: hrd rdn 2f
　　　　out: kpt on ins fnl f: nrst fin) .................................................... 2.5
2291 Lord Leitrim (IRE) (48) *(NACallaghan)* 3-8-13 WRyan (7) (lw: dwlt: r.o fnl 2f: nvr
　　　　nrr) ................................................................................... hd.6
1289⁵ In a Whirl (USA) (55) *(DRLaing)* 4-9-12 TyroneWilliams (4) (swtg: hdwy ½-wy:
　　　　kpt on wl over 1f out: nt pce to chal) .......................................... 2.7
2103⁶ State Governor (51) *(DWChapman)* 4-9-8 SWood (6) (chsd ldrs: rdn 2f out: sn
　　　　btn) ................................................................................... 1.8
2280³ Strip Cartoon (IRE) (57) (bl) *(SRBowring)* 4-9-7 ‡⁷MHarris (2) (lost pl after 4f:
　　　　unbalanced ent st: sn rdn: no imp) .............................................. 3.9
353 Another Nut (44) *(PDEvans)* 3-8-9 LCharnock (0) (nvr nr ldrs) .......... 1½.10
2333⁵ Spanish Realm (42) *(MBrittain)* 5-8-13 GCarter (5) (b.hind: prom: hrd rdn over
　　　　2f out: sn wknd) ................................................................... nk.11
1427⁴ Klairover (46) *(CJHill)* 5-9-3 NAdams (12) (s.i.s: a bhd) .................. ¾.12
2366 Aegaen Lady (54) (v) *(JEtherington)* 3-9-5 TLucas (13) (plld hrd: gd spd 4f) . nk.13

9/2 Morpick, 5/1 Strip Cartoon (IRE), 6/1 JOVIAL KATE (USA), 7/1 Quinzii Martin(op 9/2), 8/1 Lord Leitrim
(IRE)(tchd 12/1), 9/1 The Dream Maker (IRE), 10/1 In a Whirl (USA), 12/1 Klairover, 14/1 Spanish Realm, 20/1
State Governor, Starchy Cove, 25/1 Aegaen Lady, 33/1 Another Nut. CSF £31.58, CT £224.75. Tote £6.50:
£2.40 £1.80 £2.70 (£17.20). Mr Philip Serbert (MALTON) bred by Northwest Farms in USA. 13 Rn
　　　　　　　　　　　　　　　　　　　　　　　　　　　　　　　　　　　　　1m 15.5 (2.1)
　　　　　　　　　　　　　　　　　　　　　　　　　　　　　　　　　　SF—41/21/–/–/–/–

## 2482 PARIS STKS (Mdn 2-Y.O) £1182.00 (£327.00: £156.00)　　6f (AWT)　　7-45 (7-48)

2024 **Astrac Trio (USA)** *(SGNorton)* 9-0 KDarley (5) (a.p: led over 1f out: r.o wl) ....... —1
Sylvan Starlight *(SirMarkPrescott)* 8-9 GDuffield (10) (lt-f: sn chsng ldrs: kpt on
　　　　ins fnl f: no ch w wnr) ........................................................... 3.2
2205² Kennedys Prima (Fav) *(AAScott)* 8-9 BRaymond (4) (led tl hdd & wknd over 1f
　　　　out) ................................................................................... 2½.3
2049⁶ Dream a Bit *(JGFitzGerald)* 8-9 KFallon (7) (lw: a.p: hrd rdn wl over 4f out: r.o
　　　　one pce) ............................................................................. s.h.4
2038² Trundley Wood *(GAPritchard-Gordon)* 8-9 WRyan (9) (prom tl wknd wl over 1f
　　　　out) ................................................................................... 3.5
Formidable Liz *(NBycroft)* 8-9 SWebster (3) (cmpt: bkwd: hdwy u.p over 1f out:
　　　　nvr nrr) .............................................................................. nk.6
1946⁶ Sian Wyn *(JBerry)* 8-9 JCarroll (8) (chsd ldrs: rdn 2f out: sn btn) ............ hd.7
2363 Ignited *(MrsNMacauley)* 9-0 NDay (6) (leggy: lt-f: bit bkwd: s.s: a outpcd & bhd:
　　　　t.o) .................................................................................... 4.8
1553⁴ Oriental Princess *(MrsSOliver)* 8-9 GCarter (1) (s.s: outpcd: a bhd: t.o) ......... 20.10

8/11 Kennedys Prima(Evens—4/6), 6/1 Trundley Wood, 10/1 ASTRAC TRIO (USA), Ignited, 12/1 Dream a
Bit(op 8/1), 14/1 Sylvan Starlight, 16/1 Sian Wyn, 25/1 Oriental Princess, 50/1 Ors. CSF £120.94, Tote £16.60:
£2.60 £2.30 £1.10 (£240.50). Mr T. L. Beecroft (BARNSLEY) bred by William Floyd in USA. 10 Rn
　　　　　　　　　　　　　　　　　　　　　　　　　　　　　　　　　　　　　1m 15.9 (2.5)
　　　　　　　　　　　　　　　　　　　　　　　　　　　　　　　　　　SF—20/3/–/–/–/–

## 2483 EAST MIDLANDS ELECTRICITY H'CAP (0-70) £1245.00 (£345.00: £165.00)
1m (AWT)　　　　　　　　　　　　　　　　　　　　　　　　　　　　8-15 (8-16)

2210 **Miss Sarajane** (45) *(RHollinshead)* 8-8-7 WRyan (2) (lw: a.p: led after 2f: hdd
　　　　& 2nd st: rallied gamely u.p to ld cl home) .................................. —1

2366⁴ No Decision (52) (bl) *(MWEasterby)* 5–9-0 TLucas (9) (a.p: led ent st: rdn over 1f out: hdd nr fin) ............................................... nk.2

2198⁵ L'Acquesiana (31) (v) *(DShaw)* 4–7-7 RStreet (5) (b: prom: 3rd st: jnd ldrs 1f out: rdn & no ex nr fin) ............................................... ³/₄.3

1721³ Premier Dance (54) *(DHaydnJones)* 5–9-2 TyroneWilliams (8) (rdn thrght: 6th st: nvr plcd to chal) ............................................... 10.4

Charly Pharly (FR) (66) (bl) *(FHLee)* 5–10-0 RLappin (4) (bit bkwd: chsd ldrs: 4th st: wknd wl over 1f out) ............................................... ¹/₂.5

Manse Key Gold (36) *(JDooler)* 5–7-9 ‡³JFanning (6) (a in rr) ............................................... 4.6

1793 Chloes Diamond (IRE) (54) *(JLSpearing)* 4–8-9 ‡⁷EHusband (7) (nvr trbld ldrs) . 5.7

1992 Crofter's Cline (60) (v) (Fav) *(ABailey)* 8–9-8 GCarter (1) (lw: led 2f: lost pl & 5th st: sn bhd) ............................................... 2¹/₂.8

1551⁶ Mushy Boff (52) *(CJHill)* 4–9-0 NAdams (3) (lost pl ¹/₂-wy: t.o ent st) ............................................... 2.9

LONG HANDICAP: L'Acquesiana 7-1.

**4/1** Crofter's Cline, **9/2** Mushy Boff, **11/2** No Decision, MISS SARAJANE, **15/2** Premier Dance, **9/1** Chloes Diamond (IRE), **10/1** L'Acquesiana, **16/1** Charly Pharly (FR), **33/1** Manse Key Gold. CSF £30.74, CT £234.59. Tote £5.70: £1.80 £1.30 £2.70 (£9.80). Mr J. Smyth (UPPER LONGDON) bred by W. and Mrs Whitehead. 9 Rn
1m 42.7 (3.4)
SF—12/18/–/–/–/–

---

**2484**     ARIES H'CAP (0-70) £1245.00 (£345.00: £165.00)     **1¹/₂m (AWT)**     8-45 (8-45)
(Weights raised 7 lb)

2218⁶ **Must Be Magical (USA) (23)** (bl) *(FHLee)* 4–8-5 RLappin (7) (lw: mde all: sn clr: styd on strly) ............................................... —1

2047⁴ Not Yet (42) *(EWeymes)* 8–9-10 DMcKeown (3) (swtg: chsd ldrs: 4th st: styd on u.p appr fnl f: nvr nrr) ............................................... 1.2

2036³ Atlantic Way (39) *(CJHill)* 4–9-7 NAdams (8) (hdwy & 5th st: rdn 2f out: styd on: nt rch ldrs) ............................................... 3.3

2156* Pie Hatch (IRE) (49) (Fav) *(SirMarkPrescott)* 3–9-5 GDuffield (4) (a.p: 2nd st: wknd 2f out) ............................................... 2.4

2367* Grey Commander (39) *(MBrittain)* 4–9-7 (5x) KDarley (5) (hld up: effrt & 8th st: hrd rdn wl over 1f out: nvr nr to chal) ............................................... 4.5

2367³ Swell Time (IRE) (30) *(CNAllen)* 4–8-5 ‡⁷GForster (9) (b.hind: hdwy 8f out: 3rd st: sn rdn & wknd) ............................................... 1¹/₂.6

2204 One for the Boys (38) *(CaptJWilson)* 5–9-6 WRyan (5) (b: lw: lost pl 5f out: t.o) 20.7

1530 Ben's Beauty (32) (bl) *(MrsSOliver)* 4–9-0 SPerks (2) (s.i.s: t.o fr ¹/₂-wy) ............... 12.8

**9/4** Pie Hatch (IRE), **100/30** Swell Time (IRE), **5/1** Grey Commander, Atlantic Way, **8/1** Not Yet, **25/1** MUST BE MAGICAL (USA), One for the Boys, **33/1** Ben's Beauty. CSF £173.35, CT £963.20. Tote £26.80: £3.70 £1.50 £2.30 (£33.40). Mr F. H. Lee (WILMSLOW) bred by Flaxman Holdings Ltd in USA. 8 Rn     2m 39.6 (5.4)
SF—7/24/15/9/15/–

T/Plpt: £149.00 (7.55 Tckts).     IM

---

## 2308—HAMILTON (R-H)

### Thursday, July 30th [Good, Good to firm patches]

Going Allowance: St: minus 0.20 sec; Rnd: nil sec per fur (F)     Wind: slt against

Stalls: low

**2485**     HYNDFORD CLAIMING STKS (3-Y.O) £2238.00 (£618.00: £294.00)     
1¹/₂m 17y     2-45 (2-46)

2111* **Grouse-N-Heather (60)** (Fav) *(MrsGRReveley)* 8-5 ‡³JFanning (3) (hld up: rdn to chal 2f out: styd on u.p to ld cl home) ............................................... —1

2148⁴ Miliyel (49) *(PMonteith)* 8-0 LCharnock (2) (chsd ldrs: qcknd to ld 8f out: rdn appr fnl f: hdd & no ex nr fin) ............................................... ¹/₂.2

2311⁵ Solstice (99) *(MrsGRReveley)* 8-11 KDarley (1) (led 4f: prom: ev ch & rdn 4f out: sn wknd & wl bhd) ............................................... 25.3

**2/7** GROUSE-N-HEATHER, **7/2** Miliyel, **16/1** Solstice. CSF £1.53, Tote £1.50 (£1.10). Mr Robbie Cameron (SALTBURN) bred by R. A. Cameron. 3 Rn     2m 42.5 (10.5)

---

**2486**     BONNINGTON (S) STKS     £2469.00 (£684.00: £327.00)     **1m 1f 36y**     3-15 (3-18)

2326⁵ Henbury Hall (IRE) (62) *(MrsGRReveley)* 4–9-7 DMcKeown (10) (a.p: led on bit wl over 1f out: sn rdn & hung lft: styd on) ............................................... —1

Persian Fleece *(MrsGRReveley)* 3–8-0 JFanning (11) (hld up: hdwy appr st: rdn 2f out: styd on wl fnl f) ............................................... s.h.2

1893⁵ Shardra *(MJCamacho)* 3–8-0 NConnorton (4) (a.p: led 4f out tl hdd 2f out: kpt on fnl f) ............................................... nk.3

**2487 — 2490**

2020 Reel of Tulloch (IRE) **(62)** (bl) *(Fav)* *(PCHaslam)* 3-8-12 KDarley (7) (w ldrs: disp ld 4f out: led 2f out: sn rdn: hdd wl over 1f out: nt qckn) 1.4
1996 Alicante **(42)** *(FJYardley)* 5-9-0 KFallon (8) (cl up: rdn 3f out: one pce) ............ 4.5
2365⁵ Capital Idea (IRE) **(50)** *(RonaldThompson)* 3-8-12 JLowe (6) (in tch: effrt over 2f out: no imp) ................................................................ nk.6
Swank Gilbert *(TAKCuthbert)* 6-9-0 LCharnock (3) (nvr trbld ldrs) ................. 2¹/₂.7
Morcinda **(50)** *(PMonteith)* 6-9-5(5) ‡7ADobbin (9) (hld up & bhd: effrt 3f out: one pce) .......................................................................... nk.8
2072⁶ Bold Mood **(40)** *(JBerry)* 3-8-5 GCarter (5) (led tl hdd 4f out: sn wknd) ............ 4.9
2209 Son of Pearl (IRE) (40/1) Withdrawn (ref to ent stalls) : not under orders

**11/10** Reel of Tulloch (IRE), **9/4** HENBURY HALL (IRE), **14/1** Capital Idea (IRE), Alicante, **16/1** Shardra, Persian Fleece, **20/1** Morcinda, **33/1** Bold Mood, **100/1** Swank Gilbert. CSF £31.44, Tote £2.70: £1.10 £9.70 £2.60 (£31.10). Mrs M. E. Gray (SALTBURN) bred by Tally Ho Stud Co (UK) Ltd & Ninevah Ltd in Ireland. 9 Rn; Bt in 3,200 gns
1m 59.6 (5.3)
SF—27/5/4/13/3/–

**2487** EARNOCK H'CAP (0-70) £2713.40 (£752.40: £360.20) **1m 65y** 3-50 (3-52)
(Weights raised 8 lb)

2311★ Bold Melody **(53)** *(Fav)* *(PCHaslam)* 3-9-5 (5x) KDarley (1) (a cl up: slt ld 4f out: rdn & r.o wl fnl f) ...................................................... —1
2291★ Champenoise **(49)** *(MBell)* 4-9-9 (5x) DMcKeown (5) (b.hind: trckd ldrs: hdwy on bit over 2f out: ev ch & rdn appr fnl f: nt r.o) ................ 2.2
2150⁵ Master Plan (FR) **(23)** *(MissLAPerratt)* 6-7-11 JFanning (3) (hld up & bhd: effrt over 2f out: styd on: nt pce to chal) ................................... 1¹/₂.3
Reza **(50)** *(JLEyre)* 4-9-5 ‡5OPears (2) (led tl hdd 4f out: one pce) ............. 1.4
2210⁴ Lombard Ships **(50)** *(MO'Neill)* 5-9-10 GCarter (4) (prom: rdn & ev ch 2f out: nt qckn) ........................................................................... nk.5

**Evens** BOLD MELODY, **2/1** Champenoise, **5/1** Lombard Ships, **14/1** Reza, **33/1** Master Plan (FR). CSF £3.23, Tote £1.60: £1.10 £2.20 (£1.90). Mrs P. Haslam (MIDDLEHAM) bred by Deepwood Farm Stud. 5 Rn
1m 53.8 (10.5)

**2488** ORBISTON AUCTION STKS (Mdn 2-Y.O) £2196.00 (£606.00: £288.00)
**6f 5y** 4-25 (4-26)

Montone (IRE) *(Fav)* *(CBBBooth)* 8-11 GOldroyd (2) (cmpt: str: trckd ldrs: hdwy to ld wl over 1f out: rn green & styd on) ....................... —1
1112 Penny Banger (IRE) *(MJohnston)* 8-3 DMcKeown (4) (a w ldrs: rdn & ev ch appr fnl f: kpt on) .......................................................... 1¹/₂.2
2176 Critical Mass *(JBerry)* 8-12 GCarter (5) (prom: effrt 2f out: one pce) .............. 1.3
1762⁶ Special Risk (IRE) *(MBell)* 8-12 KDarley (3) (led tl hdd wl over 1f out: no ex) .... nk.4
2264⁵ Sweet Poppy *(JSWainwright)* 8-3 LCharnock (1) (chsd ldrs 3f: sn wknd) ........... 3.5

**7/4** MONTONE (IRE), **2/1** Special Risk (IRE), **9/4** Critical Mass, **12/1** Penny Banger (IRE), **25/1** Sweet Poppy. CSF £16.70, Tote 2.40: £1.10 £1.40 (£17.60). Mr C. B. B. Booth (FLAXTON) bred by Sean Gorman in Ireland. 5 Rn
1m 13 (3)
SF—11/-/-/-/–

**2489** E.B.F. WALLACE STKS (Mdn 2-Y.O) £2320.00 (£640.00: £304.00)
**5f 4y** 5-00 (5-00)

917 Just Baileys *(Fav)* *(MJohnston)* 8-9 DMcKeown (4) (mde all: drew clr wl over 1f out: unchal) ...................................................... —1
807 Salt N Vinegar (IRE) *(RonaldThompson)* 9-0 JLowe (2) (chsd ldrs: rdn ¹/₂-wy: styd on: no ch w wnr) .............................................. 15.2
Coffee Mint *(JBerry)* 8-9 GCarter (3) (neat: leggy: prom: drvn along ¹/₂-wy: one pce fnl 2f) .................................................................... 3¹/₂.3
Greetland Glory *(JBerry)* 8-9 LCharnock (1) (small: str: bit bkwd: s.i.s: sn drvn along: n.d) ...................................................... 2.4

**Evens** JUST BAILEYS, **2/1** Coffee Mint(op 5/4), **6/1** Salt N Vinegar (IRE), **16/1** Greetland Glory(op 10/1). CSF £5.73, Tote £1.60 (£2.70). G. R. Bailey Ltd (Baileys Horse Feeds) (MIDDLEHAM) bred by P. and Mrs Venner. 4 Rn
60.8 sec (2.5)
SF—25/-/-/-/–

**2490** GAETAN BILLIARD CHAMPAGNE SPRINT APP'CE H'CAP (F & M) (0-80) £2322.00
(£642.00: £306.00) **5f 4y** 5-35 (5-35)

1053² Penny Hasset **(68)** *(MWEasterby)* 4-10-0 JMarshall (1) (cl up: rdn 2f out: led ent fnl f: r.o) ...................................................... —1
2214 Furiella **(67)** *(PCHaslam)* 4-9-8 ‡5NicolaHowarth (3) (led tl hdd ent fnl f: kpt on same pce) ........................................................ 2.2

2325³ Pretonic (60) (Fav) (MJohnston) 4-9-6 LNewton (2) (w ldrs: rdn 2f out: ev ch
appr fnl f: nt qckn) ...................................................................... 1¹/₂.3

**13/8** Pretonic, **2/1** PENNY HASSET & Ors. CSF £5.17, Tote £2.50 (£2.50). Mrs Anne Henson (SHERIFF HUTTON)
bred by Mrs Anne Henson. 3 Rn                                              59.8 sec (1.5)
SF—64/50/42

T/Plpt: £105.80 (10.25 Tckts).                                                          GB

## 2031—SALISBURY (R-H)
### Thursday, July 30th [Firm]
Going Allowance: minus 0.35 sec per fur (F)                              Wind: nil

Stalls: high

**2491**        NEWNHAM STKS (Mdn 2-Y-O) £1987.50 (£550.00: £262.50)     **5f**     6-15 (6-16)

2034⁶ **Top Pet (IRE)** (RHannon) 9-0 JReid (1) (lw: a.p: rdn & edgd rt over 1f out: led wl
ins fnl f: r.o) ............................................................................. —1
Sarena Lady (IRE) (PFICole) 8-9 TQuinn (7) (lt-f: unf: led tl wl ins fnl f) .............. 1.2
Don'tlie (IRE) (GBBalding) 8-9 JWilliams (2) (unf: b.nr hind: outpcd tl rapid
hdwy fnl f: fin fast) ................................................................... s.h.3
Pontevecchio Moda (DRCElsworth) 8-9 WCarson (4) (small: rdn & hdwy 2f out:
r.o ins fnl f) ............................................................................. ³/₄.4
2171⁴ Saraswati (Fav) (PJMakin) 8-9 LDettori (3) (prom: rdn over 1f out: btn whn nt clr
run ins fnl f) .......................................................................... ³/₄.5
2256³ Kildee Lad (APJones) 9-0 NAdams (5) (w ldr tl wknd over 1f out) ................... 1.6
Ivy Benson (BWHills) 8-9 DHolland (6) (cmpt: dwlt: a bhd: t.o) ......................... 12.7

**11/10** Saraswati, **5/2** Sarena Lady (IRE), **11/2** Pontevecchio Moda(4/1—6/1), **6/1** TOP PET (IRE)(4/1—13/2),
**12/1** Don'tlie (IRE), **14/1** Ivy Benson(op 6/1), **20/1** Kildee Lad. CSF £22.24, Tote £5.80: £2.10 £2.00 (£10.10).
Mrs A. Valentine (MARLBOROUGH) bred by P. Valentine in Ireland. 7 Rn              61.32 sec (1.32)
SF—39/30/29/26/23/24

**2492**        PEMBROKE H'CAP (0-70) £2784.00 (£774.00: £372.00)       **1¹/₂m**    6-45 (6-46)
                         (Weights raised 3 lb)

2305² **Rocquaine Bay** (35) (Jt-Fav) (MJBolton) 5-7-12 CRutter (2) (swtg: bhd: hdwy
3f out: swtchd 2f out: hung rt 1f out: led ins fnl f: r.o wl) ........................ —1
2036* Caspian Beluga (57) (Jt-Fav) (MrsAKnight) 4-9-6 SWhitworth (1) (lw: led: sn
clr: hdd ins fnl f) ..................................................................... 4.2
1278 Killick (36) (REPeacock) 4-7-13⁽¹⁾ DHolland (6) (chsd ldrs: hrd rdn over 2f out:
one pce) ................................................................................ 6.3
2255⁶ Bee Beat (57) (bl) (EAWheeler) 4-9-6 AClark (11) (bhd tl hdwy fnl 2f: nrst fin) .... 2.4
2255* Bold Resolution (IRE) (56) (Jt-Fav) (CACyzer) 4-9-5 (5x) TQuinn (12) (lw: rdn &
hdwy over 3f out: one pce fnl 2f) ..................................................... 1¹/₂.5
2372 Head Turner (30) (CPWildman) 4-7-7 NAdams (4) (no hdwy fnl 3f) ..................... 3.6
2036⁵ Holly Brown (42) (PJHobbs) 9-8-2 ‡³TSprake (5) (lw: rdn over 4f out: no hdwy) 1¹/₂.7
1640⁵ Arrastra (60) (IABalding) 4-9-9 JReid (13) (plld hrd: prom tl wknd over 2f out) ... 6.8
1284 Classics Pearl (IRE) (36) (NATwiston-Davies) 4-7-13 TyroneWilliams (3) (nvr nr
ldrs) .................................................................................... s.h.9
1914 Master of the Rock (66) (bl) (PJMakin) 3-9-3 LDettori (10) (prom: rdn 5f out:
wknd over 3f out) ..................................................................... ³/₄.10
2235 Q-Eight (IRE) (52) (APJarvis) 4-9-1 AMcGlone (7) (a in rr: t.o fnl 4f) ............ 15.11
1975 Alrayed (USA) (61) (MajorWRHern) 4-9-10 WCarson (9) (swtg: a in rr: t.o fnl 4f) 20.12
Come to Good (32) (MPMuggeridge) 5-7-9⁽²⁾ AMackay (8) (s.s: plld hrd: sn
prom: wknd over 4f out: t.o fnl 3f) ................................................... 6.13
LONG HANDICAP: Head Turner 7-5, Come to Good 7-6.

**9/2** ROCQUAINE BAY, Bold Resolution (IRE)(op 3/1), Caspian Beluga, **6/1** Alrayed (USA), Arrastra(op 4/1), **10/1**
Holly Brown, Master of the Rock, **12/1** Bee Beat(8/1—14/1), Q-Eight (IRE), **25/1** Head Turner, Killick, **33/1** Ors.
CSF £25.63, CT £432.56. Tote £4.30: £1.60 £1.80 £12.80 (£8.80). Mr D. C. Woollard (SHREWTON) bred by
Ann L. Woollard. 13 Rn                                                    2m 33.12 (0.52)
SF—37/51/18/35/31/–

**2493**        DOWNING CLAIMING STKS (3-Y-O) £2022.50 (£560.00: £267.50)   **6f**    7-15 (7-19)

2280⁴ **Venture Capitalist** (84) (bl) (Fav) (RHannon) 9-1 JReid (11) (mde all: clr over 1f
out: easily) ............................................................................ —1
The New Girl (69) (CCEIsey) 8-6 DHolland (3) (s.i.s: hrd rdn & hdwy over 1f out:
r.o ins fnl f) .......................................................................... 5.2
2411⁵ Lifetime Fame (76) (JWPayne) 8-11 MRoberts (9) (lw: chsd wnr: hrd rdn 2f out:
no imp) ................................................................................ hd.3

2227⁵ Leigh Crofter **(66)** (bl) *(RJHolder)* 8-1 ‡⁷SDrowne (2) (a.p: hrd rdn over 2f out: one pce) ............................................................. 2½.4
1795⁶ Orchard Bay **(46)** *(DRTucker)* 8-1 GBardwell (5) (lw: nvr nr to chal) .................. 2.5
2234 Upthorpe Girl *(APJarvis)* 8-0 AMcGlone (8) (prom: hrd rdn & wknd over 2f out) ½.6
2265⁵ Little Saboteur **(77)** (bl) *(PJMakin)* 8-5⁽¹⁾ LDettori (7) (prom over 3f) ................ 2½.7
2006⁵ Ben Bluff **(48)** *(LGCottrell)* 8-11 TRogers (10) (prom tl rdn & wknd over 2f out) nk.8
1745 Sizzling Affair **(53)** *(TCasey)* 8-4 ‡³TSprake (1) (bhd fnl 2f) ........................... 4.9
1975⁶ Joshua John (IRE) *(BRMillman)* 8-8 JWilliams (4) (lw: s.i.s: a bhd) .................. 6.10
Apache Maid *(JSMoore)* 8-3 JQuinn (6) (lengthy: a bhd) ................................. 2.11

**21/20** VENTURE CAPITALIST(4/6—11/10), **4/1** Lifetime Fame, **5/1** Little Saboteur(op 3/1), **6/1** Leigh Crofter(tchd 16/1), **12/1** The New Girl, **25/1** Joshua John (IRE), **33/1** Ben Bluff, Sizzling Affair, Upthorpe Girl, **40/1** Orchard Bay, **50/1** Apache Maid. CSF £15.01, Tote £2.00: £1.10 £2.60 £1.90 (£10.80). Mr D. K. Harris (MARLBOROUGH) bred by Brook Bloodstock Plc. 11 Rn
1m 13.54 (1.24)
SF—34/5/9/–/–/–

## 2494
OVER TO YOU JOHN H'CAP (0-80) £3418.00 (£1024.00: £492.00: £226.00)
**6f 212y**                                                          7-45 (7-52)

2254⁴ **Teanarco (IRE) (59)** *(RJHolder)* 4-8-10 MRoberts (6) (lw: hld up & plld hrd: rdn 2f out: led ins fnl f: r.o wl) .................................................. —1
2035⁴ Aitch N'Bee **(74)** *(LadyHerries)* 9-9-11 LDettori (5) (lw: hdwy over 2f out: hrd rdn over 1f out: btn whn edgd rt wl ins fnl f) ............................. 1½.2
2417⁴ Rywater Dream **(48)** *(RJHodges)* 4-7-13 WCarson (3) (led over 3f out tl ins fnl f) .............................................................................................. ¾.3
2307 Maria Cappuccini **(53)** *(KOCunningham-Brown)* 4-8-4 DHolland (9) (hdwy over 2f out: hrd rdn over 1f out: nt qckn ins fnl f) ............................. 1.4
2198★ Lucky Noire **(60)** *(GHarwood)* 4-8-4 ‡⁷GayeHarwood (8) (hld up on ins: plld out & nt olr run 2f out: r.o ins fnl f) ........................................ ¾.5
1776★ Respectable Jones **(71)** *(GBBalding)* 6-9-8 JWilliams (10) (lw: prom tl wknd fnl f) .............................................................................................. 2½.6
2268★ Dream Carrier (IRE) **(72)** (Fav) *(RHannon)* 4-9-9 (6x) PaulEddery (2) (prom: hrd rdn & wknd over 1f out) ....................................................... s.h.7
233 En Attendant (FR) **(77)** *(BHanbury)* 4-10-0 BRaymond (1) (lw: hld up & bhd: nvr plcd to chal) ....................................................................... ¾.8
2036 Hightown-Princess (IRE) **(43)** *(JSMoore)* 4-7-8⁽¹⁾ JQuinn (11) (prom 5f) ........ 1.9
2254 Bright Sea (USA) **(42)** *(WRWilliams)* 4-7-7 NAdams (7) (led over 3f: t.o) ...... 10.10
1811⁵ Hitchin a Ride **(53)** *(MPMuggeridge)* 5-8-4 AClark (4) (bhd fnl 2f) ............. 2.11
LONG HANDICAP: Hightown-Princess (IRE) 6-13.

**13/8** Dream Carrier (IRE), **11/2** Rywater Dream, **6/1** TEANARCO (IRE), **7/1** Lucky Noire(4/1—8/1), **8/1** Aitch N'Bee(op 5/1), Respectable Jones, **9/1** Maria Cappuccini(op 6/1), **10/1** En Attendant (FR), **25/1** Hitchin a Ride, **50/1** Ors. CSF £53.12, CT £261.65. Tote £7.30: £2.20 £2.30 £1.50 (£20.40). Mr B. K. Symonds (BRISTOL) bred by R. A. Collins in Ireland. 11 Rn
1m 27.56 (1.86)
SF—31/41/13/15/13/23

## 2495
TRINITY MEDIAN AUCTION GRADUATION STKS (3-Y.O.F) £2364.00 (£654.00: £312.00)
**1m 1f 209y**                                                      8-15 (8-17)

370³ **Double Flutter** *(MRChannon)* 8-8 PaulEddery (5) (hld up & bhd: hdwy over 4f out: rdn to ld 2f out: r.o wl) ............................................................. —1
1712 Hidden Laughter (USA) **(81)** *(BWHills)* 9-1 DHolland (1) (led 5f: hrd rdn & ev ch 2f out: one pce) .................................................................... 3½.2
2020³ Legal Embrace (CAN) **(76)** (Fav) *(JRFanshawe)* 9-1 WCarson (2) (plld hrd: chsd ldr: led 5f out to 2f out: one pce) ........................................... 3.3
1238 Golden Proposal **(47)** *(MJBolton)* 8-8 CRutter (4) (t.o fnl 4f) ................... 20.4
2137⁶ Private Practice *(MJHeaton-Ellis)* 8-8 JReid (3) (t.o fnl 3f) ...................... 4.5

**6/4** Legal Embrace (CAN), **13/8** DOUBLE FLUTTER, **3/1** Hidden Laughter (USA), **11/1** Private Practice, **33/1** Golden Proposal. CSF £6.74, Tote £2.60: £1.70 £2.10 (£4.50). Mr John W. Mitchell (UPPER LAMBOURN) bred by M. Channon. 5 Rn
2m 7.13 (2.43)
SF—35/35/29/–/–

## 2496
ROBINSON H'CAP (3-Y.O) (0-70) £2868.00 (£798.00: £384.00)   **1m**   8-45 (8-47)

2230⁶ **Singers Image (61)** (v) *(GBBalding)* 8-13 JWilliams (5) (hdwy over 3f out: led over 1f out: edgd lft ins fnl f: jst hld on) .................................... —1
2077⁵ Deevee **(43)** *(CJBenstead)* 7-9 TyroneWilliams (13) (lw: hdwy 2f out: ev ch ins fnl f: r.o) ............................................................................................. s.h.2
1890⁴ Wakil (IRE) **(44)** *(LGCottrell)* 7-10 NCarlisle (15) (lw: a.p: r.o ins fnl f) ......... 1.3
2006⁴ Court Minstrel **(66)** *(LJHolt)* 9-0 JReid (10) (a.p: ev ch over 1f out: one pce) ... 2½.4
1917 Silky Siren **(54)** *(EAWheeler)* 8-6 SWhitworth (12) (hld up: stdy hdwy 2f out: nvr plcd to chal) ......................................................................... 1½.5

```
1799 Norman Warrior (54) (DMorris) 8-1 ‡5StephenDavies (4) (no hdwy fnl 2f) ........ 1½.6
2184 Our Occasion (69) (RHannon) 9-7 MRoberts (1) (no hdwy fnl 2f) ................... 2.7
2230² Mustahil (IRE) (66) (bl) (RJHodges) 9-1 ‡³TSprake (17) (led over 6f) ........... ½.8
1421 Dominant Serenade (54) (PWHarris) 8-3 ‡³FNorton (11) (nvr nrr) ................. 2.9
2240∗ Lamore Ritorna (55) (KOCunningham-Brown) 8-7 (5x) DHolland (2) (prom 6f) 2½.10
1642⁶ Rockbourne (52) (Fav) (DRCElsworth) 8-4 WCarson (18) (bhd fnl 2f) .......... 1.11
1955 Aedean (56) (CAHorgan) 8-8 AMcGlone (7) (n.d) .............................. s.h.12
       Jolto (42) (KOCunningham-Brown) 7-8⁽¹⁾ JQuinn (8) (prom over 5f) ......... 2½.13
1975⁴ Tom's Apache (51) (bl) (WRWilliams) 7-12⁽²⁾ ‡5RPrice (16) (n.d) ........... hd.14
2230⁵ Duty Sergeant (IRE) (52) (bl) (MPMuggeridge) 8-4 AClark (14) (prom 5f) ....... 2.15
1589 Chinaman (46) (bl) (WGRWightman) 7-12 GBardwell (6) (t.o) ............... 20.16
2170⁶ Brave the Wind (52) (bl) (IABalding) 8-1 ‡³SO'Gorman (3) (prom 5f: t.o) ...... 1½.17
1767⁴ Athar (IRE) (50) (RJBaker) 8-2 RFox (9) (mid div: sddle slipped & uns rdr over 1f
                out) ............................................................................... 0
```
                          LONG HANDICAP: Jolto 7-3.

**9/2** Rockbourne(op 8/1), **5/1** Court Minstrel, Mustahil (IRE), **13/2** Brave the Wind, **7/1** Silky Siren(10/1—4/1), **8/1** Lamore Ritorna(op 5/1), Our Occasion(op 4/1), **9/1** Deevee(12/1—8/1), **10/1** Duty Sergeant (IRE), **11/1** Norman Warrior(8/1—12/1), **12/1** SINGERS IMAGE(8/1—14/1), **16/1** Aedean, Dominant Serenade, Tom's Apache, **20/1** Athar (IRE), Wakil (IRE), **25/1** Ors. CSF £140.73, CT £2,058.50. Tote £38.60: £5.10 £2.50 £7.90 £1.90 (£156.70). Miss B. Swire (DORCHESTER) bred by Miss B. Swire. 18 Rn        1m 42.05 (2.75)
                                                                                SF—16/–/–/5/–/–

T/Plpt: £372.00 (5.5 Tckts).                                                                KH

2283—**YARMOUTH (L-H)**

**Thursday, July 30th [Firm]**

Going Allowance: minus 0.10 sec per fur (F)                        Wind: slt across

Stalls: centre

**2497**    CARNIVAL STKS (Mdn) £2238.00 (£618.00: £294.00)    1¾m 17y    2-20 (2-21)

```
2089³ Receptionist (Fav) (HRACecil) 3-8-2 WRyan (3) (hld up: 3rd st: led 2f out: drvn
                out) .......................................................................... —1
1953⁴ Shesadelight (JLDunlop) 3-8-2 GDuffield (2) (lw: led 1f: 2nd st: led over 3f out
                to 2f out: one pce ins fnl f) ............................................. 1½.2
2287⁴ Santarem (USA) (WJHaggas) 4-9-2 NDay (1) (b: led after 1f tl over 3f out: sn
                rdn & outpcd) ............................................................. 12.3
```
**Evens** RECEPTIONIST, **11/8** Shesadelight, **4/1** Santarem (USA)(op 5/2). CSF £2.67, Tote £1.80 (£1.50). Cliveden Stud (NEWMARKET) bred by Cliveden Stud. 3 Rn            3m 6.6 (8.6)

**2498**    BRADWELL CLAIMING STKS (3-Y.O) £3124.00 (£864.00: £412.00)
            1¾m 17y                                              2-50 (2-51)

```
2057⁴ Cov Tel Lady (67) (Fav) (MHTompkins) 8-0⁽¹⁾ PRobinson (4) (lw: hld up & bhd:
                3rd st: led on bit wl ins fnl f: canter) ............................. —1
1990³ Alizari (USA) (bl) (GHarwood) 8-8 WRyan (1) (lw: chsd ldr: 2nd st: rdn to ld appr
                fnl f: hdd & no ex wl ins fnl f) ......................................... 1.2
2109⁶ Shanti Flyer (IRE) (47) (bl) (SPCWoods) 8-3 WWoods (2) (led: rdn & hdd 2f out:
                sn btn) .................................................................... 12.3
```
**4/6** COV TEL LADY(op Evens), **6/4** Alizari (USA), **10/1** Shanti Flyer (IRE)(op 6/1). CSF £1.94, Tote £1.70 (£1.10). Coventry Newspapers Limited (NEWMARKET) bred by Mrs R. Owen-George. 3 Rn        3m 6.1 (8.1)

**2499**    WOODBRIDGE H'CAP (0-70) £2928.00 (£808.00: £384.00)    5f 43y    3-25 (3-26)

```
2154² Spring High (47) (bl) (Fav) (KTIvory) 5-8-9 ‡7CScally (1) (mde most: rdn fnl f:
                led nr fin) ............................................................... —1
2206² Bells of Longwick (64) (DRLaing) 3-9-9 ‡5ATucker (3) (hld up: gd hdwy over 1f
                out: ev ch ins fnl f: r.o) ............................................. hd.2
2301∗ Ski Captain (59) (PHowling) 8-10-0 (7x) WNewnes (2) (a.p: slt ld ins fnl f:
                unable qckn cl home) ................................................ s.h.3
```
**11/10** SPRING HIGH, **2/1** Bells of Longwick, **9/4** Ski Captain. CSF £3.37, Tote £2.10 (£1.90). Mr K. T. Ivory (RADLETT) bred by Mrs P. A. Brown. 3 Rn            62.9 sec (2.6)
                                                                            SF—33/46/50

**2500**    MARINA LEISURE CENTRE (S) STKS (2-Y.O) £2364.00 (£654.00: £312.00)
            6f 3y                                              3-55 (3-57)

```
2080∗ Guv'nors Gift (Fav) (MHTompkins) 8-11 PRobinson (6) (hdwy ½-wy: rdn over
                1f out: r.o strly to ld last stride) .................................. —1
```

2284★ Red Ballet (bl) *(MrsNMacauley)* 8-6 ‡5SWilliams (7) (led: wl clr ent fnl f: wknd & ct post) ........................................................................ hd.2

19795 Stapleford Lass *(SPCWoods)* 8-6 WWoods (3) (b: hdwy wl over 1f out: kpt on ins fnl f: nvr nrr) ........................................................... 4.3

995 Baileys Colours *(BJMcMath)* 7-13 ‡7CHawksley (8) (chsd ldrs: effrt 2f out: no imp) ....................................................................... ¾.4

21952 Jasmin Isle *(MissGayKelleway)* 8-6 WNewnes (4) (chsd ldrs over 4f: sn rdn & wknd) ..................................................................... 7.5

2055 Monet Order *(JRJenkins)* 8-11 ‡5SMaloney (1) (prom over 3f: sn wknd: t.o) ....... 20.6

1170 Our Nikki (v) *(GBlum)* 8-6 AShoults (5) (swtg: s.s: a outpcd: t.o) ................. 8.7

**5/6** GUV'NORS GIFT, **11/4** Jasmin Isle, **6/1** Stapleford Lass, **13/2** Red Ballet, **20/1** Monet Order, **33/1** Ors. CSF £7.16, Tote £2.10: £1.40 £2.20 (£3.70). The Tompkins Team (NEWMARKET) bred by Stud-On-The-Chart. 7 Rn; Bt in 3,200 gns     1m 14.6 (4)
                                             SF—6/–/–/–/–/–

## 2501

E.B.F. COTMAN STKS (Mdn 2-Y.O.F) £2406.00 (£666.00: £318.00)
7f 3y                               4-30 (4-33)

16002 **Self Assured (IRE)** (Fav) *(HRACecil)* 8-11 WRyan (9) (a.p: led over 1f out: drvn clr fnl f) ..................................................................... —1

Quinsigimond *(SirMarkPrescott)* 8-11 GDuffield (4) (w'like: bit bkwd: unruly stalls: dwlt: hdwy 4f out: styd on fnl f: no ch w wnr) .............. 4.2

1867 Half a Dozen (USA) *(AAScott)* 8-11 JFortune (6) (hdwy over 2f out: styd on wl ins fnl f) ...................................................................... nk.3

13224 Don't Jump (IRE) *(MHTompkins)* 8-11 PRobinson (5) (lw: led: clr ½-wy: hdd over 1f out: sn btn) .............................................................. 2.4

La Delitzia (USA) *(PFICole)* 8-11 GBaxter (1) (leggy: lt-f: unf: prom tl wknd wl over 1f out) ................................................................. 5.5

19575 Jafetica *(DRLaing)* 0-11 NDay (2) (chsd ldrs over 4f) ...................... ¾.6

21905 Ikhtisas (USA) *(BHanbury)* 8-11 DaleGibson (7) (dwlt: a bhd) .............. 1½.7

2167 Cursory Glance (IRE) *(AAScott)* 8-11 WNewnes (8) (still bkwd: s.i.s: a bhd) ..... 3.8

Jolis Absent *(MJRyan)* 8-11 MTebbutt (3) (w'like: scope: bkwd: a bhd) ........... 2.9

**1/3** SELF ASSURED (IRE), **11/2** Ikhtisas (USA), **15/2** La Delitzia (USA), **16/1** Quinsigimond, Don't Jump (IRE), Half a Dozen (USA), **33/1** Ors. CSF £9.10, Tote £1.30: £1.00 £3.80 £6.20 (£11.90). Sheikh Mohammed (NEWMARKET) bred by Mount Coote Stud in Ireland. 9 Rn     1m 26.3 (3.5)
                               SF—34/22/21/15/–/–

## 2502

WROXHAM H'CAP (0-80) £3289.50 (£981.00: £468.00: £211.50)    7f 3y   5-05 (5-07)
(Weights raised 1 lb)

22834 Coral Flutter (51) (bl) *(JWPayne)* 5-8-2(1) GDuffield (4) (mde virtually all: rdn out) ........................................................................ —1

2283★ Queen of Shannon (IRE) (69) *(DMorris)* 4-9-6 (6x) MTebbutt (1) (lw: chsd ldrs: effrt over 1f out: rdn & no ex nr fin) .................................. 1½.2

22892 Roca Murada (IRE) (51) *(MJRyan)* 3-7-2(1) ‡7CHawksley (3) (hld up: hdwy 2f out: rdn & unable qckn fnl f) ........................................... 1½.3

22902 Farmer Jock (54) *(MrsNMacauley)* 10-8-5 PRobinson (5) (hld up: effrt u.p appr fnl f: nvr able to chal) ...................................................... 5.4

Aasff (USA) (80) *(DMorley)* 3-9-10 WNewnes (8) (bkwd: racd stands' side: hld up: nvr plcd to chal) ........................................................... 2.5

19615 Quiet Victory (50) (bl) *(MissLCSiddall)* 5-7-10(3) ‡5SMaloney (6) (chsd ldrs 5f: sn rdn & wknd) .................................................................. nk.6

9035 Vuchterbacher (49) *(PFTulk)* 6-7-7 ‡7TWilson (7) (b: bit bkwd: racd stands' side: nvr plcd to chal) .................................................. 3½.7

Saboteur (42) *(WJMusson)* 8-7-7 DaleGibson (2) (bkwd: disp ld early: lost pl 3f out: t.o) .................................................................. 20.8

LONG HANDICAP: Saboteur 6-8.

**5/4** Roca Murada (IRE), **3/1** Queen of Shannon (IRE), **5/1** Farmer Jock, **8/1** CORAL FLUTTER, **9/1** Quiet Victory, Aasff (USA)(tchd 16/1), **11/1** Vuchterbacher, **25/1** Saboteur. CSF £34.05, CT £48.04. Tote £7.50: £2.20 £1.80 £1.50 (£11.10). Mrs J. W. Payne (NEWMARKET) bred by Lady Juliet de Chair. 8 Rn    1m 25.3 (2.5)
                               SF—40/53/16/18/31/2

T/Plpt: £15.30 (144.69 Tckts).                                          IM

## 2092a—TIPPERARY (L-H)
### Thursday, July 23rd [Good to soft]

## 2503a

AER RIANTA SHANNON CHALLENGE RACE (listed race)     £8063.00    1¾m

1821a3 **Sleet Skier** *(Ireland)* 5-10-1 MJKinane ................................................. —1

Mirana (IRE) *(Ireland)* 3-8-7 DHogan ..................................................... 1.2
The Poachers Lady (IRE) *(Ireland)* 4-9-7 PVGilson ................................ ¾.3
1842 PER QUOD (USA) *(BHanbury)* 7-9-10 BRaymond (btn further 8½al) .................... 5
Tote £2.40: £1.50 £2.60 (£4.40). Mr A.J.O'Reilly (D.K.Weld,IRELAND) bred by Curative Ltd. 6 Rn    3m 8.3

## 2320a—MAISONS-LAFFITTE (L-H)

### Friday, July 24th [Good]
Going Allowance: nil sec per fur (G)

### 2504a
PRIX MAURICE DE NIEUIL (Gp 2)    £41280.00    1½m 110y

955a² **Vert Amande (FR)** *(Fav)* *(France)* 4-9-2 DBoeuf (hld up: last st: chal wl over 1f
out: led ins fnl f: r.o wl) ...................................................... —1
1929³ MASHAALLAH (USA) *(JHMGosden)* 4-9-8 JReid (a cl up: 2nd st: led wl over 1f
out: r.o one pce) ...................................................... nk.2
1499a* Songlines (FR) *(France)* 3-8-5 OBenoist (a cl up: chal fr wl over 2f out: r.o one
pce) ...................................................... 1.3
1229a² Merzouk (USA) *(France)* 3-8-5 ESaint-Martin (led tl wl over 1f out: grad wknd) . ½.4
Villandry (USA) *(France)* 4-8-13 TJarnet (mid div: sme late hdwy) ...................... 2.5
Embarcadero (GER) *(Germany)* 4-9-2 MRimmer (nvr nrr) ...................... 1.6
1644a² Lights Out (FR) *(France)* 6-9-2 GMosse (prom early: sn btn st) ...................... s.h.7
9a* Gloria Mundi (FR) *(France)* 5-8-13 BMarcus (cl up tl st: sn wknd) ...................... hd.8

24/10 VERT AMANDE (FR), 11/4 Songlines (FR), 15/4 Merzouk (USA), 17/4 Mashaallah (USA), 6/1 Villandry (USA), 10/1 Lights Out (FR), 20/1 Embarcadero (GER), 37/1 Gloria Mundi (FR). Tote 3.40f: 1.30f 1.50f 1.60f (8.30f). Mr E.Sarasola (E.Lellouche,FRANCE) bred by Baron Guy de Rothschild in France. 8 Rn   2m 36.8 (2.3)
SF—79/78/65/64/68/69

## 2318a—LEOPARDSTOWN (L-H)

### Saturday, July 25th [Good]
Going Allowance: 0.40 sec per fur (G)

### 2505a
BALLINTEER E.B.F. STKS (Mdn 2-Y.O) £5159.00    7f

**Fatherland (IRE)** *(Ireland)* 2-9-0 PVGilson ...................................................... —1
Scribe (IRE) *(Ireland)* 2-9-0 KJManning ...................................................... 2.2
Shrewd Idea *(Ireland)* 2-9-0 WJO'Connor ...................................................... 2.3
Tote £2.30: £1.20 £1.30 £2.10 (£2.20). Mrs M.V.O'Brien (M.V.O'Brien,IRELAND) bred by Ballydoyle Stud in
Ireland. 10 Rn    1m 32.7 (7.7)
SF—26/20/14

## 2319a—EVRY (R-H)

### Saturday, July 25th [Good]
Going Allowance: minus 0.20 sec per fur (F)

### 2506a
PRIX DAPHNIS (Gp 3) (3-Y.O.C) £20640.00    1m 1f

1493a² **Steinbeck (USA)** *(France)* 3-8-13 TJarnet ...................................................... —1
1198 Rainbow Corner *(France)* 3-8-13 DBoeuf ...................................................... 1½.2
1227a* Stubass (IRE) *(Italy)* 3-8-9 SSoto ...................................................... nose.3
Tote 2.90f: 1.10f 1.10f 1.30f (2.10f). Sheikh Mohammed (A.Fabre,FRANCE) bred by Edward A.Seltzer &
J.Calicchio in USA. 8 Rn    1m 51.43 (1.13)
SF—55/50/45

## ARLINGTON PARK (L-H)

### Saturday, July 25th [Soft]

### 2507a
AMERICAN DERBY (Grade 2) (3-Y.O) £96257.00    1m 1f 110y (turf)

**The Name's Jimmy (USA)** *(America)* 3-8-8 PDay ...................................................... —1
1493a³ Standiford (USA) *(France)* 3-8-2 GStevens ...................................................... 2.2
May I Inquire (USA) *(America)* 3-8-2 FTorres ...................................................... 2½.3
1876⁴ FREE FLYER (IRE) *(MMoubarak)* 3-8-2 SSellers ...................................................... nk.4
Tote 11.00 (1-2) 6.20 7.60 (1-2-3) 4.40 4.60 4.20 (47.20). Mount Joy Stables Inc. (C.Stutts,AMERICA) bred by
Triple D Stable in USA. 14 Rn    1m 59.4

## VELIEFENDI (R-H) Turkey
### Saturday, July 25th [Good to firm]

**2508a**       TOPKAPI TROPHY   £40163.00   **1m**

1644a³ **Past Master (USA)** *(France)* 4–9–7 SGuillot ..................................... —**1**
       Devir (TUR) *(Turkey)* 6–9–7 MCilgin .................................................... ½**.2**
2022★ SPEAKER'S HOUSE (USA) *(PflCole)* 3–8–13 TQuinn ......................... ½**.3**
Tote 4.20TL: 1.50TL 2.20TL (6.60TL). Sheikh Mohammed (A.Fabre,FRANCE) bred by Northridge Farm in USA. 8
Rn                                                                                    1m 35.2

**2509a**       BOSPHORUS TROPHY (C & F) £40163.00   **1½m**

1825a² **CAPTAIN HORATIUS (IRE)** *(JLDunlop)* 3–8–10 JReid ..................... —**1**
1823a⁶ Olanthe (USA) *(France)* 3–8–10 SGuillot ....................................... 5.**2**
       Prestige (TUR) *(Turkey)* 3–8–10 SAkdi ............................................ 3.**3**
Tote 1.35TL (2.75TL). Mr D.R.Hunnisett (ARUNDEL) bred by B.W.Hills & Mrs V.Shaw in Ireland. 9 Rn   2m 27

## BORDEAUX (R-H) La Teste de Buch
### Sunday, July 26th [Firm]

**2510a**       CRITERIUM DU BEQUET (listed race) (2-Y.O) £10320.00   **6f**

2010★ **SHARP PROD (USA)** *(LordHuntingdon)* 2–9–0 CAsmussen ............... —**1**
       Fleurissante (FR) *(France)* 2–8–7 PDumortier ................................... nk.**2**
       Smadoun (FR) *(France)* 2–8–9 DSicaud .......................................... ½**.3**
Tote ? 20f: ? 00f 2,40f (SF: 8.10f). The Queen (WEST ILSLEY) bred by The Queen in USA. 5 Rn  No time taken

## 845a—DUSSELDORF (R-H)
### Sunday, July 26th [Good]

**2511a**       PREIS DER PRIVATBANKIERS MERCK, FINCK & CO (Gp 1) (C & F) £70423.00
               **1½m**

957a★ **Platini (GER)** *(Germany)* 3–8–6 MRimmer ................................. —**1**
1646a⁵ SNURGE *(PflCole)* 5–9–7 TQuinn ................................................. hd.**2**
       Sugunas (GER) *(Germany)* 4–9–7 KWoodburn .................................. 4.**3**
1825a★ Lomitas *(Germany)* 4–9–7 ABoschert (btn further 1¾l) ...................... **5**
Tote 61DM: 30DM 40DM (SF: 426DM). Stall Steigenberger (B.Schultz,GERMANY) bred by Frau E & A
Steigenberger in Germany. 6 Rn                                                        2m 29.5

## 2244—EDINBURGH (R-H)
### Friday, July 31st [Firm]
Going Allowance: minus 0.20 sec per fur (F)                              Wind: almost nil

Stalls: high

**2512**       BLW STOCKTRADE CLAIMING STKS (2-Y.O) £1355.40 (£374.40: £178.20)
               **5f**                                                       6-30 (6-31)

2143⁴ Selvole *(MissLAPerratt)* 7-5 ‡7ClaireBalding (1) (racd alone centre: mde all: r.o
       wl fnl f) ........................................................................................ —**1**
2221⁴ Bright Gem (Fav) *(TFairhurst)* 8-8 JFanning (2) (hld up in tch: hdwy 2f out: rdn &
       ev ch ins fnl f: nt qckn) ........................................................... 1½**.2**
2232⁴ Domes of Silence *(JBerry)* 8-3 GCarter (4) (b.off hind: cl up: ev ch ins fnl f: no
       ex) .................................................................................................. 2.**3**
2360⁵ Sea-Ayr (IRE) *(MissLAPerratt)* 7-8⁽³⁾ ‡7RHavlin (6) (s.i.s: bhd: hdwy u.p ½-wy:
       one pce) ......................................................................................... 1.**4**
       Dashing Lady *(MJohnston)* 8-2 RPElliott (5) (s.i.s: effrt ½-wy: sn btn) ......... 7.**5**

**10/11** Bright Gem, **7/2** Sea-Ayr (IRE), **5/1** Domes of Silence(op 3/1), **9/1** Dashing Lady(op 6/1), **16/1** SELVOLE.
CSF £29.32, Tote £20.70: £7.60 £1.20 (£7.70). Mr John Muir (AYR) bred by Mrs S. Abbott. 5 Rn
                                                                                    60.4 sec (2.7)
                                                                                    SF—3/14/1/–/–

**2513**       DRUMSHEUGH GARDENS H'CAP (0-70) £1632.00 (£452.00: £216.00)
               **1m 7f 16y**                                                7-00 (7-00)
                            (Weights raised 14 lb)
2045★ **Desert Mist (43)** (bl) (Fav) *(DenysSmith)* 3–9–5 KFallon (5) (trckd ldrs gng wl:
       led over 2f out: sn pushed clr: eased ins fnl f) ...................... —**1**

2246★ Alpha Helix (26) (v) *(MissLAPerratt)* 9–9–3 (3x) JFanning (1) (hld up: pushed
along ½-wy: hdwy u.p ent st: chsd wnr fnl 2f: eased whn
btn fnl f) ............ 6.2

22613 Rexy Boy (30) *(WLBarker)* 5–9–7 SWebster (3) (led tl hdd over 2f out: sn rdn &
one pce) ............ 6.3

20455 Racing Raskal (33) *(CaptJWilson)* 5–9–10 GCarter (4) (chsd ldr: ev ch 3f out: sn
rdn & btn) ............ 1½.4

Fingers Crossed (30) *(MDHammond)* 8–9–7 DMcKeown (2) (in tch: rdn appr st:
sn wknd & bhd) ............ 8.5

**13/8** DESERT MIST, **9/4** Alpha Helix, **9/2** Racing Raskal, **6/1** Rexy Boy(op 4/1), **16/1** Fingers Crossed(tchd
10/1). CSF £5.18, Tote £2.10: £1.20 £1.70 (£2.20). Albury Racing Limited (BISHOP AUCKLAND) bred by Mrs C.
R. Philipson. 5 Rn      3m 17.8 (7.3)
SF—2/–/–/–/–

---

**2514**     BELL LAWRIE WHITE H'CAP (0-80) £1940.00 (£540.00: £260.00)     **5f**   7-30 (7-34)

22793 **Miss Vaxette (64)** (Fav) *(JLSpearing)* 3–9–1 GHind (2) (in tch: hdwy to ld appr
fnl f: rdn & r.o wl) ............ —1

1787 Super Rocky (77) *(RBastiman)* 3–9–7 ‡7HBastiman (4) (w ldr: led ½-wy: hdd
appr fnl f: no ex) ............ 2.2

23114 Bee Dee Ell (USA) (45) *(MissLAPerratt)* 3–7–10 JFanning (3) (bhd & rdn along:
styd on fnl f: nvr able to chal) ............ 3.3

24665 Kabcast (63) (bl) *(DWChapman)* 7–9–0 ‡5SMaloney (5) (led to ½-wy: wknd appr
fnl f) ............ 2.4

**11/8** MISS VAXETTE, **9/4** Kabcast, **5/2** Super Rocky(2/1–3/1), **10/1** Bee Dee Ell (USA)(8/1–16/1). CSF £4.87,
Tote £2.50 (£3.40). Vax Appliances Ltd (ALCESTER) bred by N. J. Dent. 4 Rn      59.7 sec (2)
SF—41/39/2/12

---

**2515**     STOCKBROKERS STKS (Mdn) £1506.00 (£416.00: £198.00)     **1m 3f 32y**   8-00 (8-00)

21682 **Bustinetta (80)** (Fav) *(JRFanshawe)* 3–8–5 GDuffield (2) (trckd ldrs: rdn to ld
over 2f out: hdd ent fnl f: kpt on u.p to ld wl ins fnl f) ............ —1

19582 Well Ahead *(MJohnston)* 3–8–5 DMcKeown (1) (led tl hdd appr st: rn wd st: styd
on fnl f) ............ ¾.2

22443 Super Blues *(TDBarron)* 5–9–2 AlexGreaves (3) (cl up: led appr st: hdd over 2f
out: rallied to ld ent fnl f: no ex nr fin) ............ s.h.3

**1/8** BUSTINETTA, **10/1** Super Blues, **11/1** Well Ahead. CSF £1.91, Tote £1.10 (£1.60). Mr B. E. Nielsen
(NEWMARKET) bred by Stetchworth Park Stud Ltd. 3 Rn      2m 25.8 (6.1)
SF—8/6/16

---

**2516**     BLW DISCRETIONARY PORTFOLIO MANAGEMENT (S) STKS (2-Y.O) £1317.60 (£363.60:
£172.80)    **7f 15y**                 8-30 (8-32)

22472 **Lucky Owl** *(MissLAPerratt)* 8-6 JFanning (3) (hld up: hdwy over 2f out: led ent
fnl f: sn rdn: jst hld on) ............ —1

21062 Lofty Deed (USA) *(SirMarkPrescott)* 8-11 GDuffield (4) (chsd ldrs: rdn 3f out:
n.m.r wl over 1f out: swtchd appr fnl f: r.o: jst failed) ............ s.h.2

21185 Laurel Etoile *(JBerry)* 8-6 DMcKeown (1) (prom: rdn & ev ch 2f out: styd on) .. 1½.3

21452 Daily Sport's Gift (Fav) *(JBerry)* 8-11 GCarter (6) (led tl hdd ent fnl f: kpt on same
pce) ............ 1.4

*1249 Resolution Time (8/1) Withdrawn (lame) : not under orders — Rule 4 applies*

**11/10** Daily Sport's Gift(op 4/6), **2/1** Lofty Deed (USA)(9/2—7/4), **9/2** LUCKY OWL, **20/1** Laurel Etoile. CSF
£10.87, Tote £4.50: £3.10 (£4.80). Mr William Provan Hunter (AYR) bred by R. A. Cameron. 4 Rn; No bid
1m 30.4 (4.2)
SF—8/12/2/4

---

**2517**     BLW PEP WINNERS TAXBREAK H'CAP (0-70) £1632.00 (£452.00: £216.00)
**1m 16y**                        9-00 (9-02)

1589 **Lawnswood Junior (50)** *(JLSpearing)* 5–9–5 KDarley (3) (a chsng ldrs: led
appr fnl f: drvn out) ............ —1

22024 Routing (56) (Fav) *(MDHammond)* 4–9–4 ‡7ADobbin (1) (trckd ldrs: n.m.r on ins
wl over 2f out: styd on fnl f) ............ ¾.2

23794 Sky Cat (44) (v) *(CTinkler)* 8–8–8 ‡5SMaloney (4) (hld up & bhd: hdwy over 2f
out: styd on fnl f: nt qckn) ............ 1½.3

2141 Tickham Vixen (IRE) (42) *(JDBethell)* 4–8–11 GDuffield (2) (prom: rdn over 2f
out: ev ch appr fnl f: nt qckn) ............ 1.4

2219 Thisonesforalice (51) *(AHarrison)* 4–9–6 KFallon (8) (cl up: rdn 3f out: ev ch 2f
out: one pce) ............ 2.5

2148 New Beginning **(35)** *(JSHaldane)* 9–8–4 DMcKeown (6) (b: dwlt: hdwy to ld
after 2f: hdd ent st: sn btn) ............................................................ 2.6
2160 Talish **(37)** (bl) *(TDBarron)* 4–8–6 AlexGreaves (5) (led 2f: cl up: led ent st: hdd
appr fnl f: sn wknd) ............................................ nk.7
Makeminemusic **(53)** *(FWatson)* 3–9–0 SWebster (7) (bit bkwd: bhd: rdn ent st:
sn t.o) ............................................................ 20.8

**2/1** Routing, **7/2** LAWNSWOOD JUNIOR, Sky Cat, **9/2** Tickham Vixen (IRE), **10/1** Talish, **11/1**
Thisonesforalice(8/1—12/1), **66/1** Ors. CSF £10.61, CT £22.77. Tote £4.70: £1.70 £1.40 £1.70 (£5.70). Mr
Graham Treglown (ALCESTER) bred by Chilcombe Manor Stud. 8 Rn
1m 42.7 (4.1)
SF—19/16/1/1/4/–

T/Plpt: £17.30 (46.6 Tckts). GB

## 2181—**NEWMARKET (R-H)** July Course
## **Friday, July 31st [Good to firm]**
Going Allowance: nil sec per fur (F)                                    Wind: mod against

Stalls: high

**2518**  SIDE HILL APP'CE CLAIMING STKS (3-Y.O) £2872.00 (£856.00: £408.00: £184.00)
1¹⁄₂m
6-15 (6-16)

2064* **Storm Dust (70)** (Fav) *(JRFanshawe)* 9-4 ‡6NVarley (3) (hld up: led on ins 1f
out: drvn out) ............................................................ —1
1395³ Kojiki *(LMCumani)* 9-12 JWeaver (4) (led: edgd lft & hdd 1f out: rdn & no ex) 3¹⁄₂.2
2297³ Big Pat **(56)** *(JPearce)* 8-12 RPrice (2) (chsd ldr: rdn 3f out: wknd appr fnl f) ..... 7.3
2200³ Doogie Bopper (IRE) **(63)** *(MBell)* 9-0 ‡3PTurner (1) (b.off fore: hld up & bhd: rdn
over 2f out: no imp) ............................................................ 5.4

**15/8** STORM DUST, **3/1** Boogie Bopper (IRE), Big Pat, **100/30** Kojiki. CSF £7.29, Tote £2.50 (£4.20). Mr John R.
Sims (NEWMARKET) bred by Sunley Stud. 4 Rn
2m 38.6 (9.35)
SF—10/11/–/–

**2519**  E.B.F. DEXA'TEX STKS (Mdn 2-Y.O) £3785.00 (£1130.00: £540.00: £245.00)
7f
6-45 (6-47)

1944² **Wathik (USA)** (Fav) *(HThomsonJones)* 9-0 RHills (9) (lw: a.p: rdn to ld ins fnl f:
r.o) ............................................................ —1
Kassab *(JLDunlop)* 9-0 LDettori (4) (lengthy: scope: dwlt: hdwy 2f out: led over
1f out: sn hdd: chal ins fnl f: r.o) ............................................................ hd.2
2190² Royal Roller (IRE) *(CNAllen)* 8-7 ‡7GForster (8) (hld up & bhd: hdwy 2f out: rdn &
r.o ins fnl f) ............................................................ 2.3
Almamzar (USA) *(MRStoute)* 9-0 SCauthen (1) (w'like: unf: bit bkwd: chsd ldrs:
ev ch over 1f out: unable qckn) ............................................................ 1.4
Yajeed (USA) *(AAScott)* 9-0 BRaymond (10) (leggy: bkwd: hdwy 3f out: kpt on
wl ins fnl f) ............................................................ ¹⁄₂.5
Riviere Actor (USA) *(JLDunlop)* 9-0 TQuinn (6) (tall: leggy: hdwy over 2f out:
bmpd appr fnl f: r.o) ............................................................ ¹⁄₂.6
1899³ Blue Blazer *(BHanbury)* 9-0 WRyan (2) (lw: a.p: led over 1f out: sn hdd & wknd) 2.7
1502 Prairie Grove *(RHannon)* 9-0 PRobinson (7) (led tl hdd over 2f out: grad wknd) 4.8
Sculler (USA) *(HRACecil)* 9-0 PatEddery (5) (w'like: lengthy: s.i.s: swtchd rt: sn
w ldrs: led over 2f out: sn hdd: eased) ............................................................ hd.9
Nedaarah *(AAScott)* 8-9 WRSwinburn (3) (leggy: scope: bkwd: bhd: effrt over
2f out: hmpd over 1f out: sn btn) ............................................................ 1¹⁄₂.10

**15/8** WATHIK (USA), **11/4** Sculler (USA), **5/1** Almamzar (USA)(8/1—10/1), **7/1** Royal Roller (IRE)(6/1—10/1),
**9/1** Blue Blazer, **14/1** Kassab, Riviere Actor (USA), Nedaarah, **20/1** Yajeed (USA), **33/1** Prairie Grove. CSF
£21.60, CT £28.53. Tote £2.90: £1.30 £5.10 (£1.90). Mr Hamdan Al-Maktoum (NEWMARKET) bred by
Crescent Farm in USA. 10 Rn
1m 28.18 (3.78)
SF—43/42/29/33/31/29

**2520**  MALONEY & RHODES H'CAP (0-90) £4503.00 (£1344.00: £642.00: £291.00)
6f
7-10 (7-11)

2337² **Running Glimpse (IRE) (73)** (Jt-Fav) *(MissBSanders)* 4-8-12 MRoberts (6)
(led over 3f out: hrd rdn fnl f: hld on gamely) ............................................................ —1
2003 So Rhythmical **(74)** (Jt-Fav) *(GHEden)* 8–8-13 PatEddery (4) (b.off hind: swtg:
hld up: gd hdwy appr fnl f: rdn & r.o wl) ............................................................ hd.2
2333* Fighter Squadron **(60)** (bl) *(JAGlover)* 3–7-7 (7x) JQuinn (7) (lw: hld up: effrt &
nt clr run over 1f out: fin wl) ............................................................ nk.3

2406² Easy Line **(89)** *(PJFeilden)* 9-10-0 BRaymond (8) (b: hld up & bhd: gd hdwy over 1f out: nvr nrr) ............................................. ³/4.4

2009★ Fay's Song (IRE) **(79)** (Jt-Fav) *(RAkehurst)* 4-9-4 TQuinn (3) (a.p: ev ch 1f out: no ex ins fnl f) ............................................. ³/4.5

1943 Gentle Hero (USA) **(81)** *(MPNaughton)* 6-9-1 ‡⁵JWeaver (9) (lw: led over 2f: rdn & wknd over 1f out) ............................................. 2¹/2.6

2009 Panchellita (USA) **(66)** *(JSutcliffe)* 3-7-13 BCrossley (5) (spd over 4f) ............... 1¹/2.7

2290★ Luna Bid **(66)** *(MBlanshard)* 9-8-5⁽¹⁾ (7x) RCochrane (2) (s.i.s: a bhd) ............... 1.8

624 Face North (IRE) **(56)** *(ARDavison)* 4-7-9 EJohnson (1) (bkwd: prom tl wknd qckly wl over 1f out) ............................................. 1¹/2.9

**4/1** RUNNING GLIMPSE (IRE), So Rhythmical, Fay's Song (IRE), **11/2** Easy Line, **6/1** Luna Bid, **7/1** Fighter Squadron, **9/1** Panchellita (USA), Gentle Hero (USA), **16/1** Face North (IRE). CSF £21.29, CT £104.40. Tote £4.90: £1.80 £1.80 £1.80 (£13.00). Copyforce Ltd (EPSOM) bred by B. W. Hills and Mrs V. Shaw in Ireland. 9 Rn
1m 13.60 (2.10)
SF—56/56/35/67/54/41

## 2521

BEDFORD LODGE HOTEL H'CAP (0-90) £3622.50 (£1080.00: £515.00: £232.50)
7f　　　　　　　　　　　　　　　　　　　7-40 (7-41)

1930 **Rise Up Singing (67)** (bl) *(WJMusson)* 4-9-0 PatEddery (1) (a.p: led over 2f out: rdn out) ............................................. —1

1696⁴ Sharpalto **(81)** *(MrsGRReveley)* 5-9-9 ‡⁵JWeaver (3) (lw: hld up: hdwy 2f out: hrd rdn & kpt on fnl f) ............................................. ³/4.2

1480⁶ Brown Fairy (USA) **(66)** *(MrsNMacauley)* 4-8-13 DBiggs (7) (lw: chsd ldrs: rdn over 1f out: styd on nr fin) ............................................. 2¹/2.3

2369⁶ Resolute Bay **(78)** (v) *(RMWhitaker)* 6-9-11 ACulhane (4) (s.i.s: hld up: hdwy over 2f out: rdn & one pce fnl f) ............................................. nk.4

2183⁵ Strong Suit (IRE) **(86)** *(RHannon)* 3-9-12 MRoberts (6) (lost pl 3f out: styd on ins fnl f: n.d) ............................................. ³/4.5

2283² Sugemar **(59)** (Fav) *(JARToller)* 6-8-6 PRobinson (2) (prom: outpcd appr fnl f: sn btn) ............................................. 1¹/2.6

2183⁴ Young Shadowfax **(54)** *(CNAllen)* 5-8-1 GBardwell (8) (led tl hdd & wknd over 2f out) ............................................. 3¹/2.7

**100/30** Sugemar, **7/2** RISE UP SINGING, **4/1** Strong Suit (IRE), **9/2** Sharpalto, **9/1** Ors. CSF £18.01, CT £115.31. Tote £3.60: £2.00 £2.80 (£10.00). Mrs Rita Brown (NEWMARKET) bred by B. E. Green. 7 Rn　1m 27.16 (2.76)
SF—58/65/47/58/57/32

## 2522

J.M. RATCLIFFE RUNNING GAP STKS　£4308.00 (£1284.00: £612.00: £276.00)
1¹/2m　　　　　　　　　　　　　　　　　8-10 (8-12)

1458 **Colorific (106)** *(BWHills)* 3-9-0 PatEddery (6) (stdd s: gd hdwy 2f out: led appr fnl f: r.o strly) ............................................. —1

2239★ Vratislav (USA) *(JHMGosden)* 3-8-7 RCochrane (1) (lw: hld up: jnd ldrs over 1f out: unable qckn nr fin) ............................................. 1¹/2.2

2189² Tik Fa (USA) **(100)** (Fav) *(BHanbury)* 3-8-11 WRSwinburn (3) (lw: a.p: led 3f out tl appr fnl f: one pce) ............................................. 2.3

2181⁵ Back Billy (IRE) *(CEBrittain)* 3-8-4 MRoberts (2) (lw: hld up in tch: outpcd over 2f out: styd on wl ins fnl f) ............................................. 2.4

2174³ Percy's Girl (IRE) **(97)** *(GWragg)* 4-9-7 SCauthen (4) (lw: led: hdd 3f out: sltly hmpd & swtchd over 2f out: sn btn) ............................................. nk.5

2181⁴ Sheriffmuir **(96)** *(LMCumani)* 3-9-0 LDettori (5) (lw: prom: rdn 2f out: sn btn) .... 4.6

**5/2** Tik Fa (USA), **11/4** Percy's Girl (IRE), **7/2** COLORIFIC(tchd 11/2), Sheriffmuir(5/2—4/1), **5/1** Vratislav (USA), **16/1** Back Billy (IRE). CSF £20.57, Tote £6.70: £2.80 £2.10 (£19.60). Mr K. Abdulla (LAMBOURN) bred by Juddmonte Farms. 6 Rn　2m 37.32 (8.62)
SF—14/4/4/–/9/–

## 2523

ANT AVIATION STKS (3-Y.O-F) £3975.00 (£1100.00: £525.00)　1m　　8-40 (8-41)

1975★ **Petal Girl** *(RHannon)* 8-11 MRoberts (3) (lw: hld up: hdwy to ld 2f out: hrd rdn fnl f: all out) ............................................. —1

473⁴ Waterfowl Creek (IRE) *(GWragg)* 8-11 WRSwinburn (1) (lw: hld up: ev ch appr fnl f: hrd rdn & r.o gamely) ............................................. nk.2

2189³ United Kingdom (USA) (Fav) *(HRACecil)* 9-3 SCauthen (2) (lw: set slow pce: qckn'd 3f out: hdd 2f out: sn outpcd) ............................................. 10.3

**8/11** United Kingdom (USA), **9/4** Waterfowl Creek (IRE), **3/1** PETAL GIRL. CSF £8.27, Tote £3.20 (£3.20). Mr John L. Moore (MARLBOROUGH) bred by John L. Moore. 3 Rn　1m 46.86 (9.16)
SF—5/4/–

T/Trio: Race 3: £32.80 (20.1 Tckts). T/Plpt: £1,117.70 (2.2 Tckts).　　　　　　　　IM

# NEWMARKET (R-H) July Course
## Saturday, August 1st [Good to firm]
Going Allowance: St: minus 0.25 sec; Rnd: minus 0.45 sec (F)          Wind: slt half bhd

Stalls: centre

**2524**  JIF LEMON STKS (Amateurs)    £2872.00 (£856.00: £408.00: £184.00)
1½m                                                      2-15 (2-16)

1948* **Cunning** (Fav) (*LMCumani*) 3-10-5  MrsSCumani (3) (stdd s: hdwy 7f out: led 3f out: sn clr: unchal) .................................................. —1
2228* Puritan (CAN) (76) (*GHarwood*) 3-10-11  MissAHarwood (4) (lw: led 2f: rdn & outpcd 4f out: styd on ins fnl f) ................................. 15.2
1914⁶ Mahairy (USA) (68) (*AAScott*) 3-10-0 ‡⁵MissTBracegirdle (1) (lw: chsd ldrs: styd on appr fnl f: nvr nrr) ...................................... s.h.3
2401² Line Drummer (USA) (76) (*PAKelleway*) 4-10-11 ‡⁵MissSKelleway (2) (b: swtg: hld up: hdwy to ld over 5f out: hdd 3f out: wknd fnl f) .......... 1.4
2036² Le Baron Perche (FR) (69) (*CJames*) 3-10-7 ‡⁵MrEJames (7) (swtg: pushed along ½-wy: lost tch 3f out: t.o) .............................. 10.5
2296³ Tudor Da Samba (53) (*JRFanshawe*) 3-10-0 ‡⁵MrsJFanshawe (5) (w ldrs tl wknd qckly ½-wy: t.o) .............................. 2½.6
1767⁶ Spirit Sam (18) (*PJFeilden*) 7-10-11 ‡⁵MrSRees (6) (swtg: led after 2f tl over 5f out: wknd qckly: t.o) ......................... 30.7

**4/5** CUNNING, **3/1** Puritan (CAN), **4/1** Line Drummer (USA), **16/1** Mahairy (USA)(op 10/1), **25/1** Le Baron Perche (FR), **33/1** Tudor Da Samba, **66/1** Spirit Sam. CSF £3.65, Tote £1.80: £1.50 £1.80 (£2.00). Fittocks Stud Limited (NEWMARKET) bred by R. G. Stokes. 7 Rn
2m 28.39 (2.33 under best; U.31)
SF—68/44/32/41/17/5

**2525**  ROBINSON'S FRUIT DRINKS CLAIMING STKS (3-Y.O) £3687.50 (£1100.00: £525.00: £237.50)   7f                                    2-45 (2-46)

2230³ **Lord Vivienne (IRE)** (71) (Fav) (*PFICole*) 9-1  MRoberts (4) (b: swtg: chsd ldr tl led over 3f out: sn clr: drvn out) ........................ —1
2303* Certain Lady (63) (*GBlum*) 7-7 ‡⁵DHarrison (3) (in tch: hdwy to chase wnr fnl 2f: no imp) ................................................. 3½.2
*2194³* Myasha (USA) (72) (bl) (*MrsLPiggott*) 8-8 ‡⁷GMilligan (1) (b.hind: swtg: hld up: hdwy over 2f out: one pce fnl f) ...................... 6.3
2303² Coniston Lake (IRE) (61) (*GLewis*) 7-8 ‡⁵NGwilliams (6) (b.hind: chsd ldrs: rdn over 2f out: one pce) .......................... 1.4
2079⁶ Horizontale (45) (*CEBrittain*) 7-6⁽³⁾ ‡⁵BDoyle (5) (nvr nr to chal) ............... hd.5
2237* Legend Dulac (IRE) (57) (*JLHarris*) 8-11  PRobinson (2) (bolted bef s: led over 3f: grad wknd) .......................... s.h.6

**9/4** LORD VIVIENNE (IRE)(3/1—2/1), **7/2** Coniston Lake (IRE), Certain Lady, **11/2** Legend Dulac (IRE), **9/1** Myasha (USA), **14/1** Horizontale. CSF £9.33, Tote £2.40: £1.60 £1.70 (£3.70). Mr Reg Hester (WHATCOMBE) bred by Binfield Manor Farms Ltd. in Ireland. 6 Rn
1m 26 (1.60)
SF—50/17/14/–/–/12

**2526**  E.B.F. COLMAN'S MUSTARD STKS (Mdn 2-Y.O) £3590.00 (£1070.00: £510.00: £230.00)   6f                                    3-20 (3-21)

**Desert Shot** (Fav) (*MRStoute*) 9-0  WRSwinburn (1) (w'like: scope: bit bkwd: hld up: gd hdwy 2f out: led appr fnl f: r.o strly) ........... —1
Ribbonwood (USA) (*JHMGosden*) 8-9  MHills (5) (w'like: leggy: s.s: hld up & bhd: hdwy over 2f out: chsd wnr fnl f: no imp) ............. 2.2
1170³ Formal Affair (*CACyzer*) 8-9  MRoberts (4) (led tl hdd over 2f out: ev ch 1f out: one pce) ......................... 4.3
2176³ Princely Favour (IRE) (*RHannon*) 9-0  BRouse (3) (lw: w ldrs 4f: edgd lft over 1f out: sn btn) ............................ 3.4
Absolutely Fact (USA) (*WJHaggas*) 9-0  JQuinn (2) (cmpt: bit bkwd: w ldrs: led over 2f out tl appr fnl f: carried lft: sn btn) ............ 3.5

**1/2** DESERT SHOT, **7/2** Princely Favour (IRE)(op 7/4), **7/1** Ribbonwood (USA)(3/1—15/2), **11/1** Formal Affair, **25/1** Absolutely Fact (USA). CSF £4.75, Tote £1.50: £1.30 £1.90 (£3.70). Maktoum Al Maktoum (NEWMARKET) bred by The Lavington Stud. 5 Rn
1m 12.46 (0.96)
SF—51/38/22/15/3

**2527**  ROBINSONS BARLEY WATER H'CAP (3-Y.O) (0-90) £4581.00 (£1368.00: £654.00: £297.00)   1m                                    3-50 (3-51)

2230* **Blockade (USA)** (78) (*MBell*) 8-11  MHills (7) (mde all stands' side: rdn clr fnl f) —1

2276* Northern Graduate (USA) **(62)** *(MrsGRReveley)* 7-9 JLowe (5) (hdwy ½-wy: hrd rdn over 2f out: r.o wl fnl f) ......... 2½.2

2353² Straw Thatch **(72)** *(MJohnston)* 8-5 DMcKeown (9) (a.p: ev ch over 1f out: one pce) ......... nk.3

2188 Co-Chin (IRE) **(76)** *(GLewis)* 8-9 PaulEddery (8) (a.p: ev ch over 1f out: rdn & no ex fnl f) ......... ½.4

1533⁶ Change the Will **(64)** *(MDIUsher)* 7-6 ‡⁵DHarrison (2) (lw: chsd ldrs far side: kpt on fnl 2f) ......... 4.5

2348 Baluga **(88)** *(GHarwood)* 9-7 WRSwinburn (1) (swtg: led far side: rdn 3f out: sn btn) ......... 4.6

2000³ Common Council **(76)** *(GAPritchard-Gordon)* 8-9 PRobinson (3) (w ldr far side over 5f) ......... nk.7

Alight (IRE) **(84)** *(ACStewart)* 9-3 MRoberts (6) (a in rr) ......... 3.8

2348² Wave Hill **(87)** (Fav) *(RHannon)* 9-6 LPiggott (4) (lw: swtchd stands' side ½-wy: rdn over 2f out: sn wknd) ......... 3.9

**9/4** Wave Hill, **4/1** Co-Chin (IRE), **5/1** Northern Graduate (USA), **7/1** BLOCKADE (USA), **8/1** Common Council, **9/1** Baluga, **10/1** Straw Thatch, **12/1** Alight (IRE), **16/1** Change the Will. CSF £41.12, CT £325.97. Tote £8.50: £2.20 £1.60 £2.30 (£19.90). Mr A. M. Warrender (NEWMARKET) bred by Patricia C. Warrender in USA. 9 Rn
1m 37.92 (0.22)
SF—64/40/49/51/22/39

**2528** COLMAN'S OF NORWICH NURSERY £15140.00 (£4520.00: £2160.00: £980.00)
6f
4-20 (4-22)

2108* **Tajdif (USA)** (Jt-Fav) *(DMorley)* 8-3 MHills (11) (lw: chsd ldrs stands' side: rdn to ld ins fnl f: r.o) ......... —1

2176⁶ Saint Express *(RMWhitaker)* 9-0 ACulhane (8) (a.p stands' side: led over 1f out tl ins fnl f) ......... 2.2

2242* Dark Eyed Lady (IRE) *(DWPArbuthnot)* 8-1 ‡⁵RPrice (7) (led stands' side tl over 1f out: sn rdn: no ex) ......... nk.3

2342* No Reservations (IRE) *(RFJohnsonHoughton)* 8-0 ‡⁵DHarrison (10) (hdwy over 1f out: nvr nrr) ......... nk.4

2008* Time's Arrow (IRE) *(GCBravery)* 8-6 PaulEddery (12) (a.p: r.o one pce over 1f out) ......... s.h.5

2068⁴ Sweet Romeo *(MJohnston)* 8-3 DMcKeown (4) (lw: spd far side over 4f) ......... 4.6

2143³ Caps Ninety-Two (IRE) *(DrJDScargill)* 7-10 JQuinn (9) (in tch 4f) ......... 2½.7

2175⁴ Young Ern *(SDow)* 9-7 LPiggott (3) (racd far side: nvr nr) ......... ½.8

1196⁶ Fierro (bl) *(CEBrittain)* 8-1 GCrealock (5) (led far side: swtchd rt 2f out: sn rdn & btn) ......... 2.9

619* Bonus Point (Jt-Fav) *(MrsGRReveley)* 8-4 KDarley (1) (lw: sn rdn along far side: a bhd) ......... 3½.10

2242⁵ Cliburnel News (IRE) *(MHTompkins)* 8-8 PRobinson (2) (lw: in tch far side: rdn ½-wy: sn wknd) ......... 4.11

2017³ Crusade (IRE) *(RHannon)* 9-2 MRoberts (6) (w ldrs far side over 3f: virtually p.u fnl f: t.o) ......... 30.12

**9/2** TAJDIF (USA), Bonus Point, **13/2** Time's Arrow (IRE), Dark Eyed Lady (IRE), Saint Express(op 12/1), **9/1** Crusade (IRE), **10/1** No Reservations (IRE), **12/1** Young Ern, **14/1** Sweet Romeo, Cliburnel News (IRE), **20/1** Ors. CSF £33.33, CT £175.03. Tote £4.70: £2.00 £2.40 £2.10 (£32.00). Mr Hamdan Al-Maktoum (NEWMARKET) bred by Miss Barbara Hunter in USA. 12 Rn
1m 12.69 (1.19)
SF—35/38/24/22/27/8

**2529** LADBROKE H'CAP (0-90) £4581.00 (£1368.00: £654.00: £297.00)
1¼m
4-50 (4-54)

2202* **Vallance (72)** *(PWHarris)* 4-9-1 WRSwinburn (8) (chsd ldr: rdn to ld wl over 2f out: styd on) ......... —1

2180⁴ Rising Tempo (IRE) **(58)** (Jt-Fav) *(CACyzer)* 4-8-1 DBiggs (3) (hdwy 4f out: rdn over 1f out: r.o wl ins fnl f) ......... 2.2

2054² Bescaby Boy **(67)** *(JWharton)* 6-8-5 ‡⁵SWilliams (4) (a.p: ev ch over 2f out: rdn over 1f out: sn btn) ......... nk.3

2110² Taylors Prince **(63)** *(HJCollingridge)* 5-8-6 JQuinn (5) (chsd ldrs: one pce fnl 3f) ......... 6.4

2288⁴ Busted Rock **(85)** *(MrsLPiggott)* 7-10-0 LPiggott (1) (chsd ldrs: no hdwy fnl 2f) ......... 1½.5

2473² Surrey Dancer **(68)** *(BHanbury)* 4-8-6 ‡⁵DHarrison (7) (lw: hld up: a bhd) ......... 3½.6

2184⁵ Little Rousillon **(64)** (Jt-Fav) *(ACStewart)* 4-8-7 MRoberts (6) (dwlt: nvr plcd to chal) ......... s.h.7

2295⁵ Whisper's Shadow **(68)** (v) *(MHTompkins)* 3-8-2 PRobinson (2) (set str pce tl hdd & wknd wl over 2f out) ......... 10.8

4/1 Rising Tempo (IRE)(3/1—9/2), Little Rousillon, **9/2** Surrey Dancer, **5/1** VALLANCE, Busted Rock(7/1—8/1), **8/1** Taylors Prince, **9/1** Bescaby Boy, **10/1** Whisper's Shadow. CSF £24.99, CT £162.72. Tote £6.30: £2.10 £1.60　£2.10　(£16.30). Mrs P. W. Harris (BERKHAMSTED) bred by Pendley Farm. 8 Rn
2m 2.31 (0.86 under best; U.29)
SF—59/41/44/33/52/23

**2530**　　COLMAN'S SAUCES STKS (2-Y.O) £5005.00 (£1210.00)　　**7f**　　5-25 (5-25)

1965² **Tioman Island** *(PFICole)* 9-1 TQuinn (1) (trckd ldr: rdn to ld 1f out: r.o) ............. —1
1796* Fitzcarraldo (USA) (Fav) *(LMCumani)* 9-0 LDettori (2) (lw: led: rdn & hdd 1f out:
　　　　unable qckn) ...................................................................... 3¹/₂.2

8/15 Fitzcarraldo (USA), **11/8** TIOMAN ISLAND. Tote £2.00. H. H. Sultan Ahmad Shah (WHATCOMBE) bred by
Whitsbury Manor Stud. 2 Rn
1m 25.55 (1.15)
SF—57/45

T/Trio: Race 4: £46.60 (31.4 Tckts). T/Plpt: £46.40 (149.6 Tckts).　　　　　　　　IM

---

2160—**THIRSK (L-H)**
### Friday, July 31st [Firm]
Going Allowance: minus 0.25 sec per fur (F)　　　　　　　　Wind: almost nil

Stalls: high

**2531**　　COWESBY APP'CE H'CAP (3-Y.O) (0-70) £2469.00 (£684.00: £327.00)
　　　　**1m**　　　　　　　　　　　　　　　　　　　　　　2-15 (2-17)
　　　　　　　　　　(Weights raised 2 lb)
1⁵63⁴ **Thornton Gate (55)** (bl) *(MHEasterby)* 8-8 OPears (6) (mde all: styd on wl fnl
　　　　2f) .................................................................................... —1
2186⁴ Much Sought After **(68)** *(DMorley)* 9-7 EBentley (5) (b.hind: lw: in tch: effrt over
　　　　2f out: styd on wl: nrst fin) ................................................ 1¹/₂.2
2266³ Magnetic Point (USA) **(57)** *(AAScott)* 8-10 JTate (2) (trckd ldrs: chal 2f out: rdn
　　　　& nt qckn appr fnl f) ......................................................... ¹/₂.3
2266* Cap Camarat (CAN) **(58)** (Fav) *(PFICole)* 8-11 (8x) JDSmith (8) (chsd ldrs: effrt
　　　　3f out: one pce) ................................................................. 5.4
2104* Grubby **(45)** *(RHollinshead)* 7-12 AGarth (7) (cl up tl outpcd fnl 2f) ................ ³/₄.5
2160⁵ Hot Punch **(45)** *(PCalver)* 7-5 ‡7CAdamson (1) (bhd: effrt 3f out: n.d) ............. 1¹/₂.6
1909 Capital Lad **(40)** *(MAvison)* 7-7 DarrenMoffatt (4) (chsd ldr tl rdn & wknd over 2f
　　　　out) ................................................................................... 3.7
1992 Malcesine (IRE) **(53)** *(CaptJWilson)* 7-13 ‡7AnnaLaw (3) (lw: dwlt: n.d) ............. 4.8
　　　　　　LONG HANDICAP: Capital Lad 6-13.

2/1 Cap Camarat (CAN), **3/1** Magnetic Point (USA), **6/1** Grubby, **8/1** Much Sought After, THORNTON GATE, **10/1** Hot Punch, **14/1** Malcesine (IRE), **33/1** Capital Lad. CSF £60.59, CT £211.41. Tote £6.90: £1.50 £2.30 £1.40 (£32.80). Mr T. H. Bennett (MALTON) bred by Jim Strange. 8 Rn
1m 38.5 (2.5)
SF—27/35/22/8/–/–

**2532**　　LEWIS GEIPEL MEMORIAL CHALLENGE CUP (Nursery)　£3180.60 (£881.60: £421.80)
　　　　**5f**　　　　　　　　　　　　　　　　　　　　　　　2-50 (2-51)
　　　　　　　　　　(Weights raised 12 lb)
2044* **Grinnell** *(DenysSmith)* 8-12 KFallon (1) (bhd: rdn ¹/₂-wy: styd on to ld ins fnl f:
　　　　all out) ............................................................................... —1
2264⁴ Dead Calm *(CTinkler)* 8-2 GDuffield (4) (lw: hdwy 2f out: n.m.r: ev ch wl ins fnl f:
　　　　kpt on wl) ............................................................................ s.h.2
2330² Cloudy Reef *(RHollinshead)* 8-3 ‡7AGarth (3) (prom: led wl over 1f out tl ins fnl f:
　　　　styd on wl) ......................................................................... hd.3
2085 Our Mica (bl) *(JBerry)* 8-6 GCarter (8) (lw: sn cl up: rdn & nt qckn appr fnl f) .. 2¹/₂.4
2081 Field of Vision (IRE) (bl) *(MJohnston)* 8-12 DMcKeown (2) (lw: led tl hdd wl over
　　　　1f out: grad wknd) .............................................................. hd.5
1526⁵ Bella Bambola (IRE) (Fav) *(BBeasley)* 7-8 LCharnock (5) (lw: cl up: rdn 2f out:
　　　　wknd over 1f out: eased) ....................................................... 3.6

7/2 Bella Bambola (IRE), **4/1** Field of Vision (IRE), **9/2** GRINNELL, **5/1** Cloudy Reef, Dead Calm, **6/1** Our Mica. CSF £23.04, CT £90.05. Tote £4.30: £2.10 £1.50 (£6.80). Mr David McCune (BISHOP AUCKLAND) bred by J. F. Buchanan. 6 Rn
59.6 sec (1.9)
SF—35/24/24/17/22/–

**2533**　　GOLDEN FLEECE (S) STKS (3 & 4-Y.O) £2343.00 (£648.00: £309.00)
　　　　**1¹/₂m**　　　　　　　　　　　　　　　　　　　　　3-25 (3-26)

2297⁴ **Expansionist (57)** (Jt-Fav) *(SPCWoods)* 3-8-2 WWoods (5) (lw: a.p: effrt ent
　　　　st: led appr fnl f: styd on) ................................................... —1

2069³ **Salu (52)** (v) *(JEtherington)* 3-7-8 ‡³FNorton (3) (cl up: led 3f out: hung lft: hdd over 1f out: one pce) ............................................................ nk.2

1626⁵ **Reach for Glory (61)** (Jt-Fav) *(RMWhitaker)* 3-8-8 ACulhane (4) (outpcd: hdwy u.p ent st: no imp fnl 2f) ............................................................ 5.3

2087⁵ **Major Risk (49)** *(PAKelleway)* 3-8-2 GDuffield (1) (led tl hdd & hmpd 3f out: swtchd: put hd in air: nt r.o) ............................................................ hd.4

2357² **Lord Advocate (43)** (v) *(MPNaughton)* 4-9-6 JakiHouston (2) (cl up tl wknd 3f out) ............................................................ 12.5

**9/4** Reach for Glory, EXPANSIONIST, **7/2** Salu, **5/1** Lord Advocate, **8/1** Major Risk. CSF £9.62, Tote £3.50: £1.90 £1.60 (£4.60). High Point Bloodstock Ltd (NEWMARKET) bred by N. E. and Mrs Poole. 5 Rn; No bid
2m 32.8 (2.8)
SF—30/21/25/18/12

**2534** TATTERSALLS AUCTION SERIES STKS (Qualifier) (Mdn 2-Y.O) £3080.00 (£920.00: £440.00: £200.00) **7f** 3-55 (4-02)

1937 **Cosmic Star** *(SPCWoods)* 8-4 WWoods (7) (lw: trckd ldrs: effrt over 2f out: r.o u.p to ld ins fnl f) ............................................................ —1

2264 **Sky Wish** (Fav) *(MissSEHall)* 8-5 NConnorton (3) (led: hung rt most of wy: hdd ins fnl f: kpt on) ............................................................ ¾.2

2112⁴ **Mughal Princess (IRE)** *(MrsJRRamsden)* 8-6 PBurke (11) (lw: unruly s: dwlt: hdwy ent st: styd on: nt pce to chal) ............................................................ 2½.3

2277 **Cure the King (IRE)** *(SGNorton)* 9-0 KDarley (9) (bhd tl hdwy 3f out: hung lft: r.o nr fin) ............................................................ s.h.4

2049² **Ho-Joe (IRE)** *(AHarrison)* 8-11 KFallon (10) (hld up: c wd & hdwy 3f out: nt qckn appr fnl f) ............................................................ 1½.5

2118⁴ **El Guapo** *(TFairhurst)* 8-3 ‡³FNorton (1) (w ldr tl wknd fnl 2f) ............................................................ ½.6

2074 **Contrac Countess (IRE)** *(BSRothwell)* 8-0 GHind (5) (effrt ½-wy: nvr trbld ldrs) 1½.7

Sorayah's Pet *(SirMarkPrescott)* 9-0 GDuffield (2) (cmpt: scope: bit bkwd: prom tl grad wknd fnl 2f) ............................................................ hd.8

1322 **Desert Laughter (IRE)** *(RHollinshead)* 7-13 ‡⁷AGarth (6) (s.i.s: nvr nr to chal) ... hd.9

**Efizia** *(MrsGRReveley)* 8-0 JLowe (4) (w'like: bit bkwd: sn bhd) ............................................................ 5.10

2102 **La Bonita (IRE)** *(JBerry)* 8-7 GCarter (8) (prom 2f: sn bhd) ............................................................ 1½.11

**9/2** Sky Wish, **5/1** COSMIC STAR, Cure the King (IRE)(op 3/1), **11/2** Ho-Joe (IRE), **6/1** Sorayah's Pet, **10/1** Desert Laughter (IRE)(op 20/1), **14/1** La Bonita (IRE), El Guapo, **16/1** Ors. CSF £26.69, Tote £7.40: £2.10 £2.00 £3.40 (£20.60). Mr Arashan Ali (NEWMARKET) bred by Lt-Col R. Bromley Gardner. 11 Rn 1m 27.7 (4.4)

**2535** PETER BELL MEMORIAL H'CAP (0-80) £2834.80 (£782.80: £372.40) **2m** 4-25 (4-26)
(Weights raised 12 lb)

2001² **Jack Button (IRE) (75)** *(BobJones)* 3-9-10 NDay (3) (hrd rdn & lost pl 6f out: hdwy 3f out: led appr fnl f: hung lft: styd on) ............................................................ —1

2231² **Suez Canal (IRE) (74)** (bl) (Fav) *(PWChapple-Hyam)* 3-9-6 ‡³FNorton (1) (led 7f out & qcknd clr: hrd rdn 2f out: hdd over 1f out: nt resolute) 2.2

**Vain Prince (44)** *(NTinkler)* 5-8-9 LCharnock (2) (led 9f: hrd rdn appr st: one pce fnl 2f) ............................................................ 10.3

**4/5** Suez Canal (IRE), **5/4** JACK BUTTON (IRE), **10/1** Vain Prince. CSF £2.51, Tote £2.20 (£1.10). A. and B. Racing (NEWMARKET) bred by Empress Syndicate in Ireland. 3 Rn 3m 27 (4)
SF—30/24/3

**2536** GO RACING IN YORKSHIRE H'CAP (0-70) £2427.00 (£672.00: £321.00) **6f** 4-55 (4-59)
(Weights raised 4 lb)

1333² **Our Rita (62)** *(PAKelleway)* 3-9-7 KDarley (9) (bhd: hdwy over 1f out: str run to ld nr fin) ............................................................ —1

2050⁵ **Dancing Wild (36)** *(MrsGRReveley)* 3-7-9 NCarlisle (2) (chsd ldrs: outpcd ½-wy: styd on to ld ins fnl f: hdd & nt qckn nr fin) ............................................................ 1½.2

2123 **Henry Will (39)** *(TFairhurst)* 8-8-4 NConnorton (1) (hdwy ½-wy: ev ch 1f out: nt qckn) ............................................................ 1½.3

2115³ **Rock Opera (IRE) (59)** (Jt-Fav) *(MPNaughton)* 4-9-10 GHind (7) (bhd: hdwy u.p 2f out: chal 1f out: styd on one pce) ............................................................ nk.4

2163* **Double Feature (IRE) (62)** (Jt-Fav) *(MrsJRRamsden)* 3-9-7 MBirch (3) (bhd: hdwy ½-wy: chal 1f out: no ex u.p) ............................................................ d.h.4

2234⁶ **Miss Brightside (37)** *(ASmith)* 4-7-13 ‡³FNorton (8) (in tch: nt clr run 1f out: sn btn) ............................................................ 2½.6

2066 **Mahzooz (64)** *(MMoubarak)* 3-9-9 GBaxter (5) (lw: w ldrs tl wknd 1f out) ............................................................ hd.7

2206 **Le Chic (53)** *(DWChapman)* 6-9-4 SWood (4) (cl up: led over 3f out tl ins fnl f: wknd) ............................................................ 1.8

2123 **Minizen Music (IRE) (28)** *(MBrittain)* 4-7-7 JLowe (6) (lw: led tl hdd over 3f out: wknd 2f out) ............................................................ 3.9

LONG HANDICAP: Minizen Music (IRE) 7-5.

3/1 Rock Opera (IRE), Double Feature (IRE), 11/2 OUR RITA, 7/1 Minizen Music (IRE)(op 14/1), Miss Brightside, 9/1 Dancing Wild, 12/1 Mahzooz, 20/1 Ors. CSF £48.51, CT £819.22. Tote £4.80: £2.00 £2.20 £5.00 (£40.40). Mr T. Brady (NEWMARKET) bred by Terry Brady. 9 Rn
1m 12.4 (2.2)
SF—33/1/4/20/23/–

T/Plpt: £443.20 (5.4 Tckts).                                                                AA


# THIRSK (L-H)
## Saturday, August 1st [Firm]
Going Allowance: St: minus 0.50 sec (H); Rnd: minus 0.30 sec (F)          Wind: slt bhd

Stalls: high

**2537**          TOPCLIFFE STKS (2-Y.O) £2834.80 (£782.80: £372.40)     **6f**     2-20 (2-21)

2017* **Splendent (USA)** (Fav) *(PFICole)* 9-4 AMunro (3) (lw: trckd ldr: led appr fnl f: shkn up & qcknd: comf) ..................... —1
1902* The Sharp Bidder (IRE) *(RHollinshead)* 9-4 BRaymond (1) (led tl hdd appr fnl f: r.o) ............... ¾.2
2121² Glowing Value (IRE) *(JBerry)* 9-4 JCarroll (2) (hld up: effrt 2f out: rdn & no imp) 1½.3

1/9 SPLENDENT (USA)(op 1/6), 8/1 Glowing Value (IRE)(op 5/1), 20/1 The Sharp Bidder (IRE). CSF £2.50, Tote £1.10 (£2.00). Mr Fahd Salman (WHATCOMBE) bred by Derry Meeting Farm et. al. in USA. 3 Rn  1m 11.8 (1.6)
SF—12/9/3


**2538**          SUTTON STKS (Mdn 3-Y.O) £2343.00 (£648.00: £309.00)     **7f**     2-50 (2-53)

2229³ **Turret Gates** *(JARToller)* 9-0 GDuffield (5) (mde most: styd on wl fnl f) ............. —1
2133⁴ Jahangir (IRE) *(BHanbury)* 9-0 BRaymond (7) (lw: a cl up: disp ld over 2f out: no ex ins fnl f) ............... 1.2
2165² Auction King (IRE) (60) *(ASmith)* 9-0 SWebster (3) (a chsng ldrs: rdn & one pce fnl 2f) .................. 3.3
2062⁵ Always Lynsey (IRE) *(MissLCSiddall)* 8-9 MBirch (4) (t: a.p: one pce fnl 3f) ........ 2.4
2324³ Mummy's Brew *(BBeasley)* 8-9 LCharnock (2) (chsd ldr tl grad wknd fnl 3f) ...... 2.5
Stitched Up (IRE) (Fav) *(PWChapple-Hyam)* 9-0 MTebbutt (1) (w'like: scope: s.s: nt rcvr: fin lame) ............... 3½.6
Atan's Gem (USA) *(JNorton)* 8-9 JFortune (6) (unf: bit bkwd: a bhd) ............... 3½.7

6/4 Stitched Up (IRE), 9/4 TURRET GATES, 11/4 Jahangir (IRE), 14/1 Auction King (IRE), 50/1 Ors. CSF £8.13, Tote £3.40: £1.70 £1.90 (£3.50). Duke of Devonshire (NEWMARKET) bred by Brickfield Bloodstock Agency Ltd. 7 Rn  1m 25.8 (2.5)
SF—31/28/19/8/2/–


**2539**          NARBOL (S) STKS (Ladies) (3-Y.O) £2553.00 (£708.00: £339.00)     **6f**     3-25 (3-27)

2353³ **Soba Guest (IRE)** (69) *(JBerry)* 10-0 MissDianaJones (4) (b.nr hind: lw: mde all: kpt on wl u.p fnl f) ............... —1
2029 Patience Please (76) *(MHEasterby)* 9-8⁽⁴⁾ ‡⁵MrsSEasterby (2) (a cl up: effrt 2f out: nt qckn ins fnl f) ............... 1½.2
2327³ Oyston's Life (50) *(JBerry)* 9-11⁽²⁾ ‡⁵MissLPerratt (12) (a chsng ldrs: nt qckn fnl 2f) ............... 1½.3
1750 My Grain (34) *(RHollinshead)* 9-9 MrsGRees (10) (mid div tl styd on fnl 2f) ........ 1.4
2379 Throw Away Line (42) *(REBarr)* 9-2 ‡⁷MissMCarson (7) (a chsng ldrs: rdn 2f out: one pce) ............... 1½.5
1918⁴ Ergon (62) *(DJSCosgrove)* 9-2 ‡⁷MrsDCamp-Simpson (11) (b: lw: in tch: styd on one pce fnl 2f) ............... 4.6
1896⁵ Ravecino (45) *(JSHaldane)* 9-4 ‡⁵MissPRobson (8) (chsd ldrs: sn drvn: outpcd fnl 2f) ............... nk.7
1992 Kick on Majestic (IRE) (36) (v) *(NBycroft)* 9-7 ‡⁷MissABycroft (9) (sn outpcd & bhd: sme late hdwy) ............... 1½.8
Highborn (IRE) *(PSFelgate)* 9-7 ‡⁷MrsMMorris (6) (str: bkwd: nvr wnt pce) ...... 1½.9
2237⁶ Galley Gossip (44) (v) *(RBrotherton)* 9-7 ‡⁷MissVHill (3) (s.s: a bhd) ............... 1.10
2245 Miss Narnia (42) *(MDods)* 9-9 MrsAFarrell (5) (spd to ½-wy: sn rdn & wknd) ...... nk.11
2424 True Touch *(TDBarron)* 9-9 ‡⁵MrsDKettlewell (1) (sn outpcd) ............... 3½.12

11/8 Patience Please, 3/1 SOBA GUEST (IRE), 8/1 Oyston's Life, 17/2 Ergon, 16/1 Kick on Majestic (IRE), 25/1 True Touch, My Grain, 33/1 Ravecino, Throw Away Line, Miss Narnia, 50/1 Ors. CSF £6.80, Tote £3.80: £1.50 £1.50 £2.30 (£2.90). Mr Richard Jinks (COCKERHAM) bred by Tullamaine Castle Stud in Ireland. 12 Rn; No bid
1m 11 (0.8)
SF—38/26/23/17/4/–

**2540**  BARCLAYS BANK H'CAP (0-90) £3525.00 (£1050.00: £500.00: £225.00)
1½m
4-00 (4-01)

2250* **Explosive Speed (USA) (57)** *(MDHammond)* 4–8–1 GDuffield (2) (hld up: effrt
3f out: rdn to ld ins fnl f: r.o) ............................................ —1
2332² Eire Leath-Sceal **(55)** (Fav) *(MBrittain)* 5–7–8⁽²⁾ ‡⁵SMaloney (1) (lw: hdwy 8f out:
pushed along appr st: styd on & ev ch 1f out: nt qckn nr fin) ¾.2
2357 Sapphirine **(58)** *(RMWhitaker)* 5–8–2 JFanning (4) (cl up: led wl over 1f out tl ins
fnl f: no ex) ............................................................. 2.3
1996⁶ Arabian Bold (IRE) **(73)** *(WJHaggas)* 4–9–3 NDay (6) (led tl hdd wl over 1f out:
one pce) ................................................................ 1½.4
2226⁴ Duc de Berry (USA) **(84)** *(GHarwood)* 4–10–0 MPerrett (3) (sn cl up: outpcd
appr st: no imp after) ................................................. 5.5

**9/4** Eire Leath-Sceal (55), **3/1** EXPLOSIVE SPEED (USA), Duc de Berry (USA), **5/1** Arabian Bold (IRE), **8/1** Sapphirine.
CSF £9.30, Tote £3.50: £1.60 £1.60 (£2.60). Wetherby Racing Bureau Plc (MIDDLEHAM) bred by Buckram Oak
Farm in USA. 5 Rn
2m 30.7 (0.7)
SF—44/35/39/51/52

**2541**  EUROPRINT PROMOTIONS PORTFOLIO H'CAP (0-80) £3318.75 (£990.00: £472.50:
£213.75)  1m
4-30 (4-31)

2427⁴ **Green's Cassatt (USA) (44)** *(WMBrisbourne)* 4–7–9⁽²⁾ ‡⁵SMaloney (3) (stdd s:
hld up: effrt 2f out: r.o wl fnl f to ld cl home) ................... —1
2421* Tyrian Purple (IRE) **(61)** *(RHollinshead)* 4–8–10 (6x) ‡⁷MHumphries (2) (led:
shkn up 1f out: r.o: jst ct) ........................................... ½.2
1778* Alkarif (USA) **(77)** *(MrsJRRamsden)* 3–9–12 GBaxter (6) (hld up: smooth hdwy
to chal over 1f out: rdn & nt qckn ins fnl f) .................... 1.3
2487² Champenoise **(50)** *(MBell)* 4–8–6 GDuffield (1) (b.off hind: hld up: swtchd &
effrt over 2f out: no imp) ............................................. 6.4
2263³ Tathir (CAN) **(54)** *(DMorley)* 4–8–10 MBirch (4) (b: b.hind: chsd ldrs: rdn 2f out:
grad wknd) .............................................................. 4.5
1629² Persuasius (IRE) **(56)** (bl) (Fav) *(BBeasley)* 4–8–12 DNicholls (5) (lw: chsd ldr:
effrt 3f out: sn rdn & btn) ........................................... 6.6

**3/1** Persuasius (IRE), **100/30** Tyrian Purple (IRE), **9/2** Tathir (CAN), **5/1** Champenoise, Alkarif (USA)(op 3/1), **9/1**
GREEN'S CASSATT (USA). CSF £34.71, Tote £15.70: £3.00 £2.20 (£17.50). Mr K. K. Baron (BASCHURCH) bred
by Meryl A.Tanz Racing Stable & Carole Corfman in USA. 6 Rn
1m 37.7 (1.7)
SF—20/33/46/8/–/–

**2542**  YORKSHIRE TELEVISION STKS (Mdn 3-Y.O) £2406.00 (£666.00: £318.00)
1½m
5-00 (5-01)

1470⁵ **Guilty Secret (IRE)** (Fav) *(PWChapple-Hyam)* 8-9 GDuffield (3) (lw: mde all:
easily) .................................................................. —1
Marionetta (USA) *(LMCumani)* 8-9 JFortune (2) (w'like: leggy: sn cl up: effrt u.p
3f out: kpt on: no ch w wnr) ........................................ 2.2
Redstella (USA) *(RMWhitaker)* 9-0 MBirch (4) (w'like: str: bit bkwd: hdwy appr
st: outpcd fnl 2f) ...................................................... 5.3
Forest Star (USA) *(MMoubarak)* 9-0 GBaxter (5) (w'like: scope: bit bkwd: hld
up: effrt ent st: hung lft & n.d) ................................... 1½.4
1830⁵ Tajfehn (USA) *(BHanbury)* 8-9 BRaymond (1) (bit bkwd: cl up tl outpcd ent st:
sltly hmpd 3f out: sn btn) ............................................ 4.5

**Evens** GUILTY SECRET (IRE)(op 4/6), **7/4** Marionetta (USA), **5/1** Forest Star (USA), **20/1** Redstella (USA), **25/1**
Tajfehn (USA). CSF £3.07, Tote £2.10: £1.10 £1.40 (£2.10). Mr R. E. Sangster (MARLBOROUGH) bred by
Swettenham Stud in Ireland. 5 Rn
2m 34.4 (4.4)
SF—15/11/6/3/–

**2543**  DIRECTORS TROPHY (Nursery)  £3669.75 (£1098.00: £526.50: £240.75)
7f
5-30 (5-34)
(Weights raised 5 lb)

2158² **Wishing Cap (USA)** *(SirMarkPrescott)* 8-1 GDuffield (6) (hdwy 3f out: disp ld
appr fnl f: styd on to ld nr fin) .................................... —1
2233³ Bold Face (IRE) (bl) *(RFJohnsonHoughton)* 9-0 MBirch (1) (led & sn clr: disp ld
appr fnl f: r.o u.p: hdd & no ex nr fin) ........................... nk.2
2277⁴ Pine Ridge Lad (IRE) *(BBeasley)* 8-13 DNicholls (2) (lw: chsd ldr: effrt 3f out: r.o
one pce) ................................................................ 6.3
2259² Merry Mermaid *(JFBottomley)* 7-13 PBurke (9) (lw: bhd tl styd on fnl 3f: nrst fin) nk.4
961² Whitley Gorse *(JEtherington)* 9-7 TLucas (4) (unruly in stalls: sn in tch: grad
wknd fnl 2f) ............................................................ 5.5
2360² Plum First (bl) *(NBycroft)* 8-13 NDay (5) (chsd ldrs tl rdn & wknd over 2f out) .... 5.6

2247* Allegrissima (Fav) *(JBerry)* 8-11 JCarroll (7) (unruly in stalls: prom early: lost
　　　tch appr st) ....................................................................... 3½.**7**
1860² Weaver George (IRE) *(MHEasterby)* 7-13 ‡$SMaloney (3) (cl up to st: sn bhd) .......... s.h.**8**
2068² Mohican Brave (IRE) *(JGFitzGerald)* 9-7 KFallon (8) (lw: lost tch fr ½-wy) ......... 7.**9**

**5/1** Allegrissima, **11/2** WISHING CAP (USA), Bold Face, Merry Mermaid, **9/1** Mohican Brave (IRE), **12/1** Whitley Gorse. CSF £31.02, CT £197.96. Tote £4.60: £1.70 £2.10 £2.20 (£11.50). Pinnacle Racing Stable (NEWMARKET) bred by Michael Cahan & Dr Geroulis in USA. 9 Rn　　　　　　　　　　　　　　　　　　　　　1m 26.4 (3.1)
　　　　　　　　　　　　　　　　　　　　　　　　　　SF—9/21/2/–/–/–

T/Plpt: £7.80 (353.1 Tckts).　　　　　　　　　　　　　　　　　　　　　　AA

2414—**WINDSOR　(Fig.8)**
### Saturday, August 1st [Good to firm]
Going Allowance: minus 0.30 sec per fur (F)　　　　　　　Wind: slt half bhd

Stalls: high

**2544**　　E.B.F. MOLSON SPECIAL DRY STKS (Mdn 2-Y.O) £2092.00 (£582.00: £280.00)
　　　　　　**5f 217y**　　　　　　　　　　　　　　　　　　6-00 (6-03)

1944³ **Devilry** *(GLewis)* 9-0 PaulEddery (12) (hrd rdn & hdwy 1f out: led last strides) .. —**1**
　　Angus Dundee (IRE) *(HRACecil)* 9-0 PatEddery (16) (cmpt: bit bkwd: led: hrd
　　　rdn over 1f out: hdd last strides) ........................................... hd.**2**
1056³ The Seer (Fav) *(BWHills)* 9-0 AMunro (10) (lost pl over 2f out: rallied fnl f: r.o) . hd.**3**
297⁶ Gone Prospecting (USA) *(RHannon)* 9-0 DaleGibson (6) (a.p: ev ch 1f out: r.o) nk.**4**
Stay With Me Baby *(DRCElsworth)* 8-9 DHolland (9) (w'like: bit bkwd: hdwy
　　over 1f out: r.o ins fnl f) ...................................................... 1½ **5**
　　Mind the Roof (IRE) *(DRCElsworth)* 8-9 SWhitworth (15) (leggy: dwlt: hdwy
　　over 1f out: r.o ins fnl f) ...................................................... nk.**6**
1915 Arawa *(DMarks)* 8-9 AMcGlone (2) (a.p: rdn over 1f out: one pce) ............... 1½.**7**
　　Azrag (IRE) *(TThomsonJones)* 9-0 WCarson (8) (b.hind: leggy: scope: bit
　　　bkwd: a.p: ev ch 2f out: wknd fnl f) ....................................... 3½.**8**
2233 Hotel California (IRE) *(JWHills)* 8-9 RHills (1) (prom over 3f) ....................... 1.**9**
1571 Ascom Pager Too *(PHowling)* 8-6 ‡³FNorton (7) (b) ............................... 2½.**10**
2233 Amillionmemories *(MrsBarbaraWaring)* 9-0 NHowe (11) ........................... 2½.**11**
2238² Kyrenia Game *(PMitchell)* 8-6 ‡$SO'Gorman (13) ................................. 1½.**12**
2269 Dark and Stormy *(MDixon)* 8-9 ‡$ATucker (14) (a bhd) ........................... 1½.**13**
　　Boxboy *(KOCunningham-Brown)* 8-11 ‡³RPerham (3) (leggy: prom over 2f) ... ¾.**14**
　　Swift Revenge *(MRChannon)* 8-9 BRouse (4) (w'like: bit bkwd: a bhd) .......... hd.**15**
　　Haiti Belle *(MMcCourt)* 8-9 NAdams (5) (unf: bit bkwd: a bhd) ..................... 8.**16**

**9/4** The Seer, **100/30** Angus Dundee (IRE), **4/1** DEVILRY, **6/1** Azrag (IRE), **16/1** Haiti Belle, Hotel California (IRE), Mind the Roof (IRE), Stay With Me Baby, Gone Prospecting (USA), **33/1** Arawa, Swift Revenge, Amillionmemories, **50/1** Ors. CSF £17.36, Tote £5.50: £1.80 £1.70 £1.20 (£13.10). Lady McIndoe (EPSOM) bred by Tarworth Bloodstock Investments Ltd. 16 Rn　　　　　　　1m 12 (1.5)
　　　　　　　　　　　　　　　　　　　　　　　SF—34/33/32/31/20/19

**2545**　　HOFMEISTER (S) STKS (3 & 4-Y.O) £1506.60 (£417.60: £199.80)
　　　　　　**1m 67y**　　　　　　　　　　　　　　　　　　6-30 (6-35)

2209 **Sally Fast (53)** *(BPalling)* 3-7-11 ‡$StephenDavies (11) (6th st: led 1f out: r.o wl) —**1**
736 Precious Air (IRE) (40) *(AMoore)* 4-9-0 CandyMorris (10) (hdwy 2f out: hrd rdn
　　over 1f out: r.o wl ins fnl f) ...................................................... s.h.**2**
2253⁴ Daily Sport Girl (44) *(FJYardley)* 3-8-7 JQuinn (16) (3rd st: led over 3f out to 1f
　　out: unable qckn) ............................................................... 1.**3**
　　Shalou *(RJHodges)* 3-8-12 DHolland (2) (gd hdwy over 1f out: r.o wl ins fnl f) .. 1.**4**
2079³ Honey Vision (46) (bl) *(GHEden)* 3-8-2 DaleGibson (4) (hrd rdn 2f out: hdwy
　　over 1f out: r.o) .................................................................. ¾.**5**
2254 Pine Glen Pepper (29) (bl) *(JAkehurst)* 4-9-0 SWhitworth (7) (7th st: nt clr run
　　over 1f out: one pce) ............................................................ ½.**6**
1741 Bo Knows Best (IRE) (36) *(JSutcliffe)* 3-8-7 BRouse (15) (hdwy fnl 2f: nvr nrr) .. 1.**7**
1772 Our Eddie (54) (bl) (Jt-Fav) *(BGubby)* 3-8-7 PatEddery (1) (hrd rdn & hdwy 3f
　　out: one pce) ..................................................................... 1.**8**
2251 Rapid Rosie (24) (v) *(DRLaing)* 4-8-9 TyroneWilliams (12) (4th st: one pce fnl 3f) 1.**9**
1949 Modern Art (IRE) *(RAkehurst)* 4-9-0 AMunro (17) (2nd st: wknd 2f out) .......... ¾.**10**
1912⁶ Aragona (46) *(PDCundell)* 3-8-2 RHills (9) (lw: a mid div) ....................... 2½.**11**
2297² Selaginella (52) (Jt-Fav) *(MRChannon)* 3-7-11 ‡$BDoyle (8) (lw: hdwy over 3f
　　out: wknd 2f out) ................................................................. 3½.**12**
2303 Rock Song (IRE) (54) *(PFICole)* 3-8-12 WCarson (6) (lw: a bhd) ................. hd.**13**

2240 Flying Promise (39) (RABennett) 4–9-0 WNewnes (3) (led 1f: 5th st: wknd over 2f out) ........................................................................................ 1¹/₂.14
2305 Sixofus (IRE) (48) (bl) (WGMTurner) 4–9-2 ‡³TSprake (14) (led over 7f out tl over 3f out: sn wknd) ............................................................................. s.h.15
1009 Zafra (25) (GFHCharles-Jones) 4–8-4 ‡⁵ATucker (5) (a bhd) ..................... 3¹/₂.16
　　 Abbey Green (CJHill) 4–9-0 NAdams (13) (s.s: a bhd) ........................... 7.17

**9/2** Our Eddie, Selaginella, **5/1** Rock Song (IRE), **15/2** Honey Vision, **8/1** Modern Art (IRE), Shalou, **10/1** Sixofus (IRE), **14/1** Rapid Rosie(op 33/1), Bo Knows Best (IRE)(10/1—16/1), Daily Sport Girl, Aragona(op 8/1), **16/1** Pine Glen Pepper, **20/1** SALLY FAST, **25/1** Flying Promise, **33/1** Ors. CSF £522.75, Tote £76.70: £9.10 £18.90 £5.70 (Wnr or 2nd w any £11.60). Mr W. H. Joyce (COWBRIDGE) bred by W. H. Joyce. 17 Rn; No bid
1m 43.8 (2.2)
SF—12/28/18/20/8/18

**2546**　　FOSTERS NURSERY　£2343.00 (£648.00: £309.00)　**5f 10y**　7-00 (7-03)
　　　　　　　　　　　　　(Weights raised 3 lb)
2308* **Bold County** (MJohnston) 8-6 RPElliott (5) (hld up: led over 1f out: comf) ......... —1
2080³ Infant Protege (USA) (CEBrittain) 7-6⁽⁴⁾ ‡⁵BDoyle (2) (hdwy over 1f out: r.o ins fnl f) .............................................................................................................. 2.2
2176 Grand Dancer (IRE) (bl) (RJRWilliams) 9-7 RCochrane (8) (led over 2f out tl over 1f out: unable qckn) ...................................................................... 1¹/₂.3
2286⁴ Fiveofive (IRE) (Fav) (NACallaghan) 8-6 PatEddery (7) (outpcd: hrd rdn over 2f out: hdwy over 1f out: nvr nrr) ................................................................. 3.4
2257* Wealthywoo (bl) (JSMoore) 7-8 JQuinn (1) (spd over 3f) .......................... 1¹/₂.5
2242⁴ Brigadore Gold (RHannon) 8-4 MRoberts (6) (led over 2f) ........................ 2.6
2255³ Kind of Cute (CCElsey) 8-5 DHolland (3) (prom 3f) ................................. ¹/₂.7
　2008 Brave Bidder (BGubby) 7-7 NAdams (4) (spd over 2f) ............................. nk.8
LONG HANDICAP: Infant Protege (USA) 7-3, Brave Bidder 7-5.

**6/4** Fiveofive (IRE), **3/1** BOLD COUNTY, **13/2** Brigadore Gold, **15/2** Wealthywoo(5/1—8/1), **9/1** Infant Protege (USA)(op 6/1), **10/1** Grand Dancer (IRE), **12/1** Kind of Cute, **20/1** Brave Bidder. CSF £28.25, CT £223.88. Tote £4.40: £1.70 £2.20 £2.30 (£23.70). The Fairyhouse 1992 Partnership (MIDDLEHAM) bred by Someries Stud. 8 Rn
59.9 sec (0.9)
SF—44/22/45/18/–/2

**2547**　　COURAGE BEER COMPANY H'CAP (3-Y.O) (0-90) £2880.50 (£798.00: £381.50)
　　　　　　**1m 3f 135y**　　7-30 (7-31)
　　　　　　　　　　　　　(Weights raised 9 lb)
1446 **Striking Image (IRE) (60)** (RHannon) 8-8 RCochrane (5) (w ldr: led over 8f out: hrd rdn over 1f out: r.o wl) ............................................................... —1
2241* Wassl This Then (IRE) (73) (DWPArbuthnot) 9-7 TQuinn (3) (2nd st: hrd rdn over 2f out: unable qckn) ............................................................... 5.2
2036⁶ Dajitus (63) (MJHeaton-Ellis) 8-11 DHolland (7) (b: lw: 4th st: one pce fnl 2f) . 3¹/₂.3
2334* Maestroso (IRE) (68) (Fav) (RFJohnsonHoughton) 9-2 MRoberts (4) (6th st: hrd rdn 3f out: one pce) .......................................................................... ¹/₂.4
1901² El Rabab (USA) (69) (HThomsonJones) 9-3 RHills (1) (5th st: wknd over 2f out) 8.5
2266 Headless Heights (60) (PMitchell) 8-8 PaulEddery (6) (a bhd) ................... 12.6
　788 Money Spinner (USA) (65) (LordHuntingdon) 8-8 ‡⁵DHarrison (2) (led 3f: 3rd st: wknd over 4f out) ............................................................................. 2¹/₂.7

**2/1** Maestroso (IRE), **5/2** Wassl This Then (IRE), **7/2** El Rabab (USA), **8/1** Money Spinner (USA)(10/1—12/1), **14/1** Headless Heights, **16/1** STRIKING IMAGE (IRE) & Ors. CSF £52.50, Tote £12.00: £3.60 £1.70 (£21.30). Mrs C. J. Powell (MARLBOROUGH) bred by Shanbally House Stud in Ireland. 7 Rn
2m 26.5 (4)
SF—20/23/6/10/–/–

**2548**　　WADWORTH 6X H'CAP (0-70) £2532.00 (£702.00: £336.00)　**5f 10y**　8-00 (8-04)
2153* **Dawes of Nelson (47)** (MJBolton) 7–8-5 JLowe (12) (hdwy over 1f out: led ins fnl f: all out) ..................................................................................... —1
2307 Erris Express (46) (JSMoore) 7–7-11 ‡⁷DGibbs (1) (a.p: ev ch fnl f: r.o wl) ...... s.h.2
2061² The Noble Oak (IRE) (65) (bl) (MMcCormack) 4–9-9 JReid (9) (lw: a.p: rdn over 2f out: ev ch ins fnl f: r.o) ................................................................... ³/₄.3
1415⁶ Joe Sugden (56) (PHowling) 8–9-0 MRoberts (10) (lw: a.p: hrd rdn over 1f out: ev ch ins fnl f: r.o) ...................................................................... ¹/₂.4
1756⁶ Castle Maid (38) (RJHodges) 5–7-7 ‡³FNorton (16) (gd hdwy over 1f out: hrd rdn: r.o wl) .......................................................................................... nk.5
2199 Sports Post Lady (IRE) (50) (CJHill) 4–8-8 NAdams (17) (lw: outpcd: hdwy over 1f out: r.o ins fnl f) .............................................................................. hd.6
2063⁵ Katie-a (IRE) (55) (RMWhitaker) 3–8-9 ACulhane (4) (hdwy over 1f out: r.o) ..... nk.7
1314 Calibairn (42) (DJSCosgrove) 4–8-0⁽¹⁾ AShoults (8) (hdwy over 1f out: nvr nrr) s.h.8
2229² Belthorn (49) (JJBridger) 3–8-3⁽²⁾ SWhitworth (3) (led tl ins fnl f: unable qckn) 1¹/₂.9
2279* Ganeshaya (47) (bl) (MFBarraclough) 3–8-1 NCarlisle (13) (prom over 3f) .... s.h.10

2127 Ashtina (62) (RJHodges) 7-9-6 PatEddery (5) (spd over 3f) ............... nk.11
2307 Sea Crusader (47) (bl) (MBlanshard) 3-8-1 DHolland (7) (swtg: prom over 3f) 2.12
2199⁶ Barbezieux (39) (bl) (TJNaughton) 5-7-6⁽⁴⁾ ‡5DHarrison (11) (a bhd) ............... ¾.13
2053 Wilco (52) (AndrewTurnell) 3-8-6 RHills (15) (spd over 3f) ............... 2½.14
2307 Flash of Straw (IRE) (52) (GLewis) 3-8-6 PaulEddery (14) (lw: a bhd) .......... 1½.15
Ever Sharp (74) (JWhite) 8-9-11 ‡7CAvery (2) (bit bkwd: prom over 3f) ......... ½.16
2303 Julia Sabina (43) (CCElsey) 3-7-11 JQuinn (6) (outpcd) ............... 1½.17
2051 Easy Delta (46) (MDixon) 3-7-9⁽⁷⁾ ‡5ATucker (18) (s.s: a bhd) ............... 8.18
LONG HANDICAP: Barbezieux 6-11, Easy Delta 6-12.

7/2 The Noble Oak (IRE)(5/1—11/2), 11/2 Ashtina, Ganeshaya, 9/1 DAWES OF NELSON, Joe Sugden(12/1—8/1), 10/1 Erris Express(14/1—16/1), 11/1 Wilco(7/1—12/1), 12/1 Katie-a (IRE), 14/1 Sports Post Lady (IRE), Castle Maid, 16/1 Belthorn, 20/1 Sea Crusader, 33/1 Calibairn, Julia Sabina, Barbezieux, Flash of Straw (IRE), 50/1 Ever Sharp, 66/1 Easy Delta. CSF £96.24, CT £354.95. Tote £12.10: £2.90 £2.60 £1.40 £1.70 (£112.80).
Mr A. R. M. Galbraith (SHREWTON) bred by D. Cornwall. 18 Rn    59.9 sec (0.9)
SF—43/34/58/47/25/39

**2549**    JOHN SMITH'S STKS (Mdn 3-Y.O) £1683.00 (£468.00: £225.00)
1¼m 7y    8-30 (8-38)

Fermoy (USA) (Fav) (LMCumani) 8-9 LDettori (8) (hdwy 3f out: led 1f out: pushed out) ............... —1
1476 Usaidit (68) (bl) (WCarter) 9-0 PaulEddery (13) (lw: led 9f: unable qckn) ... 1½.2
2137³ Garachico (USA) (bl) (GHarwood) 9-0 TQuinn (16) (lw: 6th st: hrd rdn over 1f out: one pce) ............... 2.3
Flamingo Rose (IRE) (HRACecil) 8-9 PatEddery (12) (bit bkwd: hdwy over 2f out: one pce) ............... 1½.4
1933⁶ Wild Applause (IRE) (JHMGosden) 8-9 MHills (22) (b.nr hind: hdwy over 1f out: r.o) ............... s.h.5
1746⁴ Pompion (USA) (JHMGosden) 9-0 RCochrane (20) (5th st: hrd rdn over 2f out: one pce) ............... ¾.6
Long Silence (USA) (MrsJCecil) 8-9 JReid (21) (unf: scope: hdwy over 2f out: one pce) ............... 1½.7
2168⁴ Bird Watcher (MajorWRHern) 9-0 WRyan (6) (4th st: wknd over 1f out) ......... 3.8
Greek Chime (IRE) (LordHuntingdon) 9-0 AMunro (1) (dwlt: nvr nrr) ............... nk.9
2293⁶ Romance (IRE) (MJHeaton-Ellis) 8-9 RHills (11) ............... 2½.10
Debacle (USA) (GHarwood) 9-0 AClark (15) (b: nvr nrr) ............... nk.11
1245 Dioman Shadeed (USA) (JRFanshawe) 9-0 DHolland (5) (2nd st: wknd over 2f out) ............... 1.12
633 Hurricane Toke (IRE) (ACStewart) 9-0 MRoberts (18) ............... 2.13
693 Brooks Express (FR) (RAkehurst) 8-11 ‡3RPerham (9) ............... 3½.14
The Grey Texan (MissBSanders) 9-0 WNewnes (4) (leggy: lt-f) ............... 4.15
Kalokagathos (CGCox) 9-0 DaleGibson (2) (lw: prom 5f) ............... 2.16
1792 Sulaah Rose (MrsJJordan) 8-2 ‡7PAllinson (14) (swtg: 3rd st: wknd over 3f out) 5.17
2239⁴ Alif (IRE) (JLDunlop) 9-0 WCarson (3) (bhd fnl 6f) ............... 1½.18
Bar Three (IRE) (LJCodd) 8-7 ‡7WHollick (19) (w'like: a bhd) ............... s.h.19
Hazy Shades (JJBridger) 8-9 SWhitworth (10) (a bhd: t.o) ............... 20

13/8 FERMOY (USA)(7/2—6/4), 5/1 Flamingo Rose (IRE)(tchd 8/1), 11/2 Bird Watcher(5/2—6/1), 13/2 Pompion (USA)(12/1—6/1), 7/1 Long Silence (USA)(4/1—8/1), 14/1 Garachico (USA)(12/1—20/1), Greek Chime (IRE)(10/1—16/1), Alif (IRE), Wild Applause (IRE), 16/1 Hurricane Toke (IRE), 25/1 Debacle (USA), 33/1 Dioman Shadeed (USA), Usaidit, 50/1 Ors. CSF £60.88, Tote £3.20: £1.50 £4.60 £3.90 (£74.10). Sheikh Mohammed (NEWMARKET) bred by Darley Stud Management Co Ltd. in USA. 20 Rn   2m 6.8 (3.8)
SF—37/35/39/27/26/29

T/Plpt: £1,191.20 (2 Tckts).    AK

## 2200—RIPON (R-H)

### Monday, August 3rd [Good to firm]

Going Allowance: St: minus 0.40 sec; Rnd: minus 0.10 sec (F)    Wind: fresh across

Stalls: low

**2550**    SEE-SAW CLAIMING STKS (2-Y.O) £2364.00 (£652.00: £312.00)   **5f**   2-30 (2-32)

1192⁴ **Lord Olivier (IRE)** (89) (Fav) (WJarvis) 8-11 MTebbutt (5) (mde all: easily) ....... —1
Out of Aces (MrsVAAconley) 7-8 LCharnock (2) (lt-f: bit bkwd: bhd: hdwy 2f out: r.o wl nr fin) ............... 2.2
2067* Classic Storm (70) (JBerry) 8-6 JCarroll (6) (chsd wnr: rdn 2f out: r.o one pce) ¾.3
2232⁶ Master Sinclair (IRE) (61) (RHollinshead) 8-4 WRyan (3) (in tch: hdwy over 1f out: styd on wl nr fin) ............... nk.4

1699 Dancing Domino *(MHEasterby)* 8-9 KDarley (4) (chsd ldrs tl wknd ins fnl f) ........ 2.5
16645 Norstano **(78)** *(MHEasterby)* 8-6 MBirch (7) (spd 3f) .............................. 1½.6
Boulmerka *(MJohnston)* 7-11 JLowe (1) (unf: bit bkwd: s.s: a bhd) ............ 10.7

**4/5 LORD OLIVIER (IRE), 2/1** Classic Storm(11/4—7/4), **10/1** Norstano, **12/1** Dancing Domino, **16/1**
Boulmerka, **25/1** Master Sinclair (IRE), **50/1** Out of Aces. CSF £27.29, Tote £1.80: £1.30 £11.80 (£72.00). Miss
V. R. Jarvis (NEWMARKET) bred by Michael Staunton in Ireland. 7 Rn                                                 59.4 sec (0.8)
SF—41/16/25/22/19/10

---

### 2551
E.B.F. TRAMPOLINE STKS (Mdn 2-Y.O) £2322.00 (£642.00: £306.00)
**5f**                                                                                                      3-00 (3-03)

23683 **Falsoola** (Fav) *(MRStoute)* 8-9 PatEddery (2) (lw: mde most: pushed along &
r.o wl fnl 2f) ..................................................................................................... —1
21614 Primula Bairn *(MrsJRRamsden)* 8-9 MBirch (3) (disp ld to ½-wy: kpt on: nt pce
of wnr) .......................................................................................................... 1½.2
2388 Grey Pride *(JBerry)* 9-0 JCarroll (6) (a chsng ldrs: sn drvn along: no imp fnl 2f) . 4.3
2024 Doc Cottrill *(MrsJRRamsden)* 9-0 PBurke (1) (s.i.s: stdy hdwy 2f out: r.o) ............ 4.4
22484 Free Dancer *(RAllan)* 8-9 SWebster (4) (rn green & sn drvn along: n.d) ............ s.h.5
2205 Bajan Affair *(MissLCSiddall)* 8-4 ‡5DHarrison (7) (lw: spd 3f: sn wknd) ................ 1.6
18545 Humber's Supreme (IRE) *(BSRothwell)* 8-9 GHind (5) (sn outpcd & bhd) .......... 15.7

**4/11 FALSOOLA, 7/2** Primula Bairn, **14/1** Free Dancer, Grey Pride, **20/1** Doc Cottrill, **33/1** Bajan Affair, **50/1**
Humber's Supreme (IRE). CSF £2.40, Tote £1.40: £1.10 £1.80 (£1.70). Sheikh Mohammed (NEWMARKET)
bred by Sheikh Mohammed bin Rashid al Maktoum. 7 Rn                                                           59.1 sec (0.5)
SF—45/39/28/12/6/–

---

### 2552
'GO RACING IN YORKSHIRE' H'CAP (3-Y.O) (0-80) £3377.25 (£1008.00: £481.50:
£218.25) **6f**                                                                                            3-30 (3-37)
(Weights raised 1 lb)

2029* **First Gold (65)** (Jt-Fav) *(JWharton)* 8-9 MBirch (4) (lw: hdwy ½-wy: wandered
u.p: led ins fnl f: all out) ..................................................................................... —1
18614 Absolutely Nuts **(73)** *(BAMcMahon)* 9-3 TQuinn (8) (lw: a chsng ldrs: chal ins
fnl f: kpt on) ...................................................................................................... nk.2
22794 Kalar **(49)** (bl) *(DWChapman)* 7-7 SWood (2) (led: hung rt most of wy: hdd ins
fnl f: r.o) ............................................................................................................ s.h.3
1926 Castlerea Lad **(77)** *(RHollinshead)* 9-7 WRyan (3) (hdwy 2f out: ev ch ins fnl f:
kpt on one pce) ................................................................................................. ½.4
17916 Gymcrak Tycoon **(75)** *(MHEasterby)* 9-5 KDarley (6) (a chsng ldrs: kpt on
same pce fnl 2f) ................................................................................................. nk.5
21403 Followmegirls **(67)** *(MrsALMKing)* 8-11 MRoberts (5) (bhd: hdwy ½-wy: sn
chsng ldrs: nt qckn fnl f) .................................................................................... 2.6
24063 Pink'n Black (IRE) **(53)** *(GBlum)* 7-6(1) ‡5DHarrison (7) (unruly gng to s: in tch:
hrd rdn 2f out: no imp) ....................................................................................... 2½.7
2300* Scala Milano **(64)** (Jt-Fav) *(KTIvory)* 8-8 GBardwell (1) (lw: chsd ldrs: sn drvn
along: wknd over 1f out) .................................................................................... 6.8
2131 Cromer's Express **(53)** (v) *(MissLCSiddall)* 7-8 ‡3FNorton (9) (spd 4f: sn wknd) . 1.9
LONG HANDICAP: Kalar 6-13.

**7/2** Scala Milano, **FIRST GOLD, 4/1** Pink'n Black (IRE), **11/2** Absolutely Nuts, **9/1** Gymcrak Tycoon(op 6/1), **12/1**
Followmegirls, Castlerea Lad, **25/1** Cromer's Express, **33/1** Kalar. CSF £20.59, CT £475.66. Tote £4.40: £1.30
£2.10 £4.60 (£7.80). Mr J. L. Ashby (MELTON MOWBRAY) bred by Messinger Stud Ltd. 9 Rn     1m 12.1 (0.4)
SF—39/46/21/47/44/28

---

### 2553
ARMSTRONG MEMORIAL CHALLENGE CUP (H'cap) (0-105) £6813.00 (£2034.00:
£972.00: £441.00) **1½m 60y**                                                                              4-00 (4-03)
(Weights raised 3 lb)

22023 **Tell No Lies (87)** (Jt-Fav) *(MHEasterby)* 5–9-10 MBirch (1) (lw: hld up: a gng
wl: led ins fnl f: shkn up & qcknd cl home) ....................................................... —1
2200* Kanvass **(79)** (Jt-Fav) *(JRFanshawe)* 3–8-5 GDuffield (3) (lw: trckd ldrs: led &
qcknd 3f out: hdd ins fnl f: rallied u.p) ............................................................. ½.2
23862 Regal Lover (IRE) **(73)** *(MBell)* 3–7-13 MRoberts (5) (led tl hdd 3f out: one pce) 7.3
2244* Latvian **(69)** (bl) *(RAllan)* 5–8-1 ‡5JWeaver (4) (cl up tl rdn & outpcd 3f out:
wandered u.p: no imp after) .............................................................................. ½.4
Corn Lily **(71)** *(MrsGRReveley)* 6–8-8 JLowe (2) (bit bkwd: trckd ldrs: chal 4f
out: wknd over 2f out) ........................................................................................ 8.5
1252* Mad Militant (IRE) **(81)** *(RHollinshead)* 3–8-7 WRyan (6) (hld up: effrt 4f out: sn
rdn & btn) .......................................................................................................... 1.6

**11/4** Kanvass, **TELL NO LIES, 100/30** Regal Lover (IRE), **5/1** Latvian, **7/1** Corn Lily, **8/1** Mad Militant (IRE). CSF
£10.58, Tote £4.10: £2.20 £2.00 (£6.30). Mrs A. Johnstone (MALTON) bred by The Dunchurch Lodge Stud Co
and Mrs A. Johnstone. 6 Rn                                                                                  2m 36.6 (2.6)
SF—72/52/32/33/24/21

**2554**　TOMMY SHEDDEN CHALLENGE TROPHY (H'cap) (0-80) £3494.25 (£1044.00: £499.50: £227.25)　**1m 1f**　4-30 (4-35)

2378⁴ **Jubran (USA) (67)** *(MPNaughton)* 6-9-7　MRoberts (3) (chsd ldrs: effrt & edgd lft over 2f out: hrd rdn to ld ins fnl f) ..................................... —1
2065* **Floating Line (60)** *(PWigham)* 4-9-0　MWigham (7) (bhd & rdn 4f out: gd hdwy 3f out: r.o nr fin) ..................................... 1.2
2327* **Jefferson Davis (IRE) (70)** *(BBeasley)* 3-9-2　DNicholls (8) (lw: led tl hdd & no ex ins fnl f) ..................................... 1½.3
2293³ **Retender (USA) (69)** *(LMCumani)* 3–8-10　‡⁵JWeaver (4) (lw: b.hind: bhd: swtchd & effrt over 2f out: nrst fin) ..................................... 2.4
2028 **Cradle of Love (USA) (74)** *(JWHills)* 4—10-0　MHills (9) (lw: in tch: effrt 4f out: rdn & nt qckn over 2f out) ..................................... 3.5
2421⁴ **Who's Tef (IRE) (62)** *(MHEasterby)* 4–8-11　‡⁵SMaloney (10) (lw: chsd ldrs tl rdn & wknd over 2f out) ..................................... 1½.6
2355³ **Master Copy (IRE) (47)** (bl) *(CBBBooth)* 3–7-7　JQuinn (5) (bhd: effrt 4f out: n.d) ..................................... 2.7
2326* **Tancred Grange (64)** *(MissSEHall)* 3–8-5　‡⁵OPears (1) (chsd ldr tl wknd 3f out) 3½.8
2384* **Waseela (IRE) (75)** (Fav) *(AAScott)* 3–9-7 (5x)　BRaymond (6) (lw: cl up tl rdn & wknd over 3f out) ..................................... 1½.9
2378² **Corcina (74)** *(MBell)* 4–9-7 ‡⁷PTurner (2) (b.off fore: chsd ldrs: rdn appr st: wknd 4f out) ..................................... 5.10

11/4 Waseela (IRE), 11/2 Retender (USA)(op 7/2), 6/1 Corcina, 7/1 JUBRAN (USA), 8/1 Floating Line, Tancred Grange, 12/1 Who's Tef (IRE), Cradle of Love (USA), 14/1 Jefferson Davis (IRE), 20/1 Master Copy (IRE). CSF £56.13, CT £692.53. Tote £9.90: £3.00 £2.80 £4.20 (£32.60). Mrs Elke Scullion (RICHMOND) bred by King Ranch, Inc. in USA. 10 Rn　　1m 52.9 (2.7)
SF—53/43/40/28/37/17

**2555**　BOUNCING CASTLE STKS (Mdn 3-Y.O) £2658.00 (£642.00)　**1m**　5-00 (5-10)

2186³ **Many a Quest (USA)** (Fav) *(LMCumani)* 8-9　‡⁵JWeaver (1) (lw: mde all: v.easily) —1
2164⁶ **Tip it In** *(ASmith)* 9-0　SWebster (3) (chsd wnr: rdn 4f out: n.d) ..................................... 4.2
Jdaayel (5/4) Withdrawn (ref to ent stalls) : not under orders — Rule 4 applies

4/7 MANY A QUEST (USA), 33/1 Tip it In. Tote £1.10. Mr Richard L. Duchossois (NEWMARKET) bred by Carolyn T. Groves in USA. 2 Rn　　1m 44.1 (6.4)

**2556**　LEVY BOARD MEDIAN AUCTION STKS (3-Y.O) £2976.00 (£888.00: £424.00: £192.00) 1½m 60y　5-30 (5-30)

1872² **Asian Punter (IRE) (68)** (Fav) *(AHide)* 8-11　WRyan (4) (hld up: hdwy 4f out: rdn to ld over 1f out: r.o) ..................................... —1
1561* **Briggs Lad (IRE) (68)** *(WJarvis)* 9-2　MTebbutt (2) (lw: trckd ldr: chal over 2f out: nt qckn fnl f) ..................................... 1½.2
2403 **Philgun (58)** *(CWCElsey)* 9-2‡⁵SMaloney (1) (led: qcknd ent st: hdd over 1f out: no ex) ..................................... hd.3
**Royal Sultan** *(DenysSmith)* 8-11　JLowe (3) (bit bkwd: cl up tl wknd over 2f out) 10.4

**Evens** ASIAN PUNTER (IRE), 11/8 Briggs Lad (IRE), 13/2 Philgun, 25/1 Royal Sultan. CSF £2.64, Tote £1.90 (£1.20). Mr Rory C. Leader (NEWMARKET) bred by Patrick Cox in Ireland. 4 Rn　　2m 43.7 (9.7)
T/Plpt: £46.20 (257.6 Tckts).　　AA

## 2232—NOTTINGHAM (L-H)

### Monday, August 3rd [Good to firm, Firm patches]
Going Allowance: St: 0.30 sec (G); Rnd: minus 0.05 sec per fur (F)　　Wind: slt against

Stalls: high

**2557**　E.B.F. MINERS STKS (Mdn 2-Y.O.F) £2042.40 (£566.40: £271.20) **6f 15y**　5-45 (5-47)

**Katiba (USA)** *(JLDunlop)* 8-11　WCarson (6) (w'like: leggy: dwlt: hld up & bhd: swtchd & hdwy over 1f out: qcknd to ld nr fin) ..................................... —1
**Blue Tess (IRE)** *(MMoubarak)* 8-11　GCarter (4) (leggy: scope: chsd ldrs: led wl ins fnl f: hdd nr fin) ..................................... ¾.2
2031³ **Clear Look** (Fav) *(PFICole)* 8-11　AMunro (8) (led: shkn up & hdd wl ins fnl f) ... nk.3
**Ajanta** *(BWHills)* 8-11　PatEddery (5) (small: lengthy: bhd: hdwy over 2f out: nvr able to chal) ..................................... 4.4
2171 **Petonellajill** *(RHannon)* 8-11　AMcGlone (7) (a chsng ldrs: rdn & outpcd appr fnl f) ..................................... 6.5
**Dancing Seer** *(MAJarvis)* 8-11　RCochrane (9) (leggy: lt-f: unf: prom over 4f) ..... 1.6

2055 Creative Flair (USA) *(PFICole)* 8-11 TQuinn (2) (hld up: hdwy over 2f out: rdn & wknd appr fnl f) ............................................. 3.7

Hush Baby (IRE) *(DMorris)* 8-6 ‡⁵StephenDavies (3) (w'like: bkwd: unruly stalls: chsd ldrs 4f: sn wknd) ............................................. 1¹/₂.8

2368⁵ Merch Fach (IRE) *(JDRoberts)* 8-11 JWilliams (1) (outpcd: a bhd) ............... nk.9

2052⁶ Tequila Twist (IRE) *(AAScott)* 8-11 JFortune (10) (prom 4f: sn lost tch) ......... ¹/₂.10

**8/11** Clear Look, **11/4** Blue Tess (IRE)(6/4—3/1), **8/1** KATIBA (USA)(op 4/1), **10/1** Ajanta(4/1—11/1), **16/1** Petonellajill, **20/1** Creative Flair (USA), Dancing Seer, **25/1** Tequila Twist (IRE), **50/1** Ors. CSF £31.48, Tote £5.60: £2.10 £1.50 £1.10 (£28.20). Mr Hamdan Al-Maktoum (ARUNDEL) bred by Foxfield in USA. 10 Rn
1m 16 (5)
SF—33/30/29/13/—/—/

**2558** MANSFIELD BREWERY NURSERY £1887.60 (£523.60: £250.80)
6f 15y
6-15 (6-17)
(Weights raised 4 lb)

2242² **Pizza Connection (84)** *(JLDunlop)* 9-7 PatEddery (1) (s.i.s: hdwy over 2f out: shkn up to ld wl ins fnl f) ............................................. —1

2010² Simmering (84) (Fav) *(GWragg)* 9-7 RHills (3) (hld up: hdwy to ld over 1f out: hdd & unable qckn nr fin) ............................................. ¹/₂.2

1748³ Heathyards Gem (65) *(RHollinshead)* 7-9 ‡⁷AGarth (6) (led tl hdd & wknd over 1f out) ............................................. 5.3

1526⁶ Annie Rose (56) (bl) *(TDBarron)* 7-9 JFanning (4) (gd spd over 4f) ............... 2¹/₂.4

2309* Palacegate Prince (73) *(JBerry)* 8-10 JCarroll (5) (lw: chsd ldrs: rdn wl over 1f out: sn btn) ............................................. hd.5

2238* Hy Wilma (64) *(RJHodges)* 8-1 WCarson (2) (swvd lft s: prom: reminders bef ¹/₂-wy: sn wknd: t.o) ............................................. 10.6

LONG HANDICAP: Annie Rose 7-6.

**7/4** Simmering, **7/2** PIZZA CONNECTION, Hy Wilma, **13/2** Palacegate Prince, **10/1** Heathyards Gem(16/1—8/1), **14/1** Annie Rose(10/1—16/1). CSF £9.40, Tote £4.30: £2.40 £1.80 (£2.80). Gerecon Italia (ARUNDEL) bred by Mrs M. de Jong. 6 Rn
1m 15.9 (4.9)
SF—45/43/7/—/11/—/

**2559** TOTE NOTTINGHAM STEWARDS CUP (H'cap) (0-100) £4566.80 (£1366.40: £655.20: £299.60) 6f 15y
6-45 (6-49)

2404* **Drum Sergeant (67)** (bl) (Jt-Fav) *(JParkes)* 5–8-0 (7x) MRoberts (6) (lw: dwlt: hld up: hdwy wl over 1f out: led ins fnl f: readily) ............... —1

2227 Baligay (73) *(RJHodges)* 7–8-3 ‡³FNorton (13) (a.p: ev ch appr fnl f: r.o) ......... 2.2

2435 Adwick Park (82) *(TDBarron)* 4–9-1 RCochrane (5) (lw: bhd: gd hdwy appr fnl f: fin wl) ............................................. 1¹/₂.3

2404 Breezy Day (81) *(BAMcMahon)* 6–8-7 ‡7JBramhill (8) (dropped rr ¹/₂-wy: gd hdwy appr fnl f: nrst fin) ............................................. 1.4

2435 Red Rosein (94) *(CaptJWilson)* 6–9-13 GCarter (4) (b.off hind: dwlt: hdwy & n.m.r wl over 1f out: r.o wl ins fnl f) ............................................. nk.5

2188³ Arabellajill (88) (Jt-Fav) *(RHannon)* 3–9-2 PatEddery (14) (lw: w ldrs tl led appr fnl f: sn hdd: unable qckn) ............................................. ¹/₂.6

2435 Letsbeonestaboutit (81) *(MrsNMacauley)* 6–9-0 DMcKeown (11) (lw: chsd ldrs: rdn along 2f out: nvr able to chal) ............................................. hd.7

2395* Iron King (75) *(JLSpearing)* 6–8-1 (7x) ‡7AGarth (9) (hdwy ¹/₂-wy: rdn to chal over 1f out: wknd fnl f) ............................................. 1¹/₂.8

2406⁴ Tigani (73) (bl) *(DWChapman)* 6–8-6 SWood (10) (lw: led tl hdd over 1f out: sn btn) ............................................. ¹/₂.9

1525* Finjan (92) *(MPNaughton)* 5–9-11 AMunro (1) (hdwy ¹/₂-wy: ev ch & rdn over 1f out: wknd fnl f) ............................................. s.h.10

2214 Tamim (USA) (94) (bl) *(HThomsonJones)* 3–9-8 RHills (3) (prom: rdn over 2f out: wknd ins fnl f) ............................................. ¹/₂.11

2003² Windpower (IRE) (86) *(JBerry)* 3–9-0 JCarroll (12) (lw: prom: ev ch appr fnl f: rdn & edgd lft: sn btn) ............................................. 3¹/₂.12

2262² Diet (65) (bl) *(MissLAPerratt)* 6–7-7 ‡⁵NKennedy (7) (lw: disp ld over 4f: wknd fnl f) ............................................. ¹/₂.13

**9/2** DRUM SERGEANT, Arabellajill(7/2—11/2), **6/1** Baligay, **7/1** Windpower (IRE), **10/1** Red Rosein, **12/1** Letsbeonestaboutit, Adwick Park(op 8/1), **14/1** Finjan(10/1—16/1), Tamim (USA)(10/1—16/1), Iron King, **16/1** Diet, **20/1** Ors. CSF £30.26, CT £276.22. Tote £7.30: £2.30 £1.80 £4.30 (£28.90). Mr W. A. Sellers (MALTON) bred by Snarehill Stud Co. 13 Rn
1m 14.6 (3.6)
SF—50/45/51/39/58/45

**2560** MINERS WELFARE (S) STKS (3 & 4-Y-O) £1674.00 (£464.00: £222.00)
1³/₄m 15y
7-15 (7-16)

2408² *Ghostly Glow (52)* (v) *(CCElsey)* 3–8-8 MRoberts (3) (led tl rn wd & hdd paddock bnd: led 10f out: clr fnl 2f: r.o) ............................................. —1

2235⁵ Ballymac Girl (50) (Fav) (CTNash) 4-9-2 WNewnes (6) (b: s.s: hdwy 7f out: 4th st: chsd wnr fnl 2f: hrd rdn: no imp) ...................................... 3.2

1951⁴ Romanian (IRE) (46) (ARDavison) 4-9-7 PatEddery (4) (hld up: 5th st: hdwy 3f out: kpt on u.p fnl f) ...................................................... 2.3

2272² Kentucky Chicken (USA) (30) (bl) (MissLCSiddall) 3-8-3 DMcKeown (1) (lft in ld paddock bnd: hdd 10f out: 2nd st: wknd over 2f out) ......... 8.4

1864 Alamshah (IRE) (51) (JAGlover) 4-9-2 ‡5SWilliams (7) (bit bkwd: chsd ldrs: 3rd st: wknd over 3f out) .................................................... 8.5

599 Hidden Flower (47) (JDRoberts) 3-8-5⁽²⁾ JWilliams (2) (bit bkwd: chsd ldrs 9f: 6th & btn st) ............................................................... s.h.6

2372 Market Trader (MFBarraclough) 3-7-10 ‡7CHawksley (5) (bkwd: lost tch 6f out: 7th st: sn t.o) .................................................. 30.7

2/1 Ballymac Girl, 9/4 Romanian (IRE), GHOSTLY GLOW(op 6/4), 11/1 Kentucky Chicken (USA), 14/1 Alamshah (IRE)(op 5/1), 33/1 Ors. CSF £7.06, Tote £2.60: £1.60 £2.20 (£3.90). Mr T. C. Marshall (LAMBOURN) bred by Mrs P. A. Clark. 7 Rn; Bt in 4,000 gns　　　　3m 5.9 (7.4)
SF—13/15/16/–/–/–

**2561**　　BRITISH COAL H'CAP (0-70) £2087.80 (£580.80: £279.40)　　**1m 54y**　　7-45 (7-52)

2541★ **Green's Cassatt (USA)** (48) (WMBrisbourne) 4-8-1 (6x) ‡5SMaloney (9) (hld up in tch: gd hdwy to ld wl ins fnl f: r.o) ........................... —1

2210★ Irish Groom (39) (bl) (JPSmith) 5-7-4 ‡7AGarth (10) (b: hdwy 3f out: ev ch ins fnl f: r.o) ........................................................... 2.2

Good for the Roses (47) (CGCox) 6-8-5 WNewnes (15) (a.p: 3rd st: led ins fnl f: sn hdd & no ex) ............................................. hd.3

2125³ Swift Romance (IRE) (63) (Jt-Fav) (BRMilliman) 4-9-7 JWilliams (6) (hld up: gd hdwy appr fnl f: fin fast) ....................................... s.h.4

2483★ Miss Carajane (51) (RHollinshead) 8-8-9 (6x) WRyan (19) (a.p: 2nd st: led 2f out tl ins fnl f) .......................................... £1/₂.5

2394 Norfolk Thatch (40) (KSBridgwater) 6-7-7⁽⁵⁾ ‡5BDoyle (14) (chsd ldrs: 5th st: rdn 2f out: kpt on) ........................................ 1/₂.6

1721⁵ Lexus (IRE) (48) (Jt-Fav) (RJRWilliams) 4-8-6⁽¹⁾ RCochrane (1) (hld up: effrt 2f out: nt pce to chal) ........................................ 1/₂.7

2276⁴ Queen of Dreams (37) (DrJDScargill) 4-7-9 JQuinn (3) (chsd ldrs: rdn 2f out: one pce) .................................................... hd.8

2160⁶ Stairway to Heaven (IRE) (51) (bl) (TDBarron) 4-8-9 AlexGreaves (11) (nvr trbld ldrs) ............................................. hd.9

2393⁵ Specialist Dream (IRE) (44) (LJCodd) 3-7-9 JLowe (12) (nvr nrr) ............ 1.10

1922 Cornhill Melody (38) (JLSpearing) 4-7-3⁽³⁾ ‡7CHawksley (17) (hdwy & 6th st: wknd over 2f out) .......................................... 1.11

572 Hold Fast (IRE) (38) (HCandy) 4-7-10 SDawson (5) (swtg: bit bkwd: plld v.hrd: nvr trbld ldrs) ............................................ 21/₂.12

2210 Sareen Express (IRE) (43) (MrsJCDawe) 4-8-1 JFanning (18) (hdwy 5f out: 4th st: rdn wl over 1f out: sn btn) ............................. hd.13

2198 Grey Illusions (35) (LJHolt) 4-7-7 NAdams (13) (m.n.s) ...................... 11/₂.14

175⁵ Ruth's Gamble (66) (DWChapman) 4-9-10 KDarley (7) (bhd: m.n.s) ...... 11/₂.15

2160³ Errema (46) (CTinkler) 7-8-4⁽¹⁾ MBirch (4) (m.n.s) ........................... 21/₂.16

1434 Tara's Girl (56) (bl) (FJYardley) 5-9-0 AClark (8) (stdd s: a in rr) ......... 5.17

2210 Cartel (49) (JLHarris) 5-8-7 TQuinn (16) (led to 2f out: wknd qckly: t.o) ...... 4.18

LONG HANDICAP: Norfolk Thatch 7-6, Cornhill Melody 6-13, Grey Illusions 7-5.
Uncertain (33/1) Withdrawn (ref to ent stalls) : not under orders

11/2 Swift Romance (IRE)(4/1—6/1), Lexus (IRE)(op 10/1), 7/1 Irish Groom, Errema, 9/1 GREEN'S CASSATT (USA), Cartel, 10/1 Stairway to Heaven (IRE), 12/1 Miss Sarajane, 14/1 Grey Illusions, Specialist Dream (IRE), 16/1 Queen of Dreams, Sareen Express (IRE), 20/1 Good for the Roses, 25/1 Hold Fast (IRE), Ruth's Gamble, Norfolk Thatch, 33/1 Ors. CSF £72.91, CT £1,162.89. Tote £15.50: £3.00 £2.20 £6.10 £2.40 (£85.20). Mr K. K. Baron (BASCHURCH) bred by Meryl A.Tanz Racing Stable & Carole Corfman in USA. 18 Rn　　1m 43.8 (4.2)
SF—18/1/15/30/10/–

**2562**　　TYREX (SHEPSHED) LTD STKS (Mdn 3-Y.O) £1718.20 (£475.20: £226.60)　**2m 9y**　　8-15 (8-18)

1704⁴ **Chatterer (USA)** (GHarwood) 9-0 AClark (1) (lw: s.s: led 7f out: clr fnl 3f: unchal) ............................................... —1

2228² Sea Plane (70) (Fav) (MajorWRHern) 9-0 WCarson (4) (led 1f: pushed along & dropped rr 10f out: 5th st: effrt u.p 3f out: no imp) .............. 7.2

2287³ Desert Peace (IRE) (PFICole) 9-0 TQuinn (2) (chsd ldrs: 2nd st: hrd rdn over 2f out: sn btn) .................................... s.h.3

2211³ Laughton Lady (42) (MrsNMacauley) 8-9 NAdams (5) (chsd ldrs: 4th st: hrd rdn & wknd over 3f out) .......................... 30.4

1068 Euroflight **(62)** *(BWHills)* 8-9 PatEddery (3) (led after 1f to 7f out: 3rd & rdn st: sn wknd: t.o) ............................................................... 30.5

**11/8** Sea Plane, **3/1** Desert Peace (IRE), **100/30** CHATTERER (USA), **4/1** Euroflight(6/1—3/1), **25/1** Laughton Lady. CSF £8.26, Tote £5.00: £1.50 £1.70 (£5.10). Sheikh Mohammed (PULBOROUGH) bred by Mrs J. G. Jones Snr in USA. 5 Rn
3m 29 (4.6)
SF—46/39/38/8/–

T/Plpt: £60.20 (32.7 Tckts). IM

## NOTTINGHAM (L-H)

### Tuesday, August 4th [Firm, Good to firm patches]

Going Allowance: St: 0.20 sec (G); Rnd: minus 0.15 sec per fur (F)     Wind: mod against

Stalls: centre

**2563**     BRUSSELS (S) STKS (2-Y.O) £1582.20 (£439.20: £210.60)     **6f 15y**     6-00 (6-01)

2389 **Walid's Princess (IRE) (44)** *(JWharton)* 8-6 AShoults (17) (lw: chsd ldrs stands' side: led wl ins fnl f: r.o) ................................ —1
22845 Good Image *(APJarvis)* 8-11 TQuinn (15) (lw: led stands' side tl hdd wl ins fnl f) ¾.2
23893 Awesome Risk **(56)** *(GLewis)* 8-6 AMcGlone (13) (hdwy ½-wy: hrd rdn over 1f out: one pce) ................................................. 1½.3
24882 Penny Banger (IRE) **(58)** (Fav) *(MJohnston)* 8-6 DMcKeown (1) (led far side: edgd rt fnl 2f: sn btn) .................................. 5.4
22846 My Miss Molly (IRE) *(MissGayKelleway)* 8-6 GayKelleway (3) (b.hind: chsd ldrs far side: rdn over 1f out: sn btn) .................... 3.5
2389 Jade Runner **(62)** *(MrsNMacauley)* 8-6 NCarlisle (2) (hdwy over 2f out: nt rch ldrs) ...................................................... ½.6
2414 Sea Strand *(MBlanshard)* 8-6 GCarter (8) (chsd ldrs: rdn over 1f out: no imp) . nk.7
23636 Summers Dream **(51)** *(BRichmond)* 8-6 AProud (12) (sme late hdwy: n.d) ...... ½.8
1349 Colonial Heights (IRE) *(RHannon)* 8-11 SRaymont (16) (s.s: hdwy 2f out: nvr nrr) ...................................................... ¾.9
2389 Hawke Bay (v) *(DHaydnJones)* 8-11 SWhitworth(14)(prom stands' side over 4f) 1½.10
2205 Desirable Miss *(MBrittain)* 8-6 SWebster (10) (nvr nr to chal) ................ ¾.11
23635 Westmead Nick **(48)** *(JBerry)* 8-11 JCarroll (5) (lw: bhd fnl 2f: t.o) ......... 8.12
20586 Stroika (IRE) (bl) *(CJames)* 8-6 WNewnes (4) (spd far side 4f: t.o) ......... 2½.13
2112 Sean's Delight *(JMCarr)* 8-6 SWood (6) (w ldr far side 3f: sn wknd: t.o) ....... ¾.14
2225 Mad March Hare *(DRTucker)* 8-6 ‡5RPrice (11) (chsd ldrs over 3f: sn wknd: t.o) nk.15
2005 Flash of Joy *(CDBroad)* 8-6 NAdams (9) (s.s: a bhd: t.o) ................. 12.16

**100/30** Penny Banger (IRE), **7/2** Awesome Risk(9/4—4/1), **15/2** WALID'S PRINCESS (IRE)(op 20/1), **8/1** Jade Runner, **10/1** Colonial Heights (IRE), Good Image, **12/1** Stroika (IRE)(op 8/1), Sea Strand, **16/1** Westmead Nick, **20/1** Summers Dream, **25/1** Desirable Miss, My Miss Molly (IRE), **33/1** Ors. CSF £77.60, Tote £18.60: £4.60 £2.60 £1.50 (£34.60). Mrs Violet J. Hannigan (MELTON MOWBRAY) bred by Mrs G. Doyle in Ireland. 16 Rn; Bt in 3,400 gns
1m 16.5 (5.5)
SF—6/8/–/–/–/–

**2564**     AIR SPEED H'CAP (0-70) £1841.40 (£510.40: £244.20)     **5f 13y**     6-30 (6-30)

21532 **Here Comes a Star (57)** *(JMCarr)* 4-9-1 WNewnes (7) (lw: hld up in tch: gd hdwy to ld ins fnl f: r.o strly) .................................. —1
25482 Erris Express **(46)** (Fav) *(JSMoore)* 7-8-4 AMcGlone (6) (s.s: pushed along thrght: hdwy to ld 1f out: hdd & no ex ins fnl f) ............ 1½.2
24662 Catherines Well **(70)** *(MWEasterby)* 9-9-7 ‡7PaulJohnson (2) (a.p: slt ld over 1f out: sn hdd: unable qckn fnl f) .................... 1.3
24664 Simmie's Special **(61)** *(RHollinshead)* 4-8-12 ‡7SWynne (5) (a.p: rdn & ev ch appr fnl f: kpt on) ........................................ ¾.4
23013 Barbara's Cutie **(36)** *(MBlanshard)* 4-7-8 NCarlisle (4) (led tl hdd over 1f out: one pce) ............................................ ½.5
2105 Petitesse **(46)** *(GBlum)* 4-8-4 AShoults (1) (w ldrs: rdn appr fnl f: one pce) ...... s.h.6
1978 Vendredi Treize **(38)** *(SRBowring)* 9-7-3(3) ‡7AGarth (3) (b: chsd ldrs: effrt over 1f out: no ex fnl f) ........................... ½.7
1729 Uppance **(35)** *(DWChapman)* 4-7-7 SWood (8) (lw: nvr nr ldrs) ............. 2½.8
2229 Laggard's Quest **(40)** *(CDBroad)* 3-7-8(1) NAdams (9) (swtg: outpcd: t.o) ....... 12.9
LONG HANDICAP: Vendredi Treize 7-0, Uppance 6-12, Laggard's Quest 6-12.

**15/8** Erris Express, **4/1** Catherines Well, **5/1** HERE COMES A STAR, **17/2** Simmie's Special, **9/1** Petitesse, **11/1** Barbara's Cutie, **16/1** Vendredi Treize, **33/1** Uppance, **50/1** Laggard's Quest. CSF £13.44, CT £34.57. Tote £4.10: £1.50 £1.60 £1.10 (£5.70). Mrs June Goodridge (MALTON) bred by A. and M. Scarfe. 9 Rn
61.9 sec (3.2)
SF—57/40/53/41/21/30

## 2565

FRANKFURT H'CAP (0-70) £1933.80 (£536.80: £257.40)     2m 9y     7-00 (7-01)

1970* **Glenstal Priory (49)** (Fav) *(PFICole)* 5-8-13 TQuinn (3) (lw: hdwy ½-wy: 3rd st: led 3f out: rdn clr fnl f) ......................... —1

2109⁴ Briggscare **(62)** *(WJarvis)* 6-9-12 MTebbutt (7) (b: hld up: hdwy & 5th st: ev ch over 1f out: rdn & hung lft: unable qckn) ........................... 3.2

1970 Cold Marble (USA) **(38)** *(DRTucker)* 7-8-2 JQuinn (1) (chsd ldrs: 4th st: rdn & one pce fnl 2f) ........................... 6.3

2397³ My Swan Song **(37)** *(JPSmith)* 7-7-8 ‡7AGarth (11) (chsd ldrs: 6th st: styd on fnl 2f: nvr nrr) ........................... ½.4

Radar Knight **(39)** *(RABennett)* 4-8-3 NAdams (4) (bit bkwd: prom: led 6f out to 3f out: grad wknd) ........................... 10.5

2101 Kanooz (IRE) **(35)** (bl) *(SMellor)* 4-7-13 DanaMellor (12) (lost pl 7f out: sme late hdwy: n.d) ........................... 2½.6

1632⁶ Delta Foxtrot (USA) **(66)** *(DWPArbuthnot)* 3-9-1 BRaymond (6) (bit bkwd: prom: 2nd st: wknd over 2f out) ........................... 1½.7

1477 Clifton Hampden **(64)** (v) *(LadyHerries)* 4-10-0 WRyan (2) (lw: lost tch ½-wy: t.o) ........................... 20.8

2294⁶ Edgewise **(42)** *(DMorris)* 9-8-1(13) ‡5StephenDavies (8) (led 1f: wknd 5f out: t.o) 5.9

2261⁶ Lyphard's Song (IRE) **(35)** (bl) *(NAGraham)* 4-7-13 MRoberts (5) (swtg: led after 1f to 6f out: wknd rapidly: t.o) ........................... 10.10

LONG HANDICAP: Edgewise 6-12

**2/1** GLENSTAL PRIORY, **9/2** Briggscare, **5/1** My Swan Song, **6/1** Lyphard's Song (IRE)(op 4/1), **12/1** Delta Foxtrot (USA), Clifton Hampden(op 8/1), **20/1** Radar Knight, Edgewise, **25/1** Cold Marble (USA), **33/1** Kanooz (IRE). CSF £10.60, CT £149.94. Tote £2.80: £1.20 £1.70 £12.60 (£4.00). Norman Hill Plant Hire Ltd (WHATCOMBE) bred by Swettenham Stud. 10 Rn                                3m 29.7 (5.3)

SF—22/32/2/–/–/–

## 2566

EAST MIDLANDS INTERNATIONAL AIRPORT H'CAP (0-70) £2164.80 (£602.80: £290.40)     1m 1f 213y     7-30 (7-32)

1298 **Don't Forsake Me (60)** *(DMorley)* 3-9-1 WRyan (5) (mde all: rdn over 1f out: hld on gamely) ........................... —1

2156³ Spray of Orchids **(49)** *(JEtherington)* 3-8-4 KDarley (14) (lw: hdwy & 7th st: effrt u.p appr fnl f: r.o wl) ........................... ¾.2

2334⁶ Irish Honey (IRE) **(43)** *(BHanbury)* 3-7-12 JQuinn (3) (lw: hld up: hdwy on ins 2f out: hrd rdn & r.o fnl f) ........................... 1.3

2054 Russian Vision **(61)** (bl) (Jt-Fav) *(AAScott)* 3-9-2 BRaymond (2) (a.p: 3rd st: rdn to chal 2f out: kpt on one pce fnl f) ........................... 1½.4

2135⁴ Altermeera **(64)** *(MrsBarbaraWaring)* 4-10-0 NHowe (1) (chsd ldrs: 6th st: wknd wl over 1f out) ........................... 1½.5

1914⁵ Eleckydo **(47)** *(RJHodges)* 3-7-13 ‡3FNorton (7) (bit rdn 3f out: nt rch ldrs) 5.6

1909⁶ Affirmed's Destiny (USA) **(49)** (Jt-Fav) *(JLDunlop)* 3-8-4 TQuinn (10) (hld up: gd hdwy 3f out: wknd appr fnl f) ........................... 5.7

2156⁴ Gallant Jack (IRE) **(55)** *(DHaydnJones)* 3-8-10 RHills (8) (chsd ldrs: 5th st: rdn & wknd 2f out) ........................... ½.8

2296⁶ Aislabie Airborne **(38)** (bl) *(MrsNMacauley)* 3-7-7 NAdams (4) (lw: nvr plcd to chal) ........................... hd.9

1079 Boldrullah **(49)** *(DWPArbuthnot)* 3-7-13 ‡5RPrice (9) (b: hld up: a in rr) ........................... 1½.10

2249⁴ Dust D'Throne (USA) **(37)** (Jt-Fav) *(MissLCSiddall)* 4-8-1 MRoberts (6) (bit bkwd: chsd wnr: 2nd st: rdn 3f out: sn btn) ........................... s.h.11

2001 Sonalto **(40)** *(DLWilliams)* 6-8-4 JLowe (13) (prom: 4th st: wknd over 2f out) 2½.12

2007 Otter Bush **(38)** (v) *(GBlum)* 3-7-7 SWood (12) (bhd & rn wd ent st: t.o) ........................... 4.13

LONG HANDICAP: Aislabie Airborne 6-13, Otter Bush 7-6.

**6/1** Dust D'Throne (USA), Affirmed's Destiny (USA)(op 4/1), Russian Vision (USA), **7/1** Eleckydo, Spray of Orchids, Altermeera, **9/1** DON'T FORSAKE ME, **14/1** Gallant Jack (IRE), Boldrullah, Irish Honey (IRE), **50/1** Ors. CSF £62.86, CT £783.91. Tote £17.10: £4.40 £1.90 £4.80 (£52.80). Lord Clinton (NEWMARKET) bred by British Thoroughbred Racing and Breeding P L C. 13 Rn                                2m 6.9 (4.4)

SF—42/29/21/36/45/6

## 2567

BUSINESS AIR STKS (Mdn 3-Y.O) £1826.00 (£506.00: £242.00)     1m 54y     8-00 (8-01)

1597³ **Lap of Luxury** (Fav) *(WJarvis)* 8-9 NDay (4) (chsd ldr: 2nd st: led appr fnl f: sn wl clr: eased nr fin) ........................... —1

Nakupita (IRE) *(ACStewart)* 8-9 MRoberts (7) (lengthy: unf: bit bkwd: s.i.s: 6th st: rdn over 3f out: styd on fnl f: a hld) ........................... 3½.2

2432 Don't Drop Bombs (USA) *(AAScott)* 9-0 BRaymond (2) (bit bkwd: a.p: 3rd st: rdn 3f out: one pce) ........................... nk.3

5915 Casting Shadows *(RDickin)* 8-9 DMcKeown (5) (bkwd: s.i.s: 7th st: styd on appr fnl f: nvr nrr) ........................... 2.4

2475³ Dam Certain (IRE) *(AWDenson)* 8-9 TQuinn (3) (led tl appr fnl f: sn outpcd: wknd nr fin) ..... ¹/₂.5

2236⁴ Spring Saint *(MJHeaton-Ellis)* 9-0 WNewnes (8) (lw: chsd ldrs: 4th st: wknd 2f out) ..... 2¹/₂.6

Form Mistress *(PTWalwyn)* 8-9 NHowe (1) (hld up: 5th st: wknd over 2f out) ..... 5.7

**11/10 LAP OF LUXURY, 100/30** Nakupita (IRE)(7/4—9/2), **6/1** Spring Saint(op 4/1), **11/1** Form Mistress(8/1—12/1), **14/1** Don't Drop Bombs (USA)(op 8/1), **18/1** Dam Certain (IRE), **33/1** Casting Shadows. CSF £4.69, Tote £1.90: £1.40 £1.60 (£2.70). Mr I. C. Hill-Wood (NEWMARKET) bred by Langham Hall Bloodstock. 7 Rn
1m 46.3 (6.7)

---

**2568**  E.B.F. ELEGANT DAYS STKS (Mdn 2-Y.O) £1992.00 (£552.00: £264.00)
6f 15y  8-30 (8-33)

2167⁵ **Regalsett** *(RHannon)* 9-0 MRoberts (2) (a w ldrs: led appr fnl f: qcknd clr fnl f) . —1

2335² Hoy-Liegh-Rag *(MJohnston)* 9-0 DMcKeown (11) (led tl appr fnl f: rdn & fnd nil) ..... 5.2

2233⁵ Saxon Magic *(JABennett)* 8-9 JQuinn (7) (chsd ldrs: kpt on u.p ins fnl f) ..... 1¹/₂.3

2233 Legal Risk *(DHaydnJones)* 8-9 RHills (6) (chsd ldrs: rdn 2f out: r.o) ..... 2.4

2208 Persiansky (IRE) *(BHanbury)* 9-0 BRaymond (5) (prom: rdn wl over 1f out: one pce) ..... 2¹/₂.5

Velasco (IRE) *(SirMarkPrescott)* 9-0 GDuffield (1) (leggy: unf: bkwd: s.s: nvr nr to chal) ..... ¹/₂.6

Omidjoy (IRE) *(SPCWoods)* 8-9 WWoods (9) (lt-f: unf: nvr trbld ldrs) ..... s.h.7

817 Moscatop (IRE) *(68)* *(RHollinshead)* 9-0 WRyan (8) (a in rr) ..... 4.8

2233 Melodic Drive *(PSFelgate)* 9-0 JLowe (3) (bit bkwd: chsd ldrs centre 4f) ..... ³/₄.9

Coalisland *(RIngram)* 9-0 WNewnes (4) (w'like: bkwd: outpcd: t.o) ..... 2¹/₂.10

**11/8 Hoy-Liegh-Rag, 11/4** REGALSETT(6/4—3/1), **8/1** Persiansky (IRE)(10/1—6/1), **9/1** Velasco (IRE), **14/1** Saxon Magic, **16/1** Moscatop (IRE)(op 8/1), **33/1** Ors. CSF £6.30, Tote £3.00: £1.60 £1.10 £2.50 (£2.90). Mr G. Z. Mizel (MARLBOROUGH) bred by Guest Leasing and Bloodstock Co. 10 Rn
1m 15.4 (4.4)
SF—36/16/5/—/—/—

T/Plpt: £10.30 (184.65 Tckts).  IM

---

## 2259—REDCAR (L-H)

### Tuesday, August 4th [Firm]

Going Allowance: St: minus 0.55 sec (H); Rnd: minus 0.15 sec (F)  Wind: fresh across

Stalls: high

**2569**  SAPPHIRE (S) STKS  £2427.00 (£672.00: £321.00)  1m 1f  2-15 (2-17)

2354★ **Kagram Queen (53)** (Fav) *(MrsGRReveley)* 4-9-0 KDarley (2) (lw: in tch: swtchd over 2f out: styd on wl to ld cl home) ..... —1

2354³ Reilton (50) *(JParkes)* 5-9-5 GDuffield (5) (hld up & bhd: hdwy 4f out: led wl over 1f out tl ct cl home) ..... ¹/₂.2

2219⁶ Young Jason (53) *(FHLee)* 9-9-0 ‡5NKennedy (3) (hld up & bhd: stdy hdwy 3f out: rdn appr fnl f: nt qckn) ..... 2¹/₂.3

2379⁵ Matts Boy (56) *(MissSEHall)* 4-9-5 NConnorton (9) (a in tch: led over 2f out tl wl over 1f out: grad wknd) ..... 3.4

1629⁵ Zinger (41) (bl) *(TFairhurst)* 4-9-5 JFanning (11) (chsd ldr tl outpcd fnl 2f) ..... 2.5

2394 Barkston Singer (44) *(JLHarris)* 5-9-0 CDwyer (1) (b.nr fore: hdwy 4f out: rdn & one pce: fnl 2f) ..... nk.6

Grondola *(DBurchell)* 5-9-0 DMcKeown (8) (led 1f: led over 3f out tl over 2f out: sn wknd) ..... 6.7

1481 Ghylldale (36) (v) *(RBastiman)* 4-8-7 ‡7HBastiman (10) (shkn up 4f out: n.d) ... hd.8

2250⁴ Mr News (IRE) (43) (v) *(BBeasley)* 3-8-6 ‡5SWilliams (7) (chsd ldr tl rdn & nt run on fnl 4f) ..... 7.9

2351⁵ Supreme Court (33) (bl) *(MDods)* 5-9-0 ‡5OPears (5) (led after 1f tl over 3f out: sn wknd: t.o) ..... 10

**2/1 KAGRAM QUEEN, 9/4** Young Jason, **100/30** Matts Boy, **8/1** Reilton, **16/1** Barkston Singer, **25/1** Mr News (IRE), **33/1** Zinger, Ghylldale, **50/1** Grondola, **66/1** Supreme Court. CSF £17.33, Tote £2.80: £1.30 £2.00 £1.20 (£10.30). Mrs E. A. Kettlewell (SALTBURN) bred by E. W. and E. A. Kettlewell. 10 Rn; No bid  1m 52.3 (3.3)
SF—30/33/20/16/10/4

---

**2570**  RUBY H'CAP (Amateurs) (0-70) £2616.00 (£726.00: £348.00)  7f  2-45 (2-51)

2144★ **Flashy's Son (48)** (Fav) *(MDHammond)* 4-10-11 MrsLPearce (2) (in tch: hdwy 3f out: led appr fnl f: r.o wl) ..... —1

1366⁶ Quinta Royale (48) *(WGMTurner)* 5-10-6 ‡5MrsJGault (15) (lw: chsd ldrs: chal & rdr lost irons appr fnl f: r.o nr fin) ................................................ hd.2

2066 Bill Moon (49) *(PJFeilden)* 6-10-12 MissJFeilden (9) (lw: in tch: effrt 3f out: rdn & nt qckn appr fnl f) .................................................................. 3½.3

2325⋆ Johnston's Express (IRE) (38) *(EJAlston)* 4-9-10 ‡5MrWilkinson (10) (a chsng ldrs: kpt on one pce fnl 2f) ............................................................ s.h.4

2289³ Night Transaction (49) *(AHide)* 5-10-7 ‡5MissLHide (14) (hdwy over 2f out: r.o nr fin) ...................................................................................... 1.5

1388 Languedoc (64) *(MPNaughton)* 5-11-8 ‡5MrRGreen (16) (led tl hdd & wknd over 1f out) ................................................................................... 5.6

2468 Gott's Desire (45) *(RBastiman)* 6-10-3 ‡5MissLRevell (8) (chsd ldrs tl outpcd wl over 2f out) ................................................................................... hd.7

1013² Malunar (65) *(MHTompkins)* 7-11-9 ‡5MrPritchard-Gordon (4) (b: nvr trbld ldrs) ...................................................................................... nk.8

2326³ No Comebacks (42) *(EJAlston)* 4-10-0 ‡5MrsSBarclay (1) (dwlt: bhd tl sme late hdwy) ..................................................................................... hd.9

2219⁴ Martini Executive (65) *(BBeasley)* 4-11-9 ‡5MrDDurrant (13) (n.d) ............ nk.10

1964⁶ Cool Enough (39) *(MrsJRRamsden)* 11-10-2 MrRHale (6) (nvr trbld ldrs) ....... ½.11

2352² Pickles (52) *(PCHaslam)* 4-11-1 MissABillot (7) (cl up 5f: sn wknd) ............ 7.12

2291 Lime Street Lil (30) *(DAWilson)* 4-9-7 MissDianaJones (5) (n.d) ............ 13

2303 Justamanda (48) *(WHolden)* 3-10-0 ‡5MissKHolden (5) (lw: dwlt: a bhd) ...... 14

2326 Barud (IRE) (42) *(DBurchell)* 4-10-0 ‡5MrNMiles (12) (spd 4f: sn lost pl) ...... 15

2326 Brown as a Berry (IRE) (31) *(v) (WStorey)* 4-9-3⁽¹⁾ ‡5MissSStorey (11) (sn bhd) .. 16

LONG HANDICAP: Lime Street Lil 9-5, Brown as a Berry (IRE) 9-3.

5/1 FLASHY'S SON, 6/1 Night Transaction, Pickles, 7/1 Bill Moon, 8/1 Johnston's Express (IRE), 10/1 Martini Executive, 12/1 Malunar, Quinta Royale, 14/1 Languedoc, No Comebacks, 16/1 Cool Enough, Barud (IRE), Lime Street Lil, 25/1 Gott's Desire, Justamanda, 33/1 Brown as a Berry (IRE). CSF £64.13, CT £402.49. Tote £5.50: £1.70 £3.30 £2.80 (£88.40). Lee Construction (Newcastle) Ltd (MIDDLEHAM) bred by Brian A. Shovelton (North Wales) Ltd. 16 Rn                    1m 23.9 (1.7)

SF—42/36/31/14/22/22

## 2571
FREEMAN JEWELLERS DIAMOND H'CAP (0-80) £3002.00 (£896.00: £428.00: £194.00)
1m 3f                                                      3-15 (3-18)

(Weights raised 3 lb)

1890 **Hester Stanhope (55)** *(PWHarris)* 3-8-7 MBirch (3) (in tch: hdwy over 2f out: led ins fnl f: styd on wl nr fin) ...................................................... —1

2326⁴ Top Scale (35) (v) *(WWHaigh)* 6-7-11 JLowe (2) (lw: chsd ldrs: led wl over 3f out tl ins fnl f: kpt on one pce) ............................................................. 1½.2

2355⋆ Talented Ting (IRE) (69) *(PCHaslam)* 3-9-7 KDarley (4) (lw: led 1f: chsd ldrs: chal 2f out: nt qckn fnl f) ................................................................. s.h.3

2332⋆ Sinclair Lad (IRE) (62) *(RHollinshead)* 4-9-10 WRyan (5) (hld up & bhd: effrt 3f out: styd on nr fin) .................................................................... 3½.4

2422² Touch Above (57) *(TDBarron)* 6-9-5 AlexGreaves (7) (led after 1f tl wl over 3f out: ev ch tl grad wknd fnl 2f) ..................................................... 2½.5

2312² Great Max (IRE) (70) (Fav) *(SirMarkPrescott)* 3-9-8 GDuffield (9) (trckd ldrs: effrt 3f out: sn rdn & grad wknd) .......................................................... 3.6

2423⁴ Sharquin (37) *(MBrittain)* 5-7-8⁽⁶⁾ ‡5SMaloney (6) (effrt 4f out: no imp) ......... nk.7

2332⁴ Barbary Reef (IRE) (41) (bl) *(GHEden)* 4-8-3 DaleGibson (1) (unruly stalls: s.s: a bhd) ......................................................................................... ½.8

1220 Paper Clip (57) *(JDBethell)* 3-8-9 DMcKeown (8) (prom tl wknd 3f out) ......... 6.9

2366 Silver Concord (44) *(GMMoore)* 4-8-6 JFanning (10) (bhd & rdn 4f out: n.d) .. 3.10

LONG HANDICAP: Sharquin 7-6.

4/1 Great Max (IRE), 9/2 Talented Ting (IRE), 5/1 Top Scale, 6/1 Sinclair Lad (IRE), Touch Above, 9/1 HESTER STANHOPE, 10/1 Barbary Reef (IRE), 16/1 Sharquin, Paper Clip, 33/1 Silver Concord. CSF £49.52, CT £209.68. Tote £13.00: £3.40 £1.70 £1.80 (£29.90). Mrs P. W. Harris (BERKHAMSTED) bred by Pendley Farm. 10 Rn
2m 20.2 (4.5)

SF—31/18/41/37/27/24

## 2572
BREITLING NURSERY    £3288.00 (£984.00: £472.00: £216.00)    7f    3-45 (3-47)

2328⋆ **Ventiquattrofogli (IRE) (83)** (Fav) *(JLDunlop)* 9-7 JReid (7) (a gng wl: led appr fnl f: sn qcknd clr) ..................................................................... —1

2259⋆ Arctic Guest (IRE) (59) *(MJohnston)* 7-11 JLowe (6) (cl up: led wl over 2f out tl over 1f out: no ch w wnr) .............................................................. 4.2

2330³ Blue Radiance (68) *(TFairhurst)* 8-6 JFanning (2) (lw: cl up: chal 3f out: nt qckn appr fnl f) ......................................................................... 3.3

1932⁶ Comtec's Legend (59) *(JFBottomley)* 7-6⁽²⁾ ‡5NKennedy (5) (sn bhd: styd on fnl 2f: nrst fin) ........................................................................... 1½.4

1296 Pinkerton's Silver (61) (bl) *(MHEasterby)* 7-8⁽⁵⁾ ‡5SMaloney (9) (led tl hdd wl over 2f out: sn rdn & btn) ........................................................... ¾.5

2374* Hot Storm (68) *(MJCamacho)* 8-6 NConnorton (4) (chsd ldrs: swtchd over 2f out: sn btn) ............................................................ 2.6
889⁴ Vardy (IRE) (56) *(PCHaslam)* 7-8 EJohnson (3) (outpcd fnl 3f) ............ 1½.7
2049³ Moonshine Dancer (67) *(MrsGRReveley)* 8-5 DaleGibson (1) (in tch 4f: sn btn) . 3.8
2389² Workingforpeanuts (IRE) (62) *(CASmith)* 8-0 RPElliott (8) (sn t.o: sme late hdwy) 2.9

**Evens** VENTIQUATTROFOGLI (IRE), **6/1** Hot Storm, **7/1** Workingforpeanuts (IRE), Arctic Guest (IRE), **12/1** Comtec's Legend, **16/1** Blue Radiance, **20/1** Moonshine Dancer, Pinkerton's Silver, **25/1** Vardy (IRE). CSF £8.39, CT £64.47. Tote £2.10: £1.30 £2.40 £3.30 (£6.60). Gerecon Italia (ARUNDEL) bred by Kiltinan Farms Inc in Ireland. 9 Rn                                                          1m 22.9 (0.7)
SF–39/3/3/–/–/–

### 2573
EMERALD CLAIMING STKS (Mdn 3-Y.O) £2259.00 (£624.00: £297.00)
**2m 4y**                                                                4-15 (4-17)

2004³ **Mystic Memory (65)** (Fav) *(SirMarkPrescott)* 8-3 GDuffield (4) (hdwy ½-wy: rdn to ld appr fnl f) ......................................................... —1
2470² Stingray City (USA) (59) (bl) *(JEtherington)* 8-10 KDarley (5) (trckd ldrs: effrt 3f out: styd on nr fin) .............................................. ½.2
1286 Notable Exception (60) *(JWHills)* 8-4 RHills (3) (hdwy 10f out: led 8f out tl appr fnl f: no ex) .......................................................... 2.3
2334⁴ Aide Memoire (IRE) (48) *(CBBBooth)* 8-3⁽²⁾ ACulhane (1) (lw: led tl hdd ½-wy: outpcd fnl 3f) .................................................. 10.4
1962⁶ Sing Another (36) *(MrsGRReveley)* 8-5 JLowe (2) (lw: hld up & bhd: effrt 4f out: sn rdn & btn) ..................................................... 12.5

**5/4** MYSTIC MEMORY, **2/1** Stingray City (USA), **7/2** Notable Exception, **20/1** Aide Memoire (IRE), **25/1** Sing Another. CSF £3.88, Tote £1.80: £1.10 £1.70 (£2.30). Mrs P. G. Goulandris (NEWMARKET) bred by Hesmonds Stud Ltd. 5 Rn; Mystic Memory clmd Mrs G Hugill £9,600                             3m 38.8 (13.8)

### 2574
OPAL GRADUATION STKS (2-Y.O) £3096.00 (£856.00: £408.00)    **6f**    4-45 (4-46)

2328² **Nominator (92)** (Fav) *(RHollinshead)* 9-4 WRyan (3) (lw: mde most: all out) ...... —1
2299* Expo Mondial (IRE) (79) *(JMPEustace)* 9-4 MTebbutt (2) (lw: trckd ldrs: hdwy ins fnl f: fin wl) ................................................. nk.2
1927⁵ Spark (IRE) (93) *(CWCElsey)* 8-8 ‡⁵SMaloney (1) (w wnr: rdn 2f out: r.o) .......... hd.3

**4/5** NOMINATOR, **2/1** Spark (IRE). **4/1** Expo Mondial (IRE). CSF £3.56, Tote £1.60 (£2.20). Mr J. D. Graham (UPPER LONGDON) bred by Auldyn Stud Ltd. 3 Rn                                        1m 10.7 (1.4)
SF–10/9/–

### 2575
LEVY BOARD H'CAP (3-Y.O) (0-70) £2954.00 (£819.00: £392.00)
**1m 5f 135y**                                                           5-15 (5-16)

(Weights raised 13 lb)
2036 **Corinthian God (IRE) (40)** *(DAWilson)* 8-8 GDuffield (2) (trckd ldr: led 2f out: r.o u.p) ............................................................ —1
2334 Kadari (53) (v) (Fav) *(AHarrison)* 9-2 ‡⁵JWeaver (4) (lw: hld up: effrt 3f out: hng lft & nt run on fnl f) ...................................... 1.2
2312³ Invisible Armour (45) *(PCHaslam)* 8-13 EJohnson (1) (led tl hdd 2f out: r.o one pce) ................................................................ hd.3
2142⁴ Tees Gazette Girl (45) *(MrsGRReveley)* 8-6 ‡⁷ClaireBalding (3) (lw: chsd ldrs: effrt 4f out: outpcd fnl f) ....................................... 6.4

**5/4** Kadari, **11/4** Tees Gazette Girl, **3/1** Invisible Armour, **7/1** CORINTHIAN GOD (IRE). CSF £15.09, Tote £7.00 (£4.70). Mr T. S. M. S. Riley-Smith (EPSOM) bred by Mrs J. McNally in Ireland. 4 Rn        2m 59.3 (8.3)
T/Plpt: £12.70 (249.46 Tckts).                                                        AA

## 2302—BRIGHTON (L-H)
### Tuesday, August 4th [Firm]
Going Allowance: minus 0.25 sec per fur (F)                    Wind: fresh half against

Stalls: low

### 2576
DOWNS (S) STKS    £2280.00 (£630.00: £300.00)    **1m 1f 209y**    2-00 (2-01)

2297⁵ **Chummy's Child (IRE) (48)** *(JSutcliffe)* 3-8-12 PatEddery (2) (lw: mde all: hrd rdn 2f out: r.o wl) .......................................... —1
2394 Beechwood Cottage (34) (bl) *(ABailey)* 9-9-2 ‡⁵ATucker (8) (lw: 6th st: chsd wnr over 1f out: no imp) ....................................... 1½.2
112 Wave Master *(RJHodges)* 5-9-4 ‡³TSprake (3) (3rd st: n.m.r on ins over 2f out: one pce) .............................................. 2.3

2303⁴ Simon Ellis (IRE) **(47)** *(DRLaing)* 3–8-12 TyroneWilliams (5) (lw: 2nd st: rdn & ev
　　ch over 2f out: wknd over 1f out) ..................................... 2¹/₂.4
2251² Moving Force **(38)** *(EAWheeler)* 5–9-7 SWhitworth (6) (5th st: one pce fnl 2f) . 2¹/₂.5
　1872 King of Normandy (IRE) **(64)** *(Fav)* *(RHannon)* 3–8-12 MRoberts (4) (lw: 4th st:
　　rdn over 3f out: nt clr run & eased over 1f out) ..................... ¹/₂.6
2287⁶ Yorkshire Fisher (IRE) *(MissGayKelleway)* 4–9-7 GBardwell (7) (a bhd: t.o fnl 4f) 30.7
　2051 Three and a Half (v) *(MissLBower)* 3–8-12 SDawson (1) (a bhd: t.o fnl 4f) .......... 2.8

**4/7** King of Normandy (IRE), **5/1** CHUMMY'S CHILD (IRE)(op 3/1), **6/1** Moving Force, **11/1** Simon Ellis (IRE)(op
7/1), **16/1** Beechwood Cottage(op 10/1), Wave Master(op 8/1), **25/1** Yorkshire Fisher (IRE), **50/1** Three and a
Half. CSF £67.10, Tote £6.50: £2.00 £2.50 £3.40 (£53.40). Mr C. Gaventa (EPSOM) bred by Peter Carroll in
Ireland. 8 Rn; No bid　　　　　　　　　　　　　　　　　　　　　　　　2m 5.2 (7.2)

---

**2577**　　E.B.F. ALFRISTON STKS (Mdn 2-Y.O) £2611.00 (£721.00: £343.00)
　　　　**5f 59y**　　　　　　　　　　　　　　　　　　　　　2-30 (2-32)

2274⁶ **Troon** *(Fav)* *(MrsLPiggott)* 9-0 LPiggott (1) (b: b.hind: lw: 5th st: hdwy over 2f
　　out: led over 1f out: r.o wl) ........................................ —1
　803 War Requiem (IRE) *(GBBalding)* 9-0 JWilliams (4) (4th st: rdn 3f out: chsd wnr
　　fnl f: r.o) ...................................................... ³/₄.2
2080 Christian Spirit **(52)** *(RHannon)* 9-0 MRoberts (3) (lw: led 4f: unable qckn) ..... 2¹/₂.3
2031 Marwell Mitzi *(WGRWightman)* 8-9 GBardwell (4) (3rd st: ev ch wl over 1f out:
　　wknd fnl f) ..................................................... 3.4
2308³ Tayish *(TThomsonJones)* 9-0 WCarson (2) (lw: w ldr 3f) ........................ 8.5

**6/4** TROON, **11/4** Tayish, **5/1** War Requiem (IRE), **7/1** Christian Spirit(op 4/1), **8/1** Marwell Mitzi(10/1—6/1).
CSF £8.04, Tote £2.40: £1.70 £1.50 (£6.30). Mr Tony Hirschfeld (NEWMARKET) bred by Senator David Seale. 5
Rn　　　　　　　　　　　　　　　　　　　　　　　　　　　　　　63.7 sec (3.4)
　　　　　　　　　　　　　　　　　　　　　　　　　　　　　　SF—7/4/–/–/–

---

**2578**　　DUKE OF NORFOLK MEMORIAL NURSERY　£6056.00 (£1808.00: £864.00: £392.00)
　　　　**6f 209y**　　　　　　　　　　　　　　　　　　　　　3-00 (3-01)

*2102*★ Noyan **(80)** *(MBell)* 8-7 MHills (3) (lw: mde virtually all: rdn out) ................ —1
2342² Zuno Warrior **(94)** *(GLewis)* 9-7 PatEddery (1) (lw: 4th st: rdn over 3f out: ev ch
　　fnl 2f: unable qckn fnl f) ......................................... 1¹/₂.2
1858★ Futurballa **(91)** *(Fav)* *(JLDunlop)* 9-4 WCarson (2) (lw: 5th st: hrd rdn over 1f
　　out: r.o one pce) ................................................ 1¹/₂.3
2037⁴ Finavon **(69)** *(IABalding)* 7-7⁽¹⁾ ‡³SO'Gorman (5) (lw: 3rd st: hrd rdn over 2f out:
　　wknd over 1f out) ............................................... 7.4
　1902 Poco Pierna (IRE) **(67)** *(WCarter)* 7-1⁽¹⁾ ‡7CHawksley (7) (lw: nvr nr to chal) ...... ³/₄.5
2052³ Bichette **(80)** *(RHannon)* 8-7 MRoberts (6) (no hdwy fnl 3f) .................... 2¹/₂.6
2462 Warm Spell **(67)** *(RSimpson)* 7-8⁽¹⁾ AMackay (6) (lw: 6th st: wknd over 2f out)　hd.7
2106★ Miss Fayruz (IRE) **(66)** *(MrsLPiggott)* 7-7 JQuinn (4) (2nd st: wknd 2f out) ....... ³/₄.8
　　LONG HANDICAP: Poco Pierna (IRE) 6-10, Warm Spell 7-6, Miss Fayruz (IRE) 7-0.

**9/4** Futurballa, **7/2** Finavon, **4/1** Zuno Warrior, **5/1** NOYAN, **11/2** Bichette(4/1—6/1), **16/1** Warm Spell, **25/1**
Miss Fayruz (IRE), **50/1** Poco Pierna (IRE). CSF £23.04, CT £51.59. Tote £6.80: £1.90 £1.30 £1.50 (£11.20). Mr
Yucel Birol (NEWMARKET) bred by Oakgrove Stud. 8 Rn　　　　　　　　　　1m 21.5 (1.5)
　　　　　　　　　　　　　　　　　　　　　　　　　　　　　　SF—44/53/45/–/–/3

---

**2579**　　SOUTH COAST STKS　£3660.00 (£1010.00: £480.00)
　　　　**7f 214y**　　　　　　　　　　　　　　　　　　　　　3-30 (3-31)

　1455 **Karinga Bay (111)** *(Fav)* *(GLewis)* 5–8-11 BRouse (2) (lw: 2nd st: led over 3f
　　out: easily) ..................................................... —1
2281² Flaming Arrow **(92)** *(HRACecil)* 4–9-0 WRSwinburn (1) (3rd st: chsd wnr fnl 3f:
　　hrd rdn over 1f out: unable qckn) ................................. 10.2
1703⁵ Line Engaged (USA) **(88)** (v) *(PTWalwyn)* 4–8-11 PatEddery (3) (led over 4f) ... 15.3

**4/6** KARINGA BAY, **6/4** Flaming Arrow, **9/1** Line Engaged (USA). CSF £1.96, Tote £1.60 (£1.30). Mr K. Higson
(EPSOM) bred by K. Higson. 3 Rn　　　　　　　　　　　　　　　　　　1m 33.8 (1.6)
　　　　　　　　　　　　　　　　　　　　　　　　　　　　　　SF—43/16/–

---

**2580**　　B.T.R.B. SUPPORTERS GROUP H'CAP (3-Y.O) (0-70) £2511.00 (£696.00: £333.00)
　　　　**1m 3f 196y**　　　　　　　　　　　　　　　　　　　4-00 (4-03)

1632² **Severine (USA) (62)** *(JLDunlop)* 8-13 PatEddery (9) (3rd st: led over 2f out:
　　hrd rdn: r.o wl) ................................................. —1
　831 Roberto's Gal **(56)** *(NCWright)* 8-7 VSmith (8) (hdwy over 1f out: r.o ins fnl f) ... ³/₄.2
2477★ Storm Drum **(56)** (bl) *(Fav)* *(PJMakin)* 8-7 (5x) MRoberts (5) (lw: 6th st: hrd rdn
　　over 1f out: nt r.o) ............................................... 1¹/₂.3
2033 The Karaoke King **(63)** *(RHannon)* 8-11 ‡RPerham (1) (lw: 5th st: one pce fnl 2f) .. 1¹/₂.4

2211 Silken Words (USA) **(58)** *(WRMuir)* 8-2 ‡7KimMcDonnell (6) (prom over 6f) ...... 10.5
2077 Murasil (USA) **(64)** *(MajorWRHern)* 9-1 WCarson (2) (lw: 4th st: eased whn btn
wl over 1f out) ..... 2¹/₂.6
1857² Kajaani (IRE) **(66)** *(PFlCole)* 9-3 TQuinn (4) (led: clr 10f out: hdd over 2f out: sn
wknd) ..... 1.7
2069⁴ Walking on Water **(70)** (bl) *(RFJohnsonHoughton)* 9-7 BRaymond (7) (lw: 2nd
st: wknd over 2f out) ..... 10.8
2296⁴ Wheeler's Wonder (IRE) **(46)** *(NCWright)* 7-6 ‡5BDoyle (3) (a bhd) ..... 12.9

**5/4** Storm Drum(6/4—2/1), **7/2** SEVERINE (USA), **9/1** Murasil (USA), **9/1** Kajaani (IRE), **10/1** The Karaoke
King, **16/1** Walking on Water, Wheeler's Wonder (IRE), **33/1** Ors. CSF £81.26, CT £195.91. Tote £4.10: £1.30
£5.70 £1.30 (£108.70). Miss K. Rausing (ARUNDEL) bred by Miss K. Rausing in USA. 9 Rn      2m 30 (3)
SF—39/31/28/31/2/10

---

**2581**      TOWN HALL H'CAP (0-70) £2532.00 (£702.00: £336.00)      **6f 209y**      4-30 (4-32)
(Weights raised 3 lb)

2307⁴ **Amethystine (USA) (58)** (Fav) *(RJHodges)* 6-8-13 ‡7SDrowne (4) (3rd st: led
over 1f out: rdn out) ..... —1
2476 Ain'tlifelikethat **(49)** (bl) *(TJNaughton)* 5-8-11 MHills (7) (lw: hdwy over 1f out:
unable qckn ins fnl f: prom 3rd, 2l: plcd 2nd) ..... 2
2343⁵ Caromish (USA) **(62)** *(MDIUsher)* 5-9-10 MWigham (2) (w ldr: led over 2f out tl
over 1f out: sn wknd: fin 4th, 7l: plcd 3rd) ..... 3
2307⁵ Restore **(49)** (bl) *(RVoorspuy)* 9-8-11 SDawson (5) (led over 4f: wknd over 1f
out: fin 5th, 1¹/₂l: plcd 4th) ..... 4
2427⁵ Dance on Sixpence **(60)** (v) *(HJCollingridge)* 4-9-8 JQuinn (8) (6th st: wknd 2f
out: fin 6th, nk: plcd 5th) ..... 5
2290 Harlequin Girl **(31)** *(KTIvory)* 4-7-7 GBardwell (3) (4th st: btn whn hmpd wl over
1f out) ..... ¹/₂.7
2303³ Red Sombrero **(59)** *(LGCottrell)* 3-9-1 AMunro (9) (lw: bhd fnl 3f) ..... hd.8
2483 Chloes Diamond (IRE) **(46)** (bl) *(JLSpearing)* 4-8-8 MRoberts (10) (a bhd) ..... 4.9
2107⁴ Millfit **(61)** *(BHanbury)* 3-9-3 WRSwinburn (1) (mid div whn hmpd on ins
wl over 1f out: nt rcvr) ..... 1¹/₂.10
2141 Juvenara **(36)** *(CJHill)* 6-7-9 ‡3Norton (6) (5th st: edgd lft wl over 1f out: ev ch
fnl f: r.o: fin 2nd, ¹/₂l: disq: plcd last) ..... 0
LONG HANDICAP: Harlequin Girl 7-5.

*Stewards Enquiry: Juvenara disq. (interference to Harlequin Girl). Norton suspended 13-16/8/92 (careless riding).*

**5/2** AMETHYSTINE (USA)(7/2—4/1), **5/1** Juvenara, **7/1** Chloes Diamond (IRE), Ain'tlifelikethat, **8/1** Caromish
(USA), **9/1** Dance on Sixpence(6/1—10/1), **10/1** Restore, Millfit (USA), **12/1** Red Sombrero, **33/1** Harlequin Girl.
CSF £19.63, CT £113.74. Tote £3.90: £1.60 £2.10 £2.90 (£9.60). Mr J. W. Mursell (SOMERTON) bred by
Hyllview Farms, Inc in USA. 10 Rn      1m 22.6 (2.6)
SF—34/14/24/16/–/8/–

---

**2582**      LEVY BOARD H'CAP (0-70) £2758.00 (£763.00: £364.00)      **7f 214y**      5-00 (5-02)
(Weights raised 8 lb)

2429² **Kingchip Boy (54)** (Fav) *(MJRyan)* 3-8-13 DBiggs (4) (6th st: led over 1f out:
rdn out) ..... —1
2060⁵ Navaresque **(42)** *(RJHodges)* 7-8-8 WCarson (1) (lw: 3rd st: led 2f out tl over 1f
out: unable qckn) ..... 3.2
2079 Flying Wind **(57)** (bl) *(JSutcliffe)* 3-9-2 BRouse (5) (swtg: hdwy over 2f out: hrd
rdn over 1f out: one pce) ..... 2¹/₂.3
2254 Old Comrades **(56)** *(LGCottrell)* 5-9-8 TRogers (3) (4th st: hrd rdn over 1f out:
one pce) ..... 2¹/₂.4
2476⁶ Aldahe **(44)** *(BRMillman)* 7-8-10 AMunro (2) (lw: nvr nr to chal) ..... 1.5
2266 Rio Trusky **(40)** *(MDIUsher)* 3-7-8⁽⁴⁾ ‡5ATucker (7) (swtg: 2nd st: led 3f out to 2f
out: sn wknd) ..... hd.6
1976 Great Hall **(45)** *(PDCundell)* 3-8-4 JWilliams (9) (a bhd) ..... 1¹/₂.7
2075 Najeb (USA) **(65)** (bl) *(BHanbury)* 3-9-10 WRSwinburn (8) (swtg: 5th st: wknd
over 3f out) ..... 12.8
2251³ Mardior **(33)** *(WGRWightman)* 4-7-13 GBardwell (6) (lw: led 5f) ..... ¹/₂.9

**9/4** KINGCHIP BOY(7/4—3/1), **7/2** Aldahe(tchd 6/1), Navaresque, **11/2** Old Comrades(op 7/2), **7/1** Mardior,
**16/1** Great Hall, **20/1** Ors. CSF £10.89, CT £107.66. Tote £3.30: £1.80 £1.10 £4.10 (£5.40). Four Jays Racing
Partnership (NEWMARKET) bred by R. M. Scott. 9 Rn      1m 36.1 (3.9)
SF—10/–/–/–/–/–

---

T/Plpt: £132.00 (27.6 Tckts).      AK

# BRIGHTON (L-H)
## Wednesday, August 5th [Firm]
Going Allowance: minus 0.30 sec per fur (F)   Wind: mod half across

Stalls: low

**2583**   STANMER CLAIMING STKS   £2385.00 (£660.00: £315.00)   **7f 214y**   2-00 (2-01)

| | | |
|---|---|---|
| 2240 | **Durneltor (63)** *(Fav) (RHannon)* 4–9-2 JReid (6) (hld up: sltly hmpd over 4f out: 5th st: led over 2f out: r.o wl) | —1 |
| 1986[4] | Dancing Beau (IRE) **(69)** *(MrsLPiggott)* 3–8-9 LPiggott (9) (lw: 2nd st: led wl over 2f out: sn hdd: one pce) | 5.2 |
| 2576[2] | Beechwood Cottage **(34)** (bl) *(ABailey)* 9–8-1 ‡⁵ATucker (4) (hld up: 7th st: hrd rdn 2f out: r.o one pce) | ³⁄₄.3 |
| 2240 | Anatroccolo **(40)** *(RABennett)* 5–8-1 PRobinson (3) (4th st: one pce fnl 2f) | 3.4 |
| 2291 | Wayward Son **(42)** *(GLewis)* 3–7-13 DBiggs (2) (dwlt: 9th st: nvr nrr) | 1¹⁄₂.5 |
| 2125 | Betalongabill **(45)** (bl) *(MMadgwick)* 3–7-12 ‡⁷CAvery (7) (8th st: a bhd) | 3¹⁄₂.6 |
| 2304[6] | Monte Bre **(60)** *(RAkehurst)* 6–8-10 TQuinn (8) (3rd st: hrd rdn over 2f out: sn wknd: b.b.v) | 1¹⁄₂.7 |
| 2343 | Up the Punjab **(53)** *(AMoore)* 3–7-11 NAdams (10) (led after 5f: sn wknd) | 2¹⁄₂.8 |
| 1912 | Little Nod **(49)** *(JWhite)* 3–8-3 GDuffield (5) (6th st: sn wknd) | 4.9 |

**85/40** DURNELTOR, **11/4** Dancing Beau (IRE), **3/1** Up the Punjab, **5/1** Monte Bre, **12/1** Beechwood Cottage, **25/1** Betalongabill, **33/1** Wayward Son, **50/1** Ors. CSF £8.30, Tote £3.00: £1.30 £1.60 £2.30 (£5.00). Mrs A. Valentine (MARLBOROUGH) bred by P. Valentine. 9 Rn   1m 34.7 (2.5)
SF—29/7/–/–/–/–

**2584**   E.B.F. BLACK ROCK STKS (Mdn 2-Y-O) £2343.00 (£648.00: £309.00)   **6f 209y**   2-30 (2-31)

| | | |
|---|---|---|
| 2130[4] | **Empire Pool** *(Fav) (LordHuntingdon)* 9-0 WRSwinburn (4) (lw: 3rd st: led ins fnl f: comf) | —1 |
| 2409[6] | Exhibit Air (IRE) *(RHannon)* 8-9 JReid (2) (2nd st: led over 2f out tl ins fnl f: unable qckn) | ³⁄₄.2 |
| 2208[6] | The Gold Souk (IRE) *(JLDunlop)* 9-0 TQuinn (7) (7th st: hrd rdn over 1f out: r.o) | 3.3 |
| 1957 | Lidoma (IRE) *(JLDunlop)* 8-9 WCarson (3) (4th st: rdn 2f out: one pce) | 1¹⁄₂.4 |
| 2193[5] | Cashable **(72)** *(JRJenkins)* 9-0 SWhitworth (8) (led over 4f: rdn over 2f out: wknd over 1f out) | 3.5 |
| 2292[3] | Keltic Danseuse (IRE) *(MrsLPiggott)* 8-2 ‡⁷GMilligan (6) (5th st: no hdwy fnl 2f) | 2.6 |
| | Bonasa (IRE) *(BWHills)* 8-9 DHolland (1) (leggy: lt-f: 6th st: hrd rdn over 2f out: sn wknd) | 5.7 |

**2/5** EMPIRE POOL, **7/1** Exhibit Air (IRE), **10/1** Bonasa (IRE)(op 5/1), Keltic Danseuse (IRE)(op 6/1), **14/1** The Gold Souk (IRE)(6/1—16/1), **16/1** Ors. CSF £4.52, Tote £1.40: £1.20 £2.80 (£4.00). The Queen (WEST ILSLEY) bred by The Queen. 7 Rn   1m 23.2 (3.2)
SF—20/13/9/–/–/–

**2585**   B.T.R.B. H'CAP (0-100) £5692.00 (£1696.00: £808.00: £364.00)   **1m 3f 196y**   3-00 (3-02)

| | | |
|---|---|---|
| 2349[6] | **Barrish (69)** *(RAkehurst)* 6–9-4 JReid (6) (2nd st: led over 1f out: drvn out) | —1 |
| 2347[6] | Prince Hannibal **(75)** *(Fav) (JLDunlop)* 5–9-10 WCarson (4) (lw: 4th st: rdn over 1f out: unable qckn) | 6.2 |
| 2518* | Storm Dust **(70)** *(JRFanshawe)* 3–8-8 GCarter (3) (3rd st: hrd rdn over 2f out: one pce) | 3.3 |
| 2012[3] | Simonov **(79)** *(GHarwood)* 3–9-3 AClark (5) (lw: led over 10f: sn wknd) | 2¹⁄₂.4 |
| 2020[5] | Eden's Close **(74)** (v) *(MHTompkins)* 3–8-12 PRobinson (2) (poor 6th st: hrd rdn over 2f out: nvr nrr) | 1.5 |
| 2305* | Scenic Dancer **(54)** (v) *(AHide)* 4–8-3 WNewnes (1) (poor 5th st: a bhd) | 7.6 |
| 2451 | Alessandrina (USA) **(79)** (v) *(MRStoute)* 3–9-3 WRSwinburn (7) (poor 7th st: a bhd) | 12.7 |

**7/4** Prince Hannibal(3/1—7/2), **7/2** BARRISH(5/1—6/1), **9/2** Simonov, **5/1** Storm Dust(op 3/1), Scenic Dancer(8/1—9/2), **9/1** Eden's Close, **16/1** Alessandrina (USA)(op 8/1). CSF £10.84, Tote £5.90: £2.50 £1.90 (£5.60). Mr A. D. Spence (EPSOM) bred by Sheikh Mohammed bin Rashid al Maktoum. 7 Rn   2m 29.9 (2.9)
SF—39/33/11/15/8/–

**2586**   GORING STKS (Mdn) £2070.00 (£570.00: £270.00)   **6f 209y**   3-30 (3-31)

| | | |
|---|---|---|
| 2053[4] | **Chance to Dream (54)** *(RHannon)* 3–8-8 JReid (4) (hld up: 4th st: led over 2f out: sn clr: pushed out) | —1 |

2393³ Mainly Me **(70)** *(PTWalwyn)* 3-8-8 PRobinson (6) (2nd st: rdn 2f out: unable qckn) .................................................................. 4.2

865² Twilight Secret **(Fav)** *(JWHills)* 3-8-8 MHills (2) (led over 4f: rdn over 2f out: eased whn btn nr fin) ............................................. 5.3

2240 Bounder Rowe **(40)** *(JFfitch-Heyes)* 5-9-5 TQuinn (1) (3rd st: rdn 2f out: one pce) .............................................................. 1½.4

Nordansk *(LJHolt)* 3-8-13 WNewnes (3) (dwlt: 6th st: a bhd) .......................... 3½.5
The Teflon Don *(RBrotherton)* 3-8-13 JWilliams (5) (5th st: wknd 3f out: t.o) ....... 30.6

**4/5** Twilight Secret, **6/4** Mainly Me, **11/2** CHANCE TO DREAM(5/1—8/1), **25/1** The Teflon Don, **66/1** Ors. CSF £14.32, Tote £5.00: £1.90 £1.70 (£5.70). Mrs D. Hammerson (MARLBOROUGH) bred by Ranston (Bloodstock) Ltd. 6 Rn                                           1m 22.4 (2.4)
SF—27/15/–/6/–/–

**2587**   JIMMY HEAL MEMORIAL TROPHY (Nursery) £3330.00 (£990.00: £470.00: £210.00)
5f 59y                                              4-00 (4-00)

2546⁴ **Fiveofive (IRE) (66)** (bl) *(NACallaghan)* 9-7 JReid (2) (lw: 3rd st: swtchd rt over 1f out: led ins fnl f: pushed out) ............................. —1

2437 Be Polite (IRE) **(56)** **(Fav)** *(MBell)* 8-11 MHills (3) (2nd st: led 2f out: hrd rdn & hdd ins fnl f: one pce) ...................................... 3.2

2500⁵ Jasmin Isle **(55)** *(MissGayKelleway)* 8-3 ‡7CHawksley (1) (lw: led over 3f: ev ch ins fnl f: one pce) .............................................. hd.3

2388⁴ Bodandere **(62)** (v) *(MJFetherston-Godley)* 9-3 TQuinn (4) (4th st: hrd rdn over 2f out: one pce) ............................................. 1½.4

**13/8** Be Polite (IRE), **15/8** Bodandere, **9/4** FIVEOFIVE (IRE), **7/1** Jasmin Isle. CSF £6.32, Tote £2.80 (£2.40). Mr T. A. Foreman (NEWMARKET) bred by Naver Enterprises Ltd in Ireland. 4 Rn          63.5 sec (3.2)
SF—13/–/–

**2588**   HASSOCKS H'CAP (3-Y.O) (0-90) £2846.00 (£848.00: £404.00: £182.00)
6f 209y                                             4-30 (4-30)

(Weights raised 11 lb)

1928 **Olette (77)** *(GWragg)* 9-6 MHills (3) (mde all: rdn ins fnl f: pushed out) ............. —1

2114* Dune River **(68)** **(Fav)** *(SirMarkPrescott)* 8-11 GDuffield (4) (lw: 2nd st: hrd rdn 2f out: unable qckn) .................................. 2½.2

2380⁴ Morsun **(77)** (bl) *(DMorley)* 9-6 WCarson (5) (lw: rdn 4f out: 4th st: one pce fnl 2f) .............................................................. 3½.3

2468 Hawa Layaam (IRE) **(78)** (v) *(AAScott)* 9-7 WRSwinburn (6) (3rd st: hrd rdn 2f out: sn wknd) ........................................... 15.4

**13/8** Dune River, **15/8** Morsun, **5/2** OLETTE, **15/2** Hawa Layaam (IRE)(7/2—8/1). CSF £6.76, Tote £3.30 (£3.80). Sir Philip Oppenheimer (NEWMARKET) bred by P. D. and Mrs Player. 4 Rn        1m 22 (2)
SF—44/25/20/–

**2589**   LEVY BOARD H'CAP (0-70) £2684.50 (£742.00: £353.50)
5f 213y                                           5-00 (5-00)

2427 **Liffey River (USA) (51)** *(MrsLPiggott)* 4-9-1 LPiggott (4) (8th st: swtchd rt over 1f out: str run fnl f: led nr fin) ......................... —1

2141⁵ Proud Brigadier (IRE) **(47)** *(WCarter)* 4-8-11 JReid (5) (5th st: led ins fnl f: sn hdd: r.o) ............................................... ½.2

2478³ Catalani **(50)** *(TJNaughton)* 7-9-0 DHolland (8) (2nd st: led 3f out: hdd ins fnl f: r.o) .............................................. ½.3

1920 Banbury Flyer **(50)** *(MrsALMKing)* 4-9-0 WRSwinburn (9) (7th st: rdn 2f out: one pce) ............................................... 1½.4

2337⁶ Lady Sabo **(69)** *(GLewis)* 3-10-0 MHills (6) (lw: dwlt: 9th st: rdn over 1f out: r.o fnl f) ................................................ 1½.5

2365* Inswinger **(33)** *(WGRWightman)* 6-7-11 GBardwell (1) (3rd st: rdn 2f out: one pce) .............................................. ½.6

2581³ Caromish (USA) **(62)** *(MDIUsher)* 5-9-12 MWigham (3) (4th st: rdn 3f out: sn wknd) ................................................... 3½.7

93 Sunley Sparkle **(50)** *(DRGandolfo)* 4-8-11 ‡3RPerham (7) (led 3f) ...................... 2.8

2141³ Scarlet Princess **(48)** **(Fav)** *(RJHodges)* 4-8-12 WCarson (2) (6th st: rdn 3f out: sn wknd) ............................................... 2.9

**3/1** Scarlet Princess(4/1—5/1), **4/1** Banbury Flyer(op 6/1), Catalani, **5/1** Lady Sabo, **6/1** Caromish (USA), **7/1** Proud Brigadier (IRE), **10/1** LIFFEY RIVER, **14/1** Inswinger(op 7/1), **25/1** Sunley Sparkle. CSF £76.56, CT £305.41. Tote £6.80: £2.10 £2.10 £1.50 (£23.70). Mrs Heather Hirschfeld (NEWMARKET) bred by Warren W. Rosenthal in USA. 9 Rn                                    1m 10 (1.6)
SF—33/27/28/22/30/–

T/Plpt: £80.30 (44.05 Tckts).                                                    SM

# BRIGHTON (L-H)
## Thursday, August 6th [Firm]
Going Allowance: minus 0.30 sec per fur (F)                    Wind: almost nil

Stalls: low

**2590**    MARINA AUCTION STKS (Mdn 2-Y.O) £2238.00 (£618.00: £294.00)
             **5f 213y**                                        2-00 (2-02)

1932[4] **After the Last** (Jt-Fav) *(RHannon)* 8-8 JReid (6) (led over 1f: 2nd st: led 2f out:
             hrd rdn: r.o wl) ............................................................... —1
  365 Perdition (IRE) *(JWHills)* 8-2 MHills (4) (5th st: chsd wnr over 1f out: unable
             qckn) ....................................................................... 2.2
2482[2] Sylvan Starlight (Jt-Fav) *(SirMarkPrescott)* 8-3 GDuffield (3) (led over 4f out to
             2f out: one pce) ......................................................... 2¹/₂.3
2306[3] Scenic Reef (IRE) (54) *(JMPEustace)* 8-3 TQuinn (2) (lw: 4th st: hrd rdn over 1f
             out: one pce) ............................................................. ¹/₂.4
2428[2] Cuddly Date (46) *(DTThom)* 8-0 DBiggs (5) (swtg: 3rd st: wknd 2f out) ............ 8.5
2306[4] Petite Vino (48) (bl) *(JJBridger)* 8-0 DaleGibson (1) (lw: 6th st: a bhd) ........... 7.6

**11/10** Sylvan Starlight, AFTER THE LAST, **10/1** Scenic Reef (IRE), **20/1** Perdition (IRE)(op 8/1), Cuddly Date(op
8/1), **66/1** Petite Vino. CSF £17.97, Tote £2.50: £1.40 £3.20 (£32.80). Mr Roger Barby (MARLBOROUGH) bred
by Sagittarius Bloodstock Agency. 6 Rn                                      1m 9.3 (0.9)
                                                                      SF—40/26/17/15/–/–

**2591**    RINGMER (S) STKS (2-Y.O) £2469.00 (£684.00: £327.00)    **5f 59y**    2-30 (2-31)

2195 **Nikki Noo Noo** (54) *(CJHill)* 8-6 GDuffield (4) (swtg: mde all: hrd rdn over 1f
             out: r.o wl) ................................................................... 1
2474[3] Lady of Shadows (48) (v) *(SDow)* 8-6 AMunro (2) (b.hind: 4th st: hrd rdn over 1f
             out: one pce) ................................................................ 5.2
2238[6] Sterling Princess (45) (bl) *(JRJenkins)* 8-1 ‡5DHarrison (5) (3rd st: hrd rdn over
             1f out: one pce) ............................................................ s.h.3
        Naughty Charlotte *(APJarvis)* 8-6 TQuinn (7) (neat: hdwy over 1f out: nvr nrr) 3¹/₂.4
2005 Hawaii Star (IRE) (Fav) *(GLewis)* 8-6 PatEddery (8) (lw: 2nd st: ev ch wl over 1f
             out: eased whn btn fnl f) ................................................. 1¹/₂.5
2005 Downlands Aris *(TJNaughton)* 8-6 DHolland (1) (6th st: no hdwy fnl 3f) .......... 2¹/₂.6
2207[4] Keamari *(BForsey)* 8-1 ‡5BDoyle (6) (reard s: a bhd) ........................... 1¹/₂.7
1764 Victorian Star (44) *(PButler)* 7-13 ‡7DToole (3) (5th st: wknd 3f out) ............... s.h.8

**5/4** Hawaii Star (IRE), **6/4** NIKKI NOO NOO, **8/1** Lady of Shadows(6/1—9/1), **12/1** Naughty Charlotte (op 6/1),
**25/1** Keamari(op 8/1), Sterling Princess, **50/1** Ors. CSF £13.03, Tote £2.70: £1.40 £1.30 £2.70 (£5.90). Mr C.
John Hill (BARNSTAPLE) bred by C. T. Olley and Robin Olley. 8 Rn; No bid          62.6 sec (2.3)
                                                                      SF—14/–/–/–/–/–

**2592**    BRIGHTON SPRINT H'CAP (0-90) £6004.00 (£1792.00: £856.00: £388.00)
             **5f 213y**                                        3-00 (3-01)

2307★ **Shikari's Son** (70) (Fav) *(JWhite)* 5–8-8 TQuinn (5) (lw: 5th st: nt clr run over 2f
             out: swtchd rt over 1f out: led nr fin) ...................................... —1
2337 Plain Fact (88) *(JWHills)* 7–9-12 MHills (1) (swtg: 2nd st: led ins fnl f: hrd rdn:
             hdd nr fin) ................................................................. nk.2
2581★ Amethystine (USA) (65) *(RJHodges)* 6–8-0 (7x) ‡3TSprake (7) (6th st: rdn over
             1f out: r.o one pce) ....................................................... 2.3
2404[6] Misdemeanours Girl (70) *(MRChannon)* 4–8-3 ‡5BDoyle (3) (led tl ins fnl f:
             unable qckn) .............................................................. ³/₄.4
2465[4] Martinosky (66) *(WGRWightman)* 6–8-4 GDuffield (6) (3rd st: one pce fnl 2f) .. 1¹/₂.5
2435 Green Dollar (90) *(EAWheeler)* 9–9-9 ‡5DHarrison (3) (4th st: one pce fnl 2f) .... s.h.6
2227 Assignment (72) *(JFfitch-Heyes)* 6–8-10 AMunro (4) (lw: hld up: nt clr run on
             ins wl over 1f out: swtchd rt: sn wknd) ................................. 2¹/₂.7

**5/2** SHIKARI'S SON, **3/1** Martinosky, **4/1** Green Dollar, **6/1** Misdemeanours Girl (IRE)(op 7/2), **15/2** Amethystine
(USA), **12/1** Ors. CSF £27.10, Tote £3.60: £2.10 £2.80 (£15.80). Mr Alan Spargo (WENDOVER) bred by W. H.
Joyce. 7 Rn                                                                1m 8.8 (0.4)
                                                                      SF—50/67/33/33/28/46

**2593**    B.T.R.B. 'HOORAY LADY' H'CAP (0-80) £2924.00 (£872.00: £416.00: £188.00)
             **1m 1f 209y**                                     3-30 (3-32)

1585★ **Avice Caro** (USA) (77) *(JHMGosden)* 3–9-7 PatEddery (4) (mde all: rdn out) ... —1
2457★ Neptune's Pet (80) (Fav) *(GLewis)* 4–10-5 (5x) JReid (3) (2nd st: rdn over 1f
             out: no imp) .................................................................. 2¹/₂.2

2305³ Tiger Claw (USA) **(50)** *(RJHodges)* 6–8-3 DHolland (1) (3rd st: rdn over 3f out:
one pce) .................................................................. 6.3
2062 Bold Steve **(63)** *(LMCumani)* 3–8-7 LDettori (2) (4th st: one pce fnl 2f) ......... 1.4

**6/5** Neptune's Pet, **3/1** AVICE CARO (USA)(op 2/1), Tiger Claw (USA)(7/2—9/2), **6/1** Bold Steve(7/2—13/2).
CSF £6.69, Tote £2.80 (£2.00). Sheikh Mohammed (NEWMARKET) bred by Darley Stud Management Co Ltd in
USA. 4 Rn
2m 1.6 (3.6)
SF—41/48/6/8

**2594**      CLIFTONVILLE STKS (Mdn) £2070.00 (£570.00: £270.00)    **1m 3f 196y**   4-00 (4-00)

1180⁶ **Fern (100)** *(Fav)* *(LMCumani)* 3–8-5 LDettori (1) (led over 5f out: r.o wl) ............ —1
21374 Constructivist (IRE) **(70)** *(BWHills)* 3–8-10 DHolland (3) (lw: led over 6f: hrd rdn
4f out: 2nd st: unable qckn fnl f) ...................................... 6.2
2252³ La Joya (IRE) *(GHarwood)* 3–8-5 AClark (2) (3rd st: wknd over 3f out) ............ 20.3

**4/9** FERN(1/4—4/7), **2/1** Constructivist (IRE), **10/1** La Joya (IRE). CSF £1.73, Tote £1.50 (£1.30). Fittocks Stud
Limited (NEWMARKET) bred by Fittocks Stud Ltd. 3 Rn
2m 29.8 (2.8)
SF—27/20/—

**2595**      EDBURTON H'CAP (3-Y.O) (0-70) £2820.00 (£840.00: £400.00: £180.00)
**5f 59y**                                        4-30 (4-31)

2303⁵ **Treasure Time (IRE) (62)** *(JWhite)* 9-5 DaleGibson (3) (lw: mde virtually all: all
out) ......................................................................... —1
2465⁶ Savalaro **(51)** *(JFfitch-Heyes)* 8-8 TQuinn (2) (lw: 3rd st: rdn over 1f out: r.o wl
ins fnl f) ................................................................... nk.2
24194 Sea-Deer **(64)** *(Fav)* *(LJHolt)* 9-7 JReid (1) (6th st: rdn over 2f out: r.o wl ins fnl f) ... hd.3
2291 Palacegate Gold (IRE) **(49)** *(RJHodges)* 8-3 ‡³TSprake (8) (4th st: rdn over 1f
out: r.o) .................................................................. ½.4
2229³ Bridle Talk (IRE) **(46)** *(MMcCormack)* 8-3 AClark (6) (lw: s.s: 5th st: ev ch over
1f out: r.o) ............................................................... nk.5
1994⁶ Miss Shadowfax **(64)** *(CNAllen)* 9-7 LDettori (7) (lw: bhd fnl 3f) ................. 10.6
2082³ Jaromic **(55)** (bl) *(PFTulk)* 8-12 GDuffield (5) (b: 2nd st: wknd over 2f out) ........ 2.7
2301⁶ Cumbrian Cavalier **(40)** *(JRBostock)* 7-4 ‡⁷CHawksley (4) (s.s: a bhd) ............ 3½.8

**9/4** Sea-Deer, **11/4** TREASURE TIME (IRE), **7/1** Palacegate Gold (IRE)(5/1—15/2), Jaromic, **15/2** Savalar
o(6/1—10/1), **10/1** Bridle Talk (IRE), **16/1** Miss Shadowfax, **25/1** Cumbrian Cavalier. CSF £21.44, CT £47.69.
Tote £4.10: £1.70 £2.00 £1.20 (£12.70). Mrs Rita Bates (WENDOVER) bred by Mrs D. Davison in Ireland. 8 Rn
61.9 sec (1.6)
SF—41/29/41/21/20/-

T/Plpt: £60.80 (47.9 Tckts).                                    AK

1952—**KEMPTON (R-H)**

**Wednesday, August 5th [Good to firm, Firm patches]**

Going Allowance: Rnd: minus 0.20 sec; Rest: minus 0.30 sec (F)      Wind: almost nil

Stalls: high

**2596**      LADBROKE APP'CE H'CAP (0-70) £2532.00 (£702.00: £336.00)    **1½m**   6-00 (6-02)
(Weights raised 11 lb)

2455⁵ **Miss Pin Up (66)** *(Jt-Fav)* *(PatMitchell)* 3–9-10 DBiggs (6) (lw: hdwy over 2f out:
hrd rdn over 1f out: led wl ins fnl f: r.o wl) ........................... —1
1760 Miss Witch **(47)** *(HCandy)* 4–8-13 ‡³AntoinetteArmes (3) (led tl wl ins fnl f: r.o) .. ½.2
232 Scotoni **(49)** *(RJO'Sullivan)* 6–9-1 ‡³CHawksley (1) (lw: hdwy over 5f out: 3rd st:
one pce fnl 2f) .......................................................... 3½.3
1637⁵ Quietly Impressive (IRE) **(49)** *(MBell)* 4–9-4 PTurner (8) (lw: 4th st: hrd rdn 2f
out: one pce) ............................................................ ½.4
2451 Beam Me Up Scotty (IRE) **(47)** *(PMitchell)* 3–8-5 DHarrison (7) (5th st: no hdwy
fnl 3f) ................................................................... 5.5
2467² Marandisa **(40)** *(MPNaughton)* 5–8-9 RPrice (2) (swtg: 2nd st: wknd over 2f
out) ..................................................................... 1½.6
2241⁶ Littleton Lullaby **(27)** *(MMadgwick)* 7–7-7(1) ‡³CAvery (2) (6th st: wknd over 2f
out) ..................................................................... 2.7
2260* Doctor's Remedy **(38)** *(Jt-Fav)* *(MrsJJordan)* 6–8-4 ‡³KimMcDonnell (4) (a bhd) nk.8
2492 Q-Eight (IRE) **(50)** *(APJarvis)* 4–9-2 ‡³PBowe (9) (bhd fnl 6f: t.o) .................. 25.9

**4/1** Doctor's Remedy, MISS PIN UP, **5/1** Beam Me Up Scotty (IRE), **11/2** Marandisa, **7/1** Miss Witch, **8/1** Quietly
Impressive (IRE), **10/1** Scotoni(8/1—12/1), **20/1** Q-Eight (IRE), **33/1** Littleton Lullaby. CSF £28.29, CT £231.27.
Tote £3.70: £1.50 £1.60 £2.80 (£11.50). Mr E. Baldwin (NEWMARKET) bred by Brook Bloodstock P L C. 9 Rn
2m 34.65 (4.45)
SF—42/30/25/27/4/5

**2597** LONDON'S FAMILY RACECOURSE NURSERY £2872.00 (£856.00: £408.00: £184.00)
6f 6-30 (6-32)
(Weights raised 11 lb)

2418* **Defenceless (76)** *(RHannon)* 9-6 (5x) BRouse (1) (swtg: mde all: rdn out) ........ —1
2418⁶ Pair of Jacks (IRE) **(69)** *(WRMuir)* 8-13 TQuinn (5) (lw: hld up: hrd rdn over 1f
out: r.o) ................................................................................. ¾.2
2368* Jarena (IRE) **(77)** (Fav) *(GLewis)* 9-7 PatEddery (3) (lw: chsd wnr: hrd rdn over
1f out: unable qckn) ....................................................... 1.3
1422⁶ Breakfast Boogie **(67)** *(JRFanshawe)* 8-4 ‡⁷NVarley (4) (dwlt: hdwy 3f out: wknd
wl over 1f out) ................................................................. 5.4

**5/4** Jarena (IRE), **5/2** DEFENCELESS, **100/30** Pair of Jacks (IRE), **15/2** Breakfast Boogie. CSF £9.42, Tote £3.10
(£6.10). Mr N. Ahamad (MARLBOROUGH) bred by Newgate Stud Co. 4 Rn
1m 14.30 (3)
SF—10/-/4/-

**2598** E.B.F. RIVERMEAD STKS (Mdn 2-Y.O) £2700.00 (£750.00: £360.00)
7f (J.C) 7-00 (7-06)

2269³ **Anaheim (IRE)** (Fav) *(RHannon)* 9-0 JReid (18) (mde virtually all: qcknd over 1f
out: easily) ....................................................................... —1
1472⁵ City Rocket *(PJMakin)* 9-0 PatEddery (13) (lw: 2nd st: rdn over 2f out: unable
qckn) ................................................................................. 4.2
Summer Pageant *(JRFanshawe)* 8-9 GDuffield (17) (unf: scope: hdwy over 3f
out: 5th st: one pce fnl 2f) ............................................. nk.3
Mutakallam (USA) *(HThomsonJones)* 9-0 RHills (8) (gd sort: 6th st: rdn over 2f
out: one pce) ................................................................... 2.4
Capablanca *(IABalding)* 9-0 RCochrane (6) (leggy: stdy hdwy on ins fnl 2f: r.o
wl: bttr for r) ............................................................... s.h.5
1260 The Executor *(RFJohnsonHoughton)* 9-0 AMunro (9) (no hdwy fnl 2f) .......... ½.6
Revelation (IRE) *(HHannon)* 9-0 BRaymont (5) (w'like: bit bkwd: stdy hdwy fnl
2f: r.o wl: bttr for r) ....................................................... s h 7
2130 Contract Court (USA) *(CACyzer)* 9-0 GCarter (3) (nvr nr to chal) ............... 2.8
Moon Carnival *(LadyHerries)* 8-9 AClark (15) (unf: bit bkwd: rdn over 4f out:
hdwy fnl 2f: r.o) ............................................................ nk.9
2444 Knobbleeneeze *(MRChannon)* 9-0 BRouse (16) (3rd st: wknd over 2f out) ... 1.10
867⁵ Erlking (IRE) *(LordHuntingdon)* 8-9 ‡5DHarrison (12) (4th st: wknd over 2f out) 4.11
Beauchamp Hero *(JLDunlop)* 9-0 TQuinn (4) (unf: scope: nvr nrr) .............. s.h.12
2269 Juliasdarkinvader *(AMoore)* 9-0 CandyMorris (10) (prom over 3f) ............. 1¹/₂.13
Bold Visit (IRE) *(DRCElsworth)* 9-0 JWilliams (19) (w'like: scope: s.s: a bhd) . nk.14
Kimberley Boy *(BWHills)* 9-0 DHolland (1) (str: scope: dwlt: a bhd) ............ nk.15
Midyan Blue (IRE) *(JMPEustace)* 9-0 MTebbutt (2) (unf: scope: a bhd) .......... nk.16
2376 Chummy's Friend (IRE) *(BWHills)* 8-9 MHills (7) (swtg: hmpd over 5f out: bhd
whn hmpd over 2f out) ..................................................... 2.17
2190 Fanfold (IRE) *(AWDenson)* 8-9 WNewnes (11) (prom over 3f: wkng whn bdly
hmpd over 2f out) ............................................................. 2.18
Lord Chief Justice *(JLDunlop)* 9-0 WCarson (14) (w'like: dwlt: rdn thrght: a
bhd) ................................................................................. 2¹/₂.19
1867 Beyond the Limit (20/1) Withdrawn (unruly gng to s) : not under orders
Stewards Enquiry: Trainer & rdr of Revelation each fined £400 under Rule 151 (failure to run horse on its merits).

**7/2** ANAHEIM (IRE)(tchd 11/2), **4/1** City Rocket(3/1—9/2), **9/2** Mutakallam (USA)(op 11/4), **10/1** Lord Chief
Justice(op 6/1), Capablanca, **12/1** Beauchamp Hero, Summer Pageant, **14/1** Kimberley Boy, **16/1** Erlking (IRE),
**20/1** Contract Court (USA), Moon Carnival, Bold Visit (IRE), Revelation (IRE), The Executor, Chummy's Friend
(IRE), **25/1** Midyan Blue (IRE), **33/1** Knobbleeneeze, **50/1** Ors. CSF £19.81, Tote £4.80: £1.90 £2.20 £4.70
(£5.10). A. F. Budge (Equine) Limited (MARLBOROUGH) bred by Scarteen Stud in Ireland. 19 Rn
1m 25.70 (1.50)
SF—46/34/28/27/26/24

**2599** LBC NEWSTALK 97.3 FM H'CAP (0-80) £3002.00 (£896.00: £428.00: £194.00)
5f 7-30 (7-36)
(Weights raised 3 lb)

2290 **Dickens Lane (45)** *(RJHodges)* 5–7-10 DBiggs (7) (gd hdwy over 1f out: led wl
ins fnl f: r.o wl) ............................................................. —1
2548 Ganeshaya **(50)** (bl) *(MFBarraclough)* 3–7-6⁽³⁾ ‡5DHarrison (10) (chsd ldr: led
over 2f out tl wl ins fnl f: r.o) ......................................... ¹/₂.2
2548 Ashtina **(62)** *(RJHodges)* 7–8-13 PatEddery (3) (lost pl over 2f out: rallied over
1f out: ev ch wl ins fnl f: r.o) ....................................... s.h.3
2206³ Rays Mead **(50)** *(LJHolt)* 4–8-1 AMunro (9) (a.p: rdn over 1f out: unable qckn) . 2.4
1576⁶ Noble Power (IRE) **(76)** *(BPalling)* 3–9-9 RCochrane (4) (lw: rdn over 2f out: gd
hdwy fnl f: r.o) ............................................................... ¾.5
2395⁴ Rhythmic Dancer **(73)** *(JLSpearing)* 4–9-9 GHind (2) (ins over 2f out: hdwy on
ins over 1f out: hrd rdn over 1f out: one pce) ............. s.h.6
2224² Consulate **(62)** (Fav) *(JBalding)* 6–8-13 JReid (11) (a.p: rdn over 1f out: one pce) 1.7
2199⁴ Frimley Parkson **(47)** (bl) *(PHowling)* 8–7-12⁽⁵⁾ MRoberts (8) (a bhd) .............. 2.8

897 Stocktina **(42)** *(RJHodges)* 5–7-7  NAdams (5) (a bhd) ............................... 4.9
24786 Shades of Jade **(56)** *(JJBridger)* 4–8-7  SWhitworth (6) (led over 2f) ............... 4.10
LONG HANDICAP: Frimley Parkson 6-11, Stocktina 7-3.

**4/1** Consulate, **9/2** Rays Mead, **11/2** Ganeshaya, **15/2** Ashtina, **8/1** Shades of Jade, **9/1** Rhythmic Dancer, **11/1**
DICKENS LANE, **14/1** Noble Power (IRE), **20/1** Ors. CSF £61.33, CT £421.27. Tote £14.10: £3.00 £1.80 £2.60
(£59.40). Bull & Bear Racing (SOMERTON) bred by Barronstown Stud. 10 Rn
59.46 sec (0.46)
SF—43/37/57/37/56/56/41

**2600**    'LOOKING FOR A HURDLER' CLAIMING STKS    £2364.00 (£654.00: £312.00)
1¼m **(J.C)**    8-00 (8-04)

24305 **Amazon Express (54)** *(CEBrittain)* 3–8-2  MRoberts (7) (lw: mde virtually all:
hrd rdn fnl f: r.o wl) ..... —1
21462 Port in a Storm **(60)** *(WJarvis)* 3–8-6  RCochrane (9) (lw: hdwy & nt clr run wl
over 1f out: r.o wl ins fnl f) ..... ¾.2
22406 Up All Night **(56)** *(JWHills)* 3–7-13  RHills (5) (4th st: hrd rdn over 1f out: r.o) .... nk.3
2416* Vanroy **(66)** (v) (Fav) *(JRJenkins)* 8–9-3  SWhitworth (8) (lw: 5th st: n.m.r on ins
over 2f out: unable qckn) ..... 4.4
Genuine Lady *(APJarvis)* 4–8-8  JReid (1) (lw: nvr nr to chal) ..... 8.5
24162 Molly Splash **(54)** *(CACyzer)* 5–8-6  GCarter (6) (rdn over 4f out: 6th st: wknd
over 2f out) ..... hd.6
21283 Regal Racer **(76)** *(DRCElsworth)* 3–8-12  WCarson (2) (3rd st: wknd over 1f out) 1½.7
24126 Formal Invitation (IRE) **(58)** *(GLewis)* 3–8-5(1)  PatEddery (4) (lw: 2nd st: wknd
over 1f out) ..... 1½.8
Be My Era (IRE) *(AWDenson)* 4–9-4  WNewnes (10) (bhd fnl 5f: t.o) ..... 25.9

**7/4** Vanroy, **3/1** Regal Racer, **13/2** Formal Invitation (IRE), **9/1** AMAZON EXPRESS (op 6/1), **10/1** Port in a Storm,
Up All Night (7/1—11/1), Molly Splash (6/1—11/1), **14/1** Genuine Lady (10/1—16/1), **33/1** Be My Era (IRE). CSF
£86.11, Tote £8.30: £1.90 £1.90 £2.80 (£28.30). Mr A. J. Richards (NEWMARKET) bred by Ewar Stud Farms. 9
Rn    2m 3.77 (1.77)
SF—40/42/34/44/19/16

**2601**    BECKFORD H'CAP (3-Y.O) (0-80) £3262.00 (£976.00: £468.00: £214.00)
1m (rnd)    8-30 (8-31)
(Weights raised 5 lb)

21705 **Muhit (USA) (74)** *(PTWalwyn)* 9-6  WCarson (3) (lw: 3rd st: led 1f out: hrd rdn:
r.o wl) ..... —1
Fit on Time (USA) **(69)** *(MRStoute)* 9-1  PatEddery (4) (lw: 2nd st: led over 2f out
to 1f out: hrd rdn: r.o) ..... ½.2
20183 Ma Bella Luna **(75)** (Fav) *(JLDunlop)* 9-7  MRoberts (2) (5th st: hrd rdn over 1f
out: r.o) ..... nk.3
23843 Red Kite **(67)** *(MBell)* 8-13  MHills (7) (lw: 4th st: n.m.r 2f out: hrd rdn over 1f out:
unable qckn) ..... 3½.4
1122 Gold Jubilee **(65)** *(PJMakin)* 8-11  JReid (6) (6th st: one pce fnl 2f) ..... 2.5
24333 Courageous Knight **(74)** *(RHannon)* 8-4  AMunro (9) (a bhd) ..... 1.6
16084 Sir Oliver (IRE) **(67)** *(RJHodges)* 8-10 ‡3FNorton (10) (a bhd) ..... 6.7
2266 Mere Chants **(68)** *(DRCElsworth)* 9-0  JWilliams (1) (a bhd) ..... 5.8
2227 Appealing Times (USA) **(69)** *(WAO'Gorman)* 8-12 ‡3EmmaO'Gorman (8) (led
over 5f) ..... 10.9

**3/1** Ma Bella Luna, **9/2** Red Kite, **5/1** MUHIT (USA), Courageous Knight, **13/2** Fit on Time (USA) (4/1—7/1), **7/1**
Mere Chants, **14/1** Sir Oliver (IRE) (op 8/1), **20/1** Ors. CSF £34.86, CT £101.78. Tote £5.80: £1.80 £2.30 £1.80
(£18.90). Mr Hamdan Al-Maktoum (LAMBOURN) bred by Shadwell Farm Incorporated in USA. 9 Rn
1m 39.57 (2.37)
SF—46/39/44/25/17/23

T/Trio: Race 4: £152.10 (9.1 Tckts). T/Plpt: £1,363.70 (2.6 Tckts).    AK

2330—**PONTEFRACT (L-H)**
**Wednesday, August 5th [Firm]**
Going Allowance: minus 0.15 sec per fur (F)    Wind: fresh half bhd
Stalls: low

**2602**    HYDE SPORTING PROMOTIONS H'CAP (Ladies) (0-70) £2553.00 (£708.00: £339.00)
1¼m 6y    2-50 (2-52)

14215 **Falcons Dawn (51)** *(ABailey)* 5–10-5  MissLEaton (2) (hld up: hdwy appr st: led
ins fnl f: r.o wl) ..... —1
20662 Brilliant **(67)** (Fav) *(JPearce)* 4–11-7  MrsLPearce (5) (trckd ldrs: hdwy to chal
over 1f out: r.o) ..... 2½.2

2422 Thunderbird One (USA) **(61)** *(DenysSmith)* 3-10-3 ‡3MissMCarson (8) (chsd ldrs tl lost pl 3f out: hdwy over 1f out: r.o u.p) ...................... 1/2.3
22813 Thundering **(38)** *(AWJones)* 7-9-6(6) MissIDWJones (10) (trckd ldrs: led wl over 3f out tl ins fnl f: no ex) .............................. 2.4
2267 Cathos (FR) **(54)** *(DAWilson)* 7-10-8 MissJAllison (12) (b: sn prom: chal 3f out: sn rdn: wknd over 1f out) .................. s.h.5
17394 Rapid Lad **(32)** *(JLSpearing)* 14-9-0 MissTSpearing (11) (lw: bhd: hdwy appr st: nvr rchd ldrs) .................................. 4.6
2561 Cornhill Melody **(35)** *(JLSpearing)* 4-9-0(3) ‡3MissCSpearing (7) (lw: prom tl outpcd fnl 3f) .............................. 1/2.7
2357 Just for Kicks **(32)** *(JJO'Neill)* 6-8-11 ‡3MrsNCraggs (3) (bhd: effrt 4f out: n.d) ... 2.8
2422 Doughman **(41)** (bl) *(JNorton)* 3-9-0 MrsAFarrell (1) (chsd ldrs tl wknd 3f out) s.h.9
2281 The Metropole (IRE) **(41)** *(AWPotts)* 3-8-11 ‡3MissSJudge (4) (b.off hind: a bhd) .............................................. 11/2.10
23544 Be the Best **(44)** *(MPNaughton)* 4-9-12 MissPRobson (6) (lw: outpcd 5f out: n.d after) ........................................ nk.11
1970 One of the Lads **(42)** *(BRCambidge)* 10-9-10(10) MissHNoonan (9) (led tl hdd wl over 3f out: sn wknd: t.o) ............................ 12

LONG HANDICAP: Thundering 8-13, Rapid Lad 8-10, Cornhill Melody 8-9, Just for Kicks 8-5, Doughman 8-13, The Metropole (IRE) 8-8, One of the Lads 8-12.

**Evens** Brilliant, **5/1** Cathos (FR), **9/1** Thundering(op 6/1), **12/1** FALCONS DAWN, Be the Best, Thunderbird One (USA), **14/1** Rapid Lad, **16/1** Cornhill Melody, **25/1** Just for Kicks, **50/1** The Metropole (IRE), **66/1** Just for Kicks, **100/1** One of the Lads. CSF £23.39, CT £148.47. Tote £18.80: £2.90 £1.20 £2.30 (£15.70). Paul Green (Huyton) & Anthony King (TARPORLEY) bred by E. A. Bourke. 12 Rn

2m 15.7 (7.4)
SF−30/41/22/7/22/−

---

**2603**    CUDWORTH CLAIMING STKS    £2322.00 (£474.00 each)    5f    3-20 (3-20)

2424* **Walking Possession (73)** (bl) *(RBoss)* 3-8-9 MTebbutt (0) (chsd ldrs: effrt & edgd lft over 1f out: qcknd to ld wl ins fnl f) ...................... −1
24243 Metal Boys **(87)** *(RHollinshead)* 5-8-12 WRyan (1) (disp ld wl over 1f: led 1/2-wy: nt qckn nr fin) .................................... 11/2.2
1598 Loose Zeus (USA) **(51)** *(CFWall)* 3-7-12 NCarlisle (5) (in tch: styd on wl fnl f: nrst fin) .......................................... d.h.2
24242 Food of Love **(96)** (Fav) *(JBerry)* 4-8-12 JCarroll (3) (led to 1/2-wy: edgd rt: nt qckn ins fnl f) ...................................... 1/2.4
22065 Lonely Lass **(42)** *(AWJones)* 6-7-11 JQuinn (2) (in tch: no hdwy fnl 2f) ........... 11/2.5
2234 Make Or Mar **(50)** *(BEllison)* 4-8-1 JLowe (4) (b: lw: a bhd: t.o) .............. 20.6

**5/4** Food of Love, **9/4** Metal Boys, **3/1** WALKING POSSESSION, **20/1** Loose Zeus, **50/1** Ors. CSF w MB £4.67, w LZ £19.37, Tote £3.40: £1.50 £0.90 MB £1.90 LZ (w MB £2.00, w LZ £6.30). Madagans Plc (NEWMARKET) bred by Downclose Stud. 6 Rn

62.9 sec (1.4)
SF−52/35/49/47/26/−

---

**2604**    PARKSIDE INNES & LEISURE H'CAP (0-90) £3622.50 (£1080.00: £515.00: £232.50)    5f    3-50 (3-51)

21924 **Forest Fairy (61)** *(RBoss)* 3-7-13 JQuinn (5) (mde all: qcknd 1/2-wy: r.o wl) ....... −1
2404 Arc Lamp **(62)** *(JAGlover)* 6-8-4 JFortune (1) (a chsng ldrs: hdwy u.p over 1f out: r.o) ................................................. 11/2.2
2376 Paley Prince (USA) **(82)** *(MDIUsher)* 6-9-10 RCochrane (2) (lw: hld up: sltly hmpd after 1f: effrt & nt clr run wl over 1f out: swtchd & r.o) nk.3
2466* Prince Belfort **(68)** (Fav) *(MPNaughton)* 4-8-5 ‡5JWeaver (6) (lw: cl up tl outpcd appr fnl f) ........................................ 11/2.4
2404 Loft Boy **(68)** (bl) *(JDBethell)* 9-8-10 BRaymond (7) (chsd ldr tl rdn & btn over 1f out) .................................................. 11/2.5
2376 Eager Deva **(86)** *(RHollinshead)* 5-9-7 ‡7SWynne (3) (lw: several positions: effrt 2f out: no imp) ....................................... 2.6

**7/4** Prince Belfort, **100/30** Eager Deva, **11/2** Paley Prince (USA), **13/2** FOREST FAIRY, **7/1** Arc Lamp, **12/1** Loft Boy. CSF £41.04, Tote £5.20: £2.20 £2.30 (£20.70). Mrs Eileen Williams (NEWMARKET) bred by Miss H. K. Monteith. 6 Rn

62.8 sec (1.3)
SF−44/43/62/37/36/39

---

**2605**    'GO RACING IN YORKSHIRE' H'CAP (0-70) £3054.00 (£912.00: £436.00: £198.00)    11/2m 8y    4-20 (4-23)

23342 **Hazaaf (USA) (59)** *(AAScott)* 3-9-2 BRaymond (5) (lw: chsd ldrs: disp ld wl over 1f out: r.o) ............................................ −1
22674 Samain (USA) **(49)** *(JAGlover)* 5-8-12 ‡5SWilliams (8) (lw: hld up & bhd: stdy hdwy on outside 5f out: disp ld over 1f out: sn hdd: r.o) ... nk.2

2420★ Escape Talk (26) (JDooler) 5–7–8 (6x) JFanning (4) (chsd ldr tl outpcd 7f out: hdwy over 1f out: fin wl) .................................................. 3½.3
2473 Checkpoint Charlie (60) (JMPEustace) 7–10–0 MTebbutt (2) (bhd: hdwy 3f out: one pce appr fnl f) ........................................................... hd.4
2204² Sweet Request (42) (JRBostock) 4–8–10 JLowe (13) (in tch: hdwy to chal 3f out: one pce appr fnl f) ...................................................... 7.5
2204⁵ Red Jam Jar (29) (JMackie) 7–7–11 JQuinn (11) (b: trckd ldrs: effrt 3f out: n.m.r ent st: sn btn) ................................................................ 4.6
2422⁵ Thimbalina (42) (Fav) (DAWilson) 6–8–5 ‡⁵OPears (10) (b: mid div: effrt 4f out: no imp) .................................................................. 2½.7
2329² Luks Akura (46) (v) (MJohnston) 4–8–7 ‡⁷MBaird (9) (led after 2f: sn clr: edgd rt ent st: sn hdd & btn) ................................................... s.h.8
2250³ Kenyatta (USA) (65) (DenysSmith) 3–9–8 NConnorton (3) (effrt on ins whn n.m.r 4f out: n.d) ................................................................. 1½.9
Bijou Princess (45) (ABailey) 4–8–13 AMackay (1) (bhd: drvn along 5f out: n.d) ½.10
2540² Eire Leath-Sceal (53) (MBrittain) 5–9–7 KDarley (7) (lw: led 2f: chsd ldrs tl wknd 4f out: eased whn btn) ...................................... 1.11
2235 Access Cruise (USA) (48) (BAMcMahon) 5–9–2 JFortune (12) (bhd: hdwy & ev ch 3f out: wknd wl over 1f out) ...................................... 2.12
1580⁶ Nipotina (36) (RHollinshead) 6–7–11 ‡⁷AGarth (6) (swtg: prom tl wknd 4f out) 12.13

9/2 Thimbalina, 6/1 Samain (USA), 7/1 Eire Leath-Sceal, Sweet Request, 15/2 HAZAAF (USA), 10/1 Kenyatta (USA), Luks Akura, Escape Talk, 14/1 Red Jam Jar, Checkpoint Charlie, 16/1 Nipotina, 25/1 Access Cruise (USA), 33/1 Bijou Princess. CSF £49.10, CT £418.40. Tote £6.70: £2.50 £2.30 £3.50 (£23.80). Maktoum Al Maktoum (NEWMARKET) bred by Bruce Hundley & W. M. Allen in USA. 13 Rn                    2m 38.5 (4)
SF—44/39/14/47/15/–

**2606**     TATTERSALLS AUCTION SERIES STKS (Qualifier) (Mdn 2-Y.O) £2978.50 (£826.00: £395.50)   **6f**                                                4-50 (4-54)

2277² Brandonhurst (Fav) (IABalding) 8–10 RCochrane (1) (lw: in tch: hdwy ent st: led over 1f out: r.o) ........................................................... —1
1171 Mena (JWPayne) 8–0 JQuinn (8) (bhd: hdwy 2f out: hung lft: r.o wl) ..... 1½.2
2350² Runrig (IRE) (MissLAPerratt) 8–1 JFanning (4) (bhd: hdwy ½-wy: nt clr run & bdly hmpd 1f out: swtchd & r.o wl) ......................................... 3½.3
Wanza (JHanson) 8–11 EJohnson (11) (w'like: str: scope: led tl hdd & no ex 1f out) ................................................................................ 3.4
2425⁴ Breaking Hearts (IRE) (APStringer) 7–10⁽¹⁾ ‡⁵SMaloney (3) (lw: chsd ldrs tl grad wknd fnl 2f) ................................................................. ½.5
1664⁴ Ann Hill (IRE) (79) (RHollinshead) 8–2⁽¹⁾ WRyan (7) (swtg: bhd: effrt ent st: no imp) ......................................................................... 2.6
2074³ Andrula Mou (RBoss) 8–5 MTebbutt (5) (cl up: disp ld over 1f out: hung lft & sn wknd) .................................................................... hd.7
Manadel (SRBowring) 8–0 AProud (2) (lengthy: bit bkwd: disp ld to ½-wy: wknd qckly 2f out) .............................................................. 25.8
287⁶ Wrightmill (IRE) (CTinkler) 8–9 MBirch (10) (a bhd) ................................. 2.9
1448 Great Mashhor (v) (JSWainwright) 8–8 LCharnock (9) (outpcd ½-wy: sn bhd) 1½.10
2002 Target Line (DMcCain) 8–1 ‡⁵NKennedy (6) (spd 3f: rdn & wknd qckly) .... 1½.11

4/6 BRANDONHURST, 7/2 Runrig (IRE), 8/1 Andrula Mou, 12/1 Wanza, 16/1 Ann Hill (IRE), 25/1 Breaking Hearts (IRE), 33/1 Wrightmill (IRE), Mena, 66/1 Manadel, 100/1 Ors. CSF £23.02, Tote £1.70: £1.50 £5.20 £1.80 (£25.50). Mr R. P. B. Michaelson (KINGSCLERE) bred by Hockley Ltd. 11 Rn                    1m 17.3 (3.3)
SF—12/–/–/–/–/–

**2607**     LEDSTONE CLAIMING H'CAP (0-60) £3036.00 (£846.00: £408.00)   **1m 4y**                                                5-20 (5-23)

2351⁴ **Imhotep (45)** (MrsGRReveley) 5–9–2 KDarley (6) (led after 1f: qcknd clr ent st: r.o wl) ........................................................................... —1
Sweet Revival (32) (JAGlover) 4–8–3 JFortune (11) (in tch: hdwy 3f out: r.o wl u.p fnl f) .................................................................. 1½.2
2253 Please Please Me (IRE) (29) (KOCunningham-Brown) 4–8–0 NCarlisle (20) (hdwy over 2f out: r.o wl fnl f) ...................................... 1½.3
2198 Kelly's Kite (33) (HJCollingridge) 4–8–4 JQuinn (4) (swtg: chsd ldrs: hmpd over 2f out: r.o u.p fnl f) .................................................. s.h.4
2413 High Baccarat (52) (v) (CCElsey) 3–9–2 TRogers (19) (a chsng ldrs: no ex appr fnl f) .................................................................... 1½.5
2413² Breezed Well (57) (CNAllen) 6–9–7 ‡⁷GForster (9) (s.i.s: bhd tl hdwy over 2f out: styd on wl nr fin) .............................................. 1.6
2291 Bobbie Bold (36) (RO'Leary) 4–8–7 MBirch (21) (bhd: hld up: swtchd & hdwy over 1f out: styd on wl) ............................................ hd.7
2517³ Sky Cat (41) (v) (CTinkler) 8–8–7 ‡⁵JWeaver (10) (swtg: hdwy & prom appr st: rdn & btn over 1f out) ...................................... nk.8

1840⁴ Honey Boy Simba (39) (v) (MO'Neill) 6–8–10 DMcKeown (14) (lw: chsd ldrs tl
      outpcd fnl 2f) .................................................................................. 3¹/₂.9
2379² Pride of Pendle (53) (PCalver) 3–8–10 ‡⁷JTate (1) (dwlt: nvr nrr) ................... 7.10
2291³ Miss Magenta (IRE) (35) (RThompson) 4–8–6 AMackay (3) (b: stumbled bnd
      after 1f: n.d) ................................................................................... 1¹/₂.11
2289 Chaff (30) (DMorris) 5–8–1 JLowe (17) (n.d) .............................................. s.h.12
2254 Lawnswood Prince (IRE) (49) (JLSpearing) 3–8–13 AlexGreaves (2) (s.i.s: n.d) ³/₄.13
1964 Chance Report (35) (FHLee) 4–8–1 ‡⁵NKennedy (18) (led 1f: chsd ldrs tl wknd
      over 2f out) ...................................................................................... 8.14
2354⁶ Simply Candy (IRE) (0) (APStringer) 4–8–6 ‡SMaloney (5) (lw: pushed along
      ¹/₂-wy: n.d) ...................................................................................... ¹/₂.15
2384 Barmbrack (44) (RMWhitaker) 3–8–8 ACulhane (8) (a bhd) ......................... 2.16
2384⁶ Phil-Man (46) (TFairhurst) 3–8–10 JFanning (22) (n.d) ................................ 2¹/₂.17
1787⁶ Dreaming Echo (300) (JBalding) 4–7–8 ‡⁷ClaireBalding (7) (a bhd) ............... 2¹/₂.18
962 Tibby Head (IRE) (45) (JMackie) 4–9–2 GBaxter (13) (in tch 5f) ..................... 2.19
2487⁴ Reza (50) (JLEyre) 4–9–2 ‡⁵OPears (15) (b: in tch & drvn along ¹/₂-wy: n.d after) 3¹/₂.20
2469* Spanish Express (51) (v) (RBoss) 3–9–1 (6x) BRaymond (12) (lw: trckd
      ldrs: effrt 3f out: wknd qckly) ............................................................ 1¹/₂.21
     2263⁴ Premier Major (IRE) (10/1) Withdrawn (lame at s) : not under orders

**5/1** Spanish Express, **6/1** Breezed Well, **8/1** IMHOTEP, Pride of Pendle, Kelly's Kite, **9/1** Miss Magenta (IRE), Sky
Cat, **12/1** Honey Boy Simba, **14/1** Bobbie Bold, Phil-Man, Sweet Revival, **16/1** Chance Report, Tibby Head (IRE),
Reza, **20/1** Chaff, **25/1** Lawnswood Prince (IRE), **33/1** Please Please Me (IRE), Barmbrack, Simply Candy (IRE),
**50/1** Ors. CSF £123.12, CT £3,287.99. Tote £9.80: £3.00 £4.60 £3.80 £2.20 (£216.70). Mrs E. A. Kettlewell
(SALTBURN) bred by Blackdown Stud. 21 Rn
                                                                     1m 44.2 (2.6)
                                                                    SF—39/21/13/16/23/25

---

**2608**    E.B.F. FEATHERSTONE STKS (Mdn 2-Y.O) £2684.50 (£742.00: £353.50)
        6f                                                                 5-50 (5-52)

1845² Goodbye Millie (Fav) (SGNorton) 8–9 JFortune (1) (lw: mde all: shkn up 2f out:
      r.o wl) ............................................................................................. —1
   Killy's Filly (JBerry) 8–9 JCarroll (2) (lengthy: scope: bit bkwd: chsd wnr: rdn 2f
      out: nt qckn) ................................................................................... 2¹/₂.2
   Light the Bay (MrsVAAconley) 8–9 LCharnock (3) (cmpt: bit bkwd: unruly s:
      chsd ldrs: rdn ¹/₂-wy: no imp) ............................................................. 3.3

**4/9** GOODBYE MILLIE, **3/1** Killy's Filly(op 2/1), **13/2** Light the Bay. CSF £1.98, Tote £1.40 (£1.20). Mr G. Corbett
(BARNSLEY) bred by G. Corbett. 3 Rn                                          1m 18.4 (4.4)
T/Plpt: £385.50 (11.95 Tckts).                                                             AA

---

# PONTEFRACT (L-H)
## Thursday, August 6th [Firm]
Going Allowance: minus 0.30 sec per fur (F)                            Wind: slt half bhd

Stalls: low

**2609**    WHITELANE-PONTEFRACT APP'CE SERIES H'CAP (Rnd 3) (0-70) £2385.00 (£660.00:
        £315.00)   1¹/₄m 6y                                              2-50 (2-50)

1143 **Vague Dancer** (60) (Jt-Fav) (MrsJRRamsden) 6–9–4 JWeaver (2) (lw: hld up:
      stdy hdwy 4f out: led over 1f out: sn clr: comf) ...................................... —1
2113⁵ Katy's Lad (67) (Jt-Fav) (BAMcMahon) 5–9–11 SSanders (7) (led tl hdd over 1f
      out: no ch w wnr) ............................................................................. 3.2
2422 Overpower (64) (MHTompkins) 8–9–4 ‡⁴MGodsafe (4) (hld up & bhd: hdwy 4f
      out: styd on fnl f: no imp) .................................................................. 3.3
2417⁶ Sean's Scholar (USA) (49) (Jt-Fav) (CNAllen) 5–8–7 GForster (3) (a.p: chal 3f
      out: rdn & btn wl over 1f out) ............................................................ 2.4
2531³ Magnetic Point (USA) (58) (AAScott) 3–8–7 JTate (5) (cl up: chal 3f out: rdn &
      fnd nil appr fnl f) ............................................................................. nk.5
2468³ Bidweaya (USA) (43) (JLEyre) 5–8–1 OPears (1) (chsd ldrs: chal 3f out: rdn &
      wknd over 1f out) ............................................................................. 7.6
2420 Millie (USA) (56) (GFleming) 4–9–0 StephenDavies (6) (cl up tl wknd 5f out: sn
      bhd) .............................................................................................. 8.7

**4/1** VAGUE DANCER, Sean's Scholar (USA), Katy's Lad, **5/1** Magnetic Point (USA), Bidweaya (USA), **7/1**
Overpower, **33/1** Millie (USA). CSF £17.97, Tote £4.00: £2.20 £2.40 (£8.40). Mr K. E. Wheldon (THIRSK) bred
by P. Haworth. 7 Rn                                                            2m 12.5 (4.2)
                                                                    SF—32/33/20/5/4/–

**2610**    E.B.F. CARLETON STKS (Mdn 2-Y.O) £2513.00 (£693.00: £329.00)    5f    3-20 (3-20)

|       | **Celestial Key (USA)** (SGNorton) 9-0 KDarley (2) (scope: bit bkwd: led early: chsd ldr: sn pushed along: led ins fnl f: r.o wl) | —1 |
|-------|------|------|
|       | Blow Dry (IRE) (Fav) (JHanson) 9-0 EJohnson (3) (gd sort: bit bkwd: sn led tl hdd ins fnl f: rdn & r.o) | 1/2.2 |
| 2381  | Beanshoot (JBerry) 8-9 JCarroll (1) (cmpt: bit bkwd: sn outpcd & bhd) | 20.3 |
|       | Super Scenario (EJAlston) 9-0 KFallon (4) (w'like: bit bkwd: sn outpcd & bhd) | 12.4 |

**11/10** Blow Dry (IRE), **2/1** CELESTIAL KEY (USA), **3/1** Beanshoot(op 2/1), **25/1** Super Scenario. CSF £4.43, Tote £3.50 (£2.10). Mr M. J. Brodrick (BARNSLEY) bred by Pillar Stud, Inc. in USA. 4 Rn    63.1 sec (1.6)
SF—38/36/–/–

**2611**    ROTHMANS ROYALS NORTH SOUTH CHALLENGE SERIES H'CAP (0-90) £4012.50 (£1200.00: £575.00: £262.50)    1m 4y    3-50 (3-51)

| 2341★ | **State Dancer (USA)** (88) (Fav) (MMoubarak) 5-9-9 ‡5StephenDavies (4) (lw: trckd ldrs: hdwy to ld over 1f out: rdn & r.o wl) | —1 |
|-------|------|------|
| 2352³ | Spanish Verdict (69) (DenysSmith) 5-8-9 KFallon (5) (lw: hld up: effrt 3f out: r.o u.p fnl f: nrst fin) | nk.2 |
| 2369² | Causley (77) (BAMcMahon) 7-9-3 BRaymond (2) (lw: led tl hdd over 1f out: one pce) | 1½.3 |
| 2184  | Elegant Friend (68) (MHTompkins) 4–8-8 PRobinson (1) (swtg: chsd ldrs: effrt & ev ch over 1f out: nt qckn) | hd.4 |
|       | Caleman (86) (RBoss) 3–9-5 MRoberts (3) (chsd ldr: effrt 2f out: sn rdn & btn) | 5.5 |

**2/1** STATE DANCER (USA), **5/2** Spanish Verdict, **9/2** Elegant Friend(6/1—4/1), **5/1** Causley, **13/2** Caleman. CSF £6.91, Tote £2.90: £1.50 £1.60 (£4.40). Ecurie Fustok (NEWMARKET) bred by Blue Grass Breeders Inc., et al. in USA. 5 Rn    1m 42.5 (0.9)
SF—59/44/47/37/33

**2612**    DIANNE NURSERY    £2820.00 (£840.00: £400.00: £180.00)    6f    4-20 (4-20)

| 2193⁶ | **Walsham Witch** (68) (MHTompkins) 8-9 PRobinson (1) (mde most: r.o u.p fnl f) | —1 |
|-------|------|------|
| 2221² | Bold Seven (IRE) (77) (FHLee) 9-4 RLappin (4) (chsd ldrs: chal 1f out: r.o) | ¾.2 |
| 2387★ | Tarnside Rosal (78) (Fav) (JEtherington) 9-5 (7x) JCarroll (3) (lw: hld up: effrt ent st: n.m.r & nt qckn) | 2.3 |
| 2223★ | Dahliz (IRE) (75) (HThomsonJones) 9-2 NCarlisle (2) (lw: chsd ldr over 4f: r.o one pce) | nk.4 |
| 2157★ | Penang Star (IRE) (80) (WAO'Gorman) 9-4 ‡3EmmaO'Gorman (5) (lw: chsd ldrs tl rdn & btn over 2f out: eased considerably fnl f) | 25.5 |

**2/1** Tarnside Rosal, **9/4** Dahliz (IRE)(op 7/2), **11/2** Bold Seven (IRE), Penang Star (IRE), **6/1** WALSHAM WITCH. CSF £30.97, Tote £5.80: £2.00 £2.70 (£17.10). Mr J. H. Ellis (NEWMARKET) bred by J. R. Mitchell. 5 Rn    1m 16.2 (2.2)
SF—15/21/14/10/–

**2613**    UPTON CLAIMING STKS (3-Y.O) £2343.00 (£648.00: £309.00)    1½m 8y    4-50 (4-53)

| 2485★ | **Grouse-N-Heather** (60) (Jt-Fav) (MrsGRReveley) 8-4 JFanning (3) (lw: a.p: rdn to ld over 1f out: styd on wl) | —1 |
|-------|------|------|
| 2533² | Salu (53) (v) (JEtherington) 7-7(1) ‡3FNorton (6) (a in tch: hdwy & ev ch over 1f out: rdn & nt r.o) | 1½.2 |
| 2430² | Silver Samurai (70) (Jt-Fav) (RHollinshead) 8-10 WRyan (4) (led early: led 5f out tl over 1f out: nt qckn) | ¾.3 |
| 2351⁶ | Clair Soleil (USA) (DenysSmith) 8-6 KFallon (8) (chsd ldrs: effrt appr st: sn outpcd) | 6.4 |
| 2392⁵ | Futures Gift (IRE) (50) (AWPotts) 8-6 SWebster (5) (prom tl lost pl 4f out: styd on wl fnl f) | s.h.5 |
|       | Croft House (JDooler) 7-12(1) ‡5OPears (2) (b.hind: unruly gng to post: s.i.s: hld up & effrt 6f out: sn btn) | 20.6 |
| 2472⁵ | Scorton (IRE) (MDods) 8-4 PBurke (7) (plld hrd: sn led: hdd 5f out: wknd qckly & sn t.o: p.u ins fnl f) | 0 |

**6/4** GROUSE-N-HEATHER, Silver Samurai, **9/2** Salu, **14/1** Futures Gift (IRE), **33/1** Clair Soleil (USA), **50/1** Croft House, **66/1** Scorton (IRE). CSF £8.05, Tote £2.40: £1.40 £1.70 (£5.10). Mr Robbie Cameron (SALTBURN) bred by R. A. Cameron. 7 Rn    2m 38.8 (4.3)
SF—11/–/12/–/–/–

**2614**　JIM GUNDILL MEMORIAL H'CAP (0-70) £3210.00 (£960.00: £460.00: £210.00)
6f
5-20 (5-23)

(Weights raised 8 lb)

22835 **Ushba (FR)** (53) (CGCox) 4-9-5 MRoberts (3) (b.hind: mde most: hung rt fnl 2f: all out) ............................................................... —1

1512* Nordan Raider (48) (Fav) (MJCamacho) 4-9-0 NConnorton (6) (lw: trckd ldrs: hdwy over 2f out: sn chsng wnr: nt qckn ins fnl f) ............... ½.2

21442 Granny Mc (58) (EJAlston) 5-9-10 PRobinson (8) (chsd ldrs: rdn over 2f out: styd on one pce) ............................................. 1½.3

2325 Blue Grit (50) (MDods) 6-9-2 KFallon (11) (outpcd tl hdwy 2f out: r.o nr fin) .... s.h.4

2481 Strip Cartoon (IRE) (53) (SRBowring) 4-9-5 JQuinn (1) (led early: cl up tl wknd 2f out) .................................................. 2.5

2361* Coolaba Prince (IRE) (60) (FHLee) 3-9-7 RLappin (7) (a chsng ldrs: rdn ½-wy: wknd over 1f out) .......................................... 4.6

25364 Double Feature (IRE) (62) (MrsJRRamsden) 3-9-9 MBirch (4) (nvr nr to chal) ... 5.7

22224 Brisas (46) (bl) (TFairhurst) 5-8-12 JFanning (10) (chsd ldrs over 4f) ............ 3.8

19185 Virginia Cottage (46) (BAMcMahon) 3-8-7 JLowe (2) (nvr plcd to chal) ........ 2½.9

2466 Dreams Eyes (31) (RBastiman) 4-7-8 ‡3FNorton (9) (hld up & bhd: n.d) .......... 2.10

2/1 Nordan Raider, 4/1 USHBA (FR), 6/1 Blue Grit, 9/1 Granny Mc, Coolaba Prince (IRE), 10/1 Strip Cartoon (IRE), 11/1 Double Feature (IRE)(8/1—12/1), 14/1 Brisas, 25/1 Ors. CSF £12.07, CT £60.10. Tote £3.80: £1.60 £1.40 £2.50 (£5.00). Mrs S. J. Stovold (LYNEHAM) bred by Darley Stud Management in France. 10 Rn
1m 15.2 (1.2)
SF—45/38/42/33/28/14

**2615**　STEWARDS STKS (Mdn 3-Y.O) £2511.00 (£696.00: £333.00)　1¼m 6y 5-50 (5-53)

**Almuhtarāma (IRE)** (ACStewart) 0 0 MRoberts (4) (w'like: cl up: led 4f out: rdn & r.o wl appr fnl f) ......................................... —1

9102 Indian Jack (IRE) (MajorWRHern) 9-0 RCochrane (3) (hld up: hdwy 4f out: chal 2f out: styd on wl) ........................................ ¾.2

12454 Kabayil (Fav) (PTWalwyn) 8-9 PRobinson (2) (lw: trckd ldr: effrt 3f out: one pce fnl 2f) ..................................................... 7.3

19035 Cheeka (MRLeach) 9-0 DNicholls (1) (reluctant to ent stalls: led tl hdd 4f out: hmpd over 3f out: sn wl bhd) ......................... dist.4

13/8 Kabayil, 2/1 Indian Jack (IRE), ALMUHTARAMA (IRE), 20/1 Cheeka. CSF £5.92, Tote £2.80 (£2.40). Sheikh Ahmed Al Maktoum (NEWMARKET) bred by R. Ades in Ireland. 4 Rn
2m 11.2 (2.9)
SF—36/39/20/–

T/Plpt: £329.70 (9.25 Tckts).　　　　　　　　　　　　　　　　　　　　　　　AA

## 2225—BATH (L-H)

### Thursday, August 6th [Firm]

Going Allowance: minus 0.25 sec per fur (F)　　　　　　　　　　　Wind: nil

Stalls: low

**2616**　PINKNEY APP'CE H'CAP (3-Y.O) (0-70) £2355.00 (£655.00: £315.00)
1m 5y
2-10 (2-24)

22662 **Emaura** (56) (KOCunningham-Brown) 8-4 ‡3MBressington (5) (led 7f out: shkn up over 1f out: r.o wl) .................................. —1

22666 Mr Tate (IRE) (59) (Fav) (RAkehurst) 8-10 LCarter (10) (hdwy over 2f out: hrd rdn over 1f out: one pce) ............................. 1½.2

18855 Spanish Glory (52) (bl) (IABalding) 8-0 ‡3DGriffiths (3) (lw: 3rd st: rdn over 1f out: nt qckn) .............................................. ½.3

2496 Athar (IRE) (50) (RJBaker) 7-12 ‡3RWaterfield (1) (hdwy 2f out: r.o one pce fnl f) 2.4

2422 Mindomica (58) (MBell) 8-9 ACairns (8) (lw: hld up: hdwy 4f out: 4th st: wknd over 1f out) ...................................................... hd.5

2496* Singers Image (66) (v) (GBBalding) 9-3 (6x) TraceyPursegloye (6) (hld up & bhd: nvr nr to chal) ......................................... 3.6

1565 My Boy Buster (42) (CJHill) 7-7 BRussell (7) (swtg: led 1f: 2nd st: wknd 2f out) ¾.7

2493 Sizzling Affair (53) (TCasey) 8-4 GMilligan (9) (5th st: wknd 2f out) ............ 2.8

1922 So Beguiling (USA) (43) (v) (MrsALMKing) 7-8(1) DCarson (11) (5th st: wknd over 2f out: t.o) ................................................ 12.9

2496 Mustahil (IRE) (70) (RJHodges) 9-7 TThompson (4) (bhd tl p.u over 3f out) .......... 0
LONG HANDICAP: My Boy Buster 7-5, So Beguiling (USA) 6-11.
2165* Edgeaway (5/1) Withdrawn (broke out of stalls) : not under orders

**100/30** Mr Tate (IRE)(3/1—9/2), **7/2** EMAURA, **9/2** Singers Image, **11/2** Spanish Glory, **6/1** Mindomica, **7/1** Mustahil (IRE), **14/1** Athar (IRE), **25/1** My Boy Buster, **33/1** Ors. CSF £15.47, CT £57.49. Tote £3.80: £1.50 £1.60 £1.80 (£10.30). Mr D. Bass (STOCKBRIDGE) bred by Mrs P. J. Van Straubenzee and C. J. R. Trotter. 10 Rn
1m 41.2 (1.9)
SF—31/32/20/12/22/21

| 2617 | AUGUST (S) STKS | £2600.00 (£725.00: £350.00) | **5f 161y** | 2-40 (2-53) |

| | | | |
|---|---|---|---|
| 2209* | **Surrey Racing (63)** (GLewis) 4–9-0 BRouse (14) (lw: hdwy 2f out: led wl ins fnl f: r.o wl) | | —1 |
| 2234⁴ | Nuclear Express (58) (RLee) 5–8-7 ‡⁷SDrowne (3) (b: a.p: led ins fnl f: sn hdd: r.o) | | 1.2 |
| 2227⁶ | Unveiled (61) (Fav) (RJHodges) 4–8-9 WCarson (15) (hdwy 2f out: ev ch ins fnl f: nt qckn) | | 1.3 |
| 2548 | Wilco (52) (AndrewTurnell) 3–8-9 RHills (7) (a.p: led over 1f out tl ins fnl f) | | hd.4 |
| 2209³ | Slip-a-Snip (64) (GBBalding) 5–8-9 JWilliams (16) (lw: hdwy wl over 1f out: nvr nr to chal) | | ½.5 |
| 2548 | Sea Crusader (47) (bl) (MBlanshard) 3–8-9 WNewnes (10) (a.p: led 2f out tl over 1f out: wknd ins fnl f) | | ½.6 |
| 1258⁵ | Forlorn Diver (45) (BGubby) 4–8-7 ‡⁷CAvery (4) (no hdwy fnl 2f) | | 1½.7 |
| 2502⁴ | Farmer Jock (57) (MrsNMacauley) 10–9-0 WWharton (5) (prom over 3f) | | ½.8 |
| 2234² | Melodic Habit (45) (MrsAKnight) 5–8-9 SWhitworth (9) (led over 3f: wknd over 1f out) | | 1½.9 |
| 1030² | Pendor Dancer (54) (bl) (BForsey) 9–9-0 NHowe (17) (prom 4f) | | s.h.10 |
| 2481 | In a Whirl (USA) (46) (DRLaing) 4–8-9 TyroneWilliams (2) (lw: prom: hrd rdn over 2f out: wknd over 1f out) | | 2.11 |
| 2493⁵ | Orchard Bay (46) (DRTucker) 3–7-13 ‡⁵ATucker (18) (bhd fnl 3f) | | ½.12 |
| 594 | Grand Time (59) (CJHill) 3–8-9 NAdams (11) (a bhd) | | ½.13 |
| 1009 | Princess Jestina (IRE) (35) (GHYardley) 4–8-9 BCrossley (6) (n.d) | | d.h.13 |
| 2493 | Ben Bluff (48) (bl) (LGCottrell) 3–8-9 TRogers (1) (a bhd) | | 1.15 |
| 2290 | Goody Four Shoes (40) (DRTucker) 4–8-9 CRutter (13) (a bhd) | | hd.16 |
| 1903 | Bella's Match (34) (bl) (BPalling) 3–8-4 AMcGlone (12) (bhd fnl 3f: t.o) | | 20.17 |

**3/1** Unveiled, **5/1** Slip-a-Snip, SURREY RACING, **6/1** Farmer Jock, **10/1** Melodic Habit(op 6/1), **11/1** Nuclear Express(7/1—12/1), **16/1** Pendor Dancer, Grand Time, Wilco, **20/1** In a Whirl (USA), **25/1** Sea Crusader, Orchard Bay, **33/1** Ben Bluff, Goody Four Shoes, **66/1** Ors. CSF £57.81, Tote £4.60: £2.30 £4.10 £2.00 (£47.70). Mr K. Higson (EPSOM) bred by W. R. Swinburn. 17 Rn; No bid
1m 11 (1.7)
SF—39/28/26/25/17/15

| 2618 | BACKHOUSE PENSIONERS SPRINT H'CAP (0-80) £3600.00 (£1080.00: £520.00: £240.00) | **5f 11y** | 3-10 (3-22) |

| | | | |
|---|---|---|---|
| 2499* | **Spring High (53)** (bl) (KTIvory) 5–8-1 (6x) GBardwell (2) (a.p: led 1f out: all out) | | —1 |
| 1755⁵ | How's Yer Father (78) (RJHodges) 6–9-12 ADicks (6) (hdwy over 1f out: n.m.r ins fnl f: r.o wl) | | hd.2 |
| 2478 | Gallant Hope (57) (LGCottrell) 10–8-5 JWilliams (1) (dwlt: hdwy on ins 2f out: swtchd rt ins fnl f: r.o wl) | | s.h.3 |
| 2227 | Cee-En-Cee (70) (bl) (Fav) (MMcCourt) 8–9-4 CRutter (8) (bhd: hmpd 2f out: gd hdwy fnl f: fin wl) | | ¾.4 |
| 2395² | Samson-Agonistes (73) (BAMcMahon) 6–9-7 WNewnes (7) (a.p: led 2f out to 1f out: no ex) | | ½.5 |
| 2589³ | Catalani (50) (TJNaughton) 7–7-12 AMcGlone (3) (b: a.p: ev ch over 1f out: one pce fnl f) | | s.h.6 |
| 2301⁵ | Maid Welcome (63) (bl) (MrsNMacauley) 5–8-11 WWharton (11) (led 3f: wknd over 1f out) | | 3.7 |
| 2494⁶ | Respectable Jones (71) (GBBalding) 6–9-5 SWhitworth (9) (nvr trbld ldrs) | | nk.8 |
| | Red River Boy (48) (RJHodges) 9–7-10 DanaMellor (5) (prom 3f) | | 1½.9 |
| 2435 | Grand Prix (80) (DRCElsworth) 7–10-0 SDawson (10) (bhd fnl 2f) | | 2½.10 |
| 2333⁴ | Oratel Flyer (45) (v) (RThompson) 5–7-7 NAdams (4) (bhd fnl 2f) | | s.h.11 |

LONG HANDICAP: Oratel Flyer 6-1.

**7/2** Cee-En-Cee, **9/2** Samson-Agonistes, **6/1** SPRING HIGH(5/1—15/2), **7/1** Catalani, Grand Prix, **8/1** Maid Welcome, **10/1** Gallant Hope, How's Yer Father, Respectable Jones, **50/1** Ors. CSF £59.85, CT £539.37. Tote £6.70: £2.40 £2.40 £2.40 (£55.10). Mr K. T. Ivory (RADLETT) bred by Mrs P. A. Brown. 11 Rn 61.5 sec (1)
SF—42/66/44/54/55/31

| 2619 | WILLESLEY STKS (Mdn 2-Y.O) £2756.00 (£766.00: £368.00) | **5f 161y** | 3-40 (3-53) |

| | | | |
|---|---|---|---|
| | **Amazing Baby (USA)** (DRCElsworth) 8-9 JWilliams (6) (unf: scope: a.p: rdn over 1f out: r.o to ld last strides) | | —1 |
| 2346 | Mawayed (USA) (Fav) (PTWalwyn) 9-0 WCarson (2) (led: rdn fnl f: hdd last strides) | | nk.2 |

1748⁵ Galejade *(DHaydnJones)* 8-9 WNewnes (7) (prom: rdn & r.o one pce fnl 2f) ..... 4.3
    Pat Poindestres *(MPMuggeridge)* 8-9 BRouse (8) (small: unf: bkwd: chsd ldrs tl
        wknd over 1f out) ..................................................................................... 3.4
    Bold a Maiden *(DRLaing)* 8-9 TyroneWilliams (5) (unf: prom: ev ch 2f out: wknd
        over 1f out) ........................................................................................... 6.5
    Monday At Three *(BRMillman)* 9-0 AMcGlone (1) (unf: rdn 3f out: sn bhd) ........ 8.6
2368  It Bites (IRE) *(APJames)* 8-9 SDawson (4) (sn outpcd) .................................... 6.7
    Over the Cliffs (IRE) *(JABennett)* 8-9 GBardwell (3) (unf: outpcd: t.o) ............... 15.8

**8/13** Mawayed (USA), **2/1** AMAZING BABY (USA), **11/1** Galejade, **14/1** Bold a Maiden, **50/1** Monday At Three, **66/1** Ors. CSF £3.48, Tote £3.30: £1.20 £1.10 £1.60 (£1.70). Sheikh Ahmed Al Maktoum (WHITSBURY) bred by Foxfield in USA. 8 Rn
                                                              1m 11.8 (2.5)
                                                          SF—18/22/1/–/–/–

## 2620
SILKWOOD STKS (Mdn 3-Y.O.F) £2756.00 (£766.00: £368.00)
1¹/₄m 46y
                                                      4-10 (4-20)

2270⁵ **Shahaamh (IRE)** *(HThomsonJones)* 8-11 RHills (1) (mde all: shkn up & qcknd
        over 1f out: readily) .............................................................................. —1
    Annacurragh (IRE) *(ACStewart)* 8-11 AMcGlone (7) (unf: scope: wnt 2nd st: rdn
        2f out: no imp) ...................................................................................... 3.2
2270² Goodniteout (IRE) **(83)** *(DRCElsworth)* 8-11 WCarson (3) (chsd wnr tl 3rd
        st: hrd rdn over 2f out) ......................................................................... 3.3
425⁵ Glacial Moon (USA) *(BWHills)* 8-11 JWilliams (4) (hld up: 6th st: no hdwy fnl 2f) 3.4
    Esprit Fort (USA) *(PWChapple-Hyam)* 8-11 WNewnes (2) (rdn & 5th st: wknd 2f
        out) ...................................................................................................... 1.5
902⁵ Hymn Book (IRE) **(72)** *(RJManning)* 8-11 BRouse (6) (hdwy 4f out: 4th st: wknd
        2f out) .................................................................................................. s.h.6
2370⁵ Alto Princess *(APJones)* 0 11 NIAdams (5) (last st: a in rr: t.o) ..................... 12.7

**1/2** Goodniteout (IRE), **11/2** Glacial Moon (USA)(3/1—6/1), **6/1** Annacurragh (IRE)(4/1—13/2), **7/1** SHAHAAMH (IRE), **16/1** Esprit Fort (USA), **50/1** Hymn Book (IRE), **66/1** Alto Princess. CSF £44.22, Tote £6.80: £2.60 £3.10 (£23.40). Mr Hamdan Al-Maktoum (NEWMARKET) bred by Shadwell Estate Company Limited in Ireland. 7 Rn
                                                           2m 9.8 (2.1)
                                                           SF—51/45/39/33/31/30

## 2621
COLERNE H'CAP (0-70) £2921.00 (£878.00: £424.00: £197.00)
1m 3f 144y
                                                      4-40 (4-46)

972 **Moon Spin (64)** *(MajorWRHern)* 3-9-10 WCarson (7) (3rd st: nt clr run
        over 2f out: qcknd to ld over 1f out: easily) ........................................... —1
2413⁶ Admiralty Way **(40)** *(RBrotherton)* 6-8-11 JWilliams (4) (lw: hld up: hdwy & 4th
        st: led 2f out tl over 1f out) .................................................................. 2¹/₂.2
2255⁴ Antico Nativo (IRE) **(54)** *(SDow)* 4-9-11 MPerrett (2) (lw: 2nd st: ev ch 2f out:
        hrd rdn: one pce) ................................................................................. 2.3
2014⁶ Baby Wizzard **(52)** *(IABalding)* 3-8-12 CRutter (6) (lw: 6th st: hrd rdn over 2f
        out: sn wknd) ....................................................................................... 5.4
2077 Finaldream (IRE) **(53)** *(AWDenson)* 4-9-10 WNewnes (1) (led over 9f: wknd
        qckly) ................................................................................................... 6.5
2413³ Now Boarding **(41)** *(RJHodges)* 5-8-5 ‡⁷SDrowne (3) (hld up: 5th st: rdn &
        wknd 2f out) ........................................................................................ 4.6
    Irene Lock **(35)** *(DCTucker)* 4-8-6 ADicks (5) (plld hrd: prom over 6f: last st: t.o
        fnl 3f) ................................................................................................... 15.7

**9/4** MOON SPIN, **3/1** Baby Wizzard, **7/2** Now Boarding, **5/1** Antico Nativo (IRE)(op 3/1), **6/1** Admiralty Way, **20/1** Finaldream (IRE), **50/1** Irene Lock. CSF £15.06, Tote £3.30: £2.10 £1.80 (£14.00). Mrs W. R. Hern (LAMBOURN) bred by Wick-Dromdiah Investments Ltd. 7 Rn
                                                           2m 30.7 (4)
                                                      SF—40/22/32/9/9/–

T/Plpt: £139.60 (22.62 Tckts).                                            KH

# VICHY (R-H)
## Friday, July 31st [Good]

## 2622a
GRAND PRIX DE VICHY (Gp 3) £25800.00 1¹/₄m

1454 **Goofalik (USA)** *(France)* 5-9-2 CAsmussen ............................................ —1
1455 Tel Quel (FR) *(France)* 4-9-2 TJarnet .................................................... hd.2
556 Daros (bl) *(France)* 3-8-7 MBoutin ..................................................... 1¹/₂.3
Tote 4.20f: 1.40f 1.20f 4.60f (3.20f). Mr David Thompson (J.E.Hammond,FRANCE) bred by Wertheimer Et Frere in USA. 9 Rn
                                                               2m 3.3

## CLAIREFONTAINE (R-H)
**Friday, July 31st [Good]**

### 2623a
PRIX DES PETUNIAS (3-Y.O) £4644.00    **1m 3f**

|  |  |  |
|---|---|---|
| **Mestre de Camp (FR)** *(France)* 3–8–9  DRegnard | —**1** |
| Force Tranquille (FR) *(France)* 3–9–0  TGillet | 4.**2** |
| Hidden Love *(France)* 3–8–6  FGrenet | nk.**3** |
| 2041  BASILICA *(CEBrittain)* 3–8–8 ‡⁶FSanchez (btn further 3l) | **6** |

Tote 37.90f: 11.70f 1.70f 3.20f. Mr R.Crepon (R.Crepon,FRANCE) bred by Comtesse Bertrand de Tarragon in France. 11 Rn                                                                 2m 42.2

## DEAUVILLE (R-H)
**Saturday, August 1st [Good to soft]**
Going Allowance: minus 0.15 sec per fur (G)

### 2624a
PRIX D'ASTARTE (Gp 2) (F & M) £25800.00    **1m**

| 1357a² | **Hydro Calido (USA)** (Fav) *(France)* 3–8–7  FHead (hld up: str run to ld ins fnl f: wnt clr: impressive) | —**1** |
|---|---|---|
| 1357a★ | Marble Maiden *(France)* 3–8–8⁽¹⁾  SCauthen (a.p: led 1f out tl ins fnl f: nt pce of wnr) | 1¹/₂.**2** |
| 1460 | Euphonic (USA) *(France)* 3–8–7  DBoeuf (cl up to 1f out: sn outpcd & wknd) | 1¹/₂.**3** |
| 2090a³ | CRYSTAL PATH (FR) *(MMoubarak)* 4–9–0  ACruz (led to 1f out: one pce) | 1¹/₂.**4** |
| 1231a | Caerlina (IRE) *(France)* 4–9–0  ELegrix (nvr nrr: one pce fnl 2f) | 1¹/₂.**5** |
|  | Pia Bride (USA) *(France)* 3–8–7  T.Jarnet (prom: btn 2f out) | s.nk.**6** |
|  | Foolish Eclipse (CAN) *(France)* 3–8–7  GMosse (n.d) | 1¹/₂.**7** |
| 1823a³ | Guislaine (FR) *(France)* 3–8–7  CAsmussen (m.n.s) | s.h.**8** |
|  | Eastern Exodus (USA) *(France)* 3–8–7  ODoleuze (a in rr) | 2.**9** |

**23/10** HYDRO CALIDO (USA), **5/2** Guislaine (FR), **19/4** Marble Maiden, **21/4** Caerlina (IRE), **29/4** Euphonic (USA), **17/2** Crystal Path (FR), **10/1** Pia Bride (USA), **32/1** Eastern Exodus (USA), **33/1** Foolish Eclipse (CAN). Tote 3.30f: 1.50f 1.70f 2.70f (6.40f). Mr S.Niarchos (F.Boutin,FRANCE) bred by Flaxman Holdings Ltd. in USA. 9 Rn                                                                 1m 35.8 (U.8)
SF—87/83/77/79/74/66

## DEAUVILLE (R-H)
**Sunday, August 2nd [Good to soft]**
Going Allowance: 0.05 sec per fur (G)

### 2625a
PRIX DE CABOURG (Gp 3) (2-Y.O) £20640.00    **6f**

| 1827a² | **Secrage (USA)** *(Italy)* 2–8–8  BJovine | —**1** |
|---|---|---|
|  | Kingmambo (USA) (bl) *(France)* 2–8–11  FHead | 1.**2** |
|  | Namaqualand *(France)* 2–8–11  SCauthen | 1.**3** |

Tote 13.60f: 6.10f 3.10f (SF: 50.30f). General Horse Advertising (F.Brogi,ITALY) bred by Lucy G.Bassett in USA. 6 Rn                                                                 1m 11.7 (2.7)
SF—46/45/41

### 2626a
PRIX MAURICE DE GHEEST (Gp 2)    £25800.00    **6f 110y**

| 1942² | **PURSUIT OF LOVE** (Fav) *(HRACecil)* 3–8–9  MJKinane (a cl up: led 2f out: r.o wl: impressive) | —**1** |
|---|---|---|
| 655 | Cardoun (FR) *(France)* 3–8–9  DBoeuf (mid div: hdwy wl over 1f out: r.o wl fnl f) | 1¹/₂.**2** |
| 1935⁴ | TWAFEAJ (USA) *(BHanbury)* 3–8–6  WRSwinburn (hld up: str late run: r.o) | 1.**3** |
| 284a⁴ | Ganges (USA) *(France)* 4–9–0  FHead (bhd early: chal wl over 1f out: one pce cl home) | ³/₄.**4** |
|  | Crack Regiment (USA) (bl) *(France)* 4–9–0  ACruz (mid div: sme late hdwy) | 1¹/₂.**5** |
| 1942⁴ | ELBIO *(PJMakin)* 5–9–0  RCochrane (mid div: effrt over 1f out: one pce fnl f) | 1¹/₂.**6** |
| 1822a² | Lion Cavern (USA) *(France)* 3–8–9  SCauthen (mid div: bmpd wl over 1f out: one pce) | 1¹/₂.**7** |
| 1222a³ | Tertian (USA) *(France)* 3–8–9  PatEddery (mid div: bmpd wl over 1f out: one pce) | nk.**8** |
| 1228a² | Reference Light (USA) *(Italy)* 5–9–0  MPlanard (prom 4f: hung sltly & outpcd wl over 1f out) | 6.**9** |
|  | Worldwide (IRE) *(France)* 3–8–9  ELegrix (broke wl: led over 4f out to 2f out: sn wknd) | ¹/₂.**10** |
| 2092a³ | Bradawn Breever (IRE) (bl) *(Ireland)* 3–8–9  RJGriffiths (led 2f: wknd qckly 2f out) | 5.**11** |

**19/10** PURSUIT OF LOVE, **9/4** Lion Cavern (USA), **52/10** Cardoun (FR), **15/2** Elbio, **39/4** Tertian (USA), **12/1** Ganges (USA), **13/1** Reference Light (USA), **29/1** Twafeaj (USA), **30/1** Crack Regiment (USA), **31/1** Worldwide (IRE), **43/1** Bradawn Breever (IRE). Tote 2.90f: 1.60f 2.00f 5.80f (11.80f). Lord Howard de Walden (NEWMARKET) bred by Lord Howard de Walden. 11 Rn                                              1m 16.3 (0.8)
SF—85/79/74/78/72/70

## 960a—MUNICH (L-H)
### Sunday, August 2nd [Good]

**2627a**    GROSSER MERCEDES BENZ PREIS-BAYERISCHES ZUCHTRENNEN (Gp 1)
£98592.00    1¼m

| | | |
|---|---|---|
| 1876★ **Kooyonga (IRE)** *(Ireland)* 4-9-2 WJO'Connor | ............................................... | —**1** |
| 1456² ZAAHI (USA) *(HThomsonJones)* 3-8-7 RHills | ...................................................... | ¾.**2** |
| 1455★ PERPENDICULAR *(HRACecil)* 4-9-6 WRyan | ..................................................... | 1¼.**3** |
| 955a★ Dear Doctor (FR) *(France)* 5-9-6 CAsmussen | ................................................ | s.h.**4** |
| 1497a⁵ Fortune's Wheel (IRE) *(France)* 4-9-6 MBoutin | ............................................ | 2½.**5** |

Tote 18DM: 11DM 12DM 15DM (SF: 84DM). Mr M.Haga (M.Kauntze,IRELAND) bred by Ovidstown Bloodstock Ltd. in Ireland. 7 Rn                                                                                     2m 5.8

## 2315a—NAPLES (R-H)
### Sunday, August 2nd [Good]

**2628a**    GRAN PREMIO CITTA DI NAPOLI (Gp 3)    £2/907.00    1¼m

| | | |
|---|---|---|
| 2315a★ **Guado d'Annibale (IRE)** *(Italy)* 3-8-3 JacquelineFreda | .......................................... | —**1** |
| 1826a³ Taff's Acre (Italy) *(Italy)* 3-8-7 LDettori | ...................................................... | 2.**2** |
| Prospective Ruler (USA) *(Italy)* 4-8-10 GPucciatti | ..................................................... | ¾.**3** |
| 2315a² MARCUS THORPE (USA) *(PAKelleway)* 4-8-10 FJovine (btn further 6½2l) | ............. | **8** |

Tote 74L: 21L 15L 43L (149L). Aterno Stud (A.Renzoni,ITALY) bred by Aterno Stud in Ireland. 11 Rn  2m 1.1

## 2388—WOLVERHAMPTON (L-H)
### Friday, August 7th [Good to firm, Good fnl 7f]
Going Allowance: St: nil sec per fur; Rnd: 0.10 sec per fur (G)                      Wind: almost nil

Stalls: high

**2629**    STARFISH STKS (Mdn 2-Y.O) £2784.00 (£774.00: £372.00)    7f    2-10 (2-16)

| | | |
|---|---|---|
| 2167 **Frivolous Air** *(IABalding)* 8-9 LDettori (11) (5th st: pushed out to ld cl home) | ... | —**1** |
| 2167³ Shamam (USA) *(PTWalwyn)* 9-0 WCarson (5) (led tl hrd rdn & hdd nr fin) | ........ | nk.**2** |
| 2130² Carelaman (Fav) *(JLDunlop)* 9-0 JReid (14) (b.off hind: lw: 6th st: ev ch over 1f out: one pce fnl f) | | 4.**3** |
| 2034 Romalito *(MBlanshard)* 9-0 GCarter (4) (s.i.s: wl bhd tl gd hdwy fnl 2f: r.o) | ...... | 1½.**4** |
| 2398⁵ Nu Shan (IRE) *(MRStoute)* 9-0 SCauthen (13) (4th st: rdn & one pce fnl 2f) | ...... | nk.**5** |
| Giordano (IRE) *(WRMuir)* 8-11 ‡³RPerham (2) (scope: bkwd: 7th st: no hdwy fnl 2f) | ..... | 4.**6** |
| 2248² Dowreyna *(MRStoute)* 8-9 PRobinson (10) (chsd ldr: 2nd st: rdn & ev ch over 1f out: wknd fnl f) | | 1.**7** |
| 1809³ Impair (USA) (bl) *(PFICole)* 9-0 AMunro (9) (8th st: a mid div) | ......................... | nk.**8** |
| 1077⁵ Royal Deed (USA) *(PMMcEntee)* 8-9 AClark (1) (s.i.s: a bhd) | .......................... | 3.**9** |
| Across the Bow (USA) *(IABalding)* 9-0 MRoberts (3) (unf: scope: lw: 5th st: wknd over 2f out) | | 1.**10** |
| Armenian Coffee (IRE) *(JLDunlop)* 9-0 AMcGlone (8) (lengthy: scope: bit bkwd: dwlt: a bhd) | | nk.**11** |
| 2398 Paper Days *(RJHolder)* 9-0 JWilliams (12) (a bhd) | .......................... | nk.**12** |
| Silvies Star *(CDBroad)* 8-9 CRutter (6) (small: scope: bkwd: a bhd: t.o) | .......... | 8.**13** |

**Evens** Carelaman(6/4—7/4), **7/2** Shamam (USA), **15/2** Dowreyna, **10/1** Impair (USA), Nu Shan (IRE)(op 4/1), **12/1** FRIVOLOUS AIR(op 7/1), **14/1** Across the Bow (USA)(op 6/1), **33/1** Armenian Coffee (IRE), Paper Days, **40/1** Giordano (IRE), **66/1** Ors. CSF £53.99, Tote £17.20: £4.30 £1.10 £1.40 (£21.40). Mr Paul Mellon (KINGSCLERE) bred by Paul Mellon. 13 Rn                                                     1m 29 (4.7)
SF—35/39/27/22/21/6

**2630**  CANDY-FLOSS (S) STKS (3 & 4-Y.O) £2385.00 (£660.00: £315.00)
1m 3f                                                           2-40 (2-40)

25183 **Big Pat (56)** *(JPearce)* 3–8–9 ‡5RPrice (1) (wnt 2nd st: led 4f out: rdn 3f out: all
         out) ....................................................................................... —1
23723 Forgetful **(54)** *(DBurchell)* 3–8–6 MRoberts (5) (3rd st: rdn 4f out: ev ch fnl f: r.o) hd.2
2397  Monorose **(53)** *(DHaydnJones)* 3–8–6 WNewnes (3) (4th st: r.o one pce fnl 3f) 2¹/2.3
24772 Blushing Belle **(52)** (v) *(FPFICole)* 4–9–5 PatEddery (7) (swtg: led 7f: rdn,
         edgd rt & wknd 2f out) ............................................................... 3.4
23943 Friendlypersuasion (IRE) **(35)** *(RHollinshead)* 4–9–3 ‡7EHusband (6) (hld up:
         5th st: wknd 4f out) ................................................................... 7.5
       Young Sam *(PDEvans)* 3–8–4 ‡7HayleyWilliams (4) (w'like: dwlt: last st: t.o fnl 4f) dist.6
2253  Mystic Panther **(50)** *(RJHolder)* 4–9–7 JWilliams (2) (6th st: hrd rdn 3f out:
         virtually p.u fnl f: dismntd cl home) ........................................... 0

**13/8** Blushing Belle, **9/4** Forgetful, **5/1** BIG PAT, **17/2** Mystic Panther, **14/1** Monorose, Friendlypersuasion
(IRE)(op 8/1), **33/1** Young Sam. CSF £15.64, Tote £5.40: £2.70 £1.90 (£5.60). Burton Park Country Club
(NEWMARKET) bred by Mrs P. J. Lewis. 7 Rn; No bid
                                                                    SF—18/14/9/16/–/–

---

**2631**  DECK-CHAIR H'CAP (3-Y.O) (0-70) £2763.00 (£768.00: £369.00)
1¹/2m 70y                                                      3-10 (3-11)

                          (Weights raised 4 lb)
2575★ **Corinthian God (IRE) (45)** *(DAWilson)* 8-0 (5x) GCarter (8) (swtg: 2nd st: led
         briefly wl over 3f out: led over 1f out: all out) ........................... —1
1446  Fly for Gold (IRE) **(56)** *(DWPArbuthnot)* 8-6 ‡5RPrice (10) (bkwd: hld up: 6th st:
         hdwy over 3f out: rdn over 2f out: ev ch ins fnl f: r.o) ......... hd.2
22463 Shayna Maidel **(41)** *(MBell)* 7-7⁽¹⁾ ‡3FNorton (3) (bhd tl gd hdwy 3f out: sn rdn:
         ev ch ins fnl f: r.o) ..................................................................... ¹/2.3
20072 Pride of Britain (CAN) **(46)** *(LGCottrell)* 8-1 AMunro (5) (hld up: 3rd st: led
         over 3f out tl over 1f out: r.o) ................................................... ¹/2.4
22115 Indian Territory **(58)** *(DHaydnJones)* 8-13 WNewnes (2) (5th st: wknd 2f out) ... 7.5
23343 Mr Ziegfeld (USA) **(65)** *(SirMarkPrescott)* 9-6 GDuffield (6) (lw: nvr nr to chal) 2¹/2.6
2496  Aedean **(56)** *(CAHorgan)* 8-11 AMcGlone (4) (nvr trbld ldrs) ................ ¹/2.7
22115 Child Star (FR) **(51)** *(DMarks)* 8-6 PRobinson (5) (led over 9f: wknd over 2f out) 3.8
1632  Erlemo **(50)** (bl) *(CJBenstead)* 8-5⁽¹⁾ JWilliams (1) (a bhd) ................. 3.9
15683 Leap in the Dark (IRE) **(66)** *(JLDunlop)* 9-7 WCarson (9) (lw: prom: stdd 6f out:
         4th st: wknd 3f out) ................................................................... 1¹/2.10

**7/2** Pride of Britain (CAN), **5/1** Leap in the Dark (IRE)(4/1—6/1), Mr Ziegfeld (USA), **6/1** Aedean, **7/1** Fly for Gold
(IRE), **8/1** Child Star (FR)(op 5/1), **10/1** Shayna Maidel, CORINTHIAN GOD (IRE)(op 6/1), **20/1** Indian Territory,
**33/1** Erlemo. CSF £72.06, CT £657.09. Tote £11.60: £1.70 £2.60 £2.40 (£52.50). Mr T. S. M. S. Riley-Smith
(EPSOM) bred by Mrs J. McNally in Ireland. 10 Rn
                                                                    2m 43.7 (12)

---

**2632**  BUCKET & SPADE H'CAP (3-Y.O) (0-70) £2763.00 (£768.00: £369.00)
1m 200y                                                        3-40 (3-45)

                          (Weights raised 1 lb)
22632 **Cachou (USA) (62)** *(JHMGosden)* 9-0 PatEddery (1) (stdd s: bhd tl plld out &
         hdwy over 2f out: hrd rdn to ld wl ins fnl f) ........................... —1
20794 Elizabethan Air **(51)** *(ANLee)* 8-4 JQuinn (13) (swtg: 5th st: hrd rdn & ev ch ins
         fnl f: nt qckn) ......................................................................... 1¹/2.2
23552 Sie Amato (IRE) **(52)** *(CaptJWilson)* 8-4 GBardwell (11) (2nd st: led over 2f out:
         hrd rdn & hdd wl ins fnl f) ......................................................... hd.3
24962 Deevee **(43)** *(CJBenstead)* 7-9 NCarlisle (3) (8th st: r.o one pce fnl 2f) ......... 3.4
2125  Prince of Darkness (IRE) **(69)** *(CAHorgan)* 9-7 GDuffield (12) (dwlt: hdwy
         3f out: rdn 2f out: one pce) ....................................................... 3¹/2.5
2429★ Tiffany's Case (IRE) **(56)** (Fav) *(CAHorgan)* 8-8 (5x) SDawson (7) (hld up &
         bhd: hdwy 2f out: nt rch ldrs) ..................................................... nk.6
23924 Tina Meena Lisa **(51)** *(EHOwenjun)* 7-10⁽⁹⁾ ‡7SSanders (4) (nvr nrr) ......... hd.7
2479★ Sirtelimar (IRE) **(62)** *(BobJones)* 9-0 (5x) VSmith (5) (led over 6f: hrd rdn &
         wknd over 1f out) ...................................................................... 2.8
20783 Continuity **(65)** *(GHarwood)* 9-3 AClark (2) (3rd st: wknd over 2f out) ......... nk.9
21033 Eriny (USA) **(67)** *(SGNorton)* 9-0 ‡5OPears (9) (4th st: wknd wl over 1f out) ..... ¹/2.10
23623 Ballyranter **(54)** *(HJCollingridge)* 8-6 MRoberts (14) (hdwy & 7th st: wknd over
         3f out) .................................................................................... 1¹/2.11
2422  Intrepid Fort **(46)** (v) *(BWMurray)* 7-9 ‡3FNorton (10) (a bhd: t.o) ........... 6.12
1213  Crackling **(49)** *(DMarks)* 8-1 WCarson (8) (6th st: wknd 3f out: t.o) .......... 6.13
1917  Jovial Man (IRE) **(48)** *(SMellor)* 8-0 CRutter (6) (a bhd: t.o) .................. 3.14

**11/4** Tiffany's Case (IRE), **5/1** CACHOU (USA), **6/1** Prince of Darkness (IRE)(10/1—11/2), **8/1** Deevee, **12/1** Crackling, **14/1** Tina Meena Lisa, Eriny (USA), Continuity, Sirtelimar (IRE), Ballyranter, Sie Amato (IRE), Elizabethan Air(op 8/1), **50/1** Ors. CSF £69.01, CT £852.71. Tote £4.90: £2.90 £3.00 £3.20 (£22.40). Mr K. Abdulla (NEWMARKET) bred by Juddmonte Farms Incorporated in USA. 14 Rn    1m 53.4 (4.9)
SF—40/24/24/6/21/7

---

**2633**    SEA BREEZE CLAIMING STKS (2-Y.0) £2511.00 (£696.00: £333.00)    **5f** 4-10 (4-14)

| | |
|---|---|
| 2257² | **Aberlady** (75) (Fav) (MAJarvis) 8-6 PRobinson (3) (mde all: rdn over 1f out: all out) ........................................ —1 |
| 2396* | Convenient Moment (63) (JBerry) 8-0 GCarter (8) (a.p: ev ch fnl f: r.o wl) ........ hd.2 |
| 2532³ | Cloudy Reef (66) (RHollinshead) 7-7 ‡⁷AGarth (2) (hdwy 2f out: r.o ins fnl f) ....... 3.3 |
| 900⁶ | Shy Romance (PMMcEntee) 8-2 MRoberts (1) (w wnr: rdn & flashed tail over 1f out: wknd ins fnl f) ........................ 2¹/₂.4 |
| 2396 | Nigels Prospect (DHaydnJones) 8-5 JWilliams (10) (nvr nr to chal) ............... 2.5 |
| 973 | Spenmax (IRE) (WGMTurner) 7-13⁽¹⁾ ‡³TSprake (6) (no hdwy fnl 2f) .............. nk.6 |
| 2396⁴ | Over the Dec (46) (BAMcMahon) 7-3 ‡⁷JBramhill (4) (prom over 3f) .............. 1¹/₂.7 |
| 2335⁶ | Magirika (IRE) (MMoubarak) 8-1 GDuffield (7) (chsd ldrs over 2f) ............... 2¹/₂.8 |
| 2619 | It Bites (IRE) (APJames) 7-12 SDawson (9) (outpcd: t.o) ....................... 6.9 |
| 2232 | Goan Girl (PSFelgate) 7-12 NAdams (5) (outpcd: t.o) ......................... nk.10 |

**13/8** ABERLADY, **5/2** Convenient Moment, **5/1** Cloudy Reef, Magirika (IRE), **16/1** Shy Romance, **20/1** Over the Dec, **33/1** Spenmax (IRE), **50/1** It Bites (IRE), Nigels Prospect, **66/1** Goan Girl. CSF £6.02, Tote £3.30: £1.10 £2.00 £2.60 (£1.60). Mr M. Sinclair (NEWMARKET) bred by Farmers Hill and Fitzroy Studs. 10 Rn
60.1 sec (2.8)
SF—36/29/10/9/4/–

---

**2634**    SAND CASTLE H'CAP (0-70) £2637.00 (£732.00: £351.00)    **7f**    4-40 (9-41)

| | |
|---|---|
| 2427² | **Glenscar** (36) (JLSpearing) 6-7-4⁽²⁾ ‡/AGarth (6) (bhd tl hdwy on ins over 2f out: led fnl f: r.o wl) ........................... —1 |
| 2394 | Homile (46) (BAMcMahon) 4-8-0 ‡⁷SSanders (5) (4th st: rdn & ev ch ins fnl f: nt qckn) ....................................... 1¹/₂.2 |
| 2476⁴ | Zinbaq (39) (CJBenstead) 6-8-0 GDuffield (10) (7th st: hdwy over 1f out: r.o ins fnl f) ........................................ s.h.3 |
| 1588⁶ | Prepare (IRE) (38) (RJHolder) 4-7-13 NAdams (11) (lw: 2nd st: ev ch ins fnl f: one pce) ..................................... 1¹/₂.4 |
| 2432* | Karen Louise (65) (Fav) (MissHCKnight) 3-9-6 (5x) MRoberts (8) (led 2f: 3rd st: led over 4f out: rdn over 2f out: hdd ins fnl f: eased whn btn) 3.5 |
| 344 | Nawwar (55) (CJBenstead) 8-9-2 JWilliams (2) (nvr nrr) ...................... s.h.6 |
| 2290⁶ | Yonge Tender (44) (bl) (CNWilliams) 5-8-5 JCurant (1) (lw: nvr trbld ldrs) ....... nk.7 |
| 2276⁵ | Wessex Milord (32) (JABennett) 7-7-7 GBardwell (12) (b: led 5f out: sn hdd: wknd over 2f out) ............................. s.h.8 |
| 2481 | Another Nut (46) (PDEvans) 3-7-10⁽²⁾ ‡⁵ATucker (7) (5th st: wknd 3f out) ...... hd.9 |
| 2394⁶ | Urshi-Jade (35) (KWhite) 4-7-3⁽²⁾ ‡⁷TWilson (4) (6th st: wknd 3f out) ......... 2.10 |
| 2013 | Highland Magic (IRE) (67) (MJFetherston-Godley) 4-10-0 CRutter (3) (lw: a bhd) ....................................... ¹/₂.11 |

LONG HANDICAP: Wessex Milord 7-1.

**7/4** Karen Louise, **9/2** GLENSCAR, **5/1** Zinbaq, Yonge Tender, **9/1** Highland Magic (IRE), **16/1** Prepare (IRE), **20/1** Nawwar, Homile, **33/1** Urshi-Jade, **50/1** Ors. CSF £77.52, CT £424.51. Tote £5.50: £1.30 £3.30 £1.90 (£39.20). Mr Stephen Borsberry (ALCESTER) bred by Mrs Kiki Ward Platt. 11 Rn    1m 28 (3.7)
SF—31/36/35/29/41/36

T/Plpt: £190.20 (13.7 Tckts).    KH

---

## 1828—HAYDOCK (L-H)

### Friday, August 7th [Good to firm]

Going Allowance: St: minus 0.20; Rnd: minus 0.05 sec per fur (F)    Wind: slt bhd

Stalls: high

**2635**    HALEWOOD STKS (Mdn 3-Y.O.F) £2040.00 (£565.00: £270.00) **1m 3f 200y**    6-10 (6-11)

| | |
|---|---|
| 1027⁶ | **Encore Une Fois** (IRE) (75) (PWChapple-Hyam) 8-11 WCarson (4) (chsd ldr: 2nd st: led over 2f out: hld on gamely) ................. —1 |
| 1948² | Rosina Mae (74) (Fav) (LordHuntingdon) 8-11 BRaymond (7) (hld up: 4th st: rdn to chal over 1f out: no ex nr fin) ................... s.h.2 |
| 2137² | Alyafill (USA) (69) (BHanbury) 8-4 ‡⁷VBray (2) (lw: a.p: 3rd st: rdn 3f out: swtchd rt over 1f out: r.o) .......................... 2.3 |

2116² Wand (IRE) *(HRACecil)* 8-6 ‡⁵StephenDavies (5) (lw: led: rdn & hdd over 2f out: r.o one pce) ............................................................................ 3.4

Adelina Patti *(ACStewart)* 8-11 MRoberts (1) (lt-f: unf: hld up: 6th st: effrt u.p 2f out: no imp) ................................................................................ 12.5

1956 Bracing (IRE) *(GHarwood)* 8-11 AClark (3) (still bkwd: chsd ldrs: lost pl & 6th st: sn btn) .................................................................................. 6.6

Colonial Beauty (FR) *(GFHCharles-Jones)* 8-11 NNewnes (6) (w'like: bkwd: s.s: wl bhd tl s.u ent st) ............................................................... 0

**2/1** Rosina Mae, **3/1** ENCORE UNE FOIS (IRE), **4/1** Wand (IRE), **5/1** Adelina Patti, **8/1** Alyafill (USA), **20/1** Bracing (IRE), **50/1** Colonial Beauty (FR). CSF £8.96. Tote £3.50: £1.50 £1.90 (£4.20). Mr R. E. Sangster (MARLBOROUGH) bred by Swettenham Stud in Ireland. 7 Rn                        2m 31.86 (3.86)
SF—52/51/40/36/17/5

**2636**   BANK QUAY AUCTION STKS (Mdn 2-Y.O) £1590.00 (£440.00: £210.00)
5f
6-40 (6-42)

2274 **Birchwood Sun (78)** *(RHollinshead)* 8-8 WRyan (1) (bhd & outpcd: rdn 2f out: str run to ld wl ins fnl f) .................................................... —1

1993³ Sicily Oak *(DMcCain)* 8-0 MRoberts (6) (bhd & outpcd tl gd hdwy appr fnl f: fin wl) ............................................................................ ½.2

1851³ Benzoe (IRE) **(71)** *(MWEasterby)* 8-9 TLucas (2) (chsd ldrs: led 1f out tl hdd & outpcd nr fin) ...................................................................... 2.3

2368⁴ Hills Raceaid (IRE) **(65)** (bl) *(JBerry)* 8-5 JCarroll (4) (lw: led to ½-wy: rdn & ev ch appr fnl f: one pce) ................................................. ½.4

1472 Magic Pearl **(84)** (Fav) *(EJAlston)* 7-12 ‡³FNorton (5) (chsd ldr: led ½-wy to 1f out: sn rdn & wknd) ......................................................... 3½.5

2551⁶ Bajan Affair (bl) *(MissLCSiddall)* 8-4 WCarson (3) (nvr nr to chal) ......................... 8.6

Cicerone *(PCalver)* 8-8 AClark (7) (lt-f: bkwd: s.s: hung bdly lft thrght: a bhd) .... 4.7

**4/6** Magic Pearl, **11/2** Benzoe (IRE), **7/1** BIRCHWOOD SUN, **9/1** Sicily Oak(op 6/1), **10/1** Hills Raceaid (IRE), **16/1** Bajan Affair, **25/1** Cicerone. CSF £57.90. Tote £7.70: £2.10 £2.40 (£23.60). Mr B. Swain (UPPER LONGDON) bred by The Hall Stud Ltd. 7 Rn                        60.63 sec (1.63)
SF—42/32/33/27/6/–

**2637**   HAYDOCK PARK LEISURE COMPANY H'CAP (0-95) £2831.50 (£784.00: £374.50)
7f 30y
7-10 (7-12)

(Weights raised 2 lb)

1403⁴ **Bold Angel (83)** *(MHEasterby)* 5–9-10 MBirch (7) (lw: a.p: 2nd st: led over 1f out: r.o wl) ................................................................................ —1

2213³ Sir Arthur Hobbs **(62)** *(FHLee)* 5–7-12 ‡⁵NKennedy (8) (lw: hld up: 6th st: styd on u.p ins fnl f) ...................................................................... nk.2

2325⁴ Glenstal Princess **(59)** *(RHollinshead)* 5–7-7 ‡⁷AGarth (1) (lw: hld up: hdwy 3f out: kpt on ins fnl f: nvr nrr) ............................................... 1½.3

2347 Bold Boss **(89)** *(BHanbury)* 3–9-10 BRaymond (5) (lw: a.p: 3rd st: rdn over 1f out: unable qckn) ................................................................. s.h.4

2262³ Profilic **(73)** *(CaptJWilson)* 7–9-0 WRyan (6) (lw: hld up & bhd: gd hdwy appr fnl f: fin wl) ..................................................................... hd.5

2202 Imperial Bid (FR) **(80)** *(DenysSmith)* 4–9-7 KFallon (2) (hld up: effrt over 2f out: rdn & one pce appr fnl f) ......................................................... 1.6

2404² Cronk's Courage **(76)** (v) *(EJAlston)* 6–9-3 JFortune (9) (led tl hdd over 1f out: hrd rdn & edgd lft fnl f: sn btn) .......................................... hd.7

2410² Annabelle Royale **(75)** (Fav) *(MrsNMacauley)* 6–9-2 MRoberts (3) (lw: hld up: rdn & n.m.r over 2f out: swtchd rt: no imp) ............................. 1½.8

2013 Prenonamoss **(80)** *(DWPArbuthnot)* 4–9-7 WCarson (4) (b.hind: chsd ldrs: 5th st: effrt & bdly hmpd ins fnl f: nt rcvr) ................................. hd.9

2404 Heaven-Liegh-Grey **(82)** *(MJohnston)* 4–9-9 RPElliott (10) (chsd ldrs: 4th st: rdn & wknd 2f out: t.o) ........................................................... 8.10

**7/2** Annabelle Royale, **4/1** Bold Boss, **6/1** BOLD ANGEL, **7/1** Prenonamoss, Sir Arthur Hobbs, **8/1** Cronk's Courage, Glenstal Princess, **9/1** Profilic, **20/1** Imperial Bid (FR), **33/1** Heaven-Liegh-Grey. CSF £44.98, CT £311.50. Tote £8.30: £2.40 £1.80 £2.70 (£38.40). Mr A. M. Wragg (MALTON) bred by A. M. Wragg. 10 Rn                        1m 29.41 (2.11)
SF—73/46/36/66/55/59

**2638**   MANCHESTER EVENING NEWS H'CAP (0-90) £2469.00 (£684.00: £327.00)
1³/₄m
7-40 (7-41)

2401³ **Lord Hastie (USA) (78)** (bl) (Fav) *(SGNorton)* 4–9-6 MRoberts (1) (lw: s.s: hld up: 3rd st: effrt 4f out: led 2f out: hung bdly lft: r.o) ............. —1

2178 Alqairawaan **(81)** *(JLDunlop)* 3-8-10  WCarson (3) (lw: led to 2f out: ev ch whn
hmpd & swtchd rt appr fnl f: r.o) ........................................ ¹/₂.2

20276 Be a Honey **(86)** *(NAGraham)* 4-10-0  WRyan (2) (chsd ldr: 2nd st: ev ch 2f out:
btn whn n.m.r appr fnl f) ...................................................... 10.3

**1/2** LORD HASTIE (USA), **3/1** Be a Honey(op 2/1), **5/1** Alqairawaan. CSF £2.85, Tote £1.50 (£2.00). Mrs Joy
Bendall (BARNSLEY) bred by Upland Farm Park Series 6 in USA. 3 Rn          3m 4.89 (6.39)
                                                                      SF—35/24/22

---

**2639**   HAYDOCK PARK PONY CLUB CLAIMING STKS (3-Y.O) £2022.50 (£560.00: £267.50)
           6f                                                               8-10 (8-11)

25524 **Castlerea Lad (77)** (Fav) *(RHollinshead)* 9-3  WRyan (2) (lw: hld up: swtchd rt
over 1f out: qcknd to ld ins fnl f) ........................................ —1

20293 Arctic Appeal (IRE) **(89)** *(JBerry)* 9-8  JCarroll (4) (lw: led: rdn over 1f out: edgd
lft & hdd ins fnl f) .......................................................... 2¹/₂.2

2432 Swinging Tich *(BAMcMahon)* 7-13  MRoberts (3) (chsd ldr: ev ch 1f out: sn rdn
& one pce) ...................................................................... ¹/₂.3

23102 Our John **(51)** *(RonaldThompson)* 8-11  AMackay (1) (lw: hld up: effrt over 2f
out: rdn & unable qckn appr fnl f) ....................................... 1.4

**11/10** CASTLEREA LAD(6/4—Evens), **15/8** Arctic Appeal (IRE), **5/1** Swinging Tich, **8/1** Our John. CSF £3.41,
Tote £2.20 (£1.80). Mrs Tess Graham (UPPER LONGDON) bred by J. D. Hurd. 4 Rn    1m 13.43 (1.73)
                                                                      SF—45/40/15/23

---

**2640**   LIZ McCOLGAN GRADUATION STKS (3-Y.O) £2196.00 (£606.00: £288.00)
           5f                                                               8-40 (8-41)

2169 **Bletchley Park (IRE) (101)** (Fav) *(AAScott)* 9-4  BRaymond (2) (lw: hld up:
hdwy over 1f out: hrd rdn to ld cl home) ........................ —1

2164* Belated **(75)** *(HThomsonJones)* 8-13  RHills (1) (lw: led: rdn & edgd lft ins fnl f:
ct cl home) ...................................................................... s.h.2

1417 Music Dancer **(57)** *(JBerry)* 9-4  JCarroll (3) (swtg: gd spd over 3f: sn rdn & btn) 7.3

**Evens** BLETCHLEY PARK (IRE), **5/4** Belated, **15/2** Music Dancer. CSF £2.38, Tote £1.90 (£1.30). Mr Paul
Moorhouse (NEWMARKET) bred by D. M. Dick in Ireland. 3 Rn              60.13 sec (1.13)
                                                                      SF—62/56/33

T/Trio: Race 3: £263.30 (4.1 Tckts). T/Plpt: £338.30 (8.05 Tckts).                        IM

---

# HAYDOCK (L-H)
## Saturday, August 8th [Good to soft]
Going Allowance: St: 0.20 sec per fur; Rnd: 0.25 sec per fur (G)     Vis: mod becoming good

Stalls: 2nd high, 6th low                                    Wind: nil becoming slt bhd

---

**2641**   JOHN MALLINSON H'CAP (0-110) £7635.00 (£2280.00: £1090.00: £495.00)
           1m 30y                                                           1-45 (1-47)

20215 **St Ninian (99)** *(MHEasterby)* 6-9-9  MBirch (4) (chsd ldr: 2nd st: rdn to ld wl ins
fnl f: r.o) ........................................................................ —1

2343* Badawi (USA) **(92)** *(JHMGosden)* 4-9-2  MHills (3) (hld up: 4th st: hdwy to ld 2f
out: hrd rdn & hdd wl ins fnl f) ......................................... ¹/₂.2

23485 Starlight Flyer **(95)** (bl) (Fav) *(MMoubarak)* 5-9-5  ACruz (5) (lw: led to 2f out:
rallied u.p fnl f: r.o) ........................................................ s.h.3

23412 Piquant **(88)** *(LordHuntingdon)* 5-8-12  BRaymond (6) (lw: chsd ldrs: 3rd st:
effrt over 2f out: one pce) .............................................. 2¹/₂.4

2400* Savoyard **(100)** (bl) *(MAJarvis)* 4-9-10  LDettori (1) (b: lw: hld up: 5th st: rdn 3f
out: no imp) .................................................................... 5.5

Rully **(88)** *(CEBrittain)* 3-8-5  WRyan (2) (h.d.w: bkwd: s.i.s: 6th st: a bhd: t.o) dist.6

**2/1** Starlight Flyer, **3/1** Piquant, **4/1** Badawi (USA)(op 5/2), **5/1** Savoyard, **13/2** ST NINIAN, **20/1** Rully. CSF
£29.42, Tote £9.20: £2.60 £2.20 (£24.60). Lady Murless (MALTON) bred by Lady Murless. 6 Rn
                                                                      1m 45.58 (5.18)
                                                                      SF—61/52/54/39/36/-

---

**2642**   CORAL BOOKMAKERS H'CAP (0-110) £9474.00 (£2832.00: £1356.00: £618.00)
           5f                                                               2-15 (2-19)

2337 **Bit of a Lark (96)** *(RHollinshead)* 4-9-2  ACruz (5) (a.p: led over 1f out: jst hld
on) ................................................................................ —1

2435 Beau Venture (USA) **(95)** *(FHLee)* 4-8-10 ‡⁵NKennedy (14) (lw: hdwy over 1f
out: fin wl: fin 3rd, ½l: plcd 2nd) ....................................... 2

2376⁶ Cumbrian Waltzer **(95)** *(MHEasterby)* 4-8-10 MBirch (17) (hdwy over 1f out: rdn
& r.o wl nr fin: fin 4th, 1½l: plcd 3rd) ....................................... 3

2435 Viceroy **(108)** (v) *(BBeasley)* 5-9-7 SWynne (1) (lw: a.p: rdn & no
ex nr fin: fin 5th, s.h: plcd 4th) ....................................... 4

Gipsy Fiddler **(98)** *(JJO'Neill)* 4-9-4 BRaymond (12) (bkwd: gd hdwy over 1f
out: unable qckn wl ins fnl f: fin 6th, hd: plcd 5th) ................ 5

2003 Gondo **(76)** (v) *(EJAlston)* 5-7-3 ‡⁷DarrenMoffatt (3) (a.p: ev ch 1f out: wknd ins
fnl f) ....................................... 1.7

2376³ Never in the Red **(90)** (bl) *(JBerry)* 4-8-10 GCarter (4) (lw: prom: hrd rdn over 1f
out: one pce) ....................................... ¾.8

2376 Lucedeo **(83)** *(JLSpearing)* 8-7-10 ‡⁷AGarth (2) (hdwy appr fnl f: nt rchd ldrs) .... s.h.9

2435 Double Blue **(94)** (Fav) *(MJohnston)* 3-8-10 LDettori (13) (lw: spd over 3f) .... 1.10

2465³ Petraco (IRE) **(73)** (bl) *(LJCodd)* 4-7-0 ‡⁷DWright (15) (nvr trbld ldrs) ............ hd.11

2400 Stack Rock **(96)** *(EJAlston)* 5-9-2 KFallon (10) (led after 1f tl over 1f out: sn
outpcd) ....................................... 1.12

2404³ Seamere **(83)** (bl) *(BRCambidge)* 9-8-3 JLowe (9) (spd over 3f) ............ s.h.13

2559 Tigani **(73)** (bl) *(DWChapman)* 6-7-7 SWood (16) (led 1f: rdn & wknd over 1f
out) ....................................... 1½.14

2443⁴ Walk in the Park **(91)** *(RSimpson)* 3-8-7 WRyan (6) (m.n.s) .................. 1½.15

2465² Fivesevenfiveo **(80)** *(RJHodges)* 4-7-7⁽⁵⁾ ‡⁷MHumphries (18) (lw: m.n.s) .. 1.16

2404⁵ Samsolom **(75)** *(JBalding)* 4-7-9⁽²⁾ AMackay (7) (outpcd) ............ s.h.17

2376⁵ Absolution **(83)** *(MPNaughton)* 8-8-3⁽¹⁾ MHills (8) (prom over 3f) ......... 1½.18

2404³ Cantoris **(88)** *(RJRWilliams)* 6-8-8 DHolland (11) (lw: hld up: swtchd rt ins fnl f:
fin fast: fin 2nd, nk: disq: plcd last) ....................................... 0

LONG HANDICAP: Samsolom 6-10.

*Stewards Enquiry: Cantoris disq. (interference to Tigani & Stack Rock 1f out). Holland suspended 17-20/8/92
(careless riding).*

**9/2** Double Blue, **15/2** Cantoris, **9/1** Cumbrian Waltzer, **10/1** Beau Venture (USA), Petraco (IRE), **11/1** Seamere,
**12/1** Absolution, Never in the Red, **14/1** Fivesevenfiveo, Stack Rock, **16/1** BIT OF A LARK, Gondo, Viceroy, Walk
in the Park, **20/1** Lucedeo, **33/1** Gipsy Fiddler, **50/1** Ors. CSF £158.38, CT £1,407.11. Tote £32.00: £6.40 £2.40
£1.90 £7.90 (£390.00). Mr R. E. Mason (UPPER LONGDON) bred by Auldyn Stud Ltd. 18 Rn　60.84 sec (1.84)
SF—85/76/76/75/80/76

---

**2643**　　BURTONWOOD BREWERY ROSE OF LANCASTER STKS (Gp 3)　£17600.00 (£6592.50:
　　　　　£3171.25: £1386.25)　　**1¼m 120y**　　　　　　　　　　　　　　2-45 (2-50)

1826a\* Half a Tick (USA) **(107)** *(PFICole)* 4-9-3 CRutter (2) (hld up: 6th st: rdn over 2f
out: str run to ld wl ins fnl f) ....................................... —1

2402⁴ Spartan Shareef (IRE) **(100)** *(CEBrittain)* 3-8-7 MBirch (5) (lw: hld up & bhd: 8th
st: hdwy to ld over 1f out tl hdd wl ins fnl f) ......................... ¾.2

2336\* Fast Manouvre (FR) **(92)** *(MMoubarak)* 3-8-7 ACruz (8) (b: a.p: 3rd st: styd on
u.p ins fnl f) ....................................... 2.3

1230a⁴ Calling Collect (USA) (Fav) *(LMCumani)* 3-8-7 LDettori (7) (w'like: lw: led 1f: 5th
st: led 2f out tl hdd & wknd over 1f out) ............................ 2.4

2220⁶ Flashfoot **(107)** *(IABalding)* 4-9-3 PRobinson (1) (lw: led after 1f to 3f out: rdn &
wknd over 1f out) ....................................... 3.5

2402\* Young Buster (IRE) **(117)** *(GWragg)* 4-9-7 MHills (3) (lw: hld up: 7th st: effrt on
ins 3f out: n.m.r over 1f out: sn btn) ................................ 10.6

1710⁴ Desert Sun **(114)** *(HRACecil)* 4-9-3 WRyan (6) (lw: chsd ldr: 2nd st: led over 3f
out to 2f out: eased whn btn fnl f) ................................... 1.7

820⁶ Top Register (USA) *(LordHuntingdon)* 3-8-7 BRaymond (4) (lw: chsd ldrs: 4th
st: rdn & wknd 2f out) ....................................... ¾.8

**7/4** Calling Collect (USA), **5/2** Young Buster (IRE), **6/1** Desert Sun, Fast Manouvre (FR), **8/1** HALF A TICK (USA),
**10/1** Top Register (USA), **16/1** Flashfoot, **25/1** Spartan Shareef (IRE). CSF £137.96, Tote £9.30: £1.90 £4.90
£2.00 (£184.30). Mr C. J. Wates (WHATCOMBE) bred by Robert Masterson in USA. 8 Rn　2m 17.01 (5.31)
SF—76/64/60/56/60/44

---

**2644**　　JUDDMONTE CLAIMING STKS　£2616.00 (£726.00: £348.00)
　　　　　**1¼m 120y**　　　　　　　　　　　　　　　　　　　　　3-20 (3-21)

2406⁵ Rambo's Hall **(91)** (Fav) *(JAGlover)* 7-9-9 DNicholls (8) (hld up & bhd: rapid
hdwy over 1f out: led wl ins fnl f: readily) ......................... —1

2378³ Eagle Feather (IRE) **(67)** *(JLDunlop)* 3-8-9 WRyan (2) (chsd ldrs: 4th st: led wl
over 1f out tl hdd nr fin) ....................................... 1.2

2294² Able Lassie **(65)** *(MrsGRReveley)* 4-8-3 ‡⁵NKennedy (6) (hld up: gd hdwy over
1f out: fin wl) ....................................... 1.3

24035 Liability Order (66) *(RBoss)* 3–8–5 BRaymond (7) (dwlt: sn rcvrd: 3rd st: rdn & no ex fnl f) ............................................................................. 2½.4
1705 Majed (IRE) (66) *(MrsGRReveley)* 4–9–0 JLowe (3) (hld up: stdy hdwy 2f out: nt rch ldrs) ............................................................................... 2.5
26093 Overpower (64) *(MHTompkins)* 8–8–4 ‡7MGodsafe (4) (lw: hld up: 6th st: shkn up over 2f out: no imp) ................................................ 1½.6
2392* Don't Smile (70) *(MHTompkins)* 3–8–1 PRobinson (1) (chsd ldrs: 5th st: wknd 2f out) ................................................................................ 5.7
19763 Shoehorn (62) *(MCPipe)* 5–8–7 MHills (5) (led tl hdd & wknd wl over 1f out) ... 1½.8
20472 Azureus (IRE) (76) *(MrsGRReveley)* 4–9–2 ‡7DarrenMoffatt (9) (w ldr: 2nd st: ev ch tl wknd 2f out) ................................................................. nk.9
The Last Washer (IRE) (44) *(MHTompkins)* 3–7–12(4) ‡7SMulvey (10) (bit bkwd: a bhd: t.o) ............................................................... 10.10

3/1 RAMBO'S HALL, 7/2 Eagle Feather (IRE), 11/2 Don't Smile, 6/1 Able Lassie(op 4/1), 8/1 Liability Order, Azureus (IRE), 12/1 Shoehorn, Majed (IRE)(op 8/1), 14/1 Overpower, 66/1 The Last Washer (IRE). CSF £13.96, Tote £4.40: £2.10 £1.60 £2.10 (£9.50). Mr B. Dixon (WORKSOP) bred by Sqdn-Ldr Frank Barrett. 10 Rn
2m 20.85 (9.15)
SF—44/36/20/17/22/9

**2645** HARVEY JONES H'CAP (0-90) £3318.75 (£990.00: £472.50: £213.75)
1m 3f 200y
3-55 (3-56)

1691 I Perceive (67) (Fav) *(FHLee)* 5–8–9 PRobinson (4) (lw: hld up & bhd: 6th st: smooth hdwy to ld wl ins fnl f: r.o wl) ..................................... —1
16325 Sastago (USA) (81) *(JHMGosden)* 3–8–12 MHills (7) (led tl hdd ins fnl f: kpt on same pce) ................................................................... 2½.2
1501 Latour (61) *(CEBrittain)* 4–8–3 GCarter (2) (chsd ldr: 2nd st: rdn 3f out: kpt on) . 2.3
19962 Muizenberg (72) *(JACEdwards)* 5–9–0 LDettori (5) (lw: stdd s: 4th st: rdn 2f out: sn btn) ...................................................................... 2½.4
9905 Holy Zeal (82) *(DWPArbuthnot)* 6–9–10 BRaymond (6) (b: bit bkwd: chsd ldrs: 3rd st: rdn & wknd over 2f out) ......................................... hd.5
20235 Uluru (IRE) (84) *(MrsJRRamsden)* 4–9–12 MBirch (1) (lw: hld up: 5th st: nvr plcd to chal: t.o) .............................................................. 20.6

11/4 I PERCEIVE, 7/2 Muizenberg, 4/1 Sastago (USA), 6/1 Uluru (IRE)(op 3/1), 13/2 Ors. CSF £12.67, Tote £4.40: £1.90 £2.40 (£11.50). Mr F. H. Lee (WILMSLOW) bred by R. Hodgins. 6 Rn
2m 37.74 (9.74)
SF—28/26/13/19/28/–

**2646** E.B.F HERMITAGE GREEN STKS (Mdn 2-Y.O) £2880.50 (£798.00: £381.50)
6f
4-25 (4-27)

24445 Bonjour *(JHMGosden)* 9–0 NDay (3) (lw: s.i.s: hdwy ½-wy: led 2f out: pushed clr fnl f) ......................................................................... —1
18322 Storm Venture (IRE) *(BBeasley)* 9–0 DNicholls (5) (a.p: slt ld over 2f out: sn hdd: rdn & no ex fnl f) ............................................................... 3.2
23383 Magic Street *(MMoubarak)* 8–9 ACruz (1) (a w ldrs: rdn over 1f out: one pce) .... ½.3
Divorce Court (IRE) *(LMCumani)* 9–0 LDettori (8) (w'like: scope: bit bkwd: bhd & outpcd: hdwy over 1f out: nt rch ldrs) ......................... 2½.4
23464 My Patriarch (Fav) *(JLDunlop)* 9–0 WRyan (2) (still bkwd: led 2f: ev ch tl rdn & wknd over 2f out) ..................................................... ¾.5
Hazard a Guess (IRE) *(MrsJRRamsden)* 9–0 MBirch (4) (wl grwn: chsd ldrs: pushed along ½-wy: nt pce to chal) ..................................... 2.6
22236 Peacefull Reply (USA) *(FHLee)* 9–0 BRaymond (7) (still bkwd: led after 2f tl hdd & wknd over 2f out) ........................................................ 2.7
Premier Blues (FR) *(RJRWilliams)* 8–9 PRobinson (6) (lt-f: bit bkwd: outpcd: a bhd) ................................................................................. 1½.8
Salik (v) *(PTWalwyn)* 9–0 GCarter (9) (lt-f: outpcd: a bhd: t.o) ................... 7.9

2/1 My Patriarch, 5/2 Magic Street, 5/1 Divorce Court (IRE), 6/1 BONJOUR(op 4/1), 8/1 Storm Venture (IRE), 14/1 Salik (IRE), 25/1 Ors. CSF £49.95, Tote £8.30: £2.20 £1.80 £1.50 (£28.60). Sheikh Mohammed (NEWMARKET) bred by Sheikh Mohammed bin Rashid al Maktoum. 9 Rn
1m 15.67 (3.97)
SF—44/32/25/20/17/9

**2647** PRESCOT H'CAP (3-Y.O) (0-90) £3552.75 (£1062.00: £508.50: £231.75)
1m 30y
4-55 (4-58)

(Weights raised 10 lb)
15165 Salda (68) *(RMWhitaker)* 8–10 GCarter (5) (lw: hld up: 5th st: shkn up over 1f out: styd on to ld nr fin) ................................................. —1
20005 Robingo (IRE) (74) *(CEBrittain)* 9–2 MBirch (8) (lw: hld up & bhd: gd hdwy 2f out: led ins fnl f tl ct cl home) ...................................... s.h.2

2399* Walimu (IRE) **(71)** (Fav) *(CFWall)* 8-13 NDay (6) (a.p: 4th st: led over 1f out tl
hdd & no ex ins fnl f) .................................................. 1½.3

2463³ Majal (IRE) **(76)** *(BHanbury)* 9-4 BRaymond (9) (lw: hld up: hdwy over 2f out: nt
pce to chal) .......................................................... 2½.4

2393 Eastleigh **(67)** *(RHollinshead)* 8-2 ‡7AGarth (3) (a.p: 3rd st: led over 2f out tl over
1f out: rdn & wknd fnl f) ............................................. 1½.5

1772² First Century (IRE) **(77)** *(BRMillman)* 9-5 LDettori (1) (chsd ldrs: 6th st: wknd wl
over 1f out) .......................................................... 5.6

2502⁵ Aasff (USA) **(77)** *(DMorley)* 9-5 PRobinson (7) (bit bkwd: led tl over 2f out:
eased whn btn appr fnl f) ............................................ 6.7

2184³ Agnes Flemming (USA) **(77)** *(PWHarris)* 9-5 WRyan (2) (w ldrs: 2nd st: wknd
over 2f out: t.o) ..................................................... 15.8

**11/4** Walimu (IRE)(3/1—2/1), **7/2** Agnes Flemming (USA)(3/1—9/2), **4/1** First Century (IRE), **5/1** Majal
(IRE)(4/1—6/1), **10/1** Eastleigh, Aasff (USA)(op 6/1), **12/1** SALDA & Ors. CSF £123.19, CT £463.71. Tote
£17.90: £2.80 £2.90 £1.50 (£65.80). Mr E. R. Thomas (WETHERBY) bred by Newtownbarry House Stud. 8 Rn
1m 45.55 (5.15)
SF—49/54/46/43/22/24

T/Trio: Race 2: £562.20 (4.1 Tckts). T/Plpt: £477.70 (16.09 Tckts). IM

2518—**NEWMARKET** **(R-H)** July Course
### Friday, August 7th [Good to firm]
Going Allowance: 0.05 sec per fur (G)                          Wind: fresh against

Stalls: high

**2648**  HEADLAND INTERNATIONAL PROPERTIES H'CAP (0-95) £4581.00 (£1368.00: £654.00:
£297.00) **2m 24y**                                            6-00 (6-02)

2401* **Mull House (73)** *(FJO'Mahony)* 5-8-6(1) (4x) WRSwinburn (5) (lw: hld up:
hdwy 3f out: led over 1f out: sn clr: comf) ........................ —1

2339² Requested **(76)** (Fav) *(RAkehurst)* 5-8-9 AMunro (6) (led 2f: led over 3f out tl
hdd over 1f out: sn btn) ............................................. 7.2

2439⁶ Access Ski **(72)** *(RBoss)* 5-8-5 NDay (4) (hld up: jnd ldr after 3f: led over 5f out tl
over 3f out: sn btn) ................................................. 10.3

2401⁴ Trojan Lancer **(60)** *(DrJDScargill)* 6-7-7 JQuinn (3) (hld up: hdwy 5f out: rdn &
wknd over 2f out) .................................................... 15.4

2139² Hidden Light (IRE) **(83)** *(MAJarvis)* 3-7-10(4) ‡5NGwilliams (2) (led after 2f: rdn &
hdd over 5f out: sn bhd) ............................................. 20.5
LONG HANDICAP: Trojan Lancer 7-6.

**15/8** Requested, **7/2** Trojan Lancer, MULL HOUSE(5/2—4/1), **5/1** Hidden Light (IRE)(op 3/1), **6/1** Access Ski(op
12/1). CSF £9.84, Tote £3.00: £1.60 £1.50 (£3.50). Mr M. Lowry (LINGFIELD) bred by D. J. and Mrs Deer. 5 Rn
3m 28.97 (5.97)
SF—40/36/22/–/–/–

**2649**  BILLINGHAM ROBINSON ACCOUNTANTS (S) STKS (2-Y.O) £3132.00 (£936.00:
£448.00: £204.00) **7f**                                       6-25 (6-28)

1899 **Kaloochi** *(RHannon)* 8-11 JLloyd (13) (hld up: hdwy 3f out: led ins fnl f: readily) —1

2428³ Mr Butch **(50)** *(MRChannon)* 8-11 AMunro (11) (trckd ldrs: ev ch over 1f out:
kpt on) .............................................................. ¾.2

2374⁴ Madam Cyn's Risk **(48)** *(NACallaghan)* 8-1 ‡5DHarrison (8) (lw: hld up: hdwy 2f
out: hmpd over 1f out: r.o ins fnl f) ................................ 1½.3

2247³ Take Your Partner (IRE) **(57)** *(MJohnston)* 8-6 AMcGlone (1) (swtg: prom: led
over 2f out tl ins fnl f: no ex) ...................................... nk.4

West End Girl *(RJRWilliams)* 8-6 RCochrane (12) (tall: rangy: dwlt: r.o fnl 2f: nrst
fin) ................................................................. ½.5

2112² Kafioca (IRE) **(55)** (v) *(MHTompkins)* 8-6 PRobinson (2) (lw: dwlt: hdwy 3f out:
nvr rchd ldrs) ...................................................... nk.6

2500⁴ Baileys Colours *(BJMcMath)* 8-6 LDettori (7) (prom tl wknd over 1f out) ............. 3.7

1296 Miss Bridge (IRE) *(MBell)* 7-13 ‡7PTurner (9) (chsd ldrs 4f) ...................... 1½.8

Adamparis *(ANLee)* 8-6 JQuinn (4) (small: unf: bkwd: dwlt: a bhd) .................. ¾.9

2232* Maribella **(82)** (Fav) *(PFICole)* 8-11 JReid (3) (b: lw: prom: ev ch wl over 1f out:
sn wknd) ........................................................... nk.10

Freckenham *(JEBanks)* 7-13 ‡7JSwinnerton (6) (lengthy: unf: dwlt: a bhd) ....... 8.11

2306 Montana D'Or *(RCurtis)* 8-1 ‡5NGwilliams (5) (prom over 3f) ..................... 1½.12

2389⁶ Water Diviner **(69)** (bl) *(RFJohnsonHoughton)* 9-2 WRSwinburn (10) (led over
4f: t.o) ............................................................. 8.13

Riflebird (IRE) *(MBell)* 8-6 MHills (14) (leggy: unf: w ldr 4f: wknd qckly: t.o) .... 15.14

4/7 Maribella, 9/1 Kafioca (IRE), 10/1 Riflebird (IRE), 12/1 Take Your Partner (IRE)(op 8/1), KALOOCHI(op 8/1), Mr Butch(op 8/1), West End Girl, 20/1 Madam Cyn's Risk, Water Diviner, 25/1 Baileys Colours, Freckenham, Adamparis, 50/1 Ors. CSF £149.46, Tote £22.70: £4.90 £2.90 £4.20 (£232.80). Lord of Lewknor (MARLBOROUGH) bred by Catridge Farm Stud Ltd. 14 Rn; No bid
1m 29.84 (5.44)
SF—20/18/3/7/5/4

## 2650
BERNARD LLOYD ASSOCIATES H'CAP (0-90) £3817.50 (£1140.00: £396.25 each)
6f
6-55 (6-57)

| | | | | |
|---|---|---|---|---|
| 2520² | So Rhythmical (74) (Fav) (GHEden) 8-8-13 AMunro (11) (b.off hind: chsd ldrs: led 1f out: drvn out) | —1 |
| 2435 | Clifton Charlie (USA) (84) (MRChannon) 4-9-9 MHills (4) (lw: hdwy over 2f out: r.o fnl f: nt rch wnr) | hd.2 |
| 2559³ | Adwick Park (82) (TDBarron) 4-9-7 RCochrane (6) (lw: squeezed out s: hdwy whn n.m.r appr fnl f: fin wl) | hd.3 |
| 2520³ | Fighter Squadron (59) (bl) (JAGlover) 3-7-7 JQuinn (1) (chsd ldrs: ev ch 1f out: no ex nr fin) | d.h.3 |
| 2521⁴ | Resolute Bay (76) (v) (RMWhitaker) 6-9-1 ACulhane (5) (lw: s.i.s: sn rdn along: r.o wl fnl f) | ¹/₂.5 |
| 2458 | Profit a Prendre (54) (DAWilson) 8-7-0 ‡7SharonMillard (9) (b: hdwy 3f out: nt qckn fnl f) | ³/₄.6 |
| 2520⁴ | Easy Line (89) (PJFeilden) 9-10-0 WRSwinburn (10) (b: hld up: r.o appr fnl f: nvr able to chal) | nk.7 |
| 2478⁵ | Sylvan Breeze (81) (bl) (PMitchell) 4-9-6 SWhitworth (3) (lw: led: sn clr: wknd & hdd 1f out) | 3¹/₂.8 |
| 2603* | Walking Possession (79) (bl) (RBoss) 3-8-13 (6x) MTebbutt (2) (chsd ldr 4f) | 2.9 |
| 2268⁵ | Prince of the Sea (IRE) (79) (DWPArbuthnot) 4-8-13 ‡5RPrice (12) (b: lw: in tch: rdn ¹/₂-wy: sn hdd) | 2¹/₂.10 |
| 2203⁴ | Filicaia (65) (DonEnricoIncisa) 6 7-11 ‡7ClaireBalding (8) (s.s: effrt over 2f out: no imp) | nk.11 |
| 1214 | Risk Zone (73) (v) (RHannon) 3-8-7 AMcGlone (7) (rdn ¹/₂-wy: sn bhd) | 2.12 |

LONG HANDICAP: Fighter Squadron 7-5.

4/1 SO RHYTHMICAL, 5/1 Fighter Squadron, 11/2 Adwick Park, 6/1 Easy Line, 8/1 Walking Possession, 12/1 Resolute Bay, Risk Zone, 14/1 Sylvan Breeze, Prince of the Sea (IRE), 16/1 Filicaia, Profit a Prendre(op 10/1), 20/1 Clifton Charlie (USA). CSF £71.91, CT £204.80 SR, CC & AP: £189.07 SR, CC & FS. Tote £4.40: £1.70 £7.90 AP £1.40, FS £0.90 (£37.10). Miss C. A. Barrow (NEWMARKET) bred by D. C. R. Allen. 12 Rn
1m 13.77 (2.27)
SF—59/68/65/37/57/25

## 2651
EMPLAS TRADE WINDOWS CLAIMING STKS £3236.00 (£896.00: £428.00)
1¹/₂m
7-25 (7-27)

| | | | |
|---|---|---|---|
| 2043* | Upper House (v) (Fav) (GWragg) 3-9-3 WRSwinburn (2) (lw: chsd ldr: rdn 3f out: ev ch: r.o u.p to ld cl home) | —1 |
| 2294³ | Kate Royale (40) (GCBravery) 3-7-6⁽¹⁾ ‡5DHarrison (3) (hld up & plld hrd: led on bit 2f out: eased ins fnl f: shkn up & ct cl home) | hd.2 |
| 2295³ | Carrolls Marc (IRE) (46) (PJFeilden) 4-8-9 ‡5JWeaver (1) (b.hind: led tl hdd & outpcd 2f out: sn wknd) | 20.3 |

4/11 UPPER HOUSE, 7/2 Carrolls Marc (IRE), 8/1 Kate Royale. CSF £2.89, Tote £1.30 (£2.00). Sir Philip Oppenheimer (NEWMARKET) bred by Hascombe and Valiant Studs. 3 Rn; Kate Royale clmd M Gillard £4,620.50
2m 37.84 (9.14)
SF—18/–/–

## 2652
TUDOR GATE HOTEL AND RESTAURANT NURSERY £4698.00 (£1404.00: £672.00: £306.00) 7f
7-55 (7-59)

(Weights raised 3 lb)

| | | | |
|---|---|---|---|
| 2193* | King Paris (IRE) (88) (Fav) (MBell) 9-7 MHills (3) (chsd ldrs: led 2f out: drvn out) | —1 |
| 1932* | Wynona (IRE) (78) (GCBravery) 8-11 WRSwinburn (5) (lw: s.s: hdwy over 2f out: r.o ev nr fin) | hd.2 |
| 2010 | Beaver Brook (70) (RHannon) 8-3 JLloyd (6) (hld up: hdwy over 3f out: ev ch 2f out: one pce) | 3¹/₂.3 |
| 2025³ | Alderney Prince (USA) (84) (PFICole) 9-3 AMunro (7) (prom 5f: one pce) | nk.4 |
| 2076⁴ | Boldville Bash (IRE) (68) (TDBarron) 8-1 KDarley (8) (lw: hld up & plld hrd: effrt 2f out: no imp fnl f) | hd.5 |
| 1923* | Milngavie (IRE) (75) (MJohnston) 8-8 DMcKeown (4) (chsd ldrs 4f) | 5.6 |
| 2158* | Another Kingdom (60) (JWharton) 7-7 JQuinn (1) (led 5f) | 4.7 |
| 2428⁵ | Canazei (60) (v) (DonEnricoIncisa) 7-7 JakiHouston (2) (plld hrd: spd 3f: sn bhd: t.o) | 15.8 |

LONG HANDICAP: Another Kingdom 7-6, Canazei 6-9.

**11/8** KING PARIS (IRE)(2/1—5/4), **5/1** Wynona (IRE)(3/1—11/2), Beaver Brook, **15/2** Another Kingdom(8/1—12/1), **8/1** Alderney Prince (USA), **9/1** Milngavie (IRE), Boldville Bash (IRE)(8/1—12/1), **50/1** Canazei. CSF £8.96, CT £25.57. Tote £2.40: £1.40 £1.50 £1.90 (£4.20). Mrs Pauline Karpidas (NEWMARKET) bred by Mrs P. Karpidas in Ireland. 8 Rn
1m 27.73 (3.33)
SF—62/51/32/45/28/20

**2653** CARWIN VENTURE STKS (Mdn 2-Y.O) £3752.50 (£1120.00: £535.00: £242.50)
7f 8-25 (8-27)

25195 **Yajeed (USA)** (Fav) *(AAScott)* 9-0 SCauthen (2) (chsd ldrs: rdn over 2f out: kpt on to ld nr fin) ............................................................ —1
19255 Declassified (USA) *(LMCumani)* 9-0 LDettori (5) (lw: chsd ldrs: led over 1f out tl hdd & no ex nr fin) ............................................................ s.h.2
Hostile Witness (IRE) *(RHannon)* 9-0 JReid (4) (scope: s.i.s: hdwy over 2f out: n.m.r over 1f out: r.o fnl f) ............................................................ 1½.3
Czar's Witness *(PFICole)* 9-0 AMunro (3) (cmpt: led over 5f) ............................ s.h.4
18686 Platinum Venture *(SPCWoods)* 9-0 WWoods (7) (prom: no hdwy fnl 2f) ............ 2.5
Piston (IRE) *(BHanbury)* 9-0 WRSwinburn (6) (cmpt: bkwd: plld hrd: w ldr 4f) .. 10.6
Chajothelytbrigade (IRE) *(CNAllen)* 8-2 ‡7GForster (1) (small: lt-f: effrt 3f out: sn bhd) ............................................................ nk.7

**Evens** YAJEED (USA)(6/4—10/11), **3/1** Declassified (USA)(op 5/1), **4/1** Czar's Witness(op 6/4), **9/1** Hostile Witness (IRE), **14/1** Piston (IRE)(10/1—16/1), **33/1** Ors. CSF £4.58, Tote £1.90: £1.50 £1.80 (£3.00). Mr A. Merza (NEWMARKET) bred by Crook Investment Company in USA. 7 Rn
1m 28.29 (3.89)
SF—46/45/40/39/33/3

T/Trio: Race 3: w AP £112.10 (5.1 Tckts); w FS £61.40 (9.3 Tckts). T/Plpt: £97.50 (36.2 Tckts). Dk

# NEWMARKET (R-H) July Course
## Saturday, August 8th [Good to firm]
Going Allowance: minus 0.15 sec per fur (F)
Wind: slt against

Stalls: centre

**2654** MONTANA WINES STKS (Mdn 3-Y.O) £3720.00 (£1110.00: £530.00: £240.00)
1¼m 2-10 (2-15)

**Mamdooh** (Fav) *(ACStewart)* 9-0 MRoberts (6) (cmpt: bit bkwd: hld up: hdwy 3f out: led over 1f out: rdn out) ............................................................ —1
22986 Anna Comnena (IRE) *(LMCumani)* 8-4 ‡5JWeaver (8) (in tch: plld out over 1f out: ev ch fnl f: r.o) ............................................................ nk.2
21862 Reflecting (IRE) **(73)** *(JHMGosden)* 9-0 WRSwinburn (4) (led tl over 1f out: one pce) ............................................................ 2½.3
25224 Back Billy (IRE) *(CEBrittain)* 9-0 WCarson (5) (prom: rdn whn sltly hmpd wl over 1f out: sn btn) ............................................................ 4.4
23992 Shakreen (USA) **(67)** *(MrsLPiggott)* 8-9 LPiggott (1) (swtg: b.hind: in tch tl wknd wl over 1f out) ............................................................ ¾.5
Patrol *(MRStoute)* 9-0 AMunro (3) (cmpt: lw: chsd ldr 8f) ............................ ¾.6
Oncilla *(ACStewart)* 8-9 AClark (7) (lengthy: unf: bit bkwd: a in rr: rdn 5f out: t.o) 15.7
Call Me Dickins *(RHollinshead)* 9-0 SPerks (2) (unf: leggy: last thrght: t.o) ....... 12.8

**7/4** MAMDOOH(5/4—2/1), **9/4** Back Billy (IRE)(7/4—3/1), **9/2** Reflecting (IRE), **10/1** Shakreen (USA)(6/1—12/1), Anna Comnena (IRE)(8/1—12/1), **12/1** Patrol(op 6/1), **33/1** Ors. CSF £18.15, Tote £2.90: £1.30 £2.00 £1.40 (£14.00). Mr Hamdan Al-Maktoum (NEWMARKET) bred by Cheveley Park Stud Ltd. 8 Rn
2m 7.03 (4.43)
SF—41/30/35/27/20/23

**2655** BROOKS OF NORWICH CLAIMING STKS (3-Y.O) £3002.00 (£896.00: £428.00: £194.00)
1m 2-40 (2-42)

2496 **Our Occasion (66)** *(RHannon)* 9-6 MRoberts (6) (hld up: hdwy over 2f out: rdn to ld jst over 1f out: sn clr: r.o wl) ............................................................ —1
2072* Round by the River **(67)** *(WWHaigh)* 8-9 DMcKeown (1) (hdwy over 2f out: ev ch appr fnl f: one pce) ............................................................ 5.2
25275 Change the Will **(61)** *(MDIUsher)* 8-5 WCarson (2) (lw: chsd ldrs: led wl over 1f out tl jst over 1f out: one pce) ............................................................ ¾.3
22493 Super Summit **(54)** *(JPearce)* 8-13 ‡5RPrice (8) (chsd ldr 6f) ............................ 8.4
22686 Spanish Miner (USA) **(77)** *(AAScott)* 8-10 WRSwinburn (3) (chsd ldrs: rdn 2f out: sn btn) ............................................................ 3.5
12845 Dublin Indemnity (USA) **(47)** *(NACallaghan)* 8-7 ‡7JTate (7) (a bhd) ................... ¾.6

2554³ Jefferson Davis (IRE) **(70)** (Fav) *(BBeasley)* 8-11 ‡⁵SWilliams (5) (lw: led: clr
over 2f out: hdd wl over 1f out: wknd qckly) ........................ 2.7
2219 Forest Dew (USA) **(63)** (v) *(MHTompkins)* 7-13 GBardwell (4) (lw: a in rr: rdn &
btn 3f out) ........................ 6.8

**100/30** Jefferson Davis (IRE), **4/1** Round by the River, **9/2** Forest Dew (USA), Spanish Miner (USA)(tchd 7/1),
**13/2** Change the Will, **10/1** OUR OCCASION, Super Summit, **33/1** Dublin Indemnity (USA). CSF £45.56, Tote
£9.20: £2.30 £1.40 £1.60 (£28.90). Simon Ellis Ltd (MARLBOROUGH) bred by Grange Thoroughbreds. 8 Rn;
Our Occasion clmd W Musson £13,300, Forest Dew (USA) clmd R Sharp £5,011    1m 41.03 (3.13)
SF—38/12/6/–/–/–

## 2656

DICKINS INVITATION H'CAP (Ladies) (0-70) £3428.50 (£1048.00: £519.00: £254.50)
**1m**    3-15 (3-20)

(Weights raised 1 lb)

2410★ **Dodgy (56)** (v) *(SDow)* 5–9-11 MissMJuster (1) (led tl over 1f out: led wl ins fnl f:
r.o wl) ........................ —1
2026⁶ Buddy's Friend (IRE) **(57)** *(RJRWilliams)* 4–9-12 MissAGiambertone (3) (trckd
ldr tl led over 1f out: rdn & hdd wl ins fnl f: r.o) ........................ s.h.2
2289⁴ Shining Jewel **(66)** *(MrsLPiggott)* 5–10-7 MrsJCrossley (6) (hdwy 2f out: n.m.r
ins fnl f: r.o cl home) ........................ ½.3
1954 Takenhall **(57)** *(MJFetherston-Godley)* 7–9-12 MrsAFarrell (7) (prom tl lost pl
over 2f out: styd on fnl f) ........................ 2.4
2427 Alnasric Pete (USA) **(54)** *(DAWilson)* 6–9-9 MissDClerc (2) (prom tl no hdwy fnl
2f) ........................ nk.5
2366³ Cee-Jay-Ay **(59)** *(JBerry)* 5–10-0 MissIDWJones (11) (hdwy over 2f out: wknd
over 1f out) ........................ 4.6
580⁵ Pims Classic **(53)** *(JLHarris)* 4–9-8 MissEOldengren (12) (prom 5f) ........................ 1½.7
2290 A Little Precious **(55)** *(JRBostock)* 6–9-10 MrsLPearce (10) (bhd: rdn 3f out: nvr
rchd ldrs) ........................ ¾.8
2013² Usa Dollar **(56)** (bl) *(BGubby)* 9–9-11 MissKSchlick (5) (prom 6f) ........................ 2½.9
2191 Ler Cru (IRE) **(67)** *(CEBrittain)* 3–10-1 MrsEMellor (4) (effrt over 2f out: btn wl
over 1f out) ........................ 1½.10
774★ Ballerina Bay **(61)** *(DTThom)* 4–10-2 MrsRVanDerKraats (8) (hld up & plld hrd
early: effrt over 2f out: sn btn) ........................ 6.11
2394² Shaffaaf (USA) (10/1) Withdrawn (bolted bef s) : not under orders

**4/1** Usa Dollar, **6/1** Cee-Jay-Ay, Buddy's Friend (IRE), DODGY, **7/1** A Little Precious, Takenhall, **8/1** Ler Cru
(IRE), **9/1** Shining Jewel, **14/1** Ballerina Bay, **33/1** Ors. CSF £39.80, CT £294.03. Tote £5.20: £1.50 £3.20 £3.60
(£17.50). Mr J. A. Redmond (EPSOM) bred by J. A. Redmond. 11 Rn    1m 42.29 (4.59)
SF—24/24/31/16/12/5

## 2657

SWEET SOLERA STKS (listed race) (2-Y.O.F) £9218.75 (£2750.00: £1312.50: £593.75)
**7f**    3-45 (3-47)

1927³ **Mystic Goddess (USA) (100)** (Fav) *(MRStoute)* 8-8 WCarson (2) (swtg: plld
hrd: set slow pace: qcknd over 1f out: r.o wl) ........................ —1
2185² Reine de Neige *(AAScott)* 8-8 WRSwinburn (5) (dwlt: sn in tch: wnt 2nd over 2f
out: ev ch appr fnl f: unable qckn) ........................ ½.2
1713³ Holly Golightly **(97)** *(RHannon)* 8-8 MRoberts (3) (hdwy 2f out: ev ch appr fnl f:
one pce) ........................ 1½.3
1845★ Love of Silver (USA) *(CEBrittain)* 8-8 GCrealock (8) (a in tch: rdn 2f out: styd on
one pce) ........................ nk.4
1553★ Mrs West (USA) *(JLDunlop)* 8-8 WNewnes (4) (hld up: hdwy over 2f out: btn
appr fnl f) ........................ 2½.5
2132³ East Liberty **(94)** *(IABalding)* 8-8 LPiggott (1) (lw: chsd ldrs: rdn wl over 1f
out: one pce) ........................ nk.6
1591⁶ Latest Flame (IRE) *(MRChannon)* 8-8 AMunro (7) (lw: prom over 4f) ........................ 5.7
2526³ Formal Affair *(CACyzer)* 8-8 DBiggs (6) (plld hrd: prom 4f) ........................ 2.8

**10/11** MYSTIC GODDESS (USA)(8/11—5/4), **9/4** Reine de Neige(7/4—11/4), **8/1** Holly Golightly, **16/1** Mrs
West (USA), East Liberty (USA)(op 10/1), Love of Silver (USA), **20/1** Latest Flame (IRE), **33/1** Formal Affair. CSF
£3.53, Tote £1.90: £1.10 £1.20 £1.50 (£1.90). Cheveley Park Stud (NEWMARKET) bred by Cheveley Park Stud
in USA. 8 Rn    1m 27.61 (3.21)
SF—30/28/23/22/14/13

## 2658

BRIERLEY INVESTMENTS H'CAP (0-115) £16570.00 (£4960.00: £2380.00: £1090.00)
**7f**    4-20 (4-24)

2400⁴ **Deprecator (USA) (91)** *(JHMGosden)* 4–9-5 WCarson (13) (b.hind: swtg:
hdwy 2f out: led jst ins fnl f: r.o wl) ........................ —1
2369★ Doulab's Image **(85)** (bl) *(JAGlover)* 5–8-8 ‡⁵SWilliams (21) (bhd tl hdwy wl over
1f out: fin wl) ........................ ½.2

24355 Hard to Figure (90) (RJHodges) 6–8-11 ‡7SDrowne (12) (hrd rdn 2f out: hdwy over 1f out: r.o nr fin) ........................................... 1¹⁄₂.3

2435 Taufan Blu (IRE) (94) (MJohnston) 3–9-2 DMcKeown (20) (hdwy over 1f out: r.o ins fnl f: nrst fin) ........................................... 1.4

11743 Crystal Heights (FR) (82) (WAO'Gorman) 4–8-10 AMunro (16) (swtg: a.p: led over 2f out tl jst ins fnl: one pce) ........................................... hd.5

25926 Green Dollar (89) (EAWheeler) 9–9-3 MTebbutt (9) (hld up: hdwy over 1f out: hrd rdn fnl f: nrst fin) ........................................... ¹⁄₂.6

1943 Ringland (USA) (83) (PCHaslam) 4–8-11 LPiggott (19) (lw: hld up: r.o appr fnl f: nvr nrr) ........................................... 1.7

2191★ Big Leap (IRE) (99) (MMoubarak) 3–9-2 ‡5JWeaver (10) (prom tl one pce fr over 1f out) ........................................... nk.8

19435 Superbrave (76) (Fav) (WJarvis) 6–8-4 MRoberts (15) (b: prom: ev ch over 1f out: eased whn btn fnl f) ........................................... s.h.9

2458★ Belfort Ruler (66) (BGubby) 5–7-8 NAdams (17) (hld up: nt clr run wl over 1f out: nt rcvr) ........................................... 2¹⁄₂.10

2348 Cheveux Mitchell (76) (v) (MRChannon) 5–7-11 ‡7PTurner (5) (led centre over 4f) ........................................... 3¹⁄₂.11

2447 Superoo (76) (JSutcliffe) 6–8-4 WNewnes (7) (dwlt: nvr able to chal) ........ 2.12

19432 Ashdren (82) (AHarrison) 5–8-10 WRSwinburn (1) (nvr gng wl: bhd fnl 3f) ...... ¹⁄₂.13

24003 Panikin (92) (JWharton) 4–9-6 JWilliams (6) (chsd ldrs: btn whn hmpd over 1f out) ........................................... 2.14

24212 Golden Chip (IRE) (77) (APStringer) 4–8-3 JQuinn (3) (bhd fnl 3f) ........... ¹⁄₂.15

2382★ Act of Union (IRE) (72) (BBeasley) 3–7-8 LCharnock (18) (swtg: led stands' side over 4f: wknd qckly over 1f out) ........................................... 3¹⁄₂.16

2435 Kayvee (97) (GHarwood) 3–9-5 AClark (14) (lw: prom 4f) ........................................... 2.17

23373 Nordic Brave (76) (MBrittain) 6–8-4 GBardwell (4) (spd far side 4f) ............ 1¹⁄₂.18

2169 Spanish Storm (IRE) (102) (SPCWoods) 3–9-10 WWoods (11) (prom tl wknd qckly 3f out: t.o) ........................................... 20.19

7/2 Superbrave(4/1—6/1), 8/1 Superoo, Kayvee, Big Leap (IRE), 10/1 Ashdren, 12/1 Hard to Figure, 16/1 DEPRECATOR (USA), Cheveux Mitchell, Golden Chip (IRE), Panikin, Taufan Blu (IRE), Doulab's Image, Ringland (USA), Crystal Heights (FR), 25/1 Nordic Brave, Belfort Ruler, Act of Union (IRE), 33/1 Ors. CSF £240.87, CT £2,894.40. Tote £19.10: £4.10 £4.60 £3.50 £3.20 (£777.60). Ms Rachel D. S. Hood (NEWMARKET) bred by Dr. Thomas F. Van Meter II in USA. 19 Rn      1m 25.48 (1.08)

SF—73/60/58/60/53/58

---

**2659**    FAY, RICHWHITE STKS (Mdn 3-Y.O) £3590.00 (£1070.00: £510.00: £230.00)
7f
            4-50 (4-52)

     Amwag (USA) (ACStewart) 8-9 MRoberts (2) (leggy: scope: dwlt: sn in tch: led wl over 1f out: qcknd clr: easily) ........................................... —1

24322 Climbing High (IABalding) 8-9 WNewnes (3) (hld up: hdwy 2f out: kpt on one pce) ........................................... 8.2

     Emir Albadou (USA) (Fav) (MRStoute) 9-0 WRSwinburn (6) (lengthy: scope: bit bkwd: prom: led briefly 2f out: one pce) ........................................... ¹⁄₂.3

25382 Jahangir (IRE) (68) (BHanbury) 9-0 AMunro (4) (chsd ldrs: rdn 2f out: sn wknd) ........................................... 4.4

24193 Nbaat (USA) (68) (CJBenstead) 9-0 WCarson (4) (prom 4f) ........................... 5.5

22934 Jumaira Star (USA) (JHMGosden) 9-0 LPiggott (1) (led 5f: eased appr fnl f) .... ¹⁄₂.6
Tamrah (IRE) (16/1) Withdrawn : not under orders

8/11 Emir Albadou (USA), 11/4 AMWAG, 11/2 Climbing High, 11/1 Nbaat (USA)(8/1—14/1), 20/1 Ors. CSF £16.98, Tote £4.40: £2.50 £1.90 (£7.60). Mr Hamdan Al-Maktoum (NEWMARKET) bred by Shadwell Farm Incorporated in USA. 6 Rn      1m 26.10 (1.70)

SF—53/29/32/20/5/3

---

**2660**    AUCKLAND H'CAP (0-90) £4695.00 (£1410.00: £680.00: £315.00)
1¹⁄₄m
            5-20 (5-24)

22883 **Kinematic (USA) (86)** (JHMGosden) 4–9-6 ‡5JWeaver (8) (lw: led after 2f: rdn 4f out: wnt clr 1f out: r.o wl) ........................................... —1

2415★ Mahsul (IRE) (64) (CJBenstead) 4–8-3 WCarson (1) (hld up: gd hdwy 2f out: one pce fnl f) ........................................... 4.2

25293 Bescaby Boy (67) (JWharton) 4–8-6 JWilliams (2) (lw: hld up: gd hdwy over 1f out: nrst fin) ........................................... ³⁄₄.3

21914 Riviera Vista (89) (Fav) (GWragg) 3–9-5 WRSwinburn (3) (lw: hld up: plld out 3f out: hdwy 2f out: btn appr fnl f) ........................................... ³⁄₄.4

2401 Madagans Grey (75) (RBoss) 4–9-0 AMunro (4) (chsd ldrs: ev ch jst over 2f out: one pce) ........................................... ³⁄₄.5

1466 Major's Law (IRE) (75) (CEBrittain) 3–8-5 BCrossley (10) (swtg: nvr nr to chal) 3¹⁄₂.6

2288⁵ Bowden Boy (IRE) **(71)** (bl) *(NACallaghan)* 4–8-3 ‡⁷JTate (11) (hld up: hdwy 3f
　　out: sn one pce) ........................................................................................................ hd.**7**
2527³ Straw Thatch **(74)** *(MJohnston)* 3–8-4⁽²⁾ AClark (5) (lw: in tch 7f) ................... 2¹/₂.**8**
1869 Rose Alto **(83)** *(JRFanshawe)* 4–9-1 ‡⁷NVarley (6) (swtg: prom 6f) ...................... 8.**9**
2191 Good Reference (IRE) **(82)** *(MBell)* 3–8-12 LPiggott (4) (led 2f: w wnr tl over 3f
　　out: eased whn btn 2f out) ............................................................................... 10.**10**

**6/4** Riviera Vista, **5/1** Mahsul (IRE), Bescaby Boy, **6/1** KINEMATIC (USA)(4/1—13/2), **10/1** Bowden Boy
(IRE)(op 6/1), **12/1** Rose Alto(op 8/1), **14/1** Good Reference (IRE), Straw Thatch, **20/1** Major's Law (IRE), **25/1**
Madagans Grey. CSF £36.15, CT £151.77. Tote £8.60: £2.80 £1.70 £1.60　(£17.80). Mr K. Abdulla
(NEWMARKET) bred by Juddmonte Farms, Inc. in USA. 10 Rn　　　　　　　2m 4.32 (1.72)
　　　　　　　　　　　　　　　　　　　　　　　　　　　　　　　　SF–74/49/50/61/54/38

T/Trio: Race 5: £3,062.90 (1.1 Tckts). T/Jkpt: Not won; £1,596.85 to Newbury 14/8/92. T/Plpt: £202.00 (36.85
Tckts).　　　　　　　　　　　　　　　　　　　　　　　　　　　　　　　　　RC

## 2569–**REDCAR (L-H)**

### Friday, August 7th [Firm, Good to firm fnl 5f]

Going Allowance: minus 0.10 sec per fur (F)　　　　　　　　Wind: slt half bhd

Stalls: high

**2661**　　BEDALE (S) STKS (2-Y.O) £2595.00 (£720.00: £345.00)　　**6f**　　2-00 (2-02)

1559² First Option **(65)** (Fav) *(MHEasterby)* 8-11 KDarley (9) (a.p: chal 1f out: styd on
　　u.p.to ld cl home) ................................................................................ —**1**
2558⁵ Palacegate Prince **(73)** *(JBerry)* 8-11 JCarroll (1) (chsd ldrs: rdn to ld jst ins fnl f:
　　kpt on: jst ct) ................................................................................................ hd.**2**
2428⁴ Monet Monet Monet *(WCarter)* 7-13 ‡⁷CHawksley (10) (led tl hdd ins fnl f. no ex) 2¹/₂.**0**
2277 Don't Be Saki (IRE) **(62)** (bl) *(JEtherington)* 8-6 KFallon (4) (s.s: styd on wl fnl 2f:
　　nrst fin) ................................................................................................... 1¹/₂.**4**
2330⁴ Hairraising **(60)** *(NACallaghan)* 8-6 WRyan (5) (lw: trckd ldrs: effrt 2f out: sn btn) 1.**5**
　　Clanrock *(RMWhitaker)* 8-11 ACulhane (8) (w'like: leggy: scope: s.i.s: stdy
　　hdwy ¹/₂-wy: nvr plcd to chal) ........................................................................ 3.**6**
2112³ Bay Rum **(50)** (bl) *(BBeasley)* 8-6 LCharnock (2) (prom tl outpcd fnl 2f) .......... 1¹/₂.**7**
1959 Sainted Sue *(JSHaldane)* 8-6 NConnorton (6) (w ldrs 2f: sn outpcd) ................ hd.**8**
1923 Newinsky **(62)** *(CTinkler)* 8-11 MBirch (3) (prom to ¹/₂-wy: sn bhd) .................. 5.**9**
2328⁴ Eightofus **(58)** *(GMMoore)* 8-11 DMcKeown (7) (sn pushed along & bhd) ...... 1¹/₂.**10**

**2/1** FIRST OPTION, **3/1** Palacegate Prince, **6/1** Monet Monet Monet, Don't Be Saki (IRE), **15/2** Hairraising, **11/1**
Newinsky, **14/1** Eightofus, Bay Rum, **25/1** Clanrock, **100/1** Sainted Sue. CSF £8.83, Tote £3.20: £1.80 £1.80
£2.20 (£3.80). Mr P. D. Savill (MALTON) bred by Dodford Stud. 10 Rn; Bt in 3,700 gns　　1m 12 (2.7)
　　　　　　　　　　　　　　　　　　　　　　　　　　　　　　　SF–31/30/8/9/–/–

**2662**　　BBC RADIO CLEVELAND H'CAP (3-Y.O) (0-80) £2976.00 (£888.00: £424.00: £192.00)
　　　　**1m**　　　　　　　　　　　　　　　　　　　　　2-30 (2-32)

　　　　　　　　　　　　　(Weights raised 9 lb)
2384⁴ Watch Me Go (IRE) **(53)** *(BobJones)* 8-3 NConnorton (4) (lw: led tl hdd over 1f
　　out: rallied u.p to ld cl home) ...................................................................... —**1**
2263* Nile Delta (IRE) **(71)** (Fav) *(HRACecil)* 9-7 WRyan (3) (cl up: led over 1f out: sn
　　hrd drvn: nt qckn & hdd nr fin) ..................................................................... hd.**2**
2384² Batabanoo **(66)** *(MrsGRReveley)* 9-2 KDarley (2) (a chsng ldrs: effrt over 2f out:
　　r.o one pce) ......................................................................................... ³/₄.**3**
2384⁵ April Shadow **(55)** *(CWThornton)* 8-5 GHind (1) (prom: effrt over 2f out: wknd
　　ins fnl f) ................................................................................................... 5.**4**

**4/11** Nile Delta (IRE), **5/1** Batabanoo, **11/2** WATCH ME GO (IRE), **16/1** April Shadow. CSF £8.04, Tote £6.40
(£2.30). 121 Racing Club (NEWMARKET) bred by Rosemount Stud in Ireland. 4 Rn　　1m 37.9 (2.9)
　　　　　　　　　　　　　　　　　　　　　　　　　　　　　　　SF–33/50/43/17

**2663**　　JOHN SMITH'S MAGNET H'CAP (3-Y.O) (0-90) £3143.25 (£936.00: £445.50: £200.25)
　　　　**5f**　　　　　　　　　　　　　　　　　　　　　3-00 (3-01)

2406 Mamma's Too **(86)** *(JBerry)* 9-7 JCarroll (3) (a chsng ldrs: drvn along ¹/₂-wy:
　　styd on to ld wl ins fnl f) ............................................................................... —**1**
2443³ Bodari **(80)** (Fav) *(DAWilson)* 8-10 †5DHarrison (6) (chsd ldrs: rdn ¹/₂-wy: r.o wl
　　nr fin) ..................................................................................................... hd.**2**
2514² Super Rocky **(77)** *(RBastiman)* 8-12 RHills (4) (chsd ldrs: rdn to ld ins fnl f: nt
　　qckn cl home) .......................................................................................... nk.**3**
2279⁵ Creche **(68)** (bl) *(MrsNMacauley)* 8-3 DMcKeown (5) (led & sn clr: hdd ins fnl f:
　　no ex) ...................................................................................................... ³/₄.**4**

2514* Miss Vaxette (70) (JLSpearing) 8-5 (7x) GHind (2) (lw: outpcd tl hdwy over 1f out: n.m.r: styd on nr fin) ............................................................ s.h.5
2115⁶ Hemsworth Lad (IRE) (58) (PCalver) 7-7 JFanning (7) (stdd s: effrt ½-wy: no imp) ............................................................ 3½.6
1871 Ned's Bonanza (75) (MDods) 8-10 JLowe (1) (prom: rdn ½-wy: wknd 1f out) ... 1.7

5/4 Bodari, 11/2 Super Rocky, Ned's Bonanza, Miss Vaxette, 10/1 Hemsworth Lad (IRE), 11/1 MAMMA'S TOO, 12/1 Creche. CSF £24.77, Tote £6.10: £2.30 £1.60 (£4.80). Mr J. K. Brown (COCKERHAM) bred by R. Brewis. 7 Rn
58.8 sec (2.1)
SF—55/43/44/32/33/7

---

**2664**  PAT PHOENIX H'CAP (0-80) £2924.00 (£872.00: £416.00: £188.00)
2m 3f
3-30 (3-32)

2397⁶ Premier Princess (38) (GAHam) 6-7-6 ‡5DHarrison (3) (lw: trckd ldrs: rdn to ld over 1f out: styd on u.p) ............................................................ —1
2261* Broctune Grey (69) (MrsGRReveley) 8-10-0 KDarley (1) (hld up: stdy hdwy 3f out: rdn & ev ch ins fnl f: nt qckn) ...................... 1.2
2261⁴ Arctic Oats (45) (WWHaigh) 7-8-4 DMcKeown (5) (lw: led: qcknd over 3f out: hdd over 1f out: no ex) ............................................................ 1½.3
2278* Smilingatstrangers (50) (v) (MrsBarbaraWaring) 4-8-2 ‡7CHawksley (4) (hld up: effrt over 3f out: styd on: nt pce to chal) ............ nk.4
2391³ Seldom In (41) (JWharton) 6-7-9 ‡5SMaloney (7) (lw: in tch: effrt 4f out: outpcd fnl 3f) ............................................................ 15.5
2391 Bar Billiards (66) (bl) (RFJohnsonHoughton) 3-8-8 RHills (6) (chsd ldrs tl rdn & btn over 2f out) ............................................................ nk.6

7/4 Broctune Grey, 11/4 Smilingatstrangers, 9/2 Seldom In, 7/1 PREMIER PRINCESS, 17/2 Arctic Oats, 12/1 Bar Billiards. CSF £18.70, Tote £7.60: £2.70 £2.00 (£9.90). Mr D. M. Drury (AXBRIDGE) bred by H. H. Aga Khan. 6 Rn
4m 12.6 (7.6)

---

**2665**  LEVY BOARD CLAIMING STKS (3-Y.O.F) £3158.00 (£944.00: £452.00: £206.00)
7f
4-00 (4-04)

2539² Patience Please (72) (Fav) (MHEasterby) 8-5 MBirch (5) (trckd ldrs: rdn to ld ins fnl f: styd on) ............................................................ —1
2539⁵ Throw Away Line (43) (REBarr) 8-4(1) SWebster (1) (led: hrd rdn & hdd ins fnl f: kpt on) ............................................................ 1½.2
2275⁵ Battuta (50) (REarnshaw) 7-9 ‡7CHawksley (4) (a chsng ldrs: styd on same pce fnl 2f) ............................................................ ½.3
2048⁶ Spanish Performer (50) (TFairhurst) 8-3 JFanning (2) (bhd: effrt over 2f out: styd on nr fin) ............................................................ nk.4
2253⁶ Grecian Belle (34) (DAWilson) 7-6 ‡5DHarrison (6) (chsd ldrs tl rdn & btn appr fnl f) ............................................................ s.h.5
2449 Greetland Folly (80) (RMWhitaker) 8-3 ACulhane (7) (lw: in tch: hdwy 3f out: rdn 2f out: sn bhd) ............................................................ 1½.6
2263⁵ Mini Fete (FR) (JParkes) 8-3 LCharnock (3) (drvn along after 2f: sn bhd) ......... 15.7

10/11 PATIENCE PLEASE, 9/4 Greetland Folly, 8/1 Battuta, 9/1 Spanish Performer(op 6/1), 16/1 Throw Away Line, 25/1 Grecian Belle, 50/1 Mini Fete (FR). CSF £14.40, Tote £1.80: £1.40 £3.90 (£15.60). Mr I. Bray (MALTON) bred by Pitts Farm Stud. 7 Rn
1m 25.6 (3.4)
SF—30/24/13/20/8/14

---

**2666**  TEESMOUTH STKS (Mdn 3-Y.O) £2070.00 (£570.00: £270.00)  6f  4-30 (4-31)

Elsals (Fav) (HThomsonJones) 9-0 RHills (1) (cmpt: scope: dwlt: hdwy u.p ½-wy: led over 1f out: styd on u.p) ............................................................ —1
2493² The New Girl (69) (CCElsey) 8-9 DHolland (2) (reluctant to ent stalls: chsd ldrs: chal 2f out: nt qckn fnl f) ............................................................ 2.2
2399⁵ Blue Is True (IRE) (48) (LJBarratt) 8-9 LCharnock (5) (lw: sn disp ld: led over 2f out tl over 1f out: nt qckn) ............................................................ ½.3
2324² Countercheck (IRE) (54) (bl) (CFWall) 9-0 SWebster (8) (lw: disp ld stands' side tl hdd over 2f out: sn outpcd: styd on fnl f) ............................................................ ½.4
1673 Noble Cause (IRE) (47) (REarnshaw) 9-0 ACulhane (6) (in tch: drvn along over 2f out: no imp after) ............................................................ 3½.5
2362⁴ Forza Azzurri (IRE) (55) (bl) (MrsNMacauley) 9-0 DMcKeown (3) (outpcd fr ½-wy) ............................................................ 2½.6
Sky Record (MissSEHall) 9-0 NConnorton (4) (cmpt: bit bkwd: nvr trbld ldrs) . 3½.7
2357 Dark Midnight (IRE) (51) (RRLamb) 8-7 ‡7RHavlin (7) (spd to ½-wy: sn bhd) ..... 7.8

**13/8** ELSALS, **7/4** The New Girl(Evens—15/8), **6/1** Countercheck (IRE), **10/1** Forza Azzurri (IRE), **20/1** Noble Cause (IRE), Blue Is True (IRE), **33/1** Sky Record, **40/1** Dark Midnight (IRE). CSF £4.57, Tote £2.40: £1.30 £1.10 £4.00 (£2.10). Mr Hamdan Al-Maktoum (NEWMARKET) bred by Home Stud Ltd. 8 Rn    1m 11.9 (2.6)
SF—36/23/21/24/10/–

---

**2667**  CLEVELAND AUCTION STKS (Mdn 2-Y.O) £2721.00 (£756.00: £363.00)
7f                                                                       5-00 (5-02)

2274² **Silverlocks** (Fav) *(MissSEHall)* 8-0 NConnorton (4) (trckd ldrs: led over 1f out:
shkn up & r.o) ............................................................................ —1
2534  Efizia *(MrsGRReveley)* 7-8 JLowe (8) (led tl hdd over 1f out: r.one pce) .......... 5.2
Jalcanto *(MrsGRReveley)* 8-5 KDarley (6) (w'like: scope: bit bkwd: a cl up: sltly
hmpd over 1f out: kpt on nr fin) ................................................ hd.3
2474⁴ Petite Jess *(WCarter)* 7-1 ‡⁷CHawksley (3) (a chsng ldrs: outpcd 2f out: no imp
after) ........................................................................................ 2¹/₂.4
1963³ Bold Philip **(74)** *(BBeasley)* 8-3⁽³⁾ ‡⁵SWilliams (1) (lw: in tch tl outpcd fnl 2f) ...... 5.5
2274  Oxrib *(CTinkler)* 7-13 LCharnock (2) (hld up & bhd: nvr nr to chal) ............... 2.6
Timber Topper *(MrsGRReveley)* 7-6 ‡⁷DarrenMoffatt (7) (w'like: unf: bit bkwd:
prom to ¹/₂-wy: sn outpcd) ........................................................ 3.7
Blakeney Boy *(RRLamb)* 7-9 ‡⁷RHavlin (5) (bit bkwd: stdd s: outpcd & lost tch fr
¹/₂-wy) ....................................................................................... dist.8

**2/5** SILVERLOCKS(1/3—1/2), **8/1** Petite Jess, **9/1** Bold Philip(op 6/1), Jalcanto, **16/1** Efizia, **20/1** Timber Topper, Oxrib, **33/1** Blakeney Boy. CSF £8.84, Tote £1.50: £1.10 £3.00 £1.60 (£12.40). Miss Betty Duxbury (MIDDLEHAM) bred by John A. Jones Morgan. 8 Rn     1m 26.8 (4.6)
SF—6/–/–/–/–/–

T/Plpt: £199.50 (14.1 Tckts).                                                        AA

---

# REDCAR (L-H)

## Saturday, August 8th [Good to firm becoming Good]

Going Allowance: 1st-4th: minus 0.10 sec (F); Rest: nil sec (G)        Wind: slt across

Stalls: high

---

**2668**  STAINTONDALE (S) STKS   £2553.00 (£708.00: £339.00)  7f      2-00 (2-03)

2216² **Inseyab (60)** (Fav) *(PCHaslam)* 4-8-10 ‡⁵DHarrison (4) (hdwy ¹/₂-wy: led wl
over 1f out: styd on) ................................................................. —1
2201⁵ Long Lane Lady **(46)** *(JMackie)* 6-9-1 GHind (10) (led: clr ¹/₂-wy: hdd wl over 1f
out: kpt on wl) ........................................................................... ³/₄.2
2183⁶ Gant Bleu (FR) **(56)** *(RMWhitaker)* 5-9-6 ACulhane (3) (hld up & bhd: hdwy 2f
out: too much to do) ................................................................... ³/₄.3
1791  Military Expert **(63)** *(CaptJWilson)* 3-9-0 JCarroll (9) (stumbled s: sn in tch: one
pce fnl 2f) ................................................................................. 4.4
2311³ Hataal (IRE) **(33)** (v) *(JBalding)* 3-9-0 ClaireBalding (5) (bhd tl styd on fnl 2f) ... 1¹/₂.5
1964  Vital Voltage (IRE) **(30)** *(MWEllerby)* 3-9-0 PBurke (6) (prom tl outpcd wl over 2f
out) ........................................................................................... 1¹/₂.6
1964  Scottish Ruby **(58)** *(CTinkler)* 3-9-0 GDuffield (2) (outpcd fr ¹/₂-wy) ............... 6.7
2502⁶ Quiet Victory **(47)** (bl) *(MissLCSiddall)* 5-8-12 ‡³FNorton (7) (spd over 4f) ....... 1¹/₂.8
1964  L'Amour Precieux **(49)** *(MWEasterby)* 3-9-0 TLucas (8) (t: early spd: bhd fnl 3f) 7.9

**8/13** INSEYAB, **5/1** Gant Bleu (FR), **9/1** Military Expert, **10/1** Quiet Victory, **14/1** Long Lane Lady, **20/1** Scottish Ruby, **25/1** Hataal (IRE), **50/1** Ors. CSF £10.10, Tote £1.60: £1.10 £2.30 £1.80 (£15.80). Mrs P. Haslam (MIDDLEHAM) bred by Gainsborough Stud Management Ltd. 9 Rn; No bid     1m 25.9 (3.7)
SF—30/33/36/18/4/11

---

**2669**  PAUL DANIELS MAGIC NURSERY   £3785.00 (£1130.00: £540.00: £245.00)
5f                                                                       2-20 (2-32)

(Weights raised 22 lb)

2437* **Zany Zanna (IRE) (72)** *(GAPritchard-Gordon)* 9-1 ‡⁵DHarrison (6) (stdd s:
hmpd after 1f & lost tch: gd hdwy ¹/₂-wy: led ins fnl f: r.o wl) —1
2264* Rhett's Choice **(69)** *(JBerry)* 9-3 JCarroll (1) (w ldr: led 2f out tl lns fnl f: r.o) ..... ¹/₂.2
2532² Dead Calm **(60)** *(CTinkler)* 8-8 TLucas (4) (lw: chsd ldrs: effrt 2f out: r.o one
pce) .......................................................................................... 2¹/₂.3
1738⁴ Make Mine a Double **(71)** *(MissSEHall)* 9-2 ‡³FNorton (3) (a.p: effrt 2f out: nt pce
to chal) ..................................................................................... 2.4
2225⁶ Rahon (IRE) **(73)** *(PWChapple-Hyam)* 9-2 ‡⁵LNewton (2) (chsd ldrs: rdn 2f out:
one pce) ................................................................................... 1.5
2489* Just Baileys **(70)** (Fav) *(MJohnston)* 9-4 GDuffield (5) (lw: led 3f: wknd 1f out) 2¹/₂.6

13/8 Just Baileys, 3/1 ZANY ZANNA (IRE), 11/2 Rhett's Choice, 13/2 Dead Calm, 7/1 Make Mine a Double, 10/1 Rahon (IRE). CSF £17.68, Tote £3.10: £1.50 £2.30 (£6.60). Mr Giles W. Pritchard-Gordon (NEWMARKET) bred by Limestone Stud in Ireland. 6 Rn
60.1 sec (3.4)
SF—23/23/4/4/–/–

**2670**    GO RACING IN YORKSHIRE APP'CE H'CAP (0-70) £2427.00 (£672.00: £321.00)
1¼m    3-00 (3-05)

25713 **Talented Ting (IRE) (69)** (PCHaslam) 3-9-5 ‡5NicolaHoward (4) (lw: cl up: led 4f out: clr 2f out: pushed out) .................................... —1

25312 Much Sought After **(69)** (Fav) (DMorley) 3-9-7 ‡3EBentley (3) (b.hind: lw: slipped appr st: hdwy 3f out: styd on: nt rch wnr) ............... 4.2

26023 Thunderbird One (USA) **(58)** (DenysSmith) 3-8-6 ‡7CTeague (7) (chsd ldrs: chal 3f out: sn rdn: outpcd fnl 2f) ................. 3½.3

2379★ Tarda **(56)** (MrsGRReveley) 5-9-3 ‡3ClaireBalding (2) (lw: hld up: effrt over 3f out: hung lft: nvr able to chal) ...................... nk.4

24086 Tempering **(48)** (DWChapman) 6-8-12 GForster (6) (swtg: sn cl up: led appr st tl hdd 4f out: sn wknd) ........................ 7.5

2596 Doctor's Remedy **(43)** (MrsJJordan) 6-8-0(5) ‡7PAllison (1) (led tl hdd appr st: wknd over 3f out) ............................. 1.6

1961 Hizeem **(29)** (MPNaughton) 6-7-7 CHawksley (5) (lw: slipped appr st: n.d) ...... 1½.7
LONG HANDICAP: Hizeem 7-6.

3/1 Much Sought After, 7/2 TALENTED TING (IRE), Tarda, 5/1 Thunderbird One (USA), 15/2 Doctor's Remedy, 12/1 Tempering, 16/1 Hizeem. CSF £13.31, Tote £4.20: £2.50 £1.90 (£8.80). Mr Martin Wickens (MIDDLEHAM) bred by R. A. Keogh. 7 Rn
2m 7.1 (4.6)
SF—49/43/21/31/12/–

**2671**    BONUSPRINT H'CAP (3-Y.O) (0-100) £3975.00 (£1100.00: £525.00)
1¼m    3-30 (3-31)
(Weights raised 8 lb)

18053 **Mathaayl (USA) (75)** (bl) (HThomsonJones) 8-12 NCarlisle (1) (trckd ldr: smooth hdwy to ld ins fnl f: r.o wl) ................... —1

2385★ Wrets **(82)** (MRStoute) 9-5 GDuffield (2) (lw: set stdy pce: qcknd 4f out: hdd ins fnl f: r.o) ................................. 1½.2

24532 Wild Fire **(84)** (Fav) (GWragg) 9-4 ‡3FNorton (3) (hld up: hdwy over 2f out: sn rdn & nt qckn) ............................... 2.3

8/13 Wild Fire, 9/4 Wrets, 7/1 MATHAAYL (USA). CSF £16.93, Tote £7.00 (£4.30). Mr Hamdan Al-Maktoum (NEWMARKET) bred by Hamdan Al Maktoum in USA. 3 Rn
2m 14.1 (11.6)

**2672**    OLD RABY CLAIMING H'CAP (0-70) £2954.00 (£819.00: £392.00)
6f    4-00 (4-03)
(Weights raised 10 lb)

1961 **Arabat (53)** (v) (MPNaughton) 5-9-10 JakiHouston (4) (chsd ldrs: led wl over 1f out: hung lft & r.o) .......................... —1

22454 Supreme Desire **(39)** (ASmith) 4-8-10 SWebster (2) (w ldrs: rdn over 2f out: r.o one pce) ................................. 2½.2

25393 Oyston's Life **(54)** (JBerry) 3-9-6 JCarroll (5) (lw: hdwy ½-wy: ev ch 2f out: nt qckn fnl f) ................................ s.h.3

23255 Miss Aragon **(49)** (MissLCSiddall) 4-9-3 ‡3FNorton (1) (chsd ldrs: rdn & one pce fnl 2f) ................................... 3½.4

2325 Don't Run Me Over **(48)** (BCMorgan) 3-9-0 GDuffield (6) (lw: mde most tl hdd & wknd wl over 1f out) ..................... nk.5

2481 Spanish Realm **(41)** (MBrittain) 5-8-12 PSedgwick (3) (b.off hind: chsd ldrs 5f) . 5.6

1625 Chester Belle **(33)** (PCHaslam) 3-7-6 ‡7NicolaHoward (11) (dwlt: hdwy ½-wy: no imp) ................................. ½.7

25362 Dancing Wild **(38)** (Fav) (MrsGRReveley) 3-8-4 NCarlisle (12) (chsd ldrs stands' side: rdn 3f out: sn btn) ............... 1.8

2325 Pipe Opener **(46)** (bl) (JLSpearing) 4-9-3 GHind (8) (no imp fr ½-wy) .............. nk.9

Nagem **(38)** (LJBarratt) 9-8-9 PBurke (10) (led stands' side: hung lft over 2f out: sn wknd) ............................... 1½.10

25363 Henry Will **(39)** (TFairhurst) 8-8-10 JFanning (7) (n.d) ...................... s.h.11

2249 Our Amber **(24)** (DWChapman) 5-7-2(2) ‡7CHawksley (9) (prom over 3f) ....... s.h.12
LONG HANDICAP: Our Amber 7-5.

3/1 Dancing Wild, 11/2 Miss Aragon, 6/1 Don't Run Me Over, 13/2 Oyston's Life, 9/1 Henry Will, 9/1 ARABAT, 12/1 Supreme Desire, 14/1 Pipe Opener, 16/1 Chester Belle, 25/1 Our Amber, Spanish Realm, 33/1 Nagem. CSF £101.15, CT £685.47. Tote £20.10: £5.20 £2.50 £2.30 (£109.30). Mrs H. H. Wane (RICHMOND) bred by Gerald W. Leigh. 12 Rn
1m 13.1 (3.8)
SF—34/10/19/4/–/–

## 2673

MIDDLETON STKS (Mdn) £2070.00 (£570.00: £270.00)    **1m 1f**    4-30 (4-32)

| | | |
|---|---|---|
| 2298[4] | **Laughsome** (Fav) *(JHMGosden)* 3–8-8 JCarroll (1) (trckd ldrs: led over 3f out: pushed clr fnl 2f) | —1 |
| 1792[4] | Clear Sound (v) *(GWragg)* 3-8-5 ‡3FNorton (3) (clr up: chal ent st: one pce wl over 2f out) | 5.2 |
| | Edirepus *(MrsGRReveley)* 4–9-7 GDuffield (4) (led tl hdd over 3f out: one pce) | 7.3 |
| 2114[5] | Sparkling Skies *(EWeymes)* 3–8-8 ACulhane (2) (unruly in stalls: a bhd: t.o) | dist.4 |

**4/7** LAUGHSOME, **5/2** Clear Sound, **7/1** Edirepus, **33/1** Sparkling Skies. CSF £2.24, Tote £1.40 (£1.60). Sheikh Mohammed (NEWMARKET) bred by White Lodge Stud Ltd. 4 Rn    1m 58.1 (9.1)

## 2674

E.B.F. SINNINGTON STKS (Mdn 2-Y.O.F) £2684.50 (£742.00: £353.50)    **6f**    5-00 (5-03)

| | | |
|---|---|---|
| 1485[6] | **Royal Diva** *(MissSEHall)* 8-11 GHind (1) (mde most: r.o wl fnl 2f) | —1 |
| 2414[3] | Fairy Story (IRE) *(JWHills)* 8-8 ‡3FNorton (2) (trckd ldrs: effrt 2f out: nt qckn) | 4.2 |
| 2190[4] | Henequin (USA) (Fav) *(JHMGosden)* 8-11 JCarroll (4) (a.p: effrt over 2f out: sn rdn & no imp) | 2½.3 |
| | Grogfryn *(JBerry)* 8-11 NCarlisle (6) (neat: scope: chsd ldrs tl outpcd fnl 2f) | hd.4 |
| 2501 | Ikhtisas (USA) *(BHanbury)* 8-11 GDuffield (5) (w wnr 4f: sn wknd) | 8.5 |
| | Final Action *(RMWhitaker)* 8-11 ACulhane (3) (neat: dwlt: nvr wnt pce) | 6.6 |

**4/7** Henequin (USA), **5/1** Fairy Story (IRE), **7/1** Ikhtisas (USA), **11/1** ROYAL DIVA(op 6/1), **20/1** 0rs. CSF £55.37, Tote £20.70: £3.30 £2.10 (£12.20). Mr R. Ogden (MIDDLEHAM) bred by R. Ogden. 6 Rn    1m 14.1 (4.8)

T/Plpt: £649.10 (3.42 Tckts).    AA

## 2350—AYR (L-H)

### Saturday, August 8th [Good]

Going Allowance: St: minus 0.10 sec (F); Rnd: 0.20 sec per fur (G)    Wind: slt across

Stalls: centre

## 2675

FULLERTON STKS (Mdn 2-Y.O) £2472.00 (£692.00: £336.00)    **7f**    2-35 (2-39)

| | | |
|---|---|---|
| 2340[4] | **Visto Si Stampi (IRE)** (Fav) *(JLDunlop)* 9-0 RHills (13) (lw: a chsng ldrs: rdn to ld wl over 1f out: sn clr: comf) | —1 |
| | I Remember You (IRE) *(FHLee)* 9-0 RLappin (7) (tall: leggy: scope: cl up: rdn & outpcd 2f out: styd on fnl f: nt rch wnr) | 4.2 |
| | Persian Charmer (IRE) *(MissLAPerratt)* 9-0 AMcGlone (1) (lengthy: leggy: bkwd: a.p: led 2f out: sn hdd: kpt on same pce) | s.h.3 |
| 2519 | Blue Blazer *(BHanbury)* 9-0 SWhitworth (3) (lw: mid div: hdwy 3f out: styd on: nt pce to chal) | 1½.4 |
| | Move Smartly (IRE) *(FHLee)* 9-0 AlexGreaves (12) (cmpt: bit bkwd: in tch: effrt over 2f out: styd on same pce) | ¾.5 |
| 2025[4] | Irish Dominion *(MissSEHall)* 9-0 NConnorton (4) (lw: in tch: hdwy & ch 2f out: sn rdn & no ex) | ½.6 |
| 2212[2] | Mondragon *(MrsGRReveley)* 9-0 KDarley (6) (cl up: effrt over 2f out: one pce) | 3½.7 |
| 2356[3] | Grand as Owt *(DenysSmith)* 9-0 JFortune (11) (bhd: styd on fnl 2f: nrst fin) | 2.8 |
| 2205 | Court Pianist (IRE) *(CWCElsey)* 9-0 GBaxter (2) (led tl hdd 2f out: grad wknd) | ½.9 |
| 1605[4] | Mad Mytton (74) (bl) *(ABailey)* 8-9 ‡5ATucker (5) (plld hrd: in tch: effrt over 2f out: btn appr fnl f) | 3.10 |
| 2248[3] | Drumdonna (IRE) *(JBerry)* 8-9 RPElliott (14) (prom to st) | 1½.11 |
| | Cornflake *(DenysSmith)* 8-9 DaleGibson (9) (cmpt: str: bkwd: s.i.s: a bhd) | 2.12 |
| 2309[3] | Anne's Bay (IRE) *(DMoffatt)* 8-4 ‡5SMaloney (8) (nvr wnt pce) | 2½.13 |
| | Try N' Fly (IRE) *(MissLAPerratt)* 8-7 ‡7RHavlin (10) (w'like: unf: bkwd: s.i.s: a bhd: t.o fnl 4f) | dist.14 |

**Evens** VISTO SI STAMPI (IRE), **5/1** Irish Dominion, **9/1** Mondragon(op 5/1), **11/1** Blue Blazer, **14/1** Persian Charmer (IRE)(op 8/1), **16/1** I Remember You (IRE), **20/1** Court Pianist (IRE), Grand as Owt, **25/1** Drumdonna (IRE), **50/1** Move Smartly (IRE), Cornflake, Mad Mytton, **100/1** Try N' Fly (IRE), **200/1** Anne's Bay (IRE). CSF £16.87, Tote £1.90: £1.10 £4.80 £3.40 (£377.30). Gerecon Italia (ARUNDEL) bred by Samac Ltd in Ireland. 14 Rn    1m 29.45 (5.45)

SF—39/27/26/21/19/17

## 2676

BELLEISLE H'CAP (0-70) £2276.00 (£636.00: £308.00)    **5f**    3-05 (3-07)

| | | |
|---|---|---|
| 2359[2] | **Ballad Dancer (54)** (Jt-Fav) *(EJAlston)* 7–8-12 GBaxter (5) (in tch: rdn along ½-wy: r.o wl to ld cl home) | —1 |
| 2478[4] | Serious Hurry (56) (bl) *(SirMarkPrescott)* 4–9-0 RHills (6) (mde most: drvn along appr fnl f: hdd & nk ex cl home) | nk.2 |

2564 Uppance **(35)** *(DWChapman)* 4–7–0 ‡⁷MBaird (8) (chsd ldrs: rdn 2f out: styd on fnl f) ............ 1.3
2359⁴ Langtonian **(63)** (bl) *(JBerry)* 3–9–3 JFortune (1) (wnt lft s: sn rcvrd: disp ld ½-wy: rdn & nt qckn fnl f) ............ hd.4
2046★ Best Effort **(68)** *(MPNaughton)* 6–9–5 ‡⁷ADobbin (4) (in tch: effrt ½-wy: r.o one pce fnl f) ............ ½.5
2224³ Hinari Video **(45)** *(MJohnston)* 7–8–3 RPElliott (3) (in tch: rdn 2 out: no ex fnl f) ½.6
1020 Parisienne King (USA) **(46)** *(FHLee)* 3–7–9⁽⁵⁾ ‡⁵SMaloney (7) (sn rdn along: nvr trbld ldrs) ............ 5.7
2245³ Cottage Gallery (IRE) **(35)** (bl) *(WAStephenson)* 4–7–7 DaleGibson (2) (prom: rdn ½-wy: wknd wl over 1f out) ............ 1½.8

LONG HANDICAP: Uppance 6-12, Cottage Gallery (IRE) 7-5.
*Stewards Enquiry: R.Hills suspended 17-20/8/92 (excessive use of whip).*

**3/1** Serious Hurry, BALLAD DANCER, **7/2** Best Effort, **9/2** Hinari Video, **8/1** Langtonian(6/1—9/1), **14/1** Cottage Gallery (IRE), **33/1** Parisienne King (USA), **66/1** Uppance. CSF £11.54, CT £416.76. Tote £3.30: £1.10 £1.40 £36.60 (£7.60). Mr Mick Graham (PRESTON) bred by Collinstown Stud Farm Ltd. 8 Rn    59.67 sec (1.67)
SF—54/55/23/53/53/35

---

**2677**  ROYAL TROON H'CAP (0-70) £2402.00 (£672.00: £326.00)  **1m 7f**  3-35 (3-39)
(Weights raised 9 lb)

1898⁵ **Fair Flyer (IRE) (47)** *(MJohnston)* 3–8–3 RPElliott (10) (a.p: led & qcknd clr ent st: drvn out) ............ —1
2485² Miliyel **(50)** *(PMonteith)* 3–8–6 KDarley (8) (hld up & bhd: hdwy 3f out: drvn along over 1f out: styd on) ............ 1½.2
312 Moment of Truth **(36)** *(PMonteith)* 8–8–6 GBaxter (1) (hld up & bhd: styd on wl fnl 2f: nrst fin) ............ 1½.3
2083² Prince Mercury **(68)** *(JLDunlop)* 3–9–10 RHills (6) (a chsng ldrs: rdn 3f out: one pce fnl 2f) ............ nk.4
2222⁶ Dollar Seeker (USA) **(50)** (bl) *(ABailey)* 8–9–1 ‡⁵ATucker (3) (prom: rdn 3f out: btn 2f out) ............ 8.5
893² Bridge Player **(46)** *(DMoffatt)* 5–9–2 JFortune (7) (in tch: hdwy & effrt on outside over 2f out: no imp) ............ ½.6
2513² Alpha Helix **(30)** (v) *(MissLAPerratt)* 9–7–7⁽²⁾ ‡⁷RHavlin (13) (hld up: hdwy 3f out: rdn & btn 2f out) ............ 1.7
2358⁴ Fairgroundprincess **(36)** *(FHLee)* 4–8–6 RLappin (9) (bhd: effrt over 2f out: n.d) nk.8
2513★ Desert Mist **(49)** (bl) (Fav) *(DenysSmith)* 3–8–5 DaleGibson (5) (in tch: rdn along ½-wy: no imp fnl 3f) ............ 1½.9
2492⁴ Bee Beat **(53)** (bl) *(EAWheeler)* 4–9–9 AMcGlone (12) (mid div: wknd ent st) ... 6.10
2122² Natral Exchange (IRE) **(55)** (v) *(JWHills)* 3–8–11 SWhitworth (4) (cl up: led 7f out: hdd ent st: sn wknd) ............ hd.11
2217⁵ Touching Times **(51)** *(TCraig)* 4–9–2 ‡⁵SMaloney (2) (a bhd) ............ s.h.12
Scalp 'em (IRE) **(49)** *(FHLee)* 4–9–5 NConnorton (11) (led to 7f out: wknd qckly 3f out) ............ 10.13

**3/1** Desert Mist(op 2/1), **11/2** Prince Mercury, **6/1** FAIR FLYER (IRE), **7/1** Natral Exchange (IRE), **8/1** Bee Beat, **12/1** Bridge Player, Alpha Helix, **14/1** Fairgroundprincess, Miliyel, **16/1** Dollar Seeker (USA), **25/1** Touching Times, **33/1** Moment of Truth, **50/1** Scalp 'em (IRE). CSF £78.41, CT £2,317.61. Tote £11.50: £2.40 £3.30 £11.30 (£87.20). Mr William Provan Hunter (MIDDLEHAM) bred by J. Mamakos in Ireland. 13 Rn
3m 25.63 (13.13)

---

**2678**  DARVEL CLAIMING STKS  £2290.00 (£640.00: £310.00)  **1m**  4-05 (4-11)

2378★ **Mbulwa (56)** (Fav) *(SEKettlewell)* 6–8–10 JFortune (3) (b: a chsng ldrs: drvn to ld wl ins fnl f: styd on) ............ —1
2463 Laurel Queen (IRE) **(63)** *(JBerry)* 4–9–5 RHills (2) (a.p: led 3f out: rdn along appr fnl f: hdd & no ex towards fin) ............ ¾.2
2469² Euroblake **(68)** *(TDBarron)* 5–9–6 AlexGreaves (7) (bhd: rdn 3f out: styd on u.p fnl f) ............ 4.3
2351² Princess Maxine (IRE) **(58)** *(MissLAPerratt)* 3–8–8 DaleGibson (1) (in tch: effrt over 2f out: ev ch wl over 1f out: one pce) ............ 1.4
2561 Ruth's Gamble **(66)** *(DWChapman)* 4–9–0 KDarley (4) (chsd ldrs: rdn 3f out: no imp) ............ 2.5
2218² Rahif **(62)** *(MrsGRReveley)* 4–9–4 GBaxter (6) (led & sn clr: hdd 3f out: sn wknd) 6.6
2487³ Master Plan (FR) **(22)** *(MissLAPerratt)* 6–8–6 AMcGlone (5) (a bhd) ............ 10.7

**3/1** MBULWA, **4/1** Laurel Queen (IRE)(op 9/4), **9/2** Rahif, Euroblake(op 9/4), **6/1** Princess Maxine (IRE), **8/1** Ruth's Gamble, **33/1** Master Plan (FR). CSF £13.80, Tote £3.70: £1.70 £2.50 (£11.00). Northumbria Leisure Ltd (MIDDLEHAM) bred by Hascombe and Valiant Studs. 7 Rn    1m 42.63 (5.43)
SF—39/46/35/20/20/6

**2679**   BARRASSIE STKS (2-Y.O) £3148.00 (£878.00: £424.00)    7f    4-35 (4-38)

24416 **Antester (IRE) (100)** *(PWChapple-Hyam)* 9-1 SWhitworth (3) (b.off hind: chsd
     ldr: led wl over 2f out: rdn & r.o wl fnl f) ............................. —1
2286* Ibraz (USA) (86) *(HThomsonJones)* 9-1 RHills (2) (trckd ldrs: rdn 2f out: styd on
     one pce) ................................................................. 1½.2
2356* Woodhaunter (USA) (91) **(Fav)** *(JHMGosden)* 9-1 AMcGlone (1) (led: rdn 3f
     out: hdd wl over 2f out: no ex fnl f) ................................. s.h.3

**Evens** Woodhaunter (USA), **9/4** ANTESTER (IRE), **5/2** Ibraz (USA). CSF £6.54, Tote £3.40 (£4.20). Mr Luciano
Gaucci (MARLBOROUGH) bred by Hadi Al Tajir in Ireland. 3 Rn                    1m 29.96 (5.96)
                                                                              SF—32/27/26

**2680**   OLD PRESTWICK H'CAP (3-Y.O) (0-70) £2402.00 (£672.00: £326.00)    5-05 (5-07)
           7f

(Weights raised 6 lb)

2531* **Thornton Gate (59)** (bl) *(MHEasterby)* 8-13 ‡⁵SMaloney (4) (mde all: rdn & r.o
     wl fnl 2f) .............................................................. —1
25523 Kalar (41) (bl) *(DWChapman)* 7-9 ‡⁵ATucker (1) (a.p: rdn 2f out: kpt on one pce)    3.2
22495 Gizlaan (USA) (56) *(BHanbury)* 9-1 AMcGlone (8) (hld up & bhd: hdwy over 2f
     out: kpt on u.p) ....................................................... ½.3
20885 Venture Fourth (50) *(EJAlston)* 8-9 GBaxter (3) (s.i.s: hdwy 2f out: styd on: nt
     rch ldrs) .............................................................. 2.4
24965 Silky Siren (54) **(Fav)** *(EAWheeler)* 8-13 SWhitworth (9) (chsd ldrs: effrt over 2f
     out: btn whn eased wl ins fnl f) ...................................... 2.5
21143 Maritime Lady (USA) (62) *(MRStoute)* 9-7 RHills (5) (chsd ldrs tl rdn & wknd
     appr fnl f) ............................................................ 3.6
2353* Rose Gem (IRE) (60) *(PCHaslam)* 9-5 DaleGibson (7) (hld up & bhd: hdwy u.p
     on outside over 2f out: eased whn btn appr fnl f) .................... hd.7
 2552 Cromer's Express (55) *(MissLCSiddall)* 8-12 KDarley (2) (s.i.s. sn in tch: offrt 3f
     out: sn wknd) .......................................................... 1.8
13286 Palacegate King (50) *(JBerry)* 8-9 JFortune (6) (chsd ldrs: rdn 3f out: wknd 2f
     out) .................................................................... 2.9

*Stewards Enquiry: Whitworth fined £185 under Rule 151 (ii) (failure to ensure best possible placing).*

**5/4** Silky Siren(Evens—6/4), **9/2** Rose Gem (IRE), **5/1** THORNTON GATE(4/1—6/1), **11/2** Kalar, **11/1** Maritime
Lady (USA)(8/1—12/1), **12/1** Gizlaan (USA)(op 8/1), **14/1** Venture Fourth, **20/1** Palacegate King, **50/1** Cromer's
Express. CSF £32.18, CT £292.59. Tote £8.40: £2.70 £2.10 £6.90 (£16.30). Mr T. H. Bennett (MALTON) bred
by Jim Strange. 9 Rn                                                        1m 29.22 (5.22)
                                                                           SF—42/15/33/21/19/18

T/Plpt: £688.60 (2.3 Tckts).                                                                   GB

## 2407—**LINGFIELD  (L-H)**

## Saturday, August 8th [Turf Good to firm, AWT Standard]
Going Allowance: Turf: minus 0.20 (F); AWT: minus 0.55 sec (FS)           Wind: nil

Stalls: high

**2681**   HEINZ SOUPS APP'CE NURSERY    £1674.00 (£464.00: £222.00)    7f    5-50 (5-55)
           (Weights raised 5 lb)

2544 **Kyrenia Game (60)** *(PMitchell)* 8-3 SO'Gorman (4) (rdn over 5f out: gd hdwy
     over 1f out: str run fnl f: led nr fin) ............................... —1
2462 Le Couteau (65) *(DWPArbuthnot)* 8-8 RPrice (6) (hld up: led 2f out: hrd rdn:
     hdd nr fin) ............................................................ 1.2
25162 Lofty Deed (USA) (61) *(SirMarkPrescott)* 8-4 DBiggs (1) (swtg: hld up: ev ch ins
     fnl f: unable qckn nr fin) ............................................ ¾.3
22853 Poly Vision (IRE) (68) *(MRChannon)* 8-11 BDoyle (7) (swtg: hdwy over 2f out:
     hrd rdn over 1f out: one pce) ........................................ 2.4
24092 Bold Acre (68) *(DRLaing)* 8-6 ‡⁵DToole (5) (lw: a.p: ev ch 2f out: edgd rt wl over
     1f out: one pce) ...................................................... nk.5
20585 Floodlight (IRE) (52) *(RJHolder)* 7-4 ‡⁵RWaterfield (3) (led over 2f: wknd over 1f
     out) .................................................................... 2.6
2248* Clear Honey (USA) (78) *(BHanbury)* 9-2 ‡⁵VBray (2) (led over 4f out to 2f out:
     wkng whn n.m.r wl over 1f out) ...................................... ¾.7
 595* Jeremiahs Boy (71) *(RJHodges)* 9-0 TSprake (8) (prom 3f: t.o) ............ 30.8

**11/4** Jeremiahs Boy(5/1—5/2), **3/1** Bold Acre, **5/1** Poly Vision (IRE), Lofty Deed (USA), **13/2** Clear Honey
(USA), **10/1** Le Couteau, **16/1** KYRENIA GAME & Ors. CSF £142.58, CT £835.95. Tote £16.10: £3.80 £2.20
£1.70 (£23.70). Mr G. V. Eliades (EPSOM) bred by George Eliades. 8 Rn       1m 24.17 (2.87)
                                                                           SF—24/26/20/21/20/–

## 2682

DAILY STAR H'CAP (0-70) £1632.00 (£452.00: £216.00)     **2m (AWT)**    6-20 (6-24)

2197* **Yenoora (IRE) (68)** (Fav) *(PFICole)* 3–9-0 MRoberts (9) (lw: led over 10f out: hrd rdn over 1f out: r.o wl) ............................... —1

2407² **Ideal Candidate (57)** *(TJNaughton)* 3–8-3 DBiggs (4) (hld up: chsd wnr over 3f out: hrd rdn & ev ch wl over 1f out: one pce ins fnl f) ....... 2½.2

2451⁴ **Springs Welcome (67)** *(CACyzer)* 6–9-7 ‡⁷TMcLaughlin (8) (lw: s.s: hdwy over 4f out: one pce fnl 3f) ........................................ 8.3

2412 **Intricacy (64)** *(CCElsey)* 4–9-6 ‡⁵DHarrison (2) (nvr nr to chal) .............. 4.4

2278⁴ **Caroles Clown (35)** *(MJHaynes)* 6–7-3 ‡⁷DToole (3) (b.hind: lw: nvr nrr) ........... 5.5

1970 **Lady Westgate (32)** *(GBBalding)* 8–7-7 NAdams (5) (b.off hind: prom over 12f)   8.6

2397 **Himlaj (USA) (40)** *(SMellor)* 7–8-1 DanaMellor (7) (hdwy 6f out: wknd over 3f out)   ¾.7

2533⁴ **Major Risk (53)** *(PAKelleway)* 3–7-8⁽⁶⁾ ‡⁵BDoyle (6) (led over 5f: wknd over 4f out) ....................................................... 6.8

2253³ **Pleasure Ahead (44)** (bl) *(MDixon)* 5–8-5 BRouse (10) (bhd fnl 4f) ................. 8.9

2367 **Erin's Town (33)** *(WCarter)* 6–7-8⁽¹⁾ JQuinn (1) (lw: 4th whn p.u over 9f out: broke shoulder: dead) ......................... 0

LONG HANDICAP: Lady Westgate 7-6, Major Risk 7-5, Erin's Town 7-6.

**5/6** YENOORA (IRE)(6/4—4/5), **5/1** Caroles Clown 6-12, Springs Welcome, **8/1** Ideal Candidate, **11/1** Pleasure Ahead, **14/1** Intricacy(op 7/1), **20/1** Erin's Town, **25/1** Major Risk, **33/1** Lady Westgate, **50/1** Himlaj (USA). CSF £8.82, CT £30.98. Tote £1.80: £1.40 £1.60 £1.80 (£4.00). Mr Reg Hester (WHATCOMBE) bred by Binfield Manor Farms Ltd in Ireland. 10 Rn       3m 20.09 (1.39 under best; U2.91)
SF—41/27/37/37/–/–

## 2683

B.S.B. DORLAND ADVERTISING AGENCY STKS (2-Y.O) £2005.00 (£555.00: £265.00) **6f**     6-50 (6-51)

2338 **Lys (IRE)** *(CEBrittain)* 8-6 MRoberts (4) (mde all: hrd rdn over 1f out: r.o wl) ..... —1

2342⁴ **Rain Splash (84)** *(RHannon)* 8-13 BRouse (2) (hld up: hrd rdn over 1f out: r.o wl ins fnl f) ........................... s.h.2

**Pipers Reel** (Fav) *(LordHuntingdon)* 8-1 ‡⁵DHarrison (1) (unf: lw: w wnr: rdn over 1f out: unable qckn) .......................... 2½.3

**Miss Delivery** *(PHowling)* 8-6 JMurray (3) (neat: bhd fnl 2f) ................... 10.4

**5/4** Pipers Reel, **7/4** Rain Splash(op 4/6), **11/4** LYS (IRE), **33/1** Miss Delivery. CSF £7.45, Tote £3.50 (£2.30). Sheikh Marwan Al Maktoum (NEWMARKET) bred by Oliver Murphy in Ireland. 4 Rn    1m 12.51 (3.91)

## 2684

FOOD SERVICES H'CAP (0-80) £2250.00 (£625.00: £300.00)   **7f**    7-20 (7-26)
(Weights raised 1 lb)

2502* **Coral Flutter (55)** (bl) (Jt-Fav) *(JWPayne)* 5–8-5 JQuinn (8) (mde all: rdn out) .. —1

2173³ **Mossy Rose (58)** (Jt-Fav) *(LordHuntingdon)* 6–8-3 ‡⁵DHarrison (3) (lw: a.p: hrd rdn over 1f out: unable qckn) ............................. 2½.2

2183 **Tender Moment (IRE) (68)** *(CEBrittain)* 4–9-4 MRoberts (4) (hdwy 2f out: one pce fnl f) ............................................ 1.3

2494* **Teanarco (IRE) (64)** *(RJHolder)* 4–8-7 ‡⁷SDrowne (2) (hld up: hrd rdn 2f out: one pce) .......................................... 1.4

2476 **Fabled Orator (45)** *(PHowling)* 7–7-9⁽²⁾ DBiggs (6) (b.nr hind: lw: nvr nr to chal)   4.5

2458 **Across the Bay (74)** *(SDow)* 5–9-3 ‡⁷AMartinez (7) (bhd fnl 3f) ............ hd.6

2410³ **Lord Oberon (IRE) (67)** *(RJO'Sullivan)* 4–9-3 AClark (9) (a bhd) ............ 2½.7

2404 **Tauber (66)** *(PatMitchell)* 8–8-13 ‡³SO'Gorman (5) (prom over 4f) ............ 6.8

2198 **Mabonne (54)** (bl) *(JLDunlop)* 3–7-12 NAdams (1) (hld up: rdn over 2f out: wknd over 1f out) ................................... 1½.9

LONG HANDICAP: Fabled Orator 6-13.

**4/1** CORAL FLUTTER, Mossy Rose(6/1—7/1), **5/1** Teanarco (IRE), Lord Oberon (IRE), **11/2** Tender Moment (IRE), **8/1** Mabonne, **9/1** Across the Bay, Tauber(6/1—10/1), **40/1** Fabled Orator. CSF £20.25, CT £82.28. Tote £3.60: £1.60 £1.70 £2.20 (£12.10). Mrs J. W. Payne (NEWMARKET) bred by Lady Juliet de Chair. 9 Rn     1m 22.39 (1.09)
SF—54/44/56/42/18/39

## 2685

HEINZ SALAD DRESSING S.I.A. (S) H'CAP (3-Y.O) (0-60) £1520.00 (£420.00: £200.00) **1¼m (AWT)**    7-50 (7-52)

1949 **Day of History (IRE) (37)** *(CACyzer)* 8-6 DBiggs (3) (lw: hdwy over 3f out: hrd rdn over 1f out led ins fnl f: r.o wl) ................. —1

2583⁵ **Wayward Son (42)** *(GLewis)* 8-6 ‡⁵DHarrison (1) (led: hrd rdn over 1f out: hdd ins fnl f: unable qckn) ........................ 1.2

2041⁶ **Highland Flame (42)** *(ANLee)* 8-6 ‡⁵StephenDavies (6) (hdwy over 4f out: hrd rdn over 1f out: one pce) ..................... ½.3

2486³ **Shardra (47)** (Fav) *(MJCamacho)* 9-2 MRoberts (10) (a.p: rdn over 4f out: eased whn btn fnl f) ............................... 7.4

2254⁶ Bishopstone Bill *(29) (SMellor)* 7-12  DanaMellor (8) (no hdwy fnl 3f) .............. 3¹/₂.5
2372² Princess of Orange *(52) (CCElsey)* 9-7  JQuinn (7) (lw: prom 7f) ......................... 4.6
2545 Selaginella *(51) (MRChannon)* 9-1 ‡⁵BDoyle (2) (lw: prom over 6f) ................... s.h.7
1890 The Dominant Gene *(35) (bl) (JRJenkins)* 8-4⁽¹⁾ AClark (5) (bhd fnl 4f) .............. 8.8
1794 Lady Risk Me *(34) (JRBostock)* 7-12⁽⁴⁾ ‡⁵RPrice (9) (swtg: a bhd) .................... 1.9
*2100* Dots Dee *(33) (JMBradley)* 8-2  NAdams (4) (lw: bhd fnl 6f) ............................ ¹/₂.10

2/1 Shardra(11/8—9/4), 11/2 Highland Flame, 13/2 DAY OF HISTORY (IRE), The Dominant Gene(12/1—6/1), 7/1 Princess of Orange(6/1—9/1), 15/2 Selaginella, 12/1 Wayward Son, 20/1 Bishopstone Bill, 25/1 Ors. CSF £72.67, CT £412.50. Tote £8.20: £2.00 £3.40 £2.20 (£75.20). Mr R. M. Cyzer (HORSHAM) bred by Mount Coote Stud in Ireland. 10 Rn; No bid                                   2m 6.17 (3.17)
                                                                      SF—5/3/2/–/–/–

**2686**    HEINZ BEANZ STKS (Mdn 2-Y.O.F) £1618.00 (£448.00: £214.00)
            **5f (AWT)**                                              8-20 (8-20)

        **Five Islands** (Fav) *(PFICole)* 8-11  MRoberts (6) (b.hind: cmpt: lw: led 4f out: qcknd over 1f out: comf) ............................................................... —1
        Seasonal Splendour (IRE) *(CACyzer)* 8-11  DBiggs (4) (unf: bit bkwd: outpcd: str run fnl f: fin wl) .................................................................... nk.2
   2285 Home Affair *(DTThom)* 8-8 ‡³SO'Gorman (5) (lw: a.p: ev ch 2f out: unable qckn) ... 2.3
  1422⁵ Rich Midas (IRE) *(61) (GLewis)* 8-6 ‡⁵DHarrison (2) (a bhd) .............................. 5.4
   1472 Comanche Companion *(TJNaughton)* 8-11  JQuinn (3) (b: wknd 1f: wknd over 1f out) .................................................................................. 2.5

Evens FIVE ISLANDS, 2/1 Comanche Companion, 6/1 Seasonal Splendour (IRE), 7/1 Rich Midas (IRE), 20/1 Home Affair. CSF £7.08, Tote £2.20: £1.40 £1.70 (£6.50). Lord Portman (WHATCOMBE) bred by Viscount Portman. 5 Rn                                                        60.04 sec (1.84)
                                                                      SF—5/4/–/–/–

T/Plpt: £555.80 (4.3 Tckts).                                                     AK

2479—**SOUTHWELL (L-H)** Fibresand
## Saturday, August 8th [Slow]
Going Allowance: St: 0.10 sec per fur; Rnd: 0.40 sec per fur (SL)      Wind: slt half against
Stalls: high

**2687**    MARSH STKS (Mdn) £1660.00 (£460.00: £220.00)    **1m (AWT)**    6-00 (6-03)

  2432⁶ **Spencer's Revenge** *(LordHuntingdon)* 3-9-0  AProud (12) (chsd ldrs: rdn to ld over 1f out: drew clr) ............................................. —1
  2252² High Savannah *(64) (MAJarvis)* 4-9-2  GCrealock (11) (hdwy to chase ldrs over 3f out: styd on one pce u.p fnl 2f) ................................. 5.2
  *2479²* Nobby Barnes *(62) (RWArmstrong)* 3-9-0  CKTse (8) (lw: trckd ldrs: led over 2f out tl over out: one pce) ......................................... nk.3
  2276² Chequers (IRE) *(74) (RJRWilliams)* 3-9-0  TRogers (3) (b.hind: effrt & chsd ldrs over 3f out: wknd 2f out) ........................................ 5.4
  2472² Secret Treaty (IRE) *(PWChapple-Hyam)* 3-8-9  KFallon (2) (s.i.s: sn drvn along: hdwy & prom 5f out: wknd over 2f out: n.d) ............... 10.5
        High Finance *(RJWeaver)* 7-9-7  JLowe (7) (dwlt s: effrt over 3f out: n.d) ......... 8.6
   2281 Lightning Decision *(JPSmith)* 4-9-0 ‡⁷SWynne (10) (plld hrd: chsd ldrs tl lost pl over 2f out) ........................................................ hd.7
  *2479⁵* Strangersinthenite *(45) (JSWainwright)* 3-9-0  EJohnson (3) (chsd ldr: sn drvn along: lost pl over 3f out) ........................................... 2.8
   1082⁶ Unique Tribute *(CACyzer)* 3-9-0  AMorris (6) (bit bkwd: drvn along: chsd ldrs tl lost pl over 3f out: sn bhd) ....................................... 2.9
   1089 Sunnyside Rock (IRE) *(41) (JEtherington)* 4-9-7  TLucas (1) (led tl hdd & wknd over 2f out) ............................................................... hd.10
   *2041* Dancing Pet *(37) (WWHaigh)* 3-8-9  AMackay (9) (b.hind: a bhd) ................... 3.11
        Dotterel (IRE) *(RGBrazington)* 4-9-7  PD'Arcy (4) (bhd & rdn 5f out) ............... 1.12

2/1 Secret Treaty (IRE), 7/2 SPENCER'S REVENGE, 9/2 Chequers (IRE), 6/1 High Savannah, 10/1 Nobby Barnes, 20/1 High Finance, 25/1 Unique Tribute, 50/1 Ors. CSF £21.99, Tote £4.80: £1.50 £2.10 £1.80 (£26.80). Lord Crawshaw (WEST ILSLEY) bred by Lord Crawshaw. 12 Rn                         1m 46.8 (7.5)
                                                                      SF—35/22/19/4/–/–

**2688**    SOUTHWELL (S) STKS (2-Y.O) £1744.00 (£484.00: £232.00)    **7f (AWT)**    6-30 (6-35)

  2157⁴ **Persian Traveller (IRE)** *(60) (CNAllen)* 8-4 ‡⁷GForster (12) (b.off hind: lw: chsd ldr: led over 3f out: rdn clr over 1f out) ....................... —1

2039³ Carnea *(JGFitzGerald)* 8-6 KFallon (4) (a chsng ldrs: kpt on u.p fnl 2f: no ch w wnr) .......... 10.2

2363² Sounds Risky **(44)** (bl) *(GMMoore)* 8-6 DMcKeown (1) (led tl over 3f out: wknd over 1f out) .......... 2¹/₂.3

2426 First Reserve (bl) *(BSRothwell)* 8-11 PD'Arcy (2) (lw: sn drvn along: kpt on fnl 2f: nvr nr to chal) .......... nk.4

2002 Lawnswood Quay *(JBerry)* 8-11 TRogers (5) (hld up & plld hrd: hdwy 3f out: styd on fnl 2f: n.d) .......... nk.5

2207 Bell Lad (IRE) *(CASmith)* 8-11 AProud (7) (sn bhd) .......... 10.6

2363 Hasta la Vista **(44)** *(MWEasterby)* 8-11 TLucas (3) (lw: sn wl bhd) .......... 1.7

2480² Palacegate Sunset (Fav) *(JBerry)* 8-11 AMackay (8) (lw: chsd ldrs: sn drvn along: lost pl 3f out) .......... 2¹/₂.8

2482 Burble (bl) *(DWChapman)* 8-6 SWood (13) (swtg: s.s: hdwy to chase ldrs over 3f out: wknd qckly 2f out) .......... hd.9

2482⁶ Formidable Liz *(NBycroft)* 8-6 SWebster (10) (bit bkwd: hdwy 5f out: wknd over 2f out) .......... hd.10

**5/2** Palacegate Sunset, **5/1** Formidable Liz, **11/2** Sounds Risky, **7/1** Carnea(op 9/2), Hasta la Vista, **8/1** PERSIAN TRAVELLER (IRE), **14/1** Lawnswood Quay, **16/1** First Reserve, **20/1** Burble, **33/1** Bell Lad (IRE). CSF £57.09, Tote £9.60: £2.60 £2.00 £1.50 (£26.90). Mr J. N. Oliver (NEWMARKET) bred by Frank Dunne in Ireland. 10 Rn; No bid                                   1m 33.4 (6.8)
SF—30/2/-/-/-/-

---

**2689**  NATIONAL PLANT & TRANSPORT H'CAP (0-70) £1730.00 (£480.00: £230.00)
7f (AWT)                                                   7-00 (7-02)

2210⁵ **Kinlacey (55)** *(BAMcMahon)* 5–8-13 ‡⁷SSanders (10) (lw: sn bhd & drvn along: hdwy 5f out: r.o wl to ld ins fnl f: sn clr) .......... —1

2481★ Jovial Kate (USA) **(63)** *(BEllison)* 5–9-9 ‡⁵SWilliams (8) (lw: led after 1f tl hdd & no ex ins fnl f) .......... 5.2

1795⁵ Have a Nightcap **(47)** *(JLHarris)* 9-8-3 DMcKeown (12) (lw: sn bhd: hdwy on outside over 2f out: styd on fnl f) .......... 1.3

2366★ Idir Linn (IRE) **(48)** *(DJGMurray-Smith)* 4–8-13 CRutter (3) (lw: hdwy 5f out: rdn 3f out: kpt on same pce fnl 2f) .......... ³/₄.4

2283³ On Y Va (USA) **(55)** (Fav) *(RJRWilliams)* 5–9-6 WNewnes (5) (hdwy over 2f out: kpt on: nvr nr to chal) .......... ¹/₂.5

2427³ Kissavos **(60)** (v) *(CCElsey)* 6–9-11 TRogers (7) (lw: hdwy over 3f out: styd on fnl 2f: nvr rchd ldrs) .......... nk.6

2361² Miss Movie World **(45)** *(NBycroft)* 3–7-13 ‡⁵NKennedy (6) (chsd ldrs tl wknd over 1f out) .......... 1.7

1797 Creego **(39)** *(JAGlover)* 3–7-12 LCharnock (9) (chsd ldrs tl lost pl 2f out) .......... 3.8

2536 Minizen Music (IRE) **(30)** *(MBrittain)* 4–7-9⁽²⁾ JLowe (4) (led 1f: sn drvn along: hmpd & lost pl 5f out: sn wl bhd) .......... 5.9

2099 One Magic Moment (IRE) **(41)** *(CACyzer)* 4–8-6⁽¹⁾ KFallon (4) (in tch tl lost pl 5f out) .......... 2¹/₂.10

2481 State Governor **(46)** *(DWChapman)* 4–8-11 SWood (2) (w ldr: hmpd & lost pl 5f out: sn wl bhd) .......... ³/₄.11

2289⁶ Share Holder **(40)** *(MissGayKelleway)* 4–7-12 ‡⁷CHawksley (11) (chsd ldrs tl lost pl 3f out) .......... 6.12
LONG HANDICAP: Minizen Music (IRE) 7-5.

**5/1** On Y Va (USA), **6/1** KINLACEY, **13/2** Miss Movie World, **7/1** Idir Linn (IRE), **8/1** Kissavos, **9/1** One Magic Moment (IRE), Jovial Kate (USA), **12/1** Creego, **16/1** State Governor, **25/1** Ors. CSF £51.85, CT £729.36. Tote £5.80: £2.60 £2.80 £4.90 (£44.40). Mr Michael G. T. Stokes (TAMWORTH) bred by J. E. Sainsbury and Mrs P. E. White. 12 Rn                        1m 33.7 (7.1)
SF—34/29/9/14/19/23

---

**2690**  DERRY BUILDING SERVICES NURSERY   £1562.00 (£432.00: £206.00)
5f (AWT)                                                   7-30 (7-31)

2387⁵ **Isotonic (77)** *(GMMoore)* 9-1 WNewnes (6) (mde virtually all: drvn clr over 1f out: eased nr fin) .......... —1

1547 Samanthas Joy **(55)** *(TFairhurst)* 7-7 JFanning (3) (unruly in stalls: reard at s: sn w wnr: edgd lft & nt qckn over 1f out) .......... 5.2

2546³ Grand Dancer (IRE) **(81)** (bl) *(RJRWilliams)* 9-5 AMunro (2) (b.hind: sltly hmpd s: sn outpcd & bhd: hdwy over 1f out: r.o u.p nr fin) .......... s.h.3

2030 Super Seve (IRE) **(81)** *(JBerry)* 9-5 JCarroll (4) (sn outpcd: rdn 3f out: n.d) .......... 1¹/₂.4

2271³ Area Girl **(83)** (Fav) *(SirMarkPrescott)* 9-7 GDuffield (1) (lw: wnt rt s: chsd ldrs: rdn ¹/₂-wy: wknd over 1f out) .......... nk.5

2055⁶ Carnbrea Snip **(75)** *(MBell)* 8-6 ‡⁷PTurner (5) (chsd ldrs: rdn ¹/₂-wy: sn lost pl) 2¹/₂.6
LONG HANDICAP: Samanthas Joy 7-6.

2/1 Area Girl, **9/2** Carnbrea Snip, **11/2** Super Seve (IRE), Grand Dancer (IRE), **6/1** Samanthas Joy, **7/1** ISOTONIC. CSF £40.00, Tote £8.40: £4.00 £2.10 (£25.20). Mr J. Burgess (MIDDLEHAM) bred by Mrs S. M. Sands and M. Yiapatos. 6 Rn
61.2 sec (3.2)
SF—47/5/30/24/25/–

**2691**    MIDLAND POWERFORM STKS (Mdn 3-Y.O) £1604.00 (£444.00: £212.00)
1¹/₂m (AWT)                                                8-00 (8-01)

| | | |
|---|---|---|
| 2422⁴ | **Cultured (73)** *(MRStoute)* 9-0 PD'Arcy (6) (lw: sn led: rdn & styd on strly fnl 2f) | —1 |
| 2089² | Blue Flag (USA) **(Fav)** *(LordHuntingdon)* 9-0 LDettori (2) (hld up & bhd: gd hdwy & wnt 2nd 6f out: ev ch & rdn 2f out: btn whn eased nr fin) | 10.2 |
| 2100⁵ | Ste-Jen (IRE) *(GMMoore)* 9-0 WNewnes (1) (chsd ldrs 7f out: brought wd st: styd on fnl f) | 2.3 |
| 2370² | Landed Gentry (USA) **(68)** *(PWChapple-Hyam)* 9-0 KFallon (5) (lw: chsd ldrs: drvn along & lost pl 7f out: c wd st: kpt on fnl f) | 5.4 |
| 1919² | Friendly House (IRE) *(MAJarvis)* 9-0 AMunro (3) (sn bhd & drvn along: sme hdwy 4f out: n.d) | 20.5 |
| 1074³ | Our Joey *(JWharton)* 8-9 ‡5SWilliams (8) (b.nr hind: in tch tl lost pl 7f out) | nk.6 |
| 2549 | Bar Three (IRE) *(LJCodd)* 8-7 ‡7WHollick (4) (bhd fnl 6f) | 8.7 |
| 2272⁴ | Whitwell Hill *(MrsVAAconley)* 8-9 LCharnock (7) (led early: sn drvn along: chsd ldrs 5f: sn wl bhd) | dist.8 |

**11/10** Blue Flag (USA), **5/2** CULTURED, **5/1** Landed Gentry, **14/1** Friendly House (IRE), **25/1** Our Joey, Ste-Jen, (IRE), **50/1** Ors. CSF £5.18, Tote £4.30: £1.40 £1.10 £3.20 (£2.70). Mrs David Thompson (NEWMARKET) bred by Cheveley Park Stud Ltd. 8 Rn
2m 43.8 (9.6)
SF—52/32/28/18/–/–

**2692**    EAST MIDLANDS ELECTRICITY H'CAP (0-70) £1660.00 (£460.00: £220.00)
1¹/₂m (AWT)                                                8-30 (8-32)

(Weights raised 4 lb)

| | | |
|---|---|---|
| 2362⋆ | **Take by Storm (IRE) (70)** *(GMMoore)* 3–9-10 WNewnes (2) (lw: trckd ldrs gng wl: clr 2nd & c wd st: r.o wl u.p to ld nr fin) | —1 |
| 2296² | Tales of Wisdom **(65)** *(SirMarkPrescott)* 3–9-5 AMunro (3) (led: c stands' side st: rdn 2f out: hung lft & hdd wl ins fnl f: styd on) | hd.2 |
| 2484⁶ | Swell Time (IRE) **(28)** *(CNAllen)* 4–7-7 GBardwell (10) (swtg: a chsng ldrs: kpt on u.p fnl 3f) | 7.3 |
| 2420 | Remwood Girl **(29)** *(KSBridgwater)* 6–7-8 SWood (6) (sn bhd: effrt 5f out: kpt on: n.d) | 8.4 |
| 2484² | Not Yet **(45)** *(EWeymes)* 8–8-10 DMcKeown (7) (prom: drvn along 5f out: no imp) | 3.5 |
| 2156⁵ | Make Me Proud (IRE) **(43)** *(RWArmstrong)* 3–7-11 RStreet (9) (sn bhd: nvr nr ldrs) | 8.6 |
| 2255² | Sharp Top **(45)** **(Fav)** *(MJRyan)* 4–8-10 GDuffield (4) (lw: chsd ldrs: drvn along ¹/₂-wy: lost pl 4f out) | 10.7 |
| 2367 | Commanche Sioux (IRE) **(44)** (v) *(KAMorgan)* 4–8-4 ‡5JWeaver (5) (chsd ldrs tl rdn & lost pl over 4f out) | hd.8 |
| 1546⁴ | Domain **(49)** (bl) *(RJWeaver)* 4–8-7 ‡7JTate (1) (lw: chsd ldrs: rdn 5f out: sn bhd) | 3¹/₂.9 |
| 2059 | Vinstan **(52)** (bl) *(CASmith)* 6–9-3 MWigham (8) (swtg: chsd ldrs: drvn along & lost pl 7f: sddle slipped: p.u over 5f out) | 0 |
| 2484⁵ | Grey Commander **(37)** (v) *(MBrittain)* 4–8-2 JLowe (11) (stumbled & uns rdr s) | 0 |

**4/1** Sharp Top, **9/2** TAKE BY STORM (IRE), **5/1** Tales of Wisdom, **7/1** Commanche Sioux (IRE), **17/2** Not Yet, **12/1** Grey Commander(op 8/1), Grey Commander(op 8/1), **14/1** Swell Time (IRE), **25/1** Make Me Proud (IRE), Remwood Girl, **33/1** Vinstan. CSF £23.67, CT £244.96. Tote £7.60: £2.20 £1.80 £2.50 (£13.00). Miss V. Foster (MIDDLEHAM) bred by Abbeville Stud in Ireland. 11 Rn
2m 45.3 (11.1)
SF—47/41/1/–/–/–

T/Plpt: £618.70 (2 Tckts).                                                WG

2427—**LEICESTER  (R-H)**
**Monday, August 10th [Good]**
Going Allowance: minus 0.10 sec per fur (F)                    Wind: slt bhd

Stalls: high

**2693**    COALVILLE H'CAP (0-80) £2847.00 (£792.00: £381.00)    **1m 1f 218y**    6-00 (6-10)

| | | |
|---|---|---|
| 2012⁴ | **Scottish Bambi (70)** *(RHannon)* 4–9-7 ‡3RPerham (4) (a.p: 3rd st: led ins fnl f: hld on gamely) | —1 |

20865 Tanoda **(46)** *(MBrittain)* 6-8-0 JLowe (7) (hld up: 5th st: str run fnl f: jst failed) . nk.2

23786 Milanese **(75)** *(DMorley)* 3-9-6 WRyan (1) (hld up: 4th st: led over 2f out tl ins fnl f: rallied nr fin) ............................................................... nk.3

2273 Inan (USA) **(72)** *(JLDunlop)* 3-9-3 WCarson (8) (lw: led tl over 2f out: kpt on one pce) .................................................................... 7.4

23475 Chatham Island **(65)** (Fav) *(CEBrittain)* 4-9-0 ‡5BDoyle (5) (lw: prom: 2nd st: rdn over 1f out: sn btn) ...................................................... ¾.5

Faaz (USA) **(57)** *(AAScott)* 3-8-2 JFortune (3) (h.d.w. bkwd: s.i.s: 6th st: lost tch fnl 3f: t.o) ..................................................... 2½.6

24316 Tomashenko **(63)** *(JMackie)* 3-8-8 GHind (6) (s.s: 7th st: gd hdwy over 3f out: rdn & wknd 2f out: t.o) ............................................ 12.7

Moonlight Shift **(52)** *(WClay)* 6-8-6 SDawson (2) (bkwd: s.i.s: bhd & outpcd: 8th st: t.o) ........................................................ 30.8

**3/1** Chatham Island, **7/2** SCOTTISH BAMBI, **4/1** Inan (USA), **7/1** Tomashenko, **8/1** Milanese(6/1—9/1), **17/2** Tanoda, **14/1** Faaz (USA), **50/1** Moonlight Shift. CSF £28.10, CT £183.64. Tote £5.30: £1.90 £1.80 £2.70 (£19.70). Mr William J. Kelly (MARLBOROUGH) bred by Cheveley Park Stud Ltd. 8 Rn       2m 8 (5.3)

SF—44/22/41/24/19/2

---

## 2694

REARSBY (S) STKS (3-Y.O) £1733.40 (£482.40: £232.20)       **7f 9y**       6-30 (6-34)

25252 **Certain Lady (61)** (Fav) *(GBlum)* 7-7 ‡5DHarrison (14) (a.p: led ½-wy: r.o wl) ..... —1

24066 Ace Girl **(52)** *(SRBowring)* 7-12 JQuinn (9) (led to ½-wy: rdn over 1f out: kpt on) 2.2

1590 Mexican Dancer **(50)** *(RJHolder)* 8-0 ‡7SDrowne (16) (hdwy 3f out: rdn over 1f out: nt pce to chal) .......................................... 3.3

2291 All Earz (IRE) **(49)** *(REarnshaw)* 7-10 ‡7CHawksley (20) (a.p: hrd rdn appr fnl f: r.o one pce) ............................................... 3.4

2582 Great Hall **(45)** (bl) *(PDCundell)* 8-3 PRobinson (18) (hdwy ½-wy: hrd rdn appr fnl f: one pce) .............................................. ½.5

2561 Specialist Dream (IRE) **(44)** *(LJCodd)* 9-1 VSmith (11) (chsd ldrs: rdn 2f out: one pce) ................................................ 3.6

20844 Dick Whittington **(48)** *(CTinkler)* 8-6 GCarter (7) (sme hdwy fnl 2f: nvr nrr) ....... 3½.7

21644 J'Arrive *(JPearce)* 7-13 ‡5RPrice (12) (nvr nr to chal) ................................... d.h.7

2545 Aragona **(44)** (bl) *(PDCundell)* 7-12 CRutter (12) (prom 5f) ................................. hd.9

2539 Highborn (IRE) *(PSFelgate)* 9-7 WRyan (3) (bit bkwd: m.n.s) ................................ ½.10

2539 Galley Gossip **(46)** (v) *(RBrotherton)* 8-5(2) AClark (4) (nvr trbld ldrs) ................ 3.11

2234 Double Lark **(43)** *(RHollinshead)* 7-10 ‡7JDennis (13) (s.s: a in rr) ....................... 2½.12

19124 Rocky Bay **(41)** *(DHaydnJones)* 7-12 JLowe (5) (nvr rchd ldrs) ............................. 6.13

2296 Petty Cash **(33)** *(DrJDScargill)* 7-12 SDawson (8) (m.n.s) ...................................... ½.14

1148 Sennon Cove *(MJCharles)* 7-11 ‡7SSanders (10) (bit bkwd: m.n.s) ........................ 1½.15

2229 Clean Gate **(42)** *(PDCundell)* 8-3 GBardwell (19) (n.d) ............................................ ½.16

21873 Relatively Risky *(JWharton)* 8-5(1) JWilliams (17) (bhd fnl 3f) ................................... nk.17

26666 Forza Azzurri (IRE) **(55)** *(MrsNMacauley)* 8-6 GHind (2) (s.s: a bhd) ..................... 5.18

1040 Moniaive *(WClay)* 8-6 JFortune (6) (bit bkwd: spd over 4f: sn lost tch) ..................... 2.19

**15/8** CERTAIN LADY, **5/1** J'Arrive, **13/2** Relatively Risky, Ace Girl, **10/1** Dick Whittington, **11/1** Rocky Bay, Specialist Dream (IRE), **20/1** Forza Azzurri (IRE), **25/1** Mexican Dancer, Aragona, Great Hall, All Earz (IRE), **33/1** Clean Gate, Double Lark, **50/1** Petty Cash, **66/1** Galley Gossip, Sennon Cove, Highborn (IRE), **100/1** Moniaive. CSF £15.69, Tote £2.70: £1.80 £2.00 £7.70 (£9.10). Mrs Bridget Blum (NEWMARKET) bred by Dunchurch Lodge Stud. 19 Rn; Bt in 4,000 gns       1m 24.8 (2.5)

SF—31/30/23/10/15/18

---

## 2695

INSTITUTE OF INSURANCE BROKERS NURSERY       £2285.00 (£635.00: £305.00)
**7f 9y**       7-00 (7-01)

25285 **Time's Arrow (IRE) (86)** *(GCBravery)* 9-7 WRSwinburn (8) (lw: hld up & bhd: gd hdwy to ld ins fnl f: hrd rdn: all out) ................................ —1

24183 Tee Gee Jay **(64)** (bl) *(CNWilliams)* 7-13 JQuinn (4) (b.hind: hld up in tch: led over 1f out tl ins fnl f: rallied gamely nr fin) ................... nk.2

2474★ Awestruck **(68)** (Fav) *(WJHaggas)* 8-3 MHills (10) (a.p: ev ch appr fnl f: rallied u.p nr fin) ........................................ ½.3

20583 Mrs Dawson **(59)** *(DrJDScargill)* 7-1(1) ‡7CHawksley (3) (led tl appr fnl f: kpt on u.p ins fnl f) ................................... ¾.4

19396 Iommelli (IRE) **(86)** *(PAKelleway)* 9-7 PatEddery (5) (hdwy over 2f out: styd on u.p ins fnl f) ................................... 1.5

2360★ Umbubuzi (USA) **(73)** *(FHLee)* 8-8 RLappin (1) (lw: w ldrs: rdn over 1f out: unable qckn) ........................................ hd.6

24266 Share a Moment (CAN) **(76)** *(RHollinshead)* 8-11 WRyan (6) (nvr trbld ldrs) ..... ½.7

24093 General Chase **(60)** *(RJHolder)* 7-9 NAdams (7) (chsd ldrs: rdn wl over 1f out: nt pce to chal) ................................ ½.8

2462 Credit Squeeze **(71)** *(RFJohnsonHoughton)* 8-6 WCarson (9) (prom tl rdn & wknd over 1f out) ................................ 1½.9

2024⁵ Magication **(80)** *(CEBrittain)* 9-1 MRoberts (2) (bhd: effrt u.p over 2f out: no imp) ......................................................................................... 2¹/₂.**10**

**6/4** Awestruck, **5/1** TIME'S ARROW (IRE), **13/2** Magication, **8/1** Tee Gee Jay, **10/1** Umbubuzi (USA), Iommelli (IRE), **11/1** Credit Squeeze, **16/1** Share a Moment (CAN), **20/1** Ors. CSF £42.57, CT £79.85. Tote £6.50: £2.30 £1.40 £1.70 (£23.70). Mr Richard J. Gray (NEWMARKET) bred by Mrs M. Lowry in Ireland. 10 Rn
1m 25.7 (3.4)
SF—46/23/25/7/38/24

**2696**　　　LANGHAM CLAIMING STKS (2-Y.O) £1814.00 (£504.00: £242.00)　　**7f 9y** 7-30 (7-33)

2232² **Sabo's Express** (Fav) *(RHannon)* 8-11 MRoberts (8) (led tl hdd appr fnl f: rallied u.p to ld wl ins fnl f) ................................................................ —**1**
2138⁴ Calisar **(64)** *(WGMTurner)* 8-6 ‡³TSprake (1) (hdwy 3f out: led over 1f out tl ins fnl f: r.o nr fin) ........................................................................ nk.**2**
　　　Eastern Glow *(SPCWoods)* 8-4 WWoods (4) (small: lt-f: hld up: hdwy 2f out: r.o wl fnl f) ............................................................................. ¹/₂.**3**
2418 Skullcap **(72)** *(TJNaughton)* 8-3 GCarter (11) (a.p: rdn over 1f out: kpt on) ..... 1¹/₂.**4**
2563★ Walid's Princess (IRE) **(44)** *(JWharton)* 8-2 AShoults (6) (a.p: ev ch 1f out: unable qckn) ......................................................................... s.h.**5**
2037⁵ Blue Sombrero (IRE) *(RJHolder)* 8-4 JWilliams (3) (hdwy 2f out: styd on ins fnl f) ³/₄.**6**
2389⁵ Duchess Dianne (IRE) **(50)** *(RJHolder)* 8-2 JQuinn (7) (prom tl wknd ent fnl f) 1¹/₂.**7**
　　　Kiawah *(JRFanshawe)* 7-12 GBardwell (2) (small: s.s: nvr nrr) ................... s.h.**8**
2572⁶ Hot Storm **(68)** *(MJCamacho)* 7-10 DBiggs (4) (s.i.s: a in rr) .................... 6.**9**
1547 Grand Game *(DHaydnJones)* 8-1 JLowe (13) (t.o) .................................. 8.**10**
2277 Certain Way (IRE) *(CTinkler)* 8-7 JFortune (5) (chsd ldrs over 4f: sn lost tch: t.o)1¹/₂.**11**
2428 Red Russian *(BJMcMath)* 7-8 ‡⁷CHawksley (14) (bit bkwd: effrt u.p 3f out: no imp: t.o) .......................................................................... ¹/₂.**12**
　　　Davrob *(BPalling)* 8-5 NAdams (9) (lt-f: s.o: a bhd: t.o) .......................... nk.**13**
2274 Fergus Garber *(JMCarr)* 8-1 CRutter (15) (bhd fr ¹/₂-wy: t.o) .................... 4.**14**

**7/2** SABO'S EXPRESS, **4/1** Hot Storm, Skullcap, **7/1** Walid's Princess (IRE), **15/2** Calisar, **9/1** Davrob(8/ 1—6/1), **16/1** Kiawah(op 8/1), **20/1** Blue Sombrero (IRE), Eastern Glow, Duchess Dianne (IRE), **33/1** Grand Game, **40/1** Red Russian, **50/1** Ors. CSF £29.20, Tote £3.50: £1.80 £2.60 £6.70 (£14.20). Miss W. M. Jones (MARLBOROUGH) bred by R. Bulfield. 14 Rn
1m 27.4 (5.1)
SF—10/4/—/—/—/

**2697**　　　CAPTAINS STKS (3-Y.O) £2259.00 (£624.00: £297.00)　　**5f 218y**　　8-00 (8-01)

2229 **Elhasna** (USA) *(MajorWRHern)* 8-2 WCarson (1) (w'like: swrvd lft s: racd alone centre: led over 2f out: clr fnl f) .................................... —**1**
2435 Wilde Rufo **(100)** (Fav) *(PAKelleway)* 9-1 PatEddery (3) (led: hdd & rdn over 2f out: edgd lft appr fnl f: sn btn) ............................................ 5.**2**
2419 Nonanno (bl) *(AJChamberlain)* 8-7 JWilliams (2) (b: bit bkwd: lost tch ¹/₂-wy: t.o) 30.**3**

**4/11** Wilde Rufo, **9/4** ELHASNA (USA), **25/1** Nonanno. CSF £3.35, Tote £2.90 (£1.10). Mr Hamdan Al-Maktoum (LAMBOURN) bred by Georgia E. Hofmann in USA. 3 Rn
1m 13.2 (3.2)
SF—12/5/

**2698**　　　EVINGTON H'CAP (0-70) £2973.00 (£828.00: £399.00)　　**1m 3f 183y**　　8-30 (8-33)
(Weights raised 3 lb)

2241★ **Incola (44)** *(HCandy)* 6-8-9 CRutter (17) (hld up: hdwy over 2f out: led 1f out: sn clr: easily) ..................................................................... —**1**
2170⁴ Diamond Wedding (USA) **(65)** *(NAGraham)* 3-9-5 PatEddery (10) (7th st: led 3f out to 1f out: sn btn) .............................................................. 4.**2**
2397⁵ Gesnera **(37)** *(KWhite)* 4-8-2 NCarlisle (11) (chsd ldrs: 5th st: styd on nr fin) ... ³/₄.**3**
2547⁴ Maestroso (IRE) **(67)** *(RFJohnsonHoughton)* 3-9-7 MRoberts (5) (hdwy over 3f out: ev ch 2f out: kpt on one pce) ......................................... ³/₄.**4**
　　　By Far (USA) **(35)** *(OO'Neill)* 6-8-0 NAdams (16) (bit bkwd: mid div: styd on fr 2f out: nrst fin) .................................................................. 2¹/₂.**5**
2358² Carol's Pet (IRE) **(44)** *(MJohnston)* 4-8-9 DMcKeown (15) (lw: sn chsng ldrs: kpt on same pce fnl 2f) ...................................................... 1¹/₂.**6**
2281⁶ Captain My Captain (IRE) **(44)** *(RBrotherton)* 4-8-9 JWilliams (14) (bhd: hdwy appr fnl f: nrst fin) ............................................................ 3¹/₂.**7**
2168⁶ Oozlem (IRE) **(68)** *(CAHorgan)* 3-9-8 AMcGlone (9) (sme hdwy fnl 2f: nvr nrr) .. 2.**8**
2605 Eire Leath-Sceal **(56)** *(MBrittain)* 5-9-7 JLowe (1) (chsd ldrs: 8th st: rdn 2f out: sn wknd) ........................................................................ s.h.**9**
1530⁶ Grove Serendipity (IRE) **(59)** *(AHide)* 4-9-10 WRyan (13) (nvr nr to chal) ....... nk.**10**
2184 Wild Strawberry **(67)** (v) *(JMPEustace)* 3-9-7 MTebbutt (6) (chsd ldrs: 6th st: wknd 2f out) ............................................................................ 1.**11**

2209 Nazare Blue **(42)** *(MrsBarbaraWaring)* 5-8-7 NHowe (7) (b: m.n.s) ................. 1.12
2492⁵ Bold Resolution (IRE) **(54)** *(CACyzer)* 4-9-5 GCarter (12) (m.n.s) ...................... 6.13
  38 Shirl **(43)** *(GFHCharles-Jones)* 3-7-6⁽⁴⁾ ‡⁵DHarrison (19) (bkwd: prom: 4th st:
      wknd over 2f out) .......................................................... 2¹/₂.14
2305 Albert **(48)** *(DAWilson)* 5-8-13 JFortune (3) (lw: a bhd) ......................... 2.15
2293 Art Critic (IRE) **(51)** *(MJHeaton-Ellis)* 3-8-5 PaulEddery (18) (bit bkwd: m.n.s) s.h.16
2476 Majestic Melody **(52)** *(WCarter)* 4-8-12 ‡⁵NGwilliams (2) (swtg: prom: 3rd st:
      wknd 3f out) ................................................................ 3.17
2492³ Killick **(33)** *(REPeacock)* 4-7-12 JQuinn (8) (chsd ldr: 2nd st: led over 3f out: sn
      hdd & wknd) ............................................................... hd.18
2484* Must Be Magical (USA) **(29)** (bl) *(FHLee)* 4-7-1⁽¹⁾ ‡⁷CHawksley (4) (lw: sn led &
      clr: hdd over 3f out: wknd qckly) ..................................... 1¹/₂.19
      LONG HANDICAP: Must Be Magical (USA) 7-2.

**4/1** Maestroso (IRE), **7/1** INCOLA, **8/1** Bold Resolution (IRE), Diamond Wedding (USA), **9/1** Killick(16/1—6/1), Carol's Pet (IRE), **12/1** Captain My Captain (IRE), Eire Leath-Sceal, **14/1** Albert, Grove Serendipity (IRE)(20/1—12/1), **16/1** Must Be Magical (USA), Nazare Blue, **25/1** Wild Strawberry, Gesnera, **33/1** Shirl, Art Critic (IRE), Oozlem (IRE), **50/1** Ors. CSF £61.78, CT £1,248.25. Tote £8.00: £2.30 £1.70 £6.50 £2.00 (£29.30). Mrs David Blackburn (WANTAGE) bred by Mrs D. Blackburn. 19 Rn 2m 33.4 (4.6)
SF—37/39/20/37/11/17

T/Plpt: £63.40 (28.2 Tckts). IM

## 2531—THIRSK (L-H)

### Monday, August 10th [Good]

Going Allowance: minus 0.10 sec per fur (F) Wind: almost nil

Stalls: high

**2699** WEST YORKSHIRE (S) H'CAP (3 & 4-Y.O) (0-60) £1800.00 (£500.00: £240.00)
1m 6-05 (6-10)

2327⁴ **Cledeschamps (39)** *(MWEllerby)* 3-8-6 PBurke (1) (a.p: rdn to ld appr fnl f: rdn
      out) ....................................................................... —1
2561 Stairway to Heaven (IRE) **(51)** (bl) (Fav) *(TDBarron)* 4-9-4 ‡⁷VHalliday (6)
      (outpcd & bhd early: hdwy ent st: r.o u.p nr fin) ....................... nk.2
2665⁵ Grecian Belle **(34)** *(DAWilson)* 3-8-1 GDuffield (2) (led early: a cl up: chal 2f
      out: one pce fnl f) ..................................................... 1¹/₂.3
2607 Chance Report **(35)** *(FHLee)* 4-8-4 ‡⁵NKennedy (15) (cl up: led over 3f out tl
      appr fnl f: no ex) ........................................................ 4.4
1964⁵ Syke Lane **(36)** *(RMWhitaker)* 3-8-3 ACulhane (12) (lw: in tch: hdwy u.p 2f out:
      no imp) ................................................................... 3.5
2634 Another Nut **(41)** *(PDEvans)* 3-8-8 BRaymond (7) (in tch: hdwy over 2f out: nvr
      able to chal) ........................................................... s.h.6
2218⁴ J P Morgan **(42)** (v) *(MPNaughton)* 4-8-11 ‡⁵JWeaver (9) (lw: nvr bttr than mid
      div) ...................................................................... 1.7
1896⁴ Mummys Rocket **(35)** (bl) *(MO'Neill)* 3-8-8 SWood (4) (b: a same pl) ............ nk.8
1294 Emerald Ears **(47)** *(EWeymes)* 3-9-0 DMcKeown (13) (sn led tl hdd over 3f out:
      grad wknd) .............................................................. ¹/₂.9
2291 Gleneliane (IRE) **(37)** (bl) *(JLHarris)* 4-8-11 KFallon (17) (b.nr fore & nr hind: lw:
      effrt ent st: n.d) ...................................................... 2¹/₂.10
2430 My Jersey Pearl (IRE) **(33)** *(DonEnricoIncisa)* 3-7-7 ‡⁷ClaireBalding (10) (n.d) . 4.11
2539 Kick on Majestic (IRE) **(36)** (v) *(NBycroft)* 3-8-3 KDarley (5) (s.i.s: n.d) .......... 3.12
2607 Phil-Man **(44)** *(TFairhurst)* 3-8-11 JFanning (8) (chsd ldrs tl wknd over 2f out) ³/₄.13
  62⁶ Whirlygig **(40)** (v) *(JSWainwright)* 3-8-7 LCharnock (16) (unruly s: s.i.s: n.d) .. 5.14
2401 Loudest Whisper **(50)** (bl) *(KSBridgwater)* 4-9-5 ‡⁵SWilliams (14) (b: prom to st) 3.15
      Kiltroum (FR) **(40)** *(CTinkler)* 3-8-7 MBirch (11) (chsd ldrs to st: wknd qckly: t.o) .
      20.16

**4/1** Stairway to Heaven (IRE), **11/2** Grecian Belle, **9/1** J P Morgan(op 6/1), **10/1** Syke Lane, **12/1** Kick on Majestic (IRE), Loudest Whisper, Kiltroum (FR), **14/1** Chance Report(op 8/1), Phil-Man, Mummys Rocket, **16/1** Emerald Ears, Gleneliane (IRE), **20/1** Another Nut, **33/1** CLEDESCHAMPS & Ors. CSF £148.79, CT £776.79. Tote £41.30: £5.70 £1.40 £1.40 £3.70 (£67.80). Mrs H. J. Ellerby (PICKERING) bred by Mrs H. J. Ellerby. 16 Rn; No bid
1m 39.9 (3.9)
SF—21/32/10/1/–/–

**2700** E.B.F. BOWNCROFT STKS (Mdn 2-Y.O) £1903.00 (£528.00: £253.00)
7f 6-35 (6-36)

2364⁴ **Just You Dare (IRE)** *(SirMarkPrescott)* 9-0 GDuffield (4) (lw: chsd ldrs: led 2f
      out: r.o u.p) ............................................................. —1

| 2426 | Red Cent (JEtherington) 8-9 ‡⁵JWeaver (6) (prom: gd hdwy to disp ld 2f out: hung lft: nt qckn fnl f) | 2¹/₂.2 |
| 2277 | Hyde's Happy Hour (NTinkler) 9-0 DNicholls (10) (in tch: hdwy & edgd lft 2f out: styd on) | 3¹/₂.3 |
| 1485 | Careless Son (Fav) (MissSEHall) 9-0 NConnorton (2) (chsd ldrs: sn pushed along: one pce fnl 3f) | hd.4 |
| | Keep Your Distance (MrsGRReveley) 9-0 KDarley (7) (leggy: scope: bit bkwd: s.i.s: bhd tl styd on wl fnl 2f) | 3.5 |
| 1071 | Steal a March (MWEasterby) 9-0 TLucas (1) (hld up & bhd: stdy hdwy 2f out: nvr plcd to chal) | 1.6 |
| 2205⁵ | Bardia (DonEnricoIncisa) 8-9 JakiHouston (8) (lw: bhd & effrt 3f out: n.d) | 2¹/₂.7 |
| | New Kid in Town (NTinkler) 9-0 LCharnock (9) (cmpt: bit bkwd: prom: ev ch 3f out: grad wknd fnl 2f) | 1¹/₂.8 |
| 2335⁵ | See Us There (IRE) (JBerry) 9-0 JCarroll (5) (disp ld tl led ent st: hdd 2f out: sn wknd) | hd.9 |
| 2292⁴ | First Affair (MRStoute) 8-9 BRaymond (3) (b.off hind: disp ld to st: sn lost pl) | hd.10 |

11/4 Careless Son, 4/1 First Affair(op 5/2), 5/1 JUST YOU DARE (IRE), 7/1 Keep Your Distance, Red Cent, 12/1 See Us There (IRE), 14/1 Bardia, 16/1 Steal a March, Hyde's Happy Hour, 20/1 New Kid in Town. CSF £37.15, Tote £4.80: £1.70 £2.00 £5.70 (£10.00). Mrs David Thompson (NEWMARKET) bred by Graigueshoneen Stud in Ireland. 10 Rn
1m 27.8 (4.5)
SF—22/9/3/2/–/–

## 2701
YORKSHIRE PUDDING CLAIMING STKS £1935.00 (£535.00: £255.00)
1¹/₂m
7-00 (7-01)

| 2613² | **Salu** (52) (bl) (Fav) (JEtherington) 3-8-1 GDuffield (3) (in tch: pushed along appr st: led 2f out: styd on) | —1 |
| 2573² | Stingray City (USA) (61) (JEtherington) 3-8-12 KDarley (9) (cl up: lod ont st & qcknd: hdd 2f out) | 3¹/₂.2 |
| 2329³ | Duggan (53) (bl) (RJWilliams) 5-9-10 BRaymond (5) (hld up: smooth hdwy 3f out: effrt over 1f out: fnd nil) | 5.3 |
| 2569 | Mr News (IRE) (43) (bl) (BBeasley) 3-8-4 ‡⁵SWilliams (7) (effrt appr st: styd on: no imp) | 5.4 |
| 1911 | Leonadis Polk (51) (bl) (JHJohnson) 3-8-6 KFallon (1) (trckd ldrs: effrt 3f out: no rspnse) | 1.5 |
| 5⁹5 | Top Prize (MBrittain) 4-9-5 PSedgwick (4) (bhd tl c wd & hdwy 3f out: nvr nrr) | ¹/₂.6 |
| 2420⁵ | Quip (26) (MPNaughton) 7-9-1 JakiHouston (6) (sn chsng ldrs: outpcd ent st: sn lost pl) | 12.7 |
| 2235 | Megan's Flight (34) (THCaldwell) 3-8-6 ‡⁵NKennedy (10) (chsd ldrs tl rdn & wknd 3f out: eased whn btn) | 7.8 |
| 2569⁵ | Zinger (41) (bl) (TFairhurst) 4-9-3 JFanning (2) (lw: lost tch fnl 4f) | 1¹/₂.9 |
| 2420 | Banker Mason (USA) (24) (bl) (WLBarker) 6-9-4 SWebster (8) (lw: led tl hdd ent st: sn wknd) | 4.10 |

9/4 SALU, 5/2 Stingray City (USA), 3/1 Duggan, 12/1 Leonadis Polk(op 8/1), 16/1 Zinger, 20/1 Quip, 25/1 Top Prize, 33/1 Megan's Flight, Mr News (IRE), 100/1 Banker Mason (USA). CSF £7.62, Tote £3.00: £1.50 £1.70 £1.40 (£3.50). Mr W. N. Lumley (MALTON) bred by W. N. Lumley. 10 Rn
2m 34.7 (4.7)
SF—28/32/34/4/4/16

## 2702
SUNDERLAND A.F.C./JOHNNY RIDLEY H'CAP (0-80) £1987.50 (£550.00: £262.50)
6f
7-30 (7-31)

| 2411⁴ | **Manuleader** (56) (bl) (BBeasley) 3-8-1 LCharnock (5) (lw: w ldr: led 2f out: hld on wl) | —1 |
| 2689 | Miss Movie World (49) (NBycroft) 3-7-8 JFanning (7) (trckd ldrs: n.m.r over 1f out: qcknd to chal wl ins fnl f: no ex nr fin) | s.h.2 |
| 2614 | Double Feature (IRE) (62) (MrsJRRamsden) 3-8-7 MBirch (4) (hld up: hdwy over 1f out: r.o nr fin) | 2.3 |
| 2280⁶ | Sully's Choice (USA) (49) (bl) (DWChapman) 11-7-13 SWood (6) (lw: led 4f: sn rdn & one pce) | ¹/₂.4 |
| 2536⁴ | Rock Opera (IRE) (59) (Fav) (MPNaughton) 4-8-4 ‡⁵JWeaver (2) (chsd ldrs: rdn over 2f out: grad wknd) | 2¹/₂.5 |
| 217 | On the Edge (74) (TDBarron) 4-9-10 AlexGreaves (3) (prom tl outpcd fnl 2f) | 2.6 |
| 2382³ | Parfait Amour (76) (RMWhitaker) 3-9-7 ACulhane (1) (chsd ldrs: rdn ¹/₂-wy: sn btn) | 5.7 |

11/4 Rock Opera (IRE), 4/1 Parfait Amour, 9/2 Double Feature (IRE), 5/1 Sully's Choice (USA), 6/1 Miss Movie World, 10/1 On the Edge(op 16/1), 11/1 MANULEADER. CSF £65.57, Tote £16.90: £4.90 £2.60 (£32.80). Manulife Group Services Limited (HAMBLETON) bred by Cobhall Court Stud. 7 Rn
1m 11.9 (1.7)
SF—41/33/38/28/23/35

**2703—2705**

**2703**  SUNDERLAND A.F.C./LADBROKES NURSERY  £2022.50 (£560.00: £267.50)
7f                                                                          8-00 (8-02)
(Weights raised 11 lb)

| | | |
|---|---|---|
| 2259³ | **Hi Nod (63)** *(MJCamacho)* 8-12 NConnorton (5) (lw: trckd ldrs: led wl over 1f out: sn rdn clr) | —1 |
| 2543⁴ | Merry Mermaid **(55)** *(JFBottomley)* 8-4 PBurke (2) (bhd tl styd on u.p fnl 2f: no ch w wnr) | 4.2 |
| 2002⁵ | Ttyfran **(72)** *(FHLee)* 9-2 ‡⁵NKennedy (3) (bhd: hdwy 3f out: styd on: no imp) .. | nk.3 |
| 2112⁶ | Fanfan (IRE) **(51)** (bl) *(Jt-Fav)* *(MHEasterby)* 8-0⁽¹⁾ KDarley (6) (lw: cl up: disp ld 3f out: outpcd fnl 2f) | hd.4 |
| 2543* | Wishing Cap (USA) **(65)** *(Jt-Fav)* *(SirMarkPrescott)* 9-0 GDuffield (7) (chsd ldrs: pushed along appr st: wknd wl over 2f out) | 5.5 |
| 2543⁵ | Whitley Gorse **(72)** *(JEtherington)* 9-2 ‡⁵JWeaver (4) (led tl hdd wl over 1f out: sn btn) | ½.6 |
| 2398 | Behaanis (USA) **(70)** *(AAScott)* 9-5 JCarroll (1) (lw: nvr wnt pce) | 4.7 |

**3/1** Fanfan (IRE), Wishing Cap (USA)(op 2/1), **7/2** HI NOD, **11/2** Ttyfran, **15/2** Whitley Gorse, **8/1** Merry Mermaid, **14/1** Behaanis (USA). CSF £28.10, Tote £4.90: £2.50 £4.30 (£21.70). Mr Brian Nordan (MALTON) bred by B. Nordan. 7 Rn                                      1m 28 (4.7)
SF—17/–/8/–/–

**2704**  SOUTH YORKSHIRE STKS (Mdn 3-Y.0) £1506.00 (£416.00: £198.00)
1m                                                                          8-30 (8-32)

| | | |
|---|---|---|
| 2385² | **So Smug (USA) (76)** *(Fav)* *(JHMGosden)* 8-9 BRaymond (1) (mde most: shkn up over 1f out: r.o) | —1 |
| 1561² | Canaan Lane **(69)** *(AHarrison)* 8-3 (trckd ldrs: chal over 1f out: r.o) . | 1.2 |
| | Jawaher (IRE) *(RJRWilliams)* 8-9 GDuffield (2) (neat: scope: in tch: shkn up over 2f out: r.o one pce) | 5.3 |
| 2549 | Dioman Shadeed (USA) *(JRFanshawe)* 8-7 ‡⁷NVarley (4) (s.s: hdwy ent st: sn prom: nt qckn appr fnl f) | 2½.4 |
| 693 | Quixotic *(PWHarris)* 9-0 MBirch (5) (disp ld 5f: sn rdn & wknd) | 7.5 |

**2/5** SO SMUG (USA), **9/2** Jawaher (IRE), **9/1** Dioman Shadeed (USA), **16/1** Canaan Lane, **33/1** Quixotic. CSF £6.33, Tote £1.40: £1.10 £2.10 (£3.10). Mrs Elizabeth Moran (NEWMARKET) bred by Edward A. Seltzer & Brushwood Stable in USA. 5 Rn                              1m 41.7 (5.7)

T/Plpt: £219.60 (8.02 Tckts).
AA

**2544—WINDSOR  (Fig.8)**

## Monday, August 10th [Good]

Going Allowance: 5f: minus 0.20 sec; Rest: nil sec per fur (F)               Wind: almost nil

Stalls: high

**2705**  STRATFIELDSAYE (S) STKS    £2658.00 (£738.00: £354.00)
1m 3f 135y                                                                  2-30 (2-35)

| | | |
|---|---|---|
| 1269⁵ | **Carousel Music (56)** *(JAkehurst)* 5-9-8 MRoberts (6) (2nd st: led over 3f out: all out) | —1 |
| 2600⁶ | Molly Splash **(55)** *(CACyzer)* 5-9-8 GCarter (12) (hdwy & 6th st: ev ch fnl 2f: hrd rdn: r.o) | ½.2 |
| 2187⁶ | Bel Baraka (IRE) **(60)** *(Fav)* *(DRCElsworth)* 3-8-13 JWilliams (7) (led tl over 3f out: one pce) | 7.3 |
| 2576³ | Wave Master *(RJHodges)* 5-9-10 ‡³TSprake (13) (5th st: one pce fnl 3f) | 5.4 |
| 2240⁵ | Count Robert (USA) **(53)** *(MissJacquelineSDoyle)* 4-9-10 JQuinn (11) (lw: 3rd st: ev ch 2f out: wknd fnl f) | ½.5 |
| 1810 | Quiet Riot **(39)** (bl) *(JWhite)* 10–9-13 DaleGibson (14) (s.s: nrst fin) | 3.6 |
| 2416⁶ | Predestine **(51)** *(MMadgwick)* 7–9-13 GBaxter (1) (b: lw: 7th st: no hdwy) | 1.7 |
| 2576⁵ | Moving Force **(36)** *(EAWheeler)* 5–9-13 SWhitworth (2) (lw: nvr nrr) | 1.8 |
| 1810 | Solid Steel (IRE) **(39)** *(AMoore)* 4-9-10 CandyMorris (10) (nvr nr ldrs) | 1½.9 |
| 2051 | Tresilian Owl *(RJHodges)* 4-9-10 DBiggs (4) (n.d) | 15.10 |
| 2343 | Marjons Boy **(27)** (bl) *(CDBroad)* 5-9-13 NCarlisle (5) (lw: n.d) | ¾.11 |
| 2416 | Sukey Tawdry **(23)** *(RABennett)* 6-9-8 WNewnes (3) (b: prom 5f) | ½.12 |
| 1917 | Forge **(50)** *(PDCundell)* 4-9-10 TRogers (8) (lw: 6th st: wknd 4f out) | ½.13 |
| 2281 | Oh so Handy *(RCurtis)* 4-9-10 GBardwell (9) (prom 4f: t.o) | 30.14 |

**3/1** Bel Baraka (IRE), **7/2** Molly Splash, Count Robert (USA)(5/2—9/2), **4/1** CAROUSEL MUSIC, **10/1** Wave Master, **11/1** Predestine(op 7/1), **16/1** Moving Force, **20/1** Quiet Riot, **33/1** Marjons Boy, Forge, **50/1** Ors. CSF £18.85, Tote £4.30: £1.90 £1.90 £1.50 (£9.20). Mr John Trickett (UPPER LAMBOURN) bred by P. Barrett. 14 Rn; Bt in 4,800 gns                          2m 31.8 (9.3)
SF—15/14–/–/–/–

**2706**    ROBERT AND NORAH WILMOT NURSERY    £2448.00 (£678.00: £324.00)
     **5f 217y**                                                    3-00 (3-03)

(Weights raised 10 lb)

2138[2] **True Story (IRE) (68)** *(RHannon)* 8-11 MRoberts (1) (rdn along: hdwy 3f out: led over 1f out: r.o wl) ............................ —1
2388* Special One **(74)** *(JWHills)* 9-3 RHills (3) (a.p: ev ch over 1f out: r.o) ................. 1.2
2350* Palm Chat **(69)** (Fav) *(LMCumani)* 8-12 LDettori (9) (lw: a.p: rdn over 2f out: one pce fnl f) ............................................ 1.3
2578 Miss Fayruz (IRE) **(61)** *(MrsLPiggott)* 8-4 JQuinn (4) (a.p: one pce fnl 2f) ........ 2½.4
2418[2] Regent's Lady **(67)** *(CJames)* 8-11 AMcGlone (5) (led over 4f) .................. 2½.5
2437 Mr Nevermind (IRE) **(67)** *(GLewis)* 8-10 BRouse (8) (a bhd) ...................... 4.6
2425* Felt Lucky (IRE) **(78)** *(MRChannon)* 9-7 PatEddery (6) (spd 4f) ................. 5.7
1657[4] Toff Sundae **(61)** *(PMMcEntee)* 7-11 ‡7AGarth (7) (lw: a bhd) ................ ¾.8

**7/4** Palm Chat, **100/30** Special One(5/1—3/1), **7/2** TRUE STORY (IRE), **15/2** Felt Lucky (IRE)(4/1—8/1), **9/1** Regent's Lady(op 6/1), **16/1** Mr Nevermind (IRE)(op 10/1), **20/1** Ors. CSF £23.43. Tote £4.60: £1.40 £1.70 £1.10 (£10.00). Mr Guy Hart (MARLBOROUGH) bred by Cecil Harris Bloodstock Ltd in Ireland. 8 Rn
                                                     1m 13.2 (2.7)
                                                SF–43/45/36/18/14/–

**2707**    ROBERT MORLEY MEMORIAL H'CAP (0-80) £3980.00 (£1190.00: £570.00: £260.00)
     **1m 67y**                                                      3-30 (3-38)

1106[6] **Salbyng (54)** *(JWHills)* 4-8-2 RHills (4) (lw: 6th st: hrd rdn over 1f out: led ins fnl f: all out) ............................ —1
2496[3] Wakil (IRE) **(52)** *(LGCottrell)* 3-7-7 NCarlisle (10) (lw: 3rd st: ev ch over 1f out: r.o wl nr fin) ........................ hd.2
2561* Green's Cassatt (USA) **(52)** *(WMBrisbourne)* 4-7-9 (5x) ‡5SMaloney (2) (lw: hdwy 2f out: r.o wl ins fnl f) ...................... nk.3
2447 Saafend **(65)** (Fav) *(JSutcliffe)* 4-8-13 MRoberts (9) (stdd s: rapid hdwy over 3f out: led 2f out tl ins fnl f) .............. ¾.4
2476[3] Royal Dartmouth (USA) **(56)** *(BRMillman)* 7-8-4[1] JWilliams (8) (b: lw: nvr nrr) . ¾.5
1612[5] Statajack (IRE) **(67)** *(DRCElsworth)* 4-9-1 BRouse (5) (gd hdwy 2f out: one pce fnl f) ........................................ 1½.6
2433[4] Grand Vitesse (IRE) **(77)** *(RHannon)* 3-9-4 JReid (11) (led 2f: 4th st: wknd 2f out) ........................................ 1½.7
2236[5] Apollo Red **(59)** *(PWHarris)* 3-7-9[3] ‡5ATucker (3) (lw: nvr nr to chal) ........ 3½.8
2341 Akkazao (IRE) **(77)** *(WCarter)* 4-9-11 WNewnes (12) (5th st: wknd 2f out) .... 3½.9
2429[5] Lake Dominion **(67)** (bl) *(PWHarris)* 3-8-8 PaulEddery (6) (wknd 3f out) ....... s.h.10
2403[4] Congress (IRE) **(58)** *(MRStoute)* 3-9-5 PatEddery (7) (led after 2f to 2f out: wknd fnl f) ........................ hd.11
1366 Red Jack (IRE) **(53)** *(JAkehurst)* 3-7-8 NAdams (1) (2nd st: wknd 2f out) ....... 1.12
                     LONG HANDICAP: Wakil (IRE) 7-2.

**11/4** Saafend, **100/30** Congress (IRE)(5/1—3/1), **4/1** Green's Cassatt (USA)(op 6/1), **7/1** Royal Dartmouth (USA), **8/1** Grand Vitesse (IRE)(6/1—9/1), **11/1** Statajack (IRE)(8/1—12/1), **14/1** SALBYNG, **16/1** Apollo Red, Akkazao (IRE), Lake Dominion, **20/1** Wakil (IRE), **33/1** Red Jack (IRE). CSF £242.50, CT £1,223.14. Tote £21.30: £3.60 £4.30 £1.70 (£313.50). Mrs P. Jubert (LAMBOURN) bred by Llety Stud. 12 Rn   1m 45.1 (3.5)
                                                     SF–35/25/26/42/31/37

**2708**    SHADWELL STUD APP'CE SERIES H'CAP (0-70) £2716.50 (£754.00: £361.50)
     **1¼m 7y**                                                      4-00 (4-04)

2417* **Santana Lady (IRE) (70)** *(MJHeaton-Ellis)* 3-9-1 ‡7RuthCoulter (9) (led over 3f out to 2f out: led last stride) ........................ —1
2413* Rival Bid (USA) **(61)** (Fav) *(MAJarvis)* 4-9-8 KRutter (8) (8th st: stdy hdwy 2f out: led ins fnl f: eased nr fin: ct post) .......... s.h.2
2417[3] Keep Your Word **(57)** *(GBBalding)* 6-8-13 ‡5TraceyPurseglove (3) (7th st: led 2f out tl ins fnl f: btn whn hmpd cl home) ............ 2½.3
1945[5] Bronze Runner **(37)** (bl) *(EAWheeler)* 8-7-7[5] ‡5JDSmith (5) (b: 5th st: ev ch 2f out: one pce) ............................ 6.4
2266[4] Missy-S (IRE) **(52)** *(GAPritchard-Gordon)* 3-8-4 DHarrison (11) (5th st: wknd over 1f out) .......................... s.h.5
1917 Bit on the Side (IRE) **(53)** *(WJMusson)* 3-8-0 ‡5DMcCabe (2) (nvr nrr) ......... nk.6
2182[5] Rive-Jumelle (IRE) **(63)** *(MBell)* 4-9-10 PTurner (1) (hdwy 3f out: wknd over 1f out) ........................... 2.7
2273[4] Supertop **(54)** *(PWHarris)* 4-9-1 ATucker (4) (3rd st: rdn & wknd over 2f out) .. hd.8
2416 Allimac Nomis **(52)** *(ICampbell)* 3-7-11[9] ‡7SMulvey (12) (nvr nr to chal) ......... nk.9
2502 Vuchterbacher **(48)** *(PFTulk)* 6-8-4 ‡5TWilson (7) (led tl wknd over 3f out) ...... 5.10
*1320* Trainee (USA) **(47)** *(WJHaggas)* 3-7-8 ‡5SallyRadford-Howes (10) (t.o) ......... 15.11
2422[3] Weeheby (USA) **(67)** *(AAScott)* 3-8-12 ‡7HazelMilligan (6) (6th st: wknd 3f out: t.o) .......................... 3.12

**5/2** Rival Bid (USA), **7/2** Bit on the Side (IRE), **5/1** Supertop, Missy-S (IRE), **13/2** Keep Your Word, SANTANA LADY (IRE), **7/1** Rive-Jumelle (IRE), **12/1** Bronze Runner, **16/1** Allimac Nomis, Weeheby (USA), **20/1** Ors. CSF £26.25, CT £111.31. Tote £8.70: £1.80 £1.90 £2.30 (£12.70). Mrs Teresa McWilliams (WROUGHTON) bred by Milltown Stud in Ireland. 12 Rn
2m 9.1 (6.1)
SF—40/46/32/—/10/5

**2709** TATTERSALLS AUCTION SERIES STKS (Qualifier) (Mdn 2-Y.O) £2807.00 (£777.00: £371.00) **5f 10y**
4-30 (4-31)

1880⁵ **Brigante Di Cielo** *(RHannon)* 8-8 JLloyd (5) (a.p: hrd rdn fnl 2f: led ins fnl f: all out) ............................................................................ —1
1538 Blazing Soul (IRE) *(Fav)* *(PAKelleway)* 8-1 MRoberts (3) (lw: led tl ins fnl f) ...... nk.2
2414⁴ Geoff's Risk *(GLewis)* 8-6 ‡⁵DHarrison (1) (a.p: r.o one pce fnl 2f) .................... 3½.3
1902 Lorins Gold *(AndrewTurnell)* 8-6 AMcGlone (4) (a.p: hrd rdn fnl 2f: one pce) .. s.h.4
Who's Tom (IRE) *(WJMusson)* 8-10 JReid (7) (b: unf: bit bkwd: a same pl) ........ 5.5
Risk Proof *(GLewis)* 8-8 RaymondBerry (2) (lw: unf: scope: s.s: a bhd) ............ 12.6
La Calderona *(AAScott)* 8-3 RHills (6) (str: bit bkwd: a outpcd) ........................ 1.7
New Rhythm *(GHEden)* 8-5 AMunro (8) (cmpt: bit bkwd: outpcd) ................ 1.8

**9/4** Blazing Soul (IRE), **5/2** Geoff's Risk, **9/2** BRIGANTE DI CIELO, **11/2** Who's Tom (IRE)(7/2—6/1), La Calderona(3/1—6/1), **9/1** Lorins Gold(6/1—10/1), **14/1** Risk Proof(10/1—16/1), **20/1** New Rhythm. CSF £16.35, Tote £7.90: £3.80 £1.60 £1.10 (£9.40). Mr P. J. Christey (MARLBOROUGH) bred by Whitsbury Manor Stud. 8 Rn
60.6 sec (1.6)
SF—42/34/25/24/8/—

**2710** PLEASURES OF AGE STKS (2-Y.O.C & G) £2950.00 (£880.00: £420.00: £190.00) **5f 217y**
5-00 (5-00)

2124★ **Realities (USA) (96)** *(GHarwood)* 9-2 JReid (2) (lw: w ldr: led 3f out: rdn fnl f: r.o wl) ............................................................................ —1
933★ Firm Pledge (USA) **(100)** *(Fav)* *(PFICole)* 9-2 AMunro (3) (lw: led 3f: hrd rdn & ev ch fnl f: r.o) ............................................................................ hd.2
Mr Vincent *(GLewis)* 8-8 PaulEddery (5) (str: outpcd) ........................ 8.3
2167 Lincoln Imp (USA) *(AMoore)* 8-11 BRouse (1) (w ldrs 3f) ........................ 12.4

**4/9** Firm Pledge (USA), **7/4** REALITIES (USA), **20/1** Mr Vincent, **50/1** Lincoln Imp (USA). CSF £2.92, Tote £3.00 (£1.10). Mr Simon Karmel (PULBOROUGH) bred by Kathleen Crompton & Russell B. Jones Jnr in USA. 4 Rn
1m 13.7 (3.2)
SF—38/37/—/—

**2711** BEAT THE DEVIL GRADUATION STKS (3 & 4-Y.O) £3002.00 (£896.00: £428.00: £194.00) **1m 67y**
5-30 (5-31)

647² **Shuailaan (USA)** *(Fav)* *(ACStewart)* 3-9-2 MRoberts (3) (3rd st: hrd rdn fnl 2f: led ins fnl f: all out) ............................................................................ —1
2343³ Reported (IRE) **(106)** *(MJHeaton-Ellis)* 3-9-5 JReid (1) (lw: 2nd st: led 2f out tl ins fnl f: r.o wl) ............................................................................ nk.2
2464³ L'Hermine **(83)** *(HCandy)* 3-9-2 WNewnes (6) (led to 2f out: r.o one pce) ........ 2.3
2433 Mougins (IRE) **(95)** *(DRCElsworth)* 3-9-2 BRouse (5) (lw: 4th st: ev ch over 1f out: eased whn btn ins fnl f) ............................................................................ 2.4
799³ Ibsen *(ICampbell)* 4-9-2 MTebbutt (4) (b: a same pl) ............................ 15.5
Wild Poppy *(EAWheeler)* 3-8-4 SWhitworth (2) (w'like: bkwd: s.s: a last: t.o) ...... 25.6

**4/9** SHUAILAAN (USA), **3/1** Reported (IRE), **10/1** Mougins (IRE)(op 6/1), **16/1** L'Hermine, **40/1** Ibsen, **66/1** Wild Poppy. CSF £2.25, Tote £1.50: £1.10 £1.40 (£1.80). Sheikh Ahmed Al Maktoum (NEWMARKET) bred by W. S. Farish & W. S. Kilroy in USA. 6 Rn
1m 45.2 (3.6)
SF—48/50/41/35/—

T/Plpt: £84.10 (49.35 Tckts). Hn

**2616—BATH (L-H)**

**Tuesday, August 11th [Firm]**

Going Allowance: 5f-5f 161y: minus 0.05; Rest: minus 0.20 sec (F)     Wind: mod against

Stalls: low

**2712** AUGUST (S) STKS (3 & 4-Y.O) £2407.50 (£670.00: £322.50)     **1m 5y**     2-00 (2-12)

2545² **Precious Air (IRE) (52)** *(AMoore)* 4-8-10 BRouse (6) (3rd st: led over 1f out: sn clr: r.o wl) ............................................................................ —1
1174 Seaside Minstrel **(44)** *(CJHill)* 4-9-1 GHind (16) (hld up in rr: hdwy 2f out: str run fnl f: fin wl) ............................................................................ 2.2

2576⁴ Simon Ellis (IRE) **(47)** *(DRLaing)* 3–8–0 ‡⁵ATucker (8) (bhd: rdn over 4f out: gd
hwdy over 1f out: fin fast) .................................................. 1.3
2303 Walkonthemoon **(50)** *(MMcCormack)* 3–8–3 CRutter (12) (2nd st: ev ch 2f out:
one pce) .......................................................................... hd.4
2607⁵ High Baccarat **(49)** (v) *(CCElsey)* 3–8–5 TRogers (9) (dwlt: hdwy & 7th st: hrd
rdn & one pce fnl 2f) ........................................................ hd.5
2291² Kathy Fair (IRE) **(43)** *(RJBaker)* 3–8–0 AMunro (4) (lw: dwlt: hdwy over 1f out: nt
rch ldrs) .......................................................................... 1.6
2392 Litmore Dancer **(47)** *(JMBradley)* 4–8–10 NAdams (3) (plld hrd: led tl hdd over
1f out: wknd fnl f) ............................................................. hd.7
2545⁴ Shalou **(60)** *(RJHodges)* 3–8–8 DBiggs (10) (lw: nvr trbld ldrs) ................... 1.8
1214 Grey But Rosy (IRE) **(50)** (bl) *(DRCElsworth)* 3–8–0 SDawson (2) (hdwy over 1f
out: bdly hmpd ins fnl f: nt rcvr) ....................................... 2.9
2545 Sixofus (IRE) **(43)** *(WGMTurner)* 4–8–8 ‡⁷SDrowne (5) (hrd rdn & wknd 3f out) hd.10
Musical Lyrics *(MrsJGRetter)* 4–8–2 ‡³TSprake (14) (4th st: wknd 2f out) ......... s.h.11
2463⁶ Lyn's Return (IRE) **(60)** (Fav) *(RSimpson)* 3–8–8 SWhitworth (11) (hdwy & 5th
st: wknd over 2f out) ................................................... 2¹⁄₂.12
1672³ Zaire *(ANLee)* 3–8–5 NCarlisle (1) (a bhd) ........................................ hd.13
2545 Rock Song (IRE) **(53)** (bl) *(PFICole)* 3–8–8 TQuinn (13) (prom: stumbled over 4f
out: 8th & wkng st: p.u over 1f out: b.b.v) ............................ 0
*Tout de Val (50/1) Withdrawn (ref to ent stalls) : not under orders*

**5/2** Lyn's Return (IRE), **4/1** Shalou(3/1—9/2), **7/1** PRECIOUS AIR (IRE)(4/1—8/1), **8/1** Kathy Fair (IRE)(op 5/1), **9/1** Zaire, **10/1** Grey But Rosy (IRE)(8/1—12/1), Rock Song (IRE)(8/1—12/1), **14/1** High Baccarat, **16/1** Walkonthemoon, **20/1** Simon Ellis (IRE), Litmore Dancer, **25/1** Sixofus (IRE), **33/1** Seaside Minstrel, **50/1** Musical Lyrics. CSF £189.00, Tote £7.00: £3.10 £8.00 £7.30 (£93.30). Mr K. Higson (BRIGHTON) bred by Dictum Enterprises Ltd in Ireland. 14 Rn; Bt in 3,000 gns                                    1m 42.7 (3.4)
SF—21/20/2/4/5/–

---

**2713**     TRIPLEPRINT MEDIAN AUCTION STKS (2-Y.O.F) £2637.00 (£732.00: £351.00)
**5f 161y**                                                             2-30 (2-37)

2450³ **Brockton Dancer (78)** (Fav) *(RHannon)* 8-8 JReid (2) (w ldr tl led over 3f out:
pushed out) .................................................................... —1
2491⁴ Pontevecchio Moda *(DRCElsworth)* 8-8 JWilliams (1) (hld up: swtchd rt & rdn
over 1f out: nt qckn) ...................................................... 2.2
Steading *(HCandy)* 8-8 CRutter (4) (cmpt: s.i.s: hld up: hdwy on ins over 1f out:
r.o one pce) .................................................................. 1.3
2557 Merch Fach (IRE) *(JDRoberts)* 8-8 TLang (3) (rdn 3f out: bhd fnl 2f) ........... 10.4
2491 Ivy Benson *(BWHills)* 8-8 TQuinn (5) (led over 2f: rdn & wknd 2f out) ....... 1¹⁄₂.5

**4/7** BROCKTON DANCER, **15/8** Pontevecchio Moda, **14/1** Steading(8/1—16/1), **16/1** Ivy Benson(op 8/1), **50/1** Merch Fach (IRE). CSF £2.05, Tote £1.50: £1.10 £1.30 (£1.20). Mrs D. A. La Trobe (MARLBOROUGH) bred by W. H. Joyce. 5 Rn                                                            1m 12 (2.7)
SF—35/27/23/–/–

---

**2714**     ROTHMANS ROYALS NORTH SOUTH CHALLENGE SERIES H'CAP (0-90) £3655.00
(£1090.00: £520.00: £235.00)   **1m 5y**                                3-00 (3-04)

2457² **Talent (USA) (82)** (v) *(LordHuntingdon)* 4–9-13 AMunro (4) (led 4f: rdn to ld 2f
out: r.o wl) ................................................................... —1
2494² Aitch N'Bee **(75)** *(LadyHerries)* 9–9-6 TQuinn (5) (swtg: hld up in rr: ran: last st:
hdwy on ins 2f out: r.o ins fnl f) ..................................... 2.2
2458 Eternal Flame **(63)** *(JWHills)* 4–8-8 WNewnes (3) (5th st: rdn & ev ch over 1f out:
nt qckn) ........................................................................ ¹⁄₂.3
2460⁴ Gilderdale **(83)** *(JWHills)* 10–9-7 ‡⁷MHenry (6) (hld up: hdwy & 3rd st: rdn & ev
ch over 1f out: one pce) ............................................... 2¹⁄₂.4
2637 Annabelle Royale **(79)** *(MrsNMacauley)* 6–9-10 JReid (8) (lw: 4th st: rdn &
wknd over 1f out) ......................................................... 1.5
2417² Sooty Tern **(55)** *(JMBradley)* 5–8-0 NAdams (9) (chsd ldr: led 4f out to 2f out:
wknd over 1f out) ......................................................... ³⁄₄.6
2427 Asterix **(59)** (v) *(JMBradley)* 4–8-4⁽²⁾ JWilliams (7) (7th st: no hdwy fnl 3f) ......... ³⁄₄.7
816 Gotcha (BAR) **(83)** *(RHannon)* 3–9-7 JLloyd (2) (hmpd after 1f: 8th & rdn st: a
bhd) .............................................................................. 6.8
2447 Field of Honour **(78)** (Fav) *(LMCumani)* 4–9-4 ‡⁵JWeaver (2) (lw: plld hrd: sddle
slipped: 5th st: eased whn btn fnl f) ............................... 5.9

**5/2** Field of Honour, **9/2** Gilderdale, **5/1** TALENT (USA), **9/1** Gotcha (BAR), **10/1** Annabelle Royale, Sooty Tern, Aitch N'Bee, **14/1** Eternal Flame, **25/1** Asterix. CSF £45.51, CT £568.29. Tote £5.10: £1.70 £2.40 £3.50 (£14.10). The Queen (WEST ILSLEY) bred by The Queen in USA. 9 Rn                          1m 40.4 (1.1)
SF—72/59/45/50/50/24

## 2715

B.B.C. RADIO BRISTOL H'CAP (0-80) £3066.00 (£851.00: £408.00)
**1m 5f 22y**

3-30 (3-31)

2412* **Chucklestone (66)** *(JSKing)* 9-9-9 TQuinn (1) (mde all: rdn over 5f out: r.o wl) — **1**
2255⁵ Spectacular Dawn **(77)** *(JLDunlop)* 3-9-8 JReid (3) (chsd wnr: 2nd st: rdn & no imp fnl 2f) .................. 2¹/₂.**2**
2226⁴ Monarda **(71)** (Fav) *(PFICole)* 5-10-0 AMunro (5) (4th st: rdn & one pce fnl 2f) 2¹/₂.**3**
2677⁴ Fair Flyer (IRE) **(53)** *(MJohnston)* 3-7-5 (6x) ‡⁷MBaird (8) (lw: lost pl 7f out: hdwy & 3rd st: one pce fnl 2f) .................. hd.**4**
790 Janiski **(54)** (v) *(MrsBarbaraWaring)* 9-8-11 NHowe (7) (hld up & bhd: hdwy & 5th st: wknd 2f out) .................. 3¹/₂.**5**
2391² White River **(43)** (v) *(DHaydnJones)* 6-8-0 NCarlisle (4) (7th st: a bhd) .................. 2.**6**
2089⁴ Dawn Flight **(74)** (bl) *(LadyHerries)* 3-9-5 JWilliams (6) (lw: 6th st: bhd fnl 2f) .... 5.**7**
597 Pinkjinski (IRE) **(66)** *(DBurchell)* 3-8-11 ADicks (2) (plld hrd: prom 9f: last st: t.o fnl f) .................. 25.**8**

**9/4** Monarda, **7/2** Fair Flyer (IRE), **5/1** Spectacular Dawn, **7/1** CHUCKLESTONE, **8/1** White River, **10/1** Dawn Flight, **14/1** Janiski(10/1—16/1), **40/1** Pinkjinski (IRE). CSF £37.11, CT £90.70. Tote £7.50: £2.10 £1.50 (£21.50). Mr Mark O'Connor (SWINDON) bred by R. B. Stokes. 8 Rn    2m 51.3 (3.6)
SF—47/41/42/4/17/2

## 2716

PENNSYLVANIA CLAIMING STKS (Mdn 3-Y.O) £2469.00 (£684.00: £327.00)
**1m 3f 144y**

4-00 (4-02)

2253 **City Line (38)** *(DRLaing)* 7-11 ‡⁵ATucker (4) (chsd ldr: 2nd & rdn st: led over 1f out: drvn out) .................. — **1**
1367² White Wedding **(60)** *(PFICole)* 8-2 CRutter (3) (b.hind: hld up: 3rd st: hrd rdn 2f out: swtchd rt over 1f out: r.o one pce) .................. 1¹/₂.**2**
1632³ Pyare Square **(70)** (bl) *(IABalding)* 8-9 JReid (1) (led tl hdd over 1f out: one pce) .................. 2.**3**
2211 Killshandra (IRE) **(40)** *(MrsBarbaraWaring)* 8-3 NHowe (2) (s.i.s: last & rdn st: bhd fnl 2f) .................. 4.**4**

**8/11** Pyare Square, **13/8** White Wedding, **9/1** CITY LINE(op 5/1), **25/1** Killshandra (IRE). CSF £21.91, Tote £9.10 (£5.90). Mr F. Hope (LAMBOURN) bred by R. Hannon and Mrs M. Hartley. 4 Rn    2m 33.1 (6.4)

## 2717

LADBROKE NURSERY    £2906.25 (£870.00: £417.50: £191.25)
**5f 161y**

4-30 (4-31)

(Weights raised 1 lb)
877³ **Northern Bird (83)** *(BWHills)* 9-7 JWilliams (2) (b.hind: bhd: swtchd rt & hdwy 2f out: led 1f out: r.o wl) .................. — **1**
2055 Lowrianna (IRE) **(60)** *(DHaydnJones)* 7-12 NCarlisle (3) (lw: rdn & outpcd in rr: gd hdwy & swtchd rt over 1f out: rdn & hng lft ins fnl f) .......... 3.**2**
2221⁵ Second Colours (USA) **(80)** *(PSFelgate)* 9-4 TQuinn (1) (lw: a.p: led over 2f out to 1f out: one pce) .................. 1.**3**
1749⁵ Homemaker **(59)** *(RJHolder)* 7-11 NAdams (6) (a.p: rdn over 1f out: one pce) nk.**4**
2371* Minshaar **(78)** (Jt-Fav) *(KSBridgwater)* 9-2 BRaymond (5) (prom: rdn over 2f out: n.m.r over 1f out: r.o one pce) .................. 1.**5**
2546* Bold County **(78)** (Jt-Fav) *(MJohnston)* 9-2 RPElliott (4) (hdwy over 2f out: hrd rdn & ev ch whn edgd lft over 1f out: wknd fnl f) .................. 2.**6**
2342⁵ Sharp Gazelle **(68)** *(BSmart)* 8-6 WNewnes (7) (led 3f) .................. 2.**7**

**3/1** Bold County, Minshaar, **5/1** NORTHERN BIRD, **6/1** Second Colours (USA)(op 4/1), **7/1** Lowrianna (IRE), **8/1** Homemaker, **12/1** Sharp Gazelle(10/1—16/1). CSF £34.19, Tote £4.70: £3.00 £3.00 (£19.30). Mr John E. Bradley (LAMBOURN) bred by S. Wingfield Digby. 7 Rn    1m 12.4 (3.1)
SF—40/5/21/−/14/6

## 2718

LEVY BOARD H'CAP (0-70) £2856.00 (£791.00: £378.00)    **5f 11y**

5-00 (5-03)

2229⁴ **Mister Jolson (51)** *(RJHodges)* 3-8-7 ‡³TSprake (3) (a.p: rdn over 1f out: r.o to ld post) .................. — **1**
2548 Belthorn **(45)** *(JJBridger)* 3-8-4 AMunro (12) (led: hrd rdn fnl f: ct post) .... s.h.**2**
2229⁶ Red Verona **(40)** *(EAWheeler)* 3-7-8⁽¹⁾ ‡⁵ATucker (7) (hdwy over 2f out: r.o one pce fnl f) .................. 2.**3**
2141 Beveled Edge **(50)** *(BPalling)* 3-8-4 ‡⁵JWeaver (11) (bhd tl hdwy 2f out: rdn over 1f out: r.o ins fnl f) .................. ¹/₂.**4**
2618³ Gallant Hope **(54)** (bl) *(LGCottrell)* 10-9-3 JWilliams (9) (bhd: swtchd rt & hdwy wl over 1f out: r.o ins fnl f) .................. nk.**5**
2548⁵ Castle Maid **(37)** *(RJHodges)* 5-8-0 DBiggs (6) (hdwy over 2f out: ev ch fnl 1f out: one pce) .................. ³/₄.**6**
2548³ The Noble Oak (IRE) **(65)** (bl) (Jt-Fav) *(MMcCormack)* 4-10-0 JReid (5) (prom: ev ch over 1f out: wknd fnl f) .................. 2.**7**

  1552 Tachyon Park **(34)** *(PHowling)* 10-7-11 CRutter (4) (no hdwy fnl 2f) ............... 1.8
  2617 Pendor Dancer **(54)** (bl) *(BForsey)* 9-9-3 SWhitworth (8) (hld up: jnd ldrs 3f out:
                 wknd wl over over 1f out) ......................................... nk.9
25548⁶ Sports Post Lady (IRE) **(49)** (Jt-Fav) *(CJHill)* 4-8-12 PaulEddery (1) (prom over
                 3f) ......................................... ³/₄.10
2565⁵ Barbara's Cutie **(36)** *(MBlanshard)* 4-7-13 NCarlisle (10) (bhd fnl 2f) ............... 3.11
2307 Fontaine Lady **(38)** *(TThomsonJones)* 5-8-1 NAdams (2) (prom: rdn over 2f
                 out: wknd wl over 1f out) ......................................... 2.12
1162 Village Pet **(45)** (bl) *(PJHobbs)* 4-8-8 AMcGlone (13) (spd over 2f) ............... 4.13

**9/2** Sports Post Lady (IRE)(tchd 3/1), The Noble Oak (IRE), **5/1** Gallant Hope, **8/1** Pendor Dancer(6/1—10/1), **9/1** MISTER JOLSON, **11/1** Fontaine Lady, **12/1** Castle Maid(op 8/1), **14/1** Red Verona, **16/1** Barbara's Cutie, **20/1** Village Pet, Belthorn, Beveled Edge, **25/1** Tachyon Park. CSF £150.93, CT £2,254.34. Tote £12.50: £3.30 £3.50 £6.60 (£45.90). Mr J. W. Mursell (SOMERTON) bred by Mrs D. D. Scott. 13 Rn      63.1 sec (2.6)
                                           SF—36/32/14/22/34/14

T/Plpt: £2,143.50 (1.4 Tckts).                                              KH

## 2466—CATTERICK (L-H)

### Tuesday, August 11th [Good]

Going Allowance: 5f-7f: nil sec; Rest: minus 0.20 sec (F)           Wind: slt half against

Stalls: low

**2719**     HASKER STREET (S) STKS (2-Y-O) £1245.00 (£345.00: £165.00)     **7f**     6-00 (6-06)

2649³ **Madam Cyn's Risk (48)** *(NACallaghan)* 8-1 ‡⁵OPears (4) (in tch: effrt ent st:
                 styd on to ld wl ins fnl f) ......................................... —1
2606⁶ Ann Hill (IRE) **(78)** (Fav) *(RHollinshead)* 7-13 ‡⁷AGarth (8) (outpcd ½-wy: hdwy
                 2f out: r.o wl nr fin) ......................................... ½.2
1670 Monastic Flight (IRE) **(8)** *(BSRothwell)* 8-11 DHolland (12) (sn led: clr ent st: hdd &
                 no ex nr fin) ......................................... ½.3
2247⁴ Society Gown (USA) *(TDBarron)* 8-11 KDarley (2) (broke wl: stdd & sn bhd:
                 hdwy 2f out: r.o) ......................................... 2¹/₂.4
2516* Lucky Owl **(56)** *(MissLAPerratt)* 8-6 JFanning (10) (lw: chsd ldrs: wnt 2nd st: sn
                 rdn & nt qckn) ......................................... 1¹/₂.5
1007⁵ Kesanta *(WGMTurner)* 8-6 GBaxter (11) (lw: chsd ldrs tl rdn & wknd over 2f out) 4.6
*2480* Libby-J *(MWEasterby)* 8-6 TLucas (13) (a same pl) ......................................... 3.7
1056 Newgatesky *(BWMurray)* 8-6 JFortune (5) (in tch tl rdn & btn appr st) ............... 5.8
2489³ Coffee Mint *(JBerry)* 8-6 JCarroll (9) (chsd ldrs tl rdn & wknd ent st) ............... 3.9
1762 Princess Nebia *(BJMcMath)* 8-6 EJohnson (6) (led early: sn bhd) ............... 2¹/₂.10
1559 Cambus Bay *(WTKemp)* 8-6 JLowe (3) (sn bhd) ......................................... 1.11

**2/1** Ann Hill (IRE), **11/4** MADAM CYN'S RISK, **5/1** Lucky Owl, **7/1** Society Gown (USA), **8/1** Kesanta, **16/1** Coffee Mint, **33/1** Libby-J, Monastic Flight (IRE), **50/1** Newgatesky, Princess Nebia, **100/1** Cambus Bay. CSF £8.13, Tote £4.50: £1.80 £1.30 £7.20 (£6.20). Roldvale Intend (NEWMARKET) bred by Roldvale Ltd. 11 Rn; Bt in 4,500 gns                                          1m 28.2 (5)
                                           SF—12/8/18/10/–/–

**2720**     MAUNBY HALL STKS (Mdn 3-Y.O) £1161.00 (£321.00: £153.00)
           1¹/₂m 44y                                  6-30 (6-31)

1962⁴ Maji **(66)** *(DMorley)* 8-9 MBirch (7) (hld up: hdwy gng wl appr st: led wl over 1f
                 out: shkn up & r.o) ......................................... —1
1891⁶ In the Money (IRE) **(62)** *(RHollinshead)* 9-0 KDarley (2) (bhd: hdwy ent st: r.o
                 u.p: nt pce of wnr) ......................................... 2.2
2170³ Dazzling Fire (IRE) **(68)** (Fav) *(BWHills)* 8-9 DHolland (8) (lw: cl up: led 4f out tl
                 wl over 1f out: hrd rdn & sn btn) ......................................... 3¹/₂.3
2542⁴ Forest Star (USA) *(MMoubarak)* 9-0 LDettori (3) (lw: a chsng ldrs: styd on one
                 pce fnl 4f) ......................................... 6.4
       Kims Selection (IRE) *(SGNorton)* 8-9 ‡⁵OPears (4) (w'like: hdwy ½-wy: one pce
                 fnl 3f) ......................................... 3¹/₂.5
2515² Well Ahead **(67)** *(MJohnston)* 8-9 DMcKeown (5) (chsd ldrs tl outpcd fnl 3f) ..... 5.6
1919³ Gaveko (USA) *(JGFitzGerald)* 9-0 KFallon (1) (bhd: sme hdwy 4f out: n.d) ..... 10.7
2116⁴ Green Flower (USA) *(MRStoute)* 8-9 JCarroll (9) (led tl hdd 4f out: wknd ent st) 1¹/₂.8
       Raith Pc *(GRichards)* 9-0 JLowe (6) (chsd ldrs tl rdn & wknd qckly 4f out) ......... 8.9

**11/10** Dazzling Fire (IRE), **4/1** Forest Star (USA), **6/1** MAJI, **8/1** Well Ahead, **17/2** Green Flower (USA), **14/1** In the Money (IRE), **33/1** Kims Selection (IRE), Gaveko (USA), **50/1** Raith Pc. CSF £73.44, Tote £7.40: £1.90 £3.20 £1.20 (£29.70). Mr Saeed Manana (NEWMARKET) bred by Sheikh Mohammed bin Rashid al Maktoum. 9 Rn
                                           2m 39.8 (5.8)
                                           SF—13/12/–/–/–/–

**2721** AMATEUR RIDERS ASSOCIATION H'CAP (0-70) £1266.00 (£351.00: £168.00)
1½m 44y
7-00 (7-01)

2540³ **Sapphirine (58)** *(RMWhitaker)* 5-12-0 MrsSWhitaker (6) (lw: a:p: led wl over 1f out: r.o wl) .................................................................. —1

2602★ Falcons Dawn (54) (Fav) *(ABailey)* 5-11-10 (3x) MissLEaton (11) (lw: hld up: gd hdwy 4f out: ev ch over 1f out: nt qckn) ..................... 1½.2

1922 Spanish Whisper (30) *(JRBostock)* 5-10-0 MrsLPearce (2) (lw: led tl hdd 5f out: kpt on u.p fnl 2f) ...................................................... 3½.3

1184 Corporate Type (IRE) (28) *(GPKelly)* 4-9-7[5] ‡⁵MrsSWalker (10) (cl up: led 5f out tl wl over 1f out: sn wknd) ................................. ¾.4

2670³ Thunderbird One (USA) (58) *(DenysSmith)* 3-10-12 ‡⁵MissMCarson (15) (bhd tl styd on fnl 3f: nrst fin) ........................................... 1½.5

2692⁵ Not Yet (42) *(EWeymes)* 8-10-12 MrJWeymes (5) (in tch: no hdwy fnl 4f) ...... ½.6

2420 Al Badeto (23) *(JNorton)* 5-9-2 ‡⁵MrGHaine (7) (styd on wl fnl 3f: nrst fin) ........ 2.7

2605³ Escape Talk (27) *(JDooler)* 5-9-6 ‡⁵MrDWilcox (3) (lw: bhd: effrt ½-wy: nvr rchd ldrs) ................................................................... 2.8

Band Sargeant (IRE) (48) *(GRichards)* 3-10-7 MrRHale (13) (in tch tl.outpcd fnl 4f) .......................................................................... 1½.9

2367 Mr Wishing Well (53) *(RJRWilliams)* 6–11-9 MrsSAstaire (12) (b.hind: racd wd: bhd: hdwy appr st: n.d) ............................................ ½.10

2261² Sexy Mover (32) *(WStorey)* 5-9-11 ‡⁵MissSStorey (1) (chsd ldrs tl wknd appr st) 7.11

2602 Be the Best (44) (v) *(MPNaughton)* 4-11-0 MissPRobson (8) (prom tl wknd ½-wy) ...................................................................... hd.12

2070⁴ Lightning Spark (45) *(MAvison)* 3–10-4 MissMJuster (4) (chsd ldrs tl wknd qckly 4f out) ........................................................ 1½.13

Schwantz (31) *(WTKemp)* 4-10-1 MrDParker (8) (prom to ½-wy) ............... 10.14

747 Nishara (39) *(NBycroft)* 4–10-4 ‡⁵MissABycroft (14) (prom early: wl bhd fnl 4f) 12.15

LONG HANDICAP. Corporate Type (IRE) 8-13, Al Badeto 9-4.

9/4 Falcons Dawn, 13/2 Escape Talk, 7/1 Spanish Whisper, 8/1 Thunderbird One (USA), 9/1 Sexy Mover, 11/1 SAPPHIRINE, 12/1 Mr Wishing Well, 14/1 Lightning Spark, Not Yet, 33/1 Band Sargeant (IRE), Be the Best, Al Badeto, 50/1 Schwantz, 66/1 Corporate Type (IRE), 200/1 Nishara. CSF £33.00, CT £175.91. Tote £12.60: £3.00 £1.80 £2.90 (£28.10). Mr Frazer Hines (WETHERBY) bred by E. J. Loder. 15 Rn    2m 41.6 (7.6)
SF—42/35/4/–/11/10

**2722** 'LEVE ET RELUIS' STKS (Mdn 3-Y.O) £1108.50 (£306.00: £145.50)    5f   7-30 (7-37)

**Amazing Feat (IRE) (71)** (Fav) *(MrsGRReveley)* 9-0 KDarley (5) (chsd ldrs: effrt whn bdly hmpd ent fnl f: swtchd & r.o: fin 2nd, ¾:l: awrdd r) —1

2406 Black Boy (IRE) *(JAGlover)* 8-9 ‡⁵SWilliams (4) (s.i.s: sn trckng ldrs: led over 1f out: hng lft: eased: fin 1st: disq: plcd 2nd) .................... 2

2119³ Nordoora (IRE) *(JHMGosden)* 8-4 ‡⁵SMaloney (3) (led tl hdd over 1f out: sn btn) .. 1½.3

2539 True Touch (45) *(TDBarron)* 9-0 AlexGreaves (1) (a chsng ldrs: kpt on fnl f) ...... 1.4

Dear Person *(JLHarris)* 8-9 LDettori (6) (small: dwlt: a outpcd & bhd) .......... 12.5

2419 Call to the Bar (IRE) (bl) *(CGCox)* 9-0 MBirch (2) (lw: bolted 7f bef s: spd to ½-wy: sn bhd) ......................................................... 5.6

*Stewards Enquiry: Obj. to Black Boy by Darley sustained. Black Boy disq. (interference to Amazing Feat fnl f).*

6/5 AMAZING FEAT (IRE)(op 4/5), 11/4 Black Boy (IRE), 7/1 Call to the Bar (IRE)(op 4/1), 15/2 Nordoora (IRE), 10/1 Dear Person, 33/1 True Touch. CSF £4.51, Tote £2.00: £1.50 £2.30 (£4.10). Mr P. D. Savill (SALTBURN) bred by Old Meadow Stud in Ireland. 6 Rn    60.4 sec (2.9)
SF—37/39/23/29/–/–

**2723** CHARLES CLINKARD FINE FOOTWEAR H'CAP (3-Y.O) (0-70) £1688.00 (£468.00: £224.00)    7f    8-00 (8-05)

(Weights raised 1 lb)

**Celestine (51)** *(TFairhurst)* 8-3 JFanning (11) (chsd ldrs: led 2f out: r.o wl) ........ —1

2075⁴ Young Valentine (63) *(RMWhitaker)* 9-1 ACulhane (12) (a.p: ev ch over 1f out: kpt on) .................................................................. 1½.2

2393⁴ Mary Macblain (49) *(JLHarris)* 7-10[3] ‡⁵SMaloney (6) (hmpd after s: bhd tl hdwy ent st: r.o nr fin) ........................................... 2.3

2479³ Kirkby Belle (48) *(EWeymes)* 7-7 ‡⁷AGarth (10) (in tch: hdwy 2f out: styd on) ... 1½.4

2107⁵ La Kermesse (USA) (60) *(JHMGosden)* 8-12 JCarroll (1) (a chsng ldrs: rdn & one pce fnl 2f) ................................................... 1.5

2668 L'Amour Precieux (49) *(MWEasterby)* 8-1 KDarley (5) (t: hmpd after s: bhd tl sme hdwy fnl 2f) ........................................... 1½.6

2443 Boy Martin (69) *(MJohnston)* 9-7 DMcKeown (8) (chsd ldrs tl outpcd appr st: n.d after) ....................................................... ½.7

2311⁶ Ivors Princess (49) *(MrsGRReveley)* 7-8 ‡⁷DarrenMoffatt (9) (dwlt: effrt ent st: nvr rch ldrs) ............................................... 1.8

2680 Rose Gem (IRE) **(60)** *(PCHaslam)* 8-12 DaleGibson (2) (led tl hdd & wknd 2f out) ............................................................................ nk.**9**
2051 Umbria **(41)** *(MPNaughton)* 7-7 JakiHouston (7) (bhd: effrt on ins whn nt clr run fnl 2f: nt rcvr) ........................................................ ½.**10**
2472⁴ Brambles Way **(55)** (v) *(WLBarker)* 8-2 ‡⁵OPears (3) (hmpd & fell after 2f) ............ 0

**3/1** Rose Gem (IRE), **9/2** La Kermesse (USA), **7/1** Brambles Way, Umbria(op 4/1), Mary Macblain, **8/1** Boy Martin, Young Valentine, **16/1** Ivors Princess, **25/1** Kirkby Belle, **33/1** CELESTINE, **66/1** L'Amour Precieux. CSF £244.48, CT £1,872.23. Tote £26.10: £6.20 £2.70 £2.40 (£179.40). Mr M. J. Grace (MIDDLEHAM) bred by J. G. and Mrs J. M. Brearley. 11 Rn     1m 27.3 (4.1)
SF—28/35/10/5/21/5

**2724**     BROUGH PARK NURSERY     £1576.00 (£436.00: £208.00)     **5f 212y**     8-30 (8-33)

2550⁴ **Master Sinclair (IRE) (62)** *(RHollinshead)* 7-4 ‡⁷AGarth (8) (s.s: hdwy on ins 2f out: led wl ins fnl f: r.o) ............................................ —**1**
1963⁵ Missed the Boat (IRE) **(65)** *(TDBarron)* 8-0 KDarley (7) (s.i.s: hdwy 2f out: r.o nr fin) ........................................................................... ¾.**2**
2067⁶ Shadow Jury **(86)** (v) *(JSWainwright)* 9-7 PBurke (4) (chsd ldrs: led over 1f out tl wl ins fnl f: no ex) ...................................................... 1.**3**
2532⁴ Our Mica **(58)** (bl) *(JBerry)* 7-7 JFanning (9) (hdwy appr st: chal 2f out: nt qckn fnl f) ...................................................................... 1½.**4**
1360⁴ Daaniera (IRE) **(82)** (bl) *(JBerry)* 9-3 JCarroll (1) (effrt & slipped appr st: hdwy whn hmpd over 1f out: nt rcvr) ............................ 1½.**5**
2076 Nutty Brown **(69)** (bl) *(SGNorton)* 7-13 ‡⁵OPears (6) (mde most tl hdd over 1f out: grad wknd) ....................................................... ¾.**6**
2532★ Grinnell **(70)** *(DenysSmith)* 8-5 KFallon (5) (in tch: effrt 2f out: n.m.r & nt qckn) . 2.**7**
2368² Action Night **(72)** (Fav) *(MMoubarak)* 8-7⁽¹⁾ LDettori (2) (prom: outpcd ent st: sn btn) .................................................................... 2½.**8**
2387³ Juliet Bravo **(77)** *(BBeasley)* 8-12 DNicholls (3) (w ldr 4f: sn wknd) ................... 2¼.**9**

**5/2** Action Night, **9/2** Grinnell, **5/1** Juliet Bravo(op 10/1), **8/1** Daaniera (IRE), MASTER SINCLAIR (IRE), **10/1** Missed the Boat (IRE), **12/1** Ors. CSF £74.94, CT £865.41. Tote £9.60: £2.10 £3.10 £2.90 (£64.90). Sinclair Developments Limited (UPPER LONGDON) bred by Kellsboro House Stud in Ireland. 9 Rn     1m 14.6 (4.1)
T/Plpt: £491.90 (4.1 Tckts).     AA

## 2497—**YARMOUTH (L-H)**

### Tuesday, August 11th [Firm]

Going Allowance: St: nil sec; Rnd: minus 0.30 sec per fur (F)     Wind: nil     Vis: poor 4th race

Stalls: centre

**2725**     MARKET GATES CLAIMING STKS (3-Y.O) £2238.00 (£618.00: £294.00)     1¼m 21y     2-20 (2-22)

2554⁴ **Retender (USA) (69)** *(LMCumani)* 8-13 LDettori (3) (b.hind: 4th st: hdwy 4f out: led 3f out: hng lft over 2f out: rdn out) .......................... —**1**
2430³ Edge of Darkness **(70)** (Fav) *(JWHills)* 8-6 RHills (4) (lw: hld up: last st: hdwy 2f out: hrd rdn: no ch w wnr) ................................... 3½.**2**
2562⁵ Euroflight **(62)** *(BWHills)* 7-7 ‡⁵DHarrison (5) (led 7f: one pce) ........................ 6.**3**
2430 Lady of Sardinia (BEL) **(66)** *(JWPayne)* 8-2 GDuffield (1) (3rd st: wknd qckly 3f out) .................................................................... 10.**4**
1921⁶ Dragon Spirit **(56)** (bl) *(SPCWoods)* 8-3 WWoods (2) (b: 2nd st: wknd over 3f out) .................................................................... 2.**5**

**2/1** Edge of Darkness, **9/4** RETENDER (USA), **3/1** Lady of Sardinia (BEL)(op 2/1), **6/1** Euroflight, **25/1** Dragon Spirit. CSF £6.54, Tote £2.50: £1.90 £1.50 (£3.70). Mr L. Gatto-Roissard (NEWMARKET) bred by Amerivest Thor'bred Partners & E.A.Seltzer in USA. 5 Rn     2m 7 (2.6)
SF—43/29/4/–/–

**2726**     FILBY BRIDGE H'CAP (0-80) £3460.00 (£1030.00: £490.00: £220.00)     6f 3y     2-50 (2-51)

(Weights raised 6 lb)
2618★ **Spring High (54)** (bl) (Fav) *(KTIvory)* 5-9-1 (6x) GBardwell (4) (lw: mde all: drvn out) ................................................................... —**1**
2449 Hi-Tech Honda (IRE) **(67)** *(CEBrittain)* 3-9-9 GDuffield (1) (lw: hdwy over 2f out: hrd rdn over 1f out: unable qckn fnl f) ..................... 1.**2**
2254 Mu-Arrik **(50)** *(DAWilson)* 4-8-11 GCarter (5) (hld up: hdwy 2f out: one pce fnl f) 2.**3**
2536★ Our Rita **(68)** *(PAKelleway)* 3-9-10 LPiggott (2) (prom 4f: one pce) ................... nk.**4**
2617 Farmer Jock **(57)** *(MrsNMacauley)* 10-9-4 DMcKeown (3) (effrt & hrd rdn over 2f out: wknd over 1f out) .......................................... 2½.**5**

85/40 SPRING HIGH, **4/1** Mu-Arrik(op 5/2), Hi-Tech Honda (IRE), Our Rita, **11/2** Farmer Jock. CSF £9.54, Tote £3.00: £2.20 £1.80 (£6.60). Mr K. T. Ivory (RADLETT) bred by Mrs P. A. Brown. 5 Rn
1m 13.6 (3)
SF—41/45/25/37/21

---

## 2727

E.B.F. MANSHIP STKS (Mdn 2-Y.O) £2259.00 (£624.00: £297.00)
**6f 3y** 3-20 (3-21)

|  |  |  |
|---|---|---|
| **Lost Soldier (USA)** *(LMCumani)* 9-0 LDettori (2) (gd sort: scope: led 2f out: pushed clr 1f out: easily) | —1 |
| 2233² Tropical Waters (USA) *(MMoubarak)* 8-9 WCarson (1) (hld up: plld hrd: ev ch wl over 1f out: wknd appr fnl f) | 4.2 |
| Mam'zelle Angot *(MRStoute)* 8-9 WRSwinburn (5) (leggy: scope: led 2f: led over 2f out to 2f out (one pce) | 2¹/₂.3 |
| 1595² Suivez (Jt-Fav) *(CEBrittain)* 9-0 GDuffield (3) (led 4f out tl over 2f out: wknd qckly) | 10.4 |
| Sing as We Go *(BobJones)* 8-9 NDay (4) (lt-f: bhd fr over 2f out) | ¹/₂.5 |

**15/8** Suivez, Tropical Waters (USA), **7/2** LOST SOLDIER (USA)(op 2/1), **9/2** Mam'zelle Angot, **33/1** Sing as We Go. CSF £10.10, Tote £4.40: £1.70 £1.70 (£3.70). Sheikh Mohammed (NEWMARKET) bred by Wimborne Farm Inc in USA. 5 Rn
1m 14 (3.4)
SF—32/11/1/–/–

---

## 2728

CAISTER CASTLE STKS (Mdn 2-Y.O) £2385.00 (£660.00: £315.00)
**7f 3y** 3-50 (3-51)

|  |  |
|---|---|
| **Ajfan (USA)** *(HThomsonJones)* 8-9 RHills (1) (str: cmpt: trckd ldrs: led over 3f out: qckned clr over 1f out: impressive) | —1 |
| 2438⁴ Magical Queen (IRE) (Fav) *(MMoubarak)* 8-9 WCarson (2) (a in tch: hdwy over 2f out: one pce appr fnl f) | 6.2 |
| 2398 Muraadi Ana (IRE) *(AAScott)* 9-0 WRSwinburn (7) (outpcd tl hdwy over 1f out: r.o ins fnl f) | 1.3 |
| 2185 Madam Caprice *(RGuest)* 8-9 MHills (4) (prom tl lost pl 4f out: hdwy over 2f out: wknd appr fnl f) | 3.4 |
| 1995⁵ Pamar *(CEBrittain)* 9-0 GCarter (3) (prom 5f) | 4.5 |
| *1549* Benevolent *(SirMarkPrescott)* 9-0 GDuffield (6) (led tl over 3f out: wknd over 2f out) | 3¹/₂.6 |
| Grey Watch *(LadyHerries)* 8-9 LDettori (8) (small: bit bkwd: a bhd) | 2¹/₂.7 |
| Marco Claudio (IRE) *(PAKelleway)* 9-0 JQuinn (10) (lt-f: dwlt: a bhd) | 4.8 |
| Baeza *(HRACecil)* 9-0 WRyan (5) (w'like: bit bkwd: a bhd) | 2.9 |
| 2292² Russia Pobeda (USA) *(MrsLPiggott)* 8-9 LPiggott (9) ‡5(b: b.hind: prom over 3f) | 2¹/₂.10 |

**7/4** Magical Queen (IRE)(tchd 3/1), **5/2** AJFAN (USA)(op 6/4), **4/1** Baeza, **6/1** Russia Pobeda (USA), **14/1** Pamar, **16/1** Benevolent, Grey Watch, Madam Caprice, **20/1** Ors. CSF £8.14, Tote £4.20: £1.30 £2.10 £6.10 (£6.60). Mr Hamdan Al-Maktoum (NEWMARKET) bred by Flaxman Holdings Ltd in USA. 10 Rn
1m 26 (5.2)
SF—17/–/–/–/–

---

## 2729

HOLIDAY PLAYGROUND (S) H'CAP (3 & 4-Y.O) (0-60) £2406.00 (£666.00: £318.00)
**1m 3y** 4-20 (4-24)

(Weights raised 2 lb)

|  |  |
|---|---|
| 2291 **Joseph's Wine (IRE) (35)** (Jt-Fav) *(RBastiman)* 3-8-8 RHills (3) (lw: hld up: hdwy over 2f out: led 1f out: all out) | —1 |
| 2326 Broad Appeal (33) *(RCSpicer)* 4-8-13 MHills (6) (s.i.s: hdwy over 2f out: ev ch ins fnl f: unable qckn cl home) | hd.2 |
| 2291 Aragon Court (38) (bl) (Jt-Fav) *(JPearce)* 4-8-13 ‡5RPrice (2) (lw: hld up: hdwy 3f out: led 2f out to 1f out: one pce) | 4.3 |
| 2394⁵ A Nymph Too Far (IRE) (38) *(DrJDScargill)* 3-8-6 ‡5KRutter (4) (a in tch: one pce fnl 2f) | 3.4 |
| 2581 Harlequin Girl (29) *(KTIvory)* 4-8-9 GDuffield (5) (nvr able to chal) | 2.5 |
| 2545³ Daily Sport Girl (50) *(FJYardley)* 3-9-9 JQuinn (7) (prom: led 3f out to 2f out: sn wknd) | 8.6 |
| 2291⁵ Tendresse (IRE) (33) *(DRTucker)* 4-8-13 GBardwell (12) (a bhd) | 4.7 |
| 1421⁶ Jolizal (36) (v) *(DMorris)* 4-8-11 ‡5StephenDavies (8) (chsd ldr over 4f) | 1¹/₂.8 |
| Indian Mohawk (IRE) (37) *(MPMuggeridge)* 4-9-3 LPiggott (11) (led 5f) | 2¹/₂.9 |
| 2655⁶ Dublin Indemnity (USA) (47) *(NACallaghan)* 3-9-6 WCarson (10) (lw: prom 4f: wknd qckly) | 3.10 |
| 2427 Candle King (IRE) (44) *(MJFetherston-Godley)* 4-9-10 WRSwinburn (9) (mid div tl wknd over 2f out) | 3¹/₂.11 |

**4/1** Aragon Court, JOSEPH'S WINE (IRE)(3/1—5/1), **6/1** Indian Mohawk (IRE)(op 10/1), Jolizal(tchd 10/1), **13/2** Tendresse (IRE), **7/1** A Nymph Too Far (IRE), Dublin Indemnity (USA), **10/1** Candle King (IRE)(op 6/1), **14/1** Daily Sport Girl, Harlequin Girl, **25/1** Broad Appeal. CSF £90.11, CT £407.30. Tote £7.70: £2.40 £7.60 £2.30 (£96.70). Mrs P. Bastiman (WETHERBY) bred by Michael Fennessy. 11 Rn; No bid
1m 40.5 (5.2)
SF—16/20/8/–/–

**2730**      LEVY BOARD H'CAP (0-70) £2406.00 (£666.00: £318.00)    **7f 3y**     4-50 (4-52)

2656³ **Shining Jewel (66)** *(MrsLPiggott)* 5-10-0 LPiggott (3) (hld up: hdwy 2f out: led
     jst fnl f: pushed out) ............................................................ —1
2581 Juvenara (36) (Fav) *(CJHill)* 6-7-12 WCarson (4) (hld up: hdwy 3f out: led over
     1f out tl jst ins fnl f: hrd rdn & unable qckn) ...................... hd.2
2684★ Coral Flutter (60) *(JWPayne)* *(CJHill)* 5-9-8 (5x) JQuinn (1) (led tl over 1f out: r.o) . hd.3
2656⁵ Alnasric Pete (USA) (54) *(DAWilson)* 6-9-2 GCarter (2) (in tch tl one pce wl over
     1f out) .................................................................................. 5.4
2570 Gott's Desire (42) (v) *(RBastiman)* 6-8-4 MHills (5) (trckd ldr 4f) ................. 4.5

**9/4** Juvenara, **11/4** Coral Flutter, SHINING JEWEL, **7/1** Alnasric Pete (USA), **8/1** Gott's Desire(tchd 12/1). CSF
£8.50, Tote £3.40: £1.30 1.60 (£3.30). Mr D. W. Rolt (NEWMARKET) bred by H. Ward. 5 Rn   1m 27 (4.2)
                                                          SF—51/20/43/22/–

**2731**      EAST COAST H'CAP (0-70) £3158.00 (£944.00: £452.00: £206.00)
         1³⁄₄m 17y                                               5-20 (5-20)

2358★ **Briggsmaid (56)** *(JMPEustace)* 4-9-0 MTebbutt (7) (hld up: 6th st: c wd &
     hdwy over 3f out: led 2f out: pushed out: jst hld on) ............ —1
2377★ Heavenly Waters (54) (Fav) *(RFJohnsonHoughton)* 3-7-13(1) RHills (1)
     (b.hind: hld up: 7th st: hdwy 2f out: ev ch ins fnl f: r.o) ..... s.h.2
2477⁴ Saif Al Adil (IRE) (48) *(KTIvory)* 3-7-7 GBardwell (8) (a.p: 2nd st: hrd rdn 2f out:
     r.o one pce) ........................................................................ 1.3
2295² Native Magic (70) *(RWArmstrong)* 6-10-0 LPiggott (3) (led 10f out to 2f out: one
     pce) ..................................................................................... 4.4
2373 Socks and Shares (50) (bl) *(PWHarris)* 3-7-9 AMackay (6) (lw: 4th st: wknd 3f
     out) ...................................................................................... 7.5
2505³ Cold Marble (USA) (38) *(DRTucker)* 7-7-10 JQuinn (4) (3rd st: ev ch over 2f
     out: sn wknd) ..................................................................... 1¹⁄₂6
2439 Skisurf (57) *(CEBrittain)* 6-9-1 GDuffield (2) (lw: 5th st: rdn & wknd 3f out) ........ 1.7
2373 Rashita (35) (bl) *(GHEden)* 5-7-7 GKing (5) (swtg: led 4f: wknd qckly 7f out: t.o) dist.8
                                 LONG HANDICAP: Rashita 6-6.

**9/4** Heavenly Waters, **3/1** BRIGGSMAID, **11/2** Skisurf, **13/2** Native Magic, **9/1** Saif Al Adil (IRE)(tchd 14/1), **12/1**
Cold Marble (USA), **14/1** Socks and Shares, **66/1** Rashita. CSF £9.27, CT £42.79. Tote £4.00: £1.90 1.50 £1.40
(£4.40). Mr F. W. Briggs (NEWMARKET) bred by John L. Moore. 8 Rn          3m 3.8 (5.8)
T/Plpt: £45.10 (51.4 Tckts).                                                       RC

## 2420— **BEVERLEY (R-H)**

### Wednesday, August 12th [Good to soft]
Going Allowance: 0.25 sec per fur (G)                             Vis:str half against

Stalls: low

**2732**      D.J. ARKSEY (S) STKS    £2637.00 (£732.00: £351.00)    **7f 100y**     2-15 (2-20)

2552⁵ **Gymcrak Tycoon (75)** (Fav) *(MHEasterby)* 3-8-10 MBirch (12) (trckd ldrs: led
     2f out: pushed clr fnl f) .................................................... —1
2209² Glenfield Greta (60) *(PSFelgate)* 4-8-11 WRyan (6) (hld up: hdwy over 2f out:
     styd on fnl f: no imp) ........................................................ 3¹⁄₂.2
1294⁵ Richmond (IRE) (54) (bl) *(BBeasley)* 4-9-2 LCharnock (10) (lw: led 6f out to 2f
     out: kpt on one pce) ......................................................... 1¹⁄₂.3
2699² Stairway to Heaven (IRE) (51) (bl) *(TDBarron)* 4-8-4 ‡⁷VHalliday (18) (a chsng
     ldrs: rdn & n.m.r 2f out: swtchd & styd on) ...................... 1¹⁄₂.4
2072³ Giddy Heights (IRE) (52) *(JPLeigh)* 3-8-1(1) PRobinson (3) (racd wd: sn w ldrs:
     one pce fnl 2f) .................................................................. nk.5
2369 Pimsboy (51) (bl) *(FJYardley)* 5-9-2 JCarroll (13) (a chsng ldrs: one pce fnl 3f) 4.6
2668⁶ Vital Voltage (IRE) (30) (v) *(MWEllery)* 3-8-5 PBurke (2) (nvr bttr than mid div) 2¹⁄₂.7
2538⁴ Always Lynsey (IRE) *(MissLCSiddall)* 3-8-0 KDarley (5) (t: chsd ldrs: effrt over
     2f out: wknd over 1f out) ................................................. 3¹⁄₂.8
2569² Reilton (50) *(JParkes)* 5-8-11 WCarson (16) (sme hdwy over 2f out: n.d) ...... 1¹⁄₂.9
2561⁶ Norfolk Thatch (32) *(KSBridgwater)* 6-8-6 ‡⁵SWilliams (8) (in tch: effrt u.p over
     2f out: nvr rchd ldrs) ....................................................... s.h.10
2486⁶ Capital Idea (IRE) (48) *(RonaldThompson)* 3-8-10 JLowe (15) (a in rr) ......... 1¹⁄₂.11
2198 Beljinski (25) *(BJMcMath)* 4-7-13 ‡⁷CHawksley (17) (led to 6f out: lost pl 3f out) 2.12
2417 Chica Mia (48) *(GAHam)* 8-8-6 ‡⁵DHarrison (7) (a bhd) ................................... 3.13
2272 Indian Heather (IRE) *(JParkes)* 4-8-1 ‡⁵OPears (14) (hld up: a in rr) ............... 1¹⁄₂.14
     Highcliffe Jester *(PBeaumont)* 3-8-5 NConnorton (9) (w'like: str: bit bkwd: s.s:
     a wl bhd) .......................................................................... 2¹⁄₂.15

**11/10** GYMCRAK TYCOON, **4/1** Stairway to Heaven (IRE), **6/1** Reilton, **7/1** Glenfield Greta, **12/1** Always Lynsey (IRE), **14/1** Norfolk Thatch, **16/1** Richmond (IRE), **20/1** Giddy Heights (IRE), Pimsboy, **33/1** Chica Mia, Highcliffe Jester, Beljinski, Capital Idea (IRE), Vital Voltage (IRE), **50/1** Indian Heather (IRE). CSF £11.52, Tote £2.10: £1.30 £2.30 £4.60 (£4.90). Gymcrak Thoroughbred Racing III Plc (MALTON) bred by Lord Halifax. 15 Rn; Bt in 5,200 gns
1m 35.6 (5.4)
SF—43/33/33/18/17

**2733**      TATTERSALLS AUCTION SERIES STKS (Qualifier) (Mdn 2-Y.O) £2924.00 (£872.00: £416.00: £188.00)    **7f 100y**                   2-45 (2-49)

2409 **Marius (IRE)** *(BWHills)* 8-8 DHolland (2) (b.hind: hld up gng wl: smooth hdwy over 2f out: r.o: pushed out to ld nr fin) ................................ —1
2534 Contrac Countess (IRE) **(55)** *(BSRothwell)* 7-9 ‡5DHarrison (3) (s.i.s: sn rcvrd: hdwy to ld 2f out: r.o) ................................ ½.2
10715 Express Mariecurie (IRE) *(PWChapple-Hyam)* 8-8 WCarson (4) (lw: sn w ldr: led over 2f out: sn hdd: nt qckn fnl f) ................................ 1½.3
2108 Ume River (IRE) *(MHTompkins)* 8-5 PRobinson (5) (chsd ldrs: no ex fnl f) ...... s.h.4
24623 Chinnery (IRE) **(79)** (Fav) *(JMPEustace)* 8-12 MTebbutt (11) (lw: hld up: effrt & n.m.r 2f out: swtchd outside & styd on) ................................ 1½.5
2534 La Bonita (IRE) *(JBerry)* 8-7 JCarroll (7) (lw: led tl over 2f out: wknd 1f out) ...... 1.6
12976 April Point (IRE) *(RHollinshead)* 8-9 WRyan (9) (prom to 3f out: rn green & grad wknd) ................................ 1½.7
22084 Mr Geneaology (USA) *(JLSpearing)* 8-10 GHind (1) (dwlt s: bhd tl kpt on fnl f) . ¾.8
25346 El Guapo **(58)** *(TFairhurst)* 8-6 JFanning (6) (chsd ldrs tl drdn & lost pl wl over 1f out) ................................ 2½.9
2068 Wild Expression *(CTinkler)* 8-13 MBirch (10) (a in rr) ................................ 2½.10
18976 Emmandee *(MWEasterby)* 8-7 TLucas (8) (plld hrd early: sn bhd) ................................ 4.11

**Evens** Chinnery (IRE), **9/2** MARIUS (IRE), **11/2** Mr Geneaology (USA), **9/1** Express Mariecurie (IRE), **14/1** April Point (IRE)(op 9/1), **20/1** Ume River (IRE), **25/1** El Guapo, Contrac Countess (IRE), Wild Expression, La Bonita (IRE), **33/1** Emmandee. CSF £93.64, Tote £6.60: £1.50 £7.30 £1.50 (£131.80). Mrs Leonard Simpson (LAMBOURN) bred by James O'Sullivan in Ireland. 11 Rn
1m 38.4 (8.2)

**2734**      CHARLES ELSEY MEMORIAL CHALLENGE TROPHY (H'cap) (0-90) £3652.00 (£1096.00: £528.00: £244.00)    **1m 3f 216y**             3-15 (3-18)

(Weights raised 8 lb)

2113³ **First Bid (50)** *(RMWhitaker)* 5-7-13 JFanning (6) (lw: trckd ldrs gng wl: led over 1f out: rdn clr fnl f) ................................ —1
2101⁵ Kinoko **(46)** *(KWHogg)* 4-7-2(1) ‡7AGarth (2) (hld up: hdwy over 2f out: nt qckn fnl f) ................................ 3.2
2222⁵ Daisy Girl **(66)** *(JMackie)* 6-9-1 MBirch (1) (hld up: smooth hdwy over 3f out: led 2f out: sn hdd: edgd rt & grad wknd) ................................ 1½.3
2423★ Bold Elect **(75)** (Fav) *(PWigham)* 4-9-10 MWigham (5) (lw: trckd ldrs: effrt & ev ch over 2f out: wknd over 1f out) ................................ 5.4
2391★ Rajai (IRE) **(83)** (bl) *(JLDunlop)* 3-9-7 WCarson (3) (hld up: effrt over 4f out: hrd drvn & wandered 2f out: sn wknd) ................................ 2.5
2204 John Shaw (USA) **(50)** *(JSWainwright)* 4-7-13 PBurke (8) (led tl over 3f out: one pce) ................................ 2.6
2273⁵ Bold Ambition **(44)** *(TKersey)* 5-7-7 JLowe (7) (trckd ldrs tl outpcd over 4f out: sn lost pl) ................................ 1½.7
2134 Castillet **(81)** *(GHarwood)* 3-9-5 AClark (4) (trckd ldrs: led over 3f out to 2f out: sn wknd) ................................ hd.8
2423² Smoke **(45)** *(JParkes)* 6-7-1(1) ‡7CHawksley (9) (lw: s.s: a bhd: edgd lft fnl f) ..... 5.9
LONG HANDICAP: Bold Ambition 7-4, Smoke 7-2.

**9/4** Bold Elect, **4/1** Rajai (IRE), **6/1** FIRST BID, **13/2** Daisy Girl, **8/1** Castillet, Smoke, **12/1** Kinoko, **16/1** Bold Ambition, **50/1** John Shaw (USA). CSF £64.62, CT £435.91. Tote £6.80: £1.70 £3.20 £2.40 (£106.50). Thomlinson's (WETHERBY) bred by R. M. Whitaker. 9 Rn
2m 40.5 (8.9)
SF—26/9/33/32/25/–

**2735**      CONTRAC COMPUTER SUPPLIES NURSERY    £3652.00 (£1096.00: £528.00: £244.00)    **7f 100y**             3-45 (3-47)

(Weights raised 1 lb)

2085² **Costa Verde (79)** *(KWHogg)* 8-9 WRyan (8) (hld up: gd hdwy over 1f out: r.o wl to ld wl ins fnl f) ................................ —1
2374⁶ Amerigue **(69)** *(MissSEHall)* 7-8 ‡5DHarrison (1) (sn rckng ldrs: led led over 1f out: nt qckn nr fin) ................................ ½.2
2112⁵ Doc Spot **(64)** *(CaptJWilson)* 7-1(1) ‡7CHawksley (4) (sltly hmpd s: hdwy & prom over 2f out: r.o one pce u.p fnl f) ................................ 2.3
2578³ Futurballa **(91)** (Fav) *(JLDunlop)* 9-7 WCarson (6) (lw: rn in snatches: effrt over 2f out: sn prom: styd on same pce fnl f) ................................ ½.4

2528 Bonus Point **(75)** *(MrsGRReveley)* 8-5 KDarley (3) (lw: sltly hmpd s: trckd ldr: led 2f out: sn hdd: hung rt & wknd fnl f) ............................ 1½.5

2076* Argyle Cavalier (IRE) **(74)** *(FHLee)* 7-13 ‡5NKennedy (7) (hld up: hdwy on ins 2f out: wknd over 1f out) ............................ 1½.6

2516³ Laurel Etoile **(66)** *(JBerry)* 7-3⁽³⁾ ‡7AGarth (9) (chsd ldrs tl wknd wl over 1f out) .. 4.7

2543³ Pine Ridge Lad (IRE) **(67)** *(BBeasley)* 7-11 LCharnock (2) (wnt rt s: led tl hdd & wknd 2f out) ............................ 2½.8

1860⁶ Kentucky Dreams **(63)** *(RonaldThompson)* 7-7 JLowe (5) (trckd ldrs tl lost pl over 2f out) ............................ 1½.9

LONG HANDICAP: Doc Spot 6-11, Laurel Etoile 6-11, Kentucky Dreams 7-4.

**13/8** Futurballa, **9/2** Bonus Point, **7/1** COSTA VERDE, Argyle Cavalier (IRE), **9/1** Amerigue, **10/1** Kentucky Dreams, **11/1** Pine Ridge Lad (IRE)(12/1—8/1), **16/1** Laurel Etoile, **20/1** Doc Spot. CSF £61.77, CT £1,092.30. Tote £7.00: £1.60 £2.40 £3.90 (£42.70). Mr Anthony White (ISLE OF MAN) bred by Auldyn Stud Ltd. 9 Rn
1m 37 (6.8)
SF—22/4/–/24/–

---

**2736**　　JOURNAL H'CAP (3-Y.O) (0-90) £3548.00 (£1064.00: £512.00: £236.00)
**2m 35y**　　　　　　　　　　　　　　　　　　　4-15 (4-16)

2575² **Kadari (58)** *(AHarrison)* 7-6⁽⁴⁾ ‡5DHarrison (6) (lw: hld up: gd hdwy 3f out: led over 2f out: clr whn swvd & hit rail over 1f out) ............................ —1

2535² Suez Canal (IRE) **(76)** *(PWChapple-Hyam)* 9-1 DHolland (7) (trckd ldrs: effrt over 4f out: kpt on fnl 2f: no ch w wnr) ............................ 7.2

2535* Jack Button (IRE) **(77)** (v) *(BobJones)* 9-2 NDay (4) (chsd ldrs: drvn along 7f out: hrd rdn to ld over 3f out: hdd over 2f out) ............................ 1.3

2470³ Gay Ming **(56)** *(RHollinshead)* 7-2⁽²⁾ ‡7AGarth (1) (bhd & outpcd 6f out: kpt on fnl 2f: n.d) ............................ 3½.4

2087⁴ Moor Lodge (USA) **(69)** *(MHTompkins)* 8-8 PRobinson (3) (effrt 5f out: sn prom: rdn & lost pl over 2f out: eased whn no ch) ............................ 12.5

2287* Betelgeuse **(81)** (Fav) *(HRACecil)* 9-6 WRyan (5) (led tl over 3f out: sn wknd & eased) ............................ 12.6

LONG HANDICAP: Kadari 7-6, Gay Ming 7-2.

**15/8** Betelgeuse(11/10—2/1), **2/1** Jack Button (IRE), **11/2** KADARI, **13/2** Suez Canal (IRE), **7/1** Moor Lodge (USA), **16/1** Gay Ming. CSF £35.21, Tote £7.40: £2.70 £1.80 (£16.30). Mr J. G. Rookes (MIDDLEHAM) bred by Lord Rotherwick. 6 Rn
3m 40.8 (10.1)
SF—17/32/32/–/8/8

---

**2737**　　EAST RIDING YEOMANRY CHALLENGE TROPHY (H'cap) (Amateurs) (0-70) £3003.00
(£833.00: £399.00)　**2m 35y**　　　　　　　　　　4-45 (4-47)

2535³ Vain Prince **(40)** *(NTinkler)* 5-9-12 MrsAFarrell (4) (lw: trckd ldrs: led over 3f out: styd on wl u.p appr fnl f) ............................ —1

2059⁴ Naseem Elbarr (USA) **(63)** *(ACStewart)* 4-11-0 ‡7MrVLukaniuk (10) (a chsng ldrs: ev ch 3f out: one pce) ............................ 5.2

2358³ Grey Power **(57)** *(MrsGRReveley)* 5-11-1 MrNWilson (6) (lw: hld up: stdy hdwy 5f out: ev ch 2f out: rdn over 1f out: edgd lft & kpt on) ....... ½.3

1241⁶ Carefree Times **(39)** *(JNorton)* 5-9-11 MissPRobson (2) (sn bhd: sme hdwy 5f out: n.d) ............................ 25.4

2664* Premier Princess **(40)** (Fav) *(GAHam)* 6-9-12 (5x) MissMJuster (8) (lw: chsd ldrs: drvn along 5f out: wknd 3f out) ............................ 5.5

2602 The Metropole (IRE) **(43)** *(AWPotts)* 3-8-7 ‡7MissSJudge (13) (b.off hind: led 4f: lost pl 6f out: n.d after) ............................ ¾.6

2197³ Afore Jane **(55)** *(GHarwood)* 3-9-12 MissAHarwood (5) (b.hind: lw: chsd ldrs: drvn along & lost pl 4f out) ............................ 20.7

2677⁵ Dollar Seeker (USA) **(50)** (bl) *(ABailey)* 8-10-8 MissIDWJones (1) (b: lw: led 10f out tl over 3f out: sn wknd) ............................ 6.8

2120⁵ Newark Antiquefair **(28)** *(BCMorgan)* 4-9-0 MissSBaxter (9) (led after 4f to 10f out: chsd ldrs tl lost pl 4f out) ............................ 8.9

Lafkadio **(52)** *(MCChapman)* 5-10-5 ‡5MrMChapman (11) (bkwd: bhd whn reminders & swvd bdly lft 11f out: racd wd & sn t.o) ............................ 1.10

2605 Bijou Princess **(45)** (bl) *(ABailey)* 4-10-3 MissLEaton (12) (w ldrs tl rdn & lost pl 9f out: sn bhd: t.o) ............................ 12.11

2484 One for the Boys **(33)** *(CaptJWilson)* 5-9-5 MrsGRees (7) (b: sn bhd: p.u wl over 1f out: lame) ............................ 0

LONG HANDICAP: The Metropole (IRE) 8-6, Newark Antiquefair 8-9.

**2/1** Premier Princess, **6/1** Afore Jane, Naseem Elbarr (USA), **13/2** Grey Power(op 10/1), **9/1** VAIN PRINCE, **12/1** Dollar Seeker (USA), **14/1** Carefree Times, **16/1** Lafkadio, **20/1** Bijou Princess, Newark Antiquefair, **40/1** One for the Boys, **100/1** The Metropole (IRE). CSF £56.97, CT £343.36. Tote £9.20: £2.00 £1.80 £2.80 (£25.20). Mr A. C. Findlay (MALTON) bred by Lodge Park Stud. 12 Rn
3m 44.1 (13.4)
SF—18/24/24/–/–/–

**2738**　　NORFOLK STREET MEDIAN AUCTION STKS (Mdn 3-Y.O) £2684.50 (£742.00: £353.50)
　　　　　　**1m 100y**　　　　　　　　　　　　　　　　　　　　　　　5-15 (5-15)

2362² **King's Guest (IRE) (62)** *(GAPritchard-Gordon)* 9-0 PRobinson (5) (mde all:
　　　　　　　　　　　　　　styd on fnl 2f) ........................................ —1
　1244² Ginger Flower (Fav) *(GWragg)* 8-9 MHills (4) (trckd ldrs: effrt u.p over 2f out: kpt
　　　　　　　　　　　　　　on: nvr able to chal) ................................... 4.2
　2687 Dancing Pet (37) *(WWHaigh)* 8-9 DMcKeown (1) (lw: chsd ldr: one pce fnl 3f) .. 5.3
　　　　Fairy Wisher (IRE) *(ACStewart)* 8-9 WRyan (2) (w'like: lw: s.i.s: hdwy & prom 4f
　　　　　　　　　　　　　　out: rdn & wknd over 2f out) ........................ 5.4
　2137 Faustnluce Lady *(GAHam)* 8-4 ‡5DHarrison (3) (bhd & rdn 5f out) ............... 5.5

**6/4** Ginger Flower, **2/1** KING'S GUEST (IRE), **33/1** Fairy Wisher (IRE), **9/4** Dancing Pet. 5 Ors. CSF £5.15, Tote £3.20: £1.30
£1.60 (£2.90). Lord Cadogan (NEWMARKET) bred by Mrs P. Grubb in Ireland. 5 Rn　　　　　1m 50.2 (7.5)
　　　　　　　　　　　　　　　　　　　　　　　　　　　　　　　　　　　　SF—19/2/–/–/–

T/Plpt: £2270.20 (1.8 Tckts).　　　　　　　　　　　　　　　　　　　　　　　　WG

# BEVERLEY (R-H)

## Thursday, August 13th [Good]

Going Allowance: 0.20 sec per fur (G)

Stalls: high

Wind: fresh against

**2739**　　　TOLL GAVEL CLAIMING STKS　　£2758.00 (£763.00: £364.00)　　2m 35y 2-10 (2-11)

2533* **Expansionist (57)** *(SPCWoods)* 3-8-2 WWoods (4) (in tch: hdwy appr st: led
　　　　　　　　　　　　　2f out: styd on wl) ........................................ —1
　2134 Rolling the Bones (USA) **(66)** (bl) (Fav) *(JRFanshawe)* 3-8-8 KDarley (8) (cl up:
　　　　　　　　　　　　　led 5f out to 2f out: kpt on wl) ..................... 1½.2
2560² Ballymac Girl (50) *(CTNash)* 4-9-4 JCarroll (6) (b: chsd ldrs: ev ch 3f out: one
　　　　　　　　　　　　　pce) ................................................... 10.3
2565² Briggscare (62) *(WJarvis)* 6-9-9 MTebbutt (2) (b: hld up: hdwy appr st: no imp
　　　　　　　　　　　　　fr wl over 2f out) .................................. s.h.4
　　　　Memphis Toes (FR) *(KSBridgwater)* 5-9-2 ‡5SWilliams (3) (bhd: gd hdwy appr
　　　　　　　　　　　　　st: one pce fnl 3f) ................................. 3½.5
2483⁶ Manse Key Gold (32) *(JDooler)* 5-8-10 DMcKeown (7) (in tch: effrt appr st: sn
　　　　　　　　　　　　　wknd) ................................................ 12.6
　2302 Rustyside *(CTNash)* 5-9-2 MWigham (5) (hdwy 6f out: sn rdn & no imp) ...... s.h.7
　2087 My Turn Next (30) *(KWHogg)* 4-8-13 JCorrigan (9) (led tl hdd 5f out: sn bhd) .. dist.8
　1907 Dont Embarrass Me *(TKersey)* 3-8-0 JLowe (1) (b: t.o fr ½-wy) ............... dist.9

**13/8** Rolling the Bones (USA), **5/2** EXPANSIONIST, Briggscare, **6/1** Ballymac Girl(op 10/1), **16/1** Memphis Toes
(FR), **25/1** Manse Key Gold, **33/1** My Turn Next, **50/1** Ors. CSF £7.40, Tote £3.90: £1.60 £1.40 £1.50 (£3.30).
High Point Bloodstock Ltd (NEWMARKET) bred by N. E. and Mrs Poole. 9 Rn; Rolling the Bones (USA) clmd M
Naughton £12,060　　　　　　　　　　　　　　　　　　　　　　　　　　　　3m 42.5 (11.8)
　　　　　　　　　　　　　　　　　　　　　　　　　　　　　　　　　　　SF—2/6/6/10/–/–

**2740**　　　ST JOHN AMBULANCE CLAIMING STKS (2-Y.O) £2758.00 (£763.00: £364.00)
　　　　　　**5f**　　　　　　　　　　　　　　　　　　　　　　　　　　　2-40 (2-42)

2661* **First Option (65)** *(MHEasterby)* 9-0 KDarley (7) (trckd ldrs gng wl: led ins fnl f:
　　　　　　　　　　　　　rdn & r.o) ............................................ —1
1235⁵ Hotaria (60) *(RMWhitaker)* 8-2 ACulhane (11) (hld up: swtchd 2f out: r.o: nt pce
　　　　　　　　　　　　　of wnr) ............................................. 1½.2
2330* Trentesimo (IRE) **(83)** *(JBerry)* 9-0 JCarroll (4) (led tl hdd & no ex ins fnl f) ...... 2.3
2690³ Grand Dancer (IRE) **(81)** (bl) (Fav) *(RJRWilliams)* 8-9 MHills (4) (lw: trckd ldr:
　　　　　　　　　　　　　effrt wl over 1f out: rdn & nt qckn) ............... 1½.4
1782⁶ Dunnington (MWEasterby) 8-4(1) MBirch (6) (gd spd to ½-wy: sn lost pl) .......... 5.5
2339⁶ Celtic Cherry (JBalding) 8-4 GHind (8) (sn in tch: grad wknd fnl 2f) ............. 1.6
　2428 Poppet Plume (52) *(GMMoore)* 8-3 JFanning (2) (sn pushed along & n.d) ........ 1.7
　2550 Boulmerka (MJohnston) 8-4 RPElliott (10) (s.i.s: hmpd & swtchd over 1f out: a
　　　　　　　　　　　　　bhd) ................................................... ½.8
2550² Out of Aces (MrsVAAconley) 8-9 LCharnock (5) (gd spd 3f: sn lost pl) .......... 1½.9

**6/4** Grand Dancer (IRE), **3/1** Trentesimo (IRE), **5/1** FIRST OPTION, **13/2** Out of Aces, **9/1** Hotaria, **14/1** Poppet
Plume, **16/1** Boulmerka, **20/1** Dunnington, **25/1** Celtic Cherry. CSF £47.46, Tote £5.70: £1.70 £1.80 £1.50
(£15.10). Mr P. D. Savill (MALTON) bred by Dodford Stud. 9 Rn　　　　　　　　65.4 sec (3.9)
　　　　　　　　　　　　　　　　　　　　　　　　　　　　　　　　　SF—42/24/28/17/–/–

**2741** STRUTHERS & CARTER SPRINT H'CAP (0-90) £3886.00 (£1168.00: £564.00: £262.00)
5f
3-10 (3-13)

      **Precentor (59)** *(JDBethell)* 6-7-13 AMunro (7) (lw: a.p: led ins fnl f: styd on wl) —1
2637 Cronk's Courage **(77)** (v) *(EJAlston)* 6-9-3 MHills (12) (led tl hdd ins fnl f: kpt on) ................................................................................................... 1.2
2564* Here Comes a Star **(64)** *(JMCarr)* 4-8-4 (7x) SMorris (13) (hdwy ½-wy: swtchd ins fnl f: r.o) ................................................................................. nk.3
2559 Iron King **(73)** *(JLSpearing)* 6-8-6 ‡7AGarth (4) (s.i.s: hdwy 2f out: r.o) ........ nk.4
2592⁴ Misdemeanours Girl (IRE) **(70)** *(Fav)* *(MRChannon)* 4-8-5 ‡5BDoyle (11) (in tch: effrt 2f out: styd on: nt pce to chal) ................................................. ¾.5
2458⁶ Bold Habit **(86)** *(BBeasley)* 7-9-7 ‡5SWilliams (8) (bhd: hdwy centre over 1f out: styd on wl) ...................................................................................... hd.6
2224* Playful Poet **(70)** *(MHEasterby)* 5-8-5 ‡5SMaloney (3) (led centre tl wknd ins fnl f) ....................................................................................................... ¾.7
2280 Gemini Fire **(79)** *(MPNaughton)* 8-9-0 ‡5JWeaver (9) (bhd tl sme late hdwy) .... 2.8
2603² Metal Boys **(86)** *(RHollinshead)* 5-9-5 ‡7SWynne (2) (lw: chsd ldrs tl rdn & btn appr fnl f) ..................................................................................... ½.9
196³ Meeson Times **(62)** *(BEllison)* 4-8-2(2) JFortune (6) (prom tl wknd over 1f out) ¹⁄₂.10
2424⁴ The Right Time **(54)** (bl) *(JParkes)* 7-7-1(1) ‡7CHawksley (10) (lw: sltly hmpd s: n.d) ............................................................................................ 1.11
2663 Ned's Bonanza **(75)** *(MDods)* 3-8-11 JLowe (5) (chsd ldrs centre over 3f) .... nk.12
2548 Katie-a (IRE) **(57)** *(RMWhitaker)* 3-7-7 JFanning (1) (dwlt: a bhd) ...................... 13
LONG HANDICAP: The Right Time 6-13, Katie-a (IRE) 7-3.

**9/2** Misdemeanours Girl (IRE), **5/1** Playful Poet, **7/1** Here Comes a Star, Cronk's Courage, **8/1** Bold Habit, **10/1** Iron King, **14/1** Gemini Fire, **16/1** Ned's Bonanza, Metal Boys, Meeson Times, PRECENTOR, Katie-a (IRE), **20/1** The Right Time. CSF £113.73, CT £1,786.80. Tote £15.40: £4.00 £2.50 £1.90 (£62.80). Lord Westbury (MIDDLEHAM) bred by Chovoloy Park Stud Ltd. 13 Rn
65.1 sec (3.6)
SF—33/47/33/34/30/45

**2742** MAX JAFFA MEMORIAL H'CAP (0-80) £3860.00 (£1160.00: £560.00: £260.00)
1m 1f 207y
3-40 (3-41)

      (Weights raised 2 lb)
2734² **Kinoko (45)** *(KWHogg)* 4-8-2 JCorrigan (2) (hld up: stdy hdwy over 2f out: led ins fnl f: rdn out) ...................................................................................... —1
2273² Top Villain **(36)** *(BSRothwell)* 6-7-7 JQuinn (1) (in tch: led & qcknd over 2f out: hdd ins fnl f: kpt on) ................................................................................. ¾.2
2571⁴ Sinclair Lad (IRE) **(62)** *(RHollinshead)* 4-9-5 WRyan (8) (stdd s: bhd tl hdwy 3f out: rdn & no imp) ......................................................................... 4.3
2288⁶ Holiday Island **(73)** *(CEBrittain)* 3-9-7 PRobinson (5) (in tch: effrt 3f out: sn rdn & outpcd: styd on nr fin) ............................................................... 2.4
2554² Floating Line **(60)** *(Fav)* *(PWigham)* 4-9-3 MWigham (3) (trckd ldrs: effrt 3f out: grad wknd fnl 2f) ............................................................................. 2½.5
2609² Katy's Lad **(67)** *(BAMcMahon)* 5-9-3 ‡7SSanders (4) (led tl hdd over 2f out: sn outpcd) ................................................................................................ s.h.6
293 Choral Sundown **(52)** *(CWCElsey)* 4-8-2 ‡7AGarth (7) (prom: effrt 3f out: no imp) 2.7
2219³ Doctor Roy **(60)** *(NBycroft)* 4-9-3 SWebster (10) (lw: hld up & bhd: effrt appr st: n.d) ................................................................................................. 3½.8
2100 Sea Lord **(53)** *(KWHogg)* 3-7-8(6) ‡7MHumphries (6) (chsd ldrs to st: sn wknd) 2½.9
1236² Scottish Park **(71)** *(JPLeigh)* 3-9-0 ‡5JWeaver (9) (bhd & rdn appr st: n.d) ....... 5.10
LONG HANDICAP: Top Villain 7-5, Sea Lord 6-11.

**7/2** Floating Line, **9/2** Katy's Lad, **11/2** Top Villain, **6/1** Doctor Roy, Sinclair Lad (IRE), **9/1** Holiday Island, **10/1** KINOKO, **14/1** Choral Sundown, Scottish Park, **50/1** Sea Lord. CSF £59.67, CT £329.74. Tote £13.00: £3.80 £1.60 £2.10 (£45.10). Mr Anthony White (ISLE OF MAN) bred by Auldyn Stud Ltd. 10 Rn
2m 8 (6)
SF—48/37/55/53/44/43

**2743** S AND C LADY TAVERNERS H'CAP (0-80) £3289.50 (£981.00: £468.00: £211.50)
7f 100y
4-10 (4-12)

2366² **Sandmoor Denim (53)** *(SRBowring)* 5-8-8 SWebster (7) (a.p: rdn to ld ins fnl f: r.o wl) ............................................................................................... —1
2541² Tyrian Purple (IRE) **(63)** *(Fav)* *(RHollinshead)* 4-8-11 ‡7MHumphries (4) (led tl hdd ins fnl f: kpt on same pce) .............................................................. 2½.2
2351³ Claudia Miss **(56)** *(WWHaigh)* 5-8-11 DMcKeown (6) (lw: cl up: chal 2f out: no ex u.p fnl f) ........................................................................................ 1.3
2732⁶ Pimsboy **(51)** (v) *(FJYardley)* 5-8-6 JQuinn (3) (bhd: hdwy 3f out: nt qckn appr fnl f) ..................................................................................................... 3½.4
2468⁶ Mca Below the Line **(58)** (bl) *(WLBarker)* 4-8-13 KDarley (9) (pushed along appr st: styd on fnl 2f: no imp) .................................................... s.h.5

25172 Routing **(58)** *(MDHammond)* 4–8-13 JCarroll (2) (lw: hld up: n.m.r 2f out: sn hrd drvn & no imp) ............................................................ 2½.6
2494 En Attendant (FR) **(73)** *(BHanbury)* 4–10-0 WRyan (8) (cl up tl grad lost pl fnl 3f) 5.7
2355 Chill Wind **(44)** (bl) *(NBycroft)* 3–7-7 LCharnock (5) (bhd: c wd & hdwy ent st: rdn & wknd 2f out) .......................................................... nk.8
14845 Lord Lambson **(55)** *(RMWhitaker)* 3–8-4 ACulhane (1) (lw: prom tl wknd 2f out) 2½.9
LONG HANDICAP: Chill Wind 6-12.

**100/30** Tyrian Purple (IRE), **4/1** SANDMOOR DENIM, **5/1** En Attendant (FR), **11/2** Routing, **7/1** Claudia Miss, **9/1** Mca Below the Line, **10/1** Lord Lambson, **14/1** Pimsboy, **50/1** Chill Wind. CSF £16.64, CT £80.77. Tote £3.70: £1.40 £1.40 £1.90 (£5.60). Mr E. H. Lunness (EDWINSTOWE) bred by Rathasker Stud. 9 Rn 1m 35.3 (5.1)
SF—40/35/32/16/22/14

**2744** FREEMEN'S STKS (Mdn) £2070.00 (£570.00: £270.00) **1m 1f 207y** 4-40 (4-41)

8655 **Romoosh** *(CEBrittain)* 3–8-5 PRobinson (2) (trckd ldrs: led wl over 1f out & qcknd: hld on wl nr fin) ............................................... —1
Mimique (Fav) *(HRACecil)* 3–8-10 WRyan (1) (lw: stdd s: plld hrd: hdwy 2f out: effrt over 1f out: r.o) ......................................... ½.2
Great Absalom *(JSWainwright)* 3–8-10 LCharnock (3) (led tl hdd wl over 1f out: sn wl outpcd) ...................................................... 15.3
Mr Sunny *(PBeaumont)* 3–8-10 PBurke (4) (w'like: bit bkwd: chsd ldr tl rdn & wknd ent st) ...................................................... 4.4

**30/100** Mimique, **3/1** ROMOOSH, **50/1** Ors. CSF £4.08, Tote £4.10 (£1.30). Mr F. M. Kalla (NEWMARKET) bred by The Overbury Stud. 4 Rn 2m 10.4 (8.4)
SF—27/31/1/–

**2745** E.B.F. ROUTH STKS (Mdn 2-Y.O.F) £2846.00 (£848.00: £404.00: £182.00)
5f 5-10 (5-13)

25583 **Heathyards Gem (65)** *(RHollinshead)* 8-11 WRyan (1) (cl up: led over 1f out: r.o u.p) ............................................................. —1
25573 Clear Look (Fav) *(PFICole)* 8-11 AMunro (5) (hld up: nt clr run & swtchd over 1f out: r.o wl nr fin) ...................................... hd.2
25512 Primula Bairn *(MrsJRRamsden)* 8-11 MBirch (2) (lw: cl up tl outpcd 2f out: hdwy 1f out: r.o nr fin) ............................................ hd.3
24056 My Cherrywell *(MrsVAAconley)* 8-11 JLowe (4) (cl up: led ½-wy: hdd wl over 1f out: wknd ins fnl f: fin faint) ............................ 1½.4
24386 Nahlati (IRE) *(CEBrittain)* 8-11 PRobinson (8) (led to ½-wy: wknd over 1f out) .. 4.5
23686 Miss Whittingham (IRE) **(60)** *(JBerry)* 8-11 JCarroll (6) (plld hrd: chsd ldrs over 3f) ................................................................ 2.6
1450 Cizard (IRE) *(AWPotts)* 8-11 SWebster (7) (prom over 3f) ............................... nk.7
Flash of Amber *(JLSpearing)* 8-11 GHind (3) (neat: s.i.s: n.d) ........................... 3.8
2551 Humber's Supreme (IRE) (bl) *(BSRothwell)* 8-11 JQuinn (9) (lw: spd over 3f: wknd qckly) ...................................................... 6.9

**6/5** Clear Look, **11/4** Primula Bairn, **100/30** Nahlati (IRE), **16/1** Flash of Amber, **20/1** HEATHYARDS GEM, Miss Whittingham (IRE), My Cherrywell, **50/1** Ors. CSF £43.78, Tote £15.60: £2.20 £1.10 £1.60 (£12.80). Mrs B. L. Morgan (UPPER LONGDON) bred by G. W. Hampson. 9 Rn 66.2 sec (4.7)
SF—23/22/21/15/–/–

T/Plpt: £308.60 (12.35 Tckts). AA

2491—**SALISBURY (R-H)**
**Wednesday, August 12th [Good]**
Going Allowance: minus 0.10 sec per fur (F)                                    Wind: fresh across

Stalls: high

**2746** E.B.F. SANDOWN STKS (Mdn 2-Y.O) £2723.20 (£755.20: £361.60) **6f** 2-00 (2-04)

2438 **Delta Downs** *(RHannon)* 8-9 BRaymond (7) (a chsng ldrs: hrd rdn 2f out: swtchd lft over 1f out: rdn to ld wl ins fnl f) .......................... —1
383 Midwinter Dream *(DRCEIsworth)* 9-0 RCochrane (6) (lw: a.p: rdn over 2f out: led over 1f out tl wl ins fnl f) ........................................ 1.2
555 Brigg Fair *(RHannon)* 9-0 JReid (12) (lw: led over 4f: ev ch ins fnl f: r.o) .......... s.h.3
24913 Don'tlie (IRE) (Fav) *(GBBalding)* 8-9 JWilliams (8) (b.nr hind: rdn & hdwy over 2f out: nt rch ldrs) ................................................. 3.4
Primocelle *(HCandy)* 8-9 CRutter (4) (unf: bkwd: hrd rdn & hdwy fnl 2f: nvr nr to chal) ......................................................................... 1.5

2409 Queens Contractor *(MJHeaton-Ellis)* 9-0 WNewnes (10) (b.hind: lw: prom 4f) .. ¾.6
2418⁵ Kintwyn **(62)** *(v)* *(DRLaing)* 9-0 SWhitworth (2) (prom 4f) ...................... 1½.7
Meritre (IRE) *(RJHolder)* 8-9 AMunro (9) (lengthy: scope: a bhd) ................... 6.8
2233 Smart Teacher (USA) *(PWHarris)* 9-0 PaulEddery (1) (a bhd) ..................... 1½.9
1742⁶ Petiole *(WRMuir)* 8-6 ‡3RPerham (11) (prom over 3f) ......................... ¾.10
Kennington Proton *(JRBosley)* 8-4 ‡5NGwilliams (5) (unf: scope: t.o fnl 3f) .... 3½.11
Flying Gabriel *(PHowling)* 8-9 JMurray (3) (w'like: scope: t.o fnl 3f) .......... 12.12

5/2 Don'tlie (IRE)(7/4—11/4), 3/1 Midwinter Dream(5/2—9/2), 7/2 DELTA DOWNS, 4/1 Queens Contractor(7/1—7/2), 12/1 Brigg Fair, Primocelle(op 6/1), 25/1 Kintwyn, 33/1 Meritre (IRE), Petiole, 50/1 Smart Teacher (USA), 66/1 Ors. CSF £14.52. Tote £6.10: £2.30 £1.80 £4.00 (£10.00). A. F. Budge (Equine) Limited (MARLBOROUGH) bred by A. F. Budge (Equine) Ltd. 12 Rn
1m 16.34 (4.04)
SF—2/3/2/–/–/–

**2747**　　FRESHWATER H'CAP (0-80) £2950.00 (£880.00: £420.00: £190.00)　**5f 2-30 (2-30)**

2520 **Face North (IRE) (52)** *(ARDavison)* 4-8-2 JLloyd (4) (swtg: bhd: hrd rdn 2f out:
rapid hdwy fnl f: led post) ............................................. —1
779⁵ Very Dicey **(78)** *(WRMuir)* 4-10-0 TQuinn (6) (led: rdn over 1f out: edgd lft ins fnl
f: ct post) ............................................. s.h.2
2599★ Dickens Lane **(52)** *(Jt-Fav)* *(RJHodges)* 5-8-2 (7x) DBiggs (2) (swtg: a chsng
ldrs: r.o ins fnl f) ............................................. 1.3
2599 Stocktina **(43)** *(RJHodges)* 5-7-7 JQuinn (3) (chsd ldr: one pce fnl f) ............. 2.4
1262⁴ Musval **(56)** *(RHannon)* 3-7-9 ‡7AWhelan (2) (hdwy over 2f out: one pce fnl f) s.h.5
2301² Trioming **(43)** *(APJones)* 6-7-7 NAdams (8) (prom: hrd rdn over 2f out: sn wknd) 3.6
2395³ Jess Rebec **(54)** *(LGCottrell)* 4-8-4 NCarlisle (5) (a bhd) ................... 3½.7
2494⁴ Maria Cappuccini **(53)** *(Jt-Fav)* *(KOCunningham-Brown)* 4-8-3 AMunro (1) (lw:
carried lft s: outpcd) ............................................. 3½.8
LONG HANDICAP: Stocktina 7-2, Trioming 7-5.

4/1 Jess Rebec, Maria Cappuccini, Dickens Lane, 13/2 Trioming, Very Dicey, 15/2 FACE NORTH (IRE), 11/1 Musval, 25/1 Stocktina. CSF £47.74, CT £190.78. Tote £14.10: £2.90 £2.00 £1.60 (£34.70). Mr Cecil Holland (CATERHAM) bred by Ciaran Quigley in Ireland. 8 Rn
62.27 sec (2.27)
SF—33/58/28/11/12/–

**2748**　　UPAVON STKS (3-Y.O.F) £4464.00 (£1332.00: £636.00: £288.00)
**1m 1f 209y**　　3-00 (3-01)

1843 **Delve (IRE) (92)** *(JLDunlop)* 9-0 TQuinn (3) (chsd ldr: led over 2f out: hrd rdn
fnl f: r.o w) ............................................. —1
2453★ Party Cited (USA) **(105)** *(Fav)* *(DRCElsworth)* 9-5 JWilliams (1) (rdn & hdwy
over 2f out: ev ch over 1f out: nt qckn fnl f) ........................ 1.2
934⁴ Never a Care (USA) **(85)** *(BWHills)* 8-5 PatEddery (5) (prom: rdn over 3f out: wknd 2f
out) ............................................. 10.3
2495★ Double Flutter **(75)** *(MRChannon)* 9-0 PaulEddery (2) (a in rr) ............... nk.4
2270★ Gong *(PTWalwyn)* 8-9 RCochrane (4) (led over 7f: wknd over 1f out) ............. ¾.5

**Evens** Party Cited (USA), 7/2 Never a Care (USA)(7/4—4/1), 4/1 Gong, 9/1 DELVE (IRE)(op 4/1), 10/1 Double Flutter(op 6/1). CSF £18.01, Tote £9.30: £3.80 £1.30 (£8.00). Sir Robin McAlpine (ARUNDEL) bred by R. A. Collins in Ireland. 5 Rn
2m 7.69 (2.99)
SF—60/64/30/33/31

**2749**　　YARMOUTH H'CAP (0-100) £3557.50 (£1060.00: £505.00: £227.50)
**1½m**　　3-30 (3-30)

(Weights raised 8 lb)
2492² **Caspian Beluga (58)** *(MrsAKnight)* 4-8-0 JQuinn (4) (mde all: sn clr: unchal) ... —1
1574³ Ivor's Flutter **(73)** *(DRCElsworth)* 8-13 JWilliams (2) (hld up: rdn along 5f
out: chsd wnr fnl 2f: no imp) ........................................ 6.2
2180★ Opera Ghost **(82)** *(PWHarris)* 6-9-10 WRSwinburn (1) (hld up: rdn over 2f
out: eased whn btn ins fnl f) ........................................ 5.3
2549³ Garachico (USA) **(72)** *(bl)* *(GHarwood)* 3-8-3 TQuinn (3) (chsd wnr: rdn over 2f
out: eased whn btn wl over 1f out) ................................. 30.4

9/4 Opera Ghost(op 6/4), 5/2 CASPIAN BELUGA, 3/1 Garachico (USA), 7/2 Ivor's Flutter(op 2/1). CSF £9.56, Tote £3.50 (£4.70). Mr L. J. Hawkings (CULLOMPTON) bred by Wretham Stud. 4 Rn
2m 35.08 (2.48)
SF—49/41/51/–

**2750**　　ISLE OF WIGHT H'CAP (0-70) £3321.50 (£924.00: £444.50)　**6f 212y　4-00 (4-01)**

2561 **Hold Fast (IRE) (38)** *(HCandy)* 4-8-0 CRutter (14) (hdwy on far side over 2f
out: r.o) ............................................. —1
2634³ Zinbaq **(40)** *(CJBenstead)* 6-8-2 PaulEddery (7) (rdn & hdwy stands' side over
1f out: r.o wl ins fnl f) ............................................. nk.2

2427* Kirriemuir **(41)** *(KOCunningham-Brown)* 4-8-3 SDawson (11) (prom: led far side over 2f out: hdd cl home) .............................................. hd.3

2601 Sir Oliver (IRE) **(67)** *(RJHodges)* 3-9-9 PatEddery (9) (led stands' side over 4f: rallied ins fnl f) .............................................. 1.4

207 Courting Newmarket **(46)** *(MrsAKnight)* 4-8-8 SWhitworth (6) (a.p: led stands' side over 2f out: hdd ins fnl f) .............................................. ½.5

2634⁶ Nawwar **(55)** *(CJBenstead)* 8-9-3 RCochrane (3) (hdwy fnl f: nvr nrr) ....... s.h.6

2582⁵ Aldahe **(42)** *(BRMillman)* 7-8-4 AMunro (10) (prom: no hdwy fnl 2f) ........ 1½.7

2586* Chance to Dream **(61)** *(Jt-Fav)* *(RHannon)* 3-9-3 (7x) JReid (1) (hdwy over 2f out: one pce fnl f) .............................................. ½.8

2013 Beatle Song **(65)** *(RJHodges)* 4-9-10 ‡³TSprake (4) (nvr nr to chal) .............. nk.9

2494 Hightown-Princess (IRE) **(37)** *(JSMoore)* 4-7-10⁽³⁾ ‡³SO'Gorman (12) (swtg: prom centre over 5f) .............................................. hd.10

2125⁴ Lord's Final **(37)** *(CRBarwell)* 5-7-8⁽²⁾ ‡⁵ATucker (2) (racd stands' side: bhd fnl 2f) .............................................. 1.11

1642⁵ Red Ink **(54)** *(Jt-Fav)* *(JSutcliffe)* 3-8-10 WNewnes (5) (swtg: nvr trbld ldrs) .. 1½.12

1238 Bright Paragon (IRE) **(46)** *(HJCollingridge)* 3-8-2 JQuinn (17) (led far side over 4f: sn wknd) .............................................. 3.13

351 Predictable **(57)** *(MrsAKnight)* 6-9-0 ‡⁵KRutter (16) (prom far side over 4f) ...... 1.14

2164⁵ So Superb **(66)** *(JLDunlop)* 3-9-8 TQuinn (15) (racd far side: bhd fnl 3f: t.o) .. 5.15

2303 Shecangosah **(37)** *(RJHodges)* 3-7-7 NAdams (13) (racd far side: bhd fnl 2f: t.o) .............................................. 2½.16

2406 Cronk's Quality **(40)** *(DCJermy)* 9-8-2 NHowe (8) (a bhd: t.o) ................. s.h.17

**11/2** Red Ink, Chance to Dream(4/1—6/1), **7/1** Zinbaq, **8/1** Kirriemuir(6/1—10/1), Aldahe(6/1—10/1), Sir Oliver, (IRE), **10/1** Lord's Final(op 6/1), **11/1** Nawwar, **14/1** So Superb(10/1—16/1), Beatle Song, **20/1** Predictable, **33/1** HOLD FAST (IRE) & Ors. CSF £230.61, CT £1,841.94. Tote £35.80: £5.80 £1.70 £2.50 £2.50 (£162.90). Kingstone Warren Partners (WANTAGE) bred by Airlie Stud in Ireland. 17 Rn   1m 30.47 (4.77)
SF—4/5/5/22/5/13

---

### 2751

BEMBRIDGE CLAIMING STKS (3-Y.O) £2343.00 (£648.00: £309.00)
1½m

4-30 (4-30)

2422 **Grog (IRE) (71)** *(Fav)* *(MRChannon)* 9-5 PatEddery (3) (chsd ldr: led over 2f out: sn clr: easily) .............................................. —1

2197⁵ Temple Knight **(52)** *(CACyzer)* 8-11 DBiggs (5) (hld up: rdn & swtchd lft over 2f out: chsd wnr wl over 1f out: no imp) .............................................. 6.2

2576⁶ King of Normandy (IRE) **(64)** (bl) *(RHannon)* 9-1 JLloyd (2) (hld up: rdn drvn over 5f out: styd on one pce fnl 2f) .............................................. 5.3

2334 Sandro **(51)** (bl) *(JRFanshawe)* 9-1 WRSwinburn (6) (led over 9f: wknd wl over 1f out) .............................................. 2.4

2576* Chummy's Child (IRE) **(48)** *(JSutcliffe)* 8-9 AMunro (4) (b: rdn 4f out: bhd fnl 3f) 8.5

Samjamalifran *(MCPipe)* 8-9 JWilliams (1) (prom tl rdn & wknd qckly over 3f out: t.o) .............................................. 15.6

**8/11** GROG (IRE), **5/1** King of Normandy (IRE)(7/2—6/1), **11/2** Chummy's Child (IRE)(op 3/1), **6/1** Sandro, **16/1** Temple Knight, **25/1** Samjamalifran. CSF £11.28, Tote £1.70: £1.20 £3.70 (£6.70). Mrs D. Hanson (UPPER LAMBOURN) bred by Michael P. Keane in Ireland. 6 Rn; Grog (IRE) clmd A Clegg £11,556.50   2m 37.76 (5.16)
SF—41/21/15/11/–/–

---

### 2752

LEVY BOARD H'CAP (0-80) £3003.00 (£833.00: £399.00)    6f

5-00 (5-03)

2307⁶ Grey Charmer (IRE) **(53)** *(CJames)* 3-7-10 DaleGibson (11) (rdn along & outpcd: rapid hdwy over 1f out: str run to ld post) .............. —1

2617³ Unveiled **(61)** *(RJHodges)* 4-8-9 RCochrane (13) (gd hdwy over 1f out: led wl ins fnl f: hdd post) .............................................. s.h.2

2618² How's Yer Father **(78)** *(Fav)* *(RJHodges)* 6-9-12 PatEddery (7) (hdwy 2f out: led ins fnl f: sn hdd: r.o) .............................................. hd.3

2465 Temple Fortune (USA) **(69)** *(RHannon)* 3-8-12 JReid (10) (hld up: stdy hdwy over 2f out: r.o ins fnl f) .............................................. nk.4

2307² Divine Pet **(63)** *(WGRWightman)* 7-8-11 JWilliams (3) (lw: hdwy over 1f out: r.o ins fnl f) .............................................. 1.5

2435 Baysham (USA) **(80)** (bl) *(BRMillman)* 6-9-9 ‡⁵JWeaver (1) (lw: racd alone stands' side: led tl wknd ins fnl f) .............................................. 2½.6

2618⁴ Cee-En-Cee **(70)** (bl) *(MMcCourt)* 8-9-4 TQuinn (14) (lw: nvr nrr) ............. 1.7

2617² Nuclear Express **(58)** *(RLee)* 5-7-13 ‡⁷SDrowne (12) (b: prom: rdn over 2f out: wknd over 1f out) .............................................. nk.8

2527⁴ Co-Chin (IRE) **(75)** *(GLewis)* 3-9-4 PaulEddery (5) (prom: ev ch over 1f out: wknd fnl f) .............................................. 3.9

2617⁵ Slip-a-Snip **(64)** *(GBBalding)* 5-8-7 ‡⁵RPrice (2) (outpcd) ......................... ½.10

2032 Thornfield Boy **(67)** *(RJHolder)* 6-9-1 AMunro (9) (prom over 4f) ................. 2.11

2617 Melodic Habit (45) *(MrsAKnight)* 5–7-7 JQuinn (8) (led far side over 4f: sn wknd) ............ 1½.**12**
2227³ John O'Dreams (45) *(MrsJCDawe)* 7–7-7 AMackay (6) (prom 4f) ................. hd.**13**
LONG HANDICAP: John O'Dreams 7-4.

**7/2** How's Yer Father, **11/2** Divine Pet, **7/1** Nuclear Express, Cee-En-Cee, **8/1** Co-Chin (IRE), Baysham (USA), **17/2** Temple Fortune (USA)(6/1—9/1), **9/1** Unveiled, **14/1** Slip-a-Snip, **16/1** GREY CHARMER (IRE), **20/1** Ors. CSF £150.11, CT £569.09. Tote £36.00: £6.10 £2.20 £1.90 (£183.10). Miss S. Previte (NEWBURY) bred by Scarteen Stud in Ireland. 13 Rn
1m 16.13 (3.83)
SF—–/5/21/6/1/3

T/Plpt: £299.00 (11.10 Tckts). KH

# SALISBURY (R-H)

## Thursday, August 13th [Good becoming Soft]

Going Allowance: 1st-5th: 0.20 sec (G); Rest: 0.40 sec per fur (Y)      Wind: mod across

Stalls: high

**2753**   BROAD CHALKE STKS (Mdn 3-Y.O) £2574.00 (£714.00: £342.00)
6f 212y                                                    2-00 (2-05)

**Sweet Jaffa** *(MajorWRHern)* 8-9 WCarson (14) (str: scope: led 5f out tl over 2f out: rdn out) ............ —**1**
2276³ Express Service **(81)** *(Fav)* *(PJMakin)* 9-0 WRSwinburn (3) (lw: a:p: rdn to ld over 2f out: hdd over 1f out: r.o) ............ ¾.**2**
2419⁶ Acara (IRE) *(CJames)* 8-9 RCochrane (2) (lw: a:p: hrd rdn & ev ch over 1f out: one pce) ............ 3.**3**
2419⁵ Efra (60) *(RHannon)* 9-0 JLloyd (12) (lw: a:p: rdn & ev ch over 1f out: r.o one pce) ............ 1½.**4**
2496 Rockbourne (47) *(DRCElsworth)* 8-9 SJWilliams (5) (swtg: hdwy 2f out: nt rch ldrs) ............ hd.**5**
2549 Brooks Express (FR) *(RAkehurst)* 8-11 ‡³RPerham (4) (prom over 5f) ............ 2.**6**
2239⁵ Sir Joey (USA) *(RJHolder)* 9-0 ADicks (8) (lw: plld hrd: hdwy over 2f out: rdn over 1f out: wknd fnl f) ............ 1.**7**
408⁵ Pleasuring (65) *(MMcCormack)* 8-9 JReid (10) (b.nr hind: lw: nvr nrr) ............ 2.**8**
2567⁵ Dam Certain (IRE) *(AWDenson)* 8-9 TQuinn (13) (n.d) ............ s.h.**9**
787 Montagne *(HCandy)* 8-9 CRutter (9) (led 2f: wknd over 2f out) ............ 2.**10**
2417 Two Birds (47) *(CAHorgan)* 8-9 AMcGlone (1) (a bhd) ............ 2.**11**
2417 Spinayab (42) *(EAWheeler)* 8-9 SWhitworth (7) (stumbled s: a in rr: t.o) ............ 12.**12**
2062 Dreams to Wotan *(MJWilkinson)* 9-0 NAdams (11) (bhd fnl 3f: t.o) ............ 13
*Seemenomore (33/1) Withdrawn (ref to ent stalls) : not under orders*

**6/5** Express Service, **7/2** SWEET JAFFA(6/1—7/1), **9/1** Rockbourne(5/1—10/1), **10/1** Efra(6/1—11/1), **12/1** Pleasuring(8/1—14/1), Acara (IRE)(op 8/1), **16/1** Montagne(op 10/1), **20/1** Dam Certain (IRE), **33/1** Ors. CSF £7.97, Tote £4.80: £1.50 £1.10 £2.80 (£4.10). Mrs C. A. Waters (LAMBOURN) bred by Brook Bloodstock P L C. 13 Rn
1m 31.12 (5.42)
SF—35/38/24/24/18/14

**2754**   AMESBURY CLAIMING STKS   £3054.00 (£912.00: £436.00: £198.00)
1m 1f 209y                                                2-30 (2-32)

2408³ **Smiling Chief (IRE) (48)** *(CACyzer)* 4–9-3 DBiggs (4) (lw: a:p: led over 1f out: rdn & edgd lft wl ins fnl f: r.o) ............ —**1**
2473* Loki (IRE) (73) *(GLewis)* 4–9-3 PaulEddery (10) (hld up: stdy hdwy over 3f out: ev ch 1f out: hrd rdn: r.o) ............ 1.**2**
2473⁵ Flying Speed (USA) (75) *(MCPipe)* 4–9-10 JReid (3) (chsd ldr tl lft in ld & hmpd 7f out: hdd 1f out: 3rd & btn whn hmpd wl ins fnl f) ............ hd.**3**
Lascar (USA) *(GThorner)* 4-8-13 ‡³RPerham (2) (bit bkwd: s.s: sn rcvrd: plld hrd: ev ch 2f out: wknd over 1f out) ............ 12.**4**
1063 Petmer (40) *(GBBalding)* 5–8-13 WNewnes (5) (b: s.s: sn rcvrd: hrd rdn & wknd over 2f out) ............ 1½.**5**
Deauville Duchess *(PJHobbs)* 5–8-12 TSprake (8) (a bhd) ............ 5.**6**
Mrs Mouse *(NATwiston-Davies)* 4–8-9 JWilliams (7) (bkwd: dwlt: rdn over 4f out: sn t.o) ............ 25.**7**
1903 Tamasha (46) *(CJHill)* 3–7-12 GBardwell (9) (plld hrd: prom tl slipped bnd 7f out: nt rcvr: t.o) ............ ½.**8**
2545 Rapid Rosie (24) (v) *(DRLaing)* 4–8-2 ‡⁵ATucker (1) (led tl s.u bnd 7f out) ............ 0
*Stewards Enquiry- Obj. to Smiling Chief by Reid overruled*

**5/4** Loki (IRE), **2/1** Flying Speed (USA), **10/1** SMILING CHIEF (IRE), **14/1** Petmer, Tamasha(op 8/1), **25/1** Deauville Duchess, **33/1** Ors. CSF £21.34, Tote £9.00: £1.60 £1.30 £1.40 (£8.70). Mr R. M. Cyzer (HORSHAM) bred by Thoroughbred Breeding Stock Agency in Ireland. 9 Rn
2m 12.39 (7.69)
SF—46/44/50/15/12/1

**2755** TOTE BOOKMAKERS H'CAP (0-100) £4542.00 (£1356.00: £648.00: £294.00)
1m 3-00 (3-13)

2341 **Two Left Feet (91)** *(SirMarkPrescott)* 5–10-0 GDuffield (3) (chsd ldr: led 2f out: rdn clr fnl f) —1
24493 Trooping (IRE) **(82)** *(GHarwood)* 3–8-12 AClark (10) (lw: hld up: rdn & ev ch over 2f out: r.o one pce) 7.2
24332 Wesaam (USA) **(96)** *(Fav) (MajorWRHern)* 3–9-12 WCarson (7) (lw: racd alone far side: led 5f out to 2f out: sn btn) 2.3
2616* Emaura **(63)** *(KOCunningham-Brown)* 3–7-7 GBardwell (1) (led 3f: one pce fnl 2f) nk.4
2341 Rose Elegance **(75)** *(WRMuir)* 3–8-5 TQuinn (9) (lw: rdn & bhd 4f out: sme hdwy fnl 2f) 2½.5
671 Kitaab (USA) **(76)** *(ACStewart)* 3–8-6 RHills (6) (bit bkwd: dwlt: nvr nr to chal) .. ½.6
2184 Diaco **(66)** *(MAJarvis)* 7–8-3 PaulEddery (5) (prom: rdn & ev ch over 2f out: sn wknd) 2½.7
1166 Pure Formality **(86)** *(DRCElsworth)* 3–9-2 JWilliams (4) (bhd fnl 4f) 2.8
21734 Absonal **(72)** *(RHannon)* 5–8-9 RCochrane (8) (a bhd) 1.9
LONG HANDICAP: Emaura 7-0.

**7/2** Wesaam (USA), **4/1** Trooping (IRE), Rose Elegance(5/1—7/1), **11/2** Kitaab (USA)(op 3/1), TWO LEFT FEET, **8/1** Absonal, **12/1** Pure Formality(8/1—14/1), **14/1** Ors. CSF £28.05, CT £82.77. Tote £6.60: £1.80 £1.80 £1.90 (£15.50). Mr P. W. W. Molins (NEWMARKET) bred by Stud-On-The-Chart. 9 Rn 1m 44.32 (5.02)
SF—63/26/34/–/–/–

**2756** WHITCHURCH STKS (2-Y.O) £5910.00 (£1635.00: £780.00) 6f 212y 3-30 (3-37)

24455 **Little Too Much (IRE) (100)** *(GHarwood)* 9-0 WCarson (3) (mde all: rdn out) ... —1
2381* Azhar *(MRStoute)* 9-0 WRSwinburn (2) (chsd wnr: ev ch ins fnl f: r.o) hd.2
2346* Rapid Success (USA) *(Fav) (DRCElsworth)* 9-5 RCochrane (1) (hld up: rdn over 2f out: wknd wl over 1f out) 10.3

**4/5** Rapid Success (USA), **5/2** LITTLE TOO MUCH (IRE), **100/30** Azhar. CSF £7.95, Tote £3.00 (£3.00). Mr J. Garcia-Roady (PULBOROUGH) bred by Bloodstock Management International in Ireland. 3 Rn
1m 31.63 (5.93)
SF—32/31/6

**2757** LESLIE JOEL BIRTHDAY CELEBRATION H'CAP (F & M) (0-70) £3370.50 (£938.00: £451.50) 1m 1f 209y 4-00 (4-05)

(Weights raised 1 lb)

21702 **Googly (58)** *(WGRWightman)* 3–8-12 GBardwell (13) (lw: hdwy 4f out: led over 1f out: r.o wl) —1
24843 Atlantic Way **(34)** *(CJHill)* 4–7-11 DBiggs (16) (led 3f: led 2f out tl over 1f out: nt qckn) 2½.2
24153 Lady Lacey **(48)** (v) *(GBBalding)* 5–8-11 JWilliams (3) (swtchd rt over 2f out: gd hdwy over 1f out: fin wl) ¾.3
2372* Misty Goddess (IRE) **(60)** *(MAJarvis)* 4–9-4 ‡5KRutter (10) (a.p: ev ch over 1f out: one pce) 1½.4
2547* Striking Image (IRE) **(66)** *(RHannon)* 3–9-6 RCochrane (6) (lw: a.p: no hdwy fnl 2f) hd.5
2621* Moon Spin **(71)** *(Fav) (MajorWRHern)* 3–9-11 (7x) WCarson (4) (lw: hdwy over 3f out: led over 2f out: sn hdd: wknd over 1f out) 2.6
2492 Arrastra **(56)** *(IABalding)* 4–9-5 JReid (9) (hdwy 3f out: wknd over 1f out) 1½.7
9106 Sheringa **(68)** *(GBBalding)* 3–9-8 WNewnes (11) (nvr trbld ldrs) 3.8
2430* Addicted to Love **(79)** *(PJMakin)* 3–9-10 TQuinn (8) (prom 8f) 3.9
12094 Sharriba **(70)** *(DRCElsworth)* 3–9-10 BRouse (2) (n.d) 2½.10
26073 Please Please Me (IRE) **(30)** *(KOCunningham-Brown)* 4–7-7 NAdams (5) (hdwy 6f out: wknd 3f out) 3.11
2198 Bellatrix **(47)** *(CEBrittain)* 4–8-10 GCrealock (12) (hdwy 4f out: wknd over 2f out) ½.12
24175 Rosietoes (USA) **(45)** *(LGCottrell)* 4–8-8 NCarlisle (15) (led 7f out: clr 4f out: hdd & wknd over 2f out) 2.13
24954 Golden Proposal **(47)** *(MJBolton)* 3–8-1 CRutter (14) (lw: plld hrd: bhd fnl 4f: t.o) 7.14
20644 Tafsir **(60)** *(HThomsonJones)* 3–9-0 RHills (7) (bhd fnl 4f: t.o) 3½.15
1885 Vellandrucha **(47)** *(JABennett)* 3–8-1 AMcGlone (1) (b: t.o fnl 5f) 2.16
LONG HANDICAP: Please Please Me (IRE) 7-6.

**11/4** Moon Spin, **4/1** GOOGLY(op 7/1), **13/2** Striking Image (IRE)(4/1—7/1), **9/1** Misty Goddess (IRE)(6/1—11/1), **10/1** Addicted to Love(op 6/1), Lady Lacey, **14/1** Tafsir(op 8/1), Sheringa, Sharriba, **20/1** Arrastra, Bellatrix, Rosietoes (USA), Atlantic Way, Please Please Me (IRE), **25/1** Golden Proposal, **33/1** Vellandrucha. CSF £82.47, CT £727.85. Tote £5.50: £1.10 £4.20 £2.00 £2.10 (£75.00). Mr A. G. Lansley (UPHAM) bred by W. G. R. Wightman and Mrs J. A. Thomson. 16 Rn 2m 11.75 (7.05)
SF—47/27/39/43/44/45

**2758**  TATTERSALLS AUCTION SERIES STKS (Qualifier) (Mdn 2-Y.O) £3076.50 (£854.00: £409.50)  **6f**  4-30 (4-32)

**Exclusively Yours** *(RGuest)* 7-10 ‡5DHarrison (9) (leggy: a.p: led 1f out: rdn out) — 1
25264 Princely Favour (IRE) **(91)** (Fav) *(RHannon)* 8-6 BRouse (11) (a.p: led 2f out tl 1f out: nt qckn) ...................... 1½.2
Weaver Bird *(HCandy)* 8-0 CRutter (6) (unf: scope: prom: lost pl over 2f out: rdn & rallied over 1f out: r.o) ...................... hd.3
22743 Look Who's Here (IRE) *(BAMcMahon)* 8-6 WCarson (14) (a.p: ev ch whn edgd lft over 1f out: nt qckn ins fnl f) ...................... hd.4
Arman's Sax (IRE) *(JLDunlop)* 8-7 AClark (12) (leggy: rdn over 2f out: hdwy over 1f out: r.o) ...................... 5.5
25445 Stay With Me Baby *(DRCElsworth)* 8-0 DHolland (13) (no hdwy fnl 2f) ............ 2½.6
2456 Sea Baron **(78)** *(MBlanshard)* 8-9 JReid (10) (led 4f) ...................... ¾.7
1610 El Nino (IRE) *(RHannon)* 8-3 ‡3RPerham (5) (dwlt: nvr nrr) ...................... ¾.8
1610 Chummy's Idea (IRE) *(JSutcliffe)* 8-2(1) SWhitworth (8) (n.d) ...................... hd.9
22083 Festin *(JLDunlop)* 8-12 AMcGlone (7) (a bhd: t.o) ...................... 7.10
9953 Welsh Pet *(PJMakin)* 8-2 TSprake (1) (a bhd: t.o) ...................... 5.11
19235 Valere Knight (IRE) *(CGCox)* 8-7 WNewnes (3) (leggy: bit bkwd: prom over 3f: t.o) ...................... 1.12
2459 Game Germaine *(BWHills)* 8-1 GDuffield (2) (prom: rdn over 2f out: sn wknd: t.o) ...................... 1.13

**13/8** Princely Favour (IRE), **2/1** EXCLUSIVELY YOURS(op 3/1), **11/2** Look Who's Here (IRE)(3/1—6/1), **6/1** Stay With Me Baby, **14/1** Festin, Welsh Pet, **16/1** Sea Baron(op 8/1), Valere Knight (IRE), Weaver Bird, **20/1** Arman's Sax (IRE), El Nino (IRE), **25/1** Ors. CSF £7.06, Tote £3.60: £2.40 £1.60 £6.20 (£7.50). Mrs Lesley Mills (NEWMARKET) bred by Brook Stud Ltd. 13 Rn  1m 17.23 (4.93)
SF—32/36/29/34/15/7

**2759**  VIOLET APPLIN CHALLENGE CUP (H'cap) (0-80) £3236.00 (£968.00: £464.00: £212.00)  **1¾m**  6 00 (6-02)

2397* Wilkins **(61)** (Jt-Fav) *(JRFanshawe)* 3-8-6 GCarter (9) (a.p: led 4f out: clr 2f out: wandered ins fnl f: r.o) ...................... — 1
23972 Polistatic **(37)** *(CAHorgan)* 5-7-9 DaleGibson (4) (hdwy 5f out: chsd wnr fnl 3f: no imp) ...................... 4.2
22352 Greenwich Bambi **(62)** *(WCarter)* 4-9-1 ‡5NGwilliams (6) (lw: hld up: hdwy 4f out: one pce fnl 3f) ...................... 3½.3
2401 Green Lane (USA) **(69)** *(IABalding)* 4-9-13 JReid (5) (a chsng ldrs: r.o one pce fnl 3f) ...................... hd.4
20574 Elite Reg **(50)** *(PFICole)* 3-7-9(1) DBiggs (1) (prom: hrd rdn 4f out: one pce) .. 3½.5
24123 Belafonte **(60)** *(RJHolder)* 5-8-13 ‡5ATucker (3) (hld up & bhd: rdn 6f out: nvr nr to chal) ...................... 3.6
24124 Smartie Lee **(52)** *(PFICole)* 5-8-10 TQuinn (12) (led 10f: wknd 3f out) ...................... hd.7
9406 Taroob (IRE) **(74)** *(JLDunlop)* 3-9-5 WCarson (13) (lw: dropped rr over 7f out: nvr nrr) ...................... 7.8
2492* Rocquaine Bay **(43)** (Jt-Fav) *(MJBolton)* 5-8-1(1) GDuffield (2) (a bhd) ...................... 6.9
22782 Intrepid Lass **(44)** *(HCandy)* 5-8-2 CRutter (11) (prom 10f) ...................... nk.10
7906 Western Dancer **(50)** *(CAHorgan)* 11-8-8 AMcGlone (7) (hdwy 6f out: wknd over 3f out: t.o) ...................... 10.11
2267 Mount Nelson **(65)** *(DWPArbuthnot)* 6-9-9 RCochrane (8) (b: b.hind: a bhd: t.o) 5.12
1891* Sadler's Way **(57)** (Jt-Fav) *(GLewis)* 3-9-6 PaulEddery (10) (hdwy 5f out: hrd rdn over 3f out: sn wknd: t.o) ...................... 4.13
25622 Sea Plane **(70)** (bl) *(MajorWRHern)* 3-9-1 WRSwinburn (14) (prom 10f: t.o) .. hd.14

**6/1** WILKINS, Rocquaine Bay, Sadler's Way, **7/1** Sea Plane, **8/1** Intrepid Lass, **9/1** Polistatic, Belafonte, **10/1** Elite Reg, Smartie Lee, **11/1** Greenwich Bambi, **12/1** Taroob (IRE), Green Lane (USA), **14/1** Mount Nelson, **16/1** Western Dancer. CSF £63.04, CT £560.38. Tote £8.10: £2.60 £4.10 £5.50 (£49.60). Lord Vestey (NEWMARKET) bred by Major J. S. R. Edmunds and J. S. Delahooke. 14 Rn  3m 8.26 (10.06)
SF—47/28/41/52/13/25

T/Plpt: £37.30 (96.4 Tckts).  KH

2505a—**LEOPARDSTOWN (L-H)**

**Monday, August 3rd [Good]**
Going Allowance: 0.10 sec per fur (G)

**2760a**  BROWNSTOWN STUD STKS (listed race) (F & M) £8621.00  **1m**

1816a4 **Via Borghese (USA)** *(Ireland)* 3-9-1 LPiggott ...................... — 1
1097a Gdansk's Honour (USA) (bl) *(Ireland)* 3-9-1 KJManning ...................... 1½.2
Darayna (IRE) *(Ireland)* 3-8-10 SCauthen ...................... 20.3

Tote £1.30 (£2.00). Mr Malcolm Parrish (M.V.O'Brien,IRELAND) bred by Panama Traders, Bedford & Skymarc Farms in USA. 3 Rn

1m 42.4 (4.4)
SF—47/42/–

## 2761a
WINNING WEST WOOD ROCHESTOWN E.B.F. STKS (listed race) (2-Y.O.F) £8061.00
7f

| | |
|---|---|
| **Chanzi** (USA) *(Ireland)* 2–8–10 SCauthen | —1 |
| Asema (USA) *(Ireland)* 2–8–10 MJKinane | nk.2 |
| Reliable (USA) *(Ireland)* 2–8–10 KJManning | 2.3 |

Tote £1.60: £1.40 £2.50 (£3.70). Sheikh Mohammed (J.M.Oxx,IRELAND) bred by Darley Stud Management Co. Ltd. in USA. 6 Rn

1m 30.9 (5.9)
SF—18/17/11

# LEOPARDSTOWN (L-H)
## Saturday, August 8th [Good]
Going Allowance: 0.20 sec per fur (G)

## 2762a
WATERFORD FOODS PHOENIX SPRINT STKS (Gp 3)    £13902.00    6f

| | | |
|---|---|---|
| | **Park Dream (IRE)** *(Ireland)* 3–8–7 CRoche (mde all: rdn over 1f out: r.o wl) | —1 |
| 2318a² | Poolesta (IRE) *(Ireland)* 3–8–7 WJO'Connor (prom: ev ch fnl 2f: no ex fnl f) | 1¹/₂.2 |
| 1467 | Street Rebel (CAN) *(Ireland)* 4–9-8 RHughes (chsd ldrs: outpcd over 1f out: styd on fnl f) | 3.3 |
| 2092a★ | Flowing (USA) (Jt-Fav) *(Ireland)* 3–8-7 MJKinane (cl up: ev ch fnl 2f: unable qckn fnl f) | d.h.3 |
| 1711² | PRINCE FERDINAND (Jt-Fav) *(Ireland)* 3–9-2 JReid (s.i.s: hdwy to trck ldrs ¹/₂-wy: rdn over 1f out: sn btn) | 2¹/₂.5 |
| 2626a | Bradawn Breever (IRE) (bl) *(Ireland)* 3–9-8 SCraine (chsd ldrs: rdn over 2f out: no imp fnl 2f) | 5¹/₂.6 |
| 2092a² | Maledetto (IRE) *(Ireland)* 3–8-10 KJManning (chsd ldrs ¹/₂-wy: no imp fnl 2f) | 5.7 |
| | Trevor's Lady (IRE) *(Ireland)* 3–8-7 EALeonard (in tch to ¹/₂-wy: n.d after) | 2¹/₂.8 |

**6/4** Prince Ferdinand, Flowing (USA), **8/1** Poolesta (IRE), **9/1** PARK DREAM (IRE), **10/1** Street Rebel (CAN), **16/1** Bradawn Breever (IRE), Maledetto (IRE), **1,000/1** Trevor's Lady (IRE). Tote £9.00: £2.40 £2.50 £2.20 £0.70 (£39.70). Mr Patrick H. Burns (J.S.Bolger,IRELAND) bred by Mrs Mary Entenmann in Ireland. 8 Rn

1m 13.3 (2.1)
SF—75/69/72/68/55/39

# LEOPARDSTOWN (L-H)
## Sunday, August 9th [Good]
Going Allowance: nil sec per fur (G)

## 2763a
BALLYROAN STKS (listed race)    £8061.00    1¹/₄m

| | | |
|---|---|---|
| | **Dabtiya (IRE)** *(Ireland)* 3–8–7 WRSwinburn | —1 |
| 1819a | Mining Tycoon (IRE) *(Ireland)* 3–8-10 KJManning | 1.2 |
| 1817a | Malvernico (IRE) *(Ireland)* 4–9-7 CRoche | ³/₄.3 |

Tote £4.30: £2.00 £5.00 £2.50 (£34.00). H.H.Aga Khan (J.M.Oxx,IRELAND) bred by H.H.Aga Khan in Ireland. 9 Rn

2m 6.7 (2.7)
SF—66/67/76/80/60

## 2764a
HEINZ 57 PHOENIX STKS (Gp 1) (2-Y.O.C & F) £81402.00    6f

| | | |
|---|---|---|
| 2441⁵ | **PIPS PRIDE** *(RHannon)* 2–9–0 LDettori (racd stands' side in tch: hdwy to ld wl over 1f out: sn u.p: r.o wl) | —1 |
| 2093a³ | Shahik (USA) *(Ireland)* 2–9-0 SCraine (racd stands' side: hmpd & swtchd ¹/₂-wy: hdwy over 1f out: chal ins fnl f: no ex) | ³/₄.2 |
| 2441⁴ | DARBONNE (USA) *(GHarwood)* 2–9-0 WCarson (cl up: hmpd ¹/₂-wy: str chal fnl f: kpt on) | nk.3 |
| 1818a★ | Ivory Frontier (IRE) *(Ireland)* 2–9-0 CRoche (led stands' side: edgd rt & lft ¹/₂-wy: hdd wl over 1f out: edgd lft 1f out: r.o) | ¹/₂.4 |
| 2537★ | SPLENDENT (USA) *(PFICole)* 2–9-0 MRoberts (prom stands' side: lost pl 2f out: no imp whn nt clr run & swtchd 1f out: r.o) | 2.5 |
| 2093a★ | Tropical (bl) *(Ireland)* 2–8-11 MJKinane (racd stands' side in rr: hdwy 2f out: sn rdn & btn) | 1¹/₂.6 |
| 2441★ | SON PARDO (Fav) *(RHannon)* 2–9-0 JReid (prom far side: no imp fr ¹/₂-wy) | 9.7 |
| 2452⁵ | Kamaatera (IRE) (bl) *(Ireland)* 2–9-0 WRSwinburn (chsd ldrs far side: sme hdwy ¹/₂-wy: n.d fnl 2f) | 1¹/₂.8 |
| 2176² | ARADANZA *(MRChannon)* 2–9-0 PaulEddery (prom far side: rdn ¹/₂-wy: sn bhd) | 5¹/₂.9 |

**2/1** Son Pardo, **100/30** Tropical, **5/1** Splendent (USA), **6/1** Ivory Frontier (IRE), **10/1** Darbonne (USA), PIPS PRIDE, **14/1** Shahik (USA), **16/1** Aradanza, **33/1** Kamaatera (IRE). Tote £22.60: £8.40 £4.10 £5.20 (£182.30). Mrs V.S.Grant (MARLBOROUGH) bred by R.A. and J.H.Popely. 9 Rn
1m 13 (1.8)
SF—64/61/60/58/50/41

## 2624a—DEAUVILLE (R-H)
### Saturday, August 8th [Good to soft]
Going Allowance: 0.80 sec per fur (S)

**2765a**   PRIX DE PSYCHE (Gp 3) (3-Y.O.F) £20640.00   1¼m

| | | |
|---|---|---|
| **Palomelle (FR)** *(France)* 3-8-9 ODoleuze | ............................................... | —1 |
| Vanille *(USA)* *(France)* 3-8-9 TJarnet | | nk.2 |
| 2091a³ Faribole (IRE) *(France)* 3-8-9 OBenoist | | ½.3 |
| 1347★ FEMININE WILES (IRE) *(PWChapple-Hyam)* 3-8-9 CBlack (btn further 2l) | | 6 |

Tote 12.60f: 3.00f 1.80f 3.40f (28.50f). Mr P.Rayaz (A.Spanu,FRANCE) bred by Mrs A.M.Balbous in France. 11 Rn
2m 12.6 (10.3)
SF—72/71/70

## DEAUVILLE (R-H)
### Sunday, August 9th [Soft]
Going Allowance: 0.90 sec per fur (S)

**2766a**   PRIX DE POMONE (Gp 2) (F & M) £25800.00   1m 5f 110y

| | | |
|---|---|---|
| 1984a² **Magic Night (FR)** *(Jt-Fav)* *(France)* 4 0 9 ABadel (hld up: rapid hdwy wl over 1f out: led ins fnl f: r.o wl: impressive) | ........................... | —1 |
| 1843⁵ Sought Out (IRE) *(France)* 4-9-2 CAsmussen (a cl up: effrt fr 2f out: r.o wl) | ..... | 1.2 |
| 1929⁴ ALWAYS FRIENDLY *(HCandy)* 4-9-2 AMunro (mid div: led wl over 1f out: r.o one pce) | | s.nk.3 |
| 2319a★ Linnga (IRE) *(France)* 3-8-7 GGuignard (a cl up: mid div st: one pce after) | ..... | 1½.4 |
| 1824a² Trampoli (USA) *(France)* 3-8-7 TJarnet (nvr nrr) | ........................................ | 2½.5 |
| 1098a Winnetka (USA) *(France)* 3-8-7 FHead (hld up: btn wl over 1f out) | ..................... | 8.6 |
| MAGNIFICENT STAR (USA) *(MMoubarak)* 4-9-2 ACruz (cl up to st: wknd qckly) | | 10.7 |
| 2231★ MISS PLUM *(HRACecil)* 3-8-7 PatEddery (led to 2f out: sn btn) | ......................... | 5.8 |
| 1231a L'Amour Fou (IRE) (bl) *(Jt-Fav)* *(France)* 4-9-2 PBruneau (a outpcd: sn btn) | .. dist.9 |

**6/10** L'Amour Fou (IRE), MAGIC NIGHT (FR), **9/2** Trampoli (USA), Linnga (IRE), **11/1** Sought Out (IRE), **13/1** Magnificent Star (USA), **16/1** Miss Plum, **18/1** Always Friendly, **27/1** Winnetka (USA). Tote 1.60f (cpld w L'Amour Fou): 1.10f 1.90f 2.40f (11.20f). Mr H.Yokoyama (P.Demercastel,FRANCE) bred by Mr & Mrs A.Simoes de Almeida in France. 9 Rn
3m 7.1 (16.6)
SF—58/56/55/43/38/22

## 2097a—HOPPEGARTEN (R-H) Germany
### Sunday, August 9th [Good]

**2767a**   GROSSER PREIS VON BERLIN (Gp 3)   £70423.00   6f 110y

| | | |
|---|---|---|
| 1942★ **MR BROOKS** *(RHannon)* 5-9-6 LPiggott | ............................................... | —1 |
| 1475 Monde Bleu *(France)* 4-9-6 SGuillot | ............................................... | ½.2 |
| 1228a★ Dream Talk (bl) *(France)* 5-9-6 GMosse | | 1.3 |

Tote 19DM: 12DM 22DM 12DM (SF: 116DM). Mr Paul Green (MARLBOROUGH) bred by Mrs J. R. Rossdale. 12 Rn
1m 14.6

## NEUSS (R-H) Germany
### Sunday, August 9th [Good]

**2768a**   DEUTSCHER BUCHMACHER STUTENPREIS VON NEUSS (Gp 3) (F & M) £24120.00   1¼m 110y

| | | |
|---|---|---|
| **Arastou (GER)** *(Germany)* 3-8-5 AHelfenbein | ............................................... | —1 |
| 2091a² SARATOGA SOURCE (USA) *(IABalding)* 3-8-5 WRyan | ........................................ | 3.2 |
| First Class (GER) *(Germany)* 3-8-7 ATylicki | | 4.3 |

Tote 47DM: 15DM 15DM 19DM (167DM). Gestut Haus Ittlingen (U.Ostmann,GERMANY) bred by Gestut Hof Ittlingen in Germany. 11 Rn
2m 7.8

2251—**FOLKESTONE (R-H)**
**Friday, August 14th [Good]**
Going Allowance: minus 0.15 sec per fur (F)                    Wind: slt half bhd

Stalls: low

**2769**    HYTHE STKS (Mdn 3-Y.O) £2070.00 (£570.00: £270.00)    **1m 1f 149y**    1-50 (1-51)

| | | |
|---|---|---|
| 2549 | **Debacle (USA)** (GHarwood) 9-0  AClark (5) (lw: led 6f out: clr over 1f out: hrd rdn ins fnl f: r.o wl) | —1 |
| 2549² | **Usaidit (73)** (Fav) (WCarter) 8-9 ‡⁵NGwilliams (3) (lw: 6th st: swtchd rt over 1f out: r.o wl ins fnl f) | 2½.2 |
| | Private Bank (USA) (ACStewart) 9-0  GCarter (4) (bit bkwd: led over 3f: 2nd st: hrd rdn over 1f out: unable qckn) | 2.3 |
| | Rutbah (ACStewart) 8-9  WRyan (6) (w'like: scope: bkwd: 5th st: one pce fnl 2f) | 1½.4 |
| | Jameel Dancer (MRStoute) 9-0  DHolland (1) (unf: scope: 3rd st: rdn over 1f out: wknd fnl f) | 1.5 |
| 979³ | Summer Cruise (ANLee) 9-0  JQuinn (2) (lw: a bhd) | 2½.6 |
| 2549 | Romance (IRE) (MJHeaton-Ellis) 8-9  JLloyd (7) (4th st: wknd 2f out) | hd.7 |

**7/4** Usaidit, **2/1** Rutbah, **4/1** Jameel Dancer(op 5/4), **13/2** Summer Cruise, **16/1** DEBACLE (USA)(8/1—20/1), **50/1** Ors. CSF £41.99, Tote £15.80: £5.30 £2.10 (£28.50). Mr David Saxby (PULBOROUGH) bred by Juddmonte Farms Incorporated in USA. 7 Rn
2m 5.9 (8.2)

**2770**    ROTHMANS ROYALS NORTH SOUTH CHALLENGE SERIES H'CAP (0-80) £3106.00 (£928.00: £444.00: £202.00)    **6f 189y**    2-20 (2-23)

| | | |
|---|---|---|
| 2617★ | **Surrey Racing (68)** (GLewis) 4-9-2 (5x)  BRouse (5) (hdwy 2f out: led 1f out: r.o wl) | —1 |
| 2449 | **Amadeus Aes (80)** (DMorris) 3-9-3 ‡⁵StephenDavies (2) (4th st: ev ch 1f out: unable qckn) | 2.2 |
| 2476 | Try Leguard (IRE) (71) (Jt-Fav) (WCarter) 3-8-13  GCarter (8) (lw: 3rd st: led over 1f out: rdn hd: one pce) | 2.3 |
| 2494 | Dream Carrier (IRE) (71) (Jt-Fav) (RHannon) 4-9-5  LPiggott (6) (5th st: one pce fnl 2f) | hd.4 |
| 2582² | Navaresque (45) (RJHodges) 7-7-7  DaleGibson (3) (6th st: one pce fnl 2f) | 2½.5 |
| 240 | Shake Town (USA) (77) (v) (MHTompkins) 4-9-11  PRobinson (4) (lw: nvr nr to chal) | 1½.6 |
| 1890 | Breakdancer (IRE) (54) (WRMuir) 3-9-10  JQuinn (7) (2nd st: led 2f out tl over 1f out: sn wknd) | nk.7 |
| 2458² | Helios (78) (RSimpson) 4-9-12  WRyan (1) (lw: a bhd) | 2½.8 |
| 2589 | Caromish (USA) (62) (MDIUsher) 5-8-10  MWigham (9) (led 5f) | 5.9 |

LONG HANDICAP: Navaresque 7-4.

**7/2** Try Leguard (IRE)(op 7/1), Dream Carrier (IRE), **11/2** SURREY RACING(4/1—6/1), Helios(7/2—6/1), **13/2** Navaresque, **12/1** Caromish (USA), Amadeus Aes, **14/1** Shake Town (USA), **16/1** Breakdancer (IRE). CSF £59.72, CT £237.95. Tote £5.90: £1.90 £3.00 £1.50 (£29.70). Mr K. Higson (EPSOM) bred by W. R. Swinburn. 9 Rn
1m 24.7 (3.1)
SF—40/35/25/30/–/23

**2771**    DUNGENESS (S) STKS (2-Y.O) £2679.00 (£744.00: £357.00)    **6f**    2-50 (2-54)

| | | |
|---|---|---|
| 2409 | **Soviet Express** (PFICole) 8-11  GBaxter (1) (a.p: hrd rdn over 1f out: led ins fnl f: drvn out) | —1 |
| 2233 | Star Minstrel (IRE) (MMcCormack) 8-11  AClark (13) (w ldr: led over 2f out tl ins fnl f: hrd rdn: r.o wl) | hd.2 |
| 2428★ | No Extras (IRE) (61) (Jt-Fav) (JSutcliffe) 8-11  BRouse (8) (rdn & hdwy 2f out: ev ch ins fnl f: r.o) | nk.3 |
| 2544 | Ascom Pager Too (PHowling) 8-6  BCrossley (9) (b: hld up: rdn over 2f out: r.o one pce) | 3¼.4 |
| 2563 | Sea Strand (MBlanshard) 8-6  DHolland (10) (a.p: hrd rdn over 1f out: wknd fnl f) | 3.5 |
| 2414⁵ | Tony's Mist (Jt-Fav) (RHannon) 8-11  LPiggott (11) (lw: led over 3f: eased whn btn fnl f) | 1½.6 |
| 2591² | Lady of Shadows (48) (SDow) 8-6  WRyan (5) (b.hind: prom over 3f) | 2½.7 |
| 2306 | Morning News (IRE) (MHTompkins) 8-11  PRobinson (12) (hdwy over 2f out: wknd over 1f out) | 1½.8 |
| 2398 | We Are Doomed (JRFanshawe) 8-11  GCarter (6) (a bhd) | 1½.9 |
| | Texas Cowgirl (IRE) (GAPritchard-Gordon) 8-6  NCarlisle (14) (scope: bit bkwd: s.s: a bhd) | 1.10 |
| 2563⁵ | My Miss Molly (IRE) (MissGayKelleway) 8-6  GayKelleway (7) (b.hind: a bhd) | hd.11 |

*2008* Golden Klair *(42)* *(CJHill)* 8-6 DBiggs (4) (a bhd) ............................................. 3¹/₂.12
2106⁴ Miss Fitness *(47)* (v) *(DrJDScargill)* 8-6 JQuinn (2) (a bhd: t.o fnl 4f) ................... 13

**7/4** Tony's Mist, No Extras (IRE), **6/1** SOVIET EXPRESS, **8/1** Star Minstrel (IRE), **12/1** Lady of Shadows(8/1—14/1), **20/1**, We Are Doomed, **25/1** Texas Cowgirl (IRE), Sea Strand, Miss Fitness(op 8/1), **33/1** Golden Klair, **50/1** Ors. CSF £53.48, Tote £4.60: £1.10 £3.80 £1.70 (£46.70). Mr Brook Land (WHATCOMBE) bred by C. J. Mason and R. J. Mason. 13 Rn; Bt in 7,200 gns
　　　　　　　　　　　　　　　　　　　　　　　　　　　　　　　　　1m 13.5 (2.8)
　　　　　　　　　　　　　　　　　　　　　　　　　　SF—23/22/21/2/–/–/

## 2772　　　　WAKEFIELD H'CAP (0-70) £2679.00 (£744.00: £357.00)　　**6f**　　　3-20 (3-26)

2581² **Ain'tlifelikethat** *(47)* (bl) *(TJNaughton)* 5-8-8 GCarter (14) (hld up: led over 1f
　　　　　out: rdn out) ................................................................................................... —1
2290⁴ Almasa *(55)* *(DMorris)* 4-8-11 ‡⁵StephenDavies (12) (lw: w ldr: led over 2f out tl
　　　　　over 1f out: unable qckn) ........................................................................ 1¹/₂.2
2009⁴ Harry's Coming *(67)* *(RJHodges)* 8-9-7 ‡⁷SDrowne (3) (hdwy over 2f out: rdn
　　　　　over 1f out: one pce) ............................................................................. 2¹/₂.3
2589* Liffey River (USA) *(55)* *(MrsLPiggott)* 4-9-2 (7x) LPiggott (8) (b: b.hind: lw: hld
　　　　　up: ev ch over 1f out: one pce) .................................................................. ¹/₂.4
2307³ My Ruby Ring *(41)* *(DRLaing)* 5-7-11 ‡⁵ATucker (1) (hld up: n.m.r wl over 1f out:
　　　　　r.o one pce) ............................................................................................... ¹/₂.5
2564⁶ Petitesse *(46)* *(GBlum)* 4-8-7 AShoults (5) (gd spd 4f) ................................. 3.6
2198 Darakah *(53)* (Fav) *(CJHill)* 5-9-0 DHolland (4) (hld up: hdwy fnl f: r.o) ........... ¹/₂.7
*2689* One Magic Moment (IRE) *(48)* *(CACyzer)* 4-8-9 DBiggs (2) (nvr nr to chal) ...... s.h.8
2603² Loose Zeus (USA) *(51)* *(CFWall)* 3-8-7 NCarlisle (9) (s.s: nvr nrr) ..................... ¹/₂.9
2589 Sunley Sparkle *(50)* *(DRGandolfo)* 4-8-8 ‡³RPerham (13) (led over 3f) ............ ¹/₂.10
*1535* Sunset Street (IRE) *(60)* *(SDow)* 4-9-0 ‡⁷AMartinez (7) (spd over 3f) ............. hd.11
*2411* Master Hyde (USA) *(49)* (bl) *(PMitchell)* 3-8-5 AClark (10) (spd 4f) ................... ¹/₂.12
　　　　　First Tradition *(33)* *(CJHill)* 7-7-8⁽¹⁾ JQuinn (6) (bhd fnl 2f) ........................ s.h.13
　　　　　Bathsheba Everdene *(40)* *(KOCunningham-Brown)* 4-8-1 SDawson (15)
　　　　　(outpcd) ..................................................................................................... ³/₄.14
2494 Hitchin a Ride *(48)* *(MPMuggeridge)* 5-8-9 MPerrett (11) (outpcd) ................. 10.15
　　　　　　　　　LONG HANDICAP: First Tradition 7-3.
　　*Stewards Enquiry: Holland fined £400 for breach of Rule 151 (ii) (failure to ride horse to it's merits)*

**100/30** Darakah, **9/2** Liffey River (USA), **11/2** My Ruby Ring(tchd 10/1), **7/1** AIN'TLIFELIKETHAT, **8/1** Loose Zeus (USA)(6/1—9/1), **9/1** Harry's Coming, **12/1** Almasa(op 8/1), **16/1** Petitesse, **20/1** Master Hyde (USA), Sunset Street (IRE), **25/1** Hitchin a Ride, One Magic Moment (IRE), **33/1** Ors. CSF £84.87, CT £701.99. Tote £6.60: £2.40 £3.30 £3.20 (£155.20). Mr D. Borrows (EPSOM) bred by Miss B. Galway-Greer. 15 Rn
　　　　　　　　　　　　　　　　　　　　　　　　　　　　　　　　　1m 12.4 (1.7)
　　　　　　　　　　　　　　　　　　　　　　　　　SF—42/39/39/32/11/9

## 2773　　　　E.B.F. DANES STKS (Mdn 2-Y-O) £2301.00 (£636.00: £303.00)　　**5f**　　3-50 (3-58)

1259 **Hello Hobson's (IRE)** *(JAkehurst)* 8-9 DHolland (1) (lw: hld up: rdn over 1f out:
　　　　　led ins fnl f: all out) ................................................................................. —1
1469 Windrush Boy *(81)* (Fav) *(MMcCormack)* 9-0 AClark (2) (led: hrd rdn over 1f
　　　　　out: hdd ins fnl f: r.o wl) ........................................................................... s.h.2
1979⁴ Gweek (IRE) *(PAKelleway)* 8-9 PRobinson (6) (lw: hld up: ev ch wl over 1f out:
　　　　　unable qckn) .............................................................................................. 4.3
2031 Imafifer (IRE) *(WRMuir)* 8-11 ‡³RPerham (3) (spd 3f) ..................................... 5.4
2225 Ambivalentattitude *(MDIUsher)* 9-0 MWigham (4) (lw: a bhd) .......................... 1¹/₂.5
2587³ Jasmin Isle *(51)* (bl) *(MissGayKelleway)* 8-9 GayKelleway (5) (spd over 2f) ...... 7.6

**8/13** Windrush Boy(2/5—4/6), **3/1** HELLO HOBSON'S (IRE), **6/1** Gweek (IRE)(7/1—10/1), **16/1** Jasmin Isle(12/1—25/1), **50/1** Imafifer (IRE), **100/1** Ambivalentattitude. CSF £4.95, Tote £4.80: £2.00 £1.30 (£3.30). Hobson's International Ltd (UPPER LAMBOURN) bred by A. W. Allen in Ireland. 6 Rn
　　　　　　　　　　　　　　　　　　　　　　　　　　　　　　　　　60.5 sec (1.7)
　　　　　　　　　　　　　　　　　　　　　　　　　SF—46/50/29/11/8/–

## 2774　　　　OAKLANDS H'CAP (0-70) £2733.50 (£756.00: £360.50)　　**1¹/₂m**　　4-20 (4-28)

2295⁴ **Prosequendo (USA)** *(64)* *(MDixon)* 5-10-0 MPerrett (8) (6th st: led over 1f out:
　　　　　rdn out) ...................................................................................................... —1
2698 Bold Resolution (IRE) *(54)* *(CACyzer)* 4-9-4 DBiggs (1) (5th st: hrd rdn over 1f
　　　　　out: unable qckn) ........................................................................................ 3¹/₂.2
2596³ Scotoni *(49)* *(RJO'Sullivan)* 6-8-13 AClark (5) (lw: a.p: led over 2f out tl over 1f
　　　　　out: one pce) .............................................................................................. s.h.3
1491 A a Bamba *(56)* *(NACallaghan)* 3-8-2 ‡⁷JTate (9) (hdwy on ins over 2f out: 4th
　•　　　 st: one pce fnl 2f) ...................................................................................... 2¹/₂.4
　　　　　Viaggio *(57)* *(JAkehurst)* 4-9-7 DHolland (3) (prom over 9f) .......................... 2¹/₂.5
2416³ Kandy Secret (USA) *(62)* *(RHannon)* 3-9-1 JLloyd (6) (nvr nr to chal) ............... 1.6
2302³ Maligned (IRE) *(51)* *(JRFanshawe)* 3-8-0 GCarter (7) (no hdwy fnl 2f) ............... nk.7
2596⁵ Beam Me Up Scotty (IRE) *(47)* (bl) *(PMitchell)* 3-8-0 NCarlisle (4) (led 8f: 2nd st:
　　　　　wknd 2f out) ............................................................................................... 1.8

2621³ Antico Nativo (IRE) **(54)** (Fav) *(SDow)* 4-9-4 LPiggott (2) (a.p: led 4f out tl over 2f out: 3rd st: wknd wl over 1f out) ...................................... ¾.**9**

**11/4** Antico Nativo (IRE)(4/1—9/2), **5/1** Viaggio(12/1—14/1), **11/2** Bold Resolution (IRE), Kandy Secret (USA)(op 3/1), Scotoni, **11/1** Maligned (IRE), PROSEQUENDO (USA), **12/1** A a Bamba, **16/1** Beam Me Up Scotty (IRE). CSF £65.99, CT £339.92. Tote £9.50: £2.70 £1.90 £1.90 (£19.60). Mr J. Daniels (EPSOM) bred by H. Turney McKnight and June H. McKnight in USA. 9 Rn      2m 39.2 (5.7)
                                                    SF—39/22/16/–/14/6

T/Plpt: £102.20 (22.55 Tckts).                                                  AK

## 2635—HAYDOCK (L-H)
### Friday, August 14th [Good]
Going Allowance: nil sec per fur (G)                                      Wind: almost nil

Stalls: high

**2775**      LITTLE STANNYLANDS STUD APPCE H'CAP (0-70) £2763.00 (£768.00: £369.00)
            1¼m 120y                                                  5-45 (5-46)

2182⁶ **Light Hand (64)** *(MHTompkins)* 6-9-4 ‡⁷SMulvey (6) (s.s: hdwy 3f out: styd on to ld wl ins fnl f) ................................................ —**1**
2273³ Mingus (USA) **(56)** (Fav) *(MrsJRRamsden)* 5-9-3 JWeaver (12) (lw: hld up: hdwy to ld over 2f out: hrd rdn & ct nr fin) ..................... 1½.**2**
2570 No Comebacks **(42)** *(EJAlston)* 4-7-10 ‡⁷NVarley (14) (s.s: hdwy over 2f out: fin wl) ............................................................. hd.**3**
893 Mac Rambler **(32)** *(NBycroft)* 5-7-4 ‡³AGarth (10) (bit bkwd: styd on fnl 2f: nvr nrr) ............................................................. 3¼.**4**
880 Pennine Star (IRE) **(58)** *(CWCElsey)* 4-9-5 JFanning (1) (bkwd: hdwy over 2f out: hrd rdn appr fnl f: kpt on) ............................ 3.**5**
2554 Master Copy (IRE) **(54)** (bl) *(CBBBooth)* 3-7-12⁽⁷⁾ ‡⁷GParkin (2) (chsd ldrs: 5th st: rdn over 1f out: one pce) ........................ 1½.**6**
2634 Urshi-Jade **(41)** *(KWhite)* 4-7-9⁽⁸⁾ ‡⁷JDennis (9) (effrt u.p over 2f out: nt rch ldrs) 4.**7**
2394* Sanawi **(52)** *(PDEvans)* 5-8-6 ‡⁷DWright (15) (chsd ldrs: 6th st: hrd rdn 2f out: sn btn) ........................................................ 1.**8**
2483⁵ Charly Pharly (FR) **(48)** (bl) *(FHLee)* 5-8-9 NKennedy (8) (bit bkwd: led tl hdd & wknd over 2f out) ........................................ 3.**9**
2420 Queens Tour **(39)** *(MBrittain)* 7-7-11⁽⁷⁾ ‡³LNewton (11) (m.n.s) .................. 1½.**10**
2571 Sharquin **(41)** (v) *(MBrittain)* 5-7-9⁽⁹⁾ ‡⁷JMarshall (7) (chsd ldrs: 4th st: rdn & wknd over 2f out) ...................................... 1½.**11**
2721 Mr Wishing Well **(53)** *(RJWilliams)* 6-8-7 ‡⁷GMitchell (5) (hld up: hdwy 3f out: wknd appr fnl f) ...................................... 1.**12**
Ella Street **(35)** *(CaptJWilson)* 5-7-3⁽³⁾ ‡⁷AnnaLaw (13) (bkwd: a bhd: t.o) ...... 15.**13**
2739 My Turn Next **(45)** *(KWHogg)* 4-7-13⁽¹³⁾ ‡⁷DCarson (4) (a bhd: t.o) ............ 2½.**14**
2200 Waaza (USA) **(65)** (bl) *(AAScott)* 3-8-9 ‡⁷HazelMilligan (16) (prom: 2nd st: wknd over 2f out: t.o) ......................................... 8.**15**
2427 Regal Romper (IRE) **(38)** *(MrsSJSmith)* 4-7-6⁽⁶⁾ ‡⁷JBramhill (3) (bit bkwd: prom: 3rd st: wknd over 3f out: t.o) .......................... 4.**16**
         LONG HANDICAP: Mac Rambler 7-3, Queens Tour 7-5, Sharquin 7-5, Ella Street 6-13,
                             My Turn Next 7-5.

**3/1** Mingus (USA), **5/1** Charly Pharly (FR), **7/1** Sanawi, **8/1** No Comebacks, LIGHT HAND, **10/1** Mr Wishing Well, Waaza (USA), **12/1** Master Copy (IRE), **14/1** Pennine Star (IRE), **16/1** Queens Tour, **20/1** Sharquin, **50/1** Ors. CSF £31.49, CT £186.08. Tote £6.90: £1.90 £1.50 £2.10 £7.10 (£9.40). Mr John A. Furze (NEWMARKET) bred by The Dunchurch Lodge Stud Co and Mrs A. Johnstone. 16 Rn      2m 17.15 (5.45)
                                                SF—49/45/23/10/33/9

**2776**      COUNTRYWIDE FREIGHT AUCTION STKS (2-Y.O) £1730.00 (£480.00: £230.00)
            6f                                                  6-15 (6-16)

2558² **Simmering (84)** (Fav) *(GWragg)* 8-3 MHills (6) (dwlt: hdwy ½-wy: led ent fnl f: r.o wl) ................................................................ —**1**
2612² Bold Seven (IRE) **(77)** *(FHLee)* 7-13 ‡⁵NKennedy (10) (led 1f: led over 1f out tl ent fnl f: one pce) ...................................... 2.**2**
1046⁶ I'M a Dreamer (IRE) **(8)** *(WWHaigh)* 8-3 DMcKeown (2) (bit bkwd: a.p: rdn over 1f out: one pce) .................................... 3½.**3**
2452 Marchwell Lad **(89)** *(MRChannon)* 8-10 KDarley (3) (lw: led after 1f tl over 1f out: sn rdn & btn) ..................................... 4.**4**
2405 Noteability **(59)** *(JBerry)* 8-2⁽¹⁾ JCarroll (4) (lw: chsd ldrs over 4f: sn outpcd) .. 5.**5**
Target Time *(DMcCain)* 7-11 JFanning (8) (w'like: bkwd: s.s: outpcd) ............ 1½.**6**

Rum Tempest *(CTinkler)* 8-5[(2)] MBirch (5) (lt-f: unf: bit bkwd: in tch: rdn 2f out:
no imp) ..................................................................... $^1/_2$.7
1524[3] Paajib (IRE) **(80)** *(CTinkler)* 8-8 TLucas (1) (lw: outpcd) ......................... $^1/_2$.8
Andrew's Express (IRE) *(SEKettlewell)* 8-4 JFortune (11) (w'like: scope: bkwd:
outpcd: t.o) ................................................................. 7.9

**6/5** SIMMERING, **7/2** Marchwell Lad, Bold Seven (IRE), **14/1** Noteability, **16/1** Paajib (IRE), **20/1** I'M A Dreamer (IRE), Rum Tempest, **50/1** Ors. CSF £5.71, Tote £2.00: £1.10 £1.40 £2.70 (£3.00). Mrs G. Wragg (NEWMARKET) bred by P. D. and Mrs Player. 9 Rn
1m 14.50 (2.80)
SF—33/21/11/2/–/–

---

**2777**　　CLAUDE HARRISON MEMORIAL CHALLENGE TROPHY (H'cap) (0-90) £2954.00
(£819.00: £392.00)　　**1m 30y**　　6-45 (6-46)

(Weights raised 5 lb)
2609★ **Vague Dancer (60)** *(Fav)* *(MrsJRRamsden)* 6–8–6 ‡[5]JWeaver (4) (chsd ldrs: 4th
st: led wl over 1f out: hrd rdn fnl f: hld on gamely) ................ —1
2656 Shaffaaf (USA) **(58)** *(PDEvans)* 4–8–9 DMcKeown (6) (a.p: 3rd st: jnd wnr over
1f out: r.o) ..................................................................... s.h.2
2403 Aljernaas **(80)** *(LMCumani)* 3–9–10 LDettori (5) (bit bkwd: hld up: 6th st: hdwy
over 2f out: hrd rdn appr fnl f: one pce) ........................... 2$^1/_2$.3
2637[2] Sir Arthur Hobbs **(62)** *(FHLee)* 3–8–6 ‡[5]NKennedy (5) (lw: hld up: 5th st: effrt u.p
2f out: nvr able to chal) ................................................. 1.4
2432 Under the Bridge *(PWHarris)* 3–9–3 WRSwinburn (3) (led over 4f: wknd qckly
over 1f out) ................................................................... 6.5
2431[4] Brambleberry **(72)** *(MrsSJSmith)* 3–8–9 ‡[7]JMarshall (2) (chsd ldr: 2nd st: led
over 3f out tl over 1f out: sn rdn & btn) ......................... s.h.6

**5/4** VAGUE DANCER, **2/1** Sir Arthur Hobbs, **7/1** Aljernaas, **8/1** Shaffaaf (USA), **16/1** Under the Bridge, **25/1** Brambleberry. CSF £10.32, Tote £2.10: £1.50 £2.60 (£7.00). Mr K. E. Wheldon (THIRSK) bred by P. Haworth. 6 Rn
1m 45.96 (5.56)
SF—9/11/18/–/–/–

---

**2778**　　BODDINGTON'S BITTER CLAIMING STKS (3-Y.O) £1548.00 (£428.00: £204.00)
**1m 30y**　　7-15 (7-17)

2687[4] **Chequers (IRE) (74)** *(RJRWilliams)* 8-9 MHills (6) (hld up: 4th st: led 2f out: hrd
rdn: r.o) ........................................................................ —1
2699 Mummys Rocket **(35)** *(MO'Neill)* 7-7 ‡[5]NKennedy (4) (b: hld up: 5th st: gd hdwy
over 1f out: r.o) ............................................................ 1.2
1533 Rafah **(76)** *(Fav)* *(BHanbury)* 8-9 WRSwinburn (3) (lw: a.p: 2nd st: ev ch over 1f
out: unable qckn) .......................................................... 1$^1/_2$.3
Notrella (IRE) *(MissLAPerratt)* 7-12 JFanning (1) (w'like: bkwd: s.s: 6th st: hdwy
to jn ldrs 3f out: rdn & wknd over 1f out) ...................... 12.4
2742 Sea Lord **(35)** *(KWHogg)* 8-7 JCorrigan (5) (prom: 3rd st: rdn & wknd over 2f
out) .............................................................................. 6.5
2672[3] Oyston's Life **(54)** *(JBerry)* 9-0 JCarroll (2) (led to 2f out: sn hrd rdn & wknd) 2$^1/_2$.6

**11/8** Rafah(10/11—6/4), **7/4** CHEQUERS (IRE), **6/1** Oyston's Life, **9/1** Mummys Rocket(12/1—14/1), **16/1** Notrella (IRE), **33/1** Sea Lord. CSF £15.04, Tote £2.60: £1.40 £2.20 (£13.20). Mr D. A. Johnson (NEWMARKET) bred by J. Ryan in Ireland. 6 Rn
1m 46.36 (5.96)
SF—5/–/–/–/–

---

**2779**　　MOTORCIRCLE GARAGES (STOKE) NURSERY　£1604.00 (£444.00: £212.00)
**5f**　　7-45 (7-47)
(Weights raised 4 lb)
2546[2] **Infant Protege (USA) (63)** *(CEBrittain)* 7-8[(3)] ‡[5]BDoyle (4) (bhd: hdwy & swtchd
rt 1f out: str rn to ld nr fin) ......................................... —1
2221 Mistertopogigo (IRE) **(85)** *(BBeasley)* 9-7 DNicholls (5) (lw: led: shkn up ent fnl
f: ct nr fin) ................................................................... hd.2
2633[3] Cloudy Reef **(67)** *(RHollinshead)* 7-10 ‡[7]AGarth (9) (bhd: gd hdwy & ev ch wl ins
fnl f: no ex cl home) ..................................................... nk.3
2328[3] Margaret's Gift **(78)** *(JBerry)* 9-0 JCarroll (6) (lw: chsd ldrs: effrt & ev ch appr fnl
f: unable qckn) ............................................................. 1$^1/_2$.4
2717[5] Minshaar **(78)** *(Fav)* *(KSBridgwater)* 9-0 WCarson (8) (effrt 2f out: hrd rdn over
1f out: nt pce to chal) ................................................... 1$^1/_2$.5
2543[6] Plum First **(70)** (bl) *(NBycroft)* 8-6 SWhitworth (1) (lw: prom on outside: rdn wl
over 1f out: sn btn) ....................................................... 1$^1/_2$.6
2500[2] Red Ballet **(63)** (bl) *(MrsNMacauley)* 7-13 CRutter (7) (swtg: spd 3f: sn rdn &
lost tch) ........................................................................ $^3/_4$.7
2735★ Costa Verde **(85)** *(KWHogg)* 9-6 (6x) LDettori (3) (chsd ldrs: effrt & ev ch appr
fnl f: sn outpcd) ............................................................ s.h.8
2390[4] Luckifosome **(57)** *(PDEvans)* 7-0 ‡[7]DWright (2) (s.i.s: sn rdn along: a bhd) ........ 1.9
LONG HANDICAP: Luckifosome 7-5.

3/1 Minshaar, **9/2** Margaret's Gift, **6/1** Red Ballet, **15/2** Costa Verde, **8/1** INFANT PROTEGE (USA), Mistertopogigo (IRE), **17/2** Cloudy Reef, **12/1** Ors. CSF £63.19, CT £507.06. Tote £7.10: £2.10 £2.40 £1.90 (£42.60). Mrs Celia Miller (NEWMARKET) bred by Don Dick in USA. 9 Rn
61.53 sec (2.53)
SF—29/55/29/41/35/21

## 2780
SWAN WITH TWO NECKS STKS (Mdn 3-Y.O) £1660.00 (£460.00: £220.00)
1¼m 120y
8-15 (8-17)

| | | |
|---|---|---|
| 2298³ | **Whirl (77)** *(JRFanshawe)* 8-9 KDarley (3) (hld up: 6th st: rdn to chal 1f out: styd on to ld wl ins fnl f) | —1 |
| 2336⁴ | Triennium (USA) **(80)** *(Fav)* *(LMCumani)* 9-0 LDettori (11) (lw: led after 2f: hrd rdn over 1f out: hdd & no ex wl ins fnl f) | 1.2 |
| | Janaat *(AAScott)* 8-9 WRSwinburn (2) (unf: scope: bkwd: hld up: stdy hdwy fnl 2f: nrst fin) | 3.3 |
| 2615³ | Kabayil *(PTWalwyn)* 8-9 WCarson (5) (prom: 4th st: one pce appr fnl f) | ¾.4 |
| | Draft Board *(JHMGosden)* 8-9 PatEddery (4) (leggy: bit bkwd: hdwy & 3rd st: wknd wl over 1f out) | 3½.5 |
| 2432⁴ | Gunner's Daughter *(HCandy)* 8-9 CRutter (7) (bkwd: hld up: 7th st: effrt 3f out: wknd over 1f out) | 1½.6 |
| 2399³ | Raheena (USA) *(JHMGosden)* 8-9 JCarroll (6) (bkwd: styd on fnl 2f: nvr nrr) .. | s.h.7 |
| 2429 | Be My Everything (IRE) **(63)** *(RHollinshead)* 8-2 ‡7DCarson (9) (chsd ldrs: 5th st: wknd over 2f out) | 6.8 |
| 902⁴ | Heniu (USA) *(LordHuntingdon)* 9-0 DMcKeown (10) (bit bkwd: led 2f: hrd rdn 3f out: sn wknd) | 2½.9 |
| 2549 | Hurricane Toke (IRE) *(ACStewart)* 9-0 SWhitworth (1) (a bhd) | hd.10 |
| | Mistress Minx *(LJCodd)* 8-2 ‡7WHollick (8) (w'like: leggy: bkwd: s.s: sn rcvrd: 2nd st: wknd over 3f out: t.o) | dist.11 |

**3/1** Triennium (USA), **7/2** WHIRL, **6/1** Draft Board, Kabayil, **13/2** Janaat(4/1—7/1), **10/1** Hurricane Toke (IRE)(14/1—16/1), Raheena (USA), **12/1** Gunner's Daughter, **14/1** Heniu (USA), **20/1** Be My Everything (IRE), **50/1** Mistress Minx. CSF £15.02, Tote £5.90: £2.10 £1.70 £2.10 (£7.20). Lord Halifax (NEWMARKET) bred by Marquess of Hartington and the Earl of Halifax. 11 Rn
2m 16.22 (4.52)
SF—50/53/42/40/33/30

T/Plpt: £100.70 (32.35 Tckts).　　　　　　　　　　　　　　　　　　　　　　　　　　　　　　IM

## 2687—SOUTHWELL (L-H) Fibresand
### Friday, August 14th [Standard]
Going Allowance: minus 0.10 sec per fur (FS)　　　　　　　　Wind: slt half bhd

Stalls: 1st & 6th high, remainder low

## 2781
REELPAPERS STKS (Mdn 2-Y.O) £2469.00 (£684.00: £327.00)
5f (AWT)
2-30 (2-34)

| | | |
|---|---|---|
| 1764² | **Prince Manki** *(RHannon)* 9-0 AMcGlone (14) (lw: cl up: led wl over 1f out: r.o u.p) | —1 |
| 2471⁵ | Hickory Blue (Fav) *(SGNorton)* 8-9 ‡5OPears (5) (cl up centre: led ½-wy tl wl over 1f out: nt qckn) | 2.2 |
| 2491⁶ | Kildee Lad **(63)** *(APJones)* 9-0 NAdams (11) (a chsng ldrs: kpt on u.p fnl f) | ¾.3 |
| 2544 | Arawa *(DMarks)* 8-9 JLowe (4) (lw: chsd ldrs: styd on one pce fnl 2f) | s.h.4 |
| 2074 | Comet Whirlpool (IRE) *(BBeasley)* 9-0 LCharnock (7) (w ldrs tl rdn & btn over 1f out) | hd.5 |
| 2471⁶ | Mdm Racer (IRE) *(JBerry)* 9-0 JCarroll (12) (a chsng ldrs: rdn ½-wy: kpt on one pce) | s.h.6 |
| 1851⁶ | Rose Flyer (IRE) *(MCChapman)* 8-9 SWebster (9) (in tch: hrd rdn over 1f out: styd on one pce) | 1½.7 |
| 2568⁶ | Velasco (IRE) *(SirMarkPrescott)* 9-0 GDuffield (13) (lw: s.s: outpcd & wl bhd tl r.o fnl f) | 2½.8 |
| 2074 | Apollo de Oriente (v) *(JSWainwright)* 9-0 DLee (10) (cl up 3f: wknd qckly) | hd.9 |
| 2274 | Glow of Hope *(EJAlston)* 8-2 ‡7SKnott (8) (led to ½-wy: sn wknd) | 1½.10 |
| 2195⁶ | Conbrio Star **(47)** (bl) *(CGCox)* 9-0 TRogers (3) (b.hind: spd 3f) | 2.11 |
| 2512³ | Domes of Silence **(49)** *(JBerry)* 9-0 MBirch (6) (sn outpcd & wl bhd: sme late hdwy) | 1½.12 |
| | She's a Breeze *(ASmith)* 8-9 DMcKeown (1) (leggy: unf: s.s: a bhd) | 2.13 |
| | Hershebar *(SRBowring)* 9-0 CDwyer (2) (leggy: scope: outpcd & bhd fr ½-wy) | 1½.14 |

**3/1** Hickory Blue(op 6/1), **9/2** PRINCE MANKI(op 3/1), **5/1** Velasco (IRE)(op 5/2), **7/1** Kildee Lad, **8/1** Domes of Silence, Arawa(10/1—12/1), **16/1** Glow of Hope, Mdm Racer (IRE), **20/1** Hershebar, **25/1** Rose Flyer (IRE), Apollo de Oriente, **33/1** Ors. CSF £18.29, Tote £4.10: £1.80 £1.30 £2.80 (£10.60). Roldvale Limited (MARLBOROUGH) bred by Roldvale Ltd. 14 Rn
61.1 sec (3.1)
SF—28/15/17/11/15/14

## 2782

ENSO UK (S) STKS (2-Y.O) £2616.00 (£726.00: £348.00)    **7f (AWT)**    3-00 (3-04)

| | | | |
|---|---|---|---|
| 1675[4] | **Mighty Miss Magpie (IRE) (51)** *(MRChannon)* 8-6 DMcKeown (6) (w ldr: led over 2f out: styd on u.p) | | —1 |
| 2543 | Allegrissima **(56)** *(JBerry)* 8-11 JCarroll (7) (lw: a chsng ldrs: kpt on u.p fnl 2f: nvr able to chal) | | 4.2 |
| 2688* | Persian Traveller (IRE) **(60)** (Fav) *(CNAllen)* 8-9 ‡7GForster (5) (b.off hind: led tl hdd over 2f out: one pce) | | 2.3 |
| 2008 | Daring King *(DSasse)* 8-6 ‡5RPrice (12) (lw: in tch: hdwy u.p over 2f out: nvr rchd ldrs) | | s.h.4 |
| 2480[3] | Yeveed (IRE) **(55)** *(MHEasterby)* 8-1 ‡5SMaloney (1) (lw: w ldrs tl bdly hmpd & lost pl after 2f: drvn along & no imp after) | | 3½.5 |
| 2688[2] | Carnea *(JGFitzGerald)* 8-6 KFallon (9) (lw: s.i.s: hdwy ent st: nrst fin) | | hd.6 |
| 2085[6] | Sure Risk **(55)** *(RHannon)* 8-6 AMcGlone (8) (in tch: outpcd appr st: styd on fnl f) | | 2½.7 |
| 2363[4] | Egg **(48)** *(TDBarron)* 8-11 AlexGreaves (15) (s.i.s: nvr nr to chal) | | 2½.8 |
| 2277 | Irish Roots (IRE) **(62)** *(CTinkler)* 8-11 TLucas (14) (chsd ldrs to st) | | hd.9 |
| 2688[4] | First Reserve (bl) *(BSRothwell)* 8-11 GHind (2) (s.i.s: gd hdwy ½-wy: wknd wl over 1f out) | | ½.10 |
| 2480[4] | Alice Bay **(49)** *(DHaydnJones)* 8-6 JLowe (3) (nvr trbld ldrs) | | 2½.11 |
| 1848[6] | Peak Fitness *(JAGlover)* 8-11 JFortune (11) (outpcd fr ½-wy) | | 2.12 |
| 2381[3] | Sophie's Boy **(67)** *(MHEasterby)* 8-11 MBirch (13) (lw: dwlt: a bhd) | | nk.13 |
| 2649 | Water Diviner **(69)** (bl) *(RFJohnsonHoughton)* 9-2 AMunro (10) (lw: n.d) | | 2.14 |
| 2488[5] | Sweet Poppy *(JSWainwright)* 8-6 LCharnock (4) (chsd ldrs to st: wknd qckly) | | 12.15 |

**9/4** Persian Traveller (IRE), **5/1** Allegrissima(op 3/1), **9/1** Yeveed (IRE), MIGHTY MISS MAGPIE (IRE), Sure Risk(op 6/1), **12/1** Water Diviner(op 7/1), Egg, **14/1** Carnea, Sophie's Boy, **20/1** Alice Bay, **25/1** Peak Fitness, First Reserve, Irish Roots (IRE), **33/1** Ors. CSF £52.27, Tote £9.40: £2.60 £2.40 £1.80 (£44.00). Mighty Quinn Racing (II) Limited (UPPER LAMBOURN) bred by Rathasker Stud in Ireland. 15 Rn; No bid    1m 30.5 (3.9)
                                         CF 23/16/8/4/–/–

## 2783

SOTTRICI BINDA UK H'CAP (3-Y.O) (0-70) £2616.00 (£726.00: £348.00)
**1¾m (AWT)**    3-30 (3-32)

(Weights raised 3 lb)

| | | | |
|---|---|---|---|
| 1850[3] | **Witches Coven (50)** *(MBell)* 8-7 GDuffield (6) (lw: chsd ldrs: effrt 4f out: styd on to ld ins fnl f) | | —1 |
| 2575[3] | Invisible Armour **(45)** *(PCHaslam)* 8-2 EJohnson (10) (lw: mde most tl hdd & no ex ins fnl f) | | 1.2 |
| 2120[4] | Thor Power (IRE) **(52)** *(DTThom)* 8-9 AMunro (4) (lw: mid div & pushed along ½-wy: styd on fnl f: nrst fin) | | 2.3 |
| 2467* | Seraphim (FR) **(48)** (Jt-Fav) *(TDBarron)* 8-5 AlexGreaves (2) (lw: a chsng ldrs: one pce fnl 3f) | | ¾.4 |
| 2631 | Child Star (FR) **(51)** *(DMarks)* 8-8 JLowe (7) (hdwy ½-wy: sn chsng ldrs: one pce fnl 3f) | | 2.5 |
| 2272[3] | King Optimist **(37)** *(ASmith)* 7-8(1) AMackay (11) (chsd ldrs: chal ½-wy: outpcd fnl 3f) | | 2.6 |
| 1888[1] | Whatcomesnaturally (USA) **(50)** *(MCChapman)* 8-7 SWebster (5) (outpcd & bhd tl styd on fnl 3f) | | 7.7 |
| 1914 | Suzie Sue (IRE) **(54)** *(DWPArbuthnot)* 8-6 ‡5RPrice (1) (lw: hld up & bhd: gd hdwy 8f out: ev ch & rdn 4f out: sn wknd) | | 6.8 |
| 2423[5] | Iron Baron (IRE) **(64)** *(RHollinshead)* 9-7 SPerks (12) (lw: hdwy ½-wy: drvn along 4f out: no imp) | | 2.9 |
| 2386[3] | Top Table **(64)** (Jt-Fav) *(MRStoute)* 9-7 PD'Arcy (9) (lw: chsd ldrs: sn drvn along: lost tch ½-wy) | | 5.10 |
| 2296[5] | Princess Evita (FR) **(38)** *(RGuest)* 7-2(1) ‡7CHawksley (3) (chsd ldrs tl rdn & wknd ½-wy) | | 1½.11 |
| 2630[3] | Monorose **(50)** (v) *(DHaydnJones)* 8-7 SWhitworth (8) (disp ld to ½-wy: sn wknd) | | 1½.12 |

LONG HANDICAP: King Optimist 7-6.

**5/1** Seraphim (FR), Top Table, **7/1** Thor Power (IRE), Invisible Armour, WITCHES COVEN, **10/1** Child Star (FR), **12/1** Iron Baron (IRE), **16/1** King Optimist, **20/1** Monorose, Whatcomesnaturally (USA), **25/1** Suzie Sue (IRE). CSF £46.81, CT £296.88. Tote £5.20: £1.70 £1.60 £1.50 (£20.60). Hambleton Thoroughbreds Plc (NEWMARKET) bred by Glazeley Stud. 12 Rn    3m 8.8 (9.5)

## 2784

PAPER COMPANY H'CAP (0-70) £2532.00 (£702.00: £336.00)
**1½m (AWT)**    4-25 (4-25)

(Weights raised 9 lb)

| | | | |
|---|---|---|---|
| 2698 | **Must Be Magical (USA) (29)** (bl) *(FHLee)* 4–7-13 RLappin (4) (lw: mde all: sn clr: styd on wl fnl 3f) | | —1 |

2656 Pims Classic **(54)** *(JLHarris)* 4–9-5 ‡[5]SMaloney (9) (bhd: hdwy 6f out: styd on: no ch w wnr) .................. 8.2

2692 Grey Commander **(37)** (v) *(MBrittain)* 4–8-7 JLowe (5) (in tch: drvn along 7f out & lost pl: styd on fnl 2f) ................. 2.3

2692[2] Tales of Wisdom **(65)** *(SirMarkPrescott)* 3–9-10 AMunro (2) (lw: a chsng ldrs: drvn along 5f out: r.o one pce) ........... 1½.4

2367[6] Affa **(50)** *(TThomsonJones)* 3–8-9 SWhitworth (6) (a chsng ldrs: effrt 4f out: outpcd fnl 3f) ............... 3½.5

2420[3] Jarras **(37)** (bl) *(CASmith)* 7–8-7 GDuffield (10) (prom: drvn along 5f out: wknd 3f out) ............... 10.6

2103[4] Lunagraphe (USA) **(28)** *(BobJones)* 4–7-5 ‡[7]CHawksley (8) (chsd ldrs tl outpcd 5f out) .................. 6.7

2607 Simply Candy (IRE) **(48)** *(APStringer)* 4–8-13 ‡[5]SWilliams (3) (chsd ldrs tl rdn & outpcd 7f out: sn bhd) .............. 10.8

　　　Colorado Insight **(42)** *(MrsVAAconley)* 4–8-12 LCharnock (1) (t.o ½-wy: n.d after) ................. 1½.9

1889[6] Emma Victoria **(25)** *(TKersey)* 4–7-9[(1)] AMackay (7) (b: lw: t.o ½-wy: n.d) ...... ½.10

**Evens** Tales of Wisdom(op 7/4), **7/1** Grey Commander, **8/1** Jarras, **9/1** Affa, **10/1** MUST BE MAGICAL (USA)(op 5/1), **16/1** Lunagraphe (USA), Pims Classic(op 10/1), **25/1** Simply Candy (IRE), **33/1** Colorado Insight, **50/1** Emma Victoria. CSF £128.52, CT £1,069.05. Tote £9.30: £2.00 £2.70 £1.80 (£67.30). Mr F. H. Lee (WILMSLOW) bred by Flaxman Holdings Ltd in USA. 10 Rn　　2m 40.4 (6.2)
SF—11/15/–/13/–/–

---

**2785**　　UK VEHICLE RENTALS (NOTTINGHAM) CLAIMING STKS　£2910.00 (£810.00: £390.00)　**7f (AWT)**
　　　　　　　　　　　　　　　　　　　　　　　　　　　　　　　4-55 (4-58)

2607 **Spanish Express (47)** *(RBoss)* 3–8-5 AMunro (3) (lw: w ldrs: led ½-wy: r.o u.p fnl 2f) ............... —1

2665★ Patience Please **(70)** (Fav) *(MHEasterby)* 3–7-10[(1)] ‡[5]SMaloney (10) (in tch: hdwy to chase wnr 2f out: r.o: nvr able to chal) ............... 2.2

2688[2] Long Lane Lady **(40)** *(JMackie)* 6–8-0 GHind (9) (a chsng ldrs: styd on fnl 3f: no imp) ............... 3½.3

2614[5] Strip Cartoon (IRE) **(56)** (bl) *(SRBowring)* 4–8-6 ‡[7]MHarris (5) (led to ½-wy: grad wknd) ............... 1½.4

2201[6] Gallery Artist **(60)** *(RGuest)* 4–8-0 ‡[7]SEiffert (8) (chsd ldrs: rdn & c wd st: grad wknd) ............... hd.5

2100[4] Tanana **(47)** *(JGFitzGerald)* 3–8-4[(2)] KFallon (14) (in tch & rdn appr st: no imp after) ............... 2½.6

　　　Lock Keeper (USA) **(58)** *(JMackie)* 6–8-5 LCharnock (11) (t: in tch: rdn 4f out: one pce) ............... 2.7

2469[4] Station Express (IRE) **(28)** *(BEllison)* 4–8-5 GDuffield (1) (nvr nr ldrs) ............... ¾.8

2366[5] Wellsy Lad (USA) **(58)** *(DWChapman)* 5–8-10 SWood (6) (chsd ldrs over 4f: sn wknd) ............... 5.9

2099[6] Hubbers Favourite **(46)** *(MrsNMacauley)* 4–8-4 NDay (15) (n.d) ............... 1.10

2607 Reza **(48)** (bl) *(JLEyre)* 4–8-8 ‡[5]OPears (12) (s.i.s: a bhd) ............... 1½.11

2694 Sennon Cove **(89)** *(MJCharles)* 3–7-8 JLowe (4) (s.i.s: a outpcd & bhd) ............... ½.12

　　　Smiling Sun (IRE) **(89)** *(WAO'Gorman)* 4–8-8 ‡[3]EmmaO'Gorman (2) (b: cl up tl wknd over 2f out) ............... ½.13

2689[3] Have a Nightcap **(47)** *(JLHarris)* 3–7-10 ‡[5]RPrice (13) (nvr wnt pce) ............... nk.14

**5/2** Patience Please, **7/1** Smiling Sun (IRE)(op 7/2), Wellsy Lad (USA), **9/1** SPANISH EXPRESS, **10/1** Long Lane Lady, **14/1** Reza(op 33/1), Strip Cartoon (IRE), **16/1** Tanana, Hubbers Favourite, Gallery Artist (IRE), Have a Nightcap, **20/1** Lock Keeper (USA), **33/1** Ors. CSF £29.49, Tote £6.90: £2.00 £2.00 £1.90 (£10.80). Mr P. Asquith (NEWMARKET) bred by I. W. T. and Mrs Loftus. 14 Rn; Spanish Express clmd Agency FIPS £7,100
1m 29.2 (2.6)
SF—41/26/19/20/13/9

---

**2786**　　GAS WARM HOMES APP'CE H'CAP (0–70) £2532.00 (£702.00: £336.00)　**5f (AWT)**
　　　　　　　　　　　　　　　　　　　　　　　　　　　　　　5-25 (5-32)

2481[3] **The Dream Maker (IRE) (44)** *(MrsNMacauley)* 3–7-7[(5)] ‡[5]MHumphries (8) (a w ldrs: led 2f out: r.o) ............... —1

　　　Imco Double (IRE) **(60)** *(WHolden)* 4–9-4 PTurner (1) (a cl up: disp ld 2f out: r.o) ............... nk.2

2539★ Soba Guest (IRE) **(70)** *(JBerry)* 3–9-3 ‡[7]ADaly (14) (b.nr hind: a chsng ldrs: kpt on wl fnl f) ............... 1.3

2672[5] Don't Run Me Over **(49)** *(BCMorgan)* 3–7-12[(1)] ‡[5]SSanders (10) (led 3f: r.o one pce) ............... 2.4

1853[2] The Shanahan Bay **(56)** (v) *(MrsNMacauley)* 7–9-0 SWynne (6) (b: chsd ldrs tl outpcd 2f out) ............... 1½.5

2310[3] Miss Siham (IRE) **(45)** *(JBalding)* 3–7-8 ‡[5]ClaireBalding (4) (w ldrs tl outpcd fnl f) s.h.6

2680² Kalar (45) (DWChapman) 3-7-13 SMaloney (3) (cl up: kpt on one pce fnl f) .... hd.7
2650³ Fighter Squadron (57) (bl) (Fav) (JAGlover) 3-8-11 SWilliams (7) (outpcd &
bhd: styd on towards fin) .................................................. 1½.8
629⁴ Merryhill Maid (IRE) (70) (JLHarris) 4–10-0 OPears (12) (b.nr fore: sn outpcd &
nvr trbld ldrs) ................................................................... 2½.9
1924⁴ Johanna Thyme (37) (RBastiman) 5–7-4⁽²⁾ ‡⁵TWilson (9) (s.i.s: a outpcd & bhd) ½.10
First Flush (50) (KTIvory) 6–8-3⁽¹²⁾ ‡⁵CScally (13) (b: nvr wnt pce) ................. 2.11
2000 My Abbey (64) (EJAlston) 3–8-11 ‡⁷SKnott (5) (swtg: dwlt: a bhd) .................... 4.12
LONG HANDICAP: The Dream Maker (IRE) 7-3, Johanna Thyme 7-6.
2747 Trioming (10/1) Withdrawn (bolted bef s) : not under orders

2/1 Fighter Squadron, 8/1 Don't Run Me Over, Merryhill Maid (IRE), Soba Guest (IRE), 9/1 The Shanahan Bay,
10/1 Kalar, 12/1 Johanna Thyme, THE DREAM MAKER (IRE), 14/1 Imco Double (IRE), Miss Siham (IRE), 20/1
My Abbey, 25/1 First Flush. CSF £151.31, CT £1,298.82. Tote £17.60: £5.00: £1.60 £2.60 (£715.30). Mr Robert
Dixon (MELTON MOWBRAY) bred by T. Connolly in Ireland. 12 Rn          60.6 sec (2.6)
SF–17/41/36/13/19/3

T/Plpt: £1,152.40 (1 Tckt).                                                              AA

## 2167—NEWBURY (L-H)

### Friday, August 14th [Good to soft, Soft back st]

Going Allowance: 0.30 sec per fur (G)                              Wind: slt half against

Stalls: centre

| **2787** | JACK COLLING POLAR JEST APP'CE H'CAP (3-Y.O) (0-90) £3704.00 (£1112.00: £536.00: £248.00)  **6f 8y** | 2-05 (2-07) |

2227⁴ **Nagida (73)** (JAHToller) 8-6 JWeaver (10) (hdwy £f out: hrd rdn & led over 1f
out: r.o wl) ..................................................................... —1
2663² Bodari (80) (Jt-Fav) (DAWilson) 8-13 DHarrison (9) (a.p: hrd rdn & ev ch 2f out:
r.o ins fnl f) ..................................................................... 1½.2
2559⁶ Arabellajill (88) (RHannon) 9-2 ‡⁵DGibbs (7) (lw: rdn & hdwy 2f out: chal wnr fnl
f: r.o) ............................................................................. hd.3
2411⁶ Walstead (IRE) (61) (DAWilson) 7-11 ‡⁷SharonMillard (11) (lw: lost pl over 3f out:
rallied over 1f out: r.o.) ........................................................ 2.4
2073 Memsahb (80) (JBerry) 8-6 ‡⁷BethanPrys-Jones (1) (led 4f out to 2f out: wknd
over 1f out) ..................................................................... 2.5
2419 Batchworth Bound (64) (bl) (EAWheeler) 7-6⁽⁴⁾ ‡⁵JDSmith (8) (a.p: led 2f out: sn
hdd & wknd) ...................................................................... ¾.6
1870⁵ Lady Roxanne (70) (LordHuntingdon) 7-10 ‡⁷JWilkinson (6) (prom 1t hung lft &
wknd 2f out) ..................................................................... nk.7
833 Beyond the Moon (IRE) (60) (MJFetherston-Godley) 7-7 BDoyle (4) (rdn over
3f out: bhd fnl 2f) .............................................................. ¾.8
2449 The Old Chapel (85) (Jt-Fav) (BAMcMahon) 8-13 ‡⁵SSanders (3) (lw: led 2f: hrd
rdn & wknd 2f out) .............................................................. ½.9
LONG HANDICAP: Batchworth Bound 6-12, Beyond the Moon (IRE) 7-6.

7/2 Bodari(op 2/1), The Old Chapel, 9/2 NAGIDA(op 11/4), 13/2 Memsahb(4/1—7/1), 7/1 Arabellajill(op 4/1),
15/2 Lady Roxanne, 14/1 Walstead (IRE)(op 8/1), 20/1 Ors. CSF £19.48, CT £95.39. Tote £5.00: £5.00 £1.50
£1.90 (£5.70). Miss U. D. Toller (NEWMARKET) bred by Mrs John Trotter. 9 Rn          1m 17.28 (5.48)
SF–18/19/21/–/–/–

| **2788** | NEWTOWN STKS (3-Y.O) £5428.00 (£1508.00: £724.00)  **1½m 5y** | 2-40 (2-41) |

2298* **Million in Mind (IRE)** (MrsJCecil) 9-2 WNewnes (2) (led after 1f: rdn 3f out: r.o
wl) ............................................................................... —1
1447* Welsh Mill (IRE) (88) (Fav) (LordHuntingdon) 9-0 WRSwinburn (1) (lw: 3rd st:
chal wnr 3f out: rdn wl over 1f out: no imp) ...................................... 2½.2
2036 Matching Green (69) (GBBalding) 8-10 JWilliams (3) (led 1f: 2nd st: rdn 4f out:
wknd 2f out) ..................................................................... 7.3

10/11 Welsh Mill (IRE), 13/8 MILLION IN MIND (IRE)(Evens—7/4), 9/2 Matching Green(6/1—7/1). CSF £3.27,
Tote £2.60 (£1.50). The Million in Mind Partnership (NEWMARKET) bred by William Farish in Ireland. 3 Rn
2m 39.02 (9.32)
SF–45/38/20

| **2789** | GARDNER MERCHANT HUNGERFORD STKS (Gp 3)  £19612.80 (£7286.99: £3456.00: £1457.21)  **7f 64y (rnd)** | 3-10 (3-11) |

1253 Mojave (104) (MRStoute) 3-8-8 WRSwinburn (5) (lw: 9th st: rdn 4f out: rapid
hdwy & swtchd over 1f out: led ins fnl f: r.o wl) ................................. —1

2626a\* Pursuit of Love (120) (Fav) *(HRACecil)* 3–8-13 PatEddery (10) (lw: 10th st: rdn 4f out: hdwy 2f out: ev ch ins fnl f: unable qckn) .................... 2.2

1926² Night Manoeuvres (107) *(HCandy)* 3–8-8 CRutter (8) (lw: 7th st: rdn 4f out: hdwy over 1f out: hung rt & r.o ins fnl f) ............................... ¹/₂.3

1817a³ Rami (USA) (110) (bl) *(DKWeld,Ireland)* 5–9-3 MJKinane (6) (6th st: hdwy 2f out: ev ch 1f out: unable qckn) ..................... 1.4

2447⁵ Band on the Run (98) *(BAMcMahon)* 5–9-0 TQuinn (2) (rdn 5f out: 4th st: led over 1f out: sn hdd: one pce) ........................... ³/₄.5

2640\* Bletchley Park (IRE) (101) *(AAScott)* 3–8-8 BRaymond (9) (5th st: led 1f out: sn hdd & wknd) ................................. 1.6

827 Norwich *(BWHills)* 5–9-0 MHills (7) (led over 3f: ev ch over 1f out: wknd fnl f) 1¹/₂.7

2464\* River Falls (113) *(RHannon)* 3–8-13 JReid (4) (lw: 3rd st: ev ch 2f out: wknd over 1f out) .............................. 1¹/₂.8

1197⁶ Sylva Honda (107) *(CEBrittain)* 4–9-3 WCarson (3) (chsd ldr: led 4f out tl wknd over 1f out) ........................... 1¹/₂.9

673² Night Jar (98) *(LordHuntingdon)* 5–8-11 LDettori (1) (8th st: a bhd) ................. 1.10

**4/6** Pursuit of Love, **11/2** Night Manoeuvres, **10/1** Norwich(op 5/1), **11/1** River Falls, Rami (USA), Night Jar, **16/1** MOJAVE(12/1—20/1), **25/1** Sylva Honda, Band on the Run, **33/1** Bletchley Park (IRE). CSF £28.01, Tote £41.90: £6.70 £1.20 £1.60 (£36.10). Sultan Mohammed (NEWMARKET) bred by The Lavington Stud. 10 Rn
1m 31.99 (4.69)
SF—57/56/49/55/50/41

**2790** WASHINGTON SINGER STKS (listed race) (2-Y.O. C & G) £8395.00 (£2500.00: £1190.00: £535.00) **7f (st)** 3-40 (3-41)

2456\* **Tenby (100)** (Fav) *(HRACecil)* 9-0 PatEddery (1) (mde all: rdn 3f out: r.o wl) ..... —1

1944\* Right Win (IRE) (100) *(RHannon)* 8-11 JReid (3) (jnd wnr 3f out: one pce fnl 2f) 4.2

1995⁴ Civil Law (IRE) *(RHollinshead)* 8-11 WRSwinburn (2) (no hdwy fnl 2f) ................. 6.3

2568\* Regalsett (84) *(RHannon)* 8-11 WCarson (4) (spd 4f: wl bhd fnl 2f) ................ 20.4

**4/9** TENBY, **11/4** Right Win (IRE), **7/1** Regalsett, **25/1** Civil Law (IRE). CSF £2.14, Tote £1.40 (£1.50). Mr K. Abdulla (NEWMARKET) bred by Juddmonte Farms. 4 Rn
1m 28.59 (4.09)
SF—70/55/37/—

**2791** LADBROKE RACING H'CAP (0-100) £8025.00 (£2400.00: £1150.00: £525.00) **1¹/₄m 6y** 4-10 (4-14)

(Weights raised 2 lb)

368² **Mesleh (94)** (Fav) *(JHMGosden)* PatEddery (3) (4th st: rdn 4f out: swtchd rt 1f out: led ins fnl f: r.o wl) ................... —1

2529\* Vallance (77) *(PWHarris)* 4–8-7 PaulEddery (7) (2nd st: hrd rdn 3f out: led over 1f out tl ins fnl f: unable qckn) .................... 1¹/₂.2

440\* Muhayaa (USA) (93) *(AAScott)* 3–9-0 WRSwinburn (4) (5th st: hrd rdn over 1f out: one pce fnl f) ............................. 2¹/₂.3

1955³ Shrewd Partner (IRE) (82) *(DRCElsworth)* 3–8-3(1) TQuinn (6) (rdn over 5f out: 6th st: r.o one pce fnl 3f) ..................... 2¹/₂.4

2453⁴ In the Picture (IRE) (82) *(RHannon)* 3–8-3 RHills (9) (7th st: rdn & hdwy over 2f out: wknd fnl f) ................................. ³/₄.5

2347 Sharp Dream (66) *(BSmart)* 4–7-10(3) CRutter (1) (sn led: hdd over 1f out: wknd fnl f) ............................. nk.6

2202² Sovereign Page (USA) (81) *(BHanbury)* 3–7-11 ‡5DHarrison (5) (3rd st: wknd 2f out) ............................... ³/₄.7

LONG HANDICAP: Sharp Dream 7-1.

**5/2** MESLEH, **11/4** In the Picture (IRE), **13/2** Vallance, Sovereign Page (USA), Shrewd Partner (IRE), **7/1** Muhayaa (USA), **33/1** Sharp Dream. CSF £16.72, CT £84.06. Tote £3.40: £2.20 £3.20 (£16.50). Sheikh Ahmed Al Maktoum (NEWMARKET) bred by Barronstown Stud. 7 Rn
2m 9.65 (6.65)
SF—73/53/55/39/38/30

**2792** SPARSHOLT STKS (Mdn 2-Y.O.F) £4337.50 (£1300.00: £625.00: £287.50) **6f 8y** 4-45 (4-49)

2526² **Ribbonwood (USA)** (Fav) *(JHMGosden)* 8-11 WRSwinburn (16) (lw: a.p: led over 1f out: shkn up: easily) ........................ —1

2438 Catherineofaragon (83) *(WGRWightman)* 8-11 JWilliams (10) (a.p: chsd wnr over 1f out: no imp) ........................... 5.2

Dancing Spirit (IRE) *(DRCElsworth)* 8-11 RCochrane (9) (unf: bit bkwd: dwlt: rdn 3f out: hdwy over 1f out: r.o ins fnl f) ............... 1¹/₂.3

2444⁴ Lamu Lady (IRE) *(PWChapple-Hyam)* 8-11 PaulEddery (4) (lw: a.p: led over 2f out tl over 1f out: unable qckn) ................. ³/₄.4

I'M Yours *(RHannon)* 8-11 BRaymond (12) (unf: outpcd: hdwy over 1f out: nvr nrr) .......................... 1¹/₂.5

19574 Newington Butts (IRE) *(RAkehurst)* 8-4 ‡⁷LCarter (8) (a.p: led wl over 1f out: sn hdd & wknd) ............................................................................................ 2¹/₂.6
　　High Finish *(HCandy)* 8-11 WNewnes (15) (lt-f: unf: dwlt: hdwy 2f out: nvr nr to chal) ............................................................................................ nk.7
1591 Ballet *(LordHuntingdon)* 8-11 MJKinane (5) (led over 3f) ........................ ³/₄.8
　　Amrah *(JLDunlop)* 8-11 RHills (7) (unf: bit bkwd: dwlt: rdn 4f out: nvr nrr) .......... 3.9
25575 Petonellajill *(RHannon)* 8-11 JReid (4) (prom 2f) ........................ 1.10
23382 City Times (IRE) *(BAMcMahon)* 8-11 WCarson (6) (prom 4f) ........................ ³/₄.11
　　Misty Jenni (IRE) *(RAkehurst)* 8-11 CRutter (13) (cmpt: bit bkwd: bhd fnl 2f) .... 1.12
　　Guanhumara *(PTWalwyn)* 8-11 NHowe (14) (neat: dwlt: a bhd:) ................ 1¹/₂.13
　　Brightside (IRE) *(PFICole)* 8-11 TQuinn (2) (w'like: bit bkwd: prom over 3f) .... hd.14
　　Diplomatist *(IABalding)* 8-11 LDettori (1) (lw: unf: scope: prom 3f) ................ 1¹/₂.15
　　Apache Myth *(RHannon)* 8-11 PatEddery (11) (w'like: scope: bkwd: t.o fnl 4f) 10.16

**6/5** RIBBONWOOD (USA)(7/4—11/10), **9/2** Lamu Lady (IRE), **8/1** Ballet(12/1—7/1), City Times (IRE)(op 5/1), **12/1** Brightside (IRE)(op 6/1), **14/1** Diplomatist, Dancing Spirit (IRE), Petonellajill(op 8/1), **16/1** Apache Myth(op 10/1), **20/1** I'M Yours, High Finish(8/1—25/1), Catherineofaragon, **33/1** Amrah, **50/1** Ors. CSF £30.70, Tote £2.20: £1.30 £7.50 £4.00 (£89.80). Sheikh Mohammed (NEWMARKET) bred by Darley Stud Management Company Ltd in USA. 16 Rn
　　　　　　　　　　　　　　　　　　　　　　　　　　　　　　1m 16.45 (4.65)
　　　　　　　　　　　　　　　　　　　　　　　　　　　　SF—40/20/14/11/5/–

---

**2793**　　LEVY BOARD H'CAP (3-Y.O) (0-90) £4659.00 (£1392.00: £666.00: £303.00)
　　　　　**2m**　　　　　　　　　　　　　　　　　　　　　5-15 (5-16)

(Weights raised 1 lb)
2497* **Receptionist (74)** *(HRACecil)* 8-11 PatEddery (1) (led 1f: 3rd st: hrd rdn & led wl over 1f out: r.o wl) ............................................................ —1
*2682** Yenoora (IRE) **(68)** *(PFICole)* 8-5 (5x) TQuinn (6) (led after 1f tl over 1f out: unable qckn) ............................................................ 4.2
25242 Puritan (CAN) **(76)** *(GHarwood)* 8-13 WCarson (9) (4th st: r.o one pce fnl 3f) ............................................................ ³/₄.3
2323a3 For Mog (USA) **(84)** *(CEBrittain)* 9-7 BRaymond (3) (lw: 8th st: hrd rdn & hdwy over 2f out: styd on fnl f) ............................................................ ³/₄.4
22673 Newton Point **(74)** *(GAPritchard-Gordon)* 8-11 RCochrane (2) (lw: 5th st: hrd rdn over 2f out: wknd fnl f) ............................................................ 1¹/₂.5
15924 Lobinda **(80)** *(JLDunlop)* 9-3 JReid (4) (9th st: rdn 3f out: nvr nr to chal) .......... 4.6
22283 Highland Battle (USA) **(68)** *(IABalding)* 8-5 PaulEddery (5) (lw: 2nd st: wknd over 2f out: t.o) ............................................................ 12.7
23703 Anditisitis (USA) **(64)** *(DWPArbuthnot)* 7-10 ‡5DHarrison (7) (lw: 7th st: wl bhd fnl 3f: t.o) ............................................................ 5.8
26646 Bar Billiards **(67)** (bl) *(RFJohnsonHoughton)* 8-4⁽¹⁾ JWilliams (8) (lw: 6th st: wknd over 3f out: t.o) ............................................................ 2.9

**100/30** Puritan (CAN)(5/1—3/1), **4/1** Newton Point, Yenoora (IRE), **11/2** For Mog (USA), **6/1** RECEPTIONIST, **9/1** Highland Battle (USA), **10/1** Lobinda, **20/1** Bar Billiards, **25/1** Anditisitis (USA). CSF £29.31, CT £86.04. Tote £6.70: £1.70 £1.60 £2.10 (£19.70). Cliveden Stud (NEWMARKET) bred by Cliveden Stud. 9 Rn
　　　　　　　　　　　　　　　　　　　　　　　　　　　　　　3m 36.32 (9.62)
　　　　　　　　　　　　　　　　　　　　　　　　　SF—49/39/46/53/41/43

T/Trio: Race 3: £62.50 (21.1 Tckts); Race 5: £19.70 (50.7 Tckts). T/Jkpt: Not won; £3,434.85 to Newbury 15/8/92. T/Plpt: £27.60 (215.8 Tckts).　　　　　　　　　　　　　　　　　LMc

---

# NEWBURY (L-H)
## Saturday, August 15th [Good]
Going Allowance: 0.20 sec per fur (G)　　　　　　　　　　　Wind: mod across

Stalls: centre

**2794**　　ST HUGH'S STKS (listed race) (2-Y.O.F) £8941.00 (£2668.00: £1274.00: £577.00)
　　　　　**5f 34y**　　　　　　　　　　　　　　　　　　2-00 (2-01)

24522 **Palacegate Episode (IRE) (100)** (Fav) *(JBerry)* 8-8 GCarter (5) (mde all: clr 2f out: unchal) ............................................................ —1
2452 Hamsah (IRE) **(94)** *(DRCElsworth)* 8-8 JWilliams (2) (outpcd: rdn over 2f out: hdwy over 1f out: nvr nrr) ............................................................ 5.2
2176 Risk Me's Girl (bl) *(RHannon)* 8-8 WRSwinburn (6) (chsd wnr tl wknd fnl f) 2.3
2002 Ballon *(CEBrittain)* 8-8 RCochrane (4) (outpcd: hrd rdn over 1f out: n.d) ........ 2¹/₂.4
2414* Bangles **(80)** *(LordHuntingdon)* 8-8 MRoberts (1) (prom: rdn 2f out: wknd fnl f) ¹/₂.5
1635* Chatterberry **(93)** *(LJHolt)* 8-8 LDettori (3) (lw: prom: rdn & hung rt over 2f out: sn wknd & eased) ............................................................ 20.6

5/6 PALACEGATE EPISODE (IRE), 7/2 Chatterberry, 13/2 Bangles, 8/1 Risk Me's Girl(6/1—9/1), 10/1 Hamsah (IRE), 33/1 Ballon. CSF £8.92, Tote £1.80: £1.20 £5.20 (£9.90). Palacegate Corporation Ltd (COCKERHAM) bred by Brendan and Sheila Powell in Ireland. 6 Rn
63.28 sec (2.58)
SF—62/42/34/24/22/–

**2795**   EUROLINK SILVER TROPHY (H'cap) (3-Y.O) (0-90) £8344.00 (£2512.00: £1216.00: £568.00)   **7f (st)**
2-30 (2-34)

19285 **Louisville Belle (IRE) (64)** *(MDIUsher)* 7-8 ‡5DHarrison (1) (hdwy over 2f out: led over 1f out: edgd bdly rt: r.o) ....................... —1

2126 Ahbab (IRE) (76) *(PTWalwyn)* 8-11 RCochrane (16) (hdwy 2f out: ev ch over 1f out: btn whn hmpd ins fnl f: fin 3rd, 2l: plcd 2nd) ................. 2

1974* Laundry Maid (82) *(HCandy)* 9-3 CRutter (11) (led: hdd over 1f out: edgd rt ins fnl f: r.o: fin 2nd, btn ¾l: disq: plcd 3rd) ............. 3

2655* Our Occasion (74) *(WJMusson)* 8-9 WRSwinburn (15) (hdwy 2f out: one pce fnl f) ........................ 2.4

850 Abbey Strand (USA) (72) *(LordHuntingdon)* 8-7 LDettori (4) (a.p: ev ch 2f out: one pce) ........................ 1.5

1533 Clare Kerry Lass (77) *(JRFanshawe)* 8-5 ‡7NVarley (5) (hdwy over 1f out: nvr nrr) ........................ ½.6

2723 Boy Martin (69) *(MJohnston)* 8-4 DMcKeown (6) (a.p: no hdwy fnl 2f) ........... 2½.7

2666² The New Girl (62) *(CCElsey)* 7-11 NAdams (9) (w ldr: ev ch 2f out: sn wknd) .. nk.8

2275* Lady Debra Darley (84) (Fav) *(RHannon)* 9-5 MRoberts (3) (hdwy 3f out: ev ch 2f out: wknd over 1f out) ........................ 2½.9

983 Magnificent (74) *(MAJarvis)* 8-4 ‡5RCutter (7) (swtg: n.d) ............... nk.10

2552* First Gold (68) *(JWharton)* 8-3 JQuinn (2) (lw: hdwy 3f out: ev ch 2f out: sn wknd) ........................ 1½.11

2449 Threepence (86) *(JBerry)* 9-7 GCarter (13) (bhd fnl 2f) ............... ¾.12

2341 Haroldon (IRE) (81) *(BPalling)* 8-11 ‡5StephenDavies (14) (prom: rdn & wknd over 2f out) ........................ 3.13

2787⁴ Walstead (IRE) (61) *(DAWilson)* 7-10 NCarlisle (8) (prom: hrd rdn 3f out: sn wknd) ........................ nk.14

1941 Risk Master (80) *(CAHorgan)* 9-1 AMcGlone (12) (lw: prom over 4f) ........... 1½.15

2268 Sylvan Sabre (IRE) (82) *(PMitchell)* 9-3 SWhitworth (10) (rdn 3f out: sn bhd) .. ¾.16

*Stewards Enquiry: Laundry Maid disq. (interference to Ahbab (IRE)). C Rutter suspended 24-27/8/92 (careless riding).*

13/2 Lady Debra Darley, 8/1 Abbey Strand (USA), 10/1 Our Occasion, Magnificent, Laundry Maid, Haroldon (IRE), First Gold(8/1—12/1), 12/1 Risk Master, Clare Kerry Lass, 14/1 Michael (IRE), The New Girl, Threepence, 16/1 LOUISVILLE BELLE (IRE), 20/1 Boy Martin, 33/1 Ors. CSF £197.15, CT £2,121.65. Tote £17.30: £2.80 £3.60 £2.30 £2.00 (£162.00). Mrs M. P. Pearson (EAST GARSTON) bred by Ballydoyle Partnership in Ireland. 16 Rn
1m 28.12 (3.62)
SF—47/68/59/50/45/41

**2796**   IBN BEY GEOFFREY FREER STKS (Gp 2) £43976.40 (£16395.12: £7822.56: £3349.92)   **1m 5f 61y**
3-00 (3-03)

1842 **Shambo** *(CEBrittain)* 5-9-3 MRoberts (4) (hld up: last st: hdwy 2f out: led over 1f out: drvn out) ........................ —1

2345⁴ Sapience (v) *(DRCElsworth)* 6-9-6 RCochrane (3) (chsd ldr: 2nd st: led 3f out tl over 1f out: r.o) ........................ ½.2

2345⁵ Rock Hopper (Fav) *(MRStoute)* 5-9-6 PatEddery (2) (hld up: 3rd st: rdn & outpcd over 2f out: rallied & ev ch 1f out: r.o) ........................ ¾.3

2136* Michelozzo (USA) *(RHannon)* 6-9-9 JLloyd (1) (led tl hdd 3f out: sn rdn: wknd 2f out: eased fnl f) ........................ 12.4

11/10 Rock Hopper, 6/4 Sapience, 9/1 SHAMBO, 10/1 Michelozzo (USA). CSF £20.58, Tote £8.50: (£6.40). Mrs C. E. Brittain (NEWMARKET) bred by Mrs C. E. Brittain. 4 Rn
3m 1.98 (16.28)

**2797**   STRATTON H'CAP (0-90) £3720.00 (£1110.00: £530.00: £240.00)   **5f 34y**
3-35 (3-37)

(Weights raised 2 lb)

2192² **Cradle Days (88)** *(RHannon)* 3-9-10 MRoberts (7) (hdwy 2f out: led ins fnl f: drvn out) ........................ —1

2290 Yes (53) *(DTThom)* 4-7-0 ‡7KimMcDonnell (3) (hdwy over 2f out: led over 1f out tl hdd & edgd rt ins fnl f) ........................ 1½.2

2395⁶ Darussalam (67) (Fav) *(RLee)* 5-8-7 PatEddery (10) (hdwy 2f out: hrd rdn & ev ch over 1f out: nt qckn ins fnl f) ........................ ½.3

2465 Olifantsfontein (79) *(RSimpson)* 4-9-5 GCarter (2) (a.p: hrd rdn over 1f out: nt qckn) ........................ 1½.4

2650 Sylvan Breeze (78) (bl) *(PMitchell)* 4-9-4 SWhitworth (9) (no hdwy fnl 2f) ......... ¾.5

1631 Seneca Reef (IRE) (79) *(IABalding)* 4-9-5 RCochrane (1) (spd 3f) ............... 1½.6

2476⁵ Ballasecret **(72)** *(RDickin)* 4–8–12 JWilliams (5) (w ldr over 2f: sn wknd) ......... 2¹/₂.**7**
2642 Petraco (IRE) **(73)** (bl) *(LJCodd)* 4–8–6 ‡⁷WHollick (6) (spd 3f) ......................... nk.**8**
2604³ Paley Prince (USA) **(82)** *(MDIUsher)* 6–9–8 WRSwinburn (4) (a bhd) ................. hd.**9**
2127² Gone Savage **(77)** *(GBBalding)* 4–9–3 LDettori (8) (led over 3f: wknd qckly) . 2¹/₂.**10**

**7/2** Darussalam, **6/1** CRADLE DAYS, Seneca Reef (IRE), Gone Savage(op 4/1), **7/1** Petraco (IRE), **8/1** Olifantsfontein(6/1—9/1), **12/1** Paley Prince (USA)(op 8/1), Ballasecret, **14/1** Ors. CSF £74.44, CT £306.46. Tote £5.60: £2.20 £3.70 £2.20 (£47.30). Mr T. A. Johnsey (MARLBOROUGH) bred by T. A. Johnsey. 10 Rn
63.79 sec (3.09)
SF—68/24/43/49/45/40

**2798**  AUGUST STKS (H'cap) (3-Y.O) (0-105) £7304.00 (£2192.00: £1056.00: £488.00)
1¹/₂m 5y                                                                                      4-10 (4-10)

2331* Last Embrace (IRE) **(80)** *(LordHuntingdon)* 7-12 ‡⁵DHarrison (1) (hld up: last
st: stdy hdwy 3f out: rdn to ld ins fnl f: r.o wl) ......................... —**1**
1346 Poinciana **(72)** *(RHannon)* 7-9 NCarlisle (5) (lw: hld up: 4th st: rdn over 2f out:
styd on ins fnl f) ........................................................ 1¹/₂.**2**
2453 Let's Get Lost **(73)** *(WJHaggas)* 7-10 JQuinn (7) (led tl ins fnl f) ......................... ¹/₂.**3**
2434⁴ Milzig (USA) **(98)** *(DRCElsworth)* 9-7 JWilliams (4) (lw: 3rd st: one pce fnl 2f) .... 2.**4**
2178² Crystal Cross (USA) **(83)** *(IABalding)* 8-6 RCochrane (2) (lw: hld up: 6th st: rdn
& wknd over 2f out) .................................................. 2¹/₂.**5**
1997³ Greek Gold (IRE) **(87)** (Fav) *(MRStoute)* 8-10 PatEddery (3) (chsd ldr: 2nd st:
hung lft 3f out: eased over 1f out: fin lame) .................... 7.**6**
2168² Tafrah (IRE) **(79)** *(MajorWRHern)* 8-2 GCarter (6) (hld up: 5th st: wknd over 2f
out: sn t.o) ..................................................... 15.**7**

**3/1** Greek Gold (IRE), **7/2** LAST EMBRACE (IRE), Tafrah (IRE), **11/2** Crystal Cross (USA), **8/1** Let's Get Lost(6/1—9/1), Poinciana, **11/1** Milzig (USA)(8/1—12/1). CSF £27.69, Tote £5.50: £2.90 £3.80 (£27.30). Mr E. J. Loder (WEST ILCLEY) bred by E. J. Loder. 7 Rn
2m 37.74 (8.04)
SF—28/22/22/43/23/13

**2799**  E.B.F. YATTENDON STKS (Mdn 2-Y.O. C & G) £4175.00 (£1250.00: £600.00: £275.00)
7f (st)                                                                                       4-45 (4-48)

Eurolink Thunder *(JLDunlop)* 9-0 LDettori (9) (lenghty: a.p: led over 1f out: r.o) —**1**
Mujaazafah (USA) *(JHMGosden)* 9-0 WRSwinburn (14) (w'like: scope: gd
hdwy over 1f out: r.o ins fnl f) ................................... 1.**2**
Frescade (USA) *(PFICole)* 9-0 DMcKeown (2) (gd sort: led over 3f: rallied fnl f:
r.o) ......................................................... s.h.**3**
Wootton Rivers *(PWChapple-Hyam)* 9-0 SWhitworth (7) (w'like: a.p: ev
ch 1f out: r.o) .............................................. hd.**4**
2456² Pistol (IRE) **(93)** (Fav) *(PFICole)* 9-0 TQuinn (11) (led over 3f out tl over 1f out: nt
qckn ins fnl f) ............................................... 1¹/₂.**5**
Ecu de France (IRE) *(JLDunlop)* 9-0 NCarlisle (6) (cmpt: stdy hdwy fnl 2f: r.o) s.h.**6**
2598⁶ The Executor *(RFJohnsonHoughton)* 9-0 JLloyd (15) (a.p: no hdwy fnl 2f) ...... ³/₄.**7**
Bitter's End (IRE) *(RHannon)* 9-0 MRoberts (1) (w'like: scope: prom over 5f) ... hd.**8**
American Swinger (USA) *(PWHarris)* 9-0 JQuinn (5) (w'like: scope: prom over 4f) 5.**9**
9885 Law Commission *(DRCElsworth)* 9-0 JWilliams (12) (hdwy 3f out: wknd over 1f
out) ......................................................... nk.**10**
Euphonic *(IABalding)* 9-0 RCochrane (10) (unf: scope: s.s: a bhd) ............... s.h.**11**
Mislemani (IRE) *(MRStoute)* 9-0 PatEddery (17) (unf: scope: bhd fnl 2f) ......... 4.**12**
1610 Akenside *(DRCElsworth)* 9-0 GCarter (4) (n.d) ........................................... nk.**13**
Ground Nut (IRE) *(HCandy)* 9-0 CRutter (4) (w'like: prom over 4f) ............... 2.**14**
Sheer Ecstasy *(RCharlton)* 9-0 SRaymont (13) (w'like: n.d) ...................... 1.**15**
2398⁴ Glorious Island *(RFJohnsonHoughton)* 8-9 ‡⁵DHarrison (16) (m.n.s) ............ s.h.**16**
2167 Highland Host *(JLDunlop)* 9-0 AMcGlone (18) (n.d) ................................ 2.**17**
My Harvinski *(PWChapple-Hyam)* 8-11 ‡³RPerham (3) (unf: prom 4f: t.o) ........... **18**

**3/1** Pistol (IRE)(tchd 6/1), **4/1** EUROLINK THUNDER, **5/1** Mislemani (IRE), **10/1** Bitter's End (IRE), Euphonic(7/1—12/1), **11/1** Mujaazafah (USA)(6/1—12/1), **12/1** Law Commission, **16/1** Wootton Rivers (USA), **20/1** Frescade (USA), **25/1** Ground Nut (IRE), The Executor, **33/1** Ors. CSF £44.91, Tote £5.00: £1.90 £4.00 £4.10 (£45.50). Eurolink Computer Services Ltd (ARUNDEL) bred by Genesis Green Stud. 18 Rn
1m 29.85 (5.35)
SF—40/37/36/35/30/29

**2800**  LEVY BOARD NURSERY  £4581.00 (£1368.00: £654.00: £297.00)
7f 64y (rnd)  (Weights raised 3 lb)                                           5-15 (5-17)

2590* After the Last **(69)** (Fav) *(RHannon)* 7-10 NCarlisle (3) (hld up: 3rd st: shkn up
to ld over 1f out: sn clr) ...................................... —**1**
2462⁴ Embankment (IRE) **(81)** *(RHannon)* 8-8 MRoberts (7) (lw: led tl rdn & hdd over
1f out: nt qckn) ............................................. 3¹/₂.**2**

2387² Captain le Saux (IRE) **(94)** *(MBell)* 9-7  MHills (1) (last st: hdwy 2f out: nt rch ldrs) .......... 6.3
2130  Hawl (USA) **(86)** *(AAScott)* 8-13  WRSwinburn (5) (4th st: rdn 4f out: wknd 2f out) .......... 3.4
2462  Premium **(74)** *(WJHaggas)* 8-1  JQuinn (4) (6th st: a bhd) .......... 2.5
2456⁴ Aberdeen Heather **(88)** *(DRCElsworth)* 9-1  JWilliams (2) (5th st: a bhd) .......... 1½.6
2577² War Requiem (IRE) **(70)** *(GBBalding)* 7-11  NAdams (6) (2nd st: rdn & wknd 2f out) .......... ½.7

5/2 AFTER THE LAST, 4/1 Embankment (IRE), 11/2 Captain le Saux (IRE), 13/2 Premium, 7/1 War Requiem (IRE), Hawl (USA), 8/1 Aberdeen Heather. CSF £12.09, Tote £3.00: £2.00 £1.90 (£4.80). Mr Roger Barby (MARLBOROUGH) bred by Sagittarius Bloodstock Agency. 7 Rn    1m 31.89 (4.59)
SF—34/35/30/14/–/4

T/Trio: Race 2: £414.40 (6.1 Tckts). T/Jkpt: Not won; £6,680.40 to York 18/8/92. T/Plpt: £9,540.40 (1.05 Tckts).
KH

2681—**LINGFIELD (L-H)**

## Saturday, August 15th [AWT Standard, Turf Good, Good to firm back st]

Going Allowance: Turf: minus 0.20 (F); AWT: minus 0.40 sec (FS)    Wind: almost nil

Stalls: centre

**2801**  TWENTY-ONE TODAY STKS (Mdn 3-Y.O) £2385.00 (£660.00: £315.00)
2m
2-20 (2-22)

2562³ **Desert Peace (IRE) (72)** (bl) *(PFICole)* 9-0  TQuinn (7) (led 7f out: rdn clr 3f out: eased ins 1nl f) .......... —1
2497² Shesadelight (Fav) *(JLDunlop)* 8-9  GDuffield (2) (lw: led 9f: 3rd st: hrd rdn 3f out: styd on fnl 2f) .......... 3.2
2455⁶ Super Sarena (IRE) **(75)** *(RSimpson)* 8-9  BRouse (11) (chsd wnr 6f out: 2nd st: hrd rdn 2f out: one pce) .......... 1½.3
2687  Unique Tribute *(CACyzer)* 9-0  DBiggs (9) (4th st: no hdwy fnl 3f) .......... 3.4
857  Rose of Macmillion *(MrsBarbaraWaring)* 8-9  NHowe (6) (rdn 6f out: 5th & btn st) .......... ½.5
1800  Bashamah (IRE) **(49)** *(CEBrittain)* 8-9  GCrealock (8) (nvr nr to chal) .......... 7.6
2498³ Shanti Flyer (IRE) **(47)** (bl) *(SPCWoods)* 8-2  ‡⁷ALiggins (4) (prom 11f: 6th & wkng st) .......... 8.7
256  Copy Lane (IRE) **(52)** *(MRChannon)* 9-0  LornaVincent (10) (a bhd) .......... 3½.8
2549  The Grey Texan *(MissBSanders)* 9-0  MHills (5) (lw: a bhd) .......... 5.9
2549  Kalokagathos *(CGCox)* 9-0  DaleGibson (4) (a bhd: t.o) .......... 10.10
2239⁶ Alton Belle **(50)** *(PHowling)* 8-9  JMurray (1) (a bhd: t.o fnl 4f) .......... 20.11

8/11 Shesadelight(op 5/4), 100/30 DESERT PEACE (IRE)(2/1—7/2), 9/2 Super Sarena (IRE), 20/1 Bashamah (IRE), 33/1 Unique Tribute, Copy Lane (IRE), 50/1 The Grey Texan, Alton Belle, Rose of Macmillion, Shanti Flyer (IRE), 66/1 Kalokagathos. CSF £5.83, Tote £3.50: £1.40 £1.00 £2.30 (£2.50). Mr Yahya Nasib (WHATCOMBE) bred by Hamilton Bloodstock (UK) Ltd in Ireland. 11 Rn    3m 35.22 (11.22)

**2802**  CROCKHAM HILL (S) STKS (2-Y.O) £2658.00 (£738.00: £354.00)
6f (AWT)
2-50 (2-54)

2563  **Stroika (IRE)** *(CJames)* 8-6  GBaxter (2) (lw: a.p: led over 1f out: drvn out) .......... —1
2681⁴ Poly Vision (IRE) **(68)** *(MRChannon)* 8-11  TQuinn (1) (swtg: hdwy 3f out: r.o one pce fnl 2f) .......... 4.2
2299³ The Wend **(54)** *(DTThom)* 8-3  ‡3SO'Gorman (9) (a.p: one pce fnl 2f) .......... s.h.3
703  Always Risky **(57)** *(PAKelleway)* 8-6  GayKelleway (8) (lw: led over 4f: wknd ins fnl f) .......... nk.4
1036² By Rubies (Fav) *(BWHills)* 8-6  MHills (11) (rdn & hdwy over 1f out: nvr nrr) .......... 2½.5
2500³ Stapleford Lass *(SPCWoods)* 8-6  WWoods (10) (swtg: hdwy 3f out: nvr nr to chal) .......... 2½.6
2516⁴ Daily Sport's Gift **(56)** *(JBerry)* 8-11  GDuffield (5) (lw: dwlt: hdwy 4f out: wknd over 1f out) .......... ½.7
1170⁶ Swiftlet (IRE) **(66)** *(DJSCosgrove)* 8-6  AShoults (3) (prom 3f) .......... 1.8
2598  Fanfold (IRE) *(AWDenson)* 8-1  ‡5BDoyle (6) (rdn 4f out: wknd wl over 1f out) .......... 4.9
2488³ Critical Mass **(57)** *(JBerry)* 8-11  MTebbutt (5) (bhd fnl 2f) .......... 1½.10
2008⁵ Melisio *(CPWildman)* 8-6  DBiggs (14) (a bhd) .......... hd.11
Generous Ben *(JSutcliffe)* 8-11  BRouse (4) (lw: neat: bhd fnl 2f) .......... s.h.12
973  Young Absalom *(LGCottrell)* 8-11  TRogers (13) (dwlt: a bhd) .......... 6.13

2/1 By Rubies, 11/4 Poly Vision (IRE)(9/4—4/1), 9/1 Melisio(op 16/1), 10/1 Critical Mass(8/1—12/1), 12/1 Generous Ben(op 8/1), Stapleford Lass(op 8/1), 14/1 Daily Sport's Gift(10/1—16/1), 16/1 Always Risky, 25/1 STROIKA (IRE), Swiftlet (IRE), The Wend, 50/1 Ors. CSF £88.55, Tote £39.70: £11.70 £1.50 £3.20 (£90.20). Mr Barry J. Ross (NEWBURY) bred by T. C. Butler in Ireland. 13 Rn; Bt in 5,200 gns    1m 13.34 (2.74)

## 2803

TANIA ANSLOW STKS (Mdn 3-Y.O.F) £2469.00 (£684.00: £327.00)　　**7f**　3-20 (3-24)

1086² **Arboretum (IRE) (67)** *(RCharlton)* 8-11 TQuinn (2) (racd alone far side: mde virtually all: clr fnl f: easily) ............................ —1

2659² Climbing High *(IABalding)* 8-8 ‡³SO'Gorman (9) (lw: hdwy 3f out: led stands' side over 1f out: no ch w wnr) ............................ 6.2

2293⁵ Mashaaer (USA) *(RWArmstrong)* 8-11 BCrossley (7) (swtg: led stands' side over 5f: unable qckn) ............................ hd.3

Hamaya (USA) (Fav) *(JHMGosden)* 8-11 MHills (6) (unf: scope: hdwy 3f out: one pce fnl 2f) ............................ 1.4

2654⁵ Shakreen (USA) (67) *(MrsLPiggott)* 8-11 MTebbutt (3) (prom 5f) ......... 1½.5

2567⁴ Casting Shadows *(RDickin)* 8-11 AClark (10) (rdn over 2f out: nvr nrr) ............ 1½.6

*1852²* Nellie Dean (71) *(JARToller)* 8-11 GDuffield (5) (prom 5f) ............ 2½.7

2432 Guiting Girl *(HCandy)* 8-11 SDawson (4) (nvr nr to chal) ............ nk.8

510 Our Emma (50) *(MrsBarbaraWaring)* 8-11 NHowe (8) (spd over 3f) ............ 3.9

1577 Red-Michelle *(EAWheeler)* 8-11 GBardwell (1) (prom over 3f) ............ 10

**15/8** Hamaya (USA), **2/1** Climbing High, **6/1** ARBORETUM (IRE), **7/1** Mashaaer (USA)(8/1—12/1), **12/1** Casting Shadows, **16/1** Nellie Dean, **20/1** Guiting Girl, Shakreen (USA), **66/1** Ors. CSF £17.54, Tote £5.40: £1.80 £1.10 £2.70 (£6.60). Exors of the late Mrs J. de Rothschild (BECKHAMPTON) bred by Mount Coote Stud in Ireland. 10 Rn
　　　　　　　　　　　1m 23.05 (1.75)
　　　　　　　　　　　SF—50/29/31/28/23/18

## 2804

FELIXSTOWE H'CAP (0-90) £2924.00 (£872.00: £416.00: £188.00)
6f (AWT)　　　　　　　3-50 (3-53)

2772³ **Harry's Coming (70)** *(RJHodges)* 8-8-7 ‡⁷SDrowne (1) (lw: mde virtually all: rdn out) ............................ —1

2592 Assignment (72) *(JFfitch-Heyes)* 6-9-2 AClark (8) (lw: prom whn hmpd 5f out: hrd rdn & rallied over 1f out: r.o) ............................ 2.2

2472³ Ponsardin (83) (Fav) *(SirMarkPrescott)* 3-9-8 GDuffield (9) (outpcd: hdwy 2f out: hrd rdn over 1f out: r.o ins fnl f) ............................ hd.3

2772 One Magic Moment (IRE) (51) *(CACyzer)* 4-7-9⁽²⁾ DBiggs (10) (a.p: ev ch wl over 1f out: unable qckn) ............................ hd.4

515 Sally's Son (81) *(WAO'Gorman)* 6-9-8 ‡³EmmaO'Gorman (4) (bit bkwd: rdn over 2f out: nvr nr to chal) ............................ 4.5

*2411²* Palacegate Racing (72) *(JBerry)* 3-8-11 MTebbutt (5) (spd over 4f) ............ 1.6

2604⋆ Forest Fairy (65) *(RBoss)* 3-8-4 NDay (6) (no hdwy fnl 3f) ............ 1½.7

1576 Trove (82) *(MrsNMacauley)* 3-9-4 ‡³SO'Gorman (3) (spd 4f) ............ ½.8

2141 Super Heights (56) (bl) *(MissAJWhitfield)* 4-8-0 DaleGibson (2) (lw: a bhd) ............ 3.9

2410 Toshiba Comet (77) (bl) *(BBeasley)* 5-9-7 DNicholls (7) (swtg: rn wd bnds: a bhd) ............ 5.10

**LONG HANDICAP:** One Magic Moment (IRE) 6-12.

**7/2** Ponsardin, **4/1** Forest Fairy, **5/1** Palacegate Racing(op 9/1), **7/1** HARRY'S COMING, **10/1** Assignment, Sally's Son, **14/1** Toshiba Comet(op 8/1), **16/1** Trove, **33/1** One Magic Moment (IRE). CSF £63.44, CT £253.26. Tote £7.80: £2.20 £2.50 £1.50 (£46.60). Mrs D. A. Wetherall (SOMERTON) bred by T. E. Herring. 10 Rn
　　　　　　　　　　　1m 11.98 (1.38)
　　　　　　　　　　　SF—17/18/23/—/6/—

## 2805

SAXBY H'CAP (0-80) £2962.80 (£820.80: £392.40)　　**1¼m (AWT)**　　4-25 (4-27)

2754⋆ **Smiling Chief (IRE) (58)** (Fav) *(CACyzer)* 4-9-0 (4x) DBiggs (10) (lw: hdwy 5f out: chsd ldr 2f out: hrd rdn fnl f: led last stride) ............................ —1

225 Belmoredean (72) *(RJO'Sullivan)* 7-10-0 AClark (6) (a.p: led 3f out: clr over 1f out: hrd rdn fnl f: ct last stride) ............................ s.h.2

2125⁶ Tiger Shoot (50) (v) *(DJSCosgrove)* 5-8-6 AShoults (5) (swtg: rdn 5f out: gd hdwy 2f out: r.o) ............................ 6.3

2607⁶ Breezed Well (65) *(CNAllen)* 6-9-0 ‡⁷GForster (1) (nvr nrr) ............ 7.4

2656 Usa Dollar (72) (bl) *(BGubby)* 5-10-0 GBaxter (12) (lw: hdwy 3f out: nvr nr to chal) ............ s.h.5

*2407* Slight Risk (72) *(PAKelleway)* 3-9-5 GayKelleway (11) (eyeshield: led 5f out to 3f out: wknd 2f out) ............ 3½.6

777⁵ Tenayestelign (45) *(DMarks)* 4-8-1 GDuffield (7) (prom 8f) ............ s.h.7

2483⁴ Premier Dance (51) *(DHaydnJones)* 5-8-2 ‡⁵RPrice (2) (bhd fnl 4f) ............ 1.8

2403 Gachette (62) *(JSutcliffe)* 3-8-9 BRouse (3) (lw: prom 6f) ............ 1.9

2413 Dr Zeva (44) *(MDixon)* 6-7-9⁽¹⁾ ‡⁵ATucker (8) (lw: rdn 7f out: a bhd) ............ 4.10

2476 Cheveley Dancer (USA) (70) *(AWDenson)* 4-9-12 NHowe (4) (led 5f: t.o) ...... 15.11

Haverton (40) *(TCasey)* 5-7-10 DaleGibson (9) (bit bkwd: prom 4f: wl bhd fnl 4f: t.o) ............ 2.12

4/1 SMILING CHIEF (IRE), 5/1 Tiger Shoot, 11/2 Gachette(10/1—5/1), 6/1 Usa Dollar(op 10/1), 7/1 Premier Dance, 11/1 Slight Risk, Breezed Well, 14/1 Belmoredean, Dr Zeva, Tenayestelign, 33/1 Cheveley Dancer (USA), 40/1 Haverton. CSF 53.30, CT £263.13. Tote £5.20: £1.70 £5.40 £1.90 (£30.10). Mr R. M. Cyzer (HORSHAM) bred by Thoroughbred Breeding Stock Agency in Ireland. 12 Rn
2m 5.24 (2.24)
SF—38/51/17/11/24/8

**2806**   ANZANI H'CAP (0-80) £2988.00 (£828.00: £396.00)   1m 3f 106y   5-00 (5-01)

| | | |
|---|---|---|
| 2355⁵ | **Sword Master (68)** *(BobJones)* 3–9-2 NDay (1) (lw: chsd ldr: led 3f out: drvn out) | —1 |
| 2529² | Rising Tempo (IRE) **(59)** (Fav) *(CACyzer)* 4–9-3 DBiggs (2) (lw: 4th st: hrd rdn & ev ch fnl f: r.o) | ½.2 |
| 2415⁶ | L'Uomo Classics **(65)** *(RRowe)* 5–9-9 GBaxter (3) (3rd st: one pce fnl 2f) | 5.3 |
| 2685² | Wayward Son **(49)** *(GLewis)* 3–7-6⁽⁴⁾ ‡⁵BDoyle (5) (hld up: 7th st: rdn over 3f out: styd on fnl f) | 3.4 |
| 2602⁵ | Cathos (FR) **(53)** *(DAWilson)* 7–8-11 BRouse (7) (b: rdn 6f out: nvr nr to chal) | 1.5 |
| 2600* | Amazon Express **(58)** *(CEBrittain)* 3–8-6 GDuffield (4) (led over 8f: wknd 2f out) | hd.6 |
| | Absent Relative **(66)** *(MissBSanders)* 4–9-10 MTebbutt (8) (lw: 5th st: no hdwy fnl 3f) | 1.7 |
| | Royal Verse (FR) **(48)** *(RCurtis)* 5–8-6 GBardwell (9) (bkwd: a bhd) | 6.8 |
| 2255 | Snickersnee **(55)** (bl) *(MDixon)* 4–8-13 AClark (6) (lw: hdwy 5f out: 6th st: wknd 3f out: t.o) | 25.9 |

LONG HANDICAP: Wayward Son 7-4.

9/4 Rising Tempo (IRE), 5/2 Amazon Express, 5/1 Cathos (FR), 8/1 Wayward Son, 17/2 SWORD MASTER, 10/1 L'Uomo Classics(op 6/1), 20/1 Absent Relative, 33/1 Snickersnee, 50/1 Royal Verse (FR). CSF £26.61, CT £179.27. Tote £10.60: £1.70 £1.10 £4.10 (£13.10). Mr Ian A. Vogt (NEWMARKET) bred by A. Carr and Son (Hexham) Ltd. 9 Rn
2m 29.36 (7.36)
SF—6/6/2/–/–/–

**2807**   BLACKBERRY LANE APP'CE H'CAP (0-70) £2448.00 (£678.00: £324.00)
7f 140y   5-30 (5-33)

| | | |
|---|---|---|
| 2570⁵ | **Night Transaction (47)** *(AHide)* 5–9-1 NVarley (13) (hld up: led over 2f out: comf) | —1 |
| 2750 | Hightown-Princess (IRE) **(34)** (v) *(JSMoore)* 4–8-2 RossBerry (10) (stdy hdwy 3f out: chsd wnr over 1f out: no imp) | 3.2 |
| 2666⁴ | Countercheck (IRE) **(55)** *(CFWall)* 3–9-2 TWilson (9) (lost pl 3f out: rallied over 1f out: r.o) | 2½.3 |
| 2650⁶ | Profit a Prendre **(55)** *(DAWilson)* 8–9-4 ‡SharonMillard (11) (hdwy 2f out: r.o one pce fnl f) | s.h.4 |
| 2561 | Lexus (IRE) **(45)** *(RJRWilliams)* 4–8-13 GMitchell (7) (lw: a.p: one pce fnl 2f) | 5.5 |
| 2545 | Our Eddie **(50)** *(BGubby)* 3–8-11 CAvery (6) (lw: prom over 5f) | nk.6 |
| 2689 | Share Holder **(34)** *(MissGayKelleway)* 4–8-2 MSimpson (2) (b.hind: spd over 5f) | ¾.7 |
| 2541⁵ | Tathir (CAN) **(49)** *(DMorley)* 4–9-2 EBentley (14) (b: b.hind: lw: led 5f: wknd fnl f) | s.h.8 |
| 2494⁵ | Lucky Noire **(60)** (Fav) *(GHarwood)* 4–10-0 GayeHarwood (5) (lw: hld up: swtchd rt 5f out: swtchd lft 3f out: hdwy 2f out: nvr nr to chal) | ½.9 |
| 2541⁴ | Champenoise **(50)** *(MBell)* 4–8-13 ‡⁵TO'Leary (4) (swtg: s.s: a bhd) | 4.10 |
| 2494³ | Ryewater Dream **(48)** *(RJHodges)* 4–9-2 SDrowne (3) (spd 5f) | 3.11 |
| 2427 | Harry's Lady (IRE) **(35)** (bl) *(TThomsonJones)* 4–8-3⁽²⁾ LMahoney (1) (bhd fnl 3f) | 5.12 |
| | Riviera Scene **(46)** *(PJMakin)* 9–8-9 ‡⁵DMiddleton (12) (s.s: a bhd: t.o) | 20.13 |
| 2427⁶ | Fast Operative **(38)** *(KOCunningham-Brown)* 5–8-6 MBressington (8) (b: lw: t.o fnl 4f) | 10.14 |

9/2 Lucky Noire, 5/1 NIGHT TRANSACTION, Profit a Prendre, 6/1 Ryewater Dream, 10/1 Lexus (IRE)(8/1—12/1), 12/1 Fast Operative(op 8/1), 14/1 Countercheck (IRE), 16/1 Tathir (CAN), 20/1 Our Eddie, 25/1 Riviera Scene, Hightown-Princess (IRE), 33/1 Ors. CSF £105.54, CT £1,483.97. Tote £5.00: £2.10 £6.60 £4.70 (£54.50). Mr Anthony Hide (NEWMARKET) bred by Alan Gibson. 14 Rn
1m 31.42 (2.92)
SF—35/13/19/15/–/–

T/Plpt: £49.10 (70.3 Tckts).
LMc

## 2550—RIPON (R-H)

### Saturday, August 15th [Good]

Going Allowance: St: minus 0.50; Rnd: minus 0.20 sec per fur (F)   Wind: almost nil

Stalls: low

**2808**   WIN WITH THE WEBB SEAL APP'CE H'CAP (0-70) £2560.00 (£760.00: £360.00: £160.00)   6f   2-15 (2-18)

| | | |
|---|---|---|
| 2570* | **Flashy's Son (53)** *(MDHammond)* 4–9-1 ‡⁷ALakeman (2) (lw: mde most: r.o wl fnl 2f) | —1 |

2614² Nordan Raider **(50)** (Fav) *(MJCamacho)* 4–8-12 ‡⁷SMulvey (10) (b.nr hind: lw: disp ld 4f: nt qckn ins fnl f) .................................... 1¹/₂.2

2672⁴ Miss Aragon **(48)** *(MissLCSiddall)* 4–9-3 SWilliams (8) (lw: hld up: effrt & nt clr run 2f out: r.o u.p fnl f) ................................................. 3.3

1999⁵ R a Express **(37)** (bl) *(BAMcMahon)* 7–8-6 SSanders (14) (a chsng ldrs: kpt on fnl f) ............................................................................. 2.4

2552⁶ Followmegirls **(64)** *(MrsALMKing)* 3–10-0 AGarth (12) (bhd tl styd on u.p fnl f) . ³/₄.5

2481⁴ Starchy Cove **(39)** *(BRCambidge)* 5–8-8 DWright (7) (chsd ldrs: one pce fnl 2f) 2¹/₂.6

2672 Our Amber **(24)** (bl) *(DWChapman)* 5–7-7 DarrenMoffatt (7) (cl up tl outpcd fnl 2f) ...................................................................................... 1.7

2607 Dreamtime Echo **(24)** (bl) *(JBalding)* 4–7-7 ClaireBalding (6) (w ldrs over 3f: grad wknd) ........................................................................... 1.8

2672⁶ Spanish Realm **(38)** *(MBrittain)* 5–8-7 JMarshall (1) (lw: b.hind: chsd ldrs 4f) ..... 2.9

2406 Premier Envelope (IRE) **(48)** *(NTinkler)* 3–8-12 GParkin (4) (gd spd over 3f) . 2¹/₂.10

2665² Throw Away Line **(50)** *(REBarr)* 3–9-0 PBowe (5) (lw: outpcd fr ¹/₂-wy) ....... nk.11

2290³ Coat of Dreams **(44)** (bl) *(RBastiman)* 3–8-8 HBastiman (13) (swtg: disp ld to ¹/₂-wy: sn rdn & wknd) ............................................................... nk.12

2672★ Arabat **(59)** (v) *(MPNaughton)* 5–10-0 OPears (9) (s.i.s: a bhd) ..................... nk.13

LONG HANDICAP: Our Amber 7-3, Dreamtime Echo 7-6.
*2614³ Granny Mc Withdrawn (no jockey available) : not under orders*

**9/4** Nordan Raider, **11/2** Arabat, **6/1** FLASHY'S SON, **8/1** Miss Aragon, Coat of Dreams, **14/1** Starchy Cove, Followmegirls, **16/1** Throw Away Line, **20/1** Premier Envelope (IRE), **25/1** Spanish Realm, R a Express, **50/1** Ors. CSF £18.36, CT £98.98. Tote £5.70: £1.80 £1.40 £1.90 (£6.90). Lee Construction (Newcastle) Ltd (MIDDLEHAM) bred by Brian A. Shovelton (North Wales) Ltd. 13 Rn     1m 11.5 (U.2)
SF—45/36/29/10/29/–

**2809**     WHARFEDALE (S) STKS (3-Y.O) £2595.00 (£720.00: £345.00)    1¹/₄m    2-45 (2-50)

2662³ **Batabanoo (66)** (Fav) *(MrsGHHeveley)* 9–2 KDarley (6) (lw: hld up & bhd: swtchd & effrt 3f out: led over 1f out: sn rdn clr) ................. — 1

2566² Spray of Orchids **(51)** *(JEtherington)* 8-6 JCarroll (2) (lw: mid div: hdwy & ev ch over 1f out: kpt on) .................................................. 2.2

2486² Persian Fleece **(48)** *(MrsGRReveley)* 7-13 ‡⁷DarrenMoffatt (3) (a chsng ldrs: effrt 3f out: r.o one pce) .................................................. 4.3

2467⁴ Chantry Bellini **(44)** (bl) *(CWThornton)* 8-6 GHind (14) (cl up: led over 4f out: qcknd clr: hdd appr fnl f: sn btn) .................................... 1¹/₂.4

1288 Dara Melody (IRE) **(50)** *(JGFitzGerald)* 8-11 KFallon (13) (swtchd & effrt over 3f out: n.m.r: styd on: nt pce to chal) ................................ 2¹/₂.5

2778⁵ Sea Lord **(35)** *(KWHogg)* 8-11 JCorrigan (11) (bhd tl styd on fnl 4f) ............... 3¹/₂.6

2311² Blunham Express **(44)** *(TFairhurst)* 8-6 JFanning (10) (lw: chsd ldrs: one pce fnl 4f) ........................................................................... 2¹/₂.7

Gymcrak Cyrano (IRE) **(59)** *(MHEasterby)* 8-6 MBirch (12) (bit bkwd: led 1f: chsd ldr tl wknd fnl 4f) ............................................... 2.8

Petite Belle **(55)** *(RMWhitaker)* 7-13 ‡⁷GParkin (8) (hld up & nvr plcd to chal) .... ³/₄.9

2630² Forgetful **(50)** (bl) *(DBurchell)* 8-6 LCharnock (1) (plld hrd: led after 1f tl over 4f out: sn wknd) ............................................................ 2¹/₂.10

2539⁴ My Grain **(40)** *(RHollinshead)* 8-6 WRyan (4) (nvr bttr than mid div) ................. 1.11

2004⁴ Drop a Curtsey **(40)** *(JDBethell)* 8-6 BRaymond (5) (s.i.s: n.d) ................... 1.12

2555² Tip it In *(ASmith)* 8-11 SWebster (7) (prom to st) .................................... 1¹/₂.13

2420⁴ Stratford Lady **(40)** *(JAGlover)* 8-6 JFortune (9) (chsd ldrs tl wknd fnl out) ...... 2.14

**Evens** BATABANOO(op 6/4), **6/1** Forgetful, Spray of Orchids, **13/2** Persian Fleece, **10/1** Gymcrak Cyrano (IRE), **14/1** Blunham Express, **16/1** My Grain, **20/1** Petite Belle, Chantry Bellini, Drop a Curtsey, Dara Melody (IRE), **25/1** Stratford Lady, **33/1** Tip it In, **50/1** Sea Lord. CSF £9.56, Tote £2.50: £1.40 £2.00 £2.00 (£6.70). Mr P. D. Savill (SALTBURN) bred by Clover Stud. 14 Rn; Bt in 9,600 gns     2m 7.2 (3.7)
SF—45/31/16/20/20/13

**2810**     SWALEDALE H'CAP (0-80) £4175.00 (£1250.00: £600.00: £275.00) 1¹/₂m 60y     3-15 (3-21)

2742★ Kinoko **(52)** *(KWHogg)* 4–8-2⁽¹⁾ (6x) JCorrigan (11) (lw: hld up: hdwy 4f out: led jst ins fnl f: rdn & r.o) .......................................... — 1

2442 Westholme (USA) **(72)** *(MHEasterby)* 4–9-8 MBirch (10) (trckd ldrs: led & qcknd 2f out: hdd ins fnl f: r.o) .............................................. 1¹/₂.2

2148⁵ Young George **(57)** *(MDods)* 5–8-7 KFallon (7) (lw: bhd: drvn along 4f out: styd on wl: nrst fin) ....................................................... 3¹/₂.3

2734★ First Bid **(56)** *(RMWhitaker)* 5–8-6 (6x) ACulhane (9) (lw: a.p: effrt 4f out: styd on) ............................................................................... hd.4

2605★ Hazaaf (USA) **(64)** (Fav) *(AAScott)* 3–8-3 JFortune (15) (trckd ldrs: effrt 3f out: one pce) ............................................................................. 2.5

2553⁵ Corn Lily **(69)** *(MrsGRReveley)* 6–9-5 JLowe (6) (bit bkwd: w ldrs: chal wl over 3f out tl outpcd fnl 2f) ................................................... ³/₄.6

*2367* Cheeky Pot **(43)** (v) *(DenysSmith)* 4-7-7 LCharnock (14) (mid div: effrt 4f out:
nvr able to chal) ............................................................... 2½.7

Masai Mara (USA) **(78)** *(PCHaslam)* 4-10-0 KDarley (8) (bit bkwd: in tch: rdn
over 3f out: no imp) ...................................................... 3.8

*2698* Eire Leath-Sceal **(54)** *(MBrittain)* 5-7-11 ‡⁷JMarshall (12) (nvr bttr than mid div) . 1.9

Burn Bridge (USA) **(47)** *(MDHammond)* 6-7-11 JFanning (16) (bit bkwd: n.d) . 1.10

*2012⁶* Desert Force (IRE) **(72)** *(MMoubarak)* 3-8-11 PRobinson (3) (lw: chsd ldrs tl
wknd fnl 3f) ................................................................. hd.11

*2515³* Super Blues **(64)** *(TDBarron)* 3-8-9 AlexGreaves (1) (swtg: led wl over 1f tl hdd
& wknd 2f out) ............................................................. ¾.12

All Welcome **(47)** *(GMMoore)* 5-7-11 PBurke (5) (effrt 4f out: sn rdn & btn) ... nk.13

*184* Castleacre **(48)** *(CASmith)* 6-7-5⁽⁵⁾ ‡⁷AGarth (13) (n.d) ......................... ½.14

*2692* Vinstan **(43)** (bl) *(CASmith)* 6-7-0 ‡⁷DWright (2) (s.s: rdn 4f out: n.d) ............... 8.15

*2556³* Philgun **(58)** *(CWCElsey)* 3-7-6 ‡⁵NKennedy (4) (led wl over 1f: cl up: c wd st:
wknd over 3f out) ....................................................... 1.16

LONG HANDICAP: Castleacre 7-3, Vinstan 7-4.

**9/2** Hazaaf (USA), **11/2** First Bid, Westholme (USA), **6/1** Corn Lily, **8/1** Desert Force (IRE), **10/1** Philgun,
KINOKO, **14/1** Young George, Cheeky Pot, **16/1** Eire Leath-Sceal, All Welcome, Super Blues, **20/1** Masai Mara
(USA), **33/1** Burn Bridge (USA), **66/1** Ors. CSF £64.71, CT £730.27. Tote £16.80: £2.80 £1.80 £3.70 £1.50
(£96.20). Mr Anthony White (ISLE OF MAN) bred by Auldyn Stud Ltd. 16 Rn　　　　2m 36.5 (2.5)
SF—38/55/33/31/24/38

# 2811

RIPON HORN BLOWER STKS (2-Y.O) £5026.00 (£1498.00: £714.00: £322.00)
**5f**　　　　　3-45 (3-49)

*2161²* Lucky Parkes **(95)** *(JBerry)* 8-12 JCarroll (6) (lw: mde all: hld on wl fnl f) .......... —1

*2342³* Ansellman **(95)** *(MJHaynes)* 8-11 PRobinson (7) (lw: a cl up: hrd rdn fnl f: r.o) nk.2

*2271\** Night Melody (IRE) **(100)** (Fav) *(RHannon)* 9-3 KDarley (4) (lw: a chsng ldrs:
effrt 2f out: nt qckn fnl f) ................................................ 2.3

*2437³* Classic Story (USA) **(91)** *(MMoubarak)* 8-11 WRyan (2) (trckd ldrs: effrt 2f out:
r.o one pce) ............................................................... 3.4

*2551\** Falsoola **(73)** *(MRStoute)* 8-6 PaulEddery (3) (swtchd & effrt ½-wy: sn hrd rdn
& no imp) ................................................................. ¾.5

*2724³* Shadow Jury **(86)** (v) *(JSWainwright)* 9-3 PBurke (5) (sn pushed along: nvr
trbld ldrs) ................................................................. ¾.6

*1963²* Scored Again *(RMWhitaker)* 8-6 ACulhane (1) (lw: plld hrd: trckd ldrs: btn whn
hmpd over 1f out) ......................................................... 2½.7

**2/1** Night Melody (IRE), **100/30** Classic Story (USA), **7/2** Falsoola, **4/1** LUCKY PARKES, **9/1** Ansellman, **20/1**
Scored Again, **33/1** Shadow Jury. CSF £34.29, Tote £4.60: £2.00 £3.30 (£27.30). Mr Joseph Heler
(COCKERHAM) bred by Joseph Heler. 7 Rn　　　　　　　　　　　　　58.1 sec (U.5)
SF—58/56/54/36/28/36

# 2812

WENSLEYDALE STKS (Mdn 2-Y.O) £2742.00 (£762.00: £366.00)　　**6f**　　4-20 (4-26)

*2335³* Fyfield Flyer (IRE) *(PWChapple-Hyam)* 9-0 PaulEddery (12) (lw: mde most:
qcknd clr fr ½-wy: r.o wl) ................................................ —1

*2444* Easy Access (IRE) *(RHannon)* 9-0 BRaymond (1) (b.off hind: a chsng ldrs: r.o
fnl 2f: no ch w wnr) ...................................................... 8.2

*2675⁶* Irish Dominion *(MissSEHall)* 9-0 NConnorton (16) (a chsng ldrs: kpt on same
pce fnl 2f) ................................................................. 2.3

*2544²* Angus Dundee (IRE) (Fav) *(HRACecil)* 9-0 WRyan (4) (lw: w wnr to ½-wy: sn
rdn & no ex) .............................................................. 1.4

Silky Heights (IRE) *(MJCamacho)* 8-9 JLowe (2) (rangy: scope: bit bkwd: hdwy
½-wy: styd on: no imp) .................................................. 1.5

Cubist (IRE) *(DMorley)* 8-9 MBirch (9) (leggy: scope: a chsng ldrs: no hdwy fnl
2f) ......................................................................... hd.6

Dutosky *(MJCamacho)* 8-9 KFallon (15) (w'like: scope: bit bkwd: s.i.s: hdwy
½-wy: nvr trbld ldrs) .................................................... 1.7

Northern Judy (IRE) *(RHollinshead)* 8-2 ‡⁷AGarth (10) (lt-f: leggy: outpcd & bhd
tl hdwy 2f out: r.o) ....................................................... s.h.8

Tykeyvor (IRE) *(MHTompkins)* 9-0 PRobinson (3) (leggy: scope: bit bkwd:
s.i.s: nvr plcd to chal) .................................................. 1½.9

Northern Chief *(MHEasterby)* 8-9 ‡⁵SMaloney (5) (w'like: scope: nvr trbld ldrs) 2.10

*2205* Codden Lad *(NTinkler)* 9-0 LCharnock (17) (bit bkwd: in tch tl outpcd fr ½-wy) 5.11

*2686³* Home Affair *(DTThom)* 8-4 ‡⁵JWeaver (7) (prom ovr 3f) ......................... hd.12

*2205* I Do Care **(55)** *(JBerry)* 9-0 JCarroll (8) (effrt ½-wy: n.d) ....................... 1½.13

Auntie Chris *(AWPotts)* 8-9 SWebster (6) (unf: bit bkwd: dwlt: a outpcd & bhd) nk.14

Moss Pageant *(MrsPABarker)* 9-0 ACulhane (14) (wl grwn: lengthy: bkwd: s.i.s:
n.d) ....................................................................... 7.15

One for Tondy *(NBycroft)* 8-9 JFanning (11) (neat: bit bkwd: unruly s: a bhd) 3½.16

RIPON, August 15—HAMILTON, August 17, 1992

**2813—2814**

**Evens** Angus Dundee (IRE)(tchd 6/4), **6/1** Cubist (IRE), Easy Access (IRE), **7/1** FYFIELD FLYER (IRE), **10/1** Irish Dominion, **12/1** Tykeyvor (IRE), **20/1** I Do Care, Home Affair, **25/1** Moss Pageant, **33/1** Ors. CSF £49.70, Tote £6.10: £2.10 £2.10 £2.50 (£17.40). Mr R. E. Sangster (MARLBOROUGH) bred by Swettenham Stud in Ireland.
16 Rn
1m 11.7 (equals standard)
SF—40/18/10/6/–/–

## 2813

NIDDERDALE H'CAP (0-70) £2973.00 (£828.00: £399.00)    **1m**    4-55 (5-02)

| | | |
|---|---|---|
| 2668* | Inseyab (60) (Fav) (PCHaslam) 4–8-13 ‡⁵JWeaver (17) (lw: trckd ldrs: led over 2f out: qcknd clr: edgd rt & drvn out) | —1 |
| 2184 | Roseate Lodge (68) (RWArmstrong) 6–9-12 CKTse (4) (a chsng ldrs: hdwy u.p over 1f out: r.o nr fin) | nk.2 |
| 2468 | Roar on Tour (60) (v) (MHEasterby) 3–8-11 MBirch (5) (trckd ldrs gng wl: led wl over 3f out tl over 2f out: kpt on nr fin) | ½.3 |
| 2035 | Spring to the Top (51) (JWPayne) 5–8-9 PRobinson (20) (led tl hdd wl over 3f out: r.o) | 1½.4 |
| 2607 | Pride of Pendle (52) (PCalver) 3–8-3 PaulEddery (1) (a chsng ldrs: effrt over 3f out: r.o one pce) | 1.5 |
| 2561 | Errema (44) (CTinkler) 7–7-11 ‡⁵SMaloney (7) (bhd: effrt on outside 3f out: nt pce nr chal) | 1.6 |
| 2662* | Watch Me Go (IRE) (56) (BobJones) 3–8-7 NConnorton (15) (lw: w ldrs: nt qckn fnl 2f) | ½.7 |
| 2642 | Samsolom (62) (JBalding) 4–9-6 GHind (18) (lw: stdd s: hdwy on ins ½-wy: one pce fnl 2f) | 1.8 |
| | Huso (70) (PCHaslam) 4–10-0 KDarley (14) (bkwd: bhd tl swtchd & hdwy 2f out: r.o) | nk.9 |
| £076? | Allegramente (55) (RO'Leary) 3–8-6 LCharnock (8) (lw: hld up: nvr nr to chal) | ½.10 |
| 2449 | Thewaari (USA) (67) (AAScott) 3–9-4 DRaymond (11) (mid div & rdn ½-wy: n.d) | hd.11 |
| 2429³ | Cappahoosh (IRE) (56) (HJCollingridge) 3–8-7 WRyan (3) (lw: chsd ldrs tl wknd over 2f out) | ¾.12 |
| 2634² | Homile (47) (BAMcMahon) 4–7-12 ‡⁷SSanders (16) (lw: prom tl wknd 3f out) | nk.13 |
| 2203⁶ | Northern Spark (56) (CWThornton) 4–9-0 JCarroll (9) (lw: n.d) | hd.14 |
| 2394⁴ | Winged Whisper (USA) (62) (CASmith) 3–8-13 MWigham (12) (b.off hind: hld up & bhd: nvr plcd to chal) | hd.15 |
| 2567³ | Don't Drop Bombs (USA) (56) (AAScott) 3–8-7 JFortune (2) (lw: n.d) | nk.16 |
| 1185 | Kentucky Rain (59) (JGFitzGerald) 3–8-10 KFallon (13) (cl up to ½-wy: sn wknd) | s.h.17 |
| 2332³ | North Esk (USA) (70) (JWWatts) 3–9-7 JLowe (10) (hmpd appr st: nvr nr to chal) | 1½.18 |
| 2556⁴ | Royal Sultan (50) (DenysSmith) 3–8-1 JFanning (19) (chsd ldrs 5f: sn wknd) | 3.19 |
| 401 | Stormswept (USA) (64) (MBrittain) 3–8-8 ‡⁷JMarshall (6) (chsd ldrs to ½-wy: sn bhd) | 1½.20 |

**4/1** INSEYAB(tchd 8/1), **8/1** Roseate Lodge, **17/2** Spring to the Top, Homile, **10/1** Cappahoosh (IRE), Watch Me Go (IRE), Errema, **12/1** Thewaari (USA), **14/1** Roar on Tour, Don't Drop Bombs (USA), Pride of Pendle, North Esk (USA), **16/1** Allegramente, Kentucky Rain, Northern Spark, **20/1** Winged Whisper (USA), **33/1** Ors. CSF £39.31, CT £402.96. Tote £5.30: £1.70 £2.20 £4.00 £2.70 (£12.00). Mrs P. Haslam (MIDDLEHAM) bred by Gainsborough Stud Management Ltd. 20 Rn
1m 41.1 (3.4)
SF—24/36/18/11/–/–

T/Trio: Race 3: £1,233.80 (1.1 Tckts). T/Plpt: £98.10 (56.85 Tckts).     AA

## 2485—HAMILTON (R-H)

### Monday, August 17th [Good, Good to soft patches]

Going Allowance: 0.20 sec per fur (G)     Wind: almost nil

Stalls: low

## 2814

PETTINAIN H'CAP (0-70) £2654.00 (£744.00: £362.00)    **1m 65y**    2-15 (2-18)
(Weights raised 2 lb)

| | | |
|---|---|---|
| 1960³ | Sweet Mignonette (52) (MrsGRReveley) 4–8-12 KDarley (13) (lw: bhd: hdwy whn nt clr run 3f out: swtchd & r.o u.p to ld wl ins fnl f) | —1 |
| 2517* | Lawnswood Junior (53) (JLSpearing) 5–8-13 GHind (11) (bhd: hdwy on ins 4f out: chal ins fnl f: r.o) | ¾.2 |
| 2249² | The Dandy Don (IRE) (52) (DenysSmith) 3–8-6 NConnorton (10) (cl up: led wl over 1f out: sn rdn: hdd & no ex wl ins fnl f) | 1.3 |
| 2609⁶ | Bidweaya (USA) (42) (JLEyre) 5–7-11 ‡⁵OPears (12) (mid div: hdwy 3f out: styd on u.p fnl f) | ¾.4 |

Page 977

2670 Hizeem **(33)** (v) *(MPNaughton)* 6–7–7 JakiHouston (14) (lw: hdwy 4f out: effrt & hung lft over 2f out: r.o one pce) .............................................. ³/₄.5
2607 Sky Cat **(40)** (v) *(CTinkler)* 8–7–9 ‡⁵SMaloney (8) (swtg: trckd ldrs: chal 3f out: hrd rdn appr fnl f: nt qckn) ........................................... nk.6
913⁶ Miss Knight **(38)** *(RBastiman)* 5–7–12 PBurke (15) (bhd tl styd on fnl 3f) ........ 2.7
377 Arrow Dancer **(33)** *(JJO'Neill)* 6–7–7 JFanning (3) (bhd: effrt ¹/₂-wy: no imp) .... nk.8
2413 Manulife **(60)** (v) *(BBeasley)* 3–9–0 LCharnock (7) (chsd ldrs: led 3f out tl wl over 1f out: sn wknd) ............................................................ nk.9
1890 Tahitian **(48)** (bl) *(MrsJRRamsden)* 3–8–2⁽¹⁾ JCarroll (2) (nvr nr to chal) .......... ³/₄.10
2517⁵ Thisonesforalice **(47)** *(AHarrison)* 4–8–7 KFallon (1) (a bhd) .......................... nk.11
2529 Little Rousillon **(62)** (Fav) *(ACStewart)* 4–9–8 SWhitworth (5) (mid div: effrt ¹/₂-wy: no imp) ............................................................... 2.12
2486 Swank Gilbert **(33)** *(TAKCuthbert)* 6–7–0 ‡⁷DarrenMoffatt (9) (led tl hdd 3f out: sn wknd) ........................................................... 1¹/₂.13
2468⁵ Kummel King **(64)** *(EJAlston)* 4–9–10 JFortune (4) (lw: chsd ldrs 5f: sn wknd) . 1.14
2487* Bold Melody **(58)** *(PCHaslam)* 3–8–7 ‡⁵JWeaver (6) (lw: prom: effrt 3f out: sn rdn & wknd) ............................................................... 2¹/₂.15

LONG HANDICAP: Hizeem 6-13, Arrow Dancer 7-6, Swank Gilbert 7-1.

**5/2** Little Rousillon, **5/1** SWEET MIGNONETTE, **17/2** Bidweaya (USA), **9/1** The Dandy Don (IRE), **12/1** Thisonesforalice, **14/1** Lawnswood Junior, Tahitian, **16/1** Kummel King, **20/1** Manulife, Sky Cat, **25/1** Miss Knight, **33/1** Hizeem, **50/1** Arrow Dancer, **100/1** Swank Gilbert. CSF £65.62, CT £618.29. Tote £4.80: £2.10 £4.40 £3.10 (£48.00). Mr M. J. Ogden (SALTBURN) bred by Countess of Durham. 15 Rn  1m 49.8 (6.5)
SF—26/25/15/4/–/–

**2815**          HAZELBANK (S) STKS (3 & 4-Y.O) £2318.00 (£648.00: £314.00)
                 **1m 1f 36y**                                        2-45 (2-46)

2486⁴ **Reel of Tulloch (IRE) (58)** *(PCHaslam)* 3–8–8 DMcKeown (9) (lw: hld up: effrt whn hmpd wl over 2f out: qcknd to ld wl ins fnl f) ................ —1
2732³ Richmond (IRE) **(54)** (bl) (Jt-Fav) *(BBeasley)* 4–9–1 LCharnock (10) (chsd ldrs: led 3f out & hung rt: hdd wl ins fnl f: r.o) ........................... ¹/₂.2
2486* Henbury Hall (IRE) **(60)** *(MrsGRReveley)* 4–9–4 KDarley (5) (lw: led 1f: cl up: rdn over 2f out: r.o one pce) ...................................... 5.3
2569 Ghylldale **(34)** (v) *(RBastiman)* 4–8–4⁽¹⁾ ‡⁷HBastiman (6) (hdwy 3f out: styd on: nvr able to chal) ........................................... 1.4
2677² Miliyel **(52)** (Jt-Fav) *(PMonteith)* 3–7–8 ‡⁵NKennedy (1) (chsd ldrs: hmpd wl over 2f out: one pce after) ...................................... nk.5
1562⁶ Stoproveritate **(48)** *(SGNorton)* 3–7–10⁽²⁾ ‡⁵SMaloney (8) (cl up early: sn lost pl: effrt 4f out: no imp) ...................................... 4.6
2785 Reza **(46)** *(JLEyre)* 4–8–6 ‡⁵OPears (4) (led after 1f tl hmpd 3f out: wkng whn hmpd wl over 1f out) .......................................... 4.7
2072⁴ Fairford **(58)** *(JGFitzGerald)* 3–8–4 KFallon (7) (in tch: effrt over 3f out: hung rt: wknd over 2f out) ..................................... ¹/₂.8
2249 Shadaylou (IRE) **(40)** *(MissLAPerratt)* 3–7–13 JLowe (3) (lw: in tch tl outpcd ent st: n.d after) ........................................... nk.9
2699 J P Morgan **(42)** (v) *(MPNaughton)* 4–8–6 ‡⁵JWeaver (2) (w ldrs: wkng whn hmpd wl over 2f out) ..................................... ¹/₂.10

**7/2** Richmond (IRE), Miliyel, **5/1** REEL OF TULLOCH (IRE), Fairford, Henbury Hall (IRE), **10/1** Stoproveritate, **16/1** J P Morgan, **20/1** Reza, **25/1** Ghylldale, **33/1** Shadaylou (IRE). CSF £22.26, Tote £6.10: £1.90 £1.20 £2.00 (£9.20). Lord Scarsdale (MIDDLEHAM) bred by J. Cummins in Ireland. 10 Rn; Bt in 6,000 gns  2m 0.2 (5.9)
SF—33/38/26/9/–/–

**2816**          ROYAL SCOTS DRAGOON GUARDS H'CAP (0-70) £2500.00 (£700.00: £340.00)
                 **6f 5y**                                             3-15 (3-19)

2548* **Dawes of Nelson (50)** *(MJBolton)* 7–8–13 JLowe (7) (lw: bhd: hdwy 2f out: styd on to ld wl ins fnl f) .......................................... —1
2676⁶ Hinari Video **(43)** *(MJohnston)* 7–8–6 DMcKeown (10) (hdwy ¹/₂-wy: disp ld ins fnl f: nt qckn nr fin) ...................................... 1.2
2559 Diet **(62)** (v) (Jt-Fav) *(MissLAPerratt)* 6–9–4 ‡⁷RHavlin (9) (lw: led tl hdd & no ex wl ins fnl f) .......................................... nk.3
2046⁴ Lift Boy (USA) **(43)** *(DenysSmith)* 4–8–2 NConnorton (12) (chsd ldrs: effrt 2f out: grad wknd fnl f) ..................................... 3.4
2614⁴ Blue Grit **(49)** (Jt-Fav) *(MDods)* 6–8–12 KFallon (2) (lw: in tch: drvn along ¹/₂-wy: one pce) ......................................... hd.5
2469³ Say You Will **(33)** (v) *(MPNaughton)* 8–7–10 JakiHouston (8) (chsd ldrs: rdn ¹/₂-wy: no imp after) .................................. 1¹/₂.6
2361⁴ High Principles **(63)** *(JBerry)* 3–9–8 JCarroll (6) (chsd ldrs tl outpcd fnl 2f) ...... 3¹/₂.7
2570⁴ Johnston's Express (IRE) **(38)** *(EJAlston)* 4–8–1 JFortune (5) (lw: trckd ldrs: shkn up ¹/₂-wy: sn btn) ....................................... 1¹/₂.8

2521 Young Shadowfax **(53)** *(CNAllen)* 5–8-9 ‡⁷GForster (1) (b.nr hind: outpcd fr
     ¹/₂-wy) ............................................................................................ s.h.**9**
2672 Chester Belle **(34)** *(PCHaslam)* 3–7-7 LCharnock (4) (bhd fr ¹/₂-wy) ............. 1.**10**
2676³ Uppance **(34)** *(TCraig)* 4–7-4 ‡⁷DarrenMoffatt (3) (spd to ¹/₂-wy: sn bhd) .......... 7.**11**
1618⁴ Nevada Mix **(45)** *(MissLAPerratt)* 8–8-8 JFanning (11) (b: a bhd) ...................... 3.**12**
               LONG HANDICAP: Chester Belle 7-1.

**9/2** Blue Grit(op 3/1), Diet(op 3/1), **11/2** Johnston's Express, **6/1** Hinari Video, **7/1** DAWES OF NELSON, **8/1** High Principles, **12/1** Young Shadowfax(op 8/1), Nevada Mix, **14/1** Lift Boy (USA), **20/1** Uppance, Say You Will, **66/1** Chester Belle. CSF £46.32, CT £194.46. Tote £6.30: £2.20 £2.20 £1.80 (£13.80). Mr A. R. M. Galbraith (SHREWTON) bred by D. Cornwall. 12 Rn             1m 14.4 (4.4)
                                                 SF—35/24/35/7/16/–

**2817**     ROSEBANK CLAIMING STKS (3-Y.O) £2290.00 (£640.00: £310.00)
        **6f 5y**                                                 3–45 (3-46)

2639² **Arctic Appeal (IRE) (87)** *(Fav)* *(JBerry)* 8-11 JCarroll (5) (lw: cl up: led ¹/₂-wy:
     r.o fnl f) ................................................................................................... —**1**
2702* **Manuleader (56)** (bl) *(BBeasley)* 8-11 ‡⁵SWilliams (6) (lw: hdwy ¹/₂-wy: chsd wnr
     fnl 2f: sn rdn & nt qckn) .......................................................................... 2¹/₂.**2**
2702³ **Double Feature (IRE) (60)** *(MrsJRRamsden)* 8-9 MBirch (3) (lw: a.p: effrt 2f out:
     no ex fnl f) ................................................................................................ 1.**3**
1018 **Rural Lad (68)** *(MrsJRRamsden)* 8-13 DMcKeown (2) (lw: hld up: stdy hdwy
     after 2f: shkn up over 1f out: sn btn) ....................................................... 5.**4**
2062⁶ **Fort Derry (IRE) (82)** *(EJAlston)* 8-12 KFallon (1) (prom early: outpcd & bhd fr ¹/₂-wy) 2¹/₂.**5**
2613 **Scorton (IRE) (MDods)** 8-12 LCharnock (4) (led to ¹/₂-wy: sn wknd) .................. 6.**6**

**2/5** ARCTIC APPEAL (IRE), **6/1** Double Feature (IRE)(tchd 10/1), **8/1** Manuleader, Rural Lad, **20/1** Scorton (IRE), **66/1** Fort Derry (IRE). CSF £4.43, Tote £1.30: £1.10 £2.10 (£3.80). Mr Yahya Nasib (COCKERHAM) bred by Hamilton Bloodstock (UK) Ltd. in Ireland. 6 Rn              1m 14.5 (4.5)
                                                CF   31/21/15/–/–/–

**2818**     E.B.F. WILLIAM PEARCE MEMORIAL STKS (Mdn 2-Y.O) £2654.00 (£744.00: £362.00)
        **6f 5y**                                                 4-15 (4-17)

     **Bold Amusement** *(MrsGRReveley)* 9-0 KDarley (1) (w'like: scope: bit bkwd:
     a.p: rdn to ld ins fnl f: r.o wl) ................................................................. —**1**
877 **Robix (IRE)** *(CTinkler)* 9-0 MBirch (4) (lw: mde most tl hdd ins fnl f: no ex) .... 2.**2**
2727³ **Mam'zelle Angot** *(Fav)* *(MRStoute)* 8-4 ‡⁵JJones (6) (b.hind: a w ldrs: rdn over 1f
     out: nt qckn) ............................................................................................ 2¹/₂.**3**
2335⁴ **Best Appearance (IRE)** *(JGFitzGerald)* 9-0 KFallon (5) (hdwy ¹/₂-wy: styd on:
     nrst fin) .................................................................................................... ¹/₂.**4**
     **High Romance** *(DMoffatt)* 8-2 ‡⁷DarrenMoffatt (3) (cmpt: lw: sn trckng ldrs: effrt
     stands' side ¹/₂-wy: rdn & btn over 1f out) .............................................. 1¹/₂.**5**
2667⁵ **Bold Philip (69)** *(BBeasley)* 8-9 ‡⁵SWilliams (8) (lw: nvr trbld ldrs) ................ 10.**6**
2745 **Flash of Amber** *(JLSpearing)* 8-9 GHind (9) (cl up to ¹/₂-wy: sn wknd) ............ 5.**7**
     **The Loon** *(JJO'Neill)* 9-0 TLucas (7) (b: leggy: s.i.s: a outpcd & bhd) ............. s.h.**8**
     **Friendly Knight** *(JSHaldane)* 9-0 LCharnock (10) (w'like: bkwd: prom to ¹/₂-wy:
     sn bhd) ..................................................................................................... 3.**9**
2610⁴ **Super Scenario** *(EJAlston)* 9-0 JFortune (2) (bit bkwd: a outpcd & bhd) ........ 10.**10**

**Evens** Mam'zelle Angot(4/5–5/4), **5/1** Best Appearance (IRE), BOLD AMUSEMENT(7/1—8/1), **11/2** High Romance, **14/1** Bold Philip, Robix (IRE), **20/1** The Loon, Flash of Amber, **100/1** Friendly Knight, **200/1** Super Scenario. CSF £65.62, Tote £7.30: £2.10 £7.70 £1.30 (£92.40). Mr David Bell (SALTBURN) bred by Cheveley Park Stud Ltd. 10 Rn             1m 15 (5)
                                                 SF—24/16/–/–/–/–

**2819**     LEVY BOARD MEDIAN AUCTION STKS (Mdn 2-Y.O) £2346.00 (£656.00: £318.00)
        **5f 4y**                                                 4-45 (4-46)

2471⁴ **Pilgrim Bay (IRE) (66)** *(JBerry)* 8-10 JCarroll (1) (trckd ldrs: hdwy 2f out: led
     ins fnl f: r.o) ............................................................................................ —**1**
2646⁶ **Hazard a Guess (IRE)** *(MrsJRRamsden)* 8-10 MBirch (7) (bit bkwd: bhd: hdwy
     over 1f out: r.o wl nr fin) ......................................................................... 2.**2**
416² **Peedie Peat** *(Fav)* *(JJO'Neill)* 9-0 TLucas (4) (lw: s.i.s: outpcd tl hdwy over 1f
     out: r.o nr fin) ......................................................................................... 1.**3**
2532⁶ **Bella Bambola (IRE) (50)** (bl) *(BBeasley)* 8-10 LCharnock (2) (led tl hdd & wknd
     ins fnl f) ................................................................................................... hd.**4**
     **Sporting Spirit** *(DWChapman)* 9-0 SWood (5) (cmpt: bkwd: s.i.s: wnt prom
     ¹/₂-wy: outpcd appr fnl f) ......................................................................... 6.**5**
2414 **Grab Sunday Sport** *(MissGayKelleway)* 8-7 GHind (3) (w ldrs tl wknd qckly over
     1f out) ...................................................................................................... nk.**6**
2425⁵ **Oscars Quest (53)** *(JBerry)* 8-7 DMcKeown (6) (spd over 3f) ........................... 3.**7**

11/8 Peedie Peat(op 9/4), 2/1 PILGRIM BAY (IRE), 3/1 Hazard a Guess (IRE), 20/1 Bella Bambola (IRE), Grab Sunday Sport, 33/1 Ors. CSF £8.27, Tote £3.60: £2.00 £1.60 (£4.60). Mr Frank A. McNulty (COCKERHAM) bred by Ennistown Stud in Ireland. 7 Rn

62.9 sec (4.6)
SF—24/16/16/10/–/–

**2820**　　CARSTAIRS APP'CE H'CAP (0-70) £2318.00 (£648.00: £314.00)
　　　　　　1½m 17y

5-15 (5-15)

| | | |
|---|---|---|
| 2313⁴ **Hamilton Lady (IRE)** (32) (DMoffatt) 4–7-3 ‡⁴DarrenMoffatt (9) (lw: chsd ldrs: led over 3f out tl over 2f out: rallied to ld wl ins fnl f: lame) | .. —1 |
| 2045 **Brilliant Disguise** (42) (PMonteith) 3–7-7 NKennedy (6) (bhd: hdwy over 2f out: r.o nr fin) | ³/₄.2 |
| 2644³ **Able Lassie** (63) (Fav) (MrsGRReveley) 3–8-9 JFanning (5) (lw: hld up: stdy hdwy to ld over 2f out: rdn appr fnl f: hdd & wknd wl ins fnl f) | hd.3 |
| 2113⁴ **Carlingford (USA)** (61) (MPNaughton) 6–9-8 SMaloney (4) (cl up tl outpcd fnl 2f) | 2½.4 |
| 2391⁶ **West Stow** (66) (MRStoute) 3–9-3 JJones (8) (in tch: effrt & swtchd over 2f out: one pce) | hd.5 |
| 2339 **Magic Secret** (67) (PCHaslam) 4–10-0 JWeaver (2) (prom: effrt over 3f out: sn outpcd) | ½.6 |
| 2166* **Golden Torque** (67) (RBastiman) 5–9-10 ‡⁴HBastiman (1) (lw: hld up: effrt 3f out: sn rdn & one pce) | ½.7 |
| 2670⁵ **Tempering** (45) (bl) (DWChapman) 6–8-6 OPears (7) (led tl hdd over 3f out: sn lost pl: sddle slipped) | 12.8 |
| 2698⁶ **Carol's Pet (IRE)** (44) (MJohnston) 4–8-1 ‡⁴MBaird (3) (lw: reluctant to r: a wl t.o) | 9 |

LONG HANDICAP: Hamilton Lady (IRE) 7-4, Brilliant Disguise 7-2.

5/2 Able Lassie, 7/2 Magic Secret, 5/1 West Stow, 6/1 Golden Torque, 8/1 Tempering(op 12/1), Carol's Pet (IRE), Carlingford (USA), 16/1 HAMILTON LADY (IRE), 66/1 Brilliant Disguise. CSF £421.31, CT £3,142.61. Tote £15.20: £3.00 £7.70 £2.00 (£92.80). Haydock Exhibitions Ltd (CARTMEL) bred by Citadel Stud Establishment in Ireland. 9 Rn

2m 40.3 (8.3)
SF—16/18/48/41/35/45

T/Plpt: £14.40 (191 Tckts).

AA

---

2705—**WINDSOR (Fig.8)**

**Monday, August 17th [Good to soft]**

Going Allowance: 5f 10y: minus 0.25 sec (F); Rest: nil sec (G)　　　　　　Wind: nil

Stalls: high

**2821**　　ADDITIONAL APP'CE H'CAP (0-70) £2595.00 (£720.00: £345.00)
　　　　　　5f 10y

2-30 (2-36)

| | | |
|---|---|---|
| 2599² **Ganeshaya** (52) (bl) (MFBarraclough) 3–8-7 EHusband (4) (a.p: led & bmpd wl over 1f out: hrd rdn: edgd lft: all out) | —1 |
| 2747⁴ **Stocktina** (38) (RJHodges) 5–7-10 SDrowne (15) (swtg: a.p: r.o wl ins fnl f) | s.h.2 |
| 2548⁴ **Joe Sugden** (55) (PHowling) 8–8-13 DebbieBiggs (12) (lw: led tl wnt lft & bmpd wl over 1f out: r.o) | 2.3 |
| 2564² **Erris Express** (48) (Fav) (RHannon) 7–8-6 DGibbs (2) (b: outpcd: hdwy over 2f out: hrd rdn: nrst fin) | s.h.4 |
| 2718 **Fontaine Lady** (38) (v) (TThomsonJones) 5–7-10 JDSmith (6) (a.p: r.o one pce fnl 2f) | hd.5 |
| 1978 **Stormbuster** (46) (PSFelgate) 3–7-10 ‡⁵DToole (16) (swtg: nvr nrr) | 2.6 |
| 2603⁵ **Lonely Lass** (44) (AWJones) 6–8-2 DWright (5) (a.p: one pce fnl 2f) | s.h.7 |
| 2718 **Barbara's Cutie** (35) (MBlanshard) 4–7-7 CAvery (17) (lw: no hdwy fnl 2f) | 1.8 |
| 2548 **Barbezieux** (43) (bl) (TJNaughton) 5–7-10⁽⁸⁾ ‡⁵TAshley (3) (hdwy 2f out: r.o one pce) | nk.9 |
| 2548 **Calibairn** (40) (DJSCosgrove) 4–7-12 DMcCabe (10) (s.s: nrst fin) | s.h.10 |
| 2617⁴ **Wilco** (55) (AndrewTurnell) 3–8-5 ‡⁵MarkDenaro (9) (spd 3f) | s.h.11 |
| 2481 **Klairover** (46) (CJHill) 5–8-4 TWilson (1) (n.d) | 1.12 |
| 1716 **Fay Eden (IRE)** (41) (RJHodges) 4–7-13 DCarson (11) (lw: n.d) | s.h.13 |
| 2617 **Forlorn Diver** (47) (BGubby) 4–8-0⁽²⁾ ‡⁵WAldwinkle (7) (lw: n.d) | hd.14 |
| 2006⁶ **Paradise Forum** (64) (CAHorgan) 3–9-0 ‡⁵DFifield (14) (lw: n.d) | ³/₄.15 |
| 2617 **Goody Four Shoes** (38) (DRTucker) 4–7-10 BRussell (18) (n.d) | nk.16 |
| 1434 **Greetland Rock** (39) (PHowling) 4–7-11 LCarter (8) (swtg: n.d) | 1½.17 |
| 2548 **Ever Sharp** (70) (JWhite) 8–10-0 PBowe (13) (bit bkwd: w ldr tl wknd 2f out) | 2½.18 |

LONG HANDICAP: Barbara's Cutie 7-5, Barbezieux 6-11.

7/2 Erris Express, 11/2 Joe Sugden, 13/2 GANESHAYA, 8/1 Stocktina, 9/1 Wilco, 10/1 Klairover(8/1—12/1), 12/1 Paradise Forum, Barbara's Cutie, 20/1 Fontaine Lady, Stormbuster, Fay Eden (IRE), Calibairn, 25/1 Lonely Lass, 33/1 Ors. CSF £55.88, CT £281.19. Tote £7.10: £1.90 £1.60 £1.60 £1.40 (£30.40). Abbots Salford Caravan Park (CLAVERDON) bred by Campbell Stud. 18 Rn
　　　　61.6 sec (2.6)
　　　　SF—16/4/13/5/–/–

## 2822

BELMEAD (S) STKS (3-Y.O) £2658.00 (£738.00: £354.00)　　5f 217y　　3-00 (3-03)

| 2196⁵ | **Easy Does it (48)** (MrsAKnight) 8-9 JQuinn (14) (lw: mde all: r.o wl) ............................ —1 |
| 1794 | Roxy Music (IRE) (49) (bl) (GAPritchard-Gordon) 9-2 PRobinson (3) (hdwy over 2f out: hrd rdn over 1f out: r.o ins fnl f) ...................... 1½.2 |
| 2429⁶ | Sure Shot Norman (47) (JSutcliffe) 9-0 TQuinn (15) (lw: a.p: r.o one pce fnl 2f) ½.3 |
| 2552 | Pink'n Black (IRE) (58) (GBlum) 8-11 ‡5DHarrison (2) (a.p: hrd rdn over 1f out: nt qckn) .......................................................... ¾.4 |
| 2525⁴ | Coniston Lake (IRE) (61) (bl) (GLewis) 9-0 BRouse (4) (b.hind: a.p: no hdwy fnl 2f) .................................................... hd.5 |
| 2694 | Highborn (IRE) (PSFelgate) 9-0 WRyan (12) (hdwy over 1f out: r.o ins fnl f) .. s.h.6 |
| 2595⁴ | Palacegate Gold (IRE) (49) (RJHodges) 9-7 TSprake (6) (nvr nr to chal) ............. 1.7 |
| 2525³ | Myasha (USA) (70) (bl) (Fav) (MrsLPiggott) 9-7 LPiggott (11) (b.hind: hld up: rdn over 1f out: no rspnse) ................................. 2.8 |
| 2493 | Little Saboteur (65) (bl) (PJMakin) 9-2 AMunro (5) (lw: hld up: hrd rdn over 1f out: no rspnse) ........................................... nk.9 |
| 2718³ | Red Verona (39) (EAWheeler) 8-9 JWilliams (9) (swtg: s.s: nvr nrr) ................ 2.10 |
| 2365⁶ | Fourofus (56) (RBoss) 9-0 BRaymond (7) (n.d) ............................................ 2½.11 |
| 2617⁶ | Sea Crusader (47) (MBlanshard) 9-7 WNewnes (1) (spd 3f) ........................... 2½.12 |
| 2617 | Grand Time (54) (CJHill) 9-7 ADicks (13) (lw: spd 3f) ................................... ¾.13 |
| 2493 | Apache Maid (JSMoore) 8-9 AMcGlone (8) (t.o) ................................................ 6.14 |
| 2564 | Laggard's Quest (30) (CDBroad) 9-0 NAdams (10) (s.s: a bhd: t.o) ................ nk.15 |

100/30 Myasha (USA), 9/2 Coniston Lake (IRE)(6/1—4/1), 5/1 Sure Shot Norman, 6/1 Little Saboteur, 15/2 Pink'n Black (IRE), 10/1 Red Verona(8/1—12/1), 14/1 Fourofus, Palacegate Gold (IRE), 16/1 Sea Crusader, Highborn (IRE), Grand Time, 20/1 Easy Does It, 25/1 Roxy Music (IRE), 33/1 Ors. CSF £411.83, Tote £18.10: £4.70 £9.10 £1.80 (£280.90). Mr Derek V. Bolt (CULLOMPTON) bred by B. E. Green. 15 Rn; No bid; Roxy Music (IRE) clmd K Cunningham-Brown £6,011
　　　　1m 13.7 (3.2)
　　　　SF—31/32/28/22/24/23

## 2823

THEALE GRADUATION STKS (3 & 4-Y.O) £3158.00 (£944.00: £452.00: £206.00)　　1¼m 7y　　3-30 (3-33)

| 812⁴ | **Pabouche (USA) (92)** (bl) (HRACecil) 3-9-2 PatEddery (7) (mde virtually all: hrd rdn fnl 3f: swvd lft ins fnl f: all out) ................ —1 |
| 2137* | North Russia (CAN) (77) (JHMGosden) 3-9-2 RCochrane (6) (lw: 2nd st: jnd wnr 3f out: bmpd ins fnl f: r.o) ............... 1.2 |
| | Big Beat (USA) (60) (DRCElsworth) 4-9-0 JWilliams (2) (swtg: bit bkwd: 3rd st: one pce fnl 3f) ........................................ 10.3 |
| 1956 | Vanuatu (IRE) (TThomsonJones) 3-8-1 NAdams (9) (b: 6th st: nvr nr to chal) ...... 4.4 |
| | Fermain (LordHuntingdon) 3-8-6 AMunro (10) (unf: scope: s.s: nvr nr ldrs) ..... 2½.5 |
| | Lady Marriott (LMCumani) 4-8-9 LDettori (5) (bit bkwd: s.s: nvr nr ldrs) ............. 1.6 |
| | Chandigarh (RLee) 4-9-0 BRaymond (1) (bit bkwd: 4th st: wknd 3f out) .............. 10.7 |
| 440⁵ | Highland Fantasy (USA) (Fav) (BWHills) 3-8-1 WCarson (3) (b.hind: a bhd) ... 3½.8 |
| | Symmetrical (BWHills) 3-8-6 MHills (4) (bit bkwd: 5th st: wknd 3f out) ............... 4.9 |
| 2137 | Corpus (RJHodges) 3-8-3 ‡3FNorton (8) (bit bkwd: a bhd: t.o) ........................ 10.10 |

Stewards Enquiry: Obj. to Pabouche (USA) by Cochrane overruled.

2/1 Highland Fantasy (USA)(op 7/2), 9/4 North Russia (CAN)(op 6/4), PABOUCHE (USA)(6/4—5/2), 12/1 Lady Marriott, 16/1 Fermain, 25/1 Symmetrical, 33/1 Big Beat (USA), 50/1 Chandigarh, 100/1 Ors. CSF £7.57, Tote £3.20: £1.60 £1.10 £3.20 (£4.30). Sheikh Mohammed (NEWMARKET) bred by Darley Stud Management Co Ltd. in USA. 10 Rn
　　　　2m 9.7 (6.7)
　　　　SF—35/33/11/–/–/–

## 2824

RUSSELL NURSERY　£3184.00 (£952.00: £456.00: £208.00)　　5f 10y　　4-00 (4-03)

| 2690⁶ | **Carnbrea Snip (71)** (MBell) 8-7 MHills (1) (a.p: led over 2f out: all out) ........... —1 |
| 2577* | Troon (75) (MrsLPiggott) 8-11 LPiggott (3) (b: b.hind: lw: gd hdwy over 1f out: hrd rdn & r.o wl ins fnl f) ............................ s.h.2 |
| 2390² | My Bonus (85) (DJSCosgrove) 9-2 ‡5DHarrison (2) (b.hind: hdwy over 1f out: nt qckn ins fnl f) ...................................... 2.3 |
| 2371⁴ | Second Chance (IRE) (72) (PMitchell) 8-8 PatEddery (5) (lw: a.p: one pce fnl 2f) .................................................... 2.4 |
| 2256⁵ | Bellsabanging (63) (DRLaing) 7-8⁴ ‡5ATucker (7) (nvr nr to chal) ................ nk.5 |
| 2437 | Sea Exhibition (IRE) (73) (MBlanshard) 8-9 RCochrane (6) (no hdwy fnl 2f) ..... hd.6 |
| 2143² | Tuscan Dawn (83) (JBerry) 9-5 GCarter (4) (led over 2f) .............................. 3½.7 |

2085[5] Formaestre (IRE) **(69)** *(MHTompkins)* 8-5 PRobinson (8) (outpcd) ............... 4.8
2597[3] Jarena (IRE) **(77)** (Fav) *(GLewis)* 8-5 PaulEddery (9) (lw: prom 3f) ............... s.h.9
2546[5] Wealthywoo **(57)** (bl) *(JSMoore)* 7-7 JQuinn (10) (lw: spd 3f) ............... 1¹/₂.10
LONG HANDICAP: Wealthywoo 7-5.

**7/2** Jarena (IRE), **11/2** Tuscan Dawn, Second Chance (IRE)(4/1—6/1), **6/1** My Bonus, **7/1** Bellsabanging, **8/1** Troon, **9/1** CARNBREA SNIP, **12/1** Formaestre (IRE)(8/1—14/1), **14/1** Ors. CSF £73.62, CT £429.47. Tote £10.80: £3.50 £2.60 £2.10 (£42.80). Mrs S. M. Crompton (NEWMARKET) bred by Mrs J. R. Hine and Miss J. Bunting. 10 Rn
60.9 sec (1.9)
SF—30/33/30/14/–/3

**2825** ROTHMANS ROYALS NORTH SOUTH CHALLENGE SERIES H'CAP (0-90) £4435.00
(£1330.00: £640.00: £295.00) **1m 67y** 4-30 (4-33)

Croft Valley **(74)** *(RAkehurst)* 5-9-5 TQuinn (19) (lw: mde all: r.o wl) ............. —1
2813[2] Roseate Lodge **(68)** *(RWArmstrong)* 6-8-13 CKTse (7) (lw: hdwy 2f out: r.o ins fnl f) ............. 1¹/₂.2
2601[4] Red Kite **(66)** *(MBell)* 3-8-5 MHills (18) (lw: 2nd st: r.o one pce fnl 2f) ....... 2¹/₂.3
2707[4] Saafend **(65)** (Fav) *(JSutcliffe)* 4-8-10 MRoberts (5) (gd hdwy over 2f out: hrd rdn: one pce) ............. 2.4
2502[2] Queen of Shannon (IRE) **(70)** *(DMorris)* 4-9-1 MTebbutt (1) (lw: 5th st: one pce fnl 2f) ............. ¹/₂.5
2567* Lap of Luxury **(72)** *(WJarvis)* 3-8-11 NDay (3) (nvr nr to chal) ............. ¹/₂.6
2476 Sovereign Rock (IRE) **(74)** *(RHannon)* 3-8-13 JLloyd (4) (lw: nvr nr ldrs) .......... 1.7
2658[5] Crystal Heights (FR) **(82)** *(WAO'Gorman)* 4-9-13 AMunro (10) (4th st: wknd 2f out) ............. 2.8
Scales of Justice **(79)** *(JWHills)* 6-9-10 JWilliams (15) (s.s: nrst fin) ............. hd.9
2463[2] Domicksky **(75)** *(RSimpson)* 4-9-6 WRyan (14) (lw: a mid div) ............. ³/₄.10
2611[4] Elegant Friend **(67)** *(MHTompkins)* 4-8-12 PRobinson (6) (n.d) ............. nk.11
2561[4] Swift Romance (IRE) **(63)** *(BRMilliman)* 4-8-8 GBardwell (11) (n.d) ............. s.h.12
2422[6] Self Expression **(76)** *(IABalding)* 4-9-7 RCochrane (12) (lw: n.d) ............. 2.13
2453 Swallowcliffe **(78)** *(PTWalwyn)* 3-9-3 GDuffield (16) (lw: 3rd st: wknd over 2f out) ............. 2¹/₂.14
2449 Shaping Up (USA) **(85)** *(IABalding)* 3-9-10 JReid (9) (n.d) ............. ³/₄.15
2453 Tissisat (USA) **(83)** *(IABalding)* 3-9-8 PatEddery (20) (hld up & bhd: nvr plcd to chal) ............. ¹/₂.16
1382[5] Shirley's Train (USA) **(78)** *(LordHuntingdon)* 3-8-12 ‡5DHarrison (17) (n.d) ............. 1.17
2230[4] Thinking Twice (USA) **(69)** *(PWHarris)* 3-8-8 PaulEddery (2) (n.d) ............. 2.18
1275[3] Handsome Gent **(80)** *(LordHuntingdon)* 3-9-5 BRaymond (21) (swtg: 6th st: wknd over 3f out) ............. ¹/₂.19
2658 Cheveux Mitchell **(76)** (v) *(MRChannon)* 5-9-7 WNewnes (13) (prom whn hmpd after 2f: nt rcvr) ............. 3¹/₂.20
1129[2] Alycida (USA) **(84)** *(LMCumani)* 3-9-9 LDettori (8) (prom 4f: t.o) ............. 21

**6/1** Saafend, **13/2** Roseate Lodge, **7/1** Lap of Luxury, **8/1** Alycida (USA), **9/1** Tissisat (USA), **10/1** Domicksky, **12/1** Elegant Friend, Swift Romance (IRE), **14/1** Handsome Gent, **16/1** Shirley's Train (USA)(op 10/1), Sovereign Rock (IRE)(op 10/1), Queen of Shannon (IRE), Crystal Heights (FR), **20/1** Red Kite, Thinking Twice (USA), Cheveux Mitchell, **25/1** Shaping Up (USA), **33/1** CROFT VALLEY, Swallowcliffe, Self Expression, **40/1** Scales of Justice. CSF £242.28, CT £4,075.08. Tote £57.60: £17.40 £2.20 £3.70 £1.70 (£546.30). Miss Vivian Pratt (EPSOM) bred by Mrs M. Pratt. 21 Rn
1m 45.7 (4.1)
SF—44/33/17/16/19/13

**2826** BRACKNELL MEDIAN AUCTION STKS (Mdn 2-Y-O) £3036.00 (£846.00: £408.00)
**5f 10y** 5-00 (5-11)

2171[5] Simply Sooty **(82)** *(BRMilliman)* 8-2(2) GBaxter (2) (w ldrs: led 2f out: drvn out) . —1
Go Flightline (IRE) *(MBell)* 8-3 MHills (1) (unf: hdwy over 2f out: r.o ins fnl f) ..... 6.2
2459[4] Show Faith (IRE) (Fav) *(RHannon)* 8-2 MRoberts (25) (led 3f: swvd lft ins fnl f) nk.3
2619[4] Pat Poindestres *(MPMuggeridge)* 7-11 GBardwell (11) (nrst fin) ............. s.h.4
2414[2] Karukera *(MJHeaton-Ellis)* 7-11 WCarson (14) (a.p: r.o one pce fnl 2f) ............. s.h.5
2274 Folly Vision (IRE) *(RHannon)* 8-0 SRaymont (5) (nvr nrr) ............. 1¹/₂.6
1300[3] Avril Etoile *(LJHolt)* 7-10 ‡7CAvery (7) (a.p: one pce fnl 2f) ............. nk.7
1591 Sparky's Song *(JWHills)* 7-11 SDawson (8) (nvr nr to chal) ............. 3.8
Trinity Hall *(CAHorgan)* 7-12(1) AMcGlone (3) (unf: bkwd: hdwy fnl f: r.o) ........ s.h.9
2501[6] Jafetica *(DRLaing)* 7-8(2) ‡5ATucker (18) (spd 3f) ............. 1.10
2491[5] Saraswati *(PJMakin)* 8-0 AMunro (16) (n.d) ............. s.h.11
1283[5] Aragrove *(LJHolt)* 8-6(1) JReid (24) (n.d) ............. nk.12
Diskette *(LordHuntingdon)* 7-6 ‡5DHarrison (23) (unf: hdwy fnl f: r.o) ............. ¹/₂.13
Felice's Pet *(GLewis)* 8-0 PaulEddery (12) (leggy: n.d) ............. 1.14
Hobey Cat *(DRCEIsworth)* 7-7(1) ‡5BDoyle (6) (unf: bit bkwd: n.d) ............. 1.15
Persian Melody (IRE) *(DRCEIsworth)* 8-9 JWilliams (10) (unf: scope: n.d) ....... ¹/₂.16
2008 Pondering (v) *(SDow)* 8-2 JLloyd (13) (hmpd s: n.d) ............. ¹/₂.17

| 889 | Hohne Garrison (JWhite) 8-2 DaleGibson (4) (n.d) | 1.18 |
| 2709⁶ | Risk Proof (GLewis) 8-2 PRobinson (19) (a bhd) | nk.19 |
| | Lughnasa (JJBridger) 7-11 NAdams (21) (w'like: v.bkwd: outpcd) | s.h.20 |
| | The Golden Sport (GLewis) 8-2 GDuffield (9) (unf: a bhd) | hd.21 |
| 2773⁴ | Imafifer (IRE) (WRMuir) 8-2 ‡³RPerham (20) (spd 3f) | 3¹/₂.22 |
| 2633⁴ | Shy Romance (64) (bl) (PMMcEntee) 7-11 DBiggs (15) (w ldrs 3f: wknd qckly) | 1¹/₂.23 |

*Jest Rosie (33/1) Withdrawn (rdr inj in parade ring) : not under orders*

**13/8** Show Faith (IRE), **11/2** Karukera, **13/2** Saraswati(7/2—7/1), **9/1** Diskette(tchd 14/1), **10/1** SIMPLY
SOOTY, **16/1** Avril Etoile(op 10/1), **20/1** Go Flightline (IRE), Aragrove, **25/1** Felice's Pet, Persian Melody (IRE),
**33/1** Ors. CSF £168.19, Tote £11.60: £2.40 £3.70 £1.30 (£31.20). Mrs S. Joint (CULLOMPTON) bred by Mrs S.
Joint. 23 Rn            60.1 sec (1.1)
SF—41/18/16/10/9/6

---

**2827**    QUORTINA CHALLENGE CUP (H'cap) (0-85) £3340.00 (£1000.00: £480.00: £220.00)
       1m 3f 135y            5-30 (5-36)

(Weights raised 13 lb)

| 2357* | **Swift Silver (57)** (WJMusson) 5–9-0 JReid (4) (7th st: led ins fnl f: r.o wl) | —1 |
| 1044⁵ | Full Quiver (50) (v) (MrsBarbaraWaring) 7–8-7 NHowe (13) (b.off fore: 6th st: led over 1f out tl ins fnl f) | 1.2 |
| 2670⁶ | Doctor's Remedy (36) (bl) (MrsJJordan) 6–7-0 ‡7KimMcDonnell (14) (5th st: r.o one pce fnl 2f) | 3.3 |
| 2757⁵ | Striking Image (IRE) (66) (RHannon) 3–8-13 LDettori (9) (lw: led after 2f tl over 1f out) | 3.4 |
| 2677 | Bee Beat (49) (bl) (EAWheeler) 4–8-6 WNewnes (7) (lw: dwlt: nrst fin) | s.h.5 |
| 2312⁴ | Arfey (68) (TThomsonJones) 3–9-1 WCarson (11) (b: nvr nrr) | 8.6 |
| 2133⁵ | Heavyweight (IRE) (60) (CAHorgan) 3–8-7 AMcGlone (3) (lost pl 3f out: sme late hdwy) | 1¹/₂.7 |
| | Ketti (42) (DLWilliams) 7–7-13 NAdams (2) (blkwd: nvr nr to chal) | ³/₄.8 |
| 2698² | Diamond Wedding (USA) (65) (Fav) (NAGraham) 3–8-12 PatEddery (10) (lw: 8th st: no hdwy) | hd.9 |
| 2241⁴ | Mahrajan (66) (CJBenstead) 8–9-9 RCochrane (5) (sme hdwy 3f out: sn wknd) | 1¹/₂.10 |
| 2527 | Alight (74) (ACStewart) 3–9-7 MRoberts (12) (3rd st: wknd over 2f out) | hd.11 |
| | Smiles Ahead (67) (PJBevan) 4–9-10 BCrossley (1) (led 2f: 2nd st: wknd over 2f out) | 2.12 |
| | Jarzon Dancer (50) (DAWilson) 4–8-7 GCarter (8) (4th st: wknd over 2f out) | ³/₄.13 |
| | Viking Venture (40) (MrsLCJewell) 7–7-6⁽⁴⁾ ‡5DHarrison (6) (b: bit bkwd: a bhd: t.o fnl 4f) | dist.14 |

LONG HANDICAP: Doctor's Remedy 7-5, Viking Venture 7-6.

**3/1** Diamond Wedding (USA)(2/1—100/30), **9/2** Alight (IRE)(op 8/1), **5/1** Striking Image, IRE), **6/1** Mahrajan,
**13/2** SWIFT SILVER, **11/1** Arfey (IRE)(8/1—14/1), **14/1** Doctor's Remedy, **16/1** Bee Beat, Full Quiver, Jarzon
Dancer, **25/1** Smiles Ahead, **33/1** Heavyweight (IRE), **40/1** Ors. CSF £101.67, CT £1,304.60. Tote £5.50: £1.90
£4.60 £4.90 (£37.70). The Hon Mr John Corbett (NEWMARKET) bred by Dr O. Zawawi. 14 Rn   2m 31 (8.5)
SF—15/6/–/–/–/–

T/Plpt: £181.50 (22.25 Tckts).                  Hn

---

2769—**FOLKESTONE (R-H)**

### Tuesday, August 18th [Good to firm]

Going Allowance: minus 0.10 sec per fur (F)         Wind: almost nil

Stalls: low

**2828**    KENT MESSENGER GROUP H'CAP (0-70) £2742.00 (£762.00: £366.00)
       1m 1f 149y            1-45 (1-50)

(Weights raised 1 lb)

| 2707⁴ | **Wakil (IRE) (47)** (Fav) (LGCottrell) 3–7-12 NCarlisle (1) (2nd st: led over 1f out: edgd lft: rdn out) | —1 |
| 2583⁴ | Anatroccolo (40) (RABennett) 5–7-13 CRutter (10) (led 8f: unable qckn) | 3¹/₂.2 |
| 2805⁴ | Breezed Well (57) (CNAllen) 6–8-9 ‡7GForster (13) (6th st: r.o one pce fnl 2f) | 2.3 |
| 2684 | Lord Oberon (IRE) (65) (RJO'Sullivan) 4–9-10 WRyan (12) (4th st: one pce fnl 2f) | 2¹/₂.4 |
| 2708³ | Keep Your Word (57) (GBBalding) 6–8-9 ‡TraceyPurseglove (4) (hdwy over 1f out: nvr nrr) | s.h.5 |
| 2707³ | Green's Cassatt (USA) (55) (WMBrisbourne) 4–8-7 ‡7CHawksley (14) (hdwy over 1f out: r.o) | ¹/₂.6 |
| 2621² | Admiralty Way (41) (RBrotherton) 6–8-0 SDawson (6) (hdwy 5f out: 5th st: wknd over 1f out) | 2.7 |
| 2473⁴ | My Alibi (IRE) (42) (SDow) 4–8-1 JQuinn (9) (nvr nr to chal) | 8.8 |

| | | |
|---|---|---|
| 2413 | Simply George **(55)** (bl) *(RBoss)* 3–8–6 MTebbutt (7) (prom over 6f) | hd.9 |
| 2567⁶ | Spring Saint **(59)** *(MJHeaton-Ellis)* 3–8–10 GDuffield (11) (3rd st: wknd wl over 1f out) | 2.10 |
| 2184 | Brightness **(69)** *(MMoubarak)* 3–9-6 RCochrane (2) (b.hind: bhd fnl 4f) | 1.11 |
| 899 | Alice's Mirror **(53)** *(TPMcGovern)* 3–8–4 NAdams (8) (a bhd) | 2.12 |
| 2632 | Continuity **(59)** (bl) *(GHarwood)* 3–8–10 AClark (3) (prom over 6f) | 7.13 |
| 2135⁵ | Dominant Force **(57)** *(RHannon)* 3–8–8 JLloyd (5) (a bhd) | hd.14 |
| 2805 | Tenayestelign **(40)** *(DMarks)* 4–7-13 GBardwell (15) (a bhd) | 3.15 |

**11/4** WAKIL (IRE), **5/1** Green's Cassatt (USA), **10/1** Keep Your Word(op 6/1), Breezed Well, **11/1** Admiralty Way(op 7/1), **12/1** Lord Oberon (IRE)(op 8/1), **14/1** Brightness(op 8/1), Tenayestelign, Continuity, My Alibi (IRE), **16/1** Dominant Force, Simply George, Spring Saint(op 10/1), **40/1** Ors. CSF £94.19, CT £911.60. Tote £3.10: £1.50 £20.70 £2.90 (£160.60). Mr E. J. S. Gadsden (CULLOMPTON) bred by Rocklow Stud in Ireland. 15 Rn                                                                    2m 2.3 (4.6)
SF—28/22/28/38/22/19

### 2829
KENT TODAY (S) STKS (3 & 4-Y.O) £2427.00 (£672.00: £321.00)
**1m 1f 149y**                                                           2-15 (2-19)

| | | |
|---|---|---|
| 2729³ | **Aragon Court (38)** *(JPearce)* 4–9-0 RCochrane (3) (lw: 4th st: led over 1f out: r.o wl) | —1 |
| 2705⁵ | Count Robert (USA) **(53)** *(MissJacquelineSDoyle)* 4–9-0 JQuinn (8) (lw: hdwy over 3f out: 2nd st: led 2f out tl over 1f out: unable qckn) | 4.2 |
| 2600 | Formal Invitation (IRE) **(48)** (bl) *(GLewis)* 3–8-6 BRouse (2) (b: b.nr hind: rdn & hdwy 5f out: led over 2f out: sn hdd: one pce) | 1¹/₂.3 |
| 2251⁶ | Bengal Tiger (IRE) **(53)** (bl) *(JAkehurst)* 4–9-0 WRyan (1) (rdn over 2f out: 5th st: r.o one pce fnl f) | hd.4 |
| 2033 | High Post **(47)** *(DMarks)* 3–8-6 GDuffield (10) (hdwy on ins wl over 1f out: nvr nrr) | hd.5 |
| 2712 | Zaire *(ANLee)* 3–8-6 NCarlisle (4) (lw: nvr nr to chal) | ³/₄.6 |
| 1504 | China Sky **(41)** *(CNAllen)* 4–8–7 ‡7GForster (9) (6th st: no hdwy fnl 2f) | 2.7 |
| 2331⁴ | Soul Trader (bl) *(BWHills)* 3–8-1 DLee (7) (prom over 6f) | 2.8 |
| 2712⁵ | High Baccarat **(50)** (v) *(CCElsey)* 3–8-6 TRogers (6) (lw: led 7f: 3rd st: wknd wl over 1f out) | 2.9 |

**5/2** Bengal Tiger (IRE), **7/2** ARAGON COURT(op 7/1), **5/1** Count Robert (USA), **13/2** Soul Trader, **7/1** Formal Invitation (IRE), **8/1** High Post, **10/1** High Baccarat, **20/1** China Sky, **33/1** Zaire. CSF £20.91, Tote £4.10: £1.60 £1.50 £2.80 (£19.60). Mr Jeff Pearce (NEWMARKET) bred by Mrs K. W. Sneath. 9 Rn; No bid  2m 5.9 (8.2)

### 2830
SHEPWAY FESTIVAL H'CAP (0-70) £2784.00 (£774.00: £372.00)
**6f 189y**                                                             2-50 (2-57)

| | | |
|---|---|---|
| 2750³ | **Kirriemuir (41)** *(KOCunningham-Brown)* 4–8-1 NCarlisle (12) (b.nr hind: hdwy 2f out: led ins fnl f: rdn out) | —1 |
| 2770* | Surrey Racing **(68)** (Fav) *(GLewis)* 4–10-0 (5x) BRouse (15) (6th st: r.o one pce fnl 2f) | 3.2 |
| 2458 | Pigalle Wonder **(48)** *(RJO'Sullivan)* 4–8–8 AClark (4) (2nd st: led over 1f out tl ins fnl f: one pce) | s.h.3 |
| 2689⁶ | Kissavos **(51)** *(CCElsey)* 6–8–10 TRogers (11) (b.hind: lw: swtchd lft 2f out: hdwy over 1f out: r.o) | ¹/₂.4 |
| 2772 | Sunset Street (IRE) **(60)** *(SDow)* 4–8-13 ‡7AMartinez (5) (hdwy fnl 2f: r.o) | hd.5 |
| 2707 | Red Jack (IRE) **(53)** *(JAkehurst)* 3–8–8 SWhitworth (10) (hdwy fnl 2f) | s.h.6 |
| 2254³ | Spanish Love **(40)** *(CGCox)* 6–7–9(7) ‡5ATucker (7) (nvr nr to chal) | nk.7 |
| 2561 | Queen of Dreams **(34)** *(DrJDScargill)* 4–7-8 JQuinn (3) (lw: 3rd st: one pce fnl 2f) | nk.8 |
| 2496 | Chinaman **(38)** *(WGRWightman)* 3–7-7 GBardwell (6) (hdwy over 1f out: r.o) | 1.9 |
| 2750 | Cronk's Quality **(40)** (bl) *(DCJermy)* 9–8-0 SDawson (9) (led over 5f out tl over 1f out: sn wknd) | 1¹/₂.10 |
| 2752 | Slip-a-Snip **(58)** *(GBBalding)* 3–8-8 ‡5RPrice (8) (lw: bhd fnl 3f) | 1¹/₂.11 |
| 2053 | Blue Drifter (IRE) **(53)** *(JSutcliffe)* 3–8-8 NAdams (2) (s.i.s: a bhd) | hd.12 |
| 2449 | Kentucky Starlet (USA) **(58)** *(RHannon)* 3–8-13 BRaymond (16) (led over 1f: 5th st: wknd 2f out) | ¹/₂.13 |
| 2088 | Tadora (IRE) **(52)** *(CJBenstead)* 3–8-7 CRutter (1) (lw: 4th st: wknd over 1f out) | 1.14 |
| 2432⁵ | Sudanor (IRE) **(59)** (bl) *(MJHeaton-Ellis)* 3–9-0 PRobinson (14) (bhd fnl 2f) | 1¹/₂.15 |
| | The Cuckoo's Nest **(68)** *(CEBrittain)* 4–10-0 RCochrane (13) (bit bkwd: prom over 4f) | 2¹/₂.16 |

LONG HANDICAP: Spanish Love 7-6.

**15/8** Surrey Racing(11/4—7/4), **5/1** KIRRIEMUIR, **7/1** Kentucky Starlet (USA), **8/1** Spanish Love, **9/1** Kissavos, **12/1** Sudanor (IRE), **16/1** Slip-a-Snip, Tadora (IRE), **20/1** Pigalle Wonder, The Cuckoo's Nest, **25/1** Sunset Street (IRE), Queen of Dreams, **50/1** Ors. CSF £14.56, CT £164.66. Tote £4.90: £1.60 £1.30 £6.80 £1.70 (£5.80). Mr R. N. Short (STOCKBRIDGE) bred by Dr W. J. Heffernan. 16 Rn                                     1m 24.8 (3.2)
SF—58/46/25/26/27/21

## 2831

KENTISH EXPRESS STKS (Mdn 3-Y.O) £2070.00 (£570.00: £270.00)   6f 3-20 (3-26)

2753⁴ **Efra (60)** *(RHannon)* 9-0 JLloyd (10) (lw: rdn & hdwy over 2f out: led ins fnl f:
hdd nr fin: fin 2nd, hd: awrdd r) ......................................................................... —1

2419 Cashmiriana (IRE) **(53)** *(MissHCKnight)* 8-9 SWhitworth (8) (led tl ins fnl f: r.o:
fin 3rd, ³⁄₄l: plcd 2nd) ............................................... 2

2063 Jucea **(61)** *(DWPArbuthnot)* 8-9 PRobinson (6) (a.p: rdn over 2f out: r.o: fin 4th,
¹⁄₂l: plcd 3rd) ............................................... 3

2659⁵ Nbaat (USA) **(67)** *(CJBenstead)* 9-0 RCochrane (7) (lw: hld up: rdn over 2f out:
unable qckn fnl f: fin 5th, 1l: plcd 4th) ............................................... 4

2419² Sure Lord (IRE) **(68)** (v) *(WRMuir)* 9-0 GDuffield (9) (lw: a.p: ev ch over 1f out:
one pce: fin 6th, 1l: plcd 5th) ............................................... 5

2586⁵ Nordansk **(45)** *(LJHolt)* 9-0 MPerrett (11) (lw: spd over 4f) ......................... 3¹⁄₂.7

2419 Night Gown *(MissGayKelleway)* 8-9 GayKelleway (4) (b: lw: a.p: rdn over 2f out:
wkng whn hmpd over 1f out) ......................... 8.8

Ballygriffin Belle *(TPMcGovern)* 8-9 NAdams (1) (b.hind: w'like: bit bkwd: s.s: a
bhd) ......................................................................... 1¹⁄₂.9

2726² Hi-Tech Honda (IRE) **(67)** (Fav) *(CEBrittain)* 9-0 BRaymond (2) (rdn over 2f out:
swtchd & hdwy over 1f out: led nr fin: fin 1st: disq: plcd last) . 0

*Stewards Enquiry: Hi-Tech Honda (IRE) disq. (interference to Night Gown over 1f out). Raymond suspended
27/8-1/9/92 (careless riding).*

**15/8** Hi-Tech Honda (IRE), **2/1** Sure Lord (IRE), **6/1** Nbaat (USA), **9/1** Jucea, **12/1** EFRA(op 7/1), **14/1**
Cashmiriana (IRE)(op 6/1), **33/1** Ors. CSF £137.85, Tote £10.70: £2.90 £3.50 £1.30 (£128.40). Mr Paul Jubert
(MARLBOROUGH) bred by Mrs B. Alexander. 9 Rn                                    1m 13.1 (2.4)
SF—40/39/36/34/35/31

## 2832

RADIO KENT AUCTION STKS (Mdn 2-Y.O) £2805.00 (£780.00: £375.00)
**6f**                                                                      3-55 (3-59)

2285² **Snowy River (FR)** (Fav) *(DiJD Cargill)* 0 1□ RCochrane (?) (mde all:
wandered over 1f out: comf) ......................................................................... —1

2285⁵ Daring Past *(RBoss)* 8-6 MTebbutt (6) (hrd rdn over 1f out: unable qckn) 3¹⁄₂.2

My Best Valentine *(PWHarris)* 8-9 SWhitworth (4) (w'like: bit bkwd: hdwy over
2f out: hrd rdn over 1f out: one pce) ............................................... ¹⁄₂.3

2598 Erlking (IRE) *(LordHuntingdon)* 8-9 WRyan (10) (hmpd s: a.p: one pce fnl 2f) 1¹⁄₂.4

1902 Charrua *(JRFanshawe)* 8-13 GDuffield (1) (a.p: one pce fnl 2f) ......................... ¹⁄₂.5

791² Rough Guess (IRE) *(LordHuntingdon)* 8-4 PRobirison (5) (outpcd: hrd rdn over
3f out: nvr nrr) ......................................................................... 8.6

339 Persian Gusher (IRE) *(SDow)* 7-13 ‡7AMartinez (7) (spd 4f) ......................... nk.7

1991 Recit D'Argent *(CJames)* 8-6 JQuinn (11) (lw: spd over 4f) ......................... 2¹⁄₂.8

Formalin *(WAO'Gorman)* 8-6 NAdams (9) (str: bit bkwd: spd over 3f) ......................... 3.9

2696 Red Russian (bl) *(BJMcMath)* 8-6 EJohnson (8) (swvd rt & hmpd s: a wl bhd) 1¹⁄₂.10

2474⁵ Recipdico Mist (IRE) *(TJNaughton)* 7-12 ‡3FNorton (3) (lw: bhd fnl 3f) ............... 7.11

**10/11** SNOWY RIVER (FR), **5/2** Rough Guess (IRE)(9/4—4/1), **8/1** Daring Past, Erlking (IRE), **16/1** Formalin(op
10/1), Charrua(op 10/1), **50/1** Ors. CSF £9.24, Tote £1.90: £1.10 £2.40 £5.50 (£6.30). M. Reditt & Son Ltd
(NEWMARKET) bred by Stavros Niarchos in France. 11 Rn                                    1m 13.3 (2.6)
SF—34/14/15/9/11/–

## 2833

DAVE AUSTIN BREAKFAST SHOW H'CAP (0-70) £2954.00 (£819.00: £392.00)
**1¹⁄₂m**                                                                      4-25 (4-25)

2477 **Island Blade (IRE) (48)** *(RAkehurst)* 3–8-5 ‡3RPerham (4) (lw: 3rd st: hrd rdn
over 1f out: led nr fin) ......................................................................... —1

2806⁵ Cathos (FR) **(53)** *(DAWilson)* 7–9-9 BRouse (1) (b: rdn over 5f out: 2nd st: led
over 1f out: hdd nr fin) ......................................................................... ¹⁄₂.2

2580* Severine (USA) **(66)** (Jt-Fav) *(JLDunlop)* 3–9-12 WRyan (6) (5th st: hrd rdn over
1f out: r.o one pce) ......................................................................... 2¹⁄₂.3

2197⁴ Jupiter Moon **(63)** *(CEBrittain)* 3–9-9 BRaymond (7) (lw: led over 10f) ......... 2.4

2701³ Duggan **(53)** *(RJRWilliams)* 5–9-9 RCochrane (3) (6th st: no hdwy fnl 2f) ......... 7.5

2631³ Shayna Maidel **(42)** (Jt-Fav) *(MBell)* 3–8-2 GDuffield (5) (lw: 4th st: wknd over 1f
out) ......................................................................... 1¹⁄₂.6

2413 Moreirwen **(25)** *(JO'Donoghue)* 5–7-9 NAdams (2) (a bhd: t.o) ......................... 25.7

**3/1** Shayna Maidel(tchd 9/2), Severine (USA)(op 7/4), **7/2** Duggan(5/1—3/1), **11/2** Jupiter Moon, **6/1** Cathos
(FR), **13/2** ISLAND BLADE (IRE), **33/1** Moreirwen. CSF £41.22, Tote £10.70: £3.30 £3.20 (£8.80). The Lime
Street Racing Syndicate (EPSOM) bred by Waverton Stud Ltd in Ireland. 7 Rn                2m 40.3 (6.8)
SF—11/28/26/19/5/–

## 2834

PAT MARSH APP'CE H'CAP (0-70) £2385.00 (£660.00: £315.00)
**2m 93y**                                                                      4-55 (4-55)

2692 **Sharp Top (52)** *(MJRyan)* 4–9-12 PMcCabe (2) (hld up: led over 2f out: clr over
1f out: comf) ......................................................................... —1

2373* Arctic Splendour (USA) **(56)** (Jt-Fav) *(PWChapple-Hyam)* 3–9-2 DCarson (8)
(b.off hind: hdwy 5f out: 3rd st: chsd wnr fnl 2f: no imp) ...... **7.2**
20833 Podrida **(48)** *(RJO'Sullivan)* 6–9-8 GMitchell (7) (6th st: r.o one pce fnl 2f) ........ 1/2.**3**
25473 Dajitus **(60)** *(MJHeaton-Ellis)* 3–9-6 RuthCoulter (5) (b: 4th st: one pce fnl 2f)  11/2.**4**
26826 Lady Westgate **(23)** *(GBBalding)* 8–7-6 ‡5IonaWands (9) (hdwy over 1f out: nvr
nrr) ........................................................... 1/2.**5**
20836 Trojan Envoy **(25)** *(WCarter)* 4–7-13 AMartinez (4) (nvr nr to chal) ................... 6.**6**
22672 Scent of Battle **(42)** *(MJHaynes)* 4–9-2 DToole (1) (lw: led over 6f out tl over 2f
out: 2nd st: wknd over 1f out) ..................................... 8.**7**
2565* Glenstal Priory **(54)** (Jt-Fav) *(PFICole)* 5–9-9 ‡5PMcCormick (6) (lw: 5th st: wknd
wl over 1f out) ............................................... 1/2.**8**
25655 Radar Knight **(35)** *(RABennett)* 4–8-9 NVarley (3) (lw: led over 9f: wknd 4f out) 10.**9**

**3/1** Arctic Splendour (USA), Glenstal Priory, **4/1** Scent of Battle, **7/1** SHARP TOP, Podrida(5/1—15/2), **8/1**
Radar Knight(tchd 14/1), **12/1** Trojan Envoy(op 8/1), **16/1** Dajitus(op 10/1), **33/1** Lady Westgate. CSF £28.20,
CT £143.56. Tote £7.90: £1.70 £1.70 £2.50 (£13.50). Malpass Bros Ltd (NEWMARKET) bred by Limestone
Stud. 9 Rn
3m 41.1 (8.6)

T/Plpt: £3,007.30 (0.3 Tckts); £2,844.77 to York 19/8/92.
AK

---

## 2017—YORK (L-H)

### Tuesday, August 18th [Good]

Going Allowance: 6f 214y: minus 0.20 (F); Rest: minus 0.05 sec (G)        Wind: almost nil

Stalls: high

**2835**  DEPLOY ACOMB STKS (2-Y.O) £14750.00 (£4400.00: £2100.00: £950.00)
6f 214y
2-05 (2-07)

2034* **Woodchat** (USA) **(94)** (Fav) *(PFICole)* 9-5 AMunro (3) (lw: chsd ldrs: n.m.r &
swtchd over 1f out: r.o wl to ld cl home) .............................. —**1**
2340* Salatin (USA) **(100)** *(PTWalwyn)* 9-5 WCarson (8) (lw: a cl up: slt ld 1f out: r.o:
no ex nr fin) ................................................. hd.**2**
2501* Self Assured (IRE) **(92)** *(HRACecil)* 9-0 SCauthen (9) (lw: cl up: led wl over 1f
out: hdd 1f out: r.o) ........................................ 3/4.**3**
Newton's Law (IRE) **(88)** *(PWChapple-Hyam)* 8-12 PaulEddery (4) (w'like: scope:
hld up & bhd: hdwy 3f out: rdn & nt qckn appr fnl f) ........ 21/2.**4**
2584* Empire Pool **(100)** *(LordHuntingdon)* 9-5 WRSwinburn (1) (a chsng ldrs: rdn
over 2f out: r.o one pce) ...................................... 11/2.**5**
2375* Persian Brave (IRE) **(100)** *(MBell)* 9-5 MHills (5) (lw: chsd ldrs tl outpcd 1/2-wy:
no imp after) .............................................. s.h.**6**
2598* Anaheim (IRE) **(100)** *(RHannon)* 9-5 JReid (7) (lw: led tl hdd wl over 1f out: grad
wknd) ..................................................... 11/2.**7**
25742 Expo Mondial (IRE) **(91)** *(JMPEustace)* 9-5 MRoberts (2) (sn pushed along: no
imp fr 1/2-wy) .............................................. 2.**8**

2790³ Civil Law (IRE) (50/1) Withdrawn (lame at s) : not under orders

**3/1** WOODCHAT (USA), **100/30** Salatin (USA), **4/1** Self Assured (IRE), **5/1** Anaheim (IRE), **15/2** Persian Brave
(IRE), **12/1** Newton's Law (IRE)(op 8/1), **20/1** Ors. CSF £12.57, Tote £3.50: £1.30 £1.40 £1.50 (£5.30). Mr
Fahd Salman (WHATCOMBE) bred by Oak Crest Farm in USA. 8 Rn
1m 23.65 (1.25)
SF—65/64/57/47/49/48

**2836**  RACECALL MELROSE H'CAP (3-Y.O) (0-115) £15270.00 (£4560.00: £2180.00:
£990.00)
1m 5f 194y
2-35 (2-40)

2451* **Daru** (USA) **(80)** (v) *(JHMGosden)* 8-10 SCauthen (12) (lw: a in tch: hdwy
4f out: led over 1f out: r.o: comf) .................................. —**1**
2442 Al Karnak (IRE) **(84)** *(MMoubarak)* 9-0 LDettori (6) (hdwy ent st: qcknd to ld wl
over 1f out: wknd 1f out) ...................................... 1.**2**
24553 Three Wells **(89)** *(JLDunlop)* 9-5 JReid (10) (lw: hld up & bhd: hdwy on outside
4f out: hung lft: nvr able to chal) ............................... 31/2.**3**
1990* Teddy's Play (USA) **(80)** *(JWHills)* 8-10 MHills (4) (hdwy & prom 7f out: led 3f
out tl wl over 1f out: one pce) .................................. 21/2.**4**
2314a5 Flight Lieutenant (USA) **(85)** *(PMitchell)* 9-1 LPiggott (8) (hld up & bhd: effrt ent
st: r.o u.p: nvr rchd ldrs) ..................................... 5.**5**
24122 Farmer's Pet **(81)** *(GAPritchard-Gordon)* 8-11 GCarter (7) (a cl up: led 4f out: sn
hdd & one pce) .............................................. 31/2.**6**
2736* Kadari **(67)** *(AHarrison)* 7-6(4) (4x) ‡5DHarrison (11) (lw: hld up: hmped ent st: effrt
& n.m.r 3f out: hung lft & n.d) .................................. 1.**7**
25532 Kanvass **(82)** *(JRFanshawe)* 8-12 PatEddery (14) (a.p: effrt 4f out: rdn & btn
over 2f out) ................................................ 2.**8**
2178* Spikenard **(91)** *(PTWalwyn)* 9-7 TQuinn (6) (lw: cl up tl rdn & btn over 2f out) .. s.h.**9**

*2692* Take by Storm (IRE) *(76)* *(GMMoore)* 8-6 DMcKeown (1) (lw: trckd ldrs tl outpcd fnl 4f) ............................................................. ¹/₂.**10**

2349⁴ Green Lane (IRE) *(78)* *(RCharlton)* 8-8 WCarson (2) (lw: hdwy ent st: sn drvn along: eased whn btn appr fnl f) .............................. 4.**11**

2736² Suez Canal (IRE) (v) *(PWChapple-Hyam)* 8-6 PaulEddery (13) (led tl hdd 4f out: sn lost pl) ....................................................... 2¹/₂.**12**

2596² Miss Pin Up *(71)* *(PatMitchell)* 8-1 DBiggs (15) (effrt on outside 4f out: sn rdn & btn) .............................................................. nk.**13**

2336³ Lobilio (USA) *(86)* *(CEBrittain)* 9-2 MRoberts (9) (chsd ldrs tl wknd over 4f out) 5.**14**

2455⁴ Faugeron *(85)* *(GWragg)* 9-1 WRSwinburn (3) (sn drvn along: bhd tl sme hdwy u.p 4f out: sn wknd) ....................................... ³/₄.**15**

LONG HANDICAP: Kadari 7-2.

**5/1** DARU (USA), **6/1** Kanvass, **8/1** Three Wells, **10/1** Faugeron, Farmer's Pet, Green Lane (IRE), **11/1** Spikenard, **12/1** Teddy's Play (USA), Lobilio (USA), **14/1** Al Karnak (IRE), Miss Pin Up, **16/1** Kadari, Take by Storm (IRE), **20/1** Ouns. CSF £69.25, CT £509.25. Tote £4.60: £2.10 £6.10 £3.00 (£141.00). Sheikh Mohammed (NEWMARKET) bred by Albert G. Clay & Charlotte Clay Buxton in USA. 15 Rn      2m 57.60 (4)
SF–49/51/49/35/30/19

**2837**    JUDDMONTE INTERNATIONAL STKS (Gp 1)    £164852.00 (£60668.00: £28834.00: £11470.00: £4235.00: £1341.00)    1¹/₄m 85y      3-10 (3-21)

1456⁴ **Rodrigo de Triano (USA)** *(PWChapple-Hyam)* 3–8-12 LPiggott (12) (hld up & bhd: hdwy 4f out: smooth progress to ld over 1f out: pushed out) .......................................................... —**1**

2461² All At Sea (USA) *(HRACecil)* 3–8-9 PatEddery (2) (in tch: hdwy on bit 3f out: led over 2f out tl appr fnl f: r.o) ....................................... 1.**2**

2022² Seattle Rhyme (USA) *(DRCElsworth)* 3–8-12 CAsmussen (3) (swtg: hld up: gd hdwy 3f out: hrd rdn appr fnl f: kpt on) ............................ 3.**3**

1819a² Dr Devious (IRE) *(PWChapple-Hyam)* 3–8-12 JReid (8) (lw: a.p: ev ch & rdn 2f out: no ex) .............................................. s.n.**4**

2189³ Masad (IRE) *(LMCumani)* 3–8-12 LDettori (5) (lw: hld up: effrt over 3f out: wnt prom 2f out: sn rdn & btn) ...................................... 3.**5**

1876⁶ Zoman (USA) *(PFICole)* 5–9-6 AMunro (9) (lw: chsd ldrs: pushed along over 4f out: grad wknd fnl 3f) ...................................... 2¹/₂.**6**

1198 Alnasr Alwasheek *(MRStoute)* 3–8-12 SCauthen (1) (lw: led tl hdd over 2f out: sn rdn & btn) .................................................. 1¹/₂.**7**

2461* Ruby Tiger *(PFICole)* 5–9-3 TQuinn (10) (lw: in tch: rdn 4f out: sn btn) ................ 8.**8**

2461⁶ Gussy Marlowe *(CEBrittain)* 4–9-3 WCarson (7) (lw: bhd: effrt 4f out: no imp) .... 5.**9**

2345³ Terimon *(CEBrittain)* 6–9-6 MRoberts (6) (cl up tl wknd 4f out) ...................... hd.**10**

2316a Bobzao (IRE) *(WCarter)* 3–8-12 JCarroll (4) (chsd ldrs tl wknd qckly over 3f out) 3.**11**

2627a* Kooyonga (IRE) (Fav) *(MKauntze, Ireland)* 4–9-3 WJO'Connor (11) (lw: sn pushed along: bhd & rdn 4f out: wandered 3f out & virtually p.u) ............................................... dist.**12**

**2/1** Kooyonga (IRE), **5/1** All At Sea (USA), **7/1** Alnasr Alwasheek, **8/1** Dr Devious (IRE), RODRIGO DE TRIANO (USA), **9/1** Ruby Tiger, **16/1** Seattle Rhyme (USA), Masad (IRE)(op 25/1), **20/1** Zoman (USA), **25/1** Terimon, **100/1** Gussy Marlowe, **200/1** Bobzao (IRE). CSF £43.37, Tote £8.80: £2.40 £1.60 £2.80 (£28.50). Mr R. E. Sangster (MARLBOROUGH) bred by Swettenham Stud in USA. 12 Rn      2m 7.19 (U.31)
SF–96/91/88/87/81/84

**2838**    GREAT VOLTIGEUR STKS (Gp 2) (3-Y.O.C & G) £49572.00 (£18447.60: £8773.80: £3726.60)    1m 3f 195y      3-45 (3-53)

2434* **Bonny Scot (IRE)** (Fav) *(LMCumani)* 8-9 LDettori (1) (lw: hld up: effrt over 3f out: led appr fnl f: r.o wl) ............................. —**1**

1458⁴ Sonus (IRE) *(JHMGosden)* 8-9 SCauthen (5) (trckd ldrs: chal over 2f out: led wl over 1f out: sn hdd & hrd rdn) ....................... 1¹/₂.**2**

1198 Assessor (IRE) *(RHannon)* 8-9 JReid (3) (lw: a.p: effrt 3f out: r.o fnl f) ............ 2¹/₂.**3**

2432⁴ Alflora (IRE) *(CEBrittain)* 8-9 MRoberts (2) (lw: led: qcknd over 3f out: hdd wl over 1f out: sn btn) ................................. 2.**4**

2174⁴ Host (IRE) *(CEBrittain)* 8-9 WCarson (4) (lw: cl up: rdn 3f out: sn btn) .............. 25.**5**

2522* Colorific *(BWHills)* 8-9 PatEddery (6) (hld up: broke down over 3f out: p.u) ............ 0

**11/8** BONNY SCOT (IRE), **7/2** Sonus (IRE), **9/2** Assessor (IRE), **5/1** Colorific, **8/1** Alflora (IRE), **50/1** Host (IRE). CSF £6.32, Tote £2.30: £1.40 £2.00 (£4.80). Lord Weinstock (NEWMARKET) bred by Ballymacoll Stud Farm Ltd. in Ireland. 6 Rn      2m 30.22 (3.22)
SF–57/54/49/45/–/

**2839**    EAGLE LANE H'CAP (0-110) £13110.00 (£3930.00: £1890.00: £870.00)    6f      (Weights raised 1 lb)      4-15 (4-25)

2435⁶ **Master Planner (97)** *(CACyzer)* 3–9-3 DBiggs (18) (lw: mde all stands' side: r.o wl fnl f) .............................................. —**1**

2642 Stack Rock (94) *(EJAlston)* 5-8-13 ‡⁵JWeaver (20) (a cl up stands' side: nt qckn ins fnl f) ............................................................................................ 1.2
2262⁶ Densben (81) *(DenysSmith)* 8-8-5 KFallon (13) (lw: chsd ldrs centre: rdn 2f out: r.o nr fin) ......................................................................... ³/₄.3
2658³ Hard to Figure (91) *(RJHodges)* 6-9-1 JWilliams (16) (lw: bhd: hdwy 2f out: r.o wl fnl f) ..................................................................................... hd.4
2435 Bold Lez (98) *(MJHaynes)* 5-9-8 SCauthen (12) (lw: led centre: rdn 2f out: kpt on) ......................................................................................... s.h.5
2559 Finjan (89) *(MPNaughton)* 5-8-13 AMunro (23) (chsd ldrs stands' side: styd on one pce fnl 2f) ..................................................................... s.h.6
2435 Appledorn (83) *(BAMcMahon)* 5-8-7 JReid (9) (in tch: hdwy over 1f out: styd on) .............................................................................................. s.h.7
2188* Rose Indien (FR) (96) *(MMoubarak)* 3-9-2 LDettori (10) (lw: chsd ldrs far side: chal 2f out: wknd ins fnl f) .................................................. nk.8
2435 Milagro (85) *(RHannon)* 3-8-5 PatEddery (17) (chsd ldrs centre tl wknd fnl f) 1¹/₂.9
2658 Panikin (92) *(JWharton)* 4-8-11 ‡⁵SWilliams (5) (lw: disp ld far side tl rdn & btn over 1f out) ............................................................................ s.h.10
2697² Wilde Rufo (100) *(PAKelleway)* 3-9-6 JCarroll (11) (a in tch: effrt over 2f out: nt qckn) ............................................................................................. nk.11
2592² Plain Fact (90) *(JWHills)* 7-9-0 MHills (22) (racd stands' side: nvr trbld ldrs) .. nk.12
2449 Claybank (USA) (86) *(BWHills)* 3-8-6 WCarson (7) (disp ld far side tl rdn & btn appr fnl f) ........................................................................................ s.h.13
2435 Bertie Wooster (85) *(RJHolder)* 9-8-9 WRSwinburn (21) (lw: racd stands' side: effrt ¹/₂-wy: no imp) ....................................................................... ³/₄.14
2642³ Cumbrian Waltzer (95) (Fav) *(MHEasterby)* 7-9-5 MBirch (4) (hdwy far side 2f out: nvr plcd to chal) ...................................................................... ¹/₂.15
1875⁴ Sir Harry Hardman (100) (bl) *(FHLee)* 4-9-5 ‡⁵NKennedy (8) (hdwy 2f out: n.d) s.h.16
2658⁶ Green Dollar (88) *(EAWheeler)* 9-8-12 LPiggott (6) (nvr plcd to chal) ............ hd.17
2650³ Adwick Park (84) *(TDBarron)* 4-8-8 KDarley (19) (lw: swtchd lft s: racd centre: n.d) ..................................................................................................... 1.18
1931³ Dominuet (86) *(JLSpearing)* 7-8-10 GHind (1) (lw: n.d) .................................. 1.19
2376⁴ Allinson's Mate (IRE) (78) *(TDBarron)* 4-8-2 AlexGreaves (2) (lw: chsd ldrs far side: rdn 2f out: sn wknd) .................................................................. s.h.20
2520⁶ Gentle Hero (USA) (79) *(MPNaughton)* 6-8-3 MRoberts (14) (cl up 4f) ........... ¹/₂.21
2650² Clifton Charlie (USA) (86) *(MRChannon)* 4-8-10 TQuinn (15) (rdn & bhd fr ¹/₂-wy) ............................................................................................................. 6.22
2435 Orthorhombus (99) (bl) *(GLewis)* 3-9-5 PaulEddery (3) (sn outpcd & bhd) ...... 4.23

**5/1** Cumbrian Waltzer, **10/1** Rose Indien (FR)(9/1—14/1), **12/1** Hard to Figure, Claybank (USA), **14/1** Adwick Park, Bold Lez, Dominuet, Allinson's Mate (IRE), Densben, **16/1** Gentle Hero (USA), Clifton Charlie (USA), Finjan, MASTER PLANNER, Plain Fact, **20/1** Orthorhombus, Bertie Wooster, Appledorn, Green Dollar, Milagro, **25/1** Panikin, **33/1** Sir Harry Hardman, Stack Rock, **50/1** Wilde Rufo. CSF £426.82, CT £6,678.77. Tote £26.90: £6.40 £12.00 £2.80 £2.90 (£394.50). Mr R. M. Cyzer (HORSHAM) bred by C. A. Cyzer. 23 Rn　　1m 11.02 (0.82)
SF—81/73/62/71/77/67

**2840**　　LONSDALE STKS (listed race)　　£18112.50 (£5400.00: £2575.00: £1162.50)
　　　　　　1m 7f 195y
　　　　　　　　　　　　　　　　　　　　　　　　　　　　　4-45 (4-53)

2446* **Further Flight** (114) (Fav) *(BWHills)* 6-9-5 MHills (6) (lw: b.hind: hld up: styd hdwy to ld wl over 1f out: shkn up & sn qcknd clr) .............. —1
2446³ Landowner (IRE) (110) *(JHMGosden)* 3-8-5 WCarson (4) (lw: hld up: hdwy 6f out: ev ch & rdn over 2f out: edgd lft & r.o one pce) ......... 2¹/₂.2
2446 Tyrone Bridge (106) *(MCPipe)* 6-9-3 MRoberts (7) (w ldr: led wl over 2f out tl wl over 1f out: sn outpcd) .................................................................. 2.3
826 Nibbs Point (IRE) (105) *(LMCumani)* 4-8-12 LDettori (5) (chsd ldrs: rdn 3f out: one pce fnl 2f) .................................................................................... 2.4
2323a² Silvernesian (USA) *(JLDunlop)* 3-8-0 AMunro (2) (lw: led tl hdd wl over 2f out: sn outpcd) ........................................................................................ 3¹/₂.5
2542³ Redstella (USA) *(RMWhitaker)* 3-8-0 GCarter (1) (lost tch 6f out) ................. 20.6
2737 Lafkadio (52) (bl) *(MCChapman)* 5-9-0 SWebster (3) (prom to ¹/₂-wy: sn rdn: wknd qckly appr st) ........................................................................... 12.7

**5/6** FURTHER FLIGHT, **3/1** Landowner (IRE), **8/1** Tyrone Bridge, **10/1** Nibbs Point (IRE), Silvernesian (USA), **100/1** Redstella (USA), **200/1** Lafkadio. CSF £3.51, Tote £1.80: £1.30 £1.40 (£2.00). Mr S. Wingfield Digby (LAMBOURN) bred by S. Wingfield Digby. 7 Rn　　　　　　3m 25.64 (5.64)
SF—41/24/34/27/11/–

**2841**　　EGLINTON NURSERY　　£12135.00 (£3630.00: £1740.00: £795.00)
　　　　　　6f 214y
　　　　　　　　　　　　　(Weights raised 1 lb)　　　　5-15 (5-23)

2578* **Noyan** (89) *(MBell)* 8-10 MHills (7) (led 3f: chsd ldrs: r.o u.p to ld last stride) .... —1
2528⁴ No Reservations (IRE) (85) *(RFJohnsonHoughton)* 8-1 ‡⁵DHarrison (14) (lw: hdwy ¹/₂-wy: led ins fnl f: r.o: jst ct) .................................................. s.h.2

2462 Hung Parliament **(73)** *(BWHills)* 7-8 DaleGibson (3) (hdwy 3f out: hrd rdn fnl f: r.o nr fin) .................................................................. nk.3

23446 Carranita (IRE) **(88)** *(BPalling)* 8-4 ‡5StephenDavies (11) (w ldr: led 4f out tl ins fnl f: kpt on wl) ............................................... hd.4

2462* Marillette (USA) **(100)** (Fav) *(JHMGosden)* 9-7 SCauthen (10) (lw: hdwy over 2f out: edgd lft: r.o nr fin) ....................................... 1.5

2706* True Story (IRE) **(74)** *(RHannon)* 7-9 (6x) DBiggs (1) (lw: a chsng ldrs: outpcd over 2f out: styd on fnl f) ....................................... 3.6

23752 Wufud (USA) **(95)** *(JLDunlop)* 9-2 TQuinn (5) (in tch: outpcd 2f out: r.o fnl f) .. 2½.7

19653 Mhemeanles **(92)** *(MHEasterby)* 8-13 MBirch (9) (lw: trckd ldrs tl hmpd & lost pl ½-wy) ............................................................... 2.8

23753 Cardinal Dogwood (USA) **(76)** *(MBrittain)* 7-11 JLowe (4) (bhd: sme hdwy 2f out: n.d) ........................................................ s.h.9

26462 Storm Venture (IRE) **(79)** *(BBeasley)* 8-0 LCharnock (13) (chsd ldrs: hung lft ½-wy: sn rdn & no imp after) ...................................... s.h.10

2528* Tajdif (USA) **(89)** *(DMorley)* 8-10 WCarson (6) (lw: chsd ldrs over 5f: eased whn btn) ............................................................ 3.11

2667* Silverlocks **(87)** *(MissSEHall)* 8-3 ‡5JWeaver (8) (trckd ldrs: effrt 3f out: hung lft & sn wknd) ............................................... nk.12

2335* Garp (FR) **(86)** *(MRStoute)* 8-7 PatEddery (12) (lw: effrt on outside ½-wy: sn wknd & eased) ..................................................... nk.13

2068* Persian Fountain (IRE) **(72)** *(BSRothwell)* 7-7 SWood (2) (lw: in tch 4f) ......... ½.14

**7/2** Marillette (USA), **4/1** Tajdif (USA), **15/2** NOYAN, Garp (FR), **8/1** True Story (IRE), **11/1** Persian Fountain (IRE), **12/1** Hung Parliament, Silverlocks, No Reservations (IRE), Carranita (IRE), **14/1** Storm Venture (IRE), Wufud (USA), **16/1** Mhemeanles, **33/1** Cardinal Dogwood (USA). CSF £96.18, CT £1,009.80. Tote £10.00: £2.80 £3.00 £3.60 (£89.50). Mr Yucel Birol (NEWMARKET) bred by Oakgrove Stud. 14 Rn 1m 24.60 (2.20)
                                                              SF—42/32/24/33/47/12

1/Trio. Race 2. £001.40 (8.2 Tckts), Race 3: £65.10 (47.1 Tckts) & Race 5: £1,818.70 (3 Tckts). T/Jkpt: Not won; £12,639.00 to York 19/8/92. T/Plpt: £156.90 (148.55 Tckts).    AA

## YORK (L-H)
### Wednesday, August 19th [Good to firm]
Going Allowance: minus 0.15 sec per fur (F)
                                                      Wind: slt across

Stalls: high

**2842**    ROUS (S) STKS (2-Y-O) £8350.00 (£2500.00: £1200.00: £550.00)    **6f**   2-05 (2-14)

27762 Bold Seven (IRE) **(82)** (Fav) *(FHLee)* 8-1 ‡5NKennedy (18) (w ldrs: led 2f out: r.o strly: eased nr fin) ......................................... —1

2598 Knobbleeneeze *(MRChannon)* 8-11 PatEddery (1) (lw: w ldr far side: kpt on wl fnl f) ................................................................ 1½.2

27796 Plum First **(70)** *(RHannon)* 8-11 SWebster (2) (led far side: kpt on same pce fnl f) nk.3

26612 Palacegate Prince **(65)** *(JBerry)* 8-11 TQuinn (13) (led 4f: r.o same pce) ......... ½.4

2758 El Nino (IRE) *(RHannon)* 8-11 BRouse (9) (lw: a.p: rdn & nt qckn fnl 2f) ......... nk.5

26616 Clanrock *(RMWhitaker)* 8-11 AMunro (2) (blind off eye: racd far side: chsd ldrs: styd on one pce appr fnl f) ............................... 1½.6

2176 Florac (IRE) *(MJHeaton-Ellis)* 8-6 BRaymond (16) (b.hind: chsd ldrs: drvn along over 2f out: no imp) ....................................... 1.7

2274 Scoffera *(NTinkler)* 8-6 LCharnock (20) (in tch: no imp fnl 2f) ......................... 1½.8

15793 Ban Ri (IRE) *(MHTompkins)* 8-6 PRobinson (10) (chsd ldrs tl wknd 2f out) ...... 1½.9

2544 Hotel California (IRE) **(66)** *(JWHills)* 8-6 MHills (12) (lw: swtchd rt s: nvr rchd ldrs) ............................................................... ¾.10

2700 New Kid in Town *(NTinkler)* 8-11 RCochrane (8) (nvr nr to chal) ................ ¾.11

27761 I'M a Dreamer (IRE) *(WWHaigh)* 8-11 DMcKeown (19) (chsd ldrs: drvn along & hung bdly lft ½-wy: sn lost pl) ......................... nk.12

27095 Who's Tom (IRE) *(WJMusson)* 8-11 JReid (7) (b: sn outpcd) ......................... hd.13

1902 Strephon (IRE) (v) *(MHTompkins)* 8-11 GDuffield (11) (chsd ldrs: rdn ½-wy: sn wknd) ............................................................. 1.14

2688 Formidable Liz *(NBycroft)* 8-6 JLowe (4) (racd far side: prom 4f) ................. s.h.15

2205 Challenger Row (IRE) *(CWThornton)* 8-11 RPElliott (15) (b.hind: n.d) ............ s.h.16

      Simply Superb *(MWEasterby)* 8-11 TLucas (5) (w'like: leggy: racd far side: plld hrd: outpcd fr ½-wy) .................................. nk.17

25446 Mind the Roof (IRE) *(DRCEllsworth)* 8-6 WCarson (17) (sn bhd & drvn along) ¾.18

25122 Bright Gem **(58)** (bl) *(TFairhurst)* 8-6 JFanning (6) (racd far side: chsd ldrs tl wknd over 2f out) .................................. nk.19

      Quick Victory *(PCHaslam)* 8-6 DaleGibson (14) (unf: scope: dwlt: a bhd) ...... 8.20

26883 Sounds Risky **(47)** (bl) *(GMMoore)* 8-1 ‡5DHarrison (21) (wl bhd fnl 2f) ........... 5.21

3/1 BOLD SEVEN (IRE), **100/30** Mind the Roof (IRE), **8/1** Florac (IRE), Palacegate Prince, **10/1** Knobbleeneeze, **12/1** El Nino (IRE), **14/1** Who's Tom (IRE), I'M a Dreamer (IRE), **16/1** Ban Ri (IRE), **20/1** Bright Gem, Sounds Risky, Hotel California (IRE), **25/1** Quick Victory, Challenger Row (IRE), Clanrock, Plum First, New kid in Town, **33/1** Ors. CSF £37.39, Tote £3.80: £1.80 £3.10 £10.10 (£38.00). Mr F. H. Lee (WILMSLOW) bred by Airlie Stud in Ireland. 21 Rn; Bt in 16,200 gns

1m 13.14 (2.94)
SF—10/14/13/11/10/4

**2843** ASTON UPTHORPE YORKSHIRE OAKS (Gp 1) (F & M) £77728.00 (£28552.00: £13526.00: £5330.00: £1915.00: £549.00) **1m 3f 195y** 2-35 (2-47)

2094a* **User Friendly** *(Fav) (CEBrittain)* 3–8-11 GDuffield (3) (lw: s.s: sn rcvrd: effrt, hung lft & swtchd 3f out: led over 1f out: r.o strly) ............... —1

2094a[4] Bineyah (IRE) *(MRStoute)* 3–8-11 PatEddery (2) (lw: sn outpcd & bhd: hdwy 3f out: hrd rdn & styd on wl fnl f: no ch w wnr) ..................... 2½.2

2542* Guilty Secret *(PWChapple-Hyam)* 3–8-11 PaulEddery (4) (trckd ldr: led over 2f out tl over 1f out: r.o same pce) ..................... s.h.3

1843* Niodini (USA) (v) *(MRStoute)* 3–8-11 SCauthen (1) (trckd ldrs: effrt & ev ch over 2f out: kpt on same pce) ..................... nk.4

1470 Pearl Angel *(MissBSanders)* 3–8-11 LPiggott (7) (lw: hld up & bhd: effrt over 3f out: nvr rchd ldrs) ..................... 10.5

1646a[3] Lara's Idea (bl) *(LuigiCamici,Italy)* 4–9-7 JReid (6) (lw: trckd ldrs: drvn along & outpcd over 3f out: sn lost pl) ..................... ¾.6

717[4] Midnight Air (USA) *(HRACecil)* 3–8-11 RCochrane (5) (lw: led tl over 2f out: sn wknd & eased) ..................... s.h.7

2766a Magnificent Star (USA) *(MMoubarak)* 4–9-7 LDettori (8) (lw: hld up: effrt over 4f out: wknd over 2f out) ..................... 2.8

**8/11** USER FRIENDLY, **8/1** Magnificent Star (USA), Niodini (USA), Midnight Air (USA), Bineyah (IRE), **12/1** Lara's Idea, **33/1** Ors. CSF £7.18, Tote £1.70: £1.10 £1.90 £3.20 (£5.10). Mr W. J. Gredley (NEWMARKET) bred by Stetchworth Park Stud Ltd. 8 Rn

2m 29.41 (2.41)
SF—55/50/49/48/28/20

**2844** TOTE EBOR H'CAP (0-115) £67709.25 (£20349.00: £9824.50: £4562.25) **1m 5f 194y** 3-10 (3-25)

(Weights raised 2 lb)

2442[5] **Quick Ransom (81)** *(MJohnston)* 4–8-3 DMcKeown (1) (led 1f: trckd ldrs: led over 2f out: hrd rdn & hld on wl fnl f) ..................... —1

2442[3] Brier Creek (USA) **(92)** *(JHMGosden)* 3–8-2 PaulEddery (6) (lw: mid div: effrt & pushed along 4f out: r.o wl fnl f) ..................... hd.2

2028[3] Steerforth (IRE) **(99)** *(ACStewart)* 4–9-7 MRoberts (11) (lw: trckd ldrs: effrt over 2f out: n.m.r: styd on strly fnl f) ..................... ½.3

1002[5] Whitechapel (USA) **(80)** *(LordHuntingdon)* 4–8-2 AMunro (12) (trckd ldrs: ev ch over 2f out: edgd lft u.p: r.o one pce fnl f) ..................... ¾.4

2339 Star Player **(82)** *(RJBaker)* 6–7-13 ‡5SMaloney (15) (hld up: effrt 3f out: styd on wl fnl f: nt rch ldrs) ..................... hd.5

2645[5] Holy Zeal **(82)** *(DWPArbuthnot)* 6–8-4 TQuinn (14) (hld up & bhd: gd hdwy over 2f out: n.m.r: r.o wl nr fin) ..................... nk.6

2442[2] Castoret **(77)** *(JWHills)* 6–7-8 ‡5DHarrison (16) (lw: sn bhd: hdwy & nt cl run over 2f out: styd on strly cl home) ..................... hd.7

2442 Deposki **(90)** (bl) *(MRStoute)* 4–8-12 LDettori (9) (trckd ldrs & plld hrd: effrt over 2f out: kpt on: nvr rchd ldrs) ..................... 3.8

2349[3] Hajaim (IRE) **(86)** *(CEBrittain)* 4–8-8 SCauthen (8) (hld up: effrt & nt clr run over 3f out: styd on strly: nt rch ldrs) ..................... 2.9

2442[6] Kiveton Kabooz **(80)** *(LMCumani)* 4–8-8 JFortune (3) (bhd tl styd on wl fnl 2f) ..................... s.h.10

8615 Jackson Flint **(81)** (bl) *(HThomsonJones)* 4–8-3 GDuffield (5) (dwlt: bhd tl kpt on fnl 2f) ..................... ¾.11

2451[2] Storm Crossing (USA) **(90)** *(Fav) (GHarwood)* 3–8-0 AMcGlone (21) (trckd ldrs: ev ch tl rdn & wknd 3f out) ..................... hd.12

1697[3] Satin Lover **(92)** *(NTinkler)* 4–9-0 RCochrane (19) (lw: trckd ldrs: led over 3f out tl over 2f out: wknd over 1f out) ..................... ½.13

2442 Castle Courageous **(91)** *(LadyHerries)* 4–8-13 JReid (2) (lw: trckd ldrs: bdly hmpd over 12f out: nt rcvr) ..................... 3.14

2460 Grand Hawk (USA) **(79)** *(MMoubarak)* 4–8-1 PRobinson (10) (bhd: effrt on ins whn bdly hmpd over 3f out: nt rcvr) ..................... 3½.15

1697[4] Hawait Al Barr **(98)** *(MRStoute)* 4–9-6 PatEddery (13) (b.off hind: led after 1f tl over 3f out: wknd 2f out) ..................... 2½.16

990 Star Quest **(79)** *(JRJenkins)* 5–8-1 KDarley (18) (lw: in tch: effrt over 4f out: sn lost pl) ..................... 3½.17

2347[2] Gulf Sailor (IRE) **(82)** *(MRStoute)* 4–8-4 MHills (7) (bhd: effrt on outside over 3f out: sn wknd) ..................... 1.18

2222[3] Itqan (IRE) **(84)** *(BWHills)* 4–8-6 WCarson (4) (lw: hld up & bhd: sme hdwy 2f out: n.d) ..................... hd.19

2446 Parting Moment (USA) **(102)** *(IABalding)* 5–9–10 BRaymond (22) (w ldrs tl
wknd over 2f out) .......................................................................... nk.**20**
2638★ Lord Hastie (USA) **(78)** *(SGNorton)* 4–8–0 DaleGibson (20) (swtg: a in rr) ...... hd.**21**
2172 First Victory **(88)** *(RHannon)* 6–8–10 BRouse (17) (b: bhd & drvn along 6f out) 3.**22**

**7/1** Storm Crossing (USA), **8/1** Brier Creek (USA), Hawait Al Barr, **10/1** Castoret, **11/1** Whitechapel
(USA)(8/1—12/1), **12/1** Hajaim (IRE), Steerforth (IRE), **16/1** QUICK RANSOM, First Victory, Satin Lover,
Itqan (IRE), **18/1** Lord Hastie (USA), **20/1** Kiveton Kabooz, Deposki, Gulf Sailor (IRE), **25/1** Jackson Flint, **33/1** Parting
Moment (USA), Castle Courageous, Grand Hawk (USA), Holy Zeal, **40/1** Star Player, **50/1** Star Quest. CSF
£129.35, CT £1,474.18. Tote £29.80: £5.50 £2.30 £4.10 £2.50 (£139.90). Mr J. S. Morrison (MIDDLEHAM)
bred by Benham Stud. 22 Rn                                                               2m 55.48 (1.88)
                                                                     SF—49/47/65/44/40/44/33

**2845**   SCOTTISH EQUITABLE GIMCRACK STKS (Gp 2) (2-Y.O.C & G) £61353.00 (£22917.40:
£10971.20: £4738.40)   **6f**                                                        3-45 (3-56)

2764a⁵ **Splendent (USA)** *(PFICole)* 9-0 AMunro (1) (b.off hind: lw: w ldrs: rdn to ld over
1f out: r.o wl) ............................................................................ —**1**
2441³ Green's Bid *(PFICole)* 9-0 TQuinn (2) (w ldrs: ev ch & rdn over 1f out: edgd lft,
hmpd & styd on: fin 3rd, hd: plcd 2nd) ............................................... 2
2177★ Silver Wizard *(GLewis)* 9-0 PatEddery (6) (chsd ldrs: effrt & n.m.r 1f out:
squeezed thro: r.o: fin 2nd, ½l: disq: plcd 3rd) ................................. 3
2764a³ Darbonne (USA) *(GHarwood)* 9-0 SCauthen (8) (led: hung lft ½-wy: hdd &
wknd over 1f out) ...................................................................... 1½.**4**
2764a Son Pardo *(RHannon)* 9-5 JReid (3) (a chsng ldrs: effrt u.p ½-wy: nt pce to
chal) ...................................................................................... 1½.**5**
2610² Blow Dry (IRE) *(JHanson)* 9-0 EJohnson (5) (trckd ldrs tl wknd over 2f out) .. 2.**6**
1930⁵ Fortune Cay (IRE) *(RHannon)* 9-0 WCarson (7) (plld hrd: trckd ldrs to ½-wy: sn
lost pl) ................................................................................... s.h.**7**
1457★ Petardia (Fav) *(GWragg)* 9-3 MHills (4) (hld up: effrt & hung lft ½ wy: edgd bdly
lft over 1f out: sn wknd) .............................................................. 3.**8**
*Stewards Enquiry: Silver Wizard (USA) disq. (interference to Green's Bid over 1f out). Eddery suspended*
*28/8-1/9/92 (careless riding).*

**2/1** Petardia, **3/1** Silver Wizard (USA), **4/1** Son Pardo, **7/1** Green's Bid, **8/1** SPLENDENT (USA), Darbonne (USA),
**14/1** Fortune Cay (IRE), **100/1** Blow Dry (IRE). CSF £57.77, Tote £16.30: £2.80 £2.40 £1.20 (£36.70). Mr Fahd
Salman (WHATCOMBE) bred by Derry Meeting Farm et. al. in USA. 8 Rn                          1m 11.42 (1.22)
                                                                     SF—58/56/55/49/48/35/34

**2846**   ANDY CAPP H'CAP (0-110) £12330.00 (£3690.00: £1770.00: £810.00)
**1m 205y**                                                                          4-15 (4-35)

2641² **Badawi (USA) (93)** *(JHMGosden)* 4–8-13 SCauthen (16) (swtg: trckd ldrs: rdn
to ld over 1f out: r.o wl) ............................................................... —**1**
824⁵ Military Fashion **(99)** *(LMCumani)* 6–9-5 LDettori (3) (a chsng ldrs: effrt 2f out:
r.o fnl f) .................................................................................. 2½.**2**
2220⁴ Ile de Chypre **(108)** *(GHarwood)* 7–10-0 TQuinn (9) (b.hind: led tl over 1f out:
kpt on same pce u.p) .................................................................. hd.**3**
2380² Cumbrian Challenge (IRE) **(88)** *(MHEasterby)* 3–7-10 ‡5SMaloney (1) (lw: plld
hrd: trckd ldrs: r.o same pce u.p fnl 2f) ........................................... nk.**4**
2460⁶ Lucky Guest **(90)** *(JLDunlop)* 5–8-10 WCarson (7) (hld up: hdwy on ins 3f out:
nt clr run fr wl over 1f out: nt rcvr) ................................................ 1½.**5**
2433⁵ Juniper Berry (IRE) **(88)** *(PWChapple-Hyam)* 3–8-1 PaulEddery (14) (s.i.s: sn
in tch & drvn along: styd on same pce fnl 2f) .................................... hd.**6**
Mellottie **(96)** *(MrsGRReveley)* 7–9-2 JLowe (8) (bit bkwd: hld up & bhd: stdy
hdwy 2f out: r.o fin) .................................................................... 2½.**7**
2644 Azureus (IRE) **(73)** *(MrsGRReveley)* 4–7-7 DaleGibson (2) (lw: sn bhd: styd on
fnl 2f: nt rch ldrs) ...................................................................... 1½.**8**
2554⁵ Jubran (USA) **(76)** *(MPNaughton)* 6–7-10(3) MRoberts (17) (lw: plld hrd: chsd
ldrs tl rdn & lost pl over 1f out) .................................................... 1½.**9**
2457³ Pay Homage **(94)** *(IABalding)* 4–9-0 RCochrane (11) (bhd: sme hdwy 2f out:
n.d) ........................................................................................ hd.**10**
2447⁴ Camden's Ransom (USA) **(78)** *(DRCEIsworth)* 5–7-7(5) ‡5BDoyle (6) (swtg: in
tch tl lost pl 5f out: sme hdwy 2f out: n.d) ....................................... s.h.**11**
1280² Cezanne **(85)** *(MRStoute)* 3–7-12 AMunro (10) (in tch: effrt & drvn along 3f out:
sn lost pl) ................................................................................ 4.**12**
479 Virkon Venture (IRE) **(73)** *(MHTompkins)* 4–7-7 AMackay (15) (a in rr) ............ 5.**13**
1480★ Major Mouse **(78)** *(WWHaigh)* 4–7-9 ‡3FNorton (5) (bhd: sme hdwy u.p over 3f) 3.**14**
2643 Top Register (USA) **(101)** *(LordHuntingdon)* 3–9-0 JReid (12) (prom tl lost pl 3f
out: sn eased) ........................................................................... 1.**15**
2447² Mudaffar (IRE) **(93)** (Fav) *(RWArmstrong)* 4–8-13 LPiggott (4) (a bhd: shkn up
3f out: no rspnse: eased) ............................................................. 10.**16**
LONG HANDICAP: Azureus (IRE) 7-6, Jubran (USA) 7-5, Camden's Ransom (USA) 7-6.

**6/1** Mudaffar (IRE), **13/2** BADAWI (USA), **9/1** Lucky Guest, Camden's Ransom (USA), **10/1** Pay Homage, **12/1** Cezanne, Azureus (IRE), **14/1** Jubran (USA), Cumbrian Challenge (IRE), Major Mouse, Ile de Chypre, Military Fashion, **16/1** Juniper Berry (IRE), Top Register (USA), **20/1** Ors. CSF £87.61, CT £1,124.14. Tote £6.20: £1.80 £4.70 £4.10 £3.10 (£81.40). Sheikh Mohammed (NEWMARKET) bred by Mill Ridge Farm Ltd in USA. 16 Rn
1m 48.91 (U.09)
SF—80/78/86/53/62/52/59

## 2847

ROSES STKS (listed race) (2-Y.O.C & G) £14100.00 (£4200.00: £2000.00: £900.00)
5f
4-45 (4-59)

| | | | |
|---|---|---|---|
| 2452 | **Sabre Rattler (99)** (JBerry) 8-12 PatEddery (2) (lw: mde all: r.o strly fnl f) | | —1 |
| 2528² | Saint Express (96) (RMWhitaker) 8-12 AMunro (4) (unruly in stalls: trckd ldrs gnl wl: effrt over 1f out: unable qckn) | | 1.2 |
| 2574* | Nominator (92) (RHollinshead) 8-12 GDuffield (8) (sn outpcd: hung lft thrght: hdwy u.p over 1f out: swtchd & styd on nr fin) | | ¾.3 |
| 2550* | Lord Olivier (IRE) (98) (WJarvis) 8-12 MTebbutt (3) (w ldrs tl rdn & wknd over 1f out) | | 3½.4 |
| 2710* | Realities (USA) (96) (GHarwood) 8-12 JReid (6) (v.unruly in stalls: w ldrs: drvn along 2f out: wknd over 1f out) | | nk.5 |
| 2190* | Normanton Park (88) (RHannon) 8-12 BRaymond (7) (s.i.s: a outpcd: swtchd lft ½-wy: n.d) | | 5.6 |
| 1469⁴ | Elle Shaped (IRE) (100) (RHannon) 8-12 LPiggott (5) (chsd ldrs tl lost pl ½-wy: sn eased) | | 6.7 |

**11/8** Realities (USA), **7/2** Elle Shaped (IRE), **9/2** Normanton Park, **13/2** SABRE RATTLER, **10/1** Saint Express, Lord Olivier, **14/1** Nominator. CSF £59.64, Tote £7.10: £2.30 £4.30 (£34.50). Mr H. B. Hughes (COCKERHAM) bred by H. B. Hughes. 7 Rn
58.99 sec (1.49)
SF—53/49/46/32/31/11

## 2848

FALMOUTH H'CAP (3-Y.O) (0-110) £11160.00 (£3330.00: £1590.00: £720.00)
5f
5-15 (5-25)
(Weights raised 3 lb)

| | | | |
|---|---|---|---|
| 2448 | **Western Approach (USA)** (101) (Fav) (JHMGosden) 9-7 PatEddery (3) (lw: mde all: drvn clr over 1f out: r.o wl) | | —1 |
| 1994⁶ | Bunty Boo (86) (BAMcMahon) 8-6 TQuinn (11) (lw: a chsng wnr: r.o u.p fnl f) | | 3½.2 |
| 2493* | Venture Capitalist (86) (bl) (RHannon) 8-6 LPiggott (13) (sn outpcd & bhd: hdwy u.p over 1f out: styd on nr fin) | | 1.3 |
| 2443² | Saddlehome (USA) (77) (RMWhitaker) 7-11 JFanning (4) (a chsng ldrs: no imp fnl 2f) | | nk.4 |
| 2787² | Bodari (81) (DAWilson) 7-10 ‡5DHarrison (1) (lw: chsd wnr: rdn 2f out: r.o one pce) | | 2½.5 |
| 2663³ | Super Rocky (77) (RBastiman) 7-11 DaleGibson (6) (lw: chsd ldrs tl wknd 2f out) | | 1½.6 |
| | Storm Melody (USA) (100) (AAScott) 9-6 BRaymond (2) (b: b.hind: w ldrs: ev ch & rdn 2f out: sn lost pl) | | ½.7 |
| 2741 | Ned's Bonanza (73) (MDods) 7-7 JLowe (7) (bhd tl styd on appr fnl f) | | nk.8 |
| 2359* | Echo-Logical (89) (RHannon) 8-9 KDarley (12) (sn bhd: sme hdwy 2f out: nvr nr to chal) | | 2½.9 |
| 2443 | Nifty Fifty (IRE) (87) (JBerry) 8-7 LCharnock (8) (a bhd) | | 1.10 |
| 2443⁵ | Allthruthenight (IRE) (86) (LJHolt) 8-6⁽¹⁾ JReid (5) (swtg: sltly hmpd s: a in rr) | | ½.11 |
| 2639* | Castlerea Lad (81) (RHollinshead) 8-1 AMunro (10) (a outpcd) | | 1.12 |
| 2376 | Educated Pet (78) (MJohnston) 7-9 ‡3FNorton (9) (lw: s.i.s: a bhd) | | 2.13 |

**9/2** WESTERN APPROACH (USA), **11/2** Saddlehome (USA), **13/2** Venture Capitalist, **7/1** Bodari, **9/1** Bunty Boo, **10/1** Echo-Logical, Allthruthenight (IRE), **11/1** Educated Pet, Super Rocky, **14/1** Nifty Fifty (IRE), **16/1** Castlerea Lad, **33/1** Ors. CSF £42.00, CT £240.52. Tote £3.60: £2.00 £3.00 £2.30 (£33.10). Mr K. Abdulla (NEWMARKET) bred by Juddmonte Farms Incorporated in USA. 13 Rn
57.76 sec (0.26)
SF—87/58/54/44/33/28

T/Trio: Race 3: £761.70 (6.2 Tckts), Race 5: £778.60 (4.1 Tckts), Race 7: £50.30 (47.1 Tckts). T/Jkpt: Not won; £21,826.21 to York 20/8/92. T/Plpt: £615.40 (50.2 Tckts).
WG

# YORK  (L-H)

## Thursday, August 20th [Good to firm]

Going Allowance: minus 0.10 sec per fur (F)　　　　　　　　Wind: almost nil

Stalls: high

## 2849

MOORESTYLE CONVIVIAL STKS (Mdn 2-Y.O) £7505.00 (£2240.00: £1070.00: £485.00)
6f
2-05 (2-06)

| | | | |
|---|---|---|---|
| 2598 | **Revelation (IRE)** (RHannon) 9-0 PatEddery (2) (a.p: chal over 2f out: led over 1f out: sn clr) | | —1 |

Map of Stars (USA) *(Fav) (MRStoute)* 9-0 SCauthen (7) (w'like: unf: lw: cl up: slt
ld after 2f: rdn over 2f out: outpcd appr fnl f) ...................... 5.2
York Hill *(PAKelleway)* 9-0 GayKelleway (4) (rangy: scope: bit bkwd: s.i.s: sn
outpcd: gd hdwy over 2f out: kpt on) .................................. 1.3
Society Lady (USA) *(AAScott)* 8-9 BRaymond (3) (lengthy: scope: s.s: rn green
to ½-wy: hdwy 2f out: n.d) .......................... 1½.4
Sarangani Bay (USA) *(PWChapple-Hyam)* 9-0 PaulEddery (6) (w'like: scope:
hung lft virtually thrght: slt ld 2f: cl up tl wknd 2f out) .......... 6.5
Bend Sable (IRE) *(PCHaslam)* 9-0 RCochrane (5) (str: cmpt: bit bkwd: prom to
½-wy: grad wknd) .................................. 6.6

**4/5** Map of Stars (USA), **100/30** REVELATION (IRE), **11/2** Sarangani Bay (USA), **7/1** Society Lady (USA), **25/1**
Ors. CSF £6.34, Tote £3.00: £1.70 £1.10 (£2.10). Mr J. G. Davis (MARLBOROUGH) bred by A. L. and J.
Chapman in Ireland. 6 Rn                                    1m 12.25 (2.05)
SF—47/27/23/12/–/–

---

**2850**     LOWTHER STKS (Gp 2) (2-Y.O.F) £38502.00 (£14342.85: £6833.93: £2916.22)
             **6f**                                              2-35 (2-37)

2452³ **Niche** *(RHannon)* 9-0 LPiggott (4) (lw: mde all: shkn up 2f out: r.o strly fnl f:
readily) ..................................... —1
1939⁵ Shamisen *(CEBrittain)* 8-11 SCauthen (5) (prom: rdn & sltly outpcd 2f out: styd
on fnl f: no ch w wnr) ..................................... 4.2
1927² Toocando (IRE) *(Fav) (CNAllen)* 8-11 RCochrane (2) (trckd ldrs: rdn & ev ch
over 2f out: unable qckn fnl f: fin lame) ..................... 1½.3
2717* Northern Bird *(BWHills)* 8-11 WCarson (3) (trckd ldrs: outpcd & hrd rdn 2f out:
kpt on ins fnl f) ..................................... ¾.4
£7041³ Risk Me's Girl *(RHannon)* 8-11 WRSwinburn (1) (cl up tl rdn & wknd appr fnl f) ¾.5
2724 Juliet Bravo *(BBeasley)* 8-11 LCharnock (7) (unruly gng to s: o.o: a bhd: t o fnl
2f) ..................................... 30.6

**7/4** Toocando (IRE)(op Evens), **2/1** NICHE, **9/2** Northern Bird, **13/2** Shamisen, **14/1** Risk Me's Girl, **100/1** Juliet
Bravo. CSF £13.12, Tote £2.70: £1.60 £2.80 (£10.20). Lord Carnarvon (MARLBOROUGH) bred by Highclere
Stud Ltd. 6 Rn                                    1m 11.61 (1.41)
SF—60/41/35/32/29/–

---

**2851**     KEENELAND NUNTHORPE STKS (Gp 1)     £93528.00 (£34742.40: £16471.20:
             £6938.40)     **5f**                                 3-10 (3-12)

2176* **Lyric Fantasy (IRE)** *(Fav) (RHannon)* 2-7-8⁽¹⁾ MRoberts (10) (lw: a.p: led 2f
out: r.o strly fnl f) ..................................... —1
2767a* Mr Brooks *(RHannon)* 5-9-6 LPiggott (8) (lw: hdwy 2f out: kpt on wl u.p ins fnl f:
nt qckn cl home) ..................................... ½.2
Diamonds Galore (CAN) *(DanielVella,Canada)* 7-9-6 AGryder (5) (swtg: w ldrs:
slt ld & rdn over 2f out: sn hdd: kpt on fnl f) ..................... 1½.3
2626a⁶ Elbio *(PJMakin)* 5-9-6 WRSwinburn (1) (lw: wnt lft s: hdwy over 2f out: r.o wl fnl
f) ..................................... nk.4
2448⁴ Freddie Lloyd (USA) *(NACallaghan)* 3-9-3 PatEddery (7) (led tl disp ld ½-wy:
hdd over 2f out: unable qckn) ..................................... nk.5
2448 Paris House *(JBerry)* 3-9-3 SCauthen (4) (a chsng ldrs: rdn & edgd lft over 1f
out: no ex) ..................................... 2½.6
2448⁶ Farfelu (bl) *(WRMuir)* 5-9-6 TQuinn (3) (in tch: rdn ½-wy: nvr able to chal) ..... 1½.7
2448⁵ Harvest Girl (IRE) *(GAPritchard-Gordon)* 3-9-0 WCarson (6) (chsd ldrs over 3f:
grad wknd) ..................................... hd.8
2169 Medaille D'Or (v) *(JWPayne)* 4-9-6 LDettori (2) (outpcd fr ½-wy) ............... 1.9
2448 El Yasaf (IRE) *(MCPipe)* 4-9-6 JWilliams (11) (in tch 3f) ..................... 3½.10
2448² Blyton Lad *(MJCamacho)* 6-9-6 SWebster (9) (lw: sn drvn along & nvr wnt pce)2½.11

**8/11** LYRIC FANTASY (IRE), **9/2** Mr Brooks, **8/1** Freddie Lloyd (USA), **10/1** Elbio, **11/1** Paris House, **25/1** Blyton
Lad, **33/1** Diamonds Galore (CAN), **50/1** Medaille D'Or, **66/1** Ors. CSF £4.53, Tote £1.80: £1.20 £1.80 £3.90
(£3.40). Lord Carnarvon (MARLBOROUGH) bred by Minch Bloodstock in Ireland. 11 Rn
57.39 sec (0.45 under 2y best; U.11)
SF—72/96/90/89/85/75

---

**2852**     BRADFORD & BINGLEY H'CAP (0-115) £25635.00 (£7680.00: £3690.00: £1695.00)
             **7f 202y**                                         3-45 (3-47)

(Weights raised 5 lb)

2658² **Doulab's Image (89)** (bl) *(JAGlover)* 5-8-11 ‡5SWilliams (2) (dwlt: hld up:
smooth hdwy 3f out: led over 1f out: r.o strly) .................... —1

2658★ Deprecator (USA) **(96)** *(JHMGosden)* 4–9-9 WCarson (8) (b.hind: hdwy & n.m.r over 2f out: styd on strly u.p ins fnl f) ......................... ¹/₂.2

1870★ Noble Pet **(89)** *(PJMakin)* 3–8-10 LPiggott (16) (bhd: swtchd & hdwy over 2f out: styd on wl & hung bdly lft tl no ex cl home) ............... nk.3

2433★ Philidor **(88)** *(JMPEustace)* 3–8-9 RCochrane (18) (lw: bhd: gd hdwy 2f out: r.o ins fnl f) ....................................................... 1¹/₂.4

2400² Gymcrak Premiere **(94)** *(MHEasterby)* 4–9-7 MBirch (21) (in tch: rdn to chal over 2f out: nt qckn fnl f) ........................................ 1¹/₂.5

2527★ Blockade (USA) **(84)** *(MBell)* 3–8-0 ‡5JWeaver (5) (t: led tl sddle slipped & hdd over 2f out: eased fnl f) ....................................... hd.6

2447⁶ Magnified (USA) **(96)** *(BWHills)* 3–9-3 PatEddery (19) (bhd: gd hdwy over 3f out: hrd rdn & sltly hmpd ins fnl f: no ex) .......................... ³/₄.7

2400⁵ Rocton North (IRE) **(89)** (bl) *(RHannon)* 4–9-2 JReid (20) (hdwy ¹/₂-wy: sn chsng ldrs: hrd rdn 2f out: sltly hmpd ins fnl f) ................... nk.8

1906★ Big Blue **(90)** *(CEBrittain)* 3–8-11 MRoberts (23) (bhd tl styd on wl fnl 3f: nt rch ldrs) ....................................................... 3¹/₂.9

2380⁵ Killy **(83)** *(FHLee)* 3–8-4 AMunro (9) (chsd ldrs: rdn & nt clr run 3f out: grad wknd) ........................................................ nk.10

2658 Golden Chip (IRE) **(77)** *(APStringer)* 4–8-4 PaulEddery (11) (n.d) .......... 1¹/₂.11

2343⁴ Lead the Dance **(103)** *(HRACecil)* 3–9-10 SCauthen (4) (prom: led over 2f out: sn hrd rdn: hdd over 1f out: wknd) .......................... 3¹/₂.12

1930 Venus Observed **(89)** *(HCandy)* 4–8-9 ‡7AntoinetteArmes (22) (bhd: hdwy on outside over 3f out: sn rdn & no imp) ........................ 2.13

Double Entendre **(71)** *(MBell)* 6–7-12 EJohnson (13) (in tch: effrt over 3f out: nt clr run & wknd over 2f out) ................................ 3.14

2658 Ashdren **(81)** *(AHarrison)* 5–8-8 WRSwinburn (1) (prom early: sn lost pl: n.d after) ...................................................... 2.15

2447 Jalmusique **(90)** *(MHEasterby)* 6–8-12 ‡5SMaloney (12) (b.hind: chsd ldrs tl wknd u.p wl over 2f out) ...................................... nk.16

2447★ Little Bean **(94)** (Fav) *(GWragg)* 3–9-1 MHills (15) (hdwy over 3f out: n.m.r & outpcd over 2f out: eased whn btn) ........................ nk.17

2647★ Salda **(75)** *(RMWhitaker)* 3–7-5⁽³⁾ ‡5NKennedy (10) (nvr nr to chal) ............... 1¹/₂.18

2541³ Alkarif (USA) **(77)** *(MrsJRRamsden)* 3–7-12 AMackay (17) (hdwy on outside appr st: sn rdn & btn) .................................... 5.19

2447 Main Bid (IRE) **(92)** *(MMoubarak)* 3–8-13 LDettori (6) (in tch tl wknd over 3f out) hd.20

2527 Wave Hill **(86)** *(RHannon)* 3–8-7 BRaymond (14) (in tch over 4f) ................. hd.21

2028⁶ Arany **(91)** *(MHTompkins)* 5–9-4 PRobinson (7) (prom to st: sn lost pl: t.o) ... 20.22

LONG HANDICAP: Salda 7-6.

**5/1** Little Bean, **7/1** Magnified (USA), **8/1** Blockade (USA), **11/1** Jalmusique, **12/1** Gymcrak Premiere, **13/1** Lead the Dance, **14/1** Deprecator (USA), Philidor, Main Bid (IRE), DOULAB'S IMAGE, **16/1** Noble Pet, Salda, Alkarif (USA), **20/1** Big Blue, Ashdren, Wave Hill, **25/1** Arany, Rocton North (IRE), **33/1** Venus Observed, Golden Chip (IRE), Double Entendre, **50/1** Killy. CSF £193.44, CT £2,909.84. Tote £20.80: £3.90 £3.10 £3.70 £5.10 (£96.90). Claremont Management Services (WORKSOP) bred by Hadi Al Tajir. 22 Rn     1m 37.02 (1.02)
SF—70/80/66/60/67/46

2749³ **Opera Ghost (82)** *(PWHarris)* 6–8-13 WRSwinburn (9) (lw: bhd: hdwy & nt clr run 3f out: styd on strly u.p fnl 2f tl to ld cl home) ................ —1

2721★ Sapphirine **(65)** *(RMWhitaker)* 5–7-3⁽³⁾ (4x) ‡7AGarth (5) (lw: mid div: rdn & hdwy over 3f out: styd on gamely to ld ins fnl: hdd nr fin) . nk.2

2453⁵ Scrutineer (USA) **(90)** (Fav) *(JHMGosden)* 3–8-11 SCauthen (7) (lw: chsd ldr: led wl over 3f out: clr over 2f out: wknd & hdd ins fnl f) .... 2¹/₂.3

2442⁴ Seal Indigo (IRE) **(83)** *(RHannon)* 4–9-0 JReid (11) (lw: bhd tl hdwy appr st: sn prom & drvn along: edgd lft & no ex fnl 2f) ................... 2¹/₂.4

2451⁶ Simply-H (IRE) **(79)** *(MBell)* 3–7-9 ‡5SMaloney (4) (hdwy fr rr over 3f out: n.m.r 2f out: kpt on) ................................................ 1¹/₂.5

2749² Caspian Beluga **(62)** *(MrsAKnight)* 4–7-7 (4x) JQuinn (8) (lw: lad tl hdd wl over 3f out: sn wknd: eased fnl f) ............................... 1¹/₂.6

2442 Highbrook (USA) **(78)** *(MHTompkins)* 4–8-9 PRobinson (3) (b: in tch: rdn 4f out: sn outpcd) ..................................................... 1¹/₂.7

2553⁵ Tell No Lies **(93)** *(MHEasterby)* 5–9-10 MBirch (14) (lw: hld up: sme hdwy over 3f out: sn rdn & no imp) ...................................... 7.8

2524⁴ Line Drummer (USA) **(76)** *(PAKelleway)* 4–8-7 GayKelleway (6) (chsd ldrs: hrd drvn 4f out: wknd 3f out) ...................................... 4.9

2349★ Libk **(94)** *(HThomsonJones)* 4–9-11 WCarson (10) (hld up & bhd: sme hdwy over 3f out: n.d) ................................................ 2.10

2742 Doctor Roy **(62)** *(NBycroft)* 4–7-7 LCharnock (12) (n.d) .................... nk.**11**
2645* I Perceive **(72)** *(FHLee)* 5–8-3 PaulEddery (17) (s.i.s: a in rr) ........................ 1¹/₂.**12**
Sarawat **(88)** *(MrsGRReveley)* 4–9-5 BRaymond (1) (chsd ldrs tl lost pl over 5f out) ................................................................ 1¹/₂.**13**
2451³ Western Dynasty **(72)** *(MJRyan)* 6–8-3 MRoberts (13) (lw: in tch to st) ........... 2.**14**
2020² Kinglow (USA) **(86)** (bl) *(MrsJCecil)* 3–8-7 LDettori (16) (bhd: effrt appr st: sn btn) ........................................................................ hd.**15**
2451⁵ Legion of Honour **(73)** *(WJarvis)* 4–8-4 AMunro (15) (lw: chsd ldrs tl wknd over 3f out) ..................................................................... 1.**16**
342 Munday Dean **(66)** *(DWPArbuthnot)* 4–7-11 JLowe (2) (b: b.hind: chsd ldrs: pushed along 6f out: wknd 4f out) ........................... 4.**17**
LONG HANDICAP: Doctor Roy 7-5.

**5/1** Scrutineer (USA), **11/2** Seal Indigo (IRE), **8/1** Kinglow (USA), Libk, **9/1** Tell No Lies, **10/1** Legion of Honour, Highbrook (USA), **12/1** Caspian Beluga, **14/1** Western Dynasty, I Perceive, OPERA GHOST, **16/1** Sapphirine, **20/1** Simply-H (IRE), **25/1** Line Drummer (USA), **33/1** Munday Dean, Sarawat, **50/1** Doctor Roy. CSF £207.98, CT £1,175.85. Tote £18.70: £3.20 £5.40 £1.80 £1.90 (£212.70). Mrs P. W. Harris (BERKHAMSTED) bred by Pendley Farm. 17 Rn
2m 29.10 (2.10)
SF–66/41/58/56/34/29

---

**2854** GALTRES STKS (listed race) (F & M) £15140.00 (£4520.00: £2160.00: £980.00)
1m 3f 195y
4-45 (4-51)

2524* **Cunning (88)** (Fav) *(LMCumani)* 3–8-8 LDettori (3) (lw: hld up: hdwy on bit to ld wl over 2f out: sn clr: v.impressive) ........................... —**1**
2522⁵ Percy's Girl (IRE) **(97)** *(GWragg)* 4–9-4 SCauthen (4) (hld up & bhd: hdwy 2f out. kpt on: no ch w wnr) .................................. 6.**2**
2431* Shirley Valentine *(HRACecil)* 3–8-8 PatEddery (7) (trckd ldrs: disp wl over 2f out: sn hdd: hung lft & one pce appr fnl f) ........................ 8.**3**
2407* Ardisia (USA) **(86)** *(PFICole)* 3–8-8 AMunro (6) (chsd ldr: chal 3f out: wknd over 2f out) ............................................................... 4.**4**
717* Aquamarine *(BWHills)* 3–9-0 PaulEddery (2) (trckd ldrs: pushed along 5f out: lost tch 2f out) ....................................................... 2¹/₂.**5**
1843 Sea Goddess **(90)** *(WJarvis)* 4–9-7 JReid (5) (led: disp ld wl over 2f out: sn hdd & btn) ............................................................... hd.**6**
2744 Romoosh *(CEBrittain)* 3–8-8 PRobinson (1) (lw: in tch: rdn 4f out: wknd over 2f out) ......................................................................... 15.**7**

**4/5** CUNNING(op 5/4), **7/2** Shirley Valentine(9/4—4/1), **8/1** Ardisia (USA), **9/1** Percy's Girl (IRE), **10/1** Aquamarine(op 6/1), **12/1** Sea Goddess, **25/1** Romoosh. CSF £8.89, Tote £1.90: £1.50 £2.30 (£7.10). Fittocks Stud Limited (NEWMARKET) bred by R. G. Stokes. 7 Rn
2m 28.57 (1.57)
SF–66/64/38/30/31/37

---

**2855** CITY OF YORK STKS (listed race) £11842.50 (£3540.00: £1695.00: £772.50)
6f 214y
5-15 (5-15)

2711² **Reported (IRE) (106)** *(MJHeaton-Ellis)* 3–8-9 PatEddery (1) (lw: led & sn clr: rdn over 1f out: kpt on wl nr fin) ............................ —**1**
2435³ Consigliere **(93)** *(RCharlton)* 4–9-0 PaulEddery (2) (b: lw: trckd ldrs: hdwy over 2f out: ev ch 1f out: unable qckn nr fin) ......................... 2.**2**
2463* Knight of Mercy **(99)** *(RHannon)* 6–9-0 WCarson (10) (lw: in tch: effrt over 3f out: styd on same pce fnl 2f) ...................................... 3¹/₂.**3**
2169* Montendre **(112)** *(MMcCormack)* 3–9-0 JReid (3) (prom: hdwy to chse clr ldr ¹/₂-wy: sn rdn: wknd over 1f out) .................................. hd.**4**
1926⁵ Fylde Flyer **(102)** *(JBerry)* 3–9-0 WCarson (4) (chsd wnr to ¹/₂-wy: sn drvn along: hung lft & no ex fnl 2f) ....................................... ¹/₂.**5**
2383* Casteddu **(115)** (bl) *(JWPayne)* 3–9-3 RCochrane (6) (lw: trckd ldrs: drvn along 3f out: no imp) .............................................. hd.**6**
2641⁵ Savoyard **(100)** (bl) *(MAJarvis)* 4–9-0 LPiggott (5) (b: lw: bhd: effrt 3f out: no imp: eased ins fnl f) ........................................... 7.**7**

**5/4** Casteddu, **5/1** Montendre, REPORTED (IRE), **6/1** Knight of Mercy, **8/1** Savoyard, **17/2** Consigliere, **12/1** Fylde Flyer(op 8/1). CSF £42.09, Tote £5.90: £2.50 £3.50 (£19.70). Mr F. J. Sainsbury (WROUGHTON) bred by John Byrne in Ireland. 7 Rn
1m 23.05 (0.65)
SF–75/74/63/67/60/62

---

T/Trio: Race 3: £26.50 (135.2 Tckts), Race 4: £1,363.40 (3.1 Tckts) & Race 5: £610.30 (6.1 Tckts) T/Jkpt: £23,732.20 (1.2 Tckts). T/Plpt: £101.20 (231 Tckts).
O'R

2596—**KEMPTON (R-H)**
**Wednesday, August 19th [Good]**
Going Allowance: St: minus 0.05 sec: Rest: minus 0.20 sec (F)        Wind: nil

Stalls: high

**2856**    FORESTER APP'CE H'CAP (0-80) £3106.00 (£928.00: £444.00: £202.00)
         1¼m (J.C)                         5-40 (5-41)

2754² **Loki (IRE) (73)** (GLewis) 4-9-3 ‡⁷BRussell (1) (lw: hdwy 6f out: 3rd st: led over
         1f out: r.o wl) .................................................................................... —1
2757³ Lady Lacey (51) (v) (GBBalding) 5–7-11⁽³⁾ ‡⁵DO'Neill (2) (2nd st: ev ch over 1f
         out: unable qckn) ............................................................................. 1½.2
2660 Bowden Boy (IRE) (69) (bl) (NACallaghan) 4-8-13 ‡⁷JTate (5) (5th st: hrd rdn
         over 2f out: swtchd lft ins fnl f: r.o) ............................................... nk.3
2415⁴ Celia Brady (55) (HCandy) 4–7-13 ‡⁷AntoinetteArmes (9) (led over 8f: one pce) 1.4
2415 Sarah-Clare (57) (Fav) (RAkehurst) 4-8-1 ‡⁷LCarter (6) (hdwy 6f out: 4th st: one
         pce fnl 2f) ......................................................................................... 2.5
2600³ Up All Night (52) (JWHills) 3–7-2 ‡⁷MHenry (4) (nvr nr to chal) ................. 2½.6
2687² High Savannah (64) (MAJarvis) 4-9-1 KRutter (8) (lw: a bhd) ..................... 2.7
2417 Jimlil (76) (BPalling) 4-9-13 PTurner (7) (swtg: rdn over 3f out: 6th st: wknd
         over 2f out) ....................................................................................... 4.8
     Wednesdays Auction (IRE) (55) (BHanbury) 4–7-13 ‡⁷VBray (3) (swtg: bhd fnl
         4f) .................................................................................................... 1½.9

7/2 Sarah-Clare, 9/2 Lady Lacey, LOKI (IRE), 5/1 Celia Brady, 7/1 Up All Night, 9/1 Jimlil, Bowden Boy (IRE),
High Savannah, 25/1 Wednesdays Auction (IRE). CSF £24.55, CT £162.19. Tote £4.80: £1.70 £1.70 £1.90
(£11.30). Mr T. K. Laidlaw (EPSOM) bred by Abbey Lodge Stud in Ireland. 9 Rn    2m 6.50 (4.50)
                                                   SF–45/12/27/8/3/–

**2857**    WIGAN NURSERY   £2595.00 (£720.00: £345.00)    **6f**        6-10 (6-11)
                               (Weights raised 9 lb)

2597² **Pair of Jacks (IRE) (71)** (WRMuir) 8-4 WWoods (12) (a.p: led over 1f out: r.o
         wl) ................................................................................................... —1
2482³ Kennedys Prima (70) (AAScott) 8-3 GHind (8) (b.off hind: a.p: led over 3f out tl
         over 1f out: r.o) ................................................................................ 1½.2
2649² Mr Butch (61) (MRChannon) 7-1 ‡⁷KimMcDonnell (10) (lw: hld up: rdn over 2f
         out: r.o wl ins fnl f) ......................................................................... ¾.3
2491* Top Pet (IRE) (85) (RHannon) 9-4 JLloyd (7) (hdwy 2f out: r.o ins fnl f) ......... 1½.4
2528 Caps Ninety-Two (IRE) (66) (DrJDScargill) 7-13 JQuinn (13) (a.p: hrd rdn over
         1f out: unable qckn) ......................................................................... ½.5
1657³ Kingsdown Cavalier (72) (RHannon) 7-12⁽³⁾ ‡⁵DO'Neill (9) (hdwy over 2f out:
         one pce) .......................................................................................... 2.6
2450* Hallorina (68) (WGRWightman) 8-1 GBardwell (1) (swtg: led over 2f: wknd over
         1f out) ............................................................................................. ½.7
2450² Simply Finesse (75) (RAkehurst) 8-8 JWilliams (4) (nvr nr) ........................ 2.8
2646⁴ Bonjour (88) (Fav) (JHMGosden) 9-7 WRSwinburn (11) (prom over 3f: rdn over
         4f out) ............................................................................................. hd.9
2686⁴ Rich Midas (IRE) (63) (GLewis) 7-3⁽²⁾ ‡⁷CHawksley (6) (bhd fnl 2f) ........... 2½.10
2587* Fivefive (IRE) (69) (bl) (NACallaghan) 7-9 ‡⁷JTate (3) (a bhd) ..................... ½.11
2528 Fierro (74) (CEBrittain) 8-7 GCrealock (2) (outpcd) ....................................... 7.12
2587⁴ Bodandere (60) (bl) (MJFetherston-Godley) 7-0 ‡⁷AntoinetteArmes (5) (prom
         over 2f) ............................................................................................. 2.13
               LONG HANDICAP: Bodandere 7-3.

7/4 Bonjour(op 11/4), 7/1 Hallorina, 8/1 PAIR OF JACKS (IRE), 9/1 Top Pet (IRE), Simply Finesse, 10/1 Caps
Ninety-Two (IRE), Kennedys Prima, Fivefive (IRE), 14/1 Kingsdown Cavalier, Mr Butch, 20/1 Fierro, 25/1
Rich Midas (IRE), 40/1 Bodandere. CSF £95.77, CT £1,223.96. Tote £7.40: £2.40 £5.50 £3.80 (£101.60). Mr
Russ Dalton (LAMBOURN) bred by Loan and Development Corporation in Ireland. 13 Rn    1m 13.88 (2.58)
                                                   SF–32/25/13/31/10/1

**2858**    CUNLIFFE STKS (Mdn 3-Y.O) £2532.00 (£702.00: £336.00)    **1m (rnd)**    6-40 (6-41)

2659⁴ **Jahangir (IRE) (68)** (BHanbury) 9-0 JLloyd (3) (2nd st: led over 2f out: r.o wl) . —1
2432³ Hameem (IRE) (74) (Fav) (AAScott) 9-0 WRSwinburn (10) (led over 5f: unable
         qckn) ................................................................................................ 7.2
2432 Face the Future (PWHarris) 9-0 JQuinn (2) (5th st: r.o one pce 2nd 3f) ............ 8.3
4935 Grey Cphas (MMcCormack) 9-0 MPerrett (9) (nvr nr to chal) .......................... 2.4
     Amlak (USA) (ACStewart) 9-0 MRoberts (5) (w'like: scope: bit bkwd: 3rd st:
         wknd over 2f out) ............................................................................. 4.5

Aquado *(WJarvis)* 9-0 RCochrane (7) (unf: scope: bit bkwd: rdn over 5f out: 4th
st: wknd over 2f out) ...................................................................................... s.h.6
2711⁶ Wild Poppy *(EAWheeler)* 8-9 SWhitworth (8) (6th st: no hdwy fnl 3f) ................. s.h.7
Bayin (USA) *(RWArmstrong)* 9-0 JWilliams (1) (leggy: unf: reluctant to r: a wl
bhd) ...................................................................................................................... nk.8
*715³ Anima (7/1) Withdrawn (lame at s) : not under orders*

5/2 Hameem (IRE), **3/1** Bayin (USA), Amlak (USA), **5/1** Aquado, **13/2** JAHANGIR (IRE), **25/1** Face the Future,
**33/1** Ors. CSF £22.57, Tote £7.30: £1.70 £1.40 £3.20 (£7.60). Mr J. R. Ali (NEWMARKET) bred by Mrs A. W.
Riddell-Martin in Ireland. 8 Rn                                    1m 39.53 (2.33)
SF—41/20/–/–/–/–

**2859**  LBC NEWSTALK 97.3 FM STKS (2-Y.O) £2763.00 (£768.00: £369.00)
7f (J.C)                                                                    7-10 (7-14)

2346² **Abtaal** (Fav) *(HThomsonJones)* 8-12 WCarson (4) (lw: 2nd st: led 2f out: rdn
out) ........................................................................................................................ —1
2653⁶ Piston (IRE) *(BHanbury)* 8-5 ‡⁷VBray (2) (led 5f: ev ch ins fnl f: r.o wl) ........... hd.2
2444⁶ Bobbie Dee *(DRCElsworth)* 8-7 SWhitworth (11) (6th st: rdn over 1f out: unable
qckn) .................................................................................................................. 2¹/₂.3
Hard Task *(RFJohnsonHoughton)* 8-7 JLloyd (3) (w'like: scope: bit bkwd:
hdwy fnl 2f: r.o) .................................................................................................. ¹/₂.4
Kinema Red (USA) *(JHMGosden)* 8-12 LDettori (13) (w'like: scope: rdn & hdwy
over 2f out: one pce) ........................................................................................ ³/₄.5
Marco Magnifico (USA) *(BWHills)* 8-12 MHills (16) (unf: s.s: swtchd lft over 2f
out: hdwy over 1f out: nvr nrr) ......................................................................... 3¹/₂.6
2746⁴ Don'tlie (IRE) *(GRRalding)* 8-7 JWilliams (5) (b.nr hind: swtg: no hdwy fnl 3f) .... 2.7
Fire in My Body (USA) *(PWChapple-Hyam)* 8-12 PaulEddery (12) (w'like:
scope: 5th st: wknd 2f out) ................................................................................ hd.0
Shamgaan (USA) *(MRStoute)* 8-12 WRSwinburn (10) (unf: 3rd st: eased whn
btn fnl f) ............................................................................................................... s.h.9
Hatta River (USA) *(MajorWRHern)* 8-12 RCochrane (8) (leggy: scope: bit bkwd:
nvr nr to chal) ..................................................................................................... 2¹/₂.10
Westray (FR) *(DrJDScargill)* 8-12 JWilloyd (14) (w'like: s.i.s: a bhd) ................... 2.11
Red Whirlwind *(MRStoute)* 8-12 SCauthen (1) (w'like: scope: mid div over 4f:
eased whn btn fnl 2f) .......................................................................................... 6.12
Farley (DEN) *(RAkehurst)* 8-12 AClark (9) (neat: a bhd) ....................................... 1¹/₂.13
Western Valley *(KOCunningham-Brown)* 8-7 GBardwell (6) (unf: 4th st: wknd
over 2f out) ......................................................................................................... 2.14
Darsing *(MJWilkinson)* 8-12 GHind (15) (wl grwn: bit bkwd: a bhd) ................. 2.15

5/4 ABTAAL, **6/1** Fire in My Body (USA)(8/1—12/1), **13/2** Shamgaan (USA)(8/1—5/1), **9/1** Red Whirlwind,
**10/1** Kinema Red (USA)(7/1—12/1), Hatta River (USA)(op 6/1), **12/1** Bobbie Dee, **16/1** Marco Magnifico (USA),
**20/1** Piston (IRE), **25/1** Don'tlie (IRE), **50/1** Ors. CSF £27.83, Tote £2.10: £1.30 £12.20 £4.00 (£69.40). Mr
Hamdan Al-Maktoum (NEWMARKET) bred by Cheveley Park Stud Ltd. 15 Rn          1m 26.03 (1.83)
SF—50/42/36/34/37/29

**2860**  PREMIER MARKETS H'CAP (0-80) £3158.00 (£944.00: £452.00: £206.00)
1¹/₂m                                                                    7-40 (7-43)

2086 **Quadrireme** (72) *(MajorWRHern)* 3-9-4 WCarson (2) (5th st: hrd rdn over 1f
out: led ins fnl f: r.o wl) ................................................................................... —1
2451 Mahfil (71) (Fav) *(RAkehurst)* 4-9-13 TQuinn (10) (hdwy 6f out: led over 5f out:
hrd rdn 2f out: hdd ins fnl f: unable qckn) .................................................... 1.2
1302³ Lemon's Mill (USA) (78) *(JHMGosden)* 3-9-10 WRSwinburn (6) (rdn over 3f
out: hdwy over 2f out: hrd rdn over 1f out: one pce) ................................... 2.3
2556⋆ Asian Punter (IRE) (68) *(AHide)* 3-9-0 JWilliams (11) (lw: 3rd st: hrd rdn over 1f
out: one pce) ....................................................................................................... s.h.4
1025⁶ Esbooain (FR) (71) *(LMCumani)* 3-9-3 LDettori (4) (4th st: hrd rdn over 1f out:
one pce) ............................................................................................................... 3.5
2600² Port in a Storm (60) *(WJarvis)* 3-8-6 RCochrane (5) (nvr nr to chal) ............... nk.6
1955 Cosmic Future (68) *(SPCWoods)* 3-9-0 WWoods (3) (lw: 6th st: wknd over 1f
out) ...................................................................................................................... 1.7
2204 Horizon (IRE) (49) (bl) *(TThomsonJones)* 4-8-5 SWhitworth (1) (led over 6f:
2nd st: wknd over 2f out) ................................................................................. 7.8
Crown Baladee (USA) (67) *(MDIUsher)* 5-9-9 JReid (9) (bit bkwd: a bhd) .......... 1.9
2596⁴ Quietly Impressive (IRE) (49) *(MBell)* 4-7-12‡⁷PTurner (7) (lw: hdwy over 5f out:
wknd over 3f out) ............................................................................................... 4.10
2645³ Latour (60) *(CEBrittain)* 4-9-2 MRoberts (8) (bhd fnl 5f) .................................... 8.11

**4/1** Mahfil, **9/2** Port in a Storm, Cosmic Future, **6/1** Latour, Lemon's Mill (USA), **9/1** Esbooain (FR), **10/1** Asian Punter (IRE), **14/1** Quietly Impressive (IRE), QUADRIREME, **25/1** Horizon (IRE), **33/1** Crown Baladee (USA). CSF £67.61, CT £350.52. Tote £23.90: £4.50 £2.20 £3.80 (£66.40). Mr R. D. Hollingsworth (LAMBOURN) bred by R. D. Hollingsworth. 11 Rn

2m 34.51 (4.31)

SF—37/44/37/26/23/11

## 2861

CONFEDERACY H'CAP (0-90) £3184.00 (£952.00: £456.00: £208.00)
6f

8-10 (8-12)

27973 **Darussalam (67)** (Fav) *(RLee)* 5–8-8 WCarson (16) (lw: hld up: led over 1f out: rdn out) .................................................. —1

25592 Baligay **(76)** *(RJHodges)* 7–9-3 MHills (14) (a.p: hrd rdn over 1f out: unable qckn) .......................................... 2½.2

25895 Lady Sabo **(67)** *(GLewis)* 3–8-4 PaulEddery (17) (rdn & hdwy over 2f out: one pce fnl f) ...................................... ¾.3

2795 Sylvan Sabre (IRE) **(82)** (bl) *(PMitchell)* 3–9-5 SWhitworth (15) (led over 4f: one pce) ............................................. ½.4

24583 Blue Topaze **(69)** *(RJHolder)* 4–8-10 LDettori (10) (hdwy over 1f out: r.o) ...... 1½.5

16143 Zeboim **(67)** (bl) *(WRMuir)* 6–8-1 ‡7KimMcDonnell (13) (lw: a.p: hrd rdn 2f out: one pce) ................................. nk.6

2786 Merryhill Maid (IRE) **(70)** *(JLHarris)* 4–8-11 JLloyd (7) (nvr nr to chal) .............. nk.7

25925 Martinosky **(64)** *(WGRWightman)* 6–8-5 JWilliams (12) (nvr nrr) .......................... 2½.8

24655 Coppermill Lad **(53)** *(LJHolt)* 9–7-1(1) ‡7CHawksley (4) (nvr nrr) ......................... 4.9

1368★ Rainbow Fleet **(57)** *(DMarks)* 4–7-12 JQuinn (9) (nvr nrr) ............................ ¾.10

2520★ Running Glimpse (IRE) **(75)** *(MissBSanders)* 4–9-2 MRoberts (5) (spd 4f) ........ 2.11

25205 Fay's Song (IRE) **(77)** *(RAkehurst)* 4–9-4 TQuinn (11) (prom 4f) ...................... ½.12

27526 Baysham (USA) **(80)** (bl) *(BRMillman)* 6–9-2 ‡5JWeaver (3) (lw: bhd fnl 3f) ...... ¾.13

2520 Luna Bid **(67)** *(MBlanshard)* 9–8-8 RCochrane (1) (s.s: a bhd) ............................ 1.14

2435 Masnun (USA) **(84)** *(RJO'Sullivan)* 7–9-11 JReid (8) (a bhd) .......................... 1½.15

1445 Holetown **(84)** *(RHannon)* 3–9-7 WRSwinburn (6) (spd over 3f) ...................... 1.16

2747 Maria Cappuccini **(53)** *(KOCunningham-Brown)* 4–7-8 GBardwell (2) (lw: bhd fnl 3f) .......................................... 2½.17

LONG HANDICAP: Coppermill Lad 7-4.

**4/1** DARUSSALAM, **7/1** Blue Topaze, **8/1** Baligay, Fay's Song (IRE), Running Glimpse (IRE), **9/1** Masnun (USA)(12/1—8/1), **11/1** Lady Sabo, **12/1** Rainbow Fleet, Zeboim, **14/1** Martinosky, **20/1** Coppermill Lad, Baysham (USA), Sylvan Sabre (IRE), **25/1** Merryhill Maid (IRE), Holetown, Luna Bid, **33/1** Maria Cappuccini. CSF £36.83, CT £318.04. Tote £5.00: £1.30 £2.60 £2.60 £6.20 (£22.90). Foxley Saddlery and Countrywear (PRESTEIGNE) bred by Mrs I. M. Raine. 17 Rn

1m 12.53 (1.23)

SF—63/62/46/59/44/34

T/Trio: Race 6: £161.70 (10.3 Tckts). T/Plpt: £236.50 (12.4 Tckts).

AK

## 2725—YARMOUTH (L-H)

### Wednesday, August 19th [Good]

Going Allowance: minus 0.15 sec per fur (F)　　　　Wind: mod half against

Stalls: high

## 2862

EVE APP'CE STKS (Mdn 3-Y.O) £2301.00 (£636.00: £303.00)　　1m 3y　　2-20 (2-22)

26012 **Fit on Time (USA) (71)** (Fav) *(MRStoute)* 8-9 ‡5KPattinson (3) (lw: trckd ldrs: led over 2f out: pushed out) .............. —1

27043 Jawaher (IRE) *(RJRWilliams)* 8-4 ‡5GMitchell (5) (led over 5f: rdn & kpt on) ........ 2.2

434 Euridice (IRE) *(LMCumani)* 8-4 ‡5JCHarris (1) (swvd lft s: sn prom: ev ch 3f out: rdn, edgd lft & no rspnse appr fnl f) .................. 2.3

2186 Top Sire *(JHMGosden)* 9-0 DDunnachie (4) (prom over 4f: sn rdn & wknd qckly) 25.4

Join the Clan *(MrsNMacauley)* 8-10(1) SWynne (2) (lt-f: unf: plld hrd: spd 3f: sn t.o: virtually p.u fnl 2f) ...................................... dist.5

**4/11** FIT ON TIME (USA), **15/2** Euridice (IRE)(op 5/1), **8/1** Jawaher (IRE), **12/1** Top Sire(op 7/1), **33/1** Join the Clan. CSF £3.47, Tote £1.40: £1.10 £2.00 (£2.10). Miss H. Al Maktoum (NEWMARKET) bred by Gainsborough Stud Management Ltd. in USA. 5 Rn

1m 39.4 (4.1)

SF—15/2/–/–/–/–

## 2863

PLEASURE BEACH (S) STKS (2-Y.O) £2679.00 (£744.00: £357.00)
5f 43y

2-50 (2-54)

25905 Cuddly Date **(57)** *(DTThom)* 8-6 DBiggs (7) (chsd ldrs: rdn to ld ins fnl f) .......... —1

25872 Be Polite (IRE) **(53)** (bl) *(MBell)* 8-6 KFallon (12) (a.p: ev ch fnl f: no ex nr fin) .. nk.2

25632 Good Image **(62)** *(APJarvis)* 8-11 WRyan (14) (a.p: r.o ins fnl f) .................. hd.3

1991³ Red Leader (IRE) **(74)** *(PFICole)* 8-11 GBaxter (4) (lw: w ldr: led 2f out tl hdd &
no ex ins fnl f) .......... hd.4
2661³ Monet Monet Monet **(55)** *(WCarter)* 7-13 ‡⁷CHawksley (8) (r.o fnl 2f: nrst fin) ..... 3.5
2563⁶ Jade Runner **(47)** *(MrsNMacauley)* 8-6 NDay (2) (chsd ldrs: rdn 2f out: sn btn) nk.6
2232 The Institute Boy **(66)** *(KRBurke)* 8-6 ‡⁵JWeaver (1) (swtg: chsd ldrs: no ex ins
fnl f) .......... hd.7
2633² Convenient Moment **(71)** (Fav) *(JBerry)* 8-6 GCarter (3) (spd over 3f) .......... ½.8
2745 Cizard (IRE) *(AWPotts)* 8-6 SWhitworth (9) (n.d) .......... s.h.9
2330⁵ Tropical Tia (IRE) **(52)** *(RVoorspuy)* 8-6 SDawson (11) (dwlt: nvr nr to chal) .... 1.10
2591⁴ Naughty Charlotte *(APJarvis)* 8-6 WRadmore (13) (dwlt: a bhd) .......... s.h.11
1895⁵ Spanish Thread **(66)** *(GAPritchard-Gordon)* 8-6 JQuinn (10) (lw: chsd ldrs 3f) 1½.12
2124 Tee-Emm *(PHowling)* 8-11 BCrossley (6) (led 3f: eased whn btn ins fnl f) ...... nk.13

**Evens** Convenient Moment(6/4 – 10/11), **7/2** Red Leader (IRE), **10/1** Good Image, **11/1** Be Polite (IRE)(op 6/1),
**14/1** The Institute Boy(10/1 – 16/1), **16/1** Spanish Thread, Monet Monet Monet, **20/1** CUDDLY DATE, **25/1**
Naughty Charlotte, Tropical Tia (IRE), Jade Runner, **50/1** Ors. CSF £39.00: £5.30 £1.70 £2.50
(£104.70). Mr D. T. Thom (NEWMARKET) bred by D. R. Botterill. 13 Rn; No bid 63.8 sec (3.5)
SF—7/6/10/9/–/–

---

**2864** BRITANNIA PIER STKS (Mdn 2-Y.O.F) £2700.00 (£750.00: £360.00)
7f 3y
3-25 (3-29)

**Iviza (IRE)** (Fav) *(MRStoute)* 8-11 PD'Arcy (14) (rangy: scope: dwlt: trckd ldrs:
n.m.r over 1f out: qcknd to ld post) .......... —1
2438⁵ Nicer (IRE) *(BWHills)* 8-11 WRyan (15) (hld up: hdwy over 2f out: led over 1f
out: ct post) .......... s.h.2
1538⁵ Lakab (USA) *(HThomsonJones)* 8-11 NCarlisle (9) (chsd ldrs: rdn & r.o appr fnl
f) .......... 6.3
2338⁴ Mataris *(PTWalwyn)* 0 11 GBaxter (10) (prom: ev ch over 1f out: one pce) ........ ½.4
Grove Daffodil (IRE) *(MHTompkins)* 8-4 ‡⁷SMulvey (11) (b.nr hind: leggy: blwdr
r.o fnl 2f: nrst fin) .......... nk.5
Solartica (USA) *(JRFanshawe)* 8-11 GCarter (2) (w'like: scope: bit bkwd: in tch:
r.o fnl 2f) .......... 2.6
1957 Heretical Miss *(RHannon)* 8-8 ‡⁹RPerham (13) (led over 5f) .......... 1½.7
Fair Maid of Kent (USA) *(JHMGosden)* 8-11 GHind (3) (lengthy: scope: s.i.s:
nvr trbld ldrs) .......... ¾.8
Pearly Mist (IRE) *(CEBrittain)* 8-8 ‡³RonHillis (6) (leggy: unf: prom: ev ch wl over
1f out: sn btn) .......... 3½.9
Serotina (IRE) *(WJarvis)* 8-6 ‡⁵JWeaver (4) (unf: bit bkwd: n.d) .......... 3½.10
2171 Barassie *(PMitchell)* 8-8 ‡³SO'Gorman (12) (chsd ldrs 4f) .......... 3½.11
Emerald Sands *(ACStewart)* 8-11 SWhitworth (1) (lengthy: unf: a bhd) .......... 1.12
2269⁶ Seren Quest *(AWDenson)* 8-11 DBiggs (4) (prom 4f) .......... ½.13
Manaarah (USA) *(AAScott)* 8-11 GKing (7) (scope: bit bkwd: chsd ldrs over 4f) 5.14
2501³ Half a Dozen (USA) *(AAScott)* 8-11 NDay (5) (rdn 3f out: a bhd) .......... 2.15

**7/4** IVIZA (IRE), **9/2** Mataris, **6/1** Lakab (USA)(op 3/1), **7/1** Nicer (IRE)(op 3/1), **8/1** Fair Maid of Kent
(USA)(5/1 – 10/1), **10/1** Half a Dozen (USA), **12/1** Emerald Sands, **20/1** Solartica (USA), **25/1** Serotina (IRE),
Manaarah (USA), Pearly Mist (IRE), **33/1** Grove Daffodil (IRE), Seren Quest, **50/1** Barassie. CSF
£16.27, Tote £2.30: £1.30 £2.60 £3.10 (£8.20). Sheikh Mohammed (NEWMARKET) bred by Kiltinan Farms Inc.
in Ireland. 15 Rn 1m 25.9 (3.1)
SF—35/34/16/14/6/7

---

**2865** LOWESTOFT H'CAP (0-70) £3392.00 (£1016.00: £488.00: £224.00)
7f 3y
4-00 (4-07)

2502³ Roca Murada (IRE) **(54)** (Jt-Fav) *(MJRyan)* 3–8-12 DBiggs (10) (a.p: led 1f out:
rdn out) .......... —1
2570³ Bill Moon **(49)** (Jt-Fav) *(PJFeilden)* 6–8-7 ‡⁵StephenDavies (3) (hld up: hdwy 2f
out: no ex ins fnl f) .......... 1.2
2687³ Nobby Barnes **(60)** *(RWArmstrong)* 3–9-4 CKTse (11) (chsd ldrs: ev ch over 1f
out: no ex ins fnl f) .......... hd.3
2496 Tom's Apache **(44)** *(WRWilliams)* 3–8-2 NAdams (6) (lw: swtg: hld up: hdwy &
n.m.r wl over 1f out: swtchd r & r.o fnl f) .......... hd.4
2369⁵ Bernstein Bette **(65)** *(PSFelgate)* 6–10-0 WRyan (8) (hld up & bhd: hdwy over
1f out: nrst fin) .......... 1½.5
2300² Rock Band (IRE) **(65)** *(LMCumani)* 3–9-4 ‡⁵JWeaver (14) (net-muzzle: chsd
ldrs: one pce fnl f) .......... 1½.6
2607⁴ Kelly's Kite **(33)** *(HJCollingridge)* 4–7-10 JQuinn (4) (swtg: nvr nrr) .......... s.h.7
2502 Saboteur **(31)** *(WJMusson)* 8–7-8⁽¹⁾ NCarlisle (7) (bit bkwd: led tl hdd & wknd
over 1f out) .......... 3.8
2592³ Amethystine (USA) **(63)** *(RJHodges)* 6–9-5 ‡⁷SDrowne (5) (prom tl rdn & wknd
over 1f out) .......... nk.9

2538* Turret Gates (70) *(JARToller)* 3-9-9 ‡⁵RPrice (12) (chsd ldrs: led over 1f out: sn hdd & btn) ............................................. nk.10
26806 Maritime Lady (USA) (59) (v) *(MRStoute)* 3-9-3 GCarter (9) (lw: chsd ldrs 4f) .. 6.11
2634 Yonge Tender (41) (bl) *(CNWilliams)* 5-8-4 JCurant (13) (a bhd) ................. ¾.12
2618 Red River Boy (45) *(RJHodges)* 9-8-8 TSprake (1) (a bhd) ........................ nk.13
26005 Genuine Lady (53) *(APJarvis)* 4-9-2 TRogers (2) (b.nr hind: dwlt: rdn ½-wy: sn wl bhd) ................................................................. 12.14

LONG HANDICAP: Saboteur 7-6.

**6/1** ROCA MURADA (IRE), Bill Moon, **13/2** Kelly's Kite, Rock Band (IRE), **7/1** Amethystine (USA), **9/1** Yonge Tender, **12/1** Maritime Lady (USA)(op 7/1), Bernstein Bette, **14/1** Nobby Barnes, Turret Gates, **16/1** Red River Boy, **20/1** Tom's Apache, Saboteur, **25/1** Genuine Lady. CSF £40.40, CT £452.03. Tote £6.40: £1.80 £2.00 £4.50 (£22.90). Mr Tim Corby (NEWMARKET) bred by John Houghton in Ireland. 14 Rn 1m 25.6 (2.8)
SF—40/32/42/25/45/30

## 2866

BUNGAY H'CAP (0-90) £3817.50 (£1140.00: £545.00: £247.50)     **6f 3y**   4-30 (4-33)

2227 **Truthful Image (76)** (bl) *(MJRyan)* 3-8-13 DBiggs (9) (a.p: rdn to ld over 1f out: no ex & ct nr fin: fin 2nd, s.h: awrdd r) ............................ —1
2650 Risk Zone (70) (bl) *(RHannon)* 3-8-4 ‡³RPerham (7) (a.p: no ex fnl f: fin 3rd: 1½el: plcd 2nd) ............................................................. 2
2650 Easy Line (87) *(PJFeilden)* 9-9-7 ‡⁷MichaelDenaro (4) (stdd s: hdwy over 1f out: nrst fin: fin 4th, 1½el: plcd 3rd) ....................................... 3
19312 No Quarter Given (72) *(PSFelgate)* 7-8-13 WRyan (1) (chsd ldrs: rdn & ev ch over 1f out: fin 5th, ½el: plcd 4th) ............................ 4
27522 Unveiled (62) *(RJHodges)* 4-7-10⁽⁴⁾ ‡⁷SDrowne (10) (led over 4f: fin 6th, 1½el: plcd 5th) ................................................................. 5
2411 Badawiah (70) *(WAO'Gorman)* 3-8-7 GCarter (3) (in tch: btn whn bdly hmpd wl over 1f out) ............................................................. 2.7
15254 Pop to Stans (73) *(JPearce)* 3-8-5 ‡⁵RPrice (8) (spd 4f) ................................ 1.8
2559 Letsbeonestaboutit (79) (bl) *(MrsNMcauley)* 6-9-6 NAdams (2) (prom 3f) ........ ½.9
2494 Bright Sea (USA) (53) (bl) *(WRWilliams)* 4-7-8⁽¹⁾ NCarlisle (5) (hmpd & uns rdr after 1f) .......................................................................... 0
2787* Nagida (73) (Fav) *(JARToller)* 3-8-5 ‡⁵JWeaver (6) (hld up: swtchd over 2f out: rdn & r.o to ld nr fin: fin 1st: disq: plcd last) ...................... 0

LONG HANDICAP: Bright Sea (USA) 6-3.

*Stewards Enquiry: Nagida disq. (interference to Badawiah 2f out). Weaver suspended 28/8-1/9/92 (careless riding).*

**3/1** Nagida(op 2/1), **4/1** Unveiled, **6/1** Easy Line, TRUTHFUL IMAGE, **7/1** No Quarter Given, **15/2** Letsbeonestaboutit, **12/1** Risk Zone(op 8/1), **14/1** Pop to Stans(op 8/1), **16/1** Badawiah, **50/1** Bright Sea (USA). CSF £67.54, CT £411.81. Tote £9.30: £2.80 £4.30 £1.70 (£87.20). Mrs Margaret Baxter (NEWMARKET) bred by A. Bromley. 10 Rn 1m 12.7 (2.1)
SF—31/38/27/38/28/5

## 2867

BOTTON BROTHERS H'CAP (Ladies) (0-70) £2595.00 (£720.00: £345.00) 1¾m 17y     5-00 (5-06)

21783 **Bandoline (66)** *(BWHills)* 3-11-2 MissEJohnsonHoughton (8) (swtg: chsd ldrs: 6th st: r.o to ld ins fnl f) ............................................... —1
8736 Bayadere (USA) (55) (v) *(MRStoute)* 3-10-5 MissMJuster (10) (led: sn clr: hdd over 2f out: rallied fnl f) ....................................................... ¾.2
26513 Carrolls Marc (IRE) (46) *(PJFeilden)* 4-10-8 MissJFeilden (6) (b.hind: bhd: hdwy & 7th st: led over 2f out tl hdd & wknd ins fnl f) ........ nk.3
25562 Briggs Lad (IRE) (68) (Fav) *(WJarvis)* 3-11-4 MrsLPearce (1) (lost pl 7f out: rallied & wandered 3f out: no imp fnl f: fin 5th, s.h: plcd 4th) .. 4
25804 The Karaoke King (63) *(RHannon)* 3-10-13 MrsJBoggis (7) (plld hrd: in tch: nt clr run 3f out: nvr rchd ldrs: fin 6th, 2½el: plcd 5th) ................. 5
25243 Mahairy (USA) (68) *(AAScott)* 3-11-4 MissTBracegirdle (3) (prom: 2nd st: wknd 2f out) ......................................................................... 8.7
590 Gulfland (31) *(GAPritchard-Gordon)* 11-9-7 MissLStopford-Sackville (12) (hdwy 4f out: no imp appr fnl f) ............................................. 1½.8
26312 Fly for Gold (IRE) (59) *(DWPArbuthnot)* 3-10-9 MrsDArbuthnot (13) (b.hind: prom: 5th st: sn wknd) .............................................................. 3.9
27313 Saif Al Adil (IRE) (48) *(KTIvory)* 3-9-12 MrsEMellor (4) (lw: prom: 3rd st: wknd 3f out) ....................................................................... s.h.10
2054 Someone Brave (42) *(BobJones)* 4-10-4 MissDianaJones (11) (swtg: chsd ldrs: 4th st: sn wknd) .................................................................. 3.11
937 Jokers Patch (57) *(WRWilliams)* 5-11-2 ‡³MissAYardley (2) (bhd fr ½-wy) ...... ½.12
Golden Main (43) *(SMellor)* 6-10-5 MissKMarks (14) (a bhd) ...................... nk.13
26054 Checkpoint Charlie (59) *(JMPEustace)* 7-11-4 ‡³MissJSlater (9) (lw: s.s: a wl bhd) .............................................................................. nk.14

*2783\** Witches Coven **(50)** *(MBell)* 3–9–11 (4x) ‡³MrsGBell (5) (hdwy 4f out: nvr nrr: fin 4th, 2½l: disq: plcd last) ....................................................... 0

*Stewards Enquiry: Obj. to Witches Coven by Clerk of the Scales sustained. Mrs G. Bell fined £100 (failure to weigh-in). Miss J. Feilden suspended 28-31/8/92 (excessive use of whip).*

2/1 Briggs Lad (IRE)(op 6/1), **5/1** Saif Al Adil (IRE), **7/1** BANDOLINE(op 3/1), **15/2** Fly for Gold (IRE), **8/1** Witches Coven, **14/1** The Karaoke King, Checkpoint Charlie, **16/1** Mahairy (USA), Bayadere (USA), **20/1** Carrolls Marc (IRE), **33/1** Ors. CSF £103.05, CT £1,921.30. Tote £7.40: £1.80 £3.70 £3.60 (£84.60). Sheikh Mohammed (LAMBOURN) bred by Sheikh Mohammed bin Rashid al Maktoum. 14 Rn　　　　3m 6.9 (8.9)
　　　　　　　　　　　　　　　　　　　　　　　　　　　　　　　SF–20/7/9/–/–/–

---

**2868**　　COBHOLM H'CAP (F & M) (0-70) £2574.00 (£714.00: £342.00)
　　　　　**1m 3f 101y**　　　　　　　　　　　　　　　　　　　　5-30 (5-35)

23574 **Shadow Bird (50)** *(GAPritchard-Gordon)* 5–9–6 NDay (1) (lw: hld up: wnt 4th st: rdn & qcknd to ld ins fnl f) ..................................... —1

　728 Positive Aspect **(41)** *(JPearce)* 3–7–11 ‡⁵RPrice (8) (prom: 5th st: led over 2f out tl ins fnl f: unable qckn) ............................................ ¾.2

*2004²* Lady Dundee (USA) **(65)** *(MrsJCecil)* 3–9–12 KFallon (7) (7th st: rdn 4f out: styd on appr fnl f) ................................................... 2.3

2228⁴ Swan Heights **(60)** *(JRFanshawe)* 3–9–7 GCarter (2) (lw: led tl over 2f out: one pce) .................................................................. nk.4

23315 Jade Mistress **(58)** *(AHide)* 3–9–5 TSprake (10) (dwlt: hdwy over 3f out: ev ch 2f out: wknd ins fnl f) ......................................... 2½.5

2571\* Hester Stanhope **(60)** *(Fav)* *(PWHarris)* 3–9–7 WRyan (4) (hld up: hdwy 4f out: wknd over 1f out) .................................... 2½.6

1976 Always Alex **(28)** *(PDEvans)* 5–7–12 NCarlisle (6) (plld hrd: w ldrs: 2nd st: wknd 3f out) ................................................................ ¾.7

*2562⁴* Laughton Lady **(42)** *(MrsNMacauley)* 3–8–3 NAdams (3) (lw: prom: 3rd st: wknd over 2f out) ...................................... 1½.8

*1548\** Shakinski **(51)** *(MJRyan)* 3–8–12 DBiggs (9) (6th st: rdn over 2f out: sn btn) ... 3½.9

2/1 Hester Stanhope, **4/1** Shakinski(7/1–3/1), **6/1** Lady Dundee (USA)(op 7/2), SHADOW BIRD, **7/1** Swan Heights(op 9/2), **12/1** Positive Aspect, **14/1** Laughton Lady(op 8/1), **16/1** Always Alex(12/1–33/1), **20/1** Jade Mistress. CSF £66.26, CT £411.03. Tote £3.90: £1.10 £9.00 £2.40 (£35.30). Mr A. G. Don (NEWMARKET) bred by Whitsbury Manor Stud. 9 Rn　　　　　　　　　　　　　　　　　2m 29.6 (5.6)
　　　　　　　　　　　　　　　　　　　　　　　　　　SF–34/9/34/28/21/18

T/Plpt: £323.10 (9.4 Tckts).　　　　　　　　　　　　　　　　　　　　　　Dk

---

# YARMOUTH (L-H)
## Thursday, August 20th [Good to soft]
Going Allowance: 0.40 sec per fur (Y)　　　　　　　　　Wind: mod across

Stalls: high

**2869**　　PEDDARS CROSS STKS (Mdn 3-Y.O) £2448.00 (£678.00: £324.00)
　　　　　**1m 3f 101y**　　　　　　　　　　　　　　　　　2-20 (2-23)

　　**Irish Stamp (IRE)** *(JPearce)* 8–9 ‡⁵RPrice (4) (lengthy: 6th st: led wl over 2f out: hdd 2f out: led 1f out: r.o wl) ..................................... —1

2615² Indian Jack (IRE) *(MajorWRHern)* 9–0 SDawson (6) (s.i.s: hld up: hdwy 4f out: led 2f out to 1f out: one pce) ................................. 3½.2

　Neieb (USA) *(BHanbury)* 8–9 GBaxter (1) (dwlt: hdwy & 4th st: led 3f out: sn hdd & no ex) ...................................................................... 2.3

2549⁴ Flamingo Rose (IRE) *(Fav)* *(HRACecil)* 8–9 WRyan (3) (lw: lost pl & 7th st: hdwy 3f out: nvr able to chal) ..................................... 2½.4

2542² Marionetta (USA) *(LMCumani)* 8–9 JFortune (7) (chsd ldrs: 5th st: faded fnl 3f) 10.5

　Storm Gauge (USA) *(MrsJCecil)* 8–9 AMcGlone (8) (rangy: unf: trckd ldrs: 3rd st: wknd over 3f out) .................................................. 2.6

2654⁶ Patrol *(MRStoute)* 9–0 GDuffield (2) (led over 7f: sn wknd) ..................... 2½.7

2122⁴ Rampal (IRE) *(GWragg)* 8–11 ‡³FNorton (5) (lw: w ldr: 2nd st: led 4f out to 3f out: wknd qckly) .................................................... 10.8

7/4 Flamingo Rose (IRE), **2/1** Indian Jack (IRE), **4/1** Marionetta (USA)(op 5/2), **8/1** Patrol, **20/1** Rampal (IRE), Storm Gauge (USA), **33/1** IRISH STAMP (IRE) & Ors. CSF £94.23, Tote £53.00: £5.20 £1.30 £5.80 (£44.30). Mr Jeff Pearce (NEWMARKET) bred by H. H. Aga Khan in Ireland. 8 Rn　　　　　　2m 35.1 (11.1)
　　　　　　　　　　　　　　　　　　　　　　　　SF–30/28/19/14/–/–

---

**2870**　　JOHN BECKETT CLAIMING STKS (3-Y.O) £3028.00 (£904.00: £432.00: £196.00)
　　　　　**1¾m 17y**　　　　　　　　　　　　　　　　　2-50 (2-50)

2739\* Expansionist **(57)** *(SPCWoods)* 8–10 WWoods (2) (chsd ldr: 2nd st: led over 4f out: clr over 1f out: rdn out) ................................ —1

2630* Big Pat **(58)** *(JPearce)* 8-9 ‡⁵RPrice (4) (chsd ldrs: 3rd st: rdn 2f out: no ex appr fnl f) .................................................................................................. 10.2

2498* Cov Tel Lady **(66)** (Fav) *(MHTompkins)* 8-10 ‡⁷SMulvey (1) (s.i.s: hdwy & 4th st: ev ch over 3f out: sn rdn & btn) ................................... 12.3

2566⁴ Russian Vision **(60)** (v) *(AAScott)* 9-4 JFortune (3) (led 10f: wknd qckly) ........ dist.4

2691⁵ Friendly House (IRE) **(62)** (bl) *(MAJarvis)* 8-3 ‡⁵KRutter (5) (rdn ½-wy: last st: sn t.o) ........................................................................................ 12.5

**7/4** Cov Tel Lady, **5/2** EXPANSIONIST, **9/2** Big Pat, **5/1** Russian Vision, **11/1** Friendly House (IRE). CSF £12.02, Tote £2.50: £1.50 £1.40 (£5.00). High Point Bloodstock Ltd (NEWMARKET) bred by N. E. and Mrs Poole. 5 Rn
3m 13.2 (15.2)

## 2871
HMS CROMER H'CAP (3-Y.O) (0-70) £2511.00 (£696.00: £333.00)
**1m 3y**      3-25 (3-28)

(Weights raised 2 lb)

2184* **Buzzards Bellbuoy (66)** *(HJCollingridge)* 9-7 VSmith (10) (racd alone stands' side: mde all: rdn out) ................................................ —1

2632⁶ Tiffany's Case (IRE) **(59)** *(CAHorgan)* 9-0 AMcGlone (7) (hld up: hdwy 2f out: r.o fnl f: nt rch wnr) ........................................................ 1.2

2632² Elizabethan Air **(54)** *(ANLee)* 8-2 ‡⁷CHawksley (2) (chsd ldrs: rdn 2f out: no ex fnl f) ................................................................. 2¹/₂.3

2616 Edgeaway **(65)** (v) *(JWHills)* 9-6 WRyan (12) (a.p: one pce appr fnl f) ............... 2.4

1642² Mastamist **(42)** (bl) *(RVoorspuy)* 7-11 SDawson (11) (bhd tl r.o fnl 2f) ............... 1¹/₂.5

2548 Flash of Straw (IRE) **(47)** (Fav) *(GLewis)* 7-13 ‡³FNorton (6) (lw: chsd ldrs tl rdn & btn over 2f out) ............................................... 2.6

2750⁴ Sir Oliver (IRE) **(65)** *(RJHodges)* 9-6 JFortune (4) (lw: prom tl rdn & wknd over 2f out) ...................................................................... 5.7

1807³ Wafi (USA) **(65)** *(BHanbury)* 9-6 GBaxter (3) (lw: hdwy 4f out: wknd over 2f out) 3.8

2616⁵ Mindomica **(54)** (bl) *(MBell)* 8-2 ‡⁷PTurner (9) (lw: reard s: hld up: hdwy 4f out: wknd over 2f out) ...................................... nk.9

2582* Kingchip Boy **(60)** *(MJRyan)* 9-1 DBiggs (8) (hld up: effrt & wnt lft over 2f out: sn no imp) ...................................................... 7.10

1673⁴ Douraj (IRE) **(63)** *(CEBrittain)* 9-0 GDuffield (5) (bit bkwd: bhd fnl 3f) ............... 1¹/₂.11

2252⁶ Guesstimation (USA) **(45)** *(JPearce)* 8-0 GBardwell (1) (lw: plld hrd: led centre 5f) ........................................................................ 2.12

**4/1** Flash of Straw (IRE), **6/1** Kingchip Boy(4/1—13/2), **13/2** Tiffany's Case (IRE)(op 4/1), **7/1** Elizabethan Air, **8/1** Mastamist(tchd 14/1), **17/2** BUZZARDS BELLBUOY(6/1—9/1), Douraj (IRE), **12/1** Mindomica(op 6/1), **16/1** Wafi (USA), Edgeaway(op 10/1), **20/1** Sir Oliver (IRE), **33/1** Guesstimation (USA). CSF £57.91, CT £373.70. Tote £11.90: £3.70 £3.20 £3.00 (£51.90). Mr N. H. Gardner (NEWMARKET) bred by N. H. Gardner. 12 Rn
1m 42.2 (6.9)
SF—51/41/21/33/5/1

## 2872
FRITTON LAKE NURSERY    £3523.50 (£1053.00: £504.00: £229.50)
**7f 3y**      4-00 (4-01)

2695³ **Awestruck (68)** (Fav) *(WJHaggas)* 8-1 GDuffield (6) (mde all: rdn clr fnl f) ......... —1

2500* Guv'nors Gift **(71)** *(MHTompkins)* 7-11⁽⁷⁾ ‡⁷SMulvey (7) (lw: hld up: hdwy 2f out: ev ch 1f out: edgd lft & no rspnse fnl f) .................. 4.2

2544* Devilry **(88)** *(GLewis)* 9-7 WRyan (4) (plld hrd: trckd ldrs: outpcd over 2f out: r.o wl fnl f) ............................................................. hd.3

2488⁴ Special Risk (IRE) **(62)** *(MBell)* 7-2⁽²⁾ ‡⁷CHawksley (1) (hdwy 3f out: no ex appr fnl f) ............................................................. 1.4

2717³ Second Colours (USA) **(80)** *(PSFelgate)* 8-13 GHind (2) (chsd ldr: rdn over 2f out: sn btn) ................................................... 8.5

2285 Mister Blake **(66)** (bl) *(WAO'Gorman)* 7-13 DBiggs (5) (a bhd) ......................... 3¹/₂.6

LONG HANDICAP: Special Risk (IRE) 7-3.

**5/2** AWESTRUCK, **3/1** Guv'nors Gift, **9/2** Devilry(3/1—5/1), **13/2** Special Risk (IRE)(op 4/1), **7/1** Ors. CSF £9.58, Tote £2.80: £1.50 £2.00 (£6.00). Mrs David Thompson (NEWMARKET) bred by Cheveley Park Stud Ltd.
6 Rn
1m 29.1 (6.3)
SF—35/19/42/6/7/–

## 2873
E.B.F. WELLINGTON PIER STKS (Mdn 2-Y.O.C & G) £2406.00 (£666.00: £318.00)
**7f 3y**      4-30 (4-33)

2728⁶ **Benevolent** *(SirMarkPrescott)* 9-0 GDuffield (5) (stdd s: hdwy 4f out: led 2f out: edgd lft & sn clr) ................................................ —1

Shareek (USA) *(MRStoute)* 9-0 WRyan (8) (leggy: unf: hld up: hdwy 2f out: kpt on fnl f) .......................................................... 4.2

2286² Fortensky (USA) (Fav) *(LMCumani)* 9-0 JFortune (1) (hdwy 3f out: ev ch 2f out: sn outpcd) ................................................... nk.3

Nessun Dorma *(GWragg)* 8-11 ‡³FNorton (11) (scope: bit bkwd: chsd ldrs: outpcd 2f out: kpt on wl fnl f) ............................................... hd.4

2286³ Rusty Reel *(CEBrittain)* 9-0 GCrealock (3) (lw: chsd ldrs: outpcd 2f out: r.o fnl f) ...................................................................................... 1.5

2398⁶ Dusty Point (IRE) *(BHanbury)* 9-0 GBaxter (10) (w ldrs tl wknd 2f out) ............. s.h.6

2653⁵ Platinum Venture *(SPCWoods)* 9-0 WWoods (7) (led 4f) .................................... 5.7

2598⁴ Mutakallam (USA) *(HThomsonJones)* 9-0 NCarlisle (9) (bhd: effrt 3f out: nvr trbld ldrs) .................................................................................. 3.8

Horseradish *(DMorley)* 9-0 MTebbutt (4) (rangy: scope: s.s: a bhd) ............ 1.9

2526⁵ Absolutely Fact (USA) *(WJHaggas)* 9-0 NDay (6) (w ldrs: led 3f out to 2f out: sn wknd) ............................................................................ 1½.10

Fabulous Way *(MRStoute)* 9-0 CDwyer (2) (unf: bkwd: w ldrs over 3f: sn wknd) 12.11

**5/4** Fortensky (USA), **9/4** Mutakallam (USA), **5/1** Shareek (USA)(op 3/1), **12/1** Rusty Reel, **14/1** Platinum Venture, **20/1** Horseradish, BENEVOLENT, **25/1** Dusty Point (IRE), Nessun Dorma, **33/1** Ors. CSF £116.96, Tote £27.80: £3.80 £2.20 £1.20 (£147.30). Mr Fahd Salman (NEWMARKET) bred by Lt-Col R. Bromley Gardner. 11 Rn     1m 29.5 (6.7)
SF—41/29/28/24/23

## 2874
MUNDESLEY H'CAP (0-70) £3028.00 (£904.00: £432.00: £196.00)
1¼m 21y        5-00 (5-05)

2529⁶ **Surrey Dancer (68)** *(BHanbury)* 4-9-12 NCarlisle (2) (lw: trckd ldrs: 5th st: led on bit over 1f out: shkn up & r.o) ..................................... —1

2518⁴ Boogie Bopper (IRE) (62) *(MBell)* 3-8-9 ‡³FNorton (1) (bhd: last st: rdn & hdwy over 1f out: no imp ins fnl f) ................................................. 1.2

2805³ Tiger Shoot (50) (v) *(DJSCosgrove)* 5-8-8 AShoults (3) (swtg: chsd ldr: 2nd st: led 3f out tl over 1f out: one pce) ................................. ¾.3

£666* Don't Forsake Me (63) *(DMorley)* 3-8-13 WRyan (5) (led over 7f: ev ch over 1f out: sn wknd) ............................................................. 6.4

1150 Callipoli (USA) (63) *(RGuest)* 5-9-7 GBaxter (4) (bit bkwd: prom: 3rd st: wknd 2f out) .............................................................................. 1½.5

2580² Roberto's Gal (58) (Fav) *(NCWright)* 3-8-8 GDuffield (6) (dwlt: rdn 4f out: a bhd) 2.6

2585⁶ Scenic Dancer (53) (v) *(AHide)* 4-8-11 WWoods (7) (lw: plld hrd: chsd ldrs: 4th & c wd st: rdn & wknd over 2f out) .................................. 2½.7

**5/2** Roberto's Gal, **4/1** Tiger Shoot, **9/2** Boogie Bopper (IRE), **11/2** Don't Forsake Me, SURREY DANCER, **7/1** Scenic Dancer, **14/1** Callipoli (USA)(op 8/1). CSF £28.41, CT £99.45. Tote £5.50: £2.50 £2.40 (£15.10). Cronk Thoroughbred Racing Ltd (NEWMARKET) bred by Fonthill Stud. 7 Rn     2m 14.4 (10)
SF—52/33/30/23/28/11

T/Plpt: £308.10 (7.8 Tckts).                  Dk

## 2675–AYR (L-H)
### Thursday, August 20th [Good to soft]
Going Allowance: St: 0.15 sec (G); Rnd: 0.50 sec per fur (Y)     Wind: slt across

Stalls: high

## 2875
ST QUIVOX CLAIMING STKS    £2221.50 (£624.00: £304.50)    **5f**    2-30 (2-31)

2265² **Another Episode (IRE) (88)** (Fav) *(JBerry)* 3-9-7 GCarter (3) (lw: mde all: rdn clr appr fnl f) ................................................................... —1

1333⁶ Francis Ann (47) *(MissLAPerratt)* 4-8-5 JFanning (1) (sn outpcd & bhd: styd on fnl 2f: no ch w wnr) ................................................... 6.2

2333⁶ North of Watford (49) *(MPNaughton)* 7-8-12 DMcKeown (2) (chsd wnr: rdn over 2f out: sn btn) ......................................................... 2.3

**1/3** ANOTHER EPISODE (IRE), **9/2** North of Watford, **6/1** Francis Ann. CSF £2.39, Tote £1.30 (£4.60). Palacegate Corporation Ltd (COCKERHAM) bred by Brendan and Sheila Powell in Ireland. 3 Rn
61.79 sec (3.79)
SF—47/7/6

## 2876
GREENWELL MONTAGU NURSERY    £2169.00 (£609.00: £297.00)    **5f**    3-00 (3-01)

2740* **First Option (71)** (Fav) *(MHEasterby)* 9-2 (5x) KDarley (5) (hld up: stdy hdwy to ld 1f out: rdn & r.o wl: comf) ..................................... —1

2221⁶ Cockerham Ranger (76) *(JBerry)* 9-7 GCarter (3) (lw: trckd ldrs: rdn to ld over 1f out: sn hdd & nt qckn) ....................................... 3.2

2488* Montone (IRE) (72) *(CBBBooth)* 9-3 GOldroyd (1) (lw: sn bhd: rdn ½-wy: styd on: nrst fin) ....................................................... 2½.3

2512★ Selvole (52) *(MissLAPerratt)* 7-4 ‡[7]ClaireBalding (4) (cl up tl rdn & wknd over 1f out) ................................................................ ½.4

2221[3] Stardust Express (70) *(MJohnston)* 9-1 DMcKeown (2) (led tl hdd & wknd over 1f out) ................................................................ 1½.5

**5/4** FIRST OPTION, **2/1** Montone (IRE), **8/1** Stardust Express, **10/1** Selvole(op 5/1), **16/1** Cockerham Ranger(op 8/1). CSF £13.91, Tote £1.80: £1.50 £1.40 (£5.70). Mr P. D. Savill (MALTON) bred by Dodford Stud. 5 Rn
61.80 sec (3.80)
SF—41/34/20/–/10

---

**2877**    BELMONT H'CAP (0-80) £2801.00 (£848.00: £414.00: £197.00)
         2m 1f 105y                         3-30 (3-31)

2739[2] **Rolling the Bones (USA) (66)** *(MPNaughton)* 3-8-2 KDarley (7) (lw: hld up: hdwy ent st: led appr fnl f: r.o) ................................ —1

2222[4] Attadale (56) *(LLungo)* 4-8-6 KFallon (8) (a.p: led wl over 2f out: sn rdn: hdd appr fnl f: one pce) ................................ 1½.2

2222[2] Aahsaylad (78) (v) *(FHLee)* 6-10-0 RLappin (3) (lw: s.i.s: bhd & drvn along 6f out: styd on fnl 2f: nvr able to chal) ................................ 2.3

2677 Alpha Helix (43) (v) *(MissLAPerratt)* 9-7-7 JFanning (2) (chsd ldrs: rdn ent st: r.o one pce) ................................ ½.4

2677[3] Moment of Truth (43) *(PMonteith)* 8-7-7 DaleGibson (6) (lw: hld up & bhd: hdwy u.p 3f out: nvr rchd ldrs) ................................ ½.5

234 Jinxy Jack (78) *(GRichards)* 8-10-0 DNicholls (9) (trckd ldrs: led on bit appr st: hdd wl over 2f out: wknd wl over 1f out) ................................ 12.6

2737 Newark Antiquefair (43) *(BCMorgan)* 4-7-0 ‡[7]DarrenMoffatt (4) (cl up: led 6f out tl hdd appr st: sn wknd) ................................ 2½.7

2677 Scalp 'em (IRE) (43) *(FHLee)* 4-7-7 SWood (1) (led tl hdd 6f out: wknd ent st) ................................ ¾.8

1126[4] Native Crown (IRE) (54) *(MrsSCBradburne)* 4-8-4 NConnorton (5) (chsd ldrs tl wknd over 3f out) ................................ 8.9

LONG HANDICAP: Alpha Helix 6-6, Moment of Truth 7-0, Newark Antiquefair 6-1, Scalp 'em (IRE) 7-6.

**6/5** Aahsaylad, **5/1** ROLLING THE BONES (USA), Attadale, **15/2** Moment of Truth, **14/1** Jinxy Jack(op 8/1), **16/1** Native Crown (IRE), **33/1** Alpha Helix, **50/1** Scalp 'em (IRE), **66/1** Newark Antiquefair. CSF £26.30, CT £39.27. Tote £6.10: £1.10 £1.60 £1.30 (£15.60). Mr M. F. Hyman (RICHMOND) bred by Holtsinger Incorporated in USA. 9 Rn
4m 2.28 (16.78)
SF—8/10/30/–/–/16

---

**2878**    BURNS CLAIMING STKS    £2263.50 (£636.00: £310.50)    **7f**      4-05 (4-07)

2678[2] **Laurel Queen (IRE) (63)** (Fav) *(JBerry)* 4-9-3 GCarter (1) (lw: hld up & bhd: hdwy on bit to ld over 1f out: hung lft: sn rdn clr) ................................ —1

2637 Heaven-Liegh-Grey (76) *(MJohnston)* 4-9-5 RPElliott (6) (lw: chsd ldrs: chal 2f out: nt qckn fnl f) ................................ 2.2

2689★ Kinlacey (60) *(BAMcMahon)* 5-8-12 ‡[7]SSanders (2) (effrt ½-wy: styd on wl fnl f: nvr able to chal) ................................ 1.3

2816[3] Diet (62) (v) *(MissLAPerratt)* 6-9-0 NConnorton (7) (lw: led tl hdd over 1f out: sn btn) ................................ 5.4

2678[4] Princess Maxine (IRE) (57) *(MissLAPerratt)* 3-8-4 DaleGibson (5) (chsd ldrs: rdn 3f out: wknd wl over 1f out) ................................ 5.5

2514[3] Bee Dee Ell (USA) (42) *(MissLAPerratt)* 3-8-11 JFanning (3) (prom tl outpcd wl over 2f out) ................................ 1.6

2785[2] Patience Please (67) (bl) *(MHEasterby)* 3-8-8 KDarley (4) (trckd ldrs: effrt 3f out: sn btn) ................................ 4.7

**9/4** LAUREL QUEEN (IRE), **5/2** Patience Please, **11/2** Kinlacey(4/1—6/1), **6/1** Princess Maxine (IRE)(op 4/1), **9/1** Diet(op 6/1), **14/1** Heaven-Liegh-Grey(op 8/1), **66/1** Bee Dee Ell (USA). CSF £25.57, Tote £2.70: £1.80 £3.80 (£22.30). Laurel (Leisure) Limited (COCKERHAM) bred by E. Lonergan in Ireland. 7 Rn 1m 31.64 (7.64)
SF—41/37/27/14/–/–

---

**2879**    KIRKOSWALD STKS (Mdn 2-Y.O) £2368.50 (£666.00: £325.50)    **7f**      4-35 (4-45)

2675 **Drumdonna (IRE)** *(JBerry)* 8-9 SWood (9) (bhd: c wd & hdwy 3f out: r.o wl to ld wl ins fnl f) ................................ —1

2223[4] Eleusis (FR) (Fav) *(PWChapple-Hyam)* 9-0 DMcKeown (11) (lw: cl up: led wl over 2f out: sn hrd drvn & r.o: hdd & no ex wl ins fnl f) ................................ ¾.2

Beauman *(BAMcMahon)* 8-7 ‡[7]SSanders (10) (leggy: scope: a chsng ldrs: rdn to chal ent fnl f: nt qckn) ................................ nk.3

2629[2] Shamam (USA) *(PTWalwyn)* 9-0 GCarter (1) (led tl hdd over 2f out: r.o one pce) 2½.4

2606[3] Runrig (IRE) *(MissLAPerratt)* 8-9 JFanning (4) (chsd ldrs tl outpcd over 2f out: kpt on fnl f) ................................ 2.5

| | | |
|---|---|---|
| 2629⁵ | Nu Shan (IRE) *(MRStoute)* 9-0 DaleGibson (6) (lw: bhd & pushed along: hdwy u.p 2f out: nvr nrr) | 2¹/₂.6 |
| 1995³ | Totally Unique (USA) **(90)** *(EWeymes)* 9-0 PD'Arcy (8) (lw: chsd ldrs tl rdn & wl outpcd wl over 2f out) | 2¹/₂.7 |
| 877 | Master Fiddler *(EWeymes)* 9-0 RLappin (7) (in tch tl rdn & outpcd fnl 3f) | 1¹/₂.8 |
| 2675 | Cornflake *(DenysSmith)* 8-9 KFallon (5) (a bhd) | 1¹/₂.9 |
| 2700⁴ | Careless Son *(MissSEHall)* 9-0 NConnorton (3) (nvr nr to chal) | ¹/₂.10 |
| 2024 | Shomberg (IRE) *(PCalver)* 9-0 DNicholls (2) (in tch 4f: eased whn btn) | 6.11 |
| | Roscommon Joe (IRE) *(JJO'Neill)* 9-0 TLucas (12) (w'like: in tch: rn wd st: wknd over 2f out) | hd.12 |

*Lucky Domino (66/1) Withdrawn (unruly in stalls) : not under orders*

**5/2** Eleusis (FR), **3/1** Shamam (USA)(op 2/1), **9/2** Totally Unique (USA)(op 3/1), **7/1** Runrig (IRE), **14/1** Careless Son(op 8/1), Shomberg (IRE)(op 8/1), **16/1** Nu Shan (IRE)(op 8/1), **20/1** Beauman, **33/1** DRUMDONNA (IRE), **50/1** Ors. CSF £105.43, Tote £41.90: £4.70 £1.10 £6.50 (£252.70). Mrs Norma Peebles (COCKERHAM) bred by B. Ryan in Ireland. 12 Rn

1m 32.09 (8.09)
SF—26/29/12/20/7/4

---

**2880**  GOUKSCROFT H'CAP (0-70) £2253.00 (£633.00: £309.00)  1¹/₄m  5-05 (5-08)

(Weights raised 16 lb)

| | | |
|---|---|---|
| 2775⁶ | **Master Copy (IRE) (43)** (bl) *(CBBBooth)* 3-8-12 GOldroyd (6) (hld up & bhd: smooth hdwy to ld ent fnl f: shkn up & qcknd) | —1 |
| 2632³ | Sie Amato (IRE) **(55)** (Fav) *(CaptJWilson)* 3-9-10 GCarter (3) (disp ld tl led appr st: hdd & no ex ins fnl f) | 1¹/₂.2 |
| 2814⁵ | Hizeem **(25)** *(MPNaughton)* 6-8-2 JakiHouston (1) (lw: s.i.s: sn prom: chal over 1f out: hung lft & nt qckn) | 1¹/₂.3 |
| 1311 | Reklaw **(31)** *(MDHammond)* 5-8-8 JFanning (2) (prom: hdwy & ev ch 3f out: sn rdn & one pce) | 2.4 |
| 2486 | Morcinda **(49)** *(PMonteith)* 6-9-5⁽⁴⁾ ¥ADOLDIN (4) (hld up: hdwy ent st: outpcd wl over 2f out) | l2.5 |
| 1518 | Sir Norman Holt (IRE) **(55)** *(FHLee)* 3-9-10 DMcKeown (7) (disp ld tl hdd appr st: wknd over 2f out) | 2¹/₂.6 |
| 797 | Tidal River **(43)** *(DenysSmith)* 3-8-5 ⁷CTeague (5) (trckd ldrs: c wd st: sn wknd) | 6.7 |

**11/4** Sie Amato (IRE), **7/2** MASTER COPY (IRE), **4/1** Reklaw, **5/1** Sir Norman Holt (IRE), **7/1** Hizeem(op 9/2), **14/1** Morcinda, **50/1** Tidal River. CSF £11.94, Tote £4.40: £1.70 £2.80 (£6.90). Blacktype Racing Partnership (FLAXTON) bred by Pegasus Farm in Ireland. 7 Rn

2m 15.21 (9.91)
SF—49/58/33/35/22/22

T/Plpt: £31.00 (43.64 Tckts). AA

---

## 2746-SALISBURY (R-H)

### Thursday, August 20th [Good to soft, Soft patches]

Going Allowance: St: 0.40 sec (Y); Rnd: 0.25 sec per fur (G)  Wind: almost nil

Stalls: high

**2881**  WOODFORD APP'CE H'CAP (0-70) £2679.00 (£744.00: £357.00)
6f 212y  5-30 (5-33)

| | | |
|---|---|---|
| 2369³ | Hawaii Storm (FR) **(50)** *(MissAJWhitfield)* 4-8-13 ATucker (15) (lw: a.p: led ins fnl f: r.o wl) | —1 |
| 2496 | Jolto **(40)** *(KOCunningham-Brown)* 3-7-9⁽³⁾ ‡³BThomas (14) (led tl ins fnl f: r.o wl) | s.h.2 |
| 2634 | Highland Magic (IRE) **(65)** *(MJFetherston-Godley)* 4-10-0 MichaelDenaro (19) (a.p: hrd rdn over 1f out: unable toppl) | 1¹/₂.3 |
| 2684² | Mossy Rose **(59)** (Fav) *(LordHuntingdon)* 6-9-8 DHarrison (5) (lw: hdwy over 2f out: hrd rdn over 1f out: one pce) | 2¹/₂.4 |
| 2807 | Lucky Noire **(60)** *(GHarwood)* 4-9-6 ‡³PHoughton (18) (b: lw: hdwy 3f out: hrd rdn over 1f out: one pce) | nk.5 |
| 2787⁶ | Batchworth Bound **(51)** (bl) *(EAWheeler)* 3-8-9 JDSmith (20) (swtg: a.p: one pce fnl 2f) | 2.6 |
| 2601⁵ | Gold Jubilee **(61)** *(PJMakin)* 3-9-5 RPerham (11) (lw: hdwy over 2f out: one pce) | 2¹/₂.7 |
| 2730² | Juvenata **(39)** *(CJHill)* 6-8-2 BDoyle (16) (hrd rdn & hdwy over 2f out: one pce) | ³/₄.8 |
| 2607 | Miss Magenta (IRE) **(32)** *(RThompson)* 4-7-6 ‡³NicolaHowarth (17) (prom over 5f) | ¹/₂.9 |
| 2634⁴ | Prepare (IRE) **(36)** *(RJHolder)* 4-7-10 ‡³SDrowne (7) (prom over 4f) | nk.10 |
| 2583* | Durneltor **(63)** *(RHannon)* 4-9-5 ‡⁷AWhelan (3) (nvr nrr) | s.h.11 |

2752 John O'Dreams (42) (MrsJCDawe) 7-8-5 GForster (1) (s.s: nvr nrr) ............... 2.12
27705 Navaresque (42) (RJHodges) 7-8-2 ‡3PBowe (10) (a mid div) ................ ¾.13
28074 Profit a Prendre (55) (DAWilson) 8-8-11 ‡7SharonMillard (13) (b: prom over 4f) s.h.14
27304 Alnasric Pete (USA) (52) (DAWilson) 6-9-1 SO'Gorman (9) (b: hdwy over 2f
　　　　out: wknd over 1f out) .......................................................... nk.15
2694 Aragona (44) (PDCundell) 3-7-13 ‡3DGibbs (4) (bhd fnl 3f) ............... 4.16
2757 Golden Proposal (47) (MJBolton) 3-8-5 StephenDavies (12) (bhd fnl 3f) ..... ½.17
2620 Alto Princess (42) (APJones) 3-8-0 JTate (2) (prom over 4f) ............... 15.18
　　　　Oscilante (45) (RAkehurst) 4-8-5 ‡3LCarter (8) (bhd fnl 3f) ............... 19

7/2 Mossy Rose, 7/1 Durneltor(4/1—8/1), 15/2 HAWAII STORM (FR), 11/1 Alnasric Pete (USA)(10/1—16/1), Juvenara(8/1—12/1), 12/1 Profit a Prendre(op 7/1), 14/1 Navaresque(8/1—16/1), Lucky Noire, Prepare (IRE), 16/1 Gold Jubilee, Batchworth Bound, 20/1 Highland Magic (IRE), 25/1 Oscilante, John O'Dreams, 33/1 Aragona, Golden Proposal, Jolto, Miss Magenta (IRE), 50/1 Alto Princess. CSF £204.64, CT £4,282.09. Tote £6.00: £2.10 £13.90 £7.80 £1.30 (Wnr or 2nd w any £3.50). Mr Andreas Sofroniou (LAMBOURN) bred by Horse France in France. 19 Rn
1m 32.21 (6.51)
SF—43/24/52/38/35/15

**2882**　ODSTOCK CLAIMING STKS (3-Y.O) £2320.00 (£645.00: £310.00)
　　　　6f 212y
　　　　　　　　　　　　　　　　　　　　　　　　　　　　6-00 (6-03)

12196 **Salisong** (71) (PFICole) 9-0 ‡7JDSmith (8) (gd hdwy over 1f out: led ins fnl f:
　　　　edgd lft: drvn out) .......................................................... —1
27535 Rockbourne (47) (DRCElsworth) 8-4 JWilliams (11) (gd hdwy over 1f out: ev ch
　　　　ins fnl f: carried lft: r.o wl) ........................................... hd.2
26163 Spanish Glory (52) (bl) (IABalding) 8-5 ‡3SO'Gorman (1) (lw: a.p: hrd rdn over 1f
　　　　out: unable qckn) .......................................................... 7.3
2187 Sandcastle City (59) (bl) (RHannon) 8-11 JLloyd (15) (a.p: hrd rdn over 1f out:
　　　　one pce) .................................................................... s.h.4
2694* Certain Lady (61) (GBlum) 8-2 ‡5DHarrison (12) (lw: a.p: led over 1f out tl ins fnl
　　　　f: sn wknd) ................................................................. ½.5
2617 Orchard Bay (47) (DRTucker) 7-10(1) ‡7SDrowne (14) (a.p: hrd rdn over 2f out:
　　　　wknd ins fnl f) ............................................................. 1.6
26945 Great Hall (40) (bl) (PDCundell) 8-4 ‡3RPerham (7) (a.p: hrd rdn over 2f out:
　　　　wknd ins fnl f) ............................................................. ½.7
2545* Sally Fast (50) (BPalling) 8-3 ‡5StephenDavies (19) (nvr nr to chal) ............... 1½.8
2787 Beyond the Moon (IRE) (59) (MJFetherston-Godley) 8-1 ‡5BDoyle (18) (nvr nrr) ... ½.9
910 Morgans Ace (BRMillman) 8-13 NHowe (17) (nvr nrr) ............................... ½.10
2525* Lord Vivienne (IRE) (80) (bl) (PFICole) 9-7 TQuinn (4) (swtg: led over 5f) .......... s.h.11
2496 Lamore Ritorna (55) (KOCunningham-Brown) 9-0 SWhitworth (5) (prom over
　　　　5f) ......................................................................... ¾.12
27516 Samjamalifran (MCPipe) 8-2 BCrossley (13) (a mid div) ......................... hd.13
496 Ceatharlach (47) (RJHolder) 8-13 NAdams (6) (prom over 5f) ..................... 2.14
26495 Marvelous Molly (49) (IABalding) 7-13 ‡7DGriffiths (3) (lw: bhd fnl 3f) ........... s.h.15
2632 Crackling (40) (DMarks) 8-9 ‡7GForster (9) (a bhd) ............................. nk.16
2549 Hazy Shades (JJBridger) 8-12 MPerrett (16) (hdwy over 2f out: wknd over 1f
　　　　out) ........................................................................ 7.17
2753 Two Birds (47) (CAHorgan) 8-2 TSprake (2) (a bhd) .............................. 3.18
　　　　Mcnab (IRE) (CPWildman) 8-9 CRutter (10) (leggy: s.s: a bhd) .................. 10.19
　　　　　　　　*Stewards Enquiry: Obj. to Salisong by Williams overruled.*

9/4 Lord Vivienne (IRE), 9/2 Certain Lady, 13/2 Rockbourne, 9/1 Spanish Glory(6/1—10/1), 10/1 Sandcastle City, Lamore Ritorna(8/1—12/1), 12/1 SALISONG(op 8/1), Marvelous Molly, 14/1 Sally Fast(10/1—16/1), 20/1 Great Hall, Two Birds, 25/1 Samjamalifran, Orchard Bay, Beyond the Moon (IRE), Ceatharlach, 33/1 Ors. CSF £95.28, Tote £13.20: £3.90 £2.30 £2.80 (£27.40). Mrs Martyn Arbib (WHATCOMBE) bred by Mrs J. R. Hine and Miss J. Bunting. 19 Rn; Spanish Glory clmd K Cunningham-Brown £6,013, Rockbourne clmd O Stokes £4,600
1m 32.44 (6.74)
SF—41/30/10/15/4/-

**2883**　BBC WILTSHIRE SOUND NURSERY £2511.00 (£696.00: £333.00)
　　　　6f 212y
　　　　　　　　　　　　　(Weights raised 8 lb)　　　　　　6-30 (6-34)

21385 **Spring Sunrise** (59) (MBlanshard) 7-9 ‡5DHarrison (8) (hdwy 2f out: led ins fnl f:
　　　　r.o wl) ..................................................................... —1
22773 Rockover (71) (Fav) (RHannon) 8-12 JLloyd (2) (lw: hld up: led over 1f out tl ins
　　　　fnl f: r.o wl) .............................................................. nk.2
2681* Kyrenia Game (67) (PMitchell) 8-5 ‡3SO'Gorman (6) (hdwy 2f out: ev ch 1f out:
　　　　unable qckn) ............................................................... 2.3
2572 Workingforpeanuts (IRE) (59) (CASmith) 7-9 ‡5ATucker (11) (lw: s.s: hdwy over
　　　　1f out: r.o) ................................................................ ½.4
26812 Le Couteau (70) (DWPArbuthnot) 8-11 TQuinn (9) (a.p: rdn over 4f out: one
　　　　pce) ....................................................................... 3½.5

2606² Mena **(73)** *(JWPayne)* 9-0 JWilliams (10) (s.s: nvr nr to chal) ............... ½.6

1762⁴ Raging Thunder **(80)** *(GLewis)* 9-7 CRutter (7) (lw: a:p: ev ch over 1f out: sn wknd) ............... 3.7

2717⁴ Homemaker **(58)** *(RJHolder)* 7-13 NAdams (3) (prom over 4f) ............... ½.8

2374² Daisy James (IRE) **(61)** *(JMPEustace)* 8-2 SWhitworth (5) (a.p: led 2f out tl over 1f out: sn wknd) ............... nk.9

2590⁶ Petite Vino **(56)** (bl) *(JJBridger)* 7-6⁽⁴⁾ ‡5BDoyle (1) (lw: led 5f) ............... 1.10

2558⁶ Hy Wilma **(58)** *(RJHodges)* 7-13 TSprake (4) (lw: prom over 3f) ............... 5.11

LONG HANDICAP: Petite Vino 7-0.

**3/1** Rockover(4/1—5/1), **7/1** Mena, SPRING SUNRISE(8/1—12/1), **8/1** Hy Wilma(6/1—9/1), Kyrenia Game, **10/1** Homemaker, Le Couteau(op 6/1), Raging Thunder(6/1—11/1), **12/1** Workingforpeanuts (IRE)(8/1—14/1), **14/1** Daisy James (IRE), **33/1** Petite Vino. CSF £26.29, CT £157.05. Tote £10.00: £2.20 £1.70 £3.30 (£13.60). Mr R. J. Campbell (UPPER LAMBOURN) bred by Littleton Stud. 11 Rn    1m 32.90 (7.20)

SF—15/31/18/6/11/12

---

**2884**    NIGHTFALL STKS (2-Y.O) £2872.00 (£856.00: £408.00: £184.00)    **5f**   7-00 (7-01)

2811³ **Night Melody (IRE) (100)** (Fav) *(RHannon)* 9-5 MHills (4) (hld up: led on bit 2f out: v.easily) ............... —1

Esthal (IRE) *(RJHodges)* 8-4 ‡7SDrowne (8) (unf: hld up: chsd wnr over 1f out: no imp) ............... 2½.2

Air Command (BAR) *(RHannon)* 8-8 ‡9RPerham (6) (cmpt: bit bkwd: lost pl over 2f out: rallied fnl f: r.o) ............... ¾.3

Bright Spells *(DRCElsworth)* 8-6 JWilliams (5) (unf: bit bkwd: outpcd: gd hdwy fnl f: r.o wl) ............... 2.4

1744⁴ Bonita Bee *(LJHolt)* 8-6 NAdams (9) (nvr nr to chal) ............... nk.5

1135 Coopers Delight *(GLewis)* 8-6 ‡5DHarrison (3) (prom over 3f) ............... 2.6

2727⁵ Sing as We Go *(BJDJones)* 8-6 TQuinn (1) (led 4f out to 2f out: sn wknd) ...... 1½.7

2031 Step on it *(CPWildman)* 8-6 CRutter (2) (led 1f: wknd over 2f out) ............... 2.8

**2/5** NIGHT MELODY (IRE), **7/1** Esthal (IRE)(16/1—20/1), **15/2** Bright Spells(5/1—8/1), **12/1** Bonita Bee(op 8/1), **14/1** Air Command (BAR)(op 8/1), **25/1** Sing as We Go, **33/1** Ors. CSF £4.43, Tote £1.60: £1.30 £1.60 £2.10 (£5.00). Mr P. D. Savill (MARLBOROUGH) bred by Leo Collins in Ireland. 8 Rn    64.30 sec (4.30)

SF—59/34/35/25/24/16

---

**2885**    NETTON H'CAP (0-90) £3132.00 (£936.00: £448.00: £204.00)

   **1m 1f 209y**    (Weights raised 3 lb)    7-30 (7-30)

**C U Coral (55)** *(MCPipe)* 3–7-5⁽²⁾ ‡5BDoyle (1) (lw: a.p: hrd rdn 2f out: edgd lft 1f out: led ins fnl f: r.o wl) ............... —1

2714 Gotcha (BAR) **(83)** (bl) *(RHannon)* 3–9-7 ‡3RPerham (9) (a.p: led 3f out tl ins fnl f: unable qckn) ............... 2.2

2660² Mahsul (IRE) **(65)** *(CJBenstead)* 4–9-0 TQuinn (7) (lw: hdwy over 2f out: 3rd & btn whn hmpd 1f out) ............... 3½.3

2413 Capital Bond (IRE) **(47)** *(RJHolder)* 4–7-10 NAdams (6) (hld up: hrd rdn over 3f out: one pce) ............... ¾.4

2708* Santana Lady (IRE) **(70)** (Fav) *(MJHeaton-Ellis)* 3–8-11 WRSwinburn (2) (lw: a.p: hrd rdn 4f out: one pce) ............... nk.5

2062* Second Call **(67)** *(HCandy)* 3–8-8 CRutter (5) (hld up: rdn over 3f out: one pce) ............... s.h.6

2413⁵ Samurai Gold (USA) **(51)** (v) *(PTWalwyn)* 4–7-9⁽²⁾ ‡5ATucker (4) (nvr nr to chal) ............... nk.7

Front Page **(55)** *(JAkehurst)* 5–8-4 SWhitworth (10) (bit bkwd: led 7f) ............... 2½.8

Woodside Heath **(55)** *(JSMoore)* 5–8-4 JWilliams (3) (b: a bhd: t.o) ............... 9

**3/1** Santana Lady (IRE)(op 2/1), **7/2** Mahsul (IRE), **9/2** Second Call(4/1—6/1), **11/2** Samurai Gold (USA), **10/1** Gotcha (BAR)(5/1—11/1), **12/1** Capital Bond (IRE), **16/1** Front Page(10/1—20/1), C U CORAL, **33/1** Woodside Heath. CSF £138.72, CT £620.35. Tote £25.20: £3.80 £3.00 £1.60 (£128.90). Mr D. E. McDowell (WELLINGTON) bred by Cleaboy Farms Co. 9 Rn    2m 13.28 (8.58)

SF—20/46/32/12/26/22

---

**2886**    NETHERAVON STKS (Mdn 3-Y.O.F) £2145.00 (£595.00: £285.00)    **1½m** 8-00 (8-01)

2780³ **Janaat** (Jt-Fav) *(AAScott)* 8-11 WRSwinburn (3) (lw: a.p: rdn over 4f out: edgd rt over 2f out: led ins fnl f: r.o wl) ............... —1

2757 Sheringa **(68)** *(GBBalding)* 8-11 JWilliams (9) (gd hdwy over 1f out: r.o wl ins fnl f) ............... 2½.2

1746⁵ Etiquette *(LordHuntingdon)* 8-6 ‡5DHarrison (7) (hld up: led over 2f out tl ins fnl f: unable qckn) ............... 2.3

Surf Boat *(BWHills)* 8-11 MHills (1) (b.hind: a.p: led over 3f out tl over 2f out: one pce) ............... 3½.4

2757 Sharriba **(70)** *(DRCElsworth)* 8-6 ‡5BDoyle (2) (nvr nr to chal) ............... 1½.5

1720⁵ Oribi *(PFICole)* 8-11 TQuinn (11) (hld up: shkn up over 2f out: eased whn btn over 1f out) ............... 3½.6

2616⁴ Athar (IRE) **(47)** *(RJBaker)* 8-11 NHowe (5) (lw: nvr nrr) ................................ 2.7
2654² Anna Comnena (IRE) (Jt-Fav) *(LMCumani)* 8-6 ‡⁵JWeaver (10) (lw: a.p: led 5f
out tl over 3f out: wkng whn hmpd over 2f out) ................... 3.8
1207⁴ Shameem (USA) *(MRStoute)* 8-11 JLloyd (8) (led 7f: wknd 3f out) .................. 1¹⁄₂.9
2298 Place Mat *(DrJDScargill)* 8-11 CRutter (6) (a bhd) ...................................... 12.10
Broadway Ruckus (CAN) *(DRLaing)* 8-11 SWhitworth (4) (bit bkwd: a bhd) ... 12.11

**9/4** JANAAT(7/4—6/4), Anna Comnena (IRE)(6/4—5/2), **4/1** Oribi(8/1—10/1), **7/1** Etiquette, **9/1** Sheringa(12/
1—8/1), **10/1** Shameem (USA)(7/1—11/1), **16/1** Surf Boat(op 10/1), Sharriba(10/1—20/1), **33/1** Place Mat,
**50/1** Athar (IRE), **66/1** Broadway Ruckus (CAN). CSF £24.18, Tote £3.50: £1.50 £2.50 £2.10 (£26.90).
Maktoum Al Maktoum (NEWMARKET) bred by Hesmonds Stud Ltd. 11 Rn 2m 40.88 (8.28)
SF—44/39/30/23/20/18

T/Plpt: £349.70 (5.45 Tckts). AK

---

### 2093a—CURRAGH (R-H)
**Saturday, August 15th [Good to soft becoming Soft]**
Going Allowance: 0.10 sec per fur (G)

#### 2887a
MITSUBISHI ELECTRIC E.B.F. TYROS STKS (listed race) (2-Y.O) £8061.00 7f

2505a\* **Fatherland (IRE)** *(Ireland)* 2-8-11 LPiggott .......................................... —1
Frenchpark *(Ireland)* 2-8-11 PShanahan .................................... 1¹⁄₂.2
Earl of Barking (IRE) *(Ireland)* 2-8-11 RJGriffiths ............................ 1.3
Tote £1.30: £1.20 £2.00 (£3.60). Mrs M. V. O'Brien (M.V.O'Brien,IRELAND) bred by Ballydoyle Stud in Ireland. 6
Rn 1m 26.9 (3.7)
SF—52/47/44

#### 2888a
CARMELITES KILDARE 7th CENTENARY DESMOND STKS (Gp 3) £10748.00 1m

2760a\* **Via Borghese (USA)** (Fav) *(Ireland)* 3-8-5 WCarson (disp ld tl led over 1f out:
hld on wl) .............................. —1
2760a² Gdansk's Honour (USA) (bl) *(Ireland)* 3-8-5 CRoche (prom tl lost pl 2f out: r.o
u.p fnl f: jst failed) ......................... hd.2
2383² SURE SHARP (USA) *(BWHills)* 5-9-7 DHolland (disp ld tl hdd over 1f out: no ex) 1¹⁄₂.3
1817a Approach The Bench (IRE) *(Ireland)* 4-9-3 LPiggott (chsd ldrs: no imp tl hrd rdn
& kpt on u.p fnl f) ........................... 2.4
1817a⁵ Tarwiya (IRE) *(Ireland)* 3-8-9 MJKinane (trckd ldrs: effrt over 1f out: sn btn) .... s.h.5
2762a³ Street Rebel (CAN) *(Ireland)* 4-9-7 RHughes (mid div: effrt over 1f out: sn wknd) 2.6
Stark Contrast (USA) (bl) *(Ireland)* 3-8-8 PShanahan (bhd fnl 2f) ...................... 10.7

**6/4** VIA BORGHESE (USA), **4/1** Sure Sharp (USA), **5/1** Tarwiya (IRE), **6/1** Gdansk's Honour (USA), **7/1** Approach
The Bench (IRE), **12/1** Street Rebel (CAN), **33/1** Stark Contrast (USA). Tote £2.20: £1.50 £1.80 (£5.70). Mr
Malcolm Parrish (M.V.O'Brien,IRELAND) bred by Panama Traders, Bedford & Skymarc Farms in USA. 7 Rn
1m 41 (4)
SF—43/42/53/43/34/40

#### 2889a
ROYAL WHIP STKS (Gp 3) £10748.00 1¹⁄₂m

2454² **JAHAFIL** (Fav) *(MajorWRHern)* 4-9-4 WCarson (mde all: clr after 3f: easily) ...... —1
2763a² Mining Tycoon (IRE) *(Ireland)* 3-8-7 CRoche (chsd wnr tl lost pl ¹⁄₂-wy: rdn &
styd on wl fnl 2f: no ch w wnr) ............. 6.2
1229a\* In a Tiff (IRE) *(Ireland)* 3-9-3 MJKinane (in rr tl sme hdwy 2f out: kpt on) ........... 3.3
Ebaziya (IRE) *(Ireland)* 3-8-4 RHughes (chsd wnr fr ¹⁄₂-wy: rdn & no imp over 2f
out: wknd fnl f) ............................. 4¹⁄₂.4
2763a³ Malvernico (IRE) *(Ireland)* 4-9-4 KJManning (mid div: rdn & wknd 2f out) ........... 8.5

**6/4** JAHAFIL, **11/4** Ebaziya (IRE), **4/1** In a Tiff (IRE), Mining Tycoon (IRE), **12/1** Malvernico (IRE). Tote £2.20:
£1.30 £2.20 (£6.50). Mr Hamdan Al-Maktoum (LAMBOURN) bred by Hesmonds Stud Ltd. 5 Rn 2m 36.2 (5.9)
SF—57/34/38/16/14

---

### 2765a—DEAUVILLE (R-H)
**Saturday, August 15th [Soft]**
Going Allowance: 0.90 sec per fur (S)

#### 2890a
PRIX GUILLAUME D'ORNANO (Gp 2) (3-Y.O) £30960.00 1¹⁄₄m

2316a² **GREAT PALM (USA)** *(PFICole)* 3-8-11 AMunro (mde all: hrd rdn fnl f: r.o wl) ... —1
2220\* SHARPITOR (IRE) (v) *(WJarvis)* 3-8-11 JReid (mid div: 3rd st: hdwy 2f out: ev
ch 1f out: no ex) ............................. nk.2

2627a[2] ZAAHI (USA) (Fav) *(HThomsonJones)* 3–8–11 RHills (a.p: 2nd st: ev ch over 1f
out: one pce fnl f) ............................................................................................ 2.3
2765a[6] FEMININE WILES (IRE) *(PWChapple-Hyam)* 3–8–8 CAsmussen (6th st: hdwy
2f out: kpt on: nvr able to chal) ........................................................................... 3.4
2316a[3] Fast Cure (USA) *(France)* 3–8–11 ELegrix (5th st: nvr nr to chal) ........................ 4.5
843a[4] Cristofori (USA) *(France)* 3–8–11 TJarnet (prom tl lost pl end st: wknd qckly) ...... 8.6
1823a Johann Quatz (FR) *(France)* 3–9–4 FHead (mid div: 4th st: sn wknd) .............. s.nk.7
1823a[4] Adieu Au Roi (IRE) *(France)* 3–9–2 MBoutin (ref to r: t.n.p) ............................. 0

**2/1** Zaahi (USA), **4/1** Cristofori (USA), **44/10** GREAT PALM (USA), **11/2** Adieu Au Roi (IRE), **27/4** Johann Quatz
(FR), **8/1** Fast Cure (USA), **37/4** Sharpitor (IRE), **18/1** Feminine Wiles (IRE). Tote 5.40f: 1.60f 2.60f 1.40f
(22.30f). Mr Fahd Salman (WHATCOMBE) bred by Bertram M. Linder & Peter Brant in USA. 8 Rn
2m 12.7 (10.4)
SF—83/82/78/72/64/48

# DEAUVILLE (R-H)
## Sunday, August 16th [Soft]
Going Allowance: St: 0.45 sec (Y); Rnd: 1.00 sec per fur (S)

## 2891a
PRIX GONTAUT-BIRON (Gp 3)   £20640.00   1¼m

648 **CORRUPT (USA)** *(PWChapple-Hyam)* 4–8–9 LDettori ................................................. —1
956a[2] Sillery (USA) *(France)* 4–8–11 FHead ................................................................ 1½.2
2643★ HALF A TICK (USA) *(PFICole)* 4–9–1 CRutter ...................................................... s.nk.3
2627a[3] PERPENDICULAR *(HRACecil)* 4–9–4 PatEddery ................................................... 2½.4
Tote 10.00f: 3.50f 1.70f (SF: 32.40f). Mr F. M. Kalla (MARLBOROUGH) bred by Claremont Green in USA. 6 Rn
2m 14.4 (12.1)
3f—74/70/76/71

## 2892a
PRIX DU HARAS DE FRESNAY-LE-BUFFARD JACQUES LE MAROIS (Gp 1) (C & F)
£103199.00   1m (st)

1454[4] **Exit to Nowhere (USA)** (Jt-Fav) *(France)* 4–9–4 CAsmussen (hld up: hdwy 2f
out: qcknd to ld 1f out: r.o strly) .......................................................................... —1
1454★ LAHIB (USA) *(JLDunlop)* 4–9–4 WCarson (mid div: effrt 2f out: r.o wl) .................. 1.2
2626a[2] Cardoun (FR) *(France)* 3–8–11 DBoeuf (hld up: hdwy & nt clr run on rails over 1f
out: squeezed thro 1f out: fin wl) ...................................................................... hd.3
2440[6] Star of Cozzene (USA) *(France)* 4–9–4 GMosse (hld up in rr: hdwy fnl 2f: r.o wl:
nrst fin) ........................................................................................................ nk.4
958a[6] Hatoof (USA) *(France)* 3–8–8 WRSwinburn (hld up & bhd: effrt wl over 1f out: r.o
one pce) ...................................................................................................... 2.5
2626a Lion Cavern (USA) *(France)* 3–8–11 TJarnet (a.p: led 3f out to 1f out: sn btn) .. 1½.6
2220[5] El Prado (IRE) *(Ireland)* 3–8–11 CRoche (prom: ev ch 2f out: grad wknd) ........ 1½.7
1359a★ Misil (Italy) *(Italy)* 4–9–4 LDettori (prom 8f out) ............................................ 1½.8
2090a★ Take Risks (FR) *(France)* 3–8–11 MBoutin (mid div: one pce fnl 2f) ................... nk.9
2624a★ Hydro Calido (USA) (Jt-Fav) *(France)* 3–8–8 FHead (hld up: hmpd whn hdwy
over 1f out: nt rcvr) ....................................................................................... 1½.10
2440[5] SIKESTON (USA) *(CEBrittain)* 6–9–4 MRoberts (w ldr to ½-wy: sn btn) ........... 4.11
1926 HAZM (USA) *(HThomsonJones)* 3–8–11 RHills (led 5f: sn wknd) ..................... 2.12
1823a[2] Kitwood (USA) *(France)* 3–8–11 PatEddery (chsd ldrs tl wknd over 2f out) ...... 1.13
1822a★ DILUM (USA) *(PFICole)* 3–8–11 AMunro (prom tl wknd over 2f out) ............... 1.14

**23/10** Hydro Calido (USA), EXIT TO NOWHERE (USA), **4/1** Misil (USA), **19/4** Lion Cavern (USA), Kitwood (USA),
**5/1** Dilum (USA), **37/4** Cardoun (FR), **10/1** Sikeston (USA), **13/1** Hazm (USA), Lahib (USA), **16/1** Hatoof (USA),
Take Risks (FR), **27/1** El Prado (IRE), **36/1** Star of Cozzene (USA). Tote 3.30f (cpld w Hydro Calido): 3.60f 4.70f
2.50f (67.20f). Mr S.Niarchos (F.Boutin,FRANCE) bred by Flaxman Holdings Ltd. in USA. 14 Rn 1m 40.8 (4.2)
SF—95/92/84/90/74/72

2767a—**HOPPEGARTEN (R-H)** Germany
## Saturday, August 15th [Good]
## 2893a
SCHWARZGOLD-RENNEN (listed race) (F & M) £21127.00   1m

1058[4] **ARBUSHA (USA)** *(LordHuntingdon)* 3–8–10 WNewnes ....................................... —1
Ligona *(Germany)* 3–8–10 ABoschert .................................................................. 3.2
Beyond the Lace (IRE) *(Sweden)* 4–9–7 GNordling ............................................. 1¼.3
Tote 19DM: 11DM 10DM 13DM (SF: 53DM). Mr Henryk De Kwiatkowski (WEST ILSLEY) bred by Kennelot
Stables Ltd. in USA. 7 Rn
1m 37.1

# HOPPEGARTEN (R-H) Germany
## Sunday, August 16th [Good]

### 2894a
BMW EUROPACHAMPIONAT (Gp 3) (3-Y.O) £140845.00    1½m

2511a* **Platini (GER)** *(Germany)* 3-9-2 MRimmer ....................................................... —1
24343 BEYTON (USA) *(RHannon)* 3-9-2 JLloyd .................................................................... 4.2
1498a5 Rosefinch (USA) *(France)* 3-8-11 RCochrane ............................................................ hd.3
2323a* JAPE (USA) *(PFICole)* 3-9-2 AClark (btn further 7½l) ............................................ 5
2509a* CAPTAIN HORATIUS (IRE) *(JLDunlop)* 3-9-2 JReid (btn 14½l by wnr) ................. 6
Tote 27DM: 14DM 26DM 18DM (SF: 223DM). Stall Steigenberger (B.Schutz,GERMANY) bred by A & Mrs
E.Steigenberger in Germany. 9 Rn                                                                    2m 28.7

# GELSENKIRCHEN-HORST (R-H) Germany
## Sunday, August 16th [Good]

### 2895a
ARAL-POKAL (Gp 1) £82746.00    1½m

2622a2 **Tel Quel (FR)** *(France)* 4-9-6 MJKinane ............................................................. —1
2511a2 SNURGE *(PFICole)* 5-9-6 TQuinn .......................................................................... hd.2
845a2 Chesa Plana *(Germany)* 3-8-2 ABest ...................................................................... ¾.3
Tote 120DM: 46DM 19DM (SF: 319DM). Sheikh Mohammed (A.Fabre,FRANCE) bred by Marystead Farm Ltd. in
France. 6 Rn                                                                                       2m 40.5

## 1992—CHESTER (L-H)
### Friday, August 21st [Good to firm]
Going Allowance: minus 0.40 sec per fur (F)                                              Wind: slt across

Stalls: low

### 2896
WIRRAL APP'CE H'CAP (0-70) £3003.00 (£833.00: £399.00)
1¼m 75y                                                                                2-30 (2-31)

(Weights raised 8 lb)
905 **Salman (USA) (40)** *(SGNorton)* 6–8-7 GParkin (3) (swtg: bit bkwd: mde all: sn
    wl clr: unchal) ............................................................................................ —1
736 Al Skeet (USA) **(30)** *(RJPrice)* 6–7-11 PMcCabe (7) (bit bkwd: hld up: hdwy
    over 3f out: 2nd st: no imp) ...................................................................... 7.2
27753 No Comebacks **(42)** *(EJAlston)* 4–8-9 NVarley (4) (s.s: bhd: hdwy & 5th st: styd
    on ins fnl f) ............................................................................................... 1.3
23542 Princess Roxanne **(57)** (bl) *(ABailey)* 5–9-7 ‡3WHollick (5) (lost tch ½-wy:
    hdwy & 3rd st: nvr nr to chal) ................................................................ nk.4
2775 Sanawi **(52)** *(PDEvans)* 5–9-5 DWright (8) (s.i.s: hld up & bhd: sme hdwy fnl 2f:
    nvr nrr) ..................................................................................................... 1.5
25615 Miss Sarajane **(46)** *(RHollinshead)* 8–8-10 ‡3JDennis (1) (swtg: chsd wnr 7f: 4th
    & btn st) ................................................................................................... 2.6
2571 Paper Clip **(52)** *(JDBethell)* 3–8-8 ‡3KateDovey (6) (chsd ldrs: rdn 3f out: 6th &
    btn st) ...................................................................................................... hd.7
2805 Premier Dance **(42)** (v) *(DHaydnJones)* 5–8-6 ‡3SianWilliams (2) (swtg: chsd
    ldrs to ½-wy: grad wknd) ......................................................................... 7.8
2632 Tina Meena Lisa **(42)** *(EHOwenjun)* 3–8-1 JBramhill (10) (a bhd) ............... 3½.9
14406 Ten High (IRE) **(38)** *(JDooler)* 3–7-8 ‡3ADaly (9) (a bhd) ........................... 3.10
3/1 Princess Roxanne, 4/1 No Comebacks, 6/1 Miss Sarajane, 7/1 Sanawi, 8/1 Tina Meena Lisa, 10/1 Paper
Clip, Premier Dance, 14/1 SALMAN (USA), 20/1 Ten High (IRE), 50/1 Al Skeet (USA). CSF £358.18, CT
£2,955.41. Tote £27.50: £4.20 £13.10 £1.70 (£124.00). Mr S. G. Norton (BARNSLEY) bred by Mr Nelson
McMakin in USA. 10 Rn                                                                  2m 11.52 (1.52)
                                                                               SF—36/12/22/33/29/16

### 2897
E.B.F. COMBERMERE STKS (Mdn 2-Y.O) £3687.50 (£1100.00: £525.00: £237.50)
5f 16y                                                                                 3-00 (3-03)

568 **Local Heroine** *(JBerry)* 8-9 GCarter (3) (a.p: led appr fnl f: r.o wl) ............... —1
    Yakin (USA) (Fav) *(HThomsonJones)* 8-9 RHills (8) (w'like: scope: lw: a.p: effrt
    & ev ch appr fnl f: unable qckn) ............................................................. 1.2
26365 Magic Pearl **(70)** *(EJAlston)* 8-9 DHolland (2) (a.p: ev ch wl over 1f out: kpt on nr
    fin) ........................................................................................................... hd.3
20444 Pure Madness (USA) *(DrJDScargill)* 9-0 JQuinn (7) (chsd ldrs: hrd rdn 2f out:
    no imp) ..................................................................................................... 5.4

2773² Windrush Boy **(81)** *(MMcCormack)* 9-0 JReid (9) (swtg: led over 3f: wknd fnl f) ..... 1.5
Well Tried (IRE) *(RHollinshead)* 8-9 WRyan (5) (w'like: scope: bit bkwd: s.s: a outpcd) ................................................................................. nk.6
1699 Cracker Jack (bl) *(TFairhurst)* 9-0 JFanning (4) (swtg: chsd ldrs: rdn along ½-wy: wknd 2f out) ................................................................ 2.7
2568⁴ Legal Risk *(DHaydnJones)* 8-9 JLowe (6) (outpcd) ........................................... hd.8
Freddie Jack *(FHLee)* 9-0 BRaymond (1) (lt-f: bit bkwd: outpcd) ............... 3½.9

**9/4** Yakin (USA), **3/1** Windrush Boy, **6/1** Freddie Jack, **13/2** Magic Pearl, **10/1** Pure Madness (USA), **14/1** LOCAL HEROINE, **16/1** Well Tried (IRE), Legal Risk, **50/1** Cracker Jack. CSF £42.10, Tote £12.20: £2.00 £1.40 £1.90 (£45.30). Mrs L. J. Meylan (COCKERHAM) bred by Mrs L. Meylan. 9 Rn                    61.74 sec (1.14)
SF—32/28/27/12/8/2

---

## 2898
KIDSONS IMPEY BONUS SERIES FINAL (H'cap) (0-100) £9910.00 (£2980.00: £1440.00: £670.00)  **7f 2y**                                    3-30 (3-35)

2447³ Polonez Prima **(81)** *(JEBanks)* 5–8-10 ‡5JWeaver (15) (hld up: hdwy 2f out: r.o to ld nr fin) ..................................................................................... —1
2658 Belfort Ruler **(66)** *(BGubby)* 5–8-0 JQuinn (8) (a.p: led ½-wy: hrd rdn & ct nr fin) nk.2
2463⁴ Cape Pigeon (USA) **(87)** *(LGCottrell)* 7–9-7 AMunro (12) (lw: mid div: hdwy over 1f out fin wl) ................................................................ 2½.3
2637⁵ Profilic **(73)** *(CaptJWilson)* 7–8-7 WRyan (6) (lw: hld up: gd hdwy fnl f: fin fast) hd.4
2447 Heart of Darkness **(90)** (v) *(IABalding)* 4–9-10 RCochrane (5) (hdwy 3f out: rdn appr fnl f: unable qckn) ................................................... hd.5
2219⁵ Habeta (USA) **(69)** *(JWWatts)* 6–8-3 JLowe (1) (chsd ldrs: kpt on one pce ins fnl f) ................................................................................... 2.6
1926 Jade Vale **(75)** *(JWHills)* 3–8-4 RHills (10) (s.i.s: hdwy 3f out: rdn & no ex appr fnl f) ............................................................................. nk.7
2447 Parliament Piece **(93)** *(MrsONovoley)* 6–9-13 DMcKeown (3) (lw: sme hdwy appr fnl f: nvr nrr) ...................................................... nk.8
2214³ Never so Sure **(88)** (bl) *(ABailey)* 4–9-8 AMackay (9) (chsd ldrs: effrt 2f out: sn rdn & wknd) ................................................................ s.h.9
2637⁶ Imperial Bid (FR) **(78)** *(DenysSmith)* 4–8-12 KFallon (14) (lw: s.i.s: nvr nr to chal) 2.10
1393⁴ Colossus **(73)** *(CEBrittain)* 4–8-7 JReid (7) (bit bkwd: chsd ldrs: rdn over 2f out: sn btn) ................................................................. ½.11
242 Amthaal (USA) **(73)** *(MRStoute)* 3–8-2 DHolland (16) (bit bkwd: nvr nr ldrs) .. 1½.12
2468⁴ Leave it to Lib **(65)** *(PCalver)* 5–7-13 JFanning (4) (lw: led to ½-wy: wknd over 2f out) ....................................................................... 2½.13
2658 Ringland (USA) **(82)** (Fav) *(PCHaslam)* 4–9-2 KDarley (2) (lw: m.n.s) ............... 3.14
2449⁴ High Sevens **(91)** *(HCandy)* 3–9-6 CRutter (11) (chsd ldrs over 4f: sn lost tch) s.h.15

**7/1** Ringland (USA), **8/1** POLONEZ PRIMA, Never so Sure, **10/1** Colossus, **11/1** Profilic, **12/1** Heart of Darkness, Cape Pigeon (USA), High Sevens, Leave it to Lib, Parliament Piece, **14/1** Belfort Ruler, Amthaal (USA), **16/1** Habeta (USA), **25/1** Jade Vale, **33/1** Imperial Bid (FR). CSF £98.67, CT £1,203.76. Tote £8.10: £2.80 £8.60 £3.70 (£57.50). Mr B. J. Butterworth (NEWMARKET) bred by D. M. Dick. 15 Rn            1m 25.30 (0.90)
SF—67/56/69/54/70/43

---

## 2899
BLACK FRIARS H'CAP (0-100) £7720.00 (£2320.00: £1120.00: £520.00)  **1m 7f 195y**                                    4-00 (4-25)

(Weights raised 2 lb)
1938 Our Aisling **(74)** *(SGNorton)* 4–8-4 ‡5OPears (9) (hld up & bhd: gd hdwy 3f out: r.o to ld wl ins fnl f) ................................................... —1
2339⁴ Aude la Belle (FR) **(75)** (Fav) *(MrsAKnight)* 4–8-7 ‡3FNorton (2) (lw: hld up: gd hdwy 5f out: ev ch ins fnl f: styd on) ................................. 1½.2
2339 Jungle Dancer (IRE) **(85)** *(MRStoute)* 4–9-6 DHolland (6) (swtg: led after 1f tl hdd & no ex wl ins fnl f) ................................................ ¾.3
2439* Bardolph (USA) **(81)** *(PFICole)* 5–8-11 ‡5DHarrison (8) (b.off hind: a.p: ev ch over 1f out: one pce) .......................................... 4.4
718⁴ Welshman **(66)** *(MBlanshard)* 6–8-1 JQuinn (10) (bkwd: prom tl wknd 2f out) .. ¾.5
2339³ Brandon Prince (IRE) **(82)** (bl) *(IABalding)* 4–9-3 RCochrane (4) (lw: chsd ldrs: rdn over 1f out: sn wknd) ................................... 3½.6
2648³ Access Ski **(69)** *(RBoss)* 5–8-4 AMunro (3) (lw: prom over 12f) ...................... 5.7
2339 My Desire **(68)** *(MrsGRReveley)* 4–8-3 JLowe (5) (chsd ldrs: rdn 3f out: sn btn) 1½.8
2439 My Chiara **(65)** *(PJBevan)* 6–8-0⁽⁴⁾ BCrossley (7) (a bhd: t.o) ........................ 7.9
2339* Gay Glint **(89)** *(NAGraham)* 5–9-5 ‡5JWeaver (1) (led 1f: jnd ldr 9f out: wknd over 2f out: t.o) ................................................ 7.10

**9/2** Aude la Belle (FR)(op 3/1), **5/1** Bardolph (USA), **6/1** Brandon Prince (IRE), **7/1** Welshman, **8/1** Gay Glint, **9/1** OUR AISLING, **11/1** My Desire, **12/1** My Chiara, **14/1** Ors. CSF £43.77, CT £505.16. Tote £9.90: £2.60 £1.80 £4.20 (£15.50). Mr A. K. Smeaton (BARNSLEY) bred by A. K. Smeaton. 10 Rn            3m 25.81 (0.81)
SF—18/19/31/18/7/19

**2900**    EASTGATE NURSERY   £4503.00 (£1344.00: £642.00: £291.00)
      5f 16y                                              4-30 (4-53)

2437[2] **Riston Lady (IRE) (77)** *(BSRothwell)* 8-5 ‡5DHarrison (4) (lw: mde all: qcknd 1f
      out: eased nr fin) ..................................................................... —1
   2418 Waterlord (IRE) (72) *(CGCox)* 8-5 AClark (6) (a.p: ev ch over 1f out: r.o strly u.p
      ins fnl f) ..................................................................... 1/2.2
   2390* Charity Express (IRE) (84) *(JBerry)* 9-3 GCarter (1) (bhd & outpcd: gd hdwy
      over 1f out: fin wl) ..................................................................... hd.3
   2608* Goodbye Millie (68) *(SGNorton)* 8-1(1) JFortune (8) (chsd ldrs: rdn & outpcd 2f
      out: kpt on u.p ins fnl f) ..................................................................... 1.4
   2876* First Option (73) **(Fav)** *(MHEasterby)* 8-6 (7x) KDarley (9) (prom: chal 1f out:
      wknd nr fin) ..................................................................... 1.5
   2055 Stormy Heights (73) *(JRJenkins)* 8-6 GBaxter (3) (chsd ldrs: hmpd & snatched
      up 2f out: rallied appr fnl f: r.o) ..................................................................... hd.6
   2636* Birchwood Sun (75) *(RHollinshead)* 8-8 WRyan (2) (outpcd) ..................... 3.7
   2717[2] Lowrianna (IRE) (61) *(DHaydnJones)* 7-8(1) JLowe (5) (chsd ldrs: hrd rdn 2f
      out: sn wknd) ..................................................................... nk.8
   1489[2] Mysterious Ways (FR) (74) *(MrsJCecil)* 8-7 PaulEddery (10) (bit bkwd: chsd
      ldrs: rdn 1/2-wy: sn btn) ..................................................................... 5.9

**3/1** First Option(op 6/4), **4/1** Charity Express (IRE), **5/1** RISTON LADY (IRE), **8/1** Mysterious Ways (FR), **9/1**
Goodbye Millie, **10/1** Birchwood Sun, Stormy Heights, **12/1** Lowrianna (IRE), **33/1** Waterlord (IRE). CSF
£106.22, CT £635.07. Tote £4.60: £1.60 £6.20 £1.50 (£138.10). Mrs G. M. Z. Spink (CATWICK) bred by D.
Cordell-Lavarack in Ireland. 9 Rn                                 61.98 sec (1.38)
                                           SF—23/31/32/12/13/12

**2901**    GREY FRIARS STKS (Mdn 2-Y.O) £4012.50 (£1200.00: £575.00: £262.50)
      7f 2y                                              5-00 (5-24)

2438[3] **Abury (IRE) (Fav)** *(PWChapple-Hyam)* 8-9 PaulEddery (10) (s.i.s: rdn along
      thrght: hdwy 1/2-wy: 3rd st: led ins fnl f: r.o) ..................................... —1
   1396[4] Nemea (USA) *(JRFanshawe)* 8-9 GCarter (5) (bit bkwd: mid div: 6th st: styd on
      strly ins fnl f) ..................................................................... 1/2.2
   Johns Act (USA) *(DHaydnJones)* 9-0 JLowe (6) (w'like: bkwd: bhd: hdwy appr
      fnl f: fin wl) ..................................................................... 1/2.3
   2426[3] Almansour (USA) (99) *(HRACecil)* 9-0 WRyan (1) (led tl hdd & no ex ins fnl f) .. 1/2.4
   2438 Don't Forget Marie (IRE) *(RHannon)* 8-9 BRaymond (8) (chsd ldrs: 5th st:
      swtchd outside 1f out: no imp) ..................................................................... 11/2.5
   2653[4] Czar's Witness *(PFICole)* 9-0 AMunro (7) (lw: chsd ldrs: 4th st: ev ch 1f out:
      eased whn btn) ..................................................................... 21/2.6
   2584[5] Cashable (70) (bl) *(JRJenkins)* 9-0 GBaxter (4) (w ldr: 2nd & rdn st: sn wknd) .. 3.7
   Arc Bright (IRE) *(RHollinshead)* 9-0 KDarley (3) (w'like: leggy: bit bkwd: s.s: a
      bhd) ..................................................................... 8.8
   1424 Rare Occurance *(MJCharles)* 9-0 DMcKeown (2) (bit bkwd: a bhd: t.o) .............. 9
   2719[3] Monastic Flight (IRE) *(BSRothwell)* 9-0 DHolland (9) (chsd ldrs over 4f: sn
      wknd: t.o) ..................................................................... 10

**11/10** ABURY (IRE), **11/4** Czar's Witness, **9/2** Almansour (USA), **12/1** Nemea (USA)(op 8/1), **25/1** Don't Forget
Marie (IRE), Cashable, **33/1** Ors. CSF £14.17, Tote £2.10: £1.30 £2.80 £4.90 (£12.20). Mr R. E. Sangster
(MARLBOROUGH) bred by Swettenham Stud in Ireland. 10 Rn             1m 27.42 (1.22)
                                           SF—35/33/36/34/24/21

T/Trio: Race 3: £824.80 (2.1 Tckts). T/Plpt: £297.40 (21.6 Tckts).                       IM

# CHESTER (L-H)
## Saturday, August 22nd [Good to firm]
Going Allowance: minus 0.20 sec per fur (F)       Wind: mod half bhd    Vis: 7th race v.bad

Stalls: low

**2902**    TRICITY BENDIX SENATOR H'CAP (0-100) £6644.50 (£1996.00: £963.00: £446.50)
      5f 16y                                            1-40 (1-43)

   2435 **Crystal Jack (FR) (81)** *(FHLee)* 4-8-10 WRSwinburn (10) (chsd ldrs: shkn up
      to ld ins fnl f: r.o) ..................................................................... —1
   2741 Metal Boys (83) *(RHollinshead)* 5-8-12 KDarley (2) (gd hdwy appr fnl f: fin wl) .. 1.2
   2642 Cantoris (91) *(RJRWilliams)* 6-9-6 RCochrane (6) (hdwy wl over 1f out: r.o nr fin) nk.3
   2741* Precentor (64) *(JDBethell)* 6-7-7 LCharnock (7) (hdwy wl over 1f out: fin fast) .. 1/2.4
   2642 Never in the Red (88) (bl) *(JBerry)* 4-8-10 ‡7AGarth (1) (lw: w ldr: led 2f out tl hdd
      & no ex ins fnl f) ..................................................................... 1.5

2741² Cronk's Courage **(78)** (v) *(EJAlston)* 6–8-4 ‡³FNorton (3) (prom: rdn over 2f out: eased whn btn fnl f) .................................................. 2¹/₂.6

2747² Very Dicey **(80)** (Jt-Fav) *(WRMuir)* 4–8-9 JReid (5) (lw: chsd ldrs: rdn over 1f out: sn btn) .................................................. s.h.7

2359³ Ever so Lonely **(67)** (bl) *(ABailey)* 3–7-0 ‡⁷DWright (8) (led 3f: wknd u.p appr fnl f) .................................................. 1¹/₂.8

2839 Plain Fact **(90)** *(JWHills)* 7–9-5 MHills (12) (s.s: effrt & bdly hmpd 1f out: nt rcvr) .. s.h.9

2642⁵ Gipsy Fiddler **(98)** (Jt-Fav) *(JJO'Neill)* 4–9-13 WCarson (4) (chsd ldrs over 3f) 3.10

2804 Forest Fairy **(67)** *(RBoss)* 3–7-7 JQuinn (13) (m.n.s) .................................................. 1¹/₂.11

2395 Lonsom Lass **(66)** *(LJBarratt)* 4–7-9 JLowe (9) (outpcd: a bhd) .................................................. s.h.12

2559⁴ Breezy Day **(80)** *(BAMcMahon)* 6–8-2 ‡⁷SSanders (15) (lw: outpcd: a bhd) ... 1¹/₂.13

2642 Absolution **(80)** *(MPNaughton)* 8–8-9 AMunro (11) (a bhd) .................................................. 1.14

LONG HANDICAP: Precentor 7-6, Ever so Lonely 7-1, Forest Fairy 7-5.

**6/1** Very Dicey, Gipsy Fiddler, **7/1** Cantoris, **9/1** Never in the Red, CRYSTAL JACK (FR), **11/1** Precentor, Cronk's Courage, **14/1** Absolution, Breezy Day, **16/1** Plain Fact, Metal Boys, **20/1** Forest Fairy, Ever so Lonely, **33/1** Lonsom Lass. CSF £121.86, CT £959.40. Tote £7.10: £2.20 £7.50 £2.30 (£137.90). Mrs B. Facchino (WILMSLOW) bred by Daniel Fernandez and Paul Vuillard in France. 14 Rn
61.20 sec (0.60)
SF—64/62/69/40/53/37

---

**2903**  TRICITY BENDIX PRESIDENT NURSERY  £6735.50 (£2024.00: £977.00: £453.50)
7f 2y  2-10 (2-11)

(Weights raised 13 lb)

2800★ **After the Last (79)** (Fav) *(RHannon)* 8-13 WCarson (1) (lw: bhd: hdwy on ins & 6th st: styd on to ld last stride) .................................................. —1

2537³ Glowing Value (IRE) **(87)** *(JBerry)* 9-4 MHills (5) (lw: a.p: led over 2f out: clr ent fnl f: rdn & ct last stride) .................................................. s.h.2

2121³ Conspicuous (IRE) **(77)** *(PFICole)* 8-11 AMunro (2) (lw: hld up: 5th st: swtchd outside appr fnl f: nvr able to chal) .................................................. 4.0

2606★ Brandonhurst **(86)** *(IABalding)* 9-6 RCochrane (6) (bhd: rdn 2f out: 7th st: nt clr run appr fnl f: nvr able to chal) .................................................. ¹/₂.4

877 Warkworth (USA) **(71)** (v) *(JWWatts)* 8-5 JLowe (9) (lw: swtg: s.s: led after 1f tl over 2f out: 3rd st: r.o one pce) .................................................. s.h.5

2802★ Stroika (IRE) **(64)** *(CJames)* 7-12 JQuinn (3) (led 1f: rdn along ¹/₂-wy: 4th & wkng st) .................................................. 3¹/₂.6

2703³ Ttyfran **(68)** *(FHLee)* 7-13 ‡³FNorton (7) (prom: 2nd st: rdn & wknd appr fnl f) ...... 7

**6/4** AFTER THE LAST, **11/2** Conspicuous (IRE), **6/1** Brandonhurst, **7/1** Glowing Value (IRE), Ttyfran, **10/1** Stroika (IRE), **20/1** Warkworth (USA). CSF £10.83, CT £34.69. Tote £2.00: £1.30 £3.70 (£7.20). Mr Roger Barby (MARLBOROUGH) bred by Sagittarius Bloodstock Agency. 7 Rn
1m 28.33 (2.13)
SF—46/53/31/38/22/4

---

**2904**  TRICITY BENDIX SERIES SIX CHESTER STKS (listed race) £15215.00 (£4240.00: £2045.00)  1m 5f 89y  2-40 (2-42)

2889a★ **Jahafil (110)** (Fav) *(MajorWRHern)* 4–9-7 WCarson (3) (lw: mde all: qcknd 2f out: r.o strly) .................................................. —1

2454³ Surrealist (IRE) **(107)** *(BWHills)* 4–9-5 JReid (1) (lw: chsd wnr: 2nd & rdn st: kpt on one pce) .................................................. 2¹/₂.2

2454★ Spinning **(108)** *(IABalding)* 5–9-5 RCochrane (2) (lw: hld up: 3rd st: rdn over 1f out: sn btn) .................................................. 6.3

**11/10** JAHAFIL, **7/4** Spinning, **100/30** Surrealist (IRE). CSF £4.07, Tote £2.10 (£2.80). Mr Hamdan Al-Maktoum (LAMBOURN) bred by Hesmonds Stud Ltd. 3 Rn
2m 53.63 (4.23)
SF—38/31/19

---

**2905**  LINENHALL GRADUATION STKS (2-Y.O) £5114.00 (£1532.00: £736.00: £338.00)
6f 18y  3-15 (3-19)

2526★ **Desert Shot (100)** (Fav) *(MRStoute)* 9-4 WRSwinburn (1) (hld up: 3rd st: qcknd to ld 1f out: sn clr) .................................................. —1

867★ Zimzalabim **(94)** *(BWHills)* 9-4 WCarson (4) (bit bkwd: hld up: 4th st: rdn & r.o fnl f: no ch w wnr) .................................................. 3.2

2669² Rhett's Choice **(74)** *(JBerry)* 8-13 MHills (4) (lw: chsd ldr: led ent st to 1f out: sn rdn & outpcd) .................................................. nk.3

1690³ Exodus (IRE) **(88)** *(MHEasterby)* 8-11 KDarley (3) (bit bkwd: led tl hdd & 2nd st: sn wknd) .................................................. 8.4

**4/9** DESERT SHOT, **4/1** Zimzalabim, **7/1** Rhett's Choice, **20/1** Exodus (IRE). CSF £2.42, Tote £1.50 (£1.60). Maktoum Al Maktoum (NEWMARKET) bred by The Lavington Stud. 4 Rn
1m 15.91 (2.61)
SF—28/16/10/–

**2906** PARADISE CLAIMING STKS £3882.50 (£1160.00: £555.00: £252.50)
1¼m 75y

3-45 (3-49)

26133 **Silver Samurai (67)** (RHollinshead) 3-7-5 ‡7AGarth (11) (lw: s.i.s: sn chsng
ldrs: 3rd st: led ins fnl f: r.o) ....................................................................... —1

26113 Causley **(76)** (Jt-Fav) (BAMcMahon) 7-7-13 ‡7SSanders (5) (led tl hdd wl ins fnl
f) ........................................................................................................................ ¾.2

26445 Majed (IRE) **(63)** (MrsGRReveley) 4-8-7 JLowe (4) (hld up & bhd: gd hdwy &
5th st: r.o ins fnl f) ............................................................................................ nk.3

24574 Danzarin (IRE) **(71)** (RHannon) 4-8-8 WCarson (3) (prom: 4th & rdn st: one
pce) .................................................................................................................. 2½.4

6723 Lost Reputation (IRE) **(87)** (Jt-Fav) (BWHills) 3-8-8 MHills (9) (bit bkwd: bhd:
styd on fnl 2f: nvr nrr) ........................................................................................ 2.5

26444 Liability Order **(67)** (bl) (RBoss) 3-8-6(1) JReid (8) (prom: 2nd st: rdn & wknd
over 1f out: eased whn btn) ............................................................................... 2½.6

27782 Mummys Rocket **(45)** (bl) (MO'Neill) 3-7-7 JQuinn (2) (b: chsd ldrs tl 6th &
wkng st) ............................................................................................................. 3.7

1692 Lara's Baby (IRE) **(64)** (NTinkler) 4-8-1 LCharnock (6) (bit bkwd: chsd ldrs: rdn
along ½-wy: nvr nr to chal) ................................................................................ hd.8

24865 Alicante **(42)** (FJYardley) 5—7-13 ‡7JDennis (1) (a bhd: t.o) ......................... 12.9

2483 Crofter's Cline **(50)** (ABailey) 8—7-13 ‡7WHollick (7) (lw: chsd ldrs 7f: sn lost tch:
t.o) .................................................................................................................... 7.10

1551 More Larks (IRE) **(41)** (MBJames) 4-8-6 AProud (10) (bit bkwd: s.s: a bhd: t.o) 15.11

**7/2** Lost Reputation (IRE), Causley, **5/1** Danzarin (IRE), **7/1** SILVER SAMURAI, **8/1** Lara's Baby (IRE)(op 20/1),
Majed (IRE), **9/1** Liability Order, **20/1** Mummys Rocket, **25/1** Crofter's Cline, **50/1** Ors. CSF £29.80, Tote £6.90:
£1.50 £1.90 £2.80 (£14.10). Mrs B. Facchino (UPPER LONGDON) bred by Elisha Holdings. 11 Rn; Causley clmd
Miss A Keen £10,879
2m 11.61 (1.61)
SF—40/46/53/49/45/38

**2907** ROUGE ROSE STKS (Mdn 3-Y.O.F) £3655.00 (£1090.00: £520.00: £235.00)
1¼m 75y

4-20 (4-23)

19173 Yildiz **(93)** (Fav) (BWHills) 8-11 MHills (3) (mde all: drvn clr over 2f out: unchal) —1

19566 First Fling (IRE) **(81)** (RCharlton) 8-11 WRSwinburn (2) (a.p: 3rd st: r.o one pce fnl f:
fin 3rd, 3l: plcd 2nd) ........................................................................................... 2

22363 Queen Caroline (USA) (HRACecil) 8-6 ‡5StephenDavies (6) (lw: hdwy to chse
wnr fnl 4f: 2nd st: rdn & no imp: fin 2nd, 5l: disq: plcd 3rd) ........................... 3

14322 Donia (USA) **(74)** (PFICole) 8-11 AMunro (1) (lw: hld up: hdwy 4f out: 4th & rdn
st: no imp) ......................................................................................................... 1½.4

Lady Dominion (ABailey) 8-11 AMackay (5) (cmpt: bkwd: s.s: sn chsng ldrs:
lost tch 4f out: 5th & btn st) ................................................................................ 7.5

2538 Atan's Gem (USA) (JNorton) 8-11 JLowe (4) (swtg: bit bkwd: chsd wnr over 5f:
sn lost tch: 6th & t.o st) ..................................................................................... 15.6

Stewards Enquiry: Queen Caroline disq. (interference to First Fling 1f out).Davies suspended 31/8/92 (careless
riding)

**10/11** YILDIZ, **4/1** Donia (USA), First Fling (IRE), **6/1** Queen Caroline (USA), **25/1** Lady Dominion, **40/1** Atan's
Gem (USA). CSF £4.90, Tote £1.80: £1.30 £1.60 (£2.80). Mr S. Mino (LAMBOURN) bred by Charlton Down
Stud. 6 Rn
2m 12.12 (2.12)
SF—55/40/39/36/22/–

**2908** LEVY BOARD H'CAP (0-90) £5858.00 (£1754.00: £842.00: £386.00)
1½m 66y

4-50 (4-54)

25536 **Mad Militant (IRE) (77)** (RHollinshead) 3-9-3 RCochrane (6) (hld up & bhd:
hdwy 4f out: led over 2f out: hdd & 2nd st: led 1f out: rdn clr) —1

26454 Muizenberg **(70)** (JACEdwards) 5-9-6 AMunro (9) (lw: hld up: hdwy to ld ent st:
sn hdd: kpt on one pce) .................................................................................... 2.2

2720* Maji **(66)** (DMorley) 3-8-6 WCarson (7) (hld up: hdwy over 3f out: 3rd st: rdn &
unable qckn fnl f) ............................................................................................... 1½.3

27212 Falcons Dawn **(56)** (Fav) (ABailey) 5-8-6 AMackay (1) (hdwy 5f out: 4th & rdn
st: kpt on) .......................................................................................................... 1.4

28102 Westholme (USA) **(74)** (MHEasterby) 4-9-10 KDarley (5) (in tch: effrt & 5th st:
rdn & no imp appr fnl f) ...................................................................................... 1½.5

23672 Pippas Song **(69)** (GWragg) 3-8-9 JReid (8) (chsd ldrs: 6th & rdn st: sn btn) .... 4.6

28106 Corn Lily **(67)** (MrsGRReveley) 6-9-3 JLowe (3) (w ldr: led 7f out tl over 2f out:
wknd qckly: t.o) .................................................................................................. 20.7

26452 Sastago (USA) **(82)** (JHMGosden) 3-9-8 MHills (4) (lw: chsd ldrs 9f: grad lost
tch: t.o) .............................................................................................................. hd.8

22314 Funoon (IRE) **(78)** (MRStoute) 3-9-4 WRSwinburn (2) (led over 5f: wknd 3f out:
t.o) ..................................................................................................................... dist.9

9/2 Falcons Dawn, **5/1** Pippas Song, **6/1** Corn Lily, Westholme (USA), **13/2** Sastago (USA), **7/1** Maji, **9/1** Muizenberg, **10/1** MAD MILITANT (IRE) & Ors. CSF £85.38, CT £610.12. Tote £11.80: £2.30 £3.10 £2.00 (£63.60). Mrs B. Facchino (UPPER LONGDON) bred by Cloghran Stud Farm Co. in Ireland. 9 Rn

2m 41.68 (5.08)
SF—28/27/10/8/18/–

T/Trio: Race 1: £399.80 (4.1 Tckts). T/Plpt: £40.40 (189.35 Tckts).                                     IM

## 2265—SANDOWN (R-H)

### Friday, August 21st [Good to soft, Soft patches]

Going Allowance: 0.35 sec per fur (Y)                                              Wind: nil

Stalls: low

**2909**   REALLY USEFUL & POLYDOR RECORDS CLAIMING STKS (3-Y.O) £2385.00 (£660.00: £315.00)   **5f 6y**
2-00 (2-02)

| | | |
|---|---|---|
| 2642 | **Walk in the Park (90)** (Fav) *(RSimpson)* 7-10 ‡⁵ATucker (6) (outpcd: hdwy over 2f out: hrd rdn over 1f out: led ins fnl f: r.o wl) | —1 |
| 2663* | **Mamma's Too (88)** *(JBerry)* 8-6 TQuinn (8) (led 4f out: hrd rdn over 1f out: hdd ins fnl f: unable qckn) | 2.2 |
| 2663⁵ | **Miss Vaxette (69)** *(JLSpearing)* 7-13 MRoberts (3) (a.p: rdn over 1f out: one pce) | 2.3 |
| 2772 | **Loose Zeus (USA) (58)** *(CFWall)* 8-0 NCarlisle (1) (outpcd: swtchd rt 2f out: hdwy over 1f out: one pce) | 3.4 |
| 2599⁵ | **Noble Power (IRE) (74)** *(BPalling)* 8-7 ‡⁵StephenDavies (7) (lw: a.p: hrd rdn over 1f out: wknd fnl f) | hd.5 |
| 2552 | **Scala Milano (64)** *(KTIvory)* 7-13 GBardwell (4) (led 1f: wknd over 1f out) | 5.6 |
| 2747⁵ | **Musval (56)** *(RHannon)* 7-9 NAdams (2) (swtg: hld up: rdn over 2f out: wknd over 1f out) | ¾.7 |
| 2650 | **Walking Possession (79)** (bl) *(RBoss)* 8-5 PatEddery (9) (lw: a bhd) | nk.8 |
| 2595 | **Jaromic (50)** *(PFTulk)* 8-4 GDuffield (5) (b: lw: outpcd) | 15.9 |

**5/4** WALK IN THE PARK, **2/1** Mamma's Too, **5/1** Walking Possession, **12/1** Miss Vaxette, **16/1** Noble Power (IRE), **33/1** Loose Zeus (USA), Scala Milano, Musval, **50/1** Jaromic. CSF £4.17, Tote £2.30: £1.10 £1.10 £2.30 (£2.50). Mr M. J. Lewin (FOXHILL) bred by Rodney Meredith. 9 Rn; Mamma's Too clmd J Purcell £15,000

62.58 sec (3.08)
SF—56/58/43/32/38/10

**2910**   AMAZING JOSEPH DREAM MILE (Nursery) £3782.00 (£1136.00: £548.00: £254.00)   **1m 14y**
2-35 (2-46)

| | | |
|---|---|---|
| 2695⁵ | **Iommelli (IRE) (86)** *(PAKelleway)* 9-3 DBiggs (15) (lw: hdwy over 2f out: led ins fnl f: rdn out) | —1 |
| 2652⁴ | **Alderney Prince (USA) (83)** *(PFICole)* 9-0 TQuinn (7) (lw: 4th st: hrd rdn over 1f out: ev ch ins fnl f: r.o) | nk.2 |
| 2568⁵ | **Persiansky (IRE) (64)** *(BHanbury)* 7-9 NCarlisle (9) (hrd rdn & hdwy wl over 1f out: r.o ins fnl f) | nk.3 |
| 2652² | **Wynona (IRE) (85)** (Fav) *(GCBravery)* 9-2 WRSwinburn (3) (b.off fore: lw: 6th st: rdn over 2f out: r.o ins fnl f) | nk.4 |
| 2584² | **Exhibit Air (IRE) (78)** *(RHannon)* 8-9 PatEddery (2) (lw: swvd lft s: 2nd st: led over 2f out tl ins fnl f: r.o) | ½.5 |
| 1429² | **Lochore (66)** *(RIngram)* 7-6 ‡⁵BDoyle (12) (hdwy over 1f out: r.o wl ins fnl f) | ¾.6 |
| *2802²* | **Poly Vision (IRE) (68)** *(MRChannon)* 7-13 MRoberts (16) (3rd st: wknd over 2f out) | 3.7 |
| 2462⁵ | **Bourbon Jack (80)** *(JWPayne)* 8-11 LDettori (11) (no hdwy fnl 3f) | s.h.8 |
| 2800⁶ | **Aberdeen Heather (88)** *(DRCEIsworth)* 9-5 JWilliams (8) (nvr nrr) | 1.9 |
| 2068⁶ | **Hadeer's Dance (83)** *(RWArmstrong)* 9-0 GDuffield (10) (lw: 5th st: ev ch over 1f out: sn wknd) | ½.10 |
| 2130⁵ | **Bonar Bridge (USA) (90)** *(RHannon)* 9-4 ‡³RPerham (14) (a mid div) | 1½.11 |
| 2238³ | **De Chine (62)** *(JSMoore)* 7-7 NAdams (17) (a bhd) | 3½.12 |
| 2800⁴ | **Hawl (USA) (86)** (bl) *(AAScott)* 9-3 WCarson (1) (swtg: carried lft s: bhd fnl 3f) | nk.13 |
| 2578⁵ | **Poco Pierna (IRE) (63)** *(WCarter)* 7-1⁽¹⁾ ‡⁷CHawksley (5) (lw: dwlt: a bhd) | 5.14 |
| 2719* | **Madam Cyn's Risk (62)** *(NACallaghan)* 7-0 (5x) ‡⁷AntoinetteArmes (6) (lw: a bhd) | 1½.15 |
| 2543² | **Bold Face (IRE) (78)** (bl) *(RFJohnsonHoughton)* 8-9⁽¹⁾ SCauthen (13) (led over 5f: eased whn btn over 1f out) | 5.16 |

LONG HANDICAP: De Chine 6-6, Poco Pierna (IRE) 7-0, Madam Cyn's Risk 7-3.
*2299² Glowing Dancer (16/1) Withdrawn (uns rdr: broke loose & wnt thro rail gng to s: rdr inj): not under orders*

**100/30** Wynona (IRE), **13/2** Alderney Prince (USA), **8/1** Persiansky (IRE)(5/1—9/1), **10/1** Exhibit Air (IRE)(8/1—12/1), **11/1** Bourbon Jack, Bold Face (IRE)(8/1—12/1), **12/1** Poly Vision (IRE), IOMMELLI (IRE), Hawl (USA)(14/1—8/1), **14/1** Hadeer's Dance, **16/1** Lochore, Madam Cyn's Risk, **20/1** Aberdeen Heather, **25/1** Bonar Bridge (USA), **40/1** Poco Pierna (IRE), **66/1** De Chine. CSF £83.82, CT £617.48. Tote £21.80: £3.20 £1.60 £2.60 £1.60 (£42.00). Mr G. Mazza (NEWMARKET) bred by Frank Barry in Ireland. 16 Rn   1m 46.70 (7.50)
SF—32/28/28/19/–

---

**2911**   STARLIGHT EXPRESS ROLLER STKS (listed race) (F & M) £8595.00 (£2610.00: £1280.00: £615.00)   **1m 14y**   3-10 (3-19)

2659* **Amwag (USA)** (Fav) (ACStewart) 3-8-9 MRoberts (6) (lw: 3rd st: led 2f out: pushed out) ............ —1
Melpomene (USA) **(100)** (LordHuntingdon) 4-9-1 WRSwinburn (7) (5th st: chsd wnr over 1f out: r.o) ............ 2.2
2523* Petal Girl **(89)** (RHannon) 3-8-9 JLloyd (11) (hdwy over 1f out: r.o) ............ 3½.3
2436 Splice **(90)** (JRFanshawe) 3-8-9 NCarlisle (12) (swtg: hdwy over 1f out: hrd rdn ins f: r.o) ............ hd.4
2791⁶ Sharp Dream **(57)** (BSmart) 4-9-1 MHills (9) (4th st: hrd rdn over 1f out: wknd fnl f) ............ 4.5
2436³ Mrs Fisher (IRE) **(95)** (SirMarkPrescott) 3-8-9 GDuffield (3) (2nd st: led over 2f out: sn hdd: wknd fnl f) ............ s.h.6
1599⁶ Langtry Lady **(79)** (MJRyan) 6-9-1 DBiggs (8) (swtg: hdwy over 2f out: nt clr run on ins wknd) ............ s.h.7
2726⁴ Our Rita **(68)** (PAKelleway) 3-8-9 GBardwell (1) (s.i.s: nvr nrr) ............ 7.8
2322a² Cloud of Dust **(105)** (JLDunlop) 3-8-12 TQuinn (13) (swtg: dwlt: hdwy over 2f out: eased whn btn fnl f) ............ 1½.9
2436⁶ Miss Haggis **(87)** (RBoss) 3-8-9 PatEddery (2) (s.i.s: hdwy 5f out: 6th st: wknd over 2f out) ............ 10.10
2461⁵ Fragrant Hill **(100)** (v) (IABalding) 4-9-7 SCauthen (4) (lw: led over 5f) ............ 1½.11
Anlace **(90)** (LMCumani) 3-8-9 LDettori (5) (a bhd) ............ 1½.12
2282³ Last Exit **(85)** (WJarvis) 3-8-9 WCarson (10) (lw: bhd fnl 2f) ............ 10.13

**9/4** AMWAG (USA)(op 6/4), **5/2** Cloud of Dust, **11/2** Anlace, **8/1** Mrs Fisher (IRE)(tchd 12/1), **10/1** Melpomene (USA), **16/1** Fragrant Hill, Petal Girl, Miss Haggis(op 10/1), **20/1** Splice, **33/1** Last Exit, **50/1** Langtry Lady, **100/1** Ors. CSF £24.53, Tote £2.70: £1.70 £2.90 £3.90 (£29.00). Mr Hamdan Al-Maktoum (NEWMARKET) bred by Shadwell Farm Incorporated in USA. 13 Rn   1m 43.62 (4.42)
SF—71/71/54/53/47/40

---

**2912**   SUNSET BOULEVARD SOLARIO STKS (Gp 3) (2-Y.O) £18815.00 (£7058.25: £3404.13: £1497.62)   **7f 16y**   3-40 (3-48)

2175* **White Crown (USA)** **(100)** (BHanbury) 8-11 WRSwinburn (1) (swtg: 3rd st: led over 2f out: rdn out) ............ —1
2652* King Paris (IRE) **(88)** (MBell) 8-11 MHills (6) (lw: rdn over 2f out: hdwy over 1f out: r.o wl ins fnl f) ............ 1½.2
2530² Fitzcarraldo (USA) (LMCumani) 8-11 LDettori (2) (lw: 5th st: rdn over 2f out: r.o one pce) ............ 2½.3
2530* Tioman Island **(100)** (PFICole) 8-11 TQuinn (9) (lw: 4th st: rdn over 2f out: one pce) ............ 2.4
2756⁶ Little Too Much (IRE) **(100)** (GHarwood) 8-11 MRoberts (3) (swtg: led over 4f: wknd fnl f) ............ ¾.5
2519³ Royal Roller (IRE) (CNAllen) 8-11 WCarson (8) (hdwy on ins whn hmpd over 1f out: nt rcvr) ............ 2.6
2445 Persian Revival (FR) **(85)** (BAMcMahon) 8-11 JWilliams (7) (swtg: a bhd) ............ 1.7
2269* Mukhamedov **(97)** (Fav) (HRACecil) 8-11 PatEddery (5) (6th st: rdn over 2f out: wknd over 1f out) ............ 1½.8
2445³ Shebl (USA) **(100)** (v) (MRStoute) 8-11 SCauthen (4) (2nd st: wknd wl over 1f out) ............ nk.9

**2/1** Mukhamedov, **9/4** WHITE CROWN (USA), **7/1** Tioman Island, **8/1** Shebl (USA)(6/1—9/1), King Paris (IRE)(10/1—12/1), **11/1** Little Too Much (IRE)(8/1—12/1), **20/1** Fitzcarraldo (USA), **25/1** Royal Roller (IRE), **50/1** Persian Revival (FR). CSF £19.36, Tote £2.80: £1.30 £2.70 £4.10 (£18.00). Mr Saeed Suhail (NEWMARKET) bred by David Mowat & Fawn Leap Farm in USA. 9 Rn   1m 31.53 (4.53)
SF—66/61/53/47/45/39

---

**2913**   CATS 11TH YEAR H'CAP (3-Y.O) (0-100) £3808.00 (£1144.00: £552.00: £256.00)   **1m 1f**   4-10 (4-20)

(Weights raised 7 lb)
2231³ **Grand Master (IRE)** **(85)** (bl) (Fav) (PFICole) 9-3 TQuinn (7) (lw: mde all: hrd rdn over 1f out: r.o wl) ............ —1

1934 Anne Bonny **(84)** *(JRFanshawe)* 9-2 PatEddery (6) (lw: 5th st: hrd rdn over 1f
out: r.o wl ins fnl f ..................................................................................... 1.2
27484 Double Flutter **(75)** *(MRChannon)* 8-7 JWilliams (3) (swtchd rt & gd hdwy over
1f out: swtchd lft ins fnl f: r.o wl) ...................................................... hd.3
1466 Glide Path (USA) **(80)** *(JWHills)* 8-12 MHills (5) (lw: swtchd rt & hdwy over 1f
out: r.o wl ins fnl f) .......................................................................... ¾.4
26473 Walimu (IRE) **(71)** *(CFWall)* 8-3 NCarlisle (10) (hrd rdn & hdwy wl over 1f out: r.o
wl ins fnl f) ........................................................................................ nk.5
13466 Stani (USA) **(80)** *(BHanbury)* 8-12 WRSwinburn (1) (lw: 2nd st: ev ch over 1f
out: wknd ins fnl f) ........................................................................... 2½.6
26604 Riviera Vista **(89)** *(GWragg)* 9-7 MRoberts (8) (lw: 6th st: hrd rdn over 1f out:
one pce) ............................................................................................... 4.7
2453 The Power of One **(74)** *(RSimpson)* 8-6 GDuffield (4) (lw: 4th st: hrd rdn 3f out:
wknd over 1f out) ................................................................................. 1.8
27424 Holiday Island **(73)** *(CEBrittain)* 8-0 ‡5BDoyle (11) (swtg: 3rd st: wknd 2f out) .. nk.9
2453 Scandalmonger (USA) **(77)** *(BWHills)* 8-9 WCarson (9) (bhd fnl 2f) ................. ¾.10
24336 Savash (USA) **(78)** *(MMoubarak)* 8-10 LDettori (2) (lw: a bhd) ........................ 8.11

**4/1** GRAND MASTER (IRE)(op 7/1), **9/2** Scandalmonger (USA), **11/2** Riviera Vista, **8/1** Walimu (IRE), Glide Path
(USA), **9/1** Double Flutter, Anne Bonny, **14/1** Savash (USA), **16/1** Stani (USA), The Power of One, **25/1** Holiday
Island. CSF £36.33, CT £278.46. Tote £4.50: £2.20 £3.10 £2.60 (£41.30). Mr Fahd Salman (WHATCOMBE)
bred by Hullin Co N V in Ireland. 11 Rn          1m 57.83 (6.43)
SF—55/51/41/44/34/35

---

**2914**     ASPECTS OF LOVE GRADUATION STKS (3-Y.O.F) £3548.00 (£1064.00: £512.00:
£236.00)    **1m 3f 91y**              4-45 (4-50)

1843 **Mystery Play (IRE) (90)** *(Fav)* *(RWHills)* 9-4 SCauthen (4) (2nd st: led over 2f
out: comf) ........................................................................................... —1
19552 Zawaahy (USA) **(80)** *(AAScott)* 9-4 WRSwinburn (1) (lw: 5th st: chsd wnr over 1f
out: no imp) ......................................................................................... 4.2
Guillem (USA) *(HRACecil)* 8-11 PatEddery (5) (wl grwn: 3rd st: rdn over 2f out:
one pce) ............................................................................................... 3.3
1347 Cottonwood *(LordHuntingdon)* 9-4 MRoberts (3) (led 9f) ................................. 4.4
22985 Melody Mountain (IRE) *(CEBrittain)* 8-11 LDettori (2) (4th st: wknd over 2f out:
t.o) ...................................................................................................... 30.5

**2/1** MYSTERY PLAY (IRE), **3/1** Zawaahy (USA), **100/30** Guillem (USA)(op 2/1), **5/1** Cottonwood, **10/1** Melody
Mountain (IRE)(12/1—8/1). CSF £7.49, Tote £2.60: £1.30 £1.70 (£4.80). Sheikh Mohammed (LAMBOURN)
bred by London Thoroughbred Services Ltd in Ireland. 5 Rn      2m 30.39 (8.69)
SF—57/49/38/37/–

---

**2915**     PHANTOM STAYERS H'CAP (3-Y.O) (0-90) £3964.00 (£1192.00: £576.00: £268.00)
**1¾m**                   5-15 (5-18)

26822 **Ideal Candidate (62)** *(TJNaughton)* 7-9(2) DBiggs (4) (hdwy over 2f out: led wl
over 1f out: rdn wl) ............................................................................. —1
2109* Drought (IRE) **(65)** *(MRStoute)* 7-12 WCarson (10) (5th st: led over 2f out tl over
1f out: r.o) ........................................................................................... 1.2
27492 Ivor's Flutter **(72)** *(DRCElsworth)* 8-5 JWilliams (9) (hdwy over 2f out: r.o ins fnl
f) ......................................................................................................... 1½.3
23492 Turgenev (IRE) **(88)** *(Fav)* *(JHMGosden)* 9-7 SCauthen (1) (swtg: hdwy 6f out:
4th st: ev ch 2f out: hrd rdn over 1f out: unable qckn) ....................... 5.4
25553 Regal Lover (IRE) **(73)** (v) *(MBell)* 8-6 MHills (8) (6th st: hrd rdn 1f out: one
pce) ..................................................................................................... 4.5
2715 Dawn Flight **(74)** (bl) *(LadyHerries)* 8-7 TQuinn (2) (3rd st: wknd over 2f out) .. 25.6
2451 Resplendent **(75)** *(NCWright)* 8-8 GDuffield (7) (bhd fnl 3f) ............................. nk.7
21346 King's Treasure (USA) **(72)** *(IABalding)* 8-5 LDettori (3) (lw: a bhd) .................. hd.8
22114 Dordogne **(60)** *(RAkehurst)* 7-7 NAdams (11) (lw: led 6f: wknd over 4f out) ....... 1.9
2651* Upper House **(70)** (v) *(GWragg)* 8-3 MRoberts (5) (lw: 2nd st: wknd over 2f out) nk.10
2759 Sadler's Way **(75)** *(GLewis)* 8-8 PatEddery (6) (led 8f out tl over 2f out: sn wknd) 5.11
              LONG HANDICAP: Ideal Candidate 7-5, Dordogne 7-0.

**13/8** Turgenev (IRE), **11/2** Ivor's Flutter, **6/1** Drought (IRE), **8/1** King's Treasure (USA), **9/1** Upper House, **10/1**
Regal Lover (IRE), **12/1** IDEAL CANDIDATE, **14/1** Sadler's Way, **20/1** Resplendent, **33/1** Ors. CSF £78.34, CT
£406.25. Tote £9.50: £1.90 £2.00 £2.80 (£24.60). Mr T. O'Flaherty (EPSOM) bred by Lt-Col and Mrs D. Coker.
11 Rn               3m 6.17 (11.47)
SF—16/17/21/27/4/–

---

T/Trio: Race 5: £113.60 (15.1 Tckts). T/Jkpt: Not won; £1,606.75 to Sandown 22/8/92. T/Plpt: £41.00 (202
Tckts).                                                            AK

## SANDOWN (R-H)

**Saturday, August 22nd [Good to soft]**
Going Allowance: 0.35 sec per fur (Y)

Wind: mod across

Stalls: low

**2916**    ICI PAINTS (S) NURSERY  £2570.00 (£770.00: £370.00: £170.00)
          **7f 16y**
                                                           2-00 (2-03)

2782[5]  **Yeveed (IRE) (55)** *(MHEasterby)* 8-6  JWilliams (2) (hdwy & edgd rt over 1f out:
         led ins fnl f: rdn out) ..................................................... —1

2802[5]  **By Rubies (54)** *(BWHills)* 8-5  DHolland (10) (hdwy over 2f out: led over 1f out tl
         ins fnl f: unable qckn) ....................................................... 4.2

2563[3]  Awesome Risk (54) *(GLewis)* 8-0 ‡5DHarrison (3) (lw: jinked rt s: mid div whn
         hmpd over 1f out: gd hdwy fnl f: r.o wl) .......................... 1½.3

2557     Creative Flair (USA) (60) *(PFICole)* 8-11  TQuinn (15) (lw: 4th st: hrd rdn over 1f
         out: one pce) ........................................................... hd.4

2649     Baileys Colours (49) *(BJMcMath)* 7-7 ‡7CHawksley (14) (lw: nt clr run on ins 2f
         out: hdwy over 1f out: r.o) ................................................. nk.5

2696[4]  Skullcap (59) *(TJNaughton)* 8-10  MRoberts (1) (5th st: led wl over 1f out: sn
         hdd & wknd) ............................................................. nk.6

2695[2]  Tee Gee Jay (70) (v) (Fav) *(CNWilliams)* 9-7  PatEddery (8) (b.hind: rdn over 2f
         out: mid div whn hmpd over 1f out) ................................... 3½.7

2771     We Are Doomed (54) *(JRFanshawe)* 7-12 ‡7NVarley (6) (lw: dwlt: bhd whn
         hmpd on ins 2f out: nvr nrr) ............................................... 6.8

2118[6]  Five Clubs (IRE) (56) *(DTThom)* 8-7  CDwyer (11) (2nd st: wknd 2f out) ............ ½.9

2700     First Affair (59) (v) *(MRStoute)* 8-10  LDettori (4) (b.off hind: hmpd s: nvr nrr)  1½.10

2703[4]  Fanfan (IRE) (47) (bl) *(MHEasterby)* 7-12  SDawson (12) (led: clr 4f out: hdd wl
         over 1f out: sn wknd) .................................................... 3.11

2284[3]  Heroic Deed (62) (v) *(MHTompkins)* 8-6 ‡7SMulvey (13) (lw: 6th st: wknd 2f out)3½.12

2480*    Shades of Croft (52) *(MDIUsher)* 8-3  RHills (7) (3rd st: wknd over 2f out) ......... 6.13

2802[3]  The Wend (58) *(DTThom)* 8-6 ‡3SO'Gorman (5) (a bhd) ......................... 6.14

2450     Superensis (60) *(WRMuir)* 8-11  SCauthen (16) (lw: bhd whn hmpd on ins 2f
         out) ................................................................... 2.15

5/1 Tee Gee Jay, 11/2 By Rubies, 13/2 Fanfan (IRE), Creative Flair (USA), 7/1 Skullcap, 11/1 Awesome
Risk(8/1—12/1), Shades of Croft, 14/1 Superensis, 16/1 First Affair, 20/1 Five Clubs (IRE), Heroic Deed, 25/1
YEVEED (IRE), 33/1 Ors. CSF £145.24, CT £1,463.63. Tote £27.00: £5.50 £2.40 £2.30 (£87.30). Mrs Marjorie
Graham (MALTON) bred by Eastward Bloodstock Holdings Ltd. in Ireland. 15 Rn; No bid   1m 35.25 (8.25)
                                                                        SF—5/–/–/–/–/–

**2917**    VYMURA INTERNATIONAL STKS (Amateurs)  £2570.00 (£770.00: £370.00: £170.00)
          **1¼m 7y**
                                                           2-35 (2-38)

2460[2]  **Pharly Story (96)** (Fav) *(MCPipe)* 4-11-7  MrsLPearce (7) (hdwy 6f out: 2nd st:
         led over 1f out: rdn out) ................................................... —1

2660*    Kinematic (USA) (92) *(JHMGosden)* 4-11-12  MrJDurkan (5) (lw: hdwy 6f out:
         3rd st: hrd rdn over 2f out: ev ch fnl f: r.o) ....................... ¾.2

2707[6]  Statajack (IRE) (64) (bl) *(DRCElsworth)* 4-11-7  MrRAlner (4) (hdwy over 4f out:
         poor 4th st: r.o wl ins fnl f) ............................................... nk.3

2708[4]  Bronze Runner (32) (bl) *(EAWheeler)* 8-11-3 ‡4MissLNicoll (3) (wl bhd 6f: nvr
         nrr) .................................................................... 10.4

2460     Mellaby (USA) (93) *(MRStoute)* 4-11-12  MissMJuster (10) (lw: led over 7f) ....... ½.5

1546[6]  Cheap Metal (Rlngram) 7-11-3 ‡4MrKMannish (6) (s.s: a wl bhd: t.o) ........... 20.6

         Mr Kewmill *(JABennett)* 9-11-3 ‡4MissAPurdy (9) (b: bit bkwd: bhd fnl 5f: t.o) .... 20.7

2775     Mr Wishing Well (48) *(RJRWilliams)* 6-11-7  MrSAstaire (1) (b.hind: a wl bhd: t.o) 7.8

1640     Yeoman Bound (22) *(KTIvory)* 4-11-3 ‡4MrDMarshall (2) (lw: prom over 4f: poor
         6th st: t.o) ............................................................... 5.9

         Church Star (bl) *(JJBridger)* 8-10-12 ‡4MissMBridger (8) (bkwd: prom over 4f:
         poor 5th st: t.o) ......................................................... 2½.10

4/5 PHARLY STORY, 9/4 Kinematic (USA), 5/1 Mellaby (USA), 14/1 Statajack (IRE), 50/1 Bronze Runner, 100/1
Mr Wishing Well, 200/1 Ors. CSF £2.85, Tote £1.80: £1.20 £1.40 £1.80 (£2.00). Mr A. J. Lomas (WELLINGTON)
bred by Deepwood Farm Stud. 10 Rn                                         2m 15.27 (10.97)
                                                                        SF—60/63/57/33/41/–

**2918**    BERNARD SUNLEY CHARITABLE FOUNDATION GRADUATION STKS (2-Y.O) £3540.00
          (£1065.00: £515.00: £240.00)   **1m 14y**
                                                           3-10 (3-14)

         **Sharjah (USA)** *(MAJarvis)* 8-8  SCauthen (4) (leggy: scope: rdn over 4f out:
         hdwy over 1f out: led ins fnl f: r.o wl) .................................... —1

Elkhart (USA) *(HRACecil)* 8-8 DaleGibson (2) (str: scope: bit bkwd: rdn 3f out: hdwy over 1f out: ev ch ins fnl f: unable qckn) ...................... 1½.2

Commanche Gold (IRE) *(LordHuntingdon)* 8-8 RHills (1) (unf: scope: bit bkwd: s.s: hdwy whn hmpd on ins over 1f out: swtchd lft: r.o wl) .. 1.3

2002* Icy South (USA) **(100)** *(JHMGosden)* 9-4 DHolland (7) (led over 4f: led over 1f out tl ins fnl f: one pce) ...................... ¾.4

2340³ Darecliff (USA) *(RHannon)* 8-11 MRoberts (4) (lw: 5th st: rdn over 3f out: one pce ins fnl f) ...................... 1.5

26576 East Liberty (USA) **(94)** *(IABalding)* 8-7 ‡³SO'Gorman (11) (lw: 6th st: rdn over 2f out: 3rd whn bdly hmpd on ins fnl f) ...................... 3½.6

22695 Range Rider (IRE) *(CEBrittain)* 8-6 ‡⁵BDoyle (9) (w ldr: led over 3f out tl over 1f out: 2nd & btn whn hmpd ins fnl f) ...................... nk.7

2445 Majestic Hawk (USA) **(100)** *(MMoubarak)* 9-1 LDettori (8) (3rd st: wknd over 1f out) ...................... nk.8

2519² Kassab (Fav) *(JLDunlop)* 8-11 PatEddery (10) (lw: lost pl over 4f out: rdn over 3f out: bhd whn hmpd over 2f out) ...................... nk.9

21756 Grand Applause (IRE) *(RSimpson)* 8-6 ‡⁵ATucker (12) (a bhd) ...................... s.h.10

1322* Zilfi (USA) **(84)** *(PFICole)* 9-1 TQuinn (5) (4th st: wkng whn n.m.r over 2f out) . 8.11

**13/8** Kassab, **9/2** Darecliff (USA), **5/1** Majestic Hawk (USA)(3/1—11/2), **6/1** SHARJAH (USA)(4/1—13/2), **7/1** Icy South (USA)(5/1—15/2), **12/1** Zilfi (USA), **16/1** Elkhart (USA)(op 8/1), East Liberty (USA)(op 10/1), **33/1** Range Rider (IRE), Commanche Gold (IRE), **50/1** Grand Applause (IRE). CSF £89.62, Tote £5.90: £1.70 £4.60 £5.20 (£60.00). Sheikh Ahmed Al Maktoum (NEWMARKET) bred by John C. & Mrs Mabee in USA. 11 Rn
1m 47.38 (8.18)
SF—13/8/5/13/3/–

---

**2919** TEXAS HOMECARE H'CAP (0-90) £3215.00 (£965.00: £465.00: £215.00)
bf 6y
3-40 (3-49)

(Weights raised 1 lb)

2797 **Gone Savage (76)** *(GBBalding)* 4-9-1 PatEddery (1) (w ldr: led over 1f out: all out) ...................... —1

27415 Misdemeanours Girl (IRE) **(68)** *(MRChannon)* 4-8-2 ‡⁵BDoyle (13) (hld up: rdn over 2f out: ev ch ins fnl f: r.o wl) ...................... s.h.2

27972 Yes **(55)** *(DTThom)* 4-7-1(1) ‡⁷KimMcDonnell (10) (hdwy over 1f out: ev ch ins fnl f: r.o wl) ...................... hd.3

27473 Dickens Lane **(54)** *(RJHodges)* 5-7-7 NAdams (12) (lw: a.p: rdn over 2f out: r.o) ½.4

27974 Olifantsfontein **(78)** (bl) (Fav) *(RSimpson)* 4-9-3 TQuinn (9) (lw: led over 3f: unable qckn) ...................... 1½.5

28213 Joe Sugden **(58)** *(PHowling)* 8-7-6(3) ‡⁵DHarrison (6) (lw: a.p: rdn over 2f out: one pce) ...................... ½.6

26186 Catalani **(54)** *(TJNaughton)* 7-7-7 DaleGibson (2) (b: prom over 3f) ...................... 1½.7

2816* Dawes of Nelson **(56)** *(MJBolton)* 7-7-2 (6x) ‡⁷AntoinetteArmes (11) (no hdwy fnl 2f) ...................... nk.8

27525 Divine Pet **(62)** *(WGRWightman)* 7-8-1 SDawson (4) (outpcd: nvr nrr) ...................... 1½.9

27416 Bold Habit **(85)** *(BBeasley)* 7-9-5 ‡⁵SWilliams (14) (lw: s.s: outpcd) ...................... hd.10

2797 Paley Prince (USA) **(80)** *(MDIUsher)* 6-9-5 SCauthen (8) (prom over 3f) ...................... nk.11

2747* Face North (IRE) **(57)** *(ARDavison)* 4-7-3(2) ‡⁷CHawksley (7) (lw: s.s: outpcd) ½.12

28214 Erris Express **(60)** (bl) *(RHannon)* 7-7-6(6) ‡⁷AWhelan (3) (s.s: a bhd) ...................... ¾.13

27414 Iron King **(72)** (v) *(JLSpearing)* 6-8-11 MRoberts (3) (outpcd) ...................... 2½.14

LONG HANDICAP: Dickens Lane 7-5, Catalani 7-3, Erris Express 7-1.

**13/2** Olifantsfontein, **7/1** GONE SAVAGE, **8/1** Joe Sugden, **9/1** Iron King, **10/1** Yes, Dawes of Nelson, **11/1** Face North (IRE)(8/1—12/1), Bold Habit, **12/1** Misdemeanours Girl (IRE), **14/1** Divine Pet, **16/1** Dickens Lane, **20/1** Ors. CSF £76.48, CT £747.21. Tote £7.50: £3.00 £2.70 £3.00 (£64.00). Mr Rex L. Mead (DORCHESTER) bred by Mrs C. F. Van Straubenzee and R. Mead. 14 Rn
62.76 sec (3.26)
SF—71/57/41/45/63/36

---

**2920** WILLIAM HILL H'CAP (3-Y-O) (0-100) £4510.00 (£1360.00: £660.00: £310.00)
1¼m 7y
4-15 (4-20)

21824 **Valley of Fire (83)** *(JRFanshawe)* 8-7 MRoberts (4) (3rd st: led over 2f out: hrd rdn over 1f out: r.o wl) ...................... —1

26474 Majal (IRE) **(74)** *(BHanbury)* 7-7 ‡⁵DHarrison (3) (lw: s.s: hdwy over 4f out: 6th st: chsd wnr over 1f out: r.o) ...................... 1.2

24312 Tudor Island **(70)** *(CEBrittain)* 7-8 DaleGibson (5) (5th st: hrd rdn over 2f out: unable qckn) ...................... 3½.3

8586 Major Bugler (IRE) **(76)** *(GBBalding)* 8-0 NAdams (2) (rdn & hdwy over 1f out: r.o) ...................... nk.4

20563 Clurican (IRE) **(83)** *(DNicholson)* 8-7 JWilliams (6) (swtg: 4th st: wknd over 2f out) ...................... 5.5

19802 Anchorage (IRE) **(90)** *(HRACecil)* 9-0 LDettori (7) (lw: led over 7f) ...................... ¾.6

1387* Zalon (IRE) **(97)** (Fav) *(JHMGosden)* 9-7 SCauthen (8) (lw: rdn over 4f out: 2nd st: wknd over 1f out) ...................................................... 1¹⁄₂.7

2671² Wrets **(82)** *(MRStoute)* 8-6 PatEddery (1) (lw: a bhd) ................................. 15.8

3/1 Zalon (IRE)(2/1—100/30), **100/30** Majal (IRE)(9/2—3/1), **6/1** Anchorage (IRE), **13/2** Tudor Island, **7/1** Wrets, VALLEY OF FIRE, **11/1** Major Bugler (IRE), **20/1** Clurican (IRE). CSF £28.33, CT £143.10. Tote £7.00: £1.70 £1.80 £1.70 (£18.50). Sheikh Mohammed (NEWMARKET) bred by Sheikh Mohammed bin Rashid al Maktoum. 8 Rn
2m 13.16 (8.86)
SF—39/23/17/22/19/24

## 2921

HENKEL HOME IMPROVEMENTS H'CAP (0-90) £3215.00 (£965.00: £465.00: £215.00)
1³⁄₄m
4-45 (4-48)

(Weights raised 2 lb)

2339 **Majestic Image (72)** *(LordHuntingdon)* 6-8-8 ‡⁵DHarrison (4) (5th st: led over 2f out: rdn out) ...................................................... —1

2682⁴ Intricacy **(60)** *(CCElsey)* 4-8-1 DHolland (5) (2nd st: hrd rdn over 3f out: unable qckn fnl 2f) ...................................................... 7.2

2638³ Be a Honey **(83)** *(NAGraham)* 4-9-10 SCauthen (3) (led over 11f: one pce) .... nk.3

2698 Grove Serendipity (IRE) **(53)** (v) *(AHide)* 4-7-8 NAdams (10) (lw: 3rd st: hrd rdn over 2f out: one pce) ...................................................... 4.4

2774* Prosequendo (USA) **(68)** *(MDixon)* 5-8-9 DaleGibson (3) (rdn over 3f out: nvr nr to chal) ...................................................... ³⁄₄.5

2222* Farat (USA) **(75)** (Fav) *(JLDunlop)* 4-9-2 PatEddery (9) (b: swtg: hdwy over 5f out: rdn over 4f out: 4th st: wknd over 2f out) ................... 3¹⁄₂.6

2401⁵ Army of Stars **(75)** 7-9-3 MRoberts (1) (lw: bhd fnl 5f) ........................... 15.7

2439⁴ Master Foodbroker (IRE) **(82)** (bl) *(DRCElsworth)* 4-9-9 JWilliams (2) (a wl bhd) 2.8

2648² Requested **(76)** *(RAkehurst)* 5-9-3 TQuinn (8) (6th st: wknd over 3f out) ........... 6.9

Calicon **(77)** *(IABalding)* 6-9-4 LDettori (6) (bkwd: a wl bhd: t.o) ................ 30.10

**15/8** Farat (USA), **7/2** MAJESTIC IMAGE, **11/2** Requested, **13/2** Master Foodbroker (IRE), **8/1** Army of Stars(6/1—9/1), **12/1** Prosequendo (USA), **14/1** Intricacy, **16/1** Be a Honey, **33/1** Ors. CSF £47.29, CT £637.04. Tote £4.60: £1.50 £3.00 £3.70 (£30.40). Lord Huntingdon (WEST ILSLEY) bred by John and Mrs Van Geest. 10 Rn
3m 7.75 (13.05)
SF—13/—/14/—/-/—

## 2922

KALON GROUP STKS (Mdn 3-Y.O) £2570.00 (£770.00: £370.00: £170.00)
1¹⁄₄m 7y
5-20 (5-24)

553 **Anghaam (USA)** *(ACStewart)* 8-9 MRoberts (4) (bit bkwd: 4th st: led over 2f out: rdn out) ...................................................... —1

1383⁴ Unforgiving Minute *(PWHarris)* 8-9 ‡⁵DHarrison (7) (lw: hdwy over 2f out: hrd rdn over 1f out: r.o) ...................................................... 1¹⁄₂.2

2545⁵ Wild Applause (IRE) (Fav) *(JHMGosden)* 8-9 PatEddery (6) (b.nr hind: lw: 3rd st: ev ch over 2f out: hrd rdn over 1f out: unable qckn) ...... 1¹⁄₂.3

2549 Long Silence (USA) *(MrsJCecil)* 8-9 SCauthen (8) (hrd rdn over 4f out: hdwy over 1f out: r.o wl ins fnl f) ...................................................... s.h.4

1175 Magadeer (USA) **(73)** *(JLDunlop)* 8-9 RPElliott (13) (swtg: 5th st: ev ch over 2f out: one pce) ...................................................... 1¹⁄₂.5

2549 Greek Chime (IRE) *(LordHuntingdon)* 9-0 RHills (9) (lw: 6th st: hrd rdn over 1f out: one pce) ...................................................... 4.6

2654⁴ Back Billy (IRE) *(CEBrittain)* 9-0 LDettori (3) (led over 5f: 2nd st: led over 3f out tl over 2f out: sn wknd) ...................................................... 3.7

Fatack *(MRStoute)* 8-9 ‡JJones (5) (bit bkwd: nvr nr to chal) ................ ³⁄₄.8

2431⁵ Billy Bunter *(HCandy)* 9-0 CRutter (10) (swtg: hdwy over 2f out: wknd over 1f out) ...................................................... hd.9

Princess Ermyn *(MDixon)* 8-9 DaleGibson (14) (unf: scope: a bhd) ............. 2¹⁄₂.10

1503⁵ Captain Marmalade **(63)** *(DTThom)* 9-0 CDwyer (1) (a bhd) ................... ¹⁄₂.11

Court of Kings *(PFICole)* 9-0 TQuinn (11) (w'like: scope: w ldr: led over 4f out tl over 3f out: wknd over 2f out) ...................................................... 1.12

440 Quadrant *(BWHills)* 9-0 DHolland (15) (bit bkwd: hdwy over 5f out: wknd over 2f out) ...................................................... 8.13

Exarch (USA) *(BWHills)* 9-0 JWilliams (12) (str: scope: a bhd) ........... ¹⁄₂.14

2343 Take it in Cash *(RDickin)* 8-9 SDawson (2) (lw: bhd fnl 5f: t.o) ............ 20.15

**7/4** Wild Applause (IRE), **100/30** ANGHAAM (USA)(8/1—3/1), **9/2** Long Silence (USA), **9/1** Back Billy (IRE), Unforgiving Minute, **12/1** Court of Kings, **14/1** Billy Bunter(10/1—16/1), **20/1** Greek Chime (IRE), **25/1** Quadrant, **33/1** Captain Marmalade, Exarch (USA), Fatack, Magadeer (USA), **50/1** Ors. CSF £35.23, Tote £5.40: £2.00 £3.10 £1.90 (£30.20). Mr Hamdan Al-Maktoum (NEWMARKET) bred by Indian Creek in USA. 15 Rn
2m 14.11 (9.81)
SF—32/27/22/21/16/9

T/Trio: Race 4: £112.70 (24.4 Tckts). T/Jkpt: Not won; £4,380.95 to Goodwood 28/08/92. T/Plpt: £1,225.60 (10.55 Tckts).
AK

2808—**RIPON (R-H)**
**Saturday, August 22nd [Good becoming Good to soft]**
Going Allowance: St: minus 0.20 sec (F); Rnd: nil sec per fur (G)      Wind: fresh half bhd
Stalls: low      Vis: fair

**2923**      WOOL (S) STKS (3-Y.O) £2553.00 (£708.00: £339.00)      1¼m      2-20 (2-22)

2809² **Spray of Orchids (52)** (JEtherington) 8-6 GDuffield (8) (lw: hld up: hdwy & n.m.r over 3f out: led over 1f out: hld on nr fin) ..................... —1

2809³ Persian Fleece (48) (MrsGRReveley) 8-6 JFanning (5) (trckd ldrs: hdwy & ev ch over 1f out: r.o u.p) ............................................... s.h.2

2298 Charmed Life (Fav) (HRACecil) 8-11 AMcGlone (10) (lw: led: hrd drvn 4f out: hdd over 1f out: wandered & nt qckn in fnl f) ................. 1½.3

2699 Emerald Ears (43) (EWeymes) 8-6 GHind (2) (unruly gng to s: reard s: hld up: hdwy on ins & prom whn hmpd 2f out: one pce) ........... 6.4

2809 Petite Belle (52) (RMWhitaker) 8-6 ACulhane (4) (bit bkwd: hld up: effrt & n.m.r over 3f out: wknd over 2f out) ......................... 7.5

2809 Tip it In (ASmith) 8-11 SWebster (7) (lw: chsd ldrs tl wknd over 3f out) ........... 2½.6

1850 Super Charge (33) (bl) (MWEllerby) 8-11 SMorris (6) (chsd ldrs: rdn & wknd over 1f out) ................................................... 5.7

2566 Boldrullah (40) (DWPArbuthnot) 8-11 MBirch (3) (b: chsd ldrs: effrt u.p 4f out: sn lost pl) ............................................... 6.8

2738³ Dancing Pet (34) (WWHaigh) 8-6 DMcKeown (9) (chsd ldrs: drvn along 5f out: wknd over 3f out) ...................................... ½.9

Roaring Breeze (MissSEHall) 8-6 NConnorton (1) (hld up: effrt on outside ent st: lost pl over 3f out) ................................... 1.10

**8/11** Charmed Life, **5/2** SPRAY OF ORCHIDS, **8/1** Persian Fleece, **14/1** Roaring Breeze, **16/1** Petite Belle, **20/1** Emerald Ears, **25/1** Dancing Pet, **50/1** Ors. CSF £22.77, Tote £2.80: £1.10 £1.30 £1.40 (£5.30). Mr T. A. Stephenson (MALTON) bred by Nidd Park Stud. 10 Rn; No bid      2m 9.1 (5.6)
SF—36/35/37/20/6/6

**2924**      TATTERSALLS AUCTION SERIES STKS (Qualifier) (Mdn 2-Y.O) £3392.00 (£1016.00: £488.00: £224.00)      6f      2-50 (2-53)

**Gymcrak Tiger (IRE)** (MHEasterby) 8-9 MBirch (17) (leggy: scope: w ldrs: led wl over 1f out: drvn out) ................................... —1

2758⁴ Look Who's Here (IRE) (84) (Fav) (BAMcMahon) 8-7 JFortune (8) (lw: chsd ldrs centre: rdn & hung bdly lft over 1f out: nt qckn wl ins fnl f) . ¾.2

2657 Formal Affair (80) (CACyzer) 8-6 DBiggs (4) (disp ld stands' side tl wl over 1f out: hrd rdn & nt qckn) ...................................... 5.3

2771² Star Minstrel (IRE) (62) (MMcCormack) 8-7 AClark (6) (lw: chsd ldrs: drvn along over 2f out: kpt on same pce) ........................ 1.4

2286⁵ Silver Groom (IRE) (APJarvis) 8-9 MTebbutt (10) (lw: chsd ldrs: drvn along over 2f out: one pce) ....................................... nk.5

1902⁵ Panther (IRE) (CWCElsey) 8-5 ‡⁵SMaloney (11) (lw: s.i.s: hdwy ½-wy: styd on fnl f) ..................................................... 2.6

769 Laxey Flyer (JBerry) 8-0 GCarter (7) (chsd ldrs tl wknd over 2f out) ............... 5.7

2039⁶ Colmar (RBastiman) 8-4⁽⁴⁾ DMcKeown (1) (w ldrs stands' side tl wknd 2f out) .... s.h.8

Mark's Club (IRE) (BWHills) 8-2 ‡⁷CMunday (16) (unf: disp ld stands' side tl wknd 2f out: eased whn btn) ........................... 1½.9

2118 Colonel Future (v) (JWWatts) 8-7 NConnorton (13) (w ldr centre over 3f: sn wknd) ................................................... hd.10

2606⁴ Wanza (JHanson) 8-11 EJohnson (9) (sn chsng ldrs: wknd over 2f out) ........ hd.11

2636² Sicily Oak (DMcCain) 8-0 GBardwell (18) (lw: sn drvn along: chsd ldrs tl lost pl over 2f out) ............................................. hd.12

2118 Covent Garden Girl (MWEasterby) 8-2 JFanning (5) (s.i.s: a in rr) ............... ¾.13

Who's the Best (IRE) (APJarvis) 8-0 PaulEddery (12) (w'like: scope: in tch: rn green & drvn along ½-wy: grad wknd) ................... ½.14

2606⁵ Breaking Hearts (IRE) (APStringer) 8-0 AMcGlone (14) (lw: chsd ldrs tl lost pl over 2f out) ............................................. ¾.15

Dancing Diamond (IRE) (CFWall) 8-3 NCarlisle (15) (leggy: unf: s.i.s: a outpcd) nk.16

Combellino (PWHarris) 8-10 GHind (3) (wl grwn: scope: bit bkwd: rn green & nvr wnt pce) ............................................... hd.17

2776 Rum Tempest (CTinkler) 8-7 GDuffield (2) (bit bkwd: sn drvn along: outpcd fr ½-wy) ................................................... ½.18

7/2 Look Who's Here (IRE), **4/1** Formal Affair, **9/2** GYMCRAK TIGER (IRE), **17/2** Who's the Best (IRE)(op 14/1), **10/1** Mark's Club (IRE), Sicily Oak, **12/1** Star Minstrel (IRE), Wanza, Silver Groom (IRE), Panther (IRE), **14/1** Combellino, **16/1** Breaking Hearts (IRE), **20/1** Laxey Flyer, **25/1** Colmar, **33/1** Ors. CSF £23.74, Tote £5.10: £2.30 £2.10 £2.00 (£17.70). Gymcrak Thoroughbred Racing IV Plc (MALTON) bred by David Barry in Ireland. 18 Rn
1m 13.2 (1.5)
SF—41/36/15/12/13/–

### 2925
TOTE GREAT ST WILFRID H'CAP (0-110) £15385.00 (£4630.00: £2240.00: £1045.00)
6f
3-25 (3-30)

| | | |
|---|---|---|
| 2839 | **Green Dollar (88)** *(EAWheeler)* 9–9–4 MTebbutt (10) (lw: trckd ldrs: qcknd to ld jst ins fnl f: rdn & edgd rt: r.o wl) | —1 |
| 15115 | Gorinsky (IRE) **(72)** *(JBerry)* 4–8-2 JFortune (13) (disp ld: nt qckn ins fnl f) | 1¹/₂.2 |
| 25595 | Red Rosein **(92)** *(CaptJWilson)* 6–9-8 GCarter (14) (b.off hind: lw: dwlt: hdwy ¹/₂-wy: r.o wl fnl f) | hd.3 |
| 2637 | Prenonamoss **(80)** *(Fav)* *(DWPArbuthnot)* 4–8-10 MBirch (5) (b.hind: lw: a chsng ldrs: rdn ¹/₂-wy: nt qckn fnl f) | hd.4 |
| 2642 | Gondo **(75)** *(EJAlston)* 5–8-5 GBaxter (17) (disp ld tl no ex fnl f) | ³/₄.5 |
| 2559* | Drum Sergeant **(77)** (bl) *(JParkes)* 5–8-7 PaulEddery (3) (lw: dwlt: racd stands' side: hdwy ¹/₂-wy: kpt on wl fnl f) | hd.6 |
| 28396 | Finjan **(89)** *(MPNaughton)* 5–9-0 ‡⁵JWeaver (2) (chsd ldr stands' side: nt qckn over 1f out) | s.h.7 |
| 2642 | Tigani **(70)** (bl) *(DWChapman)* 6–8-0 SWood (1) (swtg: led stands' side tl wknd jst ins fnl f) | 1¹/₂.8 |
| 26422 | Beau Venture (USA) **(97)** *(FHLee)* 4–9-8 ‡⁵NKennedy (15) (lw: trckd ldrs: ev ch over 1f out: sn wknd) | ³/₄.9 |
| 2839* | Master Planner **(101)** *(CACyzer)* 3–9-13 (4x) DBiggs (9) (lw: w ldr tl wknd over 1f out) | hd.10 |
| 2848 | Educated Pet **(78)** *(MJohnston)* 3–8-4 DMcKeown (7) (prom: drvn along ¹/₂-wy: sn outpcd) | ¹/₂.11 |
| 28393 | Densben **(81)** *(DenysSmith)* 3–8-11 KFallon (16) (chsd ldrs tl rdn & btn 2f out) | ¹/₂.12 |
| 2839 | Allinson's Mate (IRE) **(78)** *(TDBarron)* 4–8-8 AlexGreaves (6) (lw: sn outpcd) | 1¹/₂.13 |
| 2435 | Poets Cove **(83)** *(MMcCormack)* 4–8-13 GDuffield (8) (nvr rchd ldrs) | 1¹/₂.14 |
| 2650 | Filicaia **(66)** (v) *(DonEnricoIncisa)* 6–7-3⁽³⁾ ‡⁷ClaireBalding (12) (s.i.s: a in rr) | 3.15 |
| 26505 | Resolute Bay **(76)** (v) *(RMWhitaker)* 6–8-6 ACulhane (4) (sn outpcd: hrd rdn ¹/₂-wy: n.d) | 1.16 |

LONG HANDICAP: Filicaia 7-6.

**13/2** Prenonamoss, **8/1** Drum Sergeant, Densben, **9/1** Master Planner, **10/1** Red Rosein, Gondo, Allinson's Mate (IRE), **11/1** Finjan, **12/1** Beau Venture (USA), **14/1** Gorinsky (IRE), Poets Cove, Resolute Bay, **16/1** GREEN DOLLAR, **20/1** Educated Pet, **25/1** Tigani, **33/1** Filicaia. CSF £203.41, CT £2,140.76. Tote £24.70: £4.40 £3.50 £2.00 £2.20 (£173.30). Mr B. Azemoudeh (LAMBOURN) bred by Brian Gubby Ltd. 16 Rn
1m 12.3 (0.6)
SF—68/46/65/52/44/45

### 2926
COCKED HAT 'COCK OF THE NORTH' H'CAP (0-90) £4659.00 (£1392.00: £666.00: £303.00)
1¹/₄m
3-55 (3-57)

| | | |
|---|---|---|
| 2678* | **Mbulwa (56)** (Jt-Fav) *(SEKettlewell)* 6–8-4 GCarter (3) (lw: mde all: styd on strly fnl 2f) | —1 |
| 28062 | Rising Tempo (IRE) **(63)** *(CACyzer)* 4–8-11 DBiggs (6) (lw: trckd ldrs: effrt & ev ch over 1f out: r.o same pce) | 1¹/₂.2 |
| 25715 | Touch Above **(56)** *(TDBarron)* 6–8-4 AlexGreaves (4) (trckd ldrs: nt qckn fnl f) | nk.3 |
| 2660 | Rose Alto **(80)** *(JRFanshawe)* 4–10-0 GDuffield (8) (trckd ldrs: n.m.r & swtchd ins over 1f out: styd on same pce) | nk.4 |
| 26112 | Spanish Verdict **(71)** *(DenysSmith)* 5–9-5 KFallon (11) (lw: trckd ldrs: outpcd 3f out: kpt on fnl f) | 1¹/₂.5 |
| 27423 | Sinclair Lad (IRE) **(61)** *(RHollinshead)* 4–8-9 PaulEddery (10) (hld up: effrt on ins 3f out: n.m.r & swtchd 2f out: no imp) | ³/₄.6 |
| 2660 | Straw Thatch **(70)** *(MJohnston)* 3–8-10 DMcKeown (2) (lw: trckd ldrs: drvn along over 3f out: sn lost pl) | 3.7 |
| 2813 | Huso **(69)** *(PCHaslam)* 4–8-12 ‡⁵JWeaver (9) (hld up: stdy hdwy on ins over 3f out: wknd 2f out) | 1¹/₂.8 |
| 26933 | Milanese **(77)** *(DMorley)* 3–9-3 MBirch (7) (lw: plld hrd: hdwy & ev ch over 2f out: sn wknd) | nk.9 |
| 17003 | Nicely Thanks (USA) **(65)** *(TDBarron)* 3–7-12 ‡⁷VHalliday (1) (bhd: effrt over 3f out: nvr nr ldrs) | hd.10 |
| 2453 | Bayaireg (USA) **(81)** (Jt-Fav) *(AAScott)* 3–9-7 JFortune (5) (s.s: hld up & bhd: effrt over 3f out: sn btn) | 8.11 |

**5/1** Bayaireg (USA), MBULWA, **6/1** Rising Tempo (IRE), **8/1** Spanish Verdict, Huso, Sinclair Lad, **10/1** Milanese, **12/1** Straw Thatch, Nicely Thanks (USA), Touch Above, **14/1** Rose Alto. CSF £32.95, CT £313.28. Tote £6.00: £2.10 £2.00 £3.00 (£17.90). Northumbria Leisure Ltd (MIDDLEHAM) bred by Hascombe and Valiant Studs. 11 Rn
2m 8.1 (4.6)
SF—44/48/40/63/51/39

**2927**　　BILLY NEVETT MEMORIAL CHALLENGE CUP (H'cap) (0-80) £3494.25 (£1044.00: £499.50: £227.25)　　**1½m 60y**　　　　　　　　4-30 (4-32)

2670² **Much Sought After (70)** *(DMorley)* 3-9-2 PaulEddery (3) (lw: trckd ldrs: effrt over 3f out: led 2f out: sn clr: comf) ................................ —1

2246⁵ Danza Heights (41) *(MrsGRReveley)* 6-7-11 JFanning (9) (lw: hld up: stdy hdwy over 3f out: styd on u.p fnl f: no ch w wnr) ................ 3.2

2515* Bustinetta (68) *(JRFanshawe)* 3-9-0 GDuffield (7) (lw: trckd ldrs: pushed along & outpcd 3f out: styd on wl fnl f) ................ 1.3

2734 Bold Ambition (43) *(TKersey)* 5-7-8⁽⁶⁾ ‡⁵NKennedy (1) (lw: a chsng ldrs: one pce fnl 2f) ................ 2½.4

312 West With the Wind (54) *(GMMoore)* 5-8-5 ‡‡JWeaver (5) (dwlt: bhd: hdwy & prom 5f out: ev ch tl wknd over 1f out) ................ 1½.5

2820⁴ Carlingford (USA) (61) *(MPNaughton)* 6-9-3 NConnorton (6) (led to 2f out: wknd over 1f out) ................ 2½.6

2810³ Young George (56) *(MDods)* 5-8-12 KFallon (4) (lw: s.i.s: bhd: sme hdwy 4f out: n.d) ................ 2½.7

2810 Super Blues (55) *(TDBarron)* 5-8-11 AlexGreaves (11) (chsd ldrs tl outpcd fnl 3f) ................ 2½.8

2691* Cultured (73) (Fav) *(MRStoute)* 3-9-5 PD'Arcy (2) (chsd ldr: effrt & rdn over 3f out: ev ch tl wknd over 2f out) ................ s.h.9

2403⁶ Timurid (FR) (74) *(JLDunlop)* 3-9-6 MBirch (10) (chsd ldrs tl wknd 2f out) ....... 3.10

2413 Briery Fille (42) *(BJMcMath)* 7-7-12 EJohnson (8) (bit bkwd: a in rr) ................ 5.11

Valiant Warrior (72) *(MDHammond)* 4-10-0 DMcKeown (12) (bit bkwd: dwlt: a bhd) ................ 12.12

**4/1** Cultured, **5/1** Bustinetta, **11/2** Timurid (FR), **6/1** Danza Heights, **7/1** Young George, **8/1** MUCH SOUGHT AFTER, **10/1** Carlingford (USA), **14/1** Super Blues, **25/1** West With the Wind, Valiant Warrior, **33/1** Ors. CSF £51.20, OT £240.30. Tote £6.80: £2.00 £2.00 £1.90 (£27.60). The MSA Partnership (NEWMARKET) bred by Astalon Ltd. 12 Rn　　　　　　　　　　　　　　　　　　　　　　2m 40.2 (6.2)
　　　　　　　　　　　　　　　　　　　　　　　　　　　　　SF—40/15/30/5/13/20

**2928**　　SAWLEY NURSERY　£2448.00 (£678.00: £324.00)　　**6f**　　　　5-00 (5-01)

2550³ **Classic Storm (71)** *(JBerry)* 8-3 GCarter (2) (lw: chsd ldrs: rdn & edgd rt over 1f out: r.o wl to ld jst ins fnl f) ................ —1

2558* Pizza Connection (89) (Fav) *(JLDunlop)* 9-7 PaulEddery (3) (dwlt: bhd: hdwy over 2f out: ev ch 1f out: nt qckn) ................ 1½.2

2387⁴ Willshe Gan (83) *(DenysSmith)* 9-1 KFallon (1) (lw: w ldr: led & edgd rt over 1f out: hdd jst ins fnl f: kpt on same pce) ................ 1.3

2550⁶ Norstano (69) (bl) *(MHEasterby)* 7-10⁽⁴⁾ ‡⁵SMaloney (7) (led: rdn 2f out: hung rt: hdd & wknd over 1f out) ................ 3.4

2818⁶ Bold Philip (69) *(BBeasley)* 8-1 NConnorton (4) (outpcd ½-wy: n.d) ................ 5.5

2776 Paajib (IRE) (70) *(CTinkler)* 8-2 GDuffield (10) (s.i.s: sn drvn along: hdwy 2f out: styd on nr fin) ................ s.h.6

1844⁴ Key to My Heart (IRE) (88) *(DMoffatt)* 9-6 JFortune (5) (lw: chsd ldrs: rdn ½-wy: sn outpcd) ................ 1½.7

2669⁴ Make Mine a Double (67) *(MissSEHall)* 7-13 NCarlisle (8) (lw: nvr wnt pce) ....... 2.8

2396³ Bluebella (61) *(MrsPABarker)* 7-7 SWood (9) (sn outpcd) ................ 1.9

924⁵ Legendary Hero (67) *(TDBarron)* 7-13 JFanning (6) (lw: nvr plcd to chal) ..... 3½.10

1848⁵ Matthew David (63) *(MBrittain)* 7-9 GBardwell (11) (chsd ldrs: sn drvn along: lost pl ½-wy) ................ 4.11

LONG HANDICAP: Bluebella 6-10.

**13/8** Pizza Connection, **4/1** CLASSIC STORM, **9/1** Key to My Heart (IRE), Make Mine a Double, **10/1** Norstano, **11/1** Willshe Gan, **14/1** Matthew David, Paajib (IRE), **16/1** Legendary Hero, **25/1** Bold Philip, **33/1** Bluebella. CSF £10.67, CT £61.80. Tote £4.10: £1.60 £1.50 £3.50 (£3.50). Mr D. J. Ayres (COCKERHAM) bred by Concorde Breeding and Racing International P'Ship. 11 Rn　　　　　　　　　　　　　1m 12.9 (1.2)
　　　　　　　　　　　　　　　　　　　　　　　　　　　　　SF—41/53/43/12/–/–

**2929**　　LEVY BOARD APP'CE STKS　£2427.00 (£672.00: £321.00)　　**1m 1f**　　5-30 (5-30)

2579² **Flaming Arrow (92)** (Fav) *(HRACecil)* 4-9-5 GParkin (3) (lw: trckd ldr gng wl: led on bit over 2f out: canter) ................ —1

2699⁴ Chance Report (31) *(FHLee)* 4-9-0 DWright (7) (lw: hld up: styd on fnl 2f: no ch w wnr) ................ 5.2

1747 Sally Fay (IRE) (40) *(TKersey)* 4-9-0 ClaireBalding (1) (lw: hld up: effrt 3f out: kpt on one pce) ................ 1.3

1323 Tina's Game (APStringer) 4-8-9 HBastiman (5) (chsd ldrs: drvn along over 3f out: one pce) ................ 1½.4

825 Seagull Hollow (IRE) (78) *(MHEasterby)* 3-8-12 JMarshall (4) (trckd ldrs: effrt over 3f out: rdn & wknd 2f out) ................ 10.5

Nutacre *(GPKelly)* 7–9-0 PaulJohnson (2) (b: bkwd: led tl over 2f out: sn lost pl) 10.6
1597⁶ Dancing Boat *(KAMorgan)* 3–8-7 EHusband (6) (bhd fnl 4f) ...................... 2.7

**1/5** FLAMING ARROW, **6/1** Seagull Hollow (IRE), **16/1** Dancing Boat, **20/1** Chance Report, **50/1** Tina's Game, **100/1** Ors. CSF £5.67, Tote £1.30: £1.10 £3.70 (£4.80). Mr Saeed Maktoum Al Maktoum (NEWMARKET) bred by Gainsborough Stud Management Ltd. 7 Rn                                             1m 56.2 (6)

SF—15/–/–/–/–/–

T/Trio: Race 3: £386.60 (5.2 Tckts). T/Plpt: £37.30 (136.55 Tckts).                              WG

## 2557—**NOTTINGHAM (L-H)**
### Monday, August 24th [Good]
Going Allowance: 6f-1m 54y: 0.35 sec; Rest: 0.15 sec per fur (G)        Wind: slt half against

Stalls: high

**2930**   NOTTINGHAM STKS (Mdn 2-Y.O.F) £2700.00 (£750.00: £360.00)
            1m 54y                                                          2-00 (2-06)

1038⁵ **Helvellyn (USA)** *(HRACecil)* 8-11  SCauthen (3) (mde all: shkn up over 1f out:
          r.o wl) ...................................................................... —1
2657² Reine de Neige **(Fav)** *(AAScott)* 8-11  BRaymond (16) (hld up: hdwy 3f out: hrd
          rdn & kpt on fnl f) ........................................................ 1¹/₂.2
2185³ Sehailah *(MrsLPiggott)* 8-11  LPiggott (10) (a.p: 4th st: ev ch 2f out: rdn & no ex
          fnl f) ........................................................................ 2.3
1600³ Cashell *(MRStoute)* 8-11  PatEddery (17) (bit bkwd: chsd ldrs: 5th st: rdn 2f out:
          wknd over 1f out) ....................................................... 3¹/₂.4
2102⁵ Manx Monarch *(RHollinshead)* 8-11  WRyan (2) (hdwy 3f out: styd on ins fnl f) 2¹/₂.5
2674⁴ Grogfryn *(JBerry)* 8-11  JCarroll (1) (chsd ldrs: 6th st: rdn 3f out: sn btn) ...... nk.6
2277  Burning Cost *(GAPritchard-Gordon)* 8-11  NDay (5) (nvr trbld ldrs) ........ 2¹/₂.7
2405⁵ Bonny Princess *(JDBethell)* 8-11  AMunro (12) (chsd ldrs: 7th st: rdn & wknd 2f
          out) ......................................................................... 2.8
2568  Omidjoy (IRE) *(SPCWoods)* 8-11  BRouse (4) (hdwy over 2f out: nvr nr to chal) s.h.9
2696⁶ Blue Sombrero (IRE) **(60)** *(RJHolder)* 8-11  JWilliams (15) (a bhd) ........... s.h.10
      Tinstone *(JAGlover)* 8-11  DMcKeown (14) (leggy: s.s: hdwy over 3f out: wknd
          2f out) ...................................................................... 5.11
2696  Kiawah *(JRFanshawe)* 8-11  GDuffield (18) (s.s: effrt ¹/₂-wy: wknd over 2f out) . 2.12
2248⁵ Crystal Stone *(TThomsonJones)* 8-11  TQuinn (8) (lw: chsd wnr: 2nd st: wknd
          over 2f out) ............................................................... 1¹/₂.13
2629  Silvies Star *(CDBroad)* 8-11  NAdams (13) (bit bkwd: a bhd) .............. 2¹/₂.14
2428  Bold Treasure (IRE) *(MrsNMacauley)* 8-6 ‡5SWilliams (9) (bit bkwd: prom: 3rd
          st: wknd 3f out: t.o) ...................................................... 10.15
      Minteen *(JWhite)* 8-11  DaleGibson (1) (unf: scope: bit bkwd: sn outpcd: a t.o) 20.16

**8/11** Reine de Neige, **4/1** Sehailah, **15/2** HELVELLYN (USA)(op 4/1), **12/1** Cashell(op 6/1), **20/1** Burning Cost, **25/1** Grogfryn, **33/1** Crystal Stone, Manx Monarch, **50/1** Kiawah, Tinstone, Bonny Princess, Blue Sombrero (IRE), **66/1** Minteen, Omidjoy (IRE), **100/1** Ors. CSF £12.56, Tote £6.30: £1.40 £1.10 £1.40 (£3.70). Sheikh Mohammed (NEWMARKET) bred by Jonathan H. F. Davis in USA. 16 Rn          1m 46.5 (6.9)

SF—36/31/25/14/6/5

**2931**   ALVERTON (S) H'CAP (3-Y.O) (0-60) £3015.00 (£840.00: £405.00)
            1m 1f 213y                                                      2-30 (2-36)

2545  **Bo Knows Best (IRE) (39)** **(Fav)** *(JSutcliffe)* 8-3  BRouse (12) (hdwy & 7th st:
          rdn to ld ins fnl f: eased nr fin) ........................................ —1
2809  Stratford Lady **(36)** (bl) *(JAGlover)* 7-11 ‡3FNorton (3) (chsd ldrs: 5th st: led 3f
          out tl ins fnl f) .......................................................... 2.2
2809⁴ Chantry Bellini **(44)** (bl) *(CWThornton)* 8-8  GHind (14) (hdwy 3f out: r.o wl ins
          fnl f) ....................................................................... s.h.3
2481  Aegaen Lady **(47)** *(JEtherington)* 8-6 ‡5JWeaver (9) (lw: hld up: hdwy 2f out:
          nrst fin) ..................................................................... hd.4
2783  Iron Baron (IRE) **(57)** *(RHollinshead)* 9-7  WRyan (15) (bhd: effrt over 2f out:
          styd on wl fnl f) ........................................................... ¹/₂.5
2699⁶ Another Nut **(39)** *(PDEvans)* 7-10 ‡7AGarth (2) (led to 3f out: sn rdn & wknd) .. 2¹/₂.6
2291⁴ Broughton's Tango (IRE) **(43)** (bl) *(WJMusson)* 8-7  JReid (10) (b: hld up: hdwy
          4f out: ev ch 2f out: sn rdn & wknd) ................................. hd.7
2416⁴ Nomadic Rose **(44)** *(TJNaughton)* 8-8  GCarter (4) (chsd ldr: 2nd st: wknd
          over 2f out) ............................................................... 12.8
2809  Gymcrak Cyrano (IRE) **(52)** (v) *(MHEasterby)* 8-11 ‡5SMaloney (11) (lw: chsd
          ldrs over 7f) .............................................................. ¹/₂.9
      Titian Girl **(40)** *(MissLCSiddall)* 8-4  DMcKeown (20) (nvr nrr) ................ 2.10

Page 1024

| | | |
|---|---|---|
| 2481[6] | Lord Leitrim (IRE) **(42)** (NACallaghan) 8-6 GDuffield (8) (b.nr hind: n.d) | 2.11 |
| 2716[4] | Killshandra (IRE) **(40)** (MrsBarbaraWaring) 8-4 NHowe (21) (a in rr) | 2.12 |
| 2694 | Dick Whittington **(47)** (CTinkler) 8-11 MTebbutt (6) (lw: n.d) | ¾.13 |
| 2146[3] | Qualitair Idol **(41)** (JFBottomley) 8-5 PBurke (1) (n.d) | 2.14 |
| 2694 | Galley Gossip **(41)** (RBrotherton) 8-5 JWilliams (5) (plld hrd: 3rd st: wknd 3f out) | s.h.15 |
| 2783[6] | King Optimist **(35)** (bl) (ASmith) 7-13 JQuinn (7) (chsd ldrs: 4th st: wknd over 2f out) | 1.16 |
| 2708 | Trainee (USA) **(39)** (bl) (WJHaggas) 8-3[(1)] NDay (18) (a bhd: t.o) | 6.17 |
| 1128[4] | Weekend Girl **(32)** (WMBrisbourne) 7-3[(2)] ‡[7]CHawksley (13) (6th st: wknd over 3f out: t.o) | hd.18 |
| 2694 | Moniaive **(42)** (WClay) 8-6 JLowe (23) (lw: a bhd: t.o) | hd.19 |
| 2739 | Dont Embarrass Me **(30)** (TKersey) 7-8 DaleGibson (22) (s.s: a bhd: t.o) | 15.20 |
| 2829[5] | High Post **(47)** (DMarks) 8-11 TQuinn (17) (bhd fnl 3f: t.o) | 2.21 |
| 2470[6] | Soft Note (IRE) **(50)** (v) (MBell) 9-0 AMunro (16) (b.hind: bhd fnl 3f: t.o) | 4.22 |

**9/4** BO KNOWS BEST (IRE), **8/1** High Post(6/1—10/1), Lord Leitrim (IRE), **10/1** Broughton's Tango (IRE)(op 6/1), **11/1** Chantry Bellini, **12/1** Gymcrak Cyrano (IRE)(op 7/1), Soft Note (IRE)(op 8/1), **14/1** Dick Whittington(op 7/1), Iron Baron (IRE), **16/1** Nomadic Rose, **18/1** Trainee (USA), **20/1** Stratford Lady, King Optimist, **25/1** Another Nut, Aegaen Lady, **33/1** Qualitair Idol, Galley Gossip, **50/1** Ors. CSF £49.66, CT £419.11. Tote £3.20: £1.10 £4.90 £3.10 £8.60 (£144.40). Mr John Sutcliffe (EPSOM) bred by Gay O'Callaghan in Ireland. 22 Rn; Bt in 7,200 gns
    2m 10.4 (7.9)
    SF—25/15/25/22/36/6

---

**2932**    TATTERSALLS AUCTION SERIES STKS (Qualifier) (Mdn 2-Y.O) £2952.00 (£822.00: £396.00)  **6f 15y**    3-00 (3-07)

| | | |
|---|---|---|
| 2758[3] | Weaver Bird (Fav) (HCandy) 8-0 SDawson (17) (a.p stands' side: led over 1f out: r.o wl) | 1 |
| 2710[3] | Mr Vincent (GLewis) 8-5 PaulEddery (2) (mde all far side: rdn & no ex ins fnl f) | 1½.2 |
| 1422[3] | Manor Adventure **(70)** (BAMcMahon) 8-2 AMunro (16) (led stands' side after 2f: hdd over 1f out: one pce) | 2.3 |
| 2425[2] | Heart Broken **(76)** (JGFitzGerald) 8-4[(1)] KFallon (12) (led 2f: ev ch 1f out: unable qckn) | 1½.4 |
| 2108[5] | Glen Miller **(8-9)** (JWPayne) 8-9 RCochrane (15) (r.o appr fnl f: fin wl) | 2½.5 |
| 2277 | Aviator's Dream (JFBottomley) 8-5 PBurke (1) (scope: bkwd: racd far side: chsd ldrs: r.o one pce fnl f) | d.h.6 |
| | Lola Wants (CFWall) 8-1 PRobinson (18) (lt-f: unf: in tch stands' side: kpt on fnl f) | ¾.7 |
| | Spring Sixpence (JRFanshawe) 8-6 GDuffield (3) (unf: chsd ldr far side over 4f) | 1.8 |
| 856[2] | Vladivostok (BWHills) 8-10 DHolland (9) (s.i.s: sn rcvrd: chsd ldrs 4f) | 1½.9 |
| 2519 | Prairie Grove (RHannon) 9-0 BRaymond (19) | s.h.10 |
| 2832[6] | Rough Guess (IRE) (LordHuntingdon) 7-11 ‡[5]DHarrison (4) (racd far side: bhd tl sme late hdwy) | s.h.11 |
| | Secret Fantasy (IRE) (CFWall) 8-4 NCarlisle (20) (lengthy: bit bkwd: nvr trbld ldrs) | nk.12 |
| 2277 | Quick Silver Boy **(66)** (DBurchell) 8-5 MHills (5) (brght stands' side: nvr trbld ldrs) | ¾.13 |
| 2633[5] | Nigels Prospect (DHaydnJones) 8-6 JWilliams (22) (n.d) | 1.14 |
| 1728[2] | Gangleader (SPCWoods) 8-8 BRouse (11) (n.d) | nk.15 |
| 2106[3] | April Double (IRE) (MHTompkins) 7-12[(5)] ‡[7]SMulvey (10) (s.s: rdn over 2f out: no imp) | s.h.16 |
| 2758 | Valere Knight (IRE) **(58)** (CGCox) 8-7 AClark (21) (n.d) | hd.17 |
| | Tallino (CCElsey) 8-3 JLowe (8) (cmpt: str: bit bkwd: swtchd stands' side: gd spd 4f) | ½.18 |
| | Inovar (CBBBooth) 8-8[(1)] GOldroyd (14) (str: scope: s.s: a bhd) | 1½.19 |
| 2733 | April Point (IRE) (RHollinshead) 8-4 WRyan (13) (sn wl bhd) | s.h.20 |
| | Magic Fan (IRE) (PWHarris) 8-12 SWhitworth (7) (cmpt: bkwd: t.o) | 10.21 |
| | Do Tell (TWDonnelly) 8-10 NAdams (6) (unf: bit bkwd: t.o) | 20.22 |

**7/2** WEAVER BIRD, **4/1** Vladivostok(op Evens), **10/1** Prairie Grove, Heart Broken, Mr Vincent, **12/1** Rough Guess (IRE)(op 20/1), Tallino, **16/1** Gangleader, Inovar, Manor Adventure, Quick Silver Boy, **25/1** Spring Sixpence, Lola Wants, Glen Miller, **33/1** Magic Fan (IRE), Valere Knight (IRE), April Point (IRE), April Double (IRE), **50/1** Ors. CSF £39.75, Tote £3.90: £2.00 £3.00 £3.60 (£17.90). Mrs Henry Candy (WANTAGE) bred by W. and R. Barnett Ltd. 22 Rn
    1m 17.4 (6.4)

---

**2933**    BENTINCK GRADUATION STKS  £3465.00 (£1035.00: £495.00: £225.00)
    **1m 1f 213y**    3-30 (3-33)

| | | |
|---|---|---|
| 781[2] | **Tapis Rouge (IRE)** (Fav) (HRACecil) 3-9-2 SCauthen (4) (chsd ldrs: 3rd st: rdn over 1f out: r.o strlv to ld cl home) | —1 |

911* Besotted **(92)** *(BWHills)* 3-8-11 PatEddery (6) (stdd s: sn prom: 2nd st: led over 2f out tl ct nr fin) .................................................................................. hd.2

1746 Amaze **(97)** *(LadyHerries)* 3-9-2 JReid (3) (b: hld up: 6th st: hdwy over 2f out: r.o) ............................................................................................................ 4.3

2791³ Muhayaa (USA) **(93)** *(AAScott)* 3-9-2 BRaymond (7) (lw: led over 7f: sn rdn & btn) ........................................................................................................... 6.4

1751² Kasikci **(78)** *(RHollinshead)* 3-8-11 WRyan (5) (hld up: 5th st: effrt 3f out: no imp) ......................................................................................................... 15.5

Master D Dee *(PWHarris)* 4-9-9 PaulEddery (1) (chsd ldrs: 4th st: wknd over 3f out: t.o) ................................................................................................... 15.6

1862* Ajzem (USA) **(91)** *(MRStoute)* 3-9-2 MBirch (2) (b: a last: virtually p.u fnl 2f: t.o: fin lame) ................................................................................................ 30.7

**4/5** TAPIS ROUGE (IRE), **100/30** Muhayaa (USA), **7/1** Besotted(op 4/1), **10/1** Ajzem (USA), **11/1** Amaze, **66/1** Kasikci, **100/1** Master D Dee. CSF £6.48, Tote £1.90: £1.20 £2.10 (£2.80). Sheikh Mohammed (NEWMARKET) bred by Newton Stud Farm Inc in Ireland. 7 Rn 2m 8.8 (6.3)
SF—54/48/45/33/–/–

**2934** VICTORIA CENTRE H'CAP (0-70) £2952.00 (£822.00: £396.00)
1¾m 15y (Weights raised 2 lb) 4-00 (4-02)

2737* **Vain Prince (45)** (Fav) *(NTinkler)* 5-8-7 LCharnock (13) (lw: hld up: 5th st: led 2f out: all out) ................................................................................................. —1

2731* Briggsmaid **(59)** *(JMPEustace)* 4-9-7 MTebbutt (3) (hld up: hdwy 4f out: ev ch fnl f: unable qckn nr fin) ..................................................................... nk.2

2759² Polistatic **(39)** *(CAHorgan)* 5-8-1 DaleGibson (5) (hld up: hdwy ent st: rdn & r.o appr fnl f) ......................................................................................... 2.3

2397 Enfant du Paradis (IRE) *(PDEvans)* 4-7-6 ‡‡AGarth (16) (lw: hdwy & 4th st: ev ch 3f out: styd on u.p fnl f) ......................................................... 2.4

2698⁵ By Far (USA) **(34)** *(OO'Neill)* 6-7-10 NAdams (11) (hld up & bhd: hdwy 4f out: styd on ins fnl f) ...................................................................... hd.5

2698⁴ Maestroso (IRE) **(67)** *(RFJohnsonHoughton)* 3-9-3 JReid (12) (styd on fnl 2f: nvr nrr) .................................................................................................... 2.6

2810⁵ Hazaaf (USA) **(60)** *(AAScott)* 3-8-10 BRaymond (7) (prom: led over 4f out: sn hdd: rdn & wknd appr fnl f) .................................................. 7.7

2834* Sharp Top **(52)** *(MJRyan)* 4-8-7 ‡PMcCabe (18) (chsd ldr: 2nd st: led 4f out to 2f out: one pce) ................................................................ ½.8

2774 Maligned (IRE) **(47)** *(JRFanshawe)* 3-7-11 GBardwell (1) (lw: chsd ldrs: 3rd st: wknd over 2f out) ..................................................... 1.9

2774⁴ A a Bamba **(53)** *(NACallaghan)* 3-8-3 GDuffield (19) (b.hind: bhd: effrt over 3f out: nvr nr ldrs) .............................................................. hd.10

2715⁵ Janiski **(51)** (v) *(MrsBarbaraWaring)* 9-8-13 JLowe (15) (lw: nvr nr ldrs) ........... 1.11

2759 Smartie Lee **(49)** *(PFICole)* 5-8-11 TQuinn (17) (prom over 10f: sn wknd) ........ nk.12

2632 Ballyranter **(48)** *(HJCollingridge)* 3-7-12 JQuinn (6) (chsd ldrs: 7th st: wknd 2f out) ................................................................................................. 1.13

2715⁶ White River **(40)** (v) *(DHaydnJones)* 6-8-2 TyroneWilliams (14) (hdwy ½-wy: 6th st: rdn & wknd over 2f out) ......................................... 10.14

2566⁵ Altermeera **(62)** *(MrsBarbaraWaring)* 4-9-10 NHowe (10) (chsd ldrs 9f) ......... ¾.15

2698 Captain My Captain (IRE) **(43)** *(RBrotherton)* 4-8-5⁽⁴⁾ JWilliams (9) (b: a bhd) s.h.16

2605 Access Cruise (USA) **(43)** *(BAMcMahon)* 5-8-5 JFortune (8) (s.s: hld up: nvr plcd to chal) ..................................................................................... 1.17

187 Windsor Park (USA) **(47)** *(KSBridgwater)* 6-8-9 AMunro (2) (lw: chsd ldrs 8f: sn lost tch: t.o) ........................................................................... 10.18

687⁶ High Mind (FR) **(62)** *(MissLCSiddall)* 3-8-12 MBirch (4) (bit bkwd: reard s: a in rr) ................................................................................................. 8.19

2810 Vinstan **(35)** (bl) *(CASmith)* 6-7-4 ‡‡CHawksley (20) (led & sn wl clr: hdd & wknd qckly over 4f out: t.o) ....................................... 2½.20

**11/2** VAIN PRINCE, **13/2** Sharp Top, **8/1** Captain My Captain (IRE)(tchd 12/1), **10/1** Briggsmaid, Hazaaf (USA), **11/1** Maestroso (IRE), Polistatic, **14/1** Enfant du Paradis (IRE), By Far (USA), **16/1** Maligned (IRE), A a Bamba, Ballyranter, Janiski, Altermeera, **20/1** Smartie Lee, White River, **25/1** Windsor Park (USA), High Mind (FR), **33/1** Access Cruise (USA), **66/1** Vinstan. CSF £60.54, CT £564.03. Tote £7.70: £2.60 £2.40 £2.90 £4.40 (£14.80). Mr A. C. Findlay (MALTON) bred by Lodge Park Stud. 20 Rn 3m 7.4 (8.9)
SF—25/38/14/1/4/21

**2935** CENTENARY H'CAP (0-70) £2742.00 (£762.00: £366.00) 1m 54y 4-30 (4-35)

1025 **Houlston's Will (58)** *(MrsJRRamsden)* 3-9-0 GBaxter (12) (hld up: shkn up 3f out: styd on to ld wl ins fnl f) ....................................... —1

2707* Salbyng **(58)** (Fav) *(JWHills)* 4-9-6 RHills (2) (lw: chsd ldrs: 5th st: led over 1f out tl wl ins fnl f) ............................................... ½.2

2561² Irish Groom **(40)** (bl) *(JPSmith)* 5-7-9 ‡‡AGarth (15) (hld up: hdwy 3f out: ev ch fnl f: unable qckn cl home) ........................... hd.3

2755  Diaco **(63)** *(MAJarvis)* 7–9–11  AMunro (4) (hld up: stdy hdwy 3f out: ev ch ins fnl f: r.o) ............................................................................................. s.h.4
2813  Homile **(47)** *(BAMcMahon)* 4–8–9  TQuinn (16) (hld up: stdy hdwy & 7th st: led over 2f out tl appr fnl f: rdn & wknd fnl f) ............................. 4.5
2827  Ketti **(42)** (bl) *(DLWilliams)* 7–8–4  WRyan (20) (bhd: hdwy over 2f out: nvr nrr)  1½.6
2427  State of Affairs **(40)** *(CAHorgan)* 4–8–9  DaleGibson (8) (chsd ldrs: 6th st: rdn & one pce appr fnl f) ............................................................ ½.7
2369⁴  Santi Sana **(66)** (bl) *(LadyHerries)* 4–10–0  PaulEddery (5) (b.off hind: effrt over 2f out: nvr able to chal) ...................................................... 1½.8
  2687  Sunnyside Rock (IRE) **(40)** *(JEtherington)* 4–8–2  KDarley (19) (a mid div) ........ ¾.9
2032  Mariette Larkin **(60)** *(GBBalding)* 3–9–2  JWilliams (10) (hld up & bhd: nvr plcd to chal) ............................................................................................. 4.10
2813  Winged Whisper (USA) **(60)** *(CASmith)* 3–9–2  MWigham (17) (lw: s.s: a bhd) .. 2.11
2714⁶  Sooty Tern **(52)** *(JMBradley)* 5–9–0  NAdams (7) (w ldr: 2nd st: rdn & wknd 3f out) ......................................................................................................... 3½.12
2392  Northern Nation **(47)** *(WClay)* 4–8–9  JLowe (11) (n.d) ...................................... 2½.13
2561³  Good for the Roses **(47)** *(CGCox)* 6–8–9  AClark (14) (lw: sn prom: 4th st: rdn & wknd over 2f out) .................................................................................. 1½.14
2123⁴  Wild Prospect **(62)** *(CTinkler)* 4–9–10  MBirch (4) (lw: led tl hdd & wknd over 2f out) ........................................................................................................... 1.15
2813  Don't Drop Bombs (USA) **(54)** *(AAScott)* 3–8–10  BRaymond (18) (chsd ldrs 5f: sn wknd: t.o) .............................................................................................. 6.16
2827  Jarzon Dancer **(50)** *(DAWilson)* 4–8–2  GCarter (6) (lw: a in rr: t.o) .................... 2.17
2561  Uncertain **(40)** *(DHaydnJones)* 4–8–2  TyroneWilliams (9) (bit bkwd: prom: 3rd st: wknd over 3f out: t.o) ................................................................ 2½.18
1611  Miss Cresta **(62)** *(HCandy)* 3–9–4  SDawson (1) (a bhd: t.o) .............................. 2.19

**6/1** Salbyng, **15/2** Good for the Roses(op 5/1), **8/1** Sooty Tern, **17/2** Santi Sana, **9/1** Irish Groom(op 6/1), **10/1** Diaco, **12/1** HOULSTON'S WILL(9/1–14/1), Homile, **14/1** Don't Drop Bombs (USA), Wild Prospect, Miss Cresta, Mariette Larkin, **16/1** Winged Whisper (USA), Jarzon Dancer, **33/1** Ketti, Sunnyside Rock (IRE), State of Affairs, Northern Nation, **50/1** Uncertain. CSF £81.01, CT £643.40. Tote £12.80: £5.20 £2.00 £2.30 £2.30 (£975.50). Mark Houlston (Yorkshire Decorators) Ltd (THIRSK) bred by M. Houlston. 19 Rn    1m 46.4 (6.8)
SF—40/44/18/47/19/9

T/Plpt: £33.80 (128.30 Tckts).                                                                                              IM

2602—**PONTEFRACT (L-H)**
### Tuesday, August 25th [Good to firm]
Going Allowance: 5f: minus 0.40; Rest: minus 0.10 sec per fur (F)          Wind: fresh half bhd

Stalls: low

**2936**          WHITELANE-PONTEFRACT APP'CE SERIES H'CAP (Rnd 4) (0-70) £2532.00 (£702.00: £336.00)    **5f**                                                      2-45 (2-46)

2797  **Ballasecret (70)** *(RDickin)* 4–10–0  DMeredith (1) (mde all: rdn appr fnl f: r.o wl)  —1
  Banham College **(56)** *(BAMcMahon)* 6–9–0  JBramhill (4) (lw: a chsng ldrs: hdwy over 1f out: r.o wl) ................................................................................ 1½.2
2589⁴  Banbury Flyer **(47)** *(MrsALMKing)* 4–8–5  AGarth (8) (lw: hdwy 2f out: r.o wl nr fin) ...................................................................................................... 2½.3
2722⁶  Call to the Bar (IRE) **(54)** (v) *(CGCox)* 3–8–9  JWeaver (10) (lw: chsd wnr tl outpcd appr fnl f) ................................................................................... 5.4
  2786*  The Dream Maker (IRE) **(40)** *(MrsNMacauley)* 3–7–9  MHumphries (7) (bhd: hdwy & c wd st: nrst fin) ................................................................ hd.5
1054  Yours Or Mine (IRE) **(35)** *(DWChapman)* 4–7–7  DarrenMoffatt (5) (swtg: bhd: hdwy u.p 2f out: nvr rchd ldrs) .............................................................. 1.6
2718⁶  Castle Maid **(38)** *(RJHodges)* 5–7–10⁽²⁾  SDrowne (3) (nvr trbld ldrs) ............... 1½.7
2722²  Black Boy (IRE) **(66)** (v) (Fav) *(JAGlover)* 3–9–7  SWilliams (2) (lw: sn in tch: effrt ½-wy: hung lft & no imp) .................................................................. ¾.8
2466  Jive Music **(35)** (bl) *(NBycroft)* 6–7–7  TWilson (12) (chsd ldrs over 3f) ............. d.h.8
  2786⁴  Don't Run Me Over **(47)** *(BCMorgan)* 3–8–2  RHavlin (13) (lw: outpcd fr ½-wy) ½.10
2514⁴  Kabcast **(60)** (bl) *(DWChapman)* 7–9–4  ClaireBalding (3) (swtg: prom 3f) ...... 1½.11
2808⁴  R a Express **(39)** *(BAMcMahon)* 7–7–11⁽⁴⁾  SSanders (6) (lw: sn bhd & drvn along: n.d) ......................................................................................................... 2½.12
  2689²  Jovial Kate (USA) **(45)** *(BEllison)* 5–8–3  GParkin (11) (outpcd fr ½-wy) .......... 2.13
            LONG HANDICAP: Yours Or Mine (IRE) 7-5, Jive Music 6-13.

**4/1** Black Boy (IRE), **13/2** Jovial Kate (USA), **7/1** Banbury Flyer, BALLASECRET, **8/1** Castle Maid, The Dream Maker (IRE), **12/1** Don't Run Me Over, R a Express, **14/1** Kabcast, Banham College, **20/1** Call to the Bar (IRE), **50/1** Ors. CSF £88.04, CT £641.58. Tote £6.50: £2.00 £5.10 £2.30 (£39.90). Mr R. J. Adams (NEWENT) bred by Mrs D. Price. 13 Rn                                                                      62.2 sec (0.7)
SF—60/40/21/5/–/–

**2937**    TIMEFORM RACE CARD (S) STKS (3 & 4-Y.O) £2637.00 (£732.00: £351.00)
1¼m 6y                                                           3-15 (3-18)

2569* **Kagram Queen (53)** *(MrsGRReveley)* 4–8-9 KDarley (1) (lw: hld up: stdy hdwy
3f out: swtchd & qcknd to ld ins fnl f: r.o) ............................. —1

2757⁴ Misty Goddess (IRE) **(60)** (Fav) *(MAJarvis)* 4–8-4 ‡⁵KRutter (7) (b: lw: trckd ldrs:
led wl over 1f out tl ins fnl f: kpt on) ......................... 1.2

2817⁴ Rural Lad **(68)** *(MrsJRRamsden)* 3–8-1 DHolland (2) (hld up & bhd: hdwy on
ins 3f out: wnt lft over 1f out: r.o one pce) .................... 3½.3

2354⁵ Speedy Sioux **(51)** *(CWThornton)* 3–7-10 JLowe (14) (cl up: led 3f out tl wl over
1f out: sn outpcd) ................................................. 1½.4

2209⁵ Kind Style (IRE) **(30)** *(RHollinshead)* 4–9-9 WRyan (12) (hld up: hdwy over 3f
out: sn chsng ldrs: rdn & btn wl over 1f out) ......... 8.5

2427  Watermill Girl **(29)** *(DTThom)* 4–8-4 GDuffield (10) (mid div: effrt appr st: no imp) 1.6

2856  Wednesdays Auction (IRE) **(55)** *(BHanbury)* 4–9-7 RCochrane (13) (drvn
along 5f out: styd on fnl 2f: n.d) ....................... hd.7

       Ivan the Terrible (IRE) **(56)** *(MissSJWilton)* 4–9-2 ‡⁵SWilliams (4) (chsd ldr tl
wknd over 2f out) ............................................. 1½.8

2607  Bobbie Bold **(34)** *(TKersey)* 4–8-9 KFallon (11) (hld up: n.m.r appr st: sn rdn &
no imp) ...................................................... 2½.9

2784  Emma Victoria **(24)** *(TKersey)* 4–8-4 GHind (9) (b: n.d) ........... hd.10

2685⁶ Princess of Orange **(50)** *(CCElsey)* 3–7-10 JQuinn (3) (swtg: chsd ldrs: c wd
bnd 8f out: wknd 6f out) ........................... 25.11

2602  Doughman **(32)** (bl) *(JNorton)* 3–7-12 ‡³FNorton (6) (led tl hdd 3f out: sn lost pl) 3.12

2737  Bijou Princess **(35)** (bl) *(ABailey)* 4–8-4 JFortune (8) (chsd ldrs: rdn 4f out: sn
wknd) ...................................................... ½.13

2732  Highcliffe Jester *(PBeaumont)* 3–8-1 PBurke (15) (bit bkwd: racd wd: lost tch 5f
out: t.o) .................................................... dist.14

**6/5** Misty Goddess (IRE)(op 2/1), **9/2** KAGRAM QUEEN(op 3/1), Speedy Sioux, **8/1** Rural Lad(op 5/1), **12/1**
Wednesdays Auction (IRE), **20/1** Princess of Orange(op 12/1), **33/1** Bobbie Bold, Kind Style (IRE), Watermill Girl,
Bijou Princess, Ivan the Terrible (IRE), **66/1** Doughman, **100/1** Ors. CSF £9.85. Tote £5.00: £1.80 £1.50 £1.90
(£4.50). Mrs E. A. Kettlewell (SALTBURN) bred by E. W. and E. A. Kettlewell. 14 Rn; Bt in 6,600 gns; Rural Lad
clmd R Spicer £6,010                                                          2m 13.6 (5.3)
                                                                    SF—32/25/15/7/4/–

**2938**    TIMEFORM NURSERY    £3418.00 (£1024.00: £492.00: £226.00)
1m 4y                                                           3-45 (3-47)
                        (Weights raised 3 lb)

2374⁵ **Kiss in the Dark (56)** *(MrsGRReveley)* 7-10 JFanning (1) (a.p: styd on to ld wl
ins fnl f) ................................................... —1

2733³ Express Mariecurie (IRE) **(70)** *(PWChapple-Hyam)* 8-10 PaulEddery (13) (cl
up: led 1f out: wn hdd & r.o one pce) ............... ¾.2

2076⁵ Atherton Green (IRE) **(74)** *(JAGlover)* 9-0 DMcKeown (10) (a chsng ldrs: effrt 2f
out: kpt on u.p) ........................................ ½.3

2728³ Muraadi Ana (IRE) **(62)** *(AAScott)* 8-2 JFortune (12) (lw: trckd ldrs: effrt 2f out:
edgd lft & r.o one pce) ................................ 1½.4

2700² Red Cent **(68)** *(JEtherington)* 8-8 GDuffield (3) (bhd: hdwy u.p 2f out: nvr rchd
ldrs) ...................................................... 1½.5

2629* Frivolous Air **(81)** *(IABalding)* 9-7 RCochrane (1) (lw: led tl hdd & wknd 1f out) s.h.6

2652⁵ Boldville Bash (IRE) **(66)** *(TDBarron)* 8-6 KDarley (5) (lw: hld up & bhd tl r.o v.wl
fnl f) ...................................................... s.h.7

2462  Strike-a-Pose **(60)** *(CNWilliams)* 8-0 JQuinn (4) (in tch: effrt 3f out: one pce) ... hd.8

2572⁴ Comtec's Legend **(56)** *(JFBottomley)* 7-7⁽³⁾ ‡³FNorton (8) (lw: in tch tl outpcd
appr st: n.d after) ................................... 1½.9

2735³ Doc Spot **(61)** *(CaptJWilson)* 8-1 GBardwell (14) (hdwy to jn ldrs after 3f: wknd
2f out) .................................................... ¾.10

2572  Moonshine Dancer **(58)** *(MrsGRReveley)* 7-12 JLowe (9) (nvr nr ldrs) .......... 5.11

2733* Marius (IRE) **(74)** (Fav) *(BWHills)* 9-0 DHolland (5) (b.hind: bhd: effrt 3f out: n.d)1½.12

2695⁴ Mrs Dawson **(62)** *(DrJDScargill)* 7-9 ‡⁷CHawksley (7) (s.s: sme hdwy ½-wy) . nk.13

2543  Mohican Brave (IRE) **(71)** *(JGFitzGerald)* 8-11 KFallon (6) (a bhd) ......... 20.14

                        LONG HANDICAP: Comtec's Legend 7-5.

**3/1** Marius (IRE), **9/2** Muraadi Ana (IRE), **8/1** Frivolous Air, Boldville Bash (IRE)(6/1—9/1), **10/1** Express
Mariecurie (IRE), Strike-a-Pose, **11/1** Mrs Dawson, **12/1** Red Cent, **16/1** Doc Spot, Comtec's Legend, KISS IN
THE DARK, **20/1** Atherton Green (IRE), **25/1** Moonshine Dancer, **33/1** Moonshine Dancer. CSF £159.06, CT
£2,927.93. Tote £25.90: £5.30 £2.20 £6.30 (£125.80). Mr R. Meredith (SALTBURN) bred by Rodney Meredith.
14 Rn                                                               1m 46.9 (5.3)

**2939**    TIMEFORM FUTURITY (Stks) (2-Y.O) £4269.00 (£1272.00: £606.00: £273.00)
6f                                                              4-15 (4-16)

2847³ **Nominator (92)** *(RHollinshead)* 9-3 WRyan (5) (lw: w ldr: carried wd st: led over
1f out: r.o wl) ......................................... —1

2812\* Fyfield Flyer (IRE) **(90)** (Fav) *(PWChapple-Hyam)* 9-3 PaulEddery (1) (lw: led: hung rt & rn wd st: hdd over 1f out: no ex) ............................ 4.2
2724 Grinnell **(68)** *(DenysSmith)* 9-3 KFallon (2) (chsd ldrs tl outpcd ½-wy: styd on wl fnl f) .................................................................... 2½.3
2450[4] Two Moves in Front (IRE) **(81)** *(JBerry)* 9-3 JCarroll (3) (lw: prom tl outpcd ½-wy: n.d after) ................................................................ 10.4
2480[5] Buzz-B-Babe **(67)** *(BEllison)* 8-11 JFortune (4) (sn outpcd & bhd) ................. 1½.5

**4/7** Fyfield Flyer (IRE), **7/4** NOMINATOR, **25/1** Two Moves in Front (IRE), **40/1** Grinnell, **66/1** Buzz-B-Babe. CSF £2.89, Tote £2.90: £1.30 £1.10 (£1.40). Mr J. D. Graham (UPPER LONGDON) bred by Auldyn Stud Ltd. 5 Rn
1m 16.1 (2.1)
SF—49/33/23/–/–

**2940** PHIL BULL TROPHY (Stks)    £3427.50 (£1020.00: £485.00: £217.50)
**2m 1f 216y**                                                                    4-45 (4-49)

2439[2] **Farsi (85)** (bl) (Fav) *(RHollinshead)* 4–9-3 WRyan (3) (lw: hld up: led on bit 2f out: easily) ....................................................................... —1
2439[5] Retouch **(89)** *(PFlCole)* 6–9-10 PaulEddery (5) (lw: led 6f: chsd ldrs: led 3f out to 2f out: no ch w wnr) ................................................... 5.2
2439 Haitham **(86)** *(RAkehurst)* 5–9-10 RCochrane (1) (lw: hld up: hdwy 4f out: sn rdn & one pce) ...................................................................... 5.3
2899 Access Ski **(69)** *(RBoss)* 5–9-3 MTebbutt (4) (led after 6f tl hdd 3f out: sn wknd) 12.4
2373[5] Juris Prudence (IRE) **(43)** *(BAMcMahon)* 4–8-2 ‡[7]SSanders (2) (lw: jnd ldr 10f out tl rdn & wknd 6f out) ............................................. 5.5

**8/11** FARSI, **2/1** Retouch, **13/2** Haitham, **16/1** Access Ski, **100/1** Juris Prudence (IRE). CSF £2.53, Tote £1.70: £1.20 £1.30 (£1.60). Mr J. F. Bower (UPPER LONGDON) bred by Lord Howard de Walden. 5 Rn    3m 58.5 (6.3)
SF—22/24/19/–/–

**2941** TIMEFORM PERSPECTIVE H'CAP (3-Y-O) (0-70) £2973.00 (£828.00: £399.00)
**1m 4y**                                                                    5-15 (5-18)

(Weights raised 2 lb)
2814 **Tahitian (47)** *(MrsJRRamsden)* 8-2 DHolland (2) (lw: hdwy ½-wy: swtchd ins 2f out: led over 1f out: sn rdn clr) ............................................ —1
2814[3] The Dandy Don (IRE) **(52)** *(DenysSmith)* 8-7 KFallon (8) (chsd ldrs: outpcd wl over 2f out: styd on fnl f) ...................................................... 8.2
2809\* Batabanoo **(66)** (Fav) *(MrsGRReveley)* 9-7 KDarley (5) (bhd tl styd on wl fnl 3f: nrst fin) ................................................................................ hd.3
1642 Abeloni **(54)** *(JAGlover)* 8-4 ‡[5]SWilliams (15) (in tch; effrt on outside 3f out: styd on) ............................................................................... 2½.4
2829 High Baccarat **(50)** (v) *(CCElsey)* 8-5[(1)] TRogers (4) (a chsng ldrs: one pce fnl 3f) ................................................................................ 2½.5
2699\* Cledeschamps **(45)** *(MWEllerby)* 8-0[(1)] SMorris (11) (w ldr: led 2f out tl over 1f out: sn btn) ...................................................................... nk.6
2043[6] Primo Pageant **(48)** (bl) *(MJCamacho)* 8-3 NConnorton (16) (hdwy on outside ½-wy: sn rdn: hung lft & no imp appr fnl f) ................................ 1½.7
2723[3] Mary Macblain **(46)** *(JLHarris)* 7-10 ‡[5]SMaloney (10) (b.hind: w ldrs tl wknd 1f out) ..................................................................................... ½.8
2361[5] Dandy Desire **(45)** *(BCMorgan)* 8-0 JLowe (17) (hld up & bhd: nt clr run 2f out: nrst fin) ............................................................................ s.h.9
2680[4] Venture Fourth **(49)** *(EJAlston)* 8-4 GBaxter (3) (bhd: effrt 3f out: no imp) ........ 4.10
2399[4] Gold Belt (IRE) **(50)** *(RHollinshead)* 7-12 ‡[7]AGarth (1) (chsd ldrs: bdly hmpd over 2f out: n.d after) ................................................. 1½.11
2355[6] Great Lord **(64)** *(JWWatts)* 9-5 GDuffield (20) (lw: hdwy ½-wy: sn prom: btn w hmpd 1f out) ................................................................. 1½.12
2384 Essayeffsee **(50)** (bl) *(MHEasterby)* 8-5 MBirch (7) (b.hind: led tl hdd 2f out: wkng whn sltly hmpd wl over 1f out) ....................................... 1½.13
2803[6] Casting Shadows **(59)** *(RDickin)* 9-0 DMcKeown (22) (chsd ldr tl wknd 2f out) 2.14
2162\* Any Dream Would Do **(51)** *(PBeaumont)* 8-6 PBurke (14) (n.d) .................... 1½.15
2538[5] Mummy's Brew **(47)** *(BBeasley)* 8-2 LCharnock (18) (n.d) ......................... 3½.16
2707 Apollo Red **(54)** *(PWHarris)* 8-9 JQuinn (13) (n.d) ................................... 1.17
2668\* Military Expert **(56)** *(CaptJWilson)* 8-11 JCarroll (21) (chsd ldrs to ½-wy: sn wknd) ................................................................................... 1½.18
2668 Scottish Ruby **(52)** *(CTinkler)* 8-7 TLucas (9) (a in rr) .............................. nk.19
2187[4] Roly Wallace **(50)** (bl) *(KTIvory)* 9-2 GBardwell (12) (prom 4f) ................... 1½.20
2580[6] Murasil (USA) **(61)** *(MajorWRHern)* 9-2 WRyan (6) (w ldrs: wkng whn bdly hmpd over 2f out) ........................................................ nk.21
2813 Watch Me Go (IRE) **(55)** *(BobJones)* 8-10 NDay (19) (lw: racd wd: sn outpcd & bhd) ........................................................................... 3½.22

**11/2** Batabanoo, **6/1** Murasil (USA), **8/1** TAHITIAN, **11/1** Watch Me Go (IRE), **12/1** Military Expert, Essayeffsee, Any Dream Would Do, Great Lord (IRE), **14/1** Gold Belt (IRE), The Dandy Don (IRE), **16/1** Mary Macblain, Cledeschamps, **20/1** Roly Wallace, Primo Pageant, Venture Fourth, **25/1** High Baccarat, Casting Shadows, Apollo Red, Abeloni, **33/1** Ors. CSF £116.82, CT £629.87. Tote £9.80: £2.50 £2.90 £1.90 £11.50 (£117.40). Mr K. E. Wheldon (THIRSK) bred by Hesmonds Stud Ltd. 22 Rn
1m 45.2 (3.6)
SF—22/3/16/—/—/—

**2942**  TIMEFORM H'CAP (0-70) £2847.00 (£792.00: £381.00)  **6f**  5-45 (5-50)

2816⁵ **Blue Grit (49)** *(MDods)* 6–8-7 KFallon (4) (styd on to ld ins fnl f: r.o) ................ —1
2570 Cool Enough (37) *(MrsJRRamsden)* 11–7-9 PBurke (11) (bhd: c wd & hdwy 2f
out: r.o wl) ................................................................................. 1¹/₂.2
*2786* Fighter Squadron (60) (bl) *(JAGlover)* 3–8-9 ‡⁵SWilliams (5) (lw: hdwy over 2f
out: r.o u.p fnl f) ......................................................................... nk.3
2672 Henry Will (37) *(TFairhurst)* 8–7-9 JFanning (13) (sn pushed along & bhd: styd
on wl fnl 2f) ............................................................................... 1¹/₂.4
*2786* Kalar (48) (bl) *(DWChapman)* 3–8-2 SWood (1) (chsd ldrs: hrd rdn over 1f out:
nt qckn) ..................................................................................... hd.5
*2786* Johanna Thyme (40) *(RBastiman)* 5–7-5⁽⁵⁾ ‡⁷AGarth (15) (s.i.s: styd on wl fnl 2f:
nrst fin) ..................................................................................... ³/₄.6
2517⁴ Tickham Vixen (IRE) (40) *(JDBethell)* 4–7-12 JQuinn (10) (lw: styd on fnl 2f: nvr
nrr) ......................................................................................... s.h.7
2861 Luna Bid (67) *(MBlanshard)* 9–9-11 RCochrane (17) (bhd tl r.o fnl f) ............... nk.8
Farndale (35) *(BCMorgan)* 5–7-7 GBardwell (12) (bit bkwd: hdwy ¹/₂-wy: led 2f
out tl ins fnl f: wknd) ..................................................................... hd.9
2632 Intrepid Fort (40) (bl) *(BWMurray)* 3–7-8 LCharnock (7) (nvr rchd ldrs) ............ 2.10
2821 Fay Eden (IRE) (41) *(RJHodges)* 4–7-13 NAdams (9) (nvr trbld ldrs) ............... ³/₄.11
2614* Ushba (FR) (57) (Fav) *(CGCox)* 4–9-1 AClark (3) (b.hind: led tl hdd & hung rt 2f
out: sn wknd) .............................................................................. hd.12
*2481²* Morpick (51) (v) *(JPLeigh)* 5–8-9 PaulEddery (2) (hmpd 1f: cl up tl wknd wl over
1f out) ..................................................................................... 1.13
2614 Virginia Cottage (43) *(BAMcMahon)* 3–7-4⁽²⁾ ‡⁷JBramhill (16) (hdwy ¹/₂-wy:
wknd over 1f out) ........................................................................ 2.14
2816⁴ Lift Boy (USA) (43) *(DenysSmith)* 3–7-11 JLowe (8) (prom 4f) .................... ¹/₂.15
2808 Granny Mc (58) *(EJAlston)* 5–9-2 GDuffield (18) (lw: in tch: effrt over 2f out:
wknd over 1f out) ........................................................................ 2¹/₂.16
2680 Cromer's Express (47) (bl) *(MissLCSiddall)* 3–8-1 KDarley (14) (lw: in tch 4f) .. 4.17
2672 Nagem (39) *(LJBarratt)* 9–7-8⁽⁴⁾ ‡³FNorton (6) (w wnr over 4f: eased whn btn) . 1.18
LONG HANDICAP: Johanna Thyme 7-6, Farndale 7-5.

**4/1** Ushba (FR), **6/1** Fighter Squadron, **13/2** Morpick, BLUE GRIT, **8/1** Granny Mc, **10/1** Lift Boy (USA), **14/1** Cool Enough, Tickham Vixen (IRE), Kalar, **16/1** Luna Bid, Johanna Thyme, Fay Eden (IRE), **33/1** Henry Will, Cromer's Express, Intrepid Fort, Nagem, **50/1** Virginia Cottage, **100/1** Farndale. CSF £91.50, CT £540.79. Tote £7.20: £1.90 £3.90 £1.60 £8.40 (£74.30). Mr C. Michael Wilson (DARLINGTON) bred by Collinstown Stud Farm Ltd. 18 Rn
1m 16 (2)
SF—41/23/36/16/22/8

T/Plpt: £99.70 (58.12 Tckts).  AA

2576—**BRIGHTON (L-H)**

**Tuesday, August 25th [Good to firm]**
Going Allowance: 0.10 sec per fur (G)  Wind: fresh half against

Stalls: low

**2943**  1892 MAYOR EWART MEDIAN AUCTION GRADUATION STKS (3-Y.O) £2984.00
(£824.00: £392.00)  **7f 214y**  2-00 (2-01)

2464² **John Rose (100)** *(PAKelleway)* 9-7 GayKelleway (3) (2nd st: led over 1f out:
rdn out) .................................................................................... —1
2475* Blue Marine (Fav) *(ACStewart)* 9-2 MRoberts (1) (lw: led over 6f: unable qckn
fnl f) ....................................................................................... 2¹/₂.2
2750 Chance to Dream (63) *(RHannon)* 9-2 JReid (2) (3rd st: wknd over 2f out: t.o) 30.3

**8/13** Blue Marine, **6/4** JOHN ROSE, **14/1** Chance to Dream(op 8/1). CSF £2.68, Tote £2.10 (£1.10). Mr Lewis H. Norris (NEWMARKET) bred by John Rose. 3 Rn
1m 37.5 (5.3)
SF—40/27/—

**2944**  PEPPER POT APP'CE (S) H'CAP (0-60) £2553.00 (£708.00: £339.00)
**1m 3f 196y**  2-30 (2-32)

2698 **Shirl (37)** *(GFHCharles-Jones)* 3–7-7⁽⁴⁾ ‡⁴PMcCabe (11) (4th st: led 2f out: r.o
wl) ......................................................................................... —1

2734⁶ John Shaw (USA) **(44)** *(JSWainwright)* 4–9–0 MichaelDenaro (6) (hdwy over 2f out: r.o wl ins fnl f) ..................................................................... ¹/₂.2
2815⁴ Ghylldale **(33)** (v) (Fav) *(RBastiman)* 4–8–3 HBastiman (14) (lw: hdwy over 2f out: hrd rdn over 1f out: unable qckn) ............................ 1¹/₂.3
2828³ Breezed Well **(57)** *(CNAllen)* 4–8–2 GForster (16) (hdwy over 4f out: 5th st: hrd rdn over 1f out: wknd fnl f) ................................................ 6.4
2805 Dr Zeva **(30)** *(MDixon)* 6–7–10 ‡⁴DToole (3) (lw: nvr nr to chal) .............. 2¹/₂.5
268⁵³ Highland Flame **(43)** (v) *(ANLee)* 3–8–3 StephenDavies (17) (led 10f) .... 1¹/₂.6
2705 Solid Steel (IRE) **(37)** (v) *(AMoore)* 4–8–7 PBowe (12) (nvr nrr) .......... s.h.7
2596 Littleton Lullaby **(23)** *(EAWheeler)* 7–7–7 AntoinetteArmes (15) (lw: hdwy 2f out: one pce) ................................................................... ¹/₂.8
Mick's Tycoon (IRE) **(58)** (bl) *(MCPipe)* 4–10–0 EHusband (2) (nvr nrr) ..... 1.9
2705 Marjons Boy **(27)** (bl) *(CDBroad)* 5–7–11 CAvery (9) (lw: 2nd st: wknd over 2f out) ......................................................................................... 2.10
2682 Pleasure Ahead **(29)** *(MDixon)* 5–7–13 NGwilliams (10) (a mid div) ...... 6.11
2630⁴ Blushing Belle **(48)** (bl) *(PFlCole)* 4–9–4 JDSmith (1) (6th st: wknd over 3f out) 2¹/₂.12
2621 Irene Lock **(30)** *(DCTucker)* 4–7–10 ‡⁴RWaterfield (13) (a bhd) ........... 2.13
2806⁴ Wayward Son **(42)** *(GLewis)* 3–7–12 ‡⁴BRussell (5) (bhd fnl 4f) ........... 12.14
2754 Rapid Rosie **(24)** (v) *(DRLaing)* 4–7–8 KimMcDonnell (4) (3rd st: wknd over 3f out) ......................................................................................... 1¹/₂.15
2394 Hills of Hoy **(35)** *(KCBailey)* 6–8–5 CMunday (8) (prom 7f) ................. 6.16
1366 Excelsis **(47)** *(JRJenkins)* 6–8–13 ‡⁴CAddington (7) (lw: a bhd) ........ 15.17

LONG HANDICAP: Shirl 7-6.

**9/2** Ghylldale, **5/1** Blushing Belle, Breezed Well(op 3/1), **7/1** Mick's Tycoon (IRE), **15/2** Wayward Son, **8/1** Highland Flame(op 5/1), **10/1** Dr Zeva, **12/1** Pleasure Ahead, **14/1** John Shaw (USA)(10/1—16/1), Hills of Hoy, **16/1** Solid Steel (IRE), **20/1** Excelsis, **25/1** Marjons Boy, Littleton Lullaby, **33/1** SHIRL & Ors. CSF £437.01, CT £2,267.14. Tote £56.40: £8.90 £2.50 £1.40 £1.60 (£1,349.00). Mr P. H. Wafford (WANTAGE) bred by The Overbury Stud. 17 Rn; No bid                                          2m 35.2 (8.2)
                                                        SF—9/29/15/27/–/–

**2945**     QUEEN'S PARK CENTENARY CHALLENGE CUP (H'cap) (0-80) £3882.50 (£1160.00:
            £555.00: £252.50)     **6f 209y**                          3-00 (3-05)

2714 **Field of Honour (78)** (Fav) *(LMCumani)* 4–9–13 LDettori (3) (lw: hdwy 2f out: led ins fnl f: pushed out) ...................................................... —1
2830⁵ Sunset Street (IRE) **(58)** *(SDow)* 4–8–7 TQuinn (8) (5th st: ev ch ins fnl f: unable qckn) ..................................................................... ³/₄.2
1110⋆ Ikteshaf **(75)** *(BHanbury)* 4–9–10 BRaymond (6) (4th st: led 2f out tl ins fnl f: one pce) ...................................................................... 1.3
2730⋆ Shining Jewel **(69)** *(MrsLPiggott)* 5–9–4 LPiggott (1) (hdwy over 1f out: r.o) .... nk.4
1412³ Mogwai (IRE) **(66)** (bl) *(RFJohnsonHoughton)* 3–8–10 AMunro (7) (6th st: r.o one pce fnl 2f) ................................................................. 1¹/₂.5
2770 Helios **(77)** *(RSimpson)* 4–9–12 JReid (5) (lw: led 2f: 2nd st: ev ch 2f out: one pce) ................................................................................ 1.6
2752³ How's Yer Father **(79)** *(RJHodges)* 6–10–0 WCarson (4) (hrd rdn over 1f out: nvr nr to chal) ................................................................ nk.7
2866² Risk Zone **(70)** (bl) *(RHannon)* 3–8–11 ‡³RPerham (10) (lw: led 5f) .......... ¹/₂.8
1174 Gabbiadini **(71)** *(MHTompkins)* 3–9–6 PRobinson (2) (c centre st: bhd fnl 3f) ..... 3.9
1994³ Sharling **(72)** *(JHMGosden)* 3–9–2 AMcGlone (9) (3rd st: wknd wl over 1f out) nk.10

**11/4** FIELD OF HONOUR(2/1—3/1), **6/1** Risk Zone, **13/2** Helios, **7/1** Shining Jewel, **8/1** How's Yer Father(op 5/1), **9/1** Ikteshaf(6/1—10/1), Sharling, Sunset Street (IRE), **12/1** Mogwai (IRE)(14/1—20/1), **25/1** Gabbiadini. CSF £25.99, CT £181.53. Tote £2.80: £1.50 £1.90 £2.30 (£15.60). Lord Portsmouth (NEWMARKET) bred by T. M. Saud. 10 Rn                                                      1m 24.6 (4.6)
                                                        SF—54/32/46/39/26/39

**2946**     BRIGHTON H'CAP (Ladies) (0-70) £2490.00 (£690.00: £330.00)
            **1m 1f 209y**                                            3-30 (3-35)

                        (Weights raised 5 lb)
211³ **Strat's Legacy (40)** *(DWPArbuthnot)* 5–9–13 MrsDArbuthnot (4) (b.hind: hdwy 6f out: 4th st: led ins fnl f: r.o wl) ............................................ —1
2202 Elegant Touch **(70)** *(MMoubarak)* 3–11–2 ‡⁵MissLFoustok (15) (2nd st: led over 1f out tl ins fnl f: unable qckn) ............................... 5.2
2708 Weeheby (USA) **(62)** *(AAScott)* 3–10–13 MissTBracegirdle (13) (lw: a.p: led over 4f out tl over 1f out: one pce) ........................ 1.3
2305⁴ Long Furlong **(52)** (Fav) *(MCPipe)* 4–10–11 MrsLPearce (9) (lw: hdwy 3f out: hrd rdn over 1f out: one pce) ....................................... hd.4
2705² Molly Splash **(53)** *(CACyzer)* 5–10–12 MissMCornelius (11) (hdwy over 2f out: hrd rdn over 1f out: one pce) ....................................... 3.5
2867⁵ The Karaoke King **(63)** *(RHannon)* 3–11–0 MrsJBoggis (1) (lw: 6th st: no hdwy fnl 3f) ............................................................................ 1.6

2833² Cathos (FR) **(51)** *(DAWilson)* 7-10-10 MissJAllison (8) (b: hdwy over 5f out: 5th st: wknd 3f out) ........................... ½.7
2602⁴ Thundering (33) *(AWJones)* 7-9-6⁽¹⁾ MissIDWJones (2) (nvr nrr) ................... ½.8
2593³ Tiger Claw **(47)** *(RJHodges)* 6-10-6 MrsJHembrow (14) (a mid div) ......... 1½.9
2566 Sonalto **(30)** *(DLWilliams)* 6-9-3 MissDPomeroy (6) (a bhd) ..................... 5.10
2678 Master Plan (FR) **(45)** *(DLWilliams)* 6-9-13⁽¹⁸⁾ ‡⁵MissVHaigh (3) (a bhd) ......... nk.11
2586² Mainly Me **(67)** *(PTWalwyn)* 3-10-13 ‡⁵MissATurner (12) (prom 5f: sddle slipped) .................... 5.12
2583 Up the Punjab **(50)** *(AMoore)* 3-9-10 ‡⁵MrsJMoore (7) (led over 5f: 3rd st: wknd over 3f out) .......................... 15.13
1952 Christian Warrior **(60)** *(REPeacock)* 3-10-6 ‡⁵MrsCPeacock (5) (a bhd) ........... 8.14
Hung Over **(32)** (bl) *(RChampion)* 6-9-0 ‡⁵MrsCWatkinson (10) (virtually ref to r) 15
LONG HANDICAP: Master Plan (FR) 8-9.

**2/1** Long Furlong, **4/1** Cathos (FR)(6/1—7/2), **8/1** Tiger Claw (USA)(op 5/1), **9/1** Thundering, **12/1** Molly Splash(op 8/1), Weeheby (USA)(op 8/1), Elegant Touch(op 7/1), Mainly Me(8/1—14/1), **14/1** The Karaoke King(10/1—16/1), **16/1** STRAT'S LEGACY, **25/1** Up the Punjab, **33/1** Hung Over, Christian Warrior, **50/1** Ors. CSF £186.61, CT £2,180.43. Tote £17.50: £4.00 £4.00 £4.40 (£340.80). Mr Jack Blumenow (COMPTON) bred by Exors of the late A. Stratton Smith. 15 Rn 2m 8 (10)
SF—23/30/25/22/17/17

## 2947
E.B.F. GARDENER WARD STKS (Mdn 2-Y.O.C & G) £2427.00 (£672.00: £321.00)
**6f 209y** 4-00 (4-01)

2269² **Ihtiraz (94)** (Fav) *(HThomsonJones)* 9-0 RHills (4) (lw: 3rd st: led on bit over 2f out: v.easily) ............................ —1
2629⁶ Giordano (IRE) *(WRMuir)* 8-11 ‡³RPerham (3) (4th st: hrd rdn over 1f out: unable qckn) ........................ 5.2
2746⁶ Queens Contractor *(MJHeaton-Ellis)* 9-0 LPiggott (5) (b.hind: led over 4f: hrd rdn over 1f out: one pce) ............... 2.3
1873 Mr Copyforce *(MissBSanders)* 9-0 MPerrett (1) (lw: lost pl over 4f out: 5th st: one pce fnl 3f) ...................... 2½.4
2584³ The Gold Souk (IRE) *(JLDunlop)* 9-0 TQuinn (2) (2nd st: wknd over 2f out) ..... 15.5

**1/5** IHTIRAZ(4/11—2/5), **13/2** The Gold Souk (IRE)(7/2—7/1), **8/1** Queens Contractor, **33/1** Giordano (IRE), **66/1** Mr Copyforce. CSF £7.30, Tote £1.20: £1.10 £4.60 (£6.40). Mr Hamdan Al-Maktoum (NEWMARKET) bred by Shadwell Estate Company Limited. 5 Rn 1m 26 (6)
SF—20/2/–/–/–

## 2948
QUEEN'S PARK SPA STKS (Mdn 2-Y.O) £2070.00 (£570.00: £270.00)
**5f 213y** 4-30 (4-36)

2108³ **Jallaaf (USA)** *(LMCumani)* 9-0 LDettori (2) (lw: 4th st: led over 1f out: r.o wl) .... —1
2459⁶ Inderaputeri *(MissGayKelleway)* 8-9 AMunro (6) (b.nr hind: 6th st: hrd rdn over 1f out: r.o wl ins fnl f) ................. 3.2
2619² Mawayed (USA) (Fav) *(PTWalwyn)* 9-0 WCarson (8) (3rd st: ev ch over 1f out: unable qckn) ............................. 2.3
2459³ Tajarib (IRE) *(JLDunlop)* 8-9 TQuinn (4) (5th st: n.m.r over 2f out: one pce) ....... 3.4
2577⁴ Marwell Mitzi **(55)** *(WGRWightman)* 8-9 (dwlt: nvr nr to chal) ................. 5.5
2826⁴ Pat Poindestres *(MPMuggeridge)* 8-9 BRouse (7) (led over 4f) .................... 2.6
1384 Mouchez le Nez (IRE) *(JAkehurst)* 8-9 JReid (10) (a bhd) ............................ 2.7
2619⁵ Bold a Maiden *(DRLaing)* 8-9 TyroneWilliams (1) (lw: 2nd st: wknd over 2f out) . 6.8
Dance Magical *(MDixon)* 8-9 DaleGibson (5) (unf: bit bkwd: s.s: a wl bhd: t.o fnl 4f) ................................. 30.9
*2826 Jest Rosie (50/1) Withdrawn (ref to ent stalls) : not under orders*

**11/8** Mawayed (USA)(op 5/2), **3/1** Tajarib (IRE)(9/4—4/1), **9/2** Inderaputeri(8/1—4/1), **6/1** JALLAAF (USA)(op 3/1), **16/1** Pat Poindestres(op 8/1), **25/1** Marwell Mitzi, **50/1** Ors. CSF £30.53, Tote £5.50: £1.70 £1.10 £1.30 (£16.10). Sheikh Ahmed Al Maktoum (NEWMARKET) bred by Four Fifths Stable in USA. 9 Rn 1m 12.3 (3.9)
SF—34/17/14/–/–/–

## 2949
FRIENDS OF QUEEN'S PARK H'CAP (3-Y.O) (0-70) £2364.00 (£654.00: £312.00)
**5f 213y** 5-00 (5-01)

2831⁵ **Sure Lord (IRE) (68)** *(WRMuir)* 9-5 WCarson (1) (lw: 4th st: led 1f out: r.o wl) .. —1
2595² Savalaro **(52)** *(JFfitch-Heyes)* 8-3 TQuinn (8) (lw: led 5f: unable qckn) .............. 2.2
2496 Duty Sergeant (IRE) **(49)** (bl) *(MPMuggeridge)* 7-9 ‡⁵DHarrison (9) (hdwy over 2f out: hrd rdn over 1f out: one pce) ...................... 1½.3
2520 Panchellita (USA) **(62)** (bl) (Fav) *(JSutcliffe)* 8-13 BRouse (3) (lw: hdwy 2f out: hrd rdn over 1f out: one pce) ............. ¾.4
2822 Myasha (USA) **(70)** (bl) *(MrsLPiggott)* 9-7 LPiggott (4) (b.hind: lw: nvr nr to chal) ...................... 3½.5
2808⁵ Followmegirls **(62)** *(MrsALMKing)* 8-13 JReid (2) (5th st: wknd over 2f out) .... 2½.6

2822　Red Verona **(48)** *(EAWheeler)* 7-8[6] ‡5ATucker (6) (lw: 6th st: wknd over 2f out) .... ½.7
2821　Paradise Forum **(64)** (v) *(CAHorgan)* 9-1 AMunro (5) (lw: 3rd st: wknd over 2f
out) ......................................................................................................................................... 3.8
2595★　Treasure Time (IRE) **(64)** *(JWhite)* 9-1 DaleGibson (10) (lw: 2nd st: wknd over
1f out) ................................................................................................................................... nk.9
2303　Smudgemupum **(47)** (v) *(MissBSanders)* 7-5 ‡7AntoinetteArmes (7) (a bhd) .... 6.10
LONG HANDICAP: Red Verona 7-5.

**11/8** Panchellita (USA), **5/1** Treasure Time (IRE), **13/2** Savalaro, **7/1** SURE LORD (IRE), **12/1** Myasha (USA)(op
8/1), Paradise Forum, **14/1** Followmegirls, **16/1** Duty Sergeant (IRE), Red Verona, **25/1** Smudgemupum. CSF
£49.52, CT £647.90. Tote £7.00: £1.80 £2.40 £2.70 (£17.50). The Sussex Stud Limited (LAMBOURN) bred by
Dana Stud Ltd and Sussex Stud Ltd in Ireland. 10 Rn　　　　　　　　　　　　　　　　1m 12.2 (3.8)
SF—41/17/8/18/12/–

T/Plpt: £1,344.10 (2.35 Tckts).　　　　　　　　　　　　　　　　　　　　　　　　　　　　　　　　AK

# BRIGHTON (L-H)
## Wednesday, August 26th [Good to firm]
Going Allowance: nil sec per fur (G)　　　　　　　　　　　　Wind: fresh half against

Stalls: low

**2950**　　SEAGULLS STKS (Mdn) £2070.00 (£570.00: £270.00)　　**5f 213y**　　2-15 (2-16)

2475[2]　**Silica (USA) (63)** (Fav) *(JHMGosden)* 3-8-9 SCauthen (4) (lw: 3rd st: led over
2f out: rdn out) ...................................................................................................................... —1
1320　N̶e̶s̶t̶ **(58)** *(LordHuntingdon)* 3-8-9 MRoberts (3) (lw: 2nd st: led over 3f out tl
over 2f out: ev ch ins fnl f: unable qckn) ................................................................... 2.2
2680[3]　Gizlaan (USA) **(56)** *(BHanbury)* 3-8-9 LPiggott (5) (4th st: nrd rdn over 1f out:
one pce) ............................................................................................................................. 2½.3
2545　Abbey Green *(CJHill)* 4-9-4 NAdams (2) (lw: s.s: 5th st: a bhd) .......................... 6.4
2866　Bright Sea (USA) **(34)** (bl) *(WRWilliams)* 4-9-4 NHowe (1) (lw: led over 2f) ...... 10.5

**4/5** SILICA (USA)(4/6—Evens), **11/4** Nest, **3/1** Gizlaan (USA), **100/1** Ors. CSF £3.23, Tote £1.70: £1.50 £2.20
(£2.20). Sheikh Mohammed (NEWMARKET) bred by Kentucky Heritage T'bred Breeding Prtnrs II in USA. 5 Rn
1m 11.7 (3.3)
SF—29/21/11/–/–/–

**2951**　　SADDLESCOMBE STKS (Mdn 2-Y.O) £2616.00 (£726.00: £348.00)
**6f 209y**　　2-45 (2-47)

2653[2]　**Declassified (USA)** (Fav) *(LMCumani)* 9-0 LDettori (10) (lw: 5th st: led 2f out:
rdn out) ................................................................................................................................ —1
　　　Stitchcombe *(PWChapple-Hyam)* 9-0 WCarson (1) (str: bkwd: 3rd st: hrd rdn
over 1f out: r.o wl ins fnl f) ......................................................................................... 1½.2
2405[3]　Royal Flex (USA) *(MrsLPiggott)* 8-9 LPiggott (5) (4th st: ev ch whn n.m.r 1f out:
unable qckn) ....................................................................................................................... ½.3
2426[4]　Leave a Kiss *(IABalding)* 8-9 AMunro (3) (lw: led 5f: one pce fnl f) ............... s.h.4
1635[5]　Villavina *(SDow)* 8-9 JWilliams (6) (6th st: rdn over 1f out: r.o ins fnl f) ............... ¾.5
2584[4]　Lidoma (IRE) *(JLDunlop)* 8-9 GDuffield (4) (lw: rdn & no hdwy fnl 3f) ................... 5.6
　　　Candarela *(PHowling)* 8-9 JQuinn (9) (leggy: dwlt: a bhd) ................................. 4.7
2802　Generous Ben *(JSutcliffe)* 9-0 BRouse (8) (a bhd) ............................................. 8.8
2438　Malzeta (IRE) *(MJHeaton-Ellis)* 8-9 LPiggott (7) (lw: 2nd st: wknd over 2f out) .... 6.9
　　　Sea Syrah (IRE) *(MBlanshard)* 9-0 NCarlisle (2) (w'like: bkwd: s.s: a wl bhd) ... 3.10

**4/9** DECLASSIFIED (USA)(op 4/6), **5/1** Royal Flex (USA), **8/1** Stitchcombe(op 7/1), **12/1** Leave a Kiss(op 7/1),
**20/1** Villavina(op 8/1), Lidoma (IRE)(op 8/1), **50/1** Malzeta (IRE), **100/1** Ors. CSF £5.15, Tote £1.50: £1.10
£1.40 £1.20 (£4.50). Mr Edward P. Evans (NEWMARKET) bred by E.P.Evans, Foxfield T'breds Inc & P.M.Brant in
USA. 10 Rn　　　　　　　　　　　　　　　　　　　　　　　　　　　　　　　　　　　　1m 24.7 (4.7)
SF—30/25/18/17/15/–

**2952**　　NEWHAVEN (S) H'CAP (3, 4 & 5-Y.O) (0-60) £2679.00 (£744.00: £357.00)
**7f 214y**　　3-15 (3-18)

2828[2]　**Anatroccolo (40)** *(RABennett)* 5–9-1 LDettori (2) (mde all: hrd rdn over 1f out:
all out) ................................................................................................................................. —1
2712[2]　Seaside Minstrel **(50)** (Fav) *(CJHill)* 4-9-11 WCarson (10) (lw: gd hdwy over 1f
out: str run fnl f: fin wl) .............................................................................................. s.h.2
2729[2]　Broad Appeal **(38)** *(RCSpicer)* 4-8-13 GDuffield (12) (3rd st: hrd rdn over 1f
out: r.o wl ins fnl f) ...................................................................................................... hd.3

2770 Breakdancer (IRE) **(51)** *(WRMuir)* 3–9-3 ‡³RPerham (6) (6th st: hrd rdn over 1f out: r.o one pce) .................................................................................................. 2.4

2712* Precious Air (IRE) **(52)** *(AMoore)* 4–9-13 BRouse (15) (swtg: 5th st: hrd rdn over 1f out: one pce) ........................................................................................ hd.5

2729 Dublin Indemnity (USA) **(42)** *(NACallaghan)* 3–8-4 ‡⁷JTate (9) (hdwy 2f out: hrd rdn over 1f out: r.o one pce) ................................................................... 1¹/₂.6

2865 Genuine Lady **(53)** *(APJarvis)* 4–10-0 LPiggott (5) (hdwy 2f out: nvr nrr) ......... 1¹/₂.7

2772 Sunley Sparkle **(46)** *(DRGandolfo)* 4–9-7 JQuinn (13) (lw: nvr nr to chal) ...... 1.8

2712 Litmore Dancer **(46)** *(JMBradley)* 4–9-7 JWilliams (14) (hdwy over 2f out: wknd over 1f out) ......................................................................................... 3¹/₂.9

2829 China Sky **(41)** *(CNAllen)* 4–8-9 ‡⁷GForster (8) (a mid div) ............................. 3.10

2712³ Simon Ellis (IRE) **(47)** *(DRLaing)* 3–8-11 ‡⁵ATucker (17) (lw: nvr nrr) ............. 2.11

2705 Moving Force **(40)** *(EAWheeler)* 5–8-12 ‡³FNorton (16) (lw: bhd fnl 2f) ......... 2¹/₂.12

2881 Golden Proposal **(42)** *(MJBolton)* 3–8-11 AMunro (11) (lw: 2nd st: wknd over 2f out) ........................................................................................................ 1¹/₂.13

2708 Allimac Nomis **(43)** *(ICampbell)* 3–8-5 ‡⁷SMulvey (1) (4th st: wknd over 2f out) 12.14

2882 Two Birds **(43)** (bl) *(CAHorgan)* 3–8-12 TyroneWilliams (7) (a bhd) ............... 15.15

2586⁴ Bounder Rowe **(40)** *(JFfitch-Heyes)* 5–8-10 ‡⁵DHarrison (3) (mid div whn fell over 4f out) .................................................................................................... 0

**11/2** Seaside Minstrel(4/1—6/1), **13/2** ANATROCCOLO, **7/1** Precious Air (IRE)(op 9/2), Allimac Nomis(5/1—8/1), **8/1** Simon Ellis (IRE), **9/1** Broad Appeal, **10/1** Dublin Indemnity (USA), **12/1** Genuine Lady, **14/1** Moving Force, Breakdancer (IRE), Litmore Dancer, **20/1** China Sky, Bounder Rowe, **25/1** Ors. CSF £42.31, CT £301.45. Tote £6.50: £1.40 £1.40 £2.60 £3.30 (£6.70). Miss Samantha Dare (MAIDENHEAD) bred by Thoroughbred Holdings International. 16 Rn; No bid　　　　　　　　　　　　　　　　　　　　　　1m 37.4 (5.2)

SF—23/32/19/17/26/–

**2953**　　GEORGE ROBEY CHALLENGE TROPHY (H'cap) (0-70) £3288.00 (£984.00: £472.00: £216.00)　**6f 209y**　　　　　　　　　　　　　　　　　　　3-45 (3-49)
　　　　　　(Weights raised 3 lb)

2822⁵ **Coniston Lake (IRE) (61)** (bl) *(GLewis)* 3–9-4 BRouse (15) (b.hind: lw: hdwy over 1f out: rdn fnl f: led nr fin) ..................................................................... —1

2772* Ain'tlifelikethat **(54)** (bl) *(TJNaughton)* 5–9-2 GCarter (11) (hdwy over 2f out: led over 1f out: hrd rdn fnl f: hdd nr fin) ............................................. ¹/₂.2

2822³ Sure Shot Norman **(47)** *(JSutcliffe)* 3–7-11 ‡⁷JTate (10) (lw: 4th st: led 2f out tl over 1f out: one pce) ....................................................................... 2¹/₂.3

2582⁴ Old Comrades **(54)** *(LGCottrell)* 5–9-2 TRogers (13) (lw: hdwy over 1f out: r.o ins fnl f) ........................................................................................ ³/₄.4

1947 Charmed Knave **(52)** *(DRLaing)* 7–9-0 TyroneWilliams (4) (6th st: ev ch over 1f out: one pce) ............................................................................................ s.h.5

2865⁶ Rock Band (IRE) **(65)** *(LMCumani)* 3–9-8 LDettori (14) (5th st: one pce fnl 2f) s.h.6

2750 Aldahe **(40)** (Jt-Fav) *(BRMillman)* 7–8-2 AMunro (9) (lw: nvr nr to chal) ...... 1.7

2583² Dancing Beau (IRE) **(61)** *(MrsLPiggott)* 3–9-4 LPiggott (7) (lw: nvr nrr) ........ 2.8

2881 Juvenara **(38)** (Jt-Fav) *(CJHill)* 6–8-0 WCarson (16) (nvr nrr) ....................... 1.9

2714 Asterix **(54)** (v) *(JMBradley)* 4–9-2 JWilliams (3) (lw: nvr nrr) .................... ¹/₂.10

2581⁴ Restore **(47)** (bl) *(RVoorspuy)* 9–8-9 SDawson (18) (lw: nvr nrr) ............... 1¹/₂.11

2865⁴ Tom's Apache **(44)** *(WRWilliams)* 3–8-1 NAdams (2) (nvr nrr) ................... 1.12

2468² Susanna's Secret **(46)** (bl) *(WCarter)* 5–8-13 ‡⁵NGwilliams (5) (led 5f) ....... ¹/₂.13

2752* Grey Charmer (IRE) **(55)** *(CJames)* 3–8-12 DaleGibson (1) (lw: a bhd) ......... 2¹/₂.14

2770 Caromish (USA) **(57)** *(MDIUsher)* 5–9-2 ‡³RPerham (17) (3rd st: wknd over 2f out) ............................................................................................................. nk.15

2723⁵ La Kermesse (USA) **(59)** *(JHMGosden)* 3–9-2 SCauthen (6) (lw: hdwy over 2f out: eased whn btn over 1f out) ........................................................... 2¹/₂.16

2632⁵ Prince of Darkness (IRE) **(67)** *(SirMarkPrescott)* 3–9-10 GDuffield (12) (2nd st: wknd over 2f out) ........................................................................ 7.17

**7/1** Aldahe, Juvenara, **8/1** Sure Shot Norman, **9/1** Ain'tlifelikethat, **10/1** Prince of Darkness (IRE), Dancing Beau (IRE), Rock Band (IRE), **12/1** Grey Charmer (IRE), Susanna's Secret, Old Comrades, La Kermesse (USA), **14/1** Charmed Knave, **16/1** Caromish (USA), CONISTON LAKE (IRE), Tom's Apache, **20/1** Restore. CSF £153.84, CT £1,151.42. Tote £52.20: £10.90 £1.70 £2.30 £3.90 (£148.50). Mr K. Higson (EPSOM) bred by K. Molloy in Ireland. 17 Rn　　　　　　　　　　　　　　　　　　　　　　　　1m 23.9 (3.9)

SF—46/42/15/32/29/36

**2954**　　LANCING STKS (Mdn) £2070.00 (£570.00: £270.00)　　**1m 1f 209y**　　4-15 (4-17)

1971 **Busman (IRE) (64)** *(MajorWRHern)* 3–8-13 WCarson (6) (mde all: rdn out) ....... —1

Brecon Beacons (IRE) *(RCharlton)* 3–8-8 LDettori (1) (5th st: rdn over 2f out: unable qckn) ........................................................................................ 6.2

2620² Annacurragh (IRE) (Fav) *(ACStewart)* 3–8-8 MRoberts (5) (2nd st: hrd rdn over 4f out: one pce) .............................................................................. 1.3

302 Tiffany Gem (IRE) *(LordHuntingdon)* 3–8-8 DaleGibson (7) (lw: 3rd st: hrd rdn over 2f out: one pce) ............................................................................... 2.4

2769⁶ Summer Cruise *(ANLee)* 3-8-13 JQuinn (4) (nvr nr to chal) ............................... 6.5
　　　Jackson Square (IRE) *(WGMTurner)* 4-9-7 TSprake (3) (str: scope: bit bkwd:
　　　　4th st: wknd over 2f out) ............................................................. 2½.6
　2254 Pearl Ransom **(46)** *(WGRWightman)* 5-9-2 JWilliams (2) (lw: 6th st: wknd over
　　　2f out) ................................................................................. 3½.7

**8/11** Annacurragh (IRE), **9/4** Brecon Beacons (IRE)(6/4—5/2), **13/2** BUSMAN (IRE), **33/1** Summer Cruise,
Tiffany Gem (IRE), **100/1** Ors. CSF £19.71, Tote £7.60: £2.00 £1.40 (£6.50). Lord Weinstock (LAMBOURN)
bred by Ballymacoll Stud Farm Ltd in Ireland. 7 Rn 　　　　　　　　　　　　　　　　2m 7.3 (9.3)
　　　　　　　　　　　　　　　　　　　　　　　　　　　　　　　SF—6/–/–/–/–/–

**2955**　　　ROTTINGDEAN H'CAP (0-70) £2553.00 (£708.00: £339.00)　**1m 3f 196y** 4-45 (4-49)
　　　　　　　　　(Weights raised 5 lb)

2757² **Atlantic Way (36)** *(CJHill)* 4-7-11 ‡³FNorton (4) (2nd st: led 2f out: comf) .......... —1
　2759 Rocquaine Bay **(42)** *(MJBolton)* 5-8-6 JWilliams (2) (5th st: r.o one pce fnl 2f) .. 6.2
　2255³ Shamshom Al Arab (IRE) **(38)** *(WCarter)* 4-8-2 DBiggs (3) (lw: 3rd st: ev ch 2f
　　　out: one pce) ......................................................................... nk.3
25756 Moon Spin **(70)** *(MajorWRHern)* 3-9-10 WCarson (6) (a.p: led over 4f out to 2f
　　　out: one pce) ......................................................................... ½.4
*2484*⁴ Pie Hatch (IRE) **(45)** **(Fav)** *(SirMarkPrescott)* 3-7-13 GDuffield (1) (lw: 4th st:
　　　wknd over 2f out) .................................................................... 15.5
1766* Snow Blizzard **(57)** *(SDow)* 4-9-7 LPiggott (5) (lw: led over 7f: 6th st: t.o) ........ 30.6

**3/1** Pie Hatch (IRE), **7/2** Moon Spin(op 2/1), **9/2** Snow Blizzard, ATLANTIC WAY, **6/1** Shamshom Al Arab (IRE),
**13/2** Rocquaine Bay. CSF £28.28, Tote £6.00: £2.00 £2.00 £3.90 (£15.80). Mr C. John Hill (BARNSTAPLE) bred by
Mrs M. L. Parry and P. M. Steele-Mortimer. 6 Rn 　　　　　　　　　　　　　　　2m 32.6 (5.6)
　　　　　　　　　　　　　　　　　　　　　　　　　　　　　SF—27/24/19/39/–/–

T/Plpt: £126.50 (32.25 Tckts).　　　　　　　　　　　　　　　　　　　　　　　　　AK

2661—**REDCAR (L-H)**

**Wednesday, August 26th [Good to firm becoming Good]**

Going Allowance: Races 1-5: minus 0.30 sec; Race 6: minus 0.05 (F)　Wind: fresh half bhd

Stalls: high

**2956**　　FURNITURE FACTORS RACING SCHOOLS APP'CE H'CAP (0-80) £3080.00 (£920.00:
　　　　　£440.00: £200.00)　**6f**　　　　　　　　　　　2-00 (2-01)

　　　　　　　　　(Weights raised 1 lb)

2808* **Flashy's Son (60)** **(Fav)** *(MDHammond)* 4-8-6 ‡⁴ALakeman (4) (b.off hind:
　　　chsd ldrs: led over 1f out: r.o wl) ................................................. —1
2772² Almasa **(58)** *(DMorris)* 4-8-8 StephenDavies (1) (lw: sn wl outpcd: hdwy 2f out:
　　　nt qckn fnl f) ....................................................................... 1½.2
*2786*³ Soba Guest (IRE) **(70)** *(JBerry)* 3-8-8 ‡⁸SPorritt (8) (b.nr hind: led tl over 1f out:
　　　one pce) ............................................................................. ½.3
　2925 Educated Pet **(78)** *(MJohnston)* 3-9-6 ‡⁴MBaird (3) (s.i.s: hdwy ½-wy: ev ch
　　　over 1f out: kpt on same pce) ..................................................... 1.4
　2604² Arc Lamp **(62)** *(JAGlover)* 6-8-12 SMaloney (9) (sn chsng ldrs: effrt over 2f out:
　　　nt qckn over 1f out) ................................................................ ¾.5
　2406 State Flyer **(64)** **(v)** *(CBBooth)* 4-9-0 FArrowsmith (7) (lw: s.s: outpcd & bhd:
　　　hdwy over 1f out: styd on wl nr fin) ............................................. nk.6
　2604⁴ Prince Belfort **(69)** *(MPNaughton)* 4-9-5 JWeaver (5) (chsd ldrs: edgd lft u.p 2f
　　　out: sn lost pl) ..................................................................... 1½.7
　2564⁴ Simmie's Special **(60)** *(RHollinshead)* 4-8-10 AGarth (10) (chsd ldrs: edgd lft
　　　thrght: wknd 2f out) ................................................................ ½.8
2942⁴ Henry Will **(43)** *(TFairhurst)* 8-7-3 ‡⁴ClaireBalding (6) (sn outpcd & bhd) ........... 3.9
　2813 Stormswept (USA) **(59)** *(MBrittain)* 3-8-5 JMarshall (2) (lw: s.i.s: a outpcd &
　　　bhd) ................................................................................. 7.10

　　　　　　　　LONG HANDICAP: Henry Will 7-1.

**11/4** FLASHY'S SON, **5/1** Almasa, **7/1** Arc Lamp, Prince Belfort, **15/2** Soba Guest (IRE), **8/1** State Flyer, **11/1**
Educated Pet, **12/1** Simmie's Special, **14/1** Henry Will, **20/1** Stormswept (USA). CSF £16.21, CT £84.69. Tote
£3.90: £1.90 £1.90 £2.70 (£8.60). Lee Construction (Newcastle) Ltd (MIDDLEHAM) bred by Brian A. Shovelton
(North Wales) Ltd. 10 Rn 　　　　　　　　　　　　　　　　　　　　　　　　　1m 10.6 (1.3)
　　　　　　　　　　　　　　　　　　　　　　　　　　　　　　SF—30/26/24/32/21/22

**2957**　　RUNSWICK BAY CLAIMING STKS　£2637.00 (£732.00: £351.00)
　　　　　**1m 5f 135y**　　　　　　　　　　　　　　　2-30 (2-31)

2870* **Expansionist (62)** **(Fav)** *(SPCWoods)* 3-8-4 WRyan (1) (chsd ldrs: led over 3f
　　　out: hld on wl cl home) ............................................................ —1

2870³ Cov Tel Lady (66) *(MHTompkins)* 3-8-7 PRobinson (6) (hld up: hdwy over 3f
out: ev ch ins fnl f: nt qckn nr fin) ....................................... s.h.2

2906* Silver Samurai (67) *(RHollinshead)* 3-7-13 ‡⁷AGarth (11) (lw: hld up: stdy hdwy
on outside 3f out: nt qckn fnl f) .............................. 1½.3

2613* Grouse-N-Heather (65) *(MrsGRReveley)* 3-8-7 JFanning (5) (lw: trckd ldrs:
effrt & ev ch 2f out: no imp) ................................ hd.4

2820⁶ Magic Secret (67) *(PCHaslam)* 4-8-13 ‡⁵JWeaver (7) (lw: plld hrd: trckd ldrs:
effrt over 2f out: one pce) .................................. 3.5

2836 Suez Canal (IRE) (75) *(PWChapple-Hyam)* 3-9-0 PaulEddery (10) (trckd ldrs:
drvn along over 2f out: no imp) ........................... ¾.6

1866 Topcliffe (37) (v) *(MrsVAAconley)* 5-8-13 LCharnock (2) (lw: led & plld hrd: hdd
over 3f out: sn wknd) ......................................... 8.7

2701⁴ Mr News (IRE) (42) (v) *(BBeasley)* 3-8-4⁽⁵⁾ ‡⁵SWilliams (4) (lw: plld hrd: trckd
ldrs: drvn along over 3f out: nt r.o) ...................... 1½.8

1976 Izitallworthit *(JMackie)* 3-8-1 GHind (12) (s.i.s: a in rr) .................. 3.9

1520 Grey Realm (30) *(REBarr)* 4-8-9 SWebster (1) (a in rr) .................. 6.10

1510² Double Sherry *(RMWhitaker)* 3-7-12⁽⁴⁾ ‡⁷GParkin (3) (plld hrd: chsd ldrs tl lost pl
6f out) ............................................................ 1.11

Dancing Days (bl) *(JParkes)* 6-8-7 ‡⁷VHalliday (8) (bhd: sme hdwy 5f out: wknd
over 3f out) ..................................................... 2½.12

Magdalene Heights (26) *(DRFranks)* 4-8-10 DMcKeown (9) (plld hrd: hdwy &
in tch ½-wy: lost pl over 5f out: sn wl bhd: dead) ........... 30.13

11/4 EXPANSIONIST, 7/2 Grouse-N-Heather, 9/2 Suez Canal (IRE), 6/1 Silver Samurai, Magic Secret, 10/1 Cov
Tel Lady, 33/1 Double Sherry, 50/1 Izitallworthit, Topcliffe, Mr News (IRE), 66/1 Dancing Days, 100/1 Grey
Realm, 150/1 Magdalene Heights. CSF £27.36, Tote £3.70: £2.10 £2.10 £1.70 (£23.90). High Point Bloodstock
Ltd (NEWMARKET) bred by N. E. and Mrs Poole. 13 Rn; Magic Secret clmd P Douglas £8,005,
Grouse-N-Heather clmd D. Fairbairn £11,100, Expansionist clmd R Hale £8,010　　　　　2m 59.9 (8.9)

---

**2958**　　　TETLEY BITTER H'CAP (0-90) £4142.50 (£1240.00: £595.00: £272.50)
　　　　　　7f

　　　　　　　　　　　　　　　　　　　　　　　　　　　　　　3-00 (3-02)

(Weights raised 2 lb)

2813 **Thewaari (USA) (65)** *(AAScott)* 3-8-8 BRaymond (10) (lw: s.i.s: hld up: hdwy
over 2f out: r.o wl u.p to ld wl ins fnl f) ...................... —1

2684³ Tender Moment (IRE) (67) *(CEBrittain)* 4-9-1 RCochrane (3) (lw: chsd ldrs: led
over 1f out: r.o u.p) ............................................ ½.2

2676* Ballad Dancer (56) *(EJAlston)* 7-8-4 GBaxter (14) (chsd ldrs stands' side:
hdwy over 1f out: styd on wl nr fin) ...................... nk.3

2732* Gymcrak Tycoon (74) *(MHEasterby)* 3-9-3 MBirch (1) (hld up: hdwy & prom
½-wy: nt qckn fnl f) ......................................... s.h.4

2813 Northern Spark (53) *(CWThornton)* 4-8-1 GHind (13) (lw: led stands' side to
½-wy: led over 2f out tl over 1f out: r.o same pce) ...... ½.5

2126 La Bamba (74) *(GAPritchard-Gordon)* 6-8-9 WHood (8) (lw: dwlt: bhd tl hdwy
over 2f out: rdn & r.o fnl f: nt rch ldrs) ................... s.h.6

2770⁶ Shake Town (USA) (73) (v) *(MHTompkins)* 4-9-7 PRobinson (2) (sn bhd: hdwy
over 2f out: kpt on u.p: nvr able to chal) ................ ½.7

2722* Amazing Feat (IRE) (71) (Fav) *(MrsGRReveley)* 3-9-0 KDarley (9) (lw: trckd
ldrs: effrt & outpcd over 2f out: styd on fnl f) .......... ½.8

2714⁵ Annabelle Royale (76) *(MrsNMacauley)* 6-9-5 ‡⁵SWilliams (6) (w ldrs tl lost pl 2f
out) .............................................................. 1½.9

1508 Super Benz (76) *(TFairhurst)* 6-9-10 JFanning (11) (stumbled & lost pl ½-wy:
n.d after) ...................................................... 2½.10

2668 Quiet Victory (45) (v) *(MissLCSiddall)* 5-7-7 JLowe (5) (gd spd far side 4f) .... s.h.11

2785³ Long Lane Lady (50) *(JMackie)* 6-7-12 SWood (4) (chsd ldrs far side tl lost pl
over 2f out) ................................................... ½.12

2637³ Glenstal Princess (59) *(RHollinshead)* 5-8-0 ‡⁷AGarth (12) (lw: hdwy ½-wy: lost
pl 2f out) ...................................................... nk.13

2658 Act of Union (IRE) (72) *(BBeasley)* 3-9-1 LCharnock (15) (chsd ldr stands'
side: led ½-wy tl over 2f out: sn wknd) ................. ½.14

2723² Young Valentine (65) *(RMWhitaker)* 3-8-8 AClhane (7) (bhd fnl 2f) ....... 12.15

4/1 Amazing Feat (IRE)(op 6/1), 6/1 Shake Town (USA), 8/1 La Bamba, Gymcrak Tycoon, 9/1 Tender Moment
(IRE), 10/1 Northern Spark, Ballad Dancer, 12/1 Glenstal Princess, Annabelle Royale, Act of Union (IRE), 14/1
Young Valentine, THEWAARI (USA), Super Benz, 25/1 Ors. CSF £134.47, CT £1,222.40. Tote £15.10: £5.80
£2.80 £3.80 (£68.50). Mr Saeed Suhail (NEWMARKET) bred by John Franks in USA. 15 Rn　1m 23.8 (1.6)
　　　　　　　　　　　　　　　　　　　　　　　　　　SF—39/44/32/44/26/46/40

---

**2959**　　　YORKSHIRE TELEVISION H'CAP (0-70) £2616.00 (£726.00: £348.00)
　　　　　　1m 3f

　　　　　　　　　　　　　　　　　　　　　　　　　　　　　　3-30 (3-33)

(Weights raised 5 lb)

2926⁶ Sinclair Lad (IRE) (61) *(RHollinshead)* 4-9-10 WRyan (11) (lw: hld up: stdy
hdwy 3f out: rdn & swtchd appr fnl f: styd on to ld nr fin) .... —1

2725* Retender (USA) **(70)** (Fav) *(LMCumani)* 3–9-5 ‡⁵JWeaver (6) (b.hind: lw: trckd ldrs: bdly hmpd ent st: rdn to ld over 1f out: r.o) ............... nk.**2**

2810⁴ First Bid **(56)** *(RMWhitaker)* 5–9-5 JFanning (8) (trckd ldrs: led over 4f out tl over 2f out one pce) ........................................ 5.**3**

2357⁵ Marowins **(50)** *(EJAlston)* 3–8-4 KFallon (12) (sn bhd: styd on wl u.p fnl 2f: nt rch ldrs) ................................................................. nk.**4**

2775 Sharquin **(30)** *(MBrittain)* 5–7-7 JLowe (5) (trckd ldrs: rdn to ld over 2f out: hdd & wknd over 1f out) ................................................. 3.**5**

2677 Fairgroundprincess **(32)** *(FHLee)* 4–7-9 GBardwell (1) (b: lw: chsd ldrs: stumbled bdly ent st: kpt on same pce fnl 3f) ................ s.h.**6**

2605⁶ Red Jam Jar **(30)** *(JMackie)* 3–7-7 SWood (7) (b: lw: chsd ldrs: ev ch tl rdn & outpcd fnl 2f) ................................................... 1.**7**

2698 Wild Strawberry **(61)** (v) *(JMPEustace)* 3–9-1 MTebbutt (14) (hld up & plld hrd: slipped bdly ent st: sme hdwy 2f out: n.d) ............ 3½.**8**

2732 Reilton **(56)** *(JParkes)* 5–9-0 ‡⁵OPears (13) (sn bhd) .......................... 8.**9**

Dara Loch (IRE) **(39)** *(MrsJRRamsden)* 4–8-2 GBaxter (3) (mid div: plld hrd: effrt & rdn over 2f out: sn wknd) ................................. 5.**10**

*1850*⁵ Miss Hyde (USA) **(55)** (bl) *(JAGlover)* 3–8-9 JFortune (4) (trckd ldr: led & slipped bdly ent st: sn hdd & wknd) ....................... 1½.**11**

Rudda Cass **(30)** *(MrsVAAconley)* 6–8-7-7 LCharnock (2) (led tl hdd, slipped bdly & bdly hmpd ent st: sn bhd) ................................ 20.**12**

Fiery Sun **(37)** (v) *(REBarr)* 7–7-7⁽⁵⁾ ‡⁷AGarth (9) (chsd ldrs tl stumbled bdly appr st: sn lost pl) .................................................. 13

2775 Waaza (USA) **(60)** (bl) *(AAScott)* 3–9-0 BRaymond (10) (lw: reard bdly s: a wl t.o) ......................................................................... 14

LONG HANDICAP: Red Jam Jar 7-2.

**6/4** Retender (USA), **6/1** First Bid, **15/2** SINCLAIR LAD (IRE), **9/1** Fairgroundprincess, **11/1** Marowins, **12/1** Miss Hyde (USA), Waaza (USA), **14/1** Wild Strawberry, **20/1** Dara Loch (IRE), Sharquin, Red Jam Jar, Reilton, **50/1** Fiery Sun, **100/1** Rudda Cass. CCF £10.07, CT £72.58. Tote £7.50: £2.50 £1.40 £1.60 (£8.30). Sinclair Developments Limited (UPPER LONGDON) bred by John Burns in Ireland. 14 Rn        2m £0.5 (4.8)
SF—29/23/13/–/–/–

---

**2960**        ANDERSONS NURSERY   £2831.50 (£784.00: £374.50)   **5f**        4-00 (4-06)

2418⁴ Sheila's Secret (IRE) **(84)** (Fav) *(WCarter)* 9-2 KDarley (6) (b.nr hind: chsd ldrs: r.o u.p to ld jst ins fnl f) .......................... —**1**

2437⁶ Trevorsninepoints **(64)** *(MJRyan)* 7-10 GBardwell (7) (led: rdn & hung lft ½-wy: nt qckn fnl f) ............................................. 1.**2**

2740² Hotaria **(70)** *(RMWhitaker)* 8-2 ACulhane (10) (lw: stdd & swtchd lft s: hdwy ½-wy: rdn & nt qckn over 1f out) ......................... 3.**3**

2532⁵ Field of Vision (IRE) **(61)** *(MJohnston)* 7-0 ‡⁷MBaird (1) (cl up tl lost pl over 1f out: kpt on nr fin) ....................................... 1.**4**

2264⁶ Arkendale Diamond (USA) **(66)** *(BBeasley)* 7-12 LCharnock (8) (chsd ldrs: nt qckn fnl f) ........................................................ 1.**5**

*2482*⁴ Dream a Bit **(70)** *(JGFitzGerald)* 7-11 ‡⁵SMaloney (4) (kpt on u.p fnl 2f: nvr nr to chal) ...................................................... 1½.**6**

1886⁵ Coconut Johnny **(62)** *(GMMoore)* 7-8 JLowe (2) (chsd ldrs: rdn ½-wy: sn wknd) ¾.**7**

2152³ Make it Happen (IRE) **(70)** (bl) *(JBerry)* 8-2⁽¹⁾ JCarroll (9) (nvr wnt pce) ............ 2.**8**

2811⁵ Shadow Jury **(89)** (v) *(JSWainwright)* 9-0 ‡⁷MichaelDenaro (5) (lw: sltly hmpd s: sn outpcd & rdn along) ................................ 2½.**9**

2733 El Guapo **(61)** (bl) *(TFairhurst)* 7-7 JHanning (11) (sn wl outpcd) ........ 2½.**10**

1192 Whisperdales **(71)** (bl) *(MWEllerby)* 8-3 SMorris (3) (swtg: racd wd: prom to ½-wy: sn lost pl) ................................................. ¾.**11**

LONG HANDICAP: Field of Vision (IRE) 7-6, El Guapo 7-4.

**4/1** SHEILA'S SECRET (IRE), **5/1** Trevorsninepoints, Make it Happen (IRE), **6/1** Hotaria, **9/1** Field of Vision (IRE), **12/1** Arkendale Diamond (USA), Coconut Johnny, Shadow Jury, **33/1** Dream a Bit, **20/1** El Guapo, **33/1** Whisperdales. CSF £21.93, CT £105.86. Tote £3.80: £1.60 £1.90 £1.70 (£9.70). Sherwoods Transport Ltd (EPSOM) bred by A. F. O'Callaghan in Ireland. 11 Rn        58.1 sec (1.4)
SF—44/20/14/–/2/–

---

**2961**        NORTON FOODS SUPPLIES LTD AUCTION STKS (Mdn 2-Y.O) £2532.00 (£702.00: £336.00)   **1m**        4-30 (4-42)

2409 Home From the Hill (IRE) *(MBell)* 8-9 MHills (9) (b.off hind: trckd ldrs: styd on u.p fnl 2f: led nr fin) ........................................ —**1**

2675³ Persian Charmer (IRE) *(MissLAPerratt)* 9-0 AMcGlone (13) (lw: led after 2f: clr over 2f out: rdn & no ex nr fin) ............................ ½.**2**

2274⁵ Fort Vally **(67)** *(BWMurray)* 8-9 GBaxter (2) (sn bhd: hdwy 2f out: kpt on fnl f) ... 3.**3**

2629⁴ Romalito *(MBlanshard)* 9-0 RCochrane (14) (lw: sn bhd & drvn along: hdwy over 2f out: hrd rdn & r.o one pce) ........................... 2.**4**

1899 Stevie's Wonder (IRE) *(WCarter)* 9-0 PaulEddery (8) (w ldrs: nt qckn fnl 2f) ...... hd.**5**
2024⁶ Olivadi (IRE) *(Fav) (LMCumani)* 9-0 JFortune (5) (lw: trckd ldrs: effrt over 2f out:
      one pce) ................................................................................................... 2¹/₂.**6**
2733⁴ Ume River (IRE) *(MHTompkins)* 9-0 PRobinson (4) (outpcd & drvn along ¹/₂-wy:
      kpt on fnl 2f: nvr nr to chal) ....................................................... 1¹/₂.**7**
2667² Efizia *(MrsGRReveley)* 8-9 JLowe (3) (trckd ldrs: no imp fnl 2f) .................. ³/₄.**8**
2826 Pondering *(SDow)* 9-0 DMcKeown (12) (nvr nr ldrs) ....................................... 5.**9**
      Aberlemno *(JBerry)* 9-0 JCarroll (6) (w'like: bit bkwd: chsd ldrs: drvn along
      ¹/₂-wy: sn lost pl) ........................................................................ 1.**10**
27005 Keep Your Distance *(MrsGRReveley)* 9-0 KDarley (16) (trckd ldrs: effrt over 2f
      out: grad wknd) ...................................................................... nk.**11**
2733 Wild Expression *(CTinkler)* 9-0 BRaymond (15) (hld up: a bhd) ................. 1¹/₂.**12**
2534 Desert Laughter (IRE) *(RHollinshead)* 9-0 WRyan (10) (bit bkwd: n.d) ........ s.h.**13**
2842 Simply Superb *(MWEasterby)* 9-0 TLucas (7) (hld up & plld hrd: in rr fr ¹/₂-wy) nk.**14**
2606 Wrightmill (IRE) *(CTinkler)* 9-0 MBirch (11) (led 2f: lost pl 3f out: sn bhd) ...... nk.**15**
287 Miramichi Bay *(MrsVAAconley)* 8-7 ‡⁷GParkin (1) (unruly s: ducked bdly lft &
      uns rdr s) .......................................................................................... 0
2667³ Jalcanto (10/1) Withdrawn (broke out of stalls) : not under orders — Rule 4 applies

**9/4** Olivadi (IRE)(3/1—4/1), **5/1** Keep Your Distance(op 8/1), HOME FROM THE HILL (IRE)(3/1—5/2), **11/2** Persian Charmer (IRE), **10/1** Ume River (IRE), Romalito, **20/1** Efizia, **25/1** Fort Vally, Stevie's Wonder (IRE), Aberlemno, **33/1** Desert Laughter (IRE), Simply Superb, **50/1** Wrightmill (IRE), Wild Expression, Pondering, **100/1** Miramichi Bay. CSF £30.05, Tote £4.00: £1.80 £2.30 £16.00 (£16.60). Capt B. W. Bell (NEWMARKET) bred by R. M. Fox in Ireland. 16 Rn                                                    1m 38.3 (3.3)
                                                                                        SF—40/43/29/26/25/17

**2962**    JOSHUA TETLEY STKS (Mdn)  *(1¹/₄m)*  5-00 - **Abandoned**—home bnd unsafe

T/Plpt: £58.60 (73.2 Tckts).                                                              WG

## 2512-EDINBURGH (R-H)
**Thursday, August 27th [Soft]**
Going Allowance: St: 0.50 sec (Y); Rnd: 0.20 sec per fur (G)        Wind: slt almost against
Stalls: high

**2963**    PERGODA APP'CE H'CAP (0-70) £2380.80 (£668.80: £326.40)    **5f**    2-10 (2-11)

29093 **Miss Vaxette (69)** *(JLSpearing)* 3-9-10 MHumphries (7) (chsd ldrs: carried lft
      appr fnl f: r.o wl to ld cl home) ........................................................ —**1**
2689 Minizen Music (IRE) **(38)** *(MBrittain)* 4-7-10⁽³⁾ JMarshall (6) (s.i.s: bhd: hdwy to
      ld ent fnl f: hdd & no ex nr fin) ...................................................... hd.**2**
2741 The Right Time **(45)** (bl) *(JParkes)* 7-8-3 VHalliday (5) (s.i.s: hdwy 2f out: ev ch
      ent fnl f: styd on) ............................................................................ 1.**3**
2816 Uppance **(35)** (bl) *(TCraig)* 4-7-7 DarrenMoffatt (11) (hld up: hdwy ¹/₂-wy: kpt
      on one pce appr fnl f) ............................................................... 1¹/₂.**4**
26764 Langtonian **(62)** (bl) *(JBerry)* 3-9-3 SHaworth (10) (cl up: ev ch whn hung lft
      appr fnl f: no ex) ........................................................................... 3.**5**
25643 Catherines Well **(70)** *(MWEasterby)* 9-10-0 PaulJohnson (12) (in tch: effrt
      ¹/₂-wy: no ex fnl f) ........................................................................ ³/₄.**6**
26765 Best Effort **(67)** *(Fav) (MPNaughton)* 9-9-0 ADobbin (8) (chsd ldrs: drvn along
      ¹/₂-wy: one pce appr fnl f) ............................................................. nk.**7**
27866 Miss Siham (IRE) **(44)** *(JBalding)* 3-7-13 ClaireBalding (1) (spd on outside over
      3f) ................................................................................................ 3¹/₂.**8**
26636 Hemsworth Lad (IRE) **(58)** *(PCalver)* 3-8-9 JTate (3) (mid div: styd on fnl f: nt trble
      ldrs) .......................................................................................... nk.**9**
2536 Le Chic **(51)** *(DWChapman)* 6-8-9 MHarris (9) (led tl hdd ent fnl f: sn wknd) 3¹/₂.**10**
2902 Lonsom Lass **(66)** *(LJBarratt)* 4-9-10 DWright (4) (prom tl sddle slipped 2f out:
      n.d after) .................................................................................... ¹/₂.**11**
                  LONG HANDICAP: Minizen Music (IRE) 6-12, Uppance 7-6.

**4/1** Best Effort, **5/1** Catherines Well, **11/2** Langtonian, **6/1** MISS VAXETTE, The Right Time, **10/1** The Right Time, **14/1** Le Chic, **16/1** Hemsworth Lad (IRE), **20/1** Miss Siham (IRE), **25/1** Minizen Music (IRE), **50/1** Lonsom Lass. CSF £112.71, CT £837.36. Tote £5.10: £1.40 £2.80 £1.60 (£45.00). Vax Appliances Ltd (ALCESTER) bred by N. J. Dent. 11 Rn                                                                   63.1 sec (5.4)
                                                                                        SF—52/23/26/10/22/30

**2964**    SALAMANCA (S) STKS  £2403.20 (£675.20: £329.60)    **1m 7f 16y**    2-40 (2-40)

27012 **Stingray City (USA) (60)** *(Fav) (JEtherington)* 3-8-4 KDarley (1) (a trckng ldrs:
      led on bit 3f out: drew clr wl over 1f out: v.easily) ................... —**1**

2513⁴ Racing Raskal **(30)** *(CaptJWilson)* 5–9–3 ‡⁷SWynne (5) (bhd: drvn along ½-wy: hdwy ent st: ev ch 2f out: no ch w wnr) ............................................ 5.2
    Coopers Spot-on (IRE) *(PMonteith)* 4–9–4⁽¹⁾ ‡⁷ADobbin (2) (cl up: led ent st: hdd 3f out: one pce) ....................................................... 3.3
2533⁵ Lord Advocate **(44)** (v) *(MPNaughton)* 4–9–5 ‡⁵JWeaver (4) (led tl hdd ent st: btn whn eased fnl 2f) ....................................... 12.4
2701⁶ Top Prize **(44)** *(MBrittain)* 4–9–3 JLowe (3) (prom tl rdn & wknd ent st) ...... 2.5
2420⁶ Janeswood (IRE) **(26)** (bl) *(JParkes)* 4–8–12 LCharnock (6) (bhd & drvn along ½-wy: t.o fnl 3f) ............................................... 25.6

**2/5** STINGRAY CITY (USA), **7/1** Lord Advocate, **9/1** Top Prize, Coopers Spot-on (IRE)(op 6/1), **14/1** Racing Raskal, **33/1** Janeswood (IRE). CSF £6.69, Tote £1.50: £1.10 £1.70 (£2.80). Mr P. D. Savill (MALTON) bred by Rolling Meadows Farm in USA. 6 Rn; Bt in 6,400 gns     3m 32.2 (21.7)

---

**2965**    E.B.F. ROYAL SCOTS CLUB STKS (Mdn 2-Y.O) £2448.00 (£688.00: £336.00)
      5f                                                  3-10 (3-12)

2819⁵ **Sporting Spirit** *(DWChapman)* 9-0 SWood (3) (hdwy on stands' side ½-wy: kpt on wl to ld nr fin) .............................................. —1
2818⁵ High Romance *(DMoffatt)* 8-2 ‡⁷DarrenMoffatt (8) (prom: led ½-wy: hdd & no ex wl ins fnl f) .............................................. 1½.2
2274⁴ Racing Telegraph **(77)** (Fav) *(JPearce)* 9-0 KDarley (13) (a.p: rdn & ev ch appr fnl f: nt qckn) .............................................. ¾.3
2636³ Benzoe (IRE) **(71)** *(MWEasterby)* 9-0 TLucas (10) (s.i.s: bhd tl styd on wl fnl f: nrst fin) .............................................. 1½.4
2745⁶ Miss Whittingham (IRE) **(56)** *(JBerry)* 8-9 DMcKeown (9) (gd spd over 3f: one pce) .............................................. 1½.5
2207³ General Brooks (IRE) **(51)** (v) *(JBerry)* 9-0 JCarroll (1) (w ldrs: ev ch wl over 1f out: no ex) .............................................. 2½.6
    Evahart *(JHJohnson)* 0-4 ‡⁵JWeaver (7) (small: hkwd: s.i.s: bhd: styd on fnl f: nt rch ldrs) .............................................. nk.7
2471² Hawaymyson (IRE) **(68)** *(JHJohnson)* 9-0 JFortune (12) (sn rdn along: nvr trbld ldrs) .............................................. 2.8
1524⁴ Principal Player (USA) **(70)** *(PMonteith)* 9-0 MBirch (6) (led to ½-wy: sn btn) ... ½.9
2818 The Loon *(JJO'Neill)* 8-7 ‡⁷AGarth (5) (in tch: effrt ½-wy: sn btn) .............. 2½.10
2740⁶ Celtic Cherry *(JBalding)* 8-9 GHind (2) (in tch tl rdn & wknd ½-wy) .............. ¾.11
2897 Cracker Jack (bl) *(TFairhurst)* 9-0 JFanning (4) (w ldr tl ½-wy: wknd qckly) .... 12
    Pretty Average *(TCraig)* 8-9 LCharnock (11) (w'like: bkwd: stdd s: a bhd) .......... 13

**7/4** Racing Telegraph, **5/2** Benzoe (IRE), **11/2** Principal Player (USA), **9/1** Hawaymyson (IRE)(op 5/1), **16/1** General Brooks (IRE), High Romance, **25/1** Evahart, Cracker Jack, **33/1** SPORTING SPIRIT, Miss Whittingham (IRE), **66/1** Celtic Cherry, **100/1** Ors. CSF £412.71, Tote £60.30: £10.40 £5.00 £1.70 (Wnr or 2nd w any £3.80). Mr Phillip Kneafsey (YORK) bred by Phillip Kneafsey. 13 Rn     64.2 sec (6.5)
                                                       SF—20/2/11/5/–/–

---

**2966**    EDMONDS H'CAP (0-70) £2860.40 (£804.40: £393.20)     **7f 15y**     3-40 (3-44)

2680* **Thornton Gate (66)** (bl) (Fav) *(MHEasterby)* 3-9-2 ‡⁵SMaloney (14) (mde all: brought stands' side ent st: kpt on wl fnl f) .............................................. —1
2814² Lawnswood Junior **(53)** *(JLSpearing)* 5–8-13 GHind (4) (hdwy 3f out: chal appr fnl f: styd on) .............................................. 2.2
2808 Spanish Realm **(33)** *(MBrittain)* 5–7-7 JLowe (16) (a.p: ev ch 2f out: one pce) .. s.h.3
2878⁴ Diet **(62)** (v) *(MissLAPerratt)* 6–9-8 NConnorton (6) (chsd ldrs far side: kpt on u.p fnl f) .............................................. ½.4
2723* Celestine **(57)** *(TFairhurst)* 3–8-12 JFanning (1) (in tch: effrt over 2f out: nt qckn appr fnl f) .............................................. 2½.5
2421³ Verdant Boy **(49)** *(MPNaughton)* 3–8-9 KFallon (13) (hdwy over 3f out: styd on appr fnl f: nt rch ldrs) .............................................. ½.6
2814 Swank Gilbert **(36)** *(TAKCuthbert)* 6–7-3⁽³⁾ ‡⁷ClaireBalding (9) (styd on fnl 2f: n.d) .............................................. 7.7
2678⁵ Euroblake **(66)** *(TDBarron)* 5–9-7 ‡⁵OPears (11) (nvr bttr than mid div) ............ hd.8
1441 Jane's Brave Boy **(34)** *(TCraig)* 10–7-1⁽¹⁾ ‡⁷DarrenMoffatt (5) (chsd ldrs: racd far side: wknd 2f out) .............................................. 1½.9
2678⁵ Ruth's Gamble **(56)** *(DWChapman)* 4–8-9 KDarley (10) (nvr trbld ldrs) ............ 2.10
2517⁶ New Beginning **(33)** *(JSHaldane)* 9–7-7 SWood (8) (rdn along ½-wy: n.d) .... hd.11
2216⁴ Valley of Time (FR) **(44)** *(TCraig)* 4–8-4 LCharnock (3) (cl up tl wknd qckly fnl out) .............................................. 3½.12
2539 Ravecino **(43)** *(JSHaldane)* 3–7-5⁽³⁾ ‡⁷AGarth (8) (in tch: racd alone centre: btn over 2f out) .............................................. 1½.13
915⁵ Rage **(62)** (bl) *(TCraig)* 5–9-8 SWebster (7) (in tch to st: sn bhd) .................... ½.14
903 Monti Beppo **(52)** *(LJBarratt)* 3–8-0 ‡⁷DWright (12) (reard s: a t.o) ................... 10.15
    LONG HANDICAP: Swank Gilbert 7-1, Jane's Brave Boy 6-8, New Beginning 7-5.

**5/2** THORNTON GATE, **11/2** Lawnswood Junior, **6/1** Euroblake(op 4/1), **8/1** Celestine, Verdant Boy, Ruth's Gamble, **12/1** Diet, **14/1** Valley of Time (FR), **33/1** Jane's Brave Boy, New Beginning, Ravecino, Spanish Realm, **40/1** Swank Gilbert, **50/1** Monti Beppo, **66/1** Rage. CSF £16.07, CT £344.36. Tote £4.20: £2.10 £1.10 £5.80 (£7.10). Mr T. H. Bennett (MALTON) bred by Jim Strange. 15 Rn      1m 31.1 (4.9)
SF—49/40/19/46/28/23

---

**2967**    GALLIPOLI CLAIMING STKS (Mdn 3-Y.O.C & G) £2291.20 (£643.20: £313.60)
       **1m 16y**                                    4-10 (4-11)

2655⁴ **Super Summit (54)** (Fav) *(JPearce)* 9-0 KDarley (3) (a cl up: led wl over 1f out: sn pushed clr) ............................................................. —1
1293⁴ Arjiil *(MHTompkins)* 8-8 MBirch (5) (chsd ldrs: ev ch 2f out: kpt on same pce) .. 3.2
1852 Milton Rooms (IRE) **(56)** (bl) *(CBBBooth)* 8-9 GOldroyd (2) (bhd & drvn along ent st: styd on u.p fnl f: nrst fin) ............................................. 6.3
2878⁶ Bee Dee Ell (USA) **(42)** *(MissLAPerratt)* 8-8 JFanning (6) (led after 2f tl hdd wl over 1f out: sn wknd) ........................................................ 8.4
2334 Fait Accompli (FR) **(40)** *(JJO'Neill)* 7-11 ‡⁷AGarth (4) (led 2f: w ldr tl wknd over 2f out) .......................................................................... 7.5

**7/4** SUPER SUMMIT(op 4/5), **2/1** Arjiil, **9/2** Milton Rooms (IRE), **5/1** Bee Dee Ell (USA), **25/1** Fait Accompli (FR). CSF £5.25, Tote £2.00: £1.10 £1.80 (£2.20). Mr D. J. Maden (NEWMARKET) bred by S. J. Mear. 5 Rn
1m 44.5 (5.9)
SF—35/20/3/–/–

---

**2968**    LADBROKE H'CAP (0-70) £2840.00 (£860.00: £420.00: £200.00)
       **1½m 31y**                                   4-40 (4-41)

                         (Weights raised 7 lb)
2815 **J P Morgan (39)** (v) *(MPNaughton)* 4-8-7 KFallon (6) (a chsng ldrs: led ent st: rdn & styd on fnl f) ............................................................ —1
2775² Mingus (USA) **(56)** (Fav) *(MrsJRRamsden)* 5-9-5 ‡⁵JWeaver (1) (hld up: prom: smooth hdwy to chal over 1f out: sn rdn & nt r.o) ............... ¾.2
2693² Tanoda **(48)** *(MBrittain)* 6-9-2 JLowe (2) (chsd ldrs: rdn & ev ch over 2f out: one pce) ......................................................................... 6.3
2877⁴ Alpha Helix **(28)** (v) *(MissLAPerratt)* 9-7-10 JFanning (7) (rdn along 7f out: styd on fnl 2f: n.d) ...................................................... 12.4
2815⁵ Miliyel **(52)** *(PMonteith)* 3-8-10 LCharnock (4) (chsd ldrs: rdn & outpcd wl over 2f out) ............................................................................. 8.5
2677⁶ Bridge Player **(44)** *(DMoffatt)* 5-8-5 ‡⁷DarrenMoffatt (3) (s.s: hdwy appr st: sn btn) ...................................................................................... 5.6
2820 Carol's Pet (IRE) **(42)** *(MJohnston)* 4-8-10 DMcKeown (4) (virtually ref to r: a t.o) 20.7
2820 Tempering **(45)** (bl) *(DWChapman)* 6-8-13 SWood (5) (w ldr tl wknd qckly ent st: sn t.o) ............................................................................ 12.8
2737 Dollar Seeker (USA) **(44)** (bl) *(ABailey)* 8-8-12 JCarroll (8) (led tl hdd ent st: sn bhd: broke down & dismntd over 1f out) ............................ 0

**2/1** Mingus (USA), **7/2** Tanoda(op 2/1), **6/1** Carol's Pet (IRE), **8/1** Alpha Helix, Dollar Seeker (USA), **9/1** Miliyel, **10/1** Bridge Player, **20/1** Tempering, **33/1** J P MORGAN. CSF £95.37, CT £279.66. Tote £16.80: £3.60 £1.70 £1.30 (£41.80). Mr Raymond Miquel (RICHMOND) bred by The Mount Coote Partnership. 9 Rn    2m 43 (10.5)
SF—12/22/7/–/–/–

T/Plpt: £10.20 (222.7 Tckts).                                         GB

---

2801—**LINGFIELD (L-H)**

## Thursday, August 27th [Turf Good, Good to firm patches back st, AWT Standard]

Going Allowance: Turf: 0.15 sec (G); AWT: minus 0.10 sec (FS)      Wind: str half bhd
Stalls: high

**2969**    SANDERSTEAD STKS (Mdn 3-Y.O) £2217.00 (£612.00: £291.00)
       **7f (AWT)**                                      2-00 (2-02)

       **Albert the Bold** *(MrsLPiggott)* 9-0 LDettori (6) (eyeshield: b: a.p: led over 1f out: rdn out) .................................................................................... —1
2128 Harcliff *(DJSCosgrove)* 9-0 GDuffield (5) (b.hind: rdn thrght: hdwy over 1f out: r.o wl ins fnl f) ................................................................... s.h.2
5116 Gold Blade *(NAGraham)* 9-0 RCochrane (3) (b.nr fore: lw: dwlt: hdwy over 1f out: ev ch ins fnl f: r.o) ........................................................ nk.3
2053 Grand Fellow (IRE) **(51)** (v) *(JDBethell)* 9-0 AMunro (2) (hld up: rdn over 3f out: unable qckn ins fnl f) ..................................................... 2½.4

2831 Night Gown (bl) *(MissGayKelleway)* 8-9 GayKelleway (4) (b: lw: led 6f out tl over
1f out: wknd ins fnl f) ........................................................ 3.5
2865³ Nobby Barnes (62) (Fav) *(RWArmstrong)* 9-0 LPiggott (7) (hdwy over 4f out:
hrd rdn over 1f out: eased whn btn fnl f) ............................. 2.6
2229⁵ Double Shift *(JWhite)* 8-9 DaleGibson (1) (led 1f: wknd over 2f out) .............. 8.7

7/4 Nobby Barnes(op Evens), 3/1 Double Shift, 13/2 Harcliff, 8/1 Gold Blade, ALBERT THE BOLD(op 9/2), 20/1
Ors. CSF £48.36, Tote £8.70: £2.90 £3.40 (£38.10). Miss J. Semple (NEWMARKET) bred by Doverlodge Stud. 7
Rn
1m 27.37 (3.37)
SF—38/37/36/28/14/13

## 2970

ARDINGLY (S) STKS    £2553.00 (£708.00: £339.00)    2m    2-30 (2-30)

1239* **The Last Empress (IRE) (66)** (Fav) *(PFICole)* 4-9-8 TQuinn (9) (b.hind: hld up:
led over 4f out: clr over 2f out: easily) ................................. —1
2560* Ghostly Glow (54) (v) *(CCEIsey)* 3-8-13 PatEddery (3) (lw: led over 11f out tl
over 4f out: 2nd st: hrd rdn over 2f out: no imp) ................. 12.2
2867 Jokers Patch (57) *(WRWilliams)* 5-9-13 NAdams (6) (hdwy over 4f out: 3rd st:
hrd rdn over 2f out: one pce) ............................................... 2.3
1977⁶ Rich Pickings (36) *(CACyzer)* 3-8-4 AMorris (1) (hrd rdn over 5f out: 4th st: one
pce fnl 3f) ....................................................................... 1½.4
2692⁶ Make Me Proud (IRE) (43) (bl) *(RWArmstrong)* 3-8-4 GDuffield (8) (lw: led over
4f: wknd over 4f out: 5th st: t.o) ......................................... 25.5
2477 Soft Verges *(WCarter)* 4-8-13 ‡5NGwilliams (5) (bhd fnl 8f: t.o) ..................... 12.6
Written Agreement *(REPeacock)* 4-9-9 JWilliams (4) (lw: s.s: a bhd: t.o fnl 8f) ... 4.7
2651² Kate Royale (44) *(MCPipe)* 3-8-4 JQuinn (7) (bhd fnl 6f: poor 6th st: t.o) ....... 20.8

**Evens** THE LAST EMPRESS (IRE), **100/30** Ghostly Glow, **5/1** Kate Royale, **10/1** Rich Pickings, **16/1** Soft Verges,
**20/1** Make Me Proud (IRE), **33/1** Ors. CSF £4.73, Tote £2.00: £1.30 £1.10 £4.90 (£2.70). Mr Reg Hester
(WHATCOMBE) bred by Binfield Manor Farms Ltd in Ireland. 8 Rn, 3uld A 0 noid 8,200 gns  3m 42.96 (18.96)

## 2971

NICHOLSON, GRAHAM & JONES H'CAP (0-90) £3021.00 (£836.00: £399.00)
1m 3f 106y
3-00 (3-02)

**Canny Chronicle (80)** *(MHTompkins)* 4-10-0 PRobinson (9) (hdwy over 1f
out: led wl ins fnl f: r.o wl) ................................................ —1
2460³ Pelorus (80) *(DRCEIsworth)* 7-9-7 ‡7JHunter (1) (lw: 3rd st: led over 1f out: hrd
rdn & hdd wl ins fnl f: r.o) ................................................. nk.2
2408* Princess Moodyshoe (62) (Jt-Fav) *(MCPipe)* 4-8-10 LPiggott (6) (lw: hrd rdn
over 2f out: hdwy over 1f out: r.o one pce) ......................... 3.3
1955 Aremef (USA) (80) *(MrsJCecil)* 3-9-5 PaulEddery (3) (led 10f: one pce) .......... 1½.4
2827³ Doctor's Remedy (45) (bl) *(MrsJJordan)* 6-7-0 ‡7KimMcDonnell (8) (2nd st: ev
ch over 1f out: wknd ins fnl f) ............................................ 1.5
2806 Sword Master (73) *(BobJones)* 3-8-12 NDay (4) (4th st: hrd rdn over 2f out:
wknd over 1f out) ............................................................. 2.6
2805* Smiling Chief (IRE) (69) *(CACyzer)* 3-8-9 DBiggs (2) (lw: 6th st: no hdwy fnl 3f) ½.7
202² Rapporteur (USA) (70) *(CCEIsey)* 6-9-4 PatEddery (5) (b: 5th st: wknd
over 2f out) ..................................................................... 12.8
LONG HANDICAP: Doctor's Remedy 6-10.

4/1 Rapporteur (USA), Princess Moodyshoe, 9/2 Sword Master, 11/2 Aremef (USA), 6/1 Pelorus, Smiling Chief
(IRE), 14/1 CANNY CHRONICLE, 20/1 Doctor's Remedy. CSF £84.13, CT £362.18. Tote £17.80: £3.20 £1.80
£1.10 (£35.70). Newcastle Evening Chronicle (NEWMARKET) bred by Fonthill Stud. 8 Rn  2m 34.14 (12.14)

## 2972

CRANLEIGH STKS (2-Y.O) £2736.00 (£756.00: £360.00)    1m (AWT)    3-30 (3-31)

2462² **Foolish Heart (IRE) (88)** *(NAGraham)* 8-13 MRoberts (5) (mde all: r.o wl) ........ —1
2445 Known Approach (USA) **(100)** (Fav) *(PFICole)* 9-4 TQuinn (6) (lw: chsd wnr 6f
out: hrd rdn & ev ch over 3f out: unable qckn fnl 2f) ........... 1½.2
2195 Balustrade Boy (IRE) *(BStevens)* 8-11 MTebbutt (7) (wl bhd 6f: hdwy over 1f
out: nvr nrr) ..................................................................... 8.3
2306 Dhahran *(PFICole)* 8-11 AMunro (1) (lw: prom 3f) ...................................... 4.4
2910 Poly Vision (IRE) (63) *(MRChannon)* 8-11 PatEddery (8) (prom 4f) ............... 1½.5
2190⁶ Early to Rise *(CACyzer)* 8-11 DBiggs (2) (lw: a wl bhd) ............................... 7.6
2771 My Miss Molly (IRE) *(MissGayKelleway)* 8-6 GayKelleway (3) (b.hind: swtg:
s.i.s: a wl bhd) ................................................................ hd.7
1442 Kill the Plague (USA) (42) (bl) *(APJones)* 8-11 NAdams (4) (lw: outpcd) ......... 2¹/₂.8

**Evens** Known Approach (USA)(op 4/6), **11/8** FOOLISH HEART (IRE), **10/1** Poly Vision (IRE), **14/1** Dhahran, **33/1**
Early to Rise, **100/1** Ors. CSF £2.92, Tote £2.50: £1.80 £1.10 £6.60 (£1.70). Mr Richard Berenson
(NEWMARKET) bred by Gerry Canavan in Ireland. 8 Rn
1m 40.76 (4.06)
SF—26/26/-/-/-/-

## 2973

TONBRIDGE NURSERY   £2658.00 (£738.00: £354.00)   7f   4-00 (4-02)
(Weights raised 9 lb)

2674² **Fairy Story (IRE) (66)** *(JWHills)* 8-2 RHills (1) (racd alone: mde virtually all: r.o wl) ......................................................................................................... —1

2010 Final Frontier (IRE) (69) *(RAkehurst)* 8-2 ‡³FNorton (9) (a.p: ev ch over 1f out: unable qckn) ....................................................................................... 2.2

2703⁵ Wishing Cap (USA) (65) *(SirMarkPrescott)* 8-1 GDuffield (12) (hld up: ev ch over 1f out: one pce) ............................................................................... ½.3

2824⁶ Sea Exhibition (IRE) (71) *(MBlanshard)* 8-7 RCochrane (3) (hdwy over 1f out: r.o) ......................................................................................................... 2.4

2482⁵ Trundley Wood (73) *(GAPritchard-Gordon)* 8-9 LDettori (14) (hld up: ev ch over 1f out: one pce) ................................................................................ ½.5

1899⁶ Jonsalan (75) *(WCarter)* 8-11 PaulEddery (2) (lw: a.p: hrd rdn over 1f out: one pce) ............................................................................................... 1½.6

1586² Ombre Darme (IRE) (62) (bl) *(JWPayne)* 7-12⁽²⁾ AMunro (11) (lw: nvr nr to chal) 2½.7

2363\* Jordywrath (58) *(ICampbell)* 7-8 JQuinn (7) (no hdwy fnl 2f) ......................... 2.8

2800⁵ Premium (70) (bl) (Fav) *(WJHaggas)* 8-6 PatEddery (13) (lw: spd over 4f) ..... 2½.9

2501⁴ Don't Jump (IRE) (83) *(MHTompkins)* 9-5 PRobinson (10) (lw: outpcd) ......... ¾.10

2706⁶ Mr Nevermind (IRE) (60) *(GLewis)* 7-10 DBiggs (5) (a bhd) ..................... s.h.11

2857³ Mr Butch (67) *(MRChannon)* 8-3⁽¹⁾ TQuinn (8) (a.p: hrd rdn & ev ch over 1f out: wknd fnl f) ................................................................................................ 1½.12

2577⁵ Tayish (57) (bl) *(TThomsonJones)* 7-7 NAdams (6) (bhd fnl 2f) ..................... 3.13
LONG HANDICAP: Tayish 7-5.

9/2 Premium, 11/2 Jordywrath, 7/1 Mr Butch, 8/1 Wishing Cap (USA), FAIRY STORY (IRE)(op 5/1), 9/1 Mr Nevermind (IRE)(8/1—12/1), 10/1 Final Frontier (IRE), 12/1 Jonsalan(op 7/1), 14/1 Trundley Wood, Ombre Darme (IRE), 16/1 Sea Exhibition (IRE)(op 10/1), 20/1 Don't Jump (IRE), 25/1 Tayish. CSF £79.09, CT £677.61. Tote £6.30: £2.60 £3.20 £3.10 (£48.00). The Fairy Story Partnership (LAMBOURN) bred by Deepwood Farm Stud in Ireland. 13 Rn
1m 25.54 (4.24)
SF—40/34/31/31/31/28

## 2974

PEMBURY H'CAP (0-70) £2469.00 (£684.00: £327.00)   6f (AWT)   4-30 (4-33)

2702² **Miss Movie World (43)** (Fav) *(NBycroft)* 3–8-5 AMunro (4) (a.p: led 1f out: rdn out) ................................................................................................................. —1

2772⁵ My Ruby Ring (39) *(DRLaing)* 5–8-5 TyroneWilliams (10) (a.p: led wl over 1f out to 1f out: unable qckn) ........................................................................... 1.2

2772⁴ Liffey River (USA) (54) *(MrsLPiggott)* 4–9-6 LPiggott (3) (eyeshield: b: b.hind: lw: hdwy over 1f out: r.o ins fnl f) ................................................... 2½.3

2589⁶ Inswinger (41) *(WGRWightman)* 6–8-7 JWilliams (7) (outpcd: hdwy over 2f out: one pce) .................................................................................................. 2½.4

2804⁴ One Magic Moment (IRE) (50) *(CACyzer)* 4–9-2 DBiggs (1) (rdn & no hdwy fnl 2f) 1.5

1552 Ever so Artistic (44) *(PHowling)* 5–8-10 LDettori (9) (lw: led over 4f) ............... 3.6

2786² Imco Double (62) *(WHolden)* 4–9-7 ‡⁷PTurner (11) (lw: spd 4f) ........................ 1.7

2718 Sports Post Lady (IRE) (55) *(CJHill)* 4–9-7 PaulEddery (2) (lw: bhd fnl 2f) ....... nk.8

2712 Sixofus (IRE) (43) *(WGMTurner)* 4–8-9 TSprake (5) (a bhd) ............................ ¾.9

2830 Cronk's Quality (40) (bl) *(DCJermy)* 9-8-6 SDawson (6) (outpcd) ................... 1½.10

2786⁵ The Shanahan Bay (54) (v) *(MrsNMacauley)* 7–9-1 ‡⁵SWilliams (8) (b: a bhd: t.o) 11

11/4 MISS MOVIE WORLD, 13/2 Liffey River (USA), 7/1 Inswinger, 8/1 One Magic Moment (IRE), My Ruby Ring, Imco Double (IRE), Sports Post Lady (IRE), 10/1 The Shanahan Bay, 25/1 Ever so Artistic, Sixofus (IRE), 33/1 Cronk's Quality. CSF £22.96, CT £118.78. Tote £3.40: £1.70 £2.20 £2.20 (£15.00). Mr Stephen Johnson (BRANDSBY) bred by J. Williams. 11 Rn
1m 12.96 (2.36)
SF—32/28/33/10/15/–

T/Plpt: £337.80 (10.85 Tckts).   AK

## KLAMPENBORG (R-H) Denmark
## Sunday, August 2nd [Good to firm]

## 2975a

DANSK OAKS (3-Y.O.F)   £13575.00   1½m

**Saucy Girl (FR)** *(Sweden)* 3–9-0 GNordling ...................................................... —1

Recent Therm *(Denmark)* 3–9-0 FJohansson ................................................. nk.2

Cantata (DEN) *(Denmark)* 3–9-0 OLarsen ..................................................... ½.3

2297\* BY ARRANGEMENT (IRE) *(RGuest)* 3–9-0 CHawksley (btn further 5¾l) ......... 8

Tote 62Kr: 25Kr 56Kr 28Kr (691 Kr). Hb Skattkistan (Mrs E.Nordling,SWEDEN) bred by Darley Stud Management Co. Ltd. in France. 14 Rn
2m 32.3

## 2890a—DEAUVILLE (R-H)
**Wednesday, August 19th [Soft]**
Going Allowance: 0.70 sec per fur (Y)

### 2976a          PRIX DE MEAUTRY (Gp 3)    £20640.00    6f

2626a³ **TWAFEAJ (USA)** *(BHanbury)* 3-8-6 WRSwinburn ............................. —**1**
2440  THOURIOS (bl) *(GHarwood)* 3-8-9 AClark ..................................... s.h.**2**
2169  AMIGO MENOR (bl) *(DJGMurray-Smith)* 6-9-0 CRutter ..................... 1¹/₂.**3**
2435  NOTLEY *(RHannon)* 5-9-0 GMosse (btn further 5¹/₂l) .......................... **9**
27896 BLETCHLEY PARK (IRE) *(AAScott)* 3-8-9 CAsmussen (btn 8¹/₂l by wnr) ....... **10**
Tote 3.20f: 2.00f 5.80f 10.80f (32.00f). Mr Abdullah Ali (NEWMARKET) bred by Bill H.Melton in USA. 11 Rn
1m 14 (5)
SF—76/78/76

## 2887a—CURRAGH (R-H)
**Saturday, August 22nd [Soft]**
Going Allowance: 0.45 sec per fur (Y)

### 2977a          MELD STKS (Gp 3) (F & M) £10748.00    1¹/₂m

2094a² **Market Booster (USA)** *(Ireland)* 3-9-0 MJKinane (hld up: hdwy 4f out: chal 2f
out: sn disp ld: led over 1f out: rdn clr fnl f) ........................... —**1**
2763a★ Dabtiya (IRE) *(Ireland)* 3-8-7 JPMurtagh (a.p: led over 2f out: sn jnd: hdd over
1f out: r.o: no ch w wnr) .................................................. 3.**2**
2503a² Mirana (IRE) *(Ireland)* 3-8-7 DHogan (trckd ldr: lost pl over 2f out: r.o one pce
fnl 2f) ........................................................................ 5.**3**
1353a² Pollys Glow (IRE) *(Ireland)* 3-8-7 KJManning (led over 9f: kpt on one pce fnl 2f) 1.**4**
2094a³ Arrikala (IRE) (Fav) *(Ireland)* 3-8-7 CRoche (plld hrd: bhd: rdn 3f out: no imp fnl
2f) ......................................................................... 2¹/₂.**5**
Hazaradjat (IRE) *(Ireland)* 3-8-7 RHughes (mid div: rdn 3f out: sn btn & bhd) .. 20.**6**

**11/10** Arrikala (IRE), **5/2** MARKET BOOSTER (USA), **9/2** Dabtiya (IRE), **10/1** Pollys Glow (IRE), **12/1** Hazaradjat (IRE), **25/1** Mirana (IRE). Tote £4.00: £1.80 £4.00 (£10.00). Moyglare Stud Farms Ltd. (D.K.Weld,IRELAND) bred by Moyglare Stud Farms Ltd. in USA. 6 Rn
2m 39.9 (9.6)
SF—58/45/35/33/28/–

### 2978a          E.B.F. ANGLESEY STKS (Gp 3) (2-Y.O) £14369.00    6f 63y

**Basim (USA)** *(Ireland)* 2-8-10 CRoche (mde all: drew clr fnl f) ................ —**1**
Up and At'em *(Ireland)* 2-8-10 LPiggott (trckd ldr: rdn to chal & ev ch over 1f
out: no ex: eased whn btn) .............................................. 6.**2**
El Zorro Dorado (IRE) (Fav) *(Ireland)* 2-8-10 SCraine (hld up: hdwy to chal 2f
out: sn rdn & btn: eased) .............................................. 6.**3**

**Evens** El Zorro Dorado (IRE), **2/1** Up and At'em, **5/2** BASIM (USA). Tote £5.00 (£6.90). Maktoum Al Maktoum (J.S.Bolger,IRELAND) bred by Calumet Farm and Kingston Park Stud in USA. 3 Rn
1m 18.6 (4.1)
SF—68/44/20

## 2976a—DEAUVILLE (R-H)
**Saturday, August 22nd [Heavy]**
Going Allowance: St: 0.40 sec (Y); Rnd: 1.10 sec per fur (S)

### 2979a          CHALLENGE D'OR PIAGET (listed-restricted race) (2-Y.O) £154799.00    7f (st)

**Master Peace (FR)** *(France)* 2-9-0 ELegrix ................................. —**1**
Top Salse (FR) *(France)* 2-9-0 CAsmussen ................................. 2¹/₂.**2**
Marchand de Sable (USA) *(France)* 2-9-0 DBoeuf ........................... ³/₄.**3**
21854 DARSHAY (FR) *(RHannon)* 2-8-10 BRaymond (btn further 14³/₄l) ......... **10**
2653★ YAJEED (USA) *(AAScott)* 2-9-0 WRyan (btn more than 17³/₄l by wnr) ...... **11**
Tote 4.80f: 2.00f 3.20f 2.20f (28.90f). Mr J.D.Schiefelbein (J-C Cunnington,FRANCE) bred by Haras du Bois Roussel in France. 18 Rn
1m 27.6 (4.6)
SF—73/65/63

### 2980a          PIAGET D'OR (listed-restricted race) (3-Y.O) £206398.00    1¹/₄m

2319a² **Urban Sea (USA)** *(France)* 3-8-10 MBoutin ............................. —**1**
1498a² Sheba Dancer (FR) *(France)* 3-8-10 DBoeuf ........................... 2¹/₂.**2**

Mariage Secret (FR) *(France)* 3–8–10 FHead ....................................... nk.3
2453 KING'S LOCH (IRE) *(HRACecil)* 3–9–0 WRyan (btn further 11l) ................ 5
Tote 7.60f: 1.50f 1.10f 1.20f (4.10f). Mr D.Tsui (J.Lesbordes,FRANCE) bred by Marystead Farm in USA. 11 Rn
2m 14.4 (12.1)
SF—86/81/80/64/58

# DEAUVILLE (R-H)
## Sunday, August 23rd [Heavy]
Going Allowance: St: 0.75 sec per fur; Rnd: 0.85 sec per fur (S)

## 2981a     PRIX MORNY AGENCE FRANCAISE (Gp 1) (2-Y.O.C & F) £103199.00    6f (st)

Zafonic (USA) *(France)* 2–8–11 PatEddery (mid div: hdwy over 2f out: led over
1f out: r.o wl) .......................................................... —1
2625a* Secrage (USA) *(Italy)* 2–8–8 BJovine (prom: led over 2f out tl over 1f out: t.o) ... ³/₄.2
2344* MARINA PARK *(MJohnston)* 2–8–8 DMcKeown (broke wl: prom: chal over 1f
out: kpt on) .................................................................. ¹/₂.3
Wixon (FR) *(France)* 2–8–8 ESaint-Martin (in rr: hdwy 2f out: r.o one pce) ... 1¹/₂.4
2320a* Didyme (USA) (Fav) *(France)* 2–8–11 GMosse (mid div: effrt over 1f out: unable
qckn) .................................................................. nose.5
2625a² Kingmambo (USA) *(France)* 2–8–11 FHead (hld up in rr: effrt over 2f out: styd on
nr fin) .................................................................. 1.6
2625a³ Namaqualand (USA) *(France)* 2–8–11 SCauthen (nvr nr to chal) ................ nk.7
1496a* Future Storm (USA) *(Italy)* 2–8–11 VMessatesta (mid div: effrt ¹/₂-wy: sn btn) .. 1¹/₂.8
2445 PORT LUCAYA (bl) *(RHannon)* 2–8–11 JReid (led over 3f: sn wknd) ............. nk.9
2320a² Creaking Board *(France)* 2–8–8 ELegrix (a bhd) .............................. 3.10

5/4 Didyme (USA), 27/10 ZAFONIC (USA), 11/2 Creaking Board, Future Storm (USA), 7/1 Kingmambo (USA),
11/1 Secrage (USA), 12/1 Namaqualand (USA), 16/1 Marina Park, 23/1 Wixon (FR), 56/1 Port Lucaya. Tote
3.70f: 2.00f 3.90f 4.80f (43.20f). Mr K.Abdulla (A.Fabre,FRANCE) bred by Juddmonte Farms in USA. 10 Rn
1m 14.8 (5.8)
SF—71/65/62/56/58/54

## 2982a     PRIX KERGORLAY (Gp 2) £25800.00    1m 7f

2766a² Sought Out (IRE) *(France)* 4–9–1 CAsmussen (mde all: qcknd over 2f out:
unchal) .................................................................. —1
1468* DRUM TAPS (USA) (Fav) *(LordHuntingdon)* 6–9–11 LDettori (a.p: 3rd st: chsd
wnr fr over 1f out: no imp) .................................................. 5.2
2796⁴ MICHELOZZO (USA) *(RHannon)* 6–9–4 JReid (hld up & bhd: hdwy & 5th st:
styd on fnl 2f) .......................................................... 4.3
2096a² In-Quarto (bl) *(France)* 3–8–7 DBoeuf (trckd ldr: 2nd st: one pce fnl 2f) ........... 1¹/₂.4
2796* SHAMBO *(CEBrittain)* 5–9–8 MRoberts (hld up: hdwy 4f out: 4th st: one pce fnl
2f) .................................................................. 5.5
1468³ Turgeon (USA) *(France)* 6–9–11 SCauthen (rdn & 7th st: one pce) ............. 5.6
2027² HATEEL *(PTWalwyn)* 6–9–4 WCarson (a in rr: 8th st: n.d) .................... 6.7
1059 SUPREME CHOICE (USA) *(BWHills)* 4–9–4 PatEddery (prom tl 6th & wkng st) ... 8.8
1492a² Triple Tiara (USA) *(France)* 3–8–4 TJarnet (bhd: 9th st: effrt over 2f out: sn
wknd) .................................................................. 8.9

Evens Drum Taps (USA), 29/10 SOUGHT OUT (IRE), 4/1 Triple Tiara (USA), Turgeon (USA), 13/2 In-Quarto,
10/1 Shambo, 13/1 Supreme Choice (USA), 33/1 Hateel, 41/1 Michelozzo. Tote 3.90f: 1.50f 1.40f 3.90f
(3.50f). Lord Weinstock (J.E.Hammond,FRANCE) bred by Ballymacoll Stud Farm Ltd. in Ireland. 9 Rn
3m 25.4 (14.4)
SF—84/89/78/65/76/73/60

## 2699—THIRSK (L-H)
## Friday, August 28th [Good to firm]
Going Allowance: nil sec per fur (G)                                         Wind: slt bhd

Stalls: high

## 2983     TOMMY FAIRHURST (S) STKS (2-Y.O) £2742.00 (£762.00: £366.00)    7f 2-20 (2-30)

2782³ Persian Traveller (IRE) (59) *(CNAllen)* 8-4 ‡⁷PMcCabe (1) (lw: a.p: styd on to
ld jst ins fnl f: r.o wl) .................................................. —1
2649⁴ Take Your Partner (IRE) (57) *(MJohnston)* 8-6 RPElliott (16) (led: rdn 2f out:
hdd & no ex ins fnl f) .................................................. 2¹/₂.2

2259⁶ Touch N' Glow **(57)** *(NTinkler)* 8-6  NConnorton (11) (s.i.s: hdwy 3f out: r.o wl nr
　　fin) ............................................................................................................ 2.**3**

2842⁴ Palacegate Prince **(65)** *(JBerry)* 9-3  JCarroll (7) (lw: a cl up: effrt 3f out: btn appr
　　fnl f) ........................................................................................................... 1.**4**

2735² Amerigue **(77)** *(MissSEHall)* 8-7 ‡⁵NKennedy (10) (bhd: hdwy 3f out: nrst fin) .... 1.**5**

2719⁵ Lucky Owl **(56)** *(MissLAPerratt)* 8-6  JFanning (2) (s.i.s: hdwy 3f out: nvr rchd
　　ldrs) ........................................................................................................... s.h.**6**

1605⁶ Panic Button (IRE) **(71)** *(MHEasterby)* 8-6  MBirch (9) (bit bkwd: chsd ldrs tl
　　wknd over 2f out) ...................................................................................... 3¹/₂.**7**

2696³ Eastern Glow (Jt-Fav) *(SPCWoods)* 8-6  WRyan (6) (b.hind: lw: bhd: hdwy 2f
　　out: nvr rchd ldrs) ...................................................................................... 3.**8**

 2782 Sophie's Boy **(67)** *(MHEasterby)* 8-8 ‡³SMaloney (3) (bhd: hdwy u.p 2f out: n.d) ¹/₂.**9**

2661⁴ Don't Be Saki (IRE) **(55)** *(JEtherington)* 8-6  MHills (15) (lw: bhd: hdwy over 2f
　　out: sn rdn & n.d) ..................................................................................... 3¹/₂.**10**

2550⁵ Dancing Domino **(63)** (Jt-Fav) *(MHEasterby)* 8-11  KDarley (13) (outpcd ent st:
　　n.d) ........................................................................................................... 1¹/₂.**11**

 2782 Irish Roots (IRE) **(62)** *(CTinkler)* 8-11  GDuffield (12) (chsd ldrs tl wknd over 2f
　　out) ........................................................................................................... 1¹/₂.**12**

2688 Hasta la Vista **(44)** *(MWEasterby)* 8-11  TLucas (8) (prom to st) ...................... hd.**13**

Jim Cantle *(MWEasterby)* 8-12⁽¹⁾ DNicholls (5) (leggy: scope: bit bkwd: s.i.s:
　　n.d) ........................................................................................................... 3¹/₂.**14**

2608³ Light the Bay *(MrsVAAconley)* 8-6  JLowe (4) (dwlt: a bhd) ............................. hd.**15**

2928⁵ Bold Philip **(69)** *(BBeasley)* 8-11  LCharnock (14) (prom to st: sn bhd) ............ 1¹/₂.**16**

**4/1** Eastern Glow, Dancing Domino, **6/1** Palacegate Prince, **13/2** Amerigue, **7/1** PERSIAN TRAVELLER (IRE),
**10/1** Panic Button (IRE), **11/1** Don't Be Saki (IRE), **14/1** Lucky Owl, Take Your Partner (IRE), **20/1** Sophie's Boy,
Light the Bay, Bold Philip, **25/1** Touch N' Glow, **33/1** Jim Cantle, Irish Roots (IRE), **40/1** Hasta la Vista. CSF
£101.40, Tote £10.00: £3.10 £7.60 £6.00 (£142.80). Mr J. N. Oliver (NEWMARKET) bred by Frank Dunne in
Ireland. 16 Rn; Sold J Ramsden 6,200 gns
1m 28.1 (4.8)
SF—18/12/6/14/1/–

**2984**　　LYNDA RAMSDEN H'CAP (0-70) £2700.00 (£750.00: £360.00)　**6f**　　2-50 (2-58)
**(Weights raised 4 lb)**

2936⁶ Yours Or Mine (IRE) **(33)** *(DWChapman)* 4–8-1  NConnorton (15) (chsd ldrs
　　stands' side: led ins fnl f: r.o) ...................................................................... —**1**

2750 Bright Paragon (IRE) **(43)** *(HJCollingridge)* 3–8-7  VSmith (13) (led stands' side
　　tl ins fnl f: no ex) ..................................................................................... 2¹/₂.**2**

2723 Umbria **(41)** (Jt-Fav) *(MPNaughton)* 3–8-5  KDarley (10) (lw: cl up: led far side:
　　r.o u.p) ...................................................................................................... ¹/₂.**3**

2821⁶ Stormbuster **(46)** (Jt-Fav) *(PSFelgate)* 3–8-10  WRyan (23) (lw: in tch stands'
　　side: styd on wl fnl f) ................................................................................. ¹/₂.**4**

2672² Supreme Desire **(39)** *(ASmith)* 4–8-7  SWebster (4) (cl up: led far side to ¹/₂-wy:
　　r.o one pce) ............................................................................................... 1¹/₂.**5**

2699⁵ Syke Lane **(36)** *(RMWhitaker)* 3–8-0⁽¹⁾ AShoults (12) (hdwy stands' side over 1f
　　out: nrst fin) ............................................................................................... 2.**6**

2672 Dancing Wild **(37)** (Jt-Fav) *(MrsGRReveley)* 3–8-1  NCarlisle (19) (lw: chsd ldrs
　　stands' side: nt qckn appr fnl f) ................................................................... ¹/₂.**7**

2567 Form Mistress **(49)** *(PTWalwyn)* 3–8-13  MBirch (21) (lw: spd stands' side over
　　4f) ............................................................................................................. 1¹/₂.**8**

2821 Lonely Lass **(44)** *(AWJones)* 6–8-12  GDuffield (11) (nvr trbld ldrs) ................... s.h.**9**

2795 The New Girl **(59)** (v) *(CCElsey)* 3–9-6 ‡³SMaloney (5) (racd far side: in tch & rdn
　　¹/₂-wy: no imp) ........................................................................................... s.h.**10**

2722⁴ True Touch **(44)** *(TDBarron)* 3–8-8  AlexGreaves (18) (lw: spd over 4f) ............. 1.**11**

2666⁵ Noble Cause (IRE) **(47)** *(REarnshaw)* 3–8-11  JCarroll (20) (lw: dwlt: sme late
　　hdwy: n.d) .................................................................................................. ¹/₂.**12**

2159⁶ Reina **(30)** (bl) *(JDBethell)* 4–7-5 ‡⁷KateDovey (7) (b.nr hind: racd far side: n.d) ¹/₂.**13**

1924 Kabera **(25)** (bl) *(DWChapman)* 4–7-7  SWood (3) (racd far side: outpcd fr
　　¹/₂-wy) ...................................................................................................... ³/₄.**14**

2935 Sunnyside Rock (IRE) **(40)** (bl) *(JEtherington)* 4–8-8  MHills (2) (racd far side:
　　n.d) ........................................................................................................... ¹/₂.**15**

2743 Chill Wind **(35)** (bl) *(NBycroft)* 3–7-13  LCharnock (22) (n.d) ......................... 1¹/₂.**16**

2536 Mahzooz **(60)** (bl) *(MMoubarak)* 3–9-10  GBaxter (16) (nvr wnt pce) ............. 1¹/₂.**17**

2809 Blunham Express **(40)** (bl) *(TFairhurst)* 3–8-4  JFanning (17) (cl up over 3f) ...... 5.**18**

2676 Parisienne King (USA) **(37)** (v) *(FHLee)* 3–7-10 ‡⁵NKennedy (8) (racd far side:
　　spd 4f: eased whn btn) ............................................................................... 1.**19**

1328³ Legitim **(37)** *(JMJefferson)* 3–8-1  JLowe (9) (wl outpcd far side fr ¹/₂-wy) ....... ³/₄.**20**

2639³ Swinging Tich **(55)** *(BAMcMahon)* 3–9-5  JFortune (6) (lw: s.s: a bhd) .......... 2¹/₂.**21**

2517 Makeminemusic **(48)** *(FWatson)* 3–8-12⁽²⁾ DNicholls (1) (bhd far side fr ¹/₂-wy) 2.**22**

1075 Kashgar **(29)** *(DWChapman)* 3–7-0 ‡⁷DarrenMoffatt (14) (n.d) ...................... 3¹/₂.**23**

LONG HANDICAP: Kabera 7-5, Kashgar 7-3.

8/1 Stormbuster, Umbria, Dancing Wild, **10/1** Supreme Desire, The New Girl, **11/1** True Touch, **12/1** Swinging Tich, Noble Cause (IRE), **14/1** Form Mistress, Lonely Lass, Blunham Express, Legitim, Chill Wind, Syke Lane(op 8/1), **16/1** Mahzooz, **20/1** Reina, Bright Paragon (IRE), **25/1** Sunnyside Rock (IRE), YOURS OR MINE (IRE), **33/1** Parisienne King (USA), Makeminemusic, **50/1** Ors. CSF £452.18, CT £3,390.45. Tote £36.50: £6.80 £2.60 £4.50 £2.40 (£935.70). Mrs J. M. Davenport (YORK) bred by Gorden Patterson in Ireland. 23 Rn   1m 12.3 (2.1)
SF—45/41/37/40/31/16

**2985**  SALLY HALL H'CAP (3-Y.O) (0-70) £3446.60 (£957.60: £459.80)   1½m 3-20 (3-26)
(Weights raised 4 lb)

27154 **Fair Flyer (IRE)** (53) (MJohnston) 8-8 RPElliott (2) (lw: stdd after s: hdwy ent st: led ins fnl f: r.o wl) ............................... —1
27202 In the Money (IRE) **(62)** (RHollinshead) 9-3 WRyan (5) (lw: trckd ldrs: led over 2f out: hung lft: hrd rdn, hdd & no ex ins fnl f) ................... 1½.2
18412 Tempelhof (IRE) **(63)** (Fav) (JWHills) 9-4 GBaxter (7) (cl up: led 4f out tl over 2f out: one pce) ............... 6.3
2470* Kayartis (41) (MrsGRReveley) 7-10 JLowe (4) (a in tch: effrt appr st: hrd rdn & one pce fnl 2f) ............... 1½.4
25246 Tudor Da Samba (53) (JRFanshawe) 8-8 KDarley (8) (mid div tl styd on u.p fnl 3f: nrst fin) ............... hd.5
2701* Salu (54) (bl) (JEtherington) 8-9 JCarroll (13) (hld up: stdy hdwy ent st: effrt 2f out: sn rdn & btn) ............... 2½.6
2868 Shakinski (51) (MJRyan) 7-13 ‡7PMcCabe (11) (bhd: hdwy on outside 3f out: no imp) ............... ½.7
25475 El Rabab (USA) **(66)** (HThomsonJones) 9-7 NCarlisle (6) (lw: effrt appr st: sn rdn: nvr trbld ldrs) ............... 2.8
28205 West Stow **(66)** (MRStoute) 9-7 MBirch (3) (led tl hdd 4f out: sn btn) ............... nk.9
2605 Kenyatta (USA) **(62)** (DenysSmith) 9-3 NConnorton (4) (lw: chsd ldrs tl rdn & wknd wl over 2f out) ............... 7.10
26316 Mr Ziegfeld (USA) **(62)** (SirMarkPrescott) 9-3 GDuffield (1) (lw: nvr nr ldrs) ..... ½.11
2531 Capital Lad (38) (MAvison) 7-0 ‡7DarrenMoffatt (12) (a bhd: t.o) ............... 12
29083 Maji **(66)** (DMorley) 9-7 MHills (9) (sddle slipped & p.u 6f out) ............... 0
LONG HANDICAP: Capital Lad 7-1.

**9/2** Tempelhof (IRE), **6/1** Maji, In the Money (IRE), Kayartis, **13/2** Salu, **10/1** FAIR FLYER (IRE), West Stow, **12/1** Mr Ziegfeld (USA), **14/1** Tudor Da Samba, El Rabab (USA), **16/1** Shakinski, Kenyatta (USA), **50/1** Capital Lad. CSF £67.26, CT £288.54. Tote £13.90: £5.00 £2.20 £1.40 (£30.10). Mr William Provan Hunter (MIDDLEHAM) bred by J. Mamakos in Ireland. 13 Rn   2m 35.1 (5.1)
SF—43/49/38/13/24/20

**2986**  E.B.F. MARY REVELEY STKS (Mdn 2-Y.O) £2784.00 (£774.00: £372.00)
6f
3-50 (3-56)

361 **Latin Leader** (MrsJRRamsden) 9-0 GBaxter (16) (bit bkwd: trckd ldrs: chal over 1f out: styd on to ld wl ins fnl f) ............... —1
2646 Peacefull Reply (USA) **(FHLee)** 8-9 ‡5NKennedy (11) (mde most tl hdd wl ins fnl f: rallied nr fin) ............... hd.2
Ribhi (USA) (Fav) (DMorley) 9-0 MHills (14) (lt-f: a chsng ldrs: nt qckn ins fnl f) 1½.3
2405 Queen of the Quorn (GMMoore) 8-9 JFanning (13) (a w ldrs: drvn along ½-wy: r.o one pce) ............... 4.4
Somnifere (USA) (PWChapple-Hyam) 8-9 WRyan (2) (lt-f: unf: cl up tl rdn & btn appr fnl f) ............... nk.5
15915 Moon Watch (JRFanshawe) 8-9 KDarley (1) (lw: chsd ldrs: one pce fnl 2f) ........ ½.6
17794 Cinders Girl (JMPEustace) 8-9 MTebbutt (3) (lw: in tch: effrt ½-wy: no imp) .. 1.7
23812 Ashover (TDBarron) 9-0 AlexGreaves (9) (lw: nvr trbld ldrs) ............... 1.8
26463 Magic Street (MMoubarak) 8-9 JFortune (5) (lw: sn drvn along: nvr trbld ldrs) .. ¾.9
Lida's Delight (USA) (MWEasterby) 9-0 TLucas (8) (b: wl grwn: unf: bit bkwd: s.s: nvr nr to chal) ............... 2½.10
2781 Velasco (IRE) (SirMarkPrescott) 8-9 GDuffield (6) (lw: hld up: nvr plcd to chal) nk.11
Kira (MissLCSiddall) 8-9 NCarlisle (18) (leggy: a outpcd & bhd) ............... 1.12
2812 Northern Chief (MHEasterby) 9-0 MBirch (4) (n.d) ............... hd.13
Hung Hing (IRE) (bl) (JDBethell) 9-0 RPElliott (10) (w'like: w ldrs: hung bdly lft to ½-wy: sn lost pl) ............... 2½.14
23566 Blakes Reach (RRLamb) 8-7 ‡7RHavlin (17) (s.i.s: a bhd) ............... 2½.15
Corona Gold (JGFitzGerald) 9-0 DNicholls (15) (lengthy: scope: bkwd: in tch 4f) ............... s.h.16
2038 River Fire (IRE) (JBerry) 8-9 JCarroll (19) (sn outpcd & bhd) ............... ¾.17
2776 Andrew's Express (IRE) (SEKettlewell) 9-0 SWebster (7) (n.d) ............... 0

**7/4** Ribhi (USA), **4/1** Magic Street, **6/1** Moon Watch, Somnifere, USA)(op 4/1), **14/1** LATIN LEADER, Cinders Girl, Ashover, **16/1** Velasco (IRE), **20/1** River Fire (IRE), Northern Chief, Corona Gold, Hung Hing (IRE), **25/1** Kira, **33/1** Lida's Delight (IRE), Peacefull Reply (USA), **40/1** Ors. CSF £391.44, Tote £50.10: £8.90 £9.40 £1.50 (£615.20). Mr David Thompson (THIRSK) bred by Cheveley Park Stud Ltd. 18 Rn   1m 13.5 (3.3)
SF—34/28/27/6/5/3

## 2987

MARK JOHNSTON H'CAP (0-80) £3606.20 (£1003.20: £482.60)    1m    4-20 (4-27)

(Weights raised 5 lb)

27324 **Stairway to Heaven (IRE) (55)** (bl) *(TDBarron)* 4–8-5 ‡7VHalliday (11) (hdwy ent st: led over 1f out: rdn & r.o wl) .................................. —1

2862* Fit on Time (USA) (71) (Jt-Fav) *(MRStoute)* 3–9-8 WRyan (6) (lw: hdwy over 3f out: hrd rdn appr fnl f: styd on: nt pce of wnr) ............. 3½.2

28286 Green's Cassatt (USA) (55) (Jt-Fav) *(WMBrisbourne)* 4–8-9 ‡3SMaloney (2) (a in tch: effrt 3f out: styd on one pce appr fnl f) ..................... 4.3

25213 Brown Fairy (USA) (65) *(MrsNMacauley)* 4–9-8 MTebbutt (16) (lw: s.i.s: hdwy 3f out: styd on) ....................... 3.4

27433 Claudia Miss (56) (v) *(WWHaigh)* 5–8-13 GDuffield (4) (s.i.s: hdwy 3f out: nvr able to chal) ............................ 3½.5

2554 Waseela (IRE) (73) *(AAScott)* 3–9-10 JFortune (1) (lw: chsd ldr: led wl over 2f out tl over 1f out: sn wknd) .................... nk.6

25693 Young Jason (53) *(FHLee)* 9–8-5 ‡5NKennedy (14) (hld up & bhd: hdwy whn nt clr run 2f out: swtchd: nt rcvr) ................... 1½.7

*1996*3 Queen Warrior (70) *(PTWalwyn)* 3–9-7 MBirch (7) (in tch: effrt ent st: sn rdn & one pce) .................... ½.8

2814 Manulife (60) (v) *(BBeasley)* 3–8-11 LCharnock (10) (chsd ldrs: ev ch 3f out: wknd over 1f out) ..................... s.h.9

14804 Star Connection (66) *(RMWhitaker)* 4–9-9 ACulhane (9) (bhd: sme hdwy 2f out: n.d) ..................... 1½.10

2647 Aasff (USA) (71) (bl) *(DMorley)* 3–9-8 MHills (3) (swtg: led tl hdd wl over 2f out: sn btn) .................. 2½.11

23796 Flying Down to Rio (IRE) (49) *(MPNaughton)* 4–8-6 KDarley (8) (lw: chsd ldrs 5f) ..................... 2½.12

27322 Glenfield Greta (60) *(PSFelgate)* 4–9-3 JLowe (5) (lw: s.i.s: effrt & nt clr run 2f out: n.d) ..................... hd.13

1960 Dawn Success (56) (bl) *(DWChapman)* 0–0-10 EWood (13) (lw: n d) ............. hd.14

2676 Cottage Gallery (IRE) (36) *(WAStephenson)* 4–7-7 JFanning (12) (prom to st) 5.15

LONG HANDICAP: Cottage Gallery (IRE) 7-2.

5/1 Green's Cassatt (USA)(8/1—9/1), Fit on Time (USA), **8/1** STAIRWAY TO HEAVEN (IRE), **9/1** Brown Fairy (USA), **10/1** Waseela (IRE), **11/1** Young Jason, **12/1** Flying Down to Rio (IRE), Star Connection, Claudia Miss, Queen Warrior, Glenfield Greta, **14/1** Dawn Success, Aasff (USA), **25/1** Manulife, **33/1** Cottage Gallery (IRE). CSF £47.43, CT £209.75. Tote £13.50: £4.40 £1.30 £2.70 (£47.70). Mr Liam Moroney (THIRSK) bred by Peter Doyle in Ireland. 15 Rn     1m 39.9 (3.9)

SF—32/38/13/17/–/7

## 2988

COLIN TINKLER APP'CE STKS (Mdn 3-Y.O) £2364.00 (£654.00: £312.00)    7f    4-55 (4-56)

2780 **Be My Everything (IRE) (63)** *(RHollinshead)* 8-2 ‡7JDennis (4) (hld up: qcknd to ld over 2f out: edgd rt: sn clr) ..................... —1

28032 Climbing High (68) (Fav) *(IABalding)* 8-2 ‡7DGriffiths (6) (lw: w ldrs: chal ent st: sn rdn & r.o one pce) ..................... 8.2

26624 April Shadow (51) *(CWThornton)* 8-2 ‡7KSked (3) (cl up: hmpd appr st: effrt whn sltly hmpd 2f out: rdn & nt qckn) ..................... 1½.3

25383 Auction King (IRE) (60) *(ASmith)* 9-0 VHalliday (2) (lw: led tl hdd & hung rt over 2f out: sn btn) ..................... ½.4

2732 Always Lynsey (IRE) (49) *(MissLCSiddall)* 8-9 GParkin (1) (t: bhd: effrt over 2f out: hrd rdn & no imp) ..................... nk.5

2666 Dark Midnight (IRE) (45) *(RRLamb)* 9-0 RHavlin (5) (cl up to st: hrd rdn & sn wknd) ..................... 25.6

*Stewards Enquiry: Havlin suspended 6-7/9/92 (excessive use of the whip).*

**8/15** Climbing High, **5/1** BE MY EVERYTHING (IRE), **8/1** April Shadow, Auction King (IRE), **20/1** Always Lynsey (IRE), **33/1** Dark Midnight (IRE). CSF £7.87, Tote £5.70: £1.90 £1.10 (£3.00). Mrs B. Facchino (UPPER LONGDON) bred by Barronstown Bloodstock in Ireland. 6 Rn     1m 27.7 (4.4)

SF—22/–/–/–/–/–

T/Plpt: £2,064.00 (1.25 Tckts).        AA

## 2433—GOODWOOD (R-H)

**Friday, August 28th [Good to soft, Soft patches]**

Going Allowance: 5f: 0.40 sec per fur; Rest: 0.60 sec per fur (Y)     Wind: mod half against

Stalls: low

## 2989

OAKLEY APP'CE H'CAP (0-80) £4127.75 (£1232.00: £588.50: £266.75)    5f    2-10 (2-10)

(Weights raised 6 lb)

2936* **Ballasecret (77)** *(RDickin)* 4–10-0 (7x) ‡3DMeredith (4) (chsd ldr: led over 1f out: hrd rdn: r.o wl) ..................... —1

2499² Bells of Longwick (64) *(DRLaing)* 3–9-1 ATucker (7) (hld up: ev ch ins fnl f: r.o) ¾.2
2861 Coppermill Lad (49) (Jt-Fav) *(LJHolt)* 9–8-0 ‡³CAvery (3) (lw: outpcd: gd hdwy fnl f: fin wl) ............... 1.3
2821² Stocktina (39) (Jt-Fav) *(RJHodges)* 5–7-7 AGarth (4) (hld up: rdn over 2f out: unable qckn) ............ ¾.4
2718 The Noble Oak (IRE) (64) (bl) *(MMcCormack)* 4–9-4 StephenDavies (5) (lw: hld up: hrd rdn over 2f out: one pce) ............ 2½.5
2902 Ever so Lonely (61) (bl) *(ABailey)* 3–8-9 ‡³PBowe (6) (led over 3f) ............ 3½.6
2817² Manuleader (59) (bl) *(BBeasley)* 3–8-5 ‡⁵GMacDonald (1) (a bhd) ............ 4.7

**3/1** Stocktina, Coppermill Lad, **5/1** The Noble Oak (IRE), **11/2** BALLASECRET, **6/1** Manuleader, **7/1** Bells of Longwick(5/1—8/1), **12/1** Ever so Lonely. CSF £38.73, Tote £9.50: £3.60 £2.90 (£66.40). Mr R. J. Adams (NEWENT) bred by Mrs D. Price. 7 Rn
62.27 sec (4.67)
SF—61/45/26/16/31/8

**2990** SCHRODER INVESTMENT MANAGEMENT H'CAP (0-90) £8025.00 (£2400.00: £1150.00: £525.00) **1m**
2-40 (2-42)

2858* Jahangir (IRE) (73) *(BHanbury)* 3–8-12 (5x) LPiggott (8) (lw: 4th st: led 3f out: rdn out) ............ —1
2347 Green's Ferneley (IRE) (81) (bl) (Jt-Fav) *(RCharlton)* 4–9-12 MRoberts (2) (b: lw: 3rd st: hrd rdn over 1f out: unable qckn) ............ 3½.2
2935² Salbyng (58) (Jt-Fav) *(JWHills)* 4–8-3 RHills (6) (lw: 6th st: hrd rdn over 1f out: one pce) ............ ¾.3
2417 Ghurrah (IRE) (62) *(CJBenstead)* 3–8-1 TyroneWilliams (10) (lw: rdn 5f out: hdwy 2f out: one pce) ............ hd.4
2755² Trooping (IRE) (82) *(GHarwood)* 3–9-7 AClark (9) (lw: 5th st: rdn over 2f out: one pce) ............ ½.5
2825 Domicksky (75) *(RSimpson)* 4–9-1 ‡⁵ATucker (1) (nvr nr to chal) ............ 1.6
2473 Northern Conqueror (IRE) (54) *(TJNaughton)* 4–7-13 DBiggs (11) (nvr nrr) .... 1½.7
2707⁵ Royal Dartmouth (USA) (55) *(BRMillman)* 7–8-0 TSprake (3) (b: lw: nvr nrr) .... nk.8
2795 Magnificent (78) *(MAJarvis)* 3–8-11 PRobinson (5) (bhd fnl 2f) ............ 10.9
2755⁴ Emaura (60) *(KOCunningham-Brown)* 3–7-13 GBardwell (4) (lw: 2nd st: wknd over 2f out) ............ 7.10
2252* Agincourt Song (USA) (81) *(JLDunlop)* 3–9-6 SCauthen (7) (lw: led 5f) ............ 4.11

**11/2** Green's Ferneley (IRE), Salbyng, **7/1** Magnificent, JAHANGIR (IRE), Trooping (IRE), **10/1** Agincourt Song (USA), Royal Dartmouth (USA), **12/1** Domicksky, **14/1** Ghurrah (IRE), **16/1** Emaura, **20/1** Northern Conqueror (IRE). CSF £39.48, CT £199.41. Tote £6.00: £2.00 £2.30 £2.30 (£13.60). Mr J. R. Ali (NEWMARKET) bred by Mrs A. W. Riddell-Martin in Ireland. 11 Rn
1m 44.12 (6.52)
SF—72/75/50/47/65/56

**2991** BUTLINS SOUTHCOAST WORLD PRESTIGE STKS (Gp 3) (2-Y.O.F) £13360.00 (£4998.00: £2399.00: £1043.00) **7f**
3-10 (3-14)

2657⁴ Love of Silver (USA) (100) *(CEBrittain)* 8-9 MRoberts (5) (lw: led 6f out: drvn out) ............ —1
2338* Dancing Bloom (IRE) *(MRStoute)* 8-9 LPiggott (1) (lw: led 1f: 2nd st: hrd rdn & ev ch fnl f: r.o) ............ nk.2
2728* Ajfan (USA) (96) *(HThomsonJones)* 8-9 RHills (4) (lw: 6th st: rdn over 2f out: r.o) ............ 1½.3
2792* Ribbonwood (USA) (100) (Fav) *(JHMGosden)* 8-9 SCauthen (3) (swtg: 4th st: rdn over 2f out: r.o one pce) ............ s.h.4
2859³ Bobbie Dee *(DRCElsworth)* 8-9 JWilliams (7) (lw: hdwy over 1f out: r.o) ............ ¾.5
2841⁴ Carranita (IRE) (88) *(BPalling)* 8-9 StephenDavies (6) (3rd st: one pce fnl 2f) .... ¾.6
2344³ Lake Pleasant (IRE) (100) *(RHannon)* 8-9 PRobinson (2) (5th st: wknd over 2f out) ............ 8.7

**11/8** Ribbonwood (USA), **5/2** Dancing Bloom (IRE)(7/4—11/4), **11/2** Ajfan (USA), **9/1** Lake Pleasant (IRE), LOVE OF SILVER (USA)(tchd 14/1), **20/1** Bobbie Dee, **33/1** Carranita (IRE). CSF £29.96, Tote £7.40: £2.40 £1.90 (£9.90). Mr Ali Saeed (NEWMARKET) bred by Brylynn Farm in USA. 7 Rn
1m 32.14 (7.44)
SF—47/46/41/40/38/36

**2992** HORSE RACING ABROAD H'CAP (3-Y.O) (0-80) £4077.50 (£1220.00: £585.00: £267.50) **1½m**
3-40 (3-46)

(Weights raised 2 lb)
2134³ Top Royal (74) *(JLDunlop)* 9-3 BCrossley (8) (hdwy over 2f out: led wl over 1f out: r.o wl) ............ —1
2757* Googly (64) (Jt-Fav) *(WGRWightman)* 8-7 GBardwell (7) (lw: hdwy over 2f out: ev ch wl over 1f out: unable qckn fnl f) ............ 2.2
2769² Usaidit (73) *(WCarter)* 9-2 JWilliams (13) (lw: 4th st: led over 2f out tl wl over 1f out: one pce) ............ 5.3

2915* Ideal Candidate (63) (TJNaughton) 8-6 (5x) DBiggs (3) (hdwy over 2f out: one pce) ............................................................................................................. 3.4

2860³ Lemon's Mill (USA) (78) (Jt-Fav) (JHMGosden) 9-7 SCauthen (2) (6th st: one pce fnl 3f) ..................................................................................................... 1¹/₂.5

512⁵ Indian Decision (71) (JLDunlop) 9-0 PRobinson (1) (swtg: nvr nr to chal) ......... ³/₄.6

2585³ Storm Dust (72) (JRFanshawe) 8-8 ‡⁷NVarley (14) (no hdwy fnl 3f) .................... ¹/₂.7

2631 Erlemo (50) (bl) (CJBenstead) 7-0 ‡⁷AntoinetteArmes (4) (led 9f out tl over 2f out: sn wknd) .......................................................................................... 3¹/₂.8

2631* Corinthian God (IRE) (52) (DAWilson) 7-9⁽²⁾ TyroneWilliams (12) (led 2f: 2nd st: wknd over 2f out) ......................................................................................... 2¹/₂.9

2698 Oozlem (IRE) (63) (CAHorgan) 8-6 AMcGlone (11) (rdn 7f out: bhd fnl 5f) ... 1¹/₂.10

2660⁶ Major's Law (IRE) (70) (CEBrittain) 8-13 MRoberts (10) (swtg: led 10f out to 9f out: 3rd st: wknd over 2f out) ....................................................................... ¹/₂.11

2693⁶ Faaz (USA) (53) (AAScott) 7-10 SDawson (5) (bhd fnl 3f) ............................... nk.12

2769⁹ Debacle (USA) (77) (GHarwood) 9-6 AClark (9) (b: a bhd) ............................. ³/₄.13

2791 Sovereign Page (USA) (78) (BHanbury) 9-7 LPiggott (6) (lw: hdwy 5f out: 5th st: wknd over 2f out) ................................................................................... 10.14

LONG HANDICAP: Erlemo 7-2, Corinthian God (IRE) 7-6.

11/2 Lemon's Mill (USA), Googly, 6/1 Ideal Candidate, Major's Law (IRE), 8/1 Debacle (USA), 12/1 Oozlem (IRE), 14/1 TOP ROYAL, Corinthian God (IRE), Usaidit, Storm Dust, 16/1 Sovereign Page (USA), 20/1 Faaz (USA), Indian Decision, 33/1 Erlemo. CSF £83.68, CT £1,016.63. Tote £17.40: £4.30 £2.00 £4.70 (£96.00). Mr Aubrey Ison (ARUNDEL) bred by Miss G. Abbey. 14 Rn

2m 44.77 (13.07)

SF—44/30/29/13/25/16

---

**2993**    ST ROCHES CLAIMING H'CAP (3-Y.O) (0-70) £2721.00 (£756.00: £363.00)
             1¹/₄m                                                                    4-15 (4-20)

(Weights raised 2 lb)

2931* Bo Knows Best (IRE) (43) (Fav) (JSutcliffe) 7-9 (4x) ‡⁵ATucker (0) (6th st: led over 2f out: drvn out) ......................................................................................... —1

2882 Crackling (40) (DMarks) 7-4 ‡⁷AGarth (4) (hdwy over 2f out: hrd rdn & ev ch ins fnl f: r.o) .......................................................................................................... ³/₄.2

2685* Day of History (IRE) (40) (CACyzer) 7-11 DBiggs (18) (hrd rdn & hdwy over 2f out: unable qckn) ............................................................................................ 5.3

2580³ Storm Drum (58) (bl) (PJMakin) 9-1 SCauthen (6) (hdwy over 2f out: hrd rdn over 1f out: one pce) ............................................................................................ 2.4

2566⁶ Eleckydo (43) (RJHodges) 8-0 TSprake (14) (swtchd lft 3f out: hdwy over 2f out: nvr nrr) ................................................................................................... 3.5

2871⁶ Flash of Straw (IRE) (47) (GLewis) 8-4 AMcGlone (12) (a.p: one pce fnl 3f) ....... 2.6

2806⁶ Amazon Express (57) (CEBrittain) 9-0 MRoberts (17) (lw: 3rd st: wknd over 1f out) ................................................................................................................ ¹/₂.7

2725² Edge of Darkness (58) (JWHills) 9-1 RHills (5) (no hdwy fnl 3f) .......................... 3.8

2601 Mere Chants (64) (DRCElsworth) 9-7 JWilliams (8) (nvr nr to chal) ................... 2¹/₂.9

2680⁵ Silky Siren (53) (EAWheeler) 8-10 SWhitworth (11) (nvr nrr) ........................... 1¹/₂.10

2685 Selaginella (50) (MRChannon) 8-2 ‡⁵BDoyle (2) (6th st: wknd over 1f out) nk.11

2302⁵ My Senor (39) (MMadgwick) 7-10 SDawson (10) (nvr nrr) .............................. 4.12

2632⁴ Deevee (46) (CJBenstead) 8-3 TyroneWilliams (13) (s.s: nvr nrr) ..................... hd.13

2805⁶ Slight Risk (63) (PAKelleway) 9-6 GayKelleway (3) (eyecover: led 1f: led over 4f out tl over 2f out: sn wknd) ...................................................................................... 1.14

2882 Lamore Ritorna (55) (KOCunningham-Brown) 8-12 LPiggott (15) (led 9f out tl over 4f out: 2nd st: wknd over 2f out) ........................................................................ ³/₄.15

2801 Alton Belle (44) (bl) (PHowling) 8-1⁽¹⁾ BCrossley (1) (4th st: wknd over 2f out) 5.16

2830 Chinaman (38) (bl) (WGRWightman) 7-9 GBardwell (7) (hdwy 5f out: wknd over 3f out) ....................................................................................................... 5.17

52³ Lizzie Drippin (CAN) (45) (MDIUsher) 8-2 PRobinson (16) (a bhd: t.o whn virtually p.u over 3f out) .................................................................................... 18

7/4 BO KNOWS BEST (IRE), 6/1 Edge of Darkness, 7/1 Storm Drum, 10/1 Amazon Express(op 6/1), 11/1 Silky Siren, 12/1 Day of History (IRE), Deevee, 16/1 Flash of Straw (IRE)(op 10/1), Slight Risk, Mere Chants, 20/1 My Senor, Lamore Ritorna, Lizzie Drippin (CAN), 25/1 Selaginella, 33/1 Crackling, Chinaman, 50/1 Alton Belle. CSF £64.28, CT £593.60. Tote £2.90: £1.40 £12.70 £3.10 £1.90 (£126.60). Mr John Sutcliffe (EPSOM) bred by Gay O'Callaghan in Ireland. 18 Rn

2m 15.77 (10.77)

SF—33/26/23/37/16/16

---

**2994**    COWDRAY (S) STKS (2-Y.O) £2868.00 (£798.00: £384.00)    6f    4-45 (4-56)

2826 Risk Proof (GLewis) 8-11 SCauthen (20) (hdwy over 1f out: led ins fnl f: r.o wl) —1

2863² Be Polite (IRE) (53) (bl) (MBell) 8-6 RHills (17) (a.p: ev ch ins fnl f: r.o) ........... ¹/₂.2

2842⁵ El Nino (IRE) (Fav) (RHannon) 8-11 BCrossley (7) (hdwy over 1f out: r.o ins fnl f) nk.3

2005⁴ My Godson (61) (bl) (BBeasley) 8-11 ‡⁵SWilliams (15) (led: hrd rdn & edgd rt over 1f out: hdd ins fnl f: r.o) ................................................................... nk.4

2771⁵ Sea Strand *(MBlanshard)* 8-6 GBardwell (11) (lost pl 3f out: rallied fnl f: r.o wl) .......................... nk.5
2857 Bodandere **(56)** *(MJFetherston-Godley)* 8-6 MRoberts (9) (hld up: rdn over 1f out: r.o) ........................... 1.6
1989³ Risky Number **(56)** *(JSMoore)* 8-11 DBiggs (13) (lw: a.p: hrd rdn over 1f out: one pce) ....................... ³⁄₄.7
2195⁵ Arctic Agnes (USA) *(RAkehurst)* 7-13 ‡7LCarter (16) (prom 4f) .......................... 3.8
2396 Purbeck Centenary *(MRChannon)* 8-13⁽²⁾ LornaVincent (10) (hld up: rdn over 1f out: wknd ins fnl f) ........................ hd.9
1251 Miss Otter (IRE) *(GAPritchard-Gordon)* 8-6 SWhitworth (2) (n.d) ........................ 4.10
2544 Dark and Stormy *(MDixon)* 8-11 MPerrett (14) (outpcd) ........................ s.h.11
Duke of Budworth *(MHTompkins)* 8-11 PRobinson (21) (leggy: prom over 4f) ¹⁄₂.12
2591 Keamari **(43)** *(BForsey)* 8-1 ‡5ATucker (3) (prom 3f) .......................... 2.13
Arras Royale *(JELong)* 8-11 CandyMorris (19) (unf: bit bkwd: outpcd) ........ hd.14
1764 All Promises **(40)** *(PButler)* 7-13 ‡7SDrowne (12) (prom over 3f) .......................... ¹⁄₂.15
Gerski *(RHannon)* 7-13 ‡7DGibbs (4) (unf: bkwd: outpcd) ........................ s.h.16
Capten Morgan (IRE) *(WJHaggas)* 8-11 JWilliams (18) (cmpt: bit bkwd: a bhd) ¹⁄₂.17
2863 Tropical Tia (IRE) **(52)** *(RVoorspuy)* 8-6 SDawson (8) (n.d) .......................... 1.18
1300 Don't Tell Dick *(DRLaing)* 8-6 TyroneWilliams (5) (n.d) .......................... 8.19
2746 Petiole (bl) *(WRMuir)* 8-7⁽¹⁾ LPiggott (1) (a bhd) .......................... 4.20
828 Midget Gem *(NAGraham)* 8-11 AMcGlone (6) (n.d) .......................... 10.21

**2/1** El Nino (IRE), **5/1** Be Polite (IRE), **8/1** Bodandere, **10/1** Risky Number, Duke of Budworth(12/1—8/1), **14/1** Capten Morgan (IRE), Miss Otter (IRE), Petiole, RISK PROOF, My Godson, **16/1** Gerski, **20/1** Midget Gem, Tropical Tia (IRE), Sea Strand, All Promises, Arctic Agnes (USA), **33/1** Purbeck Centenary, **50/1** Dark and Stormy, Don't Tell Dick, Keamari, **66/1** Arras Royale. CSF £88.99, Tote £18.60: £5.10 £1.70 £1.80 (£68.60). Roldvale Limited (EPSOM) bred by Roldvale Ltd. 21 Rn; Sold K Cunningham-Brown 6,500 gns; El Nino (IRE) clmd M Dixon £6,050

1m 17.47 (7.07)
SF—28/21/25/24/18/14

**2995** WEST DEAN STKS (Mdn 3-Y-O) £2385.00 (£660.00: £315.00) 7f 5-20 (5-25)

2858² **Hameem (IRE) (74)** (bl) *(AAScott)* 9-0 RHills (3) (lw: mde all: clr over 4f out: r.o wl) .......................... —1
2753² Express Service **(79)** (Fav) *(PJMakin)* 9-0 MRoberts (5) (3rd st: chsd wnr fnl 3f: no imp) .......................... 6.2
2704⁵ Quixotic *(PWHarris)* 9-0 SWhitworth (7) (5th st: one pce fnl 3f) .......................... 3.3
Concinnity (USA) *(LJHolt)* 9-0 AMcGlone (2) (unf: bkwd: s.s: 6th st: nvr nr to chal) .......................... 7.4
Great Splendour *(CEBrittain)* 8-9 PRobinson (4) (unf: bit bkwd: 2nd st: wknd over 2f out) .......................... 2.5
King's Signet (USA) *(JHMGosden)* 9-0 SCauthen (6) (cmpt: bit bkwd: 4th st: hrd rdn over 2f out: eased whn btn over 1f out) .......................... 10.6
2780 Mistress Minx *(LJCodd)* 8-2 ‡7WHollick (1) (a bhd) .......................... 5.7

**5/4** Express Service(6/4—Evens), **5/2** HAMEEM (IRE), **3/1** King's Signet (USA)(6/4—4/1), **12/1** Great Splendour(op 8/1), **50/1** Quixotic, Concinnity (USA), **66/1** Mistress Minx. CSF £5.64, Tote £4.00: £1.60 (£2.80). Maktoum Al Maktoum (NEWMARKET) bred by The Sussex Stud in Ireland. 7 Rn 1m 32.77 (8.07)
SF—41/23/14/—/—/—

T/Trio: Race 4: £205.30 (7.1 Tckts); Race 5: £317.30 (4.1. T/Jkpt: Not won; £5,924.40 to Goodwood 29/08/92. T/Plpt: £213.50 (33.6 Tckts). AK

# GOODWOOD (R-H)

## Saturday, August 29th [Good to soft, Good patches]
Going Allowance: 0.40 sec per fur (Y) Wind: almost nil

Stalls: 2nd & 6th low, remainder high

**2996** MARCH STKS (listed race) (3-Y-O) £10770.00 (£3210.00: £1530.00: £690.00) 1³⁄₄m 2-00 (2-02)

1940★ Rain Rider (Fav) *(JLDunlop)* 9-1 WCarson (4) (2nd st: led over 1f out: drvn out) —1
652★ Allegan (USA) *(HRACecil)* 8-11 SCauthen (3) (led tl over 1f out: hrd rdn: r.o) ... hd.2
1464⁴ Currency Basket (IRE) *(PO'Leary,Ireland)* 8-11 LPiggott (1) (4th st: one pce fnl 3f) .......................... 15.3
2836 Spikenard **(89)** *(PTWalwyn)* 8-6 RCochrane (2) (3rd st: wknd 2f out) .......................... 4.4

**11/10** RAIN RIDER, **6/5** Allegan (USA), **8/1** Spikenard(12/1—20/1), **16/1** Currency Basket (IRE). CSF £2.71, Tote £2.00 (£1.20). Mrs E. M. H. Ogden White (ARUNDEL) bred by Ash Hill Stud. 4 Rn 3m 7.71 (8.71)
SF—70/65/35/22

## 2997

SPORT ON 5 H'CAP (0-105) £12135.00 (£3630.00: £1740.00: £795.00)
**6f**                                                                    2-30 (2-48)
(Weights raised 2 lb)

2650★ **So Rhythmical (77)** (GHEden) 8–8–8 WCarson (13) (b.off hind: hdwy 2f out: led ins fnl f: all out) ...... —1

28394 Hard to Figure **(91)** (Jt-Fav) (RJHodges) 6–9–8 RCochrane (11) (nt clr run over 2f out: swtchd & hdwy over 1f out: fin wl) .......... s.h.2

2898 Never so Sure **(87)** (bl) (ABailey) 4–9–4 LPiggott (14) (a.p: led over 1f out tl ins fnl f: r.o) .......... nk.3

2804² Assignment **(69)** (JFfitch-Heyes) 6–8–0 TyroneWilliams (15) (lw: broke loose fr stalls: hdwy over 2f out: hrd rdn over 1f out: r.o) .......... 1.4

24354 Heather Bank **(94)** (JBerry) 3–9–7 GCarter (7) (a.p: nt qckn fnl f) .......... ¾.5

2909★ Walk in the Park **(90)** (RSimpson) 3–8–12 ‡5ATucker (9) (lw: nvr nrr) .......... ½.6

2925★ Green Dollar **(93)** (EAWheeler) 9–9–10 MTebbutt (3) (gd hdwy fnl f: r.o) .......... ½.7

2861 Masnun (USA) **(82)** (Jt-Fav) (RJO'Sullivan) 7–8–13 PaulEddery (4) (hdwy over 1f out: nvr nr to chal) .......... 2.8

2337 Choir Practice **(76)** (WJHaggas) 5–8–7 JQuinn (6) (nvr nr ldrs) .......... ½.9

2861 Martinosky **(63)** (bl) (WGRWightman) 6–7–8 GBardwell (12) (led over 1f out) .......... 1.10

2919² Misdemeanours Girl (IRE) **(69)** (Jt-Fav) (MRChannon) 4–7–9 ‡5BDoyle (2) (bhd fnl 3f) .......... 1.11

2658 Kayvee **(96)** (GHarwood) 3–9–9 AClark (10) (lw: w ldrs tl wknd 2f out) .......... 2.12

2435 Aughfad **(93)** (v) (TCasey) 6–9–10 JReid (8) (spd 4f) .......... nk.13

2797 Petraco (IRE) **(72)** (bl) (LJCodd) 4–7–10 ‡7WHollick (5) (stumbled 5f out: hmpd 4f out: a wl bhd) .......... 1½.14

**7/1** Hard to Figure, Misdemeanours Girl (IRE), Masnun (USA), **8/1** SO RHYTHMICAL, Heather Bank, **10/1** Aughfad, **11/1** Never so Sure, Kayvee, **14/1** Green Dollar, Petraco (IRE), **16/1** Walk in the Park, Martinosky, **20/1** Assignment, **33/1** Choir Practice. CSF £56.72, CT £562.39. Tote £6.80: £2.00 £2.60 £4.20 (£24.30). Miss C. A. Barrow (NEWMARKET) bred by D. C. R. Allen. 14 Rn
1m 14.05 (3.65)
SF—69/82/77/55/73/62

## 2998

BEEFEATER GIN CELEBRATION MILE (Stks) (Gp 2) £50035.00 (£18686.75: £8943.38: £3859.87)   **1m**                                         3-10 (3-21)

2440² **Selkirk (USA)** (Fav) (IABalding) 4–9–3 RCochrane (1) (hld up in rr: hdwy over 2f out: led ins fnl f: easily) .......... —1

2506a★ Steinbeck (USA) (AFabre,France) 3–8–8 SCauthen (4) (5th st: outpcd over 2f out: hdwy over 1f out: r.o ins fnl f) .......... 2½.2

2440 Rudimentary (USA) (HRACecil) 4–9–3 LPiggott (3) (led 1f: led 4f out: sn clr: hdd & wknd ins fnl f) .......... hd.3

1823a Alhijaz (JLDunlop) 3–9–0 WCarson (5) (6th st: nrst fin) .......... nk.4

26435 Flashfoot (IABalding) 4–9–0 PaulEddery (2) (3rd st: wknd over 2f out) .......... 10.5

8495 Mystiko (USA) (CEBrittain) 4–9–0 JReid (7) (led after 1f to 4f out: 2nd st: wknd over 2f out) .......... hd.6

2789 Sylva Honda (CEBrittain) 4–9–0 GCarter (6) (4th st: wknd over 2f out) .......... 3½.7

**1/2** SELKIRK (USA), **5/1** Steinbeck (USA), **7/1** Rudimentary (USA), **10/1** Mystiko (USA), **20/1** Alhijaz, **50/1** Flashfoot, **100/1** Sylva Honda. CSF £3.51, Tote £1.50: £1.30 £1.80 (£2.60). Mr George Strawbridge (KINGSCLERE) bred by George Strawbridge Jnr in USA. 7 Rn
1m 41.72 (4.12)
SF—89/72/80/76/46/45

## 2999

RICHMOND-BRISSAC TROPHY (H'cap) (Amateurs) (0-90) £3557.50 (£1060.00: £505.00: £227.50)   **1m 1f**                                   3-40 (3-45)

2874★ **Surrey Dancer (71)** (BHanbury) 4–10–13 MrFGrassoCaprioli (2) (6th st: led wl over 1f out: r.o wl) .......... —1

2825² Roseate Lodge **(72)** (RWArmstrong) 6–11–0 MrLMaynard (10) (8th st: hdwy over 1f out: nt qckn fnl f) .......... 1½.2

27144 Gilderdale **(82)** (JWHills) 10–11–10 MrCVigors (7) (5th st: r.o ins fnl f) .......... s.h.3

2707 Akkazao (IRE) **(75)** (WCarter) 4–11–3 MrSSwiers (4) (3rd st: led over 2f out tl wl over 1f out) .......... 3½.4

2946 Tiger Claw (USA) **(51)** (RJHodges) 6–9–7 MrOFrei (9) (last & wd st: gd hdwy 2f out: one pce fnl f) .......... ¾.5

23436 Berlin Wall (IRE) **(72)** (Jt-Fav) (PWChapple-Hyam) 4–11–0 MrJDurkan (6) (2nd st: led over 3f out tl over 2f out) .......... 1.6

28285 Keep Your Word **(55)** (GBBalding) 6–9–11 MrJRees (5) (4th st: one pce fnl 2f) .......... s.h.7

2846 Virkon Venture (IRE) **(70)** (Jt-Fav) (MHTompkins) 4–10–12 MrMArmytage (3) (9th st: hdwy over 3f out: wknd 2f out) .......... ½.8

2825 Swift Romance (IRE) **(62)** (BRMillman) 4–10–4 MrDSalter (1) (7th st: wknd over 2f out) .......... 8.9

2917 Yeoman Bound **(58)** (KTIvory) 4–10–0(7) MrKSantana (8) (led tl wknd qckly over 3f out: t.o) .......... 15.10

LONG HANDICAP: Tiger Claw (USA) 9-3, Yeoman Bound 7-6.

**7/2** Berlin Wall (IRE), Virkon Venture (IRE), **9/2** SURREY DANCER, **5/1** Roseate Lodge, Gilderdale, **12/1** Keep Your Word, **16/1** Akkazao (IRE)(op 8/1), **25/1** Swift Romance, Tiger Claw (USA), **100/1** Yeoman Bound. CSF £26.13, CT £107.38. Tote £4.50: £1.40 £1.70 £2.10 (£7.20). Cronk Thoroughbred Racing Ltd (NEWMARKET) bred by Fonthill Stud. 10 Rn 2m 3.24 (12.54)
SF—2/–/7/–/–/–

**3000**     SOLENT STKS (Mdn 2-Y.O) £4077.50 (£1220.00: £585.00: £267.50)     **7f** 4-10 (4-12)

2799⁴ **Wootton Rivers (USA)** *(PWChapple-Hyam)* 9-0 PaulEddery (12) (6th st: led over 1f out: r.o wl) ......................... —1

2799⁶ Ecu de France (IRE) (Jt-Fav) *(JLDunlop)* 9-0 WCarson (9) (4th st: ev ch over 1f out: r.o wl) ......................... 3½.2

2728 Grey Watch *(LadyHerries)* 8-9 JWilliams (4) (wl bhd tl gd hdwy over 1f out: fin wl) ......................... 1.3

1899 Coppot Tel (IRE) *(CEBrittain)* 8-9 ‡⁵BDoyle (5) (2nd st: r.o one pce fnl 2f) ......... 2.4

2456³ Lt Welsh (USA) *(IABalding)* 9-0 RCochrane (8) (3rd st: led 2f out: sn hdd & wknd) ......................... s.h.5

Cameo Kirby (FR) *(AAScott)* 9-0 GCarter (3) (w'like: 5th st: ev ch 2f out: nt qckn) ... s.h.6

2653³ Hostile Witness (IRE) (Jt-Fav) *(RHannon)* 9-0 JReid (6) (7th st: rdn over 2f out: no hdwy) ......................... 1½.7

Starlight Rose (IRE) *(CAHorgan)* 8-9 DaleGibson (11) (lengthy: a bhd) ............. ½.8

Wordsmith (IRE) *(GHarwood)* 9-0 MPerrett (2) (str: scope: a bhd) ......................... 1.9

1709 October Brew (USA) *(GLewis)* 9-0 AClark (7) (hdwy on ins & nt clr run 2f out: nt rcvr) ......................... 1½.10

2799 American Swinger (USA) *(PWHarris)* 9-0 SWhitworth (10) (led tl wknd 2f out) .. 2.11

**11/4** Hostile Witness (IRE), Ecu de France (IRE), **3/1** Lt Welsh (USA), **100/30** WOOTTON RIVERS (USA), **16/1** Cameo Kirby (FR), **33/1** Ors. CSF £12.54, Tote £4.20: £1.60 £1.20 £6.90 (£5.60). Mr R. E. Sangster (MARLBOROUGH) bred by Swettenham Stud in USA. 11 Rn 1m 32.02 (7.32)
SF—32/21/13/7/11/10

**3001**     RAUGHMERE NURSERY   £3915.00 (£1170.00: £560.00: £255.00)     **6f** 4-45 (4-45)
(Weights raised 5 lb)

2557★ **Katiba (USA) (80)** (Fav) *(JLDunlop)* 9-6 WCarson (3) (dwlt: hdwy 2f out: led ins fnl f: r.o wl) ......................... —1

2824⁴ Second Chance (IRE) **(71)** *(PMitchell)* 8-11 AClark (6) (a.p: led over 2f out tl ins fnl f) ......................... nk.2

2709³ Geoff's Risk **(67)** *(GLewis)* 8-7 PaulEddery (7) (a.p: ev ch 1f out: nt qckn) ...... 2½.3

2612★ Walsham Witch **(74)** *(MHTompkins)* 9-0 DaleGibson (2) (chsd ldrs: rdn 2f out: r.o one pce) ......................... ½.4

2928★ Classic Storm **(78)** *(JBerry)* 9-4 GCarter (8) (prom over 4f) ......................... 4.5

2474² Musical Prospect (USA) **(81)** *(RHannon)* 9-7 RCochrane (4) (prom 4f) ......................... ½.6

2683★ Lys (IRE) **(78)** *(CEBrittain)* 8-13 ‡⁵BDoyle (5) (dwlt: a bhd) ......................... nk.7

2706 Felt Lucky (IRE) **(74)** *(MRChannon)* 8-9 ‡⁵ATucker (1) (led over 3f) ......................... 4.8

**5/4** KATIBA (USA), **9/2** Classic Storm, **11/2** Geoff's Risk(4/1—6/1), **8/1** Musical Prospect (USA)(14/1—16/1), **10/1** Lys (IRE), **12/1** Second Chance (IRE), **16/1** Walsham Witch, **20/1** Felt Lucky (IRE). CSF £15.55, CT £58.50. Tote £2.30: £1.10 £3.20 £1.50 (£23.00). Mr Hamdan Al-Maktoum (ARUNDEL) bred by Foxfield in USA. 8 Rn 1m 15.11 (4.71)
SF—60/43/29/34/22/23

**3002**     PILLEY GREEN H'CAP (0-80) £4370.00 (£1310.00: £630.00: £290.00)
**7f**     5-15 (5-17)

2772 **Darakah (53)** *(CJHill)* 5-8-5 AClark (19) (rapid hdwy over 1f out: str run to ld wl ins fnl f) ......................... —1

1992 Veloce (IRE) **(53)** *(ABailey)* 4-7-12 ‡⁷WHollick (8) (5th st: led over 1f out tl wl ins fnl f) ......................... nk.2

2935 State of Affairs **(41)** *(CAHorgan)* 5-7-7 DaleGibson (12) (hdwy 2f out: r.o wl ins fnl f) ......................... ¾.3

2060³ Garth **(73)** (v) *(PJMakin)* 4-9-11 SWhitworth (4) (gd hdwy 2f out: r.o ins fnl f) ... ¾.4

2825 Cheveux Mitchell **(76)** *(MRChannon)* 5-9-11 ‡³RPerham (1) (3rd st: ev ch over 1f out: nt qckn) ......................... nk.5

2750² Zinbaq **(42)** *(CJBenstead)* 6-7-8(1) TyroneWilliams (3) (hdwy over 2f out: ev ch over 1f out: nt qckn) ......................... s.h.6

2898² Belfort Ruler **(71)** *(BGubby)* 5-9-6 ‡³RonHillis (11) (9th st: hrd rdn over 1f out: one pce) ......................... s.h.7

2684⁵ Fabled Orator **(41)** *(PHowling)* 7-7-0 ‡⁷DWright (10) (led 4f out tl wknd over 1f out) ......................... 1½.8

2616 Mustahil (IRE) **(65)** *(RJHodges)* 3-8-5 ‡⁷CAvery (7) (nvr nr to chal) ......................... 1½.9

2795⁴ Louisville Belle (IRE) **(70)** *(MDIUsher)* 3-9-3 RCochrane (16) (nvr nr ldrs) ......... 1.10

```
2945³  Ikteshaf (75) (BHanbury) 4–9-13 AShoults (5) (7th st: wknd 2f out) .............. hd.11
2830*  Kirriemuir (48) (KOCunningham-Brown) 4–8-0 SDawson (9) (8th st: wknd 2f
         out) ............................................................................................. hd.12
2726³  Mu-Arrik (48) (DAWilson) 4–8-0 GCarter (2) (a bhd) ............................. 2¹⁄₂.13
2881*  Hawaii Storm (FR) (54) (MissAJWhitfield) 4–8-1 ‡5ATucker (18) (4th st: wknd
         over 2f out) ..................................................................................... 2¹⁄₂.14
2898   Colossus (71) (CEBrittain) 4–9-4 ‡⁶BDoyle (13) (6th st: wknd over 2f out) ....... 1.15
       Young Duke (IRE) (74) (bl) (MMcCormack) 4–9-12 MPerrett (17) (a bhd) ...... nk.16
800    Dawn's Delight (41) (KTIvory) 14–7-7 GBardwell (15) (a bhd) ................... 1¹⁄₂.17
2753*  Sweet Jaffa (74) (Fav) (MajorWRHern) 3–9-7 WCarson (6) (a wl bhd) ............. 2.18
2752   Co-Chin (IRE) (73) (bl) (GLewis) 3–9-6 PaulEddery (14) (led 4f: 2nd st: wknd
         qckly) ............................................................................................. 8.19
       LONG HANDICAP: State of Affairs 7-6, Fabled Orator 7-1, Dawn's Delight 7-3.
```

**9/2** Sweet Jaffa(7/1—8/1), **6/1** Hawaii Storm (FR), **8/1** DARAKAH, Louisville Belle (IRE), **10/1** Kirriemuir, **11/1** Zinbaq, **12/1** Belfort Ruler(op 8/1), **14/1** Ikteshaf, Mu-Arrik, **16/1** Garth, Colossus, Co-Chin (IRE), **25/1** Mustahil (IRE), State of Affairs, **33/1** Veloce (IRE), Young Duke (IRE), Cheveus Mitchell, **50/1** Dawn's Delight, **66/1** Fabled Orator. CSF £219.64, CT £5,640.98. Tote £10.10: £2.70 £9.90 £11.50 £3.20 (£123.40). Mr C. John Hill (BARNSTAPLE) bred by Yeomanstown Lodge Stud. 19 Rn    1m 31.42 (6.72)
SF—32/24/17/47/46/14

T/Trio: Race 2: £70.00 (31.4 Tckts) & Race 7: £780.50 (22.2 Tckts). T/Jkpt: £6,242.90 (1.05 Tckts). T/Plpt: £37.30 (226.6 Tckts).    Hn

## 2648—NEWMARKET (R-H) July Course

### Friday, August 28th [Good]

Going Allowance: minus 0.05 sec per fur (G)    Wind: fresh across

Stalls: 2nd – 4th low, remainder high

---

**3003**    BEAUFORT (S) STKS (3-Y-O) £3418.00 (£1024.00: £492.00: £226.00)
7f    2-00 (2-01)

```
2882   Lord Vivienne (IRE) (80) (Jt-Fav) (PFICole) 9-6 TQuinn (1) (swtg: chsd ldrs:
         led 2f out: veered bdly lft over 1f out: jst hld on) ................ —1
2778³  Rafah (72) (Jt-Fav) (BHanbury) 9-1 WCarson (4) (lw: chsd ldrs: hrd rdn fnl f: r.o)  ¹⁄₂.2
2655³  Change the Will (56) (MDIUsher) 8-9 RCochrane (6) (dwlt: rdn & hdwy ¹⁄₂-wy:
         styd on one pce) ............................................................... 3.3
2694   J'Arrive (JPearce) 8-4 ‡⁵RPrice (3) (prom: rdn & ev ch over 2f out: one pce) ... 2¹⁄₂.4
2639⁴  Our John (51) (RonaldThompson) 9-6 LDettori (8) (chsd ldrs: rdn 2f out: sn
         btn) .............................................................................. 4.5
2935   Winged Whisper (USA) (60) (CASmith) 9-6 MWigham (9) (bhd: styd on fnl 2f:
         nvr nrr) .......................................................................... 1¹⁄₂.6
2712⁴  Walkonthemoon (47) (bl) (MMcCormack) 9-1 JReid (11) (lw: led & sn clr: hdd &
         wknd 2f out) .................................................................... 2.7
2822   Fourofus (56) (RBoss) 8-11 ‡³RPerham (5) (chsd ldr over 3f: wknd wl over 1f
         out) ............................................................................ s.h.8
2909⁶  Scala Milano (64) (KTIvory) 9-1 AMunro (2) (chsd ldrs 5f) ....................... nk.9
2882⁴  Sandcastle City (59) (bl) (RHannon) 9-6 JLloyd (12) (prom: rdn ¹⁄₂-wy: sn
         wknd) .......................................................................... 1¹⁄₂.10
2922   Captain Marmalade (63) (DTThom) 9-0 CDwyer (10) (s.i.s: a bhd) ............... 1.11
2469   Vandervally (RMWhitaker) 9-0 DaleGibson (7) (a bhd: rdn 3f out: no rspnse) .. 7.12
```

**9/4** Rafah, LORD VIVIENNE (IRE)(op 6/4), **7/1** Change the Will, **8/1** Our John(tchd 20/1), **10/1** Sandcastle City, **14/1** Scala Milano, **16/1** Winged Whisper (USA), **20/1** Captain Marmalade, Vandervally, **25/1** Walkonthemoon, **33/1** Ors. CSF £7.91, Tote £3.10: £1.50 £1.40 £1.60 (£2.90). Mr Reg Hester (WHATCOMBE) bred by Binfield Manor Farms Ltd in Ireland. 12 Rn; Sold J Purcell 7,000 gns    1m 26.90 (2.54)
SF—62/55/40/27/31/26

---

**3004**    SHALFLEET H'CAP (3-Y-O) (0-90) £5010.00 (£1500.00: £720.00: £330.00)
6f    2-35 (2-37)

```
2787³  Arabellajill (88) (RHannon) 9-7 JLloyd (18) (lw: hld up: hdwy ¹⁄₂-wy: led appr
         fnl f: r.o wl) ................................................................. —1
2053   Peerage Prince (64) (PatMitchell) 7-4⁽⁴⁾ ‡⁷CHawksley (14) (a.p: hrd rdn over 1f
         out: kpt on) ................................................................. 2.2
2393⁶  Southwold Air (69) (JLDunlop) 8-2 GCarter (15) (gd hdwy appr fnl f: fin wl) ..... nk.3
2795   First Gold (68) (bl) (JWharton) 8-1 JQuinn (3) (a.p far side: hrd rdn fnl f: unable
         qckn) ........................................................................ 1.4
2795   Boy Martin (66) (bl) (MJohnston) 7-10 ‡³FNorton (8) (lw: chsd ldrs: rdn over 1f
         out: one pce) ............................................................... nk.5
```

2866 Nagida **(79)** *(JARToller)* 8-12 DHolland (16) (lw: a.p: ev ch over 1f out: unable
qckn) .................................................................................................................. s.h.6
2666* Elsals **(70)** (Fav) *(HThomsonJones)* 8-3 WCarson (2) (lw: hdwy 2f out: kpt on
ins fnl f: nvr nrr) ................................................................................. 1¹⁄₂.7
2275⁶ Thrie-Na-Helah (IRE) **(70)** (v) *(RMWhitaker)* 8-3 DaleGibson (13) (led 4f: rdn &
wknd appr fnl f) .................................................................................... 1.8
2188⁶ Jigsaw Boy **(75)** *(RJHolder)* 8-8 AMunro (4) (nvr trbld ldrs) ......................... nk.9
2640³ Music Dancer **(60)** *(JBerry)* 7-7 NAdams (9) (n.d) ........................................ 2.10
2131* Invigilate **(64)** *(MPNaughton)* 7-11 JakiHouston (19) (w ldrs: rdn 2f out: sn btn) nk.11
28614 Sylvan Sabre (IRE) **(76)** (bl) *(PMitchell)* 8-9 PaulEddery (6) (s.i.s: a bhd) ..... nk.12
2449 Castilian Queen (USA) **(78)** *(JHMGosden)* 8-13 JReid (7) (in tch far side 4f) .. nk.13
452 Doesyoudoes **(60)** *(DTThom)* 7-0 ‡7KimMcDonnell (12) (swtg: led far side over
4f: sn wknd) .................................................................................... ¹⁄₂.14
2911 Miss Haggis **(87)** *(RBoss)* 9-6 TQuinn (10) (spd far side 4f) ......................... 1¹⁄₂.15
2337 Ghalyoon (USA) **(82)** *(PTWalwyn)* 9-1 LDettori (5) (n.d) ................................ 2.16
1410* Hardliner **(76)** *(CFWall)* 8-9 NDay (1) (outpcd) ........................................ 3¹⁄₂.17
2656 Ler Cru (IRE) **(65)** (bl) *(CEBrittain)* 7-12 GCrealock (11) (a in rr) .................... nk.18
2419* Wandering Stranger **(72)** *(PJMakin)* 8-5 RCochrane (17) (bhd fr ¹⁄₂-wy: t.o) .... 6.19
LONG HANDICAP: Peerage Prince 7-2, Music Dancer 7-4, Doesyoudoes 7-6.

5/1 Elsals(op 9/1), 8/1 Sylvan Sabre (IRE), Nagida, 9/1 Castilian Queen (USA), Wandering Stranger(12/1—8/1),
12/1 Invigilate, 14/1 Jigsaw Boy, First Gold, ARABELLAJILL, 16/1 Miss Haggis, 20/1 Ghalyoon (USA), Hardliner,
Boy Martin, Ler Cru (IRE), 25/1 Thrie-Na-Helah (IRE), Southwold Air, 33/1 Music Dancer, 50/1 Ors. CSF
£470.82, CT £14,358.28. Tote £19.90: £3.70 £5.70 £5.90 £2.20 (£262.40)? Mrs J. Cash (MARLBOROUGH)
bred by Mrs J. Cash. 19 Rn                                                    1m 13.78 (2.28)
SF—55/16/27/22/16/31

**3005**        PORT OF TILBURY STKS (Mdn 2-Y.O) £4207.50 (£1260.00: £605.00: £277.50)
            **7f**                                                          3-05 (3-10)

**Emperor Jones (USA)** *(JHMGosden)* 9-0 RCochrane (10) (cmpt: scope: a.p:
led wl over 1f out: pushed clr: impressive) ................................ —1
Dixieland Melody (USA) *(BHanbury)* 9-0 DMcKeown (4) (w'like: gd hdwy over
1f out: fin fast) .................................................................... 4.2
Rain Brother (USA) *(PWChapple-Hyam)* 9-0 PaulEddery (13) (w'like: scope:
led after 2f tl wl over 1f out: r.o one pce) ............................... nk.3
Western Cape (USA) *(RCharlton)* 9-0 TQuinn (16) (cmpt: scope: bkwd: hdwy 3f
out: rdn & no ex appr fnl f) .............................................. ¹⁄₂.4
Desert Secret (IRE) (Fav) *(MRStoute)* 9-0 JReid (14) (gd sort: scope: 2f: kpt
on one pce appr fnl f) ........................................................ 1¹⁄₂.5
2356² Manila Bay (USA) *(MBell)* 9-0 AMunro (11) (prom tl rdn & wknd appr fnl f) ... 2.6
Coneybury (IRE) *(LMCumani)* 9-0 LDettori (6) (w'like: scope: bit bkwd: chsd
ldrs 5f: grad wknd) ............................................................ ³⁄₄.7
Yahmi (IRE) *(MajorWRHern)* 9-0 BProcter (9) (gd sort: bkwd: chsd ldrs over 4f) nk.8
Son of Sharp Shot (IRE) *(JLDunlop)* 9-0 NDay (2) (neat: s.s: effrt ¹⁄₂-wy: n.d) .. nk.9
Pistol River (IRE) *(RHannon)* 9-0 JLloyd (5) (neat: s.s: nvr nr to chal) ......... s.h.10
Cyrus the Bold (IRE) *(BWHills)* 9-0 DHolland (3) (leggy: scope: bkwd: chsd ldrs
4f) .................................................................................. 1.11
1397³ Blue Laws (IRE) *(JGFitzGerald)* 9-0 KFallon (8) (chsd ldrs over 4f) ................ 1.12
Gustavia (IRE) *(RWArmstrong)* 8-9 RStreet (7) (wl grwn: bkwd: chsd ldrs: hmpd
& lost pl over 2f out: sn bhd) ............................................ nk.13
Sun Grebe (IRE) *(JLDunlop)* 8-9 GCarter (15) (w'like: leggy: s.s: a bhd) ......... 3.14
Wings Cove *(MRStoute)* 9-0 PD'Arcy (12) (cmpt: scope: bkwd: a bhd) ......... s.h.15
Dyab (USA) *(PTWalwyn)* 9-0 WCarson (5) (wl grwn: bit bkwd: prom over 4f:
eased whn btn) .................................................................. ³⁄₄.16

7/2 Desert Secret (IRE)(3/1—9/2), 4/1 EMPEROR JONES (USA), **9/2** Manila Bay (USA)(tchd 8/1), 7/1
Coneybury (IRE)(op 9/2), 10/1 Western Cape (USA), 12/1 Yahmi (IRE)(op 8/1), 14/1 Rain Brother (USA), 16/1
Pistol River (IRE), Cyrus the Bold (IRE)(8/1—20/1), 20/1 Dixieland Melody (USA), Dyab (USA), Son of Sharp
Shot (IRE), Wings Cove, 33/1 Ors. CSF £80.83, Tote £6.10: £2.10 £4.80 £4.50 (£165.60). Sheikh Mohammed
(NEWMARKET) bred by Cherry Valley Farm Inc. & E. A. Cox Jnr in USA. 16 Rn          1m 28.25 (3.85)
SF—37/25/24/22/17/11

**3006**        HOPEFUL STKS (listed race)    £9625.00 (£2875.00: £1375.00: £625.00)
            **6f**                                                          3-35 (3-39)

2839 **Rose Indien (FR) (96)** *(MMoubarak)* 3-8-8 LDettori (1) (a.p: led 2f out: sn clr:
unchal) ............................................................................ —1
2383⁴ Hamas (IRE) **(104)** *(PTWalwyn)* 3-8-10 WCarson (13) (racd centre: hdwy over
2f out: r.o fnl f: no ch w wnr) ............................................ 2¹⁄₂.2
2855⁵ Fylde Flyer **(102)** *(JBerry)* 3-9-2 DMcKeown (5) (led 4f: kpt on u.p ins fnl f) ...... ¹⁄₂.3

2925³ Red Rosein (92) (CaptJWilson) 6-8-9 GCarter (4) (b.off hind: lw: s.s: hdwy appr fnl f: r.o wl ins fnl f) .................................................... ¹/₂.4
2855² Consigliere (93) (Fav) (RCharlton) 4-9-0 PaulEddery (3) (b: lw: chsd ldrs: hrd drvn 2f out: nvr able to chal) .................................................... hd.5
2839² Stack Rock (94) (EJAlston) 5-8-9 AMunro (7) (in tch: rdn 2f out: kpt on nr fin) .. 1.6
2642² Bit of a Lark (100) (RHollinshead) 4-9-0 CRutter (9) (chsd ldrs 4f) .................... ¹/₂.7
1096a³ Chicarica (USA) (110) (JHMGosden) 4-9-4 DHolland (2) (swtg: racd centre: nvr rchd ldrs) .................................................... 1.8
2855⁴ Montendre (112) (MMcCormack) 5-9-6 JReid (10) (a bhd) .................... nk.9
429⁵ Herora (IRE) (105) (NAGraham) 3-8-8 RCochrane (11) (lw: dwlt: nvr nr ldrs) .. s.h.10
2169 Sunday's Hill (99) (MBlanshard) 3-8-10 JQuinn (2) (spd 4f: sn wknd) ......... hd.11
2976a Notley (107) (RHannon) 5-9-6 JLloyd (8) (lw: bhd: rdn 2f out: no imp) ......... hd.12
2839⁵ Bold Lez (98) (MJHaynes) 5-9-0 TQuinn (6) (prom tl wknd 2f out: eased whn btn: t.o) .................................................... 12.13

5/1 Consigliere, 13/2 Montendre, 7/1 Hamas (IRE), 8/1 Bold Lez, Stack Rock, 17/2 Notley, Chicarica (USA)(6/1—9/1), 12/1 ROSE INDIEN (FR), 14/1 Bit of a Lark, 16/1 Red Rosein, Herora (IRE), 20/1 Fylde Flyer, 33/1 Sunday's Hill. CSF £85.33, Tote £11.30: £3.30 £2.10 £4.70 (£40.90). Ecurie Fustok (NEWMARKET) bred by Francois Geffroy in France. 13 Rn                                         1m 12.60 (1.10)
SF—66/58/62/53/57/46

## 3007

BREHENY H'CAP (0-90) £4815.00 (£1440.00: £690.00: £315.00)
1³/₄m 175y                                                              4-05 (4-10)

2635* Encore Une Fois (IRE) (75) (PWChapple-Hyam) 3-8-9 PaulEddery (10) (a.p: led over 2f out tl over 1f out: rallied u.p to ld cl home) ................ —1
2329* Persian Fantasy (82) (JLDunlop) 3-9-2 JReid (9) (lw: hld up: hdwy 4f out: led over 1f out tl cl last stride) .................................................... s.h.2
2385³ Nijmegen (65) (JGFitzGerald) 4-8-12 KFallon (5) (lw: hdwy 3f out: styd on ins fnl f: nvr nrr) .................................................... 6.3
2455 Dime Bag (70) (BWHills) 3-8-4 DHolland (3) (hdwy 5f out: rdn & wknd fnl f) ..... 1.4
1874⁵ Mootawel (USA) (76) (HThomsonJones) 3-8-10 AMunro (1) (chsd ldrs tl wknd over 3f out) .................................................... ³/₄.5
2648* Mull House (79) (Fav) (FJO'Mahony) 5-9-12 WCarson (11) (hld up & bhd: rdn 3f out: styd on: nvr nrr) .................................................... ¹/₂.6
2089* Free Mover (IRE) (80) (NAGraham) 3-9-0 LDettori (1) (chsd ldrs 11f: sn lost tch) ³/₄.7
2235³ Lookingforarainbow (IRE) (58) (BobJones) 4-8-5 JQuinn (4) (led over 7f out: sn clr: hdd & wknd over 2f out: t.o) .................................................... 20.8
2540* Explosive Speed (USA) (61) (MDHammond) 4-8-8 DMcKeown (2) (hld up in tch: wknd 4f out: t.o) .................................................... 9
2793⁵ Newton Point (73) (bl) (GAPritchard-Gordon) 3-8-7 RCochrane (8) (prom: rdn 4f out: sn wknd: t.o) .................................................... 10
1534 Rajanpour (USA) (49) (bl) (RCurtis) 7-7-7³ ‡³FNorton (12) (led 7f: rdn & wknd over 4f out: t.o) .................................................... 11

4/1 Mull House, 6/1 ENCORE UNE FOIS (IRE), Free Mover (IRE)(4/1—13/2), 7/1 Persian Fantasy(op 9/2), Newton Point, 8/1 Explosive Speed (USA), Mootawel (USA), 14/1 Lookingforarainbow (IRE), 16/1 Dime Bag, 20/1 Nijmegen, 33/1 Rajanpour (USA). CSF £42.88, CT £711.50. Tote £6.80: £2.20 £2.70 £2.50 (£16.50). Mr R. E. Sangster (MARLBOROUGH) bred by Swettenham Stud in Ireland. 11 Rn   3m 10.21 (.37 under best; 4.21)
SF—46/32/42/33/38/53

## 3008

BLUE PETER STKS (2-Y.O) £4306.50 (£1287.00: £616.00: £280.50)       6f  4-35 (4-39)

2727* Lost Soldier (USA) (97) (Fav) (LMCumani) 9-5 LDettori (9) (a.p: led 2f out: drvn clr fnl f) .................................................... —1
Pluck (RCharlton) 8-6 TQuinn (8) (lt-f: hdwy 2f out: kpt on fnl f: nvr nrr) ............. 3.2
2795² I'M Yours (RHannon) 8-6 JReid (6) (lw: led 4f: rdn & no ex appr fnl f) ............. 2¹/₂.3
Factual (USA) (BWHills) 8-11 PaulEddery (7) (w'like: scope: sn w ldrs: ev ch 2f out: wknd appr fnl f) .................................................... 2.4
Lailati (USA) (MRStoute) 8-6 RCochrane (4) (gd sort: dwlt: chsd ldrs 4f: sn wknd) .................................................... 2.5
Matron of Honor (NCWright) 8-6 GCarter (2) (w'like: b.hind: outpcd) ................ 1.6
Beggarman Thief (JHMGosden) 8-11 WCarson (1) (w'like: scope: w ldrs tl wknd qckly wl over 1f out) .................................................... 1.7
Iolite (MAJarvis) 8-6 GCrealock (3) (cmpt: scope: outpcd: a bhd) .................... 5.8
Kelly Mac (NACallaghan) 8-11 AMunro (5) (str: cmpt: bkwd: s.i.s: outpcd: a bhd) .................................................... ³/₄.9

Evens LOST SOLDIER (USA)(op 7/4), 2/1 Beggarman Thief (USA), 10/1 I'M Yours, Factual (USA)(8/1—14/1), 11/1 Lailati (USA)(op 6/1), 14/1 Pluck, 20/1 Iolite, 25/1 Kelly Mac, 33/1 Matron of Honor. CSF £16.89, Tote £2.20: £1.40 £2.70 £2.10 (£15.70). Sheikh Mohammed (NEWMARKET) bred by Wimborne Farm Inc in USA. 9 Rn                                   1m 14.62 (3.12)
SF—37/12/2/–/–/–

**3009** SAXHAM APP'CE H'CAP (0-90) £4698.00 (£1404.00: £672.00: £306.00)
1m

5-10 (5-10)

2777* **Vague Dancer** (66) *(MrsJRRamsden)* 6-8-12 ‡³StephenDavies (4) (lw: hld up: hdwy to ld ins fnl f: r.o) .......... —1

2656* Dodgy (59) (v) *(SDow)* 5-8-8 FNorton (12) (racd alone stands' side: mde most tl ins fnl f) .......... 1.2

2236⁶ Pelargonia (75) *(RCharlton)* 3-9-4 RPrice (8) (lw: hdwy over 2f out: styd on nr fin) .......... 2.3

2896⁶ Miss Sarajane (47) *(RHollinshead)* 8-7-7⁽¹⁾ ‡³MHumphries (5) (a.p: ev ch over 1f out: wknd nr fin) .......... nk.4

2656 Ballerina Bay (56) (v) *(DTThom)* 4-7-12 ‡⁷KimMcDonnell (7) (hld up: hdwy over 2f out: rdn & nt qcknd fnl f) .......... 4.6

1146⁵ Karamoja (75) *(NAGraham)* 3-9-4 SO'Gorman (11) (bhd tl styd on appr fnl f) .... 4.6

2852⁶ Blockade (USA) (84) (Fav) *(MBell)* 3-9-3 ‡¹⁰TO'Leary (3) (t: w ldr: rdn 3f out: sn btn) .......... ³/₄.7

2403² Bentico (65) *(MAJarvis)* 3-8-5 ‡³KRutter (1) (a in rr) .......... hd.8

2660⁵ Madagans Grey (72) *(RBoss)* 4-9-7 RPerham (2) (lw: chsd ldrs: ev ch 2f out: sn rdn & wknd) .......... 1¹/₂.9

Palmas Pride (63) *(MDHammond)* 5-8-2⁽⁵⁾ ‡¹⁰ALakeman (9) (a bhd) .......... 2.10

2807* Night Transaction (55) *(AHide)* 5-7-11⁽¹⁾ ‡⁷DCarson (10) (chsd ldrs 5f: wknd 2f out: t.o) .......... 10.11

801 Waveband (73) *(BWHills)* 3-8-6 ‡¹⁰SMcCarthy (6) (chsd ldrs 5f: sn wknd: t.o) .... 12

**5/2** Blockade (USA), **4/1** Pelargonia(3/1—9/2), **11/2** VAGUE DANCER(4/1—6/1), **13/2** Bentico, **8/1** Dodgy, **11/1** Night Transaction, **12/1** Madagans Grey, **14/1** Ballerina Bay, Miss Sarajane, **20/1** Palmas Pride, Karamoja, **33/1** Waveband. CSF £49.19, CT £184.76. Tote £5.90: £2.30 £2.10 £2.00 (£13.60). Mr K. E. Wheldon (THIRSK) bred by P. Haworth. 12 Rn
1m 41.69 (3.99)
SF—32/25/29/3/5/13

T/Trio: Race 2: £888.20 (1.1 Tckts); Race 5: £239.90 (3.1. T/Plpt: £2,570.90 (2.15 Tckts). IM

## NEWMARKET (R-H) July Course
### Saturday, August 29th [Good]

Going Allowance: St: nil (G); Rnd: minus 0.20 sec per fur (F) Wind: slt half bhd

Stalls: 1st - 4th high, remainder low

**3010** LAGRANGE CLAIMING STKS (3-Y.O) £3132.00 (£936.00: £448.00: £204.00)
1¹/₂m

2-15 (2-18)

2751² **Temple Knight** (52) *(CACyzer)* 9-2 DBiggs (2) (chsd ldrs: led over 1f out: r.o wl) .......... —1

2757 Addicted to Love (62) *(PJMakin)* 9-1 TQuinn (9) (a.p: rdn over 3f out: ev ch 1f out: unable qckn) .......... 1.2

2926⁶ Greek Chime (IRE) (Jt-Fav) *(LordHuntingdon)* 9-6 MRoberts (4) (lw: led tl hdd over 1f out: one pce) .......... 2.3

1319 Maradonna (USA) *(LMCumani)* 9-7 LDettori (1) (hld up & bhd: rdn 5f out: styd on fnl 2f: nvr nrr) .......... 1¹/₂.4

2870² Big Pat (58) *(JPearce)* 8-3 ‡⁵RPrice (5) (prom: rdn jst over 1f out: sn btn) ........ 3¹/₂.5

2868² Positive Aspect (43) *(JPearce)* 8-1 GDuffield (8) (hld up: effrt 2f out: no imp appr fnl f) .......... ¹/₂.6

2784⁴ Tales of Wisdom (63) (bl) (Jt-Fav) *(SirMarkPrescott)* 8-9 AMunro (7) (lw: chsd ldrs: hrd rdn & wknd over 2f out) .......... 5.7

2419 Mansber (IRE) (50) *(PatMitchell)* 8-2 PRobinson (a bhd: t.o) .......... 25.8

Pip's Optimist *(PJFeilden)* 8-6 NDay (3) (prom 9f: wknd qckly: t.o) .......... 9

**5/2** Tales of Wisdom, Greek Chime (IRE), **5/1** Addicted to Love, **7/1** Maradonna (USA), **8/1** Big Pat, **12/1** Positive Aspect, **25/1** Mansber (IRE), TEMPLE KNIGHT, **50/1** Pip's Optimist. CSF £130.77, Tote £24.20: £3.30 £2.00 £1.50 (£58.50). Mr S. Wingfield Digby (HORSHAM) bred by S. Wingfield Digby. 9 Rn
2m 35.59 (6.89)
SF—9/6/7/5/–/–

**3011** E.B.F. PARK LODGE STKS (Mdn 2-Y.O) £4077.50 (£1220.00: £585.00: £267.50)
6f

2-45 (2-46)

**Inchinor** *(RCharlton)* 9-0 TQuinn (8) (gd sort: lw: chsd ldrs: chal 1f out: rdn to ld ins fnl f: hld on) .......... —1

Mithl Al Hawa *(JRFanshawe)* 8-9 GDuffield (2) (w'like: scope: a.p: led jst ins fnl f: sn hdd: r.o) .......... nk.2

Blues Traveller (IRE) *(BWHills)* 9-0 DHolland (3) (str: cmpt: s.s: gd hdwy 2f out: r.o ins fnl f) .......... 3¹/₂.3

Dahyah (USA) *(Fav) (MRStoute)* 9-0 MRoberts (6) (gd sort: wl grwn: bkwd: led: rdn along over 2f out: hdd ins fnl f: one pce) .................. 1½.4
2746³ Brigg Fair *(RHannon)* 9-0 BRouse (5) (lw: w ldr tl wknd appr fnl f) .................. 3½.5
Jackpot Star *(RHannon)* 9-0 PRobinson (4) (neat: scope: nvr plcd to chal) ..... 2½.6
Jobie *(WJHaggas)* 9-0 NDay (11) (str: cmpt: lw: s.s: hdwy ½-wy: sn rdn: r.o one pce) .................. s.h.7
Ocara (USA) *(HRACecil)* 8-9 WRyan (13) (w'like: scope: prom 4f) .................. 1.8
Secret Assignment (USA) *(CACyzer)* 9-0 DBiggs (7) (w'like: chsd ldrs over 3f) 2½.9
Desert Nomad *(AMunro)* 8-9 AMunro (1) (cmpt: s.s: a bhd) .................. ¾.10
2346⁶ Anaxagoras *(AAScott)* 9-0 JFortune (9) (w ldrs to ½-wy: sn rdn & wknd) ........ ½.11
Tabkir (USA) *(JLDunlop)* 9-0 LDettori (12) (w'like: unf: bhd: hrd rdn 2f out: no imp) .................. 1.12
Little Osborne (IRE) *(MBell)* 8-9 MHills (10) (b: b.hind: leggy: scope: bhd: rdn & rn green 3f out: sn t.o) .................. 15.13

**11/10** Dahyah (USA)(4/5—5/4), **13/2** Ocara (USA)(10/1—6/1), **7/1** Brigg Fair, **10/1** Mithl Al Hawa, Tabkir (USA), **12/1** INCHINOR, **14/1** Blues Traveller (IRE), **16/1** Anaxagoras, **25/1** Desert Nomad, Secret Assignment (USA), **33/1** Ors. CSF £121.02, Tote £10.90: £3.20 £4.40 £4.50 (£205.70). Sir Philip Oppenheimer (BECKHAMPTON) bred by Hascombe and Valiant Studs. 13 Rn
1m 14.39 (2.89)
SF—42/36/27/21/7/–

---

**3012** PHILIP CORNES NICKEL ALLOYS NURSERY £15400.00 (£4600.00: £2200.00: £1000.00) **6f** 3-20 (3-22)

2811⁵ **Falsoola (82)** *(MRStoute)* 8-13 MRoberts (2) (a.p: led ins fnl f: rdn out) ............ —1
1957* White Shadow (IRE) **(86)** *(RCharlton)* 9-3 WRyan (3) (a.p: led over 1f out tl ins fnl f: rdn out) .................. nk.2
2842* Bold Seven (IRE) **(82)** *(FHLee)* 8-8 ‡⁵NKennedy (9) (bhd: gd hdwy 2f out: nvr nr to chal) .................. 3½.3
2371⁵ Maybe Gold **(72)** *(DWPArbuthnot)* 8-3⁽¹⁾ TQuinn (8) (b: b.hind: chsd ldrs: rdn jst over 1f out: one pce) .................. 3½.4
2537² The Sharp Bidder (IRE) **(87)** *(RHollinshead)* 9-4 LDettori (1) (lw: prom tl wknd appr fnl f) .................. 1½.5
2850⁶ Juliet Bravo **(72)** *(BBeasley)* 8-3 DHolland (7) (led tl hdd & wknd over 1f out) .... 1.6
2857² Kennedys Prima **(76)** *(AAScott)* 8-7 JFortune (6) (hdwy jst over 1f out: rdn & kpt on fnl f) .................. 1.7
2243³ Moving Image (IRE) **(77)** *(MBell)* 8-8 MHills (12) (b: b.hind: nvr trbld ldrs) .......... 1.8
2745² Clear Look **(73)** (Fav) *(PFICole)* 7-11 ‡⁷JDSmith (10) (lw: chsd ldrs: rdn along ½-wy: no imp) .................. hd.9
2900³ Charity Express (IRE) **(87)** *(JBerry)* 9-4 DMcKeown (14) (s.s: sn chsng ldrs: no imp fnl 2f) .................. ½.10
2758² Princely Favour (IRE) **(86)** *(RHannon)* 9-3 BRouse (13) (m.n.s) .................. 1½.11
2812 Home Affair **(68)** (v) *(DTThom)* 7-13 DBiggs (11) (spd over 3f) .................. 2.12
2857* Pair of Jacks (IRE) **(80)** *(WRMuir)* 8-11 AMunro (4) (lw: spd over 3f) .......... 2½.13
2274* Heavenly Risk **(90)** *(RHannon)* 9-7 RHills (5) (in tch 4f: eased whn btn: t.o) ..... 8.14

**3/1** Clear Look(tchd 7/2), **11/2** The Sharp Bidder (IRE), **15/2** Maybe Gold, **8/1** White Shadow (IRE), **9/1** FALSOOLA, Pair of Jacks (IRE), **11/1** Charity Express (IRE)(8/1—12/1), **12/1** Heavenly Risk, Bold Seven (IRE), **14/1** Princely Favour (IRE), **16/1** Moving Image (IRE), **20/1** Kennedys Prima, **33/1** Ors. CSF £76.09, CT £800.50. Tote £8.90: £3.00 £3.40 £4.20 (£24.00). Sheikh Mohammed (NEWMARKET) bred by Sheikh Mohammed bin Rashid al Maktoum. 14 Rn
1m 14.35 (2.85)
SF—42/45/22/3/12/–

---

**3013** DANEPAK BACON H'CAP (0-110) £11160.00 (£3330.00: £1590.00: £720.00) **1¼m** 3-50 (3-53)

2654* Mamdooh **(88)** *(ACStewart)* 3-8-11 MRoberts (2) (a.p: led over 1f out: r.o wl) ... —1
2220³ Inner City (IRE) **(105)** (Fav) *(LMCumani)* 3-10-0 LDettori (5) (hld up: hdwy over 2f out: ev ch 1f out: rdn & r.o) .................. 1½.2
2554 Corcina **(72)** *(MBell)* 4-8-3 MHills (7) (b.off fore: led tl over 1f out: kpt on gamely) .................. 2.3
2647² Robingo (IRE) **(76)** *(CEBrittain)* 3-7-13 AMunro (11) (lw: gd hdwy appr fnl f: fin wl) .................. ½.4
2671* Mathaayl (USA) **(78)** (bl) *(HThomsonJones)* 3-8-1 NCarlisle (3) (plld hrd: chsd ldrs: ev ch over 1f out: wknd ins fnl f) .................. 2.5
824 Selaah **(90)** *(MRStoute)* 5-9-2 ‡⁵JJones (1) (lw: pushed along & bhd ½-wy: effrt 2f out: r.o) .................. ½.6
2913 Riviera Vista **(86)** (bl) *(GWragg)* 3-8-9 RHills (8) (hdwy over 4f out: ev ch jst over 1f out: sn rdn & wknd) .................. 1½.7
Roll a Dollar **(90)** *(DRCElsworth)* 6-9-7 BRouse (4) (lw: a bhd) .................. 2½.8
Halkopous **(88)** *(MHTompkins)* 6-9-5 PRobinson (6) (bhd: effrt 4f out: no imp) 1½.9

2844 Gulf Sailor (IRE) **(82)** *(MRStoute)* 4-8-13 DHolland (9) (jnd ldr after 3f: wknd
over 2f out) ............................................................................................... hd.**10**
19345 Jumaira Shark (CAN) **(80)** *(JHMGosden)* 3-8-3 GHind (10) (chsd ldrs 7f) ..... 1½.**11**
25472 Wassl This Then (IRE) **(73)** *(DWPArbuthnot)* 3-7-10 DBiggs (12) (b: b.hind:
prom tl rdn & wknd over 4f out) ............................................... 3½.**12**

**7/2** Inner City (IRE), **4/1** Robingo (IRE)(6/1—8/1), **11/2** MAMDOOH(7/2—6/1), **15/2** Jumaira Shark
(CAN)(5/1—8/1), **8/1** Gulf Sailor (IRE), **9/1** Corcina(14/1—8/1), **12/1** Riviera Vista, Wassl This Then (IRE), **14/1**
Mathaayl (USA), **16/1** Halkopous, **20/1** Selaah, **25/1** Roll a Dollar. CSF £25.19, CT £162.75. Tote £4.00: £2.30
£1.90 £2.50 (£7.60). Mr Hamdan Al-Maktoum (NEWMARKET) bred by Cheveley Park Stud Ltd. 12 Rn
2m 4.20 (1.60)
SF—61/75/46/41/39/53

## 3014
FREEMASON LODGE H'CAP (3-Y.O) (0-100) £4893.00 (£1464.00: £702.00: £321.00)
7f
4-20 (4-21)

29136 **Stani (USA) (77)** *(BHanbury)* 8-5 WRyan (11) (lw: a.p: led jst over 1f out: rdn
out) .......................................................................................................... —**1**
29092 Mamma's Too **(88)** *(MBell)* 9-2 LDettori (13) (s.s: racd centre: gd hdwy appr fnl
f: fin wl) ............................................................................................... 1.**2**
2642 Double Blue **(93)** *(MJohnston)* 9-7 DMcKeown (8) (led far side: ev ch over 1f
out: unable qckn) .......................................................... ½.**3**
2898 Jade Vale **(72)** *(JWHills)* 8-0 RHills (7) (prom tl rdn & outpcd 2f out: styd on ins
fnl f) ............................................................................... nk.**4**
23824 By Hand **(76)** *(WJHaggas)* 8-4 NDay (5) (chsd ldr far side: rdn & no imp appr fnl
f) ........................................................................................ 2½.**5**
2803* Arboretum (IRE) **(76)** *(RCharlton)* 8-4 TQuinn (12) (led centre over 5f: sn wknd) hd.**6**
1706 Hopeful Bid (IRE) **(73)** *(RHannon)* 8-1 BCrossley (10) (lw: racd centre: spd 5f) ½.**7**
2898 Amthaal (USA) **(70)** *(MRStoute)* 7-12 DHolland (2) (prom 5f: eased whn btn
appr fnl f) ........................................................................ nk.**8**
27954 Our Occasion **(74)** *(Fav)* *(WJMusson)* 8-2 MRoberts (4) (lw: hld up: stdy hdwy
appr fnl f: nvr nrr) ................................................................ s.h.**9**
26475 Eastleigh **(72)** *(RHollinshead)* 7-7(7) ‡7MHumphries (1) (a in rr) ......................... 1½.**10**
22282 Majboor (IRE) **(92)** *(PTWalwyn)* 9-6 AMunro (6) (in tch: rdn & wknd over 2f out) 1½.**11**
Magic Steps **(77)** *(CEBrittain)* 8-5 DBiggs (9) (chsd ldrs 4f: sn wknd) ............ 2½.**12**
28033 Mashaaer (USA) **(68)** *(RWArmstrong)* 7-10 NCarlisle (3) (a bhd) ................. 1½.**13**

**4/1** Our Occasion(6/1—3/1), **5/1** Arboretum (IRE), **6/1** STANI (USA), **9/1** Double Blue, **10/1** Jade Vale, Amthaal
(USA), **11/1** Mamma's Too, **12/1** By Hand, Magic Steps, **16/1** Majboor (IRE), **20/1** Ors. CSF
£65.73, CT £538.03. Tote £6.70: £2.50 £2.50 £3.40 (£50.50). Mr Saeed Suhail (NEWMARKET) bred by Glen Hill
Farm in USA. 13 Rn
1m 27.07 (2.67)
SF—50/58/61/39/35/34

## 3015
LADBROKES H'CAP (0-90) £7960.00 (£2380.00: £1140.00: £520.00)
5f
4-50 (4-52)

21923 **Inherent Magic (IRE) (77)** *(MMcCormack)* 3-9-0 MRoberts (8) (a.p: hrd rdn 1f
out: r.o to ld post) ................................................................ —**1**
2478* Sigama (USA) **(80)** *(FHLee)* 6-9-1 ‡5NKennedy (2) (mde most: hrd rdn fnl f: jst
ct) ...................................................................................... s.h.**2**
29255 Gondo **(74)** **(v)** *(EJAlston)* 5-9-0 DHolland (10) (swvd rt s: a chsng ldrs: kpt on
ins fnl f) ............................................................................. 1½.**3**
28664 No Quarter Given **(70)** *(PSFelgate)* 7-8-10 TQuinn (12) (chsd ldrs: rdn & r.o wl
ins fnl f) ............................................................................ nk.**4**
29564 Educated Pet **(76)** *(MJohnston)* 3-8-13 DMcKeown (6) (outpcd tl r.o appr fnl f) 1½.**5**
1400 Branston Abby (IRE) **(85)** *(MJohnston)* 3-9-8 RHills (1) (gd spd 4f) ................. nk.**6**
29193 Yes **(55)** *(Fav)* *(DTThom)* 4-7-2 ‡7KimMcDonnell (9) (r.o appr fnl f: nvr nrr) ... 1.**7**
2902 Very Dicey **(78)** *(WRMuir)* 4-9-4 AMunro (7) (w ldrs over 3f: rdn & no ex fnl f) . hd.**8**
29022 Metal Boys **(85)** *(RHollinshead)* 5-9-11 WRyan (3) (chsd ldrs over 3f) ............. hd.**9**
25996 Rhythmic Dancer **(70)** *(JLSpearing)* 4-8-10 GHind (4) (s.i.s: nvr trbld ldrs) ... s.h.**10**
2866* Truthful Image **(79)** **(bl)** *(MJRyan)* 3-9-2 DBiggs (5) (lw: spd over 3f) ............. hd.**11**
20164 Born to Be **(79)** *(SDow)* 3-9-2 BRouse (11) (bhd fr ½-wy) ......................... 3.**12**
2642 Seamere **(83)** **(bl)** *(BRCambidge)* 9-9-4 ‡5RPrice (15) (a bhd) ....................... s.h.**13**
2902 Absolution **(78)** *(MPNaughton)* 8-9-4 JFortune (13) (a bhd) ......................... nk.**14**

**6/1** Yes(8/1—10/1), **7/1** No Quarter Given, **9/1** INHERENT MAGIC (IRE), Gondo, Metal Boys, **11/1** Seamere,
Very Dicey, Sigama (USA)(8/1—12/1), **12/1** Truthful Image, **14/1** Educated Pet, Branston Abby (IRE),
Absolution, **20/1** Rhythmic Dancer, **25/1** Born to Be. CSF £91.81, CT £831.60. Tote £8.60: £2.80 £2.50 £3.00
(£35.90). Orchid Racing & Bloodstock Limited (WANTAGE) bred by Mrs M. McStay in Ireland. 14 Rn
60.72 sec (1.72)
SF—66/66/59/54/51/59

**3016**    STANLEY HOUSE STKS (Mdn 3-Y.O) £3785.00 (£1130.00: £540.00: £245.00)
1m                  5-25 (5-29)

441³ **Talb** (USA) *(Jt-Fav)* *(JLDunlop)* 9-0 TQuinn (2) (a.p: led wl over 1f out: r.o wl) .. —1
938⁵ Thames Glow *(DRCElsworth)* 8-9 BRouse (6) (lw: hld up: hdwy 3f out: rdn &
       unable qckn fnl f) ................................................ 1.2
2871 Wafi (USA) **(57)** *(BHanbury)* 9-0 WRyan (3) (led tl hdd & wknd wl over 1f out) ... 8.3
Grand Honda (IRE) *(CEBrittain)* 9-0 AMunro (1) (w'like: prom 5f: grad wknd: t.o) 7.4
Wainwright (USA) *(JHMGosden)* 9-0 DHolland (4) (bkwd: chsd ldrs tl
       rdn & wknd 3f out: eased whn btn: t.o) ..................... 15.5
2858 Bayin (USA) *(RWArmstrong)* 9-0 BCrossley (7) (chsd ldrs: rdn ½-wy: sn lost
       tch: t.o) ............................................................... 20.6
*Utrillo (USA) (20/1) Withdrawn (ref to ent stalls) : not under orders*

7/4 TALB (USA)(5/4—2/1), Wainwright (USA)(Evens—2/1), **5/1** Grand Honda (IRE)(10/1—9/2), **10/1** Thames
Glow, **16/1** Bayin (USA), **20/1** Wafi (USA). CSF £15.77, Tote £2.20: £1.50 £2.10 (£8.80). Mr Hamdan
Al-Maktoum (ARUNDEL) bred by B & D.Taylor, N.Brooks, Brooks & Maberry in USA. 6 Rn   1m 41.13 (3.43)
                                                        SF—49/41/22/1/–/–

T/Trio: Race 4: £151.80 (9 Tckts) & Race 6: £140.10 (10.2 Tckts). T/Plpt: £1,782.60 (5.05 Tckts).     IM

---

2821—**WINDSOR** (Fig.8)
## Saturday, August 29th [Good]
Going Allowance: 5f 217y: minus 0.10 sec; Rest: nil sec per fur (G)        Wind: almost nil

Stalls: high

**3017**    BRADFIELD (S) STKS (3 & 4-Y.O) £1898.00 (£528.00: £254.00)
1m 67y                  5-20 (5-24)

     **Prince Rooney** (IRE) *(PButler)* 4-8-1 ‡⁷SDrowne (18) (bit bkwd: 5th st: led over
       2f out: hrd rdn: r.o wl) ....................................... —1
2581 Red Sombrero **(59)** *(LGCottrell)* 3-8-4⁽²⁾ JLloyd (10) (lw: hdwy over 2f out: hrd
       rdn over 1f out: r.o one pce) ............................. 2¹/₂.2
1426⁵ Toss the Dice **(57)** *(Fav)* *(MAJarvis)* 3-8-2 GDuffield (3) (lw: 4th st: hrd rdn over
       1f out: one pce) ................................................ 3.3
2694³ Mexican Dancer **(54)** *(RJHolder)* 3-7-11 NAdams (14) (3rd st: hrd rdn over 2f
       out: one pce) .................................................... s.h.4
868 Wise Portia **(47)** *(HCandy)* 3-7-11 CRutter (9) (hdwy over 2f out: nvr nrr) .... 1¹/₂.5
Almost a Princess (bl) *(JAkehurst)* 4-8-0⁽²⁾ ‡⁵Pears (4) (hdwy 3f out: shkn up
       2f out: one pce) ................................................ s.h.6
1811⁶ Persian Bud (IRE) **(32)** *(JRBosley)* 4-8-3 ‡⁵NGwilliams (20) (2nd st: wknd wl
       over 1f out) ...................................................... 1.7
2539⁶ Ergon **(57)** *(DJSCosgrove)* 3-7-5⁽¹⁾ ‡⁷PMcCabe (19) (nvr nr to chal) ........... s.h.8
Telephus *(BJMcMath)* 3-8-2 EJohnson (17) (leggy: unf: bit bkwd: nvr nrr) ... nk.9
2545 Flying Promise **(39)** *(RABennett)* 4-8-8 NHowe (13) (led 6f) ...................... 2¹/₂.10
2729 Jolizal **(34)** *(DMorris)* 4-8-9 MTebbutt (21) (mid div whn hmpd 6f out) ...... 1.11
2946 Up the Punjab **(50)** *(AMoore)* 3-8-3 CandyMorris (15) (hdwy over 3f out: wknd
       over 1f out) ...................................................... nk.12
2937⁶ Watermill Girl **(30)** (v) *(DTThom)* 4-7-13⁽¹⁾ ‡⁵KRutter (8) (nvr nrr) ................ 1¹/₂.13
2712 Musical Lyrics **(35)** *(MrsJGRetter)* 4-8-3 TSprake (11) (prom 4f) ............... 10.14
2583 Little Nod **(47)** *(JWhite)* 3-8-2 PRobinson (1) (6th st: wknd over 4f out) ...... 2.15
2882 Sally Fast **(50)** *(BPalling)* 3-7-10 ‡⁷PBowe (5) (a bhd) ............................ ³/₄.16
2882 Beyond the Moon (IRE) **(50)** *(MJFetherston-Godley)* 3-7-11 JQuinn (2) (a bhd) ¹/₂.17
2416 Evening Dress **(38)** *(ICampbell)* 3-7-12⁽⁸⁾ ‡⁷SMulvey (6) (a bhd) ................ ¹/₂.18
Renta Kid **(67)** *(PJHobbs)* 3-8-3 AMcGlone (12) (prom 4f) ...................... 4.19
Maoujoud *(RPCHoad)* 4-8-5 ‡³SO'Gorman (16) (bhd fnl 3f) ...................... 6.20
2822 Apache Maid *(JSMoore)* 3-7-11 RStreet (7) (a bhd) .................................. 1.21

2/1 Toss the Dice, **8/1** Red Sombrero(5/1—9/1), PRINCE ROONEY (IRE)(12/1—14/1), **10/1** Mexican
Dancer(op 6/1), **12/1** Ergon(op 8/1), Beyond the Moon (IRE)(8/1—14/1), Telephus, Sally Fast(8/1—14/1), **14/1**
Renta Kid, Up the Punjab, **16/1** Almost a Princess, **20/1** Little Nod, Jolizal, **25/1** Flying Promise, **33/1** Ors. CSF
£72.58, Tote £20.20: £5.30 £3.10 £2.00 (£129.10). Mr D. J. Perry (LEWES) bred by Miss E. C. Holdsworth in
Ireland. 21 Rn; No bid                                             1m 45.9 (4.3)
                                                        SF—22/17/6/–/–/–

**3018**    LORDS TAVERNERS STKS (2-Y.O) £2658.00 (£738.00: £354.00)
5f 217y                  5-45 (5-49)

2776* **Simmering** **(92)** *(GWragg)* 8-6 MHills (1) (hld up: led over 1f out: comf) ........... —1

2452 Greenlet (IRE) **(97)** (Fav) *(MRStoute)* 8-8⁽²⁾ SCauthen (9) (lw: a.p: ev ch over 1f
out: unable qckn) ...................................................................................... 5.2
Primo Figlio *(RHannon)* 8-11 JLloyd (4) (leggy: unf: hld up: rdn over 2f out: one
pce) ...................................................................................................... 2.3
2629 Royal Deed (USA) *(PMMcEntee)* 8-6 PRobinson (5) (a.p: one pce fnl 2f) ........... 2.4
1378 Auntie Ginger *(PButler)* 8-6 AProud (6) (led over 4f) .................................. 7.5
Ice Rebel *(MissBSanders)* 8-11 GDuffield (2) (w'like: bkwd: a bhd) ............... nk.6
Al Moulouki *(JWPayne)* 8-11 WHood (7) (w'like: bkwd: s.s: a bhd) ............... 3¹⁄₂.7
Gallop to Glory *(PMitchell)* 8-8 ‡³SO'Gorman (8) (w'like: bhd fnl 3f) ............ s.h.8

**6/5** Greenlet (IRE), **11/8** SIMMERING(Evens—6/4), **10/1** Primo Figlio(8/1—12/1), **16/1** Auntie Ginger, **25/1** Ice
Rebel, **33/1** Gallop to Glory, Al Moulouki, **50/1** Royal Deed (USA). CSF £3.23, Tote £2.60: £1.10 £1.10 £1.70
(£1.60). Mrs G. Wragg (NEWMARKET) bred by P. D. and Mrs Player. 8 Rn                1m 12.6 (2.1)
SF—38/20/15/2/–/–

**3019** STAR AND GARTER NURSERY  £2847.00 (£792.00: £381.00)
5f 217y
6-10 (6-15)
(Weights raised 5 lb)

2306* **Yours by Right (69)** *(WGMTurner)* 8-7 TSprake (13) (a.p: led over 2f out: hrd
rdn & hung lft ins fnl f: r.o wl) .................................................................. —1
791* Moon Over Miami **(75)** *(CJames)* 8-13 JQuinn (7) (hdwy & bmpd wl over 1f out:
r.o wl ins fnl f) ....................................................................................... 1.2
2709* Brigante Di Cielo **(75)** *(RHannon)* 8-13 JLloyd (1) (a.p: rdn & edgd rt wl over 1f
out: unable qckn) ................................................................................... 2¹⁄₂.3
2824² Troon **(82)** (Fav) *(MrsLPiggott)* 9-6 LPiggott (10) (b: b.hind: hld up: one pce fnl
2f) ........................................................................................................ ¹⁄₂.4
2528 Cliburnel News (IRE) **(80)** *(MHTompkins)* 9-4 PRobinson (12) (hld up: hrd rdn
over 1f out: one pce) ............................................................................... ³⁄₄.5
2030⁵ In Case (USA) **(83)** *(RCharlton)* 9-7 MHills (6) (lw: hdwy over 2f out: one pce) .. ¹⁄₂.6
2857 Bonjour **(82)** (v) *(JHMGosden)* 9-6 SCauthen (2) (lw: hld up: hrd rdn over 2f
out: btn whn hmpd wl over 1f out) ............................................................ ³⁄₄.7
2138⁶ Simply Amiss **(75)** *(SirMarkPrescott)* 8-13 GDuffield (11) (led over 3f) ............. 1¹⁄₂.8
877⁶ Nitouche **(79)** *(PatMitchell)* 9-3 JReid (4) (a mid div) ............................... 1.9
2437 Polar Storm (IRE) **(78)** *(LadyHerries)* 9-2 JWilliams (5) (a bhd) ...................... 1¹⁄₂.10
2781* Prince Manki **(72)** *(RHannon)* 8-10 AMcGlone (8) (a bhd) .......................... 3.11
659² Wahem (IRE) **(68)** *(CEBrittain)* 8-6 MRoberts (3) (lw: prom over 4f) .............. ¹⁄₂.12
2916 The Wend **(75)** *(DTThom)* 7-7 NAdams (9) (bhd fnl 2f) ............................... 4.13
LONG HANDICAP: The Wend 7-6.

**5/1** Troon(tchd 8/1), **11/2** Brigante Di Cielo, **6/1** Simply Amiss, Bonjour, **7/1** YOURS BY RIGHT, Wahem (IRE)(op
12/1), **9/1** In Case (USA)(op 6/1), **11/1** Polar Storm (IRE)(8/1—12/1), Moon Over Miami, **16/1** Prince Manki,
Cliburnel News (IRE), **20/1** Nitouche, **33/1** The Wend. CSF £80.47, CT £426.98. Tote £9.40: £2.80 £3.00 £2.30
(£49.40). Mr John Turner (SHERBORNE) bred by R. J. Turner. 13 Rn                1m 12.1 (1.6)
SF—49/51/41/46/31/42

**3020** WINTER HILL STKS (listed race) £9707.50 (£2935.00: £1430.00: £677.50)
1¹⁄₄m 7y
6-40 (6-43)

2711* **Shuailaan (USA)** *(ACStewart)* 3-8-10 MRoberts (6) (4th st: rdn over 3f out: led
over 2f out: r.o wl) ................................................................................. —1
2174* Adam Smith **(106)** *(LMCumani)* 4-9-4 LDettori (2) (lw: 5th st: rdn over 1f out: r.o
wl ins fnl f) .......................................................................................... hd.2
1200⁴ Knifebox (USA) **(98)** *(JHMGosden)* 4-9-7 WCarson (1) (led over 7f: unable qckn) 5.3
1869 Royal Seaton **(86)** *(BRMillman)* 3-8-6 JWilliams (3) (nvr nr to chal) ............... hd.4
2174* Peto **(106)** (Fav) *(HRACecil)* 3-8-10 SCauthen (2) (3rd st: rdn over 2f out: one
pce) ...................................................................................................... 1¹⁄₂.5
2460 Fire Top **(93)** *(RAkehurst)* 7-9-4 RCochrane (5) (2nd st: rdn over 2f out: wknd
over 1f out) .......................................................................................... 6.6
855 Run Don't Fly **(109)** *(PFICole)* 6-9-10 TQuinn (4) (6th st: a bhd) ................... 5.7

**7/4** Peto, **2/1** SHUAILAAN (USA)(op 5/4), **3/1** Adam Smith, **10/1** Fire Top(8/1—12/1), **12/1** Run Don't Fly
(USA), **16/1** Knifebox (USA), **33/1** Royal Seaton. CSF £8.67, Tote £2.60: £2.10 £1.80 (£5.20). Sheikh Ahmed Al
Maktoum (NEWMARKET) bred by W. S. Farish & W. S. Kilroy in USA. 7 Rn                2m 6.5 (3.5)
SF—61/68/61/45/46/38

**3021** HARPOON LOUIE'S H'CAP (0-80) £2847.00 (£792.00: £381.00)
1m 3f 135y
7-10 (7-13)

(Weights raised 2 lb)

2836 **Green Lane (IRE) (76)** (bl) (Jt-Fav) *(RCharlton)* 3-9-6 SCauthen (15) (lw: mde
all: hrd rdn over 1f out: r.o wl) .................................................................. —1
2708⁶ Bit on the Side (IRE) **(51)** *(WJMusson)* 3-7-9 JQuinn (17) (5th st: hrd rdn over 1f
out: r.o) ................................................................................................ ³⁄₄.2

2596[2] Miss Witch **(49)** *(HCandy)* 4–7–10 ‡[7]AntoinetteArmes (9) (2nd st: ev ch 2f out: hrd rdn over 1f out: unable qckn) ...................... 3[1/2].3
2827* Swift Silver **(62)** *(Jt-Fav) (WJMusson)* 5–9–2 JReid (14) (hdwy 2f out: r.o ins fnl f) 3[1/2].4
2860* Quadrireme **(76)** *(Jt-Fav) (MajorWRHern)* 3–9–6 WCarson (7) (4th st: rdn 3f out: one pce) .................... nk.5
2915 Upper House **(66)** (v) *(GWragg)* 3–8–10 MRoberts (12) (3rd st: wknd over 3f out) 10.6
2827 Mahrajan **(64)** *(CJBenstead)* 8–9–4 TQuinn (8) (hdwy over 2f out: hrd rdn over 1f out: eased whn btn ins fnl f) .................... 2.7
2833* Island Blade (IRE) **(50)** *(RAkehurst)* 3–7–8 NAdams (10) (lw: no hdwy fnl 3f) ..... [3/4].8
Mahong **(63)** (bl) *(MrsHParrott)* 4–9–3 JWilliams (4) (a mid div) .................... hd.9
27494 Garachico (USA) **(70)** (bl) *(GHarwood)* 3–9–0 RCochrane (3) (a mid div) .......... 2.10
2827 Viking Venture **(39)** *(DAWilson)* 7–7–0 ‡[7]SharonMillard (2) (b: nvr nrr) ............ 1[1/2].11
2971[5] Doctor's Remedy **(39)** (bl) *(MrsJJordan)* 6–7–0 ‡[7]KimMcDonnell (6) (a mid div) [1/2].12
2827[2] Full Quiver **(53)** (v) *(MrsBarbaraWaring)* 7–8–7 NHowe (5) (lw: 6th st: wknd wl over 1f out) .................... nk.13
2754[6] Deauville Duchess **(40)** *(PJHobbs)* 5–7–8 RStreet (13) (a bhd) .................... [3/4].14
2711[5] Ibsen **(67)** *(ICampbell)* 4–9–7 MTebbutt (16) (a bhd) .................... 1.15
Sulli Boy (NOR) **(46)** *(MissBSanders)* 7–8–6 CRutter (1) (a bhd) .................... 6.16
1047 Myfontaine **(70)** *(KTIvory)* 5–9–10 GBardwell (11) (bhd fnl 2f) .................... 1.17
LONG HANDICAP: Viking Venture 7-0, Doctor's Remedy 7-4.

**5/1** Swift Silver, Quadrireme, GREEN LANE (IRE), **7/1** Island Blade (IRE), **8/1** Full Quiver, **10/1** Mahrajan, Miss Witch, **12/1** Upper House(op 8/1), **14/1** Garachico (USA), Bit on the Side (IRE), **20/1** Myfontaine, Sulli Boy (NOR), Ibsen, **25/1** Mahong, **33/1** Doctor's Remedy, Deauville Duchess, **50/1** Viking Venture. CSF £74.81, CT £649.70. Tote £6.60: £2.00 £3.00 £1.60 £1.70 (£110.30). Lord Weinstock (BECKHAMPTON) bred by Ballymacoll Stud Farm Ltd in Ireland. 17 Rn                2m 30.1 (7.6)
SF—30/2/–/9/12/–

**3022**    RFD SPINNERS GRADUATION STKS (3-Y.O) £2574.00 (£714.00: £342.00)
1m 3f 135y                                                    7-40 (7-42)

711[3] **Mack the Knife (111)** *(Fav) (MajorWRHern)* 9–4 WCarson (2) (swtg: mde all: rdn out) .................... —1
1015[2] Anchorite **(100)** *(PTWalwyn)* 9–4 LDettori (7) (2nd st: rdn over 3f out: unable qckn) .................... 4.2
1198 Young Freeman (USA) **(90)** *(GHarwood)* 9–4 RCochrane (3) (lw: 3rd st: ev ch over 1f out: one pce) .................... s.h.3
Time for a Flutter *(DRCElsworth)* 8–6 JWilliams (8) (leggy: bit bkwd: s.s: 6th st: shkn up over 2f out: one pce) .................... 5.4
864[3] Beauchamp Grace *(JLDunlop)* 8–7[(1)] JReid (4) (nvr nr to chal) .................... 7.5
1319 Aldavera *(MDixon)* 8–6 ‡[5]NGwilliams (1) (4th st: wknd over 3f out) .................... 2.6
1953 River Hawk *(RFJohnsonHoughton)* 8–11 TQuinn (5) (5th st: wknd over 3f out) .... 7.7
1986[5] Hullo Mary Doll *(RIngram)* 7–13 ‡[7]RossBerry (6) (lw: s.s: a bhd: t.o) .................... dist.8

**Evens** MACK THE KNIFE(tchd 8/13), **11/4** Young Freeman (USA), **11/2** Anchorite(4/1—6/1), **7/1** Beauchamp Grace, **10/1** Time for a Flutter(op 16/1), **50/1** River Hawk, **100/1** Ors. CSF £7.11, Tote £1.70: £1.20 £1.50 £1.30 (£3.70). Sir John Astor (LAMBOURN) bred by Sir John Astor. 8 Rn                2m 31.7 (9.2)
SF—12/4/3/–/–/–

T/Trio: Race 5: £425.40 (2 Tckts). T/Plpt: £14.50 (168.4 Tckts).                    AK

2374—**NEWCASTLE (L-H)**
## Saturday, August 29th [Good]
Going Allowance: 5f-8f: minus 0.05 sec (G); Rest: minus 0.20 sec (F)    Wind: slt half against

Stalls: high

**3023**    ARMADA NURSERY    £5344.50 (£1596.00: £763.00: £346.50)    **5f**    2-20 (2-21)
(Weights raised 6 lb)

2794[5] **Bangles (77)** *(LordHuntingdon)* 9–2 KFallon (6) (lw: disp ld tl led over 1f out: r.o: eased nr fin) .................... —1
2842[3] Plum First **(66)** *(NBycroft)* 8–2 ‡[3]SMaloney (8) (disp ld tl hdd over 1f out: kpt on wl) .................... [3/4].2
2471* Sea Gazer (IRE) **(75)** *(Fav) (TDBarron)* 9–0 KDarley (7) (lw: disp ld over 3f: styd on wl) .................... s.h.3
2669* Zany Zanna (IRE) **(82)** *(GAPritchard-Gordon)* 9–4 ‡[3]FNorton (1) (in tch: hdwy 2f out: nt qckn wl ins fnl f) .................... [1/2].4
2669[3] Dead Calm **(58)** *(CTinkler)* 7–11 JLowe (5) (a chsng ldrs: effrt 2f out: r.o one pce) .................... 1[1/2].5
2779[3] Cloudy Reef **(69)** *(RHollinshead)* 8–1 ‡[7]AGarth (9) (lw: s.i.s: hdwy 2f out: n.m.r: kpt on) .................... [1/2].6

2824* Carnbrea Snip **(78)** *(MBell)* 9-3 GBaxter (4) (disp ld over 3f: eased whn btn) ..... 3.7
2857⁵ Caps Ninety-Two (IRE) **(66)** *(DrJDScargill)* 7-12 ‡⁷CHawksley (3) (lw: s.i.s: styd on fnl 2f: n.d) ...................................................................................... s.h.8
2703⁶ Whitley Gorse **(59)** *(JEtherington)* 7-12 LCharnock (10) (spd over 3f: sn wknd) 2.9
2928⁴ Norstano **(65)** (bl) *(MHEasterby)* 8-4 MBirch (12) (lw: nvr wnt pce) ............. ¹/₂.10
2905³ Rhett's Choice **(78)** *(JBerry)* 9-3 JCarroll (2) (b.hind: s.i.s: a bhd) ................ 4.11

**5/1** Sea Gazer (IRE), **6/1** BANGLES, Norstano, Whitley Gorse, **7/1** Zany Zanna (IRE), **8/1** Rhett's Choice, **12/1** Dead Calm, **14/1** Carnbrea Snip, Plum First, Cloudy Reef, **16/1** Caps Ninety-Two (IRE). CSF £74.80, CT £407.53. Tote £6.20: £2.30 £2.10 £3.30 (£30.90). Mr J. Rose (WEST ILSLEY) bred by John Rose. 11 Rn
61.44 sec (3.04)
SF—36/19/30/32/5/7

---

## 3024

ROTHMANS ROYALS NORTH SOUTH CHALLENGE SERIES H'CAP (0-90) £4077.50
(£1220.00: £585.00: £267.50)   **7f**
2-50 (2-56)

2878* **Laurel Queen (IRE) (66)** *(JBerry)* 4-8-5 JCarroll (9) (swtchd s: hld up & bhd: stdy hdwy over 2f out: r.o to ld wl ins fnl f: hung lft) .......................... —1
2956⁵ Flashy's Son **(60)** **(Fav)** *(MDHammond)* 4-7-10 ‡³SMaloney (17) (b.off hind: disp ld tl led over 1f out: hrd rdn & hdd wl ins fnl f) .................. nk.2
2463⁵ King Al **(89)** *(DrJDScargill)* 5-10-0 SWebster (12) (b: lw: outpcd & bhd 3f out: hdwy over 1f out: r.o u.p) ......................................................... 4.3
2348⁵ Desert Splendour **(73)** *(CEBrittain)* 4-8-12 GCrealock (18) (lw: outpcd tl hdwy 2f out: styd on) ........................................................... ¹/₂.4
2958  Super Benz **(76)** *(TFairhurst)* 6-9-1 JFanning (6) (a in tch: styd on wl fnl 2f) ...... 1.5
2521² Sharpalto **(84)** *(MrsGRReveley)* 5-9-2 ‡⁷GForster (2) (lw: hdwy 3f out: sn prom: nt qckn u.p fnl f) ......................................................... ³/₄.6
2926* Mbulwa **(60)** *(SEKettlewell)* 6-7-10 ‡³FNorton (10) (disp ld over 5f: nt qckn) ..... ¹/₂.7
1934  Calpella **(79)** *(JARToller)* 3-8-13 GBaxter (13) (effrt 3f out: styd on: no imp) .... nk.8
2417  Foolish Touch **(58)** *(WJMusson)* 10-7-4⁴ ‡⁷CHawksley (3) (b: sn bhd: hdwy centre mid-race: r.o) ................................................. nk.9
2348  High Low (USA) **(86)** *(WJHaggas)* 4-9-11 KDarley (8) (effrt 3f out: btn whn hmpd over 1f out) ...................................................... nk.10
2898⁶ Habeta (USA) **(67)** *(JWWatts)* 6-8-6 JLowe (15) (lw: a chsng ldrs: drvn along ¹/₂-wy: no imp) ............................................................... nk.11
2925  Filicaia **(62)** *(DonEnricoIncisa)* 6-7-8 ‡⁷ClaireBalding (16) (lw: sn outpcd & bhd: swtchd 2f out: n.d) ................................................... 3¹/₂.12
2925  Allinson's Mate (IRE) **(76)** *(TDBarron)* 4-9-1 AlexGreaves (11) (lw: n.d) .......... nk.13
2926⁵ Spanish Verdict **(70)** *(DenysSmith)* 5-8-9 KFallon (7) (lw: sn drvn along: n.d) .... 1.14
2898  Leave it to Lib **(63)** *(PCalver)* 5-7-9 ‡⁷JTate (14) (lw: disp ld over 4f: sn wknd) ³/₄.15
2958⁵ Northern Spark **(54)** *(CWThornton)* 4-7-7 LCharnock (1) (lw: disp ld over 4f: sn wknd) ³/₄.16
2521* Rise Up Singing **(72)** (bl) *(WJMusson)* 4-8-11 JHBrown (7) (disp ld 4f: sn wknd) ................................................................ 1¹/₂.17
2852  Jalmusique **(87)** *(MHEasterby)* 6-9-12 MBirch (4) (b.hind: prom to ¹/₂-wy) .. 10.18
LONG HANDICAP: Northern Spark 7-6.

**6/1** Flashy's Son, **15/2** Mbulwa, Calpella, **8/1** Desert Splendour, **9/1** Jalmusique, **11/1** Sharpalto, LAUREL QUEEN (IRE), **12/1** Habeta (USA), Rise Up Singing, **14/1** Allinson's Mate (IRE), High Low (USA), **16/1** Spanish Verdict, Foolish Touch, **20/1** Leave it to Lib, **25/1** Super Benz, Northern Spark, **33/1** King Al, **50/1** Filicaia. CSF £74.53, CT £1,977.63. Tote £8.90: £2.00 £1.50 £4.80 £2.50 (£19.40). Laurel (Leisure) Limited (COCKERHAM) bred by E. Lonergan in Ireland. 18 Rn
1m 26.60 (2.30)
SF—51/41/61/43/43/42

---

## 3025

NEWGATE APP'CE STKS (Mdn) £2070.00 (£570.00: £270.00)
**1¹/₂m 93y**
3-25 (3-26)

2628a **Marcus Thorpe (USA) (102)** **(Fav)** *(PAKelleway)* 4-9-4 ‡³ABates (6) (b: a gng wl: led over 3f out: sn clr: pushed out) ................................... —1
989  Charolles *(HRACecil)* 3-8-6 StephenDavies (10) (hld up: hdwy 5f out: styd on: no ch w wnr) .................................................... 12.2
2869³ Neieb (USA) *(BHanbury)* 3-8-3 ‡³CHawksley (4) (a chsng ldrs: effrt ent st: one pce) ..................................................................... 4.3
1330ª Storm Gayle (IRE) *(CWThornton)* 3-8-6 LNewton (2) (mde most tl hdd over 3f out: sn outpcd) .................................................... 3¹/₂.4
2064⁵ Only a Rose *(CWThornton)* 3-7-13 ‡⁷KSked (1) (chsd ldrs: rdn appr st: sn btn) . 3.5
2673³ Edirepus *(MrsGRReveley)* 4-9-0 ‡⁷SCopp (5) (w ldr tl wknd appr st) ............. 20.6
2929⁴ Tina's Game *(APStringer)* 4-8-13 ‡³HBastiman (3) (prom: pushed along ¹/₂-wy: sn wknd) ................................................................ 6.7
Heliopsis *(MDHammond)* 4-9-0 ‡⁷ALakeman (1) (cmpt: bit bkwd: sn wl bhd) .. 5.8
Finalto *(RHollinshead)* 4-9-7 AGarth (3) (wl grwn: s.i.s: a wl bhd) ................. 8.9
2807  Tathir (CAN) **(44)** (bl) *(DMorley)* 4-9-0 ‡⁵EBentley (8) (b: b.hind: hld up: effrt 5f out: rdn & no rspnse appr st) ........................................... 10.10

**6/5** MARCUS THORPE (USA), **5/2** Charolles, **5/1** Neieb (USA), **20/1** Storm Gayle (IRE), **25/1** Tathir (CAN), **33/1** Only a Rose, Edirepius, **50/1** Finalto, **66/1** Ors. CSF £4.07, Tote £2.10: £1.50 £1.10 £1.70 (£3.10). Mr G. Mazza (NEWMARKET) bred by Stonereath Farms Inc in USA. 10 Rn                2m 39.65 (1.15)
SF—68/32/21/17/4/–

---

**3026**  THOMAS LONSDALE GALLAGHER H'CAP (0-80) £3622.50 (£1080.00: £515.00: £232.50)   **1¼m 32y**                                4-00 (4-04)

(Weights raised 4 lb)

| | |
|---|---|
| 2527² **Northern Graduate (USA) (62)** (Fav) *(MrsGRReveley)* 3-9-1 KDarley (3) (chsd ldrs: pushed along over 3f out: r.o gamely fnl f to ld cl home) —1 | |
| 2810 Cheeky Pot **(40)** (bl) *(DenysSmith)* 4-8-1 LCharnock (2) (lw: disp ld tl led 3f out: qcknd clr over 1f out: no ex cl home) .................. 1.2 | |
| 2926 Nicely Thanks (USA) **(61)** *(TDBarron)* 3-8-7 ‡⁷VHalliday (4) (bhd: hdwy on ins 3f out: styd on wl) ..................... 2.3 | |
| 2926³ Touch Above **(56)** *(TDBarron)* 6-9-3 AlexGreaves (6) (disp ld tl hdd 3f out: one pce) ........................... hd.4 | |
| 2571² Top Scale **(37)** (v) *(WWHaigh)* 6-7-12 JLowe (10) (b.hind: lw: in tch: effrt 3f out: styd on: nt pce to chal) ............ 1½.5 | |
| 2927 Young George **(54)** *(MDods)* 5-9-1 KFallon (5) (in tch: rdn over 2f out: no imp) 2.6 | |
| 2926 Straw Thatch **(69)** *(MJohnston)* 3-9-8 RPElliott (8) (hld up: shkn up over 2f out: nvr nr to chal) ............ 2½.7 | |
| 2929³ Sally Fay (IRE) **(35)** *(TKersey)* 4-7-3⁽²⁾ ‡⁷ClaireBalding (9) (bhd: hdwy appr st: sn btn) ................. ½.8 | |
| 2852 Salda **(71)** *(RMWhitaker)* 3-9-10 ACulhane (11) (prom tl rdn & btn 2f out) ......... 3.9 | |
| 2959⁵ Sharquin **(38)** *(MBrittain)* 5-7-10⁽⁶⁾ ‡³SMaloney (1) (b.hind: chsd ldrs tl wknd 3f out) ............... 10.10 | |
| 1850 Linpac Express **(59)** (bl) *(CWCElsey)* 3-8-11 JCarroll (7) (lw: a bhd) ............... 8.11 | |

LONG HANDICAP: Sharquin 7-5.

**7/4** NORTHERN GRADUATE (USA), **5/1** Top Scale, **7/1** Touch Above, **10/1** Young George, Nicely Thanks (USA), Salda(op 6/1), **12/1** Straw Thatch, **20/1** Sharquin, Cheeky Pot, **25/1** Sally Fay (IRE), **33/1** Linpac Express. CSF £32.29, CT £254.87. Tote £2.30: £1.20 £5.10 £3.00 (£29.40). Mr P. D. Savill (SALTBURN) bred by Ann Trimble & Donald T. Johnson in USA. 11 Rn                  2m 10.02 (3.32)
SF—48/32/34/43/21/34

---

**3027**  WIDE OPEN H'CAP (0-110) £7635.00 (£2280.00: £1090.00: £495.00)  **1m**                           4-30 (4-33)

| | |
|---|---|
| 2846⁴ **Cumbrian Challenge (IRE) (88)** (Fav) *(MHEasterby)* 3-8-13 MBirch (3) (chsd ldrs: led 1f out: shkn up & qcknd) —1 | |
| 2846 Mellottie **(96)** *(MrsGRReveley)* 7-9-13 JLowe (5) (hld up & bhd: hdwy over 2f out: r.o: nt pce of wnr ins fnl f) ............... 2.2 | |
| 2611★ State Dancer (USA) **(91)** *(MMoubarak)* 5-9-3 ‡⁵StephenDavies (6) (in tch: shkn up over 2f out: styd on) ...... 2½.3 | |
| 1391³ Cool Luke (IRE) **(78)** *(GMMoore)* 3-8-3 JCarroll (2) (bit bkwd: cl up: slt ld over 2f out: hung lft: hdd 1f out: sn btn) .... ½.4 | |
| Knock to Enter (USA) **(90)** *(MRStoute)* 4-9-7 KDarley (4) (hld up: effrt 2f out: no imp) ............... 1.5 | |
| 2852 Alkarif (USA) **(77)** *(MrsJRRamsden)* 3-8-2⁽¹⁾ GBaxter (1) (led tl hdd & sltly hmpd over 2f out: sn btn) .... nk.6 | |

**100/30** CUMBRIAN CHALLENGE (IRE), **7/2** Alkarif (USA), Mellottie, **4/1** State Dancer (USA), **5/1** Knock to Enter (USA), **12/1** Cool Luke (IRE). CSF £14.15, Tote £4.30: £1.20 £2.50 (£4.90). Cumbrian Industrials Ltd (MALTON) bred by Major V. McCalmont in Ireland. 6 Rn                     1m 40.22 (1.22)
SF—75/83/65/49/64/44

---

**3028**  GALLOWGATE CLAIMING STKS (3-Y.O) £2490.00 (£690.00: £330.00)  **1m**                           5-00 (5-07)

| | |
|---|---|
| 2967★ **Super Summit (54)** *(JPearce)* 8-13 MBirch (3) (a cl up: led 1f out: rdn & r.o) .... —1 | |
| 2906 Mummys Rocket **(46)** (bl) *(MO'Neill)* 7-7⁽¹⁾ ‡³FNorton (5) (b: a.p: effrt over 2f out: styd on) ...... 1.2 | |
| 2665³ Battuta **(48)** *(REarnshaw)* 7-4 ‡⁷CHawksley (4) (a chsng ldrs: nt clr run 2f out tl r.o cl home) ............ nk.3 | |
| 2778★ Chequers (IRE) **(74)** *(RJRWilliams)* 8-13 JCarroll (11) (hld up: effrt on outside 3f out: hrd rdn 2f out: nt pce to chal) ..... ½.4 | |
| 1986³ Hot Prospect *(JEtherington)* 8-1 KDarley (6) (effrt 3f out: hdwy over 1f out: styd on) ........... hd.5 | |
| 2808 Throw Away Line **(46)** *(REBarr)* 8-4 SWebster (2) (led tl hdd 1f out: one pce) .... 2.6 | |
| 2655² Round by the River **(65)** *(WWHaigh)* 8-11 ‡³SMaloney (12) (c wd & effrt st: rdn over 2f out: nt qckn) ............... 1½.7 | |

*2687* Strangersinthenite **(42)** (v) *(JSWainwright)* 8-2 LCharnock (9) (bhd: effrt over 2f
out: n.d) ............................................................................................... 1.8
*2950³* Gizlaan (USA) **(56)** *(BHanbury)* 8-3 GBaxter (10) (chsd ldrs tl rdn & wknd 2f out) 1.9
*2665⁴* Spanish Performer **(48)** *(TFairhurst)* 8-2 JFanning (1) (nvr trbld ldrs) ............... 5.10
*2699* My Jersey Pearl (IRE) **(28)** *(DonEnricoIncisa)* 7-7 ‡7ClaireBalding (13) (a bhd) ³/₄.11
*167* Dream Sweet Dreams (USA) *(BHanbury)* 7-7 JLowe (8) (chsd ldrs tl lost pl ent
st) ..................................................................................................... 6.12

**85/40** Chequers (IRE), **5/1** SUPER SUMMIT, **6/1** Round by the River, **13/2** Gizlaan (USA), **8/1** Mummys
Rocket(op 5/1), **9/1** Battuta, **12/1** Hot Prospect, **14/1** Spanish Performer, **16/1** Dream Sweet Dreams (USA),
**20/1** Throw Away Line, **33/1** Strangersinthenite, **50/1** My Jersey Pearl (IRE). CSF £43.96, Tote £5.80: £2.60
£2.70 £2.10 (£39.10). Mr D. J. Maden (NEWMARKET) bred by S. J. Mear. 12 Rn                    1m 42.91 (3.91)
SF—34/11/7/28/15/12

T/Plpt: £85.80 (39.85 Tckts).                                                                AA

# NEWCASTLE (L-H)
## Monday, August 31st [Good]
Going Allowance: St: 0.30 sec; Rnd : 0.10 sec per fur (G)                    Wind: str against

Stalls: high

**3029**    RAFA WINGS APPEAL NURSERY    £3200.00 (£950.00: £450.00: £200.00)
7f                                                          2-15 (2-16)

(Weights raised 1 lb)

*2695⁶* Umbubuzi (USA) **(74)** *(FHLee)* 8-6 PaulEddery (9) (in tch: hdwy to ld ins fnl f:
hld on wl) ............................................................................................ —1
*1471⁶* Jervia **(89)** *(JWWatts)* 9-7 WRyan (13) (hld up: nt clr run & swtchd 1f out: qcknd
to chal wl ins fnl f: nt qckn nr fin) ......................................................... s.h.2
*2462* Dalalah **(78)** *(HThomsonJones)* 8-10 RHills (11) (led tl hdd ins fnl f: kpt on same
pce) ................................................................................................. 1¹/₂.3
*2612³* Tarnside Rosal **(79)** *(JEtherington)* 8-11 KFallon (7) (in tch: hdwy & ev ch over
1f out: nt qckn) .................................................................................... 2.4
*2790⁴* Regalsett **(84)** *(RHannon)* 9-2 MHills (12) (lw: a.p: effrt 2f out: kpt on one pce fnl
f) ..................................................................................................... s.h.5
*2700³* Hyde's Happy Hour **(63)** *(NTinkler)* 7-7 LCharnock (6) (lw: bhd: hdwy over 1f
out: nvr nr to chal) .............................................................................. 3.6
*2782★* Mighty Miss Magpie **(66)** *(MRChannon)* 7-7⁽⁵⁾ ‡5BDoyle (4) (chsd ldrs:
chal 2f out: wknd 1f out) ...................................................................... hd.7
*2928⁶* Paajib (IRE) **(65)** *(CTinkler)* 7-11 JLowe (3) (lw ldrs over 5f: wknd) .................. 2.8
*2482★* Astrac Trio (USA) **(83)** *(SGNorton)* 8-10 ‡5OPears (8) (lw: prom tl rdn & btn wl
over 1f out) ........................................................................................ s.h.9
*2924⁶* Panther (IRE) **(79)** *(CWCElsey)* 8-11 LDettori (10) (effrt ¹/₂-wy: rdn & wknd appr
fnl f) ................................................................................................ 1.10
*2873★* Benevolent **(81)** (Fav) *(SirMarkPrescott)* 8-13 GDuffield (5) (hld up & bhd: effrt
3f out: sn rdn & btn) ........................................................................... nk.11
*2735⁵* Bonus Point **(72)** *(MrsGRReveley)* 8-4 KDarley (1) (lw: hld up: effrt 3f out: hung
lft & sn btn) ...................................................................................... 3¹/₂.12

**3/1** Benevolent, **11/2** Regalsett, **13/2** Jervia, **9/1** Astrac Trio (USA), Bonus Point, Mighty Miss Magpie (IRE), **10/1**
Tarnside Rosal, **12/1** Dalalah, UMUBUZI (USA), **14/1** Panther (IRE), **16/1** Hyde's Happy Hour, **25/1** Paajib
(IRE). CSF £84.05, CT £885.49. Tote £21.30: £5.50 £2.20 £4.70 (£123.00). Semi-Chem Bargain Centres
(WILMSLOW) bred by Glencrest Farm in USA. 12 Rn                                1m 31.38 (7.08)
SF—17/31/15/10/14/–

**3030**    E.B.F. HEDGEHOPE STKS (Mdn 2-Y.O) £2826.00 (£786.00: £378.00)    7f 2-50 (2-54)

*2340²* Blush Rambler (USA) (Fav) *(MRStoute)* 9-0 WRyan (7) (lw: a gng wl far side:
led 2f out: sn clr) ............................................................................... —1
*2859⁶* Marco Magnifico (USA) **(89)** *(BWHills)* 9-0 MHills (9) (lw: prom far side: kpt on fnl 2f:
no ch w wnr) ..................................................................................... 7.2
Blue Grotto (IRE) *(JWWatts)* 9-0 GBaxter (12) (gd sort: bhd stands' side: hdwy
2f out: r.o wl) .................................................................................... hd.3
*2534⁴* Cure the King (IRE) *(SGNorton)* 8-9 ‡5OPears (5) (in tch far side: stdy hdwy over
1f out: r.o: nvr plcd to chal) ................................................................. 1¹/₂.4
*2924* Who's the Best (IRE) *(APJarvis)* 8-9 ‡5BDoyle (6) (led far side tl hdd 2f out: sn
outpcd) ............................................................................................ nk.5
*2924⁵* Silver Groom (IRE) *(APJarvis)* 9-0 MTebbutt (4) (chsd ldrs far side: nt qckn fnl
2f) .................................................................................................. hd.6

2812 Dutosky *(MJCamacho)* 8-9 ACulhane (15) (prom: led stands' side over 2f out: sn rdn & btn) .................................................................. 4.7
23983 Tajdid (IRE) *(HThomsonJones)* 9-0 RHills (19) (lw: led stands' side tl hdd over 2f out: sn wknd) ...................................................... 2.8
Demurrer *(JGFitzGerald)* 9-0 KFallon (8) (leggy: scope: s.s: bhd far side tl sme late hdwy) ............................................................ 3.9
Stage Artist *(JEtherington)* 8-9 GDuffield (1) (w'like: leggy: chsd ldrs far side 5f) nk.10
Stephanentse *(WWHaigh)* 8-9 SWebster (2) (w'like: unf: bit bkwd: a outpcd & bhd far side) .................................................... 1½.11
2879 Roscommon Joe (IRE) *(JJO'Neill)* 9-5(12) ‡7ADobbin (3) (cl up far side 5f) 1½.12
2859 Fire in My Body (USA) *(PWChapple-Hyam)* 9-0 PaulEddery (14) (lw: s.i.s: hdwy stands' side ½-wy: wknd wl over 1f out) ......................... ¾.13
29054 Exodus (IRE) **(68)** *(MHEasterby)* 9-0 KDarley (11) (spd stands' side over 4f) .. 1.14
Ranunculus *(JBerry)* 9-0 LDettori (18) (cmpt: scope: prom stands' side 4f) .... 1½.15
2812 Codden Lad *(NTinkler)* 9-0 LCharnock (10) (spd far side 4f: wknd qckly) ...... 1½.16
2205 Song in Your Heart *(AHarrison)* 9-0 MWood (16) (a bhd stands' side) ............ nk.17
Innocent Abroad (DEN) *(CBBBooth)* 8-9 GOldroyd (17) (neat: scope: racd stands' side: a bhd) ............................................... 1½.18
2879 Cornflake *(DenysSmith)* 8-9 JLowe (13) (chsd ldrs stands' side to ½-wy: sn wknd) ............................................................. 7.19

**6/4** BLUSH RAMBLER (USA)(op Evens), **7/2** Marco Magnifico (USA), **8/1** Fire in My Body (USA), **9/1** Tajdid (IRE), **10/1** Blue Grotto (IRE), **16/1** Cure the King (IRE), **20/1** Demurrer, Exodus (IRE), **25/1** Dutosky, Silver Groom (IRE), Ranunculus, Stage Artist, **33/1** Cornflake, **50/1** Ors. CSF £7.77, Tote £2.00: £1.20 £2.10 £3.20 (£4.10). Sheikh Mohammed (NEWMARKET) bred by Holtsinger Inc. in USA. 19 Rn    1m 29.17 (4.87)
SF—58/37/36/26/25/29

---

**3031**   CHEVIOT H'CAP (0–100) £7570.00 (£2260.00: £1080.00 £490.00)   **6f**   3-20 (3-23)

28483 **Venture Capitalist (86)** (bl) *(RHannon)* 3-8-13 RHills (6) (lw: trckd ldrs gng wl: led 1f out: rdn & r.o) ..................................... —1
2839 Claybank (USA) **(84)** (Fav) *(BWHills)* 3–8–11 MHills (4) (chsd ldrs: rdn to ld wl over 1f out: sn hdd: kpt on) .................................. 1.2
2925 Densben **(81)** *(DenysSmith)* 8–8-12 KFallon (8) (in tch: effrt over 1f out: r.o) .... ¾.3
22624 Love Jazz (USA) **(82)** *(TDBarron)* 3–8–9 KDarley (3) (in tch: hdwy 2f out: styd on wl) ........................................................ 1½.4
2902* Crystal Jack (FR) **(86)** *(FHLee)* 4–9-3 PaulEddery (7) (in tch: hdwy 2f out: nvr nr to chal) ...................................................... 3.5
1393 Amron **(81)** *(JBerry)* 5–8-12 LDettori (5) (w ldr tl wknd wl over 1f out) ........... 4.6
2902 Gipsy Fiddler **(97)** *(JJO'Neill)* 4–9-7 ‡7ADobbin (9) (led tl hdd & wknd wl over 1f out) ..................................................... ½.7
2848 Storm Melody (USA) **(97)** *(AAScott)* 3-9-10 WRyan (1) (b: b.hind: nvr wnt pce) 8.8
2839 Clifton Charlie (USA) **(84)** *(MRChannon)* 4–9-1 MTebbutt (2) (a outpcd & bhd) . 1.9

**4/1** Claybank (USA), **9/2** VENTURE CAPITALIST, **6/1** Crystal Jack (FR), Densben, **8/1** Amron, Clifton Charlie (USA), **9/1** Gipsy Fiddler, **10/1** Love Jazz (USA), **12/1** Storm Melody (USA). CSF £21.35, CT £97.84. Tote £5.00: £2.00 £2.20 £2.10 (£10.00). Mr D. K. Harris (MARLBOROUGH) bred by Brook Bloodstock Plc. 9 Rn    1m 15.60 (4.10)
SF—53/37/35/26/22/1

---

**3032**   VIRGINIA STKS (listed race) (F & M) £9706.25 (£2900.00: £1387.50: £631.25) 1¼m 32y   3-55 (3-58)

24364 **Red Slippers (USA) (100)** *(LMCumani)* 3–8-6 LDettori (9) (hld up: swtchd outside 2f out: r.o wl to ld ins fnl f) ............................... —1
2386* Citiqueen (IRE) **(84)** *(HRACecil)* 3–8–6 KDarley (5) (lw: pushed along: hdwy 3f out: styd on wl to ld ins fnl f: sn hdd: kpt on) .................. 1½.2
2843 Midnight Air (USA) **(93)** *(HRACecil)* 3–8-6 WRyan (3) (trckd ldrs: led 2f out tl ins fnl f: no ex) ............................................. 1½.3
2914* Mystery Play (IRE) **(95)** *(BWHills)* 3–8-6 GDuffield (6) (sn cl up: led 3f out to 2f out: nt qckn) .................................................. 2.4
2890a4 Feminine Wiles (IRE) **(107)** *(PWChapple-Hyam)* 3–8-12 PaulEddery (2) (lw: trckd ldrs: effrt 3f out: one pce) ................................ 1½.5
29133 Double Flutter **(78)** *(MRChannon)* 3–8-6 KFallon (1) (bhd: hdwy appr st: sn rdn & nvr able to chal) ........................................ 1½.6
19352 LoveEaloch (IRE) **(109)** (Fav) *(MBell)* 4–9-0 MHills (4) (lw: in tch: effrt ent st: rdn & no imp) ...................................................... 2½.7
26823 Springs Welcome **(66)** *(CACyzer)* 6–9-0 LCharnock (8) (lw: a outpcd & bhd) .. 15.8
2461 Gai Bulga **(97)** (bl) *(GWragg)* 3–8-6 RHills (7) (led tl hdd 3f out: sn wknd) ....... 4.9

**100/30** Lovealoch (IRE), **4/1** RED SLIPPERS (USA), **9/2** Mystery Play (IRE), **11/2** Midnight Air (USA), **13/2** Feminine Wiles (IRE), **8/1** Citiqueen (IRE), **14/1** Gai Bulga, **20/1** Double Flutter, **66/1** Springs Welcome. CSF £31.83, Tote £3.70: £1.60 £2.00 £1.80 (£17.00). Sheikh Mohammed (NEWMARKET) bred by Swettenham Stud in USA. 9 Rn                                     2m 9.52 (2.82)
SF—74/71/68/64/67/58

## 3033      LEAF (S) STKS (2-Y.O) £2595.00 (£720.00: £345.00)      **5f**      4-30 (4-31)

| | | |
|---|---|---|
| **Norling (IRE)** *(BBeasley)* 8-6 LCharnock (4) (cmpt: scope: trckd ldrs: effrt over 1f out: r.o to ld wl ins fnl f) | —1 |
| 29005 First Option **(85)** (Fav) *(MHEasterby)* 8-11 KDarley (3) (a cl up: led over 1f out: hrd rdn & r.o: jst ct) | hd.2 |
| 28426 Clanrock *(RMWhitaker)* 8-6 ACulhane (9) (bhd: hdwy whn hmpd over 1f out: r.o wl nr fin) | ¾.3 |
| 2598 Chummy's Friend (IRE) *(BWHills)* 8-1 MHills (7) (a chsng ldrs: kpt on same pce fnl f) | 3.4 |
| 27244 Our Mica **(54)** (bl) *(JBerry)* 8-6 LDettori (6) (led tl hdd over 1f out: sn btn) | 3.5 |
| 2863 Cizard (IRE) *(AWPotts)* 8-1 RHills (11) (effrt ½-wy: nvr able to chal) | 4.6 |
| 28765 Stardust Express **(70)** *(MJohnston)* 8-6 JLowe (1) (prom tl outpcd fnl 2f) | hd.7 |
| 20673 Purchased by Phone (IRE) **(73)** *(JSWainwright)* 7-8 ‡7DarrenMoffatt (10) (cl up: wkng whn hmpd over 1f out) | nk.8 |
| Master Peckitt *(SEKettlewell)* 8-6 SWebster (12) (unf: bit bkwd: dwlt: n.d) | 3.9 |
| 28633 Good Image **(64)** *(APJarvis)* 8-11 WRyan (5) (s.i.s: a bhd) | ¾.10 |
| Another Jade *(APJarvis)* 7-10 ‡5BDoyle (2) (neat: lw: dwlt: hdwy ½-wy: sn wknd) | ¾.11 |
| 2363 I'Ll Risk it *(JBerry)* 8-2(1) PaulEddery (8) (sn bhd: t.o) | 12 |

**4/5** First Option(Evens—6/4), **11/2** Another Jade(4/1—6/1), **6/1** Chummy's Friend (IRE), **7/1** Purchased by Phone (IRE), Clanrock(op 7/2), **8/1** NORLING (IRF)(op 16/1), **16/1** Good Image, Stardust Express, Our Mica, **50/1** Ors. CSF £17.15, Tote £28.00: £4.50 £1.50 £2.40 (£28.20). Mr Peter Tierney (HAMBLETON) bred by Mrs A. Whitehead in Ireland. 12 Rn; No bid                                     63.97 sec (5.57)
SF—10/14/6/–/–/–

## 3034      PERKINS MEMORIAL CUP (H'cap) (0-80) £3054.00 (£912.00: £436.00: £198.00)      2m 19y      5-05 (5-06)

| | | |
|---|---|---|
| 2934* **Vain Prince (48)** (Fav) *(NTinkler)* 5-8-4 (3x) LCharnock (7) (lw: hld up: hdwy 10f out: led over 2f out: hld on gamely cl home) | —1 |
| 29342 Briggsmaid **(59)** *(JMPEustace)* 4-9-1 MTebbutt (2) (lw: hld up: stdy hdwy 2f out: swtchd ins & chal wl ins fnl f: nt qckn nr fin) | s.h.2 |
| 28772 Attadale **(56)** *(LLungo)* 4-8-12 KFallon (6) (bhd: hdwy 3f out: r.o u.p: nrst fin) | 1.3 |
| 6832 Sillars Stalker (IRE) **(49)** *(MrsJRRamsden)* 4-8-5 GBaxter (4) (trckd ldrs: led ent st tl over 2f out: no ex) | 8.4 |
| 2877* Rolling the Bones (USA) **(68)** *(MPNaughton)* 3-8-10 KDarley (8) (bhd: shkn up over 2f out: no imp) | 7.5 |
| 22783 Shoofe (USA) **(72)** *(DMorley)* 4-10-0 WRyan (1) (cl up: disp ld 6f out tl wknd over 2f out) | nk.6 |
| 23734 Moving Out **(71)** *(SirMarkPrescott)* 4-9-13 GDuffield (2) (led tl hdd ent st: sn wknd) | 15.7 |
| 2877 Native Crown (IRE) **(49)** *(MrsSCBradburne)* 4-8-5 PaulEddery (3) (prom to st: sn bhd) | 2½.8 |

*Stewards Enquiry: Tebbutt suspended 9-12/9/92 (excessive use of whip).*

**100/30** VAIN PRINCE, **4/1** Sillars Stalker (IRE), **9/2** Rolling the Bones (USA), Moving Out, **11/2** Briggsmaid, **7/1** Attadale, **11/1** Shoofe (USA), **25/1** Native Crown (IRE). CSF £20.56, CT £108.88. Tote £3.70: £1.60 £1.90 £2.20 (£6.80). Mr A. C. Findlay (MALTON) bred by Lodge Park Stud. 8 Rn                      3m 36.63 (11.13)
T/Plpt: £105.30 (27.2 Tckts).                                                                                  AA

## 2136—CHEPSTOW  (L-H)

### Monday, August 31st [Soft, Heavy patches]

Going Allowance: 1st race: 0.60 sec (Y); Rest: 0.80 sec per fur (S)        Wind: mod half bhd

Stalls: high

## 3035      E.B.F. ROMEO STKS (Mdn 2-Y.O C & G) £2724.90 (£756.40: £362.70)      1m 14y      2-20 (2-24)

| | | |
|---|---|---|
| 2225 **World Express (IRE)** (v) *(BRMillman)* 9-0 JWilliams (10) (plld hrd: a.p: rdn 3f out: r.o strly to ld ins fnl f: r.o wl) | —1 |
| Lyford Cay (IRE) *(PWChapple-Hyam)* 9-0 RCochrane (6) (unf: scope: bkwd: hld up: hdwy 4f out: led over 2f out tl rdn & hdd ins fnl f) | 2½.2 |

2799 The Executor *(RFJohnsonHoughton)* 9-0 WCarson (12) (led over 5f: r.o one pce) ............................................................................ 2½.3

Biljan (USA) (Fav) *(PFICole)* 9-0 TQuinn (8) (str: rangy: hdwy 4f out: ev ch 2f out: one pce) ....................................................... 1½.4

828 C D Shareplan (USA) *(MRChannon)* 8-11 ‡³RPerham (11) (w ldrs: one pce fnl 2f) ............................................................................. 2.5

2799 Ground Nut (IRE) *(HCandy)* 9-0 CRutter (9) (bhd tl rdn & hdwy fnl 2f: nvr nr to chal) ........................................................................ 1½.6

2444 Pistols At Dawn (USA) *(RHannon)* 9-0 TyroneWilliams (3) (hdwy over 3f out: hrd rdn & wknd over 2f out) ............................... 6.7

2799 Sheer Ecstasy *(RCharlton)* 9-0 TRogers (13) (no hdwy fnl 2f) ............... 2.8

Its Unbelievable *(JWhite)* 8-7 ‡⁷TWilson (5) (lt-f: a bhd) ...................... 2.9

Prince of Music (USA) *(PFICole)* 8-7 ‡⁷JDSmith (14) (w'like: sn rdn along: a bhd)    5.10

2629 Armenian Coffee (IRE) *(JLDunlop)* 9-0 BRouse (1) (swvd lft s: a bhd) ............. hd.11

2802 Young Absalom *(LGCottrell)* 9-0 NCarlisle (7) (prom 5f) ....................... hd.12

2728 Baeza *(HRACecil)* 9-0 AMcGlone (4) (prom: rdn 3f out: wknd qckly: t.o) ......... 5.13

2037 Baulking Towers *(MMcCormack)* 8-7 ‡⁷SDrowne (2) (bhd fnl 4f: t.o) ........... 12.14

**9/4** Biljan (USA), **5/2** Lyford Cay (IRE), **7/2** The Executor, **12/1** Baeza(op 7/1), **16/1** Pistols At Dawn (USA), **20/1** Ground Nut (IRE), Prince of Music (USA), Sheer Ecstasy, Armenian Coffee (IRE), **33/1** Baulking Towers, **50/1** C D Shareplan (USA), Its Unbelievable, **66/1** WORLD EXPRESS (IRE), **100/1** Young Absalom. CSF £213.80, Tote £51.90: £9.40 £1.70 £1.50 (£967.00). World Express Limited (CULLOMPTON) bred by D. Twomey in Ireland.
14 Rn                                                                      1m 41.6 (9.1)
SF—35/27/19/14/5/3

---

**3036**      E.B.F. JULIET STKS (Mdn 2-Y.O.F) £2811.70 (£781.20: £375.10)
**1m 14y**                                                              2-50 (2-56)

**Comme D'Habitude (USA)** *(PFICole)* 8-11 TQuinn (8) (scope: a.p: led over 1f out: rdn out) ....................................................... —1

27282 Magical Queen (IRE) (Fav) *(MMoubarak)* 8-11 WCarson (3) (iw: nld up: hdwy 3f out: rdn over 1f out: ev ch ins fnl f: nt qckn) ............... 1½.2

22694 Gold Tassel *(RHannon)* 8-11 TyroneWilliams (1) (rdn & hdwy over 2f out: ev ch ins fnl f: no ex) .................................................... 1.3

2657 Latest Flame (IRE) **(84)** *(MRChannon)* 8-11 BRouse (11) (a.p: led over 2f out tl over 1f out: one pce) ............................................. ¾.4

2438 Olympic Run *(JLDunlop)* 8-11 AMcGlone (13) (led over 5f: wknd over 1f out) .... 4.5

Singer on the Roof *(IABalding)* 8-11 RCochrane (4) (b.hind: w'like: scope: prom 6f) .............................................................. nk.6

2444 On Request (IRE) *(IABalding)* 8-4 ‡⁷DGriffiths (12) (hdwy over 2f out: nvr trbld ldrs) ....................................................... 1½.7

Ample (IRE) *(PFICole)* 8-11 CRutter (2) (lengthy: scope: prom 5f) ........... nk.8

1591 Honorary Guest *(DJGMurray-Smith)* 8-11 TRogers (5) (no hdwy fnl 2f) ...... 2½.9

2389 Arewenearlythere (IRE) *(MBlanshard)* 8-11 NCarlisle (7) (a bhd) ............ ½.10

2746 Meritre (IRE) *(RJHolder)* 8-4 ‡⁷SDrowne (14) (a bhd) ...................... ½.11

1957 Bright Wales *(MMcCormack)* 8-4 ‡⁷PBowe (6) (rdn 4f out: sn wl bhd) ........ 2½.12

Apachee Flower *(JDRoberts)* 8-11 TLang (10) (w'like: bkwd: bhd fnl 3f: t.o) .... 6.13

Perfect Set (IRE) *(MRChannon)* 8-8 ‡³RPerham (9) (lengthy: bit bkwd: t.o fnl 4f) 1½.14

**7/4** Magical Queen (IRE), **11/2** Singer on the Roof, **6/1** COMME D'HABITUDE (USA)(op 5/2), Gold Tassel, **8/1** Latest Flame (IRE), **10/1** Olympic Run, **20/1** Ample (IRE), **25/1** On Request (IRE), **33/1** Meritre (IRE), Perfect Set (IRE), **40/1** Honorary Guest, Bright Wales, **66/1** Ors. CSF £16.08, Tote £8.20: £2.50 £1.30 £2.10 (£7.50). Mr Christopher Wright (WHATCOMBE) bred by Amerivest T-Bred Partners 3 in USA. 14 Rn      1m 42.9 (10.4)
SF—37/32/29/27/15/14

---

**3037**      JOHN HYLTON WATTS MEMORIAL H'CAP (0-70) £3566.50 (£994.00: £479.50)
**7f 16y**                                                             3-20 (3-26)

2830 **Spanish Love (37)** *(CGCox)* 6—7-3 ‡⁷DWright (15) (a.p: led over 2f out: rdn out) —1

2823 Chandigarh **(53)** *(RLee)* 4—8-5 ‡⁷PBowe (16) (a.p: led over 3f out tl over 2f out: rallied ins fnl f) ........................................... 1½.2

28304 Kissavos **(50)** *(CCElsey)* 6—8-9 TRogers (11) (hdwy over 3f out: ev ch ins fnl f: nt qckn) ........................................................ 1.3

30026 Zinbaq **(41)** *(CJBenstead)* 6—8-0 TyroneWilliams (6) (hdwy wl over 1f out: rdn & r.o one pce fnl f) ......................................... nk.4

2410 Abso **(66)** *(RHannon)* 4—9-8 ‡³RPerham (13) (hdwy fnl 2f: nt rch ldrs) ...... 3½.5

2750★ Hold Fast (IRE) **(40)** *(HCandy)* 4—7-13 CRutter (9) (a.p: no hdwy fnl 2f) .......... 2.6

2656 A Little Precious **(54)** *(JRBostock)* 6—8-13 TQuinn (2) (nvr nrr) ............. 1½.7

27506 Nawwar **(52)** (Fav) *(CJBenstead)* 8—8-11 RCochrane (17) (hdwy over 1f out: n.d) ......................................................... hd.8

2750 Beatle Song **(64)** *(RJHodges)* 4—9-2⁽¹⁾ ‡⁷TThompson (14) (prom 4f) ........... 3½.9

2684 Mabonne **(51)** (v) *(JLDunlop)* 3—8-5 AMcGlone (4) (hdwy over 3f out: wknd 2f out) ........................................................ 1½.10

2881 Alnasric Pete (USA) **(49)** *(DAWilson)* 6–8–8 JWilliams (2) (s.i.s: a bhd) .......... 3½.**11**
2493⁴ Leigh Crofter **(64)** (bl) *(RJHolder)* 3–8–11 ‡7SDrowne (3) (a bhd) .................. hd.**12**
2750⁵ Courting Newmarket **(45)** *(MrsAKnight)* 4–7–13 ‡5LNewton (10) (led over 3f) 2½.**13**
2953* Coniston Lake (IRE) **(64)** (bl) *(GLewis)* 3–9–4 (6x) BRouse (4) (bhd: swtchd to
race alone far side 3f out: n.d) .................... ½.**14**
2410⁴ Fair Enchantress **(54)** *(JABennett)* 4–8–13 NCarlisle (18) (prom over 3f) ...... nk.**15**
2634 Wessex Milord **(39)** *(JABennett)* 7–7–5⁽⁵⁾ ‡7TWilson (12) (b: a bhd) .................. ½.**16**
2151⁵ Lingdale Lass **(44)** *(MWEckley)* 3–7–12 WCarson (8) (a bhd) ............................ 3.**17**
1032 Treasure Court **(41)** *(PBurgoyne)* 5–7–7⁽⁷⁾ ‡7PMcCabe (1) (a bhd) .................. 4.**18**
LONG HANDICAP: Wessex Milord 6-13, Treasure Court 7-1.

11/2 Nawwar(op 10/1), 7/1 Zinbaq, Hold Fast (IRE), 9/1 A Little Precious, 10/1 Coniston Lake (IRE), Courting Newmarket, Lingdale Lass, 11/1 Kissavos, 12/1 Chandigarh, Abso, 14/1 Leigh Crofter, 16/1 Beatle Song, Alnasric Pete (USA), Mabonne, SPANISH LOVE, 20/1 Fair Enchantress, 50/1 Ors. CSF £195.95, CT £2,033.86. Tote £35.20: £5.30 £4.00 £2.00 £1.90 (£136.00). Orchid Racing & Bloodstock Limited (LYNEHAM) bred by Southcourt Stud. 18 Rn
1m 28.8 (8.3)
SF—34/45/46/36/47/18

**3038** FRANKIE DETTORI TON-UP STKS (3-Y.O.F) £3448.00 (£999.00: £477.00: £216.00)
7f 16y
3-50 (3-51)

**Well Beyond (IRE) (101)** *(BWHills)* 9-3 TQuinn (plld hrd: a.p: led over 1f
out: hrd rdn & edgd rt ins fnl f: all out) ......................................... —**1**
1935⁶ Ships Lantern **(91)** *(CFWall)* 9-0 NCarlisle (5) (led over 5f: hrd rdn whn jinked rt
ins fnl f: r.o) ............................................ ¾.**2**
2795² Ahbab (IRE) **(79)** (v) *(PTWalwyn)* 8-11 WCarson (7) (chsd ldr: ev ch over 1f out:
btn whn nt clr run ins fnl f) ........................... 2.**3**
2846⁶ Juniper Berry (IRE) **(87)** *(PWChapple-Hyam)* 9-0 JWilliams (6) (hld up: wl bhd
over 2f out: gd hdwy fnl f: fin wl) ...................... ½.**4**
2523² Waterfowl Creek (IRE) (Fav) *(GWragg)* 9-0 RCochrane (3) (prom: hrd rdn over
2f out: wknd over 1f out) ............................... 8.**5**
1611 Star Goddess (USA) **(83)** *(MRChannon)* 9-0 BRouse (4) (prom 5f) ............... 7.**6**
2753 Seememore *(RJPrice)* 8-11 CRutter (1) (w'like: a bhd: t.o fnl 2f) ............... 7.**7**

11/10 Waterfowl Creek (IRE)(6/4—7/4), 9/2 Ahbab (IRE), 5/1 Juniper Berry (IRE), 7/1 Ships Lantern(op 4/1), Star Goddess (USA), 8/1 WELL BEYOND (IRE), 50/1 Seememore. CSF £56.83, Tote £12.20: £4.70 £2.80 (£51.20). Mr K. Abdulla (LAMBOURN) bred by Melchester Stud Ltd. in Ireland. 7 Rn
1m 29 (8.5)
SF—59/54/45/46/22/1

**3039** BANK HOLIDAY NURSERY £4110.00 (£1230.00: £590.00: £270.00)
6f 16y
4-25 (4-28)

(Weights raised 12 lb)
2233* Shiro **(78)** (Fav) *(RJRWilliams)* 9-7 RCochrane (5) (lw: hld up: hdwy over 2f
out: led over 1f out: hdd fnl f: rallied to ld cl home) ................... —**1**
795³ Victoria Hall **(60)** *(WGMTurner)* 7-10 ‡7TWilson (6) (led tl over 1f out: r.o wl) ½.**2**
2771³ No Extras (IRE) **(69)** *(JSutcliffe)* 8-12 BRouse (4) (hld up: hdwy over 2f out: led
ins fnl f: hdd nr fin) ..................................... nk.**3**
2841⁶ True Story (IRE) **(72)** *(RHannon)* 8-12 ‡3RPerham (2) (lw: a.p: ev ch over 1f out:
nt qckn fnl f) ............................................. 1½.**4**
2800 War Requiem (IRE) **(66)** *(GBBalding)* 8-9 JWilliams (4) (nvr nrr) ................ 2½.**5**
2842² Knobbleeneeze **(71)** *(MRChannon)* 9-0 WCarson (8) (lw: prom nrr) ............... 1½.**6**
2900 Lowrianna (IRE) **(59)** *(DHaydnJones)* 8-2 TyroneWilliams (3) (lw: prom: nt clr
run 2f out: sn wknd) ..................................... 1.**7**
2883⁵ Le Couteau **(67)** *(DWPArbuthnot)* 8-10 TQuinn (8) (a bhd) ...................... nk.**8**
2781³ Kildee Lad **(63)** *(APJones)* 8-6 CRutter (1) (prom 4f) ............................. 4.**9**

9/4 SHIRO, 9/2 Victoria Hall, 11/2 Knobbleeneeze(op 7/2), 13/2 True Story (IRE)(op 4/1), 8/1 No Extras (IRE)(op 5/1), 11/1 Le Couteau(op 6/1), 14/1 War Requiem (IRE)(op 8/1), Lowrianna (IRE)(op 8/1), 25/1 Kildee Lad. CSF £11.95, CT £60.48. Tote £3.20: £1.50 £1.90 £2.50 (£13.90). Mr Saeed Manana (NEWMARKET) bred by Sheikh Mohammed bin Rashid al Maktoum. 9 Rn
1m 17.2 (8.2)
SF—39/12/27/21/8/7

**3040** SEVERN BRIDGE H'CAP (0-90) £3728.25 (£1116.00: £535.50: £245.25)
1¼m 36y
4-55 (4-56)

2457⁵ **Gueca Solo (78)** *(HRACecil)* 4–10-0 AMcGlone (7) (dwlt: sn rcvrd: 4th st: led 2f
out: jst hld on) .......................................... —**1**
2920⁴ Major Bugler (IRE) **(74)** (Jt-Fav) *(GBBalding)* 3–9-2 JWilliams (4) (hdup: last st:
hdwy 3f out: r.o strly ins fnl f: jst failed) ............. s.h.**2**
2180 Dovale **(68)** *(WJarvis)* 4–9-4 RCochrane (5) (hld up: 5th st: hdwy over 2f out: ev
ch over 1f out: one pce) ................................. 2½.**3**
2594² Constructivist (IRE) **(70)** *(BWHills)* 3–8-12 TQuinn (1) (led 8f: one pce) .......... 1½.**4**

2871 Sir Oliver (IRE) **(63)** *(RJHodges)* 3–7-12 ‡⁷SDrowne (6) (chsd ldr: 2nd st: ev ch
     2f out: sn wknd) ............................................................................. hd.5
2693⁴ Inan (USA) **(71)** (bl) (Jt-Fav) *(JLDunlop)* 3–8-13 WCarson (3) (lw: plld hrd:
     fly-jumped after 2f: 3rd st: rdn & wknd over 2f out: t.o) ...... 25.6
2352 Spanish Grandee (USA) **(76)** *(PWChapple-Hyam)* 4–9-7 ‡⁵LNewton (2) (6th st:
     rdn & lost tch over 2f out) ............................................................ 7.7

**100/30** Major Bugler (IRE), Inan (USA), **9/2** Dovale, **13/2** GUECA SOLO, Constructivist (IRE), **8/1** Sir Oliver
(IRE)(op 16/1), **9/1** Spanish Grandee (USA)(op 6/1). CSF £26.05, Tote £7.30: £4.20 £2.10 (£15.90). Exors of
the late Mr C. A. B. St. George (NEWMARKET) bred by O. and Mrs Fox-Pitt. 7 Rn      2m 18.5 (14.2)
                                                   SF—52/39/36/27/12/–

## 3041
CAERWENT APP'CE H'CAP (0-70) £2532.00 (£702.00: £336.00)
1½m 23y                                        5-25 (5-27)

(Weights raised 4 lb)
2886 **Athar (IRE) (47)** *(RJBaker)* 3–8-4 RWaterfield (5) (4th st: led 3f out: clr 2f out:
     rdn out) ...................................................................................... —1
2896² Al Skeet (USA) **(32)** *(RJPrice)* 6–7-13⁽¹⁾ RossBerry (2) (hdwy on ins & 6th st:
     chsd wnr over 2f out: no imp) ...................................................... 8.2
2739³ Ballymac Girl **(52)** *(CTNash)* 4–9-5 SWynne (10) (hdwy & 4th st: one pce fnl 3f) 4.3
2698³ Gesnera **(37)** *(KWhite)* 4–8-4 TWilson (6) (led 9f: sn wknd) ........................ 2.4
2759⁶ Belafonte **(57)** *(RJHolder)* 5–9-10 SDrowne (4) (prom: 7th st: wknd over 3f out) 2½.5
2834⁵ Lady Westgate **(26)** *(GBBalding)* 8–7-7 IonaWands (3) (hdwy 3f out: nvr trbld
     ldrs) ............................................................................................ 4.6
2784⁵ Affa **(52)** *(TThomsonJones)* 3–8-9 JDSmith (11) (b: 3rd st: wknd 3f out) .......... 1½.7
2944⁎ Shirl **(39)** *(GFHCharles-Jones)* 3–7-10 (7x) PMcCabe (9) (hdwy & 5th st: wknd
     3f out) ........................................................................................ s.h.8
2885⁎ C U Coral **(61)** (Fav) *(MCPipe)* 3–9-4 EHusband (8) (hrd rdn & lost tch over 3f
     out: r.o) ...................................................................................... 8.9
     As Good as Gold **(38)** *(TMJones)* 6–8-5 GayeHarwood (1) (plld hrd: 2nd st.
     wknd over 4f out: t.o) .................................................................. s.h.10
     Out of Stock **(30)** *(RJHodges)* 9–7-11 SMulvey (7) (s.s: a t.o) ...................... dist.11
     LONG HANDICAP: Lady Westgate 7-2.

**11/8** C U Coral(op 2/1), **6/1** Belafonte, **7/1** Shirl, Gesnera, **17/2** Ballymac Girl(12/1—8/1), **12/1** Affa, Al Skeet
(USA)(op 8/1), **20/1** Lady Westgate, **25/1** As Good as Gold, ATHAR (IRE), **33/1** Out of Stock. CSF £263.93, CT
£2,500.61. Tote £30.90: £4.80 £2.40 £3.40 (£136.20). Mr J. W. Buxton (TIVERTON) bred by Shadwell Estate
Company Ltd. in Ireland. 11 Rn      2m 47.6 (16.3)
                                                   SF—23/2/14/–/10/–

T/Plpt: £529.10 (5.45 Tckts).                                                 KH

## 2368—WARWICK (L-H)
### Monday, August 31st [Good]
Going Allowance: 5f: minus 0.20; Rest: minus 0.10 sec per fur (F)      Wind: mod bhd

Stalls: low

## 3042
GAYDON STKS (Mdn 3 & 4-Y.O) £1380.00 (£380.00: £180.00)   **5f**    2-00 (2-03)

     **Honey Seeker** *(TThomsonJones)* 3–8-11 SCauthen (11) (w'like: neat: in tch:
     str run appr fnl f: led post) ............................................................ —1
2718² Belthorn **(48)** *(JJBridger)* 3–8-6 SWhitworth (1) (led: clr over 1f out: rdn fnl f: ct
     post) .......................................................................................... s.h.2
2936 Black Boy (IRE) **(66)** (Fav) *(JAGlover)* 3–8-6 ‡⁵SWilliams (14) (w ldrs: one pce fnl
     2f) .............................................................................................. 2½.3
2941 Casting Shadows **(59)** *(RDickin)* 3–8-6 NHowe (9) (lw: chsd ldrs: no hdwy fnl
     2f) .............................................................................................. 1½.4
     Join the Clan *(MrsNMacauley)* 3–8-6 TSprake (2) (dwlt: nvr nrr) ...................... 1½.5
2821 Barbara's Cutie **(32)** *(MBlanshard)* 4–8-2 ‡⁷CAvery (5) (lw: chsd ldrs 3f) .......... 3½.6
2803 Nellie Dean **(60)** *(JARToller)* 3–8-6 DBiggs (7) (n.d) ...................................... 1½.7
2881 Alto Princess **(37)** *(APJones)* 3–8-1 ‡⁵RPrice (15) (chsd ldrs 3f: sn wknd) ........ s.h.8
2399⁶ Oriental Song **(38)** *(KSBridgwater)* 3–8-6 PD'Arcy (6) (spd over 2f) ................ 2.9
2722³ Nordoora (IRE) *(JLHarris)* 3–8-6 JQuinn (8) (lw: chsd ldr 3f) ........................ 1½.10
2229 Queen Canute (IRE) **(FHLee)** 3–8-6 JFortune (3) (rdn ½-wy: n.d) .................... 11
     Jinsky's Jewel *(RThompson)* 4–8-7 ‡⁷TAshley (12) (swtg: bit bkwd: a bhd) ......... 12
     Sharp Fairy *(ABailey)* 4–8-2 ‡⁷WHollick (4) (wl grwn: s.i.s: a wl bhd) ............ 13
252 Dilkush *(LJHolt)* 3–8-8 ‡³RonHillis (10) (bkwd: a bhd) .................................. 14
2586⁵ The Teflon Don *(RBrotherton)* 3–8-11 GCrealock (13) (lt-f: unf: bit bkwd: in tch tl
     rn wd over 2f out: sn bhd) ............................................................ 15

**100/30** Black Boy (IRE), **9/2** Belthorn(op 5/2), **5/1** HONEY SEEKER(op 10/1), **11/2** Nellie Dean, **9/1** Nordoora (IRE), **10/1** Casting Shadows, **20/1** Queen Canute (IRE), Barbara's Cutie, Sharp Fairy(op 8/1), **50/1** Ors. CSF £24.68, Tote £7.30: £3.00 £1.80 £1.60 (£21.70). Mrs T. Thomson Jones (UPPER LAMBOURN) bred by Mrs D. Whittingham. 15 Rn
        60.2 sec (2.2)
        SF—33/27/17/11/5/–

---

### 3043
BARFORD STKS (Mdn 3-Y.O.F) £1380.00 (£380.00: £180.00)    **1m**    2-30 (2-34)

| | | |
|---|---|---|
| 2780[6] | **Gunner's Daughter** *(HCandy)* 8-11 SCauthen (6) (mde all: rdn 2f out: hld on wl ins fnl f) | —1 |
| 1935[3] | Wiedniu (USA) **(107)** (Fav) *(LordHuntingdon)* 8-11 LPiggott (3) (trckd ldrs gng wl: 3rd st: rdn to chal appr fnl f: fnd nil) | ¾.2 |
| 2862[3] | Euridice (IRE) *(LMCumani)* 8-11 JFortune (10) (bhd: 7th & hdwy st: r.o appr fnl f) | 4.3 |
| 2882[2] | Rockbourne **(53)** *(WGMTurner)* 8-11 TSprake (7) (hdwy & 5th st: one pce appr fnl f) | 3½.4 |
| 2687[5] | Secret Treaty (IRE) *(PWChapple-Hyam)* 8-11 SWhitworth (8) (prom: 2nd st: wknd over 1f out) | hd.5 |
| 2803 | Guiting Girl *(HCandy)* 8-11 NHowe (9) (a.p: rdn 2f out: sn btn) | 3.6 |
| | Worthy Memories *(CFWall)* 8-11 DBiggs (4) (effrt & 6th st: no imp fnl 2f) | 6.7 |
| 2722[5] | Dear Person *(JLHarris)* 8-11 JQuinn (1) (dwlt: a bhd) | 8 |
| 2858 | Wild Poppy *(EAWheeler)* 8-6 ‡5RPrice (5) (chsd wnr over 3f: sn bhd) | 9 |

**1/6** Wiedniu (USA)(op 1/9), **7/1** GUNNER'S DAUGHTER(op 16/1), **11/1** Euridice (IRE)(op 7/1), Secret Treaty (IRE)(op 7/1), **20/1** Rockbourne, **33/1** Guiting Girl, Worthy Memories, Dear Person, **50/1** Wild Poppy. CSF £9.29, Tote £7.60: £2.00 £1.00 £1.90 (£3.00). Mr P. G. Goulandris (WANTAGE) bred by Whitsbury Manor Stud. 9 Rn
        1m 39.4 (2.4)
        SF—49/47/35/24/23/14

---

### 3044
PINLEY NURSERY    £2763.00 (£768.00: £369.00)    **1m**    3-00 (3-04)

| | | |
|---|---|---|
| 2938[2] | **Express Mariecurie (IRE) (71)** *(PWChapple-Hyam)* 7-11[(1)] ‡5RPrice (11) (lw: plld hrd: led after 2f: rdn fnl f: jst hld on) | —1 |
| 2973[6] | Jonsalan **(75)** *(WCarter)* 8-6 JFortune (2) (dwlt: gd hdwy appr fnl f: fin fast) | hd.2 |
| 2696* | Sabo's Express **(69)** *(RHannon)* 8-0 DBiggs (3) (led 2f: 2nd st: ev ch over 1f out: unable qckn) | ¾.3 |
| 2972[5] | Poly Vision (IRE) **(65)** *(MRChannon)* 7-10 JQuinn (5) (bhd: hdwy on ins fnl 2f: nrst fin) | 3.4 |
| 2779 | Costa Verde **(84)** *(KWHogg)* 9-1 JCorrigan (8) (hdwy & 5th st: ev ch 2f out: one pce) | 1.5 |
| 2758 | Festin **(78)** *(JLDunlop)* 8-9[(1)] SCauthen (10) (prom: 3rd & rdn st: wknd over 1f out) | 4.6 |
| 2735 | Laurel Etoile **(62)** *(JBerry)* 7-0 ‡7ADaly (4) (chsd ldrs: 4th st: wknd 2f out) | s.h.7 |
| 2277[5] | Cherubini **(67)** *(JRFanshawe)* 7-5 ‡7Warley (12) (b.hind: nvr nr to chal) | 1.8 |
| 2782[4] | Daring King **(62)** *(DSasse)* 7-0 ‡7MBaird (1) (b: prom tl 7th & wkng st) | nk.9 |
| 2696[2] | Calisar **(68)** *(WGMTurner)* 7-13[(2)] TSprake (9) (6th st: sn wknd) | 5.10 |
| 2037* | Cissbury Ring **(90)** (Fav) *(LadyHerries)* 9-7 LPiggott (7) (lw: a bhd: faltered & p.u ins fnl f) | 0 |

LONG HANDICAP: Laurel Etoile 6-13, Daring King 7-4.

**7/2** Cissbury Ring, **4/1** EXPRESS MARIECURIE (IRE), **5/1** Sabo's Express, **8/1** Festin, **9/1** Costa Verde, Calisar, **10/1** Cherubini, **12/1** Poly Vision (IRE), Jonsalan, **25/1** Daring King, **33/1** Laurel Etoile. CSF £47.08, CT £225.95. Tote £3.80: £1.30 £6.40 £1.80 (£77.30). Express Marie Curie Racing Club (MARLBOROUGH) bred by Swettenham Stud in Ireland. 11 Rn
        1m 41.3 (4.3)
        SF—7/15/7/–/10/–

---

### 3045
ST NICHOLAS (S) H'CAP (0-60) £1898.00 (£528.00: £254.00)
**1¼m 169y**    3-30 (3-32)

| | | |
|---|---|---|
| 2829[3] | **Formal Invitation (IRE) (48)** *(GLewis)* 3-8-5 ‡7BRussell (3) (b: b.nr hind: hdwy 2f out: led ins fnl f: pushed out) | —1 |
| 2946[5] | Molly Splash **(53)** *(CACyzer)* 5-9-12 DBiggs (5) (hdwy over 2f out: r.o wl ins fnl f) | 2.2 |
| 2427 | Salinger **(47)** *(JWHills)* 4-9-6 SCauthen (10) (a.p: led over 3f out tl wknd & hdd ins fnl f) | s.h.3 |
| 2372[4] | Primera Ballerina **(37)** *(JRBosley)* 4-8-10 RStreet (2) (led 1f: rdn 5f out: 5th st: ev ch over 1f out: one pce) | 1½.4 |
| 2944[4] | Breezed Well **(55)** *(CNAllen)* 6-9-7 ‡7GForster (13) (prom: 3rd st: one pce) | 3.5 |
| 2952 | Moving Force **(40)** *(EAWheeler)* 5-8-13 TSprake (1) (lw: kpt on fnl 2f: nt rch ldrs) | s.h.6 |
| 2829[2] | Count Robert (USA) **(49)** *(MissJacquelineSDoyle)* 4-9-8 JQuinn (4) (b.hind: bhd: r.o fnl 3f: nvr rchd ldrs) | 5.7 |

27385 Faustnluce Lady **(46)** (v) *(GAHam)* 3–8-3 ‡7NVarley (9) (nvr nrr) .......... 6.8
2784⁶ Jarras **(42)** (bl) *(CASmith)* 7–8-8 ‡7PTurner (3) (chsd ldrs: 6th st: sn btn) ........ 2½.9
2906 Alicante **(42)** *(FJYardley)* 5–8-8 ‡7JDennis (11) (wl bhd tl effrt 4f out: nvr rchd
    ldrs) ............................................................................................. 2½.10
2829★ Aragon Court **(53)** *(JPearce)* 4–9-7 ‡5RPrice (6) (chsd ldrs: 2nd st: wknd wl over
    1f out) ........................................................................................... 6.11
28136 Errema **(43)** (Fav) *(CTinkler)* 7–9-2 JFortune (14) (chsd ldrs 6f) .............. 3½.12
21356 Trendy Auctioneer (IRE) **(37)** (bl) *(MCPipe)* 4–8-10 LPiggott (15) (lw: prom: led
    4f out: sn hdd: 4th & wkng st) ..................................................... hd.13
    Stapleford Lady **(42)** *(RJManning)* 4–9-1 NHowe (17) (chsd ldrs: rdn 4f out: no
    imp) ............................................................................................. hd.14
2775 Charly Pharly (FR) **(42)** (bl) *(FHLee)* 5–9-1 RLappin (16) (bit bkwd: led aft 1f to
    4f out: sn wknd) ........................................................................... s.h.15
2699 Loudest Whisper **(49)** *(KSBridgwater)* 4–9-3 ‡5SWilliams (7) (b: prom 6f) ...... nk.16
    Mrs Claypool **(42)** *(MAJarvis)* 4–9-1 GCrealock (19) (bkwd: a bhd) ............ nk.17
1184 Noushy **(35)** *(KSBridgwater)* 4–8-1 ‡7DMcCabe (18) (t.o) ..................... 20.18
2937 Bijou Princess **(35)** (bl) *(ABailey)* 4–8-1 ‡7WHollick (20) (t.o fnl 4f) ......... s.h.19
2805 Haverton **(35)** (v) *(TCasey)* 5–8-8 JHBrown (12) (bit bkwd: a bhd: t.o) .......... ¾.20

7/2 Errema, **6/1** Charly Pharly (FR), **8/1** Aragon Court(op 5/1), Molly Splash, **9/1** Trendy Auctioneer (IRE), **10/1**
Breezed Well(op 8/1), **12/1** FORMAL INVITATION (IRE), Salinger, Count Robert (USA), **16/1** Loudest Whisper,
Moving Force, Jarras, **20/1** Mrs Claypool, Stapleford Lady, Alicante, **25/1** Faustnluce Lady, **33/1** Ors. CSF
£110.78, CT £1,111.46. Tote £19.80: £3.90 £1.60 £3.70 £4.90 (£61.60). Mrs N. Lewis (EPSOM) bred by
Patrick Eddery Ltd in Ireland. 20 Rn; Bt in 5,400 gns
                                                                            2m 20.6 (7.1)
                                                                            SF—9/26/19/6/11/2

## 3046
WARWICK CESAREWITCH H'CAP (0-80) £4050.00 (£1215.00: £585.00: £270.00)
2m 20y                                                               4-00 (4-03)

2834² **Arctic Splendour (USA) (56)** *(PWChapple-Hyam)* 3 7 9 JQuinn (14) (lw: rdn
    5f out: hdwy & 5th st: led wl over 1f out: sn clr) ................................. —1
27594 Green Lane (USA) **(68)** *(IABalding)* 4–8-13 ‡7FArrowsmith (4) (hdwy 7f out: 3rd
    st: led 2f out: sn hdd & nt qckn) ..................................................... 3.2
2677⁴ Prince Mercury **(68)** *(JLDunlop)* 3–8-6 LPiggott (12) (a.p: 4th st: ev ch over 1f
    out: r.o) ........................................................................................ ¾.3
2793³ Puritan (CAN) **(76)** (Fav) *(GHarwood)* 3–9-0 SCauthen (1) (chsd ldr: led 9f out
    to 2f out: kpt on same pce) ........................................................... nk.4
2664³ Smilingatstrangers **(50)** (v) *(MrsBarbaraWaring)* 4–8-2 NHowe (8) (hdwy 6f
    out: 2nd st: ev ch 2f out: r.o ins fnl f) ............................................... s.h.5
28276 Arfey (IRE) **(64)** *(TThomsonJones)* 3–8-2 TSprake (2) (b: chsd ldrs: 6th st: btn
    whn n.m.r over 1f out) .................................................................. 6.6
2687⁶ High Finance **(53)** *(RJWeaver)* 7–7-12(12) ‡7GForster (10) (s.s: effrt & mod 7th
    st: no imp) ................................................................................... 3½.7
2921² Intricacy **(60)** *(CCElsey)* 4–8-12 JFortune (3) (b.off hind: chsd ldrs tl 8th & btn
    st) .............................................................................................. 1½.8
2715★ Chucklestone **(72)** *(JSKing)* 9–9-10 DBiggs (13) (led 7f: rdn & wknd 5f out) .. 8.9
27376 Premier Princess **(51)** *(GAHam)* 6–7-12(10) ‡5RPrice (5) (prom tl rdn & wknd 5f
    out) ............................................................................................ 4.10
    Gaelgoir **(50)** *(CFCJackson)* 8–7-9(5) ‡7CAvery (9) (a bhd) ..................... 1½.11
2111⁴ Media Star **(42)** *(TKersey)* 7–7-8(1) RStreet (6) (b: in tch 10f) ............... s.h.12
    Siesta Key **(76)** *(TKersey)* 7–9-7 ‡7MHarris (7) (b: a bhd: t.o fr ½-wy: fin lame) ... 13
    LONG HANDICAP: High Finance 7-1, Media Star 6-5.

**15/8** Puritan (CAN)(3/1—7/4), **9/2** ARCTIC SPLENDOUR (USA), **8/1** Prince Mercury, Chucklestone,
Smilingatstrangers, **9/1** Green Lane (USA), **11/1** Intricacy, **12/1** Premier Princess(op 8/1), Arfey (IRE)(op 8/1),
**50/1** Ors. CSF £43.45, CT £291.12. Tote £5.10: £2.00 £2.90 £2.30 (£37.20). Mr R. E. Sangster
(MARLBOROUGH) bred by Swettenham Stud in USA. 13 Rn
                                                                            3m 3.4 (7.6)

## 3047
HARBURY GRADUATION STKS (2-Y.O) £3052.00 (£847.00: £406.00)    5f 4-30 (4-35)

2794² **Hamsah (IRE) (94)** (Jt-Fav) *(DRCElsworth)* 8–13 SCauthen (1) (a.p: led ins fnl
    f: rdn out) .................................................................................... —1
2939² Fyfield Flyer (IRE) **(90)** *(PWChapple-Hyam)* 9-4 LPiggott (12) (lw: neat: str:
    chsd ldrs: r.o fnl f) ........................................................................ 1½.2
23716 Laurel Delight **(65)** *(JBerry)* 8–13 JFortune (3) (led over 4f: one pce) .......... ¾.3
859² Peperonata (IRE) **(81)** (Jt-Fav) *(BWHills)* 8–13 DBiggs (11) (bit bkwd: w ldr: ev
    ch 1f out: sn btn) .......................................................................... ½.4
2912 Persian Revival (FR) **(85)** *(BAMcMahon)* 8–13 ‡5SWilliams (8) (chsd ldrs: no imp
    appr fnl f) .................................................................................... 3.5
    Sandswift *(RFJohnsonHoughton)* 8–6 TSprake (4) (leggy: r.o fnl 2f: nvr able to
    chal) ........................................................................................... 1½.6
2781 Hershebar *(SRBowring)* 8–11 JQuinn (10) (chsd ldrs 3f) ........................... 5.7

2884⁶ Coopers Delight *(GLewis)* 8-11 NHowe (2) (sn rdn & outpcd) ........................ 1½.8
2405 Inonder *(MDIUsher)* 8-1 ‡⁵RPrice (7) (nvr nr to chal) .................................. hd.9
1913 Rusty Raja *(RHannon)* 8-4 ‡⁷DO'Neill (9) (outpcd) ................................ 3½.10
     Ilmenite *(MAJarvis)* 8-6 GCrealock (6) (neat: bit bkwd: sn t.o) .............. 15.11
     Young Geninsky *(RJWeaver)* 7-13 GReaver (5) (w'like: scope: bkwd: s.s: a t.o) . 12

**9/4** Peperonata (IRE)(7/2—7/4), HAMSAH (IRE)(5/4—5/2), **3/1** Fyfield Flyer (IRE), **8/1** Laurel Delight(op 14/1), **10/1** Persian Revival (FR), **25/1** Ilmenite, **40/1** Coopers Delight, **50/1** Sandswift, Rusty Raja, **66/1** Ors. CSF £9.22, Tote £3.30: £1.60 £1.60 £1.60 (£2.90). Sheikh Ahmed Al Maktoum (WHITSBURY) bred by Sheikh Ahmed bin Rashid al Maktoum in Ireland. 12 Rn
         59.4 sec (1.4)
         SF—51/50/42/40/28/15

---

**3048**      RUGBY H'CAP (3-Y.O) (0-70) £2931.00 (£816.00: £393.00)    **7f**      5-00 (5-07)
                           (Weights raised 4 lb)

2881² **Jolto (43)** *(KOCunningham-Brown)* 7-6 ‡⁷NVarley (4) (a.p: led ent st: pushed
     out) ............................................................................... —1
2694² Ace Girl **(51)** *(SRBowring)* 8-7 JQuinn (17) (prom: 3rd st: chsd wnr fnl 2f: no imp
     fnl f) ............................................................................... ½.2
2941 Military Expert **(56)** *(CaptJWilson)* 8-5 ‡⁷JMarshall (11) (led 2f: 5th st: r.o same
     pce fnl 2f) ......................................................................... 3.3
2882 Great Hall **(46)** (bl) *(PDCundell)* 8-2 GCrealock (15) (gd hdwy wl over 1f out:
     nrst fin) ........................................................................... 1.4
2942⁵ Kalar **(48)** *(DWChapman)* 7-11 ‡⁷MBaird (12) (led after 2f tl hdd & 2nd st: one
     pce) ............................................................................... 4.5
2361³ Honey Heather (IRE) **(57)** *(CFWall)* 8-13 DBiggs (8) (b.off fore: in tch: r.o fnl f) hd.6
2803⁵ Shakreen (USA) **(65)** *(MrsLPiggott)* 9-7 LPiggott (13) (lw: in tch: no hdwy fnl 2f) s.h.7
2830 Kentucky Starlet (USA) **(57)** (bl) *(RHannon)* 8-6 ‡⁷AWhelan (12) (r.o fnl 2f: nrst
     fin) ............................................................................... s.h.8
2881⁶ Batchworth Bound **(49)** *(EAWheeler)* 8-0 ‡⁵RPrice (1) (rdn & hdwy fnl 2f: nvr
     able to chal) ...................................................................... ½.9
2593⁴ Bold Steve **(59)** *(LMCumani)* 9-1 JFortune (19) (n.d) ............................ nk.10
2882 Ceatharlach **(46)** *(RJHolder)* 7-9⁽²⁾ ‡⁷JDennis (6) (chsd ldrs: 6th st: sn btn) ... nk.11
2871⁴ Edgeaway **(63)** (v) **(Fav)** *(JWHills)* 9-5 SCauthen (10) (bhd: rdn over 2f out: no
     imp) .............................................................................. ¾.12
2830⁶ Red Jack (IRE) **(50)** *(JAkehurst)* 7-13 ‡⁷LCarter (2) (n.d) .................... nk.13
2290 Kipini **(49)** *(WJMusson)* 8-5 JHBrown (3) (chsd ldrs: 8th st: wknd over 1f out) s.h.14
2429 Ming Blue **(56)** *(PJMakin)* 8-12 TSprake (14) (bit bkwd: n.d) ................ 1½.15
1905 Bold Setko (IRE) **(59)** *(JMPEustace)* 8-12 ‡³RonHillis (9) (a bhd) ............ 1½.16
2803 Our Emma **(50)** *(MrsBarbaraWaring)* 8-6 NHowe (5) (hdwy & 4th st: rdn & wknd
     2f out) ............................................................................ 1½.17
2077 Sharp Dance **(47)** *(BSmart)* 8-3 RStreet (16) (lw: rdn over 2f out: a bhd) ........ nk.18
2816 High Principles **(61)** *(JBerry)* 8-12 ‡⁵SWilliams (18) (bhd fnl 3f) .............. 4.19
1246⁶ Buddy (IRE) **(54)** (v) *(MBell)* 8-3 ‡⁷PTurner (20) (bit bkwd: 7th st: wknd qckly) . 8.20

**5/1** Edgeaway, **13/2** JOLTO, **7/1** Bold Steve, **10/1** Ace Girl, Shakreen (USA), Honey Heather (IRE), **12/1** Red Jack (IRE), High Principles, **14/1** Ming Blue, **16/1** Kentucky Starlet (USA), Batchworth Bound, Bold Setko (IRE), Buddy (IRE), Kipini, **20/1** Military Expert, **25/1** Kalar, Sharp Dance, Great Hall, **33/1** Ors. CSF £73.01, CT £1,177.19. Tote £6.90: £2.10 £2.20 £9.80 £11.70 (£40.30). Mrs G. M. Gooderham (STOCKBRIDGE) bred by Mrs G. Gooderham. 20 Rn
         1m 28.1 (3.9)
         SF—9/22/11/5/–/–

T/Plpt: £59.10 (37.55 Tckts).                                          Dk

---

2629—**WOLVERHAMPTON (L-H)**

**Monday, August 31st [Good]**

Going Allowance: 5f-7f: 0.05 sec; Rest 0.20 sec per fur (G)      Wind: mod half bhd

Stalls: high

**3049**      MEREVALE NURSERY     £1744.00 (£484.00: £232.00)    **5f**      2-10 (2-12)

2046⁴ **Magic Orb (64)** *(JLSpearing)* 7-4⁽⁴⁾ ‡⁷CHawksley (2) (chsd ldrs: qcknd to ld ins
     fnl f: r.o) ......................................................................... —1
2636⁴ Hills Raceaid (IRE) **(69)** (bl) *(JBerry)* 7-9⁽³⁾ ‡⁷PRoberts (4) (lw: a w ldrs: ev ch ins
     fnl f: unable qckn) ................................................................ 1½.2
2773* Hello Hobson's (IRE) **(60)** **(Fav)** *(JAkehurst)* 7-7 NAdams (9) (lw: led tl hdd & no
     ex ins fnl f) ....................................................................... 1½.3
2591* Nikki Noo Noo **(63)** *(CJHill)* 7-7⁽³⁾ ‡³FNorton (6) (hdwy appr fnl f: kpt on ins fnl f:
     nvr nrr) ............................................................................ 2.4
2824³ My Bonus **(88)** *(DJSCosgrove)* 9-0 ‡⁷GForster (1) (b.hind: chsd ldrs over 3f) ... hd.5

2826 Imafifer (IRE) **(60)** (bl) *(WRMuir)* 7-0 ‡⁷KimMcDonnell (8) (lw: spd 3f) ................ 1.6
2745★ Heathyards Gem **(66)** *(RHollinshead)* 7-6 ‡⁷AGarth (3) (nvr nr to chal) ................ 3.7
2824 Wealthywoo **(60)** *(JSMoore)* 7-7 DaleGibson (7) (hmpd s: a bhd & outpcd) ..... 3.8
2863 Convenient Moment **(67)** (bl) *(JBerry)* 8-0 GCarter (5) (lw: sn pushed along: a
outpcd) ........................................................................................ 2¹/₂.9
LONG HANDICAP: Magic Orb 7-0, Nikki Noo Noo 7-2, Imafifer (IRE) 7-2, Wealthywoo 7-0.

**11/10** Hello Hobson's (IRE), **5/1** Nikki Noo Noo, Heathyards Gem(4/1—6/1), **7/1** My Bonus, Convenient Moment(op 4/1), **16/1** Hills Raceaid (IRE)(op 10/1), **25/1** Wealthywoo, MAGIC ORB, **33/1** Imafifer (IRE). CSF £308.65, CT £742.87. Tote £35.10: £6.40 £4.30 £1.50 (£185.60). Mr M. Olden (ALCESTER) bred by Glazeley Stud. 9 Rn
60.5 sec (3.2)
SF—17/16/8/–/20/–

## 3050 SPINNEY (S) NURSERY £1884.00 (£524.00: £252.00) **7f** 2-40 (2-45)

2782² **Allegrissima (68)** *(JBerry)* 9-7 GCarter (9) (b.hind: mde all: hrd rdn fnl f: jst hld
on) ........................................................................................ —1
2938 Doc Spot **(57)** *(CaptJWilson)* 8-3 ‡⁷AGarth (7) (lw: chsd ldrs: 5th st: rdn 2f out:
str chal fnl f: jst failed) .......................................................... s.h.2
2782 Alice Bay **(49)** *(DHaydnJones)* 8-1 †⁵NGwilliams (8) (chsd ldrs: 6th st: styd on
fnl 2f: nvr able to chal) ............................................................ 3.3
2916⁵ Baileys Colours **(49)** *(BJMcMath)* 8-2 EJohnson (14) (chsd wnr: 2nd st: rdn
over 1f out: one pce) ............................................................... 3.4
2058 Bohemian Queen **(50)** *(JLSpearing)* 8-3 GHind (12) (hdwy over 2f out: r.o ins
fnl f: nvr nrr) ......................................................................... 2¹/₂.5
2675 Mad Mytton **(64)** *(ABailey)* 8-10 ‡⁷SSanders (5) (hld up: hdwy 3f out: rdn appr fnl
f: one pce) ............................................................................. hd.6
2883⁴ Workingforpeanuts (IRE) **(56)** *(CASmith)* 8-9 MWigham (6) (bhd: carried wd 3f
out: nt rcvr) ........................................................................... 2.7
2284 Midarida (IRE) **(46)** *(BRouseyJ)* 7-0 ‡⁷OllawIoloy (2) (a bhd) .................... nk.8
2916² By Rubies **(Fav)** *(BWHills)* 8-10 DaleGibson (13) (a bhd) ......................... nk.9
2802 Swiftlet (IRE) **(54)** *(DJSCosgrove)* 8-7 AShoults (11) (lw: a bhd) .............. 2.10
2681⁶ Floodlight (IRE) **(50)** *(RJHolder)* 8-3 NAdams (2) (prom: 4th st: rdn over 2f out:
sn btn) ................................................................................. 2.11
2696 Duchess Dianne (IRE) **(49)** *(RJHolder)* 7-13 ‡⁹FNorton (10) (a in rr) ............ ¹/₂.12
2910 De Chine **(47)** *(JSMoore)* 7-7 ‡⁷KimMcDonnell (1) (prom: 3rd st: wknd 2f out) . 1.13
2688 Palacegate Sunset **(49)** *(JBerry)* 7-9⁽²⁾ ‡⁷PRoberts (4) (sddle slipped after 2f:
almost uns rdr over 3f out: sn bhd: t.o) ...................................... 15.14

**3/1** By Rubies, **5/1** Workingforpeanuts (IRE), **6/1** Baileys Colours, **8/1** ALLEGRISSIMA(op 5/1), **9/1** Palacegate Sunset, **10/1** Floodlight (IRE), Mad Mytton, **11/1** Duchess Dianne (IRE), **12/1** Midarida (IRE)(op 8/1), **16/1** Doc Spot, De Chine, **20/1** Ors. CSF £127.85, CT £2,258.74. Tote £8.00: £2.70 £3.20 £6.00 (£67.60). Mr P. E. T. Chandler (COCKERHAM) bred by G. C. Hughes. 14 Rn; Bt in 3,400 gns
1m 29.3 (5)
SF—37/18/3/–/–/–

## 3051 E.B.F. ASTON STKS (Mdn 2-Y-O) £2197.50 (£610.00: £292.50) **5f** 3-15 (3-18)

2405² **Abbey's Gal (79)** **(Fav)** *(IABalding)* 8-9 AClark (6) (lw: hdwy appr fnl f: shkn up
to ld wl ins fnl f) ...................................................................... —1
1915⁶ Newbury Coat *(MMcCormack)* 9-0 AShoults (4) (a.p: led over 1f out: hrd rdn &
ct wl ins fnl f) ......................................................................... 1.2
2932 Tallino *(CCElsey)* 8-9 DaleGibson (10) (bit bkwd: hdwy over 1f out: fin wl) ..... 1.3
2171 Kimbolton Korker *(AAScott)* 8-9 GHind (1) (chsd ldrs: kpt on u.p ins fnl f) ......... 1.4
2897³ Magic Pearl **(70)** *(EJAlston)* 8-9 NAdams (11) (led over 3f: wknd ins fnl f) ....... 3.5
986 Melodys Daughter *(RFJohnsonHoughton)* 8-6 ‡³FNorton (2) (prom: rdn ¹/₂-wy:
wknd over 1f out) .................................................................. 1¹/₂.6
Disco Boy *(BAMcMahon)* 8-7 ‡⁷SSanders (7) (w'like: bkwd: nvr trbld ldrs) ....... 2.7
1526 Shotley Again *(NBycroft)* 9-0 MWigham (5) (bhd fnl 2f) ............................... 2¹/₂.8
1902 Altruistic (IRE) *(CFWall)* 8-9 NDay (2) (dwlt: a bhd) ................................... hd.9
1506⁵ Bergliot **(67)** *(JBerry)* 8-9 GCarter (9) (bit bkwd: spd 3f: sn rdn & wknd) ......... 3.10
2818 Super Scenario *(EJAlston)* 8-7 ‡⁷CHawksley (3) (outpcd: t.o) ...................... 12.11

**4/7** ABBEY'S GAL, **11/2** Magic Pearl, **11/1** Bergliot, **12/1** Tallino, Kimbolton Korker, **14/1** Melodys Daughter, **33/1** Altruistic (IRE), Newbury Coat, **50/1** Disco Boy, **100/1** Ors. CSF £20.36, Tote £1.60: £1.10 £5.50 £2.90 (£20.00). Mr Jerrard Williamson (KINGSCLERE) bred by Summertree Stud. 11 Rn
60.8 sec (3.5)
SF—30/31/22/18/6/–

## 3052 COPSE H'CAP (0-70) £2052.00 (£572.00: £276.00) **1m 200y** 3-45 (3-52)

2708² **Rival Bid (USA) (63)** **(Fav)** *(MAJarvis)* 4-9-10 NDay (6) (chsd ldrs: led 2f out:
hld on gamely) ...................................................................... —1
1971⁵ Forelino (USA) **(58)** *(JLDunlop)* 3-8-12 NAdams (12) (hdwy 3f out: ev ch ins fnl
f: unable qckn nr fin) ............................................................. 1.2

2896⁵ Sanawi **(50)** *(PDEvans)* 5-8-11　MWigham (7) (hld up: hdwy 2f out: fin wl) ......... 2.3
2880⁴ Reklaw **(41)** (bl) *(MDHammond)* 5-7-9⁽⁹⁾ ‡7JTate (17) (hdwy to ld over 2f out: sn hdd: rdn & wknd fnl f) .......... 2.4
2602 Cornhill Melody **(41)** *(JLSpearing)* 4-7-9⁽⁹⁾ ‡7PRoberts (23) (hdwy over 2f out: styd on wl ins fnl f) .......... ¾.5
2881 Miss Magenta (IRE) **(36)** *(RThompson)* 4-7-4⁽⁴⁾ ‡7CHawksley (2) (hdwy over 2f out: nvr nrr) .......... 2.6
2952² Seaside Minstrel **(50)** *(CJHill)* 4-8-8 ‡3FNorton (24) (sme hdwy appr fnl f: nvr nrr) .......... s.h.7
2946 Thundering **(32)** *(AWJones)* 7-7-0 ‡7KimMcDonnell (15) (hdwy 2f out: nt rch ldrs) .......... nk.8
2885⁴ Capital Bond (IRE) **(45)** *(RJHolder)* 4-8-6 ADicks (13) (nvr trbld ldrs) .......... 1½.9
1008³ Phil-Blake **(47)** *(SMellor)* 5-8-1⁽⁶⁾ ‡7CMunday (16) (bkwd: prom: led over 3f out tl over 2f out: grad wknd) .......... s.h.10
2656⁶ Cee-Jay-Ay **(57)** *(JBerry)* 5-9-4　GCarter (4) (chsd ldrs over 6f) .......... 1½.11
2935³ Irish Groom **(40)** (bl) *(JPSmith)* 5-7-8 ‡7AGarth (18) (in tch: rdn over 2f out: sn wknd) .......... ½.12
2742⁶ Katy's Lad **(67)** *(BAMcMahon)* 5-9-7 ‡7SSanders (8) (led 5f out tl over 3f out: rdn & wknd) .......... 1½.13
2896 Tina Meena Lisa **(45)** *(EHOwenjun)* 3-7-6⁽⁶⁾ ‡7JBramhill (10) (chsd ldrs 6f) .......... ¾.14
2885 Woodside Heath **(46)** *(JSMoore)* 5-8-7 ADicks (9) (b: n.d) .......... 6.15
1188 Clean Singer **(46)** *(NBycroft)* 3-7-7⁽⁷⁾ ‡7MHumphries (20) (lw: n.d) .......... 3.16
2531 Malcesine (IRE) **(47)** *(CaptJWilson)* 3-8-1　EJohnson (3) (led 4f: sn rdn & wknd) .......... 6.17
2814 Little Rousillon **(60)** (bl) *(ACStewart)* 4-9-7 AClark (19) (n.d) .......... nk.18
2785 Have a Nightcap **(49)** *(JLHarris)* 3-7-10⁽⁴⁾ ‡7DCarson (14) (prom 6f: sn lost tch) 2.19
2807³ Countercheck (IRE) **(54)** *(CFWall)* 3-8-8　GHind (5) (prom over 5f: sn wknd: to) 10.20
LONG HANDICAP: Reklaw 7-2, Cornhill Melody 7-2, Miss Magenta (IRE) 7-6, Tina Meena Lisa 7-3, Clean Singer 7-6.

*2698 Majestic Melody (33/1) Withdrawn (ref to ent stalls) : not under orders*

**5/1** RIVAL BID (USA), **3/1** Sanawi, **7/1** Seaside Minstrel, **9/1** Katy's Lad, Sanawi, **11/1** Forelino (USA), **12/1** Cee-Jay-Ay, **14/1** Countercheck (IRE), **16/1** Capital Bond (IRE), Reklaw, **20/1** Phil-Blake, Thundering, **25/1** Miss Magenta (IRE), Tina Meena Lisa, **33/1** Malcesine (IRE), Have a Nightcap, **40/1** Cornhill Melody, **66/1** Ors. CSF £58.12, CF £505.05. Tote £7.50: £2.20 £3.70 £3.50 £5.10 (£43.90). Mr David Altham (NEWMARKET) bred by Marvin L. Warner Jnr. in USA. 20 Rn
　　　　　　　　　　　　　　　　　　　　　　　　1m 54.8 (6.3)
　　　　　　　　　　　　　　　　　　　　　SF−43/28/21/−/−/−

---

**3053**　COPPICE STKS (Mdn 3 & 4-Y.O) £1660.00 (£460.00: £220.00)
　　　　**2m 201y**　　　　　　　　　　　　　　　4-20 (4-23)

1026⁵ Two and Sixpence (USA) *(BWHills)* 3-8-2　DaleGibson (2) (chsd ldrs: led appr fnl f: styd on strly) —1
2801² Shesadelight (bl) **(Fav)** *(JLDunlop)* 3-8-2　GCarter (9) (lw: hld up: hdwy to ld 4f out: rdn & hdd appr fnl f: kpt on u.p) 4.2
2867² Bayadere (USA) **(56)** (v) *(MRStoute)* 3-8-2　PD'Arcy (4) (chsd ldr tl led 8f out: hdd 4f out: kpt on u.p) 1.3
2940⁵ Juris Prudence (IRE) **(43)** *(BAMcMahon)* 4-8-9 ‡7SSanders (6) (chsd ldrs: hrd rdn over 3f out: kpt on one pce) 2½.4
288 Peatswood *(MRChannon)* 4-9-7　GHind (10) (bit bkwd: wl bhd tl styd on fnl 3f: nvr nrr) 3.5
Miss Marigold *(RJHodges)* 3-8-4⁽²⁾ ADicks (3) (w'like: snppy: bkwd: a bhd) 7.6
2691⁴ Landed Gentry (USA) **(68)** *(PWChapple-Hyam)* 3-8-2　AClark (5) (led 9f: prom tl wknd over 3f out: t.o) 12.7
2635⁵ Adelina Patti *(ACStewart)* 3-7-13 ‡3FNorton (7) (a bhd: t.o) 25.8
2566 Aislabie Airborne **(30)** (bl) *(MrsNMacauley)* 3-8-7　NAdams (1) (lw: lost tch 4f out: t.o) 12.9
The Gorrock *(AJChamberlain)* 3-8-7　AShoults (8) (b: bkwd: a bhd: to fr ½-wy) dist.10

**Evens** Shesadelight(op 7/4), **11/2** Bayadere (USA), **6/1** Landed Gentry (USA)(op 4/1), **7/1** TWO AND SIXPENCE (USA)(8/1−14/1), **17/2** Adelina Patti, **20/1** Peatswood, **33/1** Juris Prudence (IRE), **66/1** Ors. CSF £13.45, Tote £10.90: £2.50 £1.30 £1.40 (£9.30). Mr D. J. Deer (LAMBOURN) bred by John C. & Mrs Mabee in USA. 10 Rn
　　　　　　　　　　　　　　　　　　　　　　　　3m 49.9 (13.2)

---

**3054**　STEWARDS H'CAP (0-70) £1996.00 (£556.00: £268.00)　1½m 70y　4-50 (4-52)
　　　　　　　　　　(Weights raised 11 lb)

2868★ Shadow Bird **(54)** **(Fav)** *(GAPritchard-Gordon)* 5-9-9　NDay (4) (hdwy ½-wy: 5th st: led 2f out: rdn out) —1
2370⁴ Speedo Movement **(55)** *(BAMcMahon)* 3-8-7 ‡7SSanders (6) (hdwy 3f out: jnd wnr ent fnl f: rdn & no ex nr fin) nk.2
2775⁴ Mac Rambler **(28)** *(NBycroft)* 5-7-11　DaleGibson (14) (hdwy over 3f out: styd on appr fnl: nvr nrr) 3½.3

2874³ Tiger Shoot **(49)** *(DJSCosgrove)* 5–9-4 GCarter (3) (lw: hld up: hdwy over 4f out: nt rch ldrs) ........................................................ 5.4
*2784*² Pims Classic **(50)** *(JLHarris)* 4–8-12 ‡⁷AGarth (10) (chsd ldrs: 6th st: one pce fnl 2f) ............................................................. 6.5
2860 Horizon (IRE) **(45)** (bl) *(TThomsonJones)* 4–9-0 NAdams (1) (led to 2f out: sn rdn & wknd) ........................................... nk.6
2868³ Lady Dundee (USA) **(65)** *(MrsJCecil)* 3–9-7 ‡³FNorton (15) (lw: chsd ldr: 2nd st: rdn & wknd over 2f out) ................................. 7.7
2937 Wednesdays Auction (IRE) **(49)** *(BHanbury)* 4–9-4 MWigham (16) (mid div: effrt 3f out: no imp) ........................................ 2.8
2605 Nipotina **(34)** *(RHollinshead)* 6–7-10⁽³⁾ ‡⁷DCarson (9) (s.s: a in rr) .................... nk.9
2867 Mahairy (USA) **(65)** (bl) *(AAScott)* 3–9-10 GHind (7) (prom: 3rd st: wknd over 3f out: t.o) .......................................................... 7.10
Ternimus (USA) **(50)** *(BPreece)* 5–8-12 ‡⁷MHumphries (12) (bkwd: a bhd: t.o) . 2.11
Tulfarris **(37)** *(MDHammond)* 5–7-13 ‡⁷JTate (5) (bkwd: a bhd: t.o) .............. 3¹/₂.12
2927 Briery Fille **(36)** *(BJMcMath)* 7–8-5 EJohnson (11) (a bhd: t.o) ................. 10.13
2566 Gallant Jack (IRE) **(50)** *(DHaydnJones)* 3–8-9 AClark (2) (chsd ldrs 8f: t.o) ... 1¹/₂.14
2305⁶ Casilla **(24)** *(HCandy)* 4–7-0 ‡⁷AntoinetteArmes (13) (prom: 4th st: wknd over 3f out: t.o) .......................................................... 5.15
LONG HANDICAP: Casilla 7-4.

**11/4** SHADOW BIRD, **7/2** Lady Dundee, **10/1** Speedo Movement, Pims Classic, **11/1** Mac Rambler, **12/1** Nipotina, **14/1** Mahairy (USA), Wednesdays Auction (IRE), **16/1** Horizon (IRE), **20/1** Gallant Jack (IRE), Casilla, **25/1** Tulfarris, Ternimus (USA), **50/1** Briery Fille. CSF £33.27, CT £267.78. Tote £4.00: £2.60 £4.30 £2.30 (£71.70). Mr A. G. Don (NEWMARKET) bred by Whitsbury Manor Stud. 15 Rn     2m 44.7 (13)
T/Plpt: £92.90 (19.7 Tckts).                                                                IM

---

2473—**EPSOM (L-H)**

**Monday, August 31st [Good to soft]**

Going Allowance: St: 0.40 sec (Y); Rnd: 0.30 sec per fur (G)                Wind: almost nil

Stalls: high

**3055**        LADAS STKS (Mdn 2-Y.O) £2700.00 (£750.00: £360.00)      **6f**        2-05 (2-08)

2124³ **Iron Merchant (IRE) (96)** *(RAkehurst)* 9-0 MRoberts (3) (lw: mde all: drvn out)    —1
2557² Blue Tess (IRE) **(Fav)** *(MMoubarak)* 8-9 DHolland (5) (3rd st: swtchd rt over 1f out: r.o wl ins fnl f) .......................................... nk.2
2544⁴ Gone Prospecting (USA) **(81)** *(RHannon)* 9-0 JLloyd (2) (2nd st: hrd rdn over 1f out: unable qckn) ............................................. 4.3
1902⁴ Soldiers Bay **(82)** *(LordHuntingdon)* 9-0 AMunro (10) (lw: 6th st: one pce fnl 3f) 3.4
Bajka *(WJarvis)* 8-6 ‡³EmmaO'Gorman (6) (scope: bkwd: 5th st: one pce fnl 3f) 4.5
2713² Pontevecchio Moda *(DRCEisworth)* 8-10⁽⁸⁾ ‡⁷JHunter (4) (nvr nr to chal) ......... s.h.6
2832 Persian Gusher (IRE) *(SDow)* 8-7 ‡⁷AMartinez (9) (a mid div) ...................... 2¹/₂.7
1867⁶ Dragonmist (IRE) *(GLewis)* 8-9 WHood (1) (nvr nrr) ................................. 2.8
2826 Aragrove *(LJHolt)* 9-0 JReid (11) (lw: a mid div) ................................. ³/₄.9
2700 See Us There (IRE) *(JBerry)* 9-0 GayKelleway (8) (4th st: wknd over 2f out) ..... 3.10
1202 Wickins *(GLewis)* 8-9 ‡⁵ATucker (7) (a bhd) ..................................... 2.11
2124⁵ Delay No More *(PMitchell)* 8-11 ‡³SO'Gorman (12) (swtg: bhd fnl 3f) ............. 4.12
423 Arogant Fool *(DAWilson)* 8-9 ‡⁵NKennedy (13) (b.nr fore: a bhd) ................. 4.13

**7/4** Blue Tess (IRE), **5/2** IRON MERCHANT (IRE), **15/2** Soldiers Bay(op 5/1), **8/1** Gone Prospecting (USA), Pontevecchio Moda(op 5/1), **14/1** Aragrove, **20/1** See Us There (IRE), Bajka, **25/1** Delay No More, Dragonmist (IRE), **50/1** Ors. CSF £7.49, Tote £2.80: £1.40 £1.20 £2.00 (£2.90). C. F. Sparrowhawk Ltd (EPSOM) bred by Martyn J. McEnery in Ireland. 13 Rn     1m 12.64 (4.64)
SF—43/37/26/14/–/–

**3056**        SHERWOOD STKS (Mdn 3-Y.O.F) £2196.00 (£606.00: £288.00)      **7f**        2-35 (2-39)

2555 **Jdaayel (Fav)** *(ACStewart)* 8-11 MRoberts (2) (w'like: scope: 2nd st: led over 2f out: r.o wl)    —1
Rustaka (USA) *(BWHills)* 8-11 DHolland (3) (led over 4f: unable qckn) .............. 5.2
2753 Pleasuring **(57)** *(MMcCormack)* 8-11 JReid (4) (b.nr hind: lw: 3rd st: one pce fnl 3f) .................................................... 4.3
*944* French Revolution (FR) *(PAKelleway)* 8-11 GayKelleway (1) (lw: 4th st: a in rr) 15.4

**4/5** JDAAYEL, **3/1** Pleasuring, **7/2** Rustaka (USA)(5/2—4/1), **20/1** French Revolution (FR). CSF £3.62, Tote £1.60 (£2.00). Mr Hamdan Al-Maktoum (NEWMARKET) bred by Floors Farming. 4 Rn     1m 26.89 (6.39)
SF—32/17/5/–

**3057**
MOET & CHANDON SILVER MAGNUM (H'cap) (Amateurs) (0-90) £8302.50 (£2520.00: £1235.00: £592.50) 1¹/₂m 10y
3-10 (3-15)

29173³ **Statajack (IRE)** (64) (DRCElsworth) 4-10-9 MrSSwiers (7) (lw: hdwy over 4f out: 6th st: led wl over 1f out: r.o wl) ..................... —1

27882² Welsh Mill (IRE) (84) (LordHuntingdon) 3-11-5 MrLMaynard (1) (3rd st: ev ch over 1f out: r.o) ........................... ¹/₂.2

2844 Castoret (79) (Fav) (JWHills) 6-11-10 MrCVigors (5) (gd hdwy over 1f out: r.o w ins fnl f) ......................... ³/₄.3

29153³ Ivor's Flutter (72) (DRCElsworth) 3-10-7 MrFSchafer (8) (lw: droppd rr over 7f out: rallied over 2f out: r.o one pce) ............... 3.4

2078* Blazon of Troy (68) (TThomsonJones) 3-10-3 MrFGrassoCaprioli (6) (led over 6f out tl wl over 1f out: sn wknd) ........... 4.5

28535⁵ Simply-H (IRE) (76) (MBell) 3-10-11 MrOFrei (9) (lw: 5th st: wknd over 2f out) .. 7.6

27153³ Monarda (71) (PFICole) 5-11-2 MrMArmytage (3) (lw: 2nd st: wknd over 2f out) 2¹/₂.7

2946 Cathos (FR) (55) (DAWilson) 7-10-0 MrDSalter (4) (b: 4th st: wknd over 2f out) ³/₄.8

2580 Walking on Water (65) (bl) (RFJohnsonHoughton) 3-10-0 MrGJohnsonHoughton (2) (lw: leadd over 5f: t.o fnl 3f) ........ dist.9
LONG HANDICAP: Cathos (FR) 9-13, Walking on Water 9-13.

2/1 Castoret, 5/1 STATAJACK (IRE), Welsh Mill (IRE), 11/2 Monarda, 15/2 Simply-H (IRE)(op 5/1), Ivor's Flutter, 12/1 Blazon of Troy(op 8/1), 25/1 Cathos (FR), 33/1 Walking on Water. CSF £28.96, CT £60.46. Tote £6.30: £1.70 £2.20 £1.50 (£16.70). Mrs M. E. Slade (WHITSBURY) bred by Princess Oettingen-Spielberg in Ireland. 9 Rn
2m 46.51 (11.51)
SF—44/53/56/33/21/15

**3058**
TADWORTH H'CAP (3-Y.O.F) (0-90) £3720.00 (£1110.00: £530.00: £240.00) 7f
(Weights raised 1 lb) 3-40 (3-40)

2018 **Rocality** (75) (RHannon) 9-0 JLloyd (1) (5th & styd far side st: led ins fnl f: all out) ............................ —1

30032² Rafah (72) (BHanbury) 8-11 MRoberts (3) (led: styd far side st: hdd ins fnl f: r.o wl) ....................... s.h.2

27956⁶ Clare Kerry Lass (75) (Fav) (JRFanshawe) 9-0 AMunro (2) (4th st: hrd rdn over 1f out: unable qckn) ............... 7.3

2588* Olette (82) (GWragg) 9-7 JReid (4) (2nd st: rdn over 2f out: one pce) ............. s.h.4

21073³ Hand on Heart (IRE) (63) (WJHaggas) 8-2 DHolland (5) (3rd st: rdn over 2f out: one pce) .......................... 2¹/₂.5

2/1 Clare Kerry Lass, 5/2 Olette, 4/1 Rafah, 5/1 Hand on Heart (IRE), 13/2 ROCALITY. CSF £28.13, Tote £9.20: £3.00 £2.00 (£15.20). Mr G. Z. Mizel (MARLBOROUGH) bred by Guest Leasing and Bloodstock Co. 5 Rn
1m 25.25 (4.75)
SF—60/56/38/44/17

**3059**
TOTE BOOKMAKERS SPRINT H'CAP (0-105) £8675.00 (£2600.00: £1250.00: £575.00) 5f
4-15 (4-16)

25993³ **Ashtina** (65) (RJHodges) 7-7-5(¹) ‡5NKennedy (8) (mde virtually all: drvn out) .. —1

2861 Running Glimpse (IRE) (74) (MissBSanders) 4-8-5 MRoberts (1) (a.p: ev ch fnl 2f: r.o wl) .......................... hd.2

29025⁵ Never in the Red (87) (v) (JBerry) 4-9-4 AMunro (2) (lw: a.p: hrd rdn over 1f out: r.o wl) ........................ s.h.3

2848⁵ Bodari (81) (DAWilson) 3-8-9 DHolland (5) (hld up: hrd rdn over 1f out: unable qckn) ............................ 1.4

2839 Orthorhombus (97) (v) (GLewis) 3-9-6 ‡5ATucker (7) (lw: a.p: hrd rdn over 2f out: one pce: sddle slipped) ........... 1.5

2848 Allthruthenight (IRE) (84) (LJHolt) 3-8-12 JReid (6) (swtg: nvr nr to chal) ......... hd.6

2179 Miami Banker (67) (bl) (PHowling) 6-7-9(⁴) ‡3SO'Gorman (9) (lw: bhd fnl 2f) ....... 7.7

2797* Cradle Days (93) (Fav) (RHannon) 3-9-7 JLloyd (4) (lw: bhd whn stumbled & uns rdr over 3f out) ......................... —

4/1 Cradle Days, 5/1 Never in the Red, ASHTINA, 11/2 Running Glimpse (IRE), Bodari, 6/1 Allthruthenight (IRE), 9/1 Orthorhombus, 14/1 Miami Banker. CSF £29.75, CT £129.86. Tote £5.90: £1.60 £2.00 £1.40 (£11.90). Ms S. A. Joyner (SOMERTON) bred by D. R. and Mrs Fairbairn. 8 Rn
57.75 sec (3.25)
SF—52/65/77/64/71/62

**3060**
CICERO CLAIMING STKS £3002.00 (£896.00: £428.00: £194.00) 1¹/₄m 18y
4-45 (4-52)

2856* **Loki (IRE)** (75) (Fav) (GLewis) 4-8-10 JReid (8) (lw: hdwy over 2f out: led wl over 1f out: rdn out) ................. —1

29064⁴ Danzarin (IRE) (67) (RHannon) 4-9-4 JLloyd (9) (swtg: 2nd st: ev ch over 1f out: unable qckn ins fnl f) ............... 2¹/₂.2

| | | |
|---|---|---|
| 2906[6] | Liability Order **(66)** *(RBoss)* 3–8–1 ‡[5]NKennedy (7) (lw: led over 8f: one pce) ..... | 2.3 |
| 2860 | Quietly Impressive (IRE) **(45)** *(MBell)* 4–8–1 AMunro (5) (lw: 4th st: one pce fnl 2f) | ³⁄₄.4 |
| 2754[4] | Lascar (USA) *(GThorner)* 4–8–5 ‡[3]SO'Gorman (1) (lw: 3rd st: one pce fnl 2f) .... | hd.5 |
| 2886[5] | Sharriba **(60)** *(DRCElsworth)* 3–7–10 ‡[5]ATucker (3) (lw: s.s: nvr nr to chal) ..... | 2.6 |
| 2807 | Share Holder **(30)** *(MissGayKelleway)* 4–8–9 GayKelleway (4) (b: b.hind: 6th st: wknd over 2f out) ................... | 5.7 |
| 2990 | Northern Conqueror (IRE) **(54)** *(TJNaughton)* 4–8–8 DHolland (6) (5th st: wknd over 2f out) ................... | hd.8 |
| 2600[4] | Vanroy **(67)** (v) *(JRJenkins)* 8–9–8 SWhitworth (2) (a bhd) ................... | 3.9 |

**5/6** LOKI (IRE), **6/1** Liability Order, **13/2** Sharriba(5/1—8/1), **15/2** Vanroy(5/1—8/1), **9/1** Danzarin (IRE), **14/1** Northern Conqueror (IRE), **16/1** Quietly Impressive (IRE), **33/1** Lascar (USA), **66/1** Share Holder. CSF £9.44, Tote £1.80: £1.20 £2.40 £1.80 £6.0 (£6.70). Mr T. K. Laidlaw (EPSOM) bred by Abbey Lodge Stud in Ireland. 9 Rn
2m 13.59 (9.09)
SF—35/38/17/15/18/–

---

**3061**  RANMORE H'CAP (0-90) £3882.50 (£1160.00: £555.00: £252.50)
1m 114y
5-15 (5-22)

| | | |
|---|---|---|
| 2913* | Grand Master (IRE) **(91)** (Fav) *(PFICole)* 3–10–0 AMunro (5) (lw: 5th st: led ins fnl f: rdn out) ................... | —1 |
| 2714[3] | Eternal Flame **(63)** *(JWHills)* 4–8–7 DHolland (9) (3rd st: led 2f out tl ins fnl f: r.o) | ³⁄₄.2 |
| 2805 | Gachette **(62)** *(JSutcliffe)* 3–7–8 ‡[5]ATucker (7) (led over 6f: unable qckn) .......... | 4.3 |
| 2770[4] | Dream Carrier (IRE) **(70)** *(RHannon)* 4–9–0 JLloyd (1) (lw: 6th st: hrd rdn over 1f out: nvr nrr) ................... | 8.4 |
| 2616[2] | Mr Tate (IRE) **(60)** *(RAkehurst)* 3–7–6 ‡[5]NKennedy (8) (lw: 5th st: wknd over 2f out) ................... | 2.5 |
| 2413 | Kingsfold Pet **(59)** *(M.IHaynes)* 3–7–2[(2)] ‡[7]DToole (2) (4th st: wknd over 2f out) | 2¹⁄₂.6 |
| 2593[2] | Neptune's Pet **(58)** *(GLewis)* 4–10–0 JReid (4) (lw: a bhd) ................... | 8.7 |
| 2012 | Valiant Words **(57)** *(RAkehurst)* 5–7–12 ‡[3]SO'Gorman (6) (2nd st: wknd 3f out) | 3¹⁄₂.8 |
| 2755[6] | Kitaab (USA) **(75)** *(ACStewart)* 3–8–12 MRoberts (3) (a bhd) ................... | 7.9 |

LONG HANDICAP: Kingsfold Pet 7-3.

**3/1** GRAND MASTER (IRE), **5/1** Kitaab (USA), **11/2** Mr Tate (IRE), **13/2** Eternal Flame, **7/1** Dream Carrier (IRE), **8/1** Neptune's Pet, **10/1** Valiant Words, **20/1** Ors. CSF £20.39, CT £289.37. Tote £3.20: £1.40 £2.10 £3.10 (£13.80). Mr Fahd Salman (WHATCOMBE) bred by Hullin Co N V in Ireland. 9 Rn    1m 48.14 (7.14)
SF—45/22/–/–/–/–

T/Trio: Race 5: £23.30 (83.3 Tckts) & Race 7: £84.20 (25.1. Tckts) T/Jkpt: £1,630.90 (0.35 Tckts); £1,432.60 to Epsom 1/9/92. T/Plpt: £46.80 (161.9 Tckts).    AK

---

# EPSOM (L-H)

## Tuesday, September 1st [Good]

Going Allowance: St: 0.40 (Y); Rnd: 0.25 sec per fur (G)    Wind: mod half against

Stalls: 4th high, remainder low

**3062**  CHESSINGTON STKS (Mdn 3-Y.O) £2469.00 (£684.00: £327.00)
1¹⁄₄m 18y
2-15 (2-20)

| | | |
|---|---|---|
| 1953 | Belle Isis (USA) *(LordHuntingdon)* 8–9 AMunro (10) (lw: 5th st: led ins fnl f: drvn out) ................... | —1 |
| 2836 | Lobilio (USA) **(84)** (Fav) *(CEBrittain)* 9-0 TQuinn (3) (lw: led tl ins fnl f) ............. | ¹⁄₂.2 |
| 2769[3] | Private Bank (USA) *(ACStewart)* 9-0 RHills (2) (lw: 3rd st: one pce fnl 3f) ......... | 15.3 |
| 2769[5] | Jameel Dancer (USA) *(MRStoute)* 9-0 LDettori (7) (lw: 4th st: one pce fnl 3f) ......... | 1¹⁄₂.4 |
| 2823[4] | Vanuatu (IRE) *(TThomsonJones)* 8–9 SWhitworth (4) (2nd st: wknd 2f out) ......... | 2.5 |
| 2922 | Princess Ermyn *(MDixon)* 8–9 DaleGibson (8) (lw: a bhd) ................... | 2¹⁄₂.6 |
| 2362[6] | Heavy Rock (IRE) *(DJSCosgrove)* 8-6 ‡[3]RonHillis (5) (bhd fnl 5f) ................... | 1.7 |
| 899 | Fighting Ajdal (IRE) *(ACStewart)* 9-0 AMcGlone (6) (bit bkwd: 6th st: wknd over 3f out) ................... | 2.8 |
| 2495[5] | Private Practice *(MJHeaton-Ellis)* 8–9 JWilliams (9) (a bhd) ................... | 8.9 |
| | Sting in the Tail *(GLewis)* 8–9 MHills (1) (unf: scope: dwlt: wl bhd fnl 3f: t.o) . | 20.10 |
| 2704[4] | Dioman Shadeed (USA) **(59)** *(JRFanshawe)* 9-0 GCarter (1) (ref to s: virtually t.n.p) ................... | 0 |

**4/6** Lobilio (USA), **13/2** Private Bank (USA)(4/1—7/1), Jameel Dancer(9/2—7/1), **14/1** Fighting Ajdal (IRE)(op 8/1), **16/1** BELLE ISIS (USA)(op 10/1), **20/1** Sting in the Tail, Vanuatu (IRE), **25/1** Private Practice, **33/1** Dioman Shadeed (USA), **50/1** Ors. CSF £26.17, Tote £17.80: £3.80 £1.10 £1.90 (£12.20). Lord Carnarvon (WEST ILSLEY) bred by Ryver Meadows Farms in USA. 11 Rn    2m 11.86 (7.36)
SF—46/49/19/16/7/2

**3063**  HEATHCOTE NURSERY   £3106.00 (£928.00: £444.00: £202.00)
1m 114y                                                          2-45 (2-51)

2735⁴ **Futurballa (90)** (Fav) *(JLDunlop)* 9-7 TQuinn (1) (lw: mde all: edgd bdly rt fnl 2f: r.o wl) ............................................................................... —1
2832⁴ Erlking (IRE) **(68)** *(LordHuntingdon)* 7-13 AMunro (10) (a 2nd: rdn 2f out: no imp) ............................................................................... 3½.2
 3019 Wahem (IRE) **(68)** *(CEBrittain)* 7-8 ‡5BDoyle (11) (lw: a 3rd: one pce fnl 2f) ..... 3½.3
 2285 Shynon **(62)** *(MHTompkins)* 7-7 DaleGibson (12) (6th st: styd on one pce fnl 2f) nk.4
2883³ Kyrenia Game **(68)** *(PMitchell)* 7-10 ‡3SO'Gorman (2) (nrst fin) ....................... nk.5
2374³ George Roper **(65)** *(MRChannon)* 7-10 TyroneWilliams (6) (lw: 8th st: no hdwy fnl 2f) ............................................................................... 7.6
2916³ Awesome Risk **(62)** *(GLewis)* 7-0 ‡7DWright (5) (lw: hdwy over 2f out: wknd over 1f out) ............................................................................... 2.7
2649⁴ Kaloochi **(67)** *(RHannon)* 7-12 AMcGlone (7) (a bhd) ....................................... s.h.8
2681³ Lofty Deed (USA) **(63)** *(SirMarkPrescott)* JFanning (9) (lw: 5th st: wknd 3f out) ............................................................................... nk.9
 2910 Poco Pierna (IRE) **(65)** *(WCarter)* 7-3⁽3⁾ ‡7CHawksley (8) (lw: 7th st: wknd 3f out) 1.10
2910⁶ Lochore **(69)** *(Ringram)* 7-9 ‡5NGwilliams (4) (4th st: wknd 3f out) ................ nk.11
2857⁶ Kingsdown Cavalier **(72)** *(RHannon)* 8-3⁽3⁾ RHills (3) (a bhd: t.o) ................... 25.12
LONG HANDICAP: Awesome Risk 6-13, Poco Pierna (IRE) 7-0.

**9/2** FUTURBALLA, **11/2** Lochore, Kaloochi, **6/1** Erlking (IRE), **13/2** Kyrenia Game, **7/1** Lofty Deed (USA), **8/1** George Roper, **12/1** Kingsdown Cavalier, **14/1** Awesome Risk, **20/1** Wahem (IRE), Shynon, **50/1** Poco Pierna (IRE). CSF £31.28, CT £461.20. Tote £6.00: £2.30 £2.50 £3.40 (£32.90). Gerecon Italia (ARUNDEL) bred by J. L. Woolford. 12 Rn                                                          1m 47.24 (6.24)
SF—46/13/–/–/–/–

**3064**  STEVE DONOGHUE APP'CE H'CAP (0-80) £3557.50 (£1060.00: £505.00: £227.50)
1½m 10y                                                          3-20 (3-28)

2698⋆ **Incola (53)** *(HCandy)* 6–8-9 ‡3AntoinetteArmes (2) (lw: hld up in rr: wnt 6th st: r.o strly to ld wl ins fnl f) ............................................................. —1
2571⁶ Great Max (IRE) **(67)** *(SirMarkPrescott)* 3–9-3 JFanning (7) (led over 5f out: clr over 2f out: hdd wl ins fnl f) ............................................ 2½.2
2955⋆ Atlantic Way **(42)** (Fav) *(CJHill)* 4–8-1 (6x) FNorton (4) (lw: wnt 2nd st: hrd rdn over 2f out: one pce) ................................................... 12.3
 2605 Thimbalina **(39)** *(DAWilson)* 6–7-12 NKennedy (1) (b: 4th st: one pce fnl 3f) ..... ½.4
2391⁴ Marine Society **(69)** (v) *(PTWalwyn)* 4–10-0 ATucker (3) (lw: 3rd st: wknd over 2f out) ............................................................................... 5.5
 2913 Holiday Island **(70)** *(CEBrittain)* 3–9-3 ‡3BDoyle (6) (5th st: wknd 3f out) ......... 12.6
 2774 Beam Me Up Scotty (IRE) **(43)** *(PMitchell)* 3–7-7 AGarth (5) (led over 6f: wknd & 6th st) ............................................................................... 10.7

**2/1** Atlantic Way, **4/1** Thimbalina(op 6/1), **5/1** Great Max (IRE), INCOLA(op 3/1), **13/2** Holiday Island, **12/1** Marine Society(10/1—16/1), **20/1** Beam Me Up Scotty (IRE). CSF £26.95, Tote £4.50: £2.40 £2.10 (£11.80). Mrs David Blackburn (WANTAGE) bred by Mrs D. Blackburn. 7 Rn
2m 42.16 (7.16)
SF—53/56/16/12/32/–

**3065**  REDHILL CLAIMING STKS (3-Y.O) £2238.00 (£618.00: £294.00)   5f   3-50 (3-52)

2875⋆ **Another Episode (IRE) (88)** (Fav) *(JBerry)* 9-6 GCarter (2) (lw: led 4f out: easily) —1
 2861 Holetown **(81)** (bl) *(RHannon)* 9-0 JReid (3) (led 1f: rdn over 2f out: no imp) .. 3½.2
 2909 Walking Possession **(77)** (bl) *(RBoss)* 8-9 MTebbutt (5) (a same pl: outpcd over 3f out: styd on fnl f) ................................................... nk.3
 2949 Paradise Forum **(60)** *(CAHorgan)* 8-4 DaleGibson (1) (lw: bhd fnl 3f) ............... 10.4
  65⁴ Fort Hope **(50)** (bl) *(TJNaughton)* 8-6 ‡3RPerham (4) (a bhd) ....................... ½.5

**1/2** ANOTHER EPISODE (IRE), **4/1** Walking Possession, **9/2** Holetown, **33/1** Paradise Forum, **50/1** Fort Hope. CSF £3.10, Tote £1.50: £1.20 £1.40 (£1.90). Palacegate Corporation Ltd (COCKERHAM) bred by Brendan and Sheila Powell in Ireland. 5 Rn                                                          58.64 sec (4.14)
SF—63/43/37/–/–

**3066**  CHALK LANE H'CAP (0-90) £3947.50 (£1180.00: £565.00: £257.50)
1¼m 18y                                                          4-20 (4-23)

2791⁴ **Shrewd Partner (IRE) (79)** *(DRCElsworth)* 3–9-8 YOkabe (1) (lw: mde virtually all: drvn out) ................................................................. —1
2913⁴ Glide Path (USA) **(81)** (Fav) *(JWHills)* 3–9-10 MHills (2) (lw: 6th st: ev ch 1f out: r.o) ............................................................................... 2.2
 2806 Absent Relative **(63)** *(MissBSanders)* 4–8-13 GCarter (5) (lw: 2nd st: ev ch over 1f out: nt qckn) ........................................................... ¾.3

2856⁵ Sarah-Clare (55) *(RAkehurst)* 4-8-2 ‡³RPerham (3) (4th st: nt clr run over 2f out: ev ch over 1f out: one pce) ........................................................ s.h.4
2708  Rive-Jumelle (IRE) (57) *(MBell)* 4-8-0 ‡⁷PTurner (7) (lw: 3rd st: one pce fnl 2f) 1¹/₂.5
2453  Misty View (71) *(MAJarvis)* 3-9-0 LDettori (9) (hdwy 2f out: nvr nr to chal) ........ 1.6
3060  Vanroy (67) (v) *(JRJenkins)* 8-9-3 SWhitworth (4) (lw: a bhd) ......................... 1.7
2885²  Gotcha (BAR) (84) *(RHannon)* 3-9-13 JReid (8) (5th st: wknd over 2f out) ....... hd.8
2885  Samurai Gold (USA) (50) (v) *(PTWalwyn)* 4-7-9⁽⁵⁾ ‡⁵ATucker (10) (prom 6f: nt r.o) ............................................................................................... 4.9
2698  Albert (46) *(DAWilson)* 5-7-5⁽²⁾ ‡⁵NKennedy (6) (lw: a bhd: t.o fnl 3f) .......... 30.10

**9/4** Glide Path (USA), **6/1** Gotcha (BAR), **13/2** SHREWD PARTNER (IRE), Sarah-Clare, **8/1** Misty View, Rive-Jumelle (IRE), **10/1** Vanroy, Albert, **12/1** Samurai Gold (USA), **25/1** Absent Relative. CSF £21.37, CT £324.96. Tote £8.90: £2.70 £1.50 £3.80 (£11.40). Mr Yoshiki Akazawa (WHITSBURY) bred by B. R. and Mrs Firestone in Ireland. 10 Rn                                    2m 13.01 (8.51)
                                                                         SF—48/46/33/21/21/28

---

**3067**     RUBBING HOUSE H'CAP (0-90) £3785.00 (£1130.00: £540.00: £245.00)
             6f                                                          4-50 (4-52)

2752⁴ **Temple Fortune (USA) (69)** *(RHannon)* 3-8-11 RHills (12) (3rd st: led over 2f out: drvn out) ......................................................................... —1
2945  How's Yer Father (79) *(RJHodges)* 6-9-10 AMunro (3) (6th st: hrd rdn over 1f out: r.o ins fnl f) ....................................................................... 1.2
2861³ Lady Sabo (67) *(GLewis)* 3-8-9 MHills (9) (hld up: hdwy & ev ch over 1f out: nt qckn) ...................................................................................... hd.3
3059² Running Glimpse (IRE) (74) *(MissBSanders)* 4-8-12 ‡⁷AntoinetteArmes (6) (5th st: ev ch over 1f out: nt qckn) ................................................... ¹/₂.4
2953² Ain'tlifelikethat (54) (bl) (Fav) *(TJNaughton)* 5—7-13 GCarter (8) (gd hdwy on ins over 1f out: wknd ins fnl f) ...................................................... 2.5
2919  Divine Pet (61) *(WGRWightman)* 7-8-6 JWilliams (13) (outpcd & wl bhd: gd hdwy fnl f) .............................................................................. ¹/₂.6
2589² Proud Brigadier (IRE) (48) *(WCarter)* 4-7-7 GBardwell (4) (lw: nvr nr to chal) 2¹/₂.7
2861  Fay's Song (IRE) (75) *(RAkehurst)* 4-8-13 ‡⁷LCarter (1) (lw: led over 4f out tl over 2f out) ........................................................................ 1.8
2650  Prince of the Sea (74) *(DWPArbuthnot)* 4-9-5 TQuinn (2) (b: 4th st: wknd 2f out) ........................................................................................ ³/₄.9
2956³ Soba Guest (IRE) (70) *(JBerry)* 3-8-12 LDettori (5) (lw: led over 1f out: 2nd st: wknd 2f out) .................................................................... 1.10
2925  Poets Cove (81) *(MMcCormack)* 4-9-12 JReid (11) (hmpd over 4f out: sn bhd) ¹/₂.11

**9/2** Ain'tlifelikethat, **6/1** Running Glimpse (IRE), **7/1** Soba Guest (IRE), How's Yer Father, **8/1** Poets Cove, Lady Sabo, **9/1** TEMPLE FORTUNE (USA), **10/1** Divine Pet(8/1—12/1), Fay's Song (IRE), **14/1** Ors. CSF £66.04, CT £483.03. Tote £9.50: £1.50 £2.70 £3.00 (£54.20). Mr L. H. J. Ward (MARLBOROUGH) bred by Dr E. W. Thomas in USA. 11 Rn                                   1m 11.90 (3.90)
                                                                         SF—49/58/42/43/22/27

T/Trio: Race 5: £77.90 (13.2 Tckts) & Race 6: £97.80 (8.1 Tckts) T/Jkpt: Not won; £2,520.45 to York 2/9/92. T/Plpt: £56.50 (85.9 Tckts).                                                          Hn

---

2923—**RIPON (R-H)**
**Monday, August 31st [Soft]**
Going Allowance: St: 0.35 sec per fur; Rnd: 0.55 sec per fur (Y)          Wind: slt half bhd
Stalls: low

**3068**     BONUSPRINT H'CAP (0-75) £4272.50 (£1280.00: £615.00: £282.50)
             6f                                                          2-00 (2-02)

2984★ **Yours Or Mine (IRE) (40)** *(DWChapman)* 4-7-7 (5x) SWood (11) (a.p: qcknd to ld wl over 1f out: eased nr fin: comf) .................................. —1
2808³ Miss Aragon (46) *(MissLCSiddall)* 4-7-10 ‡³SMaloney (12) (dwlt: sn prom: chal over 2f out: kpt on sme pce fnl f) ...................................... ¹/₂.2
2997  Petraco (IRE) (72) *(LJCodd)* 4-9-4 ‡⁷GParkin (1) (mde most tl hdd wl over 1f out: rallied u.p nr fin) ............................................... s.h.3
2817³ Double Feature (IRE) (60) *(MrsJRRamsden)* 3-8-9 DMcKeown (4) (rdn ¹/₂-wy: hdwy & hung rt 2f out: kpt on wl fnl f) .................................. 1¹/₂.4
2490★ Penny Hasset (73) (Fav) *(MWEasterby)* 4-9-12 TLucas (8) (prom: rdn over 2f out: wknd wl over 1f out) ........................................... 2¹/₂.5
2898⁴ Profilic (73) *(CaptJWilson)* 7-9-12 RPElliott (14) (hdwy 2f out: nvr able to chal) nk.6
2956  Henry Will (40) *(TFairhurst)* 8-7-7 JFanning (13) (sme hdwy 2f out: n.d) ........ 1¹/₂.7
2958  Act of Union (IRE) (72) (v) *(BBeasley)* 3-9-7 DNicholls (15) (chsd ldrs 4f) ........ ¹/₂.8

2741³ Here Comes a Star **(64)** *(JMCarr)* 4-9-3 SMorris (5) (in tch: effrt wl over 2f out:
no imp) ........................................................................ 3½.9
2808 Arabat **(59)** (v) *(MPNaughton)* 5-8-12 JakiHouston (10) (in tch: sn pushed
along: outpcd fnl 2f) ................................................... s.h.10
2956 Stormswept (USA) **(59)** (bl) *(MBrittain)* 3-8-8 NConnorton (6) (bhd fr ½-wy) 2½.11
*2689* State Governor **(55)** *(DWChapman)* 4-8-8 PBurke (7) (sn outpcd) ............... 2½.12
1961 Victoria Road (IRE) **(60)** (bl) *(MHEasterby)* 4-8-13 MBirch (3) (t.o & eased fnl 2f) 13
LONG HANDICAP: Yours Or Mine (IRE) 7-5, Henry Will 7-4.
*2821* ★ Ganeshaya (8/1) Withdrawn (no suitable rdr available) : not under orders
*2963²* Minizen Music (IRE) (16/1) Withdrawn (no suitable rdr available) : not under orders

**4/1** Penny Hasset, **5/1** Miss Aragon, **8/1** Here Comes a Star, Petraco (IRE), Profilic, Double Feature (IRE), **10/1**
YOURS OR MINE (IRE), **11/1** Arabat, **20/1** Act of Union (IRE), **25/1** Henry Will, Victoria Road (IRE), Stormswept
(USA), **33/1** State Governor. CSF £54.02, CT £384.78. Tote £9.80: £2.30 £2.00 £2.40 (£19.20). Mrs J. M.
Davenport (YORK) bred by Gorden Patterson in Ireland. 13 Rn
1m 15.9 (4.2)
SF—37/38/59/44/51/50

**3069** RIPON ROWELS H'CAP (0-100) £7765.00 (£2320.00: £1110.00: £505.00)
**1m**
2-30 (2-32)

2755★ **Two Left Feet (97)** (Fav) *(SirMarkPrescott)* 5-9-9 ‡5KRutter (6) (trckd ldrs: gd
hdwy to ld over 1f out: wnt rt: r.o strly) ................................ —1
2852⁵ Gymcrak Premiere **(92)** (v) *(MHEasterby)* 4-9-9 MBirch (7) (trckd ldr gng wl:
disp ld 3f out: sn led & rdn: hng rt & hdd over 1f out: no ex) 3.2
2852 Arany **(88)** *(MHTompkins)* 5-9-5 PRobinson (1) (led tl jnd 3f out: sn hdd: styd
on same pce) ............................................................... 1½.3
2191 Trafalgar Boy (USA) **(80)** *(JEtherington)* 3-8-5 JCarroll (5) (in tch: effrt 3f out:
kpt on one pce fnl 2f) ..................................................... 2.4
2447 Sagebrush Roller **(75)** *(JWWatts)* 4-8-6 NConnorton (4) (hld up in tch: effrt &
n.m.r 3f out: sn rdn & no imp) .......................................... 1½.5
2846 Mudaffar (IRE) **(92)** *(RWArmstrong)* 4-9-9 BCrossley (3) (hld up & bhd: hdwy 3f
out: sn rdn & nvr able to chal) .......................................... 2.6
2813⁵ Pride of Pendle **(68)** *(PCalver)* 3-7-7 SWood (8) (prom tl wknd wl over 2f out) 1½.7
2846 Major Mouse **(75)** *(WWHaigh)* 4-8-6 DMcKeown (2) (hld up: rn sltly wd st:
wknd over 2f out: eased) ................................................... 15.8
LONG HANDICAP: Pride of Pendle 6-4.

**100/30** TWO LEFT FEET, **5/1** Gymcrak Premiere, **11/2** Trafalgar Boy (USA), Sagebrush Roller, **6/1** Mudaffar
(IRE), **13/2** Arany, **11/1** Major Mouse, **33/1** Pride of Pendle. CSF £17.87, CT £82.17. Tote £3.80: £1.30 £1.90
£2.10 (£7.50). Mr P. W. W. Molins (NEWMARKET) bred by Stud-On-The-Chart. 8 Rn
1m 43.7 (6)
SF—85/76/67/47/43/54

**3070** BONUSPRINT CHAMPION TROPHY (Stks) (listed race) (2-Y.O) £9218.75 (£2750.00:
£1312.50: £593.75) **6f**
3-00 (3-02)

1461 **Star Family Friend (IRE) (95)** *(MHTompkins)* 8-6 PRobinson (3) (trckd ldrs:
led over 1f out: r.o wl) ...................................................... —1
2924★ Gymcrak Tiger (IRE) **(85)** *(MHEasterby)* 8-11 MBirch (5) (sn outpcd & pushed
along: gd hdwy appr fnl f: styd on: nt rch wnr) ......................... 2½.2
2939★ Nominator **(100)** *(RHollinshead)* 8-11 TLucas (10) (a.p: rdn over 2f out: kpt on
same pce fnl f) ............................................................... s.h.3
2847★ Sabre Rattler **(100)** *(JBerry)* 9-2 JCarroll (8) (trckd ldrs: effrt over 2f out: one
pce fnl f) ....................................................................... hd.4
2811² Ansellman **(95)** *(MJHaynes)* 8-11 GBardwell (9) (sn pushed along: hdwy over
1f out: kpt on nr fin) ........................................................ 1½.5
2850⁵ Risk Me's Girl **(90)** (bl) *(RHannon)* 8-6 DMcKeown (2) (led tl hdd & wknd over 1f
out) ............................................................................. nk.6
*2690*★ Isotonic **(67)** *(GMMoore)* 8-6 JFanning (1) (w ldr tl hung rt & wknd wl over 1f
out) ............................................................................. 4.7
2344⁴ Urry Urry Urry **(97)** (Fav) *(MJCamacho)* 8-6 NConnorton (6) (a outpcd) ......... 3.8
2764a Aradanza **(98)** *(MRChannon)* 8-11 BCrossley (7) (nvr nr ldrs) .................... 2½.9
2960 Shadow Jury **(89)** (v) *(JSWainwright)* 8-11 PBurke (4) (chsd ldrs to ½-wy: sn
lost pl) ......................................................................... 6.10

**7/2** Urry Urry Urry, **9/2** Nominator, **5/1** STAR FAMILY FRIEND (IRE), **11/2** Sabre Rattler, **8/1** Ansellman, Gymcrak
Tiger (IRE), **10/1** Risk Me's Girl, **11/1** Aradanza, **16/1** Isotonic, **33/1** Shadow Jury. CSF £41.83, Tote £7.20:
£1.90 £2.10 £1.80 (£51.10). Sheffield Newspapers Limited (NEWMARKET) bred by Mrs J. Corcoran in Ireland.
10 Rn
1m 15.4 (3.7)
SF—60/55/54/58/47/41

**3071** STAINLEY (S) NURSERY £2805.00 (£780.00: £375.00) **6f**
3-30 (3-34)
(Weights raised 10 lb)

*2782* Egg **(48)** (bl) *(TDBarron)* 8-0 ‡7VHalliday (17) (s.i.s: sn bhd: gd hdwy far side
over 2f out: led ins fnl f: wandered & r.o wl) .......................... —1

2563⁴ Penny Banger (IRE) **(49)** (Fav) *(MJohnston)* 8-8 DMcKeown (10) (a.p centre: hrd rdn wl over 1f out: nt qckn ins fnl f) ............................ 2.2

2876³ Selvole **(52)** *(MissLAPerratt)* 8-4 ‡7ClaireBalding (2) (led stands' side: hung rt 2f out: hdd ins fnl f: r.o) ........................................ ¹/2.3

2983 Hasta la Vista **(45)** (bl) *(MWEasterby)* 8-4⁽¹⁾ TLucas (14) (led far side: rdn over 2f out: no ex fnl f) ....................................... 1.4

2842 Ban Ri (IRE) **(57)** *(MHTompkins)* 9-2 PRobinson (16) (effrt & hdwy far side over 2f out: kpt on same pce fnl f) ........................ 2¹/2.5

2994⁴ My Godson **(62)** (bl) *(BBeasley)* 9-7 DNicholls (11) (w ldrs centre: hrd rdn & edgd rt 2f out: no ex fnl f) ................... nk.6

2690² Samanthas Joy **(56)** *(TFairhurst)* 9-1 JFanning (20) (trckd ldrs far side: rdn & unable qckn appr fnl f) ................. nk.7

2396⁵ Clangold **(42)** *(JBerry)* 8-1 AlexGreaves (18) (prom far side over 4f) ............... 2¹/2.8

2928 Bluebella **(50)** (v) *(MrsPABarker)* 8-9 SWood (4) (w ldrs to ¹/2-wy: sn rdn & grad wknd) ............................................... nk.9

2652 Canazei **(42)** *(DonEnricoIncisa)* 8-1 JakiHouston (8) (n.d) .................. nk.10

2572⁵ Pinkerton's Silver **(50)** (bl) *(MHEasterby)* 8-9 MBirch (19) (prom far side over 4f) .................................... 1¹/2.11

2661 Eightofus **(50)** *(GMMoore)* 8-6 ‡3SMaloney (1) (chsd ldrs stands' side over 3f) 2.12

1623³ Suitability (IRE) **(49)** *(PCHaslam)* 8-8 NConnorton (13) (n.d) ............. ³/4.13

2387⁶ Sefio **(54)** (v) *(JBerry)* 8-6 ‡7SPorritt (15) (bhd fnl 2f) ...................... 3¹/2.14

2802 Daily Sport's Gift **(56)** *(JBerry)* 9-1 JCarroll (12) (in tch far side to ¹/2-wy) .... nk.15

2238⁵ Admiral Frobisher (USA) **(52)** *(CFWall)* 8-11 BCrossley (7) (wl outpcd fnl 2f) 1¹/2.16

2740 Poppet Plume **(47)** (bl) *(GMMoore)* 8-1⁽¹⁾ ‡5KRutter (6) (bhd fr ¹/2-wy) ... 1.17

1526 Hot Off the Press **(55)** *(RMWhitaker)* 8-7 ‡7GParkin (9) (sn outpcd) ....... hd.18

2771 Miss Fitness **(42)** (v) *(DrJDScargill)* 8-1 GBardwell (3) (hrd rdn & btn ¹/2-wy) .. 2.19

2782 Sure Risk **(51)** *(MWEasterby)* 8-10 RPElliott (5) (in tch sf hung badly rt ¹/2-wy: sn btn) ............................................ 2.20

**4/1** Penny Banger (IRE), **13/2** My Godson(tchd 12/1), **7/1** Ban Ri (IRE), **10/1** Hot Off the Press, Clangold, Pinkerton's Silver, **12/1** Daily Sport's Gift, **14/1** Admiral Frobisher (USA), Suitability (IRE), **16/1** EGG, Poppet Plume, Eightofus, Selvole, Samanthas Joy, **20/1** Sefio, Sure Risk, Bluebella, Hasta la Vista, **33/1** Ors. CSF £85.10, CT £1,019.38. Tote £19.30: £4.50 £1.70 £4.50 £4.50 (£39.30). David Barron Racing Club (THIRSK) bred by Hever Castle Stud. 20 Rn; No bid
1m 16.5 (4.8)
SF—32/32/26/22/24/28

---

## 3072

PATELEY STKS (Mdn 3-Y.O) £2679.00 (£744.00: £357.00)   **1¹/2m 60y**   4-00 (4-02)

2922⁴ Long Silence (USA) (Jt-Fav) *(MrsJCecil)* 8-9 PRobinson (8) (trckd ldrs tl outpcd & lost pl 6f out: hdwy 4f out: led 2f out: sn clr) ......... —1

2780 Raheena (USA) *(JHMGosden)* 8-9 JCarroll (1) (hdwy to chse ldr 6f out: rdn & ev ch over 2f out: no ch w wnr) ............................. 8.2

2336⁵ Hierarch (USA) **(83)** (Jt-Fav) *(LordHuntingdon)* 9-0 DMcKeown (2) (hdwy to ld over 6f out: sn qcknd clr: hdd 2f out: nt r.o) ................. 1¹/2.3

Zafarrancho (IRE) *(JGFitzGerald)* 9-0 DNicholls (7) (s.s: bhd tl hdwy 4f out: nvr trbld ldrs) ..................................... 6.4

2549 Bird Watcher (bl) *(MajorWRHern)* 9-0 BProcter (9) (in tch tl wknd over 4f out: n.d after) .......................................... 2.5

2200³ Shadanza (IRE) *(APStringer)* 9-0 TLucas (8) (nvr trbld ldrs) ............ hd.6

2931 Titian Girl **(40)** *(MissLCSiddall)* 8-9 BCrossley (5) (led tl hdd over 6f out: wknd 4f out) ............................................ 8.7

2431 Kickcashtal *(BAMcMahon)* 8-9 ‡5KRutter (4) (prom tl outpcd 6f out: sn bhd) ..... 5.8

Eastern Phoebe *(ACStewart)* 8-9 MBirch (6) (sme hdwy 7f out: wknd over 4f out) ............................................ s.h.9

**15/8** LONG SILENCE (USA), Hierarch (USA), **7/1** Raheena (USA), **8/1** Eastern Phoebe, **9/1** Bird Watcher, **16/1** Shadanza (IRE), **20/1** Zafarrancho (IRE), **50/1** Kickcashtal, **66/1** Titian Girl. CSF £14.72, Tote £2.40: £1.30 £1.90 £1.30 (£11.40). Mr W. S. Farish III (NEWMARKET) bred by W. S. Farish, E. J. Hudson and E. J. Hudson in USA. 9 Rn
2m 48.9 (14.9)
SF—13/-/-/-/-/-

---

## 3073

TOPCLIFFE H'CAP (3-Y.O) (0-70) £3321.50 (£924.00: £444.50)   **1¹/4m**   4-30 (4-33)
(Weights raised 5 lb)

2923* Spray of Orchids **(52)** *(JEtherington)* 8-8 TLucas (5) (bhd: stdy hdwy over 4f out: styd on wl u.p to ld ins fnl f) ........................ —1

2880² Sie Amato (IRE) **(55)** *(CaptJWilson)* 8-11 GBardwell (14) (chsd ldrs: led 3f out: hrd rdn 2f out: hdd & no ex ins fnl f) .................... 1¹/2.2

2874² Boogie Bopper **(62)** (Fav) *(MBell)* 8-13 ‡5KRutter (13) (bhd: hdwy on outside over 2f out: styd on u.p fnl f: nrst fin) ............. 2¹/2.3

2620⁵ Esprit Fort (USA) **(64)** *(PWChapple-Hyam)* 9-6 BCrossley (4) (chsd ldrs: hrd rdn 3f out: wknd wl over 1f out) ................... 3¹/2.4

2729* Joseph's Wine (IRE) **(43)** *(RBastiman)* 7-10[(2)] ‡³SMaloney (3) (s.s: bhd tl hdwy 3f out: nvr trbld ldrs) ........................................... ¹/₂.5
2874⁴ Don't Forsake Me **(61)** *(DMorley)* 9-3 MBirch (12) (led tl hdd 3f out: sn btn) .... 2.6
2236⁶ Mist of the Marsh (USA) **(50)** *(JHMGosden)* 8-6 PRobinson (10) (nvr nr ldrs) .. 2¹/₂.7
2923⁴ Emerald Ears **(41)** *(EWeymes)* 7-11 JFanning (15) (chsd ldrs: ev ch 3f out: wknd over 1f out) ..................................................... hd.8
2942 Cromer's Express **(47)** *(MissLCSiddall)* 8-3 AlexGreaves (1) (effrt 4f out: n.d) ... 2.9
2880* Master Copy (IRE) **(50)** (bl) *(CBBBooth)* 7-13[(3)] ‡⁷GParkin (16) (sme hdwy 3f out: wandered & sn btn) ............................................ 2¹/₂.10
2156⁶ Nectar Collector **(65)** *(CFWall)* 9-7 NConnorton (2) (chsd ldrs tl wknd qckly over 2f out) ........................................................ 2¹/₂.11
2815⁶ Reel of Tulloch (IRE) **(61)** *(PCHaslam)* 9-3 DMcKeown (9) (hld up: effrt over 3f out: no imp) ........................................................ 5.12
1962 Rap Up Fast (USA) **(43)** *(CWThornton)* 7-6 ‡⁷KSked (8) (in rr most of wy) ..... 2¹/₂.13
2252⁵ Mayaasa (USA) **(63)** *(RWArmstrong)* 8-12 ‡⁷WAldwinckle (11) (in tch tl wknd 3f out) ...................................................... hd.14
2723 Ivors Princess **(46)** *(MJohnston)* 8-2 RPElliott (17) (a in rr) ............................ 6.15
2607 Barmbrack **(39)** (v) *(RMWhitaker)* 7-9 SWood (6) (a bhd) ............................ 1¹/₂.16

**7/2** Boogie Bopper (IRE)(3/1—9/2), **6/1** SPRAY OF ORCHIDS, **8/1** Master Copy (IRE), Reel of Tulloch (IRE)(op 5/1), **17/2** Sie Amato (IRE), **10/1** Don't Forsake Me, **11/1** Joseph's Wine (IRE), **12/1** Emerald Ears, Mist of the Marsh (USA)(op 8/1), **14/1** Mayaasa (USA), Esprit Fort (USA), **16/1** Nectar Collector, **20/1** Ivors Princess, **25/1** Cromer's Express, Barmbrack, **33/1** Rap Up Fast (USA). CSF £57.73, CT £197.20. Tote £5.60: £1.60 £2.00 £1.50 £2.70 (£27.20). Mr T. A. Stephenson (MALTON) bred by Nidd Park Stud. 16 Rn    2m 13.4 (9.9)
                                                   SF—50/50/47/47/22/39

T/Plpt: £59.60 (104.6 Tckts).                                       O'R

# RIPON (R-H)
## Tuesday, September 1st [Good to soft]
Going Allowance: St: nil sec (G); Rnd: 0.40 sec per fur (Y)       Wind: fresh across

Stalls: low

**3074**     BOROUGHBRIDGE CLAIMING STKS    £2805.00 (£780.00: £375.00)    6f 2-30 (2-33)

3031 **Clifton Charlie (USA) (84)** *(MRChannon)* 4-8-7 PaulEddery (1) (lw: shkn up after s: mde all: eased ins fnl f) ........................................ —1
2817* Arctic Appeal (IRE) **(84)** (Fav) *(JBerry)* 3-8-4 JCarroll (11) (lw: a chsng wnr: rdn 2f out: no imp) ..................................................... 2¹/₂.2
2956² Almasa **(58)** *(DMorris)* 4-7-11 ‡⁵StephenDavies (2) (lw: prom tl outpcd after 2f: styd on appr fnl f: nvr able to chal) ................................. 1.3
686 Dokkha Oyston (IRE) **(74)** *(JBerry)* 4-8-9 MRoberts (8) (lw: s.i.s: hdwy & prom after 2f out: wknd over 1f out) .......................................... 3.4
2809 My Grain **(47)** *(RHollinshead)* 3-7-7[(7)] ‡⁷MHumphries (7) (in tch: effrt ¹/₂-wy: no imp) ...................................................... 6.5
2468 Coastal Express **(64)** *(EWeymes)* 3-8-4 WCarson (5) (chsd ldr tl outpcd fnl 2f) 1¹/₂.6
2804 Toshiba Comet **(73)** (bl) *(BBeasley)* 5-8-5 ‡⁵SWilliams (4) (nvr trbld ldrs) ........ 3¹/₂.7
748 Borocay *(MJCamacho)* 4-8-1 NConnorton (3) (bkwd: s.i.s: nvr nr to chal) ...... 2¹/₂.8
     Phineas T Barnum (IRE) *(JJO'Neill)* 4-8-7 TLucas (6) (bkwd: s.i.s: a bhd) ........ 8.9
2752 Thornfield Boy **(63)** *(RJHolder)* 6-7-12 ‡⁷SDrowne (9) (sn outpcd & bhd) ........ 7.10

**1/2** Arctic Appeal (IRE)(op Evens), CLIFTON CHARLIE (USA)(op 5/1), **10/1** Dokkha Oyston (IRE), Thornfield Boy, **14/1** Coastal Express, **16/1** Toshiba Comet, **33/1** Borocay, **66/1** Ors. CSF £12.74, Tote £6.60: £1.50 £1.10 £1.50 (£4.70). Mr John W. Mitchell (UPPER LAMBOURN) bred by J. I. Racing Inc in USA. 10 Rn
                                          1m 13.9 (2.2)
                                          SF—49/36/25/25/–/–

**3075**     RUSHLEVEL CONSTRUCTION STAYERS H'CAP (0-70) £3027.50 (£840.00: £402.50)
        **2m 1f 203y**                                          3-00 (3-04)

2295⁶ **Merton Mill (62)** (bl) *(DMorley)* 5-9-8 PaulEddery (4) (lw: hdwy 10f out: effrt 3f out: styd on to ld ins fnl f) ............................................ —1
2246⁴ Brusque (USA) **(33)** *(DonEnricoIncisa)* 8-7-0 ‡⁷ClaireBalding (13) (hld up & bhd: gd hdwy on outside to ld over 2f out: hdd & no ex ins fnl f) ...................................................... 2.2
2783³ Thor Power (IRE) **(48)** *(DTThom)* 3-7-0 ‡⁷KimMcDonnell (2) (lw: a.p: ev ch 3f out: styd on) .................................................. ³/₄.3
2737² Naseem Elbarr (USA) **(63)** (Jt-Fav) *(ACStewart)* 4-9-9 MRoberts (6) (lw: mde most: hdd over 2f out: kpt on) .......................................... ³/₄.4
2059 Angelica Park **(40)** *(JWharton)* 6-8-0 JQuinn (7) (hld up: nt clr run ent st: hdwy over 2f out: nvr able to chal) ....................................... 2¹/₂.5

2498² Alizari (USA) **(66)** *(GHarwood)* 3–8–11 AClark (5) (a in tch: sn pushed along: kpt
on one pce fnl 4f) ..................................................... ½.6

2731⁴ Native Magic **(68)** *(RWArmstrong)* 6–9–7 ‡7WAldwinckle (1) (hld up: hdwy appr
st: chal over 2f out: sn wknd) ..................................... 1½.7

2968⁴ Alpha Helix **(33)** (v) *(MissLAPerratt)* 9–7–7 LCharnock (12) (bhd: hdwy ent st:
wknd over 2f out) .................................................... 3.8

2944² John Shaw (USA) **(44)** *(JSWainright)* 4–8–4 PBurke (9) (lw: nvr trbld ldrs) .... 2½.9

2836 Kadari **(62)** (Jt-Fav) *(AHarrison)* 3–8–7 WCarson (10) (lw: trckd ldrs tl rdn &
wknd 3f out) ......................................................... 1½.10

2737⁴ Carefree Times **(34)** *(JNorton)* 5–7–8⁽¹⁾ JLowe (11) (outpcd & bhd ½-wy: n.d) hd.11

2775 My Turn Next **(40)** *(KWHogg)* 4–7–7⁽⁷⁾ ‡7MHumphries (8) (trckd ldrs: effrt 4f out:
hung rt: sn wknd) .................................................... 2½.12

2959 Fiery Sun **(33)** (v) *(REBarr)* 7–7–7 NAdams (14) (prom tl wknd 4f out) ........... 12.13

2877 Scalp 'em (IRE) **(39)** *(FHLee)* 4–7–10⁽⁴⁾ ‡3SMaloney (3) (cl up tl wknd 4f out) .. ½.14

2929⁶ Nutacre **(33)** *(GPKelly)* 7–7–7 SWood (15) (b: bit bkwd: cl up 6f: sn t.o) ............. 15

LONG HANDICAP: Brusque (USA) 7-0, Thor Power (IRE) 7-3, Alpha Helix 7-4, My Turn Next 7-2,
Fiery Sun 7-6, Nutacre 6-10.

**100/30** Naseem Elbarr (USA), Kadari, **7/1** MERTON MILL, **8/1** Thor Power (IRE), **14/1** Alpha
Helix, Native Magic, John Shaw (USA), Carefree Times, **20/1** Angelica Park, **25/1** Brusque (USA), **33/1** Scalp 'em
(IRE), **50/1** Fiery Sun, My Turn Next, **66/1** Nutacre. CSF £145.77, CT £1,581.79. Tote £10.10: £2.90 £8.40
£2.50 (£1,275.80). Lord Clinton (NEWMARKET) bred by Greenland Park Stud. 15 Rn          4m 5.6 (14.3)
SF—37/–/–/34/8/18

---

**3076**      STEVE NESBITT CHALLENGE TROPHY (H'cap) (0-80) £5049.00 (£1512.00: £726.00:
£333.00)      1½m 60y                                        3-30 (3-35)

2820 **Golden Torque (64)** *(RBastiman)* 5–9–0 ‡7HBastiman (4) (b: racd wd: hld up:
hdwy to ld wl over 1f out: wandered u.p: all out) .................... —1

2780⁴ Kabayii **(70)** *(PTWalwyn)* 3 0 1 WCarson (8) (a.p: chal over 2f out: r.o u.p fnl f) hd.2

2927⁴ Bold Ambition **(37)** *(TKersey)* 5–7–8 JLowe (11) (lw: lft in ld 10f out tl had wl over
1f out: kpt on same pce) ............................................ 2½.3

2721⁵ Thunderbird One (USA) **(55)** *(DenysSmith)* 3–8–3 KFallon (5) (lw: a.p: effrt over
3f out: one pce fnl 2f) .............................................. s.h.4

2810★ Kinoko **(56)** *(KWHogg)* 4–8–13 JCorrigan (9) (lw: hld up: hdwy ent st: hrd rdn 2f
out: r.o one pce) ................................................... s.h.5

2896³ No Comebacks **(44)** *(EJAlston)* 4–7–8⁽²⁾ ‡7GMitchell (7) (hmpd 10f out: hdwy 4f
out: styd on) ....................................................... 4.6

2927⁵ West With the Wind **(51)** *(GMMoore)* 5–8–8 JQuinn (10) (s.i.s: bhd tl styd on fnl
3f) ................................................................. 3.7

2204⁶ Eurotwist **(71)** *(TDBarron)* 3–9–5 AlexGreaves (3) (hld up & bhd: effrt to ins whn
n.m.r 4f out: n.d) .................................................. ¾.8

2775 Queens Tour **(36)** *(MBrittain)* 7–7–7 NCarlisle (6) (n.d) ....................... hd.9

2660³ Bescaby Boy **(65)** *(JWharton)* 6–9–8 MBirch (13) (lw: trckd ldrs: effrt over 3f out:
wknd over 2f out) .................................................. s.h.10

2927★ Much Sought After **(76)** (Fav) *(DMorley)* 3–9–10 PaulEddery (14) (lw: nvr trbld
ldrs) .............................................................. 2.11

2927 Valiant Warrior **(68)** *(MDHammond)* 4–9–11 DMcKeown (2) (bit bkwd: in tch to
st) ................................................................ 3½.12

805 Don't Cry **(40)** *(DonEnricoIncisa)* 4–7–11 JakiHouston (15) (a bhd) ............ 2.13

562⁶ Fassfern (USA) **(74)** (bl) *(MrsJCecil)* 3–9–8 WRyan (12) (led tl faltered & lost pl
after 2f: chsd ldrs tl wknd over 3f out) ........................... 12.14

Damart (USA) **(36)** *(MissLCSiddall)* 8–7–7 NAdams (1) (s.i.s: gd hdwy ent st: sn
lost pl) ........................................................... ¾.15

LONG HANDICAP: Queens Tour 7-1, Damart (USA) 7-3.
*Stewards Enquiry: Bastiman suspended 10-11/9/92 (excessive use of whip).*

**5/1** Much Sought After, **6/1** West With the Wind, **7/1** Kinoko, **8/1** Kabayii, GOLDEN TORQUE, **9/1** Bescaby Boy,
**10/1** Eurotwist, **11/1** Fassfern (USA), **12/1** Thunderbird One (USA), **14/1** No Comebacks, **20/1** Bold Ambition,
**33/1** Don't Cry, Queens Tour, Valiant Warrior, **50/1** Damart (USA). CSF £65.37, CT £1,134.12. Tote £11.30:
£3.10 £2.50 £5.60 (£103.70). Mr Trevor J. Smith (WETHERBY) bred by H. F. Craig Harvey. 15 Rn
2m 46.4 (12.4)
SF—26/29/–/8/17/—

---

**3077**      TATTERSALLS AUCTION SERIES STKS (Qualifier) (Mdn 2-Y.O) £3782.00 (£1136.00:
£548.00: £254.00)      **6f**                                  4-00 (4-08)

2960³ **Hotaria (70)** *(RMWhitaker)* 8–4 ACulhane (1) (lw: mde all: r.o wl fnl 2f) .............. —1

2590² Perdition (IRE) **(60)** *(JWHills)* 8–2 MRoberts (7) (lw: a chsng wnr: nt qckn fnl 2f) .... 2½.2

2832³ My Best Valentine **(70)** *(PWHarris)* 8–0 PaulEddery (20) (lw: a cl up centre: kpt on
fnl f) .............................................................. ½.3

2932⁵ Aviator's Dream *(JFBottomley)* 8–6 PBurke (3) (lw: chsd ldrs: sn drvn along: kpt
on fnl 2f) ......................................................... 2½.4

26082 Killy's Filly *(JBerry)* 8-2(1) JCarroll (14) (b: lw: chsd ldrs centre: nt qckn appr fnl
f) .......................................................................................................... ¾.5
*2781* She's a Breeze *(ASmith)* 8-0 NAdams (4) (kpt on u.p fnl 2f: nvr nrr) ............... 1½.6
2425 Minster Man (IRE) *(BSRothwell)* 8-6 DHolland (12) (chsd ldrs: one pce appr fnl
f) .......................................................................................................... 2.7
Beckyhannah *(RBastiman)* 8-3(2) DMcKeown (19) (unf: b.hind: chsd ldrs
centre over 4f) ............................................................................... s.h.8
Splash of Salt (IRE) *(WJHaggas)* 8-8 JQuinn (21) (lw: w ldrs centre: rdn over 2f
out: grad wknd) ............................................................................. 2½.9
25342 Sky Wish **(72)** *(MissSEHall)* 8-5 SWebster (17) (chsd ldrs centre over 4f) ..... s.h.10
Epsom Dream *(JEtherington)* 8-8 KDarley (13) (w'like: scope: bhd: stdy hdwy
2f out: nvr nr to chal) ...................................................................... ¾.11
2916 Five Clubs (IRE) **(54)** *(DTThom)* 7-7 ‡7KimMcDonnell (24) (nvr trbld ldrs) ....... nk.12
Bonarme (IRE) *(MHEasterby)* 8-5 ‡3SMaloney (23) (lt-f: unf: hdwy ½-wy: n.d) s.h.13
28456 Blow Dry (IRE) **(Fav)** *(JHanson)* 8-11 EJohnson (11) (lw: stumbled bdly s: nt
rcvr) ............................................................................................... s.h.14
2812 Northern Judy (IRE) *(RHollinshead)* 8-2(1) WRyan (10) (n.d) ............................. nk.15
Backstabber *(DrJDScargill)* 8-5 SWood (5) (wl grwn: scope: bit bkwd: hdwy
½-wy: nvr plcd to chal) .................................................................... 1½.16
1299 Blakes Beau *(MHEasterby)* 8-11 MBirch (8) (in tch 4f) ................................... ½.17
2842 Scoffera *(NTinkler)* 8-3 LCharnock (9) (bhd fr ½-wy) ....................................... ½.18
16383 Spicy Affair *(DrJDScargill)* 8-8 JFortune (22) (chsd ldrs far side over 3f) ........ s.h.19
2961 Simply Superb *(MWEasterby)* 8-11 TLucas (6) (hld up: a bhd) ........................ 1.20
2932 Secret Fantasy (IRE) *(CFWall)* 8-9 NCarlisle (16) (n.d) ................................... 1½.21
7513 Public Way (IRE) *(NChamberlain)* 8-8 JLowe (18) (n.d) ................................... nk.22
20746 Viv's Pet *(AHide)* 8-8 GBaxter (15) (n.d) ......................................................... 4.23
2812 Moss Pageant *(MrsPABarker)* 8-11 KFallon (2) (bit bkwd: spd to ½-wy: sn bhd) 6.24

**7/4** Blow Dry (IRE), **6/1** Perdition (IRE), **8/1** Aviator's Dream, **11/1** Splash of Salt (IRE), **14/1** Sky Wish, **16/1**
HOTARIA, Killy's Filly, Spicy Affair, My Best Valentine, **25/1** Secret Fantasy (IRE), Epsom Dream, Northern Judy
(IRE), **33/1** Five Clubs (IRE), Viv's Pet, Bonarme (IRE), Public Way (IRE), Simply Superb, Backstabber, Blakes
Beau, **50/1** Ors. CSF £108.81, Tote £16.10: £3.40 £2.30 £3.50 (£26.90). Mrs Julia Richmond (WETHERBY)
bred by Mrs B. Skinner and D. F. Powell. 24 Rn                                                1m 14.9 (3.2)
SF—26/14/20/6/–/–

**3078**          HARROGATE STKS (Mdn 3-Y.O) £2910.00 (£810.00: £390.00)     1¼m    4-30 (4-43)

27442 **Mimique** **(Fav)** *(HRACecil)* 9-0 WRyan (3) (lw: mde all: pushed along & r.o fnl
2f) ..................................................................................................... —1
El Taranda *(GWragg)* 8-9 PaulEddery (10) (chsd ldrs: effrt over 3f out: styd on:
nt pce of wnr) ................................................................................. 3½.2
22704 Shimmer *(LordHuntingdon)* 8-9 DMcKeown (7) (hld up: hdwy 3f out: shkn up 2f
out: no rspnse) ............................................................................... 6.3
2654 Call Me Dickins *(RHHollinshead)* 9-0 KDarley (11) (s.i.s: hmpd over 4f out: styd
on wl fnl 3f) ..................................................................................... 10.4
30164 Grand Honda (IRE) *(CEBrittain)* 9-0 MBirch (2) (lw: chsd ldrs: outpcd ent st: no
imp after) ........................................................................................ 2.5
27694 Rutbah *(ACStewart)* 8-9 MRoberts (1) (lw: chsd wnr tl rdn & btn 3f out) ............ 1.6
2815 Shadaylou (IRE) **(34)** *(MissLAPeratt)* 8-2 ‡7RHavlin (9) (outpcd appr st: n.d) ... 15.7
Peacock Throne *(MrsJRRamsden)* 9-0 GBaxter (5) (w'like: bit bkwd: prom st:
sn lost pl) ....................................................................................... 3.8
27444 Mr Sunny *(PBeaumont)* 9-0 PBurke (8) (bhd: hung rt over 4 out: t.o) ............... 25.9
West Auckland *(NChamberlain)* 9-0 JLowe (6) (unf: bkwd: s.s: wl t.o) ............ 3.10
26916 Our Joey *(JWharton)* 8-9 ‡5SWilliams (4) (s.n drvn along: wl t.o) .......... 11

**11/10** MIMIQUE(op 7/4), **5/2** Rutbah, **6/1** Shimmer(op 4), **11/1** Grand Honda (IRE), El Taranda(8/1—12/1), **33/1**
Peacock Throne, **50/1** Call Me Dickins, **66/1** Mr Sunny, Our Joey, **100/1** Shadaylou (IRE), **200/1** West Auckland.
CSF £13.13, Tote £2.10: £1.10 £2.20 £1.90 (£9.70). Sheikh Mohammed (NEWMARKET) bred by La Grange Ltd.
11 Rn                                                                                        2m 12.7 (9.2)
SF—48/36/24/9/5/–

**3079**          CURFEW H'CAP (0-70) £2782.50 (£770.00: £367.50)    **5f**      5-00 (5-17)
(Weights raised 3 lb)

23653 **Lincstone Boy (IRE) (45)** (bl) *(SRBowring)* 4–8-7 SWebster (5) (mde all: clr
½-wy: drvn out) ............................................................................. —1
29633 The Right Time **(45)** (bl) *(JParkes)* 7–8-7 WCarson (2) (lw: a.p: hdwy u.p over 1f
out: styd on) .................................................................................. 3½.2
3068* Yours Or Mine (IRE) **(38)** **(Fav)** *(DWChapman)* 4–8-0 (5x) SWood (6) (lw: chsd
ldrs: kpt on u.p fnl f) ...................................................................... s.h.3
28162 Hinari Video **(44)** *(MJohnston)* 7–8-6 DMcKeown (1) (lw: chsd ldrs: outpcd
½-wy: no imp after) ........................................................................ nk.4

| | | | | |
|---|---|---|---|---|
| 2958³ | Ballad Dancer **(56)** *(EJAlston)* 7-9-4 GBaxter (9) (lw: bhd: hdwy 2f out: nvr rchd ldrs) | | | 2.5 |
| 2936⁵ | The Dream Maker (IRE) **(40)** *(MrsNMacauley)* 3-8-0 JQuinn (3) (chsd ldrs tl outpcd ½-wy: n.d) | | | 1.6 |
| 2919⁴ | Dickens Lane **(53)** *(RJHodges)* 5-9-1 NAdams (8) (lw: sn pushed along: no imp fr ½-wy) | | | 1½.7 |
| 2702⁵ | Rock Opera (IRE) **(57)** *(MPNaughton)* 4-9-5 MRoberts (10) (spd centre 3f) | | | 3.8 |
| 2936 | Jovial Kate (USA) **(45)** *(BEllison)* 5-8-7 JFortune (7) (b.nr hind: gd spd 3f) | | | 2½.9 |
| 3068 | Minizen Music (IRE) **(32)** *(MBrittain)* 4-7-8⁽¹⁾ JLowe (11) (spd centre 3f) | | | ¾.10 |
| 2151⁴ | Murray's Mazda (IRE) **(64)** *(JBerry)* 3-9-10 JCarroll (4) (sltly hmpd s: a bhd) | | | 4.11 |
| | LONG HANDICAP: Minizen Music (IRE) 7-2. | | | |

**5/2** Yours Or Mine (IRE), **13/2** Dickens Lane, The Right Time, **9/1** Rock Opera (IRE), **10/1** Ballad Dancer, Minizen Music (IRE), Hinari Video, **16/1** The Dream Maker (IRE), Jovial Kate (USA), **20/1** LINCSTONE BOY (IRE) & Ors. CSF £126.89, CT £397.71. Tote £39.00: £6.20 £2.00 £1.80 (£76.80). Mrs J. Addleshaw (EDWINSTOWE) bred by Ardenode Stud Ltd. in Ireland. 11 Rn

60.4 sec (1.8)
SF—57/43/35/40/44/22

T/Trio: Race 3: £13.50 (29 Tckts). T/Plpt: £365.20 (12.92 Tckts).                                  AA

## 2835—YORK (L-H)

### Wednesday, September 2nd [Good]
Going Allowance: St: 0.20 sec per fur; Rnd: 0.30 sec per fur (G)           Wind: fresh half bhd

Stalls: high

**3080**     WACHENFELD GERMAN WINES STKS (Mdn 3-Y-O) £4464.00 (£1332.00: £636.00: £288.00)   **7f 202y**                                    2-00 (2-01)

| | | | | |
|---|---|---|---|---|
| | **What Katy Did (USA)** *(JHMGosden)* 8-9 SCauthen (8) (b.hind: w'like: leggy: trckd ldr: shkn up over 2f out: r.o wl to ld nr fin) | | | —1 |
| 2659³ | Emir Albadou **(Fav)** *(MRStoute)* 9-0 PatEddery (4) (led: rdn 1f out: no ex nr fin) | | | ¾.2 |
| | Alhaajib (USA) *(JLDunlop)* 9-0 WCarson (3) (w'like: lw: s.i.s: sn bhd & drvn along: hdwy & ev ch over 3f out: kpt on) | | | 5.3 |
| 433 | Leif the Lucky (USA) *(WJarvis)* 9-0 RCochrane (1) (plld hrd: trckd ldrs: stumbled after 1f: kpt on fnl f) | | | 3.4 |
| | Quest for the Best *(ACStewart)* 8-9 MRoberts (2) (w'like: unf: lw: trckd ldrs & plld hrd: outpcd fnl 3f) | | | 8.5 |
| | Majestic Sinclair (IRE) *(RHollinshead)* 9-0 WRyan (7) (bit bkwd: dwlt: nvr nr ldrs) | | | 2½.6 |
| | Bilhab (USA) *(ACStewart)* 9-0 RHills (5) (w'like: lengthy: bit bkwd: chsd ldrs tl lost pl over 3f out) | | | 5.7 |
| | Lahoob (USA) *(BHanbury)* 9-0 LPiggott (6) (b.hind: w'like: str: effrt & prom 3f out: sn lost pl) | | | 6.8 |

**11/8** Emir Albadou (USA), **5/2** Alhaajib (USA), **7/1** WHAT KATY DID (USA), **8/1** Quest for the Best(op 5/1), Leif the Lucky (USA), **14/1** Lahoob (USA), **20/1** Bilhab (USA), **33/1** Majestic Sinclair (IRE). CSF £17.10, Tote £5.90: £1.50 £1.10 £1.50 (£7.30). Sheikh Mohammed (NEWMARKET) bred by Mareco Ltd in USA. 8 Rn

1m 42.25 (6.25)
SF—37/40/25/16/–/–

**3081**     BEST BUY PRODUCTS STKS (2-Y-O) £4844.00 (£1442.00: £686.00: £308.00)   **5f**                                    2-30 (2-30)

| | | | | |
|---|---|---|---|---|
| 2794* | **Palacegate Episode (IRE) (100) (Fav)** *(JBerry)* 8-13 JCarroll (5) (mde all: rdn 2f out: hld on wl) | | | —1 |
| 2093a⁵ | Satank (USA) **(100)** *(JWWatts)* 9-4 PatEddery (1) (w wnr over 1f out: nt qckn nr fin) | | | nk.2 |
| 2847⁴ | Lord Olivier (IRE) **(95)** *(WJarvis)* 9-0 MTebbutt (7) (lw: hdwy 2f out: swtchd lft & styd on wl ins fnl f) | | | ½.3 |
| 2928³ | Willshe Gan **(85)** *(DenysSmith)* 8-9 KFallon (6) (lw: a chsng ldrs: rdn ½-wy: kpt on wl fnl f) | | | ¾.4 |
| 2847 | Elle Shaped (IRE) **(100)** *(RHannon)* 9-0 MRoberts (3) (swvd lft s: edgd lft thrght: racd wd: chsd ldrs tl rdn & wknd over 1f out) | | | 3.5 |
| | Suragon *(JWharton)* 8-7 JWilliams (2) (w'like: lengthy: s.i.s: sn wl outpcd) | | | 20.6 |

**2/5** PALACEGATE EPISODE (IRE), **6/1** Satank (USA), **8/1** Elle Shaped (IRE), **12/1** Lord Olivier (IRE), **16/1** Willshe Gan, **50/1** Suragon. CSF £3.42, Tote £1.40: £1.20 £2.10 (£2.40). Palacegate Corporation Ltd (COCKERHAM) bred by Brendan and Sheila Powell in Ireland. 6 Rn

60.70 sec (3.20)
SF—55/59/53/45/38/–

**3082** BATLEYS CASH & CARRY H'CAP (0-100) £8220.00 (£2460.00: £1180.00: £540.00)
1m 5f 194y
3-00 (3-01)

2836* **Daru (USA) (86)** (v) (Fav) (JHMGosden) 3-8-9 SCauthen (8) (trckd ldrs: led over 2f out: r.o wl u.p) .................................................. —1

2899³ Jungle Dancer (IRE) **(86)** (MRStoute) 4-9-6 PatEddery (10) (trckd ldr: chal over 2f out: r.o u.p) .................................................. 1½.2

2926² Rising Tempo (IRE) **(64)** (CACyzer) 4-8-12 DBiggs (5) (lw: hld up: hdwy on ins over 3f out: r.o same pce fnl 2f) .................................................. 5.3

2844 Jackson Flint **(78)** (bl) (HThomsonJones) 4-8-12 RHills (6) (lw: hld up: hdwy on bit ent st: shkn up over 2f out: nt qckn) .................................................. 1½.4

2844⁶ Holy Zeal **(83)** (DWPArbuthnot) 6-9-3 TQuinn (3) (hld up: effrt over 3f out: rdn & wknd over 1f out) .................................................. 4.5

2921⁶ Farat (USA) **(74)** (JLDunlop) 4-8-8 WCarson (7) (b: plld hrd: trckd ldrs tl outpcd 4f out: n.d after) .................................................. 4.6

2853 Doctor Roy **(59)** (NBycroft) 4-7-7 LCharnock (4) (trckd ldrs tl wl outpcd 4f out) ½.7

2129 Hebridean **(94)** (HCandy) 5-10-0 CRutter (2) (hld up: effrt over 3f out: sn lost pl) 1½.8

2970* The Last Empress (IRE) **(69)** (ASReid) 4-8-3 (3x) NAdams (1) (b.hind: hld up: hdwy & prom 9f out: led over 3f out tl over 2f out: sn wknd) 1.9

2495² Hidden Laughter (USA) **(77)** (BWHills) 3-8-0 DHolland (9) (led tl over 3f out: sn wknd) .................................................. ½.10

LONG HANDICAP: Doctor Roy 7-5.

**7/4** DARU (USA), **13/2** Holy Zeal, **9/1** Jungle Dancer (IRE), Jackson Flint(12/1—8/1), Farat (USA), Hebridean, **11/1** Rising Tempo (IRE), Hidden Laughter (USA), **16/1** The Last Empress (IRE), **33/1** Doctor Roy. CSF £16.50, CT £121.38. Tote £2.50: £1.30 £2.50 £2.50 (£7.50). Sheikh Mohammed (NEWMARKET) bred by Albert G. Clay & Charlotte Clay Buxton in USA. 10 Rn
3m 5.70 (12.10)
SF—16/24/–/–/–/–

**3083** LAWRENCE BATLEY H'CAP (0-115) £15660.00 (£4680.00: £2240.00: £1020.00)
6f
3-30 (3-34)

2997³ **Never so Sure (87)** (v) (Fav) (ABailey) 4-8-8 LPiggott (2) (trckd ldrs: qcknd to ld over 1f out: sn clr: pushed out) .................................................. —1

2839 Bertie Wooster **(85)** (RJHolder) 9-8-6[1] LDettori (13) (lw: sn bhd: hdwy over 2f out: r.o fnl f) .................................................. 2½.2

2925² Gorinsky (IRE) **(73)** (JBerry) 4-7-8 NAdams (4) (chsd ldrs: kpt on same pce fnl f) .................................................. 1½.3

3014³ Double Blue **(93)** (MJohnston) 3-8-11 DMcKeown (9) (chsd ldrs: effrt over 2f out: r.o same pce) .................................................. s.h.4

2383⁶ Colway Bold **(101)** (v) (JWWatts) 3-9-5 PatEddery (5) (led tl over 1f out: kpt on) 1½.5

2839 Dominuet **(80)** (JLSpearing) 7-8-5 GHind (7) (s.i.s: hdwy ½-wy: styd on fnl f: nt rch ldrs) .................................................. nk.6

2925⁶ Drum Sergeant **(78)** (JParkes) 5-7-13[1] MRoberts (12) (lw: s.i.s: bhd tl hdwy ½-wy: effrt over 1f out: unable qckn) .................................................. nk.7

2925 Master Planner **(102)** (CACyzer) 3-9-6 DBiggs (8) (in tch: effrt over 2f out: nt rch ldrs) .................................................. 1.8

2892a Hazm (USA) **(88)** (HThomsonJones) 3-8-6 RHills (11) (chsd ldrs over 3f) ....... 3½.9

2839 Appledorn **(83)** (bl) (BAMcMahon) 5-8-4 TQuinn (7) (s.i.s: bhd: sme hdwy u.p over 2f out: n.d) .................................................. ½.10

3015⁵ Educated Pet **(76)** (MJohnston) 3-7-8 JLowe (6) (nvr nr ldrs) .................................................. ¾.11

1014² Sea Devil **(83)** (MJCamacho) 6-8-4 NConnorton (14) (b.off hind: hld up & bhd: sme hdwy over 2f out: sn wknd) .................................................. s.h.12

2861 Merryhill Maid (IRE) **(74)** (JLHarris) 4-7-2[2] ‡7CHawksley (3) (lw: a in rr) ....... hd.13

2559 Windpower (IRE) **(84)** (v) (JBerry) 3-8-2[1] JCarroll (1) (lw: chsd ldrs tl outpcd 2f out) .................................................. ½.14

2400 Norton Challenger **(107)** (v) (MHEasterby) 5-10-0 MBirch (15) (racd stands' side: sn wl bhd) .................................................. 8.15

2839 Sir Harry Hardman **(97)** (bl) (FHLee) 4-9-4 WCarson (16) (racd stands' side: a wl bhd) .................................................. 4.16

LONG HANDICAP: Merryhill Maid (IRE) 7-3.

**6/1** NEVER SO SURE, **13/2** Double Blue, **15/2** Drum Sergeant, **9/1** Gorinsky (IRE), Dominuet, **10/1** Sea Devil, **12/1** Appledorn, Norton Challenger, **14/1** Windpower (IRE), **16/1** Educated Pet, Master Planner, Colway Bold, Sir Harry Hardman, Hazm (USA), **20/1** Bertie Wooster, **25/1** Merryhill Maid (IRE). CSF £110.82, CT £996.20. Tote £5.50: £1.70 £2.90 £2.30 £1.60 (£127.50). Mrs M. O'Donnell (TARPORLEY) bred by Mrs P. A. Clark. 16 Rn
1m 12.01 (1.81)
SF—82/70/52/68/70/55/48

**3084** CAPOLINI ITALIAN WINES H'CAP (0-100) £7635.00 (£2280.00: £1090.00: £495.00)
1m 205y (Weights raised 1 lb)
4-00 (4-01)

2219² **Forever Diamonds (64)** (MHEasterby) 5-7-7 JQuinn (3) (lw: hld up: hdwy & nt clr run over 2f out: swtchd outside: led 1f out: hld on wl) .... —1

2602[2] Brilliant **(68)** *(JPearce)* 4–7–11[(1)] WCarson (2) (hld up: hdwy on ins & n.m.r over 2f out: hmpd: r.o wl fnl f: nt rch wnr) .................................. nk.2

2173★ Eclipsing (IRE) **(83)** *(RCharlton)* 4–8–12 PatEddery (5) (hld up: stdy hdwy over 3f out: ev ch 1f out: rdn & nt qckn) ....................... ¹/₂.3

1463 Double Echo (IRE) **(67)** *(JDBethell)* 4–7–10 JLowe (1) (lw: trckd ldrs: n.m.r over 2f out: led over 1f out: sn hdd: edgd rt & no ex) ................. ¹/₂.4

2846 Jubran (USA) **(71)** *(MPNaughton)* 6–8–0 AMunro (4) (led tl over 7f out: chsd ldrs: ev ch 2f out: sn btn) .......................................... 2.5

479★ Revif (FR) **(95)** **(Fav)** *(ACStewart)* 4–9–10 MRoberts (7) (bit bkwd: trckd ldrs: drvn along over 3f out: ev ch tl wknd over 1f out) ............. nk.6

28232 North Russia (CAN) **(85)** (v) *(JHMGosden)* 3–8–8 SCauthen (6) (dwlt: sn rcvrd: led over 7f out tl hdd & wknd over 1f out) .......................... 6.7

**7/4** Revif (FR), **5/1** Eclipsing (IRE), **11/2** Brilliant, North Russia (CAN), **6/1** Jubran (USA), **8/1** FOREVER DIAMONDS, **9/1** Double Echo (IRE). CSF £47.63, Tote £7.70: £2.40 £1.90 (£13.50). Mrs J. B. Russell (MALTON) bred by J. B. Russell. 7 Rn
1m 53.69 (4.69)
SF–49/52/65/47/45/68/34

---

**3085**   BATLEYS CATERING RANGE STKS (Mdn 3-Y.O) £4659.00 (£1392.00: £666.00: £303.00)   **1¹/₄m 85y**
4-30 (4-34)

1933[4] **Larrikin (USA)** *(LordHuntingdon)* 8-9 AMunro (2) (trckd ldrs: effrt & chal over 2f out: led 1f out: drvn out) .................................... —1

29222 Unforgiving Minute 9-0 PaulEddery (9) (trckd ldrs: led 3f out: r.o u.p: nt qckn nr fin) .............................................. ¹/₂.2

22982 Alum Bay **(Fav)** *(HRACecil)* 9-0 PatEddery (1) (reluctant to go to s: hld up: rdn along over 0f out: hrd rdn & kpt on appr fnl f) ..................... 6.3

27776 Brambleberry **(67)** *(MrsSJSmith)* 8-7 ‡7JMarshall (6) (w'like: trckd ldrs: effrt over 2f out: rdn & wknd over 1f out) ....................... 3¹/₂.4

27805 Draft Board *(JHMGosden)* 8-9 MHills (7) (b.nr hind: lw: trckd ldrs: effrt 2f out:sn wknd) .......................................... 1¹/₂.5

707 Kasisi (IRE) *(ACStewart)* 8-9 MRoberts (8) (hld up: effrt 4f out: sn wl outpcd) .... 7.6

2654 Oncilla *(ACStewart)* 8-9 RHills (3) (led to 3f out: sn wknd) ............. 6.7

Boyhood (IRE) (v) *(JHMGosden)* 9-0 RCochrane (5) (w'like: str: bit bkwd: s.i.s: sn rdn: reminder 7f out: rdn & hung 3f out: sn bhd) .......... 20.8

*Fort Shirley (IRE) (5/1) Withdrawn (lame at s) : not under orders — Rule 4 applies*

**13/8** Alum Bay, **4/1** Unforgiving Minute, **9/2** LARRIKIN (USA), **5/1** Draft Board, **7/1** Boyhood (IRE), **16/1** Kasisi (IRE), **25/1** Ors. CSF £22.10, Tote £5.80: £1.70 £1.30 £1.10 (£9.00). Maverick Productions Ltd (WEST ILSLEY) bred by Maverick Production Limited in USA. 8 Rn
2m 15.98 (8.48)
SF–40/43/31/17/16/2

---

**3086**   LEVY BOARD McIVOR SCOTCH WHISKY CLAIMING STKS   £5390.00 (£1610.00: £770.00: £350.00)   **7f 202y**
5-00 (5-07)

26683 **Gant Bleu (FR) (56)** *(RMWhitaker)* 5–8–7 ACulhane (2) (lw: plld hrd: n.m.r over 2f out: swtchd ins over 1f out: sn led: fin strly) .................... —1

1696 Tusky **(79)** *(MJCamacho)* 4–9–4 SMorris (3) (bit bkwd: led: rdn & edgd rt over 1f out: kpt on same pce) ........................... 3.2

28783 Kinlacey **(60)** *(BAMcMahon)* 5–8–9 TQuinn (5) (lw: sn w ldr: ev ch tl wknd over 1f out) ...................................... 1¹/₂.3

Broughtons Turmoil *(WJMusson)* 3–8–12 JHBrown (6) (b: w'like: chsd ldrs: effrt over 2f out: nt qckn over 1f out) ...................... 3.4

2855 Savoyard **(99)** **(Fav)** *(MAJarvis)* 4–9–5 LPiggott (7) (b: trckd ldrs: effrt & rdn over 2f out: wknd 1f out) ......................... 5.5

2896 Ten High (IRE) **(31)** *(JDooler)* 3–7–13 JLowe (1) (in tch: effrt over 3f out: no imp) 2.6

532 Blanc Seing (FR) *(MWEasterby)* 5–9–2 TLucas (8) (b: sn bhd) ............ 10.7

2582 Najeb (USA) **(55)** *(BHanbury)* 3–8–2 ‡5NKennedy (4) (swtg: sn drvn along: chsd ldrs tl lost pl appr st: sn bhd) .......................... 5.8

**5/4** Savoyard(op 4/5), **5/2** Kinlacey(op 4/1), **11/2** Tusky, **8/1** GANT BLEU (FR)(op 5/1), **12/1** Najeb (USA)(op 8/1), **16/1** Broughtons Turmoil, **33/1** Blanc Seing (FR), **50/1** Ten High (IRE). CSF £47.76, Tote £8.70: £1.60 £2.00 £1.30 (£26.50). Mr E. C. Alton (WETHERBY) bred by Souren Vanian in France. 8 Rn   1m 41.61 (5.61)
SF–45/47/33/27/19/–

T/Trio: Race 3: £36.70 (43.3 Tckts) & Race 4: £289.10 (8.3 Tckts) T/Jkpt: Not won; £5,168.10 to York 3/9/92. T/Plpt: £22.40 (453.3 Tckts).
WG

## 3087–3089

# YORK (L-H)
## Thursday, September 3rd [Good]
Going Allowance: 6f 214y: 0.20 sec; Rest: 0.40 sec per fur (G)　　　Wind: fresh across

Stalls: high

---

**3087**　　'GO RACING IN YORKSHIRE' APP'CE STKS (Mdn 3-Y.O) £4644.00 (£1284.00: £612.00)
　　　　　**1m 3f 195y**　　　　　　　　　　　　　　　　　　　　　　　　　2-00 (2-01)

2336² **Kasmayo** (Fav) (JHMGosden) 8-10 ‡4SWynne (1) (lw: mde all: drew clr over 4f
　　　　　out: v easily) ........................................................................................ —1

2720⁶ Well Ahead (55) (MJohnston) 8-5 ‡4MBaird (2) (swtg: chsd wnr tl outpcd 6f out:
　　　　　n.d after) ............................................................................................... 15.2

2738⁴ Fairy Wisher (IRE) (ACStewart) 8-2 ‡7ElizabethForletta (3) (wnt 2nd 6f out: rdn &
　　　　　btn over 4f out) ....................................................................................... 4.3

**1/8** KASMAYO, **20/1** Ors. CSF £1.71, Tote £1.10 (£1.40). Sheikh Ahmed Al Maktoum (NEWMARKET) bred by
Stonethorn Stud Farms Ltd. 3 Rn　　　　　　　　　　　　　　　　　　　　　　2m 39.59 (12.59)
　　　　　　　　　　　　　　　　　　　　　　　　　　　　　　　　　　　　SF—18/–/–

---

**3088**　　QUINTIN GILBEY SILVER TROPHY (H'cap) (0-90) £6524.00 (£1952.00: £936.00:
　　　　　£428.00)　　**6f 214y**　　　　　　　　　　　　　　　　　　　　2-30 (2-31)

2656⁴ **Takenhall** (57) (MJFetherston-Godley) 7-7-13 MRoberts (12) (lw: in tch: sn
　　　　　pushed along: hdwy centre to ld ent fnl f: r.o wl) ........................................ —1

3004⁵ Boy Martin (66) (MJohnston) 3-8-4 DMcKeown (13) (lw: racd centre: hdwy u.p
　　　　　2f out: styd on nrst fin) .......................................................................... 3.2

2881³ Highland Magic (IRE) (65) (MJFetherston-Godley) 4-8-2 ‡5DHarrison (2) (lw:
　　　　　b.off hind: effrt ½-wy: styd on: nvr nrr) ..................................................... nk.3

3024⁶ Sharpalto (84) (MrsGRReveley) 5-9-12 JLowe (9) (hld up: hdwy & swtchd 2f
　　　　　out: styd on nr fin) ................................................................................. ¾.4

2658 Superbrave (76) (WJarvis) 6-9-4 MHills (8) (b: lw: hld up: shkn up 3f out: styd
　　　　　on: nt pce to chal) ................................................................................. hd.5

2956⁶ State Flyer (65) (v) (CBBBooth) 4-8-0(1) ‡7GForster (3) (hld up & bhd: shkn up
　　　　　2f out: nrst fin) ..................................................................................... nk.6

3024⁵ Super Benz (76) (TFairhurst) 6-9-4 JFanning (7) (in tch: effrt 3f out: nt qckn fnl
　　　　　f) ........................................................................................................ hd.7

2830 The Cuckoo's Nest (63) (CEBrittain) 4-8-5 MBirch (11) (chsd ldrs: c wd & led
　　　　　over 2f out tl ent fnl f: sn btn) ................................................................. s.h.8

2839 Gentle Hero (USA) (77) (MPNaughton) 6-8-12 ‡7SWynne (6) (lw: led over 2f: cl
　　　　　up tl wknd over 1f out) ........................................................................... 2.9

3068⁶ Profilic (73) (CaptJWilson) 7-8-10 ‡5KRutter (5) (lw: trckd ldrs tl lost pl 2f out: n.d
　　　　　after) .................................................................................................. hd.10

2449⁵ La Dama Bonita (USA) (83) (DWPArbuthnot) 3-9-7 BRaymond (10) (w ldrs: btn
　　　　　whn squeezed out ins fnl f) ..................................................................... 1½.11

2990⁶ Domicksky (73) (RSimpson) 4-9-1 LDettori (4) (plld hrd: led wl over 4f out tl
　　　　　over 2f out: sn lost pl) ............................................................................ 12.12

2813³ Roar on Tour (62) (v) (Fav) (MHEasterby) 3-7-11 ‡3SMaloney (1) (lw: chsd ldrs:
　　　　　rdn over 2f out: sn wknd) ........................................................................ 5.13

**4/1** Roar on Tour(op 6/1), **9/2** TAKENHALL, **8/1** Superbrave, **10/1** Gentle Hero (USA), Highland Magic (IRE),
**11/1** Sharpalto, Domicksky, **12/1** Profilic, **14/1** Super Benz, La Dama Bonita (USA), **16/1** Boy Martin, State Flyer,
**20/1** The Cuckoo's Nest. CSF £66.87, CT £629.70. Tote £4.30: £1.70 £7.40 £2.40 (£67.50). Mr Craig Pearman
(EAST ILSLEY) bred by Ballymacarney Stud. 13 Rn　　　　　　　　　　　　　　1m 26.09 (3.69)
　　　　　　　　　　　　　　　　　　　　　　　　　　　　　　SF—50/46/43/65/56/37

---

**3089**　　REFERENCE POINT STRENSALL STKS (listed race)　£11355.00 (£3390.00: £1620.00:
　　　　　£735.00)　　**1m 205y**　　　　　　　　　　　　　　　　　　　3-00 (3-01)

2643² **Spartan Shareef (IRE) (103)** (CEBrittain) 3-8-9 MRoberts (4) (lw: trkd ldrs: led
　　　　　4f out: r.o wl fnl 2f) ................................................................................ —1

2846* Badawi (USA) (100) (JHMGosden) 4-8-10 SCauthen (3) (lw: trckd ldrs: effrt &
　　　　　ev ch over 2f out: hrd rdn & nt qckn appr fnl f) ........................................... 3.2

2220 Polish Blue (USA) (100) (MRStoute) 3-8-9 LDettori (5) (bhd: hdwy 4f out: rdn &
　　　　　styd on fnl 2f) ....................................................................................... 3.3

Lech (USA) (MrsLPiggott) 4-9-7 LPiggott (1) (b: led tl hdd ent st: ev ch tl outpcd
　　　　　wl over 2f out) ....................................................................................... 3.4

2789⁵ Band on the Run (98) (BAMcMahon) 5-9-1 MHills (6) (lw: cl up tl outpcd 3f out:
　　　　　sn btn) ................................................................................................. 8.5

2402² Twist and Turn (119) (Fav) (HRACecil) 3-9-1 BRaymond (2) (w ldr: led ent st:
　　　　　hdd 4f out: sn rdn & btn) ......................................................................... 3½.6

2472* Ernestan **(100)** *(MHEasterby)* 3–8–9 MBirch (7) (in tch: shkn up over 3f out: sn btn) ............................................................. 12.7

**11/8** Twist and Turn, **9/4** Badawi (USA), **6/1** SPARTAN SHAREEF (IRE), **9/1** Polish Blue (USA), **12/1** Band on the Run, **16/1** Ernestan, **20/1** Lech (USA). CSF £19.20, Tote £7.10: £2.40 £1.70 (£9.50). Mr C. T. Olley (NEWMARKET) bred by Melchester Ltd in Ireland. 7 Rn       1m 53.31 (4.31)
SF—84/76/66/69/39/28

---

**3090**   SUN LIFE OF CANADA GARROWBY H'CAP (3-Y.O) (0-115) £15140.00 (£4520.00: £2160.00: £980.00)   **1m 3f 195y**   3-30 (3-31)

(Weights raised 20 lb)

2453 **Duke of Eurolink (91)** *(LMCumani)* 9-7 LDettori (4) (lw: hld up & bhd: stdy hdwy on bit 3f out: led ins fnl f: shkn up & r.o wl) ................ —1
2403³ Billy Blazer **(72)** *(MHTompkins)* 8-2 KDarley (5) (lw: hld up: stdy hdwy over 3f out: led 2f out: hdd ins fnl f: r.o) ..................... 1¹⁄₂.2
2780* Whirl **(77)** *(JRFanshawe)* 8-7 MHills (6) (trckd ldrs: effrt & ev ch 2f out: rdn & r.o one pce) ............................. 3.3
2886* Janaat **(74)** *(AAScott)* 8-4 JFortune (3) (hld up: stdy hdwy to chal over 2f out: sn hrd rdn & nt qckn) ..................... 2¹⁄₂.4
2615* Almuhtarama (IRE) **(80)** *(ACStewart)* 8-10 MRoberts (9) (cl up: led over 6f out tl hdd 2f out: grad wknd) ............... 1¹⁄₂.5
2798² Poinciana **(74)** *(RHannon)* 8-4 BRaymond (8) (trckd ldrs: effrt over 3f out: grad wknd) ........................... hd.6
2798* Last Embrace (IRE) **(85)** *(LordHuntingdon)* 8-10 ‡⁵DHarrison (2) (lw: hld up: hdwy 3f out: rdn over 2f out: nvr able to chal) ................ hd.7
1996⁴ Truben (USA) **(84)** *(HRACecil)* 9-0 AMcGlone (1) (cl up tl rdn & wknd 2f out) .. nk.8
2788* Million in Mind (IRE) **(88)** (Fav) *(MrsJCecil)* 9-4 PaulEddery (7) (led tl hdd over 6f out: cl up tl wknd 2f out) ..................... 2.9

**4/1** Million in Mind (IRE), **6/1** Last Embrace (IRE), DUKE OF EUROLINK, Janaat, **7/1** Almuhtarama (IRE), **8/1** Poinciana, Billy Blazer, **9/1** Ors. CSF £48.15, CT £389.82. Tote £6.00: £2.00 £2.00 £3.30 (£18.80). Eurolink Computer Services Ltd (NEWMARKET) bred by A. G. Antoniades. 9 Rn       2m 36.91 (9.91)
SF—56/34/33/25/28/21

---

**3091**   DORMAN SMITH NURSERY   £7830.00 (£2340.00: £1120.00: £510.00)   **7f 202y**   4-00 (4-02)

2872³ **Devilry (84)** *(GLewis)* 8-8 PaulEddery (4) (mid div: drvn along ¹⁄₂-wy: c wd & r.o wl fnl f to ld post) ....................... —1
2277* Chevrotain **(84)** *(JWWatts)* 8-8 SCauthen (13) (lw: trckd ldrs: rdn to ld ins fnl f: jst ct) ......................... s.h.2
2928 Key to My Heart (IRE) **(81)** *(DMoffatt)* 8-5 DMcKeown (5) (lw: a.p: ev ch & rdn over 1f out: kpt on wl) ..................... hd.3
2800² Embankment (IRE) **(85)** *(RHannon)* 8-9 MRoberts (1) (trckd ldrs: led over 4f out tl ins fnl f: no ex) ..................... 1.4
2735⁶ Argyle Cavalier (IRE) **(72)** *(FHLee)* 7-5 ‡⁵NKennedy (8) (dwlt: bhd tl hdwy over 1f out: r.o wl nr fin) ..................... nk.6
2841 Mhemeanles **(87)** *(MHEasterby)* 8-11 MBirch (14) (lw: cl up tl outpcd over 2f out: styd on nr fin) ..................... 2.7
2818⁴ Best Appearance (IRE) **(69)** *(JGFitzGerald)* 7-7 JFanning (3) (lw: trckd ldrs: disp ld 3f out: sn rdn: wknd 1f out) ..................... 1.8
2841* Noyan **(97)** *(MBell)* 9-7 MHills (2) (lw: led tl hdd over 4f out: kpt on same pce) .. 1.8
2938 Boldville Bash (IRE) **(69)** (Fav) *(TDBarron)* 7-7 JLowe (10) (lw: bhd: effrt 4f out: hrd rdn & styd on: no imp) ..................... hd.9
3044⁵ Costa Verde **(84)** *(KWHogg)* 8-8 JCorrigan (12) (hld up & bhd: effrt over 3f out: hrd rdn & wnt tl fnl: no imp) ..................... 1¹⁄₂.10
1690⁴ Razaroo (USA) **(76)** *(JEtherington)* 8-0⁽¹⁾ KDarley (9) (outpcd ¹⁄₂-wy: n.d after) 4.11
2864 Half a Dozen (USA) **(79)** *(AAScott)* 8-3 JFortune (6) (lost tch fr ¹⁄₂-wy: t.o) ......... 12
LONG HANDICAP: Best Appearance (IRE) 7-5, Boldville Bash (IRE) 7-6.

**9/2** Boldville Bash (IRE), **5/1** Embankment (IRE), **11/2** Chevrotain, **13/2** DEVILRY, **7/1** Best Appearance (IRE), **15/2** Noyan, **8/1** Mhemeanles, **11/1** Key to My Heart (IRE), **14/1** Argyle Cavalier (IRE), **16/1** Half a Dozen (USA), **20/1** Ors. CSF £42.51, CT £361.14. Tote £6.30: £2.30 £1.90 £2.20 (£12.30). Lady McIndoe (EPSOM) bred by Tarworth Bloodstock Investments Ltd. 12 Rn       1m 42.32 (6.32)
SF—47/46/42/43/22/41

---

**3092**   HUNTINGTON GRADUATION STKS (2-Y.O) £5162.50 (£1540.00: £735.00: £332.50)   **6f 214y**   4-30 (4-30)

**Kusamba (USA)** *(RCharlton)* 8-6 MHills (6) (small: neat: lw: hld up: effrt over 2f out: led over 1f out: rdn & r.o wl) ................ —1

Black Dragon (IRE) *(BWHills)* 8-8(2) SCauthen (5) (cmpt: unf: cl up: led 2f out: hdd appr fnl f: r.o u.p) ............................................ 1/2.2

Yawl (Fav) *(BWHills)* 8-1 DHolland (7) (leggy: scope: hld up: hdwy to chal 1/2-wy: rdn & nt qckn appr fnl f) ............................................ 5.3

2835 Anaheim (IRE) **(91)** *(RHannon)* 9-2 BRaymond (3) (led tl hdd 2f out: sn outpcd) 3.4

2912⁶ Royal Roller (IRE) **(94)** *(CNAllen)* 8-11 LPiggott (5) (lw: chsd ldrs tl rdn & btn 2f out) ............................................ 1½.5

Hatta Sunshine (USA) *(JHMGosden)* 8-6 LDettori (4) (lengthy: unf: prom tl outpcd fnl 3f) ............................................ 8.6

Trachelium *(JHanson)* 8-1 EJohnson (1) (rangy: bit bkwd: s.i.s: outpcd & bhd) 30.7

**11/4** Yawl, **3/1** Royal Roller (IRE), **4/1** KUSAMBA (USA), Hatta Sunshine (USA), **5/1** Black Dragon (IRE), **6/1** Anaheim (IRE), **20/1** Trachelium. CSF £24.75, Tote £5.60: £2.70 £2.80 (£17.70). Mr S. S. Niarchos (BECKHAMPTON) bred by Flaxman Holdings Limited in USA. 7 Rn 1m 26.89 (4.49)
SF—46/46/24/30/20/–

T/Trio: Race 2: £162.60 (8.2 Tckts) & Race 4: £181.80 (7 Tckts). T/Jkpt: Not won; £8,199.20 to York 4/9/92. T/Plpt: £445.70 (16.6 Tckts). AA

---

2881—**SALISBURY (R-H)**

**Thursday, September 3rd [Good to soft becoming Soft]**

Going Allowance: St: 0.70; Rnd: 0.50 sec per fur (Y) Wind: mod against

Stalls: centre

**3093** E.B.F. QUIDHAMPTON STKS (I) (Mdn 2-Y.O.F) £3174.50 (£882.00: £423.50)
**6f 212y** 2-20 (2-23)

2338⁵ **Thawakib (IRE)** *(JLDunlop)* 8-11 WCarson (3) (lw: led over 4f out: pushed out) —1

2438² Zenith (Fav) *(IABalding)* 8-11 JReid (11) (a.p: rdn over 2f out: ev ch over 1f out: r.o) ............................................ 1½.2

2930⁴ Cashell *(MRStoute)* 8-11 BRouse (5) (rdn over 3f out: hdwy over 2f out: r.o one pce) ............................................ 8.3

2792 Diplomatist *(IABalding)* 8-11 RCochrane (2) (lw: a.p: no hdwy fnl 2f) ............ 1/2.4

2459 Glimpse of Heaven *(DRCElsworth)* 8-11 MTebbutt (4) (hld up: no hdwy fnl 2f) 1.5

Amistina *(RCharlton)* 8-11 PatEddery (13) (leggy: hld up: shkn up over 2f out: clearfvd over 1f out) ............................................ 8.6

1591 Tartouka *(GLewis)* 8-11 AClark (10) (nvr trbld ldrs) ............................................ 3/4.7

Bronze Maquette (IRE) *(PFICole)* 8-11 TQuinn (7) (unf: scope: bit bkwd: prom 5f: eased whn btn over 1f out) ............................................ 5.8

933 Fir Copse *(PRHedger)* 8-11 DBiggs (12) (lw: bmpd s: sn rcvrd: wknd over 1f out) ............................................ 3/4.9

Fast Fiesta *(MRChannon)* 8-8 ‡3RPerham (1) (str: dwlt: a bhd) ............ 2.10

2826 Jafetica *(DRLaing)* 8-6 ‡5ATucker (9) (plld hrd: led over 2f: wknd over 2f out) .. 1/2.11

1342 Is She Quick *(MrsJCDawe)* 8-11 NHowe (6) (prom over 3f) ............................................ 2.12

Tempesta Rossa (IRE) *(BWHills)* 8-11 RHills (4) (unf: scope: bit bkwd: a bhd) nk.13

Clearfoot *(RJHolder)* 8-11 JWilliams (6) (leggy: a bhd) ............................................ 1.14

**2/1** Zenith, **3/1** Cashell(op 5/1), **5/1** THAWAKIB (IRE)(op 3/1), **13/2** Bronze Maquette (IRE), **10/1** Tempesta Rossa (IRE)(op 6/1), **12/1** Amistina(op 6/1), **16/1** Diplomatist, **20/1** Fast Fiesta, Tartouka, Glimpse of Heaven, **33/1** Ors. CSF £16.39, Tote £5.00: £1.90 £1.40 £1.60 (£4.70). Mr Hamdan Al-Maktoum (ARUNDEL) bred by Barronstown & Gainesway T'bred Ltd in Ireland. 14 Rn 1m 33.74 (8.04)
SF—50/45/21/19/16/–

**3094** H.S. LESTER MEMORIAL CHALLENGE CUP (H'cap) (0-90) £3915.00 (£1170.00: £407.50 each) **1m 1f 209y** 2-50 (2-53)

(Weights raised 7 lb)

2806³ L'Uomo Classics **(64)** *(RRowe)* 5-9-0 GBaxter (5) (led 2f: led over 1f out: drvn out) ............................................ —1

Cadency **(69)** *(MHTompkins)* 4-9-5 RCochrane (3) (hld up & bhd: hdwy over 2f out: hrd rdn & ev ch ins fnl f: r.o) .. nk.2

2788³ Matching Green **(69)** (Fav) *(GBBalding)* 3-8-12 JWilliams (1) (prom: rdn over 2f out: swtchd rt over 1f out: r.o wl ins fnl f) ............................................ s.h.3

2780 Heniu (USA) **(65)** *(LordHuntingdon)* 3-8-8 TQuinn (4) (led after 2f tl over 1f out: r.o) ............................................ d.h.3

2693∗ Scottish Bambi **(74)** *(RHannon)* 4-9-7 ‡3RPerham (6) (lw: hld up: hdwy 3f out: rdn 1f out: wknd fnl f) ............................................ 7.5

2846 Camden's Ransom (USA) **(72)** *(DRCElsworth)* 5-9-8 WCarson (2) (hld up & plld hrd: bhd fnl 2f) ............................................ 3½.6

11/4 Matching Green, 3/1 Camden's Ransom (USA), 7/2 Scottish Bambi, 11/2 L'UOMO CLASSICS(8/1—5/1), 13/2 Heniu (USA)(op 4/1), 10/1 Cadency(6/1—12/1). CSF £45.28, Tote £8.70: £3.20 £2.30 (£35.90). Mrs Ann Galvanoni (PULBOROUGH) bred by W. and Mrs Whitehead. 6 Rn

2m 19.02 (14.32)

SF—7/11/3/–/–/–

**3095**     E.B.F. 'WESSEX STALLIONS' H'CAP (F & M) (0-90) £9650.00 (£2900.00: £1400.00: £650.00))   **6f 212y**

3-20 (3-26)

2825⁵ **Queen of Shannon (IRE) (70)** *(DMorris)* 4–9-3 MTebbutt (14) (chsd ldr far side: hrd rdn over 1f out: edgd lft fnl f: led cl home) .......... —1

2795⁵ Abbey Strand (USA) **(70)** *(LordHuntingdon)* 3–8-13 JReid (13) (led far side group: led 1f out: hdd nr fin) ................................................. 1.2

2601* Muhit (USA) **(77)** *(PTWalwyn)* 3–9-6 WCarson (11) (lw: a.p: hrd rdn 2f out: r.o ins fnl f) ....................................................................... nk.3

1755² Jaldi (IRE) **(70)** (bl) *(JSutcliffe)* 4–9-3 PatEddery (1) (led: clr stands' side & rdn 2f out: hdd over 1f out: no ex ins fnl f) ............................... 1¹/₄.4

2795 Lady Debra Darley **(83)** *(RHannon)* 3–9-9 ‡³RPerham (3) (lw: hdwy over 3f out: hrd rdn 2f out: r.o one pce) ........................................ hd.5

2753³ Acara (IRE) **(58)** *(CJames)* 3–8-1 JQuinn (4) (hdwy 3f out: wknd over 1f out) .... 6.6

2755 Pure Formality **(80)** (bl) *(DRCElsworth)* 3–9-9 TQuinn (6) (hdwy 3f out: wknd over 1f out) ............................................................................ hd.7

2861⁵ Blue Topaze **(68)** *(RJHolder)* 4–9-1 JWilliams (5) (lw: hld up: hdwy 3f out: rdn & wknd over 1f out) ...................................................... 2¹/₂.8

2229⁹ Sunley Silks **(78)** *(MRChannon)* 3–9-2 ‡⁵ATucker (8) (prom 4f) ........... 3¹/₂.9

2861² Baligay **(78)** *(RJHodges)* 7–9-4 ‡7SDrowne (2) (spd over 3f: t.o) ...................... 7.10

2684⁴ Teanarco (IRE) **(63)** *(RJHolder)* 4–8-10 DBiggs (12) (bhd fnl 3f: t.o) ................ 2¹/₂.11

2825 Shaping Up **(79)** (bl) *(IABalding)* 3–9-8 RCochrane (9) (a bhd: t.o) ............ ¹/₂.12

2958² Tender Moment (IRE) **(67)** *(Fav)* *(CEBrittain)* 4–9-0 RHills (10) (a bhd: t.o) ... 1¹/₂.13

1403 Morgannwg (IRE) (20/1) Withdrawn (uns rdr & bolted gng to s) : not under orders

4/1 Tender Moment (IRE)(6/1—13/2), 9/2 Jaldi (IRE), 5/1 Blue Topaze, 8/1 Abbey Strand (USA), 9/1 Sunley Silks, 10/1 Muhit (USA), 12/1 Baligay, QUEEN OF SHANNON (IRE), 14/1 Lady Debra Darley, 16/1 Pure Formality, Shaping Up (USA), Teanarco (IRE), 20/1 Acara (IRE). CSF £102.23, CT £926.45. Tote £20.20: £5.20 £3.20 £2.70 (£181.80). The Killoughery Family (NEWMARKET) bred by George Killoughery in Ireland. 13 Rn

1m 35.36 (9.66)

SF—32/25/31/23/28/–

**3096**     DICK POOLE STKS (2-Y.O.F) £7497.50 (£2255.00: £1090.00: £507.50)   **6f**

3-50 (3-51)

2792² **Catherineofaragon (79)** *(WGRWightman)* 8-9 JWilliams (7) (w ldr tl led 3f out: drew clr fnl f) ................................................................... —1

2686² Seasonal Splendour (IRE) *(CACyzer)* 8-9 DBiggs (9) (rdn & lost pl over 3f out: rallied fnl f) ............................................................................... 10.2

2826* Simply Sooty **(84)** *(BRMillman)* 8-12 GBaxter (4) (led 3f out: ev ch over 1f out: one pce) ................................................................................ hd.3

1925⁴ Cristal Flite *(RHannon)* 8-9 RHills (6) (a.p: ev ch wl over 1f out: one pce) ........ nk.4

2452⁶ Anonymous **(95)** *(CEBrittain)* 9-4 GCrealock (8) (no hdwy fnl 2f) ..................... 7.5

Barboukh *(DRCElsworth)* 8-9 TQuinn (2) (w'like: scope: bit bkwd: hdwy 2f out: wknd fnl f) ................................................................................... hd.6

2657⁵ Mrs West (USA) **(95)** *(JLDunlop)* 8-12 JReid (5) (lw: hld up: hdwy 2f out: eased whn btn fnl f) ............................................................................ hd.7

2171* Poker Chip **(79)** *(Fav)* *(IABalding)* 8-12 RCochrane (1) (lw: rdn & hdwy over 2f out: wknd over 1f out) ..................................................... ³/₄.8

2850⁴ Northern Bird **(91)** *(BWHills)* 9-1 WCarson (2) (b.hind: lw: prom 4f: t.o) .......... 5.9

11/4 Poker Chip, 3/1 Northern Bird, 4/1 Barboukh, 6/1 Simply Sooty, 8/1 Mrs West (USA), Anonymous, 12/1 CATHERINEOFARAGON, Cristal Flite(op 8/1), 16/1 Seasonal Splendour (IRE). CSF £164.73, Tote £9.80: £2.40 £2.90 £1.60 (£62.90). Mr T. R. Mountain (UPHAM) bred by T. R. Mountain. 9 Rn

1m 20.41 (8.11)

SF—17/–/–/–/–/–

**3097**     SALISBURY FESTIVAL H'CAP (0-70) £3199.00 (£889.00: £427.00)   **1¹/₂m**

4-20 (4-21)

2886² **Sheringa (65)** *(GBBalding)* 3–9-6 JWilliams (13) (hld up: hdwy over 3f out: led over 2f out: r.o wl) ......................................................... —1

2993* Bo Knows Best (IRE) **(45)** *(Fav)* *(JSutcliffe)* 3–7-9⁽¹⁾ (5x) ‡⁵ATucker (8) (hld up & bhd: stdy hdwy fnl 2f: too much to do) .............................. 5.2

3064⁴ Thimbalina **(39)** *(DAWilson)* 6–8-3 WCarson (10) (b: prom: ev ch over 2f out: one pce) ................................................................................... 5.3

2993⁵ Eleckydo **(49)** *(RJHodges)* 3–7-11⁽⁶⁾ ‡7SDrowne (11) (hdwy 5f out: one pce fnl 2f) ............................................................................................... ¹/₂.4

2827⁴ Striking Image (IRE) **(64)** *(RHannon)* 3-9-5 PatEddery (5) (lw: led 3f: led over 3f out tl over 2f out: sn wknd) ...................................... 6.5
2391⁵ Moot Point (USA) **(52)** (bl) *(JRJenkins)* 4-9-2 GBaxter (3) (lw: nvr nrr) .............. 2.6
2934³ Polistatic **(39)** *(CAHorgan)* 5-8-3 DaleGibson (2) (prom: rdn 4f out: wknd 3f out) 8.7
2823³ Big Beat (USA) **(60)** *(DRCElsworth)* 4-9-10 TQuinn (1) (led 9f out tl over 4f out: wknd 3f out) .................................................. 1½.8
2774⁵ Viaggio **(55)** (bl) *(JAkehurst)* 4-9-5 RCochrane (12) (prom: led over 4f out tl over 3f out: sn wknd) ...................................... hd.9
2860 Latour **(56)** *(CEBrittain)* 4-9-6 GCrealock (4) (prom: rdn & wknd over 2f out) 3½.10
2828 Tenayestelign **(32)** *(DMarks)* 4-7-10 SDawson (6) (hdwy 5f out: wknd over 2f out) ........................................................... 1.11
2882 Morgans Ace **(47)** *(BRMillman)* 3-8-2 JQuinn (7) (lw: a bhd: t.o) .................... 7.12
Golden Gunner (IRE) **(58)** *(MMcCourt)* 4-9-8 MPerrett (9) (t.o fnl 4f) ............ dist.13

2/1 Bo Knows Best (IRE), 9/2 Thimbalina(7/1—8/1), 5/1 SHERINGA, 9/1 Striking Image (IRE)(op 6/1), 10/1 Polistatic(op 6/1), Latour, 11/1 Viaggio(7/1—12/1), 12/1 Big Beat (USA), 20/1 Ors. CSF £15.81, CT £43.80. Tote £6.10: £2.20 £1.80 £2.00 (£7.70). Mr David Shering (DORCHESTER) bred by Ron Fear. 13 Rn
2m 44 (11.40)
SF—52/17/15/8/18/11

---

**3098**  BLANDFORD H'CAP (0-80) £3450.75 (£1032.00: £494.50: £225.75)  **5f** 4-50 (4-51)

2989² **Bells of Longwick (64)** (v) *(Fav)* *(DRLaing)* 3-8-7 ‡5ATucker (11) (a.p: led over 1f out: rdn & edgd lft wl ins fnl f: r.o) ................ —1
2919 Face North (IRE) **(55)** *(ARDavison)* 4-8-5 TQuinn (3) (rdn & hdwy 2f out: ev ch over 1f out: btn whn nt clr run nr fin) ..................... 1.2
2997 Martinosky **(63)** *(WGRWightman)* 6-8-13 JWilliams (2) (bhd tl hdwy over 1f out: r.o ins fnl f) ....................................... ³⁄₄.3
2881 John O'Dreams **(44)** *(MrsJCDawe)* 7-7-8(¹) JQuinn (8) (led over 3f: one pce) 2¹⁄₂.4
2963* Miss Vaxette **(70)** *(JLSpearing)* 3-8-11 ‡7MHumphries (10) (prom over 3f) ........ ¹⁄₂.5
2952 Golden Proposal **(46)** *(MJBolton)* 3-7-8(¹) DaleGibson (4) (prom tl hrd rdn & wknd over 1f out) ......................................... 1.6
2866⁵ Unveiled **(62)** *(RJHodges)* 4-8-12 PatEddery (5) (sme hdwy whn nt clr run over 1f out: n.d) .................................... 2.7
1474 Pharaoh's Dancer **(73)** *(EAWheeler)* 5-9-9 MWigham (9) (a bhd) .................... ³⁄₄.8
2906² Noble Power (IRE) **(74)** *(BPalling)* 3-9-8 RHills (6) (bhd fnl 2f) ..................... 1¹⁄₂.9
2642 Fivesevenfiveo **(75)** *(RJHodges)* 4-9-4 ‡7SDrowne (1) (a bhd) .................... 2¹⁄₂.10
2779⁶ Seneca Reef (IRE) **(76)** (v) *(IABalding)* 4-9-12 RCochrane (7) (prom 3f) ........ 1.11
LONG HANDICAP: John O'Dreams 7-2, Golden Proposal 7-4.

*Stewards Enquiry: Trainer & rdr of Pharaoh's Dancer each fined £350 under Rule 151 (ii) (failure to ensure best possible placing).*

4/1 BELLS OF LONGWICK, 9/2 Unveiled, 5/1 Miss Vaxette, 6/1 Seneca Reef (IRE), 7/1 Pharaoh's Dancer, 9/1 Martinosky(op 6/1), 10/1 Face North (IRE), 14/1 Fivesevenfiveo, Noble Power (IRE), John O'Dreams, 33/1 Golden Proposal. CSF £41.51, CT £316.86. Tote £5.70: £1.70 £4.10 £2.40 (£42.50). Mrs Marion Wickham (LAMBOURN) bred by Mrs Wickham. 11 Rn
66.08 sec (6.08)
SF—41/35/40/11/26/5

---

**3099**  E.B.F. QUIDHAMPTON STKS (II) (Mdn 2-Y.O.F) £3150.00 (£875.00: £420.00)
6f 212y  5-20 (5-23)

Forthwith *(RHannon)* 8-11 BRouse (12) (lt-f: hdwy 2f out: led ins fnl f: r.o wl) .... —1
2884⁴ Bright Spells *(Fav)* *(DRCElsworth)* 8-11 JWilliams (6) (led tl ins fnl f) ................ 2¹⁄₂.2
Forest Song *(RCharlton)* 8-11 DaleGibson (2) (neat: hdwy over 2f out: hrd rdn over 1f out: r.o one pce) ....................... ³⁄₄.3
2598 Beyond the Limit *(LadyHerries)* 8-11 AClark (7) (dwlt: hdwy over 3f out: one pce fnl 2f) .............................................. 3.4
2438 Smart Daisy *(IABalding)* 8-11 RCochrane (4) (prom: rdn over 3f out: wknd fnl f) 1¹⁄₂.5
2544 Swift Revenge *(MRChannon)* 8-11 JQuinn (9) (plld hrd: no hdwy fnl 2f) ............. 7.6
2864³ Lakab (USA) *(HThomsonJones)* 8-11 RHills (3) (lw: hdwy 4f out: wknd 2f out) nk.7
Swiss Mountain *(DRLaing)* 8-6 ‡5ATucker (10) (neat: bit bkwd: bhd fnl 2f) ........ ³⁄₄.8
1279⁶ Summit Fever (IRE) *(PFICole)* 8-11 TQuinn (11) (prom over 4f) .................... 5.9
Admired *(MRChannon)* 8-11 PatEddery (8) (unf: bit bkwd: prom 4f) ............... nk.10
Shalholme *(RJHolder)* 8-11 JReid (13) (neat: dwlt: a bhd) ..................... 3.11
Alwal *(CJames)* 8-11 GBaxter (5) (leggy: prom 3f: t.o) .......................... 5.12
2713⁴ Merch Fach (IRE) **(56)** *(JDRoberts)* 8-11 TLang (1) (dwlt: a bhd: t.o) ............. 15.13

9/4 Bright Spells, 4/1 Smart Daisy, Lakab (USA)(3/1—9/2), 11/2 Beyond the Limit(5/1—8/1), 15/2 Admired(5/1—12/1), 9/1 Summit Fever (IRE)(4/1—10/1), 14/1 Forest Song, FORTHWITH, 25/1 Shalholme, 33/1 Alwal, Swift Revenge, Swiss Mountain, 50/1 Merch Fach (IRE). CSF £47.39, Tote £19.50: £6.30 £1.60 £4.00 (£49.60). Mr L. H. J. Ward (MARLBOROUGH) bred by L. H. J. Ward. 13 Rn
1m 35.26 (9.56)
SF—28/20/18/9/4/–

T/Plpt: £595.60 (5.05 Tckts).
KH

3049—**WOLVERHAMPTON (L-H)**
**Thursday, September 3rd [Good]**
Going Allowance: 0.10 sec per fur (G)

Wind: fresh bhd

Stalls: high

**3100**   CANAL BARGE STKS (I) (Mdn 2-Y.O) £2574.00 (£714.00: £342.00)   **7f**   2-10 (2-13)

2629³ **Carelaman** (JLDunlop) 9-0 WRyan (6) (4th st: shkn up 2f out: led appr fnl f: comf) ....................................................................................................... —1
828³ The Informer (USA) (Fav) (PFICole) 9-0 AMunro (3) (bit bkwd: led: rdn over 2f out: hdd 1f out: rallied nr fin) ............................................................... ¹/₂.2
1348⁵ Bagalino (USA) (RCharlton) 9-0 GCarter (9) (bit bkwd: chsd ldrs: 3rd st: one pce fnl 2f) ................................................................................................ 5.3
446 Roger the Butler (IRE) (MBell) 9-0 GDuffield (12) (bkwd: 6th st: rdn & effrt over 2f out: nt rch ldrs) ....................................................................................... 2.4
2426⁵ Native Trio (USA) (PWHarris) 9-0 SWhitworth (1) (chsd ldr: rdn over 2f out: edgd rt: sn btn) ............................................................................................... 2.5
2733 Mr Geneaology (USA) (JLSpearing) 9-0 GHind (2) (in tch: effrt 3f out: nvr nr to chal) .................................................................................................................. ¹/₂.6
2728 Russia Pobeda (USA) (MrsLPiggott) 8-9 PRobinson (5) (b.hind: 5th st: wknd 3f out) ............................................................................................................ nk.7
2002⁴ Turfmans Vision (RHollinshead) 8-7 ‡AGarth (4) (dwlt: a in rr: t.o) .................. 10.8
Ark Celeste (WWHaigh) 8-9 SWebster (7) (leggy: lt-f: s.i.s: a bhd: t.o) ............ 1¹/₂.9
Annyban (EJAlston) 8-9 KFallon (8) (scope: bkwd: a bhd: t.o) ........................... 3.10
2947² Giordano (IRE) (WRMuir) 9-0 JLloyd (10) (chsd ldrs 5f: sn lost tch: t.o) ........ 2¹/₂.11
2396 Ess-Pee-Cee (WClay) 0-4 ‡NPrice (11) (sn bhd & t.o) ..................................... 12.12

10/11 The Informer (USA), 11/2 Bagalino (USA), CARELAMAN, 11/1 Native Trio (USA), 14/1 Giordano (IRE)(op 8/1), 16/1 Russia Pobeda (USA)(op 10/1), 25/1 Roger the Butler (IRE), Turfmans Vision, 33/1 Mr Geneaology (USA), 50/1 Annyban, Ark Celeste, 100/1 Ess-Pee-Cee. CSF £10.30, Tote £5.90: £1.90 £1.10 £1.70 (£3.20). Mr P. G. Goulandris (ARUNDEL) bred by Hesmonds Stud Ltd. 12 Rn                                     1m 28.8 (4.5)
SF—43/41/26/20/14/12

**3101**   VALLEY PARK CLAIMING STKS   £2973.00 (£828.00: £399.00)   **1m**   2-40 (2-44)

2755 **Absonal** (70) (Jt-Fav) (RHannon) 5-8-13 GDuffield (1) (hld up: hdwy over 2f out: led 1f out: r.o wl) .......................................................................................... —1
2814 Kummel King (62) (EJAlston) 4-8-13 KFallon (12) (hdwy 3f out: rdn & ev ch 2f out: unable qckn fnl f) ................................................................................... 1¹/₂.2
2581 Chloes Diamond (IRE) (43) (JLSpearing) 4-8-2 AlexGreaves (20) (hdwy to ld over 2f out: hdd 1f out: one pce) ....................................................................... 2¹/₂.3
2630⁵ Friendlypersuasion (IRE) (38) (RHollinshead) 4-8-9 WRyan (10) (hdwy over 2f out: nrst fin) ......................................................................................................... 1¹/₂.4
2644 Shoehorn (55) (REPeacock) 5-8-5 GCarter (17) (b: hdwy over 2f out: nt rch ldrs) 4.5
Yankee Flyer (57) (MissSJWilton) 5-8-6 ‡SWilliams (4) (bit bkwd: effrt & swtchd ins over 3f out: r.o one pce) .......................................................... 1¹/₂.6
3052³ Sanawi (50) (PDEvans) 5-8-8 ‡⁵LNewton (13) (r.o appr fnl f: nvr nrr) .............. hd.7
2416 Willesdon (USA) (39) (v) (ABarrow) 8-8-11 NAdams (5) (b.hind: hdwy u.p 3f out: nt pce to chal) ............................................................................................ 3¹/₂.8
2953⁶ Rock Band (IRE) (63) (Jt-Fav) (LMCumani) 3-8-5 ‡⁵JWeaver (8) (prom: 4th st: ev ch 2f out: eased whn btn fnl f) ............................................................... ¹/₂.9
Brenda From Huby (41) (BCMorgan) 4-8-2 GBardwell (9) (bkwd: chsd ldrs: 5th st: wknd over 2f out) ..................................................................................... hd.10
2935⁵ Homile (47) (BAMcMahon) 4-9-1 AMunro (2) (chsd ldrs 5f) ........................... 1.11
2712 Shalou (56) (RJHodges) 3-8-5 ‡³FNorton (3) (prom: 6th st: rdn & wknd 2f out) hd.12
2967² Arjjil (v) (MHTompkins) 3-8-6 PRobinson (15) (b.bhd: t.o) ............................. 1¹/₂.13
3073 Cromer's Express (47) (MissLCSiddall) 3-7-13 ‡⁷SMulvey (18) (s.s: a bhd) .... ¹/₂.14
2931⁶ Another Nut (39) (PDEvans) 3-7-4 ‡⁷AGarth (7) (chsd ldr: 2nd st: wknd over 2f out) ..................................................................................................................... 2.15
Apple (53) (WHolden) 3-8-12 NCarlisle (14) (b: bkwd: m.n.s) ......................... 2¹/₂.16
2729⁴ A Nymph Too Far (IRE) (37) (v) (DrJDScargill) 3-7-4⁽²⁾ ‡⁷CHawksley (11) (b.hind: prom: 3rd st: wknd wl over 2f out) ...................................................... ¹/₂.17
2958 Quiet Victory (45) (MissLCSiddall) 5-8-6 TyroneWilliams (6) (led: sn wl clr: rdn 3f out: hdd & wknd over 2f out: t.o) ........................................................... 7.18
2753 Sir Joey (USA) (RJHolder) 3-8-12 ADicks (19) (t.o) ........................................ 1¹/₂.19
2933⁶ Master D Dee (PWHarris) 4-9-3 SWhitworth (16) (a bhd: t.o) ........................ 4.20

**3102—3103**

**4/1** Rock Band (IRE)(op 6/1), ABSONAL(op 9/4), **11/2** Sanawi, **11/1** Arjjil(8/1—12/1), **12/1** Homile, Kummel King(8/1—14/1), Shoehorn(op 7/1), **16/1** Shalou, **25/1** Friendlypersuasion (IRE), Chloes Diamond (IRE), Quiet Victory, **33/1** Another Nut, Yankee Flyer, Sir Joey (USA), **40/1** A Nymph Too Far (IRE), Apple, **50/1** Ors. CSF £47.02, Tote £2.70: £2.10 £4.50 £16.00 (£29.20). Capt R. W. Hornall (MARLBOROUGH) bred by Mrs Nerys Dutfield. 20 Rn
1m 42.7 (5.4)
SF—30/25/6/8/–/–

**3102**  SMESTOW BROOK H'CAP (3-Y.O) (0-70) £2553.00 (£708.00: £339.00)
1¾m 134y                                                        3-10 (3-14)

27312 **Heavenly Waters (55)** *(RFJohnsonHoughton)* 8-6 GDuffield (5) (b.hind: bhd: hdwy over 2f out: led ins fnl f: r.o wl) ......................... —1

28334 Jupiter Moon (60) *(CEBrittain)* 8-11 AMunro (7) (prom: 4th st: led 1f out: sn hdd & one pce) ............................................... 2½.2

26315 Indian Territory (55) *(DHaydnJones)* 8-6 TyroneWilliams (9) (hdwy & 3rd st: led over 3f out tl ins fnl f: one pce) ......................... 1½.3

25805 Silken Words (USA) (54) *(WRMuir)* 8-6 JLloyd (13) (hdwy over 2f out: styd on appr fnl f: nvr nrr) ............................................... 2½.4

2985★ Fair Flyer (IRE) (57) *(Fav) (MJohnston)* 8-8 (4x) RPElliott (3) (lw: hdwy 3f out: rdn over 1f out: sn wknd) ......................... 2.5

27162 White Wedding (51) *(PFICole)* 8-2 CRutter (12) (b.off hind: sme late hdwy: nvr nrr) ............................................... 4.6

2992 Corinthian God (IRE) (49) *(DAWilson)* 8-0 GBardwell (4) (a in rr: t.o) ............ 15.7

2759 Taroob (IRE) (70) *(JLDunlop)* 9-7 GHind (11) (chsd ldrs over 10f: grad wknd: t.o) ............................................... ½.8

2783⁵ Child Star (FR) (49) *(DMarks)* 7-7 ‡⁷AGarth (1) (led over 7f: led ent st tl over 3f out: sn wknd: t.o) ............................................... 2.9

28684 Swan Heights (59) *(JRFanshawe)* 8-10 GCarter (10) (chsd ldrs: 5th st: rdn & wknd 3f out: t.o) ............................................... 8.10

29152 Drought (IRE) (67) *(MRStoute)* 9-4 WRyan (14) (chsd ldr: led 7f out tl hdd & 2nd st: wknd 3f out: t.o) ............................................... 2½.11

2793 Highland Battle (USA) (64) *(IABalding)* 9-1 PRobinson (6) (a bhd: t.o) ............ 2.12

28674 Briggs Lad (IRE) (68) (bl) *(WJarvis)* 9-5 JCarroll (8) (chsd ldrs: 6th st: rdn 3f out: sn wknd: t.o) ............................................... 2.13

2915 Dordogne (49) *(RAkehurst)* 7-11 ‡³FNorton (2) (opt pl ½-wy: t.o) ............ 2.14

**100/30** Fair Flyer (IRE)(5/1—3/1), **9/2** Drought (IRE), **13/2** HEAVENLY WATERS, **8/1** White Wedding, **9/1** Highland Battle (USA), **12/1** Briggs Lad (IRE), **14/1** Jupiter Moon, Corinthian God (IRE), **16/1** Child Star (FR), Taroob (IRE), Swan Heights, **20/1** Dordogne, **25/1** Indian Territory, **33/1** Silken Words (USA). CSF £87.41, CT £1,957.94. Tote £10.30: £3.10 £3.00 £8.00 (£221.80). Mr R. Crutchley (DIDCOT) bred by R. E. Crutchley. 14 Rn
3m 13.7 (7.7)
SF—29/29/21/14/14/–

**3103**  AUTUMN H'CAP (0-70) £2595.00 (£720.00: £345.00)   **5f**   3-40 (3-50)

2234 **Cranfield Comet (60)** *(JBerry)* 3-9-2 JCarroll (3) (a.p: led appr fnl f: rdn out) ... —1

2822 Little Saboteur (55) *(PJMakin)* 3-8-11 TSprake (1) (hdwy 2f out: rdn & r.o wl nr fin) ............................................... 1½.2

2989★ Ballasecret (70) *(RDickin)* 4-9-7 ‡⁷DMeredith (19) (led tl appr fnl f: kpt on u.p ins fnl f) ............................................... ¾.3

29894 Stocktina (41) *(RJHodges)* 5-7-10 ‡³FNorton (6) (chsd ldrs: kpt on ins fnl f: nvr able to chal) ............................................... 2.4

2984 Lonely Lass (41) *(AWJones)* 6-7-6 ‡⁷ClaireBalding (9) (lw: hdwy over 1f out: kpt on ins fnl f) ............................................... ½.5

29362 Banham College (56) *(BAMcMahon)* 6-9-0 AMunro (11) (a.p: rdn over 1f out: no exl fnl f) ............................................... 1½.6

27265 Farmer Jock (54) (bl) *(MrsNMacauley)* 10-8-7 ‡⁵SWilliams (7) (b: lw: outpcd tl r.o ins fnl f) ............................................... ½.7

5912 We're All Game (60) *(BCMorgan)* 3-9-2 PRobinson (18) (bkwd: nvr nrr) ............ 2.8

2909 Musval (52) *(RHannon)* 3-8-8 JLloyd (14) (spd over 3f) ............ ½.9

3079★ Lincstone Boy (IRE) (52) (bl) *(SRBowring)* 4-8-10 (7x) SWebster (20) (in tch over 3f) ............................................... 1½.10

2747 Jess Rebec (53) *(LGCottrell)* 4-8-11 NCarlisle (17) (nvr trbld ldrs) ............ 3.11

2963 Lonsom Lass (41) *(LJBarratt)* 4-9-8 LCharnock (5) (gd spd 3f) ............ 2½.12

2718 Pendor Dancer (52) (bl) *(BForsey)* 9-8-10 SWhitworth (15) (n.d) ............ ½.13

2861 Maria Cappuccini (50) *(KOCunningham-Brown)* 4-8-8 GBardwell (16) (w ldrs 3f: sn outpcd) ............................................... hd.14

29196 Joe Sugden (55) *(PHowling)* 8-8-13 GDuffield (13) (gd spd 3f) ............ 1.15

2772 Hitchin a Ride (43) (bl) *(MPMuggeridge)* 5-8-1 TyroneWilliams (10) (m.n.s) .... 1.16

27726 Petitesse (43) *(GBlum)* 4-8-1 AShoults (12) (m.n.s) ............ 1.17

3068 *Ganeshaya (11/1) Withdrawn (ref to ent stalls) : not under orders — Rule 4 applies*

**3/1** Ballasecret, **5/1** Lincstone Boy (IRE), **9/1** Banham College, **12/1** Joe Sugden, Stocktina, **16/1** Farmer Jock, Pendor Dancer, Jess Rebec, Hitchin a Ride, Petitesse, **20/1** Musval, CRANFIELD COMET, **25/1** We're All Game, Maria Cappuccini, **33/1** Little Saboteur, Lonely Lass, **50/1** Lonsom Lass. CSF £439.34, CT £1,995.84. Tote £21.30: £3.30 £5.20 £1.50 £1.70 (£209.40). Cranfield Industries Limited (COCKERHAM) bred by J. R. C. and Mrs Wren. 17 Rn
60.4 sec (3.1)
SF—50/39/46/13/7/23

---

## 3104

WATERBRIDGE CLAIMING STKS    £2637.00 (£732.00: £351.00)
1½m 70y                                                              4-10 (4-16)

29233 **Charmed Life** (HRACecil) 3-8-11  WRyan (8) (b.nr fore: hld up: hdwy 3f out: sn
rdn: led appr fnl f: r.o) ......................................... —1
26353 Alyafill (USA) (70) (Fav) (BHanbury) 3-8-3 ‡7PTurner (14) (chsd ldrs: 4th st: c
wd & led over 3f out: hdd over 1f out: one pce) .................. 2.2
26924 Remwood Girl (29) (KSBridgwater) 6-8-7 PD'Arcy (5) (hdwy & 6th st: ev ch 3f
out: one pce appr fnl f) ........................................... 3½.3
29333 Kasikci (78) (RHollinshead) 3-8-6 GDuffield (9) (hdwy 3f out: kpt on one pce
appr fnl f) ........................................................ 2.4
2957 Izitallworthit (JMackie) 3-8-4 GCarter (13) (chsd ldrs: 7th st: one pce fnl 2f) .... 6.5
2937 Ivan the Terrible (IRE) (56) (MissSJWilton) 4-8-11 ‡5SWilliams (2) (b: chsd ldrs:
5th st: ev ch over 3f out: sn rdn & wknd) ........................ 8.6
Skimmer Hawk (BobJones) 3-8-11 NDay (11) (w'like: swtg: bit bkwd: nvr nr to
chal) ............................................................. 1½.7
2868 Always Alex (25) (PDEvans) 5-8-1 ‡5LNewton (10) (prom: 3rd st: wknd 3f out) .. 6.8
27513 King of Normandy (IRE) (53) (bl) (RHannon) 3-8-9 JLloyd (16) (led & sn clr:
wknd & hdd over 3f out) .......................................... 1½.9
Snooker Table (TBHallett) 9-9-10 NAdams (4) (bkwd: á bhd) ............. 1½.10
2705* Carousel Music (56) (JAkehurst) 5-8-9 SWhitworth (6) (prom: 2nd st: rdn &
wknd over 2f out) ................................................. 3.11
1976 Medbourne (IRE) (39) (JLHarris) 3-8-2(2) JCarroll (1) (a bhd) ......... nk.12
2716* City Line (48) (DRLaing) 3-8-3 GBardwell (12) (prom to ½-wy: sn lost tch: t.o) 10.13
2694 Petty Cash (36) (bl) (DrJDScargill) 3-7-4(3) ‡7CHawksley (7) (b.hind: bhd fr
½-wy: t.o) ........................................................ 7.14
1362 Tauzio (IRE) (JMackie) 4-9-6 GHind (3) (bkwd: a bhd: t.o) ............. 1½.15
Hillcrest Girl (TWDonnelly) 3-7-4 ‡7AGarth (15) (w'like: bkwd: dwlt: a bhd: t.o) 30.16

**7/4** Alyafill (USA), **7/2** CHARMED LIFE, **4/1** Kasikci, **6/1** Carousel Music, **10/1** Always Alex, **14/1** City Line, **16/1** King of Normandy (IRE), **25/1** Skimmer Hawk, **33/1** Medbourne (IRE), **50/1** Ors. CSF £10.36, Tote £3.40: £1.20 £1.30 £7.60 (£3.60). Mr L. Marinopoulos (NEWMARKET) bred by Stilvi Compania Financiera S A. 16 Rn; Charmed Life clmd A Barrow £8,001
2m 43.9 (12.2)

---

## 3105

SEPTEMBER H'CAP (0-70) £2973.00 (£828.00: £399.00)    7f    4-40 (4-44)

2032 **Millsolin (IRE) (50)** (Fav) (RAkehurst) 4-8-12 GCarter (3) (5th st: led appr fnl f:
sn clr: v.easily) ................................................. —1
20096 Quick Steel (53) (bl) (TPMcGovern) 4-9-1 NAdams (9) (a.p: 3rd st: c wd & led
over 3f out: hdd appr fnl f) ...................................... 8.2
2958 Glenstal Princess (59) (RHollinshead) 5-9-7 WRyan (8) (hdwy over 2f out: r.o
fnl f: nvr nrr) ................................................... 1½.3
2941 Dandy Desire (45) (BCMorgan) 3-8-3 PRobinson (15) (chsd ldrs: 4th st: rdn 2f
out) .............................................................. s.h.4
18145 Judgement Call (57) (PHowling) 5-9-5 GDuffield (6) (bit bkwd: led 1f: 2nd st:
rdn & wknd over 1f out) .......................................... 1½.5
2013 Jokist (63) (WJarvis) 9-9-11 AMunro (17) (hdwy 2f out: r.o ins fnl f: nvr nrr) .... hd.6
2589 Scarlet Princess (47) (RJHodges) 4-8-6 ‡3FNorton (2) (nvr plcd to chal) ......... s.h.7
28222 Roxy Music (IRE) (51) (KOCunningham-Brown) 3-8-9 SWhitworth (13) (6th st:
rdn & ev ch over 2f out: sn wknd) ............................... 1½.8
2831* Efra (64) (RHannon) 3-9-8 JLloyd (7) (hld up: nvr plcd to chal) ......... nk.9
2952 Sunley Sparkle (46) (DRGandolfo) 4-8-3 ‡5JWeaver (11) (nvr nr ldrs) ........... nk.10
2634* Glenscar (41) (JLSpearing) 6-7-10 ‡7AGarth (12) (s.i.s: a in rr) ......... 6.11
27854 Strip Cartoon (IRE) (52) (bl) (SRBowring) 4-8-7 ‡7MHarris (16) (led after 1f: racd
alone far side: hdd over 3f out: sn btn) ......................... 4.12
2953 Susanna's Secret (46) (WCarter) 5-8-1 ‡7CHawksley (5) (m.n.s) ......... ½.13
29535 Charmed Knave (52) (DRLaing) 7-9-0 TyroneWilliams (8) (m.n.s) ......... 2.14
2906 Crofter's Cline (43) (v) (ABailey) 8-7-12 ‡7WHollick (10) (t.o) ......... 5.15
24696 Whippet (60) (JABennett) 8-9-8 JCarroll (14) (t.o) ......... nk.16
2966 Monti Beppo (52) (LJBarratt) 3-8-10 LCharnock (4) (t.o) ......... 1½.17

**100/30** MILLSOLIN (IRE)(6/1—3/1), **9/2** Glenscar, **9/1** Efra, **10/1** Glenstal Princess(7/1—11/1), **11/1** Jokist, **12/1** Scarlet Princess, **14/1** Strip Cartoon (IRE), Quick Steel, Dandy Desire, **16/1** Charmed Knave, Roxy Music (IRE), **20/1** Judgement Call, Susanna's Secret, **25/1** Crofter's Cline, Whippet, **40/1** Sunley Sparkle, **50/1** Monti Beppo. CSF £48.09, CT £406.94. Tote £2.90: £1.30 £9.90 £3.00 £3.40 (£11.90). Normandy Developments (London) (EPSOM) bred by Lhasa Trading Ltd. in Ireland. 17 Rn    1m 27.8 (3.5)
SF—56/35/36/17/28/33

**3106**    CANAL BARGE STKS (II) (Mdn 2-Y.O) £2553.00 (£708.00: £339.00)    7f  5-10 (5-19)

|  |  |  |  |  |
|---|---|---|---|---|
| | **Frontier Flight (USA)** (RCharlton) 9-0 GCarter (9) (w'like: leggy: bit bkwd: mde most: rn green appr fnl f) | | | —1 |
| 3011⁶ | Jackpot Star (Fav) (RHannon) 9-0 PRobinson (2) (6th st: effrt over 2f out: sn ev ch: rdn & unable qckn) | | | 2.2 |
| | Doctoor (USA) (WJarvis) 9-0 AMunro (5) (w'like: str: bit bkwd: chsd ldrs: 5th st: shkn up over 2f out: one pce) | | | 3½.3 |
| 2080⁴ | Pickupadailysport (51) (MissGayKelleway) 8-9 ‡5JWeaver (3) (4th st: effrt 2f out: hrd rdn & sn btn) | | | 8.4 |
| 2776⁵ | Noteability (58) (JBerry) 8-9 JCarroll (4) (lw: chsd ldrs: 3rd st: rdn 2f out: sn btn) | | | 2.5 |
| 2818 | Flash of Amber (JLSpearing) 8-9 GHind (10) (styd on fnl 2f: nvr nrr) | | | ½.6 |
| 1409 | Knyaz (LGCottrell) 9-0 NCarlisle (7) (bit bkwd: a bhd) | | | 5.7 |
| 1670 | Merryhill Kerry (IRE) (JLHarris) 8-6 ‡3FNorton (1) (s.i.s: a bhd) | | | ½.8 |
| 2994 | Capten Morgan (IRE) (WJHaggas) 9-0 GDuffield (6) (outpcd) | | | 1½.9 |
| 807 | Form Secret (IRE) (LJBarratt) 8-9 LCharnock (11) (s.s: a bhd & outpcd) | | | 1½.10 |
| 2482 | Oriental Princess (MrsSOliver) 8-2 ‡7DCarson (8) (bolted bef s: chsd wnr: 2nd st: wknd 3f out: t.o) | | | 25.11 |

**11/8** Jackpot Star(5/4—2/1), **2/1** Doctoor (USA), **6/1** FRONTIER FLIGHT (USA)(op 4/1), **10/1** Noteability( 16/1—8/1), **33/1** Knyaz, **40/1** Flash of Amber, Capten Morgan (IRE), **50/1** Oriental Princess, Merryhill Kerry (IRE), Pickupadailysport, **66/1** Form Secret (IRE). CSF £13.35, Tote £9.60: £1.40 £1.40 £1.30 (£7.20). Dr Carlos E. Stelling (BECKHAMPTON) bred by Aaron U. Jones in USA. 11 Rn    1m 30.1 (5.8)
SF—24/18/7/–/–/–

T/Plpt: £215.00 (9.6 Tckts).    IM

**1232a—BADEN-BADEN (L-H)**

**Friday, August 28th [Good]**

**3108a**    SPRETI-RENNEN (Gp 3) £26408.00    1¼m

|  |  |  |  |
|---|---|---|---|
| 2579★ | **KARINGA BAY** (GLewis) 5-8-9 BRouse | | —1 |
| 2511a³ | Sugunas (GER) (Germany) 4-8-11 ABoschert | | ½.2 |
| 2508a★ | Past Master (USA) (France) 4-9-0 SGuillot | | ¾.3 |

Tote 87DM: 22DM 20DM 35DM (SF: 425DM). Mr K. Higson (EPSOM) bred by K.Higson. 10 Rn    2m 3.6

**2979a—DEAUVILLE (R-H)**

**Saturday, August 29th [Soft]**

Going Allowance: 0.70 sec per fur (Y)

**3109a**    PRIX QUINCEY (Gp 3)    £20640.00    1m (st)

|  |  |  |  |
|---|---|---|---|
| | **Dampierre (USA)** (France) 4-9-0 TJarnet | | —1 |
| | Burdur (France) 4-9-0 CLeScrill | | 1½.2 |
| 842a | Bakari (IRE) (France) 3-8-8 DBoeuf | | 1.3 |

Tote 2.60f: 2.40f 5.70f (SF: 85.50f). Mr D. Wildenstein (A.Fabre,FRANCE) bred by Allez France Stables Ltd. in USA. 5 Rn    1m 44.6 (8)
SF—64/59/50

**DEAUVILLE (R-H)**

**Sunday, August 30th [Soft]**

Going Allowance: St: 0.70 sec (Y); Rnd: 1.20 sec per fur (S)

**3110a**    PRIX DE LA NONETTE (Gp 3) (3-Y.O.F) £20640.00    1¼m

|  |  |  |  |
|---|---|---|---|
| | **River Nymph (USA)** (France) 3-9-2 GMosse | | —1 |
| 1824a★ | Trishyde (USA) (France) 3-9-2 FHead | | 1.2 |
| | Revasser (USA) (bl) (France) 3-9-2 TJarnet | | 1½.3 |
| 2461⁴ | OUMALDAAYA (USA) (bl) (JLDunlop) 3-9-2 WCarson | | 1½.4 |

Tote 9.80f: 3.40f 1.70f (SF: 53.40f). Mrs C.Thieriot (J de Roualle,FRANCE) bred by Cormal Investments Inc. in USA. 7 Rn    2m 18.7 (16.4)
SF—58/56/53/50

## 3111a　　GRAND PRIX DE DEAUVILLE LANCEL (Gp 2)　£51600.00　1½m 110y

1356a⁵ **Modhish (IRE)** *(France)* 3–8-7 TJarnet (hld up: hdwy & 5th st: hmpd whn chal over 1f out: led 1f out: r.o) ........................................................ —1
2895a² SNURGE (Fav) *(PFICole)* 5–9-2 TQuinn (hld up: 4th st: effrt 2f out: ev ch 1f out: r.o one pce) ............................................................................. 1½.2
2096a³ Djais (FR) *(France)* 3–8-7 CBlack (led to 1f out: one pce) ........................... nk.3
2504a\* Vert Amande (FR) *(France)* 4–9-5 DBoeuf (prom: 3rd st: styd on one pce: nvr nrr) ................................................................................................... 1½.4
2643³ FAST MANOUVRE (FR) *(MMoubarak)* 3–8-7 LDettori (mid div: hdwy over 2f out: 6th st: sn btn) ..................................................................................... 8.5
2316a Dadarissime (FR) *(France)* 3–8-7 RBriard (chsd ldr: 2nd st: effrt 2f out: wknd qckly) .................................................................................................. 3.6
　Justice (FR) *(France)* 4–9-2 SCauthen (prom tl 7th & wkng st) ........................... 20.7

**5/4** Snurge, **11/4** Vert Amande (FR), **41/10** MODHISH (IRE), **5/1** Dadarissime (FR), **13/1** Fast Manouvre (FR), Djais (FR), **16/1** Justice (FR). Tote 5.10f: 1.90f 1.20f (SF: 15.60f). Sheikh Mohammed (A.Fabre,FRANCE) bred by Kilfrush Stud Farm in Ireland. 7 Rn
2m 55.5 (18)
SF—63/69/59/68/40/34

## 3112a　　PRIX DU CALVADOS (Gp 3) (2-Y.O.F) £20640.00　7f (st)

　**Cox Orange (USA)** *(France)* 2–8-9 SCauthen ...................................................... —1
2320a³ Rouquette *(France)* 2–8-9 ABadel ............................................................... ¾.2
　Sissingaya (USA) *(France)* 2–8-9 FHead ........................................................ 2.3

Tote 2.40f: 1.60f 1.90f (SF: 9.40f). Sheikh Mohammed (A.Fabre,FRANCE) bred by East American Breeding Co. in USA. 5 Rn
1m 30 (7)
SF—63/61/55

## 2977a—CURRAGH (R-11)

### Sunday, August 30th [Soft]
Going Allowance: 0.40 sec per fur (Y)

## 3113a　　E.B.F. FUTURITY STKS (Gp 3) (2-Y.O) £13435.00　7f

2887a\* **Fatherland (IRE)** (Fav) *(Ireland)* 2–8-10 LPiggott (hld up: smooth hdwy 2f out: led 1f out: comf) ........................................................................................ —1
2835⁴ NEWTON'S LAW (IRE) *(PWChapple-Hyam)* 2–8-10 RCochrane (prom: led over 2f out to 1f out: no ex) .............................................................................. 1½.2
　Colour Party (USA) *(Ireland)* 2–8-10 WJO'Connor (led over 4f: kpt on one pce) 4.3
1818a⁴ Staviski *(Ireland)* 2–8-10 KJManning (sme hdwy over 2f out: no imp fnl 2f) ........ 4.4
　Ignatius (USA) *(Ireland)* 2–8-10 CRoche (prom tl rdn & btn 2f out) .................. 2½.5

**4/7** FATHERLAND (IRE), **7/2** Ignatius (USA), **5/1** Newton's Law (IRE), **8/1** Colour Party (USA), **33/1** Staviski. Tote £1.30: £1.10 £2.10 (£3.80). Mrs M.V.O'Brien (M.V.O'Brien,IRELAND) bred by Ballydoyle Stud in Ireland. 5 Rn
1m 28.2 (5)
SF—63/58/46/34/26

## 2775—HAYDOCK (L-H)

### Friday, September 4th [Soft]
Going Allowance: 0.55 sec per fur (Y)　　　　　　　　　　　Wind: fresh half against

Stalls: low

## 3114　　SUTTON LEACH STKS (Mdn 3-Y.O) £2364.00 (£654.00: £312.00)　1¾m 2-15 (2-17)

2635⁴ **Wand (IRE)** *(HRACecil)* 8-9 WRyan (4) (a.p: 2nd st: c stands' side: led 3f out: r.o wl) ...................................................................................................... —1
　Hit the Fan *(RCharlton)* 9-0 PaulEddery (5) (w'like: bkwd: hdwy 6f out: 5th st: styd on u.p fnl f) ................................................................................... 2½.2
2886⁴ Surf Boat *(BWHills)* 8-9 MHills (8) (chsd ldrs: 3rd st: ev ch 1f out: unable qckn) hd.3
　Nemir *(JHMGosden)* 9-0 GHind (7) (b: w'like: scope: bkwd: hdwy & 6th st: rdn 2f out: styd on: nvr able to chal) ............................................................... 7.4
2801³ Super Sarena (IRE) (70) *(RSimpson)* 8-4 ‡⁵ATucker (9) (led tl hdd 3f out: sn btn) 15.5
2869 Patrol (v) *(MRStoute)* 9-0 AMunro (6) (chsd ldrs: 4th st: wknd over 2f out) ....... 1.6
2431³ Fortune Star (IRE) (Fav) *(JLDunlop)* 9-0 MRoberts (1) (hld up: effrt over 3f out: no imp) .............................................................................................. hd.7
2549 Alif (IRE) *(JLDunlop)* 9-0 JLowe (10) (a bhd) ............................................. 3.8
　Farmer's Fire (IRE) *(CFWall)* 9-0 GDuffield (3) (b: bkwd: chsd ldrs to ½-wy: grad wknd) ............................................................................................ 8.9
2934 High Mind (FR) (62) *(MissLCSiddall)* 9-0 DMcKeown (2) (s.s: a bhd) ............... 3.10
*2691* Bar Three (IRE) (bl) *(LJCodd)* 9-0 JCarroll (11) (bkwd: a bhd: t.o) ................... 11

2/1 Fortune Star (IRE), 11/4 Surf Boat, 5/1 WAND (IRE), 10/1 Nemir, Hit the Fan, 12/1 Super Sarena (IRE), 14/1 Patrol, 20/1 Farmer's Fire (IRE), 25/1 Alif (IRE), 50/1 Ors. CSF £50.31, Tote £4.60: £1.70 £1.40 £1.80 (£16.60). Cliveden Stud (NEWMARKET) bred by Lyonstown Stud in Ireland. 11 Rn　　　　3m 11.20 (12.70)
SF–45/45/39/30/–/–

### 3115　　BOLD HEATH CLAIMING STKS (2-Y.O) £2700.00 (£750.00: £360.00)　　6f 2-50 (2-55)

| | | |
|---|---|---|
| 2826 | **Diskette** (*LordHuntingdon*) 8-0 MRoberts (13) (chsd ldrs: led over 1f out: r.o wl) | —1 |
| 2818³ | Mam'zelle Angot (Fav) (*MRStoute*) 7-7(1) ‡³FNorton (14) (b.hind: hdwy 2f out: ev ch ins fnl f: unable qckn) | 1.2 |
| 2826 | Sparky's Song (*JWHills*) 7-7 SDawson (11) (chsd ldrs: rdn over 1f out: one pce) | 6.3 |
| 3033³ | Clanrock (*RMWhitaker*) 7-13(1) DHolland (9) (lw: in tch: effrt u.p appr fnl f: styd on) | s.h.4 |
| 2724⁵ | Daaniera (IRE) (78) (*JBerry*) 8-12 JCarroll (7) (lw: w ldrs tl rdn & wknd appr fnl f) | 1.5 |
| 2557 | Hush Baby (IRE) (*DMorris*) 8-8(2) MTebbutt (16) (hdwy 2f out: nvr able to chal) | ¾.6 |
| 2924 | Mark's Club (IRE) (*BWHills*) 8-2 MHills (6) (bit bkwd: hdwy 2f out: styd on one pce fnl f) | 1½.7 |
| 2779 | Red Ballet (61) (bl) (*MrsNMacauley*) 8-2 AMunro (12) (led tl hdd & wknd over 1f out) | ½.8 |
| 1749 | Calenick Lass (*DHaydnJones*) 7-9 TyroneWilliams (5) (bit bkwd: nvr wnt pce) | s.h.10 |
| 2932 | April Point (IRE) (*RHollinshead*) 7-4 ‡⁷AGarth (10) (spd stands' side 4f) | s.h.10 |
| 2819⁶ | Grab Sunday Sport (*MissGayKelleway*) 8-2 GHind (8) (s.i.s: a bhd) | 1½.11 |
| 2776⁶ | Target Time (*DMcCain*) 8-0 JFanning (15) (bit bkwd: s.s: a bhd) | 3.12 |
| 3050⁶ | Mad Mytton (66) (bl) (*ABailey*) 8-6 GBaxter (2) (racd far side: a outpcd) | 2.13 |
| 3039⁴ | True Story (72) (bl) (*RHannon*) 8-11 GCarter (4) (racd far side: a outpcd) | 6.14 |
| 3019 | Simply Amiss (75) (*SirMarkPrescott*) 8-3 GDuffield (3) (racd far side: bhd fr ½-wy) | 2½.15 |
| 1782⁴ | Jocks Joker (*CaptJWilson*) 7-12 JLowe (1) (bit bkwd: racd far side: a bhd) | 1.16 |

7/2 Mam'zelle Angot, 9/2 DISKETTE, 11/2 Clanrock, 8/1 Simply Amiss, 15/2 True Story (IRE), 9/1 Daaniera (IRE), 10/1 Mark's Club (IRE), 12/1 Red Ballet, 14/1 Sparky's Song, 25/1 Grab Sunday Sport, Hush Baby (IRE), Mad Mytton, Jocks Joker, 33/1 Ors. CSF £22.13, Tote £5.70: £2.30 £2.40 £8.50 (£14.10). Mr M. L. Oberstein (WEST ILSLEY) bred by Maverick Productions Ltd. 16 Rn　　　　1m 18.28 (6.58)
SF–20/9/–/–/–/

### 3116　　BIRKDALE H'CAP (0-90) £4012.50 (£1200.00: £575.00: £262.50)
　　1m 3f 200y　　　　　　　　　　　　　　　　　　　3-25 (3-26)

(Weights raised 8 lb)

| | | |
|---|---|---|
| 3021★ | **Green Lane (IRE) (80)** (bl) (Jt-Fav) (*RCharlton*) 3-9-7 (4x) PaulEddery (1) (lw: mde all: shkn up appr fnl f: r.o wl nr fin) | —1 |
| 1665⁴ | Bigwheel Bill (IRE) (74) (*JWWatts*) 3-9-1 JLowe (4) (a.p: 2nd st: hrd rdn appr fnl f: r.o wl nr fin) | ¾.2 |
| 2908★ | Mad Militant (IRE) (81) (*RHollinshead*) 3-9-8 WRyan (3) (lw: s.i.s: 4th st: effrt over 1f out: kpt on) | ¾.3 |
| 2734⁵ | Rajai (IRE) (81) (bl) (*JLDunlop*) 3-9-8 MRoberts (2) (b.nr fore: lw: a.p: 3rd st: rdn over 1f out: one pce) | 2½.4 |
| 681³ | Admirals Seat (63) (Jt-Fav) (*MrsJRRamsden*) 4-8-13 GBaxter (7) (bkwd: hld up: 5th st: kpt on same pce fnl 2f) | 4.5 |
| 2827 | Smiles Ahead (63) (*PJBevan*) 4-8-13 BCrossley (5) (still bkwd: hld up: 6th st: rdn over 2f out: sn btn) | 3.6 |
| 1968² | Hillzah (USA) (74) (*RBastiman*) 4-9-10 MHills (6) (bit bkwd: hld up: hdwy & 5th st: wknd over 2f out) | 5.7 |

5/2 Admirals Seat, GREEN LANE (IRE), 5/1 Mad Militant (IRE), 13/2 Rajai (IRE), 7/1 Hillzah (USA), 9/1 Bigwheel Bill (IRE), 14/1 Smiles Ahead. CSF £22.37, Tote £2.80: £2.10 £3.10 (£13.80). Lord Weinstock (BECKHAMPTON) bred by Ballymacoll Stud Farm Ltd. in Ireland. 7 Rn　　　2m 42.88 (14.88)
SF–24/16/21/16/–/–

### 3117　　E.B.F. BIRKENHEAD STKS (Mdn 2-Y.O) £3465.00 (£1035.00: £495.00: £225.00)
　　5f　　　　　　　　　　　　　　　　　　　　　　　4-00 (4-02)

| | | |
|---|---|---|
| 2444² | **Carbon Steel (IRE)** (Fav) (*BWHills*) 9-0 DHolland (4) (hld up: led appr fnl f: edgd lft: v.easily) | —1 |
| 2826⁶ | Folly Vision (IRE) (*RHannon*) 8-9 KDarley (1) (hld up: effrt u.p over 1f out: r.o wl) | 1½.2 |
| 2024 | Northern Bluff (*JWWatts*) 9-0 WRyan (12) (outpcd tl styd on u.p appr fnl f) | 2.3 |
| 1742³ | Russia With Love (*JDBethell*) 8-9 DMcKeown (11) (chsd ldrs: kpt on u.p ins fnl f) | ¾.4 |
| | Safe Bid (*RHollinshead*) 8-3(1) ‡⁷CarlLlewellyn (8) (lt-f: bkwd: s.s: hdwy 2f out: fin wl) | 2.5 |

2811 Scored Again **(73)** *(RMWhitaker)* 9-0 ACulhane (10) (led ½-wy tl appr fnl f: sn rdn & wknd) ................................................................................ 1.6

2932³ Manor Adventure **(70)** *(BAMcMahon)* 8-9 AMunro (7) (lw: led over 2f: wknd appr fnl f) ............................................................................ s.h.7

772³ Mr Dingle *(WJHaggas)* 9-0 MRoberts (5) (still bkwd: s.i.s: a bhd) ...................... ³/₄.8

2388⁶ Musical Times *(MrsNMacauley)* 8-9 NCarlisle (3) (a in rr) ................................ 1.9

2965⁵ Miss Whittingham (IRE) **(56)** (v) *(JBerry)* 8-9 JCarroll (2) (lw: spd 3f) .......... hd.10
City Lighter *(EJAlston)* 8-9 GBaxter (9) (w'like: scope: bkwd: s.s: a bhd & outpcd) ...................................................................................... 6.11

**5/6** CARBON STEEL (IRE), **5/1** Mr Dingle(op 3/1), **8/1** Scored Again, Manor Adventure, **14/1** Northern Bluff, Russia With Love, **16/1** Folly Vision (IRE)(op 10/1), **25/1** Miss Whittingham (IRE), **33/1** Ors. CSF £15.63, Tote £1.80: £1.20 £3.80 £3.80 (£32.80). Mr Howard Kaskel (LAMBOURN) bred by W. Lazy and C. H. Wacker III in Ireland. 11 Rn 64.65 sec (5.65)
SF—42/31/28/20/6/13

---

**3118** KIRKBY H'CAP (0-85) £3728.25 (£1116.00: £535.50: £245.25) **2m 45y** 4-30 (4-31)

2736³ Jack Button (IRE) **(75)** *(BobJones)* 3-8-6 NDay (7) (lw: hld up: hdwy over 3f out: rdn to ld 2f out: styd on) .......................................... —1

2759* Wilkins **(68)** (Fav) *(JRFanshawe)* 3-7-13 GCarter (6) (led 1f: 3rd st: led over 2f out: sn hdd: r.o one pce: fin 3rd, 3l: plcd 2nd) ..................... 2

2793* Receptionist **(80)** *(HRACecil)* 3-8-11 WRyan (2) (a.p: 5th st: kpt on one pce fnl f: fin 4th, 4l: plcd 3rd) ................................................ 3

1372* Five to Seven (USA) **(75)** *(SGNorton)* 3-8-6 KDarley (5) (bit bkwd: chsd ldr: 2nd st: rdn & wknd over 2f out: fin 5th, 5l: plcd 4th) ..................... 4

354³ Maamur (USA) **(70)** *(DBurchell)* 4-8-9 ‡⁵StephenDavies (11) (bkwd: led after 1f tl over 2f out: sn hrd rdn & btn: fin 6th, 2¹/₂l: plcd 5th) ........... 5

£400? Good Hand (USA) **(84)** *(JMWatts)* 6–10-0 NConnorton (3) (hld up: a bhd) ........ 2,7

2759 Mount Nelson **(57)** *(DWPArbuthnot)* 6-8-1 AMunro (1) (b: b.hind: swtg: prom: 4th st: wknd over 3f out) ............................................ 5.8

2638² Alqairawaan **(82)** *(JLDunlop)* 3-8-13 MRoberts (10) (lw: chsd ldrs 10f: grad wknd) ......................................................... 2¹/₂.9

2439 Go South **(63)** (bl) *(JRJenkins)* 8-8-7 NCarlisle (4) (a bhd: t.o) ...................... 20.10
Kausar (USA) **(67)** *(GMMoore)* 5-8-11 DMcKeown (8) (bkwd: lost pl over 5f out: t.o) .................................................................... 11

2867* Bandoline **(68)** *(BWHills)* 3–7-13 DHolland (9) (hld up: hdwy & 6th st: styd on u.p ins fnl f: fin 2nd, 2¹/₂l: disq: plcd last) .......................... 0
*Stewards Enquiry: Obj. to Bandoline by Clerk of Scales sustained. Holland fined £315 (failure to weigh in).*

**5/2** Wilkins, **7/2** Receptionist, **13/2** Alqairawaan, **9/1** Five to Seven (USA), JACK BUTTON (IRE), **14/1** Good Hand (USA), Go South, **20/1** Maamur (USA), **25/1** Ors. CSF £31.06, CT £87.55. Tote £8.50: £2.20 £1.60 £1.70 (£15.90). A. and B. Racing (NEWMARKET) bred by Empress Syndicate in Ireland. 11 Rn 3m 41.26 (14.06)
SF—40/30/27/35/25/25

---

**3119** CLOCK FACE STKS (Mdn) £2385.00 (£660.00: £315.00) **7f 30y** 5-05 (5-06)

Key Suspect (USA) *(JHMGosden)* 3-9-0 GHind (3) (w'like: bit bkwd: hld up: hdwy to ld 2f out: sn clr: unchal) .................................... —1

2950² Nest **(58)** (Fav) *(LordHuntingdon)* 3-8-9 MRoberts (10) (lw: a.p: 3rd st: rdn 2f out: kpt on: no ch w wnr) .............................. 6.2

2942 Tickham Vixen (IRE) **(40)** *(JDBethell)* 4-8-13 DMcKeown (2) (hld up: hdwy u.p wl over 1f out: nvr nrr) ........................... 3¹/₂.3

Indica (USA) *(JHMGosden)* 3-8-9 JCarroll (1) (lengthy: unf: s.i.s: hdwy over 2f out: nvr nr to chal) ..................................... 1.4

2995³ Quixotic *(PWHarris)* 3-9-0 SWhitworth (9) (chsd ldrs: 4th st: rdn appr fnl f: sn btn) ....................................................... ¹/₂.5

2941 Gold Belt (IRE) **(50)** *(RHollinshead)* 3-8-9 WRyan (5) (chsd ldrs: 5th st: led over 2f out: sn hdd & wknd) ............................ 5.6

2687 Lightning Decision *(JPSmith)* 4-9-4 PaulEddery (6) (bit bkwd: led over 4f: rdn & wknd fnl 2f) ........................................... 3.7

2922 Court of Kings (bl) *(PFICole)* 3-9-0 AMunro (7) (bkwd: chsd ldr: 2nd st: rdn & wknd over 3f out) ........................................ s.h.8

1918 Joie de Patina *(SGNorton)* 3-8-9 JFortune (4) (bit bkwd: 6th st: rdn & wknd over 2f out) ...................................................... nk.9

2942 Virginia Cottage **(41)** *(BAMcMahon)* 3-8-2 ‡⁷JBramhill (8) (lw: a in rr) .......... 2.10

**13/8** Nest(9/4—6/4), **4/1** Court of Kings, **5/1** KEY SUSPECT (USA), **7/1** Indica (USA), **8/1** Gold Belt (IRE), **17/2** Quixotic, **16/1** Tickham Vixen (IRE), **33/1** Virginia Cottage, **50/1** Ors. CSF £13.42, Tote £6.10: £1.90 £1.40 £2.70 (£9.90). Mr Landon Knight (NEWMARKET) bred by Landon Knight in USA. 10 Rn 1m 36.51 (9.21)
SF—20/-/-/-/-/-

**3120**    MELLING H'CAP (0-90) £3435.75 (£1026.00: £490.50: £222.75)    **5f**    5-35 (5-36)

3068³ **Petraco (IRE) (72)** *(LJCodd)* 4–8–12 GDuffield (4) (a.p: rdn appr fnl f: led ins fnl
f: r.o) ...................................................................................................................... —1

2848² Bunty Boo **(88)** *(BAMcMahon)* 3–9–5 ‡⁷SSanders (2) (lw: a.p: led 2f out tl ins fnl
f) ...................................................................................................................... 1¹/₂.2

3079⁵ Ballad Dancer **(56)** *(EJAlston)* 7–7–10 TyroneWilliams (8) (hld up: hdwy over 1f
out: fin wl) .......................................................................................................... 2.3

2956⁵ Arc Lamp **(62)** *(JAGlover)* 6–8–2 JFortune (7) (chsd ldrs: rdn over 1f out: kpt on) hd.4

2214* Big Hand (IRE) **(90)** *(JWWatts)* 3–10–0 JLowe (3) (lw: chsd ldrs: no hdwy fnl f) 1¹/₂.5

2741 Gemini Fire **(77)** *(Fav)* *(MPNaughton)* 8–9–3 MRoberts (9) (led 3f: wknd qckly) . 2.6

2599 Consulate **(60)** *(JBalding)* 6–7–7 ‡⁷ClaireBalding (5) (nvr nr to chal) ...................... 7

2741 Meeson Times **(59)** *(BEllison)* 4–7–13 AMunro (6) (b: a bhd) ............................... 8

1752⁴ Tino Tere **(82)** *(JBerry)* 3–9–6 JCarroll (1) (bit bkwd: racd alone far side: bhd fr
¹/₂-wy) ................................................................................................................ 9

**2/1** Gemini Fire, **9/2** PETRACO (IRE), **5/1** Bunty Boo, **6/1** Ballad Dancer, **13/2** Big Hand (IRE), **12/1** Tino Tere,
**14/1** Consulate, **16/1** Ors. CSF £26.63, CT £126.27. Tote £4.90: £1.70 £1.90 £1.50 (£16.70). Mr B. W.
Hampson (NANTWICH) bred by Mrs M. Beaumont in Ireland. 9 Rn                    64.12 sec (5.12)
                                                                                                        SF—51/52/21/26/46/27

T/Trio: Race 5: £8.50 (93.5 Tckts). T/Plpt: £31.50 (148.5 Tckts).                                        IM

# HAYDOCK (L-H)

## Saturday, September 5th [Soft, Good to soft patches]
Going Allowance: St: 0.30 sec (G); Rnd: 0.55 sec per fur (Y)                          Wind: almost nil

Stalls: high

**3121**    LADBROKE H'CAP (0-110) £7960.00 (£2380.00: £1140.00: £520.00)
            **7f 30y**                                                                2-00 (2-03)

(Weights raised 6 lb)

3027⁴ **Cool Luke (IRE) (77)** *(GMMoore)* 3–8–0 JFanning (5) (hld up: gd hdwy to ld
appr fnl f: r.o wl) .............................................................................................. —1

2447 Marine Diver **(71)** *(BRMillman)* 6–7–12 DaleGibson (1) (hdwy over 2f out: hrd
rdn whn stumbled & swvd bdly lft ins fnl f: nt rcvr) ........................................... 1¹/₂.2

3069* Two Left Feet **(102)** *(Fav)* *(SirMarkPrescott)* 5–10–1 (5x) GDuffield (11) (lw:
chsd ldrs: 4th st: n.m.r appr fnl f: r.o wl ins fnl f) ............................................ s.h.3

2925⁴ Prenonamoss **(80)** *(DWPArbuthnot)* 4–8–6 ‡³FNorton (8) (b.hind: chsd ldrs: 5th
st: led over 2f out tl wknd appr fnl f: one pce) ................................................ ¹/₂.4

2997 Green Dollar **(92)** *(EAWheeler)* 9–9–5 MTebbutt (3) (hld up: hdwy whn bdly
hmpd 1f out: nt rcvr) ....................................................................................... 1¹/₂.5

2919 Bold Habit **(84)** *(BBeasley)* 7–8–6 ‡⁵JWeaver (7) (lw: hld up: swtchd rt appr fnl f:
r.o) .................................................................................................................. s.h.6

2795 Threepence **(83)** *(JBerry)* 3–8–6 JCarroll (4) (in tch: 6th st: effrt over 2f out: no
imp) ................................................................................................................. 2.7

2852³ Noble Pet **(93)** *(PJMakin)* 3–9–2 LPiggott (2) (hld up: effrt over 2f out: btn whn
hmpd ins fnl f: eased) ..................................................................................... 1¹/₂.8

3014* Stani (USA) **(81)** *(BHanbury)* 3–8–4 PaulEddery (9) (chsd ldr: 2nd st: rdn 2f out:
sn btn) ............................................................................................................. s.h.9

3069³ Arany **(88)** *(MHTompkins)* 5–9–1 PRobinson (10) (lw: led tl hdd & wknd over 2f
out) ................................................................................................................. hd.10

Mentalasanythin **(85)** *(ABailey)* 3–8–3 ‡⁵ATucker (6) (swtg: bit bkwd: prom: 3rd
st: wknd over 2f out) ........................................................................................ 4.11

**5/2** Two Left Feet, **4/1** Noble Pet, **7/1** Stani (USA), **8/1** Mentalasanythin, Arany, **10/1** Prenonamoss, **14/1** Bold
Habit, COOL LUKE (IRE), **20/1** Marine Diver, Green Dollar, **25/1** Threepence. CSF £218.35, CT £843.67. Tote
£17.50: £3.60 £6.40 £1.70 (£136.90). Mr B. Batey (MIDDLEHAM) bred by Lodge Park Stud in Ireland. 11 Rn
                                                                                        1m 33.40 (6.10)
                                                                                        SF—53/46/76/49/59/45

**3122**    WEBSTER'S YORKSHIRE BITTER H'CAP (0-115) £11355.00 (£3390.00: £1620.00:
            £735.00)    **1¹/₄m 120y**                                                2-30 (2-37)

(Weights raised 7 lb)

2028* **Mr Confusion (IRE) (86)** *(SGNorton)* 4–9–6 LPiggott (8) (a.p: 2nd st: led over
1f out: r.o wl) .................................................................................................. —1

3013 Halkopous **(83)** *(v)* *(MHTompkins)* 6–9–3 PRobinson (2) (lw: s.i.s: hld up: hdwy
over 2f out: rdn & r.o wl fnl f) .......................................................................... ³/₄.2

2914² Zawaahy (USA) **(83)** *(AAScott)* 3–8–9 BRaymond (1) (a.p: 3rd st: ev ch appr fnl
f: unable qckn) ................................................................................................ 2.3

2853 Tell No Lies **(90)** *(MHEasterby)* 5–9–10 MBirch (5) (chsd ldrs: 4th st: rdn over 1f out: nt pce to chal) ......................................................... 2.4

1723★ Dress Sense (IRE) **(94)** *(LMCumani)* 3–9–1 ‡⁵JWeaver (3) (lw: hld up: effrt 3f out: rdn & btn appr fnl f) ............................................... 3.5

2914⁴ Cottonwood *(LordHuntingdon)* 3–8–9 JReid (7) (hdwy & 5th st: rdn wl over 1f out: no imp) ............................................................... s.h.6

2853³ Scrutineer (USA) **(90)** (Fav) *(JHMGosden)* 3–9–2 SCauthen (6) (lw: led: rdn 2f out: sn hdd & wknd) ............................................ 2¹/₂.7

2028 Andrath (IRE) **(74)** *(CEBrittain)* 4–8–8 PaulEddery (4) (lw: in tch: 6th st: wknd over 2f out) ...................................................... 3¹/₂.8

**15/8** Scrutineer (USA), **4/1** MR CONFUSION (IRE)(3/1—9/2), **5/1** Dress Sense (IRE), **6/1** Halkopous, **7/1** Tell No Lies, **9/1** Zawaahy (USA), **14/1** Ors. CSF £27.20, CT £188.80. Tote £3.70: £1.50 £2.20 £2.00 (£14.10). Mr R. Fenwick-Gibson (BARNSLEY) bred by D. P. O'Brien in Ireland. 8 Rn                   2m 21.32 (9.62)
SF—68/63/51/62/47/40

---

**3123**          FLANGEFITT STAINLESS NURSERY      £3947.50 (£1180.00: £565.00: £257.50)
                  **6f**                                                                   3-00 (3-05)

2924² Look Who's Here (IRE) **(82)** *(BAMcMahon)* 9-0 BRaymond (8) (hdwy appr fnl f: led & qcknd clr ins fnl f) ...................................... —1

2205★ Storiths (IRE) **(87)** (Jt-Fav) *(JWWatts)* 9-5 LPiggott (4) (a.p: led appr fnl f: hung rt & hdd ins fnl f) ................................... 3.2

2812² Easy Access (IRE) **(78)** *(RHannon)* 8-10 JReid (6) (b.off hind: hld up: ev ch over 1f out: hmpd & unable qckn fnl f) .......................... nk.3

2841 Tajdif (USA) **(89)** (Jt-Fav) *(DMorley)* 9-7 PaulEddery (5) (hld up: gd hdwy over 1f out: fin wl) ............................................. ¹/₂.4

2551⁴ Doc Cottrill **(64)** *(MrsJRRamsden)* 7-10 JFanning (10) (lw: hdwy over 1f out: nvr nrr) ............................................................ hd.5

2900⁴ Goodbye Millie **(67)** *(SGNorton)* 7-10 ‡³FNorton (7) (r.o appr fnl f: nrst fin) ........ 3.6

2619³ Galejade **(72)** *(DHaydnJones)* 7-13(11) ‡⁵ATucker (15) (nvr nr to chal) ............... nk.7

2900 Birchwood Sun **(69)** *(RHollinshead)* 7-8 ‡⁷AGarth (3) (lw: nvr trbld ldrs) ............... 3¹/₂.8

2883 Raging Thunder **(72)** (bl) *(GLewis)* 8-4 KDarley (2) (gd spd 4f) ....................... ³/₄.9

2690⁴ Super Seve (IRE) **(78)** *(JBerry)* 8-10 GDuffield (9) (prom 4f: sn wknd) ............... 5.10

2779⁴ Margaret's Gift **(77)** *(JBerry)* 8-9 JCarroll (13) (lw: led over 4f: wknd qckly) ... 1¹/₂.11

2612⁴ Dahliz (IRE) **(73)** *(HThomsonJones)* 8-5 RHills (1) (lw: jnd ldrs ¹/₂-wy: rdn & wknd 2f out) ............................................................ ³/₄.12

3071⁵ Ban Ri (IRE) **(61)** (v) *(MHTompkins)* 7-7 DaleGibson (12) (spd to ¹/₂-wy: sn lost tch) ............................................................... ³/₄.13

2471³ Milbank Challenger **(67)** *(MHEasterby)* 7-10(3) ‡³SMaloney (14) (w ldrs to ¹/₂-wy: sn outpcd) ............................................................ hd.14

2781 Glow of Hope **(66)** *(EJAlston)* 7-7(5) ‡⁵BDoyle (11) (outpcd: t.o) ...................... 15
LONG HANDICAP: Ban Ri (IRE) 7-3, Glow of Hope 6-12.

**5/1** Tajdif (USA), Storiths (IRE), **6/1** Doc Cottrill, Margaret's Gift, **10/1** Raging Thunder, **11/1** Milbank Challenger, Easy Access (IRE), LOOK WHO'S HERE (IRE), **12/1** Dahliz (IRE), **14/1** Super Seve (IRE), Birchwood Sun, **16/1** Galejade, Ban Ri (IRE), **33/1** Glow of Hope. CSF £64.40, CT £500.23. Tote £10.30: £3.00 £2.60 £2.90 (£19.90). Mr S. L. Edwards (TAMWORTH) bred by Hollyhill Stud in Ireland. 15 Rn    1m 16.14 (4.44)
SF—47/40/30/39/13/1

---

**3124**          HAYDOCK PARK SPRINT CUP (Stks) (Gp 1) £72595.00 (£26605.00: £12552.50:
                  £4887.50: £1693.75: £416.25)   **6f**                                  3-30 (3-32)

2440⁴ **Sheikh Albadou** (Jt-Fav) *(AAScott)* 4–9–9 BRaymond (1) (lw: hld up gng wl: qcknd to ld ins fnl f: clr whn edgd rt: impressive) .......................... —1

2851² Mr Brooks (Jt-Fav) *(RHannon)* 5–9–9 LPiggott (4) (lw: hld up: hdwy 2f out: rdn over 1f out: r.o: no ch w wnr) ...................................... 2¹/₂.2

1942⁶ Wolfhound (USA) *(JHMGosden)* 3–9–9 SCauthen (6) (lw: chsd ldrs: outpcd 2f out: styd on nr fin) ............................................ 6.3

1942 Shalford (IRE) *(RHannon)* 4–9–9 JReid (8) (lw: wnt lft s: led tl hdd & outpcd ins fnl f) .............................................................. nk.4

2839 Wilde Rufo *(PAKelleway)* 3–9–6 KDarley (2) (outpcd tl r.o ins fnl f) ....................... 2¹/₂.5

2169 Sizzling Saga (IRE) *(JBerry)* 4–9–9 JCarroll (7) (lw: w ldrs: rdn 2f out: sn btn) .. 2¹/₂.6

2435 Tbab (IRE) *(CEBrittain)* 4–9–9 MBirch (5) (hld up: effrt 2f out: nvr able to chal) ... 5.7

2976a Bletchley Park (IRE) *(AAScott)* 3–9–6 RHills (3) (b.nr fore: spd 4f: sn outpcd: t.o) 10.8

**9/4** SHEIKH ALBADOU, Mr Brooks, **5/2** Shalford (IRE), **7/1** Wolfhound (USA), **33/1** Tbab (IRE), **66/1** Sizzling Saga (IRE), Bletchley Park (IRE), **100/1** Wilde Rufo. CSF £6.98, Tote £3.00: £1.30 £1.30 £1.10 (£2.90). Mr Hilal Salem (NEWMARKET) bred by Highclere Stud Ltd. 8 Rn    1m 14.17 (2.47)
SF—96/86/59/61/48/41

### 3125

JUDDMONTE CLASSIC CLAIMING STKS   £10965.00 (£3270.00: £1560.00: £705.00)
1¼m 120y
4-05 (4-06)

2644* **Rambo's Hall (87)** (Fav) *(JAGlover)* 7-9-4 DNicholls (4) (lw: hld up: 6th st: swtchd rt 2f out: led on bit 1f out: rdn out) ............................ —1

2775* Light Hand **(66)** *(MHTompkins)* 6-8-0 PRobinson (2) (lw: hld up & bhd: gd hdwy to chal 1f out: r.o) ............................ 1.2

2644² Eagle Feather (IRE) **(74)** *(JLDunlop)* 4-8-8 JReid (8) (a.p: 5th st: ev ch 1f out: unable qckn) ............................ 1½.3

2820³ Able Lassie **(62)** *(MrsGRReveley)* 4-8-1 JFanning (3) (a.p: 3rd st: led 2f out tl over 1f out: one pce) ............................ 1½.4

2100² Firefighter **(70)** *(RHollinshead)* 3-8-3 PaulEddery (1) (lw: hld up: effrt 3f out: no imp) ............................ 10.5

2644 Don't Smile **(64)** *(MHTompkins)* 3-8-6 DaleGibson (5) (chsd ldrs: 2nd st: wknd wl over 1f out) ............................ 1½.6

2774⁶ Kandy Secret (USA) **(58)** (bl) *(RHannon)* 3-7-12 AMcGlone (6) (chsd ldrs: 4th st: wknd 3f out: t.o) ............................ 12.7

2644⁶ Overpower **(62)** *(MHTompkins)* 8-8-5 RHills (7) (lw: led tl hdd & wknd 2f out: t.o) 8

**6/4** RAMBO'S HALL, **3/1** Light Hand, **4/1** Eagle Feather, **8/1** Firefighter, **10/1** Able Lassie, **12/1** Kandy Secret (USA), **20/1** Don't Smile, **25/1** Overpower. CSF £6.74, Tote £2.60: £1.30 £1.50 £1.60 (£4.50). Mr B. Dixon (WORKSOP) bred by Sqdn-Ldr Frank Barrett. 8 Rn; Eagle Feather (IRE) clmd S Bjorling £10,100, Able Lassie clmd C Bjorling £8,010
    2m 19.69 (7.99)
SF—82/62/67/57/39/39

### 3126

LADBROKE RACING APP'CE H'CAP (0-90) £8350.00 (£2500.00: £1200.00: £550.00)
6f
4-35 (4-38)
(Weights raised 4 lb)

2808² **Nordan Raider (52)** *(MJCamacho)* 4-7-8 JFanning (5) (lw: hld up: hdwy 2f out: led wl ins fnl f: r.o) ............................ —1

2861* Darussalam **(74)** *(RLee)* 5-8-13 ‡³SWynne (11) (lw: hld up: hdwy to ld ins fnl f: sn hdd: r.o) ............................ 1½.2

3002² Veloce (IRE) **(61)** *(ABailey)* 4-7-10(5) ‡⁷WHollick (3) (a.p: ev ch ins fnl f: unable qckn) ............................ ½.3

2919 Iron King **(71)** *(JLSpearing)* 6-8-13 AGarth (2) (hld up: gd hdwy appr fnl f: fin wl) nk.4

2848 Echo-Logical **(85)** *(RHannon)* 3-9-10 RPerham (13) (a.p: led over 2f out tl ins fnl f) ............................ hd.5

2902 Breezy Day **(78)** *(BAMcMahon)* 6-9-3 ‡³JBramhill (12) (hld up: effrt & n.m.r 1f out: nt pce to chal) ............................ ¾.6

2777⁴ Sir Arthur Hobbs **(62)** *(FHLee)* 5-8-4 ATucker (4) (lw: gd hdwy appr fnl f: fin wl) 1½.7

3002⁴ Darakah **(57)** *(CJHill)* 5-7-13 FNorton (7) (s.s: nvr nr to chal) ............................ s.h.8

2275⁴ Devon Dancer **(74)** (v) *(MHEasterby)* 3-8-13 SMaloney (8) (dwlt: hdwy ½-wy: wknd over 1f out) ............................ ¾.9

2614⁶ Coolaba Prince (IRE) **(60)** *(FHLee)* 3-7-13 NKennedy (6) (chsd ldrs over 4f) .. ¾.10

2902⁴ Precentor **(64)** *(JDBethell)* 6-8-6 BDoyle (10) (hld up: hdwy & n.m.r over 1f out: nt rcvr) ............................ 1½.11

3015 Yes **(54)** *(DTThom)* 4-7-7 ‡³KimMcDonnell (9) (m.n.s) ............................ ¾.12

2902⁶ Cronk's Courage **(77)** (v) *(EJAlston)* 6-9-5 JWeaver (14) (lw: led over 3f: sn wknd) ............................ 3½.13

3068² Miss Aragon **(51)** *(MissLCSiddall)* 4-7-4 ‡³TWilson (1) (prom over 3f: wknd qckly) ............................ 10.14

LONG HANDICAP: Miss Aragon 7-2.

**11/2** Darakah, **15/2** Darussalam, **8/1** Precentor, Cronk's Courage, Yes, **9/1** NORDAN RAIDER, **10/1** Veloce (IRE), Echo-Logical, **11/1** Breezy Day, **12/1** Sir Arthur Hobbs, **14/1** Coolaba Prince (IRE), **16/1** Devon Dancer, **20/1** Iron King, **25/1** Miss Aragon. CSF £71.42, CT £638.51. Tote £9.50: £3.00 £2.50 £3.10 (£44.30). Mrs J. A. Camacho (MALTON) bred by B. Nordan. 14 Rn
    1m 15.66 (3.96)
SF—37/50/31/47/57/47

### 3127

ALTRINCHAM GRADUATION STKS (2-Y.O) £4045.00 (£1210.00: £580.00: £265.00)
1m 30y
5-05 (5-07)

2675* **Visto Si Stampi (IRE) (88)** (Fav) *(JLDunlop)* 8-11 JReid (7) (hld up & bhd: hdwy 2f out: sustained chal u.p to ld nr fin) ............................ —1

2505a³ Shrewd Idea *(MKauntze,Ireland)* 8-11 GDuffield (2) (lw: led 1f: 2nd st: led 1f out tl ct nr fin) ............................ s.h.2

2679² Ibraz (USA) **(84)** *(HThomsonJones)* 8-11 RHills (8) (led after 1f to 1f out) ............ 2.3

2918 Majestic Hawk (USA) **(96)** (bl) *(MMoubarak)* 8-11 GBaxter (1) (a.p: 5th st: effrt u.p appr fnl f: sn rdn: unable qckn) ............................ ¾.4

2918⁴ Icy South (USA) **(97)** *(JHMGosden)* 9-1 SCauthen (9) (b.nr fore: lw: a.p: 3rd st: ev ch over 1f out: rdn & one pce) ............................ 3.5

2175³ Prevene (IRE) **(100)** *(PFICole)* 8-11 PaulEddery (3) (chsd ldrs: 4th st: rdn & btn appr fnl f) ............................ 3.6

2002² Bristol Fashion *(MBell)* 8-7 PRobinson (4) (hld up: nvr trbld ldrs) ........................ 3.7
2426 Bollin Duncan *(MHEasterby)* 8-7 MBirch (6) (a bhd) ........................................ 6.8
2879★ Drumdonna (IRE) (77) *(JBerry)* 8-6 JCarroll (5) (lw: dwlt: sn chsng ldrs: 6th st: wknd over 2f out) ...................................................... 3¹/₂.9

**5/2** VISTO SI STAMPI (IRE), **11/4** Shrewd Idea, **5/1** Prevene (IRE), Icy South (USA), **7/1** Majestic Hawk (USA), **10/1** Bristol Fashion, **11/1** Ibraz (USA), **16/1** Drumdonna (IRE), **33/1** Bollin Duncan. CSF £10.50, Tote £3.70: £1.20 £1.70 £3.10 (£5.50). Gerecon Italia (ARUNDEL) bred by Samac Ltd in Ireland. 9 Rn 1m 48.28 (7.88)
SF—45/44/38/36/31/18

T/Trio: Race 1: £172.70 (8.3 Tckts). T/Plpt: £52.90 (216.65 Tckts). IM

## 2856—KEMPTON (R-H)

### Friday, September 4th [Good]

Going Allowance: Rnd: 0.10 sec per fur; Rest: 0.40 sec per fur (G)      Wind: mod across

Stalls: 2nd low, remainder high

**3128**      WATFORD H'CAP (0-90) £3552.75 (£1062.00: £508.50: £231.75)
1³/₄m                                                          2-05 (2-14)

2267⁵ **Empire Blue (65)** *(PFICole)* 9-8-7 BRaymond (2) (b: lw: hdwy & 7th st: hrd rdn over 2f out: r.o to ld nr fin) ...................................................... —1
937 Subsonic (IRE) **(77)** *(JLDunlop)* 4-9-5 BRouse (5) (hdwy 6f out: 5th st: wkd ins fnl f tl nr fin) ................................................................ nk.2
2001⁵ Broom Isle (62) *(MrsAKnight)* 4-7-13(1) ‡5OPears (11) (4th st: ev ch fnl f: r.o) .... ¹/₂.3
£006 Miss Pin I Ip (69) *(PatMitchell)* 3-8-0 DBiggs (1) (hdwy & 2nd st: led 2f out tl wkd ins fnl 1) ..................................................................... nk.4
2836⁶ Farmer's Pet (79) (Jt-Fav) *(GAPritchard-Gordon)* 3-8-10 LDettori (3) (led after 1f to 2f out: ev ch ins fnl f: nt qckn) ........................................ 3.5
2793⁶ Lobinda (78) *(JLDunlop)* 3-8-9 WCarson (8) (rdn 5f out: 6th st: no hdwy) ...... 3¹/₂.6
2899⁶ Brandon Prince (IRE) (82) (bl) *(IABalding)* 4-9-10 RCochrane (4) (nvr nr to chal) 1.7
2226³ Elaine Tully (IRE) (76) *(MJHeaton-Ellis)* 4-9-4 PatEddery (13) (prom tl rdn & wknd 5f out) ...................................................................... 8.8
2920⁵ Clurican (IRE) (76) *(DNicholson)* 3-8-7 AClark (7) (lw: 3rd st: wknd over 2f out) 1¹/₂.9
2921 Master Foodbroker (IRE) (81) *(DRCElsworth)* 4-9-9 JWilliams (6) (a bhd) ...... 12.10
2899⁵ Welshman (66) (Jt-Fav) *(MBlanshard)* 6-8-8 JQuinn (12) (led 1f: wknd 6f out: t.o fnl 4f) ............................................................................ 25.11
2451 Shahdjat (IRE) (72) *(KCBailey)* 4-9-0 MPerrett (9) (lw: a bhd: t.o fnl 5f) ............ 12

**11/2** Farmer's Pet, Welshman, **6/1** Lobinda(op 4/1), **15/2** Brandon Prince (IRE), **8/1** Elaine Tully (IRE)(tchd 12/1), **10/1** Miss Pin Up, **12/1** EMPIRE BLUE, Broom Isle, **16/1** Subsonic (IRE), **20/1** Master Foodbroker (IRE), **25/1** Clurican (IRE), **50/1** Shahdjat. CSF £150.88, CT £1,912.71. Tote £16.80: £4.10 £4.30 £3.90 (£128.20). Richard Green (Fine Paintings) (WHATCOMBE) bred by Guiting Stud Ltd. 12 Rn 3m 4.50 (7.90)
SF—28/39/18/18/22/14

**3129**      STANMORE NURSERY   £3915.00 (£1170.00: £560.00: £255.00)   **6f**   2-40 (2-43)
(Weights raised 8 lb)

3049³ **Hello Hobson's (IRE) (63)** (Fav) *(JAkehurst)* 7-11(3) WCarson (6) (lw: a.p: qcknd to ld ins fnl f: r.o) .................................................... —1
2779★ Infant Protege (USA) (67) *(CEBrittain)* 7-10 ‡5BDoyle (8) (hld up: led over 1f out tl ins fnl f) ..................................................................... ³/₄.2
2409 Steppin High (68) *(LordHuntingdon)* 7-11 ‡5DHarrison (4) (a.p: r.o in once pce fnl 2f) ........................................................................... 3.3
2799⁵ Pistol (IRE) (84) *(PFICole)* 9-4 CRutter (3) (lw: a.p: hrd rdn over 1f out: nt qckn) nk.4
2994 Risky Number (59) *(JSMoore)* 7-7 DaleGibson (9) (w ldrs: led over 2f out tl over 1f out) ............................................................................ ¹/₂.5
2225★ Chili Heights (77) *(GBBalding)* 8-11 JWilliams (1) (b.hind: nrst fin) ................ hd.6
2081⁶ Kensworth Lady (67) *(MBlanshard)* 8-1 JQuinn (7) (reard s: nvr nr to chal) ........ 6.7
2900² Waterlord (IRE) (75) *(CGCox)* 8-9 AClark (5) (lw: led over 2f: wknd 2f out) ...... 5.8
2776⁴ Marchwell Lad (78) *(MRChannon)* 8-12 PatEddery (2) (dwlt: wknd over 3f out tl over 2f out) ................................................................ 1¹/₂.9
2857⁴ Top Pet (IRE) (87) *(RHannon)* 9-7 JLloyd (11) (outpcd) ................................ 2¹/₂.10
2414 Venture Prints (59) *(RChampion)* 7-7 NAdams (10) (spd 3f) ...................... 1¹/₂.11
LONG HANDICAP: Risky Number 7-4, Venture Prints 7-6.

**4/1** HELLO HOBSON'S (IRE), **9/2** Pistol (IRE), **13/2** Marchwell Lad, **7/1** Infant Protege (USA), Steppin High, Chili Heights, **9/1** Top Pet (IRE), **12/1** Waterlord (IRE), Kensworth Lady, **20/1** Risky Number, **50/1** Venture Prints. CSF £30.51, CT £175.80. Tote £4.40: £2.10 £3.00 £2.10 (£9.30). Hobson's International Ltd (UPPER LAMBOURN) bred by A. W. Allen in Ireland. 11 Rn 1m 15.63 (4.33)
SF—45/41/30/50/23/40

## 3130—3132

**3130**　MILCARS CHERTSEY LOCK STKS (2-Y.O.C & G) £4597.50 (£1380.00: £665.00: £307.50)　**7f (J.C)**
3-10 (3-12)

**Pembroke (USA)** *(JHMGosden)* 8-11 SCauthen (7) (w'like: scope: lw: 5th st: led 1f out: pushed out) ............................................................. —1
Flashfeet *(IABalding)* 8-11 LDettori (2) (leggy: scope: lw: 6th st: led over 1f out: sn hdd: r.o) ....................................................................... ½.2
Baron Ferdinand *(RCharlton)* 8-11 JLloyd (9) (w'like: scope: lw: 3rd st: ev ch 1f out: nt qckn) .......................................................................... 1.3
2849* Revelation (IRE) (Fav) *(RHannon)* 9-4 PatEddery (8) (led after 2f tl wknd over 1f out) .................................................................................. 1½.4
Bixby (USA) *(DRCElsworth)* 8-11 RCochrane (10) (unf: scope: s.s: 7th st: hrd rdn over 2f out: r.o one pce) .................................................... 5.5
2568 Coalisland *(RIngram)* 8-6 ‡5JWeaver (5) (led 2f: 2nd st: wknd over 1f out) ....... 2½.6
Monsieur Dupont (IRE) *(BWHills)* 8-11 JWilliams (1) (str: scope: bkwd: nvr nr to chal) .......................................................................................... hd.7
Jihaad (USA) *(JLDunlop)* 8-11 WCarson (11) (w'like: scope: bkwd: s.s: a bhd) ¾.8
Allensea (IRE) *(CAHorgan)* 8-11 DaleGibson (4) (unf: a bhd) ......................... hd.9
Bransby Road (IRE) *(RAkehurst)* 8-8 ‡3RPerham (6) (str: lw: outpcd) ........... hd.10
Chummy's Saga *(BWHills)* 8-11 PRobinson (3) (w'like: scope: j.path after 2f: 4th st: wknd over 1f out) ...................................................... 2.11

**10/11** Revelation (IRE), **4/1** PEMBROKE (USA), Flashfeet(op 5/1), Jihaad (USA)(op 5/1), **16/1** Baron Ferdinand, **33/1** Ors. CSF £46.13, Tote £4.10: £1.50 £2.20 £3.20 (£27.40). Sheikh Mohammed (NEWMARKET) bred by Stonereath Farm Inc in USA. 11 Rn
1m 30.34 (6.14)
SF—50/48/45/47/25/12

**3131**　MILCARS TEMPLE FORTUNE STKS (listed race) £8976.25 (£2710.00: £1317.50: £621.25)　**1m (J.C)**
3-40 (3-41)

2643⁴ **Calling Collect (USA)** (Fav) *(LMCumani)* 3-8-9 LDettori (7) (stdy hdwy over 2f out: led ins fnl f: pushed out) ......................................... —1
2789³ Night Manoeuvres (107) *(HCandy)* 3-9-1 RCochrane (9) (lw: hdwy over 1f out: r.o wl ins fnl f) ......................................................................... 2.2
1596* Hazaam (USA) *(MRStoute)* 3-8-9 SCauthen (1) (lw: 4th st: led over 1f out tl ins fnl f) ...................................................................................... s.h.3
849 Mukaddamah (USA) (116) *(PTWalwyn)* 4-9-0 WCarson (6) (lw: 5th st: ev ch 2f out: wknd 1f out) .......................................................... 3.4
2641* St Ninian (101) *(MHEasterby)* 6-9-0 MBirch (3) (2nd st: led over 2f out tl over 1f out) ........................................................................ hd.5
983³ Modernise (USA) (100) *(RCharlton)* 3-8-9 PatEddery (5) (lw: 6th st: wknd over 1f out) ............................................................................. 1½.6
2522³ Tik Fa (96) *(BHanbury)* 3-8-9 BRaymond (8) (3rd st: wknd over 2f out) ... 3.7
2789 River Falls (110) *(RHannon)* 3-8-9 PRobinson (2) (lw: a bhd) ..................... ½.8
2097a² Flying Brave (110) (v) *(JLDunlop)* 4-9-0 JWilliams (4) (led: sn clr: hdd & wknd qckly over 2f out) ...................................................... 12.9

**5/2** CALLING COLLECT (USA), **9/2** Hazaam (USA)(7/2—11/2), **5/1** Night Manoeuvres(op 8/1), **6/1** Modernise (USA), **9/1** Mukaddamah (USA), **10/1** St Ninian, **12/1** Flying Brave, **14/1** River Falls, **20/1** Tik Fa (USA). CSF £14.52, Tote £3.40: £1.80 £1.90 £2.00 (£9.00). Miss G. Gatto Roissard (NEWMARKET) bred by B & R Partners in USA. 9 Rn
1m 41.26 (4.66)
SF—75/75/68/64/63/53

**3132**　MILCARS STKS (2-Y.O.F) £4760.00 (£1430.00: £690.00: £320.00)　**7f (J.C)**
4-10 (4-17)

**Athens Belle (IRE)** *(RCharlton)* 8-8 PatEddery (16) (unf: scope: gd hdwy 2f out: hrd rdn 1f out: led wl ins fnl f: r.o) ................................. —1
2849⁴ Society Lady (USA) *(AAScott)* 8-8 SCauthen (10) (5th st: led over 1f out tl wl ins fnl f) ................................................................................... ¾.2
Miss Fascination *(MAJarvis)* 8-8 PRobinson (4) (w'like: scope: 8th st: hdwy 2f out: r.o ins fnl f) ...................................................................... 3.3
Sooty Swift (IRE) *(CEBrittain)* 8-8 MBirch (11) (unf: bit bkwd: led tl over 1f out) ¾.4
Modi (USA) *(LordHuntingdon)* 8-8 LDettori (6) (unf: hdwy over 2f out: styd on) . 1.5
2859⁴ Hard Task *(RFJohnsonHoughton)* 8-8 JLloyd (19) (7th st: no hdwy fnl 2f) ...... 1½.6
Midnight Heights *(JWPayne)* 8-8 JQuinn (7) (leggy: a mid div: no hdwy fnl 2f) . ½.7
2792³ Dancing Spirit (IRE) (Fav) *(DRCElsworth)* 8-8 RCochrane (14) (4th st: wknd over 1f out) .................................................................................. 3½.8
Katie Eileen (USA) *(RHannon)* 8-8 AClark (2) (w'like: scope: hdwy over 2f out: wknd over 1f out) ............................................................. ½.9

Kryptos (USA) *(LordHuntingdon)* 8-3 ‡5DHarrison (13) (unf: scope: nvr nrr) .. s.h.10
Bobbysoxer *(JLDunlop)* 8-8 AMcGlone (1) (leggy: scope: bit bkwd: nrst fin) .. ½.11
Canadian Eagle *(GLewis)* 8-5 ‡3RPerham (3) (w'like: nvr nrr) ......................... s.h.12
Seek the Pearl *(MRStoute)* 8-8 PD'Arcy (8) (leggy: n.d) ............................... nk.13
Lake Poopo (IRE) *(BWHills)* 8-8 WCarson (12) (w'like: scope: bit bkwd: 6th st:
    n.m.r & eased 2f out) ......................................................... 5.14
Mim *(GBBalding)* 8-8 JWilliams (15) (unf: a bhd) ........................................ hd.15
Breeze by *(IABalding)* 8-5 ‡3SO'Gorman (9) (leggy: a bhd) ......................... 1½.16
25983 Summer Pageant *(JRFanshawe)* 8-8 BRouse (20) (3rd st: wknd over 2f out) ... 1.17
Dana Springs (IRE) *(RHannon)* 8-8 BRaymond (17) (leggy: bit bkwd: 2nd st:
    wknd over 2f out) .............................................................. ½.18
2792 Guanhumara *(PTWalwyn)* 8-8 DBiggs (18) (s.s: a bhd) ............................... 3½.19

**3/1** Dancing Spirit (IRE)(op 2/1), **5/1** Miss Fascination(7/2—11/2), **13/2** Society Lady (USA), **7/1** Hard Task, **8/1** ATHENS BELLE (IRE)(5/1—9/1), **10/1** Summer Pageant(op 6/1), **12/1** Dana Springs (IRE)(op 7/1), **14/1** Sooty Swift (IRE), Seek the Pearl, Lake Poopo (IRE)(op 7/1), **16/1** Katie Eileen (USA), Kryptos (USA)(10/1—20/1), **20/1** Modi (USA), Breeze by, **25/1** Midnight Heights, **33/1** Bobbysoxer, **50/1** Ors. CSF £64.97, Tote £8.60: £3.00 £2.00 £2.20 (£36.30). Lord Weinstock (BECKHAMPTON) bred by Ballymacoll Stud Farm Ltd in Ireland. 19 Rn
1m 30.09 (5.89)
SF—48/46/37/35/32/27

**3133**   RADLETT H'CAP (3-Y.O) (0-80) £3816.00 (£1143.00: £549.00: £252.00)
       **7f (rnd)**                                 4-40 (4-45)
                       (Weights raised 5 lb)
2825 **Sovereign Rock (IRE) (72)** *(RHannon)* 9-5 LDettori (4) (lw: hdwy over 1f out:
    led ins fnl f: all out) .......................................................... —1
2993 Silky Siren (53) (bl) *(EAWheeler)* 7-9 ‡5DHarrison (16) (2nd st: led over 2f out tl
    ins fnl f: r.o) ............................................................... s.h.2
2865* Roca Murada (IRE) **(67)** *(Jt-Fav)* *(MJRyan)* 8-4 DBiggs (3) (7th st: ev ch 1f out:
    r.o) ......................................................................... ¾.3
17242 Morocco (IRE) (74) *(RCharlton)* 9-7 PatEddery (14) (lw: 8th st: ev ch ins fnl f:
    wknd nr fin) ................................................................ 1½.4
2882* Salisong (71) *(PFICole)* 8-11 ‡7JDSmith (1) (9th st: styd on fnl 2f) ............... s.h.5
29455 Mogwai (IRE) (66) (bl) *(RFJohnsonHoughton)* 8-13 RCochrane (5) (nvr nrr) .... nk.6
2995* Hameem (IRE) (74) (bl) *(AAScott)* 9-7 (6x) BRaymond (9) (lw: 5th st: ev ch 2f
    out: wknd fnl f) ............................................................. ¾.7
26596 Jumaira Star (USA) (70) *(JHMGosden)* 9-3 SCauthen (8) (lw: hrd rdn 2f out: no
    hdwy) ..................................................................... 2½.8
2795 Walstead (IRE) (60) *(DAWilson)* 8-7 JWilliams (6) (styd hvly fnl 2f: r.o) .......... nk.9
3052 Countercheck (IRE) (54) *(CFWall)* 8-1 PRobinson (13) (lw: n.d) ................ s.h.10
2881 Gold Jubilee (58) *(PJMakin)* 8-5 TSprake (15) (lw: n.d) ............................ 1½.11
24496 Super Serenade (IRE) **(GBBalding)* 9-6 BRouse (2) (b: lw: 6th st: wknd fnl f) ¾.12
30043 Southwold Air (69) *(JLDunlop)* 9-2 WCarson (7) (lw: n.d) ........................ 6.13
2831 Hi-Tech Honda (IRE) (68) *(CEBrittain)* 9-1 MBirch (11) (4th st: wknd over 2f out)1½.14
24964 Court Minstrel (62) *(LJHolt)* 8-9 AMcGlone (10) (n.d) ......................... hd.15
2966* Thornton Gate (72) (bl) *(MHEasterby)* 9-2 (6x) ‡3SMaloney (12) (led tl hrd rdn &
    wknd over 2f out) ........................................................... ½.16
2787 Lady Roxanne (67) *(LordHuntingdon)* 8-7 ‡7DSalt (17) (a bhd) ................... ½.17
30042 Peerage Prince (55) *(Jt-Fav)* *(PatMitchell)* 7-13 ‡3SO'Gorman (18) (lw: 3rd st:
    wknd over 2f out) ......................................................... 2½.18

**7/1** Roca Murada (IRE), Peerage Prince, **8/1** Hameem (IRE), Thornton Gate, **10/1** Silky Siren, **11/1** Southwold Air, **12/1** Hi-Tech Honda (IRE), Jumaira Star (USA), Morocco (IRE), **14/1** SOVEREIGN ROCK (IRE), **16/1** Salisong, **20/1** Super Serenade, Court Minstrel, Gold Jubilee, **25/1** Mogwai (IRE), **33/1** Ors. CSF £136.45, CT £972.03. Tote £28.20: £5.30 £3.70 £1.80 £2.10 (£130.00). Mr P. A. Howell (MARLBOROUGH) bred by K. Molloy in Ireland. 18 Rn
1m 27.45 (3.45)
SF—64/39/46/58/47/48

T/Trio: Race 6: £801.60 (1.1 Tckts). T/Jkpt: Not won; £10,544.30 to Kempton 5/9/92. T/Plpt: £1,929.50 (3.6 Tckts).
Hn

# KEMPTON (R-H)

## Saturday, September 5th [Good]

Going Allowance: nil sec per fur (G)                        Wind: almost nil

Stalls: low

**3134**   TEDDINGTON GRADUATION STKS (3-Y.O.F) £3231.00 (£963.00: £459.00: £207.00)
       **6f**                                     2-10 (2-12)

2851 **Harvest Girl (IRE) (100)** (Fav) *(GAPritchard-Gordon)* 9-4 LDettori (6) (hld up:
    led over 1f out: comf) ...................................................... —1

2697* Elhasna (USA) *(MajorWRHern)* 9-4 WCarson (1) (lw: hld up: led over 2f out tl over 1f out: unable qckn) ............ 6.2

2640² Belated (79) *(HThompsonJones)* 9-4 PatEddery (3) (lw: chsd ldr: ev ch wl over 1f out: one pce) ............ 3½.3

2898 High Sevens (89) *(HCandy)* 9-4 CRutter (2) (led over 3f: one pce) ............ nk.4

3004 Castilian Queen (76) *(JHMGosden)* 9-4 RCochrane (5) (lw: bhd fnl 3f) ............ 6.5

*2882 Hazy Shades (100/1) Withdrawn : not under orders*

**Evens** HARVEST GIRL (IRE), **5/2** Elhasna (USA), **8/1** High Sevens(5/1—9/1), Belated, **14/1** Castilian Queen (USA)(8/1—16/1). CSF £3.58, Tote £1.70: £1.10 £1.50 (£2.10). Mr Giles W. Pritchard-Gordon (NEWMARKET) bred by Corduff Stud in Ireland. 5 Rn                              1m 13.43 (2.13)

SF—61/37/23/22/–

---

**3135**     ARION H'CAP (3-Y.O.F) (0-90) £3699.00 (£1107.00: £531.00: £243.00)
**1m (J.C)**

2-40 (2-43)

2825⁶ **Lap of Luxury (70)** *(WJarvis)* 8-5 NDay (6) (6th st: led 2f out: hrd rdn: r.o wl) ....—1

2990⁴ Ghurrah (IRE) (62) *(CJBenstead)* 7-11 TyroneWilliams (11) (lw: rdn & hdwy over 3f out: 4th st: hrd rdn over 2f out: r.o) ............ 1½.2

2825 Swallowcliffe (72) (v) *(PTWalwyn)* 8-7 LDettori (1) (lw: hld up: hrd rdn over 1f out: r.o) ............ s.h.3

2871² Tiffany's Case (IRE) (62) (Fav) *(CAHorgan)* 7-11 SDawson (10) (hdwy over 1f out: r.o wl ins fnl f) ............ 1.4

2140² Hugging (77) *(MMcCormack)* 8-12 CAsmussen (9) (swtg: hrd rdn & hdwy on ins over 1f out: r.o one pce) ............ 1.5

3058⁴ Olette (82) *(GWragg)* 9-3 RCochrane (13) (led 6f: one pce) ............ s.h.6

2988* Be My Everything (IRE) (69) *(RHollinshead)* 7-11 ‡7JDennis (5) (swtg: nvr nr to chal) ............ 1.7

2586³ Twilight Secret *(JWHills)* 8-2 GCarter (3) (nvr nrr) ............ 1.8

242 Sylvan (IRE) (86) *(CFWall)* 9-7 JWilliams (12) (hdwy 2f out: wknd over 1f out) ... 2.9

2725⁴ Lady of Sardinia (BEL) (61) *(JWPayne)* 7-10(1) DBiggs (2) (a mid div) ............ hd.10

2704* So Smug (USA) (74) *(JHMGosden)* 8-9 PatEddery (4) (5th st: wknd over 2f out)2½.11

2854 Romoosh *(CEBrittain)* 8-5 GCrealock (7) (2nd st: wknd 2f out) ............ hd.12

2935 Mariette Larkin (58) *(GBBalding)* 7-7 NAdams (8) (hdwy over 4f out: wknd over 3f out) ............ 2.13

2403 Enaya (78) *(RWArmstrong)* 8-13 WCarson (14) (3rd st: eased whn btn over 1f out) ............ 2.14

LONG HANDICAP: Mariette Larkin 7-5.

**11/2** Tiffany's Case (IRE), **15/2** Ghurrah (IRE)(12/1—7/1), **8/1** Hugging, Romoosh, So Smug (USA), **9/1** Twilight Secret, **10/1** LAP OF LUXURY, Olette, Enaya, **14/1** Be My Everything, **16/1** Lady of Sardinia (BEL), Swallowcliffe, **25/1** Ors. CSF £77.83, CT £1,086.32. Tote £10.90: £3.20 £4.30 £5.60 (£152.90). Mr I. C. Hill-Wood (NEWMARKET) bred by Langham Hall Bloodstock. 14 Rn                    1m 39.74 (3.14)

SF—44/31/40/27/39/43

---

**3136**     BONUSPRINT SIRENIA STKS (listed race) (2.Y.O) £7253.75 (£2180.00: £1052.50: £488.75)   **6f**

3-10 (3-11)

2845³ **Silver Wizard (USA) (100)** (Fav) *(GLewis)* 9-5 PatEddery (1) (lw: hld up: led over 1f out: comf) ............—1

2459* Forest Wind (USA) *(MMoubarak)* 9-1 LDettori (5) (led 5f out tl over 1f out: unable qckn) ............ 2½.2

2444* Liyakah (USA) (90) *(MajorWRHern)* 8-10 WCarson (2) (lw: led 1f: rdn over 1f out: one pce) ............ 2.3

2619² Amazing Baby (USA) (73) *(DRCElsworth)* 8-6 CAsmussen (4) (nvr nr to chal) 1½.4

2960* Sheila's Secret (IRE) (92) *(WCarter)* 8-6 JWilliams (6) (a bhd) ............ 1.5

237* Other One (84) *(NCWright)* 8-6 GCarter (3) (a bhd) ............ 8.6

**13/8** SILVER WIZARD (USA), **9/4** Liyakah (USA), **11/4** Forest Wind (USA), **14/1** Amazing Baby (USA), Sheila's Secret (IRE), **66/1** Other One. CSF £6.10, Tote £2.30: £1.50 £2.10 (£2.90). Mrs Shirley Robins (EPSOM) bred by Bounding Basque Breeding Syndicate in USA. 6 Rn                              1m 13.17 (1.87)

SF—67/53/40/30/26/–

---

**3137**     GEOFFREY HAMLYN H'CAP (0-90) £3728.25 (£1116.00: £535.50: £245.25)
**1m (J.C)**

3-40 (3-42)

2714² **Aitch N'Bee (76)** *(LadyHerries)* 9–9-5 LDettori (6) (gd hdwy over 1f out: led ins fnl f: drvn out) ............—1

1870 Merlins Wish (USA) (80) *(RHannon)* 8-9-4 GBardwell (5) (hrd rdn & hdwy over 1f out: r.o wl ins fnl f) ............ hd.2

2581⁵ Dance on Sixpence (57) (v) *(HJCollingridge)* 4–8-0 CRutter (4) (3rd st: led over 1f out tl ins fnl f: r.o) ............ hd.3

2881⁴ Mossy Rose **(59)** *(LordHuntingdon)* 6–7–11 ‡5DHarrison (8) (lw: gd hdwy over
        1f out: r.o wl ins fnl f) ................................................................................ 2.4
2828⁴ Lord Oberon (IRE) **(63)** *(RJO'Sullivan)* 4–8–6 AClark (3) (hdwy over 1f out: r.o
        ins fnl f) .............................................................................................. 1¹/₂.5
3088 Domicksky **(73)** *(RSimpson)* 4–9–2 WCarson (9) (lw: hdwy over 1f out: r.o) .... nk.6
2647⁶ First Century (IRE) **(72)** *(BRMillman)* 3–8–10 JWilliams (18) (4th st: one pce fnl f) s.h.7
2458⁴ Hamadryad (IRE) **(76)** *(WCarter)* 4–9–5 CAsmussen (16) (no hdwy fnl 3f) ....... nk.8
2410⁶ Vanborough Lad **(64)** *(MJHaynes)* 3–8–2 GCarter (11) ............ s.h.9
2935 Santi Sana **(65)** *(LadyHerries)* 4–8–8 NDay (2) (b.off hind: nvr nrr) ............. nk.10
2911 Langtry Lady **(79)** *(MJRyan)* 6–9–8 DBiggs (7) (hdwy over 2f out: wknd over 1f
        out) ...................................................................................................... ¹/₂.11
2987³ Green's Cassatt (USA) **(55)** *(WMBrisbourne)* 4–7–5(1) ‡7CHawksley (5) (lw: nvr
        nrr) ..................................................................................................... s.h.12
2971² Pelorus **(82)** *(DRCElsworth)* 7–9–4 ‡7JHunter (13) (hdwy & nt clr run on ins over
        1f out: nvr nrr) ...................................................................................... s.h.13
2958 Shake Town (USA) **(71)** (v) *(MHTompkins)* 4–9–0 RCochrane (12) (lw: a bhd) hd.14
2825⁴ Saafend **(65)** *(JSutcliffe)* 4–8–1 ‡7JTate (1) (led over 4f out tl over 1f out: sn
        wknd) .................................................................................................. s.h.15
2473³ Texan Tycoon **(66)** *(RAkehurst)* 4–8–2 ‡7TAshley (10) (lw: a bhd) .............. 2.16
2825 Scales of Justice **(78)** *(JWHills)* 6–9–7 BRouse (14) (6th st: wknd over 2f out) 3¹/₂.17
2990² Green's Ferneley (IRE) **(83)** (bl) (Fav) *(RCharlton)* 4–9–12 PatEddery (17) (b:
        lw: 5th st: wknd wl over 1f out) ................................................................ 2.18
2078⁵ Traders Dream **(58)** *(TThomsonJones)* 3–7–10 NAdams (19) (led over 3f: 2nd
        st: wknd over 2f out) ............................................................................... 2.19

**5/1** Green's Ferneley (IRE), **8/1** Mossy Rose, **10/1** Shake Town (USA), **11/1** Scales of Justice, **12/1** Langtry
Lady, Saafend, **14/1** Lord Oberon (IRE), Pelorus, AITCH N'BEE, **16/1** Domicksky, Hamadryad (IRE), **20/1** Santi
Sana, Texan Tycoon, **25/1** First Century (IRE), Dance on Sixpence, Green's Cassatt (USA), **33/1** Ors. CSF
£342.24, CT £9,746.20. Tote £9.20: £2.30 £8.20 £5.00 £2.00 (£356.40). Lady Herries (LITTLEHAMPTON) bred
by Liam Ward. 19 Rn                                                                    1m 39.83 (3.23)
                                                                           SF—57/55/36/27/31/40

**3138**          BONUSPRINT SEPTEMBER STKS (Gp 3) £21573.00 (£7992.15: £3771.08: £1568.77)
                 **1m 3f 30y**                                                          4-10 (4-12)

2345 Jeune **(113)** *(GWragg)* 3–8–6 RCochrane (1) (lw: 4th st: qcknd & led over 1f
        out: pushed out) ....................................................................................... —1
557² Red Bishop (USA) **(111)** *(JHMGosden)* 4–9–0 WCarson (4) (rdn over 4f out: 3rd
        st: one pce fnl 2f) ................................................................................... 3¹/₂.2
2837³ Seattle Rhyme (USA) **(120)** (Fav) *(DRCElsworth)* 3–8–6 CAsmussen (3) (lw: 5th
        st: rdn over 2f out: r.o one pce) ................................................................ nk.3
2891a* Corrupt (USA) **(110)** *(PWChapple-Hyam)* 4–9–5 LDettori (2) (b: 2nd st: led over
        2f out tl over 1f out: one pce) ................................................................. 1¹/₂.4
2846³ Ile de Chypre **(108)** *(GHarwood)* 7–9–7 AClark (5) (led over 8f) .................... 10.5

**8/11** Seattle Rhyme (USA), **11/2** Corrupt (USA), Red Bishop (USA), **6/1** JEUNE, **16/1** Ile de Chypre. CSF £30.89,
Tote £6.30: £2.10 £1.60 (£14.80). Sir Robin McAlpine (NEWMARKET) bred by Sir Robin McAlpine. 5 Rn
                                                                                   2m 22.61 (5.01)
                                                                           SF—42/43/34/44/26

**3139**          SPELTHORNE H'CAP (0-90) £8180.00 (£2465.00: £1195.00: £560.00)
                 **1¹/₂m**                                                              4-40 (4-43)

2734³ Daisy Girl **(65)** *(JMackie)* 6–8–6 GCarter (4) (4th st: led over 1f out: drvn out) ... —1
657² Laburnum **(84)** (Fav) *(LMCumani)* 4–9–11 LDettori (9) (rdn over 2f out: hdwy
        over 1f out: str run ins fnl f: fin wl) ........................................................... hd.2
3013 Roll a Dollar **(86)** *(DRCElsworth)* 6–9–13 BRouse (5) (6th st: rdn over 1f out: r.o
        wl ins fnl f) ........................................................................................... s.h.3
2853 Western Dynasty **(68)** *(MJRyan)* 6–8–9 DBiggs (11) (lw: 5th st: hrd rdn over 1f
        out: r.o) ................................................................................................ ³/₄.4
3013⁴ Robingo (IRE) **(75)** *(CEBrittain)* 3–8–7 GCrealock (12) (hdwy over 1f out: r.o
        one pce) ............................................................................................... 1¹/₂.5
2853* Opera Ghost **(86)** *(PWHarris)* 6–9–13 RCochrane (7) (hdwy over 1f out: r.o ins
        fnl f) ................................................................................................... s.h.6
2860⁴ Asian Punter (IRE) **(68)** *(AHide)* 3–7–7 ‡7NVarley (6) (lw: 2nd st: led over 2f out tl
        over 1f out: one pce) .............................................................................. s.h.7
605³ Equity Card (IRE) **(70)** *(GAPritchard-Gordon)* 4–8–6 ‡5DHarrison (8) (nvr nrr) ..... 2.8
1a³ Specificity (USA) **(86)** *(JHMGosden)* 4–9–13 NDay (1) (b.hind: swtg: nvr nrr) ... nk.9
1318⁵ Rare Detail (IRE) **(72)** *(DRCElsworth)* 4–8–6 ‡7JHunter (10) (b: lw: nvr nrr) ... ³/₄.10
2853 Kinglow (USA) **(81)** (bl) *(MrsJCecil)* 3–8–13 PatEddery (2) (lw: 3rd st: wknd over
        2f out) .................................................................................................. 2.11

Vintage **(87)** *(MajorWRHern)* 7–10-0 JWilliams (14) (bit bkwd: swtg: a bhd) ..... 1.12
2885⁵ Santana Lady (IRE) **(70)** *(MJHeaton-Ellis)* 3–8-2 CRutter (3) (led over 9f) ......... 2.13
2806 Royal Verse (FR) **(52)** *(RCurtis)* 5–7-7 GBardwell (15) (prom 9f) ...................... 5.14
2885³ Mahsul (IRE) **(63)** *(CJBenstead)* 4–8-4 WCarson (6) (a bhd) .......................... 2.15
LONG HANDICAP: Royal Verse (FR) 6-9.

**4/1** Laburnum, **11/2** Robingo, **7/1** Opera Ghost, **8/1** Kinglow (USA), **10/1** Roll a Dollar, Mahsul (IRE), **12/1** DAISY GIRL, **14/1** Santana Lady (IRE), **16/1** Asian Punter (IRE), Specificity (USA), **20/1** Western Dynasty, Rare Detail (IRE), **25/1** Vintage, **33/1** Equity Card (IRE), **100/1** Royal Verse (FR). CSF £54.72, CT £463.12. Tote £14.30: £3.30 £1.70 £4.30 (£23.80). Mr S. Taberner (CHURCH BROUGHTON) bred by S. Taberner. 15 Rn
2m 34.44 (4.24)
SF—50/68/69/49/44/63

**3140**    GREBE APP'CE H'CAP (0-70) £2721.00 (£756.00: £363.00)
      1m 1f (rnd)                                          5-10 (5-14)

2911⁵ **Sharp Dream (64)** (Fav) *(BSmart)* 4–9-8 StephenDavies (4) (lw: 6th st: hrd rdn over 1f out: led wl ins fnl f: r.o wl) ................................................................ —1
3045³ Breezed Well (53) *(CNAllen)* 6–8-11 GForster (5) (lw: hdwy over 1f out: r.o wl ins fnl f) ........................................................................................................ s.h.2
2999 Keep Your Word (53) *(GBBalding)* 6–8-6 ‡⁵TraceyPurseglove (8) (4th st: led over 2f out: clr over 1f out: hdd wl ins fnl f: r.o) ....................... s.h.3
2825 Elegant Friend (65) *(MHTompkins)* 4–9-2 ‡⁷SMulvey (18) (lw: hdwy over 1f out: r.o wl ins fnl f) ........................................................................................ 1.4
3009⁵ Ballerina Bay (56) (v) *(DTThom)* 4–8-9 ‡⁵FArrowsmith (3) (hdwy over 1f out: r.o ins fnl f) ................................................................................................ 1½.5
2033⁴ Super Morning (49) *(JPearce)* 6–8-7 PTurner (19) (lw: hdwy over 1f out: r.o)˙ . s.h.6
1252⁴ Will Soon (68) *(HCandy)* 3–9-3 ‡³AntoinetteArmes (6) (b: lw: nvr nr to chal) ..... s.h.7
1150³ Joli's Great (51) *(MJRyan)* 4–8-4 ‡⁵PMcCabe (9) (hdwy fnl 2f: r.o) ................... s.h.8
3021⁴ Swift Silver (61) *(WJMusson)* 5–9-0 ‡⁵PBowe (2) (a mid div) ............................. ½.9
3060² Danzarin (IRE) (67) *(RHannon)* 4–9-4 ‡⁷MarkDenaro (12) (lw: a.p: led over 3f out: tl over 2f out: sn wknd) ........................................................ s.h.10
2946³ Weeheby (USA) (62) *(AAScott)* 3–8-11 ‡³JTate (13) (a mid div) .......................... 1.11
800 Possessive Lady (45) *(MBell)* 5–7-12 ‡⁵NVarley (11) (a mid div) ...................... 1.12
2554⁵ Cradle of Love (USA) (70) (bl) *(JWHills)* 4–10-0 KRutter (10) (5th st: wknd wl over 1f out) ............................................................................. 1½.13
2757 Rosietoes (USA) (42) *(LGCottrell)* 4–7-9 ‡⁵CAvery (15) (3rd st: wknd over 2f out) ½.14
2941 Roly Wallace (60) (bl) *(KTIvory)* 3–8-7⁽¹⁾ 7–⁵CScally (14) (b.hind: a bhd) ......... ¾.15
3009⁴ Miss Sarajane (46) *(RHollinshead)* 3–8-1 ‡³MHumphries (16) (a bhd) ............... 2.16
2935 Good for the Roses (46) *(CGCox)* 6–7-13 ‡⁵DWright (1) (lw: bhd fnl 3f) ............... 6.17
2829⁴ Bengal Tiger (IRE) (48) (bl) *(JAkehurst)* 4–8-6 CHawksley (7) (led over 5f) ......... 1.18
Majority Holding (46) *(MJWilkinson)* 7–7-11⁽⁶⁾ ‡⁷DGriffiths (17) (a bhd) .............. 2.19
3735 Solid (IRE) (53) *(JRJenkins)* 4–8-4 ‡⁷CAddington (20) (a bhd) .......................... 3.20

**100/30** SHARP DREAM, **8/1** Will Soon, **10/1** Keep Your Word, Danzarin (IRE), **11/1** Weeheby (USA), **12/1** Swift Silver, Possessive Lady, **14/1** Super Morning, **16/1** Miss Sarajane, Elegant Friend, Ballerina Bay, Cradle of Love (USA), **20/1** Bengal Tiger (IRE), Good for the Roses, Joli's Great, Breezed Well, **25/1** Solid (IRE), **33/1** Roly Wallace, Rosietoes (USA), **66/1** Majority Holding. CSF £68.27, CT £594.06. Tote £4.90: £2.10 £3.70 £2.50 £8.40 (£54.40). Mrs L. M. Dresher (LAMBOURN) bred by Aston Park Stud. 20 Rn    1m 53.40 (3.40)
SF—57/45/39/46/34/31

T/Trio: Race 4: Any 2 fr 1st 3 w any £57.60 (30.4 Tckts) & Race 6: £161.80 (11 Tckts). T/Jkpt: Not won; £16,011.85 to Doncaster 9/9/92. T/Plpt: £634.40 (13.75 Tckts).               AK

## 2983—THIRSK (L-H)

### Saturday, September 5th [Good to firm]
Going Allowance: St: minus 0.15; Rnd: minus 0.05 sec per fur (F)      Wind: almost nil

Stalls: high

**3141**    FALCON CLAIMING STKS    £2553.00 (£708.00: £339.00)    1½m    2-15 (2-15)

3010³ **Greek Chime (IRE)** (Jt-Fav) *(LordHuntingdon)* 3–8-6 DMcKeown (7) (lw: a.p: chal & wnt lft 3f out: sn drvn along: styd on wl u.p to ld nr fin) —1
2957³ Silver Samurai (67) (Jt-Fav) *(RHollinshead)* 3–8-6 WRyan (9) (hld up: gd hdwy appr st: led 2f out: hdd & no ex nr fin) ................................. hd.2
2985⁶ Salu (53) (bl) *(JEtherington)* 3–8-1⁽¹⁾ GHind (11) (hld up: smooth hdwy on outside 2f out: sn ev ch: edgd lft u.p & nt qckn nr fin) ....... hd.3
2923² Persian Fleece (49) (Jt-Fav) *(MrsGRReveley)* 3–7-7 JLowe (8) (in tch: effrt 3f out: kpt on same pce fnl 2f) ................................................ 2.4
3072⁶ Shadanza (IRE) *(APStringer)* 3–8-4 TLucas (12) (hld up: stdy hdwy over 2f out: nvr plcd to chal) ...................................................................... 5.5

2923⁵ Petite Belle **(56)** *(RMWhitaker)* 3-8-2(16) ‡⁷GParkin (2) (sme hdwy 3f out: sn drvn
along: nvr able to chal) .................................................. 4.6
Eastern Pleasure **(44)** *(MDHammond)* 5-8-7 KFallon (3) (hld up: effrt 3f out: n.d) ³/4.7
Clovermill **(42)** (v) *(WBentley)* 4-8-6 NConnorton (4) (lw: trckd ldrs: effrt 5f out:
wknd 3f out) .................................................. 1¹/2.8
Jubilata (USA) *(MPNaughton)* 4-8-6 JakiHouston (1) (a in rr) ...................... ¹/2.10
2957 Mr News (IRE) **(35)** (v) *(BBeasley)* 3-8-0 LCharnock (10) (lw: chsd ldrs to st: sn
lost pl) .................................................. ¹/2.10
2691 Whitwell Hill *(MrsVAAconley)* 3-7-8(1) NCarlisle (5) (led tl hdd & wknd 2f out) .. 4.11
2809⁶ Sea Lord **(37)** *(KWHogg)* 3-8-2(2) JCorrigan (6) (w ldr tl wknd & sltly hmpd 3f
out) .................................................. 15.12

**11/4** Persian Fleece, Silver Samurai, **GREEK CHIME (IRE), 8/1** Salu, **9/1** Shadanza (IRE), **25/1** Jubilata (USA),
Petite Belle, **33/1** Mr News (IRE), **50/1** Sea Lord, Eastern Pleasure, **66/1** Ors. CSF £10.14, Tote £3.30: £1.60
£1.20 £2.40 (£4.20). Lord Weinstock (WEST ILSLEY) bred by Ballymacoll Stud Farm Ltd. in Ireland. 12 Rn
2m 34.9 (4.9)
SF—37/36/30/18/19/9

---

**3142**     SAXTY WAY STKS (Mdn) £2280.00 (£630.00: £300.00)     **6f**     2-45 (2-47)

2995⁶ **King's Signet (USA)** (Fav) *(JHMGosden)* 3-8-11 GHind (4) (mde all: wnt clr
over 2f out: unchal) .................................................. —1
2750 So Superb **(64)** (bl) *(JLDunlop)* 3-8-11 WRyan (2) (sn chsng wnr: rdn & no imp
fnl 2f) .................................................. 8.2
2777⁵ Under the Bridge **(69)** *(PWHarris)* 3-8-11 SWhitworth (5) (prom: drvn along
¹/2-wy: sn outpcd) .................................................. 2.3
Miss Limelight *(ASmith)* 3-8-6 SWebster (1) (leggy: unf: s.i.s: a outpcd) .......... 10.4
Chandni (IRE) *(BHanbury)* 3-8-6 JFortune (3) (leggy: scope: wnt lft s: sme
hdwy after 2f: sn btn) .................................................. 4.5

**9/4** KING'S SIGNET (USA), **5/2** Under the Bridge, **11/4** So Superb, **5/1** Chandni (IRE), **25/1** Miss Limelight. CSF
£7.85, Tote £2.50: £1.40 £1.60 (£4.50). Sheikh Mohammed (NEWMARKET) bred by Darley Stud Management
Co Ltd. in USA. 5 Rn
1m 11.5 (1.3)
SF—53/20/12/–/–

---

**3143**     HAMBLETON CUP (H'cap) (0-80) £4240.00 (£1270.00: £610.00: £280.00)
**1¹/2m**     3-15 (3-20)

2908 Corn Lily **(65)** *(MrsGRReveley)* 6-9-0 ‡⁷DarrenMoffatt (2) (lw: mde all: rdn clr
appr st: hld on wl fnl 2f) .................................................. —1
2329⁴ Stapleton (IRE) **(73)** *(JWWatts)* 3-9-6 WRyan (5) (lw: chsd ldrs: rdn over 2f out:
kpt on fnl f) .................................................. 2.2
3076⁵ Kinoko **(56)** *(KWHogg)* 4-8-12 JCorrigan (3) (hld up: smooth hdwy appr st:
hung bdly lft fnl 2f: styd on) .................................................. ¹/2.3
2496 Dominant Serenade **(49)** *(MDHammond)* 3-7-10 EJohnson (6) (bhd: hdwy
over 2f out: kpt on wl u.p fnl f) .................................................. s.h.4
2742² Top Villain **(40)** *(BSRothwell)* 6-7-10 NCarlisle (12) (a chsng ldrs: effrt 4f out:
kpt on same pce fnl 2f) .................................................. 1.5
2927² Danza Heights **(42)** (Fav) *(MrsGRReveley)* 6-7-12 JLowe (4) (lw: hld up mid
div: effrt over 3f out: nvr rchd ldrs) .................................................. 1.6
2959³ First Bid **(55)** *(RMWhitaker)* 5-8-4 ‡⁷GParkin (7) (lw: bhd: sme hdwy 3f out: n.d) ¹/2.7
3026⁶ Young George **(52)** *(MDods)* 5-8-8 KFallon (13) (bhd: pushed along 7f out:
hdwy on outside 2f out: n.d) .................................................. 5.8
2869★ Irish Stamp (IRE) **(79)** *(JPearce)* 3-9-7 ‡⁵RPrice (11) (lw: chsd ldrs tl wknd appr
st) .................................................. s.h.9
2959⁶ Fairgroundprincess **(37)** *(FHLee)* 4-7-7 LCharnock (8) (prom: hrd rdn 3f out:
wknd 2f out) .................................................. 3¹/2.10
3026⁴ Touch Above **(55)** *(TDBarron)* 6-8-11 DMcKeown (1) (hld up & bhd: gd hdwy
on outside over 2f out: sn rdn & btn) .................................................. 1.11
2927 Super Blues **(51)** *(TDBarron)* 5-8-0 ‡⁷VHalliday (9) (a in rr) .................. 4.12
3024 Mbulwa **(60)** *(SEKettlewell)* 6-9-2 JFortune (10) (chsd ldr tl wknd 3f out) ....... 12.13
LONG HANDICAP: Fairgroundprincess 7-0.

**6/1** Danza Heights, **7/1** Irish Stamp (IRE), **15/2** Mbulwa, **8/1** Kinoko, **9/1** Fairgroundprincess(14/1—8/1), Top
Villain, Touch Above, First Bid, **10/1** Young George, **CORN LILY, 12/1** Stapleton (IRE), **25/1** Super Blues, **33/1**
Dominant Serenade. CSF £112.68, CT £920.64. Tote £9.50: £3.10 £3.60 £2.80 (£73.10). Mrs Susan McDonald
(SALTBURN) bred by Countess of Durham. 13 Rn
2m 33.7 (3.7)
SF—57/59/50/33/31/31

---

**3144**     CRATHORNE H'CAP (0-80) £3366.90 (£1006.20: £481.60: £219.30)     **5f** 3-45 (3-50)

2618⁵ **Samson-Agonistes (73)** *(BAMcMahon)* 6-9-7 ‡⁷SSanders (4) (chsd ldrs: led 2f
out: qcknd clr: hld on wl nr fin) .................................................. —1

3024 Allinson's Mate (IRE) **(73)** *(TDBarron)* 4–10–0 WRyan (2) (racd far side: chsd ldr: gd hdwy over 1f out: styd on strly ins fnl f) .................... ½.**2**

2702⁶ On the Edge **(72)** *(TDBarron)* 4–9–6 ‡?VHalliday (8) (hdwy & swtchd lft 2f out: styd on wl fnl f) ................................. 2½.**3**

2925 Tigani **(67)** (v) *(DWChapman)* 6–9–8 SWebster (15) (swtg: w ldr tl hrd rdn 2f out: styd on same pce) ................................. nk.**4**

2604⁵ Loft Boy **(64)** *(JDBethell)* 9–8–12 ‡?KateDovey (14) (lw: s.s: swtchd lft & gd hdwy over 1f out: styd on wl nr fin) ................. hd.**5**

2848⁶ Super Rocky **(75)** *(RBastiman)* 3–9–7 ‡?HBastiman (1) (lw: led far side 3f: unable qckn) ................................. s.h.**6**

3068⁵ Penny Hasset **(73)** *(MWEasterby)* 4–10–0 TLucas (12) (effrt & n.m.r over 2f out: kpt on u.p fnl f) ......................... 1½.**7**

2395⁵ Pallium (IRE) **(69)** *(MPNaughton)* 4–9–10 KFallon (5) (lw: hdwy on outside 2f out: nt rch ldrs) .......................... nk.**8**

2878² Heaven-Liegh-Grey **(67)** (Fav) *(MJohnston)* 4–9–8 RPElliott (16) (lw: mde most tl hdd & wknd 2f out) ......................... ¾.4**9**

2848 Ned's Bonanza **(70)** *(MDods)* 3–9–4 ‡$OPears (9) (spd over 3f) ................. nk.**10**

2956 Prince Belfort **(67)** *(MPNaughton)* 4–9–8 NConnorton (10) (lw: prom tl wknd over 1f out) ......................... ½.**11**

2153⁵ Chateau Nord **(54)** *(JBerry)* 3–8–0 ‡?PRoberts (11) (nvr trbld ldrs) ................. 1.**12**

2663⁴ Creche **(67)** *(MrsNMacauley)* 3–9–6 DMcKeown (7) (chsd ldrs 3f) ................. 2.**13**

2963⁴ Uppance **(39)** (bl) *(TCraig)* 4–7–8⁽¹⁾ NCarlisle (3) (bhd fnl 2f) ............. 1½.**14**

1281* Just Bob **(70)** (bl) *(SEKettlewell)* 3–9–9 JFortune (6) (b.hind: nvr wnt pce) ...... ¾.**15**

LONG HANDICAP: Uppance 7-1.

**9/4** Heaven-Liegh-Grey(4/1—2/1), **6/1** Penny Hasset, **8/1** Tigani, **11/1** Prince Belfort, **14/1** Just Bob, SAMSON-AGONISTES, Chateau Nord, Creche, Super Rocky, **16/1** Loft Boy, Ned's Bonanza, **20/1** Allinson's Mate (IRE), On the Edge, Pallium (IRE), **33/1** Uppance. CSF £238.33, CT £4,975.31. Tote £17.20: £5.00 £4.20 £9.50 (£126.70). Mr J. B. Wilcox (TAMWORTH) bred by D. W. Pike. 15 Rn                    59.3 sec (1.6)
SF—60/65/47/48/37/45

---

**3145**      HIGHFLYER STKS    £2994.40 (£828.40: £395.20)    7f        4-15 (4-19)

3083⁴ **Double Blue (93)** (Fav) *(MJohnston)* 3–9–1 DMcKeown (6) (lw: disp ld tl rn wd appr st: led wl over 1f out: rdn & r.o wl) .................... —**1**

2637⁴ Bold Boss **(89)** *(BHanbury)* 3–9–1 NCarlisle (4) (lw: outpcd tl c wd & hdwy 2f out: ev ch ins fnl f: r.o) ......................... ½.**2**

2825 Crystal Heights (FR) **(81)** *(WAO'Gorman)* 4–9–5 JFortune (3) (mde most over 5f: kpt on one pce) ......................... 1½.**3**

2943² Blue Marine **(ACStewart)* 3–8–10 WRyan (1) (lw: trckd ldrs: swtchd & effrt 2f out: edgd rt & nt qckn) ......................... hd.**4**

2029 Boursin (IRE) **(83)** *(PCalver)* 3–9–1 GHind (2) (a outpcd & bhd) ................. 10.**5**

2958 Young Valentine **(63)** *(RMWhitaker)* 3–9–4 AClhane (5) (lw: cl up tl rdn & wknd 3f out) ......................... 5.**6**

**2/1** DOUBLE BLUE, **3/1** Blue Marine, **100/30** Bold Boss, **6/1** Crystal Heights (FR), **10/1** Boursin (IRE), **33/1** Young Valentine. CSF £8.13, Tote £1.90: £1.10 £1.90 (£4.10). Mr R. W. Huggins (MIDDLEHAM) bred by The Queen. 6 Rn                                         1m 26 (2.7)
SF—55/53/52/42/17/5

---

**3146**      UNDERWOOD STKS (I) (Mdn 2-Y.0) £2511.00 (£696.00: £333.00)    1m    4-45 (4-49)

2918² **Elkhart (USA)** (Fav) *(HRACecil)* 9–0 WRyan (6) (lw: trckd ldrs: chal over 2f out: sn rdn: r.o u.p to ld nr fin) .................... —**1**

2910³ Persiansky (IRE) **(70)** *(BHanbury)* 9–0 NCarlisle (8) (lw: trckd ldrs: hdwy to ld wl over 1f out: r.o u.p: jst ct) ......................... nk.**2**

2456 Safir (USA) *(JLDunlop)* 9–0 JLowe (1) (lw: led tl hdd wl over 1f out: rallied & ev ch ins fnl f: kpt on) ......................... s.h.**3**

2185 Gypsy Crystal (USA) *(RMWhitaker)* 8–9 AClhane (5) (a chsng ldrs: one pce fnl 2f) ......................... 4.**4**

Young Tess *(MissSEHall)* 8–9 SWebster (3) (lengthy: bit bkwd: bhd: swtchd & effrt 2f out: r.o wl nr fin) ......................... 7.**5**

2675 Grand as Owt **(79)** *(DenysSmith)* 9–0 KFallon (4) (chsd ldrs tl outpcd fnl 2f) ... 1½.**6**

2269 Greystoke *(LordHuntingdon)* 9–0 DMcKeown (2) (hdwy appr st: outpcd fnl 3f) .. 5.**7**

I'M No Fool *(MHEasterby)* 9–0 NConnorton (10) (rangy: scope: bit bkwd: sn bhd: sme late hdwy) ......................... ½.**8**

2986 Blakes Reach *(RRLamb)* 8-7 ‡?RHavlin (11) (chsd ldrs over 4f: sn wknd) .......... ½.**9**

Deacon Brodie *(MWEasterby)* 9–0 TLucas (9) (leggy: scope: bit bkwd: s.i.s: plld hrd & hung rt: a bhd) ......................... 1½.**10**

2961 Miramichi Bay (bl) *(MrsVAAconley)* 9-0 LCharnock (7) (dwlt: hdwy & in tch appr
st: wknd over 2f out) .................................................................. 3.11
*Stewards Enquiry:* Havlin suspended 14-17/9/92 (excessive use of whip).

**1/5** ELKHART (USA)(2/7 –1/6), **10/1** Safir (USA)(op 6/1), **14/1** Greystoke, Persiansky (IRE), **25/1** I'M No Fool,
**66/1** Grand as Owt, Young Tess, **100/1** Deacon Brodie, Blakes Reach, Gypsy Crystal (USA), **150/1** Miramichi
Bay. CSF £4.63, Tote £1.20: £1.10 £1.60 £1.50 (£3.80). Sheikh Mohammed (NEWMARKET) bred by W Lazy T
Ltd. in USA. 11 Rn     1m 41.3 (5.3)
SF–14/13/12/–/–/–

**3147**     UNDERWOOD STKS (II) (Mdn 2-Y.O) £2511.00 (£696.00: £333.00)   **1m** 5-15 (5-18)

3005² **Dixieland Melody (USA)** (Fav) *(BHanbury)* 9-0 WRyan (5) (lw: hld up: hdwy
ent st: led over 2f out: pushed along: r.o wl) ....................... —1
2864 Manaarah (USA) *(AAScott)* 8-9 JFortune (2) (s.i.s: hdwy 3f out & c wd: ev ch
over 1f out: r.o) ...................................................................... 3.2
2873 Mutakallam (USA) *(HThomsonJones)* 9-0 NCarlisle (6) (lw: led tl hdd over 2f
out: kpt on one pce) .............................................................. 5.3
2924 Wanza *(JHanson)* 9-0 EJohnson (7) (lw: a chsng ldrs: nt qckn fnl 2f) .......... ¾.4
2879 Master Fiddler *(EWeymes)* 9-0 GHind (10) (uns rdr & bolted gng to s: cl up tl
wknd over 2f out) ................................................................... 7.5
Karibuni *(DRFranks)* 9-0 DMcKeown (8) (neat: bit bkwd: s.s: hdwy appr st: nvr
nr to chal) ............................................................................. 8.6
2700⁶ Steal a March *(MWEasterby)* 9-0 TLucas (1) (s.i.s: n.d) ............................. 4.7
1734⁵ Sandmoor Satin *(MHEasterby)* 8-9 NConnorton (9) (b.hind: n.d) ............... nk.8
2563 Sean's Delight *(JMCarr)* 8-9 SMorris (3) (a outpcd & wl bhd) ..................... 10.9
1191 Native Worth *(JMJefferson)* 9-0 AShoults (4) (swtg: unruly s: in tch to st: sn
bhd) ................................................................................... hd.10

**2/5** DIXIELAND MELODY (USA), **9/2** Mutakallam (USA), **16/1** Manaarah (USA), **20/1** Wanza, **33/1** Sandmoor
Satin, Steal a March, **40/1** Master Fiddler, **66/1** Ors. CSF £7.63, Tote £1.40: £1.10 £1.80 £1.30 (£5.00). Mr
Saeed Suhail (NEWMARKET) bred by Franklin N. Groves in USA. 10 Rn     1m 40.8 (4.8)
SF–22/8/–/–/–/–

**3148**     PHOENIX NURSERY   £3659.40 (£1018.40: £490.20)   **7f**     5-45 (5-52)
(Weights raised 8 lb)

2703★ **Hi Nod (64)** (Fav) *(MJCamacho)* 8-1 NConnorton (3) (lw: trckd ldrs: rdn to ld
ins fnl f: r.o wl) ..................................................................... —1
2938⁴ Muraadi Ana (IRE) **(65)** (bl) *(AAScott)* 8-2 ACulhane (13) (hdwy to jn ldrs ent st:
led wl over 1f out: hdd ins fnl f: no ex) .................................. 1½.2
3091 Costa Verde **(84)** *(KWHogg)* 9-7 JCorrigan (10) (lw: hld up: swtchd ins 2f out:
effrt over 1f out: hrd rdn & styd on) ......................................... ¾.3
2360⁶ Contract Elite (IRE) **(65)** *(CWThornton)* 8-9 GHind (8) (bhd tl gd hdwy 2f out: r.o
wl) .................................................................................... 1½.4
2973⁴ Sea Exhibition (IRE) **(67)** *(MBlanshard)* 8-4 DMcKeown (16) (bhd: hdwy 2f out:
r.o wl) .................................................................................. 1.5
2706³ Palm Chat **(70)** *(LMCumani)* 8-7 JFortune (1) (lw: in tch: effrt 3f out: rdn & nt pce
to chal) ................................................................................ s.h.6
2910 Bold Face (IRE) **(73)** (bl) *(RFJohnsonHoughton)* 8-5 ‡⁵RPrice (2) (cl up: effrt 3f
out: grad wknd fnl 2f) ............................................................. 2.7
2983⁴ Palacegate Prince **(65)** *(JBerry)* 8-2 LCharnock (5) (led tl hdd wl over 1f out:
grad wknd) ........................................................................... ½.8
3023⁵ Dead Calm **(58)** *(CTinkler)* 7-9 PBurke (12) (lw: racd wd: prom tl edgd lft &
wknd over 2f out) .................................................................. nk.9
1788² Charlies Reward **(56)** *(TFairhurst)* 7-0 ‡7ClaireBalding (7) (w ldrs tl wknd 2f out) ¾.10
1036 Ruby Cooper **(62)** *(JWharton)* 7-13 AShoults (11) (nvr trbld ldrs) .................. 2.11
2901⁴ Almansour (USA) **(84)** *(HRACecil)* 9-7 WRyan (9) (bhd: effrt over 2f out: n.d) 1½.12
2903⁵ Warkworth (USA) **(70)** *(JWWatts)* 8-7 JLowe (4) (unruly bef s: broke wl: sn lost
pl) ...................................................................................... nk.13
2938⁵ Red Cent **(68)** (bl) *(JEtherington)* 8-5 TLucas (6) (hld up: effrt ent st: sn wknd) 3.14
1959 Lettermore **(58)** *(RMWhitaker)* 7-9 EJohnson (15) (lw: a bhd) ..................... 1½.15
2901 Monastic Flight (IRE) **(61)** (bl) *(BSRothwell)* 7-12 NCarlisle (14) (racd wd: prom
to st: sn wknd & eased) ......................................................... 16

**2/1** HI NOD, **5/1** Palm Chat, **11/1** Bold Face (IRE), Almansour (USA), **12/1** Muraadi Ana (IRE), **14/1** Palacegate
Prince, Sea Exhibition (IRE), Costa Verde, **16/1** Warkworth (USA), Red Cent, **20/1** Ruby Cooper, Dead Calm,
Monastic Flight (IRE), **25/1** Charlies Reward, **33/1** Ors. CSF £26.85, CT £262.91. Tote £3.50: £1.70 £2.90 £2.90
£6.70 (£29.20). Mr Brian Nordan (MALTON) bred by B. Nordan. 16 Rn     1m 27.2 (3.9)
SF–24/20/37/13/12/14

T/Plpt: £380.00 (9.4 Tckts).     O'R/AA

2814—**HAMILTON (R-H)**

## Monday, September 7th [Good to soft becoming Soft]
Going Allowance: 1st-3rd: 0.60 sec (Y); Rest: 0.75 sec per fur (S)     Wind: fresh across

Stalls: low

**3149**     W H ROBERTSON-AIKMAN MEMORIAL H'CAP (3 & 4-Y.O) (0-70) £2542.00 (£712.00: £346.00)     **1m 1f 36y**
2-15 (2-19)

| | | |
|---|---|---|
| 3076[6] | **No Comebacks** (42) *(EJAlston)* 4-8-6 KFallon (8) (bhd: gd hdwy on ins over 2f out: led ins fnl f: eased fr fin) | —1 |
| 2814 | **Thisonesforalice** (43) *(AHarrison)* 4-8-7 JCarroll (13) (lw: a chsng ldrs: led 2f out tl ins fnl f: nt pce of wnr) | 2½.2 |
| 3073[5] | **Joseph's Wine (IRE)** (41) *(RBastiman)* 3-7-10 ‡3SMaloney (1) (a chsng ldrs: effrt 3f out: styd on fnl f) | 2½.3 |
| 806[5] | **Ready to Draw (IRE)** (62) *(RonaldThompson)* 3-9-6 JLowe (14) (hdwy 4f out: styd on one pce fnl 2f) | nk.4 |
| 3026 | **Straw Thatch** (68) *(MJohnston)* 3-9-12 DMcKeown (15) (led early: chsd ldrs: no ex fnl 2f) | 1½.5 |
| 2941[2] | **The Dandy Don (IRE)** (53) *(DenysSmith)* 3-8-11 BRaymond (12) (chsd ldr tl outpcd wl over 2f out) | 3½.6 |
| 2926 | **Huso** (64) *(PCHaslam)* 4-9-9 ‡5JWeaver (10) (hdwy ent st: ev ch 3f out: sn rdn & grad wknd) | nk.7 |
| 3026[2] | **Cheeky Pot** (42) (bl) *(Fav)* *(DenysSmith)* 4-8-6 LCharnock (5) (hdwy to jn ldrs ent st: led 4f out to 2f out: grad wknd) | 2.8 |
| 3026★ | **Northern Graduate (USA)** (68) *(MrsGRReveley)* 3-9-12 KDarley (9) (hdwy ent st: shkn up 4f out: nvr plcd to chal) | 1½.9 |
| 3025 | **Tina's Game** (36) *(APStringer)* 4-8-0(2) GDuffield (6) (sn led: hdd 4f out: wknd 3f out) | s.h.10 |
| 2941 | **Mummy's Brew** (44) *(BBeasley)* 3-8-2(2) JFortune (11) (a bhd) | 12.11 |
| 891[2] | **Aragon Ayr** (46) *(PMonteith)* 4-8-10 PBurke (7) (n.d) | 10.12 |
| 2967[3] | **Milton Rooms (IRE)** (53) (bl) *(CBBBooth)* 3-8-11(1) GOldroyd (2) (hdwy ent st: wknd over 3f out: t.o) | 13 |
| 2721 | **Nishara** (36) *(NBycroft)* 4-7-9(1) ‡5NKennedy (3) (t.o) | 14 |
| 2959 | **Dara Loch (IRE)** (34) *(MrsJRRamsden)* 4-7-12 JFanning (4) (chsd ldrs to st: t.o) | 15 |

**4/1** Cheeky Pot, **9/2** Northern Graduate (USA), **6/1** The Dandy Don (IRE), **7/1** Huso, Joseph's Wine (IRE), **10/1** NO COMEBACKS, Thisonesforalice, **16/1** Aragon Ayr, Ready to Draw (IRE)(op 10/1), **20/1** Straw Thatch, Dara Loch (IRE), **25/1** Milton Rooms (IRE), **33/1** Tina's Game, **50/1** Mummy's Brew, **100/1** Nishara. CSF £99.99, CT £690.06. Tote £10.60: £2.90 £2.80 £3.10 (£145.30). Mr Lionel Snowden (PRESTON) bred by Newmarket Thoroughbred Breeders P L C. 15 Rn
2m 3.4 (9.1)
SF—36/29/10/33/34/8

**3150**     HAMILTON PALACE STKS (Mdn) £2080.00 (£580.00: £280.00)     **1m 65y** 2-45 (2-49)

| | | |
|---|---|---|
| 3080 | **Lahoob (USA)** *(BHanbury)* 3-8-9 BRaymond (8) (b.hind: mde all: shkn up nr fin) | —1 |
| | **Royal Comedian** *(BWMurray)* 3-8-4 JFortune (9) (unruly in paddock: sn chsng ldrs: rdn 2f out: r.o: edgd rt nr fin) | ¾.2 |
| 3025 | **Heliopsis** *(MDHammond)* 4-9-0 JCarroll (7) (bhd tl styd on fnl 2f: nrst fin) | 12.3 |
| 3052 | **Tina Meena Lisa** (35) *(EHOwenjun)* 3-8-4 JLowe (4) (cl up tl outpcd wl over 2f out) | 1.4 |
| 2967[4] | **Bee Dee Ell (USA)** (42) *(MissLAPerratt)* 3-8-9 JFanning (6) (b.hind: cl up tl wknd 3f out) | 1½.5 |
| 2985 | **Kenyatta (USA)** (57) (bl) *(Fav)* *(DenysSmith)* 3-8-9 KFallon (2) (prom: effrt over 3f out: sn btn) | 3.6 |
| 3042 | **Sharp Fairy** *(ABailey)* 4-8-9 NConnorton (5) (hld up: stdy hdwy 4f out: grad lost pl fnl 2f) | s.h.7 |
| 3073 | **Ivors Princess** (46) *(MJohnston)* 3-8-4 DMcKeown (1) (a bhd: t.o) | 30.8 |

**13/8** Kenyatta (USA), **100/30** LAHOOB (USA)(op 2/1), **15/2** Sharp Fairy, **8/1** Tina Meena Lisa, **10/1** Ivors Princess, **14/1** Bee Dee Ell (USA), Heliopsis, **16/1** Royal Comedian. CSF £43.68, Tote £4.00: £2.60 £8.30 £1.40 (£42.90). Mr B. Hanbury (NEWMARKET) bred by Pillar Stud Incorporated in USA. 8 Rn
1m 52.6 (9.3)
SF—28/21/-/-/-/-

**3151**     'WIN WITH THE TOTE' CLAIMING STKS     £2738.00 (£768.00: £374.00)     **1m 65y**
3-15 (3-29)

| | | |
|---|---|---|
| 1849★ | **Quantity Surveyor** (67) *(Fav)* *(SirMarkPrescott)* 3-8-12 GDuffield (5) (drvn along most of wy: a.p: led 3f out: hung rt: styd on wl) | —1 |
| 2966[6] | **Verdant Boy** (47) *(MPNaughton)* 9-8-7 NConnorton (9) (a chsng ldrs: styd on fnl 2f: nt pce of wnr) | 2.2 |

2941 Mary Macblain (46) *(JLHarris)* 3-8-4(1) DMcKeown (8) (bhd: effrt over 3f out: styd on wl fnl 2f) ............................................................... 5.3

2814 Bold Melody (57) *(PCHaslam)* 3-7-12 ‡5NKennedy (7) (a chsng ldrs: ev ch 4f out: one pce fnl 2f) .................................................. 3/4.4

2966 Jane's Brave Boy (20) *(TCraig)* 10-8-7 LCharnock (10) (led tl hdd 3f out: grad wknd) .................................................... 6.5

2814 Miss Knight (36) *(RBastiman)* 5-8-2 PBurke (6) (c wd & effrt 4f out: sn rdn & no imp) ................................................ 1/2.6

*2785* Station Express (IRE) (28) *(BEllison)* 4-8-7 JFortune (1) (in tch tl outpcd fnl 3f) 8.7

3086 Blanc Seing (FR) *(MWEasterby)* 5-9-7 TLucas (2) (b: sn wl bhd: sme late hdwy) 2.8

364 Great Service (44) *(MDods)* 5-8-13 KFallon (4) (lw: a bhd) ....................... 7.9

23275 Lowlands Boy (46) *(TFairhurst)* 3-8-8 JFanning (3) (prom tl wknd 4f out) ..... 31/2.10
      *Miss Mac (200/1) Withdrawn (broke out of stalls) : not under orders*

**9/4** QUANTITY SURVEYOR, **4/1** Miss Knight(op 6/1), **9/2** Bold Melody(op 5/2), Verdant Boy, **8/1** Mary Macblain, **20/1** Great Service, **25/1** Blanc Seing (FR), **33/1** Lowlands Boy, Station Express (IRE), **66/1** Jane's Brave Boy. CSF £11.83, Tote £3.60: £1.10 £2.30 £2.50 (£5.30). Lady Fairhaven (NEWMARKET) bred by Lord Fairhaven. 10 Rn
           1m 52.4 (9.1)
           SF—33/22/4/-/-/-

---

**3152**    MACALLAN SINGLE HIGHLAND MALT SCOTCH WHISKY H'CAP (3 & 4-Y.O.) (0-70)
        £2752.00 (£772.00: £376.00)    1¹/₂m 17y           3-45 (3-54)

10255 **Sunderland Echo (46)** (Fav) *(MrsGRReveley)* 3-8-10 JLowe (9) (hld up & bhd: hdwy on ins 4f out: led 2f out: eased ins fnl f: pushed out nr fin) .................................................................................................. —1

25734 Aide Memoire (IRE) (47) *(CBBBooth)* 3-8-11(1) GOldroyd (4) (bhd tl hdwy over 2f out; r.o wl) ................................................................................. 3/4.2

29594 Marowins (48) *(EJAlston)* 3-8-12 KFallon (11) (bhd: hdwy 4f out: styd on one pce appr fnl f) .............................................................................. 6.3

28336 Shayna Maidel (39) *(MBell)* 3-8-0 ‡3SMaloney (10) (hdwy 5f out: ev ch over 2f out: one pce) ................................................................................. 4.4

3052 Clean Singer (38) *(NBycroft)* 3-8-2 LCharnock (8) (cl up: ev ch 4f out: wknd 2f out) ............................................................................................... 1.5

27214 Corporate Type (IRE) (25) *(GPKelly)* 4-7-12 SWood (14) (hdwy 4f out: styd on) hd.6

3078 Shadaylou (IRE) (34) *(MissLAPerratt)* 3-7-5 ‡7ClaireBalding (6) (hdwy 5f out: sn prom: grad wknd fnl 2f) .............................................................. nk.7

30254 Storm Gayle (IRE) (64) *(MJohnston)* 3-9-9 ‡5LNewton (18) (chsd ldrs tl wknd wl over 2f out) ...................................................................................... 10.8

*27832* Invisible Armour (45) *(PCHaslam)* 3-8-4 ‡5JWeaver (13) (disp ld tl led 8f out: clr ent st: hdd 2f out: wknd qckly) ...................................................... 5.9

20715 Hthaal (USA) (55) *(LLungo)* 4-10-0 JFortune (3) (chsd ldrs tl wknd over 2f out) . 10

2968 Carol's Pet (IRE) (37) *(MJohnston)* 4-8-10 RPElliott (12) (reluctant to r: t.o tl sme late hdwy) ....................................................................................... 11

3017 Watermill Girl (29) *(DTThom)* 4-8-2 GDuffield (17) (prom to st: sn rdn & btn) ...... 12

Cyrill Henry (IRE) (48) *(MDods)* 3-8-7 ‡NKennedy (7) (cl up tl wknd over 3f out: t.o) ................................................................................................. 13

18946 Caithness Rock (49) *(CParker)* 3-8-13 JCarroll (16) (prom to st: t.o) .................. 14

Mangrove Mist (IRE) (51) *(PMonteith)* 4-9-3(1) ‡7ADobbin (3) (t.o) ...................... 15

3034 Native Crown (49) (bl) *(MrsSCBradburne)* 4-9-3 ‡5OPears (15) (disp ld 4f: cl up tl wknd 4f out: t.o) ........................................................... 16

25733 Notable Exception (60) *(SEKettlewell)* 3-9-10 JFortune (5) (t.o) ...................... 17

2699 Gleneliane (IRE) (34) *(JLHarris)* 4-8-7 DMcKeown (1) (lw: p.u lame 7f out) ........... 0

**4/1** SUNDERLAND ECHO, **5/1** Marowins, **6/1** Shayna Maidel, **7/1** Invisible Armour, Carol's Pet (IRE), **8/1** Corporate Type (IRE), **12/1** Caithness Rock, Notable Exception, **16/1** Watermill Girl, Storm Gayle (IRE), **20/1** Aide Memoire (IRE), **25/1** Gleneliane (IRE), **33/1** Shadaylou (IRE), Mangrove Mist (IRE), Native Crown (IRE), Hthaal (USA), Cyrill Henry (IRE), **66/1** Clean Singer. CSF £82.43, CT £398.10. Tote £3.80: £1.30 £7.10 £2.00 £1.50 (£82.80). Northeast Press Limited (SALTBURN) bred by B. E. Green. 18 Rn
          2m 48 (16)
          SF—26/25/14/-/-/-

---

**3153**    SOUTER OF STIRLING H'CAP (3-Y.O.) (0-70) £2570.00 (£720.00: £350.00)
        6f 5y                                4-15 (4-29)

             (Weights raised 7 lb)

29665 **Celestine (56)** *(TFairhurst)* 9-0 JFanning (1) (in tch: rdn ¹/₂-wy: styd on to ld ins fnl f) .............................................................................................................. —1

2942 Lift Boy (USA) (40) *(DenysSmith)* 7-5 ‡7CTeague (5) (led tl hdd ins fnl f: kpt on one pce) ................................................................................................ 1¹/₂.2

2813 Kentucky Rain (54) *(JGFitzGerald)* 8-5 ‡7MichaelHunt (8) (a in tch: styd on fnl f) 3/4.3

30485 Kalar (47) *(DWChapman)* 8-5 SWood (6) (chsd ldrs: effrt 2f out: kpt on one pce) nk.4

3052 Malcesine (IRE) **(47)** *(CaptJWilson)* 8-5 JFortune (3) (a chsng ldrs: kpt on same pce fnl 2f) .................................................................. nk.5

2984 Chill Wind **(40)** (bl) *(NBycroft)* 7-7[5] ‡[5]NKennedy (2) (outpcd & bhd tl styd on wl fnl f) ............................................................................... 1½.6

2942 Intrepid Fort **(37)** (bl) *(BWMurray)* 7-9[1] LCharnock (11) (hdwy to disp ld ½-wy: sn rdn & no imp) .......................................................... 2.7

2778[6] Oyston's Life **(52)** *(JBerry)* 8-10 JCarroll (9) (chsd ldrs: rdn ½-wy: btn appr fnl f) nk.8

3004 Invigilate **(63)** *(MPNaughton)* 9-2 ‡[5]JWeaver (4) (effrt ½-wy: no imp: eased ins fnl f) ...................................................................... hd.9

3003[2] Our John **(55)** *(RonaldThompson)* 8-13 JLowe (7) (outpcd fr ½-wy) .............. 3½.10

3016[3] Wafi (USA) **(57)** (Fav) *(BHanbury)* 9-1 BRaymond (10) (lw: spd to ½-wy: sn bhd) 4.11

LONG HANDICAP: Chill Wind 7-2.

**3/1** Wafi (USA), **5/1** Invigilate(op 3/1), **6/1** CELESTINE, Our John, **8/1** Oyston's Life, **10/1** Kalar, **12/1** Lift Boy (USA), **14/1** Intrepid Fort, **20/1** Kentucky Rain, **25/1** Malcesine (IRE), **66/1** Chill Wind. CSF £65.26, CT £1,210.76. Tote £6.90: £2.40 £5.80 £2.70 (£103.00). Mr M. J. Grace (MIDDLEHAM) bred by J. G. and Mrs J. M. Brearley. 11 Rn

1m 17.9 (7.9)

SF—32/3/14/13/12/–

**3154** LEVY BOARD CLAIMING STKS £2248.00 (£628.00: £304.00) **6f 5y** 4-45 (4-51)

2875[2] **Francis Ann (47)** *(MissLAPerratt)* 4-8-0 JFanning (1) (cl up: led 2f out: styd on wl) ................................................................................. —1

2966[4] Diet **(63)** (v) *(MissLAPerratt)* 6-8-11 GDuffield (3) (a cl up: rdn 2f out: styd on one pce fnl f) ....................................................................... 2.2

3074[4] Dokkha Oyston (IRE) **(74)** (Fav) *(JBerry)* 4-9-3 JCarroll (5) (chsd ldrs: effrt & ev ch 2f out: nt qckn) .................................................................. 2.3

3074 Borocay *(MJCamacho)* 4-9-1 NConnorton (2) (outpcd & bhd tl styd on appr fnl f) ................................................................................... 2½.4

159[3] Miss Calculate *(CaptJWilson)* 4-8-8 JFortune (4) (cl up: chal wl over 2f out: wknd over 1f out) ................................................................ 6.5

3074 Toshiba Comet **(73)** (v) *(BBeasley)* 5-9-0 ‡[5]SWilliams (6) (led 4f: sn rdn & wknd) 4.6

**6/4** Dokkha Oyston (IRE), **15/8** Diet, **4/1** FRANCIS ANN, **9/1** Toshiba Comet, **14/1** Miss Calculate, **50/1** Borocay. CSF £11.51, Tote £7.70: £2.50 £1.80 (£3.90). Miss L. A. Perratt (AYR) bred by Mrs H. T. Jones. 6 Rn

1m 17.2 (7.2)

SF—32/35/33/21/–/–

**3155** LORD HAMILTON OF DALZELL NURSERY £2416.00 (£676.00: £328.00) **6f 5y**

5-15 (5-22)

(Weights raised 9 lb)

3071* **Egg (55)** (bl) *(TDBarron)* 8-3 (7x) JLowe (1) (dwlt: bhd tl hdwy 2f out: led ins fnl f: r.o wl) .................................................................... —1

2572[3] Blue Radiance **(63)** *(TFairhurst)* 9-11 JFanning (2) (chsd ldrs: rdn to ld over 1f out: hdd ins fnl f) ........................................................... 2.2

2842 Formidable Liz **(50)** *(NBycroft)* 7-7 ‡[5]NKennedy (3) (uns rdr & bolted gng to s: hdwy 2f out: ev ch 1f out: edgd lft & nt qckn) ..................... 1.3

2563 Desirable Miss **(51)** (bl) *(MBrittain)* 7-10[3] ‡[3]SMaloney (5) (cl up: wandered u.p 2f out: no ex fnl f) ....................................................... 2.4

2960 Make it Happen (IRE) **(67)** *(JBerry)* 9-1 DMcKeown (6) (cl up: rdn 2f out: one pce) ................................................................................. 1½.5

2818[2] Robix (IRE) **(73)** (Fav) *(JBerry)* 9-7 JCarroll (4) (cl up stands' side: led 2f out tl appr fnl f: edgd rt & nt qckn) ....................................... ½.6

3071[3] Selvole **(52)** *(MissLAPerratt)* 7-7 ‡[7]ClaireBalding (9) (racd centre: led 4f: grad wknd) ................................................................... 1½.7

2629 Dowreyna **(66)** *(MRStoute)* 9-0 GDuffield (7) (spd centre tl wknd appr fnl f) .. 1½.8

2928 Make Mine a Double **(62)** (v) *(MissSEHall)* 8-10 NConnorton (7) (lw: prom centre over 4f) ........................................................ 1½.9

2965* Sporting Spirit **(72)** *(DWChapman)* 9-6 SWood (8) (lost tch fr ½-wy) .......... 8.10

**7/2** Robix (IRE)(op 7/1), **4/1** EGG, **9/2** Dowreyna, **6/1** Sporting Spirit, **8/1** Selvole(op 5/1), Blue Radiance, Make Mine a Double, **16/1** Desirable Miss, **20/1** Make it Happen (IRE), **33/1** Formidable Liz. CSF £34.13, CT £852.64. Tote £4.40: £2.70 £5.20 £4.40 (£36.30). David Barron Racing Club (THIRSK) bred by Hever Castle Stud. 10 Rn

1m 17.2 (7.2)

SF—35/35/13/8/21/25

T/Plpt: £1,095.90 (2.8 Tckts).

AA

## 3100—**WOLVERHAMPTON (L-H)**
### Monday, September 7th [Good]
Going Allowance: 0.10 sec per fur (G)

Wind: str bhd

Stalls: high

**3156**  HAGLEY STKS (Mdn 2-Y.O.F) £2805.00 (£780.00: £375.00)  **5f**  2-30 (2-32)

| | | |
|---|---|---|
| 2897² | **Yakin (USA)** (Fav) *(HThomsonJones)* 8-11 RHills (2) (lw: a.p: led over 1f out: sn clr: v.easily) | —1 |
| | The Ordinary Girl (IRE) *(TCasey)* 8-11 JReid (4) (cmpt: bit bkwd: hdwy over 1f out: r.o fnl f: no ch w wnr) | 4.2 |
| 2924 | Sicily Oak (66) *(DMcCain)* 8-11 MRoberts (3) (bhd tl hdwy over 1f out: r.o) | ½.3 |
| 3012 | Home Affair (62) (v) *(DTThom)* 8-11 DBiggs (5) (led ½-wy tl appr fnl f: rdn & no ex fnl f) | ½.4 |
| 2826⁵ | Karukera *(MJHeaton-Ellis)* 8-11 DHolland (1) (chsd ldrs: no hdwy fnl 2f) | 1½.5 |
| 1635⁶ | Patong Beach *(JWHills)* 8-11 MHills (8) (sme hdwy fnl f: nvr nrr) | 1½.6 |
| 3033 | Another Jade *(APJarvis)* 8-11 MTebbutt (6) (bit bkwd: nvr trbld ldrs) | ¾.7 |
| 1538 | Early Song *(PTWalwyn)* 8-11 RCochrane (10) (bit bkwd: nvr nr to chal) | s.h.8 |
| 2897⁶ | Well Tried (IRE) *(RHollinshead)* 8-11 WRyan (9) (a in rr) | 1½.9 |
| 2863⁶ | Jade Runner (51) (v) *(MrsNMacauley)* 8-11 NCarlisle (12) (led to ½-wy: sn rdn & wknd) | 4.10 |
| 2863 | Naughty Charlotte *(APJarvis)* 8-11 SWhitworth (7) (outpcd) | 4.11 |
| | Dutch Dancer (BAR) *(JBerry)* 8-11 GCarter (11) (scope: bkwd: outpcd: a bhd: t.o) | 7.12 |

**4/7** YAKIN (USA), **15/2** The Ordinary Girl (IRE), **9/1** Early Song(op 4/1), **10/1** Karukera, **12/1** Sicily Oak(op 7/1), Patong Beach(op 8/1), **14/1** Dutch Dancer (BAR)(op 8/1), Well Tried (IRE)(op 7/1), **50/1** Ors. CSF £6.80, Tote £1.50: £1.30 £1.50 £3.50 (£15.90). Mr Hamdan Al-Maktoum (NEWMARKET) bred by Cormal Investments Inc. in USA. 12 Rn
60.9 sec (3.6)
SF—35/19/17/15/9/3

**3157**  BEWDLEY (S) STKS (3 & 4-Y.O) £2511.00 (£696.00: £333.00)
**1¾m 134y**  3-00 (3-02)

| | | |
|---|---|---|
| 2867³ | **Carrolls Marc (IRE)** (46) *(PJFeilden)* 4-9-5 MRoberts (13) (b.hind: lw: hld up & bhd: hdwy 4f out: led wl over 1f out: eased nr fin) | —1 |
| 2964* | Stingray City (USA) (60) (Fav) *(JEtherington)* 3-8-12 WRyan (11) (a.p: 3rd st: led over 2f out: sn hdd: styd on fnl f) | 1.2 |
| 1667² | Elsa (40) *(RJHolder)* 3-7-9 ‡7SDrowne (7) (hdwy & 6th st: led 2f out: sn hdd: kpt on nr fin) | nk.3 |
| 2868 | Laughton Lady (39) *(MrsNMacauley)* 3-8-2 NAdams (14) (hdwy 9f out: rdn & 4th st: wknd over 1f out) | 8.4 |
| 2793 | Bar Billiards (60) (bl) *(RFJohnsonHoughton)* 3-8-12 JReid (1) (lw: chsd ldr: 2nd st: led 4f out tl over 2f out: sn rdn & wknd) | 4.5 |
| 2934⁴ | Enfant du Paradis (IRE) *(PDEvans)* 4-8-7 ‡7AGarth (2) (prom: 5th & rdn st: sn btn) | 8.6 |
| 2970 | Kate Royale (40) *(MCPipe)* 3-7-11 ‡5DHarrison (10) (effrt & 7th st: no imp: t.o) | 10.7 |
| 3072 | Titian Girl (32) *(MissLCSiddall)* 3-8-2 BCrossley (5) (a bhd: t.o) | ½.8 |
| 2937 | Emma Victoria (22) *(TKersey)* 4-9-0 GHind (12) (b: chsd ldrs 10f: sn rdn & wknd: t.o) | ¾.9 |
| 2970² | Ghostly Glow (54) (v) *(CCElsey)* 3-8-12 RCochrane (6) (lw: a bhd & t.o) | 4.10 |
| 1898 | Sioux Perfick (40) *(CWThornton)* 3-8-2 JQuinn (4) (bhd fr ½-wy: t.o) | 6.11 |
| 2783 | Monorose (47) (v) *(DHaydnJones)* 3-8-2 TyroneWilliams (8) (b.nr hind: mde most 10f: sn rdn & wknd: t.o) | 2.12 |
| 1905 | Sly Prospect (USA) (56) (v) *(KWhite)* 4-9-5 RWernham (3) (chsd ldrs 8f: wknd qckly) | 1½.13 |
| 2931 | Dont Embarrass Me (20) (v) *(TKersey)* 3-8-7 SWebster (9) (b: lost pl ½-wy: t.o) | 14 |

**9/4** Stingray City (USA), **6/1** CARROLLS MARC (IRE), **15/2** Ghostly Glow, **8/1** Enfant du Paradis (IRE), Bar Billiards, **14/1** Elsa, **16/1** Kate Royale(op 10/1), Monorose, **20/1** Laughton Lady, **25/1** Sioux Perfick, Sly Prospect (USA), **50/1** Titian Girl, **100/1** Ors. CSF £17.42, Tote £7.10: £1.70 £1.40 £5.40 (£7.50). Mr Lou Carroll (NEWMARKET) bred by John Connaughton in Ireland. 14 Rn; No bid
3m 15.7 (9.7)
SF—22/13/–/–/–/–

**3158**  BREWOOD H'CAP (0-70) £2805.00 (£780.00: £375.00)  **2m 201y**  3-30 (3-32)
(Weights raised 9 lb)

| | | |
|---|---|---|
| 3046³ | **Prince Mercury (68)** (Fav) *(JLDunlop)* 3-9-10 JReid (9) (hld up: 3rd st: rdn 2f out: wandered & led ent fnl f: sn clr) | —1 |

2759 Intrepid Lass (41) *(HCandy)* 5–8-3 ‡7AntoinetteArmes (13) (led: rdn 2f out: hdd appr fnl f: one pce) ........................................................ 8.2

30753 Thor Power (IRE) (44) *(DTThom)* 3–9-0 DBiggs (12) (wl bhd tl hdwy 3f out: nvr nrr) ....................................................................................... 4.3

30534 Juris Prudence (IRE) (43) *(BAMcMahon)* 4–8-12 MRoberts (5) (hdwy 6f out: kpt on one pce fnl 2f) ...................................................................... 5.4

2867 Witches Coven (46) *(MBell)* 3–7-13 ‡3FNorton (14) (hld up mid div: effrt & 4th st: wknd over 3f out) ....................................................................... 5.5

3046 Gaelgoir (45) *(CFCJackson)* 8–8-7 ‡7CAvery (1) (b: bkwd: wl bhd tl styd on fnl 2f) .................................................................................................... 2.6

28344 Dajitus (58) *(MJHeaton-Ellis)* 3–9-0 DHolland (10) (lw: chsd ldrs: 2nd st: wknd 3f out) ................................................................................................. 4.7

2565 Delta Foxtrot (USA) (60) *(DWPArbuthnot)* 3–9-2 GBaxter (8) (lw: hld up mid div: nt rch ldrs) ............................................................................................. 2.8

26645 Seldom In (38) *(JWharton)* 8–8-7 JQuinn (6) (hdwy 7f out: 5th st: wknd fnl 3f) .... s.h.9

25654 My Swan Song (35) *(JPSmith)* 7–8-4 NAdams (7) (hdwy 7f out: 6th st: wknd over 3f out) ......................................................................................... ³/₄.10

2867 Saif Al Adil (IRE) (47) *(KTIvory)* 3–8-3 GBardwell (11) (a bhd) ....................... 5.11

28015 Rose of Macmillion (60) *(MrsBarbaraWaring)* 3–9-2 NHowe (2) (chsd ldr 12f: sn wknd: t.o) ....................................................................................... 20.12

Sterling Buck (USA) (34) *(GHYardley)* 5–7-12(10) ‡5RPrice (4) (bkwd: stumbled s: hdwy 8f out: wknd 5f out: t.o) .............................................. 15.13

3021 Deauville Duchess (37) (bl) *(PJHobbs)* 5–8-6 DaleGibson (3) (prom tl wknd qckly 7f out: t.o) ....................................................................................... 14

**5/1** PRINCE MERCURY, **13/2** Thor Power (IRE), Witches Coven, **7/1** Juris Prudence (IRE), **9/1** My Swan Song, Intrepid Lass, **10/1** Seldom In, Dajitus, **16/1** Saif Al Adil (IRE), Delta Foxtrot (USA), **20/1** Rose of Macmillion, **33/1** Deauville Duchess, **66/1** Ors. CSF £43.71, CT £265.68. Tote £5.80: £2.20 £1.60 £1.70 (£37.60). Duke of Marlborough (ARUNDEL) bred by The Duke of Marlborough. 14 Rn
3m 37.7 (11)
SF—17/–/–/–/–/

---

**3159**
BLOXWICH H'CAP (3-Y.O.F) (0-70) £2889.00 (£804.00: £387.00)
1m 200y
4-00 (4-03)

(Weights raised 1 lb)

29932 **Crackling** (45) (Jt-Fav) *(DMarks)* 7-11 SDawson (15) (hld up: gd hdwy 3f out: wandered appr fnl f: led fns fnl f: r.o) .................................. —1

3041 Affa (52) *(TTThomsonJones)* 7-11 ‡7JDSmith (19) (b: hdwy to ld 3f out: hdd & no ex ins fnl f) ...................................................................................... 2.2

27085 Missy-S (IRE) (48) *(GAPritchard-Gordon)* 7-9 ‡5DHarrison (14) (hdwy 2f out: r.o wl ins fnl f) ........................................................................... 2¹/₂.3

30174 Mexican Dancer (50) *(RJHolder)* 8-2 NAdams (18) (hdwy over 2f out: nrst fin) 1¹/₂.4

2018 Remany (66) *(JRFanshawe)* 9-4 GCarter (17) (hdwy on outside 2f out: nvr nrr) 1¹/₂.5

29314 Aegaen Lady (47) *(JEtherington)* 7-10 ‡3FNorton (9) (lw: in tch: effrt 3f out: nt trble ldrs) ........................................................................................... 3¹/₂.6

29313 Chantry Bellini (44) (bl) *(CWThornton)* 7-10 JQuinn (7) (b.hind: lw: prom: 6th st: ev ch 3f out: wknd appr fnl f) ............................................... 2.7

2959 Wild Strawberry (57) (v) *(JMPEustace)* 8-9 MTebbutt (5) (dwlt: hdwy ¹/₂-wy: wknd wl over 1f out) ..................................................................... nk.8

2355 Kelimutu (46) *(CFWall)* 7-12 NCarlisle (4) (lw: 7th st: wknd fnl 2f) ............. 1¹/₂.9

28686 Hester Stanhope (59) *(PWHarris)* 8-11 PaulEddery (10) (m.n.s) .............. 1¹/₂.10

2993 Selaginella (47) *(MRChannon)* 7-8(2) ‡5BDoyle (3) (prom: 3rd st: led 4f out to 3f out: grad wknd) ............................................................................. ³/₄.11

3068 Stormswept (USA) (54) *(MBrittain)* 8-6 SWebster (16) (m.n.s) ................. 1.12

2757 Tafsir (52) *(HThomsonJones)* 8-4 RHills (11) (chsd ldrs: 8th st: wknd 3f out) 2¹/₂.13

27856 Tanana (50) *(JGFitzGerald)* 8-2 GBaxter (12) (prom: 4th st: wknd over 2f out) . 6.14

3017 Sally Fast (49) *(BPalling)* 7-10(2) ‡5StephenDavies (13) (m.n.s) ................ ¹/₂.15

2813 Cappahoosh (IRE) (54) (Jt-Fav) *(HJCollingridge)* 8-6 MRoberts (8) (chsd ldrs: 5th st: wknd over 2f out) ............................................................. ¹/₂.16

1921 Penny Orchid (IRE) (69) (bl) *(BBeasley)* 9-7 RCochrane (6) (prom 5f: sn wknd) 8.17

3048 Kentucky Starlet (USA) (57) (bl) *(RHannon)* 8-6 ‡3RPerham (1) (lw: chsd ldr: 2nd st: wknd over 3f out: t.o) .................................................... 2.18

2769 Romance (IRE) (57) *(MJHeaton-Ellis)* 8-9 WRyan (20) (prom to ¹/₂-wy: t.o) .... 15.19

25315 Grubby (46) *(RHollinshead)* 7-5(5) ‡7AGarth (2) (led 5f: sn lost tch: t.o) ............. 1.20

**6/1** CRACKLING, Cappahoosh (IRE), **10/1** Missy-S (IRE), Remany, **12/1** Affa, Chantry Bellini, **14/1** Grubby, Kentucky Starlet (USA), Hester Stanhope, Wild Strawberry, Penny Orchid (IRE), **16/1** Romance (IRE), Tanana, **20/1** Mexican Dancer, Aegaen Lady, Tafsir, **25/1** Kelimutu, Sally Fast, **33/1** Ors. CSF £74.57, CT £667.38. Tote £6.40: £2.10 £3.70 £2.00 £6.70 (£45.60). Mr Denis Marchant (UPPER LAMBOURN) bred by Miss S. McCreery and Stowell Hill Ltd. 20 Rn
1m 54.2 (5.7)
SF—11/5/–/–/–/

**3160** PELSALL MEDIAN AUCTION STKS (2-Y.O) £2952.00 (£822.00: £396.00)
7f

4-30 (4-32)

2799* **Eurolink Thunder (91)** (Fav) *(JLDunlop)* 9-0 LDettori (6) (hld up: 5th st: led
over 2f out: rn green: pushed out) ................................................ —1
2918 Range Rider (IRE) *(CEBrittain)* 8-1 MRoberts (9) (3rd st: rdn & ev ch whn hung
lft over 1f out: r.o) .................................................................. nk.2
1342⁵ Fleur Power (IRE) **(64)** *(BPalling)* 7-10⁽⁵⁾ ‡5StephenDavies (8) (led tl hdd over 2f
out: wkng whn bmpd appr fnl f) ................................................. 7.3
2225⁵ Daily Sport Don *(RHannon)* 8-1 AMcGlone (5) (prom: 4th st: rdn & ev ch 2f out:
sn wknd) ........................................................................... ½.4
3035 Pistols At Dawn (USA) *(RHannon)* 8-6 JReid (4) (hld up: 7th st: effrt 3f out: nvr
able to chal) ....................................................................... 3.5
Heathyards Boy *(RHollinshead)* 8-4 WRyan (7) (w'like: bit bkwd: s.s: last st: nvr
nr to chal) ......................................................................... 1.6
Rad *(SPCWoods)* 8-0 GCarter (2) (w'like: bkwd: 6th st: wknd over 2f out) ......... 2.7
2633 Goan Girl *(PSFelgate)* 7-12 NAdams (3) (a bhd: 8th st: t.o) .................. 15.8
2812 Auntie Chris *(AWPotts)* 7-10⁽¹⁾ TyroneWilliams (1) (dwlt: sn chsng ldr: 2nd st:
sn wknd: t.o) ...................................................................... 12.9

**1/2** EUROLINK THUNDER, **3/1** Range Rider (IRE), **20/1** Pistols At Dawn (USA), Fleur Power (IRE), **25/1** Daily
Sport Don, **33/1** Heathyards Boy, **50/1** Rad, **100/1** Ors. CSF £2.27, Tote £1.40: 1.00 £1.30 £2.40 (£1.30).
Eurolink Computer Services Ltd (ARUNDEL) bred by Genesis Green Stud. 9 Rn     1m 28.6 (4.3)
SF–46/32/6/9/5/–

**3161** LEVY BOARD CLAIMING STKS £2784.00 (£774.00: £372.00) **1m 3f** 5-00 (5-05)

2754³ **Flying Speed (USA) (75)** (Fav) *(MCPipe)* 4-9-10 MRoberts (11) (b: hld up &
bhd: hdwy over 3f out: led wl lns fnl f: r.o) ................................... —1
2959 Waaza (USA) **(55)** *(AAScott)* 3-8-12 RHills (6) (lw: 4th st: led over 2f out tl wl ins
fnl) ................................................................................ ¾.2
2931⁵ Iron Baron (IRE) **(56)** *(RHollinshead)* 3-8-8 WRyan (15) (hld up: styd on fnl 2f:
nvr nrr) ........................................................................... 3.3
2712 Lyn's Return (IRE) **(56)** *(RSimpson)* 3–8-11 ‡5ATucker (4) (hld up & bhd: swtchd
ins over 2f out: styd on fnl f) .................................................. nk.4
3101⁵ Shoehorn **(55)** *(REPeacock)* 5-8-8 GCarter (10) (b: a.p: 2nd st: led 4f out tl over
2f out: rdn & wknd appr fnl f) .................................................. 1½.5
3104³ Remwood Girl **(29)** *(KSBridgwater)* 6-8-7 PD'Arcy (13) (hdwy & 5th st: hrd rdn
2f out: one pce) .................................................................. ¾.6
3104⁶ Ivan the Terrible (IRE) **(46)** *(MissSJWilton)* 4-9-4 LDettori (9) (b: chsd ldrs: 6th
st: hrd rdn & wknd over 1f out) ................................................ 1½.7
3026 Sally Fay (IRE) **(30)** *(TKersey)* 4-8-9 JQuinn (14) (b: 8th st: effrt & hrd rdn over
3f out: sn btn) ................................................................... 4.8
2775 Urshi-Jade **(30)** *(KWhite)* 4-8-0 ‡7JDennis (16) (hdwy & 7th st: rdn over 2f out:
sn btn) ........................................................................... 1½.9
2937⁵ Kind Style (IRE) **(30)** *(RHollinshead)* 4-8-10 RCochrane (7) (m.n.s) ........... 3.10
3010 Pip's Optimist *(PJFeilden)* 3–8-6 NDay (5) (prom 6f) ......................... 1½.11
2954⁶ Jackson Square (IRE) *(WGMTurner)* 4-9-3 ‡7PMcCabe (1) (prom: 3rd st: wknd
over 2f out) ...................................................................... ¾.12
2613⁵ Futures Gift (IRE) **(50)** *(AWPotts)* 3–8-12 SWebster (2) (rdn along ½-wy: a bhd:
t.o) ............................................................................... 6.13
2754 Mrs Mouse *(NATwiston-Davies)* 4–8-9 JWilliams (3) (dwlt: a bhd: t.o) ......... 10.14
3104 Tauzio (IRE) *(JMackie)* 4-9-6 GHind (12) (led tl hdd 4f out: sn rdn & wknd: t.o) 10.15
2209 Quarrington Hill *(KSBridgwater)* 3–8-8 AProud (8) (unruly s: prom tl wknd 5f
out: t.o) ......................................................................... 16

**8/11** FLYING SPEED (USA), **9/2** Iron Baron (IRE), **8/1** Shoehorn(op 5/1), **12/1** Remwood Girl, **16/1** Waaza
(USA)(op 10/1), **20/1** Lyn's Return (IRE)(op 10/1), Ivan the Terrible (IRE)(op 10/1), **25/1** Kind Style (IRE), **33/1**
Futures Gift (IRE), **50/1** Jackson Square (IRE), Sally Fay (IRE), **66/1** Ors. CSF £14.51, Tote £1.60: £1.10 £4.10
£1.80 (£15.10). Mr F. Barr (WELLINGTON) bred by Buckram Oak Farm in USA. 16 Rn; Shoehorn clmd Mrs A
Turner £2,001     2m 27.2 (12.2)

**3162** NEWPORT NURSERY £2637.00 (£732.00: £351.00) **5f** 5-30 (5-33)
(Weights raised 4 lb)

3047³ **Laurel Delight (65)** *(JBerry)* 8-11 GCarter (2) (mde all: clr fr ½-wy: eased cl
home) ............................................................................ —1
3001³ Geoff's Risk **(66)** *(GLewis)* 8-12 PaulEddery (11) (hdwy appr fnl f: r.o ins fnl f: no
ch w wnr) ........................................................................ 4.2
1973⁴ Alasib **(74)** (Jt-Fav) *(MMoubarak)* 9-6 LDettori (3) (chsd ldrs: rdn over 1f out: r.o
one pce) ......................................................................... ½.3
3019 Nitouche **(75)** *(PatMitchell)* 9-2 ‡5DHarrison (9) (lw: hdwy over 1f out: nvr nrr) . nk.4

2863★ Cuddly Date (61) *(DTThom)* 8-4 ‡³SO'Gorman (10) (nvr nr to chal) .............. 1½.5
2960² Trevorsninepoints (69) *(MJRyan)* 9-1 DBiggs (4) (a.p: rdn appr fnl f: kpt on) .. s.h.6
2437 Press the Bell (63) *(JBerry)* 8-9 RHills (12) (spd stands' side over 3f) ............. ½.7
3049★ Magic Orb (60) (Jt-Fav) *(JLSpearing)* 7-13 (7x) ‡⁷CHawksley (5) (rdn along
         ½-wy: a struggling) ................................................. ½.8
3001⁶ Musical Prospect (USA) (73) (bl) *(RHannon)* 9-5 MRoberts (1) (lw: swvd lft s: sn
         rdn along: a bhd) ............................................. 2.9
3012⁶ Juliet Bravo (72) *(BBeasley)* 9-4 RCochrane (7) (prom over 3f) ................ 1½.10
2779⁵ Minshaar (74) *(KSBridgwater)* 9-6 JReid (13) (spd stands' side 3f) .............. s.h.11
2960⁵ Arkendale Diamond (USA) (63) *(BBeasley)* 8-9 MTebbutt (14) (outpcd) ......... 5.12
3001 Felt Lucky (IRE) (71) *(MRChannon)* 9-3 SWhitworth (6) (lw: bhd fnl 2f) ......... ¾.13
2558⁴ Annie Rose (50) (bl) *(TDBarron)* 7-10 DaleGibson (8) (dwlt: a bhd) ............. 4.14

**4/1** Magic Orb(7/2—6/1), Alasib(op 12/1), **5/1** LAUREL DELIGHT, **6/1** Geoff's Risk, **9/1** Trevorsninepoints, **10/1**
Musical Prospect (USA), **11/1** Nitouche, **14/1** Minshaar, Press the Bell, **25/1** Ors. CSF £33.92, CT £118.37. Tote
£6.80: £2.30 £2.00 £1.80 (£20.50). Laurel (Leisure) Limited (COCKERHAM) bred by G. Blum and Ridge Barn
Farm Ltd. 14 Rn
                                               60.4 sec (3.1)
                                       SF—45/30/36/31/13/23

T/Plpt: £439.06 (17 Tckts).
                                                   IM

## 2324—CARLISLE (R-H)

### Tuesday, September 8th [Good, Good to soft patches]

Going Allowance: 5f-7f: minus 0.05 (G); Rest: minus 0.25 sec (F)       Wind: str across

Stalls: high

**3163**      BRENT STKS (I) (Mdn 2-Y.O) £1702.00 (£472.00: £226.00)    **5f 207y**   2-10 (2-12)

    Doulabella (IRE) *(SirMarkPrescott)* 8-9 GDuffield (8) (neat: unf: a chsng ldrs:
         rdn over 1f out: r.o to ld cl home) .......................................... —1
2986² Peacefull Reply (USA) (84) (Jt-Fav) *(FHLee)* 8-9 ‡⁵NKennedy (6) (lw: led tl hdd
         over 1f out: kpt on wl) ......................................................... hd.2
361³ Reasons for Love (IRE) (Jt-Fav) *(JJO'Neill)* 8-9 MBirch (9) (lw: a chsng ldrs: ev
         ch ins fnl f: r.o) .................................................................. nk.3
3008 Iolite *(MAJarvis)* 8-9 LDettori (1) (a cl up: led over 1f out tl hdd nr fin) ........... hd.4
3030 Dutosky *(MJCamacho)* 8-9 NConnorton (12) (chsd ldrs: chal over 1f out: no ex
         wl ins fnl f) ......................................................................... s.h.5
2983 Don't Be Saki (IRE) (52) (v) *(JEtherington)* 8-9 KFallon (11) (lw: prom: effrt 2f
         out: one pce appr fnl f) ........................................................ 1.6
    Bold Flash *(PCHaslam)* 9-0 DMcKeown (4) (w'like: bit bkwd: in tch tl grad wknd
         fr ½-wy) ............................................................................. 5.7
2965 Pretty Average *(TCraig)* 8-9 PBurke (5) (w ldrs 4f) ................................. 5.8
    Ultrakay (IRE) *(JBerry)* 9-0 JCarroll (3) (w'like: sn outpcd) ..................... ½.9
1531 Pressure Off *(JHJohnson)* 9-0 SWood (10) (reminders after 1f: bhd fr ½-wy) .. 6.10
    Choker *(CWThornton)* 8-9 GHind (2) (leggy: unf: s.s: a bhd) ................... 3.11
    Oubeck *(EWeymes)* 8-9 JFanning (7) (cmpt: str: bit bkwd: s.i.s: sme hdwy
         ½-wy: sn wknd) .................................................................. nk.12

**3/1** Peacefull Reply (USA), Reasons for Love (IRE), **11/2** Dutosky, DOULABELLA (IRE), **10/1** Iolite, **12/1** Oubeck,
Ultrakay (IRE), **25/1** Don't Be Saki, Bold Flash, Pressure Off, **100/1** Pretty Average. CSF
£20.98, Tote £7.30: £1.80 £1.50 £1.60 (£8.60). Mrs David Thompson (NEWMARKET) bred by Yeomanstown
Lodge Stud in Ireland. 12 Rn
                                              1m 16.2 (3.9)
                                       SF—11/10/9/8/7/3

**3164**      BRENT STKS (II) (Mdn 2-Y.O) £1688.00 (£468.00: £224.00)    **5f 207y**   2-40 (2-42)

1409³ Rocket to the Moon (IRE) (86) *(PWChapple-Hyam)* 8-9 ‡⁵DHarrison (2) (a.p:
         led appr fnl f: styd on) ......................................................... —1
2038³ Tanagome (USA) *(SGNorton)* 8-9 ‡⁵OPears (4) (cl up: led wl over 1f out: hdd
         appr fnl f: kpt on) .............................................................. 1½.2
    Missa Brevis (USA) (bl) (Fav) *(JWWatts)* 8-9 GDuffield (11) (lw: in tch: effrt
         ½-wy: styd on: nt pce to chal) ............................................. 3.3
2948⁴ Tajarib (IRE) *(JLDunlop)* 8-9 LDettori (6) (lw: cl up: rdn 2f out: one pce) ....... 3.4
2841 Cardinal Dogwood (USA) (71) *(MBrittain)* 9-0 MBirch (9) (w ldrs: rdn 2f out: sn
         btn & eased) ...................................................................... 6.5
2428 Go Orange *(JLSpearing)* 8-9 GHind (4) (in tch 4f) .............................. ½.6
    Dancing Haze *(MissSEHall)* 9-0 SWebster (10) (w'like: bit bkwd: b.nr hind:
         s.i.s: nvr wnt pce) .............................................................. 3.7
2965 Evahart *(JHJohnson)* 8-9 SWood (5) (led tl hdd wl over 1f out: sn wknd) ........ 2½.8
2102⁶ Prime Painter (72) *(RFFisher)* 9-0 KFallon (3) (a bhd) ........................... 9

2719 Cambus Bay *(WTKemp)* 8-2 ‡7JTate (1) (drvn along after 2f: sn bhd) .................. **10**
3030 Roscommon Joe (IRE) *(20/1) Withdrawn (broke out of stalls) : not under orders*

**6/4** Missa Brevis (USA), **15/8** ROCKET TO THE MOON (IRE), **4/1** Tajarib (IRE), **20/1** Tanagome (USA), Prime
Painter, Cardinal Dogwood (USA), **25/1** Evahart, **100/1** Go Orange, Dancing Haze, **500/1** Cambus Bay. CSF
£33.28, Tote £3.00: £1.10 £4.00 £1.30 (£17.20). Mrs Jane Chapple-Hyam (MARLBOROUGH) bred by Ian
Calder in Ireland. 10 Rn                                          1m 15.6 (3.3)
                                                            SF—23/17/5/–/–/–


# 3165

SNOW GOOSE AUCTION STKS (2-Y.O) £1786.00 (£496.00: £238.00)     **5f** 3-10 (3-13)

2939⁴ **Two Moves in Front (IRE) (72)** *(JBerry)* 8-6 DMcKeown (5) (a cl up: led ins fnl
         f: rdn & r.o) ......................................................... —1
         Baliana *(CBBBooth)* 8-1⁽³⁾ GHind (2) (w'like: scope: in tch: hdwy ¹/₂-wy: r.o wl
         fnl f) ..................................................................... s.h.2
1461 Moodiesburn (IRE) **(88)** (Fav) *(ABailey)* 7-5 ‡7DWright (12) (h.d.w: led tl hdd ins
         fnl f: kpt on) ........................................................... 1¹/₂.3
2965 Principal Player (USA) **(69)** *(PMonteith)* 7-12⁽⁴⁾ ‡5OPears (8) (prom: drvn along
         ¹/₂-wy: sdn on fnl f) ................................................... 1.4
2819² Hazard a Guess (IRE) *(MrsJRRamsden)* 7-13 PBurke (10) (in tch: effrt ¹/₂-wy:
         styd on sme pce) ..................................................... 2¹/₂.5
2960 Whisperdales **(65)** *(MWEllerby)* 8-4 SMorris (9) (chsd ldrs: drvn along: edgd lft
         ¹/₂-wy: no imp) ....................................................... ³/₄.6
751⁶ Supreme Soviet *(JSHaldane)* 7-10 ‡3SMaloney (4) (cl up: rdn 2f out: no ex) ... d.h.6
         Jotra *(RMWhitaker)* 7-8 ‡5DHarrison (3) (b: w'like: s.s: bhd tl styd on fnl 2f: nrst
         fin) ..................................................................... 1¹/₂.8
1092 Lady Adaro (IRE) *(LJO'Neill)* 7-8 JFanning (6) (bhd fr ¹/₂-wy) .................. 3.9
3030 Song in Your Heart (v) *(AHarrison)* 7-13 GLuffield (7) (lw: spd to ¹/₈ wy) ...... hd.10
2405 Don't Tell Jean **(67)** *(NBycroft)* 7-7⁽²⁾ ‡5NKennedy (1) (n.d) .................. 1.11
2965 The Loon *(JJO'Neill)* 7-13 SWood (10) (a bhd) ................................. 2¹/₂.12
2965⁶ General Brooks (IRE) **(64)** *(JBerry)* 8-3 JCarroll (11) (spd to ¹/₂-wy) .......... nk.13

**7/4** Moodiesburn (IRE), **7/1** Baliana, Hazard a Guess (IRE)(op 4/1), TWO MOVES IN FRONT (IRE)(10/1—12/1),
**12/1** General Brooks (IRE), **20/1** Principal Player (USA), Song in Your Heart, **25/1** Jotra, Don't Tell Jean, **33/1**
Lady Adare (IRE), Whisperdales, **100/1** Ors. CSF £45.14, Tote £5.60: £1.80 £2.90 £1.30 (£32.60). Mr Robert
Aird (COCKERHAM) bred by Newlands House Stud in Ireland. 13 Rn         62.5 sec (2.3)
                                                            SF—41/35/19/22/13/7


# 3166

MATTHEW BROWN H'CAP (0-70) £2122.00 (£592.00: £286.00)     **5f**     3-40 (3-43)

2984⁵ **Supreme Desire (44)** *(ASmith)* 4-8-3⁽⁷⁾ SWebster (6) (a chsng ldrs: hrd rdn to
         ld wl ins fnl f) ......................................................... —1
3126 Miss Aragon **(46)** *(MissLCSiddall)* 4-8-0 ‡5DHarrison (11) (in tch: ev ch ins fnl f:
         r.o) ..................................................................... s.h.2
2741 Katie-a (IRE) **(53)** *(RMWhitaker)* 3-8-10 ACulhane (5) (hld up & bhd: hdwy over
         1f out: fin fast) ....................................................... nk.3
3144 Pallium (IRE) **(69)** *(MPNaughton)* 4-9-7 ‡7SWynne (4) (lw: bhd & swtchd rt after
         s: hdwy 2f out: kpt on wl) ............................................. s.h.4
2942 Farndale **(34)** *(BCMorgan)* 5-7-0 ‡7DarrenMoffatt (12) (lw: cl up: led ¹/₂-wy tl hdd
         wl ins fnl f) ........................................................... hd.5
3079⁴ Hinari Video **(44)** *(MJohnston)* 7-7-10 ‡7MBaird (8) (chsd ldrs: effrt 2f out: styd
         on) ..................................................................... ¹/₂.6
2490³ Pretonic **(58)** (bl) *(MJohnston)* 4-9-3 DMcKeown (2) (in tch: one pce fnl 2f) .... nk.7
2424⁵ Swinging Lady **(51)** *(WWHaigh)* 4-8-10 LDettori (3) (b.off hind: lw: in tch: no
         imp fnl 2f) ............................................................. ¹/₂.8
3079² The Right Time **(45)** (Fav) *(JParkes)* 7-8-4 GDuffield (7) (bhd: sme hdwy fnl
         2f: n.d) ................................................................. 2¹/₂.9
2936 Kabcast **(58)** (bl) *(DWChapman)* 7-8-12 ‡5OPears (1) (cl up over 3f) ............... 1.10
2936 Jive Music **(34)** *(NBycroft)* 6-7-7 JFanning (9) (lw: led to ¹/₂-wy: sn btn) ......... ³/₄.11
2942* Blue Grit **(55)** (bl) *(MDods)* 6-8-9 ‡5NKennedy (15) (w ldrs: rdn ¹/₂-wy: sn wknd) nk.12
2151⁶ Melody Anne **(36)** *(JSHaldane)* 3-7-7 SWood (10) (b.hind: w ldrs 3f) ........... 7.13
3079 Minizen Music (IRE) **(40)** *(TCraig)* 4-7-10⁽²⁾ ‡3SMaloney (14) (n.d) ............ ³/₄.14
1439 Minsk **(38)** (bl) *(TCraig)* 6-7-11⁽⁴⁾ PBurke (13) (spd to ¹/₂-wy: sn bhd) ............ nk.15
         LONG HANDICAP: Farndale 7-6, Jive Music 7-0, Melody Anne 7-2, Minsk 6-9.

**6/1** The Right Time, **15/2** Pretonic, **8/1** Swinging Lady, Blue Grit, Hinari Video, Miss Aragon, **11/1** SUPREME
DESIRE, **12/1** Minizen Music (IRE)(op 16/1), **14/1** Farndale, **16/1** Pallium (IRE), **20/1** Katie-a (IRE), **25/1** Kabcast,
**33/1** Jive Music, **50/1** Ors. CSF £82.91, CT £1,551.74. Tote £17.80: £3.70 £3.00 £5.50 (£67.30). Miss J. F.
Craze (BEVERLEY) bred by John E. and Mrs Wilkinson. 15 Rn         62.5 sec (2.3)
                                                            SF—38/34/43/53/17/25

**3167**  GREYLAG CLAIMING STKS (I) (3-Y.O) £1618.00 (£448.00: £214.00)
6f 206y

4-10 (4-11)

2815[6]  **Stoproveritate (44)** *(SGNorton)* 8-2 NConnorton (6) (effrt over 2f out: gd hdwy over 1f out: led wl ins fnl f) .................................. —1

2729[6]  Daily Sport Girl (48) (bl) *(RTJuckes)* 8-0 GHind (5) (chsd ldrs: led wl over 1f out: nt qckn nr fin) ................................................. nk.2

2699  Phil-Man (43) *(TFairhurst)* 8-5 JFanning (1) (a chsng ldrs: kpt on u.p fnl f) ...... 2½.3

2655  Jefferson Davis (IRE) (70) *(BBeasley)* 8-12 ‡[5]SWilliams (7) (led tl hdd wl over 1f out: r.o one pce) ............................ nk.4

3028[3]  Battuta (47) *(REarnshaw)* 8-2 JCarroll (11) (lw: hdwy ent st: sn rdn: styd on nr fin) ................................................. hd.5

2882[5]  Certain Lady (59) (Fav) *(GBlum)* 7-8 ‡[3]DHarrison (8) (in tch tl outpcd ent st: rdn & no imp after) .............................. 12.6

3073  Barmbrack (39) *(RMWhitaker)* 8-7 ACulhane (4) (hdwy ent st: sn rdn & btn) .. 8.7

2817[5]  Fort Derry (IRE) *(EJAlston)* 8-9 KFallon (2) (a bhd) .......................... nk.8

3028  My Jersey Pearl (IRE) (28) *(DonEnricoIncisa)* 7-7 ‡[7]ClaireBalding (9) (a bhd) .. 1½.9

2923  Super Charge (33) (bl) *(MWEllerby)* 8-13 SMorris (3) (chsd ldrs: rdn over 3f out: sn wknd) .................................... 6.10

**6/4** Certain Lady, **3/1** Jefferson Davis (IRE), **7/2** Battuta, **10/1** STOPROVERITATE, Daily Sport Girl, **20/1** Phil-Man, Barmbrack, **33/1** Super Charge, **100/1** Ors. CSF £95.00, Tote £11.50: £2.10 £4.10 £6.30 (£79.80). Mr John D. Clark (BARNSLEY) bred by Dr and Mrs J. D. Royle. 10 Rn

1m 29 (3.8)

SF—26/23/20/26/15/–

---

**3168**  GREYLAG CLAIMING STKS (II) (3-Y.O) £1618.00 (£448.00: £214.00)
6f 206y

4-40 (4-42)

3058[5]  **Hand on Heart (IRE) (63)** (Fav) *(WJHaggas)* 8-4 GDuffield (5) (chsd ldrs: led 2f out: rdn & r.o wl) .............................. —1

2878  Patience Please (60) *(MHEasterby)* 8-4 MBirch (1) (lw: in tch: stdy hdwy 3f out: ev ch 1f out: rdn & r.o) ...................... 1½.2

2984[6]  Syke Lane (33) *(RMWhitaker)* 7-12 PBurke (7) (a in tch: effrt 3f out: styd on: no imp) ................................................. 5.3

3017[3]  Toss the Dice (55) *(MAJarvis)* 8-9 LDettori (11) (lw: led tl hdd 2f out: one pce) .. 1.4

3028[6]  Throw Away Line (46) *(REBarr)* 8-5 SWebster (4) (a chsng ldrs: hrd rdn over 2f out: grad wknd) ....................... 1½.5

2987  Manulife (54) (v) *(BBeasley)* 8-10 ‡[5]SWilliams (6) (bhd: hdwy u.p 3f out: n.d) ..... 1.6

2966  Ravecino (41) *(JSHaldane)* 7-10[(1)] ‡[3]SMaloney (9) (cl up tl wknd over 2f out) .. 7.7

2699  Kick on Majestic (IRE) (33) *(NBycroft)* 8-0 ‡[5]NKennedy (3) (s.i.s: n.d) ............ 1½.8

2699  Whirlygig (38) (bl) *(JSWainwright)* 8-1[(2)] SMorris (8) (bhd: hdwy 4f out: sn wknd) ................................................. 2.9

1918  Liberty Glen *(JLEyre)* 7-13 ‡[5]OPears (2) (dwlt: a bhd) .................... s.h.10

2114[4]  Stamshaw (45) *(BAMcMahon)* 7-11 ‡[7]JBramhill (10) (sn chsng ldrs: wknd 3f out) ................................................. 1½.11

**15/8** HAND ON HEART (IRE), **3/1** Toss the Dice, **7/2** Patience Please, **12/1** Throw Away Line, Syke Lane, **16/1** Manulife, **20/1** Kick on Majestic (IRE), Stamshaw, **50/1** Whirlygig, Ravecino, **66/1** Liberty Glen. CSF £8.54, Tote £2.00: £1.50 £1.10 £1.70 (£3.60). Mrs M. M. Haggas (NEWMARKET) bred by Kellsboro House Stud in Ireland. 11 Rn; Hand on Heart (IRE) clmd T Littleton £6,500

1m 28.2 (3)

SF—40/35/14/22/13/15

---

**3169**  WHITE FRONT STKS (Mdn) £1548.00 (£428.00: £204.00)  1¾m 32y  5-10 (5-14)

3022[5]  **Beauchamp Grace** (Fav) *(JLDunlop)* 3-8-5 GDuffield (8) (lw: cl up: led 5f out: rdn & styd on) ................................. —1

Shadows of Silver *(BAMcMahon)* 4-9-2 MBirch (7) (wl grwn: plld hrd & jnd ldrs 10f out: ev ch 2f out: nt qckn fnl f) .............. 2½.2

3053  Landed Gentry (USA) (68) *(PWChapple-Hyam)* 3-8-5 ‡[5]DHarrison (3) (hdwy appr st: styd on fnl f: nvr able to chal) ........... 2½.3

3010[4]  Maradonna (USA) *(LMCumani)* 3-8-10 LDettori (2) (lw: in tch: effrt 4f out: one pce) ................................................. 6.4

2720[5]  Kims Selection (IRE) *(SGNorton)* 3-8-5 ‡[5]OPears (9) (hld up: bdly hmpd appr st: nt rcvr) ...................... 3½.5

747[5]  Acquisition (46) *(SGPayne)* 5-9-7 SWebster (5) (t.o fr ½-wy) ............... dist.6

3025[5]  Only a Rose (60) *(CWThornton)* 3-8-5 GHind (6) (prom: outpcd whn b.d over 3f out) ................................................. 0

3087[2]  Well Ahead (55) *(MJohnston)* 3-8-5 DMcKeown (1) (led tl hdd 5f out: 2nd whn hmpd & fell over 3f out) ............................ 0

Queen Buzzard (50/1) Withdrawn (lame at s) : not under orders

10/11 BEAUCHAMP GRACE, 5/2 Maradonna (USA), 9/1 Shadows of Silver(8/1—12/1), 14/1 Landed Gentry (USA)(op 8/1), 16/1 Well Ahead(op 10/1), 25/1 Kims Selection (IRE), 33/1 Only a Rose, 66/1 Acquisition. CSF £8.91, Tote £2.10: £1.10 £1.30 £3.10 (£32.30). Mr E. Penser (ARUNDEL) bred by E. Penser. 8 Rn
3m 10.4 (13.4)

**3170**     BARNACLE H'CAP (0-70) £2346.00 (£656.00: £318.00)    **7f 214y**    5-40 (5-49)

| | | |
|---|---|---|
| 2966 | **Ruth's Gamble (52)** *(DWChapman)* 4-9-1 SWood (10) (hdwy over 3f out: r.o u.p fnl f to ld cl home) | —1 |
| 2588² | Dune River **(68)** *(SirMarkPrescott)* 3-9-12 GDuffield (12) (lw: chsd ldrs: led wl over 2f out: r.o: jst ct) | nk.2 |
| 2570 | Martini Executive **(64)** (bl) *(BBeasley)* 4-9-8 ‡⁵SWilliams (5) (lw: mid div tl swtchd over 1f out: r.o wl nr fin) | 1½.3 |
| 2987 | Flying Down to Rio (IRE) **(46)** *(MPNaughton)* 4-8-4 ‡⁵DHarrison (9) (in tch: rdn over 3f out: styd on wl) | ½.4 |
| 2935⁴ | Diaco **(65)** (Fav) *(MAJarvis)* 7-10-0 LDettori (6) (lw: bhd: gd hdwy to chal over 1f out: sn rdn & nt qckn) | 1½.5 |
| 3045 | Errema **(43)** *(CTinkler)* 7-8-6 MBirch (18) (bhd & rdn appr st: styd on strly fnl 2f) | 1½.6 |
| 2693 | Tomashenko **(53)** *(JMackie)* 3-8-11 PBurke (3) (lw: hld up: hdwy on bit to chal over 2f out: wandered bdly u.p & wknd fnl f) | ¾.7 |
| 2941 | Watch Me Go (IRE) **(54)** *(BobJones)* 3-8-12 NConnorton (2) (lw: chsd ldr tl grad wknd fnl 2f) | 2.8 |
| 2966² | Lawnswood Junior **(57)** *(JLSpearing)* 5-8-13⁽²⁾ ‡⁷SWynne (4) (bhd: hdwy on ins 2f out: n.d) | 1½.9 |
| 2554⁶ | Who's Tef (IRE) **(59)** *(MHEasterby)* 4-9-5 ‡³SMaloney (7) (chsd ldrs tl wknd over 1f out) | s.h.10 |
| 2987 | Young Jason **(52)** *(FHLee)* 9-8-10 ‡⁵NKennedy (19) (effrt appr st: n.d) | 1.11 |
| | Stay Awake **(43)** *(JJO'Neill)* 6-8-6 JFanning (8) (prom tl wknd over 2f out) .... nk.12 | |
| | Avishayes (USA) **(55)** *(MDHammond)* 5-9-4 JCarroll (14) (s.i.s: rvr tn to chal) 1½.13 | |
| 2554 | Tancred Grange **(62)** *(MissSEHall)* 3-9-1 ‡⁵OPears (17) (led tl hdd & wknd over 2f out) | 7.14 |
| 3074⁶ | Coastal Express **(64)** *(EWeymes)* 3-9-8 KFallon (13) (cl up tl wknd over 2f out) | 2.15 |
| 2561 | Tara's Girl **(47)** (v) *(RTJuckes)* 5-8-3 ‡⁷GParkin (16) (cl up tl wknd 3f out) | 16 |
| 3009 | Palmas Pride **(57)** *(MDHammond)* 5-8-13 ‡⁷ALakeman (11) (dwlt: a wl bhd) | 17 |

11/2 Diaco, 7/1 Lawnswood Junior, Dune River, 9/1 Who's Tef (IRE), 10/1 Young Jason, 11/1 Tancred Grange, Martini Executive, 12/1 Errema, 14/1 Flying Down to Rio (IRE), 16/1 Tomashenko, Coastal Express, RUTH'S GAMBLE, 20/1 Watch Me Go (IRE), Avishayes (USA), 33/1 Ors. CSF £116.01, CT £1,176.96. Tote £32.40: £3.90 £2.60 £2.20 £3.30 (£183.00). Mr P. D. Savill (YORK) bred by D. W. Chapman. 17 Rn   1m 41.1 (2.4)
SF—35/45/36/16/35/8

T/Plpt: £932.20 (2.6 Tckts).      GB/AA

**2693—LEICESTER (R-H)**
**Tuesday, September 8th [Good]**
Going Allowance: 0.05 sec per fur (G)      Wind: fresh half bhd
Stalls: high

**3171**     E.B.F. FILBERT STKS (I) (Mdn 2-Y.O.F) £2807.00 (£777.00: £371.00)
     **1m 8y**      1-50 (1-53)

| | | |
|---|---|---|
| 2864 | **Fair Maid of Kent (USA)** (Fav) *(JHMGosden)* 8-11 SCauthen (2) (lw: a.p: led 4f out to 1f out: qcknd to ld nr fin) | —1 |
| 2930 | Omidjoy (IRE) *(SPCWoods)* 8-11 GCarter (9) (hld up: hdwy over 2f out: led 1f out tl ct last stride) | s.h.2 |
| | Puget Dancer (USA) *(MBell)* 8-11 NDay (11) (leggy: scope: bit bkwd: s.s: hdwy over 2f out: nvr able to chal) | 2½.3 |
| 1538⁶ | Baydon Belle (USA) *(GLewis)* 8-11 PaulEddery (8) (bhd: hdwy 2f out: styd on ins fnl f) | ¾.4 |
| 2951⁵ | Villavina *(SDow)* 8-11 RProbinson (9) (hdwy ½-wy: wknd appr fnl f) | ¾.5 |
| 2792 | High Finish *(HCandy)* 8-11 CRutter (7) (chsd ldrs: rdn over 2f out: sn btn) | 4.6 |
| 3036 | Perfect Set (IRE) *(MRChannon)* 8-11 DHolland (5) (led 4f: hrd rdn over 2f out: sn wknd) | 2½.7 |
| 2864 | Heretical Miss *(RHannon)* 8-11 JReid (10) (nvr trbld ldrs) | nk.8 |
| | Endearing Val *(CNAllen)* 8-8⁽⁴⁾ ‡⁷MichaelDenaro (3) (lt-f: hld up: a bhd) | 5.9 |
| 2864 | Emerald Sands *(ACStewart)* 8-11 RHills (1) (bhd fnl 3f) | 2½.10 |
| 3036 | Apachee Flower *(JDRoberts)* 8-8 ‡³FNorton (4) (still bkwd: a bhd) | 6.11 |

**4/5** FAIR MAID OF KENT (USA)(op 7/4), **7/2** High Finish, **7/1** Baydon Belle (USA), **10/1** Villavina(op 5/1), **12/1** Emerald Sands, **14/1** Omidjoy (IRE), Heretical Miss, **16/1** Puget Dancer (USA)(10/1—20/1), **33/1** Endearing Val, **50/1** Apachee Flower, **100/1** Perfect Set (IRE). CSF £15.14, Tote £2.10: £1.10 £6.80 £5.40 (£17.50). Sheikh Mohammed (NEWMARKET) bred by Hickory Tree Farm Inc. in USA. 11 Rn

1m 40.6 (5.6)

SF—19/18/10/8/6/–

## 3172
E.B.F. FILBERT STKS (II) (Mdn 2-Y.O.F) £2782.50 (£770.00: £367.50)
**1m 8y**                                                                                      2-20 (2-21)

2792 **Brightside (IRE)** (PFICole) ·8-11 TQuinn (5) (a.p: led over 2f out: rdn clr: eased
nr fin) ................................................................................................ —1

2864 Pearly Mist (IRE) (CEBrittain) 8-6 ‡⁵BDoyle (9) (bit bkwd: w ldrs: ev ch over 2f
out: hrd rdn over 1f out: one pce) ...................................................... 4.2

Abet (USA) (MajorWRHern) 8-11 SCauthen (4) (scope: bit bkwd: hld up: jnd
ldrs 3f out: shkn up over 2f out: r.o one pce) .................................. 1½.3

3036 On Request (IRE) (IABalding) 8-11 RCochrane (6) (hdwy over 1f out: r.o fnl f) .. ¾.4

2864⁶ Solartica (USA) (Fav) (JRFanshawe) 8-11 GCarter (3) (lw: hld up: chsd ldrs: no
hdwy fnl 2f) ...................................................................................... 1½.5

3036 Honorary Guest (DJGMurray-Smith) 8-11 TRogers (1) (nvr plcd to chal) ............ ¾.6

2519 Nedaarah (AAScott) 8-11 JFortune (8) (hld up in tch: rdn & effrt 3f out: wknd fnl
f) ...................................................................................................... 2½.7

1748⁶ Petite Louie (WCarter) 8-6 ‡⁵NGwilliams (2) (led over 5f: hrd rdn & wknd 2f out:
t.o) ................................................................................................... 12.8

3047 Young Geninsky (RJWeaver) 8-11 JLowe (10) (dwlt: sn prom: wknd 3f out: t.o) 12.9

My Sister Lucy (APJarvis) 8-11 MTebbutt (7) (unf: scope: bhd: rdn ½-wy: t.o) 8.10

**2/1** Solartica (USA)(6/4—9/4), **5/2** Abet (USA)(op 6/4), **7/2** BRIGHTSIDE (IRE)(5/1—3/1), **8/1** Nedaarah, On Request (IRE), **12/1** Pearly Mist (IRE), **50/1** Petite Louie, Honorary Guest, My Sister Lucy, **100/1** Young Geninsky. CSF £41.25, Tote £4.80: £1.30 £3.30 £1.30 (£23.60). Mr Faisal Salman (WHATCOMBE) bred by Barronstown Bloodstock Ltd. in Ireland. 10 Rn

1m 40.4 (5.4)

SF—22/5/5/3/–/–

## 3173
RANCLIFFE (S) NURSERY £2763.00 (£768.00: £369.00) **1m 8y**         2-50 (2-54)

2695 **General Chase (59)** (RJHolder) 8-6 PRobinson (20) (hdwy 3f out: carried rt
appr fnl f: r.o u.p to ld nr fin) ....................................................... —1

3050² Doc Spot (57) (CaptJWilson) 7-11 ‡7AGarth (2) (a.p: led & hung rt over 2f out:
veered bdly rt fnl f: ct nr fin) ........................................................ s.h.2

2947⁵ The Gold Souk (IRE) (60) (JLDunlop) 8-7 JReid (19) (chsd ldrs: kpt on same
pce ins fnl f) ................................................................................... 4.3

2961 Pondering (56) (SDow) 8-3 GCarter (17) (hdwy fnl 2f: fin wl) ........................ ½.4

3063⁶ George Roper (65) (v) (MRChannon) 8-7 ‡⁵RPrice (16) (a.p: ev ch whn bmpd 2f
out: nt rcvr) .................................................................................... ¾.5

1932 Hallplace (61) (MRChannon) 8-8 CRutter (6) (in tch: rdn over 1f out: nt pce to
chal) ............................................................................................... 2½.6

3050 Workingforpeanuts (IRE) (56) (CASmith) 7-10 ‡7CHawksley (10) (r.o over 1f
out: nvr nrr) .................................................................................... nk.7

2409⁵ Galactic Fury (63) (BStevens) 8-10 MTebbutt (4) (chsd ldrs: no hdwy fnl 2f) ...... 3.8

2719⁴ Society Gown (USA) (56) (Fav) (TDBarron) 8-3 KDarley (14) (hdwy whn bdly
hmpd over 2f out: nt rcvr) ............................................................... 1.9

2543 Weaver George (IRE) (53) (MHEasterby) 7-11 ‡³FNorton (3) (led over 5f: sn rdn
& wknd) .......................................................................................... 2.10

2916 Superensis (56) (WRMuir) 8-3 AClark (18) (m.n.s) ...................................... 3½.11

2973 Ombre Darme (IRE) (58) (bl) (JWPayne) 8-5(1) RCochrane (11) (m.n.s) ........... hd.12

2842 Challenger Row (IRE) (56) (CWThornton) 8-3 RPElliott (1) (b.hind: rdn ½-wy: a
bhd) ............................................................................................... 1½.13

2930 Bonny Princess (61) (JDBethell) 8-8 JLowe (8) (m.n.s) .................................. ¾.14

2916⁴ Creative Flair (60) (PFICole) 8-7 TQuinn (9) (w ldrs: hmpd 2f out: nt rcvr) 2.15

2910 Madam Cyn's Risk (58) (NACallaghan) 8-5 DHolland (9) (m.n.s) ...................... 3.16

2961⁵ Stevie's Wonder (IRE) (74) (WCarter) 9-2 ‡⁵NGwilliams (15) (prom: hrd rdn 3f
out: sn wknd) ................................................................................... 1½.17

2938 Mrs Dawson (55) (DrJDScargill) 8-2 SDawson (5) (a bhd) ............................. hd.18

3047 Coopers Delight (62) (GLewis) 8-9 PaulEddery (12) (plld hrd: prom 5f: sn wknd) 5.19

2983³ Touch N' Glow (52) (NTinkler) 7-13 LCharnock (13) (virtually ref to r: t.o) ......... 20.20

Stewards Enquiry: Gwilliams suspended 23-24/9/92 (excessive use of whip), Garth suspended 17-19/9/92 (careless riding)

**7/1** Society Gown (USA), **8/1** Creative Flair (USA)(op 5/1), Doc Spot, **9/1** Mrs Dawson(25/1—8/1), Workingforpeanuts (IRE), George Roper(12/1—8/1), **10/1** Ombre Darme (IRE), Touch N' Glow(op 16/1), The Gold Souk (IRE)(8/1—12/1), **14/1** GENERAL CHASE(10/1—16/1), Coopers Delight(8/1—16/1), **16/1** Galactic Fury, Madam Cyn's Risk, Weaver George (IRE), Hallplace, Bonny Princess, **20/1** Pondering, Challenger Row (IRE), **25/1** Stevie's Wonder (IRE), **33/1** Su perensis. CSF £131.62, CT £1,118.46. Tote £45.30: £9.10 £2.40 £2.00 £5.60 (£59.60). Mrs Marigold West (BRISTOL) bred by R. M. West. 20 Rn; No bid

1m 40.4 (5.4)

SF—17/7/5/–/1/–

## 3174

STAG H'CAP (0-70) £3419.50 (£952.00: £458.50)  1m 1f 218y  3-20 (3-32)

(Weights raised 2 lb)

| | | |
|---|---|---|
| 2708 | **Supertop (51)** *(PWHarris)* 4–8–11 PaulEddery (14) (chsd ldrs: 8th st: rdn to ld appr fnl f: hdd ins fnl f: rallied to ld nr fin) | —1 |
| 2959* | Sinclair Lad (IRE) **(64)** *(RHollinshead)* 4–9–3 ‡7EHusband (19) (chsd ldrs: 4th st: led ins fnl f tl nr fin) | nk.2 |
| 1292* | I'M Electric **(57)** *(RCurtis)* 6–9–3 NDay (4) (chsd ldrs: 7th st: kpt on ins fnl f) | 1½.3 |
| | Hostile Act **(45)** *(KAMorgan)* 7–8–5 AClark (5) (b: bkwd: bhd: styd on fnl 2f: nvr nrr) | 2.4 |
| 2885⁶ | Second Call *(HCandy)* 3–9–3 CRutter (9) (hdwy over 2f out: nt rch ldrs) | hd.5 |
| 2987 | Aasff (USA) **(65)** *(DMorley)* 3–9–4 RHills (17) (lw: hld up & bhd: hdwy 3f out: hrd rdn over 1f out: nvr nrr) | hd.6 |
| 3045 | Alicante **(44)** *(MCChapman)* 5–7–13⁽²⁾ ‡5RPrice (18) (a.p: 2nd st: led over 3f out tl over 2f out: sn rdn & btn) | ¾.7 |
| 2670⁴ | Tarda **(55)** *(MrsGRReveley)* 5–9–1 KDarley (8) (hld up: effrt over 2f out: nvr nrr) | 1.8 |
| 3137 | Green's Cassatt (USA) **(54)** *(WMBrisbourne)* 4–8–7 ‡7CHawksley (10) (nvr nr to chal) | 1½.9 |
| 2753 | Montagne **(52)** *(HCandy)* 3–8–5 SDawson (16) (led tl hdd over 3f out: wkng whn bmpd appr fnl f) | 2½.10 |
| 3048 | Ming Blue **(56)** (bl) *(PJMakin)* 3–8–9 TSprake (15) (swtg: m.n.s) | 2.11 |
| 2874⁶ | Roberto's Gal (57) (v) *(NCWright)* 3–8–10 TQuinn (2) (prom: 6th st: wknd over 2f out) | 1½.12 |
| 626⁵ | Hamanaka (USA) **(70)** *(JRFanshawe)* 3–9–9 GCarter (6) (mid div tl wknd over 2f out) | hd.13 |
| 3060⁴ | Quietly Impressive (IRE) **(45)** *(MBell)* 4–8–5 JFortune (7) (chsd ldrs over 7f) | s.h.14 |
| 2868⁵ | Jade Mistress **(56)** *(AHide)* 3–8–9 RCochrane (1) (hld up: effrt over 3f out: wknd 2f out) | ¾.15 |
| 2941⁴ | Aboloni **(52)** *(IAGlover)* 3–8–2 ‡3FNorton (13) (m.n.s) | 1½.16 |
| 482 | Cretoes Dancer (USA) **(66)** *(WHMuir)* 3–9–5 JReid (0) (m.n.s) | ¾.17 |
| 3054⁵ | Pims Classic **(50)** *(JLHarris)* 4–8–10 PRobinson (12) (prom: 5th st: wknd 3f out) | hd.18 |
| 2874⁵ | Callipoli (USA) **(58)** (Fav) *(RGuest)* 5–9–4 SCauthen (11) (lw: prom: 3rd st: wknd 2f out) | 19 |

11/2 Callipoli (USA), 6/1 I'M Electric(7/1—9/1), 9/1 Tarda, SUPERTOP, Sinclair Lad (IRE), 10/1 Second Call, 12/1 Quietly Impressive (IRE), Hamanaka (USA)(7/1—14/1), Roberto's Gal, 14/1 Abeloni(op 9/1), Jade Mistress(op 8/1), 16/1 Green's Cassatt (USA), 20/1 Aasff, 25/1 Pims Classic, Ming Blue, 33/1 Montagne, Cretoes Dancer (USA), 50/1 Ors. CSF £85.18, CT £492.10. Tote £8.20: £2.60 £2.90 £1.70 £16.10 (£52.90). Mrs G. A. Godfrey (BERKHAMSTED) bred by Limestone Stud. 19 Rn  2m 8.7 (6)

SF—42/47/44/28/39/39

## 3175

TATTERSALLS AUCTION SERIES STKS (I) (Qualifier) (Mdn 2-Y.O) £3106.00 (£928.00: £444.00: £202.00)  7f 9y  3-50

| | | |
|---|---|---|
| 2758⁵ | **Arman's Sax (IRE)** (Jt-Fav) *(JLDunlop)* 8-7 JReid (8) (lw: a.p: led over 2f out: r.o wl) | —1 |
| 3036⁴ | Latest Flame (IRE) **(84)** *(MRChannon)* 8-4 TQuinn (5) (lw: led over 4f: r.o one pce) | 2.2 |
| 2842 | Mind the Roof (IRE) *(DRCElsworth)* 8-2 RHills (1) (chsd ldr: ev ch 2f out: r.o one pce) | hd.3 |
| 2883⁶ | Mena (72) *(JWPayne)* 8-0 GCarter (15) (hdwy over 3f out: one pce fnl 2f) | 2.4 |
| 3000 | Wordsmith (IRE) *(GHarwood)* 8-9 AClark (7) (lw: a.p: no hdwy fnl 2f) | nk.5 |
| 2932² | Mr Vincent (IRE) (Jt-Fav) *(GLewis)* 8-5 PaulEddery (13) (lw: rdn over 3f out: wknd over 1f out) | 2½.6 |
| 2409 | Supreme Master *(RHannon)* 8-9 NCarlisle (16) (no hdwy fnl 2f) | 1½.7 |
| 2932 | Lola Wants *(CFWall)* 8-1 PRobinson (11) (prom 5f) | 1½.8 |
| 3030⁶ | Silver Groom (IRE) **(71)** *(APJarvis)* 8-7 MTebbutt (3) (hdwy over 3f out: wknd 2f out) | ¾.9 |
| 2986 | Ashover *(TDBarron)* 8-11 KDarley (12) (lw: n.d) | 3.10 |
| | Natasha North *(TCasey)* 7-12 ‡3FNorton (14) (w'like: bkwd: a bhd) | 10 |
| | Lunar Risk *(WRMuir)* 8-8 RCochrane (9) (str: scope: bhd fnl 2f) | nk.12 |
| 2932 | Vladivostok *(BWHills)* 8-10 DHolland (6) (lw: prom over 4f) | hd.13 |
| 2932 | April Double (IRE) *(MHTompkins)* 7-10⁽³⁾ ‡7SMulvey (4) (n.d) | 3½.14 |
| | Please Say Yes (IRE) *(CNAllen)* 7-12 ‡7GForster (17) (prom over 4f) | nk.15 |
| 2008⁶ | Beat the Bagman (IRE) *(LJHolt)* 8-0 ‡7CAvery (10) (a bhd) | hd.16 |
| 2696 | Certain Way (IRE) (v) *(CTinkler)* 8-6 LCharnock (2) (t.o) | 17 |

9/4 ARMAN'S SAX (IRE), Mr Vincent, 8/1 Latest Flame (IRE), Vladivostok(op 5/1), Vladivostok(op 4/1), Lola Wants, 12/1 Wordsmith (IRE)(op 8/1), 14/1 Mind the Roof (IRE)(op 8/1), Mena, 20/1 Silver Groom (IRE), 25/1 Supreme Master, 33/1 Beat the Bagman (IRE), Certain Way (IRE), Lunar Risk, Ashover, 50/1 Ors. CSF £23.23, Tote £4.00: £1.90 £2.10 £2.70 (£19.80). Gerecon Italia (ARUNDEL) bred by J. Cummins in Ireland. 17 Rn  1m 27.4 (5.1)

SF—22/13/10/2/10/–

## 3176

LEICESTERSHIRE CLAIMING STKS (3-Y.O) £2742.00 (£762.00: £366.00)
1m·8y
4-20 (4-31)

| | | | | | |
|---|---|---|---|---|---|
| 3014⁴ | **Jade Vale (71)** (Jt-Fav) *(JWHills)* 9-5 RHills (4) (a.p: led ins fnl f: r.o wl) | | | | —1 |
| 2228 | Eiras Mood *(BPalling)* 7-12 ‡⁵StephenDavies (15) (hdwy over 2f out: ev ch over 1f out: nt qckn) | | | | 2.2 |
| 1085⁶ | Tyrone Flyer **(45)** *(MCPipe)* 8-2 DHolland (1) (led tl ins fnl f) | | | | 3½.3 |
| 268⁵⁴ | Shardra **(47)** *(MFBarraclough)* 7-13 JLowe (12) (a.p: r.o one pce fnl 2f) | | | | 1.4 |
| 2866 | Badawiah **(67)** *(WAO'Gorman)* 8-7 GCarter (9) (b: nvr nrr) | | | | 2.5 |
| 3014 | Eastleigh **(65)** *(RHollinshead)* 9-0 KDarley (6) (hdwy over 2f out: wknd fnl f) | | | | nk.6 |
| 2453 | Bid for Six (USA) **(73)** (Jt-Fav) *(RHannon)* 8-4 PaulEddery (2) (no hdwy fnl 2f) | | | | 1½.7 |
| 3004 | Hardliner **(73)** *(CFWall)* 8-6 PRobinson (8) (plld hrd: prom over 5f) | | | | ¾.8 |
| 3028⁴ | Chequers (IRE) **(63)** (v) *(RJRWilliams)* 8-10 RCochrane (11) (n.d) | | | | ¾.9 |
| 2831 | Nordansk **(45)** *(LJHolt)* 9-0 JReid (16) (bit bkwd: prom tl wknd over 1f out) | | | | ½.10 |
| 1907⁵ | Shafayif **(43)** *(ICampbell)* 8-12 ‡⁷SMulvey (10) (a bhd) | | | | 4.11 |
| 1109⁶ | Jalore **(50)** *(RHollinshead)* 7-11 ‡⁷MHumphries (3) (hdwy: prom 6f) | | | | 11 |
| 1034 | Lady Randolph **(37)** *(ICampbell)* 8-9 MTebbutt (5) (a bhd) | | | | ¾.13 |
| 1005⁶ | Swynford Flyer *(JFBottomley)* 8-13 LCharnock (13) (bit bkwd: t.o) | | | | 20.14 |
| 2293 | Groovey Dancer *(BJMcMath)* 8-6 EJohnson (14) (prom over 4f: t.o) | | | | 7.15 |
| 38 | Daily Sport August **(39)** *(MCChapman)* 8-0 ‡⁵RPrice (7) (prom 4f: t.o) | | | | ¾.16 |

**3/1** Bid for Six (USA), JADE VALE(tchd 5/1), **5/1** Chequers (IRE), **8/1** Badawiah(5/1—9/1), **9/1** Hardliner(op 4/1), Eastleigh, **12/1** Tyrone Flyer, **20/1** Shardra, **33/1** Shafayif, **50/1** Nordansk, Eiras Mood, **66/1** Ors. CSF £14.57, Tote £3.80: £1.70 £6.90 £2.00 (Wnr or 2nd w any £1.80). Major Brijendra Singh (LAMBOURN) bred by Maj B. Singh. 16 Rn
1m 38.5 (3.5)
SF—58/31/24/18/20/26

## 3177

SWAN H'CAP (3-Y.O) (0-70) £3419.50 (£952.00: £458.50)
1m 3f 183y
4-50 (4-58)
(Weights raised 4 lb)

| | | | | | |
|---|---|---|---|---|---|
| 3021² | **Bit on the Side (IRE) (54)** (Fav) *(WJMusson)* 8-9 JReid (9) (hld up: stdy hdwy over 2f out: led over 1f out: r.o wl) | | | | —1 |
| 3054² | Speedo Movement **(55)** *(BAMcMahon)* 8-3 ‡⁷SSanders (18) (hdwy 3f out: r.o fnl f: nt trble wnr) | | | | 3.2 |
| 2810 | Philgun **(55)** *(CWCElsey)* 8-10 KDarley (20) (5th st: r.o one pce fnl 2f) | | | | 2.3 |
| 2228⁶ | Post Impressionist (IRE) **(60)** *(BWHills)* 9-1 DHolland (11) (hdwy fnl 2f: nvr nrr) | | | | ½.4 |
| 3026³ | Nicely Thanks (USA) **(61)** *(TDBarron)* 8-9 ‡⁷VHalliday (22) (hrd rdn & gd hdwy 2f out: r.o) | | | | 1½.5 |
| 2985² | In the Money (IRE) **(64)** *(RHollinshead)* 8-12 ‡⁷AGarth (10) (4th st: led 3f out tl over 1f out) | | | | ½.6 |
| 2992 | Faaz (USA) **(50)** (bl) *(AAScott)* 8-5 JFortune (15) (bhd tl hdwy 3f out: rdn 2f out: n.d) | | | | ½.7 |
| 3073 | Mist of the Marsh (USA) **(50)** *(JHMGosden)* 8-5 PRobinson (5) (bhd tl hdwy over 2f out: nrst fin) | | | | hd.8 |
| 1909⁵ | Bilberry **(48)** *(CWCElsey)* 8-3 LCharnock (7) (led 7f out to 3f out: wknd 2f out) | | | | 7.9 |
| 2860⁶ | Port in a Storm **(54)** *(WJarvis)* 8-9 RCochrane (6) (n.d) | | | | 1.10 |
| 2985 | Shakinski **(47)** *(MJRyan)* 7-9 ‡⁷PMcCabe (8) (n.d) | | | | 2½.11 |
| 2946⁶ | The Karaoke King **(59)** *(RHannon)* 9-0 SCauthen (14) (6th st: wknd over 2f out) | | | | ¾.12 |
| 2580 | Wheeler's Wonder **(41)** (v) *(NCWright)* 7-10 SDawson (21) (n.d) | | | | 1½.13 |
| | Bonzer **(42)** *(JGFitzGerald)* 7-8 ‡³FNorton (1) (bit bkwd: prom tl 7th st: eased whn btn over 1f out) | | | | ¾.14 |
| 2896 | Paper Clip **(47)** *(JDBethell)* 8-2 JLowe (1) (lw: n.d) | | | | ½.15 |
| 2621⁴ | Baby Wizzard **(49)** *(IABalding)* 8-4 PD'Arcy (19) (n.d) | | | | ¾.16 |
| 2867 | Fly for Gold (IRE) **(57)** *(DWPArbuthnot)* 8-12 TQuinn (13) (b.hind: led 2f: 3rd st: wknd 3f out) | | | | ½.17 |
| 2922 | Billy Bunter **(66)** *(HCandy)* 9-7 CRutter (3) (a bhd) | | | | nk.18 |
| 2780 | Hurricane Toke (IRE) **(60)** *(ACStewart)* 9-1 RHills (2) (t.o) | | | | 19 |
| 3073² | Sie Amato (IRE) **(55)** *(CaptJWilson)* 8-10 GCarter (12) (led after 2f out to 7f out: 2nd st: wknd 3f out) | | | | 20 |

**3/1** BIT ON THE SIDE (IRE), **8/1** Sie Amato (IRE)(tchd 12/1), Hurricane Toke (IRE)(12/1—14/1), Nicely Thanks (USA), **9/1** Speedo Movement(op 6/1), The Karaoke King, **10/1** Fly for Gold (IRE), **12/1** Port in a Storm, **14/1** In the Money (IRE), Post Impressionist (IRE)(op 8/1), **16/1** Mist of the Marsh (USA)(op 10/1), Baby Wizzard, **20/1** Philgun, Faaz (USA), Shakinski, **25/1** Paper Clip, **33/1** Ors. CSF £34.02, CT £466.86. Tote £3.40: £1.50 £3.00 £4.90 £5.60 (£10.60). Mr Mike Hawkett (NEWMARKET) bred by Stallion Development Group in Ireland. 20 Rn
2m 34 (5.2)
SF—49/37/40/44/35/37

## 3178

TATTERSALLS AUCTION SERIES STKS (II) (Qualifier) (Mdn 2-Y.O) £3106.00 (£928.00: £444.00: £202.00)
7f 9y
5-20 (5-30)

| | | | | | |
|---|---|---|---|---|---|
| | **Instant Affair (USA)** *(PFICole)* 8-8 TQuinn (4) (lt-f: a.p: led & flashed tail over 1f out: drvn out) | | | | —1 |

28832 Rockover **(77)** (Jt-Fav) *(RHannon)* 8-9(1) SCauthen (11) (a.p: ev ch over 1f out: r.o) .................................................................................................................. 1.2
28645 Grove Daffodil (IRE) (Jt-Fav) *(MHTompkins)* 8-0 PRobinson (14) (gd hdwy over 1f out: fin wl) ............................................................................................. 1/2.3
Prima Sinfonia *(SMHillen)* 8-4 JLowe (5) (scope: a.p: led 2f out tl over 1f out: one pce) ............................................................................................................... 3/4.4
2649 Adamparis *(ANLee)* 8-3 JFortune (4) (bit bkwd: hdwy over 2f out: ev ch over 1f out: wknd fnl f) ............................................................................................. 21/2.5
30305 Who's the Best (IRE) *(APJarvis)* 8-7 MTebbutt (17) (a.p: ev ch over 1f out: wknd fnl f) .................................................................................................................... 1.6
28125 Silky Heights (IRE) *(MJCamacho)* 8-4 LCharnock (6) (bkwd: hdwy 3f out: one pce fnl f) ......................................................................................................... 1.7
2225 Body Language *(IABalding)* 8-4 RHills (10) (stdd s: plld hrd: nvr trbld ldrs) ..... 21/2.8
Sellafield (IRE) *(WRMuir)* 8-6 AClark (15) (leggy: lt-f: prom 5f) ............................. nk.9
Clar Dubh (IRE) *(MHTompkins)* 7-10(3) ‡7SMulvey (8) (leggy: bkwd: n.d) ............. hd.10
27332 Contrac Countess **(65)** *(BSRothwell)* 8-0 DHolland (9) (led centre 5f) ......... 1/2.11
2883 Daisy James (IRE) **(53)** *(JMPEustace)* 7-12 ‡3FNorton (16) (n.d) .................. 1/2.12
3029 Panther (IRE) **(79)** *(CWCElsey)* 8-7 KDarley (3) (bhd fnl 2f) ............................. 1.13
2961 Desert Laughter (IRE) *(RHollinshead)* 8-5 PaulEddery (12) (n.d) ......................... 2.14
2758 Sea Baron **(76)** *(MBlanshard)* 8-9 RCochrane (1) (racd alone stands' side: led 5f: wknd qckly) ............................................................................................. 1/2.15
26495 West End Girl *(RJRWilliams)* 8-1 CRutter (7) (n.d) ............................................. hd.16
30504 Baileys Colours **(49)** *(BJMcMath)* 7-8 ‡7CHawksley (2) (spd 4f) .................. s.h.17

**3/1** Grove Daffodil (IRE)(op 2/1), Rockover(9/4—4/1), **7/1** Adamparis(33/1—4/1), **8/1** INSTANT AFFAIR (USA)(op 4/1), Prima Sinfonia(14/1—20/1), **12/1** Silky Heights (IRE)(op 6/1), **14/1** Body Language, Contrac Countess (IRE), Who's the Best (IRE), West End Girl(op 6/1), **16/1** Panther (IRE)(op 10/1), **20/1** Sea Baron(op 5/1), **33/1** Desert Laughter (IRE), Baileys Colours (IRE), Daisy James (IRE), **50/1** Ors. CSF £34.56, Tote £7.20: £6.00 £2.10 £1.90 (£17.70) Mr Athos Christodoulou (WHATCOMBE) bred by Gallagher's Stud in USA. 17 Rn
1m 27.3 (5)
SF—24/22/11/13/4/5

T/Plpt: £1,016.10 (2.3 Tckts). IM/KH

---

2969—**LINGFIELD (L-H)**

### Tuesday, September 8th [Good to soft, AWT standard]
Going Allowance: Turf: 0.15 sec (G); AWT: minus 0.30 sec (FS)  Wind: slt across

Stalls: 6th centre, remainder high

**3179**   ABBEY WELL MINERAL WATER STKS (Mdn 2-Y-O) £2700.00 (£750.00: £360.00)
5f                                                                                   2-00 (2-05)

28262 **Go Flightline (IRE)** *(MBell)* 8-9 MHills (17) (a.p: led ins fnl f: drvn out) .............. —1
2900 Mysterious Ways (FR) **(70)** *(MrsJCecil)* 9-0 WRyan (9) (lw: a.p: led over 1f out tl ins fnl f: r.o wl) ....................................................................................... s.h.2
30514 Kimbolton Korker *(AAScott)* 8-9 BRaymond (11) (b.hind: led over 3f: unable qckn) ......................................................................................................... 11/2.3
29325 Glen Miller *(JWPayne)* 9-0 AMunro (13) (lw: rdn over 2f out: hdwy over 1f out: r.o) ................................................................................................................... 1.4
Most Eminent *(PWHarris)* 9-0 SWhitworth (7) (unf: scope: bit bkwd: s.s: hdwy 2f out: r.o) ...................................................................................................... 3/4.5
3011 Desert Nomad *(SDow)* 8-9 JQuinn (20) (hdwy over 1f out: r.o) ........................ s.h.6
2746 Kintwyn **(63)** (v) *(DRLaing)* 9-0 TyroneWilliams (19) (a.p: hrd rdn over 1f out: one pce) ........................................................................................................ nk.7
30553 Gone Prospecting (USA) **(81)** (Jt-Fav) *(RHannon)* 9-0 WCarson (18) (lw: prom 3f) ............................................................................................................... 11/2.8
River Refuge *(JARToller)* 9-0 DaleGibson (14) (leggy: bit bkwd: nvr nr to chal) ... hd.9
Crime Ofthecentury (Jt-Fav) *(PFICole)* 8-9 PatEddery (8) (b.hind: unf: bit bkwd: s.s: hdwy over 3f out: wknd over 1f out) ....................................................... 3.10
2826 Persian Melody (IRE) *(DRCElsworth)* 8-9 JWilliams (12) (lw: a mid div) ............ 1.11
2986 Velasco (IRE) *(SirMarkPrescott)* 9-0 CNutter (16) (nvr nrr) ............................ 11/2.12
19915 Sui Generis (IRE) *(CGCox)* 8-9 GBaxter (5) (prom over 3f) ............................. 1/2.13
2842 Who's Tom (IRE) *(WJMusson)* 9-0 JHBrown (1) (b: s.s: a bhd) ...................... 4.14
3018 Gallop to Glory *(PMitchell)* 8-11 ‡3SO'Gorman (6) (outpcd) ......................... 2.15
French Heiress *(CEBrittain)* 8-9 GCrealock (3) (lt-f: a bhd) ............................. 1.16
1601 Generally *(PatMitchell)* 8-9 DBiggs (15) (bhd fnl 2f) ...................................... nk.17
26834 Miss Delivery *(PHowling)* 8-9 BCrossley (4) (outpcd) .................................... 1.18
1057 Ascom Pager (IRE) *(GLewis)* 8-9 BRouse (2) (b.hind: bit bkwd: a bhd) ........... 1/2.19

5/2 Crime Ofthecentury(5/4—3/1), Gone Prospecting (USA)(7/2—4/1), **4/1** GO FLIGHTLINE (IRE), **8/1** Kimbolton Korker(5/1—9/1), **16/1** Glen Miller, **20/1** Mysterious Ways (FR), **33/1** Desert Nomad, French Heiress, River Refuge, Soul Generis (IRE), Persian Melody (IRE), **50/1** Ors. CSF £72.14, Tote £4.90: £1.80 £5.10 £3.00 (£46.90). Mr Ian K. I. Stewart (NEWMARKET) bred by Kieran and Robert Ryan in Ireland. 19 Rn
60.72 sec (3.72)
SF—35/39/28/29/26/20

## 3180

HENKEL ECOLAB (S) STKS  £2490.00 (£690.00: £330.00)
1¼m (AWT)

2-30 (2-34)

|  |  |  |
|---|---|---|
| | **Jo N Jack (IRE)** *(RIngram)* 4-9-4 CDwyer (2) (a.p: led over 1f out: rdn out) ...... | —1 |
| 2413⁴ | May Square (IRE) (56) *(MrsAKnight)* 4-9-10 WRyan (11) (a.p: led over 2f out tl over 1f out: unable qckn) ................................................................ | 2½.2 |
| 477 | Awesome Power (70) *(CRNelson)* 6-9-10 NAdams (13) (hdwy over 3f out: hrd rdn over 2f out: one pce) ................................................ | 1.3 |
| 2993 | Amazon Express (52) (Fav) *(CEBrittain)* 3-9-3 MRoberts (1) (led over 7f) ........... | 4.4 |
| 2952⁴ | Breakdancer (IRE) (50) *(WRMuir)* 3-9-0 ‡³RPerham (9) (nvr nr to chal) .............. | 2.5 |
| 3054 | Casilla (21) *(HCandy)* 4-8-13 AMunro (12) (rdn & no hdwy fnl 3f) ................. | 2.6 |
| 2829 | Soul Trader (bl) *(BWHills)* 3-8-6 PatEddery (3) (prom over 6f) ..................... | ½.7 |
| 2931 | High Post (49) *(DMarks)* 3-8-12 ‡⁵ATucker (8) (nvr nrr) ........................... | s.h.8 |
| 2729 | Indian Mohawk (IRE) (32) *(DRCEisworth)* 4-9-4 JWilliams (14) (nvr nrr) ......... | 6.9 |
| *2785* | Hubbers Favourite (43) (v) *(MrsNMacauley)* 4-8-13 BCrossley (10) (a.p: ev ch over 3f out: wknd over 2f out) ................................................ | nk.10 |
| 1366 | Saysana (26) *(AMoore)* 5-9-5 CandyMorris (5) (prom 5f) ......................... | 10.11 |
| 3017 | Maoujoud (RPCHoad) 4-9-1 ‡³SO'Gorman (4) (prom over 4f: t.o) ................... | 20.12 |
| 2705⁴ | Wave Master (50) *(RJHodges)* 5-9-10 MHills (6) (a bhd: t.o) ...................... | ½.13 |
| | Forever Tweeky *(PRHedger)* 3-8-6 AMcGlone (7) (w'like: bit bkwd: a bhd: t.o) | ½.14 |

**9/4** Amazon Express(op 4/1), **7/2** Awesome Power, **6/1** May Square (IRE), **9/1** Breakdancer (IRE), **10/1** High Post, Indian Mohawk (IRE)(12/1—7/1), **12/1** Soul Trader(op 8/1), Wave Master(op 8/1), **20/1** Casilla, **33/1** JO N JACK (IRE) & Ors. CSF £216.63, Tote £42.80: £7.70 £2.20 £1.90 (£123.00). Mrs M. T. Morgan (EPSOM) bred by East Riding Sack and Paper Co in Ireland. 14 Rn; No bid   2m 7.32 (4.32)
SF—31/32/30/15/8/3

## 3181

G. G. BAXTER LTD STKS (I) (Mdn 2-Y.O) £2924.80 (£812.80: £390.40)
7f

3-00 (3-04)

|  |  |  |
|---|---|---|
| | **Burooj** *(DMorley)* 9-0 WCarson (12) (unf: scope: a.p: led over 1f out: rdn out) .. | —1 |
| | Mullitover *(MJHeaton-Ellis)* 9-0 WRyan (13) (w'like: a.p: led over 2f out tl over 1f out: unable qckn) ............................................ | 1½.2 |
| 2948² | Inderaputeri (Fav) *(MissGayKelleway)* 8-9 JQuinn (14) (b: a.p: hrd rdn over 1f out: one pce) .................................................... | 1.3 |
| 2598 | Beauchamp Hero *(JLDunlop)* 9-0 MHills (5) (hdwy over 1f out: r.o) ............... | ¾.4 |
| 3000⁶ | Cameo Kirby (FR) *(AAScott)* 9-0 BRaymond (7) (hrd rdn & no hdwy fnl 2f) ...... | 6.5 |
| 2799 | Akenside *(DRCEisworth)* 9-0 JWilliams (17) (spd over 5f) ........................ | ³⁄₄.6 |
| | Season's Star *(HCandy)* 8-9 AMunro (4) (unf: lw: prom over 5f) ................ | 2.7 |
| 1957 | So Saucy *(CEBrittain)* 8-9 GBaxter (18) (spd 4f) ................................. | 1.8 |
| 3018⁶ | Ice Rebel *(MissBSanders)* 9-0 GBardwell (20) (nvr nrr) .......................... | 2.9 |
| 2233⁶ | Smarginato (IRE) *(JLDunlop)* 9-0 MRoberts (10) (s.s: shkn up over 3f out: nvr nrr) ............................................................ | ³⁄₄.10 |
| | Kawasir (CAN) *(PTWalwyn)* 9-0 BRouse (11) (leggy: unf: s.s: nvr nrr) ......... | 3½.11 |
| 3018 | Al Moulouki *(JWPayne)* 9-0 WHood (16) (nvr nrr) ............................... | 1½.12 |
| 2649 | Freckenham *(JEBanks)* 8-4 ‡⁵JWeaver (15) (outpcd) ............................ | 1½.13 |
| 2864 | Barassie *(PMitchell)* 8-6 ‡³SO'Gorman (19) (rdn over 3f out: nvr nrr) .......... | ³⁄₄.14 |
| 1610 | Take the Mick *(AWheeler)* 9-0 SWhitworth (8) (outpcd) ......................... | ½.15 |
| 2501 | Jolis Absent *(MJRyan)* 8-9 DBiggs (6) (outpcd) .................................. | nk.16 |
| | Ansillo *(JHMGosden)* 9-0 PatEddery (2) (w'like: bit bkwd: led over 4f) ......... | ½.17 |
| | Fitzroy Lad *(MRChannon)* 8-11 ‡³RPerham (3) (unf: scope: a bhd) ............. | 2½.18 |
| 2826 | The Golden Sport *(GLewis)* 9-0 AMcGlone (1) (bhd fnl 4f) ...................... | 12.19 |
| 2994 | Arras Royale *(JELong)* 9-0 NAdams (4) (bhd fnl 3f) ............................. | 3½.20 |

**7/2** Inderaputeri, **4/1** Smarginato (IRE)(op 7/1), Ansillo(2/1—5/1), **11/2** BUROOJ, **6/1** Cameo Kirby (FR), **12/1** Beauchamp Hero(tchd 8/1), **14/1** Kawasir (CAN)(op 8/1), Akenside, **16/1** Season's Star, **20/1** So Saucy, Ice Rebel, **25/1** Mullitover, **33/1** Fitzroy Lad, **50/1** Ors. CSF £135.34, Tote £6.10: £2.80 £23.60 £1.70 (£533.00). Mr Hamdan Al-Maktoum (NEWMARKET) bred by Shadwell Estate Company Limited. 20 Rn   1m 26.69 (5.39)
SF—35/30/22/25/7/5

## 3182

RATIONAL COMBI STEAMER H'CAP (0-95) £3106.00 (£928.00: £444.00: £202.00)
7f 140y

3-30 (3-37)

|  |  |  |
|---|---|---|
| 2458 | **Caroles Express (69)** *(RAkehurst)* 4-8-5 MRoberts (9) (hdwy over 1f out: hrd rdn fnl f: led nr fin) ...................................... | —1 |

2898* Polonez Prima **(87)** *(JEBanks)* 5-9-4 ‡⁵JWeaver (3) (hld up: rdn over 3f out: led wl over 1f out tl hdd nr fin) .................................................. 1.2

3004 Sylvan Sabre (IRE) **(76)** *(PMitchell)* 3-8-7 JWilliams (10) (hdwy over 1f out: r.o ins fnl f) ............................................................. 2¹/₂.3

3009² Dodgy **(62)** (v) *(SDow)* 5-7-12 JQuinn (8) (led 6f: one pce) .................. 1¹/₂.4

3121⁵ Green Dollar **(92)** *(EAWheeler)* 9-10-0 WCarson (2) (nvr nr to chal) ............... ¹/₂.5

2830² Surrey Racing **(72)** *(GLewis)* 4-8-8 BRouse (4) (hld up: rdn over 2f out: wknd over 1f out) ................................................... 1¹/₂.6

2898³ Cape Pigeon (USA) **(87)** *(LGCottrell)* 7-9-9 AMunro (6) (lw: prom 5f) ......... 1¹/₂.7

2958 Annabelle Royale **(75)** *(MrsNMacauley)* 6-8-11 DBiggs (1) (a.p: ev ch over 2f out: wknd over 1f out) .................................. 2¹/₂.8

3002⁵Cheveux Mitchell **(75)** (v) *(Fav)* *(MRChannon)* 5-8-11 PatEddery (7) (spd over 5f) .................................................... 3¹/₂.9

2521⁶ Sugemar **(59)** *(JARToller)* 6-7-9 GBardwell (5) (a bhd) ........................... 8.10

**7/2** Cheveux Mitchell, **4/1** CAROLES EXPRESS, **6/1** Polonez Prima, **7/1** Cape Pigeon (USA), **15/2** Dodgy(5/1—8/1), **8/1** Sugemar, **10/1** Annabelle Royale, Surrey Racing(op 6/1), **14/1** Green Dollar(op 8/1), **20/1** Sylvan Sabre (IRE). CSF £27.22, CT £395.94. Tote £5.20: £1.60 £2.20 £4.80 (£20.80). Mrs Susan Crane (EPSOM) bred by W. L. Caley. 10 Rn

1m 33.70 (5.20)

SF−30/40/21/7/35/10

## 3183

FALCON CATERING EQUIPMENT H'CAP (0-80) £3473.20 (£965.20: £463.60)
6f

4-00 (4-08)

1878⁵ **Fascination Waltz (67)** *(DShaw)* 5-9-4 BRaymond (13) (hld up: led ins fnl f: r.o wl) .................................................................. −1

2865 Amethystine (USA) **(63)** *(RJHodges)* 6-8-7 ‡⁷SDrowne (1) (racd far side: a.p: led over 2f out tl ins fnl f: unable qckn) .................... 3.2

?8??* Easy Does it **(48)** (Jt-Fav) *(MrsAKnight)* 3-7-10 JQuinn (14) (a.p: hrd rdn over 1f out: one pce) ....................................... 1.3

2726* Spring High **(58)** (bl) (Jt-Fav) *(KTIvory)* 5-8-9 GBardwell (6) (b: racd far side: a.p: hrd rdn over 1f out: one pce) ............... s.h.4

2404 Ayr Raider **(67)** *(WRMuir)* 5-9-4 MRoberts (5) (racd far side: hdwy 2f out: one pce) ......................................................... s.h.5

2861 Rainbow Fleet **(55)** *(DMarks)* 4-8-6 MHills (10) (hdwy over 1f out: r.o) ............ ³/₄.6

2830³ Pigalle Wonder **(49)** *(RJO'Sullivan)* 4-7-9⁽¹⁾ ‡⁵ATucker (17) (lw: a.p: one pce fnl 2f) ..................................................... 1¹/₂.7

3105² Quick Steel **(53)** (bl) *(TPMcGovern)* 4-8-6 NAdams (9) (nvr nr to chal) ........... 1¹/₂.8

2942 Luna Bid **(65)** (Jt-Fav) *(MBlanshard)* 9-9-2 WRyan (18) (nvr nrr) .................. 1¹/₂.9

3067 Fay's Song (IRE) **(75)** (Jt-Fav) *(RAkehurst)* 4-9-5 ‡⁷LCarter (19) (lw: a mid div) .................................................. ¹/₂.10

2949³ Duty Sergeant (IRE) **(48)** (bl) *(MPMuggeridge)* 3-7-10⁽¹⁾ TyroneWilliams (16) (a mid div) .................................................. 1¹/₂.11

2718⁵ Gallant Hope **(55)** (bl) *(LGCottrell)* 10-8-6⁽¹⁾ JWilliams (20) (b: outpcd) nk.12

3015 Born to Be **(77)** *(SDow)* 3-9-11 BRouse (12) (prom 4f) .................. s.h.13

2953 Grey Charmer (IRE) **(55)** *(CJames)* 3-8-3 DaleGibson (7) (outpcd) ........... 2.14

3015 Truthful Image **(78)** (bl) *(MJRyan)* 3-9-12 DBiggs (11) (s.s: a bhd) ......... s.h.15

3105 Efra **(64)** *(RHannon)* 3-8-12 AMcGlone (15) (outpcd) .................... s.h.16

2684 Tauber **(66)** *(PatMitchell)* 8-9-0 ‡³SO'Gorman (8) (spd over 4f) .......... 6.17

2919 Dawes of Nelson **(55)** (Jt-Fav) *(MJBolton)* 7-8-6 WCarson (2) (racd far side: a bhd) ................................................... 6.18

2599 Shades of Jade **(54)** *(JJBridger)* 4-8-5 SWhitworth (4) (racd far side: led over 3f) 4.19

**10/1** Dawes of Nelson, Gallant Hope, Spring High, Easy Does it, Fay's Song (IRE)(8/1—12/1), Luna Bid, **11/1** Ayr Raider, Pigalle Wonder, **12/1** Quick Steel, Tauber, Truthful Image, **14/1** FASCINATION WALTZ, Rainbow Fleet, Efra, **16/1** Duty Sergeant (IRE), **20/1** Grey Charmer (IRE), Born to Be, **25/1** Ors. CSF £303.94, CT £3,308.70. Tote £19.20: £3.80 £8.60 £2.40 £2.70 (£1,476.80). Mr Fred A. Havercroft (ASHINGTON) bred by Ballymacarney Stud. 19 Rn

1m 12.84 (4.24)

SF−37/14/−/11/19/4

## 3184

BARTON QUALITY FOODS STKS (Mdn 3-Y.O) £2238.00 (£618.00: £294.00)
1¹/₂m (AWT)

4-30 (4-32)

2922 **Quadrant** *(BWHills)* 9-0 PatEddery (5) (chsd ldr: led over 3f out: r.o wl) ........... −1

Alkhafji *(HRACecil)* 9-0 WRyan (2) (wl grwn: s.s: hdwy over 4f out: ev ch 1f out: r.o) .............................................................. 1.2

2907⁴ Donia (USA) **(69)** *(PFICole)* 8-9 AMunro (3) (a.p: one pce fnl 2f) ............. 4.3

2798³ Let's Get Lost **(74)** (Fav) *(WJHaggas)* 9-0 MRoberts (1) (b: b.hind: led over 8f) . 2.4

2922⁵ Magadeer (USA) **(73)** *(JLDunlop)* 8-9 BRaymond (4) (rdn 5f out: bhd fnl 4f) ... s.h.5

**11/8** Let's Get Lost(Evens—7/4), **3/1** QUADRANT, **4/1** Magadeer (USA)(op 9/4), **11/2** Donia (USA), **10/1** Alkhafji(op 6/1). CSF £23.76, Tote £6.20: £2.10 £1.70 (£8.70). Mr R. D. Hollingsworth (LAMBOURN) bred by R. D. Hollingsworth. 5 Rn

2m 32.78 (3.38)

SF−30/28/15/16/10

## 3185

BEEFEATER GIN H'CAP (0-80) £2962.80 (£820.50: £392.40)  **7f (AWT)**  5-00 (5-02)

| | | |
|---|---|---|
| 2969* | **Albert the Bold (63)** *(MrsLPiggott)* 3-8-7 LPiggott (8) (eyeshield: b: a.p: led over 2f out: drvn out) | —1 |
| 2945² | Sunset Street (IRE) **(58)** *(Fav) (SDow)* 4-8-6 AMunro (5) (b: hdwy on ins over 2f out: n.m.r wl over 1f out: squeezed thro ins fnl f) | ½.2 |
| 2303⁶ | Whitehall (IRE) **(64)** *(CRNelson)* 3-8-8 NAdams (12) (hld up: hrd rdn over 1f out: r.o wl ins fnl f) | ½.3 |
| 2750 | Predictable **(64)** *(MrsAKnight)* 6-8-12 JQuinn (9) (a.p: ev ch over 2f out: unable qckn) | 1.4 |
| 2974⁵ | One Magic Moment (IRE) **(48)** *(CACyzer)* 4-7-10 DBiggs (4) (hdwy over 1f out: r.o) | ¾.5 |
| 2974² | My Ruby Ring **(52)** *(DRLaing)* 5-7-9⁽⁷⁾ ‡5ATucker (1) (b: nt clr run on ins wl over 1f out: hdwy fnl f) | hd.6 |
| 3067⁵ | Ain'tlikelikethat **(56)** (bl) *(TJNaughton)* 5-8-4 MHills (11) (b: s.s: hdwy over 1f out: r.o) | hd.7 |
| 2804* | **Harry's Coming (76)** *(RJHodges)* 8-9-3 ‡7SDrowne (10) (nvr nr to chal) | nk.8 |
| 3105 | Roxy Music (IRE) **(49)** *(KOCunningham-Brown)* 3-7-7 GBardwell (3) (led 6f out tl over 2f out: wknd over 1f out) | 1½.9 |
| 2993 | Slight Risk **(69)** *(PAKelleway)* 3-8-13 GayKelleway (7) (eyecover: led 1f: ev ch over 2f out: wknd over 1f out) | 4.10 |
| 2830 | Tadora (IRE) **(58)** *(CJBenstead)* 3-8-2 TyroneWilliams (6) (outpcd) | 4.11 |
| 1266 | Looting (USA) **(45)** *(MDIUsher)* 6-7-7 DaleGibson (2) (prom over 3f) | 3½.12 |

LONG HANDICAP: My Ruby Ring 7-4, Looting (USA) 7-6.

**5/2** Sunset Street (IRE), **5/1** ALBERT THE BOLD(6/1—8/1), Ain'tlikelikethat, **8/1** Harry's Coming, **10/1** My Ruby Ring, Roxy Music (IRE), **12/1** One Magic Moment (IRE), **14/1** Whitehall (IRE), Predictable, **20/1** Slight Risk, **25/1** Ors. CSF £17.72, CT £152.81. Tote £3.90: £1.50 £1.90 £4.60 (£7.10). Miss J. Semple (NEWMARKET) bred by Doverlodge Stud. 12 Rn
1m 25.97 (1.97)
SF—32/29/29/30/12/10

## 3186

G. G. BAXTER LTD STKS (II) (Mdn 2-Y.O) £2924.80 (£812.50: £390.40)
**7f**
5-30 (5-35)

| | | |
|---|---|---|
| | **Urgent Request (IRE)** *(BWHills)* 9-0 PatEddery (2) (b: leggy: racd far side: mde all: clr over 2f out: unchal) | —1 |
| | Dukrame *(HCandy)* 8-9 AMunro (14) (unf: scope: hld up: edgd lft wl over 1f out: unable qckn) | 10.2 |
| 1845³ | Yfool *(JRFanshawe)* 8-9 BRaymond (17) (lw: hld up: hrd rdn over 1f out: one pce) | ¾.3 |
| | Barik (IRE) *(Fav) (ACStewart)* 9-0 MRoberts (18) (w'like: scope: a.p: one pce fnl 2f) | 2.4 |
| 2758⁶ | Stay With Me Baby *(DRCElsworth)* 8-9 JWilliams (13) (a.p: one pce fnl 2f) | 1.5 |
| 2598⁵ | Capablanca *(IABalding)* 9-0 MHills (5) (lw: spd over 5f) | 1½.6 |
| 2771⁴ | Ascom Pager Too **(57)** *(PHowling)* 8-9 BCrossley (16) (no hdwy fnl 2f) | 2.7 |
| | Time Honored (USA) *(SirMarkPrescott)* 9-0 CNutter (19) (unf: nvr nr to chal) | 5.8 |
| 2947⁴ | Mr Copyforce *(MissBSanders)* 9-0 MPerrett (6) (prom over 4f) | nk.9 |
| 2598 | Lord Chief Justice *(JLDunlop)* 9-0 AMcGlone (3) (prom 3f) | 3½.10 |
| 2812⁴ | Angus Dundee (IRE) *(HRACecil)* 9-0 WRyan (1) (racd far side: outpcd) | hd.11 |
| | Get Sunday Sport (IRE) *(MissGayKelleway)* 9-0 GBaxter (20) (leggy: bit bkwd: a mid div) | hd.12 |
| | Halham Tarn *(PTWalwyn)* 9-0 NHowe (7) (w'like: bit bkwd: a mid div) | s.h.13 |
| | Doodies Pool (IRE) *(GLewis)* 9-0 BRouse (11) (w'like: bit bkwd: outpcd) | ½.14 |
| | Lady All Star (USA) *(AAScott)* 8-9 DaleGibson (4) (leggy: lt-f: outpcd) | s.h.15 |
| 2171 | Dotty's Walker (FR) *(CACyzer)* 8-9 DBiggs (4) (racd far side: outpcd) | ¾.16 |
| 2409 | Soojama (USA) *(RVoorspuy)* 9-0 NAdams (9) (outpcd) | 2.17 |
| 1178 | Tudela **(48)** *(MrsAKnight)* 8-9 JQuinn (8) (outpcd) | s.h.18 |
| | Supper With Susie *(TJNaughton)* 8-6 ‡3RPerham (12) (leggy: s.s: a bhd) | ¾.19 |
| 2859 | Farley (DEN) *(RAkehurst)* 9-0 SWhitworth (15) (a bhd) | ½.20 |

**5/4** Barik (IRE)(4/5—7/4), **5/1** URGENT REQUEST (IRE)(tchd 8/1), **6/1** Capablanca(op 7/2), **8/1** Angus Dundee (IRE)(5/1—9/1), **12/1** Stay With Me Baby, **14/1** Yfool, **20/1** Lady All Star (USA), Dukrame, **25/1** Doodies Pool (IRE), Time Honored (USA), Lord Chief Justice, **33/1** Mr Copyforce, Farley (DEN), Get Sunday Sport (IRE), **50/1** Ors. CSF £100.41. Tote £6.50: £2.40 £5.50 £1.80 (£109.40). Mr K. Abdulla (LAMBOURN) bred by Juddmonte Farms in Ireland. 20 Rn
1m 24.93 (3.63)
SF—61/25/23/22/14/14

T/Plpt: £1,065.00 (2.95 Tckts).

AK

2400—**DONCASTER (L-H)**
**Wednesday, September 9th [Good]**
Going Allowance: 5f-8f: nil sec (G); Rest: minus 0.20 sec (F)          Wind: str half against

Stalls: high

**3187**     E.B.F. NURSERY (F) £19575.00 (£5850.00: £2800.00: £1275.00)
             **6f 110y**                                                      2-00 (2-07)

(Weights raised 1 lb)

3012* **Falsoola (91)** (Jt-Fav) *(MRStoute)* 9-5 SCauthen (8) (lw: hld up & bhd: stdy
          hdwy over 2f out: led jst ins fnl f: r.o wl u.p) ......................... —1
28413 Hung Parliament (80) *(BWHills)* 8-3 ‡5DHarrison (15) (h.d.w. lw: hld up & bhd:
          gd hdwy over 2f out: ev ch ins fnl f: r.o) .......................... 1.2
2883* Spring Sunrise (69) *(MBlanshard)* 7-8(4) ‡3FNorton (10) (hdwy 2f out: n.m.r:
          styd on wl fnl f) ......................................................... hd.3
29324 Heart Broken (76) *(JGFitzGerald)* 8-4 KFallon (14) (lw: trckd ldrs: led over 1f
          out tl jst ins fnl f: no ex) ........................................... s.h.4
30123 Bold Seven (IRE) (82) *(FHLee)* 8-5 ‡5NKennedy (6) (bhd: gd hdwy 2f out: nt
          qckn ins fnl f) ........................................................... ½.5
2713* Brockton Dancer (78) *(RHannon)* 8-4 JReid (16) (hld up: hdwy on ins & nt clr
          run over 2f out: r.o fnl f) .......................................... 2.6
30234 Zany Zanna (IRE) (82) (Jt-Fav) *(GAPritchard-Gordon)* 8-5 ‡JWeaver (11) (lw:
          chsd ldrs: effrt 2f out: r.o fnl f) ................................. 3.7
30184 Royal Deed (USA) (70) *(PMMcEntee)* 7-12 JLowe (9) (unruly gng to s: mid div:
          effrt & hung lft ½-wy: n.d) ......................................... 4.8
21324 Where's the Dance (77) *(CEBrittain)* 8-5 MRoberts (4) (in tch: effrt ½-wy: sn
          wknd) ..................................................................... 2.9
3012 Clear Look (73) *(PFICole)* 8-1 AMunro (1) (chsd ldrs: rdn over 2f out: sn wknd) 2.10
2746* Delta Downs (77) *(RHannon)* 8-5 BRaymond (7) (chsd ldrs tl lost pl over 2f out) ¾.11
28412 No Reservations (IRE) (93) *(RFJohnsonHoughton)* 9-7 TQuinn (12) (lw: w ldr:
          led ½-wy tl over 1f out: sn wknd) .............................. 1.12
2857 Hallorina (68) *(WGRWightman)* 7-10 GBardwell (13) (chsd ldrs: sn drvn along:
          wknd 2f out) ......................................................... 1½.13
3077* Hotaria (75) *(RMWhitaker)* 8-3 (5x) ACulhane (3) (lw: led to ½-wy: wknd 2f out) 1½.14
28722 Guv'nors Gift (68) *(MHTompkins)* 7-10 DaleGibson (2) (bhd fr ½-wy) ............. 2.15
2973* Fairy Story (IRE) (71) *(JWHills)* 7-13 RHills (5) (hung lft thrght: wl bhd fr ½-wy) 7.16

7/1 FALSOOLA, Zany Zanna (IRE), 8/1 Fairy Story (IRE), 9/1 Hung Parliament, 11/1 Brockton Dancer, Hallorina,
12/1 Guv'nors Gift, Clear Look, Where's the Dance, 14/1 No Reservations (IRE), Bold Seven (IRE), Spring
Sunrise, 16/1 Hotaria, Delta Downs, 20/1 Heart Broken, 50/1 Royal Deed (USA). CSF £63.72, CT £792.31. Tote
£5.50: £1.60 £2.20 £6.10 £5.40 (£20.80). Sheikh Mohammed (NEWMARKET) bred by Sheikh Mohammed bin
Rashid al Maktoum. 16 Rn                                              1m 21.02 (3.82)
                                                                     SF—29/9/—/8/7/—

**3188**     TOTE-PORTLAND H'CAP (0-115) £19690.00 (£5920.00: £2860.00: £1330.00)
             **5f 140y**                                                      2-35 (2-40)

(Weights raised 4 lb)

2435* **Lochsong (88)** (Fav) *(IABalding)* 4-8-12 WCarson (16) (lw: mde virtually all:
          drvn along & r.o wl fnl f) ........................................... —1
3031* Venture Capitalist (93) (bl) *(RHannon)* 3-9-0 (7x) RHills (17) (bhd: gd hdwy
          over 2f out: r.o wl u.p fnl f) ...................................... nk.2
29023 Cantoris (92) *(RJRWilliams)* 6-9-2 DHolland (22) (gd hdwy ½-wy: nt qckn fnl f) 1½.3
29976 Walk in the Park (89) *(RSimpson)* 3-8-5 ‡5ATucker (3) (lw: racd far side: hdwy to
          ld over 2f out: r.o fnl f) ............................................ 1½.4
2465* Paddy Chalk (82) *(LJHolt)* 6-8-6 JReid (8) (b: hdwy ½-wy: styd on u.p appr fnl f) hd.5
16885 Love Returned (80) *(WJarvis)* 5-8-4 PRobinson (20) (hld up: hdwy & nt clr run
          over 1f out: r.o nr fin) .............................................. hd.6
2642 Lucedeo (82) *(JLSpearing)* 8-7-13 ‡7AGarth (19) (hld up: hdwy over 1f out: r.o
          nr fin) ................................................................... ¾.7
29975 Heather Bank (92) (bl) *(JBerry)* 3-8-13 JCarroll (15) (lw: w wnr: rdn over 1f out:
          sn btn) .................................................................. hd.8
30066 Stack Rock (96) *(EJAlston)* 5-9-1 ‡JWeaver (7) (lw: chsd ldrs: effrt 2f out: styd
          on same pce) ......................................................... hd.9
21793 Terrhars (IRE) (99) *(RHannon)* 4-9-6 ‡3RPerham (14) (chsd ldrs tl wknd over 1f
          out) ....................................................................... sh.10
26584 Taufan Blu (IRE) (94) (bl) *(MJohnston)* 3-9-1 MRoberts (9) (lw: s.i.s: swtchd rt
          s: nt clr run fnl f: nt rcvr) .......................................... nk.11
3083* Never so Sure (98) (v) *(ABailey)* 4-9-8 (10x) LPiggott (5) (racd far side: effrt 2f
          out: kpt on: nvr able to chal) ..................................... hd.12

2902 Plain Fact (88) *(JWHills)* 7-8-12 MHills (10) (nvr rchd ldrs) .............. 1½.13
1688 Fangio (87) *(WGMTurner)* 3-8-8 TSprake (6) (swtchd rt s: chsd ldrs tl wknd 2f out) ............................................................................................ 1½.14
3006 Bit of a Lark (100) *(RHollinshead)* 4-9-10 PatEddery (1) (nvr bttr than mid div) nk.15
3059⁵ Orthorhombus (97) (v) *(GLewis)* 3-9-4 PaulEddery (2) (racd far side: chsd ldrs 4f) ................................................................................................... nk.16
2848 Nifty Fifty (IRE) (83) *(JBerry)* 3-8-4 NCarlisle (12) (chsd ldrs tl wknd over 2f out) ¾.17
3015⁶ Branston Abby (IRE) (84) *(MJohnston)* 3-8-5 DMcKeown (13) (s.i.s: n.d) ..... s.h.18
2919★ Gone Savage (78) *(GBBalding)* 4-8-2 NAdams (21) (chsd ldrs: wkng whn squeezed out on ins over 1f out) .................................................... 1.19
3031 Gipsy Fiddler (97) *(JJO'Neill)* 4-9-7 BRaymond (1) (led far side over 3f: sn wknd) ............................................................................................... nk.20
2925 Beau Venture (USA) (97) *(FHLee)* 4-9-2 ‡5NKennedy (5) (racd far side: bhd fnl 2f) ..................................................................................................... 1½.21
3074★ Clifton Charlie (USA) (91) *(MRChannon)* 4-9-1 (7x) TQuinn (18) (p.u after wl over 1f: dead) ..................................................................................... 0

**4/1** LOCHSONG, **9/1** Cantoris, **10/1** Never so Sure, **11/1** Paddy Chalk, Taufan Blu (IRE), Heather Bank, **14/1** Venture Capitalist, **16/1** Gone Savage, **20/1** Love Returned, Bit of a Lark, Terrhars (IRE), Stack Rock, Plain Fact, **25/1** Beau Venture (USA), Fangio, Lucedeo, Branston Abby (IRE), **33/1** Orthorhombus, Walk in the Park, Clifton Charlie (USA), **40/1** Nifty Fifty (IRE), **50/1** Gipsy Fiddler. CSF £55.06, CT £451.49. Tote £4.20: £1.50 £4.00 £1.90 £8.60 (£42.50). Mr J. C. Smith (KINGSCLERE) bred by Littleton Stud. 22 Rn          1m 7.78 (0.78)
SF—82/83/79/62/62/59

---

**3189** DONCASTER BLOODSTOCK SALES SCARBROUGH STKS (listed race) £11160.00
(£3330.00: £1590.00: £720.00)  **5f**          3-10 (3-12)

3006 **Notley (106)** (bl) *(RHannon)* 5-9-7 BRaymond (6) (chsd ldrs: sn pushed along: n.m.r & swtchd over 1f out: r.o wl u.p to ld nr fin) ............. —1
3134★ Harvest Girl (IRE) (100) *(GAPritchard-Gordon)* 3-9-1 LDettori (1) (chsd ldrs: led jst ins fnl f: r.o u.p) ................................................................ nk.2
2851 Blyton Lad (110) *(MJCamacho)* 6-9-7 SWebster (9) (lw: chsd ldrs: drvn along & hung lft ½-wy: led over 1f out tl nt qckn ins fnl f) ............. 2½.3
2443³ Silca-Cisa (93) *(MRChannon)* 3-9-1 PatEddery (12) (swtchd lft s: gd hdwy & ev ch over 1f out: sn wknd) .................................................... 3.4
2851 Medaille D'Or (108) (v) *(JWPayne)* 4-9-11 AMunro (8) (s.i.s: bhd: styd on fnl 2f: nt rch ldrs) .............................................................................. nk.5
2443⁶ Master of Passion (90) (v) *(JMPEustace)* 3-9-2 LPiggott (4) (led over 1f: led ½-wy tl over 1f out: kpt on) ....................................................... hd.6
2642⁴ Viceroy (100) (v) (Fav) *(BBeasley)* 5-9-8 RCochrane (11) (hld up: effrt u.p over 1f out: nvr nr to chal) ........................................................... 1½.7
2851 Farfelu (101) (bl) *(WRMuir)* 5-9-4 TQuinn (3) (lw: hdwy 2f out: kpt on fnl f: eased nr fin) ............................................................................ 1½.8
Sovereign Grace (IRE) *(JGBurns,Ireland)* 3-9-1 JReid (7) (lw: w ldrs 3f: sn wknd) ............................................................................................. 1½.9
2851⁶ Paris House (114) (v) *(JBerry)* 3-9-12 JCarroll (5) (lw: sn w ldrs: led over 3f out tl over 2f out: sn lost pl) ................................................... 5.10
1535 Regal Scintilla (100) *(GBBalding)* 3-9-3 SCauthen (10) (lw: hld up: hdwy 2f out: sn wknd) ........................................................................ hd.11
3070⁶ Risk Me's Girl (90) (bl) *(RHannon)* 2-7-7 GBardwell (2) (lw: chsd ldrs early: sn lost pl & wl bhd) .................................................................. 15.12

**4/1** Viceroy, **6/1** Blyton Lad, Paris House, **7/1** NOTLEY, Harvest Girl (IRE), **15/2** Silca-Cisa, **8/1** Farfelu, **16/1** Risk Me's Girl, Medaille D'Or, **20/1** Sovereign Grace (IRE), Regal Scintilla, **25/1** Master of Passion. CSF £51.88, Tote £10.70: £2.80 £2.60 £1.90 (£38.40). Mr D. F. Cock (MARLBOROUGH) bred by Grange Stud (UK). 12 Rn
60.29 sec (1.59)
SF—75/68/64/46/55/45

---

**3190** A. F. BUDGE PARK HILL STKS (Gp 3) (F & M) £24693.00 (£9169.65: £4344.83:
£1827.52)  **1¾m 132y**          3-40 (3-43)

2843⁴ **Niodini (USA) (108)** *(MRStoute)* 3-8-5 PaulEddery (4) (trckd ldrs: led 2f out: drvn out) ...................................................................................... —1
2843³ Guilty Secret (IRE) *(PWChapple-Hyam)* 3-8-5 WCarson (8) (chsd ldrs: kpt on wl u.p fnl 2f) ............................................................................ ¾.2
2455² Anna of Saxony (92) *(JHMGosden)* 3-8-6(1) JReid (5) (lw: hld up & bhd: gd hdwy 3f out: hung lft u.p & nt qckn fnl f) ................................. ¾.3
2854³ Shirley Valentine *(HRACecil)* 3-8-5 PatEddery (11) (led tl over 3f out: r.o one pce) ........................................................................................... 3.4
2843² Bineyah (IRE) (110) *(MRStoute)* 3-8-5 BRaymond (9) (lw: effrt & pushed along 7f out: edgd rt u.p over 2f out: nvr nr to chal) ...................... 2.5

2766a³ Always Friendly (110) (Fav) (HCandy) 4-9-3 AMunro (12) (hld up: effrt 4f out: n.m.r over 2f out: kpt on: nvr able to chal) .................... 1½.6

2620⁎ Shahaamh (IRE) (HThomsonJones) 3-8-5 RHills (7) (trckd ldr: led over 3f out to 2f out: sn wknd) ................................ 2.7

2840⁴ Nibbs Point (IRE) (105) (LMCumani) 4-9-3 LDettori (6) (bhd & drvn along 8f out: n.d) .................................................... 3½.8

2843 Magnificent Star (USA) (119) (MMoubarak) 4-9-8 TQuinn (1) (hld up: hdwy 7f out: lost pl over 3f out) ................................ 2½.9

2854⁵ Aquamarine (BWHills) 3-8-5 RCochrane (2) (a in rr) ............................ 1½.10

2907⁎ Yildiz (93) (BWHills) 3-8-5 MHills (10) (chsd ldrs tl rdn & outpcd 4f out: n.m.r & wknd over 2f out) .................................... 4.11

2927³ Bustinetta (68) (JRFanshawe) 3-8-5 GDuffield (3) (lw: hmpd & uns rdr after 1f) .... 0

4/1 Always Friendly, 9/2 Bineyah (IRE), 11/2 NIODINI (USA), 6/1 Guilty Secret (IRE), 15/2 Nibbs Point (IRE), 11/1 Anna of Saxony, Yildiz, 12/1 Shirley Valentine, 20/1 Magnificent Star (USA), 25/1 Aquamarine, 50/1 Ors. CSF £34.84, Tote £7.80: £2.40 £2.20 £3.30 (£39.70). Sheikh Mohammed (NEWMARKET) bred by Triple C Thorostock in USA. 12 Rn     3m 7.11 (3.51)

SF—27/25/24/17/13/22

---

**3191**    MAY HILL STKS (Gp 3) (2-Y.O.F) £16236.00 (£6038.80: £2869.40: £1215.80)
      1m (rnd)                                           4-10 (4-14)

2841⁵ **Marillette (USA) (100)** (JHMGosden) 8-8 PatEddery (7) (lw: hld up & bhd: hdwy over 2f out: qcknd to ld jst ins fnl f: r.o wl) .............. —1

2835³ Self Assured (IRE) (92) (Fav) (HRACecil) 8-8 SCauthen (8) (trckd ldrs: led over 1f out: r.o u.p) .................................... 3.2

2344⁵ Ivanka (IRE) (100) (CEBrittain) 8-8 MRoberts (6) (lw: hld up: effrt & swtchd outside over 2f out: r.o same pce fnl f) ............... 1.3

2991⁵ Bobbie Dee (DRCElsworth) 8-8 JWilliams (5) (otyd on u.p fnl 2f: nt rch ldrs) ... 2½.4

2979a Darshay (FR) (RHannon) 8-8 JReid (9) (lw: hdwy & prom over 3f out: r.o same pce appr fnl f) ................................... ¾.5

2918⁶ East Liberty (USA) (94) (IABalding) 8-8 RCochrane (2) (led 1f: led over 2f out tl over 1f out: one pce) .......................... ¾.6

2901⁎ Abury (IRE) (PWChapple-Hyam) 8-8 PaulEddery (11) (lw: effrt 3f out: sn rdn: nvr nr to chal) .................................... 3.7

3132² Society Lady (USA) (AAScott) 8-8 BRaymond (12) (lw: hdwy & prom over 3f out: wknd over 1f out) ............................. 2½.8

2930³ Sehailah (MrsLPiggott) 8-8 LPiggott (1) (hdwy to ld after 1f: hdd over 2f out: sn wknd) .............................................. ¾.9

2901² Nemea (USA) (JRFanshawe) 8-8 GDuffield (3) (lw: chsd ldrs: rdn over 2f out: wkng whn sltly hmpd over 1f out) ................. 5.10

3001⁎ Katiba (USA) (79) (JLDunlop) 8-8 WCarson (4) (sn bhd: hdwy on ins over 3f out: hmpd & wknd over 1f out) ....................... 1½.11

Nanny Margaret (IRE) (PAKelleway) 8-8 KDarley (10) (lengthy: scope: a in rr) . 5.12

7/4 Self Assured (IRE), 4/1 Katiba (USA), 9/2 Ivanka (IRE), 9/1 Society Lady (USA), 10/1 Abury (IRE), 14/1 Bobbie Dee, 16/1 Nemea (USA), 20/1 Darshay (FR), Sehailah, 25/1 East Liberty (USA), 50/1 Nanny Margaret (IRE). CSF £12.42, Tote £4.90: £1.60 £1.40 £2.40 (£4.80). Sheikh Mohammed (NEWMARKET) bred by Robert Clay & Rogers Trust in USA. 12 Rn     1m 38.56 (2.26)

SF—60/51/48/40/37/35

---

**3192**    FESTIVAL H'CAP (0-80) £4890.00 (£1470.00: £710.00: £330.00)
      1¼m 60y                                             4-40 (4-45)

2693⁵ **Chatham Island (61)** (CEBrittain) 4-9-0 PatEddery (16) (chsd ldrs: styd on wl u.p to ld ins fnl f) ..................................... —1

2968² Mingus (USA) (56) (Jt-Fav) (MrsJRRamsden) 5-8-9 MRoberts (11) (lw: hld up: gd hdwy over 2f out: styd on to chal wl ins fnl f: no ex nr fin) nk.2

3013 Jumaira Shark (CAN) (78) (v) (JHMGosden) 3-9-10 SCauthen (10) (trckd ldrs: rdn to ld over 1f out: nt qckn ins fnl f) ................. ¾.3

3027⁶ Alkarif (USA) (74) (MrsJRRamsden) 3-9-6 GBaxter (21) (hld up: hdwy over 3f out: styd on wl fnl f) ..................................... ½.4

2807⁵ Lexus (IRE) (42) (RJRWilliams) 4-7-9 JQuinn (18) (mid div whn carried rt over 3f out: styd on wl nr fin) .............................. nk.5

2813⁴ Spring to the Top (51) (JWPayne) 5-8-4 AMunro (24) (chsd ldrs: r.o one pce fnl 2f) .................................................. 1½.6

716² Touch Paper (USA) (79) (BWHills) 3-9-11 MHills (25) (stdd s: bhd: gd hdwy over 3f out: swtchd ins: several positions: r.o wl nr fin) ...... nk.7

2941³ Batabanoo (67) (MrsGRReveley) 3-8-13 KDarley (6) (hld up: nt clr run several times fnl 3f: styng on strly whn snatched up nr fin) ............. ½.8

| | | |
|---|---|---|
| 2987⁴ | Brown Fairy (USA) **(63)** *(MrsNMacauley)* 4–9-2 DBiggs (7) (stdd s: hld up & plld hrd: hdwy u.p 3f out: wnt lft: nt qckn fnl f) | ½.9 |
| 3043⁵ | Secret Treaty (IRE) **(61)** *(PWChapple-Hyam)* 3–8-7 PaulEddery (20) (effrt & swtchd rt over 3f out: hrd rdn & kpt on: nvr able to chal) | hd.10 |
| 617³ | Margs Girl **(52)** *(TFairhurst)* 5–8-5 JFanning (22) (b: styd on fnl 3f: nt rch ldrs) | 1.11 |
| 2585⁵ | Eden's Close **(72)** *(MHTompkins)* 3–9-4 PRobinson (4) (led: clr over 2f out: wknd & hdd over 1f out) | ¾.12 |
| 2403² | Drummer Hicks **(77)** (Jt-Fav) *(EWeymes)* 3–9-9 DMcKeown (14) (chsd ldrs: effrt & ev ch over 3f out: wknd & eased ins fnl f) | 2.13 |
| 3021 | Mahong **(60)** *(MrsHParrott)* 4–8-13 JWilliams (12) (n.d) | ½.14 |
| 125² | Qualitair Sound (IRE) **(57)** *(JFBottomley)* 4–8-10 GCarter (9) (bit bkwd: in tch tl grad wknd fnl 3f) | nk.15 |
| 2927 | Timurid (FR) **(71)** *(JLDunlop)* 3–9-3 MBirch (8) (hdwy over 3f out: rdn & wknd wl over 1f out) | 2.16 |
| 3073★ | Spray of Orchids **(57)** *(JEtherington)* 3–8-0 (5x) ‡³FNorton (5) (chsd ldrs: effrt & n.m.r on ins over 2f out: sn lost pl) | 1½.17 |
| | Shaffic (FR) **(63)** *(MDHammond)* 5–9-2 JCarroll (13) (bit bkwd: bhd tl sme late hdwy) | hd.18 |
| 2926 | Bayaireg (USA) **(79)** *(AAScott)* 3–9-11 BRaymond (2) (chsd ldrs tl rdn & wknd over 2f out) | 1½.19 |
| 2988⁴ | Auction King (IRE) **(59)** *(ASmith)* 3–8-5 SWebster (19) (bhd: effrt & hrd drvn over 3f out: n.d) | nk.20 |
| 3105³ | Glenstal Princess **(57)** *(RHollinshead)* 5–8-10 WRyan (3) (sn wl bhd) | 1½.21 |
| 2415 | Execution Only (IRE) **(59)** *(JWWatts)* 4–8-12 GDuffield (17) (a bhd) | 3½.22 |
| 2827 | Alight (IRE) **(69)** *(ACStewart)* 3–8-8 ‡²ElizabethForletta (1) (chsd ldrs tl lost pl over 3f out: sn bhd) | 15.23 |
| 2698 | Art Critic (IRE) **(48)** *(MJHeaton-Ellis)* 3–7-8(1) NCarlisle (15) (wl bhd fnl 2f) | 2.24 |

LONG HANDICAP: Art Critic (IRE) 7-6.

15/2 Mingus (USA), Drummer Hicks, 17/2 Jumaira Shark (CAN), 9/1 Spring to the Top, 11/1 Spray of Orchids, Batabanoo, 12/1 CHATHAM ISLAND, 14/1 Timurid (FR), Bayaireg, 16/1 Alkarif (USA), Touch Paper (USA), 20/1 Brown Fairy (USA), Glenstal Princess, Secret Treaty (IRE), 25/1 Eden's Close, Qualitair Sound (IRE), Execution Only (IRE), 33/1 Mahong, Margs Girl, Lexus (IRE), Alight (IRE), 50/1 Shaffic (FR), Auction King (IRE), 100 /1 Art Critic (IRE). CSF £95.30, CT £760.41. Tote £14.20: £3.30 £1.60 £2.40 £13.20 (£34.80). Mr B. H. Voak (NEWMARKET) bred by G. C. Hughes. 24 Rn                     2m 8.91 (1.91)

                                                       SF—61/55/68/63/37/43

T/Trio: Race 2: £90.10 (17 Tckts); Race 4: £161.60 (6 Tckts) & Race 6: £38.90 (22.1 Tckts). Jkpt: Not won; £18,444.30 to Doncaster 10/9/92. T/Plpt: £141.40 (76.65 Tckts).          WG

# DONCASTER (L-H)

## Thursday, September 10th [Good to firm]

Going Allowance: minus 0.20 sec per fur (F)                               Wind: mod against

Stalls: high

**3193**     QUEEN'S OWN YORKSHIRE DRAGOONS GRADUATION STKS (2-Y.O) £3882.50
               (£1160.00: £555.00: £252.50)     **7f**             2-00 (2-01)

| | | |
|---|---|---|
| 2812 | Tykeyvor (IRE) *(MHTompkins)* 8-11 PRobinson (6) (hld up: hdwy to ld fnl f: rdn & r.o wl) | —1 |
| | Great Steps *(EWeymes)* 8-2 MRoberts (7) (rangy: scope: bit bkwd: cl up: stdd: hdwy 2f out: r.o wl nr fin) | 1½.2 |
| 3000★ | Wootton Rivers (USA) **(93)** (Fav) *(PWChapple-Hyam)* 9-1 PaulEddery (3) (trckd ldrs: outpcd & n.m.r 2f out: styd on nr fin) | hd.3 |
| 2930⁵ | Manx Monarch *(RHollinshead)* 8-6 AMunro (4) (chsd ldrs: disp ld 2f out tl ins fnl f: no ex) | s.h.4 |
| | Dig in the Ribs (IRE) *(RHollinshead)* 8-7 RCochrane (8) (w'like: unf: bhd tl gd hdwy to jn ldrs after 3f: hung rt: wknd 1f out) | nk.5 |
| 2426★ | Qaffal (USA) **(94)** *(DMorley)* 9-1 WCarson (5) (lw: mde most tl hdd & wknd ins fnl f) | ¾.6 |
| | Waaree (USA) *(AAScott)* 8-7 BRaymond (2) (cmpt: scope: bit bkwd: prom tl rdn & btn wl over 1f out) | 3.7 |
| | Olicana (IRE) *(BWHills)* 8-7 EJohnson (1) (rangy: unf: trckd ldrs: hmpd 4f out: lost pl fnl 2f) | ¾.8 |

4/9 Wootton Rivers (USA), 6/1 Qaffal (USA), 8/1 Waaree (USA), 12/1 Olicana (IRE), 25/1 TYKEYVOR (IRE) & Ors. CSF £367.06, Tote 34.70: £4.80 £2.60 £1.10 (£160.10). Mr H. Key (NEWMARKET) bred by H. Key in Ireland. 8 Rn                                           1m 30.55 (7.15)

## 3194

MALLARD H'CAP  £9396.00 (£2808.00: £1344.00: £612.00)
1³/₄m 132y

2-35 (2-37)

2844² **Brier Creek (USA) (94)** (Fav) *(JHMGosden)* 3-8-3 MRoberts (12) (lw: hld up & bhd: effrt over 3f out: r.o wl to ld ins fnl f) ................................ —1

2844 Kiveton Kabooz (78) (bl) *(LMCumani)* 4-7-13 AMunro (6) (sn trckng ldrs: led wl over 2f out: qcknd clr: hdd ins fnl f) .................................... ³/₄.2

2836² Al Karnak (IRE) (88) *(MMoubarak)* 3-7-6 ‡⁵DHarrison (11) (hld up & bhd: effrt over 3f out: gd hdwy 2f out: r.o) ............................... 3.3

3046² Green Lane (USA) (72) *(IABalding)* 4-7-7 JLowe (4) (hld up & bhd: hdwy 4f out: nt pce to chal) .................................................. 6.4

2844 Castle Courageous (89) *(LadyHerries)* 5-8-10 JReid (7) (lw: trckd ldrs: effrt 3f out: sn outpcd: styd on appr fnl f) ........................... s.h.5

2844 Satin Lover (89) *(NTinkler)* 4-8-10 RCochrane (5) (lw: sn trckng ldrs: effrt 3f out: one pce fnl 2f) .......................................... 2¹/₂.6

2853 Sarawat (80) *(MrsGRReveley)* 4-8-1 JFanning (8) (hld up: hdwy ent st: ch 2f out: grad wknd) .............................................. 2.7

2178⁴ Not in Doubt (USA) (89) *(HCandy)* 3-7-12 CRutter (1) (lw: drvn along appr st: nvr trbld ldrs) ............................................... 5.8

3007* Encore Une Fois (IRE) (87) *(PWChapple-Hyam)* 3-7-7⁽³⁾ ‡³FNorton (10) (effrt 4f out: nvr nr ldrs) ............................................. 4.9

2844⁵ Star Player (82) *(RJBaker)* 6-8-0 ‡³SMaloney (13) (racd wd: trckd ldrs: effrt 3f out: sn wknd) ............................................ hd.10

2982a Hateel (107) *(PTWalwyn)* 6-10-0 WCarson (9) (lw: bhd: rdn ent st: n.d) ......... ¹/₂.11

2854⁶ Sea Goddess (90) *(WJarvis)* 4-8-11 SCauthen (14) (led after 2f tl hdd wl over 2f out: eased whn btn) ....................................... ¹/₂.12

2921³ Be a Honey (84) *(NAGraham)* 4-8-5⁽²⁾ PatEddery (3) (led 2f: cl up tl wknd over 3f out) ................................................... 2¹/₂.13

2844 Itqan (IRE) (80) *(BWHills)* 4-8-1 GDuffield (2) (trckd ldrs & plld hrd tl wknd over 3f out) ................................................... 8.14

LONG HANDICAP: Green Lane (USA) 7-3, Encore Une Fois (IRE) 7-3.

**11/4 BRIER CREEK (USA), 5/1** Al Karnak (IRE), **7/1** Kiveton Kabooz, **9/1** Not in Doubt (USA)(14/1—8/1), **10/1** Star Player, **12/1** Encore Une Fois, Castle Courageous, **14/1** Satin Lover, Itqan (IRE), **16/1** Be a Honey, **20/1** Sea Goddess, Hateel, **25/1** Ors. CSF £22.23, CT £86.39. Tote £4.00: £1.60 £2.70 £1.90 (£12.50). Sheikh Mohammed (NEWMARKET) bred by Allen E Paulson in USA. 14 Rn             3m 2.22 (0.7 under best; U1.38)
SF–74/68/55/44/60/55

## 3195

KIVETON PARK STKS (Gp 3)  £23733.00 (£8820.15: £4185.08: £1766.77)
7f

3-10 (3-12)

2789² **Pursuit of Love (121)** *(HRACecil)* 3-9-3 RCochrane (7) (lw: chsd ldrs: sn pushed along: hdwy u.p 2f out: led over 1f out: r.o v.wl) ..... —1

2762a⁵ Prince Ferdinand (118) *(MMcCormack)* 3-9-0 JReid (5) (lw: trckd ldrs: smooth hdwy to ld wl over 1f out: sn hdd & nt qckn) ................... 2.2

2436* Storm Dove (USA) (109) *(RCharlton)* 3-8-7 PatEddery (2) (lw: bhd: hdwy u.p 3f out: hrd rdn & one pce appr fnl f) ........................ nk.3

2892a Dilum (USA) (119) *(PFICole)* 3-9-0 AMunro (10) (effrt 3f out: hdwy u.p 2f out: styd on nr fin) .......................................... s.h.4

2789 Norwich *(BWHills)* 5-9-4 SCauthen (8) (lw: s.s: hld up & bhd: swtchd & hdwy over 2f out: nvr nr to chal) ............................... 3¹/₂.5

3131 River Falls (110) (bl) *(RHannon)* 3-8-10 BRaymond (9) (chsd ldrs: hrd rdn ¹/₂-wy) .................................................... 2¹/₂.6

2011⁴ Bog Trotter (USA) (110) *(WJHaggas)* 4-9-4 LPiggott (6) (led over 5f: sn wknd) s.h.7

3124⁵ Wilde Rufo (100) *(PAKelleway)* 3-8-10 JCarroll (1) (in tch: drvn along ¹/₂-wy: grad wknd) ................................................ 2.8

2855* Reported (IRE) (106) *(MJHeaton-Ellis)* 3-8-10 PaulEddery (3) (cl up tl wknd over 2f out) ............................................ 1¹/₂.9

2998 Sylva Honda (107) *(CEBrittain)* 4-9-4 GDuffield (4) (lw: cl up tl wknd & n.m.r over 2f out) ......................................... ¹/₂.10

**9/4** Storm Dove (USA), **7/2** Dilum (USA), **4/1** PURSUIT OF LOVE(3/1—9/2), **5/1** Prince Ferdinand, **12/1** Bog Trotter (USA), **14/1** Norwich, **16/1** Reported (IRE), **25/1** River Falls, **50/1** Sylva Honda, **100/1** Wilde Rufo. CSF £22.62, Tote £4.20: £1.20 £1.90 £1.50 (£12.10). Lord Howard de Walden (NEWMARKET) bred by Lord Howard de Walden. 10 Rn             1m 23.95 (0.55)
SF–74/65/57/63/56/40

## 3196

SEPTEMBER H'CAP (3-Y.O) (0-85) £4893.00 (£1464.00: £702.00: £321.00)
6f

3-40 (3-43)

3014⁶ **Arboretum (IRE) (73)** (Fav) *(RCharlton)* 8-7 ‡⁵DHarrison (15) (cl up: led wl over 1f out: r.o wl) .............................................. —1

2974* Miss Movie World **(54)** *(NBycroft)* 7-7 JFanning (17) (lw: trckd ldrs: effrt 2f out: r.o) ...... 2.2
2411* Tate Dancer (IRE) **(77)** *(RWArmstrong)* 9-2 SCauthen (16) (led over 4f: hrd drvn & r.o one pce) ...... 1½.3
2848 Castlerea Lad **(78)** *(RHollinshead)* 9-3 PatEddery (5) (mid div: hdwy 2f out: styd on) ...... 1.4
2831³ Jucea **(56)** *(DWPArbuthnot)* 7-9 JLowe (10) (cl up tl outpcd 2f out: sn btn) .... 2½.5
3153 Invigilate **(63)** *(MPNaughton)* 8-2 WCarson (2) (hdwy ½-wy: sn prom: no ex appr fnl f) ...... ½.6
3103 Ganeshaya **(56)** (bl) *(MFBarraclough)* 7-9 NCarlisle (14) (cl up tl outpcd fnl 2f) .. s.h.7
3067³ Lady Sabo **(67)** *(GLewis)* 8-6 PaulEddery (6) (hdwy 2f out: nvr trbld ldrs) ........ ¾.8
3031⁴ Love Jazz (USA) **(82)** *(TDBarron)* 9-7 BRaymond (11) (prom tl outpcd over 2f out: n.d after) ...... nk.9
1791³ Debsy Do (USA) **(68)** *(SGNorton)* 8-2 ‡⁵OPears (7) (cl up 4f) ...... ¾.10
3133⁴ Sovereign Rock (IRE) **(77)** *(RHannon)* 8-13 (5x) ‡³RPerham (13) (sn drvn along & bhd: n.d) ...... hd.11
2989 Manuleader **(67)** (bl) *(BBeasley)* 8-1 ‡5JWeaver (8) (prom 3f) ...... ¾.12
2105 Indian Endeavour **(65)** *(RGuest)* 8-4 MHills (1) (lw: spd 4f) ...... s.h.13
3083 Educated Pet **(75)** *(MJohnston)* 9-0 DMcKeown (9) (lw: stdd s: effrt ½-wy: n.d) ½.14
2949⁴ Panchellita (USA) **(60)** *(JSutcliffe)* 7-13 MRoberts (3) (s.i.s: swtchd stands' side after 2f: nvr nr to chal) ...... ½.15
2073³ Pageboy **(82)** *(PCHaslam)* 9-7 LPiggott (4) (s.i.s: a bhd) ...... 6.16
2743 Lord Lambson **(57)** *(RMWhitaker)* 7-3(3) ‡⁷AGarth (12) (prom 2f: sn outpcd) .... 5.17

LONG HANDICAP: Miss Movie World 7-4, Lord Lambson 7-3.

**7/1** ARBORETUM (IRE), **8/1** Sovereign Rock (IRE), **9/1** Tate Dancer (IRE), Panchellita (USA), Lady Sabo, **10/1** Ganeshaya, Castlerea Lad, Miss Movie World, Jucea, **12/1** Jucea, **14/1** Educated Pet, Invigilate, Love Jazz (USA), **16/1** Pageboy, **20/1** Indian Endeavour, Debsy Do (USA), Manuleader, **50/1** Lord Lambson. CSF £72.71, CT £595.98. Tote £5.90: £1.90 £2.20 £1.90 £3.10 (£30.20). Exors of the late Mrs J. de Rothschild (BECKHAMPTON) bred by Mount Coote Stud in Ireland. 17 Rn

1m 12.32 (1.32)
SF—43/21/38/35/3/8

---

**3197** DONCASTER CUP (Stks) (Gp 3)  £20493.00 (£7578.15: £3564.08: £1469.77)
2¼m 4-10 (4-10)

2840* **Further Flight (114)** **(Fav)** *(BWHills)* 6—9-3 MHills (6) (b.hind: hld up: stdy hdwy 3f out: r.o u.p fnl f to ld post) ...... —1
2446² Witness Box (USA) **(108)** *(JHMGosden)* 5—9-0 SCauthen (3) (lw: led: qcknd 3f out: hrd rdn fnl f: jst ct) ...... s.h.2
11a² Hieroglyphic (IRE) **(103)** *(PWChapple-Hyam)* 4—9-0 WCarson (1) (hld up: plld wd & effrt 3f out: styd on: no ch w ldrs) ...... 8.3
2899² Aude la Belle (FR) **(75)** *(MrsAKnight)* 4—8-11 FNorton (4) (trckd ldrs: ev ch over 4f out: outpcd fnl 2f) ...... ¾.4
3007⁶ Mull House **(79)** *(FJO'Mahony)* 5—9-0 PaulEddery (5) (cl up: pushed along over 3f out: one pce) ...... 2½.5

**8/15** FURTHER FLIGHT, **9/4** Witness Box (USA), **10/1** Hieroglyphic (IRE), **40/1** Mull House, **50/1** Aude la Belle (FR). CSF £2.03, Tote £1.50: £1.10 £1.40 (£1.50). Mr S. Wingfield Digby (LAMBOURN) bred by S. Wingfield Digby. 5 Rn

3m 55.60 (0.43 under best: 2.90)
SF—38/34/26/22/22

---

**3198** KYOTO H'CAP (0-90) £5283.00 (£1584.00: £762.00: £351.00)  7f  4-40 (4-42)

2743 En Attendant (FR) **(71)** *(BHanbury)* 4—8-12 BRaymond (8) (in tch: hdwy 2f out: r.o wl to ld post) ...... —1
2852 Rocton North (IRE) **(87)** (bl) *(RHannon)* 4—10-0 JReid (2) (racd far side: led: hrd rdn fnl f: jst ct) ...... hd.2
2945 Risk Zone **(69)** (bl) *(RHannon)* 3—9-0 AMcGlone (10) (racd alone centre: chsd ldrs: kpt on wl fnl f) ...... ¾.3
2795³ Laundry Maid **(85)** *(HCandy)* 3—9-8 CRutter (12) (led stands' side: kpt on u.p fnl 2f) ...... s.h.4
3086* Gant Bleu (FR) **(60)** *(RMWhitaker)* 5—8-1 (4x) ACulhane (15) (in tch: hdwy & ev ch 2f out: nt qckn) ...... 1.5
2658 Superoo **(74)** **(Fav)** *(JSutcliffe)* 6—9-1 MRoberts (20) (bhd: hdwy 2f out: styd on wl nr fin) ...... hd.6
3121⁶ Bold Habit **(84)** *(BBeasley)* 7—9-6 ‡5JWeaver (7) (s.i.s: hdwy 3f out: nvr able to chal) ...... nk.7
2201* Royal Girl **(65)** *(MissSEHall)* 5—8-1 ‡5DHarrison (17) (in tch: effrt 3f out: no hdwy after) ...... 1.8
1707⁶ Corn Futures **(76)** *(JPLeigh)* 4—9-3 DMcKeown (21) (in tch: no hdwy fr wl over 2f out) ...... ¾.9

**3199**

| | |
|---|---|
| 3088⁶ | State Flyer (65) (v) *(CBBBooth)* 4-7-13⁽²⁾ ‡⁷GForster (9) (dwlt: hdwy u.p over 2f out: n.d) ............................................ ¾.10 |
| 2447 | Set Table (USA) (79) (v) *(JHMGosden)* 3-9-2 SCauthen (6) (chsd ldrs: effrt & ch over 2f out: rdn & wknd) ............ hd.11 |
| 3002 | Colossus (69) *(CEBrittain)* 4-8-10 AMunro (16) (prom over 4f) .............. hd.12 |
| 2743* | Sandmoor Denim (59) *(SRBowring)* 5-7-11 ‡³FNorton (3) (n.d) ......... 1½.13 |
| 2958⁶ | La Bamba (73) *(GAPritchard-Gordon)* 6-9-0 WHood (4) (hld up & bhd: n.d) .. ¾.14 |
| 2449 | Sir Boudle (IRE) (82) *(CRNelson)* 3-9-5 PatEddery (11) (a in rr) .......... hd.15 |
| 3120³ | Ballad Dancer (56) *(EJAlston)* 7-7-11 TyroneWilliams (19) (in tch tl outpcd wl over 2f out) ............... 1½.16 |
| 2079² | May Hills Legacy (IRE) (72) *(DWPArbuthnot)* 3-8-9 LPiggott (18) (b: chsd ldrs over 4f: sn btn) .................... ¾.17 |
| 3083 | Merryhill Maid (IRE) (68) *(JLHarris)* 4-8-9 PaulEddery (13) (chsd ldrs over 4f) 2½.18 |
| 3003* | Lord Vivienne (IRE) (80) *(RCSpicer)* 3-9-3 GDuffield (14) (cl up tl wknd qckly over 2f out) ........................ 1.19 |
| 626 | Lucknam Style (65) *(MrsBarbaraWaring)* 4-8-6 NHowe (1) (racd far side: rdn & bhd fr ½-wy) ......................... 5.20 |

4/1 Superoo(op 6/1), 9/1 La Bamba, Gant Bleu (FR), 10/1 Set Table (USA), 11/1 Royal Girl, Ballad Dancer, 12/1 Laundry Maid, 16/1 Bold Habit, Sir Boudle (IRE), Sandmoor Denim, Rocton North (IRE), May Hills Legacy (IRE), 20/1 EN ATTENDANT (FR), Colossus, State Flyer, Risk Zone, 25/1 Lord Vivienne (IRE), 33/1 Corn Futures, Merryhill Maid (IRE), 100/1 Lucknam Style. CSF £287.28, CT £5,758.60. Tote £53.60: £11.20 £4.80 £8.40 £2.80 (£460.20). Exors of the late Mr Bernard Newton (NEWMARKET) bred by Marystead Farm in France. 20 Rn
1m 24.86 (1.46)
SF—55/70/46/61/37/50

---

**3199** LEVY BOARD NURSERY £5361.00 (£1608.00: £774.00: £357.00)
1m (st) 5-10 (5-13)
(Weights raised 6 lb)

| | |
|---|---|
| 3063³ | **Wahem (IRE) (64)** *(CEBrittain)* 7-13 MRoberts (7) (mde all far side: drvn along over 1f out: eased nr fin) ............ —1 |
| 3091² | Chevrotain (84) *(Fav)* *(JWWatts)* 9-5 SCauthen (12) (lw: hdwy ½-wy: styd on u.p to ld stands' side ins fnl f: no imp on wnr) ............ 2½.2 |
| 2879² | Eleusis (FR) (81) *(PWChapple-Hyam)* 9-2 PaulEddery (17) (led stands' side: rdn over 2f out: hdd & no ex ins fnl f) ............ nk.3 |
| 2903* | After the Last (86) *(RHannon)* 9-7 LPiggott (9) (lw: a chsng ldrs stands' side: chal over 1f out: nt qckn) ............ 2½.4 |
| 2961³ | Fort Vally (72) *(BWMurray)* 8-7 JFortune (16) (a chsng ldrs stands' side: kpt on u.p fnl 2f) ............ 2½.5 |
| 2986* | Latin Leader (85) *(MrsJRRamsden)* 9-6 GBaxter (10) (lw: a in tch stands' side: shkn up over 2f out: nvr able to chal) ............ 1½.6 |
| 2703 | Behaanis (USA) (58) *(AAScott)* 7-7 SWood (2) (racd far side: chsd ldrs: no imp wl over 2f out) ............ 1½.7 |
| 2652⁶ | Milngavie (IRE) (68) *(MJohnston)* 8-3 JLowe (3) (racd far side: hdwy ½-wy: nvr able to chal & eased) ............ ½.8 |
| 2961* | Home From the Hill (IRE) (79) *(MBell)* 9-0 MHills (6) (lw: hdwy stands' side 3f out: nvr rch ldrs) ............ 1½.9 |
| 1273⁵ | Preston Guild (IRE) (60) *(MissSEHall)* 7-9 TyroneWilliams (18) (bhd stands' side tl styd on fnl 2f: n.d) ............ 1.10 |
| 3044⁴ | Poly Vision (IRE) (65) *(MRChannon)* 7-11 ‡³FNorton (15) (cl up stands' side tl wknd over 2f out) ............ ¾.11 |
| 2938⁶ | Frivolous Air (81) *(IABalding)* 9-2 RCochrane (19) (bhd & drvn along stands' side: nvr nrr) ............ ½.12 |
| 2879 | Careless Son (60) (v) *(MissSEHall)* 7-9 NCarlisle (13) (sn outpcd & bhd stands' side: sme late hdwy) ............ 1½.13 |
| 3063 | Lochore (69) *(RIngram)* 7-13 ‡⁵NKennedy (11) (unruly bef s: prom stands' side to ½-wy: eased whn btn) ............ 7.14 |
| 2938³ | Atherton Green (IRE) (80) *(JAGlover)* 9-1 DMcKeown (8) (racd stands' side: nvr nr ldrs) ............ 1½.15 |
| 2873 | Platinum Venture (77) *(SPCWoods)* 8-12 JReid (20) (prom stands' side 3f) ... hd.16 |
| 2681 | Clear Honey (USA) (68) *(BHanbury)* 8-3 AMunro (21) (chsd ldrs stands' side 5f) ............ hd.17 |
| 2932 | Rough Guess (IRE) (63) *(LordHuntingdon)* 7-7 ‡⁵DHarrison (4) (drvn along & bhd) ............ ¾.18 |
| 3029⁶ | Hyde's Happy Hour (63) *(NTinkler)* 7-12 LCharnock (5) (dwlt: racd stands' side: a bhd) ............ 1½.19 |
| 2841 | Garp (FR) (80) *(MRStoute)* 9-1 PatEddery (14) (racd stands' side: a bhd) .... 1.20 |
| 2939⁵ | Buzz-B-Babe (63) *(BEllison)* 7-12 JFanning (1) (swtg: racd far side: chsd wnr to ½-wy) ............ 4.21 |

LONG HANDICAP: Behaanis (USA) 7-6.

5/2 Chevrotain, 9/2 After the Last, 8/1 Latin Leader, 9/1 Home From the Hill (IRE), 10/1 Garp (FR), Eleusis (FR), 14/1 Atherton Green (IRE), WAHEM (IRE), Clear Honey (USA), 18/1 Frivolous Air, 20/1 Rough Guess (IRE), Fort Vally, Lochore, Milngavie (IRE), Poly Vision (IRE), 25/1 Careless Son, Preston Guild (IRE), 33/1 Behaanis (USA), Hyde's Happy Hour, Platinum Venture, 50/1 Buzz-B-Babe. CSF £54.62, CT £382.76. Tote £15.60: £2.90 £1.10 £2.10 £1.70 (£20.40). Mr F. M. Kalla (NEWMARKET) bred by E. J. Loder in Ireland. 21 Rn
1m 39.08 (0.82 under best; 2.58)
SF—22/34/30/27/5/13

T/Trio: Race 2: £37.30 (24.9 Tckts), Race 4: £43.00 (21.4 Tckts) & Race 6: Any 2 fr 1st 3 w any £60.30 (13.9 Tckts). T/Jkpt: Not won; £24,027 to Doncaster 11/9/92. T/Plpt: £53.00 (192.75 Tckts). AA

# DONCASTER (L-H)
## Friday, September 11th [Good to firm]
Going Allowance: 5f-8f: nil; Rest: minus 0.20 sec per fur (F)     Wind: fresh half against

Stalls: high

**3200**   LAURENT-PERRIER ROSE CHAMPAGNE STKS (I) (Mdn 2-Y.O) £2560.00 (£760.00: £360.00: £160.00)   **1m (st)**   1-05 (1-06)

| | | |
|---|---|---|
| **Dakar Rally** (Fav) *(HRACecil)* 8-10 SCauthen (12) (gd sort: scope: w ldrs: led wl over 1f out: r.o wl fnl f: edgd lft nr fin) | | —1 |
| 3005⁵ Desert Secret (IRE) *(MRStoute)* 9-0 PatEddery (3) (hld up: hdwy on outside over 2f out: chal appr fnl f: wnt rt: r.o u.p) | | hd.2 |
| 3005 Cyrus the Bold (IRE) *(BWHills)* 9-0 MHills (11) (lw: hld up: swtchd & gd hdwy over 2f out: ev ch & sltly hmpd ins fnl f: kpt on) | | 2.3 |
| Zind (IRE) *(PWChapple-Hyam)* 8-10 PaulEddery (4) (gd sort: bit bkwd: rdn along & hdwy 3f out: kpt on nr fin: nt pce to chal) | | 2.4 |
| Mountain High (FR) *(JGFitzGerald)* 8-10 KFallon (13) (w'like: in tch: rdn along ½-wy: hdwy & nt clr run over 1f out: kpt on same pce) | | ¾.5 |
| Setta *(MMoubarak)* 8-5 LDettori (9) (leggy: bit bkwd: dwlt: plld hrd & sn in tch: effrt over 2f out: wknd over 1f out) | | 1.6 |
| Amiarge *(MBrittain)* 8-10 DMcKeown (6) (unf: bhd: hdwy over 2f out: n.d) | | 1½.7 |
| 2646⁵ My Patriarch *(JLDunlop)* 9-0 WCarson (2) (lw: plld hrd: trckd ldrs: effrt 3f out: wknd over 1f out: hmpd whn btn) | | 3½.8 |
| 3005 Yahmi (IRE) *(MajorWRHern)* 9-0 RHills (10) (w ldrs over 5f: grad lost pl) | | ½.9 |
| 2799 Euphonic *(IABalding)* 9-0 BRaymond (1) (prom over 5f) | | 1½.10 |
| 1623 Raggerty (IRE) *(JBerry)* 9-0 JCarroll (7) (sn rdn along & outpcd) | | ½.11 |
| 2700 Bardia *(DonEnricoIncisa)* 8-9 JakiHouston (8) (chsd ldrs to ½-wy: sn lost pl) | | 2.12 |
| 2675² I Remember You (IRE) *(FHLee)* 9-0 AMunro (5) (w ldr 5f: sn wknd: eased whn btn fnl f) | | 8.13 |

7/4 DAKAR RALLY, 9/2 Zind (IRE)(4/1—6/1), 11/2 Desert Secret (IRE)(2/1—6/1), 8/1 My Patriarch, 10/1 Yahmi (IRE), I Remember You (IRE), 12/1 Setta, 14/1 Cyrus the Bold (IRE), 20/1 Euphonic, 33/1 Mountain High (FR), 50/1 Raggerty (IRE), Amiarge, 100/1 Bardia. CSF £12.19, Tote £2.70: £1.40 £1.50 £6.70 (£3.80). Sheikh Mohammed (NEWMARKET) bred by Cliveden Stud Ltd. 13 Rn     1m 40.78 (4.28)
SF—31/34/28/18/6/8

**3201**   SUN PRINCESS GRADUATION STKS (3-Y.O) £4480.00 (£1330.00: £630.00: £280.00)   **1m (rnd)**   1-35 (1-38)

| | | |
|---|---|---|
| 3131 **Tik Fa** (USA) **(96)** (v) *(BHanbury)* 9-2 LDettori (6) (hld up & bhd: hdwy on ins 3f out: swtchd 2f out: qcknd to ld ins fnl f: r.o wl) | | —1 |
| 2711³ L'Hermine **(87)** *(HCandy)* 9-2 PatEddery (3) (led: rdn wl over 2f out: hdd ins fnl f: unable qckn) | | 3.2 |
| 3016* Talb (USA) (Fav) *(JLDunlop)* 9-2 WCarson (5) (hld up: effrt over 3f out: styd on appr fnl f: nt pce to chal) | | ¾.3 |
| 3006 Herora (IRE) **(101)** *(NAGraham)* 9-0 MRoberts (4) (hld up gng wl: stdy hdwy & n.m.r on ins 3f out: ev ch over 1f out: nt qckn) | | 3½.4 |
| 1460 King Olaf (IRE) **(103)** *(PWChapple-Hyam)* 9-5 PaulEddery (1) (trckd ldrs: effrt 3f out: nvr able to chal: wknd over 1f out) | | 7.5 |
| 2933⁴ Muhayaa (USA) **(92)** *(AAScott)* 9-5 BRaymond (8) (lw: plld hrd & prom early: outpcd ½-wy & sn drvn along: no imp fnl 3f) | | 4.6 |
| 869* Dawaahi (USA) **(85)** *(JHMGosden)* 9-2 SCauthen (2) (prom tl wknd 3f out: eased whn btn) | | 2½.7 |
| 1467 Beware of Agents **(96)** *(MJohnston)* 9-5 DMcKeown (7) (prom tl wknd over 3f out) | | 7.8 |

5/2 Talb (USA), 5/1 Dawaahi (USA), King Olaf (IRE), Herora (IRE), 8/1 Muhayaa (USA), 9/1 Beware of Agents(12/1—14/1), 10/1 TIK FA (USA), 12/1 L'Hermine. CSF £102.02, Tote £9.90: £1.80 £2.90 £1.40 (£50.10). Mr Abdullah Ali (NEWMARKET) bred by Hardie Scott in USA. 8 Rn     1m 39.16 (2.86)
SF—43/34/32/19/3/–

**3202**  LAURENT-PERRIER ROSE CHAMPAGNE STKS (II) (Mdn 2-Y.O) £2560.00 (£760.00: £360.00: £160.00)  **1m (st)**  2-05 (2-08)

Taos (IRE) *(JHMGosden)* 8-10 SCauthen (12) (cmpt: hld up & bhd: smooth hdwy 2f out: qcknd to ld ins fnl f: readily) .............................. —1

Planetary Aspect (USA) *(PWChapple-Hyam)* 8-10 PaulEddery (6) (w'like: str: trckd ldrs: led over 1f out tl ins fnl f: nt pce of wnr) ............ 1½.2

1936⁶ Aljazzaf (Fav) *(CEBrittain)* 9-0 LDettori (10) (bit bkwd: mde most tl hdd over 1f out: kpt on same pce) .................................................... 4.3

2901 Arc Bright (IRE) *(RHollinshead)* 9-0 KDarley (11) (in tch: effrt & n.m.r over 2f out: kpt on fnl f) ....................................................... 3.4

Soul Emperor *(MBell)* 8-10 AMunro (1) (str: scope: bit bkwd: prom tl outpcd ½-wy: sme hdwy over 1f out: no imp) ............................ nk.5

Desert Challenger (IRE) *(ACStewart)* 8-10 MRoberts (7) (gd sort: cmpt: w ldrs: rdn along ½-wy: wnt rt & wknd over 2f out) ...................... s.h.6

2918 Grand Applause (IRE) (77) *(RSimpson)* 8-9 ‡5ATucker (4) (w ldrs 5f) ......... 2½.7

2879³ Beauman *(BAMcMahon)* 9-0 WCarson (3) (in tch: pushed along over 3f out: sn btn) ............................................................................... 6.8

3030 Stage Artist *(JEtherington)* 8-9 NConnorton (2) (a in rr) ..................... ¾.9

Fabfer (IRE) *(PWChapple-Hyam)* 8-10 PatEddery (5) (w'like: scope: prom on outside tl wknd over 3f out: eased fnl f) ........................ 5.10

Tioga (IRE) *(RHannon)* 8-10 BRaymond (9) (gd sort: trckd ldrs: hdwy to ld over 1f out: faltered & sn hdd: p.u lame nr fin) ..................... 0

7/2 Aljazzaf, 4/1 Desert Challenger (IRE)(op 9/4), 11/2 Fabfer (IRE), TAOS (IRE), 6/1 Planetary Aspect (USA), 8/1 Soul Emperor, 10/1 Tioga (IRE), 14/1 Beauman, 25/1 Stage Artist, 33/1 Ors. CSF £37.36, Tote £5.70: £1.90 £2.90 £1.60 (£50.60). Sheikh Mohammed (NEWMARKET) bred by Barronstown Bloodstock in Ireland. 11 Rn
1m 42.01 (5.51)
SF—13/8/–/–/–/–

**3203**  POLYPIPE H'CAP (3-Y.O) (0-90) £3200.00 (£950.00: £450.00: £200.00)  **1m (st)**  2-35 (2-38)

(Weights raised 5 lb)

2191 **Nashville Blues (IRE)** (83) *(JWHills)* 9-7 MHills (8) (hld up & bhd: gd hdwy to ld ins fnl f: r.o strly) ........................................... —1

2941* Tahitian (59) *(MrsJRRamsden)* 7-11 JFanning (9) (hld up: rdn to ld 1f out: sn hdd: unable qckn) .................................................. 1½.2

2555* Many a Quest (USA) (80) *(LMCumani)* 9-4 LDettori (12) (lw: hld up: effrt & nt clr run 2f out: swtchd outside & r.o wl ins fnl f) ............ 1½.3

3137² Merlins Wish (USA) (80) (Fav) *(RHannon)* 9-4 PatEddery (6) (a.p: rdn & ev ch appr fnl f: unable qckn) .................................... 2½.4

1758⁴ Pippin Park (USA) (75) *(HCandy)* 8-13 CRutter (11) (led 1f: led 3f out to 1f out: no ex) ........................................................ nk.5

3013 Riviera Vista (83) *(GWragg)* 9-7 RHills (4) (w ldrs: rdn over 2f out: ev ch tl wknd fnl f) ....................................................... 1½.6

2913 Scandalmonger (USA) (76) *(BWHills)* 9-0 WCarson (13) (hld up in tch gng wl: effrt over 1f out: hmpd & nt rcvr) ......................... nk.7

2935* Houlston's Will (62) *(MrsJRRamsden)* 8-0 AMunro (5) (effrt & hdwy on outside over 2f out: hmpd over 1f out: nt rcvr) ................. ¾.8

2958 Amazing Feat (IRE) (69) *(MrsGRReveley)* 8-7 KDarley (10) (trckd ldrs: rdn over 3f out: grad wknd) ................................... 1.9

2969³ Gold Blade (61) *(NAGraham)* 7-13 MRoberts (2) (b.nr fore: prom 5f: grad wknd) 2.10

3088² Boy Martin (66) *(MJohnston)* 8-4 DMcKeown (1) (lw: in tch: hdwy over 2f out: sn rdn & btn) ...................................................... hd.11

2958⁴ Gymcrak Tycoon (74) *(MHEasterby)* 8-12 MBirch (7) (plld hrd: led after 1f to 3f out: wknd 2f out) ................................... 1½.12

3119⁶ Gold Belt (IRE) (58) *(RHollinshead)* 7-3⁽³⁾ ‡7AGarth (3) (in tch 5f) ...... 7.13

LONG HANDICAP: Gold Belt (IRE) 7-1.

7/2 Merlins Wish (USA), 7/1 Many a Quest (USA), Tahitian, 15/2 Scandalmonger (USA), 8/1 Boy Martin, 9/1 Riviera Vista(12/1—8/1), 12/1 Gold Blade, Houlston's Will, 14/1 Amazing Feat (IRE), Gymcrak Tycoon, NASHVILLE BLUES (IRE), 25/1 Pippin Park (USA), 100/1 Gold Belt (IRE). CSF £99.57, CT £683.81. Tote £15.50: £3.80 £3.00 £2.90 (£83.10). Mrs S. Bosher (LAMBOURN) bred by Mrs Larry Walsh in Ireland. 13 Rn
1m 41.08 (4.58)
SF—38/9/25/17/11/14

**3204**  TROY STKS (listed race) (3-Y.O) £8975.00 (£2675.00: £1275.00: £575.00)  **1½m**  3-05 (3-06)

3087* **Kasmayo** *(JHMGosden)* 8-11 SCauthen (4) (lw: mde virtually all: qcknd over 3f out: rdn & r.o wl fnl 2f) .............................................. —1

3090* Duke of Eurolink **(91)** (Fav) *(LMCumani)* 8-11 LDettori (5) (lw: hld up: effrt over 1f out: r.o wl: too much to do) .................... 1½.2

3089³ Polish Blue (USA) **(100)** *(MRStoute)* 8-11 BRaymond (3) (lw: bhd: effrt over 3f out: styd on: no imp) .................... 6.3

3022² Anchorite **(100)** *(PTWalwyn)* 8-11 MRoberts (1) (led early: chsd ldr tl outpcd fnl 2f) .................... hd.4

3020⁴ Royal Seaton **(86)** *(BRMillman)* 8-11 MBirch (6) (hld up: plld hrd & hdwy appr st: wknd 3f out) .................... 15.5

11/8 Duke of Eurolink, 9/4 KASMAYO, 9/2 Polish Blue (USA), 7/1 Anchorite, 14/1 Royal Seaton. CSF £5.50, Tote £2.90: £1.40 £1.30 (£2.20). Sheikh Ahmed Al Maktoum (NEWMARKET) bred by Stonethorn Stud Farms Ltd. 5 Rn
2m 31.69 (1.09)
SF—62/59/47/46/16

**3205**　　LAURENT-PERRIER CHAMPAGNE STKS (Gp 2) (2-Y.O.C & G) £42840.00 (£16052.00: £7726.00: £3382.00)　**7f**
3-35 (3-37)

2845 **Petardia** *(GWragg)* 9-0 MHills (6) (lw: hld up & bhd: hdwy on bit over 2f out: led 1f out: shkn up & r.o) .................... —1

1349² Needle Gun (IRE) *(CEBrittain)* 8-11 SCauthen (8) (hld up & bhd: nt clr run & swtchd 2f out: r.o wl) .................... 1½.2

2912³ Fitzcarraldo (USA) *(LMCumani)* 8-11 LDettori (7) (trckd ldrs: stdy hdwy to ld over 1f out: rdn & kpt on wl) .................... nk.3

2912 Mukhamedov *(HRACecil)* 8-11 PatEddery (3) (lw: hld up: hdwy 3f out: rdn 2f out: nt qckn) .................... 2.4

1925* Lord President (USA) (Fav) *(PFICole)* 8-11 AMunro (5) (lw: cl up: led over 2f out: sn hdd, rdn & btn) .................... 5.5

3047⁵ Persian Revival (FR) *(BAMcMahon)* 8-11 MBirch (2) (led over 4f: sn outpcd) ..... 3.6

3113a² Newton's Law (IRE) *(PWChapple-Hyam)* 8-11 PaulEddery (9) (lw: chsd ldrs: pushed along ½-wy: wknd 2f out) .................... 2½.7

2790² Right Win (IRE) *(RHannon)* 8-11 MRoberts (4) (chsd ldrs over 4f: sn wknd) .................... 7.8

2947* Ihtiraz *(HThomsonJones)* 8-11 RHills (1) (cl up tl rdn & wknd 3f out) .................... 5.9

6/4 Lord President (USA)(op Evens), 11/2 PETARDIA, 6/1 Mukhamedov, 7/1 Newton's Law (IRE), 8/1 Right Win (IRE), 16/1 Ihtiraz(12/1—20/1), 20/1 Needle Gun (IRE), 50/1 Persian Revival (FR). CSF £86.61, Tote £5.90: £2.10 £3.10 £2.40 (£61.90). Mollers Racing (NEWMARKET) bred by Highfield Stud Ltd and The Glen Andred Stud. 9 Rn
1m 25.86 (2.46)
SF—63/55/54/48/33/24

**3206**　　DERWENT MACDEE H'CAP (0-100) £3200.00 (£950.00: £450.00: £200.00)　**1½m**
4-10 (4-11)

2853⁴ **Seal Indigo (IRE) (82)** (Fav) *(RHannon)* 4-9-3 PatEddery (8) (lw: hld up & bhd: hdwy 3f out: swtchd ins: qcknd to ld ins fnl f: cleverly) .................... —1

2853 Libk **(92)** *(HThomsonJones)* 4-9-13 RHills (2) (trckd ldrs: smooth hdwy 3f out: rdn 2f out: styd on nr fin) .................... ¾.2

2920³ Tudor Island **(73)** (bl) *(CEBrittain)* 4-9-7 MRoberts (3) (chsd ldrs: effrt over 2f out: sn hrd drvn: styd on ins fnl f) .................... s.h.3

2853⁶ Caspian Beluga **(62)** *(MrsAKnight)* 4-7-8 ³FNorton (4) (lw: led: qcknd over 2f out: hdd & no ex ins fnl f) .................... nk.4

2442 Secret Society **(85)** *(MJCamacho)* 5-9-6 NConnorton (10) (lw: hld up: hdwy 4f out: shkn up over 2f out: no imp) .................... 4.5

Top Spin **(78)** *(MajorWRHern)* 3-8-4 MHills (9) (chsd ldrs: effrt over 3f out: wknd over 2f out) .................... 4.6

3076³ Bold Ambition **(58)** *(TKersey)* 5-7-7 JLowe (5) (lw: sme hdwy 4f out: nvr trbld ldrs) .................... 5.7

2810 Eire Leath-Sceal **(58)** *(MBrittain)* 5-7-7 LCharnock (7) (chsd ldrs tl wknd 3f out) .................... 7.8

880² Vasiliev **(79)** *(JPLeigh)* 4-9-0 DNicholls (6) (lw: s.s: a bhd) .................... 5.9

LONG HANDICAP: Bold Ambition 6-0, Eire Leath-Sceal 7-0.

9/4 SEAL INDIGO (IRE), 4/1 Tudor Island(6/1—7/1), 11/2 Secret Society(4/1—6/1), 6/1 Libk(op 4/1), 7/1 Caspian Beluga, 10/1 Top Spin, 16/1 Vasiliev, 20/1 Eire Leath-Sceal, 50/1 Bold Ambition. CSF £14.97, CT £45.45. Tote £2.60: £1.40 £2.20 £1.40 (£7.00). Mr G. Howard-Spink (MARLBOROUGH) bred by Mrs M. P. Pitt in Ireland. 9 Rn
2m 31.02 (0.42)
SF—75/83/54/48/66/42

**3207**　　PRINCE OF WALES H'CAP (0-90) £5127.00 (£1536.00: £738.00: £339.00)　**5f**
4-40 (4-50)

(Weights raised 1 lb)
2963⁶ **Catherines Well (69)** *(MWEasterby)* 9-8-10 TLucas (14) (lw: in tch: hdwy to ld ins fnl f: r.o) .................... —1

3144 Heaven-Liegh-Grey (67) (bl) *(MJohnston)* 4-8-8 MRoberts (10) (cl up: led over 1f out tl ins fnl f: r.o) .................... ½.2

2813 Samsolom (60) *(JBalding)* 4-8-1 KDarley (9) (lw: a.p: hdwy 2f out: hrd rdn & kpt on wl fnl f) ........................ nk.3

3144³ On the Edge (72) *(TDBarron)* 4-8-13 LDettori (15) (lw: swtg: hdwy 2f out: r.o) .... nk.4

3126⁴ Iron King (71) *(JLSpearing)* 6-8-5 ‡7AGarth (13) (bhd tl hdwy 2f out: fin wl) ...... hd.5

3015³ Gondo (74) (v) *(EJAlston)* 5-9-1 KFallon (4) (racd far side: hdwy 2f out: styd on wl) ........................ ½.6

2919 Paley Prince (USA) (78) *(MDIUsher)* 4-9-5 SCauthen (5) (lw: led far side: rdn 2f out: nt qckn ins fnl f) .......... 2.7

3144⁴ Tigani (67) *(DWChapman)* 6-8-8 SWood (8) (lw: racd centre: cl up tl rdn & btn wl over 1f out) ................. nk.8

3144* Samson-Agonistes (80) *(BAMcMahon)* 6-9-0 (7x) ‡7SSanders (17) (lw: chsd ldrs: rdn ½-wy: nt qckn) .......... s.h.9

3144⁶ Super Rocky (75) *(RBastiman)* 3-9-0 DMcKeown (3) (stdd s: bhd far side tl r.o wl appr fnl f) ................ hd.10

3015² Sigama (USA) (83) (Fav) *(FHLee)* 6-9-5 ‡5NKennedy (16) (lw: led tl hdd & wknd over 1f out) ............... nk.11

2603⁴ Food of Love (80) *(JBerry)* 4-9-7 JCarroll (11) (chsd ldrs over 3f) ........ 2½.12

3144 Prince Belfort (67) *(MPNaughton)* 4-8-3 ‡5JWeaver (1) (cl up far side over 3f: eased whn btn) .............. nk.13

2989⁵ The Noble Oak (IRE) (62) (bl) *(MMcCormack)* 4-8-3 CRutter (12) (dwlt: a bhd) 3½.14

3120 Meeson Times (59) *(BEllison)* 4-8-0 AMunro (7) (racd centre: nvr wnt pce) .. s.h.15

2848⁴ Saddlehome (USA) (77) *(RMWhitaker)* 3-9-2 WCarson (2) (racd far side: prom over 3f) ..................... ¾.16

3144 Ned's Bonanza (70) *(MDods)* 3-8-9 JLowe (6) (lw: racd far side: spd over 3f) 2½.17

**11/2** Sigama (USA), **8/1** On the Edge, **9/1** Heaven-Liegh-Grey, **10/1** Samson-Agonistes, **11/1** Gondo, **12/1** Iron King, Saddlehome (USA)(op 8/1), **14/1** Food of Love, Tigani, CATHERINES WELL, **16/1** Paley Prince (USA), The Noble Oak (IRE), **20/1** Samsolom, Super Rocky, 25/1 Prince Belfort, **33/1** Ors. OCT £110.16, CT £2,266.59. Tote £17.20: £3.40 £1.50 £5.10 £2.00 (£48.50). Mr K. Hodgson (SHERIFF HUTTON) bred by R. J. Powell. 17 Rn

60.48 sec (1.78)

SF—60/56/48/59/50/58

T/Trio: Race 4: £126.50 (7 Tckts); Race 8: Any 2 fr 1st 3 £20.50 (16 Tckts). T/Jkpt: Not won; £31,090.45 to Doncaster 12/9/92. T/Plpt: £239.00 (30.95 Tckts).　　　　　　O'R/AA

# DONCASTER (L-H)

## Saturday, September 12th [Good to firm]

Going Allowance: St: 0.10 sec per fur; Rnd: nil sec per fur (G)　　　　Wind: fresh against

Stalls: high

**3208**　　BATTLE OF BRITAIN NURSERY　£4045.00 (£1210.00: £580.00: £265.00)
　　　　　6f　　　　　　　　　　　　　　　　　　　　　　　　　2-05 (2-07)

(Weights raised 7 lb)

3011⁵ **Brigg Fair** (80) *(RHannon)* 9-4 JReid (7) (lw: hld up & bhd: stdy hdwy to disp ld ins fnl f: rdn to ld cl home) .................... —1

3019⁶ In Case (USA) (83) *(RCharlton)* 9-7 PatEddery (9) (led: qcknd over 2f out: hrd drvn fnl f: r.o: jst ct) ........... hd.2

3129⁶ Chili Heights (76) *(GBBalding)* 9-0 JWilliams (3) (b.hind: hld up & bhd: hdwy 2f out: kpt on: no imp) ............. 6.3

3129² Infant Protege (USA) (72) (Jt-Fav) *(CEBrittain)* 8-10 MRoberts (2) (lw: bhd: hdwy ½-wy: rdn wl over 1f out: sn outpcd) ............ 1½.4

3033* Norling (IRE) (68) (Jt-Fav) *(NTinkler)* 8-6 LCharnock (8) (trckd ldrs: effrt 2f out: sn btn) ....................... 5.5

3123 Super Seve (IRE) (74) *(JBerry)* 8-12 JCarroll (11) (in tch tl outpcd fnl 2f) .. 2.6

2724* Master Sinclair (IRE) (68) *(RHollinshead)* 7-13 ‡7AGarth (12) (s.i.s: effrt ½-wy: no imp) .................... hd.7

2948³ Mawayed (USA) (72) *(PTWalwyn)* 8-10 WCarson (10) (in tch 4f: sn wknd) ...... 1½.8

988 Touch Silver (76) *(BWHills)* 9-0 SCauthen (5) (prom 4f) .............. 2.9

3117² Folly Vision (IRE) (78) *(RHannon)* 9-2 LPiggott (6) (lw: prom 4f: eased whn btn) 6.10

2225⁴ Allez Bianco (66) *(RJHolder)* 8-4 NAdams (4) (prom over 3f: sn rdn & wknd) nk.11

**9/2** Norling (IRE), Infant Protege (USA), **5/1** Mawayed (USA), **6/1** In Case (USA), **8/1** Touch Silver, **10/1** Chili Heights, BRIGG FAIR, **12/1** Folly Vision (IRE), Master Sinclair (IRE), **20/1** Allez Bianco, **25/1** Super Seve (IRE). CSF £64.51, CT £566.64. Tote £22.00: £4.60 £2.30 £2.90 (£48.10). Mr John Norman (MARLBOROUGH) bred by Roldvale Ltd. 11 Rn

1m 14.39 (3.39)

SF—48/50/19/9/–/–

## 3209

ROTHMANS ROYALS NORTH SOUTH CHALLENGE SERIES H'CAP (Semi-Final) (0-100) £16050.00 (£4800.00: £2300.00: £1050.00)　**1m (rnd)**　　　　2-35 (2-38)

2468* **Indian Slave (IRE) (64)** (RGuest) 4–7–7 ‡5DHarrison (7) (mid div: effrt 3f out: r.o wl to ld cl home) ..................................................................... —1

2825* Croft Valley (80) (Fav) (RAkehurst) 5–9–0 WCarson (6) (lw: led: qcknd over 2f out: hrd rdn fnl f: no ex cl home) ............................................... ¾.2

3027³ State Dancer (USA) (90) (MMoubarak) 5–9–5 ‡5StephenDavies (2) (chsd ldrs: effrt over 2f out: kpt on fnl f) ................................................... ½.3

2825 Self Expression (70) (bl) (IABalding) 4–8–4 MHills (14) (hld up & bhd: effrt over 2f out: r.o) .................................................................... nk.4

2852* Doulab's Image (94) (bl) (JAGlover) 5–9–9 ‡5SWilliams (10) (lw: bhd: hdwy 3f out: nrst fin) ....................................................................... 1.5

3088⁴ Sharpalto (83) (MrsGRReveley) 5–9–3 JLowe (9) (hld up & bhd: effrt 3f out: n.m.r: nvr able to chal) ...................................................... 3.6

3088* Takenhall (65) (MJFetherston-Godley) 7–7–13 NAdams (13) (lw: hdwy u.p over 1f out: nrst fin) ................................................................ nk.7

3024 Spanish Verdict (69) (DenysSmith) 5–8–3 KFallon (1) (lw: chsd ldrs: drvn along over 2f out: no imp after) ............................................... nk.8

2611⁵ Caleman (81) (RBoss) 3–8–10 GDuffield (20) (chsd ldr tl rdn & btn wl over 1f out) ...................................................................................... 1½.9

2825 Alycida (USA) (84) (LMCumani) 3–8–13 LDettori (4) (swtg: chsd ldrs tl grad wknd fnl 2f) .................................................................... 2½.10

3137⁴ Aitch N'Bee (80) (LadyHerries) 9–9–0 SCauthen (3) (hld up: effrt 3f out: n.m.r & n.d) .................................................................................... 2.11

3024³ King Al (89) (DrJDScargill) 5–9–9 SWebster (21) (b: effrt u.p 3f out: n.d) ........ hd.12

3024 Habeta (USA) (65) (JWWatts) 6–7–13 JFanning (19) (bhd: effrt ½-wy: n.d) .... nk.13

3024⁴ Desert Splendour (72) (CEBrittain) 4–8–6 MRoberts (11) (prom 5f: btn whn hmpd over 1f out) ................................................................ nk.14

2825 Shirley's Train (USA) (74) (LordHuntingdon) 3–8–3 DMcKeown (15) (hld up & bhd: n.d) ................................................................................. s.h.15

2641⁴ Piquant (87) (LordHuntingdon) 5–9–7 PatEddery (12) (lw: hdwy ½-wy: sn prom: wknd over 1f out) .................................................... nk.16

2656² Buddy's Friend (IRE) (59) (RJRWilliams) 4–7–7 DaleGibson (17) (in tch 5f) ..... ½.17

3024 Rise Up Singing (72) (bl) (WJMusson) 4–8–6⁽¹⁾ JReid (18) (sn chsng ldrs: wknd 2f out) ............................................................................... 7.18

3024⁴ Laurel Queen (73) (JBerry) 4–8–7 JCarroll (8) (bhd: effrt ½-wy: n.d) ....... 5.19

7/1 Croft Valley, 9/1 Piquant, 10/1 Doulab's Image, Laurel Queen (IRE), 12/1 Aitch N'Bee, INDIAN SLAVE (IRE), Self Expression, 14/1 Alycida (USA), Takenhall, State Dancer (USA), King Al, Desert Splendour, 16/1 Sharpalto, 20/1 Habeta (USA), Shirley's Train (USA), Buddy's Friend (IRE), Rise Up Singing, 25/1 Spanish Verdict, 33/1 Caleman. CSF £88.23, CT £1,106.23. Tote £11.90: £2.50 £1.70 £4.60 £2.80 (£27.10). Mr R. Axford (NEWMARKET) bred by Ivan W. Allan in Ireland. 19 Rn　　　　　　　　　　1m 38.45 (2.15)
SF—47/66/69/53/69/54

## 3210

FLYING CHILDERS STKS (Gp 2) (2-Y.O) £22680.00 (£8416.50: £3983.25: £1670.25)
**5f**　　　　　　　　　　　　　　　　　　　　　　　3-05 (3-08)

3096 **Poker Chip** (IABalding) 8-6 MHills (2) (lw: sn outpcd & bhd: hdwy 2f out: r.o wl to ld cl home) ................................................................. —1

2847² Saint Express (RMWhitaker) 8-11 ACulhane (5) (a in tch: swtchd & effrt 2f out: squeezed thro to chal ins fnl f: r.o) ............................ ¾.2

3081² Satank (USA) (JWWatts) 8-11 PatEddery (7) (lw: led: qcknd ½-wy: edgd lft & hrd rdn fnl f: r.o gamely) .................................... s.h.3

3047⁴ Peperonata (IRE) (BWHills) 8-6 JLowe (6) (chsd ldrs: pushed thro to chal wl over 1f out: wknd ins fnl f) ........................................ 2½.4

2452* Millyant (Fav) (RGuest) 8-11 MRoberts (4) (b.hind: cl up: rdn 2f out: wknd 1f out) ............................................................................ 3½.5

2850⁴ Niche (RHannon) 8-11 LPiggott (1) (lw: cl up tl rdn & wknd over 1f out) ......... 1½.6

3070⁴ Sabre Rattler (JBerry) 8-11 JCarroll (3) (lw: gd spd over 3f) ...................... 1.7

10/11 Millyant, 3/1 Niche, 11/2 Satank (USA), 17/2 Sabre Rattler, 20/1 Saint Express, 25/1 Peperonata (IRE), 33/1 POKER CHIP. CSF £385.83, Tote £32.40: £6.30 £5.90 (£178.40). Mr J. C. Smith (KINGSCLERE) bred by Littleton Stud. 7 Rn　　　　　　　　　　　　　60.56 sec (1.86)
SF—65/67/66/51/42/36

## 3211

COALITE ST LEGER STKS (Gp 1) (3-Y.O,C & F) £161368.00 (£59812.00: £28781.00: £11855.00: £4802.50: £1981.50)　**1¾m 132y**　　　3-40 (3-42)

2843* **User Friendly** (Fav) (CEBrittain) 8-11 GDuffield (2) (lw: trckd ldrs: led 2f out: r.o v.wl) ........................................................................ —1

2838² Sonus (IRE) *(JHMGosden)* 9-0 SCauthen (1) (lw: trckd ldr: rdn to ld over 2f out: sn hdd: r.o) .................................................................... 3¹/₂.2

2838★ Bonny Scot (IRE) *(LMCumani)* 9-0 LDettori (6) (lw: trckd ldrs: effrt over 3f out: r.o u.p: nt pce to chal) ......................................................... nk.3

3020★ Shuailaan (USA) *(ACStewart)* 9-0 MRoberts (7) (hld up & bhd: gd hdwy over 2f out: nt qckn kns fnl f) ................................................................. ³/₄.4

3022★ Mack the Knife *(MajorWRHern)* 9-0 LPiggott (3) (led: qcknd over 3f out: hdd over 2f out: sn outpcd) ............................................................... 6.5

2838³ Assessor (IRE) *(RHannon)* 9-0 JReid (8) (b: bhd: effrt appr st: rdn & no imp fnl 4f) .............................................................................................. 5.6

2996★ Rain Rider *(JLDunlop)* 9-0 WCarson (5) (lw: prom: effrt 4f out: sn rdn & btn) .... ³/₄.7

**7/4** USER FRIENDLY, **5/2** Bonny Scot (IRE), **5/1** Rain Rider, **15/2** Sonus (IRE), **14/1** Mack the Knife, Assessor (IRE), **18/1** Shuailaan (USA). CSF £13.63, Tote £2.60: £1.80 £3.10 (£8.40). Mr W. J. Gredley (NEWMARKET) bred by Stetchworth Park Stud Ltd. 7 Rn          3m 5.48 (1.88)
SF—78/74/73/71/59/49/47

---

**3212**          COALITE H'CAP (0-115) £23150.00 (£6950.00: £3350.00: £1550.00)
1m (st)          4-15 (4-17)

(Weights raised 2 lb)

30272 **Mellottie (98)** *(MrsGRReveley)* 7–9-10 JLowe (9) (lw: hld up & bhd: hdwy on bit 2f out: qcknd to ld wl ins fnl f) ............................................... —1

2852 Double Entendre (70) *(MBell)* 6–7-10 EJohnson (6) (hdwy over 2f out: led over 1f out: r.o: nt pce cl wnr cl home) .................................................. 1.2

30844 Double Echo (IRE) (67) *(JDBethell)* 4–7-7 LCharnock (14) (lw: in tch: hdwy to chal over 1f out: nt qckn) ......................................................... 1¹/₂.3

2898 Parliament Piece (91) *(MrsGRReveley)* 6–8-10 ‡DarrenMoffatt (4) (lw: led & sn clr: rdn 3f out: hdd over 1f out: kpt on) ...................................... 1¹/₂.4

2348★ Colour Sergeant (90) *(LordHuntingdon)* 4–9-2 LPiggott (8) (lw: chsd ldrs tl lost pl over 2f out: styd on fnl f) ................................................... 1¹/₂.5

31212 Marine Diver (74) *(BRMillman)* 6–8-0 DaleGibson (15) (hld up & bhd: hdwy 2f out: rdn & nvr able to chal) ..................................................... ¹/₂.6

30692 Gymcrak Premiere (94) *(MHEasterby)* 4–9-6 KDarley (13) (chsd ldrs tl outpcd over 2f out: n.d after) ........................................................ 1.7

30142 Mamma's Too (90) *(MBell)* 3–8-11 MHills (12) (hld up & bhd: hdwy over 2f out: nvr rchd ldrs) ............................................................... ³/₄.8

27553 Wesaam (USA) (95) *(MajorWRHern)* 3–9-2 WCarson (7) (lw: drvn along over 3f out: no imp) ..................................................................... 1¹/₂.9

2846 Pay Homage (92) *(IABalding)* 4–9-4 GDuffield (1) (hld up: effrt over 2f out: rdn & sn btn) ......................................................................... hd.10

30275 Knock to Enter (USA) (88) *(MRStoute)* 4–9-0 PatEddery (5) (hdwy 3f out: sn rdn & btn) ................................................................................ ³/₄.11

2990★ Jahangir (IRE) (80) **(Fav)** *(BHanbury)* 3–8-1 MRoberts (3) (lw: chsd ldrs tl grad lost pl wl over 2f out) ......................................................... s.h.12

3027★ Cumbrian Challenge (IRE) (94) *(MHEasterby)* 3–9-1 MBirch (11) (lw: chsd ldrs: outpcd ¹/₂-wy: n.d after) ................................................. hd.13

2447 Daswaki (CAN) (80) *(RHannon)* 4–8-6 BRouse (2) (chsd ldrs 6f: sn wknd) .... 1¹/₂.14

**3/1** Jahangir (IRE)(op 5/1), **6/1** Colour Sergeant, **13/2** MELLOTTIE, **10/1** Cumbrian Challenge (IRE), Knock to Enter (USA), **11/1** Wesaam (USA), **11/1** Wesaam (USA), Daswaki (CAN), **14/1** Mamma's Too, Pay Homage, Marine Diver, **20/1** Parliament Piece, **25/1** Ors. CSF £139.84, CT £3,459.39. Tote £8.30: £2.70 £7.20 £7.90 (£172.40). Mrs J. G. Fulton (SALTBURN) bred by Mrs G. R. Reveley and partners. 14 Rn          1m 38.61 (2.11)
SF—90/69/61/73/74/56

---

**3213**          REFERENCE POINT SCEPTRE STKS (listed race) (F & M) £9462.50 (£2825.00: £1350.00: £612.50)          1m (st)          4-45 (4-46)

1217 **Perfect Circle (118)** **(Fav)** *(MRStoute)* 3–8-5 WCarson (6) (lw: hdwy 3f out: pushed along & r.o wl to ld ins fnl f) ................................... —1

30323 Midnight Air (USA) (98) *(HRACecil)* 3–8-5 AMcGlone (5) (trckd ldrs: led wl over 1f out tl ins fnl f: no ex) ............................................................. 1.2

30892 Badawi (USA) (100) *(JHMGosden)* 4–8-10 SCauthen (1) (cl up: disp ld wl over 1f out: nt qckn fnl f) ........................................................... 2.3

29113 Petal Girl (90) *(RHannon)* 3–8-5 MRoberts (4) (bhd: effrt 3f out: styd on: nvr able to chal) ................................................................. 2.4

3038★ Well Beyond (IRE) (100) *(BWHills)* 3–8-5 PatEddery (8) (hld up: effrt over 2f out: sn rdn: edgd lft & no imp) .............................................. ³/₄.5

6724 Cambrian Hills (IRE) (100) *(PWChapple-Hyam)* 3–8-6(¹) JReid (7) (b.hind: hld up & bhd: hdwy over 2f out: sn rdn & nvr able to chal) ............... 1.6

2768a2 Saratoga Source (USA) (105) *(IABalding)* 3–8-9 MHills (2) (led tl hdd wl over 1f out: sn btn) ............................................................... 3¹/₂.7

2911[4] Splice (89) *(JRFanshawe)* 3–8-5 GDuffield (3) (swtg: chsd ldrs tl rdn & wknd
over 2f out) ............................................................................................. 8.8

7/4 PERFECT CIRCLE, 2/1 Badawi (USA), 11/2 Midnight Air (USA), 8/1 Well Beyond (IRE), 10/1 Petal Girl, 12/1
Saratoga Source (USA), 20/1 Splice, 33/1 Cambrian Hills (IRE). CSF £11.93, Tote £2.80: £1.40 £1.80 £1.50
(£9.00). Hanson Leigh Racing (NEWMARKET) bred by Gerald W. Leigh and Sven Hanson. 8 Rn
1m 39.03 (2.53)
SF—65/62/61/50/48/46

**3214**      ROUS GRADUATION STKS (2-Y.O) £3687.50 (£1100.00: £525.00: £237.50)
6f                                                                    5-15 (5-15)

3008[4] **Factual (USA)** *(BWHills)* 8-11 PatEddery (2) (lw: trckd ldrs: effrt over 1f out:
hung rt: led ins fnl f: r.o) ........................................................ —1
3055★ Iron Merchant (IRE) (94) *(RAkehurst)* 9-4 MRoberts (3) (led tl hdd ins fnl f: kpt
on wl) .................................................................................................. 1.2
30125 The Sharp Bidder (IRE) (87) *(RHollinshead)* 9-4 LDettori (8) (cl up: chal over 1f
out: edgd lft & nt qckn) ...................................................................... 1.3
Hejraan (USA) (Fav) *(MRStoute)* 8-6 WCarson (4) (neat: scope: lw: plld hrd:
hdwy 2f out: sn hrd drvn: squeezed out over 1f out) ............... 1¼.4
3047★ Hamsah (IRE) (94) *(DRCElsworth)* 9-2 SCauthen (6) (chsd ldrs tl lost pl 2f out:
styd on nr fin) ..................................................................................... ¾.5
Scusi *(WJarvis)* 8-11 JReid (5) (gd sort: hld up: effrt & kpt on same pce fnl 2f) hd.6
30183 Primo Figlio *(RHannon)* 8-11 BRouse (7) (bhd: shkn up 2f out: nvr plcd to chal) 1½.7
10566 Cutthroat Kid (IRE) *(SGNorton)* 8-11 KDarley (1) (bit bkwd: sn outpcd & wl bhd:
r.o fnl f) .............................................................................................. 1.8

13/8 Hejraan (USA), 11/4 Hamsah (IRE), 13/2 FACTUAL (USA), 13/2 Iron Merchant (IRE), 8/1 Scusi, 10/1 Primo
Figlio, 12/1 The Sharp Bidder (IRE), 25/1 Cutthroat Kid (IRE). CSF £5.30: £1.80 £1.90 £2.90
(£16.40). Mr K. Abdulla (LAMBOURN) bred by Juddmonte Farms in USA. 8 Rn
1m 14.21 (3.21)
SF—45/48/44/26/34/28

T/Trio: Race 2: £417.70 (3.1 Tckts); Race 5: £650.90 (3.1 Tckts). T/Jkpt: Not won; £44,474.95 to Sandown
15/9/92. T/Plpt: £11,230.30 (1.6 Tckts). AA

2828—**FOLKESTONE (R-H)**
**Thursday, September 10th [Good]**
Going Allowance: St: minus 0.20 sec; Rest: minus 0.10 sec (F)        Wind: almost nil
Stalls: low

**3215**      DEAL APP'CE H'CAP (0-70) £2490.00 (£690.00: £330.00)   **1m 1f 149y** 1-50 (1-52)
(Weights raised 10 lb)
2931 **Broughton's Tango (IRE)** (40) *(WJMusson)* 3–8-1 DMcCabe (6) (b: gd hdwy
2f out: led over 1f out: r.o wl) ..................................................... —1
3060 Share Holder (30) *(MissGayKelleway)* 4–7-12 MBaird (10) (b: b.hind: led over
7f out tl over 1f out: unable qckn) ............................................. 5.2
3140 Joli's Great (51) *(MJRyan)* 4–9-5 PMcCabe (2) (hdwy over 1f out: r.o one pce) ¾.3
1434 Liu Liu San (IRE) (30) *(PButler)* 4–7-12 DToole (11) (lw: lost pl over 3f out: r.o
one pce fnl 2f) ................................................................................... 3½.4
30736 Don't Forsake Me (61) *(DMorley)* 3–9-8 EBentley (7) (lw: 3rd st: wknd over 1f
out) ..................................................................................................... 2½.5
30405 Sir Oliver (IRE) (63) *(RJHodges)* 3–9-10 TThompson (3) (5th st: wknd over 1f
out) ..................................................................................................... hd.6
30525 Cornhill Melody (27) *(JLSpearing)* 4–7-9 DWright (4) (lw: led 2f: 6th st: wknd wl
over 1f out) ....................................................................................... nk.7
3140 Weeheby (USA) (62) *(AAScott)* 3–9-4 ‡5HazelMilligan (9) (lw: a bhd) ............. 4.8
30664 Sarah-Clare (55) (Fav) *(RAkehurst)* 4–9-9 LCarter (5) (s.s: hdwy over 3f out: 4th
st: hrd rdn over 1f out: eased whn btn fnl f) ............................... 1½.9
2415 Anguish (IRE) (54) *(NACallaghan)* 3–8-10 ‡5AWhelan (1) (2nd st: wknd over 1f
out) ..................................................................................................... 2½.10
606 Sally Forth (37) *(JRBostock)* 6–8-5 TWilson (8) (b: a bhd) ........................... 5.11

9/4 Sarah-Clare, 4/1 Joli's Great, 13/2 Anguish (IRE), 7/1 Don't Forsake Me, 8/1 Cornhill Melody(6/1—12/1),
BROUGHTON'S TANGO (IRE), 11/1 Weeheby (USA)(op 6/1), 14/1 Sir Oliver (IRE)(op 8/1), 25/1 Share Holder,
33/1 Sally Forth, 50/1 Liu Liu San (IRE). CSF £156.80, CT £837.27. Tote £12.90: £3.00 £4.00 £1.80 (£121.10).
Broughton Thermal Insulation (NEWMARKET) bred by Mrs D. Rudkin in Ireland. 11 Rn  2m 5.8 (8.1)

**3216**      WALMER STKS (Mdn 3-Y.O.F) £2070.00 (£570.00: £270.00)   **6f 189y** 2-20 (2-23)

30162 **Thames Glow** (Fav) *(DRCElsworth)* 8-11 JWilliams (1) (3rd st: led 1f out: r.o wl) —1

2988² Climbing High **(68)** (bl) *(IABalding)* 8-11 TQuinn (2) (2nd st: led over 1f out: sn hdd: unable qckn) .......................................................................... 3.2

3014 Mashaaer (USA) **(64)** *(RWArmstrong)* 8-11 RHills (7) (5th st: r.o one pce fnl 2f) . 1.3

2882³ Spanish Glory **(51)** *(KOCunningham-Brown)* 8-11 DBiggs (5) (6th st: r.o one pce fnl 2f) .......................................................................... nk.4

3028 Gizlaan (USA) **(53)** (bl) *(BHanbury)* 8-11 LDettori (3) (swtg: 4th st: hrd rdn over 1f out: one pce) .......................................................................... 2.5

3042 Alto Princess **(37)** *(APJones)* 8-11 NAdams (4) (led over 5f) ........................ 4.6

Dancing Miss (IRE) *(PRHedger)* 8-11 MPerrett (9) (unf: s.s: a bhd) ........... ½.7

Jupiter Rising *(DWPArbuthnot)* 8-6 ‡⁵RPrice (8) (w'like: bit bkwd: a bhd) ........ s.h.8

3142⁵ Chandni (IRE) *(BHanbury)* 8-11 WRyan (6) (lw: a bhd) ........................... 1.9

**4/5** THAMES GLOW, **7/2** Climbing High, **5/1** Mashaaer (USA), **14/1** Spanish Glory(7/1—16/1), **16/1** Gizlaan (USA)(op 8/1), **33/1** Jupiter Rising, **50/1** Ors. CSF £4.02, Tote £1.80: £1.10 £1.60 £1.80 (£2.60). Mr A. C. Morgan (WHITSBURY) bred by A. Morgan. 9 Rn    1m 25.5 (3.9)
SF—28/19/16/15/9/–

---

**3217**    SCOTTISH EQUITABLE STKS (2-Y.O) £2954.00 (£819.00: £392.00)    **6f**   2-50 (2-51)

2792 Misty Jenni (IRE) *(RAkehurst)* 8-6 TQuinn (2) (mde all: all out) ................ —1

2948★ Jallaaf (USA) **(82)** *(LMCumani)* 9-4 LDettori (1) (lw: a.p: ev ch fnl 2f: hrd rdn: r.o wl) .......................................................................... hd.2

2884★ Night Melody (IRE) **(100)** (Fav) *(RHannon)* 9-7 KDarley (8) (hld up: hrd rdn over 1f out: r.o) .......................................................................... ½.3

2758 Chummy's Idea (IRE) *(JSutcliffe)* 8-6 BRouse (4) (lw: lost pl over 3f out: nvr nr to chal) .......................................................................... 8.4

1208 Silent Prince *(MissBSanders)* 8-6 MPerrett (6) (spd 4f) ........................... 2.5

Serious Result *(RAkehurst)* 8-6 GCarter (7) (leggy: lt-f: spd 4f) ................. 10.6

Azure Royal *(GLewis)* 8-11 RaymondBerry (5) (leggy: bit bkwd: s.s: a bhd) ..... 3.7

**4/6** Night Melody (IRE), **11/8** Jallaaf (USA), **33/1** Serious Result, MISTY JENNI (IRE), **50/1** Ors. CSF £75.61, Tote £15.30: £3.40 £1.50 (£9.90). Mr P. F. Roberts (EPSOM) bred by William Flood in Ireland. 7 Rn   1m 13.8 (3.1)
SF—6/17/18/–/–/–

---

**3218**    EAST WEAR BAY (S) STKS (2-Y.O) £2700.00 (£750.00: £360.00)    **5f**   3-20 (3-24)

3033² First Option **(85)** (Fav) *(MHEasterby)* 9-4 KDarley (18) (lw: led over 3f out: hrd rdn over 1f out: r.o wl) .......................................................................... —1

2924 Covent Garden Girl *(MWEasterby)* 8-6 WRyan (11) (hdwy over 1f out: r.o) ........ 2.2

2857 Rich Midas (IRE) **(54)** *(GLewis)* 7-13 ‡⁷BRussell (1) (a.p: hrd rdn over 1f out: unable qckn) .......................................................................... ¾.3

2578 Warm Spell **(62)** *(RSimpson)* 9-4 BRouse (19) (hdwy over 1f out: r.o) ............ nk.4

2916⁶ Skullcap **(59)** *(TJNaughton)* 8-13 ‡⁵ATucker (2) (s.s: hdwy over 1f out: r.o) .... ½.5

3129⁵ Risky Number **(59)** *(JSMoore)* 8-11 DaleGibson (17) (lw: a.p: one pce fnl 2f) . s.h.6

2863⁴ Red Leader (IRE) **(63)** (bl) *(PFICole)* 8-11 TQuinn (6) (lw: a.p: one pce fnl 2f) .. ½.7

2948 Mouchez le Nez (IRE) *(JAkehurst)* 8-6 DHolland (16) (nvr nr to chal) ........... ¾.8

2238 Gaynor Goodman (IRE) **(50)** *(JSMoore)* 8-6 DBiggs (20) (led over 1f: wknd over 1f out) .......................................................................... nk.9

2883 Hy Wilma **(55)** *(RJHodges)* 8-6 ‡⁷SDrowne (7) (lw: no hdwy fnl 2f) ........... nk.10

Mississipi Maid *(WGMTurner)* 8-6 TSprake (14) (w'like: bit bkwd: outpcd) ..... s.h.11

2551³ Grey Pride **(64)** *(JBerry)* 8-11 GCarter (9) (prom over 2f) ....................... 1.12

2826 Shy Romance **(60)** *(PMMcEntee)* 8-6 JWilliams (13) (outpcd) ............... 1½.13

2863⁵ Monet Monet Monet **(55)** *(WCarter)* 8-6 LDettori (4) (lw: prom over 3f) ...... hd.14

2706⁵ Regent's Lady **(69)** *(CJames)* 8-11 MPerrett (3) (prom 3f) ..................... hd.15

3049⁶ Imafifer (IRE) **(55)** (bl) *(WRMuir)* 8-11 AClark (12) (bhd fnl 2f) ................. 1.16

3019 Prince Manki **(66)** *(RHannon)* 9-4 RHills (15) (outpcd) ......................... 2.17

2930 Bold Treasure (IRE) (bl) *(MrsNMacauley)* 8-6 NAdams (8) (s.s: a bhd) ......... 1.18

2802⁴ Always Risky **(57)** *(PAKelleway)* 8-6 GayKelleway (5) (lw: prom over 3f) ... 1½.19

2649 Montana D'Or *(RCurtis)* 8-6 GBardwell (10) (outpcd) ...................... 2½.20

**3/1** FIRST OPTION(op 2/1), **4/1** Skullcap(op 8/1), **6/1** Regent's Lady, Red Leader (IRE), Grey Pride, **9/1** Prince Manki(6/1—10/1), **10/1** Monet Monet Monet, **14/1** Warm Spell, **20/1** Hy Wilma, Always Risky, Rich Midas (IRE), **25/1** Shy Romance, Mouchez le Nez (IRE), **25/1** Ors. CSF £88.61, Tote £3.40: £2.00 £8.50 £8.80 (£45.20). Mr P. D. Savill (MALTON) bred by Dodford Stud. 20 Rn; Bt in 8,600 gns    60.9 sec (2.1)
SF—42/22/12/30/23/20

---

**3219**    K & V LIPSCOMB (MOTORS) LTD H'CAP (0-70) £2490.00 (£690.00: £330.00)
**1m 7f 92y**    3-50 (3-52)

(Weights raised 1 lb)

2992⁴ Ideal Candidate **(63)** *(TJNaughton)* 3-9-4 GCarter (8) (hdwy over 3f out: 2nd st: led over 2f out: r.o wl) .......................................................................... —1

2992 Erlemo **(45)** (bl) *(CJBenstead)* 3-7-7 ‡7AntoinetteArmes (3) (lw: 3rd st: hrd rdn over 1f out: unable qckn) ...................................................... 6.2

2934 Sharp Top **(55)** *(MJRyan)* 4-9-1 ‡7PMcCabe (4) (hdwy 3f out: 5th st: one pce fnl 2f) .......................................................... 1½.3

3102* Heavenly Waters **(59)** *(Fav)* *(RFJohnsonHoughton)* 3-9-0 (4x) WRyan (5) (b.hind: 6th st: nvr nr to chal) ............................................. 3.4

2759 Sea Plane **(69)** (bl) *(MajorWRHern)* 3-9-10 JWilliams (9) (lw: chsd ldr: led 5f out tl over 2f out: sn wknd) ............................................. 2½.5

2985³ Tempelhof (IRE) **(61)** *(JWHills)* 3-9-2 RHills (10) (led over 10f: 4th st: wknd over 2f out) ...................................................... 15.6

3041⁶ Lady Westgate **(26)** *(GBBalding)* 8-7-7 JQuinn (2) (bhd fnl 5f) ............................................ 6.7

3010* Temple Knight **(61)** *(CACyzer)* 3-9-2 DBiggs (1) (a bhd) ...................................................... 2½.8

2455 Mr Poppleton **(55)** *(DWPArbuthnot)* 3-8-10 TQuinn (6) (b.hind: lw: bhd fnl 4f) ... 6.9

331 Lady Poly **(39)** *(MissFSanders)* 4-8-6 GBardwell (7) (bhd fnl 4f) ............................................ 2½.10

LONG HANDICAP: Lady Westgate 7-2.

**9/4 Heavenly Waters, 9/2 IDEAL CANDIDATE, 5/1 Temple Knight, 6/1 Sharp Top(op 4/1), Tempelhof (IRE), 12/1 Sea Plane(op 6/1), 14/1 Mr Poppleton(op 8/1), 33/1 Ors. CSF £105.50, CT £798.01. Tote £5.90: £1.90 £6.30 £1.90 (£61.00). Mr T. O'Flaherty (EPSOM) bred by Lt-Col and Mrs D. Coker. 10 Rn**    3m 24.2 (5.2)
SF—37/6/26/22/29/6

---

**3220**    ST MARGARET'S BAY H'CAP (0-70) £2532.00 (£702.00: £336.00)    **5f**   4-20 (4-21)
(Weights raised 3 lb)

3042⁶ **Barbara's Cutie (35)** (v) *(MBlanshard)* 4-7-8⁽³⁾ ‡7AVery (9) (lw: a:p: led over 2f out: r.o wl) ...................................................... —1

3103² Little Saboteur **(55)** (Jt-Fav) *(PJMakin)* 3-9-5 TSprake (14) (lw: a:p: hrd rdn over 1f out: ev ch ins fnl f: r.o) ........................... ½.2

2936⁴ Call to the Bar (IRE) **(50)** *(CGCox)* 3-8-7 ‡7DWright (15) (a:p: hrd rdn over 1f out: ev ch ins fnl f: unable chal) ..................... 2.3

2599 Frimley Parkson **(32)** (bl) *(PHowling)* 8-7-12 JQuinn (1) (a.p: one pce fnl 2f) ..... 2.4

2949² Savalaro **(53)** (Jt-Fav) *(JFitch-Heyes)* 3-9-3 TQuinn (6) (lw: a:p: one pce fnl 2f) ½.5

3103 We're All Game **(60)** *(BCMorgan)* 3-9-10 DHolland (7) (nvr nr to chal) ............................. 5.6

2936 Castle Maid **(38)** *(RJHodges)* 5-7-11⁽³⁾ ‡7SDrowne (2) (lw: nvr nrr) ............................. s.h.7

2718 Tachyon Park **(29)** *(PHowling)* 10-7-9 DBiggs (11) (no hdwy fnl 2f) ...................................... 1.8

2989³ Coppermill Lad **(49)** (Jt-Fav) *(LJHolt)* 9-9-1 LDettori (4) (lw: outpcd) ....................... ½.9

3004 Doesyoudoes **(50)** *(DTThom)* 3-8-13 ‡7FArrowsmith (8) (outpcd) ...................... nk.10

2984 Form Mistress **(45)** (v) *(PTWalwyn)* 3-8-9 GCarter (13) (bhd fnl 2f) .................. s.h.11

2821 Wilco **(52)** *(AndrewTurnell)* 3-9-2 RHills (12) (lw: outpcd) ...................................... 1.12

2821 Barbezieux **(30)** (bl) *(TJNaughton)* 5-8-9 NAdams (4) (outpcd) ...................... 1½.13

3098⁶ Golden Proposal **(37)** *(MJBolton)* 3-8-1 DaleGibson (3) (lw: bhd fnl 2f) ............ 1.14

3065⁵ Fort Hope **(50)** (bl) *(TJNaughton)* 3-8-9 ‡5StephenDavies (16) (lw: led over 2f) 1½.15

2949 Red Verona **(40)** *(EAWheeler)* 3-8-4 SWhitworth (10) (outpcd) ...................... 1.16

**9/2 Savalaro, Little Saboteur(op 3/1), Coppermill Lad, 10/1 Wilco(op 6/1), 12/1 Form Mistress(op 8/1), 14/1 Red Verona, Doesyoudoes, Castle Maid, Call to the Bar (IRE), 16/1 We're All Game, BARBARA'S CUTIE, 20/1 Ors. CSF £85.92, CT £957.87. Tote £20.60: £3.10 £1.50 £2.70 £2.60 (£58.50). Mr Alan Fearn (UPPER LAMBOURN) bred by Pinfold Stud and Farms Ltd. 16 Rn**    60.2 sec (1.4)
SF—32/55/35/18/35/36

---

**3221**    LEVY BOARD H'CAP (0-70) £3101.00 (£861.00: £413.00)    **1½m**    4-50 (4-54)

2993³ **Day of History (IRE) (43)** *(CACyzer)* 3-7-9⁽²⁾ DBiggs (15) (2nd st: led over 1f out: drvn out) ...................................................... —1

2955² Rocquaine Bay **(41)** *(MJBolton)* 5-8-2 TSprake (10) (hdwy over 1f out: r.o wl ins fnl f) ...................................................... hd.2

2529⁴ Taylors Prince **(60)** *(Fav)* *(HJCollingridge)* 5-9-7 JQuinn (12) (lw: 4th st: hrd rdn over 1f out: r.o) ...................................................... ½.3

2921⁵ Prosequendo (USA) **(67)** *(MDixon)* 5-10-0 MPerrett (9) (lw: hdwy over 1f out: r.o) 1.4

2757 Arrastra **(51)** *(IABalding)* 4-8-12 JWilliams (1) (hdwy over 1f out: nvr nr to chal) nk.5

3021³ Miss Witch **(48)** *(HCandy)* 4-8-2 ‡7AntoinetteArmes (8) (led over 10f) ............... 5.6

2874 Scenic Dancer **(51)** (v) *(AHide)* 4-8-12 DaleGibson (4) (lw: nvr nr to chal) ...... 2½.7

2731⁵ Socks and Shares **(46)** (bl) *(PWHarris)* 3-7-12 NAdams (2) (lw: 3rd st: wknd over 1f out) ...................................................... 8.8

3073 Mayaasa (USA) **(63)** *(RWArmstrong)* 3-9-4 RHills (11) (6th st: wknd over 1f out) 7.9

3021 Island Blade (IRE) **(49)** *(RAkehurst)* 3-8-1 GCarter (6) (lw: hdwy over 3f out: 5th st: wknd over 1f out) ...................................................... 5.10

2853 Munday Dean **(60)** *(DWPArbuthnot)* 4-9-7 TQuinn (4) (b.hind: lw: prom 9f) ... 10.11

3021 Sulli Boy (NOR) **(41)** *(MissBSanders)* 7-8-2 GBardwell (3) (a bhd) ...................... 4.12

3025³ Neieb (USA) **(68)** *(HBanbury)* 4-9-9 LDettori (5) (prom over 9f) ...................... 6.13

2134⁵ Themeda **(70)** *(CRNelson)* 3-9-8 DHolland (14) (lw: prom 7f) ...................... 5.14

LONG HANDICAP: Day of History (IRE) 7-6.

**5/1** Taylors Prince, **11/2** Island Blade (IRE), **13/2** Miss Witch(4/1—7/1), Rocquaine Bay, **7/1** Prosequendo (USA), DAY OF HISTORY (IRE)(4/1—8/1), **9/1** Munday Dean(tchd 14/1), **10/1** Neieb (USA)(8/1—12/1), **12/1** Themeda(8/1—14/1), Scenic Dancer(op 8/1), **20/1** Arrastra, **25/1** Mayaasa (USA), Socks and Shares, **33/1** Sulli Boy (NOR). CSF £53.09, CT £236.61. Tote £10.90: £2.70 £2.90 £1.80 (£28.40). Mr R. M. Cyzer (HORSHAM) bred by Mount Coote Stud in Ireland. 14 Rn                                                 2m 38 (4.5)
SF—24/30/48/53/36/16

T/Plpt: £314.00 (7.9 Tckts).                                                                                  AK

### 3108a—BADEN-BADEN (L-H)
### Tuesday, September 1st [Soft]

**3222a**　　　OETTINGEN-RENNEN (Gp 3)　　£26408.00　　**1m**

2317a★ **Acteur Francais (USA)** *(France)* 4-9-2 SGuillot ........................................... —1
1100a★ Young Moon (bl) *(Norway)* 6-9-2 ABond ........................................... 1¼.2
2097a★ Irish Stew (GER) (bl) *(Germany)* 4-9-2 ATylicki ........................................... ½.3
2888a³ SURE SHARP (USA) *(BWHills)* 5-9-2 SCauthen (btn further 11¼l) ..................... 6
Tote 79DM: 24DM 43DM 17DM (SF: 1477DM). Mr Paul de Moussac (A.Fabre,FRANCE) bred by Marylands Stud in USA. 9 Rn                                                                 1m 43.1

### BADEN-BADEN (L-H)
### Wednesday, September 2nd [Soft]

**3223a**　　　JACOBS GOLDENE PEITSCHE (Gp 2)　　£33451.00　　**6f**

2851¹ **ELBIO** (bl) *(P.IMakin)* 5-9-3 JReid ........................................... —1
2976a★ TWAFEAJ (USA) *(BHanbury)* 3-8-7 DNaymond ........................................... 1.2
1983a★ Wedding of the Sea (USA) *(France)* 3-8-7 TJarnet ........................................... 1¾.3
2449★ ROCKY WATERS (USA) *(GLewis)* 3-8-11 BRouse (btn further 6¾l) ..................... 6
Tote 48DM: 21DM 23DM 17DM (SF: 347DM). Mr Brian Brackpool (MARLBOROUGH) bred by D.W.Samuel. 9 Rn
1m 12.9

### BADEN-BADEN (L-H)
### Friday, September 4th [Heavy]

**3224a**　　　MOET & CHANDON-RENNEN (Gp 2) (2-Y.O) £35211.00　　**6f**

2510a★ **SHARP PROD (USA)** *(LordHuntingdon)* 2-9-2 LPiggott ........................................... —1
2320a⁵ Glorieux Dancer (FR) *(France)* 2-9-2 MBoutin ........................................... ¾.2
Nasr Allah (USA) *(Germany)* 2-9-2 DIlic ........................................... 1.3
2845⁵ SON PARDO *(RHannon)* 2-9-2 JReid ........................................... 1½.4
Tote 44DM: 25DM 30DM (SF: 236DM). The Queen (WEST ILSLEY) bred by The Queen in USA. 6 Rn  1m 17.1

### BADEN-BADEN (L-H)
### Sunday, September 6th [Heavy]

**3225a**　　　GROSSER PREIS VON BADEN (Gp 1)　　£105634.00　　**1½m**

2504a² **MASHAALLAH (USA)** *(JHMGosden)* 4-9-6 JReid ........................................... —1
2894a★ Platini (GER) *(Germany)* 3-8-9 MRimmer ........................................... 1¼.2
2796² SAPIENCE *(DRCElsworth)* 6-9-6 WCarson ........................................... 1½.3
Tote 70DM: 23DM 14DM (SF: 212DM). Sheikh Ahmed Al Maktoum (NEWMARKET) bred by W.S.Farish, W.T.Carter, & E.J.Hudson Jnr in USA. 5 Rn                                           2m 37.8

### 3113a—CURRAGH (R-H)
### Saturday, September 5th [Soft]
Going Allowance: 0.75 sec per fur (S)

**3226a**　　　TRUSTED PARTNER MATRON STKS (Gp 3) (F & M) £13435.00　　**1m**

2911 **CLOUD OF DUST** *(JLDunlop)* 3-8-7 MRoberts (hld up: hdwy to chal over 2f out: led over 1f out: edgd rt: kpt on wl) ............................... —1
1462 SOIREE (IRE) *(BWHills)* 3-8-7 DHolland (hld up in rr: hdwy wl over 1f out: r.o fnl f: nt rch wnr) ........................................... 2.2
2888a⁵ Tarwiya (IRE) (bl) *(Ireland)* 3-8-11 RHughes (mid div: effrt 2f out: no ex fnl f: fin 4th, s.h: plcd 3rd) ........................................... 3

631 MUSICALE (USA) (Fav) *(HRACecil)* 3-9-0 MJKinane (a.p: ev ch 2f out: n.m.r over 1f out: btn whn hmpd fnl f: fin 5th, 2l: plcd 4th) ............. **4**
2888a² Gdansk's Honour (USA) (bl) *(Ireland)* 3-8-7 CRoche (led tl over 1f out: sn rdn & edgd lft: wknd fnl f: fin 6th, 2½l: plcd 5th) ............................. **5**
Winning Heart (bl) *(Ireland)* 5-9-1 KJManning (prom: chal 2f out: 2nd, rdn & no ex fnl f: wnt rt: fin 3rd, ½l: disq: plcd last) ............................. **0**
*Stewards Enquiry: Winning Heart disq. (interference to Musicale (USA) ins fnl f).*

**4/6** Musicale (USA), **7/2** Gdansk's Honour (USA), **6/1** Tarwiya (IRE), **8/1** Soiree (IRE), **9/1** CLOUD OF DUST, **20/1** Winning Heart. Tote £14.20: £6.50 £6.70 (£40.50). Miss Peggy Kwoh (ARUNDEL) bred by The Duke of Marlborough. 6 Rn
1m 44.5 (7.5)
SF—71/65/71/66/63/54

## 3227a
MOYGLARE STUD STKS (Gp 1) (2-Y.O.F) £81869.00 **7f**

1927* **SAYYEDATI** (Fav) *(CEBrittain)* 2-8-11 MRoberts (cl up: chal 2f out: led over 1f out: kpt on wl) ............................. **—1**
2132* BRIGHT GENERATION (IRE) *(PFICole)* 2-8-11 AMunro (prom: led over 2f out tl over 1f out: no ex) ............................. 1½.**2**
Alouette *(Ireland)* 2-8-11 KJManning (hld up: rdn over 2f out: no imp tl styd on ins fnl f) ............................. 1½.**3**
2445⁴ ANCESTRAL DANCER *(MBell)* 2-8-11 MHills (cl up: no hdwy fnl 2f) ............................. 1½.**4**
2864² NICER (IRE) *(BWHills)* 2-8-11 DHolland (swvd lft s: sn led: hdd over 2f out: sn rdn & btn) ............................. 2.**5**
Special Pageant (IRE) *(Ireland)* 2-8-11 CRoche (in rr: rdn ½-wy: no imp fnl 2f) . 3.**6**
2792 CITY TIMES (IRE) *(BAMcMahon)* 2-8-11 WJO'Connor (a in rr) ............................. 4.**7**
Babushka (IRE) *(Ireland)* 2-8-11 SCraine (mid div: rdn over 2f out: sn btn & bhd) 8.**8**
*2761a² Asema (USA) (9/1) Withdrawn (bolted bef s) : not under orders*

**11/10** SAYYEDATI, **5/2** Bright Generation (IRE), **9/2** Ancestral Dancer, **12/1** Nicer (IRE), **20/1** City Times (IRE), Babushka (IRF), Special Pageant (IRE), **25/1** Alouette. Tote £1.70: £1.20 £1.20 £4.80 (£1.90). Mr Mohamed Obaida (NEWMARKET) bred by Gainsborough Stud Management Ltd. 8 Rn
1m 31.5 (8.3)
SF—51/46/41/36/30/21

## 2507a—ARLINGTON PARK (L-H)
### Saturday, September 5th [Firm]

## 3228a
BEVERLEY D STKS (Grade 1) (F & M) £160428.00 **1m 1f 110y**

**Kostroma** *(America)* 6-8-11 KDesormeaux ............................. **—1**
2837 RUBY TIGER *(PFICole)* 5-8-11 TQuinn ............................. 1½.**2**
Dance Smartly (CAN) *(Canada)* 4-8-11 PDay ............................. nk.**3**
2624a⁴ Crystal Path (FR) *(MMoubarak)* 4-8-11 EFires (btn further 6¼l) ............................. **9**
Tote 7.00 (1-2) 4.40 5.80 (1-2-3) 3.00 3.40 2.60. W de Burgh, R.Sangster & Prestonwood Farm (G.Jones,AMERICA) bred by T. Stack & Valerio Ltd. 13 Rn
1m 54

## ARLINGTON PARK (L-H)
### Sunday, September 6th [Firm]

## 3229a
ARLINGTON MILLION (Grade 1) £319149.00 **1¼m (Turf)**

2627a⁴ **Dear Doctor** (FR) *(France)* 5-9-0 CAsmussen ............................. **—1**
Sky Classic (CAN) *(Canada)* 5-9-0 PDay ............................. hd.**2**
10* Golden Pheasant (USA) *(America)* 6-9-0 GStevens ............................. nk.**3**
2892a* Exit to Nowhere (USA) *(France)* 4-9-0 FHead ............................. 2¼.**4**
2440³ SECOND SET (IRE) *(LMCumani)* 4-9-0 LDettori (btn further 5l) ............................. **8**
2943* JOHN ROSE *(PAKelleway)* 3-8-8 GayKelleway (btn 24½l by wnr) ............................. **12**
Tote 29.80 (1-2) 10.60 3.80 (1-2-3) 6.80 2.80 5.60. Mr Henri Chalhoub (J.E.Hammond,FRANCE) bred by Amerigroup Leasing in France. 12 Rn
1m 59.8

## 2095a—LONGCHAMP (R-H)
### Sunday, September 6th [Soft]
Going Allowance: St: 0.10 sec per fur; Rnd: 0.25 sec per fur (G)

## 3230a
PRIX D'ARENBERG (Gp 3) (2-Y.O) £20640.00 **5f (st)**

**Zieten** (USA) *(France)* 2-8-9 SCauthen ............................. **—1**
2981a⁴ Wixon (FR) *(France)* 2-8-6 ESaint-Martin ............................. ¾.**2**

Ski Paradise (USA) *(France)* 2-8-6 TJarnet .................................................. 1½.3
Tote 1.60f: 1.10f 1.20f (SF: 4.50f). Sheikh Mohammed (A.Fabre,FRANCE) bred by Darley Stud Managemant in USA. 5 Rn
58.9 sec (1.9)
SF—67/61/55

**3231a** EMIRATES PRIX DU MOULIN DE LONGCHAMP (Gp 1) (C & F) £92879.00
**1m (Grande)**

2837² **ALL AT SEA (USA)** *(HRACecil)* 3-8-8 PatEddery (broke wl: a.p: 2nd st: qcknd
to ld over 1f out: hld on wl) ................................ —1
1456* Brief Truce (USA) (bl) (Jt-Fav) *(Ireland)* 3-8-11 MJKinane (hld up: 6th st: hrd
rdn & hdwy on outside over 1f out: styd on wl u.p) ............ nk.2
2892a⁵ Hatoof (USA) *(France)* 3-8-8 GMosse (mid div: 7th st: r.o fnl 2f) .................... 2½.3
2892a Misil (USA) *(Italy)* 4-9-2 RCochrane (prom: 4th st: r.o one pce fnl 2f) ............ 2.4
2892a Kitwood (USA) *(France)* 3-8-11 TJarnet (a mid div: 5th st: effrt 2f out: one pce) 1.5
2892a³ Cardoun (FR) (bl) *(France)* 3-8-11 DBoeuf (plld hrd: mid div: 8th st: effrt 2f out:
n.d) ......................................... ¾.6
2892a Take Risks (FR) *(France)* 3-8-11 MBoutin (hld up: 9th st: n.d) ...................... ½.7
1230a³ Shanghai (USA) *(France)* 3-8-11 ALequeux (a bhd: last st: n.d) ................... 2.8
Sharp Review (IRE) (Jt-Fav) *(Ireland)* 4-9-2 PShanahan (led over 6f: wknd qckly) 1.9
2892a El Prado (IRE) *(Ireland)* 3-8-11 LPiggott (chsd ldr over 5f: 3rd st: grad wknd) .. 4.10

2/1 Sharp Review (IRE), Brief Truce (USA), **29/10** ALL AT SEA (USA), **6/1** Kitwood (USA), **25/4** Hatoof (USA), **7/1** Cardoun (FR), **8/1** Shanghai (USA), **11/1** Misil (USA), **20/1** El Prado (IRE), **25/1** Take Risks (FR). Tote 3.90f: 1.60f 1.40f 1.70f (5.30f). Mr K.Abdulla (NEWMARKET) bred by Juddmonte Farms in USA. 10 Rn 1m 40.7 (3)
SF—79/81/70/72/64/62

1496a—**CAPANNELLE (R-H)**
**Sunday, September 6th [Good]**

**3232a** PREMIO ANIENE (listed race) (2-Y-O) £20930.00 **6f**

1496a **Mister Naif (USA)** *(Italy)* 2-8-10 LSorrentino ........................................ —1
2928² PIZZA CONNECTION *(JLDunlop)* 2-8-7 WRyan ..................................... s.nk.2
Pinta (IRE) *(Italy)* 2-8-4 VMessatesta ................................................. ¾.3
Tote 21L: 12L 13L 13L (45L). Scuderia Cieffedi (L.Brogi,ITALY) bred by Pine View Partners Inc. in USA. 8 Rn
1m 9.9

**FLORENCE (R-H)**
**Sunday, September 6th [Good]**

**3233a** PREMIO TOSCANA (listed race) (2-Y-O) £20930.00 **7f 110y**

2572* **VENTIQUATTROFOGLI (IRE)** *(JLDunlop)* 2-8-9 BRaymond ....................... —1
Zlata Husa (IRE) *(Italy)* 2-8-9 AHerrera ................................................ 2½.2
Campalto (IRE) *(Italy)* 2-8-9 OFancera .................................................. 2½.3
Tote 20L: 14L 41L 33L (148L). Gerecon Italia (ARUNDEL) bred by Kiltinan Inc. in Ireland. 12 Rn 1m 33

2989—**GOODWOOD (R-H)**
**Friday, September 11th [Good]**
Going Allowance: 0.45 sec per fur (Y) Wind: v.str half against

Stalls: low

**3234** ORIEL GROUP H'CAP (0-90) £3622.50 (£1080.00: £515.00: £232.50)
**1½m** 2-10 (2-14)

3116* **Green Lane (IRE) (85)** (bl) *(RCharlton)* 3-9-13 (5x) ‡⁵DHarrison (1) (lw: mde all:
rdn out) .................................................. —1
2992* Top Royal (79) (Jt-Fav) *(JLDunlop)* 3-9-12 TQuinn (5) (hdwy over 2f out: hrd
rdn over 1f out: r.o wl ins fnl f) ............................... nk.2
3097² Sheringa (70) (Jt-Fav) *(GBBalding)* 3-9-3 (5x) JWilliams (4) (5th st: hrd rdn
over 1f out: unable qckn) ..................................... 2½.3
2971 Rapporteur (USA) (67) *(CCElsey)* 6-9-9 JReid (2) (lw: 2nd st: r.o one pce fnl 2f) ½.4
2992 Debacle (USA) (75) *(GHarwood)* 3-9-8 AClark (3) (3rd st: hrd rdn over 1f out:
wknd fnl f) .................................................. 2½.5
2920² Majal (IRE) (78) *(BHanbury)* 3-9-11 RCochrane (7) (lw: 4th st: wknd 2f out) .... hd.6

2860 Cosmic Future **(65)** *(SPCWoods)* 3–8-12 BRouse (6) (6th st: hrd rdn over 3f
out: wknd over 1f out) ................................................ $3^{1}/_{2}$.**7**
3076 Fassfern (USA) **(74)** *(MrsJCecil)* 3–9-7 WRyan (8) (a bhd) ................................. **8.8**

**11/4** Sheringa, Top Royal, **9/2** GREEN LANE (IRE), **6/1** Cosmic Future, **15/2** Majal (IRE), **14/1** Rapporteur (USA),
**25/1** Ors. CSF £15.91, CT £34.97. Tote £4.40: £1.40 £1.10 £1.50 (£5.90). Lord Weinstock (BECKHAMPTON)
bred by Ballymacoll Stud Farm Ltd in Ireland. 8 Rn      2m 44.68 (12.98)
SF—37/35/21/26/20/22

## 3235

STARDOM STKS (listed race) (2-Y.O) £11355.00 (£3390.00: £1620.00: £735.00)
**1m**      2-40 (2-42)

3030* **Blush Rambler (USA) (100)** *(MRStoute)* 8-11 CAsmussen (4) (5th st: led over
1f out: pushed out) ................................................ **—1**
3070³ Nominator **(100)** *(RHollinshead)* 8-11 WRyan (3) (4th st: led over 2f out tl over
1f out: unable qckn) ................................................ **4.2**
2835* Woodchat (USA) **(100)** (Fav) *(PFICole)* 8-11 TQuinn (5) (lw: 2nd st: ev ch over
2f out: hrd rdn over 1f out: one pce) ................................ nk.**3**
3092⁵ Royal Roller (IRE) **(94)** *(CNAllen)* 8-11 RCochrane (2) (s.s: 6th st: wknd 2f out) 10.**4**
3063* Futurballa **(90)** *(JLDunlop)* 8-11 JReid (1) (lw: led over 5f) ................... $1^{1}/_{2}$.**5**
2903² Glowing Value (IRE) **(93)** *(JBerry)* 8-11 GCarter (6) (3rd st: wknd over 3f out:
t.o) ................................................ 30.**6**

**8/11** Woodchat (USA), **3/1** BLUSH RAMBLER (USA), **11/2** Futurballa, **16/1** Nominator(op 10/1), **20/1** Royal
Roller (IRE), **33/1** Glowing Value (IRE). CSF £34.85, Tote £4.10: £1.60 £2.80 (£18.90). Sheikh Mohammed
(NEWMARKET) bred by Holtsinger Inc in USA. 6 Rn      1m 43.55 (5.95)
SF—61/49/48/18/13/—

## 3236

COUNTRY GENTLEMEN'S ASSOCIATION H'CAP (0-80) £4699.75 (£1408.00: £676.50:
£310.75)   **1m 1f**      3-10 (3-15)

3137 **Hamadryad (IRE) (76)** *(WCarter)* 4–9-5 ‡⁵NGwilliams (12) (hdwy 2f out: led 1f
out: rdn out) ................................................ **—1**
3061⁵ Mr Tate (IRE) **(60)** *(RAkehurst)* 3–8-2 JFortune (9) (lw: 5th st: led over 1f out: sn
hdd: unable qckn) ................................................ **5.2**
2990³ Salbyng **(60)** *(JWHills)* 4–8-8 DHolland (3) (hdwy over 1f out: r.o wl ins fnl f) ... $^{1}/_{2}$.**3**
2856² Lady Lacey **(51)** (v) *(GBBalding)* 5–7-13 DaleGibson (11) (hdwy over 1f out: r.o) $^{1}/_{2}$.**4**
2999² Roseate Lodge **(72)** (Fav) *(RWArmstrong)* 6–9-6 RCochrane (2) (nt clr run over
2f out: gd hdwy over 1f out: fin wl) ................................ $^{3}/_{4}$.**5**
3054⁴ Tiger Shoot **(49)** *(DJSCosgrove)* 5–7-6 ‡⁵DHarrison (7) (lw: n.m.r over 1f out:
nvr nr to chal) ................................................ **2.6**
2880⁶ Sir Norman Holt (IRE) **(52)** (bl) *(FHLee)* 3–7-8 NAdams (13) (led over 7f) ......... hd.**7**
2999* Surrey Dancer **(75)** *(BHanbury)* 4–9-9 WRyan (4) (lw: hdwy 2f out: one pce) $^{1}/_{2}$.**8**
3066³ Absent Relative **(63)** *(MissBSanders)* 4–8-11 GCarter (14) (lw: no hdwy fnl 2f) .. **1.9**
2990 Royal Dartmouth (USA) **(53)** *(BRMillman)* 7–8-1 NCarlisle (1) (b: 6th st: wknd fnl
f) ................................................ **2.10**
Forge Bay **(49)** *(HJCollingridge)* 5–7-4⁽⁴⁾ ‡⁷CHawksley (4) (a mid div) ......... $1^{1}/_{2}$.**11**
2987² Fit on Time (USA) **(73)** *(MRStoute)* 3–9-1 CAsmussen (15) (lw: a mid div) ... **1.12**
2944⁵ Dr Zeva **(47)** *(MDixon)* 6–7-2⁽²⁾ ‡⁷DToole (8) (lw: nvr nrr) ................................. nk.**13**
1877 Cru Exceptionnel **(70)** *(PJMakin)* 4–9-4 GDuffield (5) (hdwy over 2f out: wknd
over 1f out) ................................................ $1^{1}/_{2}$.**14**
3021 Garachico (USA) **(66)** (bl) *(GHarwood)* 3–8-8 TQuinn (16) (lw: 4th st: wknd over
2f out) ................................................ 6.**15**
2707 Grand Vitesse (IRE) **(76)** (bl) *(RHannon)* 3–9-4 JReid (10) (2nd st: wknd over 2f
out) ................................................ **1.16**
2971 Smiling Chief (IRE) **(65)** *(CACyzer)* 4–8-13 DBiggs (17) (lw: prom over 5f) ..... 10.**17**
3009 Bentico **(64)** *(MAJarvis)* 3–8-6 JQuinn (18) (3rd st: wknd over 2f out) .............. $^{1}/_{2}$.**18**
LONG HANDICAP: Forge Bay 7-3, Dr Zeva 6-4.

**5/1** Roseate Lodge(tchd 10/1), **7/1** Fit on Time (USA), **8/1** Surrey Dancer, **10/1** Cru Exceptionnel, **12/1** Lady
Lacey, Salbyng(op 8/1), **14/1** Bentico, Absent Relative, Grand Vitesse, Tiger Shoot(10/1—16/1), **20/1** Mr
Tate (IRE), Royal Dartmouth (USA), Garachico (USA), Smiling Chief (IRE), **25/1** Sir Norman Holt (IRE),
HAMADRYAD (IRE), **66/1** Forge Bay, **200/1** Dr Zeva. CSF £386.78, CT £5,556.64. Tote £49.20: £8.20 £4.10
£2.30 £3.00 (£892.50). Miss Maha Kalaji (EPSOM) bred by P. Myerscough in Ireland. 18 Rn   1m 59.42 (8.72)
SF—31/–/3/–/11/–

## 3237

ABTRUST SELECT STKS (Gp 3) £18350.00 (£6880.00: £3315.00: £1455.00)
**1¼m**      3-40 (3-44)

3020³ **Knifebox (USA) (104)** *(JHMGosden)* 4–9-0 DHolland (1) (lw: mde all: hrd rdn
2f out: r.o wl) ................................................ **—1**
3138* Jeune **(113)** (Jt-Fav) *(GWragg)* 3–8-10 RCochrane (2) (lw: hdwy 2f out: r.o wl
ins fnl f) ................................................ $^{1}/_{2}$.**2**

2748² Party Cited (USA) **(103)** *(DRCElsworth)* 3–8–4 JWilliams (4) (6th st: rdn over 1f out: unable qckn) ............................................................................ 2.3
2891a⁴ Perpendicular **(118)** *(HRACecil)* 4–9-5 WRyan (10) (hdwy over 1f out: one pce) 1¹/₂.4
2622a⋆ Goofalik (USA) (Jt-Fav) *(JEHammond,France)* 5–9-3 CAsmussen (9) (lw: 5th st: hrd rdn over 1f out: one pce) ............................................ 1¹/₂.5
551 Environment Friend **(125)** *(JRFanshawe)* 4–9-0 GDuffield (8) (lw: 4th st: wknd 2f out) ............................................................................................ 2.6
3025⋆ Marcus Thorpe (USA) **(102)** *(PAKelleway)* 4–9-0 DBiggs (3) (b: nvr nr to chal) .. 1.7
2402⁵ Lucky Lindy (IRE) *(RHannon)* 3–8-7 JReid (6) (3rd st: wknd 2f out) ............... nk.8
2837 Bobzao (IRE) **(102)** *(WCarter)* 3–8-7 BRouse (7) (2nd st: wknd over 1f out) ....... 5.9
3020 Run Don't Fly (USA) **(100)** *(PFICole)* 6–9-0 TQuinn (5) (a bhd: t.o) ................. 25.10

**9/4** Goofalik (USA), Jeune, **11/2** Perpendicular, **7/1** Lucky Lindy (IRE), **11/1** Environment Friend, **16/1** Party Cited (USA), **25/1** KNIFEBOX (USA), Bobzao (IRE), **33/1** Run Don't Fly (USA), **66/1** Marcus Thorpe (USA). CSF £75.55, Tote £23.30: £3.90 £1.40 £2.30 (£22.90). Sheikh Mohammed (NEWMARKET) bred by Barbara Hunter in USA.
10 Rn                                  2m 12.54 (7.54)
SF–70/65/55/67/62/55

---

**3238**       ANNE FRANCES STEVENS MEMORIAL STKS (Mdn 3-Y.O) £2954.00 (£819.00: £392.00)
                **1m**                                      4-10 (4-15)

        **Fraam** *(AAScott)* 9-0 JFortune (1) (str: 4th st: led over 1f out: rdn out) ........ —1
3080⁴ Leif the Lucky (USA) *(WJarvis)* 9-0 RCochrane (2) (gd hdwy over 1f out: r.o wl ins fnl f) ................................................................................. 1¹/₂.2
440³ Barahin (IRE) (Fav) *(JLDunlop)* 9-0 JReid (12) (stumbled over 5f out: 5th st: rdn & nt clr run over 2f out: unable qckn fnl f) ............................ 6.3
        Cormorant Bay *(FHLee)* 8-9 WRyan (11) (b.nr hind: unf: hdwy over 1f out: one pce) ..................................................................................................... nk.4
2707 Lake Dominion **(60)** *(PWHarris)* 9-0 JQuinn (4) (6th st: hrd rdn over 1f out: one pce) ................................................................................................. 3.5
2538⁶ Stitched Up (IRE) *(PWChapple-Hyam)* 9-0 DHolland (8) (lw: led over 6f) ......... s.h.6
1025 Vernonia **(71)** *(JHMGosden)* 3-8-9 GDuffield (9) (3rd st: wknd over 1f out) ......... 2¹/₂.7
2995⁴ Concinnity (USA) *(LJHolt)* 9-0 AMcGlone (1) (nvr nr to chal) ...................... 2.8
        Emily Allan (IRE) *(KOCunningham-Brown)* 8-9 SWhitworth (13) (unf: bit bkwd: a mid div) ................................................................................. 1.9
        Our Man in Havana *(PFICole)* 9-0 TQuinn (3) (2nd st: wknd over 1f out) ... 4.10
        I'M Curious *(RThompson)* 8-9 JWilliams (6) (neat: bit bkwd: dwlt: a bhd) ...... nk.11
        Lloyds Dream *(DShaw)* 9-0 GCarter (5) (cmpt: bkwd: a bhd) .................. 7¹/₂.12
441 Nasseer *(PMitchell)* 9-0 AClark (7) (s.s: a bhd) .......................... 11¹/₂.13

**13/8** Barahin (IRE)(4/6—7/4), **7/2** FRAAM, **5/1** Leif the Lucky (USA), **7/1** Stitched Up (IRE)(op 9/2), **12/1** Our Man in Havana, **14/1** Vernonia(op 8/1), **16/1** Cormorant Bay, **20/1** Lake Dominion, **33/1** I'M Curious, Concinnity (USA), **50/1** Ors. CSF £21.25, Tote £6.20: £2.30 £1.70 £1.50 (£16.00). Maktoum Al Maktoum (NEWMARKET) bred by Gainsborough Stud Management Ltd. 13 Rn              1m 44.80 (7.20)
SF–46/41/23/17/13/12

---

**3239**       HIGH WOOD CLAIMING H'CAP (0-70) £2658.00 (£738.00: £354.00)
                **1m**                                      4-45 (4-49)

                           (Weights raised 8 lb)
2952³ **Broad Appeal (39)** *(RCSpicer)* 4–8-0 ‡5DHarrison (10) (hdwy 2f out: led over 1f out: r.o wl) ............................................................................. —1
3140³ Keep Your Word **(53)** *(GBBalding)* 6–9-5 JWilliams (17) (gd hdwy over 1f out: r.o wl ins fnl f) ............................................................................. 3¹/₂.2
2881⁵ Lucky Noire **(58)** *(GHarwood)* 4–9-10 AClark (3) (b: lw: hdwy over 3f out: rdn over 2f out: unable qckn) ......................................................... 2¹/₂.3
2954 Pearl Ransom **(46)** *(WGRWightman)* 5–8-12 GCarter (7) (rdn over 2f out: hdwy over 1f out: r.o wl) ................................................................. ³/₄.4
3037 Nawwar **(52)** *(CJBenstead)* 8–9-4 RCochrane (16) (lw: hdwy over 1f out: r.o) ... ¹/₂.5
3140² Breezed Well **(53)** *(CNAllen)* 6–8-12 ‡7GForster (11) (hld up: nt clr run over 2f out: hrd rdn over 1f out: one pce) .................................. s.h.6
3045³ Salinger **(47)** *(JWHills)* 4–8-13 SDawson (2) (a.p: led over 3f out tl over 1f out: sn wknd) ................................................................................... 1.7
3024 Foolish Touch **(54)** *(WJMusson)* 10–9-6 JReid (5) (b: hdwy over 1f out: nvr nrr) ³/₄.8
3002 Dawn's Delight **(35)** (v) *(KTIvory)* 14–8-1 GBardwell (8) (b: b.hind: a mid div) .... 2.9
3037³ Kissavos **(50)** *(CCElsey)* 6–9-2 TRogers (1) (6th st: wknd over 1f out) .......... s.h.10
2865 Kelly's Kite **(31)** *(HJCollingridge)* 4–7-11 JQuinn (15) (a mid div) ................ 1¹/₂.11
1911 Mofador (GER) **(47)** (v) *(FHLee)* 8–8-13 TyroneWilliams (9) (b: 5th st: wknd over 2f out) ................................................................................. 8.12
2885 Front Page **(50)** (Fav) *(JAkehurst)* 5–9-2 SWhitworth (6) (3rd st: wknd over 1f out) ..................................................................................... ¹/₂.13
*2786* First Flush **(31)** *(KTIvory)* 6–7-11 DaleGibson (12) (b: 2nd st: wknd over 2f out) 6.14

2807 Ryewater Dream **(47)** *(RJHodges)* 4–8-6 ‡⁷SDrowne (4) (led 1f: wknd over 2f out) ............................................................................................................. hd.**15**

　　Heroes Sash (USA) **(55)** *(AMoore)* 7–9-7 NAdams (13) (bhd fnl 3f) ................ ³/₄.**16**

2935 Jarzon Dancer **(42)** (bl) *(DAWilson)* 4–8-8 GDuffield (14) (led over 4f: 4th st: wknd over 2f out) ............................................................................................... 3.**17**

**100/30** Front Page(7/1–3/1), **6/1** Keep Your Word, **8/1** Breezed Well, **9/1** Foolish Touch, **10/1** Nawwar, Kissavos(8/1—12/1), **12/1** Salinger(op 8/1), Lucky Noire(op 8/1), **14/1** Kelly's Kite(op 8/1), BROAD APPEAL(op 8/1), **16/1** Mofador (GER)(op 10/1), **20/1** Pearl Ransom, Jarzon Dancer, Ryewater Dream, **33/1** Ors. CSF £94.76, CT £967.89. Tote £16.70: £3.00 £1.60 £1.70 £9.00 (£31.70). Mr John Purcell (SPALDING) bred by A. W. J. Perry. 17 Rn　　　　　　　　　　　　　　　　　　　　　　　　　　　　　1m 44.28 (6.68)

SF—40/48/45/31/35/28

**3240**　　CARNES SEAT STKS (Mdn 2-Y.O) £3174.50 (£882.00: £423.50)　　**6f**　　5-20 (5-25)

3005³ **Rain Brother (USA)** (Fav) *(PWChapple-Hyam)* 9-0 DHolland (16) (lw: mde all: hrd rdn over 1f out: r.o wl) ........................................................................................ —**1**

　　Desert Venus *(BHanbury)* 8-9 WRyan (14) (leggy: lt-f: a.p: ev ch ins fnl f: r.o) .... 1.**2**

2799 Law Commission *(DRCElsworth)* 9-0 JWilliams (4) (hld up: swtchd rt over 2f out: ev ch ins fnl f: r.o) ....................................................................................... s.h.**3**

　　Nabjelsedr *(CJBenstead)* 9-0 GDuffield (5) (leggy: hld up: swtchd rt over 2f out: one pce) ........................................................................................................... 3¹/₂.**4**

2884² Esthal (IRE) *(RJHodges)* 8-7 ‡⁷SDrowne (15) (a.p: one pce fnl 2f) ................ 2¹/₂.**5**

2799 My Harvinski *(PWChapple-Hyam)* 9-0 SWhitworth (1) (nvr nr to chal) ............. ¹/₂.**6**

　　Hard Eight *(ACStewart)* 9-0 JQuinn (12) (unf: bit bkwd: no hdwy fnl 2f) .......... s.h.**7**

2746² Midwinter Dream *(DRCElsworth)* 8-7 ‡⁷JHunter (9) (hld up: nvr nrr) ................. 1.**8**

2884⁵ Bonita Bee **(67)** *(LJHolt)* 8-9 AMcGlone (7) (prom over 4f) ............................... 1.**9**

2826³ Show Faith (IRE) *(RHannon)* 9-0 JReid (11) (prom over 4f) ............................ 2.**10**

3047⁶ Sandswift *(RFJohnsonHoughton)* 8-9 RCochrane (6) (a mid div) ..................... s.h.**11**

　　Tickerty's Gift *(RHannon)* 9-0 BRouse (2) (str: outpcd) ...................................... ³/₄.**12**

　　Il Moro Di Venezia (IRE) *(JLDunlop)* 9-0 TQuinn (10) (unf: scope: bit bkwd: a bhd) ......................................................................................................................... 2¹/₂.**13**

　　Infantry Glen *(MDIUsher)* 8-9 MWingham (8) (cmpt: bkwd: bhd fnl 2f) ............ 1.**14**

　　Tell Mama *(HCandy)* 8-9 SDawson (13) (b.nr hind: w'like: a bhd) .................... 1¹/₂.**15**

　　Mauser *(JLDunlop)* 9-0 GCarter (17) (unf: scope: hdwy 3f out: eased whn btn over 1f out) ......................................................................................................... hd.**16**

3055 Delay No More *(PMitchell)* 9-0 AClark (3) (a bhd) ......................................... 17

**5/4** RAIN BROTHER (USA), **4/1** Desert Venus(op 7/4), **8/1** Esthal (IRE), **10/1** Law Commission, **14/1** Show Faith (IRE), **16/1** Midwinter Dream(op 10/1), Sandswift, **20/1** Il Moro Di Venezia (IRE), **33/1** Hard Eight, Mauser, My Harvinski, Nabjelsedr, **50/1** Ors. CSF £6.90, Tote £2.60: £1.60 £2.00 £3.30 (£4.80). Mr Luciano Gaucci (MARLBOROUGH) bred by Gainesway Thoroughbreds Ltd in USA. 17 Rn　　　　　　1m 15.77 (5.37)

SF—46/37/41/30/13/18

T/Trio: Race 3: Wnr & 2nd w any £27.80 (44.2 Tckts); Race 4: £58.60 (15.1 Tckts). T/Plpt: £179.40 (37.25 Tckts).

AK

# GOODWOOD (R-H)

## Saturday, September 12th [Good]

Going Allowance: 6f-10f: 0.20 sec; Rest: 0.05 sec per fur (G)　　　　Wind: slt across

Stalls: high

**3241**　　ANC 'EXPRESS DELIVERY' TROPHY (H'cap) (3-Y.O) (0-90) £7830.00 (£2340.00: £1120.00: £510.00)　　**1m**　　2-00 (2-04)

2795 **Risk Master (79)** *(CAHorgan)* 8-11 DHolland (5) (s.s: rapid hdwy over 1f out: led ins fnl f: r.o) ...................................................................................................... —**1**

3137 Vanborough Lad **(63)** *(MJHaynes)* 7-9 DBiggs (12) (hld up: hdwy 2f out: ev ch ins fnl f: r.o) .............................................................................................................. 1.**2**

3066★ Shrewd Partner (IRE) **(83)** *(DRCElsworth)* 9-1 TQuinn (9) (bmpd over 2f out: hdwy over 1f out: r.o ins fnl f) ......................................................................... 2¹/₂.**3**

2990⁵ Trooping (IRE) **(82)** *(GHarwood)* 9-0 AClark (8) (lw: hdwy over 2f out: led wl over 1f out tl ins fnl f) ............................................................................................ nk.**4**

3135⁴ Tiffany's Case (IRE) **(66)** (Fav) *(CAHorgan)* 7-7⁽⁴⁾ ‡⁵BDoyle (10) (bdly hmpd over 2f out: swtchd lft: r.o: nrst fin) ................................................................... ¹/₂.**5**

3145² Bold Boss **(89)** *(BHanbury)* 9-7 BRaymond (3) (swtg: 6th st: ev ch 1f out: nt qckn) ....................................................................................................................... 1¹/₂.**6**

2871★ Buzzards Bellbuoy **(71)** *(HJCollingridge)* 8-3 JQuinn (1) (led tl wknd wl over 1f out) ................................................................................................................................ ³/₄.**7**

3133⁵ Salisong **(70)** *(PFICole)* 7-9 ‡⁷JDSmith (2) (4th st: wknd over 1f out) .................. 1.**8**

2825³ Red Kite **(66)** *(MBell)* 7-9 ‡³FNorton (7) (bhr: 3rd st: wknd over 1f out) ......... s.h.**9**

3014 Hopeful Bid (IRE) (71) (RHannon) 8-3 GCarter (11) (lw: 5th st: wknd over 1f out) s.h.10
3014 Majboor (IRE) (88) (PTWalwyn) 9-6 RHills (6) (lw: 2nd st: wknd 2f out) ............. 2.11
3014 Our Occasion (72) (WJMusson) 8-4 PaulEddery (4) (a bhd) .................... ¹/₂.12

11/2 Tiffany's Case (IRE), 6/1 Bold Boss, 7/1 Shrewd Partner (IRE), Buzzards Bellbuoy, 8/1 Red Kite, 9/1 Salisong, 10/1 Trooping (IRE)(8/1—12/1), 12/1 Our Occasion, 14/1 Vanborough Lad, 16/1 Hopeful Bid (IRE), 20/1 Majboor (IRE), 33/1 RISK MASTER. CSF £358.09, CT £3,218.64. Tote £47.70: £9.60 £3.90 £2.00 (£305.30). Mrs B. Sumner (BILLINGBEAR) bred by Arthur E. Smith. 12 Rn
1m 42.74 (5.14)
SF—44/25/37/35/12/35

**3242**    HIGHLAND SPRING/ROA NURSERY    £4175.00 (£1250.00: £600.00: £275.00)
7f      (Weights raised 3 lb)      2-30 (2-36)

3063⁵ **Kyrenia Game (64)** (PMitchell) 7-11 ‡3SO'Gorman (4) (lw: hdwy 2f out: swvd bdly lft ins fnl f: led last stride) ........................ —1
2903⁴ Brandonhurst (85) (Fav) (IABalding) 9-7 RCochrane (5) (hdwy 2f out: led ins fnl f tl last stride) ........................ s.h.2
2910 Aberdeen Heather (85) (DRCElsworth) 9-0 ‡7JHunter (12) (rapid hdwy over 1f out: ev ch ins fnl f: nt qckn) ........................ 1¹/₂.3
2695 Credit Squeeze (67) (RFJohnsonHoughton) 8-3 DHolland (9) (lw: led over 5f out: hrd rdn 2f out: hdd ins fnl f) ........................ 1.4
2973 Mr Butch (66) (MRChannon) 8-2 JQuinn (7) (6th st: r.o one pce fnl 2f) ........................ 4.5
3129³ Steppin High (68) (LordHuntingdon) 8-4 AMunro (8) (led over 1f: 3rd st: wknd over 1f out) ........................ nk.6
2994* Risk Proof (66) (KOCunningham-Brown) 8-2 GBardwell (4) (hrd rdn over 2f out: nvr nr ldrs) ........................ 2¹/₂.7
3029* Umbubuzi (USA) (79) (FHLee) 9-1 PaulEddery (3) (lw: 4th st: wknd 2f out) ........................ ¹/₂.8
3148² Muraadi Ana (IRE) (68) (AAScott) 8-4 JFortune (10) (2nd st: wknd over 2f out) ........................ ³/₄.9
2824 Formaestre (IRE) (64) (MHTompkins) 8-0 RHills (11) (5th st: wknd over 2f out) nk.10
3039⁵ War Requiem (IRE) (63) (GBBalding) 7-13 SDawson (0) (a bhd) ........................ 1.11
2910⁵ Exhibit Air (IRE) (80) (RHannon) 9-2 BRaymond (1) (bhd fnl 3f) ........................ 1.12

9/2 Brandonhurst, 9/1 Steppin High, 7/1 Exhibit Air (IRE), 8/1 Muraadi Ana (IRE), 9/1 Umbubuzi (USA), 10/1 KYRENIA GAME, 11/1 Aberdeen Heather(8/1—12/1), 12/1 War Requiem (IRE), 14/1 Formaestre (IRE), Risk Proof, Credit Squeeze, 20/1 Mr Butch. CSF £49.42, CT £459.60. Tote £13.90: £3.20 £1.90 £3.90 (£35.50). Mr G. V. Eliades (EPSOM) bred by George Eliades. 12 Rn
1m 31.39 (6.69)
SF—3/26/14/–/–/–

**3243**    LADBROKE RACING SPRINT H'CAP (0-110) £15530.00 (£4640.00: £2220.00: £1010.00)    6f      3-00 (3-06)

2997⁴ **Assignment (68)** (JFfitch-Heyes) 6-8-2 TyroneWilliams (16) (a.p: hrd rdn: edgd lft & led over 1f out: all out) ........................ —1
2997² Hard to Figure (93) (Fav) (RJHodges) 6-9-13 RCochrane (17) (gd hdwy over 1f out: ev ch ins fnl f: r.o) ........................ nk.2
2997* So Rhythmical (80) (GHEden) 8-9-0 AMunro (4) (b.off hand: swtg: hdwy over 2f out: ev ch whn hmpd over 1f out: r.o) ........................ 1.3
3183⁴ Fascination Waltz (71) (DShaw) 5-8-5 (4x) DBiggs (3) (a.p: led 2f out tl over 1f out) ........................ ³/₄.4
3182⁵ Green Dollar (92) (EAWheeler) 9-9-12 TSprake (18) (gd hdwy fnl 2f: nvr nrr) .. nk.5
3004* Araballajill (95) (RHannon) 3-9-9 ‡3RPerham (11) (nrst fin) ........................ ¹/₂.6
3006 Sunday's Hill (97) (v) (MBlanshard) 3-9-9 ‡5JWeaver (19) (no hdwy fnl 2f) ........................ ¹/₂.7
3067⁴ Running Glimpse (IRE) (75) (MissBSanders) 4-8-2 ‡7AntoinetteArmes (14) (gd spd 4f) ........................ hd.8
2997 Kayvee (93) (bl) (GHarwood) 3-9-10 AClark (13) (lw: prom over 4f) ........................ 2.9
2337⁵ Massiba (IRE) (90) (MJHeaton-Ellis) 3-9-7 TQuinn (15) (lw: racd alone far side: spd over 4f) ........................ ¹/₂.10
3103³ Ballasecret (87) (RDickin) 4-9-0⁽⁷⁾ ‡7DMeredith (2) (led 4f) ........................ hd.11
3031⁵ Crystal Jack (FR) (86) (FHLee) 4-9-6 PaulEddery (4) (n.d) ........................ 1.12
3120* Petraco (IRE) (78) (LJCodd) 4-8-12 DHolland (5) (spd over 3f) ........................ 1¹/₂.13
3002 Belfort Ruler (70) (BGubby) 5-8-4 JQuinn (9) (n.d) ........................ hd.14
3133 Hameem (IRE) (77) (bl) (AAScott) 3-8-8 BRaymond (8) (prom 4f) ........................ 2¹/₂.15
2787⁵ Memsahb (79) (JBerry) 3-8-10 JFortune (6) (lw: s.s: a bhd) ........................ 1.16
3006⁴ Red Rosein (93) (CaptJWilson) 6-9-13 GCarter (10) (b.off hind: n.d) ........................ ³/₄.17
3121 Mentalasanythin (85) (ABailey) 3-9-2 NDay (1) (swtg: n.d) ........................ 1.18
2997 Aughfad (91) (v) (TCasey) 6-9-8 ‡3FNorton (7) (lw: spd 3f) ........................ 7.19

9/2 Hard to Figure(tchd 7/1), 8/1 Fascination Waltz, 10/1 So Rhythmical, 11/1 ASSIGNMENT, 12/1 Petraco (IRE), 14/1 Running Glimpse (IRE), 16/1 Red Rosein, Araballajill, Green Dollar, Aughfad, Mentalasanythin, Kayvee, 20/1 Massiba (IRE), Hameem (IRE), 25/1 Crystal Jack (FR), Sunday's Hill, Belfort Ruler, 33/1 Ors. CSF £54.45, CT £473.15. Tote £13.00: £3.10 £1.70 £2.00 £2.30 (£18.50). Mr Alex Gorrie (LEWES) bred by Lord Porchester. 19 Rn
1m 13.11 (2.71)
SF—58/82/65/53/73/68

## 3244

SERVISAIR STAYERS' TROPHY (H'cap) (0-90) £3752.50 (£1120.00: £535.00: £242.50)
2m                                            3-30 (3-49)

3219* **Ideal Candidate (67)** (Fav) *(TJNaughton)* 3-7-9 (4x) DBiggs (7) (a gng wl: 4th
st: led 2f out: v.easily) ........................................................................ −1

3082⁶ Farat (USA) **(72)** *(JLDunlop)* 4-8-13 GCarter (6) (b: 3rd st: led over 3f out to 2f
out: no ch w wnr) ........................................................................ 2½.2

3046⁴ Puritan (CAN) **(75)** *(GHarwood)* 3-8-3 AClark (4) (2nd st: ev ch 3f out: r.o one
pce) ........................................................................ 5.3

3139 Rare Detail (IRE) **(70)** *(DRCElsworth)* 4-8-4 ‡⁷JHunter (9) (b: s.s: gd hdwy 2f
out: nvr nr to chal) ........................................................................ 2½.4

3128* Empire Blue **(68)** *(PFICole)* 9-8-9 TQuinn (1) (b: 6th st: no hdwy fnl 3f) ........ 1½.5

2373 Mrs Barton (IRE) **(59)** *(BWHills)* 4-8-0 DHolland (8) (led 8f out tl over 3f out) .... 5.6

2798⁵ Crystal Cross (USA) **(80)** *(IABalding)* 3-8-8 RCochrane (5) (7th st: no hdwy) .. s.h.7

Muse **(73)** *(DRCElsworth)* 5-8-7 ‡⁷RossBerry (11) (a bhd) ........................ 4.8

3046⁵ Smilingatstrangers **(55)** (v) *(MrsBarbaraWaring)* 4-7-3⁽³⁾ ‡⁷CHawksley (2) (a bhd) 5.9

2940³ Haitham **(88)** *(RAkehurst)* 5-9-3 ‡⁷LCarter (10) (led: wknd over 3f out) ....... 10.10

3046 Chucklestone **(70)** *(JSKing)* 9-8-11 PaulEddery (3) (led 8f) ....................... nk.11

LONG HANDICAP: Smilingatstrangers 7-4.

**9/4** IDEAL CANDIDATE, **13/2** Empire Blue, **7/1** Farat (USA), Puritan (CAN)(op 9/2), **8/1** Crystal Cross (USA),
**10/1** Smilingatstrangers, **12/1** Mrs Barton (IRE), Haitham, **14/1** Rare Detail (IRE), Chucklestone, **25/1** Muse. CSF
£26.90, CT £18.05. Tote £3.20: £1.90 £3.20 £2.40 (£23.90). Mr T. O'Flaherty (EPSOM) bred by Lt-Col and Mrs
D. Coker. 11 Rn                                       3m 30.57 (3.97)

SF−49/64/49/47/50/36

## 3245

BATTLE OF BRITAIN WESTHAMPNETT H'CAP (Amateurs) (0-70) £2763.00 (£768.00:
£369.00)   7f                                         4-10 (4-22)

2777² **Shaffaaf (USA) (63)** *(PDEvans)* 4-10-9 ‡⁵MrWMcLaughlin (14) (lw: gd hdwy
over 1f out: r.o wl to ld last strides) ........................................................ −1

2953⁴ Old Comrades **(53)** *(LGCottrell)* 5-9-13 ‡⁵MrDSalter (1) (hdwy over 3f out: led 2f
out tl fnl strides) ........................................................................ s.h.2

3037 Alnasric Pete (USA) **(46)** *(DAWilson)* 6-9-11 MrsJCrossley (9) (b: lw: wl bhd tl
rapid hdwy over 1f out: fin wl) ........................................................ ¾.3

3140⁵ Ballerina Bay **(56)** (v) *(DTThom)* 4-10-7 MissIDWJones (13) (b: gd hdwy over
1f out: ev ch wl ins fnl f: r.o) ........................................................ s.h.4

2969⁶ Nobby Barnes **(59)** *(DAWilson)* 3-10-6 MissJAllison (11) (b: hdwy over 2f out:
rdn over 1f out: one pce) ........................................................ 5.5

2570² Quinta Royale **(53)** *(WGMTurner)* 5-9-13 ‡⁵MrsJGault (5) (hdwy 2f out: styd on
one pce) ........................................................................ ½.6

2865² Bill Moon **(49)** *(PJFeilden)* 6-10-0 MissJFeilden (19) (lw: hdwy 2f out: nt rch ldrs) ¾.7

3105⁵ Judgement Call **(55)** *(PHowling)* 5-10-6 MissYHaynes (8) (b: lw: led over 5f out
to 2f out) ........................................................................ s.h.8

3185² Sunset Street (IRE) **(60)** *(SDow)* 4-10-6 ‡⁵MrTCuff (10) (b: hdwy & hmpd over 1f
out: nvr nr to chal) ........................................................ ½.9

2946 Mainly Me **(64)** *(PTWalwyn)* 3-10-6 ‡⁵MissATurner (12) (n.d) ........................ 1.10

2999⁶ Berlin Wall (IRE) **(70)** *(PWChapple-Hyam)* 4-11-2 ‡⁵MrsJChapple-Hyam (2)
(6th st: wknd 2f out) ........................................................ ½.11

2689⁴ Idir Linn (IRE) **(44)** *(DJGMurray-Smith)* 4-9-4 ‡⁵MissEFolkes (7) (5th st: wknd
over 1f out) ........................................................................ 2.12

3037² Chandigarh **(68)** (Fav) *(RLee)* 4-10-7 MrMArmytage (17) (3rd st: wknd 2f out) 3.13

3037* Spanish Love **(43)** *(CGCox)* 6-9-8 MissABillot (16) (prom over 3f) ............... 2.14

3065⁴ Paradise Forum **(57)** *(CAHorgan)* 3-9-13 ‡⁵MissDPomeroy (6) (n.d) ................ 2.15

3061⁴ Dream Carrier (IRE) **(68)** (bl) *(RHannon)* 4-11-0 ‡⁵MrRHannon (18) (n.d) ....... 3.16

3048* Jolto **(49)** *(KOCunningham-Brown)* 3-9-10 MissMJuster (15) (2nd st: wknd 2f
out) ........................................................................ 2.17

2945 Gabbiadini **(68)** *(MHTompkins)* 5-11-0 ‡⁵MrPPritchard-Gordon (20) (n.d) ..... s.h.18

2830 Sudanor (IRE) **(57)** *(MJHeaton-Ellis)* 3-9-13 ‡⁵MissFHaynes (3) (n.d) ............. ¾.19

3183 Pigalle Wonder **(48)** *(RJO'Sullivan)* 4-9-8 ‡⁵MrSGault (4) (led over 1f: 4th st:
wknd over 2f out) ........................................................ 2½.20

**5/1** Chandigarh, **7/1** Jolto, **8/1** Old Comrades(op 14/1), **9/1** Sunset Street (IRE), **10/1** Bill Moon, **12/1** Berlin Wall
(IRE), SHAFFAAF (USA), Spanish Love(op 8/1), **14/1** Ballerina Bay(op 8/1), Alnasric Pete (USA), **16/1** Pigalle
Wonder, Quinta Royale, **20/1** Dream Carrier (IRE), Judgement Call, Idir Linn (IRE), **25/1** Gabbiadini, Mainly Me,
Nobby Barnes, **33/1** Ors. CSF £105.35, CT £1,274.69. Tote £13.00: £3.10 £3.10 £3.00 £4.70 (£168.60). Mr R.
Cave (WELSHPOOL) bred by Maverick Production & Derry Meeting Farm in USA. 20 Rn    1m 31.11 (6.41)

SF−49/37/33/42/26/17

## 3246

FOXHALL CLAIMING STKS (3-Y.O) £2511.00 (£696.00: £333.00)    1¼m 4-40 (4-53)

3161⁴ **Lyn's Return (IRE) (56)** *(RSimpson)* 7-11 ‡⁵BDoyle (1) (lw: 4th st: led over 2f
out: r.o) ........................................................................ −1

2975a By Arrangement (IRE) (63) (RGuest) 7-3[(1)] ‡[7]CHawksley (5) (3rd st: r.o ins fnl f) 2.2
2869 Rampal (IRE) (GWragg) 8-7 RCochrane (4) (2nd st: ev ch 2f out: one pce) ...... 1½.3
25854 Simonov (77) (Fav) (GHarwood) 8-12 AClark (3) (b: led tl over 2f out) ............... ¾.4
30226 Aldavera (MDixon) 8-7 ‡[5]NGwilliams (6) (lw: 6th st: a bhd: t.o) .......................... 20.5
560 Canadian Boy (IRE) (DShaw) 8-4 DBiggs (7) (lw: 5th st: wknd over 3f out: t.o) .. 4.6
3043 Wild Poppy (45) (EAWheeler) 7-11[(4)] TSprake (2) (a bhd: last st: t.o) ............... 7.7

**11/8** Simonov, **15/8** By Arrangement (IRE), **100/30** LYN'S RETURN (IRE), **10/1** Rampal (IRE), **50/1** Ors. CSF
£9.72, Tote £4.50: £1.80 £1.70 (£5.30). Mr Rod Simpson (FOXHILL) bred by Hamwood Stud in Ireland. 7 Rn; By
Arrangement (IRE) clmd C Challis £8,565
2m 15.16 (10.16)
SF—2/–/5/8/–/–

**3247**          E.B.F. GOLDINGS STKS (Mdn 2-Y.O) £3106.00 (£928.00: £444.00: £202.00)
1m                                                                                      5-10 (5-21)

Palace Pageant (USA) (Jt-Fav) (IABalding) 9-0 RCochrane (3) (str: scope: 6th
st: led 2f out: rdn ins fnl f: r.o) ............ —1
Marastani (USA) (Jt-Fav) (GHarwood) 9-0 MPerrett (5) (w'like: scope: 5th st:
outpcd over 2f out: one pce) ................ ¾.2
Jizyah (HThomsonJones) 8-9 RHills (2) (cmpt: bit bkwd: 2nd st: led over 3f out
to 2f out) ..................... 4.3
Chouette (WJMusson) 8-9 PaulEddery (1) (scope: 3rd st: ev ch 2f out: sn
wknd) ................... hd.4
Acanthus (IRE) (JLDunlop) 9-0 TQuinn (6) (unf: scope: bit bkwd: led over 4f) .... 6.5
Flying Amy (RCurtis) 8-9 GBardwell (7) (leggy: scope: 4th st: wknd over 2f out) 1.6

**2/1** PALACE PAGEANT (USA)(11/10—9/4), Marastani (USA)(11/4—7/4), **11/4** Jizyah(2/1—3/1), **8/1** Acanthus
(IRE)(op 5/1), **25/1** Chouette, **33/1** Flying Amy. CSF £6.09, Tote £2.90: £1.90 £2.20 (£5.30). Mr Paul Mellon
(KINGSCLERE) bred by Paul Mellon in USA. 6 Rn          1m 48.78 (11.18)

T/Trio: Race 3 £82.90 (20.2 Tckts) & Race 4: £26.90 (37.2 Tckts). T/Plpt: £396.60 (21.6 Tckts).          H11

---

**3035—CHEPSTOW (L-H)**

**Saturday, September 12th [Soft]**
Going Allowance: 1.00 sec per fur (S)                                    Wind: slt half against

Stalls: high

**3248**          BRECON APP'CE STKS   £2469.00 (£684.00: £327.00)   1¼m 36y   2-15 (2-17)

30384 Juniper Berry (IRE) (87) (PWChapple-Hyam) 3-8-2 LNewton (7) (hld up: 4th
st: stdy hdwy 4f out: led 2f out: r.o wl) ..................... —1
3041* Athar (IRE) (52) (RJBaker) 3-7-9 ‡[7]RWaterfield (5) (w ldr: 2nd & carried wd st:
rdn & ev ch over 2f out: one pce) .......................... 8.2
2917* Pharly Story (95) (Fav) (MCPipe) 4-8-12[(1)] ‡[3]EHusband (4) (lw: 3rd st: rdn 3f
out: one pce) ................... 1½.3
2446 Tetradonna (IRE) (RHannon) 4-8-1 ‡[3]DGibbs (1) (lw: led: c wd st: hung lft & hdd
2f out: swvd bdly rt over 1f out: nt rcvr) ..................... nk.4
28236 Lady Marriott (LMCumani) 4-8-3[(6)] ‡[7]JCHarris (3) (poor 6th st: stdy hdwy fnl 2f:
nvr plcd to chal) ................. 1½.5
Celtic Banjo (JDRoberts) 7-8-1 ‡[3]TWilson (6) (bit bkwd: reluctant to r: a t.o) .... 15.6
Coney Dove (RJPrice) 7-8-1 ‡[3]PBowe (2) (bkwd: poor 5th st: t.o) ................... dist.7

**7/4** Pharly Story, **9/4** Tetradonna (IRE), **5/2** JUNIPER BERRY (IRE), **16/1** Athar (IRE), **20/1** Lady Marriott, **100/1**
Ors. CSF £31.12, Tote £4.10: £2.30 £2.70 (£20.30). Mr R. E. Sangster (MARLBOROUGH) bred by Swettenham
Stud in Ireland. 7 Rn          2m 19.4 (15.1)
SF—37/14/28/16/15/–

**3249**          CLEARWELL H'CAP (0-90) £3523.50 (£1053.00: £504.00: £229.50)
1¼m 36y                                                                2-45 (2-46)

(Weights raised 3 lb)
3060* Loki (IRE) (75) (GLewis) 4-9-3 ‡[7]BRussell (6) (swtg: hld up: 5th st: hdwy over 3f
out: swtchd over 1f out: led fnl f: rdn out) ..................... —1
3057* Statajack (IRE) (68) (bl) (Fav) (DRCElsworth) 4-9-3 SWhitworth (5) (hld up: last
st: hdwy 3f out: led over 1f out: sn hdd: nt qckn) ................. 2.2
31404 Elegant Friend (67) (MHTompkins) 4-9-2 PRobinson (4) (swtg: 4th st: rdn 2f
out: led 1f out: hdd & wknd ins fnl f) ................... 3.3
30613 Gachette (61) (JSutcliffe) 3-7-12 ‡[5]ATucker (3) (led over 8f: wknd fnl f) ............ 6.4
30625 Vanuatu (IRE) (58) (TThomsonJones) 3-8-0 NCarlisle (1) (3rd st: hrd rdn &
wknd over 2f out) ................... 5.5

2856³ Bowden Boy (IRE) **(69)** (bl) *(NACallaghan)* 4-9-4 WRyan (2) (2nd st: rdn 4f out: wknd over 2f out) .......... 2¹/₂.6

6/4 Statajack (IRE)(op 5/2), 4/1 LOKI (IRE), 5/1 Elegant Friend, 6/1 Gachette(4/1—7/1), Bowden Boy (IRE), 14/1 Vanuatu (IRE). CSF £9.99, Tote £3.50: £2.10 £1.40 (£3.00). Mr Michael H. Watt (EPSOM) bred by Abbey Lodge Stud in Ireland. 6 Rn
    2m 19.9 (15.6)
    SF—47/43/36/6/–/–

---

**3250**    TATTERSALLS AUCTION SERIES STKS (Qualifier) (Mdn 2-Y.O) £2616.00 (£726.00: £348.00)   **7f 16y**    3-20 (3-25)

**Surprise Surprise** *(HCandy)* 8-2 CRutter (5) (scope: bit bkwd: a gng wl: hdwy to ld on bit 2f out: sn clr) .......... —1
   Blue Nova (IRE) *(PWChapple-Hyam)* 8-12 SWhitworth (10) (w'like: bit bkwd: dwlt: sn rcvrd: led over 2f out: sn hdd: no ch w wnr) .......... 5.2
3036 Ample (IRE) *(PFICole)* 8-7 GHind (6) (hdwy over 1f out: r.o) .......... 6.3
3093⁵ Glimpse of Heaven (Fav) *(DRCElsworth)* 7-10 ‡5NKennedy (3) (prom: ev ch whn n.m.r over 2f out: sn wknd) .......... 1¹/₂.4
2802 Melisio **(50)** *(CPWildman)* 8-0 NCarlisle (2) (prom 5f) .......... 5.5
3055 Wickins (bl) *(GLewis)* 8-8 PRobinson (8) (led: sn clr: wknd & hdd over 2f out) .......... 2¹/₂.6
1715⁴ Junction Twentytwo **(58)** *(CDBroad)* 8-7⁽¹⁾ MWigham (9) (prom over 3f) .......... s.h.7
3093 Fast Fiesta *(MRChannon)* 7-9 ‡5ATucker (11) (rdn over 3f out: a bhd) .......... 5.8
2619⁶ Monday At Three (v) *(BRMillman)* 8-7 GBaxter (7) (prom over 3f) .......... 3.9
   Murphy's Hope (IRE) *(MJHeaton-Ellis)* 8-11 WRyan (1) (w'like: scope: prom 4f) .......... 1.10
   Shamrock Dancer (IRE) *(RJBaker)* 7-13⁽⁴⁾ ‡5RPrice (4) (str: bkwd: s.s: a wl bhd: t.o) .......... 8.11

9/4 Glimpse of Heaven(op 5/4), 9/2 SURPRISE SURPRISE, 6/1 Blue Nova (IRE)(op 3/1), 7/1 Ample (IRE)(op 4/1), 8/1 Murphy's Hope(6/1—10/1), 12/1 Junction Twentytwo, 20/1 Melisio, 28/1 Monday At Three, 33/1 Shamrock Dancer (IRE), Fast Fiesta, 40/1 Wickins. CSF £27.47, Tote £6.00: £2.10 £2.20 £2.30 (£10.40). Mrs J. E. L. Wright (WANTAGE) bred by Wheelersland Stud. 11 Rn
    1m 31.3 (10.8)
    SF—31/26/3/–/–/–

---

**3251**    HEATHER (S) STKS   £2952.00 (£822.00: £396.00)   **7f 16y**    4-00 (4-06)

3017★ **Prince Rooney (IRE) (61)** *(PButler)* 4-8-12 ‡7SDrowne (11) (lw: a.p: led 2f out: rdn out) .......... —1
2283⁶ Dorking Lad **(50)** *(MHTompkins)* 10-9-5 PRobinson (22) (gd hdwy over 1f out: hrd rdn fnl f: r.o wl) .......... ³/₄.2
2561 Sareen Express (IRE) *(MrsJCDawe)* 4-9-0 ‡5ATucker (10) (a chsng ldrs: r.o ins fnl f) .......... hd.3
3017² Red Sombrero **(59)** *(LGCottrell)* 3-8-10 NCarlisle (7) (a.p: ev ch 2f out: wknd fnl f) .......... 6.4
3074⁵ My Grain **(40)** *(RHollinshead)* 3-8-5 WRyan (19) (hdwy over 1f out: nvr nrr) .... nk.5
2209⁶ Just a Step **(77)** (Fav) *(MMcCormack)* 6-9-5 CRutter (5) (lw: prom tl wknd over 1f out) .......... nk.6
3180 Hubbers Favourite **(32)** (v) *(MrsNMacauley)* 4-8-9 BCrossley (4) (prom: led over 3f out to 2f out: wknd over 1f out) .......... 4.7
3067 Prince of the Sea (IRE) **(71)** *(DWPArbuthnot)* 4-9-0 ‡5RPrice (6) (nvr trbld ldrs) .. 2.8
2958 Long Lane Lady **(48)** *(JMackie)* 6-9-0 GHind (13) (prom over 4f) .......... 1¹/₂.9
3042 Jinsky's Jewel *(RThompson)* 4-8-7 ‡7TAshley (20) (swtg: n.d) .......... 1.10
2931 Galley Gossip **(35)** *(RBrotherton)* 3-8-10 GCrealock (1) (racd far side: a bhd) . 4.11
2941⁵ High Baccarat **(45)** (v) *(AJChamberlain)* 3-8-10 TRogers (3) (prom far side 4f) .. 2¹/₂.12
2644 The Last Washer (IRE) **(40)** *(RJBaker)* 3-8-10 NHowe (2) (s.s: a bhd) .......... 2.13
2950⁴ Abbey Green *(CJHill)* 4-9-0 SWhitworth (15) (lw: s.s: a bhd) .......... 1¹/₂.14
   Mr Smiley *(RJBaker)* 5-8-7 ‡7DWright (18) (bit bkwd: bhd fnl 3f) .......... 3¹/₂.15
2942 Fay Eden (IRE) **(36)** *(RJHodges)* 4-8-9 ‡5NKennedy (14) (n.d) .......... s.h.16
2087 Salmon Dancer (IRE) **(30)** *(MFBarraclough)* 3-8-3 ‡7MHumphries (8) (n.d) .......... ¹/₂.17
2882 Mcnab (IRE) *(CPWildman)* 3-8-5 ‡5RKutter (12) (t.o) .......... 5.18
2694 Rocky Bay **(40)** *(DHaydnJones)* 3-8-3 ‡7BRussell (16) (prom 4f: t.o) .......... ¹/₂.19
   Davamal *(JMBradley)* 3-7-12 ‡7MichaelBradley (9) (bhd fnl 3f: t.o) .......... 8.20
2974 Cronk's Quality **(36)** (bl) *(DCJermy)* 9-9-5 MWigham (17) (led over 3f: wknd qckly: t.o) .......... 6.21
   Singing Sarah *(JDRoberts)* 4-8-9 TLang (21) (bkwd: t.o) .......... 2.22

2/1 Just a Step(tchd 3/1), 13/2 Prince of the Sea (IRE)(3/1—7/1), 8/1 PRINCE ROONEY (IRE)(op 5/1), Red Sombrero, 9/1 Long Lane Lady, 12/1 Dorking Lad(op 8/1), 14/1 Abbey Green(op 8/1), My Grain, 20/1 Sareen Express (IRE), Fay Eden (IRE), Rocky Bay, High Baccarat, 25/1 Cronk's Quality, 33/1 Hubbers Favourite, 50/1 Ors. CSF £98.86, Tote £9.30: £2.90 £2.20 £7.90 (£46.40). Mr D. J. Perry (LEWES) bred by Miss E. C. Holdsworth in Ireland. 22 Rn; Bt in 4,000 gns
    1m 31.5 (11)
    SF—38/43/37/15/9/22

## 3252

RYEFORD STKS (Mdn 3-Y.O) £2406.00 (£666.00: £318.00)     **6f 16y**    4-30 (4-34)

1368[6] **Neither Nor (71)** *(RJHolder)* 8-9 JWilliams (5) (hld up: hdwy over 2f out: rdn wl
over 1f out: led ins fnl f: r.o wl) .................................................... —1

3080[2] Emir Albadou (USA) *(Fav) (MRStoute)* 9-0 WRyan (9) (a.p: led over 2f out: hdd
& nt qckn ins fnl f) .................................................................. 2.2

3048 Batchworth Bound (46) *(EAWheeler)* 8-9 SWhitworth (1) (a.p: rdn over 1f out:
ev ch ins fnl f: nt qckn) ........................................................... 1.3

3042[4] Casting Shadows (53) (bl) *(RDickin)* 8-9 NHowe (7) (led over 3f: r.o one pce) .. 2.4

2757 Vellandrucha (39) *(JABennett)* 8-9 NCarlisle (8) (sn pushed along: hdwy over
1f out: r.o) ................................................................................ ³/₄.5

3056[3] Pleasuring (57) *(MMcCormack)* 8-9 GBaxter (6) (b.nr hind: prom over 3f) ........ 4.6

2984 The New Girl (55) *(CCElsey)* 8-9 PRobinson (3) (prom over 3f) ..................... 1.7

Hall's Creek (IRE) (bl) *(DWPArbuthnot)* 8-9 ‡5RPrice (4) (str: b.hind: w ldrs over
3f) ........................................................................................... 5.8

3042[5] Join the Clan *(MrsJMacauley)* 8-9 BCrossley (2) (prom over 3f) .................... 2.9

3038 Seemenomore *(RJPrice)* 8-9 CRutter (10) (a bhd) ..................................... 3.10

**1/3** Emir Albadou (USA)(2/9—2/5), **6/1** NEITHER NOR(5/1—8/1), **20/1** Pleasuring, Casting Shadows, The New
Girl, **33/1** Join the Clan, **50/1** Hall's Creek (IRE), **66/1** Batchworth Bound, Vellandrucha, Seemenomore. CSF
£7.71, Tote £5.80: £1.50 £1.00 £6.20 (£2.50). Mr D. Tylden-Wright (BRISTOL) bred by D. Tylden-Wright. 10 Rn
1m 19.3 (10.3)
SF—9/6/–/–/–/–

## 3253

REDBROOK H'CAP (0-90) £3289.50 (£981.00: £468.00: £211.50)
**5f 16y**              5-00 (5-01)

3004 **Jigsaw Boy (72)** *(RJHolder)* 3-8-10 JWilliams (2) (bhd tl hdwy over 1f out: r.o
to ld cl home) ........................................................................... —1

3098 Fivesevenfiveo (73) *(RJHodges)* 4-8-6 ‡7SUrowne (4) (rdn over 2f out: hdwy fnl
f: r.o wl) .................................................................................... nk.2

3059★ Ashtina (67) *(Fav) (RJHodges)* 7-8-2 ‡5NKennedy (3) (led tl ct nr fin) ............. hd.3

2861 Baysham (USA) (76) (v) *(BRMillman)* 6-8-11 ‡5RPrice (1) (a chsng ldrs: r.o ins
fnl f) ........................................................................................ nk.4

3015 Metal Boys (84) *(RHollinshead)* 5-9-3 ‡7SWynne (5) (a chsng ldrs: styd on fnl f) 1.5

3098[★] Bells of Longwick (68) (v) *(DRLaing)* 3-8-6 TyroneWilliams (7) (chsd ldr: eased
whn btn ins fnl f) ..................................................................... 5.6

3059 Miami Banker (59) *(PHowling)* 6-7-13 CRutter (8) (spd over 2f) .................... hd.7

3098 Noble Power (IRE) (71) *(BPalling)* 3-8-9 WRyan (6) (a bhd) ......................... 6.8

3103 Jess Rebec (54) *(LGCottrell)* 4-7-8(1) NCarlisle (9) (hdwy 3f out: hrd rdn &
wknd wl over 1f out) ................................................................ 4.9

LONG HANDICAP: Jess Rebec 7-5.

**3/1** Ashtina, **7/2** Bells of Longwick, **9/2** Baysham (USA)(3/1—5/1), **6/1** JIGSAW BOY, **12/1** Noble Power
(IRE)(op 8/1), Miami Banker, Metal Boys(op 8/1), **16/1** Fivesevenfiveo(op 10/1), **20/1** Jess Rebec. CSF £78.12,
CT £307.49. Tote £7.00: £2.10 £2.40 £1.90 (£43.00). All Eight Club (BRISTOL) bred by Mrs J. A. Rawding. 9 Rn
64.5 sec (7.5)
SF—46/41/36/44/46/15

T/Plpt: £257.20 (9.2 Tckts).                                             KH

## 2712—**BATH (L-H)**

### Monday, September 14th [Good]

Going Allowance: 5f 161y: 0.40 sec; Rest 0.10 sec per fur (G)      Wind: mod against

Stalls: low

## 3254

AUTUMN (S) H'CAP (3 & 4-Y.O) (0-60) £2740.00 (£765.00: £370.00)
**1m 5y**                2-00 (2-04)

3052 **Seaside Minstrel (52)** *(Fav) (CJHill)* 4-9-10 WCarson (9) (gd hdwy 2f out: str
run fnl f: led last strides) ......................................................... —1

2705[3] Bel Baraka (IRE) (53) *(DRCElsworth)* 3-9-6 JWilliams (18) (hdwy 3f out: led wl
over 1f out: hrd rdn fnl f: hdd last strides) ............................... hd.2

1004[6] Time Lapse (57) *(PJMakin)* 3-9-10 PatEddery (14) (outpcd: plld out & rapid
hdwy over 1f out: fin wl) ........................................................... 1.3

3101[3] Chloes Diamond (IRE) (43) *(JLSpearing)* 4-8-12 ‡3EmmaO'Gorman (11) (hdwy
3f out: ev ch wl over 1f out: unable qckn) ................................ nk.4

3105 Sunley Sparkle (42) *(DRGandolfo)* 4-9-0 TQuinn (16) (lw: rdn & hdwy over 2f
out: one pce fnl f) .................................................................. 1¹/₂.5

3180[4] Amazon Express (52) (bl) *(CEBrittain)* 3-9-5 MRoberts (3) (rdn over 3f out:
n.m.r 2f out: nvr nr to chal) ..................................................... 2¹/₂.6

3180⁵ Breakdancer (IRE) **(50)** *(WRMuir)* 3-9-0 ‡³RPerham (4) (2nd st: led 3f out tl wl over 1f out: wknd fnl f) .................. 1.**7**

3043⁴ Rockbourne **(53)** *(WGMTurner)* 3-9-6 TSprake (17) (lw: 5th st: wknd over 2f out) 5.**8**

2952 Litmore Dancer **(43)** *(JMBradley)* 4-8-8 ‡⁷MichaelBradley (6) (a mid div) .......... nk.**9**

2712 Grey But Rosy (IRE) **(49)** *(PMMcEntee)* 3-8-9 ‡⁷PBowe (5) (carried rt wl over 1f out: a mid div) .................... ½.**10**

2993 Lamore Ritorna **(49)** *(KOCunningham-Brown)* 3-9-0 SWhitworth (10) (4th st: wknd 3f out) ...................... 3.**11**

3003⁶ Winged Whisper (USA) **(57)** *(CASmith)* 3-9-0 MWigham (7) (s.i.s: rdn 4f out: a bhd) ....................... nk.**12**

891 Victor Romeo **(50)** *(RCSpicer)* 3-8-12 ‡⁵DHarrison (1) (prom over 3f) ......... 3½.**13**

3048 Buddy (IRE) **(49)** (bl) *(MBell)* 3-9-2 JCarroll (3) (led over 5f out to 3f out: wknd 2f out) .................... 1½.**14**

3159 Sally Fast **(47)** (bl) *(BPalling)* 3-9-0 DHolland (15) (bhd fnl 3f) ............ 1.**15**

Coochie **(47)** *(RJBaker)* 3-9-0 NHowe (13) (bit bkwd: a wl bhd) ........... 1.**16**

3003 Walkonthemoon **(47)** (bl) *(MMcCormack)* 3-9-0 JFortune (8) (6th st: wknd over 3f out) ...................... 1½.**17**

594 Corley Flower **(46)** *(PDCundell)* 3-8-13 LDettori (12) (led over 2f: 3rd st: wknd 3f out) ...................... 4.**18**

**100/30 SEASIDE MINSTREL, 4/1 Amazon Express, 15/2 Rockbourne, 9/1 Bel Baraka (IRE), 10/1 Time Lapse, Chloes Diamond (IRE), 14/1 Buddy (IRE), Breakdancer (IRE), 20/1 Sally Fast, 25/1 Grey But Rosy (IRE), Lamore Ritorna, Litmore Dancer, 33/1 Victor Romeo, Winged Whisper (USA), Walkonthemoon, Sunley Sparkle, 66/1 Ors. CSF £32.02, CT £258.02. Tote £3.90: £1.40 £2.50 £2.90 £2.20 (£13.40). Mr C. John Hill (BARNSTAPLE) bred by J. S. Bell. 18 Rn; No bid** 1m 45.9 (6.6)
SF–23/18/19/6/3/–

**3255** E.B.F. TORMARTON STKS (I) (Mdn 2-Y.O) £2840.00 (£790.00: £380.00)
5f 161y 2-30 (2-33)

3008² **Pluck** (Fav) *(RCharlton)* 8-9 PatEddery (8) (hld up: led wl over 1f out: pushed out) .................... —1

Landrail (USA) *(BWHills)* 8-9 DHolland (7) (unf: scope: lost pl over 2f out: rallied 1f out: r.o) ...................... 2.**2**

2897 Legal Risk **(58)** *(DHaydnJones)* 8-9 MRoberts (3) (w ldrs: ev ch 2f out: unable qckn fnl f) ...................... nk.**3**

3012 Kennedys Prima **(76)** *(AAScott)* 8-9 JFortune (2) (chsd ldr: led 2f out: sn hdd: wknd fnl f) ...................... 2½.**4**

2832 Recit D'Argent **(47)** *(CJames)* 9-0 DaleGibson (5) (no hdwy fnl 2f) ......... 3½.**5**

3051⁶ Melodys Daughter *(RFJohnsonHoughton)* 8-9 GDuffield (1) (led over 3f) ........ 2½.**6**

2675 Court Pianist (IRE) *(SMHillen)* 9-0 JLowe (10) (bhd fnl 3f) .............. 2.**7**

Duveen (IRE) *(CRNelson)* 9-0 PaulEddery (4) (str: scope: bkwd: s.s: a wl bhd) . 5.**8**

Sparky's Girl *(RJBaker)* 8-9 NHowe (9) (leggy: unf: bit bkwd: t.o fnl 3f) ........... 30.**9**

2826 Lughnasa (66/1) Withdrawn (lame at s) : not under orders

**2/5 PLUCK, 11/2 Landrail (USA)(op 7/2), 8/1 Kennedys Prima, 14/1 Duveen (IRE)(10/1—16/1), 20/1 Legal Risk, Melodys Daughter, 50/1 Court Pianist (IRE), 66/1 Ors. CSF £3.55, Tote £1.40: £1.10 £1.60 £1.80 (£2.60). Lord Derby (BECKHAMPTON) bred by Exors of the late Lady Derby. 9 Rn** 1m 15.5 (6.2)
SF–17/9/8/–/–/–

**3256** VICTORIA HOUSE H'CAP (0-80) £3406.75 (£1024.00: £494.50: £229.75)
1m 3f 144y 3-00 (3-05)
(Weights raised 4 lb)

2971³ **Princess Moodyshoe** **(61)** *(MCPipe)* 4-9-2 MRoberts (16) (3rd st: led over 1f out: comf) .................... —1

2971⁶ Sword Master **(72)** *(BobJones)* 3-9-4 NDay (15) (lw: led 1f: 2nd st: led over 2f out tl over 1f out: unable qckn) ............... 2½.**2**

2401⁶ Good for a Loan **(64)** *(RLee)* 5-9-5 JWilliams (20) (hdwy 5f out: 5th st: hrd rdn 2f out: r.o ins fnl f) .................. hd.**3**

3021 Full Quiver **(50)** (v) *(MrsBarbaraWaring)* 7-8-5 NHowe (10) (lw: hdwy over 2f out: hrd rdn wl over 1f out: r.o) ........... ½.**4**

2917⁴ Bronze Runner **(38)** (bl) *(EAWheeler)* 8-7-0 ‡⁷AntoinetteArmes (14) (in rr 6f: gd hdwy over 2f out: r.o) ................ ½.**5**

3057⁵ Blazon of Troy **(64)** *(TThomsonJones)* 3-8-10 TQuinn (17) (lw: 4th st: one pce fnl 2f) ...................... 1.**6**

2934 Captain My Captain (IRE) **(43)** *(RBrotherton)* 4-7-7⁽⁵⁾ ‡⁵DHarrison (18) (hdwy 4f out: hrd rdn 2f out: one pce) ......... 2.**7**

2734 Castillet **(76)** *(GHarwood)* 3-9-8 AClark (4) (hdwy over 2f out: rdn wl over 1f out: sn wknd) .................... 4.**8**

2305 Sky Train **(69)** *(JLDunlop)* 3-9-1 AMunro (13) (swtg: a abt same pl) ....... 1½.**9**

2955⁴ Moon Spin **(68)** *(MajorWRHern)* 3-9-0 WCarson (2) (no hdwy fnl 3f) ........... s.h.**10**

573 Eleganza (IRE) **(70)** *(SMHillen)* 3-9-2 JLowe (8) (a mid div) ............... 8.**11**

2370★ Resounding Success (IRE) **(72)** (Fav) *(BWHills)* 3-9-4 PatEddery (6) (6th st: wknd over 3f out) ................... 1½.**12**

30412 Al Skeet (USA) (43) (RJPrice) 6-7-5(5) ‡7CHawksley (3) (lw: bhd fnl 5f) ............ 5.13
3114 Farmer's Fire (IRE) (55) (CFWall) 3-8-1(2) GDuffield (9) (b: wl bhd fnl 8f) ............ 5.14
13243 Modesto (USA) (66) (KOCunningham-Brown) 4-9-7 SWhitworth (19) (b: led
     after 1f tl wknd over 2f out) ............................................. ¾.15
27514 Sandro (51) (bl) (RJBaker) 3-7-11 DaleGibson (5) (prom tl 7th & wkng st) ..... 10.16
18825 Judge and Jury (59) (bl) (MJFetherston-Godley) 3-8-5 DHolland (1) (bhd fnl 4f) 5.17
3022 River Hawk (50) (RFJohnsonHoughton) 3-7-10 GBardwell (7) (prom 6f) ..... 1½.18
    Tonkawa (69) (JMBradley) 7-9-10 NAdams (11) (b: bkwd: s.s: a wl bhd) .... s.h.19
2935 Uncertain (45) (DHaydnJones) 4-7-7(7) ‡7CAvery (12) (bit bkwd: t.o fnl 4f) ..... 25.20
    LONG HANDICAP: Bronze Runner 7-1, Al Skeet (USA) 7-2, Uncertain 7-2.

**9/2** Resounding Success (IRE), **11/2** PRINCESS MOODYSHOE, **7/1** Blazon of Troy(5/1—8/1), **8/1** Moon Spin, **12/1** Good for a Loan, **14/1** Sword Master, Modesto (USA), Judge and Jury, Eleganza (IRE), Sky Train (IRE), **16/1** Full Quiver, Castillet, **20/1** Bronze Runner, Al Skeet (USA), Captain My Captain (IRE), **33/1** Farmer's Fire (IRE), **40/1** Sandro, River Hawk, **66/1** Ors. CSF £78.45, CT £838.64. Tote £5.00: £1.60 £3.20 £2.80 £3.90 (£48.90). Mrs Alison C. Farrant (WELLINGTON) bred by Mrs E. Allwood and Mrs A. C. Farrant. 20 Rn    2m 33.4 (6.7)
                                                                      SF—46/43/43/28/8/30

---

**3257**     GWR FM RADIO H'CAP (0-70) £3270.25 (£982.00: £473.50: £219.25)
         **5f 161y**                                                          3-30 (3-36)

30676 **Divine Pet (60)** (WGRWightman) 7-9-4 JWilliams (2) (lw: outpcd: rapid hdwy
     over 1f out: str run fnl f: led nr fin) ..................................... —1
29363 Banbury Flyer (46) (Fav) (MrsALMKing) 4-8-4 MRoberts (11) (lw: hdwy 2f out:
     hrd rdn & ev ch ins fnl f: r.o) ........................................... ¾.2
30984 John O'Dreams (39) (MrsJCDawe) 7-7-11 JLowe (10) (a.p: ev ch ins fnl f: r.o) hd.3
2718* Mister Jolson (55) (RJHodges) 3-8-10 RCochrane (17) (lw: led over 2f out: hrd
     rdn fnl f: ct nr fin) ...................................................... s.h.4
2752 Cee-En-Cee (60) (bl) (MMcCourt) 8-9-13 TQuinn (14) (mid div whn hrd rdn
     over 2f out: r.o wl ins fnl f) ............................................. 1.5
3183 Gallant Hope (54) (bl) (LGCottrell) 10-8-12 NCarlisle (18) (a.p: rdn 2f out:
     unable qckn fnl f) ....................................................... s.h.6
3048 Ceatharlach (42) (bl) (RJHolder) 3-7-11 NAdams (3) (hrd rdn & hdwy over 1f
     out: one pce fnl f) ...................................................... ¾.7
3103* Cranfield Comet (65) (JBerry) 3-9-6 JCarroll (19) (a.p: ev ch 2f out: wknd fnl f) 1.8
3042* Honey Seeker (62) (TThomsonJones) 3-9-3 PaulEddery (1) (lw: nt clr run 2f
     out: nvr nrr) ............................................................ ¾.9
2617 Ben Bluff (46) (LGCottrell) 3-7-10 ‡5DHarrison (15) (rdn 3f out: nvr nr to chal) ¾.10
    Amour du Soir (USA) (59) (RLee) 5-9-3 PatEddery (7) (b: bkwd: s.s: wl bhd 3f:
     stdy hdwy over 1f out: nvr nrr) .......................................... 2.11
3098 Unveiled (60) (RJHodges) 4-9-4 WCarson (8) (a mid div) ......................... nk.12
2881 Oscilante (39) (RAkehurst) 4-7-6(4) ‡5NKennedy (9) (outpcd: nvr nrr) ............. nk.13
3220 Castle Maud (35) (bl) (RJHodges) 5-7-7 DaleGibson (5) (b: gd spd 3f) ............ ¾.14
28826 Orchard Bay (44) (DRTucker) 3-7-13 GBardwell (13) (prom over 3f) ............... ¾.15
24782 Cheshire Annie (IRE) (56) (WCarter) 3-8-11 AMunro (16) (spd 4f) ................ 2.16
1144 Life's a Breeze (49) (MRChannon) 3-8-4 GDuffield (4) (prom 3f: wkng whn
     hmpd 2f out) ........................................................... nk.17
2822 Grand Time (50) (CJHill) 3-8-5 DHolland (12) (w ldrs tl hrd rdn & wknd wl over
     1f out: eased whn btn) .................................................. s.h.18
3134 Hazy Shades (38) (JJBridger) 3-7-7 JFanning (6) (led 3f: t.o) ..................... 8.19
    LONG HANDICAP: Hazy Shades 7-4.

**5/1** Banbury Flyer(op 8/1), **7/1** Mister Jolson, **8/1** Cranfield Comet, **9/1** Cee-En-Cee, Unveiled, Honey Seeker, **10/1** DIVINE PET, Cheshire Annie (IRE), John O'Dreams, **16/1** Gallant Hope, Castle Maud(12/1—20/1), **20/1** Oscilante, Amour du Soir (USA), Grand Time, **25/1** Life's a Breeze, **33/1** Ben Bluff, Orchard Bay, Ceatharlach, **66/1** Hazy Shades. CSF £60.14, CT £494.77. Tote £8.30: £1.90 £1.80 £2.20 £2.30 (£30.10). Mrs A. J. Taylor (UPHAM) bred by Mrs R. Newton. 19 Rn                                   1m 14.2 (4.9)
                                                                  SF—52/35/27/39/52/36

---

**3258**     SHERSTON CLAIMING STKS (Mdn 3-Y.O) £2442.50 (£680.00: £327.50)
         **1m 3f 144y**                                                       4-00 (4-05)

27203 **Dazzling Fire (IRE) (64)** (Fav) (BWHills) 8-9 PatEddery (10) (led 7f out: hrd rdn
     ins fnl f: jst hld on) .................................................... —1
29936 Flash of Straw (IRE) (42) (bl) (GLewis) 7-7 ‡5DHarrison (2) (lost pl over 4f out:
     rallied over 2f out: hrd rdn over 1f out: r.o wl nr fin) .................... s.h.2
28566 Up All Night (46) (JWHills) 7-7 DaleGibson (12) (lw: plld hrd: 2nd st: rdn over 2f
     out: ev ch over 1f out: nt qckn) ......................................... 1.3
31612 Waaza (USA) (55) (AAScott) 7-12 JFanning (5) (lw: 3rd st: rdn 2f out: wknd fnl f) 6.4
3045 Faustnluce Lady (40) (v) (GAHam) 7-0 ‡7DWright (9) (hdwy & hrd rdn 2f out: nvr
     nr ldrs) ................................................................ 3.5
31573 Elsa (46) (RJHolder) 7-6(6) ‡7CHawksley (8) (7th st: wknd over 2f out) ............ 1.6
3097 Morgans Ace (40) (BRMillman) 8-2 TSprake (6) (swtg: n.d) ........................ 4.7

3104 Skimmer Hawk (BobJones) 8-0 GDuffield (13) (rdn & 4th st: wknd 3f out) ........ nk.8
2993 Chinaman (28) (WGRWightman) 7-12 GBardwell (4) (a in rr) .......................... 1½.9
Ice Strike (USA) (CRNelson) 9-0 DHolland (1) (str: scope: bit bkwd: dwlt: a bhd) 8.10
2823⁵ Fermain (LordHuntingdon) 9-0 MRoberts (7) (hdwy over 4f out: 5th st: wknd 3f out) .................................................................................................................. 1.11
2725³ Euroflight (43) (DRTucker) 7-7 NAdams (11) (prom: rdn 6f out: 6th & wkng st: t.o) .................................................................................................................... 20.12
1758⁵ Lycian Moon (MrsJCDawe) 7-7 JLowe (3) (led over 4f: wknd 4f out: t.o) ....... 30.13

11/8 DAZZLING FIRE (IRE)(op 2/1), 4/1 Fermain, 5/1 Waaza (USA)(7/2—11/2), 9/1 Up All Night(5/1—10/1), 10/1 Elsa, 14/1 Flash of Straw (IRE), 20/1 Euroflight, 25/1 Ice Strike (USA), 33/1 Skimmer Hawk, 50/1 Ors. CSF £20.79, Tote £2.60: £1.50 £3.20 £2.60 (£17.80). Mr N. N. Browne (LAMBOURN) bred by Iris Company in Ireland. 13 Rn; Waaza (USA) clmd Miss L Siddall £7,013
2m 35.4 (8.7)
SF—18/1/–/–/–/–/–

## 3259

FAULKLAND STKS (Mdn 3-Y.O) £2784.00 (£774.00: £372.00)
1¹/₄m 46y
4-30 (4-40)

Caspian Tern (USA) (HCandy) 8-9 AMunro (4) (wl grwn: gd hdwy over 2f out: led ins fnl f: r.o wl) .......................................................................................... —1
1842 Fieldridge (89) (Fav) (CRNelson) 9-0 DHolland (2) (hdwy 6f out: 4th st: ev ch ins fnl f: nt qckn) ............................................................................................ 2½.2
2992³ Usaidit (72) (WCarter) 9-0 PaulEddery (14) (lw: 2nd st: led 3f out tl ins fnl f) .. 1½.3
2993 Miss Rita (CFWall) 8-9 GDuffield (12) (hdwy & 5th st: one pce fnl 2f) ............... 2.4
649 Jazz (79) (LMCumani) 8-9 LDettori (10) (7th st: r.o one pce fnl 2f) ................... 1½.5
Roxy River (RHannon) 8-6 ‡³RPerham (3) (unf: scope: nvr nrr) ............................ 3.6
2907² First Fling (IRE) (RCharlton) 8-9 TQuinn (11) (prom tl 8th & wkng st) ............... 4.7
3119 Court of Kings (PFICole) 9-0 AClark (15) (lw: a bhd) ......................................... hd.8
3062⁴ Jameel Dancer (MRStoute) 9-0 RCochrane (6) (3rd st: hrd rdn 2f out: sn wknd) ¾.9
1079³ Vagrancy (BWHills) 8-9 PatEddery (7) (led over 7f: wknd qckly) ....................... 1½.10
1033⁵ Tradition (MajorWRHern) 8-9 WCarson (5) (6th st: wknd 3f out) ........................ hd.11
3053⁶ Miss Marigold (RJHodges) 8-9 ADicks (9) (reluctant to r: a t.o) ...................... 10.12
2056⁵ Woodcock Wendy (MJBolton) 8-9 JLowe (13) (swtg: a in rr: reluctant to r 5f out: t.o) ...................................................................................................................... 30.13
2803 Red-Michelle (30) (EAWheeler) 8-9 SWhitworth (8) (bhd: t.o 4f out: p.u 1f out: lame) ........................................................................................................................ 0
*3016 Utrillo (USA) (9/1) Withdrawn (ref to ent stalls) : not under orders — Rule 4 applies*

7/2 Fieldridge(3/1—5/1), 9/2 Tradition, 5/1 First Fling (IRE)(6/1—8/1), 11/2 Jazz(op 7/2), 6/1 Vagrancy(op 7/2), 10/1 Usaidit, 12/1 CASPIAN TERN (USA)(op 6/1), 16/1 Jameel Dancer(11/1—20/1), 25/1 Court of Kings, Roxy River, 50/1 Ors. CSF £47.11, Tote £15.70: £3.60 £1.80 £2.70 (£21.50). Mr Fahd Salman (WANTAGE) bred by Wimborne Farm Incorporated in USA. 14 Rn
2m 14.1 (6.4)
SF—41/41/38/29/26/17

## 3260

BATHFORD NURSERY £3384.00 (£1017.00: £491.00: £228.00)
1m 5y
(Weights raised 8 lb)
5-00 (5-09)

3063² Erliking (IRE) (68) (Fav) (LordHuntingdon) 8-8 MRoberts (6) (3rd st: led over 2f out: all out) ................................................................................................................ —1
2578⁴ Finavon (68) (v) (IABalding) 8-8 RCochrane (1) (hdwy 3f out: ev ch whn hung rt 1f out: r.o wl nr fin) ............................................................................................ s.h.2
3148⁵ Sea Exhibition (IRE) (65) (MBlanshard) 8-0 ‡⁵DHarrison (3) (6th st: nt clr run ins fnl f: r.o) .............................................................................................................. 2.3
3173★ General Chase (66) (RJHolder) 8-6 (7x) JWilliams (4) (gd hdwy over 1f out: r.o) ½.4
3035³ The Executor (76) (RFJohnsonHoughton) 9-2 WCarson (12) (4th st: one pce fnl 2f) ............................................................................................................................... 3.5
2930 Blue Sombrero (IRE) (60) (RJHolder) 8-0 NAdams (11) (lw: nvr nrr) ............... nk.6
3036³ Gold Tassel (81) (RHannon) 9-7 PatEddery (2) (wl bhd tl hdwy over 2f out: one pce fnl f) ............................................................................................................... 1.7
3029 Mighty Miss Magpie (IRE) (61) (MRChannon) 8-1 AMunro (8) (5th st: hrd rdn & wknd 2f out) ...................................................................................................... 2.8
2972³ Balustrade Boy (IRE) (65) (BStevens) 8-5 DaleGibson (15) (n.d) ....................... s.h.9
3115³ Sparky's Song (63) (JWHills) 8-3 SDawson (13) (bhd fnl 4f) ........................... s.h.10
3050³ Alice Bay (60) (DHaydnJones) 7-7⁽⁷⁾ ‡⁷CAvery (9) (2nd st: led 3f out: sn hdd: hrd rdn & wknd 2f out) ....................................................................................... s.h.11
2052 Trepidation (IRE) (57) (MJFetherston-Godley) 7-6⁽⁴⁾ ‡⁵NKennedy (14) (hld up: hdwy over 3f out: hung lft & wknd wl over 1f out) .......................................... nk.12
3063 Lofty Deed (USA) (62) (SirMarkPrescott) 8-2 GDuffield (5) (a bhd) ............... ½.13
2572⁴ Arctic Guest (IRE) (57) (MJohnston) 7-11 JLowe (7) (lw: led 5f) ...................... 6.14
2972 Kill the Plague (USA) (58) (bl) (APJones) 7-5⁽⁵⁾ ‡⁷CHawksley (10) (7th & wkng st: t.o) .......................................................................................................................... 20.15

LONG HANDICAP: Alice Bay 7-1, Trepidation (IRE) 7-4, Kill the Plague (USA) 6-10.
*Stewards Enquiry: Cochrane suspended 23-26/9/92 (excessive use of whip).*

**2/1** ERLKING (IRE)(3/1—7/2), **6/1** Arctic Guest (IRE), **7/1** Finavon, **8/1** The Executor(5/1—9/1), Sea Exhibition (IRE), **9/1** Gold Tassel, **10/1** General Chase, Mighty Miss Magpie (IRE), **12/1** Blue Sombrero (IRE)(op 8/1), **16/1** Lofty Deed (USA)(10/1—20/1), Sparky's Song(op 10/1), **33/1** Balustrade Boy (IRE), Alice Bay, **50/1** Ors. CSF £18.67, CT £98.33. Tote £2.90: £1.30 £2.50 £2.30 (£13.90). Lady Newman (WEST ILSLEY) bred by Mrs P. Grubb in Ireland. 15 Rn                                                                                      1m 47 (7.7)

**3261**　　E.B.F. TORMARTON STKS (II) (Mdn 2-Y.O) £2840.00 (£790.00: £380.00)
　　　　　　**5f 161y**　　　　　　　　　　　　　　　　　　　　　　　　　　　　5-30 (5-35)

| | | |
|---|---|---|
| 2176[5] | **Surprise Offer (100)** (bl) (Fav) *(RHannon)* 9-0 LDettori (4) (mde all: clr 3f out: unchal) | —1 |
| 1946[3] | Sophisticated Air *(IABalding)* 8-9 RCochrane (2) (chsd wnr fnl 3f: no imp) | 8.2 |
| | Gentle Moment *(HCandy)* 8-9 AMunro (5) (str: scope: bhd tl hdwy over 1f out: r.o) | hd.3 |
| 2826 | Hobey Cat *(DRCElsworth)* 8-9 JWilliams (8) (hdwy over 1f out: nvr nrr) | 3½.4 |
| 3156 | Another Jade *(APJarvis)* 8-9 SWhitworth (9) (prom over 3f) | 5.5 |
| *1848* | Dorazine *(CJHill)* 8-9 GBardwell (6) (a bhd) | hd.6 |
| 1378 | Right Will Prevail *(GLewis)* 8-9 ‡5DHarrison (10) (a bhd) | 2.7 |
| 2884 | Step on it *(CPWildman)* 8-9 TQuinn (1) (a bhd: t.o) | 15.8 |
| 3099 | Shalholme *(RJHolder)* 8-9 GDuffield (3) (prom over 3f: t.o) | 4.9 |
| 3077 | Spicy Affair *(DrJDScargill)* 8-9 DHolland (7) (prom tl broke down over 2f out: sn p.u) | 0 |

**8/15** SURPRISE OFFER(1/3—4/7), **3/1** Sophisticated Air(5/2—9/2), **10/1** Gentle Moment(op 6/1), **20/1** Hobey Cat, **25/1** Spicy Affair, **33/1** Shalholme, **50/1** Ors. CSF £2.64, Tote £1.50: £1.10 £1.10 £2.10 (£1.80). Lord Carnarvon (MARLBOROUGH) bred by Woodditton Stud Ltd. 10 Rn                                                     1m 15 (5.7)

　　　　　　　　　　　　　　　　　　　　　　　　　　　　　　　　　　　　　SF—32/-/-/-/-/-

T/Plpt· £109.20 (30.75 Tckts).　　　　　　　　　　　　　　　　　　　　　　　　LMc/KH

3171—**LEICESTER (R-H)**

**Monday, September 14th [Good to firm]**

Going Allowance: St: minus 0.05 sec; Rnd: minus 0.20 sec (F)　　　　　Wind: slt half bhd

Stalls: high

**3262**　　E.B.F. KEGWORTH STKS (Mdn 2-Y.O.C) £3496.00 (£1048.00: £504.00: £232.00)
　　　　　　**7f 9y**　　　　　　　　　　　　　　　　　　　　　　　　　　　　2-10 (2-13)

| | | |
|---|---|---|
| | **True Hero (USA)** (Fav) *(JHMGosden)* 9-0 SCauthen (6) (lengthy: scope: bkwd: s.i.s: hdwy 2f out: r.o wl to ld nr fin) | —1 |
| 3100[4] | Roger the Butler (IRE) *(MBell)* 9-0 MHills (7) (led tl wl ins fnl f) | nk.2 |
| | Chummy's Pal (USA) *(BWHills)* 9-0 JReid (13) (unf: scope: bit bkwd: hld up: effrt 2f out: r.o wl ins fnl f) | 1½.3 |
| 2388[5] | Ok Bertie *(DMorris)* 9-0 MTebbutt (11) (a.p: ev ch over 1f out: rdn & no ex fnl f) | s.h.4 |
| | Fourforfun *(RHannon)* 9-0 BRaymond (10) (unf: prom: styd on one pce fnl f) | 5.5 |
| | Harry *(PAKelleway)* 9-0 KDarley (5) (b: unf: sme hdwy fnl 2f: nvr nrr) | 1½.6 |
| | M'Bebe *(BWHills)* 9-0 RStreet (4) (leggy: lt-f: s.s: hdwy 2f out: nrst fin) | s.h.7 |
| 1873 | Koa *(MJHeaton-Ellis)* 9-0 WRyan (9) (b: bit bkwd: prom 5f) | ¾.8 |
| | Pero *(BWHills)* 9-0 GBaxter (3) (neat: bkwd: mdn to tch to ½-wy: r.o fnl 2f) | 2.9 |
| 2932 | Magic Fan (IRE) *(PWHarris)* 8-11 ‡3FNorton (15) (effrt ½-wy: nt trble ldrs) | 1½.10 |
| 3175 | Supreme Master *(RHannon)* 9-0 BRouse (1) (nvr trbld ldrs) | 2½.11 |
| | Legal Artist (IRE) *(NAGraham)* 9-0 DMcKeown (16) (w'like: str: bkwd: dwlt: m.n.s) | hd.12 |
| | Restitution *(JRFanshawe)* 9-0 GCarter (12) (tall: scope: bit bkwd: s.i.s: m.n.s) | 1.13 |
| | Todden *(CFWall)* 9-0 PRobinson (2) (leggy: unf: prom 4f) | 1½.14 |
| 3035 | Baulking Towers *(MMcCormack)* 9-0 CRutter (8) (chsd ldrs 5f: wknd qckly) | 1½.15 |
| | Rubidian *(SirMarkPrescott)* 9-0 CNutter (14) (lengthy: bit bkwd: sn pushed along: bhd fr ½-wy) | ¾.16 |

**2/5** TRUE HERO (USA), **10/1** Roger the Butler (IRE), Chummy's Pal (USA), **12/1** Fourforfun(op 8/1), **14/1** Restitution, **20/1** Pero, Supreme Master, **25/1** Todden, Legal Artist (IRE), **33/1** Harry, Koa, Rubidian, M'Bebe, Ok Bertie, **50/1** Ors. CSF £7.68, Tote £1.30: £1.10 £2.40 £2.80 (£4.90). Sheikh Mohammed (NEWMARKET) bred by Mrs George Proskauer & Warren Rosenthal in USA. 16 Rn                                     1m 25.7 (3.4)

　　　　　　　　　　　　　　　　　　　　　　　　　　　SF—44/43/38/37/22/17

**3263**　　GOLDEN HAND (S) STKS (3-Y.O) £2574.00 (£714.00: £342.00)
　　　　　　**1m 1f 218y**　　　　　　　　　　　　　　　　　　　　　　　　　2-40 (2-44)

| | | |
|---|---|---|
| 3017 | **Telephus** *(BJMcMath)* 8-11 EJohnson (3) (hld up: hdwy 3f out: str run to ld ins fnl f) | —1 |
| 3159[6] | Aegaen Lady (47) *(JEtherington)* 8-1 ‡5JWeaver (16) (hld up: 7th st: hdwy 2f out: led appr fnl f: hdd & no ex ins fnl f) | 2.2 |

31574 Laughton Lady **(39)** (bl) *(MrsNMacauley)* 8-6 DBiggs (4) (lw: chsd ldr: 2nd st: led over 2f out tl appr fnl f: one pce) ............................................. 1½.3

30106 Positive Aspect **(43)** *(JPearce)* 8-1 ‡5RPrice (14) (hdwy over 2f out: styd on ins fnl f) ............................................. 1½.4

800 Desired Guest **(75)** (Fav) *(MRStoute)* 9-2 JReid (11) (bit bkwd: chsd ldrs: 5th st: rdn over 2f out: no imp) ............................................. s.h.5

31763 Tyrone Flyer **(45)** *(MCPipe)* 8-11 BRaymond (2) (racd wd: led: sn clr: hdd over 2f out: one pce) ............................................. 3.6

31594 Mexican Dancer **(50)** *(RJHolder)* 7-13 ‡7SDrowne (6) (chsd ldrs: 6th st: one pce fnl 2f) ............................................. ¾.7

31613 Iron Baron (IRE) **(56)** *(RHollinshead)* 8-4 WRyan (18) (nvr nr to chal) ............................................. 1½.8

2937 Princess of Orange **(45)** *(WMBrisbourne)* 7-13 ‡7AGarth (8) (hdwy 4f out: no imp fnl 2f) ............................................. 3.9

*2689* Creego **(39)** *(JAGlover)* 8-6 ‡5SWilliams (7) (lw: plld hrd: chsd ldrs 7f) ............................................. 1.10

3104 King of Normandy (IRE) **(50)** (bl) *(RHannon)* 8-11 BRouse (5) (lw: prom: 3rd st: wknd 2f out) ............................................. nk.11

24966 Norman Warrior **(51)** *(DMorris)* 8-11 MTebbutt (10) (m.n.s) ............................................. 1.12

15174 Kaytura *(MHTompkins)* 8-6 PRobinson (19) (a bhd) ............................................. 3½.13

31684 Toss the Dice **(55)** (bl) *(MAJarvis)* 8-11 MHills (9) (effrt 2f out: n.d) ............................................. hd.14

3028 Strangersinthenite **(42)** *(JSWainwright)* 8-11 GBaxter (12) (s.s: hld up: plld hrd: a in rr) ............................................. s.h.15

3167 Fort Derry (IRE) **(41)** *(EJAlston)* 8-11 KFallon (4) (m.n.s) ............................................. 5.16

29885 Always Lynsey (IRE) **(49)** *(MissLCSiddall)* 8-6 DMcKeown (15) (t: m.n.s) ..... 2½.17

28584 Grey Cphas *(MMcCormack)* 8-11 SCauthen (1) (m.n.s) ............................................. 18

749 Fletchinni (IRE) **(34)** *(ABailey)* 8-11 GCarter (13) (bit bkwd: prom: 4th st: wknd over 2f out) ............................................. 19

**4/1** Desired Guest, **9/2** TELEPHUS(7/1—4/1), **8/1** Grey Cphas, **9/1** Iron Baron (IRE), Kaytura(op 5/1), **10/1** Mexican Dancer(7/1—11/1), Toss the Dice(op 6/1), Tyrone Flyer, **12/1** Positive Aspect, **16/1** Norman Warrior(op 10/1), **20/1** King of Normandy (IRE), Aegaen Lady, Laughton Lady, **25/1** Always Lynsey (IRE), Princess of Orange, **33/1** Strangersinthenite, Creego, **50/1** Ors. CSF £93.35, Tote £5.60: £2.40 £9.80 £5.80 (£99.90). Back Hill Bloodstock Ltd (NEWMARKET) bred by B. Alexander. 19 Rn; at 6,500 gns 2m 7.2 (4.5)
SF—32/18/21/13/27/16

---

**3264** LEICESTER SOUND FM H'CAP (0-70) £3346.00 (£931.00: £448.00)
5f 218y

3-10 (3-16)

30793 **Yours Or Mine (IRE) (45)** (Fav) *(DWChapman)* 4-8-3 SWood (13) (a.p: rdn to ld ins fnl f: all out) ............................................. —1

2752 Nuclear Express **(56)** *(RLee)* 5-8-7 ‡7SDrowne (4) (a.p: ev ch ins fnl f: r.o) ....... nk.2

*3185*6 My Ruby Ring **(39)** *(DRLaing)* 5-7-11 TyroneWilliams (15) (hdwy & nt clr run 1f out: swtchd & r.o strly nr fin) ............................................. hd.3

28665 Bernstein Bette **(64)** *(PSFelgate)* 6-9-8 WRyan (12) (hdwy over 1f out: fin fast) hd.4

3067 Proud Brigadier (IRE) **(47)** *(WCarter)* 4-8-0 ‡5NGwilliams (21) (lw: gd hdwy appr fnl f: no ex nr fin) ............................................. nk.5

3105 Strip Cartoon (IRE) **(50)** (bl) *(SRBowring)* 4-8-8 GBaxter (14) (led over 4f out: r.o ins fnl f) ............................................. hd.6

*2974*3 Liffey River (USA) **(54)** *(MrsLPiggott)* 4-8-5 ‡7GMilligan (22) (b: b.hind: chsd ldrs: led over 1f out tl ins fnl f) ............................................. 1.7

3002 Mu-Arrik **(47)** (b) *(DAWilson)* 4-8-5 GCarter (3) (bhd tl r.o fnl 2f) ............................................. 1.8

30376 Hold Fast (IRE) **(40)** *(HCandy)* 4-7-12 CRutter (6) (dwlt: nvr nrr) ............................................. 3.9

3037 Courting Newmarket **(46)** *(MrsAKnight)* 4-7-13(3) ‡5OPears (19) (nvr trbld ldrs) hd.10

*3185* Harry's Coming **(67)** *(RJHodges)* 8-9-8 ‡3FNorton (17) (chsd ldrs: no hdwy fnl 2f) ............................................. s.h.11

3183 Tauber **(66)** *(PatMitchell)* 8-9-7 ‡3SO'Gorman (10) (spd 4f) ............................................. nk.12

1379 Kaths Choice **(36)** *(HJCollingridge)* 4-7-8 JQuinn (20) (m.n.s) ............................................. 3.13

2984 Swinging Tich **(50)** *(BAMcMahon)* 3-8-5 MBirch (11) (s.s: a bhd) ............................................. 1.14

3088 The Cuckoo's Nest **(61)** *(MWilliams)* 4-9-5 BRaymond (18) (hdwy 2f out: n.d) ¾.15

3037 Lindgale Lass **(41)** (v) *(MWEckley)* 3-7-10(1) DBiggs (16) (s.s: a bhd) ............................................. ¾.16

3119 Lightning Decision **(44)** *(JPSmith)* 4-8-2 PRobinson (8) (outpcd) ............................................. nk.17

3101 Quiet Victory **(40)** *(MissLCSiddall)* 5-7-12 BCrossley (2) (spd stands' side 4f) . 3.18

28215 Fontaine Lady **(42)** *(TThomsonJones)* 5-7-7(6) ‡7JDSmith (1) (prom 4f: sn lost tch) ............................................. 1.19

29496 Followmegirls **(59)** *(MrsALMKing)* 3-8-7 ‡7AGarth (8) (in tch to ½-wy: sn wknd) 1½.20

**7/2** YOURS OR MINE (IRE)(5/1—6/1), **9/2** Bernstein Bette, **17/2** Mu-Arrik(6/1—9/1), **12/1** The Cuckoo's Nest, Liffey River (USA), My Ruby Ring, Hold Fast (IRE), Harry's Coming(op 8/1), **14/1** Proud Brigadier (IRE), Nuclear Express, **20/1** Swinging Tich, Tauber, Kaths Choice, Fontaine Lady, Courting Newmarket, Quiet Victory, **33/1** Followmegirls, **50/1** Lightning Decision. CSF £54.19, CT £527.59. Tote £5.00: £1.90 £4.80 £1.90 £2.60 (£68.00). Mrs J. M. Davenport (YORK) bred by Gorden Patterson in Ireland. 20 Rn
1m 12.6 (2.6)
SF—31/34/23/47/24/31

## 3265  WREN STKS  £2846.00 (£848.00: £404.00: £182.00)  1m 8y  3-40 (3-41)

3038⁵ **Waterfowl Creek (IRE)** (87) *(GWragg)* 3–8-5 MHills (1) (lw: hld up: hdwy over
1f out: qcknd to ld ins fnl f) ................................................................... —1

2929\* Flaming Arrow (92) *(HRACecil)* 4–9-1 BRaymond (5) (lw: hld up: plld out & led
2f out: hdd & no ex ins fnl f) ................................................. 1½.2

3119\* Key Suspect (USA) (80) *(Fav)* *(JHMGosden)* 3–8-11 SCauthen (4) (w ldr: rdn 2f
out: r.o one pce) ............................................................ 12.3

3101² Kummel King (62) *(EJAlston)* 4–9-3 KFallon (2) (disp ld 6f: sn rdn & btn) ...... 1.4

702 La Raptotte (28) (bl) *(MJCharles)* 5–8-7 DMcKeown (3) (a bhd) ................... 2.5

**11/8** Key Suspect (USA), **13/8** Flaming Arrow(5/4—15/8), **11/4** WATERFOWL CREEK (IRE), **20/1** Kummel King,
**100/1** La Raptotte. CSF £7.43, Tote £4.60: £2.00 £1.10 (£3.00). Sir Philip Oppenheimer (NEWMARKET) bred by
Hascombe and Valiant Studs in Ireland. 5 Rn   1m 38.5 (3.5)
SF—32/37/–/–/–/

## 3266  CHARNWOOD CLAIMING STKS (3 & 4-Y.O) £2679.00 (£744.00: £357.00)
1m 3f 183y  4-10 (4-13)

3010⁵ **Big Pat** (58) *(JPearce)* 3–8-2 ‡⁵RPrice (11) (a.p: 2nd st: led over 4f out: sn rdn
clr: hld on) ................................................................. —1

3104⁴ Kasikci (70) *(RHollinshead)* 3–7-7 ‡⁷AGarth (4) (led aftr 3f tl over 4f out: rdn &
r.o fnl f) ..................................................................... 2.2

3141³ Salu (56) (bl) *(JEtherington)* 4–8-1 ‡³FNorton (2) (hdwy & 6th st: rdn over 3f out:
styd on fnl f) ............................................................... 3½.3

3141² Silver Samurai (67) *(Fav)* *(RHollinshead)* 3–8-9 WRyan (13) (s.s: hdwy & 5th st:
kpt on appr fnl f: nvr able to chal) ............................... hd.4

3060⁵ Lascar (USA) *(OThorner)* 4–8-13 ‡³SO'Gorman (3) (hdwy 3f out: styd on appr
fnl f: nvr nrr) ................................................................. 1.5

2993⁴ Storm Drum (57) (bl) *(PJMakin)* 3–8-13 JReid (12) (chsd ldrs: 4th st: wknd over
2f out) ........................................................................ 3.6

2420 Amalfi (41) *(JPearce)* 3–7-12 DBiggs (6) (nvr plcd to chal) ................... s.h.7

2957 Double Sherry *(RMWhitaker)* 3–8-8 ACulhane (1) (s.s: a bhd) ................ 8.8

2929 Dancing Boat *(KAMorgan)* 3–8-9 DMcKeown (9) (a in rr) ...................... 5.9

1367⁵ Everso Irish (53) *(MHTompkins)* 3–8-5 PRobinson (7) (b.nr fore: a bhd) ....... hd.10

3104 City Line (45) (v) *(DRLaing)* 3–7-10 ‡⁵ATucker (5) (swtg: chsd ldrs tl 7th & wkng
st) ......................................................................... ½.11

3157 Titian Girl (32) (bl) *(MissLCSiddall)* 3–8-0 BCrossley (10) (led 3f: 3rd st: wknd
over 3f out) ................................................................. 1½.12

**13/8** Silver Samurai, **9/2** Storm Drum, Salu(3/1—5/1), **6/1** Kasikci(op 4/1), **8/1** BIG PAT, **11/1** Lascar (USA),
**14/1** Everso Irish, **20/1** City Line, **25/1** Amalfi, **33/1** Titian Girl, Double Sherry, **50/1** Dancing Boat. CSF £56.30,
Tote £8.70: £1.90 £2.10 £1.60 (£49.20). Burton Park Country Club (NEWMARKET) bred by Mrs P. J. Lewis. 12
Rn   2m 35.9 (7.1)

## 3267  RIVER NURSERY  £2805.00 (£780.00: £375.00)  5f 218y  4-40 (4-43)

3039\* **Shiro** (82) *(Fav)* *(RJRWilliams)* 9-6 SCauthen (2) (hld up: hdwy to ld over 1f out:
sn clr: eased nr fin) ...................................................... —1

3123 Birchwood Sun (66) *(RHollinshead)* 8-4 WRyan (9) (gd hdwy over 2f out: ev ch
1f out: r.o) .................................................................. 2.2

3039³ No Extras (IRE) (71) *(JSutcliffe)* 8-9 BRouse (5) (hld up: hdwy 2f out: ev ch appr
fnl f: unable qckn) ......................................................... ¾.3

2799 Glorious Island (66) *(RFJohnsonHoughton)* 8-4 MHills (12) (a.p: ev ch over 1f
out: kpt on same pce) .................................................... 3.4

2951³ Royal Flex (USA) (74) *(MrsLPiggott)* 8-12 BRaymond (15) (a.p: ev ch appr fnl f:
one pce) .................................................................... 1½.5

2872⁵ Second Colours (USA) (77) *(PSFelgate)* 9-1 KDarley (1) (led ½-wy tl wknd over
1f out) ...................................................................... 1½.6

2897⁴ Pure Madness (USA) (63) *(DrJDScargill)* 8-1 JQuinn (3) (chsd ldrs over 4f) ...... hd.7

2269 Boisterous (56) (bl) *(WRMuir)* 7-1 ‡⁷KimMcDonnell (8) (spd over 3f) ........ 1½.8

3175 Beat the Bagman (IRE) (60) *(LJHolt)* 7-12 AMcGlone (10) (in tch: carried rt 2f
out: nt rcvr) ................................................................ 2.9

2973 Tayish (62) (bl) *(TThomsonJones)* 7-7⁽⁷⁾ ‡⁷JDSmith (11) (led to ½-wy: rdn & wnt
bdly rt 2f out: sn btn) .................................................... s.h.10

3063 Kingsdown Cavalier (66) *(RHannon)* 8-4 DBiggs (7) (lw: m.n.s) .............. ½.11

3019 The Wend (58) *(DTThom)* 7-7⁽³⁾ ‡³FNorton (13) (outpcd) .................... 2½.12

3001⁴ Walsham Witch (72) *(MHTompkins)* 8-10 PRobinson (4) (spd over 3f) ......... hd.13

2986 Cinders Girl (68) *(JMPEustace)* 8-6 MTebbutt (6) (b: a bhd: t.o) ............ 15.14
LONG HANDICAP: Tayish 7-2, The Wend 7-2.

**13/8** SHIRO, **9/2** Birchwood Sun, **13/2** Walsham Witch, **8/1** Royal Flex (USA), No Extras (IRE)(op 5/1), **14/1** Glorious Island, Kingsdown Cavalier, Second Colours (USA), **16/1** Pure Madness (USA), **20/1** Beat the Bagman (IRE), Boisterous, Cinders Girl, **25/1** Ors. CSF £11.02, CT £49.28. Tote £2.70: £1.80 £2.60 £2.50 (£15.50). Mr Saeed Manana (NEWMARKET) bred by Sheikh Mohammed bin Rashid al Maktoum. 14 Rn     1m 13 (3)
SF—40/16/18/1/3/–

T/Plpt: £488.50 (24.3 Tckts).                                        IM

## 2909—SANDOWN (R-H)

### Tuesday, September 15th [Good, Good to firm back st]

Going Allowance: St: 0.30 sec per fur; Rnd: 0.10 sec per fur (G)        Wind: almost nil

Stalls: high

**3268**     E.B.F. HEATHER STKS (Mdn 2-Y.O) £2862.50 (£860.00: £415.00: £192.50)
                5f 6y                                     2-20 (2-21)

3011  **Jobie** (WJHaggas) 9-0 MHills (7) (hdwy 2f out: led over 1f out: pushed out) ...... —1
2792  Ballet (LordHuntingdon) 8-9 MRoberts (4) (w ldrs: led wl over 1f out: sn hdd:
              r.o) ........................................................................................ 1½.2
2826  Avril Etoile (66) (Fav) (LJHolt) 8-9 JReid (6) (a.p: rdn over 1f out: nt qckn) ....... nk.3
3008  Kelly Mac (NACallaghan) 9-0 PatEddery (9) (led over 3f) ................................. 3½.4
3178  Sea Baron (75) (MBlanshard) 9-0 RCochrane (3) (lw: hdwy 2f out: one pce fnl f)  nk.5
2452  Perfect Passion (JJBridger) 8-9 LDettori (2) (no hdwy fnl 2f) ........................... 2½.6
3055⁵  Bajka (WJarvis) 8-9 SCauthen (5) (lw: w ldrs tl wknd 2f out) ........................... 1½.7
2826  Saraswati (67) (PJMakin) 8-9 TQuinn (1) (lw: outpcd) .................................... 5.8
           *Mustakim (IRE) Withdrawn (injured in box) : not under orders*

**11/4** Avril Etoile, **100/30** Ballet(7/4—7/2), **7/2** Bajka, **5/1** JOBIE, **8/1** Kelly Mac, **12/1** Saraswati, **16/1** Sea Baron, **20/1** Perfect Passion. CSF £21.29, Tote £6.90: £1.80 £1.10 £1.70 (£8.30). Mr J. A. Redmond (NEWMARKET) bred by J. A. Redmond. 8 Rn                                   64.60 sec (5.10)
SF—28/17/16/7/6/–

**3269**     WESTMINSTER-MOTOR (TAXI) INSURANCE H'CAP (3-Y.O.F) (0-90) £3783.75
              (£1140.00: £552.50: £258.75)   **1m 14y**                2-50 (2-55)
                          (Weights raised 9 lb)

3056*  **Jdaayel** (79) (Fav) (ACStewart) 9-6 MRoberts (11) (3rd st: led 2f out: r.o wl) ..... —1
3135  Sylvan (IRE) (80) (CFWall) 9-7 JWilliams (14) (gd hdwy on ins over 1f out: fin wl) 1½.2
1533  She's Pleased (USA) (78) (LMCumani) 9-5 LDettori (10) (gd hdwy 2f out: r.o
             one pce) ........................................................................................ ½.3
3002  Sweet Jaffa (72) (MajorWRHern) 8-13 WCarson (3) (hdwy over 1f out: r.o ins fnl
             f) ................................................................................................ s.h.4
3135  So Smug (USA) (69) (v) (JHMGosden) 8-10 PatEddery (12) (s.s: bhd & rdn
             along: hdwy on ins over 1f out: r.o) ............................................. ¾.5
3058³  Clare Kerry Lass (74) (JRFanshawe) 9-1 AMunro (2) (swtg: nrst fin) ................. hd.6
3135⁵  Hugging (76) (MMcCormack) 9-3 JReid (13) (swtg: 5th st: one pce fnl 2f) ....... 1½.7
3135  Twilight Secret (64) (JWHills) 8-5 MHills (8) (swtg: hdwy 2f out: hmpd 1f out: nt
             rcvr) ........................................................................................... ¾.8
3135³  Swallowcliffe (74) (v) (PTWalwyn) 9-1 TQuinn (4) (led 1f: 2nd st: led 3f out to 2f
             out) ............................................................................................. ½.9
3058*  Rocality (78) (RHannon) 9-5 RCochrane (6) (6th st: wknd over 1f out) .......... 1½.10
3058²  Rafah (75) (BHanbury) 9-2 BRaymond (1) (lw: nvr trbld ldrs) ............................ 2.11
2987⁶  Waseela (IRE) (71) (AAScott) 8-9 ‡³FNorton (9) (4th st: wknd over 2f out) ...... 1½.12
2647  Agnes Flemming (USA) (75) (PWHarris) 9-2 PaulEddery (5) (a bhd: t.o) ........ 12.13
2707  Congress (IRE) (76) (v) (MRStoute) 9-3 SCauthen (7) (lw: led after 1f tl wknd
             qckly 3f out: t.o) .......................................................................... 12.14

**4/1** JDAAYEL, **7/1** Twilight Secret, **9/1** Swallowcliffe, Agnes Flemming (USA)(8/1—12/1), **10/1** Rafah, So Smug (USA), She's Pleased (USA), Rocality, **12/1** Congress (IRE), Hugging, Sweet Jaffa, **14/1** Waseela (IRE), **16/1** Clare Kerry Lass, **33/1** Sylvan (IRE). CSF £112.15, CT £1,156.29. Tote £3.70: £2.10 £7.70 £3.20 (£136.40). Mr Hamdan Al-Maktoum (NEWMARKET) bred by Floors Farming. 14 Rn          1m 43.90 (4.70)
SF—47/43/39/32/27/31

**3270**     WOODCHESTER L.M.S. H'CAP (3-Y.O) (0-90) £3829.25 (£1154.00: £559.50: £262.25)
              **1¼m 7y**                          3-25 (3-31)

2913⁵  **Walimu (IRE)** (71) (CFWall) 8-7 RCochrane (13) (gd hdwy to ld wl over 1f out:
             jst hld on) ................................................................................... —1
3090⁵  Almuhtarama (IRE) (77) (ACStewart) 8-13 MRoberts (2) (3rd st: led 2f out: sn
             hdd: rallied ins fnl f: r.o) ............................................................ s.h.2

3066² Glide Path (USA) **(82)** *(JWHills)* 9-4 MHills (5) (lw: hdwy 3f out: one pce fnl 2f) .. 3.3
2593* Avice Caro (USA) **(85)** (Jt-Fav) *(JHMGosden)* 9-7 SCauthen (9) (lw: 4th st: hrd
            rdn over 1f out: r.o ins fnl f) ....................................... ¾.4
2971⁴ Aremef (USA) **(78)** *(MrsJCecil)* 9-0 PaulEddery (8) (led to 2f out: r.o one pce) s.h.5
2992 Sovereign Page (USA) **(76)** *(BHanbury)* 8-12 BRaymond (3) (lw: 2nd st: ev ch
            2f out: one pce) ....................................... nk.6
1275 Thamestar (IRE) **(80)** *(JLDunlop)* 9-2 TQuinn (12) (lw: nvr nrr) ........................ 1½.7
3009⁶ Karamoja **(73)** *(NAGraham)* 8-9 WCarson (7) (6th st: wknd over 1f out) .......... 1½.8
3137 First Century (IRE) **(71)** *(BRMillman)* 8-7 JWilliams (11) (nvr nr to chal) ............. ¾.9
1941 Showgi (USA) **(84)** *(JRFanshawe)* 9-6 PatEddery (10) (swtg: n.d) ..................... ½.10
2777³ Aljernaas **(80)** (Jt-Fav) *(LMCumani)* 9-2 LDettori (4) (swtg: nvr bttr than mid div)1½.11
3073³ Boogie Bopper **(61)** *(MBell)* 7-8 ‡³FNorton (6) (n.d) ..................................... s.h.12
3174 Cretoes Dancer (USA) **(66)** *(WRMuir)* 8-2 CRutter (1) (5th st: wknd 2f out) ..... nk.13
2239 Snappy's Boy Josh **(57)** *(PJFeilden)* 7-7 NAdams (14) (s.s: a bhd: t.o) .......... 20.14
          LONG HANDICAP: Snappy's Boy Josh 6-1.

**5/1** Aljernaas, Avice Caro (USA), **11/2** Glide Path (USA), **6/1** Almuhtarama (IRE), **15/2** WALIMU (IRE), **9/1** Sovereign Page (USA)(12/1—8/1), **10/1** Karamoja(14/1—16/1), **11/1** Boogie Bopper (IRE), **14/1** Aremef (USA), Showgi (USA), **16/1** Thamestar (IRE), First Century (IRE), **25/1** Cretoes Dancer (USA), **100/1** Snappy's Boy Josh. CSF £52.59, CT £254.24. Tote £10.40: £2.70 £2.50 £2.10 (£45.30). Sheikh Ahmed Al Maktoum (NEWMARKET) bred by Sheikh Ahmed bin Rashid al Maktoum in Ireland. 14 Rn     2m 9.72 (5.42)
                                               SF—49/54/53/54/46/43

---

**3271**    WILLOW CLAIMING STKS (3-Y.O) £2862.50 (£860.00: £415.00: £192.50)
        **5f 6y**                                              3-55 (4-01)

2911 **Our Rita (66)** *(PAKelleway)* 8-0 AMunro (5) (hld up: qcknd ins fnl f: led cl home)  —1
3188 Branston Abby (IRE) **(84)** (Fav) *(MJohnston)* 8-1 MRoberts (4) (led 3f out: shkn
            up wl ins fnl f: hdd nr fin) ....................................... hd.2
2493³ Lifetime Fame **(72)** *(JWPayne)* 8-5 RCochrane (6) (hdwy fnl f: first fin) ............. 2⅛.3
3031 Storm Melody (USA) **(92)** *(AAScott)* 8-9 BRaymond (2) (b.hind: hld up: ev ch 1f
            out: nt qckn) ....................................... nk.4
3183 Born to Be **(77)** *(SDow)* 8-8 TQuinn (1) (b: ev ch over 1f out: wknd fnl f) ......... 2½.5
2909⁴ Loose Zeus (USA) **(56)** *(CFWall)* 7-8 ‡TWilson (7) (gd spd 4f) ........................... ½.6
3048 High Principles **(60)** *(JBerry)* 8-7 JCarroll (8) (led 2f: bhd fnl 2f) ........................ 8.7

**11/10** Branston Abby (IRE), **4/1** Storm Melody (USA), **5/1** OUR RITA, **8/1** High Principles, **9/1** Lifetime Fame, **20/1** Loose Zeus (USA), **33/1** Born to Be. CSF £10.50, Tote £5.40: £2.00 £1.50 (£5.40). Mr T. Brady (NEWMARKET) bred by Terry Brady. 7 Rn; Our Rita clmd A Edwards £9,000        63.02 sec (3.52)
                                          SF—46/46/34/40/43/32/16

---

**3272**    'BLUE RIBAND FUTURITY' STKS (2-Y.O) £4250.00 (£1280.00: £620.00: £290.00)
        **1m 14y**                                             4-30 (4-31)

2175² **Geisway (CAN) (100)** (Fav) *(RHannon)* 9-4 PatEddery (6) (4th st: led 1f out:
            pushed out) ....................................... —1
2912 Shebl (USA) **(99)** *(MRStoute)* 9-4 SCauthen (3) (led 6f out tl over 2f out: hrd rdn:
            r.o) ....................................... 2.2
2951* Declassified (USA) **(86)** *(LMCumani)* 9-4 LDettori (4) (led 2f: 2nd st: led over 2f
            out to 1f out) ....................................... s.h.3
2175⁵ Ericolin (IRE) *(CEBrittain)* 8-12 MRoberts (1) (dwlt: 6th st: hdwy fnl f: r.o) .......... hd.4
2799³ Frescade (USA) *(PFICole)* 8-12 AMunro (2) (lw: 3rd st: rdn over 2f out: wknd
            over 1f out) ....................................... 2.5
2756³ Rapid Success (USA) **(93)** *(DRCElsworth)* 9-4 RCochrane (5) (5th st: wknd 2f
            out) ....................................... 7.6

**9/4** GEISWAY (CAN), **5/2** Rapid Success (USA), **4/1** Frescade (USA)(op 9/4), **6/1** Shebl (USA), **10/1** Declassified (USA)(op 6/1), **14/1** Ericolin (IRE)(12/1—20/1). CSF £13.88, Tote £2.60: £1.60 £2.00 (£6.70). A. F. Budge (Equine) Limited (MARLBOROUGH) bred by Michael Byrne in Canada. 6 Rn    1m 44.58 (5.38)
                                          SF—35/29/28/21/15/–

---

**3273**    TAXINEWS H'CAP (0-80) £3783.75 (£1140.00: £552.50: £258.75)
        **1¾m**                                              5-00 (5-02)

2774² **Bold Resolution (IRE) (53)** *(CACyzer)* 4–8-9 MRoberts (2) (hdwy 5f out: led wl
            over 1f out: comf) ....................................... —1
3143 Irish Stamp (IRE) **(76)** *(JPearce)* 3–9-7 SCauthen (10) (lw: hdwy over 2f out: rdn
            over 1f out: r.o ins fnl f) ....................................... 2.2
2921⁴ Grove Serendipity (IRE) **(51)** (v) *(AHide)* 4–8-7 NAdams (5) (lw: 2nd st: led over
            3f out tl wknd wl over 1f out) ....................................... 1.3
3128⁴ Miss Pin Up **(69)** (Fav) *(PatMitchell)* 3–9-0 BRaymond (9) (lw: hdwy & n.m.r
            over 1f out: styd on) ....................................... ¾.4

2944 Blushing Belle **(45)** *(PFICole)* 4-8-1 CRutter (8) (swtg: 4th st: r.o one pce fnl 2f)  1.5
2992[6] Indian Decision **(69)** *(JLDunlop)* 3-9-0 JReid (4) (swtg: nvr nrr) ........................ hd.6
*2783* Top Table **(64)** (v) *(MRStoute)* 3-8-9 PaulEddery (3) (3rd st: wknd 2f out) ...... 3¹/₂.7
3141★ Greek Chime (IRE) **(68)** *(LordHuntingdon)* 3-8-13 AMunro (6) (5th st: wknd 2f
                                                   out) .......................................................... 4.8
2648[4] Trojan Lancer **(57)** *(DrJDScargill)* 6-8-13 RCochrane (7) (nvr nr to chal) ........... 2.9
      Jinga **(72)** *(LadyHerries)* 7-10-0 JWilliams (1) (bit bkwd: nrst fin) ................... ¹/₂.10
3021[5] Quadrireme **(75)** *(MajorWRHern)* 3-9-6 WCarson (13) (prom 8f) .................. ³/₄.11
3040[4] Constructivist (IRE) **(68)** *(BWHills)* 3-8-13 PatEddery (15) (b.off hind: 6th st:
                                                   wknd over 3f out) ................................. 2¹/₂.12
2921 Calicon **(72)** *(IABalding)* 6-10-0 LDettori (12) (bit bkwd: a wl bhd) ................ ¹/₂.13
3021 Mahrajan **(63)** *(CJBenstead)* 8-9-5 TQuinn (11) (a wl bhd) ...................... s.h.14
2605 Luks Akura **(44)** (v) *(MJohnston)* 4-7-7 ‡7MBaird (14) (lw: led tl wknd qckly over
                                                   3f out) ............................................... ³/₄.15

**5/1** Miss Pin Up, **11/2** Greek Chime (IRE), **13/2** Irish Stamp (IRE), **7/1** Quadrireme, **8/1** Indian Decision,
Constructivist (IRE), **10/1** BOLD RESOLUTION (IRE), **14/1** Top Table, Grove Serendipity (IRE), Trojan Lancer(op
8/1), Mahrajan, **20/1** Luks Akura, **25/1** Blushing Belle, Jinga, **33/1** Calicon. CSF £72.89, CT £855.35. Tote
£10.60: £3.00 £4.30 £5.40 (£44.70). Mr R. M. Cyzer (HORSHAM) bred by G. O'Brien in Ireland. 15 Rn
                                                                      3m 4.73 (10.03)
                                                                      SF—9/17/1/6/–/3

**3274**         WEY NURSERY     £3670.00 (£1105.00: £535.00: £250.00)     **1m 1f**     5-30 (5-44)
                 (Weights raised 8 lb)
2938 **Marius (IRE) (74)** *(BWHills)* 8-7 PatEddery (8) (b.hind: lw: hdwy 3f out: led over
                                                   1f out: r.o wl) ................................................ —1
2910[2] Alderney Prince (USA) **(88)** *(PFICole)* 9-7 AMunro (3) (5th st: led 2f out tl over 1f
                                                   out: hrd rdn: r.o) ............................................ 1.2
2973[2] Final Frontier (IRE) **(70)** (Fav) *(RAkehurst)* 8-0 ‡3FNorton (10) (lw: 4th st: r.o one
                                                   pce fnl 2f) ................................................ 3¹/₂.3
3000[4] Coppot Tel (IRE) **(80)** *(CEBrittain)* 8-13 MRoberts (6) (lw: 2nd st: led over 2f out:
                                                   sn hdd: one pce) ........................................ 2¹/₂.4
3035★ World Express (IRE) **(83)** (v) *(BRMillman)* 9-2 JWilliams (1) (nrst fin) ............. 2.5
3063[4] Shynon **(66)** *(MHTompkins)* 7-6[6] ‡7MHumphries (2) (6th st: one pce fnl 2f) ... nk.6
2901[5] Don't Forget Marie (IRE) **(75)** *(RHannon)* 8-8 AMcGlone (7) (a mid div) ......... nk.7
2879[6] Nu Shan (IRE) **(69)** (v) *(MRStoute)* 8-2 WCarson (12) (dwlt: bhd tl sme hdwy &
                                                   hrd rdn over 2f out: nt r.o) .......................... ³/₄.8
2409 Hillsdown Boy **(63)** *(SDow)* 7-3[3] ‡7AGarth (11) (a bhd) ...................... 1¹/₂.9
1932 Miss Ribbons **(60)** *(PatMitchell)* 7-0 ‡7DWright (9) (led tl wknd qckly over 2f out) 3.10
3035[5] C D Shareplan (USA) **(72)** *(MRChannon)* 8-5 PaulEddery (5) (lw: 7th st: wknd
                                                   over 2f out) ............................................ 7.11
3055 Arogant Fool **(60)** *(DAWilson)* 7-0 ‡7SharonMillard (4) (swtg: 3rd st: wknd over
                                                   3f out: t.o fnl 2f) ...................................... 20.12
                 LONG HANDICAP: Shynon 7-4, Miss Ribbons 7-0.

**3/1** Final Frontier (IRE)(4/1—9/2), **5/1** Alderney Prince (USA), **11/2** Coppot Tel (IRE), **13/2** MARIUS (IRE), **8/1**
World Express (IRE), Shynon(op 5/1), **11/1** Nu Shan (IRE), **16/1** C D Shareplan (USA), Don't Forget Marie (IRE),
**50/1** Ors. CSF £36.10, CT £105.67. Tote £6.80: £2.60 £2.10 £1.50 (£23.50). Mrs Leonard Simpson
(LAMBOURN) bred by James O'Sullivan in Ireland. 12 Rn                 1m 57.74 (1.04 under 2y best: 6.34)
                                                                      SF—18/29/–/3/–/–

T/Trio: Race 3: £57.50 (22.1) & Race 6: £212.20 (5 Tckts). T/Jkpt: Not won; £60,299.84 to Sandown 16/9/92.
T/Plpt: £131.60 (51.45 Tckts).                                                                          Hn

# SANDOWN  (R-H)

## Wednesday, September 16th [Good, Good to firm patches back st]
Going Allowance: St: minus 0.05 sec; Rnd: nil sec per fur (G)                          Wind: nil

Stalls: high

**3275**         OXSHOTT NURSERY     £3761.00 (£1133.00: £549.00: £257.00)     **5f 6y**     2-20 (2-25)

3136[5] **Sheila's Secret (IRE) (89)** *(WCarter)* 8-12 JReid (4) (a.p: led over 2f out: all out) —1
3070[5] Ansellman **(98)** (Fav) *(MJHaynes)* 9-2 ‡5JWeaver (3) (lw: a.p: ev ch fnl f: r.o) . hd.2
3162[2] Geoff's Risk **(73)** *(GLewis)* 7-3[3] ‡7CHawksley (10) (b.hind: hdwy 2f out: r.o ins
                                                   fnl f) ................................................... nk.3
2824 Tuscan Dawn **(80)** *(JBerry)* 8-3[2] TQuinn (1) (lw: hld up: ev ch over 1f out: nt
                                                   qckn) ................................................ 1¹/₂.4
3162[5] Cuddly Date **(70)** *(DTThom)* 7-0 ‡7KimMcDonnell (9) (spd 4f) .................. 1¹/₂.5
2824[5] Bellsabanging **(77)** *(DRLaing)* 7-9[7] ‡5ATucker (8) (s.s: hdwy on ins 2f out: nt clr
                                                   run over 1f out: nt rcvr) ............................. nk.6
3129 Waterlord (IRE) **(73)** *(CGCox)* 7-10 NAdams (12) (gd spd over 3f) ............... hd.7

2883 Petite Vino **(70)** *(JJBridger)* 7-0 ‡7AntoinetteArmes (2) (dwlt: nvr nrr) ................. 2.8
3179 Kintwyn **(72)** *(DRLaing)* 7-9(2) TyroneWilliams (3) (a bhd) ................................... 2.9
3012 Moving Image (IRE) **(77)** *(MBell)* 8-0 CRutter (11) (b.hind: led over 2f) .......... hd.10
3001² Second Chance (IRE) **(73)** *(PMitchell)* 7-10 DBiggs (6) (bhd fnl 2f) ................. hd.11
3018⁵ Auntie Ginger **(72)** *(PButler)* 7-2(2) ‡7DToole (7) (lw: bhd fnl 2f) .................. 1½.12
3129 Kensworth Lady **(71)** *(MBlanshard)* 7-8(1) JQuinn (5) (lw: a bhd) .................. 1½.13
LONG HANDICAP: Geoff's Risk 7-3, Cuddly Date 6-12, Bellsabanging 7-0, Petite Vino 5-10,
Kintwyn 7-0, Auntie Ginger 7-5, Kensworth Lady 7-1.

**11/4** Ansellman, **13/2** SHEILA'S SECRET (IRE), Geoff's Risk, Second Chance (IRE), **8/1** Auntie Ginger(6/1—10/
1), **10/1** Waterlord (IRE), **12/1** Moving Image (IRE)(8/1—14/1), Tuscan Dawn(op 8/1), **16/1** Kensworth Lady,
**20/1** Cuddly Date, **25/1** Bellsabanging, **33/1** Kintwyn, **100/1** Petite Vino. CSF £23.29, CT £112.85. Tote £7.10:
£2.30 £1.50 £1.80 (£9.90). Sherwoods Transport Ltd (EPSOM) bred by A. F. O'Callaghan in Ireland. 13 Rn
61.95 sec (2.45)
SF—49/52/24/32/9/17

---

**3276** ALINGTON STKS (Mdn 2-Y.O) £3057.50 (£920.00: £445.00: £207.50)
7f 16y
2-50 (2-55)

3005 **Gustavia (IRE)** *(RWArmstrong)* 8-9 NDay (14) (3rd st: led wl over 1f out: r.o wl) .....—1
Trippiano **(Fav)** *(HRACecil)* 9-0 PatEddery (6) (gd sort: lw: racd wd: 6th st:
hdwy over 2f out: r.o ins fnl f) ........................................ 3½.2
2859² Piston (IRE) *(BHanbury)* 9-0 BRaymond (11) (swtg: led over 5f) ...................... 1.3
2346⁵ Eastern Memories (IRE) *(RHannon)* 9-0 SWhitworth (2) (hdwy fnl 2f: nvr nrr) .. 1½.4
3132⁶ Hard Task *(RFJohnsonHoughton)* 8-9 TQuinn (1) (swtg: 2nd st: wknd over 1f
out) ...................................................................... nk.5
3005 Son of Sharp Shot (IRE) *(JLDunlop)* 9-0 CRutter (10) (5th st: one pce fnl 2f) ...... nk.6
3000³ Grey Watch *(LadyHerries)* 8-9 JWilliams (13) (nrst fin) ............................ 1½.7
3005 Sun Grebe (IRE) *(JLDunlop)* 8-9 GBaxter (4) (a abt same pl) ...................... 1½.8
Captain Jack *(LMCumani)* 8-9 ‡JWeaver (2) (w'like: scope: bit bkwd: a bhd) .. nk.9
Moujeeb (USA) *(MRStoute)* 9-0 PD'Arcy (5) (w'like: scope: a bhd) .............. 1½.10
3130⁶ Coalisland *(RIngram)* 9-0 JQuinn (12) (a bhd) ................................. 5.11
2884³ Air Command (BAR) *(RHannon)* 9-0 BRouse (8) (4th st: wknd 2f out) ............ 10.12

**5/4** Trippiano, **9/4** Piston (IRE), **12/1** Eastern Memories (IRE)(10/1—16/1), Grey Watch(op 7/1), Captain
Jack(10/1—20/1), **16/1** Son of Sharp Shot (IRE)(12/1—20/1), Air Command (BAR)(10/1—20/1), **20/1**
Moujeeb (USA), Hard Task, **33/1** GUSTAVIA (IRE) & Ors. CSF £75.92, Tote £127.60: £12.20 £1.50 £1.40
(£205.10). Mrs Robert Armstrong (NEWMARKET) bred by Lodge Park Stud in Ireland. 12 Rn 30.70 (3.70)
SF—39/33/30/25/19/23

---

**3277** IAN GREIG BENEFIT H'CAP (0-100) £4354.00 (£1312.00: £636.00: £298.00)
1m 14y
3-20 (3-27)

(Weights raised 5 lb)
3061 **Neptune's Pet (82)** *(GLewis)* 4-9-3 JReid (5) (hld up: hdwy over 1f out: qcknd
ins fnl f: led last strides) ........................................... —1
3094⁶ Camden's Ransom (USA) **(70)** *(DRCElsworth)* 5-8-5(3) JWilliams (10) (in rr tl
hdwy over 2f out: r.o u.p fnl f) ...................................... hd.2
2999⁴ Akkazao (IRE) **(74)** *(WCarter)* 4-8-9 BRouse (1) (2nd st: led over 3f out tl last
strides) ............................................................. hd.3
722⁵ For Reg (IRE) **(93)** **(Fav)** *(ACStewart)* 3-9-10 PatEddery (4) (3rd st: ev ch & hrd
rdn fnl f: r.o) ....................................................... s.h.4
3137 Langtry Lady **(77)** (v) *(MJRyan)* 6-8-12 DBiggs (8) (5th st: r.o one pce fnl 2f) . 1½.5
2852 Big Blue **(87)** *(CEBrittain)* 3-9-4 TQuinn (9) (lw: hdwy & hrd rdn over 2f out: one
pce) ................................................................. 6.6
3137³ Dance on Sixpence **(60)** (v) *(HJCollingridge)* 4-7-9 JQuinn (7) (swtg: 4th st: ev
ch over 1f out: wknd fnl f) .......................................... nk.7
2527⁶ Baluga **(87)** *(GHarwood)* 3-9-4 AClark (6) (lw: led over 4f) ..................... 5.8
2521⁵ Strong Suit (IRE) **(85)** (bl) *(RHannon)* 3-9-2 SWhitworth (3) (6th st: wknd 2f out) 2½.9
1926 Berseto (USA) **(80)** *(HRACecil)* 3-8-11 BRaymond (2) (wl bhd fnl 3f) .......... 3½.10

**100/30** For Reg (IRE), **5/1** Camden's Ransom (USA), **8/1** Akkazao (IRE), Dance on Sixpence, NEPTUNE'S PET,
Big Blue, **10/1** Strong Suit (IRE), **11/1** Langtry Lady, **14/1** Ors. CSF £43.34, CT £299.26. Tote £8.30: £2.20
£2.40 £2.70 (£21.40). K. B. Symonds and Partners (EPSOM) bred by D. G. Mason. 10 Rn 1m 42.76 (3.56)
SF—50/37/40/54/37/25

---

**3278** ROOKERY CLAIMING STKS £2921.00 (£878.00: £424.00: £197.00)
5f 6y
3-50 (3-55)

3188 **Gone Savage (78)** **(Fav)** *(GBBalding)* 4-8-7 PatEddery (6) (mde all: easily) ...... —1
3183 Fay's Song (IRE) **(73)** *(RAkehurst)* 4-8-2 JQuinn (7) (lw: hld up: ev ch over 1f
out: hrd rdn: nt qckn) ............................................... 1½.2
Lyndon's Linnet **(65)** *(RIngram)* 4-8-9 CDwyer (5) (a.p: one pce fnl 2f) .......... 3.3

3079 Dickens Lane **(52)** *(RJHodges)* 5-8-3 DBiggs (3) (lw: a.p: one pce fnl 2f) ....... s.h.4
 Black Jewel *(MDIUsher)* 9-8-1 CRutter (2) (a bhd) ............................................ 2.5
 Al Billal *(JJBridger)* 4-8-9 TyroneWilliams (4) (lw: a bhd) ................................. 6.6

**4/7** GONE SAVAGE, **7/4** Fay's Song (IRE), **14/1** Dickens Lane, **20/1** Lyndon's Linnet, **66/1** Ors. CSF £1.98, Tote
£1.60: £1.20 £1.20 (£1.50). Mr Rex L. Mead (DORCHESTER) bred by Mrs C. F. Van Straubenzee and R. Mead. 6
Rn
61.49 sec (1.99)
SF—53/42/37/30/20/4

**3279** HEADWAY PROPERTY INITIATIVES H'CAP (0-80) £4011.25 (£1210.00: £587.50:
£276.25) **1m 3f 91y**
4-20 (4-24)

30972 **Bo Knows Best (IRE) (49)** *(JSutcliffe)* 3-7-7 NAdams (13) (5th st: led over 2f
out: sn clr: drvn out) ...................................................................................... —1
31743 I'M Electric **(57)** *(RCurtis)* 6-8-8 NDay (6) (gd hdwy 2f out: r.o: nt rch wnr) .... 2¹/₂.2
31394 Western Dynasty **(70)** *(MJRyan)* 6-9-2 ‡5JWeaver (10) (lw: hdwy 2f out: r.o one
pce fnl f) ........................................................................................................ 1¹/₂.3
3139 Mahsul (IRE) **(61)** *(CJBenstead)* 4-8-12 TQuinn (1) (hdwy fnl 2f: nvr nrr) ....... 1¹/₂.4
30762 Kabayil **(73)** *(PTWalwyn)* 3-9-3 BRouse (9) (2nd st: ev ch over 2f out: one pce) 3¹/₂.5
3097 Viaggio **(54)** *(JAkehurst)* 4-8-5⁽⁴⁾ JWilliams (2) (nrst fin) ........................... 1.6
3177★ Bit on the Side (IRE) **(57)** *(Fav)* *(MJMusson)* 3-8-1 (3x) TyroneWilliams (4)
(hdwy & 6th st: ev ch over 2f out: sn wknd) ................................................ ³/₄.7
3094★ L'Uomo Classics **(67)** *(RRowe)* 5-9-4 GBaxter (15) (nvr nr to chal) ............. nk.8
31745 Second Call **(64)** *(HCandy)* 3-8-8 CRutter (14) (lw: nvr trbld ldrs) .............. s.h.9
30402 Major Bugler (IRE) **(76)** *(GBBalding)* 3-9-6 PatEddery (7) (lw: a bhd) ........... ¹/₂.10
2585★ Barrish **(77)** *(RAkehurst)* 6-10-0 JReid (5) (led after 2f to 6f out: 3rd st: wknd 3f
out) ................................................................................................................ nk.11
30823 Rising Tempo (IRE) **(62)** *(CACyzer)* 4-8-13 DBiggs (12) (lw: prom tl wknd & 7th
st) .................................................................................................................. nk.12
 Castle Clown **(71)** *(LadyHerries)* 7-9-8 JQuinn (3) (led 6f out tl wknd over 2f
out) ................................................................................................................ 1¹/₂.13
30904 Janaat **(72)** *(AAScott)* 3-9-2 BRaymond (11) (lw: led 2f: 4th st: wknd 3f out) .. nk.14
 Duke of Monmouth (USA) **(77)** *(SESherwood)* 4-10-0 MPerrett (8) (a bhd) ..... ³/₄.15

**3/1** Bit on the Side (IRE), **6/1** BO KNOWS BEST (IRE), **13/2** Major Bugler (IRE)(8/1—10/1), **8/1** Janaat, I'M
Electric, **9/1** Rising Tempo (IRE), **10/1** Barrish(8/1—12/1), **14/1** Western Dynasty, **16/1** Kabayil, **20/1** Second
Call, **25/1** Mahsul (IRE), **33/1** L'Uomo Classics, Viaggio, **40/1** Ors. CSF £50.80, CT £595.48. Tote £6.90: £2.00
£3.10 £4.60 (£31.80). Mr John Sutcliffe (EPSOM) bred by Gay O'Callaghan in Ireland. 15 Rn  2m 25.88 (4.18)
SF—37/47/52/45/43/29

**3280** MITRE GRADUATION STKS (3-Y.O.F) £3510.75 (£1056.00: £510.50: £237.75)
**1¹/₄m 7y**
4-55 (4-57)

29132 **Anne Bonny (87)** *(JRFanshawe)* 9-4 TQuinn (3) (lw: 2nd st: led over 2f out: sn
clr: r.o wl) ..................................................................................................... —1
29332 Besotted **(98)** *(Fav)* *(BWHills)* 9-4 PatEddery (2) (3rd st: chsd wnr fnl 2f: hrd rdn:
no imp) .......................................................................................................... 6.2
 788 Sea Clover (IRE) **(80)** *(MajorWRHern)* 9-4 JReid (1) (led tl wknd over 2f out) ..... 5.3
 Natchez Trace *(JLDunlop)* 8-11 AClark (4) (unf: scope: a last: t.o) ................... 30.4

**8/13** Besotted, **5/2** ANNE BONNY, **11/1** Natchez Trace(14/1—8/1), **12/1** Sea Clover (IRE)(7/1—14/1). CSF
£4.19, Tote £3.40 (£1.50). Mr David Thompson (NEWMARKET) bred by R. H. Cowell. 4 Rn  2m 8.45 (4.15)
SF—62/50/34/–

**3281** HERSHAM APP'CE H'CAP (3-Y.O) (0-80) £2999.00 (£902.00: £436.00: £203.00)
**7f 16y**
5-30 (5-32)

30145 **By Hand (74)** *(WJHaggas)* 8-8 ‡7SallyRadford-Howes (4) (lw: led over 5f: led
ins fnl f: r.o wl) ............................................................................................. —1
31334 Morocco (IRE) **(73)** *(RCharlton)* 8-7 ‡7RhonaGent (2) (lw: 3rd st: led over 1f out tl
fnl f) .............................................................................................................. hd.2
3241 Hopeful Bid (IRE) **(71)** (bl) *(RHannon)* 8-5 ‡7MarkDenaro (3) (lw: hdwy over 2f
out: ev ch over 1f out: nt qckn) ....................................................................... ¹/₂.3
23432 Confronter **(80)** *(Fav)* *(PFICole)* 9-4 ‡3JDSmith (5) (lw: 5th st: hrd rdn over 2f out:
one pce) ......................................................................................................... 1¹/₂.4
3133 Countercheck (IRE) **(56)** *(CFWall)* 7-4⁽⁴⁾ ‡7TWilson (6) (lw: nvr nrr) ............ 3.5
30484 Great Hall **(52)** (bl) *(PDCundell)* 7-7 AntoinetteArmes (9) (dwlt: a bhd) ........... ¹/₂.6
3159 Cappahoosh (IRE) **(54)** *(HJCollingridge)* 7-6 ‡3CHawksley (8) (lw: 6th st: wknd
3f out) ............................................................................................................ 4.7
3037 Coniston Lake (IRE) **(66)** (bl) *(GLewis)* 8-0 ‡7AmandaBowen (1) (b.hind: 4th &
rn wd st: wknd over 2f out) ............................................................................. nk.8
2949 Smudgemupum **(52)** *(MissBSanders)* 7-3 ‡4DToole (7) (2nd st: wknd 3f out) ... nk.9
 LONG HANDICAP: Countercheck (IRE) 7-6, Great Hall 7-4, Smudgemupum 6-13.
*Stewards Enquiry: Smith suspended 25-26/9/92 (excessive use of whip).*

**11/8** Confronter, **11/2** Morocco (IRE), **7/1** Cappahoosh (IRE), **8/1** BY HAND(op 5/1), Hopeful Bid (IRE), **10/1** Countercheck (IRE)(8/1—14/1), Coniston Lake (IRE), **20/1** Great Hall, **33/1** Smudgemupum. CSF £47.95, CT £332.46. Tote £7.60: £1.80 £2.00 £1.70 (£14.10). Mrs M. M. Haggas (NEWMARKET) bred by Woodditton Stud Ltd. 9 Rn　　　　　　　1m 30.58 (3.58)
　　　　　　　　　　　　　　　　　　　　　　　　　　　　　　　　SF—40/38/34/42/5/6

T/Trio: Race 3: £83.60 (15.3 Tckts) & Race 5: £223.20 (7.1 Tckts). T/Jkpt: Not won; £96,027.50 to Newbury 18/9/92. T/Plpt: £81.10 (83.40 Tckts).　　　　　　　　　　　　　　　　　　　Hn


## 2862—YARMOUTH (L-H)
### Tuesday, September 15th [Good]
Going Allowance: nil sec per fur (G)　　　　　　　　　　　　Wind: str against

Stalls: high

**3282**　　REGENT STKS (Mdn 3-Y-O) £2385.00 (£660.00: £315.00)　**1³⁄₄m 17y**　2-10 (2-12)

2823 **Highland Fantasy (USA)** *(BWHills)* 8-9　DHolland (5) (a.p: 2nd st: led 4f out: rdn out) ...................................................................................................... —1

3114⁴ Nemir *(JHMGosden)* 9-0　GHind (8) (b: hld up: hdwy 3f out: hrd rdn & unable qckn fnl f) ........................................................................................ 2¹⁄₂.2

2869⁴ Flamingo Rose (IRE) *(HRACecil)* 8-9　WRyan (10) (b.nr hind: chsd ldrs: 4th st: jnd wnr over 2f out: rdn & no ex fnl f) ......................................... 2¹⁄₂.3

2635² Rosina Mae (74) (Fav) *(LordHuntingdon)* 8-6　‡3DHarrison (4) (hld up & bhd: hdwy 3f out: styd on: nvr able to chal) .................................. nk.4

2783 Whatcomesnaturally (USA) (46) *(MCChapman)* 8-5(1)　‡5RPrice (2) (prom: 3rd st: wknd over 1f out) ........................................................... 3¹⁄₂.5

3158 Saif Al Adil (IRE) (47) *(RIvory)* 9-0　GBardwell (1) (lw: chsd ldrs: 5th st: rdn & wknd over 2f out) ...................................................... 5.6

3053² Shesadelight (bl) *(JLDunlop)* 8-9　GDuffield (11) (effrt & 6th st: rdn & wknd 3f out) ................................................................................. s.h.7

2783 Princess Evita (FR) (37) *(RGuest)* 8-2　‡7SEiffert (7) (led 10f: wknd wl over 2f out) 3.8
　　　Sea Pet *(MissGayKelleway)* 8-9　GayKelleway (6) (leggy: lt-f: dwlt: a bhd) ......... sh.9

3016⁶ Bayin (USA) *(RWArmstrong)* 9-0　RHills (9) (lw: hdwy ent st: wknd wl over 2f out) ³⁄₄.10

1940⁵ Free Transfer (IRE) (67) *(PFTulk)* 9-0　LPiggott (3) (hld up: effrt 3f out: no imp: eased whn btn) ................................................................. 1¹⁄₂.11

**9/4** Rosina Mae, **3/1** Nemir, **9/1** Shesadelight, **13/2** HIGHLAND FANTASY (USA)(5/1—8/1), **9/1** Flamingo Rose (IRE)(op 6/1), **10/1** Free Transfer (IRE), **20/1** Bayin (USA), **33/1** Saif Al Adil (IRE), Sea Pet, **50/1** Whatcomesnaturally (USA), **66/1** Princess Evita (FR). CSF £24.94, Tote £13.20: £2.90 £1.40 £2.30 (£25.30). Mr A. B. Weller (LAMBOURN) bred by Golden Park Ltd in USA. 11 Rn　　　　3m 7.4 (9.4)

**3283**　　BROOKE (S) STKS (2-Y-O) £2973.00 (£828.00: £399.00)　**6f 3y**　2-40 (2-46)

2233 **Palacegate Touch** *(JBerry)* 8-11　GCarter (10) (s.i.s: hld up: rapid hdwy over 1f out: qcknd to ld wl ins fnl f) ...................................................... —1

2771 Texas Cowgirl (IRE) *(GAPritchard-Gordon)* 8-6　WHood (8) (s.s: hdwy to ld over 1f out: hdd nr fin) ........................................................ 1¹⁄₂.2

2994 Duke of Budworth *(MHTompkins)* 8-11　PRobinson (7) (hdwy ¹⁄₂-wy: rdn over 1f out: r.o) ...................................................................... 1¹⁄₂.3

2973 Mr Nevermind (IRE) (55) (bl) *(GLewis)* 8-11　BRouse (3) (a.p: led centre ¹⁄₂-wy tl over 1f out: kpt on one pce) ....................................... nk.4

2928 Legendary Hero (64) (v) (Jt-Fav) *(TDBarron)* 8-11　KDarley (20) (w ldrs stands' side: rdn over 1f out: unable qckn) ...................................... 1.5

3155 Dowreyna (66) *(MRStoute)* 8-6　GDuffield (6) (prom tl rdn & wknd over 1f out) . hd.6

2706⁴ Miss Fayruz (IRE) (59) *(MrsLPiggott)* 8-11　LPiggott (12) (nvr trbld ldrs) ......... 2¹⁄₂.7

2994² Be Polite (IRE) (60) (v) (Jt-Fav) *(MBell)* 8-6　RHills (15) (b.nr hind: r.o appr fnl f: nvr nrr) ................................................................. ³⁄₄.8

3136⁶ Don't Be Saki (IRE) (52) (v) *(JEtherington)* 8-6　KFallon (13) (hdwy u.p 2f out: nvr nr to chal) ........................................................ hd.9

2863 The Institute Boy (54) *(KRBurke)* 8-11　AShoults (14) (m.n.s) ........................ nk.10

2994⁵ Sea Strand (57) *(MBlanshard)* 8-6　GBardwell (5) (spd 4f) ............................ nk.11

3156 Jade Runner (51) (bl) *(MrsNMacauley)* 8-6　NCarlisle (19) (m.n.s) ............... 1¹⁄₂.12

Nightmare Lady *(WHolden)* 8-11(1)　MTebbutt (18) (unf: bkwd: s.i.s: a in rr) ...... nk.13

3050 Swiftlet (IRE) (48) *(DJSCosgrove)* 8-3　‡3DHarrison (17) (chsd ldrs 4f) ........... nk.14

3148 Charlies Reward (52) *(TFairhurst)* 8-11　JFanning (4) (m.n.s) ...................... hd.15

3077 Backstabber *(DrJDScargill)* 8-11　JQuinn (10) (bit bkwd: prom 4f) .............. 1¹⁄₂.16

3115 Red Ballet (61) (bl) *(MrsNMacauley)* 8-11　DBiggs (1) (racd alone far side: led over 3f) ............................................................................ nk.17

Blue Trumpet (bl) *(AHide)* 8-11　DaleGibson (16) (w'like: bit bkwd: dwlt: a bhd) 1¹⁄₂.18

| | | |
|---|---|---|
| 3033 | Good Image (64) (APJarvis) 8-11 WRyan (9) (lw: m.n.s) | 1.19 |
| 2409 | Tresaria (IRE) (PHowling) 8-6 DHolland (2) (m.n.s) | 2½.20 |

6/1 Legendary Hero(op 4/1), Be Polite (IRE), 13/2 Dowreyna(op 4/1), 9/1 Don't Be Saki (IRE), 10/1 Miss Fayruz (IRE), Sea Strand, 12/1 Good Image(op 8/1), Red Ballet, 14/1 Mr Nevermind (IRE), Texas Cowgirl (IRE), 16/1 Duke of Budworth, 20/1 PALACEGATE TOUCH, 25/1 The Institute Boy, Blue Trumpet, Backstabber, Nightmare Lady, Charlies Reward, 33/1 Ors. CSF £266.29, Tote £27.40: £5.70 £6.10 £6.30 (£352.60). Palacegate Corporation Ltd (COCKERHAM) bred by The Woodhaven Stud. 20 Rn; Bt in 6,750 gns          1m 15.3 (4.7)

SF—3/-/-/-/-/-

**3284**  BRIAN TAYLOR MEMORIAL H'CAP (3-Y-O) (0-90) £4971.00 (£1488.00: £714.00: £327.00)  **6f 3y**      3-10 (3-14)

(Weights raised 3 lb)

| | | |
|---|---|---|
| 3142* | **King's Signet (USA) (86)** (Fav) (JHMGosden) 9-7 GHind (2) (lw: a.p: led over 2f out: rdn clr wl ins fnl f) | —1 |
| 1598 | Sasparella (65) (bl) (WJarvis) 8-0 PRobinson (1) (hld up: gd hdwy appr fnl f: r.o nr fin) | 1½.2 |
| 3004⁶ | Nagida (78) (JARToller) 8-8 ‡⁵JWeaver (3) (chsd ldrs centre: effrt & ev ch 1f out: hrd rdn: unable qckn) | 1½.3 |
| 3133 | Hi-Tech Honda (IRE) (67) (CEBrittain) 8-2 GDuffield (5) (a.p: rdn over 1f out: one pce) | 3.4 |
| 2911 | Last Exit (82) (WJarvis) 9-3 DHolland (4) (rdn along ½-wy: kpt on ins fnl f: nvr nrr) | 1½.5 |
| 2411³ | Waders Dream (IRE) (76) (JEBanks) 8-6 ‡⁵StephenDavies (9) (lw: spd over 4f) | nk.6 |
| 3196³ | Tate Dancer (IRE) (77) (RWArmstrong) 8-12 LPiggott (8) (led centre over 3f: wknd over 1f out) | 1.7 |
| 3183 | Truthful Image (78) (v) (MJRyan) 8-13 DBiggs (6) (bhd fr ½-wy) | ¾.8 |
| 3004⁴ | First Gold (68) (bl) (JWharton) 8-3 JQuinn (7) (spd 4f: sn rdn & wknd) | 3.9 |
| 3133 | Walstead (IRE) (60) (DAWilson) 7-9 GBardwell (10) (racd stands' side: bhd fnl 2f) | 3.10 |
| 2902 | Forest Fairy (63) (RBoss) 7-9 ‡3DHarrison (12) (dwlt: sn rcvrd: led stands' side ½-wy: no ch fnl 2f) | 2½.11 |
| 2804⁶ | Palacegate Racing (71) (JBerry) 8-6 GCarter (11) (led stands' side to ½-wy: sn wknd: t.o) | 25.12 |

3/1 KING'S SIGNET (USA), 5/1 Tate Dancer (IRE), 13/2 First Gold, 7/1 Waders Dream (IRE), Truthful Image, 9/1 Nagida, 10/1 Hi-Tech Honda (IRE), 14/1 Walstead (IRE), 16/1 Palacegate Racing, 20/1 Sasparella, 25/1 Ors. CSF £56.10, CT £449.71. Tote £4.20: £2.00 £3.80 £3.20 (£34.60). Sheikh Mohammed (NEWMARKET) bred by Darley Stud Management Co Ltd in USA. 12 Rn          1m 12.3 (1.7)

SF—73/46/48/30/39/27

**3285**  TATTERSALLS AUCTION SERIES STKS (Qualifier) (Mdn 2-Y-O) £3106.00 (£928.00: £444.00: £202.00)  **6f 3y**      3-40 (3-47)

| | | |
|---|---|---|
| 2965³ | **Racing Telegraph (77)** (JPearce) 8-0 ‡⁵RPrice (2) (a.p: led 1f out: r.o wl) | —1 |
| 3077² | Perdition (IRE) (64) (JWHills) 8-1 RHills (1) (a.p: led 2f out to 1f out: unable qckn fnl f) | 1.2 |
| 3115 | Mark's Club (IRE) (BWHills) 8-7 DHolland (3) (chsd ldrs: kpt on ins fnl f: nvr nrr) | 2½.3 |
| 1192⁵ | Bob's Return (IRE) (Fav) (MHTompkins) 8-11 PRobinson (12) (hdwy over 1f out: rdn & r.o nr fin) | hd.4 |
| 2425⁶ | Our Shadee (USA) (64) (KTIvory) 8-6 GBardwell (13) (led 4f: sn rdn: no ex appr fnl f) | ¾.5 |
| 2932 | Spring Sixpence (JRFanshawe) 8-6 GDuffield (4) (chsd ldrs: rdn over 1f out: sn btn) | ¾.6 |
| | Sassamouse (RGuest) 7-7 ‡⁷CHawksley (8) (lt-f: unf: dwlt: r.o appr fnl f: nrst fin) | hd.7 |
| | Smith N'Allan (BobJones) 8-8 NDay (5) (w'like: str: bkwd: s.s: hdwy 2f out: wknd appr fnl f) | hd.8 |
| | Trianglepoint (IRE) (GAPritchard-Gordon) 7-13 ‡3DHarrison (14) (w'like: leggy: s.s: a in rr) | 2½.9 |
| 3156⁴ | Home Affair (62) (DTThom) 8-0 DBiggs (9) (chsd ldrs tl wknd wl over 1f out) | hd.10 |
| 2932 | Gangleader (60) (SPCWoods) 8-8 WWoods (10) (spd over 3f) | 1½.11 |
| 3077 | Splash of Salt (IRE) (WJHaggas) 8-4 JQuinn (16) (chsd ldrs 4f) | ¾.12 |
| 2185 | More Than Love (PAKelleway) 8-1 KDarley (6) (w ldrs 3f: sn rdn & wknd) | 1½.13 |
| | Access Festivals (RBoss) 8-7 MTebbutt (11) (lt-f: unf: s.s: a bhd) | nk.14 |
| 2285 | Distant Spring (IRE) (GAPritchard-Gordon) 8-8 JFanning (7) (bit bkwd: sn.s) | 3.15 |
| 3178⁶ | Who's the Best (IRE) (70) (APJarvis) 8-7 WRyan (15) (lw: chsd ldrs 4f: sn wknd) | 3.16 |

9/4 Bob's Return (IRE)(9/2—5/1), 5/1 RACING TELEGRAPH, 6/1 Perdition (IRE), 9/1 Spring Sixpence(op 6/1), Splash of Salt (IRE), 10/1 Who's the Best (IRE), 12/1 Gangleader(14/1—8/1), 14/1 Mark's Club (IRE)(8/1—16/1), 20/1 Home Affair, Sassamouse, 25/1 Our Shadee (USA), Access Festivals, Trianglepoint (IRE), 33/1 Smith N'Allan, Distant Spring (IRE), 50/1 More Than Love. CSF £35.78, Tote £5.70: £1.90 £2.10 £4.80 (£8.20). Mr Cliff Woof (NEWMARKET) bred by Mottramcourt Ltd. 16 Rn          1m 14 (3.4)

SF—18/15/11/14/6/3

**3286**    JACK LEADER MEMORIAL CHALLENGE TROPHY (Nursery)    £6160.00 (£1840.00:
£880.00: £400.00)    **7f 3y**      4-10 (4-14)

(Weights raised 9 lb)

29735 **Trundley Wood** (68) *(GAPritchard-Gordon)* 8-5 ‡3DHarrison (4) (hld up: hdwy
3f out: rdn & edgd rt 1f out: led ins fnl f: r.o) ....................... —1

2872★ **Awestruck** (73) (Fav) *(WJHaggas)* 8-13 NDay (5) (led tl hdd ins fnl f) ............. 1½.2

2010 Silent Expression (71) *(DMorris)* 8-11 MTebbutt (1) (a.p: rdn & n.m.r 1f out: nt
rcvr) ............................................................................ ¾.3

2938 Strike-a-Pose (59) *(CNWilliams)* 7-13 JQuinn (3) (a.p: effrt appr fnl f: unable
qckn) ........................................................................... nk.4

30554 Soldiers Bay (78) *(LordHuntingdon)* 9-4 LPiggott (9) (hld up: r.o ins fnl f: nvr
nrr) ............................................................................ 1½.5

3242 Formaestre (IRE) (64) *(MHTompkins)* 8-4 PRobinson (8) (hld up & bhd: swtchd
lft & hdwy 2f out: r.o) ........................................................ nk.6

31626 Trevorsninepoints (66) *(MJRyan)* 8-6 DBiggs (7) (plld hrd: chsd ldrs: shkn up
2f out: no imp) ............................................................... nk.7

29733 Wishing Cap (USA) (65) *(SirMarkPrescott)* 8-5 GDuffield (2) (prom: rdn 2f out:
sn btn) ........................................................................ 3.8

**15/8** Awestruck(6/4—9/4), **9/2** Silent Expression, **13/2** Wishing Cap (USA), Soldiers Bay, **9/1** Strike-a-Pose,
**10/1** Trevorsninepoints(16/1—8/1), **11/1** TRUNDLEY WOOD & Ors. CSF £30.62, CT £99.21. Tote £17.20:
£2.60 £1.10 £2.50 (£18.20). Mrs E. H. Vestey (NEWMARKET) bred by Mrs A. M. Vestey. 8 Rn   1m 28.1 (5.3)
                                   SF—11/14/10/–/11/–/

**3287**    YARMOUTH ROADS H'CAP (0-70) £3470.00 (£1040.00: £500.00: £230.00)
**1m 3y**      4-40 (4-46)

3009 **Night Transaction** (53) *(AHide)* 5-8-5 ‡7NVarley (4) (lw: hld up: hdwy 2f out:
rdn to ld wl ins fnl f) ....................................................... —1

27303 Coral Flutter (61) *(JWPayne)* 5-8-13 ‡6LBlane (9) (a.p: led 3f out tl hdd nr fin) 1½.2

2865 Yonge Tender (41) (bl) *(CNWilliams)* 5-8-0(3) JCurant (2) (chsd ldrs: hrd rdn
ins fnl f: r.o) ................................................................ s.h.3

2993 Deevee (42) *(CJBenstead)* 3-7-7(1) ‡3DHarrison (10) (lw: hdwy 2f out: styd on
ins fnl f) ..................................................................... 3.4

29454 Shining Jewel (69) *(MrsLPiggott)* 5-10-0 LPiggott (a.p: effrt over 2f out: wknd
ins fnl f) ..................................................................... hd.5

30023 State of Affairs (42) *(CAHorgan)* 5-8-1 DaleGibson (14) (lw: hld up: effrt u.p
over 1f out: nt pce to chal) ................................................. 1½.6

31333 Roca Murada (IRE) (58) *(MJRyan)* 3-8-12 DBiggs (6) (chsd ldrs over 6f: sn hrd
rdn & wknd) .................................................................. nk.7

831 Case for the Crown (USA) (41) (Fav) *(BJCurley)* 5-8-0 GCarter (16) (b: bit
bkwd: bhd: swtchd rt & effrt over 1f out: nvr nr to chal) ...... ¾.8

2607 Chaff (39) *(DMorris)* 5-7-5(6) ‡7CHawksley (5) (mde most 5f: sn rdn & btn) ..... 3½.9

2830 Blue Drifter (IRE) (50) *(JSutcliffe)* 3-8-4(1) BRouse (17) (nvr trbld ldrs) ........ nk.10

2935 Don't Drop Bombs (USA) (48) *(AAScott)* 3-8-2 JFortune (8) (m.n.s) ............ nk.11

3140 Possessive Lady (44) *(MBell)* 5-8-3(1) GDuffield (13) (lw: prom over 5f) ........ 3.12

3048 Edgeaway (61) (v) *(JWHills)* 3-9-1 RHills (3) (prom over 4f) ...................... 1½.13

1544 Sockem (34) *(CNWilliams)* 5-7-7 JQuinn (7) (disp ld to ½-wy: sn rdn & wknd:
t.o) ........................................................................... 12.14

3068 Henry Will (36) (bl) *(TFairhurst)* 8-7-9 JFanning (12) (spd to ½-wy: sn lost tch:
t.o) ........................................................................... s.h.15

LONG HANDICAP: Chaff 6-12, Sockem 7-3.

**3/1** Case for the Crown (USA)(5/1—5/2), **5/1** Roca Murada (IRE), **6/1** Shining Jewel, State of Affairs, **9/1** Coral
Flutter(5/1—10/1), **10/1** Possessive Lady, **11/1** Edgeaway, **12/1** Deevee, NIGHT TRANSACTION(op 8/1), **14/1**
Yonge Tender, **20/1** Blue Drifter (IRE), Henry Will, Don't Drop Bombs (USA), **33/1** Ors. CSF £119.68, CT
£1,429.52. Tote £24.00: £5.10 £4.30 £6.10 (£90.90). Mr Anthony Hide (NEWMARKET) bred by Alan Gibson. 15
Rn                                               1m 40 (4.7)
                                SF—20/28/9/–/27/–

T/Plpt: Not won; £5,156.30 to Yarmouth 16/9/92.                        IM

# YARMOUTH (L-H)
## Wednesday, September 16th [Good to firm]
Going Allowance: St: minus 0.20 sec; Rnd: minus 0.30 sec (F)      Wind: slt half bhd

Stalls: high

**3288**    NEWTOWN (S) STKS (3 & 4-Y.O) £2469.00 (£684.00: £327.00)    **1m 3y**   2-10 (2-14)

1417 **Saifan** (63) (bl) *(DMorris)* 3-8-5 ‡5StephenDavies (6) (s.i.s: hdwy ½-wy: led ins
fnl f: sn clr) ................................................................. —1

2750 Red Ink (52) *(JSutcliffe)* 3–8-10 PaulEddery (5) (hld up: hdwy 2f out: rdn & r.o fnl f) ............ 2.2

2952 Genuine Lady (47) *(APJarvis)* 4–8-9 WRyan (3) (a.p: led over 2f out tl ins fnl f) . ¾.3

3048² Ace Girl (56) *(SRBowring)* 3–8-5(1) ‡7MHarris (8) (led tl over 2f out: rdn & wknd appr fnl f) ............ 2½.4

3003⁴ J'Arrive (53) (Fav) *(JPearce)* 3–8-5 MRoberts (9) (chsd ldrs: hrd rdn appr fnl f: sn btn) ............ nk.5

2101 Armashocker (44) *(DSasse)* 4–8-9 ‡5RPrice (7) (hld up: effrt 3f out: nvr able to chal) ............ 3.6

2993 Alton Belle (35) (bl) *(PHowling)* 3–8-5 BCrossley (10) (in tch: rdn over 2f out: no imp) ............ 5.7

2862⁴ Top Sire *(JHMGosden)* 3–8-10 WCarson (4) (a bhd: t.o) ............ 10.8

3101 Arjiil *(MHTompkins)* 3–8-10 GDuffield (1) (lw: prom 5f: sn lost tch: t.o) ............ 3½.9

3176 Chequers (IRE) (63) *(RJRWilliams)* 3–9-2 RCochrane (2) (hmpd & fell wl after 1f) 0

**9/4** J'Arrive(tchd 7/2), **5/1** Red Ink, **11/2** Ace Girl, Chequers (IRE), **10/1** SAIFAN, **11/1** Genuine Lady(7/1—12/1), **12/1** Arjiil(7/1—14/1), Top Sire(7/1—14/1), **50/1** Armashocker, **66/1** Alton Belle. CSF £53.59, Tote £12.20: £3.20 £1.90 £3.10 (£43.60). Mrs Rosalie Hawes (NEWMARKET) bred by M. M. Nashar. 10 Rn; Bt in 3,600 gns

1m 39.3 (4)
SF–7/6/3/–/–/–

## 3289

LIFEBOAT STKS (Mdn 2-Y.O.C & G) £2490.00 (£690.00: £330.00)     **7f 3y** 2-40 (2-45)

3008 **Beggarman Thief (USA)** *(JHMGosden)* 9-0 RCochrane (9) (plld hrd: hld up & bhd: gd hdwy to ld ins fnl f: r.o) ............ —1

2873² Shareek (USA) *(MRStoute)* 9-0 AMunro (7) (a.p: ev ch 1f out: unable qckn ins fnl f) ............ 1½.2

3005 Coneybury (IRE) *(LMCumani)* 9-0 LDettori (10) (bit bkwd: hld up: r.o appr fnl f: fin wl) ............ 2½.3

2873⁴ Nessun Dorma (Fav) *(GWragg)* 9-0 MRoberts (6) (chsd ldrs: effrt over 1f out: nt pce to chal) ............ 1½.4

Press Gallery *(MrsJTCecil)* 9-0 PaulEddery (1) (gd sort: bit bkwd: s.s: sn chsng ldrs: ev ch 1f out: one pce) ............ 1½.5

Yeltsin *(HRACecil)* 9-0 WRyan (3) (w'like: bit bkwd: chsd ldrs over 5f: sn wknd) 4.6

Barraak *(MajorWRHern)* 9-0 WCarson (8) (w'like: bit bkwd: hld up: hdwy 2f out: hrd rdn appr fnl f: sn btn) ............ nk.7

3186 Time Honored (USA) *(SirMarkPrescott)* 9-0 GDuffield (4) (hld up: hdwy to ld over 2f out: hdd & wknd qckly fnl f) ............ 1½.8

1701 Scorcher (IRE) *(CEBrittain)* 8-9 ‡5BDoyle (5) (prom: led 3f out: sn hdd & wknd) nk.9

2482 Ignited *(MrsNMacauley)* 9-0 NCarlisle (12) (b: led 4f: rdn & wknd over 2f out: t.o) ............ 6.10

2108 Side Bar *(MJRyan)* 9-0 MTebbutt (2) (spd 4f: lost tch: t.o) ............ nk.11

**3/1** Nessun Dorma, **9/2** Shareek (USA)(op 3/1), Press Gallery(7/1—4/1), **5/1** Coneybury (IRE)(4/1—6/1), **11/2** Yeltsin(3/1—6/1), **13/2** BEGGARMAN THIEF (USA)(5/1—8/1), **12/1** Time Honored (USA), **16/1** Barraak(op 10/1), **50/1** Ors. CSF £35.76, Tote £11.90: £3.10 £1.50 £1.70 (£28.30). Mr Landon Knight (NEWMARKET) bred by Landon Knight in USA. 11 Rn

1m 26 (3.2)
SF–31/26/18/13/8/–

## 3290

SHADWELL STUD APP'CE SERIES H'CAP (0-70) £2723.20 (£755.20: £361.60)
**7f 3y**     3-10 (3-14)

3245⁴ **Ballerina Bay (56)** (v) *(DTThom)* 4–8-13 ‡5FArrowsmith (5) (hld up: hdwy 3f out: jnd ldr ins fnl f: led cl home) ............ —1

2871 Guesstimation (USA) (35) *(JPearce)* 3–7-2 ‡5DWright (2) (a.p: led over 1f out: rdn & edgd lft fnl f: hdd nr fin) ............ s.h.2

3245 Judgement Call (55) *(PHowling)* 5–8-12 ‡5CAvery (9) (led over 4f: kpt on one pce fnl 2f) ............ 3.3

2865 Saboteur (35) *(WJMusson)* 8–7-6(4) ‡5DMcCabe (1) (prom: led over 2f out tl over 1f out: one pce) ............ hd.4

3024² Flashy's Son (66) *(MDHammond)* 4–9-7 ‡7ALakeman (3) (hdwy ½-wy: rdn & wknd over 1f out) ............ 3½.5

3133² Silky Siren (56) (bl) (Fav) *(EAWheeler)* 3–9-0 DHarrison (11) (chsd ldrs over 4f: sn rdn & btn) ............ 1½.6

3133 Peerage Prince (64) *(PatMitchell)* 3–9-8 RPerham (12) (chsd ldrs 5f: sn wknd) . ½.7

2427 Affordable (63) *(WCarter)* 4–9-11 NGwilliams (6) (nvr trbld ldrs) ............ nk.8

2953³ Sure Shot Norman (47) *(JSutcliffe)* 3–8-2 ‡³JTate (10) (prom over 5f) ............ nk.9

2757 Bellatrix (45) *(CEBrittain)* 4–8-7 BDoyle (4) (effrt over 2f out: hrd rdn & no imp) 1½.10

3287² Coral Flutter (61) (bl) *(JWPayne)* 5–9-6 ‡³BLane (14) (s.s: nvr nr to chal) ........ hd.11

2187 Executive Spirit (65) *(DSasse)* 3–9-9 RPrice (8) (swvd rt s: a bhd) ............ 2.12

3074³ Almasa (60) *(DMorris)* 4–9-8 StephenDavies (13) (a bhd) ............ 4.13

2871 Mindomica (51) (v) *(MBell)* 3–8-9 KRutter (7) (prom 5f: wknd qckly: t.o) ............ ¾.14

LONG HANDICAP: Saboteur 7-4.

**5/1** Silky Siren, **11/2** Coral Flutter(4/1—6/1), Flashy's Son(4/1—6/1), **7/1** Almasa, BALLERINA BAY, **11/1** Sure Shot Norman, **12/1** Bellatrix, Judgement Call, **14/1** Mindomica(op 8/1), **16/1** Saboteur, Affordable, **20/1** Peerage Prince, **33/1** Ors. CSF £182.06, CT £2,462.48. Tote £8.20: £2.10 £13.60 £4.20 (£261.90). Mrs Carol Whitwood (NEWMARKET) bred by Mrs C. Whitwood and N. E. C Sherwood. 14 Rn     1m 24.7 (1.9)
SF—49/23/38/17/35/23

### 3291

NORFOLK FARMERS CLAIMING STKS (2-Y.O) £3036.00 (£846.00: £408.00)
7f 3y
3-40 (3-44)

| | | |
|---|---|---|
| 3055[6] | **Pontevecchio Moda** (DRCElsworth) 7-7 ‡⁵BDoyle (11) (hdwy over 1f out: str run & veered bdly lft fnl f: led cl home) | —1 |
| 3115[2] | **Mam'zelle Angot (Fav)** (MRStoute) 7-12 WCarson (3) (b.hind: led far side: hrd drvn fnl f: ct last stride) | nk.2 |
| 3186 | **Ascom Pager Too (57)** (PHowling) 8-6 BCrossley (10) (gd hdwy appr fnl f: fin fast) | 3.3 |
| 2973 | **Premium (65)** (bl) (WJHaggas) 8-7 MRoberts (9) (hdwy ½-wy: r.o one pce appr fnl f) | 1.4 |
| 3077 | **Secret Fantasy (IRE)** (CFWall) 8-0 NCarlisle (2) (lw: chsd ldrs: rdn 2f out: kpt on) | 1.5 |
| 3093 | **Tartouka (GLewis)** 7-9 ‡³DHarrison (7) (chsd ldrs: hrd rdn & no ex appr fnl f) | 1½.6 |
| 3283 | **Miss Fayruz (IRE) (60)** (MrsLPiggott) 8-8(1) LPiggott (17) (chsd ldrs stands' side: styd on ins fnl f) | ½.7 |
| 3008[6] | **Matron of Honor** (NCWright) 8-2 PaulEddery (13) (b.hind: bit bkwd: hdwy 3f out: hrd rdn over 1f out: sn btn) | 1½.8 |
| 3178 | **Clar Dubh (IRE)** (MHTompkins) 8-2(4) GDuffield (15) (styd on fnl 2f: nvr nrr) | 1½.9 |
| 3050* | **Allegrissima (73)** (JBerry) 8-2 GCarter (6) (b.hind: lw: led stands' side: sn rdn & btn) | s.h.10 |
| 2781 | **Rose Flyer (IRE)** (MCChapman) 8-6 SWebster (12) (m.n.s) | 3½.11 |
| 2916 | **Heroic Deed (65)** (MHTompkins) 7-12(6) ‡⁷SMulvey (14) (m.n.s) | hd.12 |
| | **Imperial Forte** (RJRWilliams) 8-6 WRyan (19) (lt-f: ohsd ldrs stands' side 4f) | s.h.13 |
| 2719 | **Princess Nebia** (BJMcMath) 7-9(1) EJohnson (8) (m.n.s) | 2.14 |
| 3106 | **Capten Morgan (IRE)** (WJHaggas) 7-13 AMunro (4) (prom far side over 4f) | hd.15 |
| 3156 | **Naughty Charlotte** (APJarvis) 7-1 ‡⁷DWright (5) (m.n.s) | 1½.16 |
| 1502 | **Honour and Glory** (BobJones) 7-12 GBardwell (16) (bkwd: t.o) | 17 |

**9/4** Mam'zelle Angot(op 7/2), **3/1** Allegrissima, **11/2** PONTEVECCHIO MODA(3/1—6/1), **6/1** Matron of Honor, **8/1** Premium, **12/1** Miss Fayruz (IRE), **20/1** Imperial Forte, Heroic Deed, **25/1** Clar Dubh (IRE), Tartouka, **33/1** Naughty Charlotte, Princess Nebia, Rose Flyer (IRE), Honour and Glory, Secret Fantasy (IRE), **50/1** Ors. Tote £7.10: £2.00 £1.20 £17.40 £1.10 (£19.39). Mr Walter Mariti (WHITSBURY) bred by Walter Mariti. 17 Rn     1m 26.1 (3.3)
SF—8/12/11/9/–/–

### 3292

GOLDEN JUBILEE CHALLENGE TROPHY (H'cap) (0-100) £7765.00 (£2320.00: £1110.00: £505.00)    1¼m 21y
4-10 (4-13)

| | | |
|---|---|---|
| 2671[3] | **Wild Fire (82)** (GWragg) 3-8-12 WRyan (1) (hld up: 7th st: stdy hdwy to ld ins fnl f: r.o wl) | —1 |
| 2791[2] | **Vallance (79)** (PWHarris) 4-9-4 PaulEddery (8) (lw: a.p: 3rd st: led 3f out tl ins fnl f) | 1.2 |
| 2529[5] | **Busted Rock (81)** (MrsLPiggott) 7-9-3 LPiggott (9) (lw: hld up: last st: gd hdwy over 2f out: nt rch ldrs) | 1½.3 |
| 2460[5] | **Barford Lad (79)** (JRFanshawe) 5-9-1 LDettori (3) (lw: chsd ldrs: 4th st: rdn over 1f out: one pce) | 1½.4 |
| 2920 | **Zalon (IRE) (95)** (JHMGosden) 3-9-11 WCarson (6) (hld up: 8th st: styd on fnl 2f: nvr nrr) | 5.5 |
| 3013[3] | **Corcina (72)** (MBell) 4-8-8 GDuffield (4) (b: chsd ldr: 2nd st: wknd over 2f out) | 2.6 |
| 2823* | **Pabouche (USA) (90)** (bl) (HRACecil) 3-9-1 ‡⁵StephenDavies (2) (lw: led 7f: wknd over 1f out: eased whn btn fnl f) | 2.7 |
| 3013* | **Mamdooh (95) (Fav)** (ACStewart) 3-9-11 MRoberts (7) (chsd ldrs: 5th st: wknd 3f out) | 3.8 |
| 3021 | **Myfontaine (66)** (KTIvory) 5-8-2 GBardwell (5) (lw: hld up: 6th st: wknd over 3f out: t.o) | 10.9 |

**11/8** Mamdooh, **5/1** Zalon (IRE), **11/2** WILD FIRE, **17/2** Corcina, **10/1** Busted Rock, **11/1** Vallance, **12/1** Pabouche (USA), **14/1** Barford Lad, **33/1** Myfontaine. CSF £57.26, CT £537.69. Tote £5.60: £2.00 £2.40 £1.80 (£58.70). Sir Philip Oppenheimer (NEWMARKET) bred by Hascombe and Valiant Studs. 9 Rn     2m 5.1 (0.7)
SF—61/62/61/56/56/35

### 3293

NORTH SEA H'CAP (0-90) £4464.00 (£1332.00: £636.00: £288.00)
1m 3f 101y
4-40 (4-42)

| | | |
|---|---|---|
| 2926[4] | **Rose Alto (80)** (JRFanshawe) 4-9-8 GDuffield (3) (a.p: 3rd st: led 3f out: sn drvn clr: v.easily) | —1 |

2992 Major's Law (IRE) **(67)** *(CEBrittain)* 3-8-2 MRoberts (10) (a.p: 4th st: styd on u.p fnl f: no ch w wnr) ............................................ 2.2
2985 El Rabab (USA) **(62)** (Fav) *(HThomsonJones)* 3-7-11[(1)] WCarson (1) (lw: hld up: wnt 6th st: rdn over 1f out: kpt on) ............................ nk.3
1891[5] Alderbrook **(60)** *(MrsJCecil)* 3-7-9 NCarlisle (7) (bit bkwd: a.p: 2nd st: hrd rdn 2f out: sn btn) ............................................ 7.4
2926 Milanese **(74)** *(DMorley)* 3-8-9 MTebbutt (6) (lw: hld up: hdwy over 2f out: nvr nr to chal) ........................................ 1½.5
3139 Vintage **(86)** *(MajorWRHern)* 7-10-0 AMunro (4) (still bkwd: s.i.s: sn chsng ldrs: 7th st: btn over 2f out) .................... 3.6
2908 Sastago (USA) **(81)** *(JHMGosden)* 3-9-2 PaulEddery (5) (led over 8f: sn rdn & wknd: t.o) .................................. 10.7
2673[2] Clear Sound **(63)** *(GWragg)* 3-7-9 ‡DHarrison (9) (chsd ldrs: 5th st: wknd over 2f out: t.o) .................................. nk.8
3040* Gueca Solo **(81)** *(HRACecil)* 4-9-9 WRyan (8) (lw: hld up: hdwy over 3f out: rdn 2f out: sn wknd: t.o) ........................ s.h.9
Black Sapphire **(68)** *(MHTompkins)* 5-8-3 ‡SMulvey (2) (bkwd: a bhd: t.o) .. 1½.10

**4/1** El Rabab (USA), **5/1** ROSE ALTO, **6/1** Gueca Solo(op 4/1), **7/1** Major's Law (IRE), **8/1** Sastago (USA)(9/2—9/1), Vintage(6/1—9/1), **9/1** Milanese(op 5/1), **10/1** Clear Sound, **16/1** Alderbrook, **33/1** Black Sapphire. CSF £35.34, CT £136.91. Tote £6.80: £2.00 £1.80 £1.60 (£17.80). T. & J. Vestey (NEWMARKET) bred by T. R. G. Vestey. 10 Rn 2m 24.7 (0.7)
SF—66/42/36/20/31/44

**3294** HALVERGATE H'CAP (0-70) £3114.00 (£927.00: £441.00: £198.00)
5f 43y 5-10 (5-11)

3103 **Joe Sugden (52)** *(PHowling)* 8-9-8 MRoberts (3) (hld up: gd hdwy over 1f out: led ins fnl f: r.o) ..................................... —1
3183[4] Spring High **(58)** (bl) *(KTIvory)* 5-10-0 GBardwell (1) (b: a.p: led over 1f out tl ins fnl f: rallied u.p cl home) .................... ½.2
3220* Barbara's Cutie **(39)** (v) *(MBlanshard)* 4-8-2 (7x) ‡CAvery (6) (lw: a.p: led 2f out tl over 1f out: rallied nr fin) .................... nk.3
2963 Le Chic **(48)** *(DWChapman)* 6-9-4 LDettori (4) (lw: gd hdwy appr fnl f: fin wl) .... 1.4
2245[5] Tommy Tempest **(46)** *(KRBurke)* 3-9-0 AShoults (7) (led 3f: rdn over 1f out: unable qckn) .................................. ¾.5
2465 Ski Captain **(58)** *(PHowling)* 8-10-0 GDuffield (2) (prom: rdn along ½-wy: outpcd appr fnl f) ............................ 1½.6
3103 Lincstone Boy (IRE) **(53)** (bl) *(SRBowring)* 4-9-9 SWebster (5) (lw: chsd ldrs: rdn 2f out: sn btn) ................................ 6.7

**5/2** Spring High, **5/1** Barbara's Cutie, **11/2** Lincstone Boy (IRE)(op 7/2), JOE SUGDEN, **6/1** Ski Captain(op 4/1), Le Chic(10/1—5/1), **12/1** Tommy Tempest. CSF £18.34, Tote £4.10: £1.90 £2.00 (£8.10). Mr J. J. Amass (GUILDFORD) bred by J. Jack. 7 Rn 62.4 sec (2.1)
SF—46/52/25/37/30/42

T/Plpt: £448.00 (33.15 Tckts). IM

# YARMOUTH (L-H)
## Thursday, September 17th [Good to firm]
Going Allowance: minus 0.20 sec per fur (F)                    Wind: str half against

Stalls: high

**3295** GORLESTON STKS (Mdn 2-Y.O.F) £3003.00 (£833.00: £399.00) 6f 3y 2-10 (2-19)

3132[4] **Sooty Swift (IRE)** (Jt-Fav) *(CEBrittain)* 8-11 MRoberts (2) (mde all: qcknd clr 1f out: unchal) .............................. —1
3055[2] Blue Tess (IRE) *(MMoubarak)* 8-11 AMunro (11) (b.hind: racd stands' side: a.p: ev ch tl outpcd fnl f) ....................... 3½.2
2674[5] Ikhtisas (USA) *(BHanbury)* 8-11 WRyan (4) (swtg: a.p: rdn over 1f out: sn outpcd) ................................... 2½.3
Saja (USA) (Jt-Fav) *(HThomsonJones)* 8-11 RHills (1) (w'like: bkwd: s.i.s: sn rcvrd: prom tl wknd over 1f out) .............. 2½.4
Golden Guest *(MrsJCecil)* 8-11 PaulEddery (10) (leggy: lf-t: hld up: sme hdwy appr fnl f: nvr plcd to chal) ..................... ¾.5
La Menorquina (USA) *(LMCumani)* 8-11 LDettori (7) (w'like: scope: bhd: effrt & rdn along 2f out: no imp) ..................... nk.6
Mrs Jekyll (IRE) *(CFWall)* 8-11 NCarlisle (5) (lf-t: dwlt: sn chsng ldrs: rdn & wknd appr fnl f) ......................... ¾.7
Agenda One *(MissAJWhitfield)* 8-11 DaleGibson (3) (leggy: lf-t: bit bkwd: chsd ldrs: rdn 2f out: sn btn) ................. 6.8

```
         Episode One (GLewis) 8-11 JQuinn (8) (lt-f: unf: nvr trbld ldrs) ........................ nk.9
         Burning Sand (bl) (JMPEustace) 8-11 MHills (6) (leggy: lt-f: unruly bef s: a bhd)3¹/₂.10
   3047 Ilmenite (MAJarvis) 8-11 GCrealock (9) (bhd fr ¹/₂-wy) .................................. 4.11
```

**5/2** SOOTY SWIFT (IRE), Saja (USA)(3/1—4/1), **7/2** Blue Tess (IRE)(9/4—4/1), **10/1** Agenda One, La Menorquina (USA)(op 7/2), **16/1** Golden Guest(op 7/1), **25/1** Mrs Jekyll (IRE), **33/1** Ikhtisas (USA), Burning Sand, **50/1** Episode One, **66/1** Ilmenite. CSF £10.95, Tote £2.80: £1.30 £1.60 £3.80 (£3.80). Sheikh Mohammed (NEWMARKET) bred by Sheikh Mohammed bin Rashid al Maktoum in Ireland. 11 Rn  1m 12.6 (2)

SF—33/19/9/–/–/–

## 3296

BREYDON WATER H'CAP (0-70) £3080.00 (£920.00: £440.00: £200.00)
**6f 3y**                                                                     2-40 (2-44)

```
  3183⁶ Rainbow Fleet (55) (Fav) (DMarks) 4–9-2 MHills (5) (hdwy 2f out: hrd rdn to ld
         nr fin) ...........................................................................  —1
  2858³ Face the Future (55) (PWHarris) 3–8-13 WRyan (3) (hdwy ¹/₂-wy: led 2f out tl nr
         fin) ........................................................................... s.h.2
  3183⁵ Ayr Raider (67) (WRMuir) 5–10-0 MRoberts (11) (outpcd tl r.o ins fnl f) ......... 6.3
  3002 Fabled Orator (39) (bl) (PHowling) 7–8-0⁽¹⁾ BCrossley (6) (b.nr hind: lw: disp ld:
         hrd rdn appr fnl f: no ex) ................................................... ³/₄.4
  2984² Bright Paragon (IRE) (44) (HJCollingridge) 3–8-2 JQuinn (2) (led 3f: rdn & btn
         appr fnl f) ................................................................. 1¹/₂.5
  3220 Doesyoudoes (56) (DTThom) 3–9-0 LDettori (7) (chsd ldrs over 4f) ................ 1.6
  3220 Tachyon Park (36) (v) (PHowling) 10–7-6⁽⁴⁾ ‡⁵BDoyle (10) (nvr nr to chal) ....... 1.7
  3264 Fontaine Lady (41) (bl) (TThomsonJones) 5–7-9⁽⁵⁾ ‡⁷JDSmith (4) (in tch over 3f:
         sn outpcd) ................................................................. 1¹/₂.8
  3294² Spring High (58) (bl) (KTIvory) 5–8-12 ‡⁷CScally (9) (chsd ldrs 4f: sn lost tch) .. 1¹/₂.9
  2822⁴ Pink'n Black (IRE) (51) (GBlum) 3–8-4 ‡⁵StephenDavies (1) (lost pl ¹/₂-wy) ...... 6.10
```

LONG HANDICAP: Tachyon Park 7-4.

**7/2** RAINBOW FLEET, **4/1** Spring High, Bright Paragon (IRE), **5/1** Ayr Raider, **7/1** Pink'n Black (IRE), **12/1** Fabled Orator, **14/1** Fontaine Lady, Face the Future, **25/1** Doesyoudoes, **33/1** Tachyon Park. CSF £45.85, CT £224.47. Tote £5.10: £1.90 £2.90 £1.90 (£34.00). Mr R. J. F. Brothers (UPPER LAMBOURN) bred by Colin G. R. Booth. 10 Rn                                                                      1m 12.8 (2.2)

SF—34/30/21/–/–/–

## 3297

E.B.F. HASTINGS STKS (Mdn 2-Y.O) £2898.00 (£864.00: £412.00: £186.00)
**1m 3y**                                                                     3-10 (3-12)

```
  2519⁴ Almamzar (USA) (Fav) (MRStoute) 9-0 PaulEddery (3) (lw: mde all: shkn up
         ins fnl f: hld on wl) .......................................................  —1
         Dragon's Teeth (IRE) (LMCumani) 9-0 LDettori (4) (w'like: scope: a.p:
         sustained chal fnl f: r.o) ................................................. nk.2
  2185⁵ Marros Mill (MBell) 8-9 MHills (9) (chsd ldrs: r.o one pce appr fnl f) ......... 3¹/₂.3
  2398 Genseric (FR) (RWArmstrong) 9-0 RHills (2) (w wnr: rdn 2f out: sn btn) ......... 2.4
         Anchor Stone (HRACecil) 9-0 WRyan (5) (w'like: leggy: bit bkwd: dwlt: hdwy 3f
         out: nt pce to chal) ....................................................... 4.5
  2951 Candarela (PHowling) 8-9 JQuinn (8) (rdn along over 2f out: nvr nr ldrs) ....... 5.6
  2873 Horseradish (DMorley) 9-0 AMunro (6) (chsd ldrs: rdn ¹/₂-wy: sn wknd: t.o) .... 15.7
         Teejayem (IRE) (MCChapman) 8-9 BCrossley (7) (unf: bkwd: s.s: a bhd: t.o) .. 20.8
```

**8/11** ALMAMZAR (USA)(Evens—4/6), **9/2** Anchor Stone(op 3/1), **5/1** Marros Mill, **10/1** Dragon's Teeth (IRE)(op 11/2), **20/1** Horseradish, **33/1** Genseric (FR), Candarela, **50/1** Teejayem (IRE). CSF £8.40, Tote £1.80: £1.10 £2.20 £1.50 (£5.80). Sheikh Ahmed Al Maktoum (NEWMARKET) bred by G.W.Humphrey, Jnr., L.I.Humphrey & P.Firman in USA. 8 Rn                                                           1m 40.2 (4.9)

SF—2/1/–/–/–/–

## 3298

GREAT YARMOUTH STAYERS' H'CAP (0-90) £4269.00 (£1272.00: £606.00: £273.00)
**2¹/₄m 51y**                                                                 3-40 (3-42)

```
  3118³ Receptionist (79) (Fav) (HRACecil) 3–9-2 WRyan (4) (a.p: 3rd st: qcknd to ld 1f
         out) .........................................................................  —1
  2339⁶ Cabochon (77) (DMorley) 5–10-0 PaulEddery (5) (hld up & bhd: 5th st: effrt 2f
         out: styd on strly fnl f) ................................................... ³/₄.2
  3053* Two and Sixpence (USA) (68) (BWHills) 3–8-5 DaleGibson (3) (set v.slow pce
         7f: 2nd st: led over 2f out tl hdd & outpcd fnl f) ......................... 3¹/₂.3
  2840 Lafkadio (48) (bl) (MCChapman) 5–7-13 AMunro (2) (led & qcknd after 7f: hrd
         rdn & btn over 2f out: sn wknd) ........................................... 2¹/₂.4
  2739⁴ Briggscare (58) (WJarvis) 6–8-9 MHills (1) (b: lw: hld up: 4th st: rdn 3f out: sn
         t.o) ....................................................................... 12.5
```

**5/2** RECEPTIONIST, **11/4** Cabochon, Two and Sixpence (USA), **4/1** Briggscare, **12/1** Lafkadio. CSF £8.95, Tote £2.80: £1.60 £2.00 (£4.80). Cliveden Stud (NEWMARKET) bred by Cliveden Stud. 5 Rn          4m 14

```
```

**3299**　　　NORFOLK STKS (3-Y.O.F) £7530.00 (£2080.00: £990.00)　　1¹/₄m 21y　　4-10 (4-12)

2549* **Fermoy (USA) (80)** *(Fav) (LMCumani)* 8-9　LDettori (3) (lw: hld up: 3rd st: hdwy
to ld ent fnl f: pushed out) ...................................................... —1

 1935 Katakana (USA) **(108)** *(MRStoute)* 8-7　PaulEddery (2) (led after 2f to 1f out: sn
rdn & no ex) ...................................................... 2¹/₂.2

2854⁴ Ardisia (USA) **(89)** *(PFICole)* 9-4　AMunro (1) (led 2f: 2nd st: jnd ldr 4f out: rdn
appr fnl f: one pce) ...................................................... nk.3

**10/11** FERMOY (USA)(6/4—4/5), **9/4** Katakana (USA)(6/4—5/2), **3/1** Ardisia (USA). CSF £2.95, Tote £1.90
(£1.90). Sheikh Mohammed (NEWMARKET) bred by Darley Stud Management Co Ltd. in USA. 3 Rn
　　　　　　　　　　　　　　　　　　　　　　　　　　　　　　　　2m 7.4 (3.0)
　　　　　　　　　　　　　　　　　　　　　　　　　　　　　　　　SF—45/38/48

**3300**　　　LOTTIE AND ALBERT BOTTON MEMORIAL NURSERY　　£3882.50 (£1160.00: £555.00:
　　　　　£252.50)　　**1m 3y**　　　　　　　　　　　　　　　　　　　4-40 (4-47)

2910 **Hawl (USA) (80)** *(AAScott)* 8-10　RHills (7) (hld up: hdwy 2f out: r.o strly to ld wl
ins fnl f) ...................................................... —1

3030⁴ Cure the King (IRE) **(73)** *(SGNorton)* 8-3　MHills (1) (lw: chsd ldrs: rdn to ld over
1f out tl nr fin) ...................................................... nk.2

2835 Expo Mondial (IRE) **(91)** *(JMPEustace)* 9-7　LDettori (5) (hld up: hdwy appr fnl f:
styd on u.p ins fnl f) ...................................................... 2.3

3146² Persiansky (IRE) **(73)** *(Fav) (BHanbury)* 8-3　NCarlisle (6) (lw: s.i.s: sn wnt prom:
ev ch over 1f out: unable qckn) ...................................................... ¹/₂.4

2873⁵ Rusty Reel **(68)** *(CEBrittain)* 9-4　MRoberts (2) (lw: a.p: led over 2f out tl over 1f
out: sn rdn & wknd) ...................................................... ³/₄.5

3100 Russia Pobeda (USA) **(65)** *(MrsLPiggott)* 7-9　JQuinn (3) (b: b.hind: led over 5f:
rdn & wknd appr fnl f) ...................................................... 1¹/₂.6

3063 Kaloochi **(67)** *(RHannon)* 7-4 ‡7AWhelan (4) (s.i.s: a bhd) ...................................................... 2¹/₂.7

**9/4** Persiansky (IRE)(7/4—11/4), **3/1** Cure the King (IRE), **100/30** Rusty Reel, **7/1** Kaloochi(10/1—12/1), Expo
Mondial (IRE), **16/1** HAWL (USA), **20/1** Russia Pobeda (USA). CSF £59.43, Tote £17.60: £7.50 £2.10 (£19.70).
Mr Hamdan Al-Maktoum (NEWMARKET) bred by Shadwell Estate Co Ltd. in USA. 7 Rn　　1m 38.9 (3.6)
　　　　　　　　　　　　　　　　　　　　　　　　　　　　　　SF—18/10/22/–/–/–/

T/Plpt: £80.80 (35.05 Tckts).　　　　　　　　　　　　　　　　　　　　　　　　　IM

2732—**BEVERLEY (R-H)**

**Wednesday, September 16th [Good to firm]**

Going Allowance: 5f-1m 100y: minus 0.20; Rest: minus 0.30 sec (F)　　　　Wind: almost nil

Stalls: high

**3301**　　　HUMBER ESTUARY (S) NURSERY　.　£1884.00 (£524.00: £252.00)
　　　　　**7f 100y**　　　　(Weights raised 1 lb)　　　　　　　　2-30 (2-33)

2842 **Hotel California (IRE) (57)** *(JWHills)* 9-4　RHills (17) (in tch: effrt & swtchd over
1f out: styd on wl to ld last strides) ...................................................... —1

2703² Merry Mermaid **(48)** *(Fav) (JFBottomley)* 8-9　PBurke (19) (lw: chsd ldrs: led wl
over 1f out: r.o u.p) ...................................................... hd.2

2938 Comtec's Legend **(51)** *(JFBottomley)* 8-7 ‡5NKennedy (1) (lw: hdwy on outside
over 2f out: hng lft u.p: styd on: nt rch 1st 2) ...................................................... 3¹/₂.3

1660 Crab 'n Lobster (IRE) **(48)** *(MrsJRRamsden)* 8-9　KFallon (5) (in tch: kpt on
same pce fnl 2f) ...................................................... 2¹/₂.4

3199 Poly Vision (IRE) **(60)** *(MRChannon)* 9-7　DHolland (12) (chsd ldrs: hng bdly
lft u.p 3f out: ev ch tl wknd over 1f out) ...................................................... 1.5

3071² Penny Banger (IRE) **(50)** *(MJohnston)* 8-11　DMcKeown (2) (sn bhd: hdwy over
1f out: styd on nr fin) ...................................................... s.h.6

2802⁶ Stapleford Lass **(51)** *(SPCWoods)* 8-12　WWoods (7) (swtg: unruly in stalls: in
tch: no imp fnl 2f) ...................................................... nk.7

3173 Weaver George (IRE) **(53)** *(MHEasterby)* 9-0　MBirch (10) (chsd ldrs tl wknd
over 1f out) ...................................................... 1.8

3033 Stardust Express **(57)** *(MJohnston)* 9-4　RPElliott (14) (lw: led tl wl over 1f out:
sn wknd) ...................................................... hd.9

3071 Hot Off the Press **(49)** *(RMWhitaker)* 8-10　ACulhane (11) (nvr bttr than mid div) nk.10

3148 Lettermore **(53)** *(RMWhitaker)* 8-7 ‡7GParkin (4) (sn bhd: rdn & edgd lft 2f out:
n.d) ...................................................... 2.11

2842 Strephon (IRE) **(52)** *(MHTompkins)* 8-13　PRobinson (6) (chsd ldrs tl lost pl over
2f out) ...................................................... ³/₄.12

3147 Steal a March **(56)** *(MWEasterby)* 9-3　TLucas (15) (s.i.s: hld up: stdy hdwy over
2f out: nvr plcd to chal) ...................................................... ¹/₂.13

3173 Society Gown (USA) **(56)** (bl) *(TDBarron)* 9-3　KDarley (8) (in tch: effrt u.p 2f out:
sn wknd) ...................................................... s.h.14

2733 Emmandee (57) (bl) (MWEasterby) 9-4 LCharnock (9) (s.i.s: a in rr) .............. 1.15
2983⁶ Lucky Owl (50) (MissLAPerratt) 8-11 JFanning (18) (chsd ldrs tl lost pl 2f out) 4.16
3106⁶ Flash of Amber (50) (JLSpearing) 8-11 GHind (3) (a bhd) ............................ hd.17
2428⁶ Forthemoment (52) (bl) (PCalver) 8-13 DaleGibson (13) (sn bhd) .............. 2½.18

5/1 Merry Mermaid, 6/1 Society Gown (USA), 8/1 Penny Banger (IRE)(op 5/1), 9/1 HOTEL CALIFORNIA (IRE),
12/1 Comtec's Legend, Poly Vision (IRE), 14/1 Stapleford Lass, Steal a March(op 8/1), Weaver George (IRE),
Crab 'n Lobster (IRE), Lucky Owl, Hot Off the Press, 16/1 Strephon (IRE), Stardust Express, 25/1 Ors. CSF
£52.54, CT £503.94. Tote £9.80: £2.00 £1.70 £6.20 £5.30 (£41.60). Mr Christopher Wright (LAMBOURN) bred
by Kilcarn Stud in Ireland. 18 Rn; Sold D Chapman 6,000 gns                              1m 34.5 (4.3)
                                                                                        SF—17/7/–/–/–/–

## 3302
HUMBERSIDE SEAHAWKS H'CAP (0-80) £3236.00 (£968.00: £464.00: £212.00)
1m 100y                                                                    3-00 (3-03)

1739 **Cold Shower (IRE) (60)** (JAGlover) 3-8-5 ‡⁵SWilliams (11) (lw: in tch: stdy
hdwy ins 2f out: led jst ins fnl f: edgd rt: r.o u.p nr fin) .... —1
3170 Lawnsmood Junior (55) (JLSpearing) 3-8-7 KDarley (10) (hld up: gd hdwy 2f
out: styng on whn nt clr run & swtchd ins fnl f) .............. ¾.2
3192 Eden's Close (72) (MHTompkins) 3-9-8 PRobinson (12) (hdwy over 2f out: led
over 1f out: hdd & nt qckn ins fnl f) .............. s.h.3
368 Shabanaz (71) (SGNorton) 7-9-6 ‡⁵OPears (8) (lw: hld up & bhd: gd hdwy 2f
out: styng on wl whn hmpd & snatched up ins fnl f) .............. 2.4
3101⁴ Friendlypersuasion (IRE) (42) (RHollinshead) 4-7-3⁽³⁾ ‡⁷AGarth (13) (sme hdwy
2f out: kpt on: nvr nr to chal) .............. 7.5
3021 Doctor's Remedy (39) (MrsJJordan) 6-7-0 ‡⁷CTeague (6) (sn bhd: hld up:
hdwy on outside over 2f out: nvr rchd ldrs) .............. 2½.6
2743² Tyrian Purple (64) (Jt-Fav) (RHollinshead) 4-8-11 ‡⁷MHumphries (9) (lw:
led tl hdd over 1f out: sn wknd) .............. ½.7
3170 Young Jason (52) (FHLee) 9-8-1 ‡³NKennedy (4) (hld up & bhd: sme hdwy on
outside 2f out: n.d) .............. ¾.8
3149 Huso (64) (Jt-Fav) (PCHaslam) 4-9-4 DHolland (15) (chsd ldrs: rdn over 3f out:
wknd 2f out) .............. ½.9
1310 Crail Harbour (49) (PCHaslam) 6-8-3 DMcKeown (2) (s.i.s: a bhd) .............. 1.10
3069 Pride of Pendle (51) (PCalver) 3-8-1 DaleGibson (7) (nvr nr ldrs) .............. 1½.11
Bold Arabella (63) (JLSpearing) 4-9-3 GHind (14) (hdwy 4f out: wknd over 2f
out) .............. hd.12
3170 Who's Tef (IRE) (59) (MHEasterby) 4-8-10 ‡³SMaloney (5) (chsd ldrs tl wknd 2f
out) .............. nk.13
2743⁶ Routing (58) (MDHammond) 4-8-9 ‡³RonHillis (3) (dwlt: gd hdwy to jn ldr 5f out:
wknd qckly over 2f out) .............. 8.14
LONG HANDICAP: Doctor's Remedy 7-3.

11/2 Tyrian Purple (IRE), Huso, 8/1 Friendlypersuasion (IRE)(op 12/1), Lawnsmood Junior, Eden's Close, 10/1
Routing, Who's Tef (IRE), 11/1 Young Jason, 12/1 COLD SHOWER (IRE), Shabanaz, 14/1 Pride of Pendle, 20/1
Crail Harbour, 25/1 Doctor's Remedy, 33/1 Bold Arabella. CSF £97.92, CT £751.47. Tote £14.70: £3.70 £2.90
£3.20 (£24.40). Claremont Management Services (WORKSOP) bred by Leinster Stud in Ireland. 14 Rn
                                                                                        1m 45.2 (2.5)
                                                                                        SF—28/30/42/34/–/–

## 3303
HUMBERSIDE LEISURE SERVICES AUCTION STKS (Mdn 2-Y.O) £2700.00 (£750.00:
£360.00)   7f 100y                                                      3-30 (3-36)

3175² **Latest Flame (IRE) (80)** (Fav) (MRChannon) 8-8 DHolland (2) (chsd ldrs: rdn
to ld over 1f out: styd on wl) .............. —1
2879⁵ Runrig (IRE) (66) (MissLAPerratt) 8-1 JFanning (3) (a chsng ldrs: styd on wl ins
fnl f) .............. 1.2
3077 Sky Wish (64) (MissSEHall) 8-5 NConnorton (11) (in tch: effrt 2f out: hung rt:
kpt on) .............. 1½.3
3077 Bonarme (IRE) (MHEasterby) 8-8 MBirch (10) (in tch: swtchd ins & styd on fnl
2f: nt rch ldrs) .............. 1.4
2961 Ume River (IRE) (67) (MHTompkins) 8-5 PRobinson (7) (in tch: effrt u.p 2f out:
nvr able to chal) .............. 1½.5
3077⁵ Killy's Filly (JBerry) 8-2⁽¹⁾ JCarroll (9) (b.hind: chsd ldrs: no hdwy fnl 2f) .............. 1.6
3077 Scoffera (NTinkler) 8-3 LCharnock (4) (in tch: no imp fnl 2f) .............. 1.7
2080 Moonstruck Bard (45) (SPCWoods) 8-5 WWoods (12) (led tl over 1f out: sn
wknd) .............. hd.8
3077⁴ Aviator's Dream (JFBottomley) 8-6 PBurke (6) (lw: effrt over 2f out: nvr able to
chal) .............. 2.9
2832² Daring Past (69) (RBoss) 8-3 ‡⁵NKennedy (18) (nvr rchd ldrs) .............. 1½.10
2961 Wrightmill (IRE) (v) (CTinkler) 8-9 TLucas (8) (chsd ldrs tl rdn & lost pl over 2f
out) .............. 1½.11

3178 West End Girl *(RJRWilliams)* 8-2 KDarley (16) (s.i.s: n.d) .............................. 1½.**12**
2534⁵ Ho-Joe (IRE) **(66)** *(AHarrison)* 8-11 KFallon (5) (lw: s.s: a bhd) ....................... 2.**13**
3165 Lady Adare (IRE) *(JJO'Neill)* 8-0 SWood (2) (unruly s: n.d) ............................. 1.**14**
3147 Native Worth *(JMJefferson)* 8-6 MWood (14) (a bhd) ............................... s.h.**15**
3146 Miramichi Bay (bl) *(MrsVAAconley)* 8-8 ACulhane (15) (chsd ldrs tl lost pl over
2f out) .................................................................................................. 5.**16**
Cyrano Diamond (IRE) *(RonaldThompson)* 8-5 JLowe (13) (w'like: bit bkwd:
s.i.s: sn bhd & drvn along) ............................................. 1½.**17**
2259⁵ Jasilu *(MWEasterby)* 7-13 ‡³SMaloney (4) (bhd fnl 2f) ......................... 2½.**18**

5/2 LATEST FLAME (IRE), 7/1 Daring Past, 8/1 Aviator's Dream, Runrig (IRE), Ume River (IRE), Sky Wish, 9/1 Killy's Filly, 12/1 West End Girl, Ho-Joe (IRE), 14/1 Bonarme (IRE), 20/1 Moonstruck Bard, 33/1 Ors. CSF £23.98, Tote £2.70: £1.50 £1.40 £4.60 (£4.60). Miss Juliet E. Reed (UPPER LAMBOURN) bred by The Woodhaven Stud in Ireland. 18 Rn                                                              1m 33.9 (3.7)
SF—14/4/3/3/–/–

**3304**     RAFFINGORA SPRINT H'CAP (0-95) £3561.00 (£1068.00: £514.00: £237.00)
5f
4-00 (4-05)

(Weights raised 4 lb)
3166⁴ **Pallium (IRE) (67)** *(MPNaughton)* 4-8-7 KFallon (16) (lw: hdwy ½-wy: r.o wl to
ld wl ins fnl f) ......................................................................... —**1**
3068 Here Comes a Star **(64)** *(JMCarr)* 4-8-4 SMorris (7) (lw: hdwy over 1f out: r.o wl
u.p nr fin) ..................................................................................... nk.**2**
3207∗ Catherines Well **(74)** (Jt-Fav) *(MWEasterby)* 9-9-0 (5x) TLucas (14) (lw: a
chsng ldrs: nt qckn ins fnl f) ...................................................... 1.3
2997 Misdemeanours Girl (IRE) **(68)** (Jt-Fav) *(MRChannon)* 4-8-8 DHolland (15) (lw:
w ldr: led 2f out: edgd lft 1f out: hdd & wknd ins fnl f) ........ nk.**4**
1688 African Chimes **(76)** *(WAO'Gorman)* 5-8-13 ‡³EmmaO'Gorman (10) (lw: a
chsng ldrs: styng on wl whn hmpd ins fnl f) ......................... hd.**5**
3083 Drum Sergeant **(76)** (bl) *(JParkes)* 5-8-11 ‡⁵OPears (12) (lw: hld up: hdwy 2f
out: n.m.r & nt qckn ins fnl f) ................................................... s.h.**6**
3207⁴ On the Edge **(72)** *(TDBarron)* 4-8-5 ‡⁷VHalliday (11) (a chsng ldrs: rdn 2f out:
kpt on same pce) ..................................................................... ¾.**7**
3253⁵ Metal Boys **(84)** *(RHollinshead)* 5-9-3 ‡⁷SWynne (2) (w ldrs tl wknd fnl f) ....... s.h.**8**
3188 Lucedeo **(82)** *(JLSpearing)* 8-9-1 ‡⁷AGarth (1) (s.i.s: bhd tl some late hdwy) .. 1½.**9**
3098⁵ Miss Vaxette **(70)** *(JLSpearing)* 3-8-8 KDarley (9) (led to 2f out: wknd over 1f
out) ............................................................................................ hd.**10**
3144⁵ Loft Boy **(63)** *(JDBethell)* 9-7-10 ‡⁷KateDovey (13) (lw: nvr nr ldrs) ................ 1½.**11**
3079 Rock Opera (IRE) **(55)** *(MPNaughton)* 4-7-9 JakiHouston (6) (chsd ldrs tl lost
pl 2f out) .................................................................................... 1½.**12**
3015 Seamere **(81)** (bl) *(BRCambidge)* 9-9-7 JLowe (4) (lw: hld up in rr: n.m.r over 1f
out: n.d) ..................................................................................... 1½.**13**
3144 Just Bob **(68)** (bl) *(SEKettlewell)* 3-8-6 JFortune (5) (s.i.s: n.d) ........................ ¾.**14**
1053⁴ Singing Star **(80)** *(JBalding)* 6-9-6 PRobinson (3) (b: lw: plld hrd: trckd ldrs:
hmpd after 2f: sn bhd) .............................................................. ¾.**15**
2201 Glencroft **(56)** (bl) *(DWChapman)* 8–7-10 SWood (8) (t: led stands' side:
swtchd lft to r alone 3f out: wknd qckly over 1f out) .......... 7.**16**

6/1 Misdemeanours Girl (IRE), Catherines Well, 13/2 On the Edge, 8/1 Drum Sergeant, PALLIUM (IRE), 10/1 Miss Vaxette, 11/1 African Chimes, 12/1 Seamere, Here Comes a Star, 14/1 Lucedeo, 16/1 Metal Boys, Loft Boy, 20/1 Just Bob, Singing Star, Rock Opera (IRE), 33/1 Glencroft. CSF £97.83, CT £577.71. Tote £6.60: £1.40 £3.50 £1.60 £1.90 (£291.80). Mr W. J. Kelly (RICHMOND) bred by North Ridge Farm Inc in Ireland. 16 Rn
62.3 sec (0.8)
SF—57/53/59/52/56/53

**3305**     SNOWY GRAY MEMORIAL H'CAP (0-80) £3132.00 (£936.00: £448.00: £204.00)
2m 35y
4-30 (4-31)

(Weights raised 1 lb)
2957² **Cov Tel Lady (68)** *(MHTompkins)* 3-8-10 PRobinson (4) (hld up & bhd: gd
hdwy 2f out: qcknd to ld jst ins fnl f: r.o wl) ........................ —**1**
426∗ Avro Anson **(51)** (Fav) *(MJCamacho)* 4-8-5 NConnorton (1) (bit bkwd: trckd
ldrs: effrt over 3f out: rdn to ld over 1f out: sn hdd & nt qckn) 1.**2**
9516 Yorkshire Holly **(47)** *(MAvison)* 9–8-1 AProud (3) (hld up: effrt over 2f out: r.o
one pce appr fnl f) .................................................................... ¾.**3**
2664² Broctune Grey **(70)** *(MrsGRReveley)* 8-9-10 KDarley (5) (trckd ldrs: effrt & hrd
rdn over 2f out: r.o one pce: nvr able to chal) ...................... 3.**4**
3075⁶ Alizari (USA) **(64)** *(GFleming)* 3-8-6 RPElliott (7) (chsd ldrs: drvn along 5f out:
n.m.r & swtchd 1f out: sn wknd) ............................................ 1½.**5**
2513³ Rexy Boy **(39)** *(WLBarker)* 5-7-7 JLowe (6) (led tl hdd & wknd over 1f out) ....... 7.**6**
LONG HANDICAP: Rexy Boy 6-9.

6/4 Avro Anson, 5/2 COV TEL LADY, 3/1 Broctune Grey, 12/1 Alizari (USA), 14/1 Yorkshire Holly, 20/1 Rexy Boy. CSF £6.45, CT £34.52. Tote £3.30: £1.60 £1.40 (£6.10). Coventry Newspapers Limited (NEWMARKET) bred by Mrs R. Owen-George. 6 Rn

3m 49.1 (18.4)

## 3306

BURTON AGNES STKS (Mdn 3-Y.O.F) £2215.00 (£615.00: £295.00)
1m 1f 207y

5-00 (5-14)

| 3159⁵ | **Remany (66)** *(JRFanshawe)* 8-11 RHills (12) (lw: trckd ldrs gng wl: swtchd over 1f out: led jst ins fnl f: readily) | −1 |
| 2862² | Jawaher (IRE) *(RJRWilliams)* 8-11 KDarley (1) (hdwy over 2f out: styng on whn hmpd ins fnl f: no ch w wnr) | 3½.2 |
| 2954² | Brecon Beacons (IRE) *(RCharlton)* 8-11 DaleGibson (5) (chsd ldrs: led 5f out tl jst ins fnl f: one pce) | ½.3 |
| 2200⁴ | Portree *(HRACecil)* 8-11 AMcGlone (13) (lw: hdwy to chse ldrs 4f out: rdn over 2f out: r.o one pce fnl f) | hd.4 |
| 3078² | El Taranda (Jt-Fav) *(GWragg)* 8-8 ‡3FNorton (9) (lw: chsd ldrs: rdn & wandered over 1f out: wknd ins fnl f) | ½.5 |
| 1740² | Oak Apple (USA) (62) *(BHanbury)* 8-11 MBirch (3) (b: chsd ldrs tl rdn & wknd over 2f out) | 7.6 |
| 3221 | Neieb (USA) (68) *(BHanbury)* 8-11 DMcKeown (4) (bhd: sme hdwy over 2f out: sn wknd) | hd.7 |
| 553 | Barga *(WClay)* 8-11 JLowe (10) (nvr nr ldrs) | 2½.8 |
| 2620⁴ | Glacial Moon (USA) (66) (Jt-Fav) *(BWHills)* 8-11 DHolland (2) (jnd ldrs 5f out: drvn along over 2f out: sn lost pl) | 3½.9 |
| | Ice Walk *(WJarvis)* 8-11 PRobinson (6) (hdwy to jn ldrs 5f out: drvn along & wknd over 2f out) | 8.10 |
| £011⁵ | Melody Mountain (IRE) *(CEBrittain)* 8-11 GCrealock (11) (a in rr) | 3.11 |
| 2907⁶ | Atan's Gem (USA) *(JNorton)* 8-11 NConnorton (7) (a bhd) | hd.12 |
| 3056⁴ | French Revolution (FR) *(PAKelleway)* 8-11 WWoods (8) (uns rdr & bolted hef s; led to 5f out: wknd over 3f out) | hd.13 |

3/1 El Taranda, Glacial Moon (USA), 5/1 Brecon Beacons, 13/2 Portree, 9/1 Oak Apple (USA), 10/1 REMANY, Jawaher (IRE), 16/1 Melody Mountain (IRE), 20/1 Neieb (USA), 25/1 Ice Walk, 33/1 French Revolution (FR), 50/1 Ors. CSF £102.68, Tote £12.80: £3.20 £2.30 £2.20 (£62.70). Mr A. C. Hall (NEWMARKET) bred by Pinfold Stud and Farms Ltd. 13 Rn

2m 4.7 (2.7)

SF−40/33/32/32/27/16

## 3307

E.B.F. GARROWBY STKS (Mdn 2-Y.O.C & G) £2469.00 (£684.00: £327.00)
1m 100y

5-35 (5-41)

| 2544³ | **The Seer (82)** (Jt-Fav) *(BWHills)* 9-0 DHolland (1) (bhd: effrt & pushed along 4f out: led over 1f out: one pce) | −1 |
| 3146³ | Safir (USA) (Jt-Fav) *(JLDunlop)* 9-0 RHills (9) (lw: chsd ldrs: led 5f out tl over 1f out: one pce) | 4.2 |
| 2456 | Mahogany Light (USA) (bl) *(GHarwood)* 9-0 KDarley (3) (hdwy 4f out: sn hrd rdn: one pce) | 2½.3 |
| 3147⁵ | Master Fiddler *(EWeymes)* 9-0 GHind (6) (chsd ldrs: one pce fnl 2f) | 3½.4 |
| 3163 | Bold Flash *(PCHaslam)* 9-0 DMcKeown (10) (effrt over 3f out: kpt on: nvr rchd ldrs) | 2.5 |
| | Never so Brave *(MissSEHall)* 9-0 NConnorton (8) (leggy: unf: sn bhd: stdy hdwy 2f out: styd on wl nr fin) | 1½.6 |
| | Vaigly Sunthyme *(JMCarr)* 9-0 SMorris (7) (unf: scope: bit bkwd: effrt over 2f out: styd on one pce) | ½.7 |
| 3164 | Prime Painter (68) *(RFFisher)* 9-0 KFallon (2) (chsd ldrs tl hrd rdn & lost pl over 2f out) | 7.8 |
| 2961 | Aberlemno *(JBerry)* 9-0 JCarroll (12) (chsd ldrs tl wknd over 2f out) | 6.9 |
| 2873⁶ | Dusty Point (IRE) *(BHanbury)* 9-0 MBirch (4) (lw: bhd: effrt on outside 3f out: hung rt: n.d) | nk.10 |
| 3146 | Deacon Brodie *(MWEasterby)* 9-0 TLucas (11) (led to 5f out: rdn & wknd over 2f out) | 1.11 |
| 2782 | First Reserve (47) (bl) *(BSRothwell)* 8-11 ‡3FNorton (13) (sn drvn along: chsd ldrs tl lost pl over 2f out) | 2½.12 |
| 1689 | Daves Chance *(TFairhurst)* 9-0 JFanning (5) (rr div whn hmpd over 5f out: sn wl bhd) | 25.13 |

7/4 THE SEER, Safir (USA), 7/1 Mahogany Light (USA), 10/1 Dusty Point (IRE), 20/1 Aberlemno, 33/1 Deacon Brodie, Master Fiddler, Bold Flash, Vaigly Sunthyme, Never so Brave, Prime Painter, 50/1 Ors. CSF £4.98, Tote £3.10: £1.10 £1.20 £1.20 (£2.80). Mr A. R. B. Aspinall (LAMBOURN) bred by Mrs B. Skinner. 13 Rn

1m 46.9 (4.2)

SF−11/−/−/−/−/−

WG

T/Plpt: £188.30 (14 Tckts).

# BEVERLEY (R-H)

**Thursday, September 17th [Good to firm]**

Going Allowance: minus 0.20 sec per fur (F)

Wind: mod half bhd

Stalls: high

**3308**   DRIFFIELD ALL-AGED (S) STKS   £2511.00 (£696.00: £333.00)   **5f**   2-30 (2-34)

3166 **Pretonic (58)** *(MJohnston)* 4-9-9 DMcKeown (13) (lw: gd hdwy over 1f out: r.o
wl to ld post) ............................................................................................................ —1
3103⁶ Banham College **(57)** *(BAMcMahon)* 6-9-7 ‡7SSanders (17) (chsd ldrs tl
outpcd ½-wy: swtchd lft & styd on wl to ld wl ins fnl f: jst ct) ........ s.h.2
3166 The Right Time **(46)** (bl) *(JParkes)* 7-9-7 ‡7ADobbin (8) (lw: chsd ldrs: led ins fnl
f: sn hdd & no ex nr fin) .................................................................................... ¾.3
3115⁴ Clanrock **(65)** (Fav) *(RMWhitaker)* 2-7-13 JFanning (11) (a chsng ldrs: nt qckn
fnl f) ............................................................................................................................ nk.4
3207 Tigani **(66)** (bl) *(DWChapman)* 6-10-0 SWebster (3) (sn bhd: gd hdwy u.p over
1f out: styd on wl nr fin) ................................................................................ s.h.5
2781⁶ Mdm Racer (IRE) *(JBerry)* 2-8-2(3) JFortune (14) (led tl ins fnl f: kpt on u.p) .... d.h.5
3218³ Rich Midas (IRE) **(54)** *(GLewis)* 2-7-1 ‡7CTeague (1) (hdwy on outside ½-wy:
kpt on: nvr nr to chal) .................................................................................... 1½.7
3047 Hershebar *(SRBowring)* 2-7-10 ‡3FNorton (16) (styd on fnl 2f: nrst fin) ............ s.h.8
3077 Minster Man (IRE) (bl) *(BSRothwell)* 2-8-0(1) GHind (2) (kpt on fnl 2f: n.d) ...... 2½.9
3168 Stamshaw **(45)** *(BAMcMahon)* 3-8-7 ‡7JBramhill (12) (sn outpcd & bhd: rdn
½-wy: styd on appr fnl f) .................................................................................... ½.10
2936 Don't Run Me Over **(45)** *(BCMorgan)* 3-9-7 ‡5JWeaver (10) (chsd ldrs over 3f) nk.11
3071 Clangold **(36)** *(JBerry)* 2-7-8 LCharnock (7) (chsd ldrs tl wknd over 1f out:
eased whn btn) .................................................................................................... ½.12
3042 Nordoora (IRE) *(JLHarris)* 3-8-11 ‡3SMaloney (18) (chsd ldrs 3f: sn lost pl) .... nk.13
3144 Chateau Nord *(JBerry)* 3-9-5 ‡7PRoberts (4) (sn wl outpcd) ................................ nk.14
2694⁴ All Earz (IRE) **(47)** *(REarnshaw)* 3-8-12 ‡7CHawksley (5) (s.i.s: a in rr) ...... s.h.15
5413 Twilight Falls **(53)** *(MJCamacho)* 7-10-0 NConnorton (15) (bit bkwd: hld up &
bhd: nvr plcd to chal) .................................................................................... 1½.16
2842 Quick Victory *(PCHaslam)* 2-7-2(1) ‡7NicolaHowarth (9) (s.i.s: a bhd) ................ 1.17

**4/1** Clanrock, **9/2** Banham College, **5/1** PRETONIC, **15/2** Twilight Falls, **10/1** Tigani, Rich Midas (IRE), **16/1**
Minster Man (IRE), Clangold, The Right Time, Don't Run Me Over, **20/1** Nordoora (IRE), Chateau Nord, Mdm
Racer (IRE), **25/1** Stamshaw, Hershebar, **33/1** Ors. CSF £28.63, Tote £5.50: £1.70 £2.70 £4.40 (£11.30). Brian
Yeardley Continental Ltd (MIDDLEHAM) bred by Brian Yeardley. 17 Rn; No bid   63.6 sec (2.1)
SF—47/44/41/18/46/20

**3309**   BEVERLEY RUGBY UNION CLUB APP'CE H'CAP (0-80) £2385.00 (£660.00: £315.00)
**1m 3f 216y**   3-00 (3-01)

3143 **First Bid (53)** *(RMWhitaker)* 5-9-0 JFanning (3) (lw: trckd ldr: effrt & hmpd 1f
out: swtchd & r.o wl to ld jst ins fnl f: all out) ...................................... —1
2860⁵ Esbooain (FR) **(69)** *(LMCumani)* 3-9-8 JWeaver (6) (led: drvn clr 3f out: swvd lft
1f out: wandered & hdd jst ins fnl f: kpt on wl) .................................... nk.2
3076 Much Sought After **(75)** *(DMorley)* 3-9-10 ‡4EBentley (4) (trckd ldrs: effrt over 2f
out: one pce) ........................................................................................................ 10.3
3026⁵ Top Scale **(35)** (v) *(WWHaigh)* 6-7-10 SMaloney (5) (hld up: styd on u.p fnl 3f:
nvr nr to chal) ........................................................................................................ 2.4
3045★ Formal Invitation (IRE) **(52)** *(GLewis)* 3-8-1 ‡4BRussell (8) (b: effrt over 4f out: sn
drvn along: n.d) .................................................................................................. nk.5
3266³ Salu **(56)** (bl) *(JEtherington)* 3-8-9 FNorton (2) (bhd: effrt over 3f out: nvr trbld
ldrs) .......................................................................................................................... 1.6
3177² Speedo Movement **(58)** *(BAMcMahon)* 3-8-7 ‡4SSanders (1) (effrt 5f out: wknd
over 2f out) .......................................................................................................... 2½.7
3128³ Broom Isle **(62)** (Fav) *(MrsAKnight)* 4-9-9 OPears (9) (chsd ldrs: drvn along 5f
out: wknd over 3f out) ...................................................................................... nk.8
3054 Nipotina **(36)** *(RHollinshead)* 6-7-7(4) ‡4MHumphries (7) (a in rr) ...................... 1½.9
LONG HANDICAP: Nipotina 7-5.

**9/2** Broom Isle, **5/1** Speedo Movement, **11/2** Formal Invitation (IRE), Much Sought After, **6/1** Salu, Esbooain
(FR), FIRST BID, **17/2** Top Scale, **33/1** Nipotina. CSF £39.81, CT £192.95. Tote £6.10: £3.00 £2.10 £1.50
(£28.70). Thomlinson's (WETHERBY) bred by R. M. Whitaker. 9 Rn   2m 43.3 (11.7)

**3310**   TETLEY BITTER H'CAP (0-90) £3785.00 (£1130.00: £540.00: £245.00)
**7f 100y**   3-30 (3-31)

3198★ **En Attendant (FR) (76)** (Fav) *(BHanbury)* 4-10-0 (5x) JReid (6) (trckd ldrs gng
wl: led on bit jst ins fnl f: sn clr: easily) ................................................ —1

2906² Causley **(75)** *(BAMcMahon)* 7-9-6 ‡⁷SSanders (9) (lw: led tl hdd jst ins fnl f: kpt on: no ch w wnr) .......................... 5.2

3052 Cee-Jay-Ay **(53)** *(JBerry)* 5-8-5 JFortune (7) (s.i.s: hdwy to chse ldrs 5f out: hrd rdn & styd on fnl 2f) .......................... 1¹/₂.3

3209 Spanish Verdict **(69)** *(DenysSmith)* 5-9-0 ‡⁷GForster (3) (lw: hdwy over 2f out: kpt on one pce over 1f out) .......................... 2.4

3198 Sandmoor Denim **(59)** *(SRBowring)* 5-8-11 SWebster (10) (lw: chsd ldrs tl rdn & wknd over 1f out) .......................... 1.5

3088 Profilic **(71)** *(CaptJWilson)* 7-9-2 ‡⁷SWynne (2) (hld up: hdwy on ins 2f out: hmpd & swtchd ins fnl f: n.d) .......................... ³/₄.6

3088 Super Benz **(74)** *(TFairhurst)* 6-9-12 JFanning (11) (lw: trckd ldrs tl lost pl over 2f out) .......................... 1¹/₂.7

3069 Major Mouse **(74)** *(WWHaigh)* 4-9-12 DMcKeown (5) (hld up & bhd: sme hdwy over 2f out: nvr nr to chal) .......................... 2.8

1700 Doyce **(60)** *(JEtherington)* 3-8-8 NConnorton (1) (sn bhd: sme hdwy over 2f out: n.d) .......................... s.h.9

3105⁴ Dandy Desire **(46)** *(BCMorgan)* 3-7-8⁽¹⁾ LCharnock (4) (chsd ldrs: drvn along 3f out: sn wknd) .......................... 4.10

2588³ Morsun **(75)** (bl) *(DMorley)* 3-9-9 GHind (8) (chsd ldrs: ev ch 2f out: sn wknd) .......................... 5.11

LONG HANDICAP: Dandy Desire 7-5.

**5/1** EN ATTENDANT (FR), **6/1** Causley, **13/2** Super Benz, Cee-Jay-Ay, **7/1** Major Mouse, **8/1** Sandmoor Denim, **17/2** Morsun, **10/1** Spanish Verdict, **14/1** Profilic, **16/1** Ors. CSF £32.81, CT £180.46. Tote £4.70: £1.80 £2.00 £2.60 (£11.60). Exors of the late Mr Bernard Newton (NEWMARKET) bred by Marystead Farm in France. 11 Rn
1m 31.7 (1.5)
SF—69/46/26/29/23/26

## 3311

SANDSFIELD GRAVEL H'CAP (0-70) £3816.00 (£1143.00: £549.00: £252.00)
1m 1f 207y
4-00 (4-04)

3149★ No Comebacks **(47)** *(EJAlston)* 4-8-2 (5x) ‡⁵JWeaver (18) (swtg: hld up & bhd: effrt on ins 2f out: r.o wl u.p to ld ins fnl f) .......................... —1

3052★ Rival Bid (USA) **(68)** (Fav) *(MAJarvis)* 4-10-0 NDay (13) (chsd ldrs: led over 1f out tl nt qckn ins fnl f) .......................... 2¹/₂.2

3174⁶ Aasff (USA) **(65)** *(DMorley)* 3-9-5 JFortune (9) (s.i.s: hdwy & prom 6f out: styd on u.p appr fnl f) .......................... ³/₄.3

3174² Sinclair Lad (IRE) **(64)** *(RHollinshead)* 4-9-3 ‡⁷EHusband (7) (hld up: hdwy & ev ch 2f out: wknd fnl f) .......................... 1.4

2896★ Salman (USA) **(47)** *(SGNorton)* 6-8-0 ‡⁷GParkin (12) (swtg: led: edgd lft & hdd over 1f out: kpt on same pce) .......................... nk.5

2959 Rudda Cass **(34)** *(MrsVAAconley)* 8-7-8⁽¹⁾ LCharnock (11) (a chsng ldrs: kpt on wl fnl 2f) .......................... nk.6

3143⁵ Top Villain **(40)** *(BSRothwell)* 6-8-0⁽¹⁾ GHind (15) (trckd ldrs: effrt 2f out: nvr able to chal) .......................... 1.7

3076⁴ Thunderbird One (USA) **(55)** *(DenysSmith)* 3-8-2 ‡⁷GForster (16) (chsd ldrs: drvn along 5f out: wknd over 1f out) .......................... 4.8

2959 Reilton **(50)** *(JParkes)* 5-8-5 ‡⁵OPears (8) (sn bhd: sme hdwy 2f out: n.d) .......................... 1¹/₂.9

3180★ Jo N Jack (IRE) **(57)** *(RIngram)* 4-9-3 (5x) CDwyer (1) (mid div: effrt on outside over 2f out: sn rdn: n.d) .......................... 2.10

Lodging **(37)** *(BEllison)* 5-7-4⁽⁴⁾ ‡⁷CHawksley (4) (nvr nr to chal) .......................... 2.11

3177 Sie Amato (IRE) **(57)** *(CaptJWilson)* 3-8-11 JReid (5) (chsd ldrs tl wknd 2f out) nk.12

3073 Reel of Tulloch (IRE) **(60)** *(PCHaslam)* 3-9-0 DMcKeown (3) (sn bhd: sme hdwy 2f out: n.d) .......................... 4.13

3114 High Mind (FR) **(57)** (bl) *(MissLCSiddall)* 3-8-11 AMcGlone (6) (bolted bef s: dwlt: a in rr) .......................... 1¹/₂.14

3168 Whirlygig **(42)** *(JSWainwright)* 3-7-7⁽³⁾ ‡³FNorton (10) (a bhd) .......................... hd.15

3159 Stormswept (USA) **(54)** *(MBrittain)* 3-8-8 SWebster (2) (b: a in rr) .......................... 2¹/₂.16

2701 Zinger **(35)** *(TFairhurst)* 4-7-9 JFanning (14) (chsd ldrs tl wknd wl over 2f out) 1¹/₂.17

3149² Thisonesforalice **(43)** *(AHarrison)* 4-8-0 ‡³SMaloney (17) (sn drvn along: chsd ldrs tl lost pl over 3f out) .......................... 1¹/₂.18

LONG HANDICAP: Rudda Cass 6-13, Whirlygig 7-4.

**4/1** Rival Bid (USA), **6/1** Top Villain, **7/1** Salman, **15/2** Sinclair Lad (IRE), **8/1** NO COMEBACKS, **10/1** Jo N Jack (IRE), **11/1** Sie Amato (IRE), **12/1** Thunderbird One (USA), Thisonesforalice, **14/1** Aasff (USA), **16/1** Reel of Tulloch (IRE), **20/1** Reilton, **33/1** High Mind (FR), Lodging, **40/1** Zinger, **50/1** Whirlygig, **66/1** Rudda Cass. CSF £40.06, CT £427.41. Tote £8.40: £2.20 £1.60 £3.50 £1.80 (£16.70). Mr Lionel Snowden (PRESTON) bred by Newmarket Thoroughbred Breeders P L C. 18 Rn
2m 5.1 (3.1)
SF—17/38/27/23/5/—

## 3312

C.N.W-S 80th BIRTHDAY STKS (Mdn 2-Y.O) £2448.00 (£678.00: £324.00)
5f
4-30 (4-33)

2735 Pine Ridge Lad (IRE) **(63)** *(MJohnston)* 9-0 DMcKeown (5) (chsd ldrs: styd on u.p fnl f: led post) .......................... —1

3165² Baliana *(Fav) (CBBBooth)* 8-9 GOldroyd (9) (lw: trckd ldrs: led 2f out: edgd lft fnl f: nt qckn nr fin: jst ct) ..................................................... hd.2
3117 Musical Times *(MrsNMacauley)* 8-9 NDay (7) (sn bhd: hdwy & hrd rdn over 1f out: r.o strly: nt rch ldrs) ..................................................... ¹/₂.3
Epsom Dream *(JEtherington)* 8-9 JReid (2) (in tch: hdwy over 1f out: nvr nr to chal) ..................................................... 2¹/₂.4
General Link *(PAKelleway)* 9-0 WWoods (8) (lengthy: scope: bit bkwd: chsd ldrs: effrt ¹/₂-wy: kpt on same pce appr fnl f) ..................................................... ³/₄.5
2157³ Colfax Starlight **(61)** *(BSRothwell)* 8-9 GHind (6) (chsd ldrs: rdn ¹/₂-wy: sn lost pl) 5.6
Larn Fort *(TFairhurst)* 9-0 JFanning (1) (leggy: unf: bit bkwd: s.i.s: sn outpcd) .. 1.7
811⁴ Lucky Mill *(FHLee)* 8-9 RLappin (4) (slt ld 3f: edgd lft & wknd qckly) ............... 1¹/₂.8
Gold Fort *(BWMurray)* 9-0 JFortune (10) (unf: scope: bit bkwd: a wl outpcd) ..... 7.9
3156 Dutch Dancer *(BAR) (JBerry)* 8-9 LCharnock (3) (w ldr: rdn & hung lft ¹/₂-wy: wandered & wknd qckly 2f out) ..................................................... 6.10

**5/4** Baliana, **4/1** Lucky Mill(op 7/4), **5/1** PINE RIDGE LAD (IRE)(7/1—8/1), **7/1** General Link, **10/1** Epsom Dream, Colfax Starlight, **14/1** Dutch Dancer (BAR), **20/1** Larn Fort, Gold Fort, **25/1** Musical Times. CSF £12.64, Tote £10.00: £2.60 £1.10 £7.30 (£9.70). Mr R. Jenkinson (MIDDLEHAM) bred by Whitechurch Stud in Ireland. 10 Rn
63.6 sec (2.1)
SF—38/32/30/20/22/—

## 3313
E.B.F. WILLERBY STKS (Mdn 2-Y.O.F) £2637.00 (£732.00: £351.00)
1m 100y
5-00 (5-03)

3093² **Zenith** *(Fav) (IABalding)* 8-11 JReid (2) (lw: sn trckng ldrs: led over 1f out: pushed out) ..................................................... —1
Seama *(USA) (SirMarkPrescott)* 8-6 ‡⁵KRutter (8) (lengthy: scope: in tch tl lost pl ¹/₂-wy: hdwy 2f out: edgd rt & styd on fnl f) ..................................................... 2¹/₂.2
3171² Omidjoy *(IRE)* **(81)** *(SPCWoods)* 8-11 WWoods (11) (a chsng ldrs: r.o same pce u.p fnl 2f) ..................................................... 1.3
Cromarty *(HRACecil)* 8-11 AMcGlone (5) (cmpt: dwlt: hdwy over 3f out: ev ch 2f out: one pce) ..................................................... nk.4
Jendorcet *(TFairhurst)* 8-11 JFanning (9) (cmpt: bit bkwd: s.i.s: bhd tl kpt on fnl 2f) ..................................................... 5.5
3156 Early Song *(PTWalwyn)* 8-11 LCharnock (3) (chsd ldrs: wnt 2nd over 2f out: sn hrd drvn & wknd) ..................................................... nk.6
3100 Ark Celeste *(WWHaigh)* 8-11 SWebster (10) (nvr rchd ldrs) ..................................................... 2¹/₂.7
3132 Breeze by *(IABalding)* 8-8 ‡³SO'Gorman (7) (chsd ldrs tl lost pl over 2f out) ... s.h.8
3178 Contrac Countess *(IRE)* **(65)** *(BSRothwell)* 8-9 GHind (1) (bhd: sme hdwy 3f out: sn rdn & wknd) ..................................................... nk.9
3193⁴ Manx Monarch **(85)** *(RHollinshead)* 8-4 ‡7DCarson (13) (nvr nr to chal) ........... 1.10
3030 Stephanentse *(WWHaigh)* 8-11 DMcKeown (4) (bit bkwd: sn wl bhd) ..................................................... 2.11
2374 Rose of Man *(JBerry)* 8-11 JFortune (6) (chsd ldrs tl lost pl over 3f out) ........ 3¹/₂.12
2986 Kira *(MissLCSiddall)* 8-6 ‡JWeaver (12) (led: clr over 3f out: hdd & wknd qckly over 1f out) ..................................................... s.h.13

**8/13** ZENITH, **5/1** Cromarty(op 3/1), **8/1** Omidjoy (IRE), **10/1** Seama (USA), **14/1** Manx Monarch, **20/1** Early Song, **25/1** Contrac Countess (IRE), Rose of Man, Breeze by, **50/1** Ors. CSF £8.87, Tote £1.60: £1.10 £3.20 £1.80 (£12.30). The Queen (KINGSCLERE) bred by The Queen. 13 Rn
1m 47.7 (5)
T/Plpt: £66.20 (41.55 Tckts).
WG

## 3179—LINGFIELD (L-H)

## Thursday, September 17th [Good, Rnd Good to firm patches, AWT Standard]

Going Allowance: Turf: nil sec (G); AWT: minus 0.10 sec (FS)
Wind: almost nil
Stalls: high

## 3314
E.B.F. PUTNEY STKS (I) (Mdn 2-Y.O) £2658.00 (£738.00: £354.00)
7f
2-20 (2-22)

1120⁵ **Cropton** *(MrsJCecil)* 8-9 RCochrane (5) (racd far side: mde virtually all: hrd rdn over 1f out: r.o wl) ..................................................... —1
Triple *(BWHills)* 9-0 GBaxter (1) (unf: a.p far side: ev ch ins fnl f: r.o) ................. ¹/₂.2
Amaam Amaam *(Fav) (JHMGosden)* 9-0 SCauthen (13) (unf: scope: a.p: hung lft over 1f out: unable qckn) ..................................................... 2¹/₂.3
2598² City Rocket **(90)** *(PJMakin)* 9-0 TSprake (16) (a.p: hrd rdn over 1f out: one pce) ¹/₂.4
2598 Moon Carnival *(LadyHerries)* 8-9 JWilliams (11) (a.p: one pce fnl 2f) ............... hd.5
Sea Siren *(HCandy)* 8-9 CRutter (12) (w'like: no hdwy fnl 2f) ..................................................... 1¹/₂.6
Rispoto *(SirMarkPrescott)* 8-9 CNutter (9) (leggy: lt-f: nvr nr to chal) ..................................................... 1¹/₂.7
Rakis *(IRE)* *(CJBenstead)* 9-0 WCarson (10) (str: bkwd: a mid div) ..................................................... 3.8

2629 Across the Bow (USA) *(IABalding)* 9-0 SWhitworth (8) (outpcd) ...................... hd.9
3000 Starlight Rose (IRE) *(CAHorgan)* 8-9 SDawson (4) (racd far side: prom over 4f) 1½.10
2456 Night Edition *(SDow)* 9-0 BRouse (15) (a bhd) ............................................... 1.11
    Kitoto (IRE) *(PFICole)* 9-0 TQuinn (3) (leggy: lt-f: racd far side: prom over 5f) hd.12
 988 Restart *(LordHuntingdon)* 8-11 ‡³DHarrison (6) (bit bkwd: racd far side: a bhd) ½.13
2951 Sea Syrah (IRE) *(MBlanshard)* 9-0 GBardwell (7) (racd far side: a bhd) ............ 8.14
    Don Tocino *(JLDunlop)* 9-0 AClark (14) (w'like: scope: s.s: a bhd) ................. ½.15
3186 Get Sunday Sport (IRE) *(MissGayKelleway)* 9-0 GCarter (2) (racd far side: a
    bhd) ............................................................................................................. 16

**5/6** Amaam Amaam, **7/1** City Rocket(op 4/1), Sea Siren(tchd 16/1), **10/1** Moon Carnival(8/1—14/1), **20/1** Triple, Restart, Rakis (IRE), Kitoto (IRE), **33/1** CROPTON & Ors. CSF £483.45, Tote £30.70: £4.20 £6.00 £1.10 (£128.60). Lady Murless (NEWMARKET) bred by Lady Murless. 16 Rn         1m 25 (3.70)
SF—39/42/34/32/26/21

**3315**     BIFFA RECYCLING (S) STKS (2-Y.O) £2679.00 (£744.00: £357.00)
          6f (AWT)                                                       2-50 (2-53)

2948⁶ **Pat Poindestres (60)** *(MPMuggeridge)* 8-6 BRouse (4) (led 1f: led over 1f out:
    comf) ............................................................................................................. —1
3218⁵ Skullcap (59) *(TJNaughton)* 8-11 RCochrane (11) (hld up: rdn over 2f out: r.o
    one pce fnl f) ................................................................................................ 3½.2
3283 The Institute Boy (54) (bl) *(KRBurke)* 8-11 AShoults (6) (led 5f out tl over 1f out:
    one pce) ...................................................................................................... hd.3
2396² Girl Next Door (59) *(NAGraham)* 8-6 AClark (1) (a.p: rdn over 1f out: one pce) .. 1.4
2872⁶ Mister Blake (69) (bl) *(WAO'Gorman)* 8-8 ‡³Emma O'Gorman (2) (swtg: hdwy
    over 1f out: one pce) ..................................................................................... 1½.5
3148 Palacegate Prince (61) (bl) *(Fav)* *(JBerry)* 8-11 GCarter (5) (rdn thrght: hdwy fnl
    f: nvr nrr) ........................................................................................................ 4.6
3218⁶ Risky Number (58) *(JSMoore)* 0 11 DBiggs (14) (lw: no hdwy fnl 2f) ................ ½.7
2903⁶ Stroika (IRE) (64) *(CJames)* 8-8 GBaxter (8) (swtg: prom over 2f) ................... 4,8
3162 Annie Rose (50) (bl) *(TDBarron)* 8-6 JWilliams (13) (s.s: hdwy over 2f out: wknd
    wl over 1f out) ............................................................................................... ¾.9
3173 Creative Flair (USA) (60) *(PFICole)* 8-6 TQuinn (7) (bhd fnl 2f) ....................... 1½.10
2994 All Promises (40) *(PButler)* 7-13 ‡⁷SDrowne (10) (bhd fnl 2f) ....................... 6.11
2591 Victorian Star (40) *(PButler)* 7-13 ‡⁷DToole (12) (swtg: a bhd) ..................... ¾.12
2863 Tee-Emm (bl) *(PHowling)* 8-11 TyroneWilliams (9) (prom tl rn wd bnd & wknd
    wl over 1f out) ............................................................................................... 1½.13
2916 Shades of Croft (49) *(MDIUsher)* 8-11 MWigham (12) (a bhd) ....................... 1½.14

**7/2** Palacegate Prince, **5/1** Stroika (IRE), Skullcap, **6/1** Girl Next Door(8/1—10/1), **10/1** Creative Flair (USA)(5/1—12/1), Mister Blake(8/1—12/1), **12/1** PAT POINDESTRES, **20/1** Annie Rose, The Institute Boy, Risky Number, **25/1** Shades of Croft, **33/1** Ors. CSF £66.62, Tote £23.40: £4.80 £1.70 £7.30 (£108.70). Mr J. K. Grimes (MARLBOROUGH) bred by Bar Equipment and Refridgeration Co Ltd. 14 Rn; Sold J Daniels 5,800 gns
1m 13.98 (3.38)
SF—12/3/3/2/–/–/–

**3316**     JARDINE INSURANCE BROKERS H'CAP (0-70) £2385.00 (£660.00: £315.00)
          2m                       (Weights raised 1 lb)                             3-20 (3-21)

2934 **Janiski (47)** (v) *(MrsBarbaraWaring)* 9–8-11 NHowe (1) (lw: s.s: 5th st: led 1f
    out: rdn out) ................................................................................................... —1
3102⁴ Silken Words (USA) (53) *(WRMuir)* 3–8-5 WCarson (3) (chsd ldr: led over 6f out
    to 1f out: r.o) ................................................................................................ ½.2
3118 Go South (60) *(JRJenkins)* 8–9-10 GBaxter (4) (hrd rdn over 5f out: hdwy over
    1f out: r.o ins fnl f) ....................................................................................... nk.3
3244* Ideal Candidate (68) *(Fav)* *(TJNaughton)* 3–9-6 (5x) GCarter (7) (4th st: hrd rdn
    over 1f out: unable qckn) ............................................................................... hd.4
 585⁶ Mediator (53) *(AMoore)* 3–8-5 NAdams (2) (6th st: no hdwy fnl 3f) .............. 8.5
3219 Lady Poly (39) *(MissBSanders)* 4–8-3 GBardwell (5) (3rd st: wknd wl over 1f
    out) ............................................................................................................... 2½.6
3215² Share Holder (30) *(MissGayKelleway)* 3–7-9 ‡⁷MBaird (8) (b: b.hind: led over 9f:
    2nd st: wknd over 2f out) .............................................................................. 6.7
3219² Erlemo (45) (bl) *(CJBenstead)* 3–7-4 ‡⁷AntoinetteArmes (6) (lw: bhd fnl 6f) ........ 5.8

**2/5** Ideal Candidate, **7/1** Silken Words (USA), **10/1** Erlemo(op 6/1), **12/1** Share Holder(op 8/1), Go South, **20/1** JANISKI, **50/1** Ors. CSF £135.54, CT £1,589.02. Tote £21.50: £3.20 £1.70 £2.30 (£29.80). Mrs Barbara Waring (CHIPPENHAM) bred by Dayspring Co Ltd. 8 Rn         3m 35.35 (11.35)

**3317**     WALTON HILL H'CAP (0-90) £3366.80 (£934.80: £448.40)     **7f 140y**    3-50 (4-17)

3126 **Darakah (57)** *(CJHill)* 5–7-12 WCarson (3) (lw: a.p: hrd rdn over 1f out: led last
    strides) .......................................................................................................... —1

3105 Charmed Knave **(53)** *(DRLaing)* 7–7–8[(1)] TyroneWilliams (2) (a.p: led over 4f out: hrd rdn fnl f: hdd last strides) .............................................. hd.2

3198[3] Risk Zone **(69)** (bl) *(RHannon)* 3–8–3 ‡[3]RPerham (15) (swtg: racd stands' side: a.p: rdn over 1f out: r.o ins fnl f) ................................................ s.h.3

3182★ Caroles Express **(75)** (Fav) *(RAkehurst)* 4–9–2 (6x) TQuinn (7) (a.p: hrd rdn over 1f out: eased whn btn ins fnl f) ................................. 3½.4

3182[4] Dodgy **(62)** (v) *(SDow)* 5–8–3 GCarter (14) (racd stands' side: hdwy 3f out: wknd over 1f out) ...................................................................... 5.5

3098 Pharaoh's Dancer **(73)** *(EAWheeler)* 5–9–0 MWigham (5) (nvr nr to chal) ........ 1½.6

3182 Cape Pigeon (USA) **(87)** *(LGCottrell)* 7–9–7 ‡[7]CAvery (13) (lw: racd stands' side: prom over 5f) .......................................................... nk.7

3137[4] Mossy Rose **(59)** *(LordHuntingdon)* 6–7–11 ‡[3]DHarrison (10) (lw: racd stands' side: outpcd) ................................................................ 4.8

Old Glory **(65)** *(RJHolder)* 4–8–6 JWilliams (6) (outpcd) ............................ 1.9

3037 Fair Enchantress **(52)** (bl) *(JABennett)* 4–7–7 GBardwell (8) (outpcd) ............ nk.10

3198 Lucknam Style **(65)** *(MrsBarbaraWray)* 4–8–6 NHowe (12) (racd stands' side: led 3f: wknd over 2f out) ............................................... ¾.11

3133 Southwold Air **(69)** *(JLDunlop)* 3–8–6 AClark (9) (lw: a bhd) ....................... ½.12

3182 Cheveux Mitchell **(75)** (v) *(MRChannon)* 5–9–2 RCochrane (11) (lw: racd stands' side: a bhd) ........................................................... 5.13

3236 Cru Exceptionnel **(70)** (bl) *(PJMakin)* 4–8–11 SCauthen (4) (lw: spd 5f) ............. 14
LONG HANDICAP: Charmed Knave 7-5, Fair Enchantress 7-6.

**4/1** Caroles Express, **5/1** DARAKAH, Risk Zone(tchd 8/1), **9/2** Dodgy, **9/1** Mossy Rose, **10/1** Dodgy, Cheveux Mitchell, **16/1** Cape Pigeon (USA), Pharaoh's Dancer, **25/1** Fair Enchantress, Southwold Air, **33/1** Ors. CSF £133.63, CT £786.47. Tote £7.20: £2.20 £4.50 £2.70 (£69.70). Mr C. John Hill (BARNSTAPLE) bred by Yeomanstown Lodge Stud. 14 Rn                                       1m 32.48 (3.98)
SF—24/19/27/29/1/7

---

## 3318 KINGSTON H'CAP (0-80) £2811.60 (£777.60: £370.80) **5f (AWT)** 4-20 (4-42)

3257 **Cranfield Comet (65)** (Jt-Fav) *(JBerry)* 3–8–11 GCarter (1) (rdn over 2f out: hdwy over 1f out: led ins fnl f: r.o wl) ......................................... —1

3015 Very Dicey **(80)** *(WRMuir)* 4–10–0 TQuinn (10) (lw: a.p: led over 1f out tl ins fnl f: unable qckn) .............................................. 2½.2

3207 Paley Prince (USA) **(78)** *(MDIUsher)* 6–9–12 RCochrane (4) (hdwy over 1f out: r.o) ............................................................................... ¾.3

2676[2] Serious Hurry **(56)** (Jt-Fav) *(SirMarkPrescott)* 4–8–4 CNutter (7) (a.p: led over 2f out tl over 1f out: one pce) .................................... hd.4

2974[6] Ever so Artistic **(48)** *(PHowling)* 5–7–10[(3)] DBiggs (5) (lw: a.p: one pce fnl 2f) ... ¾.5

3103 Pendor Dancer **(55)** (bl) *(BForsey)* 9–7–12[(5)] ‡[5]RPrice (9) (a.p: ev ch over 1f out: one pce) ...................................................... ¾.6

2797[5] Sylvan Breeze **(73)** (bl) *(PMitchell)* 4–9–9 SWhitworth (2) (nvr nr to chal) .......... ½.7

1138 Factuelle **(45)** *(CJHill)* 5–7–7 GBardwell (3) (lw: a bhd) .............................. 2½.8

415[6] Ipsilante **(51)** *(ASReid)* 3–7–11 NAdams (8) (outpcd) .................................. 1½.9

3183 Shades of Jade **(54)** *(JJBridger)* 4–8–2 TyroneWilliams (6) (led over 2f) ......... nk.10
LONG HANDICAP: Ever so Artistic 7-3, Factuelle 7-3.

**7/2** CRANFIELD COMET(9/4—4/1), Serious Hurry, **9/2** Very Dicey, **11/2** Paley Prince (USA), **6/1** Sylvan Breeze(op 4/1), **10/1** Shades of Jade, **11/1** Factuelle, **14/1** Pendor Dancer, **20/1** Ors. CSF £20.02, CT £78.78. Tote £4.40: £1.80 £2.30 £2.70 (£21.60). Cranfield Industries Limited (COCKERHAM) bred by J. R. C. and Mrs Wren. 10 Rn                                                      59.72 sec (1.52)
SF—57/64/59/36/25/24

---

## 3319 BARNES GRADUATION STKS (3-Y.O) £2454.40 (£678.40: £323.20) 1m 3f 106y 4-55 (5-04)

2933★ **Tapis Rouge (IRE)** (Fav) *(HRACecil)* 9-5 SCauthen (3) (lw: 2nd st: led 2f out: shkn up 1f out: comf) ............................................ —1

2798[4] Milzig (USA) **(96)** *(DRCElsworth)* 9-1 TQuinn (2) (chsd ldr: led over 4f out to 2f out: eased whn btn ins fnl f) ................................... 5.2

1414★ Rainridge **(85)** (v) *(JLDunlop)* 9-5 WCarson (1) (led 7f) ............................ 15.3

**4/9** TAPIS ROUGE (IRE), **7/2** Milzig (USA), **5/1** Rainridge(4/1—6/1). CSF £2.10, Tote £1.60 (£1.60). Sheikh Mohammed (NEWMARKET) bred by Newton Stud Farm Inc. in Ireland. 3 Rn                  2m 27.21 (5.21)
SF—53/39/13

---

## 3320 E.B.F. PUTNEY STKS (II) (Mdn 2-Y.O) £2637.00 (£732.00: £351.00) 7f 5-25 (5-34)

**Taahhub (IRE)** *(BWHills)* 9-0 WCarson (5) (str: scope: a.p: led over 1f out: pushed out) ......................................................... —1

3000[2] Ecu de France (IRE) (Fav) *(JLDunlop)* 9-0 SCauthen (15) (lw: a.p: rdn over 3f out: r.o ins fnl f) ........................................................ 2.2

| | | |
|---|---|---|
| 2901³ | Johns Act (USA) (DHaydnJones) 9-0 JWilliams (14) (rdn over 3f out: hdwy over 1f out: r.o) | 2½.3 |
| 2857 | Simply Finesse (75) (RAkehurst) 9-0 TQuinn (3) (led 5f out tl over 1f out: sn wknd) | 2½.4 |
| 3000⁵ | Lt Welsh (USA) (IABalding) 9-0 RCochrane (4) (led 2f: rdn over 2f out: unable qckn) | hd.5 |
| 3099 | Swiss Mountain (DRLaing) 8-9 TyroneWilliams (6) (rdn & no hdwy fnl 2f) | 3.6 |
| 2930 | Crystal Stone (TThomsonJones) 8-9 SWhitworth (10) (lw: prom 5f) | hd.7 |
| 3181 | Fitzroy Lad (MRChannon) 8-9 ‡⁵RPrice (1) (nvr nr to chal) | 1.8 |
| | Sir Thomas Beecham (SDow) 9-0 BRouse (7) (unf: nvr nrr) | 2.9 |
| 2948 | Dance Magical (MDixon) 8-4 ‡⁵NGwilliams (11) (outpcd) | ¾.10 |
| 2859 | Darsing (MJWilkinson) 9-0 CRutter (2) (a bhd) | 3½.11 |
| 2930 | Silvies Star (CDBroad) 8-9 NAdams (9) (a mid div) | 1½.12 |
| 2306⁵ | Kismetim (71) (GLewis) 9-0 AClark (14) (a bhd) | 10.13 |
| 3130 | Allensea (IRE) (CAHorgan) 9-0 SDawson (12) (a bhd) | 1.14 |
| | Arabian Castle (MJHeaton-Ellis) 9-0 GCarter (13) (w'like: bit bkwd: a bhd) | 10.15 |
| 2746 | Flying Gabriel (PHowling) 8-9 DBiggs (8) (outpcd) | 8.16 |

**2/1** Ecu de France (IRE)(11/10—5/2), **11/4** Lt Welsh (USA), **4/1** Simply Finesse(op 8/1), **6/1** Johns Act (USA), TAAHHUB (IRE)(5/1—8/1), **20/1** Kismetim, **33/1** Allensea (IRE), Arabian Castle, **50/1** Ors. CSF £18.82, Tote £6.50: £2.50 £1.20 £2.10 (£7.80). Mr Hamdan Al-Maktoum (LAMBOURN) bred by Roland H. Alder in Ireland. 16 Rn
1m 25.78 (4.48)
SF—33/27/19/11/10/—

T/Plpt: Not won; £2,391.90 to Newbury 18/9/92.
AK

3228a—**ARLINGTON PARK** (L-H)
**Monday, September 7th [Firm]**

## 3321a
NEWBURY H'CAP   £24064.00   **1m 110y**

| | | |
|---|---|---|
| | **Zeeruler (USA)** (America) 4-8-1 GGomez | —1 |
| | Evanescent (USA) (America) 5-8-1⁽¹⁾ CSilva | hd.2 |
| | Aptakisic (IRE) (America) 4-8-0⁽¹⁾ JVelasquez | hd.3 |
| 2097a³ | ENHARMONIC (USA) (LordHuntingdon) 5-8-4 SSellers (btn further 3l) | 7 |
| 2641³ | STARLIGHT FLYER (MMoubarak) 5-8-0⁽¹⁾ MSmith (btn 7½l by wnr) | 11 |

Tote 36.40 (1-2) 18.60 12.60 (1-2-3) 8.80 9.60 6.60. J and J Racing Stable (D Von Hemel,AMERICA) bred by D. Johnson in USA. 12 Rn
1m 41

## 3322a
SECRETARIAT STKS (Grade 1) (3-Y.O) £96257.00   **1¼m**

| | | |
|---|---|---|
| | **Ghazi (USA)** (America) 3-8-2 RDavis | —1 |
| | Paradise Creek (USA) (America) 3-8-11 MSmith | ½.2 |
| | Tango Charlie (USA) (America) 3-8-5 ASorrows | 1¾.3 |
| 2507a⁴ | FREE FLYER (IRE) (MMoubarak) 3-8-2 HMcCauley (btn further 1½l) | 8 |

Tote 35.20 (1-2) 13.00 4.60 (1-2-3) 10.00 3.20 5.80. Mr H. Shoaib (D.Carroll,AMERICA) bred by Deer Lawn Farm in USA. 10 Rn
2m 1

3230a—**LONGCHAMP** (R-H)
**Tuesday, September 8th [Good]**
Going Allowance: 0.10 sec per fur (G)

## 3323a
PRIX GLADIATEUR (Gp 3)   £22704.00   **1m 7f 110y (Grande)**

| | | |
|---|---|---|
| 1221a³ | **Le Montagnard (FR)** (France) 4-9-0 CPhelippeau | —1 |
| 2096a★ | Dajraan (IRE) (France) 3-8-11 TJarnet | s.nk.2 |
| | Thunder Grey (FR) (France) 6-9-0 TGillet | 2½.3 |

Tote 8.10f: 2.50f 1.30f (SF: 25.10f). Mr J. Blandin (G.Henrot,France) bred by R.Hesketh, Mrs M.Bryant & Ecurie Balwell in France. 6 Rn
3m 26.7 (7.7)
SF—38/34/34

# CRAON (R-H) France
**Saturday, September 12th [Good]**

## 3324a
PRIX HOLST HARAS DU POITS GASNIER-CRITERIUM DE L'OUEST (listed race) (2-Y.O)
£10314.00   **1m**

| | | |
|---|---|---|
| | **Sawasdee (FR)** (France) 2-8-11 JBoisnard | —1 |
| 3224a² | Glorieux Dancer (FR) (France) 2-9-2 MBoutin | ½.2 |

2510a³ Smadoun (FR) *(France)* 2-8-11 DSicaud ................................................ nk.3
2835⁵ EMPIRE POOL *(LordHuntingdon)* 2-8-11 CAsmussen (btn further 4l) ................. 5
Tote 9.90f: 2.10f 1.70f 1.90f (12.20f). Mr G.Samama (J-P Pelat,FRANCE) bred by G.Samama in France. 10 Rn
No time taken

## 2760a—LEOPARDSTOWN (L-H)

### Sunday, September 13th [Good to soft]
Going Allowance: St: nil sec (G); Rnd: 0.55 sec per fur (Y)

### 3325a
TATTERSALLS BREEDERS STKS (listed-restricted race) (2-Y.O) £91589.00   **6f**

2193² **MR MARTINI (IRE)** (bl) *(CEBrittain)* 2-8-10 MRoberts ............................... —1
2800³ CAPTAIN LE SAUX (IRE) *(MBell)* 2-8-10 MHills ........................................ hd.2
  My-O-My (IRE) *(Ireland)* 2-8-7 SCraine ................................................ ¹/₂.3
3044* EXPRESS MARIECURIE (IRE) *(PWChapple-Hyam)* 2-8-7 JReid (btn further 7l) .... 8
2717⁶ BOLD COUNTY *(MJohnston)* 2-8-7 RPElliott (btn 8³/₄l by wnr) ..................... 10
2528³ DARK EYED LADY (IRE) *(DWPArbuthnot)* 2-8-7 TQuinn (btn 13¹/₄l by wnr) ........ 11
2794⁴ BALLON *(CEBrittain)* 2-8-7 GBaxter (btn 14³/₄l by wnr) ......................... 15
2528⁶ SWEET ROMEO *(MJohnston)* 2-8-7 DMcKeown (btn 25³/₄l by wnr) ................... 19
Tote £4.70: £2.30 £3.20 £4.70 (£16.80). Circlechart Ltd. (NEWMARKET) bred by Mrs W.Hanson in Ireland. 19
Rn
          1m 15.3 (4.1)
          SF—14/13/8

### 3326a
MEADOW MEATS E.B.F. FLYING FIVE (Stks) (Gp 3)   £13902.00   **5f**

2762a³ **Flowing (USA)** (Fav) *(Ireland)* 4-9-10 PShanahan (trckd ldrs: chal & led 1f out:
  sn clr: eased nr fin) ........................................................ —1
2762a* Park Dream (IRE) *(Ireland)* 3-9-7 CRoche (led 4f: no ex) ........................ 1¹/₂.2
2762a² Poolesta (IRE) (bl) *(Ireland)* 3-9-2 WJO'Connor (in tch: effrt over 1f out: kpt on) hd.3
2978a² Up and At'em *(Ireland)* 2-8-0 NMcCullagh (in tch: effrt over 1f out: one pce) .... ¹/₂.4
  Moumayaz (USA) *(Ireland)* 2-8-0 MRoberts (chsd ldrs: no hdwy fnl f) ............. 1¹/₂.5
3113a⁴ Staviski *(Ireland)* 2-8-0 DManning (bhd: n.d) ................................... 7.6
2762a⁶ Bradawn Breever (IRE) (bl) *(Ireland)* 3-10-2 RJGriffiths (prom tl wknd over 1f out) ...
          1¹/₂.7
  Lute and Lyre (IRE) (bl) *(Ireland)* 3-9-2 JReid (cl up tl wknd over 1f out) ....... 4.8
2452⁴ Preponderance (IRE) *(Ireland)* 2-7-11 WJSupple (in tch: effrt ¹/₂-wy: btn &
  wknd over 1f out) ........................................................ 2¹/₂.9

13/8 FLOWING (USA), 5/2 Park Dream (IRE), 5/1 Poolesta (IRE), 6/1 Moumayaz (USA), 9/1 Preponderance
(IRE), 10/1 Up and At'em, 16/1 Bradawn Breever (IRE), 20/1 Lute and Lyre (IRE), 33/1 Staviski. Tote £2.60:
£1.40 £1.60 £2.00 (£5.20). Mrs J.Maxwell Moran (D.K.Weld,IRELAND) bred by Tommy Stack in USA. 9 Rn
          60.4 sec (1.4)
          SF—82/73/67/49/43/15

### 3327a
KERRY GROUP IRISH CHAMPION STKS (Gp 1) (C & F) £80654.00   **1¹/₄m**

2837⁴ **DR DEVIOUS (IRE)** *(PWChapple-Hyam)* 3-8-11 JReid (hld up: hmpd 7f out:
  hdwy 4f out: rdn to jn ldr 1f out: r.o to ld last stride) ............. —1
2345* St Jovite (USA) (Fav) *(Ireland)* 3-8-11 CRoche (led 1f: w ldr: led 3f out: rdn 2f
  out: jnd 1f out: edgd lft u.p fnl f: jst ct) ............................ s.h.2
2838⁴ ALFLORA (IRE) *(CEBrittain)* 3-8-11 MRoberts (hld up: hdwy on outside 7f out:
  effrt 3f out: one pce) ................................................ 9.3
2837 Kooyonga (IRE) *(Ireland)* 4-9-3 WJO'Connor (in tch: sme hdwy over 2f out: nvr
  able to chal) ........................................................ 6.4
2889a⁵ Malvernico (IRE) *(Ireland)* 4-9-6 KJManning (chsd ldrs: effrt over 2f out: sn rdn
  & one pce) .......................................................... 2.5
2890a* GREAT PALM (USA) *(PFICole)* 3-8-11 TQuinn (cl up: led 6f out to 3f out: sn rdn
  & wknd) ............................................................. 15.6
1351a³ Dowland (USA) *(Ireland)* 4-9-6 PVGilson (mid div tl rdn & wknd 4f out: sn bhd)   8.7
  Magic Carr (USA) (bl) *(Ireland)* 3-8-11 CEverard (s.s: led after 1f tl wknd qckly
  6f out) ............................................................. dist.8

4/7 St Jovite (USA), 7/2 DR DEVIOUS (IRE), 4/1 Kooyonga (IRE), 11/1 Great Palm (USA), 50/1 Alflora (IRE),
100/1 Malvernico (IRE), 200/1 Ors. Tote £6.90: £1.50 £1.20 £3.00 (£3.50). Mr Sidney H.Craig
(MARLBOROUGH) bred by Lyonstown Stud in Ireland. 8 Rn
          2m 10 (6)
          SF—92/91/73/67/66/27

### 3328a
MEADOW MEATS E.B.F. KILLAVULLAN STKS (Gp 3) (2-Y.O.F) £13902.00   **1m**

3227a **Asema (USA)** *(Ireland)* 2-8-7 PShanahan (in tch: hdwy 2f out: led 1f out: r.o wl) —1

3227a³ Alouette *(Fav)* *(Ireland)* 2-8-7 CRoche (cl up: rdn ½-wy: sn lost pl: hdwy u.p over 1f out: kpt on: nt trble wnr) ............................................ 2.2

1985a² JUST SPECULATION (IRE) *(PFICole)* 2-8-7 TQuinn (cl up: ev ch 2f out: no ex fnl f) .......................... 1.3

Lady Ounavarra (IRE) *(Ireland)* 2-8-7 MRoberts (mid div: rdn 2f out: no ex fnl f) 2.4

Tbaareeh (USA) *(Ireland)* 2-8-7 KJManning (led 7f: sn wknd) ..................... 1.5

3029² JERVIA *(JWWatts)* 2-8-7 LPiggott (in rr ½-wy: hdwy 2f out: no imp u.p fr over 1f out) ............ 7.6

Atsuko (IRE) *(Ireland)* 2-8-7 SCraine (hld up: rdn over 2f out: sn wknd) .......... 1½.7

**11/10** Alouette, **7/2** ASEMA (USA), **9/2** Jervia, **11/2** Just Speculation (IRE), **8/1** Atsuko (IRE), **10/1** Tbaareeh (USA), **11/1** Lady Ounavarra (IRE). Tote £4.90: £2.30 £1.60 (£3.50). Mr Allen E.Paulson (D.K.Weld,IRELAND) bred by Landon Knight Stables in USA. 7 Rn      1m 44.4 (6.4)
                 SF−63/57/54/48/45/24

3323a—**LONGCHAMP (R-H)**
**Sunday, September 13th [Good]**
Going Allowance: 0.10 sec per fur (G)

## 3329a
PRIX NIEL ESCADA (Gp 2) (3-Y.O.C & F) £41270.00   **1½m (Grande)**

2504a³ Songlines (FR) *(France)* 3-9-2 OBenoist (mde virtually all: hrd rdn over 1f out: hld on gamely) ................... —1

Petit Loup (USA) *(France)* 3-9-2 CAsmussen (mid div: 4th st: chal over 1f out: r.o: jst failed) ........................ nose.2

1356a Apple Tree (FR) *(France)* 3-9-2 TJarnet (a.p: 3rd st: r.o wl fnl f) ...................... ½.3

1819a9³ Contested Bid (USA) *(France)* 3-9-2 PatEddery (chsd wnr: 2nd st: one pce fnl f) 1.4

1819a6 Marignan (USA) *(France)* 3-9-2 DBoeuf (hld up: 7th st: hdwy fnl f: nvr able to chal) ............ 2.5

2316a Glanville (USA) (bl) *(France)* 3-9-2 ELegrix (mid div: 5th st: one pce) .............. hd.6

2890a Johann Quatz (FR) *(France)* 3-9-2 FHead (hld up: last st: n.d) ................. hd.7

1356a★ Polytain (FR) *(Fav)* *(France)* 3-9-2 LDettori (mid div: 6th st: outpcd fnl f) ......... 2.8

**6/4** Polytain (FR), **3/1** Marignan (USA), **15/4** Contested Bid (USA), **25/4** Petit Loup (USA), **15/2** Apple Tree (FR), **12/1** SONGLINES (FR), **15/1** Johann Quatz (FR), **41/1** Glanville (USA). Tote 12.80f: 3.30f 2.20f 2.70f (40.90f). Sir Robin McAlpine (E.Bartholomew,FRANCE) bred by Sir Robin McAlpine in France. 8 Rn    2m 32.8 (2.8)
                 SF−86/85/84/82/78/77

## 3330a
PRIX VERMEILLE ESCADA (Gp 1) (3-Y.O.F) £103199.00   **1½m (Grande)**

1498a★ Jolypha (USA) *(Fav)* *(France)* 3-9-2 PatEddery (hld up: 8th st: gd hdwy on ins over 1f out: n.m.r 1f out: led ins fnl f: r.o wl) ........... —1

2854★ CUNNING *(LMCumani)* 3-9-2 LDettori (trckd ldr: 4th st: hdwy to ld 1f out: hdd ins fnl f: r.o) ................... hd.2

2980a★ Urban Sea (USA) *(France)* 3-9-2 MBoutin (led to 1f out: styd on) ................... ½.3

1823a5 Verveine (USA) *(France)* 3-9-2 DBoeuf (prom: 5th st: r.o fnl 2f) ................... nose.4

2977a★ Market Booster (USA) *(Ireland)* 3-9-2 MJKinane (hld up: 9th st: hdwy on ins 2f out: n.m.r over 1f out: r.o) ........... hd.5

3110a² Trishyde (USA) *(France)* 3-9-2 FHead (hld up & bhd: last st: r.o fnl 2f: nt rch ldrs) .......... s.nk.6

2765a★ Palomelle (FR) *(France)* 3-9-2 TJarnet (mid div: 6th st: one pce fnl 2f) ........... 2½.7

3110a★ River Nymph (USA) *(France)* 3-9-2 ELegrix (mid div: 7th st: no hdwy fnl 2f) .... 1½.8

2766a4 Linnga (IRE) *(France)* 3-9-2 GGuignard (w ldr: 2nd st: rdn 2f out: sn btn) ......... 1.9

Ionian Sea *(France)* 3-9-2 CBlack (cl up: effrt 3f out: 3rd st: rdn & btn 2f out) 1½.10

**16/10** JOLYPHA (USA), **5/2** Market Booster (USA), **11/2** Cunning, **10/1** Trishyde (USA), Verveine (USA), **12/1** Linnga (IRE), **17/1** Palomelle (FR), River Nymph (USA), **31/1** Ionian Sea. Tote 2.60f: 1.40f 2.70f 3.50f (10.40f). Mr K.Abdulla (A.Fabre,FRANCE) bred by Juddmonte Farms in USA. 10 Rn   2m 32.8 (2.8)
                 SF−86/85/84/83/82/81

## 3331a
PRIX DE LA SALAMANDRE (Gp 1) (2-Y.O.C & F) £51600.00   **7f (Nouvelle)**

2981a★ Zafonic (USA) *(Fav)* *(France)* 2-8-11 PatEddery (hld up: 5th st: qcknd to ld over 1f out: sn clr: impressive) ........... —1

2981a6 Kingmambo (USA) *(France)* 2-8-11 FHead (led: rdn 2f out: hdd over 1f out: r.o one pce) ................... 3.2

2845★ SPLENDENT (USA) *(PFICole)* 2-8-11 AMunro (prom: 3rd st: effrt & ev ch over 1f out: one pce) ................... ½.3

2441² CANASKA STAR *(PAKelleway)* 2-8-11 SCauthen (mid div: 4th st: n.m.r wl over 1f out: sn swtchd: r.o ins fnl f) ........... 1½.4

2981a[5] Didyme (USA) *(France)* 2–8–11 ELegrix (trckd ldr: 2nd st: rdn over 1f out: sn
wknd) .................................................................................................. s.h.**5**

Tenga (USA) *(France)* 2–8–8 ESaint-Martin (stdd s: a last: n.d) .............. 3.**6**

**1/2** ZAFONIC (USA), **4/1** Splendent (USA), **17/4** Didyme (USA), **11/1** Kingmambo (USA), Canaska Star, **12/1**
Tenga (USA). Tote 1.50f: 1.10f 1.20f (SF: 14.10f). Mr K.Abdulla (A.Fabre,FRANCE) bred by Juddmonte Farms in
USA. 6 Rn
1m 23.3 (3.3)
SF—58/49/47/42/41/29

### 3332a
PRIX FOY ESCADA (Gp 3) (C & F) £20640.00 **1½m (Grande)**

2766a★ **Magic Night (FR)** *(Fav) (France)* 4–8–13 ABadel (trckd ldr: 3rd st: hdwy on ins
over 1f out: qcknd to ld ins fnl f: r.o wl) ........................................ —**1**
1984a[3] Subotica (FR) *(France)* 4–9–2 TJarnet (trckd ldrs: hdwy 3f out: 2nd st: ev ch 2f
out: r.o ins fnl f) ............................................................................ ¾.**2**
2895a★ Tel Quel (FR) *(France)* 4–9–2 SCauthen (set slow pce: qcknd 2f out: hdd ins fnl
f: hrd rdn & no ex) ...................................................................... s.h.**3**
1984a[4] Saganeca (USA) *(France)* 4–8–13 CAsmussen (a in rr: last st: outpcd fnl 2f) ...... 4.**4**

**7/10** MAGIC NIGHT (FR), **6/4** Subotica (FR), **9/2** Tel Quel (FR), **9/1** Saganeca (USA). Tote 1.70f: 1.10f 1.10f (SF:
2.80f). Mr H.Yokohama (P.Demercastel,FRANCE) bred by Mr & Mrs Armenio Simoes de Almeida in France. 4 Rn
2m 40.5 (10.5)
SF—6/7/6/–

---

## 1985a—SAN SIRO (R-H)
### Sunday, September 13th [Good to soft]

### 3333a
PREMIO MOTTALCIATA (F & M) £9302.00 **1¼m**

2170★ **ONLY ROYALE (IRE)** *(LMCumani)* 3–8–7 GDettori .................................... —**1**
Cividale (IRE) *(Italy)* 3–8–7 MPlanard .................................................. 1.**2**
Siddharta (USA) *(Italy)* 4–8–13 SSoto ................................................... 5.**3**
Tote 12L: 11L 14L (24L). Mr G. Sainaghi (NEWMARKET) bred by Barronstown Stud in Ireland. 6 Rn 2m 11.4

### 3334a
PREMIO PIETRO BESSERO (listed race) (F & M) £20930.00 **1m**

2911[2] **MELPOMENE (USA)** *(LordHuntingdon)* 4–8–8 RCochrane .......................... —**1**
2322a★ Mountain Ash *(Italy)* 3–8–8 MTellini .............................................. 8.**2**
2911 ANLACE *(LMCumani)* 3–8–4 GDettori ............................................. ¾.**3**
Tote 17L: 12L 17L (29L). Lord Carnarvon (WEST ILSLEY) bred by Lord Porchester in USA. 7 Rn 1m 38.7

### 3335a
PREMIO DEL PIAZZALE MEMORIAL E CAMICI (listed race) £20930.00 **1m 1f**

3013[2] **INNER CITY (IRE)** *(LMCumani)* 3–8–7 GDettori ................................... —**1**
2998[5] FLASHFOOT *(IABalding)* 4–8–11 RCochrane ..................................... 4.**2**
Capolago *(Italy)* 5–8–9 MTellini ...................................................... ¾.**3**
Tote 16L: 11L 12L 13L (20L). Sheikh Mohammed (NEWMARKET) bred by Ballynagran Bloodstock Ltd. in Ireland.
9 Rn
1m 49.9

### 3336a
PREMIO FEDERICO TESIO (Gp 3) £27907.00 **1m 3f**

1358a★ **Erdelistan (FR)** *(Italy)* 5–8–11 SSoto ........................................... —**1**
2891a[3] HALF A TICK (USA) *(PFICole)* 4–8–11 CRutter ................................... 1.**2**
Cherry Grove Lad (IRE) *(Ireland)* 4–8–11 RCochrane ............................. 1½.**3**
1226a★ SECRET HAUNT (USA) *(LMCumani)* 4–9–1 GDettori (btn further 8l) ......... **4**
Tote 43L: 21L 15L (44L). Allevamento Cavalli da Corsa (M.D'Auria,ITALY) bred by H.H.Aga Khan in France. 7 Rn
2m 18.6

---

## TABY (L-H) Sweden
### Sunday, September 13th [Good]

### 3337a
STOCKHOLM CUP INTERNATIONAL £48216.00 **1½m**

**Silvestro** *(Norway)* 7–9–8 KAndersen ................................................ —**1**
Pearl Panther *(Norway)* 4–9–8 TFrick ................................................ ½.**2**
2504a Gloria Mundi (FR) *(France)* 5–9–4 OPoirier .................................... 4.**3**
2894a[6] CAPTAIN HORATIUS (IRE) *(JLDunlop)* 3–8–11 WRyan (btn further ½l) .......... **6**
Tote 60.90Kr: 20Kr 20Kr 46Kr (272.30Kr). Stall Nor (T.Dahl,NORWAY) bred by Citadel Stud Establishment. 15
Rn
2m 29.2

2875—**AYR (L-H)**

## Thursday, September 17th [Soft]

Going Allowance: St: 0.35 sec (Y); Rnd: 0.75 sec per fur (S)　　　　Wind: slt across

Stalls: high

**3338**　　E.B.F. HALL FARM STUD STKS (Mdn 2-Y.O.F) £2752.00 (£772.00: £376.00)
　　　　　7f
　　　　　　　　　　　　　　　　　　　　　　　　　　　　　　　2-00 (2-02)

　1461　**Toledo Queen (IRE)** (Fav) *(PWChapple-Hyam)* 8-11 DHolland (6) (a.p: hdwy
　　　　　　on outside to ld appr fnl f: styd on u.p) ....................... —1
　2973　Don't Jump (IRE) **(73)** *(MHTompkins)* 8-11 PRobinson (4) (lw: led tl hdd over 2f
　　　　　　out: disp ld over 1f out: kpt on gamely) ........................... s.h.2
　29306　Grogfryn *(JBerry)* 8-11 JCarroll (7) (swtg: bhd: effrt 3f out: no imp) ...... 5.3
　31633　Reasons for Love (IRE) *(JJO'Neill)* 8-11 MBirch (5) (cl up: hung rt ent st: sn rdn
　　　　　　& nt qckn) ................................... nk.4
　25012　Quinsigimond *(SirMarkPrescott)* 8-11 GDuffield (2) (lw: cl up: slt ld over 2f out tl
　　　　　　hdd & wknd over 1f out) ........................... ½.5
　3163　Oubeck *(EWeymes)* 8-11 BRaymond (3) (s.i.s: sn rcvrd & prom: wknd wl over
　　　　　　1f out) ........................................ 10.6
　　　　　Nellie Hen *(ABailey)* 8-11 KDarley (1) (cmpt: s.i.s: n.d) ............. 7.7

**4/7** TOLEDO QUEEN (IRE), **7/2** Quinsigimond, **6/1** Reasons for Love (IRE), **33/1** Oubeck, Don't Jump (IRE),
Grogfryn, **50/1** Nellie Hen. CSF £15.84, Tote £1.50: £1.10 £5.20 (£12.80). Mr R. E. Sangster (MARLBOROUGH)
bred by Swettenham Stud in Ireland. 7 Rn　　　　　　　　　　　　　　　1m 35.12 (11.12)
　　　　　　　　　　　　　　　　　　　　　　　　　　　SF—8/7/-/-/-/-

**3339**　　BOGSIDE CUP (H'cap) (0-100) £3403.75 (£1030.00: £502.50: £238.75)
　　　　　1m 7f
　　　　　　　　　　　　　　　　　　　　　　　　　　　　　　　2-35 (2-36)

　3118　**Bandoline (70)** (Fav) *(BWHills)* 3-8-5 DHolland (2) (hld up & bhd: hdwy to ld
　　　　　　over 1f out: hdd ins fnl f: rallied to ld cl home) ................... —1
　28773　Aahsaylad **(75)** (v) *(FHLee)* 6-9-7 BRaymond (1) (in tch: hrd rdn 2f out: led ins
　　　　　　fnl f: ct cl home) .............................. nk.2
　3194　Sarawat **(80)** *(MrsGRReveley)* 4-9-12 KDarley (3) (hld up: effrt whn nt clr run &
　　　　　　swtchd over 1f out: styd on: nvr able to chal) ..................... 5.3
　31162　Bigwheel Bill (IRE) **(76)** *(JWWatts)* 3-8-11 JLowe (5) (trckd ldrs: effrt & ev ch
　　　　　　over 2f out: wknd 1f out) ....................... nk.4
　3118　Good Hand (USA) **(82)** *(JWWatts)* 6—10-0 MBirch (8) (lw: led tl hdd wl over 1f
　　　　　　out: grad wknd) ............................ 5.5
　3118　Kausar (USA) **(63)** *(GMMoore)* 5-8-9 JCarroll (4) (trckd ldrs: effrt 3f out: wknd
　　　　　　over 1f out) ................................ 7.6
　1073　Family Line **(82)** *(MissLAPerratt)* 4-10-0 GDuffield (7) (lost tch fnl 3f) ......... 7.7
　3206　Eire Leath-Sceal **(55)** *(MBrittain)* 5-8-1(4) PRobinson (6) (cl up tl wknd 3f out) .. ½.8

**7/4** BANDOLINE, **100/30** Sarawat, **9/2** Aahsaylad, **6/1** Bigwheel Bill (IRE), **20/1** Good Hand (USA), Eire
Leath-Sceal, **33/1** Kausar (USA), **40/1** Family Line. CSF £8.71, CT £16.51. Tote £2.10: £1.30 £1.30 £1.60
(£4.20). Sheikh Mohammed (LAMBOURN) bred by Sheikh Mohammed bin Rashid al Maktoum. 8 Rn
　　　　　　　　　　　　　　　　　　　　　　　　　　　3m 30.81 (18.31)
　　　　　　　　　　　　　　　　　　　　　　　　　　　SF—22/37/37/21/33/7

**3340**　　TIMEFORM HARRY ROSEBERY TROPHY (Stks) (listed race) (2-Y.O) £7050.00
　　　　　(£2100.00: £1000.00: £450.00)　5f
　　　　　　　　　　　　　　　　　　　　　　　　　　　3-10 (3-13)

　30472　**Fyfield Flyer (IRE) (90)** *(PWChapple-Hyam)* 8-11 DHolland (3) (lw: cl up: led
　　　　　　2f out: edgd lft: r.o wl fnl f) ........................ —1
　30813　Lord Olivier (IRE) **(98)** *(WJarvis)* 8-11 MTebbutt (1) (lw: chsd ldr: ev ch 2f out: nt
　　　　　　qckn fnl f) ................................. 2½.2
　30814　Willshe Gan **(90)** *(DenysSmith)* 8-6 KFallon (5) (a chsg ldrs: sn drvn along:
　　　　　　hung lft fr ½-wy: kpt on one pce) ................... 4.3
　3162*　Laurel Delight **(84)** *(JBerry)* 8-6 JCarroll (2) (lw: led 3f: grad wknd) ......... 2.4
　32173　Night Melody (IRE) **(100)** (Fav) *(RHannon)* 8-11 KDarley (4) (hld up: effrt 2f out:
　　　　　　sn rdn & fnd nil) ........................... nk.5

**7/4** Night Melody (IRE), **4/1** Lord Olivier (IRE), FYFIELD FLYER (IRE), **9/2** Laurel Delight, **7/1** Willshe Gan. CSF
£17.09, Tote £3.90: £1.70 £1.90 (£7.60). Mr R. E. Sangster (MARLBOROUGH) bred by Swettenham Stud in
Ireland. 5 Rn　　　　　　　　　　　　　　　　　　　　　61.44 sec (3.44)
　　　　　　　　　　　　　　　　　　　　　　　　　　　SF—63/53/32/24/28

**3341**　　WEIR MEMORIAL TROPHY (H'cap) (0-80) £2853.00 (£864.00: £422.00: £201.00)
　　　　　5f
　　　　　　　　　　　　　　　　　　　　　　　　　　3-40 (3-44)

　32206　**We're All Game (57)** *(BCMorgan)* 3-8-8 PRobinson (12) (a.p: racd stands'
　　　　　　side: led ins fnl f: r.o wl) ......................... —1

1512⁵ B Grade **(42)** *(JBalding)* 7–7–2⁽²⁾ ‡⁷ClaireBalding (13) (dwlt: bhd to hdwy over 1f
out: r.o wl) .................................................................................. 2.2

3144 Penny Hasset **(71)** *(MWEasterby)* 4–9–10 TLucas (6) (a chsng ldrs: rdn ½-wy:
styd on fnl f) ........................................................................ ½.3

3166³ Katie-a (IRE) **(53)** (Fav) *(RMWhitaker)* 3–8–4 ACulhane (4) (stdd s: bhd: gd
hdwy 2f out: chal 1f out: rdn & no ex fnl f) ....................... hd.4

3154² Diet **(63)** (v) *(MissLAPerratt)* 6–8–11 ‡⁵NKennedy (3) (in tch: styd on fnl f: nvr
able to chal) .......................................................................... ½.5

3196² Miss Movie World **(51)** *(NBycroft)* 3–8–2 SWood (9) (chsd ldrs: effrt 2f out: one
pce) ..................................................................................... 1½.6

2963 Best Effort **(65)** *(MPNaughton)* 6–9–4 DHolland (14) (lw: hdwy u.p 2f out: no imp) ½.7

2963⁵ Langtonian **(59)** (bl) *(JBerry)* 3–8–10 JCarroll (7) (led & clr centre tl hdd & wknd
ins fnl f) ............................................................................... ½.8

3150⁵ Bee Dee Ell (USA) **(42)** (bl) *(MissLAPerratt)* 3–7–0 ‡⁷DarrenMoffatt (2) (chsd ldrs
centre tl outpcd fnl 2f) ........................................................ ½.9

618 Crestwood Lad (USA) **(59)** *(MrsGRReveley)* 3–8–10 KDarley (10) (lw: drvn
along ½-wy: nvr trbld ldrs) ................................................ ½.10

3166⁶ Hinari Video **(44)** *(MJohnston)* 7–7–11 PBurke (8) (nvr trbld ldrs) ................... nk.11

3154* Francis Ann **(54)** *(MissLAPerratt)* 4–8–7 (7x) GDuffield (11) (sn pushed along:
n.d) ...................................................................................... 1½.12

3166 Minizen Music (IRE) **(41)** (bl) *(MBrittain)* 4–7–8⁽¹⁾ JLowe (4) (outpcd fr ½-wy) nk.13

3120 Consulate **(58)** *(JBalding)* 6–8–11 BRaymond (5) (sn outpcd & bhd) ........... 1½.14
LONG HANDICAP: B Grade 7-4, Minizen Music (IRE) 6-13.

**9/2** Katie-a (IRE), **5/1** Miss Movie World, **11/2** Penny Hasset, **9/1** Consulate, **10/1** Francis Ann, **12/1** Best Effort,
Diet, **14/1** Langtonian, Hinari Video, **16/1** WE'RE ALL GAME, **33/1** Crestwood Lad (USA), B Grade, **40/1** Minizen
Music (IRE), **100/1** Bee Dee Ell (USA). CSF £351.74, CT £2,913.27. Tote £29.30: £5.90 £5.20 £1.90 (£361.60).
Mr G. Whitaker (BURTON-ON-TRENT) bred by Hever Castle Stud. 14 Rn
62.29 sec (4.29)
SF—43/15/49/28/33/18

**3342**      BRODICK CLAIMING STKS      £2430.00 (£680.00: £330.00)      **1m**      4-10 (4-16)

3203 **Houlston's Will** **(62)** *(MrsJRRamsden)* 3–8–5 KFallon (5) (lw: outpcd & bhd: gd
hdwy 2f out: r.o to ld wl ins fnl f) .................................... —1

3069⁵ Sagebrush Roller **(73)** (Fav) *(JWWatts)* 4–8–11 BRaymond (1) (a.p: effrt over 2f
out: led wl ins fnl f: sn hdd & btn) .................................... 1½.2

2987* Stairway to Heaven (IRE) **(64)** (bl) *(TDBarron)* 4–7–10 ‡⁷VHalliday (11) (hdwy to
ld over 2f out: hng bdly lft: hdd & wknd wl ins fnl f) ...... 3½.3

3168³ Syke Lane **(33)** *(RMWhitaker)* 3–7–0 ‡⁷DWright (3) (a in tch: effrt over 2f out: one
pce) ...................................................................................... 4.4

2814 Arrow Dancer **(31)** *(JJO'Neill)* 6–8–3⁽¹⁾ MBirch (10) (led tl hdd over 2f out: one
pce) ...................................................................................... s.h.5

966 Ace Reporter *(MHTompkins)* 3–8–0⁽¹⁾ PRobinson (8) (chsd ldrs: racd stands'
side fnl 3f: no imp) ............................................................ 3½.6

3167³ Phil-Man **(43)** *(TFairhurst)* 3–7–7 ‡⁵NKennedy (7) (chsd ldr tl outpcd fnl 2f) ......... 4.7

2815³ Henbury Hall (IRE) **(59)** *(MrsGRReveley)* 4–8–4 KDarley (9) (lw: effrt over 3f out:
sn rdn & n.d) ...................................................................... 1½.8

3151² Verdant Boy **(47)** *(MPNaughton)* 9–8–2 DHolland (2) (chsd ldrs tl wknd over 2f
out) ...................................................................................... 2.9

3150³ Heliopsis *(MDHammond)* 4–9–3 ‡⁷ALakeman (6) (sn wl bhd) ......................... 5.10

3159 Penny Orchid (IRE) **(69)** (bl) *(BBeasley)* 3–8–0 JLowe (12) (s.s: a bhd) .......... 2.11

2880⁵ Morcinda **(40)** *(PMonteith)* 6–8–10 PBurke (4) (hrd drvn over 2f out: sn bhd) .. 4.12

**2/1** Sagebrush Roller, **11/2** Stairway to Heaven (IRE), **6/1** HOULSTON'S WILL, **13/2** Henbury Hall (IRE), **8/1** Ace
Reporter, **10/1** Verdant Boy, **14/1** Penny Orchid (IRE), **25/1** Phil-Man, **33/1** Syke Lane, Morcinda, **66/1** Heliopsis,
**100/1** Arrow Dancer. CSF £16.75, Tote £7.00: £2.10 £1.50 £1.70 (£6.90). Mark Houlston (Yorkshire
Decorators) Ltd (THIRSK) bred by M. Houlston. 12 Rn
1m 46.82 (9.62)
SF—37/38/12/–/–/–

**3343**      TATTERSALLS AUCTION SERIES STKS (Qualifier) (Mdn 2-Y.O) £2710.00 (£760.00:
£370.00)      **6f**      4-40 (4-44)

2965⁴ **Benzoe (IRE)** **(71)** *(MWEasterby)* 8–9 TLucas (6) (w ldr: led ½-wy: shkn up
appr fnl f: r.o) .................................................................... —1

3178 Panther (IRE) **(71)** *(CWCElsey)* 8–10 KDarley (12) (lw: a in tch: hdwy over 1f out:
r.o: nrst fin) ........................................................................ 4.2

2709² Blazing Soul (IRE) (Fav) *(RHannon)* 8–2 DHolland (5) (lw: a chsng ldrs: rdn
½-wy & nt qckn fnl f) ......................................................... 1½.3

2733⁶ La Bonita (IRE) (v) *(JBerry)* 8–7 JCarroll (10) (led to ½-wy: rdn & btn over 1f out) 2.4

2826 Felice's Pet *(MHTompkins)* 8–6 PRobinson (7) (a in tch: one pce fnl 2f) ......... 2½.5

3165⁴ Principal Player (USA) **(65)** *(PMonteith)* 8–9 PBurke (11) (chsd ldr tl outpcd fnl
2f) ........................................................................................ 2.6

Silver Standard *(JWWatts)* 8-8 MBirch (1) (neat: scope: bhd: hdwy 2f out: nvr nr
   to chal) ..................................................................... 1½.7
3033⁶ Cizard (IRE) **(45)** *(AWPotts)* 8-0 JLowe (4) (drvn along ½-way: nvr trbld ldrs) .... 1.8
Fortis Pavior (IRE) *(RMWhitaker)* 8-10 ACulhane (3) (cmpt: str: nvr wnt pce) ... hd.9
3164 Dancing Haze *(MissSEHall)* 8-7⁽¹⁾ MTebbutt (9) (sn drvn along: n.d) ............... ½.10
3117³ Northern Bluff **(79)** *(JWWatts)* 9-0 BRaymond (13) (in tch: rdn ½-wy: sn wknd) ½.11
3155³ Formidable Liz **(50)** *(NBycroft)* 7-10 ‡⁵NKennedy (8) (outpcd after 2f) ............ 3½.12
Bee Dee Dancer *(MissLAPerratt)* 8-2 GDuffield (2) (lengthy: unf: n.d) .............. 6.13

**6/4** Blazing Soul (IRE), **11/4** Northern Bluff, **8/1** BENZOE (op 8/1), **12/1** Felice's Pet(op 8/1), **14/1** La Bonita (IRE),
Panther (IRE), Principal Player (USA)(10/1—20/1), **20/1** Fortis Pavior (IRE), Dancing Haze, **33/1** Silver
Standard, Formidable Liz, Bee Dee Dancer, **66/1** Cizard (IRE). Tote £11.00: £2.40 £5.10 £1.60
(£123.40). Mr Tony Fawcett (SHERIFF HUTTON) bred by Mrs P. Grubb in Ireland. 13 Rn   1m 15.63 (5.23)
SF—33/18/4/1/–/–

---

**3344**   JACK JARVIS MEMORIAL H'CAP (0-90) £3615.00 (£1095.00: £535.00: £255.00)
   7f   5-10 (5-14)

3209⁶ **Sharpalto (83)** *(MrsGRReveley)* 5-10-0 KDarley (8) (hld up: hdwy over 2f out:
   led ins fnl f: r.o wl) ............................................................ —1
3002 Ikteshaf **(75)** *(BHanbury)* 4-9-6 BRaymond (5) (lw: in tch: hdwy to chal over 1f
   out: nt qckn) ...................................................................... 1½.2
3095 Teanarco (IRE) **(62)** *(RJHolder)* 4-8-7 GDuffield (11) (a.p: led wl over 1f out tl
   ins fnl f: no ex) ................................................................... hd.3
3121★ Cool Luke (IRE) **(82)** (Fav) *(GMMoore)* 3-9-9 JCarroll (9) (lw: hld up: hdwy 3f
   out: ev ch wl over 1f out: rdn & nt qckn) ............................ 2.4
3126³ Veloce (IRE) **(61)** *(ABailey)* 4-8-6 PRobinson (1) (a.p: effrt over 2f out: nt qckn
   appr fnl f) ........................................................................... nk.5
3170★ Ruth's Gamble **(57)** *(DWChapman)* 4-8-2 (5v) SWood (7) (hdwy ent st: rdn &
   one pce fnl 2f) ................................................................. 1½.6
3126 Devon Dancer **(72)** (v) *(MHEasterby)* 3-8-13 MBirch (12) (chsd ldrs: effrt over
   2f out: grad wknd) .............................................................. 1.7
3198 Royal Girl **(65)** *(MissSEHall)* 5-8-10 MTebbutt (4) (lw: shkn up 3f out: no imp) 3½.8
2570⁶ Languedoc **(61)** *(MPNaughton)* 5-8-6 DHolland (13) (cl up: led 3f out tl wl over
   1f out) ................................................................................ 5.9
3126 Sir Arthur Hobbs **(61)** *(FHLee)* 5-8-1 ‡NKennedy (2) (bhd: effrt 3f out: n.d) .... ½.10
2966³ Spanish Realm **(48)** (bl) *(MBrittain)* 5-7-7 JLowe (10) (prom 4f) ...................... s.h.11
3151⁵ Jane's Brave Boy **(48)** *(TCraig)* 10-7-0 ‡⁷DarrenMoffatt (3) (led 1f: cl up tl wknd
   3f out) ............................................................................... ½.12
3068 Act of Union (IRE) **(69)** (v) *(BBeasley)* 3-8-5 ‡⁵SWilliams (6) (led after 1f: racd
   alone far side st: hdd 3f out: wknd qckly 2f out) ................ 5.13
LONG HANDICAP: Spanish Realm 6-8, Jane's Brave Boy 5-7.

**5/1** Cool Luke (IRE), **11/2** Veloce (IRE), Ikteshaf(8/1—5/1), **6/1** SHARPALTO, **7/1** Ruth's Gamble, **12/1** Royal
Girl, Teanarco (IRE), **14/1** Languedoc, Sir Arthur Hobbs, **16/1** Devon Dancer(op 10/1), **20/1** Spanish Realm, Act
of Union (IRE), **200/1** Jane's Brave Boy. CSF £35.82, CT £350.87. Tote £7.80: £3.40 £2.20 £2.60 (£40.20). Mr
T. J. Prew (SALTBURN) bred by E. A. Badger. 13 Rn   1m 32.11 (8.11)
SF—71/58/44/54/36/27

T/Plpt: £44.80 (81.6 Tckts).   AA

---

# AYR (L-H)
## Friday, September 18th [Soft]
Going Allowance: 0.55 sec per fur (Y)   Wind: almost nil

Stalls: high

**3345**   ROYAL CALEDONIAN HUNT CUP/DOONSIDE CUP (Stks) (listed race)   £9137.50
   (£2725.00: £1300.00: £587.50)  **1¼m 192y**   2-00 (2-01)

1869 **Linpac West (97)** *(CWCElsey)* 6-8-11 JCarroll (2) (lw: trckd ldr: led wl over 1f
   out: hung rt: r.o u.p fnl f) ................................................. —1
2854² Percy's Girl (IRE) **(97)** *(GWragg)* 4-8-6 MHills (4) (hld up: outpcd over 2f out:
   hdwy over 1f out: styd on wl) ............................................ 1½.2
3190² Guilty Secret (IRE) (Fav) *(PWChapple-Hyam)* 3-8-2 MRoberts (1) (lw: led: rdn
   2f out: sn hdd: kpt on wl) ................................................... s.h.3
3194 Hateel **(107)** *(PTWalwyn)* 6-8-11 RHills (3) (lw: trckd ldrs tl rdn & outpcd fnl 2f) 15.4

**6/4** Guilty Secret (IRE), **9/4** Percy's Girl (IRE), **4/1** LINPAC WEST, **7/1** Hateel. CSF £11.26, Tote £4.80 (£9.50).
Linpac Group Limited (MALTON) bred by Lin Pac Containers Ltd. 4 Rn   2m 25.85 (12.15)
SF—37/29/24/3

**3346**  E.B.F. H'CAP (F & M) (0-90) £10437.50 (£3125.00: £1500.00: £687.50)
1¼m

2-30 (2-36)

3122⁴ **Tell No Lies (89)** *(MHEasterby)* 5-10-0 MBirch (6) (hld up: smooth hdwy to ld over 1f out: pushed along & r.o) ............................ —1

2853 Highbrook (USA) **(75)** *(MHTompkins)* 4-9-0 PRobinson (4) (lw: hld up & bhd: hdwy over 2f out: chal ins fnl f: r.o wl) .................... s.h.2

821 Zamirah (IRE) **(72)** *(GWragg)* 3-8-5 MHills (3) (lw: a chsng ldrs: chal 2f out: no ex ins fnl f) ............................................................. 2.3

3090³ Whirl **(78)** *(JRFanshawe)* 3-8-11 KDarley (1) (trckd ldrs: led wl over 2f out tl appr fnl f: one pce) ............................................. 3½.4

3040³ Dovale **(68)** *(WJarvis)* 4-8-7 RCochrane (7) (lw: chsd ldrs: ev ch over 2f out: wknd appr fnl f) ................................................ 1½.5

2968³ Tanoda **(54)** *(MBrittain)* 6-7-7 JLowe (12) (a.p: one pce fnl 3f) .............. ½.6

2922³ Wild Applause (IRE) **(75)** *(JHMGosden)* 3-8-8 PatEddery (8) (b.nr hind: bhd: hdwy appr st: no imp) ................................................... 1.7

3192 Margs Girl **(54)** *(TFairhurst)* 5-7-7 JFanning (8) (b: chsd ldr: rdn over 2f out: wknd over 1f out) ................................................ 3½.8

2814* Sweet Mignonette **(57)** *(MrsGRReveley)* 4-7-7 ‡³DHarrison (9) (in rr: effrt 3f out: n.d) ............................................................. 1.9

2922* Anghaam (USA) **(83)** *(Fav)* *(ACStewart)* 3-9-2 MRoberts (5) (lw: in tch tl outpcd fnl 2f) .......................................................... 2.10

2748⁵ Gong **(80)** *(PTWalwyn)* 3-8-13 GDuffield (2) (led: hdd wl over 2f out: sn wknd) 2.11

3342* Houlston's Will **(67)** *(MrsJRRamsden)* 3-8-0 (5x) DHolland (10) (bhd: effrt 3f out: n.d) ........................................................... 1.12

LONG HANDICAP: Tanoda 6-12, Margs Girl 7-5, Houlston's Will 7-9.

**9/4** Anghaam (USA), **8/1** Houlston's Will, Highbrook (USA), **10/1** Wild Applause (IRE), Whirl, Zamirah (IRE), TELL NO LIES, **11/1** Sweet Mignonette, **12/1** Dovale, **14/1** Gong, **16/1** Margs Girl, **40/1** Tanoda. CSF £80.43, CT £751.14. Tote £8.80: £2.80 £2.70 £2.90 (£23.20). Mrs A. Johnstone (MALTON) bred by The Dunchurch Lodge Stud Co and Mrs A. Johnstone. 12 Rn                                                              2m 14.51 (9.21)
SF—77/62/49/48/41/26

**3347**  LADBROKE RACING NURSERY   £3777.50 (£1145.00: £560.00: £267.50)
6f

3-05 (3-09)

(Weights raised 2 lb)

2841 **Silverlocks (85)** *(MissSEHall)* 9-4 NConnorton (11) (lw: hdwy ½-wy: led over 1f out: styd on wl) ..................................................... —1

3155* Egg **(60)** (bl) *(Fav)* *(TDBarron)* 7-7 (7x) JLowe (7) (lw: s.i.s: outpcd & bhd tl gd hdwy 2f out: ev ch ins.fnl f: kpt on) ......................... ½.2

2674* Royal Diva **(74)** *(MissSEHall)* 8-7 GHind (12) (lw: prom: hdwy & ev ch 1f out: nt qckn) ................................................................. 1½.3

3019⁵ Cliburnel News (IRE) **(79)** *(MHTompkins)* 8-12 PRobinson (10) (racd stands' side: a chsng ldrs: ev ch fnl f: nt qckn) ............................. 2.4

*2364⁵* Abergele **(81)** *(JGFitzGerald)* 9-0 KFallon (13) (chsd ldrs: ev ch 2f out: r.o one pce) .......................................................... 1½.5

2779 Luckifosome **(60)** *(PDEvans)* 7-0 ‡⁷DarrenMoffatt (1) (lw: chsd ldrs centre: ev ch 2f out: nt qckn) ......................................... 1.6

2939³ Grinnell **(68)** *(DenysSmith)* 8-1 MRoberts (6) (lw: hdwy u.p 2f out: kpt on one pce fnl f) ........................................................ hd.7

3012 Heavenly Risk **(88)** *(RHannon)* 9-4 7⁸ PatEddery (3) (hld up & bhd: swtchd & effrt 2f out: nt qckn fnl f) ........................................ ¾.8

3187 Hotaria **(67)** *(RMWhitaker)* 7-11 ‡³DHarrison (9) (led tl hdd over 1f out: sn wknd) ............................................................. 1½.9

2444³ Garnock Valley **(78)** *(JBerry)* 8-11 JCarroll (8) (chsd ldrs: chal 2f out: wknd over 1f out) ........................................................ 1.10

3199 Milngavie (IRE) **(64)** *(MJohnston)* 7-11 JFanning (4) (w ldrs 4f: sn wknd) ...... 2½.11

3051 Shotley Again **(61)** *(NBycroft)* 7-8⁽¹⁾ LCharnock (5) (cl up 4f: sn lost pl) .......... 4.12

3162 Juliet Bravo **(73)** *(BBeasley)* 8-1⁽⁷⁾ +5 JWeaver (2) (spd 4f) ..................... hd.13

LONG HANDICAP: Luckifosome 6-11, Shotley Again 6-13.

**4/1** Egg, **6/1** Garnock Valley, **13/2** Royal Diva, Grinnell, **9/1** Hotaria, Milngavie (IRE), **11/1** Cliburnel News (IRE), **12/1** Abergele, **14/1** Heavenly Risk, **20/1** Juliet Bravo, **25/1** Luckifosome, **33/1** SILVERLOCKS, **100/1** Shotley Again. CSF £144.31, CT £894.04. Tote £35.10: £7.90 £1.80 £2.20 (£146.60). Miss SE Hall (MIDDLEHAM) bred by John A. Jones Morgan. 13 Rn                                     1m 16.74 (6.34)
SF—43/16/24/21/17/–

**3348**  SHADWELL STUD FIRTH OF CLYDE STKS (listed race) (2-Y.O.F) £19334.00 (£5852.00: £2856.00: £1358.00) 6f

3-35 (3-39)

3012² **White Shadow (IRE) (94)** *(RCharlton)* 8-9 PatEddery (1) (prom: outpcd ½-wy: hdwy over 1f out: hrd rdn & r.o to ld cl home) ................. —1

3156* Yakin (USA) **(76)** *(HThomsonJones)* 8-9 RHills (3) (led: rdn appr fnl f: r.o: jst ct) nk.2
3070* Star Family Friend (IRE) **(100)** *(Fav)* *(MHTompkins)* 9-1 PRobinson (4) (lw: hld up: effrt & swtchd 2f out: ev ch ins fnl f: r.o) ......................... hd.3
2991⁶ Carranita (IRE) **(98)** *(BPalling)* 8-9 MRoberts (5) (lw: a chsng ldrs: edgd rt 2f out: r.o u.p) ......................... ¹/₂.4
3018* Simmering **(92)** *(GWragg)* 8-9 MHills (1) (lw: hld up: effrt over 2f out: rdn & no imp) ......................... 6.5
2897* Local Heroine **(74)** *(JBerry)* 8-9 JCarroll (2) (spd 4f: sn wknd) ......................... 3.6

**2/1** Star Family Friend (IRE), **5/2** WHITE SHADOW (IRE), **7/2** Simmering, **9/1** Carranita (IRE), **10/1** Yakin (USA), **33/1** Local Heroine. CSF £21.03, Tote £3.20: £1.80 £2.10 (£7.10). Mr K. Abdulla (BECKHAMPTON) bred by Juddmonte Farms in Ireland. 6 Rn 1m 16.71 (6.31)
SF—35/34/39/31/7/–

## 3349

LADBROKES AYRSHIRE H'CAP (0-90) £15045.00 (£4560.00: £2230.00: £1065.00)
1m                                                                4-05 (4-17)

3084³ **Eclipsing (IRE)** **(84)** *(RCharlton)* 4-9-12 PatEddery (13) (lw: hdwy 3f out: led over 1f out: rdn & r.o wl) ......................... —1
3084* Forever Diamonds **(66)** *(MHEasterby)* 5-8-8 KDarley (8) (lw: hld up: effrt over 2f out: r.o: nt pce of wnr ins fnl f: r.o) ......................... 1¹/₂.2
3084⁵ Jubran (USA) **(69)** *(MPNaughton)* 6-8-11 DHolland (2) (cl up: led over 2f out tl ins fnl f: nt qckn) ......................... 1.3
3236⁵ Roseate Lodge **(72)** *(Fav)* *(RWArmstrong)* 6-9-0 PRobinson (3) (hdwy 3f out: styd on u.p fnl f) ......................... hd.4
3245* Shaffaaf (USA) **(63)** *(PDEvans)* 4-8-5 MRoberts (15) (c wd & hdwy 3f out: styd on wl: nrst fin) ......................... ¹/₂.5
3170⁰ Martini Executive **(66)** (bl) *(BBeasley)* 4-8-3⁽²⁾ ‡5SWilliams (9) (hdwy over 3f out: rdn & one pce appr fnl f) ......................... 2.6
3212 Jahangir (IRE) **(80)** *(BHanbury)* 3-9-4 GDuffield (6) (a.p: chal over 2f out: rdn & btn appr fnl f) ......................... ³/₄.7
3121 Arany **(86)** *(MHTompkins)* 5-9-7 ‡7SMulvey (20) (a chsng ldrs: one pce fnl 2f) nk.8
3088³ Highland Magic (IRE) **(65)** *(MJFetherston-Godley)* 4-8-4 ‡3DHarrison (18) (bhd: hdwy 3f out: rdn & no imp appr fnl f) ......................... ³/₄.9
3342³ Stairway to Heaven (IRE) **(64)** (bl) *(TDBarron)* 4-7-13 ‡7VHalliday (7) (hdwy & prom 2f out: wknd over 1f out) ......................... 1¹/₂.10
3344⁶ Ruth's Gamble **(52)** *(DWChapman)* 4-7-8 SWood (19) (bhd: effrt & brght wd over 3f out: nt rch ldrs) ......................... 2.11
3192² Mingus (USA) **(56)** *(MrsJRRamsden)* 5-7-12 PBurke (12) (hld up & bhd: n.d) s.h.12
2569⁴ Matts Boy **(52)** (v) *(MissSEHall)* 4-7-8 JLowe (10) (a in rr) ......................... 3.13
3069⁴ Trafalgar Boy (USA) **(78)** (bl) *(JEtherington)* 3-8-11 ‡5JWeaver (14) (n.d) ......................... 1.14
2852⁴ Philidor **(88)** *(JMPEustace)* 3-8-11 RCochrane (16) (lw: n.d) ......................... s.h.15
3149 Aragon Ayr **(52)** *(PMonteith)* 4-7-8⁽¹⁾ LCharnock (4) (s.s: a bhd) ......................... 3¹/₂.16
3167⁴ Jefferson Davis (IRE) **(70)** *(BBeasley)* 3-8-8 GHind (1) (led tl hdd & wknd over 1f out) ......................... 1.17
3086² Tusky **(76)** (v) *(MJCamacho)* 4-9-4 SMorris (11) (lw: cl up tl rdn & wknd 3f out) ¹/₂.18
3083 Windpower (IRE) **(79)** *(JBerry)* 3-9-3 JCarroll (17) (lw: a bhd) ......................... nk.19

LONG HANDICAP: Aragon Ayr 7-2.

3026 Salda (25/1) Withdrawn : not under orders

**7/1** Roseate Lodge, **8/1** Shaffaaf (USA), **9/1** Forever Diamonds, Jahangir (IRE), Philidor, **10/1** ECLIPSING (IRE), Mingus (USA), **14/1** Ruth's Gamble, **16/1** Tusky, **20/1** Trafalgar Boy (USA), Arany, Jubran (USA), Martini Executive, Highland Magic (IRE), **25/1** Stairway to Heaven (IRE), Matts Boy, **40/1** Windpower (IRE), **50/1** Jefferson Davis (IRE), **100/1** Aragon Ayr. CSF £85.99, CT £1,606.19. Tote £9.30: £2.30 £1.90 £5.20 £1.70 (£21.00). Mr Jeremy Tree (BECKHAMPTON) bred by S. Niarchos in Ireland. 19 Rn 1m 44.99 (7.79)
SF—61/38/38/40/29/21

## 3350

WESTERN MEETING (S) STKS (3-Y.O) £2290.00 (£640.00: £310.00)
1¹/₄m 192y                                                       4-35 (4-46)

3141⁴ **Persian Fleece (49)** *(MrsGRReveley)* 8-6 KDarley (2) (trckd ldrs: led over 2f out: r.o strly) ......................... —1
2533³ Reach for Glory **(58)** *(RMWhitaker)* 9-2 ACulhane (5) (a.p: effrt over 2f out: r.o: nt pce of wnr) ......................... 3¹/₂.2
3149⁴ Ready to Draw (IRE) **(62)** *(Fav)* *(RonaldThompson)* 9-2 JLowe (6) (hld up: hdwy 3f out: rdn & one pce appr fnl f) ......................... 1¹/₂.3
3028⁵ Hot Prospect **(49)** *(JEtherington)* 8-6 MRoberts (7) (a.p: effrt over 2f out: rdn & nt qckn) ......................... 4.4
2937⁴ Speedy Sioux **(51)** *(CWThornton)* 8-6 GHind (4) (lw: cl up: chal 3f out: wknd 2f out) ......................... 7.5
2968⁵ Miliyel **(49)** *(PMonteith)* 8-6 LCharnock (3) (led tl hdd & wknd over 2f out) ......................... 10.6
2668⁵ Hataal (IRE) **(33)** (v) *(JBalding)* 7-13 ‡7ClaireBalding (1) (s.s: effrt ent st: n.d) ..... 3.7

3152⁵ Clean Singer (32) *(NBycroft)* 8-6 NConnorton (11) (chsd ldrs tl wknd wl over 2f
out) .................................................................................................................. 2¹/₂.8
* 3152 Shadaylou (IRE) (34) *(MissLAPerratt)* 8-6 GDuffield (8) (drvn along appr st: a
bhd) .................................................................................................................. hd.9
891 Stag Night (39) *(AWPotts)* 8-11 KFallon (10) (n.d) ........................................... ³/₄.10
Rusheen Na Corra (IRE) *(JJO'Neill)* 8-6 MBirch (9) (prom tl wknd qckly 6f out:
sn wl t.o) ........................................................................................................ dist.11

**9/4** Ready to Draw (IRE), **100/30** PERSIAN FLEECE, **9/2** Speedy Sioux, **6/1** Hot Prospect, **9/1** Reach for Glory(op
6/1), **12/1** Miliyel, **20/1** Hataal (IRE), **25/1** Clean Singer, **33/1** Rusheen Na Corra (IRE), Shadaylou (IRE), **50/1**
Stag Night. CSF £31.31, Tote £3.80: £1.20 £2.40 £1.40 (£30.40). Miss S. Hainey (SALTBURN) bred by Ewar
Stud Farms. 11 Rn; Sold Mrs M O'Donnell 8,000 gns                                  2m 28.87 (15.17)
SF—1/4/1/–/–/–/

**3351** ROYAL CALEDONIAN HUNT H'CAP (0-75) £3940.00 (£1195.00: £585.00: £280.00)
2m 1f 105y                                                                           5-05 (5-19)

3034⁴ **Sillars Stalker (IRE) (47)** *(Fav)* *(MrsJRRamsden)* 4–8-3 MRoberts (14) (hld
up: hdwy appr st: r.o u.p to ld cl home) ......................................... —1
3075 Kadari (59) *(AHarrison)* 3–8-0 ‡³DHarrison (9) (trckd ldrs: led 2f out: hung lft: nt
qckn nr fin) ..................................................................................................... ¹/₂.2
3152² Aide Memoire (IRE) (49) *(CBBBooth)* 3–7-7 JFanning (5) (a.p: effrt & ev ch 1f
out: kpt on) .................................................................................................... nk.3
3034 Moving Out (67) *(SirMarkPrescott)* 4-9-9 GDuffield (19) (jnd ldrs 10f out: led
appr st to 2f out: kpt on u.p) ...................................................................... 1¹/₂.4
3075² Brusque (USA) (39) *(DonEnricoIncisa)* 8-7-2⁽²⁾ ‡⁷ClaireBalding (13) (bhd:
hdwy 2f out: styd on wl) ............................................................................... 1¹/₂.5
3157² Stingray City (USA) (60) *(JEtherington)* 3–8-4 KDarley (12) (hld up: hdwy appr
st: sn chsng ldrs: rdn & one pce appr fnl f) ............................................ ¹/₂.6
Ambuscade (USA) (54) *(MrsGRReveley)* 6–8-10 KFallon (16) (lw: hld up: effrt 6f
out: rdn & one pce) ....................................................................................... ¹/₂.7
3194⁴ Green Lane (USA) (69) *(IABalding)* 4-9-4 ‡⁷FArrowsmith (18) (bhd: effrt 3f out:
r.o: nrst fin) .................................................................................................... hd.8
3046* Arctic Splendour (USA) (62) *(PWChapple-Hyam)* 3–8-1 ‡⁵JWeaver (15) (bhd:
effrt ent st: no imp) ...................................................................................... 2.9
3046 Intricacy (58) *(CCElsey)* 4–9-0 JLowe (17) (nvr trbld ldrs) ......................... 8.10
3034² Briggsmaid (62) *(JMPEustace)* 4–9-9 MTebbutt (10) (hld up: hdwy ent st: rdn &
btn 2f out) ...................................................................................................... ³/₄.11
Mr Optimistic (48) *(JJO'Neill)* 5-8–4 MBirch (2) (lw: cl up: led after 5f tl hdd appr
st: sn outpcd) ................................................................................................. 12.12
2877⁵ Moment of Truth (40) *(PMonteith)* 8–7-10⁽³⁾ PBurke (8) (bhd: effrt whn hmpd
appr st: n.d) ................................................................................................... nk.13
3076 Don't Cry (37) *(DonEnricoIncisa)* 4–7-7 JakiHouston (4) (cl up tl wknd 3f out) nk.14
3026 Linpac Express (50) *(CWCElsey)* 3–7-8 SWood (11) (bhd: effrt appr st: n.d) . 12.15
Super Ritchart (47) *(BPalling)* 4–8-3 JCarroll (3) (prom tl wknd qckly 6f out) ....... 16
3152 Mangrove Mist (IRE) (50) *(PMonteith)* 4–8-6 LCharnock (6) (a bhd) ................ 17
2677 Touching Times (47) (bl) *(TCraig)* 4–7-10 ‡⁷DWright (20) (prom to ¹/₂-wy: t.o ent
st) ................................................................................................................... 18
Hunted (62) *(ARDavison)* 5–9-4 DHolland (7) (led 5f: cl up tl wknd qckly appr st:
sn t.o) ............................................................................................................ 19

LONG HANDICAP: Aide Memoire (IRE) 7-4, Brusque (USA) 7-4, Moment of Truth 7-6, Don't Cry 7-4.

**5/2** SILLARS STALKER (IRE), **7/2** Arctic Splendour (USA), **9/1** Briggsmaid, **10/1** Aide Memoire (IRE),
Ambuscade (USA)(op 16/1), **11/1** Moving Out, **14/1** Intricacy, Brusque (USA), Kadari, Green Lane (USA), **16/1**
Stingray City (USA), **20/1** Hunted, **33/1** Linpac Express, Moment of Truth, Super Ritchart, **50/1** Ors. CSF £40.14,
CT £302.89. Tote £3.60: £1.50 £3.80 £2.60 £3.00 (£51.30). Sillars Civil Engineering (THIRSK) bred by Martyn J.
McEnery in Ireland. 19 Rn                                                            4m 6.48 (20.98)

T/Trio: Race 5: £880.00 (1.1 Tckts). T/Plpt: £886.50 (5.6 Tckts).                    AA

# AYR (L-H)

## Saturday, September 19th [Soft]

Going Allowance: St: 0.60 sec (Y); Rnd: 0.70 sec per fur (S)              Wind: almost nil

Stalls: high

**3352** ESTEE LAUDER SPELLBOUND CUP (Stks) (Amateurs)    £2570.00 (£720.00: £350.00)
1m 5f 13y                                                                           2-05 (2-07)

812² **Antiguan Flyer (84)** *(Fav)* *(BWHills)* 3–10-7 MissEJohnsonHoughton (12) (lw:
mde all: clr to st: qcknd clr again 3f out: hld on wl cl home) —1
3118⁴ Five to Seven (USA) (74) *(SGNorton)* 3–10-8⁽¹⁾ MrSSwiers (7) (a in tch: hdwy 3f
out: disp ld ins fnl f: styd on wl) ................................................................. s.h.2

Staunch Friend (USA) *(MHTompkins)* 4–11-2 MrsLPearce (4) (lw: hld up: mid div: hdwy 3f out: ev ch appr fnl f: nt qckn) ............................ 5.3

2120 Bay Tern (USA) **(40)** *(MHEasterby)* 6–10-4 ‡5MrRDyer (5) (gd hdwy to chse ldrs ent st: rdn & r.o one pce fnl 2f) ................................... 6.4

2968* J P Morgan **(41)** (v) *(MPNaughton)* 4–11-2 MissPRobson (14) (lw: a.p: effrt over 2f out: no ex) ............................................................ 1½.5

Marilyn (IRE) *(MKauntze,Ireland)* 3–10-2 MissSKauntze (11) (prom tl rdn & btn over 2f out) ......................................................... 1½.6

3139 Equity Card (IRE) **(68)** *(GAPritchard-Gordon)* 4–10-4 ‡5MrPPritchard-Gordon (10) (lw: mid div tl one pce fnl 3f) ....................................... 3½.7

Willie Sparkle *(MrsSCBradburne)* 6–10-12(3) MrJBradburne (8) (b: chsd ldrs: rdn & btn 3f out) ......................................................... nk.8

Young Pokey *(OSherwood)* 7–10-9 MrJDurkan (13) (in tch tl rdn & btn ent st) . hd.9

Menaghi *(RThompson)* 5–9-13 ‡5MrDWebb (1) (mid div tl rdn & wknd ent st) ... 5.10

Rabsha (IRE) *(DenysSmith)* 4–10-6 ‡5MissMCarson (6) (prom tl rdn & wknd over 2f out) ......................................................... hd.11

Maelkar (FR) *(JJO'Neill)* 8–10-4 ‡5MissSNichol (9) (mid div: bhd ent st) .......... hd.12

Pit Pony *(MissLAPerratt)* 8–11-11(11) ‡5MrMLightbody (2) (bit bkwd: chsd ldrs: lost pl 6f out: t.o fnl 2f) ................................................ 13

Caproni *(MissLAPerratt)* 5–10-4 ‡5MissLRobertson (3) (bit bkwd: a bhd: t.o fr ½-wy) ......................................................... 14

**15/8** ANTIGUAN FLYER, **4/1** Staunch Friend (USA), **5/1** Five to Seven (USA)(6/1—4/1), **8/1** Equity Card (IRE), Marilyn (IRE), **14/1** Maelkar (FR), **20/1** Young Pokey, **25/1** J P Morgan, **33/1** Bay Tern (USA), **50/1** Rabsha (IRE), **100/1** Caproni, Willie Sparkle, **200/1** Ors. CSF £10.73, Tote £2.70: £1.50 £1.70 £1.80 (£5.80). Mr K. Abdulla (LAMBOURN) bred by Crest Stud Ltd. 14 Rn
3m 1.76 (15.56)
SF–57/57/55/31/40/23

---

**3353**    E.B.F. TOP FLIGHT LEISURE STKC (Mdn 2-Y.O C & G) £2724.00 (£764.00: £372.00)
7f
2-40 (2-45)

**Colway Rock (USA)** *(JWWatts)* 9-0 NConnorton (7) (b.hind: w'like: scope: stdy hdwy 3f out: styd on to ld wl ins fnl f) ............................. —1

3035² Lyford Cay (IRE) (Fav) *(PWChapple-Hyam)* 9-0 DHolland (11) (cl up: led 3f out: sn rdn clr: hdd & no ex cl home) ...................................... nk.2

2961² Persian Charmer (IRE) *(MissLAPerratt)* 9-0 MHills (3) (lw: chsd ldrs: rdn & ev ch appr fnl f: nt qckn) ................................................ 1½.3

3077 Blakes Beau *(MHEasterby)* 9-0 MBirch (5) (in tch: rdn over 2f out: kpt on same pce) ......................................................... 8.4

1738² Lancaster Pilot **(69)** *(RMWhitaker)* 9-0 ACulhane (9) (in tch: effrt over 2f out: one pce) ......................................................... ¾.5

1299 Sudden Spin *(JBerry)* 9-0 JCarroll (4) (hdwy ent st: rdn & no imp fnl 2f) ....... 3.6

2456⁶ Southern Memories (IRE) *(RHannon)* 9-0 RHills (2) (chsd ldrs: rdn & btn wl over 1f out) ......................................................... 2½.7

3163² Peacefull Reply (USA) **(71)** *(FHLee)* 9-0 PaulEddery (8) (prom tl wknd over 2f out) ......................................................... 4.8

2360 Caldervale **(72)** (bl) *(ABailey)* 8-9 ‡5OPears (6) (bhd & rdn ent st: n.d) ......... 1½.9

Rosmarino *(CWThornton)* 9-0 GHind (10) (leggy: bit bkwd: s.s: a wl bhd) ..... 12.10

2986 Andrew's Express (IRE) *(SEKettlewell)* 9-0 TyroneWilliams (1) (b.hind: led tl hdd 3f out: sn wknd) ................................................ 5.11

**2/1** Lyford Cay (IRE)(op 5/4), **100/30** Persian Charmer (IRE), **7/2** Southern Memories (IRE), **10/1** Peacefull Reply (USA), **12/1** COLWAY ROCK (USA)(op 7/1), **16/1** Caldervale, **20/1** Lancaster Pilot, Rosmarino, **33/1** Blakes Beau, Sudden Spin, **100/1** Andrew's Express (IRE). CSF £34.17, Tote £29.10: £4.70 £1.10 £1.40 (£25.90). Mr R. Coleman (RICHMOND) bred by John W. Rooker in USA. 11 Rn
1m 32.80 (8.80)
SF–41/40/35/11/9/–

---

**3354**    AUCHINLECK WATER DICK PEACOCK GRADUATION STKS (2-Y.O) £3501.25 (£1060.00: £517.50: £246.25) **1m**
3-10 (3-11)

3193³ **Wootton Rivers (USA) (94)** *(PWChapple-Hyam)* 9-4 DHolland (2) (a trckng ldrs: rdn to ld ins fnl f: cleverly) ............................... —1

Flame of Persia (IRE) (Fav) *(MKauntze,Ireland)* 8-13 WJO'Connor (3) (led: rdn appr fnl f: hdd ins fnl f: styd on nr fnl) ............................. nk.2

2859* Abtaal **(87)** *(HThomsonJones)* 9-4 RHills (1) (trckd ldr: effrt & n.m.r over 1f out: sn swtchd & styd on same pce) ................................... 3.3

3127 Drumdonna (IRE) **(77)** *(JBerry)* 8-13 SWood (4) (hdwy ent st: ev ch over 1f out: sn rdn & btn) ................................................ 7.4

**5/4** Flame of Persia (IRE), **13/8** WOOTTON RIVERS (USA), **7/2** Abtaal, **33/1** Drumdonna (IRE). CSF £3.80, Tote £2.80 (£2.10). Mr R. E. Sangster (MARLBOROUGH) bred by Swettenham Stud in USA. 4 Rn
1m 48.37 (11.17)
SF–20/14/10/–

**3355**
LADBROKES (AYR) SILVER CUP (H'cap)     £12427.50 (£3720.00: £1785.00: £817.50)
6f
3-40 (3-47)

(Weights raised 1 lb)

3067² **How's Yer Father (79)** *(RJHodges)* 6–9-6 MHills (11) (drvn along 4f out: hdwy
& squeezed thro over 1f out: styd on strly to ld cl home) .... —1

3341⁵ Diet (62) (v) *(MissLAPerratt)* 6–7-10 ‡7JMarshall (14) (lw: led: clr 2f out: hdd & no
ex wl ins fnl f) ................................................. hd.2

3243* Assignment (76) *(JFfitch-Heyes)* 6–7-12 (7x) TyroneWilliams (7) (a chsng ldrs:
rdn & ev ch appr fnl f: kpt on) ................................ 1.3

3196 Love Jazz (USA) (82) *(TDBarron)* 3–9-6 KDarley (10) (in tch: effrt 2f out: styd on
same pce) ....................................................... 1½.4

3344³ Teanarco (IRE) (63) *(RJHolder)* 4–8-4 NAdams (13) (hdwy 2f out: styd on) ... nk.5

3121⁴ Prenonamoss (80) *(DWPArbuthnot)* 4–9-7 MBirch (28) (b.hind: in tch: drvn
along ½-wy: styd on: nrst fin) .................................. ½.6

3144² Allinson's Mate (IRE) (76) *(TDBarron)* 4–9-3 NConnorton (3) (hdwy ½-wy: kpt
on u.p fnl f) .................................................... nk.7

3188⁶ Love Returned (80) *(WJarvis)* 5–9-7 MTebbutt (16) (lw: a chsng ldrs: rdn & one
pce fnl 2f) ...................................................... hd.8

3126² Darussalam (74) *(RLee)* 5–9-1 DNicholls (9) (in tch: effrt 2f out: styd on same
pce) ............................................................. nk.9

3243 Ballasecret (70) *(RDickin)* 4–8-4 ‡7PTurner (25) (lw: w ldrs: no ex appr fnl f) ... hd.10

3068⁴ Double Feature (IRE) (60) (v) *(MrsJRRamsden)* 3–7-12 SWood (23) (in tch &
racd alone stands' side: kpt on fnl f) .......................... ½.11

3015* Inherent Magic (IRE) (82) *(MMcCormack)* 3–9-6 (5x) PVGilson (8) (lw: in tch:
styd on fnl f) ................................................... s.h.12

3088 Gentle Hero (USA) (77) *(MPNaughton)* 6–9-4 KFallon (24) (lw: bhd & rdn
½-wy: hdwy 2f out: styd on: nrst fin) ........................... nk.13

629 Snowgirl (IRE) (75) *(JBerry)* 4–8-13 ‡3EmmaO'Gorman (4) (lw: w ldrs: rdn & no
ex appr fnl f) ................................................... ¾.14

3304 Rock Opera (IRE) (57) *(MPNaughton)* 4–7-12 JakiHouston (21) (prom: effrt
over 2f out: one pce) ........................................... nk.15

3243 Petraco (IRE) (72) *(LJCodd)* 4–8-13 WJO'Connor (12) (in tch: rdn 2f out: no ex) nk.16

3083³ Gorinsky (IRE) (73) (Fav) *(JBerry)* 4–9-0 NCarlisle (2) (in tch to ½-wy: sn
outpcd) ......................................................... nk.17

3207⁵ Iron King (71) *(JLSpearing)* 6–8-12 GHind (15) (bhd & rdn ½-wy: n.d) ........ s.h.18

3207 Meeson Times (62) *(BEllison)* 4–7-12⁽³⁾ ‡5OPears (5) (rdn along ½-wy: no imp) 1.19

3121 Threepence (83) *(JBerry)* 3–9-7 JCarroll (18) (w ldrs: rdn 2f out: wkng whn
hmpd over 1f out) ............................................... s.h.20

3304 Just Bob (70) (bl) *(SEKettlewell)* 3–8-3 ‡5RPrice (17) (s.i.s: nvr trbld ldrs) ....... hd.21

2839 Milagro (83) *(RHannon)* 3–9-7 RHills (26) (lw: sn bhd) ...................... ½.22

3341 Best Effort (67) *(MPNaughton)* 6–8-8 DHolland (6) (lw: chsd ldrs tl wknd wl over
1f out) .......................................................... s.h.23

3198 State Flyer (65) (v) *(CBBBooth)* 4–7-13⁽¹⁾ ‡7GForster (1) (lw: a bhd) .............. ½.24

3196 Educated Pet (76) *(MJohnston)* 3–8-9 ‡5NGwilliams (22) (a in rr) ............ 1½.25

2852 Ashdren (79) *(AHarrison)* 5–9-6 PaulEddery (27) (lw: mid div & drvn along
½-wy: sn btn) ................................................... 1.26

3154³ Dokkha Oyston (IRE) (74) *(JBerry)* 4–9-1 GCarter (20) (s.i.s: a in rr) .............. 1.27

3044 Misdemeanours Girl (IRE) (69) *(MRChannon)* 4–8-5 ‡5BDoyle (29) (n.d) ....... ½.28

3344 Sir Arthur Hobbs (62) *(FHLee)* 5–7-12 ‡5NKennedy (19) (bhd fr ½-wy) ............ 4.29

**12/1** Gorinsky (IRE), **14/1** Ashdren, Ballasecret, Darussalam, Assignment, **16/1** Allinson's Mate (IRE), Inherent
Magic (IRE), Petraco (IRE), **20/1** Gentle Hero (USA), HOW'S YER FATHER, Prenonamoss, Misdemeanours Girl
(IRE), Double Feature (IRE), Teanarco (IRE), **22/1** Milagro, **25/1** Love Returned, Threepence, Iron King, Diet, **33/1**
Snowgirl (IRE), State Flyer, Best Effort, Love Jazz (USA), Dokkha Oyston (IRE), Educated Pet, **50/1** Rock Opera
(IRE), Sir Arthur Hob bs, Meeson Times, **66/1** Just Bob. CSF £383.40, CT £6,347.62. Tote £11.90: £2.70 £2.40
£2.50 £11.90 (£105.70). Unity Farm Holiday Centre Ltd (SOMERTON) bred by Lord Edwin McAlpine. 29 Rn
1m 15.57 (5.17)
SF—74/49/66/63/46/61

**3356**
LADBROKES (AYR) GOLD CUP (H'cap) (0-115) £50817.50 (£15290.00: £7395.00:
£3447.50)     6f
4-15 (4-22)

(Weights raised 2 lb)

3188* **Lochsong (95)** *(IABalding)* 4–9-0 (7x) ‡7FArrowsmith (28) (lw: racd stands'
side: cl up: led after 2f: clr ½-wy: styd on) ................... —1

3126⁵ Echo-Logical (85) *(RHannon)* 3–8-8 KDarley (8) (lw: in tch: rdn 2f out: styd on
strly nr fin) .................................................... 2.2

3188 Heather Bank (94) (v) *(JBerry)* 3–9-3 GCarter (25) (chsd ldrs: rdn ½-wy: no ex) 1½.3

3083⁶ Dominuet (84) *(JLSpearing)* 7–8-10 GHind (3) (hdwy ½-wy: rdn & nt qckn fnl f) ½.4

3074² Arctic Appeal (IRE) (84) *(JBerry)* 3–8-4 ‡3EmmaO'Gorman (11) (a chsng ldrs:
one pce fnl 2f) ................................................. s.h.5

3031³ Densben (81) *(DenysSmith)* 8–8-7 KFallon (2) (lw: mid div: styd on appr fnl f) 1½.6

3242² Hard to Figure **(91)** *(RJHodges)* 6–8-10 ‡7SDrowne (15) (rr div: hdwy 2f out: styd on fnl f) .................................................................................................... s.h.**7**

2839 Cumbrian Waltzer **(93)** *(MHEasterby)* 7–9-5 MBirch (16) (hld up & bhd: effrt 2f out: styd on: nvr nr to chal) ........................................................................ ³/₄.**8**

3188 Taufan Blu (IRE) **(94)** (bl) *(MJohnston)* 3–9-3 ACulhane (6) (bhd: effrt ¹/₂-wy: nvr trbld ldrs) ........................................................................................................... s.h.**9**

Dashing Colours (IRE) **(86)** *(DanielJMurphy,Ireland)* 3–8-2 ‡7RVSkelly (9) (in tch: kpt on same pce fnl f) ........................................................................................ nk.**10**

3188 Never so Sure **(94)** (v) *(ABailey)* 4–9-1 (7x) ‡5OPears (20) (chsd ldrs: nt qckn fnl f) ..................................................................................................................... s.h.**11**

3006³ Fylde Flyer **(101)** *(JBerry)* 3–9-10 JCarroll (5) (lw: w ldrs: rdn 2f out: no ex) .. s.h.**12**

3189⁴ Silca-Cisa **(93)** *(MRChannon)* 3–9-2 PaulEddery (18) (chsd ldrs: rdn 2f out: grad wknd) ............................................................................................................. 1¹/₂.**13**

3243³ So Rhythmical **(84)** *(GHEden)* 8–8-5 (7x) ‡5BDoyle (13) (b.off hind: bhd: hdwy ¹/₂-wy: wknd appr fnl f) ................................................................................... ³/₄.**14**

3083² Bertie Wooster **(84)** *(RJHolder)* 9–8-10 NAdams (1) (lw: effrt 2f out: btn appr fnl f) ................................................................................................................................ hd.**15**

2435² Duplicity (IRE) **(97)** *(LJHolt)* 4–9-9 PVGilson (10) (mid div: no imp fnl 2f) ....... s.h.**16**

3188³ Cantoris **(92)** *(RJRWilliams)* 6–9-4 DHolland (27) (chsd ldrs stands' side: rdn over 2f out: sn btn) .......................................................................................................... 1.**17**

1535 Cindora (IRE) **(93)** *(MHTompkins)* 3–8-9 ‡7SMulvey (12) (lw: effrt ¹/₂-wy: nvr trbld ldrs) .......................................................................................................................... ¹/₂.**18**

3145★ Double Blue **(93)** *(MJohnston)* 3–9-2 RPElliott (21) (prom 4f: sn wknd) .......... s.h.**19**

3083 Sir Harry Hardman **(97)** *(FHLee)* 4–9-4 ‡5NKennedy (8) (bhd fr ¹/₂-wy) ............ nk.**20**

3031⁶ Amron **(81)** *(JBerry)* 5–8-7 NCarlisle (14) (a in rr) ............................................... nk.**21**

3188 Stack Rock **(96)** (v) *(EJAlston)* 5–9-8 DNicholls (4) (lw: led centre 2f: wknd wl over 1f out) ............................................................................................................................ 2.**22**

3188² Venture Capitalist **(91)** (bl) (Fav) *(RHannon)* 3–9-0 (5x) RHills (17) (lw: effrt ¹/₂-wy: r.u.) .............................................................................................................................. nk.**23**

3243 Mentalasanythin **(85)** *(ABailey)* 3–8-1 ‡7DWright (29) (racd stands' side: sn outpcd) .................................................................................................................................... nk.**24**

3031² Claybank (USA) **(84)** (bl) *(BWHills)* 3–8-7 MHills (23) (lw: in tch: rdn over 2f out: sn wknd) .................................................................................................................................. 2.**25**

3083 Sea Devil **(83)** *(MJCamacho)* 6–8-9 NConnorton (24) (racd stands' side: rdn wl over 2f out: sn bhd) .............................................................................................................. hd.**26**

2851 El Yasaf (IRE) **(94)** *(MCPipe)* 4–9-6 WJO'Connor (26) (spd stands' side to ¹/₂-wy: sn outpcd) .................................................................................................................. ³/₄.**27**

1535 Bold Memory **(93)** *(MJohnston)* 3–8-11 ‡5NGwilliams (22) (wl bhd fr ¹/₂-wy) .... 3.**28**

**8/1** Venture Capitalist, **10/1** Hard to Figure, Never so Sure, LOCHSONG, **12/1** Cumbrian Waltzer, **14/1** Claybank (USA), Sea Devil, **16/1** Double Blue, Silca-Cisa, **18/1** Amron, **20/1** Cantoris, Stack Rock, Duplicity (IRE), Dashing Colours (IRE), **22/1** So Rhythmical, **25/1** Bertie Wooster, Taufan Blu (IRE), **28/1** Dominuet, **33/1** Heather Bank, Echo-Logical, Mentalasanythin, Fylde Flyer, **40/1** Arctic Appeal (IRE), Densben, **50/1** Ors. CSF £272.92, CT £9,094.39. Tote £9.70: £3.10 £5.70 £10.40 £13.00 (£243.90). Mr J. C. Smith (KINGSCLERE) bred by Littleton Stud. 28 Rn    1m 15.51 (5.11)

SF—70/56/59/50/43/40

---

**3357**    JOHNNIE WALKER WHISKY H'CAP (0-100) £4221.00 (£1278.00: £624.00: £297.00)
1¹/₄m 192y    4-45 (4-52)

3090² **Billy Blazer (77)** (Fav) *(MHTompkins)* 3–8-6 KDarley (1) (a in tch: hdwy over 2f out: led ent fnl f: styd on) ........................................................................................ —**1**

2836 Take by Storm (IRE) **(73)** *(GMMoore)* 3–8-2 JCarroll (4) (prom: led 2f out: hdd ent fnl f: no ex) ......................................................................................................... 1¹/₂.**2**

3177³ Philgun **(64)** *(CWCElsey)* 3–7-7 SWood (6) (chsd ldrs: rdn 2f out: kpt on u.p) .. 1.**3**

2917² Kinematic (USA) **(92)** *(JHMGosden)* 4–10-0 PaulEddery (3) (in tch: rdn along ent st: styd on fnl f: nvr able to chal) ........................................................................ nk.**4**

815³ Comstock **(79)** *(NTinkler)* 5–9-1⁽¹⁾ DNicholls (2) (wl bhd ent st: hdwy over 2f out: nrst fin) ................................................................................................................................ ¹/₂.**5**

3116⁵ Admirals Seat **(63)** *(MrsJRRamsden)* 4–7-13 DHolland (8) (led to 2f out: sn btn) ¹/₂.**6**

3248★ Juniper Berry (IRE) **(87)** *(PWChapple-Hyam)* 3–9-2 MHills (5) (chsd ldrs: rdn 3f out: wknd 2f out) ............................................................................................................. 5.**7**

2908⁴ Falcons Dawn **(57)** *(ABailey)* 5–7-0 ‡7DWright (7) (disp ld ent st: rdn & wknd over 2f out) ...................................................................................................................... 1.**8**

LONG HANDICAP: Philgun 6-11, Falcons Dawn 7-5.

**5/2** BILLY BLAZER, **7/2** Juniper Berry (IRE), **4/1** Admirals Seat, **5/1** Kinematic (USA), **10/1** Take by Storm (IRE), Falcons Dawn, **16/1** Comstock, **33/1** Philgun. CSF £24.30, CT £591.73. Tote £3.00: £1.30 £2.10 £3.20 (£15.90). Mr P. D. Savill (NEWMARKET) bred by Wheelersland Stud. 8 Rn    2m 28.51 (14.81)

SF—21/14/3/37/23/6

**3358**          COURVOISIER COGNAC NURSERY    £2840.00 (£860.00: £420.00: £200.00)
                 **5f**                                                                    5-15 (5-21)

(Weights raised 4 lb)

3023  **Carnbrea Snip (78)** *(MBell)* 9-4  MHills (3) (mde all: rdn ent fnl f: hld on gamely
      nr fin) ..................................................................................... —1
3218*  First Option **(70)** (Fav) *(MHEasterby)* 8-10  KDarley (4) (hld up: hdwy ½-wy: hrd
      rdn & r.o wl ins fnl f) ........................................................... hd.2
3218²  Covent Garden Girl **(57)** *(MWEasterby)* 7-6(4) ‡5BDoyle (5) (cl up: rdn & ev ch
      appr fnl f: styd on same pce) ...................................................... ½.3
3070  Isotonic **(77)** *(GMMoore)* 9-3  NCarlisle (6) (chsd ldrs: rdn ½-wy: one pce) .. 3½.4
3165*  Two Moves in Front (IRE) **(78)** *(JBerry)* 9-4  GCarter (7) (in tch tl rdn & outpcd
      ½-wy: styd on fnl f) ................................................................. s.h.5
2876²  Cockerham Ranger **(81)** *(JBerry)* 9-7  JCarroll (1) (prom: effrt & edgd lft wl over
      1f out: sn btn) ...................................................................... 4.6
3165³  Moodiesburn (IRE) **(67)** *(ABailey)* 8-0 ‡7DWright (2) (spd to ½-wy: sn wknd) .. 3½.7
3155  Sporting Spirit **(69)** *(DWChapman)* 8-9  SWood (8) (dwlt: a bhd) ................ 3.8
            LONG HANDICAP: Covent Garden Girl 7-6.

2/1 First Option, **100/30** Moodiesburn (IRE), 13/2 Isotonic, 7/1 Two Moves in Front (IRE), Covent Garden Girl,
15/2 CARNBREA SNIP, 12/1 Cockerham Ranger, 20/1 Sporting Spirit. CSF £22.61, CT £102.69. Tote £12.80:
£2.00 £1.10 £2.40 (£21.80). Mrs S. M. Crompton (NEWMARKET) bred by Mrs J. R. Hine and Miss J. Bunting. 8
Rn                                                                               63.23 sec (5.23)
                                                                            SF—59/50/30/41/41/28

T/Trio: Race 4: £214.60 (6.2 Tckts) & Race 5: Any 2 fr 1st 3 w any £42.50 (48.7 Tckts). T/Plpt: £491.60 (18.60
Tckts).                                                                                      GB

## 2787—NEWBURY (L-H)

### Friday, September 18th [Good]

Going Allowance: St: 0.05 sec; Rnd: minus 0.10 sec per fur (G)           Wind: almost nil

Stalls: centre

**3359**          WINCHESTER ASSET MANAGEMENT H'CAP (0-105) £4971.00 (£1488.00: £714.00:
                 £327.00)  **7f 64y (rnd)**                                              2-05 (2-09)

(Weights raised 2 lb)

3088  **La Dama Bonita (USA) (80)** *(DWPArbuthnot)* 3-8-2  GBardwell (16) (lw: hdwy
      over 1f out: led ins fnl f: r.o wl) .................................................. —1
2945⁶  Helios **(77)** *(RSimpson)* 4-8-3(1)  WRyan (3) (lw: hdwy over 1f out: r.o ins fnl f) 1½.2
983⁶  Sand Table **(83)** *(LordHuntingdon)* 3-8-5  AMunro (17) (hdwy over 1f out: ev ch
      ins fnl f: unable qckn) ............................................................ hd.3
3243  Kayvee **(93)** (bl) *(GHarwood)* 3-9-1  JReid (12) (lw: hdwy 2f out: led over 1f out tl
      ins fnl f: one pce) ................................................................. s.h.4
2449²  Shati (IRE) **(92)** *(HThomsonJones)* 3-9-0  NCarlisle (13) (swtg: hdwy over 1f
      out: r.o) ............................................................................ 1½.5
2997  Choir Practice **(72)** *(WJHaggas)* 5—7-12  CRutter (11) (n.m.r 2f out: hdwy over 1f
      out: r.o) ............................................................................ hd.6
3133  Super Serenade **(71)** *(GBBalding)* 3-7-7  DaleGibson (10) (swtg: 6th st: one
      pce fnl 2f) ......................................................................... hd.7
3038³  Ahbab (IRE) **(82)** (v) *(PTWalwyn)* 3-8-4  WCarson (15) (swtg: 2nd st: ev ch over
      1f out: wknd fnl f) ................................................................. 3½.8
3198  Bold Habit **(82)** *(BBeasley)* 7—8-8  LPiggott (2) (lw: hmpd s: nt clr run 2f out: nvr
      nr to chal) ......................................................................... ¾.9
3095  Tender Moment (IRE) **(71)** *(CEBrittain)* 4—7-6(4) ‡5BDoyle (14) (led 6f) ........... nk.10
3098  Seneca Reef (IRE) **(72)** (bl) *(IABalding)* 4—7-9 ‡3SO'Gorman (7) (nvr nrr) ........ hd.11
3198  Sir Boudle (IRE) **(82)** *(CRNelson)* 3-8-4  TQuinn (8) (4th st: wknd fnl f) ............ 1.12
2855³  Knight of Mercy **(98)** (Fav) *(RHannon)* 6-9-10  BRaymond (9) (rdn over 3f out:
      bhd fnl 2f) ......................................................................... ¾.13
1943  Mango Manila **(86)** *(CAHorgan)* 7—8-12  SCauthen (4) (b: hmpd s: a bhd) ........ 1.14
2852  Venus Observed **(85)** *(HCandy)* 4—8-4 ‡7AntoinetteArmes (6) (lw: 7th st: wkng
      whn hmpd on ins wl over 1f out) ................................................. 1½.15
3243  Belfort Ruler **(70)** *(BGubby)* 5—7-10  JQuinn (5) (5th st: wknd wl over 1f out) 1½.16
3085⁵  Superbrave **(75)** *(WJarvis)* 6—7-12 ‡3FNorton (1) (b: 3rd st: wknd wl over 1f out) 3½.17

6/1 Knight of Mercy, **13/2** Mango Manila, 10/1 Superbrave, 10/1 Bold Habit(op 6/1), Shati (IRE), Ahbab (IRE),
12/1 Venus Observed, Seneca Reef (IRE), **14/1** Choir Practice(10/1—16/1), Kayvee(op 8/1), Sand Table, 16/1
Super Serenade, 20/1 Tender Moment (IRE), Sir Boudle (IRE), Helios, Belfort Ruler, 25/1 LA DAMA BONITA
(USA). CSF £414.30, CT £6,410.36. Tote £47.40: £9.40 £4.40 £4.60 £3.60 (£889.40). Mr Christopher Wright
(COMPTON) bred by Edward A. Seltzer in USA. 17 Rn                                      1m 30.76 (3.46)
                                                                            SF—26/22/23/32/26/9

**3360**   JOCK COLLIER MEMORIAL STKS (2-Y.O.F) £8155.00 (£2440.00: £1170.00: £535.00)
**7f (st)**   2-40 (2-44)

Sueboog (IRE) (Jt-Fav) *(CEBrittain)* 8-8 LDettori (6) (str: scope: a.p: led 3f out: comf) ............................................................... —1

Suntara (IRE) *(BWHills)* 8-8 RStreet (8) (unf: scope: bkwd: gd hdwy 2f out: chsd wnr over 1f out: r.o) ............................................... 2½.2

Susquehanna Days (USA) *(IABalding)* 8-8 SO'Gorman (12) (leggy: gd hdwy over 1f out: r.o ins fnl f) ........................................... 6.3

Bawaeth (USA) *(BWHills)* 8-8 WCarson (2) (unf: bit bkwd: a.p: one pce fnl 2f) .. s.h.4

Princess Tateum (IRE) *(MRChannon)* 8-8 JQuinn (7) (unf: hdwy over 1f out: nvr nrr) ........................................................................ nk.5

Welsh Heritage (IRE) *(LordHuntingdon)* 8-8 AMunro (11) (leggy: scope: a.p: one pce fnl 2f) ...................................................... 1½.6

3036⁶ Singer on the Roof *(IABalding)* 8-8 BRaymond (17) (hdwy over 1f out: nvr nrr) 1½.7

Ringlet (USA) *(BWHills)* 8-8 SCauthen (9) (unf: scope: bit bkwd: a mid div) ....... 4.8

Desert Girl *(JRFanshawe)* 8-8 GCarter (1) (unf: bit bkwd: hdwy over 2f out: wknd over 1f out) ...................................................... nk.9

3132 Mim *(GBBalding)* 8-8 CRutter (13) (lw: outpcd) ................................ 2.10

3099★ Forthwith *(RHannon)* 8-13 BRouse (3) (prom: led over 3f out: sn hdd: wknd 2f out) ................................................................... 1½.11

3093 Tempesta Rossa (IRE) *(BWHills)* 8-8 JWilliams (10) (outpcd) ............... 8.12

Icterina (USA) (.Jt-Fav) *(PWChapple-Hyam)* 8-8 JReid (15) (scope: bit bkwd: s.s: outpcd) .............................................................. 2.13

Tahdid *(PTWalwyn)* 8-8 WRyan (4) (unf: bit bkwd: spd over 4f) .................... 1½.14

3175 Natasha North *(TCasey)* 8-8 FNorton (5) (led over 3f) ....................... 2.15

Proud Moment (BAR) *(RHannon)* 8-8 RPerham (14) (unf: bit bkwd: hdwy over 4f out: wknd over 2f out) ....................................... 10.16

**11/2** SUEBOOG (IRE), Icterina (USA)(op 12/1), **6/1** Forthwith(op 3/1), Bawaeth (USA), **8/1** Ringlet (USA)(op 5/1), **10/1** Singer on the Roof, **14/1** Susquehanna Days (USA), Princess Tateum (IRE), **16/1** Welsh Heritage (IRE), **20/1** Tahdid, **25/1** Proud Moment (BAR), **33/1** Suntara (IRE), Tempesta Rossa (IRE), Mim, **66/1** Natasha North. CSF £155.43, Tote £7.80: £2.50 £12.50 £7.30 (£318.20). Mr Mohamed Obaida (NEWMARKET) bred by Shutford Stud in Ireland. 16 Rn   1m 28.44 (3.94)
SF—40/32/8/7/6/1

**3361**   TONY STRATTON SMITH MEMORIAL STKS (3-Y.O) £6966.00 (£2088.00: £1004.00: £462.00)   **5f 34y**   3-10 (3-13)

3124³ Wolfhound (USA) **(114)** (Fav) *(JHMGosden)* 8-11 SCauthen (4) (hld up: led 1f out: r.o wl) ................................................................. —1

2448³ Artistic Reef **(106)** *(GHEden)* 8-11 WCarson (11) (led 4f: unable qckn) ............. 2.2

3253⁶ Bells of Longwick **(68)** *(DRLaing)* 8-6 TyroneWilliams (5) (hdwy 2f out: r.o one pce) ......................................................................... ½.3

3188⁴ Walk in the Park **(89)** *(RSimpson)* 8-6 ATucker (7) (hdwy over 1f out: r.o) ......... ½.4

3083⁵ Colway Bold **(99)** (v) *(JWWatts)* 9-2 JReid (9) (hdwy over 1f out: nvr nrr) ......... 1.5

3189 Regal Scintilla **(100)** *(GBBalding)* 8-11 AMunro (8) (a.p: ev ch over 1f out: wknd fnl f) .................................................................. 2.6

3124 Bletchley Park (IRE) **(97)** *(AAScott)* 9-2 BRaymond (2) (hdwy over 2f out: wknd over 1f out) ........................................................ 6.7

3042² Belthorn **(53)** *(JJBridger)* 8-2 JQuinn (1) (prom over 3f) ........................... 5.8

834⁵ Power Lake **(102)** *(RHannon)* 8-11 LDettori (6) (a.p: ev ch over 1f out: sn wknd) 1½.9

3189⁶ Master of Passion **(90)** (v) *(JMPEustace)* 8-11 LPiggott (12) (prom over 3f) .... hd.10

Affair of State (IRE) *(MRChannon)* 8-11 TQuinn (3) (outpcd) ..................... 2½.11

3065★ Another Episode (IRE) **(90)** *(JBerry)* 9-2 GCarter (10) (spd 3f) ..................... 5.12

**6/5** WOLFHOUND (USA), **100/30** Artistic Reef, **9/1** Walk in the Park, **12/1** Another Episode (IRE), **14/1** Colway Bold, Power Lake, **20/1** Master of Passion, Bletchley Park (IRE), Regal Scintilla, **25/1** Affair of State (IRE), **50/1** Bells of Longwick, **66/1** Belthorn. CSF £5.66, Tote £1.90: £1.10 £2.00 £4.80 (£3.60). Sheikh Mohammed (NEWMARKET) bred by W. S. Farish III and W. S. Kilroy in USA. 12 Rn   62.27 sec (1.57)
SF—71/63/56/54/60/47

**3362**   HAYNES, HANSON AND CLARK STKS (2-Y.O.C & G) £7375.00 (£2200.00: £1050.00: £475.00)   **1m (st)**   3-40 (3-42)

3130★ Pembroke (USA) (Fav) *(JHMGosden)* 9-2 SCauthen (6) (lw: a.p: shkn up over 1f out: led ins fnl f: r.o wl) .................................................... —1

3100² The Informer (USA) *(PFICole)* 8-11 AMunro (7) (led tl ins fnl f: unable qckn) ... 1½.2

White Muzzle *(PWChapple-Hyam)* 8-11 JReid (4) (w'like: scope: bit bkwd: hdwy over 2f out: rdn over 1f out: one pce) ....................... hd.3

Green Kilt *(LordHuntingdon)* 8-11 LDettori (2) (str: scope: bit bkwd: hld up: rdn
over 1f out: one pce) ........................................................... 3.4
3106² Jackpot Star *(RHannon)* 8-11 LPiggott (3) (nvr nr to chal) ................ 1½.5
2918   Kassab *(JLDunlop)* 8-11 WCarson (5) (a bhd) ............................. 2.6
2598   Kimberley Boy *(BWHills)* 8-11 JWilliams (8) (bhd fnl 3f) ................... 5.7
Circus Colours *(JLDunlop)* 8-11 TQuinn (1) (unf: scope: spd over 6f) ......... 8

**4/5 PEMBROKE (USA), 5/1** White Muzzle(op 3/1), **13/2** The Informer (USA), Kassab, **14/1** Green Kilt(op 8/1),
**20/1** Jackpot Star, **25/1** Circus Colours, **33/1** Kimberley Boy. CSF £6.69, Tote £1.70: £1.10 £1.50 £1.70
(£3.90). Sheikh Mohammed (NEWMARKET) bred by Stonereath Farm Inc in USA. 8 Rn    1m 44.47 (7.47)

---

**3363**     ALPHA SUISSE GROUP H'CAP (3-Y.O) (0-90) £6092.50 (£1840.00: £895.00: £422.50)
             **1m 1f**                                                         4-10 (4-14)

3080* **What Katy Did (USA) (80)** *(JHMGosden)* 8-11 SCauthen (4) (b.hind: 3rd st:
led ins fnl f: rdn out) .......................................................... —1
2992² Googly (67) *(WGRWightman)* 7-12 GBardwell (6) (lw: 4th st: hrd rdn 2f out: r.o
wl ins fnl f) .................................................................. nk.2
3140  Will Soon (68) *(HCandy)* 7-6 ‡7AntoinetteArmes (2) (lw: 2nd st: led 2f out tl ins fnl
f: unable qckn) ............................................................. 2½.3
2838⁵ Host (IRE) (90) *(CEBrittain)* 9-7 TQuinn (8) (led 7f: ev ch ins fnl f: one pce) .. 1.4
3203³ Many a Quest (USA) (80) (Fav) *(LMCumani)* 8-11 LDettori (1) (5th st: hrd rdn
over 1f out: one pce) ........................................................ ½.5
3122⁶ Cottonwood (78) *(LordHuntingdon)* 8-9 AMunro (3) (6th st: no hdwy fnl 3f) ... 2½.6
2230  Maple Bay (IRE) (70) *(PJMakin)* 8-1 GCarter (5) (a bhd) .................. 3½.7
3135² Ghurrah (IRE) (64) *(CJBenstead)* 7-9 WCarson (11) (lw: a bhd) ............ 7.8
2825  Thinking Twice (USA) (66) *(PWHarris)* 7-11 JQuinn (9) (a bhd) ............. 4.9
2616⁶ Singers Image (65) (v) *(GBBalding)* 7-10 SDawson (7) (a bhd) ............. 5.10

**2/1** Many a Quest (USA), **7/2 WHAT KATY DID (USA)**(3/1—5/1), **13/2** Googly, **7/1** Ghurrah (IRE), **10/1** Will
Soon, Cottonwood, **20/1** Host (IRE), Thinking Twice, Singers Image, **33/1** Maple Bay (IRE). CSF £24.49,
CT £188.05. Tote £3.20: £1.80 £1.50 £2.40 (£6.70). Sheikh Mohammed (NEWMARKET) bred by Mareco Ltd in
USA. 10 Rn                                                              1m 54.27 (5.07)
                                                                        SF—7/-/-/-/-/-

---

**3364**     JOHN HOLLINS SPORTS MANAGEMENT NURSERY     £5192.00 (£1556.00: £748.00:
             £344.00)   **7f 64y (rnd)**                                       4-40 (4-45)
                                        (Weights raised 6 lb)
2879⁴ **Shamam (USA) (77)** *(PTWalwyn)* 9-0 WCarson (4) (lw: 2nd st: led over 1f out:
rdn out) ...................................................................... —1
3019³ Brigante Di Cielo (76) *(RHannon)* 8-13 BRaymond (6) (5th st: n.m.r over 2f out:
hrd rdn over 1f out: r.o ins fnl f) .......................................... ¾.2
3199⁴ After the Last (84) (Fav) *(RHannon)* 9-7 JReid (3) (nt clr run on ins over 1f out:
hdwy fnl f: r.o wl) .......................................................... s.h.3
3051⁴ Abbey's Gal (81) *(IABalding)* 9-4 SCauthen (4) (nt clr run over 1f out: hdwy fnl f:
r.o) .......................................................................... ¾.4
3039⁶ Knobbleeneeze (67) *(MRChannon)* 8-4 JQuinn (2) (lw: 3rd st: one pce fnl 2f) ... 3.5
2903³ Conspicuous (IRE) (77) *(PFICole)* 9-0 AMunro (8) (lw: no hdwy fnl 3f) ........ ½.6
3242  War Requiem (IRE) (63) *(GBBalding)* 8-0 SDawson (1) (led over 6f out tl over 1f
out: sn wknd) ................................................................ 2.7
3012⁴ Maybe Gold (71) *(DWPArbuthnot)* 8-8 TQuinn (5) (b.hind: lw: led fnl 1f: 4th st:
wknd over 1f out) ........................................................... 6.8

**100/30** After the Last(2/1—7/2), **7/2** Abbey's Gal, **5/1** Brigante Di Cielo, SHAMAM (USA), **8/1** Conspicuous
(IRE), Knobbleeneeze, **9/1** Maybe Gold, **16/1** War Requiem (IRE). CSF £28.15, CT £85.96. Tote £5.90: £1.70
£2.00 £1.80 (£24.00). Mr Hamdan Al-Maktoum (LAMBOURN) bred by Shadwell Farm Inc in USA. 8 Rn
                                                                        1m 33.42 (6.12)

---

**3365**     VICTOR CHANDLER SILVER CLEF H'CAP (Ladies) (0-75) £3057.00 (£852.00: £411.00)
             **1m 7y (rnd)**                                                    5-15 (5-22)
                                        (Weights raised 6 lb)
2422* **Lots of Luck (57)** (Fav) *(JPearce)* 9-10-9 MrsLPearce (2) (hdwy 2f out: led
over 1f out: r.o wl) .......................................................... —1
3119² Nest (58) *(LordHuntingdon)* 3–10-6 MissJAllison (9) (hdwy 2f out: r.o one pce) 3½.2
3245  Bill Moon (49) *(PJFeilden)* 6-10-1 MissJFeilden (15) (lw: 5th st: led over 3f out tl
over 1f out: one pce) ....................................................... s.h.3
3140* Sharp Dream (69) *(BSmart)* 4-11-2 ‡5MissVMarshall (1) (hdwy over 1f out: r.o) s.h.4
3245³ Alnasric Pete (USA) (46) *(DAWilson)* 6-9-12 MrsJCrossley (7) (b: lw: n.m.r over
2f out: swtchd rt: hmpd wl over 1f out: hdwy & r.o one pce) 1½.5
2807  Champenoise (49) *(MBell)* 4-9-10 ‡5MrsLLawson (13) (swtg: nvr nr to chal) .. 2½.6
3290* Ballerina Bay (56) (v) *(DTThom)* 4-10-8 MissIDWJones (5) (no hdwy fnl 2f) .... s.h.7
2881  Durneltor (63) *(RHannon)* 4-10-10 ‡5MissSDalton (3) (led over 6f out tl over 3f
out: wknd over 1f out) ....................................................... ¾.8

32393 Lucky Noire **(58)** *(GHarwood)* 4–10-10 MissAHarwood (12) (lw: hrd rdn 2f out:
              nvr nrr) ............................................................. 2.9
 3066 Albert **(43)** *(DAWilson)* 5–9-9 MrsEMellor (8) (nvr nrr) .............................. 1.10
2958* Thewaari (USA) **(68)** *(AAScott)* 3–11-2 MissTBracegirdle (6) (lw: nvr nrr) ....... 3/4.11
3239* Broad Appeal **(44)** *(RCSpicer)* 4–9-5 (5x) ‡5MrsGBell (4) (s.s: nvr nrr) ............ 1.12
 3014 Amthaal (USA) **(67)** (v) *(MRStoute)* 3–11-1 MissMJuster (19) (4th st: wknd 2f
              out) ................................................................. 1/2.13
 3245 Mainly Me **(57)** *(PTWalwyn)* 3–10-7 ‡5MrsATurner (11) (led over 1f: 2nd st: wknd
              2f out) ............................................................. nk.14
 3241 Salisong **(70)** (bl) *(PFICole)* 3–11-4 MissMClark (16) (6th st: wknd over 2f out) 11/2.15
27703 Try Leguard (IRE) **(69)** *(JSMoore)* 3–10-12 ‡5MrsSMoore (10) (bhd fnl 3f) .. s.h.16
31056 Jokist **(61)** *(WJarvis)* 9–10-8 ‡5MrsARutherford (20) (3rd st: wknd 2f out) ...... s.h.17
32392 Keep Your Word **(57)** *(GBBalding)* 6–10-9 MissJSouthcombe (18) (bhd fnl 3f) hd.18
 3002 Hawaii Storm (FR) **(54)** *(MissAJWhitfield)* 4–10-1 ‡5MrsFWhitfield (17) (bhd fnl
              3f) .................................................................. 5.19
  215 Level Up **(55)** *(CDBroad)* 3–9-12 ‡5MissVSnowdon (14) (bhd fnl 3f) .................. 20

**5/1** LOTS OF LUCK, **11/2** Alnasric Pete (USA), **15/2** Broad Appeal, **10/1** Lucky Noire, Sharp Dream(op 5/1), **11/1** Amthaal (USA)(op 7/1), Ballerina Bay, **12/1** Keep Your Word, Thewaari (USA), **14/1** Nest, **16/1** Bill Moon, **20/1** Salisong, Try Leguard (IRE), Durneltor, Hawaii Storm (FR), Jokist, Champenoise, **25/1** Albert, **33/1** Ors. CSF £77.06, CT £1,009.15. Tote £4.40: £1.90 £4.90 £6.20 £4.90 (£37.50). Burton Park Country Club (NEWMARKET) bred by Mrs C. M. Allan. 20 Rn
                                                 1m 40.48 (4.48)
                                             SF–43/29/23/37/14/4

T/Trio: Race 3: £67.00 (15.1 Tckts). T/Jkpt: £108,511.60 (0.6 Tckts); £58,654.94 to Newbury 19/9/92. T/Plpt: £1,854.50 (6.6 Tckts).
                                                       AK

# NEWBURY (L-H)

## Saturday, September 19th [Good]

Going Allowance: St: 0.10 sec per fur; Rnd: nil sec per fur (G)       Wind: almost nil

Stalls: 1st, 2nd & 7th centre, remainder high

**3366**     HIGHCLERE NURSERY    £7200.00 (£2160.00: £1040.00: £480.00)
            **5f 34y**                                                1-30 (1-33)

                   (Weights raised 5 lb)
3208* **Brigg Fair (90)** *(RHannon)* 9-4 ‡3RPerham (4) (hld up: qcknd to ld over 1f out:
              sn clr) ............................................................. —1
 3187 Zany Zanna (IRE) **(80)** *(GAPritchard-Gordon)* 8-8 ‡3DHarrison (1) (hdwy fnl 2f:
              nvr nrr) ............................................................ 4.2
3023b Bangles **(82)** *(LordHuntingdon)* 8-13 AMunro (11) (a.p: ev ch over 1f out: one
              pce) ................................................................. 11/2.3
 3055 Aragrove **(70)** *(LJHolt)* 7-8(4) ‡7CAvery (7) (a.p: one pce fnl 2f) ..................... 11/2.4
 3275 Second Chance (IRE) **(73)** *(PMitchell)* 8-4 DBiggs (9) (led 3f) ....................... 1.5
17134 Petite Epaulette **(87)** *(WJarvis)* 9-4 LDettori (10) (lw: w ldrs: led 2f out tl over 1f
              out) ................................................................. hd.6
 3187 Where's the Dance **(73)** *(CEBrittain)* 8-4 MRoberts (3) (nvr nr to chal) ........... 1/2.7
 3012 Charity Express (IRE) **(86)** *(JBerry)* 9-3 DMcKeown (6) (s.s: hdwy 2f out: wknd
              1f out) ............................................................. 1/2.8
3179b Go Flightline (IRE) **(72)** (Fav) *(MBell)* 8-3 JQuinn (5) (lw: spd over 3f) .......... 11/2.9
 3187 Hallorina **(66)** *(WGRWightman)* 7-11 GBardwell (2) (w ldrs tl wknd 2f out) ...... 4.10
2669b Just Baileys **(64)** *(MJohnston)* 7-9 SDawson (8) (lw: outpcd) ....................... 8.11

**7/2** Go Flightline (IRE), **5/1** Bangles(op 3/1), **13/2** BRIGG FAIR, **7/1** Zany Zanna (IRE), **10/1** Where's the Dance, **12/1** Hallorina, Charity Express (IRE), **16/1** Petite Epaulette, Just Baileys, Second Chance (IRE), **20/1** Aragrove. CSF £44.52, CT £216.77. Tote £7.70: £2.40 £2.60 £1.70 (£25.70). Mr John Norman (MARLBOROUGH) bred by Roldvale Ltd. 11 Rn
                                                 63.35 sec (2.65)
                                             SF–61/35/34/9/15/28

**3367**     ROKEBY FARMS MILL REEF STKS (Gp 2) (2-Y.O) £30715.80 (£11450.64: £5462.82:
            £2338.74)    **6f 8y**                                    2-00 (2-02)

31362 **Forest Wind (USA)** *(MMoubarak)* 8-11 LDettori (4) (gd hdwy over 1f out: r.o to
              ld nr fin) .......................................................... —1
2981a3 Marina Park (Fav) *(MJohnston)* 8-6 DMcKeown (7) (lw: led 1f: led over 3f out:
              hrd rdn & edgd lft ins fnl f: hdd cl home) ............................. 1/2.2
3224a* Sharp Prod (USA) *(LordHuntingdon)* 9-1 AMunro (3) (lw: a.p: ev ch over 1f out:
              nt qckn) ............................................................ 2.3
2764a* Pips Pride *(RHannon)* 9-1 BRaymond (1) (lw: a.p: one pce fnl 2f) ..................... 1.4

3117* Carbon Steel (IRE) *(BWHills)* 8-11 PRobinson (5) (swtg: a abt same pl) ............ 1.5
3070 Aradanza *(MRChannon)* 8-11 JWilliams (6) (lw: a bhd) ................................ 3¹/₂.6
2845² Green's Bid *(PFICole)* 8-11 MRoberts (2) (lw: led after 1f tl over 3f out: wknd 2f
out) .................................................................................................... 2.7

**5/4** Marina Park, **7/2** Green's Bid, **11/2** FOREST WIND (USA), **6/1** Sharp Prod (USA), **8/1** Pips Pride, **12/1** Carbon Steel (IRE), **50/1** Aradanza. CSF £12.76, Tote £5.90: £2.40 £1.70 (£7.70). Ecurie Fustok (NEWMARKET) bred by Buckram Oak Farm in USA. 7 Rn
                                       1m 14.80 (3)
                                  SF—49/42/43/39/31/17

---

**3368**     COURAGE H'CAP (0-115) £18237.50 (£5525.00: £2700.00: £1287.50)
          **1¹/₄m 6y**                                       2-30 (2-37)

2347³ **Montpelier Boy (80)** *(LordHuntingdon)* 4-8-0 AMunro (4) (6th st: led over 2f
out: clr over 1f out: r.o) ................................................................. —1
3137 Pelorus (81) *(DRCElsworth)* 7-7-12 ‡³DHarrison (6) (lw: s.s: wl bhd tl hdwy 3f
out: nt clr run 2f out: gd late hdwy) ............................................... 1¹/₂.2
3131⁵ St Ninian (100) *(MHEasterby)* 6-9-6 JWilliams (8) (lw: hdwy 2f out: r.o ins fnl f) 3¹/₂.3
3013⁶ Selaah (86) *(MRStoute)* 5-8-6 MRoberts (7) (rdn over 3f out: hdwy over 1f out:
r.o) ................................................................................................. 1¹/₂.4
3022³ Young Freeman (USA) (99) *(GHarwood)* 3-8-13 MPerrett (9) (lw: 3rd st: ev ch
2f out: one pce) .............................................................................. ¹/₂.5
2933³ Amaze (96) *(LadyHerries)* 3-8-10 JQuinn (3) (b: no hdwy fnl 3f) ................. 3.6
2347 Charlo (97) *(JHMGosden)* 4-9-3 BRaymond (11) (lw: 5th st: wknd 3f out) ..... ¹/₂.7
3020⁶ Fire Top (93) *(RAkehurst)* 7-8-6 ‡⁷LCarter (13) (lw: 2nd st: wknd 3f out) ..... hd.8
3248³ Pharly Story (94) *(MCPipe)* 4-9-0 DMcKeown (2) (nvr nr to chal) ............... nk.9
3138⁵ Ile de Chypre (108) *(GHarwood)* 7-10-0 AClark (10) (lw: led tl wknd over 2f out) ¹/₂.10
3237 Bobzao (IRE) (100) *(WCarter)* 3-9-0 BRouse (1) (lw: 4th st: wknd 3f out) .... ¹/₂.11
2460* Knock Knock (92) *(IABalding)* 7-8-9 ‡³SO'Gorman (5) (lw: a bhd) ................. 7.12
3062² Lobilio (USA) (86) *(CEBrittain)* 3-8-0 PRobinson (12) (lw: bhd fnl 4f) .......... 5.13
3122⁵ Dress Sense (IRE) (91) (Fav) *(LMCumani)* 3-8-5⁽¹⁾ LDettori (14) (hdwy 5f out:
wknd 3f out) ................................................................................... 1¹/₂.14
             LONG HANDICAP: Montpelier Boy 7-12, Lobilio (USA) 7-12.

**11/2** Dress Sense (IRE), **7/1** MONTPELIER BOY, Selaah, Charlo, **9/1** Knock Knock, **11/1** Fire Top, **12/1** Pharly Story, St Ninian, **14/1** Pelorus, Lobilio (USA), **16/1** Bobzao (IRE), Young Freeman, **20/1** Ors. CSF £90.37, CT £1,041.62. Tote £6.90: £1.90 £4.00 £5.70 (£42.30). Sir Michael Sandberg (WEST ILSLEY) bred by M. Sandberg. 14 Rn
                                       2m 6.25 (3.25)
                                  SF—54/49/64/47/53/44

---

**3369**     'CORAL' AUTUMN CUP (H'cap) (0-110) £18318.75 (£5550.00: £2712.50: £1293.75)
          **1m 5f 61y**                                      3-00 (3-08)

3057³ **Castoret (80)** *(JWHills)* 6-7-13 ‡³DHarrison (2) (hdwy 3f out: led over 1f out: r.o
wl) ................................................................................................. —1
3057² Welsh Mill (IRE) (85) *(LordHuntingdon)* 3-7-12 AMunro (14) (lw: 6th st: led over
2f out tl one 1f out: r.o) .................................................................. 3.2
3194³ Al Karnak (IRE) (89) *(MMoubarak)* 3-7-11 ‡⁵StephenDavies (13) (hdwy 3f out:
ev ch over 1f out: nt qckn) ............................................................ 2.3
3139 Specificity (USA) (85) (Jt-Fav) *(JHMGosden)* 4-8-2 ‡⁵JWeaver (5) (b.hind:
hdwy 3f out: ev ch over 1f out: one pce) ......................................... hd.4
2844 Hajaim (IRE) (86) (Jt-Fav) *(CEBrittain)* 4-8-8 MRoberts (8) (rdn along: hdwy on
ins 3f out: one pce fnl 2f) ................................................................ ³/₄.5
3082 Hebridean (92) *(HCandy)* 5-8-7 ‡⁷AntoinetteArmes (12) (lw: nvr nrr) ............ 1¹/₂.6
2349 Close Friend (IRE) (93) *(BWHills)* 4-9-1 BRaymond (9) (nvr nr to chal) ......... 8.7
815 Lift and Load (91) *(RHannon)* 5-8-10 ‡³RPerham (15) (nvr nr ldrs) .......... 1¹/₂.8
2844 Parting Moment (USA) (97) (v) *(IABalding)* 5-9-2 ‡³SO'Gorman (16) (lw: led
after 1f tl wknd over 2f out) ............................................................. 4.9
2982a Supreme Choice (USA) (106) *(BWHills)* 4-10-0 JWilliams (10) (a bhd) .......... 5.10
3279 Rising Tempo (IRE) (73) *(CACyzer)* 4-7-9⁽²⁾ DBiggs (6) (a bhd) ................. sh.11
2446 Le Corsaire (USA) (98) *(LMCumani)* 4-9-6 LDettori (4) (lw: 5th st: wknd 3f out) 1¹/₂.12
2971* Canny Chronicle (84) *(MHTompkins)* 4-8-6 PRobinson (7) (dwlt: hdwy on ins
3f out: sn wknd) .............................................................................. hd.13
2136³ Fly Away Soon (USA) (95) *(PFICole)* 4-9-3 AClark (11) (n.d) ...................... nk.14
3139³ Roll a Dollar (89) *(DRCElsworth)* 6-8-11 BRouse (1) (dwlt: a bhd) ............. 1¹/₂.15
1464⁶ Ambiguously Regal (83) *(MrsJCecil)* 3-7-10 JQuinn (3) (led 1f: 3rd st:
led over 3f out: hdd & wknd over 2f out) .......................................... 3.16
3279 Barrish (77) *(RAkehurst)* 6-7-13 SDawson (18) (4th st: wknd over 3f out) ........ 7.17
3082⁵ Holy Zeal (81) *(DWPArbuthnot)* 6-8-3 DMcKeown (17) (2nd st: wknd over 3f out) 18
             LONG HANDICAP: Rising Tempo (IRE) 6-12.

7/1 Hajaim (IRE), Specificity (USA), **15/2** Welsh Mill (IRE), **8/1** CASTORET, **9/1** Al Karnak (IRE), Roll a Dollar, **10/1** Canny Chronicle, **14/1** Holy Zeal, **16/1** Le Corsaire (USA), Close Friend (IRE), **20/1** Barrish, **25/1** Ambiguously Regal (USA), Supreme Choice (USA), **33/1** Parting Moment (USA), Fly Away Soon (USA), Hebridean, Lift and Load (USA), **50/1** Rising Tempo (IRE). CSF £60.05, CT £506.60. Tote £9.60: £2.30 £1.70 £2.50 £2.80 (£25.20). Lady D'Avigdor-Goldsmid (LAMBOURN) bred by Mrs R. Owen-George. 18 Rn
2m 50.46 (4.76)
SF—38/31/25/29/33/29

## 3370
ROTHMANS ROYALS NORTH SOUTH CHALLENGE SERIES H'CAP (Semi-Final) (0-100)
£15140.00 (£4520.00: £2160.00: £980.00)     1m 7y (rnd)     3-35 (3-42)

| | | | |
|---|---|---|---|
| 3135* | **Lap of Luxury (76)** (WJarvis) 3–8-13 NDay (8) (6th st: led over 1f out: r.o wl) .... | | —1 |
| 3239 | Foolish Touch (53) (WJMusson) 10–7-8 JQuinn (4) (b: gd hdwy 2f out: r.o) ... | | 2¹/₂.2 |
| 3137 | Saafend (64) (Fav) (JSutcliffe) 4–8-5 MRoberts (14) (hdwy 2f out: r.o ins fns f) .. | | 2.3 |
| 3095* | Queen of Shannon (IRE) (74) (DMorris) 4–8-10 ‡⁵StephenDavies (5) (lw: 4th st: led 2f out tl over 1f out) | | 2.4 |
| 3209 | Takenhall (65) (MJFetherston-Godley) 7–8-6 LDettori (7) (lw: nvr nrr) ............. | | hd.5 |
| 2999³ | Gilderdale (82) (JWHills) 10–9-6 ‡³DHarrison (17) (lw: hdwy over 2f out: nvr nr to chal) | | s.h.6 |
| 3198 | La Bamba (72) (GAPritchard-Gordon) 6–8-13 WHood (13) (nvr trbld ldrs) ......... | | ³/₄.7 |
| 3209⁴ | Self Expression (70) (bl) (IABalding) 4–8-8 ‡³SO'Gorman (10) (lw: nvr nr ldrs) . nk.8 |
| 2999 | Swift Romance (IRE) (59) (BRMillman) 4–8-0 GBardwell (15) (lw: nrst fin) ......... | | ³/₄.9 |
| 3137 | Scales of Justice (73) (JWHills) 6–9-0 JWilliams (9) (stdy hdwy fnl 2f: r.o) ... | | 1¹/₂.10 |
| 3024 | Calpella (79) (JARToller) 3–8-11 ‡⁵JWeaver (2) (3rd st: led & hrd rdn over 2f out: sn hdd & wknd) | | ¹/₂.11 |
| 3209 | Habeta (USA) (63) (JWWatts) 6–8-4 DMcKeown (11) (n.d) ............................ | | 1¹/₂.12 |
| 0249³ | Elegant Friend (65) (v) (MHTompkins) 4–8-6 PRobinson (16) (lw: nvr nrr) .... s.h.13 |
| 2714* | Talent (USA) (87) (v) (LordHuntingdon) 4–10-0 AMunro (6) (led 4f: wknd 2f out)2¹/₂.14 |
| 2825 | Handsome Gent (76) (LordHuntingdon) 3–8-13 BRaymond (18) (n.d) ...... nk.15 |
| 3066 | Gotcha (BAR) (80) (bl) (RHannon) 3–8-12 ‡⁵JJones (12) (n.d) ..................... | | 1¹/₂.16 |
| 2684⁶ | Across the Bay (73) (v) (SDow) 5–9-0 MPerrett (3) (2nd st: led 4f out tl wknd over 2f out) | | ³/₄.17 |
| 3024 | High Low (USA) (84) (WJHaggas) 4–9-11 BRouse (5) (5th st: wknd 3f out) .. 2¹/₂.18 |

**11/2** Saafend, **15/2** Talent (USA), **8/1** Self Expression, **9/1** LAP OF LUXURY, **11/1** Queen of Shannon (IRE), **12/1** La Bamba, Elegant Friend, Takenhall, **14/1** Scales of Justice, Calpella, **16/1** Habeta, High Low (USA), Gilderdale, **20/1** Gotcha (BAR), Swift Romance (IRE), **25/1** Foolish Touch, Handsome Gent, **33/1** Across the Bay. CSF £195.86, CT £1,247.19. Tote £8.60: £2.20 £7.00 £1.60 £2.70 (£340.80). Mr I. C. Hill-Wood (NEWMARKET) bred by Langham Hall Bloodstock. 18 Rn
1m 37.74 (1.74)
SF—73/46/51/50/45/58

## 3371
ARLINGTON STKS     £4958.00 (£1484.00: £712.00: £326.00)
1m 7y (rnd)     4-10 (4-12)

| | | | |
|---|---|---|---|
| 3201* | **Tik Fa (USA) (102)** (v) (BHanbury) 3–9-0 BRaymond (6) (6th st: hdwy over 1f out: qcknd to ld ins fnl f) .................................................... | | —1 |
| 3131³ | Hazaam (USA) (Fav) (MRStoute) 3–9-2 MRoberts (4) (3rd st: led wl over 1f out tl ins fnl f) | | 2¹/₂.2 |
| 3006² | Hamas (IRE) (104) (PTWalwyn) 3–9-0 AMunro (5) (5th st: ev ch 1f out: nt qckn) s.h.3 |
| 3080³ | Alhaajib (USA) (JLDunlop) 3–8-6 LDettori (3) (4th st: rdn over 2f out: r.o ins fnl f) s.h.4 |
| 3043* | Gunner's Daughter (HCandy) 3–8-5 PRobinson (1) (b.hind: led 5f) ................. | | 5.5 |
| 3195⁶ | River Falls (105) (RHannon) 3–9-2 AClark (2) (2nd st: led 3f out tl wknd qckly wl over 1f out) | | 4.6 |

**Evens** Hazaam (USA), **9/2** Hamas (IRE), **5/1** Alhaajib (USA)(op 8/1), TIK FA (USA)(op 5/2), **12/1** River Falls, **16/1** Gunner's Daughter. CSF £10.40, Tote £5.20: £2.00 £1.40 (£4.20). Mr Abdullah Ali (NEWMARKET) bred by Hardie Scott in USA. 6 Rn
1m 38.33 (2.33)
SF—65/59/56/47/31/30

## 3372
E.B.F. HARWELL STKS (Mdn 2-Y.O) £4370.00 (£1310.00: £630.00: £290.00)
6f 8y     4-40 (4-40)

| | | | |
|---|---|---|---|
| 3011³ | **Blues Traveller (IRE)** (Fav) (BWHills) 9-0 AMunro (8) (lw: a:p: qcknd ins fnl f: led cl home) | | —1 |
| | Petersford Girl (IRE) (MissJacquelineSDoyle) 8-9 SDawson (18) (unf: hld up: led over 1f out tl nr fin) | | ¹/₂.2 |
| 2849⁵ | Sarangani Bay (USA) (PWChapple-Hyam) 9-0 AClark (10) (led tl over 1f out: nt qckn) | | 1¹/₂.3 |
| 3240 | Tickerty's Gift (RHannon) 9-0 BRouse (6) (prom 3f: r.o fnl f) ...................... | | 4.4 |
| 3035⁶ | Ground Nut (IRE) (HCandy) 9-0 CRutter (9) (lw: a:p: r.o ins fnl f) ................. | | ¹/₂.5 |
| | Pocket Piece (USA) (MRStoute) 8-9 PRobinson (7) (unf: scope: a:p: rdn & no hdwy fnl 2f) | | ³/₄.6 |

3096² Seasonal Splendour (IRE) *(CACyzer)* 8-9　DBiggs (19) (nvr nrr) .......................... hd.7
　　　Mansard (IRE) *(JHMGosden)* 9-0　MRoberts (14) (unf: prom over 4f) ................. ¹/₂.8
3160² Range Rider (IRE) **(73)** *(CEBrittain)* 9-0　JQuinn (11) (spd 4f) .......................... 1.9
　　　Top Cees *(PWHarris)* 9-0　SWhitworth (3) (leggy: n.d) ...................................... 1.10
2438 Allesca *(MDIUsher)* 8-6 ‡³DHarrison (4) (n.d) ................................................. hd.11
　　　Danny Boy *(RHannon)* 8-11 ‡³RPerham (15) (w'like: bkwd: spd over 3f) ......... hd.12
　　　Blushing Barada (USA) *(AAScott)* 8-9　BRaymond (2) (unf: b.hind: n.d) ......... 1¹/₂.13
3093 Fir Copse *(PRHedger)* 8-6·‡³SO'Gorman (13) (n.d) ..................................... 3¹/₂.14
3240 Infantry Glen *(MDIUsher)* 9-0　MWigham (17) (spd over 3f) .......................... hd.15
　　　Jadirah *(JLDunlop)* 8-9　LDettori (16) (w'like: scope: n.d) ......................... s.h.16
2948 Bold a Maiden *(DRLaing)* 8-9　GBardwell (1) (n.d) ........................................ 1.17
　　　Jewel Thief *(GBBalding)* 9-0　JWilliams (12) (w'like: bkwd: n.d) ................... ¹/₂.18
　　　Bang on Time *(GBBalding)* 9-0　MPerrett (20) (s.s: a bhd) ......................... 1¹/₂.19
　　　Roadrunner *(WGRWightman)* 9-0　TRogers (5) (unf: bit bkwd: n.d) .................. 20

**11/10** BLUES TRAVELLER (IRE), **9/2** Mansard (IRE), **9/1** Range Rider (IRE)(op 5/1), **10/1** Jadirah (USA), **12/1** Danny Boy, Sarangani Bay (USA), Seasonal Splendour (IRE), **14/1** Pocket Piece (USA)(op 7/1), **16/1** Blushing Barada (USA)(op 8/1), **20/1** Ground Nut (IRE), **33/1** Roadrunner, Petersford Girl (IRE), **50/1** Ors. CSF £42.32, Tote £2.50: £1.40 £7.60 £3.70 (£167.20). Mr Wafic Said (LAMBOURN) bred by Naver Enterprises Ltd in Ireland.
20 Rn　　　　　　　　　　　　　　　　　　　　　　　　　　　　　　1m 16.42 (4.62)
　　　　　　　　　　　　　　　　　　　　　　　　　　　　　　　　SF—20/13/12/–/–/–

T/Trio: Race 4: £80.10 (20.2 Tckts). T/Jkpt: Not won; £74,099.67 to Kempton 22/9/92. T/Plpt: £149.40 (75.59 Tckts).　　　　　　　　　　　　　　　　　　　　　　　　　　　　　　　　　　Hn

---

2781—**SOUTHWELL (L-H)** Fibresand

## Friday, September 18th [Standard]
Going Allowance: minus 0.40 sec per fur (FS)　　　　　　　　Wind: almost nil

Stalls: low

**3373**　FORD GLASS AND GLAZING LTD RACING SCHOOLS' APP'CE H'CAP (0-70) £2553.00
　　　　(£708.00: £339.00)　**7f (AWT)**　　　　　　　　　　　　　　2-30 (2-34)

3263⁶ **Tyrone Flyer (54)** *(MCPipe)* 3-9-4　StephenDavies (6) (mde all: hrd rdn over 1f
　　　out: r.o wl) ............................................................................................... —1
3017 Little Nod (59) *(JWhite)* 3-9-5 ‡⁴GMilligan (4) (4th & rdn st: edgd lft over 1f out:
　　　chsd wnr fnl f: no imp) ................................................................................. 2.2
3101 Brenda From Huby (38) *(BCMorgan)* 4-8-2 ‡⁴JTate (5) (3rd st: chsd wnr over 2f
　　　out: one pce fnl f) ................................................................................... 1¹/₂.3
3086³ Kinlacey (60) (Fav) *(BAMcMahon)* 5-9-10 ‡⁴SSanders (1) (lw: 6th & rdn st: r.o
　　　one pce fnl 2f) ............................................................................................ 2.4
3045 Charly Pharly (FR) (54) (bl) *(FHLee)* 5-9-8　NKennedy (7) (lost pl 5f out: r.o fnl
　　　2f: nvr nr to chal) ....................................................................................... 2.5
3048³ Military Expert (55) *(CaptJWilson)* 3-9-5　KRutter (11) (rdn & 7th st: no hdwy fnl
　　　2f) .............................................................................................................. ¹/₂.6
2814⁴ Bidweaya (USA) (44) *(JLEyre)* 5-8-5⁽²⁾ ‡⁷ALakeman (3) (b.nr hind: nvr nr to
　　　chal) ........................................................................................................... 1.7
2481⁵ Quinzii Martin (51) (v) *(DHaydnJones)* 4-9-1 ‡⁴PBowe (2) (8th st: no hdwy) ...... ¹/₂.8
1676⁴ In the Game (IRE) (59) *(MissAJWhitfield)* 3-9-5 ‡⁴MHarris (12) (2nd st: wknd
　　　over 2f out) ................................................................................................ 3.9
2942⁶ Johanna Thyme (36) *(RBastiman)* 5-7-11⁽³⁾ ‡⁷JAWilliams (8) (s.s: a bhd) ......... 1.10
2561 Cartel (53) *(JLHarris)* 5-9-7　SMaloney (9) (lw: 5th st: wknd 2f out) ................. ¹/₂.11
1550 Qualitair Rhythm (IRE) (50) *(ICampbell)* 4-8-11 ‡⁷GMitchell (13) (dwlt: a bhd) 1¹/₂.12
2882 Samjamalifran (36) *(MCPipe)* 3-7-10 ‡⁴SDrowne (10) (a bhd) ......................... ³/₄.13

**9/2** Kinlacey(op 11/4), **5/1** Quinzii Martin, **13/2** Charly Pharly (FR), TYRONE FLYER(4/1—15/2), **8/1** Military Expert(op 5/1), **9/1** Bidweaya (USA), **14/1** Brenda From Huby(op 50/1), **16/1** Qualitair Rhythm (IRE), **20/1** In the Game (IRE), Little Nod, Cartel, Johanna Thyme, **25/1** Samjamalifran. CSF £109.36, CT £1,583.95. Tote £7.60: £2.20 £6.10 £5.40 (£327.30). Mr J. Naughton (WELLINGTON) bred by Aston House Stud Co. 13 Rn
　　　　　　　　　　　　　　　　　　　　　　　　　　　　　　　　1m 27.9 (1.3)
　　　　　　　　　　　　　　　　　　　　　　　　　　　　　　SF—42/37/15/31/23/18

**3374**　ROYAL MOAT HOUSE STKS (Mdn 3-Y.O) £2070.00 (£570.00: £270.00)
　　　　**1m (AWT)**　　　　　　　　　　　　　　　　　　　　　　3-00 (3-03)

3192 **Auction King (IRE) (59)** (Jt-Fav) *(ASmith)* 9-0　SWebster (1) (a.p: led 4f out: rdn
　　　out) ............................................................................................................ —1
　　　Gold Surprise (IRE) *(JGFitzGerald)* 9-0 8-11 ‡³SMaloney (4) (leggy: 4th st: rdn over
　　　1f out: r.o one pce) ..................................................................................... 2.2
2237 North Flyer (60) *(BAMcMahon)* 8-7 ‡⁷SSanders (6) (wnt 2nd st: hrd rdn over 1f
　　　out: one pce) ............................................................................................. nk.3

Literary Critic (IRE) *(JARToller)* 9-0 GBaxter (7) (str: scope: dwlt: hdwy & 7th st: rdn fnl f: nt rch ldrs) ...... 2.4

2723⁴ Kirkby Belle **(46)** *(EWeymes)* 8-9 WWoods (3) (dwlt: hdwy & 6th st: one pce fnl 2f) ...... 4.5

2993 Lizzie Drippin (CAN) **(49)** *(MDIUsher)* 8-10⁽¹⁾ MWigham (11) (swtg: nvr nrr) ...... 2.6

3203 Gold Belt (IRE) **(47)** (Jt-Fav) *(RHollinshead)* 8-9 PaulEddery (9) (5th st: wknd over 2f out) ...... 1¹⁄₂.7

2969⁵ Night Gown **(45)** (v) *(MissGayKelleway)* 8-2 ‡⁷MGodsafe (8) (b: b.hind: led 4f: 3rd st: wknd 2f out) ...... 6.8

2075 Denim Blue **(54)** *(CWThornton)* 9-0 DMcKeown (12) (prom 4f: 8th & wkng st) ...... 2.9

2479⁴ Mondova (IRE) *(FHLee)* 8-9 RLappin (10) (a bhd) ...... 2.10

Damistress *(MissAJWhitfield)* 8-9 JFortune (2) (unf: dwlt: a bhd) ...... 2¹⁄₂.11

3142⁴ Miss Limelight *(ASmith)* 8-9 NAdams (5) (a bhd) ...... 4.12

5/1 Gold Belt (IRE), AUCTION KING (IRE), 6/1 Denim Blue(op 4/1), 8/1 North Flyer(5/1—10/1), Lizzie Drippin (CAN), 10/1 Literary Critic (IRE), 12/1 Gold Surprise (IRE)(op 6/1), 14/1 Kirkby Belle(op 8/1), Night Gown(op 8/1), 16/1 Mondova (IRE)(op 8/1), 20/1 Ors. CSF £55.26, Tote £5.50: £2.20 £3.10 £3.00 (£44.80). Mr David Tate (BEVERLEY) bred by Dollys Grove Stud in Ireland. 12 Rn    1m 42.8 (3.5)

## 3375

CHESHIRES OF NOTTINGHAM CLAIMING STKS (I)    £2385.00 (£660.00: £315.00)
7f (AWT)      3-30 (3-33)

1500⁵ **Skipper to Bilge (67)** *(MAJarvis)* 5-8-5 ‡⁵KRutter (6) (5th st: hdwy over 1f out: led last strides) ...... —1

3203 Gymcrak Tycoon **(74)** *(MHEasterby)* 3-8-5 ‡³SMaloney (8) (s.s: gd hdwy over 1f out: ev ch wl ins fnl f: r.o) ...... s.h.2

2898 Ringland (USA) **(80)** (Fav) *(PCHaslam)* 4-9-0 DMcKeown (7) (2nd st: led 2f out tl last strides) ...... hd.3

2804⁵ Sally's Son **(80)** (bl) *(WAO'Gorman)* 6-8-7 ‡³EmmaO'Gorman (1) (led 5f out to 2f out: one peo) ...... 5.4

2742 Scottish Park **(67)** *(JPLeach)* 3-7-10 ‡⁵NKennedy (9) (6th st: no hdwy fnl 2f) ..... hd.5

3185³ Whitehall (IRE) **(64)** *(CRNelson)* 3-8-3 NAdams (10) (5th & rdn st: no hdwy fnl 2f) ...... 1¹⁄₂.6

2937 Bobbie Bold **(33)** *(TKersey)* 4-8-3⁽¹⁾ SWebster (11) (b: nvr nrr) ...... nk.7

3182 Annabelle Royale **(75)** *(MrsNMacauley)* 6-9-2 DBiggs (2) (lw: nrst fin) ...... ³⁄₄.8

2680 Palacegate King **(57)** *(JBerry)* 3-8-5 JFortune (5) (led 2f: 4th & rdn st: wknd 2f out) ...... 3.9

3042 Nellie Dean **(58)** *(JARToller)* 3-7-8 EJohnson (3) (8th & wkng whn hmpd on ins st) ...... hd.10

2352⁵ Creselly **(58)** *(JGFitzGerald)* 5-8-2 PaulEddery (4) (b.off hind: 7th & wkng st) hd.11

9/4 Ringland (USA)(6/4—5/2), 7/1 Sally's Son, 8/1 SKIPPER TO BILGE, Gymcrak Tycoon(op 5/1), Palacegate King(op 12/1), 10/1 Nellie Dean(op 5/1), Creselly, 12/1 Scottish Park(op 8/1), Annabelle Royale, Whitehall (IRE)(op 8/1), 50/1 Bobbie Bold. CSF £64.80, Tote £9.90: £2.80 £2.50 £1.50 (£20.70). Mrs J. R. Collins (NEWMARKET) bred by J. R. Collins. 11 Rn    1m 28 (1.4)

## 3376

HALL & CO STKS (Mdn 2-Y.O) £2553.00 (£708.00: £339.00)    **6f (AWT)** 4-00 (4-04)

3163⁴ **Iolite** *(MAJarvis)* 8-9 GCrealock (2) (mde all: rdn over 1f out: r.o wl) ...... —1

3055 Persian Gusher (IRE) *(SDow)* 9-0 GBaxter (9) (5th st: hdwy 2f out: chsd wnr fnl f: r.o) ...... 1¹⁄₂.2

3115 Jocks Joker *(CaptJWilson)* 8-9 ‡⁵KRutter (6) (2nd st: r.o one pce fnl 2f) ...... 1¹⁄₂.3

2986⁴ Queen of the Quorn **(70)** *(GMMoore)* 9-0 DMcKeown (10) (4th st: one pce fnl 2f) ...... 5.4

3051 Disco Boy *(BAMcMahon)* 8-7 ‡⁷SSanders (11) (7th st: no hdwy fnl 2f) ...... s.h.5

3044 Daring King **(57)** *(DSasse)* 8-9 ‡⁵RPrice (1) (b: nvr nr to chal) ...... 1¹⁄₂.6

3156⁶ Patong Beach (Fav) *(JWHills)* 8-9 PaulEddery (3) (3rd st: wknd 2f out) ...... 6.7

3077⁶ She's a Breeze *(ASmith)* 8-9 NAdams (4) (8th st: no hdwy) ...... 1.8

3117 Mr Dingle *(WJHaggas)* 9-0 NDay (8) (b: n.d) ...... ¹⁄₂.9

2842 Sounds Risky **(47)** *(MissSJWilton)* 8-2 ‡⁷CHawksley (15) (dwlt: a bhd) ...... nk.10

2960 El Guapo **(64)** *(TFairhurst)* 9-0 DBiggs (13) (a bhd) ...... nk.11

900⁴ Broadstairs Beauty (IRE) *(MCChapman)* 9-0 SWebster (16) (dwlt: a bhd) ...... s.h.12

Scottish Temptress *(JPLeigh)* 8-4 ‡⁵NKennedy (14) (neat: bkwd: s.s: a bhd) ...... 4.13

3172 Young Geninsky (bl) *(RJWeaver)* 8-2 ‡⁷PBowe (5) (s.s: a bhd) ...... 2.14

759 Prawn Cracker (IRE) **(45)** *(JLEyre)* 8-4 ‡⁵OPears (12) (6th st: wknd over 2f out) ...... ¹⁄₂.15

5/2 Patong Beach, 3/1 IOLITE(op 7/4), 5/1 Mr Dingle(op 3/1), 10/1 Queen of the Quorn, 12/1 Daring King(op 20/1), 14/1 Disco Boy, Persian Gusher (IRE), Broadstairs Beauty (IRE), 16/1 Scottish Temptress, She's a Breeze, 20/1 Sounds Risky, Young Geninsky, El Guapo, Jocks Joker, 33/1 Prawn Cracker (IRE). CSF £48.12, Tote £3.60: £1.50 £2.30 £2.10 (£19.80). Mr R. P. Marchant (NEWMARKET) bred by Red House Stud. 15 Rn    1m 14.9 (1.5)

**3377** NATIONAL PLANT & TRANSPORT PLC H'CAP (0-70) £2511.00 (£696.00: £333.00)
2m (AWT)
4-30 (4-32)

(Weights raised 11 lb)

3177 **Shakinski (56)** (v) (Fav) (MJRyan) 3-8-13 DBiggs (7) (gd hdwy 7f out: led 4f out: comf) .................................................. —1

362 Peak District (38) (KSBridgwater) 6-8-7 NAdams (3) (hdwy 6f out: wnt 2nd st: r.o one pce fnl 2f) .................................................. 2.2

3075 Scalp 'em (IRE) (31) (FHLee) 4-8-0(1) RLappin (8) (led 8f out to 4f out: 3rd st: wknd 2f out) .................................................. 6.3

2467³ Escadaro (USA) (39) (v) (SGNorton) 3-7-3 ‡⁷CHawksley (1) (wl bhd 8f out: r.o fnl 2f: nrst fin) .................................................. 5.4

1002 Suluk (USA) (44) (RHollinshead) 7-8-6 ‡⁷MHumphries (6) (hld up & plld hrd: wl bhd 8f out: nvr nrr) .................................................. 2.5

3282 Free Transfer (IRE) (67) (PFTulk) 3-9-10 AShoults (4) (prom: 4th & wkng st) ... 12.6

22785 Count My Blessings (43) (JLEyre) 7-8-7 ‡⁵OPears (10) (b: prom: wkng from st: poor 5th st) .................................................. 5.7

3053³ Bayadere (USA) (56) (v) (MRStoute) 3-8-13 PaulEddery (9) (prom along: led after 3f to 8f out: wknd qckly over 4f out: poor 6th st) ...... 1½.8

3174 Pims Classic (53) (JLHarris) 4-9-8 DMcKeown (12) (prom 11f) .................................................. s.h.9

2687 Dotterel (IRE) (36) (RGBrazington) 4-8-5 BCrossley (5) (wl bhd 8f out: t.o) ... 30.10

Clwyd Lodge (40) (bl) (RTJuckes) 5-8-9 AMcGlone (2) (led 3f: wl bhd 8f out: t.o) .................................................. 15.11

1977 Sir Vidar (IRE) (56) (bl) (MBell) 3-8-13 JFortune (11) (p.u & collapsed after 4f: dead) .................................................. 0

11/4 SHAKINSKI, 3/1 Bayadere (USA)(op 7/4), 13/2 Escadaro (USA), 8/1 Peak District, 10/1 Suluk (USA)(op 6/1), 12/1 Free Transfer (IRE), 14/1 Dotterel (IRE), 16/1 Pims Classic, Sir Vidar (IRE)(op 10/1), 20/1 Count My Blessings, Clwyd Lodge, 25/1 Scalp 'em (IRE). CSF £24.69, CT £431.90. Tote £4.70: £1.50 £1.90 £3.90 (£25.20). Mr N. H. Tampkins (NEWMARKET) bred by Miss K. Rausing. 12 Rn 3m 40.6 (14.6)

**3378** CHESHIRES OF NOTTINGHAM CLAIMING STKS (II) £2385.00 (£660.00: £315.00)
7f (AWT)
5-00 (5-07)

27855 **Gallery Artist (IRE) (57)** (RGuest) 4-8-0(1) ‡⁷SEiffert (6) (wnt 2nd & rdn st: led over 2f out: clr over 1f out: r.o) .................................................. —1

31766 Eastleigh (70) (Jt-Fav) (RHollinshead) 3-8-8 PaulEddery (7) (6th st: hdwy over 1f out: r.o ins fnl f) .................................................. 1½.2

472 Empeeka (USA) (86) (h) (WAO'Gorman) 3-8-7 ‡³EmmaO'Gorman (2) (bhd tl gd hdwy over 1f out: rdn & r.o one pce fnl f) .................................................. hd.3

3290 Executive Spirit (65) (DSasse) 3-8-5 ‡⁵RPrice (3) (7th st: hdwy over 1f out: nt rch ldrs) .................................................. 3.4

2785 Lock Keeper (USA) (55) (JMackie) 3-8-8 NDay (5) (rdn along & sn lost pl: rallied & nt clr run 2f out: r.o one pce) .................................................. ¾.5

3170 Coastal Express (77) (Jt-Fav) (EWeymes) 3-8-9 WWoods (4) (led 1f: 8th & wkng st) .................................................. 2.6

2804 Trove (79) (MrsNMacauley) 3-8-1 ‡⁷MadeleineSmith (1) (4th st: wknd 2f out) .. hd.7

2785 Wellsy Lad (56) (DWChapman) 5-8-8 GBaxter (10) (a bhd) .................................................. 3.8

31672 Daily Sport Girl (49) (bl) (RTJuckes) 3-7-12(1) AMcGlone (11) (prom: led 3f out: sn hdd & wknd) .................................................. 2.9

3151 Lowlands Boy (46) (TFairhurst) 3-7-11 ‡⁵NKennedy (9) (5th st: wknd over 2f out) 3.10

2984 Parisienne King (USA) (33) (bl) (FHLee) 3-8-0(2) RLappin (8) (led after 1f to 3f out: 3rd st: wknd qckly: t.o) .................................................. 15.11

3/1 Eastleigh(7/2—5/1), Coastal Express(5/1—5/2), 5/1 Empeeka (USA)(2/1—11/2), 7/1 Lock Keeper (USA)(10/1—12/1), 10/1 Wellsy Lad (USA), Daily Sport Girl, 12/1 Executive Spirit(op 8/1), Trove, GALLERY ARTIST (IRE), 20/1 Lowlands Boy, 25/1 Parisienne King (USA). CSF £49.13, Tote £17.20: £3.60 £1.50 £2.10 (£37.60). Mr Rae Guest (NEWMARKET) bred by Viscount de Vesci in Ireland. 11 Rn 1m 28.7 (2.1)
SF—12/15/13/2/3/—

**3379** EAST MIDLANDS ELECTRICITY H'CAP (0-70) £2532.00 (£702.00: £336.00)
1½m (AWT)
5-30 (5-33)

3057 **Cathos (FR) (51)** (DAWilson) 7-8-11 MWigham (3) (b: dwlt: 8th st: gd hdwy over 1f out: led ins fnl f: r.o) .................................................. —1

15666 Sea Paddy (50) (RBastiman) 4-8-3 ‡⁷HBastiman (10) (hdwy & 6th st: ev ch fnl f: r.o) .................................................. 1.2

27216 Not Yet (42) (EWeymes) 8-8-2 JFortune (1) (sn rdn along: 5th st: ev ch ins fnl f: hrd rdn & r.o) .................................................. 1.3

2896 Premier Dance (47) (DHaydnJones) 5-8-2 ‡⁵NGwilliams (4) (3rd st: led wl over 1f out tl ins fnl f) .................................................. 2.4

2968 Tempering (68) (DWChapman) 6-10-0 GBaxter (11) (swtg: chsd ldr: 2nd st: led over 2f out tl wl over 1f out: wknd ins fnl f) .................................................. nk.5

3192 Qualitair Sound (IRE) **(60)** *(JFBottomley)* 4-9-6 DMcKeown (6) (4th st: one pce fnl 2f) ........................................................................................ 3.6

2828 Admiralty Way **(40)** *(RBrotherton)* 6-8-0 DBiggs (5) (lw: 7th st: no hdwy fnl 2f) nk.7

2784* Must Be Magical (USA) **(40)** (bl) *(Fav)* *(FHLee)* 4-8-0[5] RLappin (2) (led over 9f: wknd qckly) ........................................................................ 6.8

31616 Remwood Girl **(33)** *(KSBridgwater)* 6-7-7 NAdams (8) (rdn 7f out: bhd fnl 3f) . 2¹/₂.9

3076 Queens Tour **(39)** *(MBrittain)* 7-7-10[6] ‡3SMaloney (9) (b: b.hind: rdn 8f out: a bhd) ............................................................................................ ³/₄.10

Kronprinz (IRE) **(43)** *(MCChapman)* 4-8-3 SWebster (7) (a in rr: t.o) ............... 30.11

LONG HANDICAP: Remwood Girl 7-0, Queens Tour 7-4.

**3/1** Must Be Magical (USA), **6/1** Sea Paddy(op 4/1), Qualitair Sound (IRE), **7/1** Not Yet, **8/1** Tempering, **9/1** Admiralty Way, CATHOS (FR), **10/1** Premier Dance, **11/1** Remwood Girl, **14/1** Ors. CSF £61.71, CT £375.70. Tote £7.80: £2.70 £3.00 £2.20 (£65.40). Mr Peter J. Allen (EPSOM) bred by M. Olivier Nicol in France. 11 Rn

2m 40.1 (5.9)

T/Plpt: £1,370.20 (1 Tckt). KH

---

2719—**CATTERICK (L-H)**

**Saturday, September 19th [Good]**

Going Allowance: 5f: minus 0.10 sec (F); Rest: 0.10 sec per fur (G) Vis:mod

Stalls: low Wind: slt across

**3380** L.J.A. H'CAP (Ladies) (0-70) £2679.00 (£744.00: £357.00) 1¹/₂m 44y 2-15 (2-17)

3157* **Carrolls Marc (IRE) (50)** *(P.IFeilden)* 4-10-4 MissJFeilden (14) (b.hind: hdwy 7f out: rdn to ld jst ins fnl f: r.o) ............................ —1

31434 Dominant Serenade **(49)** *(MDHammond)* 3-9-9 MissIDWJones (3) (stdy hdwy 3f out: r.o wl fnl f: nt rch wnr) ...................................... ³/₄.2

3177 The Karaoke King **(54)** (bl) *(RHannon)* 3-9-9 ‡5MrsJBoggis (11) (led: sn clr: hdd over 5f out: rallied appr fnl f) ........................... 2¹/₂.3

29854 Kayartis **(40)** *(Fav)* *(MrsGRReveley)* 3-9-0 MissMJuster (8) (lw: sn chsng ldr: led over 5f out: rdn clr 3f out: hdd & wknd jst ins fnl f) ........ ¹/₂.4

3141 Jubilata (USA) **(40)** *(MPNaughton)* 4-9-8 MrsAFarrell (12) (styd on fnl 2f: nt rch ldrs) ...................................................................... 5.5

32565 Bronze Runner **(38)** (bl) *(EAWheeler)* 8-8-13[6] ‡7MissLNicoll (10) (hdwy 5f out: one pce fnl 2f) ....................................................... s.h.6

23312 Iota **(62)** *(MrsJCecil)* 3-10-8 MrsJCrossley (9) (lw: hdwy 5f out: no imp fnl 3f) . ¹/₂.7

25534 Latvian **(67)** *(RAllan)* 5-11-7 MissJThurlow (5) (chsd ldrs tl lost pl 5f out: sme hdwy over 2f out: n.d) ............................................ 1.8

27755 Pennine Star (IRE) **(54)** *(CWCleary)* 4-10-1 ‡7MissAElsey (1) (bhd: effrt on outside over 2f out: n.d) ...................................... 1¹/₂.9

3170 Watch Me Go (IRE) **(51)** *(RHannon)* 3-9-6 ‡5MissDianaJones (7) (plld hrd: trckd ldrs: effrt over 3f out: sn wknd) .......................... nk.10

31526 Corporate Type (IRE) **(32)** *(GPKelly)* 4-8-7 ‡7MrsMSandercock (4) (a in rr) .. 1¹/₂.11

2867 Gulfland **(33)** *(GAPritchard-Gordon)* 11-8-8[1] ‡7MissCPreston (2) (s.i.s: a bhd) ¹/₂.12

3073 Rap Up Fast (USA) **(40)** *(CWThornton)* 3-8-7 ‡7MissDWilkinson (6) (a bhd) ..... 12.13

Shawiniga **(38)** *(LLungo)* 6-9-1 ‡5MrsLLeggat (16) (chsd ldrs tl lost pl over 2f out) ...................................................................... hd.14

3101 Apple **(38)** *(WHolden)* 3-9-8 ‡5MissKHolden (13) (chsd ldrs tl wknd 5f out) ...... 15

30973 Thimbalina **(36)** *(DAWilson)* 6-8-13 ‡5MissLHide (15) (b: sddle slipped: bhd fnl 5f) ...................................................................... 16

LONG HANDICAP: Kayartis 8-13, Corporate Type (IRE) 8-4, Gulfland 8-9, Rap Up Fast (USA) 8-8.

**5/1** Kayartis, **13/2** Thimbalina, The Karaoke King, CARROLLS MARC (IRE), **15/2** Dominant Serenade, **8/1** Iota, **9/1** Bronze Runner, **10/1** Latvian, **24/1** Pennine Star (IRE), **16/1** Watch Me Go (IRE), Jubilata (USA), **25/1** Shawiniga, **33/1** Ors. CSF £305.73, Tote £9.00: £1.90 £3.00 £2.50 £1.50 (£53.78). Mr P. Panayiotou (NEWMARKET) bred by John Connaughton in Ireland. 16 Rn 2m 43.3 (9.3)

SF—37/26/21/11/9/–

**3381** SKYRAM H'CAP (0-70) £3288.00 (£984.00: £472.00: £216.00)
1m 5f 175y 2-50 (2-52)

3143* **Corn Lily (69)** *(Fav)* *(MrsGRReveley)* 6-9-7 ‡7DarrenMoffatt (6) (lw: s.i.s: hdwy & prom 7f out: led 5f out: styd on wl fnl 2f: jst hld on) .......... —1

3206 Bold Ambition **(37)** *(TKersey)* 5-7-10 JLowe (2) (lw: w ldrs: led 8f out to 5f out: styd on wl fnl f) ........................................ hd.2

2985 Maji **(66)** *(DMorley)* 3-9-1 GDuffield (4) (a.p: hrd drvn 3f out: styd on wl fnl f: nt qckn nr fin) ....................................... nk.3

2244² Northern Kingdom (USA) **(67)** *(SGNorton)* 3-9-2 JFortune (1) (led to 8f out: ev ch tl outpcd fnl f) .................................................................. ³/₄.4

3177 Bilberry **(45)** *(CWCElsey)* 3-7-8⁽¹⁾ EJohnson (15) (trckd ldrs: brought wd ent st: edgd lft & kpt on wl fnl f) ....................................................... nk.5

3169³ Landed Gentry (USA) **(64)** *(PWChapple-Hyam)* 3-8-10 ‡³FNorton (3) (hdwy & prom 6f out: styd on fnl 2f: nt rch ldrs) ................................. 1.6

2470⁴ Anar (IRE) **(47)** *(WCarter)* 3-7-3⁽²⁾ ‡⁷CHawksley (9) (trckd ldrs: drvn along 7f out: styd on same pce fnl 2f) ............................................... ¹/₂.7

3177⁵ Nicely Thanks (USA) **(59)** *(TDBarron)* 3-8-8 JFanning (12) (bhd: drvn along 6f out: prom over 1f out: sn wknd) ............................................ 4.8

3075 Fiery Sun **(36)** (v) *(REBarr)* 7-7-2⁽²⁾ ‡⁷ClaireBalding (13) (a in rr) ............. 7.9

3149 Cheeky Pot **(40)** (bl) *(DenysSmith)* 4-7-13 LCharnock (5) (lw: trckd ldrs tl lost pl over 2f out) ........................................................................ 3.10

2964⁵ Top Prize **(40)** *(MBrittain)* 4-7-13 AMcGlone (7) (bhd fnl 5f) ............... 2.11

892³ Litho Bold Flasher **(52)** *(CaptJWilson)* 3-7-12 ‡³SMaloney (8) (a in rr: drvn along 5f out) ..................................................................... s.h.12

3102 Highland Battle (USA) **(63)** *(IABalding)* 3-8-12 WRyan (11) (chsd ldrs tl lost pl 6f out) .............................................................................. 5.13

2957 Dancing Days **(35)** (bl) *(JParkes)* 6-7-8 DaleGibson (10) (b: bhd & hrd drvn 5f out) ............................................................................... hd.14

2204⁴ Statia (IRE) **(38)** *(DonEnricoIncisa)* 4-7-4⁽⁴⁾ ‡⁷NicolaHowarth (14) (b: a wl bhd) 1.15

LONG HANDICAP: Fiery Sun 6-13, Statia (IRE) 7-0.

**11/8** CORN LILY, **8/1** Maji, **10/1** Landed Gentry (USA), Highland Battle (USA), Nicely Thanks (USA), Northern Kingdom (USA), Anar (IRE), Cheeky Pot, **16/1** Bold Ambition, **25/1** Top Prize, Bilberry, Dancing Days, **33/1** Statia (IRE), Litho Bold Flasher, **50/1** Fiery Sun. CSF £25.87, CT £142.81. Tote £2.40: £1.10 £3.80 £3.50 (£17.00). Mrs Susan McDonald (SALTBURN) bred by Countess of Durham. 15 Rn           3m 3.6 (8.4)

SF—37/11/29/28/5/19

---

## 3382

E.B.F. ASKRIGG STKS (Mdn 2-Y.O) £2880.50 (£798.00: £381.50)  **5f**  3-25 (3-26)

**Dr Lechter** *(SMHillen)* 9-0 JLowe (6) (leggy: unf: scope: sn bhd: gd hdwy over 1f out: fin fast to ld post) ................................................. —1

3049² Hills Raceaid (IRE) **(67)** (bl) *(JBerry)* 8-9 GDuffield (10) (led over 1f out: r.o u.p: eased nr fin & jst ct) ............................................... s.h.2

2781⁵ Comet Whirlpool (IRE) *(BBeasley)* 8-9 ‡⁵SWilliams (9) (w ldrs: led ¹/₂-wy tl over 1f out: kpt on u.p nr fin) .................................................. ³/₄.3

3179³ Kimbolton Korker **(68)** *(AAScott)* 8-9 JFortune (8) (b.hind: a chsng ldrs: rdn 2f out: kpt on same pce) ...................................................... 1¹/₂.4

3179² Mysterious Ways (FR) **(76)** (Fav) *(MrsJCecil)* 9-0 WRyan (1) (chsd ldrs: rdn 2f out: wknd over 1f out) ................................................... 2.5

3123 Milbank Challenger **(62)** (bl) *(MHEasterby)* 8-11 ‡³SMaloney (3) (w ldrs tl wknd over 1f out) ............................................................ ¹/₂.6

2965² High Romance *(DMoffatt)* 8-2 ‡⁷DarrenMoffatt (5) (s.i.s: sn chsng ldrs: outpcd ¹/₂-wy: kpt on fnl f) .................................................... s.h.7

1435⁴ Meconopsis *(TFairhurst)* 8-9 JFanning (7) (s.i.s: sn in tch: kpt on fnl f: n.d) ..... hd.8

3163 Pretty Average *(TCraig)* 8-9 LCharnock (4) (led to ¹/₂-wy: wknd 2f out) ....... 2¹/₂.9

1923 Honeymoon Dawn *(RMWhitaker)* 8-2 ‡⁷GParkin (2) (chsd ldrs tl wknd 2f out) .. ¹/₂.10

*Stewards Enquiry: Duffield fined £750 under Rule 151 (ii) (failure to ensure best possible placing).*

**2/1** Mysterious Ways (FR), **3/1** Hills Raceaid (IRE), **7/2** High Romance, **9/2** Kimbolton Korker, **12/1** Milbank Challenger, **16/1** Meconopsis, **25/1** DR LECHTER, Comet Whirlpool, **33/1** Ors. CSF £98.90, Tote £32.60: £4.30 £1.80 £6.20 (£154.40). Skyline Racing Ltd (CORSE LAWN) bred by C. A. Blackwell. 10 Rn   60.5 sec (3)

SF—30/24/21/15/12/7

---

## 3383

JOHN SMITH'S BITTER H'CAP (0-70) £3496.00 (£1048.00: £504.00: £232.00)  **7f**  4-00 (4-04)

3166 **Blue Grit (55)** *(MDods)* 6-9-5 JLowe (8) (in tch: hdwy & brought wd over 2f out: r.o wl tl to ld wl ins fnl f) ................................................ —1

2987 Glenfield Greta **(57)** *(PSFelgate)* 4-9-7 WRyan (10) (hld up: brought wd st: hdwy & sltly hmpd over 1f out: wl on wl fnl f) ............................ ³/₄.2

2366⁶ Gallery Note (IRE) **(48)** *(BWHills)* 3-8-8 GBaxter (14) (chsd ldrs: swtchd stands' side over 2f out: r.o u.p fnl f) ................................................ s.h.3

3287 Henry Will **(36)** *(TFairhurst)* 8-7-11 ‡³FNorton (5) (styd on fnl 2f: nt rch ldrs) .. 1¹/₂.4

2942² Cool Enough **(39)** *(MrsJRRamsden)* 11-8-3 PBurke (2) (lw: hld up: hdwy to ld jst ins fnl f: hdd & wknd nr fin) ............................................... ¹/₂.5

2966 Euroblake **(64)** *(TDBarron)* 5-10-0 JFanning (6) (swtg: styd on wl appr fnl f: nt rch ldrs) ............................................................................ 1.6

3024 Leave it to Lib **(61)** *(PCalver)* 5-9-4 ‡⁷JTate (15) (stdy hdwy 2f out: r.o nr fin) ... nk.7

3105 Susanna's Secret **(42)** (bl) *(WCarter)* 5-8-6 DaleGibson (11) (chsd ldrs: nt qckn fnl 2f) ............................................................................ 1.8

2984 Legitim **(34)** *(JMJefferson)* 3–7–1 ‡[7]DarrenMoffatt (13) (styd on fnl 2f: nvr nr to chal) ........................................................................................................................ s.h.9

2952* Anatroccolo **(43)** (Fav) *(RABennett)* 5–8–7 GDuffield (19) (chsd ldrs tl wknd over 1f out) ........................................................................................... hd.10

1791[2] Most Surprising (IRE) **(57)** *(RMWhitaker)* 3–8–10 ‡[7]GParkin (16) (nvr rchd ldrs) .. nk.11

2730[5] Gott's Desire **(46)** *(RBastiman)* 6–8–3[(6)] ‡[7]HBastiman (17) (led over 5f out: rdn & edgd rt over 1f out: hdd & wknd jst ins fnl f) ...................... ½.12

3153 Oyston's Life **(48)** (bl) *(JBerry)* 3–8–8 JFortune (4) (s.i.s: a in rr) ........................ 1.13

3153[5] Malcesine (IRE) **(45)** (v) *(CaptJWilson)* 3–8–2 ‡[3]SMaloney (3) (s.i.s: sn rcvrd: chsd ldrs tl lost pl 2f out) ................................................... s.h.14

     Diamond Inthe Dark (USA) **(63)** *(CTinkler)* 4–9–13 TLucas (12) (led over 1f: chsd ldrs tl wknd 2f out) ............................................................ ½.15

2988[3] April Shadow **(51)** *(CWThornton)* 3–8–11 AMcGlone (18) (in tch tl lost pl over 2f out) ...................................................................................................... nk.16

2723 Brambles Way **(55)** *(WLBarker)* 3–8–8 ‡[7]CHawksley (9) (hld up: a bhd) ......... 1½.17

3196 Manuleader **(63)** (bl) *(BBeasley)* 3–9–4 ‡[5]SWilliams (1) (w ldrs tl lost pl 2f out: eased whn no ch) .................................................................................. 1½.18

2966 New Beginning **(32)** *(JSHaldane)* 9–7–10[(3)] LCharnock (20) (in tch tl wknd over 2f out) ...................................................................................................... 5.19

    86 Sno Serenade **(63)** *(MDods)* 6–9–13 SWebster (7) (nvr nr ldrs) ........................... 1.20

          LONG HANDICAP: New Beginning 7-6.

**6/1** Anatroccolo, **15/2** Cool Enough, **9/1** Euroblake, **11/1** Most Surprising (IRE), **14/1** Glenfield Greta, BLUE GRIT, Gott's Desire, Susanna's Secret, Oyston's Life, Leave it to Lib, **16/1** Manuleader, Malcesine (IRE), Brambles Way, April Shadow, **20/1** Gallery Note (IRE), Legitim, **25/1** Sno Serenade, Henry Will, **33/1** Ors. CSF £183.28, CT £3,533.49. Tote £10.20: £2.50 £4.30 £6.40 £4.50 (£105.10). Mr C. Michael Wilson (DARLINGTON) bred by Collinstown Stud Farm Ltd. 20 Rn        1m 28.3 (5.1)
                                           SF–39/39/25/9/13/35

---

## 3384     MIDDLEHAM CLAIMING STKS (3-Y.O) £2448.00 (£678.00: £324.00)
           **1m 5f 175y**                                   4-30 (4-33)

3021[6] **Upper House (62)** *(GWragg)* 9-2 GDuffield (4) (lw: chsd ldrs: brought stands' side: led over 1f out: drvn clr) ............................................... —1

3246* Lyn's Return (IRE) **(60)** *(RSimpson)* 8-10 ‡[5]ATucker (2) (hld up: gd hdwy on ins over 2f out: kpt on: no ch w wnr) ............................. 6.2

3266[2] Kasikci **(74)** *(RHollinshead)* 7-6[(4)] ‡[7]MHumphries (3) (mde most tl over 1f out: one pce) ........................................................................... 1½.3

3263 Iron Baron **(54)** *(RHollinshead)* 8-6 WRyan (1) (effrt 5f out: kpt on fnl 2f) 1½.4

3141[5] Shadanza (IRE) **(63)** *(APStringer)* 8-3 ‡[3]SMaloney (7) (chsd ldrs tl wknd over 1f out) ¾.5

3114[3] Surf Boat **(67)** (Fav) *(BWHills)* 8-4 GBaxter (5) (b.hind: swtg: chsd ldrs: effrt over 2f out: sn wknd) ......................................................... 10.6

3141 Mr News (IRE) **(35)** (v) *(BBeasley)* 8-2 JLowe (9) (racd wd: jnd ldr 7f out: lost pl & eased over 2f out) ...................................................... 12.7

     Mistic Glen (IRE) *(JParkes)* 7-10 LCharnock (6) (rangy: unf: bit bkwd: chsd ldrs tl lost pl 5f out: sn bhd) ............................................ 5.8

3062 Heavy Rock **(58)** *(DJSCosgrove)* 8-7 DaleGibson (8) (trckd ldrs tl wknd over 4f out: sn bhd) ..................................................................... 5.9

3078 West Auckland *(NChamberlain)* 8-4 SWebster (10) (bit bkwd: racd wd: sn bhd: t.o fnl f) ........................................................................................... 10

**5/4** Surf Boat, **7/2** Kasikci, **13/2** UPPER HOUSE, **15/2** Shadanza (IRE), **17/2** Lyn's Return (IRE), **12/1** Iron Baron (IRE), Mr News (IRE), **50/1** Mistic Glen (IRE), Heavy Rock (IRE), **66/1** West Auckland. CSF £57.16, Tote £5.50: £2.20 £2.10 £2.00 (£12.10). Sir Philip Oppenheimer (NEWMARKET) bred by Hascombe and Valiant Studs. 10 Rn                                                3m 4.9 (9.7)
                                               SF–19/1/–/–/–/–

---

## 3385     BEDALE NURSERY   £3392.00 (£1016.00: £488.00: £224.00)    **7f**      5-00 (5-03)

3148* **Hi Nod (67)** (Jt-Fav) *(MJCamacho)* 8-2 LCharnock (7) (trckd ldrs: led over 1f out: pushed out) ...................................................................... —1

3218[4] Warm Spell **(65)** *(RSimpson)* 7-9[(3)] ‡[5]ATucker (6) (sn bhd: gd hdwy 2f out: styd on wl fnl f: nt rch wnr) ...................................... 1.2

3148 Dead Calm **(58)** *(CTinkler)* 7-7 JLowe (4) (hdwy & ev ch 2f out: r.o same pce appr fnl f) ............................................................................... 1½.3

3148 Warkworth (USA) **(67)** (bl) *(JWWatts)* 8-2 GDuffield (8) (led after 1f: hrd rdn & hdd over 1f out: kpt on) ......................................... ¾.4

3148[4] Contract Elite (IRE) **(61)** *(CWThornton)* 3-7 ‡[7]CHawksley (10) (a chsng ldrs: kpt on same pce fnl 2f) ................................................................ ½.5

3164* Rocket to the Moon (IRE) **(83)** (Jt-Fav) *(PWChapple-Hyam)* 9-1 ‡[3]FNorton (12) (chsd ldrs: effrt 2f out: styd on same pce) .......................... hd.6

2724[2] Missed the Boat (IRE) **(66)** *(TDBarron)* 8-1 JFanning (14) (hld up: stdy hdwy 2f out: nvr plcd to chal) ..................... 1½.**7**

3123[6] Goodbye Millie **(67)** *(SGNorton)* 8-2[(2)] JFortune (1) (chsd ldrs: racd far side: lost pl over 1f out) ..................... 4.**8**

3077 Public Way (IRE) **(61)** *(NChamberlain)* 7-10 DaleGibson (13) (in tch tl lost pl over 2f out) ..................... ½.**9**

2983★ Persian Traveller (IRE) **(66)** *(MrsJRRamsden)* 8-1 PBurke (11) (lw: chsd ldrs tl wknd 2f out) ..................... nk.**10**

2285[4] Nancy (IRE) **(66)** *(CWCElsey)* 8-1 EJohnson (9) (a in rr) ..................... 1½.**11**

3091[6] Mhemeanles **(86)** *(MHEasterby)* 9-4 ‡[3]SMaloney (3) (a bhd) ..................... nk.**12**

2546[6] Brigadore Gold **(58)** *(RHannon)* 7-0 ‡[7]DarrenMoffatt (2) (chsd ldr: racd far side: lost pl 2f out) ..................... 2½.**13**

2951[4] Leave a Kiss **(74)** *(IABalding)* 8-9 WRyan (5) (led 1f: chsd ldrs tl wknd qckly over 2f out) ..................... 5.**14**

LONG HANDICAP: Dead Calm 7-4.

**4/1** Rocket to the Moon (IRE), HI NOD, **13/2** Persian Traveller (IRE), **7/1** Contract Elite, **8/1** Missed the Boat (IRE), **9/1** Mhemeanles, **12/1** Nancy (IRE), Goodbye Millie, **14/1** Leave a Kiss, Brigadore Gold, **16/1** Warm Spell, **20/1** Warkworth (USA), **25/1** Dead Calm, **33/1** Public Way (IRE). CSF £65.74, CT £1,350.88. Tote £3.10: £2.30 £4.40 £4.70 (£41.60). Mr Brian Nordan (MALTON) bred by B. Nordan. 14 Rn ..................... 1m 27.7 (4.5)
SF—31/21/14/21/6/31

## 3386

LEVY BOARD STKS (Mdn 3-Y.O) £2637.00 (£732.00: £351.00)     **7f**     5-30 (5-34)

3198 **Set Table (USA) (75)** (bl) (Fav) *(JHMGosden)* 9-0 AMcGlone (7) (lw: chsd ldrs: brought stands' side: led 2f out: drvn clr fnl f) ..................... —**1**

    **Affidare (IRE)** *(SMHillen)* 9-0 JLowe (12) (b.hind: trckd ldrs: hdwy stands' side & ev ch 2f out: sn rdn: wknd fnl f) ..................... 5.**2**

3080[6] Majestic Sinclair (IRE) *(RHollinshead)* 8-7 ‡[7]DCarson (6) (s.i.s: bhd tl gd hdwy over 1f out: r.o nr fin) ..................... 1½.**3**

3238[6] Stitched Up (IRE) *(PWChapple-Hyam)* 8-11 ‡[3]FNorton (13) (lw: chsd ldrs tl rdn & wknd over 1f out) ..................... ½.**4**

3216[2] Climbing High **(68)** (v) *(IABalding)* 8-9 WRyan (5) (led over 5f to 2f out: sn wknd) ..................... 5.**5**

2923 Roaring Breeze **(40)** *(MissSEHall)* 8-6 ‡[3]SMaloney (9) (chsd ldrs tl wknd 2f out) ½.**6**

    **Father Dan (IRE)** *(DMoffatt)* 8-7 ‡[7]DarrenMoffatt (8) (cmpt: bit bkwd: dwlt: sn wl bhd: sme hdwy fnl 2f: n.d) ..................... 1.**7**

2366 Crimson Consort (IRE) **(33)** *(DonEnricoIncisa)* 8-7 ‡[7]ClaireBalding (3) (sn wl bhd) ..................... ¾.**8**

1276 Super Marco **(43)** *(WWHaigh)* 9-0 RLappin (1) (hld up: sn bhd) ..................... hd.**9**

2969[4] Grand Fellow (IRE) **(56)** (v) *(JDBethell)* 9-0 LCharnock (11) (chsd ldrs: drvn along ½-wy: sn wknd) ..................... 4.**10**

3168[5] Throw Away Line **(46)** (v) *(REBarr)* 8-9 SWebster (10) (led over 1f: chsd ldrs tl wknd over 2f out) ..................... ½.**11**

1933 Music in My Life (IRE) **(61)** *(WJarvis)* 8-9 JFortune (4) (w ldrs tl eased after 1f: sn p.u: lame) ..................... 0

**7/4** SET TABLE (USA)(Evens—2/1), **5/2** Climbing High, **6/1** Stitched Up (IRE), **13/2** Affidare (IRE), **10/1** Music in My Life (IRE), **14/1** Grand Fellow (IRE), **16/1** Majestic Sinclair (IRE), **25/1** Father Dan (IRE), **33/1** Roaring Breeze, Throw Away Line, **50/1** Ors. CSF £14.33, Tote £2.90: £1.40 £1.70 £7.10 (£11.70). Sheikh Mohammed (NEWMARKET) bred by J. S. MacDonald Holdings in USA. 12 Rn ..................... 1m 28.3 (5.1)
SF—34/19/7/9/–/–

T/Plpt: £265.40 (8.3 Tckts).         WG

## 3215—FOLKESTONE (R-H)

### Monday, September 21st [Good to firm becoming Good to soft]

Going Allowance: 1st-3rd: 0.05 sec; Rest: 0.30 sec per fur (G)     Wind: fresh half against

Stalls: low

## 3387

DEAL H'CAP (0-70) £1716.00 (£476.00: £228.00)    **1m 1f 149y**    1-50 (1-52)
(Weights raised 3 lb)

2054[3] **Plan Ahead (67)** *(GLewis)* 3–9-3 ‡[7]BRussell (4) (lw: gd hdwy over 1f out: str run fnl f: led last strides) ..................... —**1**

2738★ King's Guest (IRE) **(62)** *(GAPritchard-Gordon)* 3–9-5 NDay (13) (lw: led: hrd rdn ins fnl f: hdd last strides) ..................... nk.**2**

3174 Montagne **(45)** *(HCandy)* 3–8-2 CRutter (12) (2nd st: rdn over 1f out: unable qckn) ..................... 1.**3**

3073[4] Esprit Fort (USA) **(60)** *(PWChapple-Hyam)* 3–9-3 LPiggott (8) (4th st: hrd rdn over 1f out: one pce) ..................... 1.**4**

2566 Affirmed's Destiny (USA) **(45)** *(JLDunlop)* 3–8-2 NCarlisle (1) (hdwy on ins over 1f out: r.o) .......................................................................... hd.5
3102 Swan Heights **(54)** *(JRFanshawe)* 3–8-11 GCarter (10) (lw: nvr nr to chal) ..... 1¹⁄₂.6
3052 Phil-Blake **(40)** *(SMellor)* 5–8-3 NAdams (6) (hdwy 4f out: 5th st: one pce fnl 2f) 1¹⁄₂.7
3236² Mr Tate (IRE) **(61)** *(RAkehurst)* 3–9-4 JReid (9) (no hdwy fnl 2f) ...................... 1¹⁄₂.8
3045² Molly Splash **(54)** *(CACyzer)* 5–9-3 MRoberts (7) (nvr nrr) ................................ hd.9
3294 Pearl Ransom **(45)** *(WGRWightman)* 5–8-8 JWilliams (2) (lw: nvr nrr) ............ nk.10
3239⁶ Breezed Well **(53)** *(CNAllen)* 6–8-9 ‡7GForster (14) (6th st: wknd over 1f out) .. 1.11
3159² Affa **(55)** *(TThomsonJones)* 3–8-12 AMcGlone (3) (lw: a bhd) ........................ 6.12
3140⁶ Super Morning **(49)** (Fav) *(JPearce)* 6–8-12 TQuinn (5) (3rd st: wknd over 1f out) .................................................................................. 2.13
3245 Sunset Street (IRE) **(60)** *(SDow)* 4–9-9 BRouse (5) (b: a bhd) ........................ 2.14
3073 Nectar Collector **(57)** (bl) *(CFWall)* 3–9-0 TyroneWilliams (11) (prom 7f) ....... 12.15

**11/2** Super Morning, **6/1** Molly Splash, **13/2** Mr Tate (IRE), **15/2** King's Guest (IRE), **9/1** Esprit Fort (USA), PLAN AHEAD, Sunset Street (IRE), **10/1** Breezed Well, **11/1** Nectar Collector, **12/1** Affa(op 8/1), **16/1** Swan Heights, Affirmed's Destiny (USA), **20/1** Montagne, **25/1** Pearl Ransom, **33/1** Phil-Blake. CSF £75.03, CT £1,234.01. Tote £11.50: £3.20 £3.20 £21.90 (£60.00). Planflow (Leasing) Ltd (EPSOM) bred by R. F. and Mrs Knipe. 10 Rn
2m 4.6 (6.9)
SF–39/40/21/34/18/24

---

**3388**    HASTINGS (S) STKS (3 & 4-Y.O) £1234.50 (£342.00: £163.50)
        1m 1f 149y                        2-20 (2-23)

3254⁶ **Amazon Express (52)** *(CEBrittain)* 3–8-8 MRoberts (2) (2nd st: hrd rdn over 1f out: led nr fin) ......................................................................... —1
3135 Lady of Sardinia (BEL) **(53)** *(JWPayne)* 3–8-3 AMcGlone (9) (led over 7f out: hrd rdn over 1f out: hdd nr fin) ............................................... nk.2
3240⁶ Bowdon Boy (IRE) **(66)** (Fav) *(NACallaghan)* 4–9-0 LPiggott (5) (4th st: hrd rdn over 1f out: one pce) ............................................................ 2¹⁄₂.3
3177 Fly for Gold (IRE) **(54)** *(DWPArbuthnot)* 3–8-3 TQuinn (7) (b.hind: 3rd st: hrd rdn over 1f out: one pce) ............................................. hd.4
3045 Aragon Court **(53)** *(JPearce)* 4–9-0 GCarter (3) (lw: 5th & rn wd st: hrd rdn over 1f out: wknd) .................................................................. 8.5
3017⁵ Wise Portia **(46)** *(HCandy)* 3–8-3 CRutter (8) (stumbled s: 6th st: nvr nr to chal) 10.6
3017 Evening Dress **(30)** (v) *(ICampbell)* 3–8-3 NAdams (4) (led 2f: wknd over 4f out) 8.7
1759 Aspirant *(KGWingrove)* 4–8-9 ‡5RPrice (6) (t: a bhd) ........................................ nk.8
2944 Rapid Rosie **(20)** (v) *(DRLaing)* 4–8-9 TyroneWilliams (1) (bhd fnl 5f: t.o) ......... 25.9
3259 Woodcock Wendy *(MJBolton)* 3–7-12 ‡5NGwilliams (10) (a bhd: t.o) ......... 2¹⁄₂.10

**6/4** Bowdon Boy (IRE), **7/2** Fly for Gold (IRE), **11/2** Lady of Sardinia (BEL), **6/1** AMAZON EXPRESS, Aragon Court, **7/1** Wise Portia, **33/1** Ors. CSF £39.38, Tote £5.90: £2.00 £2.60 £1.50 (£26.60). Mr A. J. Richards (NEWMARKET) bred by Ewar Stud Farms. 10 Rn; Sold I Moss 3,400 gns
2m 6.2 (8.5)
SF–14/8/14/2/–/–

---

**3389**    LYSANDER INSURANCE STKS (Mdn 3-Y.O.F) £1576.00 (£436.00: £208.00)
        1¹⁄₂m                                   2-50 (2-51)

3085⁶ **Kasisi (IRE)** *(ACStewart)* 8–11 MRoberts (1) (mde all: hrd rdn over 1f out: r.o wl) ................................................................................................. —1
2566³ Irish Honey (IRE) **(41)** *(BHanbury)* 8–11 NCarlisle (2) (4th st: hrd rdn over 1f out: ev ch ins fnl f: r.o) ...................................................... ¹⁄₂.2
3022⁴ Time for a Flutter **(39)** *(DRCElsworth)* 8–11 JWilliams (5) (rdn over 3f: 3rd st: hrd rdn over 1f out: unable qckn) ........................................ 2¹⁄₂.3
3025² Charolles *(HRACecil)* 8–11 AMcGlone (3) (2nd st: hrd rdn over 1f out: one pce) nk.4
3054 Lady Dundee (USA) **(62)** *(MrsJCecil)* 8–11 JReid (7) (6th st: hrd rdn over 1f out: one pce) ........................................................................... 2.5
3062⁶ Princess Ermyn *(MDixon)* 8–11 BRouse (7) (5th st: wknd over 1f out) ................ 3.6
3180 Forever Tweeky *(PRHedger)* 8–11 NAdams (4) (a bhd: t.o) .............................. 20.7

**13/8** Time for a Flutter, **7/4** Charolles, **5/1** Lady Dundee (USA), **10/1** KASISI (IRE), **12/1** Princess Ermyn, **14/1** Irish Honey (IRE), **66/1** Forever Tweeky. CSF £107.31, Tote £11.60: £4.00 £2.50 £2.50 (£24.70). Mrs H. R. Slack (NEWMARKET) bred by John Kelly in Ireland. 7 Rn
2m 45.2 (11.7)

---

**3390**    WALMER STKS (2-Y.O) £2057.50 (£570.00: £272.50)    **6f**        3-20 (3-23)

3240★ **Rain Brother (USA) (90)** *(PWChapple-Hyam)* 9-2 LPiggott (6) (mde all: hrd rdn over 1f out: r.o wl) ................................................................... —1
2847⁵ Realities (USA) **(100)** (Fav) *(GHarwood)* 9-2 JReid (1) (chsd wnr: hrd rdn & ev ch fnl f: r.o) .............................................................. hd.2
3276 Air Command (BAR) *(RHannon)* 8–11 AMcGlone (5) (a.p: rdn over 2f out: sn wknd) .......................................................................................... 12.3

Abjar *(PAKelleway)* 8-11 GayKelleway (7) (b: w'like: bit bkwd: racd far side: prom 4f) ............................................................................................................ ³/₄.4

A Secret Weapon (USA) *(JMPEustace)* 8-11 MTebbutt (2) (w'like: a bhd) .............. ³/₄.5

3217* Misty Jenni (IRE) **(87)** *(RAkehurst)* 8-11 TQuinn (4) (prom over 3f) ................... 5.6

3181 Arras Royale (bl) *(JELong)* 8-11 NAdams (3) (prom over 3f) ............................... 4.7

**8/11** Realities (USA)(11/10—5/4), **2/1** RAIN BROTHER (USA), **7/1** Misty Jenni (IRE), **20/1** Air Command (BAR), **25/1** A Secret Weapon (USA), **33/1** Abjar, **66/1** Arras Royale. CSF £3.80, Tote £2.50: £1.60 £1.10 (£2.30). Mr Luciano Gaucci (MARLBOROUGH) bred by Gainesway Thoroughbreds Ltd in USA. 7 Rn             1m 15.1 (4.4)

SF—50/49/–/–/–/–

---

## 3391

WESTENHANGER H'CAP (0-70) £1828.00 (£508.00: £244.00)     **6f**     3-50 (3-53)

2861⁶ **Zeboim (65)** (bl) (Fav) *(WRMuir)* 6-10-0 MRoberts (9) (lw: a.p: led over 2f out: pushed out) ........................................................................................... —1

3264⁵ Proud Brigadier (IRE) **(47)** *(WCarter)* 4-8-5 ‡⁵NGWilliams (3) (a.p: ev ch over 1f out: unable qckn) ..................................................................................... 1¹/₂.2

3245 Idir Linn (IRE) **(44)** *(DJGMurray-Smith)* 4-8-7 CRutter (4) (a.p: hrd rdn over 1f out: one pce) ........................................................................................... 2.3

3373² Little Nod **(42)** *(JWhite)* 3-7-9 ‡⁷GMilligan (7) (hdwy over 1f out: r.o ins fnl f) .... hd.4

3098³ Martinosky **(63)** *(WGRWightman)* 6-9-12 JWilliams (8) (a.p: one pce fnl 2f) ....... nk.5

3185 Ain'tlifelikethat **(56)** (bl) *(TJNaughton)* 5-9-5 GCarter (6) (hdwy 2f out: one pce fnl f) ............................................................................................................ 1.6

3196 Panchellita (USA) **(58)** *(JSutcliffe)* 3-9-4 BRouse (2) (lw: nvr nr to chal) ............. 5.7

3264 Liffey River (USA) **(54)** *(MrsLPiggott)* 4-9-3 LPiggott (1) (b: b.hind: spd over 4f) 4.8

3220⁴ Frimley Parkson **(30)** (bl) *(PHowling)* 8-7-7 NCarlisle (10) (prom over 3f) ........... 2.9

3257 Oscilante **(35)** *(RAkehurst)* 4-7-12 NAdams (5) (a bhd) ..................................... ¹/₂.10

Party Treat (IRE) **(39)** *(DMarks)* 4-8-2 TyroneWilliams (11) (led over 3f) ........ 1¹/₂.11

LONG HANDICAP: Frimley Parkson 7-6.

**3/1** ZEBOIM(tchd 5/1), **9/2** Martinosky, **6/1** Proud Brigadier (IRE), Panchellita (USA), **15/2** Ain'tlifelikethat, **8/1** Liffey River (USA)(op 5/1), Idir Linn (IRE), **9/1** Little Nod, **14/1** Frimley Parkson, Oscilante, **25/1** Party Treat (IRE). CSF £22.92, CT £129.64. Tote £4.80: £2.20 £3.50 £4.10 (£35.90). Mr David J. Muir (LAMBOURN) bred by Noel Finegan. 11 Rn             1m 15.8 (5.1)

SF—48/19/13/–/30/19

---

## 3392

PEDLINGE STKS (Amateurs) (Mdn 3-Y.O) £1171.50 (£324.00: £154.50) **1m 7f 92y**     4-20 (4-23)

3114 **Fortune Star (IRE)** (Fav) *(JLDunlop)* 10-5 MissEJohnsonHoughton (5) (hdwy over 2f out: 5th st: led over 1f out: hung lft: r.o wl) .............. —1

2240 Royal Glint **(40)** *(MJHeaton-Ellis)* 9-12⁽¹⁾ ‡³MissFHaynes (1) (2nd st: led 2f out tl over 1f out: unable qckn) ..................................................................... 10.2

3259 Court of Kings *(PFICole)* 10-2 ‡³MissMClark (6) (lw: led over 13f) .................. 7.3

2682 Major Risk **(45)** *(PAKelleway)* 10-2 ‡³MissSKelleway (4) (b: lw: 3rd st: wknd over 1f out) ........................................................................................................ ³/₄.4

2594³ La Joya (IRE) **(54)** *(GHarwood)* 10-0 MissAHarwood (8) (lw: 4th st: wknd over 1f out) ........................................................................................................ 7.5

Blue Lyzander *(RBrotherton)* 9-11 ‡³MissVHill (3) (w'like: bit bkwd: a bhd) ....... 15.6

3282 Sea Pet *(MissGayKelleway)* 9-11 ‡³MrVLukaniuk (7) (bhd fnl 5f: poor 6th st) ... 2¹/₂.7

2970⁴ Rich Pickings **(36)** *(DRTucker)* 9-11 ‡³MissSRowe (2) (bhd fnl 6f) .................. 10.8

**30/100** FORTUNE STAR (IRE), **4/1** La Joya (IRE), **16/1** Court of Kings(op 8/1), **20/1** Rich Pickings, **25/1** Royal Glint, Sea Pet, Major Risk, **33/1** Blue Lyzander. CSF £10.82, Tote £1.60: £1.10 £3.80 £2.50 (£20.40). Mr Cyril Humphris (ARUNDEL) bred by Newtownbarry House Stud in Ireland. 8 Rn             3m 42.5 (23.5)

T/Plpt: £531.60 (4.15 Tckts).                                                                                         AK

---

## 2936—PONTEFRACT (L-H)

### Monday, September 21st [Firm, Good to firm patches]

Going Allowance: 1st race: minus 0.35 sec; Rest: minus 0.25 sec (F)     Wind: slt half against

Stalls: low

---

## 3393

AMATEUR RIDERS ASSOCIATION H'CAP (Amateurs) (0-70) £2343.00 (£648.00: £309.00)     **1¹/₂m 8y**     2-15 (2-16)

2737³ **Grey Power (54)** *(MrsGRReveley)* 5-11-0 MrJDurkan (3) (hld up: hdwy 6f out: led wl ins fnl f: sn qcknd clr) .......................................................... —1

3054⁶ Horizon (IRE) **(42)** (bl) *(TThomsonJones)* 4-10-2 MrGHaine (7) (b: led: qcknd appr st: hdd & no ex wl ins fnl f) ....................................................... 6.2

1967[3] Brodessa **(68)** *(MrsGRReveley)* 6–12-0 MrMBuckley (10) (trckd ldrs: effrt wl over 1f out: edgd lft: styd on one pce) ............................ hd.3

2721 Al Badeto **(33)** *(JNorton)* 5–9-7 MrDParker (8) (a chsng ldrs: effrt 3f out: one pce appr fnl f) ............................ nk.4

3054★ Shadow Bird **(59)** (Fav) *(GAPritchard-Gordon)* 5–11-5 MrPPritchard-Gordon (9) (a chsng ldrs: effrt appr st: no ex appr fnl f) ................ 1½.5

Chantry Bartle **(39)** *(CWThornton)* 6–9-13[(1)] MrJWeymes (6) (swtg: cl up tl rdn & wknd over 1f out) ............................ 2.6

2367[4] Master's Crown (USA) **(45)** *(MCChapman)* 4–10-5 MrMChapman (5) (a bhd) .... 5.7

3066 Samurai Gold (USA) **(43)** *(CJames)* 4–10-3 MrEJames (4) (bhd: hdwy 6f out: wknd 3f out) ............................ 5.8

518[4] Sovereign Niche (IRE) **(44)** *(MrsJRRamsden)* 4–10-4 MrRHale (1) (bit bkwd: a bhd) ............................ ½.9

LONG HANDICAP: Al Badeto 8-8.

**2/1** Shadow Bird, **3/1** GREY POWER, **5/1** Brodessa, **7/1** Master's Crown (USA), **14/1** Sovereign Niche (IRE), Samurai Gold (USA), Horizon (IRE), **25/1** Chantry Bartle, **33/1** Al Badeto. CSF £37.59, CT £182.87. Tote £3.30: £1.40 £2.50 £2.10 (£16.10). J. P. S. Racing (SALTBURN) bred by Littleton Stud. 9 Rn    2m 39.1 (4.6)
SF—40/16/41/5/28/4

## 3394     NEW HALL CLAIMING STKS (2-Y.O) £2700.00 (£750.00: £360.00)    6f   2-45 (2-46)

3242[5] **Mr Butch (61)** *(MRChannon)* 8-0 JQuinn (1) (trckd ldrs: led over 1f out: r.o wl) . —1

3283[4] Mr Nevermind (IRE) **(55)** (bl) *(GLewis)* 7-11 ‡[3]DHarrison (12) (in tch: styd on wl fnl f: no ch w wnr) ............................ 3½.2

3218 Mississipi Maid *(WGMTurner)* 7-2 ‡[7]DarrenMoffatt (18) (led over 4f: r.o one pce) 1½.3

1623[5] Sunshine in Ramsey **(45)** (bl) *(TFairhurst)* 7-9 JFanning (10) (a chsng ldrs: kpt on u.p fnl f) ............................ 2.4

3267[0] Second Colours (USA) **(77)** *(PSFelgate)* 8-6 KDarley (9) (lw: w ldrs: slt ld wl over 1f out: sn hdd, rdn & btn) ............................ 3.5

3267 Walsham Witch **(75)** (Fav) *(MHTompkins)* 8-0[(3)] PRobinson (2) (a chsng ldrs: no hdwy fnl 2f) ............................ 1.6

2667[6] Oxrib *(JBerry)* 8-1 LCharnock (14) (lw: chsd ldrs: nt qckn fnl 2f) ............. 1½.7

3308 Minster Man (IRE) (bl) *(BSRothwell)* 8-6 JFortune (6) (in tch: drvn along ½-wy: no imp) ............................ 1.8

3070 Shadow Jury **(86)** (v) *(CTinkler)* 8-7 PBurke (7) (w ldrs 4f: sn wknd) ............. 1.9

2983[2] Take Your Partner (IRE) **(56)** *(MJohnston)* 7-2 ‡[7]MBaird (15) (cl up 4f: wknd qckly) ............................ 3.10

2363 Big Gem *(MCChapman)* 8-2 SWood (11) (a bhd) ............................ hd.11

3115 April Point (IRE) *(RHollinshead)* 7-5[(3)] ‡[7]AGarth (16) (n.d) ............................ 1½.12

2983 Light the Bay (bl) *(MrsVAAconley)* 7-7[(5)] ‡[7]MHumphries (3) (a bhd) ............... 2.13

2158[3] Laurel King *(JBerry)* 8-4 JCarroll (4) (lw: a bhd) ............................ nk.14

3036 Arewenearlythere (IRE) *(MBlanshard)* 7-10 GBardwell (8) (a bhd) ............... s.h.15

2719 Newgatesky **(46)** (bl) *(BWMurray)* 7-7[(1)] ‡[3]FNorton (5) (dwlt: a bhd) .............. 1½.16

**5/2** Walsham Witch, **4/1** Second Colours (USA), **8/1** Shadow Jury(op 5/1), Take Your Partner (IRE), MR BUTCH, **10/1** Mr Nevermind (IRE), **16/1** Laurel King, **20/1** Mississipi Maid, Oxrib, **25/1** Minster Man (IRE), **33/1** Arewenearlythere (IRE), April Point (IRE), Sunshine in Ramsey, Light the Bay, **66/1** Ors. CSF £79.44, Tote £7.00: £1.80 £2.20 £7.30 (£15.90). Mr G. Herridge (UPPER LAMBOURN) bred by G. Herridge. 16 Rn   1m 16.2 (2.2)
SF—12/-/-/-/-/-

## 3395     NEAT MARKET (S) H'CAP (3 & 4-Y.0) £2931.00 (£816.00: £393.00)   1m 4y    3-15 (3-20)

(Weights raised 2 lb)

3236 **Sir Norman Holt (IRE) (50)** (bl) (Fav) *(FHLee)* 3–9-6 DMcKeown (12) (mde all: kpt on wl fnl f) ............................ —1

2729 Tendresse (IRE) **(32)** *(CJHill)* 4–8-6 JCarroll (19) (lw: bhd: hdwy 2f out: r.o u.p: nrst fin) ............................ ¾.2

2123 Colonel Fairfax **(32)** (v) *(JWWatts)* 4–8-6 NConnorton (8) (trckd ldrs: swtchd & effrt over 1f out: rdn & nt r.o) ............................ hd.3

3239 Kelly's Kite **(29)** *(HJCollingridge)* 4–8-3 JQuinn (16) (in tch: hdwy to disp ld 2f out: rdn & no ex ins fnl f) ............................ 1.4

2297 Speed Oil **(45)** *(RBastiman)* 3–8-8 ‡[7]HBastiman (20) (s.i.s: gd hdwy on outside ½-wy: chal 2f out: nt qckn ins fnl f) ............................ 2.5

2607 Premier Major (IRE) **(41)** (v) *(BBeasley)* 3–8-11 LCharnock (13) (cl up tl rdn & btn appr fnl f) ............................ hd.6

3170[4] Flying Down to Rio (IRE) **(45)** *(MPNaughton)* 4–9-5 KFallon (6) (lw: hmpd & bhd ½-wy: hdwy 2f out: r.o) ............................ 1.7

2941[6] Cledeschamps **(44)** *(MWEllerby)* 3–9-0 SMorris (18) (hdwy & prom ½-wy: one pce fnl 2f) ............................ 2½.8

3251 Hubbers Favourite **(32)** (v) *(MrsNMacauley)* 4–8-6 BCrossley (15) (chsd ldr tl outpcd fnl 2f) ............................ 6.9

3251⁵ My Grain **(40)** *(RHollinshead)* 3-8-10 RCochrane (1) (bhd & hmpd ½-wy: n:d) 5.10
1421 Preamble **(43)** *(MrsJRRamsden)* 3-8-13 GBaxter (22) (nvr nr to chal) .......... 2½.11
3074 Phineas T Barnum (IRE) **(40)** *(JJO'Neill)* 4-9-0 BRaymond (17) (hdwy ½-wy: wknd 2f out) ............................................................................................ 1.12
2723⁶ L'Amour Precieux **(43)** *(MWEasterby)* 3-8-13 KDarley (3) (t: hld up & bhd: sme hdwy 3f out: n:d) ...................................................................... ½.13
3086⁶ Ten High (IRE) **(31)** (bl) *(JDooler)* 3-8-1 JFanning (10) (prom 6f) ............... ¾.14
3159 Selaginella **(43)** (v) *(MRChannon)* 3-8-8 ‡5BDoyle (14) (chsd ldrs 6f) ..... nk.15
Merls Pearl **(48)** *(JAGlover)* 3-8-13 ‡5SWilliams (4) (n:d) ................. 6.16
*3374* Denim Blue **(54)** *(CWThornton)* 3-9-10 PRobinson (9) (lw: prom over 5f) ... nk.17
3028 Spanish Performer **(45)** *(TFairhurst)* 3-8-12 ‡3FNorton (2) (n:d) ............ 2.18
3263 Always Lynsey (IRE) **(49)** *(MissLCSiddall)* 3-9-5 MBirch (11) (t: s.i.s: hmpd ½-wy: n:d) ............................................................................................. s.h.19
*901* Masaken **(44)** *(TKersey)* 4-9-4 SWebster (21) (b: bhd whn hmpd ½-wy: n:d) .... 20
*3176*⁴ Shardra (12/1) Withdrawn (ref to ent stalls) : not under orders — Rule 4 applies
*Stewards Enquiry: Bastiman suspended 30/9-3/10/92 (excessive use of whip).*

**5/1** SIR NORMAN HOLT (IRE)(op 10/1), **13/2** Flying Down to Rio (IRE), Kelly's Kite, **8/1** Tendresse (IRE), **10/1** Premier Major (IRE), Cledeschamps, **12/1** Speed Oil, **14/1** My Grain, Selaginella, L'Amour Precieux, Colonel Fairfax, **16/1** Preamble, Phineas T Barnum (IRE)(op 8/1), Denim Blue, **20/1** Spanish Performer, **25/1** Merls Pearl, Always Lynsey (IRE), **33/1** Hubbers Favourite, Ten High (IRE), **100/1** Masaken. CSF £45.48, CT £453.37. Tote £7.00: £2.00 £2.00 £3.50 £2.30 (£39.80). Mr D. Holt (WILMSLOW) bred by Ovidstown Investments Ltd. in Ireland. 20 Rn; Bt in 5,400 gns
1m 44.4 (2.8)
SF—34/18/17/11/10/12

**3396**
ROBERT BOWETT SAAB LEEDS H'CAP (3-Y.O) (0-90) £2436.25 each (£535.00: £242.50) **1m 4y**
3-45 (3-47)

3121 **Stani (USA) (80)** *(BHanbury)* 9-7 BRaymond (5) (cl up: chal 2f out: slt ld ins fnl f: r.o) ........................................................................................................ —1
3203² **Tahitian (60)** (Fav) *(MrsJRRamsden)* 8-1 KDarley (3) (lw: hld up: effrt 2f out: r.o u.p fnl f) .................................................................................................. —1
2990 Agincourt Song (USA) **(75)** *(JLDunlop)* 9-2 JCarroll (2) (lw: led: rdn over 2f out: r.o: hdd ins fnl f) ........................................................................................ 1½.3
*3378*² Eastleigh **(63)** *(RHollinshead)* 7-11 ‡7AGarth (4) (lw: chsd ldrs: effrt over 2f out: r.o one pce) ...................................................................................... 1½.4
3269² Sylvan (IRE) **(80)** *(CFWall)* 9-7 RCochrane (6) (lw: cl up tl rdn & btn ent fnl f) .. hd.5
3241 Our Occasion **(70)** *(WJMusson)* 8-11 JHBrown (1) (hld up & bhd: effrt over 2f out: sn outpcd) ............................................................................................ 6.6

**6/4** TAHITIAN, **3/1** STANI (USA), **7/2** Sylvan (IRE), **10/1** Agincourt Song (USA), Our Occasion, **16/1** Eastleigh. CSF £3.77 S & T, £3.04 T & S, Tote £2.00 S £1.20 T: £1.70 S £1.50 T (£3.90). Stani (USA): Mr Saeed Suhail (NEWMARKET) bred by Glen Hill Farm in USA. Tahitian: Mr K. E. Wheldon (THIRSK) bred by Hesmonds Stud Ltd. 6 Rn
1m 44.8 (3.2)
SF—29/9/19/–/18/–

**3397**
NEVISON H'CAP (0-80) £2616.00 (£726.00: £348.00) **5f**
4-15 (4-17)

3207 **Samson-Agonistes (78)** *(BAMcMahon)* 6-9-7 ‡7SSanders (2) (lw: mde all: clr 1f out: jst hld on) ...................................................................................... —1
3304⁵ African Chimes **(76)** *(WAO'Gorman)* 5-9-9 ‡3EmmaO'Gorman (12) (lw: in tch: hdwy over 1f out: wandered u.p: styd on strly cl home) .... hd.2
2956 Simmie's Special **(58)** *(RHollinshead)* 4-8-8 RCochrane (14) (wnt lft after s: a chsng ldrs: r.o nr fin) ........................................................................ hd.3
3166⁵ Farndale **(43)** *(BCMorgan)* 5-7-7 GBardwell (3) (in tch: hdwy u.p over 1f out: r.o) ................................................................................................................ hd.4
3196 Ganeshaya **(54)** (bl) *(MFBarraclough)* 3-7-7 ‡3DHarrison (8) (a chsng ldrs: outpcd 2f out: styd on fnl f) .............................................................. 2½.5
3304² Here Comes a Star **(64)** (Jt-Fav) *(JMCarr)* 4-9-0 SMorris (11) (mid div: effrt 2f out: n.m.r: styd on wl fnl f) ........................................................ hd.6
3126 Precentor **(63)** (Jt-Fav) *(JDBethell)* 6-8-13 BRaymond (13) (racd wd: styd on fnl 2f: no imp) ...................................................................................... 2.7
3207 Super Rocky **(73)** *(RBastiman)* 3-9-7 DMcKeown (4) (lw: stdd s: wl bhd tl shkn up & r.o fnl 2f) ................................................................................ hd.8
3166 Swinging Lady **(49)** *(WWHaigh)* 4-7-10 ‡3FNorton (5) (b.hind: in tch: effrt 2f out: no imp) .......................................................................................... 2.9
3207² Heaven-Liegh-Grey **(69)** (bl) *(MJohnston)* 4-9-5 JCarroll (15) (wnt lft after s: chsd wnr over 3f: sn wknd) ...................................................... hd.10
3196⁶ Invigilate **(61)** *(MPNaughton)* 3-7-7 KFallon (1) (chsd ldrs: wknd tl sme late hdwy) ......... hd.11
3015 Absolution **(75)** (v) *(MPNaughton)* 8-9-4 ‡7SWynne (10) (hmpd after s: prom tl wknd wl over 1f out) .......................................................... hd.12
3166 Kabcast **(55)** (bl) *(DWChapman)* 7-8-5 SWood (7) (n:d) ................. 5.13

3257 Grand Time **(50)** *(CJHill)* 3-7-7 ‡⁵NKennedy (9) (a bhd) ................................. 5.14
1865⁴ Baladee Pet **(52)** (bl) *(MrsVAAconley)* 3-8-0 PBurke (6) (a bhd) .................... 25.15
LONG HANDICAP: Farndale 6-12.

**6/1** Here Comes a Star, Precentor, **7/1** Heaven-Liegh-Grey, **8/1** Ganeshaya, Invigilate, **17/2** Super Rocky, **9/1** SAMSON-AGONISTES, **10/1** African Chimes, **12/1** Absolution, **16/1** Swinging Lady, Simmie's Special, **20/1** Grand Time, Farndale, **25/1** Kabcast, **33/1** Baladee Pet. CSF £91.81, CT £1,311.93. Tote £9.40: 2.80 £4.60 £4.70 (£53.20). Mr J. B. Wilcox (TAMWORTH) bred by D. W. Pike. 15 Rn
62.4 sec (0.9)
SF—64/65/49/33/29/43/34

**3398**  FRIER WOOD STKS (Mdn) £2658.00 (£738.00: £354.00)  1½m 8y  4-45 (4-50)

3169² **Shadows of Silver** *(BAMcMahon)* 4-9-2 MBirch (10) (w ldr: led 4f out: kpt on wl
fnl 2f) .............................................................................................................. —1
3072² Raheena (USA) **(Fav)** *(JHMGosden)* 3-8-8 JCarroll (3) (trckd ldrs: chal 2f out:
rdn & nt qckn appr fnl f) ............................................................................... ½.2
*3184*⁵ Magadeer (USA) **(73)** *(JLDunlop)* 3-8-8 BRaymond (1) (a chsng ldrs: effrt 3f
out: one pce) .................................................................................................. 3.3
Deduce *(GWragg)* 3-8-13 PRobinson (4) (wl grwn: dwlt: hdwy 4f out: rdn & r.o
one pce fnl 2f) ................................................................................................ 1.4
2287⁵ Debt Swap (USA) **(67)** *(JHMGosden)* 3-8-13 RCochrane (9) (a chsng ldrs:
outpcd over 2f out: no imp after) ................................................................ 3½.5
3311 High Mind (FR) **(57)** *(MissLCSiddall)* 3-8-13 DeanMcKeown (2) (hld up & bhd:
effrt over 3f out: n.d) ..................................................................................... 15.6
3078 Peacock Throne *(MrsJRRamsden)* 3-8-8 KDarley (8) (pushed along over 3f
out: n.d) ........................................................................................................ 2½.7
1288 Dartington Blake *(JDooler)* 8-9-7 JFanning (7) (led tl hdd 4f out: wknd qckly) . 15.8
*3078* Mr Sunny *(PBeaumont)* 3-8-13 PBurke (5) (rdn & lost tch fnl 5f) .................. 2½.9
Glowing Darkness *(JMCarr)* 7-9-? SWebster (6) (wl bhd fr ½-wy) .................... 1.10

**5/2** Raheena (USA), **3/1** Deduce, SHADOWS OF SILVER, **9/2** Magadeer (USA), **9/1** Debt Swap (USA)(op 6/1), **25/1** Peacock Throne, **50/1** Glowing Darkness, High Mind (FR), **100/1** Ors. CSF £10.34, Tote £4.10: £1.60 £1.40 £1.60 (£3.60). Mrs R. C. Mayall (TAMWORTH) bred by J. E. Sainsbury and Mrs P. E. White. 10 Rn
2m 37.7 (3.2)
SF—40/31/25/28/21/–

**3399**  E.B.F POPPIN LANE STKS (Mdn 2-Y.O) £3027.50 (£840.00: £402.50)
**6f**  5-15 (5-18)

828⁵ **Tychonic** **(Fav)** *(BWHills)* 9-0 RCochrane (11) (lw: trckd ldrs: led 1f out: rdn &
r.o) .................................................................................................................. —1
2308² Wolf Power (IRE) **(73)** *(TThomsonJones)* 9-0 KDarley (12) (hdwy ½-wy: sn
prom: styd on u.p fnl f) ................................................................................. ¾.2
3039² Victoria Hall **(63)** *(WGMTurner)* 8-2 ‡⁷DarrenMoffatt (2) (led tl hdd 1f out: kpt on
same pce) ...................................................................................................... 1½.3
2951² Stitchcombe *(PWChapple-Hyam)* 8-11 ‡³FNorton (8) (a chsng ldrs: rdn along
½-wy: kpt on fnl f) ......................................................................................... 3½.4
2674³ Henequin (USA) *(JHMGosden)* 9-0 BRaymond (4) (in tch: hdwy ½-wy: one
pce appr fnl f) ............................................................................................... 3½.5
Procada *(JEtherington)* 9-0 JQuinn (9) (w'like: leggy: scope: bit bkwd: bhd &
hmpd wl after 1f: styd on wl fnl 2f) ............................................................... hd.6
2568² Hoy-Liegh-Rag **(74)** *(MJohnston)* 9-0 JCarroll (14) (lw: w ldr: effrt wl over 1f out:
sn btn) ........................................................................................................... hd.7
Dances With Gold *(MJohnston)* 8-9 DMcKeown (5) (cmpt: bit bkwd: hmpd wl
after 1f: bhd tl sme late hdwy) ...................................................................... nk.8
3117⁴ Russia With Love *(JDBethell)* 8-6 ‡³DHarrison (6) (chsd ldrs over 4f: sn wknd) .. ½.9
Quessong (bl) *(FHLee)* 9-0 PRobinson (10) (lengthy: bit bkwd: bhd & hmpd wl
after 1f: n.d) .................................................................................................. 4.10
3156 Well Tried (IRE) *(RHollinshead)* 8-2 ‡⁷MHumphries (3) (outpcd after 2f) ........... ¾.11
Bloomsbury Square *(JWWatts)* 9-0 NConnorton (7) (w'like: str: scope: s.i.s:
hmpd wl after 1f: n.d) .................................................................................... 2½.12
Can Can Charlie *(MJohnston)* 9-0 RPElliott (13) (tall: unf: bit bkwd: outpcd &
bhd fr ½-wy) .................................................................................................. nk.13
3164 Roscommon Joe (IRE) *(JJO'Neill)* 9-0 JFortune (1) (n.m.r, hit rail & swvd rt wl
after 1f: a bhd) .............................................................................................. 7.14

**10/11** TYCHONIC, **7/2** Stitchcombe, **8/1** Henequin (USA)(op 5/1), **11/1** Hoy-Liegh-Rag, **12/1** Procada, Bloomsbury Square, **14/1** Russia With Love, **16/1** Victoria Hall, **20/1** Wolf Power (IRE), **33/1** Well Tried (IRE), **50/1** Ors. CSF £23.38, Tote £2.10: £1.50 £3.50 £2.40 (£23.90). Mr K. Abdulla (LAMBOURN) bred by Juddmonte Farms. 14 Rn
1m 16 (2)
SF—30/27/9/4/–/–

T/Plpt: £395.10 (7.45 Tckts).
AA

2930—**NOTTINGHAM (L-H)**

**Monday, September 21st [Good to firm becoming Good]**

Going Allowance: St: minus 0.15 sec (F); Rnd: 0.10 sec per fur (G)　　Wind: almost nil

Stalls: high

**3400**　　　　　GRACE H'CAP (0-70) £2721.00 (£756.00: £363.00)　　**6f 15y**　　　2-00 (2-04)

1776⁵ **Everglades (IRE) (65)** *(RCharlton)* 4-9-12 PatEddery (1) (hld up: hdwy over 2f
　　　　out: led ins fnl f: r.o wl) ......................................................... —1
3153³ Kentucky Rain **(54)** *(JGFitzGerald)* 3-8-9 ‡³SMaloney (4) (lw: a.p: r.o ins fnl f) ... 1.2
3264 Mu-Arrik **(47)** (bl) *(DAWilson)* 4-8-8 GDuffield (3) (lw: a.p: r.o wl ins fnl f) ........ s.h.3
3133⁶ Mogwai (IRE) **(65)** (bl) *(RFJohnsonHoughton)* 3-9-9 WRyan (16) (prom: led
　　　　stands' side over 1f out: r.o one pce) ............................... 1¹/₂.4
3264⁶ Strip Cartoon (IRE) **(52)** (bl) *(SRBowring)* 4-8-6⁽²⁾ ‡⁷MHarris (9) (led stands'
　　　　side over 4f: r.o fnl f) ................................................. hd.5
3257³ John O'Dreams **(39)** *(MrsJCDawe)* 7-8-0 JLowe (8) (lw: hdwy over 1f out: r.o) s.h.6
2366 C Sharp **(44)** *(WRMuir)* 5-8-5⁽²⁾ AClark (13) (lw: prom stands' side over 4f) ....... 3.7
2752 Melodic Habit **(40)** *(MrsAKnight)* 5-8-1 DBiggs (10) (nvr nrr to chal) ............. 1¹/₂.8
3196 Indian Endeavour **(61)** *(RGuest)* 3-9-5 MHills (12) (nvr trbld ldrs) ................. ¹/₂.9
3183² Amethystine (USA) **(64)** (Fav) *(RJHodges)* 6-9-11 WCarson (11) (lw: n.d) .... 2¹/₂.10
3183 Luna Bid **(63)** *(MBlanshard)* 9-9-10 LDettori (15) (s.i.s: a bhd) .................. ³/₄.11
3167 Barmbrack **(35)** *(RMWhitaker)* 3-7-0 ‡⁷DWright (14) (lw: dwlt: nvr nrr) ........... s.h.12
2595⁶ Miss Shadowfax **(59)** *(CNAllen)* 3-8-12 ‡⁵JWeaver (17) (spd stands' side 4f) .. ³/₄.13
3264 Lightning Decision **(44)** *(JPSmith)* 4-8-5 SDawson (6) (a bhd) .................... ¹/₂.14
3278³ Lyndon's Linnet **(65)** *(RIngram)* 4-9-12 CDwyer (7) (led far side: clr 2f out:
　　　　wknd & hdd ins fnl f) .................................................. ³/₄.15
3003 Sandcastle City **(54)** (bl) *(RHannon)* 3-8-12 RHills (2) (spd over 3f) ............ 2¹/₂.16
1417³ Night Asset **(68)** (bl) *(GLewis)* 3-9-8 PaulEddery (5) (bkwd: t.o) .................. 7.17
　　　　　　　　　　　LONG HANDICAP: Barmbrack 7-2.

5/1 Amethystine (USA), **8/1** EVERGLADES (IRE)(op 9/2), Luna Bid, Lyndon's Linnet(op 12/1), **9/1** Night
Asset(op 5/1), Strip Cartoon (IRE)(6/1—10/1), **10/1** Mu-Arrik, John O'Dreams, **14/1** Melodic Habit(8/1—16/1),
Sandcastle City, Mogwai (IRE), Indian Endeavour, **16/1** Kentucky Rain, **20/1** Miss Shadowfax, **40/1** Barmbrack,
**50/1** Ors. CSF £123.10, CT £1,195.62. Tote £11.10: £2.40 £4.20 £3.40 £3.90 (£57.70). Miss Sophie
Oppenheimer (BECKHAMPTON) bred by Hascombe and Valiant Studs in Ireland. 17 Rn　　1m 13 (2)
　　　　　　　　　　　　　　　　　　　　　　　　　　　　　SF—54/33/31/40/22/15/8

**3401**　　　E.B.F. FERAG - RMO STKS (Mdn 2-Y.O.C & G) £2880.50 (£798.00: £381.50)
　　　　　**6f 15y**　　　　　　　　　　　　　　　　　　　　　　　　　　2-30 (2-33)

2986³ **Ribhi (USA)** (Fav) *(DMorley)* 9-0 WCarson (6) (hld up: nt clr run wl over 1f out:
　　　　qcknd to ld ins fnl f: comf) ........................................... —1
3179⁴ Glen Miller **(71)** *(JWPayne)* 9-0 GDuffield (2) (lw: w ldrs: hrd rdn to ld 1f out: sn
　　　　hdd & nt qckn) ...................................................... 2.2
3148 Bold Face (IRE) **(70)** *(RFJohnsonHoughton)* 9-0 MHills (8) (led 5f: hrd rdn: nt
　　　　qckn) .............................................................. ³/₄.3
1832³ Flashman *(FHLee)* 9-0 LDettori (8) (swtg: bit bkwd: prom tl wknd fnl f) ........... 4.4
3179 Gone Prospecting (USA) **(81)** *(RHannon)* 9-0 PatEddery (5) (w ldr: n.m.r over
　　　　1f out: wknd fnl f) ................................................... 2.5
3181⁶ Akenside *(DRCElsworth)* 9-0 PaulEddery (1) (swtg: hrd rdn 2f out: a bhd) ........ 1¹/₂.6
2544 Azrag (IRE) *(TThomsonJones)* 9-0 RHills (4) (bit bkwd: a bhd) ..................... nk.7
　　　　Shalako *(RHollinshead)* 9-0 WRyan (3) (cmpt: bkwd: outpcd: t.o) ................. 6.8

7/4 RIBHI (USA), **7/2** Gone Prospecting (USA), **4/1** Glen Miller, **7/1** Flashman, **10/1** Bold Face (IRE), Akenside,
**16/1** Azrag (IRE)(op 10/1), **25/1** Shalako. CSF £9.24, Tote £1.90: £1.30 £1.30 £1.80 (£11.70). Mr Hamdan
Al-Maktoum (NEWMARKET) bred by Shadwell Estate Company Ltd in USA. 8 Rn　　1m 13.9 (2.9)
　　　　　　　　　　　　　　　　　　　　　　　　　　　　　SF—24/16/3/–/–/–

**3402**　　　NOTTINGHAM EVENING POST STKS (Mdn 2-Y.O.C & G) £3915.00 (£1170.00: £560.00:
　　　　£255.00)　**1m 54y**　　　　　　　　　　　　　　　　　　　　3-00 (3-07)

3100³ **Bagalino (USA)** (Fav) *(RCharlton)* 9-0 PatEddery (12) (lw: mde all: hrd rdn over
　　　　1f out: r.o) ......................................................... —1
3106³ Doctoor (USA) *(WJarvis)* 9-0 AMunro (9) (3rd st: hrd rdn & ev ch over 1f out: r.o
　　　　wl cl home) ......................................................... ¹/₂.2
3035 Armenian Coffee (IRE) *(JLDunlop)* 9-0 MHills (10) (sn prom: 2nd st: ev ch over
　　　　1f out: r.o) ......................................................... 1.3
　　　　Sylvania (IRE) *(RHannon)* 9-0 LDettori (6) (w'like: leggy: bit bkwd: 6th st: hdwy
　　　　2f out: ev ch over 1f out: nt r.o) ...................................... ³/₄.4
2598 Contract Court (USA) **(83)** *(CACyzer)* 9-0 DBiggs (2) (lw: plld hrd: 5th st: hrd
　　　　rdn over 2f out: wknd ins fnl f) ...................................... 2¹/₂.5

25196 Riviere Actor (USA) *(JLDunlop)* 9-0 WCarson (11) (hld up: 7th st: hdwy 3f out: eased whn btn ins fnl f) ............................................................ 1½.**6**

Naawy *(MRStoute)* 9-0 WRSwinburn (13) (w'like: scope: bit bkwd: s.s: 8th st: hdwy 2f out: nvr nrr) ........................................................... 2.**7**

Dodgy Dancer *(MrsLPiggott)* 9-0 PaulEddery (7) (b: w'like: leggy: bkwd: sn rdn along: 4th st: wknd 2f out) ......................................... 1½.**8**

3193 Olicana (IRE) *(BWHills)* 9-0 EJohnson (3) (hdwy 4f out: wknd over 1f out) ...... 1½.**9**

Dormston Boyo *(JLSpearing)* 9-0 AClark (4) (lt-f: bkwd: dwlt: a bhd: t.o) ...... 12.**10**

Barton Royal (IRE) *(RHollinshead)* 9-0 WRyan (5) (w'like: str: bkwd: s.s: a in rr: t.o) ........................................................................................ 2½.**11**

3262 Rubidian *(SirMarkPrescott)* 9-0 GDuffield (1) (bit bkwd: a bhd: t.o) .............. 3½.**12**

Troy Boy *(RHannon)* 9-0 RHills (8) (w'like: scope: sn bhd: 9th st: t.o) .............. 1.**13**

**11/8** BAGALINO (USA), **5/1** Riviere Actor (USA)(op 3/1), **11/2** Doctoor (USA)(op 3/1), **8/1** Naawy(9/2—9/1), **14/1** Sylvania (IRE)(8/1—16/1), **16/1** Olicana (IRE)(op 8/1), Contract Court (USA)(op 10/1), **20/1** Troy Boy, **33/1** Barton Royal (IRE), Dodgy Dancer, Armenian Coffee (IRE), **50/1** Rubidian, **66/1** Dormston Boyo. CSF £9.28, Tote £2.40: £1.50 £1.60 £10.20 (£3.10). Mr K. Abdulla (BECKHAMPTON) bred by Juddmonte Farms Inc in USA. 13 Rn 1m 47.4 (7.8)

**3403** HARLAND SIMON CLAIMING H'CAP (0-70) £3057.00 (£852.00: £411.00)
**1m 1f 213y** 3-30 (3-39)

(Weights raised 1 lb)

3192 **Mahong (53)** *(MrsHParrott)* 4-9-2 MWigham (21) (gd hdwy over 1f out: str run to ld last strides) ............................................................ —**1**

31762 Eiras Mood (51) *(BPalling)* 3-8-3 ‡5StephenDavies (16) (hdwy 2f out: hrd rdn to ld cl home: hdd last strides) ........................................... nk.**2**

19714 Pusey Street Boy (39) *(JRBosley)* 5-8-2 AMunro (12) (t: hdwy ins fnl f: ev ch ins fnl f: nt qckn) ................................................................ 1.**3**

30102 Addicted to Love (62) (Jt-Fav) *(PJMakin)* 3-9-6 PatEddery (15) (hdwy 2f out: hrd rdn & r.o wl ins fnl f) ....................................... nk.**4**

32463 Rampal (IRE) (60) *(GWragg)* 3-9-3 RHills (4) (3rd st: led ins fnl f: sn hdd & nt qckn) .......................................................................... hd.**5**

28095 Dara Melody (IRE) (46) *(JGFitzGerald)* 3-8-0 ‡3SMaloney (3) (lw: led 3f: 2nd st: led 1f out: sn hdd & no ex) ..................................... ¾.**6**

30665 Rive-Jumelle (IRE) (55) *(MBell)* 4-9-4 MHills (13) (led 7f out to 1f out) .............. 3½.**7**

Millrous (40) *(RGuest)* 4-7-10 ‡7CHawksley (18) (bit bkwd: s.i.s: nvr nrr) .......... 1½.**8**

3192 Brown Fairy (USA) (61) *(MrsNMacauley)* 4-9-10 DBiggs (1) (n.d) ................... ¾.**9**

32513 Sareen Express (IRE) (46) *(MrsJCDawe)* 4-8-4 ‡5ATucker (8) (m.n.s) ........... 1½.**10**

3176 Jalore (47) *(RHollinshead)* 3-8-4(3) WRyan (10) (m.n.s) ................................ 1½.**11**

31926 Spring to the Top (50) (Jt-Fav) *(JWPayne)* 5-8-13 GDuffield (11) (nvr nr ldrs) 1½.**12**

32585 Faustnluce Lady (40) *(GAHam)* 3-7-4 ‡7TWilson (14) (n.d) ........................ 1½.**13**

3076 Damart (USA) (30) *(MissLCSiddall)* 8-7-7 JLowe (22) (dwlt: a bhd) ............... ¾.**14**

3256 Al Skeet (USA) (35) *(RJPrice)* 6-7-12(2) TSprake (20) (4th st: wknd over 2f out) nk.**15**

3161 Urshi-Jade (40) *(KWhite)* 4-7-10(10) ‡7JDennis (19) (8th st: wknd over 2f out) nk.**16**

1813 Lord Neptune (59) *(MAJarvis)* 3-9-2 GCrealock (2) (bit bkwd: 7th st: wknd 3f out) ........................................................................................ 2½.**17**

2086 Be My Habitat (58) *(MissLCSiddall)* 3-8-10 ‡5JWeaver (9) (bkwd: bhd fnl 4f) 2.**18**

3105 Whippet (55) *(JABennett)* 8-9-4 MPerrett (17) (t.o) ...................................... 7.**19**

31016 Yankee Flyer (52) *(MissSJWilton)* 5-9-1 LDettori (7) (5th st: wknd 3f out: t.o) nk.**20**

3062 Private Practice (41) (v) *(MJHeaton-Ellis)* 3-7-12 DaleGibson (5) (6th st: wknd 3f out) ........................................................................................ ¾.**21**

16296 Beija Flor (42) *(FJordan)* 5-8-5 AClark (6) (bkwd: prom: hrd rdn 6f out: wknd qckly 5f out: t.o) ........................................................... 30.**22**

LONG HANDICAP: Damart (USA) 7-6, Urshi-Jade 7-4.

**11/2** Spring to the Top(4/1—6/1), Addicted to Love(7/2—6/1), **13/2** Rive-Jumelle (IRE), **10/1** Pusey Street Boy, Rampal (IRE), MAHONG(op 20/1), **11/1** Eiras Mood, **12/1** Sareen Express (IRE)(op 8/1), Brown Fairy (USA), **14/1** Yankee Flyer, Dara Melody (IRE), **16/1** Lord Neptune, **20/1** Be My Habitat, Al Skeet (USA), **25/1** Private Practice, **33/1** Jalore, Beija Flor, Faustnluce Lady, Whippet, Damart (USA), Millrous, **50/1** Urshi-Jade. CSF £120.35, CT £1,073.30. Tote £23.80: £3.80 £2.90 £1.90 £1.50 (£336.10). Mr T. J. Parrott (COOMBE HILL) bred by Highfield Stud and R. G. Percival. 22 Rn 2m 9.5 (7)

SF—42/28/25/41/38/19

**3404** USHER WALKER STKS (2-Y.O.F) £3216.40 (£959.20: £457.60: £206.80)
**1m 54y** 4-00 (4-05)

25574 **Ajanta** *(BWHills)* 8-8 PatEddery (5) (hld up: last st: hdwy over 2f out: qcknd to ld 1f out: r.o wl) ............................................................... —**1**

Kinchenjunga (Fav) *(HRACecil)* 8-8 WRyan (2) (leggy: scope: bit bkwd: w ldr: led 5f out: hrd rdn & hdd 1f out: nt qckn) ......................... 3.**2**

29243 Formal Affair (72) *(CACyzer)* 8-8 DBiggs (6) (3rd st: rdn 3f out: r.o one pce fnl 2f) ........................................................................................... 1½.**3**

3171⁴ Baydon Belle (USA) *(GLewis)* 8-8 PaulEddery (1) (chsd ldrs: 4th st: n.m.r wl
over 1f out: one pce) .................................................................................. s.h.4

3186⁵ Stay With Me Baby **(64)** *(DRCElsworth)* 8-8 GDuffield (4) (6th st: no hdwy fnl 2f) . ¹/₂.5

3181 So Saucy *(CEBrittain)* 8-8 WCarson (led over 3f: 2nd st: wknd over 2f out:
t.o) ...................................................................................................... 25.6

3260 Gold Tassel **(81)** *(RHannon)* 8-8 LDettori (3) (s.i.s: 5th st: bhd fnl 2f: t.o) ......... 10.7

**9/4** Kinchenjunga(6/4—Evens), **11/4** Gold Tassel(2/1—7/2), **9/2** AJANTA, **11/2** Baydon Belle (USA)(7/1—4/1),
**9/1** Formal Affair, **12/1** Ors. CSF £14.68, Tote £5.00: £2.50 £1.50 (£2.90). Mr K. Abdulla (LAMBOURN) bred by
Juddmonte Farms. 7 Rn                                                                                 1m 47.4 (7.8)

---

**3405**    CANADIAN PACIFIC GRADUATION STKS    £3159.20 (£941.60: £448.80: £202.40)
            **1m 1f 213y**                                                       4-30 (4-32)

3237 **Marcus Thorpe (USA) (102)** *(PAKelleway)* 4-9-0 WCarson (4) (b: 2nd st: led
over 3f out: clr over 2f out: unchal) ................................................................ —1

3234 Cosmic Future **(60)** (bl) *(SPCWoods)* 3-8-8 WWoods (2) (led after 1f: hdd over
3f out: hrd rdn over 2f out: no ch w wnr) ............................................................ 25.2

2632 Sirtelimar (IRE) **(57)** *(RCSpicer)* 3-8-13 VSmith (3) (hld up: 4th st: one pce fnl
3f) ........................................................................................................ 8.3

2980a⁵ King's Loch (IRE) **(100)** (Fav) *(HRACecil)* 3-8-8 PatEddery (1) (lw: led 1f: 3rd st:
rdn 4f out: sn lost tch: t.o) ............................................................................. 30.4

**1/2** King's Loch (IRE), **7/4** MARCUS THORPE (USA), **25/1** Cosmic Future, **33/1** Sirtelimar (IRE). CSF £18.12,
Tote £2.20 (£13.10). Mr G. Mazza (NEWMARKET) bred by Stonereath Farms Inc in USA. 4 Rn    2m 8.1 (5.6)
                                                                                          SF—54/—/—/—

---

**3406**    KODAK H'CAP (0-70) £2679.00 (£744.00: £357.00)    **2m 9y**    5-00 (5-02)

1286³ **Snow Board (55)** *(BWHills)* 4-9-5 WCarson (15) (hdwy 7f out: 6th st: hrd rdn 2f
out: str run to ld last strides) ......................................................................... —1

3244 Smilingatstrangers **(49)** (v) *(MrsBarbaraWaring)* 4-8-3 ‡⁷CHawksley (4) (dwlt:
hdwy 8f out: rdn & 7th st: led over 1f out tl ct last strides) . hd.2

3169★ Beauchamp Grace **(68)** (Fav) *(JLDunlop)* 3-9-3 PatEddery (5) (3rd st: hrd rdn
& ev ch 1f out: one pce) .............................................................................. 4.3

3177 Faaz (USA) **(47)** (v) *(AAScott)* 3-7-10 SDawson (7) (lw: in tch: hdwy 7f out: 5th
st: led over 3f out tl over 1f out: one pce) ........................................................ 1¹/₂.4

3075★ Merton Mill **(66)** (bl) *(DMorley)* 5-9-13 PaulEddery (2) (hdwy fnl 2f: nvr nrr) ..... 12.5

3157⁶ Enfant du Paradis (IRE) *(PDEvans)* 4-7-10⁽¹⁾ ‡³SMaloney (13) (hdwy 7f out: wnt
2nd st: wknd over 3f out) ............................................................................. 7.6

2759⁵ Elite Reg **(47)** *(PFICole)* 3-7-10 DBiggs (6) (nvr nrr) ....................................... 3.7

3273 Top Table **(64)** (v) *(MRStoute)* 3-8-13 WRyan (11) (prom: led 5f out tl over 3f
out: sn wknd) ........................................................................................... 6.8

3046 Premier Princess **(41)** *(GAHam)* 6-8-2 GDuffield (3) (lw: nvr nr ldrs) ............... hd.9

3158⁴ Juris Prudence (IRE) **(40)** (bl) *(BAMcMahon)* 4-8-1 JLowe (8) (prom 10f) ...... ³/₄.10

3239 Jarzon Dancer **(34)** *(DAWilson)* 4-7-9 DaleGibson (16) (a bhd) ..................... 2.11

3246⁵ Aldavera **(52)** *(MDixon)* 3-7-10⁽²⁾ ‡⁵ATucker (9) (lw: a bhd) ......................... 2¹/₂.12

3158 Delta Foxtrot (USA) **(56)** *(DWPArbuthnot)* 3-8-5 MHills (1) (lw: led 11f) ........... 3.13

*3180* Wave Master **(43)** *(RJHodges)* 5-8-4 TSprake (14) (a bhd: t.o) ..................... 6.14

3128 Shahdjat (IRE) **(64)** (bl) *(KCBailey)* 4-9-11 MPerrett (10) (w ldr: 4th st: wknd
qckly 4f out: t.o) ....................................................................................... 1¹/₂.15

Belpenel **(45)** *(CASmith)* 6-8-1⁽²⁾ ‡⁵KRutter (12) (bit bkwd: a bhd: t.o) ............. 1¹/₂.16

**2/1** Beauchamp Grace(9/4—3/1), **5/1** SNOW BOARD(4/1—6/1), **7/1** Merton Mill, Shahdjat (IRE)(op 25/1), **10/1**
Elite Reg, Smilingatstrangers(9/2—12/1), Premier Princess, **12/1** Enfant du Paradis (IRE)(10/1—16/1), Juris
Prudence (IRE)(op 8/1), **14/1** Top Table, **16/1** Faaz, Jarzon Dancer, Wave Master, **20/1** Delta Foxtrot
(USA), **25/1** Aldavera, **50/1** Belpenel. CSF £62.29, CT £131.84. Tote £6.80: £1.30 £2.10 £1.30 £6.50
(£128.50). Mr J. Hanson (LAMBOURN) bred by Juddmonte Farms. 16 Rn                    3m 32.3 (7.9)
                                                                                    SF—27/25/35/12/31/—

T/Plpt: £102.00 (21.45 Tckts).                                                                KH

---

## NOTTINGHAM (L-H)

### Tuesday, September 22nd [Good, Good to soft patches]

Going Allowance: St: nil sec per fur (G); Rnd: 0.35 sec per fur (Y)        Wind: almost nil

Stalls: high

**3407**    SIBTHORPE (S) STKS (2-Y-O) £2826.00 (£786.00: £378.00)    **1m 54y**    2-00 (2-06)

3218 **Always Risky (49)** *(PAKelleway)* 8-6 GayKelleway (13) (hld up: hdwy 3f out:
qcknd to ld over 1f out: sn clr) ...................................................................... —1

3301² Merry Mermaid **(48)** *(JFBottomley)* 8-6  PBurke (17) (swtg: hdwy over 2f out: sn
ev ch: r.o ins fnl f: no ch w wnr) .......................... 1¹/₂.2
3071 Pinkerton's Silver **(44)** (bl) *(MHEasterby)* 8-11  MBirch (14) (led 1f: 2nd st: led
over 3f out tl over 2f out: one pce) .......................... 7.3
2563 Summers Dream **(51)** *(BRichmond)* 8-1 ‡5StephenDavies (18) (prom: 3rd st:
led over 2f out tl appr fnl f: sn outpcd) .......................... nk.4
3115⁶ Hush Baby (IRE) *(DMorris)* 8-8⁽²⁾ MTebbutt (3) (gd hdwy appr fnl f: nrst fin) ...... hd.5
3146⁴ Gypsy Crystal (USA) *(RMWhitaker)* 8-6  ACulhane (9) (hdwy ent st: rdn & btn
over 1f out) .......................... s.h.6
2916 We Are Doomed **(52)** *(JRFanshawe)* 8-11  RHills (16) (hdwy over 2f out: nt rch
ldrs) .......................... 1¹/₂.7
2782⁶ Carnea **(47)** *(JGFitzGerald)* 8-6  KFallon (6) (prom: 4th st: rdn & wknd 2f out) .... ³/₄.8
3173³ The Gold Souk (IRE) **(60)** *(JLDunlop)* 8-11  JReid (20) (chsd ldrs: 5th st: wknd
over 2f out) .......................... 1.9
3106 Merryhill Kerry (IRE) *(JLHarris)* 8-6  DHolland (19) (swtg: chsd ldrs: 7th st: rdn &
wknd 2f out) .......................... s.h.10
1959⁴ Karinska *(SirMarkPrescott)* 8-6  GDuffield (5) (plld hrd: hld up: effrt 2f out: hrd
rdn & wknd over 1f out) .......................... nk.11
2983 Eastern Glow *(SPCWoods)* 8-6  WWoods (10) (b.hind: chsd ldrs: 6th st: rdn
over 2f out: sn btn) .......................... ¹/₂.12
2696 Hot Storm **(64)** *(MJCamacho)* 8-6  NConnorton (7) (m.n.s) .......................... 2¹/₂.13
3164⁶ Go Orange **(48)** *(JLSpearing)* 7-13 ‡7CHawksley (15) (effrt 3f out: no imp) ...... 3.14
3283 Don't Be Saki (IRE) **(55)** (v) *(JEtherington)* 8-6  NDay (2) (swtg: m.n.s) ...... 1¹/₂.15
3175 April Double (IRE) **(56)** *(MHTompkins)* 8-6  PRobinson (4) (bhd fr ¹/₂-wy) ...... 2.16
3250³ Ample (IRE) **(Fav)** *(PFICole)* 8-6  TQuinn (11) (chsd ldrs: effrt over 3f out: sn
wknd) .......................... s.h.17
3301 Emmandee **(57)** (bl) *(MWEasterby)* 8-11  TLucas (12) (lw: led after 1f tl over 3f
out: sn wknd: t.o) .......................... 8.18
1442 Krayyan Dawn **(42)** (bl) *(RVoorspuy)* 8-11  SDawson (8) (bkwd: t.o) ............ 30.19
2994³ El Nino (IRE) (7/1) Withdrawn (lame at s) : not under orders

**7/2** Ample (IRE), **11/2** The Gold Souk (IRE), Gypsy Crystal (USA), **6/1** Karinska, **13/2** Hush Baby (IRE), **11/1**
Eastern Glow, **12/1** Hot Storm, Merry Mermaid, **16/1** Pinkerton's Silver, We Are Doomed, **20/1** Don't Be Saki
(IRE), April Double (IRE), **25/1** Carnea, **33/1** ALWAYS RISKY, Go Orange, Emmandee, Summers Dream, **50/1**
Ors. CSF £390.73, Tote £183.10: £33.00 £3.40 £23.70 (£184.60). Mr P. A. Kelleway (NEWMARKET) bred by
Roldvale Ltd. 19 Rn; Bt in 4,000 gns                     1m 47.2 (7.6)
SF—20/15/–/–/–/–

**3408**     HAWTHORNE PRINTERS NURSERY     £3925.90 (£1178.20: £567.60: £262.30)
**1m 54y**                                     2-30 (2-40)

3091 **Boldville Bash (IRE) (65)** *(TDBarron)* 7-10  JFanning (10) (bhd: rdn & hdwy
over 2f out: led ins fnl f: styd on) .......................... —1
2675⁴ Blue Blazer **(83)** *(BHanbury)* 9-0  GDuffield (20) (lw: hld up & bhd: hdwy 2f out:
ev ch ins fnl f: r.o) .......................... nk.2
3160⁵ Pistols At Dawn (USA) **(65)** *(RHannon)* 7-10⁽¹⁾ TyroneWilliams (18) (a.p: 6th st:
ev ch 1f out: unable qckn) .......................... 3¹/₂.3
3199⁶ Latin Leader **(75)** **(Fav)** *(MrsJRRamsden)* 8-6  GBaxter (1) (chsd ldrs: 6th st: rdn
& ev ch 2f out: no ex fnl f) .......................... 2¹/₂.4
3044⁶ Festin **(72)** (bl) *(JLDunlop)* 8-3  DHolland (12) (led: wnt clr 3f out: hdd jst ins fnl f:
one pce) .......................... hd.5
3385⁵ Contract Elite (IRE) **(65)** *(CWThornton)* 7-3⁽³⁾ ‡7CHawksley (5) (lw: b.off hind:
sme hdwy fnl 2f: nvr nrr) .......................... ¹/₂.6
2652³ Beaver Brook **(75)** *(RHannon)* 8-6  BRaymond (6) (chsd ldrs: 7th st: effrt over 2f
out: no imp) .......................... 1¹/₂.7
2285⁶ Manon Lescaut **(62)** *(APJarvis)* 7-0 ‡7DWright (14) (nvr nrr) .......................... 1¹/₂.8
3193⁶ Qaffal (USA) **(90)** *(DMorley)* 9-7  PRobinson (15) (nvr nr to chal) .......................... 1¹/₂.9
3199 Atherton Green (IRE) **(70)** *(JAGlover)* 7-12 ‡3SMaloney (13) (prom: 2nd st: rdn
& wknd 2f out) .......................... hd.10
3171⁵ Villavina **(74)** *(SDow)* 8-5  TQuinn (4) (hld up: hdwy 3f out: wknd over 1f out) . nk.11
3100 Turfmans Vision **(72)** *(RHollinshead)* 8-3⁽²⁾ WRyan (9) (a bhd) .......................... nk.12
2972⁴ Dhahran **(67)** *(PFICole)* 7-12⁽²⁾ AMunro (2) (prom to ¹/₂-wy) .......................... hd.13
3148 Red Cent **(64)** *(JEtherington)* 7-9  LCharnock (7) (hdwy over 3f out: swtchd rt
over 2f out: no imp) .......................... ³/₄.14
3173 Stevie's Wonder (IRE) **(66)** (bl) *(WCarter)* 7-11  JLowe (16) (m.n.s) .......................... 3.15
2961⁴ Romalito **(72)** *(MBlanshard)* 8-3  DMcKeown (19) (m.n.s) .......................... hd.16
3030 Tajdid (IRE) **(70)** *(HThomsonJones)* 8-1  RHills (8) (mid div tl wknd over 3f out:
t.o) .......................... ³/₄.17
3172⁴ On Request (IRE) **(73)** *(IABalding)* 8-4  MHills (3) (t.o) .......................... 2.18
3307 Dusty Point (IRE) **(66)** (bl) *(BHanbury)* 7-11  EJohnson (11) (prom: 4th st: wknd
over 2f out: t.o) .......................... 2¹/₂.19

3250 Junction Twentytwo (69) (v) (CDBroad) 7-7(7) ‡7CAvery (17) (plld hrd: 4th st: sn
          rdn & wknd: t.o) ............................................................. 4.20
          LONG HANDICAP: Contract Elite (IRE) 7-6, Manon Lescaut 7-2, Junction Twentytwo 7-2.

7/2 Latin Leader(5/2—9/2), 7/1 BOLDVILLE BASH (IRE)(6/1—9/1), 8/1 Festin, 10/1 Beaver Brook, 12/1 Blue
Blazer, Contract Elite (IRE), 14/1 Qaffal (USA), On Request (IRE), Atherton Green (IRE), 16/1 Tajdid (IRE),
Romalito, 20/1 Villavina, Dhahran, Pistols At Dawn (USA), 25/1 Red Cent, Dusty Point (IRE), Stevie's Wonder
(IRE), 33/1 Ors. CSF £87.21, CT £1,490.26. Tote £9.30: £2.60 £3.30 £3.10 £1.40 (£31.10). Mr P. D. Savill
(THIRSK) bred by Louis A. Walshe in Ireland. 20 Rn                                    1m 46.3 (6.7)
                                                                              SF—23/40/11/13/9/–

**3409**     NOTTINGHAM GOOSE FAIR H'CAP (0-70) £2931.00 (£816.00: £393.00)
             1¾m 15y                                                        3-00 (3-07)

3075 **John Shaw (USA) (44)** (CTinkler) 4-8-2 PBurke (2) (in tch: hdwy 4f out: led
          over 1f out: all out) ....................................................... —1
32446 Mrs Barton (IRE) (56) (bl) (BWHills) 4-9-0 GDuffield (18) (hld up: hdwy 7f out:
          6th st: rdn & ev ch fnl f: no imp) ................................. s.h.2
3381 Anar (IRE) (49) (WCarter) 3-7-8(4) ‡3FNorton (20) (a.p: 3rd st: rdn to ld 3f out:
          hdd over 1f out: no ex fnl f) .................................. 2½.3
32194 Heavenly Waters (59) (Fav) (RFJohnsonHoughton) 3-8-7 WRyan (13) (b.hind:
          hld up: hdwy fnl 2f: fin wl: too much to do) ................... 2.4
3102 Taroob (IRE) (65) (JLDunlop) 3-8-13 RHills (12) (lw: hld up: hdwy over 2f out:
          styd on fnl f) .................................................. 2.5
30346 Shoofe (USA) (70) (v) (DMorley) 4-10-0 BRaymond (19) (hld up: hdwy over 2f out:
          rdn 2f out: no imp) ........................................... 4.6
31023 Indian Territory (55) (DHaydnJones) 3-8-3 TyroneWilliams (6) (chsd ldrs: 4th
          st: wknd 2f out) ............................................... s.h.7
3143 Young George (49) (MDods) 5-8-7 JReid (3) (nvr nrr) .................... 1.8
31045 Izitallworthit (45) (JMackie) 3-7-7 SWood (8) (nvr trbld ldrs) ........ 1½.9
          Emperors Warrior (45) (CDBroad) 6-7-10 ‡7CAvery (16) (a in rr) ........ hd.10
30414 Gesnera (39) (KWhite) 4-7-4(3) ‡7AGarth (5) (chsd ldrs: effrt & 5th st: wknd over
          2f out) ....................................................... ¾.11
32214 Prosequendo (USA) (67) (MDixon) 9-9-11 MPerrett (4) (m.n.s) ........... ½.12
3256 Judge and Jury (59) (MJFetherston-Godley) 3-8-7 TQuinn (11) (prom:
          pushed along ½-wy: rdn & wknd ent st: t.o) ................... 15.13
29404 Access Ski (64) (RBoss) 5-9-8 MTebbutt (14) (bkwd: chsd ldrs 9f: sn wknd: t.o) 2.14
29155 Regal Lover (IRE) (70) (v) (MBell) 3-9-4 MHills (1) (lw: prom: led ent st to 3f out:
          sn rdn & wknd: t.o) ........................................... 1½.15
          Wylam (43) (GHEden) 5-8-1(3) PRobinson (9) (bkwd: propped s: a bhd: t.o) nk.16
          Sole Control (49) (HCandy) 4-8-7 SDawson (15) (bkwd: a bhd: t.o) ....... 1½.17
3139 Royal Verse (FR) (40) (RCurtis) 5-7-5 ‡7CHawksley (10) (led: clr 10f out: wknd,
          hdd & 2nd st: t.o) ............................................ 15.18
20873 Handy Lass (57) (MrsJRRamsden) 3-8-5 GBaxter (7) (swtg: t.o) ............ 6.19
          Tarmon (IRE) (38) (ABarrow) 4-7-10 JLowe (17) (bkwd: t.o fnl 5f) ........ 10.20

7/2 Heavenly Waters, 7/1 Mrs Barton (IRE), 8/1 Regal Lover (IRE), 9/1 Handy Lass(op 6/1), Prosequendo (USA),
10/1 Shoofe (USA), JOHN SHAW (USA), Access Ski, 12/1 Indian Territory(op 8/1), 14/1 Taroob (IRE), Gesnera, 16/1 Izitallworthit, Anar (IRE),
Young George, JOHN SHAW (USA), Access Ski, 21/1 Judge and Jury, 25/1 Sole Control, 33/1 Royal Verse (FR),
50/1 Ors. CSF £127.41, CT £1,710.07. Tote £21.00: £4.30 £2.10 £3.40 £1.70 (£57.50). Mrs Sheila Walker
(MALTON) bred by Flaxman Holdings Ltd. in USA. 20 Rn                         3m 8.7 (10.2)
                                                                    SF—35/46/21/30/32/39

**3410**     TATTERSALLS AUCTION SERIES STKS (Qualifier) (Mdn 2-Y.O) £3057.00 (£852.00:
             £411.00)  6f 15y                                               3-30 (3-37)

3285 **Gangleader (60)** (SPCWoods) 8-8 WWoods (14) (a.p stands' side: led 2f out:
          r.o wl) ......................................................... —1
3214 Primo Figlio (RHannon) 8-7 BRaymond (8) (a.p: rdn & ev ch appr fnl f: r.o) .... 2½.2
          Nico Mike (Fav) (PWChapple-Hyam) 8-10 JReid (16) (lw: gd sort: dwlt: hdwy
          ½-wy: ev ch 2f out: one pce) ................................... 1½.3
3275 Kensworth Lady (64) (MBlanshard) 8-2 DHolland (1) (hdwy ½-wy: ev ch appr
          fnl f: unable qckn) ........................................... hd.4
28325 Charrua (JRFanshawe) 8-5 GDuffield (3) (chsd ldrs: rdn & no hdwy fnl f) ..... nk.5
2924 Dancing Diamond (IRE) (CFWall) 8-1 PRobinson (10) (hdwy 2f out: unable
          qckn fnl f) ................................................... hd.6
21182 Mr Cube (60) (PFICole) 8-9 TQuinn (4) (a.p centre: rdn over 1f out: one pce) .. 2.7
3175 Silver Groom (IRE) (71) (APJarvis) 8-0 ‡7DWright (3) (hld up: hdwy on outside 2f
          out: nt rch ldrs) ............................................. hd.8
3303 Wrightmill (IRE) (v) (CTinkler) 8-7 MBirch (24) (led stands' side 4f) ...... s.h.9
3130 Bransby Road (IRE) (RAkehurst) 8-5 ‡3RPerham (9) (chsd ldrs centre over 4f) 2½.10

3285 More Than Love *(PAKelleway)* 8-2[1] JCarroll (17) (chsd ldrs stands' side: rdn 2f
out: sn btn) ............................................................................. ½.11
Precussion *(RWArmstrong)* 8-9 BCrossley (20) (lengthy: m.n.s) ............... 1½.12
3214 Cutthroat Kid (IRE) *(SGNorton)* 8-11 KDarley (19) (prom stands' side over 4f) . 1.13
Bold Line *(RJRWilliams)* 8-7 MHills (7) (w'like: led centre 4f) ...................... s.h.14
2074 Ring Tom (IRE) *(MWEasterby)* 8-6 TLucas (11) (m.n.s) ........................... ½.15
3077 Simply Superb *(MWEasterby)* 8-8 LCharnock (15) (m.n.s) ...................... s.h.16
2274 Dontbetalking (IRE) *(JWharton)* 8-0 JFanning (18) (s.s: a bhd) ............... s.h.17
847 Honey Juice *(MFetherston-Godley)* 8-2 RHills (23) (prom stands' side over 3f) ½.18
3240 Il Moro Di Venezia (IRE) *(JLDunlop)* 8-6 AClark (22) (m.n.s) ................. nk.19
2758 Welsh Pet *(PJMakin)* 8-2 AMunro (5) (n.d) ...................................... 2½.20
3055 Dragonmist (IRE) *(GLewis)* 8-2 JLowe (2) (n.d) ................................. s.h.21
3077 Beckyhannah *(RBastiman)* 8-3[3] DMcKeown (6) (a bhd) ...................... hd.22
The Country Dancer *(MrsLPiggott)* 8-0 SDawson (12) (b: b.hind: lengthy: unf:
s.s: a bhd) .......................................................................... 2½.23
3208 Allez Bianco (62) (v) *(RJHolder)* 7-13 ‡³FNorton (21) (m.n.s) .................. ¾.24

9/2 Nico Mike(6/1—4/1), 11/2 Primo Figlio(9/4—6/1), 8/1 Cutthroat Kid (IRE), 9/1 Il Moro Di Venezia
(IRE)(20/1—8/1), 10/1 Charrua, Mr Cube (IRE), 12/1 Bransby Road (IRE)(op 5/1), 14/1 Bold Line, Kensworth
Lady, 16/1 Allez Bianco, Silver Groom (IRE), 20/1 Precussion, 25/1 GANGLEADER, Dragonmist (IRE), Honey
Juice, 33/1 Welsh Pet, Ring Tom (IRE), Wrightmill (IRE), The Country Dancer, Dontbetalking (IRE), Beckyhannah,
50/1 0 rs. CSF £160.55, Tote £120.30: £24.85 £2.10 £3.10 (£29.40). Mr Victor Sujanani (NEWMARKET) bred
by Dodford Stud. 24 Rn
1m 14.4 (3.4)
SF—26/15/12/3/5/2

---

## 3411

COLWICK MEDIAN AUCTION STKS (2-Y.O) £2826.00 (£786.00: £378.00)
6f 15y                                                              4-00 (4-01)

2832★ Snowy River (FR) (85) *(DrJDScargill)* 9-2 LPiggott (6) (mde all: qcknd over 1f
out: comf) ........................................................................... —1
3181 Smarginato (IRE) *(JLDunlop)* 8-11 JReid (4) (hld up & bhd: hdwy wl over 1f out:
r.o ins fnl f) ......................................................................... 2.2
3385⁶ Rocket to the Moon (83) *(PWChapple-Hyam)* 8-11 ‡⁵JWeaver (2) (chsd
wnr: rdn over 1f out: no ex fnl f) .................................................. 1.3
3049 Heathyards Gem (59) *(RHollinshead)* 8-11 WRyan (7) (prom tl wknd over 1f out) 5.4
3160 Rad *(SPCWoods)* 8-11 WWoods (3) (hld up: effrt 2f out: nt pce to chal) ........... 1.5
3255★ Pluck (83) (Fav) *(RCharlton)* 8-11 TQuinn (1) (chsd ldrs: rdn over 2f out: sn btn:
t.o) ................................................................................. 6.6
2010 Sober Lad (IRE) (80) *(JBerry)* 9-7 JCarroll (5) (a bhd: t.o) ..................... ½.7

10/11 Pluck, 3/1 SNOWY RIVER (FR)(op 2/1), 13/2 Rocket to the Moon (IRE)(op 4/1), 10/1 Sober Lad (IRE)(op
6/1), 20/1 Smarginato (IRE), Heathyards Gem, 25/1 Rad. CSF £43.91, Tote £3.10: £2.50 £7.40 (£27.10). M.
Reditt & Son Ltd (NEWMARKET) bred by Stavros Niarchos in France. 7 Rn
1m 14.1 (3.1)
SF—40/27/23/3/–/–

---

## 3412

FISKERTON STKS (Mdn 3-Y.O) £2616.00 (£726.00: £348.00)     6f 15y     4-30 (4-33)

3133 Jumaira Star (USA) (68) (v) (Fav) *(JHMGosden)* 9-0 LPiggott (13) (lw: a.p: rdn
to ld over 1f out: edgd rt fnl f: drvn out) .......................................... —1
2206⁴ Admirals Realm (50) *(BAMcMahon)* 9-0 MBirch (8) (lw: a.p: hrd rdn appr fnl f:
unable qckn) ...................................................................... 2.2
Alfaari (USA) *(MajorWRHern)* 9-0 RHills (6) (lengthy: scope: dwlt: hdwy 2f out:
r.o ins fnl f) ........................................................................ 2.3
Ulladulla *(RAkehurst)* 8-11 ‡³RPerham (4) (lt-f: hdwy over 1f out: r.o ins fnl f) ...... ½.4
2666³ Blue Is True (IRE) (51) *(LJBarratt)* 8-9 LCharnock (15) (chsd ldrs: swtchd rt over
1f out: one pce) ................................................................... hd.5
3252⁶ Pleasuring (51) *(MMcCormack)* 8-9 AClark (9) (b.nr hind: prom over 4f) ........ 2.6
3142² So Superb (66) (v) *(JLDunlop)* 9-0 JReid (10) (led tl over 1f out: sn rdn & wknd) ¾.7
3252 Join the Clan *(MrsNMacauley)* 8-9 TSprake (2) (prom 4f) ...................... ½.8
Access Voyager *(RBoss)* 9-0 MTebbutt (11) (lw: a bhd) .......................... nk.9
3119 Virginia Cottage (36) *(BAMcMahon)* 8-9 JFortune (1) (chsd ldrs on outside: rdn
over 2f out: no imp) ............................................................... 1½.10
3252⁵ Vellandrucha (46) *(JABennett)* 8-9 JCarroll (7) (a bhd) ........................ 2.11
3238 Our Man in Havana *(PFICole)* 9-0 TQuinn (9) (nvr trbld ldrs) ................... 3.12
3042 Queen Canute (IRE) *(FHLee)* 8-9 DMcKeown (5) (prom to ½-way: sn wknd) 1½.13
Poyle Amber *(MBlanshard)* 8-9 DHolland (12) (w'like: bkwd: outpcd: t.o) ...... dist.14

2/1 JUMAIRA STAR (USA)(6/4—9/4), 7/2 So Superb(4/1—6/1), 7/1 Alfaari (USA)(op 2/1), 8/1 Access
Voyager(4/1—10/1), Our Man in Havana(12/1—16/1), 14/1 Ulladulla, 16/1 Pleasuring,
20/1 Admirals Realm, 25/1 Blue Is True (IRE)(12/1—16/1), 33/1 Virginia Cottage, Queen Canute (IRE), Join the Clan, 50/1 Poyle
Amber. CSF £42.21, Tote £2.70: £1.40 £3.50 £2.20 (£16.20). Sheikh Ahmed Al Maktoum (NEWMARKET) bred
by Seahorse 84 in USA. 14 Rn
1m 14.4 (3.4)
SF—32/24/16/11/8/–

## 3413
BUNNY SPRINT H'CAP (F & M) (0-70) £3078.00 (£858.00: £414.00)
6f 15y
5-00 (5-05)

3264³ **My Ruby Ring (39)** (DRLaing) 5–7-13 TyroneWilliams (7) (chsd ldrs: rdn to ld ins fnl f: r.o wl) ...... —1

3290 Almasa (60) (DMorris) 4–9-1 ‡⁵StephenDavies (18) (hdwy over 1f out: fin wl) ..... 2.2

3264 Swinging Tich (50) (BAMcMahon) 3–8-7 MBirch (17) (bhd: gd hdwy appr fnl f: fin wl) .......... 1½.3

3294³ Barbara's Cutie (41) (v) (MBlanshard) 4–7-8⁽³⁾ ‡⁷CAvery (1) (led tl hdd & wknd ins fnl f) .......... s.h.4

2984 Dancing Wild (36) (MrsGRReveley) 3–7-0 ‡⁷DarrenMoffatt (6) (hld up: gd hdwy appr fnl f: nrst fin) .......... ¾.5

2881 Prepare (IRE) (37) (RJHolder) 4–7-8⁽²⁾ ‡³FNorton (3) (lw: prom: rdn over 1f out: sn btn) .......... ¾.6

3341⁴ Katie-a (IRE) (53) (RMWhitaker) 3–8-10 ACulhane (19) (lw: chsd ldrs: no hdwy fnl 2f) .......... ½.7

3264⁴ Bernstein Bette (64) (PSFelgate) 6–9-10 WRyan (16) (swtchd centre sn after s: effrt appr fnl f: no imp) .......... 1.8

3198 Merryhill Maid (IRE) (65) (JLHarris) 4–9-11 GBaxter (4) (b: nvr nrr) .................. 1.9

2931 Weekend Girl (38) (WMBrisbourne) 3–7-9⁽²⁾ LCharnock (8) (m.n.s) .......... 1½.10

3119³ Tickham Vixen (IRE) (47) (JDBethell) 4–8-7 GDuffield (14) (lw: nvr plcd to chal) .... nk.11

3166² Miss Aragon (47) (MissLCSiddall) 4–8-2 ‡⁵JWeaver (13) (spd 4f) .......... nk.12

3079⁶ The Dream Maker (IRE) (43) (MrsNMacauley) 3–7-7⁽⁶⁾ ‡⁷MHumphries (20) (w ldrs stands' side over 4f) .......... 1.13

2536⁶ Miss Brightside (36) (ASmith) 4–7-10 JLowe (5) (w ldrs 4f) .......... hd.14

3239 Ryewater Dream (44) (bl) (RJHodges) 4–8-4 TSprake (2) (swtg: outpcd) ........ ½.15

2945 Sharling (70) (JHMGosden) 3–9-13 PRobinson (15) (swtg: dwlt: a in rr) ........ hd.16

3105 Scarlet Princess (45) (RJHodges) 4–8-5 DHolland (10) (prom over 3f: sn lost tch) .......... ½.17

LONG HANDICAP: Dancing Wild 7-6, Weekend Girl 6-8.

*Stewards Enquiry: Weaver fined £100 under Rule 161 (III) (failure to draw correct weight).*

**4/1** Bernstein Bette(6/1—7/2), **7/1** Katie-a (IRE), **8/1** MY RUBY RING(op 12/1), **9/1** Scarlet Princess, **10/1** Miss Aragon(op 6/1), Almasa(op 6/1), Sharling, **12/1** Barbara's Cutie(op 6/1), **14/1** Merryhill Maid (IRE), **16/1** Dancing Wild, **20/1** Miss Brightside, Prepare (IRE), The Dream Maker (IRE), Swinging Tich, Tickham Vixen (IRE), Ryewater Dream, **50/1** Weekend Girl. CSF £83.12, CT £1,437.95. Tote £7.60: £1.50 £2.50 £5.20 £5.40 (£31.80). Mrs Marion Wickham (LAMBOURN) bred by Mrs Wickham. 17 Rn

1m 13.9 (2.9)

SF—27/35/21/7/–/–

T/Plpt: £429.50 (5.95 Tckts).

IM

---

### Tuesday, September 22nd [Good becoming Good to soft]
Going Allowance: 1st: 0.15 sec; 2-4: 0.30 sec (G); 5 & 6: 0.60 sec (Y)          Wind: nil

Stalls: high

## 3414
E.B.F. DUXFORD STKS (Mdn 2-Y.O.F) £2805.00 (£780.00: £375.00)
6f 2-15 (2-18)

3011² **Mithl Al Hawa** (Fav) (JRFanshawe) 8-11 WRSwinburn (13) (b.hind: a.p: led over 1f out: comf) .......... —1

Woodwardia (USA) (BWHills) 8-8 PatEddery (14) (unf: a.p: led 2f out tl over 1f out: unable qckn) .......... 3.2

Vayavaig (JRFanshawe) 8-8 BRouse (10) (unf: scope: a.p: rdn over 1f out: one pce) .......... 2.3

2459⁵ Oare Sparrow (PTWalwyn) 8-11 LDettori (3) (a.p: hrd rdn over 1f out: one pce) 3.4

2859 Western Valley (KOCunningham-Brown) 8-11 SWhitworth (18) (spd over 4f) .... 2.5

3099³ Forest Song (RCharlton) 8-11 PaulEddery (17) (led 4f) .......... s.h.6

2338⁶ Dittisham (USA) (RHannon) 8-11 RCochrane (4) (nvr nr to chal) .......... 1½.7

Sky Burst (LGCottrell) 8-8 NCarlisle (6) (neat: nvr nrr) .......... 6.8

1913 Dents du Midi (USA) (RWArmstrong) 8-11 GBardwell (2) (lw: outpcd) ........... s.h.9

Zhaab (MMadgwick) 8-8 AMcGlone (12) (str: bit bkwd: prom 4f) .......... nk.10

3181 Jolis Absent (MJRyan) 8-11 DBiggs (5) (outpcd) .......... ½.11

3261⁶ Dorazine (CJHill) 8-11 NAdams (11) (outpcd) .......... nk.12

2546 Brave Bidder (BGubby) 8-11 JQuinn (16) (prom over 3f) .......... s.h.13

2994 Petiole (WRMuir) 8-11 CRutter (8) (swtg: bhd fnl 2f) .......... ¾.14

Rosscoyne (WRMuir) 8-8 MRoberts (9) (b.hind: w'like: bit bkwd: a bhd) ...... 2½.15

Pink Orchid (MPMuggeridge) 8-8 JWilliams (4) (unf: a bhd) .......... 2½.16

3186 Dotty's Walker (FR) (CACyzer) 8-11 GCarter (1) (outpcd: t.o) .......... 20.17

5/6 MITHL AL HAWA, **4/1** Woodwardia (USA), **10/1** Forest Song(op 4/1), **12/1** Dittisham (USA)(6/1—14/1),
**20/1** Oare Sparrow, Vayavaig, **33/1** Dents du Midi (USA), **50/1** Rosscoyne, Sky Burst, Zhaab(op 8/1), Pink
Orchid, **100/1** Ors. CSF £4.27, Tote £1.80: £1.10 £1.50 £5.20 (£3.20). Mr Mohamed Suhail (NEWMARKET)
bred by Gainsborough Stud Management Ltd. 17 Rn
1m 14.79 (3.49)
SF—45/30/22/13/5/4

## 3415
TANGMERE H'CAP (0-90) £3640.50 (£1089.00: £522.00: £238.50)
1¾m
2-45 (2-46)

3206⁶ **Top Spin (76)** *(MajorWRHern)* 3–9–0 JWilliams (2) (hdwy 5f out: 6th st: hrd rdn
fnl f: led last stride) ............................................................ —1
3007² Persian Fantasy **(86)** *(JLDunlop)* 3–9–10 WCarson (4) (5th st: led 2f out: hrd rdn
ins fnl f: hdd last stride) .................................................... hd.2
3007⁴ Dime Bag **(68)** *(BWHills)* 3–8–3 ‡3DHarrison (12) (hdwy over 2f out: hrd rdn over
1f out: one pce) ................................................................ 3.3
3244 Haitham **(80)** *(RAkehurst)* 5–10–0 RCochrane (3) (2nd st: led over 2f out: sn
hdd: one pce) .................................................................. 5.4
2934⁶ Maestroso (IRE) **(67)** (bl) *(RFJohnsonHoughton)* 3–8–5 PaulEddery (5) (lost pl
over 3f out: r.o one pce fnl 2f) ........................................... 2½.5
3273⁴ Miss Pin Up **(69)** *(PatMitchell)* 3–8–7 DBiggs (8) (nvr nr to chal) .................. 2.6
269¹² Blue Flag (USA) **(78)** *(LordHuntingdon)* 3–9–2 LDettori (7) (lw: no hdwy fnl 3f) .. 4.7
2992 Storm Dust **(69)** *(JRFanshawe)* 3–8–7 GCarter (6) (3rd st: wknd 2f out) ......... 6.8
3007⁵ Mootawel (USA) **(75)** *(HThomsonJones)* 3–8–13 PatEddery (9) (swtg: led over
11f) .............................................................................. 2.9
700★ Pica **(81)** (Fav) *(HRACecil)* 3–9–5 SCauthen (11) (lw: rdn 4f out: bhd fnl 2f) .. 1½.10
3256 Tonkawa **(69)** *(JMBradley)* 7–9–3 NAdams (1) (b: dwlt: a bhd) ................... nk.11
3293² Major's Law (IRE) **(67)** *(CEBrittain)* 3–8–5 MRoberts (10) (swtg: 4th st: wknd
over 2f out) .................................................................... 2.12
3221 Themeda **(68)** *(CHNelson)* 3–8–0 OWhitworth (13) (a bhd) ..................... 7.13

**4/1** Pica(3/1—9/2), **6/1** Miss Pin Up, Major's Law (IRE), **13/2** Persian Fantasy, **8/1** Mootawel (USA), **9/1**
Maestroso (IRE), **14/1** Dime Bag, TOP SPIN, Blue Flag (USA), Storm Dust, **16/1** Haitham, **33/1** Themeda, **66/1**
Tonkawa. CSF £93.68, CT £1,187.95. Tote £22.10: £6.10 £2.00 £3.40 (£97.10). Mrs Hugh Dalgety
(LAMBOURN) bred by Wick-Dromdiah Investments Ltd and R. J. McCreery. 13 Rn
3m 7.94 (11.34)
SF—29/38/11/26/–/–

## 3416
HIPPODROME D'EVRY STKS (Mdn 3-Y.O.F) £2511.00 (£696.00: £333.00)
1m (J.C)
3-15 (3-18)

1532² **Galactic Miss** *(JLDunlop)* 8–11 GCarter (2) (swtg: 4th st: chsd ldr over 2f out:
hrd rdn over 1f out: led ins fnl f: r.o wl) ............................... —1
3085⁵ Draft Board (Fav) *(JHMGosden)* 8–11 RCochrane (5) (a.p: led over 3f out:
qcknd over 2f out: hdd ins fnl f: unable qckn) ...................... 3.2
Littlewick (IRE) *(GWragg)* 8–11 PaulEddery (4) (w'like: bit bkwd: hdwy over 2f
out: one pce) .................................................................. 8.3
3174 Hamanaka (USA) **(65)** *(JRFanshawe)* 8–11 RRouse (17) (5th st: wknd over 2f
out) .............................................................................. 4.4
3203⁵ Pippin Park (USA) **(72)** *(HCanty)* 8–11 CRutter (11) (2nd st: wknd 2f out) ......... 2.5
2886 Broadway Ruckus (CAN) *(DRLaing)* 8–11 JWilliams (14) (nvr nr to chal) ......... 4.7
3216 Dancing Miss (IRE) *(PRHedger)* 8–11 AMcGlone (10) (nvr nrr) .................. 4.7
Ballet Society (FR) *(JHMGosden)* 8–11 GHind (15) (str: s.s: nvr nrr) ......... 1½.8
3216⁴ Spanish Glory **(56)** *(KOCunningham-Brown)* 8–11 DBiggs (9) (nvr nrr) ........... nk.9
3238 Emily Allan (IRE) *(KOCunningham-Brown)* 8–11 SWhitworth (16) (swtg: a mid
div) .............................................................................. ¾.10
3022 Hullo Mary Doll (bl) *(RIngram)* 8–4 ‡7RossBerry (3) (reluctant to r: nvr nrr) ...... 2½.11
2995⁵ Great Splendour *(CEBrittain)* 8–11 SCauthen (8) (6th st: wknd 3f out) .......... 3.12
2987 Queen Warrior **(64)** *(PTWalwyn)* 8–11 PatEddery (12) (bhd fnl 3f) ............... 2½.13
Modern Dance (USA) *(LMCumani)* 8–11 LDettori (6) (leggy: prom over 4f) ...... 8.14
3078⁶ Rutbah *(ACStewart)* 8–11 MRoberts (13) (led over 4f: 2nd st: wknd 3f out) ...... ½.15
3216 Chandni (IRE) *(BHanbury)* 8–11 WRSwinburn (7) (bhd fnl 4f) ................... 12.16

**3/1** Draft Board, **6/1** Pippin Park (USA)(3/1—7/1), **7/1** Queen Warrior(op 4/1), **8/1** Great Splendour, GALACTIC
MISS, **9/1** Littlewick (IRE)(5/1—10/1), Modern Dance (USA)(6/1—10/1), **12/1** Rutbah(op 8/1), Hamanaka
(USA), **14/1** Ballet Society (FR)(8/1—16/1), **20/1** Spanish Glory, **50/1** Ors. CSF £31.81, Tote £5.00: £1.90
£1.80 £4.90 (£14.90). Mr P. G. Goulandris (ARUNDEL) bred by Hesmonds Stud Ltd. 16 Rn
1m 43.01 (6.41)
SF—37/28/4/–/–/–

## 3417
BIGGIN HILL H'CAP (0-80) £3816.00 (£1143.00: £549.00: £252.00)
7f (rnd)
3-45 (3-47)

3105★ **Millsolin (IRE) (65)** (Fav) *(RAkehurst)* 4–9–3 GCarter (8) (5th st: led over 1f out:
hrd rdn: r.o wl) .............................................................. —1

3203⁴ Merlins Wish (USA) **(80)** *(RHannon)* 3–10-0 PatEddery (7) (hrd rdn & hdwy over 1f out: r.o) .................................................................. 2¹/₂.2

2687★ Spencer's Revenge **(69)** *(LordHuntingdon)* 3–9-0 ‡³DHarrison (13) (lw: hdwy 2f out: r.o) ......................................................... ³/₄.3

3002⁴ Garth **(73)** (v) *(PJMakin)* 4–9-11 LDettori (4) (hdwy 2f out: r.o) ............... 2¹/₂.4

3245⁵ Nobby Barnes **(57)** *(DAWilson)* 3–8-5 GBardwell (2) (b: hdwy fnl 2f: nvr nrr) .. 1¹/₂.5

3317★ Darakah **(63)** *(CJHill)* 5–9-1 (6x) WCarson (6) (lw: outpcd: nvr nrr) ......... ³/₄.6

3277 Dance on Sixpence **(58)** *(HJCollingridge)* 4–8-10 JQuinn (15) (3rd st: ev ch over 1f out: sn wknd) ............................................................ hd.7

3004 Ler Cru (IRE) **(61)** *(CEBrittain)* 3–8-9 MRoberts (1) (lw: 2nd st: wknd wl over 1f out) ............................................................................... 1¹/₂.8

3253⁴ Baysham (USA) **(76)** (bl) *(BRMillman)* 6–10-0 JWilliams (12) (lw: hdwy over 3f out: 4th st: wknd over 2f out) ................................................ nk.9

3198 May Hills Legacy (IRE) **(69)** *(DWPArbuthnot)* 3–9-3 RCochrane (3) (b: lw: nvr nrr) ..................................................................................... ¹/₂.10

3198⁵ Gant Bleu (FR) **(62)** *(RMWhitaker)* 5–9-0 PaulEddery (14) (lw: hdwy over 2f out: wknd over 1f out) ..................................................... ¹/₂.11

3182⁶ Surrey Racing **(71)** *(GLewis)* 4–9-9 BRouse (17) (nvr nrr) ...................... 2¹/₂.12

3243 Hameem (IRE) **(74)** (bl) *(AAScott)* 3–9-8 WRSwinburn (5) (ldw over 5f) ....... s.h.13

3137⁶ Domicksky **(72)** *(RSimpson)* 4–9-10 DBiggs (16) (lw: 6th st: wknd over 1f out) 2.14

3251⁶ Just a Step **(73)** *(MMcCormack)* 6–9-11 SCauthen (11) (prom over 3f) ........ 15

3257⁵ Cee-En-Cee **(69)** (bl) *(MMcCourt)* 8–9-2 ‡⁵ATucker (18) (bhd fnl 3f) ........... 16

1411★ Canadian Capers **(70)** *(MRChannon)* 3–9-4 SWhitworth (9) (a bhd) ........... 17

1636 Gemini Bay **(63)** (bl) *(RVoorspuy)* 3–8-11 NAdams (10) (prom over 3f) ....... 18

**9/2** MILLSOLIN (IRE), **11/2** Spencer's Revenge, **8/1** Darakah, **10/1** Garth, Merlins Wish (USA), **14/1** Gant Bleu (FR), **16/1** Cee-En-Cee(op 10/1), Dance on Sixpence, Domicksky, **20/1** Surrey Racing, Baysham (USA), Just a Step, Hameem, **25/1** Nobby Barnes, **33/1** Ler Cru (IRE), Canadian Capers, May Hills Legacy (IRE), **66/1** Gemini Bay. CSF £43.67, CT £232.17. Tote £3.70: £1.80 £2.50 £1.80 £1.90 (£23.30). Normandy Developments (London) (EPSOM) bred by Lhasa Trading Ltd. in Ireland. 18 Rn       1m 29.28 (5.28)

SF—55/58/42/45/20/28

## 3418

HENDON CLAIMING STKS       £2742.00 (£762.00: £366.00)       **1m 1f**       4-15 (4-19)

3277⁵ **Langtry Lady (77)** (v) *(MJRyan)* 6–8-11 DBiggs (9) (hdwy over 2f out: led over 1f out: r.o wl) ......................................................................... —1

3137 Green's Ferneley (IRE) **(81)** (bl) *(Fav)* RCharlton) 4–8-13 PatEddery (11) (b: 4th st: ev ch over 1f out: unable qckn) ........................................ 5.2

3198 Lord Vivienne (IRE) **(80)** *(RCSpicer)* 3–8-5 ‡³DHarrison (14) (2nd st: ev ch over 1f out: one pce) ............................................................... 2.3

3212 Daswaki (CAN) **(76)** *(RHannon)* 4–9-1 BRouse (17) (swtg: led over 7f: one pce) nk.4

3125 Overpower **(60)** *(MHTompkins)* 8–8-0 ‡⁷SMulvey (10) (nvr nr to chal) ......... 3.5

3145³ Crystal Heights (FR) **(83)** *(WAO'Gorman)* 4–8-13 LDettori (3) (swtg: hdwy over 2f out: not rdn o/er 1f out: sn wknd) .................................... 4.6

3101★ Absonal **(70)** *(RHannon)* 5–8-11 RCochrane (8) (6th st: hrd rdn over 1f out: sn wknd) ................................................................................... ¹/₂.7

3066 Vanroy **(63)** (v) *(JRJenkins)* 8–8-13 SWhitworth (2) (no hdwy fnl 2f) ........... nk.8

3052 Majestic Melody **(44)** *(WCarter)* 4–7-10 ‡⁵NGwilliams (16) (s.s: nvr nrr) ....... ¹/₂.9

3264 Kaths Choice **(36)** *(HJCollingridge)* 4–8-4 NHowe (7) (prom over 5f) ......... s.h.10

3251⁴ Red Sombrero **(57)** *(LGCottrell)* 3–8-2 NCarlisle (1) (5th st: wknd 2f out) ... s.h.11

3236 Absent Relative **(61)** *(MissBSanders)* 4–8-8 MRoberts (13) (3rd st: wknd over 2f out) ............................................................................... 10.12

3238 Lloyds Dream *(DShaw)* 3–8-11 GCarter (7) (a bhd) ................................ 1.13

622⁴ Kashan (IRE) *(JMBradley)* 4–9-7 NAdams (6) (b: bhd fnl 2f) ................... ¹/₂.14

3037 Wessex Milord **(26)** *(JABennett)* 7–7-13 ‡⁷ClaireBalding (12) (b: a bhd) .... ³/₄.15

2871⁵ Mastarnist **(39)** (bl) *(RVoorspuy)* 3–7-12 ‡⁵BDoyle (15) (s.s: a bhd) ........ 15.16

3264 Courting Newmarket **(43)** *(MrsAKnight)* 4–8-8 JQuinn (18) (bhd fnl 3f) ....... ³/₄.17

Tinas Lass *(RCurtis)* 3–8-1 GBardwell (5) (w'like: a bhd) ....................... 15.18

**5/2** Green's Ferneley (IRE)(7/2—4/1), **11/2** LANGTRY LADY, **13/2** Daswaki (CAN), **8/1** Crystal Heights (FR)(op 5/1), Absent Relative, Absonal(op 5/1), **12/1** Lord Vivienne (IRE), **16/1** Overpower(op 10/1), **20/1** Kashan (IRE), Vanroy, Red Sombrero, **40/1** Mastarnist, **66/1** Ors. CSF £19.12, Tote £5.50: £1.60 £1.70 £5.50 (£5.50). Mrs Teresa Baron (NEWMARKET) bred by Stud-On-The-Chart. 18 Rn       1m 58.39 (8.39)

SF—52/39/55/34/10/11

## 3419

E.B.F. KENLEY STKS (Mdn 2-Y.O) £2700.00 (£750.00: £360.00)
**1m (J.C)**       4-45 (4-50)

2918³ **Commanche Gold (IRE)** *(Fav)* *(LordHuntingdon)* 9-0 PatEddery (10) (3rd st: led 2f out: rdn out) ............................................................ —1

Spring to Action *(IABalding)* 8-11 GCarter (14) (leggy: bit bkwd: hdwy over 2f out: ev ch 1f out: unable qckn) ................................................ 2.2

BRIGHTON, September 23, 1992

**3420 — 3421**

Star of China *(CCElsey)* 8-6 PaulEddery (6) (unf: scope: bit bkwd: hdwy 2f out:
r.o one pce) ........................................................... 3½.3
2859 Hatta River (USA) *(MajorWRHern)* 9-0 SCauthen (9) (lw: 5th st: one pce fnl 2f) .. 2.4
3000 Hostile Witness (IRE) *(RHannon)* 9-0 BRouse (1) (gd hdwy over 1f out: r.o wl
ins fnl f) ............................................................... s.h.5
Phrose *(RHannon)* 8-11 JQuinn (8) (scope: nvr nr to chal) ............ 2½.6
Tinsashe (IRE) *(MMoubarak)* 8-6 LDettori (7) (wl grwn: led 6f) ........... ¾.7
1635 Hariti (IRE) *(DRCElsworth)* 8-9 JWilliams (11) (hdwy over 2f out: one pce) ..... ¾.8
3130⁵ Bixby (USA) *(DRCElsworth)* 9-0 RCochrane (15) (2nd st: wknd over 2f out) .... 1½.9
3181 Ice Rebel *(MissBSanders)* 9-0 GBardwell (12) (prom over 4f) ............... hd.10
3275 Petite Vino (45) *(JJBridger)* 8-2 ‡7AntoinetteArmes (2) (prom over 4f) ........... s.h.11
2771 Golden Klair (42) *(CJHill)* 8-9 NAdams (13) (a bhd) ...................... hd.12
3132 Bobbysoxer *(JLDunlop)* 8-9 AMcGlone (5) (bhd fnl 5f) ..................... 1.13
3186 Soojama (IRE) *(RVoorspuy)* 9-0 CRutter (17) (4th st: wknd over 2f out) ......... nk.14
3130 Jihaad (USA) *(JLDunlop)* 9-0 WCarson (16) (hdwy over 3f out: 6th st: wknd wl
over 1f out) ........................................................... s.h.15
3099 Alwal *(CJames)* 8-9 DaleGibson (3) (swtg: prom over 4f) ................. 8.16

**11/8** COMMANCHE GOLD (IRE), **11/2** Tinsashe (IRE)(10/1—9/1), Bixby (USA), **10/1** Hostile Witness
(IRE)(7/1—12/1), **11/1** Spring to Action(5/1—12/1), **12/1** Jihaad (USA)(op 8/1), **14/1** Hatta River
(USA)(10/1—16/1), **16/1** Bobbysoxer(tchd 33/1), Phrose(op 8/1), **20/1** Hariti (IRE), **33/1** Star of China, Ice
Rebel, **66/1** Ors. CSF £18.50, Tote £1.90: £1.20 £2.80 £14.60 (£11.40). Lord Weinstock (WEST ILSLEY) bred
by Ballymacoll Stud Farm Ltd. in Ireland. 16 Rn                                    1m 44.77 (8.17)
                                                                   SF—49/43/27/29/28/17

T/Trio: £42.60 (19.2 Tckts). T/Jkpt: Not won; £106,662.68 to Ascot 24/09/92. T/Plpt: £61.10 (111.59 Tckts).
                                                                                                     AK

## 2943—BRIGHTON (L-H)
### Wednesday, September 23rd [Good to soft]
Going Allowance: 0.10 sec per fur (G)                                    Wind: mod half against

Stalls: low

**3420**    RACE HILL STKS (2-Y-O) £2709.00 (£749.00: £357.00)    **5f 59y**    1-50 (1-52)

3261* **Surprise Offer (100)** (Fav) *(RHannon)* 9-3 LDettori (6) (4th st: rdn over 2f out:
led ins fnl f: all out) ................................................... —1
3019⁴ Troon (82) *(MrsLPiggott)* 9-3 LPiggott (4) (b: b.hind: lw: 5th st: hrd rdn over 1f
out: ev ch wl ins fnl f: r.o wl) ......................................... s.h.2
2740³ Trentesimo (IRE) (78) *(JBerry)* 9-7 JCarroll (3) (lw: led over 4f out tl ins fnl f:
unable qckn) ........................................................... 2½.3
3250⁶ Wickins (bl) *(GLewis)* 8-11 PaulEddery (2) (6th st: nvr nr to chal) .................. 3½.4
3115 Grab Sunday Sport (bl) *(MissGayKelleway)* 8-11 GHind (1) (3rd st: wknd over
1f out) .................................................................. 7.5
3218 Gaynor Goodman (IRE) (49) *(JSMoore)* 8-6 DBiggs (5) (led 1f: 2nd st: wknd 2f
out) .................................................................... ¾.6

**1/8** SURPRISE OFFER(op 1/4), **7/1** Troon(op 5/2), **20/1** Trentesimo (IRE)(op 6/1), **100/1** Wickins, **200/1** Ors.
CSF £1.55, Tote £1.10: £1.10 £1.70 (£1.60). Lord Carnarvon (MARLBOROUGH) bred by Woodditton Stud Ltd. 6
Rn                                                                              64.4 sec (3.1)
                                                                   SF—51/50/44/20/–/–

**3421**    WATERHALL (S) H'CAP (0-60) £2805.00 (£780.00: £375.00)    **7f 214y**    2-20 (2-25)

3288³ **Genuine Lady (47)** *(APJarvis)* 4-9-8 TQuinn (10) (2nd & styd far side st: led
over 3f out: rdn out) ................................................... —1
3254⁵ Sunley Sparkle (42) (bl) *(DRGandolfo)* 4-8-12 ‡5JWeaver (3) (6th st: ev ch over
2f out: unable qckn) ................................................... 2.2
3254 Breakdancer (IRE) (50) *(WRMuir)* 3-9-7 WCarson (4) (hdwy over 2f out: one
pce fnl f) .............................................................. ¾.3
2953 Aldaha (38) *(BForsey)* 7-8-13 (hdwy over 2f out: one pce) ....... 1½.4
2952 Bounder Rowe (40) *(JFitch-Heyes)* 5-9-1 TyroneWilliams (14) (4th st: one pce
fnl 2f) ................................................................. 3½.5
3278⁵ Black Jewel (50) *(MDIUsher)* 9-9-11 MWigham (5) (hdwy fnl 2f: nvr nrr) ........ ¾.6
3254 Lamore Ritorna (49) *(KOCunningham-Brown)* 3-9-6 SWhitworth (15) (led over
4f) ..................................................................... nk.7
3288² Red Ink (52) *(JSutcliffe)* 3-9-9 MRoberts (13) (lw: no hdwy fnl 2f) ............ ½.8
3060 Northern Conqueror (IRE) (47) *(TJNaughton)* 4-9-8 GCarter (7) (lw: nvr nrr) .. s.h.9
3254³ Time Lapse (57) (Fav) *(PJMakin)* 3-10-0 PatEddery (2) (lw: styd far side st:
hdwy 3f out: wknd over 1f out) ......................................... 1.10

| | | |
|---|---|---|
| 3101 | Shalou (52) (RJHodges) 3-9-9 TSprake (12) (a mid div) | 2½.11 |
| 3254 | Walkonthemoon (47) (bl) (MMcCormack) 3-9-4 JReid (4) (lw: 5th & styd far side st: wknd 3f out) | 1½.12 |
| 3185⁵ | One Magic Moment (IRE) (47) (CACyzer) 4-9-8 DBiggs (17) (a mid div) | ¾.13 |
| 3281⁶ | Great Hall (45) (bl) (PDCundell) 3-9-2 PRobinson (9) (bhd fnl 3f) | ¾.14 |
| 3239 | Heroes Sash (USA) (50) (AMoore) 7-9-0 ‡5StephenDavies (8) (3rd & styd far side st: wknd over 2f out) | 2.15 |
| 525 | Heard it Before (FR) (38) (RPCHoad) 7-8-13 GDuffield (11) (bhd fnl 5f) | 10.16 |
| 3254⁴ | Chloes Diamond (IRE) (43) (JLSpearing) 4-9-1 ‡3EmmaO'Gorman (1) (ref to r: t.n.p) | 0 |

**100/30** Time Lapse(9/4—7/2), **7/2** Red Ink, **13/2** Northern Conqueror (IRE)(6/1—9/1), **8/1** One Magic Moment (IRE), **9/1** Aldhae(12/1—8/1), **14/1** Great Hall(10/1—16/1), Chloes Diamond (IRE)(10/1—16/1), GENUINE LADY, Breakdancer (IRE), **25/1** Lamore Ritorna, Heroes Sash (USA), **33/1** Ors. CSF £368.38, CT £5,767.43. Tote £21.90: £2.80 £2.40 £2.10 £2.00 (£161.10). Mrs D. Brazier (ASTON UPTHORPE) bred by S. Petterson. 17 Rn; No bid

1m 38.6 (6.4)
SF—24/8/15/2/–/–

---

## 3422

ERIC SIMMS MEMORIAL H'CAP (0-80) £3184.00 (£952.00: £456.00: £208.00)
**7f 214y** 2-50 (2-52)

(Weights raised 3 lb)

| | | |
|---|---|---|
| 2952⁵ | **Precious Air (IRE) (51)** (AMoore) 4-8-6 BRouse (1) (lw: led 6f out: comf) | —1 |
| 3061² | Eternal Flame (66) (Fav) (JWHills) 4-9-7 RHills (8) (hdwy over 2f out: hrd rdn over 1f out: unable qckn) | 2.2 |
| 3287⁵ | Shining Jewel (69) (MrsLPiggott) 5-9-10 LPiggott (10) (hdwy over 1f out: r.o) | 1.3 |
| 3245² | Old Comrades (56) (LGCottrell) 5-8-11 TRogers (9) (lost pl over 5f out: rallied over 1f out: r.o) | 2.4 |
| 2953 | Juvenara (38) (CJHill) 6-7-7 JQuinn (5) (hdwy on ins over 2f out: n.m.r wl over 1f out: nvr nrr) | 1½.5 |
| 3270 | Cretoes Dancer (USA) (60) (bl) (WHMuir) 3-8-11 CRutter (2) (3rd & hrd rdn over 1f out: sn wknd) | ½.6 |
| 3133 | Court Minstrel (60) (LJHolt) 3-8-11 JReid (13) (nvr nr to chal) | 2.7 |
| 2463 | Marzocco (50) (JFfitch-Heyes) 4-8-5 PaulEddery (12) (b.nr hind: lw: 6th st: wknd over 1f out) | ¾.8 |
| 3215⁶ | Sir Oliver (IRE) (61) (RJHodges) 3-8-12 PatEddery (7) (led 2f: 2nd st: wknd 2f out) | ½.9 |
| 2753⁶ | Brooks Express (FR) (53) (RAkehurst) 3-8-4 TQuinn (11) (4th st: wknd over 1f out) | 3.10 |
| 3216³ | Mashaaer (USA) (64) (RWArmstrong) 3-9-1 WCarson (4) (lw: 5th st: wknd 2f out) | 6.11 |

LONG HANDICAP: Juvenara 7-6.

**11/4** Eternal Flame, **4/1** Old Comrades, **8/1** Mashaaer (USA), Brooks Express (FR), Shining Jewel, **9/1** Marzocco, **10/1** Court Minstrel, Sir Oliver (IRE), **12/1** PRECIOUS AIR (IRE), **14/1** Juvenara, **16/1** Cretoes Dancer (USA). CSF £46.03, CT £271.56. Tote £17.30: £6.00 £1.90 £2.30 (£47.50). Mr K. Higson (BRIGHTON) bred by Dictum Enterprises Ltd in Ireland. 11 Rn

1m 38.2 (6.0)
SF—14/23/23/4/–/–

---

## 3423

WIN WITH THE TOTE H'CAP (0-70) £2490.00 (£690.00: £330.00)
**5f 59y** 3-20 (3-23)

| | | |
|---|---|---|
| 1551³ | **Waverley Star (47)** (KOCunningham-Brown) 7-8-7 PatEddery (14) (c stands' side st: hrd rdn & hdwy over 1f out: led wl ins fnl f) | —1 |
| 3304 | Miss Vaxette (70) (JLSpearing) 3-9-7 ‡7MHumphries (8) (hdwy over 2f out: led ins fnl f: sn hdd: r.o) | nk.2 |
| 3257⁴ | Mister Jolson (55) (RJHodges) 3-8-13 WCarson (16) (hdwy over 2f out: n.m.r over 1f out: one pce) | 2½.3 |
| 3220² | Little Saboteur (57) (Fav) (PJMakin) 3-9-1 AMunro (6) (hdwy over 2f out: ev ch over 1f out: one pce) | 2.4 |
| 3318⁴ | Serious Hurry (57) (bl) (SirMarkPrescott) 4-9-3 GDuffield (5) (led over 4f out tl ins fnl f: sn wknd) | ¾.5 |
| 3251 | Cronk's Quality (35) (bl) (DCJermy) 9-7-9⁽²⁾ SDawson (11) (5th & c stands' side st: wknd 2f out) | 2.6 |
| 3103⁴ | Stocktina (44) (RJHodges) 5-7-11⁽⁵⁾ ‡7SDrowne (15) (c stands' side st: outpcd) | ¾.7 |
| 3220⁵ | Savalaro (52) (JFfitch-Heyes) 3-8-10 TyroneWilliams (9) (led 1f: 2nd st: ev ch 2f out: wknd over 1f out) | 2½.8 |
| 2599⁴ | Rays Mead (49) (LJHolt) 4-8-9 JReid (7) (6th st: wknd 2f out) | ¾.9 |
| 3251 | Mr Smiley (33) (RJBaker) 5-7-7 NAdams (3) (always bhd) | nk.10 |
| 3318⁵ | Ever so Artistic (36) (PHowling) 5-7-7⁽²⁾ ‡3DHarrison (10) (3rd st: wknd over 2f out) | ½.11 |
| 3103 | Hitchin a Ride (39) (MPMuggeridge) 5-7-13 GBardwell (1) (4th st: wknd 2f out) | 5.12 |

3/1 Little Saboteur, **5/1** Serious Hurry(op 10/1), Mister Jolson, **6/1** Savalaro, **8/1** Stocktina, **10/1** WAVERLEY STAR, **12/1** Rays Mead, **14/1** Ever so Artistic, Miss Vaxette, **33/1** Hitchin a Ride, **40/1** Cronk's Quality, **66/1** Mr Smiley. CSF £125.43, CT £713.85. Tote £8.50: £2.70 £4.00 £2.40 (£117.60). Mr S. Pedersen (STOCKBRIDGE) bred by Ballyrogan Stud. 12 Rn
64.2 sec (3.9)
SF—45/58/40/34/33/3

---

**3424**  E.B.F. KEMP TOWN STKS (Mdn 2-Y.O) £3366.00 (£1008.00: £484.00: £222.00)
**6f 209y**  3-50 (3-53)

2873³ **Fortensky (USA)** (LMCumani) 9-0 LDettori (3) (hdwy over 2f out: led over 1f out: r.o wl) ............................................................................ —1
3132⁵ Modi (USA) (LordHuntingdon) 8-9 WRSwinburn (2) (hdwy over 2f out: rdn over 1f out: unable qckn) ............................................................ 2.2
3132 Dana Springs (IRE) (RHannon) 8-9 BRaymond (7) (hdwy over 1f out: r.o) ...... 3.3
3240⁶ My Harvinski (PWChapple-Hyam) 9-0 SWhitworth (9) (hdwy over 1f out: nvr nrr) ¹/₂.4
New Quest (PFICole) 9-0 AMunro (5) (leggy: rdn over 2f out: hdwy over 1f out: r.o) .................................................................................... 2¹/₂.5
2773³ Gweek (IRE) (PAKelleway) 8-9 PRobinson (4) (lw: led over 5f) ................. 1.6
3100⁵ Native Trio (USA) (PWHarris) 9-0 PaulEddery (12) (3rd st: ev ch over 1f out: one pce) .................................................................................. 1¹/₂.7
3285 Who's the Best (IRE) **(70)** (APJarvis) 9-0 SCauthen (13) (2nd st: wknd over 1f out) ............................................................................................ ³/₄.8
3186⁴ Barik (IRE) **(Fav)** (ACStewart) 9-0 MRoberts (1) (lw: 5th st: nt clr run on ins fnl 2f: nt rcvr) .................................................................................. 2.9
2773⁵ Ambivalentattitude (MDIUsher) 9-0 MWigham (6) (6th st: wknd over 2f out) .. 1¹/₂.10
2710⁴ Lincoln Imp (USA) **(67)** (AMoore) 9-0 BRouse (8) (a bhd) ............................. ¹/₂.11
3217⁵ Silent Prince (MissBSanders) 9-0 MPerrett (14) (4th st: wknd over 2f out) ........ 4.12
3250 Shamrock Dancer (IRE) (RJBaker) 8-9 NHowe (15) (bhd fnl 3f) .................... 1¹/₂.13
3320 Arabian Castle (MJHeaton Ellis) 9 0 JReid (10) (a bhd) ,,...................... 2.14

**5/4** Barik (IRE), **5/2** Modi (USA)(2/1—3/1), **5/1** FORTENSKY (USA), **14/1** New Quest(op 3/1), **16/1** Who's the Best (IRE)(33/1—14/1), **20/1** Dana Springs (IRE), Lincoln Imp (USA), My Harvinski(op 8/1), **33/1** Native Trio (USA), Gweek (IRE), **50/1** Arabian Castle, Shamrock Dancer (IRE), Silent Prince, **66/1** Ambivalentattitude. CSF £18.09, Tote £4.90: £1.30 £1.70 £5.80 (£8.30). Mr Gerald Leigh (NEWMARKET) bred by Gerald W. Leigh in USA. 14 Rn
1m 26.1 (6.1)
SF—19/8/–/–/–/–

---

**3425**  STEINE STKS (Mdn 3-Y.O) £2070.00 (£570.00: £270.00)  **1m 1f 209y**  4-20 (4-22)

3238³ **Barahin (IRE)** **(Fav)** (JLDunlop) 9-0 WCarson (2) (4th st: rdn over 2f out: led ins fnl f: r.o wl) .......................................................................... —1
2954³ Annacurragh (IRE) (ACStewart) 8-9 MRoberts (8) (2nd st: led over 3f out tl ins fnl f: unable qckn) ................................................................... 2.2
1770⁶ Impeccable Charm (USA) (JHMGosden) 8-9 PatEddery (5) (3rd st: rdn over 2f out: one pce) ............................................................................ 6.3
3238 Concinnity (USA) (LJHolt) 9-0 AMcGlone (3) (nvr nr to chal) .......................... 1¹/₂.4
Summer Reading (USA) (LMCumani) 8-9 LDettori (1) (leggy: 5th st: no hdwy fnl 3f) ............................................................................................. hd.5
2869² Indian Jack (IRE) **(74)** (MajorWRHern) 9-0 SCauthen (7) (led over 6f) .............. 7.6
3238 I'M Curious (RThompson) 8-9 JWilliams (4) (bhd fnl 5f) ........................... 1¹/₂.7
2954⁴ Tiffany Gem (IRE) (LordHuntingdon) 8-9 DaleGibson (6) (lw: 6th st: wknd over 3f out) ............................................................................................. 1.8

**10/11** BARAHIN (IRE), **11/4** Indian Jack (IRE), **7/1** Annacurragh (IRE)(op 4/1), Summer Reading (USA)(3/1—8/1), **10/1** Impeccable Charm (USA)(6/1—12/1), **50/1** Tiffany Gem (IRE), **66/1** Ors. CSF £7.98, Tote £2.10: £1.20 £1.60 £2.00 (£3.80). Mr Hamdan Al-Maktoum (ARUNDEL) bred by Stowell Hill Ltd and A. J. Tree in Ireland. 8 Rn
2m 7.7 (9.7)
SF—13/4/–/–/–/–

---

**3426**  FRIEND-JAMES MEMORIAL H'CAP (0-70) £2679.00 (£744.00: £357.00)
**1m 3f 196y**  4-50 (4-53)

3137 **Texan Tycoon (63)** (RAkehurst) 4–9-6 ‡7TAshley (11) (5th st: led over 1f out: r.o wl) ............................................................................................. —1
3258² Flash of Straw (IRE) **(42)** (bl) **(Fav)** (GLewis) 3–7-9 ‡3DHarrison (7) (lw: 2nd st: led over 3f out tl over 1f out: unable qckn) ......................... 1¹/₂.2
3159★ Crackling **(52)** (DMarks) 3–8-8 SDawson (3) (6th st: hrd rdn over 1f out: one pce) ............................................................................................. 6.3
1390 Thin Red Line **(47)** (v) (JRJenkins) 8-8-11 GBaxter (10) (hdwy over 2f out: hrd rdn over 1f out: wknd fnl f) ............................................ 2¹/₂.4
3221★ Day of History (IRE) **(46)** (CACyzer) 3-8-2 DBiggs (12) (a.p: led over 4f out tl over 3f out: wknd wl over 1f out) ........................................... 5.5

2178⁶ Court Circular **(63)** (v) *(LordHuntingdon)* 3-9-5 WRSwinburn (2) (lw: hdwy 5f out: 3rd st: wknd 2f out) .................. ¹/₂.**6**

3104 Carousel Music **(54)** *(JAkehurst)* 5-8-13 ‡5JWeaver (13) (led over 7f) ............ 15.**7**

3064³ Atlantic Way **(42)** *(CJHill)* 4-8-6 JQuinn (1) (hdwy over 3f out: wknd wl over 1f out) .................. ¹/₂.**8**

Ilewin **(45)** *(JRJenkins)* 5-8-2⁽¹⁶⁾ ‡7CAddington (9) (bhd fnl 3f) ............... 2¹/₂.**9**

3254 Coochie **(47)** *(RJBaker)* 3-8-3 NHowe (4) (lw: a bhd) .................. 10.**10**

1341 Sam the Man **(35)** *(JFfitch-Heyes)* 5-7-13 TyroneWilliams (5) (4th st: wknd over 2f out) .................. 8.**11**

3215⁴ Liu Liu San (IRE) **(30)** *(PButler)* 4-7-1 ‡7DToole (8) (lw: s.s: a bhd) .............. s.h.**12**

LONG HANDICAP: Ilewin 6-12.

**5/2** Flash of Straw (IRE), **7/2** Atlantic Way, TEXAN TYCOON, **5/1** Crackling, **13/2** Day of History (IRE), **12/1** Court Circular(8/1–14/1), **20/1** Carousel Music, Thin Red Line, **50/1** Liu Liu San (IRE), **66/1** Coochie, Sam the Man, **100/1** Ilewin. CSF £12.80, CT £41.85. Tote £5.50: £2.00 £2.10 £2.60 (£12.60). Normandy Developments (London) (EPSOM) bred by Clearwood Thoroughbred Stud Ltd. 12 Rn 2m 35.1 (8.1)

SF—37/9/10/8/–/–

T/Plpt: £174.80 (21.2 Tckts). AK

---

## 2336—ASCOT (R-H)

### Thursday, September 24th [Soft]

Going Allowance: St: 0.50 sec (Y); Rnd: 0.80 sec per fur (S)  Wind: almost nil

Stalls: centre

**3427**  CLARENCE HOUSE GRADUATION STKS (3-Y.O) £8538.00 (£2544.00: £121C.00: £546.00)  **7f**  2-00 (2-11)

Lord Chickney (USA) *(JHMGosden)* 8-11 SCauthen (6) (cmpt: a.p: led wl over 1f out: pushed out) .................. —**1**

3201³ Talb (USA) *(JLDunlop)* 9-4 WCarson (8) (hld up: ev ch over 1f out: unable qckn) ... 2.**2**

1136 Bold Pursuit (IRE) **(96)** *(RHannon)* 9-4 JReid (2) (lw: hld up: rdn over 3f out: r.o one pce fnl 2f) .................. ³/₄.**3**

3195 Wilde Rufo **(97)** *(PAKelleway)* 9-4 AMunro (7) (w ldr: ev ch over 2f out: one pce). 1¹/₂.**4**

3238* Fraam (Fav) *(AAScott)* 9-4 WRSwinburn (4) (lw: a.p: led over 2f out tl wl over 1f out: one pce: lame) .................. ¹/₂.**5**

Balzino (USA) *(LMCumani)* 8-11 LDettori (5) (unf: s.s: rdn over 2f out: nvr nr to chal) .................. 3.**6**

3356 Bold Memory **(93)** *(MJohnston)* 9-4 JWilliams (1) (lw: rdn wl over 1f out: sn wknd) .................. 2.**7**

3150* Lahoob (USA) **(63)** *(BHanbury)* 9-4 LPiggott (3) (b.hind: lw: led over 4f) ........... 5.**8**

**11/4** Fraam, **7/2** Talb (USA), **9/2** LORD CHICKNEY (USA)(op 6/4), **7/1** Wilde Rufo, Lahoob (USA), **10/1** Bold Pursuit (IRE), **14/1** Balzino (USA)(op 6/1), **33/1** Bold Memory. CSF £18.60, Tote £5.70: £1.70 £1.60 £2.70 (£10.20). Sheikh Mohammed (NEWMARKET) bred by Ms. Emory Alexander in USA. 8 Rn  1m 32.62 (6.12)

SF—58/59/57/52/50/34/35

**3428**  HOOVER H'CAP (0-110) £11452.50 (£3420.00: £1635.00: £742.50)  **1m (st)**  2-30 (2-41)

3125* Rambo's Hall **(88)** (Jt-Fav) *(JAGlover)* 7-8-12 DMcKeown (7) (swtg: a.p: hrd rdn & led over 1f out: r.o wl) .................. —**1**

3209² Croft Valley **(82)** *(RAkehurst)* 5-8-6 TQuinn (4) (lw: led over 2f: led over 3f out tl over 1f out: unable qckn) .................. 2¹/₂.**2**

3212⁶ Marine Diver **(73)** *(BRMillman)* 6-7-11 DaleGibson (10) (hdwy over 3f out: one pce fnl 2f) .................. 4.**3**

3277² Camden's Ransom (USA) **(74)** *(DRCEIsworth)* 5-7-7⁽⁵⁾ ‡5BDoyle (8) (hdwy over 2f out: hrd rdn over 1f out: one pce) .................. 1.**4**

2658 Big Leap (IRE) **(99)** *(MMoubarak)* 3-9-5 LDettori (1) (hrd rdn & hdwy over 1f out: nvr nrr) .................. 3¹/₂.**5**

2852 Wave Hill **(82)** *(RHannon)* 3-8-2 MRoberts (6) (lw: rdn & no hdwy fnl 2f) ......... hd.**6**

3121³ Two Left Feet **(104)** (Jt-Fav) *(SirMarkPrescott)* 5-10-0 GDuffield (12) (a.p: rdn over 2f out: wknd over 1f out) .................. 7.**7**

2341³ Sabotage (FR) **(87)** *(MRStoute)* 6-8-6 ‡5JJones (2) (b: lw: nvr nrr) .............. 1¹/₂.**8**

3310* En Attendant (FR) **(81)** *(BHanbury)* 4-8-5 (5x) BRaymond (3) (lw: hld up: rdn over 2f out: sn wknd) .................. 1.**9**

3241 Majboor (IRE) **(84)** *(PTWalwyn)* 3-8-4 WCarson (5) (lw: prom 5f) .............. ³/₄.**10**

3209 Piquant **(85)** *(LordHuntingdon)* 5-8-9 AMunro (11) (prom over 4f) .............. 5.**11**

3009 Blockade (USA) **(83)** *(MBell)* 3-8-3 MHills (13) (swtg: led over 5f out tl over 3f out: sn wknd) .................. 4.**12**

3188 Orthorhombus **(95)** *(GLewis)* 3–9–1 PaulEddery (9) (lw: a bhd) ........................ 5.13
LONG HANDICAP: Camden's Ransom (USA) 7-5.

**9/2** Two Left Feet, RAMBO'S HALL, **11/2** En Attendant (FR), **13/2** Croft Valley, **10/1** Piquant, **12/1** Marine Diver, Camden's Ransom (USA), **14/1** Wave Hill, Big Leap (IRE), **16/1** Blockade (USA), **20/1** Majboor (IRE), **25/1** Sabotage (FR), **33/1** Orthorhombus. CSF £31.51, CT £301.98. Tote £5.00: £1.80 £2.70 £3.60 (£17.80). Mr B. Dixon (WORKSOP) bred by Sqdn-Ldr Frank Barrett. 13 Rn
1m 44.24 (4.84)
SF—85/71/50/43/58/40/45

---

**3429**  HOOVER CUMBERLAND LODGE STKS (Gp 3)   £26640.00 (£9842.00: £4621.00: £1897.00)  1½m
3-05 (3-07)

2345³ **Opera House (123)** (Fav) *(MRStoute)* 4–9–5 SCauthen (5) (lw: 2nd st: led over
2f out tl over 1f out: led ins fnl f: r.o wl) .................................... —1
3138² Red Bishop (USA) **(111)** *(JHMGosden)* 4–9–0 PatEddery (1) (rdn over 4f out:
4th st: led over 1f out tl ins fnl f: unable qckn) .................... 1½.2
2133★ Garden of Heaven **(121)** *(CEBrittain)* 3–8–6 MRoberts (2) (lw: 5th st: hrd rdn
over 1f out: one pce) ........................................................... ¾.3
3211³ Bonny Scot (IRE) **(119)** *(LMCumani)* 3–8–11 LDettori (3) (swtg: 3rd st: rdn over
2f out: one pce) ................................................................ 1½.4
3225a³ Sapience **(122)** (v) *(DRCElsworth)* 6–9–5 WCarson (4) (lw: led over 9f) ......... 7.5

**9/4** OPERA HOUSE, **5/2** Red Bishop (USA), **3/1** Bonny Scot (IRE), **4/1** Sapience, **25/1** Garden of Heaven (USA). CSF £7.54, Tote £2.80: £1.40 £1.90 (£3.00). Sheikh Mohammed (NEWMARKET) bred by Meon Valley Stud. 5 Rn
2m 40.47 (10.97)
SF—91/83/75/69

---

**3430**  BLUE SEAL STKS (2-Y.O.F) £9080.50 (£2704.00: £1287.00: £578.50)
6f
3-40 (3-42)

**Queen's View (FR)** *(LMCumani)* 8-8 LDettori (4) (unf: scope: a.p: led ins fnl f:
rdn out) ........................................................................ —1
Felawnah (USA) *(JHMGosden)* 8-8 WRSwinburn (8) (leggy: scope: hdwy over
1f out: r.o wl ins fnl f) ..................................................... ¾.2
Felucca (Fav) *(HRACecil)* 8-8 PatEddery (7) (unf: scope: led tl ins fnl f: unable
qckn) ........................................................................... 3.3
3096⁶ Barboukh *(DRCElsworth)* 8-8 TQuinn (6) (a.p: rdn over 1f out: one pce) ...... 1½.4
3214⁴ Hejraan (USA) *(MRStoute)* 8-8 SCauthen (3) (a.p: hrd rdn over 1f out: one pce) ½.5
Ibtikar (USA) *(PTWalwyn)* 8-8 WCarson (5) (unf: hdwy over 2f out: wknd over 1f
out) ............................................................................ 4.6
3132 Midnight Heights *(JWPayne)* 8-8 AMunro (2) (swtg: chsd ldr over 3f) ........... 1½.7
Hoosie *(CEBrittain)* 8-8 MRoberts (1) (cmpt: bit bkwd: s.s: hdwy over 3f out:
wknd over 2f out) ............................................................ 4.8

**15/8** Felucca, **5/2** Hejraan (USA), **6/1** Felawnah (USA), **13/2** Hoosie(op 4/1), **10/1** QUEEN'S VIEW (FR)(6/1—12/1), **14/1** Barboukh(op 8/1), **16/1** Ors. CSF £63.24, Tote £10.00: £2.20 £2.10 £1.30 (£40.50). Sheikh Mohammed (NEWMARKET) bred by Darley Stud Management in France. 8 Rn
1m 19.23 (5.63)
SF—41/38/26/20/18/2

---

**3431**  GORDON CARTER H'CAP (0-110) £10416.00 (£3108.00: £1484.00: £672.00)
2m 45y
4-10 (4-11)

3273★ **Bold Resolution (IRE) (58)** (Fav) *(CACyzer)* 4–7–12⁽²⁾ (3x) MRoberts (2) (5th
st: led over 2f out: clr over 1f out: comf) ............................... —1
3082² Jungle Dancer (IRE) **(88)** *(MRStoute)* 4–10–0 PatEddery (3) (4th st: squeezed
thro over 2f out: chsd wnr over 1f out: no imp) ...................... 8.2
2899⁴ Bardolph (USA) **(81)** *(PFICole)* 5–9–7 TQuinn (5) (b.off hind: led over 7f: 3rd st:
hmpd over 2f out: r.o ins fnl f) ......................................... nk.3
3316³ Go South **(60)** *(JRJenkins)* 8–8–0 TyroneWilliams (9) (rdn over 4f out: 6th st: r.o
one pce fnl 2f) ................................................................ 4.4
3244 Muse **(70)** *(DRCElsworth)* 5–8–10 SCauthen (4) (led 9f out tl over 6f out: led
over 3f out tl over 2f out: sn wknd) .................................... s.h.5
2921 Requested **(75)** *(RAkehurst)* 5–9–1 AMunro (7) (lw: led over 6f out tl over 3f out:
2nd st: hmpd over 2f out: sn wknd) ................................... 1½.6
3197⁴ Aude la Belle (FR) **(78)** *(MrsAKnight)* 4–9–4 LPiggott (8) (hdwy over 4f out:
bmpd over 2f out: sn wknd) ............................................. 15.7
3128 Welshman **(64)** *(MBlanshard)* 6–8–4 JQuinn (1) (lw: rdn over 6f out: bhd fnl 3f) . 7.8
2836³ Three Wells **(89)** *(JLDunlop)* 3–9–3 WCarson (6) (lw: bhd fnl 3f: t.o) ............. 25.9

**5/1** BOLD RESOLUTION (IRE), **11/2** Muse, **6/1** Welshman, **13/2** Three Wells, **7/1** Bardolph (USA), Aude la Belle (FR), Requested, **10/1** Ors. CSF £47.16, CT £315.34. Tote £5.60: £1.80 £2.70 £3.40 (£16.60). Mr R. M. Cyzer (HORSHAM) bred by G. O'Brien in Ireland. 9 Rn
3m 43.31 (16.81)
SF—44/66/58/33/42/45/33

**3432** GOLDEN GATES NURSERY £9006.00 (£2688.00: £1284.00: £582.00)
6f
(Weights raised 7 lb) 4-40 (4-49)

3019* **Yours by Right (77)** *(WGMTurner)* 8-8 ‡5ATucker (5) (a.p: led ins fnl f: all out) .. —1
3129 Top Pet (IRE) **(85)** *(RHannon)* 9-7 MRoberts (11) (hmpd st: hrd rdn & hdwy
over 1f out: r.o wl ins fnl f) ............................................ s.h.2
3267* Shiro **(89)** (Fav) *(RJRWilliams)* 9-11 (7x) SCauthen (1) (hdwy over 2f out: led 1f
out tl ins fnl f: r.o) ...................................... nk.3
3019² Moon Over Miami **(81)** *(CJames)* 9-3 JQuinn (12) (lw: hld up: led wl over 1f out:
sn hdd: unable qckn) ................................ 1½.4
3205⁶ Persian Revival (FR) **(83)** *(BAMcMahon)* 9-5 TQuinn (10) (a.p: hrd rdn over 2f
out: ev ch over 1f out: one pce) ............................ 2½.5
3208³ Chili Heights **(76)** *(GBBalding)* 8-12 JWilliams (4) (nvr nr to chal) ............... 1½.6
3424² Credit Squeeze **(68)** *(RFJohnsonHoughton)* 8-4 JLowe (7) (lw: led over 4f) .... nk.7
3187⁶ Brockton Dancer **(78)** *(RHannon)* 9-0 JReid (2) (b.hind: lw: nvr nrr) ................ 1.8
3129* Hello Hobson's (IRE) **(70)** *(JAkehurst)* 8-6 WCarson (3) (lw: hdwy 3f out: wknd
over 1f out) ................................... 6.9
3162⁴ Nitouche **(75)** *(PatMitchell)* 8-8 ‡3DHarrison (8) (lw: prom 3f) .................... 5.10
3208 Touch Silver **(68)** *(BWHills)* 8-4 DHolland (3) (bhd fnl 2f) ......................... 1½.11
3175⁶ Mr Vincent **(79)** *(GLewis)* 9-1 PaulEddery (9) (lw: prom over 3f) ............... 3.12

**15/8** Shiro(7/4—7/2), **7/1** Moon Over Miami, **15/2** Brockton Dancer, **8/1** Hello Hobson's (IRE), **9/1** YOURS BY
RIGHT, **10/1** Chili Heights, **12/1** Nitouche, Touch Silver(16/1—10/1), **14/1** Persian Revival (FR), **16/1** Mr
Vincent, **33/1** Ors. CSF £216.66, CT £717.55. Tote £9.40: £2.40 £5.30 £1.80 (£105.30). Mr John Turner
(SHERBORNE) bred by R. J. Turner. 12 Rn 1m 19.47 (5.87)
SF—37/49/52/38/30/17

**3433** BISHOPSGATE APP'CE STKS £3590.00 (£1070.00: £510.00: £230.00)
7f
5-10 (5-12)

2911⁶ **Mrs Fisher (IRE) (92)** (Fav) *(SirMarkPrescott)* 3-8-2 JWeaver (2) (a.p: led over
2f out: drvn out) ......................................... —1
3135⁶ Olette **(81)** *(GWragg)* 3-7-13 ‡3FNorton (3) (bit broke s: led over 4f: rallied fnl f) nk.2
3241⁶ Bold Boss **(88)** *(BHanbury)* 3-7-13 ‡8VBray (4) (a.p: ev ch 2f out: wknd 1f out) 10.3
3359² Helios **(76)** *(RSimpson)* 4-8-8 ‡3ATucker (1) (rdn over 3f out: bhd fnl 2f) ........ 2½.4

**6/5** MRS FISHER (IRE), **9/4** Bold Boss, **5/1** Olette, **6/1** Helios. CSF £6.25, Tote £2.30 (£3.90). Mr G. D. Waters
(NEWMARKET) bred by G. D. Waters in Ireland. 4 Rn 1m 31.97 (5.47)
SF—48/44/14/15

T/Trio: Race 2 £88.30 (22.4 Tckts); & Race 5: £72.30 (22.1 Tckts). T/Jkpt: £56,931.00 (2.84 Tckts). T/Plpt:
£69.80 (211.3 Tckts). AK

# ASCOT (R-H)
## Friday, September 25th [Soft]
Going Allowance: St: 0.45 sec (Y); Rnd: 0.80 sec per fur (S) Wind: almost nil

Stalls: centre

**3434** SHADWELL ESTATES PRIVATE H'CAP 1¼m
1-30 (1-33)

3061 **Kitaab (USA) (70)** *(ACStewart)* 3-10-13 BroughScott (3) (2nd st: led 1f out: r.o
wl) ................................... —1
3215 Weeheby (USA) **(64)** *(AAScott)* 3-10-7 JoeMercer (2) (lw: 3rd st: shkn up over
2f out: r.o ins fnl f) .......................... 2½.2
2540⁵ Duc de Berry (USA) **(79)** (bl) (Jt-Fav) *(GHarwood)* 4-12-0 GrevilleStarkey (6)
(lw: led 9f: sn wknd) ................................ 2.3
3279⁵ Kabayil **(73)** *(PTWalwyn)* 3-11-2 LordOaksey (4) (bmpd s: 4th st: wknd over 2f
out) .................................. 10.4
3116⁴ Rajai (IRE) **(80)** (bl) *(JLDunlop)* 3-11-9 RobinGray (5) (bmpd s: bhd fnl 5f: 6th
st) .................................. 10.5
1275² Romansh **(80)** (Jt-Fav) *(GWragg)* 3-11-9 BillSmith (1) (lw: bhd fnl 5f: 5th st) ...... 8.6
LONG HANDICAP: Weeheby (USA) 10-2.

**5/2** Romansh, Duc de Berry (USA), **11/2** Kabayil(4/1—6/1), **7/1** Weeheby (USA), Rajai (IRE), **9/1** KITAAB
(USA)(op 5/1). CSF £55.58, Tote £14.20: £4.10 £2.60 (£44.60). Mr Hamdan Al-Maktoum (NEWMARKET) bred
by Fittocks Stud Farm in USA. 6 Rn 2m 22.88 (18.58)
SF—26/15/32/–/–/–

**3435** PERSONNEL SELECTION GRADUATION STKS (2-Y.O.C & G) £11550.00 (£3450.00:
£1650.00: £750.00) 7f 2-00 (2-04)

3011* **Inchinor** *(RCharlton)* 9-3 TQuinn (1) (lw: a.p: led over 1f out: rdn out) ............... —1

3205  Right Win (IRE) **(100)** *(RHannon)* 9-3  MRoberts (6) (a.p: led over 2f out tl over 1f
out: unable qckn ins fnl f) ......................................................... 2.2
3005★  Emperor Jones (USA) **(97)** (Fav) *(JHMGosden)* 9-3  SCauthen (2) (hld up: rdn
over 1f out: one pce) ................................................................. 4.3
2519★  Wathik (USA) **(94)** *(HThomsonJones)* 9-3  RHills (3) (lw: a.p: ev ch 2f out: wknd
over 1f out) ............................................................................. 2.4
Village Green (FR) *(CEBrittain)* 8-11  LDettori (5) (unf: scope: hld up: rdn over 2f
out: wknd over 1f out) ......................................................... ½.5
2841  Wufud (USA) **(90)** *(JLDunlop)* 9-3  WCarson (4) (bhd over 4f) ..................... 12.6

**11/10** Emperor Jones (USA), **9/4** INCHINOR, **6/1** Right Win (IRE), **12/1** Wathik (USA), **16/1** Village Green (FR),
**33/1** Wufud (USA). Tote £2.90: £1.60 £2.70 £8.70 (£13.85). Sir Philip Oppenheimer (BECKHAMPTON) bred by
Hascombe and Valiant Studs. 6 Rn                                                 1m 32.69 (6.19)
SF—58/52/40/34/26/—

**3436**    CHEVELEY PARK STUD H'CAP (3-Y.O) (0-110) £9474.00 (£2832.00: £1356.00:
£618.00)  1¼m                                                              2-30 (2-35)
(Weights raised 3 lb)

3279  **Major Bugler (IRE) (76)** *(GBBalding)* 8-1  WCarson (4) (hdwy over 5f out: led
over 1f out: rdn out) .............................................................. —1
848  Fengari **(73)** *(PTWalwyn)* 7-12  DBiggs (5) (hdwy over 2f out: hrd rdn over 1f
out: unable qckn) .................................................................... 2.2
3319²  Milzig (USA) **(96)** *(DRCElsworth)* 9-7  TQuinn (11) (lw: 6th st: rdn over 2f out:
one pce) ................................................................................ nk.3
3241★  Risk Master **(85)** *(CAHorgan)* 8-10  DHolland (8) (lw: hdwy over 2f out: one pce) 1½.4
3204⁵  Royal Seaton **(86)** *(BRMillman)* 8-11  JWilliams (1) (swtg: hdwy over 1f out: r.o) nk.5
3357★  Billy Blazer **(82)** (Fav) *(MHTompkins)* 8-7 (5x) RHills (7) (5th st: rdn over 2f out:
one pce) ................................................................................ nk.6
2920ᴬ  Valley of Fire **(89)** *(IRFanshawe)* 9-0  SCauthen (10) (led over 8f) ............... 12.7
2347  Courtline Jester **(79)** *(MAJarvis)* 8-4  JQuinn (3) (lw: wknd over 1f out) ....... 6.8
3209  Alycida (USA) **(81)** *(LMCumani)* 8-6  LDettori (9) (lw: racd wd: 2nd st: wknd over
2f out) ................................................................................... 8.9
2453  Alto Jane **(77)** *(GHarwood)* 8-2  MHills (6) (bhd fnl 5f) ........................ 2½.10
2798⁶  Greek Gold (IRE) **(86)** *(MRStoute)* 8-11  MRoberts (12) (lw: led 1f: 4th st: wknd
over 2f out) ............................................................................ 2.11
3062★  Belle Isis (USA) **(80)** *(LordHuntingdon)* 8-5  AMunro (2) (lw: bhd fnl 5f: t.o) .... 30.12

**4/1** Billy Blazer, **11/2** Royal Seaton, **7/1** Belle Isis (USA), Courtline Jester, **8/1** Valley of Fire, **10/1** MAJOR
BUGLER (IRE), Greek Gold (IRE), **12/1** Risk Master(op 8/1), Alycida (USA), **14/1** Milzig (USA), **20/1** Fengari,
**33/1** Alto Jane. CSF £163.15, CT £2,511.79. Tote £12.40: £2.90 £5.40 £6.90 (£101.30). Mr Michael
Kerr-Dineen (DORCHESTER) bred by Majors Racing International Ltd in Ireland. 12 Rn      2m 16.72 (12.42)
SF—43/36/58/44/44/39

**3437**    BERKELEY H'CAP (0-110) £17090.00 (£5120.00: £2460.00: £1130.00)
5f                                                                          3-05 (3-09)
(Weights raised 3 lb)

853⁵  **Spaniards Close (98)** *(PJMakin)* 4-9-7  WRSwinburn (11) (hdwy wl over 1f out:
led ins fnl f: r.o wl) .............................................................. —1
3253³  Ashtina **(71)** *(RJHodges)* 7-7-8⁽¹⁾  JQuinn (15) (w ldr: led over 1f out tl ins fnl f:
unable qckn) ........................................................................... 1½.2
3188  Plain Fact **(85)** *(JWHills)* 7-8-8  MHills (2) (racd stands' side: hdwy over 1f out:
r.o wl ins fnl f) ...................................................................... 1.3
3059⁴  Bodari **(80)** *(DAWilson)* 3-7-12 ‡³DHarrison (18) (led over 3f: one pce) ......... 2.4
3188  Terrhars (IRE) **(96)** *(RHannon)* 4-9-5  TQuinn (14) (lw: a.p: hrd rdn over 2f out:
one pce) ................................................................................ nk.5
3243⁴  Fascination Waltz **(73)** *(DShaw)* 5-7-10  WCarson (10) (lw: hdwy over 1f out: r.o) nk.6
3124  Tbab (IRE) **(101)** (bl) *(CEBrittain)* 4-9-10  MRoberts (12) (a.p: rdn over 2f out:
one pce) ................................................................................ nk.7
3284★  King's Signet (USA) **(93)** (Fav) *(JHMGosden)* 3-9-0 (7x) SCauthen (6) (lw: racd
stands' side: prom over 3f) .................................................... ½.8
2592★  Shikari's Son **(74)** *(JWhite)* 5-7-11  DaleGibson (1) (lw: racd stands' side: nvr
nrr) ....................................................................................... nk.9
3361⁶  Regal Scintilla **(96)** *(GBBalding)* 3-9-3  AMunro (9) (a mid div) ................ hd.10
2369  Love Legend **(84)** *(DWPArbuthnot)* 7-8-2 ‡⁵RPrice (16) (prom over 3f) ......... 2.11
2919⁵  Olifantsfontein **(77)** *(RSimpson)* 4-8-0  DHolland (3) (racd stands' side: prom
over 3f) ................................................................................. ¾.12
3095  Baligay **(78)** *(RJHodges)* 7-8-1  TSprake (17) (outpcd) ........................ hd.13
3059³  Never in the Red **(88)** (v) *(JBerry)* 4-8-11  LDettori (13) (lw: prom over 3f) ...... ¾.14
3243⁵  Green Dollar **(91)** *(EAWheeler)* 9-9-0  MTebbutt (20) (outpcd) ................. hd.15
1875⁵  Miss Nosey Parker (IRE) **(100)** *(RHannon)* 3-9-4 ‡³RPerham (4) (racd stands'
side: spd 4f) ........................................................................... 1½.16
3304⁶  Drum Sergeant **(76)** (bl) *(JParkes)* 5-7-13  DBiggs (8) (lw: a bhd) ............... hd.17

*3318*³ Paley Prince (USA) **(76)** *(MDIUsher)* 6–7-13 NCarlisle (19) (a bhd) .............. 2¹/₂.**18**
3188 Beau Venture (USA) **(95)** *(FHLee)* 4–8-13 ‡⁵NKennedy (7) (lw: racd stands' side: prom 3f) ........................... ³/₄.**19**
LONG HANDICAP: Ashtina 7-5.

**3/1** King's Signet (USA), **8/1** Tbab (IRE), **9/1** Fascination Waltz, **10/1** Olifantsfontein, **14/1** Bodari, Never in the Red, Ashtina, **16/1** Drum Sergeant, Regal Scintilla, **20/1** Green Dollar, Terrhars (IRE), SPANIARDS CLOSE, Miss Nosey Parker (IRE), Plain Fact, Love Legend, **25/1** Paley Prince (USA), Shikari's Son, **33/1** Ors. CSF £253.27, CT £5,049.16. Tote £19.00: £4.30 £2.60 £4.70 £3.20 (£66.10). Avon Industries Ltd (MARLBOROUGH) bred by Avon Industries Bath Ltd. 19 Rn
63.55 sec (3.05)
SF—91/58/68/50/70/46/73

---

**3438**    EWAR STUD FARMS APP'CE H'CAP (0-100) £4347.00 (£1296.00: £618.00: £279.00)
**1¹/₂m**                             3-35 (3-36)
(Weights raised 20 lb)

3157⁵ Bar Billiards **(52)** (bl) *(GLewis)* 3–8-0 BRussell (3) (mde all: hrd rdn over 1f out: r.o wl) ............. —**1**
395⁵ Jasoorah (IRE) **(76)** *(ACStewart)* 3–9-3 ‡⁷ElizabethForletta (7) (5th st: ev ch ins fnl f: r.o) ........................... nk.**2**
3309³ Much Sought After **(75)** *(DMorley)* 3–9-9 EBentley (6) (3rd st: ev ch 1f out: unable qckn) ........... 2.**3**
3190 Bustinetta **(68)** *(JRFanshawe)* 3–9-2 NVarley (1) (4th st: rdn over 1f out: one pce) ........... 2.**4**
3140 Swift Silver **(61)** (Fav) *(WJMusson)* 5–9-3 PBowe (2) (6th st: wknd wl over 1f out) ........... 20.**5**
3293 Black Sapphire **(68)** *(MHTompkins)* 5–9-7 ‡³SMulvey (4) (lw: 2nd st: wknd wl over 1f out) ........... 3¹/₂.**6**

**11/4** Swift Silver, **100/30** Bustinetta, **4/1** Much Sought After, **9/2** Jasoorah (IRE), **6/1** BAR BILLIARDS, **12/1** Black Sapphire. CSF £28.70, CT £100.32. Tote £8.00: £2.50 £2.00 (£12.70). Mr A. J. Richards (EPSOM) bred by Ewar Stud Farms. 6 Rn
2m 49.69 (20.19)

---

**3439**    ROSEMARY H'CAP (3-Y.O.F) (0-115) £10010.00 (£2990.00: £1430.00: £650.00)
**1m (st)**                             4-05 (4-08)
(Weights raised 14 lb)

3269★ Jdaayel **(83)** (Fav) *(ACStewart)* 8–13 (4x) MRoberts (1) (a.p: led over 1f out: rdn out) ........... —**1**
3013⁵ Mathaayl (USA) **(75)** (bl) *(HThomsonJones)* 8-5 NCarlisle (11) (hld up: ev ch ins fnl f: unable qckn) ........... 2¹/₂.**2**
3269 Hugging **(76)** *(MMcCormack)* 8-6 JReid (2) (swtg: a.p: rdn over 1f out: one pce) ........... nk.**3**
3269³ She's Pleased (USA) **(78)** *(LMCumani)* 8-8 LDettori (6) (hdwy over 1f out: r.o) . ¹/₂.**4**
3095⁵ Lady Debra Darley **(82)** *(RHannon)* 8–12 TQuinn (4) (hld up: rdn over 2f out: one pce) ........... 2.**5**
3212 Mamma's Too **(89)** *(MBell)* 9-5 LPiggott (10) (lw: hld up: nvr nr to chal) ........... 4.**6**
3014 Magic Steps **(73)** *(CEBrittain)* 8-3 DBiggs (9) (lw: a.p: rdn over 2f out: wknd over 1f out) ........... 2¹/₂.**7**
3095³ Muhit (USA) **(79)** *(PTWalwyn)* 8-9 WCarson (5) (a.p: led over 2f out tl over 1f out: sn wknd) ........... 1¹/₂.**8**
3299³ Ardisia **(89)** *(PFICole)* 9-5 AMunro (7) (led over 5f) ........... ³/₄.**9**
3082² Ships Lantern **(91)** *(CFWall)* 9-7 WRSwinburn (3) (lw: bhd fnl 2f) ........... 1.**10**
3002 Louisville Belle (IRE) **(69)** *(MDIUsher)* 7-10 ‡³DHarrison (8) (bhd fnl 2f) ........... ¹/₂.**11**

**5/2** JDAAYEL, **5/1** She's Pleased (USA), **8/1** Muhit (USA), **10/1** Hugging, Lady Debra Darley, **11/1** Louisville Belle (IRE), **12/1** Ardisia (USA) (op 8/1), **14/1** Mamma's Too, Mathaayl (USA), **33/1** Magic Steps. CSF £32.52, CT £269.77. Tote £2.60: £1.50 £5.40 £2.40 (£23.70). Mr Hamdan Al-Maktoum (NEWMARKET) bred by Floors Farming. 11 Rn
1m 48.31 (8.91)
SF—19/3/3/3/1/–

---

**3440**    KENSINGTON PALACE GRADUATION STKS (2-Y.O.F) £10507.00 (£3136.00: £1498.00: £679.00) **7f**                      4-40 (4-41)

3093★ Thawakib (IRE) (Fav) *(JLDunlop)* 9-0 WCarson (4) (lw: a.p: led over 1f out: rdn out) ........... —**1**
Criquette *(LMCumani)* 8-8 LDettori (3) (leggy: scope: hdwy over 2f out: ev ch over 1f out: r.o) ........... 1.**2**
2930★ Helvellyn (USA) **(98)** *(HRACecil)* 9-0 SCauthen (5) (led over 5f: unable qckn) ... 7.**3**
3191 Society Lady (USA) **(85)** *(AAScott)* 8-8 RHills (7) (hld up: hrd rdn over 1f out: one pce) ........... 4.**4**
3132 Dancing Spirit (IRE) *(DRCEIsworth)* 8-8 TQuinn (9) (hld up: rdn over 2f out: sn wknd) ........... 6.**5**
3136⁴ Amazing Baby (USA) **(84)** *(DRCEIsworth)* 9-0 JWilliams (2) (s.s: bhd fnl 3f) ..... nk.**6**
3372 Seasonal Splendour (IRE) *(CACyzer)* 8-8 DBiggs (1) (bhd fnl 2f) ........... 5.**7**
2256⁴ Aalu (IRE) *(CEBrittain)* 8-8 MRoberts (8) (a.p: ev ch over 2f out: sn wknd) ....... 12.**8**

**7/4** THAWAKIB (IRE), **11/4** Criquette(6/4—3/1), **4/1** Helvellyn (USA), **8/1** Society Lady (USA), **12/1** Amazing Baby (USA)(op 7/1), **14/1** Dancing Spirit (IRE), **33/1** Ors. CSF £6.70, Tote £2.60: £1.20 £1.50 £1.50 (£3.40). Mr Hamdan Al-Maktoum (ARUNDEL) bred by Barronstown & Gainesway T'bed Ltd in Ireland. 8 Rn

1m 33.08 (6.58)

SF—49/40/25/7/–/–

T/Trio: Race 3: £374.60 (5 Tckts) & Race 4: £552.60 (4 Tckts). T/Jkpt: Not won; £2,729.35 to Ascot 26/9/92. T/Plpt: Not won; £11,227.96 to Ascot 26/9/92.　　　　　　　　　　　　　　　　　　　　AK

## ASCOT (R-H)

### Saturday, September 26th [Soft]

Going Allowance: St: 0.45 sec; Rnd: 0.55 sec per fur (Y)　　　　　　　　Wind: nil

Stalls: 1st & 2nd centre, remainder high

**3441**　　FESTIVAL H'CAP　£50736.25 (£15265.00: £7382.50: £3441.25)　**7f**　1-30 (1-37)

(Weights raised 10 lb)

| | | |
|---|---|---|
| 3344* | Sharpalto (89) *(MrsGRReveley)* 5-9-3 (5x) MJKinane (1) (lw: hld up & bhd: hdwy on bit over 1f out: qcknd to ld ins fnl f) | —1 |
| 2852 | Little Bean (94) *(GWragg)* 3-9-4 MHills (5) (a.p: ev ch 1f out: nt qckn) | 3½.2 |
| 2852² | Deprecator (USA) (96) *(Jt-Fav)* *(JHMGosden)* 4-9-10 WCarson (9) (b.hind: swtg: gd hdwy over 1f out: nvr nrr) | hd.3 |
| 2889⁵ | Heart of Darkness (90) (v) *(IABalding)* 4-9-4 PatEddery (17) (hmpd 2f out: hdwy wl over 1f out: nrst fin: fin 4th, 1l & d.h: plcd 4th outright) | 4 |
| 3212 | Gymcrak Premiere (94) (v) *(MHEasterby)* 4-9-8 MBirch (15) (lw: hdwy & edgd rt 2f out: led 1f out: hdd & nt qckn: fin 4th, d.h: plcd 5th) | 5 |
| 1000 | Kimberley Park (69) *(DWPArbuthnot)* 4-7-8 ‡³FNorton (8) (a.p: r.o one pce fnl 2f) | nk.6 |
| 3095⁴ | Jaldi (IRE) (70) (bl) *(JSutcliffe)* 4-7-12 NAdams (10) (a.p: led 2f out tl wknd 1f out) | 3.7 |
| 3349 | Highland Magic (IRE) (65) *(MJFetherston-Godley)* 4-7-0 ‡⁷AntoinetteArmes (7) (nvr nr to chal) | 3.8 |
| 3209 | Rise Up Singing (72) (bl) *(WJMusson)* 4-8-0 TyroneWilliams (18) (swtg: w ldrs tl wknd over 1f out) | ¾.9 |
| 2945⁴ | Field of Honour (83) *(LMCumani)* 4-8-11 (5x) LDettori (13) (swtg: a mid div) | s.h.10 |
| 3281⁴ | Confronter (80) *(PFICole)* 3-8-4 TQuinn (12) (lw: prom 5f) | nk.11 |
| 3095² | Abbey Strand (USA) (71) (v) *(LordHuntingdon)* 3-7-6(1) ‡³DHarrison (14) (n.d) | 1½.12 |
| 3209⁵ | Doulab's Image (94) (bl) *(Jt-Fav)* *(JAGlover)* 5-9-3 (5x) ‡⁵SWilliams (21) (n.d) | ½.13 |
| 3083 | Master Planner (102) *(CACyzer)* 3-9-12 (5x) DBiggs (20) (led 5f) | 2.14 |
| 2400⁶ | Go Executive (89) *(CEBrittain)* 4-9-3 BDoyle (22) (swtg: spd over 4f) | nk.15 |
| 3198² | Rocton North (IRE) (89) (bl) *(RHannon)* 4-9-3 JReid (10) (swtg: a bhd) | nk.16 |
| 3121 | Noble Pet (89) *(PJMakin)* 3-8-13 LPiggott (11) (m.n.s) | 2.17 |
| 3251 | Prince of the Sea (IRE) (74) *(DWPArbuthnot)* 4-8-2 GBardwell (19) (n.d) | 7.18 |
| 3209 | Desert Splendour (73) *(CEBrittain)* 4-8-1 MRoberts (3) (spd 4f) | 3½.19 |
| 2191³ | Irek (91) *(Jt-Fav)* *(LordHuntingdon)* 3-9-1 SCauthen (6) (lw: spd over 4f) | 2½.20 |
| 3182³ | Sylvan Sabre (IRE) (77) *(PMitchell)* 3-8-1(1) PaulEddery (4) (swtg: n.d) | ¾.21 |

*Stewards Enquiry: Gymcrak Premiere disq. (interference to Heart of Darkness ins fnl f).*

**10/1** Irek, Doulab's Image, Deprecator (USA), **11/1** SHARPALTO, Abbey Strand (USA), **12/1** Noble Pet, Little Bean, **14/1** Heart of Darkness, Confronter, Jaldi (IRE), **16/1** Field of Honour, Desert Splendour, **20/1** Kimberley Park, Go Executive, Gymcrak Premiere, **25/1** Rocton North (IRE), Sylvan Sabre (IRE), **33/1** Rise Up Singing, Master Planner, **50/1** Highland Magic (IRE), **66/1** Prince of the Sea (IRE). CSF £119.94, CT £1,242.42. Tote £8.70: £2.00 £2.90 £2.80 £2.90 (£64.10). Mr T. J. Prew (SALTBURN) bred by E. A. Badger. 21 Rn

1m 31.08 (4.58)

SF—82/72/77/68/72/43/38

**3442**　　DIADEM STKS (Gp 3) £42660.00 (£15798.00: £7449.00: £3093.00)　**6f**　2-05 (2-11)

| | | |
|---|---|---|
| 3361* | Wolfhound (USA) (114) *(JHMGosden)* 3-8-11 SCauthen (10) (lw: a.p: led over 1f out: pushed out) | —1 |
| 3356* | Lochsong (106) *(IABalding)* 4-8-11 WCarson (1) (lw: a.p: led 3f out tl over 1f out: r.o) | 1½.2 |
| 3006 | Montendre (110) *(MMcCormack)* 5-9-0 PatEddery (5) (swtg: hdwy fnl 2f: nvr nrr) | 1.3 |
| 3223a² | Twafeaj (USA) (110) *(BHanbury)* 3-8-8 WRSwinburn (7) (swtg: led 3f: wknd over 1f out) | 1.4 |
| 2976a² | Thourios (112) (v) *(GHarwood)* 3-8-11 AClark (9) (w ldr tl wknd wl over 1f out) | 3½.5 |
| 3006* | Rose Indien (FR) (106) *(MMoubarak)* 3-8-8 LDettori (8) (swtg: hrd rdn & no hdwy fnl 2f) | 2.6 |
| 3450a⁵ | Amigo Menor (110) (bl) *(DJGMurray-Smith)* 6-9-0 CRutter (2) (lw: nvr nr to chal) | 1½.7 |
| 3124⁴ | Shalford (IRE) (126) *(Fav)* *(RHannon)* 4-9-0 MRoberts (3) (lw: spd 4f) | nk.8 |

Page 1231

2436 Misterioso **(100)** *(LordHuntingdon)* 3–8-8 AMunro (6) (swtg: outpcd) .............. d.h.**8**
2453 Artic Tracker (USA) **(93)** *(CRNelson)* 3–8-11 MHills (4) (swtg: a bhd: t.o) ....... 12.**10**
3213⁶ Cambrian Hills (IRE) **(96)** *(PWChapple-Hyam)* 3–8-8 LPiggott (11) (swtg: a
bhd: t.o) .................................................................. 2.**11**

**5/2** Shalford (IRE), **4/1** WOLFHOUND (USA), **9/2** Lochsong(op 3/1), **6/1** Twafeaj (USA), **10/1** Montendre, **12/1** Thourios, **20/1** Rose Indien (FR), Amigo Menor, **40/1** Misterioso, **50/1** Artic Tracker (USA), **66/1** Cambrian Hills (IRE). CSF £20.00, Tote £4.90: £1.80 £1.60 £4.30 (£9.80). Sheikh Mohammed (NEWMARKET) bred by W. S. Farish III and W. S. Kilroy in USA. 11 Rn 1m 17.20 (3.60)
SF—79/73/72/62/51/40/40

**3443** QUEEN ELIZABETH II STKS (Gp 1) £208339.20 (£77550.86: £36900.43: £15691.51)
1m (rnd) 2-50 (2-55)

2892a² **Lahib (USA)** *(JLDunlop)* 4–9-4 WCarson (9) (3rd st: led over 2f out: r.o wl) ...... —**1**
3231a² Brief Truce (USA) (bl) *(DKWeld,Ireland)* 3–9-0 MJKinane (2) (lw: 6th st: hdwy 2f
out: chsd wnr fnl f: no imp) .......................................... 2.**2**
2998★ Selkirk (USA) (Fav) *(IABalding)* 4–9-4 JReid (6) (lw: 8th st: hdwy on bit whn nt
clr run 2f out & over 1f out: swtchd outside: r.o) .............. 1½.**3**
3231a★ All At Sea (USA) *(HRACecil)* 3–8-11 PatEddery (7) (swtg: 5th st: rdn over 2f out:
r.o one pce) .............................................................. 2½.**4**
3229a Second Set (IRE) *(LMCumani)* 4–9-4 LDettori (8) (swtg: 4th st: hrd rdn over 1f
out: one pce) ............................................................ 3½.**5**
2998⁶ Mystiko (USA) *(CEBrittain)* 4–9-4 MRoberts (5) (2nd st: btn whn bmpd over 1f
out) ........................................................................ 8.**6**
2440★ Marling (IRE) *(GWragg)* 3–8-11 WRSwinburn (10) (swtg: 7th st: no hdwy) ....... hd.**7**
3231a Sharp Review (IRE) *(DKWeld,Ireland)* 4–9-4 PShanahan (3) (swtg: 9th st: bhd
fnl 3f) ..................................................................... 2.**8**
3371³ Hamas (IRE) *(PTWalwyn)* 3–9-0 RHills (4) (led tl wknd over 2f out) .............. 1½.**9**

**5/4** Selkirk (USA), **4/1** All At Sea (USA), **9/2** Marling (IRE), **7/1** Brief Truce (USA)(9/1—6/1), **8/1** LAHIB (USA), **14/1** Second Set (IRE), **50/1** Mystiko (USA), **200/1** Ors. CSF £56.45, Tote £10.90: £2.20 £1.40 £1.10 (£22.60). Mr Hamdan Al-Maktoum (ARUNDEL) bred by Hamdan Bin Rashid Al Maktoum in USA. 9 Rn 1m 44.50 (4.90)
SF—97/87/86/71/67/43/36

**3444** FILLIES' MILE STKS (Gp 1) (2-Y.O.F) £93015.00 (£34730.75: £16615.38: £7163.87)
1m (rnd) 3-25 (3-36)

3191³ **Ivanka (IRE)** *(CEBrittain)* 8-10 MRoberts (1) (4th st: led wl over 1f out: drvn out) —**1**
2991³ Ajfan (USA) *(HThomsonJones)* 8-10 RHills (8) (lw: 2nd st: led over 2f out tl wl
over 1f out: r.o) ........................................................ 1½.**2**
2864★ Iviza (IRE) (Fav) *(MRStoute)* 8-10 SCauthen (3) (lw: s.s: 7th st: rdn over 2f out:
styd on fnl f) ............................................................ 3.**3**
3227a² Bright Generation (IRE) *(PFICole)* 8-10 AMunro (7) (5th st: r.o one pce fnl 2f) .. ½.**4**
3191 Abury (IRE) *(PWChapple-Hyam)* 8-10 JReid (4) (6th st: styd on fnl f) ........... 1.**5**
2438★ Magique Rond Point (USA) *(HRACecil)* 8-10 PatEddery (2) (lw: 3rd st: ev ch wl
over 1f out: wknd fnl f) ............................................... ¾.**6**
2657★ Mystic Goddess (USA) *(MRStoute)* 8-10 WCarson (5) (swtg: led over 5f) ........ 7.**7**
3036★ Comme D'Habitude (USA) *(PFICole)* 8-10 TQuinn (6) (a bhd: t.o) ................. 25.**8**

**11/4** Iviza (IRE)(4/1—5/2), **7/2** Magique Rond Point (USA), Bright Generation (IRE), **11/2** Mystic Goddess (USA), **6/1** IVANKA (IRE), **14/1** Comme D'Habitude (USA), **16/1** Ajfan (USA), **33/1** Abury (IRE). CSF £77.03, Tote £6.10: £1.70 £2.60 £1.50 (£33.10). Mr Ali Saeed (NEWMARKET) bred by Stackallan Stud in Ireland. 8 Rn
1m 46.45 (7.05)
SF—56/51/42/40/37/35

**3445** KRUG TROPHY (H'cap) £60466.90 (£18155.20: £8752.60: £4051.30)
1½m 4-00 (4-07)
(Weights raised 13 lb)

2844★ **Quick Ransom (84)** *(MJohnston)* 4–9-1 (4x) DMcKeown (8) (lw: gd hdwy over
1f out: str run to ld fnl strides) ................................... —**1**
3369 Lift and Load (USA) **(91)** *(RHannon)* 5–9-8 JReid (1) (swtg: 5th st: led ins fnl f tl
last strides) ............................................................. hd.**2**
2844⁴ Whitechapel (USA) **(80)** *(LordHuntingdon)* 4–8-11 WRSwinburn (10) (2nd st:
led wl over 1f out tl ins fnl f: r.o) ................................. nk.**3**
3206⁵ Secret Society **(85)** (bl) *(MJCamacho)* 5–9-2 NConnorton (4) (hdwy fnl 2f: nrst
fin) ......................................................................... 2½.**4**
3369⁵ Hajaim (IRE) **(88)** (bl) *(CEBrittain)* 4–9-0 ‡⁵BDoyle (6) (nvr nrr) ................... ½.**5**
2844 Deposki **(84)** (bl) *(MRStoute)* 4–9-1 TQuinn (7) (4th st: wknd over 1f out) ...... 5.**6**
3234★ Green Lane (IRE) **(81)** (bl) *(RCharlton)* 3–8-4 (4x) PaulEddery (15) (swtg: led tl
wknd wl over 1f out) ................................................. 1½.**7**
3369★ Castoret **(83)** *(JWHills)* 6–8-11 (4x) ‡³DHarrison (16) (late hdwy: nvr nrr) ...... 1½.**8**
3206★ Seal Indigo (IRE) **(87)** *(RHannon)* 4–9-4 (4x) PatEddery (9) (lw: nvr nr to chal) nk.**9**

3190³ Anna of Saxony **(91)** (Fav) *(JHMGosden)* 3-9-0 SCauthen (18) (swtg: hdwy 6f out: hrd rdn & wknd 2f out) .................................................. 4.10

3122² Halkopous **(88)** (v) *(MHTompkins)* 6-9-5 PRobinson (14) (n.d) ..................... 3¹/₂.11

3122³ Zawaahy **(79)** *(AAScott)* 3-7-13 ‡³FNorton (17) (3rd st: wknd 2f out) ..... ¹/₂.12

3204² Duke of Eurolink **(95)** *(LMCumani)* 3-9-4 (4x) MRoberts (9) (n.d) ................ 8.13

3346³ Tell No Lies **(97)** *(MHEasterby)* 5-10-0 (4x) MBirch (12) (6th st: wknd 2f out) nk.14

3139² Laburnum **(84)** *(LMCumani)* 4-9-1 LDettori (2) (prom tl wknd 3f out) ............. 2¹/₂.15

3139⁶ Opera Ghost **(85)** *(PWHarris)* 6-9-2 (4x) RHills (11) (swtg: n.d) ....................... 6.16

3368 Knock Knock **(92)** *(IABalding)* 7-9-9 MHills (13) (lw: n.d) .......................... 5.17

4/1 Anna of Saxony, 11/2 Laburnum, 8/1 Castoret, Whitechapel (USA), 9/1 Green Lane (IRE), 10/1 Duke of Eurolink, 11/1 Halkopous, Deposki, 14/1 QUICK RANSOM, 16/1 Seal Indigo (IRE), 20/1 Opera Ghost, 25/1 Hajaim (IRE), Lift and Load (USA), 33/1 Secret Society, Zawaahy (USA), Tell No Lies, 40/1 Knock Knock. CSF £289.22, CT £2,708.77. Tote £19.90: £3.50 £2.30 £2.00 £6.70 (£571.00). Mr J. S. Morrison (MIDDLEHAM) bred by Benham Stud. 17 Rn

2m 39.57 (10.07)
SF—56/62/50/50/47/38

---

**3446**  ROYAL LODGE STKS (Gp 2) (2-Y.O.C & G) £66609.00 (£24978.45: £12039.23: £5288.32) **1m (rnd)**

4-35 (4-38)

3200⁸ **Desert Secret (IRE)** *(MRStoute)* 8-10 PatEddery (7) (lw: hdwy over 2f out: hrd rdn to ld wl ins fnl f) .................................................. —1

3272★ Geisway (CAN) *(RHannon)* 8-10 LPiggott (9) (2nd st: led over 2f out tl wl ins fnl f) . ¹/₂.2

3008★ Lost Soldier (USA) *(LMCumani)* 8-10 LDettori (5) (6th st: r.o one pce fnl 2f) .... 2¹/₂.3

3205² Needle Gun (IRE) *(CEBrittain)* 8-10 SCauthen (1) (5th st: hrd rdn 2f out: one pce) .................................................. ¹/₂.4

3200² Planetary Aspect (USA) *(PWChapple-Hyam)* 8-10 JReid (10) (nrst fin) ............. hd.5

1899★ Fret (USA) *(PFICole)* 8-10 AMunro (4) (lw: no hdwy fnl 2f) ............................... ³/₄.6

3448a⁵ King Paris (IRE) *(MDoll)* 8-10 MHills (2) (bhd fnl 2f) .................................... 6.7

Perfect Imposter (IRE) *(JSBolger,Ireland)* 8-10 CHoche (3) (w'like: scope: 3rd st: wknd over 1f out) .................................................. 2¹/₂.8

2849³ York Hill (IRE) *(PAKelleway)* 8-10 MRoberts (6) (4th st: wknd over 1f out) ......... 1¹/₂.9

1873★ Scottish Peak (IRE) (Fav) *(LordHuntingdon)* 8-10 WRSwinburn (8) (led tl wknd over 2f out) .................................................. 1.10

7/2 Scottish Peak (IRE), 4/1 Lost Soldier (USA), 5/1 Needle Gun (IRE), 7/1 Geisway (CAN), 8/1 King Paris (IRE), 10/1 Perfect Imposter (IRE), Planetary Aspect (USA), 12/1 Fret (USA), DESERT SECRET (IRE), 33/1 York Hill. CSF £85.62, Tote £11.00: £2.40 £2.80 £2.10 (£61.10). Maktoum Al Maktoum (NEWMARKET) bred by Swettenham Stud in Ireland. 10 Rn

1m 47.72 (8.12)
SF—59/57/49/47/46/44

T/Trio: Race 2: £56.30 (46.8 Tckts); Race 5: £3973.50 (1.1 Tckts). T/Jkpt: Not won; £10,129.58 to Newmarket 30/9/92. T/Plpt: £713.10 (60.6 Tckts).

Hn

---

2506a—**EVRY (R-H)**

**Monday, September 14th [Good]**

Going Allowance: minus 0.25 sec per fur (F)

**3447a**  PRIX DU POINT DU JOUR (listed race) £12384.00 **1m**

1645a³ **The Tender Track (USA)** *(France)* 5-8-11 ELegrix .................................... —1

3089⁴ LECH (USA) *(MrsSPiggott)* 4-8-11 LPiggott .................................................. s.nk.2

Seba le Rouge (FR) *(France)* 5-8-11 GGuignard ................................................ s.h.3

Tote 11.00f: 3.30f 2.90f 3.50f (33.50f). Mr B.Lalemant (A de Royer-Dupre,FRANCE) bred by Arlene London and Hidaway Farm in USA. 8 Rn

1m 39.27 (1.87)
SF—38/37/36

---

3329a—**LONGCHAMP (R-H)**

**Wednesday, September 16th [Good to soft]**

Going Allowance: 0.60 sec per fur (Y)

**3448a**  PRIX LA ROCHETTE (Gp 3) (2-Y.O) £20640.00 **1m (Grande)**

**Kadounor (FR)** *(France)* 2-9-2 GGuignard .................................................. —1

2979a³ Marchand de Sable (USA) *(France)* 2-9-2 DBoeuf .......................................... 1¹/₂.2

Seaton Delaval (USA) *(France)* 2-9-2 SCauthen .................................................. s.h.3

2912² KING PARIS (IRE) *(MBell)* 2-9-2 MHills (btn further ³/₄l) .................................. 5

Tote 4.00f: 2.60f 2.20f (SF: 21.20f). Mrs H. Rabatel (J.Laumain,FRANCE) bred by Mrs H. Rabatel in France. 5 Rn

1m 45.1 (7.4)
SF—63/58/57/56/54

## 3449a
PRIX D'AUMALE (Gp 3)  (2-Y.O.F) £20640.00   **1m (Grande)**

| | |
|---|---|
| **Kindergarten** *(France)* 2-8-9 SCauthen | —1 |
| Lorelie (FR) *(France)* 2-8-9 FHead | 1½.2 |
| Zigreen (FR) *(France)* 2-8-9 TJarnet | s.h.3 |

Tote 1.70f: 1.20f 2.00f 2.30f (7.40f). Sheikh Mohammed (A.Fabre,FRANCE) bred by Sheikh Mohammed bin Rashid al Maktoum. 9 Rn
1m 44.6 (6.9)
SF—64/59/58

## 2504a—MAISONS-LAFFITTE (L-H)

### Thursday, September 17th [Soft]
Going Allowance: nil sec per fur (G)

## 3450a
PRIX DE SEINE-ET-OISE (Gp 3)   £20640.00   **6f (st)**

| | |
|---|---|
| 2448  **CENTRAL CITY** *(RHannon)* 3-8-8 CBlack | —1 |
| 2767a² Monde Bleu *(France)* 4-9-4 TJarnet | ½.2 |
| 1983a³ Silicon Bavaria (FR) *(France)* 5-8-13 MBoutin | 2.3 |
| 2976a³ AMIGO MENOR (bl) *(DJGMurray-Smith)* 6-9-2 ELegrix (btn further 2¹/₄l) | 5 |

Tote 30.00f: 3.60f 1.40f 3.40f (25.80f). Mr George Strawbridge (MARLBOROUGH) bred by E.Aldridge. 11 Rn
1m 11.1 (0.6)
SF—82/90/77/75/71/66

## 3226a—CURRAGH (R-H)

### Saturday, September 19th [Soft]
Going Allowance: 6f-7f: 0.70 sec (S); Rest: 0.35 sec per fur (Y)

## 3451a
MACDONAGH BOLAND STKS (listed race)   £10748.00   **7f**

| | |
|---|---|
| 3195⁵ **NORWICH** *(BWHills)* 5-8-13 SCauthen | —1 |
| 2318a³ Miznah (IRE) *(Ireland)* 3-8-10 CRoche | 4.2 |
| 3226a³ Tarwiya (IRE) (bl) *(Ireland)* 3-8-12 PatEddery | 1.3 |

Tote £3.30: £2.20 £3.60 (£17.70). Sheikh Mohammed (LAMBOURN) bred by David & Mrs Shirley. 7 Rn
1m 29.2 (6)
SF—83/68/67

## 3452a
SMURFIT NATIONAL STKS (Gp 1)  (2-Y.O.C & F) £87477.00   **7f**

| | |
|---|---|
| 3113a* **Fatherland (IRE)** (Fav) *(Ireland)* 2-9-0 LPiggott (hld up & bhd: prog 2f out: chal 1f out: r.o wl to ld cl home) | —1 |
| 2445* MAROOF (USA) *(RWArmstrong)* 2-9-0 WCarson (led: qcknd over 2f out: hdd cl home: no ex) | ½.2 |
| Khoraz (USA) *(Ireland)* 2-9-0 MJKinane (chsd ldr tl outpcd appr fnl f: kpt on) | 3.3 |
| 2764a⁴ Ivory Frontier (IRE) *(Ireland)* 2-9-0 CRoche (prom: ev ch 2f out: no imp fnl f) | 1.4 |
| Rondelli (IRE) *(Ireland)* 2-9-0 KJManning (in tch 4f: styd on u.p appr fnl f) | ½.5 |

**4/5** FATHERLAND (IRE), **9/4** Maroof (USA), **4/1** Ivory Frontier (IRE), **14/1** Khoraz (USA), **25/1** Rondelli (IRE).
Tote £1.50: £1.20 £1.80 (£2.30). Mrs M.V.O'Brien (M.V.O'Brien,IRELAND) bred by Ballydoyle Stud in Ireland. 5 Rn
1m 33.7 (10.5)
SF—16/14/5/2/-

## 3453a
JEFFERSON SMURFIT IRISH ST LEGER (Gp 1)   £80467.00   **1³/₄m**

| | |
|---|---|
| 3225a* **MASHAALLAH (USA)** (Fav) *(JHMGosden)* 4-9-8 SCauthen (chsd ldrs: hdwy ½-wy: ld over 4f out: kpt on wl u.p fnl f) | —1 |
| 3111a² SNURGE *(PFICole)* 6-9-8 TQuinn (chsd ldr: ev ch appr fnl f: styd on wl) | nk.2 |
| 2982a² DRUM TAPS (USA) *(LordHuntingdon)* 6-9-8 JReid (cl up tl lost pl ½-wy: prog to 3rd ent st: r.o wl fnl f) | ¾.3 |
| 2796³ ROCK HOPPER *(MRStoute)* 5-9-8 PatEddery (hld up & bhd: hdwy 4f out: nvr nr to chal) | 2½.4 |
| Vintage Crop *(Ireland)* 5-9-8 MJKinane (bhd: 7th st: nvr nrr) | 2.5 |
| 2977a⁵ Arrikala (IRE) *(Ireland)* 3-8-9 CRoche (bhd tl hdwy to 4th appr st: sn wknd) | 4½.6 |
| 2977a² Dabtiya (IRE) *(Ireland)* 3-8-9 RHughes (bhd: 5th st: no imp) | 1½.7 |
| Tropicarr (USA) (bl) *(Ireland)* 3-8-12 KJManning (cl 2nd tl wknd qckly 6f out: sn t.o) | dist.8 |
| 2904* JAHAFIL *(MajorWRHern)* 4-9-8 WCarson (ld tl hdd 4f out: wknd qckly: t.o) | 15.9 |

**11/4** MASHAALLAH (USA), **9/2** Drum Taps (USA), **5/1** Snurge, **6/1** Rock Hopper, **7/1** Jahafil, Arrikala (IRE), **20/1** Dabtiya (IRE), Vintage Crop, **150/1** Tropicarr (USA). Tote £4.40: £1.80 £1.90 £2.60 (£9.20). Sheikh Ahmed Al Maktoum (NEWMARKET) bred by W.S.Farish, W.T.Carter & E.J.Hudson Jnr. in USA. 9 Rn
3m 2.1 (6.1)
SF—96/95/93/88/84/62

1355a—**BELMONT PARK** (L-H)
**Saturday, September 19th [Firm]**

**3454a**     MAN O'WAR STKS (Grade 1)     £128342.00     **1m 3f (Turf)**

|  |  |  |
|---|---|---|
| | **Solar Splendor (USA)** *(America)* 5–9–0 HMcCauley ............................................ | —1 |
| 3229a* | Dear Doctor (FR) *(France)* 5–9–0 CAsmussen ............................................ | $^{3}/_{4}$.2 |
| 29043 | SPINNING *(IABalding)* 5–9–0 RCochrane ............................................ | $2^{3}/_{4}$.3 |
| 30202 | ADAM SMITH *(LMCumani)* 4–9–0 MSmith (btn further $7^{3}/_{4}$l) ............................................ | 6 |

Tote 12.60 (1-2) 5.00 3.00 (1-2-3) 4.80 2.40 4.40 (Exacta (2 Dol) 35.20). Live Oak Plantation (P.J.Kelly,AMERICA) bred by Live Oak Stud in USA. 8 Rn                                2m 12.45

3448a—**LONGCHAMP** (R-H)
**Sunday, September 20th [Good]**
Going Allowance: 0.30 sec per fur (G)

**3455a**     PRIX DU PRINCE D'ORANGE (Gp 3)     £20640.00     **1¼m (Grande)**

|  |  |  |
|---|---|---|
| 1876 | **Arcangues (USA)** *(France)* 4–9–0 TJarnet ............................................ | —1 |
| 1356a | Prince Polino (USA) *(France)* 3–8–9 ELegrix ............................................ | 6.2 |
| 14565 | Arazi (USA) *(France)* 3–8–9 SCauthen ............................................ | hd.3 |

Tote 3.30f: 2.00f 2.80f (SF: 13.20f). Mr D.Wildenstein (A.Fabre,FRANCE) bred by Allez France Stables Ltd. in USA. 5 Rn                                                               2m 7.5 (4.3)
                                                                                SF—86/70/69

**3456a**     PRIX DE NORMANDIE (listed race)     £12384.00     **1½m (Grande)**

|  |  |  |
|---|---|---|
| 1824a3 | **Afaladja (IRE)** *(France)* 3–8–4 GGuignard ............................................ | —1 |
| 959a | Sharp Counsel (FR) *(France)* 3–8–7 DBoeuf ............................................ | 1½.2 |
| 2442 | MATADOR (USA) *(RCharlton)* 5–9–0 SCauthen ............................................ | 1.3 |

Tote 2.20f: 1.20f 2.10f 2.00f (11.40f). H.H.Aga Khan (A de Royer-Dupre,FRANCE) bred by H.H.Aga Khan in Ireland. 9 Rn                                                              2m 38.2 (8.2)
                                                                                SF—44/44/49

3333a—**SAN SIRO** (R-H)
**Sunday, September 20th [Good to soft]**

**3457a**     PREMIO NOVELLA (listed race) (2-Y.O.F) £20930.00     **7f 110y**

|  |  |  |
|---|---|---|
| 3096 | **MRS WEST (USA)** *(JLDunlop)* 2–8–7 WCarson ............................................ | —1 |
| 2972* | FOOLISH HEART (IRE) *(NAGraham)* 2–8–7 LDettori ............................................ | s.nk.2 |
| 2321a3 | Darubena (ITY) *(Italy)* 2–8–8(1) LPiggott ............................................ | 7.3 |

Tote 39L: 20L 17L (93L). Mr S.Khaled (ARUNDEL) bred by Palides Investments in USA. 6 Rn     1m 32.3

**3458a**     GRAN PREMIO D'ITALIA (Gp 1) (3-Y.O.C & F) £79070.00     **1½m**

|  |  |  |
|---|---|---|
| 28375 | **MASAD (IRE)** *(LMCumani)* 3–9–2 LDettori ............................................ | —1 |
| 3111a* | Modhish (IRE) *(France)* 3–9–2 PatEddery ............................................ | $^{3}/_{4}$.2 |
| 2889a3 | In a Tiff (IRE) *(Ireland)* 3–9–2 MJKinane ............................................ | 1.3 |
| 28405 | SILVERNESIAN (USA) *(JLDunlop)* 3–9–2 WCarson ............................................ | 3.4 |

Tote 36L: 16L 14L (26L). Mrs G.Zanocchio (NEWMARKET) bred by Azienda Agricola San Jore in Ireland. 7 Rn
                                                                                2m 30

3114—**HAYDOCK** (L-H)
**Friday, September 25th [Soft]**
Going Allowance: St: 0.30 sec per fur; Rnd : 0.20 sec per fur (G)               Wind: almost nil

Stalls: high

**3459**     STANLEY SPORTSLINE STKS (Mdn 3-Y.O) £2700.00 (£750.00: £360.00)
             **1¼m 120y**                                                       2-15 (2-19)

|  |  |  |
|---|---|---|
| 30852 | **Unforgiving Minute** (Jt-Fav) *(PWHarris)* 9–0 PaulEddery (12) (chsd ldrs: 4th st: led over 1f out: r.o wl) ............................................ | —1 |
| | Cariboo Gold (USA) *(JHMGosden)* 9-0 GCarter (9) (w'like: leggy: hld up: hdwy 3f out: r.o fnl f: no ch w wnr) ............................................ | 2½.2 |
| 25496 | Pompion (USA) *(JHMGosden)* 9-0 GHind (2) (lw: a.p: 2nd st: led 3f out tl over 1f out: one pce) ............................................ | ½.3 |
| 28863 | Etiquette *(LordHuntingdon)* 8-9 BRaymond (4) (chsd ldrs: 5th st: rdn & wknd 2f out) ............................................ | 12.4 |

With Love *(LMCumani)* 8-4 ‡5JWeaver (10) (lengthy: scope: hld up: sme hdwy fnl 2f: nvr nrr) ........................................... 1.5

2362⁵ Klingon (IRE) (65) *(RHollinshead)* 9-0 WRyan (3) (bit bkwd: nvr nr to chal) ...... 3¹⁄₂.6

Eternal (Jt-Fav) *(RCharlton)* 8-9 PatEddery (11) (lw: w'like: scope: led after 2f to 3f out: eased whn btn appr fnl f) ............................. hd.7

911 Just Hannah *(MrsBarbaraWaring)* 8-9 NHowe (1) (bkwd: a in rr) .................... 2¹⁄₂.8

Well Directed (IRE) *(JLDunlop)* 9-0 AMcGlone (5) (neat: cmpt: bkwd: s.i.s: a bhd) ............................................... 3.9

2922 Exarch (USA) *(BWHills)* 9-0 GBaxter (7) (bit bkwd: a bhd) ...................... 3.10

3072⁴ Zafarrancho (IRE) *(JGFitzGerald)* 9-0 KFallon (6) (b: bit bkwd: chsd ldrs: 6th st: wknd over 3f out) .......................... 1¹⁄₂.11

3306 Barga *(WClay)* 8-6 ‡3FNorton (8) (prom: 3rd st: rdn & wknd over 3f out) ........ 2¹⁄₂.12

5/2 UNFORGIVING MINUTE, Eternal(7/4—11/4), 7/1 Etiquette, Cariboo Gold (USA), 9/1 With Love, 10/1 Pompion (USA), 16/1 Well Directed (IRE), 20/1 Exarch (USA), 25/1 Zafarrancho (IRE), 33/1 Klingon (IRE), Just Hannah, 50/1 Barga. CSF £20.07, Tote £3.70: £1.40 £2.40 £2.00 (£19.80). Mrs P. W. Harris (BERKHAMSTED) bred by Pendley Farm. 12 Rn

2m 19.74 (8.04)

SF—41/36/35/6/–/–

---

## 3460
STANLEY CREDIT CLAIMING H'CAP (0-70) £3078.00 (£858.00: £444.00)

6f

2-45 (2-50)

**Penny Drops (47)** *(LordHuntingdon)* 3–8-5 WRyan (5) (hdwy appr fnl f: r.o to ld ins fnl f) ............................................ —1

3004 Music Dancer (56) *(JBerry)* 3–9-0 GCarter (17) (s.i.s: hdwy u.p over 1f out: fin wl) ....................................................... 2.2

3344 Languedoc (61) *(MPNaughton)* 5–9-1 ‡7SWynne (3) (led far side: clr appr fnl f: wknd & hdd ins fnl f) ................................. ³⁄₄.3

3183³ Easy Does it (48) *(MrsAKnight)* 3–8-3 ‡3FNorton (10) (lw: mde most stands' side: rdn & no ex fnl f) ................................. 3¹⁄₂.4

3042³ Black Boy (IRE) (56) *(JAGlover)* 3–8-9 ‡5OPears (15) (hdwy appr fnl f: nrst fin) 1¹⁄₂.5

3400² Kentucky Rain (54) *(JGFitzGerald)* 3–8-12 KFallon (22) (lw: w ldrs stands' side 5f) 1.6

3355 Double Feature (IRE) (59) (v) *(MrsJRRamsden)* 3–9-3 GHind (19) (hdwy appr fnl f: kpt on fnl f) ...................................... hd.7

984 Amoureuse (IRE) (60) *(THCaldwell)* 3–9-4 CDwyer (4) (bit bkwd: r.o appr fnl f: nvr nrr) .......................................... 2.8

3308 Twilight Falls (53) (Fav) *(MJCamacho)* 7–9-0 NConnorton (2) (bit bkwd: hdwy ¹⁄₂-wy: wknd over 1f out) ............................. nk.9

3196 Lord Lambson (50) *(RMWhitaker)* 3–8-1 ‡7GParkin (2) (racd far side: a bhd) .... 1.10

3198 Ballad Dancer (55) *(EJAlston)* 7–9-2 GBaxter (23) (lost pl ¹⁄₂-wy: n.d after) .... nk.11

3154⁵ Miss Calculate (52) *(CaptJWilson)* 4–8-8 ‡5JWeaver (8) (m.n.s) ............... s.h.12

3341 Hinari Video (43) *(MJohnston)* 7–8-4 PaulEddery (4) (w ldr far side to ¹⁄₂-wy) s.h.13

3310 Dandy Desire (47) *(BCMorgan)* 3–7-12(4) ‡7SSanders (9) (a bhd) ............... nk.14

3308 All Earz (IRE) (47) (bl) *(REarnshaw)* 3–8-9 ‡5StephenDavies (21) (m.n.s) ...... ³⁄₄.15

3239 First Flush (32) *(KTIvory)* 6–7-7 SWood (16) (a bhd) ......................... ¹⁄₂.16

3294⁴ Le Chic (48) *(DWChapman)* 6–8-9 BRaymond (1) (m.n.s) ....................... 2¹⁄₂.17

Berkeley Hill Boy (37) *(RHollinshead)* 5–7-5 ‡7AGarth (14) (bkwd: m.n.s) ..... nk.18

2974⁴ Inswinger (32) *(WGRWightman)* 6–7-7 GBardwell (18) (a.to) .................... 6.19

2786 Trioming (40) (bl) *(APJones)* 6–8-1 NAdams (20) (a.to) ....................... hd.20

2275 Baie Petite (44) *(AWJones)* 3–8-2 NHowe (4) (bkwd: bhd fr ¹⁄₂-wy: t.o) ....... 1¹⁄₂.21

3009 Waveband (65) (bl) *(BWHills)* 3–9-9 PatEddery (13) (spd stands' side over 3f) 6.22

LONG HANDICAP: First Flush 7-1, Inswinger 7-5.

6/1 Twilight Falls, 8/1 Kentucky Rain, Ballad Dancer, 9/1 Double Feature (IRE), Waveband, 10/1 Easy Does it, Black Boy (IRE), PENNY DROPS, 12/1 Hinari Video, 14/1 Music Dancer, 16/1 Miss Calculate, Languedoc, Inswinger, 20/1 Trioming, Le Chic, 25/1 All Earz (IRE), 33/1 Ors. CSF £141.99, CT £2,044.38. Tote £18.20: £4.40 £4.80 £6.50 £2.40 (£360.50). Mr Stanley J. Sharp (WEST ILSLEY) bred by T. M. Saud. 22 Rn

1m 15.73 (4.03)

SF—47/48/46/20/20/19

---

## 3461
STANLEY RACING H'CAP (0-90) £3640.50 (£1089.00: £522.00: £238.50)

1m 3f 200y          (Weights raised 2 lb)

3-20 (3-24)

3363² **Googly (67)** (Jt-Fav) *(WGRWightman)* 3–8-5 GBardwell (13) (a.p: 4th st: led 2f out: rdn out) ........................................ —1

3072✶ Long Silence (USA) (77) *(MrsJCecil)* 3–9-1 PaulEddery (10) (hld up: 7th st: rdn & r.o wl ins fnl f) .................................. ³⁄₄.2

3234² Top Royal (82) (Jt-Fav) *(JLDunlop)* 3–9-6 PatEddery (15) (led to 2f out: kpt on u.p fnl f) ........................................ 2¹⁄₂.3

3380 Pennine Star (IRE) (54) *(CWCElsey)* 4–8-0 SWood (1) (chsd ldrs: 6th st: hrd rdn appr fnl f: styd on) ................................ ¹⁄₂.4

2853 I Perceive (70) *(FHLee)* 5–9-2 GCarter (6) (dwlt: hdwy over 2f out: rdn appr fnl f: one pce) ........................................ nk.5

2827 Diamond Wedding (USA) (64) *(NAGraham)* 3–7-11 ‡5BDoyle (4) (hld up: hdwy over 3f out: kpt on same pce appr fnl f) ................... ¹⁄₂.6

2734[4] Bold Elect **(75)** *(PWigham)* 4–9-7 MWigham (7) (styd on fnl 2f: nvr nrr) ............. 5.7
Bollin William **(62)** *(MHEasterby)* 4–8-8 KFallon (12) (bkwd: chsd ldrs: 5th st: wknd 2f out) ............................. 3.8
1934 Sayh **(80)** *(MAJarvis)* 3–9-4 BRaymond (9) (bit bkwd: chsd ldr: 3rd st: wknd over 2f out) ............................. 2.9
3116[3] Mad Militant (IRE) **(83)** *(RHollinshead)* 3–9-7 WRyan (2) (hld up: gd hdwy & ev ch 3f out: sn rdn & wknd) ............................. 1.10
3357[5] Comstock **(78)** *(NTinkler)* 5–9-10 DNicholls (14) (a bhd) ............................. 2.11
664[2] El Nido **(71)** *(MJCamacho)* 4–9-3 NConnorton (8) (bit bkwd: mid div tl wknd over 2f out) ............................. 1¹⁄₂.12
Able Player (USA) **(47)** *(CWThornton)* 5–7-7 NAdams (3) (bkwd: in tch 9f: sn wknd) ............................. hd.13
2693 Moonlight Shift **(50)** *(WClay)* 6–7-7[(3)] ‡3FNorton (11) (bit bkwd: a bhd) ............. 3.14
La Stravaganza **(62)** *(LJCodd)* 4–8-8 GHind (5) (bkwd: prom: 2nd st: wknd 3f out) ............................. s.h.15

LONG HANDICAP: Moonlight Shift 7-2.

4/1 Top Royal, GOOGLY, 5/1 Long Silence (USA), 9/1 El Nido, 10/1 Sayh, Comstock, I Perceive, Mad Militant (IRE), 16/1 Bold Elect, Diamond Wedding (USA), 20/1 Pennine Star (IRE), 25/1 Bollin William, 33/1 La Stravaganza, Able Player (USA), 50/1 Moonlight Shift. CSF £24.68, CT £82.43. Tote £4.80: £1.70 £2.10 £1.60 (£12.70). Mr A. G. Lansley (UPHAM) bred by W. G. R. Wightman and Mrs J. A. Thomson. 15 Rn
2m 42.17 (14.17)

---

**3462**    STANLEY LEISURE ORGANISATION DREAM MILE STKS (2-Y-O) £4938.00 (£1368.00: £654.00)   **1m 30y**
3-55 (3-58)

3202★ **Taos (IRE) (100)** (Fav) *(JHMGosden)* 9-1 PaulEddery (3) (stdd s: hld up: 3rd st: smooth hdwy to ld wl ins fnl f) ............................. —1
3247★ Palace Pageant (USA) *(IABalding)* 9-1 PatEddery (1) (lw: led: shkn up appr fnl f: hdd & no ex nr fin) ............................. 2.2
2918★ Sharjah (USA) **(98)** *(MAJarvis)* 9-1 BRaymond (2) (lw: chsd ldr: 2nd st: rdn 2f out: unable qckn) ............................. hd.3

5/4 TAOS (IRE), 7/4 Sharjah (USA), 11/4 Palace Pageant (USA). CSF £4.13, Tote £2.40 (£1.80). Sheikh Mohammed (NEWMARKET) bred by Barronstown Bloodstock Ltd in Ireland. 3 Rn    1m 51.01 (10.71)

---

**3463**    STANLEY SNOOKER STKS (I) (Mdn 2-Y-O) £2427.00 (£672.00: £321.00)
**1m 30y**    4-25 (4-27)

3202[5] **Soul Emperor** (Fav) *(MBell)* 8-9 ‡5JWeaver (4) (chsd ldrs: 4th st: led wl over 1f out: all out) ............................. —1
2364[2] Soloman Springs (USA) *(SGNorton)* 9-0 ‡5OPears (9) (lw: chsd ldrs: 5th st: ev ch ins fnl f: unable qckn) ............................. ¹⁄₂.2
3005 Blue Laws (IRE) *(JGFitzGerald)* 9-0 KFallon (5) (s.s: hdwy 3f out: rdn appr fnl f: r.o) ............................. 1¹⁄₂.3
2409 Chiappucci (IRE) *(MAJarvis)* 9-0 GBardwell (8) (bit bkwd: chsd ldrs: 6th st: rdn 3f out: r.o one pce) ............................. 7.4
Wonderful Years (USA) *(MrsJRRamsden)* 9-0 GBaxter (3) (w'like: leggy: hld up: 7th st: rdn & no imp 3f out) ............................. 2¹⁄₂.5
Tremendisto *(CaptJWilson)* 9-0 GCarter (10) (w'like: s.s: effrt 3f out: nt rch ldrs) ............................. 2¹⁄₂.6
2425[3] Musical Phone **(66)** *(JPLeigh)* 9-0 NConnorton (7) (lw: prom: 2nd st: rdn & wknd appr fnl f) ............................. ¹⁄₂.7
3130 Monsieur Dupont (IRE) *(BWHills)* 9-0 PatEddery (6) (still bkwd: prom: 3rd st: wknd 2f out) ............................. ¹⁄₂.8
3202 Fabfer (IRE) *(PWChapple-Hyam)* 9-0 PaulEddery (1) (still bkwd: led tl hdd & wknd wl over 1f out) ............................. 4.9
2636[6] Bajan Affair **(50)** (bl) *(MissLCSiddall)* 8-9 AMcGlone (2) (lost pl ¹⁄₂-wy: t.o) ..... 12.10

7/4 SOUL EMPEROR, 11/4 Monsieur Dupont (IRE)(7/4—3/1), 9/2 Soloman Springs (USA), 13/2 Fabfer (IRE), 14/1 Wonderful Years (USA), 20/1 Blue Laws (IRE), Chiappucci (IRE), 25/1 Musical Phone, Tremendisto, 50/1 Bajan Affair. CSF £10.07, Tote £3.20: £1.20 £1.30 £3.30 (£4.60). Mr Fahd Salman (NEWMARKET) bred by Newgate Stud Co. 10 Rn    1m 49.75 (9.35)

---

**3464**    STANLEY CLUBS H'CAP (0-90) £3500.75 (£1046.00: £500.50: £227.75)
**5f**    5-00 (5-01)

3126[6] **Breezy Day (77)** *(BAMcMahon)* 6–9-2 BRaymond (11) (lw: hld up: rapid hdwy over 1f out: str run to ld wl ins fnl f) ............................. —1
3207[6] Gondo **(74)** (v) (Jt-Fav) *(EJAlston)* 5–8-13 KFallon (4) (a.p: led appr fnl f tl ct nr fin) ............................. ³⁄₄.2
3304★ Pallium (IRE) **(74)** *(MPNaughton)* 4–8-8 (5x) ‡5JWeaver (2) (dwlt: swtchd stands' side: gd hdwy fnl f: fin fast) ............................. s.h.3
1631 Isdar (USA) **(82)** *(HThomsonJones)* 3–9-5 WRyan (10) (bkwd: gd hdwy appr fnl f: fin wl) ............................. nk.4

3304 Metal Boys **(83)** *(RHollinshead)* 5–9-1 ‡7SWynne (1) (lw: hld up: hdwy 2f out: shkn up appr fnl f: unable qckn) .................................. 1¹/₂.5

3308⁵ Tigani **(65)** (bl) *(DWChapman)* 6–8-4 SWood (8) (chsd ldrs: rdn over 1f out: one pce) ................................................ 3¹/₂.6

3120 Tino Tere **(80)** *(JBerry)* 3–9-3 GCarter (7) (lw: led tl hdd & wknd appr fnl f) ....... ³/₄.7

3341★ We're All Game **(62)** (Jt-Fav) *(BCMorgan)* 3–7-13 (5x) GBardwell (6) (lw: hdwy ¹/₂-wy: ev ch over 1f out: wknd fnl f) .......................... s.h.8

3120⁶ Gemini Fire **(75)** *(MPNaughton)* 8–9-0 PaulEddery (3) (nvr trbld ldrs) ............. 1¹/₂.9

2466³ Last Straw **(57)** *(AWJones)* 4–7-7⁽³⁾ ‡3FNorton (9) (lw: spd over 3f: sn rdn & wknd) ...................................................... 1¹/₂.10

LONG HANDICAP: Last Straw 6-7.

**4/1** We're All Game, Gondo, **11/2** Pallium (IRE), **7/1** BREEZY DAY, Gemini Fire, **9/1** Metal Boys, **10/1** Tigani, **12/1** Tino Tere, **14/1** Isdar (USA), **25/1** Last Straw. CSF £32.98, CT £151.30. Tote £7.50: £2.20 £1.80 £2.20 (£11.80). Mrs J. McMahon (TAMWORTH) bred by John I. O'Byrne. 10 Rn       62.66 sec (3.66)
SF—59/53/47/57/47/22/32

**3465**  STANLEY SNOOKER STKS (II) (Mdn 2-Y-O) £2427.00 (£672.00: £321.00)
1m 30y                                         5-30 (5-33)

3202 **Beauman** *(BAMcMahon)* 8-7 ‡7SSanders (8) (lw: prom: 3rd st: led appr fnl f: drvn clr fnl f) .......................................... —1

3202⁴ Arc Bright (IRE) (Fav) *(RHollinshead)* 9-0 WRyan (9) (hld up: 5th st: hdwy 3f out: rdn & r.o one pce fr 2f out) ........................... 4.2

2544 Amillionmemories *(MrsBarbaraWaring)* 9-0 NHowe (5) (bhd: hdwy u.p over 1f out: styd on nr fin) .................................. s.h.3

3164⁵ Cardinal Dogwood (USA) **(69)** (bl) *(MBrittain)* 9-0 MWigham (1) (led 2f: 2nd st: rdn over 1f out: sn btn) .............................. 5.4

Safety in Numbers *(MrsJRRamsden)* 9-0 GBaxter (4) (wl grwn: bkwd: s.s: styd on fnl 2f: nvr nrr) ................................ 2¹/₂.5

2675⁵ Move Smartly (IRE) *(FHLee)* 9-0 PaulEddery (3) (bit bkwd: 6th st: led over 2f out: sn hdd & wknd) ................................ 1¹/₂.6

Civil Action (IRE) *(JHanson)* 9-0 NConnorton (6) (lt-f: bit bkwd: dwlt: nvr plcd to chal) .................................................. 5.7

3193 Waaree (USA) *(AAScott)* 9-0 BRaymond (2) (bit bkwd: chsd ldrs: 4th st: wknd over 2f out) .............................................. ³/₄.8

Altona Gold *(REarnshaw)* 8-9 AProud (7) (cmpt: bkwd: led after 2f tl over 2f out: sn wknd: t.o) ............................................ 7.9

**9/4** Arc Bright (IRE), **3/1** Move Smartly (IRE), **4/1** Waaree (USA), **5/1** BEAUMAN, **13/2** Civil Action (IRE), **14/1** Safety in Numbers, **20/1** Cardinal Dogwood (USA), **33/1** Ors. CSF £16.89, Tote £8.80: £2.00 £1.50 £7.20 (£7.60). Mrs B. Facchino (TAMWORTH) bred by Keith Freeman. 9 Rn       1m 50.17 (9.77)

T/Trio: Race 3: £9.50 (76.2 Tckts). T/Plpt: £89.60 (47.9 Tckts).       IM

# HAYDOCK (L-H)
## Saturday, September 26th [Good to soft]
Going Allowance: 0.20 sec per fur (G)                     Wind: almost nil

Stalls: high

**3466**  SALE CLAIMING STKS     £2637.00 (£732.00: £351.00)     1¹/₄m 120y     2-15 (2-17)

3125² **Light Hand (68)** (Fav) *(MHTompkins)* 6–7-13 ‡7SMulvey (6) (lw: dwlt: hdwy over 2f out: led over 1f out: rdn out) .......................... —1

3052 Katy's Lad **(66)** *(BAMcMahon)* 5–9-0 KFallon (1) (lw: a.p: 4th st: led over 2f out tl over 1f out: kpt on fnl f) .......................... 2¹/₂.2

3266⁴ Silver Samurai **(62)** *(RHollinshead)* 3–8-3 WRyan (8) (dwlt: hdwy 2f out: nt rch ldrs) ..................................................... 2¹/₂.3

3234⁶ Majal (IRE) **(76)** *(BHanbury)* 3–8-11 BRaymond (10) (lw: hld up: hdwy 3f out: ev ch over 1f out: one pce) ............................ 2.4

3384² Lyn's Return (IRE) **(60)** *(RSimpson)* 3–8-5 ‡5ATucker (14) (hdwy over 2f out: styd on u.p ins fnl f) ................................. ¹/₂.5

2934 Ballyranter **(45)** *(HJCollingridge)* 3–8-6 JQuinn (7) (chsd ldrs: 5th st: hrd rdn 2f out: sn btn) ........................................ 5.6

3180² May Square (IRE) **(56)** *(MrsAKnight)* 4–8-9 SWhitworth (13) (lw: chsd ldrs: 6th st: rdn & wknd 2f out) .......................... 2¹/₂.7

Lodestar (IRE) **(84)** *(NTinkler)* 4–9-8 DNicholls (2) (bkwd: hld up: effrt 3f out: grad wknd fnl 2f) ....................................... 5.8

2430⁴ Neltegrity **(65)** *(THCaldwell)* 3–8-3 ‡7AGarth (4) (led tl hdd & wknd wl over 2f out) 2¹/₂.9

2206⁶ Lombard Ocean **(53)** *(ABailey)* 3–7-12 ‡7WHollick (3) (swtg: a bhd) ............... nk.10

3346 Margs Girl **(47)** *(TFairhurst)* 5–8-5 JFanning (9) (b: chsd ldr: 2nd st: wknd 3f out) 4.11

3418 Kashan (IRE) *(JMBradley)* 4–9-8 JWilliams (12) (b: bit bkwd: a bhd: t.o) .......... 8.**12**
3263 Fletchinni (IRE) **(29)** (bl) *(ABailey)* 3–8-2 LCharnock (11) (prom: 3rd st: wknd
over 2f out: t.o) .................................................... 10.**13**

**4/5** LIGHT HAND(op 11/8), **11/2** Majal (IRE), **8/1** Silver Samurai, **10/1** Lyn's Return (IRE)(8/1—12/1), Katy's
Lad, **16/1** Lodestar (IRE), May Square (IRE), Margs Girl, **20/1** Neltegrity, Kashan (IRE), **50/1** Ors. CSF £11.45,
Tote £1.70: £1.30 £2.50 £1.60 (£7.50). Mr John A. Furze (NEWMARKET) bred by The Dunchurch Lodge Stud Co
and Mrs A. Johnstone. 13 Rn; Silver Samurai clmd Mrs V Aconley £8,302                2m 20.40 (8.70) .
SF—19/29/13/17/10/1

**3467**        SEPTEMBER H'CAP (0-90) £3552.75 (£1062.00: £508.50: £231.75)
        **1³/₄m**                                                                      2-45 (2-46)

(Weights raised 1 lb)

3007³ **Nijmegen (64)** *(JGFitzGerald)* 4–8-13 KFallon (5) (lw: mde all: styd on strly u.p) —**1**
3415* Top Spin **(81)** *(MajorWRHern)* 3–9-6 (5x) JWilliams (6) (hld up: 5th st: shkn up
over 2f out: styd on ins fnl f) ...................................... 1.**2**
2178 Kaiser Wilhelm **(76)** *(HRACecil)* 3–9-1 WRyan (9) (lw: a.p: 3rd st: rdn over 1f
out: nvr able to chal) ............................................... 1¹/₂.**3**
3273² Irish Stamp (IRE) **(77)** *(JPearce)* 3–8-11 ‡5RPrice (7) (chsd ldrs: 4th st: hrd rdn 2f
out: one pce) ...................................................... 3¹/₂.**4**
3339* Bandoline **(74)** (Fav) *(BWHills)* 3–8-13 DHolland (8) (plld hrd: hld up: 6th st:
effrt over 2f out: no imp) ......................................... hd.**5**
3206 Vasiliev **(75)** (v) *(JPLeigh)* 4–9-10 DNicholls (3) (lw: s.i.s: hdwy over 3f out: nt
rch ldrs) .......................................................... 10.**6**
3076 Valiant Warrior **(62)** *(MDHammond)* 4–8-11 JCarroll (4) (a bhd: t.o) ................ 5.**7**
3273 Calicon **(68)** *(IABalding)* 6–9-0 ‡3SO'Gorman (2) (bit bkwd: a bhd: t.o) ......... 2¹/₂.**8**
Tricotric **(45)** *(GMMoore)* 5–7-8(1) JQuinn (1) (bkwd: chsd wnr: 2nd st: wknd 3f
out: t.o) .......................................................... 5.**9**

LONG HANDICAP: Tricotric 7-1.

**9/4** Bandoline, **100/30** Irish Stamp (IRE), **7/2** Top Spin, **11/2** Kaiser Wilhelm, **9/1** NIJMEGEN, **20/1** Valiant
Warrior, Calicon, Vasiliev, **50/1** Tricotric. CSF £38.47, CT £174.82. Tote £8.10: £1.90 £2.00 £1.70 (£26.60). A.
F. Budge (Equine) Limited (MALTON) bred by The Overbury Stud. 9 Rn                3m 11.64 (13.14)

**3468**        LEIGH H'CAP (Amateurs) (0-90) £2574.00 (£714.00: £342.00)
        **1¹/₄m 120y**                                                                 3-15 (3-19)

(Weights raised 6 lb)

2906³ **Majed (IRE) (66)** *(MrsGRReveley)* 4–11-6 MrMBuckley (10) (lw: hld up gng wl:
stdy hdwy to ld ins fnl f: r.o) .................................... —**1**
3256² Sword Master **(73)** *(BobJones)* 3–11-3 ‡3MissDianaJones (6) (hld up: swtchd
hdwy 2f out: unable qckn fnl f) ................................... 1¹/₂.**2**
3349⁵ Shaffaaf (USA) **(66)** *(PDEvans)* 4–11-3 ‡3MrWMcLaughlin (15) (lw: hld up: gd
hdwy 2f out: unable qckn fnl f) ................................... 1¹/₂.**3**
2908⁵ Westholme (USA) **(72)** *(MHEasterby)* 4–11-9 ‡3MrsSEasterby (2) (lw: led after
2f tl hdd & no ex ins fnl f) ....................................... 4.**4**
2273 Mardessa **(56)** *(FHLee)* 4–10-10 MrsGRees (11) (swtg: hld up: stdy hdwy 3f
out: swtchd ins appr fnl f: r.o) ................................... 1¹/₂.**5**
3236 Surrey Dancer **(74)** *(BHanbury)* 4–12-0 MrMArmytage (14) (hld up: hdwy & 6th
st: ev ch over 1f out: wknd fnl f) ................................ 1¹/₂.**6**
3311 Thunderbird One (USA) **(50)** *(DenysSmith)* 3–9-8 ‡3MissMCarson (13) (lw:
chsd ldrs: 4th st: rdn & wknd 3f out) ............................ 1¹/₂.**7**
3152³ Marowins **(46)** *(EJAlston)* 3–9-4 ‡3MrRWilkinson (7) (hld up: hdwy over 2f out:
ev ch ins fnl f: sn rdn & wknd) .................................. 2.**8**
3357 Falcons Dawn **(55)** *(ABailey)* 5–10-9 MissLEaton (3) (swtg: s.s: hdwy 3f out:
wknd wl over 1f out) .............................................. hd.**9**
3256³ Good for a Loan **(64)** *(RLee)* 5–11-1 ‡3MrsCLee (12) (b: a bhd) ................ 4.**10**
3143² Stapleton (IRE) **(74)** *(JWWatts)* 3–11-4 ‡3MissLStopford-Sackville (4) (lw: prom:
5th st: ev ch 2f out: sn rdn & wknd) ............................. ¹/₂.**11**
3365* Lots of Luck **(63)** (Fav) *(JPearce)* 9–11-3 MrsLPearce (1) (lw: led 2f: 2nd st: ev
ch 2f out: sn wknd) .............................................. 1¹/₂.**12**
3311* No Comebacks **(53)** *(EJAlston)* 4–10-4 ‡3MrsSBarclay (5) (s.s: a bhd: t.o) ....... 6.**13**
3393 Samurai Gold (USA) **(48)** *(CJames)* 4–9-13(5) ‡3MrEJames (16) (s.s: hdwy 7f
out: 3rd st: wknd 3f out: t.o) .................................... 10.**14**
264 Stoneleigh Abbey (IRE) **(45)** *(BRCambidge)* 4–9-10(5) ‡3MrsHNoonan (9)
(bkwd: t.o fr ¹/₂-wy) ............................................. dist.**15**
3052² Forelino (USA) **(61)** *(JLDunlop)* 3–10-8 MissEJohnsonHoughton (8) (ref to r: t.n.p) 0

**5/2** Lots of Luck, **7/1** Forelino (USA), **15/2** MAJED (IRE), **8/1** No Comebacks, **10/1** Shaffaaf (USA), Surrey
Dancer, **14/1** Westholme (USA), Stapleton (IRE), Sword Master, **16/1** Falcons Dawn, Good for a Loan, **20/1**
Mardessa, Thunderbird One (USA), Marowins, **25/1** Samurai Gold (USA), **50/1** Stoneleigh Abbey (IRE). CSF
£105.64, CT £987.23. Tote £6.50: £1.60 £3.00 £2.60 £4.20 (£131.40). Laurel (Leisure) Limited (SALTBURN)
bred by Rowlane Investments in Ireland. 16 Rn                                        2m 22.22 (10.52)
SF—36/30/27/25/9/24

**3469**  VAUX BREWERIES H'CAP (0-100) £5010.00 (£1500.00: £720.00: £330.00)
6f

3-45 (3-50)

3083  Hazm (USA) (85) (HThomsonJones) 3-9-1 WRyan (14) (chsd ldrs: led ins fnl f: r.o wl) ......................................................................... —1
3356  Amron (78) (JBerry) 5-8-8 ‡³EmmaO'Gorman (8) (hdwy wl over 1f out: fin wl) ... 2.2
3243  Sunday's Hill (95) (v) (MBlanshard) 3-9-11 JWilliams (4) (chsd ldrs: kpt on u.p ins fnl f: nvr nrr) ................................................................ 1½.3
3464²  Gondo (74) (EJAlston) 5-8-7 DHolland (12) (hdwy 2f out: rdn & r.o ins fnl f) ... hd.4
3243  Massiba (IRE) (87) (MJHeaton-Ellis) 3-9-3 BRaymond (19) (lw: led tl hdd & wknd ins fnl f) ................................................................... s.h.5
3356⁵  Arctic Appeal (IRE) (83) (JBerry) 3-8-13 JCarroll (18) (chsd ldrs stands' side: rdn & no ex fnl f) ........................................................... 1½.6
3355  Petraco (IRE) (77) (LJCodd) 4-8-3 ‡⁷WHollick (7) (hld up: hdwy & ev ch appr fnl f: wknd fnl f) ................................................................... 1½.7
1117⁶  Isaiah (91) (MrsJCecil) 3-9-7 JQuinn (11) (bkwd: hdwy appr fnl f: nrst fin) ..... s.h.8
3355  Gentle Hero (USA) (74) (MPNaughton) 6-8-2 ‡⁵RPrice (9) (lw: chsd ldrs: effrt over 1f out: nvr able to chal) ..................................................... ½.9
2949★  Sure Lord (IRE) (73) (WRMuir) 3-7-10 ‡⁷KimMcDonnell (15) (lw: nvr nrr) ...... s.h.10
3356⁶  Densben (80) (DenysSmith) 8-8-13 KFallon (6) (m.n.s) ........................ 1½.11
3341³  Penny Hasset (71) (MWEasterby) 4-8-4 TLucas (17) (spd 4f) ..................... 1½.12
3304  On the Edge (72) (TDBarron) 4-8-5⁽¹⁾ SWhitworth (10) (m.n.s) ................ 1½.13
3243  Red Rosein (92) (CaptJWilson) 6-9-4 ‡⁷SWynne (1) (b.off hind: effrt u.p over 2f out: sn wknd) ...................................................................... 2½.14
3067★  Temple Fortune (USA) (75) (Fav) (RHannon) 3-8-2⁽¹⁾ ‡³RPerham (20) (chsd ldrs stands' side 4f) ..................................................................... 1.15
2702  Parfait Amour (73) (RMWhitaker) 3-7-10 ‡⁷AGarth (16) (b: t.o) ................... 8.16
˙984⁶  Sonderise (72) (NTinkler) 3-8-2 LCharnock (2) (bkwd: s.s: a bhd: t.o) ......... 2½.17
2552²  Absolutely Nuts (74) (BAMcMahon) 3-7-11 ‡⁷SSanders (13) (rdr lost irons s: spd 3f out: grad wknd: t.o) ...................................................... nk.18
Atall Atall (76) (GMMoore) 9-8-9 JFanning (3) (bkwd: t.o) ......................... 5.19

5/1 Temple Fortune (USA), 6/1 Arctic Appeal (IRE), 8/1 Densben, 17/2 Massiba (IRE), 9/1 Penny Hasset, 11/1 Gondo, 14/1 Atall Atall, HAZM (USA), Amron, Petraco (IRE), Absolutely Nuts, Sure Lord (IRE), Isaiah, 16/1 On the Edge, Sunday's Hill, Red Rosein, 20/1 Sonderise, Gentle Hero (USA), 25/1 Parfait Amour. CSF £205.42, CT £2,930.01. Tote £17.80: £3.00 £7.70 £10.60 £2.70 (£227.00). Mr Hamdan Al-Maktoum (NEWMARKET) bred by Skara Glen Stables in USA. 19 Rn                                              1m 14.39 (2.69)

SF—71/56/67/48/57/47

**3470**  BUGGINS FARM NURSERY  £4050.00 (£1215.00: £585.00: £270.00)
6f                        (Weights raised 1 lb)

4-20 (4-22)

3283★  Palacegate Touch (66) (JBerry) 7-12 LCharnock (10) (lw: chsd ldrs: rdn to chal fnl f: led cl home) ................................................................ —1
3262²  Roger the Butler (IRE) (85) (Fav) (MBell) 9-3 DHolland (8) (lw: mde most: hrd rdn fnl f: ct last stride) .................................................. s.h.2
3187  Guv'nors Gift (72) (MHTompkins) 7-11⁽⁸⁾ ‡⁷SMulvey (3) (lw: hdwy over 2f: hrd rdn appr fnl f: no imp) ................................................................ 5.3
3051⁵  Magic Pearl (73) (EJAlston) 8-5⁽³⁾ KFallon (4) (s.i.s: hdwy wl over 1f out: nvr nr to chal) ..................................................................... 3.4
3029⁴  Tarnside Rosal (77) (JEtherington) 8-9 TLucas (1) (lw: bhd: gd hdwy 2f out: rdn & wknd fnl f) .................................................................... ½.5
3208  Master Sinclair (IRE) (64) (RHollinshead) 7-3 ‡⁷AGarth (4) (s.i.s: hdwy fnl 2f: nvr nrr) ...................................................................... nk.6
3343²  Panther (IRE) (72) (CWCElsey) 8-4 JCarroll (5) (nvr trbld ldrs) ............... 1½.7
3424  Who's the Best (IRE) (68) (bl) (APJarvis) 7-7 ‡⁷DWright (11) (lw: w ldr 4f: grad wknd) ........................................................................ 3.8
3208  Folly Vision (IRE) (74) (RHannon) 8-3 ‡³RPerham (9) (chsd ldrs 4f: sn lost tch) .. 2.9
3187⁵  Bold Seven (IRE) (86) (FHLee) 9-4 WRyan (7) (dwlt: a bhd) ................... 3½.10
3155²  Blue Radiance (66) (TFairhurst) 7-12 JFanning (6) (a bhd) ................... ½.11

5/2 Roger the Butler (IRE), 7/2 PALACEGATE TOUCH(5/2—4/1), 8/1 Bold Seven (IRE), 9/1 Tarnside Rosal, 10/1 Blue Radiance, Folly Vision (IRE), Panther (IRE), 11/1 Guv'nors Gift, 14/1 Master Sinclair (IRE), Magic Pearl, 25/1 Who's the Best (IRE). CSF £12.79, CT £82.82. Tote £4.20: £1.90 £1.50 £3.50 (£5.60). Palacegate Corporation Ltd (COCKERHAM) bred by The Woodhaven Stud. 11 Rn                   1m 14.97 (3.27)

SF—43/61/21/17/19/–

**3471**  CASTLE IRWELL STKS (Mdn 2-Y.O.F) £2616.00 (£726.00: £348.00)
1m 30y

4-50 (4-52)

River Delta (USA) (RCharlton) 8-11 DHolland (10) (w'like: leggy: s.i.s: 7th st: led over 1f out: qcknd clr: canter) ................................... —1
3147²  Manaarah (USA) (AAScott) 8-11 BRaymond (3) (led: clr ½-wy: hdd over 1f out: sn outpcd) ....................................................................... 8.2

31723 Abet (USA) *(MajorWRHern)* 8-11 WRyan (5) (lw: chsd ldrs: 3rd st: rdn & ev ch 2f out: one pce) .......... 1.3

33603 Susquehanna Days (USA) *(Fav)* *(IABalding)* 8-8 ‡3SO'Gorman (7) (chsd ldrs: 4th st: rdn 2f out: nvr nr to chal) .......... 4.4

Trets *(PAKelleway)* 8-11 GayKelleway (6) (lt-f: unf: bkwd: styd on fnl 2f: nvr nrr) 7.5

33135 Jendorcet *(TFairhurst)* 8-11 JFanning (9) (chsd ldrs: 6th st: rdn over 2f out: sn wknd) .......... ½.6

3077 Northern Judy (IRE) *(RHollinshead)* 8-11 TLucas (1) (a bhd: t.o) .......... 6.7

3172 My Sister Lucy *(APJarvis)* 8-4 ‡7DWright (2) (bit bkwd: chsd ldrs: 5th st: wknd 2f out: t.o) .......... 1.8

3115 Target Time *(DMcCain)* 8-11 LCharnock (4) (chsd ldr: 2nd st: wknd 2f out: t.o) hd.9

3376 Scottish Temptress *(JPLeigh)* 8-11 KFallon (8) (lw: s.i.s: a bhd: t.o) .......... 7.10

**2/1** Susquehanna Days (USA), **3/1** RIVER DELTA (USA), **7/2** Manaarah (USA), **4/1** Abet (USA), **16/1** Jendorcet, **25/1** Northern Judy (IRE), Trets, **50/1** Ors. CSF £13.60, Tote £3.50: £1.40 £1.40 £1.40 (£5.80). Mr K. Abdulla (BECKHAMPTON) bred by Juddmonte Farms in USA. 10 Rn     1m 47.94 (7.54)

SF—3/–/–/–/–/–

T/Trio: Race 4: Any 2 fr 1st 3 w any £66.20 (10.3 Tckts). T/Plpt: £310.80 (21.95 Tckts).     IM

2956—**REDCAR (L-H)**

## Friday, September 25th [Good]

Going Allowance: 0.10 sec per fur (G)           Wind: almost nil

Stalls: low

**3472**     SCARBOROUGH (S) STKS (2-Y.O) £3288.00 (£918.00: £444.00)    6f    2-20 (2-25)

Call Me I'M Blue (IRE) *(Fav)* *(BBeasley)* 8-6 ‡5SWilliams (8) (w'like: mde all: sn clr: unchal) .......... —1

3283 Blue Trumpet *(AHide)* 8-11 WWoods (18) (in tch: hung lft 2f out: styd on: no ch w wnr) .......... 5.2

3260 Mighty Miss Magpie (IRE) *(61)* (v) *(MRChannon)* 8-13 CRutter (23) (hdwy 2f out: nrst fin) .......... hd.3

3301 Stardust Express *(57)* *(MJohnston)* 8-11 RPElliott (21) (hdwy stands' side over 1f out: nvr nrr) .......... hd.4

33084 Clanrock *(65)* *(RMWhitaker)* 8-11 ACulhane (19) (lw: a in tch: rdn ½-wy: styd on: no imp) .......... hd.5

2924 Colmar *(RBastiman)* 8-4⁵ ‡7HBastiman (13) (in tch: styd on fnl 2f: no imp) .......... 1.6

3283 Jade Runner *(51)* (v) *(MrsNMacauley)* 8-6 PRobinson (14) (prom: outpcd ½-wy: no imp after) .......... ¾.7

32832 Texas Cowgirl (IRE) *(GAPritchard-Gordon)* 8-6 GDuffield (6) (racd far side: chsd ldrs: rdn & no hdwy fnl 2f) .......... hd.8

33944 Sunshine in Ramsey *(45)* (bl) *(TFairhurst)* 8-6 JFanning (12) (styd on fnl 2f: n.d) ¾.9

3410 Ring Tom (IRE) *(MWEasterby)* 8-11 TLucas (16) (b.off hind: stdd s: bhd tl hdwy fnl 2f) .......... s.h.10

29606 Dream a Bit *(70)* *(JGFitzGerald)* 8-3 ‡3SMaloney (2) (disp ld far side: rdn & btn 2f out) .......... ½.11

33853 Dead Calm *(55)* *(CTinkler)* 8-11 JLowe (1) (lw: disp ld far side tl rdn & no imp fnl 2f) .......... ¾.12

3301 Society Gown (USA) *(56)* *(TDBarron)* 8-11 KDarley (4) (racd far side: n.d) .......... ½.13

3155 Selvole *(52)* *(MissLAPerratt)* 8-6 ‡7ClaireBalding (3) (racd far side: hdwy 2f out: n.d) .......... 3½.14

25125 Dashing Lady *(MJohnston)* 8-6 DMcKeown (9) (s.i.s: n.d) .......... hd.15

3071 Canazei *(36)* *(DonEnricoIncisa)* 8-6 JakiHouston (22) (n.d) .......... 2.16

2661 Sainted Sue *(JSHaldane)* 7-13 ‡7JMarshall (24) (n.d) .......... 1½.17

3315 Annie Rose *(44)* *(TDBarron)* 7-13 ‡7VHalliday (15) (n.d) .......... s.h.18

3376 Prawn Cracker (IRE) *(45)* *(JLEyre)* 8-6 MWood (26) (swtg: n.d) .......... 2½.19

26744 Final Action *(RMWhitaker)* 7-13 ‡7DWright (25) (s.s: wl bhd tl sme late hdwy) . hd.20

3173 Madam Cyn's Risk *(50)* *(NACallaghan)* 8-13 JFortune (7) (racd far side: a bhd) nk.21

3218 Monet Monet Monet *(52)* *(WCarter)* 7-13 ‡7CHawksley (17) (s.i.s: a bhd) .......... s.h.22

3163 Choker *(CWThornton)* 8-6 MBirch (10) (s.i.s: a bhd) .......... ¾.23

3343 Cizard (IRE) *(45)* *(AWPotts)* 8-6 SWebster (5) (racd far side: n.d) .......... nk.24

28194 Bella Bambola (IRE) *(50)* *(NTinkler)* 8-6 LCharnock (20) (a bhd) .......... nk.25

**5/2** CALL ME I'M BLUE (IRE)(op 4/1), **9/2** Texas Cowgirl (IRE), **7/1** Clanrock, **8/1** Stardust Express, Dream a Bit(op 5/1), **10/1** Mighty Miss Magpie (IRE), Dead Calm, Colmar, **14/1** Monet Monet Monet, **16/1** Dashing Lady, Bella Bambola (IRE), **20/1** Society Gown (USA), Jade Runner, **25/1** Selvole, **33/1** Sunshine in Ramsey, Ring Tom (IRE), Annie Rose, Madam Cyn's Risk, **50/1** Cizard (IRE), Canazei, Choker, Blue Trumpet, **100/1** Ors. CSF £138.18, Tote £3.40: £2.00 £18.90 £3.30 (£90.70). The Confederacy Ltd (HAMBLETON) bred by R. S. P. Harris and Miss E. A. M. Magor in Ireland. 25 Rn; Sold N Tinkler 9,200 gns     1m 13.3 (4)

SF—24/9/10/7/6/–

**3473**  BRITISH GAS NORTHERN H'CAP (3-Y.O) (0-90) £3210.00 (£960.00: £460.00: £210.00)
7f
2-50 (2-55)

3203 **Amazing Feat (IRE) (69)** *(MrsGRReveley)* 8-0[(1)] KDarley (12) (lw: a.p: led ins fnl f: r.o) .......................................................... —1

3188 Nifty Fifty (IRE) **(77)** *(JBerry)* 8-8 JCarroll (1) (chsd ldrs: led wl over 1f out tl ins fnl f: kpt on) ........................................... 1½.2

3365 Thewaari (USA) **(68)** *(AAScott)* 7-13 CRutter (4) (lw: hld up & bhd: stdy hdwy to chal 2f out: sn rdn & nt qckn) ................................ 1½.3

2559 Tamim (USA) **(90)** (bl) *(HThomsonJones)* 9-7 MBirch (3) (cl up: led wl over 2f out tl wl over 1f out: no pce) ...................................... 1.4

3281 Coniston Lake (IRE) **(66)** (bl) *(GLewis)* 7-4‡7CHawksley (9) (hld up: effrt over 2f out: styd on: no imp) ............................................. ½.5

3145[5] Boursin (IRE) **(80)** *(PCalver)* 8-11 JFortune (6) (hld up: stdy hdwy to chal 2f out: sn rdn & no ex) ............................................ 1½.6

3133 Thornton Gate **(72)** (bl) *(MHEasterby)* 8-0 ‡3SMaloney (5) (led over 4f: grad wknd) ........................................................ s.h.7

3203[6] Riviera Vista **(80)** (bl) (Jt-Fav) *(GWragg)* 8-11 GDuffield (10) (chsd ldrs 5f) ........ 2.8

2040 Speedy Classic (USA) **(63)** *(BWHills)* 7-8[(1)] EJohnson (2) (trckd ldrs: chal 2f out: sn rdn & wknd) .............................................. nk.9

3341 Crestwood Lad (USA) **(64)** *(MrsGRReveley)* 7-9[(2)] JLowe (8) (hld up & bhd: shkn up 3f out: n.d) .......................................... hd.10

3153★ Celestine **(62)** (Jt-Fav) *(TFairhurst)* 7-7 JFanning (7) (cl up: sn drvn along: wknd ½-wy) ......................................................... 5.11

2941 Murasil (USA) **(62)** *(MPNaughton)* 7-7 JakiHouston (11) (outpcd & bhd fr ½-wy) 8.12
LONG HANDICAP: Speedy Classic (USA) 7-5, Crestwood Lad (USA) 7-4, Murasil (USA) 7-3.

**9/2** Celestine, Riviera Vista, **6/1** Thornton Gate, **7/1** Thewaari (USA), **8/1** AMAZING FEAT (IRE), **17/2** Speedy Classic (USA), **10/1** Boursin (IRE), Coniston Lake (IRE), **14/1** Tamim (USA), **16/1** Nifty Fifty (IRE), **20/1** Crestwood Lad (USA), **25/1** Murasil (USA). CSF £115.74, CT £861.75. Tote £11.00: £2.50 £2.80 £1.80 (£85.90). Mr P. D. Savill (SALTBURN) bred by Old Meadow Stud in Ireland. 12 Rn    1m 25.7 (3.5)
SF—44/47/33/52/19/35

**3474**  TATTERSALLS AUCTION SERIES STKS (Qualifier) (Mdn 2-Y.O) £3370.50 (£938.00: £451.50) 7f
3-25 (3-29)

3178[3] **Grove Daffodil (IRE)** (Fav) *(MHTompkins)* 8-1 PRobinson (18) (hld up: smooth hdwy over 2f out: led over 1f out: rdn & r.o) ............. —1

2598 Midyan Blue (IRE) *(JMPEustace)* 8-8 DMcKeown (8) (w ldrs tl outpcd over 2f out: hdwy over 1f out: styd on wl) ........................... 2.2

3199[5] Fort Vally **(69)** *(BWMurray)* 8-3 JFortune (13) (in tch: swtchd rt after 2f: effrt & rdn 2f out: kpt on wl) ......................................... 1.3

3303[4] Bonarme (IRE) *(MHEasterby)* 8-8 MBirch (1) (cl up far side: ev ch over 1f out: r.o one pce) .............................................. ½.4

3285 Trianglepoint (IRE) *(GAPritchard-Gordon)* 8-4 KDarley (2) (bit bkwd: trckd ldrs far side: effrt over 2f out: nt qckn) .......................... ¾.5

3303[2] Runrig (IRE) **(66)** *(MissLAPerratt)* 8-1 JFanning (16) (mde most tl hdd over 1f out: no ex) ............................................... 2.6

3165[6] Supreme Soviet (IRE) *(JSHaldane)* 8-2 ‡3SMaloney (5) (chsd ldrs: ev ch 2f out: grad wknd) ........................................... ½.7

3178 Silky Heights (IRE) *(MJCamacho)* 8-8 LCharnock (9) (prom: chal over 2f out: sn rdn & grad wknd) ..................................... 1½.8

Lady Gail *(JLSpearing)* 8-5 JLowe (11) (cmpt: bit bkwd: nvr bttr than mid div) 1½.9

3261[3] Gentle Moment *(HCandy)* 8-1 CRutter (6) (sn outpcd & bhd: sme late hdwy) nk.10

3147[4] Wanza *(JHanson)* 8-11 EJohnson (14) (hld up: effrt 3f out: sn rdn & n.d) ...... 1½.11

3312[4] Epsom Dream *(JEtherington)* 8-8 JCarroll (15) (swtg: sn outpcd) ................ 1½.12

3303 Native Worth *(JMJefferson)* 8-6 MWood (12) (n.d) ............................. ½.13

O K Kealy *(JMCarr)* 8-6 SMorris (7) (unf: bkwd: s.s: a bhd) ............... 2½.14

1923 Admission (IRE) *(NChamberlain)* 8-9 SWebster (10) (w ldr to ½-wy: sn wknd) 1.15

2961 Wild Expression *(CTinkler)* 8-13 TLucas (19) (prom 4f) ...................... 3½.16

3274 C D Shareplan (USA) **(72)** *(MRChannon)* 8-11 GDuffield (4) (w ldrs far side 4f: sn wknd) .......................................... hd.17

Ragazzo (IRE) *(NTinkler)* 8-10 ABacon (3) (cmpt: bkwd: s.i.s: a wl bhd) ...... 3.18

3285 Sassamouse (20/1) Withdrawn (unruly stalls, cut & distressed) : not under orders

**6/4** GROVE DAFFODIL (IRE)(op 9/4), **5/1** Gentle Moment, **8/1** Runrig (IRE)(op 5/1), **10/1** Fort Vally, **11/1** Bonarme (IRE)(op 7/1), **12/1** Midyan Blue (IRE), Silky Heights (IRE), C D Shareplan (USA), Wanza, **25/1** Trianglepoint (IRE), Lady Gail, **50/1** Supreme Soviet, **66/1** O K Kealy, Ragazzo (IRE), Admission (IRE), Wild Expression, **100/1** Native Worth. CSF £21.28, Tote £2.50: £1.30 £4.50 £3.00 (£26.90). P. H. Betts (Holdings) Ltd (NEWMARKET) bred by Mrs Ann Galvin in Ireland. 18 Rn    1m 28 (5.8)
SF—11/12/4/7/1/–

**3475**　HARRY GEARY H'CAP (0-80) $3574.00 (£1072.00: £516.00: £238.00)
1m 1f　　　　　　　　　　　　　　　　　　　　4-00 (4-01)

(Weights raised 2 lb)

3302* **Cold Shower (IRE) (65)** *(JAGlover)* 3–8–11 (5x) ‡5SWilliams (8) (lw: hld up: hdwy on ins to ld wl over 1f out: rdn & r.o) .......................... —1
33736 Military Expert (55) *(CaptJWilson)* 3–7–13 ‡7JMarshall (16) (chsd ldrs: effrt over 3f out: sn outpcd: styd on wl fnl f) ..................... 2.2
33114 Sinclair Lad (IRE) (66) *(RHollinshead)* 4–9–8 KDarley (14) (hld up: smooth hdwy 3f out: effrt & ev ch ins fnl f: nt qckn) ........... 1.3
2990 Magnificent (68) (bl) *(MAJarvis)* 3–9–0 ‡5KRutter (10) (bhd tl hdwy 3f out: styd on wl nr fin) ............ 1.4
3302 Young Jason (50) *(FHLee)* 3–8–6 ACulhane (12) (hld up & bhd: hdwy 3f out: rdn & nt qckn appr fnl f) ............ 1.5
30783 Shimmer (59) *(LordHuntingdon)* 3–8–10 JCarroll (1) (trckd ldrs: led over 2f out tl wl over 1f out: sn btn) ........... 1½.6
3151* Quantity Surveyor (62) *(SirMarkPrescott)* 3–8–13 GDuffield (3) (lw: led tl hdd over 2f out: hrd rdn: n.m.r & grad wknd) ........ 4.7
29592 Retender (USA) (73) Jt-Fav) *(LMCumani)* 3–9–10 JFortune (6) (b.hind: trckd ldrs: hdwy 4f out: swtchd 2f out: wknd over 1f out) .... 2.8
31506 Kenyatta (USA) (50) *(DenysSmith)* 3–7–8 ‡7CTeague (2) (chsd ldrs: rdn 4f out: grad wknd) ........... 3.9
33023 Eden's Close (64) Jt-Fav) *(MHTompkins)* 3–9–1 PRobinson (13) (lw: chsd ldrs: c wd st: wknd 3f out) ......... nk.10
31675 Battuta (47) *(REarnshaw)* 3–7–5(1) ‡7CHawksley (9) (w ldrs tl wknd over 3f out) ½.11
3302 Bold Arabella (63) (bl) *(JLSpearing)* 4–9–5 JLowe (7) (swtg: n.d) ......... 1½.12
3170 Avishayes (USA) (53) *(MDHammond)* 5–8–9 DMcKeown (5) (nvr nr to chal) .. nk.13
3192 Secret Treaty (IRE) (53) *(PWChapple-Hyam)* 3–8–4 AClark (4) (trckd ldrs tl eased whn sddle slipped 2f out) ............ s.h.14
28152 Richmond (IRE) (58) *(NTinkler)* 4–9–0 LCharnock (5) (lw: prom tl wknd 4f out) 1½.15
3302 Crail Harbour (49) *(PCHaslam)* 6–8–5 JFanning (11) (a bhd) ........... 10.16

5/1 Eden's Close(op 3/1), Retender (USA), 11/2 Secret Treaty (IRE), 6/1 Quantity Surveyor, 8/1 COLD SHOWER (IRE), 10/1 Magnificent, Shimmer, 11/1 Sinclair Lad (IRE), 12/1 Richmond (IRE), 16/1 Military Expert, 20/1 Avishayes (USA), Kenyatta (USA), Battuta, 25/1 Young Jason, 33/1 Crail Harbour, 50/1 Bold Arabella. CSF £127.95, CT £1,319.66. Tote £9.30: £2.50 £3.80 £3.50 £2.00 (£280.60). Claremont Management Services (WORKSOP) bred by Leinster Stud in Ireland. 16 Rn　　　　1m 55.2 (6.2)
SF–17/–/19/8/–/–/

**3476**　MISSISSIPPI H'CAP (Amateurs) (0-70) $2931.00 (£816.00: £393.00)
1m　　　　　　　　　　　　　　　　　　4-30 (4-37)

33954 **Kelly's Kite (35)** *(HJCollingridge)* 4–8–9 ‡5MrPClose (27) (b.off fore: chsd ldrs: hdwy 2f out: r.o to ld nr fin) .......... —1
33653 Bill Moon (49) *(PJFeilden)* 6–10–0 MissJFeilden (16) (chsd ldrs: led over 2f out: sn clr: rdn & nt qckn nr fin) ......... hd.2
33103 Cee-Jay-Ay (53) *(JBerry)* 5–9–13 ‡5MrDParker (15) (in tch: styd on wl fnl f) ...... 4.3
31682 Patience Please (60) *(MHEasterby)* 3–10–2 ‡5MrsSEasterby (14) (lw: a in tch: kpt on u.p fnl 2f) ......... s.h.4
33795 Tempering (44) *(DWChapman)* 6–9–9(2) MrMBuckley (28) (bit bkwd: hdwy ½-wy: sn in tch: kpt on one pce fnl 2f) ........ 1.5
3342 Verdant Boy (49) *(MPNaughton)* 9–9–9(2) ‡5MrRGreen (7) (lw: hdwy 2f out: styd on wl) .......... ½.6
33656 Champenoise (49) *(MBell)* 4–9–9 ‡5MrsLLawson (21) (in tch: effrt 3f out: styd on one pce) ...... ½.7
3380 Watch Me Go (IRE) (51) *(BobJones)* 3–9–7 ‡5MissDianaJones (2) (lw: chsd ldrs: effrt 3f out: one pce) ....... ¾.8
31496 The Dandy Don (IRE) (51) *(DenysSmith)* 3–9–7 ‡5MissMCarson (19) (chsd ldr tl wknd 3f out) ....... nk.9
30842 Brilliant (70) (Fav) *(JPearce)* 4–11–7 MrsLPearce (8) (lw: effrt & wnt lft 2f out: nvr rchd ldrs) ......... 1.10
3140 Miss Sarajane (43) *(RHollinshead)* 8–9–8 MrsGRees (20) (swtg: in tch over 5f) 1½.11
3215 Cornhill Melody (38) *(JLSpearing)* 4–8–12(3) ‡5MissCSpearing (26) (bhd tl sme late hdwy) ......... d.h.11
3245 Berlin Wall (IRE) (68) (bl) *(PWChapple-Hyam)* 4–11–0 ‡5MrsJChapple-Hyam (9) (lw: led & sn clr: hdd over 2f out: sn wknd) ...... hd.13
3373 Bidweaya (USA) (42) *(JLEyre)* 4–9–12 ‡5MissAYardley (25) (chsd ldrs over 5f) .. ½.14
3149 Milton Rooms (IRE) (52) (bl) *(CBBBooth)* 3–9–8(6) ‡5MissCKing (12) (mid div & wandered fnl 2f: n.d) ...... 1½.15
3302 Pride of Pendle (51) *(PCalver)* 3–9–12 MrsAFarrell (5) (n.d) .......... nk.16
30524 Reklaw (35) (bl) *(MDHammond)* 5–9–0 MrsJCrossley (13) (bhd tl sme late hdwy) ........ s.h.17

3287* Night Transaction *(59)* *(AHide)* 5–10-5 (6x) ‡5MissLHide (29) (n.d) ................ hd.18
2929² Chance Report *(36)* *(FHLee)* 4–9-1⁽¹⁾ MissABillot (24) (n.d) ...................... 5.19
3311⁶ Rudda Cass *(47)* *(MrsVAAconley)* 8–9-7⁽¹²⁾ ‡5MrSWalker (3) (chsd ldrs 6f) ... 1½.20
1889* Ripsnorter (IRE) *(64)* *(JABennett)* 3–10-6 ‡5MissAPurdy (11) (s.i.s: n.d) .......... ½.21
2721 Lightning Spark *(40)* *(MAvison)* 3–9-1 MissMJuster (10) (a bhd) ................... nk.22
3263 Norman Warrior *(51)* *(DMorris)* 3–9-7 ‡5MrsLMorris (23) (n.d) ................ 2.23
2946 Master Plan (FR) *(46)* *(DLWilliams)* 6–9-6⁽¹¹⁾ ‡5MissVHaigh (18) (n.d) .......... 3.24
2775 Ella Street *(35)* *(CaptJWilson)* 5–8-9 ‡5MissJBond (4) (n.d) ............... ½.25
3245 Sudanor (IRE) *(56)* (bl) *(MJHeaton-Ellis)* 3–9-12⁽¹⁾ ‡5MissFHaynes (17) (n.d) ... 5.26
3168 Kick on Majestic (IRE) *(40)* *(NBycroft)* 3–8-10⁽¹⁾ ‡5MissABycroft (6) (n.d) ...... 2½.27
3068 State Governor *(50)* *(DWChapman)* 4–9-10 ‡5MissRClark (22) (lw: bhd fr ½-wy) 5.28
LONG HANDICAP: Kelly's Kite 8-8, Cornhill Melody 8-3, Reklaw 8-12, Chance Report 8-13,
Rudda Cass 8-4, Master Plan (FR) 8-1, Ella Street 8-3, Kick on Majestic (IRE) 8-8.

11/4 Brilliant, 7/1 Night Transaction, 10/1 Bill Moon, 11/1 Berlin Wall (IRE), Miss Sarajane, The Dandy Don (IRE), Pride of Pendle, 16/1 Watch Me Go (IRE), KELLY'S KITE, 20/1 Reklaw, Ripsnorter (IRE), Patience Please, Cee-Jay-Ay, Norman Warrior, 25/1 Champenoise, Chance Report, Verdant Boy, Tempering, Bidweaya (USA), 33/1 Kick on Majestic (IRE), Sudanor (IRE), State Governor, Lightning Spark, Rudda Cass, 50/1 Cornhill Melody, 66/1 Master Plan (FR), Milton Rooms (IRE), 100/1 Ella Street. CSF £171.23, CT £2,991.49. Tote £33.60: £6.30 £2.20 £2.30 £3.30 (£56.20). Mr H. J. Collingridge (NEWMARKET) bred by H. J. Collingridge. 28 Rn
1m 41.3 (6.5)
SF—14/32/19/21/11/9

---

**3477**   CARLTON MEDIAN AUCTION STKS (3-Y.O) £2427.00 (£672.00: £321.00)
1m 1f                                                                     5-05 (5-06)

3212 **Cumbrian Challenge (IRE) *(93)*** (Fav) *(MHEasterby)* 9-0  MBirch (3) (lw: mde
    all: shkn up over 1f out: r.o wl) ............................................. —1
3201 Beware of Agents *(94)* *(MJohnston)* 9-0  RPElliott (5) (hdwy ent st: effrt 3f out:
    one pce) ................................................................... 2.2
    South Sea *(81)* *(LMCumani)* 9-1  JFortune (4) (hld up: c wd & effrt 3f out:
    wandered u.p 2f out: nt qckn) ........................................... s.h.3
3003 Vandervally *(RMWhitaker)* 8-7  ACulhane (1) (chsd wnr tl wknd wl over 2f out) . 25.4
3150² Royal Comedian Withdrawn (inj whn uns rdr & bolted gng to s) : not under orders

1/2 CUMBRIAN CHALLENGE (IRE), 3/1 Beware of Agents, 5/1 South Sea, 200/1 Vandervally. CSF £2.31, Tote £1.40: £1.20 (£1.60). Cumbrian Industrials Ltd (MALTON) bred by Major V. McCalmont in Ireland. 4 Rn
1m 58.1 (9.1)

---

**3478**   NEWBY NURSERY (0-85) £3150.00 (£875.00: £420.00)   **5f**   5-35 (5-38)

3162 **Arkendale Diamond (USA) *(62)*** *(BBeasley)* 8-2  GDuffield (12) (chsd ldrs:
    hdwy 2f out: led ins fnl f: r.o u.p) ..................................... —1
3023 Norstano *(61)* (bl) *(MHEasterby)* 7-12 ‡3SMaloney (2) (a chsng ldrs: kpt on fnl f) 1½.2
2960⁴ Field of Vision (IRE) *(59)* (bl) *(MJohnston)* 7-13  JFanning (4) (lw: led tl hdd & no
    ex ins fnl f) ............................................................. ½.3
3208⁵ Norling (IRE) *(65)* *(NTinkler)* 8-5  LCharnock (10) (s.i.s: effrt ½-wy: styd on: nvr
    able to chal) ............................................................. hd.4
729³ Greenwich Chalenge *(81)* *(WCarter)* 9-0 ‡7CHawksley (14) (b.hind: effrt ½-wy:
    hrd rdn appr fnl f: kpt on) ................................................ nk.5
2819* Pilgrim Bay (IRE) *(66)* *(JBerry)* 8-6  JCarroll (15) (bhd: hdwy 2f out: styd on one
    pce fnl f) ................................................................ s.h.6
3071⁶ My Godson *(61)* (bl) *(BBeasley)* 8-8  (effrt ½-wy: nvr trbld ldrs) ........... hd.7
3165⁶ Whisperdales *(65)* *(MWEllerby)* 8-5  SMorris (3) (chsd ldrs over 3f: grad wknd) 1½.8
3312* Pine Ridge Lad (IRE) *(70)* *(MJohnston)* 8-10 (7x)  DMcKeown (11) (outpcd &
    bhd tl sme late hdwy) .................................................... s.h.9
3358³ Covent Garden Girl *(53)* (Fav) *(MWEasterby)* 7-0 ‡7DWright (1) (chsd ldrs:
    wandered u.p over 1f out: wknd ins fnl f) ............................... hd.10
3129 Marchwell Lad *(74)* *(MrsGRReveley)* 9-0  KDarley (9) (s.i.s: effrt 2f out: nvr nr to
    chal) .................................................................. 1½.11
3285 Home Affair *(62)* (v) *(DTThom)* 8-8  PRobinson (13) (n.d) .................... ¾.12
3283 Sea Strand *(60)* *(MBlanshard)* 7-7⁽³⁾ ‡7CAvery (6) (prom: sn drvn along: wknd
    wl over 1f out) ......................................................... 1½.13
3366 Just Baileys *(64)* (bl) *(MJohnston)* 8-4  RPElliott (7) (gd spd 3f: wknd qckly:
    eased) ................................................................... 3.14
3123 Dahliz (IRE) *(70)* (bl) *(HThomsonJones)* 8-10  MBirch (5) (prom to ½-wy) ........ 2.15
3165 Don't Tell Jean *(57)* *(NBycroft)* 7-11⁽¹⁾  PBurke (16) (b.off hind: sn bhd) .......... 8.16
LONG HANDICAP: Covent Garden Girl 7-6.

**5/1** Covent Garden Girl, **11/2** Pine Ridge Lad (IRE), **13/2** Pilgrim Bay (IRE), **7/1** Marchwell Lad, **9/1** Norling (IRE), **11/1** Norstano, Greenwich Chalenge, **12/1** My Godson, **14/1** Field of Vision (IRE), **16/1** ARKENDALE DIAMOND (USA)(op 10/1), Sea Strand, Dahliz (IRE), **25/1** Home Affair, Just Baileys, **33/1** Ors. CSF £172.21, CT £2,301.35. Tote £25.40: £4.20 £7.60 £3.90 £1.90 (£170.10). Mr S. A. Barningham (HAMBLETON) bred by John Franks in USA. 16 Rn

60.1 sec (3.4)

SF—30/20/19/24/32/23

T/Plpt: £883.40 (2.25 Tckts).

AA

# REDCAR (L-H)
## Saturday, September 26th [Soft]
Going Allowance: 0.50 sec per fur (Y)

Wind: almost nil   Vis: bad

Stalls: low

**3479**   REYNARD (S) H'CAP (0-60) £2826.00 (£786.00: £378.00)   1¼m   2-00 (2-04)

| | | | |
|---|---|---|---|
| 2944[3] | **Ghylldale (35)** (v) (RBastiman) 4-8-7 ACulhane (5) (chsd ldrs: clr ld over 3f out: eased ins fnl f) | | —1 |
| 212[5] | Our Topsie (38) (FJO'Mahony) 5-8-10 VSmith (14) (b: styd on wl fnl 3f: nrst fin) | | 5.2 |
| 3176 | Shafayif (43) (Fav) (ICampbell) 3-8-9 MTebbutt (13) (hdwy to chse ldrs over 3f out: no imp wl over 1f out) | | 1½.3 |
| 3239 | Salinger (46) (JWHills) 4-9-4 SDawson (17) (a chsng ldrs: one pce fnl 3f) | | 1½.4 |
| 3395 | Flying Down to Rio (IRE) (45) (MPNaughton) 4-9-3 AMcGlone (4) (lw: a chsng ldrs: effrt 3f out: one pce) | | ½.5 |
| 606 | Golden Ancona (42) (MBrittain) 9-9-0 MWigham (18) (kpt on fnl 2f: nvr nrr) | | ¾.6 |
| 3311 | Reel of Tulloch (IRE) (53) (PCHaslam) 3-9-6 KDarley (11) (bhd tl styd on fnl 2f) | | ½.7 |
| 3263[2] | Aegaen Lady (45) (JEtherington) 3-8-11 GCarter (16) (nvr bttr than mid div) | | s.h.8 |
| 3379[3] | Not Yet (40) (EWeymes) 8-8-12 JFortune (3) (nvr trbld ldrs) | | nk.9 |
| 3375 | Creselly (56) (JGFitzGerald) 5-9-11 ‡3SMaloney (1) (plld hrd: cl up tl outpcd fnl 3f) | | 8.10 |
| | Electrojet (34) (AWJones) 4-7-13 ‡7ClaireBalding (7) (b: n.d) | | nk.11 |
| 2813 | Allegramente (53) (RO'Leary) 3-9-5 GDuffield (10) (n.d) | | 1½.12 |
| 3177 | Paper Clip (42) (bl) (JDBethell) 3-8-8 DaleGibson (6) (lw: in tch to st) | | s.h.13 |
| 3373[5] | Charly Pharly (FR) (37) (bl) (FHLee) 5-8-4 ‡5NKennedy (2) (lw: led tl hdd early in st: sn wknd) | | 5.14 |
| 3342 | Phil-Man (45) (TFairhurst) 3-8-11 GHind (or tl wknd 3f out) | | 7.15 |
| 3254 | Victor Romeo (44) (RCSpicer) 3-8-10 JLowe (8) (n.d) | | 1½.16 |
| 2829[6] | Zaire (47) (bl) (ANLee) 3-8-13 NCarlisle (15) (n.d) | | 8.17 |
| | Yamanouchi (48) (DMoffatt) 3-8-13 ‡7DarrenMoffatt (12) (t.o) | | 18 |

**7/2** Shafayif(op 7/1), **9/2** Not Yet(op 7/1), **13/2** Flying Down to Rio (IRE), **8/1** Aegaen Lady, **9/1** Charly Pharly (FR)(op 6/1), Salinger, **10/1** Reel of Tulloch (IRE)(8/1—12/1), GHYLLDALE, **11/1** Zaire, **12/1** Allegramente, **14/1** Paper Clip, **16/1** Our Topsie, **20/1** Creselly, **25/1** Phil-Man, Golden Ancona, **50/1** Ors. CSF £169.63, CT £634.93. Tote £15.20: £2.50 £6.50 £2.10 £3.90 (£258.60). Mr M. R. Handy (WETHERBY) bred by Mrs Muriel Baldwin. 18 Rn; No bid

No time taken

**3480**   TETLEY TEA-BAG STKS (Mdn 2-Y.O.F) £3297.00 (£917.00: £441.00)   7f   2-30 (2-36)

| | | | |
|---|---|---|---|
| 3193[2] | **Great Steps** (EWeymes) 8-11 GHind (4) (chsd ldrs: led ins fnl f: r.o) | | —1 |
| | Wild Princess (USA) (Fav) (LMCumani) 8-11 JFortune (10) (leggy: scope: chsd ldrs: drvn along 3f out: ev ch 1f out: kpt on) | | 1.2 |
| 3092 | Trachelium (JHanson) 8-11 EJohnson (12) (cl up: led over 3f out: hdd ins fnl f: kpt on same pce) | | ½.3 |
| 2409 | Misbelief (JRFanshawe) 8-11 GCarter (5) (hdwy 2f out: styd on nr fin) | | nk.4 |
| 3338[5] | Quinsigimond (SirMarkPrescott) 8-11 GDuffield (15) (a chsng ldrs: one pce appr fnl f) | | 2½.5 |
| | Forever Shineing (MJCamacho) 8-11 SMorris (17) (str: scope: bkwd: nvr nrr) | | 3½.6 |
| 3146[5] | Young Tess (MissSEHall) 8-11 SWebster (11) (bhd tl r.o nr fin) | | ¾.7 |
| 3164[3] | Missa Brevis (USA) (bl) (JWWatts) 8-11 JLowe (7) (in tch: ev ch 3f out: rdn & btn appr fnl f) | | ½.8 |
| 3181 | Season's Star (HCandy) 8-11 SDawson (14) (chsd ldrs over 5f) | | hd.9 |
| 3171[9] | Puget Dancer (USA) (MBell) 8-11 GBaxter (3) (b.off hind: n.d) | | 1½.10 |
| 3202 | Stage Artist (JEtherington) 8-11 MWood (2) (n.d) | | 3½.11 |
| 3313 | Kira (MissLCSiddall) 8-11 NCarlisle (9) (prom over 4f) | | 1½.12 |
| 3047 | Inonder (MDIUsher) 8-11 tl hdd over 3f out: sn lost pl) | | 5.13 |
| | Dusky Duchess (IRE) (MissLAPerratt) 8-11 RHavlin (7) (w'like: bit bkwd: n.d) | | ¾.14 |
| | Joellise (JBalding) 8-11 KDarley (6) (b: w'like: bkwd: n.d) | | 1½.15 |
| | Broomhouse Lady (MJohnston) 8-11 RPElliott (13) (w'like: bit bkwd: a bhd) | | 1½.16 |
| 3382 | Meconopsis (TFairhurst) 8-11 PBurke (8) (bhd fr ½-wy) | | 17 |

7/4 Wild Princess (USA), 9/2 GREAT STEPS(op 3/1), 5/1 Puget Dancer (USA)(op 3/1), 13/2 Missa Brevis (USA), 9/1 Misbelief(op 5/1), 10/1 Quinsigimond, 14/1 Season's Star, 20/1 Forever Shineing, Stage Artist, 33/1 Young Tess, 50/1 Trachelium, Inonder, Joellise, Kira, Meconopsis, Broomhouse Lady, 66/1 Dusky Duchess (IRE). CSF £13.18, Tote £4.50: £1.60 £1.60 £30.90 (£7.40). Mr Norman A. Blyth (MIDDLEHAM) bred by N. A. Blyth. 17 Rn
No time taken

## 3481

GRAHAM BOSOMWORTH MEMORIAL H'CAP (0-70) £3470.00 (£1040.00: £500.00: £230.00)   7f   3-00 (3-07)

| | | |
|---|---|---|
| 3310[4] **Spanish Verdict (67)** (DenysSmith) 5-9-4 ‡[7]CTeague (4) (led to ½-wy: hdd over 1f out: rallied to ld post) | —1 |
| 3365[5] Alnasric Pete (USA) **(46)** (Jt-Fav) (DAWilson) 6-8-4 GCarter (2) (trckd ldrs gng wl: in ld over 1f out: no ex nr fin) | s.h.2 |
| 2816 Johnston's Express (IRE) **(36)** (EJAlston) 4-7-8 NCarlisle (9) (styd on fnl 3f: nrst fin) | 2½.3 |
| 3264[*] Yours Or Mine (IRE) **(48)** (Jt-Fav) (DWChapman) 4-8-6 SWood (3) (swtg: a chsng ldrs: one pce fnl 2f) | 2.4 |
| 3308[*] Pretonic **(56)** (MJohnston) 4-9-0 RPElliott (8) (trckd ldrs: nt qckn appr fnl f) | 3.5 |
| 3383 Gott's Desire **(40)** (RBastiman) 6-7-12 SDawson (13) (hdwy 3f out: nvr rchd ldrs) | 1½.6 |
| 3383 Susanna's Secret **(40)** (bl) (WCarter) 5-7-12 DaleGibson (10) (nvr nr to chal) | 3.7 |
| 3383[4] Henry Will **(39)** (TFairhurst) 8-7-6[3] ‡[5]NKennedy (12) (nvr trbld ldrs) | hd.8 |
| 3383[*] Blue Grit **(60)** (MDods) 6-9-4 JLowe (11) (n.d) | ½.9 |
| 3365 Jokist **(58)** (WJarvis) 9-9-2 MTebbutt (20) (chsd ldrs ½-wy: rdn & btn over 1f out) | ½.10 |
| 3287[3] Yonge Tender **(42)** (bl) (CNWilliams) 5-8-0 JCurant (6) (n.d) | ½.11 |
| 3192 Glenstal Princess **(55)** (RHollinshead) 5-8-13 GDuffield (1) (n.d) | hd.12 |
| 3287 Chaff **(39)** (bl) (DMorris) 5-7-4[4] ‡[7]CHawksley (21) (n.d) | ½.13 |
| 3395 Hubbers Favourite **(40)** (v) (MrsNMacauley) 4-7-12[5] TSprake (14) (led tl hdd ½-wy: grad wknd) | nk.14 |
| 3344 Royal Girl **(40)** (MissSEHall) 5-9-2 ‡[5]OPears (15) (chsd ldrs: drvn along ½-wy: sn wknd) | 3½.15 |
| 3264 Quiet Victory **(40)** (bl) (MissLCSiddall) 5-7-12[2] AMcGlone (16) (sn bhd) | 1½.16 |
| 172[*] East Barns (IRE) **(42)** (TDBarron) 4-8-0 KDarley (22) (a bhd) | ¾.17 |
| 3373[3] Brenda From Huby **(37)** (BCMorgan) 4-7-9 EJohnson (5) (n.d) | ½.18 |
| 3154[4] Borocay **(40)** (Jt-Fav) (MJCamacho) 4-8-10 ‡[3]SMaloney (17) (hdwy ½-wy: sn rdn & wknd) | hd.19 |
| 3151 Station Express (IRE) **(35)** (bl) (BEllison) 4-7-7 JakiHouston (23) (n.d) | ½.20 |
| 3383 Leave it to Lib **(60)** (PCalver) 5-8-11 ‡[7]JTate (24) (n.d) | 21 |
| 3383[5] Cool Enough **(39)** (MrsJRRamsden) 11-7-11 PBurke (7) (bhd fr ½-wy) | 22 |
| 3383 Sno Serenade **(57)** (MDods) 6-9-1 SWebster (18) (a bhd) | 23 |

LONG HANDICAP: Chaff 6-11, Hubbers Favourite 7-4, Station Express (IRE) 6-11.

6/1 Borocay(op 20/1), Alnasric Pete (USA), Yours Or Mine (IRE), 10/1 Yonge Tender, Blue Grit, Susanna's Secret, 12/1 Pretonic, Royal Girl, 14/1 Johnston's Express (IRE), Cool Enough(op 8/1), 16/1 Henry Will, Brenda From Huby, Gott's Desire, 20/1 East Barns (IRE), Glenstal Princess, SPANISH VERDICT, Jokist, Leave it to Lib, 33/1 Quiet Victory, Station Express (IRE), 50/1 Hubbers Favourite, Chaff, 66/1 Sno Serenade. CSF £144.72, CT £1,661.13. Tote £50.70: £11.20 £2.70 £5.30 £2.00 (Wnr or 2nd w any £2.90). Cox & Allen (Kendal) Ltd (BISHOP AUCKLAND) bred by Hyde Stud. 23 Rn
No time taken

## 3482

'WIN WITH THE TOTE' NURSERY   £3834.00 (£1152.00: £556.00: £258.00)   7f   3-35 (3-38)

(Weights raised 10 lb)

| | | |
|---|---|---|
| 3123[5] **Doc Cottrill (63)** (Fav) (MrsJRRamsden) 8-4 GBaxter (6) (lw: a.p: led ins fnl f: styd on wl) | —1 |
| 3173[5] George Roper **(60)** (v) (MRChannon) 8-1 DaleGibson (8) (led & sn clr: hdd ins fnl f: kpt on wl) | ¾.2 |
| 1689[*] So so **(78)** (TDBarron) 9-5 JFortune (7) (a.p: styd on wl fnl f) | 4.3 |
| 3385 Public Way (IRE) **(58)** (NChamberlain) 7-6 ‡[7]DarrenMoffatt (11) (a chsng ldrs: one pce fnl 2f) | 2.4 |
| 3163[5] Dutosky **(69)** (MJCamacho) 8-5 ‡[5]NKennedy (1) (bhd tl styd on wl fnl 2f) | s.h.5 |
| 3029[3] Dalalah **(80)** (HThomsonJones) 9-7 NCarlisle (4) (a in tch: effrt 3f out: no imp) | 1.6 |
| 3091 Razaroo (USA) **(71)** (v) (JEtherington) 8-12 GDuffield (9) (nvr trbld ldrs) | 1½.7 |
| 3260 Arctic Guest (IRE) **(57)** (MJohnston) 7-12 SWood (4) (effrt u.p ½-wy: n.d) | 1½.8 |
| 2857 Fiveofive (IRE) **(65)** (NACallaghan) 8-6 JLowe (14) (bhd tl sme late hdwy) | 1½.9 |
| 3286[3] Silent Expression **(73)** (DMorris) 9-0 MTebbutt (10) (effrt u.p ½-wy: n.d) | 2½.10 |
| 3029 Bonus Point **(71)** (MrsGRReveley) 8-12 KDarley (12) (drvn along ½-wy: n.d) | ¾.11 |
| 3155[5] Make it Happen (IRE) **(59)** (JBerry) 8-0 GCarter (5) (chsd ldrs over 4f) | 4.12 |
| 3242 Umbubuzi (USA) **(79)** (FHLee) 9-6 ACulhane (3) (sn wl bhd) | nk.13 |
| 3200 Bardia **(54)** (DonEnricoIncisa) 7-9 JakiHouston (2) (sn wl bhd) | 14 |

**3483—3485**

3/1 DOC COTTRILL(9/2—11/4), **11/2** Silent Expression, **13/2** George Roper, **8/1** Bonus Point, **9/1** Dalalah, **10/1** Dutosky(op 6/1), Fivefive (IRE), **12/1** Make it Happen (IRE), **14/1** Umbubuzi (USA), Arctic Guest (IRE), **16/1** So so, Razaroo (USA), **20/1** Bardia, **33/1** Public Way (IRE). CSF £24.05, CT £265.58. Tote £5.30: £2.30 £1.90 £3.10 (£15.20). Mr K. E. Wheldon (THIRSK) bred by M. V. B. Stimpson. 14 Rn                No time taken

**3483**     TRANSMORE VAN HIRE STKS (Mdn) £2782.50 (£770.00: £367.50)
             1m 1f                                                          4-15 (4-17)

3238² **Leif the Lucky (USA) (70)** *(Fav) (WJarvis)* 3–9-0 MTebbutt (6) (lw: a.p: led 3f out: rdn & r.o) ......................................................................................... —1

3043³ Euridice (IRE) (60) *(LMCumani)* 3–8-9 JFortune (4) (effrt 3f out: r.o u.p fnl f: nrst fin) ......................................................................................... nk.2

3062 Fighting Ajdal (IRE) *(ACStewart)* 3–9-0 AMcGlone (1) (effrt over 3f out: styd on wl: nvr nrr) ......................................................................................... 5.3

3238⁴ Cormorant Bay *(FHLee)* 3–8-9 GCarter (7) (b.nr hind: in tch: effrt 3f out: kpt on nr fin) ......................................................................................... ½.4

Albemine (USA) *(MrsJCecil)* 3–9-0 GDuffield (5) (lw: chsd ldrs: chal over 3f out: sn rdn & one pce) ......................................................................................... ½.5

Lady Donoghue (USA) *(MrsGRReveley)* 3–8-9 KDarley (2) (neat: effrt 4f out: sn rdn & no imp) ......................................................................................... 3½.6

2186⁶ Questing (USA) *(JHMGosden)* 3–9-0 GHind (8) (bit bkwd: led tl hdd & wknd 3f out) ......................................................................................... 10.7

3150 Sharp Fairy *(ABailey)* 4–9-0 GBaxter (3) (wl t.o) ......................................................................................... dist.8

**4/7 LEIF THE LUCKY (USA), 6/1** Cormorant Bay, **8/1** Albemine (USA), **9/1** Euridice (IRE)(op 6/1), **10/1** Questing (USA), **25/1** Lady Donoghue (USA), Fighting Ajdal (IRE), **100/1** Sharp Fairy. CSF £6.64, Tote £1.50: £1.10 £1.50 £2.80 (£3.20). The Singular Six Partnership (NEWMARKET) bred by Cooper Rawls & Clarence C. Lippert in USA. 8 Rn                No time taken

**3484**     E.B.F. REG BOYLE BOOKMAKERS STKS (Mdn 2-Y.O.C & G) £2831.50 (£784.00: £374.50)     5f                                                          4-45 (4-47)

3077 **Blow Dry (IRE)** *(Fav) (JHanson)* 9-0 EJohnson (6) (lw: a w ldrs: r.o wl fnl f to ld nr fin) ......................................................................................... —1

3268⁴ Kelly Mac *(NACallaghan)* 9-0 KDarley (7) (a chsng ldrs: r.o wl fnl f) ......................................................................................... nk.2

Stepanov (USA) *(JHMGosden)* 9-0 GHind (2) (str: scope: bit bkwd: trckd ldrs gng wl: led appr fnl f: hdd & no ex nr fin) ......................................................................................... hd.3

1039 Saseedo (USA) *(WAO'Gorman)* 9-0 GDuffield (8) (lw: a cl up: effrt ½-wy: nt qckn fnl f) ......................................................................................... 2.4

2414⁶ Perigord (IRE) *(MHEasterby)* 8-11 ‡³SMaloney (5) (in tch: effrt 2f out: no imp) ... 4.5

3308⁵ Mdm Racer (IRE) *(JBerry)* 9-0 GCarter (1) (slt ld tl hdd & wknd appr fnl f) ...... nk.6

3343 Silver Standard *(JWWatts)* 9-0 JLowe (4) (sn outpcd & bhd: sme late hdwy) .. 1½.7

3165 Jotra *(RMWhitaker)* 9-0 ACulhane (3) (b: dwlt: a outpcd & bhd) ......................... 4.8

**6/4** BLOW DRY (IRE), **7/4** Stepanov (USA)(op 11/10), **5/1** Kelly Mac, **8/1** Saseedo (USA), Silver Standard, **14/1** Mdm Racer (IRE), **33/1** Ors. CSF £9.59, Tote £2.70: £1.10 £1.40 £1.40 (£4.20). Mr J. Hanson (WETHERBY) bred by Miss Janet Mehigan in Ireland. 8 Rn                61.9 sec (5.2)
SF—46/45/44/36/11/13

**3485**     CLEVELAND APP'CE H'CAP (3-Y.O) (0-70) £2532.00 (£702.00: £336.00)
             1¼m                                                          5-15 (5-18)

                                    (Weights raised 2 lb)

3152* **Sunderland Echo (52)** *(Fav) (MrsGRReveley)* 8-6 DarrenMoffatt (11) (lw: plld hrd: a cl up: led wl over 2f out: drvn out) ......................................................................................... —1

3381 Nicely Thanks (USA) (56) *(TDBarron)* 8-7 ‡³VHalliday (1) (bhd & hdwy over 3f out: styd on wl fnl f) ......................................................................................... 1.2

3270 Boogie Bopper (IRE) (56) *(MBell)* 8-10 PTurner (2) (c wd & effrt 4f out: r.o u.p fnl f: nrst fin) ......................................................................................... hd.3

3135 Be My Everything (IRE) (66) *(RHollinshead)* 8-13 ‡⁷JDennis (9) (swtg: in tch: qcknd to chal 3f out: wknd over 1f out) ......................................................................................... 2½.4

3174 Jade Mistress (50) *(AHide)* 8-4 ‡⁵NVarley (4) (swtg: uns rdr & bolted gng to s: bhd tl hdwy 4f out: rdn & btn over 1f out) ......................................................................................... hd.5

3395* Sir Norman Holt (IRE) (55) (v) *(FHLee)* 8-9 (5x) OPears (6) (led tl hdd wl over 2f out: wknd over 1f out) ......................................................................................... 3½.6

3085⁴ Brambleberry (67) *(MrsSJSmith)* 9-2 ‡⁵JMarshall (10) (a chsng ldrs: effrt over 3f out: wknd over 1f out) ......................................................................................... 1.7

3350² Reach for Glory (60) *(RMWhitaker)* 8-9 ‡⁵GParkin (8) (lw: chsd ldrs tl rdn & wknd over 2f out) ......................................................................................... 3½.8

3236 Bentico (61) *(MAJarvis)* 9-1 KRutter (5) (a bhd) ......................................................................................... 2.9

2302⁴ Indian Style (IRE) (50) *(RGuest)* 8-4 CHawksley (7) (lw: cl up tl wknd over 3f out) ......................................................................................... 4.10

3102 Corinthian God (IRE) (47) *(DAWilson)* 7-8 ‡⁷SharonMillard (3) (a bhd) ........... 1½.11

**Evens** SUNDERLAND ECHO, **8/1** Nicely Thanks (USA), Sir Norman Holt (IRE), **11/1** Boogie Bopper (IRE), Reach for Glory, **12/1** Be My Everything (IRE), Bentico, **14/1** Brambleberry, **16/1** Jade Mistress, **20/1** Indian Style (IRE), **25/1** Corinthian God (IRE). CSF £10.94, CT £42.06. Tote £2.00: £1.50 £2.50 £1.30 (£9.20). Northeast Press Limited (SALTBURN) bred by B. E. Green. 11 Rn

2m 12.9 (10.4)

SF—38/37/39/37/22/25

T/Plpt: £105.70 (23.55 Tckts). AA

3254—**BATH  (L-H)**

## Monday, September 28th [Good to Soft]

Going Allowance: 5f: 0.25 sec per fur; Rest: 0.40 sec per fur (G)          Wind: nil

Stalls: low

**3486**      BLATHWAYT GRADUATION STKS (2-Y.O.F) £3338.95 (£997.60: £477.30: £217.15)
              **5f 11y**                                                           2-05 (2-07)

| | | |
|---|---|---|
| 3096[3] | Simply Sooty (84) *(BRMillman)* 9-4 GBaxter (9) (mde all: clr 2f out: r.o wl) ........ | —1 |
| 3187 | Royal Deed (USA) (66) *(PMMcEntee)* 8-8 JWilliams (5) (hdwy 3f out: chsd wnr fnl 2f: r.o one pce) | 4.2 |
| 3099 | Admired *(MRChannon)* 8-5 ‡[3]RPerham (2) (hdwy fnl 2f: r.o) | 2½.3 |
| 3217[6] | Serious Result *(RAkehurst)* 8-8 AMunro (8) (dwlt: hdwy 2f out: nvr nrr) ......... | 3½.4 |
| 3156[2] | The Ordinary Girl (IRE) (Fav) *(TCasey)* 8-8 MRoberts (3) (prom: rdn & wknd over 2f out) | nk.5 |
| 3268[6] | Perfect Passion (58) *(JJBridger)* 8-8 GBardwell (11) (swtg: spd over 2f) ........ | 1½.6 |
| 1342[6] | Fairylike (CAN) *(PFICole)* 8-8 TQuinn (10) (prom: rdn over 2f out: sn wknd) ..... | nk.7 |
| 3132 | Guanhumara *(PTWalwyn)* 8-8 LDettori (7) (a bhd) | 5.8 |
| 3360 | Proud Moment (BAR) *(RHannon)* 8-8 BRouse (1) (s.s: a bhd) | ½.9 |
| 3360 | Tempesta Rossa (IRE) *(BWHills)* 8-8 JLowe (4) (rdn over 2f out: sn bhd) | 2.10 |
| 2794[6] | Chatterberry (90) *(LJHolt)* 9-4 JReid (6) (spd over 2f) | 6.11 |

**7/4** The Ordinary Girl (IRE), **3/1** SIMPLY SOOTY, **11/2** Chatterberry(7/2—6/1), **7/1** Fairylike (CAN), **25/1** Proud Moment (BAR), Perfect Passion, Tempesta Rossa (IRE), **33/1** Ors. CSF £77.67, Tote £4.50: £1.70 £4.20 £5.20 (£30.30). Mrs S. Joint (CULLOMPTON) bred by Mrs S. Joint. 11 Rn

64.8 sec (4.3)

SF—43/17/4/-/-/-

**3487**      ALDIE APP'CE H'CAP (0-70) £2637.00 (£732.00: £351.00)      **1¼m 46y**  2-35 (2-38)

| | | |
|---|---|---|
| 3395[2] | Tendresse (IRE) (34) (Jt-Fav) *(CJHill)* 4–7-7 PMcCabe (4) (swtg: bhd tl hdwy over 3f out: led over 1f out: rdn clr fnl f) | —1 |
| 3236[4] | Lady Lacey (51) (v) (Jt-Fav) *(GBBalding)* 5–8-10 TraceyPurseglove (11) (hdwy over 3f out: r.o one pce fnl 2f) | 8.2 |
| 3215* | Broughton's Tango (IRE) (50) *(WJMusson)* 3–8-3 DMcCabe (12) (b: lw: hdwy 3f out: slt ld 2f out: sn hdd: one pce) | 3.3 |
| 3139 | Santana Lady (IRE) (69) *(MJHeaton-Ellis)* 3–9-8 RuthPurseglove (6) (lw: 3rd st: one pce fnl 2f) | 1.4 |
| 3256 | Captain My Captain (IRE) (38) *(RBrotherton)* 4–7-11 GMitchell (5) (nvr nrr) ... | 1½.5 |
| 1367[4] | Sports View (49) *(RJHolder)* 3–8-2 RWaterfield (8) (6th st: ev ch over 2f out: wknd over 1f out) | 1.6 |
| 3256 | Modesto (USA) (63) *(KOCunningham-Brown)* 4–9-5 ‡[3]WAldwinckle (1) (b: hdwy & 4th st: ev ch over 2f out: wknd wl over 1f out) | ½.7 |
| 3133 | Gold Jubilee (55) *(PJMakin)* 3–8-5 ‡[3]CWebb (10) (hdwy & 6th st: ev ch over 2f out: wknd wl over 1f out) | 2½.8 |
| 3043[6] | Guiting Girl (49) *(HCandy)* 3–7-13 ‡[3]SDrake (14) (plld hrd: 2nd st: led over 2f out: sn hdd & wknd) | 3.9 |
| | Angelo's Double (IRE) (69) *(GAHam)* 4–10-0 TThompson (2) (swtg: bit bkwd: 5th st: wknd 2f out) | 4.10 |
| 3316 | Share Holder (34) *(MissGayKelleway)* 4–7-7 GMilligan (13) (b: b.hind: led tl wknd qckly over 2f out) | ¾.11 |
| | Road to Au Bon (USA) (55) *(RJBaker)* 4–8-9 ‡[3]JDennis (3) (a bhd) ............ | 2½.12 |
| | Brigtina (53) *(JMBradley)* 4–8-9 ‡[3]MichaelBradley (9) (bit bkwd: chsd ldr 4f: wknd 4f out: wl bhd whn hung bdly rt over 2f out: t.o) | 13 |
| | Good Old George (IRE) (40) *(MJFetherston-Godley)* 3–7-4 ‡[3]AWhelan (7) (bit bkwd: t.o whn virtually p.u 3f out) | 14 |

LONG HANDICAP: Tendresse (IRE) 7-5, Share Holder 7-1, Good Old George (IRE) 7-3.

**9/2** TENDRESSE (IRE)(op 3/1), Lady Lacey, **5/1** Broughton's Tango (IRE), **9/1** Santana Lady (IRE), **10/1** Gold Jubilee, Guiting Girl, **12/1** Captain My Captain (IRE)(op 8/1), **14/1** Share Holder, Modesto (USA)(op 8/1), **16/1** Sports View, **33/1** Road to Au Bon (USA), **40/1** Good Old George (IRE), **50/1** Ors. CSF £22.67, CT £94.25. Tote £4.10: £2.10 £1.70 £1.80 (£7.10). Mr C. John Hill (BARNSTAPLE) bred by J. O'Regan in Ireland. 14 Rn
2m 16.9 (9.2)
SF—27/28/15/32/4/7

---

**3488**    MORRIS DANCER H'CAP (0-80) £3699.00 (£1107.00: £531.00: £243.00)
1m 5y                                                                3-05 (3-10)

(Weights raised 1 lb)

| | | |
|---|---|---|
| 3417[6] **Darakah (60)** (CJHill) 5–8-12 ‡[5]JWeaver (10) (gd hdwy over 1f out: str run to ld nr fin) | | —1 |
| 3236[3] Salbyng (60) (Fav) (JWHills) 4–9-3 RHills (12) (5th st: led 2f out tl hdd cl home) | | ½.2 |
| 3239 Kissavos (50) (CCElsey) 6–8-7 TQuinn (9) (4th st: led over 2f out: sn hdd: ev ch ins fnl f: nt qckn) | | ¾.3 |
| 3365 Durneltor (61) (RHannon) 4–9-4 JReid (6) (gd hdwy over 1f out: r.o) | | ½.4 |
| 2856[4] Celia Brady (54) (HCandy) 4–8-11 CRutter (13) (hdwy over 1f out: r.o ins fnl f) | | ¾.5 |
| 3137[5] Lord Oberon (IRE) (62) (RJO'Sullivan) 4–9-5 AClark (14) (hdwy 2f out: nvr nr to chal) | | 1.6 |
| 3363 Singers Image (60) (v) (GBBalding) 3–8-13 JWilliams (11) (nvr nr to chal) | | ¾.7 |
| 3137 Traders Dream (53) (TThomsonJones) 3–8-6 DHolland (15) (hdwy over 2f out: wknd over 1f out) | | s.h.8 |
| 3236 Royal Dartmouth (USA) (50) (BRMillman) 7–8-7 NCarlisle (16) (b: n.d) | | 1.9 |
| 2990 Emaura (57) (KOCunningham-Brown) 3–8-10 AMunro (2) (led over 5f) | | 3½.10 |
| 3391 Oscilante (36) (RAkehurst) 4–7-7 JLowe (17) (a bhd) | | 1.11 |
| Secret Turn (USA) (60) (AndrewTurnell) 6–9-3 AMcGlone (1) (6th st: wknd 3f out) | | 2½.12 |
| 3403 Sareen Express (IRE) (46) (MrsJCDawe) 4–7-12 ‡[5]ATucker (7) (2nd st: wknd over 2f out) | | 1½.13 |
| 2935[6] Ketti (39) (bl) (DLWilliams) 7–7-10 NAdams (8) (a bhd) | | 2.14 |
| 3317 Old Glory (62) (RJHolder) 4–9-5 ADicks (5) (dwlt: bhd fnl 3f) | | 3½.15 |
| 974 Caromandoo (IRE) (67) (ABarrow) 4–9-7 ‡[3]RPerham (3) (a bhd: t.o) | | 7.16 |
| Lihbab (36) (JMBradley) 9–7-7 GBardwell (4) (b: prom tl 3rd & wkng st: t.o) | | 1½.17 |

LONG HANDICAP: Oscilante 7-5, Lihbab 7-1.

**4/1** Salbyng(tchd 6/1), **9/2** DARAKAH, **6/1** Lord Oberon (IRE), **10/1** Royal Dartmouth (USA), **12/1** Durneltor(op 8/1), **14/1** Emaura(10/1—16/1), **16/1** Kissavos(op 10/1), Ketti(op 10/1), Singers Image, Celia Brady, Secret Turn (USA), **20/1** Traders Dream, **25/1** Oscilante, **33/1** Sareen Express (IRE), **50/1** Old Glory, **66/1** Caromandoo (IRE), **100/1** Lihbab. CSF £20.83, CT £244.87. Tote £6.50: £1.80 £1.50 £3.20 £3.10 (£7.60). Mr C. John Hill (BARNSTAPLE) bred by Yeomanstown Lodge Stud. 17 Rn
1m 46.9 (7.6)
SF—32/35/23/32/23/28

---

**3489**    DONNINGTON STKS (I) (Mdn 2-Y.O) £2553.00 (£708.00: £339.00)
1m 5y                                                                3-35 (3-39)

| | | |
|---|---|---|
| **Star Manager (USA)** (PFICole) 9-0 TQuinn (1) (gd sort: mde all: clr 2f out: eased ins fnl f) | | —1 |
| Outset (IRE) (HCandy) 9-0 AMunro (10) (w'like: 3rd st: r.o one pce fnl 2f: no ch w wnr) | | 6.2 |
| 3099[5] Smart Daisy (IABalding) 8-9 JReid (4) (4th & rdn st: outpcd over 2f out: styd on ins fnl f) | | 3.3 |
| 3186 Halham Tarn (IRE) (PTWalwyn) 9-0 LDettori (6) (chsd wnr: 2nd st: wknd fnl f) | | s.h.4 |
| Malaia (IRE) (MJHeaton-Ellis) 8-9 MHills (12) (unf: rdn over 4f out: 5th st: no hdwy fnl 3f) | | 1.5 |
| 3175 Lunar Risk (WRMuir) 8-11 ‡[3]RPerham (11) (rdn & 6th st: no hdwy fnl 3f) | | nk.6 |
| 2629 Paper Days (RJHolder) 9-0 JWilliams (8) (hdwy over 3f out: wknd over 2f out) | | 6.7 |
| 3414 Dorazine (CJHill) 8-9 NAdams (9) (nvr nr ldrs) | | 2½.8 |
| 3035 Its Unbelievable (JWhite) 9-0 NCarlisle (7) (s.i.s: a bhd) | | 1½.9 |
| 3250[2] Blue Nova (IRE) (Fav) (PWChapple-Hyam) 9-0 DHolland (5) (nvr gng wl: eased whn btn over 1f out) | | 2½.10 |
| 3173 Galactic Fury (55) (BStevens) 9-0 JLowe (3) (a bhd) | | nk.11 |
| Sunbeam Charlie (AMoore) 9-0 AClark (2) (wl grwn: a bhd: t.o) | | 12.12 |

**9/4** Blue Nova (IRE), **3/1** STAR MANAGER (USA), **7/2** Outset (IRE), **5/1** Smart Daisy(7/2—6/1), **10/1** Halham Tarn (IRE), **14/1** Malaia (IRE)(op 8/1), **33/1** Lunar Risk, Paper Days, Its Unbelievable, **50/1** Galactic Fury, Sunbeam Charlie, **66/1** Dorazine. CSF £13.92, Tote £4.70: £2.00 £1.70 £1.40 (£7.00). Mr M. Arbib (WHATCOMBE) bred by Hickory Tree Farm in USA. 12 Rn
1m 47.6 (8.3)
SF—24/6/–/–/–/–

## 3490

WESTMORELAND H'CAP (0-70) £2658.00 (£738.00: £354.00)
2m 1f 34y

4-05 (4-07)

3351 **Green Lane (USA) (68)** (IABalding) 4–9-12 JReid (12) (lw: hld up & 4th
st: led over 1f out: jst hld on) ........................................... —1
32983 Two and Sixpence (USA) (66) (BWHills) 3–8-12 DHolland (15) (led 10f to 9f out:
2nd st: led over 2f out tl over 1f out: rallied ins fnl f) ........... s.h.2
3266 City Line (54) (DRLaing) 3–7-9(7) ‡5ATucker (4) (swtg: lost pl 8f out: styd on fnl
2f) ...................................................................... 4.3
3351 Arctic Splendour (USA) (61) (PWChapple-Hyam) 3–8-2 ‡5JWeaver (14) (lw: hld
up in rr: hdwy & 5th st: one pce fnl 2f) ............................. nk.4
31582 Intrepid Lass (41) (HCandy) 5–7-6 ‡7AntoinetteArmes (8) (swtg: led 7f: led 9f
out tl over 2f out: one pce) ........................................... ¹/₂.5
3409 Judge and Jury (53) (v) (MJFetherston-Godley) 3–7-13 AMunro (3) (lw: hdwy
on ins 8f out: wknd 4f out) ............................................ 10.6
3219 Lady Westgate (36) (GBBalding) 8–7-1(1) ‡7IonaWands (6) (nvr nr to chal) ...... nk.7
2834 Glenstal Priory (50) (PFICole) 5–8-8 TQuinn (5) (droppd rr 7f out: hdwy over 4f
out: wknd 3f out) ..................................................... 8.8
32586 Elsa (47) (RJHolder) 3–7-7 NAdams (9) (prom: 6th & wkng st) ................. 2¹/₂.9
33162 Silken Words (USA) (54) (Fav) (WRMuir) 3–8-0 MRoberts (13) (rdn & 4th st:
wknd over 2f out) ..................................................... ¹/₂.10
3377* Shakinski (49) (v) (MJRyan) 3–7-9 GBardwell (11) (hld up: hdwy & 3rd st: wknd
over 2f out) .......................................................... 8.11
32735 Blushing Belle (44) (PFICole) 4–8-2 CRutter (10) (swtg: bhd fnl 2f: t.o) ....... 10.12
3256 Farmer's Fire (IRE) (51) (bl) (CFWall) 3–7-11 JLowe (1) (b: lw: prom 12f) ...... 3.13
1459 Coleridge (63) (DShaw) 4–9-7 JWilliams (7) (bkwd: t.o fnl 8f) ............... dist.14
LONG HANDICAP: City Line 7-0, Lady Westgate 6-7, Elsa 7-0.

**11/4 Silken Words (USA)**(5/1–11/2), **11/2** City Line 7-0, Lady Westgate 6-7, Elsa 7-0. (USA), Shakinski(op 4/1), **8/1 GREEN LANE (USA)**(6/1–9/1), **10/1** Glenstal Priory(op 6/1), Intrepid Lass, **16/1** Blushing Belle, Judge and Jury, **25/1** Coleridge, Farmer's Fire (IRE), Elsa, **50/1** City Line, **66/1** Lady Westgate. CSF £50.05, CT £1,916.98. Tote £7.60: £2.70 £1.70 £10.50 (£17.60). Mr Paul Mellon (KINGSCLERE) bred by Paul Mellon in USA. 14 Rn
4m 2.1 (18.1)

## 3491

DONNINGTON STKS (II) (Mdn 2-Y.O) £2553.00 (£708.00: £339.00)
1m 5y

4-35 (4-40)

31993 **Eleusis (FR) (84)** (Fav) (PWChapple-Hyam) 9-0 DHolland (1) (mde all: pushed
out) .................................................................... —1
32764 Eastern Memories (IRE) (RHannon) 9-0 BRouse (9) (2nd st: r.o one pce fnl 2f) 3¹/₂.2
3202 Grand Applause (IRE) (77) (RSimpson) 8-9 ‡5ATucker (3) (hdwy 3f out: r.o one
pce fnl 2f) ............................................................ 6.3
Two Lumps (IABalding) 9-0 JReid (10) (w'like: 3rd st: one pce fnl 2f) ...... 1.4
Allegation (PFICole) 9-0 AMunro (6) (w'like: scope: 6th st: no hdwy fnl 2f) . 2.5
3419 Golden Klair (42) (CJHill) 8-9 NAdams (11) (dwlt: nvr nr ldrs) ............... 7.6
33206 Swiss Mountain (DRLaing) 8-9 CRutter (5) (5th st: wknd over 2f out) ........ ¹/₂.7
3181 Take the Mick (EAWheeler) 9-0 JWilliams (7) (a bhd) ........................ 4.8
2598 Juliasdarkinvader (AMoore) 9-0 NCarlisle (4) (4th st: wknd 3f out) .......... 8.9
3181 Kawasir (CAN) (PTWalwyn) 9-0 RHills (2) (bhd fnl 5f) ....................... 5.10
Sure Right (IRE) (JWHills) 9-0 MHills (12) (w'like: a bhd) ................. 2¹/₂.11

**6/4 ELEUSIS (FR)**(5/2–3/1), **2/1** Eastern Memories (IRE)(tchd 7/2), **7/1** Allegation(3/1–15/2), **14/1** Two Lumps(op 8/1), **16/1** Kawasir (CAN)(op 10/1), Grand Applause (IRE)(op 6/1), **20/1** Sure Right (IRE), Swiss Mountain, **66/1** Ors. CSF £4.71. Tote £2.60: £1.10 £1.30 £3.40 (£2.80). Mr R. E. Sangster (MARLBOROUGH) bred by Eric Puerari in France. 11 Rn
1m 46.5 (7.2)
SF—40/29/6/8/2/–

## 3492

COUNTY H'CAP (3-Y.O) (0-90) £3158.00 (£944.00: £452.00: £206.00)
1m 3f 144y

5-05 (5-09)

(Weights raised 6 lb)
3244 **Crystal Cross (USA) (77)** (IABalding) 9-6 JReid (6) (hld up: 8th st: hdwy 3f out:
led ins fnl f: r.o wl) ................................................ —1
30576 Simply-H (IRE) (74) (MBell) 9-3 MRoberts (1) (lw: hld up: hdwy 4f out: 2nd st:
led 2f out tl ins fnl f) .............................................. 1¹/₂.2
27152 Spectacular Dawn (78) (JLDunlop) 9-7 TQuinn (4) (led 8f: 3rd st: r.o one pce fnl
2f) ................................................................... ³/₄.3
625* Chief Minister (IRE) (78) (Fav) (LMCumani) 9-7 LDettori (9) (lw: 7th st: ev ch 2f
out: wknd over 1f out) ............................................... 3¹/₂.4
3279 Second Call (60) (HCandy) 8-3 CRutter (2) (lw: hld up: 6th st: no hdwy fnl 2f) ... 1.5
3256 Eleganza (IRE) (68) (SMHillen) 8-11 JLowe (8) (lw: hld up & bhd: hdwy to ld
over 3f out: wknd fnl f: sn wknd) ................................... nk.6
30943 Matching Green (70) (GBBalding) 8-13 JWilliams (5) (last st: nvr nrr) ........ nk.7

1027⁵ National Emblem (FR) **(67)** *(PFICole)* 8-10 AMunro (7) (5th st: racd alone far
　　　　side: styd on fnl 2f) ....... 30.8
2908⁶ Pippas Song **(66)** (v) *(GWragg)* 8-9 MHills (3) (swtg: 4th st: wknd over 2f) ....... nk.9

**3/1** Chief Minister (IRE), **4/1** Simply-H (IRE), Matching Green, **7/1** CRYSTAL CROSS (USA), Spectacular Dawn,
**10/1** Pippas Song, **12/1** Second Call, **16/1** Ors. CSF £33.45, CT £186.86. Tote £7.60: £2.40 £1.70 £1.80
(£16.00). Mr Paul Mellon (KINGSCLERE) bred by Paul Mellon in USA. 9 Rn　　　2m 37.2 (10.5)
　　　　　　　　　　　　　　　　　　　　　　　　　　　　　　　SF–47/41/43/37/17/24

T/Plpt: £93.00 (29.15 Tckts).　　　　　　　　　　　　　　　　　　　　　　　　　　　KH

## 3149—HAMILTON (R-H)
### Monday, September 28th [Soft, Heavy patches]
Going Allowance: St: 0.50 sec per fur; Rnd: 0.60 sec per fur (Y)　　　Wind: almost nil

Stalls: low

**3493**　CAPTAIN J.C. STEWART MEMORIAL H'CAP (0-70) £2700.00 (£750.00: £165.00 each)
　　　　1½m 17y　　　　　　　　　　　　　　　　　　　　　　2-00 (2-01)

(Weights raised 2 lb)

3151 **Blanc Seing (FR) (45)** (bl) *(MWEasterby)* 5-9-1 TLucas (3) (lw: a.p: led on bit
　　　　over 2f out: shkn up & qcknd fnl f: sn clr & eased) ............. —1
3393* Grey Power **(59)** (Fav) *(MrsGRReveley)* 5-9-8 (5x) ‡7DarrenMoffatt (1) (hdwy
　　　　ent st: chal 2f out: nt qckn fnl f) ....................................... 2½.2
3352⁵ J P Morgan **(41)** (v) *(MPNaughton)* 4-8-11 KFallon (12) (styd on fnl 4f: nrst fin) 1½.3
2784³ Grey Commander **(37)** (v) *(MBrittain)* 4-8-7 KDarley (17) (cl up: chal 3f out: one
　　　　pce fnl 2f) ............................................................... d.h.3
3379 Queens Tour **(30)** *(MDrittain)* 7 8-0 LCharnock (7) (hdwy 4f out: styd on: nvr
　　　　able to chal) ........................................................... 1½.5
2783⁴ Seraphim (FR) **(48)** *(TDBarron)* 3-8-10 SWebster (16) (a chsng ldrs: effrt over
　　　　3f out: one pce) ....................................................... 1½.6
3342 Heliopsis **(42)** *(MDHammond)* 4-8-12 JCarroll (2) (lw: bhd tl styd on fnl 3f) .... 1½.7
3149 Tina's Game **(34)** *(APStringer)* 4-8-1 ‡3SMaloney (11) (cl up: chal 3f out: wknd
　　　　2f out) ................................................................. 8.8
3389² Irish Honey (IRE) **(41)** *(BHanbury)* 3-8-3 DMcKeown (4) (lw: hdwy & in tch appr
　　　　st: wknd 2f out) ....................................................... ¾.9
3351 Don't Cry **(27)** *(DonEnricoIncisa)* 4-7-4 ‡7ClaireBalding (5) (nvr trbld ldrs) ..... nk.10
2985 Mr Ziegfeld (USA) **(59)** *(SirMarkPrescott)* 3-9-7 GDuffield (13) (chsd ldrs tl
　　　　wknd 3f out) ........................................................... nk.11
3380⁵ Jubilata (USA) **(38)** *(MPNaughton)* 4-8-8 JakiHouston (18) (nvr bttr than mid
　　　　div) ................................................................... nk.12
3381 Litho Bold Flasher **(47)** *(CaptJWilson)* 3-8-2 ‡7AdelleGibbons (15) (n.d) .... 1½.13
3379 Must Be Magical (USA) **(28)** (bl) *(FHLee)* 4-7-7(5) ‡5NKennedy (14) (led tl hdd &
　　　　wknd over 2f out) ..................................................... ½.14
3219³ Sharp Top **(54)** *(MJRyan)* 4-9-10 BRaymond (10) (in tch to st) ............. 4.15
3349 Aragon Ayr **(40)** *(PMonteith)* 4-8-10 NConnorton (8) (gd hdwy 5f out: sn prom:
　　　　wknd qckly 2f out) ................................................... ¾.16
3273 Luks Akura **(41)** (v) *(MJohnston)* 4-8-4 ‡7MBaird (6) (chsd ldrs tl wknd over 3f
　　　　out) ................................................................... ½.17
3379² Sea Paddy **(50)** *(RBastiman)* 4-8-13 ‡7HBastiman (9) (swtg: bhd: sme hdwy ent
　　　　st: sn rdn & wknd) ................................................... 12.18

**7/2** Grey Power, **9/2** BLANC SEING (FR), **13/2** Irish Honey (IRE), **10/1** Sea Paddy, Sharp Top, **12/1** Heliopsis(op
8/1), **14/1** J P Morgan, **16/1** Must Be Magical (USA), Mr Ziegfeld (USA), Seraphim (FR), **20/1** Jubilata (USA),
Luks Akura, Queens Tour, **25/1** Grey Commander, Aragon Ayr, **33/1** Ors. CSF £20.90, CT £98.40 BS, GP & JPM;
£170.45 BS, GP & GC. Tote £5.80: £1.30 £1.50 £3.80 JPM £4.20 GC (£24.40). Mr J. R. Chester (SHERIFF
HUTTON) bred by Societe Aland in France. 18 Rn　　　　　　　　　　　　　2m 45.2 (13.2)
　　　　　　　　　　　　　　　　　　　　　　　　　　　　　　SF–41/43/27/23/13/20

**3494**　SHAWFIELD CLAIMING STKS (3-Y.O) £2088.80 (£576.80: £274.40)
　　　　1m 3f 16y　　　　　　　　　　　　　　　　　　　　　　2-30 (2-31)

3309⁶ Salu **(54)** (bl) (Jt-Fav) *(JEtherington)* 8-1 GDuffield (4) (hld up: effrt over 2f out:
　　　　r.o u.p to ld nr fin) ................................................... —1
3479 Reel of Tulloch (IRE) **(53)** *(PCHaslam)* 8-7 DMcKeown (5) (hld up & bhd: hdwy
　　　　2f out: rdn & r.o: jst ct) .............................................. nk.2
3384⁵ Shadanza (IRE) **(48)** *(APStringer)* 8-9 ‡3SMaloney (2) (led 1f: cl up: led 4f out to
　　　　2f out: r.o one pce) ................................................... ¾.3
3258³ Up All Night **(43)** *(JWHills)* 8-3 DaleGibson (7) (a chsng ldrs: nt clr run & swtchd
　　　　2f out: n.m.r ins fnl f: kpt on) ....................................... ½.4

3350³ **Ready to Draw (IRE) (59)** (Jt-Fav) *(RonaldThompson)* 8-3 ‡⁷ClaireBalding (1) (trckd ldrs: effrt over 2f out: r.o one pce) .................... 8.5
3395⁵ **Speed Oil (45)** *(RBastiman)* 8-5 ‡⁷HBastiman (3) (hld up & bhd: c wd st: gd hdwy 4f out: sn ev ch: btn over 2f out) .................... 12.6
3386 **Father Dan (IRE)** *(DMoffatt)* 7-11 ‡⁷DarrenMoffatt (8) (chsd ldrs tl wknd over 3f out: hmpd over 2f out) .................... 4.7
  **Peter Martin Two** *(TCraig)* 8-0 LCharnock (6) (led after 1f to 4 out: wkng whn wnt rt wl over 2f out: fin 8th, 3l: plcd last) .................... 0
  *Stewards Enquiry: Charnock suspended 7-16/10/92 (intentional interference to Father Dan (IRE)).*

**9/4** SALU, Ready to Draw (IRE), **5/1** Up All Night, **7/1** Reel of Tulloch (IRE), **10/1** Speed Oil(8/1—12/1), **12/1** Shadanza (IRE), **25/1** Father Dan (IRE), **50/1** Peter Martin Two. CSF £16.63, Tote £3.80: £1.20 £1.20 £4.10 (£7.90). Mr W. N. Lumley (MALTON) bred by W. N. Lumley. 8 Rn 2m 36 (17)

## 3495
WEEKEND TIMES STKS £2579.00 (£714.00: £341.00) **6f 5y** 3-00 (3-05)

3344² **Ikteshaf (77)** *(BHanbury)* 4-9-10 BRaymond (6) (lw: cl up: led on bit 2f out: qckbnd: comf) .................... —1
3356 **Double Blue (91)** (Fav) *(MJohnston)* 3-9-7 DMcKeown (3) (lw: led 4f: rdn & r.o one pce) .................... 3.2
3355 **Threepence (79)** *(JBerry)* 3-9-7 JCarroll (1) (w ldrs: rdn 2f out: nt qckn) .................... ¾.3
2804³ **Ponsardin (86)** *(SirMarkPrescott)* 3-9-7 GDuffield (5) (chsd ldrs tl rdn & btn over 2f out) .................... 7.4
3344 **Jane's Brave Boy (20)** *(TCraig)* 10-9-10 NConnorton (4) (nvr wnt pce) .................... 4.5
3166 **Minsk (22)** *(TCraig)* 6-8-9 LCharnock (2) (prom to ½-wy: sn rdn & wknd) .................... ¾.6

**11/10** Double Blue, **7/4** IKTESHAF, **11/2** Ponsardin, **7/1** Threepence, **100/1** Jane's Brave Boy, **150/1** Minsk. CSF £3.98, Tote £2.50: £1.80 £1.40 (£1.80). Mr B. Hanbury (NEWMARKET) bred by The Sussex Stud. 6 Rn 1m 15.9 (14.8)
SF—52/37/34/6/–/–

## 3496
N.A.R.B.O.L. H'CAP (0-90) £2668.60 (£739.60: £353.80) **6f 5y** 3-30 (3-34)
(Weights raised 1 lb)

3068 **Arabat (56)** (v) *(MPNaughton)* 5-8-2 JakiHouston (8) (chsd ldrs: led wl over 1f out: hung lft & hung on) .................... —1
3355 **Dokkha Oyston (IRE) (68)** *(JBerry)* 4-9-0 JCarroll (10) (bhd tl hdwy over 1f out: kpt on u.p) .................... 1.2
3355 **Ashdren (77)** (v) *(AHarrison)* 5-9-9 GDuffield (3) (lw: hdwy 2f out: styd on: nvr able to chal) .................... 1½.3
3344⁵ **Veloce (IRE) (60)** (Fav) *(ABailey)* 4-7-13 ‡⁷GForster (6) (lw: hdwy centre over 1f out: r.o: nrst fin) .................... 2.4
3355² **Diet (67)** (v) *(MissLAPerratt)* 6-8-6 ‡⁷JMarshall (9) (lw: led over 4f: rdn & grad wknd) .................... nk.5
3341 **Francis Ann (55)** *(MissLAPerratt)* 4-7-10 ‡⁵NKennedy (7) (a chsng ldrs: rdn ½-wy: no imp) .................... nk.6
2053* **Ingenuity (61)** *(LordHuntingdon)* 3-8-1 ‡³DHarrison (2) (chsd ldrs: rdn 2f out: sn btn) .................... 1½.7
3356 **Mentalasanythin (81)** *(ABailey)* 3-9-10 LCharnock (11) (in tch: rdn ½-wy: n.d after) .................... 2.8
3355 **Just Bob (66)** (bl) *(SEKettlewell)* 3-8-9 JFortune (5) (dwlt: a bhd) .................... 1.9
3153² **Lift Boy (USA) (50)** *(DenysSmith)* 3-7-0 ‡⁷CTeague (4) (w ldr over 3f: sn wknd) nk.10
3460 **Ballad Dancer (55)** *(EJAlston)* 7-7-12 ‡³SMaloney (1) (lw: outpcd fr ½-wy) .................... 2.11

**7/2** Veloce (IRE)(5/1—3/1), **4/1** Ingenuity, **5/1** Diet, **9/1** Ashdren, Just Bob(8/1—12/1), **11/1** Ballad Dancer, **14/1** Dokkha Oyston (IRE), Mentalasanythin, **16/1** ARABAT, **25/1** Lift Boy (USA). CSF £195.67, CT £2,131.97. Tote £53.80: £7.70 £5.20 £2.30 (£208.80). Mrs H. H. Wane (RICHMOND) bred by Gerald W. Leigh. 11 Rn 1m 15.5 (5.5)
SF—38/46/49/17/23/12

**LONG HANDICAP:** Lift Boy (USA) 6-13.

## 3497
CADZOW (S) NURSERY £2742.00 (£762.00: £366.00) **1m 65y** 4-00 (4-03)
(Weights raised 7 lb)

3050 **Palacegate Sunset (47)** *(JBerry)* 8-5 LCharnock (15) (chsd ldrs: led over 2f out: qckbnd clr: drvn out) .................... —1
3407* **Always Risky (56)** (Fav) *(PAKelleway)* 9-0 (7x) GayKelleway (10) (lw: hld up: nt clr run & swtchd over 2f out: r.o wl: too much to do) .................... ½.2
3301 **Hot Off the Press (43)** (v) *(RMWhitaker)* 9-7 DaleGibson (18) (a chsng ldrs: effrt 3f out: kpt on one pce) .................... 6.3
3173² **Doc Spot (63)** *(CaptJWilson)* 9-7 GDuffield (14) (w ldrs: effrt 3f out: one pce) .................... 2.4
3301³ **Comtec's Legend (49)** *(JFBottomley)* 8-2 ‡⁵NKennedy (8) (bhd: hdwy 5f out: nvr nrr) .................... 6.5
3407 **Carnea (48)** *(JGFitzGerald)* 8-6(1) KFallon (4) (effrt ½-wy: sn in tch: one pce appr fnl f) .................... nk.6

2983 Dancing Domino **(56)** *(MHEasterby)* 9-0 KDarley (16) (a in tch: no hdwy fnl 3f) ¾.7
3165 The Loon **(46)** *(JJO'Neill)* 8-4 SWood (5) (lw: bhd: effrt 3f out: nvr nr to chal) 3¹/₂.8
3353 Andrew's Express (IRE) **(50)** (bl) *(SEKettlewell)* 8-8 SWebster (11) (cl up over 4f: wknd) ...... ¹/₂.9
3173 Challenger Row (IRE) **(48)** *(CWThornton)* 8-6 DMcKeown (3) (b.hind: lw: bhd: effrt on outside 4f out: n.d) ...... nk.10
3343 Formidable Liz **(51)** *(NBycroft)* 8-9 JFanning (17) (mde most tl hdd & wknd over 2f out) ...... 2¹/₂.11
2983 Irish Roots (IRE) **(49)** (v) *(CTinkler)* 8-7 MBirch (2) (n.d) ...... 5.12
3303⁶ Killy's Filly **(60)** *(JBerry)* 9-4 JCarroll (13) (n.d) ...... 2¹/₂.13
3199 Rough Guess (IRE) **(55)** (v) *(LordHuntingdon)* 8-10 ‡³DHarrison (6) (n.d) ...... 2.14
3394 Newgatesky **(45)** *(BWMurray)* 7-10 ‡†DarrenMoffatt (7) (bhd: effrt ¹/₂-wy: n.d) . ¾.15
3303 Lady Adare (IRE) **(50)** *(JJO'Neill)* 8-8 JFortune (9) (jnd ldrs ent st: wknd 3f out) 2¹/₂.16
3385 Nancy (IRE) **(60)** *(CWCElsey)* 9-1 ‡³SMaloney (1) (a bhd) ...... ¹/₂.17

3/1 Always Risky, 5/1 Doc Spot, Comtec's Legend, 13/2 Rough Guess (IRE), 10/1 Carnea, 11/1 Dancing Domino, Hot Off the Press, 12/1 Killy's Filly, Irish Roots (IRE), 14/1 Challenger Row (IRE), Nancy (IRE), PALACEGATE SUNSET, 16/1 Formidable Liz, 25/1 The Loon, 33/1 Andrew's Express (IRE), 50/1 Ors. CSF £62.30, CT £484.41. Tote £22.60: £4.50 £2.20 £2.40 £1.90 (£86.20). Palacegate Corporation Ltd (COCKERHAM) bred by T. K. Knox. 17 Rn; No bid; Always Risky clmd H O'Donnell £6,200   1m 53.9 (10.6)
SF—6/13/–/–/–/–

**3498** E.B.F. BOTHWELL BRIDGE STKS (Mdn 2-Y.O) £2678.40 (£742.40: £355.20)
1m 65y                                                        4-30 (4-33)

3300² Cure the King (IRE) **(78)** *(SGNorton)* 9-0 KDarley (7) (chsd ldrs: effrt 3f out: styd on to ld ins fnl f: eased nr fnl) —1
3300⁴ Persiansky (IRE) **(73)** *(BHanbury)* 9-0 BRaymond (10) (lw: led tl hdd ins fnl f: one pce) 1.2
3362⁴ Green Kilt (Fav) *(LordHuntingdon)* 8-11 ‡⁹DHarrison (2) (lw: trckd ldrs gng wl: chal 2f out: rdn & no ex fnl f) 6.3
2818 Friendly Knight *(JSHaldane)* 9-0 LCharnock (9) (effrt ¹/₂-wy: styd on: nt pce to chal) 3.4
3338³ Grogfryn **(74)** *(JBerry)* 8-9 JCarroll (11) (swtg: chsd ldrs tl outpcd wl over 2f out) s.h.5
3353 Rosmarino *(CWThornton)* 9-0 NConnorton (3) (bhd: sme hdwy 3f out: nvr nr to chal) s.h.6
Primitive Gift *(MrsGRReveley)* 8-9 DaleGibson (4) (unf: scope: dwlt: gd hdwy 3f out: wknd wl over 1f out) 2.7
3307 Prime Painter **(60)** *(RFFisher)* 9-0 KFallon (6) (cl up tl outpcd over 3f out) 2¹/₂.8
2551⁵ Free Dancer *(RAllan)* 8-9 SWebster (8) (a bhd) nk.9
3163 Ultrakay (IRE) *(JBerry)* 9-0 DMcKeown (5) (dwlt: a bhd: t.o) dist.10

11/10 Green Kilt(8/11—6/5), 9/4 CURE THE KING (IRE), 5/1 Persiansky (IRE)(6/1—8/1), 12/1 Grogfryn(op 8/1), 33/1 Primitive Gift, Prime Painter, Rosmarino, Ultrakay (IRE), Free Dancer, 100/1 Friendly Knight. CSF £13.43, Tote £4.00: £1.50 £1.40 £1.40 (£8.60). Mr P. D. Savill (BARNSLEY) bred by Dunderry Stud in Ireland. 10 Rn   1m 53.5 (10.2)
SF—20/17/–/–/–/–

T/Plpt: £184.10 (13.3 Tckts).                                            AA

3156—**WOLVERHAMPTON (L-H)**
**Monday, September 28th [Good]**
Going Allowance: 0.60 sec per fur (Y)                Wind: almost nil  Vis:4th-6th hazy
Stalls: high

**3499** BLACK COUNTRY APP'CE H'CAP (0-70) £2721.00 (£756.00: £363.00)
5f                                                           2-20 (2-36)

3220³ Call to the Bar (IRE) **(49)** *(CGCox)* 3-8-5 ‡³DWright (8) (a.p: led over 1f out: edgd lft fnl f: r.o) —1
3412⁵ Blue Is True (IRE) **(51)** *(LJBarratt)* 3-8-7 ‡³PBowe (1) (a.p: ev ch ins fnl f: unable qckn) 1.2
3341 Langtonian **(56)** (bl) *(JBerry)* 3-9-1 EmmaO'Gorman (11) (hdwy 2f out: r.o u.p ins fnl f) s.h.3
3423 Stocktina **(39)** *(RJHodges)* 5-8-0 FNorton (12) (swtg: hld up: r.o fnl f: nvr nrr) 1¹/₂.4
3253 Noble Power (IRE) **(68)** *(BPalling)* 3-9-13 StephenDavies (5) (lw: hdwy 2f out: kpt on fnl f: nvr able to chal) 2¹/₂.5
3308³ The Right Time **(47)** (bl) *(JParkes)* 7-8-8 KRutter (10) (lw: hdwy 2f out: r.o ins fnl f: nvr nrr) s.h.6
3413⁴ Barbara's Cutie **(39)** (v) *(MBlanshard)* 4-7-11 ‡³CAvery (18) (prom: led ¹/₂-wy tl over 1f out: wknd fnl f) hd.7

Page 1253

3294 Lincstone Boy (IRE) **(51)** (bl) *(SRBowring)* 4–8–9 ‡³MHarris (6) (hung lft 2f out: nvr nr to chal) ............................................................................................ nk.8
3460⁵ Black Boy (IRE) **(56)** (Fav) *(JAGlover)* 3–9–1 SWilliams (13) (led to ½-wy: rdn & wknd over 1f out) ....................................................................................... 1.9
3067 Soba Guest (IRE) **(67)** *(JBerry)* 3–9–5 ‡⁷SPorritt (14) (b.nr hind: w ldrs over 3f: sn wknd) ..................................................................................................... 1.10
3423² Miss Vaxette **(69)** *(JLSpearing)* 3–9–11 ‡³MHumphries (20) (spd stands' side 3f) hd.11
2984⁴ Stormbuster **(44)** *(PSFelgate)* 3–7–10 ‡⁷DToole (19) (swtg: bhd fnl 2f) ........... 1½.12
2607 Lawnswood Prince (IRE) **(43)** *(JLSpearing)* 3–7–13 ‡³SSanders (9) (m.n.s) ....... 3.13
2989⁶ Ever so Lonely **(58)** *(ABailey)* 3–8–10 ‡⁷WHollick (16) (swtg: spd to ½-wy) ....... nk.14
3296⁶ Doesyoudoes **(52)** *(DTThom)* 3–8–11 SO'Gorman (2) (outpcd) ..................... d.h.16
3257 Amour du Soir (USA) **(57)** *(RLee)* 5–9–4 RPrice (7) (b: bit bkwd: outpcd) .......... 1.16
Blyton Star (IRE) **(45)** *(SRBowring)* 4–8–6 AGarth (15) (n.d) .............................. 1½.17
1144 Injaka Boy **(44)** (v) *(KWhite)* 3–8–0⁽⁵⁾ ‡³DCarson (4) (bkwd: outpcd) ............... 3½.18
*3397 Ganeshaya (8/1) Withdrawn (ref to ent stalls) : not under orders — Rule 4 applies*
*3103 Lonely Lass (20/1) Withdrawn (broke out of stalls) : not under orders*

**13/2** Black Boy (IRE), **7/1** Amour du Soir (USA), **15/2** Miss Vaxette, **9/1** Barbara's Cutie, **11/1** The Right Time, **12/1** Soba Guest (IRE), Stocktina, Stormbuster, **14/1** Langtonian, Lincstone Boy (IRE), CALL TO THE BAR (IRE), **16/1** Ever so Lonely, **20/1** Blue Is True (IRE), **25/1** Doesyoudoes, Noble Power (IRE), Lawnswood Prince (IRE), **33/1** Blyton Star (IRE), **50/1** Injaka Boy. CSF £215.53, CT £2,674.93. Tote £29.30: £5.30 £2.70 £4.00 £1.90 (£94.60). Mr Andy Robbins (LYNEHAM) bred by Somerville Stud in Ireland. 18 Rn   62.7 sec (5.4)
SF—43/41/48/27/44/24

**3500**   SEDGELEY (S) STKS   £2679.00 (£744.00: £357.00)   1½m 70y   2-50 (3-01)

2408⁴ **Allmosa (56)** *(TJNaughton)* 3–8–9 GCarter (17) (swtg: a.p: 2nd st: led appr fnl f: drew clr fnl f) ...................................................................................................... —1
1560⁶ Feeling Foolish (IRE) **(50)** *(BForsey)* 3–9–0 NHowe (18) (hdwy 6f out: 4th st: ev ch appr fnl f: unable qckn) ............................................................................ 1½.2
3387 Molly Splash **(54)** (Jt-Fav) *(CACyzer)* 3–8–9 DBiggs (7) (rdn ent st: hdwy 2f out: r.o wl ins fnl f) ........................................................................................................ nk.3
3384³ Kasikci **(55)** (Jt-Fav) *(RHollinshead)* 3–8–9 WRyan (10) (hld up: 7th st: led over 2f out tl appr fnl f: one pce) ............................................................................... nk.4
3384⁴ Iron Baron (IRE) **(50)** *(RHollinshead)* 3–8–10 ‡⁷SWynne (9) (hdwy & 6th st: rdn 2f out: nt pce to chal) ......................................................................................... 1.5
3263 Princess of Orange **(40)** *(WMBrisbourne)* 3–8–2 ‡⁷AGarth (4) (in tch: effrt 3f out: nt rch ldrs) ...................................................................................................... s.h.6
3157 Kate Royale **(37)** *(MCPipe)* 3–8–4 ‡⁵StephenDavies (14) (s.i.s: r.o fnl 3f: sn rdn: nt rch ldrs) ........................................................................................................... 2.7
3350⁵ Speedy Sioux **(48)** *(CWThornton)* 3–8–9 GHind (6) (swtg: sme late hdwy: n.d) ... 10.8
3311³ Noted Strain (IRE) **(55)** (v) *(PJMakin)* 4–9–8 TSprake (11) (bkwd: swtg: nvr trbld ldrs) .................................................................................................................. 3½.9
3045⁶ Moving Force **(34)** *(EAWheeler)* 5–9–8 SWhitworth (20) (m.n.s) ......................... 6.10
494 Needwood Poppy **(29)** *(BCMorgan)* 4–8–10 ‡⁷SSanders (19) (m.n.s) ................. hd.11
3054 Ternimus (USA) **(43)** (bl) *(BPreece)* 5–9–8 JQuinn (12) (m.n.s) ........................... 12
2810 Castleacre **(39)** *(CASmith)* 6–9–8 MWigham (3) (a bhd: t.o) ................................ 13
3104 Medbourne (IRE) **(37)** *(JLHarris)* 3–8–9 PaulEddery (5) (chsd ldrs 8f: sn wknd: t.o) ...................................................................................................................... 14
3403 Be My Habitat **(58)** (bl) *(MissLCSiddall)* 3–8–11 ‡³SO'Gorman (15) (hdwy & 5th st: rdn & wknd 3f out: t.o) ....................................................................................... 15
3263 Kaytura **(MHTompkins)** 3–8–9 PRobinson (1) (prom tl wknd ent st: t.o) .................. 16
2211 Law Faculty (IRE) **(49)** (v) *(GAHam)* 3–8–7 ‡⁷SDrowne (8) (t.o) .......................... 17
*2155* Light-of-the-Loch **(35)** *(AWPotts)* 4–9–3 CDwyer (8) (swtg: prom: 3rd st: sn wknd: t.o) ............................................................................................................... 18
2036 Woodlands Crown **(26)** *(DCTucker)* 9–9–8 RCochrane (13) (t.o fr ½-wy: p.u bef 3f out) ................................................................................................................... 0
3263³ Laughton Lady **(43)** (bl) *(MrsNMacauley)* 3–8–4 ‡⁵SWilliams (2) (led tl over 2f out: collapsed & died appr fnl f) ........................................................................... 0

**9/2** Kasikci, Molly Splash, **7/1** Iron Baron (IRE), Noted Strain (IRE), Laughton Lady, **9/1** Speedy Sioux, **10/1** Kate Royale, **12/1** ALLMOSA, Kaytura, **16/1** Feeling Foolish (IRE), **20/1** Be My Habitat, **25/1** Needwood Poppy, Moving Force, **28/1** Princess of Orange, **33/1** Law Faculty (IRE), **40/1** Woodlands Crown, **50/1** Ternimus (USA), Medbourne (IRE), **66/1** Ors. CSF £190.71, Tote £9.50: £3.00 £3.90 £3.10 (£382.60). The Durdans Four (II) Two (EPSOM) bred by Ronald Popely. 20 Rn; No bid   2m 48.1 (16.4)
SF—5/7/12/–/–/–

**3501**   CODSALL GRADUATION STKS (2-Y.O.C & G) £2856.00 (£791.00: £378.00) 1m   3-20 (3-25)

3146★ **Elkhart (USA)** (Fav) *(HRACecil)* 9–4 SCauthen (1) (mde all: pushed clr fnl f: unchal) ................................................................................................................. —1

3300∗ Hawl (USA) **(86)** *(AAScott)* 9-4 WCarson (3) (swtg: chsd wnr: 2nd st: outpcd 2f
out: sn rdn: styd on) ............................................................... 3.2

10176 Blowedifiknow *(JWharton)* 8-11 JQuinn (4) (bit bkwd: hld up: 4th st: styd on nr
fin: nvr nrr) ........................................................................ 3¹/₂.3

30443 Sabo's Express **(73)** (bl) *(RHannon)* 9-4 DBiggs (2) (swtg: chsd ldrs: 3rd st:
effrt & ev ch 2f out: rdn & wknd fnl f) ....................... hd.4

**8/13** ELKHART (USA), **7/4** Hawl (USA), **12/1** Sabo's Express(op 6/1), **50/1** Blowedifiknow. CSF £1.94, Tote
£1.50 (£1.30). Sheikh Mohammed (NEWMARKET) bred by W Lazy T Ltd in USA. 4 Rn      1m 49.6 (12.3)

## 3502 OAKEN LODGE NURSERY (F) (0-75) £2910.00 (£810.00: £390.00)   **7f**   3-50 (3-54)
(Weights raised 1 lb)

34043 **Formal Affair (72)** *(CACyzer)* 9-5 GCarter (4) (swtg: chsd ldrs: led 3f out:
qcknd clr ent fnl f: eased nr fin) .............................. —1

27404 Grand Dancer (IRE) **(70)** *(RJRWilliams)* 9-3 DBiggs (13) (hdwy on ins over 2f
out: r.o ins fnl f: no ch w wnr) ................................. 4.2

2859 Don'tlie (IRE) **(69)** *(GBBalding)* 8-11 ‡⁵RPrice (1) (lw: hdwy over 3f out: kpt on
one pce fnl f) ....................................................... 1¹/₂.3

32913 Ascom Pager Too **(60)** *(PHowling)* 8-7 BCrossley (5) (b: b.off hind: a.p: ev ch 2f
out: no ex fnl f) ..................................................... 4.4

31726 Honorary Guest **(65)** *(DJGMurray-Smith)* 8-12 TRogers (7) (lw: hdwy 2f out:
styd on appr fnl f: nvr nr to chal) ............................. 3.5

3115 Simply Amiss **(74)** *(SirMarkPrescott)* 9-2 ‡⁵KRutter (10) (sme hdwy appr fnl f:
nvr nrr) ................................................................. 1¹/₂.6

29835 Amerigue **(68)** *(MissSEHall)* 9-1 GHind (14) (styd on over 1f out: nvr nrr) ......... 1¹/₂.7

32603 Sea Exhibition (IRE) **(68)** *(MBlanshard)* 9-1 RCochrane (3) (swtg: chsd ldrs:
effrt & ev ch 3f out: grad wknd) ............................. 1¹/₂.8

01Ω3 Galejade **(67)** *(DHaydnJones)* 8-9 ‡⁵NGwilliams (8) (nvr nrr) .................. s.h.9

29866 Moon Watch **(70)** *(JH-anshawe)* 9-0 WRSwinburn (2) (nvr trbld ldrs) ............... 3.10

32953 Ikhtisas (USA) **(68)** *(BHanbury)* 9-1 WCarson (17) (stdd s: a bhd) .................. Ω.11

3199 Clear Honey (USA) **(60)** (bl) *(BHanbury)* 8-7 WRyan (15) (lw: prom: led ent st to
3f out: wknd over 1f out) ....................................... ³/₄.12

10363 Sudbury (IRE) **(66)** *(MHTompkins)* 8-13 PRobinson (12) (bit bkwd: prom 4f) .. ¹/₂.13

3320 Crystal Stone **(69)** *(TThomsonJones)* 9-2 SWhitworth (9) (a bhd) .................. ³/₄.14

3162 Musical Prospect (USA) **(68)** (bl) *(RHannon)* 9-1 PaulEddery (16) (prom tl rdn &
wknd 2f out) ......................................................... ¹/₂.15

32682 Ballet **(69)** (Fav) *(LordHuntingdon)* 9-2 SCauthen (6) (chsd ldrs over 4f: eased
whn btn) .............................................................. 4.16

31603 Fleur Power (IRE) **(64)** *(BPalling)* 8-6 ‡⁵StephenDavies (11) (led over 2f: sn rdn
& wknd: t.o) .......................................................... 5.17

**9/2** Ballet, **7/1** Moon Watch, **9/1** Ikhtisas, Amerigue, **10/1** Musical Prospect (USA), Sea Exhibition
(IRE)(8/1—12/1), Sudbury (IRE), **12/1** Don'tlie (IRE), Ascom Pager Too(op 8/1), **14/1** Clear Honey (USA),
FORMAL AFFAIR, Fleur Power (IRE), **16/1** Grand Dancer (IRE), Galejade, **20/1** Simply Amiss, **33/1** Ors. CSF
£212.37, CT £2,525.45. Tote £25.70: £3.90 £7.80 £2.90 £3.00 (£206.60). Mr R. M. Cyzer (HORSHAM) bred by
Cobhall Court Stud. 17 Rn      1m 32.9 (8.6)

SF—39/25/14/5/—/–

## 3503 E.B.F. DUDLEY STKS (Mdn 2-Y.O) £3027.50 (£840.00: £402.50)   **5f**   4-20 (4-23)

32405 **Esthal (IRE)** (Fav) *(RJHodges)* 8-7 ‡⁷SDrowne (2) (a.p: led over 1f out: pushed
out) ..................................................................... —1

18515 La Madrigal *(JWharton)* 8-9 JQuinn (3) (swtg: led tl over 1f out: rallied u.p nr fin) 1.2

32756 Bellsabanging **(66)** *(DRLaing)* 9-0 TyroneWilliams (5) (b.hind: w ldr: rdn 2f out:
r.o one pce) .......................................................... 2.3

14055 My Foxy Lady *(DHaydnJones)* 8-9 SWhitworth (1) (bit bkwd: chsd ldrs: rdn
over 1f out: nvr able to chal) ................................. 4.4

3106 Form Secret (IRE) *(LJBarratt)* 8-9 CDwyer (7) (a in rr) ........................ 1¹/₂.5

Woodlands Electric *(PAPritchard)* 9-0 PaulEddery (6) (lt-f: s.s: a outpcd) ........ 1¹/₂.6

M a El-Sahn *(RHannon)* 9-0 PRobinson (8) (w'like: chsd ldrs: swvd bdly lft over
1f out: sn btn) ...................................................... 3.7

**6/5** ESTHAL (IRE), **85/40** Bellsabanging(3/1—2/1), **7/1** M a El-Sahn(op 3/1), **16/1** La Madrigal, My Foxy Lady,
**66/1** Ors. CSF £15.72, Tote £2.30: £1.40 £3.50 (£10.30). Unity Farm Holiday Centre Ltd (SOMERTON) bred by
Gainsborough Stud Management Ltd in Ireland. 7 Rn      64.3 sec (7)

SF—13/11/8/—/–/–/

## 3504 WEST MIDLAND H'CAP (0-70) £2826.00 (£786.00: £378.00)
1³/₄m 134y   4-50 (4-53)

3380 **Iota (58)** *(MrsJCecil)* 3-8-9 SCauthen (3) (lw: a.p: 3rd st: led over 3f out: sn
drvn clr: unchal) .................................................. —1

3306 Neieb (USA) **(56)** *(BHanbury)* 3-8-7 WRSwinburn (2) (swtg: chsd ldrs: 5th st: effrt 3f out: rdn appr fnl f: kpt on one pce) .......................... 8.2
805⁴ Needwood Muppet **(54)** *(BCMorgan)* 5-9-2 GCarter (4) (bkwd: hdwy 3f out: styd on ins fnl f: nvr plcd to chal) ............................. 2.3
3380* Carrolls Marc (IRE) **(53)** *(Fav)* *(PJFeilden)* 4-9-1 RCochrane (6) (chsd ldrs: 6th st: rdn 2f out: sn btn) ............................ 1½.4
3409* John Shaw (USA) **(51)** *(CTinkler)* (7x) PBurke (4) (hld up: hdwy 3f out: sn rdn & nt rch ldrs) ............................ 2.5
2278 Shentit (FR) **(66)** (bl) *(JLDunlop)* 4-10-0 PRobinson (9) (chsd ldrs: no hdwy fnl 3f) ............................ nk.6
2477³ Dare to Dream (IRE) **(54)** *(GLewis)* 4-8-13 PaulEddery (10) (hld up & bhd: sme hdwy fnl 2f: nvr nrr) ............................ 1.7
3169 Only a Rose **(53)** *(CWThornton)* 3-8-4 GHind (5) (led 12f out to 8f out: led ent st tl over 3f out: sn wknd) ............................ 1.8
3409 Emperors Warrior **(45)** *(CDBroad)* 6-8-0 ‡⁷CAvery (1) (bkwd: a bhd) ............................ 5.9
3064⁵ Marine Society **(65)** *(RLee)* 4-9-8 ‡⁵RPrice (11) (hdwy & 4th st: wknd wl over 2f out) ............................ 2.10
3351 Briggsmaid **(61)** *(JMPEustace)* 4-9-9 MTebbutt (8) (swtg: a bhd: t.o) ............................ 8.11
3266⁵ Lascar (USA) **(49)** *(GThorner)* 4-8-8 ‡³SO'Gorman (7) (led 8f out tl hdd & 2nd st: rdn & wknd 3f out: r.o) ............................ 12
Pokey's Pride **(60)** *(JRBostock)* 4-9-8 SWhitworth (12) (bkwd: a bhd: t.o) ............................ 13
578 Fit for Life (IRE) **(47)** (bl) *(MrsNMacauley)* 4-8-4⁽⁵⁾ ‡⁵SWilliams (13) (b: bkwd: led over 2f: lost tch 6f out: t.o) ............................ 14

**100/30** Carrolls Marc (IRE), **13/2** Dare to Dream (IRE), **7/1** John Shaw (USA), **8/1** Needwood Muppet(op 12/1), Briggsmaid, **9/1** IOTA, **11/1** Lascar (USA), **12/1** Marine Society, **14/1** Shentit (FR), Neieb (USA), **33/1** Only a Rose, Fit for Life (IRE), Emperors Warrior, **50/1** Pokey's Pride. CSF £114.57, CT £956.83. Tote £7.80: £2.40 £3.00 £1.60 (£20.20). Sheikh Mohammed (NEWMARKET) bred by Sheikh Mohammed bin Rashid al Maktoum.
14 Rn　　　　　　　　　　　　　　　　　　　　　　　　　　3m 20.6 (14.6)
　　　　　　　　　　　　　　　　　　　　　　　　　　　　SF—36/18/23/19/13/27

T/Plpt: £1,292.10 (1.4 Tckts).　　　　　　　　　　　　　　　　　　　　IM

3420—**BRIGHTON (L-H)**

## Tuesday, September 29th [Good, Good to soft patches]

Going Allowance: minus 0.10 sec per fur (F)　　　　　　　　　Wind: almost nil

Stalls: low

**3505**　E.B.F. SOMPTING STKS (Mdn 2-Y.O) £2784.00 (£774.00: £372.00)
　　　　6f 209y　　　　　　　　　　　　　　　　　　1-50 (1-53)

3289³ Coneybury (IRE) *(Fav)* *(LMCumani)* 9-0 LDettori (9) (lw: hdwy over 2f out: led wl over 1f out: pushed out) ............................ —1
3360² Suntara (IRE) *(BWHills)* 8-9 SCauthen (3) (6th st: swtchd rt over 2f out: chsd wnr fnl f: no imp) ............................ 4.2
1112⁴ Royal Interval *(WGMTurner)* 9-0 TSprake (2) (led over 5f: one pce) ............................ 2½.3
3132³ Miss Fascination *(MAJarvis)* 8-9 BRaymond (5) (3rd st: one pce fnl 2f) ............................ ½.4
3295 Agenda One *(MissAJWhitfield)* 8-4 ‡⁵ATucker (7) (nvr nr to chal) ............................ 3½.5
3186 Doodies Pool (IRE) *(GLewis)* 9-0 BRouse (1) (4th st: wknd over 2f out) ............................ 1.6
3289 Scorcher (IRE) *(CEBrittain)* 9-0 GCrealock (6) (5th st: wknd over 2f out) ............................ ½.7
3314 Night Edition *(SDow)* 9-0 TQuinn (4) (2nd st: wknd over 2f out) ............................ 6.8
2930 Kiawah *(JRFanshawe)* 8-9 GBardwell (8) (a bhd) ............................ ½.9

**11/8** CONEYBURY (IRE)(5/4—2/1), **7/4** Suntara (IRE), **3/1** Miss Fascination, **20/1** Night Edition, **66/1** Ors. CSF £4.01, Tote £2.40: £1.10 £1.20 £2.40 (£1.70). Mr R. E. Sangster (NEWMARKET) bred by Swettenham Stud in Ireland. 9 Rn　　　　　　　　　　　　　　　　　　　　　　　　1m 23 (3)
　　　　　　　　　　　　　　　　　　　　　　　　　　　　SF—44/27/24/17/1/8

**3506**　LEVY BOARD STKS (Mdn 3-Y.O) £2532.00 (£702.00: £336.00)
　　　　1m 1f 209y　　　　　　　　　　　　　　　　　2-20 (2-23)

Fawz (IRE) *(RWArmstrong)* 8-9 RHills (5) (leggy: 3rd st: led over 1f out: hrd rdn: r.o wl) ............................ —1
3259⁵ Jazz **(76)** *(LMCumani)* 8-9 LDettori (4) (led over 8f: hrd rdn & unable qckn) .... 2½.2
2907³ Queen Caroline (USA) **(71)** *(Fav)* *(HRACecil)* 8-9 SCauthen (10) (lw: 2nd st: ev ch over 2f out: rdn & eased whn btn ins fnl f) ............................ 7.3
Zoom Lens (IRE) *(JLDunlop)* 8-9 TQuinn (9) (hdwy fnl f: r.o) ............................ ½.4
3258 Chinaman **(28)** *(WGRWightman)* 9-0 JWilliams (3) (nvr nrr) ............................ 1½.5
3374⁴ Literary Critic (IRE) *(JARToller)* 9-0 GBaxter (2) (6th st: no hdwy fnl 3f) ............................ 1½.6
3258 Fermain *(LordHuntingdon)* 9-0 AMunro (6) (5th st: wknd over 1f out) ............................ 2½.7

*200* Court Room **(43)** *(AMoore)* 9-0 CandyMorris (8) (a bhd) ................................ 20.8
*3412* Poyle Amber *(MBlanshard)* 8-6 ‡3DHarrison (7) (4th st: wknd over 3f out) ........ 2¹/₂.9
*3246⁶* Canadian Boy (IRE) *(DShaw)* 9-0 GCarter (1) (a wl bhd) ............................... ³/₄.10

**15/8** Queen Caroline (USA), **2/1** Jazz, **15/2** Zoom Lens (IRE)(op 5/1), Literary Critic (IRE)(10/1—12/1), **9/1** FAWZ (IRE)(op 5/1), **20/1** Fermain, **33/1** Poyle Amber, **50/1** Canadian Boy (IRE), **66/1** Ors. CSF £25.30, Tote £8.90: £2.10 £1.30 £1.10 (£18.70). Mr Hamdan Al-Maktoum (NEWMARKET) bred by Shadwell Estate Company Limited in Ireland. 10 Rn     2m 2.6 (4.6)
SF—39/34/20/19/21/18

---

**3507**    STEYNING (S) H'CAP (3-Y.O) (0-60) £2574.00 (£714.00: £342.00)
        **5f 213y**                    2-50 (2-56)

(Weights raised 4 lb)

*3254* **Rockbourne (51)** *(WGMTurner)* 9-2 TSprake (6) (hdwy 2f out: led ins fnl f: r.o wl) ............................................................................................................. —1
*2772* Master Hyde (USA) **(44)** *(PMitchell)* 8-9 MRoberts (10) (hdwy over 1f out: ev ch ins fnl f) ........................................................................................................ ³/₄.2
*2822* Palacegate Gold (IRE) **(49)** *(RJHodges)* 9-0 RCochrane (4) (4th st: led over 3f out tl ins fnl f: edgd lft: unable qckn) ...................................................... 2.3
*3257* Ceatharlach **(40)** (Fav) *(RJHolder)* 8-5 NAdams (7) (lw: rdn thrght: 5th st: ev ch over 1f out: one pce) .................................................................................. nk.4
*3257* Life's a Breeze **(46)** *(MRChannon)* 8-11 GCarter (13) (lw: nvr nr to chal) .......... ³/₄.5
*3220* Form Mistress **(40)** (v) *(PTWalwyn)* 8-5 AMunro (9) (6th st: one pce fnl 2f) ....... hd.6
*3257* Orchard Bay **(40)** (v) *(DRTucker)* 8-5 GBardwell (2) (lw: hdwy over 1f out: 5th whn hmpd ins fnl f: nt rcvr) ........................................................................ nk.7
*3413* Weekend Girl **(31)** *(WMBrisbourne)* 7-3⁽³⁾ ‡7AGarth (5) (lw: no hdwy fnl 2f) ....... ¹/₂.8
*3423* Savalaro **(52)** (bl) *(JFfitch-Heyes)* 9-3 TyroneWilliams (11) (led: c stands' side st: hdd over 3f out: wknd over 1f out) ........................................................ hd.9
*3216⁶* Alto Princess **(38)** (v) *(AFJones)* 7 12⁽¹⁾ †5RPrice (14) (prom over 4f) ............. 1¹/₂.10
*3308* Don't Run Me Over **(45)** *(BCMorgan)* 8-10 GDuffield (8) (3rd st: wknd wl over 1f out) .................................................................................................................. 2¹/₂.11
*3296* Pink'n Black (IRE) **(48)** *(GBlum)* 8-10 ‡3DHarrison (3) (hdwy over 3f out: ev ch over 1f out: btn whn bdly hmpd ins fnl f) .................................................. hd.12
*3288* Alton Belle **(35)** (bl) *(PHowling)* 8-0 BCrossley (1) (a bhd) ............................... nk.13
*3281* Smudgemupum **(44)** *(MissBSanders)* 8-4 ‡5ATucker (12) (a bhd) .................... 3¹/₂.14
*3048* Our Emma **(46)** (v) *(MrsBarbaraWaring)* 8-11 NHowe (15) (bhd fnl 2f) ............. ³/₄.15
*3003* Scala Milano **(56)** *(KTIvory)* 9-7 TQuinn (16) (2nd & c stands' side st: eased whn btn over 1f out) .............................................................................. 6.16

LONG HANDICAP: Weekend Girl 7-2.

**6/1** Ceatharlach (op 10/1), **13/2** Savalaro, **7/1** Palacegate Gold (IRE)(op 9/2), **9/1** ROCKBOURNE, Master Hyde (USA), **11/1** Pink'n Black (IRE), **12/1** Don't Run Me Over, Life's a Breeze, Scala Milano(op 8/1), **14/1** Form Mistress, **16/1** Smudgemupum (op 10/1), Orchard Bay, **33/1** Ors. CSF £78.22, CT £538.68. Tote £11.00: £2.00 £1.70 £2.00 £1.60 (£71.10). Mr J. W. Aplin (SHERBORNE) bred by Whitsbury Manor Stud. 16 Rn; No bid
            1m 11.4 (3)
SF—30/20/17/10/3

---

**3508**    BRIGHTELMSTONE NURSERY    £3574.00 (£1072.00: £516.00: £238.00)
        **6f 209y**                    3-20 (3-21)

(Weights raised 3 lb)

*3394²* **Mr Nevermind (IRE) (60)** (bl) *(GLewis)* 7-6⁽¹⁾ ‡3DHarrison (8) (hdwy 2f out: led ins fnl f: r.o wl) .................................................................................... —1
*2883* Homemaker **(58)** *(RJHolder)* 7-7 NAdams (11) (hdwy over 3f out: led over 1f out tl ins fnl f: r.o) ........................................................................................ ³/₄.2
*3029⁵* Regalsett **(82)** *(RHannon)* 9-3 RCochrane (10) (hdwy 2f out: hrd rdn over 1f out: r.o) ............................................................................................................... s.h.3
*2700\** Just You Dare (IRE) **(70)** *(SirMarkPrescott)* 8-5 GDuffield (5) (n.m.r over 3f out: swtchd rt: r.o ins fnl f) .................................................................. 1¹/₂.4
*3364* War Requiem **(58)** *(GBBalding)* 7-7 DaleGibson (12) (hdwy over 2f out: ev ch over 1f out: unable qckn) ............................................................................ s.h.5
*3217²* Jallaaf (USA) **(86)** (Fav) *(LMCumani)* 9-7 LDettori (2) (lw: hdwy over 2f out: n.m.r over 1f out: one pce) ....................................................................... ³/₄.6
*3274³* Final Frontier (IRE) **(70)** *(RAkehurst)* 8-2 ‡3FNorton (7) (led over 5f) .............. 1¹/₂.7
*3164⁴* Tajarib (IRE) **(66)** *(JLDunlop)* 8-1 RHills (4) (b.off hind: hdwy over 1f out: r.o) ... ¹/₂.8
*3408* Villavina **(74)** *(SDow)* 8-9 TQuinn (3) (6th st: one pce fnl 2f) ............................... 2¹/₂.9
*3286⁴* Strike-a-Pose **(58)** *(CNWilliams)* 7-8 NCarlisle (15) (4th st: ev ch over 1f out: wknd fnl f) .............................................................................................. s.h.10
*2781⁴* Arawa **(60)** *(DMarks)* 7-9 SDawson (18) (a mid div) ........................................... nk.11
*3274⁴* Coppot Tel (IRE) **(77)** *(CEBrittain)* 8-12 MRoberts (16) (5th st: wknd 2f out) . 1¹/₂.12
*3303* Daring Past **(60)** *(RBoss)* 7-9 JQuinn (9) (2nd st: wkng whn hmpd over 1f out) ¹/₂.13
*2901* Cashable **(70)** *(JRJenkins)* 8-5 GBaxter (17) (a bhd) ........................................ nk.14

3218 Imafifer (IRE) **(58)** *(WRMuir)* 7-0 ‡⁷KimMcDonnell (14) (3rd st: wknd over 2f out) 2¹/₂.**15**
3199 Garp (FR) **(72)** *(MRStoute)* 8-7 BRaymond (6) (a bhd) ................................ 12.**16**
3047 Rusty Raja **(60)** (bl) *(RHannon)* 7-9 GBardwell (1) (a bhd) ........................ 8.**17**
LONG HANDICAP: Homemaker 7-4, War Requiem (IRE) 7-5, Imafifer (IRE) 7-4.

**5/1** Jallaaf (USA), **6/1** Just You Dare (IRE)(op 4/1), Final Frontier (IRE), **8/1** MR NEVERMIND (IRE), Daring Past, **9/1** Regalsett(op 6/1), **10/1** Garp (FR), Coppot Tel (IRE), **12/1** Tajarib (IRE), Strike-a-Pose, **20/1** War Requiem (IRE), Homemaker, Cashable, Villavina, **33/1**·Ors. CSF £154.93, CT £1,361.76. Tote £7.00: £2.40 £9.50 £4.60 £1.80 (£143.60). Mr K. Higson (EPSOM) bred by Robert Corridan in Ireland. 17 Rn    1m 23.6 (3.6)
SF—13/12/35/18/5/31

---

**3509**      FINAL SPRINT STKS (Mdn 3-Y.O) £2070.00 (£570.00: £270.00)     **5f 59y**   3-50 (3-52)

3252³ **Batchworth Bound (55)** *(EAWheeler)* 8-9 MRoberts (5) (5th st: rdn over 1f out: led ins fnl f: r.o wl) ...................................................................... —**1**
3294⁵ Tommy Tempest **(44)** *(KRBurke)* 9-0 AShoults (7) (4th st: ev ch ins fnl f: unable qckn) ...................................................................................... 2.**2**
*3374* Night Gown **(41)** (v) *(MissGayKelleway)* 8-2 ‡⁷MGodsafe (1) (b: b.hind: led 4f out: hrd rdn over 1f out: hdd ins fnl f: one pce) ............... hd.**3**
3119⁴ Indica (USA) **(Fav)** *(JHMGosden)* 8-9 SCauthen (6) (swtg: 6th st: hrd rdn 2f out: one pce) ............................................................................. 2.**4**
2909 Jaromic **(50)** *(PFTulk)* 9-0 BRaymond (3) (b: lw: led 1f: 3rd st: wknd over 2f out) 6.**5**
3257 Hazy Shades **(31)** *(JJBridger)* 8-9 JQuinn (2) (2nd st: hrd rdn wl over 1f out: sn wknd) .................................................................................. d.h.**5**

**5/4** Indica (USA), **2/1** BATCHWORTH BOUND, **11/2** Tommy Tempest(op 12/1), **12/1** Jaromic(op 8/1), Night Gown, **33/1** Hazy Shades. CSF £12.00, Tote £2.90: £1.60 £2.60 (£6.80). Mrs Diana Price (LAMBOURN) bred by Mrs D. Price. 6 Rn                63.8 sec (3.5)
SF—15/12/-/-/-/-

---

**3510**      SALTDEAN H'CAP (0-70) £2868.00 (£798.00: £384.00)     **1m 1f 209y**   4-20 (4-22)

3221 **Mayaasa (USA) (55)** *(RWArmstrong)* 3–8-13 RHills (4) (2nd st: led ins fnl f: rdn out) ........................................................................................ —**1**
3097 Latour **(51)** *(CEBrittain)* 4–9-1 MRoberts (6) (5th & c stands' side st: hrd rdn 3f out: r.o ins fnl f) ................................................................ 1¹/₂.**2**
3403* Mahong **(58)** *(MrsHParrott)* 4–9-8 (5x) JWilliams (12) (gd hdwy over 1f out: r.o wl ins fnl f) ....................................................................... 1.**3**
3487* Tendresse (IRE) **(32)** **(Fav)** *(CJHill)* 4–7-10 TyroneWilliams (11) (hrd rdn over 2f out: hdwy over 1f out: ev ch ins fnl f: unable qckn) ............ s.h.**4**
3256 Sky Train (IRE) **(65)** *(JLDunlop)* 3–9-9 AMunro (18) (led over 8f) ...................... 7.**5**
3306 Glacial Moon (USA) **(60)** *(BWHills)* 3–9-4 SCauthen (19) (hdwy over 2f out: led over 1f out tl ins fnl f: sn wknd) .................................................. 1¹/₂.**6**
3256⁴ Full Quiver **(49)** (v) *(MrsBarbaraWaring)* 7–8-13 NHowe (8) (hdwy 3f out: wknd over 1f out) ........................................................................... nk.**7**
3287 Edgeaway **(56)** *(JWHills)* 3–9-0 TQuinn (9) (3rd st: wknd 2f out) ...................... 5.**8**
3140 Solid (IRE) **(50)** *(JRJenkins)* 4–9-0 SWhitworth (17) (lw: a mid div) ................. nk.**9**
3221 Sulli Boy (NOR) **(36)** *(MissBSanders)* 7–7-8⁽³⁾ FNorton (5) (4th st: hrd rdn over 2f out: wknd over 1f out) ...................................................... 1¹/₂.**10**
2955³ Shamshom Al Arab (IRE) **(36)** *(WCarter)* 4–8-0 DBiggs (1) (a mid div) ........... 1.**11**
1798⁵ Gerish (IRE) **(41)** *(JPearce)* 3–7-13 DaleGibson (3) (6th st: wknd over 2f out) .. 5.**12**
895⁵ Cordillero **(44)** *(AMoore)* 6-8-8 BRouse (15) (b: a bhd) ......................... 3¹/₂.**13**
3248⁵ Lady Marriott **(62)** *(LMCumani)* 4-9-12 LDettori (10) (a bhd) ...................... ³/₄.**14**
3403 Lord Neptune **(59)** *(MAJarvis)* 3–9-3 BRaymond (14) (hdwy fnl 3f) ............... 2¹/₂.**15**
3159 Kelimutu **(41)** (bl) *(CFWall)* 3–7-13 GBardwell (16) (prom 5f) ...................... 10.**16**
*1550* Vague Nancy (IRE) **(34)** *(CJHill)* 4-7-12 NAdams (13) (a bhd) ...................... 4.**17**
3245 Paradise Forum **(54)** *(CAHorgan)* 3–8-12 JQuinn (20) (a bhd) ...................... 2.**18**
831 Rock Legend **(56)** *(DShaw)* 4–9-6 GCarter (2) (a bhd) ............................. 4.**19**

**15/8** Tendresse (IRE), **7/1** Glacial Moon (USA), **15/2** Shamshom Al Arab (IRE), **10/1** Mahong, Lady Marriott(op 6/1), **14/1** Sky Train (IRE), Full Quiver(op 8/1), Latour, **16/1** Solid (IRE), **20/1** Edgeaway, **25/1** Sulli Boy (NOR), **33/1** MAYAASA (USA) & Ors. CSF £392.97, CT £4,401.50. Tote £46.90: £4.90 £2.40 £2.00 £1.60 (£72.50). Mr Hamdan Al-Maktoum (NEWMARKET) bred by Shadwell Estate Co in USA. 19 Rn    2m 2.1 (4.1)
SF—48/47/52/25/38/30

---

**3511**      EASTBOURNE H'CAP (0-70) £2805.00 (£780.00: £375.00)     **6f 209y**   4-50 (4-51)

3183 **Duty Sergeant (IRE) (45)** (bl) *(MPMuggeridge)* 3–8-0 AMunro (8) (swtchd rt & hdwy 2f out: led 1f out: r.o wl) ................................................. —**1**
3370 Across the Bay **(69)** (v) *(SDow)* 5–9-11 ‡³FNorton (14) (hdwy 2f out: ev ch 1f out: unable qckn) ...................................................................... 4.**2**

3417　Ler Cru (IRE) **(61)** (bl) *(CEBrittain)* 3–9-2 MRoberts (13) (lw: led 2f: 3rd st: one
　　　　pce fnl 2f) ................................................................... s.h.3

3317[2]　Charmed Knave **(55)** *(DRLaing)* 7–9-0 TyroneWilliams (15) (hdwy 3f out: one
　　　　pce fnl 2f) ................................................................... ¹⁄₂.4

3278[2]　Fay's Song (IRE) **(69)** *(RAkehurst)* 4–9-7 ‡7LCarter (9) (4th st: led over 1f out: sn
　　　　hdd: one pce) ................................................................... 2.5

3359　Super Serenade **(69)** *(GBBalding)* 3–9-10　SCauthen (10) (lw: nvr nr to chal) ...... ¹⁄₂.6

3421★　Genuine Lady **(52)** *(APJarvis)* 4–8-11 (5x)　TQuinn (5) (led 5f out: edgd rt over 2f
　　　　out: hdd over 1f out: sn wknd) ................................................... s.h.7

3400　Amethystine (USA) **(64)** *(RJHodges)* 6–9-2 ‡7SDrowne (7) (5th st: wknd over 1f
　　　　out) ................................................................... 1¹⁄₂.8

3391[5]　Martinosky **(63)** *(WGRWightman)* 6–9-8　JWilliams (16) (nvr nrr) ................ 1¹⁄₂.9

3365　Mainly Me **(60)** *(PTWalwyn)* 3–9-1　LDettori (18) (nvr nrr) ................ s.h.10

3176　Nordansk **(45)** *(LJHolt)* 3–8-0　NAdams (1) (2nd st: ev ch 2f out: wknd over 1f
　　　　out) ................................................................... 1¹⁄₂.11

3355[5]　Teanarco (IRE) **(Fav)** *(RJHolder)* 4–9-8　GDuffield (6) (outpcd) ................ ³⁄₄.12

3422★　Precious Air (IRE) **(56)** *(AMoore)* 4–9-1 (5x)　BRouse (17) (bhd fnl 2f) ........ ¹⁄₂.13

3153　Wafi (USA) **(52)** *(BHanbury)* 3–8-7　BRaymond (2) (6th st: wknd 2f out) ......... 3.14

3290　Sure Shot Norman **(46)** *(JSutcliffe)* 3–8-1　DBiggs (11) (lw: hdwy 3f out: wknd 2f
　　　　out) ................................................................... 1¹⁄₂.15

　　　　Lady Snooble **(39)** *(KOCunningham-Brown)* 5–7-12　NCarlisle (12) (bhd fnl 4f) ¹⁄₂.16

2804　Super Heights **(54)** (bl) *(MissAJWhitfield)* 4–8-8 ‡5ATucker (3) (lw: a bhd) ...... hd.17

**4/1** Teanarco (IRE), **8/1** Amethystine (USA), Super Serenade, Precious Air (IRE), Charmed Knave, **10/1** Fay's
Song (IRE), **11/1** Martinosky, Ler Cru (IRE), Sure Shot Norman, **12/1** Genuine Lady, **16/1** Mainly Me, Across the
Bay, DUTY SERGEANT (IRE), **20/1** Wafi (USA), Lady Snooble, **33/1** Ors. CSF £245.33, CT £2,681.57. Tote
£23.70: £4.10 £6.30 £2.30 £1.90 (£483.30). Mr W. R. Mann (MARLBOROUGH) bred by Hibernia Farm in
Ireland. 17 Rn　　　　　　　　　　　　　　　　　　　　　　　　　　　　　1m 22.5 (2.5)
　　　　　　　　　　　　　　　　　　　　　　　　　　　　　SF—38/51/41/37/38/39
　　　　　　　　　　　　　　　　　　　　　　　　　　　　　　　　　　　　　AK

T/Plpt: £36.80 (74.98 Tckts).

3023—**NEWCASTLE (L-H)**
**Tuesday, September 29th [Heavy]**
Going Allowance: St: 0.30 sec per fur (G); Rnd 0.60 sec per fur (Y)　　　Wind: almost nil

Stalls: high

**3512**　　E.B.F. PRINCES STKS (Mdn 2-Y.O) £2553.00 (£708.00: £339.00)　**1m**　2-00 (2-05)

3289[6]　**Yeltsin** *(HRACecil)* 9-0　WRyan (8) (lw: hld up: hdwy over 2f out: shkn up to ld cl
　　　　home: cleverly) ................................................................... —1

　　　　Bin Ajwaad (IRE) *(BHanbury)* 9-0　WRSwinburn (12) (w'like: scope: bit bkwd:
　　　　trckd ldrs: led over 1f out & qcknd: hdd & no ex nr fin) ...... nk.2

　　　　Araadh (USA) *(HThomsonJones)* 8-9　MHills (7) (leggy: scope: in tch: hdwy 3f
　　　　out: r.o fnl f: nrst fin) ................................................................... 3¹⁄₂.3

3320[2]　Ecu de France (IRE) **(86)** *(Fav)* *(JLDunlop)* 9-0　JReid (6) (hdwy 3f out: rdn 2f
　　　　out: styd on: nvr able to chal) ......................................... hd.4

3200[5]　Mountain High (FR) *(JGFitzGerald)* 9-0　KFallon (11) (cl up: led over 3f out tl
　　　　over 1f out: sn outpcd) ................................................................... 3¹⁄₂.5

3307[4]　Master Fiddler **(62)** *(EWeymes)* 9-0　GHind (4) (lw: prom tl outpcd fnl 2f) ......... 7.6

3030　Ranunculus *(JBerry)* 9-0　JCarroll (1) (plld hrd: chsd ldrs 5f: sn wknd) ............ 4.7

3307[6]　Never so Brave *(MissSEHall)* 9-0　NConnorton (10) (dwlt: sme hdwy 3f out: n.d) s.h.8

3030　Innocent Abroad (DEN) *(CBBBooth)* 8-9　GOldroyd (3) (hld up & bhd: nvr plcd
　　　　to chal) ................................................................... 1.9

　　　　Dancing Zena (IRE) *(MAJarvis)* 9-0　PaulEddery (9) (w'like: bkwd: mid div: shkn
　　　　up 3f out: n.d) ................................................................... 2¹⁄₂.10

2986　Hung Hing (IRE) *(JDBethell)* 9-0　DMcKeown (5) (plld hrd: hld up & bhd: n.d) s.h.11

2667　Blakeney Boy *(RRLamb)* 9-0　JFanning (2) (led tl over 3f out: wknd qckly: t.o) .... 12

**15/8** Ecu de France (IRE), **7/2** YELTSIN(2/1–4/1), **4/1** Mountain High (FR), **9/2** Bin Ajwaad (IRE), **10/1** Araadh
(USA)(op 6/1), **20/1** Dancing Zena (IRE), **33/1** Never so Brave, **50/1** Ors. CSF £18.71, Tote £4.00: £1.70 £1.70
£2.80 (£14.80). Sheikh Mohammed (NEWMARKET) bred by Cliveden Stud. 12 Rn　　　1m 48.49 (9.49)
　　　　　　　　　　　　　　　　　　　　　　　　　　　　　SF—30/29/13/17/6/–

**3513**　　NEWLANDS CLAIMING STKS (3-Y.0) £3054.00 (£912.00: £436.00: £198.00)
　　　　**1m**　　　　　　　　　　　　　　　　　　　　　　　2-30 (2-33)

3167★　**Stoproveritate (52)** *(SGNorton)* 8-1[(2)]　NConnorton (4) (hld up: hdwy on ins 3f
　　　　out: n.m.r & swtchd 2f out: led ins fnl f: r.o) ......................... —1

3374[2]　Gold Surprise (IRE) *(JGFitzGerald)* 8-5　KFallon (11) (cl up: led wl over 1f out tl
　　　　ins fnl f: no ex) ................................................................... 3¹⁄₂.2

3476 Milton Rooms (IRE) **(47)** (bl) *(CBBBooth)* 8-2⁽¹⁾ ACulhane (3) (s.i.s: gd hdwy appr st: one pce appr fnl f) ............................................... 4.3
3258* Dazzling Fire (IRE) **(64)** (Fav) *(BWHills)* 8-9 DHolland (8) (lw: led tl hdd wl over 1f out: sn outpcd) ................................................ 5.4
3170 Tancred Grange **(57)** (v) *(MissSEHall)* 8-7 PaulEddery (5) (a.p: styd on one pce fnl 2f) .......................................................... 1.5
3306 Ice Walk *(WJarvis)* 8-0 GHind (9) (hdwy 3f out: styd on one pce appr fnl f) ...... 1.6
3342⁴ Syke Lane **(40)** *(RMWhitaker)* 7-6⁽⁴⁾ ‡⁵NKennedy (16) (lw: hld up: effrt 3f out: nvr able to chal) ............................ 1½.7
3263 Toss the Dice **(51)** (bl) *(MAJarvis)* 8-3⁽²⁾ MHills (10) (cl up tl wknd 2f out) ........ hd.8
3386 Grand Fellow (IRE) **(55)** (v) *(JDBethell)* 8-3⁽²⁾ DMcKeown (7) (trckd ldrs: effrt 3f out: wknd 2f out) ................................ 6.9
3167 My Jersey Pearl (IRE) **(28)** *(DonEnricoIncisa)* 7-11 JakiHouston (2) (bhd fr ½-wy) ................................................ hd.10
3048 Bold Setko (IRE) **(57)** (bl) *(JMPEustace)* 8-7⁽¹⁾ MTebbutt (13) (bhd: effrt 3f out: n.d) ......................................... 1½.11
3263 Strangersinthenite **(38)** (v) *(JSWainwright)* 7-12 ‡³SMaloney (12) (chsd ldrs tl wknd 2f out) ........................................ ½.12
3479 Phil-Man **(45)** *(TFairhurst)* 7-12 JFanning (14) (in tch: rdn ent st: sn wknd) .. 3½.13
3386 Crimson Consort (IRE) **(33)** *(DonEnricoIncisa)* 7-7 ‡⁷ClaireBalding (1) (prom early: lost tch appr st) .............. 2.14
3466 Lombard Ocean **(53)** *(ABailey)* 9-1 WRyan (15) (a bhd) ............... 20.15
2984 Makeminemusic **(42)** (v) *(FWatson)* 8-0 LCharnock (6) (prom tl wknd qckly 3f out) .................................... 2½.16

**11/8** Dazzling Fire (IRE)(2/1—5/4), **13/2** Gold Surprise (IRE), **9/1** Tancred Grange, Syke Lane, **10/1** Toss the Dice, Bold Setko (IRE), STOPROVERITATE, **16/1** Grand Fellow (IRE), Ice Walk, **20/1** Lombard Ocean, **25/1** Phil-Man, **33/1** Milton Rooms (IRE), Strangersinthenite, **50/1** Ors. CSF £74.32, Tote £8.50: £2.30 £2.30 £14.30 (£20.20). Mr John D. Clark (BARNSLEY) bred by Dr and Mrs J. D. Royle. 16 Rn          1m 47.24 (8.24)
SF—36/29/14/6/1/–

---

**3514** NEWCASTLE MEMBERS SUBSCRIPTION H'CAP (0-100) £3557.50 (£1060.00: £505.00: £227.50)   **1m**                    3-00 (3-02)

(Weights raised 14 lb)

3349 Salda **(69)** *(RMWhitaker)* 3–9-3 MBirch (2) (mde most: wnt clr 3f out: jst hld on) —1
3192 Drummer Hicks **(74)** *(EWeymes)* 3–9-8 DMcKeown (3) (lw: hld up: stdy hdwy 2f out: r.o wl nr fin) ...................... s.h.2
3375* Skipper to Bilge **(67)** (Jt-Fav) *(MAJarvis)* 5–9-0 ‡5KRutter (4) (chsd ldrs: c wd st: outpcd 2f out: styd on wl fnl f) ...... ¾.3
3342² Sagebrush Roller **(70)** *(JWWatts)* 4–9-8 JReid (5) (lw: hld up & bhd: stdy hdwy 2f out: nt qckn ins fnl f) ...... 1½.4
3349 Tusky **(72)** *(MJCamacho)* 4–9-10 SMorris (1) (lw: cl up: c wd st: outpcd fnl 2f) . 4.5
3349³ Jubran (USA) **(70)** (Jt-Fav) *(MPNaughton)* 6–9-8 DHolland (6) (lw: racd wd thrght: w ldr tl rdn & btn 2f out) ...... 1½.6
Jim's Wish (IRE) **(58)** (bl) *(TAKCuthbert)* 4–8-10 SWebster (7) (racd wd: prom tl wknd 3f out) .............. 10.7

**7/2** Skipper to Bilge, Jubran (USA), **4/1** Sagebrush Roller, Drummer Hicks, **13/2** SALDA, **7/1** Tusky, **50/1** Jim's Wish (IRE). CSF £29.56, Tote £9.80: £2.20 £2.40 (£33.70). Mr E. R. Thomas (WETHERBY) bred by Newtownbarry House Stud. 7 Rn          1m 47.53 (8.53)
SF—48/52/42/54/35/28

---

**3515** NEWCASTLE UNIVERSITY TURF CLUB H'CAP (0-90) £3002.00 (£896.00: £428.00: £194.00)   **2m 19y**                    3-30 (3-32)

3158* **Prince Mercury (74)** *(JLDunlop)* 3–8-10 JReid (1) (trckd ldrs gng wl: led on bit ins fnl f: sn clr) ...................... —1
3351 Ambuscade (USA) **(52)** *(MrsGRReveley)* 6–8-0 KDarley (5) (lw: in tch: pushed along appr st: styd on wl fnl 3f: nrst fin) ..... 2½.2
3339⁶ Kausar (USA) **(58)** *(GMMoore)* 5–8-6 DMcKeown (4) (led: qcknd 3f out: hdd & no ex ins fnl f) ...................... s.h.3
3339⁵ Good Hand (USA) **(80)** *(JWWatts)* 6–10-0 MBirch (6) (lw: cl up tl lost pl appr st: styd on wl fnl 2f) ............ 2½.4
Hot Star **(52)** *(GMMoore)* 6–8-0 JLowe (3) (bhd: effrt appr st: styd on: no imp) . 4.5
3244³ Puritan (CAN) **(73)** *(GHarwood)* 3–8-9 AClark (2) (cl up tl wknd over 2f out) ...... 6.6
3352* Antiguan Flyer **(81)** (Fav) *(BWHills)* 3–9-3 PatEddery (9) (trckd ldrs: effrt 3f out: btn 2f out) .................... 1½.7
1466 Best Gun **(70)** *(CWCElsey)* 3–8-6 JCarroll (7) (in tch tl outpcd 5f out: n.d after) . 5.8
3351³ Aide Memoire (IRE) **(57)** *(CBBBooth)* 3–7-7 JFanning (8) (hdwy u.p appr st: wknd over 2f out) ................. 3½.9
LONG HANDICAP: Aide Memoire (IRE) 7-1.

**3/1** Antiguan Flyer, **7/2** PRINCE MERCURY, Ambuscade (USA), **4/1** Puritan (CAN), **11/1** Aide Memoire (IRE), **14/1** Good Hand (USA), **16/1** Best Gun, **25/1** Kausar (USA), **33/1** Hot Star. CSF £15.44, CT £238.02. Tote £4.00: £1.60 £1.60 £3.20 (£8.60). Duke of Marlborough (ARUNDEL) bred by The Duke of Marlborough. 9 Rn
3m 40.72 (15.22)
SF—40/27/32/51/19/22

## 3516
E.B.F. POLWARTH STKS (I) (Mdn 2-Y.O) £2343.00 (£648.00: £309.00)
**6f**
4-00 (4-03)

|  | | |
|---|---|---|
| **Spice and Sugar** (JDBethell) 8-9 JReid (3) (neat: trckd ldrs: nt clr run over 1f out: squeezed thro to ld cl home) | —1 |
| Louvre (FR) (MrsJCecil) 9-0 PaulEddery (5) (lw: unf: scope: s.i.s: sn in tch: rdn to ld wl ins fnl f: bmpd & ct cl home) | s.h.2 |
| 3343 Fortis Pavior (IRE) (RMWhitaker) 9-0 ACulhane (2) (cl up: led over 1f out: hrd rdn ins fnl f: edgd lft: nt qckn nr fin) | ½.3 |
| 3399 Dances With Gold (MJohnston) 8-9 DMcKeown (4) (hld up: effrt & swtchd over 1f out: styd on wl nr fin) | ½.4 |
| 3276³ Piston (IRE) (92) (Fav) (BHanbury) 9-0 WRSwinburn (1) (lw: led: rdn 2f out: hdd over 1f out: no ex) | nk.5 |

*Burntwood Lad (20/1) Withdrawn (lame at s) : not under orders*
*Stewards Enquiry: Obj. to Spice and Sugar by Eddery overruled.*

**1/2** Piston (IRE), **5/2** Louvre (FR), **10/1** SPICE AND SUGAR, **12/1** Dances With Gold, **20/1** Fortis Pavior (IRE). CSF £33.39, Tote £11.40: £2.10 £1.40 (£15.30). Mrs G. Fane (MIDDLEHAM) bred by Mrs G. Fane. 5 Rn
1m 17.94 (6.44)
SF—2/6/4/-/-/-

## 3517
E.B.F. POLWARTH STKS (II) (Mdn 2-Y.O) £2322.00 (£642.00: £306.00)
**6f**
4-30 (4-35)

|  | | |
|---|---|---|
| 3470² **Roger the Butler (IRE) (85)** (Fav) (MBell) 9-0 MHills (4) (lw: mde all: styd on u.p fnl f) | —1 |
| 2459 Soaking (BWHills) 9-0 PatEddery (5) (trckd ldrs: effrt over 1f out: hrd rdn: nt r.o) | 1½.2 |
| 3312 Larn Fort (TFairhurst) 9-0 JFanning (8) (chsd ldrs: outpcd over 1f out: styd on nr fin) | 1½.3 |
| 3410 Il Moro Di Venezia (IRE) (JLDunlop) 9-0 JReid (1) (a chsng ldrs: rdn & nt qckn appr fnl f) | hd.4 |
| 2842 New Kid in Town (NTinkler) 9-0 LCharnock (7) (outpcd tl styd on fnl f: n.d) | 3.5 |
| Cannon Carew (DMoffatt) 8-7 ‡7DarrenMoffatt (2) (w'like: unf: dwlt: wl bhd tl styd on fnl f) | 1.6 |
| 2636 Cicerone (PCalver) 9-0 GHind (3) (chsd ldrs tl wknd over 1f out) | ½.7 |
| Ashgore (MJohnston) 9-0 DMcKeown (6) (str: bit bkwd: s.i.s: sn wl bhd: t.o) | 15.8 |

**8/13** ROGER THE BUTLER (IRE), **5/2** Soaking, **12/1** Ashgore(op 8/1), Il Moro Di Venezia (IRE)(op 8/1), **33/1** Larn Fort, **40/1** New Kid in Town, **50/1** Ors. CSF £2.56, Tote £1.60: £1.10 £1.20 £2.50 (£1.70). Mr M. B. Hawtin (NEWMARKET) bred by Gaberson Ltd in Ireland. 8 Rn
1m 18.38 (6.88)

## 3518
LONGBENTON H'CAP (0-75) £2490.00 (£690.00: £330.00)      **5f**
5-00 (5-02)

|  | | |
|---|---|---|
| 3318* **Cranfield Comet (65)** (Fav) (JBerry) 3-9-2 JCarroll (2) (hdwy far side 2f out: led 1f out: sn rdn clr) | —1 |
| 3481⁴ Yours Or Mine (IRE) (48) (DWChapman) 4-8-1 NConnorton (9) (cl up: led stands' side over 2f out: kpt on u.p) | 1½.2 |
| 3304 Loft Boy (61) (bl) (JDBethell) 9-9-0 WRSwinburn (4) (lw: disp ld far side tl led 2f out: hdd 1f out: no ex) | 2.3 |
| 3413 Miss Aragon (47) (MissLCSiddall) 4-8-0 KDarley (6) (a in tch far side: rdn & one pce appr fnl f) | 2.4 |
| 3397 Absolution (75) (MPNaughton) 8-9-7 ‡7SWynne (1) (lw: disp ld far side 3f: rdn & one pce) | 1½.5 |
| 3341² B Grade (43) (JBalding) 7-7-3 ‡7ClaireBalding (3) (lw: bhd far side tl styd on fnl 2f) | 2½.6 |
| 3166* Supreme Desire (50) (ASmith) 4-8-3(4) SWebster (12) (chsd ldrs stands' side 3f: sn rdn & btn) | ½.7 |
| 3460 Amoureuse (IRE) (60) (THCaldwell) 4-8-11 CDwyer (5) (prom far side 3f) | nk.8 |
| 3153⁴ Kalar (46) (bl) (DWChapman) 3-7-11 SWood (11) (led stands' side tl over 2f out: sn wknd) | 3½.9 |
| 3400 Miss Shadowfax (59) (CNAllen) 3-8-3 ‡7GForster (10) (racd stands' side: n.d) | 1½.10 |
| 3355 Meeson Times (55) (BEllison) 4-8-8 MHills (7) (swtchd far side after 1f: outpcd ½-wy) | nk.11 |
| 2987 Cottage Gallery (IRE) (40) (WAStephenson) 4-7-7 JLowe (8) (spd stands' side 3f: wknd qckly) | s.h.12 |

LONG HANDICAP: Cottage Gallery (IRE) 6-12.

9/2 CRANFIELD COMET, 5/1 Yours Or Mine (IRE), 6/1 B Grade, 7/1 Miss Aragon, Loft Boy, 10/1 Absolution, Supreme Desire, 11/1 Kalar, 12/1 Meeson Times, 20/1 Miss Shadowfax, 25/1 Ors. CSF £25.87, CT £140.79. Tote £5.30: £2.00 £1.40 £2.70 (£9.70). Cranfield Industries Limited (COCKERHAM) bred by J. R. C. and Mrs Wren. 12 Rn
62.03 sec (3.63)
SF—59/38/43/21/36/–

T/Plpt: £987.00 (3 Tckts).                                                                    AA

## 3093—SALISBURY (R-H)
### Wednesday, September 30th [Soft]
Going Allowance: 1st-3rd: 0.50 sec; Rest: 0.70 sec per fur (Y)                 Wind: slt against

Stalls: high

**3519**   MARLBOROUGH STKS (I) (Mdn 2-Y.O.C & G) £2637.00 (£732.00: £351.00)
           6f 212y                                                          2-25 (2-27)

3205 **Newton's Law (IRE)** (Fav) *(PWChapple-Hyam)* 9-0 JReid (5) (mde all: clr over
           1f out: comf) .................................................................................... —1
3240³ Law Commission *(DRCEIsworth)* 9-0 JWilliams (10) (hld up: chsd wnr over 1f
           out: no imp) ...................................................................................... 4.2
3130³ Baron Ferdinand *(RCharlton)* 9-0 RCochrane (16) (lw: hld up: bdly hmpd on ins
           over 4f out: hdwy & nt clr run 2f out: r.o ins fnl) .................................. 2¹/₂.3
           Top Rank *(JSMoore)* 9-0 BRouse (2) (unf: bit bkwd: hdwy 3f out: one pce fnl 2f) 1.4
2074⁴ Anniversaire *(BobJones)* 9-0 NDay (3) (prom: hrd rdn over 2f out: wknd over 1f
           out) ................................................................................................ 3.5
           Slivovitz *(MJHeaton-Ellis)* 9-0 WRyan (13) (w'like: hld up: hdwy over 2f out:
           wknd over 1f out) ............................................................................ ³/₄.6
3402⁴ Sylvania (IRE) *(RHannon)* 9-0 BRaymond (15) (lw: no hdwy fnl 2f) .............. 3¹/₂.7
           Special Dawn (IRE) *(JLDunlop)* 9-0 AMcGlone (6) (scope: lw: nvr nrr) .............. nk.8
3320 Sir Thomas Beecham *(SDow)* 9-0 MPerrett (11) (n.d) .............................. s.h.9
           Mujawab *(HThomsonJones)* 9-0 RHills (8) (unf: bit bkwd: prom over 4f) ........ ¹/₂.10
2826 Hohne Garrison *(JWhite)* 9-0 DaleGibson (9) (a bhd) ............................. 7.11
3372 Bang on Time *(GBBalding)* 9-0 AMunro (12) (bhd fnl 3f) .......................... 2.12
2544 Boxboy *(KOCunningham-Brown)* 9-0 SWhitworth (14) (prom over 3f) ............. 1.13
           Damask Steel (IRE) *(IABalding)* 9-0 GCarter (7) (cmpt: plld hrd: rdn 3f out: mid
           div whn hmpd over 2f out) ................................................................ 2.14
           Genio *(DSasse)* 8-9 ‡⁵RPrice (1) (wl grwn: bit bkwd: dwlt: a bhd: t.o) ......... 7.15
3289 Time Honored (USA) *(SirMarkPrescott)* 9-0 GDuffield (4) (prom over 4f: t.o) .... 4.16

7/4 NEWTON'S LAW (IRE), 2/1 Baron Ferdinand, 15/2 Law Commission(op 5/1), 10/1 Sylvania (IRE), 14/1 Mujawab(op 8/1), 20/1 Special Dawn (IRE), Damask Steel (IRE), 25/1 Ors. CSF £14.93, Tote £3.10: £1.30 £1.70 £1.50 (£7.30). Mr R. E. Sangster (MARLBOROUGH) bred by Ron Con Ltd in Ireland. 16 Rn
1m 33.80 (8.10)
SF—31/19/11/8/–/–/

**3520**   FONTHILL H'CAP (0-70) £3517.50 (£980.00: £472.50)   **1m**      2-55 (3-00)

3427 **Lahoob (USA)** (66) *(BHanbury)* 3-9-6 BRaymond (12) (gd hdwy over 1f out:
           str run to ld last stride) .................................................................... —1
3203 Gold Blade (57) *(NAGraham)* 3-8-11 RCochrane (5) (lw: hld up: hdwy & nt clr
           run over 2f out: led wl over 1f out: hdd last stride) ............................... s.h.2
3363 Ghurrah (IRE) (61) *(CJBenstead)* 3-9-1 RHills (9) (lw: hrd rdn & hdwy 2f out: r.o
           one pce fnl f) .................................................................................. 2.3
2492 Master of the Rock (60) *(PJMakin)* 3-9-0 TSprake (4) (lost pl 3f out: rallied 2f
           out: one pce fnl f) ........................................................................... nk.4
3317 Mossy Rose (57) *(LordHuntingdon)* 6-9-1 AMunro (3) (lw: hdwy over 2f out:
           wknd over 1f out) ............................................................................ 6.5
3249⁴ Gachette (58) *(JSutcliffe)* 3-8-12 BRouse (7) (prom: led wl over 1f out: sn hdd
           & wknd) .......................................................................................... 2¹/₂.6
3488 Sareen Express (IRE) (46) *(MrsJCDawe)* 4-8-4 AClark (13) (prom over 6f) ....... ³/₄.7
3288* Saifan (60) (bl) *(DMorris)* 3-8-9 ‡⁵StephenDavies (6) (lw: prom over 5f) ....... s.h.8
3370 Swift Romance (IRE) (57) *(BRMillman)* 4-9-1 GBardwell (17) (b: lw: a mid div) . ¹/₂.9
3421⁶ Black Jewel (50) (v) *(MDIUsher)* 9-8-8⁽²⁾ MWigham (10) (nvr nrr) ............... hd.10
3135 Mariette Larkin (52) *(GBBalding)* 3-8-6 JWilliams (1) (nvr trbld ldrs) ........... 1.11
1947 Mulciber (70) *(GHarwood)* 4-10-0 MPerrett (16) (prom 4f) ..................... 1.12
3095⁶ Acara (IRE) (56) *(CJames)* 3-8-10 DaleGibson (18) (prom 6f) .................. ¹/₂.13
3416 Spanish Glory (56) (bl) *(KOCunningham-Brown)* 3-8-10 JReid (2) (lw: prom:
           led over 2f out tl wknd wl over 1f out) ................................................ ¹/₂.14
2828 Dominant Force (50) (bl) *(RHannon)* 3-8-4 AMcGlone (15) (led over 4f) ........ ³/₄.15
3119⁵ Quixotic (56) *(PWHarris)* 3-8-10 WRyan (11) (prom: rdn 3f out: wknd over 1f
           out) .............................................................................................. 3¹/₂.16

626 Knockavon (62) *(RJBaker)* 4–9-6 NHowe (14) (bhd fnl 4f: t.o fnl 2f) ............... 20.**17**
3387 *Affa (14/1) Withdrawn (kicked at s) : not under orders*

**11/2** Mossy Rose, **7/1** LAHOOB (USA), **9/1** Gold Blade(12/1—14/1), **10/1** Gachette, Saifan, Ghurrah (IRE), **14/1** Acara (IRE), Swift Romance (IRE), **16/1** Dominant Force, Black Jewel, **20/1** Mulciber, Quixotic, Mariette Larkin, **25/1** Spanish Glory, Sareen Express (IRE), Master of the Rock, **33/1** Knockavon. CSF £57.94, CT £500.10. Tote £6.60: £2.10 £1.90 £2.30 £6.50 (£41.30). Mr B. Hanbury (NEWMARKET) bred by Pillar Stud Incorporated in USA. 17 Rn                                                                                       1m 50.87 (11.57)

## 3521
HURDLERS CLAIMING STKS (3-Y.O) £3817.50 (£1140.00: £545.00: £247.50)
**1m 1f 209y**                                                                    3-25 (3-27)

1758* Her Honour (Fav) *(LordHuntingdon)* 8-10 JReid (7) (hld up: stdy hdwy 4f out:
 led on bit over 2f out: rdn out) ................................................ —**1**
1986* Chief of Staff (75) *(PFICole)* 9-7 AMunro (6) (lw: dwlt: hdwy 5f out: rdn over 2f
 out: r.o one pce) ............................................................. 3½.**2**
3270 Karamoja (69) *(NAGraham)* 8-9 RCochrane (1) (lw: bhd: rdn 4f out: hdwy over
 2f out: r.o one pce fnl f) ..................................................... 5.**3**
3259⁶ Roxy River *(RHannon)* 7-12 AMcGlone (5) (lw: rdn & hdwy 2f out: nvr nr to chal) .... 3.**4**
3254² Bel Baraka (IRE) (56) *(DRCEisworth)* 8-8 JWilliams (10) (lw: plld hrd: led 9f out:
 sn clr: hdd & wknd over 2f out) ............................................... 3.**5**
3259 Miss Marigold *(RJHodges)* 8-6 TSprake (8) (a bhd: t.o) ......................... 12.**6**
2254 Lily Moreton *(MJHeaton-Ellis)* 7-12 DaleGibson (3) (lw: led 1f: wknd over 4f out:
 t.o) ......................................................................... 10.**7**
3288⁵ J'Arrive (50) *(JPearce)* 7-10 GBardwell (9) (lw: prom 5f) ....................... ½.**8**
3403² Eiras Mood (55) *(BPalling)* 7-13(4) ‡$StephenDavies (2) (prom over 6f: t.o) ...... 2½.**9**
 Daring Trouble *(GFHCharles-Jones)* 9-0 EMcKinley (4) (w'like: bit bkwd: a
 bhd: t.o) .................................................................... 3½.**10**

**9/4** HER HONOUR, **5/2** Karamoja, **8/1** Roxy River, **9/1** Chief of Staff(op 6/1), **10/1** Eiras Mood, Bel Baraka (IRE), **12/1** J'Arrive, **25/1** Daring Trouble, **33/1** Ors. CSF £20.92, Tote £2.80: £1.70 £2.40 £1.30 (£5.70). Mr Jocelyn Hambro (WEST ILSLEY) bred by Waverton Farm (Stow). 10 Rn; Her Honour clmd D Pipe £15,501
2m 14.97 (10.27)
SF–43/47/25/8/12/–

## 3522
DAMERHAM H'CAP (0-70) £3652.00 (£1096.00: £528.00: £244.00)
**1½m**                                                                           3-55 (3-58)

3279* Bo Knows Best (IRE) (55) (Fav) *(JSutcliffe)* 3-8-5 BRouse (18) (lw: hld up:
 stdy hdwy to ld 2f out: shkn up wl ins fnl f: r.o wl) ......................... —**1**
2631⁴ Pride of Britain (CAN) (43) *(LGCottrell)* 3-7-7 NCarlisle (14) (lw: a.p: led 4f out
 to 2f out: hrd rdn: r.o wl) ................................................... ½.**2**
2934 Altermeera (58) *(MrsBarbaraWaring)* 4–9-2 NHowe (20) (hrd rdn & hdwy fnl 2f:
 r.o) ......................................................................... 5.**3**
3248² Athar (IRE) (64) *(RJBaker)* 3–9-0 RCochrane (11) (lw: hdwy over 4f out: one
 pce fnl 2f) .................................................................. s.h.**4**
3279 L'Uomo Classics (65) *(RRowe)* 5–9-9 GBaxter (4) (a.p: no hdwy fnl 2f) ........... nk.**5**
3387⁴ Esprit Fort (USA) (60) *(PWChapple-Hyam)* 3–8-10 JReid (3) (no hdwy fnl 2f) ..... 1.**6**
3158³ Thor Power (IRE) (44) (v) *(DTThom)* 3-7-1 ‡7KimMcDonnell (2) (hdwy over 6f
 out: wknd over 2f out) ....................................................... 10.**7**
2934 Hazaaf (USA) (60) (v) *(AAScott)* 3–8-10 BRaymond (15) (b: b.nr hind: lw: prom:
 rdn 3f out: wknd 2f out) ..................................................... 2.**8**
3263* Telephus (56) *(MJcMath)* 3–8-4 EJohnson (8) (n.d) ............................. 1½.**9**
3279⁶ Viaggio (50) *(JAkehurst)* 4–8-8 JWilliams (10) (n.d) ........................... 1.**10**
 Tomahawk (68) *(RJHolder)* 5–9-12 GDuffield (13) (lw: n.d) ..................... nk.**11**
3221² Rocquaine Bay (43) *(MJBolton)* 5–8-1 GCarter (17) (swtg: bhd most of wy) ...... s.h.**12**
3316 Erlemo (44) (bl) *(CJBenstead)* 3-7-1 ‡7AntoinetteArmes (19) (lw: hdwy 4f out:
 wknd over 2f out) ........................................................... 7.**13**
3114 Alif (IRE) (64) *(JLDunlop)* 3–9-0 RHills (5) (prom: rdn 5f out: wknd 3f out) ..... 1½.**14**
3351 Super Ritchart (42) *(BPalling)* 4–8-0 NAdams (6) (lw: reminders after 1f: a bhd) 5.**15**
3094³ Heniu (USA) (66) *(LordHuntingdon)* 3–9-2 AMunro (9) (t.o) ...................... 2.**16**
3104* Charmed Life (73) *(ABarrow)* 3–9-9 WRyan (12) (b.nr fore: lw: t.o) ............. s.h.**17**
 Grundonian (54) *(CAHorgan)* 4–8-12 AMcGlone (1) (t.o) ....................... nk.**18**
3221⁶ Miss Witch (47) *(HCandy)* 4–8-5 CRutter (16) (led 8f: t.o) ..................... 3½.**19**
 Imperial Flight (47) *(JSKing)* 7–8-5 GBardwell (7) (t.o) ...................... 2.**20**

**5/2** BO KNOWS BEST (IRE), **6/1** Telephus, **7/1** Athar (IRE), **11/1** Rocquaine Bay, **12/1** Pride of Britain (CAN), **14/1** Heniu (USA), Esprit Fort (USA), **16/1** Hazaaf (USA), Viaggio, Miss Witch, **20/1** L'Uomo Classics, Charmed Life, Thor Power (IRE), Alif (IRE), **25/1** Altermeera, Grundonian, Erlemo, **33/1** Tomahawk, Super Ritchart, **50/1** Imperial Flight. CSF £34.98, CT £627.84. Tote £3.00: £1.50 £2.40 £8.80 £1.70 (£24.30). Mr John Sutcliffe (EPSOM) bred by Gay O'Callaghan in Ireland. 20 Rn                               2m 45.11 (12.51)
SF–50/36/49/46/54/39

**3523** MARLBOROUGH STKS (II) (Mdn 2-Y.O.C & G) £2637.00 (£732.00: £351.00)
**6f 212y** 4-25 (4-27)

**Moorish** *(PFICole)* 9-0 AMunro (11) (unf: hld up: hdwy 2f out: led ins fnl f: r.o
wl) —1
3276 Captain Jack *(LMCumani)* 9-0 BRaymond (8) (lw: a.p: ev ch 1f out: nt qckn) .. 3½.2
30914 Embankment (IRE) *(85)* (Fav) *(RHannon)* 9-0 RHills (10) (plld hrd: a.p: led 2f
out: hung lft over 1f out: hung rt & hdd ins fnl f) 1.3
Chippendale Ladd (CAN) *(PWChapple-Hyam)* 9-0 JReid (16) (leggy: rdn &
hdwy 2f out: r.o one pce fnl f) 1.4
2696 Davrob *(BPalling)* 9-0 GCarter (12) (prom: hrd rdn & wknd over 1f out) 6.5
32625 Fourforfun *(RHannon)* 9-0 BRouse (7) (nvr nr to chal) ¾.6
Greenbank (USA) *(IABalding)* 9-0 RCochrane (14) (leggy: lw: prom 5f) 1½.7
3314 Don Tocino *(JLDunlop)* 9-0 AClark (4) (hdwy 3f out: wknd over 1f out) ½.8
The Where Withal *(SirMarkPrescott)* 9-0 GDuffield (6) (unf: scope: hdwy 3f out:
wknd over 1f out) 1.9
32766 Son of Sharp Shot (IRE) *(JLDunlop)* 9-0 AMcGlone (13) (led tl hdd & bmpd 3f
out) 3.10
32624 Ok Bertie *(DMorris)* 9-0 MTebbutt (9) (plld hrd: a.p: led 3f out to 2f out: sn wknd) s.h.11
3320 Fitzroy Lad *(MRChannon)* 9-0 GBardwell (5) (bhd fnl 3f) 4.12
3372 Jewel Thief *(GBBalding)* 9-0 JWilliams (15) (a bhd) 3.13
Dontdressfordinner *(DRTucker)* 9-0 NAdams (3) (unf: t.o) 5.14
3262 Legal Artist (IRE) *(NAGraham)* 9-0 WRyan (1) (lw: dwlt: t.o) 10.15
Amazing Air (USA) *(DRCElsworth)* 8-7 ‡7JHunter (2) (leggy: scope: dwlt: rdn
thrght: a bhd) 4.16

2/1 Embankment (IRE)(6/4—9/4), 9/2 Captain Jack(op 8/1), 7/1 Son of Sharp Shot (IRE), 9/2 Ok Bertie,
Greenbank (USA), 10/1 MOORISH, 14/1 Fourforfun(10/1—16/1), Chippendale Ladd (CAN), 20/1 Amazing Air
(USA), 25/1 The Where Withal, 33/1 Don Tocino, Fitzroy Lad, Jewel Thief, Legal Artist (IRE), 50/1 Ors. CSF
£53.85, Tote £11.20: £3.80 £2.00 £1.70 (£32.00). Mr Fahd Salman (WHATCOMBE) bred by Newgate Stud Co.
16 Rn 1m 35.59 (9.89)
SF—25/13/10/7/–/–

**3524** CRANBORNE H'CAP (0-70) £3272.50 (£910.00: £437.50) **6f** 4-55 (5-01)

2060 Will of Steel *(68)* *(HCandy)* 3-9-2 ‡7AntoinetteArmes (16) (a.p: led 1f out: r.o wl) —1
3101 Sir Joey (USA) *(50)* *(RJHolder)* 3-8-5 JWilliams (13) (lw: a.p: led over 2f out to
1f out: nt qckn) 2½.2
3413★ My Ruby Ring *(48)* *(DRLaing)* 5-8-6 (7x) TyroneWilliams (11) (b: rdn & hdwy
over 2f out: r.o one pce fnl f) hd.3
3183 Grey Charmer (IRE) *(53)* *(CJames)* 3-8-8 DaleGibson (15) (hdwy over 1f out:
r.o) ½.4
3220 Coppermill Lad *(47)* (Jt-Fav) *(LJHolt)* 9-7-12 ‡7CAvery (10) (lw: gd hdwy fnl f: fin
wl) s.h.5
3183 Efra *(62)* *(RHannon)* 3-9-3 BRaymond (19) (a.p: r.o one pce fnl f) s.h.6
3257 Unveiled *(58)* *(RJHodges)* 4-9-2 RCochrane (18) (lw: hdwy fnl f: r.o) s.h.7
3252 The New Girl *(51)* *(CCElsey)* 3-8-6 GDuffield (12) (swtg: hrd rdn over 1f out: no
hdwy) 1.8
3037 Leigh Crofter *(62)* (bl) *(RJHolder)* 3-8-10 ‡7SDrowne (7) (hdwy fnl f: nvr nrr) .... nk.9
3378★ Executive Spirit *(61)* *(DSasse)* 3-8-11 ‡5RPrice (1) (nvr nr to chal) 2½.10
2618 Respectable Jones *(70)* *(GBBalding)* 6-9-7 ‡7TraceyPursglove (8) (lw: w ldrs tl
wknd fnl f) ¾.11
30982 Face North (IRE) *(57)* (Jt-Fav) *(ARDavison)* 4-9-1 AMunro (14) (lw: bhd fnl 2f) ½.12
3196 Lady Sabo *(66)* *(GLewis)* 3-9-0 ‡7BRussell (6) (hdwy over 2f out: wknd over 1f
out) 5.13
3264 Harry's Coming *(65)* *(RJHodges)* 8-9-9 TSprake (9) (bhd fnl 2f) ½.14
32963 Ayr Raider *(65)* (bl) *(WRMuir)* 5-9-9 JReid (5) (lw: a bhd) 3.15
32962 Face the Future *(59)* *(PWHarris)* 3-9-0 WRyan (17) (a bhd) nk.16
3185 Roxy Music (IRE) *(50)* (bl) *(KOCunningham-Brown)* 3-8-5 NCarlisle (2) (lw: led
over 3f) 3½.17
2942 Ushba (FR) *(57)* (v) *(CGCox)* 4-8-8 ‡7DWright (4) (s.s: sn rcvrd: wknd over 2f
out) 6.18

6/1 Face North (IRE), Coppermill Lad, 13/2 Ayr Raider, 9/1 Face the Future, My Ruby Ring(12/1—8/1), 11/1
Lady Sabo, 12/1 Sir Joey (USA), 16/1 Ushba (FR), WILL OF STEEL, Unveiled, 20/1 Ors. CSF £179.67, CT £1,659.02. Tote £32.80: £5.70 £3.70 £1.60 £8.60
(£183.80). Mr P. Robinson (WANTAGE) bred by Dunchurch Lodge Stud Co. 18 Rn 1m 21.16 (8.86)
SF—9/–/–/–/–/–

T/Plpt: £50.10 (52 Tckts). KH

3003—**NEWMARKET (R-H)** Rowley Mile
## Wednesday, September 30th [Good]
Going Allowance: minus 0.30 sec per fur (F)

Wind: slt bhd

Stalls: low

**3525**  SOLTYKOFF STKS (Mdn 2-Y.O.C & G) £4893.00 (£1464.00: £702.00: £321.00)
**1m**  1-30 (1-33)

**Armiger** (HRACecil) 9-0 PatEddery (6) (gd sort: scope: a.p: led 3f out: clr fnl f: comf) ....................................................... —1
32004 Zind (IRE) (Fav) (PWChapple-Hyam) 9-0 PRobinson (15) (a.p: rdn over 2f out: sn chsng wnr: no imp fnl f) ..................... 3½.2
Scotsman (IRE) (PFICole) 9-0 TQuinn (10) (leggy: scope: unf: chsd ldrs: swtchd lft over 2f out: kpt on same pce fnl f) ............ 4.3
33625 Jackpot Star (90) (RHannon) 9-0 LPiggott (7) (lw: hdwy 2f out: edgd rt fnl f: r.o) nk4.4
League Leader (IRE) (MRStoute) 9-0 WRSwinburn (13) (w'like: bkwd: prom tl wknd appr fnl f) ...................................... 2.5
34192 Spring to Action (IABalding) 8-11 ‡³SO'Gorman (17) (led 5f: no ex appr fnl f) .... ¾.6
3000 October Brew (USA) (GLewis) 9-0 DMcKeown (2) (hdwy over 2f out: nrst fin) 1½.7
Charlie Bigtime (MissGayKelleway) 9-0 GayKelleway (1) (w'like: b.hind: s.i.s: nvr nrr) ....................................................... nk.8
Shintillo (IRE) (LMCumani) 9-0 LDettori (8) (wl grwn: s.i.s: stdy hdwy fnl 2f: r.o) 2.9
32003 Cyrus the Bold (IRE) (BWHills) 9-0 MHills (5) (nvr nr to chal) .......................... 3.10
Gradient (MrsJCecil) 9-0 PaulEddery (12) (leggy: scope: dwlt: sn pushed along: n.d) ............................................... hd.11
General Mouktar (AHide) 9-0 WWoods (4) (w'like: scope: bit bkwd: a bhd) .. 3½.12
Collier Bay (JHMGosden) 9-0 DHolland (10) (gd sort: bit hkwd: s.i.s: sn rcvrd: wknd 3f out) ......................................... 2.13
·32026 Desert Challenger (IRE) (ACStewart) 9-0 MRoberts (3) (lw: chsd ldrs over 5f) 1½.14
Fashionable Dancer (CEBrittain) 9-0 JQuinn (14) (w'like: scope: trckd ldrs over 5f) ................................................ 2.15
3289 Barraak (MajorWRHern) 9-0 WCarson (11) (lw: n.d) ..................................... ½.16
Ikhtiraa (USA) (RWArmstrong) 9-0 BCrossley (9) (w'like: scope: prom 4f: wknd qckly) ................................................ 2.17

**9/4** Zind (IRE), **7/2** ARMIGER(5/2—4/1), **6/1** Cyrus the Bold (IRE)(op 4/1), **8/1** Spring to Action, **12/1** Scotsman (IRE)(8/1—14/1), Desert Challenger (IRE), **14/1** Shintillo (IRE), Gradient, **16/1** League Leader (IRE), Jackpot Star, Collier Bay, **20/1** Barraak, **50/1** Ors. CSF £12.55, Tote £4.00: £2.10 £1.70 £3.80 (£6.80). Mr K. Abdulla (NEWMARKET) bred by Juddmonte Farms. 17 Rn
1m 37.61 (0.31)
SF—60/49/37/36/30/25

**3526**  SHADWELL STUD APP'CE SERIES H'CAP (Final) (0-90) £6524.00 (£1952.00: £936.00: £428.00) **1¼m**  2-00 (2-03)

3475★ **Cold Shower (IRE) (68)** (JAGlover) 3-8-2 (5x) ‡³SSanders (5) (lw: chsd ldrs: rdn to ld wl ins fnl f) .......................... —1
33492 Forever Diamonds (68) (MHEasterby) 5-8-11 SMaloney (11) (a.p: led over 1f out: hdd & unable qckn wl ins fnl f) ................. 1½.2
3082 Hidden Laughter (USA) (76) (BWHills) 3-8-10 ‡³JTate (14) (lw: in tch: outpcd 3f out: styd on appr fnl f) ......................... 1.3
32345 Debacle (USA) (73) (GHarwood) 3-8-10 BDoyle (7) (lw: led tl over 1f out: kpt on) ...................................................... s.h.4
33706 Gilderdale (80) (JWHills) 10-9-9 NKennedy (1) (hld up: outpcd 3f out: hdwy & nt clr run 1f out: fin wl) ...................... 2½.5
3306★ Remany (65) (Fav) (JRFanshawe) 3-7-11 ‡⁵NVarley (12) (w ldrs: rdn & ev ch over 2f out: no ex appr fnl f) ................... s.h.6
33654 Sharp Dream (69) (BSmart) 4-8-12 ATucker (13) (hld up & bhd: hdwy 4f out: wknd appr fnl f) ................................ nk.7
2999 Virkon Venture (IRE) (68) (MHTompkins) 4-8-6 ‡⁵SMulvey (9) (hld up & bhd: hdwy 4f out: wandered 1f out: r.o) ............ hd.8
33465 Dovale (64) (WJarvis) 4-8-7 OPears (4) (lw: hdwy over 3f out) ........................ nk.9
Parking Bay (72) (GAPritchard-Gordon) 5-9-1 DHarrison (10) (chsd ldrs: rdn 3f out: no imp) .......................................... hd.10
32704 Avice Caro (USA) (83) (JHMGosden) 3-9-3 ‡³FArrowsmith (8) (nvr nr to chal) ½.11
30945 Scottish Bambi (70) (RHannon) 4-8-13 RPerham (15) (chsd ldrs 7f: wkng whn hmpd 1f out) .................................... 1½.12
3236★ Hamadryad (IRE) (85) (WCarter) 4-10-0 NGwilliams (2) (swtg: s.i.s: effrt over 3f out: wknd over 2f out) ...................... 2½.13
33112 Rival Bid (USA) (70) (MAJarvis) 4-8-13 KRutter (6) (a bhd) ............................. 7.14

2987 Dawn Success **(53)** *(DWChapman)* 6–7–10 DarrenMoffatt (3) (plld hrd: prom 6f: wknd & sddle slipped) ............................................................ 4.15
*Stewards Enquiry: Tucker suspended 9-11/10/92 (excessive use of whip).*

**7/2** Remany, **8/1** COLD SHOWER (IRE), **9/1** Rival Bid (USA), **10/1** Parking Bay, Forever Diamonds, Avice Caro (USA), **11/1** Hamadryad (IRE), **12/1** Gilderdale, Sharp Dream, **14/1** Scottish Bambi, **16/1** Virkon Venture (IRE), Debacle (USA), Dovale, **20/1** Hidden Laughter (USA), **25/1** Dawn Success. CSF £81.22, CT £1,424.96. Tote £6.10: £1.90 £2.30 £6.40 (£10.60). Claremont Management Services (WORKSOP) bred by Leinster Stud in Ireland. 15 Rn
2m 5.35 (2.75)
SF–31/37/34/32/40/13

---

## 3527

HUNTER PRICE PARTNERSHIP H'CAP (3-Y.O) (0-105) £6368.00 (£1904.00: £912.00: £416.00)    **1¼m**
2-35 (2-38)

2755⁵ Rose Elegance **(74)** *(WRMuir)* 7-9 ‡3FNorton (12) (lw: bhd: rdn over 2f out: r.o wl to ld wl ins fnl f) ........................................................ —1
583² Deer Hunt **(87)** *(PJMakin)* 8-11 TQuinn (3) (lw: chsd ldrs: ev ch over 1f out: rdn ins fnl f: r.o) .................................................... ¾.2
3192³ Jumaira Shark (CAN) **(79)** (v) *(JHMGosden)* 8-3 DHolland (8) (led tl wl ins fnl f: r.o) ............................................................................ hd.3
3270⁶ Sovereign Page (USA) **(74)** (bl) *(BHanbury)* 7-9 ‡3DHarrison (7) (in tch: effrt 2f out: kpt on fnl f: nt pce to chal) .................................. 1½.4
3270* Walimu (IRE) **(75)** *(CFWall)* 7-13 JLowe (1) (hld up: hdwy 3f out: one pce appr fnl f) ............................................................................ 1.5
3192 Touch Paper (USA) **(78)** (Fav) *(BWHills)* 8-2 MHills (6) (hdwy over 2f out: nvr able to chal) .................................................................. 2.6
3139⁵ Robingo (IRE) **(75)** (bl) *(CEBrittain)* 7-13 JQuinn (4) (stdd s: plld hrd & sn chsng ldrs: wknd 2f out) ............................................ 2.7
3292 Mamdooh **(92)** *(ACStewart)* 9-2 MRoberts (10) (h.d.w: plld hrd: prom: rdn 3f out: sn btn) .......................................................... ½.8
3292* Wild Fire **(86)** *(GWragg)* 8-10 WRSwinburn (9) (hld up: hdwy 5f out: no imp fnl 2f) ..................................................................... ½.9
3212 Wesaam (USA) **(92)** *(MajorWRHern)* 9-2 WCarson (11) (lw: hld up: effrt over 3f out: nvr rchd ldrs) ........................................ hd.10
1198 Well Saddled (IRE) **(87)** *(DRCEisworth)* 8-11 PRobinson (13) (a bhd) ............ 10.11
3346 Gong **(76)** *(PTWalwyn)* 8-0 DBiggs (2) (plld hrd: prom 6f) ............................ 4.12
3368⁵ Young Freeman (USA) **(97)** *(GHarwood)* 9-7 LDettori (5) (prom 7f: sn wknd) .. nk.13
*Stewards Enquiry: Norton suspended 9-12/10/92 (excessive use of whip).*

**4/1** Touch Paper (USA), **5/1** Jumaira Shark (CAN), **11/2** Wild Fire, **13/2** Mamdooh, **10/1** Deer Hunt, **12/1** Robingo (IRE), Walimu (IRE), **14/1** Sovereign Page (USA), Wesaam (USA), Well Saddled (IRE), **20/1** Young Freeman (USA), **33/1** ROSE ELEGANCE. CSF £298.63, CT £1,760.11. Tote £35.70: £6.40 £2.80 £2.30 (£413.80). Mr A. N. Miller (LAMBOURN) bred by E. A. Badger. 13 Rn
2m 3.67 (1.07)
SF–40/54/45/34/36/35

---

## 3528

ROUS STKS (listed race)    £10867.50 (£3240.00: £1545.00: £697.50) **5f**
3-05 (3-10)

3189³ Blyton Lad **(108)** *(MJCamacho)* 6-9-0 SWebster (8) (a.p: led ins fnl f: rdn & r.o wl) .................................................................................. —1
982⁴ Garah **(113)** *(HRACecil)* 3-8-6⁽²⁾ WRSwinburn (3) (hdwy centre 2f out: ev ch 1f out: r.o) ...................................................................... 1½.2
3361² Artistic Reef **(106)** *(GHEden)* 3-8-9 WCarson (12) (led over 4f: kpt on wl) .... ½.3
3437 Miss Nosey Parker (IRE) **(100)** *(RHannon)* 3-8-4 MRoberts (4) (dwlt: swtchd rt: hdwy centre 2f out: nt ex) ................................................ ¾.4
3189² Harvest Girl (IRE) **(106)** (Fav) *(GAPritchard-Gordon)* 3-8-5⁽¹⁾ LDettori (5) (chsd ldrs centre: rdn & btn over 1f out) .................................. 1.5
3189 Farfelu **(100)** (bl) *(WRMuir)* 5-8-11 TQuinn (7) (hld up: r.o appr fnl f: nt pce to chal) ................................................................................. nk.6
3437 Regal Scintilla **(93)** *(GBBalding)* 3-8-4 MHills (9) (dwlt: sn rcvrd: no imp appr fnl f) ....................................................................................... ¾.7
3356 Cantoris **(92)** *(RJRWilliams)* 6-8-6 DHolland (11) (outpcd tl styd on fnl f) ...... nk.8
3006 Bold Lez **(96)** *(MJHaynes)* 5-8-11 PRobinson (10) (lw: sn w ldr: wknd over 1f out) .................................................................................... ½.9
3356 Silca-Cisa **(93)** *(MRChannon)* 3-8-4 PaulEddery (2) (spd centre over 3f) ........ ¾.10
3189⁵ Medaille D'Or **(106)** (v) *(JWPayne)* 4-9-0 PatEddery (1) (led centre over 3f: sn rdn & btn) ............................................................................ 2½.11
3361 Power Lake **(100)** *(RHannon)* 3-8-9 LPiggott (6) (in tch centre 3f) ................... 4.12

**3/1** Harvest Girl (IRE), **11/2** Artistic Reef(op 7/2), **6/1** Garah(op 7/2), BLYTON LAD, **10/1** Farfelu(op 16/1), **11/1** Miss Nosey Parker (IRE), **12/1** Medaille D'Or, **16/1** Bold Lez, Silca-Cisa, **20/1** Cantoris, **25/1** Ors. CSF £38.48, Tote £7.00: £2.40 £2.30 £2.00 (£27.50). Mrs J. Addleshaw (MALTON) bred by Ballinacurra Stud. 12 Rn
58.46 sec (U.94)
SF–89/79/80/72/69/74/64

**3529**    TATTERSALLS CHEVELEY PARK STKS (Gp 1) (2-Y.O.F) £74998.50 (£26128.50: £12689.25: £5358.75)    **6f**    3-40 (3-41)

3227a★ **Sayyedati** (CEBrittain) 8-11 WRSwinburn (3) (lw: mde all: r.o wl appr fnl f) ........ —**1**
2851★ **Lyric Fantasy (IRE)** (Fav) (RHannon) 8-11 MRoberts (2) (w wnr: rdn 2f out: no
imp appr fnl f) ............................................................... 2.**2**
3210★ **Poker Chip** (IABalding) 8-11 MHills (4) (chsd ldrs: rdn & no imp fnl 2f) ......... 1½.**3**
3096⁵ **Anonymous** (CEBrittain) 8-11 LDettori (1) (lw: sn pushed along & outpcd) ........ 6.**4**

**1/2** Lyric Fantasy (IRE)(op 1/3), **5/2** SAYYEDATI, **9/1** Poker Chip, **50/1** Anonymous. CSF £3.96, Tote £3.20 (£1.40). Mr Mohamed Obaida (NEWMARKET) bred by Gainsborough Stud Management Ltd. 4 Rn
1m 11.82 (0.42)
SF–53/47/41/17

**3530**    E.B.F. NURSERY (F) £20387.50 (£6100.00: £2925.00: £1337.50)    **7f**    4-10 (4-15)

2910⁴ **Wynona (IRE) (90)** (GCBravery) 9-7 LDettori (16) (b.off hind: prom tl outpcd 3f
out: rapid hdwy over 1f out: str run to ld nr fin) ................... —**1**
3187 **No Reservations (IRE) (88)** (RFJohnsonHoughton) 9-0 ‡5JWeaver (11) (prom:
led 3f out tl ct nr fin) ........................................... ½.**2**
3199 **Home From the Hill (IRE) (76)** (MBell) 8-7 MHills (15) (b.nr hind: hdwy over 2f
out: styd on fnl f) .................................................. ½.**3**
3178★ **Instant Affair (USA) (84)** (PFiCole) 9-1 TQuinn (8) (hdwy over 2f out: r.o ins fnl f) s.h.**4**
3432 **Brockton Dancer (78)** (v) (RHannon) 8-9 LPiggott (10) (b: b.hind: hdwy 3f out:
ev ch over 1f out: one pce fnl f) ............................... ½.**5**
3115★ **Diskette (78)** (LordHuntingdon) 8-6 ‡3DHarrison (18) (styd on fnl 2f: nrst fin) ..... 1.**6**
3285² **Perdition (IRE) (65)** (Jt-Fav) (JWHills) 7-10 WCarson (6) (hdwy over 2f out: one
pce appr fnl f) ..................................................... hd.**7**
3440 **Seasonal Splendour (IRE) (82)** (GACyzer) 8-13 DMcKeown (19) (bhd tl sme
late hdwy) ......................................................... nk.**8**
1742★ **Chain Dance (87)** (MRStoute) 9-4 PatEddery (3) (lw: s.i.s: r.o fnl 2f: nrst fin) ..... ½.**9**
3187² **Hung Parliament (86)** (BWHills) 9-3 DHolland (9) (w ldrs tl wknd appr fnl f) ... s.h.**10**
3187³ **Spring Sunrise (67)** (Jt-Fav) (MBlanshard) 7-9 ‡3FNorton (7) (b: b.hind: nvr nr to
chal) ............................................................... ½.**11**
3347³ **Royal Diva (74)** (Jt-Fav) (MissSEHall) 8-5 GHind (13) (b: b.hind: nvr nr to chal) hd.**12**
3186³ **Yfool (76)** (JRFanshawe) 8-7 WRSwinburn (20) (prom 5f: sn wknd) ................ ½.**13**
3242★ **Kyrenia Game (70)** (PMitchell) 7-12 ‡3SO'Gorman (2) (sn rdn along: a bhd) .. hd.**14**
3366 **Where's the Dance (70)** (CEBrittain) 8-1 MRoberts (21) (led 4f: eased ins fnl f) 2.**15**
3303★ **Latest Flame (IRE) (79)** (MRChannon) 8-0 PaulEddery (17) (a bhd) ............... 4.**16**
3267⁵ **Royal Flex (USA) (68)** (MrsLPiggott) 7-13 JQuinn (14) (n.d) ....................... 2.**17**
3187 **Delta Downs (73)** (RHannon) 8-4 PRobinson (5) (n.d) ............................... 1.**18**
3286⁶ **Formaestre (IRE) (65)** (MHTompkins) 7-5(3) ‡5NKennedy (1) (rdn ½-wy: a bhd) hd.**19**
3286⁵ **Trundley Wood (73)** (GAPritchard-Gordon) 7-13 ‡5BDoyle (4) (lw: plld hrd: bhd
fnl 3f) .............................................................. 1½.**20**
3187⁴ **Heart Broken (81)** (JGFitzGerald) 8-12 KFallon (12) (in tch 4f: sn rdn & btn) ... ½.**21**
LONG HANDICAP: Formaestre (IRE) 7-6.

**8/1** Perdition (IRE), Spring Sunrise, Royal Diva, **10/1** Chain Dance, **12/1** Instant Affair (USA), Diskette(8/1—14/1), **14/1** Hung Parliament, **16/1** Home From the Hill (IRE), Brockton Dancer, WYNONA (IRE), Kyrenia Game, Where's the Dance, Trundley Wood, **20/1** Delta Downs, Heart Broken, Latest Flame (IRE), Yfool, No Reservations (IRE), **25/1** Royal Flex (USA), Formaestre (IRE). CSF £280.25, CT £4,658.73. Tote £21.60: £4.00 £6.40 £5.80 £3.90 (£302.00). Mrs M. Wyn Griffith (NEWMARKET) bred by Rathduff Stud in Ireland. 21 Rn
1m 26.16 (2.16)
SF–42/33/24/31/23/17

T/Trio: Race 3: £548.30 (2.1 Tckts). T/Jkpt: Not won; £12,155.72 to Newmarket 1/10/92. T/Plpt: £1,065.40 (6.29 Tckts).    Dk

# NEWMARKET (R-H) Rowley Mile
## Thursday, October 1st [Good]
Going Allowance: minus 0.30 sec per fur (F)    Wind: almost nil

Stalls: 1st, 2nd & 7th low, remainder high

**3531**    TAXI NEWS WESTLEY STKS (I) (Mdn 2-Y.O) £3850.00 (£1150.00: £550.00: £250.00)
**7f**    1-30 (1-34)

**Placerville (USA)** (Fav) (HRACecil) 9-0 PatEddery (17) (b: gd sort: scope: a w
ldrs: led 3f out: rdn & r.o wl) .................................... —**1**
**Storm Canyon (IRE)** (JHMGosden) 9-0 SCauthen (10) (w'like: scope: reard s:
hdwy ½-wy: chal 2f out: r.o) ................................... 1½.**2**

| 3362² | The Informer (USA) *(PFICole)* 9-0 AMunro (3) (slt ld 4f: rdn & r.o one pce) ..... 3½.3 |
| 3372 | Danny Boy *(RHannon)* 9-0 GDuffield (1) (lw: a chsng ldrs: effrt 3f out: styd on: nt pce to chal) .................................................... 3.4 |
| | Bohemian Crown (USA) *(MRStoute)* 9-0 PRobinson (2) (gd sort: bkwd: a in tch: n.m.r over 2f out: r.o one pce) .................................... 1.5 |
| | Miss Pimpernel *(BHanbury)* 8-9 MRoberts (6) (w'like: unf: w ldrs tl outpcd fnl 2f) ½.6 |
| | Al Senafi (IRE) *(LMCumani)* 9-0 LDettori (16) (neat: scope: s.s & swtchd lft: stdy hdwy & swtchd rt 3f out: nvr plcd to chal) ................... 1½.7 |
| | Pyrrhic Dance *(JWHills)* 9-0 MHills (5) (w'like: mid div: outpcd over 2f out: styd on nr fin) ................................................. 2½.8 |
| | Kardelle *(RCharlton)* 8-9 PaulEddery (7) (w'like: scope: in tch: effrt whn n.m.r over 2f out: n.d after) ..................................... s.h.9 |
| 3372 | Blushing Barada (USA) *(AAScott)* 8-9 WRSwinburn (8) (b.hind: prom tl edgd lft & wknd over 2f out) ............................................. s.h.10 |
| | Thaleros *(GHarwood)* 9-0 LPiggott (14) (wl grwn: s.s: bhd: hdwy ½-wy: wknd 2f out) ................................................................ ½.11 |
| | He's a King (USA) *(JLDunlop)* 9-0 WCarson (9) (w'like: leggy: bhd & drvn along ½-wy: n.d) .................................................... ½.12 |
| 3132 | Lake Poopo (IRE) *(BWHills)* 8-9 DHolland (13) (prom to ½-wy: sn bhd) ..... s.h.13 |
| | Burbage (IRE) *(PWChapple-Hyam)* 9-0 JReid (11) (cmpt: in tch 4f: eased whn btn) ................................................................. hd.14 |
| | Water Skier *(BWHills)* 9-0 DMcKeown (12) (w'like: scope: prom 4f: sn lost pl) ½.15 |
| 3132 | Canadian Eagle *(GLewis)* 8-9 GCarter (15) (a bhd) ........................ nk.16 |
| | Warspite *(PTWalwyn)* 9-0 BRaymond (4) (leggy: unf: s.s: a bhd) ........... hd.17 |

**4/5** PLACERVILLE (USA) (4/7—Evens), **7/2** Storm Canyon (IRE) (op 6/1), **8/1** The Informer (USA) (op 5/1), **12/1** Burbage (IRE) (op 4/1), **14/1** Thaleros, **20/1** Al Senafi (IRE), **25/1** Kardelle, **33/1** Blushing Barada (USA), Bohemian Crown (USA), Danny Boy, He's a King (USA), Lake Poopo (IRE), Miss Pimpernel, **50/1** Ors. CSF £4.82, Tote £1.80: £1.30 £1.50 £1.90 (£4.00). Mr K. Abdulla (NEWMARKET) bred by E. A. Cox Jnr in USA. 17 Rn
1m 24.78 (0.78)
SF—57/52/41/32/29/22

---

## 3532

TAXI NEWS WESTLEY STKS (II) (Mdn 2-Y.O.) £3817.50 (£1140.00: £545.00: £247.50)
**7f**
2-00 (2-05)

| | **Barathea (IRE)** *(LMCumani)* 9-0 LDettori (4) (gd sort: sn prom: qcknd to ld ins fnl f: r.o wl) ................................................. —1 |
| | Gabr *(RWArmstrong)* 9-0 WCarson (1) (w'like: bit bkwd: a cl up: led 3f out: hrd drvn appr fnl f: sn hdd: r.o) .................................. 1½.2 |
| 3362³ | White Muzzle *(PWChapple-Hyam)* 9-0 JReid (10) (sn chsng ldrs: effrt over 2f out: r.o one pce) ............................................. ¾.3 |
| 1112⁵ | Brown's (FR) *(PWChapple-Hyam)* 9-0 MRoberts (3) (lw: led 4f: kpt on same pce) .............................................................. 1½.4 |
| 3289⁵ | Press Gallery *(MrsJCecil)* 9-0 PaulEddery (7) (chsd ldrs: chal over 2f out: rdn & btn appr fnl f) ........................................... 1½.5 |
| | Dancing Prize (IRE) *(MRStoute)* 8-9 WRSwinburn (2) (leggy: lt-f: a in tch: effrt over 2f out: styd on nr fin) ............................... s.h.6 |
| 3092⁸ | Black Dragon (IRE) (Fav) *(BWHills)* 9-0 SCauthen (12) (chsd ldrs tl outpcd fnl 2f) ............................................................. 2½.7 |
| | Mashair (USA) *(JLDunlop)* 8-9 PatEddery (5) (lt-f: scope: s.i.s: bhd tl stdy late hdwy) .................................................... nk.8 |
| | Tomos *(DMorley)* 9-0 PRobinson (8) (w'like: leggy: chsd ldrs: rdn ½-wy: sn wknd) ......................................................... hd.9 |
| | Field of Stars *(JHMGosden)* 9-0 BRaymond (6) (w'like: scope: bhd: shkn up & styd on appr fnl f) ........................................ 1½.10 |
| | Lankridge *(MajorWRHern)* 9-0 MHills (11) (cmpt: bkwd: s.i.s: outpcd & bhd fr ½-wy) .......................................................... 5.11 |
| | Cipriani Queen (IRE) *(MRStoute)* 8-9 GDuffield (9) (w'like: prom early: bhd fr ½-wy) .......................................................... 5.12 |

**11/4** Black Dragon (IRE), **3/1** White Muzzle, **9/2** Press Gallery (3/1—5/1), **11/2** Gabr (op 3/1), **10/1** Dancing Prize (IRE) (op 5/1), **12/1** BARATHEA (IRE) (10/1—20/1), **16/1** Field of Stars, **25/1** Mashair (USA), **33/1** Ors. CSF £72.18, Tote £17.00: £3.40 £2.40 £1.80 (£25.80). Sheikh Mohammed (NEWMARKET) bred by Gerald W. Leigh in Ireland. 12 Rn
1m 24.61 (0.61)
SF—60/55/53/48/43/37/34

---

## 3533

WESTMINSTER-MOTOR TAXI INSURANCE GODOLPHIN STKS (listed race) £9218.75 (£2750.00: £1312.50: £593.75) **1½m**
2-35 (2-36)

| | **Zinaad (110)** *(MRStoute)* 3-8-4⁽¹⁾ PatEddery (1) (lw: hld up & bhd: gd hdwy whn bdly hmpd wl over 2f out: led appr fnl f: r.o wl) ........... —1 |

3211² Sonus (IRE) (Fav) (JHMGosden) 3–8–3 WCarson (6) (chsd ldrs: drvn along over 4f out: styd on to chal wl over 1f out: kpt on wl) ........ 1¹/₂.2

2844³ Steerforth (IRE) (101) (ACStewart) 4–8–11 MRoberts (2) (trckd ldrs: led over 2f out tl appr fnl f: kpt on one pce) .................................. hd.3

3345² Percy's Girl (IRE) (94) (GWragg) 4–8–6 WRSwinburn (7) (lw: in tch: effrt over 4f out: hdwy 2f out: styd on wl) .................................. 1.4

3237⁶ Environment Friend (118) (JRFanshawe) 4–9–5 GDuffield (8) (lw: hld up & bhd: hdwy on ins 4f out: edgd rt appr fnl f: sn btn) ...................... 1.5

3319* Tapis Rouge (IRE) (HRACecil) 3–8–3 AMcGlone (5) (lw: in tch: rdn 4f out: btn whn hung rt appr fnl f) .................................. 1¹/₂.6

2904² Surrealist (IRE) (107) (BWHills) 4–9–3 JReid (3) (trckd ldrs: chal 4f out: btn whn hmpd over 1f out) .................................. 10.7

3292⁵ Zalon (IRE) (91) (JHMGosden) 3–8–6 DHolland (4) (led: hung lft over 2f out: sn hdd & wknd) .................................. 2¹/₂.8

**10/11** Sonus (IRE), **4/1** Steerforth (IRE), **13/2** Tapis Rouge (IRE)(op 4/1), **9/1** Surrealist (IRE), **12/1** Environment Friend(8/1—14/1), **14/1** ZINAAD, **25/1** Percy's Girl (IRE), **50/1** Zalon (IRE). CSF £26.54, Tote £9.80: £1.90 £1.10 £1.70 (£10.60). Maktoum Al Maktoum (NEWMARKET) bred by W. and R. Barnett Ltd. 8 Rn
2m 28.77 (U.53)
SF—59/57/64/57/68/49/43

---

**3534** BAILEY'S HORSE FEEDS NURSERY £5952.00 (£1776.00: £848.00: £384.00)
**5f** 3-05 (3-09)

3275* **Sheila's Secret (IRE) (89)** (Fav) (WCarter) 8-12 JReid (1) (b.nr hind: racd centre: a:p: qcknd to ld ins fnl f: r.o wl) .................................. —1

3340² Lord Olivier (IRE) (98) (WJarvis) 9-2 ‡⁵JWeaver (2) (lw: a cl up: led 2f out tl ins fnl f: r.o) .................................. 2.2

3366² Zany Zanna (IRE) (82) (GAPritchard-Gordon) 8-0 ‡⁹PDoyle (3) (sn outpcd & bhd: hdwy over 1f out: r.o v.wl) .................................. nk.3

3366³ Bangles (82) (LordHuntingdon) 8-2 ‡³DHarrison (9) (cl up tl outpcd appr fnl f: styd on nr fin) .................................. ¹/₂.4

3051² Newbury Coat (76) (MMcCormack) 7-13 AShoults (4) (chsd ldrs tl outpcd 2f out: styd on ins fnl f) .................................. 1¹/₂.5

3348⁶ Local Heroine (75) (JBerry) 7-12⁽¹⁾ CCarter (10) (led 3f: grad wknd) ............... hd.6

3214⁵ Hamsah (IRE) (96) (DRCElsworth) 9-5 SCauthen (12) (sn pushed along: cl up tl wknd over 1f out) .................................. s.h.7

3275³ Geoff's Risk (71) (GLewis) 7-8 JFanning (6) (nvr wnt pce) .................................. 2¹/₂.8

2633* Aberlady (74) (MAJarvis) 7-11 WCarson (11) (nvr trbld ldrs) .................................. 3.9

3214³ The Sharp Bidder (IRE) (88) (RHollinshead) 8-11 PaulEddery (2) (s.i.s: a outpcd) .................................. hd.10

3382⁴ Kimbolton Korker (70) (AAScott) 7-7 DaleGibson (8) (b.hind: gd spd to ¹/₂-wy: sn bhd) .................................. 1¹/₂.11

LONG HANDICAP: Kimbolton Korker 7-2.
*3189 Risk Me's Girl (12/1) Withdrawn (unruly in stalls) : not under orders*

**6/1** SHEILA'S SECRET (IRE), **13/2** The Sharp Bidder (IRE), Lord Olivier (IRE), **15/2** Aberlady, Newbury Coat, **9/1** Zany Zanna (IRE), **11/1** Hamsah (IRE), Bangles, Geoff's Risk, **12/1** Local Heroine, **20/1** Kimbolton Korker. CSF £41.50, CT £319.55. Tote £5.60: £2.10 £2.90 £3.40 (£14.40). Sherwoods Transport Ltd (EPSOM) bred by A. F. O'Callaghan in Ireland. 11 Rn
59.67 sec (0.27)
SF—63/59/42/42/33/31/51

---

**3535** NEWGATE STUD MIDDLE PARK STKS (Gp 1) (2-Y.O.C) £62948.50 (£23411.50: £11330.75: £4741.25: £1995.63: £897.37) **6f** 3-40 (3-42)

3230a* **Zieten (USA)** (AFabre,France) 9-0 SCauthen (3) (gd sort: leggy: hld up: stdy hdwy ¹/₂-wy: led wl over 1f out: r.o to ld cl home) .................................. —1

3367⁴ Pips Pride (RHannon) 9-0 LDettori (2) (lw: led: qcknd 2f out: hdd & no ex cl home) .................................. 1.2

3214* Factual (USA) (BWHills) 9-0 PatEddery (4) (lw: cl up: effrt & swtchd over 1f out: nt qckn) .................................. 2¹/₂.3

3136* Silver Wizard (USA) (Fav) (GLewis) 9-0 WCarson (1) (lw: hld up & plld hrd: effrt over 2f out: rdn & btn wl over 1f out) .................................. ³/₄.4

3354* Wootton Rivers (USA) (PWChapple-Hyam) 9-0 DHolland (5) (lw: chsd ldrs tl outpcd fnl 2f) .................................. 3.5

Virilis (CEBrittain) 9-0 MRoberts (6) (lay wl grwn: cl up to ¹/₂-wy: wknd qckly) 30.6

**8/13** Silver Wizard (USA), **5/2** ZIETEN (USA), **12/1** Pips Pride(10/1—16/1), **14/1** Factual (USA), **33/1** Wootton Rivers (USA), **33/1** Virilis. CSF £25.06, Tote £3.40: £1.40 £3.80 (£18.70). Sheikh Mohammed (FRANCE) bred by Darley Stud Management Ltd in USA. 6 Rn
1m 11.28 (U.12)
SF—66/62/52/49/37/–

## 3536

LADBROKE H'CAP (0-110) £7440.00 (£2220.00: £1060.00: £480.00)
1½m
4-10 (4-15)

(Weights raised 2 lb)

3346² **Highbrook (USA) (78)** *(MHTompkins)* 4–8-8 PRobinson (2) (lw: hld up & bhd: hdwy on bit 3f out: led wl over 1f out: rdn & r.o wl) .............. —1
3194² Kiveton Kabooz (82) (bl) *(LMCumani)* 4–8-12 LDettori (8) (hld up: stdy hdwy over 3f out: hrd rdn & r.o appr fnl f: nt qckn nr fin) .... ¾.2
3090 Million in Mind (IRE) (87) *(MrsJCecil)* 3–8-9 PaulEddery (4) (chsd ldr: led 4f out tl wl over 1f out: r.o one pce) .................... 3½.3
3139* Daisy Girl (70) *(JMackie)* 6–8-0 GCarter (3) (a.p: effrt over 2f out: rdn & r.o one pce) .................... 4.4
*3184** Quadrant (77) *(BWHills)* 3–7-13 WCarson (1) (trckd ldrs: effrt 3f out: wknd 2f out) 2.5
3368 Charlo (94) *(JHMGosden)* 4–9-10 SCauthen (8) (trckd ldrs tl wknd 2f out) ...... 8.6
3461 Sayh (80) *(MAJarvis)* 3–8-2 AMunro (6) (in tch: drvn along 4f out: sn bhd) ...... 4.7
3194 Be a Honey (80) *(NAGraham)* 4–8-10 MRoberts (9) (led tl hdd 4f out: sn outpcd) 4.8
3377⁶ Free Transfer (IRE) (71) *(PFTulk)* 3–7-7 NCarlisle (5) (a bhd) .................... 5.9
LONG HANDICAP: Free Transfer (IRE) 6-10.

9/4 Kiveton Kabooz, 11/2 Highbrook (USA), 6/1 Charlo, 13/2 Quadrant, 7/1 Daisy Girl, 8/1 Million in Mind (IRE), 14/1 Sayh, Be a Honey, 66/1 Free Transfer (IRE). CSF £16.75, CT £86.90. Tote £7.80: £2.40 £1.10 £2.90 (£6.30). Mr Nick Cook (NEWMARKET) bred by Larry Stewart in USA. 9 Rn                  2m 3u.52 (1.22)
SF—46/48/38/21/16/25

## 3537

FITZWILLIAM H'CAP (0-90) £4776.00 (£1428.00: £684.00: £312.00)     5f 4-40 (4-45)

(Weights raised 1 lb)

3437² **Ashtina (68)** (Jt-Fav) *(RJJHodges)* 7–8-8 PatEddery (1) (mde all stands' side: hld on wl fnl f) .................... —1
3341⁶ Miss Movie World (55) *(NBycroft)* 3–7-8 JFanning (7) (hdwy ½-wy: chal ins fnl f: kpt on wl) .................... ½.2
3397⁶ Here Comes a Star (67) *(JMCarr)* 4–8-7 SMorris (9) (hld up: hdwy & ch 1f out: kpt on) .................... nk.3
3397² African Chimes (76) (bl) *(WAO'Gorman)* 5–8-13 ‡³EmmaO'Gorman (6) (in tch: hdwy whn nt clr run & swtchd over 1f out: r.o) .................... 1.4
*3318²* Very Dicey (76) *(WRMuir)* 4–9-2 WCarson (11) (chsd ldrs centre: ev ch over 1f out: r.o one pce) .................... s.h.5
3284² Sasparella (68) (bl) *(WJarvis)* 3–8-7 PRobinson (10) (led centre tl outpcd ins fnl f) .................... 1.6
3464⁵ Metal Boys (83) *(RHollinshead)* 5–9-2 ‡⁷SWynne (15) (a chsng ldrs centre: nt qckn fnl f) .................... ½.7
3304 Singing Star (78) *(JBalding)* 6–9-4 JReid (3) (nvr bttr than mid div) .................... 1.8
3464³ Pallium (IRE) (71) (Jt-Fav) *(MPNaughton)* 4–8-11 MRoberts (4) (s.i.s: drvn along & sn in tch: wknd over 1f out) .................... nk.9
*3318* Sylvan Breeze (75) (bl) *(PMitchell)* 4–9-1 GDuffield (8) (racd centre & nvr wnt pce) .................... ¾.10
3126 Yes (53) *(DTThom)* 4–7-0 ‡⁷KimMcDonnell (2) (chsd ldrs tl wknd over 1f out) hd.11
3207³ Samsolom (61) (bl) *(JBalding)* 4–8-1 GHind (14) (lw: unruly in stalls: n.d) .................... ¾.12
3271² Branston Abby (IRE) (79) *(MJohnston)* 3–9-4 DMcKeown (12) (lw: hld up & bhd: effrt 2f out: n.d) .................... 1½.13
3469 Sonderise (72) *(NTinkler)* 3–8-11 LCharnock (13) (s.i.s: a outpcd & bhd) ...... 2.14
2604⁶ Eager Deva (84) *(RHollinshead)* 5–9-10 LPiggott (5) (prom to ½-wy: sn wknd & eased) .................... ½.15
LONG HANDICAP: Yes 7-6.

9/2 ASHTINA, Pallium (IRE), 8/1 Branston Abby (IRE), 9/1 African Chimes(8/1—12/1), Very Dicey, Sasparella, 12/1 Here Comes a Star, 14/1 Samsolom, 16/1 Miss Movie World, Yes, 20/1 Eager Deva, Metal Boys, Singing Star, 25/1 Sylvan Breeze, 33/1 Sonderise. CSF £68.55, CT £751.13. Tote £4.10: £1.70 £5.10 £3.80 (£53.70). Ms S. A. Joyner (SOMERTON) bred by D. R. and Mrs Fairbairn. 15 Rn            59.49 sec (0.09)
SF—62/46/58/60/62/49/52

T/Trio: Race 6: £25.50 (33.4 Tckts) & Race 7: £1,108.70 (1.1 Tckts). T/Jkpt: Not won; £19,285.32 to Newmarket 2/10/92. T/Plpt: £52.90 (143.71 Tckts).                                             AA

# NEWMARKET (R-H) Rowley Mile

## Friday, October 2nd [Good]

Going Allowance: minus 0.15 sec per fur (F)                              Wind: slt against

Stalls: 1st, 3rd & 6th high, remainder low

## 3538

STAYERS' H'CAP (3-Y.O) (0-100) £5435.50 (£1624.00: £777.00: £353.50)
2m
1-30 (1-36)

3282⁴ **Rosina Mae (67)** *(LordHuntingdon)* 8-3(¹) DMcKeown (2) (trckd ldrs: shkn up over 3f out: rdn to ld ins fnl f) .................... —1

3128⁵ Farmer's Pet **(77)** *(GAPritchard-Gordon)* 8-13 LDettori (8) (led tl hdd & unable qckn ins fnl f) .......... nk.2

3409⁴ Heavenly Waters **(59)** *(RFJohnsonHoughton)* 7-9 JLowe (7) (b.hind: hld up: rdn & hdwy 3f out: r.o wl fnl f) .......... 1½.3

3282⋆ Highland Fantasy (USA) **(72)** (Jt-Fav) *(BWHills)* 8-8 DHolland (5) (in tch: effrt 3f out: one pce fnl f) .......... nk.4

3194 Not in Doubt (USA) **(85)** (bl) *(HCandy)* 9-7 CRutter (9) (hld up: rdn & hdwy 4f out: nvr able to chal) .......... 2½.5

3118⋆ Jack Button (IRE) **(79)** *(BobJones)* 9-1 NDay (10) (swtg: bhd tl styd on fnl 2f) ... 3.6

3194 Encore Une Fois (IRE) **(80)** *(PWChapple-Hyam)* 9-2 WCarson (6) (lw: chsd ldrs: rdn 3f out: sn btn) .......... 5.7

2793² Yenoora (IRE) **(69)** *(PFICole)* 8-5 TQuinn (3) (chsd ldr tl wknd 3f out) .......... 7.8

3384⋆ Upper House **(65)** *(GWragg)* 7-12 ‡³FNorton (11) (lw: bhd: effrt 6f out: wknd 4f out) .......... 3.9

3206³ Tudor Island **(73)** *(CEBrittain)* 8-9 MRoberts (1) (prom tl wknd 3f out) .......... nk.10

3298⋆ Receptionist **(82)** (Jt-Fav) *(HRACecil)* 9-4 PatEddery (4) (prom 11f: wknd qckly) 4.11

**11/2** Receptionist, Highland Fantasy (USA)(4/1—6/1), **6/1** Upper House, **13/2** Jack Button, **15/2** Tudor Island, **8/1** Yenoora (IRE), **12/1** ROSINA MAE, Heavenly Waters, Encore Une Fois (IRE), **14/1** Ors. CSF £144.52, CT £1,853.73. Tote £14.00: £3.50 £4.70 £3.40 (£151.80). Greenland Park Ltd (WEST ILSLEY) bred by Laharna Ltd. 11 Rn
3m 25.24 (1.94)
SF—46/55/35/47/57/48

**3539**      SNOWDENS MARQUEES H'CAP (3 & 4-Y.O.F) (0-110) £5663.00 (£1694.00: £812.00: £371.00)   **6f**      2-00 (2-05)

3213 **Splice (88)** *(JRFanshawe)* 3-9-0 ‡⁷NVarley (9) (lw: hld up: hdwy to ld over 1f out: rdn out) .......... —1

3284⁵ Nagida **(70)** *(JARToller)* 3-8-6 ‡⁵JWeaver (6) (dwlt: hdwy 2f out: ev ch ins fnl f: r.o) .......... ¾.2

3095 Blue Topaze **(66)** *(RJHolder)* 4-8-1 PRobinson (13) (hld up: hdwy 2f out: kpt on fnl f) .......... 2½.3

3198⁴ Laundry Maid **(87)** *(HCandy)* 3-8-13 ‡⁷AntoinetteArmes (10) (chsd ldrs: nt clr run & swtchd lft over 1f out: r.o fnl f) .......... ¾.4

3271⋆ Our Rita **(74)** *(DrJDScargill)* 3-8-7 DHolland (12) (in tch: hmpd over 1f out: rdn & r.o appr fnl f) .......... 1½.5

3359 Ahbab (IRE) **(80)** (v) *(PTWalwyn)* 3-8-13 RHills (11) (in tch: bmpd over 1f out: r.o) .......... s.h.6

3243⁶ Arabellajill **(93)** *(RHannon)* 3-9-12 LPiggott (5) (bhd: n.m.r over 1f out: nvr rchd ldrs) .......... nk.7

3355 Snowgirl (IRE) **(72)** *(JBerry)* 4-8-7 JCarroll (1) (tongue-tied: chsd ldrs: no hdwy fnl 2f) .......... s.h.8

3196⋆ Arboretum (IRE) **(81)** (Fav) *(RCharlton)* 3-8-11 ‡³DHarrison (2) (lw: led after 2f tl over 1f out: wknd) .......... 1½.9

3469⁵ Massiba (IRE) **(87)** *(MJHeaton-Ellis)* 3-9-6 BRaymond (4) (w ldr: ev ch 2f out: hung rt & wknd wl over 1f out) .......... s.h.10

3469 Parfait Amour **(73)** *(RMWhitaker)* 3-8-6 ACulhane (3) (bhd: rdn ½-wy: styng on whn hmpd over 1f out) .......... 2½.11

3359⋆ La Dama Bonita (USA) **(84)** *(DWPArbuthnot)* 3-9-3 SCauthen (7) (bhd: effrt & n.m.r over 1f out: eased whn btn fnl f) .......... 3.12

3134² Elhasna (USA) **(90)** *(MajorWRHern)* 3-9-9 WCarson (8) (led 2f: hmpd wl over 1f out: sn bhd) .......... 2½.13

**11/2** Arboretum (IRE), **15/2** Nagida, **8/1** Massiba (IRE), SPLICE, Snowgirl (IRE), Arabellajill, **9/1** Elhasna (USA), Laundry Maid, La Dama Bonita (USA), **12/1** Blue Topaze, Our Rita, **14/1** Ahbab (IRE), **25/1** Parfait Amour. CSF £64.96, CT £668.03. Tote £11.20: £3.70 £3.20 £5.00 (£68.10). Cheveley Park Stud (NEWMARKET) bred by Cheveley Park Stud Ltd. 13 Rn
1m 11.93 (0.53)
SF—72/61/46/55/43/48

**3540**      RACING POST CLAIMING STKS   £5617.50 (£1680.00: £805.00: £367.50) **1½m**      2-35 (2-37)

3219 **Temple Knight (58)** *(CACyzer)* 3-9-1 RCochrane (7) (chsd ldrs: rdn to ld ins fnl f) .......... —1

3492² Simply-H (IRE) **(74)** *(MBell)* 3-8-10 ‡⁷PTurner (1) (plld hrd: chsd ldrs: led over 1f out: hdd & no ex ins fnl f) .......... 2.2

2828 Continuity **(52)** *(MHTompkins)* 3-8-5 PRobinson (4) (hld up: effrt over 3f out: plld out over 1f out: rdn & r.o wl fnl f) .......... s.h.3

3102 Briggs Lad (IRE) **(66)** *(WJarvis)* 3-8-12 MTebbutt (2) (hdwy over 3f out: nt rch ldrs) .......... ½.4

3461⁴ Pennine Star (IRE) **(51)** *(CWCElsey)* 4-8-13 LDettori (5) (led tl over 1f out: sn btn) .......... 3.5

3273 Greek Chime (IRE) **(65)** *(LordHuntingdon)* 3–8-12 DMcKeown (6) (chsd ldr 10f: sn btn) ............ 7.6
3266 Dancing Boat **(41)** *(KAMorgan)* 3–8-5 ‡$JWeaver (3) (prom 9f: eased whn btn fnl 2f) ............ 4.7
3161\* Flying Speed (USA) **(72)** (Fav) *(MCPipe)* 4–9-7 MRoberts (10) (prom over 9f: sn wknd) ............ hd.8
3010 Mansber (IRE) **(44)** *(PatMitchell)* 3–8-2 ‡ᐧDHarrison (9) (dwlt: a bhd) ............ nk.9
2267 Pondered Bid **(33)** (bl) *(PatMitchell)* 8–8-13 MPerrett (8) (b: swtg: t.o fnl 3f) ... 15.10

2/1 Flying Speed (USA), 11/4 Simply-H (IRE), 6/1 Greek Chime (IRE), 8/1 TEMPLE KNIGHT, 9/1 Pennine Star (IRE), 10/1 Briggs Lad (IRE), 16/1 Continuity, 33/1 Pondered Bid, 40/1 Ors. CSF £28.83, Tote £10.40: £1.90 £1.80 £4.50 (£16.40). Mr S. Wingfield Digby (HORSHAM) bred by S. Wingfield Digby. 10 Rn 2m 35.74 (6.44)
SF—19/10/4/10/5/–

## 3541
SOMERVILLE TATTERSALL STKS (listed race) (2-Y.O) £11452.50 (£3420.00: £1635.00: £742.50) **7f**
3-10 (3-12)

3235² **Nominator (100)** *(RHollinshead)* 9-1 WCarson (6) (lw: prom: led over 1f out: rdn out) ............ —1
3186\* Urgent Request (IRE) **(87)** (Fav) *(BWHills)* 8-12 PatEddery (1) (led over 6f: rdn & r.o ins fnl f) ............ nk.2
3205³ Fitzcarraldo (USA) **(100)** *(LMCumani)* 8-12 LDettori (3) (lw: trckd ldrs: plld hrd: plld out over 1f out: rdn & styd on) ............ ½.3
3289\* Beggarman Thief (USA) **(84)** *(JHMGosden)* 8-12 RCochrane (7) (lw: hld up: hmpd 2f out: r.o fnl f) ............ ½.4
2981a Port Lucaya **(100)** *(RHannon)* 8-12 LPiggott (4) (stdd & sn rdn: nvr nr: nvr trbld ldrs) 2½.5
2845⁴ Darbonne (USA) **(100)** *(GHarwood)* 8-12 SCauthen (5) (chsd ldrs: rdn, edgd lft & stumbled 2f out: one pce) ............ 1½.6
2756² Azhar **(97)** *(MRStoute)* 8-12 MRoberts (2) (bit bkwd: in tch: rdn over 2f out: sn btn) ............ 2½.7
3193⁴ Tykoyvor (IRE) **(94)** *(MHTompkins)* 8-12 PRobinson (8) (in tch 6f) ............ 1½.8

2/1 Urgent Request (IRE), 3/1 Beggarman Thief (USA)(9/4—7/2), 4/1 Fitzcarraldo (USA), 8/1 Darbonne (USA), Azhar, 16/1 NOMINATOR, 20/1 Ors. CSF £45.54, Tote £11.30: £2.10 £1.10 £1.80 (£14.10). Mr J. D. Graham (UPPER LONGDON) bred by Auldyn Stud Ltd. 8 Rn 1m 26.47 (2.47)
SF—48/44/42/40/32/27

## 3542
MAIN REEF STKS (listed race) £9462.50 (£2825.00: £1350.00: £612.50) **1m**
3-40 (3-42)

3335a\* **Inner City (IRE) (109)** (Jt-Fav) *(LMCumani)* 3–9-6 LDettori (9) (hld up: hdwy to ld wl over 1f out: sn clr: unchal) ............ —1
3226a² Soiree (IRE) **(102)** *(BWHills)* 3–8-10 DHolland (3) (dwlt: sn chsng ldrs: swtchd rt & n.m.r over 3f out: edgd lft & r.o appr fnl f) ............ 4.2
3229a John Rose **(100)** *(PAKelleway)* 3–8-10 GayKelleway (6) (lw: chsd ldrs: ev ch over 2f out: rdn & r.o one pce) ............ 2.3
3032 Lovealoch (IRE) **(109)** *(MBell)* 4–8-9 JCarroll (1) (tongue-tied: in tch: rdn 2f out: r.o fnl f) ............ 1½.4
711⁵ River Defences (USA) *(PWChapple-Hyam)* 3–8-10 LPiggott (7) (hld up & plld hrd: led over 3f out tl wl over 1f out: btn whn n.m.r 1f out) ............ s.h.5
3427\* Lord Chickney (USA) (Jt-Fav) *(JHMGosden)* 3–9-3 SCauthen (5) (s.i.s: plld hrd & sn chsng ldrs: btn over 3f out) ............ 8.6
3201² L'Hermine **(95)** *(HCandy)* 3–8-10 WCarson (4) (lw: led over 4f: sn btn) ............ 4.7
3195 Sylva Honda **(102)** *(CEBrittain)* 4–9-10 RCochrane (8) (lw: chsd ldrs 5f) ............ nk.8

11/4 Lord Chickney (USA), INNER CITY (IRE), 4/1 Soiree (IRE), 13/2 River Defences (USA), 8/1 Lovealoch (IRE), 10/1 L'Hermine(8/1—12/1), 25/1 John Rose, 33/1 Sylva Honda. CSF £13.20, Tote £2.80: £1.40 £1.60 £2.90 (£7.70). Sheikh Mohammed (NEWMARKET) bred by Ballynagran Bloodstock Ltd in Ireland. 8 Rn 1m 37.50 (0.20)
SF—85/58/57/51/51/34

## 3543
CHARLES WELLS EAGLE BITTER H'CAP (0-110) £6524.00 (£1952.00: £936.00: £428.00) **7f**
4-10 (4-14)

3417\* **Millsolin (IRE) (71)** (Fav) *(RAkehurst)* 4-8-1 (6x) GCarter (1) (prom: rdn ½-wy: led ins fnl f: r.o wl) ............ —1
3209 Caleman **(79)** *(RBoss)* 3–8-6⁽²⁾ PatEddery (11) (w ldr: led over 1f out: hdd & no ex ins fnl f) ............ 1.2
3356 Hard to Figure **(93)** *(RJHodges)* 6–9-9 LPiggott (8) (chsd ldrs: ev ch 1f out: kpt on) ............ hd.3
3355⁶ Prenonamoss **(79)** *(DWPArbuthnot)* 4–8-9 LDettori (6) (b: b.hind: chsd ldrs: kpt on one pce fnl f) ............ hd.4
3359⁴ Kayvee **(93)** *(GHarwood)* 3–9-6 MRoberts (5) (dwlt: hdwy 3f out: r.o fnl f) ............ nk.5
3198⁶ Superoo **(74)** *(JSutcliffe)* 6–8-4 RHills (16) (hld up: hdwy on far side over 2f out: rdn & r.o one pce fnl f) ............ s.h.6

3212 Knock to Enter (USA) **(84)** *(MRStoute)* 4-9-0 RCochrane (13) (swtg: dwlt: bhd tl rdn & r.o wl appr fnl f) .......... ½.**7**

3427 Bold Memory **(89)** *(MJohnston)* 3-9-2 DMcKeown (7) (plld hrd & bhd: rapid hdwy appr fnl f: fin wl) .......... hd.**8**

3317³ Risk Zone **(71)** (bl) *(RHannon)* 3-7-12 AMcGlone (14) (led far side 5f: sn btn) . hd.**9**

3359 Knight of Mercy **(98)** *(RHannon)* 6-10-0 BRaymond (10) (nvr nr to chal) .......... 1.**10**

3437 Green Dollar **(91)** *(EAWheeler)* 9-9-4 ‡³FNorton (9) (hld up: rdn over 2f out: nvr rchd ldrs) .......... ¾.**11**

3356³ Heather Bank **(94)** (v) *(JBerry)* 3-9-7 JCarroll (17) (chsd ldr far side 4f) .......... ½.**12**

3182² Polonez Prima **(90)** *(JEBanks)* 5-9-1 ‡⁵JWeaver (18) (racd far side: pushed along ½-wy: n.d) .......... 1.**13**

3400* Everglades (IRE) **(71)** *(RCharlton)* 4-8-1 (6x) DHolland (4) (lw: led over 5f) ..... ½.**14**

3212⁵ Colour Sergeant **(89)** *(LordHuntingdon)* 4-9-2 ‡³DHarrison (2) (hdwy 3f out: wknd over 1f out) .......... 1½.**15**

3284⁴ Hi-Tech Honda (IRE) **(66)** *(CEBrittain)* 3-7-7 JLowe (3) (lw: dwlt: a bhd) ........ hd.**16**

3359 Venus Observed **(82)** *(HCandy)* 4-8-5 ‡⁷AntoinetteArmes (12) (prom 4f) .......... 4.**17**

Aghaadir (USA) **(95)** *(JHMGosden)* 4-9-11 SCauthen (15) (bit bkwd: bhd fnl 2f) 1.**18**

LONG HANDICAP: Hi-Tech Honda (IRE) 7-6.

**5/2** MILLSOLIN (IRE), **7/1** Caleman(op 14/1), **9/1** Hard to Figure(14/1—8/1), **10/1** Colour Sergeant, Polonez Prima, **12/1** Kayvee, Superoo, **14/1** Venus Observed, **16/1** Risk Zone, Aghaadir (USA), Heather Bank, **20/1** Everglades (IRE), Knock to Enter (USA), Prenonamoss, Knight of Mercy, **25/1** Hi-Tech Honda (IRE), Green Dollar, **40/1** Bold Memory. CSF £21.84, CT £140.35. Tote £4.00: £1.80 £2.50 £1.90 £4.50 (£25.10). Normandy Developments (London) (EPSOM) bred by Lhasa Trading Ltd. in Ireland. 18 Rn                1m 25.12 (1.12)
SF—54/56/72/57/67/50

T/Trio: Race 6: £190.20 (10.2 Tckts). T/Jkpt: Not won; £24,139.56 to Newmarket 03/10/92. T/Plpt: £431.70 (24.2 Tckts).                Dk

---

# NEWMARKET (R-H) Rowley Mile

## Saturday, October 3rd [Good to soft]

Going Allowance: 6f-7f: 0.20 sec (G); Rest: 0.40 sec per fur (Y)        Wind: mod half against

Stalls: 5th low, remainder centre

**3544**    OH SO SHARP STKS (2-Y.O.F) £5952.00 (£1776.00: £848.00: £384.00)
7f                                                                       1-55 (1-56)

3092³ **Yawl** *(BWHills)* 8-9 DHolland (4) (led after 2f: qcknd 2f out: r.o wl) .......... —**1**

Rumpus (IRE) *(LMCumani)* 8-9 LDettori (6) (unf: scope: lw: trckd ldrs: effrt 2f out: nt qckn) .......... 6.**2**

3191² Self Assured (IRE) **(100)** (Fav) *(HRACecil)* 8-9 WCarson (5) (led 2f: cl up: rdn 3f out: outpcd fnl 2f) .......... 4.**3**

2132² Nuryandra **(94)** *(GWragg)* 8-9 MHills (7) (chsd ldrs: drvn along ½-wy: wknd over 2f out) .......... hd.**4**

Bella Ballerina *(MRStoute)* 8-9 MRoberts (3) (leggy: scope: outpcd ½-wy: sme late hdwy) .......... ½.**5**

3276* Gustavia (IRE) **(94)** *(RWArmstrong)* 8-9 NDay (1) (s.i.s: outpcd & wl bhd fr ½-wy) 5.**6**

**6/4** Self Assured (IRE), **4/1** Bella Ballerina(op 5/2), **5/1** YAWL(tchd 8/1), **15/2** Gustavia (IRE)(5/1—8/1), **8/1** Rumpus (IRE), **10/1** Nuryandra(op 5/1). CSF £35.08, Tote £8.30: £3.00 £2.30 (£41.70). Mr R. D. Hollingsworth (LAMBOURN) bred by R. D. Hollingsworth. 6 Rn                1m 28.98 (4.98)
SF—41/23/11/10/8/–

**3545**    CHOKE JADE H'CAP (0-90) £6709.50 (£2016.00: £973.00: £451.50)    7f 2-30 (2-34)
(Weights raised 3 lb)

3417 **Gant Bleu (FR) (60)** *(RMWhitaker)* 5-8-4 PaulEddery (25) (racd centre: gd hdwy over 2f out: ev ch ins fnl f: r.o: fin 2nd, 1l: awrdd r) .......... —**1**

3439⁵ Lady Debra Darley **(80)** *(RHannon)* 3-9-7 MRoberts (27) (led 2f out to 1f out: kpt on: fin 3rd,½l: plcd 2nd) .......... **2**

3365 Ballerina Bay **(61)** (v) *(DTThom)* 4-7-12 ‡⁷KimMcDonnell (22) (hdwy centre ½-wy: chal over 1f out: nt qckn nr fin: fin 4th, nk: plcd 3rd) .......... **3**

3473* Amazing Feat (IRE) **(74)** (Jt-Fav) *(MrsGRReveley)* 3-9-1 KDarley (2) (outpcd & bhd stands' side: hdwy over 1f out: fin wl: fin 5th, nk: plcd 4th) .......... **4**

3488* Darakah **(65)** (Jt-Fav) *(CJHill)* 5-8-4 (5x) ‡⁵JWeaver (7) (hdwy stands' side over 2f out: chal over 1f out: no ex) .......... 1½.**6**

3359⁶ Choir Practice **(70)** *(WJHaggas)* 5-9-0 MHills (3) (effrt stands' side ½-wy: styd on up: nrst fin) .......... 2½.**7**

3441⁶ Kimberley Park **(68)** (Jt-Fav) *(DWPArbuthnot)* 4-8-12 DMcKeown (6) (lw: racd stands'side: effrt 3f out: sn rdn & btn) .......... hd.**8**

3417 Surrey Racing **(69)** *(GLewis)* 4-8-13 GBaxter (10) (hdwy stands' side ½-wy: sn rdn & prom: wknd fnl f) .......... ¾.**9**

3287 Roca Murada (IRE) **(57)** (v) (Jt-Fav) *(MJRyan)* 3–7-12 DBiggs (13) (chsd ldrs centre: ev ch 2f out: btn wln hmpd appr fnl f) .................... ¾.**10**

3270 First Century (IRE) **(67)** *(BRMillman)* 3–8-8 DaleGibson (20) (lw: hdwy centre over 2f out: chal over 1f out: sn rdn & wknd) .................... hd.**11**

3499 Black Boy (IRE) **(54)** *(JAGlover)* 3–7-9 NCarlisle (23) (lw: effrt centre ½-wy: nvr trbld ldrs) .................... 1.**12**

3145⁶ Young Valentine **(63)** *(RMWhitaker)* 3–8-4 MBirch (21) (disp ld centre 5f: sn wknd) .................... ¾.**13**

3413 Merryhill Maid (IRE) **(63)** *(JLHarris)* 4–8-7 DHolland (26) (chsd ldrs centre tl wknd wl over 1f out) .................... 1.**14**

3386* Set Table (USA) **(75)** (bl) (Jt-Fav) *(HJMGosden)* 3–9-2 WCarson (8) (led & clr stands' side: hdd & wknd 2f out) .................... ½.**15**

3418³ Lord Vivienne (IRE) **(75)** *(RCSpicer)* 3–8-13 ‡³DHarrison (19) (lw: chsd ldrs centre: drvn along ½-wy: wknd wl over 1f out) .................... sh.**16**

3241 Buzzards Bellbuoy **(70)** *(HJCollingridge)* 3–8-11 JQuinn (16) (disp ld centre 5f: sn wknd) .................... nk.**17**

3198 Colossus **(67)** *(CEBrittain)* 4–8-6 ‡⁵BDoyle (24) (hdwy centre ½-wy: sn drvn along: ch wl over 1f out: sn wknd) .................... s.h.**18**

3396⁶ Our Occasion **(68)** *(WJMusson)* 3–8-9 NDay (28) (lw: chsd ldrs centre: hdwy u.p 3f out: rdn & btn over 1f out) .................... 1½.**19**

3469 Petraco (IRE) **(75)** *(LJCodd)* 4–9-5 LDettori (18) (lw: effrt u.p centre 3f out: n.d) 1½.**20**

Native Chieftan **(83)** *(RHannon)* 3–9-10 GBardwell (29) (bit bkwd: dwlt: racd centre: a bhd) .................... ½.**21**

3317⁴ Caroles Express **(74)** (Jt-Fav) *(RAkehurst)* 4–8-11 ‡⁷TAshley (17) (sn outpcd & bhd centre) .................... 1½.**22**

3386² Affidare (IRE) **(68)** *(SMHillen)* 3–8-9 JLowe (12) (effrt centre ½-wy: rdn & no imp) .................... nk.**23**

3270 Showgi (USA) **(80)** (bl) *(JRFanshawe)* 3–9-7 BRaymond (15) (lw: early spd centre: bhd fr ½-wy) .................... nk.**24**

3476² Bill Moon **(51)** *(PJFeilden)* 6–7-2 ‡⁷DWright (5) (racd stands' side: drvn along ½-wy: n.d) .................... hd.**25**

3349 Jahangir (IRE) **(78)** *(BHanbury)* 3–9-5 LPiggott (11) (effrt stands' side ½-wy: sn btn) .................... hd.**26**

3209 Laurel Queen (IRE) **(73)** *(JBerry)* 4–9-3 JCarroll (1) (hld up & bhd stands' side: n.d) .................... nk.**27**

3412* Jumaira Star (USA) **(67)** (v) *(JHMGosden)* 3–8-8 RCochrane (14) (lw: chsd ldrs centre tl rdn & wknd ½-wy) .................... ½.**28**

3378³ Empeeka (USA) **(70)** (h) *(WAO'Gorman)* 3–8-8 ‡³EmmaO'Gorman (4) (swtg: racd stands' side: n.d) .................... 2.**29**

1417* Hob Green **(60)** *(MrsJRRamsden)* 3–7-10 ‡⁵RBurke (9) (hdwy stands' side 3f out: led 1f out: r.o wl: fin 1st: disq: plcd last) .................... **0**

*Subsequent Stewards Enquiry: Hob Green disq. (carried incorrect weight). All bets settled on Hob Green.*

12/1 Roca Murada (IRE), Darakah, Set Table (USA), Caroles Express, Kimberley Park, Amazing Feat (IRE), 14/1 Choir Practice, Jahangir (IRE), Bill Moon, 16/1 Lady Debra Darley, Jumaira Star (USA), 20/1 Showgi (USA), Petraco (IRE), Laurel Queen (IRE), Affidare (IRE), 25/1 Buzzards Bellbuoy, Black Boy (IRE), Hob Green, GANT BLEU (FR), 33/1 Ors. CSF £471.24, CT £8,863.37. Tote £77.00: £14.20 £8.20 £3.80 £18.30 (£1,670.00). Mr E. C. Alton (WETHERBY) bred by Souren Vanian in France. 29 Rn                1m 28.32 (4.32)
SF–38/43/58/34/50/34

---

**3546** CHEVELEY PARK STUD SUN CHARIOT STKS (Gp 2) (F & M) £33678.00 (£12539.90: £5969.95: £2542.15)  1¼m                3-00 (3-05)

3032* Red Slippers (USA) **(Fav)** *(LMCumani)* 3–8-8 LDettori (2) (trckd ldrs: led 1f out: edgd rt: hld on wl cl home) .................... —**1**

3032⁵ Feminine Wiles (IRE) *(PWChapple-Hyam)* 3–8-8 LPiggott (4) (hld up: hdwy over 3f out: chal & hung lft ins fnl f: r.o) .................... hd.**2**

2436² Susurration (USA) *(JHMGosden)* 5–9-0 DHolland (7) (cl up: led 4f out tl hdd 1f out: no ex) .................... 4.**3**

2765a³ Faribole (IRE) *(EdouardBartholomew,France)* 3–8-8 MHills (3) (gd sort: lengthy: in tch: hdwy 4f out: rdn & nt qckn fnl 2f) .................... 1.**4**

3032⁴ Mystery Play (IRE) *(BWHills)* 3–8-8 PaulEddery (5) (cl up tl wknd appr fnl f) ....... 1.**5**

3213* Perfect Circle *(MRStoute)* 3–8-8 WCarson (1) (s.s: hdwy 4f out: sn drvn along: wknd wl over 1f out) .................... 7.**6**

3566a Gussy Marlowe *(CEBrittain)* 4–9-3 MRoberts (6) (lw: led tl hdd 4f out: wl outpcd fnl 3f) .................... 10.**7**

*Stewards Enquiry: Piggott suspended 12-15/10/92 (careless riding).*

6/4 RED SLIPPERS (USA), 7/2 Susurration (USA), Perfect Circle(7/4—4/1), 8/1 Faribole (IRE)(op 12/1), 14/1 Feminine Wiles (IRE), Gussy Marlowe, 25/1 Mystery Play (IRE). CSF £18.98, Tote £2.30: £1.70 £3.00 (£14.80). Sheikh Mohammed (NEWMARKET) bred by Swettenham Stud in USA. 7 Rn                2m 8.01 (5.41)
SF–80/79/77/69/67/53

**3547**  WILLIAM HILL CAMBRIDGESHIRE H'CAP (0-115) £57268.75 (£17275.00: £8387.50: £3943.75)  1m 1f
3-40 (3-46)

3428* **Rambo's Hall (92)** (Fav) *(JAGlover)* 7-9-3 (5x) DMcKeown (7) (trckd ldrs gng wl: led appr fnl f: rdn & r.o wl) .............................. —1

3368* **Montpelier Boy (83)** *(LordHuntingdon)* 4-8-8 (5x) LPiggott (2) (lw: hld up & bhd: hdwy 4f out: qcknd to chse wnr 1f out: r.o) ............. 2½.2

3212² **Double Entendre (71)** *(MBell)* 6-7-10(1) WCarson (5) (hld up: hdwy ½-wy: drvn along over 2f out: r.o: nrst fin) ............................ s.h.3

3201 **Dawaahi (USA) (85)** *(JHMGosden)* 3-8-5 DHolland (27) (bhd: effrt & n.m.r over 2f out: r.o u.p: nrst fin) ............................ 1.4

3317 **Cru Exceptionnel (72)** *(PJMakin)* 4-7-11(2) TSprake (6) (hld up: hdwy gng wl 3f out: ev ch & rdn 1f out: nt qckn) ................. ¾.5

30846 **Revif (FR) (95)** *(ACStewart)* 4-9-6 MRoberts (12) (lw: cl up: led wl over 2f out tl appr fnl f: r.o one pce) ............................ ½.6

3292⁴ **Barford Lad (79)** *(JRFanshawe)* 5-8-4 LDettori (20) (hdwy 3f out: styd on & ch 1f out: nt qckn) ............................ ½.7

3212⁴ **Mellottie (101)** *(MrsGRReveley)* 7-9-12 (5x) JLowe (24) (lw: hld up & bhd: gd hdwy 2f out: n.m.r: r.o) ............................ ½.8

3359³ **Sand Table (83)** *(LordHuntingdon)* 3-8-0 ‡³DHarrison (18) (bhd: hdwy over 2f out: nvr able to chal) ............................ 2.9

3514⁶ **Jubran (USA) (71)** *(MPNaughton)* 6-7-10 JakiHouston (11) (lw: led tl hdd wl over 2f out: kpt on one pce) ............................ ¾.10

2846⁵ **Lucky Guest (90)** *(JLDunlop)* 5-9-1 BRaymond (22) (lw: trckd ldrs: effrt & ev ch over 1f out: sn rdn & btn) ............................ nk.11

3477* **Cumbrian Challenge (IRE) (93)** *(MHEasterby)* 3-8-13 (5x) MBirch (10) (w ldr tl wknd 1f out) ............................ nk.12

3428⁵ **Marine Diver (71)** *(BRMillman)* 6-7-10 DaleGibson (3) (chsd ldrs: chal 3f out: wknd 1f out) ............................ s.h.13

3428⁴ **Camden's Ransom (USA) (73)** *(DRCElsworth)* 5-7-7(1) ‡⁵NKennedy (26) (lw: prom: outpcd whn hmpd over 1f out) ............................ ½.14

3349⁴ **Roseate Lodge (72)** *(RWArmstrong)* 6-7-11 JQuinn (21) (stdy hdwy 4f out: chal 2f out: rdn & btn 1f out) ............................ 1.15

**Lord of the Field (102)** *(JARToller)* 5-9-13 GBaxter (14) (bit bkwd: bhd tl sme late hdwy) ............................ s.h.16

3270³ **Glide Path (USA) (81)** *(JWHills)* 3-8-1 MHills (19) (effrt over 2f out: no imp) .. nk.17

3192⁴ **Alkarif (USA) (76)** *(MrsJRRamsden)* 3-7-5 ‡⁵RBurke (17) (bhd & swtchd stands' side after s: gd hdwy ½-wy: wknd 2f out) ............................ nk.18

3292 **Myfontaine (70)** (bl) *(KTIvory)* 5-7-9 GBardwell (30) (hdwy & prom over 2f out: sn hrd rdn & btn) ............................ ½.19

3370 **Scales of Justice (78)** *(JWHills)* 6-8-3 RHills (25) (lw: chsd ldrs tl wknd wl over 1f out) ............................ ½.20

3349* **Eclipsing (IRE) (88)** *(RCharlton)* 4-8-13 (5x) RCochrane (29) (swtg: jnd ldrs 4f out: wknd over 1f out) ............................ ½.21

3241⁴ **Trooping (IRE) (82)** *(GHarwood)* 3-8-2 KDarley (31) (lw: in tch: effrt 4f out: wknd 2f out) ............................ nk.22

3009* **Vague Dancer (68)** *(MrsJRRamsden)* 6-7-7 JFanning (28) (lw: chsd ldrs tl wknd fnl 2f) ............................ 3½.23

3428⁶ **Wave Hill (82)** *(RHannon)* 3-8-2 NCarlisle (4) (lw: in tch: effrt & ch 3f out: wknd 2f out) ............................ hd.24

3069⁶ **Mudaffar (IRE) (92)** *(RWArmstrong)* 4-9-3 NDay (8) (mid div: effrt 4f out: grad wknd) ............................ nk.25

3311³ **Aasff (USA) (73)** *(DMorley)* 3-7-7 SWood (23) (chsd ldrs tl wknd over 2f out) .. 1.26

3061* **Grand Master (IRE) (91)** (bl) *(PFICole)* 3-8-11 PaulEddery (1) (lw: in tch tl outpcd fnl 3f) ............................ 1.27

3277⁶ **Big Blue (87)** (bl) *(CEBrittain)* 3-8-2 ‡³BDoyle (9) (cl up tl wknd over 2f out) ... hd.28

3441 **Desert Splendour (73)** *(CEBrittain)* 4-7-12 DBiggs (15) (chsd ldrs tl wknd 3f out) ............................ hd.29

3476 **Brilliant (68)** *(JPearce)* 4-7-0 ‡⁷DWright (16) (s.i.s: hdwy stands' side: wknd 3f out) ............................ 1.30

LONG HANDICAP: Vague Dancer 7-5, Aasff (USA) 7-5, Brilliant 7-6.

9/2 RAMBO'S HALL, 8/1 Mellottie, Double Entendre, 12/1 Revif (FR)(op 8/1), Montpelier Boy, 14/1 Vague Dancer, 16/1 Grand Master (IRE), Eclipsing (IRE), 22/1 Barford Lad, Alkarif (USA), 25/1 Marine Diver, Roseate Lodge, Lucky Guest, Scales of Justice, Cumbrian Challenge (IRE), Brilliant, 33/1 Dawaahi (USA), Camden's Ransom, Wave Hill, Big Blue, Mudaffar (IRE), Desert Splendour, L ord of the Field, Cru Exceptionnel, 66/1 Ors. CSF £54.11, CT £401.76. Tote £5.90: £3.10 £2.60 £1.80 £10.30 (£30.60). Mr B. Dixon (WORKSOP) bred by Sqdn-Ldr Frank Barrett. 30 Rn
1m 54.63 (4.63)
SF—88/71/58/64/52/75

## 3548

JOCKEY CLUB CUP (Stks) (Gp 3) £17442.00 (£6454.85: £3039.93: £1258.22)
2m
                 4-15 (4-19)

3197* **Further Flight (115)** *(Fav) (BWHills)* 6–9-3 MHills (4) (b.hind: hld up: stdy hdwy to ld appr fnl f: pushed along & r.o wl) .................... —1
3369   Supreme Choice (USA) **(106)** *(BWHills)* 4–9-0 DHolland (2) (lw: led tl hdd appr fnl f: kpt on wl) .................... 5.2
2982a5 Shambo **(110)** *(CEBrittain)* 5–9-5 MRoberts (1) (hld up: hdwy 4f out: rdn & btn wl over 2f out) .................... 15.3
2844   Hawait Al Barr **(95)** *(MRStoute)* 4–8-11 BRaymond (3) (chsd ldr: effrt 4f out: sn rdn & btn) .................... 30.4

**4/6** FURTHER FLIGHT, **3/1** Shambo, **7/1** Hawait Al Barr, **9/1** Supreme Choice (USA). CSF £5.61, Tote £1.60 (£3.80). Mr S. Wingfield Digby (LAMBOURN) bred by S. Wingfield Digby. 4 Rn    3m 38.91 (15.61)
SF—11/3/–/–

## 3549

ALINGTON STKS (Mdn 2-Y.O.F) £4620.00 (£1380.00: £660.00: £300.00)
6f
                 4-45 (4-48)

3227a5 **Nicer (IRE)** *(BWHills)* 8-11 DHolland (8) (s.i.s: wnt prom ½-wy: led appr fnl f: r.o) —1
3295⁵ Golden Guest *(MrsJCecil)* 8-11 PaulEddery (1) (led tl hdd appr fnl f: no ex) .... 1½.2
3240² Desert Venus (Fav) *(BHanbury)* 8-11 BRaymond (4) (lw: w ldrs: hrd rdn over 1f out: nt qckn) .................... 1½.3
   Aneesati *(CEBrittain)* 8-11 MRoberts (10) (b: unf: scope: lw: chsd ldrs tl outpcd 2f out: kpt on ins fnl f) .................... 2½.4
3008³ I'M Yours *(RHannon)* 8-11 LPiggott (5) (in tch: effrt 2f out: no imp) .................... 1½.5
   Polanie (CAN) *(LMCumani)* 8-11 LDettori (3) (lengthy: unf: s.i.s: sn in tch: outpcd fnl 2f) .................... 3.6
   North Call *(GHEden)* 8-11 JCarroll (6) (cmpt: sn outpcd & bhd) .................... 12.7
   Nawaaya (USA) *(AAScott)* 8-11 MHills (2) (leggy: unf: s.s: n.d) .................... 6.8
588   Twitcher *(GBlum)* 8-11 AShoults (9) (bkwd: chsd ldrs tl hung bdly rt & wknd over 2f out) .................... 1½.9

**9/4** Desert Venus, **11/4** NICER (IRE), **4/1** Aneesati(op 7/4), **9/1** Polanie (CAN), **12/1** I'M Yours, Golden Guest, **14/1** Nawaaya (USA)(op 8/1), **25/1** North Call, **100/1** Twitcher. CSF £30.86, Tote £3.50: £1.40 £2.80 £1.60 (£33.00). Mrs J. M. Corbett (LAMBOURN) bred by Barronstown Bloodstock Ltd in Ireland. 9 Rn    1m 15.62 (4.22)
SF—37/31/25/15/9/–

## 3550

SUFFOLK NURSERY   £6368.00 (£1904.00: £912.00: £416.00)    6f    5-20 (5-22)
(Weights raised 1 lb)

3470* **Palacegate Touch (74)** *(JBerry)* 8-4 JCarroll (13) (trckd ldrs: effrt & swvd lft over 1f out: r.o u.p to ld wl ins fnl f) .................... —1
3394* Mr Butch **(66)** *(MRChannon)* 7-10 JQuinn (3) (lw: hld up: qcknd to ld wl over 1f out: rdn & r.o: no ex nr fin) .................... 1½.2
3123² Storiths (IRE) **(88)** (Fav) *(JWWatts)* 9-4 WCarson (7) (lw: s.i.s: pushed along & bhd: hdwy ½-wy: styd on one pce ins fnl f) .................... 1½.3
3096   Northern Bird **(89)** *(BWHills)* 9-5 DHolland (2) (b.hind: lw: bhd: hdwy ½-wy: rdn & nt qckn fnl f) .................... 2½.4
2683² Rain Splash **(85)** *(RHannon)* 9-1 BRaymond (12) (hld up & bhd: hdwy ½-wy: rdn & hung lft wl over 1f out: nvr able to chal) .................... hd.5
3432   Nitouche **(72)** *(PatMitchell)* 7-11 ‡⁵NKennedy (8) (lw: bhd tl styd on fnl 2f: n.d) .. 4.6
3366   Go Flightline (IRE) **(69)** *(MBell)* 7-13 JFanning (9) (lw: w ldrs tl wknd & eased ins fnl f) .................... ¾.7
3049⁵ My Bonus **(85)** *(DJSCosgrove)* 8-12 ‡³DHarrison (1) (b: b.hind: hld up & bhd: n.d) .................... ¾.8
3018² Greenlet (IRE) **(88)** *(MRStoute)* 8-13 ‡⁵JJones (14) (chsd ldrs: ev ch 2f out: sn rdn & btn) .................... 1½.9
3214² Iron Merchant (IRE) **(90)** *(RAkehurst)* 9-6 MRoberts (15) (lw: led tl hdd & wknd wl over 1f out) .................... 2.10
3376* Iolte **(69)** *(MAJarvis)* 7-13 GCrealock (10) (w ldrs over 4f: sn wknd) .................... 1½.11
3382⁶ Dr Lechter **(77)** *(SMHillen)* 8-7 JLowe (6) (in tch: drvn along ½-wy) .................... 1.12
3478   Pine Ridge Lad (IRE) **(72)** *(MJohnston)* 8-2 PaulEddery (4) (in tch over 3f: sn lost pl) .................... 1.13

**7/2** Storiths (IRE), **5/1** Dr Lechter, **6/1** Iron Merchant (IRE), **7/1** PALACEGATE TOUCH(op 9/2), **10/1** Iolte, Mr Butch, **11/1** Go Flightline (IRE), **12/1** Pine Ridge Lad (IRE)(op 8/1), **14/1** Nitouche, Northern Bird, Greenlet (IRE), **16/1** My Bonus, **20/1** Rain Splash. CSF £73.85, CT £268.61. Tote £5.70: £2.10 £3.10 £1.90 (£25.00). Palacegate Corporation Ltd (COCKERHAM) bred by The Woodhaven Stud. 13 Rn    1m 14.63 (3.23)
SF—50/36/52/43/38/4

T/Trio: Race 2: Any 2 fr 1st 3 w any £46.60 (26.5 Tckts); Race 4: £44.90 (83 Tckts). T/Jkpt: Not won; £30,376.22 to York 7/10/92. T/Plpt: £3,352.20 (3.75 Tckts).
                                                              AA

3314—**LINGFIELD (L-H)**

**Thursday, October 1st [Turf Soft AWT Standard]**
Going Allowance: Turf: 0.65 sec (Y); AWT: minus 0.20 sec (FS)          Wind: almost nil

Stalls: high

**3551**  E.B.F. SLEEPING PARTNER STKS (I) (Mdn 2-Y.O) £2532.00 (£702.00: £336.00)
6f                                                                    1-20 (1-25)

3012 **Princely Favour (IRE) (86)** *(RHannon)* 9-0 BRouse (13) (mde all: drvn out) ..... —1
Nafuth (USA) *(PTWalwyn)* 9-0 RHills (9) (leggy: unf: hdwy 2f out: ev ch ins fnl f:
rdn & r.o) ................................................................................. nk.2
3372 Mansard (IRE) (Fav) *(JHMGosden)* 9-0 RCochrane (14) (lw: a.p: n.m.r wl over
1f out: unable qckn fnl f) ........................................................ 2¹/₂.3
Summer Flower *(BWHills)* 8-9 RStreet (8) (dipped: lengthy: shkn up & hdwy fnl
2f: r.o) ........................................................................................... 4.4
3314 Rakis (IRE) *(CJBenstead)* 9-0 JWilliams (4) (a.p: rdn over 2f out: one pce) ........ 2.5
3255³ Legal Risk (76) *(DHaydnJones)* 8-9 JLowe (11) (a.p: ev ch 2f out: wknd over 1f
out) ............................................................................................... 1.6
3179⁶ Desert Nomad *(SDow)* 8-6 ‡³FNorton (10) (no hdwy fnl 2f) ......................... 3¹/₂.7
3410 Mr Cube (IRE) *(PFICole)* 9-0 TQuinn (7) (lw: a.p: ev ch 2f out: wknd over 1f out:
eased whn btn ins fnl f) .............................................................. 2¹/₂.8
3283 Nightmare Lady *(WHolden)* 8-9 MTebbutt (12) (a bhd) ................................. 7.9
2948 Jest Rosie *(MDIUsher)* 8-4 ‡⁵RPrice (5) (w'like: bkwd: bhd fnl 3f) ............ s.h.10
Selfish Lady *(JLSpearing)* 8-9 KDarley (2) (neat: outpcd) ....................... 2.11
Tom Parker *(PHowling)* 9-0 JQuinn (1) (w'like: scope: bkwd: swvd lft s: a bhd) 6.12
Persian Chimes (IRE) *(GAPritchard-Gordon)* 9-0 NDay (3) (w'like: bit bkwd:
prom 3f) ...................................................................................... 6.13
Hedgehog *(JO'Donoghue)* 8-9 NAdams (6) (unf: scope: bit bkwd: s.s: sme
hdwy 4f out: wknd over 2f out) ................................................. ¹/₂.14

**6/4** Mansard (IRE), **4/1** PRINCELY FAVOUR (IRE), **13/2** Nafuth (USA), **10/1** Summer Flower(op 6/1), Mr Cube
(IRE), Desert Nomad, **11/1** Legal Risk(8/1—12/1), **14/1** Persian Chimes (IRE), **16/1** Rakis (IRE), **20/1** Selfish
Lady, **33/1** Nightmare Lady, Tom Parker, **50/1** Ors. CSF £31.98, Tote £4.80: £1.70 £3.30 £1.30 (£30.70). Mr C.
M. Hamer (MARLBOROUGH) bred by Rose Bank Stud in Ireland. 14 Rn                    1m 16.32 (7.72)
SF—24/23/13/–/–/–

**3552**  E.B.F. SLEEPING PARTNER STKS (II) (Mdn 2-Y.O) £2532.00 (£702.00: £336.00)
6f                                                                    1-50 (1-57)

3179⁵ **Most Eminent** *(PWHarris)* 9-0 SWhitworth (5) (racd far side: hdwy 4f out: led wl
over 1f out: rdn out) .................................................................... —1
Chief's Song *(BWHills)* 9-0 TQuinn (4) (wl grwn: swtchd stands' side after 1f: gd
hdwy 2f out: hrd rdn: r.o ins fnl f) ............................................. 3¹/₂.2
Al Shaati (FR) (Fav) *(MRStoute)* 8-9 WRyan (10) (neat: lw: a.p: led over 2f out tl
wl over 1f out: unable qckn) ....................................................... hd.3
Record Lover (IRE) *(JHMGosden)* 9-0 RCochrane (1) (cmpt: racd far side: a.p:
chsd wnr wl over 1f out: one pce) ............................................... 1.4
3181 Al Moulouki *(JWPayne)* 9-0 WHood (6) (swtg: racd far side: no hdwy fnl 2f) ...... 6.5
3372 Jadirah (USA) *(JLDunlop)* 8-9 RHills (3) (racd far side: prom 3f) ................... hd.6
Wired for Sound *(MRChannon)* 8-11 ‡³RPerham (9) (w'like: scope: hdwy 3f out:
wknd over 1f out) ........................................................................ 2¹/₂.7
3320 Dance Magical *(MDixon)* 8-4 ‡⁵NGwilliams (12) (chsd ldr over 3f) ................... 3.8
Blues Breaker *(DSasse)* 8-4 ‡⁵RPrice (2) (w'like: racd far side: rdn 3f out: sn
wknd) ............................................................................................ 2¹/₂.9
Dance and Sing (IRE) *(DLWilliams)* 9-0 NAdams (11) (str: bit bkwd: s.s: a wl
bhd) ............................................................................................ s.h.10
St Alzina (IRE) *(GHEden)* 9-0 JWilliams (14) (w'like: led over 3f) ................... 6.11
3289 Ignited *(MrsNMacauley)* 9-0 TSprake (7) (b: spd 3f) .................................... 1.12

**6/4** Al Shaati (FR), **9/2** MOST EMINENT(op 8/1), **6/1** Record Lover (IRE)(op 3/1), Chief's Song(op 4/1), **7/1**
Jadirah (USA), **10/1** Wired for Sound, **25/1** Ignited, St Alzina (IRE), **33/1** Ors. CSF £31.25, Tote £4.40: £1.50
£2.00 £1.10 (£13.40). Twelve Of The Best (BERKHAMSTED) bred by The Lavington Stud. 12 Rn
1m 17.40 (8.80)
SF—2/–/–/–/–/–

**3553**  SIDEWALK CLAIMING STKS (I) (2-Y.O) £2574.00 (£714.00: £342.00)
6f (AWT)                                                             2-20 (2-22)

3472⁴ **Stardust Express (51)** *(MJohnston)* 8-7 RPElliott (13) (a.p: hrd rdn fnl f: led last
strides) .......................................................................................... —1

3343⁴ La Bonita (IRE) **(64)** (bl) *(JBerry)* 8-6 JCarroll (1) (led: hrd rdn fnl f: hdd last strides) ............ ¹/₂.2
2873 Absolutely Fact (USA) *(WJHaggas)* 8-11 JQuinn (7) (lw: rdn & hdwy 2f out: r.o)   2.3
3408 Dhahran **(65)** (bl) *(PFlCole)* 8-7 TQuinn (5) (a.p: hrd rdn over 3f out: one pce fnl 2f) ............ 1¹/₂.4
3343³ Blazing Soul (IRE) **(68)** (Jt-Fav) *(RHannon)* 8-4 RCochrane (12) (lw: rdn 2f out: hdwy over 1f out: nvr nrr) ............ ³/₄.5
3275⁵ Cuddly Date **(60)** (Jt-Fav) *(DTThom)* 8-0 DBiggs (3) (no hdwy fnl 2f) ............ 1¹/₂.6
3394⁵ Second Colours (USA) **(73)** *(PSFelgate)* 9-3 KDarley (10) (a abt same pl) ...... nk.7
3178 Baileys Colours **(47)** *(BJMcMath)* 8-2 EJohnson (8) (lw: hmpd leaving stalls: wl bhd over 4f: nvr nrr) ............ nk.8
3311⁵ Mister Blake **(69)** (v) *(WAO'Gorman)* 8-4 ‡³EmmaO'Gorman (14) (nvr nr to chal)   1¹/₂.10
3472 Jade Runner **(46)** (v) *(MrsNMacauley)* 7-12 TSprake (11) (prom 4f) ............ 1¹/₂.10
2771 Lady of Shadows **(47)** *(SDow)* 7-11⁽²⁾ ‡⁷AMartinez (2) (b.hind: a mid dvn) ... 1¹/₂.11
3218 Hy Wilma **(61)** *(RJHodges)* 7-11⁽⁶⁾ ‡⁷SDrowne (4) (bhd fnl 3f) ............ 5.12
2005 Screech **(56)** *(CJames)* 7-12 SDawson (6) (bhd fnl 3f) ............ 1.13
3372 Bold a Maiden (w) *(DRLaing)* 8-4 TyroneWilliams (9) (lw: prom 3f: t.o) ......... 20.14

**5/1** Blazing Soul (IRE), Cuddly Date, **6/1** La Bonita (IRE), **10/1** Second Colours (USA), STARDUST EXPRESS, Dhahran, **12/1** Hy Wilma, **11/1** Screech, **14/1** Absolutely Fact (USA), **16/1** Baileys Colours, Mister Blake, **20/1** Lady of Shadows, **25/1** Jade Runner. CSF £65.45, Tote £18.20: £3.30 £2.10 £5.10 (£29.20). Mrs R. A. Johnson (MIDDLEHAM) bred by Mrs Joan M. Martin. 14 Rn
           1m 13.33 (2.73)
SF—14/11/8/-/-/-

## 3554

AUTUMN H'CAP (3-Y.O) (0-90) £3313.60 (£919.60: £440.80)     **7f 140y**   2-50 (2-52)

3196 **Sovereign Rock (IRE) (75)** *(RHannon)* 8-12 ‡³RPerham (6) (lw: mde virtually all: rdn out) ............ —1
3241² Vanborough Lad **(65)** *(MJHaynes)* 8-5 DBiggs (2) (a.p: rdn over 2f out: r.o ins fnl f) ............ ¹/₂.2
3396⁵ Sylvan (IRE) **(81)** *(CFWall)* 9-7 GBaxter (4) (hdwy 3f out: rdn over 2f out: r.o) .... 1.3
3004 Ghalyoon (USA) **(78)** *(PTWalwyn)* 9-4 RHills (1) (n.m.r & lost pl over 2f out: rallied fnl f: r.o) ............ 2.4
3417⁵ Nobby Barnes **(57)** (Fav) *(DAWilson)* 7-11 GBardwell (12) (b: hdwy over 1f out: unable qckn: eased nr fin) ............ hd.5
3265³ Key Suspect (USA) **(80)** *(JHMGosden)* 9-6 RCochrane (3) (hld up: nt clr run over 2f out: shkn up over 1f out: one pce) ............ 1.6
2995² Express Service **(70)** *(PJMakin)* 8-10 TQuinn (11) (hdwy & nt clr run 2f out: nvr nr to chal) ............ 1¹/₂.7
3363³ Will Soon **(68)** (HCandy) 8-1 ‡⁷AntoinetteArmes (9) (lw: a.p: ev ch 2f out: wknd over 1f out) ............ nk.8
2198 Quiet Miss **(56)** *(MrsAKnight)* 7-7⁽³⁾ ‡³FNorton (8) (prom over 4f) ............ 8.9
3417 Canadian Capers **(70)** *(MRChannon)* 8-10 JQuinn (7) (prom 4f) ............ nk.10
482 Precious Wonder **(60)** *(PButler)* 8-5 TyroneWilliams (15) (hrd rdn & hdwy over 2f out: wknd over 1f out) ............ s.h.11
3252✱ Neither Nor **(47)** *(RJHolder)* 8-11 JWilliams (13) (lw: hrd rdn 3f out: a bhd) ... s.h.12
3290 Peerage Prince **(62)** *(PatMitchell)* 7-13 ‡³SO'Gorman (14) (prom over 4f) ...... 1¹/₂.13
2953 Tom's Apache **(53)** *(BillyWilliams)* 7-7 NAdams (10) (swtg: a bhd) ............ 5.14
3269⁴ Sweet Jaffa **(72)** *(MajorWRHern)* 8-12 WRyan (5) (rdn 6f out: bhd fnl 3f) ......... 8.15
        LONG HANDICAP: Quiet Miss 7-4, Tom's Apache 6-11.
*Stewards Enquiry: Bardwell fined £185 under Rule 151 (ii) (failure to ensure best possible placing).*

**9/2** Nobby Barnes(8/1—10/1), **7/1** Express Service, Will Soon, Key Suspect (USA), **8/1** Sweet Jaffa, SOVEREIGN ROCK (IRE), Vanborough Lad, **11/1** Neither Nor(8/1—12/1), **14/1** Quiet Miss, Sylvan (IRE), **16/1** Ghalyoon, **25/1** Canadian Capers, Precious Wonder, **33/1** Peerage Prince, **50/1** Tom's Apache. CSF £68.59, CT £823.68. Tote £12.30: £3.50 £2.50 £3.70 (£60.60). Mr P. A. Howell (MARLBOROUGH) bred by K. Molloy in Ireland. 15 Rn
           1m 37.47 (8.97)
SF—38/29/42/33/11/31

## 3555

UPHAM H'CAP (0-80) £3240.00 (£900.00: £432.00)     **1¹/₄m**     3-20 (3-22)
(Weights raised 3 lb)

3236⁶ **Tiger Shoot (46)** *(DJSCosgrove)* 5–8-1 JLowe (11) (b.off fore: s:i:s: hdwy 4f out: 6th st: chlr 3f out: led wl ins fnl f: drvn out) ............ —1
3215 Sarah-Clare **(52)** (Fav) *(RAkehurst)* 4–8-4 ‡³FNorton (6) (hdwy 7f out: led 4f out: hrd rdn 2f out: hdd wl ins fnl f: r.o) ............ 1.2
3389⁵ Lady Dundee (USA) **(62)** *(MrsJCecil)* 3–8-11 WRyan (1) (3rd st: ev ch 1f out: hrd rdn: r.o) ............ 1.3
3403³ Pusey Street Boy **(39)** *(JRBosley)* 5–7-8 JQuinn (8) (lw: 5th st: hrd rdn: unable qckn) ............ 1¹/₂.4
3174✱ Supertop **(55)** *(PWHarris)* 4–8-10 TQuinn (5) (4th st: wknd 2f out: eased whn btn fnl f) ............ 7.5

3269⁵ So Smug (USA) **(69)** (v) *(JHMGosden)* 3-9-4 RCochrane (7) (s.s: hdwy 5f out: 7th st: hrd rdn over 2f out: no rspnse) ..................... 5.6
3256 Castillet **(72)** *(GHarwood)* 3-9-7 AClark (9) (rdn 7f out: 8th st: nvr nr to chal) .. 3¹/₂.7
3234⁴ Rapporteur (USA) **(66)** *(CCElsey)* 6-9-7 NAdams (3) (led 8f out to 4f out: 2nd st: wknd 3f out) ..................... 10.8
3396³ Agincourt Song (USA) **(75)** *(JLDunlop)* 3-9-10 JCarroll (10) (lw: bhd fnl 7f) .... 1¹/₂.9
3180³ Awesome Power **(59)** *(CRNelson)* 6-9-0 RHills (4) (prom 5f: 9th & wkng st: eased over 2f out: t.o) ..................... 25.10
2805 Cheveley Dancer (USA) **(63)** *(AWDenson)* 4-9-4 JWilliams (2) (lw: led 2f: wknd over 4f out: t.o) ..................... 10.11

7/2 Sarah-Clare, 6/1 So Smug (USA), Rapporteur (USA)(op 4/1), 7/1 Supertop, TIGER SHOOT, 9/1 Lady Dundee (USA), 10/1 Awesome Power, Pusey Street Boy, 11/1 Agincourt Song (USA)(7/1—12/1), 14/1 Castillet, 50/1 Cheveley Dancer (USA). CSF £30.47, CT £206.92. Tote £6.10: £2.70 £1.70 £4.10 (£19.50). Mr C. V. Lines (NEWMARKET) bred by J. M. Greetham. 11 Rn
2m 17.93 (14.93)
SF—3/3/7/–/–/–

---

**3556**        LEWES H'CAP (0-70) £2679.00 (£744.00: £357.00)        **1m 3f 106y**        3-50 (3-54)
(Weights raised 4 lb)

3306⁶ **Oak Apple (USA) (56)** *(BHanbury)* 3-8-13 RCochrane (11) (lost pl 6f out: hrd rdn 5f out: rapid hdwy over 1f out: led wl ins fnl f: r.o wl) ..... —1
3221 Island Blade (IRE) **(47)** *(RAkehurst)* 3-8-1 ‡³FNorton (4) (6th st: hrd rdn over 1f out: r.o) ..................... 2.2
3236 Dr Zeva **(31)** *(MDixon)* 6-7-9⁽²⁾ SDawson (5) (7th st: hdwy over 2f out: led ins fnl f: sn hdd: unable qckn) ..................... hd.3
2698 Killick **(30)** *(REPeacock)* 4-7-8⁽¹⁾ JQuinn (6) (3rd st: led over 2f out tl ins fnl f: one pce) ..................... 1.4
388 Crabby Bill **(46)** (bl) *(MissBSanders)* 5-0-10 DBiggs (8) (rdn 7f out: hdwy 5f out: 8th st: nvr nr) ..................... 2¹/₂.5
Amigos **(56)** *(PMitchell)* 4-9-3 ‡³SO'Gorman (7) (led over 4f out tl over 2f out: wknd over 1f out) ..................... 2¹/₂.6
1063 Eastern Magic **(60)** *(JAkehurst)* 4-9-10 JWilliams (12) (rdn 8f out: nvr nr to chal) 3.7
3426² Flash of Straw (IRE) **(48)** (bl) (Fav) *(GLewis)* 3-8-0 ‡⁵ATucker (15) (2nd st: wknd wl over 1f out) ..................... ³/₄.8
2470 Clifton Chase **(49)** *(MAJarvis)* 3-8-6 GCrealock (14) (bhd fnl 5f) ..................... 10.9
3054 Mahairy (USA) **(61)** (v) *(AAScott)* 3-9-4 JFortune (9) (hdwy 5f out: 4th st: wknd over 2f out) ..................... ³/₄.10
3381³ Maji **(67)** *(DMorley)* 3-9-10 WRyan (2) (5th st: wknd over 2f out: eased whn btn over 1f out) ..................... 1¹/₂.11
3316⁶ Lady Poly **(29)** *(MissBSanders)* 4-7-7 GBardwell (3) (led over 3f: wknd 5f out) 6.12
3405³ Sirtelimar (IRE) **(57)** *(RCSpicer)* 3-9-0 VSmith (16) (sme hdwy 7f out: wknd 5f out) ..................... 3.13
3379⁴ Premier Dance **(35)** *(DHaydnJones)* 5-7-13 TyroneWilliams (10) (9th st: bhd fnl 3f) ..................... 6.14
3380 Apple **(48)** *(WHolden)* 3-8-5 JLowe (13) (mid div 5f: t.o fnl 4f) ..................... 20.15
LONG HANDICAP: Dr Zeva 7-6, Killick 7-4, Lady Poly 7-4.

7/2 Flash of Straw (IRE), 5/1 OAK APPLE (USA), 13/2 Premier Dance, 7/1 Maji, 8/1 Island Blade (IRE), 10/1 Amigos, 14/1 Clifton Chase, 16/1 Killick, 20/1 Dr Zeva, Lady Poly, Eastern Magic, Mahairy (USA), Sirtelimar (IRE), 25/1 Crabby Bill, 33/1 Apple. CSF £43.52, CT £692.67. Tote £4.70: £2.20 £3.20 £5.60 (£31.70). Mr Z. Kashiwagi (NEWMARKET) bred by Caper Hill Farm Incorporated in USA. 15 Rn
2m 39.70 (17.7)

---

**3557**        BLETCHINGLY STKS (Mdn 3-Y.O) £2070.00 (£570.00: £270.00)
**7f (AWT)**        4-20 (4-24)

2738² **Ginger Flower** *(GWragg)* 8-6 ‡³FNorton (12) (lw: rdn 5f out: hdwy 3f out: str run fnl f: led nr fin) ..................... —1
3048⁶ Honey Heather (IRE) **(56)** *(CFWall)* 8-9 DBiggs (5) (a.p: led over 2f out: hrd rdn fnl f: hdd nr fin) ..................... 1¹/₂.2
2969² Harcliff (Fav) *(DJSCosgrove)* 9-0 WRyan (7) (b.hind: a.p: ev ch 1f out: hrd rdn: r.o) ..................... nk.3
3142³ Under the Bridge **(66)** (bl) *(PWHarris)* 9-0 RCochrane (2) (led over 5f out tl over 2f out: wknd wl over 1f out) ..................... 3¹/₂.4
3412 Access Voyager *(RBoss)* 9-0 MTebbutt (13) (rdn 4f out: nvr nr to chal) ..................... 2.5
2753 Dam Certain (IRE) **(47)** *(AWDenson)* 8-9 TQuinn (9) (no hdwy fnl 3f) ..................... 2.6
2582⁶ Rio Trusky **(36)** *(MDIUsher)* 9-0 MWigham (11) (swtg: outpcd) ..................... s.h.7
3003 Captain Marmalade **(63)** *(DTThom)* 9-0 JWilliams (6) (lw: outpcd: nvr nrr) ...... 1¹/₂.8
1852 Old Fox (FR) *(DSasse)* 8-9 ‡⁵RPrice (4) (s.s: nvr nr to chal) ..................... 1/₂.9
2198 Hinton Harry (IRE) **(37)** *(SMellor)* 9-0 GBaxter (1) (dwlt: a bhd) ..................... 2.10

3042 Dilkush **(38)** *(LJHolt)* 8-7 ‡⁷CAvery (10) (bhd fnl 3f) ............................................. 3.11
*3318* Ipsilante **(47)** *(ASReid)* 8-9 RHills (4) (led over 1f: wknd over 2f out) ............. s.h.12
3037 Mabonne **(49)** (bl) *(JLDunlop)* 8-9 BRouse (3) (prom whn hmpd 6f out: nt rcvr) 2¹⁄₂.13

**11/4** Harcliff, **4/1** Under the Bridge, **9/2** GINGER FLOWER, **11/2** Honey Heather (IRE), **7/1** Access Voyager, **10/1** Mabonne, **14/1** Old Fox (FR), **20/1** Ipsilante, Dilkush, **25/1** Captain Marmalade, Dam Certain (IRE), Hinton Harry (IRE), **40/1** Rio Trusky. CSF £30.44, Tote £5.80: £1.80 £1.80 £1.70 (£8.60). Mrs H. H. Morriss (NEWMARKET) bred by H. H. Morriss. 13 Rn                    1m 26.17 (2.17)
SF–39/37/41/30/24/13

---

**3558**  SIDEWALK CLAIMING STKS (II) (2-Y.O) £2574.00 (£714.00: £342.00)
**6f (AWT)**                                                                          4-50 (4-52)

*3315* **Risky Number (57)** (bl) *(JSMoore)* 8-3 AClark (3) (lw: mde all: hrd rdn over 1f
out: r.o wl) ......................................................................... —1
34204 Wickins **(61)** (bl) *(GLewis)* 7-12 ‡³FNorton (8) (chsd wnr 3f out: rdn & ev ch 2f
out: r.o) ............................................................................ 1.2
33904 Abjar *(PAKelleway)* 9-3 GayKelleway (7) (b: dwlt: outpcd: hrd rdn 2f out: rapid
hdwy f: fin fast) ...................................................................... 1.3
33943 Mississipi Maid *(WGMTurner)* 8-0 TSprake (4) (lw: a.p: r.o one pce fnl 2f) ......... nk.4
3071 Samanthas Joy **(56)** *(TFairhurst)* 8-0 DBiggs (6) (lost pl 3f out: hrd rdn & rallied
1f out: r.o) .......................................................................... 1¹⁄₂.5
*3315★* Pat Poindestres **(66)** (Fav) *(MDixon)* 8-8 BRouse (12) (prom 4f) .................. 1¹⁄₂.6
3050 Floodlight (IRE) **(44)** *(RJHolder)* 7-10 NAdams (1) (rdn 3f out: no hdwy fnl 3f) . hd.7
*3315* Stroika (IRE) **(64)** *(CJames)* 8-0 JQuinn (9) (rdn along: a mid div) ............... 6.8
25913 Sterling Princess **(45)** (bl) *(JRJenkins)* 7-11 ‡⁵ATucker (13) (prom over 3f) ......... 2.9
3050 Midarida (IRE) **(40)** *(BForsey)* 7-10 JLowe (2) (outpcd) ............................ nk.10
3410 Welsh Pet (bl) *(PJMakin)* 8-0 CRutter (5) (a wl bhd) ................................. nk.11
32086 Super Seve (IRE) **(78)** *(JBerry)* 8-3 JCarroll (10) (lw: bhd fnl 3f) .............. 4.12
2932 Nigels Prospect *(DHaydnJones)* 8-9 JWilliams (11) (dwlt: a wl bhd) ............ s.h.13
20986 Grey Runner **(42)** *(BPalling)* 8-2 GBardwell (14) (a bhd) ...................... 1¹⁄₂.14

**7/4** Pat Poindestres, **5/1** Samanthas Joy(12/1—14/1), **7/1** Mississipi Maid(op 4/1), **8/1** Super Seve IRE(op 5/1), **10/1** Wickins, RISKY NUMBER, Stroika (IRE), **12/1** Abjar(op 8/1), **14/1** Welsh Pet, **20/1** Midarida (IRE), **25/1** Sterling Princess, **33/1** Ors. CSF £106.98, Tote £16.30: £3.30 £3.90 £3.10 (£124.20). Mrs Derek Strauss (ANDOVER) bred by Roldvale Ltd. 14 Rn                          1m 13.43 (2.83)
SF–8/–/14/–/–/–

---

**3559**  LEVY BOARD H'CAP (0-70) £3027.50 (£840.00: £402.50)   **5f**   5-20 (5-22)

32965 **Bright Paragon (IRE) (42)** *(HJCollingridge)* 3–8-2 JQuinn (5) (lw: a.p: led ins
fnl f: rdn out) .................................................................. —1
3294★ Joe Sugden **(55)** (Fav) *(PHowling)* 8–9-2 JWilliams (6) (lw: hdwy over 1f out: r.o
ins fnl f) ....................................................................... 1¹⁄₂.2
2395 My Sovereign (USA) **(68)** *(RHannon)* 3–9-11 ‡³RPerham (14) (a.p: led 1f out tl
ins fnl f: unable qckn) .......................................................... 1¹⁄₂.3
34236 Cronk's Quality **(35)** (bl) *(DCJermy)* 9-7-10⁽²⁾ SDawson (13) (racd stands'
side: a.p: r.o one pce fnl 2f) .................................................... ¹⁄₂.4
3460 Inswinger **(32)** *(WGRWightman)* 6–7-7 GBardwell (15) (racd stands' side: rdn
& hdwy 2f out: one pce fnl f) .................................................... s.h.5
2245★ Galaxy Express **(40)** *(GHEden)* 4–8-1 JCarroll (10) (b.hind: a.p: ev ch 2f out:
one pce) ......................................................................... ³⁄₄.6
*2974* Imco Double (IRE) **(51)** *(WHolden)* 4–8-12 MTebbutt (1) (gd spd over 3f) .......... 2.7
3361 Belthorn **(53)** *(JJBridger)* 3–8-13 SWhitworth (12) (racd stands' side: led 4f) ... nk.8
3391 Party Treat (IRE) **(39)** *(DMarks)* 4–8-0 JLowe (2) (spd over 2f) .................. s.h.9
2821 Calibairn **(37)** *(DJSCosgrove)* 4–7-9 ‡³FNorton (3) (prom over 2f) ................ hd.10
1978 Miss Precocious **(36)** (v) *(DShaw)* 4–7-4⁽⁴⁾ ‡⁷CHawksley (11) (s.s: a bhd) ...... 1¹⁄₂.11
3391 Frimley Parkson **(34)** (bl) *(PHowling)* 8–7-9⁽²⁾ DBiggs (7) (outpcd) ............. ³⁄₄.12
29505 Bright Sea (USA) **(34)** *(BillyWilliams)* 4–7-9 NAdams (4) (outpcd) ............... 5.13
32784 Dickens Lane **(52)** *(RJHodges)* 5–8-6 ‡⁷SDrowne (9) (outpcd) ................... 1¹⁄₂.14
LONG HANDICAP: Inswinger 7-5, Frimley Parkson 7-4.

**9/2** Joe Sugden, **5/1** Imco Double (IRE), Dickens Lane, **10/1** Belthorn(op 5/1), BRIGHT PARAGON (IRE), My Sovereign (USA)(op 6/1), **12/1** Inswinger, **14/1** Galaxy Express, **16/1** Calibairn, Frimley Parkson, Miss Precocious, **20/1** Cronk's Quality, **25/1** Ors. CSF £51.65, CT £426.12. Tote £13.30: £3.00 £1.90 £3.70 (£34.20). Mr D. C. G. Cooper (NEWMARKET) bred by B. Kennedy in Ireland. 14 Rn     62.85 sec (5.85)
SF–36/44/47/16/12/17

---

T/Plpt: £1,938.10 (0.2 Tckts); £2,095.30 to Newmarket 2/10/92.                    LMc

3450a—**MAISONS-LAFFITTE (L-H)**

**Monday, September 21st [Soft]**

Going Allowance: nil sec per fur (G)

**3560a**    LA COUPE DE MAISONS-LAFFITTE (Gp 3) £20640.00    **1¼m (st)**

  3237* **KNIFEBOX (USA)** *(JHMGosden)* 4-9-2 DHolland ............................................... —1
  2998² Steinbeck (USA) *(France)* 3-8-11 SCauthen ................................................. ¾.2
  2095a² Runyon (IRE) *(France)* 4-9-0 CAsmussen ................................................. 6.3
Tote 1.80f (cpld w Steinbeck): 2.70f 1.40f (SF: 22.20f). Sheikh Mohammed (NEWMARKET) bred by Barbara
Hunter in USA. 5 Rn                                                      2m 3.2 (1)
                                                                SF—92/85/76

3447a—**EVRY (R-H)**

**Saturday, September 26th [Good to soft]**

Going Allowance: 0.25 sec per fur (G)

**3561a**    PRIX SAINT-ROMAN (Gp 3) (2-Y.O) £20640.00    **1m 1f**

           **Richard of York** *(France)* 2-8-9 TJarnet .................................................. —1
           Devil's Rock (USA) *(France)* 2-8-9 ODoleuze ................................................. s.nk.2
           Honor and Pride (FR) *(France)* 2-8-9 ELegrix ................................................. 3.3
Tote 1.40f: 1.10f 1.60f (SF: 7.70f). Sheikh Mohammed (A.Fabre,FRANCE) bred by Hesmonds Stud Ltd. 4 Rn
                                                            1m 54.68 (4.38)
                                                                SF—64/63/54

3451a—**CURRAGH (R-H)**

**Sunday, September 27th [Soft]**

Going Allowance: 5f-8f: 0.70 sec (Y); Rest: 0.10 sec per fur (G)

**3562a**    SHAMROCK FOODS SOLONAWAY RACE (listed race) IR£8061.00    **1m**

  1816a⁵ **Equal Eloquence (USA)** *(Ireland)* 3-8-7 RHughes ................................................. —1
  1095a³ Tijara (IRE) *(Ireland)* 3-8-12 DHogan ................................................. 7.2
  1458 Thyer (USA) (bl) *(Ireland)* 3-9-1 CRoche ................................................. 3½.3
Tote £5.00: £2.40 £4.00 (£29.70). Lady Clague (J.M.Oxx,IRELAND) bred by Foxfield in USA. 5 Rn
                                                              1m 44.1 (7.1)
                                                                SF—70/54/43

**3563a**    C.L. WELD E.B.F. PARK STKS (Gp 3) (2-Y.O.F) IR£13435.00    **7f**

  3328a* **Asema (USA)** (Fav) *(Ireland)* 2-8-13 MJKinane (trckd ldrs: shkn up to ld 1f out:
                       r.o) .................................................. —1
           Miami Sands (IRE) *(Ireland)* 2-8-10 PVGilson (cl up: ev ch 1f out: r.o) ............ 1½.2
  3328a⁴ Lady Ounavarra (IRE) *(Ireland)* 2-8-10 WJSupple (in tch to ½-wy: r.o u.p fr over
                       1f out: nrst fin) .................................................. 2.3
           Riyoom (IRE) *(Ireland)* 2-8-10 CRoche (chsd ldr: rdn over 2f out: kpt on) ...... hd.4
           Tarakana (USA) *(Ireland)* 2-8-10 RHughes (led: rdn 2f out: hdd & wknd 1f out) s.h.5
           Pernilla (IRE) *(Ireland)* 2-8-10 KJManning (bhd: hdwy 2f out: sn one pce) ......... 1.6
           Dawnsio (IRE) *(Ireland)* 2-8-10 WJO'Connor (bhd tl r.o fnl 2f: nvr nrr) ......... hd.7
           Tartan Lady (IRE) *(Ireland)* 2-8-10 SCraine (in tch to ½-wy: sn rdn: kpt on same
                       pce) .................................................. ½.8

**Evens** ASEMA (USA), **3/1** Riyoom (USA), **13/2** Tarakana (USA), **10/1** Dawnsio (IRE), **12/1** Tartan Lady (IRE),
**14/1** Pernilla (IRE), Miami Sands (IRE), **16/1** Lady Ounavarra (IRE). Tote £2.00: £1.30 £3.60 £3.90 (£20.30). Mr
Allen E. Paulson (D.K.Weld,IRELAND) bred by Landon Knight Stables in USA. 8 Rn            1m 32.6 (9.4)
                                                              SF—17/9/3/2/1/—

**3564a**    R & H HALL WATERFORD TESTIMONIAL STKS (listed race) IR£8061.00    **6f**

  1467⁶ **Bezelle** *(Ireland)* 3-8-12 PShanahan ................................................. —1
  2888a⁶ Street Rebel (CAN) (bl) *(Ireland)* 4-9-5 SCraine ................................................. 1.2
  3356 TAUFAN BLU (bl) *(MJohnston)* 3-8-5 DMcKeown ................................................. 3.3
Tote £1.70: £1.50 £2.70 £2.00 (£8.10). Mr James McNeil (C.Collins,IRELAND) bred by D. A. & Mrs Hicks. 11 Rn
                                                              1m 17.3 (6.7)
                                                                SF—48/51/37

3232a—**CAPANNELLE (R-H)**
**Sunday, September 27th [Soft]**

## 3565a
PREMIO DIVINO AMORE (listed race) (2-Y.O) £20930.00   **5f**

|  |  |  |
|---|---|---|
|  | **Nord's Lucy (IRE)** *(Italy)* 2–8-8 MRoberts | —**1** |
| 3232a² | PIZZA CONNECTION *(JLDunlop)* 2–8-7 WCarson | s.nk.**2** |
|  | Biyik (USA) *(Italy)* 2–8-11 GPucciatti | 1.**3** |

Tote 122L: 18L 11L (102L). Scuderia Blueberry (V.Caruso,ITALY) bred by J. Dillon in Ireland. 6 Rn   57.5 sec

## 3566a
PREMIO LYDIA TESIO (Gp 2) (F & M) £41860.00   **1¼m**

|  |  |  |
|---|---|---|
| 3110a⁴ | **OUMALDAAYA (USA)** *(JLDunlop)* 3–8-8 WCarson | —**1** |
| 2843⁶ | Lara's Idea (Italy) 4–9-0 GDettori | ¾.**2** |
| 3110a³ | Revasser (USA) *(France)* 3–8-8 PaulEddery | ¾.**3** |
| 2893a★ | ARBUSHA (USA) *(LordHuntingdon)* 3–8-8 AMunro | 3.**4** |
| 2837 | GUSSY MARLOWE *(CEBrittain)* 4–9-0 MRoberts (btn further 7¾l) | **8** |

Tote 59L: 11L 10L 11L (55L). Mr Hamdan Al-Maktoum (ARUNDEL) bred by Shadwell Estate Company Ltd. in USA. 8 Rn   2m 1.3

## 3567a
PREMIO RUMON (listed race) (2-Y.O) £20930.00   **1m**

|  |  |  |
|---|---|---|
| 3233a★ | **VENTIQUATTROFOGLI (IRE)** *(JLDunlop)* 2–8-10 WCarson | —**1** |
| 3233a³ | Campalto (IRE) *(Italy)* 2–8-7 OFancera | 2¼.**2** |
| 2981a | Future Storm (USA) *(Italy)* 2–8-7 VMezzatesta | 2.**3** |

Tote 19L: 11L 17L 15L (103L). Gerecon Italia (ARUNDEL) bred by Kiltinan Inc. in Ireland. 8 Rn   1m 39.3

957a—**COLOGNE (R-H)**
**Sunday, September 27th [Good]**

## 3568a
PREIS VON KOLN (listed race) £21127.00   **1m**

|  |  |  |
|---|---|---|
| 2893a² | **Ligona** *(Germany)* 3–9-0 ABoschert | —**1** |
|  | Astica (GER) *(Germany)* 3–9-0 KWoodburn | 1.**2** |
| 3226a★ | CLOUD OF DUST *(JLDunlop)* 3–9-0 JReid | s.h.**3** |

Tote 113DM: 24DM 30DM 16DM (SF: 1073DM). Gestut Fahrhof (A.Wohler,GERMANY) bred by Gestut Fahrhof. 10 Rn   1m 36.9

3234—**GOODWOOD (R-H)**
**Friday, October 2nd [Good]**
Going Allowance: St: 0.25 sec (G); Rnd: 0.75 sec per fur (Y)          Wind: almost nil

Stalls: low

## 3569
ST JOHN AMBULANCE CLAIMING H'CAP (3-Y.O) (0-80) £2070.00 (£570.00: £270.00)
**1¼m**                                                                 2-15 (2-18)

(Weights raised 4 lb)

| | | |
|---|---|---|
| 3293⁴ | **Alderbrook (58)** *(MrsJCecil)* 8-8 PaulEddery (7) (3rd st: led over 2f out: hrd rdn over 1f out: r.o wl) | —**1** |
| 3363 | Maple Bay (IRE) **(66)** *(PJMakin)* 9-2 WRSwinburn (3) (2nd st: hrd rdn over 2f out: unable qckn) | 2½.**2** |
| 3221 | Socks and Shares **(43)** *(PWHarris)* 7-7 NAdams (6) (lw: rdn over 2f out: hdwy over 1f out: r.o wl ins fnl f) | 1.**3** |
|  | Fruitful Affair (IRE) **(69)** *(TThomsonJones)* 9-5 SWhitworth (2) (hdwy over 3f out: hrd rdn over 2f out: one pce) | hd.**4** |
| 3241⁵ | Tiffany's Case (IRE) **(62)** (Fav) *(CAHorgan)* 8-12 JReid (10) (b.nr hind: 6th st: hrd rdn 2f out: one pce) | ¾.**5** |
| 3370 | Handsome Gent **(71)** *(LordHuntingdon)* 9-7 AMunro (5) (swtg: nvr nr to chal) | 4.**6** |
| 3246² | By Arrangement (IRE) **(52)** *(SWoodman)* 8-2 JQuinn (8) (5th st: wknd over 3f out) | 3.**7** |
| 3287⁴ | Deevee **(43)** *(CJBenstead)* 7-7 GBardwell (11) (s.s: hdwy over 2f out: wknd over 1f out) | 1½.**8** |
| 3159 | Hester Stanhope **(57)** *(PWHarris)* 8-7 WRyan (9) (swtg: led over 7f) | 10.**9** |
| 1374² | Noel (IRE) **(60)** *(GAPritchard-Gordon)* 8-10 GDuffield (4) (swtg: 4th st: wknd over 3f out) | ¾.**10** |

LONG HANDICAP: Socks and Shares 7-4, Deevee 7-4.

2/1 Tiffany's Case (IRE)(op 3/1), **7/1 By Arrangement (IRE)**(5/1—8/1), **15/2 ALDERBROOK**, **9/1** Maple Bay (IRE), **10/1** Fruitful Affair (IRE)(7/1—12/1), **11/1** Handsome Gent(7/1—12/1), Noel (IRE), **12/1** Hester Stanhope, Deevee(op 8/1), **20/1** Socks and Shares. CSF £63.36, CT £1,157.35. Tote £8.10: £2.10 £2.90 £3.70 (£58.70). Mr James H. Stone (NEWMARKET) bred by J. H. Stone. 10 Rn     2m 19.48 (14.48)
SF—24/27/2/27/18/19

## 3570
ISLE OF WIGHT STKS (Mdn 2-Y.O.F) £3496.00 (£1048.00: £504.00: £232.00)
6f     2-45 (2-46)

| | | |
|---|---|---|
| 3099² | **Bright Spells** *(DRCElsworth)* 8-11 JWilliams (11) (hdwy over 3f out: led ins fnl f: r.o wl) | —1 |
| | Ballet Shoes (IRE) (Fav) *(RCharlton)* 8-11 WRSwinburn (3) (unf: bit bkwd: led tl ins fnl f: unable qckn) | 2.2 |
| | Lovely Bird (USA) *(MBell)* 8-11 MHills (9) (leggy: lt-f: a.p: ev ch over 1f out: one pce) | 4.3 |
| 2792 | Apache Myth *(RHannon)* 8-11 JReid (8) (a.p: rdn over 2f out: one pce) | 1½.4 |
| 3179 | Persian Melody (IRE) *(DRCElsworth)* 8-4 ‡7JHunter (10) (lw: hdwy 2f out: hrd rdn over 1f out: one pce) | 2.5 |
| 3261⁴ | Hobey Cat *(DRCElsworth)* 8-11 SWhitworth (1) (prom over 3f) | 3.6 |
| | Misty Silks *(MJRyan)* 8-11 DBiggs (6) (str: bkwd: s.s: rdn thrght: nvr nr to chal) | hd.7 |
| 3414 | Zhaab *(MMadgwick)* 8-11 JQuinn (7) (hld up: hrd rdn over 1f out: sn wknd) | 2½.8 |
| | Whimsical Notion *(MrsBarbaraWaring)* 8-11 NHowe (5) (leggy: lt-f: outpcd) | 3.9 |
| 3295 | Episode One *(GLewis)* 8-11 PaulEddery (2) (prom over 3f) | hd.10 |

2/1 Ballet Shoes (IRE), **9/4 BRIGHT SPELLS**, **4/1** Lovely Bird (USA)(op 6/1), **16/1** Hobey Cat, **20/1** Apache Myth, **33/1** Zhaab, Episode One, **50/1** Ors. CSF £6.04, Tote £3.00: £1.30 £1.40 £1.80 (£3.70). Mr C. J. Harper (WHITSBURY) bred by Whitsbury Manor Stud. 10 Rn     1m 15.76 (5.36)
SF—19/11/–/–/–/–

## 3571
R.O.A. FOUNDATION STKS (listed race)     £12678.75 (£3780.00: £1802.50: £813.75)
1¼m     3-15 (3-17)

| | | |
|---|---|---|
| 3405⁴ | **King's Loch (IRE) (100)** *(HRACecil)* 3-8-8 WRyan (7) (lw: led 8f out: hrd rdn over 1f out: r.o wl) | —1 |
| 2748* | Delve (IRE) (100) (Fav) *(JLDunlop)* 3-8-3 TQuinn (3) (3rd st: chsd wnr fnl 3f: hrd rdn over 1f out: no imp) | 2½.2 |
| 3405* | Marcus Thorpe (USA) (102) *(PAKelleway)* 4-9-0 AMunro (2) (b: 6th st: rdn over 3f out: one pce) | 1.3 |
| 3368³ | St Ninian (101) *(MHEasterby)* 6-9-0 MBirch (5) (lw: hdwy 2f out: hrd rdn over 1f out: one pce) | ¾.4 |
| 3190 | Yildiz (90) *(BWHills)* 3-8-3 MHills (4) (2nd st: hrd rdn over 2f out: wknd over 1f out) | 10.5 |
| 3204³ | Polish Blue (USA) (98) *(MRStoute)* 3-8-8 WRSwinburn (1) (lw: 5th st: rdn over 3f out: eased whn btn over 1f out) | 10.6 |
| 3204⁴ | Anchorite (97) *(PTWalwyn)* 3-8-8 PaulEddery (6) (led 2f: 4th st: wknd over 3f out: t.o) | 20.7 |
| 2911 | Fragrant Hill (99) (bl) *(IABalding)* 4-8-12 JReid (8) (a bhd: t.o) | 12.8 |

3/1 Delve (IRE)(5/2—4/1), **7/2 St Ninian**, **9/2 Polish Blue (USA)**, **13/2** Marcus Thorpe (USA), **7/1** Fragrant Hill(9/1—6/1), **10/1** Yildiz, **12/1 KING'S LOCH (IRE)**, **20/1** Anchorite. CSF £44.15, Tote £12.40: £2.60 £1.40 £1.90 (£25.40). Mr Michael Poland (NEWMARKET) bred by Michael Poland in Ireland. 8 Rn     2m 15.16 (10.16)
SF—68/58/67/65/34/19

## 3572
CHARLTON HUNT H'CAP (0-80) £3687.50 (£1100.00: £525.00: £237.50)
1½m     3-50 (3-52)

| | | |
|---|---|---|
| 3426* | **Texan Tycoon (68)** (Fav) *(RAkehurst)* 4-9-0 (5x) ‡7TAshley (7) (lw: 3rd st: led over 2f out: jinked ins fnl f: pushed out) | —1 |
| 3393² | Horizon (IRE) (42) (bl) *(TThomsonJones)* 4-7-9 NCarlisle (3) (led over 9f: ev ch ins fnl f: r.o) | nk.2 |
| 3249² | Statajack (IRE) (69) *(DRCElsworth)* 4-9-1 ‡7JHunter (4) (hrd rdn over 2f out: hdwy over 1f out: r.o wl ins fnl f) | 3.3 |
| 3279³ | Western Dynasty (68) *(MJRyan)* 6-9-7 DBiggs (6) (lw: hrd rdn & hdwy over 2f out: unable qckn) | 1½.4 |
| | Flyaway (FR) (40) *(RJWeaver)* 7-7-7 JQuinn (10) (hdwy over 3f out: hrd rdn over 2f out: one pce) | nk.5 |
| 2585² | Prince Hannibal (75) *(JLDunlop)* 5-10-0 JReid (9) (6th st: nt clr run over 3f out: one pce fnl 2f) | 2.6 |
| 3279 | Castle Clown (68) (v) *(LadyHerries)* 7-9-7 PaulEddery (11) (lw: 5th st: wknd over 3f out) | 2½.7 |
| 3273³ | Grove Serendipity (IRE) (51) (v) *(AHide)* 4-8-4 NAdams (5) (lw: 2nd st: wknd over 1f out) | 1.8 |
| 3273 | Mahrajan (61) *(CJBenstead)* 8-9-0 TQuinn (1) (a bhd) | ½.9 |

3057 Monarda **(70)** *(PFICole)* 5–9-9 AMunro (2) (lw: 4th st: wknd over 2f out) ......... ¹/₂.**10**
3387 Pearl Ransom **(45)** *(WGRWightman)* 5–7-12 GBardwell (8) (bhd fnl 4f) ............ 8.**11**
LONG HANDICAP: Flyaway (FR) 7-2.

**2/1** TEXAN TYCOON, **6/1** Statajack (IRE), **8/1** Western Dynasty(6/1—9/1), Prince Hannibal, **10/1** Monarda, **11/1** Horizon (IRE)(8/1—12/1), Grove Serendipity (IRE)(8/1—14/1), **14/1** Castle Clown, **16/1** Mahrajan, **33/1** Pearl Ransom, **100/1** Flyaway (FR). CSF £21.17, CT £100.08. Tote £2.80: £1.60 £2.50 £1.90 (£26.50). Normandy Developments (London) (EPSOM) bred by Clearwood Thoroughbred Stud Ltd. 11 Rn　　2m 46.93 (15.23)
SF—38/18/32/35/6/37

## 3573　SUPREME STKS (Gp 3)　£15300.00 (£5726.25: £2750.63: £1198.12)
7f　　　　　　　　　　　　　　　　　　　　　　　　　　　　　4-20 (4-22)

3371² **Hazaam (USA)** *(MRStoute)* 3–8-9 WRSwinburn (4) (lw: 3rd st: nt clr run over 1f
out: squeezed thro ins fnl f: led nr fin) ................................... —**1**
3195² Prince Ferdinand **(118)** (Jt-Fav) *(MMcCormack)* 3–8-13 JReid (8) (lw: 6th st:
led 1f out: rdn & hdd nr fin) ................................................. hd.**2**
655 Swing Low **(112)** *(RHannon)* 3–8-9 TQuinn (3) (lw: 4th st: led over 1f out: sn
hdd: one pce) ............................................................. 2¹/₂.**3**
3195³ Storm Dove (USA) **(109)** (Jt-Fav) *(RCharlton)* 3–8-6 PaulEddery (2) (2nd st: led
over 2f out tl over 1f out: one pce) ....................................... 2¹/₂.**4**
2789 Night Jar **(98)** *(LordHuntingdon)* 5–8-9 AMunro (7) (5th st: wknd 2f out) ............. 3.**5**
3451a★ Norwich (Jt-Fav) *(BWHills)* 5–8-12 MHills (6) (lw: led over 4f) .................. ³/₄.**6**
3083 Norton Challenger **(106)** (v) *(MHEasterby)* 5–8-12 MBirch (5) (a bhd) ............... 6.**7**

**11/4** Norwich, Prince Ferdinand, Storm Dove (USA), **7/1** Swing Low, HAZAAM (USA), **16/1** Norton Challenger, **33/1** Night Jar. CSF £24.98, Tote £6.50: £2.20 £2.40 (£12.40). Sheikh Mohammed (NEWMARKET) bred by Darley Stud Management Co Ltd in USA. 7 Rn　　1m 30.94 (6.24)
SF—80/83/71/60/54/55

## 3574　DRAWING ROOM NURSERY　£4272.50 (£1280.00: £615.00: £282.50)
1m　　　　　　　　　　　　　　　　　　　　　　　　　　　　　4-55 (4-58)

3385² **Warm Spell (65)** *(RSimpson)* 7-8 ‡⁵ATucker (12) (swtchd lft over 2f out: hdwy
over 1f out: hrd rdn to ld last strides) .................................. —**1**
2409★ Satin Dancer **(81)** *(GHarwood)* 9-1 KDarley (7) (rdn over 5f out: hdwy over 3f
out: led ins fnl f: hrd rdn & hdd last strides) ........................... nk.**2**
3146 Greystoke **(74)** (v) *(LordHuntingdon)* 8-8 WRSwinburn (13) (lw: 2nd st: led 3f
out tl ins fnl f: unable qckn) ........................................... 1¹/₂.**3**
3401⁵ Gone Prospecting (USA) **(81)** *(RHannon)* 9-1 TQuinn (8) (hdwy over 3f out: rdn
over 1f out: one pce) .................................................... ¹/₂.**4**
3408⁵ Festin **(72)** (bl) *(JLDunlop)* 8-6 JReid (9) (4th st: hrd rdn over 1f out: one pce) .. 1.**5**
3173⁶ Hallplace **(59)** (v) *(MRChannon)* 7-7 JQuinn (3) (lw: nvr nr to chal) .................. 3.**6**
3260⁴ General Chase **(68)** *(RJHolder)* 8-2 GDuffield (1) (lw: nvr nrr) .................... 1¹/₂.**7**
3307★ The Seer **(82)** (Fav) *(BWHills)* 9-2 MHills (4) (no hdwy fnl 3f) ...................... nk.**8**
3173⁴ Pondering **(63)** *(SDow)* 7-6⁽⁴⁾ ‡⁵NKennedy (10) (nvr nrr) ......................... 2.**9**
3508⁵ War Requiem (IRE) **(60)** *(GBBalding)* 7-8⁽¹⁾ NCarlisle (14) (5th st: wknd over 2f
out) ................................................................... 2.**10**
3091★ Devirly **(87)** *(GLewis)* 9-7 PaulEddery (2) (nvr nrr) ........................... s.h.**11**
3408 Romalito **(72)** *(MBlanshard)* 8-6 JWilliams (16) (s.s: nvr nrr) .................. 1.**12**
3376⁶ Daring King **(59)** *(DSasse)* 7-7 NAdams (5) (b: 6th st: wknd 3f out) ............ ³/₄.**13**
3186 Mr Copyforce **(64)** *(MissBSanders)* 7-12 GBardwell (17) (3rd st: wknd over 2f
out) .................................................................. 3.**14**
3093³ Cashell **(80)** *(MRStoute)* 9-0 WRyan (15) (led 5f) ........................... ¹/₂.**15**
3106⁴ Pickupadailysport **(63)** *(MissGayKelleway)* 7-4⁽⁴⁾ ‡⁷CHawksley (11) (a bhd) ...... 4.**16**
3260 Balustrade Boy (IRE) **(62)** *(BStevens)* 7-10 DaleGibson (6) (b: bhd fnl 4f) ...... 3¹/₂.**17**
LONG HANDICAP: Hallplace 7-4, Pondering 7-4, War Requiem (IRE) 7-4, Daring King 7-4,
Pickupadailysport 7-5.

**4/1** The Seer, **6/1** WARM SPELL, **7/1** Satin Dancer(6/1—9/1), Devirly, **9/1** Cashell(op 6/1), **10/1** General Chase, **12/1** Festin, **20/1** Greystoke, Gone Prospecting (USA), Pondering, War Requiem (IRE), **33/1** Hallplace, Romalito, **33/1** Pickupadailysport, Mr Copyforce, Daring King, **66/1** Balustrade Boy (IRE). CSF £43.84, CT £729.34. Tote £5.10: £1.80 £2.70 £3.00 £4.30 (£20.50). Mr K. Higson (FOXHILL) bred by R. H. Cowell and Mrs R. B. Collie. 17 Rn　　1m 46.60 (9)
SF—35/55/43/48/36/14

## 3575　LEVY FRIENDLY H'CAP (0-90)　£3882.50 (£1160.00: £555.00: £252.50)
5f　　　　　　　　　　　　　　　　　　　　　　　　　　　　　5-25 (5-29)

(Weights raised 4 lb)
3134³ **Belated (82)** *(HThomsonJones)* 3–9-10 MHills (12) (a.p: led over 1f out: drvn
out) .................................................................. —**1**

3423³ Mister Jolson **(56)** *(RJHodges)* 3–7-12 JQuinn (3) (a.p: hrd rdn over 1f out: ev ch ins fnl f: r.o) .......... ¹/₂.2

3059⁶ Allthruthenight (IRE) **(82)** *(LJHolt)* 3–9-10 JReid (11) (lw: hld up: rdn over 1f out: r.o one pce) .......... 1¹/₂.3

3355 Love Returned **(79)** *(WJarvis)* 5–9-8 MTebbutt (13) (hld up: rdn over 1f out: one pce) .......... ¹/₂.4

3284 Truthful Image **(76)** (bl) *(MJRyan)* 3–9-4 DBiggs (5) (a.p: rdn over 2f out: one pce) .......... 2.5

3361³ Bells of Longwick **(79)** *(DRLaing)* 3–9-7 TyroneWilliams (4) (hld up: rdn over 2f out: one pce) .......... ¹/₂.6

3518★ Cranfield Comet **(72)** (Fav) *(JBerry)* 3–9-0 (7x) GDuffield (9) (a.p: hrd rdn over 1f out: wknd fnl f) .......... 1.7

3437 Olifantsfontein **(77)** (bl) *(RSimpson)* 4–9-6 WRyan (6) (outpcd: nvr nrr) .......... hd.8

3207 The Noble Oak (IRE) **(59)** (bl) *(MMcCormack)* 4–8-2 AMunro (8) (lw: a.p: hrd rdn over 1f out: wknd fnl f) .......... 1¹/₂.9

3437 Shikari's Son **(74)** *(JWhite)* 5–9-3 TQuinn (2) (outpcd) .......... hd.10

3207 Sigama (USA) **(81)** *(FHLee)* 6–9-5 ‡⁵NKennedy (10) (lw: led over 3f) .......... nk.11

3511 Martinosky **(63)** (bl) *(WGRWightman)* 6–8-6 JWilliams (7) (a bhd) .......... hd.12

3253² Fivesevenfiveo **(74)** *(RJHodges)* 4–9-3 PaulEddery (1) (bhd fnl 2f) .......... 12.13

**4/1** Cranfield Comet, **7/1** Bells of Longwick, **15/2** Allthruthenight (IRE)(16/1—7/1), **8/1** Fivesevenfiveo, **11/1** Mister Jolson, Sigama (USA), **12/1** Olifantsfontein, **14/1** Shikari's Son, Martinosky, The Noble Oak (IRE), Love Returned, **20/1** BELATED, **25/1** Truthful Image. CSF £191.82, CT £1,624.24. Tote £20.20: £4.40 £2.80 £2.00 (£104.30). Mrs H. T. Jones (NEWMARKET) bred by Mrs H. T. Jones. 13 Rn       60.77 sec (3.17)
SF–72/44/64/60/48/49

T/Trio: Race 4: £24.60 (49.4 Tckts). T/Plpt: £240.60 (18.44 Tckts).       AK


# GOODWOOD (R-H)
## Saturday, October 3rd [Good to soft]
Going Allowance: St: 0.80 sec per fur; Rnd: 0.90 sec per fur (S)       Wind: almost nil

Stalls: low

**3576**  GEORGE TODD APP'CE H'CAP (0-70) £2826.00 (£786.00: £378.00)
1m 1f       2-15 (2-22)

3387★ **Plan Ahead (70)** (Fav) *(GLewis)* 3–9-1 ‡⁸BRussell (18) (lw: plld hrd: 2nd st: led over 2f out: rdn out) .......... —1

2632★ Cachou (USA) **(68)** *(JHMGosden)* 3–9-7 StephenDavies (7) (4th st: rdn 2f out: ev ch ins fnl f: r.o) .......... nk.2

3365 Lucky Noire **(59)** *(GHarwood)* 4–8-9⁽³⁾ ‡⁸PHoughton (15) (9th st: hdwy 2f out: rdn over 1f out: r.o) .......... 1¹/₂.3

3269 Twilight Secret **(62)** *(JWHills)* 3–9-1 FNorton (21) (led over 6f: hrd rdn 2f out: r.o) .......... ¹/₂.4

3554⁵ Nobby Barnes **(55)** *(DAWilson)* 3–7-12 ‡¹⁰SharonMillard (9) (b: dwlt: hdwy whn nt clr run over 2f out: r.o fnl f) .......... 2.5

2561 Grey Illusions **(44)** *(LJHolt)* 4–7-8⁽⁶⁾ ‡⁸CAvery (17) (hdwy 3f out: r.o one pce fnl 2f) .......... hd.6

2632 Eriny (USA) **(61)** *(SGNorton)* 3–8-11 ‡³OPears (20) (hdwy over 3f out: one pce fnl 2f) .......... 3.7

3487² Lady Lacey **(51)** (v) *(GBBalding)* 5–8-2 ‡⁷DToole (3) (5th st: hrd rdn over 1f out: wknd over 1f out) .......... 2¹/₂.8

3479² Our Topsie **(40)** *(FJO'Mahony)* 5–7-12 NGwilliams (2) (b: hdwy over 2f out: wknd over 1f out) .......... 1¹/₂.9

3159³ Missy-S (IRE) **(48)** *(GAPritchard-Gordon)* 3–8-1 ATucker (10) (hld up: brght stands' side over 3f out: nvr nrr) .......... 2¹/₂.10

3421 Northern Conqueror (IRE) **(44)** *(TJNaughton)* 4–8-2 GForster (13) (nvr nrr) .......... 3.11

3365 Albert **(39)** *(DAWilson)* 5–7-11 SO'Gorman (4) (nvr nrr) .......... 3.12

3526 Sharp Dream **(69)** *(BSmart)* 4–9-8 ‡⁵SSanders (5) (7th st: wknd over 2f out) .......... 1¹/₂.13

3170⁵ Diaco **(63)** *(MAJarvis)* 7–9-4 ‡³KRutter (16) (bhd fnl 3f) .......... 7.14

1708⁵ Little Park **(58)** *(CNWilliams)* 3–8-4⁽⁴⁾ ‡⁷TO'Leary (22) (swtg: 6th st: wknd over 2f out) .......... 7.15

3418 Absonal **(70)** *(RHannon)* 5–9-11 ‡³RPerham (8) (8th st: brght stands' side: wknd over 2f out) .......... ³/₄.16

2609⁵ Magnetic Point (USA) **(57)** *(AAScott)* 3–8-7 ‡³JTate (14) (lw: 3rd st: wknd 3f out) 2¹/₂.17

1917 Gabesia **(40)** *(HJCollingridge)* 4–7-6 ‡⁶CHawksley (1) (bhd fnl 4f) .......... 2.18

3264 Hold Fast (IRE) **(39)** *(HCandy)* 4–7-5 ‡⁶AntoinetteArmes (11) (lw: a bhd: t.o) .......... 19
LONG HANDICAP: Grey Illusions 7-2.

**4/1** PLAN AHEAD, **11/2** Albert(12/1—5/1), **9/1** Cachou (USA), Eriny (USA), **11/1** Lady Lacey, **14/1** Nobby Barnes, Twilight Secret(op 8/1), Hold Fast (IRE), Missy-S (IRE), **16/1** Our Topsie, Sharp Dream(op 8/1), **20/1** Diaco, Magnetic Point (USA), Absonal, Northern Conqueror (IRE), **25/1** Lucky Noire, **33/1** Ors. CSF £39.77, CT £752.79. Tote £3.30: £1.40 £1.80 £5.40 £3.70 (£7.50). Planflow (Leasing) Ltd (EPSOM) bred by R. F. and Mrs Knipe. 19 Rn
         2m 5.13 (14.43)
         SF—6/11/–/–/–/–

---

**3577**     BBC RADIO 5 PETER AND JANET FANNING CLAIMING H'CAP (3-Y.O) (0-80) £4971.00
        (£1488.00: £714.00: £327.00)    1½m
         2-45 (2-53)
         (Weights raised 7 lb)

3426⁵ **Day of History (IRE) (45)** (CACyzer) 7-12 TyroneWilliams (5) (5th st: led over 2f out: rdn & edgd lft over 1f out: r.o: fin 2nd, hd: awrdd r) .. —1

3426³ Crackling **(51)** (Jt-Fav) (DMarks) 8-4 SDawson (13) (6th st: led over 1f out: edgd rt ins fnl f: drvn out: fin 1st: disq: plcd 2nd) ................... 2

3406⁴ Faaz (USA) **(49)** (v) (AAScott) 8-2⁽³⁾ JFortune (1) (7th st: hdwy over 2f out: edgd rt & r.o one pce fnl f) .................................. 4.3

3466⁵ Lyn's Return (IRE) **(60)** (Jt-Fav) (RSimpson) 8-8 ‡⁵ATucker (9) (8th st: hdwy over 2f out: one pce fnl f) ................................ 4.4

3177 Port in a Storm **(50)** (WJarvis) 8-3 PRobinson (7) (9th st: r.o one pce fnl 2f) .. 1½.5

3177 Billy Bunter **(56)** (HCandy) 8-9 GCarter (2) (11th st: nvr nrr) ................. 1½.6

3426⁶ Court Circular **(59)** (v) (LordHuntingdon) 8-12 KFallon (6) (3rd st: wknd over 2f out) ................................................... 10.7

3485 Reach for Glory **(58)** (RMWhitaker) 8-11 ACulhane (12) (10th st: hdwy over 2f out: wknd wl over 1f out) ................................... hd.8

3485 Corinthian God (IRE) **(45)** (DAWilson) 7-9⁽¹⁾ ‡³SO'Gorman (10) (led over 9f) ...... 4.9

2801 Copy Lane (IRE) **(48)** (MRChannon) 7-12 ‡³FNorton (3) (4th st: wknd over 2f out) ......................................................... 3.10

3010 Tales of Wisdom **(60)** (SirMarkPrescott) 8-13 GDuffield (4) (2nd st: wknd 3f out) 12.11

*Stewards Enquiry: Obj. to Crackling by Williams sustained. Crackling disq. (interference ins fnl f).*

**9/2** Lyn's Return (IRE), Crackling, **7/1** Port in a Storm(op 4/1), **8/1** DAY OF HISTORY (IRE), **9/1** Tales of Wisdom, **12/1** Billy Bunter, Faaz (USA)(op 8/1), **14/1** Court Circular, **16/1** Reach for Glory, Copy Lane (IRE), **25/1** Corinthian God (IRE). CSF £37.16, CT 335.08. Tote £7.40: £2.00 £1.60 £4.20 (£12.90). Mr R. M. Cyzer (HORSHAM) bred by Mount Coote Stud in Ireland. 11 Rn
         2m 48.93 (17.23)
         SF—26/19/15/13/5/8

---

**3578**     CITY OF PORTSMOUTH STKS    £4230.00 (£1260.00: £600.00: £270.00)
        2m
         3-15 (3-18)

3369⁶ **Hebridean (90)** (Jt-Fav) (HCandy) 5-8-13 CRutter (1) (chsd ldr: led 3f out: hrd rdn 2f out: r.o) ............................................... —1

3194 Star Player **(80)** (RJBaker) 6-8-13 JWilliams (3) (hld up: 5th st: hdwy fnl f: r.o wl: too much to do) ............................................ ¾.2

3352³ Staunch Friend (USA) **(Jt-Fav)** (MHTompkins) 4-8-13 PRobinson (5) (hld up: 4th st: hdwy over 2f out: wknd fnl f) ................................ 8.3

3248⁴ Tetradonna (IRE) **(RHannon)** 4-8-5 ‡³RPerham (2) (3rd st: ev ch over 2f out: hrd rdn & wknd over 1f out) ..................................... 3.4

     Mrs Jawleyford (USA) (CSmith) 4-8-8 JFortune (4) (b: lt-f: led 13f) ............ dist.5

**2/1** Staunch Friend (USA), HEBRIDEAN, **3/1** Star Player, **5/1** Tetradonna (IRE), **40/1** Mrs Jawleyford (USA). CSF £7.80, Tote £3.00: £1.50 £2.00 (£4.90). Mr P. A. Deal (WANTAGE) bred by Whitsbury Manor Stud. 5 Rn
         3m 50.50 (23.90)

---

**3579**     'THE NEWS' AUCTION STKS (Mdn 2-Y.O) £8220.00 (£2460.00: £1180.00: £540.00)
        7f
         3-50 (3-54)

3178² **Rockover (78)** (RHannon) 8-12 RPerham (18) (led over 5f: led 1f out: r.o wl) .... —1

3410³ Nico Mike (PWChapple-Hyam) 9-1 SWhitworth (1) (lw: hdwy over 3f out: led over 1f out: r.o) .............................................. ½.2

3243³ Aberdeen Heather **(88)** (Fav) (DRCElsworth) 9-1 JWilliams (8) (hdwy 2f out: r.o wl ins fnl f) ............................................. ½.3

3410² Primo Figlio **(68)** (RHannon) 8-9 TyroneWilliams (16) (5th st: ev ch over 1f out: r.o) .................................................. hd.4

3372⁵ Ground Nut (IRE) (HCandy) 8-9 CRutter (14) (rdn & hdwy 2f out: r.o fnl f) ...... ¾.5

     Scorched Air (JWHills) 8-13 PRobinson (2) (cmpt: bit bkwd: 6th st: ev ch 2f out: one pce) .............................................. 2.6

     Fools Errand (IRE) (RHannon) 9-0 GHind (9) (leggy: unf: bit bkwd: hld up: hdwy over 2f out: ev ch over 1f out: wknd fnl f) ....................... 2.7

2409⁴ Formato Uni (IRE) (JLDunlop) 9-1 GCarter (10) (rdn over 4f out: nvr nrr) ......... hd.8

     Yoxall Lodge (HJCollingridge) 8-9 VSmith (13) (unf: bit bkwd: 3rd st: ev ch over 2f out: wknd over 1f out) ........................................ ¾.9

32354 Royal Roller (IRE) **(91)** *(CNAllen)* 8-9 GForster (20) (hld up: hdwy over 2f out: wknd over 1f out) ............................................................. 3.10

On Golden Pond (IRE) *(PFICole)* 9-2 ATucker (17) (w'like: b.hind: bit bkwd: 2nd st: wknd over 2f out) ........................................ hd.11

31755 Wordsmith (IRE) *(GHarwood)* 8-12 AClark (6) (dwlt: hdwy over 3f out: wknd 2f out) .............................................. s.h.12

34742 Midyan Blue (IRE) *(JMPEustace)* 8-9 MTebbutt (19) (hld up: hdwy over 2f out: rdn over 1f out: wknd fnl f) ................................... 1½.13

32976 Candarela *(PHowling)* 8-4 NHowe (15) (hdwy 3f out: wknd 2f out) ................. hd.14

3410 Honey Juice *(MJFetherston-Godley)* 8-4 NAdams (12) (a bhd) ................ 3½.15

34745 Trianglepoint (IRE) *(GAPritchard-Gordon)* 8-4 GDuffield (11) (a bhd) ............. hd.16

3186 Supper With Susie *(TJNaughton)* 8-7 AMcGlone (3) (a bhd) ............................ 12.17

3262 Magic Fan *(PWHarris)* 9-1 FNorton (7) (7th st: wknd 3f out) .................... ½.18

3171 Perfect Set (IRE) *(MRChannon)* 8-7 JFortune (4) (4th st: wknd over 2f out) ........ 19

**9/2** Aberdeen Heather, **5/1** Royal Roller (IRE), **7/1** Primo Figlio, ROCKOVER, Nico Mike(op 4/1), **8/1** Formato Uni (IRE), **10/1** Wordsmith (IRE), Trianglepoint (IRE)(14/1—8/1), **12/1** Ground Nut (IRE), **16/1** Midyan Blue (IRE), Scorched Air(op 10/1), **20/1** On Golden Pond (IRE), Fools Errand (IRE), **25/1** Yoxall Lodge, **40/1** Ors. CSF £59.00, Tote £8.50: £2.70 £2.30 £2.80 (£22.80). Mr D. B. Gallop (MARLBOROUGH) bred by B. W. Hills. 19 Rn
1m 34.55 (9.85)
SF—45/46/44/37/35/33

## 3580

SOUTH COAST RADIO CLAIMING STKS (Mdn 2-Y.O) £3548.00 (£1064.00: £512.00: £236.00) **6f** 4-20 (4-27)

3308 **Rich Midas (IRE) (56)** *(GLewis)* 7-4(2) ‡7CHawksley (13) (hdwy 2f out: rdn over 1f out: led ins fnl f: r.o wl) ............................. —1

34725 Clanrock (53) *(RMWhitaker)* 8-2 ACulhane (19) (a.p: led wl over 1f out tl ins fnl f: unable qckn) ...................................... 1½.2

3283 Be Polite (IRE) **(58)** *(MBell)* 7-10 EJohnson (14) (hdwy 2f out: r.o fnl f) ............ hd.3

18843 Heber Spring (IRE) **(60)** *(RHannon)* 8-4 TyroneWilliams (10) (hdwy 2f out: ev ch ins fnl f: unable qckn) .................................. s.h.4

31294 Pistol (IRE) **(83)** (Fav) *(PFICole)* 9-0 AClark (16) (a.p: led over 2f out tl wl over 1f out: one pce) ........................................ 2.5

1578 Hokey Pokey (FR) *(DSasse)* 8-0(2) ‡5RPrice (15) (a.p: ev ch 2f out: hrd rdn over 1f out: wknd fnl f) ......................................... 3½.6

32916 Tartouka **(45)** *(GLewis)* 7-10 NAdams (11) (nvr nrr) ................................. hd.7

3051 Altruistic (IRE) *(CFWall)* 7-5(3) ‡7TWilson (5) (a.p: rdn 2f out: one pce) ............ ½.8

3218 Grey Pride **(51)** *(JBerry)* 8-1 GCarter (17) (a.p: ev ch 1f out: eased whn btn ins fnl f) ........................................................... 2½.9

34104 Kensworth Lady **(60)** *(MBlanshard)* 7-10 ‡5ATucker (9) (a mid div) ................. 1½.10

3407 Krayyan Dawn **(42)** *(RVoorspuy)* 8-1 CRutter (1) (a mid idv) ...................... 2.11

27716 Tony's Mist *(RHannon)* 8-3 PRobinson (8) (bhd fnl 2f) .............................. s.h.12

2994 Purbeck Centenary *(MRChannon)* 8-3(4) ‡3RPerham (2) (bhd fnl 2f) ................ nk.13

33645 Knobbleeneeze **(62)** *(MRChannon)* 8-7 JWilliams (7) (prom 4f) .................... nk.14

3181 The Golden Sport (bl) *(GLewis)* 7-11 ‡3FNorton (4) (spd 4f) ....................... 1½.15

3308 Clangold **(36)** *(JBerry)* 7-10 SDawson (3) (prom over 3f) ......................... 4.16

2994 Gerski *(RHannon)* 7-12(1) AMcGlone (12) (a bhd) .................................. 3½.17

3186 Farley (DEN) *(RAkehurst)* 8-3 JFortune (18) (a bhd) ............................... 1.18

3255 Court Pianist (IRE) (bl) *(SMHillen)* 8-6 GDuffield (6) (led over 3f: sn wknd) ......... 19

**11/8** Pistol (IRE)(9/4—5/4), **8/1** Knobbleeneeze, Be Polite, (IRE), **10/1** Kensworth Lady, **12/1** Tartouka, **14/1** Clanrock, Heber Spring (IRE), **16/1** Tony's Mist, **18/1** RICH MIDAS (IRE), **25/1** Grey Pride, Farley (DEN), Court Pianist (IRE), **33/1** Hokey Pokey (FR), Clangold, The Golden Sport, Gerski, **50/1** Ors. CSF £238.26, Tote £17.00: £4.10 £4.60 £2.00 (£166.20). Mrs Sally Van Tooren (EPSOM) bred by Revival Corporation Ltd in Ireland. 19 Rn
1m 17.95 (hand) (7.55)
SF—21/28/20/27/29/1

## 3581

E.B.F. HAT HILL STKS (Mdn 2-Y.O) £2950.00 (£880.00: £420.00: £190.00) **6f** 4-55 (2-57)

32404 **Nabjelsedr** (Fav) *(CJBenstead)* 9-0 GDuffield (4) (n.m.r & swtchd rt over 2f out: rdn over 1f out: led ins fnl f: r.o wl) ................................... —1

32685 Sea Baron **(66)** *(MBlanshard)* 9-0 JWilliams (1) (hdwy rdn 1f out: ev ch ins fnl f: unable qckn) .......................................... 1½.2

19444 Bezique (USA) (v) *(JHMGosden)* 9-0 GHind (2) (bit bkwd: led over 3f: rdn 2f out: r.o one pce fnl f) ........................................... 2½.3

24505 Walnut Burl (IRE) **(71)** *(LJHolt)* 9-0 NAdams (5) (rdn over 2f out: r.o one pce fnl f) .......................................................... 1½.4

Glisso (IRE) *(LMCumani)* 9-0 JFortune (6) (cmpt: bit bkwd: a.p: led over 2f out tl hdd & wknd ins fnl f) ...................................... hd.5

Salvatore Giuliano *(SMHillen)* 9-0 GCarter (7) (w'like: bit bkwd: a.p: rdn over 2f out: wknd 1f out) ..................... 1½.6

2826 Trinity Hall *(CAHorgan)* 8-9 AMcGlone (3) (prom 3f) .................... 7.7

**7/4** NABJELSEDR, **2/1** Glisso (IRE), **7/2** Bezique (USA), **12/1** Walnut Burl (IRE), **25/1** Sea Baron, Salvatore Giuliano, **33/1** Trinity Hall. CSF £31.07, Tote £2.70: £1.40 £5.10 (£19.40). Mr Hamdan Al-Maktoum (EPSOM) bred by Sir Stanley Grinstead. 7 Rn                                      1m 18.29 (7.89)
SF—38/32/22/16/15/9

---

**3582**   GRATWICKE H'CAP (3-Y.O) (0-90) £3980.00 (£1190.00: £570.00: £260.00)
1m                                                                          5-25 (5-26)

(Weights raised 12 lb)

3236 **Grand Vitesse (IRE) (73)** *(RHannon)* 9-1 ‡³RPerham (6) (rnde all: rdn over 1f out: drvn out) ..................... —1

3365² Nest (58) *(LordHuntingdon)* 7-12 ‡⁵ATucker (7) (7th st: hdwy 3f out: hrd rdn 2f out: r.o wl ins fnl f) ..................... ¾.2

3176★ Jade Vale (71) (Fav) *(JWHills)* 9-2 SWhitworth (1) (6th st: rdn & hdwy 2f out: wknd fnl f) ..................... 7.3

3554² Vanborough Lad (65) *(MJHaynes)* 8-10 NAdams (2) (5th st: hrd rdn 3f out: wknd over 1f out) ..................... 4.4

732⁵ Prince Pericles (IRE) (72) *(HCandy)* 8-10 ‡⁷AntoinetteArmes (9) (4th st: hrd rdn over 2f out: wknd over 1f out) ..................... 2.5

3216★ Thames Glow (74) *(DRCElsworth)* 8-12 ‡⁷JHunter (5) (3rd st: hrd rdn over 2f out: wknd over 1f out) ..................... 1.6

3269 Rocality (76) *(RHannon)* 9-7 TyroneWilliams (3) (2nd st: rdn & wknd 3f out) ...... 8.7

**3/1** Jade Vale, **7/2** Vanborough Lad, **4/1** Nest, **6/1** Rocality(op 10/1), Thames Glow, **11/1** GRAND VITESSE (IRE)(7/1—12/1), **16/1** Prince Pericles (IRE). CSF £48.26, CT £140.39. Tote £11.50: £2.90 £2.00 (£22.90). Mr Robert Whitworth (MARLBOROUGH) bred by Mrs C. Martin Smith in Ireland. 7 Rn      1m 47.70 (10.10)
SF—57/38/35/17/11/10

T/Trio: Race 2: £50.60 (13.3 Tckts). T/Plpt: £53.90 (18.45 Tckts).
SM

---

3393—**PONTEFRACT (L-H)**

## Monday, October 5th [Good to soft, Soft patches]

Going Allowance: 0.45 sec per fur (Y)                              Wind: fresh half against

Stalls: low

**3583**   LEVY BOARD STKS (Mdn 3-Y.O) £2511.00 (£696.00: £333.00)   1m 4y   2-20 (2-22)

3483⁵ **Albemine (USA)** *(MrsJCecil)* 9-0 GDuffield (4) (lw: chsd ldrs: rdn to ld appr fnl f: styd on) ..................... —1

607³ Just a Mirage *(AAScott)* 8-9 JFortune (2) (b.hind: led tl hdd appr fnl f: kpt on same pce) ..................... 4.2

3416³ Littlewick (IRE) *(GWragg)* 8-9 PaulEddery (9) (bhd: hdwy u.p 3f out: nvr nrr) ...... 5.3

3412³ Alfaari (USA) (Jt-Fav) *(MajorWRHern)* 9-0 RHills (3) (chsd ldrs: rdn 3f out: sn outpcd) ..................... nk.4

3386³ Majestic Sinclair (IRE) *(RHollinshead)* 9-0 AMunro (1) (outpcd over 3f out: styd on fnl f: nrst fin) ..................... 1½.5

3427⁶ Balzino (USA) (Jt-Fav) *(LMCumani)* 9-0 LDettori (7) (bhd: effrt over 3f out: nvr nrr) ..................... ½.6

1661⁴ Isle of Innisfree (USA) (70) *(HRACecil)* 9-0 AMcGlone (8) (chsd ldrs tl rdn & btn over 2f out) ..................... 3½.7

3413⁴ Swinging Tich (48) *(BAMcMahon)* 8-9 MBirch (5) (in tch tl outpcd fnl 3f) ..................... 8.8

Petonica (IRE) *(MHTompkins)* 8-9 PRobinson (12) (in tch: effrt on outside ½-wy: sn btn) ..................... 8.9

Deer Marny *(JLSpearing)* 8-2 ‡⁷AGarth (10) (unf: bit bkwd: bhd fr ½-wy) .......... 8.10

Ferrycrosthemersey (IRE) *(GFleming)* 8-9 SWebster (11) (wl bhd fr ½-wy) ...... 3.11

1519 Gaynor's Boy (IRE) *(TKersey)* 9-0 JLowe (6) (bkwd: s.s: a wl bhd) ................. 12.12

**7/2** Balzino (USA)(op 2/1), Alfaari (USA), **4/1** Littlewick (IRE), **5/1** Just a Mirage(7/2—11/2), **8/1** Petonica (IRE), **11/1** Isle of Innisfree (USA), **16/1** Majestic Sinclair (IRE), ALBEMINE (IRE), **40/1** Swinging Tich, **100/1** Deer Marny, **250/1** Ferrycrosthemersey (IRE), **500/1** Gaynor's Boy (IRE). CSF £84.99, Tote £15.30: £3.30 £2.40 £1.70 (£242.90). Mrs Mark Burrell (NEWMARKET) bred by Peter E. Burrell Trust in USA. 12 Rn  1m 48.3 (6.7)
SF—53/36/21/25/20/15

**3584**   BUCCOO REEF (S) STKS   £2511.00 (£696.00: £333.00)   1½m 8y   2-50 (2-51)

3500⁵ **Iron Baron (IRE) (50)** *(RHollinshead)* 3–8-8 LDettori (5) (in tch: hdwy 3f out: led appr fnl f: styd on) ..................... —1

3266* Big Pat (62) (Fav) (JPearce) 3-8-11 RPrice (10) (lw: trckd ldrs: led 3f out & qcknd: hdd & no ex appr fnl f) ............................................. **5.2**

34935 Queens Tour (30) (MBrittain) 7-8-12 ‡7JMarshall (9) (effrt 4f out: styd on: nrst fin) ...................................................................... **4.3**

3479 Paper Clip (36) (JDBethell) 3-8-6 AMunro (7) (lw: a chsng ldrs: one pce fnl 3f) nk.**4**

9796 The Titan Ghost (57) (BAMcMahon) 3-8-8 MRoberts (4) (cl up: led 6f out to 3f out: sn wknd) ........................................................... **10.5**

3046 Media Star (25) (TKersey) 7-9-0 JLowe (10) (b: bhd: sme hdwy 3f out: n.d) .. **7.6**

Choir's Image (JLEyre) 5-8-11 JFortune (2) (bit bkwd: effrt & nt clr run 5f out: sme hdwy 3f out: n.d) .......................................................... **4.7**

3500 Light-of-the-Loch (35) (AWPotts) 4-8-11 SWebster (1) (dwlt: a bhd) ................ **8.8**

3467 Tricotric (32) (GMMoore) 5-9-0 MHills (3) (led tl hdd & hung rt 6f out: sn lost pl) 3½.**9**

3263 Grey Cphas (47) (MMcCormack) 3-8-8 MBirch (6) (lost tch fr ½-wy) ............ 2½.**10**

33934 Al Badeto (20) (JNorton) 5-8-6 ‡5OPears (12) (in tch to ½-wy: sn bhd) ............ **1.11**

291 Herberto (USA) (bl) (NTinkler) 5-9-2 DNicholls (11) (a bhd: t.o) ...................... **12**

35004 Kasikci (55) (RHollinshead) 3-7-13 ‡7AGarth (8) (fell after 1f) ...................... **0**

**5/4** Big Pat, **9/2** IRON BARON (IRE), **13/2** Kasikci, **7/1** The Titan Ghost, **8/1** Tricotric, **14/1** Paper Clip, **16/1** Queens Tour, Herberto (USA), **20/1** Grey Cphas, **25/1** Al Badeto, **33/1** Media Star, **50/1** Choir's Image, **66/1** Light-of-the-Loch. CSF £11.07, Tote £6.50: £1.90 £1.50 £2.20 (£4.90). Mrs B. Facchino (UPPER LONGDON) bred by Mrs D. Jackson in Ireland. 13 Rn; No bid

2m 46.3 (11.8)
SF—30/23/16/9/–/–

---

## 3585

JOHN SMITH'S BITTER H'CAP (0-80) £3980.00 (£1190.00: £570.00: £260.00)
**5f**

3-20 (3-21)

3537 **Branston Abby (IRE) (79)** (MJohnston) 3-9-12 MRoberts (6) (chsd ldrs: slt ld 1f out: r.o u.p) ...................................................... —**1**

04015 Protonio (**51**) (MJohnston) 4-8-2 GDuffield (12) (lw: a.p: effrt 2f out: kpt on one pce fnl f) ............................................................. 1½.**2**

33176 Pharaoh's Dancer (71) (Fav) (RSimpson) 5-9-5 MWigham (7) (lw: dwlt: hdwy u.p over 1f out: edgd lft: styd on) ..................................... hd.**3**

3397 Precentor (62) (bl) (JDBethell) 6-8-10 AMunro (2) (lw: in tch: effrt wl over 1f out: one pce) ................................................................... 2½.**4**

33973 Simmie's Special (59) (RHollinshead) 4-8-7 LDettori (10) (disp ld 4f: no ex) .. 1½.**5**

3464 Last Straw (48) (AWJones) 4-7-3(3) ‡7ClaireBalding (1) (a in tch: n.m.r 1f out: styd on) ................................................................... nk.**6**

3518 Kalar (46) (bl) (DWChapman) 3-7-7 SWood (5) (disp ld 4f: wknd ins fnl f) ........ ½.**7**

32572 Banbury Flyer (47) (bl) (MrsALMKing) 4-7-9 JQuinn (11) (lw: chsd ldrs tl rdn & btn over 1f out) ..................................................... hd.**8**

35184 Miss Aragon (49) (MissLCSiddall) 4-7-8(2) ‡3DHarrison (3) (bhd: sme hdwy over 1f out: n.d) ............................................... 1½.**9**

3397* Samson-Agonistes (81) (BAMcMahon) 6-9-8 ‡7SSanders (13) (disp ld over 3f: sn lost pl) .................................................................... 2½.**10**

3469 Penny Hasset (69) (MWEasterby) 4-9-3 TLucas (9) (lw: outpcd fr ½-wy) .. 2.**11**

265 Angels Answer (IRE) (67) (MrsGRReveley) 3-8-7 ‡7DarrenMoffatt (4) (b.off fore: drvn along ½-wy: n.d after) ................................................. 1.**12**

3304 Seamere (79) (BRCambidge) 9-9-13 JLowe (8) (lw: hld up: effrt over 1f out: sn wknd) ...................................................................... ¾.**13**

LONG HANDICAP: Last Straw 7-2.

**7/2** Pharaoh's Dancer, **11/2** Precentor, **8/1** Banbury Flyer, **9/1** Samson-Agonistes, Pretonic, **11/1** Simmie's Special, BRANSTON ABBY (IRE), Penny Hasset, **12/1** Miss Aragon, **14/1** Angels Answer (IRE), **16/1** Seamere, Last Straw, **25/1** Kalar. CSF £106.24, CT £426.01. Tote £9.60: £2.90 £2.80 £1.70 (£39.30). Mr J. David Abell (MIDDLEHAM) bred by John David Abell in Ireland. 13 Rn

66.1 sec (4.6)
SF—67/37/53/34/25/6

---

## 3586

TRINIDAD & TOBAGO H'CAP (0-70) £2574.00 (£714.00: £342.00)
**2m 1f 22y**

3-50 (3-52)

(Weights raised 4 lb)

35152 Ambuscade (USA) (52) (MrsGRReveley) 6-9-4 KDarley (2) (a.p: led over 2f out: sn pushed clr: eased ins fnl f) ................................. —**1**

33512 Kadari (61) (AHarrison) 3-8-13 ‡3DHarrison (4) (in tch: hdwy 5f out: styd on fnl 2f: no imp) .................................................... 2½.**2**

3493* Blanc Seing (FR) (49) (bl) (MWEasterby) 5-9-1 (4x) TLucas (5) (lw: hld up & bhd: hdwy 5f out: kpt on u.p fnl 2f: nvr nrr) .......................... ½.**3**

35153 Kausar (USA) (58) (GMMoore) 5-9-10 MHills (11) (chsd ldr: led 5f out tl over 2f out: sn outpcd) ........................................................ 2½.**4**

3351* Sillars Stalker (IRE) (51) (MrsJRRamsden) 4-9-3 MRoberts (9) (hld up & bhd: hdwy 5f out: shkn up 2f out: no imp) ............................ 1½.**5**

33773 Scalp 'em (IRE) (32) (FHLee) 4-7-7(2) ‡5NKennedy (10) (chsd ldr: drvn along 7f out: sn wknd) ...................................................... 30.**6**

3298⁴ Lafkadio (45) (bl) (MCChapman) 5–8–11 AMunro (3) (a bhd) ............... 6.7
3351⁵ Brusque (USA) (37) (DonEnricoIncisa) 8–7–10 ‡⁷ClaireBalding (8) (b: bhd fr
¹/₂-wy) ..................... 2¹/₂.8
2968⁶ Bridge Player (40) (DMoffatt) 5–7–13 ‡⁷DarrenMoffatt (6) (b: chsd ldrs tl wknd 6f
out) ...................... 4.9
2609 Millie (USA) (45) (GFleming) 4–8–6 ‡⁵OPears (1) (drvn along ¹/₂-wy: sn wl bhd) 7.10
3398⁶ High Mind (FR) (49) (MissLCSiddall) 3–8–4 MBirch (7) (led tl hdd 5f out: wknd
qckly) ....................... 2¹/₂.11

**13/8** Blanc Seing (FR), **7/2** Sillars Stalker (IRE), **4/1** AMBUSCADE (USA), **8/1** Kadari, **10/1** Kausar (USA), **12/1** Lafkadio, **16/1** Brusque (USA), **25/1** Bridge Player, **33/1** Scalp 'em (IRE), **50/1** Ors. CSF £35.05, CT £66.45. Tote £4.80: £1.40 £2.60 £1.70 (£20.80). Mrs Lynne Firth (SALTBURN) bred by Keswick Stables in USA. 11 Rn
3m 58.3 (18.3)

**3587**  CARONI NURSERY (0-85) £2847.00 (£792.00: £381.00)   **1m 4y**   4-20 (4-22)
(Weights raised 6 lb)

3408* Boldville Bash (IRE) (70) (Fav) (TDBarron) 8-12 KDarley (11) (lw: hld up:
hdwy over 2f out: led appr fnl f: r.o) ....................... —1
3091⁵ Argyle Cavalier (IRE) (71) (FHLee) 8-13 GCarter (8) (bhd: hdwy over 2f out: r.o
u.p fnl f: nrst fin) ....................... 1.2
3029 Benevolent (76) (SirMarkPrescott) 9-4 AMunro (18) (a.p: slt ld appr fnl f: sn hdd
& nt qckn) ....................... 2¹/₂.3
3199 Preston Guild (IRE) (56) (MissSEHall) 7-12 NCarlisle (10) (chsd ldrs tl lost pl 3f
out: styd on wl appr fnl f) ....................... 3¹/₂.4
3173 Bonny Princess (53) (JDBethell) 7-9 LCharnock (16) (in tch: hdwy over 2f out:
one pce appr fnl f) ....................... 1¹/₂.5
3465² Arc Bright (IRE) (79) (RHollinshead) 9-7 LDettori (17) (lw: a.p: effrt 3f out: btn
whn hmpd over 1f out) ....................... 1¹/₂.6
3274⁶ Shynon (59) (MHTompkins) 8-1⁽²⁾ PRobinson (14) (effrt appr st: rdn & nvr rchd
ldrs) ....................... nk.7
3408 Tajdid (IRE) (66) (bl) (HThomsonJones) 8-8 RHills (2) (led tl hdd & wknd appr
fnl f) ....................... 1¹/₂.8
3347 Milngavie (IRE) (58) (MJohnston) 8-0 JLowe (5) (lw: chsd ldrs: wknd whn
hmpd 2f out) ....................... 7.9
2916* Yeveed (IRE) (64) (MHEasterby) 8-6 MBirch (6) (a mid div) ....................... nk.10
3482⁴ Public Way (56) (NChamberlain) 7-5 ‡⁷DarrenMoffatt (19) (chsd ldrs tl
wknd wl over 1f out) ....................... ³/₄.11
3325a Express Mariecurie (IRE) (77) (PWChapple-Hyam) 9-2 ‡³DHarrison (15) (chsd
ldrs 6f) ....................... 2.12
2938* Kiss in the Dark (64) (MrsGRReveley) 8-6 MRoberts (13) (bhd: effrt on outside
appr st: sn rdn & n.d) ....................... ³/₄.13
3301* Hotel California (IRE) (62) (DWChapman) 8-4 SWood (9) (a bhd) ....................... ¹/₂.14
3385 Persian Traveller (IRE) (62) (MrsJRRamsden) 8-4 PBurke (1) (nvr trbld ldrs) 2¹/₂.15
3394 Big Gem (55) (MCChapman) 7-4 ‡⁷AntoinetteArmes (4) (sn outpcd & bhd) ... 1¹/₂.16
2649 Miss Bridge (IRE) (52) (MBell) 7-8⁽¹⁾ JQuinn (3) (chsd ldrs 5f: wknd qckly) ......... 17
3199 Behaanis (USA) (56) (AAScott) 7-7⁽⁵⁾ ‡⁵NKennedy (12) (a bhd) ....................... 18
LONG HANDICAP: Miss Bridge (IRE) 7-4, Behaanis (USA) 7-5.

**6/1** BOLDVILLE BASH (IRE), **7/1** Express Mariecurie (IRE), **15/2** Kiss in the Dark, **8/1** Shynon(op 12/1), Argyle Cavalier (IRE), **10/1** Yeveed (IRE), **11/1** Benevolent, **12/1** Hotel California (IRE), **14/1** Persian Traveller (IRE), Preston Guild (IRE), Behaanis (USA), Arc Bright (IRE), **16/1** Tajdid (IRE), Milngavie (IRE), **20/1** Public Way (IRE), Miss Bridge (IRE), **33/1** Bonny Princess, **66/1** Big Gem. CSF £55.48, CT £415.72. Tote £9.10: £1.90 £2.10 £3.50 £3.10 (£26.70). Mr P. D. Savill (THIRSK) bred by Louis A. Walshe in Ireland. 18 Rn   1m 49.6 (8)
SF—32/30/27/–/–/10

**3588**  CLAXTON BAY GRADUATION STKS (2-Y.O) £3087.40 (£920.20: £438.60: £197.80)
**5f**   4-50 (4-51)

3367⁶ Aradanza (88) (MRChannon) 9-4 MRoberts (6) (lw: in tch: hdwy to ld over 1f
out: rdn & r.o) ....................... —1
3312² Baliana (CBBBooth) 8-6 ACulhane (7) (sn bhd: gd hdwy over 1f out: r.o) ...... 1¹/₂.2
3340³ Willshe Gan (89) (v) (DenysSmith) 8-13 KFallon (3) (a chsng ldrs: ev ch over 1f
out: nt qckn) ....................... 2.3
3070² Gymcrak Tiger (IRE) (100) (Fav) (MHEasterby) 9-4 MBirch (9) (lw: a.p: effrt 2f
out: styd on one pce) ....................... ¹/₂.4
2610* Celestial Key (USA) (90) (SGNorton) 9-4 KDarley (8) (a.p: effrt 2f out: styd on
same pce) ....................... nk.5
3366⁶ Petite Epaulette (84) (WJarvis) 8-13 AMunro (2) (prom tl outpcd fnl 2f) .......... 2¹/₂.6
3275⁴ Tuscan Dawn (74) (JBerry) 9-4 GCarter (1) (unruly s: led after 2f tl appr fnl f:
wknd) ....................... 3¹/₂.7
3411 Sober Lad (IRE) (80) (JBerry) 9-7 LCharnock (4) (led 2f: cl up tl wknd wl over 1f
out) ....................... 2.8

Target Zero (USA) *(MJHeaton-Ellis)* 8-11 MHills (5) (lengthy: dwlt: a outpcd & bhd) .................................................................. 10.9

**5/6** Gymcrak Tiger (IRE), **8/1** Celestial Key (USA), Willshe Gan, **9/1** Petite Epaulette, ARADANZA, **14/1** Tuscan Dawn, **20/1** Target Zero (USA), Baliana, **33/1** Sober Lad (IRE). CSF £135.12, Tote £8.50: £2.20 £2.80 £1.50 (£84.60). Mrs P. Lewis (UPPER LAMBOURN) bred by Mrs P. Lewis. 9 Rn
66.3 sec (4.8)
SF—53/35/34/37/36/21

---

**3589**   MARAVAL H'CAP (0-70) £2847.00 (£792.00: £381.00)   **1m 4y**   5-20 (5-23)

3140 **Good for the Roses (42)** *(MMcCormack)* 6-8-2 MRoberts (15) (mde all: styd on wl fnl f) ........................................................ —1

3466⁶ Ballyranter (46) *(HJCollingridge)* 3-8-2(1) PaulEddery (14) (a.p: chsd wnr fnl f: kpt on wl) ........................................................ 1¹/₂.2

3302² Lawnswood Junior (56) *(JLSpearing)* 5-9-2 KDarley (11) (bhd: gd hdwy 3f out: sn chsng ldrs: styd on one pce ins fnl f) ............... 2.3

3479 Creselly (54) *(JGFitzGerald)* 5-9-0 KFallon (10) (a chsng ldrs: rdn & one pce fnl 2f) ........................................................ 2.4

All Greek to Me (IRE) (55) *(CWThornton)* 4-9-1 ACulhane (21) (outpcd & bhd tl styd on wl fnl 3f) ........................................ 6.5

3383 Brambles Way (53) (v) *(WLBarker)* 3-8-4‡⁵OPears (18) (a chsng ldrs: hrd rdn 2f out: nt qckn) ........................................ ¹/₂.6

3370² Foolish Touch (56) *(WJMusson)* 10-9-2 JQuinn (20) (b: hdwy ¹/₂-wy: prom over 1f out: no ex) ........................................ 1¹/₂.7

3476 Miss Sarajane (42) *(RHollinshead)* 8-8-2 AMunro (7) (cl up tl wknd wl over 1f out) ........................................................ 3¹/₂.8

3349 Stairway to Heaven (IRE) (60) (bl) *(TDBarron)* 4-8-13 ‡⁷VHalliday (17) (in tch: effrt over 2f out: no imp) ........................ 2¹/₂.9

3365 Broad Appeal (46) *(RCSpicer)* 4-8-0 ‡⁹DHarrison (9) (s.s: hdwy on outside ent st: nvr rchd ldrs) .................................... hd.10

3481 Henry Will (36) *(TFairhurst)* 8-7-10 JFanning (5) (cl up tl wknd 2f out) .......... hd.11

3513* Stoproveritate (56) (Fav) *(SGNorton)* 3-8-12 (6x) NConnorton (1) (lw: chsd ldrs: rdn over 3f out: sn wknd) ........................ ¹/₂.12

3481 Borocay (49) *(MJCamacho)* 4-8-9 LCharnock (12) (in tch tl rdn & wknd 3f out) 2¹/₂.13

2483² No Decision (47) *(MWEasterby)* 5-8-7 TLucas (6) (hld up & bhd: n.d) ........... 5.14

3287 Don't Drop Bombs (USA) (41) *(AAScott)* 3-7-11 DaleGibson (22) (a bhd) ...... nk.15

Jungle Knife (68) *(MHTompkins)* 6-10-0 PRobinson (4) (in tch over 5f) ........... 4.16

3088 Roar on Tour (62) *(MHEasterby)* 3-9-4 MBirch (16) (hdwy ¹/₂-wy: sn chsng ldrs: wknd 2f out) ........................................ 1¹/₂.17

2815 Reza (40) *(JLEyre)* 4-7-7 ‡⁷DarrenMoffatt (13) (bit bkwd: n.d) ................... 1¹/₂.18

3481 Cool Enough (39) *(MrsJRRamsden)* 11-7-13 PBurke (8) (a bhd) ................. 19

3509⁵ Jaromic (50) *(PFTulk)* 3-8-6 GCarter (19) (b: a bhd) ........................... 20

3170 Palmas Pride (49) (bl) *(MDHammond)* 5-8-9 GDuffield (3) (cl up to ¹/₂-wy: sn wknd) ........................................................ 21

3460 Baie Petite (39) *(AWJones)* 3-7-9 JLowe (2) (s.i.s: a bhd) ...................... 22

**7/2** Stoproveritate, **7/1** GOOD FOR THE ROSES, **8/1** Broad Appeal(op 12/1), **9/1** Foolish Touch, **10/1** Lawnswood Junior, **11/1** Roar on Tour, **12/1** Ballyranter, **14/1** No Decision, Stairway to Heaven (IRE), Miss Sarajane, Jungle Knife, **20/1** Creselly, Borocay, Reza, Cool Enough, Don't Drop Bombs (USA), Henry Will, **25/1** Brambles Way, **33/1** Palmas Pride, Jaromic, All Greek to Me (IRE), **100/1** Baie Petite. CSF £94.26, CT £812.10. Tote £11.40: £2.50 £2.30 £2.40 £16.40 (£63.90). Orchid Racing & Bloodstock Limited (WANTAGE) bred by Octram Ltd. 22 Rn
1m 49.1 (7.5)
SF—29/24/32/24/7/–

T/Plpt: £303.20 (13.8 Tckts).
AA

---

## 3042—**WARWICK (L-H)**
### Monday, October 5th [Soft]
Going Allowance: 0.70 sec per fur (S)                        Wind: fresh half against

Stalls: low

**3590**   OCTOBER NURSERY (0-75) £2994.00 (£834.00: £402.00)   **5f**   2-00 (2-05)
(Weights raised 4 lb)

3049 **Convenient Moment (60)** *(JBerry)* 8-11 JWilliams (19) (hdwy 2f out: led ins fnl f: r.o wl) ........................................ —1

3470⁴ Magic Pearl (70) (Jt-Fav) *(EJAlston)* 9-7 LPiggott (17) (a.p: ev ch 1f out: hrd rdn: r.o) ........................................ ¹/₂.2

3478 Covent Garden Girl (55) (Jt-Fav) *(MWEasterby)* 8-6 AClark (20) (a.p: ev ch 1f out: unable qckn) ................................ nk.3

3218 Red Leader (IRE) (56) *(PFICole)* 8-7 TQuinn (11) (a.p: led stands' side over 1f out: sn hdd & one pce) ........................... ¹/₂.4

3286 Trevorsninepoints (62) (Jt-Fav) *(MJRyan)* 8-13 DBiggs (3) (led on ins: rdn & edgd rt appr fnl f: hdd over 1f out) .......... 4.5

3162 Magic Orb (66) *(JLSpearing)* 8-10 ‡7CHawksley (10) (chsd ldrs: rdn & no ex appr fnl f) ........................... 1.6

3275 Moving Image (IRE) (69) *(MBell)* 9-6 WRSwinburn (15) (b.hind: chsd ldrs tl rdn & wknd over 1f out) ........................... 2¹/₂.7

2306 Steven's Dream (IRE) (50) *(JWhite)* 8-1 DaleGibson (16) (hdwy appr fnl f: nvr nrr) ........................... ¹/₂.8

2274 Sweetings Scampy (IRE) (60) *(MHEasterby)* 8-8 ‡3SMaloney (12) (prom over 3f) 1.9

32615 Another Jade (62) *(APJarvis)* 8-6 ‡7DWright (5) (nvr trbld ldrs) ........................... nk.10

3463 Musical Phone (66) *(JPLeigh)* 9-3 DMcKeown (6) (lw: m.n.s) ........................... nk.11

3030 Codden Lad (60) *(NTinkler)* 8-11 MTebbutt (9) (m.n.s) ........................... nk.12

3039 Lowrianna (IRE) (53) (Jt-Fav) *(DHaydnJones)* 8-4 TyroneWilliams (18) (a bhd) hd.13

3315⁴ Girl Next Door (57) *(NAGraham)* 8-8 WCarson (7) (prom over 3f) ........................... 2.14

3478 Sea Strand (55) *(MBlanshard)* 8-6 DHolland (8) (m.n.s) ........................... 1¹/₂.15

32835 Legendary Hero (58) (bl) *(TDBarron)* 8-9 AlexGreaves (13) (w ldrs 3f: sn lost tch) ........................... nk.16

3162 Press the Bell (63) *(JBerry)* 9-0 JCarroll (1) (spd on ins 3f) ........................... s.h.17

3315³ The Institute Boy (63) *(KRBurke)* 9-0 AShoults (2) (lw: outpcd) ........................... 1¹/₂.18

3420⁶ Gaynor Goodman (IRE) (49) *(JSMoore)* 7-11 ‡3FNorton (4) (outpcd) ........................... hd.19

3285 *Our Shadee (USA)* Withdrawn (veterinary advice) : not under orders

**8/1** Covent Garden Girl, Trevorsninepoints, Magic Pearl(op 12/1), Lowrianna (IRE)(op 20/1), **9/1** Moving Image (IRE), Red Leader (IRE), **10/1** Another Jade, Legendary Hero, **11/1** Magic Orb, **14/1** Codden Lad, **16/1** Girl Next Door(op 10/1), CONVENIENT MOMENT(op 10/1), **20/1** Sea Strand, Musical Phone, Sweetings Scampy (IRE), Gaynor Goodman (IRE), **25/1** Ors. CSF £140.21, CT £1,025.94. Tote £17.80: £5.00 £2.80 £2.10 £2.30 (£62.20). Mr David Fish (COCKERHAM) bred by D. Gill. 19 Rn

64.8 sec (6.8)

SF—31/39/23/22/12/5

---

**3591**

QUEEN BESS STKS   £3552.75 (£1062.00: £508.50: £231.75)   7f   2-30 (2-35)

3441⁴ **Heart of Darkness (89)** (v) *(IABalding)* 4–9-0 RCochrane (2) (lw: hld up: 7th st: swtchd rt to ld appr fnl f: sn clr) ........................... —1

3427² Talb (USA) *(JLDunlop)* 3–9-4 WCarson (7) (lw: chsd ldrs: 6th st: chsd wnr appr fnl f: no imp) ........................... 3.2

3265* Waterfowl Creek (IRE) (91) *(GWragg)* 3-8-10 WRSwinburn (11) (hld up: r.o over 1f out: nvr nrr) ........................... 3.3

1934 Fair Crack (IRE) (101) *(RHannon)* 3–9-4 LPiggott (1) (w ldr: led 4f out tl appr fnl f: one pce) ........................... 2.4

3201⁴ Herora (IRE) (95) *(NAGraham)* 3-8-13 DHolland (5) (bhd: gd hdwy over 1f out: nvr nrr) ........................... 1.5

3418* Langtry Lady (78) (v) *(MJRyan)* 6–9-2 DBiggs (3) (dwlt: sn rcvrd: 4th st: wknd over 1f out) ........................... hd.6

3198 Corn Futures (73) *(JPLeigh)* 4–8-9 DMcKeown (9) (hld up: effrt 2f out: no imp) . 3.7

879² Lee Artiste (99) *(PFICole)* 4–9-2 TQuinn (4) (chsd ldrs: 5th st: wknd over 1f out) ¹/₂.8

3089 Ernestan (94) *(MHEasterby)* 3–9-1 ‡3SMaloney (8) (prom: 3rd st: wknd 2f out) 1¹/₂.9

3371⁵ Gunner's Daughter *(HCandy)* 4-8-10 CRutter (6) (b.hind: led 3f: 2nd st: wknd 2f out) ........................... 3.10

3278⁶ Al Billal *(JJBridger)* 4–9-0 GBardwell (10) (a bhd: t.o) ........................... 8.11

**11/4** HEART OF DARKNESS, **3/1** Waterfowl Creek (IRE), **4/1** Talb (USA), **8/1** Herora (IRE)(op 5/1), **9/1** Lee Artiste, **12/1** Fair Crack (IRE), **14/1** Ernestan(op 8/1), **16/1** Gunner's Daughter, **25/1** Langtry Lady, **33/1** Corn Futures, **100/1** Al Billal. CSF £13.82. Tote £3.40: £1.60 £1.60 £2.00 (£7.60). Mr Paul Mellon (KINGSCLERE) bred by Paul Mellon. 11 Rn

1m 30.5 (6.3)

SF—79/74/57/59/51/53

---

**3592**

WROXHALL STKS (Mdn 3-Y.O) £2616.00 (£726.00: £348.00)   6f   3-00 (3-09)

3416² **Draft Board** (Fav) *(JHMGosden)* 8-9 RCochrane (1) (b.nr hind: a.p: 3rd st: led wl over 1f out: pushed clr) ........................... —1

3386⁴ Stitched Up (IRE) *(PWChapple-Hyam)* 9-0 LPiggott (16) (led after 1f tl appr fnl f: sn outpcd) ........................... 8.2

3412² Admirals Realm (60) *(BAMcMahon)* 9-0 TQuinn (15) (led 1f: 2nd st: one pce fnl 2f) ........................... ³/₄.3

3473 Speedy Classic (USA) (57) *(BWHills)* 9-0 DHolland (12) (chsd ldrs: 4th st: one pce fnl 2f) ........................... 2.4

3499² Blue Is True (IRE) (51) *(LJBarratt)* 8-2 ‡7PBowe (9) (5th st: rdn wl over 1f out: no imp) ........................... 1¹/₂.5

3513 Toss the Dice (49) *(MAJarvis)* 9-0 WRyan (14) (chsd ldrs: 6th st: no hdwy fnl 2f) 1¹/₂.6

Gushing *(RCharlton)* 8-9 TSprake (5) (cmpt: bkwd: dwlt: effrt over 1f out: nvr nrr) ............................................................................................................... ³/₄.7

32906 **Silky Siren (56)** (bl) *(EAWheeler)* 8-9 SWhitworth (11) (nvr nrr) ............... ³/₄.8

3251 Galley Gossip *(33)* *(RBrotherton)* 8-9 GCrealock (2) (s.s: nvr nr ldrs) ............... ¹/₂.9

25455 Honey Vision *(45)* (bl) *(GHEden)* 8-9 JCarroll (17) (nvr nr ldrs) ............... 1¹/₂.10

34124 Ulladulla *(RAkehurst)* 8-11 ‡³RPerham (6) (lw: chsd ldrs: 7th st: wknd 2f out) ... 2.11

35065 Chinaman *(28)* *(WGRWightman)* 9-0 JWilliams (3) (outpcd) .......................... nk.12

35095 Hazy Shades *(31)* *(JJBridger)* 8-9 GBardwell (10) (m.n.s) .......................... 8.13

Divine Glory *(RVoorspuy)* 8-9 SDawson (8) (lengthy: a bhd) .......................... nk.14

3499 Injaka Boy *(39)* (v) *(KWhite)* 9-0 NAdams (4) (a bhd) .......................... 2.15

2493 Joshua John (IRE) *(BRMillman)* 9-0 MTebbutt (13) (outpcd: a bhd) ......... hd.16

72 Floating Rate *(48)* *(JWhite)* 8-4 ‡⁵ATucker (7) (bkwd: outpcd) .......................... ³/₄.17

**8/11 DRAFT BOARD**(op 5/4), **7/1** Stitched Up (IRE)(op 4/1), Admirals Realm, **8/1** Ulladulla(op 5/1), **10/1** Silky Siren, **14/1** Blue Is True (IRE), Gushing(op 4/1), **16/1** Speedy Classic (USA)(op 10/1), **20/1** Toss the Dice, **33/1** Divine Glory, **50/1** Honey Vision, **66/1** Floating Rate, Chinaman, Galley Gossip, **100/1** Ors. CSF £8.17, Tote £1.80: £1.20 £2.30 £2.50 (£6.20). Lord Derby (NEWMARKET) bred by Stanley Estate and Stud Co. 17 Rn
1m 18.4 (6.4)
SF—51/24/21/13/–/1

## 3593

MOP STKS (Mdn 2-Y.O) £2070.00 (£570.00: £270.00)    **1m**    3-30 (3-40)

2519 **Sculler (USA) (Fav)** *(HRACecil)* 9-0 WRyan (14) (led over 4f out: hdd & 2nd st: led 2f out: r.o strly) ........................................................................................ —1

33994 Stitchcombe *(PWChapple-Hyam)* 9-0 LPiggott (15) (led over 3f: 3rd st: ev ch over 1f out: one pce) ................................................................................ 3.2

3276 Moujeeb (USA) *(MRStoute)* 8-9 ‡5JJones (18) (a.p: 4th st: effrt over 1f out: nvr able to chal) .......................................................................................... nk.3

34915 Allegation *(PFICole)* 9-0 WCarson (13) (hdwy fnl 2f: nrst fin) .......................... nk.4

Moussahim (USA) *(MRStoute)* 9-0 WRSwinburn (8) (unf: scope: chsd ldrs: rdn 2f out: styd on) .......................................................................................... 3.5

3200 Euphonic *(IABalding)* 9-0 RCochrane (20) (chsd ldrs: 8th st: kpt on same pce) . 4.6

Flaming Miracle (IRE) *(PFICole)* 9-0 TQuinn (5) (unf: scope: chsd ldrs: 5th st: wknd wl over 1f out) ................................................................................ ³/₄.7

Steppe Closer *(LordHuntingdon)* 8-9 DMcKeown (17) (scope: bkwd: s.s: hdwy fnl 2f: nvr nrr) .......................................................................................... ¹/₂.8

3402 Dodgy Dancer *(MrsLPiggott)* 9-0 MTebbutt (1) (b: nvr nrr) .......................... hd.9

32474 Chouette *(MRMusson)* 8-9 NDay (21) (chsd ldrs over 5f) ................................ 1¹/₂.10

Boltrose *(KWhite)* 9-0 NAdams (2) (leggy: unf: bkwd: m.n.s) ................................ 1¹/₂.11

32476 Flying Amy *(RCurtis)* 8-4 ‡5ATucker (19) (m.n.s) .......................................... s.h.12

Danroy (USA) *(GHarwood)* 8-9 AClark (9) (w'like: scope: hdwy to ld ent st: hdd 2f out: wknd qckly) ................................................................................ s.h.13

Electrolyte *(BPalling)* 9-0 DBiggs (4) (w'like: leggy: bkwd: a bhd) .......................... 1¹/₂.14

2409 Lake Princess (IRE) *(52)* *(SDow)* 8-6 ‡3FNorton (7) (chsd ldrs: 7th st: wknd 2f out) .......................................................................................... nk.15

Sea Viking *(MBlanshard)* 9-0 GBardwell (16) (wl grwn: bkwd: m.n.s) .......................... ³/₄.16

3005 Wings Cove *(MRStoute)* 9-0 JCarroll (12) (bhd fr ¹/₂-wy: t.o) ................................ 7.17

2034 Alaska Bay *(RJHolder)* 9-0 JWilliams (11) (t.o) .......................................... 10.18

Kings Water (IRE) *(APJarvis)* 8-7 ‡7DWright (22) (w'like: t.o fr ¹/₂-wy) ............... 2¹/₂.19

2901 Rare Occurance *(MJCharles)* 9-0 DHolland (6) (prom: 6th & rdn st: wknd qckly: t.o) .......................................................................................... nk.20

3240 Sandswift (bl) *(RFJohnsonHoughton)* 9-0 TSprake (3) (t.o) .......................... 1¹/₂.21

35035 Form Secret (IRE) *(LJBarratt)* 8-9 CDwyer (10) (swvd s: a t.o) .......................... 8.22

**11/4 SCULLER (USA), 4/1** Moussahim (USA)(3/1—5/1), **6/1** Stitchcombe, **8/1** Chouette, **12/1** Allegation, **14/1** Danroy (USA)(op 8/1), Steppe Closer(op 6/1), **20/1** Sandswift, Flaming Miracle (IRE), Euphonic, Dodgy Dancer, **25/1** Wings Cove, **33/1** Electrolyte, Sea Viking, Lake Princess (IRE), **50/1** Alaska Bay, Boltrose, Rare Occurance, Kings Water (IRE), **66/1** Ors. CSF £20.81, Tote £3.70: £2.40 £2.00 £8.70 (£12.60). Mr K. Abdulla (NEWMARKET) bred by Juddmonte Farms Incorporated in USA. 22 Rn 1m 46.8 (9.8)
SF—37/28/22/26/17/5

## 3594

ARDEN STKS   £3514.50 (£972.00: £463.50)   **1¹/₄m 169y**   4-00 (4-04)

10154 **Balnibarbi (Fav)** *(HRACecil)* 3-8-11 WRyan (3) (chsd ldr 6f out: 2nd st: led over 1f out: sn clr) .......................................................................................... —1

3425★ Barahin (IRE) *(JLDunlop)* 3-8-11 WCarson (1) (led over 7f out tl hdd & no ex appr fnl f) ................................................................................ 5.2

333 Monscoma (IRE) *(48)* *(RIngram)* 4-8-5⁽⁵⁾ AClark (2) (led over 3f: lost tch 4f out: 3rd & t.o ent st) ................................................................................ dist.3

**8/13 BALNIBARBI, 11/8** Barahin (IRE), **100/1** Monscoma (IRE). CSF £1.63, Tote £1.70 (£1.10). Mr K. Abdulla (NEWMARKET) bred by Juddmonte Farms. 3 Rn 2m 30.4 (16.9)
SF—5/–/–

**3595** KINGSBURY APP'CE H'CAP (0-70) £3870.00 (£1161.00: £559.00: £258.00)

**7f** 4-30 (4-33)

3476³ **Cee-Jay-Ay (52)** *(JBerry)* 5–8–7 ‡⁵PRoberts (20) (dwlt: sn wl bhd: rapid hdwy to
ld ins fnl f: r.o) ............................................................. —1

3373* **Tyrone Flyer (45)** *(MissGayKelleway)* 3–8–2 MGodsafe (7) (led 5f out: sn clr:
wknd & hdd ins fnl f) ........................................ 1¹/₂.2

3245 **Spanish Love (42)** *(CGCox)* 6–8–2 DWright (2) (chsd ldrs: 3rd st: ev ch 1f out:
unable qckn) ................................................. s.h.3

3400⁵ **Strip Cartoon (IRE) (51)** (bl) *(SRBowring)* 4–8–11⁽¹⁾ MHarris (13) (led 2f: 5th st:
styd on ins fnl f) ............................................... 2.4

3263 **Mexican Dancer (44)** *(RJHolder)* 3–8–1 RWaterfield (19) (lost pl ¹/₂-wy: r.o appr
fnl f) ............................................................. ¹/₂.5

3422⁴ **Old Comrades (54)** *(LGCottrell)* 5–9–0 TAshley (14) (b.hind: a.p: 2nd st: rdn &
wknd over 1f out) ......................................... ¹/₂.6

1544 **Verro (USA) (42)** (bl) *(JABennett)* 5–8–2 DCarson (1) (bit bkwd: chsd ldrs: 6th
st: kpt on one pce appr fnl f) ....................... 1¹/₂.7

3422³ **Shining Jewel (68)** *(MrsLPiggott)* 5–10–0 GMilligan (9) (lw: bhd: r.o fnl f: nvr nrr) 1¹/₂.8

3378* **Gallery Artist (IRE) (53)** *(RGuest)* 4–8–13 SEiffert (16) (prom: 4th st: wknd 2f out) hd.9

3485⁴ **Be My Everything (IRE) (65)** *(RHollinshead)* 3–9–8 JDennis (17) (m.n s) ........ ¹/₂.10

3245 **Chandigarh (55)** *(RLee)* 4–9–1 DMcCabe (11) (m.n s) ............................ nk.11

3263 **Creego (41)** *(JAGlover)* 3–7–12⁽²⁾ GMitchell (14) (m.n s) ...................... hd.12

3383 **Diamond Inthe Dark (USA) (59)** *(CTinkler)* 4–9–5 ADobbin (10) (chsd ldrs: 7th
st: sn wknd) ................................................. hd.13

2941 **Venture Fourth (50)** *(EJAlston)* 3–8–2⁽³⁾ ‡⁸SKnott (18) (m.n s) ............... 1¹/₂.14

3251² **Dorking Lad (53)** *(MHTompkins)* 10–8–13 SMulvey (4) (m.n s) ............... ¹/₂.15

3383² **Glenfield Greta (60)** (Fav) *(PSFelgate)* 4–9–6 DMeredith (8) (m.n s: t.o) ..... 7.16

1306 **Sirmoor (IRE) (62)** *(RHannon)* 3–9–0 ‡⁵WendyJones (3) (bkwd: t.o) ......... 2.17

3460 **All Earz (IRE) (43)** *(REarnshaw)* 3–8–0 DGibbs (5) (t.o) ...................... ¹/₂.18

3259 **Jameel Dancer (63)** *(MRStoute)* 3–9–6 KPattinson (6) (s.s: a bhd: t.o) ...... 2¹/₂.19

**6/1** Glenfield Greta, **13/2** Tyrone Flyer(op 4/1), **7/1** Be My Everything (IRE)(10/1—16/1), **8/1** CEE-JAY-AY(6/1—
10/1), Old Comrades, **9/1** Gallery Artist (IRE), Chandigarh(12/1—8/1), **10/1** Dorking Lad, **11/1** Strip Cartoon
(IRE), **12/1** Shining Jewel, **16/1** Spanish Love, Jameel Dancer, **25/1** Venture Fourth, Diamond Inthe Dark (USA),
**33/1** Mexican Dancer, All Earz (IRE), Sirmoor (IRE), Creego, **50/1** Verro (USA). CSF £61.23, CT £782.07. Tote
£7.70: £2.30 £1.60 £4.60 £4.80 (£28.60). Mr Richard Jinks (COCKERHAM) bred by B. Minty. 19 Rn
1m 32.9 (8.7)
SF—36/26/25/28/16/27

**3596** PRINCE RUPERT H'CAP (0-70) £2910.00 (£810.00: £390.00) **5f** 5-00 (5-05)

*(Weights raised 5 lb)*

3400⁶ **John O'Dreams (39)** *(MrsJCDawe)* 7–8–2 TSprake (10) (hdwy 2f out: led ins fnl
f: comf) ........................................................ —1

3499³ **Langtonian (56)** (bl) *(JBerry)* 3–9–1 ‡³EmmaO'Gorman (12) (lw: hdwy on
outside 2f out: ev ch whn edgd lft ins fnl f: r.o) ............... 1.2

3499 **Lincstone Boy (IRE) (51)** (v) *(SRBowring)* 4–9–0 SWebster (13) (w ldr: led over
1f out: sn hdd: r.o) .................................... hd.3

3308² **Banham College (57)** *(BAMcMahon)* 6–9–6 TQuinn (11) (a chsng ldrs: r.o u.p
ins fnl f) ..................................................... 1¹/₂.4

3397⁴ **Farndale (44)** *(BCMorgan)* 5–8–7 GBardwell (16) (prom: hrd rdn & ev ch over 1f
out: btn whn hmpd ins fnl f) .......................... nk.5

3499 **Barbara's Cutie (39)** (v) *(MBlanshard)* 4–7–9 ‡⁷CAvery (3) (led tl hdd appr fnl f:
no ex) ......................................................... ³/₄.6

3559² **Joe Sugden (55)** (Fav) *(PHowling)* 8–9–4 RCochrane (4) (w ldrs over 3f) ..... 2.7

3559 **Frimley Parkson (31)** (v) *(PHowling)* 8–7–8⁽¹⁾ TyroneWilliams (8) (dwlt: hdwy
over 1f out: fin wl) ....................................... s.h.8

3499 **Amour du Soir (USA) (57)** *(RLee)* 5–9–6 JWilliams (14) (b: nvr trbld ldrs) ..... ³/₄.9

3559 **Party Treat (IRE) (36)** *(DMarks)* 4–7–13 SDawson (2) (nvr trbld ldrs) ........ nk.10

3042 **Oriental Song (35)** *(KSBridgwater)* 3–7–11 NAdams (15) (m.n s) ............. 4.11

3499* **Sakharov (51)** *(MAJarvis)* 3–8–13 WRyan (6) (bkwd: m.n s) ................. ¹/₂.12

3499* **Call to the Bar (IRE) (49)** *(CGCox)* 3–8–4 ‡⁷DWright (7) (w ldrs 3f) ......... hd.13

3464 **We're All Game (62)** *(BCMorgan)* 3–9–0 LPiggott (17) (spd 3f) ............... 1.14

1167 **Lost Moment (46)** *(HJCollingridge)* 8–8–9⁽⁹⁾ VSmith (5) (b.hind: m.n s) ..... 2.15

1167 **Supreme Optimist (35)** (bl) *(REPeacock)* 8–7–5⁽⁵⁾ ‡⁷GMilligan (1) (bkwd: s.i.s:
t.o) ............................................................. 10.16

1144⁶ **It's Only Money (53)** *(THCaldwell)* 3–8–12 ‡³FNorton (9) (bit bkwd: sn outpcd:
t.o) ............................................................. 5.17

LONG HANDICAP: Frimley Parkson 7-3, Supreme Optimist 7-6.

**3597 — 3598**

**9/2** Joe Sugden(6/1—4/1), **6/1** Call to the Bar (IRE)(9/2—7/1), **7/1** Banham College(op 9/2), **9/1** We're All Game, **10/1** Barbara's Cutie, JOHN O'DREAMS, Lincstone Boy (IRE), **12/1** Farndale, Langtonian, **14/1** Amour du Soir (USA), **25/1** Sakharov, **33/1** Lost Moment, Party Treat (IRE), **50/1** Ors. CSF £110.36, CT £1,109.73. Tote £10.20: £1.90 £2.20 £2.50 £2.50 (£66.20). Miss Katie Redgate (BRIDGWATER) bred by Stephen Stanhope. 17 Rn

64.5 sec (6.5)
SF—28/37/35/35/21/6

T/Plpt: £24.70 (89.64 Tckts).        IM

## WARWICK (L-H)
**Tuesday, October 6th [Soft]**
Going Allowance: 7f-8f: 0.45 sec (Y); Rest: 0.75 sec per fur (S)      Wind: mod half against

Stalls: low

### 3597
E.B.F. BRINKLOW STKS (I) (Mdn 2-Y.O.C & G) £2782.50 (£770.00: £367.50)
7f                                                   2-00 (2-03)

| | | |
|---|---|---|
| 3181² | **Mullitover** *(MJHeaton-Ellis)* 9-0 RCochrane (5) (lw: mde all: qcknd over 1f out: comf) | —1 |
| 2398² | Semillon *(GHarwood)* 9-0 PatEddery (4) (4th st: hrd rdn & ev ch whn jinked lft 1f out: nt rcvr) | 3.2 |
| 3491² | Eastern Memories (IRE) **(81)** (Fav) *(RHannon)* 9-0 JReid (10) (w wnr: 2nd st: rdn over 1f out: nt qckn) | ½.3 |
| 3424⁵ | New Quest *(PFICole)* 9-0 AMunro (2) (b.hind: 3rd st: one pce fnl 2f) | ¾.4 |
| 3262 | Restitution *(JRFanshawe)* 9-0 GCarter (7) (bit bkwd: prom: rdn 4f out: 6th & wkng sl) | 8.5 |
| 3255 | Duveen (IRE) *(CRNelson)* 9-0 SCauthen (1) (dwlt: 5th & rdn st: wknd 2f out) | 3.0 |
| 3402 | Rubidian *(SirMarkPrescott)* 9-0 CNutter (9) (7th st: no hdwy) | 1.7 |
| | Kadastrof (FR) *(RDickin)* 9-0 SDawson (8) (w'like: leggy: bkwd: s.s: a bhd) | 6.8 |
| | Cavalier Prince (IRE) *(APJarvis)* 8-7 ‡7DWright (6) (w'like: bkwd: a bhd) | ¾.9 |
| 581 | Nordic Spirit (IRE) *(CFWall)* 9-0 MHills (3) (bkwd: a in rr: t.o) | 12.10 |

**9/4** Eastern Memories (IRE), **5/2** MULLITOVER, Semillon(7/4—11/4), **6/1** New Quest(4/1—13/2), **14/1** Restitution, **50/1** Rubidian, Kadastrof (FR), Duveen (IRE), **66/1** Ors. CSF £8.82, Tote £3.70: £1.10 £1.70 £1.10 (£5.70). Mrs D. B. Mulley (WROUGHTON) bred by Mrs D. B. Mulley. 10 Rn

1m 31.1 (6.9)
SF—44/35/33/31/7/-

### 3598
ALLIED DUNBAR NURSERY    £4020.75 (£1206.00: £580.50: £267.75)
1m                                               2-30 (2-36)

(Weights raised 6 lb)

| | | |
|---|---|---|
| 3502 | **Sudbury (IRE) (66)** *(MHTompkins)* 8-7 PatEddery (15) (lw: led 2f: 2nd st: led 2f out: drvn out) | —1 |
| 3408 | Manon Lescaut **(57)** *(APJarvis)* 7-5 ‡7DWright (18) (3rd st: hrd rdn 2f out: r.o one pce) | 2.2 |
| 3148 | Almansour (USA) **(80)** *(HRACecil)* 9-7 SCauthen (14) (4th st: one pce fnl 2f) | 2¹/₂.3 |
| 3260² | Finavon **(75)** (bl) *(IABalding)* 9-2 RCochrane (1) (s.i.s: hdwy to ld 4f out: hdd 2f out: one pce) | 1¹/₂.4 |
| 2951⁶ | Lidoma (IRE) **(64)** *(JLDunlop)* 8-5 MHills (17) (lw: rdn & lost pl 4f out: styd on fnl 2f) | 3.5 |
| 3491³ | Grand Applause **(77)** *(RSimpson)* 8-13 ‡5ATucker (12) (hdwy 2f out: nvr nr to chal) | 2.6 |
| 3502³ | Don'tlie (IRE) **(69)** *(GBBalding)* 8-10 RPrice (13) (lw: nvr nrr) | 2.7 |
| 3063 | Awesome Risk **(58)** *(GLewis)* 7-6⁽⁴⁾ ‡7CHawksley (5) (lw: hdwy 4f out: 6th st: wknd 2f out) | 1.8 |
| 3260 | Trepidation (IRE) **(53)** *(MJFetherston-Godley)* 7-8⁽¹⁾ JQuinn (6) (n.d) | 2¹/₂.9 |
| 3315 | Shades of Croft **(52)** *(MDIUsher)* 7-7 RStreet (2) (led 6f out to 5f out: 5th st: wknd 2f out) | 4.10 |
| 3508² | Homemaker **(55)** *(RJHolder)* 7-10 NAdams (4) (hrd rdn & hdwy 4f out: wknd 2f out) | 2.11 |
| 3501⁴ | Sabo's Express **(73)** (bl) *(RHannon)* 9-0 LPiggott (9) (bhd fnl 3f) | 1¹/₂.12 |
| 3300 | Kaloochi **(65)** *(RHannon)* 8-6 AMunro (7) (a bhd) | 1¹/₂.13 |
| 3424⁴ | My Harvinski **(79)** *(PWChapple-Hyam)* 9-6 JReid (8) (lw: a bhd) | nk.14 |
| 3315 | Creative Flair (USA) **(53)** (bl) *(PFICole)* 7-8 GBardwell (10) (led 5f out to 4f out: wknd qckly 3f out) | nk.15 |
| 3178 | Daisy James (IRE) **(57)** *(JMPEustace)* 7-7⁽⁴⁾ ‡5NKennedy (16) (s.i.s: a bhd: t.o) | 5.16 |
| 3414 | Petiole **(56)** *(WRMuir)* 7-11⁽⁴⁾ CRutter (3) (a bhd: t.o) | 3.17 |
| 3402⁵ | Contract Court (USA) **(80)** *(CACyzer)* 9-7 GCarter (11) (a bhd: t.o) | 15.18 |

LONG HANDICAP: Trepidation (IRE) 7-5, Shades of Croft 7-4, Petiole 7-1.

**6/1** Finavon, **8/1** My Harvinski(op 4/1), Sabo's Express(6/1—9/1), Don'tlie (IRE), Almansour (USA)(6/1—10/1), **9/1** Homemaker, **11/1** SUDBURY (IRE), **12/1** Creative Flair (USA), Awesome Risk(op 8/1), **14/1** Lidoma (IRE), Manon Lescaut, **16/1** Contract Court (USA), Kaloochi, **20/1** Grand Applause (IRE), Daisy James (IRE), **25/1** Trepidation (IRE), Shades of Croft, **33/1** Petiole. CSF £154.01, CT £1,211.39. Tote £9.30: £2.90 £2.50 £2.80 £2.30 (£573.60). Mr John Wimbs (NEWMARKET) bred by Ballykisteen Stud Ltd in Ireland. 18 Rn   1m 45 (8)
SF—27/5/27/17/–/–

---

### 3599        AUTUMN STKS (2-Y.O.F) £3132.00 (£936.00: £448.00: £204.00)        **7f**   3-00 (3-07)

3314* **Cropton (83)** *(MrsJCecil)* 9-1  RCochrane (4) (chsd ldr: 2nd st: led 2f out & r.o wl) ............................................................................................ **—1**

3502* Formal Affair **(72)** *(CACyzer)* 9-1  GCarter (2) (led 5f: r.o one pce) ...................... 3.2

3404* Ajanta **(81)** *(Fav)* *(BWHills)* 9-4  PatEddery (3) (sn pushed along: 4th st: one pce fnl 2f) ............................................................................... 1½.3

2864⁴ Mataris *(PTWalwyn)* 8-11  AMunro (6) (6th st: styd on fnl 2f) ...................... ½.4

2986⁵ Somnifere (USA) *(PWChapple-Hyam)* 8-11  JReid (7) (rdn & 3rd st: wknd over 1f out) ............................................................................................ 1½.5

Coven Moon *(HJCollingridge)* 8-8  JQuinn (5) (leggy: scope: bkwd: s.s: hdwy & 5th st: wknd 2f out) ........................................................................... 6.6

2482 Sian Wyn *(KRBurke)* 8-11  AShoults (8) (bit bkwd: bhd: rdn 4f out: 7th st: t.o) ..... 8.7

2746 Kennington Proton *(JRBosley)* 8-6  ‡⁵NGwilliams (1) (bkwd: prom 3f: wknd qckly: last st: t.o) ...................................................................... 4.8

**11/10** Ajanta(tchd 7/4), **7/2** CROPTON, **4/1** Formal Affair, **7/1** Somnifere (USA)(10/1—16/1), Mataris, **25/1** Coven Moon, **66/1** Ors. CSF £17.87, Tote £4.60: £1.70 £1.50 £1.50 (£6.90). Lady Murless (NEWMARKET) bred by Lady Murless. 8 Rn   1m 32.3 (8.1)
SF—27/18/16/7/2/–

---

### 3600        RACING SCHOOLS TOTE APP'CE H'CAP (0-70) £2733.50 (£756.00: £360.50)
**1½m 115y**        3-30 (3-30)
(Weights raised 1 lb)

3373 **Qualitair Rhythm (IRE) (50)** *(Fav)* *(ICampbell)* 4-8-2 ‡⁷GMitchell (9) (sn chsng ldr: led over 3f out: sn clr: easily) ................................................. **—1**

1970 Singing Reply (USA) **(34)** *(DMarks)* 4-9-10 ‡³ClaireBalding (10) (bit bkwd: 5th st: hdwy 2f out: r.o ins fnl f: no ch w wnr) ................................... 7.2

3504 Marine Society **(65)** *(RLee)* 4-9-10  ATucker (2) (hdwy 5f out: 4th st: one pce fnl 2f) ............................................................................................... 1.3

3158 My Swan Song **(38)** *(JPSmith)* 7-7-11⁽⁴⁾  SSanders (3) (hdwy 5f out: 6th st: one pce fnl 2f) .................................................................................. ¾.4

3556 Eastern Magic **(60)** *(JAkehurst)* 4-9-5  JTate (11) (3rd st: wknd 2f out) ............... 6.5

Wotamona **(42)** *(BPalling)* 4-8-1⁽⁵⁾  PTurner (1) (b.nr hind: bkwd: nvr nrr) .......... ½.6

3493 Must Be Magical (USA) **(34)** (bl) *(FHLee)* 4-7-7  NKennedy (7) (led over 9f: 2nd st: wknd qckly 2f out) ................................................................... 8.7

3309 Nipotina **(34)** *(RHollinshead)* 6-7-7  AGarth (4) (hdwy 5f out: wknd over 3f out) nk.8

Inkala **(55)** *(WRMuir)* 4-8-11 ‡³KimMcDonnell (6) (bkwd: prom 7f) ............... ¾.9

3409 Tarmon (IRE) **(45)** (bl) *(ABarrow)* 4-7-11⁽¹¹⁾ ‡⁷RWaterfield (5) (bit bkwd: prom 6f: wknd qckly: sn t.o) ................................................................ 25.10

Rimouski **(57)** *(BRCambidge)* 4-9-2  KRutter (8) (bkwd: s.s: a bhd: t.o fnl 5f) . 12.11

LONG HANDICAP: Singing Reply (USA) 7-3, My Swan Song 7-5, Must Be Magical 6-10, Nipotina 7-3, Tarmon (IRE) 7-6.

**7/4** QUALITAIR RHYTHM (IRE), **100/30** Eastern Magic, **5/1** My Swan Song, **7/1** Marine Society(5/1—8/1), **10/1** Inkala, **14/1** Must Be Magical (USA)(op 8/1), **16/1** Singing Reply (USA), Nipotina, **25/1** Rimouski, **33/1** Ors. CSF £29.50, CT £155.47. Tote £2.50: £1.50 £6.80 £3.90 (£36.30). Mr R. A. Newson (NEWMARKET) bred by Brendan Powell in Ireland. 11 Rn   2m 52.4 (14.9)
SF—33/7/39/10/20/1/–

---

### 3601        GUYS CLIFFE S' H'CAP (3 & 4-Y.O) (0-60) £2889.00 (£804.00: £387.00)
**1¼m 169y**        4-00 (4-03)

2059 **Drinks Party (IRE) (31)** *(JWharton)* 4-8-2  JQuinn (3) (hdwy & 6th st: hrd rdn 2f out: led nr fin) ...................................................................... **—1**

3510⁴ Tendresse (IRE) **(34)** *(Fav)* *(CJHill)* 4-8-5  NAdams (7) (hdwy to ld 3f out: hdd cl home) ........................................................................................ 1½.2

3421³ Breakdancer (IRE) **(50)** *(WRMuir)* 3-9-0  RCochrane (4) (lw: hdwy 4f out: 4th st: ev ch 1f out: nt qckn) ................................................................. nk.3

3403 Jalore **(41)** *(RHollinshead)* 3-7-12 ‡⁷MHumphries (5) (hld up & bhd: hdwy fnl 2f: r.o) .................................................................................. 3½.4

2607² Sweet Revival **(35)** *(JAGlover)* 4-8-6  JFortune (10) (5th st: no hdwy fnl 2f) ...... hd.5

3500⁶ Princess of Orange **(40)** *(WRMbbourne)* 3-7-11 ‡⁷AGarth (9) (3rd & rdn st: wknd wl over 1f out) ............................................................ 2.6

3373 Samjamalifran **(38)** *(MCPipe)* 3-7-9⁽²⁾ ‡⁷JTate (13) (bhd: hdwy 3f out: nvr trbld ldrs) ................................................................................... 6.7

3263⁴ Positive Aspect **(41)** *(JPearce)* 3–8-5 RPrice (17) (prom 6f) .......................... 1½.**8**
2582 Mardior **(31)** (bl) *(WGRWightman)* 4–8-2 GCarter (12) (bit bkwd: led over 2f: led
      6f out to 3f out: 2nd st: wknd qckly 2f out) ....................... 4.**9**
3350⁴ Hot Prospect **(44)** (bl) *(JEtherington)* 3–8-8 PatEddery (2) (prom tl 6th & wkng
      st) ................................................................................ hd.**10**
3461 La Stravaganza **(57)** *(LJCodd)* 4–9-7 ‡⁷SWynne (6) (n.d) ...................... 10.**11**
3282⁶ Saif Al Adil (IRE) **(41)** (bl) *(KTIvory)* 3–8-5 GBardwell (15) (prom 5f) ......... 6.**12**
3479⁴ Salinger **(44)** *(JWHills)* 4–9-1 MHills (11) (plld hrd: a bhd) ..................... 1½.**13**
3500² Feeling Foolish (IRE) **(50)** *(BForsey)* 3–8-9 ‡⁵ATucker (5) (b.off hind: n.d) ... 2½.**14**
3487 Good Old George (IRE) **(36)** *(MJFetherston-Godley)* 3–8-0 AMunro (1) (prom
      5f) ................................................................................ 1½.**15**
3388⁶ Wise Portia **(42)** *(HCandy)* 3–8-6 CRutter (18) (swtg: a bhd) ................ hd.**16**
3500 Kate Royale **(37)** *(MCPipe)* 3–7-10 ‡⁵NGwilliams (16) (n.d) ................... 3.**17**
3494² Reel of Tulloch (IRE) **(49)** *(PCHaslam)* 3–8-13 LPiggott (20) (bhd fnl 5f: t.o) ... 12.**18**
3426 Coochie **(36)** (bl) *(RJBaker)* 3–7-7⁽⁴⁾ ‡⁷CHawksley (8) (s.s: rapid hdwy to ld 8f
      out: hdd 6f out: wknd qckly: t.o) ..................................... 12.**19**

**2/1** Tendresse (IRE), **4/1** Reel of Tulloch (IRE)(op 7/1), **6/1** Sweet Revival(op 4/1), **8/1** Salinger(op 5/1), **14/1**
Positive Aspect, Wise Portia, Breakdancer (IRE), Mardior, DRINKS PARTY (IRE), **16/1** Feeling Foolish (IRE), Kate
Royale, **20/1** Saif Al Adil (IRE), **25/1** Hot Prospect, La Stravaganza, **33/1** Ors. CSF £46.17, CT £411.36. Tote
£22.80: £3.90 £1.10 £3.60 £10.70 (£48.90). Mr David Edge (MELTON MOWBRAY) bred by Patrick Murnaghan
in Ireland. 19 Rn; No bid
               2m 28.3 (14.8)
               SF—22/22/30/7/14/1

## 3602
    E.B.F. BRINKLOW STKS (II) (Mdn 2-Y.O.C & G) £2758.00 (£763.00: £364.00)
    7f
                        4-30 (4-33)

3011 **Anaxagoras** *(AAScott)* 9-0 JFortune (2) (hld up: hdwy & 3rd st: hrd rdn over 1f
      out: led ins fnl f: r.o wl) ......................................... —**1**
3289⁴ Nessun Dorma (Fav) *(GWragg)* 9-0 MHills (5) (led: ran over 1f out: hdd ins fnl f) 1½.**2**
3011 Secret Assignment (USA) *(CACyzer)* 9-0 GCarter (3) (bkwd: 2nd st: ev ch 2f
      out: one pce) ................................................................ 6.**3**
Major Yaasi (USA) *(JRFanshawe)* 9-0 RCochrane (6) (cmpt: str: bkwd: s.s: last
      st: hdwy 2f out: nvr nr to chal) ..................................... 4.**4**
Tejano Gold (USA) *(JMPEustace)* 9-0 MTebbutt (4) (leggy: scope: bit bkwd:
      last st: a bhd) ....................................................... ¾.**5**
Yunus Emre (IRE) *(MBell)* 9-0 SCauthen (1) (gd sort: bkwd: chsd ldr: 4th &
      wkng st: eased whn btn over 1f out) ............................... 8.**6**

**4/7** Nessun Dorma, **7/2** Yunus Emre (IRE), **7/1** ANAXAGORAS(10/1—6/1), **14/1** Major Yaasi (USA)(op 8/1),
**20/1** Ors. CSF £11.47, Tote £10.10: £1.60 £1.30 (£6.30). Abigail Limited (NEWMARKET) bred by Cheveley Park
Stud Ltd. 6 Rn
               1m 33.5 (9.3)
               SF—8/3/-/-/-/-

## 3603
    ANN HATHAWAY H'CAP (3-Y.O) (0-70) £2763.00 (£768.00: £369.00)
    2m 20y
                        5-00 (5-03)

3102 **Child Star (FR) (45)** *(DMarks)* 8-3 SDawson (16) (s.i.s: stdy hdwy on ins 6f out:
      4th st: led ins fnl f: r.o wl) ......................................... —**1**
3487⁶ Sports View **(49)** *(RJHolder)* 8-7 NAdams (3) (hld up: led 3f out tl ins fnl f) ........ 2.**2**
3504* Iota **(63)** (Fav) *(MrsJCecil)* 9-7 (5x) SCauthen (19) (lw: 2nd st: rdn 2f out: one
      pce) .............................................................................. 3.**3**
3409 Izitallworthit **(40)** *(JMackie)* 7-7 ‡⁵NKennedy (4) (gd hdwy 6f out: hrd rdn & 3rd
      st: wknd over 1f out) .................................................... 5.**4**
2736⁴ Gay Ming **(46)** *(RHollinshead)* 7-11 ‡⁷AGarth (5) (hdwy 6f out: 6th st: one pce fnl
      2f) ................................................................................. 1.**5**
3409³ Anar (IRE) **(48)** *(WCarter)* 8-1 ‡⁵NGwilliams (5) (lw: hdwy 8f out: wknd 3f out) .... 7.**6**
3381⁶ Landed Gentry (USA) **(63)** *(PWChapple-Hyam)* 9-7 JReid (10) (sme hdwy 6f
      out: nvr nr to chal) ...................................................... 1½.**7**
3577³ Faaz (USA) **(46)** (v) *(AAScott)* 8-4 JFortune (12) (dwlt: styd on fnl 2f: nvr nrr) ... ½.**8**
3282⁵ Whatcomesnaturally (USA) **(45)** *(MCChapman)* 8-3 RPrice (2) (prom: led over
      5f to 3f out: 5th & wkng st) ......................................... 2.**9**
3493⁶ Seraphim (FR) **(48)** *(TDBarron)* 8-6 AlexGreaves (1) (prom 11f) ................ 10.**10**
3522 Erlemo **(44)** (bl) *(CJBenstead)* 8-2 GCarter (13) (led 10f out tl over 5f out: sn
      wknd) ......................................................................... 8.**11**
*2197²* Perforate **(53)** *(SirMarkPrescott)* 8-11 CNutter (18) (b.hind: led over 6f: wknd
      over 4f out) ............................................................... 3.**12**
3392³ Court of Kings **(43)** *(PFlCole)* 8-1 AMunro (14) (prom 9f) ..................... s.h.**13**
3381⁵ Bilberry **(44)** *(CWCElsey)* 8-2 MHills (9) (hdwy 9f out: wknd 7f out) ............ 5.**14**
3490⁶ Judge and Jury **(52)** (v) *(MJFetherston-Godley)* 8-10 RCochrane (8) (a bhd) ... nk.**15**
3409⁵ Taroob (IRE) **(63)** *(JLDunlop)* 9-7 PatEddery (11) (prom 11f) ................... 1½.**16**
3406 Elite Reg **(44)** *(PFlCole)* 8-2 CRutter (17) (a in rr) ............................... nk.**17**

3395 Merls Pearl *(41)* *(JAGlover)* 7-13 JQuinn (7) (bit bkwd: sn bhd) ............... ¾.18
3392² Royal Glint *(39)* *(MJHeaton-Ellis)* 7-11 GBardwell (15) (t.o fnl 9f) ............... dist.19

**Evens** Iota(op 6/4), **9/1** Faaz (USA), **12/1** Landed Gentry (USA)(op 8/1), Taroob (IRE), **14/1** Whatcomesnaturally (USA), Gay Ming, Perforate, Bilberry, Court of Kings, Anar (IRE)(op 8/1), **16/1** Elite Reg, **20/1** CHILD STAR (FR), **25/1** Royal Glint, Sports View, Seraphim (FR), **33/1** Ors. CSF £436.28, CT £887.72. Tote £75.10: £9.80 £4.30 £1.20 £17.10 (£765.30). Mr P. J. Pearson (UPPER LAMBOURN) bred by Sheikh Mohammed bin Rashid al Maktoum in France. 19 Rn
3m 45.8 (19.8)
SF—11/13/24/–/–/–

T/Plpt: £14.40 (154.05 Tckts).

KH

3387—**FOLKESTONE (R-H)**

## Tuesday, October 6th [Good to soft becoming Soft]
Going Allowance: St: 0.55 sec per fur (Y);Rnd: 0.90 sec per fur (S)

Wind: str half bhd

Stalls: low

### 3604
SEDLESCOMBE (S) STKS (3 & 4-Y.O) £1245.00 (£345.00: £165.00)
1m 1f 149y

1-50 (1-52)

April City *(MJHeaton-Ellis)* 3-8-3 DHolland (5) (leggy: hdwy over 4f out: led over 2f out: hrd rdn over 1f out: r.o) ............... —1
3342⁶ Ace Reporter *(58)* *(MHTompkins)* 3-7-11⁽¹⁾ ‡⁷SMulvey (7) (3rd st: ev ch ins fnl f: r.o) ............... ¾.2
3510 Solid (IRE) *(50)* *(JRJenkins)* 4-9-0 SWhitworth (13) (rdn & lost pl 5f out: rallied over 1f out: r.o one pce) ............... 8.3
3479 Zaire *(40)* *(ANLee)* 3-8-8 AMcGlone (14) (lw: led 7f: 2nd st: wknd wl over 1f out) 8.4
3180 Indian Mohawk (IRE) *(32)* *(DRCElsworth)* 4-9-0 JWilliams (3) (lw: hdwy over 1f out: nvr nrr) ............... hd.5
3403 Millrous *(36)* *(RGuest)* 4-8-9 MRoberts (4) (4th st: wknd over 1f out) ............... 3.6
2952 Simon Ellis (IRE) *(45)* *(DRLaing)* 3-8-8 TyroneWilliams (9) (lw: 6th st: wknd 2f out) ............... nk.7
3251* Prince Rooney (IRE) *(60)* *(PButler)* 4-8-7 ‡⁷SDrowne (2) (hdwy 4f out: 5th st: wknd over 1f out) ............... 2½.8
3425 I'M Curious *(RThompson)* 3-8-3 TSprake (1) (a bhd) ............... 3.9
409 Carlowitz (USA) *(38)* *(AMoore)* 4-9-0 BRouse (10) (b: bhd fnl 3f) ............... 1½.10
3507 Alton Belle *(35)* (bl) *(PHowling)* 3-7-10 ‡⁷KateMason (12) (bhd fnl 3f) ............... 12.11
3388⁵ Aragon Court *(48)* (bl) *(JPearce)* 4-9-0 GDuffield (8) (lw: plld hrd: prom 7f) .... ½.12
3540 Mansber (IRE) *(44)* *(PatMitchell)* 3-8-8 DBiggs (6) (a bhd: t.o) ............... 25.13
Cherrywood Lass *(48)* *(RCurtis)* 4-8-6 ‡³DHarrison (11) (bit bkwd: prom 5f: t.o) 25.14

**9/4** Prince Rooney (IRE), **7/2** Solid (IRE)(6/1—8/1), **5/1** Indian Mohawk (IRE), **6/1** Millrous (op 7/2), **8/1** Ace Reporter, Aragon Court(op 9/2), **14/1** Mansber (IRE), Simon Ellis (IRE)(op 8/1), **16/1** APRIL CITY (op 10/1), **33/1** Ors. CSF £139.86, Tote £91.20: £14.40 £2.00 £1.20 (£173.70). Mr Michael P. Holmes (WROUGHTON) bred by N. Miller. 14 Rn; No bid
2m 13.4 (15.7)
SF—22/14/15/–/–/–

### 3605
BREDE APP'CE H'CAP (0-70) £1329.00 (£369.00: £177.00) **6f** 2-20 (2-23)
(Weights raised 4 lb)

2821 **Goody Four Shoes** *(35)* *(DRTucker)* 4-8-5 PMcCabe (3) (a.p: led over 2f out: clr over 1f out: r.o wl) ............... —1
3391² Proud Brigadier (IRE) *(48)* (Jt-Fav) *(WCarter)* 4-9-4 TAshley (14) (b.off hind: a.p: chsd wnr fnl 2f: r.o) ............... 2.2
3290³ Judgement Call *(54)* *(PHowling)* 5-9-10 LCarter (12) (b.hind: a.p: one pce fnl 2f) 10.3
3183 Quick Steel *(53)* (bl) (Jt-Fav) *(TPMcGovern)* 4-9-9 PBowe (9) (a.p: one pce fnl 2f) ............... ½.4
3037⁴ Zinbaq *(41)* (Jt-Fav) *(CJBenstead)* 6-8-11 TWilson (10) (lw: hdwy over 1f out: r.o) ............... ½.5
3509* Batchworth Bound *(60)* *(EAWheeler)* 3-9-9 (5x) ‡WHollick (1) (nvr nr to chal) 1½.6
3391³ Idir Linn (IRE) *(43)* *(DJGMurray-Smith)* 4-8-13 NVarley (5) (nvr nrr) ............... hd.7
3391⁴ Little Nod *(41)* *(JWhite)* 3-8-9 DCarson (6) (lw: outpcd) ............... nk.8
3559 Miss Precocious *(32)* (v) *(DShaw)* 4-8-2 DGibbs (15) (spd 4f) ............... nk.9
3296⁴ Fabled Orator *(37)* (bl) *(PHowling)* 7-8-7 DToole (4) (b.nr hind: led over 3f) .. 1.10
3509³ Night Gown *(41)* (v) *(MissGayKelleway)* 3-8-9 MGodsafe (11) (b: lw: prom over 3f) ............... ¾.11
3296 Fontaine Lady *(35)* (v) *(TThomsonJones)* 5-8-5 JDennis (2) (bhd fnl 2f) ......... ½.12
3251 Jinsky's Jewel *(33)* *(RThompson)* 4-8-3 SMulvey (7) (a bhd) ............... ½.13
3400 Indian Endeavour *(56)* (bl) *(RGuest)* 3-9-10 SEiffert (8) (prom over 3f) ............... 1½.14
3048 Kipini *(47)* *(WJMusson)* 3-9-1 DMcCabe (13) (a bhd) ............... 4.15

11/2 Quick Steel, Proud Brigadier (IRE)(4/1—6/1), Zinbaq(4/1—6/1), **8/1** Idir Linn (IRE), Little Nod, **10/1** Judgement Call, **12/1** Indian Endeavour(op 8/1), Batchworth Bound, **14/1** Fabled Orator, Kipini, **16/1** GOODY FOUR SHOES, **20/1** Night Gown, Fontaine Lady, **25/1** Miss Precocious, **33/1** Jinsky's Jewel. CSF £98.39, CT £866.80. Tote £22.40: £4.20 £1.80 £3.40 (£139.50). Mr D. R. Tucker (CULLOMPTON) bred by T. Anthony. 15 Rn

1m 17.5 (6.8)

SF—21/26/-/-/-/-

## 3606   NORTHIAM NURSERY (0-75) £2530.00 (£705.00: £340.00)   6f   2-50 (2-57)

| | | | | |
|---|---|---|---|---|
| 3470³ | **Guv'nors Gift (72)** *(MHTompkins)* 8-12 ‡⁷SMulvey (20) (a.p: led 2f out: rdn out) | | | —1 |
| 3472 | Texas Cowgirl (IRE) **(57)** *(GAPritchard-Gordon)* 8-4 GDuffield (7) (lw: hdwy over 2f out: ev ch ins fnl f: r.o) | | | 1.2 |
| 3410★ | Gangleader **(70)** (Fav) *(SPCWoods)* 9-3 WWoods (17) (hdwy 2f out: rdn over 1f out: r.o) | | | 1½.3 |
| 2686⁵ | Comanche Companion **(69)** *(TJNaughton)* 9-2 DHolland (10) (lw: a.p: ev ch 2f out: one pce) | | | 1½.4 |
| 3268³ | Avril Etoile **(68)** *(LJHolt)* 9-1 MRoberts (6) (led 4f out to 2f out: one pce) | | | hd.5 |
| 3267 | Beat the Bagman (IRE) **(56)** *(LJHolt)* 7-10 ‡⁷CAvery (18) (nvr nr to chal) | | | 4.6 |
| 3508 | Cashable **(70)** (bl) *(JRJenkins)* 9-3 WCarson (12) (led 2f: wknd over 1f out) | | | 1½.7 |
| 3217⁴ | Chummy's Idea (IRE) **(57)** *(JSutcliffe)* 8-4 BRouse (2) (lw: no hdwy fnl 2f) | | | 2.8 |
| 2649 | Maribella **(66)** *(PFiCole)* 8-6 ‡⁷JDSmith (4) (lw: a mid div) | | | hd.9 |
| 3419 | Soojama (IRE) **(53)** *(RVoorspuy)* 7-9⁽³⁾ ‡⁵BDoyle (14) (nvr nrr) | | | hd.10 |
| 3414 | Jolis Absent **(50)** *(MJRyan)* 7-11 DBiggs (15) (outpcd) | | | 2.11 |
| 3364 | Maybe Gold **(69)** *(DWPArbuthnot)* 9-2 TQuinn (16) (b.hind: lw: outpcd) | | | 2.12 |
| 2951 | Malzeta (IRE) **(56)** *(MJHeaton-Ellis)* 8-3⁽¹⁾ AClark (3) (outpcd) | | | 1½.13 |
| 3019 | Polar Storm (IRE) **(74)** *(LadyHerries)* 9-7 JWilliams (1) (outpcd) | | | 1½.14 |
| 3320 | Kismetim **(71)** *(GLewis)* 9-1 ‡³DHarrison (11) (a bhd) | | | 1.15 |
| 2994 | Arctic Agnes (USA) **(51)** *(RAkehurst)* 7-12⁽¹⁾ TSprake (19) (bhd fnl 3f) | | | ¾.16 |
| 2832 | Recipdico Mist (IHE) **(50)** *(TJNaughton)* 7 11 EJohnson (5) (lw: bhd fnl 2f) | | | 2.17 |
| 3376² | Persian Gusher (IRE) **(73)** *(SDow)* 9-6 GBaxter (8) (spd 4f) | | | ½.18 |
| 3077 | Viv's Pet **(58)** (bl) *(AHide)* 8-5 AMcGlone (13) (a bhd) | | | 12.19 |
| 3115 | *True Story (IRE)* **(10/1)** Withdrawn (ref to ent stalls) : not under orders — Rule 4 applies | | | |

**5/1** Gangleader, **7/1** Avril Etoile, Comanche Companion(10/1—14/1), **8/1** Maybe Gold, **9/1** GUV'NORS GIFT, **10/1** Maribella(op 6/1), Texas Cowgirl (IRE), **11/1** Chummy's Idea (IRE), Cashable, **14/1** Polar Storm (IRE)(op 8/1), Persian Gusher (IRE), **16/1** Kismetim, **20/1** Beat the Bagman (IRE), Soojama (IRE), **25/1** Jolis Absent, **33/1** Ors. CSF £93.20, CT £410.18. Tote £7.20: £1.70 £3.80 £2.20 £2.10 (£6.20). The Tompkins Team (NEWMARKET) bred by Stud-On-The-Chart. 19 Rn

1m 18.9 (8.2)

## 3607   E.B.F. HURST GREEN STKS (Mdn 2-Y.O.C & G) £2180.00 (£605.00: £290.00)   6f   3-20 (3-25)

| | | | | |
|---|---|---|---|---|
| 3424 | **Barik (IRE)** (Fav) *(ACStewart)* 9-0 MRoberts (2) (hld up: led on bit ins fnl f: easily) | | | —1 |
| 1485⁴ | Chiltern Hundreds (USA) *(MrsJVCecil)* 9-0 GDuffield (1) (hld up: led over 2f out tl ins fnl f: unable qckn) | | | 1.2 |
| 3268 | Mustakim (IRE) *(RWArmstrong)* 9-0 WCarson (10) (str: scope: a.p: ev ch 2f out: one pce) | | | 2½.3 |
| 3505³ | Royal Interval *(WGMTurner)* 9-0 TSprake (8) (lw: w ldr: led over 3f out tl over 2f out: hrd rdn over 1f out: one pce) | | | 1½.4 |
| 3399² | Wolf Power (IRE) **(73)** *(TThomsonJones)* 9-0 SWhitworth (9) (no hdwy fnl 2f) | | | 5.5 |
| | Tawajjah *(PTWalwyn)* 9-0 DHolland (4) (scope: nvr nr to chal) | | | 2.6 |
| | Billyback *(MJRyan)* 9-0 DBiggs (3) (cmpt: spd 4f) | | | 2½.7 |
| | Solo Charter *(MHTompkins)* 8-7 ‡⁷SMulvey (13) (leggy: outpcd) | | | hd.8 |
| | Karachi *(CEBrittain)* 9-0 GBaxter (11) (lw'like: outpcd) | | | 2½.9 |
| 3186 | Angus Dundee (IRE) (bl) *(HRACecil)* 9-0 AMcGlone (7) (bhd fnl 2f) | | | 1.10 |
| 3523 | Dontdressfordinner *(DRTucker)* 9-0 JWilliams (5) (outpcd) | | | 8.11 |
| | Bevanno (IRE) *(PatMitchell)* 9-0 WWoods (12) (w'like: bit bkwd: outpcd) | | | 2½.12 |
| 1322⁵ | Green Sword *(WAO'Gorman)* 8-11 ‡³EmmaO'Gorman (6) (bit bkwd: led over 2f) | | | ¾.13 |

**11/8** BARIK (IRE), **5/1** Wolf Power (IRE), **6/1** Mustakim (IRE), **10/1** Angus Dundee (IRE), Chiltern Hundreds (USA), **12/1** Tawajjah, **14/1** Royal Interval, Karachi, **33/1** Dontdressfordinner, **50/1** Ors. CSF £15.50, Tote £2.90: £1.40 £3.80 £3.20 (£13.60). Mr Hamdan Al-Maktoum (NEWMARKET) bred by Barronstown Stud in Ireland. 13 Rn

1m 18.9 (8.2)

SF—2/-/-/-/-/-

## 3608   E.B.F. ASHFORD STKS (Mdn 2-Y.O) £2057.50 (£570.00: £272.50)   5f   3-50 (3-51)

| | | | | |
|---|---|---|---|---|
| | **Wintering (IRE)** *(SirMarkPrescott)* 9-0 GDuffield (8) (w'like: hld up: led wl over 1f out: rdn out) | | | —1 |
| 3401² | Glen Miller **(68)** (Fav) *(JWPayne)* 9-0 WCarson (1) (lw: a.p: ev ch wl over 1f out: r.o ins fnl f) | | | 1½.2 |

33664 Aragrove **(68)** *(LJHolt)* 9-0 AMcGlone (6) (a.p: ev ch wl over 1f out: unable
qckn) ............................................................................................................ ¾.3
34866 Perfect Passion **(58)** *(JJBridger)* 8-9 SWhitworth (5) (a.p: one pce fnl 2f) .......... 4.4
25974 Breakfast Boogie **(60)** *(JRFanshawe)* 8-2 ‡7NVarley (4) (nvr nr to chal) ............ 1½.5
Walk the Beat *(RSimpson)* 9-0 BRouse (2) (str: bit bkwd: s.s: a bhd) .............. nk.6
Ginnyfasure (IRE) *(DRCElsworth)* 8-9 JWilliams (3) (lw: w'like: a bhd) ............ 2½.7
3218 Shy Romance **(49)** *(PMMcEntee)* 8-9 MRoberts (7) (led over 3f) .......................... 7.8

**2/1** Glen Miller, **7/2** WINTERING (IRE)(op 2/1), **4/1** Walk the Beat(10/1—12/1), **6/1** Aragrove(op 4/1), **8/1**
Ginnyfasure (IRE), **10/1** Breakfast Boogie, **14/1** Perfect Passion(op 8/1), **16/1** Shy Romance. CSF £11.26, Tote
£5.40: £1.40 £1.40 £2.20 (£2.70). Mrs David Thompson (NEWMARKET) bred by Rosemount House Stud in
Ireland. 8 Rn                                                                                        64.5 sec (5.7)
SF—41/35/32/11/–/9

## 3609          LEVY BOARD STKS (Mdn 3-Y.O) £1744.00 (£484.00: £232.00)      1½m    4-20 (4-23)

804 **River Anchor** *(RCharlton)* 8-9 TSprake (12) (5th st: led ins fnl: r.o wl) ................ —1
3368 Lobilio (USA) **(78)** *(Fav)* *(CEBrittain)* 9-0 MRoberts (6) (lw: led: hrd rdn over 1f
out: hdd ins fnl f: unable qckn) ...................................................................... 2½.2
29156 Dawn Flight **(68)** *(LadyHerries)* 9-0 JWilliams (7) (lw: hdwy 5f out: 6th st: rdn
over 1f out: r.o ins fnl f) ................................................................................ nk.3
33062 Jawaher (IRE) **(61)** *(RJRWilliams)* 8-6 ‡3DHarrison (3) (4th st: hrd rdn over 1f
out: one pce) .................................................................................................. 2½.4
33982 Raheena (USA) *(JHMGosden)* 8-9 WCarson (8) (lw: 2nd st: hrd rdn over 1f out:
wknd fnl f) ...................................................................................................... 1.5
9323 Sir Pageant **(70)** *(PFICole)* 9-0 TQuinn (5) (bit bkwd: 3rd st: wknd over 1f out) .. 8.6
3258 Ice Strike (USA) *(CRNelson)* 9-0 SWhitworth (11) (nvr nr to chal) ...................... 7.7
3306 French Revolution (FR) *(PAKelleway)* 8-9 GayKelleway (10) (lw: hdwy 3f out:
wknd 2f out) .................................................................................................. 5.8
3459 Well Directed (IRE) *(JLDunlop)* 9-0 AMcGlone (9) (lw: bhd fnl 4f) ...................... 1½.10
614 And Me **(43)** *(DTThom)* 8-9 CDwyer (2) (a bhd) ............................................ 1½.10
3418 Lloyds Dream *(DShaw)* 9-0 BRouse (4) (a bhd) ............................................ 20.11
2801 Kalokagathos **(40)** *(CGCox)* 9-0 MPerrett (1) (bhd fnl 4f) .............................. 3.12
Public Appeal **(59)** *(PFICole)* 9-0 AClark (13) (bhd fnl 6f: t.o) .......................... 25.13

**2/1** Lobilio (USA)(6/4—9/4), **7/2** Raheena (USA), **5/1** Jawaher (IRE)(op 3/1), **8/1** Sir Pageant, **12/1** RIVER
ANCHOR(op 8/1), Dawn Flight, **16/1** Public Appeal, Well Directed (IRE), **20/1** Ice Strike (USA), **33/1** Ors. CSF
£35.73, Tote £21.40: £4.30 £1.30 £3.10 (£60.70). Mr R. S. Dawes (BECKHAMPTON) bred by Aston House Stud
Co. 13 Rn                                                                                            2m 50 (16.5)
SF—38/38/37/24/25/14

## 3610          ROBERTSBRIDGE H'CAP (0-70) £2337.50 (£650.00: £312.50)      1½m    4-50 (4-54)

33876 **Swan Heights (51)** *(JRFanshawe)* 3–8-2 GDuffield (4) (lw: a.p: led over 2f out:
rdn out) .......................................................................................................... —1
3493 Sharp Top **(54)** *(MJRyan)* 4–8-13 DBiggs (3) (hdwy over 1f out: r.o ins fnl f) ...... 5.2
3177 Mist of the Marsh (USA) **(46)** *(JHMGosden)* 3–7-11(2) WCarson (16) (lw: 4th st:
hrd rdn over 1f out: unable qckn) .................................................................... 2.3
32213 Taylors Prince **(61)** *(HJCollingridge)* 5–9-6 VSmith (13) (lw: 5th st: hrd rdn &
edgd lft over 1f out: one pce) ........................................................................ 2.4
3387 Phil-Blake **(40)** *(SMellor)* 5–7-8(6) ‡5BDoyle (11) (led: led over 9f tl over 2f out:
2nd st: wknd fnl f) ........................................................................................ 1½.5
3406 Jarzon Dancer **(34)** *(DAWilson)* 4–7-0 ‡7SharonMillard (1) (lw: nvr nr to chal) .. ¾.6
3522* Bo Knows Best (IRE) **(59)** *(Fav)* *(JSutcliffe)* 3–8-10 (4x) BRouse (14) (3rd st:
eased whn btn over 1f out) ............................................................................ 3.7
3406 Aldavera **(47)** *(MDixon)* 3–7-12(2) TSprake (2) (lw: nvr nrr) ............................ 2½.8
33875 Affirmed's Destiny (USA) **(44)** *(JLDunlop)* 3–7-9(1) TyroneWilliams (7) (6th st:
wknd over 1f out) .......................................................................................... 1½.9
Letts Green (IRE) **(42)** *(MJHaynes)* 4–8-1 EJohnson (9) (lw: a bhd) ................ 1.10
*3379*\* Cathos (FR) **(51)** *(DAWilson)* 4–8-10 MWigham (8) (b: lw: a bhd) .................... 1.11
35102 Latour **(51)** (bl) *(CEBrittain)* 4–8-10 MRoberts (10) (led over 2f: wknd over 2f out) 2.12
3282 Princess Evita (FR) **(42)** *(RGuest)* 3–7-0 ‡7AntoinetteArmes (5) (bhd fnl 3f) ...... 6.13
24155 Nothing Doing (IRE) **(50)** *(WJMusson)* 3–7-8 ‡7DMcCabe (12) (b: lw: a bhd) .. 10.14
LONG HANDICAP: Jarzon Dancer 7-3, Princess Evita (FR) 7-2.

**6/4** Bo Knows Best (IRE), **9/2** Latour, **13/2** Mist of the Marsh (USA)(5/1—8/1), **10/1** Sharp Top, **12/1** Taylors
Prince(op 8/1), Affirmed's Destiny (USA)(op 7/1), **14/1** SWAN HEIGHTS(op 8/1), **16/1** Cathos (FR)(op 10/1),
**20/1** Phil-Blake, Nothing Doing (IRE), **25/1** Princess Evita (FR), **33/1** Ors. CSF £142.08, CT £916.72. Tote
£16.40: £3.30 £3.00 £1.80 (£63.30). Mr Peter Wetzel (NEWMARKET) bred by A. R. Jones Morgan. 14 Rn
2m 50.4 (16.9)
SF—27/28/8/27/–/–

T/Plpt: £76.70 (24.8 Tckts).                                                                                 AK

3472—**REDCAR (L-H)**
**Tuesday, October 6th [Good to soft]**
Going Allowance: 0.55 sec per fur (Y)

Wind: fresh against

Stalls: centre

**3611**   MALTON (S) STKS (2-Y.O) £3120.00 (£870.00: £420.00)   **7f**   2-15 (2-20)

1559[6] **Nellie's Gamble (43)** *(APStringer)* 8-6  SWood (9) (hdwy over 2f out: r.o to ld wl
ins fnl f) ..................................................................... —1

3291★ Pontevecchio Moda **(74)** (Fav) *(DRCElsworth)* 8-11  RHills (23) (lw: w ldr: led
¹/₂-wy: tl hdd & no ex wl ins fnl f) ......................... ³/₄.2

2124 The Premier Expres **(70)** *(CBBBooth)* 8-11  GOldroyd (16) (hld up: effrt over 2f
out: styd on wl nr fin) .......................................... ³/₄.3

3291 Honour and Glory *(BobJones)* 8-7[(1)]  NDay (11) (outpcd tl hdwy & edgd lft over
2f out: styd on wl nr fin) ..................................... 1.4

North Ardar *(MJohnston)* 8-11  RPElliott (21) (w'like: scope: bit bkwd: dwlt:
hdwy ¹/₂-wy: ev ch over 1f out: nt qckn) .................. 1¹/₂.5

2986 Northern Chief *(MHEasterby)* 8-11  BRaymond (26) (prom stands' side: rdn
over 2f out: styd on: no imp) ................................. hd.6

3472[3] Mighty Miss Magpie (IRE) **(57)** *(MRChannon)* 8-8 ‡[3]FNorton (29) (lw: chsd ldrs:
hung lft ¹/₂-wy: one pce fnl 2f) ............................ ³/₄.7

3497 Irish Roots (IRE) **(49)** (v) *(CTinkler)* 8-11  TLucas (15) (mid div: hdwy u.p 2f out:
n.m.r & no imp) ................................................. ³/₄.8

3407[3] Pinkerton's Silver **(46)** (bl) *(MHEasterby)* 8-11  MBirch (18) (led to ¹/₂-wy: styd
on one pce) ..................................................... s.h.9

3497[3] Hot Off the Press **(43)** (v) *(RMWhitaker)* 8-11  ACulhane (20) (in tch: effrt u.p
over 2f out: sn btn) ........................................... nk.10

3283[3] Duke of Budworth *(MHTompkins)* 8-11 (lw: in tch: tl outpcd fnl
2f) .............................................................. 1¹/₂.11

2284[4] Abilene **(53)** *(JARToller)* 8-6  DaleGibson (1) (racd far side: cl up tl outpcd fnl 2f) hd.12

3474 Supreme Soviet *(JSHaldane)* 8-6 ‡[5]SWilliams (22) (nvr wnt pce) ............. 2¹/₂.13

3301 Flash of Amber **(44)** (bl) *(JLSpearing)* 8-6  GHind (19) (outpcd & wl bhd tl r.o wl
fnl f) .......................................................... 2.14

3472[6] Colmar **(51)** *(RBastiman)* 8-6  KFallon (28) (b.hind: in tch: rdn 3f out: eased whn
btn fnl f) ..................................................... ¹/₂.15

3472 Sunshine in Ramsey **(49)** (bl) *(TFairhurst)* 8-6  JFanning (6) (hdwy ¹/₂-wy: sn rdn
& btn) ......................................................... s.h.16

2924 Laxey Flyer *(JBerry)* 8-6  JCarroll (24) (outpcd fr ¹/₂-wy) ...................... 1.17

Mzuri Sands *(MJCamacho)* 8-6  NConnorton (14) (leggy: lt-f: bit bkwd: dwlt: a
bhd) ........................................................... s.h.18

Social Vision (IRE) (v) *(MAvison)* 8-11  LCharnock (8) (lengthy: bit bkwd: n.d) nk.19

3155[4] Desirable Miss **(45)** (bl) *(MBrittain)* 7-13 ‡[7]JMarshall (17) (n.d) ............... 1.20

3407 We Are Doomed **(46)** (v) *(JRFanshawe)* 8-11  KDarley (5) (prom to ¹/₂-wy: sn
wknd) ......................................................... 2.21

2667 Timber Topper *(MrsGRReveley)* 8-11  LDettori (30) (bit bkwd) ............. 3¹/₂.22

3283 Charlies Reward **(49)** *(TFairhurst)* 8-11  SWebster (4) (racd far side: cl up over
4f: sn wknd) ................................................... 1¹/₂.23

3410 Beckyhannah *(RBastiman)* 8-6  PBurke (7) (chsd ldrs over 4f) ............. hd.24

3472 Selvole **(53)** *(MissLAPerratt)* 8-11  WRyan (13) (lw: n.d) ..................... ³/₄.25

3472 Canazei **(36)** (v) *(DonEnricoIncisa)* 8-6  JakiHuston (2) (racd far side: sn
outpcd) ........................................................ ¹/₂.26

3093[6] Amistina *(RCharlton)* 8-6  PaulEddery (3) (lw: n.d) ......................... 1.27

3394 Laurel King *(JBerry)* 8-11  NCarlisle (25) (in tch 4f) ......................... 1¹/₂.28

3071 Bluebella **(44)** *(MrsPABarker)* 8-6  JLowe (27) (swtg: n.d) ................. 1.29

3147 Sandmoor Satin *(MHEasterby)* 8-3 ‡[3]SMaloney (12) (b.hind: eased & wl bhd fnl
2f) ............................................................ 30

**5/2** Pontevecchio Moda, **7/1** The Premier Expres, **10/1** Duke of Budworth, Amistina, Mighty Miss Magpie (IRE),
**12/1** North Ardar(op 8/1), Colmar, **14/1** Northern Chief(op 8/1), **16/1** Supreme Soviet, **20/1** Pinkerton's Silver,
We Are Doomed, Abilene, Beckyhannah, Timber Topper, Mzuri Sands, Desirable Miss, **25/1** Laxey Flyer, Hot Off
the Press, **33/1** Charlies Reward, Selvole, Sunshine in Ramsey, **50/1** NELLIE'S GAMBLE & Ors. CSF £189.39,
Tote £35.20: £6.60 £1.50 £4.80 (£235.00). Mr Bill Grainger (THIRSK) bred by Highfield Stud Ltd. 30 Rn; no bid
1m 31.3 (9.1)
SF—8/17/15/8/7/6

**3612**   SCARBOROUGH H'CAP (0-90) £3470.00 (£1040.00: £500.00: £230.00)
**7f**   2-45 (2-48)

3370 **La Bamba (70)** (Jt-Fav) *(GAPritchard-Gordon)* 6-8-13  WHood (4) (b: s.i.s: wl
bhd tl hdwy 3f out: r.o to ld wl ins fnl f) ................... —1

3281² Morocco (IRE) **(74)** *(RCharlton)* 3–9–0 PaulEddery (10) (lw: chsd ldrs: led wl over 1f out tl hdd & no ex wl ins fnl f) ................................... 2¹/₂.2

3355⁴ Love Jazz (USA) **(82)** (Jt-Fav) *(TDBarron)* 3–9–8 KDarley (9) (lw: a.p: effrt 2f out: kpt on u.p) ................................... 1.3

3203 Boy Martin **(66)** *(MJohnston)* 3–8–6 RPElliott (7) (bhd & pushed along: hdwy 2f out: styd on wl) ................................... 3.4

3359 Bold Habit **(83)** *(SEKettlewell)* 3–8–6 JWeaver (8) (lw: hld up & bhd: hdwy 3f out: n.m.r: swtchd & nt qckn) ................................... 1.5

3481* Spanish Verdict **(71)** *(DenysSmith)* 5–8–7 ‡7CTeague (11) (lw: cl up: led 3f out tl wl over 1f out: sn btn) ................................... s.h.6

3496³ Ashdren **(77)** (v) *(AHarrison)* 5–9–6 LDettori (16) (hld up: effrt over 2f out: rdn & no imp) ................................... 1¹/₂.7

3004 Elsals **(68)** (Jt-Fav) *(HThomsonJones)* 3–8–8 RHills (13) (hdwy after 2f: sn drvn along: btn 2f out) ................................... 1¹/₂.8

3476⁴ Patience Please **(59)** *(MHEasterby)* 3–7–10 ‡3SMaloney (17) (hdwy to jn ldrs 3f out: sn rdn & wknd) ................................... 4.9

3310 Super Benz **(72)** *(TFairhurst)* 6–9–1 JFanning (5) (chsd ldrs tl wknd 2f out) .... hd.10

3473² Nifty Fifty (IRE) **(79)** *(JBerry)* 3–9–5 JCarroll (12) (lw: hdwy & prom ¹/₂-wy: wknd 2f out) ................................... ¹/₂.11

3349 Ruth's Gamble **(56)** *(DWChapman)* 4–7–13 SWood (2) (chsd ldrs tl wknd 2f out) ................................... ³/₄.12

2645 Pesidanamich (IRE) **(62)** (bl) *(JPLeigh)* 4–8–5 JLowe (14) (led 4f: sn wknd) ..... 2.13

3251 Long Lane Lady **(55)** *(JMackie)* 6–7–9⁽⁵⁾ ‡3FNorton (6) (prom over 4f) ............ ¹/₂.14

3545* Gant Bleu (FR) **(60)** (Jt-Fav) *(RMWhitaker)* 5–8–3 ACulhane (3) (lw: hdwy & ev ch 2f out: sn wknd) ................................... 1¹/₂.15

2549 Sulaah Rose **(54)** *(MrsJJordan)* 3–7–8⁽¹⁾ NCarlisle (1) (in tch to ¹/₂-wy) ........... hd.16 Hard Sell **(60)** *(JGFitzGerald)* 5–8–3 LCharnock (15) (bkwd: prom to ¹/₂-wy: sn wknd) ................................... 12.17

LONG HANDICAP: Long Lane Lady 7-2, Sulaah Rose 6-8.

**7/1** Gant Bleu (FR), Elsals, LA BAMBA, Love Jazz (USA), **9/1** Nifty Fifty (IRE), Bold Habit, Morocco (IRE), **10/1** Ashdren, **14/1** Super Benz, Patience Please, Spanish Verdict, **16/1** Boy Martin, **25/1** Ruth's Gamble, Hard Sell, **33/1** Pesidanamich (IRE), Long Lane Lady, **100/1** Sulaah Rose. CSF £65.98, CT £429.06. Tote £9.10: £1.80 £2.20 £3.10 £4.50 (£37.90). Miss M. C. MacRae (NEWMARKET) bred by Golden Vale Stud. 17 Rn
1m 28.5 (6.3)
SF—62/55/60/35/47/32

## 3613

BROTTON SEAFOODS H'CAP (0-80) £3132.00 (£936.00: £448.00: £204.00)
2m 4y
3-15 (3-16)

3305² Avro Anson **(53)** (Fav) *(MJCamacho)* 4–8–2 NConnorton (11) (lw: a.p: led over 2f out: hld on wl fnl f) ................................... —1

3351⁶ Stingray City (USA) **(60)** *(JEtherington)* 3–7–9⁽²⁾ ‡3FNorton (5) (trckd ldrs: effrt & ev ch over 1f out: hung rt & lft: nt r.o) ................................... 1.2

3339³ Sarawat **(79)** *(MrsGRReveley)* 4–10–0 KDarley (1) (lw: trckd ldrs gng wl: led over 4f out: rdn 3f out: sn hdd & no ex) ................................... 3.3

3406⁵ Merton Mill **(64)** (bl) *(DMorley)* 5–8–13 PaulEddery (6) (sn pushed along: hdwy ent st: styd on: no imp) ................................... 2.4

3352 Equity Card (IRE) **(65)** *(GAPritchard-Gordon)* 4–9–0 PRobinson (9) (lw: bhd tl styd on fnl 3f: nrst fin) ................................... 5.5

3316* Janiski **(53)** (v) *(MrsBarbaraWaring)* 9–8–2⁽⁴⁾ NHowe (10) (effrt appr st: rdn 3f out: no imp) ................................... 5.6

3046 High Finance **(44)** *(RJWeaver)* 7–7–7 JLowe (3) (chsd ldrs: shkn up 7f out: wknd 4f out) ................................... 8.7

3515 Best Gun **(70)** *(CWCElsey)* 3–8–8 JCarroll (7) (effrt whn n.m.r ent st: n.d) ......... ³/₄.8

3504⁶ Shentit (FR) **(66)** (bl) *(JLDunlop)* 4–9–1 LDettori (4) (led tl hdd over 4f out: sn wknd) ................................... 1.9

3381 Top Prize **(44)** *(MBrittain)* 4–7–7 SWood (8) (hdwy & prom appr st: wknd 4f out) 6.10

3034⁵ Rolling the Bones (USA) **(68)** *(MPNaughton)* 3–8–6 JakiHouston (2) (chsd ldrs tl wknd 4f out) ................................... 6.11

LONG HANDICAP: High Finance 6-12, Top Prize 6-13.

**15/8** AVRO ANSON, **4/1** Sarawat, **7/1** Merton Mill, **8/1** Stingray City (USA), **10/1** Rolling the Bones (USA), Shentit (FR), **11/1** Janiski, **14/1** Equity Card (IRE), **20/1** Best Gun, **33/1** High Finance, **66/1** Top Prize. CSF £16.89, CT £51.39. Tote £2.60: £1.50 £2.80 £1.90 (£10.50). Mr B. P. Skirton (MALTON) bred by B. P. Skirton and Mrs S. Camacho. 11 Rn
3m 38.4 (13.4)
SF—42/34/64/47/63/26

## 3614

PICKERING AUCTION STKS (Mdn 2-Y-O) £2679.00 (£744.00: £357.00)
1m
3-45 (3-52)

3474⁴ **Bonarme (IRE) (68)** *(MHEasterby)* 8-8 MBirch (14) (in tch: hdwy 3f out: styd on wl in to ld cl home) ................................... —1

3283 Backstabber (DrJDScargill) 8-5 SWood (17) (cl up: led over 3f out tl ct cl home) ............... nk.2
3175⁴ Mena (71) (JWPayne) 7-11 ‡³SO'Gorman (2) (lw: chsd ldrs: ev ch ins fnl f: kpt on) ............... s.h.3
3419³ Star of China (Fav) (CCElsey) 8-2 PaulEddery (19) (lw: in tch: drvn along ¹/₂-wy: kpt on wl fnl f) ............... 2.4
2961 Jalcanto (MrsGRReveley) 8-11 KFallon (6) (lw: in tch: hdwy 2f out: styd on wl) ............... s.h.5
3193⁵ Dig in the Ribs (IRE) (RHollinshead) 8-10 KDarley (10) (lw: bhd: hdwy & swtchd over 2f out: styd on wl nr fin) ............... 2¹/₂.6
3175 Certain Way (IRE) (v) (CTinkler) 8-7 LCharnock (20) (hdwy over 2f out: nvr nrr) ...... hd.7
3300⁵ Ume River (IRE) (64) (v) (MHTompkins) 8-5 PRobinson (14) (a.p: rdn over 2f out: r.o one pce) ............... ¹/₂.8
3471⁵ Trets (PAKelleway) 8-0 GHind (7) (a chsng ldrs: nt qckn fnl 2f) ............... hd.9
3307 Vaigly Sunthyme (JMCarr) 8-6 SMorris (15) (lw: bhd tl swtchd & hdwy 2f out: r.o wl) ............... nk.10
2930 Burning Cost (GAPritchard-Gordon) 7-12 ‡³FNorton (22) (prom tl wknd wl over 1f out) ............... 1¹/₂.11
3512 Never so Brave (MissSEHall) 8-6 NConnorton (16) (hld up: stdy hdwy 3f out: n.m.r & nvr able to chal) ............... ³/₄.12
Zonk (JPearce) 8-12 DaleGibson (21) (unf: w ldrs 5f: grad wknd) ............... ³/₄.13
3410 Silver Groom (IRE) (64) (APJarvis) 8-9 RHills (8) (lw: prom over 5f) ............... ¹/₂.14
3472 Dead Calm (60) (CTinkler) 8-6 TLucas (5) (hdwy 3f out: wknd over 1f out) ..... ¹/₂.15
3376 She's a Breeze (ASmith) 7-7 ‡⁷DarrenMoffatt (18) (n.d) ............... 1¹/₂.16
1264 Andrea's Girl (JBerry) 8-2 JCarroll (9) (n.d) ............... 2.17
3497⁴ Doc Spot (63) (CaptJWilson) 8-6 JLowe (1) (lw: outpcd fr ¹/₂-wy) ............... 1.18
3497 Andrew's Express (IRE) (50) (bl) (SEKettlewell) 8-9 SWebster (11) (a bhd) ...... 1.19
3480 Dusky Duchess (IRE) (MissLAPerratt) 7-13 ‡³SMaloney (12) (led tl hdd over 3f out: sn lost pce) ............... s.h.20
3463⁴ Chiappucci (IRE) (MJJarvis) 8-9 BRaymond (3) (lw: hdwy u.p ¹/₂-wy: sn wknd) 1.21
3472 Final Action (RMWhitaker) 8-1 JFanning (4) (n.d) ............... 1 22
Wyndom Earle (IRE) (REarnshaw) 8-6 ACulhane (23) (w'like: bit bkwd: prom to ¹/₂-wy: sn t.o) ............... 20.23

**100/30** Star of China(op 2/1), **7/1** Mena(op 7/2), **10/1** Chiappucci (IRE), Jalcanto(op 6/1), Dig in the Ribs (IRE)(op 5/1), Silver Groom (IRE), BONARME (IRE), **12/1** Ume River (IRE)(op 8/1), Doc Spot, **16/1** Burning Cost, **20/1** Trets, **25/1** Dead Calm, Never so Brave, Vaigly Sunthyme, **33/1** Zonk, **40/1** She's a Breeze, **66/1** Ors. CSF £477.29, Tote £10.90: £3.00 £17.50 £3.70 (Wnr or 2nd w any £5.20). Mr M. H. Easterby (MALTON) bred by Kellsboro House Stud in Ireland. 23 Rn
1m 45.3 (10.3)
SF—5/1/–/–/–/–/

---

**3615** GUISBOROUGH H'CAP (0-70) £2910.00 (£810.00: £390.00) **1m 1f** 4-15 (4-20)

3468 No Comebacks (51) (EJAlston) 4–9-2 KFallon (16) (bhd: shkn up & hdwy 4f out: r.o wl tl to ld wl ins fnl f) ............... —1
3338⁷² King's Guest (IRE) (64) (GAPritchard-Gordon) 3–9-10 NDay (15) (lw: trckd ldrs gng wl: led 2f out: sn hrd drvn: hdd wl ins fnl f: no ex) ...... 1¹/₂.2
3476 Watch Me Go (IRE) (48) (BobJones) 3–8-8 NConnorton (4) (lw: s.i.s: drvn along & sn rcvrd: prom: kpt on one pce fnl 2f) ............... 2.3
3380 Shawiniga (35) (LLungo) 6–7-7 ‡⁷DarrenMoffatt (3) (bit bkwd: trckd ldrs: rdn over 2f out: styd on same pce) ............... ³/₄.4
3479⁵ Flying Down to Rio (IRE) (42) (MPNaughton) 4–8-7 PaulEddery (12) (lw: effrt 4f out: gd hdwy 2f out: no imp fnl f) ............... 1.5
3475⁵ Young Jason (49) (FHLee) 9–9-0 ACulhane (14) (hld up & bhd: hdwy 3f out: nvr trbld ldrs) ............... nk.6
3025⁶ Edirepus (49) (MrsGRReveley) 4–9-0 KDarley (7) (swtg: sme hdwy fnl 2f: nvr trbld ldrs) ............... hd.7
2941 Essayeffsee (47) (bl) (MHEasterby) 3–8-4 ‡³SMaloney (13) (b.hind: nvr bttr than mid div) ............... 3.8
3215⁵ Don't Forsake Me (59) (DMorley) 3–9-5 MBirch (9) (lw: cl up: led over 4f out to 2f out: sn wknd) ............... hd.9
3475² Military Expert (57) (CaptJWilson) 3–8-10 ‡⁷JMarshall (6) (lw: chsd ldrs tl outpcd wl over 2f out) ............... 2.10
3485² Nicely Thanks (USA) (58) (Fav) (TDBarron) 3–9-4 LDettori (5) (lw: hdwy 4f out: rdn & wknd 2f out) ............... 2¹/₂.11
2075⁵ Canbrack (IRE) (52) (WAStephenson) 3–8-12 JLowe (11) (s.i.s: n.d) ............... 6.12
3475 Kenyatta (USA) (44) (v) (DenysSmith) 3–8-4 LCharnock (1) (led tl hdd over 4f out: sn lost pce) ............... 13
3374⁵ Kirkby Belle (46) (EWeymes) 3–8-6 DaleGibson (8) (bhd fr ¹/₂-wy) ............... 14
3403 Spring to the Top (48) (JWPayne) 5–8-13 BRaymond (10) (a bhd) ............... 15
157³ Peace Formula (IRE) (60) (RHollinshead) 3–9-6 WRyan (2) (a bhd) ............... 16

**7/2** Nicely Thanks (USA), **13/2** NO COMEBACKS, **7/1** King's Guest (IRE), **8/1** Spring to the Top, **10/1** Flying Down to Rio (IRE), Military Expert, **12/1** Watch Me Go (IRE), **14/1** Don't Forsake Me, **16/1** Young Jason, **20/1** Edirepus, Peace Formula (IRE), Shawiniga, **25/1** Essayeffsee, **33/1** Ors. CSF £48.26, CT £486.34. Tote £5.60: £1.90 £1.80 £3.80 £8.60 (£20.00). Mr Lionel Snowden (PRESTON) bred by Newmarket Thoroughbred Breeders P L C. 16 Rn
1m 58.3 (9.3)
SF—37/40/18/1/12/18

**3616**   CASTLETON STKS (Mdn) £2070.00 (£570.00: £270.00)   1¾m 19y   4-45 (4-46)

31042 **Alyafill (USA) (68)** *(BHanbury)* 3–8-7 BRaymond (11) (lw: trckd ldrs: led over 2f out: hld on wl fnl f) ............................................................... —1

32822 Nemir *(JHMGosden)* 3–8-12 LDettori (9) (b: lw: chsd ldrs: chal over 1f out: nt qckn cl home) ......................................................................... nk.2

3118 Alqairawaan (80) *(JLDunlop)* 3–8-12 RHills (8) (in tch: hdwy 4f out: styd on: nt pce to chal) ............................................................................ 8.3

31142 Hit the Fan (Fav) *(RCharlton)* 3–8-12 PaulEddery (10) (lw: sn trckng ldrs: led over 4f out tl hdd over 2f out: sn wknd) ........................................ 1½.4

34596 Klingon (IRE) (65) *(RHollinshead)* 3–8-12 KDarley (13) (bhd: effrt ent st: styd on: nvr rch ldrs) .................................................................... 3.5

Loch Clair (IRE) *(MrsJCecil)* 3–8-7 PRobinson (12) (stdy hdwy appr st: effrt 3f out: no imp) ............................................................................. 10.6

29855 Tudor Da Samba (50) *(JRFanshawe)* 3–8-12 NDay (6) (effrt on outside 4f out: sn rdn & n.d) ......................................................................... 1.7

2036 Ross Graham (60) *(MrsBarbaraWaring)* 4–9-7 NHowe (14) (chsd ldrs tl outpcd fnl 3f) ............................................................................... 1.8

11943 Shirley Ann *(RJWeaver)* 9–9-2 JLowe (5) (b: s.i.s: n.d) ............................... 15.9

Aal El Aal *(PJHobbs)* 5–9-7 JCarroll (4) (cl up: led 8f out tl over 4f out: sn wknd) .................................................................................. 6.10

10554 Glasgow *(EJAlston)* 3–8-12 KFallon (2) (pushed along appr st: n.d) ............. 3.11

32823 Flamingo Rose (IRE) *(HRACecil)* 3–8-7 WRyan (1) (lw: prom to st: sn bhd) ...... 6.12

627 Utamaro *(BWHills)* 3–8-7 MBirch (3) (led tl hdd 8f out: wknd qckly ent st: t.o) ..... 13

**9/4** Hit the Fan, **3/1** Nemir, **11/2** Aal El Aal, **9/1** Alqairawaan, **10/1** ALYAFILL (USA), Flamingo Rose (IRE), **14/1** Loch Clair (IRE), **16/1** Utamaro, **20/1** Glasgow, Klingon (IRE), **33/1** Ross Graham, Tudor Da Samba, **66/1** Shirley Ann. CSF £40.27, Tote £5.50: £2.50 £1.70 £2.60 (£12.80). Mr Abdullah Ali (NEWMARKET) bred by Nelson McMakin in USA. 13 Rn
3m 11.9 (14.3)
SF—27/31/15/12/6/–

**3617**   SETTRINGTON STKS (Mdn 2-Y.O.F) £2700.00 (£750.00: £360.00)   7f   5-15 (5-16)

28126 **Cubist (IRE)** *(DMorley)* 8-11 WRyan (6) (b.off hind: a.p: led 2f out: rdn & r.o wl) —1

32956 La Menorquina (USA) *(LMCumani)* 8-11 LDettori (13) (b.off hind: lw: hdwy ½-wy: sn trckng ldrs: styd on one pce ins fnl f) ................ 2½.2

33605 Princess Tateum (IRE) (Fav) *(MRChannon)* 8-11 PaulEddery (2) (hdwy & prom 3f out: nt qckn fnl f) ................................................ ¾.3

3480 Young Tess *(MissSEHall)* 8-11 SWebster (1) (bhd: swtchd & hdwy 2f out: r.o) 2½.4

3295 Mrs Jekyll (IRE) *(CFWall)* 8-11 NCarlisle (7) (lw: in tch: effrt 2f out: one pce) ... 2½.5

32954 Saja (USA) *(HThomsonJones)* 8-11 RHills (11) (lw: hld up: hdwy gng wl 3f out: shkn up 2f out: sn btn) ............................................... nk.6

3268 Bajka *(WJarvis)* 8-6 ‡5StephenDavies (12) (lw: a.p: effrt over 2f out: sn btn) ... 1½.7

35164 Dances With Gold *(MJohnston)* 8-11 RPElliott (9) (lw: chsd ldrs: n.m.r 3f out: grad wknd) .................................................................... hd.8

33382 Don't Jump (IRE) (81) *(MHTompkins)* 8-11 PRobinson (8) (led 5f: eased whn btn) ......................................................................... 1½.9

34716 Jendorcet *(TFairhurst)* 8-11 JFanning (4) (effrt ½-wy: n.d) ............................ 1½.10

34106 Dancing Diamond (IRE) *(CFWall)* 8-11 BRaymond (5) (prom 5f) ..................... 1½.11

3480 Broomhouse Lady *(MJohnston)* 8-11 JCarroll (10) (cl up over 4f: sn lost pl) .. 15.12

23506 Tri My Way (IRE) *(RRLamb)* 8-11 PBurke (14) (swtg: sn rdn along: bhd fr ½-wy) nk.13

3376 Young Geninsky (bl) *(RJWeaver)* 8-11 JLowe (3) (w ldrs to ½-wy: sn wknd) s.h.14

**5/2** Princess Tateum (IRE), **9/2** Saja (USA), **5/1** Don't Jump (IRE), La Menorquina (USA), **13/2** Dances With Gold, **12/1** CUBIST (IRE), **16/1** Mrs Jekyll (IRE), Young Tess, **20/1** Dancing Diamond (IRE), Bajka, **33/1** Jendorcet, **50/1** Broomhouse Lady, **100/1** Ors. CSF £70.10, Tote £35.20: £4.30 £1.40 £1.70 (£68.80). Lord Hartington (NEWMARKET) bred by David A. Clarke in Ireland. 14 Rn
1m 30.1 (7.9)
SF—36/28/26/18/10/9

T/Plpt: £213.40 (10.4 Tckts).
AA

## 3459—HAYDOCK (L-H)
### Wednesday, October 7th [Good to soft]
Going Allowance: St: 0.30 sec (G); Rnd: 0.45 sec per fur (Y)　　Wind: slt across

Stalls: high

**3618**　WALNUT GRADUATION STKS　£3084.75 (£918.00: £436.50: £195.75)
　　　　　5f　　　　　　　　　　　　　　　　　　　　　　　　　　　2-10 (2-10)

3528³ **Artistic Reef (106)** (Fav) (GHEden) 3–9-6 WCarson (2) (led over 2f out: clr ent
　　　　fnl f: easily) ...................................................................... —1
　3528 Silca-Cisa (93) (MRChannon) 3–9-4 TQuinn (1) (hld up: hdwy to chse wnr 2f
　　　　out: rdn appr fnl f: no imp) ................................................ 5.2
　3469 Absolutely Nuts (73) (BAMcMahon) 3–9-4 BRaymond (3) (led to ½-wy: outpcd
　　　　2f out: kpt on ins fnl f) ........................................................ ½.3
3495³ Threepence (79) (bl) (JBerry) 3–9-9 JCarroll (4) (prom: hrd rdn appr fnl f: sn
　　　　btn) ...................................................................................... 1½.4

**1/2** ARTISTIC REEF, **3/1** Silca-Cisa, **6/1** Threepence, **16/1** Absolutely Nuts. CSF £2.45, Tote £1.30 (£1.60). Mr
R. Mohammed (NEWMARKET) bred by Ruffiek A. Mohammed. 4 Rn
　　　　　　　　　　　　　　　　　　　　　　　　　62.12 sec (3.12)
　　　　　　　　　　　　　　　　　　　　　　　　　SF—74/52/50/49

**3619**　WHITEBEAM STKS (I) (Mdn 2-Y.O) £2427.00 (£672.00: £321.00)
　　　　　1m 30y　　　　　　　　　　　　　　　　　　　　　　2-40 (2-41)

3160⁶ Heathyards Boy (RHollinshead) 9-0 WRyan (1) (bit bkwd: chsd ldrs: 5th st: rdn
　　　　2f out: styd on to ld ins fnl f) ............................................ —1
3402³ Armenian Coffee (IRE) (86) (Jt-Fav) (JLUnIop) 9-0 WOarson (5) (lw: led after
　　　　2f tl over 2f out: led appr fnl f tl ins fnl f) .......................... 1½.2
　　　Mountain Willow (LordHuntingdon) 8-9 LDettori (8) (w'like: bit bkwd: s.s: hdwy
　　　　& 4th st: ev ch 2f out: kpt on nr fin) .................................. s.h.3
3247³ Jizyah (Jt-Fav) (HThomsonJones) 8-9 RHills (6) (led 2f: 3rd st: led over 2f out tl
　　　　ins fnl f: sn wknd) .............................................................. 3.4
3465³ Amillionmemories (79) (MrsBarbaraWaring) 9-0 NHowe (4) (2nd st: ev ch over
　　　　2f out: sn rdn & wknd) ........................................................ 1½.5
　3313 Stephanentse (WWHaigh) 8-9 SWebster (2) (a bhd) ................ 2½.6
　　　Personimus (CaptJWilson) 9-0 JFortune (7) (wl grwn: bkwd: s.s: hdwy & 6th st:
　　　　rdn & wknd 3f out: t.o) ........................................................ 7.7
　3117 City Lighter (EJAlston) 8-9 NCarlisle (3) (a bhd: rdn ½-wy: no imp: t.o) ...... 20.8

**5/2** Armenian Coffee (IRE), Jizyah, **7/2** Mountain Willow, **6/1** Amillionmemories(8/1–5/1), **10/1** HEATHYARDS
BOY, **20/1** Personimus, **33/1** Ors. CSF £32.88, Tote £12.50: £2.00 £1.10 £1.60 (£25.10). Mr L. A. Morgan
(UPPER LONGDON) bred by G. W. Hampson. 8 Rn
　　　　　　　　　　　　　　　　　　　　　　　　　1m 49.54 (9.14)
　　　　　　　　　　　　　　　　　　　　　　　　　SF—17/13/6/–/–/–

**3620**　CHAMPAGNE BOLLINGER H'CAP (0-90) £3947.50 (£1180.00: £565.00: £257.50)
　　　　　6f　　　　　　　　　　　　　　　　　　　　　　　　　3-10 (3-12)
　　　　　　　　　　　　　　(Weights raised 4 lb)

3524³ **My Ruby Ring (50)** (DRLaing) 5–7-0 ‡7KimMcDonnell (14) (a.p: led ins fnl f: r.o
　　　　wl) ........................................................................................ —1
　3469 Gentle Hero (USA) (71) (MPNaughton) 6–9-0 TQuinn (6) (chsd ldrs: rdn 2f out:
　　　　fin wl) .................................................................................. ¾.2
　3355 Darussalam (74) (RLee) 5–9-3 JWilliams (4) (hdwy appr fnl f: rdn & r.o wl cl
　　　　home) ................................................................................... hd.3
3437⁶ Fascination Waltz (72) (Jt-Fav) (DShaw) 5–9-1 AClark (10) (hld up: swtchd rt 2f
　　　　out: r.o wl fnl f) ................................................................... nk.4
3126* Nordan Raider (57) (MJCamacho) 4–8-0 JFanning (2) (lw: hdwy 2f out: ev ch
　　　　fnl f: unable qckn) ............................................................... s.h.5
3496⁴ Veloce (IRE) (60) (ABailey) 4–7-12 ‡5ATucker (1) (hdwy over 1f out: r.o wl nr fin) 1½.6
3460⁴ Easy Does it (56) (MrsAKnight) 3–7-8⁽⁴⁾ ‡3FNorton (7) (led tl hdd & wknd ins fnl f) 1.7
　3545 Jahangir (IRE) (78) (bl) (BHanbury) 3–9-5 LDettori (8) (lw: w ldrs over 4f) ...... ¾.8
3469² Amron (80) (JBerry) 3–9-9 NCarlisle (5) (chsd ldrs: rdn over 1f out: sn wknd) s.h.9
　3437 Love Legend (81) (DWPArbuthnot) 7–9-10 AMunro (12) (b: b.hind: a in rr) ... 1½.10
3518² Yours Or Mine (IRE) (50) (Jt-Fav) (DWChapman) 4–7-0 JLowe (3) (spd 4f) ...... 2.11
　3349 Windpower (IRE) (74) (JBerry) 3–9-1 JCarroll (9) (lw: m.n.s) ............... 1½.12
3464* Breezy Day (80) (BAMcMahon) 6–9-9 BRaymond (15) (lw: spd over 3f: sn lost
　　　　tch) ...................................................................................... 2½.13
3464⁴ Isdar (USA) (82) (HThomsonJones) 3–9-9 RHills (11) (outpcd: a bhd) ............ ¾.14
3196⁴ Castlerea Lad (77) (RHollinshead) 3–9-4 WRyan (13) (dwlt: a bhd) ............... 3½.15
　　　LONG HANDICAP: My Ruby Ring 7-2, Easy Does it 7-2, Yours Or Mine (IRE) 7-5.

**6/1** Fascination Waltz, Yours Or Mine (IRE)(op 10/1), **13/2** Nordan Raider, **7/1** Isdar (USA), **9/1** Breezy Day, **10/1** Darussalam, Amron, **11/1** Jahangir (IRE), **14/1** Windpower (IRE), **16/1** Gentle Hero (USA), Veloce (IRE), Castlerea Lad, Love Legend, **20/1** MY RUBY RING, **33/1** Easy Does it. CSF £281.81, CT £3,064.42. Tote £24.50: £5.30 £5.30 £3.40 (£368.40). Mrs Marion Wickham (LAMBOURN) bred by Mrs Wickham. 15 Rn　1m 16 (4.3)
SF—22/47/49/46/30/22

## 3621　　KING'S REGIMENT CUP (H'cap) (0-90) £3377.25 (£1008.00: £481.50: £218.25)
2m 45y　　　　　　　　　　　　　　　　　　　　　3-40 (3-41)

2899 **My Chiara (61)** *(PJBevan)* 6-8-9 BCrossley (1) (a.p: 3rd st: led over 3f out: sn clr: unchal) .................................................................. —1

3515⁵ Hot Star **(52)** *(GMMoore)* 6-8-0 JLowe (9) (lw: s.s: hld up & bhd: styd on fnl 2f: nvr nrr) ................................................................. 5.2

3431 Aude la Belle (FR) **(75)** *(MrsAKnight)* 4-9-6 ‡3FNorton (5) (hld up & bhd: 6th st: hdwy 3f out: sn rdn & one pce) ................................. 1½.3

2844 Lord Hastie (USA) **(80)** *(SGNorton)* 4-10-0 BRaymond (8) (lw: chsd ldrs: 5th st: effrt 3f out: wknd wl over 1f out) ............................. 2.4

3406² Smilingatstrangers **(52)** (v) *(MrsBarbaraWaring)* 4-7-7 ‡7CHawksley (3) (hdwy ½-wy: rdn 3f out: nvr nr to chal) ................................. 3½.5

3490 Coleridge **(63)** (v) *(DShaw)* 4-8-6 ‡5SWilliams (7) (bit bkwd: chsd ldrs: 4th st: rdn & wknd over 2f out) ............................................. 4.6

1256 Just My Bill **(67)** (bl) *(NTinkler)* 6-9-1 DNicholls (6) (bkwd: chsd ldr: 2nd st: wknd over 3f out: t.o) ............................................ 25.7

3461 Moonlight Shift **(46)** *(WClay)* 6-7-8⁽¹⁾ NAdams (4) (led tl hdd & wknd over 3f out: t.o) ............................................................. hd.8

3504³ Needwood Muppet **(55)** (Fav) *(BCMorgan)* 5-8-3⁽¹⁾ TQuinn (2) (lost pl 6f out: hrd rdn ent st: t.o) ............................................. 25.9
LONG HANDICAP: Needwood Muppet 6-13.

**9/4** Needwood Muppet, **9/2** Smilingatstrangers, **6/1** Hot Star, **13/2** Lord Hastie (USA), **7/1** Aude la Belle (FR), **8/1** MY CHIARA, **11/1** Just My Bill, **20/1** Coleridge, **50/1** Moonlight Shift. CSF £49.99, CT £319.10. Tote £10.50: £2.90 £2.50 £2.20 (£36.40). Mr A. Eaton (UTTOXETER) bred by Henry Cecil Bloodstock Ltd. 9 Rn
3m 44.12 (16.92)

## 3622　　RACING SCHOOLS APP'CE H'CAP (0-70) £2637.00 (£732.00: £351.00)
1¼m 120y　　　　　　　　　　　　　　　　　　　4-10 (4-12)

3466* **Light Hand (68)** (Fav) *(MHTompkins)* 6-9-10 ‡3SMulvey (5) (s.s: hld up & bhd: gd hdwy 2f out: shkn up to ld ins fnl f: comf) ............ —1

3468⁵ Mardessa **(52)** *(FHLee)* 4-8-11 NKennedy (8) (swtg: s.s: bhd: effrt & n.m.r wl over 1f out: rapid hdwy appr fnl f: fin fast) ....................... ½.2

3192 Spray of Orchids **(53)** *(JEtherington)* 3-8-5 DHarrison (7) (lw: hld up: hdwy over 2f out: r.o wl fnl f) ............................................. nk.3

3393 Sovereign Niche (IRE) **(40)** *(MrsJRRamsden)* 4-7-13 JTate (3) (bit bkwd: s.s: bhd: hdwy & 6th st: kpt on wl ins fnl f) ......................... s.h.4

1317 Always Ready **(37)** *(RLee)* 6—7-10 ATucker (1) (b: bit bkwd: led 4f: 2nd st: led 2f out tl ins fnl f) ............................................. 5.5

3350* Persian Fleece **(55)** *(ABailey)* 3-8-4 ‡3PBowe (4) (prom: 3rd st: ev ch 2f out: wknd fnl f) ...................................................... 1.6

3381 Statia (IRE) **(34)** *(DonEnricoIncisa)* 4-7-4 ‡3ClaireBalding (2) (prom: led over 6f out: rdn & hdd 2f out: sn btn) ........................... 1½.7

3459 Barga **(45)** *(WClay)* 3—7-11 AGarth (6) (chsd ldrs: 5th st: rdn & wknd 2f out) ... 3½.8

3479⁶ Golden Ancona **(40)** *(MBrittain)* 9-7-10⁽²⁾ ‡3JMarshall (10) (lw: prom: 4th st: wknd over 2f out) ..................................................... 3½.9

3475⁴ Magnificent **(67)** (bl) *(MAJarvis)* 3-9-5 KRutter (9) (lw: a in rr) ........................ ½.10
LONG HANDICAP: Statia (IRE) 7-0.

**2/1** LIGHT HAND, **5/1** Magnificent, Spray of Orchids, **13/2** Persian Fleece, Mardessa, **14/1** Always Ready, Sovereign Niche (IRE), **20/1** Golden Ancona, **33/1** Ors. CSF £14.66, CT £50.95. Tote £2.70: £1.40 £1.80 £1.70 (£8.70). Mr John A. Furze (NEWMARKET) bred by The Dunchurch Lodge Stud Co and Mrs A. Johnstone. 10 Rn
2m 25.32 (13.62)
SF—21/7/–/–/–/–

## 3623　　MAPLE (S) NURSERY　£2616.00 (£726.00: £348.00)　1¼m 120y　　4-40 (4-43)
(Weights raised 5 lb)

3301 **Stapleford Lass (45)** *(SPCWoods)* 8-6 WWoods (17) (hld up: 7th st: c wd: led over 2f out: r.o strly) ...................................... —1

3497* Palacegate Sunset **(52)** *(JBerry)* 8-13 (5x) JCarroll (14) (lw: chsd ldrs: 4th st: ev ch over 1f out: kpt on) ....................................... 1½.2

3497 Challenger Row (IRE) **(48)** *(CWThornton)* 8-9 WRyan (7) (b.hind: lw: prom: 6th st: outpcd over 2f out: swtchd rt & r.o wl fnl f) .................. hd.3

3071⁴ Hasta la Vista **(43)** *(MWEasterby)* 8-4 TQuinn (8) (hld up: hdwy 3f out: hrd rdn appr fnl f: kpt on) .................................................... s.h.4

3301 Strephon (IRE) **(46)** *(MHTompkins)* 8-0 ‡⁷SMulvey (16) (chsd ldrs: 3rd st: hrd rdn over 1f out: one pace) .................................................... ¾.5

3407⁵ Hush Baby (IRE) **(43)** (bl) *(DMorris)* 8-4 JFanning (10) (lw: hld up: hdwy over 2f out: rdn & wknd fnl f) .................................................... 2½.6

3050⁵ Bohemian Queen **(44)** *(JLSpearing)* 8-5 GHind (13) (hdwy over 2f out: nt rch ldrs) .................................................... 2½.7

3407 Hot Storm **(41)** *(MJCamacho)* 8-2 JLowe (1) (lw: s.s: bhd tl r.o ins fnl f) .......... hd.8

3407² Merry Mermaid **(52)** (Fav) *(JFBottomley)* 8-13 PBurke (2) (hld up: effrt 3f out: rdn over 1f out: no imp) .................................................... nk.9

2782 Peak Fitness **(45)** *(JAGlover)* 8-6 JFortune (11) (led tl hdd & wknd over 2f out) 1.10

3260⁶ Blue Sombrero (IRE) **(58)** *(RJHolder)* 9-5 NAdams (5) (m.n.s: t.o) ................ 10.11

2058 Lady Argent (IRE) **(44)** *(APJarvis)* 7-12 ‡⁷DWright (6) (bkwd: w ldr: 2nd st: rdn 3f out: sn wknd: t.o) .................................................... 5.12

3303 West End Girl **(52)** *(RJRWilliams)* 8-13 RHills (4) (hdwy & 5th st: wknd over 2f out: t.o) .................................................... hd.13

3407⁴ Summers Dream **(41)** *(BRichmond)* 8-2 NCarlisle (14) (t.o) ................ 2½.14

3408 Red Cent **(60)** *(JEtherington)* 9-7 TLucas (3) (dwlt: a bhd: t.o) .......... 2.15

2277 Snug Surprise **(46)** (bl) *(JSWainwright)* 8-4 ‡³FNorton (12) (bit bkwd: t.o) .... 2.16

3301 Lettermore **(47)** (v) *(RMWhitaker)* 8-5 ‡³DHarrison (9) (a bhd: t.o) ......... 8.17

**4/1** Merry Mermaid(tchd 6/1), **9/2** Palacegate Sunset, **5/1** Hush Baby (IRE), **6/1** Blue Sombrero (IRE), **11/1** Hot Storm, **12/1** Hasta la Vista, West End Girl, Bohemian Queen, **16/1** Summers Dream, **20/1** Red Cent, Strephon (IRE), Lettermore, STAPLEFORD LASS, **25/1** Peak Fitness, Challenger Row (IRE), **33/1** Ors. CSF £111.15, CT £2,140.30. Tote £34.10: £4.80 £1.50 £6.50 £2.30 (£106.10). High Point Bloodstock Ltd (NEWMARKET) bred by R. Searle. 17 Rn; No bid
2m 23.45 (11.75)
SF—22/26/21/15/9/8

---

**3624**     WHITEBEAM STKS (II) (Mdn 2-Y.O) £2427.00 (£672.00: £321.00)
1m 30y                      5-10 (5-12)

3408² **Blue Blazer (87)** *(BHanbury)* 9-0 BRaymond (6) (a.p: 3rd st: led appr fnl f: r.o wl) .................................................... —1

3320³ Johns Act (USA) *(DHaydnJones)* 9-0 JLowe (5) (plld hrd: disp ld: led 2f out: sn hdd: r.o one pce) .................................................... 2.2

3132 Kryptos (USA) *(LordHuntingdon)* 8-9 AMunro (3) (bit bkwd: chsd ldrs: 5th st: styd on ins fnl f: nvr nrr) .................................................... 4.3

3297² Dragon's Teeth (IRE) (Fav) *(LMCumani)* 9-0 LDettori (4) (lw: led 6f: rdn & wknd over 1f out) .................................................... 1.4

3419 Jihaad (USA) *(JLDunlop)* 9-0 RHills (2) (bit bkwd: chsd ldrs: 4th & rdn st: wknd 2f out: t.o) .................................................... 10.5

     Bomoh *(SPCWoods)* 9-0 WWoods (7) (lt-f: bit bkwd: hld up & bhd: 7th st: lost tch over 2f out: t.o) .................................................... 4.6

3353⁶ Sudden Spin *(JBerry)* 9-0 JCarroll (1) (hld up: 6th st: wknd over 2f out: t.o) ...... 6.7

**8/11** Dragon's Teeth (IRE), **11/4** BLUE BLAZER, **8/1** Kryptos (USA), **12/1** Johns Act (USA), **14/1** Jihaad (USA), **25/1** Ors. CSF £30.16, Tote £3.50: £1.90 £3.70 (£12.30). McHalapar Syndicate (NEWMARKET) bred by Oak Bloodstock Ltd. 7 Rn
1m 47.97 (7.57)
SF—40/34/17/19/–/–

T/Plpt: £462.50 (8 Tckts).                          IM

---

# HAYDOCK (L-H)
## Thursday, October 8th [Good to soft]
Going Allowance: 0.30 sec per fur (G)         Wind: slt half against

Stalls: high

**3625**     STANDARD LIFE STKS (2-Y.O.F) £3231.00 (£963.00: £459.00: £207.00)
1m 30y                      2-10 (2-11)

     **Lead Note (USA)** (Fav) *(HRACecil)* 8-8 PatEddery (1) (scope: lw: 2nd st: led over 2f out: easily) .................................................... —1

3172⁵ Solartica (USA) *(JRFanshawe)* 8-8 WRSwinburn (5) (hld up: 4th st: shkn up & hdwy over 2f out: chsd wnr fnl f: no imp) .................................................... 3.2

     Swift Spring (FR) *(PFICole)* 8-8 (b.off fore: w'like: bkwd: prom: 3rd st: rdn appr fnl f: one pce) .................................................... 2½.3

3191 Nanny Margaret (IRE) *(PAKelleway)* 8-8 GayKelleway (3) (bit bkwd: led tl hdd over 2f out: sn rdn & btn) .................................................... 5.4

3471 Target Time (bl) *(DMcCain)* 8-8 LDettori (2) (s.s: 5th st: rdn 2f out: no imp) ...... 8.5

**1/2** LEAD NOTE (USA), **4/1** Swift Spring (FR), **11/2** Solartica (USA), **14/1** Nanny Margaret (IRE), **66/1** Target Time. CSF £3.62, Tote £1.30: £1.10 £1.50 (£2.00). Mr K. Abdulla (NEWMARKET) bred by Juddmonte Farms Inc in USA. 5 Rn
1m 49.44 (9.04)

## 3626

FARRELLS FLYER STKS (Mdn 2-Y.O) £2742.00 (£762.00: £366.00)    **6f**   2-40 (2-44)

| | | |
|---|---|---|
| 3414³ | **Vayavaig** (Fav) *(JRFanshawe)* 8-9 WRSwinburn (10) (hld up: hdwy to ld ins fnl f: sn clr) | —1 |
| 3390⁵ | A Secret Weapon *(JMPEustace)* 9-0 MTebbutt (5) (chsd ldrs: rdn over 1f out: styd on) | 5.2 |
| 3312⁵ | General Link *(PAKelleway)* 9-0 GayKelleway (4) (b: bit bkwd: a.p: led wl over 1f out tl ins fnl f) | s.h.3 |
| 3267⁴ | Glorious Island (63) *(RFJohnsonHoughton)* 9-0 MHills (7) (a.p: rdn appr fnl f: r.o one pce) | hd.4 |
| 3000 | American Swinger (USA) *(PWHarris)* 9-0 SWhitworth (17) (styd on ins fnl f: nvr nrr) | 2½.5 |
| 3127 | Bollin Duncan *(MHEasterby)* 9-0 MBirch (6) (still bkwd: chsd ldrs: rdn ½-wy: kpt on ins fnl f) | hd.6 |
| 3551⁶ | Legal Risk (76) (bl) *(DHaydnJones)* 8-9 JLowe (9) (hdwy appr fnl f: nt rch ldrs) | ¾.7 |
| 3491 | Swiss Mountain *(DRLaing)* 8-9 TyroneWilliams (1) (chsd ldrs: rdn 2f out: ev ch 1f out: no ex fnl f) | nk.8 |
| 3376⁵ | Disco Boy *(BAMcMahon)* 9-0 TQuinn (16) (w ldrs over 4f) | 4.9 |
| 3551³ | Mansard (IRE) *(JHMGosden)* 9-0 PatEddery (19) (led over 4f: sn rdn & wknd) | s.h.10 |
| 3399 | Quessong *(FHLee)* 9-0 ACulhane (2) (still bkwd: m.n.s) | 2½.11 |
| | Whyalla Rain *(RHollinshead)* 8-9 LDettori (11) (w'like: leggy: bit bkwd: m.n.s) | ½.12 |
| | Alamel (USA) *(HThomsonJones)* 8-9 RHills (18) (w'like: lengthy: bit bkwd: chsd ldrs 4f: sn wknd) | 1½.13 |
| | Ever so Lyrical *(PWHarris)* 9-0 GHind (3) (w'like: bkwd: a bhd) | 4.14 |
| | Shillelagh Bay (IRE) *(PWHarris)* 9-0 NAdams (8) (gd sort: bkwd: m.n.s) | ½.15 |
| | Sabo the Hero *(SirMarkPrescott)* 9-0 GDuffield (12) (w'like: scope: bit bkwd: s.s: a bhd) | 1.16 |
| 3156³ | Sicily Oak (63) *(DMcCain)* 8-9 GBardwell (14) (s.s: a bhd) | 5.17 |
| 3055 | See Us There (IRE) *(JBerry)* 9-0 JCarroll (15) (lw: a bhd) | 1.18 |
| 3338 | Nellie Hen *(ABailey)* 8-4 ‡⁵ATucker (13) (bit bkwd: a bhd) | nk.19 |

**13/8** VAYAVAIG, **7/2** Mansard (IRE), **7/1** Alamel (USA)(4/1—8/1), **8/1** Sabo the Hero, **16/1** Legal Risk, General Link, **20/1** Glorious Island, Sicily Oak, Whyalla Rain, American Swinger (USA), **25/1** Shillelagh Bay (IRE), **33/1** Ors. CSF £67.13, Tote £2.40: £1.30 £17.30 £5.20 (£116.80). Dexa'tex Limited (NEWMARKET) bred by Genesis Green Stud. 19 Rn
1m 17.77 (6.07)
SF—10/-/-/-/-/-

## 3627

FORWARD SUPPORT GROUP H'CAP (0-80) £3933.00 (£1179.00: £567.00: £261.00)
**1¼m 120y**    3-10 (3-12)

| | | |
|---|---|---|
| 3302⁴ | **Shabanaz (71)** *(SGNorton)* 7-9-9 ‡⁵OPears (8) (hld up & bhd: nt clr run 2f out: gd hdwy appr fnl f: led nr fin) | —1 |
| 3468² | Sword Master (74) *(BobJones)* 3-9-10 NDay (13) (hld up: 7th st: led over 1f out: sn clr: wknd & ct cl home) | 1.2 |
| 3468 | Falcons Dawn (52) *(ABailey)* 5-8-9 JCarroll (14) (lw: hdwy fnl 2f: nvr nrr) | 4.3 |
| 3466² | Katy's Lad (66) *(BAMcMahon)* 5-9-9 LDettori (10) (lw: in tch: rdn 3f out: kpt on ins fnl f) | ¾.4 |
| 3270 | Thamestar (IRE) (75) *(JLDunlop)* 3-9-11 MHills (1) (chsd ldrs: 6th st: rdn 2f out: r.o one pce) | ¾.5 |
| 3526 | Virkon Venture (IRE) (68) *(MHTompkins)* 4-9-11 RHills (2) (lw: hld up: effrt over 2f out: nt rch ldrs) | 3½.6 |
| 3346⁶ | Tanoda (47) *(MBrittain)* 6-8-4 GDuffield (6) (in tch: 8th st: rdn 3f out: wknd appr fnl f) | ½.7 |
| 3475 | Secret Treaty (IRE) (53) *(PWChapple-Hyam)* 3-8-3 DHolland (12) (hld up: effrt over 2f out: eased whn btn fnl f) | 1.8 |
| 3485★ | Sunderland Echo (57) (Fav) *(MrsGRReveley)* 3-8-7 JLowe (11) (plld hrd: in tch: rdn over 2f out: no imp) | 1.9 |
| | Achelous (58) *(JAGlover)* 5-8-10 ‡⁵SWilliams (9) (bit bkwd: prom: 4th st: rdn & wknd 3f out: t.o) | 10.10 |
| 3311 | Sie Amato (IRE) (51) *(CaptJWilson)* 3-8-1 GBardwell (5) (prom: 3rd st: led over 2f out tl over 1f out: wknd qckly: t.o) | s.h.11 |
| 3357⁶ | Admirals Seat (62) *(MrsJRRamsden)* 4-9-5 GBaxter (4) (lw: dwlt: effrt on ins 3f out: no imp: t.o) | ½.12 |
| 3461 | El Nido (70) *(MJCamacho)* 4-9-13 SMorris (3) (lw: s.s: a bhd: t.o) | ½.13 |
| 3417 | May Hills Legacy (IRE) (66) *(DWPArbuthnot)* 3-9-2 TQuinn (7) (b: chsd ldr: 2nd st: wknd over 2f out: t.o) | 5.14 |
| 3526 | Dawn Success (53) (v) *(DWChapman)* 6-8-10 SWood (15) (lw: led tl hdd & wknd over 2f out: t.o) | hd.15 |

## 3628 — 3630

100/30 Sunderland Echo, 6/1 Secret Treaty (IRE), Katy's Lad, Virkon Venture (IRE), 8/1 Sword Master, 9/1 Admirals Seat, 12/1 Thamestar (IRE), El Nido, 14/1 SHABANAZ, 16/1 Tanoda, 20/1 Falcons Dawn, Sie Amato (IRE), May Hills Legacy (IRE), 33/1 Ors. CSF £122.14, CT £2,070.58. Tote £15.60: £3.50 £2.60 £10.10 (£103.70). Mr Peter Hayes (BARNSLEY) bred by The Overbury Stud. 15 Rn — 2m 19.72 (8.02)
SF—60/59/36/48/48/41

### 3628
STANDARD LIFE H'CAP (0-100) £3752.50 (£1120.00: £535.00: £242.50)
1m 3f 200y
(Weights raised 9 lb)
3-40 (3-42)

| | | |
|---|---|---|
| 2915⁴ | **Turgenev (IRE) (86)** *(JHMGosden)* 3-9-10 DHolland (5) (lw: hld up: 4th st: rdn to ld ins fnl f: sn clr) | —1 |
| 3078* | **Mimique (75)** *(Fav) (HRACecil)* 3-8-13 PatEddery (4) (lw: led tl hdd ins fnl f: edn & r.o) | 1¹/₂.2 |
| 2054⁶ | **Rousitto (70)** *(RHollinshead)* 4-9-2 LDettori (2) (hld up: 5th st: styd on ins fnl f: nvr nrr) | 1¹/₂.3 |
| 3346⁴ | **Whirl (76)** *(JRFanshawe)* 3-9-0 MHills (3) (chsd ldr: 2nd st: ev ch appr fnl f: sn rdn & no ex) | hd.4 |
| 3461 | **Bollin William (58)** *(MHEasterby)* 4-8-4 MBirch (1) (bit bkwd: chsd ldrs: 3rd st: wknd 2f out: t.o) | 15.5 |
| 2020⁶ | **Inchcailloch (IRE) (84)** *(RCharlton)* 3-9-8 WRSwinburn (6) (bit bkwd: hld up & bhd: 6th st: effrt 3f out: sn rdn: t.o) | 2.6 |

7/4 Mimique, 4/1 Inchcailloch (IRE), 5/1 Whirl, 11/2 Rousitto, TURGENEV (IRE), 14/1 Bollin William. CSF £14.60, Tote £5.50: £2.30 £1.50 (£3.20). Sheikh Mohammed (NEWMARKET) bred by Paolo Tomei in Ireland. 6 Rn — 2m 39.18 (11.18)
SF—34/20/20/17/–/–

### 3629
STANDARD LIFE HIGH STANDARD (S) STKS (3-Y.O) £2322.00 (£642.00: £306.00)
1¹/₄m 120y
4-10 (4-10)

| | | |
|---|---|---|
| 3494⁵ | **Ready to Draw (IRE) (59)** *(RonaldThompson)* 9-2 RPElliott (2) (lw: s.i.s: hld up: 5th st: hdwy 3f out: led ins fnl f: r.o) | —1 |
| 3479 | **Aegaen Lady (41)** *(JEtherington)* 8-1 ‡JWeaver (5) (lw: prom: 3rd st: led over 2f out tl ins fnl f) | 3¹/₂.2 |
| 3073 | **Emerald Ears (35)** (bl) *(EWeymes)* 8-11 GHind (4) (led tl over 2f out: r.o one pce) | 2¹/₂.3 |
| 3395 | **Preamble (40)** *(MrsJRRamsden)* 8-6 GBaxter (1) (hld up & bhd: 6th st: effrt over 2f out: no imp) | 2¹/₂.4 |
| 3266 | **Titian Girl (32)** *(MissLCSiddall)* 8-6 GDuffield (6) (chsd ldr: 2nd st: wknd 2f out) | 3¹/₂.5 |
| 566⁴ | **Repledge (IRE) (69)** (bl) *(Fav) (PFICole)* 8-11 TQuinn (3) (bkwd: hld up: 4th st: rdn over 2f out: sn btn) | ³/₄.6 |

4/5 Repledge (IRE), 4/1 READY TO DRAW (IRE), 5/1 Preamble(12/1—14/1), 6/1 Aegaen Lady(op 4/1), 14/1 Emerald Ears, 33/1 Titian Girl. CSF £25.00, Tote £4.60: £1.80 £2.10 (£6.60). M. D. M. Racing (Thoroughbreds) Limited (DONCASTER) bred by Aidan Sexton in Ireland. 6 Rn; No bid — 2m 23.22 (11.52)
SF—18/–/1/–/–/–

### 3630
GLOBAL ADVANTAGE NURSERY £3640.50 (£1089.00: £522.00: £238.50)
5f
4-40 (4-42)

| | | |
|---|---|---|
| 3023³ | **Sea Gazer (IRE) (79)** *(TDBarron)* 9-4 AlexGreaves (10) (lw: mde all: hrd rdn fnl f: hld on gamely) | —1 |
| 3534³ | **Zany Zanna (IRE) (82)** *(Fav) (GAPritchard-Gordon)* 9-4 ‡DHarrison (7) (hld up: hdwy over 2f out: swtchd lft appr fnl f: r.o) | ¹/₂.2 |
| 3503³ | **Bellsabanging (66)** *(DRLaing)* 8-5 TyroneWilliams (9) (lw: a.p: rdn over 1f out: r.o one pce) | 4.3 |
| 3358* | **Carnbrea Snip (82)** *(MBell)* 9-7 MHills (11) (lw: a.p: rdn appr fnl f: r.o one pce) | 5.4 |
| 3358⁶ | **Cockerham Ranger (70)** *(JBerry)* 8-9 JCarroll (8) (lw: dwlt: effrt u.p 2f out: nt pce to chal) | 1¹/₂.5 |
| 3478² | **Norstano (65)** (bl) *(MHEasterby)* 8-4⁽²⁾ MBirch (1) (nvr nr to chal) | 2¹/₂.6 |
| 3478* | **Arkendale Diamond (USA) (68)** *(CBBBooth)* 8-7 GDuffield (6) (lw: chsd ldrs: hrd rdn 2f out: sn btn) | ¹/₂.7 |
| 2928 | **Matthew David (56)** *(MHBrittain)* 7-9 JLowe (2) (bkwd: outpcd) | 1¹/₂.8 |
| 1251² | **Dayjuz (IRE) (76)** *(FHLee)* 9-1 LDettori (4) (bkwd: nvr nr ldrs) | 1.9 |
| 3382 | **High Romance (64)** *(DMoffatt)* 9-3 JBerry (3) (lw: outpcd) | ¹/₂.10 |
| 3003⁵ | **Our Mica (55)** (bl) *(JBerry)* 7-8⁽¹⁾ NAdams (5) (outpcd) | hd.11 |

3/1 Zany Zanna (IRE)(op 9/2), 11/2 Arkendale Diamond (USA), 6/1 Carnbrea Snip(op 4/1), 15/2 SEA GAZER (IRE), 9/1 Norstano, 10/1 Dayjuz (IRE), 11/1 Bellsabanging, 14/1 Cockerham Ranger, 20/1 Our Mica, High Romance, 25/1 Matthew David. CSF £27.39, CT £222.79. Tote £8.30: £2.20 £1.80 £4.90 (£11.70). Mr P. D. Savill (THIRSK) bred by D. Twomey in Ireland. 11 Rn — 63.29 sec (4.29)
SF—48/46/17/13/–/–

T/Plpt: £110.20 (33.55 Tckts).

IM

3080—**YORK (L-H)**

**Wednesday, October 7th [Good to soft]**

Going Allowance: 0.85 sec per fur (S)

Wind: mod half against

Stalls: high

**3631**  MONKGATE MEDIAN AUCTION STKS (Mdn 2-Y.O) £5010.00 (£1500.00: £720.00: £330.00)  **6f 214y**  2-00 (2-02)

3353² **Lyford Cay (IRE)** (Fav) (PWChapple-Hyam) 8-10 DHolland (4) (trckd ldrs gng wl: shkn up to ld over 1f out: pushed out) .............................. —1

3005 Pistol River (IRE) (RHannon) 8-10 JReid (10) (hmpd s: hdwy ½-wy: styd on fnl f: no ch w wnr) ............................................................. 1½.2

2675 Mondragon (MrsGRReveley) 9-0 KDarley (12) (hld up & bhd: hdwy over 1f out: r.o wl nr fin) ...................................................................... 1½.3

Bay Queen (MBell) 8-5 MHills (2) (leggy: unf: w ldrs: led over 2f out tl wknd over 1f out: wknd ins fnl f) ............................................. 1½.4

Meant to Be (HJCollingridge) 8-2 JQuinn (1) (unf: sn chsng ldrs: wknd 2f out) .. 7.5

3465⁶ Move Smartly (IRE) (FHLee) 8-10 PaulEddery (5) (in tch: drvn along ½-wy: no imp) ....................................................................................... 3.6

3399⁶ Procada (JEtherington) 8-10 RCochrane (8) (sn drvn along: chsd ldrs tl outpcd fnl 2f) .................................................................................. d.h.6

2683³ Pipers Reel (LordHuntingdon) 8-5 PatEddery (3) (hld up: hmpd after 1f: nvr nr to chal) .................................................................................... 1.8

3399 Can Can Charlie (MJohnston) 8-7 RPElliott (14) (trckd ldrs tl rn green & wknd over 2f out) ........................................................................... ½.9

3307⁵ Bold Flash (PCHaslam) 8-10 DaleGibson (6) (led tl over 2f out: sn lost pl) ..... 1.10

3353⁴ Blakes Beau (MHEasterby) 8-10 MBirch (7) (hld up: hdwy over 2f out: styd on wl nr fin) ............................................................................ nk.11

2819³ Peedie Peat (JJO'Neill) 8-10 MRoberts (9) (lw: outpcd fr ½-wy) ............. 3½.12

*3376* Broadstairs Beauty (IRE) (MCChapman) 8-7 KFallon (13) (swvd lft s: chsd ldrs tl wknd 3f out) .......................................................................... 2.13

Citizen King (GAPritchard-Gordon) 8-7 PRobinson (11) (w'like: bit bkwd: s.i.s: a wl outpcd) ....................................................................... 12.14

**13/8** LYFORD CAY (IRE), **5/1** Pistol River (IRE), **6/1** Pipers Reel, **7/1** Peedie Peat, **10/1** Procada, Bay Queen, **12/1** Mondragon, **14/1** Move Smartly (IRE), **20/1** Blakes Beau, **25/1** Can Can Charlie, Citizen King, Meant to Be, **33/1** Ors. CSF £11.60, Tote £2.30: £1.10 £2.10 £5.20 (£7.00). Mr R. E. Sangster (MARLBOROUGH) bred by J. Hayden in Ireland. 14 Rn
1m 32.68 (10.28)
SF—30/25/24/10/–/–

**3632**  MICKLEGATE (S) STKS  £5361.00 (£1608.00: £774.00: £357.00)  **6f**  2-30 (2-58)

3437 **Drum Sergeant (74)** (bl) (JParkes) 5–9-6 MRoberts (11) (lw: hld up: hdwy over 2f out: led 1f out: all out) ................................................... —1

3418⁶ Crystal Heights (FR) (80) (bl) (WAO'Gorman) 4–9-6 RCochrane (6) (trckd ldrs: led over 2f out: edgd rt u.p 1f out: r.o) .................................. s.h.2

3476⁶ Verdant Boy (47) (MPNaughton) 9–9-6 JakiHouston (9) (sn outpcd: hdwy over 1f out: styd on) ....................................................................... 2.3

3196 Debsy Do (USA) (65) (SGNorton) 3–8-8 ‡⁵OPears (4) (w ldrs: nt qckn fnl f) ..... 1½.4

3359 Superbrave (73) (WJarvis) 6–9-6 MTebbutt (8) (b: lw: trckd ldrs: hmpd over 2f out: kpt on one pce fnl f) ....................................................... s.h.5

3413² Almasa (61) (DMorris) 4–9-1 GDuffield (2) (chsd ldrs: effrt & sltly hmpd over 2f out: one pce) ...................................................................... 3.6

3004 Thrie-Na-Helah (IRE) (67) (v) (RMWhitaker) 3–8-13 ACulhane (10) (chsd ldrs: hmpd & lost pl over 2f out: styd on fnl f) .......................... nk.7

3499 Soba Guest (IRE) (67) (JBerry) 3–8-11 ‡⁷PRoberts (3) (led tl over 2f out: sn wknd) ..................................................................................... 1.8

3496² Dokkha Oyston (IRE) (68) (JBerry) 4–9-6 GCarter (16) (sn drvn along: nvr rchd ldrs) ...................................................................................... 3.9

3359 Sir Boudle (IRE) (79) (CRNelson) 3–9-4 JReid (1) (chsd ldrs tl wknd over 1f out) nk.10

3400 Lightning Decision (38) (JPSmith) 4–9-0 JQuinn (14) (in tch over 3f) ............ 3½.11

3518³ Loft Boy (61) (bl) (JDBethell) 9–9-6 PatEddery (5) (w ldrs tl wknd over 1f out) hd.12

3499⁶ The Right Time (47) (bl) (JParkes) 7–8-13 ‡⁷VHalliday (18) (chsd ldrs tl lost pl over 2f out) ............................................................................ 1.13

Believe in Me (IRE) (BAMcMahon) 3–8-5 ‡⁷SSanders (15) (b: s.s: a bhd) ... 1.14

2300³ Black Coral (IRE) (60) (CFWall) 3–8-7 PaulEddery (13) (chsd ldrs: edgd lft over 2f out: sn wknd) ...................................................................... nk.15

3196 Pageboy (79) (Fav) (PCHaslam) 3–9-4 LPiggott (2) (chsd ldrs over 2f: sn lost pl) 4.16

Bold Celt (CBBBooth) 9–9-0 GOldroyd (19) (swtg: nvr wnt pce) ................. 5.17

3413 Katie-a (IRE) **(53)** (v) *(RMWhitaker)* 3–8-13 MBirch (17) (lw: ref to r: t.n.p) ............ 0
3466 Fletchinni (IRE) **(29)** (bl) *(ABailey)* 3–8-12 KFallon (12) (Withdrawn under
Starter's orders: collapsed in stalls: dead: all stakes refunded) 0

5/1 Pageboy, 6/1 Sir Boudle (IRE), Superbrave, DRUM SERGEANT, 7/1 Crystal Heights (FR), 9/1 Dokkha Oyston (IRE), Almasa, 12/1 Thrie-Na-Helah (IRE), 14/1 Black Coral (IRE), 16/1 Loft Boy, Debsy Do (USA), 25/1 Katie-a (IRE), Soba Guest (IRE), Believe in Me (IRE), 33/1 The Right Time, Verdant Boy, 50/1 Bold Celt, Fletchinni (IRE), 66/1 Lightning Decision. CSF £49.65, Tote £5.90: £2.70 £2.50 £19.50 (£19.40). Mr W. A. Sellers (MALTON) bred by Snarehill Stud Co. 19 Rn; No bid
1m 19.40 (9.20)
SF—24/23/15/–/8/–

**3633**  NEWINGTON HOTEL YORK RACEGOERS' H'CAP (0-100) £6160.00 (£1840.00: £880.00: £400.00) 5f
3-00 (3-26)

3120² **Bunty Boo (89)** *(BAMcMahon)* 3–8-13 ‡7SSanders (6) (lw: trckd ldrs: led ½-wy: sn clr: hung lft: drvn out) ................................. —1
3356 Never so Sure **(96)** (v) *(ABailey)* 4–10-0 LPiggott (4) (trckd ldrs: effrt over 1f out: r.o u.p: nt rch wnr) .......................... 1½.2
3469⁴ Gondo **(74)** (v) *(EJAlston)* 5–8-6 KFallon (9) (lw: sn wl outpcd & bhd: gd hdwy over 1f out: r.o u.p fnl f) .................... nk.3
3437 Never in the Red **(84)** (v) *(JBerry)* 4–9-2 GCarter (11) (stdd s: sn bhd: kpt on appr fnl f: nrst fin) ................... 2.4
3460³ Languedoc **(61)** *(MPNaughton)* 5–7-7 JakiHouston (3) (sn outpcd: styd on appr fnl f: nt rch ldrs) .............. nk.5
3469 On the Edge **(70)** *(TDBarron)* 4–8-2 AlexGreaves (10) (sn wl bhd: hdwy over 1f out: r.o nr fin) ............. 1.6
3207 Prince Belfort **(64)** (v) *(MPNaughton)* 4–7-10 DBiggs (5) (chsd ldrs tl wknd over 1f out) ........ d.h.6
3464⁶ Tigani **(62)** (v) *(DWChapman)* 6–7-8 SWood (1) (led to ½-wy: wknd over 1f out) ..... hd.8
3518⁵ Absolution **(72)** *(MPNaughton)* 8–8-4 GDuffield (8) (lw: sn wl outpcd) ........... 2½.9
3397 Super Rocky **(72)** *(RBastiman)* 3–8-3 JQuinn (7) (lw: w ldrs over 3f: sn wknd) 1½.10
3564a³ Taufan Blu (IRE) **(92)** (bl) **(Fav)** *(MJohnston)* 3–9-9 MRoberts (12) (sn bhd & drvn along: hung rt ½-wy & fnd nil) ........ 7.11

4/1 Taufan Blu (IRE), 11/2 Never so Sure, 6/1 BUNTY BOO, 7/1 Never in the Red, Gondo, 9/1 Absolution, 12/1 Super Rocky, 14/1 On the Edge, Languedoc, 16/1 Tigani, 20/1 Prince Belfort. CSF £35.55, CT £213.90. Tote £5.70: £2.00 £1.80 £2.70 (£20.10). Mrs R. C. Mayall (TAMWORTH) bred by Mrs J. McMahon. 11 Rn
63.62 sec (6.12)
SF—62/71/50/52/28/33

**3634**  GOODRAMGATE H'CAP (0-100) £5253.50 (£1568.00: £749.00: £339.50) 1¼m 85y
3-30 (3-52)

3468★ **Majed (IRE) (69)** *(MrsGRReveley)* 4–7-4 ‡7DarrenMoffatt (1) (lw: dwlt s: hld up: effrt over 2f out: led over 1f out: r.o) ............. —1
3345★ Linpac West **(100)** *(CWCElsey)* 6–10-0 MRoberts (4) (trckd ldrs: rdn to ld 2f out: r.o fnl f) ........... ½.2
3292⁴ Vallance **(81)** *(PWHarris)* 4–8-9 PaulEddery (2) (led to 2f out: kpt on same pce) 5.3
3468⁴ Westholme (USA) **(71)** *(MHEasterby)* 4–7-10⁽²⁾ ‡3SMaloney (5) (hld up: effrt & outpcd over 2f out: kpt on u.p ins fnl f) ........ hd.4
3526★ Cold Shower (IRE) **(71)** **(Fav)** *(JAGlover)* 3–7-7 JQuinn (3) (trckd ldrs: ev ch over 2f out: rdn & wknd over 1f out) ............ nk.5

5/2 Cold Shower (IRE), 3/1 MAJED (IRE), Linpac West, 5/1 Vallance, 7/1 Westholme (USA). CSF £10.98, Tote £3.60: £1.50 £1.50 (£4.50). Laurel (Leisure) Limited (SALTBURN) bred by Rowlane Investments in Ireland. 5 Rn
2m 20.47 (12.97)
SF—36/72/43/29/25

**3635**  WALMGATE NURSERY £5663.00 (£1694.00: £812.00: £371.00) 6f 214y
4-00 (4-18)
(Weights raised 8 lb)

3482⁵ **Dutosky (67)** *(MJCamacho)* 8-10 NConnorton (2) (chsd ldrs: rdn & edgd rt over 1f out: led ins fnl f: styd on wl) ........... —1
3401★ Ribhi (USA) **(74)** **(Fav)** *(DMorley)* 9-3 WCarson (4) (lw: unruly s: hld up: hdwy over 2f out: swtchd 1f out & sn ev ch: nt qckn nr fin) ....... 1½.2
3347⁵ Abergele **(76)** *(JGFitzGerald)* 9-5 KFallon (3) (w ldrs: led ½-wy: clr over 1f out: hung lft & hdd ins fnl f: sn btn) ........ 2.3
3482³ So so **(78)** *(TDBarron)* 9-2 AlexGreaves (8) (sn chsng ldrs: nt qckn fnl 2f) ......... 7.4
2049★ Harpoon Louie **(75)** *(MHEasterby)* 9-4 KDarley (11) (lw: hld up & bhd: stdy hdwy 2f out: nvr plcd to chal) ......... 2½.5
3530 Royal Diva **(74)** *(MissSEHall)* 9-3 PatEddery (10) (in tch tl outpcd ½-wy: n.d after) 5.6
3160⁴ Daily Sport Don **(58)** *(RHannon)* 8-1 GDuffield (9) (hld up & bhd: effrt ½-wy: wandered: n.d) ....... hd.7

2876³ Montone (IRE) (72) *(CBBBooth)* 9-1 GOldroyd (1) (hld up: effrt ¹/₂-wy: n.d) ..... hd.**8**
3482² George Roper (66) (v) *(MRChannon)* 8-9 BRouse (6) (w ldrs tl wknd over 2f out) ...................................................................................... nk.**9**
3358 Sporting Spirit (60) *(DWChapman)* 8-3 SWood (12) (lw: sn bhd) ................... ¹/₂.**10**
3482 Arctic Guest (IRE) (52) *(MJohnston)* 7-9 DBiggs (13) (sn bhd & rdn along) ... 10.**11**
3338⁴ Reasons for Love (IRE) (69) *(JJO'Neill)* 8-12 MRoberts (7) (lw: led to ¹/₂-wy: sn lost pl & eased) ....................................................... 1¹/₂.**12**
3303 Aviator's Dream (64) *(JFBottomley)* 8-7 GBardwell (5) (lw: s.i.s: sn trckng ldrs: rdn & wknd over 2f out) ................................................. 4.**13**

15/8 Ribhi (USA), 6/1 Daily Sport Don, 13/2 Royal Diva, 7/1 George Roper, 9/1 Abergele, 10/1 Reasons for Love (IRE), 11/1 Harpoon Louie (USA), 12/1 DUTOSKY, So so, 14/1 Montone (IRE), 16/1 Arctic Guest (IRE), 20/1 Ors. CSF £38.08, CT £217.21. Tote £17.10: £3.50 £1.50 £3.50 (£22.80). Lord Matthews (MALTON) bred by Lord Victor Matthews. 13 Rn
1m 31.92 (9.52)
SF—43/45/41/22/11/–

**3636** GILLYGATE GRADUATION STKS (3-Y.O) £5922.00 (£1428.00)
1m 5f 194y
4-30 (4-36)

2996² Allegan (USA) *(Fav)* *(HRACecil)* 9-3 PatEddery (1) (mde all: clr 6f out: canter) . —**1**
2836 Faugeron (82) *(GWragg)* 9-1 MHills (2) (drvn along & lost tch over 5f out) ...... dist.**2**

1/12 ALLEGAN (USA), 7/1 Faugeron. Tote £1.10. Mr K. Abdulla (NEWMARKET) bred by Juddmonte Farms, Inc. in USA. 2 Rn
3m 10.8 (hand)

**3637** E.B.F. SPURRIERGATE STKS (Mdn 2-Y.O) £4542.00 (£1356.00: £648.00: £294.00)
6f
5-00 (5-01)

Soviet Secret *(Fav)* *(BHanbury)* 9-0 MRoberts (3) (b: w'like: leggy: trckd ldrs: effrt over 2f out: led over 1f out: drvn clr) ............................. —**1**
3401⁴ Flashman *(FHLee)* 9-0 WCarson (2) (led: drvn along over 2f out: hdd over 1f out: one pce) ................................................. 3.**2**
3175 Lola Wants *(CFWall)* 8-9 PRobinson (4) (hld up: effrt 2f out: kpt on same pce fnl f) ................................................. ³/₄.**3**
Lamsonetti *(RMWhitaker)* 8-9 ACulhane (5) (neat: scope: dwlt s: sn trckng ldrs: effrt & rn green 2f out: wknd over 1f out) ..................... 2¹/₂.**4**
3517 Ashgore *(MJohnston)* 9-0 RPElliott (1) (w ldrs tl wknd 2f out) ..................... 3.**5**

15/8 SOVIET SECRET(op Evens), 85/40 Lamsonetti(op 4/1), 4/1 Flashman, 11/2 Lola Wants, 10/1 Ashgore. CSF £8.88, Tote £2.00: £1.20 £1.50 (£2.30). Mr Hamad Ali (NEWMARKET) bred by Petra Bloodstock Agency Ltd. 5 Rn
1m 21.56 (11.36)

T/Trio: Race 3: £38.60 (40.3 Tckts). T/Jkpt: £29,817.40 (1.1 Tckts). T/Plpt: £50.10 (132.55 Tckts).     WG

# YORK (L-H)
## Thursday, October 8th [Good to soft]
Going Allowance: St: 0.80 sec (S); Rest: 0.60 sec per fur (Y)     Wind: slt across

Stalls: high

**3638** JOSHUA TETLEY STKS (2-Y.O.F) £6248.00 (£1728.00: £824.00)
6f 214y
2-00 (2-00)

3480* Great Steps (82) *(Fav)* *(EWeymes)* 8-13 MRoberts (2) (mde virtually all: qcknd 2f out: rdn & r.o wl fnl f) ................................. —**1**
Black Mischief *(HRACecil)* 8-8 WRyan (1) (neat: bit bkwd: trckd ldrs: chal over 1f out: nt qckn nr fin) ................................. ¹/₂.**2**
Sunrise Morning (USA) *(PWChapple-Hyam)* 8-8 JReid (3) (lt-f: s.i.s: sn rcvrd & cl up: rdn 2f out: sn outpcd) ............................. 2¹/₂.**3**

Evens GREAT STEPS(op 6/4), 2/1 Black Mischief(op Evens), 7/2 Sunrise Morning (USA). CSF £2.91, Tote £2.00 (£1.40). Mr Norman A. Blyth (MIDDLEHAM) bred by N. A. Blyth. 3 Rn
1m 29.91 (7.51)
SF—49/42/34

**3639** AINSTY (S) H'CAP (3-Y.O) (0-90) £4386.00 (£1308.00: £624.00: £282.00)
1¹/₄m 85y
2-30 (2-31)

2993 Edge of Darkness (54) *(JWHills)* 7-9 ‡3DHarrison (7) (hld up: effrt over 2f out: led ins fnl f: hld on wl) ................................. —**1**
3485³ Boogie Bopper (IRE) (57) *(Fav)* *(MBell)* 7-12 ‡3FNorton (2) (hld up: stdy hdwy over 2f out: chal u.p ins fnl f: nt qckn nr fin) ...................... nk.**2**

3461⁶ Diamond Wedding (USA) **(63)** (bl) *(NAGraham)* 8-7 WCarson (3) (a.p: led wl over 2f out: rdn & hung lft 1f out: sn hdd & btn) .................. 3.3

3266 Double Sherry **(49)** *(RMWhitaker)* 7-0 ‡7DWright (6) (cl up: chal 4f out: rdn & btn appr fnl f) .................. 4.4

*3378* Trove **(77)** *(MrsNMacauley)* 9-7 DMcKeown (5) (s.s: sme hdwy 3f out: n.d) ....... 5.5

3405² Cosmic Future **(60)** (bl) *(SPCWoods)* 8-4 WWoods (1) (led tl hdd 4f out: wknd wl over 2f out) .................. 15.6

3494³ Shadanza (IRE) **(49)** *(APStringer)* 7-7 JQuinn (4) (lw: trckd ldrs: led 4f out tl wl over 2f out: sn rdn & wknd) .................. 1.7

LONG HANDICAP: Double Sherry 7-2, Shadanza (IRE) 7-6.

**3/1** Boogie Bopper (IRE), **7/2** Diamond Wedding (USA), **4/1** EDGE OF DARKNESS, Shadanza (IRE), **5/1** Cosmic Future, **16/1** Trove, **33/1** Double Sherry. CSF £15.30, Tote £4.30: £1.90 £1.80 (£5.90). Mrs S. Bosher (LAMBOURN) bred by Mrs M. Tinkler. 7 Rn; Sold C Tinkler Snr 6,000 gns                    2m 20.17 (12.67)
SF—17/19/22/–/18/–

---

**3640**  ALLIED DUNBAR H'CAP (0-100) £7765.00 (£2320.00: £1110.00: £505.00)
**7f 202y**                                                                3-00 (3-04)

(Weights raised 9 lb)

3526² **Forever Diamonds (68)** (Fav) *(MHEasterby)* 5-8-4 ‡3SMaloney (1) (hld up: hdwy on bit to ld over 2f out: rdn & r.o wl) .................. —1

3468³ Shaffaaf (USA) **(66)** (bl) *(PDEvans)* 4-8-5 MRoberts (4) (hld up & bhd: hdwy 3f out: styd on: nvr able to chal) .................. 3.2

3428 En Attendant (FR) **(85)** *(BHanbury)* 4-9-10 BRaymond (13) (hld up: stdy hdwy 3f out: shkn up appr fnl f: hung lft & styd on) .................. nk.3

3212³ Double Echo (IRE) **(68)** *(JDBethell)* 4-8-7 AMunro (5) (lw: hld up: hdwy 3f out: rdn 2f out: kpt on one pce) .................. 3¹/₂.4

3473⁴ Tamim (USA) **(88)** *(HThomsonJones)* 3-9-9 NCarlisle (6) (lw: led tl hdd over 2f out: on outpcd) .................. s.h.5

3143 Mbulwa **(58)** *(SEKettlewell)* 6-7-8⁽¹⁾ ‡3FNorton (3) (chal over 2f out: sn rdn & grad wknd) .................. 1.6

3349 Arany **(84)** *(MHTompkins)* 5-9-9 PRobinson (12) (lw: bhd: effrt over 3f out: nvr able to chal) .................. 3.7

3135 Enaya **(73)** *(RWArmstrong)* 3-8-8 WCarson (7) (w ldrs: rdn 3f out: wknd 2f out) 1¹/₂.8

983 Cambrian **(84)** *(MrsJCecil)* 3-9-5 SCauthen (10) (prom tl rdn & wknd wl over 2f out) .................. 12.9

2852 Killy **(80)** *(FHLee)* 3-9-1 PaulEddery (8) (chsd ldrs tl wknd 3f out) .................. hd.10

398 Cashtal Dazzler **(62)** *(NTinkler)* 5-8-1 JFanning (2) (prom tl wknd 3f out) ......... 5.11

3514* Salda **(75)** *(RMWhitaker)* 3-8-10 (6x) GCarter (11) (hdwy on outside 4f out: sn rdn & wknd) .................. 4.12

3277 Berseto (USA) **(74)** *(HRACecil)* 3-8-9 WRyan (9) (chsd ldrs tl wknd 3f out) ...... 8.13

**3/1** FOREVER DIAMONDS, **5/1** Double Echo (IRE), **7/1** Shaffaaf (USA), **8/1** Salda, **10/1** En Attendant (FR), Cambrian, **12/1** Mbulwa, Berseto (USA), **14/1** Enaya, Arany, **16/1** Tamim (USA), **20/1** Killy, **33/1** Cashtal Dazzler. CSF £24.05, CT £178.00. Tote £3.60: £1.50 £2.20 £3.50 (£8.10). Mrs J. B. Russell (MALTON) bred by J. B. Russell. 13 Rn                    1m 42.66 (6.66)
SF—62/54/72/44/59/27

---

**3641**  BRITISH GAS N.E. APP'CE H'CAP (0-90) £6056.00 (£1808.00: £864.00: £392.00)
**1m 3f 195y**                                                            3-30 (3-33)

3339⁴ **Bigwheel Bill (IRE) (75)** *(JWWatts)* 3-9-6 StephenDavies (13) (sn led: rdn & r.o wl fnl 2f) .................. —1

3438³ Much Sought After **(75)** *(DMorley)* 3-9-3 ‡3EBentley (4) (hld up: smooth hdwy over 3f out: hrd rdn over 1f out: kpt on) .................. 1.2

3540² Simply-H (IRE) **(74)** *(MBell)* 3-9-2 ‡3PTurner (1) (a.p: effrt 3f out: kpt on: nt pce to chal) .................. 3.3

3309* First Bid **(57)** *(RMWhitaker)* 5-8-7 ‡3GParkin (2) (led early: chsd ldrs: rdn & styd on one pce fnl 3f) .................. hd.4

3357³ Philgun **(64)** *(CWCElsey)* 3-8-6 ‡3MHumphries (15) (a chsng ldrs: rdn & r.o one pce wl over 2f out) .................. 4.5

3461 Comstock **(75)** (Fav) *(NTinkler)* 5-9-11 ‡3SWynne (6) (hld up: hdwy on ins ent st: rdn over 2f out: sn rdn & no ex) .................. 2.6

3436⁶ Billy Blazer **(80)** *(MHTompkins)* 3-9-8 ‡3SMulvey (11) (hld up & bhd: effrt over 3f out: nvr rchd ldrs) .................. 2.7

3116⁶ Smiles Ahead **(60)** *(PJBevan)* 4-8-13 NGwilliams (9) (prom tl wknd fnl 3f) .... 1¹/₂.8

3076 Eurotwist **(68)** *(TDBarron)* 3-8-10 ‡3VHalliday (12) (in tch: effrt 4f out: no imp) . 10.9

892* White Willow **(58)** *(MrsGRReveley)* 3-9-4 ‡3DarrenMoffatt (5) (bit bkwd: nvr nr to chal) .................. hd.10

3461⁵ I Perceive **(69)** *(FHLee)* 5-9-5 ‡3GForster (14) (n.d) .................. 1.11

2070³ Cutleaf **(80)** *(WJarvis)* 3-9-11 KRutter (10) (in tch tl wknd over 3f out) ............ ¹/₂.12

3357² Take by Storm (IRE) **(75)** *(GMMoore)* 3–9–3 ‡³SSanders (3) (cl up tl wknd over
3f out) .................................................................................................................. nk.**13**
3116 Hillzah (USA) **(73)** *(RBastiman)* 4–9–9 ‡³HBastiman (8) (hung rt appr st: a bhd) s.h.**14**

**11/2** Comstock, **6/1** Simply-H (IRE), Billy Blazer, **7/1** First Bid, **8/1** BIGWHEEL BILL (IRE), **9/1** White Willow, **10/1**
I Perceive, Take by Storm (IRE), **12/1** Eurotwist, Philgun, Cutleaf, **14/1** Hillzah (USA), Much Sought After, **25/1**
Smiles Ahead. CSF £113.97, CT £676.28. Tote £8.40: £2.90 £6.90 £2.20 (£107.00). Mr Gerald Cooper
(RICHMOND) bred by Mrs T. V. Ryan in Ireland. 14 Rn                                     2m 39.78 (12.78)
SF—51/46/39/29/20/35

## 3642

TETLEY BITTER NURSERY    £7375.00 (£2200.00: £1050.00: £475.00)
**6f**                                                                      4-00 (4-01)

3267² **Birchwood Sun (70)** *(RHollinshead)* 8-3(3) WRyan (1) (lw: hdwy ½-wy: led
over 1f out: swvd rt ins fnl f: kpt on wl cl home) ............................... —**1**
2724⁶ Nutty Brown **(69)** *(SGNorton)* 7-13 ‡³FNorton (3) (chsd ldrs: swtchd rt over 1f
out: kpt on wl nr fin) ............................................................................. nk.**2**
3347² Egg **(62)** (bl) *(TDBarron)* 7-9 JFanning (5) (outpcd & bhd: hdwy 2f out: kpt on
wl nr fin) ............................................................................................... nk.**3**
3550² Mr Butch **(66)** *(MRChannon)* 7-13 JQuinn (11) (bhd stands' side: hdwy 2f out:
rdn & kpt on wl fnl f) ............................................................................. 2.**4**
3478⁶ Pilgrim Bay (IRE) **(66)** *(JBerry)* 7-13 GCarter (2) (w ldr: led over 1f out: sn hdd:
wkng whn hmpd ins fnl f) ...................................................................... 1.**5**
3347 Grinnell **(62)** *(DenysSmith)* 7-9 DaleGibson (8) (outpcd & bhd tl sme late hdwy) 4.**6**
3472★ Call Me I'M Blue (IRE) **(67)** (Fav) *(NTinkler)* 8-0(1) KDarley (4) (led tl hdd & wknd
over 1f out) ........................................................................................... 1½.**7**
3347★ Silverlocks **(88)** *(MissSEHall)* 9-7 NConnorton (7) (in tch 4f: sn rdn & btn) ....... nk.**8**
3353 Peacefull Reply (USA) **(71)** *(FHLee)* 8-4 PaulEddery (6) (chsd ldrs 4f: sn wknd) 8.**9**
3123⁴ Tajdif (USA) **(88)** *(DMorley)* 9-7 WCarson (9) (effrt ½-wy: rdn & n.d) ............... 1½.**10**
1396★ Ten to Six **(79)** *(EWeymes)* 8-12 DMcKeown (10) (bit bkwd: sn outpcd stands'
side & a bhd) ........................................................................................ 10.**11**

**85/40** Call Me I'M Blue (IRE), **100/30** Mr Butch, **13/2** Tajdif (USA), **15/2** Egg, **8/1** Silverlocks, **12/1** Pilgrim Bay (IRE), **14/1** BIRCHWOOD SUN, **16/1** Peacefull Reply (USA), Grinnell, **20/1** Nutty Brown. CSF
£234.96, CT £2,062.35. Tote £21.30: £3.30 £7.30 £2.20 (£106.30). Mr B. Swain (UPPER LONGDON) bred by
The Hall Stud Ltd. 11 Rn                                                         1m 17.18 (6.98)
SF—45/40/35/31/27/7

## 3643

GREEN HOWARDS CUP (Claiming Stks) (2-Y.O) £5435.50 (£1624.00: £777.00:
£353.50)    **1m 205y**                                                      4-30 (4-33)

3385 **Mhemeanles (83)** *(MHEasterby)* 8-6 ‡³SMaloney (4) (cl up: disp ld over 3f out:
led over 2f out: drvn out) .................................................................... —**1**
3498★ Cure the King (IRE) **(78)** *(SGNorton)* 9-3 KDarley (5) (chsd ldrs: effrt 3f out: styd
on wl u.p fnl f) ...................................................................................... 1½.**2**
3502² Grand Dancer (IRE) **(70)** *(RJRWilliams)* 8-4 RCochrane (3) (a.p: kpt on u.p fnl
2f: nt pce to chal) ................................................................................. 1½.**3**
3274★ Marius (IRE) **(81)** (Fav) *(BWHills)* 8-12 SCauthen (1) (b.hind: lw: led tl hdd over
2f out: grad wknd) ................................................................................ 2.**4**
3364⁶ Conspicuous **(72)** *(PFICole)* 9-0 AMunro (10) (hld up: gd hdwy 4f out: nt
qckn fnl 2f) ........................................................................................... ½.**5**
3474³ Fort Vally **(69)** *(BWMurray)* 8-2 JFortune (2) (dwlt: hdwy ent st: sn hrd drvn:
styd on: nt pce to chal) ......................................................................... nk.**6**
3512 Innocent Abroad (DEN) *(CBBBooth)* 7-7 JFanning (6) (trckd ldrs: effrt 3f out: sn
rdn & one pce) .................................................................................... 2½.**7**
3303 Moonstruck Bard **(45)** *(SPCWoods)* 8-2 WWoods (12) (broke wl: stdd: effrt 3f
out: sn rdn & btn) ................................................................................. 10.**8**
3480⁶ Forever Shineing *(MJCamacho)* 8-1 NConnorton (9) (chsd ldrs tl wknd fnl 3f) ... 1.**9**
3291 Clar Dubh (IRE) *(MHTompkins)* 7-9 DaleGibson (8) (prom: rdn 4f out: sn wknd) 5.**10**
Tom the Tank *(NTinkler)* 7-12 JQuinn (11) (w'like: bkwd: a bhd) ....................... 3.**11**

**7/4** Marius (IRE), **4/1** MHEMEANLES, **6/1** Grand Dancer (IRE), **15/2** Cure the King (IRE), **8/1** Conspicuous (IRE),
**11/1** Forever Shineing, **14/1** Fort Vally, **25/1** Clar Dubh (IRE), Innocent Abroad (DEN), **33/1** Ors. CSF £32.52,
Tote £5.40: £1.80 £2.40 £1.80 (£19.60). Mr Les Ford (MALTON) bred by Miss J. Chaplin. 11 Rn; Cure The King
(IRE) clmd C Bjorling £20,150                                                    1m 59.33 (10.33)
SF—18/24/6/8/8/—

## 3644

E.B.F. SANCTON STKS (Mdn 2-Y.O.C & G) £4347.00 (£1296.00: £618.00: £279.00)
**7f 202y**                                                                  5-00 (5-01)

3512² **Bin Ajwaad (IRE)** (Fav) *(BHanbury)* 9-0 BRaymond (1) (a gng wl: led ins fnl f:
impressive) ........................................................................................... —**1**
3314³ Amaam Amaam *(JHMGosden)* 9-0 SCauthen (3) (b: led tl hdd ins fnl f: no ch w
wnr) ...................................................................................................... 3½.**2**

34022 Doctoor (USA) *(WJarvis)* 9-0 AMunro (4) (lw: trckd ldrs: chal 3f out: sn rdn & r.o one pce) .................................................................................................. nk.3
3030 Demurrer *(JGFitzGerald)* 9-0 KFallon (2) (outpcd & bhd: styd on fnl 3f: n.d) ...... 6.4
3200 Amiarge *(MBrittain)* 9-0 KDarley (6) (cl up tl wknd wl over 1f out) ..................... s.h.5
George Dillingham *(PWHarris)* 9-0 WRyan (7) (w'like: bit bkwd: prom tl rdn & btn over 2f out) ......................................................................................... nk.6

**11/10** BIN AJWAAD (IRE), **7/4** Amaam Amaam, **6/1** Doctoor (USA), **10/1** Amiarge, **20/1** Demurrer, **25/1** George Dillingham. CSF £3.49, Tote £2.40: £1.40 £1.30 (£1.50). Mr A. Merza (NEWMARKET) bred by Tullamaine Castle Stud and Partners in Ireland. 6 Rn
1m 47 (11)
SF—7/–/–/–/–/–

T/Trio: Race 3: £51.70 (25.3 Tckts). T/Jkpt: Not won; £1,266.71 to Ascot 9/10/92. T/Plpt: £287.10 (19.65 Tckts).
AA

## BAY MEADOWS  (L-H)
### Saturday, September 19th [Firm]

**3645a**    ASCOT H'CAP (3-Y.O) £29412.00    **1m 110y**

31316 **MODERNISE (USA)** *(RCharlton)* 3-8-1 CNakatani ..................................... —1
Major Impact (USA) *(America)* 3-8-5 GStevens .............................................. nose.2
Don's Terry (USA) *(America)* 3-8-4 RSabille ................................................. nose.3
Tote 15.40 (1-2) 5.40 2.60 (1-2-3) 4.60 2.60 4.80. Mr K.Abdulla (BECKHAMPTON) bred by Rhydian Morgan-Jones in USA. 8 Rn
1m 43

## 2893a—HOPPEGARTEN  (R-H)
### Saturday, October 3rd [Good]

**3646a**    PRIX ZINO DAVIDOFF - PREIS DER DEUTSCHEN EINHEIT (Gp 3) £98592.00    **1¼m**

32374 **PERPENDICULAR** *(HRACecil)* 4-9-6 WRyan ........................................... —1
2768a* Arastou (GER) *(Germany)* 3-8-8 AHelfenbein ........................................ 1½.2
32375 Goofalik (USA) *(France)* 5-9-6 GDubroeucq ......................................... 3½.3
3108a* KARINGA BAY *(GLewis)* 5-9-6 BRouse (btn more than 7½l by wnr) .................... 8
Tote 52DM: 17DM 16DM 26DM (SF: 248DM). Lord Howard de Walden (NEWMARKET) bred by Lord Howard de Walden. 11 Rn
2m 0.9

## 3454a—BELMONT PARK  (L-H)
### Saturday, October 3rd [Turf Firm, Dirt Fast]

**3647a**    VOSBURGH STKS (Grade 1)    £64171.00    **7f (dirt)**

**Rubiano (USA)** *(America)* 5-9-0 JulieKrone ............................................. —1
3124* SHEIKH ALBADOU *(AAScott)* 4-9-0 WRSwinburn ........................................ ¾.2
Salt Lake (USA) *(America)* 3-8-11 MSmith ................................................. 1¼.3
Tote 5.20 (1-2) 2.40 3.20 (1-2-3) 2.20 2.80 3.40. Centennial Farms (F.Schulhofer,AMERICA) bred by Kirsmith Racing Associates in USA. 8 Rn
1m 22.8

**3648a**    TURF CLASSIC INVITATIONAL STKS (Grade 1)    £160428.00    **1½m (turf)**

3229a2 **Sky Classic (CAN)** *(Canada)* 5-9-0 PDay ............................................ —1
Fraise (USA) *(America)* 4-9-0 PValenzuela .............................................. 1¾.2
3454a* Solar Splendor (USA) *(America)* 5-9-0 HMcCauley ................................... 2½.3
3332a3 Tel Quel (FR) *(France)* 4-9-0 WRSwinburn .......................................... nk.4
Libor (USA) *(America)* 5-9-0 J-LSamyn ................................................... 7½.5
3454a6 ADAM SMITH *(LMCumani)* 4-9-0 MSmith ............................................... ¾.6
Tote 4.00 (1-2) 2.60 4.00 (1-2-3) 2.10 2.10 2.10. Sam Son Farm (J.Day,CANADA) bred by Sam Son Farm in Canada. 6 Rn
2m 24.4 (0.4 under best)

## 3455a—LONGCHAMP  (R-H)
### Saturday, October 3rd [Soft]
Going Allowance: 0.95 sec per fur (S)

**3649a**    CIGA PRIX DE ROYALLIEU (Gp 2) (F & M) £30960.00    **1½m 110y (Grande)**

1497a6 **Fabulous Hostess (USA)** *(France)* 4-9-0 ODoleuze (hld up in rr: hdwy 2f out: hrd rdn fnl f: led last strides) .................................................. —1

1498a Good to Dance (IRE) *(France)* 3–8-8 GMosse (hld up: hdwy & nt clr run 2f out:
led 1f out tl no ex last strides) .................................... nose.2

2181* SPRING *(JLDunlop)* 3–8-8 SCauthen (a.p: 4th st: hrd rdn over 1f out: r.o one
pce) ............................................................................. 2.3

3190⁶ ALWAYS FRIENDLY *(HCandy)* 4–9-0 AMunro (8th st: n.m.r on ins 2f out: r.o fnl
f) .................................................................................. ½.4

3456a* Afaladja (IRE) (Fav) *(France)* 3–8-8 GGuignard (led to 1f out: one pce) .......... 1½.5

3337a³ Gloria Mundi (FR) *(France)* 5–9-0 WMongil (bhd tl hdwy fnl 2f: nrst fin) .......... nk.6

La Monalisa (FR) *(France)* 4–9-0 FHead (9th st: gd hdwy 2f out: ev ch appr fnl f:
sn wknd) .......................................................... hd.7

1824a⁴ Halesia (USA) *(France)* 3–8-8 DBoeuf (prom: 5th st: wknd over 1f out) .......... 1½.8

1824a⁶ Berceau (USA) *(France)* 3–8-8 PatEddery (prom: 6th st: one pce fnl 2f) ....... s.nk.9

3330a River Nymph (USA) *(France)* 3–8-8 ELegrix (prom: 3rd st: wknd fnl 2f) ............ 6.10

2504a⁵ Villandry (USA) *(France)* 4–9-0 TJarnet (7th st: wknd 2f out) ................... 1½.11

Gold Script (FR) *(France)* 3–8-8 MBoutin (2nd st: hrd rdn & wknd 2f out) ........ 5.12

11/4 Afaladja, 7/2 Always Friendly, 4/1 Villandry (USA), Halesia (USA), 56/10 FABULOUS HOSTESS
(USA), 13/2 Spring, 16/1 River Nymph (USA), 17/1 La Monalisa (FR), 19/1 Gloria Mundi (FR), 21/1 Good to
Dance (IRE), 22/1 Ors. Tote 6.60f: 3.10f 5.90f 3.30f (95.70f). Mr J.Wertheimer (Mrs C.Head,FRANCE) bred by
Wertheimer & Frere in USA. 12 Rn                              2m 53.8 (17.2)
SF–47/40/36/41/32/37

## 3650a
CIGA PRIX DU CADRAN (Gp 1)   £51600.00   2¹/₂m (Nouv & Grande)

2982a* **Sought Out (IRE)** (Fav) *(France)* 4–8-13 CAsmussen (mde all: hrd rdn &
flashed tail fnl 2f: easily) ........................................... —1

3453a³ DRUM TAPS (USA) *(LordHuntingdon)* 5–9-2 AMunro (trckd ldrs: 3rd st: rdn to
chse wnr 2f out: no imp) ................................. 4.2

Dariyoun (USA) *(France)* 4–9-2 FHead (mid div: 4th st: styd on one pce) ...... 1½.3

3197² WITNESS BOX (USA) *(JHMGosden)* 5–9-2 SCauthen (chsd wnr: 2nd st: rdn &
wknd 2f out) ........................................................ 2½.4

1477³ Great Marquess (bl) *(France)* 5–9-2 MJKinane (hld up: 5th st: nvr nr ldrs) ........ 5.5

3323a* Le Montagnard (FR) *(France)* 4–9-2 CPhelippeau (hld up: sme hdwy 4f out: 6th
st: sn wknd) .......................................... hd.6

644a² Proud Panther (FR) *(France)* 6–9-2 ABadel (nvr gng wl: a last: t.o fnl 4f) ......... dist.7

11/10 SOUGHT OUT (IRE), 7/4 Drum Taps (USA), 7/2 Great Marquess, Witness Box (USA), 9/1 Le Montagnard
(FR), 16/1 Proud Panther (FR), 24/1 Dariyoun (USA). Tote 2.10f: 1.40f 1.50f (SF: 5.80f). Lord Weinstock
(J.E.Hammond,FRANCE) bred by Ballymacoll Stud Farm in Ireland. 7 Rn                    4m 41.1 (23.1)
SF–58/57/55/52/47/46

## 3651a
CIGA GRAND CRITERIUM (Gp 1) (2-Y.O.C & F) £123839.00   1m (Grande)

2790* **TENBY** (Fav) *(HRACecil)* 2–8-11 PatEddery (a.p: racd wd: 2nd st: led 2f out: sn
rdn: r.o wl) .................................................... —1

3235* BLUSH RAMBLER (USA) *(MRStoute)* 2–8-11 SCauthen (chsd ldrs: 6th st: hrd
rdn & hdwy 2f out: r.o: nt rch wnr) ......................... 2¹/₂.2

2978a* Basim (USA) *(Ireland)* 2–8-11 CRoche (w ldrs: led 3f out to 2f out: sn hrd rdn: r.o
one pce fnl f) .......................................... s.h.3

3448a³ Seaton Delaval *(France)* 2–8-11 TJarnet (a.p: 5th st: styd on fnl f) .......... 2¹/₂.4

3331a² Kingmambo (USA) *(France)* 2–8-11 FHead (hld up in rr: outpcd ½-wy: 8th st:
sme hdwy fnl 2f: nvr nr to chal) ........................ 1½.5

1605* LINDON LIME (USA) *(PFICole)* 2–8-11 TQuinn (last tl sme late hdwy: nvr nrr) .... 3.6

3331a⁴ CANASKA STAR *(PAKelleway)* 2–8-11 MJKinane (s.s: 10th st: hdwy 2f out: no
hdwy fnl f) ...................................................... 1.7

3331a³ SPLENDENT (USA) *(PFICole)* 2–8-11 AMunro (hld up: 4th st: sme hdwy on ins
2f out: wknd) ................................................ 8.8

3448a* Kadounor (FR) *(France)* 2–8-11 GGuignard (led 5f: 3rd st: sn wknd) ........... nose.9

2979a* Master Peace (FR) *(France)* 2–8-11 ELegrix (prom to ½-wy: 7th & wkng st) 1½.10

Fastness (IRE) *(France)* 2–8-11 CAsmussen (prom tl lost pl 3f out: 9th & btn st) 1½.11

17/10 TENBY, 7/2 Fastness (IRE), 4/1 Blush Rambler (USA), Seaton Delaval, 5/1 Kadounor (USA), 10/1
Kingmambo (USA), 14/1 Master Peace (FR), 15/1 Splendent (USA), Lindon Lime (USA), 17/1 Basim (USA),
42/1 Canaska Star. Tote 2.70f: 1.70f 2.30f 4.50f (8.50f). Mr K.Abdulla (NEWMARKET) bred by Juddmonte
Farms. 11 Rn                                                      1m 46.9 (9.2)
SF–73/65/64/56/51/42

## 3652a
CIGA PRIX DOLLAR (Gp 2)   £30960.00   1m 1f 165y (Grande)

2891a² **Sillery (USA)** (Fav) *(France)* 4–9-0 FHead (broke wl: stdd: 6th st: smooth hdwy
on bit 2f out: led 1f out: easily) ........................................... —1

2095a* Wiorno *(France)* 4-9-0 TJarnet (hld up: 7th st: stdy hdwy fr 2fout: ev ch 1f out: nt rch wnr) ....................................................... 1.2
3138⁴ CORRUPT (USA) *(PWChapple-Hyam)* 4-9-0 CAsmussen (5th st: hdwy 2f out: ev ch 1f out: one pce) .................................................. 1¹/₂.3
3336a² HALF A TICK (USA) *(PFICole)* 4-9-0 TQuinn (3rd st: led 2f out to 1f out: sn wknd) ....................................................................... 5.4
3089* SPARTAN SHAREEF (IRE) *(CEBrittain)* 3-8-9 AMunro (a mid div: 4th st: no hdwy fnl 2f) ................................................................. nk.5
3560a* KNIFEBOX (USA) *(JHMGosden)* 4-9-0 MJKinane (8th st: n.d) ............... 10.6
2837 ALNASR ALWASHEEK *(MRStoute)* 3-9-0 PatEddery (chsd ldrs: 3rd st: sn hrd rdn, btn & eased) .................................................... 1¹/₂.7
2316a* POLLEN COUNT (USA) *(JHMGosden)* 3-9-0 SCauthen (led 8f: eased whn btn) 1¹/₂.8

2/1 SILLERY (USA), 5/2 Pollen Count (USA), Knifebox (USA), 7/2 Alnasr Alwasheek, 4/1 Corrupt (USA), 8/1 Wiorno, 11/1 Half a Tick (USA), 26/1 Spartan Shareef (IRE). Tote 3.00f: 1.20f 1.50f 1.60f (11.40f). Mrs A.Head (Mrs C.Head,FRANCE) bred by Alec Head in USA. 8 Rn
2m 11.6 (12.1)
SF—74/72/69/59/53/38

### 3653a
CIGA PRIX DE LUTECE (Gp 3) (3-Y.O) £22704.00 1m 7f *(Moyenne)*

3111a⁶ **Dadarissime (FR)** *(France)* 3-8-11 CAsmussen ................................... —1
1356a Jamshid (JPN) *(France)* 3-8-9 TJarnet ........................................... 1¹/₂.2
3211⁶ ASSESSOR (IRE) *(RHannon)* 3-9-0 TQuinn ......................................... ³/₄.3
2840² LANDOWNER (IRE) *(JHMGosden)* 3-9-0 MJKinane (btn further 7¹/₂l) ................ 6
3190* NIODINI (USA) *(MRStoute)* 3-8-13 PatEddery (btn 12³/₄l by wnr) ................. 7
Tote 13.50f: 3.10f 1.60f 2.70f (36.30f). Sir J.Goldsmith (G.Bridgland,FRANCE) bred by J de Souza Lage in France. 9 Rn
3m 30 (18)
SF—60/56/59

## LONGCHAMP (R-H)
### Sunday, October 4th [Soft]
Going Allowance: 0.70 sec per fur (S)

### 3654a
CIGA PRIX DU ROND-POINT (Gp 2) £41280.00 1m **(Grande)**

3455a³ **Arazi (USA)** (Fav) *(France)* 3-8-11 SCauthen (hld up in tch: 6th st: qcknd to ld 2f out: eased nr fin: impressive) ....................................... —1
3131* CALLING COLLECT (USA) *(LMCumani)* 3-8-11 LDettori (hld up: 8th st: effrt 2f out: r.o wl) ........................................................... 4.2
2998⁴ ALHIJAZ *(JLDunlop)* 3-9-4 JReid (in tch: 7th st: hdwy over 1f out: r.o wl) ........ hd.3
3237 LUCKY LINDY (IRE) (bl) *(RHannon)* 3-8-11 MJKinane (prom: 4th st: styd on one pce fnl 2f) ................................................... 1¹/₂.4
3222a* Acteur Francais (USA) *(France)* 4-9-0 DBoeuf (bhd early: 10th st: r.o wl fnl 2f: nrst fin) ............................................................... 1.5
3109a* Dampierre (USA) *(France)* 4-9-0 TJarnet (a.p: 3rd st: sn outpcd) ................. 1¹/₂.6
3371* TIK FA (USA) (bl) *(BHanbury)* 3-8-11 WRSwinburn (chsd ldr tl lost pl 4f out: 5th st: sn btn) .................................................... ¹/₂.7
1356a Silver Kite (USA) *(France)* 3-8-11 GMosse (w ldr: 2nd st: sn btn) ............... nk.8
Primer Amor (SPA) *(Spain)* 5-9-0 WCarson (9th st: n.d) ........................... 5.9
Code Breaker (FR) *(France)* 3-8-11 ELegrix (a in rr: 11th st: n.d) ............... s.nk.10
2789* MOJAVE *(MRStoute)* 3-8-11 PatEddery (mde most 6f: wknd qckly) ............... 2¹/₂.11

6/5 ARAZI (USA), 13/4 Dampierre (USA), 23/4 Calling Collect (USA), 15/2 Mojave, 14/1 Lucky Lindy (IRE), Tik Fa (USA), 17/1 Acteur Francais (USA), 25/1 Alhijaz, 26/1 Silver Kite (USA), 31/1 Primer Amor (SPA), 34/1 Code Breaker (FR). Tote 2.20f: 1.70f 2.20f 4.70f (12.20f). Sheikh Mohammed (F.Boutin,FRANCE) bred by Ralph Wilson Jnr. in USA. 11 Rn
1m 44 (6.3)
SF—86/74/80/68/67/62

### 3655a
PRIX MARCEL BOUSSAC (Gp 1) (2-Y.O.F) £82559.00 1m **(Grande)**

**Gold Splash (USA)** *(France)* 2-8-11 GMosse (trckd ldr: 2nd st: led 2f out: r.o wl) —1
3449a* Kindergarten (Jt-Fav) *(France)* 2-8-11 SCauthen (mid div: 6th st: hdwy 2f out: r.o wl fnl f: jst failed) .............................................. s.nk.2
2991* LOVE OF SILVER (USA) *(CEBrittain)* 2-8-11 MRoberts (prom: 5th st: chal over 1f out: no ex fnl f) ..................................................... ³/₄.3
3112a² Rouquette *(France)* 2-8-11 ABadel (hld up: 9th st: gd hdwy fr over 1f out: r.o: nrst fin) .................................................................. 1.4
3191* MARILLETTE (USA) *(JHMGosden)* 2-8-11 PatEddery (hld up & bhd: 11th st: hmpd whn hdwy 2f out: r.o) ................................. hd.5
3449a² Lorelie (FR) *(France)* 2-8-11 FHead (bhd: 8th st: sme late hdwy) ............... 2¹/₂.6

| | | |
|---|---|---|
| 2981a² | Secrage (USA) *(Italy)* 2–8–11 BJovine (a mid div: 7th st: effrt 2f out: n.d) | hd.7 |
| 3112a³ | Sissingaya (USA) *(France)* 2–8–11 DBoeuf (prom: 3rd st: grad wknd) | ½.8 |
| | Marviah (USA) *(France)* 2–8–11 CAsmussen (led 6f: wknd qckly) | 1.9 |
| 3191 | NEMEA (USA) *(JRFanshawe)* 2–8–11 LDettori (10th st: n.d) | ½.10 |
| 3112a* | Cox Orange (USA) (Jt-Fav) *(France)* 2–8–11 TJarnet (prom: 4th st: wknd qckly & eased) | 15.11 |

**1/2** Cox Orange (USA), Marillette (USA), Kindergarten, **4/1** Secrage (USA), **27/4** Love of Silver (USA), **11/1** GOLD SPLASH (USA), **17/1** Rouquette, Lorelie (FR), **25/1** Marviah (USA), **35/1** Sissingaya (USA), **70/1** Nemea (USA). Tote 12.40f: 2.80f 1.70f 2.40f (29.60f). Mr J.Wertheimer (Mrs C.Head,FRANCE) bred by Wertheimer & Frere in USA. 11 Rn

1m 44.9 (7.2)

SF—73/72/70/67/66/58

## 3656a
CIGA PRIX DE L'ABBAYE DE LONGCHAMP (Gp 1)  £72239.00  **5f (st)**

| | | |
|---|---|---|
| 3124² | **MR BROOKS** (Fav) *(RHannon)* 5–9–11 LPiggott (prom: led over 1f out: sn clr: eased nr fin) | —1 |
| 1060⁶ | KEEN HUNTER (USA) *(JHMGosden)* 5–9–11 SCauthen (a.p: ev ch tl outpcd fnl f) | 2.2 |
| 3223a* | ELBIO (bl) *(PJMakin)* 5–9–11 JReid (hmpd s: gd hdwy fnl f: fin fast) | nk.3 |
| 3564a* | Bezelle *(Ireland)* 3–9–7 PShanahan (chsd ldrs: kpt on fnl f) | 1.4 |
| 3326a* | Flowing (USA) *(Ireland)* 4–9–7 MJKinane (hld up: no imp tl r.o nr fin) | s.nk.5 |
| | Bold N' Flashy (CAN) *(Canada)* 3–9–11 RDosRamos (broke wl & wnt lft s: led over 3f: one pce) | nk.6 |
| 3442⁴ | TWAFEAJ (USA) *(BHanbury)* 3–9–7 WRSwinburn (a bhd: n.d) | 2.7 |
| 2767a³ | Dream Talk (bl) *(France)* 5–9–11 GMosse (spd 3f) | 1½.8 |
| 3210⁴ | PEPERONATA (IRE) *(BWHills)* JLowe (broke wl: sn in rr & bhd) | 3.9 |

**9/10** MR BROOKS, **11/4** Keen Hunter (USA), **23/4** Elbio, **27/4** Flowing, **13/1** Bold N' Flashy (CAN), **17/1** Dream Talk, **27/1** Twafeaj (USA), **39/1** Bezelle, **64/1** Peperonata (IRE). Tote 1.90f: 1.10f 1.50f 1.40f (4.60f). Mr Paul Green (MARLBOROUGH) bred by Mrs J.R.Rossdale. 9 Rn

62.3 sec (5.3)

SF—75/67/66/59/58/60

## 3657a
CIGA PRIX DE L'ARC DE TRIOMPHE (Gp 1) (C & F) £515996.00  **1½m (Grande)**

| | | |
|---|---|---|
| 3332a² | **Subotica (FR)** *(France)* 4–9–4 TJarnet (mid div: 8th st: effrt 2f out: r.o wl u.p to ld ins fnl f: r.o) | —1 |
| 3211* | USER FRIENDLY (Fav) *(CEBrittain)* 3–8–8 GDuffield (broke wl: stdd & plld hrd: 4th st: led 2f out tl ins fnl f: r.o) | nk.2 |
| 3111a⁴ | Vert Amande (FR) *(France)* 4–9–4 ELegrix (hld up: 16th st: gd hdwy over 1f out: r.o) | 2.3 |
| 3327a² | St Jovite (USA) *(Ireland)* 3–8–11 CRoche (a.p: 2nd st: led over 2f out: sn hdd: hrd rdn & kpt on) | 1½.4 |
| 3332a⁴ | Saganeca (USA) *(France)* 4–9–1 WMongil (last early: 13th st: r.o fnl 2f: nrst fin) | s.h.5 |
| 3327a* | DR DEVIOUS (IRE) *(PWChapple-Hyam)* 3–8–11 JReid (a in tch: 7th st: hdwy 2f out: no ex appr fnl f) | ¾.6 |
| 3455a* | Arcangues (USA) *(France)* 4–9–4 GMosse (hld up: 14th st: sme hdwy over 1f out: r.o) | 2.7 |
| 3330a* | Jolypha (USA) *(France)* 3–8–8 PatEddery (hmpd s & lost pl: 17th st: r.o fnl f) | nk.8 |
| 3330a⁴ | Verveine (USA) *(France)* 3–8–8 DBoeuf (mid div: 10th st: wknd fnl f) | nose.9 |
| 3454a² | Dear Doctor (FR) *(France)* 5–9–4 CAsmussen (hld up: 18th st: n.d) | ¾.10 |
| 3453a* | MASHAALLAH (USA) *(JHMGosden)* 4–9–4 SCauthen (stdd s: prom: 6th st: sn outpcd & btn) | ½.11 |
| 3329a² | Petit Loup (USA) *(France)* 3–8–11 WRSwinburn (prom: 5th st: effrt 2f out: sn btn) | nk.12 |
| 3332a* | Magic Night (FR) *(France)* 4–9–1 ABadel (hld up: 15th st: n.m.r & hmpd 2f out: nt rcvr) | nk.13 |
| 3429⁵ | SAPIENCE *(DRCElsworth)* 6–9–4 TQuinn (led after 2f tl over 2f out) | 1½.14 |
| 2345² | SADDLERS' HALL (IRE) *(MRStoute)* 4–9–4 WCarson (led 2f: a.p: 3rd st: sn btn) | 1½.15 |
| 3330a⁵ | Market Booster (USA) *(Ireland)* 3–8–8 MJKinane (nvr m.r: 11th st: sn wknd) | 1½.16 |
| 3138³ | SEATTLE RHYME (USA) *(DRCElsworth)* 3–8–11 MRoberts (prom over 8f: 9th & wkng st) | ½.17 |
| 3329a | Polytain (FR) *(France)* 3–8–11 LDettori (hld up: 12th & btn st: t.o fnl 2f) | 18 |

**13/4** User Friendly, **9/2** Magic Night (FR), **11/2** Jolypha (USA), **13/2** St Jovite (USA), **7/1** Dr Devious (IRE), **88/10** SUBOTICA (FR), **12/1** Arcangues (USA), Verveine (USA), **16/1** Dear Doctor (FR), **21/1** Saddlers' Hall (IRE), **26/1** Mashaallah (USA), **31/1** Petit Loup (USA), **36/1** Market Booster (USA), **37/1** Polytain (FR), **55/1** Seattle Rhyme (USA), **75/1** Vert Amande (FR), **104/1** Saganeca (USA), **133/1** Sapience. Tote 9.80f: 3.00f 3.10f 10.50f (30.00f). Mr O.Lecerf (A.Fabre,FRANCE) bred by Paul de Moussac in France. 18 Rn

2m 39 (9)

SF—98/87/93/80/83/77/80

## 3658a
CIGA PRIX DE L'OPERA (Gp 2) (F & M) £41280.00    **1m 1f 55y (Grande)**

3231a[3] **Hatoof (USA)** (Fav) (France) 3-9-0 WRSwinburn (hld up: 11th st: gd hdwy 2f out: led nr fin: r.o wl) ................................................ **—1**

La Favorita (FR) (France) 3-8-9 GMosse (hld up: 8th st: rapid hdwy to ld 1f out: hdd & no ex nr fin) ....................................... ½.**2**

3228a[2] RUBY TIGER (PFlCole) 5-9-2 TQuinn (w ldr: 2nd st: sn led: hdd 1f out: styd on one pce) ......................................... **1.3**

Sporades (USA) (France) 3-8-9 TJarnet (a: 4th st: one pce fnl 2f) ........... nose.**4**

1231a Leariva (USA) (France) 5-9-0 CAsmussen (bhd: last st: rapid late hdwy: nt rch ldrs) ............................................................... s.h.**5**

3330a Palomelle (FR) (France) 3-8-9 LDettori (mid div: 9th st: styd on one pce fnl f) ... **2.6**

381a[2] Wedding Ring (IRE) (France) 3-8-9 MBoutin (in tch: 5th & hmpd st: gd late hdwy) ................................................... nk.**7**

3330a[6] Trishyde (USA) (France) 3-8-11 FHead (in rr: 10th st: effrt over 1f out: sn one pce) .......................................................... **1.8**

3334a★ MELPOMENE (USA) (LordHuntingdon) 4-9-0 MRoberts (mid div: 6th st: sn outpcd) ............................................................. ¾.**9**

2894a[3] Rosefinch (USA) (France) 3-9-0 SCauthen (mid div: 7th st: n.d) ............... **1.10**

1498a Garendare (France) 3-8-9 DBoeuf (mde most tl over 2f out: sn wknd) ............... **11**

2091a★ Formidable Flight (France) 3-8-9 ELegrix (prom early: 3rd st: wknd qckly) ........ **12**

**18/10** HATOOF (USA), **2/1** Leariva (USA), **19/4** Ruby Tiger, **5/1** Sporades (USA), **25/4** Rosefinch (USA), **15/2** Trishyde (USA), **12/1** Melpomene (USA), **29/1** Formidable Flight, **34/1** Wedding Ring (IRE), **36/1** Palomelle (FR), **55/1** Garendare, **57/1** La Favorita (FR). Tote 2.80f: 1.70f 6.00f 1.80f (59.50f). Maktoum Al Maktoum (Mrs C.Head,FRANCE) bred by Gainsborough Farm Inc. in USA. 12 Rn                    2m 2.5 (9.2)
SF—60/54/57/50/53/43


1645a—## DORTMUND (R-H)
### Sunday, October 4th [Good to firm]

## 3659a
GROSSER PREIS DER CONTINENTALE (Gp 2) (3-Y.O.C & F) £42254.00    **1¾m**

2316a[4] **Non Partisan (USA)** (France) 3-9-2 PaulEddery ..................................... **—1**

2895a[3] Chesa Plana (Germany) 3-8-11 MRimmer ................................................ nk.**2**

Protektor (GER) (Germany) 3-9-2 THellier ............................................... nk.**3**

3458a[4] SILVERNESIAN (USA) (JLDunlop) 3-9-2 AMunro ............................... ½.**4**

Tote 33DM: 17DM 18DM 52DM (SF: 149DM). Mr K.Abdulla (A.Fabre,FRANCE) bred by Juddmonte Farms in USA. 12 Rn                    2m 55.6


3457a—## SAN SIRO (R-H)
### Sunday, October 4th [Heavy]

## 3660a
PREMIO DEL DADO (listed race) (2-Y.O) £20930.00    **1m**

3175★ **ARMAN'S SAX (IRE)** (JLDunlop) 2-8-7 WRyan ..................................... **—1**

3233a[2] Zlata Husa (IRE) (Italy) 2-8-7 AHerrera ....................................... 1½.**2**

Pelder (IRE) (Italy) 2-8-9 SSoto ...................................................... **2.3**

Tote 27L: 24L 33L 20L (713L). Gerecon Italia (ARUNDEL) bred by J.Cummins in Ireland. 11 Rn    1m 49.1


3233a—## FLORENCE (R-H)
### Sunday, October 4th [Heavy]

## 3661a
PREMIO CASCINE (listed race)    £20930.00    **7f 110y**

3447a[2] **LECH (USA)** (MrsLPiggott) 4-8-7 BRaymond ..................................... **—1**

Amandhla (IRE) (Austria) 4-8-9 WLord ................................................ **5.2**

Il Corsair (IRE) (Italy) 4-8-7 SLandi ................................................ **3.3**

Tote 28L: 16L 26L 22L (68L). Mr Henryk De Kwiatkowski (NEWMARKET) bred by Kennelot Stables Ltd. in USA. 12 Rn                    1m 38

3427—**ASCOT (R-H)**
**Friday, October 9th [Good to soft, Soft patches]**
Going Allowance: St: 0.10 sec per fur; Rnd: 0.30 sec per fur (G)　　　Wind: str half bhd

Stalls: centre

**3662**　　DUKE OF EDINBURGH STKS (Mdn 2-Y.O.C & F) £8460.00 (£2520.00: £1200.00:
　　　　　£540.00)　**6f**　　　　　　　　　　　　　　　　2-00 (2-01)

　　**Rustic Craft (IRE)** *(DRCElsworth)* 9-0 JWilliams (4) (str: scope: dwlt: lost pl
　　　　　over 2f out: rallied over 1f out: led ins fnl f: r.o) ................... —1
　　Khattat (USA) *(Fav)* *(JLDunlop)* 9-0 WCarson (1) (w'like: scope: hld up: led on
　　　　　bit over 2f out: shkn up & hdd ins fnl f: no ex) ..................... 1½.2
　　Aghar (IRE) *(DRCElsworth)* 9-0 TQuinn (7) (w'like: scope: a.p: ev ch over 1f
　　　　　out: one pce) .......................................................... 2½.3
　　Wali (USA) *(PTWalwyn)* 9-0 RHills (6) (cmpt: bit bkwd: a.p: ev ch over 1f out:
　　　　　one pce) ................................................................ 2½.4
　　Wisham (USA) *(BHanbury)* 9-0 BRaymond (5) (leggy: scope: a.p: ev ch over 1f
　　　　　out: sn wknd) .......................................................... 4.5
　　Frosty Morning *(CEBrittain)* 8-9 MRoberts (3) (neat: led over 3f) ........... 5.6
　　Correspondence (CAN) *(JHMGosden)* 9-0 SCauthen (2) (cmpt: dwlt: bhd fnl
　　　　　3f) .................................................................... 3½.7

**6/5** Khattat (USA), **7/2** Wisham (USA), **13/2** Correspondence (CAN), **11/1** Frosty Morning(8/1—12/1), **12/1**
Wali (USA)(op 5/1), RUSTIC CRAFT (IRE), **16/1** Aghar (IRE)(op 6/1). CSF £25.26, Tote £14.50: £3.40 £1.40
(£7.40). Mr D. R. C. Elsworth (WHITSBURY) bred by Exors of the late Comdr H. Grenfell in Ireland. 7 Rn
　　　　　　　　　　　　　　　　　　　　　　　　　　1m 16.67 (3.07)
　　　　　　　　　　　　　　　　　　　　　　　　　SF—50/44/34/24/8/–

**3663**　　MITRE H'CAP (0-110) £8541.50 (£2552.00: £1221.00: £555.50)　**1¼m** 2-30 (2-33)
　　　　　　　　　　　　　　　　　(Weights raised 4 lb)

3576* **Plan Ahead (70)** *(GLewis)* 3–7-7 ‡DHarrison (7) (lw: rdn over 3f out: hdwy over
　　　　　1f out: led ins fnl f: r.o wl) ......................................... —1
3333a* Only Royale (IRE) **(89)** *(LMCumani)* 3–9-1 LDettori (6) (lw: hld up: led
　　　　　over 1f out: sn hdd: r.o one pce) ..................................... 1½.2
3293* Rose Alto **(85)** *(JRFanshawe)* 4–9-3 GDuffield (3) (lw: hdwy 2f out: led 1f out tl
　　　　　ins fnl f: one pce) .................................................... ¾.3
3368 Fire Top **(92)** *(RAkehurst)* 7–9-10 TQuinn (4) (lw: led 6f: led 3f out tl over 1f out:
　　　　　sn wknd) .............................................................. 5.4
3368⁴ Selaah **(85)** *(MRStoute)* 5–9-3 PatEddery (1) (5th st: wknd over 1f out) ........... ¾.5
3369 Canny Chronicle **(84)** *(MHTompkins)* 4–9-2 PRobinson (2) (nvr nr to chal) ...... nk.6
3445 Seal Indigo **(85)** *(RHannon)* 4–9-3 JReid (11) (lw: nt clr run wl over 1f out:
　　　　　nvr nrr) ............................................................... nk.7
3363⁴ Host (IRE) **(89)** *(CEBrittain)* 3–9-1 MRoberts (5) (led 4f out to 3f out: 2nd st:
　　　　　wknd over 1f out) ..................................................... 2½.8
3436² Fengari **(74)** *(PTWalwyn)* 3–8-0 DBiggs (9) (swtg: 6th st: wknd over 2f out) ... 2½.9
3363⁶ Cottonwood **(75)** *(LordHuntingdon)* 3–8-1 AMunro (8) (4th st: wknd 2f out) .... hd.10
3436³ Milzig (USA) **(96)** *(DRCElsworth)* 3–9-8 SCauthen (10) (3rd st: wknd wl over 1f
　　　　　out) ................................................................... 1½.11

**7/4** Only Royale (IRE), **11/2** PLAN AHEAD, **8/1** Selaah, **10/1** Fengari, Fire Top, **14/1** Milzig (USA), Seal Indigo
(IRE), Rose Alto, **16/1** Canny Chronicle, **20/1** Ors. CSF £14.70, CT £111.95. Tote £4.50: £1.40 £1.50 £4.70
(£4.40). Planflow (Leasing) Ltd (EPSOM) bred by R. F. and Mrs Knipe. 11 Rn　　2m 10.82 (6.52)
　　　　　　　　　　　　　　　　　　　　　　　　　SF—44/63/63/60/51/49

**3664**　　OCTOBER STKS (listed race) (3-Y.O.F) £10867.50 (£3240.00: £1545.00: £697.50)
　　　　　**1m (rnd)**　　　　　　　　　　　　　　　　　　3-05 (3-08)

3213⁵ **Well Beyond (IRE) (96)** *(BWHills)* 8-11 PatEddery (2) (lw: mde virtually all: hrd
　　　　　rdn over 1f out: r.o wl) ............................................... —1
3439* Jdaayel **(88)** *(ACStewart)* 8-11 MRoberts (6) (2nd st: ev ch fnl f: r.o wl) ........... hd.2
1462² Culture Vulture (USA) **(120)** *(PFICole)* 9-3 TQuinn (3) (lw: 4th st: ev ch ins fnl f:
　　　　　r.o) ................................................................... ½.3
3213² Midnight Air (USA) **(104)** *(Fav)* *(HRACecil)* 8-11 WRyan (7) (lw: 5th st: ev ch ins
　　　　　fnl f: unable qckn) .................................................... 2½.4
3203* Nashville Blues (IRE) **(88)** *(JWHills)* 8-11 MHills (1) (lw: 6th st: rdn over 2f out:
　　　　　one pce) .............................................................. ½.5
3442 Cambrian Hills (IRE) **(96)** *(PWChapple-Hyam)* 8-11 JReid (4) (lw: 3rd st: rdn
　　　　　over 2f out: one pce) .................................................. ¾.6
2496 Brave the Wind **(45)** *(IABalding)* 8-11 RCochrane (5) (s.s: bhd fnl 3f) ................ 8.7

**13/8** Midnight Air (USA), **2/1** Culture Vulture (USA)(op 11/10), **7/2** Jdaayel, **12/1** WELL BEYOND (IRE), **16/1** Nashville Blues (IRE)(op 10/1), **50/1** Cambrian Hills (IRE), **150/1** Brave the Wind. CSF £47.89, Tote £13.00: £3.30 £2.00 (£13.90). Mr K. Abdulla (LAMBOURN) bred by Melchester Ltd in Ireland. 7 Rn   1m 46.99 (7.39)
SF—22/21/25/9/7/5

## 3665

AIM AVIATION NURSERY    £11235.00 (£3360.00: £1610.00: £735.00)
7f                                      3-40 (3-44)

| | | |
|---|---|---|
| 3364² | **Brigante Di Cielo (79)** *(RHannon)* 8-5 BRaymond (12) (a.p: hrd rdn over 1f out: led ins fnl f: drvn out) | —1 |
| 3530 | Chain Dance **(87)** *(MRStoute)* 8-13 WRSwinburn (16) (hld up: hrd rdn over 1f out: r.o wl ins fnl f) | ½.2 |
| 3530² | No Reservations (IRE) **(88)** *(RFJohnsonHoughton)* 8-9 ‡5JWeaver (5) (hld up: led over 1f out tl ins fnl f: unable qckn) | ½.3 |
| 3364* | Shamam (USA) **(80)** *(PTWalwyn)* 8-6 RHills (13) (lw: hdwy 2f out: r.o ins fnl f) | ¾.4 |
| 3181* | Burooj **(85)** *(DMorley)* 8-11 WCarson (6) (hrd rdn & hdwy over 1f out: r.o ins fnl f) | nk.5 |
| 3200 | My Patriarch **(80)** *(JLDunlop)* 8-6 TQuinn (17) (lw: hdwy over 2f out: hrd rdn over 1f out: r.o one pce) | s.h.6 |
| 2597* | Defenceless **(79)** *(RHannon)* 8-5 BRouse (11) (swtg: led over 5f out tl over 1f out: one pce) | ½.7 |
| 3240 | Midwinter Dream **(75)** *(DRCElsworth)* 8-1 PaulEddery (2) (nvr nr to chal) | nk.8 |
| 3300³ | Expo Mondial (IRE) **(92)** *(JMPEustace)* 9-4 LDettori (4) (nvr nrr) | hd.9 |
| 3574² | Satin Dancer **(81)** (Fav) *(GHarwood)* 8-7 KDarley (1) (nvr nrr) | 1½.10 |
| 3530³ | Home From the Hill (IRE) **(76)** *(MBell)* 8-2 MHills (7) (b.nr hind: nvr nrr) | 1½.11 |
| 3324a⁵ | Empire Pool **(93)** *(LordHuntingdon)* 9-5 LPiggott (14) (lw: spd 5f) | s.h.12 |
| 3286² | Awestruck **(77)** *(WJHaggas)* 8-3 GDuffield (8) (led over 1f: wkng whn hmpd over 1f out) | 1.13 |
| 3372 | Range Rider (IRE) **(77)** (bl) *(CEBrittain)* 8-3 PRobinson (10) (prom 4f: wkng whn hmpd over 1f out) | 1½.14 |
| 3419⁵ | Hostile Witness (IRE) **(83)** *(RHannon)* 8-5 BRouse (11) (a bhd) | 12.15 |
| 2462 | Regal Aura (IRE) **(95)** *(GHarwood)* 9-7 AClark (5) (lw: a bhd) | 2½.16 |

*3199² Chevrotain (13/2) Withdrawn (broke out of stalls) : not under orders — Rule 4 applies*
*3530 Seasonal Splendour (IRE) (14/1) Withdrawn (on veterinary advice) : not under orders*

**5/1** Satin Dancer, **13/2** Burooj, **8/1** Midwinter Dream, **11/1** Home From the Hill (IRE), Chain Dance, **12/1** No Reservations (IRE), **14/1** Hostile Witness (IRE), Defenceless, **20/1** BRIGANTE DI CIELO, Awestruck, My Patriarch, Shamam (USA), Empire Pool, **33/1** Expo Mondial (IRE), Range Rider (IRE), **50/1** Regal Aura (IRE). CSF £166.43, CT £1,835.48. Tote £28.50: £4.40 £2.90 £2.90 £5.70 (£153.40). Mr P. J. Christey (MARLBOROUGH) bred by Whitsbury Manor Stud. 16 Rn     1m 29.92 (3.42)
SF—50/56/50/45/49/43

## 3666

WYNDHAM H'CAP (0-110) £10143.00 (£3024.00: £1442.00: £651.00)
2m 45y                                    4-15 (4-18)

| | | |
|---|---|---|
| 3431* | **Bold Resolution (IRE) (65)** (Fav) *(CACyzer)* 4-8-5 MRoberts (2) (hdwy over 5f out: 5th st: led wl over 1f out: pushed out) | —1 |
| 3467* | Nijmegen **(68)** *(JGFitzGerald)* 4-8-8 KFallon (11) (lw: hdwy 2f out: hrd rdn over 1f out: r.o) | 1½.2 |
| 3431² | Jungle Dancer (IRE) **(87)** *(MRStoute)* 4-9-13 PatEddery (12) (swtg: hrd rdn & hdwy 2f out: unable qckn) | 1.3 |
| 3515* | Prince Mercury **(77)** *(JLDunlop)* 3-8-6 (3x) JReid (10) (lw: rdn & hdwy wl over 1f out: r.o one pce) | 1.4 |
| 3445³ | Whitechapel (USA) **(82)** *(LordHuntingdon)* 4-9-8 WRSwinburn (7) (4th st: ev ch over 1f out: one pce) | ½.5 |
| 2899* | Our Aisling **(78)** *(SGNorton)* 4-8-13 ‡5OPears (1) (lw: s.s: nvr nrr) | 7.6 |
| 3352² | Five to Seven (USA) **(80)** *(SGNorton)* 3-8-9 LPiggott (5) (lw: led over 14f) | 8.7 |
| 3415⁴ | Haitham **(79)** *(RAkehurst)* 5-9-5 RCochrane (3) (2nd st: wknd wl over 1f out) | 6.8 |
| 3431 | Welshman **(61)** *(MBlanshard)* 6-8-1 JQuinn (4) (lw: 3rd st: wknd over 2f out) | 4.9 |
| 3467 | Calicon **(63)** *(IABalding)* 6-8-3 MHills (8) (lw: 6th st: wknd over 2f out) | 3.10 |
| 3438⁶ | Black Sapphire **(63)** *(MHTompkins)* 5-8-3 PRobinson (6) (lw: prom 10f) | 20.11 |
| 2899 | Gay Glint **(88)** *(NAGraham)* 5-10-0 SCauthen (9) (lw: hdwy over 5f out: wknd over 3f out) | nk.12 |

**11/4** BOLD RESOLUTION (IRE), **7/2** Prince Mercury, **10/1** Nijmegen, Whitechapel (USA), Jungle Dancer (USA), **12/1** Haitham, Five to Seven (USA), **14/1** Our Aisling, Welshman, **16/1** Gay Glint, **40/1** Ors. CSF £28.35, CT £219.35. Tote £3.80: £1.70 £3.10 £2.10 (£26.80). Mr R. M. Cyzer (HORSHAM) bred by G. O'Brien in Ireland. 12 Rn     3m 36.09 (9.59)
SF—43/44/62/40/55/39

**3667**    MAYFLOWER APP'CE STKS    £3655.00 (£1090.00: £520.00: £235.00)
1m (st)

4-45 (4-49)

3433² **Olette (84)** *(GWragg)* 3-8-2 JWeaver (2) (a.p: led over 3f out: pushed out) ....... —1
3427³ Bold Pursuit (IRE) **(94)** (Fav) *(RHannon)* 3-8-7 ‡³RPerham (4) (hld up: hrd rdn 2f
    out: unable qckn) ....................................................................... 1¹/₂.2
3439  Muhit (USA) **(77)** *(PTWalwyn)* 3-8-2 KRutter (8) (a.p: ev ch over 2f out: wknd fnl
    f) ...................................................................................... 10.3
3265² Flaming Arrow **(90)** *(HRACecil)* 4-8-8 ‡³StephenDavies (1) (rdn over 4f out: nvr
    nr to chal) ........................................................................... 2.4
    Disputed Call (USA) *(JWHills)* 3-8-7 DHarrison (3) (str: rdn & no hdwy fnl 2f) .. hd.5
2807² Hightown-Princess (IRE) **(35)** (v) *(MPMuggeridge)* 4-8-1 ‡⁵RossBerry (7)
    (swtg: bhd fnl 2f) .................................................................. 8.6
3511* Duty Sergeant (IRE) **(45)** (bl) *(MPMuggeridge)* 3-8-4 ‡³BRussell (5) (led over 4f) 4.7
3287⁶ State of Affairs **(41)** *(CAHorgan)* 5-8-11 SMaloney (6) (s.s: bhd fnl 4f) ............. 6.8
    Johns Joy *(DRCElsworth)* 7-8-5 ‡⁶JHunter (9) (bit bkwd: a bhd) ..................... s.h.9

7/4 Bold Pursuit (IRE), 9/4 OLETTE, 100/30 Flaming Arrow, 10/1 Muhit (USA), 20/1 Johns Joy, 25/1 Disputed Call (USA), 50/1 State of Affairs, Duty Sergeant (IRE), 100/1 Hightown-Princess (IRE). CSF £6.09, Tote £3.00: £1.40 £1.20 £2.20 (£3.30). Sir Philip Oppenheimer (NEWMARKET) bred by P. D. and Mrs Player. 9 Rn
1m 42.05 (2.65)
SF—60/60/25/25/23/–

**3668**    CORINTHIAN H'CAP (Amateurs)    £3720.00 (£1110.00: £530.00: £240.00)
1¹/₂m

5-15 (5-17)

3057⁴ **Ivor's Flutter (72)** *(DRCElsworth)* 3-10-1⁽¹⁾ MrCVigors (2) (lw: hdwy over 3f
    out: 4th st: edgd lft over 1f out: led ins fnl f: r.o wl) ..................... —1
3118⁵ Maamur (USA) **(65)** (Fav) *(DBurchell)* 4-10-2 MrNMiles (9) (led: clr 8f out: hdd
    ins fnl f: r.o) ........................................................................ 1.2
3393⁵ Shadow Bird **(57)** *(GAPritchard-Gordon)* 5-9-8 MrPPritchard-Gordon (6) (lw:
    3rd st: rdn over 1f out: unable qckn) ................................... 2¹/₂.3
3610⁴ Taylors Prince **(61)** *(HJCollingridge)* 5-9-12 MrPClose (8) (lw: 2nd st: hung lft
    2f out: sn wknd) .................................................................. 12.4
3357⁴ Kinematic (USA) **(91)** *(JHMGosden)* 4-12-0 MrJDurkan (4) (lw: rdn over 3f out:
    5th st: wknd over 2f out) .................................................... 4.5
3520  Black Jewel **(60)** *(MDIUsher)* 9-9-11⁽⁴⁾ MrGShenkin (5) (nvr nr to chal) ......... 2.6
3101  Sanawi **(57)** *(PDEvans)* 5-9-8⁽¹⁾ MrWMcLaughlin (7) (lw: 6th st: wknd over 2f
    out) ................................................................................. 20.7
1970  Coxann **(56)** *(JCMcConnochie)* 6-9-7 MrETolhurst (10) (lw: bhd fnl 6f) ........... 10.8
    Christmas Hols **(57)** (bl) *(MissLBower)* 6-9-8⁽¹⁾ MrMMannish (3) (a bhd: t.o fnl
    6f) ................................................................................. dist.9
LONG HANDICAP: Black Jewel 8-12, Sanawi 9-0, Coxann 7-5, Christmas Hols 8-7.

11/4 Maamur (USA), 3/1 Kinematic (USA)(op 2/1), 100/30 IVOR'S FLUTTER, 4/1 Shadow Bird, 11/1 Taylors Prince(8/1–12/1), 25/1 Sanawi, 50/1 Christmas Hols, 66/1 Black Jewel, 150/1 Coxann. CSF £11.68, CT £31.16. Tote £3.50: £1.30 £1.50 £1.10 (£11.20). Mr W. I. M. Perry (WHITSBURY) bred by W. I. M. Perry. 9 Rn
2m 39.23 (9.73)
SF—52/51/38/18/40/5

T/Trio: Race 2: £23.50 (39.4 Tckts) & Race 5: £63.10 (23.2 Tckts). T/Jkpt: Not won; £3,281.81 to Ascot 10/10/92. T/Plpt: £641.80 (14.15 Tckts).
AK

## ASCOT (R-H)

### Saturday, October 10th [St course Good, Rnd Good to soft]

Going Allowance: St: minus 0.15 sec (F); Rnd: 0.20 sec per fur (G)      Wind: slt half bhd

Stalls: 3rd, 4th & 6th centre, remainder high

**3669**    AUTUMN STKS (listed race) (2-Y.O) £11452.50 (£3420.00: £1635.00: £742.50)
1m (rnd)

2-00 (2-01)

3462* **Taos (IRE) (100)** (Fav) *(JHMGosden)* 8-11 SCauthen (1) (6th st: rdn over 1f
    out: led ins fnl f: r.o wl) ....................................................... —1
3272³ Declassified (USA) **(100)** *(LMCumani)* 8-11 LDettori (3) (lw: 4th st: ev ch over 1f
    out: r.o) ............................................................................. 3.2
3205⁴ Mukhamedov **(100)** *(DRLoder)* 8-11 CAsmussen (6) (prom 3f: dropped rr 4f
    out: gd hdwy over 1f out: r.o) ............................................ hd.3
3444³ Iviza (IRE) **(100)** *(MRStoute)* 8-6 PatEddery (7) (lw: led after 1f tl ins fnl f) ...... nk.4
3160* Eurolink Thunder **(91)** *(JLDunlop)* 8-11 JReid (5) (hdwy 2f out: nvr nr to chal) 1¹/₂.5
3435⁵ Village Green (FR) **(100)** *(CEBrittain)* 8-11 AMunro (9) (2nd st: wknd over 1f out) ..... 3¹/₂.6

3519⁴ Top Rank *(JSMoore)* 8-11 BRouse (2) (a bhd) ........................................ 2.7
3489★ Star Manager (USA) **(89)** *(PFICole)* 8-11 TQuinn (8) (led 1f: 3rd st: wknd 2f out) ³/₄.8
3242² Brandonhurst **(91)** *(IABalding)* 8-11 MHills (4) (5th st: wknd over 2f out) .......... nk.9

**15/8** TAOS (IRE), **2/1** Iviza (IRE), **8/1** Mukhamedov, **9/1** Star Manager (USA), **10/1** Eurolink Thunder, **14/1** Declassified (USA), **25/1** Brandonhurst, **33/1** Village Green (FR), **66/1** Top Rank. CSF £24.37, Tote £2.80: £1.40 £2.40 £2.50 (£24.20). Sheikh Mohammed (NEWMARKET) bred by Barronstown Bloodstock Ltd in Ireland. 9 Rn
1m 43.34 (3.74)
SF—65/56/55/49/49/38

## 3670

PRINCESS ROYAL STKS (Gp 3) (F & M) £27720.00 (£10256.00: £4828.00: £1996.00)
1¹/₂m
2-30 (2-32)

3330a² **Cunning (119)** (Fav) *(LMCumani)* 3-8-9 LDettori (5) (4th st: led 2f out: rdn ins fnl f: r.o) ........................................ —1
3445 Anna of Saxony **(110)** *(JHMGosden)* 3-8-6 JReid (8) (hld up in rr: hdwy 2f out: ev ch fnl f: r.o) ..................... nk.2
3280★ Anne Bonny **(87)** *(JRFanshawe)* 3-8-6 TQuinn (6) (5th st: ev ch over 1f out: nt qckn) ........................................ 2¹/₂.3
1556★ Up Anchor (IRE) **(104)** *(PFICole)* 3-8-6 AMunro (7) (3rd st: hrd rdn over 1f out: one pce) ........................................ 1.4
3533⁴ Percy's Girl **(94)** *(GWragg)* 3-8-6 SCauthen (2) (lw: hld up: hdwy & hrd rdn 2f out: one pce) ..................... s.h.5
3345³ Guilty Secret (IRE) *(PWChapple-Hyam)* 3-8-6 CAsmussen (4) (lw: led 1f: 2nd st: led over 2f out: sn hdd & wknd) .......... 3.6
3190⁵ Bineyah (IRE) **(110)** *(MRStoute)* 3-8-6 PatEddery (1) (prom tl wknd & 6th st) .. 10.7
2843⁵ Pearl Angel **(100)** *(MissBSanders)* 3-8-6 MHills (9) (lw: bhd fnl 3f) ................ ³/₄.8
2594★ Fern **(86)** *(LMCumani)* 3-8-6 JWeaver (3) (led after 1f tl wknd over 2f out) ...... 12.9

**0/10** CUNNING, **8/1** Bineyah (IRE), **9/1** Guilty Secret (IRE), **12/1** Anne Bonny, **16/1** Percy's Girl (IRE), **20/1** Anna of Saxony, Up Anchor (IRE), **33/1** Fern, **40/1** Pearl Angel. CSF £12.38, Tote £1.50: £1.20 £3.20 £2.90 (£13.30). Fittocks Stud Limited (NEWMARKET) bred by R. G. Stokes and Fittocks Stud. 9 Rn
2m 36.19 (6.69)
SF—52/48/43/41/48/34

## 3671

BOVIS H'CAP (0-115) £16700.00 (£5000.00: £2400.00: £1100.00)
5f
3-00 (3-04)

3537★ **Ashtina (74)** *(RJHodges)* 7-7-8 JQuinn (11) (mde all: clr over 1f out: r.o wl) ..... —1
3437★ Spaniards Close **(105)** (Fav) *(PJMakin)* 4-9-11 CAsmussen (6) (hld up: hdwy over 1f out: r.o wl: nt rch wnr) ........................................ 3.2
3278★ Gone Savage **(79)** *(GBBalding)* 4-7-13 DBiggs (2) (a.p: nt qckn fnl f) ............ 1.3
3437⁴ Bodari **(79)** *(DAWilson)* 3-7-9 ‡³DHarrison (10) (chsd wnr 4f: nt qckn) ............ s.h.4
3528 Regal Scintilla **(92)** (v) *(GBBalding)* 3-8-11 SCauthen (14) (lw: a.p: hrd rdn fnl 2f: one pce) ........................................ ¹/₂.5
3356 So Rhythmical **(80)** *(GHEden)* 8-8-0 CRutter (13) (b.off hind: nvr nrr) ............ ¹/₂.6
3189 Viceroy **(108)** *(MrsLPiggott)* 5-10-0 LDettori (12) (a abt same pl) ................ nk.7
3437 Tbab (IRE) **(100)** *(CEBrittain)* 4-9-1 ‡⁵BDoyle (9) (nrst fin) ........................ hd.8
3356 Stack Rock **(94)** *(EJAlston)* 5-8-9 ‡⁵JWeaver (8) (lw: no hdwy fnl 2f) ............ 1.9
3575³ Allthruthenight (IRE) **(82)** *(LJHolt)* 3-8-1 AMunro (1) (lw: prom over 3f) ......... hd.10
3437⁵ Terrhars (IRE) **(94)** *(RHannon)* 4-8-11 ‡³RPerham (16) (swtg: a bhd) .......... hd.11
3437³ Plain Fact **(86)** *(JWHills)* 7-8-6 MHills (7) (hld up: nt clr run over 1f out: nt rcvr) nk.12
3539² Nagida **(81)** *(JARToller)* 3-8-0 DaleGibson (3) (outpcd) ........................ ¹/₂.13
3575 Olifantsfontein **(77)** (bl) *(RSimpson)* 4-7-4⁽²⁾ ‡⁷CHawksley (15) (a bhd) ........ 3.14
3528 Cantoris **(91)** *(RJRWilliams)* 6-8-11 PatEddery (5) (b: outpcd) .................. s.h.15
3243 Aughfad **(89)** (v) *(TCasey)* 6-8-9 JReid (4) (spd 3f) ................................ 8.16

**9/2** Spaniards Close, **8/1** Plain Fact, **9/1** Cantoris, ASHTINA, **10/1** Terrhars (IRE), **14/1** Tbab (IRE), **16/1** Allthruthenight (IRE), Nagida, Gone Savage, Bodari, Regal Scintilla, **20/1** Stack Rock, So Rhythmical, Viceroy, **25/1** Ors. CSF £43.27, CT £573.41. Tote £7.20: £1.70 £1.40 £3.00 £3.10 (£10.30). Ms S. A. Joyner (SOMERTON) bred by D. R. and Mrs Fairbairn. 16 Rn
60.72 sec (0.22)
SF—61/80/50/45/59/46

## 3672

CORNWALLIS STKS (Gp 3) (2-Y.O) £22140.00 (£8209.50: £3879.75: £1620.75)
5f
3-35 (3-37)

3326a⁴ **Up and At 'em** *(JGCoogan,Ireland)* 8-13 BJCoogan (4) (neat: a gng wl: led over 1f out: easily) ........................................ —1
3517★ Roger the Butler **(98)** *(MBell)* 8-13 MHills (7) (lw: a.p: r.o fnl f: no ch w wnr) ³/₄.3
3420★ Surprise Offer **(100)** (bl) *(RHannon)* 8-13 LDettori (13) (led over 3f) ............ ³/₄.3
3275² Anselman **(97)** *(MJHaynes)* 8-13 CAsmussen (10) (mid div tl styd on fnl f) ...... ³/₄.4
3390² Realities (USA) **(94)** *(GHarwood)* 8-13 JReid (6) (lw: rdn over 2f out: hdwy over 1f out: r.o) ........................................ hd.5
3534² Lord Olivier (IRE) **(100)** *(WJarvis)* 8-13 MTebbutt (11) (no hdwy fnl 2f) .......... 1¹/₂.6
3531³ The Informer (USA) *(PFICole)* 8-13 AMunro (12) (lw: a mid div) .................... ¹/₂.7

3295* Sooty Swift (IRE) **(91)** *(CEBrittain)* 8-8 SCauthen (5) (outpcd: bhd tl r.o fnl f) .... ³/₄.**8**
3340* Fyfield Flyer (IRE) **(100)** *(PWChapple-Hyam)* 8-13 PatEddery (1) (lw: prom
　　　　over 3f) ................................................ ¹/₂.**9**
3534* Sheila's Secret (IRE) **(95)** *(WCarter)* 8-8 BRouse (3) (nvr nr to chal) .............. s.h.**10**
3486* Simply Sooty **(84)** *(BRMillman)* 8-8 GBaxter (9) (prom over 2f) ................. ¹/₂.**11**
3366* Brigg Fair **(100)** (Fav) *(RHannon)* 8-13 TQuinn (8) (bhd fnl 2f) ................. 2.**12**
3348² Yakin (USA) **(96)** *(HThomsonJones)* 8-8 RHills (2) (outpcd) ................. 3¹/₂.**13**

**7/2** Brigg Fair, **5/1** Fyfield Flyer (IRE), **11/2** UP AND AT 'EM, **8/1** Sheila's Secret (IRE), Yakin (USA), **10/1** Sooty Swift (IRE), **16/1** Lord Olivier (IRE), Realities (USA), **20/1** Roger the Butler (IRE), Surprise Offer, The Informer (USA), Anselliman, **33/1** Simply Sooty. CSF £94.59, Tote £6.90: £2.00 £4.90 £4.60 (£153.50). Mrs A. Hughes (IRELAND) bred by Mrs Susan Feddern. 13 Rn
　　　　　　　　　　　　　　　　　　　　　　　　　61.03 sec (0.53)
　　　　　　　　　　　　　　　　　　　　　　　　　SF—73/63/60/57/56/50

**3673**　　BROCAS H'CAP (0-110) £9240.00 (£2760.00: £1320.00: £600.00)
　　　　　　1m (rnd)　　　　　　　　　　　　　　　　4-10 (4-13)

34415 **Gymcrak Premiere (93)** (v) *(MHEasterby)* 4-9-9 KDarley (9) (lw: hdwy 3f out:
　　　　led on bit over 1f out: rdn fnl f: r.o) ................................ —**1**
33595 Shati (IRE) **(91)** *(HThomsonJones)* 3-9-3 RHills (1) (5th st: ev ch over 1f out: nt
　　　　qckn) ................................................ 2.**2**
34413 Deprecator (USA) **(98)** (Fav) *(JHMGosden)* 4-10-0 PatEddery (4) (b.hind: lw:
　　　　6th st: nt clr run 2f out: r.o ins fnl f) ............. s.h.**3**
3212 Pay Homage **(90)** (v) *(IABalding)* 4-9-6 MHills (2) (hdwy fnl 2f: nvr nrr) .......... 2.**4**
33705 Takenhall **(66)** *(MJFetherston-Godley)* 7-7-7⁽³⁾ ‡³DHarrison (8) (rdn over 3f out:
　　　　nrst fin) ................................................ ¹/₂.**5**
3293 Gueca Solo **(79)** *(DRLoder)* 4-8-8 SSanders (6) (lw: hld up in rr: hdwy & nt clr
　　　　run over 1f out: r.o ins fnl f) .................... 1.**6**
3277* Neptune's Pet **(84)** *(GLewis)* 4-9-0 JReid (10) (lw: nvr nr to chal) ........... 1¹/₂.**7**
34184 Daswaki (CAN) **(76)** (v) *(RHannon)* 4-8-6 BRouse (5) (led over 3f out tl wknd
　　　　over 1f out) ................................................ 1¹/₂.**8**
3317 Cape Pigeon (USA) **(85)** *(LGCottrell)* 7-8-8 ‡⁷CAvery (7) (lw: 4th st: wknd 2f out) ³/₄.**9**
3277 Baluga **(82)** *(GHarwood)* 3-8-8 AClark (5) (lw: led over 4f: 2nd st: wknd 2f out) s.h.**10**
34174 Garth **(72)** (v) *(PJMakin)* 4-8-2 AMunro (11) (7th st: wknd over 2f out) ........... 2.**11**
3441 Irek **(88)** *(LordHuntingdon)* 3-9-0 SCauthen (3) (3rd st: wknd qckly wl over 1f
　　　　out) ................................................ 2¹/₂.**12**

**4/1** Deprecator (USA), **5/1** Neptune's Pet, **6/1** GYMCRAK PREMIERE, **8/1** Daswaki (CAN), Irek, **9/1** Garth, **11/1** Pay Homage(8/1—12/1), **12/1** Takenhall, **16/1** Gueca Solo, **20/1** Shati (IRE), **33/1** Ors. CSF £98.89, CT £479.20. Tote £7.40: £2.30 £5.10 £1.80 (£125.70). Gymcrak Thoroughbred Racing III Plc (BREDA) bred by Cheveley Park Stud Ltd. 12 Rn
　　　　　　　　　　　　　　　　　　　　　　　　　1m 43.19 (3.59)
　　　　　　　　　　　　　　　　　　　　　　　　　SF—79/67/77/63/34/47

**3674**　　HYPERION GRADUATION STKS (2-Y.O) £8928.00 (£2664.00: £1272.00: £576.00)
　　　　　　7f　　　　　　　　　　　　　　　　　　4-40 (4-42)

34352 **Right Win (IRE) (100)** *(RHannon)* 9-5 PatEddery (1) (w ldr: led wl over 1f out:
　　　　rdn out) ................................................ —**1**
　　　　Shaiba (USA) *(MRStoute)* 8-13 CAsmussen (6) (w'like: scope: hdwy 2f out: r.o
　　　　ins fnl f: nt rch wnr) ................................ 3¹/₂.**2**
32472 Marastani (USA) *(GHarwood)* 8-13 JReid (5) (lw: led over 5f) ................. ¹/₂.**3**
3262* True Hero (USA) **(100)** (Fav) *(JHMGosden)* 9-5 SCauthen (4) (a.p: rdn 2f out:
　　　　one pce) ................................................ 4.**4**
34622 Palace Pageant (USA) **(99)** *(IABalding)* 9-5 MHills (2) (lw: no hdwy fnl 2f) ....... 2¹/₂.**5**
3096* Catherineofaragon **(95)** *(WGRWightman)* 9-0 JWilliams (7) (spd over 4f) ...... 2¹/₂.**6**
3523* Moorish **(97)** *(PFICole)* 9-5 AMunro (3) (lw: rdn over 2f out: no rspnse) ........ s.h.**7**
33543 Abtaal **(83)** *(HThomsonJones)* 9-5 RHills (8) (w ldrs tl wknd wl over 1f out) ....... ³/₄.**8**

**15/8** True Hero (USA), **11/4** RIGHT WIN (IRE), **9/2** Shaiba (USA)(5/2—5/1), **7/1** Palace Pageant (USA)(tchd 12/1), **11/1** Moorish, **14/1** Catherineofaragon, **16/1** Marastani, **25/1** Abtaal. CSF £14.87, Tote £3.20: £1.60 £2.00 £3.30 (£5.90). Mr Conal Kavanagh (MARLBOROUGH) bred by Ovidstown Investments Ltd in Ireland. 8 Rn
　　　　　　　　　　　　　　　　　　　　　　　　　1m 28.86 (2.36)
　　　　　　　　　　　　　　　　　　　　　　　　　SF—54/37/35/29/21/8

**3675**　　TANKERVILLE H'CAP (0-100) £7635.00 (£2280.00: £1090.00: £495.00)
　　　　　　1¹/₂m　　　　　　　　　　　　　　　　5-10 (5-12)

3527 **Robingo (IRE) (72)** (bl) *(CEBrittain)* 3-7-12 AMunro (4) (4th st: led ins fnl f: drvn
　　　　out) ................................................ —**1**
3461* Googly **(72)** (Fav) *(WGRWightman)* 3-7-12 GBardwell (6) (lw: 6th st: led 1f out:
　　　　sn hdd: nt qckn) ................................ 3.**2**
3555 Rapporteur (USA) **(63)** *(CCElsey)* 6-7-8 ‡³DHarrison (9) (lw: led to 1f out: r.o
　　　　one pce) ................................................ 1.**3**

3461　Mad Militant (IRE) **(80)** *(RHollinshead)* 3–8–6 LDettori (1) (lw: hdwy 2f out: r.o one pce fnl f) ...................................................... hd.4
34365　Royal Seaton **(84)** *(BRMillman)* 3–8–10 JWilliams (7) (nrst fin) ......................... 2¹⁄₂.5
3436★　Major Bugler (IRE) **(79)** *(GBBalding)* 3–8–5 PatEddery (3) (lw: 5th st: rdn 2f out: sn wknd) ...................................................... 2¹⁄₂.6
3510　Full Quiver **(63)** (v) *(MrsBarbaraWaring)* 7–7–4⁽⁴⁾ ‡7CHawksley (10) (nvr nrr) ..... nk.7
35724　Western Dynasty **(67)** *(MJRyan)* 6–8–1 DBiggs (5) (lw: 2nd st: wknd over 1f out) 1¹⁄₂.8
34452　Lift and Load (USA) **(94)** *(RHannon)* 5–10–0 JReid (2) (swtg: 3rd st: wknd wl over 1f out) ...................................................... 7.9
3370　Self Expression **(68)** (v) *(IABalding)* 4–8–2 MHills (8) (s.s: a bhd) .................... ³⁄₄.10
LONG HANDICAP: Full Quiver 6-7.

**3/1** Googly, **4/1** Major Bugler (IRE), **5/1** Lift and Load (USA), **13/2** Royal Seaton, **9/1** Western Dynasty, ROBINGO (IRE), **12/1** Mad Militant (IRE), **14/1** Self Expression, **20/1** Rapporteur (USA), **66/1** Full Quiver. CT £480.50. Tote £8.80: £4.00 £1.10 £4.40 (£32.10). Capt. M. Lemos (NEWMARKET) bred by J. J. Prendergast in Ireland. 10 Rn　　　　　　2m 37.05 (7.55)
SF—33/27/21/32/31/21

T/Trio: Race 3: £45.10 (70.7 Tckts) & Race 6: £204.90 (7.3 Tckts). T/Jkpt: £4,173.10 (1.35 Tckts). T/Plpt: £145.50 (96.50 Tckts).　　　　　　Hn

3631—**YORK (L-H)**
## Saturday, October 10th [Good]
Going Allowance: St: 0.70 sec per fur; Rest: 0.50 sec per fur (Y)　　　Wind: slt half against

Stalls: high

**3676**　　BBC RADIO 5 EMMA FORMAN GRADUATION STKS (3-Y.O) £5075.00 (£1400.00: £665.00)　**1m 3f 195y**　　　　　　　2-15 (2-16)

34382　**Jasoorah (IRE) (79)** *(ACStewart)* 8–10 MRoberts (1) (trckd ldrs: shkn up 5f out: led over 2f out: 4l clr whn eased wl ins fnl f) ........................ —1
3190　Shahaamh (IRE) **(97)** *(HThomsonJones)* 8–10 WCarson (2) (led tl over 2f out: styd on u.p ins fnl f) ...................................................... ¹⁄₂.2
3299★　Fermoy (USA) **(85)** (Fav) *(LMCumani)* 8–13 JFortune (3) (swtg: stdd s: hld up: effrt over 3f out: no imp) ...................................................... 3.3

**5/4** Fermoy (USA), **2/1** JASOORAH (IRE), **5/2** Shahaamh (IRE). CSF £5.78. Tote £2.80 (£3.00). Sheikh Ahmed Al Maktoum (NEWMARKET) bred by Miss K.Rausing, Mrs S.Rogers & M.Ryan in Ireland. 3 Rn　2m 40.63 (13.63)
SF—20/19/16

**3677**　　STAMFORD BRIDGE STKS (2-Y.O) £5744.00 (£1712.00: £816.00: £368.00)　**6f 214y**　　　　　　　2-45 (2-45)

34353　**Emperor Jones (USA) (100)** (Fav) *(JHMGosden)* 9–4 RCochrane (6) (trckd ldr: led over 2f out: drvn clr over 1f out) ...................................... —1
3320★　Taahhub (IRE) **(95)** *(BWHills)* 9–0 WCarson (5) (lw: led tl over 2f out: styd on one pce appr fnl f) ...................................................... 3¹⁄₂.2
3353★　Colway Rock (USA) **(88)** *(JWWatts)* 9–0 GDuffield (1) (lw: trckd ldrs: effrt & outpcd 3f out: styd on wl fnl f) ...................................................... s.h.3
32722　Shebl (USA) **(100)** *(MRStoute)* 9–0 WRSwinburn (2) (lw: stdd s: sn trckng ldrs: effrt over 2f out: no imp) ...................................................... 3¹⁄₂.4
　　Queens Consul (IRE) **(83)** *(BSRothwell)* 8–3 MRoberts (4) (leggy: unf: chsd ldrs tl outpcd fnl 3f) ...................................................... 7.5
32356　Glowing Value (IRE) **(93)** *(JBerry)* 9–0 JCarroll (3) (trckd ldrs tl rdn & lost pl over 2f out) ...................................................... 7.6

**Evens** EMPEROR JONES (USA), **3/1** Shebl (USA), **4/1** Taahhub (IRE), **7/1** Colway Rock (USA), **16/1** Glowing Value (IRE)(op 10/1), **33/1** Queens Consul (IRE). CSF £5.56. Tote £2.20: £1.50 £2.10 (£3.60). Sheikh Mohammed (NEWMARKET) bred by Cherry Valley Farm Inc. & E. A. Cox Jnr in USA. 6 Rn　1m 30.21 (7.81)
SF—39/24/23/12/–/–

**3678**　　CROWTHER HOMES H'CAP (3-Y.O) (0-100) £9396.00 (£2808.00: £1344.00: £612.00)　**1m 205y**　　　　　　　3-15 (3-16)

35142　**Drummer Hicks (75)** (Fav) *(EWeymes)* 8–2 DMcKeown (1) (lw: trckd ldrs: squeezed thro over 3f out: hrd rdn to ld over 1f out: r.o wl) . —1
3520★　Lahoob (USA) **(69)** *(BHanbury)* 7–10 NCarlisle (3) (lw: trckd ldrs: led over 2f out: rdn & hung lft: nt qckn fnl f) ...................................................... 1.2
35543　Sylvan (IRE) **(81)** *(CFWall)* 8–8 WRSwinburn (6) (hld up & bhd: stdy hdwy over 3f out: swtchd outside over 1f out: r.o) ...................................................... 1.3
32774　For Reg (IRE) **(94)** *(ACStewart)* 9–7 MRoberts (4) (plld hrd: trckd ldrs: effrt over 3f out: hung lft: nvr nr to chal) ...................................................... 6.4

*3184*[4] Let's Get Lost (73) *(WJHaggas)* 8-0[(1)] GDuffield (2) (led tl over 2f out: sn wknd) 3½.5
3554[4] Ghalyoon (USA) (76) *(PTWalwyn)* 8-3 WCarson (5) (sn bhd & drvn along: styd on fnl 3f: nvr rchd ldrs) ............................................................ 4.6
3545 Lord Vivienne (IRE) (73) *(RCSpicer)* 8-0 JLowe (4) (plld hrd: w ldr tl wknd over 2f out) ......................................................................... 1.7
3370 Gotcha (BAR) (78) (bl) *(RHannon)* 8-5 BRaymond (9) (sn bhd: effrt & drvn along over 4f out: n.d) ................................................... 2.8
3527[3] Jumaira Shark (CAN) (80) (v) *(JHMGosden)* 8-7 DHolland (8) (jnd ldrs 6f out: rdn & sltly hmpd over 3f out: nt r.o) ............................ 3.9

**9/4** DRUMMER HICKS, **7/2** Jumaira Shark (CAN), **4/1** For Reg (IRE), **7/1** Lahoob (USA), **10/1** Ghalyoon (USA), **11/1** Sylvan (IRE), **14/1** Let's Get Lost, **20/1** Gotcha (BAR), **33/1** Lord Vivienne (IRE). CSF £17.36, CT £130.66. Tote £2.70: £1.40 £2.40 £2.40 (£6.70). Mrs N. Napier (MIDDLEHAM) bred by Mrs N. Napier. 9 Rn
1m 55.89 (6.89)
SF—52/43/52/47/15/6

**3679**          ANC ROCKINGHAM STKS (listed race) (2-Y.O) £11550.00 (£3450.00: £1650.00: £750.00))    **6f**
3-45 (3-46)

3390★ Rain Brother (USA) (95) *(PWChapple-Hyam)* 8-12 DHolland (1) (mde all: drvn along over 2f out: hld on wl) ................................ —1
3414★ Mithl Al Hawa (94) (Fav) *(JRFanshawe)* 8-7 WRSwinburn (5) (b.off hind: chsd wnr over 3f: effrt & ev ch over 1f out: styd on wl nr fin) ...... ¾.2
3530[5] Brockton Dancer (81) *(RHannon)* 8-7 GCarter (7) (hdwy on outside over 2f out: styd on same pce fnl f) ................................... 2.3
3328a[6] Jervia (91) *(JWWatts)* 8-7 WRyan (2) (chsd ldrs tl outpcd over 2f out: kpt on) ... 4.4
3187★ Falsoola (99) *(MRStoute)* 8-7 MRoberts (3) (v.unruly in stalls: swtchd lft after 1f: sn chsng ldrs: rdn & wknd 2f out) .......................... 3.5
3123★ Look Who's Here (IRE) (89) *(BAMcMahon)* 8-12 BRaymond (8) (hld up: effrt over 2f out: nvr nr to chal) ............................. s.h.6
3136[3] Liyakah (USA) (100) *(MajorWRHern)* 8-7 WCarson (4) (swtg: hld up & bhd: effrt over 2f out: sn wknd) .......................... 1½.7
3550★ Palacegate Touch (86) *(JBerry)* 8-12 JCarroll (6) (lw: hld up & plld hrd: effrt over 2f out: sn lost pl) ................................. 1.8

**9/4** Mithl Al Hawa, **11/4** Liyakah (USA), **3/1** Falsoola, **9/2** RAIN BROTHER (USA), **12/1** Palacegate Touch, **14/1** Jervia, **16/1** Look Who's Here (IRE), **33/1** Brockton Dancer. CSF £15.55, Tote £6.20: £1.90 £1.40 £5.40 (£10.10). Mr Luciano Gaucci (MARLBOROUGH) bred by Gainesway Thoroughbreds Limited. 8 Rn
1m 16.39 (6.19)
SF—58/50/42/26/14/18

**3680**          CORAL SPRINT TROPHY (H'cap) (0-110) £13110.00 (£3930.00: £1890.00: £870.00)    **6f**
4-15 (4-19)

(Weights raised 4 lb)
3469 Densben (78) *(DenysSmith)* 8-8-6 KFallon (10) (sn bhd & drvn along: effrt & swtchd rt over 2f out: r.o wl to ld ins fnl f) ................ —1
3524[4] Will of Steel (76) *(HCandy)* 3-7-9 ‡[7]AntoinetteArmes (16) (sn bhd & pushed along: gd hdwy over 1f out: r.o wl nr fin) .............. 1.2
3356 Bertie Wooster (86) *(RJHolder)* 9-9-0 JLowe (4) (lw: sn bhd: hdwy 2f out: styd on wl fnl f) .......................................... 1½.3
3356 Sea Devil (81) *(MJCamacho)* 6-8-9 NConnorton (7) (hdwy over 2f out: nt qckn fnl f) ....................................................... s.h.4
2839 Panikin (90) *(JWharton)* 4-8-13 ‡[5]SWilliams (3) (s.i.s: sn bhd: gd hdwy & swtchd rt over 1f out: r.o strly nr fin) .................... 1.5
3207 Saddlehome (USA) (75) *(RMWhitaker)* 3-7-8 ‡[7]AGarth (6) (w ldrs: led over 2f out tl hdd & no ex ins fnl f) .......................... d.h.5
3437 King's Signet (USA) (95) *(JHMGosden)* 3-9-7 GHind (20) (chsd ldrs: effrt 2f out: r.o same pce) ....................................... hd.7
3356 Cumbrian Waltzer (91) (Fav) *(MHEasterby)* 7-9-5 MBirch (8) (hdwy over 2f out: kpt on same pce fnl f) ............................. nk.8
3355★ Allinson's Mate (IRE) (76) *(TDBarron)* 4-8-4 AlexGreaves (13) (hdwy 2f out: kpt on fnl f) ........................................ ¾.9
3553[3] Assignment (79) *(JFitch-Heyes)* 6-8-7 TyroneWilliams (2) (b.hind: w ldrs: rdn 2f out: wknd fnl f) .............................. nk.10
3620 Amron (80) *(JBerry)* 5-8-8 NCarlisle (19) (in tch over 3f) ................ 1.11
3355★ How's Yer Father (85) *(RJHodges)* 6-8-13 PaulEddery (14) (sn bhd: sme hdwy u.p over 1f out) ........................................ nk.12
3633[2] Never so Sure (96) (v) *(ABailey)* 4-9-3 ‡[7]DWright (9) (in tch: effrt over 2f out: sn wknd) ........................................ nk.13
3539 Parfait Amour (71) *(RMWhitaker)* 3-7-6[(2)] ‡[5]NKennedy (5) (sn drvn along: nvr rchd ldrs) ........................................ nk.14

3355 Gorinsky (IRE) **(71)** *(JBerry)* 4-7-13 NAdams (15) (mde most to ¹/₂-wy: wknd 2f out) .................................................................................... ¹/₂.15

3437 Baligay **(75)** *(RJHodges)* 7-8-3 DHolland (12) (w ldrs: led ¹/₂-wy: sn hdd: wknd over 1f out) ..................................................................... 2¹/₂.16

3495* Ikteshaf **(85)** *(BHanbury)* 4-8-13 BRaymond (11) (lw: w ldrs 4f: sn lost pl) ..... nk.17

3469 Red Rosein **(90)** *(CaptJWilson)* 6-9-4 GCarter (23) (b.off hind: dwlt s: a in rr) nk.18

3083 Appledorn **(81)** *(BAMcMahon)* 5-8-9 DMcKeown (18) (lw: in tch: effrt ¹/₂-wy: sn lost pl) ............................................................................................ nk.19

3495² Double Blue **(91)** *(MJohnston)* 3-9-3 MRoberts (1) (w ldrs tl lost pl 2f out: eased) ..................................................................................................... hd.20

3469³ Sunday's Hill **(95)** (v) *(MBlanshard)* 3-9-7 RCochrane (22) (lw: sn outpcd & drvn along) ................................................................................................. 2.21

3469* Hazm (USA) **(92)** *(HThomsonJones)* 3-9-4 WCarson (17) (chsd ldrs: sn drvn along: lost pl over 2f out) ............................................................ 1¹/₂.22

833* Al Sadi **(85)** *(CEBrittain)* 3-8-11 WRSwinburn (21) (lw: sn bhd) ....................... 6.23

**9/2** Cumbrian Waltzer, **17/2** King's Signet (USA), Ikteshaf, **12/1** Double Blue, **14/1** Will of Steel, Never so Sure, Assignment, **16/1** DENSBEN, Gorinsky (IRE), Sea Devil, How's Yer Father, Hazm (USA), **18/1** Allinson's Mate (IRE), **20/1** Red Rosein, Sunday's Hill, Amron, Bertie Wooster, **25/1** Al Sadi, Saddlehome (USA), **33/1** Panikin, Baligay, Appledorn, **50/1** Parfait Amour. CSF £216.33, CT £4,083.35. Tote £42.30: £6.30 £4.10 £4.90 £3.50 (£370.30). Mrs Janet M. Pike (BISHOP AUCKLAND) bred by D. W. Pike. 23 Rn     1m 15.42 (5.22)
SF—72/57/70/64/67/44

**3681**     CARLING BLACK LABEL LAGER H'CAP (0-100) £6784.00 (£2032.00: £976.00: £448.00)
6f 214y                                            4-45 (4-48)

3441 **Highland Magic (IRE) (64)** *(MJFetherston-Godley)* 4-8-0 DHolland (18) (sn drvn along: gd hdwy over 2f out: led on bit jst ins fnl f: sn clr: eased f) ............................................................................................... —1

3543⁴ Prenonamoss **(79)** *(Jt-Fav)* *(DWPArbuthnot)* 4-9-1 WCarson (15) (b.hind: sn bhd: gd hdwy & ev ch 1f out: nt qckn w whr) ................................... 1¹/₈.2

3514⁴ Sagebrush Roller **(69)** *(JWWatts)* 4-8-5 GDuffield (12) (sn bhd & pushed along: hdwy to ld wl over 1f out: hdd & no ex jst ins fnl f) .... 1.3

3640³ En Attendant (FR) **(85)** *(Jt-Fav)* *(BHanbury)* 4-9-7 BRaymond (13) (dwlt s: hld up: effrt over 2f out: r.o fnl f: nt rch ldrs) ........................................ nk.4

3375³ Ringland (USA) **(80)** *(DMoffatt)* 4-8-9 ‡7DarrenMoffatt (10) (w ldrs: ev ch over 1f out: r.o same pce) ...................................................................... 1.5

3545 Choir Practice **(69)** *(WJHaggas)* 5-8-5 WRyan (9) (hld up: gd hdwy & nt clr run over 1f out: kpt on fnl f: nt rch ldrs) ............................................ hd.6

3375² Gymcrak Tycoon **(74)** *(MHEasterby)* 3-8-7 MBirch (19) (hld up: hdwy over 2f out: kpt on: nvr able to chal) ........................................................ 3.7

3373⁴ Kinlacey **(60)** *(BAMcMahon)* 5-7-10 JLowe (6) (trckd ldrs tl grad wknd fnl 2f) .... 2.8

3310 Doyce **(60)** *(JEtherington)* 3-7-0 ‡7AntoinetteArmes (16) (sn bhd & pushed along: sme hdwy over 2f out: n.d) ...................................... 3.9

3612 Super Benz **(72)** *(TFairhurst)* 6-8-8 JFanning (14) (led after 1f tl over 3f out: sn rdn & wknd) ........................................................................................ 2.10

3612 Ashdren **(77)** *(AHarrison)* 5-8-13 GCarter (3) (w ldrs: led over 3f out tl wl over 1f out: sn wknd) ....................................................................................... hd.11

3477² Beware of Agents **(90)** *(MJohnston)* 3-9-9 RPElliott (11) (prom 4f: sn lost pl) .. 1.12

3543 Aghaadir (USA) **(91)** *(JHMGosden)* 4-9-13 RCochrane (2) (chsd ldrs: rdn over 2f out: sn wknd) ................................................................................. ¹/₂.13

3545 Colossus **(65)** *(CEBrittain)* 4-8-1 MRoberts (8) (chsd ldrs tl lost pl 2f out) ......... ¹/₂.14

3252² Emir Albadou (USA) **(83)** *(MRStoute)* 3-9-2 WRSwinburn (17) (a in rr) .............. ¹/₂.15

1314 Lord High Admiral (CAN) **(70)** *(CGCox)* 4-8-6 PaulEddery (1) (plld hrd: trckd ldrs: effrt 2f out: fnd nil) ......................................................... 1¹/₂.16

3355 State Flyer **(62)** (v) *(CBBBooth)* 4-7-12 NAdams (7) (s.i.s: hdwy on ins over 4f out: lost pl over 2f out) ........................................................................ ¹/₂.17

3344⁴ Cool Luke (IRE) **(81)** *(GMMoore)* 3-9-0 JCarroll (5) (chsd ldrs 4f: sn wknd) . 3¹/₂.18

3473 Thornton Gate **(71)** (bl) *(MHEasterby)* 3-8-1 ‡3SMaloney (4) (led 1f: w ldrs tl rdn & lost pl ¹/₂-wy: sn bhd) ................................................................. 2.19

LONG HANDICAP: Doyce 7-3.

**7/1** En Attendant (FR), Prenonamoss, **8/1** Emir Albadou (USA), **10/1** Gymcrak Tycoon, Cool Luke (IRE), Choir Practice, **12/1** HIGHLAND MAGIC (IRE), Aghaadir (USA), **14/1** Sagebrush Roller, **16/1** Thornton Gate, Ringland (USA), Kinlacey, Ashdren, **20/1** Beware of Agents, Colossus, **25/1** Super Benz, **33/1** Ors. CSF £89.76, CT £1,098.74. Tote £27.10: £4.40 £2.00 £2.30 £2.10 (£105.10). Miss N. Carroll (EAST ILSLEY) bred by W. J. Burke in Ireland. 19 Rn     1m 27.8 (hand) (5.4)
SF—57/67/54/69/54/49

**3682**     COLDSTREAM GUARDS ASSOCIATION CUP (Stks) (Mdn 3-Y.O) £6108.00 (£1824.00:
£872.00: £396.00) 1¹/₄m 85y                              5-15 (5-18)

3609² Lobilio (USA) **(78)** *(CEBrittain)* 9-0 MRoberts (8) (mde all: rdn over 2f out: styd on wl) ..................................................................................................... —1

3177[6] In the Money (IRE) **(62)** *(RHollinshead)* 9-0 WRyan (3) (chsd ldrs: effrt over 2f out: r.o u.p fnl f) .................................................... 1¹/₂.2

3459[2] Cariboo Gold (USA) *(JHMGosden)* 9-0 RCochrane (5) (chsd ldrs: ev ch & rdn over 2f out: one pce) ........................................ 1.3

3085 Fort Shirley (IRE) *(MRStoute)* 9-0 WRSwinburn (6) (w'like: leggy: scope: chsd ldrs tl wknd over 2f out) ........................................ 5.4

33714 Alhaajib (USA) **(Fav)** *(JLDunlop)* 9-0 WCarson (7) (lw: chsd ldrs: drvn along appr st: rdn over 3f out: no rspnse) ............. 1¹/₂.5

4814 Tunbridge Wells (IRE) *(JHMGosden)* 9-0 GHind (1) (stdd: effrt over 3f out: hung lft & no imp) ...................................... s.h.6

Blanchland *(PWHarris)* 9-0 PaulEddery (2) (w'like: scope: bit bkwd: dwlt s: a in rr) ........................................................... 15.7

Strathcarron *(WJarvis)* 9-0 BRaymond (4) (lengthy: s.i.s: a bhd) ........ 6.8

**4/6** Alhaajib (USA), **6/1** Cariboo Gold (USA), **13/2** LOBILIO (USA), **7/1** Fort Shirley (IRE), **16/1** Tunbridge Wells (IRE), **20/1** In the Money (IRE), **33/1** Strathcarron, **50/1** Blanchland. CSF £95.54, Tote £6.30: £1.50 £2.20 £1.60 (£43.70). The Dowager Lady Beaverbrook (NEWMARKET) bred by London Thoroughbred Services Ltd in USA. 8 Rn
2m 18.55 (11.05)
SF—42/39/37/27/24/23

T/Trio: Race 5: Any 2 fr 1st 3 w any £36.40 (62.4 Tckts) & Race 6: £204.90 (7.3 Tckts). T/Plpt: £659.60 (17.75 Tckts).
WG

## 3262—LEICESTER (R-H)

### Monday, October 12th [Good to soft]

Going Allowance: St: 0.45 sec (Y); Rnd: 0.20 sec per fur (G)          Wind: mod against

Stalls: high

## 3683

HARE STKS (I) (Mdn 2-Y.O.F) £2070.00 (£570.00: £270.00)          **7f 9y**          1-30 (1-34)

19374 **Rapid Repeat (IRE)** **(Fav)** *(MrsJCecil)* 8-11 PaulEddery (8) (a.p: rdn to ld 1f out: sn clr) ........................................ —1

3502 Ikhtisas (USA) **(68)** *(BHanbury)* 8-11 RHills (14) (hld up in tch: effrt appr fnl f: r.o wl) ...................................... 2¹/₂.2

34306 Ibtikar (USA) *(PTWalwyn)* 8-11 WCarson (15) (dwlt: rdn & hdwy over 2f out: styd on ins fnl f) ........................ ¹/₂.3

20376 Play With Me (IRE) *(JLDunlop)* 8-11 GCarter (4) (bit bkwd: hdwy ¹/₂-wy: led stands' side 2f out: r.o) ........................ nk.4

35704 Apache Myth *(RHannon)* 8-11 MRoberts (12) (led far side 6f) ......... 2.5

3276 Grey Watch **(81)** *(LadyHerries)* 8-11 JWilliams (11) (hdwy over 2f out: rdn & wknd ins fnl f) ...................................... 2¹/₂.6

Titled Girl (IRE) *(PFICole)* 8-11 TQuinn (9) (leggy: scope: bit bkwd: c stands' side: prom tl wknd over 1f out) ........ 2¹/₂.7

3410 Bold Line *(RJRWilliams)* 8-11 RCochrane (5) (bit bkwd: nvr nr to chal) ........ ³/₄.8

Glint of Ayr *(WRMuir)* 8-8 ‡3RPerham (13) (leggy: bit bkwd: nvr nr ldrs) ........ 2¹/₂.9

Austral Jane *(GHarwood)* 8-11 AClark (6) (w'like: bit bkwd: prom stands' side 5f) ...................................... ³/₄.10

3314 Rispoto *(SirMarkPrescott)* 8-11 GDuffield (16) (chsd ldrs far side 5f) ........ 1¹/₂.11

27133 Steading *(HCandy)* 8-11 CRutter (3) (hmpd s: sn led stands' side: rdn & wknd over 2f out) ...................... ¹/₂.12

Lady Arabella *(JPearce)* 8-11 RPrice (17) (leggy: lt-f: bkwd: prom 4f) ........ s.h.13

3036 Meritre (IRE) *(RJHolder)* 8-11 NAdams (1) (prom stands' side 4f) ........ 3.14

Wesshaun *(WGMTurner)* 8-11 TSprake (10) (w'like: leggy: bkwd: chsd ldrs 4f: grad wknd) ...................... 4.15

D K Daffers (IRE) *(BSmart)* 8-11 DaleGibson (7) (neat: scope: bkwd: a bhd) .. ¹/₂.16

Miss Offie *(RHollinshead)* 8-11 WRyan (6) (w'like: bkwd: bhd fr ¹/₂-wy) ........ 4.17

**13/8** RAPID REPEAT (IRE)(5/4—2/1), **7/1** Grey Watch, **8/1** Apache Myth, **9/1** Ibtikar (USA)(op 4/1), **12/1** Ikhtisas (USA)(7/1—14/1), Rispoto(op 8/1), Steading(op 7/1), Titled Girl (IRE)(op 8), **14/1** Play With Me (IRE)(op 8/1), **20/1** Austral Jane, **25/1** Bold Line, **33/1** Ors. CSF £22.06, Tote £2.10: £1.50 £4.40 £3.00 (£14.50). Lord Hartington (NEWMARKET) bred by Mrs T. V. Ryan in Ireland. 17 Rn
1m 31.3 (9)
SF—10/2/–/–/–/–

## 3684

HARE STKS (II) (Mdn 2-Y.O.F) £2070.00 (£570.00: £270.00)          **7f 9y**          2-00 (2-05)

34802 **Wild Princess (USA)** *(LMCumani)* 8-11 LDettori (11) (lw: led 4f: led wl over 1f out: sn clr: hld on) ...................... —1

Imaginary (IRE) **(Fav)** *(HRACecil)* 8-11 PatEddery (13) (lengthy: scope: s.i.s: rdn & effrt 2f out: r.o strly ins fnl f) ...................... 1.2

33604 Bawaeth (USA) *(BWHills)* 8-11 WCarson (16) (mid div: hrd rdn over 2f out: hdwy & nt clr run appr fnl f: r.o) ...................... ³/₄.3

3414⁴ Oare Sparrow *(PTWalwyn)* 8-11 RCochrane (3) (a.p: led 3f out tl wl over 1f out: one pce) .................................................................................. 2¹/₂.4
Princess Kris *(MRStoute)* 8-11 PaulEddery (14) (leggy: unf: chsd ldrs: kpt on ins fnl f: nvr nrr) ...................................................................... 1¹/₂.5
3419 Bobbysoxer *(JLDunlop)* 8-11 GCarter (5) (hdwy ¹/₂-wy: rdn over 1f out: styd on) ³/₄.6
3414⁶ Forest Song *(RCharlton)* 8-11 TSprake (9) (hld up in tch: rdn over 1f out: nt pce to chal) .................................................................................. nk.7
3099⁴ Beyond the Limit *(LadyHerries)* 8-11 AClark (10) (chsd ldrs: no hdwy fnl 2f) ... 1¹/₂.8
3570 Misty Silks *(MJRyan)* 8-11 DBiggs (2) (s.s: nvr nr ldrs) ............................... ³/₄.9
3314 Starlight Rose (IRE) *(CAHorgan)* 8-11 DaleGibson (15) (outpcd: a in rr) ........ 1¹/₂.10
3549⁵ I'M Yours *(RHannon)* 8-11 JReid (4) (w ldrs over 5f: sn wknd) ..................... 1¹/₂.11
3531⁶ Miss Pimpernel *(BHanbury)* 8-11 BRaymond (7) (prom over 4f) .................... 1¹/₂.12
*3553* Bold a Maiden *(DRLaing)* 8-11 TyroneWilliams (8) (effrt 3f out: wknd appr fnl f: t.o) ...................................................................................................... 8.13
Sense of Humour *(JWPayne)* 8-11 AMunro (1) (rangy: bkwd: s.s: a bhd: t.o) ... nk.14
2792⁶ Newington Butts (IRE) *(71)* *(RAkehurst)* 8-11 TQuinn (12) (bhd fnl 3f: t.o) ...... s.h.15
Colour of Life *(CCElsey)* 8-11 JLowe (6) (unf: unruly stalls: s.s: a bhd: t.o) ... 10.16

**3/1** Imaginary (IRE)(7/4—7/2), **7/2** WILD PRINCESS (USA)(op 9/4), **4/1** Princess Kris, **8/1** Bawaeth (USA)(op 5/1), I'M Yours(tchd 12/1), Miss Pimpernel, **12/1** Oare Sparrow (7/1), Forest Song(op 8/1), **16/1** Beyond the Limit, Bobbysoxer, **33/1** Newington Butts (IRE), Sense of Humour, Starlight Rose (IRE), **50/1** Colour of Life, Misty Silks, **66/1** Bold a Maiden. CSF £15.93, Tote £4.10: £2.00 £2.00 £2.00 (£5.50). Mr Edward P. Evans (NEWMARKET) bred by Woodrow W. Marriott in USA. 16 Rn
1m 31.5 (9.2)
SF—6/3/1/-/-/-/

## 3685

STOAT (S) STKS (2-Y.O) £2805.00 (£780.00: £375.00)   **1m 1f 218y**   2-30 (2-37)

3598 **Trepidation (IRE) (50)** (v) *(MJFetherston-Godley)* 8-11 LDettori (5) (a.p: 5th st: rdn & outpcd 3f out: styd on srtly to ld cl home) ................................ —1
3502⁵ Honorary Guest **(60)** *(DJGMurray-Smith)* 8-6 THogers (15) (hld up. 6th st. jnd ldr 3f out: led ins fnl f: ct post) ......................................................... hd.2
3574 Pondering **(56)** (Fav) *(SDow)* 8-11 TQuinn (17) (lw: hdwy ¹/₂-wy: led over 3f out tl ins fnl f: r.o) ................................................................................... hd.3
3623 Bohemian Queen **(44)** *(JLSpearing)* 8-6 KDarley (4) (chsd ldrs: hdwy 4f out: sn rdn: kpt on) ......................................................................................... 2¹/₂.4
3598 Kaloochi **(65)** (bl) *(RHannon)* 9-1 RCochrane (11) (s.s: effrt ent st: styd on fnl f: nvr nrr) .................................................................................................. 1¹/₂.5
Achy Breaky *(SRBowring)* 8-6 SWebster (14) (leggy: lt-f: s.s: bhd: hdwy over 3f out: styd on fnl f) .............................................................................. 2¹/₂.6
3606 Arctic Agnes (USA) **(50)** *(RAkehurst)* 8-3 ‡³RPerham (1) (lw: prom: 4th st: rdn & wknd over 1f out) ..................................................................... 1¹/₂.7
3491 Juliasdarkinvader *(AMoore)* 8-11 NAdams (7) (hld up in tch: effrt 2f out: nt pce to chal) .................................................................................................. 1¹/₂.8
3611⁴ Honour and Glory *(BobJones)* 8-6 NDay (9) (nvr nrr) .................................... ¹/₂.9
3410 More Than Love *(PAKelleway)* 8-6 GayKelleway (10) (nvr nr ldrs) ................. nk.10
3115 Calenick Lass *(DHaydnJones)* 8-6 TyroneWilliams (6) (lw: plld hrd: led over 6f: wknd 2f out) ........................................................................................... hd.11
2389 Longlife (IRE) **(51)** (v) *(MHTompkins)* 8-11 PRobinson (3) (prom: 2nd st: wknd 3f out) ................................................................................................... 1.12
3508 Imafifer (IRE) **(55)** *(WRMuir)* 8-11 AClark (2) (m.n.s) .................................... 8.13
2195 Freebyjove **(40)** *(PButler)* 7-13 ‡⁷SDrowne (13) (swtg: plld hrd: 3rd st: wknd 3f out: t.o) .......................................................................................... nk.14
3480 Stage Artist *(JEtherington)* 8-6 NConnorton (19) (chsd ldrs to ¹/₂-wy: hmpd & lost pl ent st: t.o) ...................................................................................... 1¹/₂.15
Eve's Treasure *(RCurtis)* 8-6 GBardwell (12) (w'like: bkwd: s.s: a bhd: t.o) ... 2¹/₂.16
3580 The Golden Sport *(GLewis)* 8-8 ‡³DHarrison (16) (prom 7f: sn wknd: t.o) ...... hd.17
3077 Five Clubs (IRE) **(54)** *(DTThom)* 8-6 DBiggs (18) (a bhd: t.o) ........................ 10.18
3307 First Reserve **(47)** (bl) *(BSRothwell)* 8-11 JFortune (8) (t.o) ........................ 15.19

**4/1** Pondering(op 6/1), **9/2** Honorary Guest(4/1—6/1), **5/1** Honour and Glory(4/1—6/1), Stage Artist, **6/1** Kaloochi(op 4/1), **10/1** TREPIDATION (IRE)(op 20/1), **12/1** Five Clubs (IRE), Longlife (IRE), **14/1** More Than Love, Arctic Agnes (USA), Bohemian Queen, **20/1** The Golden Sport, Juliasdarkinvader, Imafifer (IRE), **33/1** Achy Breaky, Calenick Lass, Eve's Treasure, **50/1** Ors. CSF £63.03, Tote £18.70: £2.90 £1.80 £2.70 (£70.60). Mrs S. C. York (EAST ILSLEY) bred by Mrs M. Mansergh in Ireland. 19 Rn; No bid
2m 15.7 (13)

## 3686

BADGER STKS (3-Y.O) £2898.00 (£864.00: £412.00: £186.00)
**1m 1f 218y**                                                          3-00 (3-03)

3259* **Caspian Tern (USA)** *(HCandy)* 8-11 AMunro (5) (chsd ldr: 2nd st: led over 1f out: qcknd clr nr fin) ........................................................................... —1
3368⁶ Amaze **(90)** *(LadyHerries)* 9-5 JReid (2) (b: lw: hld up: 4th st: hdwy over 2f out: ev ch 1f out: unable qckn) ........................................................... 1¹/₂.2

3533⁶ Tapis Rouge (IRE) **(Fav)** *(HRACecil)* 10-1  SCauthen (1) (lw: led tl hdd ent fnl f:
         kpt on u.p) ................................................................................ s.h.3
3439⁴ She's Pleased (USA) **(77)** *(LMCumani)* 8-10  LDettori (1) (lw: plld hrd: prom: 3rd
         st: rdn 2f out: one pce) ..................................................................... ³/₄.4
3583⁵ Majestic Sinclair (IRE) *(RHollinshead)* 8-11  WRyan (3) (hld up: 5th st: wknd 2f
         out: t.o) ................................................................................... 6.5

**7/4** Tapis Rouge (IRE)(11/10—2/1), **11/4** She's Pleased (USA), **3/1** Amaze, **7/2** CASPIAN TERN (USA), **50/1**
Majestic Sinclair (IRE). CSF £13.22, Tote £4.20: £2.10 £1.50 (£10.30). Mr Fahd Salman (WANTAGE) bred by
Wimborne Farm Incorporated in USA. 5 Rh                                    2m 12.3 (9.6)
                                                                          SF—21/26/35/14/3

## 3687                RABBIT H'CAP (0-70) £3713.50 (£1036.00: £500.50)    1m 3f 183y    3-30 (3-35)

3540⁵ **Pennine Star (IRE) (53)** *(CWCElsey)* 4-8-11  LDettori (5) (a gng wl: 5th st: led
         3f out: clr over 1f out: r.o wl) ............................................................ —1
3540³ Continuity **(52)** *(MHTompkins)* 3-8-2  PRobinson (21) (hdwy 3f out: r.o ins fnl f:
         nt trble wnr) ............................................................................. 5.2
3403⁴ Addicted to Love **(62)** *(PJMakin)* 3-8-12  TQuinn (1) (6th st: rdn & ev ch over 2f
         out: one pce) ............................................................................ 2.3
3610* Swan Heights **(56)** *(Fav)* *(JRFanshawe)* 3-8-6 (5x) GDuffield (3) (hld up: stdy
         hdwy 6f out: 8th st: one pce fnl 2f) ....................................................... hd.4
3279 Bit on the Side (IRE) **(58)** *(WJMusson)* 3-8-8  JReid (14) (hld up: hdwy over 3f
         out: one pce fnl 2f) ...................................................................... 2.5
2415² Hymne D'Amour (USA) **(53)** *(MissHCKnight)* 4-8-11  BRaymond (2) (7th st: hrd
         rdn & no hdwy fnl 2f) ..................................................................... 1.6
3064* Incola **(59)** *(HCandy)* 6-8-10 ‡⁷AntoinetteArmes (22) (hld up & bhd: hdwy over
         2f out: nvr nr to chal) ................................................................... s.h.7
3467⁶ Vasiliev **(69)** *(v)* *(JPLeigh)* 4-9-13  DNicholls (9) (s.s: hdwy 3f out: rdn 2f out: nt
         rch ldrs) ................................................................................ nk.8
299 Our Slimbridge **(42)** *(CNWilliams)* 4-8-0(2) JCurant (6) (lw: lost pl 6f out: hdwy
         over 2f out: rdn & wknd over 1f out) ..................................................... nk.9
3493³ J P Morgan **(40)** *(v)* *(MPNaughton)* 4-7-9 ‡³DHarrison (19) (a bhd) ............ 2¹/₂.10
3409 Regal Lover (IRE) **(65)** *(MBell)* 3-9-1  JCarroll (11) (lw: 9th st: hrd rdn & hdwy
         over 3f out: wknd 2f out) ................................................................ 5.11
3492 Pippas Song **(61)** (bl) *(GWragg)* 3-8-11  MRoberts (4) (2nd st: led over 3f out:
         sn hdd & wknd) .......................................................................... ¹/₂.12
3522³ Altermeera **(57)** *(MrsBarbaraWaring)* 4-9-1  NHowe (7) (hdwy over 4f out: wknd
         over 2f out) ............................................................................. 10.13
Mister Oddy **(43)** *(JSKing)* 6-8-1  GBardwell (8) (bkwd: prom: rdn 6f out: 4th st:
         wknd over 3f out) ....................................................................... 2¹/₂.14
3398⁵ Debt Swap (USA) **(67)** *(JHMGosden)* 3-9-3  RCochrane (16) (b.nr hind: a bhd) hd.15
3426 Atlantic Way **(40)** *(CJHill)* 4-7-12  NAdams (10) (a bhd) .......................... ¹/₂.16
3293³ El Rabab (USA) **(62)** *(HThomsonJones)* 3-8-12  RHills (17) (3rd st: wknd 2f out) hd.17
3628³ Rousitto **(70)** *(RHollinshead)* 4-10-0  WRyan (12) (a bhd) ........................ ³/₄.18
Triple Top **(40)** *(KWhite)* 7-7-12  NCarlisle (13) (bkwd: prom over 5f) ............. 1¹/₂.19
3522 Heniu (USA) **(63)** *(LordHuntingdon)* 3-8-13  DMcKeown (18) (lw: led over 8f) s.h.20
Ballystate **(55)** *(CJames)* 4-8-13  DaleGibson (20) (bkwd: bhd fnl 5f) .............. nk.21
442 James Is Special (IRE) **(61)** *(HJCollingridge)* 4-9-5  JQuinn (15) (t.o) ........... dist.22

**4/1** Swan Heights, **11/2** Continuity, **7/1** Bit on the Side (IRE), **10/1** Incola(op 6/1), Rousitto, **11/1** J P
Morgan(8/1—12/1), **14/1** Pippas Song, Addicted to Love, **16/1** El Rabab (USA), Atlantic Way, Our Slimbridge,
PENNINE STAR (IRE), **20/1** Regal Lover (IRE), Altermeera, Hymne D'Amour (USA), Debt Swap (USA), **25/1**
Heniu (USA), **33/1** Ballystate, Vasiliev, James Is Special (IRE), **100/1** Ors. CSF £105.11, CT £1,209.93. Tote
£21.20: £4.50 £1.90 £3.70 £2.40 (£77.10). Mr C. W. C. Elsey (MALTON) bred by Baronrath Stud Ltd in Ireland.
22 Rn                                                                    2m 36.7 (7.9)
                                                                        SF—42/23/29/22/20/21

## 3688        HEDGEHOG STKS (2-Y-O) £2976.00 (£888.00: £424.00: £192.00)
              5f 218y                                                    4-00 (4-00)

2528 **Young Ern (98)** *(SDow)* 9-1  TQuinn (2) (lw: chsd ldr: led over 2f out: rdn out) .. —1
1457² **So Factual (USA) (100)** *(Fav)* *(GHarwood)* 9-1  PatEddery (3) (bkwd: hld up:
         hdwy 2f out: rdn over 1f out: one pce) ................................................... 5.2
Dickins *(RHollinshead)* 8-11  WRyan (5) (cmpt: bkwd: s.i.s: rdn & outpcd over 3f
         out: sme late hdwy) ..................................................................... 10.3
3478⁵ Greenwich Chalenge **(81)** *(WCarter)* 9-1  BRouse (1) (b.hind: hld up: rdn over
         2f out: eased whn btn over 1f out) ...................................................... s.h.4
3390 Arras Royale **(50)** *(v)* *(JELong)* 8-11  NAdams (4) (led over 3f) ............... 5.5

**1/3** So Factual (USA), **11/2** Greenwich Chalenge, **6/1** YOUNG ERN, **33/1** Dickins, **100/1** Arras Royale. CSF
£8.19, Tote £6.40: £1.60 £1.20 (£1.90). Mr M. F. Kentish (EPSOM) bred by M. F. Kentish. 5 Rn  1m 16.5 (6.5)
                                                                        SF—25/5/–/–/–/–

**3689**  SHELDUCK H'CAP (0-70) £2994.00 (£834.00: £402.00)  7f 9y  4-30 (4-36)

3413 **Bernstein Bette (65)** *(PSFelgate)* 6-9-9 JWilliams (11) (hld up in rr: gd hdwy over 1f out: r.o strly to ld nr fin) ............................... —1
3545 Roca Murada (IRE) **(57)** (v) *(MJRyan)* 3-8-12 PRobinson (9) (a.p: n.m.r wl over 1f out: led ins fnl f tl nr fin) ............................... 1½.2
3545³ Ballerina Bay **(61)** (v) *(DTThom)* 4-9-5 LDettori (8) (a.p: led over 1f out tl ins fnl f: r.o) ............................... ¾.3
3460* Penny Drops **(54)** (Fav) *(LordHuntingdon)* 3-8-9 AMunro (10) (a.p: led 2f out: sn hdd: nt qckn ins fnl f) ............................... nk.4
3595* Cee-Jay-Ay **(52)** *(JBerry)* 5-8-3 ‡7PRoberts (18) (hld up: hdwy & nt clr run wl over 1f out: r.o ins fnl f) ............................... 1½.5
3002 Co-Chin (IRE) **(70)** *(GLewis)* 3-9-0 ‡3DHarrison (4) (rdn & no hdwy fnl 2f) ............ 2.6
3615 Don't Forsake Me **(59)** *(DMorley)* 3-9-0 MBirch (3) (prom 5f) ............................... 6.7
3511 Amethystine (USA) **(62)** *(RJHodges)* 6-8-13 ‡7SDrowne (2) (nvr nrr) ............................... nk.8
3481² Alnasric Pete (USA) **(50)** *(DAWilson)* 6-8-8 GCarter (5) (b: hld up: hdwy over 2f out: wknd over 1f out) ............................... 1.9
3524 Executive Spirit **(73)** *(DSasse)* 3-8-12 RPrice (6) (nvr nrr) ............................... ½.10
3511⁴ Charmed Knave **(55)** *(DRLaing)* 7-8-13 TyroneWilliams (7) (hdwy 3f out: hrd rdn & wknd 2f out) ............................... 4.11
3417 Just a Step **(70)** *(MMcCormack)* 6-10-0 AClark (13) (n.d) ............................... hd.12
Scaraben **(60)** *(HJCollingridge)* 4-9-4 VSmith (1) (swtg: bkwd: n.d) ............................... 1½.13
3396⁴ Eastleigh **(62)** *(RHollinshead)* 3-9-3 WRyan (14) (prom 5f) ............................... 1½.14
2634⁵ Karen Louise **(70)** *(MissHCKnight)* 3-9-4 ‡7AGarth (12) (bit bkwd: led 2f: led over 3f out to 2f out: sn wknd) ............................... nk.15
3317 Lucknam Style **(60)** *(MrsBarbaraWaring)* 4-9-4 NHowe (16) (plld hrd: led 5f out tl over 3f out: wknd over 2f out) ............................... ¾.16
3604 Prince Rooney (IRE) **(60)** *(PButler)* 4-8-13 ‡5JWeaver (20) (bhd fnl 3f) ............................... 2.17
3359 Seneca Reef (IRE) **(57)** (bl) *(IADalding)* 4-9-11 .IReid (17) (prom 3f) ............................... ¾.18
3576 Absonal **(69)** *(RHannon)* 3-9-3 ‡3RPerham (19) (prom 4f) ............................... ½.19
2993 Mere Chants **(59)** *(CWeedon)* 3-9-0 JLowe (15) (t.o) ............................... 4.20

**9/2** Penny Drops, **5/1** Cee-Jay-Ay, **11/2** Ballerina Bay, **7/1** Alnasric Pete (USA), **10/1** Roca Murada (IRE), BERNSTEIN BETTE, **14/1** Amethystine (USA), Charmed Knave, Eastleigh, **16/1** Absonal, Prince Rooney (IRE), **20/1** Karen Louise, Seneca Reef (IRE), Scaraben, **25/1** Co-Chin (IRE), Don't Forsake Me, **33/1** Mere Chants, Just a Step, Executive Spirit, **50/1** Lucknam Style. CSF £111.04, CT £578.56. Tote £14.30: £3.70 £2.10 £2.50 £1.80 (£154.90). Mr John Ford (MELTON MOWBRAY) bred by C. G. Reid. 20 Rn
SF—58/42/47/36/25/38

**3690**  DORMOUSE APP'CE STKS (Mdn 3-Y.O) £2553.00 (£708.00: £339.00)  1m 8y  5-00 (5-10)

3416⁵ **Pippin Park (USA) (69)** *(HCandy)* 8-2 ‡7AntoinetteArmes (5) (hld up: hdwy 3f out: led over 1f out: pushed out) ............................... —1
Whatever's Right (IRE) *(MDIUsher)* 8-7 ‡7JHunter (4) (w'like: leggy: hrd rdn & hdwy fnl 2f: r.o) ............................... 5.2
3087³ Fairy Wisher (IRE) *(ACStewart)* 8-2 ‡7ElizabethForletta (3) (hdwy over 3f out: one pce fnl 2f) ............................... s.h.3
2810 Desert Force (IRE) **(68)** *(MissGayKelleway)* 8-7 ‡7PBowe (1) (a.p: rdn 3f out: one pce fnl 2f) ............................... 4.4
3583² Just a Mirage (Fav) *(AAScott)* 8-2 ‡7JTate (12) (b.hind: led: rdn & hdd over 1f out: wknd fnl f) ............................... 2½.5
3048 Sharp Dance **(43)** *(BSmart)* 8-9 CHawksley (15) (swtg: w ldrs 6f) ............................... 1½.6
3238 Vernonia **(65)** *(JHMGosden)* 8-9 StephenDavies (11) (prom over 5f) ............................... 5.7
3583 Swinging Tich **(48)** *(BAMcMahon)* 8-2 ‡7SSanders (14) (prom over 5f) ............................... 2½.8
Chirinda (IRE) *(RJHodges)* 8-2 ‡7SDrowne (2) (lengthy: lt-f: prom 6f) ............................... ½.9
*3374* Gold Belt (IRE) **(44)** *(RHollinshead)* 8-2 ‡7DCarson (13) (dwlt: hdwy over 3f out: wknd 2f out) ............................... 1½.10
3416 Emily Allan (IRE) *(KOCunningham-Brown)* 8-2 ‡7BRussell (9) (a bhd) ............................... 3½.11
Deborah Shelley *(EAWheeler)* 8-9 SWilliams (8) (bit bkwd: a bhd) ............................... 4.12
3416 Hullo Mary Doll *(RIngram)* 8-2 ‡7TAshley (16) (swvd bdly rt s: a in rr) ............................... 2½.13
*3557* Dilkush **(38)** *(LJHolt)* 8-7 ‡7CAvery (6) (a bhd) ............................... ½.14
1159 Frankus **(46)** *(SMellor)* 8-7 ‡7PMcCabe (10) (bkwd: prom 5f) ............................... 1½.15
2162² Angel's Wing **(42)** *(RMWhitaker)* 8-2 ‡7GParkin (7) (bkwd: prom tl wknd qckly 3f out) ............................... 2½.16

**11/8** Just a Mirage(10/11—13/8), **6/1** PIPPIN PARK (USA), **13/2** Fairy Wisher (IRE)(8/1—12/1), Desert Force (IRE)(op 4/1), **8/1** Vernonia(op 5/1), **14/1** Chirinda (IRE), Swinging Tich, Gold Belt (IRE), **25/1** Angel's Wing, **33/1** Sharp Dance, **50/1** Whatever's Right (IRE), Frankus, **66/1** Ors. CSF £223.10, Tote £8.90: £5.10 £19.30 £1.10 (£634.00). Major M. G. Wyatt (WANTAGE) bred by Major Michael G. Wyatt in USA. 16 Rn   1m 42.6 (7.6)
SF—28/18/12/5/–/–

T/Plpt: £40.10 (61.9 Tckts).  IM/KH

## LEICESTER (R-H)
### Tuesday, October 13th [Good to soft]
Going Allowance: 0.30 sec per fur (G)　　　　　　　　　　Wind: almost nil

Stalls: high

**3691**　　E.B.F. SOAR STKS (Mdn 2-Y.O.C) £3370.50 (£938.00: £451.50)　　**1m 8y** 2-10 (2-14)

| | |
|---|---|
| 3005 | **Dyab (USA)** *(PTWalwyn)* 9-0 WCarson (10) (bit bkwd: hdwy ½-wy: led appr fnl f: sn clr) ........................................................... —1 |
| | Azzilfi *(JLDunlop)* 9-0 TQuinn (1) (lt-f: hld up: hdwy over 1f out: fin fast) .. 1.2 |
| 3593⁴ | Allegation *(PFICole)* 9-0 AMunro (8) (lw: chsd ldrs: effrt over 1f out: one pce) ... 3.3 |
| 3525⁵ | League Leader (IRE) *(MRStoute)* 9-0 WRSwinburn (14) (a.p: rdn over 1f out: one pce) ........................................................ 1.4 |
| 3402 | Naawy *(MRStoute)* 8-9 ‡⁵JJones (6) (still bkwd: chsd ldrs: styd on ins fnl f: nvr nrr) ................................................... 2½.5 |
| | Lord Nitrogen (USA) *(MBell)* 9-0 MHills (13) (leggy: lt-f: chsd ldrs: no hdwy fnl 2f) ........................................................ 2.6 |
| 3523 | The Where Withal *(SirMarkPrescott)* 9-0 GDuffield (7) (effrt & nt clr run over 2f out: no prog) ............................................. ¾.7 |
| 3314² | Triple (Fav) *(BWHills)* 9-0 PatEddery (11) (prom: led over 3f out tl over 1f out: sn rdn & btn) ........................................... s.h.8 |
| | Vistec Express (IRE) *(HRACecil)* 9-0 WRyan (18) (scope: unf: dwlt: hdwy ½-wy: wknd 2f out) ........................................ ¾.9 |
| 3489² | Outset (IRE) *(HCandy)* 9-0 CRutter (4) (lw: m.n.s) ............................ 2½.10 |
| 3489⁶ | Lunar Risk *(WRMuir)* 9-0 RCochrane (2) (m.n.s) .............................. ¾.11 |
| 3525 | Collier Bay *(JHMGosden)* 9-0 SCauthen (3) (bit bkwd: rdn over 2f out: nvr nr ldrs) ............................................................ nk.12 |
| 3402 | Barton Royal (IRE) *(RHollinshead)* 9-0 LDettori (5) (chsd ldrs far side 5f) ..... 3.13 |
| 3525 | Gradient *(MrsJCecil)* 9-0 PaulEddery (17) (chsd ldrs over 5f) ................ nk.14 |
| | Super Elegant *(MJFetherston-Godley)* 9-0 PRobinson (15) (wl grwn: bit bkwd: nvr nr ldrs) ...................................................... 4.15 |
| 1630⁶ | Remembrance Day (IRE) *(RHannon)* 9-0 RHills (9) (prom over 4f) ............ 1½.16 |
| | Prakash (IRE) *(CEBrittain)* 9-0 MRoberts (12) (neat: bit bkwd: dwlt: a bhd) ... ½.17 |
| 3035 | Sheer Ecstasy *(PMMcEntee)* 9-0 RPrice (16) (led tl hdd over 3f out: sn wknd) .......................................................... ½.18 |

**7/4** Triple, **7/1** League Leader (IRE)(7/2—8/1), **8/1** Gradient, **17/2** Allegation, **11/1** Vistec Express (IRE)(5/1—12/1), **12/1** DYAB (USA), Azzilfi, **14/1** Lord Nitrogen (USA), Outset (IRE), **16/1** Prakash (IRE), **20/1** Naawy, The Where Withal, Collier Bay, **25/1** Remembrance Day (IRE), **33/1** Ors. CSF £150.89, Tote £19.90: £4.20 £4.80 £3.20 (Wnr or 2nd w any £5.60). Mr Hamdan Al-Maktoum (LAMBOURN) bred by Shadwell Farm Inc in USA. 18 Rn　　　　　　　　　　　　　　　　1m 41.9 (6.9)
　　　　　　　　　　　　　　　　　　　　　　　　SF—33/30/21/18/5/4

**3692**　　WHISSENDINE (S) STKS (3-Y.O) £2721.00 (£756.00: £363.00)
　　　　　**1m 1f 218y**　　　　　　　　　　　　　　　2-40 (2-50)

| | |
|---|---|
| 3504 | **Dare to Dream (IRE) (51)** *(GLewis)* 8-3 ‡³DHarrison (4) (hdwy 3f out: hrd rdn to ld ins fnl f: r.o) .................................... —1 |
| 3569⁶ | Handsome Gent (67) (Fav) *(LordHuntingdon)* 8-6 AMunro (2) (5th st: led over 1f out tl ins fnl f: unable qckn) ...................... 1½.2 |
| 3603 | Merls Pearl (41) (bl) *(JAGlover)* 7-12 ‡³SMaloney (8) (led tl over 3f out: kpt on u.p fnl f) ........................................ 3.3 |
| 3601⁴ | Jalore (41) *(RHollinshead)* 8-6 WRyan (12) (chsd ldrs: 4th st: hrd rdn & one pce fnl f) .................................................. 2½.4 |
| 3604² | Ace Reporter (57) (v) *(MHTompkins)* 8-7 PRobinson (3) (hdwy 3f out: styd on u.p ins fnl f) ........................................ 1½.5 |
| 3629² | Aegaean Lady (41) *(JEtherington)* 8-4 ‡³FNorton (1) (in tch: 6th st: effrt over 2f out: hrd rdn & no ex ins fnl f) .................... 1½.6 |
| 3584⁵ | The Titan Ghost (57) *(BAMcMahon)* 8-6 TQuinn (5) (chsd ldr: 2nd st: led over 3f out tl over 1f out: sn wknd) ...................... ½.7 |
| 3510 | Gerish (IRE) (34) *(JPearce)* 8-1 RPrice (11) (nvr nr to chal) ................ ½.8 |
| 3521⁴ | Roxy River *(RHannon)* 9-5 MRoberts (15) (prom: 3rd st: wknd over 2f out) ....... ½.9 |
| 3601 | Feeling Foolish (IRE) (53) (bl) *(BForsey)* 8-6 RCochrane (13) (a in rr) ......... s.h.10 |
| | Sol Rouge (IRE) *(RThompson)* 8-5⁽¹⁾ KFallon (14) (small: lw: s.s: a bhd: t.o) .... 8.11 |
| 3592 | Divine Glory *(RVoorspuy)* 7-10 ‡⁵BDoyle (10) (7th st: wknd 3f out) ......... 15.12 |
| | Cool Flight *(RThompson)* 8-5⁽¹⁾ AClark (7) (lengthy: unf: bkwd: s.s: a bhd: t.o) ... ¾.13 |
| 3251 | Salmon Dancer (IRE) (30) *(MFBarraclough)* 8-12 GCarter (6) (s.s: a bhd: t.o) .. 30.14 |
| | *3409 Handy Lass (5/1) Withdrawn (insecure tack in stalls) : not under orders* |

**100/30** Handsome Gent, **4/1** DARE TO DREAM (IRE), **7/1** Ace Reporter(op 4/1), **10/1** Aegaen Lady, Jalore(op 16/1), **11/1** The Titan Ghost(7/1—12/1), Roxy River, **14/1** Feeling Foolish (IRE), **16/1** Gerish (IRE), **33/1** Sol Rouge (IRE), Cool Flight, **50/1** Ors. CSF £14.00, Tote £3.90: £1.50 £2.50 £10.70 (£7.20). Mrs Shirley Robins (EPSOM) bred by Bhima Breeding Partnership in Ireland. 14 Rn; Bt in 4,000 gns　　2m 11.8 (9.1)
SF—28/28/14/17/9/9

## 3693

E.B.F. REFERENCE POINT STKS (Mdn 2-Y.O.C) £4467.50 (£1340.00: £645.00: £297.50)
**7f 9y**　　　　　　　　　　　　　　　　　　　　　　3-10 (3-18)

3532² **Gabr** (Fav) *(RWArmstrong)* 9-0 WCarson (8) (mde msct: rdn clr fnl f) ............... —1
　　　　Bamburgh (USA) *(MRStoute)* 9-0 MRoberts (12) (w'like: leggy: bit bkwd: chsd
　　　　　ldrs: rdn over 1f out: r.o) .................................................... 2.2
3532⁵ Press Gallery *(MrsJCecil)* 9-0 PaulEddery (4) (chsd ldrs: rdn & r.o wl fnl f) ...... 1½.3
　　　　Arkaan (USA) *(MRStoute)* 9-0 WRSwinburn (11) (lt-f: hld up: hdwy 2f out: r.o
　　　　　strly ins fnl f) .............................................................. 1½.4
3372⁴ Tickerty's Gift *(RHannon)* 9-0 BRouse (15) (w ldrs: slt ld 2f out: sn hdd: one
　　　　　pce) ............................................................................ ½.5
　　　　Dover Patrol (IRE) *(HRACecil)* 9-0 WRyan (13) (w'like: scope: hdwy 2f out: styd
　　　　　on ins fnl f) .................................................................. 3½.6
3531 Pyrrhic Dance *(JWHills)* 9-0 MHills (6) (w ldrs 5f) ................................ ½.7
3531⁵ Bohemian Crown (USA) *(MRStoute)* 9-0 SCauthen (7) (chsd ldrs: rdn 2f out: sn
　　　　　btn) ........................................................................... ½.8
　　　　Missed Flight *(CFWall)* 9-0 PRobinson (5) (lt-f: s.i.s: nvr nrr) ................. 1½.9
3011 Tabkir (USA) *(JLDunlop)* 9-0 TQuinn (10) (s.s: a bhd) ............................. 1½.10
　　　　Salbus *(GHarwood)* 9-0 PatEddery (9) (gd sort: bkwd: a in rr) .................... 2.11
　　　　Ijab (CAN) *(AAScott)* 9-0 GCarter (3) (w'like: bit bkwd: m.n.s) ................. 1½.12
　　　　One Voice (USA) *(SirMarkPrescott)* 9-0 GDuffield (14) (tall: a in rr) .......... s.h.13
3552⁵ Al Moulouki *(JWPayne)* 9-0 RCochrane (1) (outpcd: a bhd) ........................ 2½.14
3465⁵ Safety in Numbers *(MrsJRRamsden)* 9-0 GBaxter (2) (bhd fnl 3f) ................. 1½.15
　　　　Labudu (USA) (16/1) Withdrawn (ref to ent stalls) : not under orders

**5/4** GABR(10/11—6/4), **7/1** Press Gallery, **8/1** Bamburgh (USA)(14/1—7/1), **9/1** Bohemian Crown (USA)(6/1—10/1), Tickerty's Gift(op 6/1), Salbus(op 6/1), **11/1** Dover Patrol (IRE)(8/1—12/1), **12/1** Arkaan (USA)(op 6/1), **16/1** Tabkir (USA), **20/1** Ijab (CAN), **33/1** Missed Flight, Al Moulouki, **50/1** Ors. CSF £13.66, Tote £1.90: £1.40 £3.50 £2.00 (£12.30). Mr Hamdan Al-Maktoum (NEWMARKET) bred by Shadwell Estate Company Limited. 15 Rn　　1m 28.1 (5.8)
SF—44/38/33/28/26/15

## 3694

WYMESWOLD CLAIMING STKS (2-Y.O) £3057.00 (£852.00: £411.00)
**5f 218y**　　　　　　　　　　　　　　　　　　　　　　3-40 (3-46)

3598 **Awesome Risk** (54) *(GLewis)* 7-7 ‡7AGarth (18) (hdwy 2f out: led ins fnl f: sn clr) —1
3553² La Bonita (IRE) (61) (v) *(JBerry)* 8-0 GCarter (15) (chsd ldrs: led over 1f out tl ins
　　　　　fnl f: one pce) ................................................................ 2½.2
3313 Manx Monarch (85) *(RHollinshead)* 8-4 WRyan (11) (hdwy over 2f out: r.o u.p
　　　　　ins fnl f) ..................................................................... s.h.3
2696⁵ Walid's Princess (IRE) (59) *(JWharton)* 8-5⁽¹⁾ AClark (20) (chsd ldrs: hrd rdn
　　　　　over 1f out: one pce) ......................................................... 2.4
3590 Girl Next Door (57) *(NAGraham)* 8-2 WCarson (9) (hdwy over 1f out: fin wl) ...... 1.5
3390³ Air Command (BAR) (72) *(RHannon)* 8-13 RHills (16) (chsd ldrs over 4f) ......... nk.6
3580* Rich Midas (IRE) (63) *(GLewis)* 7-7 ‡7CHawksley (14) (in tch: styd on ins
　　　　　fnl f: nvr nrr) ............................................................... ¾.7
3558² Wickins (57) (bl) *(GLewis)* 8-2 ‡3FNorton (4) (led tl hdd over 1f out: wknd qckly) hd.8
3410 Dontbetalking (IRE) *(JWharton)* 8-0 SSWilliams (13) (nvr nrr) ................... hd.9
3590 Musical Phone (66) *(JPLeigh)* 8-9 KFallon (17) (nvr nr to chal) ................. 2½.10
3410 Wrightmill (IRE) *(CTinkler)* 8-7 MBirch (19) (m.n.s) ............................ nk.11
2994⁶ Bodandere (55) *(MJFetherston-Godley)* 8-4 MRoberts (21) (chsd ldrs on
　　　　　outside: rdn 2f out: eased whn btn ins fnl f) ................................ 2½.12
3148 Ruby Cooper (58) *(JWharton)* 8-3 PRobinson (12) (prom over 3f) ................. 3.13
3173 Coopers Delight (54) *(GLewis)* 8-2 ‡3DHarrison (5) (m.n.s) ....................... 1½.14
3607 Green Sword (bl) *(WAO'Gorman)* 9-3 LDettori (10) (m.n.s) ........................ ¾.15
3242 Risk Proof (64) *(KOCunningham-Brown)* 8-13 PatEddery (8) (chsd ldrs to
　　　　　½-wy) ......................................................................... nk.16
3181 Freckenham (JEBanks) 7-9 ‡5NKennedy (2) (m.n.s) ................................. nk.17
2584⁶ Keltic Danseuse (IRE) (57) *(MrsLPiggott)* 7-7 ‡7GMilligan (3) (m.n.s) ......... 1½.18
3486³ Admired *(MRChannon)* 8-2 PaulEddery (6) (bhd fnl 2f) ............................ 2.19
3407 Go Orange (42) (bl) *(JLSpearing)* 8-11⁽¹⁾ GHind (7) (lt-f: m.n.s) ............... ¾.20
3106⁵ Noteability (52) (bl) *(JBerry)* 8-4 GDuffield (22) (spd 4f) ..................... 5.21
3549 Twitcher *(GBlum)* 8-0 JFanning (1) (w ldrs 4f: wknd qckly: t.o) ................. 15.22

5/1 Rich Midas (IRE), **6/1** La Bonita (IRE), **8/1** Air Command (BAR), **10/1** Manx Monarch, **12/1** Wickins(op 8/1), Risk Proof(op 8/1), Admired, Walid's Princess (IRE), **14/1** Ruby Cooper, AWESOME RISK, **16/1** Bodandere(op 8/1), Wrightmill (IRE), Girl Next Door, **20/1** Musical Phone, Noteability, Keltic Danseuse (IRE), Freckenham, Green Sword, **25/1** Dontbetalking (IRE), **33/1** Coopers Delight, Twitcher, **50/1** Go Orange. CSF £101.25, Tote £26.10: £6.90 £2.50 £2.60 (£150.90). Roldvale Limited (EPSOM) bred by Roldvale Ltd. 22 Rn   1m 14.9 (4.9)
SF—17/14/17/10/3/13

### 3695
WREAKE STKS (3-Y.O.F) £3028.00 (£904.00: £432.00: £196.00)
**1m 8y**      4-10 (4-13)

3545[2] **Lady Debra Darley (81)** *(RHannon)* 9-5 PatEddery (8) (chsd ldrs: led 2f out: rdn out) ............................................................ —1

3416* **Galactic Miss** *(JLDunlop)* 8-11 GCarter (5) (hld up: hdwy 2f out: r.o fnl f: no ch w wnr) ............................................................ 2½.2

3506[6] **Fawz (IRE) (80)** *(RWArmstrong)* 8-11 WCarson (1) (led to 2f out & kpt on appr fnl f) ............................................................ ¾.3

3269 **Rafah (70)** *(BHanbury)* 8-9 WRSwinburn (3) (lw: chsd ldr: styd on one pce appr fnl f) ............................................................ ¾.4

3334a[3] **Anlace (85)** (Fav) *(LMCumani)* 8-11 LDettori (2) (hld up in tch: rdn over 2f out: r.o one pce) ............................................................ 10.5

3269 **Swallowcliffe (71)** (v) *(PTWalwyn)* 8-11 AMunro (7) (nvr trbld ldrs) ............ nk.6

3439[3] **Hugging (76)** *(MMcCormack)* 8-10 RCochrane (4) (hld up: hrd rdn 2f out: sn btn) ............................................................ 1½.7

3416 **Great Splendour** *(CEBrittain)* 8-6 MRoberts (9) (w ldrs over 4f: sn lost tch: t.o) .. 7.8

**Noora's Rose (NZ)** *(GHarwood)* 8-6 AClark (6) (w'like: leggy: bit bkwd: s.i.s: rdn 3f out: no imp: t.o) ............................................................ 1½.9

85/40 Anlace(6/4—3/1), **3/1** Galactic Miss, **7/1** Fawz (IRE)(op 4/1), Hugging, **15/2** LADY DEBRA DARLEY, **10/1** Rafah(8/1—12/1), **20/1** Swallowcliffe(op 10/1), **25/1** Great Splendour, **33/1** Noora's Rose (NZ). CSF £28.09, Tote £7.30: £2.30 £1.30 £2.30 (£14.20). Mrs M. R. T. Rimell (MARLBOROUGH) bred by R. P. Williams. 9 Rn
1m 40.2 (5.2)
SF—63/47/45/41/13/12

### 3696
STEWARDS H'CAP (0-70) £3346.00 (£931.00: £448.00)   **1m 8y**      4-40 (4-43)

3627[3] **Falcons Dawn (52)** *(ABailey)* 5-8-10 GBaxter (7) (hld up: swtchd rt over 1f out: r.o strly to ld last stride) ............................................................ —1

3689 **Alnasric Pete (USA) (50)** *(DAWilson)* 6-8-8 GCarter (12) (b: hld up in tch: hdwy to ld ins fnl f: ct post) ............................................................ s.h.2

3520[6] **Gachette (54)** (bl) *(JSutcliffe)* 3-8-8 PatEddery (11) (a.p: led 2f out tl ins fnl f: unable qckn) ............................................................ ½.3

3520[2] **Gold Blade (59)** *(NAGraham)* 3-8-13*RCochrane (2) (b.nr fore: s.i.s: hdwy 2f out: ev ch ent fnl f: r.o) ............................................................ ¾.4

3589[3] **Lawnswood Junior (56)** *(JLSpearing)* 5-9-0 KDarley (6) (swtg: hdwy & swtchd rt 2f out: sn ev ch: no ex fnl f) ............................................................ 1.5

3422[6] **Cretoes Dancer (USA) (55)** (bl) *(WRMuir)* 3-8-6 ‡3FNorton (19) (hdwy fnl 2f: hrd rdn & r.o) ............................................................ 1.6

2525[6] **Legend Dulac (IRE) (57)** *(JLHarris)* 3-8-11 PRobinson (14) (plld hrd: led 5f: wknd over 1f out) ............................................................ 4.7

2289[5] **Kalko (64)** *(CEBrittain)* 3-9-4 MRoberts (16) (racd alone: led 3f out to 2f out: sn wknd) ............................................................ 1½.8

3485 **Brambleberry (61)** *(MrsSJSmith)* 3-9-1 MBirch (1) (w ldrs tl wknd 2f out) ........ 2.9

3310[6] **Profilic (70)** *(CaptJWilson)* 7-10-0 WCarson (20) (lw: plld hrd: prom over 5f) . nk.10

3488[6] **Lord Oberon (IRE) (61)** (Fav) *(RJO'Sullivan)* 4-9-3 ‡3DHarrison (10) (m.n.s) .. nk.11

3520[4] **Master of the Rock (60)** *(PJMakin)* 3-9-0 TQuinn (4) (m.n.s) ............ ½.12

3159 **Wild Strawberry (55)** *(DAWilson)* 3-8-9 BRouse (9) (m.n.s) ............ hd.13

3349[6] **Martini Executive (64)** (bl) *(CBBBooth)* 4-9-3 ‡5SWilliams (15) (mid div: hrd rdn & effrt 2f out: no imp) ............................................................ hd.14

3615 **Peace Formula (IRE) (60)** *(RHollinshead)* 3-9-0 WRyan (4) (m.n.s) ........ ½.15

3476 **Champenoise (47)** *(MBell)* 4-8-5 MHills (17) (m.n.s) ............ nk.16

3288 **Chequers (IRE) (63)** *(RJRWilliams)* 3-9-3 AMunro (13) (t.o) ............ 5.17

3241 **Red Kite (64)** *(MBell)* 3-9-4 LDettori (8) (lw: prom: rdn 3f out: sn btn) ........ 1½.18

2871 **Kingchip Boy (59)** *(MJRyan)* 3-8-13 GDuffield (3) (t.o) ............ 8.19

3595 **Sirmoor (IRE) (62)** *(RHannon)* 3-9-2 RHills (18) (prom to ½-wy: sn wknd: t.o) 15.20

4/1 Lord Oberon (IRE)(op 8/1), **9/2** Gold Blade, **15/2** FALCONS DAWN, **10/1** Gachette(op 6/1), Lawnswood Junior, **12/1** Alnasric Pete (USA), **14/1** Legend Dulac (IRE), Martini Executive, Profilic, **16/1** Master of the Rock, Red Kite, Kalko, Champenoise, **20/1** Wild Strawberry, Sirmoor (IRE), Chequers (IRE), **25/1** Ors. CSF £102.89, CT £864.23. Tote £9.90: £2.50 £2.30 £3.20 £1.70 (£244.20). Mr Paul Green (Huyton) (TARPORLEY) bred by E. A. Bourke. 20 Rn      1m 41.3 (6.3)
SF—37/34/32/35/33/22

T/Plpt: £262.30 (9 Tckts).      IM

3248—**CHEPSTOW (L-H)**
**Tuesday, October 13th [Good]**
Going Allowance: 0.25 sec per fur (G)                                    Wind: nil

Stalls: high

**3697**     SWETTENHAM STKS     £3850.00 (£1150.00: £550.00: £250.00)
             1½m 23y                                                  1-45 (1-46)

3211⁵ **Mack the Knife (105)** (Fav) *(MajorWRHern)* 3–8-8 BRaymond (3) (lw: mde all:
             drvn out) ...................................................................... —1
 3357  Juniper Berry (IRE) **(84)** *(PWChapple-Hyam)* 3–7-13 DHolland (2) (hld up: 5th
             & rdn st: ev ch 1f out: r.o) .......................................... 1.2
29206⁶ Anchorage (IRE) **(89)** *(HRACecil)* 3–7-13 AMcGlone (1) (3rd st: rdn 3f out: r.o
             one pce fnl 2f) ........................................................... 1.3
 2856  Jimlil **(75)** *(BPalling)* 4–8-2 ‡⁵StephenDavies (6) (hld up: last st: hdwy fnl 2f: r.o) 5.4
3571³ Marcus Thorpe (USA) **(103)** *(PAKelleway)* 4–9-2 JReid (8) (b: chsd ldr: 2nd st:
             rdn & ev ch over 2f out: wknd wl over 1f out) .................. 2½.5
22872² Hunting Ground *(REPeacock)* 4–8-8 JQuinn (7) (4th & rdn st: wknd over 3f out) 10.6
 3527  Well Saddled (IRE) **(81)** *(DRCElsworth)* 3–8-5⁽¹⁾ JWilliams (4) (b.hind: lw: 7th
             st: a bhd) ................................................................... 2½.7
  388  Wide Support **(73)** *(AMoore)* 7–9-2 CandyMorris (5) (b: bit bkwd: 6th st: wknd
             4f out: t.o) ................................................................. 12.8

**8/11** MACK THE KNIFE, **9/2** Marcus Thorpe (USA), **8/1** Juniper Berry (IRE)(op 4/1), **9/1** Well Saddled (IRE)(op
6/1), Anchorage (IRE)(op 6/1), **25/1** Jimlil, **40/1** Hunting Ground, **66/1** Wide Support. CSF £7.08, Tote £1.60:
£1.40 £1.40 £1.70 (£4.60). Sir John Astor (LAMBOURN) bred by Sir John Astor. 8 Rn     2m 41.6 (10.3)
                                                                     SF—21/10/8/1/10/–

**3698**     MINSTER H'CAP (0-70) £2721.00 (£756.00: £363.00)     1¼m 36y     2-15 (2-22)
             (Weights raised 5 lb)

34925⁵ **Second Call (57)** *(HCandy)* 3–9-0 DMcKeown (1) (led 2f: led 5f out: jst hld on) —1
 3569★ Alderbrook **(62)** (Fav) *(MrsJCecil)* 3–9-5 JCarroll (3) (3rd st: chsd wnr over 2f
             out: hrd rdn fnl f: r.o wl) ............................................. s.h.2
 3576  Lady Lacey **(51)** (v) *(GBBalding)* 5–9-0 JWilliams (16) (hdwy 2f out: r.o ins fnl f) 3½.3
2946★ Strat's Legacy **(49)** *(DWPArbuthnot)* 5–8-7 ‡⁵JWeaver (15) (b.hind: 8th st: hdwy
             3f out: one pce fnl 2f) .................................................. 3½.4
22375⁵ Nocatchim **(57)** *(BWHills)* 3–9-0 DHolland (6) (nvr nrr) ...................... ¾.5
 3488  Royal Dartmouth (USA) **(47)** *(BRMillman)* 7–8-10 TSprake (2) (b: lw: hld up &
             bhd: hdwy over 2f out: nvr nr to chal) ............................ 4.6
30975⁵ Striking Image (IRE) **(61)** *(RHannon)* 3–9-1 ‡³RPerham (14) (lw: 5th st: rdn over
             2f out: wknd wl over 1f out) ........................................... ¾.7
36003³ Marine Society **(60)** *(RLee)* 4–9-9 BRaymond (8) (b.nr fore: 6th st: wknd 3f out) 2½.8
 3488  Old Glory **(55)** *(RJHolder)* 4–9-4 JQuinn (5) (lw: 4th st: wknd 3f out) ........... hd.9
3488² Salbyng **(61)** *(JWHills)* 4–9-10 JReid (9) (7th st: wknd 3f out) ................. nk.10
35203³ Ghurrah (IRE) **(61)** *(CJBenstead)* 3–9-4 TyroneWilliams (11) (lw: s.i.s: rdn &
             hdwy over 3f out: wknd over 1f out) ................................ 4.11
 3159  Romance (IRE) **(47)** *(MJHeaton-Ellis)* 3–8-4 DaleGibson (13) (a bhd) .......... nk.12
35224² Athar (IRE) **(63)** *(RJBaker)* 3–9-6 NHowe (4) (lw: led 8f out to 5f out: 2nd st: rdn
             & wknd over 3f out) ...................................................... ½.13
 3522  Charmed Life **(64)** *(ABarrow)* 3–9-7 NAdams (12) (a bhd) ...................... 4.14
 3476  Sudanor (IRE) **(51)** (bl) *(MJHeaton-Ellis)* 3–8-8 JLowe (7) (a bhd) ............. 3½.15
 3487  Road to Au Bon (USA) **(50)** (bl) *(RJBaker)* 4–8-13 DBiggs (10) (t.o fnl 2f) ..... 12.16

**13/2** Alderbrook, **7/1** Strat's Legacy, **15/2** Lady Lacey, **8/1** Ghurrah (IRE), Athar (IRE)(op 5/1), Salbyng, **9/1**
Striking Image (IRE)(op 5/1), **12/1** Marine Society(op 8/1), Nocatchim, Royal Dartmouth (USA), **14/1** SECOND
CALL, Charmed Life, **20/1** Road to Au Bon (USA), Sudanor (IRE), Romance (IRE)(op 10/1), **25/1** Old Glory. CSF
£103.13, CT £694.68. Tote £14.50: £2.50 £1.70 £1.90 £2.30 (£53.60). Mr C. J. R. Trotter (WANTAGE) bred by
C. J. R. Trotter. 16 Rn                                               2m 14.2 (9.9)
                                                                     SF—26/30/8/4/9/–

**3699**     LESTER PIGGOTT ALL-AGED STKS     £4191.00 (£1248.00: £594.00: £267.00)
             6f 16y                                                   2-45 (2-48)

34423³ **Montendre (112)** (Fav) *(MMcCormack)* 5–10-0 JReid (2) (a.p: led over 1f out:
             rdn out) ..................................................................... —1
 3356  Fylde Flyer **(100)** *(JBerry)* 3–9-12 JWilliams (1) (lw: a.p: rdn 3f out: ev ch ins fnl
             f: r.o) ........................................................................ 1.2
3189★ Notley **(110)** *(RHannon)* 5–10-0 BRaymond (4) (hld up: plld out over 1f out: ev
             ch ins fnl f: nt qckn) ..................................................... hd.3
31246⁶ Sizzling Saga (IRE) **(104)** *(JBerry)* 4–9-5 JCarroll (3) (led over 4f) ............ ¾.4

**13/8** MONTENDRE, **5/2** Notley, **7/2** Ors. CSF £6.84, Tote £2.10 (£3.80). Mr David Mort (WANTAGE) bred by A. B. Phipps. 4 Rn
1m 14 (5)
SF—44/38/39/27

## 3700
MADEMOISELLE H'CAP (ladies) (0-70) £2679.00 (£744.00: £357.00)
6f 16y

3-15 (3-19)

3545 **Bill Moon (50)** *(PJFeilden)* 6-10-1 MissJFeilden (12) (lw: a.p: led over 1f out: drvn out) ....................................................... —1
3488³ Kissavos **(50)** (v) *(CCElsey)* 6-9-8 ‡7MissAElsey (17) (lw: w ldr: led over 3f out tl over 1f out: one pce) ................................... 3.2
3539³ Blue Topaze **(65)** (Fav) *(RJHolder)* 4-11-2 MrsEMellor (7) (lw: hdwy over 1f out: r.o ins fnl f) ......................................... 3.3
3355 Iron King **(70)** (v) *(JLSpearing)* 6-11-0 ‡7MissCSpearing (15) (hdwy over 1f out: r.o) ................................................... 1.4
3524 Ayr Raider **(62)** *(WRMuir)* 5-10-13 MissLPerratt (1) (lw: hdwy over 1f out: nvr nrr) nk.5
3575 Martinosky **(61)** *(WGRWightman)* 6-10-7 ‡5MissMClark (11) (hdwy over 2f out: wknd fnl f) ......................................... ¾.6
32576 Gallant Hope **(53)** (bl) *(LGCottrell)* 10-10-4 MrsLPearce (9) (no hdwy fnl 2f) .... 1½.7
3592² Stitched Up (IRE) **(61)** *(PWChapple-Hyam)* 4-10-3 ‡7MrsJChapple-Hyam (10) (led over 2f: wknd over 1f out) ............................. s.h.8
3511 Precious Air (IRE) **(55)** *(AMoore)* 4-9-13 ‡7MrsJMoore (18) (prom 4f) ......... 1½.9
35115 Fay's Song (IRE) **(69)** *(RAkehurst)* 4-11-6 MissJAllison (8) (swtg: prom over 3f) nk.10
3632 Soba Guest (IRE) **(64)** *(JBerry)* 3-10-13 MissIDWJones (2) (lw: prom 4f) .... s.h.11
3496 Just Bob **(63)** (bl) *(SEKettlewell)* 3-10-7 ‡5MrsDKettlewell (13) (n.d) ........... s.h.12
3600 Rimouski **(57)** *(BRCambidge)* 4-10-3 ‡5MrsHNoonan (16) (a bhd) ............... 2½.13
34004 Mogwai (IRE) **(65)** *(RFJohnsonHoughton)* 3-11-0 MissEJohnsonHoughton (4) (a bhd) .............................................. 2.14
3296★ Rainbow Fleet **(60)** *(DMarks)* 4-10-11 MissKMarks (14) (prom 3f) ........... 2½.15
3524 Unveiled **(58)** *(RJHodges)* 4-10-9 MrsJHembrow (19) (bhd fnl 2f) ............. ¾.16
3575 The Noble Oak (IRE) **(57)** (bl) *(MMcCormack)* 4-10-3 ‡5MissSFarrant (6) (lw: prom over 4f) ........................................ 1.17
3400 Luna Bid **(62)** *(MBlanshard)* 9-10-13 MissABillot (20) (dwlt: a bhd) ........... 1.18
716⁵ Tynron Doon **(65)** *(DJWintle)* 3-10-7 ‡7MissSBroadley (3) (bhd fnl 3f) ......... 5.19
3304 Glencroft **(52)** (bl) *(DWChapman)* 8-9-10 ‡7MissRClark (5) (s.s: swtchd lft: a in rr: t.o) ..................................................... 20

**4/1** Blue Topaze(op 6/1), **15/2** Gallant Hope, **8/1** Rainbow Fleet, **9/1** Stitched Up (IRE), **10/1** BILL MOON(op 6/1), **12/1** Kissavos, Unveiled, **14/1** Just Bob, Martinosky, Soba Guest (IRE), Luna Bid, Ayr Raider, Precious Air (IRE), Fay's Song (IRE), Mogwai (IRE), Iron King(10/1—16/1), **16/1** The Noble Oak (IRE)(op 10/1), **20/1** Tynron Doon, **33/1** Ors. CSF £136.16, CT £535.67. Tote £10.30: £2.30 £3.10 £1.40 £5.20 (£83.90). Mr P. J. Feilden (NEWMARKET) bred by R. S. A. Urquhart. 20 Rn
1m 13.9 (4.9)
SF—47/28/38/32/30/21

## 3701
GAINSBOROUGH CLAIMING STKS    £2889.00 (£804.00: £387.00)
1m 14y

3-45 (3-51)

3547 **Scales of Justice (71)** *(JWHills)* 6-9-2 ‡5JWeaver (19) (hld up: hdwy over 2f out: led over 1f out: pushed out) ...................... —1
3673 Cape Pigeon (USA) **(85)** (Fav) *(LGCottrell)* 7-8-12 DHolland (10) (lw: w ldrs: ev ch over 1f out: one pce) ................................. 3.2
3554 Canadian Capers **(64)** *(MRChannon)* 3-8-3 JQuinn (7) (a chsng ldrs: r.o one pce fnl 2f) ................................................. 4.3
34664 Majal (IRE) **(72)** *(BHanbury)* 3-8-12 BRaymond (13) (lw: hld up: shkn up 2f out: r.o one pce) ............................................ 1½.4
3511 Genuine Lady **(52)** *(APJarvis)* 4-7-12 ‡7DWright (17) (led over 6f) ............. 1½.5
3488 Singers Image **(59)** *(GBBalding)* 3-9-0 JWilliams (20) (nvr nrr) ................. 2.6
35143 Skipper to Bilge **(67)** *(MAJarvis)* 5-8-11 ‡5KRutter (4) (no hdwy fnl 2f) ...... nk.7
1747 Taunting (IRE) **(54)** *(MBlanshard)* 4-8-11 ‡5ATucker (22) (nvr nr to chal) .... ½.8
3601 Kate Royale **(37)** *(MCPipe)* 3-7-9 SWood (11) (prom 5f) ...................... 3.9
3592 Chinaman **(33)** *(WGRWightman)* 3-8-2 JLowe (21) (n.d) ....................... 1.10
34884 Durneltor **(61)** *(RHannon)* 4-9-0 JReid (3) (swtg: uns rdr & bolted bef s: hdwy over 3f out: wknd 2f out) ................................. 4.11
22393 Jade Green **(69)** *(PJMakin)* 3-8-4 TSprake (9) (chsd ldrs over 5f) .......... 1.12
3488 Lihbab **(26)** *(JMBradley)* 9-8-4 JCarroll (18) (b: n.d) ......................... 2.13
35826 Thames Glow **(68)** *(DRCElsworth)* 3-8-10 ‡7JHunter (14) (b: b.hind: n.d) ... 3½.14
King Parrot (IRE) *(LordHuntingdon)* 4-8-4 DMcKeown (16) (s.s: plld hrd: a bhd) nk.15
299 Ante Up (IRE) **(68)** (bl) *(JAkehurst)* 4-9-2 SWhitworth (23) (bit bkwd: s.s: a wl bhd) ................................................... ¾.16
Sweet Bloom *(APJarvis)* 4-7-7 ‡7DMcCabe (2) (bit bkwd: n.d) ................. hd.17
Tyrian **(39)** (bl) *(RJBaker)* 5-8-3(2) NHowe (8) (bit bkwd: n.d) ................. s.h.18
Budget *(AJChamberlain)* 4-8-4(3) ‡3RPerham (15) (lw: m.n.s) .................... 1.19

Rubicon Watch *(CRBarwell)* 3-8-4 TLang (12) (w'like: bit bkwd: n.d) ............ nk.**20**
2365 Three Lucky (IRE) **(31)** *(MDIUsher)* 4-8-2 DaleGibson (1) (spd 5f: t.o) ............ 8.**21**
3251 Abbey Green *(CJHill)* 4-8-4 NAdams (5) (a bhd: t.o) ....................................... 12.**22**

**3/1** Cape Pigeon (USA), **5/1** Skipper to Bilge, **7/1** Majal (IRE), SCALES OF JUSTICE, **8/1** Jade Green, **10/1** Durneltor(op 6/1), **12/1** Canadian Capers, **16/1** Thames Glow, Singers Image, King Parrot (IRE), **20/1** Taunting (IRE), **25/1** Abbey Green, Ante Up (IRE), Genuine Lady, Kate Royale, Tyrian, **33/1** Sweet Bloom, Lihbab, Three Lucky (IRE), **40/1** Rubicon Watch, **66/1** Ors. CSF £30.74, Tote £6.50: £2.30 £1.90 £6.00 (£11.90). Mr Christopher Wright (LAMBOURN) bred by Stratford Place Stud. 22 Rn; Majal (IRE) clmd J Wainwright £10,561
1m 37.6 (5.1)
SF—56/43/22/26/7/17

---

**3702**  WHITSBURY MANOR NURSERY (0-75) £2574.00 (£714.00: £342.00)
5f 16y
4-15 (4-21)

3590 **Another Jade (59)** *(APJarvis)* 8-1 ‡7DWright (1) (lw: w ldrs: led over 1f out:
pushed out) ......................................................................... —**1**
33665 Second Chance (IRE) **(70)** *(PMitchell)* 9-5 JReid (15) (lw: hdwy over 1f out: hrd
rdn: r.o) ...................................................................................... 1.**2**
35804 Heber Spring (IRE) **(66)** *(RHannon)* 8-12 ‡3RPerham (16) (s.s: swtchd lft & hdwy
2f out: hrd rdn & r.o ins fnl f) ..................................................... 1.**3**
3534 Geoff's Risk **(68)** (bl) *(GLewis)* 9-3 BRaymond (7) (b.hind: led over 3f: nt
qckn fnl f) .................................................................................. 1.**4**
3534 Aberlady **(68)** *(MAJarvis)* 8-12 ‡5KRutter (11) (hdwy over 1f out: r.o wl ins fnl f) 1½.**5**
1579 Spanish Tower **(45)** (bl) *(RJHolder)* 7-8 NAdams (14) (bit bkwd: nvr nr) ........... ¾.**6**
3218 Prince Manki **(60)** *(RHannon)* 8-9 AMcGlone (6) (prom over 3f) ....................... nk.**7**
3325a Bold County **(72)** *(MJohnston)* 9-7 DMcKeown (2) (prom over 3f) ................... hd.**8**
27736 Jasmin Isle **(47)** *(MissGayKelleway)* 7-10 JLowe (13) (prom: hrd rdn & wknd 2f
out) ........................................................................................... hd.**9**
3178 Body Language **(62)** *(IABalding)* 0-0 ‡7OO'Gorman (12) (lw: a bhd) .............. nk.**10**
2238 Apifera **(56)** *(RJHodges)* 7-12(12) ‡7SDrowne (8) (a bhd) ........................... ¾.**11**
35032 La Madrigal **(45)** *(JWharton)* 9-0 JQuinn (10) (lw: prom 3f) ......................... ¾.**12**
3580 Purbeck Centenary **(55)** *(MRChannon)* 8-4 DHolland (3) (swtg: w ldrs 3f) ..... 1½.**13**
3268 Saraswati **(58)** *(PJMakin)* 8-7 TSprake (4) (lw: outpcd) ............................ 2½.**14**
35586 Pat Poindestres **(66)** *(MDixon)* 9-1 SWhitworth (9) (a bhd) ........................ 1.**15**
3552 Dance Magical **(55)** *(MDixon)* 7-13 ‡5NGwilliams (5) (unruly stalls: a bhd) ..... 2½.**16**
LONG HANDICAP: Apifera 7-3.
*Stewards Enquiry: Holland suspended 22-25/10/92 (excessive use of whip).*

**3/1** Geoff's Risk, **13/2** Second Chance (IRE), **7/1** La Madrigal(10/1—6/1), **17/2** Aberlady(6/1—9/1), **10/1** Bold County, Body Language, Heber Spring (IRE), Saraswati, **12/1** Spanish Tower, **14/1** Pat Poindestres, Prince Manki, **16/1** ANOTHER JADE, Purbeck Centenary, **20/1** Jasmin Isle, **33/1** Dance Magical, **66/1** Apifera. CSF £120.64, CT £1,036.12. Tote £109.60: £9.10 £1.50 £1.90 £1.30 (£145.70). Mrs Rita J. Kaplan (ASTON UPTHORPE) bred by J. R. C. and Mrs Wren. 16 Rn
61.8 sec (4.8)
SF—16/30/19/20/9/—

---

**3703**  BLOOMSBURY H'CAP (0-80) £3340.00 (£1000.00: £480.00: £220.00)
5f 16y
4-45 (4-50)

3585★ **Branston Abby (IRE) (83)** *(MJohnston)* 3—10-3 (7x) JReid (2) (lw: mde virtually
all: hrd rdn fnl f: r.o wl) ............................................................ —**1**
35593 My Sovereign (USA) **(68)** *(RHannon)* 3-8-13 ‡3RPerham (5) (a.p: r.o wl ins fnl f) hd.**2**
3499 Miss Vaxette **(72)** *(JLSpearing)* 3-8-13 ‡7MHumphries (1) (a.p: r.o wl ins fnl f) s.h.**3**
3423★ Waverley Star **(51)** *(KOCunningham-Brown)* 7-8-0 DHolland (12) (a.p: nt qckn
fnl f) ........................................................................................ ½.**4**
3620 Easy Does it **(47)** *(MrsAKnight)* 3-7-9 JQuinn (8) (w ldrs: r.o one pce fnl f) ........ ¾.**5**
3575 Cranfield Comet **(71)** (bl) *(JBerry)* 3-9-5 JCarroll (10) (a.p: nt qckn fnl f) ........ hd.**6**
3417 Baysham (USA) **(76)** (v) *(BRMillman)* 6-9-6 ‡5JWeaver (17) (a.p: r.o one pce fnl
2f) ........................................................................................... ½.**7**
34995 Noble Power **(66)** *(BPalling)* 3-8-9 ‡5StephenDavies (4) (lw: nrst fin) ....... s.h.**8**
3417 Cee-En-Cee **(67)** (bl) *(MMcCourt)* 8-8-11 ‡5ATucker (3) (nvr nr to chal) ......... nk.**9**
35754 Love Returned **(78)** *(WJarvis)* 5-9-13 MTebbutt (7) (prom over 3f) ............ nk.**10**
35755 Truthful Image **(78)** (bl) *(MJRyan)* 3-9-8 DBiggs (11) (n.d) ......................... ¾.**11**
3596 Amour du Soir (USA) **(54)** *(RLee)* 5-8-3 TyroneWilliams (18) (b: n.d) ............ s.h.**12**
3253★ Jigsaw Boy **(74)** *(RJHolder)* 3-9-8 JWilliams (15) (lw: nvr nr) .................... hd.**13**
3391 Panchellita (USA) **(56)** *(JSutcliffe)* 3-8-4(1) SWhitworth (6) (n.d) ................ ¾.**14**
35853 Pharoah's Dancer **(71)** (Fav) *(RSimpson)* 5-9-6 MWigham (19) (nvr plcd to
chal) ........................................................................................ hd.**15**
35775 Very Dicey **(75)** *(WRMuir)* 4-9-10 BRaymond (14) (n.d) .............................. ½.**16**
28312 Cashmiriana (IRE) **(60)** *(MissHCKnight)* 3-8-3(5) ‡5KRutter (13) (a bhd) ........... 4.**17**
35756 Bells of Longwick **(77)** *(DRLaing)* 3-9-4 ‡7KimMcDonnell (20) (prom over 2f) .. ¾.**18**
3585 Seamere **(79)** *(BRCambidge)* 9—10-0 JLowe (9) (a bhd) ............................. nk.**19**
3397 Kabcast **(51)** (bl) *(DWChapman)* 7-8-0 SWood (16) (t.o) .............................. 10.**20**

**13/2** Pharaoh's Dancer, **7/1** Very Dicey, Love Returned(12/1—14/1), **15/2** Jigsaw Boy, **9/1** Cranfield Comet, **10/1** BRANSTON ABBY (IRE), **11/1** Baysham (USA)(12/1—8/1), **12/1** Waverley Star, **14/1** My Sovereign (USA), **16/1** Easy Does it, Bells of Longwick, **20/1** Miss Vaxette, Amour du Soir (USA), Panchellita (USA), Cashmiriana (IRE), Cee-En-Cee, **25/1** Ors. CSF £141.96, CT £2,514.71. Tote £11.60: £3.40 £3.90 £6.20 £2.80 (£117.50). Mr J. David Abell (MIDDLEHAM) bred by John David Abell in Ireland. 20 Rn                    61 sec (4)

                                                                      SF—63/43/42/27/19/42

T/Plpt: £63.60 (40.25 Tckts).                                                          KH

3611—**REDCAR (L-H)**

## Wednesday, October 14th [Good becoming Good to soft]

Going Allowance: St: 0.20 sec per fur; Rnd: 0.05 sec per fur (G)          Wind: mod against

Stalls: centre

**3704**     E.B.F. EGTON STKS (Mdn 2-Y-O) £2784.00 (£774.00: £372.00)    **6f**    2-00 (2-04)

     **Specified** (USA) (Fav) *(JHMGosden)* 9-0 PatEddery (16) (cmpt: scope: bit
       bkwd: a cl up: led wl over 2f out: pushed clr & eased fnl f) . —1
3480 Missa Brevis (USA) *(JWWatts)* 8-9 GDuffield (10) (styd on wl fnl 2f: no ch w wnr) 3½.2
3372³ Sarangani Bay (USA) *(PWChapple-Hyam)* 9-0 MRoberts (11) (a chsng ldrs:
       rdn over 2f out: one pce) ............................................ 1.3
     Anusha *(JBerry)* 8-9 JCarroll (7) (neat: unf: dwlt: bhd tl styd on wl fnl 2f) ........... 1.4
3552³ Al Shaati (FR) *(MRStoute)* 8-9 SCauthen (5) (cl up: rdn 2f out: nt qckn) ......... nk.5
2841 Storm Venture (IRE) (73) *(WJarvis)* 9-0 RCochrane (12) (a chsng ldrs: kpt on
       same pce fnl 2f) ............................................... 1½.6
3338⁶ Oubeck *(EWeymes)* 8-9 BRaymond (14) (led over 3f: grad wknd) ............... hd.7
3512 Ranunculus *(JBerry)* 9-0 GCarter (15) (chsd ldrs 4f) ........................ nk.8
     Sarah Heights *(MissLCSiddall)* 8-9 TQuinn (19) (leggy: no imp fr ½-wy) .......... ½.9
3517 Cicerone *(PCalver)* 9-0 GHind (17) (in tch: eased whn btn fnl f) ............... 1.10
3549⁶ Polanie (CAN) *(LMCumani)* 8-9 LDettori (18) (nvr nr to chal) ............... 1.11
3480³ Trachelium *(JHanson)* 8-9 EJohnson (2) (cl up to ½-wy: sn rdn & wknd) .......... 1.12
3631 Can Can Charlie *(MJohnston)* 9-0 DMcKeown (20) (outpcd & bhd tl sme late
       hdwy) ....................................................... nk.13
3399 Bloomsbury Square *(JWWatts)* 9-0 NConnorton (21) (lw: s.i.s: nvr plcd to chal) 1.14
2745³ Primula Bairn (68) *(MrsJRRamsden)* 8-9 GBaxter (4) (chsd ldrs: sn pushed
       along: wknd 2f out) ......................................... s.h.15
3312 Gold Fort *(BWMurray)* 9-0 JFortune (1) (chsd ldrs: drvn along ½-wy: sn wknd) 1.16
3312³ Musical Times (68) *(MrsNMacauley)* 8-9 MHills (3) (n.d) ...................... 5.17
3607² Chiltern Hundreds (USA) (84) *(MrsJCecil)* 9-0 PaulEddery (13) (lw: chsd ldrs:
       sn drvn along: wknd over 2f out) ............................... 1½.18
3285 Smith N'Allan *(BobJones)* 9-0 NDay (8) (bhd fr ½-wy) ...................... ½.19
3262 Todden *(CFWall)* 9-0 RHills (9) (dwlt: a bhd) .............................. 1.20
3480 Joellise *(JBalding)* 8-9 KDarley (6) (nvr wnt pce) .......................... 1½.21

**2/1** SPECIFIED (USA), **11/4** Sarangani Bay (USA)(2/1—3/1), **7/1** Polanie (CAN), **10/1** Al Shaati (FR), Trachelium, **12/1** Chiltern Hundreds (USA), **14/1** Primula Bairn, **16/1** Storm Venture (IRE), **20/1** Smith N'Allan, **25/1** Musical Times, Cicerone, **33/1** Ranunculus, Anusha, Bloomsbury Square, **40/1** Missa Brevis (USA), **50/1** Todden, Oubeck, Can Can Charlie, Sarah Heights, **66/1** Ors. CSF £83.85, Tote £3.90: £1.70 £11.80 £1.60 (£231.10). Mr K. Abdulla (NEWMARKET) bred by Juddmonte Farms in USA. 21 Rn                         1m 13.3 (4)

                                                                      SF—44/25/26/17/16/16

**3705**     CUB HUNTERS (S) H'CAP (3-Y-O) (0-60) £2658.00 (£738.00: £354.00)
     **1m 3f**
              (Weights raised 2 lb)                              2-30 (2-32)
3149³ **Joseph's Wine** (IRE) (41) (Fav) *(RBastiman)* 8-8 DMcKeown (13) (hld up: effrt
       3f out: hrd rdn & hung lft ins fnl f: styd on to ld nr fin) .......... —1
3403⁶ Dara Melody (IRE) (44) *(JGFitzGerald)* 8-11 MRoberts (10) (trckd ldrs: rdn over
       2f out: styd on wl cl home) ................................... nk.2
3603⁵ Gay Ming (46) *(RHollinshead)* 8-6 ⁷AGarth (8) (bhd: hdwy on outside 3f out: r.o
       nr fin) ..................................................... s.h.3
3615 Essayeffsee (47) (bl) *(MHEasterby)* 9-0 MBirch (2) (trckd ldrs gng wl: led on bit
       over 2f out: hrd rdn fnl f: fnd nil & jst ct) ...................... s.h.4
3603 Seraphim (FR) (45) *(TDBarron)* 8-12 AlexGreaves (14) (hdwy ent st: c wd & effrt
       over 3f out: styd on wl nr fin) ................................. nk.5
2931² Stratford Lady (37) (bl) *(JAGlover)* 8-1 ³FNorton (1) (hdwy over 4f out: sn in tch
       & rdn: nt qckn appr fnl f) ..................................... 1.6
3161 Futures Gift (IRE) (43) *(AWPotts)* 8-10 SWebster (3) (effrt 4f out: nvr rchd ldrs) 1½.7
3266 Amalfi (41) *(JPearce)* 8-8 RPrice (4) (cl up: led 4f out tl over 2f out: sn rdn & btn) 1½.8
3556 Flash of Straw (IRE) (44) (bl) *(GLewis)* 8-8 ‡³DHarrison (17) (in tch: effrt over 3f
       out: rdn & no imp) ......................................... 3½.9

3629★ Ready to Draw (IRE) **(58)** *(RonaldThompson)* 9-11 (5x) RPElliott (15) (in tch: hdwy to chase ldrs over 3f out: wknd 2f out) ................. nk.**10**
2813 Royal Sultan **(44)** *(DenysSmith)* 8-4 ‡7CTeague (12) (prom tl outpcd fnl 3f) ...... 6.**11**
1157 Jellyroll Blues **(41)** *(MrsGRReveley)* 8-8 JLowe (6) (a bhd) ........................... 10.**12**
34856 Sir Norman Holt (IRE) **(54)** (v) *(FHLee)* 9-7 WCarson (3) (led tl hdd & wknd 4f out) ................. 5.**13**
*3378* Lowlands Boy **(41)** *(TFairhurst)* 8-8 JFanning (9) (prom tl wknd over 3f out) ....... 14
1033 Alizarin **(36)** *(BCMorgan)* 8-3 GBardwell (16) (a bhd) ........................... 15
*3374* Mondova (IRE) **(36)** (bl) *(FHLee)* 7-12 ‡5NKennedy (11) (a outpcd & bhd) .......... 16

**100/30** JOSEPH'S WINE (IRE), **5/1** Flash of Straw (IRE), Dara Melody (IRE), **8/1** Ready to Draw (IRE), Stratford Lady, **9/1** Sir Norman Holt (IRE), **12/1** Essayeffsee, Gay Ming, **16/1** Amaffi, **20/1** Seraphim (FR), **25/1** Futures Gift (IRE), **33/1** Lowlands Boy, Jellyroll Blues, **50/1** Ors. CSF £20.46, CT £170.30. Tote £4.30: £1.70 £1.40 £1.50 £4.20 (£26.10). Mrs P. Bastiman (WETHERBY) bred by Michael Fennessy in Ireland. 16 Rn; No bid
2m 26.2 (10.5)

**3706** ELLERBY STKS (I) (Mdn) £2511.00 (£696.00: £333.00)   1¼m   3-00 (3-01)

**Sweet Quest** *(HRACecil)* 3-8-8 WRyan (8) (lt-f: bhd: gd hdwy 3f out: led ins fnl f: r.o wl) ........................... —**1**
33983 Magadeer (USA) **(66)** *(JLDunlop)* 3-8-8 BRaymond (1) (led tl hdd & no ex ins fnl f) ................. 4.**2**
34252 Annacurragh (IRE) **(Fav)** *(ACStewart)* 3-8-8 MRoberts (9) (trckd ldrs: effrt 3f out: hung lft & nt r.o) ................. 3.**3**
3477 Royal Comedian *(BWMurray)* 3-8-8 MFortune (6) (outpcd & lost tch 4f out: styd on wl appr fnl f: nrst fin) ................. 2.**4**
35836 Balzino (USA) *(LMCumani)* 3-8-13 LDettori (10) (in tch: effrt 4f out: one pce) .. nk.**5**
32584 Waaza (USA) **(53)** *(MissLCSiddall)* 3-8-13 RHills (5) (chsd ldrs tl wknd wl over 2f out) ................. 8.**6**
*3557*4 Under the Bridge **(60)** (bl) *(PWHarris)* 3-8-13 RCochrane (3) (cl up tl wknd wl over 2f out) ................. s.h.**7**
Local Dealer **(33)** *(JFBottomley)* 4-8-12 ‡7JMarshall (7) (chsd ldrs to st: sn wknd) ................. 2.**8**
Finneran's Fantasy *(DMorris)* 3-8-8 ‡5StephenDavies (2) (w'like: a bhd) ............. 7.**9**
Concord Wench *(PDEvans)* 4-9-0 JQuinn (4) (small: neat: a bhd) ................. 1½.**10**

**7/4** Annacurragh (IRE), **9/2** Magadeer (USA), Balzino (USA), **5/1** SWEET QUEST(op 3/1), **8/1** Royal Comedian, **12/1** Under the Bridge(op 8/1), **33/1** Waaza (USA), **66/1** Ors. CSF £25.57, Tote £4.00: £1.70 £2.10 £1.10 (£13.90). Mr Terry Ellis (NEWMARKET) bred by Patrick Eddery Ltd. 10 Rn
2m 10.6 (8.1)
SF—18/11/5/1/–/–

**3707** LESLIE PETCH MEMORIAL H'CAP (0-70) £2952.00 (£822.00: £396.00)
6f   3-30 (3-37)

3496 **Ingenuity (58)** *(LordHuntingdon)* 3-9-0 MRoberts (4) (mde most: kpt on wl fnl 2f) —**1**
3126 Coolaba Prince (IRE) **(58)** *(FHLee)* 3-9-0 WCarson (7) (a chsng ldrs: styd on same pce fnl f) ................. 1½.**2**
3585 Miss Aragon **(46)** *(MissLCSiddall)* 4-8-4 GDuffield (20) (a w ldrs: rdn 2f out: r.o one pce) ................. ¾.**3**
34602 Music Dancer **(58)** *(JBerry)* 3-9-0 JCarroll (19) (hdwy 2f out: nrst fin) ........... nk.**4**
3620★ My Ruby Ring **(56)** *(DRLaing)* 5-8-7 (7x) ‡7KimMcDonnell (15) (a chsng ldrs: effrt over 2f out: nt qckn) ................. ½.**5**
35852 Pretonic **(54)** *(MJohnston)* 4-8-12 DMcKeown (23) (a chsng ldrs: kpt on fnl f) s.h.**6**
35954 Strip Cartoon (IRE) **(50)** (bl) *(SRBowring)* 4-8-8 SWebster (24) (w ldrs stands' side: rdn 2f out: nt qckn) ................. ½.**7**
36326 Almasa **(61)** *(DMorris)* 4-9-0 ‡5StephenDavies (9) (chsd ldrs far side: no ex fnl 2f) ................. 1.**8**
3620 Yours Or Mine **(50)** *(DWChapman)* 4-8-8 SWood (17) (sn chsng ldrs: rdn & nt qckn fnl 2f) ................. 1.**9**
3499 Stormbuster **(42)** *(PSFelgate)* 3-7-12 JLowe (2) (racd far side: cl up tl wknd appr fnl f) ................. s.h.**10**
3496★ Arabat **(61)** (v) *(MPNaughton)* 5-9-5 JakiHouston (16) (a.p: effrt ½-wy: no imp) s.h.**11**
36336 On the Edge **(70)** *(TDBarron)* 4-10-0 AlexGreaves (12) (sme hdwy 2f out: n.d) nk.**12**
35965 Farndale **(43)** *(BCMorgan)* 5-8-1 GBardwell (14) (rdn ½-wy: n.d) ................. ½.**13**
3460 Twilight Falls **(51)** **(Fav)** *(MJCamacho)* 7-8-9 NConnorton (3) (nvr plcd to chal) 1.**14**
3153 Intrepid Fort **(38)** *(BWMurray)* 3-7-8(1) JQuinn (21) (nvr trbld ldrs) ................. 2.**15**
28226 Highborn **(51)** *(PSFelgate)* 3-8-7 JWilliams (11) (s.i.s: bhd tl sme late hdwy) ................. ½.**16**
3317 Southwold Air **(67)** *(JLDunlop)* 3-9-9 TQuinn (5) (n.d) ................. 2½.**17**
3460 Miss Calculate **(48)** *(CaptJWilson)* 4-8-6 GCarter (22) (n.d) ................. ½.**18**
3476 State Governor **(43)** *(DWChapman)* 4-8-1 JFanning (1) (prom far side 3f) ..... nk.**19**
3473 Crestwood Lad (USA) **(56)** *(MrsGRReveley)* 3-8-12 KDarley (6) (dwlt: a bhd) hd.**20**

Hansom Lad **(41)** *(WWHaigh)* 9–7–13 DaleGibson (10) (n.d) ............................ ½.**21**
3585 Angels Answer (IRE) **(67)** *(MrsGRReveley)* 3–9–2 ‡7DarrenMoffatt (13) (n.d) . 1½.**22**
3605 Fontaine Lady **(39)** (v) *(TThomsonJones)* 5–7–8(4) ‡3DHarrison (3) (n.d) .......... 2.**23**
3397 Swinging Lady **(47)** *(WWHaigh)* 4–8–2 ‡3FNorton (18) (n.d) ....................... 6.**24**
LONG HANDICAP: Intrepid Fort 7-3.

**7/1** Twilight Falls, **10/1** Pretonic, My Ruby Ring, Music Dancer, **11/1** Yours Or Mine (IRE), **12/1** Strip Cartoon (IRE), **14/1** Almasa, INGENUITY, **16/1** Miss Aragon, Farndale, Southwold Air, On the Edge, **20/1** Swinging Lady, Stormbuster, Arabat, Coolaba Prince (IRE), **25/1** Highborn (IRE), **33/1** Crestwood Lad (USA), Miss Calculate, **40/1** Angels Answer (IRE), **50/1** Ors. CSF £242.43, CT £4,048.36. Tote £11.30: £4.40 £5.20 £3.60 £2.50 (£118.40). The Queen (WEST ILSLEY) bred by The Queen. 24 Rn                    1m 13.4 (4.1)
SF—42/36/23/32/23/27

## 3708

REDCAR OCTOBER H'CAP (0-80) £3470.00 (£1040.00: £500.00: £230.00)
1¼m                                                                    4-05 (4-06)

3459* **Unforgiving Minute (81)** *(PWHarris)* 3–9–9 PaulEddery (8) (a.p: rdn to ld wl
over 1f out: r.o) ........................................................ —**1**
3555 Castillet **(64)** *(GHarwood)* 3–8–6 PatEddery (5) (bhd: hdwy 4f out: hrd rdn & kpt
on wl fnl 2f) ............................................................ ¾.**2**
3526⁵ Gilderdale **(80)** *(JWHills)* 10–10–0 RHills (2) (trckd ldrs: effrt & ev ch over 2f out:
styd on one pce fnl f) ................................................... hd.**3**
3434⁴ Kabayil **(70)** *(PTWalwyn)* 3–8–12 RHills (13) (a.p: effrt & ev ch 3f out: one pce) .. 5.**4**
3526⁶ Remany **(65)** *(JRFanshawe)* 3–8–7 GCarter (9) (hld up: effrt on ins 4f out: rdn &
one pce fnl 2f) ......................................................... 2½.**5**
3434* **Kitaab (USA) (70)** *(ACStewart)* 3–8–12 MRoberts (15) (cl up: led over 4f out tl wl
over 1f out: sn btn) .................................................... 3½.**6**
3475 Retender (USA) **(70)** *(LMCumani)* 3–8–12 LDettori (3) (hdwy 4f out: nvr nr to
chal) .................................................................. ½.**7**
2937* Kagram Queen **(60)** *(MrsGRReveley)* 4–8–8 KDarley (17) (hld up & bhd: swtchd
lft 3f out: nvr plcd to clal) ............................................. 3.**8**
3279⁴ Mahsul (IRE) **(59)** (Fav) *(CJBenstead)* 4–8–7 WCarson (12) (effrt 4f out: no imp) 1½.**9**
2631 Leap in the Dark (IRE) **(63)** *(JLDunlop)* 3–8–5 TQuinn (16) (w ldrs tl wknd over 2f
out) ................................................................... hd.**10**
*3375* Annabelle Royale **(74)** *(MrsNMacauley)* 6–9–8 DMcKeown (10) (nvr trbld ldrs) nk.**11**
2954* Busman (IRE) **(71)** *(MajorWRHern)* 3–8–13 JWilliams (14) (in tch: effrt 3f out: sn
btn) .................................................................... 1.**12**
2673* Laughsome **(76)** *(JHMGosden)* 3–9–4 SCauthen (6) (in tch tl wknd 3f out) ..... nk.**13**
3293⁵ Milanese **(71)** *(DMorley)* 3–8–13 JFortune (1) (effrt 4f out: sn rdn & wknd) ...... ¾.**14**
3475³ Sinclair Lad (IRE) **(66)** *(RHollinshead)* 4–9–0 WRyan (4) (bhd: effrt 4f out: no imp) ¾.**15**
1175⁵ Khrisma **(68)** *(MrsJCecil)* 3–8–10 GDuffield (11) (chsd ldrs tl wknd over 3f out) 3.**16**
3547 Jubran (USA) **(68)** *(MPNaughton)* 6–9–2 RCochrane (7) (led tl hdd over 4f out:
sn lost pl) ............................................................. 2.**17**

**7/1** Mahsul (IRE), **8/1** Remany, Kitaab (USA), Gilderdale, **9/1** Retender (USA), Laughsome, **10/1** Kagram Queen, Jubran (USA), Busman (IRE), **12/1** Sinclair Lad (IRE), UNFORGIVING MINUTE(qte 8/1), **16/1** Castillet, Kabayil, **20/1** Khrisma, Milanese, Leap in the Dark (IRE), **50/1** Annabelle Royale. CSF £185.10, CT £1,506.99. Tote £20.70: £4.50 £4.00 £2.30 £4.00 (£277.30). Mrs P. W. Harris (BERKHAMSTED) bred by Pendley Farm. 17 Rn
2m 9.3 (6.8)
SF—46/27/48/22/13/10

## 3709

E.B.F. CAPTAIN COOK STKS (Mdn 2-Y.O) £2763.00 (£768.00: £369.00)
1m                                                                     4-35 (4-37)

3532 **Tomos** *(DMorley)* 9-0 PaulEddery (14) (bhd: hdwy 2f out: hrd rdn appr fnl f:
styd on to ld nr fin) ................................................... —**1**
3030³ Blue Grotto (IRE) *(JWWatts)* 9-0 GDuffield (13) (bhd: swtchd 3f out: r.o wl fnl f:
jst failed) ............................................................. s.h.**2**
2799² Mujaazafah (USA) *(JHMGosden)* 9-0 SCauthen (15) (a.p: chal 2f out: led ins fnl
f: edgd lft & nt qckn nr fin) ........................................... nk.**3**
3307⁵ Mahogany Light (USA) *(GHarwood)* 9-0 KDarley (12) (disp ld 5f: kpt on wl u.p) hd.**4**
3200 Yahmi (IRE) *(MajorWRHern)* 9-0 RHills (9) (mde most tl hdd ins fnl f: kpt on) ... s.h.**5**
3532⁴ Brown's (FR) **(98)** (Fav) *(PWChapple-Hyam)* 9-0 MRoberts (11) (plld hrd: in
tch: rdn 3f out: hdwy u.p over 1f out: nvr able to chal) ...... 1½.**6**
3297³ Marros Mill *(MBell)* 8-9 MHills (7) (chsd ldrs tl outpcd fnl 2f) ................... 3½.**7**
Darmstadt (USA) *(JHMGosden)* 9-0 GHind (4) (lt-f: unf: b.nr fore: s.i.s: hdwy wl
over 2f out: styd on) ................................................... 3.**8**
3523² Captain Jack *(LMCumani)* 9-0 LDettori (6) (in tch: effrt ½-wy: no imp) ......... ½.**9**
3480⁴ Misbelief *(JRFanshawe)* 8-9 GCarter (2) (bhd: swtchd & effrt 3f out: rdn & n.d) ¾.**10**
3512⁵ Mountain High (FR) *(JGFitzGerald)* 9-0 KFallon (3) (outpcd & bhd most of wy) 3.**11**
3614 Zonk *(JPearce)* 9-0 RPrice (8) (chsd ldrs over 5f) ........................... 5.**12**
3463⁵ Wonderful Years (USA) *(MrsJRRamsden)* 9-0 GBaxter (10) (w ldrs over 5f: sn
wknd) ................................................................. 1½.**13**

3132 Seek the Pearl *(MRStoute)* 8-9 WRyan (17) (prom 5f) ............................. 4.14
3498⁶ Rosmarino *(CWThornton)* 9-0 NConnorton (5) (cl up tl wknd over 2f out) ....... ½.15
3517⁶ Cannon Carew *(DMoffatt)* 8-7 ‡⁷DarrenMoffatt (19) (a bhd) ......................... 1½.16
3313 Ark Celeste *(WWHaigh)* 8-9 SWebster (1) (sn outpcd & bhd) ...................... 1.17
3517³ Larn Fort *(TFairhurst)* 9-0 JFanning (18) (lost tch fr ½-wy) ..................... s.h.18
2489² Salt N Vinegar (IRE) *(RonaldThompson)* 9-0 RPElliott (16) (n.d) .............. 12.19

**15/8** Brown's (FR), **3/1** Mujaazafah (USA)(op 7/4), **7/2** Captain Jack(tchd 6/1), **8/1** Blue Grotto (IRE)(op 5/1), **10/1** TOMOS, Misbelief, **14/1** Mountain High (FR), **20/1** Yahmi (IRE), Marros Mill, Seek the Pearl, **33/1** Wonderful Years (USA), Larn Fort, Darmstadt (USA), Mahogany Light (USA), **50/1** Rosmarino, Zonk, **66/1** Cannon Carew, **100/1** Ark Celeste, **200/1** Salt N Vinegar (IRE). CSF £96.14, Tote £96.20: £8.70 £2.30 £1.60 (£74.80). Mr Saif Ali (NEWMARKET) bred by I. Stewart-Brown and M. Meacock. 19 Rn                 1m 42.8 (7.8)
SF—7/6/5/4/3/–

### 3710      LEVY BOARD STKS (Mdn 3-Y.O) £2448.00 (£678.00: £324.00)       6f      5-05 (5-06)

3416⁶ **Broadway Ruckus (CAN) (54)** *(DRLaing)* 8-9 JWilliams (2) (s.i.s: hdwy 2f out:
        r.o strly ins fnl f to ld cl home) .......................................................... —1
2831⁴ Nbaat (USA) **(63)** *(CJBenstead)* 9-0 WCarson (8) (chsd ldrs: hdwy stands' side
        over 2f out: led ins fnl f: nt qckn cl home) ................................... ½.2
3412 So Superb **(62)** (v) *(JLDunlop)* 9-0 TQuinn (6) (w ldrs: led 2f out tl ins fnl f: kpt
        on) ...................................................................................... ¾.3
3460 Dandy Desire **(42)** *(BCMorgan)* 9-0 GDuffield (3) (a chsng ldrs: ev ch 2f out: r.o
        one pce) .............................................................................. ¾.4
        Cutwater (Fav) *(JHMGosden)* 9-0 SCauthen (7) (dwlt: hdwy ½-wy: rdn & nt
        qckn appr fnl f) .................................................................. 1½.5
1310 Sammy Slew (USA) **(63)** *(CParker)* 9-0 MWood (4) (racd centre: led 4f: grad
        wknd) .................................................................................. 1½.6
3557² Honey Heather (IRE) **(56)** *(CFWall)* 8-9 BRaymond (5) (cl up tl wknd wl over 1f
        out) ..................................................................................... nk.7
3252 Hall's Creek (IRE) (bl) *(DWPArbuthnot)* 9-0 RPrice (9) (w ldrs to ½-wy: sn outpcd) 5.0
3473 Murasil (USA) **(55)** *(MPNaughton)* 9-0 MRoberts (10) (prom early: bhd fr ½-wy) 2.9
195 Aldington Peach *(PDEvans)* 8-9 JQuinn (11) (outpcd & lost tch fr ½-wy) ...... hd.10
        Henry's First *(MissLCSiddall)* 9-0 MBirch (1) (wl bhd fr ½-wy) ................ 10.11

**4/7** Cutwater, **6/1** Honey Heather (IRE), **7/1** Nbaat (USA), **12/1** So Superb(op 8/1), **14/1** Sammy Slew (USA), **20/1** Murasil (USA), **28/1** BROADWAY RUCKUS (CAN), **50/1** Ors. CSF £192.94, Tote £50.40: £5.10 £2.70 £1.90 (£249.20). Hesmonds Stud (LAMBOURN) bred by Michael Byrne in Canada. 11 Rn       1m 15.6 (6.3)

### 3711      ELLERBY STKS (II) (Mdn) £2490.00 (£690.00: £330.00)       1¼m      5-35 (5-36)

3555³ **Lady Dundee (USA) (62)** *(MrsJCecil)* 3-8-8 PaulEddery (2) (a.p: led wl over 1f
        out: rdn & styd on wl) ........................................................... —1
3483⁴ Cormorant Bay *(FHLee)* 3-8-8 WCarson (8) (chsd ldrs: effrt over 3f out: styd
        on: nt pce of wnr) ................................................................. 3½.2
2654³ Reflecting (IRE) **(80)** (Fav) *(JHMGosden)* 3-8-13 PatEddery (3) (a cl up: led wl
        over 2f out tl wl over 1f out: sn rdn & btn) .......................... 3½.3
2613⁴ Clair Soleil *(DenysSmith)* 3-8-13 KFallon (5) (a.p: one pce fnl 3f) ............ 1.4
3351 Linpac Express **(44)** *(CWCElsey)* 3-8-13 JCarroll (9) (prom tl outpcd wl over 3f
        out) ...................................................................................... 10.5
3494 Father Dan (IRE) *(DMoffatt)* 3-8-6 ‡⁷DarrenMoffatt (1) (bhd) .................. 7.6
2665 Mini Fete (FR) (bl) *(JParkes)* 3-8-8 GDuffield (4) (bhd fnl 4f) ................. s.h.7
1478⁵ Olliver Duckett *(PCalver)* 3-8-13 GHind (6) (led tl hdd wl over 2f out: rdn & wknd
        qckly) ................................................................................... 2½.8
        Melody's Honour *(JDooler)* 8-9-0 JFanning (1) (a bhd: t.o) ..................... 9

**5/6** Reflecting (IRE), **5/2** LADY DUNDEE (USA), **5/1** Cormorant Bay, **16/1** Olliver Duckett, Clair Soleil (USA), **33/1** Father Dan (IRE), Linpac Express, **100/1** Mini Fete (FR). CSF £15.05, Tote £4.00: £1.40 £2.00 £1.00 (£10.40). Mr James H. Stone (NEWMARKET) bred by Mrs Betty M. Peters in USA. 9 Rn       2m 14.4 (11.9)

T/Plpt: £626.40 (4.4 Tckts).                                                           AA

### 3525—NEWMARKET  (R-H)  Rowley Mile
### Thursday, October 15th [Good to firm]
Going Allowance: minus 0.30 sec per fur (F)                        Wind: mod half bhd

Stalls: 2nd & 3rd high, remainder low

### 3712      BUCKENHAM (S) STKS (2-Y.O) £4760.00 (£1430.00: £690.00: £320.00)
              6f                                                            2-00 (2-04)

3517² **Soaking** (Fav) *(BWHills)* 8-11 PatEddery (1) (lw: a.p: led stands' side 3f: r.o wl
        to ld ins fnl f) ...................................................................... —1

36884 Greenwich Chalenge **(81)** *(WCarter)* 9-2 BRouse (10) (b: b.hind: led stands'
    side 3f: kpt on wl fnl f) ........................................................ ³/₄.2

33854 Warkworth (USA) **(68)** (bl) *(JWWatts)* 8-11 GDuffield (28) (led: sn clr: ct nr fin)  nk.3

3285 Splash of Salt (IRE) *(WJHaggas)* 8-6 MHills (16) (a.p far side: ev ch ins fnl f: r.o)  hd.4

32912 Mam'zelle Angot **(58)** *(MRStoute)* 8-6 WCarson (8) (b: b.hind: dwlt: outpcd:
    rapid hdwy appr fnl f: fin fast) ...................................................... nk.5

3502 Sea Exhibition (IRE) **(63)** *(MBlanshard)* 8-6 DHolland (5) (a.p stands' side: r.o
    appr fnl f) .................................................................. s.h.6

3580 Knobbleeneeze **(62)** (v) *(MRChannon)* 8-11 JQuinn (25) (prom far side tl wknd
    over 1f out) ................................................................. 2.7

3635 Daily Sport Don **(58)** *(RHannon)* 8-11 WRSwinburn (24) (prom far side 4f) ...... nk.8
    Barley Cake *(WAO'Gorman)* 8-3 ‡3EmmaO'Gorman (6) (lt-f: leggy: hdwy
    stands' rail fnl 2f: nvr able to chal) .............................................. hd.9

3580 Altruistic (IRE) *(CFWall)* 8-6 GCarter (17) (chsd ldrs far side over 3f) ............... 4.10

29244 Star Minstrel (IRE) **(70)** *(MMcCormack)* 8-11 JReid (18) (in tch far side: no imp
    fnl 3f) ...................................................................... 1.11

35802 Clanrock **(65)** *(RMWhitaker)* 8-11 ACulhane (30) (chsd ldrs far side: no hdwy
    fnl 2f) ...................................................................... nk.12

*33156* Palacegate Prince **(57)** (bl) *(JBerry)* 9-2 JCarroll (22) (prom far side: eased whn
    btn ins fnl f) ................................................................ nk.13

    Hotsocks *(PatMitchell)* 8-6 LDettori (14) (leggy: w ldrs stands' side 3f: sn btn)  1.14

    Young Sparkie *(RFJohnsonHoughton)* 8-11 AMunro (4) (unf: n.d) ................ hd.15

19895 Nut Bush **(50)** *(NACallaghan)* 8-11 MRoberts (9) (b: chsd ldrs stands' side over
    3f) ........................................................................ s.h.16

    Vienna Bound *(CFWall)* 8-11 RCochrane (20) (cmpt: bkwd: s.s: a bhd) ......... hd.17

35705 Persian Melody (IRE) *(DRCElsworth)* 8-6 JWilliams (3) (b: b.hind: nvr nr to chal)  nk.18

34722 Blue Trumpet *(AHide)* 8-11 WWoods (29) (lw: chsd ldrs far side tl rdn & wknd
    over 2f out) ................................................................ nk.19

    Nomadic Fire *(DMorley)* 8-11 BRaymond (11) (lt-f: unf: dwlt: a bhd) .......... hd.20

    Broughtons Formula *(WJMusson)* 8-11 JHBrown (1) (cmpt: bit bkwd: dwlt: a
    bhd) ...................................................................... 1.21

3291 Capten Morgan (IRE) **(46)** *(WJHaggas)* 8-11 RHills (27) (rdn ¹/₂-wy: sn bhd) . hd.22

2646 Premier Blues (FR) *(RJRWilliams)* 7-13 ‡7GMitchell (13) (dwlt: a bhd) ........... ¹/₂.23

3531 Canadian Eagle *(GLewis)* 8-3 ‡3DHarrison (21) (a bhd) ...................... 2.24

3478 Don't Tell Jean **(50)** *(NBycroft)* 8-6 DMcKeown (26) (chsd ldrs far side 3f: sn
    bhd) ...................................................................... hd.25

2002 Savings Bank **(70)** *(GAPritchard-Gordon)* 8-11 WRyan (12) (chsd ldrs stands'
    side 3f) ................................................................... ¹/₂.26

    Perfectly Entitled (IRE) *(JPearce)* 8-6 RPrice (2) (prom stands' side 3f) ....... ¹/₂.27

*35536* Cuddly Date **(53)** *(DTThom)* 8-11 DBiggs (15) (racd alone centre: in tch over 3f) nk.28

    Miss Piglet (IRE) *(RIngram)* 8-6 AMcGlone (23) (small: dwlt: a bhd) .......... 4.29

**100/30** SOAKING, **4/1** Mam'zelle Angot(op 6/1), **7/1** Greenwich Chalenge(5/1—8/1), **11/1** Nut Bush, **12/1** Savings Bank, Clanrock, **14/1** Sea Exhibition (IRE), **16/1** Persian Melody (IRE), Star Minstrel (IRE)(12/1—20/1), Nomadic Fire, **20/1** Daily Sport Don, Knobbleeneeze, Canadian Eagle, Barley Cake, Young Sparkie, Splash of Salt (IRE), Vienna Bound, Warkworth (USA), Broughtons Formula, Blue Trumpet, Hotsocks, **25/1** Miss Piglet (IRE), Palacegate Prince, Pe rfectly Entitled (IRE), Premier Blues (FR), **33/1** Ors. CSF £34.37, Tote £3.10: £1.90 £3.40 £7.10 (£11.30). Mr K. Abdulla (LAMBOURN) bred by David John Brown. 29 Rn; Sold A Pitt 8,500 gns
                                  1m 12.08 (0.68)
                               SF—47/49/43/37/36/35

**3713**    GREENE KING H'CAP (0-105) £5435.50 (£1624.00: £777.00: £353.50)
        1¹/₂m
                                          2-35 (2-39)

35275 **Walimu (IRE) (73)** *(CFWall)* 3–7-13 JLowe (8) (a.p: led over 2f out: jst hld on) .. —1

2844 Storm Crossing (USA) **(89)** *(GHarwood)* 3–9-1 PatEddery (1) (lw: hld up: hdwy
    3f out: r.o wl u.p fnl f: jst failed) .................................................. hd.2

33463 Zamirah (IRE) **(73)** *(GWragg)* 3–7-10 ‡3FNorton (2) (stdd s: hdwy 2f out: r.o fnl f) 2¹/₂.3

35363 Million in Mind (IRE) **(87)** *(MrsJCecil)* 3–8-13 PaulEddery (12) (led tl over 2f out:
    kpt on) ..................................................................... 1¹/₂.4

3536* Highbrook (USA) **(83)** *(MHTompkins)* 4–9-3 PRobinson (7) (hld up & bhd: rdn
    over 2f out: r.o wl fnl f) ....................................................... 1.5

3445 Opera Ghost **(85)** *(PWHarris)* 6–9-5 WRSwinburn (9) (hdwy 4f out: r.o fnl f) .... s.h.6

3538 Tudor Island **(69)** *(CEBrittain)* 3–7-9 DBiggs (3) (chsd ldr: ev ch 3f out: sn wknd) 2¹/₂.7

3194* Brier Creek **(101)** (Fav) *(JHMGosden)* 3–9-13 SCauthen (14) (chsd ldrs:
    rdn 4f out: no imp) ........................................................... 1¹/₂.8

19553 Iftakhaar (USA) **(80)** *(MajorWRHern)* 3–8-6 WCarson (4) (prom: rdn 3f out: sn
    wknd) ..................................................................... nk.9

3369 Roll a Dollar **(86)** *(DRCElsworth)* 6–9-6 BRouse (5) (nvr nr to chal) ............. s.h.10

3445 Laburnum **(84)** *(LMCumani)* 4–9-4 LDettori (10) (chsd ldrs: rdn 4f out: sn btn) 2¹/₂.11

3527 Mamdooh **(90)** *(ACStewart)* 3–9-2 MRoberts (6) (a bhd) .................... s.h.12

3641 White Willow **(76)** *(MrsGRReveley)* 3–7-9 ‡7DarrenMoffatt (15) (a bhd) ......... 1¹⁄₂.**13**
3527⁶ Touch Paper (USA) **(76)** *(BWHills)* 3–8-2 MHills (13) (chsd ldrs tl wknd over 2f
     out) ................................................................. ¹⁄₂.**14**
3206² Libk **(94)** *(HThomsonJones)* 4–10-0 RHills (4) (chsd ldrs 9f: sn wknd) ......... 3¹⁄₂.**15**

**5/1** Brier Creek (USA), **6/1** Laburnum, **7/1** Highbrook (USA), **9/1** Touch Paper (USA), **11/1** Storm Crossing (USA), **12/1** Zamirah (IRE), Mamdooh, Tudor Island(16/1—20/1), **14/1** Opera Ghost, **16/1** WALIMU (IRE), Libk, Million in Mind (IRE), Iftakhaar (USA), **20/1** Roll a Dollar, **33/1** White Willow. CSF £164.01, CT £1,986.92. Tote £28.70: £7.20 £3.80 £3.30 (£368.10). Sheikh Ahmed Al Maktoum (NEWMARKET) bred by Sheikh Ahmed bin Rashid al Maktoum in Ireland. 15 Rn         2m 30.64 (1.34)
                                          SF—36/51/27/41/43/44

## 3714       JEYES H'CAP (0-105) £6836.00 (£2048.00: £984.00: £452.00)     **7f**     3-05 (3-09)

3545 **Hob Green (64)** *(MrsJRRamsden)* 3–7-7 JLowe (14) (hld up gng wl: hdwy wl
     over 1f out: rdn to ld ins fnl f: sn clr) .................................... —**1**
3441 Jaldi (IRE) **(69)** *(JSutcliffe)* 4–8-1 RHills (17) (hdwy over 2f out: ev ch 1f out: kpt
     on) ............................................................ 2¹⁄₂.**2**
3545⁴ Amazing Feat (IRE) **(74)** *(MrsGRReveley)* 3–8-3 KDarley (9) (outpcd tl rapid
     hdwy appr fnl f: fin wl) ................................................. ¹⁄₂.**3**
3545 Kimberley Park **(67)** *(DWPArbuthnot)* 4–7-13 WCarson (10) (hdwy & rdn 2f out:
     styd on wl nr fin) ....................................................... nk.**4**
3439⁶ Mamma's Too **(87)** *(MBell)* 3–8-9 ‡7PTurner (16) (chsd ldrs: led wl over 2f out:
     hdd ins fnl f: wknd nr fin) ............................................... s.h.**5**
3441 Rocton North (IRE) **(91)** (bl) *(RHannon)* 4–9-9 JReid (8) (hdwy 2f out: rdn & r.o
     fnl f) ................................................................. ¹⁄₂.**6**
3632² Crystal Heights (FR) **(80)** *(WAO'Gorman)* 4–8-12 PatEddery (6) (w ldrs: ev ch 3f
     out tl wknd ins fnl f) ................................................... ³⁄₄.**7**
3428 Orthorhombus **(94)** (bl) *(GLewis)* 3–9-9 PaulEddery (7) (w ldrs tl wknd appr fnl f) nk.**8**
3310 Morsun **(73)** (bl) *(DMorley)* 3–8-2 WRyan (1) (dwlt: bhd tl gd hdwy appr fnl f: fin
     wl) ................................................................... hd.**9**
3543 Bold Memory **(87)** *(MJohnston)* 3–9-2 DMcKeown (4) (stdd s: hld up: plld out
     3f out: sn rdn & no imp) ................................................ 2.**10**
    Coltrane **(70)** *(LordHuntingdon)* 4–8-2 AMunro (3) (in tch: rdn over 3f out: sn
     btn) .................................................................. 1¹⁄₂.**11**
2348⁴ Sahel (IRE) **(89)** (Fav) *(JHMGosden)* 4–9-7 SCauthen (13) (lw: rdn 3f out: n.d) nk.**12**
3545³ Kayvee **(93)** *(GHarwood)* 3–9-8 MRoberts (19) (lw: chsd ldrs: rdn 2f out: eased
     whn btn ins fnl f) ...................................................... nk.**13**
3356 Sir Harry Hardman **(94)** *(FHLee)* 4–9-12 RCochrane (2) (prom 4f) ................. hd.**14**
3441 Abbey Strand (USA) **(70)** *(LordHuntingdon)* 3–7-10 ‡3DHarrison (5) (chsd ldrs:
     rdn 3f out: sn btn) ..................................................... hd.**15**
3539⁵ Our Rita **(72)** *(DrJDScargill)* 3–8-1 JQuinn (20) (prom 5f) .................... 1¹⁄₂.**16**
3439² Mathaayl (USA) **(76)** (bl) *(HThomsonJones)* 3–8-5 NCarlisle (15) (chsd ldrs tl
     rdn & wknd 2f out) ..................................................... ¹⁄₂.**17**
3539⁴ Laundry Maid **(86)** *(HCandy)* 3–8-8 ‡7AntoinetteArmes (12) (prom 4f: sn wknd) hd.**18**
3612⁵ Bold Habit **(83)** *(SEKettlewell)* 7–8-10 ‡5JWeaver (21) (b: in tch tl rdn & wknd
     over 2f out) ........................................................... 1.**19**
3612 Gant Bleu (FR) **(62)** *(RMWhitaker)* 5–7-8 DaleGibson (22) (rdn 2f out: nvr rchd
     ldrs) ................................................................ 1¹⁄₂.**20**
3441 Go Executive **(87)** (bl) *(CEBrittain)* 4–9-5 TQuinn (18) (led over 4f) ............... 5.**21**
3469 Sure Lord (IRE) **(71)** *(WRMuir)* 3–8-0 GCarter (11) (a bhd) ........................ 3.**22**

**5/1** Sahel (IRE)(7/1—9/2), **13/2** HOB GREEN, **12/1** Bold Memory, Kayvee, Jaldi (IRE)(op 8/1), Amazing Feat (IRE), **14/1** Crystal Heights (FR), Laundry Maid, **16/1** Rocton North (IRE), Coltrane, Kimberley Park, Gant Bleu (FR), Our Rita, Mathaayl (USA), Mamma's Too, **25/1** Bold Habit, **33/1** Ors. CSF £79.08, CT £848.65. Tote £6.10: £2.10 £5.50 £3.40 £2.00 (£80.40). Mrs A. E. Sigsworth (THIRSK) bred by L. C. and Mrs A. E. Sigsworth. 22 Rn         1m 23.88 (U.12)
                                          SF—49/49/49/44/53/65

## 3715       CHALLENGE STKS (Gp 2)     £35028.00 (£13057.40: £6228.70: £2665.90)
        **7f**                                               3-40 (3-41)

3443³ **Selkirk (USA)** (Fav) *(IABalding)* 4–9-3 RCochrane (4) (lw: hld up: hdwy to ld
     over 1f out: sn pushed clr) .............................................. —**1**
3442⁵ Thourios *(GHarwood)* 3–8-11 WCarson (5) (hdwy over 3f out: led over 2f out:
     hdd over 1f out: kpt on) ................................................ 2¹⁄₂.**2**
3443⁵ Second Set (IRE) *(LMCumani)* 4–9-3 LDettori (6) (chsd ldrs: rdn 2f out: styd on
     fnl f) ................................................................ 1¹⁄₂.**3**
3573² Prince Ferdinand *(MMcCormack)* 3–8-11 JReid (7) (trckd ldrs: ev ch over 1f
     out: wknd fnl f) ......................................................... 2.**4**
3546⁶ Perfect Circle *(MRStoute)* 3–8-8 WRSwinburn (1) (bhd: rdn over 3f out: r.o fnl f) 1.**5**
3573⁶ Norwich *(BWHills)* 5–9-0 SCauthen (3) (lw: chsd ldrs tl led 3f out: sn hdd & btn) ¹⁄₂.**6**

3195⁴ Dilum (USA) *(PFlCole)* 3–8-11 AMunro (6) (lw: prom 5f) ............................ 2.7
3443⁶ Mystiko (USA) *(CEBrittain)* 4–9-3 MRoberts (8) (led 4f: wknd qckly) ............... 4.8

**5/6** SELKIRK (USA), **7/2** Second Set (IRE), **8/1** Prince Ferdinand, **9/1** Mystiko (USA), **16/1** Dilum (USA), Perfect Circle, **33/1** Ors. CSF £23.37, Tote £1.80: £1.30 £4.40 £1.60 (£32.30). Mr George Strawbridge (KINGSCLERE) bred by George Strawbridge Jnr in USA. 8 Rn
1m 22.27 (U1.73)
SF—97/83/84/72/66/70

## 3716
DAVID SWANNELL NURSERY £8675.00 (£2600.00: £912.50 each)
7f
4-10 (4-24)

3519² **Law Commission (91)** *(DRCElsworth)* 8-11 ‡⁷JHunter (11) (trckd ldrs: rdn over 1f out: r.o to ld nr fin) ..................................... —1
3516⁵ Piston (IRE) **(82)** *(BHanbury)* 8-9 WRSwinburn (24) (led tl hdd & no ex nr fin) . nk.2
3523³ Embankment (IRE) **(85)** *(RHannon)* 8-12 JReid (22) (hdwy 2f out: rdn & r.o fnl f) 1¹/₂.3
3291⁴ Premium **(66)** (bl) *(WJHaggas)* 7-0 ‡⁷AntoinetteArmes (6) (a.p: rdn & kpt on fnl f) d.h.3
3574⁵ Festin **(71)** (bl) *(JLDunlop)* 7-12⁽¹⁾ DHolland (19) (hdwy over 1f out: unable qckn ins fnl f) .................................... nk.5
3424* Fortensky (USA) **(89)** (Fav) *(LMCumani)* 9-2 LDettori (13) (trckd ldrs: rdn & swtchd over 1f out: one pce fnl f) ................ ³/₄.6
3478⁴ Norling (IRE) **(69)** *(NTinkler)* 7-7⁽³⁾ ‡³FNorton (7) (a.p: rdn & no ex appr fnl f) ... hd.7
3123 Raging Thunder **(69)** *(GLewis)* 7-7⁽²⁾ ‡³DHarrison (18) (hdwy 2f out: nt pce to chal) ............................................... 2.8
3642³ Egg **(66)** (bl) *(TDBarron)* 7-7 JLowe (3) (rdn 2f out: nvr nrr) .................. 1¹/₂.9
3482 Fiveofive (IRE) **(66)** *(NACallaghan)* 7-7 TyroneWilliams (5) (in tch: rdn over 2f out: no imp appr fnl f) ................... ¹/₂.10
3181³ Inderaputeri **(68)** *(MissGayKelleway)* 7-9 NCarlisle (21) (b.nr hind: chsd ldrs 4f) 4.11
3541 Azhar **(94)** *(MRStoute)* 9-2 ‡⁵JJones (4) (hld up: effrt over 1f out: nvr rchd ldrs) nk.12
3598 Contract Court (USA) **(75)** *(CACyzer)* 8-2 DBiggs (1) (chsd ldrs tl wknd over 2f out) ................................................. 1.13
3553³ Absolutely Fact (USA) **(66)** *(WJHaggas)* 7-7 JQuinn (2) (hld up: hdwy 3f out: rdn 2f out: sn wknd) ......................... hd.14
3574³ Greystoke **(75)** (v) *(LordHuntingdon)* 8-2 MRoberts (20) (prom over 4f: eased whn btn appr fnl f) ........................ ³/₄.15
3550⁵ Rain Splash **(82)** *(RHannon)* 8-9 PatEddery (10) (s.i.s: a bhd) .................... 1.16
3123³ Easy Access (IRE) **(78)** *(RHannon)* 8-5 WCarson (17) (b: b.hind: s.i.s: hdwy over 2f out: wknd wl over 1f out) ............ hd.17
3001 Lys (IRE) **(76)** *(CEBrittain)* 8-3 TQuinn (8) (chsd ldrs: rdn over 3f out: sn wknd) s.h.18
3482 Bonus Point **(66)** *(MrsGRReveley)* 7-0 ‡⁷DarrenMoffatt (25) (chsd ldrs tl rdn & wknd over 2f out) ..................... 1¹/₂.19
3635 Aviator's Dream **(66)** *(JFBottomley)* 7-7 GBardwell (15) (rdn ¹/₂-wy: a bhd) ... hd.20
2695 Magication **(77)** *(CEBrittain)* 7-13 ‡⁵BDoyle (16) (a bhd) ....................... ¹/₂.21
3502 Crystal Stone **(66)** *(TThomsonJones)* 7-7 NAdams (12) (a bhd) ............... 3¹/₂.22
3199 Platinum Venture **(69)** *(SPCWoods)* 7-10 EJohnson (23) (chsd ldrs 3f: sn bhd) nk.23
LONG HANDICAP: Premium 7-0, Egg 7-3, Fiveofive (IRE) 7-1, Absolutely Fact (USA) 7-3,
Aviator's Dream 6-13, Crystal Stone 7-5.
*3250* Surprise Surprise (10/1) Withdrawn (ref to ent stalls) : not under orders — Rule 4 applies*

**9/2** Fortensky (USA), **15/2** Egg, **11/1** Greystoke(8/1—12/1), **14/1** Rain Splash, Piston (IRE), Easy Access (IRE), **16/1** Embankment (IRE), Festin, Inderaputeri, **20/1** Norling (IRE), Raging Thunder, Azhar, LAW COMMISSION, Lys (IRE), **25/1** Magication, Absolutely Fact (USA), **33/1** Fiveofive (IRE), Bonus Point, Contract Court (USA), Premium, Aviator's Dream, Platinum Venture, **50/1** Crystal Stone. CSF £222.65, CT £1,535.70 LC, P & E; £2,996.73 LC, P & P. Tote £21.50: £3.50 £2.40 £4.10 £ £7.30 P (£283.40). Mr Raymond Tooth (WHITSBURY) bred by Airlie Stud. 23 Rn
1m 24.82 (0.82)
SF—53/50/48/22/33/49

## 3717
E.B.F. CHESTERTON STKS (Mdn 2-Y.O) £5010.00 (£1500.00: £720.00: £330.00)
1m
4-40 (4-54)

Bashayer (USA) *(MajorWRHern)* 8-9 WCarson (6) (leggy: scope: trckd ldrs: led 2f out: sn clr: comf) .............................. —1
Silverdale (USA) *(JHMGosden)* 9-0 SCauthen (17) (b: b.hind: leggy: scope: chsd ldrs: r.o fnl f) .................................. 2¹/₂.2
3030² Marco Magnifico (USA) *(BWHills)* 9-0 MHills (10) (prom: ev ch 2f out: unable qckn) ................................................. hd.3
Upper Mount Clair *(CEBrittain)* 8-9 MRoberts (2) (small: lt-f: prom: led 3f out to 2f out: one pce) ................................ 4.4
3579³ Aberdeen Heather **(85)** *(DRCElsworth)* 9-0 JWilliams (19) (plld hrd: prom: no hdwy fnl 2f) ..................................... ³/₄.5
Princess Borghese (USA) (Fav) *(HRACecil)* 8-9 PatEddery (16) (leggy: wl grwn: prom: rdn 3f out: eased whn btn appr fnl f) ...... 1¹/₂.6
3314⁵ Moon Carnival *(LadyHerries)* 9-0 PaulEddery (7) (nvr trbld ldrs) ............... 1¹/₂.7

Maastricht *(WJHaggas)* 9-0 JQuinn (8) (w'like: chsd ldrs 6f) .............................. ³/₄.8
3276² Trippiano *(HRACecil)* 9-0 WRyan (5) (chsd ldrs: rdn 2f out: sn btn) ................. 1.9
3525 Shintillo (IRE) *(LMCumani)* 9-0 LDettori (12) (hld up: stdy hdwy fnl 2f: n.m.r fnl f: nvr plcd to chal) ............................................................................................. nk.10
Alasad *(BHanbury)* 9-0 RHills (9) (gd sort: wl grwn: dwlt: outpcd after 3f: rdn & r.o fnl 2f) ................................................................................................... hd.11
Spanish Sahara *(PWChapple-Hyam)* 9-0 JReid (14) (b: w'like: chsd ldrs over 5f) ................................................................................................................. 1.12
3362 Circus Colours *(JLDunlop)* 9-0 TQuinn (18) (effrt 3 out: nvr trbld ldrs) .......... 5.13
Excess Baggage (IRE) *(NACallaghan)* 9-0 GDuffield (3) (neat: scope: a bhd) .. 2.14
3247⁵ Acanthus (IRE) *(JLDunlop)* 9-0 BRaymond (15) (sn rdn along: a bhd) ......... s.h.15
Commanche Creek *(LMCumani)* 9-0 JFortune (13) (w'like: scope: chsd ldrs: rdn 3f out: sn btn) ............................................................................................ ³/₄.16
3519 Sir Thomas Beecham *(SDow)* 9-0 BRouse (4) (bhd fnl 4f) ............................. 1¹/₂.17
3171 Endearing Val *(CNAllen)* 8-9 PRobinson (1) (led 5f) ....................................... 5.18
3297 Horseradish *(DMorley)* 9-0 WRSwinburn (11) (rdn after 1f: a bhd) ..................... 19

**15/8** Princess Borghese (USA), **6/1** Shintillo (IRE)(op 3/1), **7/1** Trippiano(op 7/2), **15/2** Silverdale (USA)(op 4/1), **10/1** BASHAYER (USA)(op 5/1), Commanche Creek(op 20/1), Alasad(5/1—12/1), **12/1** Marco Magnifico (USA)(op 6/1), Spanish Sahara (IRE)(6/1—14/1), **25/1** Moon Carnival, Upper Mount Clair, **33/1** Aberdeen Heather, **40/1** Acanthus (IRE), Maastricht, **50/1** Ors. CSF £85.10, Tote £7.20: £2.60 £2.90 £3.60 (£51.90). Mr Hamdan Al-Maktoum (LAMBOURN) bred by Shadwell Farm Inc & Shadwell Estate Co Ltd in USA. 19 Rn
1m 37.69 (0.39)
SF–53/50/49/32/35/25

**3718** SEVERALS APP'CE H'CAP (0-90) £5205.00 (£1560.00: £750.00: £345.00)
1¹/₄m
5-10 (5-23)

3249⋆ LOKI (IRE) (79) *(GLewis)* 4 0 1 ‡⁶ᴮRussell (7) (hld up: gd hdwy to ld 1f out: rdn out) ................................................................................................................... —1
3436 Alto Jane (70) *(GHarwood)* 3-8-9 JJones (15) (chsd ldrs: led 3f out to 1f out: r.o) ..................................................................................................................... ¹/₂.2
3403 Rive-Jumelle (IRE) (50) *(MBell)* 4-7-9 NKennedy (14) (hld up: hdwy 2f out: r.o wl fnl f) ................................................................................................................ nk.3
3627² Sword Master (74) (Fav) *(BobJones)* 3-8-13 FNorton (8) (in tch: outpcd 3f out: r.o wl appr fnl f) ......................................................................................... ¹/₂.4
3634⋆ Majed (IRE) (74) *(MrsGRReveley)* 4-9-2 (5x) ‡³DarrenMoffatt (17) (chsd ldrs: rdn 2f out: r.o ins fnl f) ...................................................................................... s.h.5
3634⁵ Cold Shower (IRE) (74) *(JAGlover)* 3-8-13 SWilliams (1) (lw: hld up: rdn & r.o appr fnl f) .......................................................................................................... 1.6
3526³ Hidden Laughter (USA) (77) *(BWHills)* 3-8-10 ‡⁶JTate (18) (in tch: rdn 3f out: no imp appr fnl f) ............................................................................................... 1¹/₂.7
3259³ Usaidit (73) *(WCarter)* 3-8-12 NGwilliams (19) (chsd ldrs: ev ch 3f out: wknd wl over 1f out) .......................................................................................................... 1¹/₂.8
3526 Parking Bay (70) *(GAPritchard-Gordon)* 5-9-1 RPerham (9) (prom over 7f) ..... hd.9
3379⁶ Qualitair Sound (IRE) (55) *(JFBottomley)* 4-8-0⁽³⁾ SMaloney (3) (nvr trbld ldrs) 3¹/₂.10
3526 Avice Caro (USA) (81) *(JHMGosden)* 3-9-6 StephenDavies (16) (lw: w ldr: rdn 4f out: sn btn) .......................................................................................................... ¹/₂.11
3526⁴ Debacle (USA) (74) *(GHarwood)* 3-8-7 ‡PHoughton (12) (lw: w ldrs 5f: sn btn) ¹/₂.12
3615⋆ No Comebacks (56) *(EJAlston)* 4-8-1 (5x) BDoyle (11) (in tch: effrt 3f out: wknd fnl f) ............................................................................................................. hd.13
3475⁶ Shimmer (55) *(LordHuntingdon)* 3-7-8 DHarrison (13) (chsd ldrs 7f: sn rdn & btn) ....................................................................................................................... 1¹/₂.14
3368² Pelorus (83) *(DRCEllsworth)* 7-9-8 ‡⁶JHunter (4) (hld up: effrt 3f out: sn rdn & btn) ........................................................................................................................ ³/₄.15
3363⁵ Many a Quest (USA) (79) *(LMCumani)* 3-9-4 JWeaver (2) (hld up: nt clr run 2f out: nvr plcd to chal) ................................................................................................ 1¹/₂.16
2836 Kanvass (80) *(JRFanshawe)* 3-8-13 ‡⁶NVarley (10) (effrt 4f out: nvr trbld ldrs) s.h.17
3690⁴ Desert Force (IRE) (68) *(MissGayKelleway)* 3-8-1 ‡⁶PBowe (6) (prom 5f) ...... 2¹/₂.18
3582⁵ Prince Pericles (IRE) (68) *(HCandy)* 3-8-4 ‡³AntoinetteArmes (5) (led 7f: sn bhd) ......................................................................................................................... 3¹/₂.19

**7/1** Sword Master, **8/1** Majed (IRE), **9/1** LOKI (IRE), Pelorus, Shimmer(8/1—12/1), Cold Shower (IRE), **10/1** Many a Quest (USA)(op 6/1), No Comebacks(8/1—12/1), **12/1** Rive-Jumelle (IRE), Hidden Laughter (USA), **14/1** Parking Bay, Avice Caro, Kanvass, **16/1** Debacle (USA), **20/1** Usaidit, **25/1** Alto Jane, Prince Pericles (IRE), Qualitair Sound (IRE), **33/1** Desert Force (IRE). CSF £210.61, CT £2,510.04. Tote £9.60: £2.50 £10.00 £2.10 £2.60 (£997.00). Mr Michael H. Watt (EPSOM) bred by Abbey Lodge Stud in Ireland. 19 Rn
2m 4.07 (1.47)
SF–59/49/34/51/53/48

T/Trio: Race 2: any 2 fr 1st 3 w any £14.70 (53.8 Tckts) & Race 3: £96.50 (8.3 Tckts). T/Jkpt: Not won; £2,152.10 to Newmarket 16/10/92. T/Plpt: £1,362.50 (5.35 Tckts). Dk

## NEWMARKET (R-H) Rowley Mile
### Friday, October 16th [Good to firm]
Going Allowance: minus 0.30 sec per fur (F)　　　　　　　Wind: mod half bhd

Stalls: centre

**3719**　　E.B.F. SNAILWELL STKS (Mdn 2-Y.O) £4932.00 (£1476.00: £708.00: £324.00)
　　　　　　**6f**　　　　　　　　　　　　　　　　　　　　　　　　2-00 (2-03)

3430³ **Felucca** (Fav) *(HRACecil)* 8-9 PatEddery (14) (lw: trckd ldrs: led over 2f out: r.o
　　　　wl) ............................................................................................... —1
3551² Nafuth (USA) *(PTWalwyn)* 9-0 WCarson (4) (a chsng ldrs: kpt on wl fnl f) ........ 1½.2
　　　　Naif (USA) *(LMCumani)* 9-0 LDettori (2) (w'like: leggy: lw: in tch: hdwy over 1f
　　　　out: styd on wl nr fin) ....................................................................... 2½.3
　　　　Dramanice (USA) *(MrsJCecil)* 9-0 SCauthen (1) (w'like: leggy: a in tch: kpt on
　　　　wl fnl f) ......................................................................................... nk.4
　　　　Logan's Luck (USA) *(MRStoute)* 9-0 KDarley (11) (w'like: scope: in tch: outpcd
　　　　2f out: hdwy appr fnl f: fin wl) ............................................................ hd.5
3214⁶ Scusi *(WJarvis)* 9-0 JReid (12) (cl up tl outpcd over 1f out) ............................ 2.6
　3523 Ok Bertie (80) *(DMorris)* 9-0 MTebbutt (8) (led tl hdd over 2f out: grad wknd) .. nk.7
　　　　Mysilv *(CFWall)* 8-9 PRobinson (7) (w'like: nvr trbld ldrs) ........................... 3½.8
　　　　Mighty Wrath *(ICampbell)* 9-0 DBiggs (10) (w'like: scope: s.i.s: sme late hdwy) 2½.9
3411⁵ Rad *(SPCWoods)* 9-0 WWoods (9) (outpcd fr ½-wy) .................................... ½.10
　　　　Bunderburg (USA) *(PWChapple-Hyam)* 9-0 DHolland (13) (b: leggy: scope: sn
　　　　pushed along: prom to ½-wy: sn wknd) ................................................ s.h.11
　　　　Calibrate *(DRCElsworth)* 9-0 JWilliams (6) (cmpt: rn green & a bhd) ............. 1½.12
　　　　Gate of Heaven *(WAO'Gorman)* 8-9 AMunro (3) (neat: prom 4f) .................... s.h.13
　　　　Mountain Spring *(MDIUsher)* 9-0 MWigham (5) (cmpt: scope: bit bkwd: s.i.s: a
　　　　bhd: t.o) ......................................................................................... 14

**8/11** FELUCCA, **7/2** Dramanice (USA), **10/1** Nafuth (USA)(op 5/1), Naif (USA)(8/1—12/1), **12/1** Scusi(op 8/1),
**20/1** Bunderburg (USA), **25/1** Logan's Luck (USA), **33/1** Calibrate, Gate of Heaven, Mysilv, **50/1** Mighty Wrath,
Mountain Spring, **66/1** Ors. CSF £10.20, Tote £1.90: £1.20 £1.80 £2.50 (£3.70). Mr K. Abdulla (NEWMARKET)
bred by Juddmonte Farms. 14 Rn　　　　　　　　　　　　　　　　　1m 11.85 (0.45)
　　　　　　　　　　　　　　　　　　　　　　　　　　　　　　　SF—50/49/39/38/37/29

**3720**　　ROCKFEL STKS (Gp 3) (2-Y.O.F) £13720.00 (£5136.00: £2468.00: £1076.00)
　　　　　　**7f**　　　　　　　　　　　　　　　　　　　　　　　　2-35 (2-40)

3544★ **Yawl** (100) *(BWHills)* 8-8 DHolland (7) (led after 1f: rdn & r.o wl fnl f) ............... —1
3430★ Queen's View (FR) *(LMCumani)* 8-8 LDettori (8) (lw: trckd ldrs: hdwy to chal ins
　　　　fnl f: rdn & nt qckn nr fin) .................................................................. ¾.2
　3444 Mystic Goddess (USA) (100) *(MRStoute)* 9-0 WRSwinburn (2) (lw: led 1f: chsd
　　　　wnr tl rdn & btn ins fnl f) ................................................................... 2.3
　3191 Katiba (USA) (90) *(JLDunlop)* 8-8 WCarson (1) (sn pushed along: prom: styd
　　　　on to chal over 1f out: wknd ins fnl f) ................................................... ½.4
3430² Felawnah (USA) (Fav) *(JHMGosden)* 8-8 SCauthen (5) (lw: dwlt: effrt 2f out: sn
　　　　rdn & no imp) ................................................................................. 1½.5
3227a⁴ Ancestral Dancer (100) *(MBell)* 8-8 MHills (6) (in tch: effrt 2f out: no imp) ....... 1½.6
3530★ Wynona (IRE) (96) *(GCBravery)* 8-8 LPiggott (3) (hld up: effrt over 2f out: n.d) .. 5.7
　　　　2758★ Exclusively Yours (16/1) Withdrawn (spread plate at s) : not under orders

**7/4** Felawnah (USA), **9/4** YAWL, **7/2** Queen's View (FR), **14/1** Mystic Goddess (USA)(op 8/1), Ancestral Dancer,
**20/1** Katiba (USA), **25/1** Wynona (IRE). CSF £9.75, Tote £3.30: £1.90 £2.30 (£5.00). Mr R. D. Hollingsworth
(LAMBOURN) bred by R. D. Hollingsworth. 7 Rn　　　　　　　　　　1m 23.81 (U.19)
　　　　　　　　　　　　　　　　　　　　　　　　　　　　　　　SF—65/63/57/55/50/45

**3721**　　BARING INTERNATIONAL DARLEY STKS (listed race)　£9462.50 (£2825.00: £1350.00:
　　　　　　£612.50)　　**1m 1f**　　　　　　　　　　　　　　3-05 (3-11)

　3547 **Mellottie** (105) *(MrsGRReveley)* 7-9-0 JLowe (2) (hld up: stdy hdwy over 2f
　　　　out: rdn to ld ins fnl f: r.o wl) ............................................................ —1
2506a² Rainbow Corner (Fav) *(HRACecil)* 3-9-3 PatEddery (4) (trckd ldrs: led over 1f
　　　　out & qcknd: hdd ins fnl f: r.o) ............................................................ 1.2
3654a² Calling Collect (USA) *(LMCumani)* 3-9-0 LDettori (6) (in tch: hdwy 3f out: hrd
　　　　rdn & ev ch over 1f out: kpt on nr fin) ................................................... s.h.3
2454⁵ Fair Average (101) *(HCandy)* 4-9-0 MRoberts (10) (a chsng ldrs: ev ch over 1f
　　　　out: styd on) ................................................................................... 2½.4
3222a⁶ Sure Sharp (USA) (111) *(BWHills)* 5-9-7 DHolland (5) (led tl hdd over 1f out: kpt
　　　　on one pce) ..................................................................................... 1½.5
3213³ Badawi (USA) (100) *(JHMGosden)* 4-8-9 SCauthen (7) (trckd ldrs: effrt over 2f
　　　　out: btn over 1f out) .......................................................................... 1.6

3654a Tik Fa (USA) (106) (v) (BHanbury) 3–8-10 WRSwinburn (3) (lw: hld up & bhd:
effrt 3f out: rdn & no imp) ................................................................... 1.7

35424 Lovealoch (IRE) (100) (MBell) 4–8-9 MHills (8) (cl up tl wknd 2f out) ............... 4.8

31314 Mukaddamah (USA) (101) (PTWalwyn) 4–9-0 WCarson (11) (hld up & bhd:
effrt 3f out: n.d) ............................................................................... 3.9

35423 John Rose (100) (PAKelleway) 3–8-10 GayKelleway (1) (hld up: efrt 4f out: rdn
& btn over 2f out) ............................................................................. 4.10

Braveboy (CEBrittain) 4–9-0 TQuinn (9) (lw: s.i.s: sn in tch: wknd over 2f out) 2$\frac{1}{2}$.11

**9/4** Rainbow Corner, **3/1** Calling Collect (USA), **7/2** MELLOTTIE, **11/1** Badawi (USA), **12/1** Tik Fa (USA),
Mukaddamah (USA), **16/1** Sure Sharp (USA), **20/1** Lovealoch (IRE), Fair Average, **50/1** John Rose, **100/1**
Braveboy. CSF £11.40, Tote £4.40: £1.50 £1.70 £1.60 (£8.60). Mrs J. G. Fulton (SALTBURN) bred by Mrs G. R.
Reveley and partners. 11 Rn                                                                    1m 48.62 (U1.38)
SF—80/80/76/68/70/55

## 3722

DEWHURST STKS (Gp 1) (2-Y.O.C & F) £95051.50 (£35588.50: £17419.25: £7508.75:
£3379.38: £1727.62)  **7f**                                                    3-40 (3-41)

3331a* **Zafonic (USA)** (Fav) (AFabre,France) 9-0 PatEddery (1) (nice colt: wl grwn: lw:
hld up: led on bit over 2f out: pushed along & r.o v.wl) ....... —1

3435* Inchinor (RCharlton) 9-0 TQuinn (11) (lw: in tch: efrt over 2f out: r.o wl: no ch w
wnr) ....................................................................... 4.2

27102 Firm Pledge (USA) (PFICole) 9-0 AMunro (7) (a chsng ldrs: effrt over 2f out: r.o) s.h.3

3360* Sueboog (IRE) (CEBrittain) 8-9 WRSwinburn (8) (led: qcknd over 2f out: sn hdd
& no ex) ................................................................... hd.4

3452a* Fatherland (IRE) (MVO'Brien,Ireland) 9-0 LPiggott (2) (gd sort: leggy: lw: hld up
& bhd: hdwy 2f out: r.o u.p: nvr able to chal) ......................... $\frac{1}{2}$.5

3205a Petardia (GWragg) 9-0 MHills (9) (h.d.w: hld up: hdwy over 2f out & no imp) 2$\frac{1}{2}$.6

35252 Zind (IRE) (PWChapple-Hyam) 9-0 MRoberts (4) (chsd ldrs tl wknd 2f out) ...... hd.7

3372* Blues Traveller (IRE) (BWHills) 9-0 DHolland (6) (effrt over 3f out: sn hd rdn &
nvr trbld ldrs) ............................................................. 1.8

29052 Zimzalabim (BWHills) 9-0 WCarson (3) (lw: hld up & bhd: effrt 3f out: n.d) ......... 3.9

34463 Lost Soldier (USA) (LMCumani) 9-0 LDettori (5) (prom tl rdn & wknd fnl 2f) ... nk.10

33675 Carbon Steel (IRE) (BWHills) 9-0 SCauthen (10) (chsd ldrs 5f: sn wknd) ......... 5.11

**10/11** ZAFONIC (USA), **5/1** Fatherland (IRE), **13/2** Inchinor, **8/1** Petardia, **12/1** Firm Pledge (USA), **14/1** Sueboog
(IRE), **33/1** Lost Soldier (USA), **50/1** Zind (IRE), **66/1** Blues Traveller (IRE), Carbon Steel (IRE), **100/1**
Zimzalabim. CSF £7.21, Tote £1.80: £1.30 £1.80 £4.70 (£6.10). Mr K. Abdulla (FRANCE) bred by Juddmonte
Farms Inc. in USA. 11 Rn                                                       1m 23.61 (U.39)
SF—74/62/61/55/58/50

## 3723

TATTERSALLS SALES NURSERY (Final) £11550.00 (£3450.00: £1650.00: £750.00)
**6f**                                                              4-15 (4-16)

36353 **Abergele (76)** (JGFitzGerald) 8-7 KFallon (13) (chsd ldrs: rdn to ld appr fnl f:
edgd lft & styd on wl) ...................................................... —1

3343* Benzoe (IRE) (77) (MWEasterby) 8-8 TLucas (4) (trckd ldrs gng wl: disp ld appr
fnl f: rdn at qckn wl ins fn f) .............................................. $\frac{1}{2}$.2

3410 Cutthroat Kid (IRE) (65) (v) (SGNorton) 7-7(1) ‡3FNorton (5) (lw: a w ldrs: rdn 2f
out: kpt on wl) .............................................................. 3$\frac{1}{2}$.3

33643 After the Last (86) (RHannon) 9-3 JReid (6) (outpcd & bhd: hdwy 2f out:
r.o wl nr fin) ............................................................... 1$\frac{1}{4}$.4

3530 Perdition (IRE) (65) (JWHills) 7-10 WCarson (14) (in tch: pushed along $\frac{1}{2}$-wy:
kpt on) ..................................................................... hd.5

3347 Hotaria (67) (RMWhitaker) 7-12 NCarlisle (8) (trckd ldrs: effrt 2f out: styd on one
pce) ........................................................................ s.h.6

3117 Manor Adventure (72) (BAMcMahon) 8-3 TQuinn (17) (cl up: led $\frac{1}{2}$-wy tl appr
fnl f: grad wknd) ........................................................... 1$\frac{1}{2}$.7

2409 Sweet Disorder (IRE) (66) (GAPritchard-Gordon) 7-6(4) ‡5BDoyle (12) (mid div:
effrt 3f out: styd on one pce) .............................................. $\frac{3}{4}$.8

3023 Caps Ninety-Two (IRE) (62) (DrJDScargill) 7-7 JQuinn (1) (prom tl wknd appr
fnl f) ....................................................................... $\frac{1}{2}$.9

3285* Racing Telegraph (71) (JPearce) 8-2 RPrice (15) (in tch 4f: grad wknd) ........ 1$\frac{1}{4}$.10

3551* Princely Favour (IRE) (86) (RHannon) 8-3 BRouse (16) (prom over 4f) ........... 1$\frac{1}{2}$.11

3534 The Sharp Bidder (IRE) (88) (RHollinshead) 9-5 LDettori (11) (dwlt: n.d) ....... 1$\frac{1}{2}$.12

36082 Glen Miller (68) (JWPayne) 7-13 AMunro (3) (in tch: pushed along $\frac{1}{2}$-wy: sn
wknd) ...................................................................... s.h.13

36063 Gangleader (70) (bl) (SPCWoods) 9-3 WWoods (2) (hld up: effrt 2f out: n.d) ... $\frac{3}{4}$.14

34746 Runrig (IRE) (66) (MissLAPerratt) 7-8 ‡3DHarrison (10) (hld up: n.d) .............. hd.15

3179 Who's Tom (IRE) (62) (WJMusson) 7-7 JLowe (9) (b: a bhd) .................. $\frac{3}{4}$.16

3411* Snowy River (FR) (90) (DrJDScargill) 9-7 LPiggott (7) (lw: led to $\frac{1}{2}$-wy: sn lost
pl) ......................................................................... s.h.17

LONG HANDICAP: Sweet Disorder (IRE) 7-5, Caps Ninety-Two (IRE) 7-6, Who's Tom (IRE) 6-9.

11/2 After the Last(7/1—8/1), 6/1 Snowy River (FR), 8/1 ABERGELE, 10/1 Benzoe (IRE)(8/1—12/1), Glen Miller, Racing Telegraph, Perdition (IRE), 11/1 Cutthroat Kid (IRE), 12/1 Gangleader, 16/1 The Sharp Bidder (IRE), Runrig (IRE), 20/1 Princely Favour (IRE), 25/1 Manor Adventure, Hotaria, Caps Ninety-Two (IRE), 33/1 Sweet Disorder (IRE), 50/1 Who's Tom (IRE). CSF £79.72, CT £815.24. Tote £8.10: £2.40 £2.30 £3.80 £2.00 (£73.20). A. F. Budge (Equine) Limited (MALTON) bred by Mrs D. O. Joly. 17 Rn     1m 11.68 (0.28)
SF—51/50/21/39/17/18

**3724**   GREENE KING H'CAP (3-Y.O) (0-100) £5617.50 (£1680.00: £805.00: £367.50)
1¾m     4-50 (4-55)

(Weights raised 1 lb)

| | | |
|---|---|---|
| 3492⁴ **Chief Minister (IRE)** (77) (bl) *(LMCumani)* 8-7 LDettori (11) (lw: a.p: effrt & wandered 2f out: led 1f out: styd on u.p) | | —1 |
| 3538⁵ Not in Doubt (USA) (87) (bl) *(HCandy)* 9-3 CRutter (14) (mid div: hdwy 4f out: ev ch over 1f out: nt qckn) | | 2.2 |
| 3438⁴ Bustinetta (66) *(JRFanshawe)* 7-10 JLowe (13) (drvn along 4f out: n.m.r: r.o wl nr fin) | | ½.3 |
| 3538★ Rosina Mae (70) (Jt-Fav) *(LordHuntingdon)* 8-0 MRoberts (6) (hld up: hdwy 4f out: rdn 2f out: nt qckn) | | 1½.4 |
| 3415 Pica (78) *(HRACecil)* 8-8⁽¹⁾ SCauthen (4) (bhd tl styd on u.p over 2f out: nrst fin) | | 1.5 |
| 3139 Asian Punter (IRE) (68) *(AHide)* 7-9 ‡³FNorton (2) (in tch: hdwy to chal 2f out: wknd appr fnl f) | | nk.6 |
| 3538⁴ Highland Fantasy (USA) (72) *(BWHills)* 8-2 DHolland (8) (b.nr hind: chsd ldrs: led over 3f out tl hdd & wknd 1f out) | | 1½.7 |
| 3090⁶ Poinciana (72) *(RHannon)* 8-2 KDarley (15) (prom: effrt on ins 4f out: btn 2f out) | | 1½.8 |
| 2996⁴ Spikenard (89) *(PTWalwyn)* 9-5 TQuinn (12) (chsd ldrs tl wknd over 2f out) | | 7.9 |
| 3461³ Top Royal (82) *(JLDunlop)* 8-12 WCarson (9) (bhd fnl 4f) | | 2.10 |
| 3538² Farmer's Pet (79) (Jt-Fav) *(GAPritchard-Gordon)* 8-6 ‡³DHarrison (3) (lw: led tl hdd over 3f out: sn wknd) | | ¾.11 |
| 3369 Ambiguously Regal (USA) (79) *(MrsJCecil)* 8-9 PaulEddery (1) (in tch: effrt 4f out: wknd wl over 2f out) | | 8.12 |
| 3536⁵ Quadrant (73) *(BWHills)* 8-3 DBiggs (7) (bhd: rdn 4f out: n.d) | | s.h.13 |
| 3613 Best Gun (68) (bl) *(CWCElsey)* 7-5⁽⁵⁾ ‡⁷AGarth (5) (a bhd) | | ¾.14 |
| 2766a Miss Plum (91) *(DRLoder)* 9-7 WRSwinburn (10) (chsd ldrs tl wknd over 3f out) | | 4.15 |

LONG HANDICAP: Best Gun 7-6.

6/1 Rosina Mae, Farmer's Pet, 7/1 Highland Fantasy (USA), Pica, CHIEF MINISTER (IRE), 8/1 Top Royal, 10/1 Miss Plum, 14/1 Bustinetta, Poinciana, 16/1 Quadrant, Ambiguously Regal (USA), 20/1 Not in Doubt (USA), Asian Punter (IRE), 25/1 Spikenard, 33/1 Best Gun. CSF £126.80, CT £1,751.50. Tote £6.30: £2.40 £7.70 £3.80 (£130.40). Mr David Thompson (NEWMARKET) bred by The Mount Coote Partnership in Ireland. 15 Rn
2m 56.19 (1.26 under best: 0.19)
SF—49/55/33/34/40/26

**3725**   NEWMARKET CHALLENGE CUP (Mdn 2-Y.O)   7f     5-15 (5-22)

| | | |
|---|---|---|
| **Munnasib (FR)** *(AAScott)* 9-0 WRSwinburn (3) (w'like: leggy: trckd ldr: rdn to ld ins fnl f) | | —1 |
| 1502 Keating (AUS) (Fav) *(MrsJCecil)* 9-0 PaulEddery (1) (led: rdn over 1f out: hdd ins fnl f: kpt on) | | ½.2 |
| Klondike (IRE) *(PTWalwyn)* 9-0 SCauthen (2) (leggy: scope: swvd bdly lft s & reluctant to r: a t.o) | | dist.3 |

10/11 Keating (AUS)(1/3—Evens), 2/1 MUNNASIB (FR)(op Evens), 5/2 Klondike (IRE)(2/1—4/1). CSF £4.14, Tote £2.60 (£2.10). Maktoum Al Maktoum (NEWMARKET) bred by Ignacio Correas in France. 3 Rn
1m 28.87 (4.87)

T/Trio: Race 4: £52.70 (18.6 Tckts) & Race 6: £338.90 (3 Tckts). T/Jkpt: £913.10 (3.5 Tckts). T/Plpt: £34.70 (280.58 Tckts).     AA

# NEWMARKET (R-H) Rowley Mile

## Saturday, October 17th [Good to firm]

Going Allowance: minus 0.35 sec per fur (F)     Wind: slt half bhd

Stalls: high

**3726**   ROTHMANS ROYALS NORTH SOUTH CHALLENGE SERIES H'CAP (Final)   £28920.00
(£8760.00: £4280.00: £2040.00)   1m     1-50 (1-53)

3370³ **Saafend (65)** *(JSutcliffe)* 4-7-10⁽¹⁾ WCarson (19) (a.p: led appr fnl f: qcknd clr)   —1

## 3727

3370★ Lap of Luxury **(84)** *(WJarvis)* 3–8-12 NDay (12) (trckd ldrs: effrt over 1f out: r.o nr fin) .......... 2¹/₂.2

3428² Croft Valley **(85)** *(RAkehurst)* 5–9-2 TQuinn (17) (led tl hdd 3f out: led 2f out tl appr fnl f: kpt on) ......... hd.3

3441★ Sharpalto **(97)** *(MrsGRReveley)* 5–9-9 ‡⁵JWeaver (18) (hld up: hdwy 3f out: nt qckn fnl f) ......... ³/₄.4

3589 Foolish Touch **(62)** *(WJMusson)* 10–7-7 JQuinn (6) (b: bhd: hdwy over 2f out: nvr able to chal) ......... ¹/₂.5

3209★ Indian Slave (IRE) **(68)** *(RGuest)* 4–7-10 ‡³DHarrison (14) (in tch: rdn 3f out: styd on: no imp) ......... 1¹/₂.6

3612★ La Bamba **(76)** *(GAPritchard-Gordon)* 6–8-7 WHood (13) (b: stdd s: hdwy 2f out: nrst fin) ......... hd.7

3441 Rise Up Singing **(69)** (bl) *(WJMusson)* 4–8-0 TyroneWilliams (10) (w ldr: led 3f out to 2f out: grad wknd) ......... nk.8

3612⁶ Spanish Verdict **(71)** *(DenysSmith)* 5–8-2 DHolland (7) (chsd ldrs: nt qckn fnl 2f) ......... nk.9

3370 Habeta (USA) **(62)** *(JWWatts)* 6–7-7 JLowe (2) (bhd tl styd on fnl 2f: nrst fin) .. d.h.9

3428 Piquant **(81)** *(LordHuntingdon)* 5–8-12 WRSwinburn (11) (cl up 6f: grad wknd) ......... s.h.11

3441 Doulab's Image **(92)** (bl) *(JAGlover)* 5–9-4 ‡⁵SWilliams (5) (bhd tl sme late hdwy) ......... hd.12

3370⁴ Queen of Shannon (IRE) **(76)** *(DMorris)* 4–8-7⁽³⁾ MTebbutt (3) (hdwy ¹/₂-wy: wknd 2f out) ......... 2¹/₂.13

3701★ Scales of Justice **(71)** (Fav) *(JWHills)* 6–8-2 RHills (8) (lw: in tch: effrt ¹/₂-wy: wknd 2f out) ......... ¹/₂.14

3673⁵ Takenhall **(62)** *(MJFetherston-Godley)* 7–7-7 NAdams (23) (prom tl rdn & wknd over 2f out) ......... hd.15

3370 High Low (USA) **(82)** *(WJHaggas)* 4–8-13 SCauthen (16) (lw: chsd ldrs over 5f) 2.16

3520 Swift Romance (IRE) **(62)** *(BRMillman)* 4–7-7 GBardwell (21) (b: lw: cl up tl wknd over 2f out) ......... 1.17

3547 Desert Splendour **(67)** *(CEDtillain)* 4–7-12 DRiggs (15) (outpcd fr ¹/₂-wy) ......... 1.18

3209 Shirley's Train (USA) **(70)** (v) *(LordHuntingdon)* 3–7-12 NCarlisle (9) (in tch tl rdn & btn over 2f out) ......... nk.19

3678 Gotcha (BAR) **(73)** (bl) *(RHannon)* 3–8-1 MRoberts (22) (lw: a outpcd & wl bhd) 5.20

3436 Alycida (USA) **(78)** *(LMCumani)* 3–8-6 LDettori (20) (chsd ldr 6f: eased whn btn) ......... ³/₄.21

3209 King Al **(87)** *(DrJDScargill)* 5–9-4 SWebster (4) (b: lw: a outpcd & bhd) ......... ¹/₂.22

LONG HANDICAP: Foolish Touch 6-12, Habeta (USA) 7-6, Swift Romance (IRE) 6-12.

7/2 Scales of Justice, 7/1 Croft Valley, Lap of Luxury, 15/2 Indian Slave (IRE), 12/1 SAAFEND, 14/1 Sharpalto, 16/1 Piquant, Doulab's Image, 20/1 High Low (USA), La Bamba, Alycida (USA), Takenhall, Rise Up Singing, Gotcha (BAR), Queen of Shannon (IRE), 25/1 Spanish Verdict, Shirley's Train (USA), 33/1 Desert Splendour, Habeta (USA), King Al, 50/1 Foolish Touch, 100/1 Swift Romance (IRE). CSF £92.33, CT £601.39. Tote £11.20: £2.40 £1.90 £2.10 £3.00 (£38.40). J. B. R. Leisure Ltd (EPSOM) bred by Edwin Turner. 22 Rn
1m 36.36 (U.94)
SF—53/61/64/69/37/35

## 3727

PHILIP CORNES HOUGHTON STKS (2-Y.O) £8850.00 (£2640.00: £1260.00: £570.00)
7f
2-20 (2-22)

3532★ **Barathea (IRE) (100)** *(LMCumani)* 9-5 LDettori (1) (trckd ldrs: effrt over 1f out: r.o u.p to ld nr fin) ......... —1

3531² Storm Canyon (IRE) (Fav) *(JHMGosden)* 8-12 SCauthen (6) (lw: trckd ldrs: led & qcknd wl over 1f out: r.o wl: jst ct) ......... nk.2

3531 Thaleros *(GHarwood)* 8-12 LPiggott (2) (hld up: hdwy ¹/₂-wy: hrd rdn & prom over 1f out: nt qckn) ......... 7.3

3531⁴ Danny Boy *(RHannon)* 8-12 GDuffield (3) (disp ld over 5f: sn outpcd) ......... nk.4

Canopus *(WJarvis)* 8-12 RCochrane (5) (lw: w'like: scope: s.i.s: effrt ¹/₂-wy: styd on one pce fnl f) ......... ³/₄.5

Northern Bred (IRE) *(LMCumani)* 8-12 JWeaver (8) (cmpt: disp ld over 5f: eased whn btn) ......... 2.6

3531 He's a King (USA) *(JLDunlop)* 8-12 WCarson (9) (lw: chsd ldrs to ¹/₂-wy: sn rdn & btn) ......... 3.7

Sun of Spring *(MRStoute)* 8-12 MRoberts (10) (cmpt: scope: bkwd: nvr trbld ldrs) ......... ³/₄.8

Eaton Row (USA) *(PWChapple-Hyam)* 8-12 JReid (7) (lt-f: scope: sn bhd: rdn ¹/₂-wy: n.d) ......... 1¹/₂.9

Noble Risk *(RHannon)* 8-12 BRaymond (4) (leggy: scope: prom 4f) ......... s.h.10

4/6 Storm Canyon (IRE), 2/1 BARATHEA (IRE), 12/1 Sun of Spring(op 6/1), 16/1 Danny Boy, 20/1 Eaton Row (USA), 25/1 Thaleros, 50/1 Ors. CSF £3.71, Tote £3.30: £1.40 £1.10 £2.60 (£1.50). Sheikh Mohammed (NEWMARKET) bred by Gerald W. Leigh in Ireland. 10 Rn
1m 23.95 (U.05)
SF—69/61/40/39/37/31

**3728**  TOTE CESAREWITCH H'CAP  £48120.00 (£14460.00: £6980.00: £3240.00)
2¹/₄m  (Weights raised 5 lb)
3-00 (3-06)

3453a⁵ **Vintage Crop (102)** (Fav) *(DKWeld,Ireland)* 5-9-6 WRSwinburn (10) (lw: hld up: hdwy 8f out: led over 1f out: styd on strly) ............................ —1

3369⁴ **Specificity (USA) (86)** *(JHMGosden)* 4-8-4 MRoberts (3) (gd hdwy 8f out: chal 3f out: rdn & nt qckn appr fnl f) ............................ 8.2

3244² **Farat (USA) (75)** *(JLDunlop)* 4-7-7 JLowe (18) (b: hdwy ¹/₂-wy: led 3f out tl over 1f out: r.o one pce) ............................ 2¹/₂.3

3621⁶ **Coleridge (75)** (bl) *(DShaw)* 4-7-0 ‡⁷DWright (20) (bhd: hdwy 8f out: styd on wl: nrst fin) ............................ 3.4

3621⁵ **Smilingatstrangers (79)** (v) *(MrsBarbaraWaring)* 4-7-4⁽⁴⁾ ‡⁷CHawksley (25) (prom: pushed along ¹/₂-wy: lost pl 6f out: styd on wl fnl 2f) ..... hd.5

3431³ **Bardolph (USA) (81)** *(PFICole)* 5-7-8 ‡⁵NKennedy (22) (b.off hind: a cl up: chal 3f out tl outpcd over 2f out) ............................ 1¹/₂.6

3538⁶ **Jack Button (IRE) (87)** *(BobJones)* 3-7-7 JQuinn (17) (mid div: effrt 8f out: sn rdn & nvr able to chal) ............................ 1¹/₂.7

3621³ **Aude la Belle (FR) (77)** *(MrsAKnight)* 4-7-6 ‡³FNorton (21) (a.p: led 5f out to 3f out: sn outpcd) ............................ hd.8

3445★ **Quick Ransom (90)** *(MJohnston)* 4-8-8 (4x) DMcKeown (13) (lw: effrt 7f out: hrd rdn 4f out: no imp) ............................ hd.9

3431⁴ **Go South (77)** (bl) *(JRJenkins)* 5-7-9⁽⁵⁾ SDawson (9) (lw: bhd: gd hdwy 8f out: hung rt 3f out: sn wknd) ............................ 1.10

3431⁵ **Muse (79)** *(DRCElsworth)* 5-7-6⁽⁴⁾ ‡⁵BDoyle (7) (prom tl outpcd & hmpd over 6f out: n.d after) ............................ ³/₄.11

3339² **Aahsaylad (77)** (v) *(FHLee)* 6-7-9 NCarlisle (23) (lw: in tch: stdy hdwy 8f out: rdn & btn over 3f out) ............................ hd.12

3298² **Cabochon (78)** *(DMorley)* 5-7-10⁽¹⁾ WCarson (12) (bhd: hdwy u.p over 6f out: btn 3f out) ............................ 4.13

3586⁴ **Kausar (USA) (75)** *(GMMoore)* 5-7-7 NAdams (6) (cl up: led over 8f out to 5f out: sn wknd) ............................ 5.14

3431 **Three Wells (89)** (v) *(JLDunlop)* 3-7-9 TyroneWilliams (14) (lw: bhd: effrt 8f out: n.d) ............................ hd.15

3197⁵ **Mull House (78)** *(FJO'Mahony)* 5-7-10 DBiggs (15) (b.hind: mid div: effrt 8f out: sn rdn & btn) ............................ nk.16

3548² **Supreme Choice (USA) (106)** *(BWHills)* 4-9-10 DHolland (8) (lw: in tch tl rdn & wknd 4f out) ............................ ¹/₂.17

3666 **Black Sapphire (81)** (v) *(MHTompkins)* 5-7-6⁽⁶⁾ ‡⁷MHumphries (11) (rdn ¹/₂-wy: a bhd) ............................ 6.18

3406 **Shahdjat (IRE) (75)** *(KCBailey)* 4-7-0 ‡⁷AntoinetteArmes (16) (a bhd) ............................ 4.19

3666 **Welshman (75)** *(MBlanshard)* 6-7-7 GBardwell (19) (led tl hdd over 8f out: grad wknd) ............................ 2.20

2921★ **Majestic Image (78)** *(LordHuntingdon)* 6-7-7 ‡³DHarrison (5) (effrt ¹/₂-wy: sn rdn & n.d) ............................ hd.21

3621⁴ **Lord Hastie (USA) (80)** *(SGNorton)* 4-7-12 JFanning (2) (hld up & bhd: effrt 7f out: sn rdn & n.d) ............................ s.h.22

3431⁶ **Requested (80)** *(RAkehurst)* 5-7-9⁽⁵⁾ ‡³SO'Gorman (24) (chsd ldr tl rdn & wknd over 5f out) ............................ 4.23

3666 **Haitham (83)** *(RAkehurst)* 5-8-1 GCarter (4) (prom tl rdn & wknd over 5f out) 2¹/₂.24

LONG HANDICAP: Farat (USA) 7-6, Coleridge 6-9, Smilingatstrangers 5-10, Jack Button (IRE) 6-9, Go South 6-9, Muse 7-5, Kausar (USA) 6-13, Black Sapphire 7-0, Shahdjat (IRE) 7-4, Welshman 6-12.

3m 49.16 (U.84)

5/1 VINTAGE CROP, **13/2** Cabochon, **10/1** Bardolph (USA), Majestic Image, **11/1** Quick Ransom, Specificity (USA), **12/1** Muse, **14/1** Aude la Belle (FR), **16/1** Mull House, Three Wells, **20/1** Go South, Farat (USA), **25/1** Supreme Choice (USA), Aahsaylad, **28/1** Jack Button (IRE), **33/1** Requested, Lord Hastie (USA), **50/1** Haitham, Welshman, **66/1** Coleridge, Black Sapphire, **100/1** Shahdjat (IRE), Kausar (USA), **150/1** Smilingatstrange rs. CSF £53.43, CT £944.85. Tote £6.40: £2.30 £2.70 £4.10 £28.40 (£30.10). Dr Michael Smurfit (IRELAND) bred by B. R. and Mrs Firestone. 24 Rn

SF—51/27/13/3/6/8

**3729**  OLIVIER DOUIEB MEMORIAL H'CAP (0-110) £8740.00 (£2620.00: £1260.00: £580.00)
6f
3-35 (3-42)

3543 **Heather Bank (94)** (v) *(JBerry)* 3-9-4 GCarter (13) (mde all: r.o wl fnl 2f) ..... —1

3620⁴ **Fascination Waltz (72)** *(DShaw)* 5-7-7 ‡⁵NKennedy (7) (hld up: hdwy 2f out: r.o wl fnl f) ............................ 2¹/₂.2

3543³ **Hard to Figure (93)** (Fav) *(RJHodges)* 6-9-5 LPiggott (22) (trckd ldrs: effrt over 1f out: rdn & styd on one pce ins fnl f) ............................ ¹/₂.3

3592★ **Draft Board (77)** *(JHMGosden)* 3-8-1 DHolland (23) (lw: a chsng ldrs: effrt 2f out: kpt on) ............................ ¹/₂.4

3681 **Colossus (67)** *(CEBrittain)* 4-7-7 GBardwell (18) (a chsng ldrs: hrd drvn 2f out: r.o one pce) ............................ s.h.5

3539* Splice **(94)** *(JRFanshawe)* 3-8-11 ‡⁷NVarley (3) (lw: hld up: gd hdwy over 2f out: nt qckn wl ins fnl f) ............................................................................... s.h.**6**
3543² Caleman **(80)** *(RBoss)* 3-8-4 GDuffield (12) (chsd wnr: rdn 2f out: one pce) ..... nk.**7**
3680⁴ Sea Devil **(81)** *(MJCamacho)* 6-8-7 NConnorton (14) (prom: effrt 2f out: styd on wl nr fin) ........................................................................... ½.**8**
3356 Venture Capitalist **(96)** (bl) *(RHannon)* 3-9-6 RHills (19) (hdwy 2f out: nvr nrr) .. ½.**9**
3680 Allinson's Mate (IRE) **(74)** *(TDBarron)* 4-8-0 JLowe (21) (in tch: effrt over 2f out: nvr able to chal) ................................................................... nk.**10**
3671⁶ So Rhythmical **(80)** *(GHEden)* 8-8-6 CRutter (20) (b.off hind: prom: drvn along ½-wy: no imp after) ..................................................................... ½.**11**
3528⁶ Farfelu **(100)** (bl) *(WRMuir)* 5-9-12 RCochrane (11) (trckd ldrs: effrt 2f out: grad wknd) ................................................................................... nk.**12**
3680 Amron **(78)** *(JBerry)* 5-8-4 NCarlisle (9) (hld up & bhd: effrt 2f out: n.d) ........ 1½.**13**
3591⁵ Herora (IRE) **(89)** *(NAGraham)* 3-8-13 MRoberts (2) (dwlt: nvr trbld ldrs) ........ ¾.**14**
3680³ Bertie Wooster **(86)** *(RJHolder)* 9-8-12 LDettori (15) (lw: bhd: effrt over 2f out: n.d) ......................................................................................... 1.**15**
3680 How's Yer Father **(83)** *(RJHodges)* 6-8-9 TSprake (4) (nvr wnt pce) .............. nk.**16**
3537 Pallium (IRE) **(74)** *(MPNaughton)* 4-7-11 ‡³DHarrison (5) (bhd: effrt u.p ½-wy: n.d) ................................................................................... 1½.**17**
3271³ Lifetime Fame **(72)** *(JWPayne)* 3-7-10 JQuinn (8) (effrt ½-wy: a bhd) ............ nk.**18**
3537 Sylvan Breeze **(76)** (bl) *(PMitchell)* 4-8-2⁽⁴⁾ SWhitworth (24) (dwlt: a bhd) .... nk.**19**
3591² Talb (USA) **(95)** *(JLDunlop)* 3-9-5 WCarson (16) (lw: chsd ldrs 4f: sn rdn & wknd) ................................................................................... nk.**20**
3680 Assignment **(77)** *(JFfitch-Heyes)* 6-8-3 TyroneWilliams (17) (drvn along thrght: spd to ½-wy: wandered & sn bhd) ..................................................... 1½.**21**
3304 Lucedeo **(80)** *(JLSpearing)* 8-8-6 DMcKeown (10) (a bhd) ............................. ½.**22**
3528 Bold Lez **(96)** *(MJHaynes)* 5-9-8 SCauthen (6) (a bhd) ................................ ½.**23**
3355 Educated Pet **(73)** *(MJohnston)* 3-7-8 ‡³FNorton (1) (a bhd) ...................... s.h.**24**
LONG HANDICAP: Colossus 7-3.

**13/2** Hard to Figure, **9/1** Caleman, Draft Board, **10/1** Splice, **12/1** Talb (USA), **14/1** Venture Capitalist, 50 Rhythmical, Bertie Wooster, Fascination Waltz, **16/1** Herora, HEATHER BANK, How's Yer Father, Pallium (IRE), Assignment, Farfelu, Bold Lez, **25/1** Lucedeo, Allinson's Mate (IRE), Lifetime Fame, **33/1** Educated Pet, Sylvan Breeze, Amron, **50/1** Colossus. CSF £263.89, CT £1,861.31. Tote £27.30: £5.20 £5.10 £1.70 £2.90 (£310.00). Mr Norman Harper (COCKERHAM) bred by Castle Farm Stud. 24 Rn 1m 11.14 (U.26)
SF—68/33/57/37/28/45

---

**3730**    DUBAI CHAMPION STKS (Gp 1) £216176.00 (£80384.00: £38892.00: £16260.00: £6830.00: £3058.00)   1¼m     4-15 (4-19)

2837* **Rodrigo de Triano (USA)** (Fav) *(PWChapple-Hyam)* 3-8-12 LPiggott (7) (b: stdd s: smooth hdwy 3f out: shkn up to ld ins fnl f: r.o) ............... —**1**
3443* Lahib (USA) *(JLDunlop)* 4-9-3 WCarson (10) (lw: chsd ldrs: led wl over 1f out & qcknd: hdd wl ins fnl f: r.o) ..................................................... nk.**2**
3533⁵ Environment Friend *(JRFanshawe)* 4-9-3 GDuffield (5) (lw: stdd s: racd centre: hdwy over 2f out: styd on wl nr fin) ............................................... 3.**3**
3211⁴ Shuailaan (USA) *(ACStewart)* 3-8-12 MRoberts (3) (led centre: drvn along 3f out: r.o one pce) ............................................................................ s.h.**4**
2890a³ Zaahi (USA) *(HThomsonJones)* 3-8-12 RHills (8) (lw: led tl hdd wl over 1f out: kpt on same pce) ............................................................... 1½.**5**
3458a* Masad (IRE) *(LMCumani)* 3-8-12 LDettori (6) (trckd ldrs centre: effrt over 2f out: no ex fnl f) ............................................................................. s.h.**6**
3560a² Steinbeck (USA) *(AFabre,France)* 3-8-12 SCauthen (9) (prom: drvn along 3f out: no imp after) ............................................................................. hd.**7**
3657a Seattle Rhyme (USA) *(DRCElsworth)* 3-8-12 JWilliams (1) (hld up centre: effrt over 3f out: wknd 2f out) ........................................................... 1½.**8**
3652a³ Corrupt (USA) *(PWChapple-Hyam)* 4-9-3 JReid (2) (chsd ldrs centre tl wknd 2f out) ............................................................................................. ¾.**9**
3652a Pollen Count (USA) *(JHMGosden)* 3-8-12 RCochrane (4) (cl up centre tl wknd 3f out) .................................................................................... 15.**10**

**11/8** RODRIGO DE TRIANO (USA), **2/1** Lahib (USA)(op 6/4), **11/1** Masad (IRE), **12/1** Steinbeck (USA), **14/1** Shuailaan (USA), **16/1** Zaahi (USA), **20/1** Seattle Rhyme (USA), Environment Friend, **40/1** Pollen Count (USA), **66/1** Corrupt (USA). CSF £4.38, Tote £2.50: £1.50 £1.40 £2.80 (£2.20). Mr R. E. Sangster (MARLBOROUGH) bred by Swettenham Stud in USA. 10 Rn       2m 2.46 (U.14)
SF—64/68/62/56/53/52

---

**3731**    BENTINCK STKS (listed race) £9706.25 (£2900.00: £1387.50: £631.25)   5f     4-45 (4-47)

3443 **Hamas (IRE) (101)** *(PTWalwyn)* 3-8-11 WCarson (4) (chsd ldrs: led 2f out: r.o wl) —**1**
3528* Blyton Lad **(113)** *(MJCamacho)* 6-9-2 SWebster (10) (lw: a.p: hmpd wl over 1f out: r.o u.p fnl f) ................................................................... 2½.**2**

3633★ Bunty Boo **(94)** *(BAMcMahon)* 3–8-6 GDuffield (2) (hmpd & stdd s: hld up & bhd tl hdwy 2f out: styd on wl) .......... hd.3

3528⁴ Miss Nosey Parker (IRE) **(98)** *(RHannon)* 3–8-6 MRoberts (7) (a chsng ldrs: rdn ½-wy: styd on wl) .......... ¾.4

3528² Garah **(107)** *(HRACecil)* 3–8-6 AMcGlone (8) (a.p: effrt ½-wy: r.o one pce) .......... nk.5

3671 Tbab (IRE) **(99)** *(CEBrittain)* 4–8-12 BRaymond (1) (lw: in tch: effrt over 2f out: styd on same pce) .......... nk.6

3671★ Ashtina **(84)** *(RJHodges)* 7–8-12 JQuinn (6) (lw: wl ldrs tl wknd appr fnl f) .......... ½.7

2848★ Western Approach (USA) **(113)** *(Fav)* *(JHMGosden)* 3–8-6 PaulEddery (11) (led 3f: sn rdn & btn) .......... ¾.8

3356⁴ Dominuet **(83)** *(JLSpearing)* 7–8-7 GHind (9) (in tch: outpcd over 2f out: n.d after) .......... 1.9

3356 El Yasaf (IRE) **(89)** *(MissGayKelleway)* 4–8-12 DHolland (3) (prom tl rdn & wknd fr ½-wy) .......... 2½.10

3356 Cindora (IRE) **(91)** *(MHTompkins)* 3–8-6 RHills (5) (a bhd) .......... 1.11

2/1 Western Approach (USA), 5/2 Garah, 7/2 Blyton Lad, 9/1 Miss Nosey Parker (IRE), 12/1 Ashtina, 16/1 HAMAS (IRE), 20/1 Tbab (IRE), 25/1 Bunty Boo, 50/1 Cindora (IRE), 66/1 Ors. CSF £68.32, Tote £21.90: £3.90 £1.80 £2.50 (£73.00). Mr Hamdan Al-Maktoum (LAMBOURN) bred by Hullin Co N V (International) in Ireland. 11 Rn
58.22 sec (U1.18)
SF—86/81/70/67/66/71

---

**3732** WESTFIELD HOUSE H'CAP (0-90) £4950.00 (£1485.00: £715.00: £330.00)
1m
5-20 (5-23)

3640 **Cambrian (80)** *(MrsJCecil)* 3–9-3 GDuffield (10) (a w ldrs centre: led centre 3f out: all out) .......... —1

3396★ Tahitian **(63)** *(Fav)* *(MrsJRRamsden)* 3–8-0 DHolland (8) (lw: effrt centre 3f out: hdwy over 1f out: fin wl) .......... s.h.2

3689³ Ballerina Bay **(61)** (v) *(DTThorn)* 4–7-8 ‡7KimMcDonnell (9) (trckd ldrs centre: hdwy over 1f out: r.o) .......... nk.3

3547 Sand Table **(82)** *(LordHuntingdon)* 3–9-5 MRoberts (22) (chsd ldrs far side: ev ch over 1f out: r.o) .......... 1½.4

3547⁵ Cru Exceptionnel **(70)** *(PJMakin)* 4–8-10 TSprake (17) (trckd ldrs far side: effrt over 1f out: r.o) .......... s.h.5

3422² Eternal Flame **(66)** *(JWHills)* 4–8-6 RHills (6) (chsd ldrs centre: outpcd over 2f out: styd on fnl f) .......... nk.6

3673 Neptune's Pet **(83)** *(GLewis)* 4–9-9 JReid (15) (in tch far side: effrt 3f out: sn btn) .......... ½.7

3543 Polonez Prima **(88)** *(JEBanks)* 5–10-0 NDay (16) (cl up far side: chal 2f out: btn ins fnl f) .......... s.h.8

3368 Dress Sense (IRE) **(86)** *(LMCumani)* 3–9-9 LDettori (3) (in tch centre: hdwy & ev ch 2f out: wknd 1f out) .......... ¾.9

3417² Merlins Wish (USA) **(81)** *(RHannon)* 3–9-4 LPiggott (23) (racd far side: effrt 3f out: no imp) .......... s.h.10

3582³ Jade Vale **(71)** *(JWHills)* 3–8-5 ‡3DHarrison (7) (racd centre: n.d) .......... ½.11

3466 May Square (IRE) **(53)** *(MrsAKnight)* 4–7-7 JQuinn (24) (led far side tl wknd over 1f out) .......... ½.12

3425⁴ Concinnity (USA) **(63)** *(LJHolt)* 3–8-0 AMcGlone (19) (racd far side: n.d) .......... 3½.13

3543 Risk Zone **(70)** *(RHannon)* 3–8-4 ‡3RPerham (1) (led centre 5f: grad wknd) .......... ½.14

3483★ Leif the Lucky (USA) **(73)** *(WJarvis)* 3–8-10 WCarson (2) (hdwy centre 3f out: wknd wl over 1f out) .......... s.h.15

3640 Killy **(75)** (v) *(FHLee)* 3–8-12 NConnorton (13) (chsd ldrs far side over 6f) .......... ½.16

3680 Al Sadi **(83)** *(CEBrittain)* 3–9-1 ‡5BDoyle (18) (cl up far side over 6f) .......... nk.17

3678³ Sylvan (IRE) **(81)** *(CFWall)* 3–9-4 GBaxter (20) (in tch far side 6f) .......... ½.18

3021 Ibsen **(63)** *(ICampbell)* 4–7-10 ‡7GMitchell (12) (racd centre: n.d) .......... 3.19

3714 Bold Memory **(87)** *(MJohnston)* 3–9-10 DMcKeown (11) (hld up far side: effrt 3f out: sn btn) .......... nk.20

3441 Sylvan Sabre (IRE) **(72)** *(PMitchell)* 3–8-9 JWilliams (14) (racd centre: n.d) .......... ½.21

3481 Chaff **(58)** (bl) *(DMorris)* 5–7-5(5) ‡7CHawksley (4) (w ldrs centre 5f) .......... ½.22

3547 Trooping (IRE) **(80)** *(GHarwood)* 3–9-3 GCarter (21) (lw: s.s: a bhd far side) .......... ½.23
LONG HANDICAP: Chaff 5-7.

11/2 Tahitian, 9/1 Leif the Lucky (USA), Sand Table, 10/1 Cru Exceptionnel, Dress Sense (IRE), 12/1 Neptune's Pet, Sylvan (IRE), Merlins Wish (USA), 14/1 Trooping (IRE), Ballerina Bay, 16/1 Polonez Prima, Bold Memory, Eternal Flame, 20/1 CAMBRIAN, Jade Vale, 25/1 Killy, Sylvan Sabre (IRE), 33/1 Concinnity (USA), May Square (IRE), Ibsen, Al Sadi, 200/1 Chaff. CSF £127.14, CT £1,513.21. Tote £32.90: £5.80 £2.10 £4.70 £2.60 (£147.00). Sheikh Mohammed (NEWMARKET) bred by Sheikh Mohammed bin Rashid al Maktoum. 23 Rn
1m 37.39 (0.09)
SF—59/41/34/54/44/39

T/Trio: Race 1: £62.40 (14.3 Tckts), Race 3: £274.40 (11.1 Tckts), Race 4: Any 2 fr 1st 3 w any £14.10 (103.8 Tckts), Race 5: £22.40 (63 Tckts) & Race 7: Any 2 fr 1st 3 w any £22.30 (51.1 Tckts). T/Jkpt: Not won; £2,859.36 to Ascot 21/10/92. T/Plpt: £85.40 (185.2 Tckts).

AA

## 2317a—**SAINT-CLOUD  (L-H)**
### Monday, October 5th [Soft]
Going Allowance: 0.45 sec per fur (Y)

**3733a**       PRIX ECLIPSE (Gp 3) (2-Y.O.F) £20640.00   **6f 110y**

|  |  |  |
|---|---|---|
| | **Elizabeth Bay (USA)** *(France)* 2–8–13  SCauthen ............................................... | —1 |
| 3230a² | Wixon (FR) *(France)* 2–8–13  FHead .......................................................... | 2.2 |
| | Firm Friend (IRE) *(France)* 2–8–13  CAsmussen ................................................ | 1½.3 |

Tote 2.50f: 1.80f 1.50f (SF: 11.50f). Sheikh Mohammed (A.Fabre,FRANCE) bred by Lazy Lane Stables, Inc. in USA. 5 Rn

1m 23.8 (4.4)<br>SF—69/61/59

**3734a**       PRIX MASSINE (listed race)    £12384.00   **1½m 110y**

|  |  |  |
|---|---|---|
| 3456a³ | **MATADOR (USA)** *(RCharlton)* 5–8–11  PatEddery ........................................ | —1 |
| 638a² | Northern Park (USA) *(France)* 4–9–2  CAsmussen ........................................... | 2.2 |
| | Valgrija (FR) *(France)* 4–8–8  ABadel ...................................................... | 1½.3 |

Tote 2.40f: 1.80f 3.30f (SF: 22.50f). Dr Carlos E.Stelling (BECKHAMPTON) bred by Flaxman Holdings Limited in USA. 7 Rn

2m 46.3 (9.3)<br>SF—60/61/50

## 3562a—**CURRAGH  (R-H)**
### Saturday, October 10th [Good to soft]
Going Allowance: 6f-8f: 0.60 sec (Y); Rest: nil sec per fur (G)

**3735a**       JUDDMUNTE E.B.F. BERESFORD STKC (Gp 3) (2-Y.O) £16121.00   **1m**

|  |  |  |
|---|---|---|
| 2887a² | **Frenchpark (Fav)** *(Ireland)* 2–8–11  PShanahan (chsd ldr: led 2f out: hdd 1f out: rallied u.p: sltly hmpd ins fnl f: led nr fin) ............... | —1 |
| 2505a² | Scribe (IRE) *(Ireland)* 2–8–11  CRoche (hld up: hdwy over 2f out: chal appr fnl f: sn led: edgd rt u.p ins fnl f: jst ct) ..................... | hd.2 |
| 3535⁵ | WOOTTON RIVERS (USA) *(PWChapple-Hyam)* 2–8–11  LPiggott (hld up: rdn & hdwy 2f out: kpt on: nvr nrr) ..................................... | 4½.3 |
| | Shandon Lake (IRE) *(Ireland)* 2–8–11  KJManning (bhd: hrd rdn over 2f out: styd on u.p fr over 1f out: nrst fin) ............................ | s.h.4 |
| | Massyar (IRE) *(Ireland)* 2–8–11  MJKinane (mid div: effrt 2f out: kpt on same pce) | s.h.5 |
| 3113a³ | Colour Party (USA) *(Ireland)* 2–8–11  WJO'Connor (led 6f: sn btn) ...................... | 3.6 |
| | I Have to Say (IRE) (bl) *(Ireland)* 2–8–8  PVGilson (chsd ldrs tl wknd 2f out) ...... | 10.7 |

2/1 FRENCHPARK, 9/4 Scribe (IRE), 7/2 Wootton Rivers (USA), 7/1 Massyar (IRE), 8/1 Colour Party (USA), 12/1 Shandon Lake (IRE), 25/1 I Have to Say (IRE). Tote £3.70: £1.40 £1.20 (£2.60). Lord Harrington (C.Collins,Ireland) bred by Lord Harrington. 7 Rn

1m 44.3 (7.3)<br>SF—60/59/45/44/43/34

## **CURRAGH  (R-H)**
### Sunday, October 11th [Good to soft]
Going Allowance: 0.40 sec per fur (Y)

**3736a**       BLANDFORD STKS (Gp 2)    £21495.00   **1½m**

|  |  |  |
|---|---|---|
| 1095a² | **Andros Bay (USA)** *(Ireland)* 3–8–7  LPiggott (led 2f: chsd ldr: led 7f out: clr over 2f out: edgd lft & rdn ins fnl f: hld on) ............... | —1 |
| 3453a⁶ | Arrikala (IRE) *(Ireland)* 3–8–5⁽¹⁾  CRoche (hld up & bhd: hdwy over 2f out: styd on wl fnl f) ................................................ | ½.2 |
| 2889a⁴ | Ebaziya (IRE) *(Ireland)* 3–8–4  DHogan (in tch: rdn 2f out: styd on one pce fnl f) | ½.3 |
| 3453a | Dabtiya (IRE) *(Ireland)* 3–8–4  RHughes (mid div: chsd wnr & effrt over 2f out: one pce fnl f) ....................................... | 2.4 |
| 2977a⁴ | Pollys Glow (IRE) *(Ireland)* 3–8–4  JHeffernan (led after 2f to 7f out: prom tl rdn & btn 2f out) ......................................... | 6.5 |
| 3562a★ | Equal Eloquence (USA) *(Ireland)* 3–8–4  SCraine (in rr: rdn over 2f out: no imp) . | 9.6 |
| 3458a³ | In a Tiff (IRE) (Fav) *(Ireland)* 3–9–1  MJKinane (chsd ldrs: pushed along 4f out: rdn & wknd over 2f out: sn bhd) ............................ | 7.7 |

5/2 In a Tiff (IRE), 100/30 Arrikala (IRE), 5/1 Dabtiya (IRE), Equal Eloquence (USA), 6/1 ANDROS BAY (USA), 9/1 Ebaziya (IRE), 16/1 Pollys Glow (IRE). Tote £7.30: £2.60 £2.20 (£13.20). Mr A.J.O'Reilly (M.V.O'Brien,IRELAND) bred by Gallagher's Stud in USA. 7 Rn

2m 37.5 (7.2)<br>SF—69/66/64/60/48/30

### 3649a—**LONGCHAMP (R-H)**
**Sunday, October 11th [Soft]**
Going Allowance: 0.40 sec per fur (Y)

## 3737a          PRIX DE CONDE (Gp 3) (2-Y.O) £20640.00     **1m 1f (Moyenne)**

**Shemaka (IRE)** *(France)* ·2-8-8 WMongil .................................... —1
3448a² Marchand de Sable (USA) *(France)* 2-8-11 DBoeuf ................... ³/₄.2
Ranger (FR) *(France)* 2-8-11 CAsmussen .................................... 3.3
Tote 6.80f: 1.70f 1.20f 1.60f (11.50f). H.H.Aga Khan (A.de Royer-Dupre,FRANCE) bred by H.H.Aga Khan in
Ireland. 9 Rn                                                                    1m 56.2 (5.8)
                                                                                SF—61/62/53

## 3738a          PRIX DE LA FORET (Gp 1) (C & F) £51600.00     **7f (Nouvelle)**

3442★ **WOLFHOUND (USA)** *(JHMGosden)* 3-9-10 PatEddery (mde all: shkn up over
1f out: r.o wl) .................................... —1
3450a³ Silicon Bavaria (FR) *(France)* 5-9-8 MBoutin (hld up & bhd: 8th st: effrt 2f out: ev
ch 1f out: no imp ins fnl f) .................................... nk.2
958a Kenbu (FR) *(France)* 3-9-6 CAsmussen (in rr: 7th st: hdwy & nt clr run 2f out: r.o
fnl f) .................................... 1¹/₂.3
2892a⁶ Lion Cavern (USA) *(France)* 3-9-10 SCauthen (a.p: 3rd st: chal 2f out: sn one
pce) .................................... 4.4
3450a² Monde Bleu *(France)* 4-9-12 TJarnet (prom: 4th st: no ex fnl f) .................................... 1¹/₂.5
3195★ PURSUIT OF LOVE (Fav) *(HRACecil)* 3-9-10 RCochrane (chsd ldr: 2nd st: hrd
rdn 2f out: wknd) .................................... nk.6
2892a Hydro Calido (USA) *(France)* 3-9-6 FHead (a bhd: 6th st: n.d) .................................... ¹/₂.7
2855⁶ CASTEDDU (IRE) *(JWPayne)* 3-9-10 AMunro (plld hrd: mid div: 5th st: sn btn) .... 5.8
**6/4** Pursuit of Love, **5/2** Hydro Calido (USA), **37/10** Lion Cavern, WOLFHOUND (USA), **21/4** Monde Bleu,
**23/4** Kenbu (FR), **26/1** Silicon Bavaria (FR), **42/1** Casteddu. Tote 4.70f (cpld w Lion Cavern): 3.70f 5.20f 2.90f
(107.50f). Sheikh Mohammed (NEWMARKET) bred by W.S.Farish III & W.S.Kilroy in USA. 8 Rn   1m 24.8 (4.8)
                                                                                SF—80/78/71/62/62/59

### 3660a—**SAN SIRO (R-H)**
**Sunday, October 11th [Heavy]**

## 3739a          PREMIO DORMELLO (Gp 3) (2-Y.O.F) £27907.00     **1m**

3457a² **FOOLISH HEART (IRE)** *(NAGraham)* 2-8-11 LDettori .................................... —1
3457a³ Darubena (ITY) *(Italy)* 2-8-11 SDettori .................................... 2¹/₂.2
2321a² Zaira da Cesena (USA) *(Italy)* 2-8-11 JReid .................................... 20.3
3457a★ MRS WEST (USA) *(JLDunlop)* 2-8-11 WCarson (btn further 13¹/₂l) .................................... 5
Tote 18L: 15L 17L (40L). Scuderia Offshore (NEWMARKET) bred by Gerry Canavan in Ireland. 5 Rn   1m

## 3740a          PREMIO VITTORIO DI CAPUA (Gp 1) (C & F) £51163.00     **1m**

3654a³ **ALHIJAZ** *(JLDunlop)* 3-8-9 WCarson .................................... —1
2998³ RUDIMENTARY (USA) *(HRACecil)* 4-8-11 JReid .................................... 3¹/₂.2
3231a⁴ Misil (USA) *(Italy)* 3-8-11 LDettori .................................... 2¹/₂.3
Tote 43L: 20L 24L (77L). Prince A.A.Faisal (ARUNDEL) bred by Nawara Stud Co Ltd. 6 Rn   1m 46.1

### 2511a—**DUSSELDORF (R-H)**
**Sunday, October 11th [Soft]**

## 3741a          GROSSER PREIS VON DUSSELDORF (Gp 2)     £28169.00     **1m 110y**

3654a⁴ **LUCKY LINDY (IRE)** (bl) *(RHannon)* 3-8-7 BRouse .................................... —1
1098a Irish Source *(France)* 3-8-3 OPeslier .................................... 2¹/₂.2
Inkognito (GER) *(Germany)* 4-9-0 THellier .................................... 1¹/₂.3
Tote 26DM: 15DM 30DM 28DM (SF: 182DM). Mr G.Howard-Spink (MARLBOROUGH) bred by Broguestown
Stud Ltd. in Ireland. 10 Rn                                                      1m 45.1

### 2627a—**MUNICH (L-H)**
**Sunday, October 11th [Soft]**

## 3742a          GROSSER SILICON BAVARIA SPRINT-PREIS (listed race) £21127.00     **6f 110y**

**Bannier (GER)** *(Germany)* 5-9-1 DWildman .................................... —1

35735 NIGHT JAR *(LordHuntingdon)* 5–8–8 BRaymond ............................................ ½.2
　　　Be Happy (GER) *(Germany)* 3–8–5 MHofer ................................................... 1¼.3
　3441 MASTER PLANNER *(CACyzer)* 3–8–9 DBiggs (btn further 3½zl) ............................. 6
Tote 92DM: 18DM 18DM 18DM (SF: 676DM). Mr M.Renner (E.Pils,GERMANY) bred by M.Renner in Germany.
10 Rn　　　　　　　　　　　　　　　　　　　　　　　　　　　　　　　　　　　　1m 21.5

## 3380—CATTERICK (L-H)
### Friday, October 16th [Good]
Going Allowance: 0.35 sec per fur (G)　　　　　　　　　　　　　Wind: fresh half against

Stalls: low

**3743**　　　　CRAVEN APP'CE GRADUATION STKS　£2427.00 (£672.00: £321.00)
　　　　　　　1½m 44y　　　　　　　　　　　　　　　　　　　　　2-15 (2-15)

35715 **Yildiz (90)** (Fav) *(BWHills)* 3–8–9 SMulvey (5) (b.off hind: chsd ldr: effrt over 3f
　　　　out: r.o u.p to ld jst ins fnl f: jst hld on) .................................... —1
3616* Alyafill (USA) (68) *(BHanbury)* 3–8–9 VBray (6) (trckd ldrs: hdwy over 2f out: r.o
　　　　wl fnl f: no ex nr fin) ........................................................ nk.2
33092 Esbooain (FR) (72) *(LMCumani)* 3–8–0 ‡7JCHarris (4) (lw: led & sn clr: hdd jst
　　　　ins fnl f: one pce) ............................................................ 4.3
　　　Film Lighting Girl (35) *(RJWeaver)* 6–8–9 JDennis (3) (nvr nr ldrs) ............... 30.4
　3583 Gaynor's Boy (IRE) *(TKersey)* 3–8–7 MHarris (2) (b: prom 3f: t.o fnl 7f) ......... dist.5

**8/13** YILDIZ, **3/1** Esbooain (FR), **9/2** Alyafill (USA), **150/1** Film Lighting Girl, **300/1** Gaynor's Boy (IRE). CSF
£3.42, Tote £1.60: £1.00 £3.80 (£1.90). Mr S. Mino (LAMBOURN) bred by Charlton Down Stud. 5 Rn
　　　　　　　　　　　　　　　　　　　　　　　　　　　　　　　　　2m 45.5 (11.5)
　　　　　　　　　　　　　　　　　　　　　　　　　　　　　　　SF—22/21/8/–/–

**3744**　　　　E.B.F. ILKLEY STKS (Mdn 2-Y.O.F) £2532.00 (£702.00: £336.00)　**7f**　2-45 (2-47)

27924 **Lamu Lady (IRE)** *(PWChapple-Hyam)* 8–11 SWhitworth (8) (lw: chsd ldrs: drvn
　　　　along & outpcd ½-wy: styd on u.p fnl 2f: led nr fin) ............................ —1
35052 Suntara (IRE) (Fav) *(BWHills)* 8–11 WRyan (3) (trckd ldrs: hdwy to ld 1f out: r.o
　　　　u.p: jst ct) ................................................................... hd.2
36173 Princess Tateum (IRE) *(MRChannon)* 8–11 GCarter (9) (led to 2f out: kpt on
　　　　same pce fnl f) ............................................................... 2½.3
　3684 Miss Pimpernel *(BHanbury)* 8–11 JCarroll (4) (s.s: bhd tl styd on fnl 2f: nt rch
　　　　ldrs) .......................................................................... nk.4
34805 Quinsigimond *(SirMarkPrescott)* 8–11 GDuffield (1) (chsd ldr: rdn to ld 2f out:
　　　　hdd 1f out: sn wknd) .......................................................... 1½.5
33995 Henequin (USA) (60) (bl) *(JHMGosden)* 8–11 BRaymond (7) (chsd ldrs tl wknd
　　　　fnl f) ......................................................................... nk.6
　3502 Ascom Pager Too (60) *(PHowling)* 8–11 BCrossley (11) (b: sn w ldrs: ev ch tl
　　　　wknd over 1f out) ............................................................. 1.7
35526 Jadirah (USA) *(JLDunlop)* 8–11 RHills (2) (drvn along & lost pl ½-wy: n.d after) ... ¾.8
23504 Apache Squaw *(CWThornton)* 8–11 DMcKeown (6) (s.i.s: bhd tl hdwy 3f out:
　　　　kpt on: nvr able to chal) ..................................................... ¾.9
　3590 Sweetings Scampy (IRE) (60) *(MHEasterby)* 8–11 MBirch (5) (chsd ldrs tl rdn &
　　　　lost pl over 3f out) .......................................................... 3½.10
　3465 Altona Gold *(REarnshaw)* 8–11 AProud (10) (chsd ldrs tl wknd qckly 3f out: sn
　　　　btn) ........................................................................... 10.11

**8/11** Suntara (IRE), **9/2** LAMU LADY (IRE)(op 9/4), **10/1** Princess Tateum (IRE), **11/1** Quinsigimond, **12/1**
Henequin (USA), **14/1** Jadirah (USA), **20/1** Miss Pimpernel, Apache Squaw, **33/1** Ascom Pager Too, **50/1**
Sweetings Scampy (IRE), **100/1** Altona Gold. CSF £8.08, Tote £5.80: £1.70 £1.10 £1.70 (£3.30). Mr R. E.
Sangster (MARLBOROUGH) bred by Swettenham Stud in Ireland. 11 Rn　　　　　1m 30 (6.8)
　　　　　　　　　　　　　　　　　　　　　　　　　　　　　SF—32/31/23/22/17/16

**3745**　　　　BRETTANBY H'CAP (0-70) £2937.40 (£816.40: £392.20)　**1m 7f 177y**　3-20 (3-23)
　　　　　　　　　　(Weights raised 2 lb)
34092 **Mrs Barton (IRE) (58)** *(BWHills)* 4–9–10 RHills (14) (a chsng ldrs: r.o gamely
　　　　u.p to ld ins fnl f: styd on wl) ............................................... —1
　3586 Bridge Player (40) *(DMoffatt)* 5–7–13 ‡7DarrenMoffatt (9) (hld up gng wl: smooth
　　　　hdwy 4f out: led 2f out: rdn & hung lft: hdd ins fnl f) ........................ 1½.2
　3515 Aide Memoire (IRE) (50) *(CBBBooth)* 3–8–6 ACulhane (11) (mid div: hdwy to ld
　　　　4f out: hdd 2f out: r.o one pce) ............................................... ½.3
　3616 Tudor Da Samba (50) *(JRFanshawe)* 3–8–6 DMcKeown (13) (trckd ldrs: hdwy
　　　　& prom 4f out: rdn & hmpd over 1f out: kpt on wl) ............................. nk.4
35843 Queens Tour (33) *(MBrittain)* 7–7–10(4) ‡3SMaloney (7) (sn bhd: some hdwy 4f
　　　　out: nvr nr ldrs) ............................................................. 8.5

3584⁴ Paper Clip **(37)** *(JDBethell)* 3–7-7 NAdams (15) (trckd ldrs: ev ch over 2f out: sn rdn & wknd) ........................................ ¾.6

3392* Fortune Star (IRE) **(62)** (Fav) *(JLDunlop)* 3–9-4 WRyan (6) (lw: mid div & drvn along 8f out: sme hdwy 4f out: n.d) ........................................ hd.7

1407³ Fanlight **(54)** *(RAkehurst)* 4–9-3 ‡³RPerham (2) (mid div: effrt 5f out: nvr able to chal) ........................................ 2½.8

3613 Top Prize **(39)** *(MBrittain)* 4–7-12⁽³⁾ ‡⁷JMarshall (4) (sn bhd: sme hdwy 5f out: n.d) ........................................ 2.9

3556 Maji **(65)** *(DMorley)* 3–9-7 GDuffield (1) (effrt 5f out: lost pl over 3f out) ........ 5.10

3613 Rolling the Bones (USA) **(68)** *(MPNaughton)* 3–9-3 ‡⁷SWynne (16) (hld up: hdwy on outside 5f out: wknd over 3f out) ........................................ 5.11

Leading Role **(40)** *(AHarrison)* 8–8-6 MWood (10) (sn bhd) ........................................ 4.12

312² Bollin Magdalene **(48)** (v) *(MHEasterby)* 4–9-0 MBirch (8) (chsd ldrs tl wknd 3f out) ........................................ 2.13

3556 Clifton Chase **(44)** (bl) *(MAJarvis)* 3–8-0⁽²⁾ GCarter (5) (chsd ldrs tl rdn & lost pl over 3f out) ........................................ 2½.14

3158 Dajitus **(55)** (v) *(MJHeaton-Ellis)* 3–8-11 JCarroll (17) (b.hind: in tch: hrd rdn 5f out: sn lost pl: t.o) ........................................ 15

3007 Rajanpour (USA) **(40)** (bl) *(RCurtis)* 7–8-6 GBardwell (12) (led to 4f out: wknd 3f out: t.o) ........................................ 16

3075 Alpha Helix **(27)** (v) *(MissLAPerratt)* 9–7-7 SWood (14) (mid div: sn drvn along: bhd fnl 5f: t.o) ........................................ 17

3305⁶ Rexy Boy **(27)** *(WLBarker)* 5–7-7 DaleGibson (3) (chsd ldrs: drvn along 10f out: lost pl 7f out: sn wl bhd: t.o) ........................................ 18

LONG HANDICAP: Paper Clip 7-6, Alpha Helix 7-5.

**5/1** Fortune Star (IRE), **6/1** Fanlight, MRS BARTON (IRE), **10/1** Aide Memoire (IRE), **11/1** Maji(8/1—12/1), **14/1** Bollin Magdalene, Rexy Boy, **16/1** Bridge Player, Clifton Chase, Tudor Da Samba, **20/1** Queens Tour, Rolling the Bones (USA), Dajitus, **25/1** Paper Clip, Alpha Helix, Rajanpour (USA), **33/1** Leading Role, **66/1** Top Prize. CSF £88.38, CT £868.62. Tote £4.60: £1.70 £3.40 £3.70 £6.50 (£29.10). Mr A. L. R. Morton (LAMBOURN) bred by B. W. Hills and Mrs V. Shaw in Ireland. 18 Rn                                                  3m 37 (16)

**3746**     HORNBY CASTLE CLAIMING STKS (2-Y.O) £3027.00 (£842.00: £405.00)
            7f                                                            3-55 (4-02)

3285³ **Mark's Club (IRE) (66)** *(BWHills)* 7-5 ‡⁷DWright (6) (s.i.s: bhd tl gd hdwy over 2f out: r.o wl jst ins fnl f) ........................................ —1

3574⁶ Hallplace **(52)** *(MRChannon)* 8-0 GDuffield (10) (lw: chsd ldrs: rdn to ld over 1f out: sn hdd & nt qckn) ........................................ 2½.2

2842 I'm a Dreamer **(70)** *(WWHaigh)* 8-4 DMcKeown (3) (in tch: styd on appr fnl f) ........................................ ¾.3

3516³ Fortis Pavior **(77)** *(RMWhitaker)* 7-7 ‡⁷MHumphries (13) (b.hind: mid div: edgd lft: styd on appr fnl f: nt rch ldrs) ........................................ 2.4

3497 Nancy (IRE) **(57)** *(CWCElsey)* 7-4⁽⁴⁾ ‡⁷ClaireBalding (20) (sn bhd: styd on fnl 2f: nt rch ldrs) ........................................ nk.5

3385 Missed the Boat (IRE) **(66)** *(TDBarron)* 8-4 AlexGreaves (14) (lw: hdwy on outside 2f out: edgd lft u.p: nvr rchd ldrs) ........................................ 1½.6

3580³ Be Polite (IRE) **(58)** *(MBell)* 7-8 GBardwell (1) (effrt appr st: kpt on fnl 2f) ........ nk.7

3050 Duchess Dianne (IRE) **(41)** *(RJHolder)* 7-7 NAdams (11) (chsd ldrs: no imp fnl 2f) ........................................ hd.8

3260 Sparky's Song **(60)** *(JWHills)* 7-11 SDawson (5) (chsd ldrs: no hdwy fnl 2f) .... s.h.9

3587 Public Way (IRE) **(56)** *(NChamberlain)* 7-13 SWood (12) (in tch tl over 2f out) 2½.10

3401³ Bold Face (IRE) **(67)** *(RFJohnsonHoughton)* 8-4 MBirch (8) (lw: led tl hdd & wknd over 1f out) ........................................ ½.11

3472 Dream a Bit **(63)** *(JGFitzGerald)* 7-6⁽³⁾ ‡⁵NKennedy (16) (chsd ldrs tl wknd 2f out) ........................................ 4.12

3480 Meconopsis **(58)** *(TFairhurst)* 7-7 JFanning (4) (uns rdr & rn loose bef s: sn bhd & drvn along: n.d) ........................................ ½.13

3291 Allegrissima **(73)** (Fav) *(JBerry)* 8-0 GCarter (17) (chsd ldrs tl wknd 2f out) ..... ½.14

3033 Master Peckitt **(58)** *(SEKettlewell)* 7-10 ‡³SMaloney (18) (chsd ldrs tl wknd over 2f out) ........................................ nk.15

3155⁶ Robix (IRE) **(73)** *(JBerry)* 8-8 JCarroll (7) (chsd ldrs tl lost pl 2f out) ........................................ s.h.16

3410 Bransby Road (IRE) **(58)** *(RAkehurst)* 8-3⁽²⁾ ‡³RPerham (9) (a in rr) ........................................ 1.17

3301 Lucky Owl **(50)** *(MissLAPerratt)* 7-11 DaleGibson (15) (s.i.s: a bhd) ........................................ 5.18

2930 Tinstone *(JAGlover)* 8-0⁽¹⁾ BCrossley (19) (in tch tl lost pl 3f out) ........................................ 4.19

3611 Timber Topper **(MrsGRReveley)** 7-5 ‡⁷DarrenMoffatt (2) (sn bhd & rdn along) 3½.20

**7/2** Allegrissima(5/1—3/1), **7/1** Fortis Pavior (IRE), MARK'S CLUB (IRE)(op 9/2), **9/1** Missed the Boat (IRE), **10/1** Bold Face (IRE), **11/1** Robix (IRE), **12/1** Be Polite (IRE), Sparky's Song(op 8/1), Bransby Road (IRE), **14/1** I'm a Dreamer (IRE), Dream a Bit, Hallplace, **33/1** Public Way (IRE), Tinstone, Lucky Owl, Duchess Dianne (IRE), Meconopsis, Nancy (IRE), **50/1** Master Peckitt, **100/1** Timber Topper. CSF £100.57, Tote £7.70: £2.30 £6.50 £2.90 (£198.40). Mr R. A. N. Bonnycastle (LAMBOURN) bred by Mrs Eilish Earley in Ireland. 20 Rn; Mark's Club (IRE) clmd Mrs S Barron £5,200                                       1m 30.6 (7.4)

SF—3/4/6/–/–/–

**3747—3748**

## 3747

ZETLAND STKS (Mdn) £2490.00 (£690.00: £165.00 each)    7f    4-30 (4-36)

| | | |
|---|---|---|
| 3375 | **Nellie Dean (53)** (bl) *(JARToller)* 3–8-6 DaleGibson (2) (mde all: sn clr: brght stands' side: kpt on ins fnl f) | —1 |
| 12876 | **Ivana (IRE) (Fav)** *(WJarvis)* 3–8-6 GDuffield (8) (hdwy over 4f out: c stands' side & chsd wnr over 2f out: sn rdn: nt qckn fnl f) | nk.2 |
| 35896 | **Brambles Way (53)** (v) *(WLBarker)* 3–8-6 ‡5OPears (7) (a chsng ldrs: ev ch & rdn over 1f out: sn wknd) | 6.3 |
| 3422 | **Brooks Express (FR) (47)** *(RAkehurst)* 3–8-8 ‡3RPerham (10) (mid div & drvn along: styd on fnl 2f: nvr nr to chal) | d.h.3 |
| 693 | **Spender** *(PWHarris)* 3–8-11 WRyan (11) (effrt u.p over 3f out: kpt on: nvr rchd ldrs) | 3.5 |
| 3511 | **Wafi (USA) (47)** *(BHanbury)* 3–8-11 BRaymond (4) (lw: chsd ldrs: effrt over 2f out: sn wknd) | 1.6 |
| 35924 | **Speedy Classic (USA) (57)** *(BWHills)* 3–8-11 RHills (5) (hdwy over 3f out: rdn & no imp fnl 2f) | 2.7 |
| 3375 | **Bobbie Bold (32)** *(TKersey)* 4–9-0 SWebster (12) (sn bhd & pushed along: styd on fnl 2f) | s.h.8 |
| 35094 | **Indica (USA)** *(JHMGosden)* 3–8-6 GHind (9) (swtg: stdd s: effrt u.p over 2f out: n.d) | 5.9 |
| 2984 | **Blunham Express (35)** *(TFairhurst)* 3–8-6 JFanning (6) (in tch tl lost pl over 3f out) | 8.10 |
| | **Life After Death** *(JBalding)* 4–8-7 ‡7JEdmunds (3) (bkwd: dwlt: sn wl bhd) | 3½.11 |
| 3557 | **Old Fox (FR) (50)** *(DSasse)* 3–8-11 GCarter (1) (chsd ldrs tl wknd qckly over 2f out: sn bhd) | 1½.12 |

2/1 Ivana (IRE), 11/2 Speedy Classic (USA), 6/1 Indica (USA), 8/1 Wafi (USA), 10/1 Brambles Way, 11/1 NELLIE DEAN, 12/1 Brooks Express (FR), Spender(op 8/1), 16/1 Old Fox (FR), 33/1 Blunham Express, 66/1 Bobbie Bold, 100/1 Life After Death. CSF £31.14, Tote £25.70: £3.60 £1.20 £1.20 BW £1.70 BE (£11.70). Mr A. J. Morrison (NEWMARKET) bred by A. J. Morrison. 12 Rn
1m 29.4 (6.2)
SF—41/40/22/24/18/15

## 3748

FAVERDALE H'CAP (0-70) £2959.80 (£822.80: £395.40)    5f    5-00 (5-04)

| | | |
|---|---|---|
| 885 | **Orient Air (51)** (bl) *(TDBarron)* 4–8-4 ‡7VHalliday (15) (sn bhd: gd hdwy 2f out: r.o wl to ld ins fnl f) | —1 |
| 3355 | **Rock Opera (IRE) (55)** *(MPNaughton)* 4–8-10 ‡5JWeaver (14) (sn bhd: gd hdwy over 1f out: r.o nr fin) | 1.2 |
| 35092 | **Tommy Tempest (46)** *(KRBurke)* 3–8-5 AShoults (10) (mde most tl hdd & wknd ins fnl f) | 2.3 |
| 3413 | **Miss Brightside (33)** *(ASmith)* 4–7-7 NAdams (7) (chsd ldrs: rdn ½-wy: kpt on one pce appr fnl f) | s.h.4 |
| 3605* | **Goody Four Shoes (36) (Fav)** *(DRTucker)* 4–7-5(1) ‡5NKennedy (6) (hdwy ½-wy: nt qckn over 1f out) | 1½.5 |
| 35594 | **Cronk's Quality (35)** (bl) *(DCJermy)* 9–7-9(2) SDawson (4) (chsd ldrs: no imp fnl 2f) | ½.6 |
| 36336 | **Prince Belfort (64)** (v) *(MPNaughton)* 4–9-3 ‡7SWynne (13) (sn bhd: hdwy over 1f out: nvr nr to chal) | 1.7 |
| 3308 | **Chateau Nord (50)** *(JBerry)* 3–8-9 JCarroll (18) (in tch: rdn 2f out: kpt on fnl f) | nk.8 |
| | **Quatre Femme (65)** *(MJohnston)* 5–9-11 DMcKeown (17) (s.i.s: bhd tl hdwy over 1f out: n.m.r: styd on nr fin) | hd.9 |
| 3460 | **Hinari Video (40)** *(MJohnston)* 7–8-0 RPElliott (11) (nvr nr ldrs) | nk.10 |
| 35856 | **Last Straw (40)** *(AWJones)* 4–7-7 ‡7ClaireBalding (1) (in tch: rdn ½-wy: n.d) | 1.11 |
| 3308 | **Nordoora (IRE) (41)** *(JLHarris)* 3–8-0(1) AProud (2) (chsd ldrs tl wknd over 1f out) | nk.12 |
| 35962 | **Langtonian (57)** (bl) *(JBerry)* 3–8-13 ‡3EmmaO'Gorman (12) (effrt ½-wy: nvr rchd ldrs) | ¾.13 |
| 3460 | **Le Chic (46)** *(DWChapman)* 6–8-6 JFanning (5) (prom to ½-wy) | 3½.14 |
| 2963 | **Miss Siham (IRE) (41)** *(JBalding)* 3–8-0 GDuffield (1) (in tch: rdn ½-wy: sn lost pl) | 3½.15 |
| 23652 | **Sobering Thoughts (38)** (bl) *(DWChapman)* 6–7-12 SWood (8) (swtg: in tch to ½-wy) | nk.16 |
| 3596 | **It's Only Money (53)** (bl) *(THCaldwell)* 3–8-12 MWood (16) (prom to ½-wy: sn lost pl) | 3.17 |

LONG HANDICAP: Miss Brightside 7-6.

15/8 Goody Four Shoes, 7/1 Langtonian, 9/1 Prince Belfort, 12/1 Rock Opera (IRE), 14/1 Last Straw, Tommy Tempest, 16/1 Hinari Video, Miss Siham (IRE), Sobering Thoughts, Le Chic, Quatre Femme, 20/1 ORIENT AIR, Nordoora (IRE), 25/1 Cronk's Quality, Miss Brightside, Chateau Nord, 66/1 It's Only Money. CSF £227.06, CT £3,148.89. Tote £33.40: £5.70 £2.50 £2.40 £6.50 (£278.80). Mrs I. M. Raine (THIRSK) bred by Mrs I. M. Raine. 17 Rn
61.6 sec (4.1)
SF—43/45/32/19/11/13
WG

## CATTERICK (L-H)
### Saturday, October 17th [Good]
Going Allowance: 0.35 sec per fur (G)            Wind: slt half against

Stalls: low

**3749**    E.B.F. NORTH RIDING STKS (I) (Mdn 2-Y.O) £2532.00 (£702.00: £336.00)
         5f                                               2-05 (2-13)

34484 **Saseedo (USA)** (WAO'Gorman) 8-11 ‡³EmmaO'Gorman (11) (chsd ldrs: rdn to ld over 1f out: r.o wl) .................................................................. —1
2437 Pirates Gold (IRE) (65) (MJHeaton-Ellis) 9-0 WRyan (15) (s.i.s: hdwy ½-wy: ev ch 1f out: r.o) ....................................................................... 2.2
32556 Melodys Daughter (62) (bl) (RFJohnsonHoughton) 8-9 KDarley (2) (led far side to ½-wy: kpt on u.p fnl f) ............................................. 2½.3
35806 Hokey Pokey (FR) (DSasse) 8-9 RPrice (5) (chsd ldrs: rdn & outpcd ½-wy: kpt on fnl f) ................................................................................ 1½.4
18684 True Precision (Fav) (JDBethell) 8-9 PRobinson (10) (b.hind: sn chsng ldrs: rdn ½-wy: no imp) ....................................................... ½.5
      Mudgee (TDBarron) 8-9 AlexGreaves (1) (lengthy: bkwd: racd far side: w ldr: led ½-wy: edgd rt: hdd over 1f out: wknd) .......................... ½.6
3611 Desirable Miss (45) (bl) (MBrittain) 8-9 MWigham (7) (hdwy ½-wy: nvr rchd ldrs) ........................................................................................ 2½.7
3630 Dayjuz (IRE) (70) (FHLee) 9-0 KFallon (8) (chsd ldrs tl wknd 2f out) ............... 2½.8
3712 Don't Tell Jean (50) (bl) (NBycroft) 8-9 PBurke (3) (unruly gng to s: racd far side: chsd ldrs tl wknd 2f out) ................................................... ½.9
2740 Out of Aces (MrsVAAconley) 8-9 LCharnock (14) (sn chsng ldrs: outpcd ½-wy: sn wknd) .................................................................................. nk.10
36374 Lamsonetti (RMWhitaker) 8-9 ACulhane (4) (s.i.s: sn wl bhd) ....................... 1½.11
3295 Ilmenite (bl) (MAJarvis) 8-4 ‡⁵KRutter (6) (sn wl bhd) ................................. hd.12
34486 Mdm Racer (IRE) (JBerry) 9-0 JCarroll (9) (stumbled s: w ldrs tl wknd 2f out) 1½.13
3484 Silver Standard (JWWatts) 9-0 AMercer (13) (sn wl bhd) .............................. ¾.14
34485 Perigord (IRE) (60) (MHEasterby) 8-11 ‡³SMaloney (12) (w ldrs tl wknd ½-wy) 2½.15

**9/4** True Precision(op 6/4), **5/1** Lamsonetti, SASEEDO (USA), **13/2** Pirates Gold (IRE), **10/1** Dayjuz (IRE), **14/1** Melodys Daughter, **20/1** Out of Aces, Mdm Racer (IRE), Perigord (IRE), Hokey Pokey (FR), **25/1** Silver Standard, **33/1** Ilmenite, Mudgee, **50/1** Ors. CSF £36.01, Tote £6.10: £1.60 1.90 4.00 (£24.40). Mr S. Fustok (NEWMARKET) bred by Audley Farm Incorporated in USA. 15 Rn      62.1 sec (4.6)
                                                   SF—40/35/20/14/12/10

**3750**    E.B.F. NORTH RIDING STKS (II) (Mdn 2-Y.O) £2511.00 (£696.00: £333.00)
         5f                                               2-35 (2-38)

34843 **Stepanov (USA)** (Fav) (JHMGosden) 9-0 GHind (8) (lw: trckd ldrs: led on bit 2f out: sn clr: eased ins fnl f: v.easily) ...................................... —1
3590 Our Shadee (USA) (64) (KTIvory) 9-0 MWigham (12) (a chsng ldrs: rdn 2f out: no ch w wnr) ............................................................................. 2½.2
3590 The Institute Boy (63) (bl) (KRBurke) 9-0 AShoults (3) (led after 1f: hdd 2f out: edgd rt u.p: kpt on) ..................................................... hd.3
3626 Sabo the Hero (SirMarkPrescott) 9-0 MBirch (10) (chsd ldrs: drvn along ½-wy: kpt on fnl f) ..................................................................... 1½.4
      Brooklands Express (JDBethell) 9-0 PRobinson (14) (lengthy: bit bkwd: s.i.s: bhd tl styd on fnl f) ......................................................... ½.5
33823 Comet Whirlpool (IRE) (73) (PatMitchell) 9-0 WWoods (13) (led 1f: chsd ldrs tl wknd 2f out) ........................................................................ 3.6
      Bold Prospect (PCalver) 9-0 DaleGibson (1) (w'like: s.i.s: sn wl bhd: hdwy 2f out: r.o fin) ....................................................................... 1½.7
3580 Grey Pride (51) (JBerry) 9-0 JCarroll (6) (chsd ldrs tl wknd 2f out) ................. 1½.8
2932 Inovar (CBBBooth) 9-0 GOldroyd (9) (w ldrs to ½-wy: sn lost pl) ..................... 2.9
36263 General Link (PAKelleway) 9-0 GayKelleway (4) (b: outpcd fr ½-wy) ............ s.h.10
3617 Young Geninsky (RJWeaver) 8-9 SWood (5) (sn bhd & drvn along) ............... 1½.11
2884 Sing as We Go (BobJones) 8-9 KFallon (7) (nvr nr ldrs) ................................. 4.12
3552 Blues Breaker (DSasse) 8-9 RPrice (2) (sn wl outpcd) ................................. ¾.13
2965 Celtic Cherry (JBalding) 8-9 KDarley (11) (prom early: bhd fr ½-wy) ............ ¾.14

**2/5** STEPANOV (USA), **7/1** General Link, **10/1** Sabo the Hero, **12/1** Comet Whirlpool (IRE), **20/1** Brooklands Express, Sing as We Go, Our Shadee (USA), **33/1** Bold Prospect, Grey Pride, Inovar, **40/1** The Institute Boy, **50/1** Blues Breaker, Celtic Cherry, **66/1** Young Geninsky. CSF £12.77, Tote £1.30: £1.10 £4.30 £5.00 (£8.10). Sheikh Mohammed (NEWMARKET) bred by Darley Stud Manaagement Company Ltd in USA. 14 Rn    62.3 sec (4.8)
                                                   SF—39/29/28/22/20/8

## 3751

NORTHERN ECHO H'CAP (0-70) £3346.00 (£931.00: £448.00)  7f  3-10 (3-13)

3174 **Abeloni (48)** (v) *(JAGlover)* 3–8–0 ‡³SMaloney (12) (chsd ldrs: hrd rdn 2f out: styd on to ld nr fin) ............................................................ —1

3595² Tyrone Flyer **(47)** (Fav) *(MissGayKelleway)* 3–7–11⁽¹⁾ ‡⁵StephenDavies (15) (led: clr over 2f out: wknd ins fnl f: jst ct) .......................... 1¹/₂.2

2987⁵ Claudia Miss **(54)** *(WWHaigh)* 5–8–12 DaleGibson (17) (a chsng ldrs: kpt on same pce u.p fnl 2f) ........................................................ 1¹/₂.3

*3375⁵* Scottish Park **(67)** *(JPLeigh)* 3–9–3 ‡⁵OPears (7) (hdwy 2f out: styd on: nvr rchd ldrs) ............................................................................ ¹/₂.4

3596 Sakharov **(47)** *(MAJarvis)* 3–8–2 PRobinson (9) (a chsng ldrs: one pce fnl 2f) .... 2.5

3383⁶ Euroblake **(62)** *(TDBarron)* 5–9–6 AlexGreaves (4) (lw: sn bhd: gd hdwy over 2f out: nrst fin) ................................................................ nk.6

3481 Blue Grit **(59)** *(MDods)* 6–9–3 KFallon (11) (sn bhd: c stands' side: styd on wl u.p fnl 2f: nt rch ldrs) .................................................. hd.7

3633⁵ Languedoc **(60)** *(MPNaughton)* 5–9–4 JakiHouston (13) (bhd tl hdwy 2f out: nvr nr to chal) ............................................................ 1.8

3612 Ruth's Gamble **(53)** *(DWChapman)* 4–8–11 SWood (14) (chsd ldrs: n.d) nk.9

2570 Pickles **(52)** *(PCHaslam)* 4–8–10 KDarley (6) (chsd ldrs tl lost pl over 2f out) 1¹/₂.10

3595 Glenfield Greta **(60)** *(PSFelgate)* 4–9–4 WRyan (10) (sn bhd: c stands' side: n.d) ......................................................................... s.h.11

3605² Judgement Call **(52)** *(PHowling)* 5–8–10 BCrossley (5) (b.hind: nvr nr ldrs) ... nk.12

3627 Dawn Success **(46)** (v) *(DWChapman)* 6–7–11 ‡⁷JMarshall (16) (chsd ldrs: c stands' side: lost pl over 2f out) ................................... 2¹/₂.13

3612⁴ Boy Martin **(65)** *(MJohnston)* 3–9–6 RPElliott (3) (lw: sn wl bhd) .................... ¹/₂.14

3481 Leave it to Lib **(60)** *(PCalver)* 5–8–11 ‡⁷JTate (2) (s.i.s: a in rr) ................... 2¹/₂.15

3696 Profilic **(70)** *(CaptJWilson)* 7–10–0 JFortune (18) (trckd ldrs: effrt u.p over 2f out: edgd rt: sn wknd) ............................................. 1¹/₂.16

2935 Wild Prospect **(60)** *(CTinkler)* 4–9–4 MBiroh (1) (chsd ldrs tl lost pl over 2f out) 2¹/₂.17

3545 Young Valentine **(60)** *(RMWhitaker)* 3–9–1 ACulhane (8) (chsd ldrs tl wknd qckly over 2f out) ........................................................ s.h.18

3615³ Watch Me Go (IRE) **(49)** (v) *(BobJones)* 3–8–4 AMercer (19) (uns rdr s: t.n.p) ..... 0

**9/2** Tyrone Flyer, **8/1** Euroblake, **10/1** Boy Martin, **12/1** Languedoc, Glenfield Greta, Wild Prospect, Leave it to Lib, Blue Grit, Dawn Success, **14/1** Watch Me Go (IRE), **16/1** Profilic, Young Valentine, Claudia Miss, Judgement Call, Ruth's Gamble, Pickles, **25/1** ABELONI & Ors. CSF £135.21, CT £1,746.96. Tote £49.60: £5.00 £1.50 £6.40 £8.30 (£149.10). A. F. Budge (Equine) Limited (WORKSOP) bred by M. Yiapatos. 19 Rn  1m 29 (5.8)

SF—36/28/38/41/20/37

## 3752

DARLINGTON AND STOCKTON TIMES CLAIMING STKS (3-Y.O) £2847.80 (£790.80: £379.40)  1¹/₂m 44y  3-40 (3-42)

3641³ **Simply-H (IRE) (74)** (Fav) *(MBell)* 8–9 ‡⁷PTurner (10) (trckd ldrs: led wl over 1f out: drvn clr) .................................................. —1

3538 Upper House **(61)** *(GWragg)* 9–1 JCarroll (4) (lw: trckd ldrs: led over 3f out: kpt on same pce u.p appr fnl f) ........................................ 4.2

3152 Notable Exception **(52)** *(MrsGRReveley)* 8–2 KDarley (9) (hdwy 5f out: one pce fnl 2f) ................................................................. 3.3

3584* Iron Baron (IRE) **(56)** *(RHollinshead)* 8–1 ‡⁷AGarth (7) (hld up & bhd: gd hdwy 4f out: no imp fnl 2f) ................................................ ¹/₂.4

3468 Marowins **(44)** *(EJAlston)* 8–5⁽¹⁾ KFallon (2) (bhd: pushed along over 4f out: kpt on: nvr nr to chal) ................................................ 3.5

3384 Mr News (IRE) **(35)** *(SEKettlewell)* 7–12 SWood (5) (hld up & bhd: sme hdwy over 2f out: n.d) ........................................................ s.h.6

3577 Reach for Glory **(53)** *(RMWhitaker)* 8–3 ACulhane (1) (chsd ldrs: drvn along 5f out: wknd 3f out) ............................................... 4.7

3258 Skimmer Hawk *(BobJones)* 8–7 DaleGibson (3) (chsd ldrs: drvn along ¹/₂-wy: lost pl over 3f out) ...................................................... s.h.8

2250² Hanley's Hands (IRE) **(61)** (v) *(MHTompkins)* 8–8 PRobinson (6) (chsd ldrs: drvn along over 3f out: sn btn) ........................................ nk.9

3311 Whirlygig **(39)** *(JSWainwright)* 7–10⁽⁶⁾ ‡³SMaloney (4) (led: rn wd paddock bnd: hdd over 3f out: sn wknd & bhd) ................................ 20.10

**11/8** SIMPLY-H (IRE), **11/4** Hanley's Hands (IRE), **4/1** Upper House, **11/1** Iron Baron (IRE), **12/1** Reach for Glory, **14/1** Notable Exception, **25/1** Marowins, **33/1** Mr News (IRE), **50/1** Ors. CSF £7.59, Tote £2.40: £1.60 £1.90 £4.20 (£3.40). Mr G. L. H. Lederman (NEWMARKET) bred by E. J. Loder in Ireland. 10 Rn  2m 48.3 (14.3)

## 3753

EVENING GAZETTE STKS (2-Y.O) £3013.20 (£835.20: £399.60)  5f 212y 4-10 (4-11)

3630* **Sea Gazer (IRE) (82)** *(TDBarron)* 9–7 KDarley (2) (mde all: c stands' side: rdn over 1f out: hld on wl) ................................................ —1

2176[4] Joyofracing **(100)** *(WAO'Gorman)* 9-4 JFortune (5) (hdwy to chse wnr after 1f:
        c stands' side: ev ch & rdn 2f out: nt qckn ins fnl f) ............ ¹/₂.2
3588[4] Gymcrak Tiger (IRE) **(100)** (Fav) *(MHEasterby)* 9-1 MBirch (1) (sn chsng ldrs:
        rdn 2f out: fnd little) ............ 7.3
3588[5] Celestial Key (USA) **(90)** *(SGNorton)* 8-10 ‡⁵OPears (3) (chsd ldrs: effrt over 2f
        out: sn wknd) ............ 1.4
3115[5] Daaniera (IRE) **(76)** *(JBerry)* 9-1 JCarroll (4) (b.nr hind: chsd ldrs tl rdn & lost pl
        over 2f out) ............ 8.5

**7/4** Gymcrak Tiger (IRE), **2/1** Joyofracing, **4/1** SEA GAZER (IRE), **11/2** Celestial Key (USA), **33/1** Daaniera (IRE).
CSF £11.35, Tote £3.90: £2.10 £1.70 (£3.50). Mr P. D. Savill (THIRSK) bred by D. Twomey in Ireland. 5 Rn
1m 15 (4.5)
SF—59/54/23/14/–

---

**3754**          SUNDERLAND ECHO (S) NURSERY    £3057.00 (£852.00: £411.00)    **7f** 4-40 (4-42)
                                    (Weights raised 2 lb)
3746 **Public Way (IRE) (54)** *(NChamberlain)* 8-11 SWood (12) (s.i.s: bhd tl gd hdwy
        2f out: r.o to ld ins fnl f) ............ —1
3407 The Gold Souk (IRE) **(57)** *(JLDunlop)* 9-0 JFortune (10) (stumbled & lost pl
        after 1f: bhd tl styd on wl fnl 2f: r.o fin) ............ ¹/₂.2
3497[5] Comtec's Legend **(50)** *(JFBottomley)* 8-7 LCharnock (14) (chsd ldrs: led 2f out
        tl ins fnl f: nt qckn) ............ ¹/₂.3
3590 Legendary Hero **(55)** *(TDBarron)* 8-12 KDarley (8) (bhd: gd hdwy on stands'
        side 2f out: r.o u.p fnl f) ............ nk.4
3558[5] Samanthas Joy **(50)** *(TFairhurst)* 8-7 PBurke (19) (chsd ldrs: ev ch & hrd rdn 2f
        out: one pce) ............ s.h.5
3611[6] Northern Chief **(52)** *(MHEasterby)* 8-9 MBirch (3) (chsd ldrs: styd on fnl f: nvr
        able to chal) ............ 1¹/₂.6
3472 Ring Tom (IRE) **(50)** *(MWEasterby)* 8-2 ‡⁵OPears (20) (chsd ldrs: ev ch & rdn 2f
        out: wknd fnl f) ............ nk.7
2649[6] Kafioca (IRE) **(51)** *(MHTompkins)* 8-8 PRobinson (16) (chsd ldrs: rdn & no imp
        fnl 2f) ............ hd.8
3407 Eastern Glow **(52)** *(SPCWoods)* 8-9 WWoods (13) (s.i.s: sn bhd: hdwy 2f out:
        n.d) ............ ¹/₂.9
3614 Dead Calm **(60)** *(CTinkler)* 9-3 TLucas (7) (sn bhd: kpt on fnl 2f: nvr nr to chal) ³/₄.10
3635 Reasons for Love (IRE) **(64)** (Fav) *(JJO'Neill)* 9-2 ‡StephenDavies (4) (hld up:
        effrt over 2f out & rdn & no imp) ............ nk.11
3044 Laurel Etoile **(54)** *(JBerry)* 8-4 ‡⁷PRoberts (11) (chsd ldrs tl lost pl 2f out) ...... 1¹/₂.12
3611 Mighty Miss Magpie (IRE) **(57)** *(MRChannon)* 9-0 DaleGibson (18) (chsd ldrs tl
        rdn & wknd 2f out) ............ ¹/₂.13
3474 Epsom Dream **(60)** (bl) *(JEtherington)* 9-3 KFallon (5) (nvr nr ldrs) ............ 1.14
3478 Just Baileys **(60)** (bl) *(MJohnston)* 9-3 RPElliott (2) (plld hrd: trckd ldrs tl lost pl
        3f out) ............ hd.15
3694 Noteability **(52)** *(JBerry)* 8-9 JCarroll (1) (chsd ldrs tl lost pl over 2f out) ...... hd.16
3517[5] New Kid in Town **(52)** (v) *(NTinkler)* 8-9 WRyan (9) (led tl hdd & wknd over 2f
        out) ............ 4.17
3218 Mouchez le Nez (IRE) **(50)** (bl) *(JAkehurst)* 8-7 BCrossley (15) (sn w ldrs: led
        over 2f out: sn hdd & wknd) ............ 2.18
3407 Merryhill Kerry (IRE) **(52)** *(JLHarris)* 8-6 ‡³SMaloney (6) (chsd ldrs tl lost pl over
        2f out: sn bhd) ............ 4.19

**11/2** Reasons for Love (IRE)(tchd 9/1), **6/1** Kafioca (IRE)(op 10/1), **13/2** Northern Chief, **9/1** The Gold Souk
(IRE), **10/1** Ring Tom (IRE), **11/1** New Kid in Town, **12/1** Mighty Miss Magpie (IRE), **14/1** Comtec's Legend,
Eastern Glow, **16/1** Mouchez le Nez (IRE), Legendary Hero, Epsom Dream, Just Baileys, Dead Calm, **20/1**
Noteability, Samanthas Joy, **25/1** Laurel Etoile, PUBLIC WAY (IRE), **33/1** Merryhill Kerry (IRE). CSF £236.69, CT
£3,016.85. Tote £85.60: £21.30 £2.20 £4.10 £4.60 (£181.20). Mr N. Chamberlain (WEST AUCKLAND) bred by
C. Farrell in Ireland. 19 Rn; No bid
1m 30.9 (7.7)
SF—19/20/11/15/9/6

---

**3755**          YORKSHIRE EVENING POST H'CAP (0-70) £3395.00 (£945.00: £455.00)
                **1m 5f 175y**
                                                                    5-10 (5-14)

3493 **Heliopsis (38)** *(MDHammond)* 4–8-2 KDarley (20) (jnd ldrs 6f out: c stands'
        side: led over 2f out: r.o u.p) ............ —1
3504[4] Carrolls Marc (IRE) **(53)** *(PJFeilden)* 4–9-3 DaleGibson (19) (b.hind: bhd: hdwy
        over 3f out: ev ch fnl f: r.o) ............ ¹/₂.2
3687[2] Continuity **(52)** (Fav) *(MHTompkins)* 3–8-7 PRobinson (8) (hld up & bhd: effrt 5f
        out: c stands' side: ev ch & rdn 1f out: hung lft: wknd) ....... ¹/₂.3

3572⁵ Flyaway (FR) **(37)** *(RJWeaver)* 7–8-1 SWood (4) (sn bhd: hdwy over 2f out & styd on: nt rch ldrs) .......................................................... 8.4

3493 Luks Akura **(41)** (v) *(MJohnston)* 4–7-12 ‡⁷MBaird (5) (led tl over 3f out: wknd over 1f out) ..................................................... 1.5

3572 Grove Serendipity (IRE) **(48)** (v) *(AHide)* 4–8-12 MBirch (14) (chsd ldrs: drvn along over 3f out: ev ch tl wknd 2f out) ................... ¹/₂.6

3603 Bilberry **(41)** *(CWCElsey)* 3–7-3⁽²⁾ ‡⁷CTeague (2) (chsd ldrs tl lost pl 3f out: sddle slipped) ............................................ hd.7

3493 Irish Honey (IRE) **(45)** *(BHanbury)* 3–8-0⁽²⁾ WWoods (9) (sn bhd: sme hdwy over 2f out: n.d) ................................................. nk.8

2833³ Severine (USA) **(65)** *(JLDunlop)* 3–9-6 WRyan (7) (chsd ldrs: c starids' side: lost pl over 2f out) .......................................... 4.9

3536 Free Transfer (IRE) **(56)** *(PFTulk)* 3–8-11 BCrossley (18) (lw: trckd ldrs: led over 3f out tl over 2f out: sn wknd) .......................... 3.10

745⁶ Mayo Man **(42)** *(MrsGRReveley)* 3–7-4 ‡⁷DarrenMoffatt (3) (sn bhd & pushed along) ............................................... 4.11

2204 Demokos (FR) **(40)** *(APStringer)* 7–8-4⁽²⁾ JFortune (12) (b.off fore: chsd ldrs tl wknd 3f out) ...................................... nk.12

3409 Royal Verse (FR) **(34)** *(RCurtis)* 5–7-12⁽²⁾ RPrice (10) (trckd ldrs tl lost pl over 4f out) ........................................ 3.13

3600 Nipotina **(33)** *(RHollinshead)* 6–7-4⁽³⁾ ‡⁷AGarth (13) (sn bhd: sme hdwy 5f out: sn wknd) ........................................ ¹/₂.14

3381² Bold Ambition **(39)** *(TKersey)* 5–8-3 ACulhane (16) (lw: chsd ldrs: drvn along 6f out: lost pl 4f out) ................................ 6.15

3493³ Grey Commander **(38)** (v) *(MBrittain)* 4–7-13 ‡³SMaloney (17) (chsd ldrs tl lost pl over 4f out) ...................................... 1.16

3409 Young George **(44)** *(MDods)* 5–8-8 JCarroll (15) (nvr nr ldrs) .............. 2¹/₂.17

3306 Atan's Gem (USA) **(44)** *(JNorton)* 3–7-6 ‡⁷ClaireBalding (11) (nvr nr ldrs) ....... 4.18

2470⁵ Haut-Brion (IRE) **(43)** *(WEtorey)* 3–7-12 PBurke (1) (a in rr) ............. 1¹/₂.19

1337⁵ Affair of Honour (IRE) **(64)** *(JJO'Neill)* 4–9-9 ‡⁵StephenDavies (6) (sn bhd & drvn along) ............................................... 8.20

**11/4** Continuity(op 5/1), **8/1** HELIOPSIS, Severine (USA), **10/1** Carrolls Marc (IRE), **12/1** Grove Serendipity (IRE)(op 8/1), Irish Honey (IRE)(op 8/1), Flyaway (FR), Bold Ambition (IRE), Young George, Haut-Brion (IRE), Affair of Honour (IRE), **14/1** Demokos (FR), Mayo Man (IRE), Bilberry, **20/1** Free Transfer (IRE), Young George, Haut-Brion (IRE), Affair of Honour (IRE), **25/1** Nipotina, Luks Akura, **40/1** Royal Verse (FR), **50/1** Atan's Gem (USA). CSF £89.23, CT £264.80. Tote £33.80: £2.70 £3.50 £1.30 £4.40 (£444.60). Maureen Godsman & Douglas Godsman (MIDDLEHAM) bred by Juddmonte Farms. 20 Rn
3m 7.3 (12.1)
SF—16/30/19/–/–/–

---

**3756**  LEVY BOARD STKS (Mdn 3-Y.O) £2616.00 (£726.00: £348.00)
1¹/₂m 44y
5-40 (5-43)

3346 **Wild Applause (IRE) (69)** (Jt-Fav) *(JHMGosden)* 8-9 JCarroll (6) (trckd ldrs: c stands' side: led jst ins fnl f: r.o wl: eased nr fin) ................. —1

3300⁴ Portree *(HRACecil)* 8-9 WRyan (9) (w ldr: led & qcknd over 5f out: clr over 2f out: styd on u.p fnl f) ............................................ 1¹/₂.2

3483² Euridice (IRE) **(60)** (Jt-Fav) *(LMCumani)* 8-9 JFortune (8) (lw: trckd ldrs tl outpcd over 4f out: hrd rdn & hung lft 2f out: kpt on same pce) ...................................................... s.h.3

3506⁴ Zoom Lens **(68)** *(JLDunlop)* 8-9 PRobinson (4) (prom tl outpcd 4f out: hdwy over 1f out: r.o wl u.p nr fin) ............................ ¹/₂.4

3718 Desert Force (IRE) **(68)** *(MissGayKelleway)* 9-0 KFallon (10) (effrt 5f out: kpt on same pce fnl 2f: nvr able to chal) ............................ 5.5

3306⁵ El Taranda *(GWragg)* 8-9 DaleGibson (1) (plld hrd & trckd ldrs: led over 6f out tl over 5f out: ev ch tl wknd over 2f out) ..................... 1.6

Media Messenger **(73)** *(DenysSmith)* 8-7 ‡⁷CTeague (3) (plld hrd: trckd ldrs tl lost pl over 3f out) ....................................... 20.7

3615 Canbrack (IRE) **(45)** *(WAStephenson)* 9-0 LCharnock (2) (led tl over 6f out: wknd qckly over 3f out: sn bhd) .................................. 7.8

Queen of the Dales *(GMMoore)* 8-9 PBurke (7) (bkwd: rn green: bhd fnl 5f) ...... 4.9

3416 Rutbah **(45)** *(ACStewart)* 8-9 MBirch (5) (hld up: effrt over 5f out: sn lost pl & bhd: t.o) ...................................................... 0

**5/2** Euridice (IRE), WILD APPLAUSE (IRE), **9/2** El Taranda, **5/1** Portree, **13/2** Zoom Lens (IRE), **16/1** Rutbah, **20/1** Media Messenger, Desert Force (IRE), **33/1** Queen of the Dales, **66/1** Canbrack (IRE). CSF £15.82, Tote £3.70: £1.20 £1.20 £1.10 (£6.20). Mr R. E. Sangster (NEWMARKET) bred by Swettenham Stud in Ireland. 10 Rn
2m 46.7 (12.7)
SF—10/7/6/5/–/–

T/Plpt: £329.00 (6.74 Tckts).   WG

2963—**EDINBURGH (R-H)**

**Monday, October 19th [Good]**

Going Allowance: St: 0.20 sec; Rnd: nil sec per fur (G)        Wind: almost nil

Stalls: high

## 3757
TOTE DUAL FORECAST MEDIAN AUCTION STKS (Mdn 3-Y.O) £1500.50 (£418.00: £201.50)   **1m 16y** ·

2-15 (2-16)

35892 **Ballyranter (49)** *(HJCollingridge)* 9-0 JQuinn (3) (cl up: led over 2f out: drvn out) ............................................................................................................... —1
37473 **Brambles Way (50)** (v) *(WLBarker)* 8-9 ‡5OPears (5) (led tl hdd over 2f out: r.o one pce) ................................................................................................ 1½.2
3513 **Phil-Man (39)** *(TFairhurst)* 9-0 JFanning (4) (trckd ldrs: effrt 3f out: no imp) ....... 7.3
3460 **Lord Lambson (46)** *(RMWhitaker)* 9-0 ACulhane (1) (bhd & rdn 3f out: n.d) ....... ¾.4
3554 **Express Service (66)** (bl) *(PJMakin)* 9-0 TSprake (2) (lw: chsd ldrs: rn wd st: sn rdn & no rspnse) ......................................................................................... hd.5

**8/11** Express Service, **2/1** BALLYRANTER, **10/1** Brambles Way, **14/1** Lord Lambson(op 8/1), **25/1** Phil-Man. CSF £16.64, Tote £3.30: £1.10 £3.50 (£4.90). Mr Graeme Short (NEWMARKET) bred by Llety Stud. 5 Rn
1m 44.7 (6.1)
SF—9/–/–/–/–/–

## 3758
TOTE EACH WAY STKS (Mdn 2-Y.O) £1595.00 (£445.00: £215.00)
**1m 16y**

2-45 (2-48)

33132 **Seama (USA)** *(SirMarkPrescott)* 8-9 JCarroll (3) (hld up: hdwy on outside 3f out: styd on wl to ld cl home) ...................................................................... —1
3474 **Lady Gail** *(JLSpearing)* 8-9 JLowe (7) (chsd ldrs: led 3f out: no ex nr fin) ....... nk.2
3643 **Forever Shineing** *(MJCamacho)* 8-9 NConnorton (4) (hld up: hdwy over 2f out: swtchd over 1f out: nt qckn) ..................................................... 1½.3
36442 **Amaam Amaam (Fav)** *(JHMGosden)* 9-0 RCochrane (5) (b: chsd ldrs: ev ch over 2f out: r.o one pce) ............................................................................ 1.4
31006 **Mr Geneaology (USA) (62)** (v) *(JLSpearing)* 9-0 KDarley (1) (dwlt: hdwy u.p 2f out: n.d) .......................................................................................... 1½.5
31815 **Cameo Kirby (FR)** *(AAScott)* 9-0 JFortune (8) (trckd ldrs: hdwy & ev ch 3f out: sn rdn & grad wknd) ............................................................................ nk.6
35983 **Almansour (USA) (80)** *(HRACecil)* 9-0 WRyan (2) (lw: cl up tl wknd 2f out) ....... ½.7
35126 **Master Fiddler (62)** *(EWeymes)* 9-0 ACulhane (6) (led tl hdd 3f out: sn lost pl) 10.8

**6/4** Amaam Amaam(4/5—7/4), **2/1** SEAMA (USA)(5/2—3/1), **4/1** Almansour (USA), **7/1** Cameo Kirby (FR), **33/1** Master Fiddler, Mr Geneaology (USA), Lady Gail, **50/1** Forever Shineing. CSF £46.67, Tote £3.60: £1.10 £21.00 £8.10 (£116.40). Mr Fahd Salman (NEWMARKET) bred by Newgate Stud Farm Inc in USA. 8 Rn
1m 45.1 (6.5)

## 3759
BET WITH THE TOTE H'CAP (0-80) £1976.50 (£554.00: £269.50)
**7f 15y**

3-15 (3-19)

3632 **Dokkha Oyston (IRE) (69)** *(JBerry)* 4-9-7 JCarroll (15) (a.p: led over 2f out: jst hld on) ..................................................................................................... —1
36965 **Lawnswood Junior (56) (Fav)** *(JLSpearing)* 5-8-8 KDarley (4) (lw: bhd: swtchd ins & hdwy over 3f out: styd on strly fnl f: jst failed) ........ s.h.2
3751 **Blue Grit (59)** *(MDods)* 6-8-11 LCharnock (14) (lw: chsd ldrs: chal over 2f out: hrd rdn: nt qckn nr fin) ....................................................... nk.3
3245 **Gabbiadini (65)** (v) *(MHTompkins)* 5-9-3 RCochrane (11) (hdwy 3f out: styd on one pce appr fnl f) ................................................................. 1½.4
3681 **Doyce (56)** (bl) *(JEtherington)* 3-8-5 NConnorton (12) (mid div & hmpd appr st: hdwy 3f out: styd on one pce fnl f) ........................ 1½.5
3383 **Malcesine (IRE) (44)** *(CaptJWilson)* 3-7-7 JFanning (1) (led tl hdd over 2f out: one pce) ...................................................................................... 2.6
36323 **Verdant Boy (53)** *(MPNaughton)* 9-8-5 JakiHouston (16) (swtchd outside & hdwy 3f out: nvr able to chal) ................................................ 1.7
2898 **Imperial Bid (FR) (76)** *(DenysSmith)* 4-10-0 KFallon (6) (effrt ent st: nvr rch ldrs) nk.8
3595 **Diamond Inthe Dark (USA) (55)** *(CTinkler)* 4-8-7 DMcKeown (8) (in tch: effrt 3f out: no imp) ....................................................................... 1.9
3751 **Dawn Success (54)** (v) *(DWChapman)* 6-7-12 SWood (13) (w ldrs tl wknd over 2f out) ...................................................................................... s.h.10
3680 **Parfait Amour (67)** *(RMWhitaker)* 3-9-2 ACulhane (9) (nvr bttr than mid div) .. nk.11
2966 **Valley of Time (FR) (43)** *(TCraig)* 4-7-9(1) NCarlisle (2) (cl up tl wknd 2f out) ..... ¾.12
3475 **Crail Harbour (47)** *(PCHaslam)* 6-7-8(6) ‡5NKennedy (5) (rn wd st: a bhd) ..... ¾.13

3514 Jim's Wish (IRE) **(51)** *(TAKCuthbert)* 4–7-10 ‡7ClaireBalding (7) (a bhd) ........... 1.14
2966 Rage **(56)** (bl) *(TCraig)* 5–8-8 PBurke (10) (a bhd) ............................................. 6.15
1090 Puffy **(48)** (bl) *(MDods)* 5–8-0 JLowe (3) (rn wd st: a bhd) ............................... hd.16
LONG HANDICAP: Malcesine (IRE) 7-6, Crail Harbour 7-6.

**3/1** Lawnswood Junior, **7/1** Verdant Boy, **8/1** Doyce, Diamond Inthe Dark (USA), **9/1** Puffy, **10/1** Blue Grit, **11/1**
DOKKHA OYSTON (IRE), **12/1** Gabbiadini, Parfait Amour, Dawn Success, **16/1** Valley of Time (FR), Malcesine
(IRE), **20/1** Imperial Bid (FR), **25/1** Crail Harbour, **50/1** Ors. CSF £44.84, CT £332.79. Tote £15.10: £3.10 £1.50
£2.40 £3.00 (£15.30). Mr Murray Grubb (COCKERHAM) bred by R. Oyston and Partners in Ireland. 16 Rn
1m 29.8 (3.6)
SF—53/39/41/42/25/7

---

**3760** TOTE PLACEPOT CLAIMING STKS (2-Y.O) £1626.50 (£454.00: £219.50)
7f 15y
3-45 (3-49)

33474 **Cliburnel News (IRE) (76)** (Fav) *(MHTompkins)* 8-8 RCochrane (8) (trckd
ldrs: led 2f out: sn qcknd clr) ............................................. —1
3614 Trets *(PAKelleway)* 8-4 WRyan (10) (bhd: hdwy on outside over 2f out: nrst fin) 2½.2
36175 **Mrs Jekyll (IRE)** *(CFWall)* 7-10 NCarlisle (11) (bhd: styd on fnl 3f: nvr nrr) ........ ¾.3
3474 Sassamouse *(RGuest)* 7-12 JLowe (1) (in tch: n.m.r 2f out: styd on u.p appr fnl
f) ................................................................................... 1½.4
3394 Take Your Partner (IRE) **(52)** *(MJohnston)* 8-2 RPElliott (12) (chsd ldrs tl rdn &
btn over 1f out) ........................................................... 1½.5
2842 Bright Gem **(58)** *(TFairhurst)* 7-12 JFanning (3) (hdwy u.p 3f out: no imp) ...... s.h.6
3611 Irish Roots (IRE) **(42)** (v) *(CTinkler)* 8-3 KDarley (9) (effrt u.p 3f out: nvr rchd
ldrs) ................................................................................ 2.7
0712 Palacegate Prince **(57)** *(JBerry)* 8-2 ‡7PRoberts (6) (a chsng ldrs: rdn & one pce
fnl 3f) ............................................................................. 1.8
3472 Sainted Sue **(49)** *(JSHaldane)* 7-114 ‡3SMaloney (5) (chsd ldrs tl wknd over 2f
out) ................................................................................. 5.9
34984 Friendly Knight *(JSHaldane)* 8-3 LCharnock (13) (hdwy ent st: sn rdn & n.d) .. ¾.10
3746 Robix (IRE) **(70)** (bl) *(JBerry)* 8-13 JCarroll (2) (led tl hdd & wknd qckly 2f out) 1½.11
3394 Oxrib **(49)** *(JBerry)* 8-7 DMcKeown (4) (in tch & rn wd st: sn bhd) ................ ¾.12

**6/5** CLIBURNEL NEWS (IRE), **5/1** Mrs Jekyll (IRE), **6/1** Robix (IRE)(op 4/1), **7/1** Sassamouse, **12/1** Take Your
Partner (IRE), Palacegate Prince, Trets(op 8/1), **14/1** Friendly Knight(op 8/1), **25/1** Irish Roots (IRE), **33/1** Ors.
CSF £17.99, Tote £1.70: £1.20 £3.60 £2.10 (£15.90). East Lancs Newspapers Readers Club (NEWMARKET)
bred by St Simon Foundation in Ireland. 12 Rn
1m 30.6 (4.4)
SF—28/16/6/3/2/–

---

**3761** TOTE PLACE ONLY (S) STKS £1455.00 (£405.00: £195.00)
1½m 31y
4-15 (4-16)

35045 **John Shaw (USA) (47)** *(CTinkler)* 4–9-3 PBurke (3) (cl up: led over 4f out: styd
on wl fnl 2f) ..................................................................... —1
3500 Noted Strain (IRE) **(50)** *(PJMakin)* 4–8-7 TSprake (12) (trckd ldrs: effrt & ev ch
over 2f out: rdn nt qckn) ................................................. 2.2
37055 Seraphim (FR) **(42)** *(TDBarron)* 3–8-0 KDarley (5) (hdwy ent st: carried wd &
racd stands' side: styd on: nvr able to chal) ...................... 3½.3
3687 J P Morgan **(40)** (v) *(MPNaughton)* 4–9-3 KFallon (6) (in tch: racd stands' side
st: hrd rdn 2f out: one pce) ............................................. 1.4
3479 Not Yet **(37)** *(EWeymes)* 8–9-3 ACulhane (9) (hld up & bhd: hdwy over 3f out:
no imp fnl 2f) .................................................................. 2½.5
35842 **Big Pat (56)** (Fav) *(JPearce)* 3–8-10 RPrice (8) (lw: chsd ldrs: effrt ent st: r.o one
pce) ................................................................................. s.h.6
3384 Mistic Glen (IRE) **(50)** *(JParkes)* 3–7-9 NCarlisle (1) (chsd ldrs: carried wd st: hung lft
& racd stands' side: no imp after) ................................... 3½.7
Felsina (IRE) *(WStorey)* 3–7-9 JFanning (7) (b: lw: trckd ldrs: effrt 3f out: sn
outpcd) ........................................................................... 1.8
2966 Swank Gilbert **(26)** *(TAKCuthbert)* 6–8-0 ‡7ClaireBalding (11) (nvr trbld ldrs) ...... 5.9
Whitworth Grey **(29)** *(MDods)* 4–8-7 JLowe (10) (a bhd) ................................ ½.10
3479 Electrojet **(27)** (bl) *(AWJones)* 4–8-7 DMcKeown (2) (b.hind: led tl hdd over 4f out:
wknd ent st) .................................................................... 25.11
3151 Great Service **(36)** (bl) *(MDods)* 5–9-3 LCharnock (4) (a bhd) .......................... 8.12

**5/2** Big Pat, **100-30** Felsina (IRE), **4/1** Seraphim (FR), **11/2** JOHN SHAW (USA)(4/1—6/1), **7/1** Noted Strain
(IRE), **9/1** J P Morgan(8/1—12/1), **14/1** Not Yet, **20/1** Great Service, **25/1** Whitworth Grey, Electrojet, **50/1** Ors.
CSF £45.02, Tote £10.00: £2.20 £2.60 £2.20 (£22.80). Mrs Sheila Walker (MALTON) bred by Flaxman Holdings
Ltd in USA. 12 Rn; Bt in 4,400 gns
2m 43.7 (11.2)

## 3762

TOTE CREDIT SPRINT H'CAP (0-70) £1924.00 (£539.00: £262.00)　　5f　4-45 (4-47)

| | | |
|---|---|---|
| 3423⁴ | **Little Saboteur (56)** *(PJMakin)* 3-9-4 TSprake (4) (cl up stands' side: led wl over 1f out: r.o wl) | —1 |
| 3585 | Kalar (43) (v) *(DWChapman)* 3-8-5 SWood (1) (led stands' side tl wl over 1f out: kpt on) | 1½.2 |
| 3632 | The Right Time (45) (bl) *(JParkes)* 7-8-8 RCochrane (3) (in tch stands' side: kpt on fnl f: nrst fin) | 2.3 |
| 801⁴ | Sartigila (60) (Fav) *(JWPayne)* 3-9-8 WRyan (2) (hdwy stands' side over 1f out: styd on nr fin) | s.h.4 |
| 3499 | Lonely Lass (39) *(AWJones)* 6-8-2 NCarlisle (9) (led centre: rdn 2f out: nt qckn) | 1.5 |
| 3748 | Langtonian (57) (bl) *(JBerry)* 3-9-2 ‡³EmmaO'Gorman (6) (hld up: effrt stands' side ½-wy: nt qckn fnl f) | nk.6 |
| 3748 | Hinari Video (40) (bl) *(MJohnston)* 3-8-13 DMcKeown (5) (chsd ldrs stands' side: outpcd over 1f out: n.d after) | s.h.7 |
| 3355 | Best Effort (64) *(MPNaughton)* 6-9-13 KFallon (7) (chsd ldrs centre: outpcd ½-wy: no imp after) | nk.8 |
| 3748* | Orient Air (58) (bl) *(TDBarron)* 4-9-0 (7x) ‡⁷VHalliday (8) (nvr wnt pce) | 1.9 |
| 3632 | Katie-a (IRE) (53) *(RMWhitaker)* 3-9-1 ACulhane (10) (s.s: wl bhd tl sme late hdwy) | hd.10 |
| 3079 | Murray's Mazda (IRE) (58) *(JBerry)* 3-8-13 ‡⁷PRoberts (11) (chsd ldrs centre 3f: sn wknd) | 3.11 |
| 2325 | Come on My Girl (IRE) (39) *(TAKCuthbert)* 4-7-9 ‡⁷ClaireBalding (12) (spd centre 3f: sn lost pl) | 7.12 |

**100/30** Sartigila, **4/1** Orient Air(3/1—5/1), LITTLE SABOTEUR, **6/1** Langtonian, **7/1** The Right Time, **12/1** Hinari Video, **14/1** Lonely Lass, Kalar, Best Effort, **25/1** Katie-a (IRE), **50/1** Come on My Girl (IRE). CSF £57.02, CT £361.61. Tote £3.60: £1.90 £4.30 £2.60 (£22.60). Mrs W. D. Blackwood (MARLBOROUGH) bred by Courtown Stud Co. 12 Rn
61.6 sec (3.9)
SF—46/27/22/35/11/24

T/Plpt: £389.80 (3.35 Tckts).

AA

## 3604—FOLKESTONE (R-H)
## Monday, October 19th [Soft]
Going Allowance: 1.10 sec per fur (S)　　　　　　　　　　　　　　Wind: almost nil

Stalls: low　　Flag start: 7th & 8th races

## 3763

HARDRES H'CAP (0-70) £2784.00 (£774.00: £372.00)　　1m 1f 149y　1-50 (1-53)

| | | |
|---|---|---|
| 3698² | **Alderbrook (62)** (Fav) *(MrsJCecil)* 3-9-4 PaulEddery (10) (2nd st: led wl over 1f out: comf) | —1 |
| 3675³ | Rapporteur (USA) (63) *(CCElsey)* 6-9-7 ‡³DHarrison (15) (lw: rdn & hdwy 3f out: 6th st: r.o ins fnl f) | 1.2 |
| 3555² | Sarah-Clare (54) *(RAkehurst)* 4-8-12 ‡³RPerham (13) (lw: 4th st: rdn over 1f out: unable qckn) | 10.3 |
| 3615² | King's Guest (IRE) (67) *(GAPritchard-Gordon)* 3-9-9 NDay (7) (lw: a.p: led over 5f out tl wl over 1f out: sn wknd) | ½.4 |
| 3416⁴ | Hamanaka (USA) (60) (v) *(JRFanshawe)* 3-9-2 GDuffield (1) (3rd st: one pce fnl 2f) | s.h.5 |
| 3403⁵ | Rampal (IRE) (58) *(GWragg)* 3-8-11 ‡³FNorton (14) (lw: nvr nr to chal) | s.h.6 |
| 3576³ | Lucky Noire (56) *(GHarwood)* 4-8-10 ‡⁷GayeHarwood (3) (lw: nvr nrr) | 7.7 |
| 3510* | Mayaasa (USA) (59) *(RWArmstrong)* 3-9-1 RHills (4) (5th st: wknd over 1f out) | 20.8 |
| 3526 | Dovale (62) *(WJarvis)* 4-9-9 JReid (12) (prom over 5f) | 2.9 |
| 3510⁵ | Sky Train (IRE) (62) *(JLDunlop)* 3-9-6 AMcGlone (5) (led 4f) | nk.10 |
| 748* | Metternich (63) *(MHTompkins)* 7-9-10 PRobinson (8) (a bhd) | 2.11 |
| 3369 | Rising Tempo (IRE) (60) *(CACyzer)* 4-9-7 MRoberts (6) (hdwy 4f out: wknd 3f out) | 3.12 |
| | Vermont Magic (62) *(RJHodges)* 4-9-2⁽²⁾ ‡⁷TThompson (9) (a bhd: t.o fnl 5f) | dist.13 |

**7/2** ALDERBROOK, **9/2** Sarah-Clare, **6/1** King's Guest (IRE), **15/2** Rising Tempo, **8/1** Dovale, **10/1** Mayaasa (USA), **12/1** Hamanaka (USA), Rampal (IRE), Metternich(op 7/1), Lucky Noire(op 8/1), **14/1** Rapporteur (USA), **16/1** Sky Train (IRE), **33/1** Vermont Magic. CSF £52.10, CT £217.56. Tote £3.60: £2.40 £2.90 £2.20 (£23.50). Mr James H. Stone (NEWMARKET) bred by J. H. Stone. 13 Rn
2m 16.8 (19.1)
SF—23/24/-/-/-

## 3764

LEVY BOARD STKS (I) (Mdn 2-Y.O) £2490.00 (£690.00: £330.00)
6f 189y
2-20 (2-30)

| | | |
|---|---|---|
| 3597² | **Semillon (80)** (bl) (Fav) *(GHarwood)* 9-0 TQuinn (2) (a gng wl: 3rd st: led on bit nr fin: hrd hld) | —1 |

3579 Yoxall Lodge *(HJCollingridge)* 9-0 VSmith (7) (w ldr: led over 4f out: hrd rdn
　　　　over 1f out: hdd nr fin) ................................................ nk.2
River North (IRE) *(MRStoute)* 9-0 PaulEddery (4) (scope: bit bkwd: hdwy 3f out:
　　　　hrd rdn over 1f out: one pce) ........................................ 2¹/₂.3
3525 Ikhtiraa (USA) *(RWArmstrong)* 9-0 RHills (9) (5th st: one pce fnl 2f) ................. 6.4
3489 Sunbeam Charlie *(AMoore)* 9-0 NAdams (1) (hdwy 2f out: wknd over 1f out) ..... 4.5
3285⁶ Spring Sixpence *(JRFanshawe)* 8-9 GCarter (3) (prom over 3f) ................... 5.6
Dance to Order (IRE) *(SirMarkPrescott)* 9-0 GDuffield (6) (str: scope: bkwd: lost
　　　　pl over 4f out: rallied 2f out: wknd over 1f out) ...................... 2.7
3250 Murphy's Hope (IRE) *(MJHeaton-Ellis)* 8-11 ‡3DHarrison (10) (6th st: wknd 2f
　　　　out) ............................................................... ³/₄.8
3419 Petite Vino (45) *(JJBridger)* 8-2 ‡7AntoinetteArmes (5) (prom 4f) ............. 2¹/₂.9
3505 Night Edition *(SDow)* 8-11 ‡3FNorton (11) (led over 2f: 4th st: wknd 2f out) ..... ¹/₂.10
3489⁴ Halham Tarn (IRE) *(PTWalwyn)* 9-0 MRoberts (8) (2nd st: wknd wl over 1f out) ¹/₂.11

11/8 SEMILLON, 9/2 Halham Tarn (IRE), 5/1 River North (IRE)(2/1—11/2), 13/2 Spring Sixpence(9/2—7/1),
9/1 Yoxall Lodge(20/1—8/1), 14/1 Dance to Order (IRE), 33/1 Ikhtiraa (USA), 40/1 Petite Vino, 50/1 Murphy's
Hope (IRE), Night Edition, 66/1 Sunbeam Charlie. CSF £13.67, Tote £2.60: £1.30 £1.30 £2.60 (£6.80). Mr K.
Abdulla (PULBOROUGH) bred by Juddmonte Farms. 11 Rn　　　　　　　　　　1m 33.5 (11.9)
　　　　　　　　　　　　　　　　　　　　　　　　　　　　　　　SF—37/36/28/10/–/–

**3765**　　LEVY BOARD STKS (II) (Mdn 2-Y.O) £2469.00 (£684.00: £327.00)
　　　　6f 189y　　　　　　　　　　　　　　　　　　2-50 (2-56)

3579² **Nico Mike** *(PWChapple-Hyam)* 9-0 PaulEddery (6) (lw: 6th st: rdn fnl f: led nr
　　　　fin) ................................................................. —1
3674³ Marastani (USA) (Fav) *(GHarwood)* 9-0 JReid (1) (lw: 3rd st: led over 1f out: rdn
　　　　fnl f: hdd nr fin) .................................................. nk.2
3579⁶ Scorched Air *(JWHills)* 8-9 RHills (4) (5th st: hrd rdn over 1f out: one pce) ...... 2¹/₂.3
3404⁵ Stay With Me Baby (71) *(DRCElsworth)* 8-9 JWilliams (10) (lw: led over 5f out tl
　　　　over 1f out: one pce) .............................................. 2.4
1944⁵ Divine Rain *(JWPayne)* 9-0 MTebbutt (3) (bit bkwd: nvr nr to chal) ............. 7.5
3289 Side Bar (50) *(MJRyan)* 9-0 PRobinson (8) (4th st: wknd over 1f out) ........... d.h.5
3491⁴ Two Lumps *(IABalding)* 9-0 MRoberts (5) (led over 1f: 2nd st: wknd over 1f out) .. 6.7
3077³ My Best Valentine *(PWHarris)* 9-0 SWhitworth (2) (prom over 4f) ............... 5.8
Medland (IRE) *(AWDenson)* 9-0 DBiggs (9) (w'like: dwlt: a bhd) .............. 2.9
Keep Breathing *(MHTompkins)* 8-7 ‡7SMulvey (7) (b.hind: w'like: s.s: a wl bhd) 5.10

**Evens** Marastani (USA), 5/2 NICO MIKE, 13/2 My Best Valentine, 10/1 Scorched Air(op 6/1), Two Lumps(op
6/1), 14/1 Stay With Me Baby, 33/1 Divine Rain, Keep Breathing, Medland (IRE), 50/1 Side Bar. CSF £5.67, Tote
£4.20: £2.00 £1.60 £2.40 (£2.30). Mr Luciano Gaucci (MARLBOROUGH) bred by D. MacRae. 10 Rn
　　　　　　　　　　　　　　　　　　　　　　　　　　　　　　　　　1m 33.9 (12.3)
　　　　　　　　　　　　　　　　　　　　　　　　　　　　　SF—31/30/17/11/–/–

**3766**　　HURSTMONCEUX H'CAP (0-70) £2658.00 (£738.00: £354.00)　6f 189y　3-20 (3-23)

3554 **Precious Wonder** (56) *(PButler)* 3-9-1 TyroneWilliams (7) (2nd st: led over 1f
　　　　out: drvn out) .................................................... —1
3595⁶ Old Comrades (53) *(LGCottrell)* 5-8-12 ‡3FNorton (15) (hdwy 2f out: hrd rdn
　　　　over 1f out: r.o ins fnl f) ......................................... 1.2
3605² Proud Brigadier (IRE) (52) *(WCarter)* 4-8-9 ‡5NGwilliams (4) (b.off hind: hdwy
　　　　over 1f out: r.o) .................................................. 2.3
3417 Dance on Sixpence (56) (v) *(HJCollingridge)* 4-9-4 VSmith (12) (a.p: led 3f out
　　　　tl over 1f out: unable qckn) ....................................... nk.4
3176⁵ Badawiah (62) *(WAO'Gorman)* 3-9-7 DHolland (3) (b: wknd over 1f out) ....... 5.5
3696³ Gachette (54) (bl) (Fav) *(JSutcliffe)* 3-8-13 BRouse (16) (3rd st: wknd over 1f
　　　　out) ............................................................. 1¹/₂.6
3700 Mogwai (IRE) (65) (bl) *(RFJohnsonHoughton)* 3-9-10 GDuffield (14) (5th st:
　　　　wknd over 1f out) ................................................ 1¹/₂.7
3689 Executive Spirit (57) *(DSasse)* 3-9-2 GCarter (11) (hdwy 2f out: wknd over 1f
　　　　out) ............................................................. 1¹/₂.8
3605⁶ Batchworth Bound (55) *(EAWheeler)* 3-9-0 SWhitworth (6) (swtg: a mid div) ..... 5.9
3359 Tender Moment (IRE) (66) *(CEBrittain)* 4-10-0 MRoberts (9) (6th st: wknd wl
　　　　over 1f out) ..................................................... 4.10
207 Lonesome Dove (IRE) (51) *(JWhite)* 4-8-8 ‡5ATucker (13) (a bhd) ............. 2¹/₂.11
3417 Gemini Bay (56) *(RVoorspuy)* 3-9-9 SDawson (1) (rdn thrght: a bhd) ......... 2.12
3555 Cheveley Dancer (USA) (53) (v) *(AWDenson)* 4-9-1 TQuinn (2) (swtg: led 4f:
　　　　4th st: wknd over 1f out) ......................................... ¹/₂.13

4/1 Gachette, 9/2 Proud Brigadier (IRE), 11/2 Old Comrades, 7/1 Tender Moment (IRE), 15/2 PRECIOUS
WONDER(op 16/1), 8/1 Dance on Sixpence, 12/1 Mogwai (IRE)(op 8/1), Badawiah, 14/1 Batchworth Bound,
25/1 Executive Spirit, Cheveley Dancer (USA), 33/1 Ors. CSF £46.60, CT £191.74. Tote £12.70: £3.80 £2.40
£1.30 (£23.30). Mr M. Murray (LEWES) bred by L. H. J. Ward. 13 Rn　　　　　　　1m 33.1 (11.5)
　　　　　　　　　　　　　　　　　　　　　　　　　　　　　SF—44/38/29/37/25/12

**3767**  BURWASH STKS (I) (Mdn 2-Y.O) £2070.00 (£570.00: £270.00)  6f  3-50 (3-52)

| | | |
|---|---|---|
| | **Fabriana** *(TJNaughton)* 8-9 GCarter (9) (w'like: rdn over 2f out: hdwy over 1f out: led wl ins fnl f: r.o wl) | —1 |
| | Domulla *(RAkehurst)* 8-11 ‡3RPerham (12) (neat: a.p: led 3f out tl wl ins fnl f: unable qckn) | 2½.2 |
| 3607⁶ | Tawajjah (Fav) *(PTWalwyn)* 9-0 RHills (3) (lw: led 3f: hrd rdn & one pce) | 3½.3 |
| | Bold Thatcher *(PWHarris)* 8-11 ‡3FNorton (4) (neat: bit bkwd: hld up: hrd rdn over 1f out: one pce) | s.h.4 |
| | Fly to the End (USA) *(AAScott)* 9-0 BRaymond (5) (w'like: a.p: rdn over 2f out: one pce) | nk.5 |
| 3607 | Billyback *(MJRyan)* 9-0 PRobinson (2) (hld up: hrd rdn over 1f out: one pce) | 2.6 |
| 3602⁶ | Yunus Emre (IRE) *(MBell)* 9-0 JReid (10) (lw: bhd fnl 2f) | 10.7 |
| 3608⁴ | Perfect Passion (56) *(JJBridger)* 8-9 SWhitworth (8) (hdwy 3f out: wknd wl over 1f out) | s.h.8 |
| | Nichodoula *(SirMarkPrescott)* 8-9 GDuffield (11) (leggy: bit bkwd: hdwy 3f out: wknd wl over 1f out) | 1.9 |
| | Doogarey *(JWhite)* 9-0 VSmith (1) (neat: a bhd) | 3.10 |
| 3505⁶ | Woodlands Electric *(PAPritchard)* 9-0 NAdams (6) (spd 3f) | 10.11 |

**4/1** Tawajjah, **5/1** Fly to the End (USA)(op 2/1), Nichodoula, Billyback(op 8/1), Yunus Emre (IRE), **11/1** Perfect Passion, Domulla, **16/1** Doogarey, Bold Thatcher, **20/1** Woodlands Electric, **33/1** FABRIANA. CSF £319.81, Tote £42.90: £7.10 £4.60 £1.20 (Wnr or 2nd w any £5.20). Mrs P. Payne (EPSOM) bred by R. M., P. J. and S. R. Payne. 11 Rn                                                1m 20.3 (9.6)
SF—35/27/16/12/14/6

**3768**  BURWASH STKS (II) (Mdn 2-Y.O) £2070.00 (£570.00: £270.00)  6f  4-20 (4-21)

| | | |
|---|---|---|
| 3531 | **Burbage (IRE)** *(PWChapple-Hyam)* 9-0 PaulEddery (11) (lw: hld up: rdn over 1f out: led ins fnl f: r.o) | —1 |
| 2590³ | Sylvan Starlight *(SirMarkPrescott)* 8-9 GDuffield (6) (a.p: led over 2f out: hrd rdn over 1f out: hdd ins fnl f: r.o) | nk.2 |
| 3581 | Trinity Hall *(CAHorgan)* 8-9 RHills (7) (hdwy over 2f out: hrd rdn over 1f out: unable qckn) | 3½.3 |
| 3626 | Swiss Mountain *(DRLaing)* 8-9 BRaymond (5) (lw: a.p: one pce fnl 2f) | 2½.4 |
| 2948⁵ | Marwell Mitzi (55) *(WGRWightman)* 8-9 JWilliams (14) (b.hind: hdwy 3f out: wknd over 1f out) | 2½.5 |
| 3171 | Heretical Miss (60) *(RHannon)* 8-6 ‡3RPerham (9) (prom over 4f) | ¾.6 |
| 3517⁴ | Il Moro Di Venezia (IRE) (Fav) *(JLDunlop)* 9-0 JReid (3) (lw: nvr nr to chal) | 1½.7 |
| 3570 | Zhaab *(MMadgwick)* 8-2 ‡7CAvery (4) (a mid div) | s.h.8 |
| 3440 | Aalu (IRE) (69) *(CEBrittain)* 8-9 MRoberts (4) (spd 4f) | 2.9 |
| 2474⁶ | July Bride *(MJHaynes)* 8-9 BRouse (13) (swtg: bhd fnl 3f) | 5.10 |
| 856⁵ | Ian's Ace *(BWHills)* 9-0 DHolland (1) (a bhd) | 3½.11 |
| 3486⁴ | Serious Result *(RAkehurst)* 8-9 TQuinn (2) (spd 3f) | 5.12 |
| 3606 | Recipdico Mist (IRE) (46) (bl) *(TJNaughton)* 8-9 GCarter (15) (lw: led over 3f) | 5.13 |

**5/2** Il Moro Di Venezia (IRE), **4/1** Sylvan Starlight(op 5/2), BURBAGE (IRE)(op 7/4), **13/2** Aalu (IRE), **10/1** Ian's Ace, **12/1** Heretical Miss, Marwell Mitzi, Serious Result, **25/1** Ors. CSF £20.63, Tote £5.30: £2.00 £1.80 £6.70 (£18.10). Mr R. E. Sangster (MARLBOROUGH) bred by S. Niarchos in Ireland. 13 Rn        1m 21.9 (11.2)
SF—8/2/–/–/–/–

**3769**  BIDDENDEN CLAIMING STKS  £2742.00 (£762.00: £366.00)  1½m  4-50 (4-51)

| | | |
|---|---|---|
| 3610² | **Sharp Top (55)** (Fav) *(MJRyan)* 4-8-9 DBiggs (15) (hld up: led over 2f out: clr over 1f out: r.o wl) | —1 |
| 3384⁶ | Surf Boat (62) *(BWHills)* 3-8-8 DHolland (8) (b.hind: hdwy over 5f out: 3rd st: chsd wnr over 1f out: r.o wl) | 1½.2 |
| 3500★ | Allmosa (53) *(TJNaughton)* 3-8-4 GCarter (11) (2nd st: one pce fnl 2f) | 8.3 |
| 3540⁴ | Briggs Lad (IRE) (64) *(WJarvis)* 3-9-3 MTebbutt (2) (lw: hdwy over 1f out: nvr nrr) | 1½.4 |
| 3506 | Fermain *(LordHuntingdon)* 3-7-12 ‡3DHarrison (4) (lw: 5th st: wknd over 1f out) | 3½.5 |
| 3072 | Eastern Phoebe *(ACStewart)* 3-8-0 MRoberts (3) (lw: 6th st: wknd 2f out) | 15.6 |
| 3521 | Lily Moreton *(MJHeaton-Ellis)* 3-7-12 TyroneWilliams (9) (lw: led over 9f: 4th st: wknd 2f out) | 3.7 |
| 3667 | Johns Joy (73) *(DRCEIsworth)* 7–9-3 ‡7JHunter (3) (a bhd) | nk.8 |
| 3576 | Our Topsie (39) *(FJO'Mahony)* 5-8-7(2) VSmith (7) (b: lw: a bhd) | 1.9 |
| 3102⁶ | White Wedding (47) *(PFICole)* 3-8-4 TQuinn (5) (b.off hind: prom: hrd rdn over 7f out: wknd qckly flat) | 15.10 |
| 3604 | Carlowitz (USA) (30) *(AMoore)* 4-8-10 BRouse (6) (a bhd) | nk.11 |
| 3403 | Private Practice (33) *(MJHeaton-Ellis)* 3-7-11 NAdams (12) (a bhd: t.o fnl 4f) | 12 |
| | Eighteenthirtyfour (IRE) *(AMoore)* 4-8-10 CandyMorris (14) (b: a bhd: t.o fnl 5f) | 13 |

**2/1** SHARP TOP(6/4—9/4), **7/2** Allmosa, **5/1** Surf Boat(op 8/1), **6/1** White Wedding, **8/1** Briggs Lad (IRE)(op 7/2), **12/1** Eastern Phoebe, Johns Joy(8/1—14/1), **14/1** Fermain, Carlowitz (USA), **16/1** Private Practice, Our Topsie(op 10/1), Lily Moreton, **33/1** Eighteenthirtyfour (IRE). CSF £15.36, Tote £2.70: £1.50 £3.10 £1.60 (£8.70). Malpass Bros Ltd (NEWMARKET) bred by Limestone Stud. 13 Rn                    2m 58.2 (24.7)

**3770**           LEEDS H'CAP (Amateurs) (0-70) £2763.00 (£768.00: £369.00)   1¹/₂m   5-20 (5-24)

| | | |
|---|---|---|
| 3522² | **Pride of Britain (CAN) (46)** (LGCottrell) 3-9-5 MrDSalter (13) (lw: hld up: led over 3f out: r.o wl) | —1 |
| 3610 | Cathos (FR) **(49)** (DAWilson) 7-10-1 MissEBronson (19) (b: hdwy over 1f out: r.o wl ins fnl f) | 2¹/₂.2 |
| 3380³ | The Karaoke King **(54)** (bl) (RHannon) 3-9-13 MrsJBoggis (14) (hdwy over 1f out: r.o one pce) | 3.3 |
| 2187⁵ | Lonesome Train (USA) **(57)** (CWeedon) 3-10-2(3) (MrRDyer (6) (lw: hdwy over 1f out: nvr nrr) | 4.4 |
| 3609³ | Dawn Flight **(68)** (LadyHerries) 3-10-13 MissMJuster (9) (3rd st: one pce fnl 2f) | hd.5 |
| 2560³ | Romanian (IRE) **(46)** (RAkehurst) 4-9-12 MrTJenks (10) (2nd st: wknd over 1f out) | 3¹/₂.6 |
| 3610 | Letts Green (IRE) **(43)** (MJHaynes) 4-9-9(4) MissYHaynes (3) (lw: 5th st: wknd over 1f out) | hd.7 |
| 3316⁵ | Mediator **(49)** (AMoore) 3-9-8 MrKGoble (18) (6th st: wkng whn hung bdly lft over 1f out) | 20.8 |
| 2086⁴ | Mysterious Maid (USA) **(56)** (JPearce) 5-10-8 MrsLPearce (11) (nvr nr to chal) | 2¹/₂.9 |
| 2955⁶ | Snow Blizzard **(55)** (SDow) 4-10-7 MrTCuff (12) (led over 8f: 4th st: wknd 2f out) | 7.10 |
| | Bold Mac **(44)** (MBlanshard) 6-9-10 MissABillot (17) (nvr nrr) | 2¹/₂.11 |
| 3591 | Al Billal **(61)** (bl) (JJBridger) 4-10-13 MissMBridger (7) (a bhd) | 3.12 |
| 3380 | Thimbalina **(36)** (DAWilson) 6-9-2 MissLEaton (20) (b: prom over 6f) | 1¹/₂.13 |
| 3468 | Samurai Gold (USA) **(46)** (v) (CJames) 4-9-12(8) MrEJames (5) (a bhd) | 7.14 |
| 2870⁴ | Russian Vision **(50)** (bl) (AAScott) 3-10-1 MrTDenne (15) (b.hind: prom 6f) | 7.15 |
| 331 | Albury Grey **(38)** (RCurtis) 5-9-8 MissEMills (1) (s.s: a t.o) | 16 |
| | Sure Pride (USA) **(55)** (AMoore) 4-10-7 MrsJMoore (4) (b: bit bkwd: s.s: a t.o) | 17 |
| 3755² | Carrolls Marc (IRE) **(53)** (Fav) (PJFeilden) 4-10-5 MissJFeilden (8) (b.hind: ref to r: t.n.p) | 0 |

**2/1** Carrolls Marc (IRE)(tchd 5/1), **7/2** Mysterious Maid (USA)(op 6/1), **6/1** Romanian (IRE)(10/1—5/1), **13/2** PRIDE OF BRITAIN (CAN)(4/1—7/1), **8/1** Dawn Flight(6/1—9/1), **10/1** Thimbalina(14/1—8/1), **12/1** Cathos (FR)(8/1—14/1), **14/1** The Karaoke King(op 8/1), Snow Blizzard, **16/1** Russian Vision(op 10/1), Lonesome Train (USA), Mediator, **20/1** Sure Pride (USA), Letts Green (IRE), **25/1** Bold Mac, **33/1** Samurai Gold (USA), Albury Grey, **50/1** Al Billal. CSF £97.53, CT £1,044.80. Tote £7.60: £2.40 £2.40 £5.80 (£31.90). Pride of Britain Limited (CULLOMPTON) bred by Blue Spruce Farm in Canada. 18 Rn                    3m 1 (27.5)

T/Plpt: £6.90 (243.73 Tckts).                                                                                          AK

3400—**NOTTINGHAM (L-H)**

## Monday, October 19th [Good to firm]

Going Allowance: St: 0.05 sec per fur; Rnd: 0.20 sec per fur (G)                    Wind: almost nil

Stalls: high

**3771**           RAINWORTH (S) H'CAP (3 & 4-Y.O) (0-60) £2868.00 (£798.00: £384.00)
                  **1m 54y**                                                          2-00 (2-04)

| | | |
|---|---|---|
| 3521 | **Eiras Mood (47)** (BPalling) 3-8-11 ‡7AGarth (4) (hld up: gd hdwy 2f out: str run to ld wl ins fnl f) | —1 |
| 3615 | Military Expert **(55)** (bl) (CaptJWilson) 3-9-5 ‡7JMarshall (16) (hdwy on outside 3f out: led ins fnl f: sn hdd: r.o) | 1.2 |
| 3705 | Sir Norman Holt (IRE) **(54)** (bl) (FHLee) 3-9-11 PatEddery (9) (lw: led after 2f: clr 3f out: hdd & no ex ins fnl f) | ¹/₂.3 |
| 3595⁵ | Mexican Dancer **(43)** (RJHolder) 3-8-7 ‡7SDrowne (12) (hdwy 3f out: rdn & hung rt appr fnl f: r.o) | s.h.4 |
| 3589 | Broad Appeal **(44)** (bl) (Fav) (RCSpicer) 4-9-4 WCarson (19) (s.s: hdwy 2f out: styd on nr fin) | hd.5 |
| 3557⁶ | Dam Certain (IRE) **(47)** (AWDenson) 3-9-4 CRutter (20) (hld up: hdwy ¹/₂-wy: rdn 2f out: one pce) | 3.6 |
| 3421² | Sunley Sparkle **(43)** (DRGandolfo) 4-9-3 AMunro (18) (r.o fnl 2f: nvr nrr) | 3.7 |
| | Lawnswood Gold (IRE) **(50)** (BAMcMahon) 4-9-3 ‡7SSanders (15) (bkwd: chsd ldrs: 6th st: wkng whn hmpd over 1f out) | 3¹/₂.8 |
| 3513 | Lombard Ocean **(45)** (ABailey) 3-9-2 GBaxter (14) (nvr nrr) | d.h.8 |
| 3615⁵ | Flying Down to Rio (IRE) **(41)** (bl) (MPNaughton) 4-8-10 ‡5JWeaver (5) (chsd ldrs: 5th st: wkng whn hmpd over 1f out) | 2¹/₂.10 |

3601 Reel of Tulloch (IRE) **(49)** (bl) *(PCHaslam)* 3-9-6 DaleGibson (1) (in tch: hdwy
3f out: btn whn hmpd appr fnl f) ............................................................ 3.11
3140 Roly Wallace **(57)** (bl) *(KTIvory)* 3-9-7 ‡7CScally (8) (effrt 4f out: nt rch ldrs) ... nk.12
3048 Red Jack (IRE) **(48)** (bl) *(JAkehurst)* 3-9-5 NHowe (11) (chsd ldrs: 4th st: wknd
over 2f out) .............................................................................................. hd.13
3520 Saifan **(57)** (bl) *(DMorris)* 3-9-9 ‡5StephenDavies (1) (m.n.s) ...................... 1½.14
3701⁵ Genuine Lady **(52)** *(APJarvis)* 4-9-5 ‡7DWright (7) (led 2f: 2nd st: btn 3f out) ... 2.15
3604 I'M Curious **(45)** *(RThompson)* 3-8-9 ‡7GForster (6) (m.n.s) ............................ ½.16
3692 The Titan Ghost **(50)** *(BAMcMahon)* 3-9-7 MBirch (10) (prom: 3rd st: wknd 2f
out: eased whn btn) ................................................................................. 1½.17
3281 Cappahoosh (IRE) **(50)** *(HJCollingridge)* 3-9-0 ‡7CHawksley (14) (a bhd) ........ 4.18
2041 Where's Ruth (IRE) **(50)** *(MWEasterby)* 3-9-7 TLucas (2) (a bhd) .................... 2½.19

**13/2** Broad Appeal, **15/2** Sir Norman Holt (IRE), **10/1** EIRAS MOOD, Flying Down to Rio (IRE), **11/1** Genuine
Lady, Saifan, **12/1** Sunley Sparkle, Mexican Dancer, **14/1** Lombard Ocean, Reel of Tulloch (IRE), **16/1** Military
Expert, The Titan Ghost, **20/1** Red Jack (IRE), Roly Wallace, Cappahoosh (IRE), **25/1** Lawnswood Gold (IRE),
Dam Certain (IRE), **33/1** Ors. CSF £147.07, CT £1,160.88. Tote £13.20: £2.30 £5.60 £2.40 £3.60 (£53.60). Mr
S. E. Salimeni (COWBRIDGE) bred by W. H. Joyce. 19 Rn; No bid
Mr 46 (6.4)
SF—25/30/34/15/25/16

**3772** WHATTON MANOR STUD STKS (2-Y.O) £3377.25 (£1008.00: £481.50: £218.25)
1m 54y
2-30 (2-33)

2398⋆ **Beneficial (90)** *(GWragg)* 9-0 MHills (5) (hld up in rr: 4th st: hdwy to ld over 1f
out: r.o) ...................................................................................................... —1
2130⋆ Double Bass (USA) **(100)** (Fav) *(HRACecil)* 9-0 SCauthen (4) (led tl hdd over 1f
out: rallied u.p cl home) .......................................................................... ½.2
Debos *(MRStoute)* 8-6 ‡5JJones (2) (rangy: scope: bit bkwd: 2nd st: jnd ldr 2f
out: unable qckn fnl f) ............................................................................. 1½.3
2979a Yajeed (USA) **(87)** *(AAScott)* 9-2 WRSwinburn (1) (lw: hld up: 3rd st: shkn up 3f
out: nvr able to chal) ................................................................................ 2½.4
3100⋆ Carelaman **(100)** *(JLDunlop)* 9-0 WCarson (3) (plld hrd: hld up: 5th st: effrt on
ins over 1f out: wknd fnl f) ...................................................................... 2.5

**7/4** Double Bass (USA), **11/4** Carelaman(2/1—3/1), **3/1** BENEFICIAL, **9/2** Yajeed (USA), **25/1** Debos. CSF
£8.18, Tote £6.20: £2.30 £1.10 (£4.10). Sir Robin McAlpine (NEWMARKET) bred by Sir Robin McAlpine. 5 Rn
1m 47.2 (7.6)
SF—10/8/–/–/–/

**3773** GAMSTON STKS (Mdn 3-Y.O) £2532.00 (£702.00: £336.00)
1³⁄₄m 15y 3-00 (3-01)

3504² **Neieb (USA) (56)** *(BHanbury)* 8-9 WRSwinburn (2) (chsd ldrs: rdn over
2f out: led ins fnl f: r.o wl) ....................................................................... —1
Indian Quest *(MajorWRHern)* 9-0 WCarson (3) (leggy: bit bkwd: s.i.s: sn chsng
ldrs: 6th st: hdwy 2f out: hrd rdn & r.o wl) ............................................. nk.2
3616² Nemir (Fav) *(JHMGosden)* 9-0 SCauthen (4) (b: lw: chsd ldrs: 4th st: led over 2f
out tl ins fnl f) ............................................................................................. 1.3
3616⁵ Klingon (IRE) **(65)** *(RHollinshead)* 9-0 LDettori (9) (hld up: 7th st: styd on fnl 2f:
nvr nrr) ....................................................................................................... 2.4
3682⁴ Fort Shirley (IRE) *(MRStoute)* 9-0 PatEddery (1) (lw: led over 11f: wknd over 1f
out) ............................................................................................................. 4.5
3219⁵ Sea Plane **(65)** (bl) *(MajorWRHern)* 9-0 AMunro (10) (plld hrd: 2nd st: wknd
over 2f out) ............................................................................................... nk.7
3609⁴ Jawaher (IRE) **(61)** *(RJRWilliams)* 8-9 MHills (8) (chsd ldrs: 5th st: wknd 3f out) nk.7
3459 Just Hannah *(MrsBarbaraWaring)* 8-9 NHowe (5) (a bhd: t.o) ...................... 30.8
3392⁶ Blue Lyzander *(RBrotherton)* 8-9 GCrealock (6) (chsd ldr to ½-wy: wknd qckly:
t.o) .............................................................................................................. 9
3459 Zafarrancho (IRE) *(JGFitzGerald)* 9-0 MBirch (7) (b: b.hind: a in rr: lost tch fnl 3f:
t.o) .............................................................................................................. 10

**11/10** Nemir, **9/2** Fort Shirley (IRE), **11/2** Jawaher (IRE), **9/1** Indian Quest(op 3/1), **12/1** NEIEB (USA), **14/1** Sea
Plane, **20/1** Klingon (IRE), **50/1** Zafarrancho (IRE), Just Hannah, **100/1** Blue Lyzander. CSF £100.69, Tote
£14.20: £1.70 £2.00 £1.40 (£31.80). Mr Saeed Suhail (NEWMARKET) bred by Guiting Stud Ltd in USA. 10 Rn
3m 6.8 (8.3)
SF—40/44/42/38/30/28

**3774** ROSELAND STKS £3059.45 (£911.60: £434.30: £195.65)
1m 1f 213y
3-30 (3-31)

3697⁵ **Marcus Thorpe (USA) (103)** *(PAKelleway)* 4-9-3 WCarson (2) (b: lw: sn bhd &
outpcd: 4th st: hdwy to ld over 2f out: pushed clr) .............................. —1
821⋆ Fetish **(89)** (Fav) *(HRACecil)* 3-8-11 PatEddery (1) (lw: dwlt: sn chsng ldr: 2nd
st: rdn & ev ch 2f out: sn outpcd) ........................................................... 10.2

3542⁵ River Defences (USA) *(PWChapple-Hyam)* 3–8-12 LPiggott (3) (set str pce: so
clr: hdd over 2f out: sn btn) .................................................. 2½.3

3571⁴ St Ninian **(102)** *(MHEasterby)* 6–9-10 MBirch (4) (lw: hld up: 3rd st: ev ch 2f out:
sn outpcd) ...................................................... hd.4

**7/4** Fetish, **9/4** River Defences (USA), **11/4** MARCUS THORPE (USA), **6/1** St Ninian. CSF £7.28, Tote £3.80
(£3.20). Mr G. Mazza (NEWMARKET) bred by Stonereath Farms Inc in USA. 4 Rn    2m 8.7 (6.2)
SF—61/35/31/42

## 3775
WOODBOROUGH STKS (I) (Mdn 2-Y.0) £2070.00 (£570.00: £270.00)
**1m 1f 213y**            4-00 (4-05)

3272⁵ **Frescade (USA)** (Fav) *(PFICole)* 9-0 AMunro (9) (mde all: veered bdly rt 6f out:
rdn out) .......................................................... —1

3602⁴ Major Yaasi (USA) *(JRFanshawe)* 9-0 WRSwinburn (7) (hld up: hdwy 3f out: hrd
rdn appr fnl f: r.o wl) ...................................... 1.2

3430 Hoosie *(CEBrittain)* 8-9 SCauthen (13) (bit bkwd: s.i.s: hdwy ent st: r.o one pce
fnl 2f) ........................................................ 2½.3

3463² Soloman Springs (USA) **(87)** *(SGNorton)* 9-0 WCarson (5) (lw: chsd ldrs: 5th
st: hrd rdn over 2f out: styd on fnl f) .................... 3½.4

2058 My Ballyboy **(43)** (bl) *(ABailey)* 8-7 ‡7PBowe (1) (prom: 2nd st: rdn 2f out: wknd
appr fnl f) ................................................. 2½.5

3274 Miss Ribbons **(50)** *(PatMitchell)* 8-9 LDettori (3) (prom: 4th st: rdn over 1f out:
sn btn) ...................................................... d.h.6

3525 General Mouktar *(AHide)* 9-0 WWoods (2) (chsd ldrs: 3rd st: rdn & wknd over 2f
out) ......................................................... s.h.7

3501³ Blowedifiknow **(67)** *(JWharton)* 8-9 ‡SWilliams (8) (nvr nr to chal) ........... ½.8

3579 Wordsmith (IRE) **(78)** *(GHarwood)* 9-0 MHills (12) (hdwy & 6th st: rdn & wknd
over 2f out) .................................................. ½.9

3593 Dodgy Dancer *(MJsLPiggott)* 9-0 LPiggott (6) (b: b hind: chsd ldrs: 7th st: wknd
over 2f out) ................................................. 1.10

3320 Allensea (IRE) *(CAHorgan)* 9-0 DaleGibson (4) (s.i.s: a bhd) ................. ¾.11

1660 Danger Baby *(BobJones)* 9-0 GBaxter (10) (a bhd) ........................... 1½.12

3593 Flying Amy *(RCurtis)* 8-9 GBardwell (14) (b.off hind: a bhd: t.o) ........... dist.13

3408³ Pistols At Dawn (USA) (10/1) Withdrawn (lame at s) : not under orders

**11/10** FRESCADE (USA), **3/1** Soloman Springs (USA)(3/1—5/1), **5/1** Hoosie(tchd 8/1), **11/1** Major Yaasi
(USA)(op 6/1), **12/1** Wordsmith (IRE), **14/1** Dodgy Dancer, **33/1** General Mouktar, **50/1** Blowedifiknow, **100/1**
Ors. CSF £12.92, Tote £1.70: £1.50 £1.70 £1.50 (£6.60). Mr Fahd Salman (WHATCOMBE) bred by Shirley N.
Lathrop in USA. 13 Rn      2m 11.2 (8.7)
SF—33/31/21/19/7/9

## 3776
WOODBOROUGH STKS (II) (Mdn 2-Y.0) £2070.00 (£570.00: £270.00)
**1m 1f 213y**            4-30 (4-35)

3471² **Manaarah (USA) (78)** (Fav) *(AAScott)* 8-9 SCauthen (3) (a.p: 2nd st: led 3f out:
clr appr fnl f: comf) ..................................... —1

3419⁶ Phrose *(RHannon)* 9-0 PatEddery (8) (b.nr hind: hld up & bhd: nt clr run & plld
out 2f out: rdn & fin wl) ................................. 2.2

3307² Safir (USA) *(JLDunlop)* 9-0 WCarson (4) (lw: led to 3f out: kpt on one pce) ... 2½.3

Valiant Commander *(PRHedger)* 9-0 GHind (5) (w'like: bit bkwd: hld up & bhd:
stdy hdwy 2f out: rdn & no ex fnl f) .................... 2½.4

3489 Galactic Fury **(55)** *(BStevens)* 8-9 ‡5JWeaver (10) (bhd: styd on fnl f: nvr nrr) .... 5.5

3574 Romalito **(64)** *(MBlanshard)* 9-0 GBardwell (11) (6th st: hrd rdn 2f out: sn btn) nk.6

3491⁶ Golden Klair **(42)** *(CJHill)* 8-9 GBaxter (6) (effrt ent st: nvr trbld ldrs) .......... nk.7

3178 Desert Laughter (IRE) *(RHollinshead)* 9-0 LDettori (12) (chsd ldrs: 5th st: wknd
over 2f out) ................................................. 1½.8

3619⁵ Amillionmemories **(75)** *(MrsBarbaraWaring)* 9-0 NHowe (9) (hdwy 6f out: 4th
st: wknd over 2f out) ..................................... ½.9

2505⁵ La Delitzia (USA) *(PFICole)* 8-9 AMunro (1) (prom: 3rd st: rdn over 3f out: sn
wknd) ...................................................... 3.10

3471 My Sister Lucy *(APJarvis)* 8-2 ‡7DWright (2) (prom tl 7th & wknd st) ........... 10.11

**6/4** MANAARAH (USA), **3/1** Safir (USA)(op 7/4), **100/30** Phrose, **10/1** La Delitzia (USA), **14/1**
Amillionmemories, **33/1** Golden Klair, Romalito, **40/1** Desert Laughter (IRE), **50/1** Galactic Fury, Valiant
Commander, **100/1** My Sister Lucy. CSF £6.64, Tote £2.90: £1.50 £1.80 £1.20 (£6.10). Sheikh Ahmed Al
Maktoum (NEWMARKET) bred by David Ringler & Nancy Ringler in USA. 11 Rn    2m 11 (8.5)
SF—30/31/26/21/6/10

## 3777
KEGWORTH H'CAP (0-70) £2805.00 (£780.00: £375.00)    **5f 13y**      5-00 (5-05)

3554 **Peerage Prince (59)** (bl) *(PatMitchell)* 3–9-2 AMunro (6) (chsd ldrs centre: hrd
rdn to ld ins fnl f) ......................................... —1

3397 Heaven-Liegh-Grey **(68)** (bl) (Fav) *(MJohnston)* 4-9-12 PatEddery (21) (b.off hind: led stands' side: rdn & hdd ins fnl f) ...................... 1½.**2**

3596⁴ Banham College **(56)** *(BAMcMahon)* 6-9-0 MBirch (13) (hdwy u.p over 1f out: fin wl) ...................... nk.**3**

3596⁶ Barbara's Cutie **(37)** (v) *(MBlanshard)* 4-7-9 GBardwell (20) (hdwy over 1f out: r.o wl ins fnl f) ...................... hd.**4**

3499 Doesyoudoes **(47)** (v) *(DTThom)* 3-7-11 ‡7KimMcDonnell (8) (chsd ldrs centre: ev ch 1f out: one pce) ...................... ½.**5**

3596³ Lincstone Boy (IRE) **(51)** (v) *(SRBowring)* 4-8-9 SWebster (2) (w ldr far side: ev ch fnl f: r.o) ...................... s.h.**6**

3748 Le Chic **(46)** *(DWChapman)* 6-8-4 GBaxter (4) (led far side: hrd rdn over 1f out: one pce) ...................... 2.**7**

3400 Lyndon's Linnet **(63)** *(RIngram)* 4-9-0 ‡7SDrowne (7) (nvr nr to chal) ...................... 1.8

3557 Ipsilante **(51)** *(ASReid)* 3-8-1 ‡7PMcCabe (3) (r.o appr fnl f: nvr nrr) ...................... hd.**9**

2922 Take in Cash **(46)** *(RDickin)* 3-8-3 CRutter (16) (nvr trbld ldrs) ...................... 1½.**10**

3605 Miss Precocious **(35)** (v) *(DShaw)* 4-7-0 ‡7DWright (5) (s.s: nvr nrr) ...................... 1½.**11**

3559★ Bright Paragon (IRE) **(48)** *(HJCollingridge)* 3-8-5 JQuinn (11) (m.n.s) ...................... 1.**12**

3252⁴ Casting Shadows **(51)** (bl) *(RDickin)* 3-8-8 NHowe (1) (s.s: n.d) ...................... ½.**13**

3341 Consulate **(55)** *(JBalding)* 6-8-13 GHind (1) (outpcd) ...................... 1.**14**

3397 Grand Time **(45)** *(CJHill)* 3-7-9 ‡7BRussell (12) (m.n.s) ...................... hd.**15**

3703 Amour du Soir (USA) **(53)** *(RLee)* 5-8-11 WCarson (19) (b: chsd ldr stands' side over 3f) ...................... s.h.**16**

3499⁴ Stocktina **(38)** *(RJHodges)* 5-7-10 DaleGibson (9) (m.n.s) ...................... 1.**17**

3537³ Here Comes a Star **(68)** *(JMCarr)* 4-9-12 SMorris (15) (m.n.s) ...................... ¾.**18**

3144 Creche **(64)** (bl) *(MrsNMacauley)* 3-9-2 ‡5SWilliams (14) (lw: spd over 3f) ...... hd.**19**

3596 Party Treat (IRE) **(41)** *(DMarks)* 4-7-6⁽⁶⁾ ‡7CHawksley (10) (t: outpcd) ...................... ½.**20**

2919 Catalani **(50)** *(JJNaughton)* 7-8-8 MHills (18) (b: swtg: outpcd) ...................... 1½.**21**

LONG HANDICAP: Miss Precocious 7-2, Party Treat (IRE) 7-5.

**5/1** Heaven-Liegh-Grey, **15/2** Here Comes a Star(op 5/1), **8/1** Bright Paragon (IRE), **9/1** Lyndon's Linnet, Banham College, **10/1** Barbara's Cutie, Lincstone Boy (IRE), **12/1** Stocktina, **20/1** Creche, Amour du Soir (USA), Catalani, Casting Shadows, PEERAGE PRINCE, Consulate, **25/1** Le Chic, Grand Time, **33/1** Ors. CSF £112.89, CT £898.93. Tote £30.30: £7.70 £1.90 £2.20 £2.60 (£142.80). Mr David A. Hobbs (NEWMARKET) bred by Tsarina Stud. 21 Rn

61.9 sec (3.2)

SF—43/47/34/10/10/21

T/Plpt: £42.60 (52.1 Tckts).

IM

3697—**CHEPSTOW (L-H)**

**Tuesday, October 20th [Good becoming Soft]**

Going Allowance: 0.65 sec per fur (Y)

Wind: fresh bhd

Stalls: high

**3778** PASTURE H'CAP (0-80) £3236.00 (£968.00: £464.00: £212.00)
1½m 23y

2-00 (2-05)

3573³ **Statajack (IRE) (69)** (bl) *(DRCElsworth)* 4-9-3 TQuinn (7) (hld up: stdy hdwy 4f out: swtchd rt over 2f out: qcknd to ld ins fnl f) ...................... —**1**

3600★ Qualitair Rhythm (IRE) **(57)** (Fav) *(ICampbell)* 4-7-12 ‡7GMitchell (13) (hld up & plld hrd: 5th st: led over 2f out tl ins fnl f) ...................... 1½.**2**

3492 Matching Green **(68)** (v) *(GBBalding)* 3-8-9 JWilliams (9) (hld up: hdwy & 7th st: r.o one pce fnl 2f) ...................... 4.**3**

3125⁵ Firefighter **(66)** *(RHollinshead)* 3-8-7 RCochrane (19) (bhd tl hdwy fnl 2f: r.o) ... 2.**4**

3459⁴ Etiquette **(68)** *(LordHuntingdon)* 3-8-7 AMunro (14) (3rd st: one pce fnl 2f) ...................... 1.**5**

3698³ Lady Lacey **(51)** (v) *(GBBalding)* 5-7-13 DaleGibson (15) (hdwy 3f out: one pce fnl 2f) ...................... ½.**6**

3409 Gesnera **(46)** *(KWhite)* 4-7-8⁽¹⁾ NCarlisle (18) (2nd st: led 3f out: sn hdd & wknd) ¾.**7**

3473 Riviera Vista **(76)** *(GWragg)* 3-9-0 ‡3FNorton (12) (hdwy 4f out: hrd rdn 3f out: wknd 2f out) ...................... 6.**8**

3600⁶ Wotamona **(48)** *(BPalling)* 4-7-10⁽³⁾ SDawson (17) (b.nr hind: 4th st: wknd over 2f out) ...................... 3½.**9**

3687 Mister Oddy **(45)** *(JSKing)* 6-7-7 GBardwell (16) (bit bkwd: led 9f) ...................... s.h.**10**

902★ Sure Haven **(75)** *(SirMarkPrescott)* 3-9-2 GDuffield (1) (6th st: wknd 3f out) 4.**11**

1626⁴ Mujid (IRE) **(65)** *(HThomsonJones)* 3-8-6 RHills (8) (bkwd: bhd fnl 3f) ...................... 5.**12**

3466 Kashan (IRE) **(80)** *(JMBradley)* 4-10-0 PaulEddery (11) (a bhd) ...................... 4.**13**

3254⁴ Seaside Minstrel **(57)** *(RJManning)* 4-8-5⁽¹⁾ ADicks (6) (a bhd) ...................... 2.**14**

Leguard Express (IRE) **(45)** *(OO'Neill)* 4-7-0 ‡7KimMcDonnell (4) (bkwd: a bhd) 1.**15**

2833⁵ Duggan **(50)** *(RJRWilliams)* 5-7-11 JQuinn (10) (t.o) ...................... 6.**16**

3697 Wide Support **(73)** *(AMoore)* 7-9-9 BRouse (2) (b: prom: 8th & wkng st: t.o) ...................... 3.**17**

Ok Records **(46)** *(OO'Neill)* 5-7-8⁽¹⁾ NAdams (5) (a bhd: t.o) ...................... 2.**18**

3701 Ante Up (IRE) **(68)** (bl) *(JAkehurst)* 4–9–2 SWhitworth (3) (bit bkwd: reluctant to
r: a t.o) ............... **19**

LONG HANDICAP: Gesnera 6-10, Wotamona 6-11, Mister Oddy 7-5, Leguard Express (IRE) 7-3,
Ok Records 6-10.

**9/4** Qualitair Rhythm (IRE)(op 9/2), **11/2** STATAJACK (IRE)(op 7/2), **13/2** Sure Haven (IRE), **9/1** Riviera Vista,
**11/1** Matching Green, Lady Lacey, **12/1** Firefighter, Etiquette, Mujid (IRE), **14/1** Duggan, Wide Support, **16/1**
Seaside Minstrel, **25/1** Ante Up (IRE), **33/1** Kashan (IRE), Gesnera, Wotamona, **50/1** Leguard Express (IRE),
Mister Oddy, **100/1** Ok Records. CSF £19.86, CT £139.50. Tote £5.10: £1.90 £1.40 £3.70 £2.20 (£11.70). Mrs
M. E. Slade (WHITSBURY) bred by Princess Oettingen-Spielberg in Ireland. 19 Rn        2m 52 (20.7)

## 3779

SPINNEY STKS     £2938.90 (£875.20: £416.60: £187.30)        **1m 14y**        2-30 (2-32)

3428 **Two Left Feet (101)** (Fav) *(SirMarkPrescott)* 5–9–10 GDuffield (2) (lw: plld hrd:
chsd ldr: led over 3f out: pushed out) ............... **—1**

3680 Sunday's Hill **(93)** *(MBlanshard)* 3–9–4 RCochrane (1) (led over 4f: rdn & one
pce fnl 2f) ............... 2½.2

3591 Lee Artiste **(94)** *(PFICole)* 4–9–5 TQuinn (4) (swtg: hld up: rdn & wknd 2f out) . 12.3

3543 Knight of Mercy **(96)** (bl) *(RHannon)* 6–9–7 BRaymond (3) (lw: s.i.s: hld up: rdn
over 4f out: sn t.o) ............... 30.4

**4/7** TWO LEFT FEET, **7/2** Knight of Mercy(op 9/4), **6/1** Lee Artiste, **10/1** Sunday's Hill. CSF £5.48, Tote £1.40
(£3.20). Mr P. W. W. Molins (NEWMARKET) bred by Stud-On-The-Chart. 4 Rn        1m 43.2 (10.7)
SF—28/10/–/–

## 3780

PAT EDDERY 200-IN-A-SEASON STKS (Mdn 2-Y.O.F) £2595.00 (£720.00: £345.00)
**7f 16y**        3-00 (3-03)

**Ivory Palm (USA)** *(JHMGosden)* 8-11 PatEddery (7) (lengthy: scope: a.p: led
over 2f out: drvn out) ............... **—1**

3683 Austral Jane *(GHarwood)* R-11 MHills (12) (a.p: jnd wnr over 2f out: hrd rdn fnl f:
r.o) ............... ½.2

3360 Tahdid *(PTWalwyn)* 8-11 WCarson (4) (hdwy 3f out: one pce fnl 2f) ............... 6.3

3549² Golden Guest (Fav) *(MrsJCecil)* 8-11 PaulEddery (10) (led over 4f: wknd over
1f out) ............... s.h.4

3440⁵ Dancing Spirit (IRE) **(86)** *(DRCElsworth)* 8-11 TQuinn (8) (prom 5f) ............... 5.5

La Posada *(RHannon)* 8-11 BRaymond (3) (lt-f: unf: s.s: nvr trbld ldrs) ............... ½.6

3414 Sky Burst *(LGCottrell)* 8-11 NCarlisle (11) (prom over 3f) ............... 10.7

3132 Katie Eileen (USA) *(RHannon)* 8-11 SWhitworth (1) (bkwd: prom 4f) ............... 8.8

3419 Hariti (IRE) *(DRCElsworth)* 8-11 JWilliams (6) (a bhd) ............... 2½.9

3414 Pink Orchid *(MPMuggeridge)* 8-11 AMunro (9) (bhd fnl 3f: t.o) ............... 8.10

3099⁶ Swift Revenge *(MRChannon)* 8-11 JQuinn (13) (dwlt: a bhd) ............... ¾.11

Habeebitti Nadia *(WJHaggas)* 8-11 BRouse (2) (w'like: bit bkwd: s.s: a bhd: t.o) 20.12

**6/4** Golden Guest(Evens—7/4), **11/4** IVORY PALM (USA)(op 6/4), **6/1** Dancing Spirit (IRE), **12/1** Hariti (IRE)(op
8/1), La Posada, **14/1** Katie Eileen (USA), Tahdid, **16/1** Habeebitti Nadia, **20/1** Swift Revenge, **25/1** Sky Burst,
Austral Jane, **33/1** Pink Orchid. CSF £65.24, Tote £3.90: £1.80 £5.30 £2.20 (£110.30). Mr K. Abdulla
(NEWMARKET) bred by Juddmonte Farms Inc in USA. 12 Rn        1m 28.5 (8)
SF—45/43/25/24/9/7

## 3781

MEADOW H'CAP (3-Y.O) (0-90) £3435.75 (£1026.00: £490.50: £222.75)
**7f 16y**        (Weights raised 6 lb)        3-30 (3-35)

3612 **Elsals (65)** (bl) *(HThomsonJones)* 8-7 RHills (7) (a.p: led 2f out: edgd rt over 1f
out: drvn out) ............... **—1**

3554* Sovereign Rock (IRE) **(79)** *(RHannon)* 9-4 ‡³RPerham (12) (a.p: led over 2f out:
sn hdd: nt qckn ins fnl f) ............... 1½.2

3554⁶ Key Suspect (USA) **(78)** *(JHMGosden)* 9-6 RCochrane (2) (dwlt: hdwy over 2f
out: rdn over 1f out: one pce) ............... 2½.3

3680² Will of Steel **(79)** (Fav) *(HCandy)* 9-0 ‡⁷AntoinetteArmes (1) (a.p: ev ch 2f out:
one pce) ............... 2.4

3582⁴ Vanborough Lad **(67)** *(MJHaynes)* 8-9 DBiggs (9) (lw: no hdwy fnl 2f) ............... 3.5

3365 Salisong **(67)** (bl) *(PFICole)* 8-9 TQuinn (8) (lw: led over 4f) ............... 1½.6

3701³ Canadian Capers **(64)** *(MRChannon)* 8-6 JQuinn (11) (prom: rdn 3f out: wknd
2f out) ............... ¾.7

3554 Neither Nor **(68)** (bl) *(RJHolder)* 8-10 JWilliams (6) (a bhd) ............... 2.8

3678² Lahoob (USA) **(71)** *(BHanbury)* 8-13 BRaymond (3) (rdn over 3f out: a bhd) ... hd.9

3511⁶ Super Serenade **(68)** *(GBBalding)* 8-10 AMunro (10) (lw: a bhd: t.o) ............... 10.10

3710² Nbaat (USA) **(63)** *(CJBenstead)* 8-5 WCarson (5) (a bhd: t.o) ............... 11

**5/2** Will of Steel, **4/1** Lahoob (USA), **8/1** Sovereign Rock (IRE), Nbaat (USA), **9/1** Key Suspect (USA)(op 6/1),
**10/1** Super Serenade, Vanborough Lad, Salisong, **12/1** Canadian Capers, **14/1** Neither Nor, **16/1** ELSALS. CSF
£133.59, CT £1,132.59. Tote £26.40: £5.20 £3.20 £3.50 (£157.10). Mr Hamdan Al-Maktoum (NEWMARKET)
bred by Home Stud Ltd. 11 Rn        1m 28.1 (7.6)
SF—47/53/47/35/21/16

**3782**    COPSE STKS (Mdn 2-Y.O.C) £2553.00 (£708.00: £339.00)    **7f 16y**    4-00 (4-05)

3551⁵ **Rakis (IRE)** *(CJBenstead)* 9-0  WCarson (4) (lw: mde all: pushed out) ............... —1
3574⁴ Gone Prospecting (USA) **(81)** *(RHannon)* 9-0  TQuinn (2) (lw: hld up: ev ch over
　　　1f out: no imp) ...................................................................................... 6.2
3516² Louvre (FR) **(Fav)** *(MrsJCecil)* 9-0  PaulEddery (8) (prom: rdn over 2f out: no
　　　rspnse) ...................................................................................... 2¹/₂.3
3491 Sure Right (IRE) *(JWHills)* 9-0  MHills (10) (bit bkwd: nvr nr to chal) ............... 8.4
3662 Correspondence (CAN) *(JHMGosden)* 9-0  RCochrane (7) (a.p: ev ch 2f out: sn
　　　wknd) .......................................................................................... nk.5
3593 Danroy (USA) *(GHarwood)* 9-0  PatEddery (6) (w wnr tl wknd 2f out) ............... 2¹/₂.6
3593 Boltrose *(KWhite)* 9-0  NAdams (1) (bkwd: rdn over 3f out: sn bhd) ............... 1¹/₂.7
3523⁶ Fourforfun *(RHannon)* 9-0  BRaymond (11) (bhd fnl 2f) .......................... 2.8
3512 Dancing Zena (IRE) *(MAJarvis)* 9-0  AMunro (5) (bkwd: bhd: nvr nr) ............... 5.9
3552 Wired for Sound *(MRChannon)* 9-0  JQuinn (3) (rdn 4f out: a in rr: t.o) ......... 1¹/₂.10

**11/8** Louvre (FR), **5/1** Gone Prospecting (USA), Danroy (USA), **13/2** Correspondence (CAN), **10/1** RAKIS (IRE),
**14/1** Fourforfun(op 8/1), Wired for Sound, **16/1** Dancing Zena (IRE), **20/1** Sure Right (IRE), **25/1** Boltrose. CSF
£58.64, Tote £14.90: £3.10 £2.30 £1.10 (£41.10). Mr Hamdan Al-Maktoum (EPSOM) bred by The Mount Coote
Partnership in Ireland. 10 Rn
　　　　　　　　　　　　　　　　　　　　　　　　　　　　　　　　　　1m 29.5 (9)
　　　　　　　　　　　　　　　　　　　　　　　　　　　　　　　SF—33/9/1/–/–/–

**3783**    ORCHARD H'CAP (0-70) £2448.00 (£678.00: £324.00)    **5f 16y**    4-30 (4-33)

3524² **Sir Joey (USA) (52)** **(Fav)** *(RJHolder)* 3–9-0  JWilliams (10) (hld up: hdwy over
　　　1f out: led ins fnl f: easily) ........................................................ —1
3748³ Tommy Tempest **(46)** *(KRBurke)* 3–8-8  AShoults (15) (hdwy over 2f out: ev ch
　　　ins fnl f: nt qckn) ...................................................................... 4.2
3703 Noble Power (IRE) **(66)** *(BPalling)* 3–9-9 ‡5JWeaver (11) (a.p: led wl over 1f out tl
　　　ins fnl f) ................................................................................ ³/₄.3
3596 Joe Sugden **(56)** *(PHowling)* 8–9-5  RCochrane (9) (a.p: r.o one pce fnl 2f) ... 2.4
3710⁴ Dandy Desire **(42)** *(BCMorgan)* 3–8-4  GDuffield (4) (nvr nr to chal) ............. nk.5
3596 Frimley Parkson **(32)** (bl) *(PHowling)* 8–7-9⁽²⁾ JQuinn (2) (led over 3f out tl wl
　　　over 1f out: one pce) ................................................................ nk.6
3596* John O'Dreams **(44)** *(MrsJCDawe)* 7–8-7  TSprake (14) (prom tl rdn & wknd
　　　over 1f out) ............................................................................ hd.7
3537 Yes **(51)** *(DTThom)* 4–8-7 ‡7KimMcDonnell (6) (dwlt: a bhd) ........................... 1.8
2617 Princess Jestina **(37)** *(GHYardley)* 4–7-7⁽²⁾ ‡7TWilson (1) (n.d) ................ 2.9
3507⁶ Form Mistress **(37)** (v) *(PTWalwyn)* 3–7-13  DBiggs (7) (prom: rdn 3f out: sn
　　　wknd) ...................................................................................... ¹/₂.10
3253 Miami Banker **(54)** (v) *(PHowling)* 6–9-3  TQuinn (9) (bhd fnl 2f) ................... ³/₄.11
3520 Mariette Larkin **(47)** *(GBBalding)* 3–8-6 ‡3SO'Gorman (8) (s.i.s: a bhd) ......... 3.12
3748⁶ Cronk's Quality **(33)** (bl) *(DCJermy)* 9–7-10  SDawson (3) (led over 1f: wknd
　　　over 2f out: t.o) ........................................................................ 6.13
　　　　　　　　LONG HANDICAP: Frimley Parkson 7-3.

**5/2** SIR JOEY (USA), **9/2** John O'Dreams(op 3/1), **13/2** Joe Sugden, **10/1** Miami Banker(op 20/1), Yes, Tommy
Tempest, **12/1** Noble Power (IRE), **14/1** Dandy Desire(op 8/1), **16/1** Form Mistress, Frimley Parkson, Mariette
Larkin, **20/1** Cronk's Quality, **33/1** Princess Jestina (IRE). CSF £27.70, CT £245.40. Tote £3.30: £1.40 £3.80
£5.40 (£24.20). Mrs A. G. Sims (BRISTOL) bred by William Plescia & Natalie Plescia in USA. 13 Rn
　　　　　　　　　　　　　　　　　　　　　　　　　　　　　　　　　　63.4 sec (6.4)
　　　　　　　　　　　　　　　　　　　　　　　　　　　　　SF—37/15/27/15/–/–

T/Plpt: £303.60 (7.31 Tckts).
　　　　　　　　　　　　　　　　　　　　　　　　　　　　　　　　　　　　KH

## 2896—CHESTER (L-H)
### Tuesday, October 20th [Good to soft]
Going Allowance: 1st-4th: 0.60 (Y); Rest: 0.80 sec per fur (S)　　　Wind: almost nil
Stalls: low

**3784**    SALTNEY STKS (I) (Mdn 2-Y.O) £3522.00 (£1056.00: £508.00: £234.00)
　　　　　　**7f 122y**　　　　　　　　　　　　　　　　　　　1-50 (1-54)

3362 **Kimberley Boy** *(BWHills)* 9-0  DHolland (5) (mde all: qcknd clr wl over 1f out) ... —1
3579 Fools Errand (IRE) *(RHannon)* 9-0  GHind (4) (hld up: effrt 3f out: styd on: no
　　　imp) .......................................................................................... 4.2
　　　Ertlon *(CEBrittain)* 9-0  MRoberts (2) (w'like: scope: chsd wnr: rdn 2f out: sn
　　　outpcd) ...................................................................................... ¹/₂.3
3164² Tanagome (USA) **(80)** *(SGNorton)* 8-9 ‡5OPears (1) (chsd ldrs tl rdn & wknd 2f
　　　out) .......................................................................................... 10.4

3498² **Persiansky (IRE) (73)** (Fav) *(BHanbury)* 9-0 LPiggott (3) (lw: unruly bef s: s.s: a
wl bhd) .................................................................. 12.5

9/4 Persiansky (IRE), **11/4** Fools Errand (IRE), **9/2** Ertlon(3/1—5/1), **5/1** KIMBERLEY BOY & Ors. CSF £17.06,
Tote £6.60: £2.10 £1.70 (£10.70). Mrs Angie Silver (LAMBOURN) bred by Kessly Bloodstock Ltd. 5 Rn
1m 41.05 (8.35)
SF—42/30/28/–/–

---

## 3785

LEVY BOARD CLAIMING STKS    £3912.00 (£1176.00: £568.00: £264.00)
**7f 2y**                                          2-20 (2-25)

3618⁴ **Threepence (74)** *(JBerry)* 3-8-7 GCarter (6) (chsd ldrs: led 3f out: styd on strly) —1
3632⁴ Debsy Do (USA) **(67)** *(SGNorton)* 3-7-13⁽²⁾ ‡⁵OPears (3) (cl up: led 4f out to 3f
out: one pce) ................................................ 5.2
3344 Devon Dancer **(70)** (v) *(MHEasterby)* 3-8-6 MBirch (7) (in tch: effrt u.p over 2f
out: wandered & styd on) ................................ hd.3
712 Troupe **(79)** (Fav) *(BWHills)* 4-9-0 DHolland (11) (dwlt: hdwy over 2f out: nrst fin) 1.4
3265⁴ Kummel King **(62)** *(EJAlston)* 4-8-6 KFallon (2) (led after 1f to 4f out: sn rdn &
styd on one pce) ........................................... hd.5
Cream and Green **(36)** *(KWhite)* 3-8-4 RPrice (16) (effrt ½-wy: styd on: no imp) 1½.6
3481 Jokist **(56)** *(WJarvis)* 9-8-7⁽¹⁾ JReid (4) (in tch: effrt 3f out: btn over 1f out) 2½.7
3518 Amoureuse (IRE) **(56)** *(THCaldwell)* 3-7-12 JFanning (15) (dwlt: hdwy 3f out:
no imp) ........................................................ hd.8
3496 Mentalasanythin **(77)** *(ABailey)* 3-8-11 LPiggott (13) (bhd tl styd on fnl f) ......... s.h.9
3689 Eastleigh **(62)** *(RHollinshead)* 3-8-4 ‡7AGarth (12) (nvr trbld ldrs) ................. 1½.10
3460⁶ Kentucky Rain **(56)** *(JGFitzGerald)* 3-7-11⁽¹⁾ ‡³SMaloney (14) (chsd ldrs: rdn to
chal 3f out: wknd ent st) .............................. 2.11
3476 Chance Report **(33)** *(FHLee)* 4-7-7⁽¹⁾ ‡⁵NKennedy (8) (s.i.s: gd hdwy ½-wy:
wknd over 2f out) ........................................ hd.12
3514⁵ Tusky **(70)** (v) *(MJCamacho)* 4-9-2 SMorris (5) (chsd ldrs tl wknd 2f out) .... 1½.13
3355 Sir Arthur Hobbs **(59)** *(FHLee)* 5-8-10 MRoberts (9) (n.d) ............................... 20.14
3400 Melodic Habit **(36)** *(MrsAKnight)* 5-7-11 JLowe (1) (led 1f: wknd ½-wy &
eased) ........................................................ nk.15
3596 Supreme Optimist **(29)** (bl) *(REPeacock)* 8-7-11 ‡⁵ATucker (10) (in tch to ½-wy:
sn wknd) ..................................................... hd.16

9/2 Troupe, **7/1** Debsy Do (USA), THREEPENCE, Mentalasanythin, **10/1** Kummel King(op 6/1), Tusky, **12/1**
Devon Dancer, **14/1** Sir Arthur Hobbs, Kentucky Rain, **16/1** Jokist, Eastleigh, **20/1** Amoureuse (IRE), **33/1**
Chance Report, Melodic Habit, **50/1** Ors. CSF £50.41, Tote £6.60: £2.20 £2.50 £3.40 (£17.80). Mr R. E.
Sangster (COCKERHAM) bred by The Overbury Stud. 16 Rn
1m 33.73 (7.53)
SF—43/20/26/31/22/15

---

## 3786

QUEENSFERRY GRADUATION STKS (2-Y.O.F) £4272.50 (£1280.00: £615.00: £282.50)
**6f 18y**                                       2-50 (2-55)

3530 **Hung Parliament (86)** (Fav) *(BWHills)* 9-2 DHolland (2) (lw: outpcd to ½-wy:
sn trckng ldrs: sltly hmpd over 1f out: led ins fnl f: comf) ..... —1
3570³ Lovely Bird (USA) **(MBell)** 8-8 MRoberts (6) (lw: cl up: led over 2f out: edgd rt
over 1f out: hdd & no ex ins fnl f) .............. ¾.2
3411⁴ Heathyards Gem **(59)** *(RHollinshead)* 9-2 WRyan (7) (chsd ldrs: effrt & ev ch
over 1f out: nt qckn) ..................................... 1½.3
3470 Folly Vision (IRE) **(70)** *(RHannon)* 8-8 JReid (4) (chsd ldrs to ½-wy: sn wl
outpcd) ........................................................ 20.4
Risk the Witch *(DJSCosgrove)* 8-8 KFallon (1) (leggy: unf: s.s: a outpcd & bhd) 1½.5
3590² Magic Pearl **(78)** *(EJAlston)* 8-8 LPiggott (3) (lw: led tl hdd over 2f out: sn wknd) 5.6

6/4 HUNG PARLIAMENT, **3/1** Lovely Bird (USA), **7/2** Magic Pearl, **9/1** Folly Vision (IRE)(op 6/1), **16/1**
Heathyards Gem(op 10/1), **20/1** Risk the Witch. CSF £5.82, Tote £2.30: £1.50 £2.00 (£3.00). Mr W. J. Gredley
(LAMBOURN) bred by Mrs P. A. Clark. 6 Rn
1m 22.53 (9.23)
SF—14/3/5/–/–/–

---

## 3787

OCTOBER H'CAP (0-90) £5504.00 (£1652.00: £796.00: £368.00)
**6f 18y**                                       3-20 (3-22)

3620⁵ **Nordan Raider (57)** (Jt-Fav) *(MJCamacho)* 4-7-10 JFanning (6) (lw: trckd ldrs:
slt ld ins fnl f: styd on u.p) ......................... —1
3243 Crystal Jack (FR) **(84)** *(FHLee)* 4-9-9 WRyan (10) (cl up: led wl over 1f out tl ins
fnl f: kpt on wl) ............................................. hd.2
3620 Love Legend **(77)** (bl) *(DWPArbuthnot)* 7-8-13 ‡³DHarrison (2) (b: in tch: styd
on u.p fnl 2f: nvr nrr) .................................... 5.3
3620 Breezy Day **(80)** *(BAMcMahon)* 6-8-12 ‡7JBramhill (14) (in tch: sn pushed
along: hdwy 2f out: no imp) ......................... s.h.4

| | | |
|---|---|---|
| 3680⁵ | Saddlehome (USA) (74) (RMWhitaker) 3–8-11 DMcKeown (9) (effrt whn hmpd appr st: hung bdly lft fnl 2f: nrst fin) | ³/4.5 |
| 3633³ | Gondo (74) (EJAlston) 5–8-13 KFallon (15) (s.i.s: hdwy 2f out: styd on) | ¹/2.6 |
| 3585⁴ | Precentor (61) (bl) (JDBethell) 6–8-0(¹) DHolland (4) (bhd: hdwy appr st: nvr nr to chal) | 4.7 |
| 3439 | Magic Steps (69) (CEBrittain) 3–8-6 GBaxter (5) (lw: sn outpcd & wl bhd: styd on fnl f) | ³/4.8 |
| 813 | The Auction Bidder (82) (RHollinshead) 5–9-7 LDettori (11) (prom tl wknd wl over 1f out) | hd.9 |
| 3680⁵ | Panikin (89) (JWharton) 4–9-9 ‡5SWilliams (3) (lw: s.i.s: hdwy ¹/2-wy: n.d) | 1¹/2.10 |
| 3618³ | Absolutely Nuts (73) (BAMcMahon) 3–8-10 MBirch (13) (racd wd: cl up: led wl over 3f out tl wl over 1f out: sn wknd) | ³/4.11 |
| 3537 | Sonderise (69) (NTinkler) 3–8-6 JReid (8) (s.i.s: n.d) | 3.12 |
| 3620 | Windpower (IRE) (69) (JBerry) 3–8-6 GCarter (1) (cl up to ¹/2-wy: sn lost pl) | 5.13 |
| 3703² | My Sovereign (USA) (68) (Jt-Fav) (RHannon) 3–8-5 MRoberts (12) (led tl hdd wl over 3f out: wknd qckly) | nk.14 |

6/1 My Sovereign (USA), NORDAN RAIDER, 8/1 Crystal Jack (FR), Panikin, Gondo, 10/1 Saddlehome (USA), Breezy Day, Precentor, 12/1 Love Legend, Windpower (IRE), 14/1 Magic Steps, Sonderise, Absolutely Nuts, 20/1 The Auction Bidder. CSF £52.55, CT £525.43. Tote £7.10: £2.50 £2.80 £2.70 (£32.10). Miss J. A. Camacho (MALTON) bred by B. Nordan. 14 Rn　　　　　1m 20.50 (7.20)

SF—34/60/49/45/42/28

**3788** TATTENHALL H'CAP (3-Y.O) (0-90) £4305.00 (£1290.00: £620.00: £285.00)
1m 7f 195y
3-50 (3-53)

| | | |
|---|---|---|
| 3603³ | Iota (64) (Jt-Fav) (MrsJCecil) 8-5 MRoberts (5) (hld up: hdwy ¹/2-wy: led wl over 1f out: styd on) | —1 |
| 3467³ | Kaiser Wilhelm (77) (HRACecil) 9-4 WRyan (6) (lw: trckd ldrs: led 4f out tl wl over 1f out: kpt on wl nr fin) | 1.2 |
| 3666 | Five to Seven (USA) (76) (SGNorton) 8-12 ‡5OPears (4) (led tl hdd 4f out: one pce) | 4.3 |
| 3666⁴ | Prince Mercury (80) (Jt-Fav) (JLDunlop) 9-7 JReid (3) (hld up: effrt over 4f out: nvr drvn along: styd on: nvr able to chal) | 1.4 |
| 3675⁴ | Mad Militant (IRE) (79) (RHollinshead) 9-6 LDettori (7) (hld up & bhd: hdwy 5f out: sn rdn & no imp) | 20.5 |
| 3586² | Kadari (62) (AHarrison) 8-0 ‡3DHarrison (1) (chsd ldrs tl rdn & wknd 5f out) | 7.6 |
| 3490² | Two and Sixpence (USA) (68) (BWHills) 8-9 DHolland (2) (prom tl outpcd 6f out: sn to & eased) | dist.7 |

7/2 Prince Mercury, IOTA, 4/1 Two and Sixpence (USA), Kaiser Wilhelm, 9/1 Kadari, 10/1 Ors. CSF £16.43, Tote £3.10: £2.00 £2.90 (£7.10). Sheikh Mohammed (NEWMARKET) bred by Sheikh Mohammed bin Rashid al Maktoum. 7 Rn　　　　　3m 51.71 (26.71)

**3789** BUNBURY H'CAP (0-80) £4825.00 (£1450.00: £700.00: £325.00)
1¹/4m 75y
4-20 (4-23)

| | | |
|---|---|---|
| 3634⁴ | Westholme (USA) (67) (MHEasterby) 4-9-7 MBirch (12) (gd hdwy 5f out: led wl over 3f out: styd on u.p fnl f) | —1 |
| 2477⁶ | Bighayir (74) (bl) (MCPipe) 5–9-11 ‡3DHarrison (2) (chsd ldrs tl outpcd over 2f out: styd on wl fnl f) | 1¹/2.2 |
| 3576² | Cachou (USA) (71) (Fav) (JHMGosden) 3–9-6 MRoberts (17) (pushed along 7f out: hdwy 4f out: kpt on one pce fnl f) | 2.3 |
| 3718 | No Comebacks (57) (EJAlston) 4–8-11 KFallon (13) (bhd tl gd hdwy 5f out: chal wl over 3f out: no ex fnl f) | hd.4 |
| 3349 | Mingus (USA) (56) (MrsJRRamsden) 5–8-5 ‡StephenDavies (5) (lw: bhd: hdwy ent st: styd on: nvr able to chal) | 2.5 |
| 3696* | Falcons Dawn (57) (ABailey) 5–8-13 (6x) GBaxter (9) (hdwy 4f out: sn chsng ldrs: one pce fnl f) | 1¹/2.6 |
| 3627⁴ | Katy's Lad (65) (BAMcMahon) 5–9-5 JFortune (8) (a chsng ldrs: rdn & one pce wl over 2f out) | hd.7 |
| 3615⁶ | Young Jason (49) (FHLee) 9–8-3(¹) ACulhane (6) (bhd: sme hdwy over 2f out: n.d) | 7.8 |
| 3040⁶ | Inan (USA) (69) (JLDunlop) 3–9-4 JReid (11) (hdwy to chse ldrs 4f out: rdn & btn over 1f out) | 3¹/2.9 |
| 3576⁴ | Twilight Secret (61) (JWHills) 3–8-10 LPiggott (16) (prom tl rdn & btn over 1f out: eased fnl f) | ³/4.10 |
| 3622³ | Mardessa (55) (FHLee) 4–8-9 LDettori (10) (lw: nvr bttr than mid div) | 1¹/2.11 |
| 2473 | Rose Glen (64) (ABailey) 6–8-13 ‡5ATucker (1) (chsd ldrs tl wknd 4f out) | 3¹/2.12 |
| 3640⁴ | Double Echo (IRE) (67) (JDBethell) 4–9-7 DMcKeown (14) (lw: chsd ldrs tl wknd 4f out) | 1¹/2.13 |

3206[4] Caspian Beluga (63) *(MrsAKnight)* 4-8-12 ‡5OPears (4) (led tl hdd 4f out: sn wknd) .................................................................. hd.14
3640[6] Mbulwa (56) *(SEKettlewell)* 6-8-10 GCarter (15) (in tch: rdn 6f out: sn lost pl) 15.15
3682[2] In the Money (IRE) (68) *(RHollinshead)* 3-9-3 WRyan (3) (disp ld after 2f: led 4f out: sn hdd & wknd) ................................................ 10.16

3/1 Cachou (USA), 13/2 Mardessa, 9/1 Falcons Dawn, 10/1 Mingus (USA), Katy's Lad, 12/1 Rose Glen, WESTHOLME (USA)(op 8/1), Twilight Secret, 14/1 No Comebacks, Caspian Beluga, Bighayir, Double Echo (IRE), 16/1 Inan (USA), 20/1 In the Money (IRE), 25/1 Ors. CSF £164.48, CT £586.39. Tote £19.00: £3.10 £3.00 £1.70 £3.50 (£151.80). Mr T. H. Bennett (MALTON) bred by Clovelly Farm Div. Gen. Agri Services in USA. 16 Rn
2m 24.72 (14.72)
SF–43/44/35/25/15/18

**3790**　　SALTNEY STKS (II) (Mdn 2-Y.O) £3522.00 (£1056.00: £508.00: £234.00)
　　7f 122y　　　　　　　　　　　　　　　　　　　　　　　　　　　4-50 (4-51)

3525[4] **Jackpot Star (90)** (Fav) *(RHannon)* 9-0 LPiggott (5) (s.s: rapid hdwy ¹/₂-wy: led wl over 2f out: sn clr) .......................................... —1
3644[4] Demurrer *(JGFitzGerald)* 9-0 KFallon (6) (sn outpcd: styd on fnl 2f: no ch w wnr) 10.2
3626[4] Glorious Island (63) *(RFJohnsonHoughton)* 9-0 DHolland (2) (chsd ldrs: effrt over 2f out: one pce) ................................................. 2¹/₂.3
3587[6] Arc Bright (IRE) (75) *(RHollinshead)* 9-0 WRyan (1) (chsd ldrs: effrt ¹/₂-wy: no imp) ..................................................................... ³/₄.4
3775[5] My Ballyboy (43) (bl) *(ABailey)* 9-0 GBaxter (4) (led & sn clr: hdd wl over 2f out: sn wknd) ............................................................. 2¹/₂.5
3523[3] Davrob *(BPalling)* 9-0 GCarter (3) (outpcd after 2f: sn t.o) ................... dist.6

10/11 JACKPOT STAR, 4/1 Arc Bright (IRE), 9/2 Glorious Island, 10/1 Demurrer, 16/1 My Ballyboy, 20/1 Davrob. CSF £9.19, Tote £1.80: £1.10 £2.70 (£5.80). N.T.C. (Racing) Limited (MARLBOROUGH) bred by The Overbury Stud. 6 Rn
1m 43.77 (11.07)
SF–24/–/–/–/–/–

T/Trio: Race 4: £225.50 (3 Tckts) & Race 6: £242.60 (3 Tckts). T/Plpt: £449.10 (9.9 Tckts).　　AA

2896—**CHESTER (L-H)**
## Wednesday, October 21st [Heavy]
Going Allowance: 1.00 sec per fur (S)　　　　　　　　　　　Wind: almost nil

Stalls: low

**3791**　　CARDEN GRADUATION STKS (2-Y.O) £3899.00 (£1172.00: £566.00: £263.00)
　　7f 2y　　　　　　　　　　　　　　　　　　　　　　　　　　　1-50 (1-52)

3619* **Heathyards Boy (85)** *(RHollinshead)* 9-4 WRyan (1) (a.p: rdn to ld over 1f out: styd on wl) ............................................................... —1
3205 Ihtiraz (94) *(HThomsonJones)* 9-4 RHills (2) (hld up: hdwy & ev ch over 1f out: rdn & nt qckn) .................................................. 3¹/₂.2
3677[3] Colway Rock (USA) (97) (Fav) *(JWWatts)* 9-4 GDuffield (6) (hld up: effrt ¹/₂-wy: sn drvn clr & nvr able to chal) ........................................ 1¹/₂.3
3753[4] Celestial Key (USA) (90) (v) *(SGNorton)* 9-4 KDarley (3) (led: qcknd after 2f: hdd over 1f out: sn btn) ...................................................... 1.4
3593[5] Moussahim (USA) *(MRStoute)* 8-11 WRSwinburn (4) (hld up: effrt over 2f out: rdn & no imp) ................................................................ 4.5
3432[2] Top Pet (IRE) (91) *(RHannon)* 9-0 MRoberts (5) (chsd ldrs tl wknd over 2f out) 2¹/₂.6

9/4 Colway Rock (USA), 11/4 Top Pet (IRE), 9/2 Ihtiraz, 13/2 Moussahim (USA), HEATHYARDS BOY, 12/1 Celestial Key (USA). CSF £31.00, Tote £5.70: £2.30 £2.50 (£20.90). Mr L. A. Morgan (UPPER LONGDON) bred by G. W. Hampson. 6 Rn
1m 36.93 (10.73)
SF–48/37/32/29/10/11

**3792**　　MARFORD STKS (Mdn 2-Y.O) £3860.00 (£1160.00: £560.00: £260.00)
　　6f 18y　　　　　　　　　　　　　　　　　　　　　　　　　　　2-20 (2-21)

**Guv's Joy (IRE)** *(BWHills)* 8-9 DHolland (6) (neat: trckd ldrs: led appr fnl f: qcknd: comf) ...................................................................... —1
3642[2] Nutty Brown (76) (Fav) *(SGNorton)* 9-0 KDarley (3) (disp ld tl hdd over 1f out: kpt on one pce) .................................................... 3¹/₂.2
3665 Range Rider (IRE) (74) *(CEBrittain)* 9-0 MRoberts (10) (in tch: effrt u.p appr st: hung lft & styd on) ................................................... 2¹/₂.3
3275 Waterlord (IRE) (62) *(CGCox)* 9-0 LDettori (5) (chsd ldrs: chal 3f out: rdn & btn 1f out) ........................................................................ ¹/₂.4

3503 M a El-Sahn *(RHannon)* 9-0 JReid (8) (bhd: stdy hdwy 2f out: rdn appr fnl f: nt qckn) ............................................................... 1½.5
3519 Mujawab *(HThomsonJones)* 9-0 RHills (2) (a.p: effrt & ch over 1f out: sn rdn & btn) ............................................................... ¾.6
3599 Sian Wyn *(KRBurke)* 8-9 AShoults (7) (nvr wnt pce) ............................................................... 7.7
3626 Mansard (IRE) **(78)** (v) *(JHMGosden)* 9-0 SCauthen (4) (disp ld tl wknd over 1f out) ............................................................... 5.8
3694² La Bonita (IRE) **(61)** (v) *(JBerry)* 8-9 JCarroll (9) (chsd ldrs 4f) ............................................................... 3½.9
3382 Honeymoon Dawn *(LJCodd)* 8-2 ‡7WHollick (1) (prom 4f: sn wknd) ............................................................... 2½.10

**100/30** Nutty Brown, **6/1** Range Rider (IRE), **13/2** Mansard (IRE), La Bonita (IRE), **7/1** GUV'S JOY (IRE)(op 4/1), Mujawab, **9/1** M a El-Sahn, **16/1** Waterlord, **50/1** Ors. CSF £26.61. Tote £6.80: £2.20 £1.50 £2.40 (£15.30). Mr Alan Lamont (LAMBOURN) bred by Curative Ltd in Ireland. 10 Rn ............ 1m 23.34 (10.04)
SF—14/8/–/–/–/–/

---

## 3793

TARPORLEY H'CAP (0-100) £5426.00 (£1628.00: £784.00: £362.00)
**7f 122y**

2-50 (2-55)

3681³ **Sagebrush Roller (69)** *(JWWatts)* 4–8-12 GDuffield (12) (bhd: hdwy appr st: led 1f out: pushed clr) ............................................................... —1
3689⁵ Cee-Jay-Ay **(56)** *(JBerry)* 5–7-13 LCharnock (9) (hdwy 4f out: chal over 1f out: kpt on one pce) ............................................................... 2½.2
3269⁶ Clare Kerry Lass **(74)** *(JRFanshawe)* 3–9-0 WRSwinburn (1) (pushed along 4f out: hdwy & ch wl over 1f out: no ex) ............................................................... 1½.3
3729⁵ Colossus **(63)** (Fav) *(CEBrittain)* 4–8-6 MRoberts (7) (lw: s.i.s: sn chsng ldrs: led wl over 1f out tl hdd 1f out: no ex) ............................................................... 2½.4
3681⁶ Choir Practice **(69)** *(WJHaggas)* 5–8-12 CRutter (11) (in tch: effrt over 3f out: one pce appr fnl f) ............................................................... 3.5
3310² Causley **(76)** *(BAMcMahon)* 7–9-5 MBirch (5) (led tl hdd wl over 1f out: grad wknd) ............................................................... ¾.6
3539 Snowgirl (IRE) **(68)** *(JBerry)* 4–8-11 JCarroll (4) (lw: chsd ldrs: chal wl over 2f out: wknd wl over 1f out) ............................................................... ½.7
858 Scarlatine (IRE) **(80)** *(JHMGosden)* 3–9-6 RCochrane (4) (bhd: hdwy ent st: nvr trbld ldrs) ............................................................... 6.8
2019³ Martina **(67)** *(JWharton)* 4–8-10 JWilliams (13) (sn outpcd & bhd: sme late hdwy) ............................................................... 1½.9
3640⁵ Tamim (USA) **(87)** *(HThomsonJones)* 3–9-13 RHills (6) (chsd ldrs tl wknd wl over 1f out) ............................................................... 7.10
3620⁶ Veloce (IRE) **(58)** (v) *(ABailey)* 4–8-1 WCarson (2) (plld hrd: cl up tl rdn & wknd qckly 3f out) ............................................................... 8.11
3185⁴ Predictable **(53)** *(MrsAKnight)* 6–7-10 JQuinn (3) (cl up tl wknd qckly 3f out) ... 4.12
3417 Domicksky **(70)** *(MRChannon)* 4–8-13 SCauthen (10) (in tch 4f: sn bhd) ...... 2½.13

**11/2** Colossus(4/1—6/1), **6/1** SAGEBRUSH ROLLER, **15/2** Cee-Jay-Ay, **8/1** Veloce (IRE), **9/1** Causley, **10/1** Choir Practice, Scarlatine (IRE), **12/1** Clare Kerry Lass, **14/1** Domicksky, Martina, **16/1** Snowgirl (IRE), **20/1** Tamim (USA), **25/1** Predictable. CSF £44.96, CT £472.74. Tote £5.70: £2.10 £2.80 £3.30 (£17.30). Mr A. K. Collins (RICHMOND) bred by Shutford Stud. 13 Rn ............ 1m 43.24 (10.54)
SF—53/32/42/26/23/28

---

## 3794

FRODSHAM H'CAP (0-95) £5426.00 (£1628.00: £784.00: £362.00)
**1¼m 75y**

3-20 (3-24)

2906⁵ Lost Reputation (IRE) **(82)** *(BWHills)* 3–8-12 DHolland (4) (chsd ldrs: drvn along 5f out: led 1f out: styd on wl) ............................................................... —1
3415 Major's Law (IRE) **(70)** *(CEBrittain)* 3–8-0(5) MRoberts (6) (led: shkn up & qcknd 4f out: hdd 1f out: no ex) ............................................................... 3.2
3547 Barford Lad **(78)** *(JRFanshawe)* 5–8-13 LDettori (8) (hld up: stdy hdwy 3f out: ch & effrt over 1f out: nt qckn) ............................................................... 2½.3
3718* Loki (IRE) **(79)** (Fav) *(GLewis)* 4–8-7 ‡7BRussell (5) (hdwy ½-wy: chsd ldrs ent st: rdn & one pce) ............................................................... 5.4
3789⁶ Falcons Dawn **(58)** *(ABailey)* 5–7-0 (6x) ‡7DWright (3) (bhd: hdwy over 3f out: no imp) ............................................................... 10.5
3785 Mentalasanythin **(77)** *(ABailey)* 3–8-7 GBaxter (2) (bhd tl styd on fnl 2f: n.d) .... hd.6
589* Rockawhile (IRE) **(96)** *(HRACecil)* 3–9-12 WRyan (7) (trckd ldrs: effrt 2f out: sn rdn & no ex) ............................................................... 2½.7
Administer **(70)** *(LJCodd)* 4–7-12 ‡7WHollick (11) (chsd ldrs tl outpcd over 2f out: n.d after) ............................................................... 2.8
3434³ Duc de Berry (USA) **(79)** (bl) *(GHarwood)* 4–9-0 WCarson (9) (prom tl wknd u.p over 3f out) ............................................................... ¾.9
3122 Scrutineer (USA) **(88)** *(JHMGosden)* 3–9-4 SCauthen (10) (chsd ldrs tl wknd over 2f out) ............................................................... 10.10
3627 El Nido **(67)** *(MJCamacho)* 4–8-2 NConnorton (1) (bhd fnl 4f) ............................................................... ½.11

LONG HANDICAP: Falcons Dawn 7-6.

11/4 Loki (IRE), 15/2 Barford Lad, 8/1 Scrutineer (USA), Rockawhile (IRE), Major's Law (IRE), 10/1 Falcons Dawn, El Nido, LOST REPUTATION (IRE), 12/1 Duc de Berry (USA), 16/1 Mentalasanythin, 33/1 Administer. CSF £77.53, CT £574.24. Tote £10.00: £2.70 £2.00 £2.10 (£40.40). Mr R. E. Sangster (LAMBOURN) bred by Seahorse Investments in Ireland. 11 Rn　　　　　　　　　　　　　　　　　　　　　　2m 25.46 (15.46)
SF—43/25/33/17/–/–

**3795**　　HESWALL GRADUATION STKS (3-Y.O) £4110.00 (£1230.00: £590.00: £270.00)
　　　　　1¹/₂m 66y　　　　　　　　　　　　　　　　　　　　　　　　　　　3-50 (3-54)

3676* Jasoorah (IRE) (86) (Fav) (ACStewart) 9-2 MRoberts (3) (lw: a.p: led over 3f out: pushed along & r.o wl) ............................................................. —1
3697³ Anchorage (IRE) (89) (HRACecil) 8-13 SCauthen (6) (dwlt: sn in tch: hdwy 3f out: no ch w wnr) .......... 12.2
3676² Shahaamh (IRE) (86) (HThomsonJones) 8-13 RHills (4) (led tl hdd over 3f out: wknd wl over 1f out) .......... 20.3
3594² Barahin (IRE) (83) (JLDunlop) 9-4 WCarson (2) (chsd ldrs tl outpcd 4f out: sn t.o) .......... 20.4
820 El Cortes (USA) (99) (PWChapple-Hyam) 9-4 JReid (5) (lost tch 4f out: sn t.o) .. 4.5
3636² Faugeron (16/1) Widdrawn (unfit to r) : not under orders

11/10 JASOORAH (IRE), 3/1 Anchorage (IRE), 13/2 El Cortes (USA), 8/1 Shahaamh (IRE), 10/1 Barahin (IRE). CSF £4.30, Tote £2.00: £1.10 £1.60 (£2.10). Sheikh Ahmed Al Maktoum (NEWMARKET) bred by Miss K.Rausing, Mrs S.Rogers & M.Ryan in Ireland. 5 Rn　　　　　　　　　2m 57.93 (21.33)
SF—12/–/–/–/–/

**3796**　　BEESTON CASTLE NURSERY　　£4662.50 (£1400.00: £675.00: £312.50)
　　　　　7f 122y　　　　　　　　　　　　　　　　　　　　　　　　　　　4-20 (4-24)

3574 The Seer (82) (BWIlills) 0 7 DHolland (2) (hdwy after 3f: chal & hung lft over 1f out: styd on to ld cl home) .......... —1
3602* Anaxagoras (80) (AAScott) 9-5 JFortune (3) (lw: led 1f: cl up: led over 2f out: hdwy rdn fnl f: jst ct) .......... hd.2
3385* Hi Nod (74) (MJCamacho) 8-13 NConnorton (10) (lw: trckd ldrs: effrt 2f out: nt qckn fnl f) .......... 3¹/₂.3
3754 Mighty Miss Magpie (IRE) (58) (MRChannon) 7-11⁽¹⁾ CRutter (8) (chsd ldrs: hdwy 2f out: one pce fnl f) .......... hd.4
3187 Fairy Story (IRE) (71) (JWHills) 8-10 JWilliams (4) (in tch: effrt 2f out: no ex fnl f) .......... 4.5
3497² Always Risky (62) (Fav) (ABailey) 8-1 WCarson (9) (led after 1f tl over 2f out: wknd wl over 1f out) .......... 1¹/₂.6
2719² Ann Hill (IRE) (58) (RHollinshead) 7-4⁽¹⁾ ‡7AGarth (7) (outpcd ¹/₂-wy: n.d after) .......... 1¹/₂.7
3274 Don't Forget Marie (IRE) (72) (RHannon) 8-11 MRoberts (5) (sn drvn along & bhd) .......... 8.8
3354⁴ Drumdonna (IRE) (75) (JBerry) 9-0 SWood (6) (dwlt: a bhd) .......... 6.9
3665 Awestruck (77) (WJHaggas) 9-2 GDuffield (1) (lw: prom tl rdn & wknd after wl over 2f: sn bhd) .......... 2.10

11/4 Always Risky, 4/1 Anaxagoras, 5/1 Hi Nod, 8/1 THE SEER(tchd 12/1), 10/1 Awestruck, Fairy Story (IRE), 12/1 Don't Forget Marie (IRE), 20/1 Ors. CSF £37.49, CT £158.53. Tote £11.80: £2.40 £2.00 £1.80 (£15.40). Mr A. R. B. Aspinall (LAMBOURN) bred by Mrs B. Skinner. 10 Rn　　1m 45.78 (13.08)
SF—23/20/3/–/–/–/

T/Trio: Race 3: 65.80 (18.2 Tckts) & Race 4: £92.30 (9.1 Tckts) T/Plpt: £211.10 (22.51 Tckts).　　　　　AA

3359—**NEWBURY (L-H)**
**Thursday, October 22nd [Soft]**
Going Allowance: St: 1.00 sec per fur; Rnd: 0.80 sec per fur (S)　　　　Wind: almost nil

Stalls: centre

**3797**　　VODAFONE BRITISH AND NORTHERN RACING SCHOOLS APP'CE H'CAP (0-80)
　　　　　£2784.00 (£774.00: £372.00)　　7f (st)　　　　　　　　　　　2-05 (2-08)

3689⁴ Penny Drops (54) (Fav) (LordHuntingdon) 3-8-4 DHarrison (9) (hdwy over 2f out: hrd rdn over 1f out: led wl ins fnl f: r.o wl) ............................................................. —1
3698⁶ Royal Dartmouth (USA) (47) (BRMillman) 7-8-0 KRutter (10) (hld up: led 2f out tl wl ins fnl f: unable qckn) .......... 1¹/₂.2
3391* Zeboim (71) (bl) (WRMuir) 6-9-10 KimMcDonnell (11) (led 5f out to 2f out: one pce) .......... 3¹/₂.3
3281³ Hopeful Bid (IRE) (71) (bl) (RHannon) 3-9-1 ‡⁶MarkDenaro (12) (lw: led 2f: one pce fnl 2f) .......... 6.4
1338 Corrin Hill (63) (BWHills) 5-8-10 ‡⁶SMcCarthy (13) (hdwy over 1f out: nvr nrr) ... 1.5

3689 Amethystine (USA) **(62)** *(RJHodges)* 6–8-9 ‡⁶WHollick (16) (nvr nr to chal) ........ 2.6
3605⁵ Zinbaq **(46)** *(CJBenstead)* 6–7-7⁽⁶⁾ ‡⁶DToole (4) (lw: prom over 5f) .................... ½.7
3689 Just a Step **(70)** *(MMcCormack)* 6–9-6 ‡³SMulvey (14) (nvr nrr) ........................ ½.8
3487 Gold Jubilee **(55)** *(PJMakin)* 3–7-13⁽³⁾ ‡⁶CWebb (21) (swtg: a mid div) ............ hd.9
3524 Leigh Crofter **(60)** *(PGMurphy)* 3–8-10 SDrowne (2) (prom over 5f) .............. 2½.12
3612² Morocco (IRE) **(75)** *(RCharlton)* 3–9-5 ‡⁶RhonaGent (3) (lw: nvr nrr) ............... 2.11
3747³ Brooks Express (FR) **(47)** *(RAkehurst)* 3–8-8 ‡³GMilligan (15) (a mid div) ...... 1½.12
3667⁶ Hightown-Princess (IRE) **(53)** (v) *(MPMuggeridge)* 4–8-0⁽¹³⁾ ‡⁶RossBerry (18)
            (nvr nrr) .............................................................................................. hd.13
3473³ Thewaari (USA) **(67)** *(AAScott)* 3–9-3 JTate (20) (outpcd) ........................... ¾.14
3681⋆ Highland Magic (IRE) **(70)** *(MJFetherston-Godley)* 4–9-9 NKennedy (7) (a bhd) 6.15
3701 Skipper to Bilge **(67)** *(MAJarvis)* 5–9-6 FArrowsmith (5) (prom over 3f) ............ 1.16
*3185* Looting (USA) **(46)** *(MDIUsher)* 6–7-10⁽⁴⁾ ‡³AMartinez (17) (bhd fnl 3f) ........... nk.17
3700⋆ Bill Moon **(56)** *(PJFeilden)* 6–8-9 (6x) StephenDavies (1) (lw: prom over 4f) .. 1½.18
3524 Roxy Music (IRE) **(47)** *(KOCunningham-Brown)* 3–7-5 ‡⁶JWilkinson (8) (prom
            over 3f) ............................................................................................... nk.19
3689 Charmed Knave **(55)** *(DRLaing)* 7–8-8 ATucker (6) (prom 4f) ............................ 3.20
         LONG HANDICAP: Zinbaq 7-6, Hightown-Princess (IRE) 7-2.

**5/1** PENNY DROPS, **6/1** Highland Magic (IRE), **8/1** Bill Moon(op 5/1), **9/1** Morocco (IRE), **10/1** Zinbaq, **12/1** Skipper to Bilge, **14/1** Thewaari (USA), Zeboim(10/1—16/1), Brooks Express (FR), **16/1** Hopeful Bid (IRE)(op 10/1), Royal Dartmouth (USA), Charmed Knave, **20/1** Leigh Crofter, **33/1** Ors. CSF £73.56, CT £939.63. Tote £4.20: £1.50 £4.40 £5.10 £3.90 (£58.70). Mr Stanley J. Sharp (WEST ILSLEY) bred by T. M. Saud. 20 Rn
                                                         1m 33.64 (9.14)
                                                    SF—58/49/62/35/27/20

---

**3798**     VODAFONE GROUP H'CAP (3-Y.O) (0-100) £3850.00 (£1150.00: £550.00: £250.00)
           **1m 5f 61y**                                                 2–40 (2-44)

3082⋆ **Daru (USA) (92)** (v) *(JHMGosden)* 8–13 SCauthen (4) (lw: hdwy ins fnl 2f
            out: led ins fnl f: rdn out) ....................................................................... —1
3668⋆ Ivor's Flutter **(77)** *(DRCElsworth)* 7–7-7⁽²⁾ ‡⁵BDoyle (1) (hdwy 3f out: led over 1f out
            tl ins fnl f: unable qckn) ...................................................................... 2½.2
3369² Welsh Mill (IRE) **(87)** *(LordHuntingdon)* 8–8 WRSwinburn (3) (led 12f: ev ch ins
            fnl f: one pce) ..................................................................................... 2.3
3743² Alyafil (USA) **(72)** *(BHanbury)* 7–7 JFanning (2) (lost pl 8f out: r.o one pce fnl 2f) ¾.4
3467² Top Spin **(83)** *(MajorWRHern)* 8–4 JWilliams (9) (lw: nvr nr to chal) ............... hd.5
3515 Antiguan Flyer **(80)** *(BWHills)* 8–1⁽¹⁾ PaulEddery (8) (2nd st: wknd wl over 1f
            out) ...................................................................................................... 10.6
3609⋆ River Anchor **(75)** *(RCharlton)* 7–7-7⁽³⁾ ‡³DHarrison (10) (6th st: wknd over 2f out) 5.7
3415 Mootawel (USA) **(72)** *(HThomsonJones)* 7–7 NCarlisle (6) (5th st: wknd over 3f
            out) ...................................................................................................... 1½.8
3492⋆ Crystal Cross **(80)** *(IABalding)* 8–1 WCarson (7) (3rd st: wknd 3f out) ...... 6.9
3032² Citiqueen (IRE) **(100)** *(HRACecil)* 9–7 LPiggott (5) (4th st: wknd over 2f out) .. 2.10
         LONG HANDICAP: Alyafil (USA) 7-5, Mootawel (USA) 7-6.

**100/30** DARU (USA), **6/1** Crystal Cross (USA), **13/2** Welsh Mill (IRE), **7/1** River Anchor, **15/2** Ivor's Flutter, Citiqueen (IRE)(op 5/1), **8/1** Alyafil (USA), Top Spin, **10/1** Antiguan Flyer, **20/1** Mootawel (USA). CSF £27.68, CT £144.53. Tote £3.90: £1.80 £3.00 £2.10 (£24.10). Sheikh Mohammed (NEWMARKET) bred by Albert G. Clay & Charlotte Clay Buxton. 10 Rn
                                                        3m 3.89 (18.19)
                                                    SF—23/–/9/–/2/–/–

---

**3799**     VODAFONE HORRIS HILL STKS (Gp 3) (2-Y.O.C & G) £25580.00 (£9559.00: £4579.50:
           £1981.50)    **7f 64y**                                            3–10 (3-14)

3541⁴ **Beggarman Thief (USA) (84)** *(JHMGosden)* 8–12 RCochrane (4) (s.s: hdwy 2f
            out: led 1f out: rdn out) ........................................................................ —1
3644⁴ Bin Ajwaad (IRE) **(82)** *(BHanbury)* 8–12 SCauthen (9) (hdwy over 2f out: led over 1f
            out: sn hdd: unable qckn) .................................................................... 2.2
3541⁵ Port Lucaya **(100)** (bl) *(RHannon)* 8–12 JReid (8) (lw: 5th st: rdn over 2f out: one
            pce) ..................................................................................................... 3.3
3541⋆ Nominator **(100)** *(RHollinshead)* 9–1 WCarson (10) (2nd st: led over 2f out tl
            over 1f out: one pce) .......................................................................... hd.4
3092⋆ Kusamba (USA) **(82)** *(RCharlton)* 8–12 MHills (6) (6th st: lost pl over 3f out: r.o one
            pce fnl 2f) .......................................................................................... 3.5
3541² Urgent Request (IRE) **(96)** *(BWHills)* 8–12 PatEddery (3) (lw: led 5f) ............ 2.6
2905⋆ Desert Shot **(100)** *(MRStoute)* 8–12 WRSwinburn (7) (hdwy over 2f out: wknd
            over 1f out) ......................................................................................... ¾.7
3722 Zimzalabim **(94)** *(BWHills)* 8–12 JWilliams (1) (a bhd) .................................. 2½.8
3367³ Sharp Prod (USA) **(100)** *(LordHuntingdon)* 9–3 LPiggott (2) (lw: 4th st: wknd 2f
            out) ...................................................................................................... 1½.9
2025⋆ New Capricorn (USA) **(100)** *(MAJarvis)* 8–12 BRaymond (11) (3rd st: wknd over
            2f out) ................................................................................................. 5.10

3693[3] Press Gallery *(MrsJCecil)* 8-12 PaulEddery (5) (swtg: hdwy over 3f out: wknd over 2f out) ............................................................ 1½.11

**3/1** Urgent Request (IRE), **5/1** Desert Shot, BEGGARMAN THIEF (USA), **7/1** Bin Ajwaad (IRE), **8/1** Sharp Prod (USA), **10/1** Nominator, **11/1** Kusamba (USA), **14/1** Zimzalabim, **25/1** Press Gallery, Port Lucaya, **33/1** New Capricorn (USA). CSF £36.22, Tote £5.00: £1.90 £2.30 £4.80 (£18.50). Mr Landon Knight (NEWMARKET) bred by Landon Knight in USA. 11 Rn
1m 35.24 (7.94)
SF—66/60/51/53/41/35

## 3800

AMEC BUILDING H'CAP (0-100) £7928.00 (£2384.00: £1152.00: £536.00)
**1m (st)**
3-40 (3-43)

3591* **Heart of Darkness (93)** (v) *(IABalding)* 4-10-0 RCochrane (11) (lw: hld up: led wl over 1f out: rdn out) ...................................................... —1

3640[2] Shaffaaf (USA) (67) (v) *(PDEvans)* 4-8-2 MHills (6) (hld up: chsd wnr over 1f out: r.o) ..................................................................... 1½.2

3543 Knock to Enter (USA) (84) *(MRStoute)* 4-9-5 WRSwinburn (10) (swtg: hld up: rdn over 2f out: one pce) ....................................... 5.3

692[2] Sharp N' Smooth (72) *(RHannon)* 5-8-7 LPiggott (12) (lw: hld up: hrd rdn over 1f out: one pce) ..................................................... s.h.4

3681 Aghaadir (USA) (84) *(JHMGosden)* 4-9-5 SCauthen (1) (lw: racd alone: a.p: hrd rdn over 1f out: wknd fnl f) ................................ 4.5

3370 Talent (USA) (86) (v) *(LordHuntingdon)* 4-9-7 BRaymond (7) (led 3f: wknd 2f out) 5.6

1463 Wild and Loose (82) *(DRCElsworth)* 4-9-3 JWilliams (8) (nvr nrr) .......................... 5.7

3690* Pippin Park (USA) (69) *(HCandy)* 3-7-8 ‡7AntoinetteArmes (4) (prom over 5f) .. hd.8

3547 Marine Diver (71) *(BRMillman)* 6-8-6 DaleGibson (9) (plld hrd: led 5f out tl wl over 1f out: sn wknd) ......................................... 1½.9

3640* Forever Diamonds (75) (Fav) *(MHEasterby)* 5-8-10 MBirch (2) (bhd fnl 2f) ....... 1.10

3686[2] Amaze (90) *(LadyHerries)* 3-9-8 JReid (5) (b: bhd fnl 2f) ............................ ¾.11

3673 Daswaki (CAN) (72) *(RHannon)* 4-0-7 DNouoo (3) (a bhd) ....................... 10.12

**7/2** Forever Diamonds, **4/1** HEART OF DARKNESS(5/1—6/1), **7/1** Amaze, **8/1** Knock to Enter (USA)(op 5/1), Shaffaaf (USA)(10/1—12/1), **9/1** Aghaadir (USA), **12/1** Pippin Park (USA), Sharp N' Smooth, Daswaki (CAN), **14/1** Marine Diver, **20/1** Ors. CSF £35.36, CT £226.25. Tote £4.40: £1.90 £2.60 £3.00 (£26.90). Mr Paul Mellon (KINGSCLERE) bred by Paul Mellon. 12 Rn
1m 48.18 (11.18)
SF—66/35/37/24/24/11

## 3801

ENBORNE STKS (Mdn 3-Y.O) £4077.50 (£1220.00: £585.00: £267.50)
**1¼m 6y**
4-10 (4-13)

**Highland Dress** *(MRStoute)* 9-0 CDwyer (7) (w'like: hdwy over 3f out: led 1f out: r.o wl) ............................................................................ —1

3682[6] Tunbridge Wells (IRE) (85) (Fav) *(JHMGosden)* 9-0 GHind (3) (2nd st: led over 4f out to 1f out: unable qckn) ....................................... 3.2

Alwatar (USA) *(ACStewart)* 8-9 AMcGlone (2) (leggy: 4th st: ev ch over 2f out: hrd rdn over 1f out: one pce) ............................. 2½.3

3389[3] Time for a Flutter *(DRCElsworth)* 8-9 AShoults (4) (hdwy over 2f out: r.o one pce) ................................................................. ¾.4

Hudud (USA) *(ACStewart)* 8-9 GCrealock (5) (unf: scope: 5th st: one pce fnl 3f) 2.5

3554 Will Soon (66) *(HCandy)* 9-0 CRutter (14) (hdwy over 2f out: wknd fnl f) ......... ¾.6

3506[6] Literary Critic (IRE) (bl) *(JARToller)* 9-0 DaleGibson (6) (3rd st: wknd over 2f out) ............................................................... 10.7

1948[5] Choppy Choppy (USA) (68) *(BWHills)* 8-9 RStreet (12) (nvr nr to chal) ............ s.h.8

3667[5] Disputed Call (USA) *(JWHills)* 9-0 GBaxter (13) (a bhd) ................................. 10.9

3273 Constructivist (IRE) (65) *(BWHills)* 9-0 MPerrett (8) (6th st: wknd 4f out) ....... 1½.10

3078[5] Grand Honda (IRE) *(CEBrittain)* 9-0 TRogers (1) (lw: led over 5f: wknd over 3f out) ....................................................... 25.11

3569[3] Socks and Shares (42) *(PWHarris)* 9-0 NHowe (10) (lw: bhd fnl 5f) ................ 8.12

3459[3] Pompion (USA) *(JHMGosden)* 9-0 BCrossley (9) (b.nr fore: bhd fnl 4f) ......... s.h.13

3609 Well Directed (IRE) (bl) *(JLDunlop)* 9-0 TyroneWilliams (11) (bhd fnl 5f: t.o) ... 25.14

**11/4** Tunbridge Wells (IRE), **5/1** HIGHLAND DRESS, **13/2** Time for a Flutter(4/1—7/1), **15/2** Will Soon, **9/1** Disputed Call (USA)(op 6/1), **10/1** Choppy Choppy (USA)(12/1—16/1), Pompion (USA), **12/1** Alwatar (USA), **16/1** Constructivist (IRE), **20/1** Hudud (USA), Literary Critic (IRE), Socks and Shares, Grand Honda, **33/1** Well Directed (IRE). CSF £19.73, Tote £5.80: £2.60 £1.70 £4.60 (£10.50). Sheikh Mohammed (NEWMARKET) bred by Meon Valley Stud. 14 Rn
2m 15.59 (12.59)
SF—54/48/38/36/32/35

## 3802

E.B.F. THEALE STKS (Mdn 2-Y.O) £4272.50 (£1280.00: £615.00: £282.50)
**6f 8y**
4-40 (4-45)

**Zarani Sidi Anna (USA)** *(MRStoute)* 8-9 PatEddery (11) (leggy: hld up: led over 1f out: rdn out) ..................................................... —1

The Little Ferret *(RHannon)* 9-0 BRouse (6) (leggy: lw: a:p: ev ch ins fnl f: r.o) .. $^3$/4.2
Complete Madness *(JWHills)* 9-0 MHills (2) (leggy: hld up: ev ch ins fnl f: r.o) .. $^3$/4.3
Quaver (USA) *(JHMGosden)* 8-9 RCochrane (16) (leggy: bit bkwd: s.s: hdwy over 2f out: r.o one pce) ............................................................. 2.4
Aroom *(CJBenstead)* 9-0 GBaxter (10) (w'like: bit bkwd: a:p: rdn 2f out: wkng whn n.m.r over 1f out) ................................................ 3.5
852² Love in the Mist (USA) *(IABalding)* 8-9 JReid (3) (a.p: ev ch 2f out: wknd fnl f) .. 1.6
Fadaki Hawaki (USA) *(AAScott)* 8-9 WRSwinburn (5) (b.hind: w'like: no hdwy fnl 2f) ........................................................ $^1$/2.7
3662⁴ Wali (USA) *(PTWalwyn)* 9-0 WCarson (12) (led over 4f) ............................ hd.8
3552 Dance and Sing (IRE) *(DLWilliams)* 9-0 NAdams (8) (nvr nrr) ..................... $^1$/2.9
Singing Mistress *(DRCElsworth)* 8-9 JWilliams (15) (lt-f: nvr nrr) ............... 3$^1$/2.10
Green Chili *(JWHills)* 8-9 PaulEddery (1) (lengthy: bit bkwd: a bhd) .............. nk.11
3662³ Aghar (IRE) *(Fav)* *(DRCElsworth)* 9-0 SCauthen (13) (spd 4f) .................... nk.12
3523 Jewel Thief *(GBBalding)* 9-0 TSprake (14) (bhd fnl 2f) ............................ nk.13
Ahjay *(DAWilson)* 9-0 MWigham (7) (wl grwn: bit bkwd: bhd fnl 3f) ............. 12.14
3360 Natasha North *(TCasey)* 8-9 MBirch (9) (bhd fnl 3f) ................................ 10.15
Bayfan (IRE) *(JSMoore)* 9-0 DaleGibson (4) (leggy: a bhd) ........................ 8.16

3/1 Aghar (IRE), 11/2 Wali (USA)(op 3/1), 6/1 Love in the Mist (USA), 13/2 ZARANI SIDI ANNA (USA), 7/1 Quaver (USA)(op 7/2), 8/1 Fadaki Hawaki (USA), 10/1 The Little Ferret(op 20/1), 16/1 Green Chili, 25/1 Jewel Thief, 33/1 Ors. CSF £63.96, Tote £4.70: £2.20 £3.30 £6.50 (£78.00). Maktoum Al Maktoum (NEWMARKET) bred by Carelaine Farm,Riordan, Phillips & Kennelot in USA. 16 Rn
1m 20.34 (8.54)
SF—44/46/43/30/23/14

### 3803

ROUND OAK H'CAP (0-100) £3980.00 (£1190.00: £570.00: £260.00)
5f 34y
5-10 (5-15)

3671¹³ Gone Savage (79) *(Fav)* *(GBBalding)* 4-9-1 PatEddery (12) (a.p: led 2f out: rdn out) .................................................................. —1
3575* Belated (85) *(HThomsonJones)* 3-9-6 MHills (8) (led 3f: unable qckn) ............. 4.2
3680 Baligay (73) *(RJHodges)* 7-8-9 TSprake (11) (hrd rdn & hdwy over 1f out: r.o) hd.3
3355 Inherent Magic (IRE) (81) *(MMcCormack)* 3-9-2 MPerrett (15) (hdwy 2f out: r.o one pce) ................................................................. 2.4
3671⁴ Bodari (79) *(DAWilson)* 3-8-11 ‡$DHarrison (2) (a.p: hrd rdn over 1f out: one pce) .................................................................... $^1$/2.5
3284 Walstead (IRE) (58) *(DAWilson)* 3-7-7 GBardwell (13) (hdwy over 1f out: nvr nrr) 2.6
3731 El Yasaf (IRE) (89) *(MissGayKelleway)* 4-9-11 GayKelleway (17) (nvr nr to chal) 1$^1$/2.7
3700⁴ Iron King (70) *(JLSpearing)* 6-8-6 PaulEddery (10) (nvr nrr) ................... s.h.8
3469 Temple Fortune (USA) (74) *(RHannon)* 3-8-9 WRSwinburn (9) (spd 3f) ........... $^3$/4.9
3731 Cindora (IRE) (91) *(MHTompkins)* 3-9-5 ‡$SMulvey (14) (nvr nrr) ............... hd.10
3671 Cantoris (89) *(RJRWilliams)* 6-9-11 RCochrane (16) (b: nvr nrr) ............... $^1$/2.11
1878⁴ Macfarlane (70) (bl) *(MJFetherston-Godley)* 4-8-6 WCarson (3) (hdwy over 2f out: wknd over 1f out) ....................................................... 1.12
3671⁵ Regal Scintilla (91) (v) *(GBBalding)* 3-9-12 SCauthen (7) (hld up: hrd rdn over 1f: sn wknd) ........................................................ $^3$/4.13
3671 Aughfad (87) *(TCasey)* 6-9-9 JReid (5) (bhd fnl 2f) ............................. s.h.14
3703 Very Dicey (75) *(WRMuir)* 4-8-4 ‡$KimMcDonnell (6) (a bhd) ................... $^3$/4.15
3575 Fivesevenfiveo (73) *(RJHodges)* 4-8-2 ‡$SDrowne (4) (a bhd) ................. $^3$/4.16
3539 Massiba (IRE) (85) *(MJHeaton-Ellis)* 3-9-6 RBaymond (1) (spd over 2f) ......... 8.17

7/2 GONE SAVAGE, 13/2 Belated, 15/2 Macfarlane, 9/1 Bodari, 10/1 Regal Scintilla, 12/1 Cantoris, Massiba (IRE), 14/1 Inherent Magic (IRE), Aughfad, 16/1 Iron King, Fiveseventiveo, Baligay, 20/1 Very Dicey, Temple Fortune (USA), Cindora (IRE), 25/1 El Yasaf (IRE), 33/1 Walstead (IRE). CSF £27.11, CT £315.74. Tote £4.50: £1.50 £1.50 £8.20 £4.20 (£8.30). Mr Rex L. Mead (DORCHESTER) bred by Mrs C. F. Van Straubenzee and R. Mead. 17 Rn
66.94 sec (6.24)
SF—76/65/53/52/45/19

T/Trio: Race 4: £197.30 (6.4 Tckts) & Race 7: £190.90 (6 Tckts). T/Jkpt: £5,632.60 (0.09 Tckts); £6,926.65 to Newbury 23/10/92. T/Plpt: £973.30 (5.8 Tckts). AK

### 3583—**PONTEFRACT (L-H)**

**Thursday, October 22nd [Good to firm, Firm patches]**
Going Allowance: nil sec per fur (G)
Wind: almost nil

Stalls: low

### 3804

BROOMFIELD STKS (Mdn 3-Y.O) £2553.00 (£708.00: £339.00)
1$^1$/2m 8y
2-25 (2-28)

3713 Iftakhaar (USA) (80) *(MajorWRHern)* 9-0 RHills (2) (lw: in tch: outpcd over 3f out: hdwy 2f out: led appr fnl f: r.o wl) ....................................... —1

3398⁴ Deduce (Jt-Fav) *(GWragg)* 9-0 PRobinson (1) (a.p: hdwy appr st: chal over 1f out: r.o) ............................................................. 1¹/₂.2

3682³ Cariboo Gold (USA) (Jt-Fav) *(JHMGosden)* 9-0 JCarroll (8) (lw: a chsng ldrs: led wl over 1f out: sn hdd & one pce) ....................... 4.3

3309 Speedo Movement (56) *(BAMcMahon)* 8-9 TQuinn (7) (cl up tl outpcd fnl 2f) .. 10.4

3062³ Private Bank (USA) (bl) *(ACStewart)* 9-0 MRoberts (3) (led tl hdd wl over 1f out: sn btn) ................................................... ³/₄.5

Fundeghe (USA) *(JEBanks)* 9-0 NDay (5) (rangy: effrt 5f out: rdn & btn appr st) 12.6

3485⁶ Lady Donoghue (USA) *(MrsGRReveley)* 8-9 KDarley (9) (cl up: chal 6f out: wknd over 2f out) .................................. 1¹/₂.7

3586 High Mind (FR) (40) *(MissLCSiddall)* 9-0 GDuffield (6) (s.i.s: jnd ldrs after wl over 1f: wknd 5f out) ................................. 20.8

3078⁴ Call Me Dickins *(RHollinshead)* 9-0 WRyan (4) (a bhd) ......................... 5.9

**9/4** Deduce, Cariboo Gold (USA), **5/2** IFTAKHAAR (USA)(7/4—11/4), **10/1** Private Bank (USA), **12/1** Fundeghe (USA), **20/1** Lady Donoghue (USA), Speedo Movement, **33/1** Call Me Dickins, **66/1** High Mind (FR). CSF £8.61, Tote £3.40: £1.30 £1.30 £1.30 (£7.50). Mr Hamdan Al-Maktoum (LAMBOURN) bred by Owens, Guida, McCarthy, et al in USA. 9 Rn                                                    2m 39.2 (4.7)
SF—53/49/42/17/20/–

**3805**    BLACKMIRES CLAIMING STKS    £2763.00 (£768.00: £369.00)    **5f**    2-55 (2-57)

3703* **Branston Abby (IRE) (85)** (Fav) *(MJohnston)* 3-8-6 MRoberts (15) (in tch: hdwy 2f out: qcknd to ld wl ins fnl f) ....................... —1

3391 Liffey River (USA) (53) *(MrsLPiggott)* 4-8-9 GDuffield (7) (b: b.hind: a chsng ldrs: kpt on wl fnl f) ............................. 2.2

3437 Paley Prince (USA) (74) *(MDIUsher)* 6-9-3 TQuinn (8) (lw: hdwy wl over 1f out: styd on strly nr fin) .......................... 1.3

3703 Love Returned (78) *(WJarvis)* 5-8-11 MTobbutt (14) (hld up: hdwy whn hmpd & carried lft over 1f out: r.o) ............... nk.4

3575 Sigama (USA) (80) *(FHLee)* 6-9-1 DMcKeown (2) (led tl hdd & no ex wl ins fnl f) nk.5

3585 Samson-Agonistes (80) *(BAMcMahon)* 6-8-2 ‡7SSanders (4) (lw: chsd ldr rdn & btn over 1f out) ................................ hd.6

3537 Metal Boys (81) *(RHollinshead)* 5-8-11 WRyan (1) (in tch: effrt 2f out: no imp) . ³/₄.7

3537⁴ African Chimes (77) (bl) *(WAO'Gorman)* 5-8-13 ‡3EmmaO'Gorman (3) (a in tch: effrt whn hung bdly lft over 1f out: wnt rt ins fnl f: styd on) s.h.8

3632 Thrie-Na-Helah (IRE) (63) (v) *(RMWhitaker)* 3-7-7 ‡7AGarth (10) (sn wl outpcd & bhd: sme late hdwy) ................. 4.9

3284 Forest Fairy (61) *(RBoss)* 3-8-5 JQuinn (12) (n.d) .......................... 2.10

3703⁶ Cranfield Comet (71) *(JBerry)* 3-8-8 JCarroll (11) (sn drvn along: n.d) ........... nk.11

1483 Sir Tasker (72) *(JLHarris)* 4-8-11 LDettori (6) (gd spd 3f: wknd qckly) ........... ³/₄.12

3710 Aldington Peach *(PDEvans)* 3-7-7⁽²⁾ ‡7MHumphries (16) (sn outpcd & bhd) .... ³/₄.13

3703 Seamere (77) *(BRCambidge)* 9-8-3 JLowe (9) (s.i.s: a bhd) ..................... 2¹/₂.14

3777 Ipsilante (53) *(ASReid)* 3-7-7⁽²⁾ ‡7PMcCabe (13) (sn bhd) .................... 1¹/₂.15

**9/4** BRANSTON ABBY (IRE), **9/2** Metal Boys, **6/1** Samson-Agonistes(op 4/1), **7/1** African Chimes, **10/1** Love Returned, **12/1** Sigama (USA), Cranfield Comet, **16/1** Seamere, **20/1** Paley Prince (USA), **25/1** Sir Tasker, Thrie-Na-Helah (IRE), **33/1** Forest Fairy, Liffey River (USA), **50/1** Ipsilante, **200/1** Aldington Peach. CSF £68.12, Tote £2.70: £1.70 £4.30 £4.70 (£119.50). Mr J. David Abell (MIDDLEHAM) bred by John David Abell in Ireland. 15 Rn                                                                       63.5 sec (2)
SF—52/47/51/44/47/33

**3806**    WHITELANE-PONTEFRACT APP'CE SERIES H'CAP (Final rnd) (0-70) £2742.00 (£762.00: £366.00)    **1¹/₄m 6y**    3-25 (3-29)

1172 **Modest Hope (USA) (43)** *(RCSpicer)* 5-8-6 AGarth (14) (lw: hld up: hdwy 4f out: led over 2f out & qcknd clr: styd on wl) ............. —1

3627 Sunderland Echo (55) *(MrsGRReveley)* 3-8-13 DarrenMoffatt (3) (lw: trckd ldrs: effrt 3f out: nt qckn ins fnl f) ................. 2¹/₂.2

3718³ Rive-Jumelle (IRE) (50) *(MBell)* 4-8-13 PTurner (2) (bhd: hdwy 3f out: r.o wl: nrst fin) ............................................. 1¹/₂.3

3487³ Broughton's Tango (IRE) (49) *(WJMusson)* 3-8-7 DMcCabe (11) (b: bhd: pushed along 5f out: styd on wl fnl 2f) ............... 4.4

3622⁴ Sovereign Niche (IRE) (41) (Fav) *(MrsJRRamsden)* 4-8-4 JWeaver (15) (hld up: hdwy over 3f out: one pce fnl 2f) ............. 1¹/₂.5

3479* Ghylldale (42) (v) *(RBastiman)* 4-8-5 HBastiman (10) (chsd ldrs: led 4f out tl over 2f out: sn btn) ..................... 1¹/₂.6

3718² Alto Jane (70) *(GHarwood)* 3-10-0 GayeHarwood (7) (effrt 5f out: styd on: no imp) ............................................ 2¹/₂.7

3547 Aasff (USA) (64) *(DMorley)* 3-9-8 EBentley (4) (lw: s.s: nvr trbld ldrs) ............... ¹/₂.8

3610 Nothing Doing (IRE) (42) *(WJMusson)* 3-8-0 PBowe (18) (bhd tl stdy late hdwy: nvr plcd to chal) ............................ hd.9

3143 Touch Above **(53)** *(TDBarron)* 6-9-2 VHalliday (19) (dwlt: n.d) ............... 1½.**10**
3479 Charly Pharly (FR) **(37)** (bl) *(FHLee)* 5-8-0[5] DCarson (12) (cl up tl wknd 3f out) 1.**11**
3600 Must Be Magical (USA) **(33)** (bl) *(FHLee)* 4-7-10[3] JMarshall (8) (led tl hdd 4f
    out: sn wknd) ..................................................................................... 5.**12**
3576 Magnetic Point (USA) **(50)** *(AAScott)* 3-8-8 MHumphries (9) (chsd ldrs tl wknd
    2f out) ............................................................................................ s.h.**13**
3476 Rudda Cass **(30)** *(MrsVAAconley)* 8-7-7 CHawksley (2) (drvn along & hdwy 8f
    out: wknd 4f out) ................................................................................. 7.**14**
3380[6] Bronze Runner **(32)** (bl) *(EAWheeler)* 8-7-9 JDSmith (17) (n.d) ............... ½.**15**
1739 Golden Beau **(36)** *(AHarrison)* 10-7-9[6] ‡4IGrantham (1) (dwlt: a bhd) ....... 2½.**16**
2941 Any Dream Would Do **(49)** *(PBeaumont)* 3-8-7 GParkin (13) (chsd ldrs tl wknd
    4f out) ............................................................................................... ¾.**17**
3387 Super Morning **(45)** *(JPearce)* 6-8-8 DWright (6) (lw: a bhd) ...................... ¾.**18**
*1548* Molten Copper (IRE) **(63)** (bl) *(MWEasterby)* 3-9-7 PaulJohnson (16) (in tch tl
    wknd 5f out) ..................................................................................... s.h.**19**
LONG HANDICAP: Must Be Magical (USA) 7-0, Golden Beau 7-0.

**3/1** Sovereign Niche (IRE)(op 5/1), **11/2** Rive-Jumelle (IRE), **8/1** Sunderland Echo, Alto Jane, **10/1** Bronze
Runner, **12/1** Ghylldale, Touch Above, Super Morning, **14/1** Nothing Doing (IRE), **16/1** Aasff (USA), MODEST
HOPE (USA), Magnetic Point (USA), Broughton's Tango (IRE), **25/1** Charly Pharly (FR), **33/1** Rudda Cass, Must
Be Magical (USA), Any Dream Would Do, **66/1** Gus. CSF £140.80, CT £749.17. Tote £40.10: £5.40 £2.10 £1.60
£3.20 (£149.80). Mr J. McManamon (SPALDING) bred by Ralph Wilson in USA. 19 Rn    2m 13.3 (5)
                                                         SF—42/44/41/27/21/19

---

**3807**    PONTEFRACT SECURITIES NURSERY   £4337.50 (£1300.00: £625.00: £287.50)
        6f                                                             4-00 (4-01)

3665 **Midwinter Dream (76)** *(DRCElsworth)* 8-9 LDettori (3) (lw: hld up: smooth
    hdwy ½-wy: led 1f out: sn qcknd clr) ...................................................... —**1**
3432 Hello Hobson's (IRE) **(70)** *(JAkehurst)* 8-3 DMcKeown (2) (a chsng ldrs: chal
    over 1f out: nt pce of wnr) .................................................................... 4.**2**
3470[5] Tarnside Rosal **(74)** *(JEtherington)* 8-7 JCarroll (8) (hdwy 2f out: styd on wl:
    nrst fin) ............................................................................................. 1.**3**
3590[5] Trevorsninepoints **(62)** *(MJRyan)* 7-9 DBiggs (1) (mde most tl hdd 1f out: no
    ex) .................................................................................................... 1.**4**
3163* Doulabella (IRE) **(75)** *(SirMarkPrescott)* 8-8 GDuffield (4) (hld up & bhd: effrt 2f
    out: r.o: nrst fin) ................................................................................ ½.**5**
3642* Birchwood Sun **(78)** *(RHollinshead)* 8-11 WRyan (14) (hmpd s: bhd tl hdwy
    over 2f out: nvr nrr) ............................................................................. ¾.**6**
3550[3] Storiths (IRE) **(88)** *(JWWatts)* 9-7 NConnorton (7) (lw: a in tch: rdn along 2f
    out: one pce) ..................................................................................... nk.**7**
3385 Goodbye Millie **(64)** *(SGNorton)* 7-8[2] ‡3FNorton (18) (styd on fnl 2f: nvr nrr) ... ¾.**8**
3382[6] Milbank Challenger **(66)** *(MHEasterby)* 7-10[1] ‡3SMaloney (11) (chsd ldrs over
    4f) .................................................................................................... hd.**9**
3642[5] Pilgrim Bay (IRE) **(66)** *(JBerry)* 7-13 LCharnock (5) (disp ld over 3f: grad wknd) 1½.**10**
3642 Peacefull Reply (USA) **(72)** *(FHLee)* 8-5[2] KFallon (16) (in tch 4f) .................. ¾.**11**
3313[6] Early Song **(69)** *(PTWalwyn)* 8-2 RHills (6) (sn bhd & drvn along: n.d) ......... nk.**12**
3606[4] Comanche Companion **(68)** *(TJNaughton)* 8-1 GCarter (9) (chsd ldrs over 4f) 1½.**13**
3598[4] Finavon **(75)** (bl) *(IABalding)* 8-8 AMunro (10) (outpcd fr ½-wy) ................... 1.**14**
3642[4] Mr Butch **(Fav)** *(MRChannon)* 8-2 JQuinn (12) (lw: wnt rt s: plld hrd: lost
    tch fr ½-wy) ...................................................................................... 2.**15**
3550 Pine Ridge Lad (IRE) **(68)** *(MJohnston)* 8-1 MRoberts (15) (lost pl after 2f: n.d) 1½.**16**
3424[6] Gweek (IRE) **(68)** *(PAKelleway)* 8-1[1] PRobinson (13) (hmpd s: n.d) ........... 1½.**17**
3607[5] Wolf Power (IRE) **(71)** *(TThomsonJones)* 8-4 KDarley (7) (hld up & a bhd) .. 2½.**18**

**5/1** Mr Butch(op 8/1), **6/1** MIDWINTER DREAM, **7/1** Storiths (IRE), **9/1** Hello Hobson's (IRE), **10/1** Pine Ridge
Lad (IRE), Doulabella (IRE), **11/1** Wolf Power (IRE), Birchwood Sun, **12/1** Finavon, Comanche Companion(op
8/1), **14/1** Tarnside Rosal, Trevorsninepoints, **16/1** Pilgrim Bay (IRE), **20/1** Early Song, Peacefull Reply (USA),
Milbank Challenger, Goodbye Millie, **25/1** Gweek (IRE). CSF £63.80, CT £707.21. Tote £5.70: £2.00 £1.70
£5.70 £3.80 (£28.40). Mr J. C. Smith (WHITSBURY) bred by Littleton Stud. 18 Rn    1m 16.8 (2.8)
                                                         SF—39/17/17/11/12/12

---

**3808**    BLUFF COVE H'CAP (0-70) £2721.00 (£756.00: £363.00)    **2m 1f 216y**   4-30 (4-30)
                             (Weights raised 6 lb)

3515[6] **Puritan (CAN) (69)** *(GHarwood)* 3-9-10 TQuinn (2) (lw: in tch: hdwy 4f out: rdn
    to ld ins fnl f: styd on strly) ................................................................... —**1**
3586* Ambuscade (USA) **(57)** **(Fav)** *(MrsGRReveley)* 6-9-10 KDarley (3) (lw: a.p: led
    3f out: rdn over 1f out: hdd ins fnl f: kpt on wl) ..................................... ¾.**2**
1866[6] Cost Effective **(36)** *(MBrittain)* 5-8-3 JLowe (6) (bhd: kpt on fnl 2f: nvr nr to chal) 20.**3**
3393 Master's Crown (USA) **(40)** *(MCChapman)* 4-8-7 KFallon (7) (sn chsng ldrs:
    led 6f out to 3f out: sn outpcd) .......................................................... 1½.**4**

3603⁴ Izitallworthit **(40)** *(JMackie)* 3-7-9 SWood (1) (chsd ldrs: outpcd 4f out: hdwy
          over 2f out: n.d) .................................................................................... 6.5
3603  Perforate **(49)** (bl) *(SirMarkPrescott)* 3-8-4 GDuffield (9) (b.hind: chsd ldrs:
          drvn along ½-wy: no imp fnl 4f) ...................................................... 15.6
33055 Alizari (USA) **(61)** (bl) *(GFleming)* 3-9-2 RPElliott (4) (cl up tl lost pl ½-wy: hdwy
          u.p 4f out: n.d) .................................................................................. 4.7
3600  Inkala **(45)** *(WRMuir)* 4-8-12 MRoberts (5) (led tl hdd 6f out: sn wknd) ............. 6.8
3504  Fit for Life (IRE) **(43)** (bl) *(MrsNMacauley)* 4-8-5⁽³⁾ ‡⁵SWilliams (10) (b: sn bhd &
          rdn along: n.d) .................................................................................. 2.9
          Rainbow Stripes **(34)** *(BSRothwell)* 5-8-1 JQuinn (8) (hld up: hdwy 6f out:
          wknd qckly 4f out) ............................................................................. 5.10

**6/5** Ambuscade (USA), **9/4** PURITAN (CAN), **10/1** Izitallworthit, Perforate, **20/1** Cost Effective, Alizari (USA),
Inkala, Master's Crown (USA), **50/1** Ors. CSF £5.08, CT £33.65. Tote £2.90: £1.40 £1.10 £2.30 (£2.20). Sheikh
Mohammed (PULBOROUGH) bred by Angus Glen Farm Ltd in Canada. 10 Rn          4m 1.4 (9.2)
                                                                              SF—18/17/–/–/–/–

## 3809
ASTA HOTEL (BARBADOS) STKS (Mdn 2-Y-O) £2973.00 (£828.00: £399.00)
1m 4y                                                                5-00 (5-03)

32854 **Bob's Return (IRE)** *(MHTompkins)* 9-0 PRobinson (13) (w ldr: led wl over 1f
          out: styd on) ...................................................................................... —1
37096 Brown's (FR) **(98)** *(PWChapple-Hyam)* 9-0 GCarter (8) (lw: mde most tl hdd
          over 1f out: kpt on wl) ....................................................................... 1.2
          Moscow Sea (USA) (Fav) *(HRACecil)* 9-0 WRyan (5) (w'like: leggy: scope: hld up in
          tch: plld wd ent st: r.o wl: too much to do) ...................................... ½.3
36696 Village Green (FR) (Fav) *(CEBrittain)* 9-0 MRoberts (14) (a chsng ldrs: drvn
          along over 2f out: styd on one pce) .................................................. 2½.4
36913 Allegation **(72)** *(PFICole)* 9-0 AMunro (12) (a.p: effrt 3f out: one pce) .......... 2½.5
1932  Sharro **(65)** *(PAKelleway)* 8-9 ‡⁵JWeaver (2) (a chsng ldrs: no hdwy fnl 2f) ...... ½.6
35593 Moujeeb (USA) *(MRStoute)* 8-9 ‡⁵JJones (21) (a.p: outpcd 3f out: no imp after) 8.7
          Burnt Imp (USA) *(GHarwood)* 9-0 TQuinn (6) (w'like: str: in tch: drvn along
          ½-wy: no imp) .................................................................................. ½.8
37094 Mahogany Light (USA) **(88)** *(GHarwood)* 9-0 KDarley (11) (lw: cl up tl outpcd &
          wknd fnl 2f) ...................................................................................... 1.9
2598  Bold Visit (IRE) *(DRCElsworth)* 9-0 LDettori (7) (chsd ldrs tl wknd wl over 1f out) 1.10
3691  Prakash (IRE) *(CEBrittain)* 9-0 DBiggs (1) (nvr nr to chal) ............................. 1½.11
36145 Jalcanto *(MrsGRReveley)* 9-0 JLowe (4) (hld up & bhd: nvr nr to chal) ......... 2½.12
3691  The Where Withal *(SirMarkPrescott)* 9-0 GDuffield (9) (bhd: stdy hdwy 2f out:
          n.d) ................................................................................................. d.h.12
3643  Tom the Tank *(NTinkler)* 9-0 JQuinn (16) (bit bkwd: in tch tl wknd over 3f out) 1.14
3313  Rose of Man *(DMoffatt)* 8-2 ‡7DarrenMoffatt (10) (bhd fr ½-wy) .................... 2½.15
2516  Resolution Time (bl) *(MrsVAAconley)* 9-0 LCharnock (3) (b.hind: s.i.s: n.d) . 1½.16
36246 Bomoh *(SPCWoods)* 9-0 WWoods (17) (a bhd) ............................................. 2½.17
3498  Ultrakay (IRE) *(JBerry)* 9-0 JCarroll (15) (prom 5f) ..................................... 5.18
3611  Mzuri Sands *(MJCamacho)* 8-9 NConnorton (19) (s.i.s: a bhd) ................... 2.19
          Kahili Ginger *(NAGraham)* 8-9 RHills (18) (lengthy: unf: in tch tl hung lft & wknd
          fr ½-wy) ........................................................................................... 3½.20
          Scottish Wedding *(JBalding)* 8-9 KFallon (20) (unf: bkwd: a outpcd & bhd) ... 3.21

**85/40** Village Green (FR)(7/2—2/1), **4/1** Brown's (FR)(3/1—9/2), **11/2** Moscow Sea (USA)(op 7/2), **11/1**
Moujeeb (USA)(8/1—14/1), Allegation(8/1—12/1), **12/1** BOB'S RETURN (IRE), Mahogany Light (USA)(op 8/1),
Burnt Imp (USA)(op 8/1), **16/1** The Where Withal, **20/1** Jalcanto, **25/1** Kahili Ginger, **33/1** Bold Visit (IRE), **50/1**
Bomoh, Mzuri Sands, Sharro, **100/1** Ors. CSF £58.96, Tote £16.20: £2.90 £2.10 £2.20 (£25.30). Mrs G. A. E.
Smith (NEWMARKET) bred by Baronrath Stud Ltd in Ireland. 21 Rn          1m 46.9 (5.3)
                                                                         SF—20/17/15/7/–/–

## 3810
LEVY BOARD STKS (Mdn 3-Y-O) £2427.00 (£672.00: £321.00)   **6f**   5-30 (5-30)

35923 **Admirals Realm (60)** *(BAMcMahon)* 9-0 TQuinn (5) (cl up: led 2f out & sn
          qcknd clr: hrd drvn fnl f: r.o) ............................................................. —1
37476 Wafi (USA) **(47)** (bl) *(BHanbury)* 9-0 WRyan (7) (hld up: hdwy 2f out: styd on: nt
          pce of wnr) ...................................................................................... 2½.2
36903 Fairy Wisher (IRE) (Fav) *(ACStewart)* 8-9 MRoberts (10) (cl up: effrt 2f out: nt
          qckn) ............................................................................................... 4.3
3524  The New Girl **(49)** *(CCElsey)* 8-9 GDuffield (6) (swtg: led 4f: sn rdn & btn) ........ 2.4
3383  Legitim **(33)** *(JMJefferson)* 9-0 JLowe (3) (s.i.s: sme hdwy u.p 2f out: n.d) ...... 1½.5
3412  Queen Canute (IRE) **(30)** *(FHLee)* 8-9 DMcKeown (8) (sn cl up: wknd wl over 1f
          out) ................................................................................................. 3½.6
3374  Miss Limelight *(ASmith)* 8-9 SWebster (9) (nvr wnt pce) ............................. 1½.7
3596  Oriental Song **(30)** *(KSBridgwater)* 8-5⁽¹⁾ ‡⁵SWilliams (4) (sn bhd) ................... ¾.8
3710  Henry's First *(MissLCSiddall)* 9-0 RHills (1) (wl bhd fr ½-wy) ...................... 20.9

**6/4** Fairy Wisher (IRE), **5/2** ADMIRALS REALM, **6/1** Wafi (USA), The New Girl, **20/1** Queen Canute (IRE), Legitim, **33/1** Oriental Song, **50/1** Ors. CSF £16.31, Tote £3.40: £1.50 £1.70 £1.30 (£7.90). Mr P. W. Leslie (TAMWORTH) bred by Hever Castle Stud Farm Ltd. 9 Rn
1m 18.2 (4.2)
SF—16/6/–/–/–/–/

T/Plpt: £90.90 (29.55 Tckts).
AA

## LAUREL PARK (L-H)
### Saturday, October 17th [Good to soft]

### 3811a
LAUREL DASH (Grade 3)  £80214.00  **6f (turf)**

| | | |
|---|---|---|
| **Glen Kate** *(America)* 5-8-7 LPincay | ............................................ | —1 |
| 3738a[2] Silicon Bavaria (FR) *(France)* 5-8-7 MBoutin | ............................................ | 3.2 |
| 3231a[6] Cardoun (FR) *(France)* 3-8-5 DBoeuf | ............................................ | nose.3 |
| 3450a★ CENTRAL CITY *(RHannon)* 3-8-4 CBlack (btn further 3¹/₄l) | ............................................ | 7 |

Tote 9.00 (1-2) 6.00 9.60 (1-2-3) 4.00 4.80 4.00. Mr B.W.McNall & Mr W.Gretzky (W.Shoemaker,AMERICA) bred by Barronstown Stud. 13 Rn
1m 10.4

### 3812a
BUDWEISER INTERNATIONAL (Grade 1)  £240642.00  **1¹/₄m (turf)**

| | | |
|---|---|---|
| 2837[6] **ZOMAN (USA)** *(PFlCole)* 5-9-0 AMunro | ............................................ | —1 |
| 3652a★ Sillery (USA) *(France)* 4-9-0 FHead | ............................................ | hd.2 |
| 3329a[4] Contested Bid (USA) *(France)* 3-8-10 PatEddery | ............................................ | 1³/₄.3 |
| 2643[6] YOUNG BUSTER (IRE) *(GWragg)* 4-9-0 MHills (btn further 9¹/₄l) | ............................................ | 8 |

Tote 17.00 (1-2) 6.00 3.00 (1-2-3) 4.00 2.40 2.80. Mr Fahd Salman (WHATCOMBE) bred by Harbor View Farm in USA. 8 Rn
2m 1.4

## NAAS (L-H)
### Saturday, October 17th [Good]
Going Allowance: minus 0.30 sec per fur (F)

### 3813a
ALI RETZA & MAMADI SOUDAVAR GARNET RACE (listed race) £8061.00  **7f**

| | | |
|---|---|---|
| **Nordic Pageant (IRE)** *(Ireland)* 3-8-8 CRoche | ............................................ | —1 |
| Lavinia Fontana (IRE) *(Ireland)* 3-8-8 PVGilson | ............................................ | 1.2 |
| Cheviot Amble (IRE) *(Ireland)* 4-8-11 WJO'Connor | ............................................ | s.h.3 |
| 3213[4] PETAL GIRL *(RHannon)* 3-8-8 SCraine (btn more than further 5¹/₂l) | ............................................ | 9 |

Tote £5.40: £2.40 £1.60 £3.50 (£13.20). Mr D.H.W.Dobson (J.S.Bolger,IRELAND) bred by D.H.W.Dobson in Ireland. 13 Rn
1m 23.7 (U.3)
SF—67/64/66

### 3737a—LONGCHAMP (R-H)
### Sunday, October 18th [Good]
Going Allowance: 0.65 sec per fur (Y)

### 3814a
PRIX DE CONSEIL DE PARIS (Gp 2)  £30960.00  **1¹/₂m (Grande)**

| | | |
|---|---|---|
| 3429[3] **GARDEN OF HEAVEN (USA)** *(CEBrittain)* 3-8-9 MRoberts (chsd ldr: 2nd st: qcknd to ld 2f out: sn clr: eased nr fin: impressive) | | —1 |
| 3649a★ Fabulous Hostess (USA) *(France)* 4-9-0 ODoleuze (hld up: last st: hdwy over 1f out: r.o wl: no ch w wnr) | | 4.2 |
| 635a[5] Dissimulateur (FR) *(France)* 3-8-9 FHead (prom: 3rd st: one pce fnl 2f) | | 2¹/₂.3 |
| 3734a[2] Northern Park (USA) (bl) *(France)* 4-9-0 GGuignard (led to 2f out: one pce) | | 1¹/₂.4 |
| 3657a Magic Night (FR) (Fav) *(France)* 4-9-1 CAsmussen (4th st: effrt 2f out: sn btn) | | 2.5 |
| Sorgho (USA) *(France)* 3-8-9 DBoeuf (5th st: a bhd) | | 3.6 |

**30/100** Magic Night (FR), **5/2** Fabulous Hostess (USA), **96/10** GARDEN OF HEAVEN (USA), **13/1** Sorgho (USA), **18/1** Dissimulateur (FR), **22/1** Northern Park (USA). Tote 10.60f: 4.30f 2.20f (SF: 28.40f). Mr B.Voak (NEWMARKET) bred by Edward A.Seltzer in USA. 6 Rn
2m 41 (11)
SF—63/61/50/52/49/37

### 3739a—SAN SIRO (R-H)
### Sunday, October 18th [Soft]

### 3815a
GRAN PREMIO DEL JOCKEY CLUB E COPPA D'ORO (Gp 1) (C & F) £162791.00  **1¹/₂m**

| | | |
|---|---|---|
| 3659a[4] **SILVERNESIAN (USA)** *(JLDunlop)* 3-8-11 LPiggott | ............................................ | —1 |
| 3429[2] RED BISHOP (USA) *(JHMGosden)* 4-9-3 WCarson | ............................................ | 1¹/₂.2 |

3336a* Erdelistan (FR) *(Italy)* 5–9-3 SSoto ........................................................... 2¹/₂.3
Tote 124L: 38L 17L (139L). Gerecon Italia (ARUNDEL) bred by Mark & Mrs Hardin in USA. 7 Rn    2m 39.9

## WOODBINE (L-H)
### Sunday, October 18th [Good to soft]

### 3816a
E.P. TAYLOR STKS (Grade 2) (F & M) £112813.00   1¹/₄m (turf)

3658a* **Hatoof (USA)** *(France)* 3–8-6 WRSwinburn ........................................ —1
3330a³ Urban Sea (USA) *(France)* 3–8-6 MBoutin ........................................ 1¹/₄.2
     Hero's Love (USA) *(Canada)* 4–8-11 DSeymour ................................ 1¹/₄.3
3658a³ RUBY TIGER *(PFICole)* 5–8-11 TQuinn ............................................ hd.4
3237³ PARTY CITED (USA) *(DRCElsworth)* 3–8-6 ASolis ............................... 2¹/₂.5
Tote 6.00 (1-2) 4.00 3.90 (1-2-3) 3.10 3.50 4.70. Maktoum Al Maktoum (Mrs C.Head,FRANCE) bred by
Gainsborough Farm Inc. in USA. 12 Rn    2m 7.8

### 3817a
ROTHMANS INTERNATIONAL (Grade 1)   £340107.00   1¹/₂m (turf)

3453a² **SNURGE** *(PFICole)* 5–9-0 TQuinn (fin 2nd, ¹/₂l: awrrd r) ................ —1
3322a* Ghazi (USA) *(America)* 3–8-7 RDavis (fin 3rd, 1¹/₄l: plcd 2nd) ............ 2
3652a² Wiorno *(France)* 4–9-0 TJarnet (fin 1st: disq: plcd 3rd) ..................... 3
3657a SADDLERS' HALL (IRE) *(MRStoute)* 4–9-0 WRSwinburn (btn further 1³/₄l) ... 5
2894a² BEYTON (USA) *(RHannon)* 3–8-7 ASolis (btn 3³/₄l by wnr) ................... 6
3657a MASHAALLAH (USA) *(JHMGosden)* 4–9-0 SCauthen (btn 8¹/₄l by wnr) ...... 11
3454a³ SPINNING *(IABalding)* 5–9-0 RCochrane (btn 9¹/₂l by wnr) ................. 12
*Stewards Enquiry: Wiorno disq. (interference to Ghazi (USA) ins fnl f).*
Tote 12.00 (1-2) 6.10 28.10 (1-2-3) 4.60 17.80 8.70. Mr M.Arbib (WHATCOMBE) bred by Kilcarn Stud. 14 Rn
2m 39

### 3187—DONCASTER (L-H)
### Friday, October 23rd [Good to firm becoming Good]
Going Allowance: 5f-8f: 0.25 sec; Rest: 0.15 sec per fur (G)      Wind: fresh half against

Stalls: high

### 3818
E.B.F. FLAXTON STKS (I) (Mdn 2-Y.O) £3669.75 (£1098.00: £526.50: £240.75)
7f      1-00 (1-06)

3011⁴ **Dahyah (USA)** *(Fav)* *(MRStoute)* 9-0 PatEddery (10) (a.p: effrt 3f out: sn hrd
     drvn & hung lft: styd on to ld wl ins fnl f) ...................................... —1
3532 Field of Stars *(JHMGosden)* 9-0 RCochrane (1) (lw: led: clr over 2f out: nt qckn
     wl ins fnl f) .................................................................................. nk.2
     Majority (IRE) *(BWHills)* 9-0 SCauthen (5) (w'like: bit bkwd: trckd ldrs: hdwy &
     ev ch over 1f out: wknd ins fnl f) .................................................. 3.3
     Nassma (IRE) *(JRFanshawe)* 8-9 WRSwinburn (11) (neat: sn outpcd & bhd:
     hdwy 2f out: styd on nr fin) ......................................................... 2¹/₂.4
     Shirley Rose *(MJohnston)* 8-9 DMcKeown (7) (cmpt: bit bkwd: swtchd rt s: bhd
     tl kpt on fnl 2f) .......................................................................... 3.5
3519⁶ Slivovitz *(MJHeaton-Ellis)* 9-0 WRyan (8) (chsd ldrs tl wknd fnl 3f) ......... 4.6
3677⁵ Queens Consul (IRE) *(BSRothwell)* 8-9 MRoberts (3) (chsd ldrs: wknd over 2f
     out) ......................................................................................... nk.7
     Follingworth Girl (IRE) *(SGNorton)* 8-9 MWood (12) (str: bkwd: s.i.s: racd
     stands' side: outpcd fr ¹/₂-wy) ...................................................... 8.8
3626 Ever so Lyrical *(PWHarris)* 9-0 PaulEddery (9) (hmpd s: sme hdwy ¹/₂-wy: n.d) 1¹/₂.9
     Poppyland *(CFWall)* 8-9 BRaymond (6) (neat: scope: sn outpcd) ......... 1.10
     Royal Executive (IRE) *(CEBrittain)* 8-9 ‡⁵BDoyle (13) (w'like: outpcd fr ¹/₂-wy) hd.11
3597 Cavalier Prince (IRE) *(APJarvis)* 8-7 ‡7DWright (14) (racd stands' side: bhd fr
     ¹/₂-wy) ...................................................................................... 1.12
3549 North Call *(GHEden)* 8-9 JCarroll (2) (a outpcd) ............................... 3.13

**11/10** DAHYAH (USA), **9/4** Majority (IRE)(3/1—7/4), **8/1** Field of Stars, **9/1** Slivovitz(12/1—7/1), **16/1** Nassma
(IRE), **20/1** Queens Consul (IRE), **25/1** Royal Executive (IRE), **33/1** Shirley Rose, North Call, **50/1** Follingworth
Girl (IRE), Poppyland, Ever so Lyrical, **100/1** Cavalier Prince (IRE). CSF £11.25, Tote £2.00: £1.30 £2.10 £1.50
(£4.20). Maktoum Al Maktoum (NEWMARKET) bred by Claiborne Farm & The Gamely Corporation in USA. 13 Rn
     1m 28.73 (5.33)
     SF—46/45/36/23/14/7

### 3819
LEVY BOARD APP'CE H'CAP (0-90) £5708.50 (£1708.00: £819.00: £374.50)
7f      1-30 (1-35)

3726 **Takenhall (62)** *(MJFetherston-Godley)* 7–8-0 FNorton (10) (sn bhd: rdn ¹/₂-wy:
     styd on appr fnl f: led nr fin) ...................................................... —1

3714* Hob Green **(69)** (Fav) *(MrsJRRamsden)* 3–8-4 (5x) JWeaver (15) (hld up: hdwy
½-wy: led 2f out: sn rdn: kpt on: hdd nr fin) .................... 1½.2

3681 Super Benz **(69)** *(TFairhurst)* 6–8-7 JFanning (5) (lw: chsd ldrs: hrd drvn ½-wy:
styd on) ...................... ¾.3

3545 Native Chieftan **(80)** *(RHannon)* 3–9-1 DHarrison (1) (a chsng ldrs: ev ch over
1f out: unable qckn) ...................... ½.4

3591 Ernestan **(90)** *(MHEasterby)* 3–9-11 SMaloney (14) (lw: s.i.s: swtchd lft s: in
tch: hrd drvn over 2f out: one pce) ...................... 1½.5

2490² Furiella **(67)** *(PCHaslam)* 4–7-12 ‡⁷TraceyLynagh (11) (led: edgd rt fr ½-wy:
hdd 2f out: sn wknd) ...................... 2.6

3511³ Ler Cru (IRE) **(62)** *(CEBrittain)* 3–7-11 BDoyle (12) (sn bhd: styd on over 1f out:
nvr rchd ldrs) ...................... s.h.7

1463³ Dorset Duke **(90)** *(GWragg)* 5–9-10 ‡⁴NHall (4) (s.s: nvr nr ldrs) ...................... 1.8

3612 Pesidanamich (IRE) **(59)** *(JPLeigh)* 4–7-11 StephenDavies (13) (nvr nr ldrs) ..... 1½.9

3479 Allegramente **(58)** *(RO'Leary)* 3–7-3 ‡⁴DWright (9) (a in rr) ...................... 1½.10

3714 Crystal Heights (FR) **(75)** (v) *(WAO'Gorman)* 4–8-13 EmmaO'Gorman (3) (s.s:
w ldrs tl wknd over 2f out) ...................... ½.11

3759⁴ Gabbiadini **(65)** (v) *(MHTompkins)* 5–7-13 ‡⁴SMulvey (8) (prom 4f: sn lost pl) .. 4.12

3759 Parfait Amour **(67)** (v) *(RMWhitaker)* 3–8-2 AGarth (6) (in tch: edgd rt ½-wy:
wandered & sn wknd) ...................... nk.13

LONG HANDICAP: Allegramente 6-13.

**11/10** Hob Green, **8/1** Native Chieftan, **10/1** Crystal Heights (FR)(7/1—11/1), **12/1** TAKENHALL, Gabbiadini, Ler
Cru (IRE)(10/1—8/1), Dorset Duke, Ernestan(op 7/1), **16/1** Super Benz, **20/1** Furiella, **25/1** Pesidanamich (IRE),
**33/1** Parfait Amour, **50/1** Allegramente. CSF £25.25, CT £219.37. Tote £12.90: £2.50 £1.50 £27.20 (£8.80). Mr
Craig Pearman (EAST ILSLEY) bred by Ballymacarney Stud. 13 Rn

     1m 29.17 (5.77)
     SF—26/25/26/32/37/4

## 3820

E.B.F. FLAXTON STKS (II) (Mdn 2-Y.O) £3640.50 (£1089.00: £522.00: £238.50)
**7f**                            2-00 (2-04)

     **Pamzig (USA)** (Fav) *(BWHills)* 8-9 TQuinn (10) (rangy: trckd ldrs: effrt &
swtchd lft over 2f out: led over 1f out: r.o wl) ...................... —1

Tajhiz (USA) *(JHMGosden)* 9-0 WCarson (2) (leggy: scope: led centre: hdd
over 1f out: r.o) ...................... 1.2

3662⁵ Wisham (USA) *(BHanbury)* 9-0 BRaymond (4) (bit bkwd: hld up: effrt 2f out: r.o
fnl f) ...................... 3.3

Brayowski *(JRFanshawe)* 9-0 PRobinson (7) (w'like: a chsng ldrs: rdn & nt
qckn fnl f) ...................... s.h.4

3704 Can Can Charlie *(MJohnston)* 9-0 RPElliott (1) (trckd ldrs tl grad wknd fnl 2f) ..... 6.5

Solomon's Dancer (USA) *(WWHaigh)* 9-0 SWebster (12) (w'like: str: sn bhd:
styd on appr fnl f) ...................... 3½.6

1701⁴ Najaran (USA) *(MRStoute)* 9-0 WRSwinburn (9) (chsd ldrs tl wknd over 2f out) . ½.7

3617 Dances With Gold *(MJohnston)* 9-0 DMcKeown (11) (led stands' side: wknd
over 2f out) ...................... 1½.8

3704 Sarah Heights *(MissLCSiddall)* 8-9 PatEddery (5) (chsd ldrs tl lost pl ½-wy: ...... 2.9

Chatoyant *(JWWatts)* 9-0 GDuffield (8) (b: gd sort: stdd s: bhd: sme hdwy 3f
out: sn wknd) ...................... s.h.10

Restraint *(PCalver)* 8-9 JFortune (6) (w'like: bit bkwd: sn wl outpcd) ................. 1.11

Elegant Ellie *(MrsLPiggott)* 8-9 LPiggott (3) (w'like: bit bkwd: prom to ½-wy: sn
lost pl) ...................... 1½.12

3691 Barton Royal (IRE) *(RHollinshead)* 9-0 LDettori (14) (sn wl outpcd & drvn along)3½.13

Mabaadi (USA) *(MAJarvis)* 9-0 SCauthen (13) (unf: scope: prom to ½-wy: sn
drvn along & wknd) ...................... 14

**3/1** PAMZIG (USA)(op 5/1), **5/1** Wisham (USA)(op 3/1), Tajhiz (USA)(op 3/1), **11/2** Najaran (USA)(4/1—6/1),
**8/1** Chatoyant, **10/1** Mabaadi (USA), Sarah Heights, **16/1** Elegant Ellie, **20/1** Dances With Gold, Brayowski, **33/1**
Can Can Charlie, Restraint, Barton Royal (IRE), **50/1** Solomon's Dancer (USA). CSF £18.73, Tote £4.40: £1.90
£2.00 £2.30 (£8.70). Mr Howard Kaskel (LAMBOURN) bred by Sugar Maple Farm in USA. 14 Rn

     1m 28.68 (5.28)
     SF—43/45/36/35/17/6

## 3821

CANTLEY PARK (S) NURSERY    £2742.00 (£762.00: £366.00)
**1m (rnd)**                        2-30 (2-36)

3754 **Reasons for Love (IRE) (64)** *(JJO'Neill)* 9-4 PatEddery (14) (lw: trckd ldr: led
3f out: sn qcknd clr : drvn out fnl f) ...................... —1

3796 Ann Hill (IRE) **(57)** *(RHollinshead)* 8-4 ‡⁷AGarth (12) (sn bhd: hdwy over 2f out:
styd on wl: nt rch wnr) ...................... 2½.2

3505 Kiawah **(54)** *(JRFanshawe)* 8-8 GBardwell (16) (hdwy 2f out: styd on strly nr fin) 2.3

889⁶ Brackenthwaite **(57)** *(TDBarron)* 8-11 AlexGreaves (13) (hdwy u.p over 2f out:
kpt on: nt rch ldrs) ...................... ½.4

3712⁶ Sea Exhibition (IRE) **(63)** (Fav) *(MBlanshard)* 9-0 ‡3DHarrison (8) (styd on fnl 2f: nvr nr to chal) ......................................................................................... hd.5
3643 Innocent Abroad (DEN) **(58)** *(CBBBooth)* 8-12 GOldroyd (18) (hdwy 2f out: nrst fin) ..................................................................................................... hd.6
3623² Palacegate Sunset **(56)** *(JBerry)* 8-10 JCarroll (3) (lw: chsd ldrs: hrd drvn over 3f out: one pce) ...................................................................................... s.h.7
3685* Trepidation (IRE) **(54)** (v) *(MJFetherston-Godley)* 8-8 (7x) LDettori (7) (hdwy & n.m.r over 2f out: kpt on: nvr nr to chal) ............................................ 1.8
3685⁵ Kaloochi **(59)** (bl) *(RHannon)* 8-13 JReid (2) (s.s: bhd tl styd on fnl 2f) ........... ¹/₂.9
3611* Nellie's Gamble **(55)** *(APStringer)* 8-9 SWood (19) (lw: hld up & bhd: sme hdwy 2f out: n.d) ........................................................................................ ¹/₂.10
3598 Don'tlie (IRE) **(67)** *(GBBalding)* 9-7 JWilliams (5) (lw: sn bhd: kpt on fnl 2f) .... 1.11
3614 Chiappucci (IRE) **(64)** *(MAJarvis)* 9-4 GCrealock (10) (sn bhd: sme hdwy 2f out: n.d) ................................................................................................... hd.12
3303 Scoffera **(60)** *(NTinkler)* 9-0 KimTinkler (6) (a in rr) ...................................... 2¹/₂.13
3685² Honorary Guest **(60)** *(DJGMurray-Smith)* 9-0 TRogers (4) (swtg: in tch: effrt over 3f out: sn wknd) ........................................................................... 1¹/₂.14
3129 Venture Prints **(52)** *(RChampion)* 8-6 JLowe (20) (trckd ldrs tl lost pl 3f out) .... 3.15
3694⁵ Girl Next Door **(56)** (v) *(NAGraham)* 8-10 WCarson (11) (nvr nr ldrs) ............... 1.16
3291 Miss Fayruz (IRE) **(55)** *(MrsLPiggott)* 8-9 LPiggott (9) (b.hind: chsd ldrs tl wknd 3f out) .................................................................................................... 2¹/₂.17
3394 Minster Man (IRE) **(52)** *(BSRothwell)* 8-6 GDuffield (17) (in tch: effrt over 3f out: sn wknd) ............................................................................................... 3.18
3617 Bajka **(62)** *(WJarvis)* 8-11 ‡5StephenDavies (15) (chsd ldrs tl wknd 3f out) .... 2¹/₂.19
3754 Just Baileys **(60)** (bl) *(MJohnston)* 9-0 RPElliott (1) (plld hrd: led to 3f out: wknd qckly) ................................................................................................ ³/₄.20

**11/2** Sea Exhibition (IRE), **6/1** Palacegate Sunset, **7/1** Girl Next Door, Trepidation (IRE), **17/2** REASONS FOR LOVE (IRE), **10/1** Honorary Guest, **11/1** Nellie's Gamble, **12/1** Miss Fayruz (IRE), Ann Hill (IRE), Kaloochi, **14/1** Don'tlie (IRE), **16/1** Brackenthwaite, Bajka, **20/1** Just Baileys, **25/1** Chiappucci (IRE), Kiawah, Minster Man (IRE), **33/1** Ors. CSF £113.75, CT £2301.21. Tote £15.40: £3.60 £2.40 £18.50 £11.00 (£83.50). Mr Jim McGrath (PENRITH) bred by Mull Enterprizes in Ireland. 20 Rn; No bid
1m 46.36 (7.06)
SF—28/6/4/5/7/4

**3822** DONCASTER WRITERS STKS £3289.50 (£981.00: £468.00: £211.50)
2m 110y
3-00 (3-01)

**Morley Street (103)** *(GBBalding)* 8-9-5 JWilliams (4) (lw: hld up: qcknd to ld over 1f out: r.o wl) .......................................................................................... —1
3666³ Jungle Dancer (IRE) **(88)** (Fav) *(MRStoute)* 4-9-5 PatEddery (2) (hld up: smooth hdwy to chal 2f out: sn rdn & nt qckn) ............................................ 3¹/₂.2
2139* Glaisdale **(90)** *(HRACecil)* 3-8-4 WRyan (3) (lw: led: qcknd 4f out: hdd over 1f out: wknd fnl f: no ex) ................................................................................ hd.3
3639⁶ Cosmic Future **(53)** *(SPCWoods)* 3-8-4 WWoods (5) (rdn 4f out: a bhd) ......... 20.4
Boarding School **(90)** *(CParker)* 5-9-0 JCarroll (1) (chsd ldrs: chal appr st: wknd wl over 2f out) ................................................................................... 12.5

**11/8** Jungle Dancer (IRE), **85/40** MORLEY STREET, **9/4** Glaisdale (IRE), **25/1** Boarding School, **100/1** Cosmic Future. CSF £5.19, Tote £3.40: £1.40 £1.50 (£4.10). Michael Jackson Bloodstock Ltd (DORCHESTER) bred by M. Parkhill. 5 Rn
3m 45.53 (16.53)

**3823** GO RACING IN YORKSHIRE H'CAP (0-90) £3786.75 (£1134.00: £544.50: £249.75)
1³/₄m 132y
3-30 (3-33)

3613³ **Sarawat (78)** *(MrsGRReveley)* 4-9-5 KDarley (6) (lw: trckd ldrs: led over 3f out: sn rdn: r.o wl) ........................................................................................ —1
3536² Kiveton Kabooz **(86)** (bl) (Fav) *(JAGlover)* 4-9-13 AMunro (2) (hld up: hdwy appr st: chal on bit 2f out: rdn & nt r.o) ...................................................... 1.2
3616³ Alqairawaan **(70)** *(JLDunlop)* 3-8-2 WCarson (11) (a chsng ldrs: outpcd 3f out: styd on fnl f) ........................................................................................... 3.3
3728 Aahsaylad **(77)** (v) *(FHLee)* 6-9-4 BRaymond (8) (pushed along & bhd: styd on fnl 4f) ................................................................................................... 3.4
3745* Mrs Barton (IRE) **(62)** (bl) *(BWHills)* 4-8-3 (4x) RHills (12) (trckd ldrs: effrt 4f out: one pce) ................................................................................................. 1¹/₂.5
3515⁴ Good Hand (USA) **(80)** *(JWWatts)* 6-9-7 NConnorton (1) (hld up & bhd: sme late hdwy) .......................................................................................... 1¹/₂.6
3755 Bold Ambition **(59)** *(TKersey)* 5-7-9⁽⁷⁾ ‡5NKennedy (7) (lw: prom: reminders 7f out: wknd 4f out) ............................................................................... 5.7
815 Balaat (USA) **(54)** *(MCChapman)* 4-7-9 TyroneWilliams (4) (hdwy 10f out: chal appr st: wknd 3f out) ................................................................................. 1.8
3468 Stapleton (IRE) **(72)** *(JWWatts)* 3-8-4 GDuffield (10) (lw: led tl hdd & wknd over 3f out) ................................................................................................ 1.9

*1002* Malenoir (USA) **(57)** *(RCSpicer)* 4–7-12[1] LCharnock (5) (prom tl rdn & wknd appr st) ...... 10

3504 Pokey's Pride **(55)** *(JRBostock)* 9–7-10 JLowe (3) (bit bkwd: a bhd) ...... 11

288[4] Signor Sassie (USA) **(65)** *(NTinkler)* 4–8-6 KimTinkler (9) (bit bkwd: rdn 9f out: sn t.o) ...... 12

LONG HANDICAP: Bold Ambition 6-8.

**4/1** Kiveton Kabooz, **9/2** Mrs Barton (IRE), **6/1** SARAWAT, **7/1** Stapleton (IRE), Aahsaylad, Alqairawaan, **9/1** Good Hand (USA), **25/1** Signor Sassie (USA), **33/1** Balaat (USA), Bold Ambition, Malenoir (USA), **50/1** Pokey's Pride. CSF £27.14, CT £154.50. Tote £8.90: £2.20 £1.60 £1.90 (£12.90). Mr S. Aitken (SALTBURN) bred by Nawara Stud Co Ltd. 12 Rn
3m 9.29 (5.69)
SF–69/75/44/54/36/51

## 3824
**6f**
WHEATLEY PARK GRADUATION STKS (2-Y.O) £3435.75 (£1026.00: £490.50: £222.75)
4-00 (4-03)

3435[4] **Wathik (USA) (100)** *(HThomsonJones)* 9-3 RHills (3) (cl up: rdn to ld ins fnl f: r.o wl) ...... —1

3704* Specified (USA) **(93)** (Fav) *(JHMGosden)* 9-3 PatEddery (2) (led: rdn 2f out: hdd & no ex ins fnl f) ...... 1.2

3541 Tykeyvor (IRE) **(94)** *(MHTompkins)* 9-3 PRobinson (4) (prom: rdn 2f out: r.o nr fin) ...... s.h.3

1844[2] Colyan (IRE) **(100)** *(MRStoute)* 9-3 WRSwinburn (1) (plld hrd: trckd ldrs: effrt over 1f out: sn btn) ...... 2[1]/4

Sunnyview Lad *(PCHaslam)* 8-11 DMcKeown (5) (w'like: bkwd: prom: outpcd 2f out: sn wknd) ...... 4.5

**1/2** Specified (USA), **4/1** Colyan (IRE), **5/1** WATHIK (USA), **16/1** Tykeyvor (IRE), **100/1** Sunnyview Lad. CSF £7.77, Tote £5.60: £1.80 £1.10 (£1.50). Mr Hamdan Al-Maktoum (NEWMARKET) bred by Crescent Farm in USA. 5 Rn
1m 15.65 (4.65)
SF–40/36/35/25/3

## 3825
**1m (rnd)**
MANSFIELD BREWERY H'CAP (0-80) £4337.50 (£1300.00: £625.00: £287.50)
4-30 (4-34)

3714[3] **Amazing Feat (IRE) (74)** (Fav) *(MrsGRReveley)* 3-9-8 KDarley (12) (lw: a.p: led over 1f out: rdn & r.o wl) ...... —1

3545 Buzzards Bellbuoy **(70)** *(HJCollingridge)* 3-9-4 JQuinn (20) (lw: in tch: hdwy 3f out: ev ch 1f out: r.o) ...... 1.2

3714 Morsun **(73)** (bl) *(DMorley)* 3-9-7 PaulEddery (14) (in tch: hdwy over 2f out: kpt on one pce fnl f) ...... 1[1]/2.3

3701[6] Singers Image **(59)** *(GBBalding)* 3-8-7 JWilliams (6) (bhd: gd hdwy 2f out: hmpd over 1f out: swtchd & r.o v.wl nr fin) ...... hd.4

3708 Leap in the Dark (IRE) **(63)** *(JLDunlop)* 3-8-11 TQuinn (11) (a chsng ldrs: sltly hmpd over 2f out: r.o one pce) ...... nk.5

2941 Great Lord (IRE) **(61)** *(JWWatts)* 3-8-9 SCauthen (10) (led tl hdd over 1f out: no ex) ...... nk.6

3576 Diaco **(59)** *(MAJarvis)* 7–8-10 AMunro (1) (mid div: effrt 3f out: n.m.r & nt qckn fnl 2f) ...... nk.7

3678 Lord Vivienne (IRE) **(70)** *(RCSpicer)* 3-9-4 LDettori (9) (hdwy 1/2-wy: hmpd over 2f out: nt qckn) ...... 3[1]/2.8

1706 Regent Lad **(67)** *(MissLCSiddall)* 8-9-4 JReid (8) (in tch: effrt 3f out: no imp) ...... 3/4.9

3387 Mr Tate (IRE) **(60)** *(RAkehurst)* 3-8-8 WCarson (16) (effrt 1/2-wy: rdn & hung lft 3f out: no imp) ...... hd.10

3696 Kalko **(64)** (bl) *(CEBrittain)* 3-8-12 MRoberts (5) (hld up: nvr trbld ldrs) ...... 3/4.11

3726 Habeta (USA) **(61)** *(JWWatts)* 6–8-12 GDuffield (15) (stdd s: effrt over 3f out: n.d) 1.12

3527 Gong **(71)** *(PTWalwyn)* 3-9-5 PatEddery (7) (chsd ldrs 5f) ...... 3/4.13

3627 May Hills Legacy (IRE) **(64)** *(DWPArbuthnot)* 3-8-12 RCochrane (4) (b: cl up tl wknd wl over 2f out) ...... 1.14

809 Birthdays' Child **(59)** *(JRFanshawe)* 4–8-10 WRSwinburn (3) (lw: n.d) ...... 1[1]/2.15

3756 Media Messenger **(73)** *(DenysSmith)* 3-9-7 KFallon (2) (s.i.s: hld up & bhd: n.d) 3.16

3751 Wild Prospect **(60)** (v) *(CTinkler)* 4–8-11 MBirch (18) (chsd ldrs: hung lft over 2f out: sn wknd) ...... 5.17

3473[6] Boursin (IRE) **(77)** *(PCalver)* 3–9-11 JFortune (13) (w ldrs tl wknd over 2f out) 1[1]/2.18

3640 Cashtal Dazzler **(56)** *(NTinkler)* 5–8-7 KimTinkler (17) (a in rr) ...... 19

797* Ballymoneyboy **(75)** *(MHTompkins)* 3-9-9 PRobinson (8) (b.nr fore: s.i.s: t.o fr 1/2-wy) ...... 20

**9/4** AMAZING FEAT (IRE), **8/1** Habeta (USA), **12/1** Ballymoneyboy, Diaco, Morsun, Gong, Mr Tate (IRE), **16/1** Buzzards Bellbuoy, Leap in the Dark (IRE), Great Lord (IRE), Lord Vivienne (IRE), Kalko, **20/1** Singers Image, Boursin (IRE), Birthdays' Child, Regent Lad, **33/1** Ors. CSF £40.31, CT £356.99. Tote £2.70: £1.60 £5.20 £3.50 £4.60 (£39.70). Mr P. D. Savill (SALTBURN) bred by Old Meadow Stud in Ireland. 20 Rn
1m 41.14 (4.84)
SF–66/59/57/42/45/42

T/Trio: Races 6: £25.30 (24.1 Tckts) & Race 8: £172.20 (3 Tckts). T/Plpt: £139.60 (26.5 Tckts). WG/AA

# DONCASTER (L-H)
## Saturday, October 24th [Good becoming Soft]
Going Allowance: 5f-8f: 0.20 sec; Rest: 0.10 sec per fur (G)

Wind: fresh across

Stalls: 2nd, 4th & 5th low, remainder high

**3826**     LEVY BOARD STKS   £5117.00 (£1526.00: £728.00: £329.00)   **7f**   1-40 (1-45)

| | | |
|---|---|---|
| 3726³ | Croft Valley (86) (RAkehurst) 5–9-8 GCarter (6) (mde all: qcknd over 2f out: r.o wl) | —1 |
| 3673³ | Deprecator (USA) (99) (Fav) (JHMGosden) 4–9-8 PatEddery (9) (b.hind: trckd ldrs: nt clr run 3f out: hdwy 2f out: r.o: nt pce of wnr) | 1½.2 |
| 3086⁵ | Savoyard (99) (bl) (MAJarvis) 4–9-8 WRyan (7) (hld up: hdwy over 2f out: kpt on one pce fnl f) | 1½.3 |
| 3591³ | Waterfowl Creek (IRE) (88) (GWragg) 3–8-8 GDuffield (2) (s.s: hld up & bhd: gd hdwy over 1f out: nvr able to chal) | nk.4 |
| 3667² | Bold Pursuit (IRE) (94) (RHannon) 3–9-5 JReid (5) (chsd ldrs: effrt over 2f out: one pce) | 2.5 |
| 404⁶ | Ruhr (IRE) (101) (bl) (BWHills) 3–8-13 JCarroll (8) (lw: stdd s: nt clr run 3f out: sn rdn & no imp) | 2.6 |
| | Thousla Rock (IRE) (97) (PWChapple-Hyam) 3–8-13 WCarson (3) (lw: hld up: hdwy over 2f out: sn rdn & btn) | 5.7 |
| 3714 | Sir Harry Hardman (91) (FHLee) 4–9-8 DMcKeown (4) (chsd ldrs tl wknd over 2f out) | 1½.8 |
| 3721 | Braveboy (CEBrittain) 4–8-12 MBirch (1) (prom tl lost tch fnl 3f) | 12.9 |

**11/8** Deprecator (USA)(Evens—6/4), **9/2** Ruhr (IRE), **13/2** Waterfowl Creek (IRE), **9/1** Bold Pursuit (IRE), CROFT VALLEY, **12/1** Savoyard, **16/1** Thousla Rock (IRE), **20/1** Sir Harry Hardman, **25/1** Braveboy. CSF £20.80, Tote £9.80: £1.90 £1.30 £3.40 (£6.90). Miss Vivian Pratt (EPSOM) bred by Mrs M. Pratt. 9 Ran  1m £7.23 (3.83)
                                                                 SF—72/67/62/47/52/40

**3827**     AUTUMN (S) STKS (3 & 4-Y.O) £3600.00 (£1080.00: £520.00: £240.00)
          1¼m 60y                                    2-10 (2-18)

| | | |
|---|---|---|
| 3302⁵ | Friendlypersuasion (IRE) (38) (RHollinshead) 4–9-0 KDarley (7) (hld up & bhd: gd hdwy over 3f out: led ins fnl f: r.o wl) | —1 |
| 3569 | Noel (IRE) (50) (GAPritchard-Gordon) 3–8-9 SCauthen (23) (swtg: hdwy 3f out: r.o wl: nrst fin) | ¾.2 |
| 3639² | Boogie Bopper (IRE) (59) (MBell) 3–8-2 ‡⁷PTurner (9) (bhd tl c wd & hdwy 3f out: r.o wl) | s.h.3 |
| 3577⁵ | Port in a Storm (45) (WJarvis) 3–8-9 PatEddery (21) (lw: trckd ldrs: n.m.r & swtchd over 1f out: sn ev ch & nt qckn) | s.h.4 |
| 1044 | Hasty Spark (33) (CFWall) 4–9-0 JLowe (12) (chsd ldrs: led over 2f out tl hdd ins fnl f: no ex) | 1.5 |
| 3701 | Taunting (IRE) (54) (MBlanshard) 4–9-0 JReid (17) (hdwy ent st: sn chsng ldrs: kpt on one pce appr fnl f) | hd.6 |
| 3692³ | Merls Pearl (38) (bl) (JAGlover) 3–8-1 ‡³SMaloney (19) (a.p: effrt 3f out: r.o one pce) | 4.7 |
| 3395 | Ten High (IRE) (27) (JDooler) 3–8-4 JFanning (2) (bdly hmpd & lost pl after s: hdwy 4f out: styd on u.p) | 1½.8 |
| 3726 | Shirley's Train (USA) (65) (Fav) (LordHuntingdon) 3–8-9 DMcKeown (5) (lw: trckd ldrs: nt clr run 3f out: hmpd over 1f out: nt rcvr) | 1½.9 |
| 3604 | Aragon Court (38) (JPearce) 4–9-0 MBirch (8) (cl up: slt ld 4f out tl over 2f out: btn whn hmpd over 1f out) | ½.10 |
| 3705 | Futures Gift (IRE) (40) (bl) (AWPotts) 3–8-9 SWebster (3) (hld up: stdy hdwy 4f out: effrt 2f out: nt r.o) | 2.11 |
| 3622 | Statia (IRE) (27) (DonEnricoIncisa) 4–8-9 KimTinkler (16) (outpcd & bhd tl sme late hdwy) | 1½.12 |
| 3604∗ | April City (MJHeaton-Ellis) 3–8-4 WRyan (4) (led tl hdd 4f out: wknd 2f out) | ¾.13 |
| 3629⁵ | Titian Girl (30) (bl) (MissLCSiddall) 3–8-4 JCarroll (1) (effrt appr st: hrd drvn & no imp) | s.h.14 |
| 3771 | I'M Curious (45) (RThompson) 3–8-4 GCarter (10) (wl bhd tl sme late hdwy) | 2½.15 |
| 3747 | Bobbie Bold (32) (TKersey) 4–8-7 ‡⁷CHawksley (15) (dwlt: n.d) | 2.16 |
| 3384 | Heavy Rock (IRE) (38) (DJSCosgrove) 3–8-4 GDuffield (18) (n.d) | nk.17 |
| 3701 | Sweet Bloom (APJarvis) 4–8-9 MTebbutt (13) (effrt u.p 4f out: sn btn) | 5.18 |
| 3639∗ | Edge of Darkness (57) (NTinkler) 3–8-9 LCharnock (6) (a outpcd & bhd) | hd.19 |
| 3513 | Strangersinthenite (38) (JSWainwright) 3–8-9 KFallon (14) (lw: chsd ldrs tl wknd 4f out) | nk.20 |
| 3639³ | Diamond Wedding (USA) (62) (bl) (NAGraham) 3–8-4 WCarson (22) (lost tch fnl 4f) | 2.21 |

3706 Concord Wench *(PDEvans)* 4-8-2 ‡7AGarth (21) (t.o) .................. **22**
3605 Jinsky's Jewel **(29)** *(RThompson)* 4-8-7 ‡7TAshley (20) (t.o) .................. **23**

**5/1** Shirley's Train (USA), **11/2** Diamond Wedding (USA), **6/1** April City, **13/2** Boogie Bopper (IRE), **7/1** Port in a Storm, Edge of Darkness, **12/1** Taunting (IRE), **14/1** Noel (IRE), **20/1** Merls Pearl, Aragon Court, **25/1** FRIENDLYPERSUASION (IRE), Futures Gift (IRE), **33/1** Hasty Spark, Heavy Rock (IRE), I'M Curious, **50/1** Ors. CSF £322.94, Tote £21.90: £4.60 £4.30 £2.30 (£93.00). Dickins Ltd (UPPER LONGDON) bred by G. J. Hamilton in Ireland. 23 Rn; No bid
2m 14.42 (7.42)
SF—36/29/21/27/30/29

**3828**  LADBROKE CHANTILLY H'CAP (0-100) £4305.00 (£1290.00: £620.00: £285.00)
**6f**
2-40 (2-40)

3543 **Everglades (IRE) (70)** *(RCharlton)* 4-8-6(1) JReid (16) (chsd ldrs stands' side: led wl over 1f out: sn clr: r.o wl) .................. **—1**
3680 Appledorn **(78)** *(BAMcMahon)* 5-9-0 GDuffield (13) (hdwy stands' side 2f out: r.o wl) .................. **3.2**
3680★ Densben **(84)** *(DenysSmith)* 8-9-6 KFallon (19) (in tch stands' side: rdn over 2f out: r.o fnl f) .................. **1½.3**
3680 Cumbrian Waltzer **(89)** *(MHEasterby)* 7-9-11 MBirch (15) (bhd stands' side tl hdwy over 1f out: fin wl) .................. **1½.4**
3539⁶ Ahbab (IRE) **(78)** (v) *(PTWalwyn)* 3-8-12 WCarson (17) (chsd ldrs stands' side: nt qckn fnl 2f) .................. **s.h.5**
3700 Fay's Song (IRE) **(67)** *(RAkehurst)* 4-8-3 SDawson (5) (racd far side: outpcd tl hdwy 2f out: styd on wl) .................. **hd.6**
3680 King's Signet (USA) **(93)** *(JHMGosden)* 3-9-13 SCauthen (7) (cl up far side: led far side ½-wy: no ch appr fnl f) .................. **¾.7**
3777★ Peerage Prince **(65)** (bl) *(PatMitchell)* 5-7-10 (6x) ‡3SO'Gorman (4) (racd far side: chsd ldrs: nt qckn appr fnl f) .................. **1½.8**
37875 Saddlehome (USA) **(74)** (v) *(RMWhitaker)* 3-8-8 DMcKeown (20) (led stands' side & clr tl hdd & wknd wl over 1f out) .................. **½.9**
3751 Profilic **(67)** *(CaptJWilson)* 7-8-3 GCarter (11) (outpcd stands' side tl styd on appr fnl f) .................. **nk.10**
3539 Arabellajill **(92)** *(RHannon)* 3-9-9 ‡3RPerham (2) (racd far side: chsd ldrs: rdn & no ch w ldrs stands' side) .................. **s.h.11**
3729² Fascination Waltz **(73)** (Jt-Fav) *(DShaw)* 5-8-4 ‡5NKennedy (3) (racd far side: hdwy over 2f out: no imp) .................. **nk.12**
3729 Lucedeo **(78)** *(JLSpearing)* 8-8-7 ‡7AGarth (18) (hdwy stands' side ½-wy: rdn & btn wl over 1f out) .................. **2½.13**
3437 Beau Venture (USA) **(92)** *(FHLee)* 4-10-0 WRyan (21) (racd far side: nvr trbld ldrs) .................. **1½.14**
3787 The Auction Bidder **(82)** *(RHollinshead)* 5-9-4 KDarley (10) (racd far side: effrt ½-wy: n.d) .................. **nk.15**
37145 Mamma's Too **(87)** *(MBell)* 3-9-0 ‡7PTurner (12) (racd stands' side: outpcd fr ½-wy) .................. **2½.16**
3024 Filicaia **(60)** *(DonEnricoIncisa)* 6-7-3 ‡7ClaireBalding (14) (a outpcd & bhd stands' side) .................. **hd.17**
3620³ Darussalam **(75)** (Jt-Fav) *(RLee)* 5-8-11 PatEddery (1) (a bhd far side) .................. **2.18**
3787 Sonderise **(69)** *(NTinkler)* 3-8-3 LCharnock (22) (prom stands' side over 3f) .................. **2½.19**
3748 Quatre Femme **(63)** *(MJohnston)* 5-7-13 JLowe (9) (led far side to ½-wy: wknd qckly) .................. **2.20**
3633 Super Rocky **(70)** *(RBastiman)* 3-8-4 NConnorton (8) (racd far side: a bhd) .................. **4.21**
3126 Cronk's Courage **(75)** (v) *(EJAlston)* 6-8-11 LPiggott (6) (spd far side to ½-wy: sn bhd) .................. **12.22**

**8/1** Fascination Waltz, Darussalam, **9/1** Cumbrian Waltzer, King's Signet (USA), **12/1** Quatre Femme, Mamma's Too, Densben, **14/1** Saddlehome (USA), **16/1** EVERGLADES (IRE), Cronk's Courage, Ahbab (IRE), **20/1** Peerage Prince, Fay's Song (IRE), Profilic, Arabellajill, **25/1** Super Rocky, **33/1** Ors. CSF £423.01, CT £5,740.49. Tote £20.00: £4.00 £7.70 £2.30 £2.40 (£458.80). Miss Sophie Oppenheimer (BECKHAMPTON) bred by Hascombe and Valiant Studs in Ireland. 22 Rn
1m 13.48 (2.48)
SF—66/62/62/61/47/37

**3829**  NORTH AMERICA TRAVEL SERVICE H'CAP (0-90) £3200.00 (£950.00: £450.00: £200.00)
**1½m**
3-10 (3-17)

(Weights raised 8 lb)

36275 **Thamestar (IRE) (72)** *(JLDunlop)* 3-9-4 LPiggott (3) (trckd ldrs: stumbled after 2f: swtchd & effrt over 1f out: str run to ld nr fin) .................. **—1**
32464 Simonov **(72)** *(GHarwood)* 3-9-4 PatEddery (11) (cl up: led over 1f out: styd on: jst ct) .................. **hd.2**
36414 First Bid **(57)** *(RMWhitaker)* 5-8-10 JFanning (12) (a cl up: effrt & ev ch over 2f out: kpt on u.p nr fin) .................. **s.h.3**

3687 Vasiliev (65) (bl) (JPLeigh) 4–9-4 DMcKeown (5) (hld up: hdwy 3f out: edgd lft u.p: styd on wl nr fin) .................................................. hd.4

3718 Kanvass (77) (JRFanshawe) 3–9-9 CAsmussen (14) (hld up & bhd: hdwy 2f out: styd on wl nr fin) .................................................. 1½.5

3628² Mimique (77) (Fav) (HRACecil) 3–9-9 SCauthen (9) (led tl over 1f out: one pce) ¾.6

3752* Simply-H (IRE) (72) (MBell) 3–8-11 ‡7PTurner (13) (hld up & bhd: effrt 3f out: styd on: nt pce to chal) .................................................. 1½.7

3713 White Willow (71) (MrsGRReveley) 3–8-10 ‡7DarrenMoffatt (15) (hdwy 8f out: wnt prom over 4f out: one pce fnl 2f) .................................................. ¾.8

View From Above (PaulGreen,Jersey) 6–9-9 SDawson (4) (in tch: effrt over 3f out: n.m.r & r.o one pce) .................................................. 1.9

3641 Eurotwist (64) (TDBarron) 3–8-3 ‡7VHalliday (8) (bhd: hdwy on ins 4f out: no imp) .................................................. hd.10

3066⁶ Misty View (68) (MAJarvis) 3–9-0 WRyan (2) (hld up & bhd: effrt 3f out: n.d) .... 2.11

3510 Rock Legend (47) (DShaw) 4–7-9 ‡5NKennedy (7) (prom tl lost pl ent st: nt clr run & nvr plcd to chal after) .................................................. ½.12

3461 Bold Elect (71) (PWigham) 4–9-10 MWigham (17) (wnt prom after 3f: rdn 4f out: wknd & eased over 1f out) .................................................. nk.13

3641² Much Sought After (78) (DMorley) 3–8-10 GDuffield (6) (chsd ldrs tl wknd fnl 3f) ½.14

3273 Trojan Lancer (54) (DrJDScargill) 6–8-7 GCarter (16) (nvr trbld ldrs) .................................................. 1½.15

3687 Rousitto (68) (RHollinshead) 4–9-7 KDarley (10) (bhd: gd hdwy 3f out: wknd 2f out) .................................................. 4.16

Emperor Alexander (IRE) (67) (NASmith) 4–9-6 JFortune (1) (hdwy appr st: rdn over 3f out: sn wknd) .................................................. 10.17

4/1 Mimique, 5/1 Simply-H (IRE), 9/1 Much Sought After, 10/1 First Bid, THAMESTAR (IRE), 11/1 View From Above, Simonov, 12/1 Kanvass, Rousitto, 14/1 Misty View, 16/1 White Willow, Trojan Lancer, Bold Elect, 20/1 Eurotwist, 33/1 Ors. CSF £113.65, CT £1,044.24. Tote £15.90: £3.00 £2.80 £2.30 £6.00 (£54.70). Mr J. E. Nash (ARUNDEL) bred by Newton Ctud Farm Inc. in Ireland 17 Rn 2m 37.02 (6.42)
SF—52/51/42/49/31/49

**3830** RACING POST TROPHY (Gp 1) (2-Y.O.C & F) £104396.50 (£38993.50: £19009.25: £8108.75: £3566.88: £1750.12) **1m (rnd)** 3-45 (3-48)

3525* **Armiger** (Fav) (HRACecil) 9-0 PatEddery (4) (lw: trckd ldrs gng wl: qcknd to ld on bit over 2f out: r.o wl) .................................................. —1

3444* Ivanka (IRE) (CEBrittain) 8-9 SCauthen (6) (trckd wnr: effrt & ev ch over 2f out: r.o: no imp) .................................................. 6.2

3722 Zind (IRE) (PWChapple-Hyam) 9-0 GDuffield (3) (lw: chsd ldrs: pushed along thrght: kpt on fnl 3f: no imp) .................................................. 4.3

3446* Desert Secret (IRE) (MRStoute) 9-0 WRSwinburn (9) (hld up: hdwy 3f out: sn rdn & no imp) .................................................. 1.4

3091 Noyan (v) (MBell) 9-0 MHills (1) (lw: led tl over 2f out: sn outpcd) .................................................. 5.5

3519* Newton's Law (IRE) (PWChapple-Hyam) 9-0 LPiggott (2) (lw: chsd ldr: effrt 4f out: sn rdn: wknd wl over 2f out) .................................................. ½.6

1595* Redenham (USA) (RHannon) 9-0 JReid (8) (lw: bhd: effrt ½-wy: nvr trbld ldrs) .. s.h.7

3669³ Mukhamedov (DRLoder) 9-0 CAsmussen (5) (bhd: effrt ½-wy: n.d) .................................................. ½.8

3655⁵ Marillette (USA) (JHMGosden) 8-9 WCarson (7) (s.i.s: effrt ½-wy: n.d) .................................................. 5.9

3199² Wahem (IRE) (CEBrittain) 9-0 KDarley (10) (cl up tl wknd over 3f out) .................................................. 15.10

5/4 ARMIGER(tchd 2/1), 9/2 Ivanka (IRE), 5/1 Marillette (USA), Desert Secret (IRE), 12/1 Redenham (USA), 14/1 Newton's Law (IRE), 25/1 Zind (IRE), 33/1 Mukhamedov, 66/1 Noyan, 100/1 Wahem (IRE). CSF £7.41, Tote £2.40: £1.40 £1.70 £4.60 (£7.60). Mr K. Abdulla (NEWMARKET) bred by Juddmonte Farms. 10 Rn 1m 39.70 (3.40)
SF—73/50/43/40/25/23

**3831** DONCASTER STKS (listed race) (2-Y.O) £7375.00 (£2200.00: £1050.00: £475.00) **5f** 4-15 (4-20)

3672⁴ **Ansellman (100)** (MJHaynes) 8-11 CAsmussen (8) (lw: led over 1f: led wl over 1f out: r.o wl) .................................................. —1

3672 Fyfield Flyer (IRE) (100) (PWChapple-Hyam) 9-1 JReid (7) (disp ld: rdn 2f out: nt qckn wl ins fnl f) .................................................. ½.2

3672³ Surprise Offer (100) (bl) (RHannon) 8-11 PatEddery (4) (a chsng ldrs: effrt 2f out: nt qckn fnl f) .................................................. 2.3

3672² Roger the Butler (IRE) (100) (MBell) 8-11 MHills (11) (lw: chsd ldrs: led over 3f tl wl over 1f out: no ex) .................................................. nk.4

3750* Stepanov (USA) (Fav) (JHMGosden) 8-11 SCauthen (2) (lw: s.i.s: hdwy to chse ldrs ½-wy: rdn, put hd in air & nt qckn appr fnl f) .................................................. 2½.5

2690⁵ Area Girl (83) (SirMarkPrescott) 8-6 GDuffield (6) (a chsng ldrs: effrt 4f out: nt qckn) .................................................. 1.6

3420² Troon **(85)** *(MrsLPiggott)* 8-11 LPiggott (1) (b: b.hind: shkn up 2f out: no imp) 1½.7

3366 Charity Express (IRE) **(83)** *(JBerry)* 8-6 JCarroll (10) (s.s. hdwy ½-wy: sn rdn & btn) ............................................................................... 2.8

3588* Aradanza **(98)** *(MRChannon)* 8-11 WCarson (5) (outpcd fr ½-wy) ............... 1½.9

3588² Baliana **(83)** (v) *(CBBooth)* 8-1 ACulhane (3) (outpcd & wl bhd fr ½-wy) ..... 10.10

**5/2** Stepanov (USA), **3/1** Roger the Butler (IRE), **9/2** Surprise Offer, **9/1** Fyfield Flyer (IRE), **10/1** ANSELLMAN, **12/1** Aradanza, **16/1** Area Girl, Baliana, **20/1** Troon, **25/1** Charity Express (IRE). CSF £87.06, Tote £10.60: £2.60 £2.90 £2.00 (£29.50). Ansells of Watford (EPSOM) bred by W. L. Caley. 10 Rn          61.18 sec (2.48)

SF—67/69/57/56/46/37

**3832**      MAZDA CARS NURSERY      £3200.00 (£950.00: £450.00: £200.00)      7f  4-45 (4-51)

3635⁴ **So so (75)** *(TDBarron)* 8-8 AlexGreaves (10) (racd centre: cl up: led over 2f out: hld on wl) .................................................................... —1

3635⁵ **Harpoon Louie (USA) (75)** *(MHEasterby)* 8-8 MBirch (2) (lw: chsd ldrs far side: chal 2f out: hrd rdn & r.o wl) ............................................ s.h.2

3482* **Doc Cottrill (68)** (Fav) *(MrsJRRamsden)* 8-1 GCarter (9) (lw: hld up & bhd centre: hdwy over 1f out: r.o wl: too much to do) ............... 1½.3

3679⁴ **Jervia (88)** *(JWWatts)* 9-7 SCauthen (3) (racd far side: hdwy 3f out: styd on one pce appr fnl f) ......................................................... 3.4

3353 **Southern Memories (IRE) (76)** *(RHannon)* 8-9 JReid (11) (led centre tl hdd over 2f out: nt qckn) ...................................................... 1½.5

3501² **Hawl (USA) (86)** *(AAScott)* 9-5 WCarson (20) (outpcd & bhd stands' side: r.o wl fnl f) ............................................................. 3½.6

3716⁵ **Festin (74)** (bl) *(JLDunlop)* 8-7 PatEddery (22) (led overall tl over 2f out: no ex) ½.7

3474 **Wanza (66)** *(JHanson)* 7-13 EJohnson (14) (lw: chsd ldr stands' side: nt qckn fnl 2f) ................................................................. 1.8

3631⁶ **Move Smartly (IRE) (65)** 7-7⁽³⁾ ‡⁵NKennedy (1) (prom far side tl outpcd fnl 2f) ........................................................................... s.h.9

3482 **Silent Expression (73)** *(DMorris)* 8-1 ‡§StephenDavies (15) (chsd ldrs stands' side tl rdn & btn over 2f out) ......................................... s.h.10

3665 **Satin Dancer (85)** *(GHarwood)* 9-4 KDarley (12) (racd centre: outpcd fr ½-wy) nk.11

3617* **Cubist (IRE) (80)** *(DMorley)* 8-13 WRyan (8) (b.off hind: racd centre: outpcd 3f out: n.d) ......................................................... 2½.12

3408 **Turfmans Vision (68)** *(RHollinshead)* 7-8 ‡7AGarth (19) (outpcd & bhd stands' side: edgd lft ½-wy: n.d) ...................................... nk.13

3465⁴ **Cardinal Dogwood (USA) (64)** (bl) *(MBrittain)* 7-11 JLowe (13) (nvr nr to chal) ¾.14

3482 **Umbubuzi (USA) (76)** *(FHLee)* 8-9 RLappin (4) (cl up far side tl wknd over 2f out) ............................................................ 1½.15

3470 **Bold Seven (IRE) (86)** *(FHLee)* 9-5 WRSwinburn (6) (racd far side: prom over 4f) .............................................................. ¾.16

3029 **Astrac Trio (USA) (78)** (v) *(SGNorton)* 8-11 NConnorton (21) (sn bhd stands' side) ....................................................... nk.17

3523 **Fitzroy Lad (65)** *(MRChannon)* 7-5⁽²⁾ ‡7CHawksley (5) (racd far side: sn bhd) nk.18

3716 **Norling (IRE) (70)** *(NTinkler)* 8-3 LCharnock (7) (led far side to ½-wy: sn wknd) nk.19

3631 **Blakes Beau (68)** *(MHEasterby)* 7-12 ‡³SMaloney (18) (pushed along stands' side & lost tch fr ½-wy) ....................................... ¾.20

3746⁶ **Missed the Boat (IRE) (62)** *(TDBarron)* 7-9 SWood (16) (bhd fnl 2f) ........... 2½.21

**9/2** Doc Cottrill, **8/1** Blakes Beau, **9/1** Harpoon Louie (USA), Cubist (IRE), Satin Dancer, **10/1** Festin, **12/1** Hawl (USA), **14/1** Jervia, **16/1** Missed the Boat (IRE), SO SO, Move Smartly (IRE), **20/1** Astrac Trio (USA), Southern Memories (IRE), Silent Expression, Norling (IRE), Bold Seven (IRE), **25/1** Fitzroy Lad, **33/1** Ors. CSF £150.89, CT £703.58. Tote £15.10: £2.90 £2.60 £1.80 £3.20 (£70.50). Mr Geoffrey Martin (THIRSK) bred by Mrs S. C. Barron. 21 Rn          1m 28.43 (5.03)

SF—40/39/27/38/21/20

T/Trio: Race 3: Wnr or 2nd w any £23.60 (43.2 Tckts) & Race 4: £400.70 (2.1 Tckts). T/Plpt: £1,206.10 (6.5 Tckts).

AA

3359—**NEWBURY (L-H)**

## Saturday, October 24th [Soft]

Going Allowance: 1.05 sec per fur (S)                Wind: slt across

Stalls: 6th & 7th centre, remainder low

**3833**      RADLEY STKS (listed race) (2-Y.O.F) £8805.00 (£2640.00: £1270.00: £585.00)      7f 64y (rnd)      1-15 (1-16)

3440² **Criquette** (Fav) *(LMCumani)* 8-8 LDettori (7) (lw: 5th st: led wl over 1f out: easily) ...................................................... —1

3570* Bright Spells **(81)** *(DRCElsworth)* 8-8 JWilliams (8) (bhd tl gd hdwy over 1f out: r.o: no ch w wnr) ............................................................................................... 5.2
36653 No Reservations (IRE) **(93)** *(RFJohnsonHoughton)* 8-8 RCochrane (6) (hdwy 2f out: r.o ins fnl f) ................................................................................................... 3.3
3549* Nicer (IRE) **(100)** *(BWHills)* 8-8 MHills (3) (dwlt: 6th st: ev ch wl over 1f out: nt qckn) ..................................................................................................................... 1½.4
36652 Chain Dance **(93)** *(MRStoute)* 8-8 WRSwinburn (1) (3rd st: ev ch over 1f out: nt qckn) ..................................................................................................................... s.h.5
30964 Cristal Flite *(RHannon)* 8-8 BRaymond (4) (led tl wknd wl over 1f out) ............... 8.6
34304 Barboukh *(DRCElsworth)* 8-8 TQuinn (2) (4th st: wknd wl over 1f out) ............... 6.7
35993 Ajanta **(81)** *(BWHills)* 8-8 PaulEddery (5) (lw: 2nd st: wknd 2f out) ................... nk.8

**8/13** CRIQUETTE, **9/2** Nicer (IRE), **8/1** Chain Dance(op 5/1), **14/1** Barboukh, Bright Spells, No Reservations (IRE), **20/1** Ajanta, **33/1** Cristal Flite. CSF £10.35, Tote £1.60: £1.20 £2.20 £2.70 (£11.60). Mr Gerald Leigh (NEWMARKET) bred by Gerald W. Leigh. 8 Rn

1m 38.32 (11.02)
SF—44/29/20/15/14/–

---

**3834**  CASTROL ST SIMON STKS (Gp 3)  £20040.00 (£7497.00: £3598.50: £1564.50)
1½m 5y                                                          1-45 (1-47)

36704 Up Anchor (IRE) **(104)** *(PFICole)* 3-8-4 AMunro (6) (mde all: all out) ............... —1
3649a3 Spring *(JLDunlop)* 3-8-4 TQuinn (8) (lw: 2nd st: ev ch fnl 2f: r.o) ....................... 1.2
35333 Zinaad **(109)** (Fav) *(MRStoute)* 3-8-7 WRSwinburn (3) (hdwy 3f out: hrd rdn fnl 2f: one pce) ............................................................................................................... 2.3
3697* Mack the Knife **(105)** *(MajorWRHern)* 3-8-7 BRaymond (2) (lw: 3rd st: rdn over 2f out: one pce) ..................................................................................................... s.h.4
3653a Niodini (USA) **(111)** *(MRStoute)* 3-8-7 PaulEddery (4) (swtg: 6th st: no hdwy fnl 2f) ......................................................................................................................... 4.5
3548* Further Flight **(116)** *(RWHills)* 6-9-3 MHills (5) (b.hind: 4th st: wknd over 3f out) 3½.6
36342 Linpac West **(101)** *(CWCElsey)* 6-9-0 LDettori (7) (hrlwy 4f out: wknd over 2f out) .......................................................................................................................... ½.7
35483 Shambo **(106)** *(CEBrittain)* 5-9-5 MRoberts (1) (lw: 5th st: wknd over 3f out) ... 20.8

**9/4** Zinaad, **11/4** Further Flight, **100/30** Spring, **10/1** Mack the Knife, **12/1** Linpac West, **20/1** Niodini (USA), **25/1** UP ANCHOR (IRE) & Ors. CSF £94.71, Tote £22.00: £2.00 £1.70 £1.50 (£43.90). Mr Fahd Salman (WHATCOMBE) bred by Universal Stables in Ireland. 8 Rn

2m 44.22 (14.52)
SF—71/69/68/67/59/62

---

**3835**  FLS AEROSPACE H'CAP (0-110) £11665.00 (£3520.00: £1710.00: £805.00)
1m 1f     (Weights raised 3 lb)                               2-15 (2-18)

3663 Host (IRE) **(82)** *(CEBrittain)* 3-9-1 MRoberts (3) (led tl wl over 1f out: led nr fin: all out) .................................................................................................................... —1
36755 Royal Seaton **(82)** *(BRMillman)* 3-9-1 SWhitworth (10) (hdwy 3f out: led wl over 1f out tl nr fin) ......................................................................................................... ¾.2
34686 Surrey Dancer **(72)** (bl) *(BHanbury)* 4-8-9 BRaymond (2) (lw: 6th st: hrd rdn over 1f out: r.o ins fnl f) ............................................................................................ nk.3
38002 Shaffaaf (USA) **(67)** (v) *(PDEvans)* 4-8-4 PRobinson (12) (lw: hdwy 3f out: one pce fnl 2f) ...................................................................................................................... 2.4
35474 Dawaahi (USA) **(87)** (Fav) *(JHMGosden)* 3-9-6 RCochrane (5) (lw: wl bhd tl rdn & hdwy over 2f out: nvr nrr) .................................................................................... 3½.5
3547 Glide Path (USA) **(79)** *(JWHills)* 3-8-12 RHills (8) (lw: 5th st: ev ch 2f out: sn wknd) .................................................................................................................... 5.6
36736 Gueca Solo **(78)** *(DRLoder)* 4-9-1 TQuinn (14) (nrst fin) .................................... 2.7
3696 Lord Oberon (IRE) **(58)** *(RJO'Sullivan)* 4-7-9 JQuinn (1) (3rd st: wknd over 2f out) ...................................................................................................................... 1.8
3714 Coltrane **(66)** (v) *(LordHuntingdon)* 4-8-3 AMunro (15) (lw: 4th st: wknd over 2f out) ...................................................................................................................... 4.9
3583* Albemine (USA) **(73)** *(MrsJCecil)* 3-8-6 PaulEddery (9) (2nd st: wknd over 2f out) ...................................................................................................................... 3.10
36864 She's Pleased (USA) **(77)** *(LMCumani)* 3-8-10 LDettori (7) (a bhd) .................. 2.11
35472 Montpelier Boy **(87)** *(LordHuntingdon)* 4-9-7 ‡3DHarrison (6) (bhd tl hdwy 3f out: wknd 2f out) ....................................................................................................... 1½.12
1597* Coniston Water (USA) **(90)** *(JHMGosden)* 3-9-9 GHind (11) (hmpd after 1f: sn bhd) ........................................................................................................................ hd.13
3663 Fengari **(68)** *(PTWalwyn)* 3-8-1 DBiggs (4) (lw: a bhd) ...................................... 1½.14
3476 Ripsnorter (IRE) **(62)** *(JABennett)* 3-7-9 GBardwell (13) (lw: a bhd: t.o fnl 3f) . 20.15

**9/2** Dawaahi (USA), **6/1** Montpelier Boy, **13/2** Albemine (USA), **11/1** Shaffaaf (USA), Coltrane, She's Pleased (USA), **12/1** Gueca Solo, Fengari, **14/1** HOST (IRE), Royal Seaton, **16/1** Surrey Dancer, **20/1** Glide Path (USA), Coniston Water (USA), Lord Oberon (IRE), **33/1** Ripsnorter (IRE). CSF £175.23, CT £2,853.82. Tote £29.10: £6.70 £4.40 £6.20 (£282.20). The Dowager Lady Beaverbrook (NEWMARKET) bred by Barronstown Stud in Ireland. 15 Rn

2m 1.14 (11.94)
SF—63/61/54/43/48/25

**3836**
NEWBURY VICTIM SUPPORT H'CAP (0-100) £3817.50 (£1140.00: £545.00: £247.50)
**1m 3f 5y**
2-50 (2-51)

(Weights raised 9 lb)

| | | |
|---|---|---|
| 3675* | Robingo (IRE) (77) (bl) (CEBrittain) 3–8-9 AMunro (6) (4th st: led 1f out: r.o wl) | —1 |
| 3445 | Castoret (86) (JWHills) 6–9-10 RHills (1) (led to 1f out: r.o) | 3¹/₂.2 |
| 3663* | Plan Ahead (76) (GLewis) 3–8-5 ‡³DHarrison (2) (lw: 6th st: hdwy on ins 3f out: ev ch 1f out: r.o) | s.h.3 |
| 3663 | Seal Indigo (IRE) (83) (RHannon) 4–9-7 TQuinn (4) (lw: nvr nrr) | 5.4 |
| 3445 | Halkopous (84) (v) (Fav) (MHTompkins) 6–9-8 PRobinson (7) (5th st: ev ch 2f out: sn wknd) | hd.5 |
| 3241³ | Shrewd Partner (IRE) (83) (DRCElsworth) 3–9-1 JWilliams (5) (2nd st: wknd over 2f out) | 10.6 |
| 3436⁴ | Risk Master (84) (CAHorgan) 3–9-2 PaulEddery (3) (a bhd) | 4.7 |
| 3436 | Valley of Fire (86) (JRFanshawe) 3–9-4 MRoberts (8) (3rd st: wknd over 2f out) | 10.8 |

**3/1** Halkopous, **100/30** Plan Ahead, **5/1** ROBINGO (IRE), **7/1** Shrewd Partner (IRE), **9/1** Valley of Fire, Castoret, **11/1** Risk Master, **12/1** Seal Indigo (IRE). CSF £42.22, CT £123.54. Tote £5.80: £1.70 £2.70 £1.50 (£36.40).
Capt. M. Lemos (NEWMARKET) bred by J. J. Prendergast in Ireland. 8 Rn
2m 31.52 (15.52)
SF—57/65/45/51/51/24

**3837**
LEVY BOARD NURSERY £4240.00 (£1270.00: £610.00: £280.00)
**7f 64y (rnd)**
3-20 (3-25)

(Weights raised 3 lb)

| | | |
|---|---|---|
| 3611² | Pontevecchio Moda (59) (DRCElsworth) 7-8 GBardwell (6) (6th st: led wl over 1f out: sn hdd: r.o to ld last strides) | —1 |
| 3240 | Show Faith (IRE) (68) (RHannon) 8-3 RHills (4) (hdwy over 2f out: led over 1f out tl last strides) | hd.2 |
| 3587³ | Benevolent (76) (SirMarkPrescott) 8-11 AMunro (2) (hdwy fnl 2f: nvr nrr) | hd.3 |
| 3712⁵ | Mam'zelle Angot (61) (Fav) (MRStoute) 7-7 ‡³DHarrison (5) (b.hind: 2nd st: led over 4f out tl wl over 1f out) | 2¹/₂.4 |
| 3746² | Hallplace (61) (MRChannon) 7-10 JQuinn (15) (hdwy 3f out: one pce fnl 2f) | 2¹/₂.5 |
| 3574 | War Requiem (IRE) (58) (GBBalding) 7-7 NAdams (3) (nrst fin) | 1.6 |
| 3704⁶ | Storm Venture (IRE) (70) (WJarvis) 8-3 MRoberts (7) (3rd st: wknd 2f out) | 4.7 |
| 3579⁵ | Ground Nut (IRE) (76) (HCandy) 8-11 CRutter (1) (4th st: wknd over 2f out) | 3¹/₂.8 |
| 3665* | Brigante Di Cielo (86) (RHannon) 9-7 BRaymond (14) (prom tl rdn & wknd over 2f out) | nk.9 |
| 3551 | Mr Cube (IRE) (65) (bl) (PFICole) 8-0 DBiggs (10) (b.off hind: n.d) | 3.10 |
| 3597⁴ | Mullitover (85) (MJHeaton-Ellis) 9-6 RCochrane (12) (led over 2f: wknd over 2f out) | 3.11 |
| 3684 | Forest Song (76) (RCharlton) 8-11 TSprake (9) (n.d) | s.h.12 |
| 3694 | Bodandere (62) (MJFetherston-Godley) 7-8⁽⁴⁾ ‡³FNorton (8) (a bhd) | ³/₄.13 |
| 2717 | Sharp Gazelle (62) (BSmart) 7-11 DaleGibson (11) (5th st: wknd 3f out) | 10.14 |
| 3508⁶ | Jallaaf (USA) (80) (LMCumani) 9-1 LDettori (13) (hrd rdn 3f out: sn bhd: t.o) | 15.15 |

LONG HANDICAP: War Requiem (IRE) 7-2, Bodandere 7-1.

**9/2** Mam'zelle Angot, **5/1** Mullitover, **8/1** Benevolent, Jallaaf (USA), Brigante Di Cielo(6/1—9/1), PONTEVECCHIO MODA, **10/1** Ground Nut (IRE)(op 16/1), **12/1** Hallplace, **14/1** Storm Venture (IRE), **16/1** Show Faith (IRE), **25/1** Mr Cube (IRE), Sharp Gazelle, **33/1** Ors. CSF £117.64, CT £959.02. Tote £7.90: £2.30 £6.70 £2.60 (£142.40). Mr Walter Mariti (WHITSBURY) bred by Walter Mariti. 15 Rn
1m 38.08 (10.78)
SF—32/40/47/21/16/10

**3838**
JULIA RIDGEWELL BIRTHDAY WHATCOMBE STKS (2-Y.O) £3915.00 (£1170.00: £560.00: £255.00) **1m (st)**
3-50 (3-53)

| | | |
|---|---|---|
| | Arusha (IRE) (DRCElsworth) 8-6 JWilliams (7) (unf: s.s: wl bhd tl gd hdwy fnl 2f: led nr fin) | —1 |
| | Andromaque (USA) (RCharlton) 8-6 TSprake (3) (unf: scope: hdwy over 2f out: led over 1f out tl nr fin) | ¹/₂.2 |
| | Tremolando (USA) (RCharlton) 8-11 PaulEddery (6) (w'like: scope: hld up: ev ch over 1f out: nt qckn) | 1.3 |
| 3674 | Moorish (90) (PFICole) 9-2 AMunro (4) (led tl rdn & wknd over 1f out) | 1¹/₂.4 |
| | Ajalan (IRE) (MRStoute) 8-6 ‡⁵JJones (8) (leggy: no hdwy fnl 2f) | 4.5 |
| | Clouded Elegance (IABalding) 8-11 RCochrane (3) (leggy: nvr nr to chal) | 2.6 |
| 3200* | Dakar Rally (100) (Fav) (HRACecil) 9-2 MRoberts (5) (lw: pushed along: prom tl hrd rdn & wknd over 2f out) | 5.7 |
| 3419 | Bixby (USA) (DRCElsworth) 8-11 TQuinn (1) (chsd ldr over 5f) | 15.8 |

**8/15** Dakar Rally, **9/2** Moorish(6/1—4/1), **9/1** Tremolando (USA)(op 6/1), **16/1** Ajalan (IRE), Clouded Elegance, **20/1** Bixby (USA)(op 6/1), **25/1** ARUSHA (IRE), **33/1** Andromaque (USA). CSF £422.34, Tote £20.10: £2.50 £7.00 £2.00 (£108.00). Mr Raymond Tooth (WHITSBURY) bred by Mrs Frances R. Hutch in Ireland. 8 Rn
1m 50.12 (13.12)
SF—21/19/21/21/–/–/

**3839**  DICK DAWSON NURSERY  £4922.50 (£1480.00: £715.00: £332.50)
6f 8y                                                    4-20 (4-27)

(Weights raised 10 lb)

3432⁶ **Chili Heights (76)** *(GBBalding)* 8-9 LDettori (7) (a.p: led over 1f out tl ins fnl f: led last strides) .................................................... —1
3702³ Heber Spring (IRE) **(70)** *(RHannon)* 8-3 TyroneWilliams (4) (hdwy 2f out: led ins fnl f tl last strides) ............................................ hd.2
3702² Second Chance (IRE) **(74)** *(PMitchell)* 8-7 MRoberts (10) (led over 4f: r.o) .... 4.3
3552★ Most Eminent **(73)** *(PWHarris)* 8-6 SWhitworth (18) (hdwy 2f out: ev ch whn hng bdly lft over 1f out: nt qckn) ........................... 1½.4
3432⁴ Moon Over Miami **(84)** *(CJames)* 8-10 ‡7AntoinetteArmes (14) (lw: a.p: nt qckn fnl f) ............................................................. ½.5
3250⁴ Glimpse of Heaven **(70)** *(DRCElsworth)* 7-12 ‡5BDoyle (2) (nrst fin) ............. nk.6
3674⁶ Catherineofaragon **(88)** *(WGRWightman)* 9-7 JWilliams (5) (no hdwy fnl 2f) ....... 1.7
3712★ Soaking **(70)** (Fav) *(GLewis)* 8-0 ‡3DHarrison (1) (hdwy 3f out: nvr nr to chal) . 2½.8
3749⁴ Hokey Pokey (FR) **(60)** *(DSasse)* 7-0 ‡7DWright (13) (prom 3f) ...................... 2.9
3470 Panther (IRE) **(69)** *(CWCElsey)* 8-2 AMunro (3) (lw: n.d) ........................ 2.10
3581⁴ Walnut Burl (IRE) **(62)** *(LJHolt)* 7-9 NAdams (11) (n.d) ......................... 2.11
3665 Defenceless **(81)** *(RHannon)* 9-0 BRouse (9) (lw: ev ch 2f out: sn wknd) ....... 1½.12
3606★ Guv'nors Gift **(78)** *(MHTompkins)* 8-11 PRobinson (16) (n.d) ..................... 7.13
3606 Maybe Gold **(65)** *(DWPArbuthnot)* 7-12 RPrice (15) (b.hind: lw: n.d) ........... ½.14
3550 Greenlet (IRE) **(84)** *(MRStoute)* 8-12 ‡5JJones (12) (n.d) ....................... ½.15
3712² Greenwich Chalenge **(74)** *(WCarter)* 8-2 ‡5NGwilliams (6) (b.hind: spd 4f) .... 1½.16
3626 Legal Risk **(69)** *(DHaydnJones)* 8-2 PaulEddery (8) (spd over 3f) ............... hd.17
2577³ Christian Spirit **(60)** *(RHannon)* 7-7 NCarlisle (17) (lw: n.d) ................. 12.18

LONG HANDICAP: Hokey Pokey (FR) 7-3, Christian Spirit 7-6.

**4/1** Soaking, **6/1** Most Eminent, **9/1** Guv'nors Gift, **10/1** Defenceless, Second Chance (IRE)(8/1—12/1), **11/1** Greenwich Chalenge, 12/1 Moon Over Miami, Catherineofaragon, **16/1** Walnut Burl (IRE), Greenlet (IRE), CHILI HEIGHTS, Heber Spring (IRE), **20/1** Christian Spirit, Glimpse of Heaven, **33/1** Ors. CCF £234.01, CT £2,437.71. Tote £17.70: £3.30 £4.20 £1.90 £2.00 (£301.10). Mr B. T. Attenborough (DORCHESTER) bred by J. Crofts. 18 Rn                                                     1m 20.99 (9.19)
SF—37/30/18/11/13/—

T/Trio: Race 3: £1,476.00 (1 Tckt). T/Jkpt: Not won; £16,147.89 to Newmarket 30/10/92. T/Plpt: £8,130.00 (0.4 Tckts); £6,591.90 to Lingfield 26/10/92.                                               Hn

3551—**LINGFIELD (L-H)**

## Monday, October 26th [Turf Soft, AWT Standard]

Going Allowance: Turf: 0.85 (S); AWT: minus 0.40 sec per fur (FS)          Wind: almost nil

Stalls: high

**3840**  LEVY BOARD CLAIMING STKS (I)  £3106.00 (£928.00: £444.00: £202.00)
7f (AWT)                                                12-45 (12-47)

3805 **African Chimes (93)** (Fav) *(WAO'Gorman)* 5-9-7 ‡3EmmaO'Gorman (13) (hdwy wl over 1f out: led ins fnl f: pushed out) ............................. —1
3781 Super Serenade **(68)** *(GBBalding)* 3-8-13 TQuinn (3) (lw: hdwy over 2f out: ev ch fnl f: r.o) ........................................................ hd.2
3751 Boy Martin **(63)** *(MJohnston)* 3-8-3 DMcKeown (10) (lw: a.p: led over 3f out tl ins fnl f: unable qckn) ......................................... 2½.3
3771⁶ Dam Certain (IRE) **(47)** *(AWDenson)* 3—7-10 DaleGibson (1) (rdn over 2f out: hdwy over 1f out: r.o) ................................................. 2½.4
3729 Sylvan Breeze **(70)** *(PMitchell)* 4—8-6 AMunro (9) (no hdwy fnl 2f) ............. 2½.5
3506 Purple Amber **(83)** *(MBlanshard)* 3—7-11 ‡3DHarrison (11) (prom over 5f) ....... 2.6
3524 Lady Sabo **(64)** *(GLewis)* 3—7-13 ‡5ATucker (9) (prom 5f) ....................... 1.7
3511 Lady Snooble **(32)** *(KOCunningham-Brown)* 5—8-1 DHolland (7) (led 4f out tl over 3f out: sn wknd) .................................................... 5.8
3017 Musical Lyrics **(35)** *(MrsJGRetter)* 4—7-11 NAdams (5) (prom 5f) ................ 1.9
3576 Little Park **(50)** *(CNWilliams)* 3—8-0 JLowe (2) (swtg: a bhd) ................. 1½.10
3771 Red Jack (IRE) **(48)** (bl) *(JAkehurst)* 3—8-5 SWhitworth (14) (prom 5f) ......... nk.11
3604 Cherrywood Lass **(40)** *(RCurtis)* 4—7-11 GBardwell (12) (outpcd) ............... 3.12
Singing Gold **(27)** (bl) *(PFTulk)* 6—8-3 ‡3TWilson (8) (b: bkwd: a bhd) ....... 3.13
Dal Miss **(30)** *(REPeacock)* 5—8-1 JFanning (6) (bit bkwd: led 3f) .............. 12.14

**13/8** AFRICAN CHIMES(11/10—7/4), **5/1** Boy Martin(op 3/1), **11/2** Sylvan Breeze, **7/1** Dam Certain (IRE)(14/1—16/1), **8/1** Super Serenade, **10/1** Lady Sabo(op 2/1), **20/1** Little Park, **33/1** Lady Snooble, **50/1** Ors. CSF £14.29, Tote £2.50: £1.50 £1.80 £1.90 (£8.60). Mr D. G. Wheatley (NEWMARKET) bred by Noel Cogan. 14 Rn                                                     1m 25.27 (1.27)
SF—46/37/19/4/6/—

## 3841

ELM H'CAP (0-90) £3047.60 (£843.60: £402.80)   **2m (AWT)**   1-15 (1-16)

(Weights raised 4 lb)

37286 **Bardolph (USA) (79)** (Fav) *(PFICole)* 5–9-10 TQuinn (4) (a.p: rdn over 3f out:
led over 2f out: eased wl ins fnl f) ................................ —1
3724 Quadrant (bl) *(BWHills)* 3–8-8 DHolland (2) (lw: hld up: led 4f out tl over 2f out:
eased whn btn ins fnl f) ................................ 1.2
3745 Rajanpour (USA) (48) *(RCurtis)* 7–7-7 GBardwell (9) (lw: led 12f: one pce) ..... 3½.3
3490 Silken Words (USA) (58) *(WRMuir)* 3–7-0 ‡7KimMcDonnell (7) (lost pl over 3f
out: r.o one pce fnl 2f) ................................ 1½.4
37565 Desert Force (IRE) (62) *(MissGayKelleway)* 3–7-11 NCarlisle (3) (lw: hld up:
rdn over 4f out: sn wknd) ................................ 12.5
37453 Aide Memoire (IRE) (58) *(CBBBooth)* 3–7-7 JFanning (5) (bhd fnl 4f) ............ 5.6
35565 Crabby Bill (54) (bl) *(MissBSanders)* 5–7-13 DBiggs (a bhd) ................... ½.7
Riyadh Lights (48) *(MDIUsher)* 7–7-7 NAdams (8) (bkwd: a bhd) ............... 12.8
1459 Row Ree (62) *(PJHobbs)* 4–8-7 JCarroll (1) (bhd tl p.u 5f out: lame) ........... 0
LONG HANDICAP: Rajanpour (USA) 6-7, Silken Words (USA) 7-1, Aide Memoire (IRE) 7-0, Riyadh Lights 6-8.

**6/4** BARDOLPH (USA)(11/10—7/4), **3/1** Quadrant, **5/1** Aide Memoire (IRE), **12/1** Silken Words (USA)(op 8/1),
Desert Force (IRE), **14/1** Row Ree(op 8/1), **16/1** Crabby Bill, **33/1** Ors. CSF £5.44, CT £66.12. Tote £2.40: £1.30
£1.50 £3.00 (£4.20). Sir George Meyrick (WHATCOMBE) bred by McMillin Bros in USA. 9 Rn  3m 23.24 (0.24)
SF—44/27/8/–/–/–

## 3842

LEVY BOARD CLAIMING STKS (II)   £3106.00 (£928.00: £444.00: £202.00)
**7f (AWT)**   1-45 (1-51)

3785★ **Threepence (74)** (Fav) *(JBerry)* 3–8-9 JCarroll (9) (a.p: led 2f out: drvn out) ..... —1
3418 Courting Newmarket (53) *(MrsAKnight)* 4–8-5(1) SWhitworth (12) (lw: hld up:
hrd rdn over 1f out: r.o) ................................ 1½.2
33754 Sally's Son (74) *(WAO'Gorman)* 6–8-7 ‡3EmmaO'Gorman (8) (a.p: ev ch over 1f
out: unable qckn) ................................ ½.3
35573 Harcliff *(DJSCosgrove)* 3–8-13 JLowe (3) (b.hind: rdn over 3f out: hdwy over 1f
out: r.o one pce) ................................ 2.4
3245 Pigalle Wonder (43) *(RJO'Sullivan)* 4–7-11 ‡5ATucker (4) (lw: led 5f) .......... 2½.5
3605 Little Nod (61) *(JWhite)* 3–8-1 DaleGibson (5) (lw: nvr nr to chal) ............. ¾.6
35072 Master Hyde (46) *(PMitchell)* 3–8-3 DHolland (1) (hld up: rdn over 2f out:
btn whn nt clr run & eased over 1f out) ................................ ½.7
3421 One Magic Moment (IRE) (47) *(CACyzer)* 4–8-7 DBiggs (10) (prom over 5f) .... 2½.8
3421 Great Hall (54) *(PDCundell)* 3–7-13 GCrealock (7) (a bhd) ................... 10.9
3507 Smudgemupum (41) *(MissBSanders)* 3–7-10 ‡3DHarrison (6) (a bhd) ......... s.h.10
3423 Mr Smiley (28) *(RJBaker)* 5–8-2 TyroneWilliams (2) (swtg: spd over 3f) ....... 3½.11
Nigels Lady *(MCPipe)* 3–7-8 GBardwell (13) (neat: dwlt: a bhd) ............... 2½.12
3690 Dilkush (38) (bl) *(LJHolt)* 3–7-13 NAdams (11) (a bhd) .................... 4.13

**Evens** THREEPENCE, **3/1** Sally's Son, **8/1** Harcliff, **10/1** Master Hyde (USA)(8/1—12/1), **16/1** Pigalle Wonder,
**20/1** Little Nod, Smudgemupum, **25/1** One Magic Moment (IRE), **33/1** Nigels Lady, Great Hall, **50/1** Ors. CSF
£47.53, Tote £2.10: £1.10 £10.90 £1.60 (£116.90). Mr R. E. Sangster (COCKERHAM) bred by The Overbury
Stud. 13 Rn  1m 25.53 (1.53)
SF—30/21/21/21/–/1

## 3843

CHAMPAGNE JACQUART NURSERY   £4370.00 (£1310.00: £630.00: £290.00)
**7f 140y**   2-15 (2-19)

(Weights raised 1 lb)

36434 **Marius (IRE) (76)** (Fav) *(BWHills)* 8-12 DHolland (9) (b.hind: lw: chsd ldr: led
over 1f out: hung rt: drvn out) ................................ —1
3574 Cashell (82) *(MRStoute)* 9-4 PaulEddery (11) (rdn & hdwy over 2f out: hrd rdn
over 1f out: ev ch ins fnl f: r.o) ................................ ¾.2
3665 Regal Aura (IRE) (85) *(GHarwood)* 9-7 MPerrett (10) (lw: a.p: nt clr run on ins 2f
out: nt clr run & snatched up ins fnl f: nt rcvr) ................................ 1½.3
37775 Miss Ribbons (57) *(PatMitchell)* 7-7 NAdams (12) (led 6f) ................... 5.4
3419 Ice Rebel (57) *(MissBSanders)* 7-7 GBardwell (7) (nvr nr to chal) ............ 1½.5
3685 Honour and Glory (58) *(BobJones)* 7-8(1) NCarlisle (4) (lw: nvr nrr) ........... hd.6
36113 The Premier Expres (58) *(CBBBooth)* 7-8 JFanning (8) (s.s: no hdwy fnl 3f) ... nk.7
3508 Tajarib (IRE) (60) *(JLDunlop)* 7-10 JLowe (6) (lw: prom 4f) ................. 3½.8
3553★ Stardust Express (59) *(MJohnston)* 7-9 TyroneWilliams (5) (prom over 6f) ..... 6.9
3611 Hot Off the Press (57) (v) *(RMWhitaker)* 7-7 DaleGibson (3) (bhd fnl 3f) ....... ½.10
36142 Backstabber (75) *(DrJDSCargill)* 8-11 AMunro (1) (lw: bhd fnl 3f) ........... 7.11
LONG HANDICAP: Miss Ribbons 7-0, Honour and Glory 7-3, Hot Off the Press 6-7.

**4/1** MARIUS (IRE), **9/2** The Premier Expres(op 3/1), **5/1** Stardust Express, **11/2** Tajarib (IRE), **7/1** Ice Rebel(op
14/1), **10/1** Regal Aura (IRE), **12/1** Cashell, **25/1** Honour and Glory, **33/1** Ors. CSF £46.72, CT
£407.23. Tote £3.90: £2.10 £2.50 £4.40 (£13.80). Mrs Leonard Simpson (LAMBOURN) bred by James
O'Sullivan in Ireland. 11 Rn  1m 38.77 (10.27)
SF—44/48/46/3/–/–

## 3844

E.B.F. WILLOW STKS (I) (Mdn 2-Y.O) £2700.00 (£750.00: £360.00)    7f  2-45 (2-48)

      **Faez** *(MajorWRHern)* 9-0 RHills (13) (w'like: hld up: led ins fnl f: r.o wl) ............ —1
37652 Marastani (USA) (Fav) *(GHarwood)* 9-0 JReid (2) (lw: racd far side: led tl ins fnl f:
      unable qckn) ..................................................................................... 2¹/₂.2
      Um Algowain (USA) *(MRStoute)* 9-0 PaulEddery (5) (leggy: scope: racd far
      side: rdn over 4f out: hdwy over 1f out: r.o wl ins fnl f) ............ 1¹/₂.3
1038 Umhambi *(BWHills)* 8-9 DHolland (12) (a.p: one pce fnl 2f) ..................... 2.4
3643 Moonstruck Bard **(45)** *(SPCWoods)* 9-0 WWoods (9) (a.p: hrd rdn over 1f out:
      one pce) ............................................................................................... 1.5
3593 Steppe Closer *(LordHuntingdon)* 8-9 DMcKeown (11) (nvr nr to chal) ............... 4.6
35524 Record Lover (IRE) *(JHMGosden)* 9-0 RCochrane (7) (s.s: racd far side: hdwy
      6f out: wknd over 1f out) ............................................................ 2¹/₂.7
37655 Divine Rain *(JWPayne)* 9-0 AMunro (6) (outpcd) ........................................ ³/₄.8
3712 Hotsocks *(PatMitchell)* 8-9 DBiggs (4) (lw: racd far side: prom over 3f) ......... 2.9
3372 Infantry Glen *(MDIUsher)* 9-0 NDay (14) (a bhd) ....................................... ³/₄.10
      Kenesha (IRE) *(SDow)* 8-9 TQuinn (1) (wl grwn: racd far side: a wl bhd) ...... ¹/₂.11
3693 Ijab (CAN) *(AAScott)* 9-0 BRaymond (3) (prom far side over 4f) ................ 1.12
36025 Tejano Gold (USA) *(JMPEustace)* 9-0 MTebbutt (8) (bhd fnl 3f) ............... 1.13
      Commanche Star *(DShaw)* 9-0 JCarroll (10) (unf: scope: a bhd) ............. 12.14

**5/4** Marastani (USA), **5/1** FAEZ(7/2—11/2), Umhambi, **7/1** Record Lover (IRE)(op 3/1), **10/1** Steppe Closer(op
5/1), Um Algowain (USA), **16/1** Ijab (CAN)(op 6/1), **33/1** Divine Rain, Moonstruck Bard, Hotsocks, **50/1** Ors. CSF
£11.88, Tote £7.70: £2.60 £1.30 £2.60 (£6.50). Mr Hamdan Al-Maktoum (LAMBOURN) bred by Shadwell
Estate Company Limited. 14 Rn                                                                          1m 30.67 (9.37)
                                                           SF—49/41/36/25/27/16

## 3845

FALLING LEAF H'CAP (0-70) £2637.00 (£732.00: £351.00)
  1¹/₄m (AWT)                                                                                    3-15 (3-18)

                            (Weights raised 3 lb)
3555 **Awesome Power (60)** *(CRNelson)* 6-9-8 PaulEddery (6) (a.p: led wl over 1f
      out: drvn out) .................................................................................. —1
36964 Gold Blade **(62)** (Fav) *(NAGraham)* 3-9-5 RCochrane (12) (lw: hdwy 3f out: hrd
      rdn over 1f out: r.o) ...................................................................... ³/₄.2
3007 Lookingforararainbow (IRE) **(55)** *(BobJones)* 4-9-3 NDay (9) (lw: hdwy over 3f
      out: rdn over 1f out: r.o) .............................................................. hd.3
3696 Kingchip Boy **(55)** (v) *(MJRyan)* 3-8-12 DBiggs (5) (a.p: led over 3f out tl wl over
      1f out: unable qckn) ...................................................................... 6.4
3259 First Fling (IRE) **(66)** *(RCharlton)* 3-9-9 TQuinn (2) (no hdwy fnl 2f) ......... 3.5
37665 Badawiah **(67)** *(WAO'Gorman)* 3-9-7 ³EmmaO'Gorman (1) (b: nvr nr to chal) .. 1.6
2451 El Volador **(59)** *(RJO'Sullivan)* 5-9-7 JReid (10) (nvr nrr) ........................ nk.7
3185 Slight Risk **(66)** *(PAKelleway)* 3-9-9 GayKelleway (3) (eyecover: led over 6f) ...... 4.8
3185 Tadora (IRE) **(53)** *(CJBenstead)* 3-8-10 TyroneWilliams (7) (lw: prom over 8f) . ³/₄.9
3576 Missy-S (IRE) **(53)** *(SPPritchard-Gordon)* 3-8-7 ³DHarrison (14) (lw: a bhd) ... 2.10
36985 Nocatchim **(53)** *(BWHills)* 3-8-10 DHolland (4) (lw: prom 6f) ................... 10.11
3256 Moon Spin **(64)** *(MajorWRHern)* 3-9-7 RHills (8) (b.hind: prom 5f) ......... 1¹/₂.12
35575 Access Voyager **(54)** *(RBoss)* 3-8-5 (s.s: a bhd) ............................... 1¹/₂.13
3105 Crofter's Cline **(49)** (bl) *(ABailey)* 8-8-11 GBaxter (11) (bhd fnl 5f) ......... ³/₄.14

**9/2** Gold Blade, **5/1** El Volador, Nocatchim, **13/2** AWESOME POWER, **7/1** Moon Spin, **12/1** Missy-S (IRE),
Access Voyager, Kingchip Boy(op 8/1), **14/1** Lookingforararainbow (IRE), First Fling (IRE), **16/1** Badawiah, **25/1**
Slight Risk, Tadora (IRE), **33/1** Crofter's Cline. CSF £36.04, CT £378.22. Tote £7.60: £2.40 £1.80 £4.60
(£18.20). Mr Garrett J. Freyne (UPPER LAMBOURN) bred by G. J. Freyne. 14 Rn                  2m 5.59 (2.59)
                                                           SF—42/37/34/17/22/18

## 3846

E.B.F. WILLOW STKS (II) (Mdn 2-Y.O) £2700.00 (£750.00: £360.00)    7f  3-45 (3-47)

35813 **Bezique (USA)** (bl) *(JHMGosden)* 9-0 RCochrane (1) (lw: racd alone: mde
      virtually all: clr over 2f out: r.o wl) ................................................ —1
37802 Austral Jane (Fav) *(GHarwood)* 8-9 JReid (3) (a.p: rdn 3f out: one pce fnl 2f) .... 8.2
37675 Fly to the End (USA) *(AAScott)* 9-0 BRaymond (2) (a.p: rdn over 2f out: one
      pce) ................................................................................................ 3¹/₂.3
      Harlestone Brook *(JLDunlop)* 8-7 ⁷KateAhern (10) (w'like: bit bkwd: hdwy over
      1f out: r.o) ...................................................................................... 3.4
3626 Shillelagh Bray (IRE) *(PWHarris)* 9-0 NAdams (5) (lw: prom 6f) ............... s.h.5
3764 Dance to Order (IRE) *(SirMarkPrescott)* 9-0 CNutter (11) (lw: nvr nrr) ........... 1.6
3171 Apachee Flower *(JDRoberts)* 8-9 TyroneWilliams (7) (lw: prom over 5f) ....... 1¹/₂.7
3684 Sense of Humour *(JWPayne)* 9-0 MTebbutt (6) (hdwy over 8f out: wknd over 1f
      out) ................................................................................................. 3.8
3551 Jest Rosie *(MDIUsher)* 8-9 RPrice (4) (spd 4f) ......................................... 12.9
3607 Bevanno (IRE) *(PatMitchell)* 9-0 WWoods (9) (a bhd) .............................. 15.10

**4/6** Austral Jane, **100/30** BEZIQUE (USA)(5/4—7/2), **7/1** Fly to the End (USA)(6/1—12/1), **12/1** Dance to Order (IRE)(8/1—14/1), **16/1** Harlestone Brook(op 8/1), **20/1** Shillelagh Bay (IRE), **50/1** Ors. CSF £5.88, Tote £3.30: £1.10 £1.10 £1.20 (£2.30). Sheikh Mohammed (NEWMARKET) bred by Prestonwood Farm in USA. 10 Rn

1m 30.49 (9.19)
SF—52/23/17/1/7/4

**3847** BURNT OAK H'CAP (0-95) £3420.00 (£950.00: £456.00) **6f** 4-15 (4-16)

37293 **Hard to Figure (93)** *(RJHodges)* 6–10-0 RCochrane (7) (a.p: led over 1f out: rdn out) ...................................................................................................... —1
3469 Isaiah **(89)** *(MrsJCecil)* 3–9-8 PaulEddery (4) (lw: led over 4f: r.o) ................ ³/₄.2
3714 Our Rita **(70)** *(DrJDScargill)* 3–8-3 DHolland (6) (hdwy 2f out: r.o ins fnl f) ...... ³/₄.3
3732 Sylvan Sabre (IRE) **(70)** *(PMitchell)* 3–8-3 AMunro (3) (hld up: hrd rdn over 1f out: r.o) ........................................................................................................ ¹/₂.4
3729 Caleman **(80)** *(RBoss)* 3–8-13 JReid (8) (a.p stands' side: one pce fnl 2f) ......... ¹/₂.5
3729 How's Yer Father **(82)** *(RJHodges)* 6–9-3 TQuinn (1) (a.p: one pce fnl 2f) ...... ³/₄.6
3707* Ingenuity **(65)** *(LordHuntingdon)* 3–7-9 ‡³DHarrison (9) (racd stands' side: prom over 4f) ................................................................................................ 3¹/₂.7
34696 Arctic Appeal (IRE) **(81)** *(Fav)* *(JBerry)* 3–9-0 JCarroll (5) (spd over 4f) ........... 1¹/₂.8
3400 Night Asset **(61)** *(bl)* *(GLewis)* 3–7-8 NAdams (4) (a bhd) ................................. 1¹/₂.9
3803 El Yasaf (IRE) **(87)** *(MissGayKelleway)* 4–9-8 GayKelleway (10) (racd stands' side: a bhd) ................................................................................................... 10.10

**7/2** Arctic Appeal (IRE), **4/1** How's Yer Father, **9/2** Caleman, **5/1** Ingenuity, **13/2** HARD TO FIGURE(op 3/1), **10/1** Isaiah, Sylvan Sabre (IRE)(op 6/1), **14/1** Our Rita, **20/1** Night Asset, **33/1** El Yasaf (IRE). CSF £64.73, CT £808.46. Tote £4.60: £1.90 £2.10 £2.50 (£42.00). Mr J. W. Mursell (SOMERTON) bred by J. W. Mursell. 10 Rn

1m 15.81 (7.21)
SF—72/63/41/39/47/48

T/Plpt: £25.80 (388.21 Tckts). AK

## 3683—LEICESTER (R-H)
### Monday, October 26th [Soft, Heavy patches]
Going Allowance: 0.95 sec per fur (S)

Wind: almost nil

Stalls: high

**3848** E.B.F. FLECKNEY STKS (Mdn 2-Y.O.F) £3125.50 (£868.00: £416.50)
**5f 218y**
1-30 (1-33)

**Siwaayib (Fav)** *(AAScott)* 8-11 WRSwinburn (9) (leggy: scope: hld up: rdn over 1f out: led ins fnl f: r.o) ................................................................... —1
37445 Quinsigimond **(74)** *(SirMarkPrescott)* 8-11 GDuffield (10) (a.p: outpcd 2f out: rdn & r.o wl cl home) ...................................................................... nk.2
34862 Royal Deed (USA) **(64)** *(PMMcEntee)* 8-6 ‡⁵JWeaver (14) (lw: led tl hdd & nt qckn ins fnl f) ........................................................................................ 2¹/₂.3
37686 Heretical Miss **(60)** *(bl)* *(RHannon)* 8-8 ‡³RPerham (11) (a.p: ev ch 2f out: sn wknd) ......................................................................................................... 3.4
37685 Marwell Mitzi **(55)** *(WGRWightman)* 8-11 JWilliams (6) (b.hind: nvr nr to chal) ... 3.5
Khubza *(HRACecil)* 8-11 SCauthen (7) (lt-f: prom: rdn & rdn 2f out) ................. ¹/₂.6
36172 La Menorquina (USA) *(LMCumani)* 8-11 LDettori (12) (lw: no hdwy fnl 2f) ...... hd.7
3683 Miss Offie *(RHollinshead)* 8-11 WRyan (5) (n.d) ........................................... 4.8
3684 Bold a Maiden *(bl)* *(DRLaing)* 8-6 ‡⁵BDoyle (4) (a bhd) ................................. ¹/₂.9
Croire (IRE) *(GWragg)* 8-11 MHills (3) (neat: bkwd: a bhd) ........................... 1¹/₂.10
36833 Ibtikar (USA) *(PTWalwyn)* 8-11 WCarson (13) (chsd ldrs: rdn 3f out: sn wknd) ¹/₂.11
Smocking *(GWragg)* 8-8 ‡³FNorton (1) (w'like: bkwd: rdn over 3f out: a bhd) 2¹/₂.12
Nikitria *(MissAJWhitfield)* 8-11 BRouse (2) (unf: bkwd: dwlt: racd alone stands' side: a bhd) ........................................................................................... hd.13
35034 My Foxy Lady *(DHaydnJones)* 8-11 NHowe (8) (t.o) ...................................... 14

**5/2** SIWAAYIB(Evens—11/4), **3/1** Ibtikar (USA)(4/1—5/1), **4/1** Khubza(7/4—5/1), **5/1** La Menorquina (USA), **10/1** Quinsigimond, **16/1** Royal Deed (USA), **20/1** Croire (IRE)(op 10/1), **33/1** Heretical Miss, My Foxy Lady, Smocking, Miss Offie, **50/1** Marwell Mitzi, Nikitria, **100/1** Bold a Maiden. CSF £27.46, Tote £3.90: £1.30 £3.90 £4.20 (£38.20). Maktoum Al Maktoum (NEWMARKET) bred by Gainsborough Stud Management Ltd. 14 Rn

1m 19 (9)
SF—31/30/15/5/–/–

**3849** SEAGRAVE APP'CE (S) H'CAP (3-Y.O) (0-60) £2658.00 (£738.00: £354.00)
**5f 218y**
2-00 (2-03)

(Weights raised 2 lb)

35074 **Ceatharlach (39)** *(bl)* *(PGMurphy)* 7-11 ‡⁵SDrowne (6) (hdwy over 2f out: led ins fnl f: r.o wl) ........................................................................................... —1

37074 Music Dancer (58) (Fav) (JBerry) 9-2 ‡5PRoberts (7) (reard stalls: led over 4f out
tl over 1f out: r.o one pce) ...................................................... 3½.2

3748 Nordoora (IRE) (39) (JLHarris) 7-11(2) ‡5JTate (15) (a.p: led over 1f out tl ins fnl f) ... s.h.3

36294 Preamble (35) (MrsJRRamsden) 7-12 StephenDavies (21) (a.p: hrd rdn over 1f
out: one pce) ............................................................. nk.4

3690 Swinging Tich (48) (BAMcMahon) 8-6 ‡5SSanders (14) (hdwy wl over 1f out: r.o
ins fnl f) .................................................................. 1.5

33833 Gallery Note (IRE) (50) (BWHills) 8-8 ‡5DWright (8) (led over 1f: ev ch 2f out: one
pce fnl f) ................................................................. s.h.6

35073 Palacegate Gold (IRE) (48) (bl) (RJHodges) 8-11 GForster (11) (plld hrd: w ldrs
tl wknd wl over 1f out) ..................................................... 3½.2.7

3511 Nordansk (41) (LJHolt) 7-13 ‡5CAvery (16) (prom: hrd rdn & wknd over 1f out) ... s.h.8

3513 Syke Lane (36) (RMWhitaker) 7-13 AGarth (19) (nvr trbld ldrs) ................. 2½.2.9

2754 Tamasha (40) (CJHill) 7-12 ‡5BRussell (3) (n.d) ............................ s.h.10

3507 Pink'n Black (IRE) (44) (GBlum) 8-7 OPears (2) (prom 4f) ................... nk.11

37594 Malcesine (IRE) (43) (CaptJWilson) 8-1 ‡5JMarshall (10) (prom over 3f) ...... 2½.12

3507 Orchard Bay (37) (v) (DRTucker) 7-9 ‡5PMcCabe (9) (b.off hind: a bhd) ...... ¾.13

3254 Buddy (IRE) (43) (MBell) 8-6 PTurner (13) (a bhd) .......................... ¾.14

3705 Jellyroll Blues (34) (MrsGRReveley) 7-11 DarrenMoffatt (17) (a bhd) ......... 2½.15

3605 Kipini (42) (bl) (WJMusson) 8-0 ‡5PBowe (4) (prom 4f) ...................... s.h.16

37515 Sakharov (43) (MAJarvis) 8-6 KRutter (1) (t.o) ............................. 15.17

3690 Deborah Shelley (39) (v) (EAWheeler) 8-2 CHawksley (5: s.s: t.o) ............ 18

**9/2** Music Dancer, **11/2** Gallery Note (IRE), Tamasha(10/1—14/1), **7/1** Sakharov, **8/1** Preamble(12/1—7/1),
**11/1** Palacegate Gold (IRE), **12/1** CEATHARLACH, **14/1** Syke Lane, Swinging Tich, **16/1** Orchard Bay, Malcesine
(IRE), **20/1** Kipini, Nordoora (IRE), **25/1** Nordansk, Pink'n Black (IRE), Jellyroll Blues, **33/1** Ors. CSF £67.92, CT
£1,029.75. Tote £20.70: £3.50 £1.40 £9.00 £1.80 (£46.10). M. & N. Plant Ltd (BRISTOL) bred by J. Neville and
R. J. Holder, 18 Rn; No bid
1m 18.7 (8.7)
SF—23/28/8/8/12/13

**3850**      WYSALL STKS      £2924.00 (£872.00: £416.00: £188.00)      1m 1f 218y   2-30 (2-32)

36952 **Galactic Miss** (Fav) (JLDunlop) 3-8-5 GCarter (4) (4th st: rdn over 2f out: led
over 1f out: sn clr: easily) .................................................. —1

36784 For Reg (IRE) (93) (ACStewart) 3-8-12 MRoberts (2) (led over 8f out tl over 1f
out: no ch w wnr) ........................................................... 6.2

3689 Scaraben (55) (HJCollingridge) 4-8-10 VSmith (5) (bit bkwd: 5th st: hdwy 3f
out: ev ch 2f out: sn wknd) ................................................. 5.3

34773 South Sea (83) (LMCumani) 3-8-9 LDettori (3) (swtg: lw: hld up & plld hrd: 3rd
st: wknd over 2f out) ....................................................... 2.4

4103 Desert Zone (USA) (JLHarris) 3-8-9 WRyan (6) (bkwd: led over 1f out: 2nd st:
wknd 2f out) ............................................................... ¾.5

157 Ossie (48) (BPalling) 3-8-0 ‡5StephenDavies (1) (bkwd: last st: rdn 4f out: t.o fnl
2f) ....................................................................... 30.6

*Stewards Enquiry: Dettori suspended 4-7/11/92 (excessive use of whip).*

**11/8** GALACTIC MISS, **15/8** For Reg (IRE)(Evens—2/1), **9/2** South Sea(op 7/1), **14/1** Scaraben(op 50/1), Desert
Zone (USA), **66/1** Ossie. CSF £4.08, Tote £2.30: £1.10 £1.70 (£3.40). Mr P. G. Goulandris (ARUNDEL) bred by
Hesmonds Stud Ltd. 6 Rn
2m 17.8 (15.1)
SF—35/30/18/13/11/1

**3851**      SQUIRREL H'CAP (0-80) £3678.00 (£1104.00: £532.00: £246.00)
**1m 3f 183y**                                                        3-00 (3-04)

36874 **Swan Heights** (58) (JRFanshawe) 3-8-2(1) GDuffield (20) (3rd st: led 3f out: sn
clr: r.o wl) ............................................................... —1

36875 Bit on the Side (IRE) (56) (WJMusson) 3-8-0 WCarson (19) (hdwy 3f out: chsd
wnr fnl 2f: eased whn btn w ins fnl f) ...................................... 5.2

33063 Brecon Beacons (IRE) (61) (RCharlton) 3-8-5(1) PatEddery (3) (4th st: one pce
fnl 2f) .................................................................... 12.3

Vado Via (48) (DJWintle) 4-7-6 ‡7ClaireBalding (11) (bkwd: wl bhd tl hdwy on
ins over 3f out: nvr nr to chal) ............................................. ¾.4

37133 Zamirah (IRE) (73) (GWragg) 3-9-3 WRSwinburn (6) (8th st: rdn over 2f out:
one pce) .................................................................. 2½.5

3696 Master of the Rock (57) (PJMakin) 3-8-1 TSprake (17) (7th st: no hdwy fnl 3f) .. 2.6

36223 Spray of Orchids (55) (JEtherington) 3-7-10 ‡3FNorton (12) (nvr nr to chal) ... ½.7

3641* Bigwheel Bill (IRE) (80) (JWWatts) 3-9-5 ‡5StephenDavies (2) (led 5f: rdn & 2nd
st: wknd 3f out) ........................................................... 2.8

36276 Virkon Venture (IRE) (63) (MHTompkins) 4-9-0 PRobinson (14) (hld up: hdwy
& hmpd over 3f out: n.d) ................................................... 3.9

3687 James Is Special (IRE) (53) *(HJCollingridge)* 4–8-4 JQuinn (4) (hld up: 6th st: wknd 3f out) ............................................. 1½.**10**
3778³ Matching Green (68) (v) *(GBBalding)* 3–8-12 JWilliams (13) (a bhd) ...... hd.**11**
3806⁵ Sovereign Niche (IRE) (42) *(MrsJRRamsden)* 4–7-7 SWood (9) (s.s: a bhd) .... 1.**12**
3755 Nipotina (42) *(RHollinshead)* 6–7-0 ‡⁷FSavage (15) (a bhd) ...................... ¾.**13**
3622 Barga (54) *(WClay)* 3–7-5⁽⁵⁾ ‡⁷AGarth (7) (a bhd) ............................. 1½.**14**
3789² Bighayir (74) (bl) (Jt-Fav) *(MCPipe)* 5–9-11 MRoberts (10) (bhd fnl 5f: t.o) ... 10.**15**
3675 Western Dynasty (65) (v) *(MJRyan)* 6–8-11 ‡⁵JWeaver (18) (chsd ldr: led 7f out: sn clr: hdd & wknd 3f out: t.o) ............................. hd.**16**
2780² Triennium (USA) (80) *(LMCumani)* 3–9-10 LDettori (16) (lw: 5th st: wknd 3f out: t.o) .............................................. 2½.**17**
3687 Altermeera (55) (v) *(MrsBarbaraWaring)* 4–8-6 NHowe (8) (chsd ldrs: rdn 6f out: sn wknd: t.o) ........................................ 15.**18**
3706★ Sweet Quest (77) (Jt-Fav) *(HRACecil)* 3–9-7 WRyan (5) (bhd fnl 3f: t.o) .......... 8.**19**
LONG HANDICAP: Sovereign Niche (IRE) 7-6, Nipotina 6-7, Barga 6-7.

**6**/1 Bighayir(tchd 9/1), Sweet Quest(4/1—13/2), **7**/1 Bit on the Side (IRE)(op 4/1), **15**/2 Virkon Venture (IRE)(9/2—8/1), **8**/1 Zamirah (IRE), **9**/1 Triennium (USA), **10**/1 Brecon Beacons (IRE), **11**/1 SWAN HEIGHTS(7/1—12/1), **12**/1 Spray of Orchids, Bigwheel Bill (IRE)(op 7/1), Sovereign Niche (IRE)(op 8/1), **16**/1 Western Dynasty, Matching Green, **25**/1 Vado Via, Master of the Rock, **33**/1 Altermeera, **50**/1 James Is Special (IRE), **66**/1 Nipotina, **100**/1 Barga. CSF £88.63, CT £758.89. Tote £9.30: £1.60 £2.30 £3.20 £20.70 (£50.80).
Mr Peter Wetzel (NEWMARKET) bred by A. R. Jones Morgan. 19 Rn                         2m 45.9 (17.1)
SF–31/19/–/–/–/–/

## 3852
JOHN O'GAUNT NURSERY  £2889.00 (£804.00: £387.00)  **7f 9y**  3-30 (3-34)
(Weights raised 6 lb)

3837³ **Benevolent (76)** *(SirMarkPrescott)* 9-3 GDuffield (11) (lw: hld up: hdwy 3f out: led over 1f out: drvn out) ....................................... —**1**
3262 Koa (65) *(MJHeaton-Ellis)* 8-6 GCarter (12) (lw: hdwy over 2f out: r.o ins fnl f) ... 4.**2**
3723 Sweet Disorder (IRE) (60) *(GAPritchard-Gordon)* 7-10 ‡⁵BDoyle (15) (hdwy over 2f out: r.o) ...................................... hd.**3**
3635² Ribhi (USA) (79) (Fav) *(DMorley)* 9-6 WCarson (6) (hrd rdn over 3f out: styd on wl fnl f) .................................... 1½.**4**
3470⁶ Master Sinclair (IRE) (64) *(RHollinshead)* 7-12 ‡⁷AGarth (17) (swtg: hdwy over 2f out: wknd over 1f out) ............................ 2.**5**
3267³ No Extras (IRE) (71) *(JSutcliffe)* 8-12 BRouse (10) (nvr nr to chal) ................. 6.**6**
3635 Sporting Spirit (52) *(DWChapman)* 7-7 SWood (14) (w ldrs tl wknd over 1f out) ¾.**7**
3754 Ring Tom (IRE) (52) *(MWEasterby)* 7-0 ‡⁷AntoinetteArmes (18) (led over 5f) ..... ½.**8**
3746 Duchess Dianne (IRE) (52) *(PGMurphy)* 7-0 ‡⁷DWright (1) (n.d) .............. 1½.**9**
3036⁵ Olympic Run (74) *(JLDunlop)* 9-1 LDettori (7) (prom: chsd ldrs' side over 4f) .. nk.**10**
3746★ Mark's Club (IRE) (66) *(TDBarron)* 8-7 AlexGreaves (4) (w ldrs stands' side over 4f) .................................... ¾.**11**
3764× Semillon (87) (bl) *(GHarwood)* 10-0 (7x) PatEddery (3) (prom bhd) ............. 5.**12**
3746⁴ Fortis Pavior (57) *(RMMWhitaker)* 7-9⁽¹⁾ ‡³FNorton (16) (prom over 4f: t.o) 12.**13**
3684⁴ Oare Sparrow (80) *(PTWalwyn)* 9-7 SCauthen (5) (led stands' side 5f: t.o) ...... 5.**14**
*3376* Sounds Risky (57) *(MissSJWilton)* 7-5⁽⁵⁾ ‡⁷CHawksley (9) (prom centre 4f: t.o) 7.**15**
3590 Lowrianna (IRE) (57) *(DHaydnJones)* 7-7⁽⁵⁾ ‡⁵NKennedy (8) (t.o) ............... 1½.**16**
3702 Apifera (53) *(RJHodges)* 7-8⁽¹⁾ JQuinn (2) (t.o) ........................ 1½.**17**
3508³ Regalsett (80) *(RHannon)* 9-7 MRoberts (19) (t.o fnl 2f) ................. 15.**18**
LONG HANDICAP: Sporting Spirit 7-6, Ring Tom (IRE) 7-4, Duchess Dianne (IRE) 6-10, Sounds Risky 7-2, Lowrianna (IRE) 7-5, Apifera 6-9.

**2**/1 Ribhi (USA), **6**/1 Semillon(4/1—13/2), **7**/1 BENEVOLENT, **11**/1 Mark's Club (IRE)(16/1—10/1), Regalsett(5/1—12/1), **12**/1 No Extras (IRE), **14**/1 Fortis Pavior (IRE), **16**/1 Oare Sparrow(op 10/1), **20**/1 Lowrianna (IRE), Olympic Run(op 10/1), **25**/1 Master Sinclair (IRE), Sweet Disorder (IRE), **33**/1 Sporting Spirit, Ring Tom (IRE), Koa, **50**/1 Ors. CSF £192.08, CT £4,877.13. Tote £6.20: £2.00 £6.60 £6.90 £1.60 (£538.10).
Mr Fahd Salman (NEWMARKET) bred by Lt-Col R. Bromley Gardner. 18 Rn                    1m 33.3 (11)
SF–38/15/4/23/–/–

## 3853
WIDMERPOOL STKS (Mdn 3-Y.O) £2658.00 (£738.00: £354.00)
**1m 1f 218y**                                                                              4-00 (4-02)

3708⁴ **Kabayil (65)** *(PTWalwyn)* 8-9 GCarter (15) (led 7f out: hrd rdn 2f out: r.o wl ins fnl f) ......................................... —**1**
Queen Leonor (IRE) *(JHMGosden)* 8-9 SCauthen (10) (w'like: bit bkwd: hld up & bhd: hdwy & 7th st: ev ch 1f out: nt qckn nr fin) ................... 1½.**2**
3616⁴ Hit the Fan *(RCharlton)* 9-0 TSprake (11) (hdwy 4f out: hrd rdn 3f out: styd on fnl f) .................................................... ¾.**3**
3706² Magadeer (USA) (66) *(JLDunlop)* 8-9 GDuffield (7) (racd wd: 3rd st: ev ch over 2f out: one pce) .................................... 1½.**4**
3682⁵ Alhaajib (USA) (Fav) *(JLDunlop)* 9-0 WCarson (8) (lw: bhd: pushed along 6f out: hdwy over 2f out: hrd rdn over 1f out: styd on) ................. 3½.**5**
3756² Portree *(HRACecil)* 8-9 WRyan (13) (4th st: wknd over 2f out) ............. 5.**6**

3713 Tudor Island **(66)** *(CEBrittain)* 9-0 MRoberts (1) (hdwy 4f out: hrd rdn 3f out: hung rt & eased whn btn over 1f out) .................................. 7.7
8813 Kate Labelle *(GWragg)* 8-9 MHills (5) (bit bkwd: 5th st: wknd over 2f out) ......... ¾.8
36902 Whatever's Right (IRE) *(MDIUsher)* 9-0 MWigham (14) (dwlt: a bhd) .................. 2.9
35062 Jazz **(73)** *(LMCumani)* 8-9 LDettori (9) (led 9f out to 7f out: 2nd st: wknd over 2f out) ...................... 1.10
37065 Balzino (USA) *(LMCumani)* 8-9 ‡5JWeaver (6) (bhd fnl 3f) ...................... 1½.11
30562 Rustaka (USA) *(BWHills)* 8-9 PatEddery (3) (prom over 5f: t.o) ..................... 20.12
37064 Royal Comedian *(BWMurray)* 8-9 KFallon (4) (lw: 6th st: wknd over 3f out: t.o) 4.13
33873 Montagne **(45)** *(HCandy)* 8-9 CRutter (2) (led 1f: wknd 4f out: t.o) ............... hd.14

**3/1** Alhaajib (USA), **7/1** KABAYIL(5/1—8/1), **8/1** Rustaka (USA)(5/1—10/1), Portree(op 12/1), **10/1** Tudor Island(16/1—8/1), **11/1** Kate Labelle(op 5/1), Queen Leonor (IRE)(op 9/2), **12/1** Hit the Fan(8/1—14/1), Jazz, **16/1** Magadeer (USA)(op 10/1), **20/1** Balzino (USA), Whatever's Right (IRE), **33/1** Ors. CSF £74.67, Tote £13.00: £4.70 £3.80 £2.40 (£85.00). Mr Hamdan Al-Maktoum (LAMBOURN) bred by Shadwell Estate Company Limited. 14 Rn
2m 20 (17.3)
SF—17/14/17/9/7/–

## 3854

THRUSSINGTON H'CAP (0-80) £2721.00 (£756.00: £363.00)  **5f 2y**   4-30 (4-33)

3703 **Jigsaw Boy (73)** *(PGMurphy)* 3-9-11 JWilliams (11) (hld up & bhd: gd hdwy & swtchd rt over 1f out: r.o strly to ld nr fin) .................................. —1
37776 Lincstone Boy (IRE) **(51)** (v) *(SRBowring)* 4-8-4 SWebster (16) (swtg: led: clr over 1f out: ct post) ................................. s.h.2
3777 Take it in Cash **(46)** *(RDickin)* 3-7-12 CRutter (14) (a.p: rdn over 1f out: r.o ins fnl f) ..................... 1½.3
37482 Rock Opera (IRE) **(58)** *(MPNaughton)* 4-8-11 KFallon (13) (hdwy over 1f out: r.o ins fnl f) ..................... hd.4
37624 Sartiqila **(60)** *(JWPayne)* 3-8-12 LDettori (12) (a.p: ev ch 2f out: hrd rdn over 1f out: r.o one pce) ...................... ½.5
37772 Heaven-Liegh-Grey **(68)** (bl) *(MJohnston)* 4-9-7 MRoberts (7) (led stands' side: one pce fnl f) ........................ ¾.6
3703 Pharaoh's Dancer **(73)** (Fav) *(RSimpson)* 5-9-12 MWigham (1) (s.s: nrst fin) .. 1½.7
2821 Klairover **(46)** *(CJHill)* 5-7-6(3) ‡7BRussell (4) (nvr nr to chal) ................. s.h.8
37876 Gondo **(74)** (v) *(EJAlston)* 5-9-8 ‡JWeaver (10) (a.p: eased whn btn ins fnl f) s.h.9
3803 Iron King **(69)** *(JLSpearing)* 6-9-8 WCarson (6) (a bhd) ........................ 1½.10
3777 Stocktina **(41)** (bl) *(RJHodges)* 5-7-8(1) JQuinn (2) (n.d) ........................ ¾.11
37775 Doesyoudoes **(47)** (v) *(DTThom)* 3-7-8 ‡5NKennedy (5) (prom far side over 2f) 2.12
3707 Stormbuster **(46)** *(PSFelgate)* 3-7-9(5) ‡3FNorton (17) (a bhd) ................. 1½.13
37033 Miss Vaxette **(74)** *(JLSpearing)* 3-9-5 ‡7MHumphries (15) (spd far side 3f) ..... nk.14
3703 Panchellita (USA) **(53)** *(JSutcliffe)* 3-8-5 BRouse (8) (a bhd) .................... ½.15
37622 Kalar **(43)** (v) *(DWChapman)* 3-7-9 SWood (3) (spd stands' side 3f) ............. nk.16
LONG HANDICAP: Stocktina 7-5, Stormbuster 7-5.

**3/1** Pharaoh's Dancer, **5/1** JIGSAW BOY(8/1—4/1), **11/2** Heaven-Liegh-Grey, **10/1** Sartiqila, Miss Vaxette(8/1—12/1), **12/1** Gondo(op 7/1), Stocktina, Lincstone Boy (IRE), Iron King, **14/1** Rock Opera, **16/1** Panchellita (USA)(12/1—20/1), Kalar, **20/1** Klairover, **25/1** Doesyoudoes, **33/1** Ors. CSF £66.04, CT £1,701.45. Tote £9.20: £3.10 £2.50 £5.70 £4.40 (£91.90). All Eight Club (BRISTOL) bred by Mrs J. A. Rawding. 16 Rn
65.5 sec (6.8)
SF—70/48/36/48/47/53/52

T/Plpt: £624.90 (4 Tckts).
KH

# LEICESTER (R-H)

## Tuesday, October 27th [Soft, Heavy patches]

Going Allowance: 0.20 sec per fur (S)                Wind: fresh bhd   Vis:mod

Stalls: high

### 3855

HOBY STKS (I) (Mdn 2-Y.O) £2070.00 (£570.00: £270.00)   **1m 8y**   12-50 (12-54)

3597 **Kadastrof (FR)** *(RDickin)* 9-0 SDawson (4) (mde virtually all: wandered u.p over 1f out: styd on) ................................. —1
3519 Sylvania (IRE) *(RHannon)* 9-0 TQuinn (11) (a.p: swtchd lft & rdn over 1f out: one pce) ..................... 3½.2
36936 Dover Patrol (IRE) (Jt-Fav) *(HRACecil)* 9-0 WRyan (8) (hdwy fnl 2f: r.o wl ins fnl f: nvr nrr) ..................... 3½.3
36193 Mountain Willow (Jt-Fav) *(LordHuntingdon)* 8-9 BRaymond (3) (in tch: effrt appr fnl f: nvr nr to chal) ..................... 1½.4
37723 Debos (Jt-Fav) *(MRStoute)* 8-9 ‡5JJones (1) (w wnr tl wknd over 1f out) ........ 2.5
Premier League (IRE) *(JEBanks)* 8-9 ‡5StephenDavies (2) (w'like: leggy: bkwd: prom: rdn over 2f out: sn btn) ..................... 5.6
Working Title (IRE) *(JWHills)* 9-0 RHills (7) (scope: bkwd: s.s: a in rr) ............. 6.7

Page 1401

Frogmarch (USA) *(MajorWRHern)* 9-0 BProcter (12) (lt-f: bkwd: prom far side over 5f: sn wknd) ............................................ ¹/₂.8

3693 One Voice (USA) *(SirMarkPrescott)* 9-0 GDuffield (5) (lw: bhd fnl 3f: t.o) .......... 10.9

3764⁵ Sunbeam Charlie *(AMoore)* 9-0 CandyMorris (6) (prom to ¹/₂-wy: sn lost tch: t.o) 4.10

Teen Jay *(GWragg)* 9-0 SCauthen (10) (w'like: lengthy: bit bkwd: bhd fr ¹/₂-wy: t.o) .......................................................................... 12.11

3683 D K Daffers (IRE) *(BSmart)* 8-9 DaleGibson (9) (s.s: a bhd: t.o fnl 3f) ............. dist.12

**3/1** Debos(op 6/4), Dover Patrol (IRE), Mountain Willow(op 2/1), **10/1** Sylvania (IRE), **11/1** Teen Jay, **12/1** Frogmarch (USA)(16/1—10/1), **20/1** One Voice (USA), **33/1** Sunbeam Charlie, Premier League (IRE), **50/1** KADASTROF (FR) & Ors. CSF £419.76, Tote £17.40: £2.90 £2.50 £1.40 (£153.00). Mr A. P. Paton (NEWENT) bred by Roland Lepeau in France. 12 Rn

1m 48.9 (13.9)

SF—35/24/13/3/–/–

**3856** HOBY STKS (II) (Mdn 2-Y.O) £2070.00 (£570.00: £270.00) **1m 8y** 1-20 (1-24)

3631² **Pistol River (IRE)** *(RHannon)* 9-0 BRaymond (6) (a.p: led 3f out: clr appr fnl f: unchal) ........................................................................... —1

3776 La Delitzia (USA) *(PFICole)* 8-9 TQuinn (11) (hdwy ¹/₂-wy: kpt on fnl 2f: no ch w wnr) ............................................................................ 15.2

3727 Sun of Spring (Fav) *(MRStoute)* 9-0 SCauthen (8) (hld up: effrt over 2f out: nvr nrr) .............................................................................. 3.3

3614 Vaigly Sunthyme *(JMCarr)* 9-0 SMorris (7) (wl bhd tl hdwy over 1f out: r.o) ....... ³/₄.4

3760² Trets *(PAKelleway)* 8-9 GayKelleway (2) (prom 6f: sn rdn & outpcd) .............. d.h.4

3614⁶ Dig in the Ribs (IRE) *(RHollinshead)* 9-0 WRyan (4) (nvr nr ldrs) .................. 6.6

3685 Juliasdarkinvader *(AMoore)* 9-0 CandyMorris (10) (prom over 5f: sn rdn & wknd) ¹/₂.7

Moonlight Eclipse *(EJAlston)* 9-0 KFallon (3) (wl grwn: bkwd: s.s: sn rcvrd: rdn & wknd 3f out: t.o) ......................................................... 15.8

3402 Olicana (IRE) *(BWHills)* 9-0 EJohnson (5) (bhd fr ¹/₂-wy: t.o) ..................... 12.9

3623 Summers Dream (35) *(BRichmond)* 8-4 ‡StephenDavies (1) (racd alone stands' side: led 5f: wknd qckly: t.o) ................................... 5.10

Steamburd *(JAGlover)* 8-5(1) ‡SWilliams (9) (leggy: lt-f: bit bkwd: s.s: a wl bhd: t.o) ........................................................................... dist.11

**7/4** Sun of Spring (IRE)(5/4—5/2), **2/1** PISTOL RIVER (IRE)(6/1—10/1), **12/1** Trets, **16/1** Steamburd, **20/1** La Delitzia (USA), Olicana (IRE), **33/1** Moonlight Eclipse, Vaigly Sunthyme, Summers Dream, **50/1** Juliasdarkinvader. CSF £35.54, Tote £3.70: £1.10 £3.40 £1.20 (£21.30). A. F. Budge (Equine) Limited (MARLBOROUGH) bred by Andrew Bradley in Ireland. 11 Rn

1m 49.8 (14.8)

SF—22/–/–/–/–/–

**3857** PYTCHLEY STKS (2-Y.O) *(7f 9y)* 1-50 - **Abandoned**—Waterlogged

**3858** BARSBY (S) H'CAP (3-Y.O) (0-60) *(1m 3f 183y)* 2-20 - **Abandoned**—Waterlogged

**3859** TUGBY STKS *(7f 9y)* 2-50 - **Abandoned**—Waterlogged

**3860** FOSSE WAY CLAIMING STKS *(1m 8y)* 3-20 - **Abandoned**—Waterlogged

**3861** ERMINE STREET H'CAP (0-80) *(1m 8y)* 3-50 - **Abandoned**—Waterlogged

**3862** CASTLE APP'CE H'CAP (0-70) *(1m 1f 218y)* 4-20 - **Abandoned**—Waterlogged

T/Plpt: £5.20 (425.28Tckts).

IM

## 3704—**REDCAR** (L-H)
### Tuesday, October 27th [Heavy]
Going Allowance: 5f-6f: 1.10 sec; Rest: 0.80 sec per fur (S)     Wind: fresh half against

Stalls: centre   Flag start: 3rd race

**3863** BRASS CASTLE CLAIMING STKS (3-Y.O) £2385.00 (£660.00: £315.00) **1m 3f** 1-00 (1-00)

3494* Salu (50) (bl) *(JEtherington)* 8-4 MBirch (2) (lw: hld up: stdy hdwy to ld over 1f out: styd on u.p) ............................................................ —1

3692² Handsome Gent (60) (LordHuntingdon) 8-6 AMunro (3) (chsd ldr: chal over 2f out: sn rdn: styd on one pce) .................................................... 2.2

3708 Milanese (64) (DMorley) 9-1 PaulEddery (6) (lw: cl up: led over 4f out tl over 1f out: sn btn) .............................................................. 3¹/₂.3

3149 Northern Graduate (USA) (65) (MrsGRReveley) 9-2 KDarley (5) (chsd ldrs: pushed along over 4f out: one pce) .......................................... 2¹/₂.4

3577⁴ Lyn's Return (IRE) (57) (RSimpson) 8-6 ‡5ATucker (7) (bhd: effrt over 4f out: n.d) ............................................................................ 25.5

3778⁴ Firefighter (66) (Fav) (RHollinshead) 8-13 RCochrane (1) (lw: drvn along over 4f: sn bhd) ................................................................. 6.6

3639⁴ Double Sherry (45) (RMWhitaker) 8-2(1) MRoberts (4) (led tl hdd & wknd over 4f out) ..................................................................... 3.7

3756 Queen of the Dales (GMMoore) 8-6 JLowe (8) (chsd ldrs to st: sn rdn & wknd) 1¹/₂.8

2/1 Firefighter, 5/1 Handsome Gent, Lyn's Return (IRE), SALU, 11/2 Northern Graduate (USA), 7/1 Milanese, 20/1 Double Sherry, 66/1 Queen of the Dales. CSF £28.33, Tote £5.70: £1.40 £1.70 £2.40 (£9.00). Mr W. N. Lumley (MALTON) bred by W. N. Lumley. 8 Rn
2m 30.7 (15)
SF—28/26/28/24/–/–

## 3864
TELEPROMPTER H'CAP (0-100) £3002.00 (£896.00: £428.00: £194.00) 1¹/₄m
1-30 (1-31)

(Weights raised 7 lb)

3718⁵ **Majed (IRE) (74)** (Fav) (MrsGRReveley) 4–8-13 ‡7DarrenMoffatt (2) (lw: hld up: effrt over 2f out: hung lft & led cl home) ..................... —1

3708* Unforgiving Minute (83) (PWHarris) 3–9-10 PaulEddery (4) (lw: chsd ldrs: slt ld over 1f out: nt qckn nr fin) .......................................... nk.2

The Goofer (65) (APStringer) 5–8-11 AMunro (3) (lw: trckd ldrs: led over 2f out tl over 1f out: no ex) .................................................... 2.3

3622* Light Hand (72) (MHTompkins) 6–9-4 PRobinson (6) (lw: hld up: effrt 4f out: ev ch over 1f out: one pce) ........................................ 1¹/₂.4

3711* Lady Dundee (USA) (62) (MrsJCecil) 3–8-0 ‡3DHarrison (5) (w ldrs: slt ld 3f out: hdd over 2f out: wknd over 1f out) ............................. 5.5

3718⁴ Sword Master (76) (BobJones) 3–9-3 NDay (1) (led tl hdd 3f out: wknd 2f out) . 2.6

3527⁴ Sovereign Page (USA) (73) (bl) (BHanbury) 3–9-0 MRoberts (7) (racd wd: prom tl outpcd fnl 2f) .......................................................... ¹/₂.7

11/4 MAJED (IRE), 7/2 Unforgiving Minute, 9/2 Light Hand, 5/1 Sword Master, 11/2 Lady Dundee (USA), 14/1 Sovereign Page (USA), 16/1 The Goofer. CSF £11.81, Tote £3.70: £1.90 £3.00 (£9.80). Laurel (Leisure) Limited (SALTBURN) bred by Rowlane Investments in Ireland. 7 Rn
2m 19.1 (16.6)
SF—13/23/6/10/–/–

## 3865
E.B.F. STKS (Mdn 2-Y.O.) £4854.00 (£1452.00: £696.00: £318.00)
5f  2-00 (2-01)

3719⁵ **Logan's Luck (USA)** (Fav) (MRStoute) 9-0 KDarley (6) (chsd ldr: led 1f out: styd on wl) ................................................................. —1

2286⁶ Romeo Oscar (BWHills) 9-0 DHolland (3) (lw: sn chsng ldrs: effrt over 2f out: kpt on) ........................................................................... 2.2

3637⁵ Ashgore (MJohnston) 9-0 DMcKeown (4) (lw: led: clr after 1f: hdd 1f out: sn btn) ............................................................................... hd.3

3749 Lamsonetti (RMWhitaker) 8-2 ‡7GParkin (2) (bhd tl styd on wl fnl 2f) ............ 5.4

Stylish Rose (IRE) (WAStephenson) 8-9 JLowe (1) (lt-f: unf: dwlt: wl bhd tl styd on fnl f) ............................................................................ 1¹/₂.5

2879 Shomberg (IRE) (PCalver) 9-0 GHind (7) (in tch: no hdwy fnl 2f) ................... hd.6

3750⁵ Brooklands Express (JDBethell) 9-0 PRobinson (11) (chsd ldrs 3f) ............. s.h.7

3704 Bloomsbury Square (JWWatts) 9-0 NConnorton (9) (b.hind: chsd ldr tl wknd wl over 1f out) .................................................................... 1¹/₂.8

3552 St Alzina (IRE) (GHEden) 9-0 JWilliams (8) (a bhd) ..................................... 12.9

3746 Master Peckitt (SEKettlewell) 9-0 SWebster (10) (bhd after 2f) ..................... 2.10

5/4 LOGAN'S LUCK (USA), 3/1 Romeo Oscar(op 2/1), 11/2 Brooklands Express, 12/1 St Alzina (IRE), 16/1 Bloomsbury Square, 20/1 Shomberg (IRE), Lamsonetti, 25/1 Ashgore, 33/1 Stylish Rose (IRE), 66/1 Master Peckitt. CSF £5.23, Tote £2.30: £1.70 £1.70 £3.10 (£4.20). Mr P. D. Savill (NEWMARKET) bred by Crystal Springs Farm in USA. 10 Rn
65.8 sec (9.1)
SF—28/20/19/–/–/–

## 3866
WESTMINSTER-MOTOR TAXI INSURANCE H'CAP (0-100) £9240.00 (£2760.00: £1320.00: £600.00) 7f
2-30 (2-32)

(Weights raised 5 lb)

3825* Amazing Feat (IRE) (82) (MrsGRReveley) 3–9-9 (7x) KDarley (10) (lw: chsd ldrs: led wl over 1f out: rdn & r.o wl) ..................................... —1

3612³ Love Jazz (USA) (81) (TDBarron) 3–9-8 MHills (6) (lw: in tch: styd on fnl 2f: no imp) ............................................................................... 8.2

3729⁴ Draft Board **(77)** *(JHMGosden)* 3–9-4 RCochrane (7) (bhd: hdwy over 2f out: styd on nr fin) .................. nk.3

3729 Sea Devil **(80)** (Fav) *(MJCamacho)* 6–9-10 NConnorton (4) (lw: pushed along ¹/₂-wy: hdwy over 2f out: rdn & btn over 1f out) .................. 3¹/₂.4

3620 Jahangir (IRE) **(76)** *(BHanbury)* 3–9-3 PRobinson (8) (led tl wl over 1f out: sn btn) .................. s.h.5

3726 Spanish Verdict **(70)** *(DenysSmith)* 5–8-7 ‡⁷CTeague (3) (cl up tl wknd 2f out) ... 3.6

3714⁴ Kimberley Park **(67)** *(DWPArbuthnot)* 4–8-11 AMunro (9) (lw: chsd ldrs over 5f) 7.7

3726 La Bamba **(76)** *(GAPritchard-Gordon)* 6–9-6 WHood (1) (b: dwlt: effrt ¹/₂-wy: rdn & btn 2f out) .................. 2.8

3620² Gentle Hero (USA) **(73)** *(MPNaughton)* 6–9-3 MRoberts (5) (cl up 5f: eased whn btn) .................. 4.9

3417³ Spencer's Revenge **(69)** *(LordHuntingdon)* 3–8-7 ‡³DHarrison (11) (a outpcd & bhd) .................. 2¹/₂.10

3785⁴ Troupe **(79)** *(BWHills)* 4–9-9 DHolland (2) (lw: prom 4f: sn wknd) .................. 7.11

3819³ Super Benz **(69)** (v) *(TFairhurst)* 6–8-13 JFanning (12) (racd around stands' side: cl up 4f: wknd qckly) .................. 2¹/₂.12

**100/30** Sea Devil, **6/1** La Bamba, **13/2** Draft Board, **7/1** AMAZING FEAT (IRE), Spencer's Revenge, **9/1** Gentle Hero (USA), **10/1** Kimberley Park, **14/1** Love Jazz (USA), **16/1** Jahangir (IRE), Troupe, **20/1** Super Benz, **33/1** Spanish Verdict. CSF £89.88, CT £609.32. Tote £10.70: £3.00 £4.70 £2.30 (£52.60). Mr P. D. Savill (SALTBURN) bred by Old Meadow Stud in Ireland. 12 Rn
1m 29.7 (7.5)
SF—80/55/50/45/37/18

---

**3867**
RACECALL GOLD TROPHY (Stks) (2-Y.O) £87786.40 (£32677.60: £15838.80: £6654.00: £2827.00: £1296.20) **6f**
3-00 (3-04)

3535² **Pips Pride** *(RHannon)* 8-5 DMcKeown (5) (lw: mde all far side: clr over 2f out: drvn out) .................. —1

3130⁴ Revelation (IRE) *(RHannon)* 8-10 PatEddery (2) (lw: hdwy far side over 2f out: styd on nr fin) .................. 1¹/₂.2

3688* Young Ern *(SDow)* 7-12 CRutter (6) (lw: in tch far side: effrt over 2f out: styd on fnl f) .................. nk.3

3716* Law Commission *(DRCElsworth)* 8-10 JWilliams (25) (s.i.s: hdwy stands' side ¹/₂-wy: nvr nrr) .................. 4.4

3753* Sea Gazer (IRE) *(TDBarron)* 8-4 KDarley (20) (lw: led & clr stands' side: no ch w far side fnl 2f) .................. 1.5

3224a⁴ Son Pardo *(RHannon)* 8-11 JReid (22) (hdwy stands' side 2f out: nvr rchd ldrs) ³/₄.6

3432⁵ Persian Revival (FR) *(BAMcMahon)* 8-7 MBirch (14) (styd on centre fnl 2f: n.d) ¹/₂.7

3799² Nominator *(RHollinshead)* 8-5⁽¹⁾ RCochrane (19) (lw: in tch stands' side: no hdwy 2f) .................. 5.8

3679² Mithl Al Hawa *(JRFanshawe)* 8-5 WRSwinburn (26) (lw: nvr trbld ldrs) ............ 2¹/₂.9

3679⁶ Look Who's Here *(BAMcMahon)* 9-2 DBiggs (15) (nvr nr to chal) ........ d.h.9

3550⁴ Northern Bird *(BWHills)* 7-7 DHarrison (9) (b.hind: n.d) .................. s.h.11

3565a² Pizza Connection (bl) *(JLDunlop)* 8-1 MHills (21) (s.i.s: n.d) .................. 1¹/₂.12

3720 Exclusively Yours *(RGuest)* 8-7 MRoberts (1) (s.i.s: sn rcvrd & chsd ldr far side: rdn & wknd over 2f out) .................. ³/₄.13

3519⁵ Anniversaire *(BobJones)* 8-4 NDay (18) (n.d) .................. nk.14

3081⁵ Elle Shaped (IRE) *(RHannon)* 8-4 GHind (16) (gd spd centre over 3f) .......... 1¹/₂.15

3411³ Rocket to the Moon (IRE) *(PWChapple-Hyam)* 8-4 PaulEddery (12) (n.d) ...... hd.16

3588³ Willshe Gan *(DenysSmith)* 7-10 LCharnock (7) (outpcd & bhd fr ¹/₂-wy) ... nk.17

3753² Joyofracing *(WAO'Gorman)* 8-4 DHolland (13) (chsd ldrs far side 4f: wknd qckly) .................. 1.18

3749⁵ True Precision *(JDBethell)* 7-7 NAdams (17) (b.nr hind: n.d) .................. nk.19

3348³ Star Family Friend (IRE) (Fav) *(MHTompkins)* 7-11⁽¹⁾ PRobinson (23) (lw: n.d) 2¹/₂.20

3719 Ok Bertie *(DMorris)* 7-12 JFanning (24) (n.d) .................. 1¹/₂.21

3348⁴ Carranita (IRE) *(BPalling)* 7-7 JQuinn (10) (lw: prom early: sn bhd) ............ 1¹/₂.22

3626* Vayavaig *(JRFanshawe)* 7-10 JLowe (4) (lw: chsd ldrs far side to ¹/₂-wy: sn wknd) .................. 3.23

3723 Gangleader (bl) *(SPCWoods)* 8-4 WWoods (11) (n.d) .................. nk.24

**5/1** Star Family Friend (IRE), **6/1** PIPS PRIDE, **9/1** Mithl Al Hawa, **10/1** Young Ern, Sea Gazer (IRE), **11/1** Exclusively Yours, **12/1** Vayavaig, **13/1** Joyofracing, Nominator, Pizza Connection, **16/1** Revelation (IRE), **20/1** Law Commission, Look Who's Here (IRE), Carranita (IRE), **25/1** Northern Bird, Son Pardo, **40/1** Elle Shaped (IRE), **50/1** Rocket to the Moon (IRE), Willshe Gan, **66/1** True Precision, Persian Revival (FR), **150/1** Ok Bertie, **200/1** Ors. CSF £92.92, Tote £7.30: £2.50 £8.50 £3.00 £5.00 (£60.70). Mrs V. S. Grant (MARLBOROUGH) bred by R. A. and J. H. Popely. 24 Rn
1m 17.2 (7.9)
SF—65/64/51/47/37/41

**3868**
REDCAR NURSERY *(1m)* 3-30 - **Abandoned**—Waterlogged

**3869**  LEVY BOARD H'CAP (0-70)  (1¾m 19y) 4-00 - **Abandoned**—Waterlogged

T/Trio: Race 5: £561.00 (1.1 Tckts). T/Plpt: £60.80 (70.9 Tckts).  AA

3282—**YARMOUTH (L-H)**
**Wednesday, October 28th [Good]**
Going Allowance: 0.35 sec per fur (G)  Wind: mod across

Stalls: high

**3870**  CALIFORNIA CLIFFS H'CAP (0-70) £2721.00 (£756.00: £363.00)  7f 3y  1-30 (1-33)

3732³ **Ballerina Bay (64)** (v) (DTThom) 4-9-11 SCauthen (4) (dwlt: hdwy 2f out: led ins fnl f: rdn out) ......... —1

3726⁵ Foolish Touch (56) (WJMusson) 10-9-3 JQuinn (6) (b: gd hdwy over 1f out: fin wl) ......... 1.2

3771 Saifan (57) (bl) (DMorris) 3-8-10 ‡5StephenDavies (2) (prom: led over 2f out: wandered u.p 1f out: sn hdd & no ex) ......... 1.3

3689² Roca Murada (IRE) (59) (v) (MJRyan) 3-9-3 PRobinson (7) (chsd ldrs: ev ch over 1f out: one pce ins fnl f) ......... nk.4

3481 Yonge Tender (42) (bl) (Fav) (CNWilliams) 5-8-3(1) MRoberts (9) (dwlt: hdwy over 3f out: outpcd over 1f out: r.o nr fin) ......... 2.5

3785 Jokist (55) (WJarvis) 9-9-2 MTebbutt (10) (hld up: kpt on appr fnl f: nvr able to chal) ......... 1½.6

3751² Tyrone Flyer (49) (MissGayKelleway) 3-8-4 ‡3DHarrison (5) (led tl over 2f out: one pce ins fnl f) ......... ½.7

2937³ Rural Lad (58) (NOOpieor) 3-9-2 RRaymond (11) (chsd ldrs: no hdwy fnl 2f) ......... 7.8

3290² Guesstimation (USA) (39) (JPearce) 3-7-4 ‡7DWright (12) (dwlt: hdwy after 2f: no ch fnl 2f) ......... s.h.9

3708 Annabelle Royale (67) (MrsNMacauley) 6-10-0 DMcKeown (3) (prom 5f) ......... nk.10

3766⁴ Dance on Sixpence (56) (v) (HJCollingridge) 4-9-3 VSmith (19) (led stands' side: no ch fnl 2f) ......... nk.11

3751 Judgement Call (51) (PHowling) 5-8-12 JWilliams (13) (lw: prom over 4f) ......... 4.12

3317 Fair Enchantress (49) (bl) (JABennett) 4-8-10 TQuinn (8) (chsd ldr 4f) ......... 2.13

3592⁶ Toss the Dice (48) (MAJarvis) 3-8-6 AMunro (16) (prom 4f) ......... ¼.14

3151³ Mary Macblain (44) (JLHarris) 3-8-2 PaulEddery (1) (chsd ldrs tl wknd over 2f out) ......... 4.15

3481⁶ Gott's Desire (39) (RBastiman) 6-8-0 SDawson (15) (prom stands' side 4f) ......... nk.16

3605 Fabled Orator (35) (bl) (PHowling) 7-7-10(1) DBiggs (18) (plld hrd: prom stands' side over 3f) ......... 1.17

3825 Birthdays' Child (59) (v) (JRFanshawe) 4-9-6 WRSwinburn (17) (a bhd) ......... 1½.18

3759 Crail Harbour (40) (v) (PCHaslam) 6-8-1 DaleGibson (14) (prom stands' side over 3f) ......... ½.19

**9/2** Yonge Tender, **11/2** Roca Murada (IRE), **8/1** BALLERINA BAY(op 5/1), Tyrone Flyer, **10/1** Guesstimation (USA), **11/1** Foolish Touch, **12/1** Dance on Sixpence, Judgement Call(op 20/1), **14/1** Annabelle Royale, **16/1** Gott's Desire(op 10/1), Crail Harbour, Toss the Dice, Jokist(op 10/1), **20/1** Mary Macblain, **25/1** Ors. CSF £91.99, CT £1,928.43. Tote £6.60: £2.20 £1.80 £16.30 £2.30 (£36.90). Mrs Carol Whitwood bred by Mrs C. Whitwood and N. E. C Sherwood. 19 Rn  1m 30.3 (7.5)
SF—36/25/15/21/1/9

**3871**  CAISTER FOR HOLIDAYS STKS (Mdn 2-Y.O.F) £2070.00 (£570.00: £270.00)
1m 3y  2-00 (2-05)

**Lille Hammer** (LMCumani) 8-11 AMunro (8) (prom: led over 1f out: rdn out) ......... —1

Tochar Ban (USA) (DRCElsworth) 8-11 JWilliams (5) (lengthy: bit bkwd: dwlt: hdwy 2f out: swtchd rt & r.o wl fnl f: jst failed) ......... s.h.2

Michaela Mia (USA) (DRLoder) 8-8 ‡3FNorton (12) (lft-f: hdwy over 2f out: r.o fnl f) 2.3

Licorne (HRACecil) 8-11 WRyan (19) (leggy: scope: hdwy 4f out: led 2f out tl over 1f out: kpt on) ......... 1½.4

Buglet (GCBravery) 8-11 NDay (1) (lft-f: unf: dwlt: sn chsng ldrs: ev ch 2f out: sn wknd) ......... 8.5

Dancing Moon (IRE) (AAScott) 8-11 WRSwinburn (9) (lengthy: scope: dwlt: hdwy 4f out: nvr rchd ldrs) ......... 1.6

3631⁴ Bay Queen (MBell) 8-11 MHills (20) (bhd tl styd on fnl 3f) ......... 2.7

Wakt (DMorley) 8-11 BRaymond (2) (unf: scope: prom 4f: eased whn btn) ......... 2.8

3512³ Araadh (USA) (Fav) (HThomsonJones) 8-11 RHills (18) (in tch: rdn over 2f out: sn btn) ......... nk.9

Rose Noble (USA) (WJarvis) 8-11 SCauthen (7) (unf: scope: bkwd: led 1f: eased whn btn appr fnl f) ......... nk.10

Dili (USA) *(ACStewart)* 8-11 MRoberts (3) (scope: bkwd: led after 4f to 2f out: sn wknd) ................................................................................ s.h.11
3685 Arctic Agnes (USA) **(43)** *(RAkehurst)* 8-11 TQuinn (11) (rdn 3f out: a bhd) ...... ¾.12
3712 Premier Blues (FR) *(RJRWilliams)* 8-4 ‡7GMitchell (2) (nvr nr to chal) .............. nk.13
3623⁶ Hush Baby (IRE) **(42)** (bl) *(DMorris)* 8-11 JFanning (6) (w ldrs over 4f) ............ 5.14
3684 Misty Silks *(MJRyan)* 8-11 DBiggs (4) (prom: ev ch 2f out: wknd) .................... hd.15
3631⁵ Meant to Be *(HJCollingridge)* 8-11 JQuinn (10) (in tch over 4f) ...................... 2.16
2728⁴ Madam Caprice *(RGuest)* 8-8 ‡3DHarrison (13) (a bhd) ............................... nk.17
3625⁴ Nanny Margaret (IRE) *(PAKelleway)* 8-11 GayKelleway (16) (n.d) ................... 3.18
Mulled Ale (IRE) *(CFWall)* 8-11 PRobinson (14) (unf: bkwd: a bhd) ............... s.h.19
Ponds (MrsJCecil) 8-11 PaulEddery (17) (unf: bit bkwd: plld hrd: w ldrs 4f) . 3½.20

**5/2 Araadh (USA), 9/2 Bay Queen**(4/1—6/1), **8/1 Licorne**(op 5/1), **9/1 Dancing Moon (IRE)**(6/1—10/1), **10/1 Ponds**(op 5/1), **LILLE HAMMER**(7/1—12/1), **Rose Noble (USA), 14/1 Tochar Ban (USA), Dili (USA)**(op 7/1), **16/1 Wakt, 20/1 Meant to Be, 25/1 Madam Caprice, 33/1** Ors. CSF £138.55, Tote £15.90: £4.80 £14.10 £15.80 (£144.50). Baron Edouard de Rothschild (NEWMARKET) bred by Mount Coote Stud. 20 Rn   1m 45.5 (10.2)

## 3872
HEMSBY HOLIDAY GRADUATION STKS £3143.25 (£936.00: £445.50: £200.25)
**1m 3y**
2-30 (2-32)

2021⁶ **Kristianstad (100)** *(MrsJCecil)* 3-9-4 PaulEddery (4) (hld up: hdwy 3f out: qcknd to ld wl ins fnl f) ........................................................................ —1
3673² Shati (IRE) **(91)** (Fav) *(HThomsonJones)* 3-9-4 RHills (3) (led 1f: chsd ldr tl led again ins fnl f: sn hdd & unable qckn) ............................................ nk.2
3710⁵ Cutwater *(JHMGosden)* 3-8-11 SCauthen (1) (led after 1f: hdd & nt qckn ins fnl f) ............................................................................................ ¾.3
3732 Chaff **(25)** (bl) *(DMorris)* 5-9-0 MRoberts (5) (in tch 5f: r.o wl fnl f) ............... 3.4
1546 Lorica D'Or *(PFTulk)* 5-9-0 WRyan (2) (chsd ldrs 6f: sn bhd) ..................... 15.5

**11/10 Shati (IRE), 9/4 Cutwater, 11/4 KRISTIANSTAD**(op 7/4), **20/1 Chaff, 100/1 Lorica D'Or**. CSF £5.98, Tote £2.40: £1.70 £1.10 (£2.30). Sheikh Mohammed (NEWMARKET) bred by Sheikh Mohammed bin Rashid al Maktoum. 5 Rn   1m 45 (9.7)

## 3873
HOPTON HOLIDAY VILLAGE CLAIMING STKS £2364.00 (£654.00: £312.00)
**1¼m 21y**
3-00 (3-03)

3732 Jade Vale **(69)** *(JWHills)* 3-9-2 MHills (4) (trckd ldrs: 5th st: led over 2f out: rdn out) ..................................................................................... —1
3604⁶ Millrous **(36)** *(RGuest)* 4-7-10 ‡7CHawksley (6) (plld hrd: 7th st: ev ch ins fnl f: r.o) ......................................................................................... ½.2
3215³ Joli's Great **(54)** *(MJRyan)* 4-8-11 DBiggs (2) (bit bkwd: hld up: nt clr run & swtchd wl over 1f out: r.o u.p fnl f) .................................................. 1½.3
3521 J'Arrive **(43)** *(JPearce)* 3-8-2 PRobinson (8) (led after 3f to 2f out: one pce) .... 2½.4
3569² Maple Bay (IRE) **(66)** *(PJMakin)* 3-9-3 WRSwinburn (5) (lw: led after 1f tl after 3f: 2nd st: ev ch 3f out tl no ex over 1f out) ........................................ 1.5
3254 Winged Whisper (USA) **(56)** *(CASmith)* 3-8-6 ‡3DHarrison (7) (b: s.i.s: bhd tl r.o fnl 3f) ........................................................................................ 6.6
3540 Flying Speed (USA) **(69)** (Fav) *(MCPipe)* 4-9-8 MRoberts (11) (in tch: effrt & 6th st: rdn 3f out: sn btn) ................................................................. 2½.7
3485⁵ Jade Mistress **(49)** (bl) *(AHide)* 3-8-5⁽¹⁾ JWilliams (9) (sn prom: 3rd st: ev ch over 2f out: sn btn) ........................................................................ 1½.8
Candesco **(38)** *(RCSpicer)* 6-8-13 KFallon (1) (bit bkwd: nt ld: 4th st: wknd over 3f out: t.o) ............................................................................ 15.9
Nutmeg Lass *(BJMcMath)* 3-7-12 EJohnson (3) (leggy: lt-f: a bhd: t.o fnl 4f) ... 6.10
2595 Cumbrian Cavalier (40/1) Withdrawn (lame at s) : not under orders

**7/4 Flying Speed (USA), 4/1 JADE VALE, 9/2 Maple Bay (IRE), 5/1 Joli's Great, 9/1 Jade Mistress**(8/1—12/1), **16/1 J'Arrive, 20/1 Winged Whisper (USA)**(op 12/1), **25/1 Nutmeg Lass, 40/1** Ors. CSF £109.72, Tote £4.40: £1.80 £7.10 £1.70 (£127.80). Mrs S. Bosher (LAMBOURN) bred by Maj B. Singh. 10 Rn; Millrous clmd M Pipe £3,000   2m 15.7 (11.3)
SF—24/3/15/1/14/–

## 3874
SEASHORE STKS (Mdn 2-Y.O.C & G) £2070.00 (£570.00: £270.00)
**6f 3y**
3-30 (3-32)

**Half Term (USA)** (Jt-Fav) *(JHMGosden)* 9-0 SCauthen (7) (w'like: scope: hld up: hdwy to ld over 1f out: sn qcknd clr: comf) ................................. —1
Castel Rosselo *(GWragg)* 9-0 RHills (4) (unf: scope: lw: s.i.s: hdwy to ld over 2f out: hung rt & hdd 1f out: nt rcvr) ............................................... 5.2
Moon Strike (FR) (Jt-Fav) *(WAO'Gorman)* 9-0 AMunro (5) (lengthy: scope: bit bkwd: dwlt: sn chsng ldrs: n.m.r over 2f out: one pce fnl f) .............. 4.3
1046⁵ Danny Blue (IRE) *(MissGayKelleway)* 9-0 KFallon (11) (hdwy over 1f out: r.o ins fnl f) ........................................................................................... 1.4

3693 Pyrrhic Dance *(JWHills)* 9-0 MHills (1) (prom: rdn over 2f out: one pce) .......... nk.5
3767⁶ Billyback *(MJRyan)* 9-0 DBiggs (8) (kpt on fnl 2f: nvr trbld ldrs) ...................... 1.6
645⁵ The Atheling (IRE) *(MHTompkins)* 9-0 PRobinson (6) (chsd ldrs over 3f: nt clr
run & sn btn) .......... 1.7
3767² Domulla *(RAkehurst)* 9-0 TQuinn (12) (prom: ev ch 2f out: sn wknd) ................. 1.8
3802 Ahjay *(DAWilson)* 9-0 JWilliams (10) (dwlt: a bhd) .......... 1.9
3581⁵ Glisso (IRE) *(Jt-Fav)* *(LMCumani)* 9-0 MRoberts (3) (w ldrs 4f) ......................... ¾.10
Convoy *(GWragg)* 8-11 ‡³FNorton (5) (unf: scope: bkwd: sn pushed along: bhd
fr ½-wy) .......... 5.11
3725² Keating (AUS) *(MrsJCecil)* 9-0 PaulEddery (9) (led over 3f: wknd qckly) .......... 3.12

7/2 Moon Strike (FR), HALF TERM (USA), Glisso (IRE), 5/1 Domulla, 10/1 Castel Rosselo, 12/1 Keating (AUS),
14/1 Pyrrhic Dance, 20/1 The Atheling (IRE), Convoy, 33/1 Billyback, Ahjay, 40/1 Danny Blue (IRE). CSF £36.97,
Tote £4.00: £1.60 £4.60 £1.90 (£27.60). Sheikh Mohammed (NEWMARKET) bred by John C. & Mrs Mabee in
USA. 12 Rn                                                                                        1m 17.3 (6.7)
SF—8/–/–/–/–/–

## 3875
VAUXHALL H'CAP (0-70) £2637.00 (£732.00: £351.00)     **1m 3f 101y**     4-00 (4-03)

3388⋆ Amazon Express (60) *(RAkehurst)* 3–8-13 TQuinn (13) (lw: rn wd 1st 5f: a.p:
3rd st: led over 3f out: clr 1f out: eased nr fin) .......... —1
3687³ Addicted to Love (62) (bl) *(PJMakin)* 3–9-1 WRSwinburn (4) (hdwy 2f out: r.o
ins fnl f) .......... 2½.2
3708² Castillet (65) (Fav) *(GHarwood)* 3–9-4 SCauthen (2) (s.s: hdwy 5f out: ev ch 2f
out: one pce appr fnl f) .......... s.h.3
2101⋆ Mizyan (IRE) (58) *(JEBanks)* 4–9-3 NDay (15) (lw: chsd ldrs: 6th st: one pce
appr fnl f) .......... 1½.4
232 Roses Have Thorns (47) *(DMorris)* 5–8-1(5) ‡⁵StephenDavies (7) (chsd ldrs: 7th
st: ev ch over 2f out: one pce) .......... nk.5
3755 Free Transfer (IRE) (50) *(PFTulk)* 3–8-3 WRyan (1) (prom: 4th st: outpcd over 3f
out: r.o fnl 2f) .......... 3½.6
3752 Skimmer Hawk (45) *(BobJones)* 3–7-12 NCarlisle (3) (nvr nrr) .......... 2.7
3829 Rock Legend (47) *(DShaw)* 4–8-1 ‡⁵NKennedy (8) (hld up: hdwy 4f out) .......... s.h.8
3668⁴ Taylors Prince (59) *(HJCollingridge)* 5–9-4 JQuinn (10) (b.nr fore: in tch: 8th st:
rdn over 2f out: sn btn) .......... 2½.9
3769⋆ Sharp Top (60) *(MJRyan)* 4–9-5 (5x) DBiggs (12) (led over 6f: 2nd st: wknd) ... 7.10
3556³ Dr Zeva (39) *(MDixon)* 6–7-9(5) ‡³FNorton (11) (b: prom: 5th st: wknd 3f out) ... 5.11
3522 Telephus (50) *(BJMcMath)* 3–8-3 EJohnson (9) (bit bkwd: rdn 3f out: n.d) ... s.h.12
578⁶ Kovalevskia (35) *(DAWilson)* 7–7-8 DaleGibson (6) (nvr trbld ldrs) .......... 3.13
3556⁴ Killick (34) *(REPeacock)* 4–7-7 JFanning (16) (b: plld hrd: prom: led 5f tl over 3f
out: wknd qckly) .......... 1½.14
905³ Petavious (69) *(LadyHerries)* 7–9-11 ‡³DHarrison (14) (a bhd) .......... 1.15
3770 Thimbalina (36) *(DAWilson)* 6–7-9 GBardwell (5) (b: a bhd) .......... nk.16
LONG HANDICAP: Dr Zeva 7-3, Killick 7-2.

11/4 Castillet, 6/1 AMAZON EXPRESS, 13/2 Sharp Top, 7/1 Addicted to Love, 9/1 Taylors Prince, Mizyan
(IRE)(14/1–8/1), 10/1 Petavious, 14/1 Dr Zeva, Thimbalina, Telephus, Rock Legend, 16/1 Free Transfer (IRE),
20/1 Roses Have Thorns, 25/1 Kovalevskia, 33/1 Ors. CSF £51.45, CT £137.14. Tote £7.30: £2.30 £2.10 £1.70
£2.60 (£19.20). Mrs Jill Moss (EPSOM) bred by Ewar Stud Farms. 16 Rn                     2m 33.5 (9.5)
SF—44/41/43/37/20/11

T/Plpt: £1,367.60 (2.4 Tckts).                                                                          Dk

## 3771—NOTTINGHAM (L-H)
### Thursday, October 29th [Good to soft]
Going Allowance: 0.90 sec per fur (S)                                        Wind: almost nil

Stalls: high

## 3876
ST ANNS (S) STKS (3-Y.O) £2322.00 (£642.00: £306.00)     **1¾m 15y**     1-20 (1-21)

3603 Judge and Jury (44) *(MJFetherston-Godley)* 9-2 MRoberts (2) (lw: hld up & wl
bhd: hdwy 3f out: styd on to ld cl home) .......... —1
3752⁴ Iron Baron (IRE) (56) *(RHollinshead)* 9-2 WRyan (9) (hdwy ½-wy: 4th st: led
appr fnl f tl nr fin) .......... nk.2
3769³ Allmosa (53) (Fav) *(TJNaughton)* 8-11 GCarter (5) (a.p: led 6f out tl appr fnl f:
one pce) .......... 5.3
3705³ Gay Ming (47) *(RHollinshead)* 8-4 ‡⁷AGarth (10) (swtg: bhd: hdwy over 2f out: nt
rch ldrs) .......... 10.4
3752 Reach for Glory (50) *(RMWhitaker)* 9-2 ACulhane (8) (bhd: styd on fnl 2f: nvr
nrr) .......... nk.5

| | | |
|---|---|---|
| 3609 | And Me **(40)** *(DTThom)* 8-6 PRobinson (4) (chsd ldrs: 5th st: wknd over 2f out) | 7.6 |
| 3769 | Lily Moreton *(MJHeaton-Ellis)* 8-6 JReid (1) (led over 8f: lost pl ent st: t.o) | 8.7 |
| 3601⁶ | Princess of Orange **(39)** *(WMBrisbourne)* 8-6 DHolland (6) (disp ld tl led 8f out: hdd 6f out: 2nd st: wknd 3f out) | 3.8 |
| 3706 | Finneran's Fantasy *(DMorris)* 8-6 ‡⁵StephenDavies (7) (chsd ldrs: 3rd st: wknd 3f out) | 3.9 |
| 3745⁶ | Paper Clip **(30)** *(JDBethell)* 8-11 NAdams (3) (prom tl 6th & wkng st: t.o) | 3.10 |
| 3601 | Good Old George (IRE) **(30)** *(MJFetherston-Godley)* 8-11 CRutter (11) (lost tch ½-wy: t.o) | dist.11 |

**7/4** Allmosa, **100/30** Gay Ming, Iron Baron (IRE), **8/1** Princess of Orange, JUDGE AND JURY, **9/1** Paper Clip(op 14/1), **12/1** Reach for Glory(op 7/1), **20/1** Lily Moreton, **25/1** And Me, **33/1** Ors. CSF £37.95, Tote £8.40: £2.30 £2.50 £1.10 (£16.50). Mr M. E. Cole (EAST ILSLEY) bred by Studcrown Ltd. 11 Rn; Bt in 3,100 gns
3m 16.9 (18.4)
SF—44/43/28/1/12

## 3877

MAPPERLEY H'CAP (0-70) £2847.00 (£792.00: £381.00)   **2m 9y**   1-50 (1-53)
(Weights raised 1 lb)

| | | |
|---|---|---|
| 3603★ | Child Star (FR) **(49)** *(DMarks)* 3–7-12 SDawson (5) (hld up: hdwy 3f out: styd on to ld ins fnl f) | —1 |
| 3603² | Sports View **(50)** (Fav) *(PGMurphy)* 3–7-13 NAdams (7) (hld up: hdwy 3f out: nt clr run appr fnl f: fin wl: unlucky) | nk.2 |
| 3621 | Needwood Muppet **(53)** *(BCMorgan)* 5–8-12 SCauthen (15) (hdwy 7f out: 4th st: led appr fnl f tl ins fnl f) | 1½.3 |
| 2120³ | Dari Sound (IRE) **(48)** *(JGFitzGerald)* 4–8-7 KFallon (18) (bit bkwd: chsd ldrs: effrt 3f out: styd on) | 1½.4 |
| 3728 | Shahdjat (IRE) **(57)** *(KCBailey)* 4–8-9 ‡⁷AntoinetteArmes (13) (a.p: 2nd st: led over 3f out tl appr fnl f: one pce) | 3½.5 |
| 3577★ | Day of History (IRE) **(49)** *(CACyzer)* 3–7-12⁽²⁾ WCarson (9) (prom: 5th st: hrd drvn & wknd over 1f out) | 1½.6 |
| 3675 | Full Quiver **(49)** (v) *(MrsBarbaraWaring)* 7–8-8 NHowe (8) (hdwy over 2f out: styd on fnl f) | 1½.7 |
| 3756⁴ | Zoom Lens (IRE) **(61)** *(JLDunlop)* 3–8-10 MRoberts (10) (hdwy 3f out: nt trble ldrs) | 5.8 |
| | Fettle Up **(35)** *(JWharton)* 4–7-8 JQuinn (11) (bkwd: chsd ldrs: hrd rdn 3f out: sn btn) | 1½.9 |
| 3745 | Fanlight **(52)** *(RAkehurst)* 4–8-11 JReid (3) (nvr plcd to chal) | nk.10 |
| 3778 | Gesnera **(35)** *(KWhite)* 4–7-8⁽¹⁾ NCarlisle (4) (bhd fnl 4f) | ½.11 |
| 3808³ | Cost Effective **(42)** *(MBrittain)* 5–7-12⁽⁶⁾ ‡³SMaloney (20) (dwlt: hdwy ½-wy: 7th st: wknd 3f out) | 1.12 |
| 2083 | Beldale Star **(47)** *(RAkehurst)* 9–8-3 ‡³RPerham (6) (b: bkwd: hdwy & 6th st: wknd over 2f out) | hd.13 |
| 3616 | Ross Graham **(50)** *(MrsBarbaraWaring)* 4–8-9 JLowe (16) (prom: 3rd st: rdn & wknd 2f out) | ½.14 |
| 3613⁴ | Merton Mill **(62)** (bl) *(DMorley)* 5–9-7 PaulEddery (1) (lw: hld up in tch: rdn over 2f out: sn wknd) | 2.15 |
| 789 | Olej (USA) **(61)** *(LordHuntingdon)* 3–8-10 DMcKeown (2) (lw: a in rr: t.o) | 10.16 |
| 990 | Officer Cadet **(47)** *(RCurtis)* 5–8-6 GBardwell (12) (bit bkwd: a bhd: t.o) | 17 |
| 3687 | Triple Top **(38)** *(KWhite)* 7–7-8⁽⁴⁾ ‡³DHarrison (14) (b: bkwd: chsd ldrs to ½-wy: grad wknd: t.o) | 18 |
| 3778 | Leguard Express (IRE) **(41)** (bl) *(OO'Neill)* 4–8-0 CRutter (19) (led tl hdd & wknd over 3f out: t.o) | 19 |
| | Grey Salute (CAN) **(65)** *(JRJenkins)* 9–9-10 JWilliams (17) (bkwd: chsd ldrs 10f: sn wknd: t.o) | 20 |

LONG HANDICAP: Triple Top 7-6.

**9/2** Sports View, **6/1** Zoom Lens (IRE), **8/1** Needwood Muppet, Fanlight, Shahdjat (IRE)(op 25/1), **17/2** CHILD STAR (FR), **9/1** Day of History (IRE), **10/1** Merton Mill, **11/1** Dari Sound (IRE), **16/1** Full Quiver, Officer Cadet, Olej (USA), **20/1** Ross Graham, Cost Effective, Beldale Star, **25/1** Gesnera, **33/1** Triple Top, Grey Salute (CAN), Leguard Express (IRE), **50/1** Fettle Up. CSF £51.18, CT £317.80. Tote £10.70: £2.80 £1.60 £1.30 £2.90 (£20.30). Mr P. J. Pearson (UPPER LAMBOURN) bred by Sheikh Mohammed bin Rashid al Maktoum in France.
20 Rn
3m 46.7 (22.3)
SF—5/5/16/9/7/–

## 3878

SNEINTON STKS   £3237.90 (£894.40: £425.70)   **6f 15y**   2-20 (2-22)

| | | |
|---|---|---|
| 3805★ | Branston Abby (IRE) **(86)** (Fav) *(MJohnston)* 3–8-13 JReid (3) (reard s: hld up & bhd: hdwy appr fnl f: led wl ins fnl f) | —1 |
| 3826 | Sir Harry Hardman **(91)** *(FHLee)* 4–8-13 WCarson (1) (led: hrd rdn fnl f: ct cl home) | nk.2 |
| | Gilt Throne **(102)** *(MHTompkins)* 5–9-9 PRobinson (2) (bkwd: chsd ldr: shkn up over 1f out: sn outpcd) | 7.3 |

**4/5** BRANSTON ABBY (IRE)(tchd 6/4), **7/4** Gilt Throne, **7/2** Sir Harry Hardman. CSF £3.54, Tote £2.00 (£1.90). Mr J. David Abell (MIDDLEHAM) bred by John David Abell in Ireland. 3 Rn 1m 20 (9)
SF—27/26/8

## 3879

NOTTINGHAM AUTUMN H'CAP (0-70) £3057.00 (£852.00: £411.00)
**6f 15y** 2-50 (2-53)

(Weights raised 4 lb)

3707[2] **Coolaba Prince (IRE) (61)** *(FHLee)* 3–9–9 WCarson (6) (chsd ldrs far side: rdn to ld ins fnl f: r.o) .......... —**1**
3854[3] Take it in Cash **(46)** *(RDickin)* 3–8–8 CRutter (22) (a.p stands' side: rdn & r.o wl fnl f) .......... ¾.**2**
3783* Sir Joey (USA) **(59)** (Fav) *(PGMurphy)* 3–9–7 (7x) JWilliams (21) (hdwy stands' side over 1f out: r.o wl nr fin) .......... ¾.**3**
3707 Strip Cartoon (IRE) **(49)** (v) *(SRBowring)* 4–8–13 GBaxter (13) (racd centre: r.o appr fnl f: nvr nrr) .......... nk.**4**
3524 Face North (IRE) **(55)** *(RAkehurst)* 4–9–5 JReid (18) (lw: chsd ldrs stands' side: kpt on u.p ins fnl f) .......... ½.**5**
3783 Mariette Larkin **(50)** *(GBBalding)* 3–8–6(3) SO'Gorman (23) (s.s: gd hdwy fnl f: fin wl) .......... hd.**6**
3707[5] My Ruby Ring **(55)** *(DRLaing)* 5–9–0 ‡[5]BDoyle (10) (b: hdwy ½-wy: led over 1f out tl ins fnl f) .......... ½.**7**
3681 State Flyer **(60)** (v) *(CBBBooth)* 4–9–3 ‡[7]GForster (25) (r.o appr fnl f: nvr nrr) ... nk.**8**
3595 Verro (USA) **(40)** (bl) *(JABennett)* 5–8–4 NCarlisle (3) (hdwy over 1f out: nrst fin) 3½.**9**
3710* Broadway Ruckus (CAN) **(60)** *(DRLaing)* 3–9–8 BRaymond (26) (nvr nrr) .......... ½.**10**
3793 Veloce (IRE) **(58)** (v) *(ABailey)* 4–9–8 WRyan (7) (lw: prom far side 4f) .......... ½.**11**
3707[6] Pretonic **(56)** *(MJohnston)* 4–9–6 DMcKeown (8) (a.p: led ½-wy tl over 1f out: sn wknd) .......... ½.**12**
3783 John O'Dreams **(44)** *(MrsJCDawe)* 7–8–8 MRoberts (15) (nvr nr to chal) .......... s.h.**13**
3803[6] Walstead (IRE) **(58)** *(DAWilson)* 3–9–8 GDuffield (24) (m.n.s) .......... ¾.**14**
3689 Lucknam Style **(54)** (v) *(MrsBarbaraWaring)* 4–9–4 NHowe (4) (prom over 4f) . ½.**15**
3707 Twilight Falls **(48)** *(MJCamacho)* 7–8–12 NConnorton (5) (lw: prom far side 4f) hd.**16**
3747[5] Spender **(46)** *(PWHarris)* 3–8–8 NAdams (19) (m.n.s) .......... hd.**17**
3378 Wellsy Lad (USA) **(50)** *(DWChapman)* 5–9–0 SWood (2) (w ldrs far side over 5f) ½.**18**
3707 Highborn (IRE) **(48)** *(PSFelgate)* 3–8–10 JLowe (17) (m.n.s) .......... nk.**19**
3400 C Sharp **(40)** *(WRMuir)* 5–8–4 JQuinn (16) (swtg: outpcd) .......... s.h.**20**
3766 Executive Spirit **(53)** (bl) *(DSasse)* 3–9–1 RPrice (20) (prom stands' side over 4f) .......... s.h.**21**
3777 Casting Shadows **(51)** *(RDickin)* 3–8–13 SDawson (14) (m.n.s) .......... s.h.**22**
3797[2] Royal Dartmouth (USA) **(45)** *(BRMillman)* 7–8–4 ‡[5]KRutter (1) (b: swtchd rt sn after s: n.d) .......... **1.23**
2582[3] Flying Wind **(55)** *(JSutcliffe)* 3–9–3 BRouse (12) (bit bkwd: bhd fr ½-wy) .......... 1½.**24**
3403 Whippet **(48)** (v) *(JABennett)* 8–8–12 DHolland (11) (led centre 3f: sn rdn & wknd) .......... **5.25**

**5/2** Sir Joey (USA), **11/4** Face North (IRE), **9/1** Royal Dartmouth (USA), **11/1** Take it in Cash, **12/1** John O'Dreams, Twilight Falls, COOLABA PRINCE (IRE), My Ruby Ring(op 8/1), **14/1** Pretonic, Broadway Ruckus (CAN), **16/1** Strip Cartoon (IRE), Walstead (IRE), **20/1** Veloce (IRE), Flying Wind, **25/1** Wellsy Lad (USA), **33/1** Ors. CSF £151.56, CT £413.32. Tote £14.00: £2.70 £3.50 £1.40 £5.10 (£175.00). Mr P. J. Cosgrove (WILMSLOW) bred by Lodge Park Stud in Ireland. 25 Rn 1m 19.6 (8.6)
SF—45/27/37/28/32/18

## 3880

E.B.F. NETHERFIELD STKS (I) (Mdn 2-Y.O) £2880.00 (£800.00: £384.00)
**1m 54y** 3-20 (3-22)

3691[2] **Azzilfi** (Fav) *(JLDunlop)* 9-0 WCarson (7) (a.p: 5th st: hrd drvn to ld 1f out: r.o) . —**1**
3531 Al Senafi (IRE) *(LMCumani)* 9-0 LDettori (6) (chsd ldrs: outpcd & rdn 3f out: styd on wl fnl f) .......... 2½.**2**
3693 Missed Flight *(CFWall)* 9-0 PRobinson (12) (chsd ldrs: 6th st: styd on u.p fnl f) ½.**3**
Haunted Wood (USA) *(HRACecil)* 8-9 SCauthen (3) (w'like: leggy: led: rdn 2f out: hdd fnl f: eased whn btn) .......... 1½.**4**
3424[3] Dana Springs (IRE) *(RHannon)* 8-9 JReid (10) (a.p: 2nd st: ev ch 2f out: sn rdn & wknd) .......... **5.5**
3531 Warspite *(PTWalwyn)* 9-0 GCarter (5) (hdwy over 2f out: nt rch ldrs) .......... 1½.**6**
Star Rage (IRE) *(JWharton)* 9-0 JWilliams (2) (scope: bit bkwd: nvr nr to chal) .. **3.7**
3553 Baileys Colours **(47)** *(BJMcMath)* 8-9 EJohnson (8) (nvr nr ldrs) .......... 2½.**8**
3782[4] Sure Right (IRE) *(JWHills)* 9-0 MHills (13) (prom: 3rd st: wknd over 2f) .......... ¾.**9**
3712 Nomadic Fire *(DMorley)* 9-0 BRaymond (9) (chsd ldrs over 5f) .......... nk.**10**
Sassiver (USA) *(RCharlton)* 9-0 PaulEddery (14) (w'like: bkwd: s.s: a bhd) ...... **1.11**
Bayrak (USA) *(ACStewart)* 9-0 MRoberts (11) (w'like: scope: bkwd: a bhd) ...... **2.12**
3717 Maastricht *(WJHaggas)* 9-0 JQuinn (1) (bit bkwd: prom: 4th st: wknd 3f out) ... **6.13**
3314 Restart *(LordHuntingdon)* 9-0 DMcKeown (4) (lw: s.i.s: a bhd: t.o) .......... **10.14**

6/4 AZZILFI, 3/1 Haunted Wood (USA)(9/4—9/2), 9/2 Al Senafi (IRE)(op 3/1), 9/1 Bayrak (USA), 10/1 Sassiver (USA), Dana Springs (IRE), 20/1 Sure Right (IRE), Nomadic Fire, Restart, Maastricht, 33/1 Ors. CSF £10.39, Tote £1.90: £1.10 £2.50 £8.80 (£4.10). Prince A. A. Faisal (ARUNDEL) bred by Nawara Stud Co Ltd. 14 Rn
1m 51.2 (11.6)
SF—37/29/27/17/2/2

**3881**   E.B.F. NETHERFIELD STKS (II) (Mdn 2-Y.O) £2857.60 (£793.60: £380.80)
1m 54y
3-50 (3-53)

**Revere (IRE)** (Fav) (PFICole) 9-0 SCauthen (10) (str: cmpt: a.p: 2nd st: led appr fnl f: drvn clr fnl f) — 1

37842 Fools Errand (IRE) (RHannon) 9-0 GHind (7) (led tl appr fnl f: sn hrd rdn: one pce) 6.2

Ajmaan (USA) (ACStewart) 9-0 MRoberts (6) (cmpt: bkwd: hld up: hdwy over 2f out: wknd appr fnl f) 1½.3

Talented (JLDunlop) 8-9 LDettori (3) (leggy: unf: a.p: 4th st: styd on same pce fnl 2f) 1.4

37904 Arc Bright (IRE) (75) (RHollinshead) 9-0 WRyan (13) (in tch: effrt 3f out: styd on one pce fnl 2f) 3½.5

Oakmead (IRE) (PWChapple-Hyam) 8-9 JReid (12) (neat: cmpt: bkwd: s.s: sme hdwy fnl 2f: nvr nrr) 2.6

2924 Combellino (PWHarris) 9-0 NAdams (2) (still bkwd: chsd ldrs: rdn over 3f out: no imp) hd.7

35055 Agenda One (MissAJWhitfield) 8-4 ‡5ATucker (8) (prom: 3rd st: wknd 2f out) ... nk.8

Altnaharra (DMorley) 8-9 MHills (9) (scope: bkwd: chsd ldrs: 5th st: wknd over 2f out) 1.9

29726 Early to Rise (CACyzer) 9-0 KFallon (1) (prom tl 6th & wkng st) 2½.10

Sir Edward Henry (IRE) (FHLee) 9-0 PaulEddery (11) (w'like: scope: bkwd: s.s: a bhd: t.o) 7.11

3491 Kawasir (CAN) (PTWalwyn) 9-0 WCarson (5) (a bhd: t.o) 15.12

3570 Whimsical Notion (MrsBarbaraWaring) 8-9 NHowe (4) (plld hrd: mid div tl wknd 3f out: t.o) 6.13

7/4 REVERE (IRE)(Evens—2/1), 9/2 Ajmaan (USA)(op 3/1), 5/1 Fools Errand (IRE), 13/2 Oakmead (IRE), 7/1 Talented, 10/1 Arc Bright (IRE), 11/1 Kawasir (CAN), Altnaharra, 14/1 Sir Edward Henry (IRE), 25/1 Combellino, Early to Rise, 33/1 Ors. CSF £13.27, Tote £2.00: £1.30 £2.00 £1.80 (£7.10). Mr Fahd Salman (WHATCOMBE) bred by Newgate Stud Co in Ireland. 13 Rn
1m 52 (12.4)
SF—25/7/2/–/–/–

**3882**   WOODTHORPE H'CAP (0-70) £3015.00 (£840.00: £405.00) 1m 54y   4-20 (4-25)

3797* Penny Drops (54) (Fav) (LordHuntingdon) 3-8-8 ‡3DHarrison (16) (hld up: hdwy over 2f out: led ins fnl f: readily) — 1

3589* Good for the Roses (47) (MMcCormack) 6-8-7 JReid (2) (a.p: 4th st: led over 2f out tl ins fnl f) 1½.2

37856 Cream and Green (38) (KWhite) 8-7-12(2) RPrice (5) (swtg: hld up: hdwy over 2f out: kpt on u.p fnl f) 2.3

3511 Sure Shot Norman (44) (JSutcliffe) 3-8-1 DHolland (10) (chsd ldrs: 7th st: rdn over 1f out: one pce) 3.4

35894 Creselly (52) (JGFitzGerald) 5-8-12 MRoberts (7) (led 3f: 2nd st: wknd over 1f out) 2½.5

2411 Pleasure Quest (45) (DWPArbuthnot) 3-8-2 JQuinn (6) (gd hdwy appr fnl f: fin wl) nk.6

3557 Captain Marmalade (57) (DTThom) 3-9-0 GDuffield (15) (hdwy fnl 2f: nrst fin) .. ½.7

3751 Watch Me Go (IRE) (49) (BobJones) 3-8-6 NConnorton (11) (lw: hdwy ½-wy: rdn 3f out: kpt on one pce) ¾.8

3137 Santi Sana (64) (LadyHerries) 4-9-10 PaulEddery (9) (b.hind: nvr nr to chal) . 1½.9

Rise Over (43) (PDEvans) 6-8-3 MHills (17) (swtg: bit bkwd: prom: 3rd st: wknd over 2f out) 2½.10

3499 Blyton Star (IRE) (43) (SRBowring) 4-8-3(2) SWebster (m.n.s) 1.11

3751* Abeloni (53) (v) (JAGlover) 3-8-7 ‡3SMaloney (8) (chsd ldrs: 6th st: rdn & wknd over 2f out) 1½.12

3732 Ibsen (58) (ICampbell) 4-8-11 ‡7GMitchell (12) (m.n.s) nk.13

Sybillin (55) (JGFitzGerald) 6-9-1 KFallon (19) (bit bkwd: a bhd) 2½.14

37666 Gachette (55) (bl) (JSutcliffe) 3-8-12 BRouse (1) (hdwy ent st: rdn & wknd 2f out) nk.15

Tilt Tech Flyer (35) (JAkehurst) 7-7-9 NAdams (13) (b: m.n.s) nk.16

3696 Legend Dulac (IRE) (55) (JLHarris) 3-8-12 PRobinson (18) (led 5f out tl over 2f out: sn wknd) 2½.17

3589 Roar on Tour (59) (v) (MHEasterby) 3-9-2 MBirch (3) (mid div: rdn 3f out: no imp) 18

1415 Very Good **(39)** *(NTinkler)* 3-7-10 GBardwell (14) (bkwd: prom: 5th st: sn wknd: t.o) ...................................................................................................... **19**

**13/8** PENNY DROPS, **6/1** Good for the Roses, **10/1** Creselly, Gachette, **11/1** Abeloni, **14/1** Watch Me Go (IRE), Roar on Tour, Sybillin, Sure Shot Norman, **16/1** Legend Dulac (IRE), **20/1** Santi Sana, Ibsen, **25/1** Rise Over, Tilt Tech Flyer, **33/1** Cream and Green, Captain Marmalade, Pleasure Quest, **50/1** Ors. CSF £13.48, CT £254.85. Tote £2.70: £1.10 £1.50 £2.70 £5.40 (£6.60). Mr Stanley J. Sharp (WEST ILSLEY) bred by T. M. Saud. 19 Rn
1m 51.1 (11.5)
SF—33/27/12/6/9/–

T/Plpt: £16.30 (147.79 Tckts).                                                                                    IM

### 3815a—SAN SIRO  (R-H)
**Wednesday, October 21st [Heavy]**

## 3883a
PREMIO CAMPOBELLO (listed race) (2-Y.O) £20930.00   **1m 1f**

3235[5] **FUTURBALLA** *(JLDunlop)* 2-8-6 TQuinn ................................................ —**1**
3643[2] Cure the King (IRE) *(Italy)* 2-8-6 FJohansson ........................... 2¹/₄.**2**
3677[4] SHEBL (USA) *(MRStoute)* 2-8-6 PaulEddery ......................... 3¹/₂.**3**
3463* SOUL EMPEROR *(MBell)* 2-8-6 AMunro (btn further 16l) ............... **8**
3624* BLUE BLAZER *(BHanbury)* 2-8-6 BRaymond (btn 24¹/₂l by wnr) ............. **10**
Tote 42L: 15L 37L 21L (346L). Gerecon Italia (ARUNDEL) bred by J. L. Woolford. 13 Rn   2m 3.5

### 3325a—LEOPARDSTOWN  (L-H)
**Saturday, October 24th [Good to soft]**
Going Allowance: 0.30 sec per fur (G)

## 3884a
E.B.F. LEOPARDSTOWN STKS (Gp 3) (2-Y.O) £13435.00   **7f**

Foresee *(Ireland)* 2-8-10 DHogan (w ldr: rdn over 1f out: r.o to ld ins fnl f: hld on wl) ...................................................................................................... —**1**
Nordic Fox (IRE) *(Ireland)* 2-8-10 CRoche (in tch on ins: swtchd rt over 1f out: r.o wl u.p fnl f) ................................................................. hd.**2**
2177[3] High Tycoon (IRE) *(Fav)* *(Ireland)* 2-8-10 PShanahan (mde most tl no ex ins fnl f) ...................................................................................................... ³/₄.**3**
Danse Royale (IRE) *(Ireland)* 2-8-7 RHughes (in tch: rdn over 1f out: nt qckn) .. 2.**4**
Fanny Blankers (IRE) *(Ireland)* 2-8-7 RJGriffiths (hld up: kpt on fnl 2f: nvr nrr) .. ¹/₂.**5**
Digpast (IRE) (bl) *(Ireland)* 2-8-10 SCraine (s.s: bhd: sme hdwy over 1f out: nrst fin) ...................................................................................................... 1.**6**
Kar Or *(Ireland)* 2-8-10 WJSupple (bhd: rdn 2f out: sn no imp) ...................... ³/₄.**7**

**2/1** High Tycoon (IRE), **5/2** Nordic Fox (IRE), **3/1** Danse Royale (IRE), **15/2** FORESEE, **16/1** Fanny Blankers (IRE), **20/1** Kar Or, **33/1** Digpast (IRE). Tote £12.30: £3.80 £1.70 (£15.00). Sheikh Mohammed (J.M.Oxx,IRELAND) bred by W.Vischer. 7 Rn
1m 33.3 (8.3)
SF—3/2/–/–/–/–/

## 3885a
TOKYO THOROUGHBREDS RACE   £7738.00   **1¹/₄m**

2889a[2] **Mining Tycoon (IRE)** *(Ireland)* 3-8-9 KJManning ......................... —**1**
3327a[4] Kooyonga (IRE) *(Ireland)* 4-9-10 WJO'Connor ........................ 2¹/₂.**2**
3736a[2] Arrikala (IRE) (bl) *(Ireland)* 3-8-10 CRoche ........................ 3¹/₂.**3**
Tote £10.20 (£31.80). Mr D.H.W.Dobson (J.S.Bolger,IRELAND) bred by Grangemore Stud in Ireland. 4 Rn
2m 9.1 (5.1)
SF—74/84/63

### KEENELAND  (L-H)
**Saturday, October 24th [Firm]**

## 3886a
QUEEN ELIZABETH II CHALLENGE CUP (Grade 1) (3-Y.O.F) £66310.00   **1m 1f (turf)**

Captive Miss (USA) *(America)* 3-8-9 JulieKrone ........................ —**1**
Suivi (USA) *(America)* 3-8-9 ASolis ........................................ nk.**2**
2766a[5] Trampoli (USA) *(America)* 3-8-9 MSmith ........................ 1.**3**
2383[3] TOUSSAUD (USA) *(JHMGosden)* 3-8-9 DFlores ........................ nk.**4**
Tote 11.80 (1-2) 5.00 4.60 (1-2-3) 3.60 3.20 4.00. Mr Z.Minassian (P.Serpe,AMERICA) bred by H.T.Mangurian Jnr. in USA. 10 Rn
1m 48.6

### 3814a—LONGCHAMP (R-H)
**Sunday, October 25th [Soft]**
Going Allowance: St: 0.55 sec (Y); Rnd: 0.70 sec per fur (S)

## 3887a
PRIX DU PETIT COUVERT (Gp 3)   £20640.00   **5f (st)**

3733a² **Wixon (FR)** *(France)* 2-8-6[1] FHead ........................................ —1
3656a² KEEN HUNTER (USA) *(JHMGosden)* 5-9-11 SCauthen ........................ ³/₄.2
          Dauberval (USA) *(France)* 3-9-11 TJarnet ................................. 6.3
Tote 4.90f: 1.30f 1.10f 1.30f (4.10f). Mr Allen E.Paulson (F.Boutin,FRANCE) bred by Allen E.Paulson in France. 9 Rn
                                                                             60.9 sec (3.9)
                                                                          SF—69/85/61

## 3888a
PRIX ROYAL-OAK (Gp 1) (C & F) £41280.00   **1m 7f 110y (Grande)**

3653a³ **ASSESSOR (IRE)** *(RHannon)* 3-8-11 TQuinn (in rr: hdwy 6f out: 2nd st: led
          over 1f out: hrd rdn & r.o wl) .................................................. —1
3649a⁴ ALWAYS FRIENDLY *(HCandy)* 4-9-0 AMunro (hld up: hdwy to ld ent st: hdd
          over ½f out: kpt on) .......................................................... 2¹/₂.2
3650a⋆ Sought Out (IRE) (Fav) *(France)* 4-9-0 CAsmussen (led tl lost pl after 2f: hdwy
          & 3rd st: one pce) ............................................................. 6.3
          Sheikh Dancer (bl) *(Spain)* 5-9-3 DBoeuf (hld up: 5th st: one pce fnl 2f) ...... 8.4
3650a⁴ WITNESS BOX (USA) *(JHMGosden)* 5-9-3 SCauthen (trckd ldrs: 4th st: unable
          qckn fnl 2f) .................................................................... 5.5
  3636⋆ ALLEGAN (USA) *(HRACecil)* 3-8-11 PatEddery (a.p: led 6f out to 4f out: sn
          wknd) ........................................................................... 8.6
3650a³ Dariyoun (USA) *(France)* 4-9-3 FHead (a mid div: nvr able to chal) ............. 5.7
 2094a Ivyanna (IRE) *(Ireland)* 3-8-8 KJManning (prom: pushed along 8f out: wknd 3f
          out) ........................................................................... 20.8
3653a² Jamshid (JPN) *(France)* 3-8-11 TJarnet (mid div tl wknd 6f out) .............. nose.9
  3594⋆ BALNIBARBI *(HRACecil)* 3-8-11 WRyan (led after 2f to 6f out: sn wknd) ....... 8.10
  3111a Justice (FR) *(France)* 4-9-3 SGuillot (mid div tl wknd 6f out: t.o) ............. 11
3653a³ Dadarissime (FR) *(France)* 3-8-11 ESaint-Martin (reluctant to r: n.d: p.u 2f out) ..... 0

**8/10** Sought Out (IRE), **19/4** Allegan (USA), Balnibarbi, **13/2** Dadarissime (FR), **15/2** Jamshid (JPN), **9/1**
Witness Box (USA), **15/1** Always Friendly, **20/1** Dariyoun (USA), **37/1** Ivyanna (IRE), **39/1** Sheikh Dancer, **43/1**
ASSESSOR (IRE), **52/1** Justice (FR). Tote 43.70f: 4.70f 2.90f 1.30f (153.70f). Mr B.E.Nielsen
(MARLBOROUGH) bred by Airlie Stud in Ireland. 12 Rn
                                                                             3m 35.8 (16.8)
                                                                       SF—38/38/32/27/22/8

## 3889a
PRIX DES RESERVOIRS (Gp3) (2-Y.O.F) £20640.00   **1m (Grande)**

          **Corrazona (USA)** *(France)* 2-8-11 ODoleuze ............................ —1
          Dancienne (FR) *(France)* 2-8-11 DBoeuf ............................... hd.2
          Borodislew (USA) *(France)* 2-8-11 ELegrix .......................... s.nk.3
Tote 4.40f: 1.80f 4.40f 5.40f (30.00f). Mr J.Wertheimer (Mrs C.Head,FRANCE) bred by Willow Wood Farm in
USA. 12 Rn
                                                                             1m 48.3 (7.7)
                                                                          SF—65/64/63

### 3883a—SAN SIRO (R-H)
**Sunday, October 25th [Heavy]**

## 3890a
PREMIO BAGUTTA MEMORIAL SERGIO CUMANI (Gp 3) (F & M) £27907.00   **1m**

3333a³ **Siddharta (USA)** *(Italy)* 4-8-8 SSoto ............................... —1
3568a³ CLOUD OF DUST *(JLDunlop)* 3-8-9 MRoberts ........................ 1¹/₂.2
3741a⁴ Irish Source *(France)* 3-8-6 OPeslier ................................. 5.3
3566a⁴ ARBUSHA (USA) *(LordHuntingdon)* 3-8-7[1] LPiggott (btn further 20l) .......... 7
 3546³ SUSURRATION (USA) *(JHMGosden)* 5-8-8 WCarson (btn 35¹/₂l by wnr) ........... 10
Tote 121L: 27L 18L 16L (436L). Ippoleasing Finanziaria (G.Verricelli,ITALY) bred by Alexander-Fairness
Thoroughbreds in USA. 11 Rn
                                                                             1m 47.8

## 3891a
GRAN CRITERIUM (Gp 1) (2-Y.O.C & F) £51163.00   **1m**

3660a³ **Pelder (IRE)** *(Italy)* 2-8-11 SSoto ................................ —1
 3674⋆ RIGHT WIN (IRE) *(RHannon)* 2-8-11 MRoberts ........................ 3¹/₂.2
3232a⋆ Mister Naif (USA) *(Italy)* 2-8-11 FJovine ............................. 3¹/₂.3
 3127⁵ ICY SOUTH (USA) *(JHMGosden)* 2-8-11 RCochrane ................... 8¹/₂.4
 3679⋆ RAIN BROTHER (USA) *(PWChapple-Hyam)* 2-8-11 JReid (btn further 4l) ....... 6

3567a★ VENTIQUATTROFOGLI (IRE) *(JLDunlop)* 2–8-11 WCarson (btn 25l by wnr) .......... **8**
3660a★ ARMAN'S SAX (IRE) *(JLDunlop)* 2–8-11 LPiggott (btn 65³/₄l by wnr) .................... **14**
Tote 108L: 29L 15L 23L (218L). Lady M Stable (L.D'Auria,ITALY) bred by Mrs M.Morris in Ireland. 14 Rn
1m 47.6

3712— **NEWMARKET (R-H)** Rowley Mile
**Friday, October 30th [Good]**
Going Allowance: 5f-6f: minus 0.10 sec (F); Rest: 0.10 sec (G)          Wind: nil

Stalls: high

**3892**          E.B.F. RED LODGE STKS (Mdn 2-Y.O) £4240.00 (£1270.00: £610.00: £280.00)
          **6f**          1-10 (1-14)

          **Serious** *(MRStoute)* 9-0 GDuffield (3) (gd sort: wl grwn: hld up: gd hdwy appr
          fnl f: r.o strly to ld nr fin) ............................................................................. —**1**
2167 Resist the Force (USA) *(CACyzer)* 9-0 MRoberts (2) (racd wd: a.p: rdn to ld ins
          fnl f: hdd cl home) ................................................................................ 1¹/₂.**2**
3802⁵ Aroom *(CJBenstead)* 9-0 RHills (10) (lw: a.p: kpt on u.p ins fnl f) ..................... ¹/₂.**3**
3719⁴ Dramanice (USA) *(MrsJCecil)* 9-0 PaulEddery (7) (led over 3f out: clr 2f out:
          hdd & no ex ins fnl f) ............................................................................ hd.**4**
          Trapezium *(LMCumani)* 8-9 LDettori (17) (gd sort: led over 2f: one pce appr fnl
          f) ....................................................................................................... 4.**5**
          Lear King (USA) *(GHarwood)* 9-0 MPerrett (11) (wl grwn: dwlt: r.o fnl 2f: nvr nrr) ¹/₂.**6**
3552² Chief's Song *(BWHills)* 9-0 DHolland (6) (hdwy over 1f out: nrst fin) ................ 1¹/₂.**7**
          Mithi Al Gamar (USA) *(MRStoute)* 8-9 BRaymond (16) (neat: chsd ldrs tl outpcd
          over 1f out) .......................................................................................... ¹/₂.**8**
          Jaazim *(MajorWRHern)* 9-0 WCarson (13) (w'like: scope: prom over 4f) ......... nk.**9**
          Alta Victoria (IRE) *(RCharlton)* 8-9 WRyan (5) (w'like: prom tl wknd over 1f out) ¹/₂.**10**
3727⁶ Northern Bred (IRE) *(LMCumani)* 9-0 JFortune (12) (lw: mid div: effrt 2f out: no
          imp) ...................................................................................................... s.h.**11**
          Anorak (USA) *(LMCumani)* 8-9 ‡5JWeaver (9) (neat: m.n.s) ............................ nk.**12**
          Learmont (USA) (Fav) *(JHMGosden)* 9-0 SCauthen (19) (gd sort: chsd ldrs 4f:
          eased whn btn) ...................................................................................... 1.**13**
3607 Karachi *(CEBrittain)* 8-9 ‡5BDoyle (18) (lw: m.n.s) ........................................ nk.**14**
3607 Solo Charter *(MHTompkins)* 9-0 PRobinson (15) (m.n.s) ............................... 2.**15**
2459 Call Me Blue *(TJNaughton)* 9-0 GCarter (8) (s.s: a bhd) ............................... s.h.**16**
          Robleu *(GHarwood)* 9-0 DMcKeown (14) (cmpt: m.n.s) ................................. 1.**17**
          Poleden (USA) *(AAScott)* 9-0 MHills (1) (wl grwn: spd centre: rdn ¹/₂-wy: sn
          wknd) .................................................................................................... 1¹/₂.**18**
          Friendly Smile *(GHEden)* 8-9 JCarroll (4) (cmpt: a bhd) .............................. s.h.**19**
          Ruano *(SPCWoods)* 9-0 WWoods (20) (w'like: unf: w ldrs to ¹/₂-wy: wknd qckly:
          t.o) ...................................................................................................... 6.**20**

**15/8** Learmont (USA)(3/1—7/2), **4/1** Dramanice (USA), Trapezium(op 5/2), **6/1** Jaazim(7/2—13/2), **12/1** Mithi
Al Gamar (USA)(op 4/1), **14/1** SERIOUS, Chief's Song(10/1—16/1), **16/1** Poleden (USA)(op 8/1), **20/1** Northern
Bred (IRE)(op 12/1), **33/1** Resist the Force (USA), Robleu, Ruano, Solo Charter, Karachi, Lear King (USA),
Friendly Smile, **50/1** Ors. CSF £395.21, Tote £30.10: £5.00 £5.80 £13.70 (£302.60). Mrs Denis Haynes
(NEWMARKET) bred by Wretham Stud. 20 Rn
1m 14.40 (3)
SF—28/22/20/19/—/1

**3893**          SOHAM HOUSE STKS (2-Y.O) £4347.00 (£1296.00: £618.00: £279.00)
          **1m**          1-40 (1-43)

3674² **Shaiba (USA)** (Fav) *(MRStoute)* 8-10 SCauthen (1) (lw: a.p: rdn 2f out: led ins
          fnl f: r.o) .............................................................................................. —**1**
          Karnak *(RCharlton)* 8-10 MHills (5) (leggy: scope: dwlt: sn chsng ldrs: styd on
          strly ins fnl f) ........................................................................................ nk.**2**
3782★ Rakis (IRE) *(CJBenstead)* 9-1 WCarson (2) (lw: a.p: led ¹/₂-wy tl ins fnl f: r.o) .. 1¹/₂.**3**
          River Boyne (USA) *(GHarwood)* 8-10 PaulEddery (3) (wl grwn: bit bkwd: chsd
          ldrs: rdn & ev ch 2f out: one pce) ........................................................... 2.**4**
3784³ Ertlon *(CEBrittain)* 8-10 MRoberts (9) (lw: racd alone far side: led 4f: one pce
          appr fnl f) ............................................................................................. nk.**5**
3717 Commanche Creek *(LMCumani)* 8-10 LDettori (4) (lw: in tch: rdn 2f out: no imp) nk.**6**
3446 York Hill *(PAKelleway)* 8-10 GayKelleway (7) (s.s: hdwy 3f out: wknd appr fnl f) ¹/₂.**7**
3809 Burnt Imp (USA) *(GHarwood)* 8-10 BRaymond (8) (bkwd: chsd ldrs: rdn 3f out:
          sn wknd) ............................................................................................... 1.**8**
          Mount Rose *(LMCumani)* 8-10 JFortune (6) (cmpt: bit bkwd: dwlt: a bhd) ......... 3.**9**

**4/9** SHAIBA (USA)(1/3—4/7), **8/1** Rakis (IRE), **9/1** Karnak(op 6/1), **10/1** Commanche Creek, Mount Rose(op 6/1), **14/1** River Boyne (USA), **16/1** Ertlon, **20/1** York Hill, **33/1** Burnt Imp (USA). CSF £6.74, Tote £1.50: £1.10 £1.80 £1.70 (£4.80). Sheikh Ahmed Al Maktoum (NEWMARKET) bred by James L. Paliafito in USA. 9 Rn
1m 42 (4.70)
SF—37/36/36/25/24/23

---

**3894**   JAMES SEYMOUR STKS (listed race) £9300.00 (£2775.00: £1325.00: £600.00)
1¼m
2-10 (2-13)

| | | |
|---|---|---|
| **Lupescu (85)** *(DRLoder)* 4-8-9 LDettori (5) (stdd s: hld up & bhd: swtchd rt & rapid hdwy 1f out: led nr fin) | —1 |
| 3721⁴ Fair Average **(105)** *(HCandy)* 4-9-0 BRaymond (3) (lw: a.p: led over 1f out tl ct last stride) | s.h.2 |
| 3721² Rainbow Corner **(Fav)** *(HRACecil)* 3-9-2 WRyan (7) (lw: hld up: pushed along 3f out: str chal fnl f: r.o) | hd.3 |
| 3801★ Highland Dress *(MRStoute)* 3-8-9 SCauthen (6) (lw: a.p: ev ch ins fnl f: unable qckn) | ¾.4 |
| 3652a⁵ Spartan Shareef (IRE) **(111)** *(CEBrittain)* 3-8-12 WCarson (2) (led tl hdd over 1f out: kpt on u.p) | s.h.5 |
| 3547⁶ Revif (FR) **(94)** *(ACStewart)* 4-9-0 MRoberts (1) (plld hrd: hld up: hdwy 2f out: unable qckn fnl f) | s.h.6 |
| 3542² Soiree (IRE) **(102)** *(BWHills)* 3-8-4 DHolland (9) (b.nr hind: hld up: hdwy 4f out: one pce fnl 2f) | 1½.7 |
| 3547 Lord of the Field **(99)** *(JARToller)* 5-9-0 GDuffield (8) (bit bkwd: hld up: effrt 2f out: sn rdn: no imp) | 1½.8 |
| Happy Smile (IRE) *(MrFDunne)* 4-8-9 BRouse (4) (hld up: effrt & rdn over 2f out: sn btn) | 1½.9 |

**15/8** Rainbow Corner, **5/1** Highland Dress, Spartan Shareef (IRE)(3/1—11/2), **7/1** Revif (FR), Soiree (IRE), **14/1** Fair Average, **16/1** Lord of the Field, **20/1** LUPESCU, **33/1** Happy Smile (IRE). CSF £218.36, Tote £22.60: £3.40 £3.40 £1.30 (£96.40). Mr Edward St George (NEWMARKET) bred by Cheveley Park Stud Ltd. 9 Rn
2m 11.85 (9.25)
SF—13/17/18/9/11/12

---

**3895**   GEORGE STUBBS STKS (listed race) £8893.75 (£2650.00: £1262.50: £568.75)
2m
2-45 (2-50)

| | | |
|---|---|---|
| 3728² **Specificity (USA) (86)** *(JHMGosden)* 4-8-10 GDuffield (2) (mde all: rdn clr appr fnl f) | —1 |
| 3415² Persian Fantasy **(89)** *(JLDunlop)* 3-8-0 WCarson (1) (hld up: plld hrd & hdwy 4f out: sn ev ch: wknd fnl f) | 4.2 |
| 3724³ Bustinetta **(67)** *(JRFanshawe)* 3-8-0 GCarter (6) (chsd ldrs: styd on u.p ins fnl f) | 4.3 |
| 2840³ Tyrone Bridge **(106)** *(MCPipe)* 6-9-4 SDawson (7) (chsd wnr to ½-wy: styd on again appr fnl f) | s.h.4 |
| 3724 Miss Plum **(85)** *(DRLoder)* 3-8-0 RHills (3) (hld up: hdwy 3f out: wknd over 1f out) | 2½.5 |
| 3666★ Bold Resolution (IRE) **(70)** *(CACyzer)* 4-9-1 MRoberts (5) (hld up & bhd: effrt 3f out: no imp: t.o) | 10.6 |
| 3653a⁶ Landowner (IRE) **(110)** **(Fav)** *(JHMGosden)* 3-8-11 SCauthen (4) (swtg: wnt 2nd ½-wy: rdn 4f out: sn lost tch: t.o) | 25.7 |

**2/1** Landowner (IRE)(5/4—5/2), **7/2** Persian Fantasy(5/1—3/1), **4/1** SPECIFICITY (USA), **5/1** Bold Resolution (IRE)(op 8/1), **7/1** Tyrone Bridge, **16/1** Bustinetta, **20/1** Miss Plum. CSF £17.43, Tote £4.20: £2.20 £2.10 (£6.50). Pin Oak Stable (NEWMARKET) bred by Pin Oak Farm in USA. 7 Rn
3m 33.40 (10.10)
SF—11/–/–/10/–/–

---

**3896**   FITZROY HOUSE H'CAP (0-90) £4628.25 (£1386.00: £665.50: £305.25)
1½m
3-15 (3-26)

| | | |
|---|---|---|
| 3521★ **Her Honour (78)** *(MCPipe)* 3-9-5 LDettori (8) (hld up: gd hdwy to ld appr fnl f: sn clr: unchal) | —1 |
| 3724⁵ Pica **(77)** *(HRACecil)* 3-9-4 WRyan (12) (rdn along 4f out: hdwy 2f out: fin wl: no ch w wnr) | 3.2 |
| 3346 Anghaam (USA) **(74)** *(ACStewart)* 3-9-1 WCarson (13) (hld up: hdwy to ld 3f out: hdd appr fnl f: one pce) | ¾.3 |
| 3090 Truben (USA) **(81)** *(DRLoder)* 3-9-8 MHills (9) (prom: lost pl 6f out: rdn & hdwy 2f out: styd on) | 1.4 |
| 3724⁶ Asian Punter (IRE) **(67)** *(AHide)* 3-8-1 ‡7NVarley (4) (lw: hdwy ½-wy: jnd ldrs 3f out: one pce fnl f) | 1½.5 |
| 3270⁵ Aremef (USA) **(76)** *(MrsJCecil)* 3-9-3 PaulEddery (11) (bhd: hdwy over 2f out: styd on fnl f) | 2.6 |
| 3713★ Walimu (IRE) **(77)** *(CFWall)* 3-9-4 JLowe (2) (chsd ldrs: no hdwy fnl 2f) | nk.7 |

3778 Sure Haven (IRE) (75) (*SirMarkPrescott*) 3-9-2 GDuffield (7) (prom: led 4f out
to 3f out: hrd rdn & wknd over 1f out) ............................................ 3.8
3778* Statajack (IRE) (73) (bl) (*DRCElsworth*) 4-9-0 (4x) ‡7JHunter (18) (dwlt: hdwy 4f
out: wknd fnl 2f) .................................................................. 1.9
3259 Tradition (68) (*MajorWRHern*) 3-8-9 RHills (1) (lw: chsd ldrs: rdn along 4f out:
sn btn) ........................................................................ 1/2.10
3713 Touch Paper (USA) (70) (bl) (*BWHills*) 3-8-11 DHolland (6) (prom: ev ch 3f out:
sn wknd) ......................................................................... 8.11
3270² Almuhtarama (IRE) (78) (Fav) (*ACStewart*) 3-9-5 MRoberts (5) (nvr nr to chal) 1.12
3713 Laburnum (80) (*MrsJRRamsden*) 4-10-0 KFallon (3) (lw: a bhd) ..................... 4.13
3718 Qualitair Sound (IRE) (47) (*JFBottomley*) 4-7-9 GBardwell (15) (prom 7f) .... 2½.14
3794 Administer (70) (*LJCodd*) 4-8-11 ‡7WHollick (10) (a bhd) ...................... s.h.15
3755⁵ Luks Akura (45) (v) (*MJohnston*) 4-7-0 ‡7DWright (17) (led 8f: sn rdn & wknd) nk.16
1894 Naseer (USA) (59) (*NACallaghan*) 3-7-11 ‡3DHarrison (16) (m.n.s) ............ s.h.17
3829⁵ Kanvass (77) (*JRFanshawe*) 3-9-4 SCauthen (14) (chsd ldrs 8f: sn lost tch) 2½.18
LONG HANDICAP: Luks Akura 7-1.

5/1 Almuhtarama (IRE), 7/1 Kanvass, 8/1 HER HONOUR, 10/1 Walimu (IRE), Statajack (IRE), Anghaam (USA),
11/1 Pica, Touch Paper (USA), 16/1 Laburnum, Aremef (USA), Sure Haven (IRE), Asian Punter (IRE), 20/1
Tradition, Qualitair Sound (IRE), 33/1 Truben (USA), Naseer (USA), 50/1 Ors. CSF £86.53, CT £819.22. Tote
£6.70: £1.70 £3.50 £3.20 £8.00 (£61.90). Mrs Alison C. Farrant (WELLINGTON) bred by Waverton Farm (Stow).
18 Rn                                                                          2m 35.38 (6.08)
SF—56/49/44/49/25/37

**3897** POTTER NURSERY £4342.25 (£1298.00: £621.50: £283.25) **5f** 3-45 (3-57)
(Weights raised 8 lb)

3749³ Melodys Daughter (58) (bl) (*RFJohnsonHoughton*) 7-8 JLowe (15) (mde
virtually all: rej't rdn fnl f: jst hld on) ......................................... —1
3749* Saseedo (USA) (73) (*WAO'Gorman*) 8-0 ‡2EmmaO'Gorman (7) (lw: dwlt: rdn
½-wy: rapid hdwy appr fnl f: fin fast) ........................................... hd.2
3702 Bold County (69) (*MJohnston*) 8-5 RPElliott (14) (chsd ldrs: hdwy to chal 1f
out: unable qckn nr fin) ......................................................... hd.3
3831 Troon (85) (*MrsLPiggott*) 9-7 JWilliams (3) (b: b.hind: hld up: gd hdwy fnl f: fin
fast) ............................................................................ hd.4
3723 Manor Adventure (70) (*BAMcMahon*) 8-7 DMcKeown (2) (lw: s.s: hdwy appr
fnl f: nrst fin) ................................................................. 1½.5
3534⁴ Bangles (82) (*LordHuntingdon*) 9-4 KFallon (6) (a.p: rdn over 1f out: no ex fnl f) hd.6
3631 Broadstairs Beauty (IRE) (59) (*MCChapman*) 7-9 SWood (4) (chsd ldrs over 3f) nk.7
3630² Zany Zanna (IRE) (84) (Fav) (*GAPritchard-Gordon*) 9-3 ‡3DHarrison (11) (nvr nr
to chal) ........................................................................ ½.8
3702* Another Jade (65) (*APJarvis*) 7-8 ‡7DWright (16) (prom tl wknd over 1f out) ..... hd.9
3156⁵ Karukera (60) (*MJHeaton-Ellis*) 7-10 JQuinn (1) (prom over 3f) ............... 1½.10
3831⁶ Area Girl (83) (*SirMarkPrescott*) 9-5 GDuffield (5) (spd 3f) ................... hd.11
3399 Russia With Love (64) (*JDBethell*) 8-0(1) RHills (9) (nvr nr ldrs) .............. ¾.12
3420³ Trentesimo (78) (*JBerry*) 9-0 JCarroll (13) (gd spd 3f) ...................... hd.13
2686* Five Islands (76) (*PFICole*) 8-5 ‡7McLaughlin (8) (b.hind: outpcd) ............ ½.14
3750² Our Shadee (USA) (64) (*KTIvory*) 8-0 GBardwell (12) (m.n.s) .................. nk.15
3750⁶ Comet Whirlpool (IRE) (70) (*PatMitchell*) 8-3 ‡3SO'Gorman (10) (outpcd) ...... 3.16

7/2 Zany Zanna (IRE), 5/1 Saseedo (USA), 8/1 Another Jade(6/1—9/1), 9/1 Area Girl, 10/1 Five Islands (op 6/1),
Bangles, 12/1 Trentesimo (IRE), 14/1 Our Shadee, MELODYS DAUGHTER, Troon, Bold County(op 8/1),
16/1 Karukera, Manor Adventure, 20/1 Russia With Love, Comet Whirlpool (IRE), 50/1 Broadstairs Beauty (IRE).
CSF £84.65, CT £826.82. Tote £13.80: £2.30 £2.10 £3.90 £3.30 (£106.20). Lord Leverhulme (DIDCOT) bred by
Viscount Leverhulme. 16 Rn                                                    61.32 sec (1.92)
SF—32/43/41/56/35/46

**3898** AVENUE APP'CE H'CAP (0-75) £4077.50 (£1220.00: £585.00: £267.50)
**1m 1f**                                                              4-15 (4-31)

3589 Jungle Knife (65) (*MHTompkins*) 6-9-3 ‡7SMulvey (9) (lw: hld up in tch: led
appr fnl f: r.o wl) ............................................................... —1
3806⁴ Broughton's Tango (IRE) (49) (*CGCox*) 3-7-11 ‡7DMcCabe (6) (in tch: styd on
strly ins fnl f) ................................................................. 1.2
3487⁴ Santana Lady (IRE) (67) (*MJHeaton-Ellis*) 3-9-1 ‡7RuthCoulter (16) (a.p: ev ch
2f out: kpt on fnl f) ............................................................ 1.3
3825 Mr Tate (IRE) (60) (*RAkehurst*) 3-8-8 ‡7LCarter (18) (hdwy 2f out: nrst fin) ........ ¾.4
3789³ Cachou (USA) (71) (*JHMGosden*) 3-9-0 ‡7SWynne (15) (hdwy to ld over 2f out:
sn hdd & edgd rt: one pce) ..................................................... 1½.5
3794⁵ Falcons Dawn (55) (*ABailey*) 5-8-4 ‡10WHollick (13) (hmpd s: r.o fnl 2f: nvr nrr) 1.6
3732⁶ Eternal Flame (66) (*JWHills*) 4-9-11 JWeaver (17) (lw: prom: led over 3f out tl
over 2f out: wknd fnl f) ......................................................... ½.7

3763 Lucky Noire **(56)** *(GHarwood)* 4–8–8 ‡⁷GayeHarwood (1) (b: prom: ev ch 2f out: sn rdn & wknd) ............................ 1.**8**
3520 Mulciber **(67)** *(GHarwood)* 4–9–5 ‡⁷PHoughton (2) (lw: prom: no hdwy fnl 2f) .. 1½.**9**
3610⁶ Jarzon Dancer **(35)** *(DAWilson)* 4–7–8⁽¹⁾ FNorton (5) (nvr nrr) ............................ 1.**10**
3582² Nest **(63)** *(Fav)* *(LordHuntingdon)* 3–9–4 DHarrison (8) (lw: nvr plcd to chal) . 1½.**11**
3797⁴ Hopeful Bid (IRE) **(71)** (bl) *(RHannon)* 3–9–5 ‡⁷MarkDenaro (7) (chsd ldrs: wknd wl over 1f out) ............................ nk.**12**
426 Lowawatha **(47)** *(DMorris)* 4–8–3 ‡³StephenDavies (11) (m.n.s) ............................ 3.**13**
3595 Shining Jewel **(67)** *(MrsLPiggott)* 5–9–5 ‡⁷GMilligan (12) (m.n.s) ............................ 4.**14**
3476⋆ Kelly's Kite **(38)** *(HJCollingridge)* 4–7–11 NKennedy (3) (dwlt: a bhd) ............ 1½.**15**
3521⁵ Bel Baraka (IRE) **(56)** *(DRCElsworth)* 3–8–4 ‡⁷JHunter (4) (led: sn wl clr: wknd & hdd over 3f out: t.o) ............................ 5.**16**
3418 Kaths Choice **(34)** *(HJCollingridge)* 4–7–7 BDoyle (10) (bhd fr ½-wy: t.o) ........ 1.**17**
*3845* Access Voyager **(54)** (v) *(RBoss)* 3–8–2 ‡⁷PMcCabe (14) (t.o) ............................ 2½.**18**
LONG HANDICAP: Jarzon Dancer 7-2, Kaths Choice 7-5.

**5/1 Nest, 11/2 Cachou (USA), 6/1 JUNGLE KNIFE, 7/1 Eternal Flame, 10/1 Kelly's Kite, Santana Lady (IRE), 12/1 Broughton's Tango (IRE), 14/1 Shining Jewel, Falcons Dawn, 16/1 Lucky Noire, Mr Tate (IRE)(op 10/1), Hopeful Bid (IRE), 20/1 Bel Baraka (IRE), Kaths Choice, 25/1 Mulciber, 33/1 Ors.** CSF £76.92, CT £667.13. Tote £7.10: £2.90 £2.60 £3.60 £2.20 (£107.80). Mr Nick Cook (NEWMARKET) bred by P. D. and Mrs Player. 18 Rn
1m 55.30. (5.30)
SF—37/14/29/20/26/8

T/Trio: Race 5: £254.80 (4 Tckts). T/Jkpt: Not won; £18,973.21 to Newmarket 31/10/92. T/Plpt: £8,063.30 (0.4 Tckts); £6,537.83 to Newmarket 31/10/92.                                                    IM

# NEWMARKET (R-H) Rowley Mile
## Saturday, October 31st [Good]
Going Allowance: nil sec per fur (G)                                                    Wind: nil

Stalls: centre

**3899**  FEDERATION OF BRITISH RACING CLUBS CLAIMING NURSERY   £4435.00 (£1330.00: £640.00: £295.00)   **6f**
1-10 (1-13)

(Weights raised 8 lb)

3590⁴ Red Leader (IRE) **(62)** *(PFICole)* 8-8 ‡⁷TMcLaughlin (4) (lw: a.p: rdn & r.o to ld ins fnl f) ............................ —**1**
3712⁴ Splash of Salt (IRE) **(62)** *(Fav)* *(WJHaggas)* 9-1 WCarson (19) (a.p: led over 2f out tl wl ins fnl f) ............................ nk.**2**
3848⁴ Heretical Miss **(60)** (bl) *(RHannon)* 8-10 ‡³RPerham (22) (a.p: led 3f out: sn hdd: ev ch 1f out: r.o) ............................ nk.**3**
3716 Fiveofive (IRE) **(60)** *(NACallaghan)* 8-13 KDarley (14) (chsd ldrs: kpt on u.p ins fnl f) ............................ nk.**4**
3716 Egg **(68)** (bl) *(TDBarron)* 9-0 ‡⁷VHalliday (14) (lw: a.p: ev ch 1f out: kpt on) ...... s.h.**5**
3630 Arkendale Diamond (USA) **(68)** *(CBBBooth)* 9-7 GOldroyd (6) (lw: hdwy over 1f out: fin wl) ............................ ½.**6**
*3376* Patong Beach **(58)** *(JWHills)* 8-11 MHills (9) (rdn ½-wy: r.o appr fnl f: nvr nrr) ... s.h.**7**
3723 Who's Tom (IRE) **(50)** *(WJMusson)* 8-3 JQuinn (5) (b: led stands' side: kpt on fnl f) ............................ hd.**8**
3611 Duke of Budworth **(60)** (v) *(MHTompkins)* 8-13 PRobinson (13) (chsd ldrs over 4f) ............................ ¾.**9**
3786³ Heathyards Gem **(68)** *(RHollinshead)* 9-7 WRyan (23) (dwlt: nvr nrr) ............ ¾.**10**
3807⁴ Trevorsninepoints **(60)** *(MJRyan)* 8-13 DBiggs (25) (spd over 3f) ............ s.h.**11**
3746³ I'M a Dreamer (IRE) **(64)** *(WWHaigh)* 9-3 DMcKeown (24) (n.d) ............ hd.**12**
3508 Arawa **(50)** *(DMarks)* 8-3 SDawson (1) (prom 4f: sn rdn & wknd) ............ 1.**13**
3760⁵ Take Your Partner (IRE) **(52)** *(MJohnston)* 8-5 JLowe (26) (led 3f: wknd over 1f out) ............................ 1.**14**
3580 Krayyan Dawn **(42)** *(RVoorspuy)* 7-9 NAdams (3) (m.n.s) ............ 1½.**15**
3301⁵ Crab 'n Lobster (IRE) **(43)** *(MrsJRRamsden)* 7-10 TyroneWilliams (10) (m.n.s) ½.**16**
3165⁵ Hazard a Guess (IRE) **(61)** *(MrsJRRamsden)* 9-0 GBaxter (16) (m.n.s) ............ ¾.**17**
3694 Dontbetalking (IRE) **(61)** *(JWharton)* 9-0 KFallon (7) (m.n.s) ............ 1½.**18**
3173 Workingforpeanuts (IRE) **(51)** *(CASmith)* 7-11 ‡⁷DMcCabe (3) (b: bhd fnl 3f) .. nk.**19**
3579 Honey Juice **(55)** *(MJFetherston-Godley)* 8-5 ‡³DHarrison (17) (a bhd) ............ ¾.**20**
3839 Christian Spirit **(55)** *(RHannon)* 8-8 RHills (2) (lw: a bhd) ............ 1½.**21**
3694³ Manx Monarch **(61)** *(RHollinshead)* 8-7 ‡⁷AGarth (18) (in tch 4f: eased whn btn) ¾.**22**
3702 La Madrigal **(61)** *(JWharton)* 9-0 JWilliams (11) (a in rr) ............ 5.**23**
3606 Viv's Pet **(52)** (bl) *(AHide)* 8-2 ‡³FNorton (21) (hmpd s: sn rcvrd: wknd over 2f out) ............................ 5.**24**
3821 Just Baileys **(53)** (bl) *(MJohnston)* 8-6 RPElliott (20) (swvd rt s: a bhd) ............ 1.**25**

4/1 Splash of Salt (IRE)(op 6/1), 8/1 Crab 'n Lobster (IRE)(tchd 20/1), 10/1 Hazard a Guess (IRE), 12/1 Egg, 14/1 Heathyards Gem, Fiveofive (IRE), Manx Monarch, 16/1 Duke of Budworth, Take Your Partner (IRE), Arawa, RED LEADER (IRE), 20/1 I'M a Dreamer (IRE), Trevorsninepoints, Heretical Miss, 25/1 Honey Juice, Patong Beach, Dontbetalking (IRE), Who's Tom (IRE), Arkendale Diamond (USA), La Madrigal, 33/1 Viv's Pet, Workingforpeanuts (IRE), Chris tian Spirit, Just Baileys, 50/1 Krayyan Dawn. CSF £79.05, CT £1,250.67. Tote £25.50: £4.30 £1.80 £3.60 £4.20 (£37.40). Generous Racing Club (WHATCOMBE) bred by Tony O'Reilly in Ireland. 25 Rn                                                                                                 1m 14.39 (2.99)
SF—34/40/34/36/41

## 3900

SPORTING LIFE ZETLAND STKS (listed race) (2-Y.O) £8850.00 (£2640.00: £1260.00: £570.00)   1¼m                                                                              1-40 (1-42)

3809* **Bob's Return (IRE)** (86) *(MHTompkins)* 8-12  PRobinson (8) (lw: mde all: rdn & styd on wl) ...................................................................................................... —1

31914 Bobbie Dee (97) *(DRCElsworth)* 8-7  JWilliams (2) (lw: hld up: hdwy over 2f out: kpt on u.p fnl f) ........................................................................................ ¾.2

34623 Sharjah (USA) (98) *(MAJarvis)* 8-12  LDettori (6) (lw: a.p: rdn & ev ch over 2f out: r.o one pce) ..................................................................................................... 2½.3

3883a3 Shebl (USA) (90) *(MRStoute)* 8-12  PaulEddery (3) (hld up: hdwy over 3f out: hrd rdn & no ex fnl f) .................................................................................. 2.4

3791* Heathyards Boy (99) *(RHollinshead)* 8-12  WRyan (1) (chsd ldrs: pushed along ½-wy: nvr nrr) .............................................................................................. 1½.5

3525 Charlie Bigtime *(MissGayKelleway)* 8-12  GayKelleway (5) (bhind: bhd tl styd on u.p fnl f) .................................................................................................. s.h.6

31276 Prevene (IRE) (95) *(PFICole)* 8-12  WCarson (9) (hld up: wnt prom 4f out: rdn & wknd over 1f out) ......................................................................................... 2.7

37762 Phrose *(RHannon)* 8-12  BRaymond (7) (lw: chsd ldrs: rdn 4f out: sn btn: t.o) .. 10.8

3501a Elkhart (USA) (Fav) *(HRACecil)* 8-12  SCauthen (4) (lw: w wnr tl wknd 3f out: eased whn but. t.o) ............................................................................................. 6.9

6/4 Elkhart (USA), 7/2 Sharjah (USA), 5/1 Heathyards Boy, 6/1 Bobbie Dee, 8/1 Prevene (IRE), 10/1 Shebl (USA), 14/1 BOB'S RETURN (IRE), 20/1 Phrose, 50/1 Charlie Bigtime. CSF £93.38, Tote £17.30: £2.90 £1.80 £1.60 (£10.30). Mrs G. A. E. Smith (NEWMARKET) bred by Baronrath Stud Ltd in Ireland. 9 Rn  2m 6.55 (3.95)
SF—59/52/52/48/45/44

## 3901

BEN MARSHALL STKS (listed race)   £9381.25 (£2800.00: £1337.50: £606.25)
1m                                                                                           2-10 (2-13)

3542* **Inner City (IRE)** (119) (Fav) *(LMCumani)* 3–9–1  LDettori (8) (lw: hld up: gd hdwy to ld wl over 1f out: clr whn edgd lft fnl f) ................................ —1

37216 Badawi (USA) (100) *(JHMGosden)* 4–8–10  SCauthen (3) (hld up: rdn & r.o wl appr fnl f) ......................................................................................................... 2½.2

35733 Swing Low (110) *(RHannon)* 3–8–9  MHills (1) (a.p: ev ch over 1f out: rdn & no ex fnl f) ................................................................................................................. 1½.3

3547 Lucky Guest (89) *(JLDunlop)* 5–8–12  WRyan (7) (lw: hdwy 3f out: styd on appr fnl f) ..................................................................................................................... 1½.4

3442 Misterioso (96) *(LordHuntingdon)* 3–8–4  DMcKeown (9) (w ldr: led over 3f tl over 1f out: sn btn) ............................................................................................... nk.5

3779* Two Left Feet (101) *(SirMarkPrescott)* 5–8–12  GDuffield (6) (chsd ldrs 6f) .......... 2.6

3654a Mojave (113) *(MRStoute)* 3–9–4  WCarson (4) (hld up & bhd: effrt over 2f out: no rspnse) .............................................................................................................. 4.7

3664* Well Beyond (IRE) (97) *(BWHills)* 3–8–10  PaulEddery (5) (led over 4f: wknd wl over 1f out) ..................................................................................................... s.h.8

3738a Casteddu (112) *(JWPayne)* 3–9–4  BRaymond (2) (a bhd: rdn 2f out: no imp) .. 2.9

8/11 INNER CITY (IRE), 9/2 Swing Low, 11/1 Mojave, Two Left Feet, Well Beyond (IRE), 16/1 Badawi (USA), 20/1 Casteddu, 33/1 Ors. CSF £4.47, Tote £1.70: £1.20 £2.60 £1.60 (£9.60). Sheikh Mohammed (NEWMARKET) bred by Ballynagran Bloodstock Ltd in Ireland. 9 Rn  1m 38.93 (1.63)
SF—77/64/58/56/47/49

## 3902

ROYSTON STKS (2 & 3-Y.O) £4347.00 (£1296.00: £618.00: £279.00)
7f                                                                                           2-40 (2-42)

Catrail (USA) *(JHMGosden)* 2–8–1  WCarson (2) (cmpt: scope: bit bkwd: s.i.s: hld up: hdwy to ld 2f out: pushed clr fnl f) .................................. —1

38264 Waterfowl Creek (IRE) (86) (Fav) *(GWragg)* 3–9–3  MHills (9) (lw: hld up: smooth hdwy 2f out: sn ev ch: outpcd fnl f) ................................................ 3½.2

38266 Ruhr (IRE) (92) (bl) *(BWHills)* 2–9–0  SCauthen (7) (led 1f: rdn 2f out: one pce) .. 2.3

3191 Sehailah (92) *(MrsLPiggott)* 2–7–8(1) ‡3DHarrison (1) (led after 1f to 2f out: grad wknd) ........................................................................................................................ 4.4

Glen Echo (IRE) *(GHarwood)* 2–8–1  WWoods (5) (leggy: scope: effrt 3f out: nvr able to chal) .............................................................................................................. ½.5

3732 Al Sadi **(79)** *(CEBrittain)* 3-9-8 BRaymond (3) (chsd ldrs over 4f) ...................... 5.6
3819[4] Native Chieftan **(79)** *(RHannon)* 3-9-5 ‡3RPerham (6) (prom tl rdn & wknd 2f out) 2.7
3704 Todden *(CFWall)* 2-8-1 PRobinson (8) (in tch tl outpcd over 2f out) ................. 4.8
3717 Excess Baggage (IRE) *(NACallaghan)* 2-8-1 GDuffield (4) (a bhd) ................. 1¹/₂.9

**100/30** Waterfowl Creek (IRE), **4/1** Catrail (USA)(3/1—9/2), Ruhr (IRE), **5/1** Sehailah(7/2—11/2), **11/2** Native Chieftain, **11/1** Al Sadi, **14/1** Glen Echo (IRE), **16/1** Excess Baggage (IRE), **50/1** Todden. CSF £17.06, Tote £3.80: £1.80 £1.40 £1.90 (£5.10). Sheikh Mohammed (NEWMARKET) bred by Calumet Farm in USA. 9 Rn
1m 26.07 (2.07)
SF—56/61/60/30/35/41

## 3903
**LADBROKE AUTUMN H'CAP** (0-115) £29535.00 (£8880.00: £4290.00: £1995.00)
1m
3-10 (3-16)
(Weights raised 8 lb)

3732★ Cambrian **(89)** *(MrsJCecil)* 3-8-7 (5x) GDuffield (11) (mde all: hld on gamely) .. —1
3664² Jdaayel **(88)** (Fav) *(ACStewart)* 3-8-6 WCarson (7) (lw: in tch: hdwy 2f out: str run u.p nr fin: jst failed) ............................................................................. hd.2
3800★ Heart of Darkness **(94)** *(IABalding)* 4-8-12 (5x) ‡3SO'Gorman (10) (lw: hdwy over 2f out: ev ch ins fnl f: nt qckn) ............................................................. ¹/₂.3
3547★ Rambo's Hall **(103)** *(JAGlover)* 7-9-10 DMcKeown (17) (chsd ldrs: rdn 2f out: styd on fnl f) ....................................................................................... ¹/₂.4
3726² Lap of Luxury **(84)** *(WJarvis)* 3-8-2 NDay (12) (prom: rdn & n.m.r ent fnl f: unable qckn) .................................................................................................. ¹/₂.5
3673★ Gymcrak Premiere **(98)** (v) *(MHEasterby)* 4-9-5 (5x) KDarley (9) (du: up: effrt over 1f out: nt rch ldrs) ..................................................................... s.h.6
3547³ Double Entendre **(75)** *(MBell)* 6-7-7 ‡3FNorton (16) (hdwy 2f out: nrst fin) ........ hd.7
3800 Marine Diver **(72)** *(BRMillman)* 6-7-7 DaleGibson (15) (s.s: styd on fnl 2f: nvr nrr) ¹/₂.8
3835 Montpelier Boy **(87)** *(LordHuntingdon)* 4-8-5 ‡3DHarrison (8) (chsd ldrs: rdn & unable qckn fnl f) ................................................................................. 1.9
3789 Double Echo (IRE) **(72)** *(JDBethell)* 4-7-7 JLowe (3) (s.s: sme hdwy fr over 1f out: nvr nrr) ......................................................................................... 2.10
3732 Trooping (IRE) **(80)** *(GHarwood)* 3-7-12 AMcGlone (6) (lw: nvr plcd to chal) ... 2.11
3732 Merlins Wish (USA) **(81)** *(RHannon)* 3-7-13 GBardwell (1) (in rr: rdn ¹/₂-wy: n.d) .................................................................................................... hd.12
3547 Camden's Ransom (USA) **(77)** *(DRCElsworth)* 5-7-7(5) ‡5BDoyle (2) (r.o fnl 2f: nvr nrr) ................................................................................................... ¹/₂.13
3356 Claybank (USA) **(85)** *(BWHills)* 3-8-3 MHills (5) (mid div: rdn ¹/₂-wy: a bhd) 1¹/₂.14
3826² Deprecator **(98)** *(JHMGosden)* 4-9-5 LDettori (18) (lw: b.hind: prom 5f) 1¹/₂.15
3726 Scales of Justice **(76)** *(JWHills)* 6—7-11 (5x) NCarlisle (4) (dwlt: a bhd) .......... 3¹/₂.16
3800⁵ Aghaadir (USA) **(91)** (v) *(JHMGosden)* 4-8-12 SCauthen (13) (prom 5f: sn lost tch) ................................................................................................... 6.17
3543★ Millsolin (IRE) **(77)** *(RAkehurst)* 4-7-12(1) GCarter (1) (b.off fore: chsd ldrs: rdn over 2f out: sn wknd) ............................................................................... 5.18

LONG HANDICAP: Marine Diver 7-6, Double Echo (IRE) 7-3, Camden's Ransom (USA) 7-6.

**4/1** Jdaayel, **5/1** Rambo's Hall, **7/1** Millsolin (IRE), **15/2** Double Entendre, Lap of Luxury, **9/1** Heart of Darkness, **10/1** Aghaadir (USA), **14/1** Gymcrak Premiere, Deprecator, **16/1** Scales of Justice, **20/1** Montpelier Boy, Merlins Wish (USA), **25/1** Claybank (USA), **33/1** Cambrian, Camden's Ransom (USA), **50/1** Marine Diver, Trooping (IRE), **66/1** Double Echo (IRE). CSF £160.61, CT £1,234.96. Tote £34.50: £5.70 £1.50 £2.90 £2.50 (£92.50). Sheikh Mohammed (NEWMARKET) bred by Sheikh Mohammed bin Rashid al Maktoum. 18 Rn
1m 38.85 (1.55)
SF—70/68/72/82/58/74

## 3904
**E.B.F. BALATON LODGE STKS** (Mdn 2-Y.O.F) £4467.50 (£1340.00: £645.00: £297.50)
7f
3-40 (3-54)

Fayfa (IRE) *(HRACecil)* 8-11 AMcGlone (4) (cmpt: a.p: shkn up to ld appr fnl f: r.o) ................................................................................................. —1
Stella Mystika (USA) *(LMCumani)* 8-11 LDettori (17) (hdwy over 1f out: sn ev ch: r.o) ............................................................................................ 1¹/₂.2
3414² Woodwardia (USA) (Fav) *(BWHills)* 8-11 PaulEddery (5) (a.p: slt ld over 1f out: sn hdd: kpt on) ........................................................................................ ¹/₂.3
Sit Alkul (USA) *(MRStoute)* 8-11 BRaymond (9) (w'like: scope: led stands' side tl over 1f out: one pce) ................................................................................ 1¹/₂.4
Ramiya *(MajorWRHern)* 8-11 WCarson (10) (cmpt: scope: a.p: ev ch 2f out: no ex fnl f) .......................................................................................... 1¹/₂.5
Chapka (IRE) *(MajorWRHern)* 8-11 BProcter (1) (neat: bit bkwd: hld up: r.o fnl f: promising) ...................................................................................... nk.6
Geordie Song *(HRACecil)* 8-6 ‡5StephenDavies (12) (cmpt: leggy: gd hdwy appr fnl f: fin wl) ................................................................................ nk.7
Dreams Are Free (IRE) *(HRACecil)* 8-11 WRyan (11) (cmpt: a.p: ev ch 2f out: eased whn btn fnl f) ......................................................................... hd.8
Hatton's Gem *(JRFanshawe)* 8-11 KDarley (24) (leggy: styd on fnl 2f: nvr nrr) .. ¹/₂.9
Meavy *(WJarvis)* 8-11 MTebbutt (8) (lt-f: scope: lw: nvr nrr) ............................ s.h.10

**3905**

3704 Polanie (CAN) *(LMCumani)* 8-11 JFortune (2) (chsd ldrs: no hdwy fnl 2f) ....... s.h.11
Princess Haifa (USA) *(MRStoute)* 8-11 CDwyer (13) (w'like: scope: nvr plcd to chal) .................................................................................................................. hd.12
3719 Mysilv *(CFWall)* 8-11 PRobinson (25) (led far side 4f: sn wknd) ........................ ½.13
Raneen Alwatar *(LMCumani)* 8-6 ‡⁵JWeaver (14) (neat: prom 5f) ...................... ½.14
Zanze (USA) *(JHMGosden)* 8-11 SCauthen (23) (cmpt: scope: chsd ldrs far side 5f: eased whn btn) ............................................................. 2.15
3818⁵ Shirley Rose *(MJohnston)* 8-11 DMcKeown (8) (lw: m.n.s) ................................ ½.16
Mow Waal (USA) *(MRStoute)* 8-5⁽¹⁾ ‡⁷KPattinson (16) (leggy: scope: m.n.s) .... ½.17
Funny Hilarious (USA) *(JRFanshawe)* 8-11 GCarter (15) (w'like: scope: chsd ldrs 4f) ......................................................................................................................... ½.18
Dusty's Darling *(MAJarvis)* 8-11 MHills (21) (lt-f: unf: prom 4f) ........................ nk.19
Magical Retreat *(CACyzer)* 8-11 KFallon (22) (w'like: scope: prom 4f: sn wknd) .................................................................................................................. ½.20
Haven of Love (IRE) *(CACyzer)* 8-11 AMorris (7) (leggy: outpcd) .................... ¾.21
Wishes *(JRFanshawe)* 8-11 GDuffield (18) (neat: outpcd) .............................. 1.22
3683 Lady Arabella *(JPearce)* 8-11 RPrice (20) (outpcd) .......................................... 1.23
Marathia *(SPCWoods)* 8-11 WWoods (19) (neat: outpcd) ............................ nk.24
*3780 La Posada (20/1) Withdrawn (unruly at s) : not under orders*

**2/1** Woodwardia (USA)(tchd 4/1), **9/1** Stella Mystika (USA)(6/1—10/1), **10/1** Zanze (USA)(5/1—12/1), Chapka (IRE)(op 16/1), Ramiya, **11/1** Dreams Are Free (IRE)(op 3/1), **12/1** Sit Alkul (USA)(6/1—14/1), **14/1** FAYFA (IRE)(op 6/1), **16/1** Raneen Alwatar(op 10/1), **20/1** Shirley Rose, Princess Haifa (USA), Mysilv, **25/1** Polanie (CAN), Funny Hilarious (USA), Wishes, Haven of Love (IRE), **33/1** Ors. CSF £136.06, Tote £30.30: £6.30 £24.00 £1.60 (£199.60). Prince A. A. Faisal (NEWMARKET) bred by Nawara Stud Co Ltd in Ireland. 24 Rn
1m 29.05 (5.05)
SF—21/16/14/9/4/3

**3905** BURROUGH GREEN H'CAP (0-80) £5469.75 (£1638.00: £786.50: £360.75)
**7f**
4-10 (4-24)

3545 **Surrey Racing (68)** *(GLewis)* 4-9-4 BRouse (8) (gd hdwy over 1f out: r.o to ld nr fin) ............................................................................................................ —1
3870 Guesstimation (USA) **(46)** *(JPearce)* 3—7-7 GBardwell (7) (a.p: led 3f out tl ct cl home) ............................................................................................................. ½.2
3797³ Zeboim **(71)** (bl) *(WRMuir)* 6-9-0 ‡⁷KimMcDonnell (20) (led 4f: kpt on one pce fnl f) ............................................................................................................... 2½.3
3209 Aitch N'Bee **(73)** *(LadyHerries)* 4-9-0 LDettori (12) (hdwy 2f out: r.o wl ins fnl f) s.h.4
3797 Highland Magic (IRE) **(70)** *(MJFetherston-Godley)* 4-9-3 ‡³DHarrison (11) (hld up: rapid hdwy fnl f: fin fast) ......................................................................... ½.5
3870⁴ Roca Murada (IRE) **(59)** (v) *(MJRyan)* 3-8-6 PRobinson (14) (dwlt: hdwy over 2f out: no ex fnl f) ................................................................................................. hd.6
3870★ Ballerina Bay **(69)** (v) *(DTThom)* 4-9-0 (5x) ‡⁵JWeaver (6) (dwlt: r.o u.p fnl f: nvr nrr) ....................................................................................................................... 1½.7
3726★ Saafend **(72)** (Fav) *(JSutcliffe)* 4-9-8 WCarson (16) (chsd ldrs: rdn 3f out: nt pce to chal) ....................................................................................................... nk.8
3797 Zinbaq **(43)** *(CJBenstead)* 6-7-7 JLowe (1) (lw: chsd ldrs: no hdwy fnl 2f) ...... 1½.9
3732 Sylvan (IRE) **(80)** *(CFWall)* 3-9-13 GBaxter (17) (bhd fnl 3f) .............................. ½.10
3847 Ingenuity **(65)** *(LordHuntingdon)* 3-8-12 DMcKeown (13) (chsd ldrs: rdn 2f out: sn btn) ............................................................................................................. hd.11
3766★ Precious Wonder **(61)** *(PButler)* 3-8-8 TyroneWilliams (10) (lw: prom: ev ch 2f out: eased whn btn) ............................................................................................ 1½.12
3673 Garth **(70)** (v) *(PJMakin)* 4-9-6 BRaymond (5) (chsd ldrs: rdn & wknd 2f out) .. 1.13
3797 Brooks Express (FR) **(47)** *(RAkehurst)* 3-7-8 JQuinn (3) (spd 4f) ...................... hd.14
*3845* Tadora (IRE) **(50)** *(CJBenstead)* 3—7-1 DBiggs (15) (disp ld 4f: sn lost tch) .. hd.15
3524⁴ Grey Charmer **(53)** *(CJames)* 3-8-0 DaleGibson (9) (outpcd) ...................... 2½.16
3002 Kirriemuir **(48)** *(KOCunningham-Brown)* 4-7-12 NCarlisle (4) (lw: spd to ½-wy: sn wknd) .......................................................................................................... ½.17
3793 Martina **(65)** *(JWharton)* 4-9-1 JWilliams (2) (prom over 4f) .............................. 3½.18
3726 Queen of Shannon (IRE) **(73)** *(DMorris)* 4-9-9 MTebbutt (18) (chsd ldrs: rdn 3f out: eased whn btn over 1f out) .................................................................... hd.19
3726 Rise Up Singing **(68)** (bl) *(WJMusson)* 4-9-4 SCauthen (19) (chsd ldrs 4f) .... 4.20
LONG HANDICAP: Guesstimation (USA) 7-0, Zinbaq 7-3.

**9/2** Saafend, **11/2** Rise Up Singing, Ballerina Bay, **10/1** Roca Murada (IRE), **12/1** Ingenuity(op 8/1), Highland Magic (IRE), **14/1** Aitch N'Bee, **16/1** Precious Wonder(op 10/1), Zeboim, Sylvan (IRE), Zinbaq, **20/1** Brooks Express (FR), Grey Charmer (FR), Kirriemuir, Garth, SURREY RACING, **25/1** Queen of Shannon (IRE), Guesstimation (USA), **33/1** Ors. CSF £424.54, CT £7,189.52. Tote £32.80: £6.80 £5.30 £4.90 £2.80 (£386.10). Mr K. Higson (EPSOM) bred by W. R. Swinburn. 20 Rn
1m 27.85 (3.85)
SF—47/20/33/46/33/21

T/Trio: Race 5: £550.60 (4 Tckts). T/Jkpt: Not won; £22,838.06 to Doncaster 6/11/92. T/Plpt: £66.80 (242.57 Tckts). IM

## 3512—NEWCASTLE (L-H)
### Monday, November 2nd [Heavy]
Going Allowance: Races 1-2: 1.30; 3-4: 1.65; 5-6: 2.00 sec (Hvy)　　Wind: str against

Stalls: 1st-4th low, remainder centre

**3906**　　　'SINGING IN THE SADDLE' H'CAP (0-70) £2700.00 (£750.00: £360.00)
　　　　　　1½m 93y
　　　　　　　　　　　　　　　　　　　　　　　　　　　　　　　　　　1-30 (1-34)

3806² **Sunderland Echo (57)** (Fav) *(MrsGRReveley)* 3-8-5 ‡⁷DarrenMoffatt (4) (trckd
　　　　ldrs: led over 2f out: sn clr) .................................................. —1
3728 Kausar (USA) **(57)** *(GMMoore)* 5-9-5 PaulEddery (6) (cl up: led appr st tl over 2f
　　　　out: one pce) ................................................................ 10.2
3756³ Euridice (IRE) **(62)** *(LMCumani)* 3-9-3 LDettori (14) (lw: stdy hdwy 5f out: wnt
　　　　prom ent st: rdn & no ex wl over 2f out) ............................ 1½.3
3493 Don't Cry **(34)** *(DonEnricoIncisa)* 4-7-3⁽³⁾ ‡⁷ClaireBalding (7) (hdwy ent st:
　　　　hung lft over 2f out: nvr rchd ldrs) .................................... 2.4
2148⁶ Deb's Ball **(55)** *(DMoffatt)* 6-9-3 JFanning (11) (hld up & bhd: hdwy appr st: rdn
　　　　3f out: no imp) ............................................................. 1.5
3755³ Continuity **(54)** *(MHTompkins)* 3-8-9 MBirch (15) (wnt prom appr st: effrt 3f out:
　　　　hung lft & nt r.o) .......................................................... 3.6
3829⁴ Vasiliev **(66)** (bl) *(JPLeigh)* 4-10-0 DMcKeown (9) (chsd ldrs tl rdn & btn wl over
　　　　2f out) ....................................................................... 8.7
2964⁴ Lord Advocate **(44)** (bl) *(MPNaughton)* 4-8-6 JakiHouston (8) (sn w ldr: wknd
　　　　ent st) ....................................................................... 10.8
3804⁵ Private Bank (USA) **(60)** (bl) *(ACStewart)* 3-9-1 RCochrane (1) (lw: led tl hdd
　　　　appr st: wknd) ............................................................. 10.9
3756 Canbrack (IRE) **(45)** *(WAStephenson)* 3-8-0 JLowe (12) (bhd: hdwy 4f out:
　　　　n.d) ..................................................................... 1½.10
3609⁵ Raheena (USA) **(68)** *(JHMGosden)* 3-9-9 JCarroll (10) (bhd & rdn 4f out: n.d) 5.11
3755 Grey Commander **(54)** (v) *(MBrittain)* 4-8-1⁽³⁾ KDarley (17) (chsd ldrs tl rdn &
　　　　wknd 4f out) ............................................................ s.h.12
3794 El Nido **(64)** *(MJCamacho)* 4-9-12 NConnorton (3) (hld up & nvr plcd to chal) 3.13
3755 Haut-Brion (IRE) **(39)** *(WStorey)* 3-7-8 JQuinn (2) (chsd ldrs tl wknd qckly appr
　　　　st) ........................................................................... 1.14
3876* Judge and Jury **(52)** *(MJFetherston-Godley)* 3-8-7⁽⁵⁾ (3x) WRyan (5) (a wl bhd:
　　　　t.o) ............................................................................ 15
　97 Camden Knight **(38)** *(NBycroft)* 7-7-7⁽¹⁾ ‡⁷AGarth (13) (b: a bhd: t.o) ........... 16
2742⁵ Floating Line **(61)** *(PWigham)* 4-9-9 MWigham (16) (bhd fr ½-wy: t.o) ......... 17
　　　　　　　　　　　LONG HANDICAP: Don't Cry 6-12.

3/1 SUNDERLAND ECHO, 5/1 Continuity, 7/1 Judge and Jury, 8/1 Kausar (USA), Euridice (IRE), 9/1 Deb's Ball,
Raheena (USA), 11/1 Vasiliev, 12/1 Floating Line, Private Bank (USA), 16/1 El Nido, 20/1 Grey Commander,
25/1 Lord Advocate, Canbrack (IRE), 33/1 Camden Knight, Haut-Brion (IRE), 66/1 Don't Cry. CSF £30.84, CT
£181.59. Tote £4.00: £1.40 £1.10 £2.50 £28.90 (£15.40). Northeast Press Limited (SALTBURN) bred by B. E.
Green. 17 Rn　　　　　　　　　　　　　　　　　　　　　　　　　　　　　　　　　2m 58.94 (20.44)
　　　　　　　　　　　　　　　　　　　　　　　　　　　　　　　　　　SF—49/43/38/6/32/18

**3907**　　　'ANYTHING GOES' STKS　　£2900.00 (£800.00: £380.00)　　1m 1f 9y
　　　　　　　　　　　　　　　　　　　　　　　　　　　　　　　　　　2-00 (2-01)

3864³ **The Goofer (65)** *(APStringer)* 5-9-11 RCochrane (1) (mde all: styd on strly fnl 3f) —1
3850* Galactic Miss (Fav) *(JLDunlop)* 3-8-10 GCarter (3) (a chsng wnr: rdn ent st: no
　　　　imp) .......................................................................... 6.2
3774² Fetish **(99)** *(HRACecil)* 3-8-13 WRyan (2) (hld up: effrt ent st: sn rdn & btn) .... 15.3

10/11 Galactic Miss, 11/10 Fetish, 10/1 THE GOOFER. CSF £17.52, Tote £5.60 (£2.40). Mrs Rowena Coleman
(THIRSK) bred by Horseshoe Agency Ltd. 3 Rn　　　　　　　　　　　　　　　2m 8.16 (15.86)
　　　　　　　　　　　　　　　　　　　　　　　　　　　　　　　　　　SF—49/16/–

**3908**　　　'THE PIRATE' CLAIMING H'CAP (3 & 4-Y.O) (0-70) £2595.00 (£720.00: £345.00)
　　　　　　1m
　　　　　　　　　　　　　　　　　　　　　　　　　　　　　　　　　　2-30 (2-34)

3898 **Lucky Noire (53)** *(GHarwood)* 4-9-2 KDarley (2) (b: lw: hld up: hdwy on bit ent
　　　　st: led 2f out: shkn up & qcknd clr appr fnl f) • ........................... —1
3849⁴ Preamble **(35)** *(MrsJRRamsden)* 3-7-9 JLowe (7) (hld up: hdwy ent st: effrt
　　　　over 1f out: nt pce of wnr) ............................................... 6.2
3589 Stoproveritate **(52)** (Fav) *(SGNorton)* 3-8-12 RCochrane (6) (hdwy 3f out: sn
　　　　rdn & styd on: nvr able to chal) ...................................... ¾.3
3346 Houlston's Will **(61)** *(MrsJRRamsden)* 3-9-7 KFallon (1) (outpcd & bhd tl styd
　　　　on fnl 3f) ..................................................................... 5.4

3785³ Devon Dancer **(68)** (v) *(MHEasterby)* 3-10-0 MBirch (4) (a chsng ldrs: one pce fnl 3f) .......... nk.5

2165³ Vanart **(54)** *(WWHaigh)* 3-9-0 DMcKeown (5) (cl up tl wknd over 2f out) .......... 4.6

3757* Ballyranter **(51)** *(HJCollingridge)* 3-8-11 JQuinn (3) (cl up: led ent st: hdd 2f out: sn rdn & btn) .......... 1½.7

3589 Borocay **(45)** *(MJCamacho)* 4-8-8 NConnorton (14) (nvr plcd to chal) .......... 2.8

3692⁵ Ace Reporter **(49)** *(MHTompkins)* 3-8-9 GDuffield (11) (racd wd: chsd ldrs to st) 25.9

3751⁴ Scottish Park **(65)** *(JPLeigh)* 3-9-6 ‡⁵JWeaver (13) (cl up tl wknd 3f out: t.o) .......... 10

3785 Eastleigh **(61)** *(RHollinshead)* 3-9-7 WRyan (12) (led tl hdd & wknd ent st: t.o) .. 11

Rossanita (IRE) **(36)** *(NBycroft)* 4-7-10⁽⁴⁾ ‡³FNorton (9) (bhd fr ½-wy: wl t.o) .......... 12

**7/2** Stoproveritate, **5/1** Ballyranter, Houlston's Will, **8/1** LUCKY NOIRE, Ace Reporter, Preamble, **10/1** Devon Dancer, Scottish Park, **11/1** Eastleigh, **14/1** Borocay, **16/1** Vanart, **50/1** Rossanita (IRE). CSF £69.91, CF £248.38. Tote £6.90: £2.30 £4.00 £1.30 (£85.30). Mrs Carol Harrison (PULBOROUGH) bred by T. J. G. Read. 12 Rn; Lucky Noire clmd Denys Smith £10,000                                     1m 55.69 (16.69)
SF—49/10/25/19/25/–

---

**3909**     'HIGH SOCIETY' STKS (Mdn) £2070.00 (£570.00: £270.00)     **1m**     3-00 (3-02)

3592 **Gushing** *(RCharlton)* 3-8-7⁽¹⁾ LDettori (2) (hld up & bhd: stdy hdwy ent st: rdn to ld ins fnl f) .......... —1

3389⁴ Charolles *(HRACecil)* 3-8-6 WRyan (5) (a.p: led wl over 1f out: sn rdn: hdd & one pce ins fnl f) .......... 2.2

3853⁴·Magadeer (USA) **(66)** *(JLDunlop)* 3-8-6 GCarter (8) (led tl hdd wl over 1f out: one pce) .......... 2½.3

Docklands (USA) (Fav) *(JHMGosden)* 3-8-6 PaulEddery (7) (b.nr fore: leggy: in tch: hdwy over 2f out: rdn & no ex appr fnl f) .......... 2.4

3513⁹ Gold Surprise (IRE) *(JGFitzGerald)* 3-8-11 KFallon (4) (bhd: effrt u.p over 3f out: n.d) .......... £0.5

3747² Ivana (IRE) *(WJarvis)* 3-8-6 JCarroll (10) (chsd ldrs: effrt 2f out: wknd over 1f out) .......... ½.6

Recording Contract *(JParkes)* 4-8-9 ‡⁵JWeaver (6) (cl up tl wknd 2f out) .......... 1.7

3695 Noora's Rose (NZ) *(GHarwood)* 3-8-6 GDuffield (1) (in tch tl rdn & wknd 3f out) 7.8

Baffie *(PMonteith)* 3-8-6 JFanning (s.s: n.d) .......... 9

3804 Lady Donoghue (USA) *(MrsGRReveley)* 3-8-6 KDarley (9) (prom tl lost tch appr st: t.o) .......... 10

**7/2** Docklands (USA), **4/1** Charolles, Magadeer (USA)(5/1—6/1), Ivana (IRE)(op 5/2), **5/1** GUSHING, **7/1** Gold Surprise (IRE), **16/1** Noora's Rose (NZ), **20/1** Lady Donoghue (USA), **25/1** Recording Contract, **33/1** Baffie. CSF £26.25, Tote £5.50: £2.20 £1.80 £1.20 (£13.10). Mrs Amanda Skiffington (BECKHAMPTON) bred by Mrs Amanda Skiffington. 10 Rn                                     1m 56.87 (17.87)
SF—22/15/7/1/–/–

---

**3910**     'YOU'LL NEVER GET RICH' H'CAP (0-90) £2950.00 (£880.00: £420.00: £190.00)
**6f**     3-30 (3-31)

3847³ **Our Rita (70)** *(DrJDScargill)* 3-8-9 RCochrane (8) (bhd: swtchd & hdwy wl over 1f out: r.o to ld wl ins fnl f) .......... —1

3879 Wellsy Lad (USA) **(53)** *(DWChapman)* 5-7-7 SWood (9) (chsd ldrs: led wl over 1f out: hdd & no ex wl ins fnl f) .......... 3.2

3828³ Densben **(84)** *(DenysSmith)* 8-9-10 KFallon (4) (in tch: hdwy 2f out: ev ch ins fnl f: nt qckn) .......... nk.3

3805⁴ Love Returned **(75)** *(WJarvis)* 5-9-1 MTebbutt (2) (trckd ldrs: chal over 1f out: rdn & wknd ins fnl f: fin 5th, 5l: plcd 4th) .......... 4

3707 Arabat **(60)** (bl) *(MPNaughton)* 5-8-0 JakiHouston (10) (led after 1f tl hdd & wknd wl over 1f out: fin 6th, 4l: plcd 5th) .......... 5

3854 Pharaoh's Dancer **(73)** (Fav) *(RSimpson)* 5-8-8 ‡⁵ATucker (5) (chsd ldrs tl rdn & btn wl over 1f out) .......... ½.7

3866 Gentle Hero (USA) **(73)** (bl) *(MPNaughton)* 6-8-13 GCarter (7) (outpcd ½-wy: sn lost tch) .......... 6.9

3732 Bold Memory **(84)** *(MJohnston)* 3-9-9 DMcKeown (1) (lw: led 1f: outpcd wl over 2f out) .......... 4.10

3591 Corn Futures **(73)** (bl) *(JPLeigh)* 4-8-8 ‡⁵JWeaver (6) (n.m.r 2f out: swtchd appr fnl f: styd on nr fin: fin 4th, 2½l: disq: plcd last) .......... 0

3866² Love Jazz (USA) **(81)** *(TDBarron)* 3-9-6 KDarley (3) (chsd ldrs: outpcd whn hmpd over 2f out: sn wknd: fin 8th, hd: disq: plcd last) .......... 0

LONG HANDICAP: Wellsy Lad (USA) 7-4.

*Stewards Enquiry: Corn Futures & Love Jazz disq. (reciprocal interference). Darley & Weaver suspended 11-20/11/92.*

5/2 Pharaoh's Dancer, 4/1 Love Jazz (USA), 11/2 Love Returned, 6/1 Densben, OUR RITA, 10/1 Gentle Hero (USA), 12/1 Arabat, Bold Memory, 16/1 Corn Futures, 33/1 Wellsy Lad (USA). CSF £143.37, CT £1,140.34. Tote £5.60: £1.60 £5.00 £2.30 (£113.60). Mr A. C. Edwards (NEWMARKET) bred by Terry Brady. 10 Rn
1m 25.93 (14.43)
SF—47/19/49/23/10/–

### 3911
'SOMETHING FOR THE BOYS' STKS (Mdn 2-Y.O.C & G) £2070.00 (£570.00: £270.00)
7f
4-00 (4-02)

| 3717 | **Shintillo (IRE)** (Fav) (*LMCumani*) 9-0 LDettori (4) (lw: a gng wl: led wl over 1f out: easily) | —1 |
| 3709 | Cannon Carew (*DMoffatt*) 8-7 ‡7DarrenMoffatt (5) (chsd ldrs: effrt 2f out: nt pce of wnr) | 6.2 |
| 3791⁵ | Moussahim (USA) (*MRStoute*) 9-0 PaulEddery (2) (lw: hld up: effrt 2f out: rdn & one pce) | 6.3 |
| 3611⁵ | North Ardar (*MJohnston*) 9-0 DMcKeown (6) (swtg: led tl hdd wl over 1f out: sn btn) | 6.4 |
| 3688³ | Dickins (*RHollinshead*) 9-0 WRyan (3) (cl up tl wknd over 1f out) | 8.5 |
| 3693 | Safety in Numbers (*MrsJRRamsden*) 9-0 KFallon (7) (chsd ldrs t| outpcd 3f out: wknd 2f out) | 1½.6 |
| 2534 | Sorayah's Pet (*SirMarkPrescott*) 9-0 GDuffield (1) (outpcd & bhd fnl 3f) | 2.7 |

4/7 SHINTILLO (IRE), 9/2 Moussahim (USA)(op 3/1), 9/1 Dickins(op 6/1), 10/1 Sorayah's Pet(op 6/1), 16/1 North Ardar, 25/1 Safety in Numbers, 50/1 Cannon Carew. CSF £20.97, Tote £1.40: £1.20 £8.40 (£13.20). Mr F. Franzi (NEWMARKET) bred by Ivan Allen in Ireland. 7 Rn
1m 43.03 (18.73)
SF—29/4/–/–/–/–

T/Plpt: £1,205.90 (1.83 Tckts).
AA

## 3493—HAMILTON (R-H)
### Tuesday, November 3rd [Heavy]
Going Allowance: St: 0.40 sec (Y); Rnd: 1.05 sec per fur (S)      Wind: almost nil

Stalls: No stalls - heavy ground

### 3912
CARFIN H'CAP (0-70) £2343.00 (£648.00: £309.00)    **1m 1f 36y**    1-00 (1-01)

| 3692⁶ | **Aegaen Lady** (41) (*JEtherington*) 3-8-4 ‡JWeaver (4) (hld up: hdwy on bit to ld wl over 1f out: shkn up & qcknd clr) | —1 |
| 3806 | Nothing Doing (IRE) (42) (*WJMusson*) 3-8-3 ‡7PBowe (5) (b: lw: bhd: effrt over 3f out: styd on: no ch w wnr) | 6.2 |
| 3752⁵ | Marowins (43) (*EJAlston*) 3-8-11 KFallon (8) (outpcd & bhd tl styd on wl fnl 2f) | nk.3 |
| 3615 | Edirepus (48) (Fav) (*MrsGRReveley*) 4-9-6 KDarley (10) (cl up: led 3f out tl wl over 1f out: one pce) | nk.4 |
| 3705⁴ | Essayeffsee (47) (bl) (*MHEasterby*) 3-9-1 MBirch (11) (b.hind: trckd ldrs: effrt over 2f out: no rspnse) | 2½.5 |
| 3311 | Thisonesforalice (42) (*AHarrison*) 4-9-0 JCarroll (3) (lw: hdwy ent st: sn prom: wknd 2f out) | hd.6 |
| 3825 | Media Messenger (60) (*DenysSmith*) 3-10-0 BRaymond (2) (cl up tl wknd over 2f out) | 1½.7 |
| 3850³ | Scaraben (55) (*HJCollingridge*) 4-9-13 VSmith (1) (b.nr hind: bhd: effrt on outside 3f out: n.d) | s.h.8 |
| | Dancing Legend (IRE) (33) (*JParkes*) 4-8-5 GDuffield (7) (prom tl wknd 3f out) | 12.9 |
| 3710 | Murasil (USA) (52) (bl) (*MPNaughton*) 3-9-6 DMcKeown (6) (led tl hdd & wknd 3f out) | 1½.10 |
| 3493 | Aragon Ayr (33) (*PMonteith*) 4-8-5 JFanning (9) (prom to ½-wy: sn wknd & wl t.o) | 11 |

7/2 Edirepus, 4/1 Scaraben, 9/2 Thisonesforalice(op 7/1), 5/1 Nothing Doing (IRE), 13/2 Essayeffsee, 10/1 AEGAEN LADY, Aragon Ayr, 12/1 Marowins(op 8/1), 16/1 Media Messenger, 20/1 Ors. CSF £61.05, CT £569.71. Tote £13.90: £3.80 £2.50 £2.40 (£28.10). Mr Ron Watkins (MALTON) bred by Messinger Stud Ltd. 11 Rn
2m 7.6 (13.3)
SF—33/14/21/29/16/14

### 3913
WHITEMOSS NURSERY (0-85) £2469.00 (£684.00: £327.00)    **1m 65y**    1-30 (1-30)

| 3754⁶ | **Northern Chief** (57) (*MHEasterby*) 7-9(2) JQuinn (9) (cl up: led 4f out: rdn & r.o wl) | —1 |
| 3091³ | Key to My Heart (IRE) (83) (Jt-Fav) (*DMoffatt*) 9-7 DMcKeown (6) (lw: trckd ldrs: effrt 3f out: nt qckn appr fnl f) | 1½.2 |
| 3587 | Shynon (55) (*MHTompkins*) 7-7 DaleGibson (4) (led tl hdd 4f out: styd on again appr fnl f) | nk.3 |

3821 Nellie's Gamble **(57)** *(APStringer)* 7-2<sup>(2)</sup> ‡<sup>7</sup>ClaireBalding (7) (bhd tl styd on wl fnl 2f) ........................................................ ¹/₂.4

3754* Public Way (IRE) **(57)** *(NChamberlain)* 7-9 SWood (11) (bhd: effrt ¹/₂-wy: no imp) 4.5

3614 Certain Way (IRE) **(56)** (v) *(CTinkler)* 7-8<sup>(1)</sup> JFanning (2) (lw: chsd ldrs: effrt 3f out: wknd over 1f out) ........................................... ¹/₂.6

3821 Palacegate Sunset **(56)** (Jt-Fav) *(JBerry)* 7-8 JakiHouston (5) (prom: effrt & ev ch 4f out: one pce wl over 2f out) ........................ 5.7

3821⁴ Brackenthwaite **(57)** *(TDBarron)* 7-9 JLowe (10) (lw: hld up: effrt ¹/₂-wy: sn rdn & n.d) ................................................................ 3¹/₂.8

3821² Ann Hill (IRE) **(60)** *(RHollinshead)* 7-5<sup>(1)</sup> ‡<sup>7</sup>AGarth (8) (a bhd) ..................... 4.9

3760 Friendly Knight **(55)** *(JSHaldane)* 7-0 ‡<sup>7</sup>DWright (3) (prom to ¹/₂-wy: sn wknd) 10.10

3809 Rose of Man **(59)** *(DMoffatt)* 7-4<sup>(4)</sup> ‡<sup>7</sup>DarrenMoffatt (1) (a bhd) ................... 3.11

LONG HANDICAP: Northern Chief 7-3, Nellie's Gamble 7-6, Certain Way (IRE) 7-2, Friendly Knight 6-11, Rose of Man 7-2.

**9/2** Palacegate Sunset(op 5/2), Key to My Heart (IRE), **5/1** Brackenthwaite, **7/1** Certain Way (IRE), **9/1** Shynon, Ann Hill (IRE), **10/1** Public Way, **12/1** NORTHERN CHIEF(op 8/1), **14/1** Nellie's Gamble(op 8/1), **33/1** Friendly Knight, **50/1** Rose of Man. CSF £58.46, CT £462.78. Tote £21.50: £4.70 £2.10 £1.60 (£62.50). Mr T. C. Chiang (MALTON) bred by Stetchworth Park Stud Ltd. 11 Rn     1m 57.2 (13.9)

SF—–/20/-/-/-/-

**3914**     WHIRLIES (S) STKS   £2301.00 (£636.00: £303.00)    **5f 4y**     2-00 (2-01)

3700 **Soba Guest (IRE) (61)** *(JBerry)* 3-9-2 JCarroll (10) (lw: mde all: rdn over 1f out: styd on) ....................................................................... —1

3879 Pretonic **(56)** *(MJohnston)* 4-8-11 DMcKeown (3) (a chsng ldrs: kpt on fnl 2f: no imp) ................................................................. 5.2

3762⁵ Lonely Lass **(37)** *(AWJones)* 6-8-6 JQuinn (7) (chsd ldrs: hdwy over 1f out: nvr able to chal) .............................................................. ¹/₂.3

3507 Don't Run Me Over **(42)** *(BCMorgan)* 3-9-2 GDuffield (9) (lw: chsd wnr: rdn & edgd rt over 1f out: sn btn) ............................................ ³/₄.4

3710⁶ Sammy Slew (USA) **(59)** *(CParker)* 3-8-11 MWood (6) (prom tl outpcd fnl 2f) . 2¹/₂.5

3762³ The Right Time **(44)** (bl) *(JParkes)* 7-8-11 BRaymond (5) (prom: rdn ¹/₂-wy: no imp after) ........................................................... hd.6

3518⁶ B Grade **(41)** *(JBalding)* 7-7-13 ‡<sup>7</sup>ClaireBalding (1) (s.i.s: effrt ¹/₂-wy: n.d) ....... 2¹/₂.7

3707 Almasa **(59)** (Fav) *(DMorris)* 4-8-1 ‡<sup>5</sup>JWeaver (2) (s.i.s: n.d) ...................... 3.8

3495⁵ Jane's Brave Boy **(20)** *(TCraig)* 10-8-4 ‡<sup>7</sup>DWright (9) (s.i.s: a outpcd & wl bhd) 1¹/₂.9

3854 Stormbuster **(39)** *(PSFelgate)* 3-8-11 JLowe (4) (sn bhd) ............................ 1.10

**11/4** Almasa, **7/2** Pretonic(op 9/4), **6/1** B Grade, SOBA GUEST (IRE), **7/1** The Right Time, **8/1** Sammy Slew (USA), **16/1** Don't Run Me Over, **33/1** Stormbuster, Lonely Lass, **66/1** Jane's Brave Boy. CSF £24.99, Tote £8.90: £3.70 £1.70 £4.30 (£18.50). Mr Richard Jinks (COCKERHAM) bred by Tullamaine Castle Stud in Ireland. 10 Rn; No bid     62.7 sec (4.4)

SF—54/29/22/29/14/13

**3915**     AUCHINGRAMONT STKS (Mdn 2-Y.O) £2448.00 (£678.00: £324.00)
    **6f 5y**     2-30 (2-30)

3704⁴ **Anusha** (Fav) *(JBerry)* 8-9 JCarroll (8) (mde all: styd on wl fnl 2f) ............... —1

3790⁵ My Ballyboy **(43)** (bl) *(ABailey)* 9-0 BRaymond (7) (a chsng ldrs: effrt 2f out: r.o one pce) ....................................................................... 3¹/₂.2

3750⁴ Sabo the Hero *(SirMarkPrescott)* 9-0 GDuffield (1) (lw: a chsng ldrs: hdwy u.p 2f out: no ex fnl f) ...................................................... ³/₄.3

3750 Bold Prospect *(PCalver)* 9-0 DaleGibson (6) (a.p: kpt on one pce fnl 2f) ........ 2¹/₂.4

3498 Primitive Gift *(MrsGRReveley)* 8-9 KDarley (2) (lw: stdd s: hdwy after 2f: rdn ¹/₂-wy: no imp) ............................................................ 2.5

3820 Sarah Heights *(MissLCSiddall)* 8-9 MBirch (4) (prom: effrt & n.m.r 2f out: sn rdn & one pce) ................................................................. ¹/₂.6

    Treble Lass *(MJohnston)* 8-9 DMcKeown (3) (neat: str: outpcd after 2f: sn bhd) 8.7

    Laid Back Ben *(BPalling)* 8-9 ‡<sup>5</sup>JWeaver (5) (w'like: hld up: swtchd & effrt over 2f out: sn btn & eased) ........................................... 3.8

**5/4** ANUSHA, **7/2** Sabo the Hero, **8/1** Treble Lass, Bold Prospect, **10/1** Sarah Heights, **12/1** Primitive Gift(op 8/1), **14/1** My Ballyboy(op 7/1), **16/1** Laid Back Ben. CSF £17.82, Tote £2.30: £1.40 £2.00 £1.30 (£9.00). Mr Yahya Nasib (COCKERHAM) bred by Hamilton Bloodstock (UK) Ltd. 8 Rn     1m 18.5 (8.5)

**3916**     BARNCLUITH SPRINT H'CAP (0-70) £2544.00 (£704.00: £336.00)
    **6f 5y**     3-00 (3-02)

(Weights raised 1 lb)

3762 **Hinari Video (37)** *(MJohnston)* 7-8-3 DMcKeown (1) (mde all: kpt on wl fnl 2f) . —1

3870 Toss the Dice **(48)** *(MAJarvis)* 3-8-13 GDuffield (5) (lw: a chsng wnr: chal wl over 1f out: no ex ins fnl f) ......................................... 1¹/₂.2

3854⁴ Rock Opera (IRE) **(58)** *(MPNaughton)* 4–9-10 KFallon (2) (bhd tl styd on u.p fnl 2f) ............ **4.3**

3879 Verro (USA) **(40)** (bl) *(JABennett)* 5–8-6 DaleGibson (3) (chsd ldrs: hrd rdn 2f out: no imp after) ............ 2¹/₂.4

3879 Highborn (IRE) **(48)** *(PSFelgate)* 3–8-13 JLowe (4) (in tch: effrt ¹/₂-wy: one pce) ³/₄.5

3481³ Johnston's Express (IRE) **(36)** (Fav) *(EJAlston)* 4–8-2 JQuinn (8) (chsd ldrs 4f: sn btn) ............ ¹/₂.7

3496⁶ Francis Ann **(53)** *(MissLAPerratt)* 4–8-12 ‡7RHavlin (6) (prom to ¹/₂-wy: sn wknd) 5.8

**5/2 Johnston's Express (IRE), 4/1 Verro (USA), 5/1 Francis Ann, Rock Opera (IRE), 8/1 Highborn (IRE), 10/1 Verdant Boy, 12/1 HINARI VIDEO(op 8/1), 14/1 Toss the Dice.** CSF £134.25, CT £858.69. Tote £12.00: £2.10 £2.40 £1.50 (£61.60). Mr L. G. McMullan (MIDDLEHAM) bred by Confey Stud Farm Ltd. 8 Rn 1m 16.8 (6.8)

SF–1/5/–/–/–/

## 3917    FINALE H'CAP (0–70) £2633.60 (£729.60: £348.80)    1¹/₂m 17y    3-30 (3-32)

3761⁴ J P Morgan **(42)** (bl) *(MPNaughton)* 4–8-5(4) KFallon (8) (chsd ldrs: led 2f out: hld on wl) ............ —1

3829 Eurotwist **(62)** *(TDBarron)* 3–8-11 ‡7VHalliday (14) (bhd: effrt 4f out: r.o strly fnl f: jst failed) ............ s.h.2

3493² Grey Power **(56)** (Fav) *(MrsGRReveley)* 5–9-5 KDarley (13) (lw: bhd: hdwy 3f out: styd on wl: nrst fin) ............ 3.3

Fishki **(42)** *(MDHammond)* 6–8-5 DMcKeown (7) (led tl hdd 2f out: kpt on same pce) ............ 4.4

3773* Neieb (USA) **(64)** *(BHanbury)* 3–9-6 BRaymond (10) (cl up: chal 3f out: rdn & btn over 1f out) ............ 7.5

3641⁵ Philgun **(61)** *(CWCElsey)* 3–9-3 JCarroll (1) (a chsng ldrs: effrt 3f out: wknd wl over 1f out) ............ 1.6

3851 Spray of Orchids **(55)** *(JEtherington)* 3–8-11 GDuffield (4) (chsd ldrs tl wknd over 2f out) ............ 2.7

3500 Needwood Poppy **(32)** *(BCMorgan)* 4–7-9(8) JLowe (12) (bhd: effrt 4f out: nvr rchd ldrs) ............ 5.8

2357³ Buzzards Crest **(30)** *(BobJones)* 7–7-7 SWood (6) (nvr trbld ldrs) ............ 1¹/₂.9

3778 Wotamona **(32)** *(BPalling)* 4–7-9(2) JQuinn (11) (b.nr hind: in tch tl wknd 3f out) 7.10

893¹⁴ Persuasive **(65)** *(MissLAPerratt)* 4–8-11 DaleGibson (3) (n.d) ............ 8.11

Invertiel **(61)** *(PMonteith)* 8–9-10 JFanning (9) (in tch tl grad wknd fnl 4f) ............ 1.12

3806 Golden Beau **(39)** *(AHarrison)* 10–7-9(9) ‡7IGrantham (5) (lost tch fnl 4f) ............ 1.13

Silver's Girl **(43)** *(DMoffatt)* 7–7-13 ‡7DarrenMoffatt (2) (chsd ldrs tl wknd 4f out) 15.14

LONG HANDICAP: Needwood Poppy 7-6, Golden Beau 7-0.

**2/1 Grey Power(3/1—7/4), 11/2 Neieb (USA), 7/1 Philgun, J P MORGAN(9/1—6/1), 8/1 Eurotwist, 12/1 Spray of Orchids(op 8/1), 14/1 Fishki, Persuasive, 16/1 Buzzards Crest(op 10/1), 20/1 Wotamona, 25/1 Silver's Girl, 33/1 Needwood Poppy, 50/1 Invertiel, 100/1 Golden Beau.** CSF £59.37, CT £142.31. Tote £9.10: £1.70 £3.40 £1.80 (£87.20). Mr Raymond Miquel (RICHMOND) bred by The Mount Coote Partnership. 14 Rn 2m 49.8 (17.8)

SF–39/44/46/24/25/20

T/Plpt: £182.60 (12.77 Tckts).

AA

## 3757—**EDINBURGH (R-H)**
### Thursday, November 5th [Good to soft]

Going Allowance: 0.50 sec per fur (Y)                                    Wind: slt against

Stalls: high

## 3918    TENNENTS LAGER STKS (Mdn 2-Y-O) £2295.00 (£645.00: £315.00)
1m 16y                                                                      1-00 (1-00)

3181 **Ansillo** (Fav) *(JHMGosden)* 9-0 PaulEddery (7) (led 2f: a gng wl: led on bit appr fnl f: v.cheekily) ............ —1

3846⁶ Dance to Order (IRE) *(SirMarkPrescott)* 9-0 GDuffield (2) (lw: led after 2f: rdn 2f out: sn hdd: r.o wl) ............ nk.2

3865⁵ Stylish Rose (IRE) *(WAStephenson)* 8-9 SWebster (6) (cl up tl lost pl after 2f: hdwy ent st: styd on: no imp) ............ 3¹/₂.3

1796³ Indian Flash (IRE) *(RGuest)* 8-9 RCochrane (5) (effrt appr st: sn chsng ldrs: one pce fnl 2f) ............ 7.4

3709 Wonderful Years (USA) *(MrsJRRamsden)* 9-0 KFallon (9) (lw: hdwy over 2f out: nvr nr to chal) ............ 3.5

3614 Andrea's Girl **(42)** *(JBerry)* 8-2 ‡7ADaly (8) (b.hind: chsd ldrs tl outpcd appr st: n.d after) ............ s.h.6

3614 Dusky Duchess (IRE) *(MissLAPerratt)* 8-2 ‡⁷RHavlin (1) (hdwy to chse ldrs ent st: sn outpcd) .............................................................................. 3.7
1036 Gold Desire *(MBrittain)* 8-7 ‡⁷JMarshall (10) (chsd ldrs to st: sn outpcd) ........... 4.8
3626 Quessong *(FHLee)* 8-9 ‡⁵NKennedy (3) (lost pl after wl over 1f: hdwy ent st: sn rdn & wknd) ............................................................................... 8.9

**2/1** ANSILLO(op Evens), **3/1** Indian Flash (IRE), **7/2** Dance to Order (IRE), **8/1** Stylish Rose (IRE), Wonderful Years (USA), **14/1** Quessong, **25/1** Gold Desire, **33/1** Andrea's Girl, **50/1** Dusky Duchess (IRE). CSF £9.28, Tote £3.10: £1.80 £1.40 £1.10 (£5.10). Mr K. Abdulla (NEWMARKET) bred by Crest Stud Ltd. 9 Rn   1m 47.6 (9)
SF—25/24/8/–/–/–

## 3919

TENNENTS NOVEMBER H'CAP (0-70) £2326.50 (£654.00: £319.50)
**1m 16y**
1-30 (1-32)

3759² **Lawnswood Junior (58)** (Fav) *(JLSpearing)* 5-9-3 KDarley (7) (hld up: effrt 3f out: led wl over 1f out: r.o) ............................................................... —1
3771² Military Expert (56) (bl) *(CaptJWilson)* 3-8-5 ‡⁷JMarshall (3) (chsd ldrs: c wd & chal 2f out: kpt on u.p fnl f) ......................................................... ¾.2
3759⁵ Doyce (54) *(JEtherington)* 3-8-10 NConnorton (2) (a.p: effrt 3f out: styd on one pce) ............................................................................................ 2.3
3757² Brambles Way (49) (v) *(WLBarker)* 3-8-0 ‡⁵OPears (8) (led tl hdd & wknd wl over 1f out) ...................................................................................... 3.4
3481 East Barns (IRE) (37) (bl) *(TDBarron)* 4—7-10 JLowe (6) (in tch tl outpcd wl over 2f out) ........................................................................................ 2.5
3793² Cee-Jay-Ay (56) *(JBerry)* 5-8-8 ‡⁷PRoberts (4) (s.s: hdwy ent st: nvr able to chal) .......................................................................................... s.h.6
2260⁵ American Hero (69) *(RAllan)* 4-9-9 ‡⁵JWeaver (5) (cl up tl wknd over 2f out) .... 20.7
875² Dancing Street (50) *(TCraig)* 4-8-9 KFallon (9) (lost tch appr st: n.d after) ........ 3.8
0000 New Beginning (34) *(JSHaldane)* 9-7-7 SWood (1) (b: dwlt: sn rcvrd & prom: rn wd appr st: sn wknd) ...................................................................... 5.9
LONG HANDICAP: New Beginning 6-13.

**2/1** LAWNSWOOD JUNIOR, **3/1** Cee-Jay-Ay, **9/2** Doyce, **9/1** Military Expert, **10/1** American Hero, **12/1** East Barns (IRE), **16/1** Brambles Way, **33/1** Dancing Street, **66/1** New Beginning. CSF £18.29, CT £64.90. Tote £3.50: £1.60 £1.80 £1.80 (£22.90). Mr Graham Treglown (ALCESTER) bred by Chilcombe Manor Stud. 9 Rn
1m 46.1 (7.5)
SF—50/36/35/16/6/17

## 3920

TENNENTS 80 SHILLING ALE CLAIMING STKS   £2274.00 (£639.00: £312.00)
**1m 3f 32y**
2-00 (2-01)

3863★ **Salu (50)** (bl) (Fav) *(JEtherington)* 3-8-8 GDuffield (2) (hld up: hdwy to chse ldr ent st: led wl over 1f out: sn clr) ................................................. —1
3350⁶ Miliyel (45) *(PMonteith)* 3-7-13 ‡³SMaloney (9) (led 8f out: sn qcknd clr: hdd wl over 1f out: no ex) ..................................................................... 3½.2
3906 Lord Advocate (44) (bl) *(MPNaughton)* 4-8-7 KFallon (1) (prom tl outpcd appr st: styd on fnl f) ...................................................................... 1½.3
3752³ Notable Exception (51) *(MrsGRReveley)* 3-9-1 KDarley (6) (bhd: effrt appr st: nvr nr to chal) .......................................................................... ¾.4
Tindari (FR) *(JMJefferson)* 4-9-1 MWood (10) (led 3f: chsd ldrs: outpcd appr st: n.d after) ............................................................................... 10.5
3711⁶ Father Dan (IRE) (v) *(DMoffatt)* 3-7-8 ‡⁷DarrenMoffatt (4) (chsd ldrs tl outpcd over 4f out: n.d after) ................................................................. 1½.6
3622 Golden Ancona (30) *(MBrittain)* 9-8-10 ‡⁷JMarshall (5) (nvr trbld ldrs) ............ 7
Persian Lion *(FWatson)* 3-8-5 JLowe (7) (b.nr hind: prom 4f: sn bhd) ............... 8
467 Sarwan (IRE) (8/1) Withdrawn (lame at s) : not under orders — Rule 4 applies

**4/6** SALU(tchd Evens), **9/4** Notable Exception, **14/1** Father Dan (IRE), Miliyel, **16/1** Lord Advocate, **20/1** Tindari (FR), **33/1** Golden Ancona, **100/1** Persian Lion. CSF £10.38, Tote £1.60: £1.10 £2.40 £2.20 (£4.50). Mr W. N. Lumley (MALTON) bred by W. N. Lumley. 8 Rn; Father Dan (IRE) clmd K Moorcroft £3,101   2m 34.3 (14.6)
SF—3/–/–/–/–

## 3921

TENNENTS L.A. AUCTION STKS (Mdn 2-Y.O) £2211.00 (£621.00: £303.00)
**5f**
2-30 (2-31)

3608⁶ **Walk the Beat** *(RSimpson)* 8-9 ‡⁵ATucker (1) (lw: reard & wnt lft s: hdwy & prom after 2f: led appr fnl f: r.o) ............................................... —1
3768² Sylvan Starlight (72) (Fav) *(SirMarkPrescott)* 8-9 GDuffield (2) (lw: a in tch: styd on u.p fnl f: nrst fin) .................................................................... ¾.2
3874⁴ Danny Blue (IRE) *(MissGayKelleway)* 9-0 KFallon (6) (lw: chsd ldrs: outpcd ½-wy: hdwy u.p 1f out: styd on) ...................................................... ¾.3
Palacegate Girl *(JBerry)* 8-9 JCarroll (8) (neat: s.i.s: sn rcvrd: led wl over 1f out: hdd appr fnl f: no ex) .............................................................. nk.4

| 3750 | Grey Pride (52) (JBerry) 8-8[1] ‡7SPorritt (7) (in tch: effrt & wnt rt over 1f out: no imp) | 3¹/2.5 |
| 3749 | Dayjuz (IRE) (67) (bl) (FHLee) 9-0 PaulEddery (4) (led over 3f: sn wknd) | 2.6 |
| 3484 | Jotra (RMWhitaker) 9-0 ACulhane (3) (b: lw: a outpcd & bhd) | 2¹/2.7 |
| 3749 | Mdm Racer (IRE) (JBerry) 8-7 ‡7PRoberts (2) (prom 3f: sn wknd) | 2¹/2.8 |

**6/5** Sylvan Starlight(4/5—5/4), **3/1** Danny Blue (IRE), **6/1** WALK THE BEAT, **7/1** Palacegate Girl(op 7/2), **14/1** Mdm Racer (IRE), Dayjuz (IRE)(op 8/1), **25/1** Jotra, **50/1** Grey Pride. CSF £13.21, Tote £10.30: £2.40 £1.10 £1.10 (£8.20). The Country Life Partnership (FOXHILL) bred by R. B. Warren. 8 Rn
63.3 sec (5.6)
SF—33/30/32/26/11/9

## 3922

TENNENTS SPECIAL H'CAP (0-70) £2389.50 (£672.00: £328.50)
1m 7f 16y

3-00 (3-00)

| 3755* | **Heliopsis** (41) (MDHammond) 4-8-4 GDuffield (13) (lw: in tch: reminders 7f out & ent st: hdwy 2f out: hrd rdn to ld ins fnl f) | —1 |
| 3804³ | Cariboo Gold (USA) (68) (JHMGosden) 3-9-8 RCochrane (7) (lw: trckd ldrs: led 3f out: wandered bdly 2f out: sn hdd: rallied u.p fnl f) | ³/4.2 |
| 3808² | Ambuscade (USA) (60) (Fav) (MrsGRReveley) 6-9-9 KDarley (8) (lw: a.p: styd on to ld over 1f out: nt qckn nr fin) | s.h.3 |
| 3755 | Bilberry (39) (CWCElsey) 3-7-7 SWood (2) (hld up & bhd: gd hdwy ¹/2-wy: wnt ech 2f out: hung rt & nt qckn) | 1¹/2.4 |
| 3877 | Cost Effective (32) (MBrittain) 5-7-9 JLowe (3) (bhd tl styd on fnl 3f: n.d) | 12.5 |
| 3724 | Best Gun (60) (bl) (CWCElsey) 3-8-9 ‡5JWeaver (5) (led tl hdd 3f out: grad wknd) | 1¹/2.6 |
| 3380 | Latvian (65) (RAllan) 5-10-0 SWebster (6) (in tch: no hdwy fnl 3f) | 7.7 |
| 3745² | Bridge Player (42) (DMoffatt) 5-7-12 ‡7DarrenMoffatt (10) (bhd: effrt appr st: n.d) | ¹/2.8 |
| 3761* | John Shaw (USA) (50) (CTinkler) 4-8-10 ‡3SMaloney (4) (chsd ldrs tl wknd wl over 2f out) | 2¹/2.9 |
| 3493 | Sea Paddy (49) (RBastiman) 4-8-5 ‡7HBastiman (14) (bhd & rdn 6f out: n.d) | 3.10 |
| 951 | Lapiaffe (40) (AHarrison) 8-8-3[1] JCarroll (9) (bhd fnl 4f) | 1¹/2.11 |
| 3745 | Alpha Helix (37) (v) (MissLAPerratt) 9-7-9[7] ‡5NKennedy (12) (nvr gng wl & a bhd) | 1.12 |
| 3745 | Rolling the Bones (USA) (62) (MPNaughton) 3-9-2 KFallon (11) (prom tl rdn & wknd appr st) | 3.13 |
| 3808 | Rainbow Stripes (35) (BSRothwell) 5-7-5[5] ‡7AGarth (1) (prom tl wknd 6f out) | 14 |
| | Another Nick (40) (JMJefferson) 6-8-3 PaulEddery (4) (b: prom to ¹/2-wy: t.o) | 15 |

LONG HANDICAP: Alpha Helix 7-2, Rainbow Stripes 7-3.
*Stewards Enquiry:* Duffield suspended 14-17/11/92 (excessive use of whip).

**9/4** Ambuscade (USA), **4/1** Cariboo Gold (USA), HELIOPSIS, **7/1** John Shaw (USA), **9/1** Bridge Player(op 5/1), **12/1** Rolling the Bones (USA), **16/1** Best Gun, Bilberry, **20/1** Sea Paddy, **25/1** Lapiaffe, Latvian, **33/1** Cost Effective, Rainbow Stripes, **66/1** Ors. CSF £21.21, CT £43.35. Tote £3.80: £2.50 £1.90 £1.80 (£10.70). Maureen Godsman & Douglas Godsman (MIDDLEHAM) bred by Juddmonte Farms. 15 Rn     3m 28.1 (17.6)

## 3923

LADBROKE ON-COURSE H'CAP (0-70) £2284.50 (£642.00: £313.50)     5f 3-30 (3-31)

| 3518 | **Supreme Desire** (46) (ASmith) 4-8-5 SWebster (1) (chsd ldrs stands' side: hrd rdn to ld ins fnl f) | —1 |
| 3854 | Kalar (46) (bl) (DWChapman) 3-8-5 SWood (2) (lw: led stands' side tl hdd & no ex ins fnl f) | 1¹/2.2 |
| 3762 | Best Effort (61) (MPNaughton) 6-9-6 KFallon (3) (chsd ldrs stands' side: rdn ¹/2-wy: kpt on nr fin) | hd.3 |
| 3879² | Take it in Cash (42) (Fav) (RDickin) 3-8-1 CRutter (5) (racd stands' side: outpcd tl styd on fnl f) | 3.4 |
| 3777 | Le Chic (43) (DWChapman) 6-8-2 KDarley (7) (led far side: wknd ins fnl f) | hd.5 |
| 3748 | Prince Belfort (61) (MPNaughton) 4-9-6 RCochrane (6) (racd far side: effrt ¹/2-wy: no imp) | 2¹/2.6 |
| 3828 | Quatre Femme (60) (MJohnston) 5-9-5 RPElliott (4) (lw: racd far side: hld up: effrt ¹/2-wy: edgd lft & no imp) | 1¹/2.7 |
| 3828 | Super Rocky (67) (RBastiman) 3-9-5 ‡7HBastiman (8) (chsd ldr far side tl wknd over 1f out) | ¹/2.8 |

**6/4** Take it in Cash, **9/2** Quatre Femme, **11/2** Kalar, **6/1** Best Effort, **17/2** SUPREME DESIRE, **11/1** Prince Belfort, Le Chic, **20/1** Super Rocky. CSF £51.34, CT £277.76. Tote £20.40: £3.40 £3.40 £2.50 (£48.90). Miss J. F. Craze (BEVERLEY) bred by John E. and Mrs Wilkinson. 8 Rn
63.3 sec (5.6)
SF—29/23/37/6/6/14

T/Plpt: £38.80 (43.10 Tckts).

AA

3840—**LINGFIELD (L-H)** Equitrack
**Thursday, November 5th [Standard]**
Going Allowance: 6f: minus 0.05 sec; Rest: minus 0.20 sec (FS)

**3924**   CAPRICORN STKS (I) (Mdn 2-Y.O) £1213.50 (£336.00: £160.50)
**1m (AWT)**                                                              12-20 (12-22)

3902 **Excess Baggage (IRE)** *(NACallaghan)* 9-0 WRyan (9) (hdwy over 3f out: led
over 1f out: rdn out) ............................................................... —1
3716 Absolutely Fact (USA) **(58)** *(CCElsey)* 9-0 JQuinn (6) (hdwy over 2f out: hrd rdn
over 1f out: r.o ins fnl f) ....................................................... 3½.2
3809⁶ Sharro **(65)** (Fav) *(PAKelleway)* 9-0 AMunro (1) (lw: w ldr: led over 2f out tl over
1f out: unable qckn) .............................................................. 1.3
3852 Duchess Dianne (IRE) **(41)** *(PGMurphy)* 8-9 NAdams (4) (swtg: led over 5f: hrd
rdn over 1f out: one pce) ....................................................... 1.4
3765 Medland (IRE) *(AWDenson)* 9-0 MHills (3) (dwlt: nvr nr to chal) .................. 1.5
One Off the Rail (USA) *(AMoore)* 9-0 BRouse (12) (leggy: bit bkwd: hdwy over
2f out: wknd wl over 1f out) .................................................... 2.6
Joy of Freedom *(CEBrittain)* 8-4 ‡§BDoyle (10) (lt-f: prom over 4f) .............. 3.7
3691 Sheer Ecstasy *(PMMcEntee)* 9-0 RPrice (11) (prom over 5f) ................... 1½.8
3685 Eve's Treasure *(RCurtis)* 8-9 GBardwell (4) (prom 5f) ......................... 6.9
3597 Rubidian *(SirMarkPrescott)* 9-0 CNutter (2) (bhd fnl 3f) ..................... 3½.10
3744 Ascom Pager Too **(60)** *(PHowling)* 8-9 DBiggs (7) (b: b.hind: bhd fnl 3f) ....... 4.11

**9/4** Sharro, **7/2** Absolutely Fact (USA), **9/2** EXCESS BAGGAGE (IRE), **7/1** Ascom Pager Too, **15/2** Joy of
Freedom(4/1—8/1), **14/1** Rubidian(op 8/1), **16/1** One Off the Rail (USA), Duchess Dianne (IRE), **25/1** Sheer
Ecstasy, Medland (IRE) **33/1** Eve's Treasure. CSF £20.57, Tote £7.00: £2.30 £1.70 £1.10 (£17.60). Mr Frank
W. Golding (NEWMARKET) bred by Miss D. Flanagan in Ireland. 11 Rn              1m 40.02 (3.32)
SF—26/15/12/4/6/–

**3925**   LEO CLAIMING STKS (I) (2-Y.O) £1192.50 (£330.00: £157.50)
**6f (AWT)**                                                              12-50 (12-52)

3712 **Nut Bush (50)** *(NACallaghan)* 7-12 TyroneWilliams (1) (b: lw: mde all: hrd rdn
2f out: r.o wl) ...................................................................... —1
3837 Mr Cube (IRE) **(60)** *(PFICole)* 7-12 JQuinn (2) (b.off hind: a.p: hrd rdn over 1f
out: unable qckn) ................................................................. 2.2
2578⁶ Bichette **(76)** *(RHannon)* 7-9 DaleGibson (8) (hld up: rdn over 3f out: r.o one
pce fnl 2f) .......................................................................... 1½.3
3843 Stardust Express **(59)** (Fav) *(MJohnston)* 8-3 DMcKeown (5) (lw: a.p: hrd rdn
over 1f out: one pce) ........................................................... nk.4
3821 Girl Next Door **(54)** (v) *(NAGraham)* 7-7 GBardwell (10) (no hdwy fnl 3f) ........ 1½.5
3712 Broughtons Formula *(WJMusson)* 8-1 ‡7DMcCabe (6) (b: lw: outpcd: nvr nrr) . 1½.6
3570⁶ Hobey Cat **(74)** *(DRCElsworth)* 7-8⁽⁴⁾ ‡§BDoyle (11) (lw: nvr nrr) ............... nk.7
3179 Miss Delivery *(PHowling)* 7-9 NCarlisle (12) (a mid div) ...................... 1.8
3844⁵ Moonstruck Bard **(45)** *(SPCWoods)* 8-3 WWoods (7) (spd over 4f) ............... 2½.9
3608 Shy Romance **(55)** *(PMMcEntee)* 7-10⁽⁶⁾ ‡3FNorton (9) (a bhd) ................. 8.10
3702⁶ Spanish Tower **(43)** (bl) *(PGMurphy)* 8-0 NAdams (4) (bhd fnl 2f) ............. 6.11
3702 Pat Poindestres **(58)** *(MDixon)* 7-11 DBiggs (3) (bhd fnl 2f) ................. 2½.12

**2/1** Stardust Express, **11/4** Bichette, **6/1** Pat Poindestres(op 4/1), **8/1** Mr Cube (IRE)(op 5/1), **10/1** Moonstruck
Bard(6/1—12/1), NUT BUSH, **14/1** Girl Next Door(op 6/1), Broughtons Formula(op 8/1), **16/1** Hobey Cat, **33/1**
Spanish Tower, **50/1** Ors. CSF £86.25, Tote £25.60: £3.00 £2.60 £1.40 (£35.00). Mrs M. E. Cooke
(NEWMARKET) bred by R. B. Warren. 12 Rn              1m 13.08 (2.48)
SF—28/20/11/18/2/4

**3926**   CAPRICORN STKS (II) (Mdn 2-Y.O) £1213.50 (£336.00: £160.50)
**1m (AWT)**                                                              1-20 (1-22)

3717⁵ **Aberdeen Heather (85)** (Fav) *(DRCElsworth)* 9-0 JWilliams (8) (hld up: led 3f
out: rdn out) ....................................................................... —1
3602³ Secret Assignment (USA) *(CACyzer)* 9-0 WRyan (2) (lw: a.p: chsd wnr over 1f
out: no imp) ....................................................................... 3½.2
3030 Fire in My Body (USA) *(PWChapple-Hyam)* 9-0 DHolland (7) (outpcd: hdwy
over 3f out: one pce fnl 2f) ................................................... 1.3
3856 Juliasdarkinvader *(AMoore)* 9-0 NAdams (5) (hdwy over 1f out: r.o) .......... ½.4
3199 Lochore **(58)** *(Ringram)* 9-0 AMcGlone (4) (a.p: one pce fnl 2f) .............. ½.5
3574 Mr Copyforce **(60)** *(MissBSanders)* 8-11 ‡3DHarrison (6) (prom 5f) .......... 3.6
3523 Legal Artist (IRE) *(NAGraham)* 9-0 DMcKeown (12) (led 1f: led over 3f out: sn
hdd: wknd over 1f out) ......................................................... ½.7

3846⁴ Harlestone Brook *(JLDunlop)* 8-7 ‡⁷KateAhern (10) (lw: nvr nrr) ...... 1¹/₂.8
3809 The Where Withal *(SirMarkPrescott)* 9-0 CNutter (9) (a bhd) ...... nk.9
3768 Zhaab *(MMadgwick)* 8-2 ‡⁷CAvery (1) (bhd fnl 2f) ...... hd.10
3880 Baileys Colours (47) *(BJMcMath)* 8-9 EJohnson (3) (lw: led 7f out tl over 3f out: wknd over 1f out) ...... s.h.11
3685 Freebyjove (40) *(PButler)* 8-2 ‡⁷SDrowne (11) (swtg: prom over 3f: t.o) ...... 12

4/5 ABERDEEN HEATHER, 9/2 Secret Assignment (USA), 10/1 The Where Withal, Harlestone Brook, Fire in My Body (USA)(op 6/1), 14/1 Baileys Colours, 16/1 Lochore, 20/1 Mr Copyforce, 50/1 Ors. CSF £5.39, Tote £1.80: £1.10 £1.90 £3.20 (£3.50). Major H. S. Cayzer (WHITSBURY) bred by D. S. Rigby. 12 Rn
1m 39.49 (2.79)
SF—34/23/20/8/6/–

**3927** LEO CLAIMING STKS (II) (2-Y-0) £1192.50 (£330.00: £157.50)
**6f (AWT)**
1-50 (1-53)

3712 **Knobbleeneeze (62)** (v) *(MRChannon)* 8-2 GCarter (6) (lw: a.p: hrd rdn over 1f out: led nr fin) ...... —1
3558* Risky Number (60) (bl) *(Fav)* *(JSMoore)* 7-9 ‡³DHarrison (3) (lw: led: clr over 3f out: hrd rdn over 1f out: hdd nr fin) ...... hd.2
3704 Chiltern Hundreds (USA) (75) *(WJMusson)* 8-6 TQuinn (1) (b: a.p: hrd rdn over 1f out: one pce) ...... 3¹/₂.3
3754⁵ Samanthas Joy (56) *(TFairhurst)* 7-7 JFanning (10) (hld up: hrd rdn over 2f out: one pce) ...... nk.4
3553 Lady of Shadows (45) *(SDow)* 7-7 JQuinn (2) (eyeshield: hld up: one pce fnl 2f) ...... ¹/₂.5
3694 Risk Proof (60) *(KOCunningham-Brown)* 8-6 DHolland (4) (lw: nvr nrr) ...... 4.6
3712 Young Sparkie *(RFJohnsonHoughton)* 8-2 WRyan (8) (lw: bhd fnl 2f) ...... nk.7
3712 Barley Cake *(WAO'Gorman)* 8-6 ‡³EmmaO'Gorman (5) (prom 4f) ...... 4.8
3824⁵ Sunnyview Lad *(PCHaslam)* 9-0 DaleGibson (7) (a bhd) ...... ³/₄.9
3712 Miss Piglet (IRE) *(RIngram)* 8-1 AMcGlone (11) (lw: a bhd) ...... 6.10

5/2 Risky Number, 7/2 Barley Cake(8/1—10/1), 4/1 KNOBBLEENEEZE(5/2—5/1), Chiltern Hundreds (USA), 6/1 Sunnyview Lad, 12/1 Samanthas Joy(op 7/1), 14/1 Risk Proof(op 7/1), Young Sparkie, 33/1 Ors. CSF £15.64, Tote £8.30: £2.80 £1.80 £1.40 (£7.00). Mr Anthony Andrews (UPPER LAMBOURN) bred by A. and Mrs Andrews. 10 Rn
1m 13.78 (3.18)
SF—18/10/7/–/–/–

**3928** GEMINI H'CAP (0-100) £2322.00 (£642.00: £306.00)
1¹/₄m (AWT)
2-20 (2-23)

3708³ Gilderdale (80) *(JWHills)* 10-8-12 MHills (4) (a.p: led ins fnl f: pushed out) ...... —1
3845⁶ Badawiah (70) *(WAO'Gorman)* 3-7-11⁽³⁾ DHolland (7) (b: a.p: led wl over 1f out tl ins fnl f: unable qckn) ...... 1¹/₂.2
3689 Absonal (65) *(RHannon)* 5-7-11 NAdams (2) (hld up: one pce fnl 2f) ...... 3.3
3293⁶ Vintage (83) *(MajorWRHern)* 7-9-1 JWilliams (1) (b: b.hind: hdwy over 3f out: one pce) ...... 3¹/₂.4
3835 Gueca Solo (76) *(DRLoder)* 4-8-8 AMunro (6) (prom over 8f) ...... s.h.5
3793 Predictable (63) *(MrsAKnight)* 6-7-9 JQuinn (5) (lw: led over 8f) ...... 1¹/₂.6
3763² Rapporteur (USA) (86) *(Fav)* *(CCElsey)* 6-9-1 ‡³DHarrison (9) (b: lw: a bhd) ...... 2.7
3237 Run Don't Fly (USA) (96) (bl) *(PFICole)* 6-10-0 TQuinn (8) (a bhd) ...... 12.8
3781 Canadian Capers (66) *(MRChannon)* 3-7-7 GBardwell (3) (prom 6f) ...... 2.9
LONG HANDICAP: Canadian Capers 7-3.

15/8 Rapporteur (USA)(5/2—13/8), 100/30 GILDERDALE(2/1—9/2), 9/2 Run Don't Fly (USA), 10/1 Canadian Capers, Predictable, Gueca Solo(6/1—12/1), 12/1 Vintage(8/1—14/1), 16/1 Ors. CSF £49.00, CT £696.97. Tote £4.30: £1.20 £4.50 £2.30 (£50.20). Abbott Racing Partners (LAMBOURN) bred by Mrs A. W. Kidd. 9 Rn
2m 4.58 (1.58)
SF—62/44/38/49/41/25

**3929** TAURUS H'CAP (0-70) £1297.50 (£360.00: £172.50)
1¹/₂m (AWT)
2-50 (2-55)

3770 **Snow Blizzard (53)** *(Fav)* *(SDow)* 4-8-11 TQuinn (12) (eyeshield: chsd ldr: hrd rdn over 1f out: led ins fnl f: r.o wl) ...... —1
3845 Slight Risk (66) *(PAKelleway)* 7-8-9 GBardwell (7) (eyecover: led: hrd rdn over 1f out: hdd ins fnl f: unable qckn) ...... 1.2
3409 Indian Territory (50) *(DHaydnJones)* 3-8-1 TyroneWilliams (5) (hdwy over 4f out: rdn over 3f out: one pce) ...... 1¹/₂.3
2944 Pleasure Ahead (37) *(MDixon)* 5-7-9 DaleGibson (13) (hdwy over 1f out: r.o wl ins fnl f) ...... 2¹/₂.4
3698⁴ Strat's Legacy (44) *(DWPArbuthnot)* 5-7-13 ‡³FNorton (1) (b.hind: hdwy over 3f out: one pce) ...... 1¹/₂.5
3853 Tudor Island (66) *(CEBrittain)* 3-8-12 ‡⁵BDoyle (14) (nvr nr to chal) ...... ³/₄.6
3863⁵ Milanese (64) *(DMorley)* 3-9-1 WRyan (8) (prom over 8f) ...... 7.7

38275 Hasty Spark (40) *(CFWall)* 4-7-12 DBiggs (10) (hdwy over 2f out: wknd wl over
1f out) ........................................................................................................ 1½.8
2867 Checkpoint Charlie (58) *(JMPEustace)* 7-9-2 MTebbutt (16) (b.hind: nvr nrr) .. hd.9
36002 Singing Reply (USA) (37) *(DMarks)* 4-7-2(2) ‡7ClaireBalding (15) (s.s: nvr nrr) nk.10
3806 Magnetic Point (USA) (47) *(AAScott)* 3-7-12 AMunro (3) (lw: prom over 9f) ...... 1.11
3221 Munday Dean (70) *(RJO'Sullivan)* 4-10-0 RPrice (11) (lw: a mid div) ............... ¾.12
Alreef (46) *(TThomsonJones)* 6-8-4 MHills (9) (bhd fnl 5f) ............................. ¾.13
3426 Carousel Music (50) *(JAkehurst)* 5-8-8 DMcKeown (6) (a bhd) ........................ 10.14
3627 Secret Treaty (IRE) (50) *(PWChapple-Hyam)* 3-8-1 DHolland (4) (prom over 7f) 10.15
38506 Ossie (43) *(BPalling)* 3-7-8 NAdams (2) (prom 6f) .............................................. 2.16

**4/1** SNOW BLIZZARD(6/1−3/1), **9/2** Strat's Legacy, **8/1** Hasty Spark, **9/1** Magnetic Point (USA), **10/1** Tudor
Island(op 6/1), Milanese, Secret Treaty (IRE)(op 5/1), **12/1** Indian Territory(op 8/1), **14/1** Carousel Music,
Munday Dean, Singing Reply (USA), **16/1** Checkpoint Charlie, **20/1** Pleasure Ahead, Alreef, **25/1** Slight Risk,
**33/1** Ossie. CSF £97.40, CT £1,064.57. Tote £4.20: £1.20: £8.30 £2.90 £4.80 (£58.50). Mr M. F. Kentish
(EPSOM) bred by M. F. Kentish. 16 Rn
2m 31.91 (2.51)
SF−48/52/33/22/23/34

---

**3930**          ARIES H'CAP (0-80) £1405.80 (£388.80: £185.40)     **2m (AWT)**     3-20 (3-23)
(Weights raised 8 lb)

34153 **Dime Bag (68)** (Fav) *(BWHills)* 3-9-10 DHolland (5) (hld up: led over 3f out:
easily) ........................................................................................................... −1
37706 Romanian (IRE) (43) *(RAkehurst)* 4-8-9 GCarter (6) (lw: hld up: chsd wnr over
1f out: no imp) .............................................................................................. 7.2
3157 Ghostly Glow (50) (v) *(CCElsey)* 3-8-3 ‡3DHarrison (7) (lw: a.p: led 6f out tl over
3f out: one pce) ........................................................................................... 1½.3
3490 Glenstal Priory (43) *(PFICole)* 5-8-9 TQuinn (8) (hld up: hrd rdn over 1f out: one
pce) .............................................................................................................. 3½.4
Sing the Blues (27) *(CJBenstead)* 8-7-7 JQuinn (4) (b: prom over 11f) ............ 1½.5
312 Cosmic Dancer (53) *(SPCWoods)* 5-9-5 WWoods (2) (a bhd) ........................ 6.6
38413 Rajanpour (USA) (34) (bl) *(RCurtis)* 7-8-0 GBardwell (3) (lw: led 10f) ............. 20.7
29703 Jokers Patch (52) *(BillyWilliams)* 5-9-4 NAdams (9) (b.off fore: lw: s.s: a bhd:
t.o) .............................................................................................................. dist.8

LONG HANDICAP: Sing the Blues 7-5.

**9/4** DIME BAG, **5/2** Romanian (IRE), **9/2** Rajanpour (USA)(3/1−5/1), **5/1** Glenstal Priory, **8/1** Ghostly Glow,
**16/1** Cosmic Dancer, Jokers Patch, **20/1** Sing the Blues. CSF £8.58, CT £35.32. Tote £2.90: £1.30 £2.20 £1.10
(£5.40). K. Al-Said (LAMBOURN) bred by Charlton Down Stud. 8 Rn
3m 25.49 (2.49)
SF−53/31/21/23/5/25

---

**3931**          SCORPIO H'CAP (0-70) £1245.00 (£345.00: £165.00)     **6f (AWT)**     3-50 (3-57)
(Weights raised 3 lb)

38403 **Boy Martin (63)** *(MJohnston)* 3-9-9 DMcKeown (5) (lw: a.p: rdn over 3f out: led
over 1f out: r.o wl) ...................................................................................... −1
3585 Banbury Flyer (45) *(MrsALMKing)* 4-8-6 AMunro (11) (hld up: hrd rdn over 1f
out: r.o) ....................................................................................................... 1½.2
37833 Noble Power (IRE) (64) *(BPalling)* 3-9-10 DBiggs (1) (lw: hdwy over 2f out: ev
ch over 1f out: unable qckn) ....................................................................... ½.3
37002 Kissavos (58) (v) *(CCElsey)* 6-9-5 TQuinn (6) (b.hind: lw: a.p: rdn over 2f out:
hmpd wl over 1f out: r.o ins fnl f) ................................................................. nk.4
3766 Mogwai (IRE) (63) (bl) *(RFJohnsonHoughton)* 3-9-9 WRyan (2) (hdwy over 1f
out: r.o) ....................................................................................................... nk.5
3870 Tyrone Flyer (61) *(MissGayKelleway)* 3-9-2 ‡5StephenDavies (4) (led over 2f:
ev ch over 1f out: wknd fnl f) ...................................................................... 3.6
3766 Gemini Bay (50) (bl) *(RVoorspuy)* 3-8-10 SDawson (9) (nvr nr to chal) ........... 1.7
38196 Furiella (61) (Fav) *(PCHaslam)* 4-9-8 DaleGibson (3) (prom over 3f) ............... 1.8
38404 Dam Certain (IRE) (45) *(AWDenson)* 3-8-2 ‡3DHarrison (13) (outpcd) ............ ½.9
3747 Speedy Classic (USA) (52) *(MJHeaton-Ellis)* 3-8-12 MHills (14) (prom 3f) ...... 2.10
37034 Waverley Star (52) *(KOCunningham-Brown)* 7-8-13 DHolland (10) (bhd fnl 2f) 2.11
33186 Pendor Dancer (50) (bl) *(BForsey)* 9-8-11 JWilliams (7) (outpcd) .................... ½.12
1685 Cellito (IRE) (53) (bl) *(WAO'Gorman)* 3-8-10 ‡EmmaO'Gorman (12) (a bhd) ... 4.13
2614 Brisas (56) (bl) *(TFairhurst)* 5-9-3 JFanning (8) (w ldr: led over 3f out tl over 1f
out: sn wknd) .............................................................................................. ½.14

**11/4** Furiella, **9/2** Kissavos, **6/1** Tyrone Flyer, Waverley Star, **7/1** Banbury Flyer, BOY MARTIN, **10/1** Mogwai
(IRE), **12/1** Noble Power (IRE), Dam Certain (IRE)(op 6/1), **14/1** Cellito (IRE), **20/1** Speedy Classic (USA),
Pendor Dancer, Brisas, **33/1** Gemini Bay. CSF £61.86, CT £566.32. Tote £8.20: £3.30 £2.30 £3.60 (£43.20).
Laharna Ltd (MIDDLEHAM) bred by Laharna Ltd. 14 Rn
1m 13.12 (2.52)
SF−53/30/46/40/43/24

T/Plpt: £66.90 (16.8 Tckts).                                              AK

3733a—**SAINT-CLOUD (L-H)**
**Monday, October 26th [Soft]**
Going Allowance: 0.70 sec per fur (S)

**3932a**     PRIX THOMAS BYRON (Gp 3) (2-Y.O.C & G) £25800.00     1m

  **Mil Foil (FR)** *(France)* 2–8–9 MBoutin ....................................................................—1
3651a⁵ Kingmambo (USA) *(France)* 2–8–9 FHead .................................................... ¹/₂.2
  Berdansk (USA) *(France)* 2–8–9 TJarnet ................................................................ 2.3
Tote 3.60f: 1.70f 1.50f (SF: 16.00f). Mr H.C.Seymour (J.E.Pease,FRANCE) bred by Mrs R.M.Pease in France. 6
Rn
                   1m 48.7 (10.1)
                   SF—28/26/20

**SAINT-CLOUD (L-H)**
**Saturday, October 31st [Soft]**
Going Allowance: 0.80 sec per fur (S)

**3933a**     PRIX DE FLORE (Gp 3) (F & M) £20640.00     1¹/₄m 110y

3658a⁴ **Sporades (USA)** *(France)* 3–8–9 SGuillot ......................................................—1
3814a² Fabulous Hostess (USA) *(France)* 4–9–2 ODoleuze ................................... s.nk.2
 641a² La Tirana (FR) *(France)* 5–8–11 WMongil .................................................... 3.3
Tote 6.60f: 1.30f 1.10f 1.60f (3.80f). Mr Paul de Moussac (A.Fabre,FRANCE) bred by Maylands Stud Ltd. in USA.
9 Rn
                   2m 21.2 (10.9)
                   SF—70/76/65

3890a—**SAN SIRO (R-H)**
**Saturday, October 31st [Heavy]**

**3934a**     PREMIO CARLO PORTA (Gp 3)     £27907.00     1¹/₄m

3652a⁶ **KNIFEBOX (USA)** *(JHMGosden)* 4–9–3 DHolland ..................................—1
1231a⁴ Funny Baby (FR) *(France)* 4–9–0 ABadel ...................................................... 2.2
2628a★ Guado d'Annibale (IRE) *(Italy)* 3–8–10 JacquelineFreda ............................. 4.3
3337a⁶ CAPTAIN HORATIUS (IRE) *(JLDunlop)* 3–9–3 JCarroll ........................... 6¹/₂.4
3652a⁴ HALF A TICK (USA) *(PFICole)* 4–9–0 CRutter (btn further 3l) ......................... 6
Tote 54L: 17L 13L 17L (48L). Sheikh Mohammed (NEWMARKET) bred by Barbara Hunter in USA. 11 Rn
                   2m 12

**GULFSTREAM PARK (L-H)**
**Saturday, October 31st [Turf Firm, Dirt Fast]**

**3935a**     BREEDERS' CUP SPRINT (Grade 1)     £267380.00     6f (dirt)

  **Thirty Slews (USA)** *(America)* 5–9–0 EDelahoussaye (chsd ldr: r.o wl to ld nr fin) —1
  Meafara (USA) (bl) *(America)* 3–8–8 JVelasquez (led tl nr fin: r.o) ..................... nk.2
3647a★ Rubiano (USA) (Fav) *(America)* 5–9–0 JulieKrone (hld up: gd hdwy fnl f: nrst fin) 3.3
3647a² SHEIKH ALBADOU *(AAScott)* 4–9–0 WRSwinburn (a.p: styd on fnl f) ............ nose.4
3656a³ ELBIO (bl) *(PJMakin)* 5–9–0 PatEddery (s.s: sn prom: kpt on fnl f) .................. 1.5
  King Corrie (CAN) *(Canada)* 4–9–0 DPenna (bhd tl r.o wl fnl f: nvr nrr) ............ ¹/₂.6
  Arrowtown (USA) (bl) *(America)* 4–9–0 LPincay (in tch: one pce fnl 2f) ............... ¹/₂.7
  Senor Speedy (USA) (bl) *(America)* 4–9–0 JChavez (wl bhd tl r.o wl fnl f: nvr nrr) 1.8
  Superstrike *(America)* 3–8–11 DSorensen (chsd ldrs over 4f) ............................ 1.9
  Furiously (USA) *(America)* 3–8–11 JBailey (a bhd) ................................. 1.10
  Gray Slewpy (USA) *(America)* 4–9–0 KDesormeaux (spd 4f) .......................... ¹/₂.11
 1060⁵ Cardmania (USA) *(America)* 6–9–0 CMcCarron (a bhd) ............................... nk.12
3647a³ Salt Lake (USA) *(America)* 3–8–11 MSmith (a bhd) ..................................... 2.13
3656a★ MR BROOKS *(RHannon)* 5–9–0 LPiggott (mid div tl faltered & fell 2f out: dead) ...... 0

21/10 Rubiano (USA), 3/1 Sheikh Albadou, 7/1 Salt Lake (USA), 71/10 Mr Brooks, 13/1 Gray Slewpy (USA),
138/10 Meafara (USA), 17/1 Senor Speedy (USA), 18/1 Superstrike, 187/10 THIRTY SLEWS (USA), 22/1
Furiously (USA), 25/1 King Corrie (CAN), 32/1 Ors. Tote 39.40 (1-2) 19.40 13.80 (1-2-3) 8.00 6.40 3.20. Mr
M.Degroot, Dutch Masters III & Mr M.Pegram (B.Baffert,AMERICA) bred by Grousemont Stud in USA. 14 Rn
                   1m 8.2

**3936a**     BREEDERS' CUP JUVENILE (Grade 1) (2-Y.O.F) £267380.00     1m 110y (dirt)

  **Eliza (USA)** (Fav) *(America)* 2–8–7 PValenzuela (a.p: led on bit 4f out: rdn 2f
    out: r.o wl) ...........................................................................................—1

|  | Educated Risk (USA) *(America)* 2-8-7 JBailey (chsd ldr: ev ch fnl f: r.o) | 1.2 |
|  | Boots 'N Jackie (USA) *(America)* 2-8-7 MLee (bhd tl swtchd & hdwy on ins fnl f: fin fast) | ½.3 |
|  | Supah Gem (USA) *(America)* 2-8-7 SMadrid (chsd ldrs: kpt on fnl f) | 5½.4 |
|  | Beal Street Blues (USA) *(America)* 2-8-7 PDay (bhd tl r.o wl fnl f) | nose.5 |
| 2981a | Creaking Board *(France)* 2-8-7 CAsmussen (bhd tl styd on fnl f) | 1½.6 |
|  | Zoonaqua (USA) *(America)* 2-8-7 CMcCarron (chsd ldrs tl wknd fnl f) | 1.7 |
|  | Liberada (USA) *(America)* 2-8-7 RHernandez (a mid div) | 1.8 |
|  | Booly (USA) (bl) *(America)* 2-8-7 EPrado (nvr nr to chal) | 1½.9 |
| 3655a³ | LOVE OF SILVER (USA) *(CEBrittain)* 2-8-7 MRoberts (chsd ldrs tl wknd 3f out) | 7.10 |
|  | Set Them Free (USA) *(America)* 2-8-7 EDelahoussaye (led over 4f: sn wknd) | nk.11 |
|  | Turkstand (USA) *(America)* 2-8-7 FAlvarado (a bhd) | 1.12 |

**6/5** ELIZA (USA), **4/1** Beal Street Blues (USA), **49/10** Zoonaqua (USA), Set Them Free (USA), **52/10** Educated Risk (USA), **71/10** Turkstand (USA), **15/1** Boots 'N Jackie (USA), **35/1** Love of Silver (USA), **68/1** Booly (USA), **76/1** Supah Gem (USA), **138/1** Creaking Board (USA), **172/1** Liberada (USA). Tote 4.40 (1-2) 3.20 4.80 (1-2-3) 2.60 3.80 4.40. Mr Allen E.Paulson (A.Hassinger Jnr,America) bred by Allen E.Paulson in USA. 12 Rn　　1m 42.8

## 3937a

BREEDERS' CUP DISTAFF (Grade 1) (F & M) £367860.00　　**1m 1f (dirt)**

|  | **Paseana (ARG)** *(America)* 5-8-11 CMcCarron (racd wd: w ldrs: led 2f out: r.o wl) | —1 |
|  | Versailles Treaty (USA) *(America)* 4-8-11 MSmith (chsd ldrs: hdwy over 1f out: no ex fnl f) | 4.2 |
|  | Magical Maiden (USA) *(America)* 3-8-7 GStevens (chsd ldrs: r.o fnl f) | ½.3 |
|  | Queen of Triumph (USA) *(America)* 3-8-7 JChavez (broke wl: chsd ldrs: styd on fnl f) | 1½.4 |
| 3443 | MARLING (IRE) *(GWragg)* 3-8-7 WRSwinburn (swtchd lft s: mid div: outpcd 3f out: rdn & n.m.r over 2f out: styd on wl fnl f) | nk.5 |
|  | Lite Light (USA) *(America)* 4-8-11 EDelahoussaye (chsd ldrs: kpt on fnl f) | ½.6 |
|  | Meadow Star (USA) *(America)* 4-8-11 PDay (hld up & bhd: sme hdwy fnl f: nvr nrr) | 1.7 |
| 21a* | Exchange (CAN) *(America)* 4-8-11 LPincay (bhd tl sme late hdwy) | 1½.8 |
|  | Fowda (USA) *(America)* 4-8-11 PValenzuela (w ldrs tl wknd fnl f) | nk.9 |
| 3664³ | CULTURE VULTURE (USA) *(PFICole)* 3-8-7 TQuinn (mid div: no hdwy fnl 2f) | ½.11 |
|  | Shared Interest (USA) *(America)* 4-8-11 JulieKrone (hld up: hdwy 2f out: wknd fnl f) | 1½.11 |
|  | Saratoga Dew (Fav) *(America)* 3-8-7 HMcCauley (led 7f: sn wknd) | 2.12 |
|  | Diamond Duo (USA) (bl) *(America)* 3-8-7 TTurner (a bhd) | 12.13 |
|  | Harbour Club (USA) *(America)* 5-8-11 JBailey (chsd ldrs tl wknd 2f out) | 1½.14 |

**2/1** Saratoga Dew (USA), **27/10** Exchange (CAN), PASEANA (ARG), **37/10** Versailles Treaty (USA), **83/10** Fowda (USA), **17/2** Marling (IRE), **15/1** Lite Light (USA), **31/1** Magical Maiden (USA), **36/1** Harbour Club (USA), **37/1** Meadow Star (USA), **44/1** Shared Interest (USA), **48/1** Culture Vulture (USA), **50/1** Ors. Tote 7.40 (cpld) (1-2) 3.80 4.00 (1-2-3) 3.00 3.20 8.60. Mr Sidney H.Craig (R.McAnally,AMERICA) bred by Haras Vacacion in Argentina. 14 Rn　　1m 48

## 3938a

BREEDERS' CUP MILE (Grade 1) £267380.00　　**1m (turf)**

|  | **Lure (USA)** *(America)* 3-8-10 MSmith (mde all: clr fnl f: easily) | —1 |
| 3322a² | Paradise Creek (USA) *(America)* 3-8-10 PDay (mid div tl hdwy 1f out: r.o wl) | 3.2 |
| 3443² | Brief Truce (USA) (bl) *(Ireland)* 3-8-10 MJKinane (s.s: hld up & bhd: gd hdwy fnl f: fin wl) | nk.3 |
|  | Val des Bois (USA) *(America)* 6-9-0 EDelahoussaye (bhd tl hdwy over 1f out: r.o wl fnl f: nrst fin) | 1½.4 |
| 3715* | SELKIRK (USA) *(IABalding)* 4-9-0 RCochrane (s.s: mid div: hdwy 1f out: nvr able to chal) | ½.5 |
|  | Luthier Enchanteur (USA) *(America)* 4-9-0 KDesormeaux (w ldrs tl one pce fnl f) | 1.6 |
|  | Forty Niner Days (USA) *(America)* 5-9-0 CNakatani (w ldr tl one pce fnl f) | 1½.7 |
| 3229a⁴ | Exit to Nowhere (USA) *(America)* 4-9-0 FHead (hld up: hdwy & n.m.r over 1f out: hmpd on ins 1f out: nt rcvr) | nose.8 |
|  | Fourstars Allstar (USA) *(America)* 4-9-0 JBailey (chsd ldrs tl wknd fnl f) | hd.9 |
|  | Lotus Pool (USA) (bl) *(America)* 5-9-0 CWoods (in tch tl wknd fnl f) | nose.10 |
| 3654a* | Arazi (USA) (Fav) *(France)* 3-8-10 PValenzuela (chsd ldrs on ins tl wknd qckly 1f out) | 1.11 |
| 3811a³ | Cardoun (FR) *(France)* 3-8-10 CAntley (hld up: bdly hmpd 3f out: nt rcvr) | 4.12 |
|  | Thunder Regent (CAN) *(America)* 5-9-0 CLopez (nvr nr ldrs) | nk.13 |
| 6a² | Bistro Garden (USA) *(America)* 4-9-0 CMcCarron (a bhd) | 4.14 |

**6/4** Arazi (USA), **38/10** Selkirk (USA), **54/10** LURE (USA), **82/10** Brief Truce (USA), **98/10** Lotus Pool (USA), **13/1** Exit to Nowhere (USA), **14/1** Val des Bois (USA), Luthier Enchanteur (USA), **20/1** Forty Niner Days (USA), **30/1** Paradise Creek (USA), Cardoun (FR), **42/1** Bistro Garden (USA), **66/1** Fourstars Allstar (USA), **75/1** Thunder Regent (CAN). Tote 12.80 (1-2) 6.40 17.60 (1-2-3) 4.60 7.80 5.00. Claiborne Farm (C.McGaughey,AMERICA) bred by Claiborne Farm & Gamely Corporation in USA. 14 Rn　　1m 32.8

## 3939a

BREEDERS' CUP JUVENILE (Grade 1) (2-Y.O.C & G) £269380.00    **1m 110y (dirt)**

| | | |
|---|---|---|
| | **Gilded Time (USA)** (Fav) *(America)* 2-8-10 CMcCarron (prom on outside: hdwy to chal 1f out: led ins fnl f: r.o wl) | —1 |
| | It'sali'Iknownfact (USA) *(America)* 2-8-10 LPincay (bhd tl rapid hdwy fnl f: fin wl) | ¾.2 |
| | River Special (USA) *(America)* 2-8-10 KDesormeaux (a.p: led over 1f out tl ins fnl f: no ex nr fin) | ½.3 |
| | Living Vicariously (USA) *(America)* 2-8-10 HMcCauley (chsd ldrs: hdwy over 1f out: no ex ins fnl f) | 5.4 |
| | Mountain Cat (USA) *(America)* 2-8-10 PDay (wl bhd tl r.o wl fnl f: nvr nr to chal) | hd.5 |
| | Caponostro (USA) *(America)* 2-8-10 JChavez (prom: led 2f out: sn hdd: one pce) | 1.6 |
| | Sea Hero (USA) (bl) *(America)* 2-8-10 JBailey (chsd ldrs: one pce fnl f) | 1½.7 |
| | Strolling Along (USA) (bl) *(America)* 2-8-10 CAntley (a mid div) | 3.8 |
| 3561a² | Devil's Rock (USA) *(France)* 2-8-10 PatEddery (bhd tl sme late hdwy) | nk.9 |
| | Secret Odds (USA) *(America)* 2-8-10 GStevens (led over 6f: sn wknd) | nose.10 |
| | Fight for Love (USA) *(America)* 2-8-10 CPerret (a bhd) | 6½.11 |
| 3722³ | FIRM PLEDGE (USA) *(PFlCole)* 2-8-10 AMunro (chsd ldrs on ins tl wknd 2f out) | 1.12 |
| | Sudden Hush (USA) *(America)* 2-8-10 PValenzuela (s.i.s: a bhd) | 7.13 |

2/1 GILDED TIME (USA), 24/10 Sea Hero (USA), 32/10 River Special (USA), 42/10 Mountain Cat (USA), 20/1 Strolling Along (USA), 29/1 Devil's Rock (USA), Secret Odds (USA), Fight for Love (USA), 38/1 Firm Pledge (USA), 47/1 It'sali'Iknownfact (USA), 49/1 Sudden Hush (USA), 52/1 Caponostro (USA), 59/1 Living Vicariously (USA). Tote 6.00 (1-2) 4.40 21.00 (1-2-3) 3.60 9.40 4.20. Mr D.Milch (D.Vienna,AMERICA) bred by Harry T.Mangurian in USA. 13 Rn
1m 43.4

## 3940a

BREEDERS' CUP TURF (Grade 1)    £534759.00    **1½m (turf)**

| | | |
|---|---|---|
| 3648a² | **Fraise (USA)** (bl) *(America)* 4-9-0 PValenzuela (bhd: hdwy on ins over 2f out: swtchd lft appr fnl f: str run to ld nr fin) | —1 |
| 3648a* | Sky Classic (CAN) (Fav) *(Canada)* 5-9-0 PDay (trckd ldrs: hdwy to ld 1f out: hdd & no ex nr fin) | nose.2 |
| | Quest for Fame (USA) *(America)* 5-9-0 PatEddery (hld up & bhd: hdwy 2f out: r.o wl fnl f) | 2.3 |
| 3657a⁶ | DR DEVIOUS (IRE) *(PWChapple-Hyam)* 3-8-9 JReid (trckd ldrs on ins: lost pl 5f out: hdwy over 2f out: kpt on fnl f) | 1.4 |
| 3657a* | Subotica (FR) *(France)* 4-9-0 TJarnet (mid div: hdwy 3f out: one pce fnl f) | ½.5 |
| 3658a | Trishyde (USA) *(France)* 3-8-6 FHead (hld up: nvr nr to chal) | 2.6 |
| | Navarone (USA) *(America)* 4-9-0 CMcCarron (chsd ldrs: jnd ldr 6f out: led appr fnl f: sn hdd & wknd) | ½.7 |
| 2622a³ | Daros (bl) *(America)* 3-8-9 EDelahoussaye (w ldr: led 6f out tl appr fnl f: wknd qckly) | 4½.8 |
| 3730 | CORRUPT (USA) *(PWChapple-Hyam)* 4-9-0 MRoberts (mid div: rdn 4f out: sn bhd) | 12½.9 |
| 3648a³ | Solar Splendor (USA) *(America)* 5-9-0 HMcCauley (led 6f: chsd ldrs tl wknd 2f out) | 3½.10 |

9/10 Sky Classic (CAN), 33/10 Navarone (USA), 15/2 Subotica (FR), 91/10 Dr Devious (IRE), 10/1 Solar Splendor (USA), 14/1 FRAISE (USA), 17/1 Quest for Fame (USA), 42/1 Daros (USA), 79/1 Trishyde (USA), 118/1 Corrupt (USA). Tote 30.00 (1-2) 6.40 2.80 (1-2-3) 4.80 2.40 5.60. Mrs Allen E.Paulson (W.Mott,AMERICA) bred by Allen E.Paulson in USA. 10 Rn
2m 24

## 3941a

BREEDERS' CUP CLASSIC (Grade 1)    £829787.00    **1¼m (dirt)**

| | | |
|---|---|---|
| 1355a* | **A P Indy (USA)** (Fav) *(America)* 3-8-9 EDelahoussaye (hld up: hdwy on ins over 1f out: led 1f out: r.o wl) | —1 |
| | Pleasant Tap (USA) *(America)* 4-9-0 GStevens (hld up: hdwy over 1f out: styd on wl ins fnl f) | 2.2 |
| 3657a | Jolypha (USA) *(France)* 3-8-6 PatEddery (mid div: lost pl 2f out: styd on wl fnl f) | ½.3 |
| | Reign Road (USA) (bl) *(America)* 4-9-0 KDesormeaux (wl bhd tl gd hdwy fnl 2f) | 1½.4 |
| | Sultry Song (USA) (bl) *(America)* 4-9-0 JBailey (prom: r.o one pce fnl f) | nk.5 |
| | Defensive Play (USA) (bl) *(America)* 5-9-0 PDay (trckd ldrs: led over 1f out: sn hdd & wknd) | hd.6 |
| | Thunder Rumble (USA) *(America)* 3-8-9 HMcCauley (led over 8f: sn wknd) | 1½.7 |
| | Strike The Gold (USA) *(America)* 4-8-9 CPerret (sn wl bhd: hdwy over 1f out: nvr nrr) | 5½.8 |
| | Twilight Agenda (USA) (bl) *(America)* 5-9-0 CMcCarron (hld up: hmpd 3f out: nt rcvr) | nk.9 |
| | Jolie's Halo (USA) *(America)* 5-9-0 EPrado (w ldr tl wknd over 1f out) | 3.10 |
| | Marquetry (USA) (bl) *(America)* 5-9-0 DFlores (hld up on outside: no hdwy fnl 2f) | 1½.11 |
| 3812a* | ZOMAN (USA) *(PFlCole)* 5-9-0 AMunro (mid div tl wknd over 1f out) | 3.12 |
| | Technology (USA) *(America)* 3-8-9 LPincay (trckd ldrs tl wknd 2f out) | 2½.13 |

3730* RODRIGO DE TRIANO (USA) *(PWChapple-Hyam)* 3-8-9 WRSwinburn (a bhd: nvr nr to chal) .................................................................................. 12.14

21/10 A P INDY (USA), 5/2 Pleasant Tap (USA), 59/10 Sultry Song (USA), 62/10 Rodrigo de Triano (USA), 77/10 Strike The Gold (USA), 15/1 Twilight Agenda (USA), 16/1 Marquetry (USA), Jolypha (USA), Defensive Play (USA), 37/1 Technology (USA), 38/1 Reign Road (USA), 41/1 Thunder Rumble (USA), 70/1 Jolie's Halo (USA), 75/1 Zoman (USA). Tote 6.20 (1-2) 3.40 3.20 (1-2-3) 2.80 2.80 3.80. T.Tsurumaki, W.S.Farish, W.S.Kilroy & H.Good (N.Drysdale,AMERICA) bred by W. S. Farish & W. S. Kilroy in USA. 14 Rn    2m 0.2

## GULFSTREAM PARK (L-H)
### Sunday, November 1st [Firm]

**3942a**    THE PEEBLES (Allowance Race) (F & M) £16043.00    1m 110y (turf)

      **Explosive Kate (USA)** *(America)* 5-8-5 CPerret ................................ —1
35734 STORM DOVE (USA) *(RCharlton)* 3-8-0 MSmith ................................ nk.2
      Little Whitey (USA) *(America)* 4-8-2 JDuarte ................................ 2½.3
Tote 4.40 (1-2) 2.60 4.20 (1-2-3) 2.40 3.40 4.20. Mr Richard L.Duchossois (L.M.Goldfine,AMERICA) bred by Hill 'N' Dale in USA. 10 Rn    1m 40.8

**3943a**    GAILY GAILY H'CAP (F & M) £80214.00    1½m (turf)

      **Rougeur (USA)** *(France)* 3-8-0 MSmith ................................ —1
36494² Good to Dance (IRE) *(France)* 3-8-1 TJarnet ................................ 1½.2
      Indian Chris (BRZ) *(America)* 3-8-1 GAlmeida ................................ 1½.3
3670² ANNA OF SAXONY *(JHMGosden)* 3-8-3(2) JReid (btn further 5¼al) ....... 11
3546* RED SLIPPERS (USA) *(LMCumani)* 3-8-2 MRoberts (btn 10¾al by wnr) ...... 12
Tote 37.00 (1-2) 16.20 12.60 (1-2-3) 10.00 9.20 5.20. Juddmonte Farms (A.Fabre,FRANCE) bred by Juddmonte Farms in USA. 13 Rn    2m 26.4

**3944a**    STEINLEN H'CAP    £80214.00    1m 110y (turf)

      **Roman Envoy (USA)** *(America)* 4-8-8 CPerret ................................ —1
      Bidding Proud (USA) *(America)* 3-8-3 NSantagata ................................ 4.2
35462 FEMININE WILES (IRE) *(PWChapple-Hyam)* 3-8-0 AMunro ................................ nose.3
Tote 3.20 (1-2) 2.60 8.60 (1-2-3) 2.40 5.00 10.80. Mr F.W.Hooper (J.E.Picou,AMERICA) bred by F.W.Hooper in USA. 10 Rn    1m 39.2

### 3565a—CAPANNELLE (L-H)
### Sunday, November 1st [Heavy]

**3945a**    PREMIO LE MARMORE (listed race) (2-Y.O) £20930.00    1m 1f

3735a³ WOOTTON RIVERS (USA) *(PWChapple-Hyam)* 2-8-7 DHolland ................ —1
      Mad Martingan *(Italy)* 2-8-7 JacquelineFreda ................................ 1½.2
3883a* FUTURBALLA *(JLDunlop)* 2-8-10 TQuinn ................................ nk.3
Tote 31L: 13L 17L 12L (329L). Mr R.E.Sangster (MARLBOROUGH) bred by Swettenham Stud in USA. 10 Rn    1m 55.4

### 3818—DONCASTER (L-H)
### Friday, November 6th [Good]
Going Allowance: 0.40 sec per fur (G)    Wind: fresh against

Stalls: high

**3946**    E.B.F. DUNKIRK STKS (I) (Mdn 2-Y.O) £2782.50 (£770.00: £367.50)    6f 1-00 (1-01)

3832⁵ **Southern Memories (IRE) (73)** *(RHannon)* 9-0 JReid (2) (hld up: hdwy 2f out: led appr fnl f: edgd rt ins fnl f: r.o) ................................ —1
3719² Nafuth (USA) (Fav) *(PTWalwyn)* 9-0 WCarson (6) (lw: chsd ldrs: effrt & ev ch appr fnl f: sn rdn: unable qckn) ................................ 2.2
3764 Murphy's Hope (IRE) *(MJHeaton-Ellis)* 9-0 WRyan (1) (prom: ev ch 2f out: one pce) ................................ 3.3
    Jalib (IRE) *(CJBenstead)* 9-0 RHills (5) (w'like: lengthy: bit bkwd: bhd: sn drvn along: styd on fnl f) ................................ 3.4
    Chilly Breeze *(SirMarkPrescott)* 8-9 GDuffield (9) (w'like: leggy: sn chsng ldrs: pushed along after 2f: outpcd fnl f) ................................ ½.5
3704 Gold Fort *(BWMurray)* 9-0 JFortune (3) (sn pushed along: outpcd fnl 2f) ........ 3½.6
2346 Red Admiral *(PCHaslam)* 9-0 DaleGibson (3) (mde most tl appr fnl f: sn rdn & btn) ................................ 1.7
3892 Poleden (USA) *(AAScott)* 9-0 MHills (8) (a in rr: rdn 2f out: no imp) ................ nk.8

2709 New Rhythm *(GHEden)* 9-0 GCarter (4) (s.i.s: a in rr: t.o) ................................. 30.9

**4/11** Nafuth (USA), **6/1** SOUTHERN MEMORIES (IRE), **11/1** Chilly Breeze, **12/1** Poleden (USA)(7/1—14/1), **20/1** Jalib (IRE), **25/1** Red Admiral, **66/1** Ors. CSF £8.25, Tote £7.80: £1.90 £1.00 £15.60 (£2.70). Mr Jim Horgan (MARLBOROUGH) bred by Jim Horgan in Ireland. 9 Rn

1m 17.66 (6.66)
SF—15/7/–/–/–/–

## 3947    WESTERN DESERT (S) H'CAP (3 & 4-Y.O) (0-60) £2784.00 (£774.00: £372.00)
1m (rnd)
1-30 (1-31)

3771⁴ **Mexican Dancer (43)** *(PGMurphy)* 3–8-1 ‡⁷SDrowne (8) (hld up: hdwy 2f out:
qcknd to ld nr fin) .................................................................................................... —1

3912⁵ Essayeffsee *(47)* (bl) *(MHEasterby)* 3–8-9 ‡³SMaloney (19) (b.hind: chsd ldrs:
rdn to ld over 1f out: hdd & no ex nr fin) ......................................................... 1.2

3494⁶ Speed Oil *(46)* (v) *(RBastiman)* 3–8-4⁽⁵⁾ ‡⁷HBastiman (7) (plld hrd: hld up: hdwy
2f out: rdn & r.o ins fnl f) ......................................................................................... 1.3

3421 Time Lapse *(58)* *(PJMakin)* 3–9-9 AMunro (14) (hld up: effrt over 2f out: unable
qckn fnl f) .................................................................................................................. 1¹/₂.4

3696 Sirmoor (IRE) *(52)* (v) *(RHannon)* 3–9-3 BRaymond (17) (w ldrs tl rdn & btn 1f
out) ............................................................................................................................. 1¹/₂.5

3732 May Square (IRE) *(51)* *(MrsAKnight)* 4–8-12 ‡⁷SWynne (9) (chsd ldrs: led over
2f out tl over 1f out: hrd rdn & wknd fnl f) ......................................................... ³/₄.6

3771* Eiras Mood *(51)* *(BPalling)* 3–8-11 ‡⁵StephenDavies (6) (r.o appr fnl f: nvr nrr) 1¹/₂.7

3827* Friendlypersuasion (IRE) *(58)* *(RHollinshead)* 4–9-12 WRyan (11) (bhd: hdwy
on outside 3f out: edgd lft & r.o) ............................................................................ 2.8

3616 Glasgow *(58)* *(EJAlston)* 3–9-5 DHolland (1) (bhd: swtchd 3f out: nt rch ldrs) .. hd.9

1663 Super-Sub *(46)* *(GFleming)* 3–8-11 PRobinson (10) (chsd ldrs 5f) ..................... ³/₄.10

3827⁶ Taunting (IRE) *(54)* *(MBlanshard)* 4–9-8 JReid (3) (prom over 5f) ....................... 2.11

3771³ Sir Norman Holt (IRE) *(54)* (bl) *(Jt-Fav)* *(FHLee)* 3–9-5 WCarson (4) (led over 5f:
hrd rdn & wknd over 1f out) .................................................................................... hd.12

3629³ Emerald Ears *(41)* *(RJHodges)* 3–8-1 TQuinn (15) (prom tl wknd over 2f out) ³/₄.13

3264 The Cuckoo's Nest *(58)* (bl) *(MWilliams)* 4–9-12 JWilliams (20) (hdwy 3f out:
rdn & wknd appr fnl f) .............................................................................................. ¹/₂.14

3771 Cappahoosh *(47)* *(HJCollinridge)* 3–8-12 MRoberts (16) (hmpd over 1f
out: n.d) ....................................................................................................................... hd.15

3707 State Governor *(39)* *(DWChapman)* 4–8-7 SWood (12) (chsd ldrs 5f) .............. hd.16

3421 Shalou *(49)* *(RJHodges)* 3–9-0 JQuinn (5) (effrt u.p 3f out: n.d) ....................... 2¹/₂.17

397 Dashing April *(41)* *(DTThom)* 4–8-9 DBiggs (13) (m.n.s) ................................. 6.18

Mitsubishi Centre (IRE) *(52)* *(APStringer)* 3–9-3 JFortune (2) (s.s: a wl bhd) ....... 19

3771⁵ Broad Appeal *(44)* (bl) *(Jt-Fav)* *(RCSpicer)* 4–8-5 ‡⁷AGarth (18) (ref to r: t.n.p) ...... 0

**6/1** Broad Appeal, Sir Norman Holt (IRE), **7/1** Eiras Mood, **10/1** MEXICAN DANCER, Friendlypersuasion (IRE),
**11/1** Cappahoosh (IRE), Taunting (IRE), **12/1** Time Lapse, Essayeffsee, Speed Oil, **14/1** Emerald Ears, Sirmoor
(IRE), May Square (IRE), Glasgow, **20/1** The Cuckoo's Nest, **25/1** Shalou, **33/1** Ors. CSF £128.36, CT
£1,359.49. Tote £12.20: £2.50 £2.40 £3.50 £4.30 (£165.40). Mrs Y. Moffatt (BRISTOL) bred by L. K. McCreery.
20 Rn; No bid

1m 44.40 (8.10)
SF—13/18/10/24/13/6

## 3948    E.B.F. DUNKIRK STKS (II) (Mdn 2-Y.O) £2782.50 (£770.00: £367.50)    6f 2-00 (2-03)

3716 **Easy Access (IRE) (78)** (Fav) *(RHannon)* 9-0 JReid (2) (hld up in tch: led ins fnl
f: rdn out) ................................................................................................................... —1

Alyakkh (IRE) *(HThomsonJones)* 8-9 RHills (1) (lt-f: a.p: led over 1f out tl ins fnl
f: rallied gamely nr fin) ............................................................................................. s.h.2

3848² Quinsigimond *(74)* *(SirMarkPrescott)* 8-9 GDuffield (11) (led wl over 3f out tl
over 1f out: no ex) ..................................................................................................... 5.3

Meesons (IRE) *(CBBBooth)* 8-9 GOldroyd (7) (leggy: scope: hdwy 2f out: nrst
fin) ............................................................................................................................... 4.4

3846 Sense of Humour *(JWPayne)* 8-9 AMunro (5) (s.i.s: hdwy ¹/₂-wy: no imp appr fnl
f) .................................................................................................................................. 1¹/₂.5

Doctor-J (IRE) *(MJHeaton-Ellis)* 9-0 GCarter (9) (cmpt: chsd ldrs: outpcd fnl 2f) 3.6

3848 Nikitria *(MissAJWhitfield)* 8-4 ‡⁵ATucker (3) (led over 2f: wknd over 2f out) 1¹/₂.7

3782⁵ Correspondence (CAN) (v) *(JHMGoodson)* 9-0 WCarson (10) (prom 3f: sn
outpcd) ....................................................................................................................... ³/₄.8

3685 Stage Artist *(JEtherington)* 8-9 NConnorton (8) (a bhd) .................................. nk.9

Needwood Nugget *(BCMorgan)* 9-0 GBardwell (6) (neat: unf: bkwd: a bhd: t.o) 8.10

3117⁵ Safe Bid *(RHollinshead)* 8-9 WRyan (4) (unruly s: dwlt: a bhd: t.o) .................. 1.11

**5/2** EASY ACCESS (IRE)(5/1—9/4), **7/2** Alyakkh (IRE)(op 7/4), Quinsigimond(5/2—4/1), **8/1** Safe Bid(op 11/2),
Correspondence (CAN), **16/1** Doctor-J (IRE), **25/1** Meesons (IRE), **33/1** Sense of Humour, Needwood Nugget,
**50/1** Ors. CSF £10.74, Tote £3.20: £1.30 £1.80 £1.30 (£6.70). Mr N. Ahamad (MARLBOROUGH) bred by
Swettenham Stud in Ireland. 11 Rn

1m 17.46 (6.46)
SF—19/13/–/–/–/–

## 3949

NORMANDY BEACHES NURSERY (0-85) £2898.00 (£864.00: £412.00: £186.00)
5f
2-30 (2-31)

3848³ **Royal Deed (USA) (64)** *(PMMcEntee)* 8-4 ‡⁵JWeaver (6) (hld up: swtchd rt & squeezed thro to ld over 1f out: sn clr) .................... —1
3897³ Bold County **(69)** (Fav) *(MJohnston)* 9-0 RPElliott (2) (hld up: hdwy over 1f out: kpt on ins fnl f) .................... 3.2
3839³ Second Chance (IRE) **(74)** *(PMitchell)* 9-5 MRoberts (3) (lw: a.p: led over 2f out tl over 1f out: one pce) .................... 1½.3
3637² Flashman **(68)** *(FHLee)* 8-13 WCarson (1) (prom tl rdn & wknd over 1f out) .................... 2½.4
3897* Melodys Daughter **(65)** (bl) *(RFJohnsonHoughton)* 8-10 (7x) JLowe (8) (led to ½-wy: hmpd over 1f out: nt rcvr) .................... nk.5
3750³ The Institute Boy **(63)** (bl) *(KRBurke)* 8-8 SWebster (4) (w ldrs over 3f) .................... hd.6
3852 Sporting Spirit **(51)** *(DWChapman)* 7-10 SWood (9) (dwlt: nvr nr to chal) .................... nk.7
3897 Another Jade **(65)** *(APJarvis)* 8-10 TQuinn (5) (chsd ldrs: drvn along ½-wy: no imp) .................... ½.8

3/1 Bold County, 4/1 Second Chance (IRE), ROYAL DEED (USA), 5/1 Melodys Daughter, 7/1 Flashman, Another Jade, 16/1 Ors. CSF £16.05, CT £46.37. Tote £5.80: £2.10 £1.60 £1.60 (£14.40). Racing Thoroughbreds Plc (WINDSOR) bred by Nydrie Stud in USA. 8 Rn
62.85 sec (4.15)
SF—47/45/44/29/25/22

## 3950

UNKNOWN SOLDIER H'CAP (0-90) £3640.50 (£1089.00: £522.00: £238.50)
2m 110y
3-00 (3-07)
(Weights raised 8 lb)

3788* **Iota (68)** *(MrsJCecil)* 3-8-6 MRoberts (11) (hld up in tch: qcknd to ld over 3f out: styd on strly) .................... —1
3728 Jack Button (IRE) **(76)** *(BobJones)* 3-9-0 NDay (2) (hld up: hdwy 4f out: chsd wnr fnl 2f: r.o) .................... 1½.2
3788² Kaiser Wilhelm **(79)** *(HRACecil)* 3-9-3 AMcGlone (13) (lw: led 3f out: effrt 3f out: styd on: nvr nrr) .................... 4.3
3621* My Chiara **(67)** *(PJBevan)* 6-9-1 BCrossley (9) (chsd ldrs: styd on fnl 2f: nvr nrr) .................... 9/4.4
3877 Fanlight **(52)** *(RAkehurst)* 4-7-11 ‡³FNorton (7) (hld up: hdwy 6f out: hrd rdn appr fnl f: kpt on) .................... 1.5
3467⁵ Bandoline **(72)** *(BWHills)* 3-8-10 DHolland (12) (lw: s.s: hld up & bhd: hdwy over 2f out: nvr plcd to chal) .................... s.h.6
3728⁴ Coleridge **(70)** (bl) *(DShaw)* 4-8-13 ‡⁵SWilliams (10) (prom: rdn over 2f out: sn btn) .................... hd.7
3728 Go South **(65)** (v) *(JRJenkins)* 8-8-13 GBaxter (1) (chsd ldrs 10f) .................... 4.8
3788⁶ Kadari **(60)** *(AHarrison)* 3-7-9⁽¹⁾ ‡³DHarrison (4) (led after 3f tl over 3f out: grad wknd) .................... hd.9
3896² Pica **(77)** (Fav) *(HRACecil)* 3-9-1 WRyan (3) (chsd ldrs 10f: grad wknd) .................... 3½.10
3728⁵ Smilingatstrangers **(54)** (v) *(MrsBarbaraWaring)* 4-8-2 JLowe (5) (drvn along & lost tch ½-wy: sn bhd) .................... 4.11
3697⁶ Hunting Ground **(67)** *(REPeacock)* 4-9-1 JQuinn (6) (prom to ½-wy: sn lost tch) .................... ¾.12
3877 Beldale Star **(47)** *(RAkehurst)* 9-7-9 NAdams (8) (b: hdwy ½-wy: wknd over 3f out) .................... 1.13
3724 Spikenard **(86)** *(PTWalwyn)* 3-9-10 TQuinn (7) (led over 3f: cl up tl wknd 4f out) .................... 2.14

4/1 Pica(op 6/1), 11/2 IOTA, 13/2 Smilingatstrangers, 8/1 Jack Button (IRE)(op 5/1), 9/1 Bandoline, 10/1 My Chiara, Kaiser Wilhelm, 14/1 Fanlight, Kadari, 16/1 Go South, Coleridge, 20/1 Spikenard, Hunting Ground, 25/1 Beldale Star. CSF £47.31, CT £401.32. Tote £4.10: £1.50 £3.30 £3.30 (£19.00). Sheikh Mohammed (NEWMARKET) bred by Sheikh Mohammed bin Rashid al Maktoum. 14 Rn
3m 45.97 (16.97)

## 3951

ROYAL BRITISH LEGION STKS £3348.00 (£999.00: £477.00: £216.00)
1¾m 132y
3-30 (3-33)

3794* **Lost Reputation (IRE) (86)** (Jt-Fav) *(BWHills)* 3-8-10 DHolland (6) (led 12f out: shkn up 3f out: sn clr: r.o) .................... —1
3823² Kiveton Kabooz **(88)** (bl) *(JAGlover)* 4-9-0 AMunro (1) (swtg: hld up: hdwy ent st: chsd wnr appr fnl f: r.o) .................... 1½.2
3773⁴ Klingon (IRE) **(63)** *(RHollinshead)* 3-8-5 WRyan (5) (hld up: styd on fnl 2f: nvr nrr) .................... 10.3
3804⁴ Speedo Movement **(53)** *(BAMcMahon)* 3-8-0 JLowe (4) (lw: a.p: chal 3f out: sn rdn: grad wknd) .................... 1½.4
3823² Glaisdale (IRE) **(87)** (Jt-Fav) *(MHTompkins)* 3-8-10 PRobinson (3) (led over 2f: wknd over 2f out) .................... 10.5
3877 Ross Graham **(50)** *(MrsBarbaraWaring)* 4-9-0 NHowe (2) (prom tl wknd 4f out) .................... s.h.6

2/1 LOST REPUTATION (IRE), Glaisdale (IRE), 9/4 Kiveton Kabooz, 25/1 Klingon (IRE), Speedo Movement, 50/1 Ross Graham. CSF £6.23, Tote £2.40: £1.60 £1.50 (£2.60). Mr R. E. Sangster (LAMBOURN) bred by Seahorse Investments in Ireland. 6 Rn
3m 15.04 (11.44)
SF—40/51/12/4/–/–

**3952** POPPY H'CAP (0-80) £4050.00 (£1215.00: £585.00: £270.00) 7f 4-00 (4-02)

3905⁵ **Highland Magic (IRE) (70)** (MJFetherston-Godley) 4-9-4 MRoberts (15) (hld up: effrt 3f out: str run to ld ins fnl f) —1

3882* Penny Drops **(64)** (Fav) (LordHuntingdon) 3-8-7 (4x) ‡DHarrison (4) (hld up: hdwy to chal ins fnl f: r.o) ³/₄.2

3793⁶ Causley **(76)** (BAMcMahon) 7-9-10 TQuinn (16) (led tl ins fnl f: r.o) 1¹/₂.3

3866 La Bamba **(76)** (GAPritchard-Gordon) 6-9-10 WHood (3) (b: hld up: rapid hdwy & n.m.r appr fnl f: fin wl) 1.4

3793* Sagebrush Roller **(73)** (JWWatts) 4-9-7 GDuffield (2) (lw: hld up: effrt & swtchd lft over 1f out: nt qckn) s.h.5

3732 Killy **(70)** (FHLee) 3-9-2 GCarter (8) (chsd ldrs: ev ch 1f out: no ex nr fin) 1.6

3681² Prenonamoss **(80)** (DWPArbuthnot) 4-9-9 ‡⁵SWilliams (20) (b.hind: hld up in tch: rdn over 1f out: nt pce to chal) 2.7

3800 Wild and Loose **(79)** (DRCElsworth) 4-9-13 JWilliams (10) (lw: hdwy over 2f out: styd on wl: nrst fin) nk.8

3620 Castlerea Lad **(75)** (RHollinshead) 3-9-7 WRyan (19) (chsd ldrs: rdn over 1f out: one pce) nk.9

3905 Ballerina Bay **(68)** (v) (DTThom) 4-8-9 (4x) ‡⁷KimMcDonnell (18) (nvr nr ldrs) nk.10

3905 Garth **(70)** (v) (PJMakin) 4-9-4 BRaymond (1) (hdwy u.p over 1f out: nvr plcd to chal) nk.11

3667³ Muhit (USA) **(76)** (PTWalwyn) 3-9-8 WCarson (7) (prom: effrt appr fnl f: unable qckn) 1¹/₂.12

3781⁴ Will of Steel **(79)** (MrsJRRamsden) 3-9-11 KFallon (6) (w ldrs: rdn over 1f out: sn btn) ³/₄.13

3797 Just a Step **(67)** (MMcCormack) 6-9-1 JReid (22) (m.n.s) s.h.14

3866 Kimberley Park **(79)** (DWPArbuthnot) 4-9-1 PRobinson (9) (prom over 5f) 1¹/₂.15

749⁵ Who's That Lady **(60)** (MHEasterby) 3-8-6 MBirch (12) (m.n.s) ³/₄.16

3828 Darussalam **(74)** (RLee) 5-9-3 ‡⁵ATucker (14) (spd 5f: sn lost tch) 1¹/₂.17

2665⁶ Greetland Folly **(74)** (RMWhitaker) 3-8-13 ‡⁷GParkin (13) (bhd fr ¹/₂-wy: t.o) 8.18

1500⁶ Mel's Rose **(68)** (DrJDScargill) 7-9-2 DHolland (21) (b.hind: bhd fr ¹/₂-wy: t.o) 19

Highest Praise (USA) **(61)** (MissSJWilton) 9-8-6 ‡³SO'Gorman (11) (spd 4f: sn wknd: t.o) 20

3825 Lord Vivienne (IRE) **(67)** (RCSpicer) 3-8-6 ‡⁷AGarth (5) (prom far side over 4f: t.o) 21

11/4 Penny Drops, 13/2 La Bamba, HIGHLAND MAGIC (IRE), 9/1 Sagebrush Roller, Prenonamoss, 12/1 Will of Steel, Kimberley Park, 14/1 Ballerina Bay, Causley, 16/1 Darussalam, Muhit (USA), Wild and Loose, 20/1 Mel's Rose, Garth, Castlerea Lad, Who's That Lady, 25/1 Greetland Folly, 33/1 Ors. CSF £27.62, CT £249.76. Tote £8.00: £2.40 £1.60 £3.70 £2.40 (£14.50). Miss N. Carroll (EAST ILSLEY) bred by W. J. Burke in Ireland. 21 Rn
1m 28.64 (5.24)
SF—68/55/67/64/60/52

T/Trio: Race 5: £63.90 (11.5 Tckts). T/Jkpt: Not won; £28,534.35 to Doncaster 7/11/92. T/Plpt: £29.10 (137.63 Tckts).
IM

# DONCASTER (L-H)

## Saturday, November 7th [Good]

Going Allowance: St: 0.30 sec; Rnd: 0.20 sec per fur (G) Wind: almost nil

Stalls: high

**3953** FLANDERS STKS (I) (Mdn 2-Y-O) £3223.50 (£896.00: £430.50) 7f 12-25 (12-27)

**Tinners Way (USA)** (JHMGosden) 9-0 PatEddery (8) (w'like: scope: sn led: shkn up over 2f out: r.o strly) —1

Kassbaan (USA) (AAScott) 9-0 WRSwinburn (1) (b.hind: w'like: leggy: sn chsng ldrs: effrt & ev ch over 2f out: kpt on) 3¹/₂.2

3693 Labudd (USA) (JHMGosden) 9-0 WCarson (5) (w'like: scope: chsd ldrs: ev ch over 2f out: unable qckn) 2¹/₂.3

Refugio (Fav) (HRACecil) 9-0 SCauthen (11) (w'like: unf: bit bkwd: w ldrs: pushed along 3f out: grad wknd) 7.4

2849⁶ Bend Sable (IRE) (PCHaslam) 9-0 DaleGibson (10) (effrt 3f out: swtchd rt appr fnl f: r.o) 1¹/₂.5

3855 Working Title (IRE) (JWHills) 9-0 MHills (6) (r.o appr fnl f: nvr nr to chal) nk.6

3880 Sassiver (USA) (RCharlton) 9-0 PaulEddery (12) (sn in tch: drvn along ¹/₂-wy: kpt on) 2¹/₂.7

3880 Nomadic Fire (DMorley) 9-0 MTebbutt (18) (hld up: effrt over 2f out: no imp) s.h.8

Turtle Power (TThomsonJones) 9-0 KDarley (3) (lt-f: nvr nrr) ³/₄.9

3855 One Voice (USA) (SirMarkPrescott) 9-0 GDuffield (4) (m.n.s) 1.10

3691⁵ Naawy (MRStoute) 9-0 BRaymond (14) (s.i.s: a bhd) 2.11

```
3881  Sir Edward Henry (IRE) (FHLee) 9-0 DMcKeown (16) (hdwy u.p over 2f out: nt
         rch ldrs) ..................................................................................... ¾.12
3782²  Gone Prospecting (USA) (81) (RHannon) 9-0 TQuinn (9) (chsd ldrs over 5f) .. ½.13
3780  Sky Burst (LGCottrell) 8-9 NCarlisle (7) (chsd ldrs 5f) ............................... 1.14
3802  Dance and Sing (IRE) (DLWilliams) 9-0 NAdams (15) (m.n.s) ....................... ½.15
3855⁴  Mountain Willow (LordHuntingdon) 8-9 AMunro (13) (m.n.s) ...................... ¾.16
3725³  Klondike (IRE) (v) (PTWalwyn) 9-0 GCarter (4) (s.i.s: a outpcd & bhd: t.o) ...... 8.17
3588  Target Zero (USA) (MJHeaton-Ellis) 9-0 WRyan (17) (gd spd 4f: wknd qckly:
         t.o) ............................................................................................ nk.18
```

**2/1** Refugio(op 5/4), **11/4** TINNERS WAY (USA)(5/2—5/1), **8/1** Kassbaan (USA)(op 5/1), Gone Prospecting (USA)(op 5/1), **12/1** Naawy, Labudd (USA)(op 7/1), Mountain Willow, **16/1** Sassiver (USA), **20/1** Nomadic Fire, **25/1** Bend Sable (IRE), **33/1** Klondike (IRE), Turtle Power, Working Title (IRE), **50/1** Ors. CSF £26.40, Tote £6.60: £2.30 £2.80 £2.90 (£32.30). Mr K. Abdulla (NEWMARKET) bred by Juddmonte Farms Inc. in USA. 18 Rn
1m 28.90 (5.50)
SF—49/38/30/9/4/3

## 3954

EL ALAMEIN NURSERY  £3991.50 (£1197.00: £576.00: £265.50)
7f  12-55 (12-56)
(Weights raised 2 lb)

```
3643*  Mhemeanles (79) (MHEasterby) 8-7 ‡³SMaloney (22) (a.p: led ½-wy: drifted rt
         fnl f: r.o u.p) ................................................................................ —1
3867  Persian Revival (FR) (82) (BAMcMahon) 8-13 TQuinn (3) (lw: a.p: chal 1f out:
         unable qckn nr fin) ........................................................................ ½.2
3867  Rocket to the Moon (IRE) (82) (PWChapple-Hyam) 8-13 PaulEddery (20) (a.p:
         styd on u.p ins fnl f) ...................................................................... 1.3
3839*  Chili Heights (83) (GBBalding) 9-0 JWilliams (19) (mid div tl styd on wl fnl f) ... 1½.4
3832  Move Smartly (IRE) (64) (FHLee) 8-13 NCarlisle (9) (hdwy over 1f out: fin wl) hd.5
3913²  Key to My Heart (IRE) (83) (DMoffatt) 9-0 DMcKeown (14) (prom: chal 3f out:
         wknd over 1f out) ........................................................................... hd.6
3760*  Cliburnel News (IRE) (76) (MHTompkins) 8-7 PRobinson (7) (chsd ldrs: hrd
         rdn over 1f out: r.o) ........................................................................ s.h.7
3635*  Dutosky (74) (Jt-Fav) (MJCamacho) 8-5 NConnorton (4) (chsd ldrs: kpt on u.p
         ins fnl f) ....................................................................................... hd.8
3631³  Mondragon (77) (Jt-Fav) (MrsGRReveley) 8-8 KDarley (12) (swtg: bhd:
         pushed along ½-wy: styng on whn hmpd appr fnl f) ................................. 1.9
3581*  Nabjelsedr (86) (CJBenstead) 9-3 WCarson (8) (b.hind: hdwy u.p over 2f out:
         n.m.r appr fnl f: nvr able to chal) ....................................................... ¾.10
3852³  Sweet Disorder (IRE) (67) (GAPritchard-Gordon) 7-7⁽⁵⁾ ‡⁵BDoyle (1) (chsd ldrs
         over 5f: sn wknd) ........................................................................... ½.11
3852*  Benevolent (82) (SirMarkPrescott) 8-13 AMunro (21) (a mid div) ................... nk.12
3899⁶  Arkendale Diamond (USA) (68) (CBBBooth) 7-13 DaleGibson (2) (effrt u.p
         ½-wy: no imp) ............................................................................... nk.13
3474  Silky Heights (IRE) (64) (MJCamacho) 7-9 JQuinn (15) (bhd fnl 2f) ................ 2.14
3899⁵  Egg (69) (bl) (TDBarron) 8-0 JLowe (13) (a in rr) ..................................... nk.15
3314⁴  City Rocket (81) (PJMakin) 8-12 SCauthen (10) (prom tl wknd qckly wl over 1f
         out) ............................................................................................ 1.16
3792³  Range Rider (IRE) (73) (bl) (CEBrittain) 8-4 MRoberts (11) (led to ½-wy: wknd
         2f out) ......................................................................................... 3.17
3832  Astrac Trio (USA) (75) (SGNorton) 8-3 ‡³FNorton (5) (m.n.s) ....................... 3.18
3807⁶  Birchwood Sun (78) (RHollinshead) 8-9 WRyan (17) (a bhd) ....................... 3½.19
3791⁴  Celestial Key (USA) (90) (SGNorton) 9-2 ‡⁵OPears (18) (prom 4f: sn lost tch) 1½.20
3855*  Kadastrof (FR) (84) (RDickin) 9-1 SDawson (6) (m.n.s) .............................. 2½.21
              LONG HANDICAP: Move Smartly (IRE) 7-5, Sweet Disorder (IRE) 7-5.
```

**15/2** Mondragon, Dutosky, **8/1** Cliburnel News (IRE), Benevolent, **10/1** Chili Heights, Persian Revival (FR), **12/1** Nabjelsedr, Egg, **14/1** City Rocket, MHEMEANLES, Key to My Heart (IRE), Range Rider (IRE), Arkendale Diamond (USA), **20/1** Rocket to the Moon (IRE), Kadastrof (FR), Birchwood Sun, Celestial Key (USA), **25/1** Ors. CSF £150.89, CT £2,577.26. Tote £22.80: £4.10 £2.90 £6.70 £4.90 (£104.40). Mr Les Ford (MALTON) bred by Miss J. Chaplin. 21 Rn
1m 28.65 (5.25)
SF—46/50/47/43/23/41

## 3955

FORTE H'CAP (Final) (0-70) (Ladies) £3078.00 (£858.00: £414.00)
1¼m 60y  1-30 (1-32)

```
3800  Pippin Park (USA) (67) (MBell) 3-10-8 ‡⁵MrsGBell (2) (a.p: led over 3f out: hld
         on gamely) ................................................................................... —1
3468  Lots of Luck (62) (Fav) (JPearce) 9-10-13 MrsLPearce (21) (hld up & bhd:
         hdwy rl out: r.o wl nr fin) ................................................................ nk.2
880  Saint Ciel (USA) (64) (FJordan) 4-11-1 MissMJuster (16) (chsd ldrs: rdn 2f out:
         kpt on strly) ................................................................................. nk.3
3778⁶  Lady Lacey (49) (v) (GBBalding) 5-9-9 ‡‡MissKGreaney (11) (hdwy 3f out: styd
         on fnl f) ....................................................................................... 1½.4
```

3789 Mardessa **(51)** *(FHLee)* 4–10-2 MrsGRees (19) (hdwy over 2f out: styd on fnl f: nvr nrr) ............... 1.5

3476 Bidweaya (USA) **(39)** *(JLEyre)* 5–8-13 ‡5MissAYardley (23) (in tch: hdwy to chal 3f out: no ex appr fnl f) ............... 3.6

3627 Achelous **(54)** (bl) *(JAGlover)* 5–10-5 MissABillot (17) (chsd ldrs: outpcd 3f out: styd on appr fnl f) ............... 1½.7

3806 Touch Above **(52)** *(TDBarron)* 6–10-3 MrsAFarrell (6) (hld up: effrt 4f out: no imp) ............... s.h.8

3823 Balaat (USA) **(49)** *(MCChapman)* 4–9-9 ‡5MissEFolkes (22) (prom: effrt ent st: wknd over 2f out) ............... 1.9

3789⁴ No Comebacks **(57)** *(EJAlston)* 4–10-3(2) ‡5MrsSBarclay (8) (nvr nr) ............... 2.10

3576⁵ Nobby Barnes **(55)** *(DAWilson)* 3–9-10 ‡5MissJSandford-Johnson (20) (b: bhd tl styd on fnl 3f) ............... 1.11

3919* Lawnswood Junior **(62)** *(JLSpearing)* 5–10-13 (4x) MissTSpearing (18) (hdwy 3f out: nvr nr to chal) ............... hd.12

3770 Carrolls Marc (IRE) **(55)** *(PJFeilden)* 4–10-6 MissJFeilden (12) (b.hind: m.n.s) ............... 1.13

3468 Thunderbird One (USA) **(44)** *(DenysSmith)* 3–8-13 ‡5MissMCarson (3) (led tl over 3f out: sn wknd) ............... 1½.14

3882 Captain Marmalade **(54)** *(DTThom)* 3–10-0 MissIDWJones (5) (m.n.s) ............... 1.15

3770³ The Karaoke King **(52)** (bl) *(RHannon)* 3–9-12 MrsJBoggis (4) (w ldrs over 7f: sn lost tch) ............... hd.16

3521³ Karamoja **(67)** (bl) *(NAGraham)* 3–10-13 MissLHide (9) (m.n.s) ............... hd.17

3708 Retender **(67)** *(MrsJRRamsden)* 3–10-13 MissTBracegirdle (1) (t.o) ............... 8.18

3511 Super Heights **(48)** *(DLWilliams)* 4–9-8 ‡5MissVHaigh (24) (t.o) ............... ½.19

3513³ Milton Rooms (IRE) **(50)** (bl) *(CBBBooth)* 3–9-5(4) ‡5MissCKing (14) (s.s: a bhd: t.o) ............... ¾.20

214 Irish Native (IRE) **(70)** *(CASmith)* 4–11-2 ‡5MrsDSmith (10) (t.o) ............... nk.21

Hemingby **(44)** *(JJO'Neill)* 5–9-4 ‡5MissSNichol (7) (prom: effrt 4f out: sn lost tch: t.o) ............... 4.22

3675 Self Expression **(64)** *(MrsJRRamsden)* 4–11-1 MissDPomeroy (13) (prom: ev ch 3f out: wknd qckly: t.o) ............... 23

3929 Hasty Spark **(40)** *(CFWall)* 4–9-0 ‡5MrsCWall (15) (b.d after 2f) ............... 0

*Stewards Enquiry: Miss C. King suspended 16-22/11/92 (careless riding).*

**4/1** Lots of Luck, **9/1** Lawnswood Junior, Mardessa, Carrolls Marc (IRE), **10/1** Retender (USA), **12/1** No Comebacks, The Karaoke King, **14/1** Lady Lacey, Achelous, Touch Above, PIPPIN PARK (USA), Karamoja, **16/1** Saint Ciel (USA), Self Expression, Nobby Barnes, **20/1** Hasty Spark, Thunderbird One (USA), **25/1** Captain Marmalade, **33/1** Milton Rooms (IRE), Hemingby, Balaat, Bidweaya (USA), **50/1** Ors. CSF £75.39, CT £900.10. Tote £32.40: £7.00 £1.60 £5.10 £4.00 (£92.20). Mr Fahd Salman (NEWMARKET) bred by Major Michael G. Wyatt in USA. 24 Rn

2m 17.54 (10.54)
SF—38/42/43/20/25/2

**3956** WILLIAM HILL NOVEMBER H'CAP (0-115) £27546.00 (£8268.00 : £3984.00 : £1842.00) 1½m
(Weights raised 3 lb) 2-05 (2-11)

3628* Turgenev (IRE) **(91)** *(JHMGosden)* 3–9-0 DHolland (21) (lw: hld up: hdwy to ld over 2f out: sn clr: r.o) ............... —1

3798* Daru (USA) **(96)** (v) (Fav) *(JHMGosden)* 3–9-5 (4x) SCauthen (20) (lw: hld up: hdwy 9f out: r.o strly fnl f: nt rch wnr) ............... 1½.2

3836² Castoret **(86)** *(JWHills)* 6–8-13 ‡3DHarrison (16) (hld up: gd hdwy appr fnl f: fin wl) ............... 2½.3

3789* Westholme (USA) **(71)** *(MHEasterby)* 4–8-1 (4x) JQuinn (15) (hld up: hdwy 4f out: sn rdn: styd on fnl f) ............... nk.4

3663³ Rose Alto **(87)** *(JRFanshawe)* 4–9-3 GDuffield (23) (chsd ldrs: ev ch 3f out: r.o one pce) ............... 1.5

3713⁵ Highbrook **(83)** *(MHTompkins)* 4–8-13 PRobinson (9) (lw: hld up: hdwy 3f out: r.o) ............... 2½.6

3896⁴ Truben (USA) **(82)** *(DRLoder)* 3–8-5(1) TQuinn (14) (swtg: chsd ldrs: effrt & ev ch 3f out: kpt on) ............... 1½.7

3572* Texan Tycoon **(74)** *(RAkehurst)* 4–8-4 GCarter (19) (hdwy 3f out: rdn over 1f out: nvr nrr) ............... ½.8

3864⁴ Light Hand **(75)** *(MHTompkins)* 6–7-12(3) ‡7SMulvey (8) (s.s: styd on fnl 3f: nvr nrr) ............... hd.9

3641⁶ Comstock **(73)** *(NTinkler)* 5–8-3(1) JFortune (24) (hdwy ent st: sn chsng ldrs: wknd over 1f out) ............... ¾.10

3666² Nijmegen **(70)** *(JGFitzGerald)* 4–7-7 ‡7DarrenMoffatt (18) (hld up: hdwy ent st: sn ev ch: wknd over 2f out) ............... ¾.11

3788³ Five to Seven (USA) **(76)** *(SGNorton)* 3–7-10 ‡3FNorton (2) (led tl over 2f out: sn rdn & wknd) ............... 2.12

3896 Administer **(70)** (bl) *(LJCodd)* 4–7-7 ‡7DWright (25) (s.s: a bhd) ............... s.h.13

3829 Rousitto **(71)** *(RHollinshead)* 4–8-1(1) KDarley (4) (m.n.s) ............... ¾.14

3666⁵ Whitechapel (USA) **(82)** *(LordHuntingdon)* 4–8–12 WRSwinburn (11) (prom: ev ch over 3f out: sn wknd) ............................................................................. 1.15

3445⁵ Hajaim (IRE) **(86)** (bl) *(CEBrittain)* 4–9–2 WCarson (7) (effrt ent st: sn ev ch: wknd 2f out) ........................................................................................... hd.16

3085⋆ Larrikin (USA) **(78)** *(LordHuntingdon)* 3–8–1 JLowe (10) (effrt 4f out: nvr able to chal) ....................................................................................................... 1½.17

3675 Lift and Load (USA) **(93)** *(RHannon)* 5–9–9 JReid (12) (prom 8f) ................... 1½.18

3829⋆ Thamestar (IRE) **(76)** *(MBell)* 3–7–13 (4x) AMunro (3) (swtg: chsd ldrs: rdn 3f out: sn btn) ............................................................................................... ½.19

3713 Brier Creek (USA) **(101)** *(JHMGosden)* 3–9–10 RCochrane (17) (m.n.s) ......... 1.20

3829 View From Above **(70)** *(PaulGreen,Jersey)* 6–8–0 SDawson (5) (m.n.s) ........... 1.21

3795⋆ Jasoorah (IRE) **(90)** *(ACStewart)* 3–8–13 (4x) MRoberts (13) (prom tl wknd over 3f out: eased whn btn) ................................................................................. 1.22

3829 Much Sought After **(79)** *(DMorley)* 3–8–2⁽¹⁾ PaulEddery (6) (chsd ldrs 9f) ......... 3.23

2805² Belmoredean **(69)** *(RJO'Sullivan)* 7–7–13 DBiggs (1) (prom tl rdn & wknd 3f out: t.o) ........................................................................................................ 6.24

1972³ Profusion **(101)** *(PFICole)* 3–9–3 ‡7TMcLaughlin (22) (sn prom: wknd over 4f out) 3.25

11/4 Daru (USA), 6/1 Jasoorah (IRE), 10/1 TURGENEV (IRE), 11/1 Larrikin (USA), 12/1 Texan Tycoon, Highbrook (USA), 14/1 Whitechapel (USA), Hajaim (IRE), 16/1 Westholme (USA), Castoret, 20/1 Thamestar (IRE), 25/1 Lift and Load (USA), Nijmegen, Comstock, 33/1 Light Hand, Brier Creek (USA), Profusion, Rose Alto, 50/1 Five to Seven (USA), View From Above, Truben (USA), Much Sought After, 100/1 Ors. CSF £36.48, CT £432.78. Tote £17.40: £3.30 £1.70 £4.70 £3.70 (£31.60). Sheikh Mohammed (NEWMARKET) bred by Paolo Tomei in Ireland. 25 Rn

2m 35.99 (5.39)
SF–70/72/61/48/62/53

## 3957

REMEMBRANCE DAY STKS (listed race) £10356.25 (£3100.00: £1487.50: £681.25)
6f

2-35 (2-40)

3731² **Blyton Lad (113)** *(MJCamacho)* 6–9–4 SWebster (11) (a cl up: led 1f out: r.o wl) —1

3887a² Keen Hunter (USA) **(118)** (Fav) *(JHMGosden)* 5–9–2 SCauthen (17) (trckd ldrs: led wl over 2f out to 1f out: no ex) ........................................................... 1.2

3731⁵ Garah **(104)** *(HRACecil)* 3–8–9 PatEddery (9) (hld up: effrt over 2f out: r.o: nvr able to chal) ............................................................................................. 1.3

3699⋆ Montendre **(112)** *(MMcCormack)* 5–9–4 JReid (8) (trckd ldrs: effrt over 2f out: nt qckn) ................................................................................................... nk.4

3671² Spaniards Close **(107)** *(PJMakin)* 4–8–11 WRSwinburn (10) (in tch: hdwy over 2f out: kpt on: nt pce to chal) ...................................................................... 3.5

3699³ Notley **(110)** (bl) *(RHannon)* 5–9–4 BRaymond (15) (sn drvn along & bhd: styd on fnl 2f: nvr nrr) ........................................................................................ 2.6

3729 Talb (USA) **(95)** (bl) *(JLDunlop)* 3–8–10 WCarson (13) (trckd ldrs: effrt ½-wy: outpcd fnl 2f) ...................................................................................... s.h.7

3878³ Gilt Throne **(102)** *(MHTompkins)* 5–8–6 PRobinson (12) (bhd: styd on u.p fnl 2f: nrst fin) ................................................................................................... nk.8

3828 Arabellajill **(90)** *(RHannon)* 3–8–5 RPerham (7) (sn pushed along: nvr trbld ldrs) 1.9

3731³ Bunty Boo **(96)** *(BAMcMahon)* 3–8–5 TQuinn (5) (prom: effrt ½-wy: wknd over 1f out) .............................................................................................. ½.10

3826 Thousla Rock (IRE) **(90)** *(PWChapple-Hyam)* 3–8–5 PaulEddery (2) (in tch: hdwy ½-wy: sn prom & rdn: wknd appr fnl f) .................................................. nk.11

3528⁵ Harvest Girl (IRE) **(105)** *(GAPritchard-Gordon)* 3–8–5 DHolland (6) (cl up tl wknd appr fnl f) ..................................................................................... 1½.12

Time to Run *(MajorWRHern)* 3–8–0 AMunro (16) (w'like: leggy: pushed along ½-wy: a rr div) ......................................................................................... 2.13

3828² Appledorn **(81)** *(BAMcMahon)* 5–8–1 KDarley (1) (spd over 4f: sn wknd) ......... ½.14

2436 Miss Bluebird (IRE) **(89)** (bl) *(PAKelleway)* 3–8–5 GDuffield (4) (led over 3f: wknd qckly) ................................................................................................ 1½.15

3731⁴ Miss Nosey Parker (IRE) **(98)** *(RHannon)* 3–8–12 MRoberts (14) (nvr wnt pce) hd.16

3828 The Auction Bidder **(79)** *(RHollinshead)* 5–8–6 WRyan (3) (sn bhd) ................. 2½.17

13/8 Keen Hunter (USA), 7/2 Spaniards Close, 10/1 Garah, Harvest Girl (IRE), 11/1 Bunty Boo, 12/1 BLYTON LAD, Montendre, 16/1 Notley, Gilt Throne, 20/1 Miss Nosey Parker (IRE), 33/1 Talb, Time to Run, 50/1 Miss Bluebird (IRE), Thousla Rock (IRE), Appledorn, Arabellajill, 100/1 The Auction Bidder. CSF £31.92, Tote £15.10: £3.20 £1.50 £3.10 (£16.70). Mrs J. Addleshaw (MALTON) bred by Ballinacurra Stud. 17 Rn

1m 13.89 (2.89)
SF–82/76/65/73/54/53

## 3958

COALITE DRAGON STKS £3611.25 (£1080.00: £517.50: £236.25)
1¼m 60y

3-05 (3-09)

3794 Rockawhile (IRE) **(89)** *(HRACecil)* 3–8–2 WRyan (15) (lw: hld up: smooth hdwy ent st: rdn to ld ins fnl f: drvn out) .......................................................... —1

3801² Tunbridge Wells (IRE) **(85)** *(JHMGosden)* 3–8–0 PRobinson (2) (hdwy 4f out: led over 2f out tl ins fnl f: kpt on wl) ...................................................... ½.2

3280² Besotted (90) *(BWHills)* 3–8-2 DHolland (13) (hld up: hdwy ent st: chal 2f out: hrd rdn & r.o one pce) .................. 2½.3

3894⁴ Highland Dress (Fav) *(MRStoute)* 3–8-12 SCauthen (7) (hmpd after 2f: sn prom: chal 3f out: one pce fnl 2f) .................. 7.4

3853★ Kabayil (65) *(PTWalwyn)* 3–8-2 GCarter (6) (led 1f: cl up: led 3f out: sn hdd & outpcd) .................. ³/₄.5

Elementary *(PaulGreen,Jersey)* 9–9-3 SDawson (8) (bkwd: cl up: led over 4f out to 3f out: sn outpcd) .................. 3.6

3896³ Anghaam (USA) (75) *(ACStewart)* 3–8-2 WCarson (3) (plld hrd: hmpd after 2f: sme hdwy 3f out: nvr trbld ldrs) .................. 1½.7

3789 In the Money (IRE) (64) *(RHollinshead)* 3–8-1⁽¹⁾ KDarley (1) (chsd ldrs: rdn 4f out: wknd 2f out) .................. ½.8

3907★ The Goofer (67) *(APStringer)* 5–9-3 AMunro (9) (lw: chsd ldrs tl wknd over 2f out) .................. 1½.9

3829 Emperor Alexander (IRE) (60) *(NASmith)* 4–8-7 ‡⁵JWeaver (5) (b: bit bkwd: in tch: effrt ent st: rdn 3f out: n.d after) .................. ³/₄.10

3583⁴ Alfaari (USA) *(MajorWRHern)* 3–8-2 RHills (4) (bhd: hdwy over 3f out: no imp) .................. ½.11

2601³ Ma Bella Luna (76) *(JLDunlop)* 3–8-2 GDuffield (14) (bit bkwd: chsd ldrs: chal 4f out: wknd 3f out) .................. ½.12

3850² For Reg (IRE) (87) *(ACStewart)* 3–8-12 MRoberts (12) (led after 1f tl over 4f out: sn lost pl) .................. 5.13

3632 Believe in Me (IRE) *(BAMcMahon)* 3–8-0 JLowe (10) (bit bkwd: s.s: plld hrd: a bhd) .................. 2½.14

3583³ Littlewick (IRE) *(GWragg)* 3–7-9⁽³⁾ ‡³FNorton (16) (a bhd: t.o) .................. 15

5/4 Highland Dress, 9/2 Besotted, 8/1 For Reg (IRE), Tunbridge Wells (IRE), ROCKAWHILE (IRE), 12/1 Ma Bella Luna, 14/1 Anghaam (USA), 16/1 Kabayil, 20/1 The Goofer, 25/1 Alfaari (USA), Littlewick (IRE), Elementary, 33/1 In the Money (IRE), 100/1 Ors. CSF £72.87, Tote £12.60: £3.10 £2.30 £1.80 (£44.50). Mr L. Marinopoulos (NEWMARKET) bred by Swettenham Stud in Ireland. 15 Rn
2m 13.69 (6.69)
SF–42/39/36/32/20/29

**3959** FLANDERS STKS (II) (Mdn 2-Y.O) £3199.00 (£889.00: £427.00)  **7f**  3-35 (3-39)

Azilian (IRE) *(JHMGosden)* 9-0 PatEddery (11) (leggy: lt-f: cl up: led 2f out: r.o) —1

Foreshore (IRE) *(ACStewart)* 8-9 MRoberts (13) (unf: scope: hld up: effrt over 2f out: r.o: nt pce of wnr) .................. 1.2

Point the Way (IRE) *(MRStoute)* 8-9 PaulEddery (17) (lt-f: unf: bkwd: hld up: hdwy 3f out: rdn & nt qckn fnl f) .................. 1½.3

3820⁶ Solomon's Dancer (USA) *(WWHaigh)* 9-0 DMcKeown (14) (bit bkwd: a cl up: effrt & ev ch 2f out: nt qckn) .................. hd.4

Stalled (IRE) *(PTWalwyn)* 9-0 RCochrane (5) (lt-f: unf: bkwd: chsd ldrs: effrt over 2f out: nt qckn ins fnl f) .................. s.h.5

Lijaam (IRE) *(AAScott)* 9-0 WRSwinburn (9) (gd sort: bit bkwd: bhd: shkn up over 2f out: r.o wl nr fin) .................. hd.6

Thunder River (IRE) *(MJHeaton-Ellis)* 9-0 GCarter (12) (w'like: leggy: bkwd: dwlt: hdwy ½-wy: styd on u.p fnl 2f) .................. 4.7

3844⁴ Umhambi *(BWHills)* 8-9 DHolland (1) (cl up tl outpcd fnl 2f) .................. 1.8

3764² Yoxall Lodge *(HJCollingridge)* 9-0 VSmith (2) (lw: cl up: chsd 3f out: wknd wl over 1f out) .................. 1½.9

Monazite *(MAJarvis)* 9-0 PRobinson (6) (gd sort: bit bkwd: outpcd fr ½-wy: nvr plcd to chal after) .................. 1½.10

Awesome Venture *(BJMcMath)* 9-0 EJohnson (3) (leggy: bkwd: s.s: stdy hdwy 2f out: nvr nr to chal) .................. hd.11

3360 Mim *(GBBalding)* 8-9 JWilliams (16) (swtg: in tch over 4f) .................. hd.12

Muhtashim (IRE) (Fav) *(JLDunlop)* 9-0 WCarson (7) (w'like: bkwd: prom: drvn along ½-wy: wknd over 2f out) .................. nk.13

Kedge *(RFJohnsonHoughton)* 9-0 JReid (18) (w'like: scope: bit bkwd: chsd ldrs 5f) .................. 1.14

3760⁴ Sassamouse *(RGuest)* 8-9 JLowe (10) (unruly bef s: dwlt: n.d) .................. 2.15

3818 Follingworth Girl (IRE) *(SGNorton)* 8-9 MWood (15) (bit bkwd: prom over 4f) .................. hd.16

3846³ Fly to the End (USA) *(AAScott)* 9-0 BRaymond (8) (led to 2f out: wknd qckly) .................. ³/₄.17

3626 Whyalla Rain *(RHollinshead)* 8-9 WRyan (4) (bit bkwd: prom to ½-wy: sn wknd) .................. 12.18

11/8 Muhtashim (IRE), 9/2 AZILIAN (IRE), 13/2 Point the Way (IRE), 10/1 Umhambi, Awesome Venture(op 16/1), Yoxall Lodge, 12/1 Fly to the End (USA), Foreshore (IRE), 16/1 Lijaam (IRE), 20/1 Kedge, Stalled (IRE), Whyalla Rain, 25/1 Follingworth Girl (IRE), Thunder River (IRE), 33/1 Ors. CSF £65.93, Tote £4.80: £1.90 £3.50 £3.50 (£26.90). Mr K. Abdulla (NEWMARKET) bred by George Strawbridge in Ireland. 18 Rn  1m 31.10 (7.70)
SF–16/8/3/7/6/5

**3960** ARMISTICE H'CAP (0-105) £3640.50 (£1089.00: £522.00: £238.50)  **5f**  4-05 (4-11)

3878★ Branston Abby (IRE) (90) (Fav) *(MJohnston)* 3–9-9 MRoberts (21) (racd stands' side: hdwy over 2f out: r.o wl to ld wl ins fnl f) .................. —1

**3961**

3633 Absolution **(69)** *(MPNaughton)* 8-8-2 NConnorton (22) (led stands' side tl ins fnl f: kpt on wl) .................................................... 1½.2

3803 Cantoris **(87)** *(RJRWilliams)* 6-9-6 RCochrane (11) (b: lw: bhd tl hdwy over 1f out: fin wl) .................................................... ½.3

3803² Belated **(86)** *(HThomsonJones)* 3-9-5 RHills (12) (a chsng ldrs: chal 1f out: r.o) .................................................... s.h.4

3854⁶ Heaven-Liegh-Grey **(68)** (bl) *(MJohnston)* 4-8-1 AMunro (20) (b.off hind: cl up stands' side: kpt on fnl f) .................................................... s.h.5

3803⁴ Inherent Magic (IRE) **(81)** *(MMcCormack)* 3-9-0 JReid (3) (cl up: led far side over 1f out: sn hrd drvn: no ex nr fin) .................................................... s.h.6

3803* Gone Savage **(90)** *(GBBalding)* 4-9-9 SCauthen (9) (chsd ldrs: hdwy to chal far side over 1f out: nt qckn nr fin) .................................................... hd.7

3731 Dominuet **(83)** *(JLSpearing)* 7-9-2 JLowe (10) (bhd tl hdwy far side over 1f out: r.o) .................................................... nk.8

3803 Cindora (IRE) **(87)** *(MHTompkins)* 3-9-6 PRobinson (16) (drvn along ½-wy: styd on: nvr able to chal) .................................................... ¾.9

3787 Panikin **(86)** *(JWharton)* 4-9-5 JWilliams (6) (effrt u.p 2f out: styd on: nt pce to chal) .................................................... nk.10

3828⁴ Cumbrian Waltzer **(88)** *(MHEasterby)* 7-9-7 MBirch (13) (lw: dwlt: bhd tl hdwy over 1f out: r.o) .................................................... s.h.11

3828 Sonderise **(66)** *(NTinkler)* 3-7-13 NCarlisle (8) (lw: shkn up ½-wy: no imp) ... nk.12

3703 Truthful Image **(72)** (bl) *(MJRyan)* 3-8-5 DBiggs (4) (lw: hdwy 2f out: nvr rchd ldrs) .................................................... 1.13

3805⁵ Sigama (USA) **(79)** *(FHLee)* 6-8-7 ‡5NKennedy (1) (led far side tl wknd over 1f out) .................................................... hd.14

3805 Metal Boys **(88)** *(RHollinshead)* 5-8-13 WRyan (15) (lw: nvr trbld ldrs) ............ ¾.15

3854 Gondo **(71)** *(EJAlston)* 5-8-4 KFallon (18) (effrt centre ½-wy: n.d) ............ nk.16

3803³ Baligay **(74)** *(RJHodges)* 7-8-7 MHills (19) (racd stands' side: outpcd fr ½-wy) 2.17

3731 Ashtina **(92)** *(RJHodges)* 7-9-11 PatEddery (14) (lw: w ldrs over 3f: sn wknd) ½.18

3828 Beau Venturo (USA) **(90)** *(FHLee)* 4-9-9 PaulEddery (17) (nvr wnt pce) .......... ½.19

3805⁵ Bodari **(79)** *(DAWilson)* 3-8-9 ‡3DHarrison (7) (lw: cl up tl wknd over 1f out) ... 1.20

3787⁴ Breezy Day **(80)** *(BAMcMahon)* 6-8-13 TQuinn (2) (lw: chsd ldrs over 3f: sn wknd) .................................................... 3½.21

3464 Gemini Fire **(71)** *(MPNaughton)* 8-8-4 DMcKeown (5) (bhd fnl 2f) ................ 1½.22

**5/1** BRANSTON ABBY (IRE), **7/1** Cumbrian Waltzer, **8/1** Gone Savage, Ashtina, **10/1** Gondo(tchd 16/1), **12/1** Belated, **14/1** Dominuet, Bodari, Baligay, Cantoris, Heaven-Liegh-Grey, **16/1** Inherent Magic (IRE), **20/1** Breezy Day, Metal Boys, Sigama (USA), Absolution, Cindora (IRE), **25/1** Panikin, Beau Venture (USA), **33/1** Gemini Fire, **40/1** Ors. CSF £105.02, CT £1,270.52. Tote £5.90: £1.60 £6.60 £4.70 £2.50 (£140.60). Mr J. David Abell (MIDDLEHAM) bred by John David Abell in Ireland. 2a Rn 61.62 sec (2.92)
SF—81/54/70/68/49/61

T/Trio: Race 4: £244.10 (7.2 Tckts); Race 8: wnr or 2nd w any £26.90 (43.5 Tckts). T/Jkpt: Not won; £31,878.48 to Cheltenham 13/11/92. T/Plpt: £1,624.40 (4.88 Tckts). IM/AA

3763—**FOLKESTONE (R-H)**

**Monday, November 9th [Heavy, Soft back st]**

Going Allowance: 6f-6f 189y: 1.15 sec (S); Rest: 1.35 sec (Hvy)            Wind: mod across

Stalls: low

**3961**          CLAYMORE H'CAP (0-70) £3272.50 (£910.00: £437.50)     **1m 1f 149y**    1-00 (1-05)

3908* **Lucky Noire (58)** *(GHarwood)* 4-8-11 (5x) ‡7PHoughton (11) (hdwy over 1f out: r.o strly fnl f to ld nr fin) .................................................... —1

3912* **Aegaen Lady (49)** (Fav) *(JEtherington)* 3-7-13⁽³⁾ (5x) ‡5JWeaver (4) (hdwy over 2f out: 6th st: led ins fnl f: hrd rdn & hdd nr fin) .................................................... ¾.2

3806* **Modest Hope (USA) (49)** *(RCSpicer)* 5-8-2 ‡7AGarth (3) (hdwy 3f out: 3rd st: led over 1f out tl wl ins fnl f: unable qckn) .................................................... 1½.3

3522⁶ **Esprit Fort (USA) (58)** *(PWChapple-Hyam)* 3-8-10 ‡3FNorton (8) (a.p: led over 3f out tl over 1f out: one pce) .................................................... 2½.4

3763³ **Sarah-Clare (52)** *(RAkehurst)* 4-8-9 ‡3RPerham (14) (2nd st: one pce fnl 2f) ... 1½.5

3825 **Ballymoneyboy (65)** *(MHTompkins)* 3-9-6 PRobinson (10) (b.nr fore: nvr nr to chal) .................................................... 3½.6

3239 **Front Page (45)** *(JAkehurst)* 5-8-5 DHolland (5) (4th st: wknd over 1f out) ...... 2½.7

2954⁵ **Summer Cruise (55)** *(ANLee)* 3-8-10 JQuinn (7) (t: a mid div) .................................................... 3.8

3845² **Gold Blade (59)** (bl) *(NAGraham)* 3-9-0 TQuinn (9) (b.nr fore: lw: 5th st: wknd over 1f out) .................................................... 6.9

3873³ **Joli's Great (54)** (v) *(MJRyan)* 4-9-0 DBiggs (6) (a bhd) .................................................... 6.10

3687 **Heniu (49)** *(LordHuntingdon)* 3-9-0 MRoberts (13) (lw: led 6f) .................................................... nk.11

**Threshfield (USA) (68)** *(BJCurley)* 6-10-0 WRyan (1) (a bhd) .................................................... nk.12

**Sharp Thistle (50)** *(WJMusson)* 6-8-3 ‡7DMcCabe (15) (b: prom over 5f) ........ ½.13

409 Victory Gate (USA) **(40)** *(AMoore)* 7–8-0(1) CandyMorris (12) (a bhd) ............... ¾.14
3778 Wide Support **(63)** (bl) *(AMoore)* 7–9-9 BRouse (2) (b: prom 6f: p.u & dismntd
2f out) ...................................................................................................... 0

**7/2** Aegaen Lady, **6/1** Front Page, Gold Blade(op 4/1), **8/1** Joli's Great, **9/1** Modest Hope (USA)(8/1—12/1),
**10/1** LUCKY NOIRE(op 5/1), Ballymoneyboy, Esprit Fort (USA)(op 5/1), Sarah-Clare(op 6/1), **12/1** Threshfield
(USA)(op 7/1), **14/1** Heniu (USA), **25/1** Wide Support, **33/1** Summer Cruise, Sharp Thistle, **50/1** Victory Gate
(USA). CSF £46.10, CT £317.99. Tote £7.30: £3.80 £1.60 £6.00 (£14.50). Mrs Carol Harrison (PULBOROUGH)
bred by T. J. G. Read. 15 Rn                                                                                      2m 17.1 (19.4)
SF–38/24/24/27/23/27

---

**3962**  FOIL (S) STKS (3 & 4-Y.O) £2574.00 (£714.00: £342.00)  **1m 1f 149y**  1-30 (1-34)

3906³ **Euridice (IRE) (62)** (Fav) *(LMCumani)* 3–7-13 ‡5JWeaver (11) (lw: 2nd st: led
over 1f out: comf) ...................................................................................... —1
3576 Northern Conqueror (IRE) **(38)** *(TJNaughton)* 4–9-0 GCarter (7) (hdwy 3f out:
3rd st: hrd rdn over 1f out: unable qckn) .................................................... 4.2
3955 Nobby Barnes **(55)** *(DAWilson)* 3–8-9 MRoberts (8) (b: hdwy 3f out: rn wd st:
hrd rdn over 1f out: one pce) ...................................................................... 2.3
3849 Nordansk **(38)** *(LJHolt)* 3–8-9 AMunro (1) (lw: plld hrd: led over 7f out tl over 1f
out: wknd fnl f) .......................................................................................... 1.4
3180 High Post **(42)** *(DMarks)* 3–8-9 GBaxter (10) (5th st: one pce fnl 2f) ............. 3.5
3370 Elegant Friend **(63)** *(MHTompkins)* 4–9-0 PRobinson (6) (lw: 6th st: wknd 2f out) 8.6
2367 Qualitair Memory (IRE) **(37)** *(JAkehurst)* 3–8-9 TQuinn (9) (4th st: wknd over 1f
out) .......................................................................................................... 2.7
3510 Lord Neptune **(50)** *(JRJenkins)* 3–8-9 JWilliams (13) (hdwy over 3f out: wknd 2f
out) .......................................................................................................... 4.8
3769 Carlowitz (USA) **(30)** *(AMoore)* 4–9-0 BRouse (4) (led 2f: wknd 3f out) ........... 4.9
3180 Maoujoud *(RPCHoad)* 4–8-7 ‡7SEiffert (12) (a bhd) .......................................... 8.10
3827 April City *(MJHeaton-Ellis)* 3–8-4 DHolland (2) (prom over 6f) ......................... 8.11
Sno Marque **(60)** (bl) *(ASReid)* 4–9-0 WRyan (3) (b: lw: a bhd) ........................ 4.12
3576 Gabesia **(32)** *(HJCollingridge)* 4–8-9 JQuinn (5) (bhd fnl 3f) ........................... 3.13

**11/10** EURIDICE (IRE), **4/1** Nobby Barnes, **11/2** Elegant Friend, **8/1** April City(6/1—9/1), **16/1** Lord Neptune, Sno
Marque, **20/1** High Post(op 10/1), Carlowitz (USA)(op 10/1), Northern Conqueror (IRE), Qualitair Memory (IRE),
**33/1** Nordansk, Maoujoud, **50/1** Gabesia. CSF £26.17, Tote £2.30: £1.40 £9.40 £1.80 (£54.90). Studcrown
Limited (NEWMARKET) bred by Equus Thirty Three in Ireland. 13 Rn; Sold W Turner 8,000 gns  2m 17.7 (20)
SF–20/27/18/16/10/–

---

**3963**  SABRE H'CAP (0-70) £2637.00 (£732.00: £351.00)  **6f 189y**  2-00 (2-08)

3870 **Rural Lad (55)** *(RCSpicer)* 3–8-4 ‡7AGarth (9) (hrd rdn & hdwy over 1f out: led
wl ins fnl f: r.o wl) .................................................................................... —1
3905 Precious Wonder **(61)** (Jt-Fav) *(PButler)* 3–9-3 TyroneWilliams (10) (3rd st: hrd
rdn over 1f out: led ins fnl f: sn hdd: unable qckn) ..................................... 2.2
3766² Old Comrades **(55)** (Jt-Fav) *(LGCottrell)* 5–8-10 ‡3FNorton (13) (4th st: one pce
fnl 2f) ...................................................................................................... 1½.3
3667 State of Affairs **(41)** *(CAHorgan)* 5–7-13 DHolland (16) (led 5f out tl ins fnl f: one
pce) .......................................................................................................... 2.4
3910² Wellsy Lad (USA) **(47)** *(DWChapman)* 5–8-0 ‡5JWeaver (15) (5th st: one pce fnl
2f) ............................................................................................................ ¾.5
3245 Jolto **(49)** *(KOCunningham-Brown)* 3–8-5 DBiggs (11) (led 2f: 2nd st: rdn over
1f out: wknd fnl f) ...................................................................................... 1.6
3700 Precious Air (IRE) **(54)** *(AMoore)* 4–8-9 ‡3DHarrison (8) (no hdwy fnl 2f) ........... ½.7
3879 Walstead (IRE) **(55)** *(DAWilson)* 3–8-11 GCarter (14) (nvr nr to chal) .................. 1½.8
3849² Music Dancer **(59)** *(RJHodges)* 3–8-8 ‡7SDrowne (3) (nvr nrr) ........................... ¾.9
3040 Spanish Grandee (USA) **(70)** *(PWChapple-Hyam)* 4–9-7 ‡7GAndrew (6) (b.off
hind: s.s: nvr nrr) ...................................................................................... s.h.10
3800 Daswaki (CAN) **(70)** *(RHannon)* 4–10-0 BRouse (5) (6th st: wknd over 1f out) 2½.11
3879 Broadway Ruckus (CAN) **(58)** *(DRLaing)* 3–9-0 JWilliams (12) (nvr nrr) ........... d.h.11
3847⁴ Sylvan Sabre (IRE) **(69)** *(PMitchell)* 3–9-11 MRoberts (1) (bhd fnl 2f) ................ 3.13
2392 Elwazir (USA) **(57)** *(DMarks)* 3–8-13 GBaxter (7) (bhd fnl 3f) ........................... 8.14
3879 Flying Wind **(52)** *(JSutcliffe)* 3–8-8 PRobinson (4) (a bhd) .............................. 2½.15
3412 Vellandrucha **(43)** *(JABennett)* 3–7-13 NCarlisle (2) (a bhd) ............................. hd.16

**5/1** Old Comrades, Precious Wonder(op 8/1), **6/1** Music Dancer, **13/2** Wellsy Lad (USA)(4/1—7/1), **7/1** Sylvan
Sabre (IRE)(op 4/1), **8/1** Daswaki (CAN)(op 4/1), **10/1** State of Affairs(op 6/1), **14/1** Precious Air (IRE),
Broadway Ruckus (CAN), **25/1** Jolto, Walstead (IRE), **25/1** Flying Wind, **33/1** Spanish Grandee (USA), Elwazir (USA),
RURAL LAD, **40/1** Vellandrucha. CSF £191.76, CT £916.99. Tote £52.30: £7.60 £1.10 £1.90 £3.40 (£268.60).
Mr John Purcell (SPALDING) bred by Derek R. Price. 16 Rn                                          1m 33.3 (11.7)
SF–35/42/30/13/12/14

**3964**　E.B.F. BROADSWORD STKS (Mdn 2-Y.O) £2658.00 (£738.00: £354.00)
6f　　2-30 (2-34)

35794 **Primo Figlio (78)** (Fav) (RHannon) 8-11 ‡3RPerham (9) (lw: led 3f: led ins fnl f: rdn out) ....................................................................................................................... —1

Land O'Lakes (IRE) (SirMarkPrescott) 9-0 GDuffield (1) (str: w ldr: led 3f out tl ins fnl f: r.o wl) ............................................................................................................ s.h.2

3904 Magical Retreat (USA) (CACyzer) 8-9 MRoberts (3) (rdn over 2f out: gd hdwy fnl f: r.o wl) ................................................................................................................... 2½.3

Patsy Grimes (MPMuggeridge) 8-9 PaulEddery (8) (w'like: bit bkwd: a.p: hrd rdn over 1f out: unable qckn) ..................................................................... 2.4

22562 Play Hever Golf (68) (TJNaughton) 9-0 GCarter (5) (swtg: a.p: hrd rdn over 1f out: one pce) ........................................................................................................... 1.5

3874 Ahjay (DAWilson) 9-0 MWigham (2) (nvr nr to chal) .................................................. 1½.6
3874 The Atheling (IRE) (MHTompkins) 9-0 PRobinson (7) (prom over 4f) .................... 1½.7
3874 Glisso (IRE) (LMCumani) 8-9 ‡5JWeaver (4) (lw: a bhd) ............................................ 12.8

Tassagh Bridge (IRE) (JWPayne) 8-9 AMunro (6) (w'like: bit bkwd: bhd fnl 3f) .. nk.9

**Evens** PRIMO FIGLIO(11/10—6/4), 4/1 Patsy Grimes(op 8/1), 6/1 Play Hever Golf, 8/1 Land O'Lakes (IRE), 10/1 The Atheling (IRE)(op 5/1), Glisso (IRE), 14/1 Magical Retreat (USA), 25/1 Ors. CSF £10.82, Tote £2.10: £1.10 £2.50 £2.10 (£11.00). Mr G. Howard-Spink (MARLBOROUGH) bred by Milton Park Stud Partners. 9 Rn
1m 20.5 (9.8)
SF—39/41/26/18/19/13

**3965**　CUTLASS NURSERY (0-85) £2978.50 (£826.00: £395.50)　6f　　3-00 (3-03)
(Weights raised 8 lb)

3899* **Red Leader (IRE) (00)** (Fav) (NTIOola) 8-6 ‡7TMcLoughlin (1) (hld up: led 2f out: comf) ........................................................................................................................... —1

3807 Comanche Companion (67) (TJNaughton) 8-13 DHolland (10) (hld up: hrd rdn over 1f out: unable qckn) ................................................................................................ 2½.2

38526 No Extras (IRE) (70) (JSutcliffe) 9-2 BRouse (9) (hld up: ev ch 2f out: one pce) 3.3

36066 Beat the Bagman (IRE) (52) (LJHolt) 7-12 NAdams (4) (hdwy over 1f out: one pce) ............................................................................................................................... 2½.4

38746 Billyback (60) (MJRyan) 8-6 DBiggs (4) (nvr nr to chal) ....................................... 2.5
39273 Chiltern Hundreds (USA) (75) (WJMusson) 9-7 JWilliams (6) (lw: nvr nrr) ......... 2½.6

3684 Newington Butts (IRE) (68) (RAkehurst) 8-7 ‡7LCarter (5) (w ldr: rdn & ev ch 2f out: sn wknd) ................................................................................................................. s.h.7

38993 Heretical Miss (62) (bl) (RHannon) 8-8 RPerham (11) (led 4f) ................................ ¾.8
36062 Texas Cowgirl (IRE) (61) (GAPritchard-Gordon) 8-2 ‡5BDoyle (2) (lw: bhd fnl 2f) 2.9
38485 Marwell Mitzi (55) (WGRWightman) 8-1 GBardwell (8) (b.hind: bhd fnl 2f) ...... 2.10
2781 Conbrio Star (50) (JRJenkins) 7-10(3) SDawson (3) (bhd fnl 2f) ......................... 15.11

**3/1** RED LEADER (IRE), 9/2 Texas Cowgirl (IRE)(op 5/2), 6/1 Heretical Miss(op 4/1), Comanche Companion, 15/2 No Extras (IRE), 10/1 Chiltern Hundreds (USA)(op 6/1), Billyback, 11/1 Marwell Mitzi, 14/1 Newington Butts (IRE), 16/1 Beat the Bagman (IRE), 33/1 Conbrio Star. CSF £21.48, CT £117.79. Tote £3.60: £1.80 £2.30 £2.30 (£10.50). Generous Racing Club (WHATCOMBE) bred by Tony O'Reilly in Ireland. 11 Rn　1m 20.8 (10.1)
SF—27/25/16/—/—/—

**3966**　EPEE STKS (Mdn 3-Y.O) £2070.00 (£570.00: £270.00)　1½m　　3-30 (3-32)

37433 **Esbooain (FR) (72)** (LMCumani) 8-9 ‡5JWeaver (8) (4th st: led wl over 1f out: r.o wl) ................................................................................................................................ —1

37566 El Taranda (GWragg) 8-6 ‡3FNorton (1) (5th st: r.o one pce fnl 2f) ................ 5.2
3853 Kate Labelle (GWragg) 8-9 AMunro (6) (2nd st: ev ch wl over 1f out: one pce) 1½.3
38013 Alwatar (IRE) (Fav) (ACStewart) 9-0 MRoberts (2) (3rd st: hrd rdn over 1f out: one pce) ................................................................................................................... s.h.4

38015 Hudud (USA) (ACStewart) 8-9 RHills (3) (bhd fnl 6f: 6th st: t.o) ........................ 20.5
3459 Exarch (USA) (MJHeaton-Ellis) 9-0 GCarter (5) (b: a bhd: t.o) ........................... 2½.6
37735 Fort Shirley (IRE) (MRStoute) 9-0 PaulEddery (4) (led over 10f: t.o) ................. ¾.7
39092 Charolles (HRACecil) 8-9 WRyan (7) (lw: bhd fnl 4f: t.o) ..................................... 10.8

**5/4** Alwatar (USA), 3/1 Charolles, 6/1 ESBOOAIN (FR)(op 7/2), Fort Shirley (IRE)(op 4/1), 9/1 El Taranda(5/1—10/1), 12/1 Kate Labelle(op 8/1), Hudud (USA)(op 7/1), 33/1 Exarch (USA). CSF £55.35, Tote £7.90: £1.90 £4.10 £2.30 (£47.50). Sheikh Ahmed Al Maktoum (NEWMARKET) bred by Dr F. Krief in France. 8 Rn
2m 58.3 (24.8)
SF—9/—/—/—/—/—

T/Plpt: £155.00 (37.1 Tckts).

AK

## SOUTHWELL (L-H) Tuesday, November 10th
**Races 3967—3973** All-Weather Racing

### 3560a—MAISONS-LAFFITTE (L-H)
**Friday, November 6th [Heavy]**
Going Allowance: 0.90 sec per fur (S)

## 3974a      CRITERIUM DE MAISONS-LAFFITTE (Gp 2) (2-Y.O.C & F) £36120.00      7f (st)

3651a **Kadounor (FR)** *(France)* 2–8–11 ODoleuze (hld up: effrt over 1f out: led ins fnl f:
        r.o wl) .............................................................................. —1
3887a* Wixon (FR) (Fav) *(France)* 2–8–8 FHead (broke wl: plld hrd: chal over 1f out: no
        ex fnl f) ............................................................................. 1½.2
    Chancetobewild (USA) *(France)* 2–8–11 CAsmussen (set slow pce: qcknd 3f
        out: hdd ins fnl f: r.o) ....................................................... ½.3
3733a³ Firm Friend (IRE) *(France)* 2–8–8 DBoeuf (hld up: sme late hdwy: nvr nr to chal) 1½.4
    Auvergne (USA) *(France)* 2–8–11 TJarnet (trckd ldr tl wknd over 1f out) .......... 2½.5

**6/4** Wixon (FR), **9/4** Chancetobewild (USA), **28/10** KADOUNOR (FR), **4/1** Auvergne (USA), **15/2** Firm Friend
(IRE). Tote 3.80f: 1.80f 1.30f (SF: 12.90f). Mrs H.Rabatel (J.Laumain,FRANCE) bred by Mrs H.Rabatel in France.
5 Rn                                                                                1m 35.4 (12.7)
                                             SF—1/-/-/-/-

### 3933a—SAINT-CLOUD (L-H)
**Sunday, November 8th [Heavy]**
Going Allowance: 1.20 sec per fur (S)

## 3975a      CRITERIUM DE SAINT-CLOUD (Gp 1) (2-Y.O.C & F) £51600.00      1¼m

3737a² **Marchand de Sable (USA)** *(France)* 2–8–11 DBoeuf (hld up: 7th st: effrt over 1f
        out: str run to ld nr fin) ..................................................... —1
    Infrasonic *(France)* 2–8–11 PatEddery (mid div: 6th st: stdy hdwy 2f out: led 1f
        out tl nr fin) ....................................................................... nk.2
    Arinthod (FR) *(France)* 2–8–11 FHead (hld up: 8th st: gd hdwy over 1f out: fin wl) hd.3
3737a³ Ranger (FR) *(France)* 2–8–11 CAsmussen (a.p: 4th st: r.o one pce fnl 2f) ........... 1.4
3735a* Frenchpark *(Ireland)* 2–8–11 PShanahan (prom: 3rd st: hdwy to ld 2f out: hdd 1f
        out: one pce) ...................................................................... 2.5
    Samakatan (IRE) (Jt-Fav) *(France)* 2–8–11 GDubroeucq (prom: 2nd st: btn over
        2f out) ................................................................................. 4.6
    Dardjini (USA) (Jt-Fav) *(France)* 2–8–8 WMongil (a.s: mid div: 5th st: sn rdn &
        btn) ..................................................................................... 2.7
    Lencloitre (FR) *(France)* 2–8–8 OPeslier (led 8f: wknd qckly) ........................... 1½.8

**5/4** Dardjini (USA), Samakatan (IRE), **3/1** Infrasonic, MARCHAND DE SABLE (USA), **11/1** Frenchpark, Ranger
(FR), **19/1** Arinthod (FR), **25/1** Lencloitre (FR). Tote 4.00f: 1.30f 1.30f 2.90f (7.10f). Mr L. De Angeli
(E.Lellouche,FRANCE) bred by Marystead Farm in USA. 8 Rn                         2m 19.1 (15.1)
                                       SF—66/65/64/62/58/50

## 3976a      PRIX PERTH (Gp 3)   £20640.00   1m

    **Northern Crystal** *(France)* 4–9–0 SGuillot ....................................................... —1
    Voleris (FR) *(France)* 3–8–11 ODoleuze ........................................................... nk.2
3658a⁵ Leariva (USA) *(France)* 5–8–10 DBoeuf ................................................... 2½.3
  2911* AMWAG (USA) *(ACStewart)* 3–8–8 MRoberts (btn further 2¼-al) ............. 5
  3903³ HEART OF DARKNESS (bl) *(IABalding)* 4–9–0 BRaymond (btn 8¾-al by wnr) ......... 8
Tote 12.50f: 2.50f 1.70f 1.50f (36.10f). Sheikh Mohammed (A.Fabre,FRANCE) bred by Mrs Y.Seydoux de
Clausonne. 12 Rn                                                                    1m 49.5 (10.9)
                                       SF—80/76/67

### 3934a—SAN SIRO (R-H)
**Sunday, November 8th [Heavy]**

## 3977a      PREMIO GIOVANNI FALCK (listed race) (F & M) £20930.00   1½m

36663² **ONLY ROYALE (IRE)** *(LMCumani)* 3–8–6 LDettori ..................................... —1
    Claw (IRE) *(Italy)* 3–8–6 JHeloury ................................................................. 5.2
3834* UP ANCHOR (IRE) *(PFICole)* 3–8–13 AMunro ............................................. ½.3

Tote 47L: 43L 67L (223L). Scuderia Emdiem (NEWMARKET) bred by Barronstown Stud in Ireland. 7 Rn
2m 41.8

### 3978a
PREMIO CHIUSURA (Gp 3)   £27907.00   **7f**

3901★ **INNER CITY (IRE)** *(LMCumani)* 3–9-6 LDettori ................................................... **—1**
13a² Punch N'Run *(Italy)* 4–9-6 MLatorre ................................................................. **4.2**
    Dominatus *(Italy)* 6–9-6 MEsposito ................................................................ **3.3**
Tote 20L: 16L 48L 72L (375L). Sheikh Mohammed (NEWMARKET) bred by Ballynagran Bloodstock Ltd. in
Ireland. 15 Rn                                                                                      1m 27.8

3945a—**CAPANNELLE  (R-H)**
**Sunday, November 8th [Heavy]**

### 3979a
PREMIO RIBOT (Gp 2)   £32558.00   **1m**

2506a³ **Stubass (IRE)** *(Italy)* 3–8-11 SSoto .......................................................... **—1**
2628a³ Prospective Ruler (USA) *(Italy)* 4–8-11 GPucciatti .................................... ½.**2**
744a³ Glacial *(Italy)* 3–8-11 EBotti ....................................................................... 3½.**3**
3774³ RIVER DEFENCES (USA) *(PWChapple-Hyam)* 3–8-11 VMezzatesta (btn further 13¾l) **8**
Tote 19L: 12L 12L 12L (67L). Scuderia Rencati (A.Botti,ITALY) bred by Joseph Crowley in Ireland. 8 Rn
1m 42.4

---

# FOREIGN RACING

Please note that foreign racing occuring after
November 8th will be included in Raceform 1993

---

# INDEX TO MEETINGS

# RETROSPECT 1992

## by Richard Onslow

The season of 1992 will probably be remembered as one in which the fillies often outshone the colts, to various extents, in four different divisions. **Marling** emerged as a top-class miler, **User Friendly** as a classic stayer, **Lochsong** made history as a sprint handicapper, and the two-year-old **Lyric Fantasy** ventured successfully into territory that has long been the preserve of the older horses. Indeed, of the colts, only **Rodrigo De Triano,** the first horse to complete the 2,000 Guineas/Champion Stakes double since Brigadier Gerard, maintained consistent, high class form to the season's end. The year also saw the introduction of Sunday Racing to England, continuing controversy over the use of the whip, an alarming decline in the bloodstock market and ongoing discussions over the creation of a British Horse Racing Board to supercede the Jockey Club as the governing authority.

**Marling**, winner of the Tattersalls Cheveley Park Stakes and her other three races as a two-year-old, is out of Marwell, winner of the Group One July Cup in 1981. A bay, with quite a bit of length about her and a fast action, Marling narrowly, and possibly unluckily, lost her unbeaten record to the French filly **Hatoof** in the 1,000 Guineas, the result only being allowed to stand after a thirty minute Stewards' Enquiry. Marling then embarked upon a triumphal summer campaign in the Goffs Irish 1,000 Guineas, the Coronation Stakes at Royal Ascot, and the Sussex Stakes at Goodwood. In the latter she obtained a significant success at the expense of colts and older horses after a sustained duel with Selkirk had tested her courage to the utmost. Second Set was third. The value of the form was solid as Second Set had been the winner of this race twelve months earlier, while Selkirk had won the Queen Elizabeth II Stakes in 1991.

### AFTER DINNER MATCH

**User Friendly**, who was unraced as a two-year-old, is a rangy bay filly by Slip Anchor out of Rostova, a mating suggested to owner-breeder Bill Gredley over the dinner table by Steve Cauthen and calculated to produce an Epsom classic winner. Making rapid progress during the Spring and early Summer, User Friendly graduated from success in maiden company to that in a classic trial and, on only her third appearance in public, in the Gold Seal Oaks. A second English Classic success was obtained in the Coalite St Leger, but she finally met with defeat in the Ciga Prix de l'Arc de Triomphe, going down narrowly after a magnificent tussle with **Subotica** throughout the final furlong.

History was made when Mr Jeff Smith's **Lochsong** became the first horse to complete the Stewards Cup, the Portland Handicap and the

Ayr Gold Cup hat-trick. As Willie Carson, who had ridden her in the first two legs of that unique treble, could not ride her in the third, the mount at Ayr was taken by Liverpool-born Francis Arrowsmith, who had been with Ian Balding since leaving school. He had won an apprentice race on her at Newbury in the Autumn of 1991, but had only ridden one previous winner in 1992. For a long time it looked long odds against Lochsong winning any race, let alone three of the most valuable handicaps of the season, as she was born with bad joints, returned with a stress fracture of her off-fore cannon-bone after her first outing, and still walked out of her box very stiff each morning.

## THE NEW MUMTAZ MAHAL?

Dubbed "The Pocket Rocket" **Lyric Fantasy,** who measures little more than 15 hands, was bought by Richard Hannon for 12,500 guineas at Doncaster on behalf of Lord Carnarvon with a view to her winning the Super Sales Sprint at Newbury, where Lord Carnarvon is Chairman. She readily achieved her primary objective, and very much more besides. At Royal Ascot this diminutive specimen of the Thoroughbred was successful in the Queen Mary Stakes, and in August she became the first two-year-old filly to win the Nunthorpe Stakes at York, defeating Mr Brooks and Canadian sprinter Diamonds Galore.

Racing under Jockey Club Rules took place on a Sunday for the first

*Lyric Fantasy (M. Roberts) trounces the older sprinters to land the Keeneland Nunthorpe Stakes.*

time on July 26th, when Doncaster attracted a highly satisfactory crowd of 23,000 people, mostly in family groups. Betting shops throughout the country were obliged to remain closed, and neither the bookmakers nor the Tote were in operation on the course, making superfluous an official announcement that betting tickets should be retained prior to the conclusion of a Stewards' Enquiry. The experiment proved a great success however. A thoroughly enjoyable day out was spent by those present, advertising how imperative it is for racing to continue to pressure Government to allow the sport to compete on an equal footing with many other areas of the leisure industry.

## CONFUSION FOR PEARS

The opening event of the Turf season was the *Raceform* Apprentice Handicap at Doncaster, won by **Mr Confusion,** trained by Steve Norton at nearby Barnsley. The successful rider was Ollie Pears, who was celebrating his 17th birthday.

Two days later Lester Piggott was unsuccessful in his bid to win the Lincoln for the first time. Riding Mudaffar for his brother-in-law Robert Armstrong, he was beaten into second place by **High Low,** trained by his son-in-law Willie Haggas.

Defeat in the Lincoln paled into complete insignificance however when Piggott landed the General Accident 2,000 Guineas on Mr Robert Sangster's **Rodrigo de Triano**. This was 56 year-old Piggott's 30th success in an English Classic, and sets a record that seems likely never to be beaten by any other rider.

The success of Rodrigo de Triano in the 2,000 Guineas was the first step taken by Peter Chapple-Hyam towards consolidating the splendid start that he made to his training career in 1991. More proof that he has already mastered the precious knack of enabling horses to retain their form from two to three came when **Dr Devious** won the Ever Ready Derby. Dr Devious, who carried the colours of Californian Sidney Craig, began his racing career as the property of Mr Sangster. In the summer of 1991 Sangster sold the colt to the Italian, Mr Luciano Gaucci, for £250,000. Having enhanced his value by winning the Three Chimneys Dewhurst Stakes, Dr Devious changed hands again in March when he was bought for $2.5 million by Mrs Jenny Craig as a 60th Birthday present for her husband.

## SPEEDY RECOVERY BY "THE DOCTOR"

The success of Dr Devious was as much a testament to the horse as to his trainer, since it followed shortly after an abortive trip to America for the Kentucky Derby which had left the colt with dirt in his lungs and an overreach on his off-hind.

A somewhat rough race for the Hanson Coronation Cup gave rise to a great deal of controversy, and much criticism of the ride that the highly regarded young French jockey Thierry Jarnet gave Subotica. While Jarnet waited for an opening to appear on the notorious Epsom camber, Saddlers' Hall edged left onto Sapience as he began to make progress on the outside two furlongs out. At the same time, Terimon, also trying to improve, was hanging right onto the hapless Sapience. With horses unexpectedly bunching in front of him, Jarnet was obliged to snatch up and although Subotica finished much the fastest of the nine runners, he was beaten into fourth place behind **Saddlers' Hall**. After a Stewards' Enquiry lasting an hour and five minutes the result stood. **Subotica** was to enjoy ample compensation in the Ciga Prix de l'Arc de Triomphe in October.

*The first of four Group One successes during the season for Rodrigo de Triano and a thirtieth Classic-winning ride for Lester Piggott — The General Accident 2,000 Guineas at Newmarket.*

The Queen enjoyed her first success at Royal Ascot for 13 years when **Colour Sergeant** beat Gymcrak Premiere by a neck in the Royal Hunt Cup. The outcome of that race represented a considerable feat on the part of Colour Sergeant's trainer, Lord Huntingdon, as the gelding had been plagued with hock trouble after winning on the All-Weather at Southwell in the August of 1991, and was having his first race of the season. In the Hunt Cup Colour Sergeant was ridden by the stable apprentice David Harrison, a 19 year-old from Rhyl.

### DRUM TAPS SCALES THE HEIGHTS

The other event landed by Lord Huntingdon at the Royal Meeting was the Gold Cup. Having taken it with Indian Queen in 1991, he won the premier race for stayers for the second year running when **Drum Taps** beat Arcadian Heights by two lengths. Drum Taps carried the colours of Mr Yoshio Asakawa, who had bought him from Lord Carnarvon in December.

Much the most eagerly anticipated race of the Royal meeting was the St James's Palace Stakes, in which Arazi, who had been acclaimed as a brilliant two-year-old, was to meet Rodrigo de Triano. The clash duly materialised, only to peter out in a bitterly disappointing anti-climax. Steve Cauthen asked Arazi for an effort shortly after making the turn into the straight, only to receive a strictly limited response, after which the $19 million colt could do no more. Meanwhile Piggott was still riding a waiting race on Rodrigo de Triano, apparently tracking Arazi. With the latter beaten, Rodrigo de Triano made late progress on the wide outside of the field but could do no better than finish fourth to the Irish outsider **Brief Truce**, who was wearing blinkers for the first time.

## FAST TIMES AT ASCOT

As well as winning the Queen Mary Stakes with Lyric Fantasy, Richard Hannon won the King Edward VII Stakes with **Beyton**, the Cork and Orrery Stakes with **Shalford** and the Norfolk Stakes with **Niche**. In the Cork and Orrey, Shalford set a new record for Ascot's six furlongs, covering it in one minute 12.53 seconds, shaving 0.13 seconds off the time returned by Ron's Victory in 1990.

A new record time for the seven-furlong course was also set as **Prince Ferdinand** won the Jersey Stakes in one minute 25.94 seconds, 0.26 seconds less than Indian Ridge had clocked in 1988. The career of Prince Ferdinand has constituted a wonderful tribute to the judgement of his trainer Matt McCormack, who bought him as a yearling for 4,000 guineas at the Doncaster sales. The Jersey Stakes was the horse's sixth success in 12 outings, and brought his earnings to more than £120,000.

Much the most unsatisfactory race at the Royal meeting was the Prince of Wales's Stakes. **Kooyonga**, who came home a length and a half ahead of Perpendicular was, on the day, clearly the best horse in the field, but hampered both Perpendicular and Young Buster as she edged right in the final furlong. Consequently she was relegated to third place, and her rider Warren O'Connor was given a six-day ban for careless riding and excessive use of the whip. Two weeks later however justice appeared to many to have been done when Kooyonga swept to an easy victory in the Coral-Eclipse Stakes at Sandown with Young Buster a well beaten tenth.

After being beaten by two lengths into second place behind Dr Devious in the Derby, the Irish-trained **St Jovite** revealed remarkable improvement. In the Budweiser Irish Derby he turned the Epsom form upside down in no uncertain terms by winning by a dozen lengths from Dr Devious without being challenged. As another horse had struck into St Jovite in running, he came back with cut heels, so briefly fears were entertained of there being insufficient time to prepare him for the King George VI and Queen Elizabeth Diamond Stakes at Ascot at the end of the following month. Such misgivings quickly proved groundless, and with Jim Bolger's stable jockey Christy Roche under suspension, Stephen Craine, who had never previously ridden a Group One winner, deputised for him at Ascot. Making all the running, St Jovite beat Saddlers' Hall by a most impressive six lengths.

## ST JOVITE SUPREMACY SHORT-LIVED

Those who accorded St Jovite Champion status after his successes at The Curragh and Ascot, soon found that they had reached their judgement prematurely when the colt was beaten a short head in the Kerry Group Irish Champion Stakes by Dr Devious, who thus confirmed suspicions that he had been a little below par in the Irish Derby. Subsequently St Jovite was only fourth in the Prix de L'Arc de Triomphe.

*St. Jovite (S. Craine) in splendid isolation in the King George VI and Queen Elizabeth Diamond Stakes at Ascot.*

Several of the leading stables encountered lean spells as a result of infection at various stages of the Summer. Jack Berry closed his Cockerham yard towards the end of May because a number of his horses were having difficulty with their breathing on account of inflamation of the larynx. Berry had been without a winner for 19 days before **Charity Express** and **Palacegate Racing** won the opening races at Catterick and Southwell respectively on June 5th.

Richard Hannon completed his fourth treble in five racing days when **Scottish Bambi**, **Risk Zone** and **Risk Me's Girl** won at Windsor on the evening of May 11th, but even his relentless progress soon received a temporary setback. He had had well over 50 runners beaten in the course of 13 days before **Port Lucaya** won at Goodwood on June 12th.

Barry Hills' stable had been through an agonisingly lean period as a result of an equine herpes infection before **Further Flight** won the Goodwood Cup for the second season in succession, beating Witness Box, ridden by Steve Cauthen, by a short head. The Stewards held that Cauthen had used his whip improperly by hitting his mount more than the permissible 10 times, five times down the shoulder. For that breach of Instruction H9, he was suspended for four days. Later in the afternoon he was held to have repeated the offence when winning the Levy Handicap on **Daru**, and was reported to Portman Square. The Jockey Club Disciplinary Committee heard the case on August 5th with the result that they extended the ban by six days, even though Pat Eddery and Michael Roberts, giving up 14 mounts between them, had given evidence on his behalf. Like Cauthen, most other jockeys resented the instructions with regard to use of the whip down the shoulder, maintaining it was the way they had been taught to ride. Accordingly the Jockeys' Association anxiously pressed for talks on this contentious issue with the Jockey Club.

After **Spinning** had won the Tote Gold Trophy on the second day of Goodwood, Ian Balding decided that if the horse had not lost too much weight he would run again two days later. As it happened Spinning actually put on one kilo, and was brought out again on the Friday to win the Schroders Glorious Stakes.

## RODRIGO SAILS HOME

On the 44th anniversary of his having ridden his first winner, **The Chase** at Haydock Park in 1948, Lester Piggott adopted waiting tactics again on Rodrigo de Triano in the Juddmonte International Stakes at York, in an attempt to overcome the disadvantage of an outside draw. They worked to perfection. Riding with the utmost confidence, he brought Rodrigo de Triano from last to first to beat All At Sea by a length and gain his fifth success in this race, following those on Dahlia in 1974 and 1975, Hawaiian Sound in 1978 and Commanche Run in 1985. The mystery of the Juddmonte was the performance of the favourite Kooyonga, who finished last of 12, being virtually pulled up. Her trainer, Michael Kauntze, subsequently announced that hormone analysis showed that she was coming into season. However the filly was never to recover her early season form.

Mark Johnston, who turned his back on a successful veterinary career to begin training in 1987, ensured the Tote Ebor Handicap prize stayed in Yorkshire when **Quick Ransom** beat Brier Creek by a head. Johnston had decided to go for the race after Quick Ransom had run Deposki to a head at Goodwood back in May 1991, so a long-term plan worked out, despite the horse chipping a hind cannon-bone in-between times.

Quick Ransom followed up by winning the Krug Handicap at Ascot's Festival of Racing on the last Saturday in September. That success brought to a sum in excess of £150,000 the prize money won by this four-year-old, whom Johnston bought for 6,000 guineas as a yearling.

## COMPENSATION FOR SHARPALTO

Yorkshire also landed the £50,000 Festival Handicap with **Sharpalto**, from Mary Reveley's increasingly successful Saltburn-on-Sea stable. The success was well-deserved compensation for Sharpalto and his connections as the gelding had been badly bumped in the corresponding event twelve months earlier. With Dean McKeown trapped in a traffic jam on the M1, top Irish jockey Mick Kinane came in for the winning ride.

One of the features of the season was the regularity with which Clive Brittain's two-year-old fillies, such as **Sayyedati**, **Ivanka** and **Love of Silver** won in the top league. Ivanka made her contribution by beating Ajfan in the Group One Fillies' Mile, a race that has been used as a stepping stone to stardom by the likes of triple classic winner Oh So Sharp and Oaks winner Diminuendo.

The climax of the Festival of Racing came when **Lahib** won the £208,000 Queen Elizabeth II Stakes for John Dunlop's Arundel stable. There was a great deal of public confidence behind Selkirk, who was dreadfully unlucky in running. After being badly buffeted at the halfway stage, Selkirk was left with far too much ground to make up in

*The race of the season? Marling fights back to deny Selkirk in the Sussex Stakes.*

the short Ascot straight, and in the circumstances did well to reach third place. Although Lahib is a four-year-old, he was having only the seventh race of his career. After needing to have a testicle removed as a two-year-old, he damaged a cartilage in a knee when winning at Newmarket in 1991.

Former jump jockey Jeremy Glover, who trains in the vast park surrounding Welbeck Abbey, for long the residence of the Dukes of Portland, in his native Nottinghamshire, won the William Hill Cambridgeshire for a third time when **Rambo's Hall** beat Montpelier Boy by two and a half lengths. Glover had previously won the race with Balthus in 1987 and Rambo's Hall in 1989. At the end of 1989 Rambo's Hall was sold to the United States for £100,000, but as he proved unable to act on the American tracks, was bought back for a quarter of that amount.

## PANIC FOR WELD

A technicality nearly foiled a huge gamble on the Irish-trained **Vintage Crop** in the Tote Cesarewitch. When trainer Dermot Weld rang Weatherbys to declare the five-year-old ten minutes before the deadline, he was informed that he could not act on behalf of owner Michael Smurfit in England. Frantically, contact was made with the office of Michael Stoute, who has the necessary authority to act for Dr Smurfit, and the declaration was made with four minutes to spare. It subsequently transpired that Weld was eligible to make it! During the previous week Vintage Crop had been backed from 25/1 to favouritism at 5/1. He ran out an easy winner under Walter Swinburn.

The Dubai Champion Stakes produced an exciting finish, with Rodrigo de Triano, again ridden by Piggott, beating Lahib by a neck. Thus Rodrigo de Triano became the first colt to complete the double of the 2,000 Guineas and the Champion Stakes since Brigadier Gerard performed the feat 21 years ago.

**Sayyedati** extended the wonderful run enjoyed by Clive Brittain's first-season fillies by depriving Lyric Fantasy of her unbeaten record in the Tattersalls Cheveley Park Stakes. Game as ever, Lyric Fantasy strove valiantly to reach the front, but could not peg back Sayyedati, who led all the way.

The outcome of the Group One races for two-year-old colts run at the back-end of the season amply demonstrated that Khaled Abdullah will hold an exceptionally strong hand for the 1993 Classics. As well as the Ciga Grand Criterium with **Tenby**, the Saudi Prince won the Dewhurst Stakes with **Zafonic** and the Racing Post Trophy at Doncaster with **Armiger**.

The Queen enjoyed, numerically speaking, her most successful season, as **Ingenuity** became her 24th winner of 1992 when beating Coolaba Prince by a length and a half in the Leslie Petch Memorial Handicap at Redcar on October 14th. Her Majesty's previous best tally of races won had been 23 in 1957.

## TRAGEDY AT GULFSTREAM

After triumphantly setting a new record in the classics at Newmarket in the Spring, Lester Piggott came within a whisker of disaster at Gulfstream Park, Florida, four days before his 57th birthday, in the Autumn. Mr Brooks, his mount in the Breeders' Cup Sprint, shattered a leg in running, and rolled on him. Fortunately the accident to Piggott was not as serious as first appeared, though it transpired he had broken a collar bone and two ribs. Announcing that he would be riding again within a few weeks, Piggott added that he had had worse falls. However poor Mr Brooks, the July Cup and Prix de l'Abbaye winner, had to be destroyed.

Apart from a short spell in the doldrums during early Summer, the new champion trainer Richard Hannon had his horses in top form from start to finish of the season. Becoming the first trainer to send out 100 winners in 1992, with the success of **Chance to Dream** at Brighton on August 5th, he reached a personal landmark when **Surprise Offer** became his 1,000th winner since he took over the East Everleigh stable from his father in 1970, by landing the E.B.F. Tormarton Stakes at Bath on September 14th. One of his finest achievements in a memorable season was to win the £90,000 Racecall Gold Trophy with **Pip's Pride** at Redcar. Therefore he completed the double in the two bonanzas designed to offer horses of relatively modest origins the chance to earn a big prize, having, as mentioned previously, already won the Newbury Super Sales Sprint with Lyric Fantasy.

Barry Hills won the 100th Pattern Race of his career when **Sure Sharp** was successful in the Group 3 Earl of Sefton Stakes at Newmarket on April 15th.

Mark Johnston sent out his 100th winner when **Luks Akura** completed a first treble for him at Carlisle in June. In July James Bethell left Chilton, Berkshire, where he had trained for 17 years, to take over the Manor House Stable, the quarters of three generations of the Peacock family, at Middleham. His first winner from his new yard was **Precentor** in the Struthers and Carter Sprint Handicap at Beverley three weeks later.

## JUST REWARD FOR EFFORT

The new Champion jockey, South African Michael Roberts, made a flying start to the season by winning on **Luchiroverte**, his first mount on the opening day at Doncaster. In the middle of May he obtained the

3,000th success of his career on **Shalford** in the Duke of York Stakes at York, and on the final day of Epsom's Derby meeting he went one ahead of Pat Eddery by winning on Mrs John Hislop's **Anonymous**. On August 8th Roberts, whose agent is Graham Rock, the freelance journalist, rode six winners in a day in England for the first time by completing a treble at Newmarket in the afternoon and another at Lingfield in the evening.

The following Tuesday he pulled muscles in his neck and back when thrown while riding work for Clive Brittain. After four days on the side-lines he resumed at Newbury, where he completed a double by winning the Group Two Ibn Bey Geoffrey Freer Stakes on **Shambo** for Brittain and the Stratton Handicap on **Cradle Days** for Richard Hannon.

Although Pat Eddery lost the championship, he was riding as well as ever, and for a long time he looked as though he would regain the lead. On June 26th he rode seven winners, three at Newmarket and four at Newcastle, and three days later he drew level with Roberts with three winners at Wolverhampton and another at Windsor, but his chances of retaining the title were virtually ruined by a five day suspension following his riding of Silver Wizard in the Scottish Equitable Gimcrack Stakes at York on August 19th. Eventually Eddery finished up with a score of 177 winners.

*A fine climax to User Friendly's domestic season — victory in the Coalite St Leger from the colts Sonus and Bonny Scot.*

Willie Carson, who was 50 on November 16th, reached the century for the 21st time in 22 years, by winning on **Burooj** at Lingfield on September 8th. Only Lester Piggott, with 25 to his credit, has notched up more centuries since the war.

After 25 seasons' riding 45 year-old George Duffield received the sort of recognition he has always deserved. Not only did he obtain his first classic successes, on **User Friendly** in the Oaks and St Leger, but he reached his first century on **Two Left Feet**, trained by Sir Mark Prescott, who has first claim on him, at Chepstow on October 20th, while earlier he had ridden his 1,600th winner in Britain on **Pie Hatch** at Pontefract on June 29th.

## ECONOMIC RECESSION HITS SALES

At a time when racing was feeling the effects of the general economic recession, further consternation was caused by the announcement that the Maktoums were reducing their commitments in England in the course of the Autumn. The brothers from the ruling family of Dubai boycotted the Newmarket yearling sales, an obvious indication of their dismay at the discriminatory VAT rate of 17.5%, that puts English breeders at such a great disadvantage with their counterparts in Ireland and France. In consequence of the absence of the Maktoums, and the extremely adverse economic situation, the yearling market was badly depressed. The 729 lots sold at Newmarket October Sales fetched 6,064,508 guineas, which was 51% down on the sum realised twelve months earlier.

The effects of the present crisis are already throwing an ominous shadow far into the future. Because of the sharp decrease in the value of Sterling, the National Stud is finding it increasingly difficult to acquire potentially top class stallions for the use of British breeders. The Stud was unsuccessful in attempts to purchase Rodrigo de Triano and Dr Devious, both of whom were sold to Japan.

However, the Stud was successful in its negotiations to obtain the 1991 Prix de l'Arc de Triomphe winner Suave Dancer, who will stand at a fee expected to be less than £15,000.

The deaths of a number of notable personalities occurred in 1992. Mr Jim Joel, that doyen of owners, died at the great age of 97 on March 23rd. A most kind and generous man, he was leading owner and leading breeder in 1967, the year that he won the 2,000 Guineas and the Derby with **Royal Palace**, whom he bred at his Childwick Bury Stud in Hertfordshire. For many years he had his horses trained in his private stable, Sefton Lodge in Newmarket, together with others in various public stables.

Mr Charles St George, a prominent figure in the insurance business, was 66 when he died suddenly on May 27th. He had horses with Henry Cecil, the late Captain Ryan Price and other trainers for nearly 40 years, winning the Oaks with **Ginevra** in 1972 as well as the St Leger with **Bruni** in 1975 and **Michelozzo** in 1989.

Mr Raymond Guest, American businessman, diplomat and politician, was 84 when he died on New Year's Day. He won the 2,000 Guineas and Derby with **Sir Ivor** in 1968.

The Earl of Iveagh was 55 at the time of his death in July. The best of the horses that he ran in England was **Karabas**, with whom the late Bernard van Cutsem won the Hardwicke Stakes at Royal Ascot in 1970. For many years Lord Iveagh owned the Kildangan Stud in Ireland.

Chummy Gaventa, who died at the age of 91 in October, was well known both as bookmaker and punter. He had horses with Ron Smyth, John Sutcliffe and other trainers, the best having been **Chummy's Special**, winner of the Norfolk Stakes at Ascot in 1980.

Former Newmarket trainer Dickie Westbrook, whose best horse **Balatina** won seven races in 1982, died at the age of 64 in July. Before taking out a licence he had been head lad to Jack Watts.

## CLASSIC JOCKEY PASSES AWAY

Billy Nevett, who died at the age of 86 in May, was for many years the leading jockey in the North, when closely associated with three generations of the Peacock family. He won substitute Derbies at Newmarket on **Owen Tudor** in 1941, **Ocean Swell** in 1944 and **Dante** in 1945, and the Oaks on **Masaka** at Epsom in 1948.

Dennis Hartigan, a member of an Irish hunting family, was 71 at the time of his death in May. Until he retired in 1990, he had been the highly regarded head lad of John Dunlop at Arundel, having joined the staff in 1947.

Major David Swannell, MBE, former senior handicapper to the Jockey Club, and Clerk of the Course at Beverley and Thirsk, died of a heart attack at the age of 73 on July 24th. A man of most original thought, Major Swannell was largely responsible for the introduction of centralised handicapping, and made an important contribution to the establishment of the National Horseracing Museum at Newmarket.

Colonel Tommy Wallis, a member of the Jockey Club, died at the age of 69 on October 21st. He had been appointed General Manager of Racecourse Holdings Trust in 1970 and Managing Director in 1975. With his soft Irish brogue, he was one of the best liked people in racing, always eager to help anyone he could, in addition to being an exceptionally capable administrator.

Sir Patrick Meaney, Deputy Chairman of the Horserace Betting Levy Board since 1985, died aged 67 in July. A Government appointee to the Board, he was a leading industrialist.

**DEATH OF A LEGEND**

Three Derby winners died during the year. Nijinsky was 25 when he had to be put down in Kentucky due to laminitis, Grundy 20 at the time of his death in Japan, and Blakeney was put down at the National Stud in November at the age of 26.

Finally, the names of the first Members of the British Horseracing Board were announced on November 3rd. Lord Hartington is to be Chairman, and Sir Nevil Macready, Deputy Chairman. Along with David Oldrey, Christopher Spence and Lord Zetland, Lord Hartington will represent the Jockey Club, while Sir Nevil, together with Lord Swaythling and Michael Darnell, have been elected to the Board by the Industry Committee. The Racecourse Association is to be represented by Sir Paul Fox and John Sanderson, and the Racehorse Owners Association by Nick Robinson and Peter Jones.

# INDEX TO PAST FLAT RACING

Figure following the horse's name indicates its age. The figures following the pedigree refer to the numbers of the races (all-weather in italics e.g. 2600) in which the horse has run; parentheses ( ) indicate a win and if followed by '*d' — disqualified; small figures 2,3,4,5,6, denote other placings. Foreign races are denoted by the suffix 'a' (not under orders) are shown thus [2600 W]. Horses withdrawn (not under orders) are shown thus [2600 W]. Figures prefixed by 1991 refer to performances at all-weather tracks during November and December of 1991, those prefixed by 1992 refer to both turf and all-weather performances from the current year. Figures without a prefix date also refer to performances from 1992 but infer that the horse did not run on an all-weather track the previous autumn.

**Cambrian Hills (IRE)** 3 b f Caerleon (USA) — My Therape (Jimmy Reppin) 429 672⁴ 3213⁶ 3442 3664⁶

**Cambus Bay** 2 b f War Hero — Harbour Girl (Quayside) 1435⁵ 1559 2719 3164

**Camden Knight** 7 b g Camden Town — Motionless (Midsummer Night II) 97 3906

**Camden's Ransom (USA)** 5 b g Hostage (USA) — Camden Court (USA) (Inverness Drive (USA)) 409 504 (912) 1106⁴ (1344) 1637⁶ 1869⁴ 2341⁶ 2447⁴ 2846 3094⁶ 3277² 3428⁴ 3547 3903

**Cameo Kirby (FR)** 2 b c Lead On Time (USA) — Nofret (FR) (Meautry (FR)) 3000⁶ 3181⁵ 3758⁶

**Camino a Ronda** 3 ch f Hallgate — Viva Ronda (Kampala) 39 96 145 778 944 1753 1912

**Camomile** 4 b f Bay Express — Hot Spice (Hotfoot) 40

**Campalto (IRE)** 2 ch c Fools Holme (USA) — Simply Gorgeous (Hello Gorgeous (USA)) 3233a³ 3567a²

**Canaan Lane** 3 gr g Northern Tempest (USA) — Milnsbridge (Dragonara Palace (USA)) 289⁵ 406⁴ 490⁴ 1049³ 1334³ 1561² 2704²

**Canaan Valley** 4 ch g Absalom — My Pink Parrot (Pirate King) [887W] 1114⁴ 1441 1847 [2123W]

**Canadian Boy (IRE)** 3 b c Commanche Run — Canadian Guest (Be My Guest (USA)) 560 3246⁶ 3506

**Canadian Capers** 3 ch f Ballacashtal (CAN) — Carolynchristensen (Sweet Revenge) 690 871³ 970 1214³ (1411) 3417 3554 3701³ 3781 3928

**Canadian Eagle** 2 ch f Risk Me (FR) — Princess Lily (Blakeney) 3132 3531 3712

**Canaska Star** 2 b c Doyoun — North Telstar (Sallust) 933² 1457⁶ 1936² 2441² 3331a⁴ 3651a

**Canazei** 2 b f Mazaad — Captain Bonnie (Captain James) 263 423 769 1296 1838³ 2428⁵ 2652 3071 3472 3611

**Canbrack (IRE)** 3 b g Glenstal (USA) — Cottage Style (Thatch (USA)) 1440 1906 2075⁵ 3615 3756 3906

**Can Can Charlie** 2 gr c Vaigly Great — Norton Princess (Wolver Hollow) 3399 3631 3704 3820⁵

**Candarela** 2 b f Damister (USA) — Guestimate (FR) (Be My Guest (USA)) 2951 3297⁶ 3579

**Candesco** 6 b m Blushing Scribe (USA) — Madame Mim (Artaius (USA)) 3873

**Candle King (IRE)** 4 b g Tender King — Candelaria (FR) (Touch Paper) 344 626 997 1133 1504 1794⁵ 1905 2427 2729

**Cannonale (IRE)** 3 b c Mummy's Treasure — Sierra Princess (Vital Season) 549 697 863 1142

**Cannon Carew** 2 ch g Gunner B — Molly Carew (Jimmy Reppin) 3517⁶ 3709 3911²

**Canny Chronicle** 4 b or br g Daring March — Laisser Aller (Sagaro) (2971) 3369 3663⁶

**Canny Lad** 2 b c Green Ruby (USA) — Young Whip (Bold Owl) 924³ 1296⁵ 2074⁵

**Canonised** 8 b g Welsh Saint — Forest Glen (Tarqogan) 59 222

**Canon Kyle (IRE)** 3 ch g Music Boy — Crymlyn (Welsh Pageant) 238⁶ 618 750³ 1484⁶ 1786⁴ 2164² (2324)

**Canopus** 2 ch c Kalaglow — Jacinth (Red God) 3727⁵

**Cantanta** 3 b or br f Top Ville — Sarah Siddons (FR) (Le Levanstell) 625⁴ 873³ 1156² (1567) 2172

**Cantata (DEN)** 3 ch f Quilted — Candy (DEN) (Caliban) 2975a³

**Cantoris** 6 b m Song — Singing Witch (Sing Sing) 2127 2404³ 2642 2902³ 3188³ 3356 3528 3671 3803 3960³

**Capablanca** 2 br g Chief Singer — Madam Trilby (Grundy) 2598⁵ 3186⁶

**Cap Camarat (CAN)** 3 ch f Miswaki (USA) — Cap d'Antibes (AUS) (Better Boy) 1428⁵ (2266) 2531⁴

**Cape Pigeon (USA)** 7 ch g Storm Bird (CAN) — Someway Somehow (USA) (What Luck (USA)) **1991:** 4020 **1992:** 626² (941) 1201⁶ 1463 (1755) 2268⁴ 2463⁴ 2898³ 3182 3317 3673 3701²

**Cape Weaver** 2 b f Pampabird — Storm Weaver (Storm Bird (CAN)) 1591³ 1937² (2405)

**Capital Bond (IRE)** 4 b c Hegemony — Have A Flutter (Auction Ring (USA)) 233 504 626 1582⁴ 1949 2413 2885⁴ 3052

**Capital Idea (IRE)** 3 b c Mister Majestic — Star Heading (Upper Case (USA)) **1991:** 4011 **1992:** 452 614 1020 1155⁴ 1625 1753 2151³ 2365⁵ 2486⁶ 2732

**Capital Lad** 3 ch g Dublin Lad — Wellington Bear (Dragonara Palace (USA)) 1909 2531 2985

**Capolago** 5 b h Horage — Panthere Rouge (ITY) (Daring Display (USA)) 3335a³

**Caponostro (USA)** 2 b c Capote (USA) — Turn it Off (USA) (Turn and Count (USA)) 3939a⁶

**Cappahoosh (IRE)** 3 ch f Salmon Leap (USA) — Tagik (Targowice (USA)) 498⁶ 1041 1371 1890³ (2075) 2429³ 2813 3159 3281 3771 3947

**Caproni** 5 b g Lomond — Helaplane (USA) (Super Concorde (USA)) 3352

**Caps Ninety-Two (IRE)** 2 b f Magical Wonder (USA) — Rahwah (Northern Baby (CAN)) 5646 782⁴ 928 (1638) 2143³ 2528 2857⁵ 3023 3723

**Captain Horatius (IRE)** 3 b c Taufan (USA) — One Last Glimpse (Relko) 389⁴ (647) (960a) 1229a 1825a² (2509a) 2894a⁶ 3337a⁶ 3934a⁴

**Captain Jack** 2 b c Salse (USA) — Sanctuary (Welsh Pageant) 3276 3523² 3709

**Captain le Saux (IRE)** 2 b c Persian Heights — Casting Couch (Thatching) 1161² (1327) (1694) 2387² 2800³ 3325a²

**Captain Marmalade** 3 ch g Myjinski (USA) — Lady Seville (Orange Bay) 433 868 1005⁴ 1268³ 1374⁵ 1503⁵ 2922 3003 3557 3882 3955

**Captain My Captain (IRE)** 4 ch g Flash of Steel — Amanzi (African Sky) 702 1063⁴ 2281⁶ 2698 2934 3256 3487⁵

**Capten Morgan (IRE)** 2 b g Governor General — Grugiar (Red Sunset) 2994 3106 3291 3712

**Creative Flair (USA) 2** gr f Seattle Dancer (USA) — Rare Thing (USA) (Grey Dawn II) 1342⁴ 1578⁵ 2055 2557 2916⁴ 3173 *3315* 3598

**Creche 3** b c Bairn (USA) — Melody Park (Music Boy) **1991:** *(4079)* **1992:** *(54) (96) 133² 217⁴ (219)* 582 [1669W] 2192⁶ 2279⁵ 2663⁴ 3144 3777

**Credit Squeeze 2** ch c Superlative — Money Supply (Brigadier Gerard) 847 1103³ 1409 (2118) 2462 2695 3242⁴ 3432

**Creeager 10** b g Creetown — Teenager (Never Say Die) (605) 805² 1290² 1459

**Creego 3** b c Creetown — Go Flamingo (Relkino) 1122 1309⁴ 1570 1797 *2689* 3263 3595

**Crept Out (IRE) 3** ch c On Your Mark — Valbona (FR) (Abdos) 242⁵ 489⁵ 1786³ (2119) 2327²

**Creselly 5** b m Superlative — Gwiffina (Welsh Saint) 1013 1157³ 1365 2352⁵ *3375* 3479 3589⁴ 3882⁵

**Crested Wave (IRE) 2** ch f Persian Heights — Sea Venture (FR) (Diatome) 439⁵ (574)

**Crestwood Lad (USA) 3** ch g Palace Music (USA) — Sweet Ellen (USA) (Vitriolic) 618 3341 3473 3707

**Cretoes Dancer (USA) 3** br g Secreto (USA) — Mary Read (USA) (Graustark) 482 3174 3270 3422⁶ 3696⁶

**Crime Ofthecentury 2** b f Pharly (FR) — Crime of Passion (Dragonara Palace (USA)) 3179

**Crimson Blade 3** ch c Crever — Red Velvet (Red God) 997 1576 2053

**Crimson Cloud (IRE) 4** ch g Red Sunset — Shangara (Credo) 761 1372⁶ 1898³

**Crimson Consort (IRE) 3** b g Red Sunset — Purple Princess (Right Tack) 3246 3746 567 904⁶ 1001³ 1440³ 2050³ 2366 3386 3513

**Criquette 2** b f Shirley Heights — Ghislaine (USA) (Icecapade (USA)) 3440² (3833)

**Crisol 3** ch f Crystal Glitters (USA) — Manora (USA) (Stop The Music (USA)) 2096a

**Cristal Flite 2** b f Niniski (USA) — Julia Flyte (Drone) 1925⁴ 3096⁴ 3833⁶

**Cristofori (USA) 3** b or br c Fappiano (USA) — Somfas (USA) (What A Pleasure (USA)) 642a⁵ 843a⁴ 2890a⁶

**Critical Mass 2** gr c Petong — Cut It Fine (USA) (Big Spruce (USA)) 255⁵ 1991⁶ 2176 2488³ 2802

**Crofter's Cline 8** b or br g Crofter (USA) — Modena (Sassafras (FR)) **1991:** *4008 4052* **1992:** 1992 *2483* 2906 3105 *3845*

**Croft House 3** b g Sizzling Melody — Isolationist (Welsh Pageant) 2613⁶

**Croft Valley 5** ch g Crofthall — Sannavally (Sagaro) **1991:** *4052* **1992:** *(2825)* 3209² 3428² 3726³ *(3826)*

**Croire (IRE) 2** b f Lomond (USA) — Fighting Run (Runnett) 3848

**Cromarty 2** b f Shareef Dancer (USA) — Forres (Thatch (USA)) 3313⁴

**Cromer's Express 3** ch c Mansingh (USA) — Sallusteno (Sallust) 506 669⁶ 1920 2131 2552 2680 2942 3073 3101

**Cronk's Courage 6** ch g Krayyan — Iresine (GER) (Frontal) **1991:** *4005² 4028⁴ (4042)* 4063 *(4081)* 4103 **1992:** 265² *(325)* 398² 478³ 629⁶ 723² 1289⁶ 2003 2203³ 2404² 2637 2741² 2902⁶ 3126 3828

**Cronk's Quality 9** b g Main Reef — Ozone (Auction Ring (USA)) 731 897⁶ 1084⁴ 2032 2406 2750 2830 *2974* 3251 3423⁶ 3559⁴ 3748⁶ 3783

**Cropton 2** b f Flash of Steel — Crymlyn (Welsh Pageant) 1120⁵ (3314) (3599)

**Crosby 6** b h Music Boy — Yelney (Blakeney) **1991:** *(4056)* 4075² 4095 **1992:** *53⁵ 77²*

**Crosby Place 6** gr m Crooner — Royal Bat (Crowned Prince (USA)) *193³* 232

**Crossillion 4** b c Rousillon (USA) — Croda Rossa (ITY) (Grey Sovereign) **1991:** *(4060)* **1992:** *88⁶* 368⁵ 477²

**Cross Mags 5** ch m Hasty Word — Red Squaw (Tribal Chief) **1991:** *4005*

**Croupier 5** b h Night Shift (USA) — Countess Walewski (Brigadier Gerard) 692 1061⁶ 1387⁶ 1706 DEAD

**Crown Baladee (USA) 5** b or br g Chief's Crown (USA) — Naseem Baladee (Kris) 2860

**Crown Reserve 4** br c Another Realm — Stardyn (Star Appeal) **1991:** *4019 4032⁴ 4073* **1992:** *115 154* 277 736⁵ 1172³ (1294) 1572

**Cruachan (USA) 4** b c Lear Fan (USA) — Sugar Hollow (USA) (Val de L'Orne (FR)) 436

**Cru Exceptionnel 4** b c Scottish Reel — Elton Abbess (Tamerlane) 626 936³ 1463⁵ 1877 3236 3317 3547⁵ 3732⁵

**Cruise Party (IRE) 4** b g Slip Anchor — Cider Princess (Alcide) 507

**Crusade (IRE) 2** b c Digamist (USA) — Theda (Mummy's Pet) 383 514² 817⁶ 1202² (1584) 2017³ 2528

**Cryptic Clue (USA) 3** b c Alleged (USA) — Nom de Plume (USA) (Nodouble (USA)) 512⁶ 1720 1917

**Crystado (FR) 3** ch c Crystal Glitters (USA) — Kantado (Saulingo) 1304³ 1862² (2186) 2464⁴

**Crystal Cross (USA) 3** b f Roberto (USA) — Crystal Cup (USA) (Nijinsky (CAN)) 695⁴ 908² (1220) 1301² 1768³ 2178² 2798⁵ 3244 (3492) 3798

**Crystal Heights (FR) 4** ch g Crystal Glitters (USA) — Fahrenheit (Mount Hagen (FR)) 1174³ 2658⁵ 2825 3145³ 3418⁶ 3632² 3714 3819

**Crystal Jack (FR) 4** b g Crystal Glitters (USA) — Cackle (USA) (Crow (FR)) 570⁵ 723⁶ (1014) (1247) 1487⁴ (1607) 2003⁶ 2435 (2902) 3031⁵ 3243 3787²

**Crystal Key 2** b f Bustino — Minor Chord (Major Portion) 1887³ 2292⁶

**Crystal Path (FR) 4** ch f Crystal Glitters (USA) — Flower Parade (Mill Reef (USA)) 343² 1816a⁶ 2090a³ 2624a⁴ 3228a

**Crystal Spirit 5** b g Kris — Crown Treasure (USA) (Graustark) 1022⁶ 1459³

**Crystal Stone 2** b f Commanche Run — Bonnie Banks (Lomond (USA)) 1957 2248⁵ 2930 3320 3502 3716

**Diet 6** b g Starch Reduced — Highland Rossie (Pablond) 796 888⁵ (1111) 1326⁴ 1512⁴ 2214 2262² 2559 2816³ 2878⁴ 2966³ 3154² 3341⁵ 3355² 3496⁵

**Digger Doyle 3** b g Cragador — Chaconia Girl (Bay Express) 939 1040⁶ *(1268)*

**Dig in the Ribs (IRE) 2** ch c Digamist (USA) — First Contact (Simbir) 3193⁵ 3614⁶ 3856⁶

**Digpast (IRE) 2** ch c Digamist (USA) — Starlit Way (Pall Mall) 3884a⁶

**Dili (USA) 2** b f Chief's Crown (USA) — Untitled (Vaguely Noble) 3871

**Dilkush 3** b g Dunbeath (USA) — Good Try (Good Bond) *182⁶* 252 3042 *3557* 3690 *3842*

**Dilum (USA) 3** br c Tasso (USA) — Yanuka (Pitcairn) 655 (1285) (1822a) 2892a 3195⁴ 3715

**Dime Bag 3** ch f High Line — Blue Guitar (Cure The Blues (USA)) 427⁶ 789 (2116) 2455 3007⁴ 3415³ *(3930)*

**Dioman Shadeed (USA) 3** b g Shadeed (USA) — Dimant Rose (USA) (Tromos) 1245 2549 2704⁴ 3062

**Diplomatist 2** b f Dominion — Dame Julian (Blakeney) 2792 3093⁴

**Disco Boy 2** b c Green Ruby (USA) — Sweet And Shiny (Siliconn) 3051 *3376⁵* 3626

**Discord 6** b g Niniski (USA) — Apple Peel (Pall Mall) **1991:** *4040⁴* **1992:** (590) *(905)* (1612)

**Diskette 3** b f Local Suitor (USA) — Last Clear Chance (USA) (Alleged (USA)) 2826 (3115) 3530⁶

**Disputed Call (USA) 3** b c Alleged (USA) — Tennis Partner (USA) (Northern Dancer) 3667⁵ 3801

**Dissimulateur (FR) 3** b c Legend of France (USA) — Dartana (FR) (Roi Dagobert) 635a⁵ 3814a³

**Distant Memory 3** gr g Don't Forget Me — Canton Silk (Runnymede) 695 942⁴ 1102⁵ 1971

**Distant Spring (IRE) 2** br g Dowsing (USA) — Fariha (Mummy's Pet) 2285 3285

**Di Stefano 4** b g Chief Singer — Doree Moisson (FR) (Connaught) 331

**Distinct Thatcher (USA) 3** b g Stifelius — Clearly Early (USA) (Distinctive (USA)) 443⁴ 549² 957a³

**Dittisham (USA) 2** b f Sir Ivor — Eltisley (USA) (Grey Sovereign) 2338⁶ 3414

**Dive for Cover (USA) 3** b c Lear Fan (USA) — Wistoral (USA) (Exceller (USA)) 1819a⁴

**Divine Glory 3** b f Valiyar — Mummy's Glory (Mummy's Pet) 3592 3692

**Divine Pet 7** br g Tina's Pet — Davinia (Gold Form) 731⁶ 1167³ 1305³ 2032 2307² 2752⁵ 2919 3067⁶ *(3257)*

**Divine Rain 2** b c Dowsing (USA) — La Reine de France (Queen's Hussar) 1502 1944³ 3765⁵ 3844

**Diving (USA) 4** br g Silver Hawk (USA) — Challenging Stage (USA) (Gold Stage (USA)) [225W] 267 326⁵ 532 DEAD

**Divorce Court (IRE) 2** b c Digamist (USA) — Centre Piece (Tompion) 2646⁴

**Dixieland Melody (USA) 2** b c Dixieland Band (USA) — Celebration Song (J O Tobin (USA)) 3005² (3147)

**Dizzy Dame 3** b f Mummy's Game — Dancing Chimes (London Bells (CAN)) 835 1033 1408

**Dizzy Penny 3** b f Pennine Walk — Tizzy (Formidable (USA)) 393²

**Dizzy (USA) 4** gr f Golden Act (USA) — Bergluft (GER) (Literat) 664

**Djais (FR) 3** ch c Vacarme (USA) — Dame de Carreau (FR) (Targowice (USA)) (1815a) 2096a³ 3111a³

**D K Daffers (IRE) 2** b f Pennine Walk — Payola (Auction Ring (USA)) 3683 3855

**Doc Cottrill 2** b g Absalom — Bridal Wave (Julio Mariner) 1699 2024 2551⁴ 3123⁵ (3482) 3832³

**Docket (USA) 4** b f Robellino (USA) — Allegedly (USA) (Sir Ivor) 536⁴ 663² 1585⁴ 1922

**Docklands (USA) 3** b f Theatrical — Dockage (USA) (Riverman (USA)) 3909⁴

**Doc Spot 2** b g Doc Marten — Detonate (Derring-Do) 571 1112 *1549⁴* 1860³ 2112⁵ 2735³ 2938 3050² 3173² 3497⁴ 3614

**Doctoor (USA) 2** ch c Cozzene (USA) — To The Top (USA) (Bold Hour) 3106³ 3402² 3644³

**Doctor-J (IRE) 2** ch c Jareer (USA) — Velvet Breeze (Windjammer (USA)) 3948⁶

**Doctor Roy 4** ch c Electric — Pushkar (Northfields (USA)) 829 1863 2026² 2219³ 2742 2853 3082

**Doctor's Remedy 6** br g Doc Marten — Champagne Party (Amber Rama (USA)) 586 *905* 9514 1125 1520⁵ 1530 1968³ (2260) 2596 2670⁶ 2827³ 2971⁵ 3021 3302⁶

**Dodger Dickins 5** gr g Godswalk (USA) — Sronica (Midsummer Night II) **1991:** *4083* **1992:** (362) 578 683 2261⁵

**Dodgy 5** b g Homing — Beryl's Jewel (Siliconn) **1991:** *4008* **1992:** 1589 1813³ 2198⁴ (2410) (2656) 3009² 3182⁴ 3317⁵

**Dodgy Dancer 2** b c Shareef Dancer (USA) — Fluctuate (Sharpen Up) 3402 3593 3775

**Doesyoudoes 3** b f Bay Express — Captain Bonnie (Captain James) **1991:** *4024⁴* *4031³ 4055³ 4079⁶* **1992:** (44) *5⁴⁵ 8⁵⁶* 163³ 227 452 3004 3220 3296⁶ 3499 3777⁵ 3854

**Dogma 3** b f Kabour — Domineering (Dominion) *61*

**Dokkha Oyston (IRE) 4** b g Prince Sabo — I Don't Mind (Swing Easy (USA)) 294⁴ (542) 686 3074⁴ 3154³ 3355 3496² 3632 (3759)

**Dollar Seeker (USA) 8** b h Buckfinder (USA) — Syrian Song (Damascus (USA)) 2001⁶ 2222⁶ 2677⁵ 2737 2968

**Dollar Wine (IRE) 3** b g Alzao (USA) — Captain's Covey (Captain James) 508 621³ 1122 1213⁶ 1572 1912⁵

**Dolly Madison (IRE) 3** b f Shirley Heights — Shellshock (Salvo) 597³ 881⁵ 1316⁶ *2043³* DEAD

**Domain 4** b c Dominion — Prelude (Troy) *90⁵⁵* 1002³ 1190³ 1564⁴ 2692

**Domes of Silence 2** b c Vin St Benet — Baby Flo (Porto Bello) *1375* 2005 2232⁴ 2512³ *2781*

**Double Bass (USA) 2** b or br c The Minstrel (CAN) — Minstrelete (USA) (Round Table) 1709² (2130) 3772²

**Double Blue 3** ch c Town And Country — Australia Fair (AUS) (Without Fear (FR)) (324) (452) (472) (535) 870² 1400² 1474² 1820a² 2435 2642 3014³ 3083⁴ (3145) 3356 3495² 3680

**Double Echo (IRE) 4** br c Glow (USA) — Piculet (Morston (FR)) **1991:** 4019 (4074) (4094) **1992:** 41² (273) 479 713² 829⁶ 1200³ 1463 3084⁴ 3212³ 3640⁴ 3789 3903

**Double Entendre 6** br m Dominion — Triumphant (Track Spare) 2852 3212² 3547³ 3903

**Double Feature (IRE) 3** ch g Exhibitioner — Elmar (Lord Gayle (USA)) 242³ 3772² 684 1040⁵ 1888⁶ (2163) 2536⁴ 2614 2702³ 2817³ 3068⁴ 3355 3460

**Double Flutter 3** b f Beldale Flutter (USA) — Perfect Double (Double Form) 370³ (2495) 2748⁴ 2913³ 3032⁶

**Double Lark 3** b c Bairn (USA) — Straffan Girl (Sallust) 808⁵ 1012 1281⁴ 1581 1918 2084 2234 2694

**Double Sherry 3** ch f Crofthall — Two's Up (Double Jump) 1510² 2957 3266 3639⁴ 3863

**Double Shift 3** b f Night Shift (USA) — Laleston (Junius (USA)) 1293² 1433² 1918² 2229⁵ 2969

**Double the Stakes (USA) 3** b c Raise A Man (USA) — Je'da Qua (USA) (Fleet Nasrullah) 375³ 457³ 766 1052 1901 2072⁵

**Doughman 3** b g Runnett — Trila Love (Lomond (USA)) 531 745 1627 1725⁶ 2066⁶ 2422 2602 2937

**Doulabella (IRE) 2** ch f Doulab (USA) — Salabella (Sallust) (3163) 3807⁵

**Doulab's Image 5** ch g Doulab (USA) — Haneena (Habitat) **1991:** 4008 4052 **1992:** (31) (50) 86 100⁶ 199² 2775 364³ 438⁵ 534⁶ (1905) (2060) (2369) 2658² (2852) 3209⁵ 3441 3726

**Douraj (IRE) 3** b g Doulab (USA) — Serraj (USA) (Seattle Slew) 471 1062 1557² 1673⁴ 2871

**Dovale 4** ch f Superlative — Astonishing (Jolly Good) 993 1555² (1879) 2180 3040³ 3346⁵ 3526 3763

**Dover Patrol (IRE) 2** b c Dancing Brave (USA) — Britannia's Rule (Blakeney) 3693⁶ 3855³

**Dowland (USA) 4** b c Sovereign Dancer (USA) — Grace Note (FR) (Top Ville) 724 954a 1351a³ 3327a

**Downlands Aris 2** b f Then Again — Pinaka (Pitcairn) 2005 2591⁶

**Dowreyna 2** br f Dowsing (USA) — Lareyna (Welsh Pageant) 859⁶ 2248² 2629 3155 3283⁶

**Doyce 3** b f Formidable (USA) — Current Raiser (Filiberto (USA)) (295) 464² 534⁵ 821 1025 1252⁵ 1700 3310 3681 3759⁵ 3919³

**Draft Board 3** b f Rainbow Quest (USA) — Selection Board (Welsh Pageant) 2780⁵ 3085⁵ 3416² (3592) 3729⁴ 3866³

**Dragonmist (IRE) 2** b f Digamist (USA) — Etage (Ile de Bourbon (USA)) 1384 1867⁶ 3055 3410

**Dragon Spirit 3** gr g Absalom — Fair Eleanor (Saritamer (USA)) **1991:** 4037 **1992:** 370 994³ 1563⁵ 1921⁶ 2725⁵

**Dragon's Teeth (IRE) 2** b c Caerleon (USA) — Scots Lass (Shirley Heights) 3297² 3624⁴

**Dramanice (USA) 2** b c Northern Fling (USA) — Almost Pure (USA) (Barrera (USA)) 3719⁴ 3892⁴

**Dramatic Pass (IRE) 3** ch g Coquelin (USA) — Miss Flirt (Welsh Pageant) 369 4882² 1025 1700⁶ 2334

**Dr Devious (IRE) 3** ch c Ahonoora — Rose of Jericho (USA) (Alleged (USA)) 444² 741a (1198) 1819a² 2837⁴ (3327a) 3657a⁶ 3940a⁴

**Dream a Bit 2** b f Dreams To Reality (USA) — On A Bit (Mummy's Pet) 1851² 2049⁶ 2482⁴ 2960⁶ 3472 3746

**Dream Carrier (IRE) 4** b g Doulab (USA) — Dream Trader (Auction Ring (USA)) 712 832 1032 1201 1500² 1716 2126² (2268) 2494 2770⁴ 3061⁴ 3245

**Dreaming Star 7** br g Star Appeal — Yea Misty (Forli (ARG)) 718

**Dream Princess 2** b f Dreams To Reality (USA) — Qualitair Princess (Bay Express) 1900 2158⁴

**Dreams Are Free (IRE) 2** b f Caerleon (USA) — Keep The Thought (USA) (Valdez (USA)) 3904

**Dreams End 4** ch c Rainbow Quest (USA) — Be Easy (Be Friendly) 1465 2347⁴

**Dreams Eyes 4** b c Dreams To Reality (USA) — Hairbrush (USA) (Sir Gaylord) 1130 1617⁴ 1978 2291 2466 2614

**Dreams to Wotan 3** b c Dreams To Reality (USA) — Olga Wagner (ITY) (Sharpen Up) 2062 2753

**Dream Sweet Dreams (USA) 3** gr or ro f Dahar (USA) — Aronia (USA) (Grey Dawn II) 167 3028

**Dream Talk 5** b h Dreams To Reality (USA) — Lala (Welsh Saint) 4a² 836a² (1228a) 2767a³ 3656a

**Dreamtime Echo 4** b f Green Ruby (USA) — Aleda Rose (Charlottown) 1427 1570 1787⁶ 2607 2808

**Dress Sense (IRE) 3** b c Top Ville — Smarten Up (Sharpen Up) 600² 835² (1505) (1723) 3122⁵ 3368 3732

**Drinks Party (IRE) 4** b f Camden Town — Holy Water (Monseigneur (USA)) **1991:** 4038 **1992:** 575⁶ 1034⁴ 1311³ 2059 (3601)

**Dr Lechter 2** b g Efisio — Ruby's Chance (Charlottesville) (3382) 3550

**Dr Maccarter (USA) 5** gr g Dr Carter (USA) — Now Voyager (USA) (Naskra (USA)) **1991:** 4019

**Drop a Curtsey 3** b f Prince Sabo — Pretty Miss (So Blessed) 1323 1682⁶ 2004⁴ 2809

**Drought (IRE) 3** b f Rainbow Quest (USA) — Short Rations (Lorenzaccio) 1872⁵ (2109) 2915² 3102

**Drumdonna (IRE) 2** b f Drumalis — Decoy Duck (Decoy Boy) 2248³ 2675 (2879) 3127 3354⁴ 3796

**Drummer Hicks 3** b or br c Seymour Hicks (FR) — Musical Princess (Cavo Doro) 268⁴ 604 1025⁴ (1335) (1700) (2018) 2403² 3192 3514² (3678)

# Index to Flat Racing

**Forty Niner Days (USA) 5** gr g Conquistador Cielo (USA) — Party Bonnet (USA) (The Axe II) 3938a

**Forza Azzurri (IRE) 3** ch c On Your Mark — Miss Legend (USA) (Bold Legend) 98⁵ 157⁴ 174 216³ 406 495⁴ 1000⁵ 1803 2015 2362⁴ 2666⁶ 2694

**Fourforfun 2** br c Midyan (USA) — Jennyjo (Martinmas) 3262⁵ 3523⁶ 3782

**Fourofus 3** b g Wassl — Que Sera (Music Boy) 582⁵ 792 1076⁵ 2365⁶ 2822 3003

**Foursingh 4** br g Mansingh (USA) — Maycrest (Imperial Fling (USA)) 31 50 66⁵ 115³ 154² 187 [422W] 616 776 1016⁶ 1362

**Fourstars Allstar (USA) 4** b c Compliance (USA) — Broadway Joan (USA) (Bold Arian (USA)) 3938a

**Fourwalk 8** br g Godswalk (USA) — Vaunt (USA) (Hill Rise) 294⁶

**Fowda (USA) 4** ch f Strawberry Road (AUS) — Al Balessa (USA) (Rare Performer (USA)) 3937a

**Fox Chapel 5** b g Formidable (USA) — Hollow Heart (Wolver Hollow) 293⁴ 368

**Foxes Diamond 4** b f Sallust — Rahesh (Raffingora) 264 359 542³ 660³ 948 1093⁵ 1271 1570 1617

**Fraam 3** b c Lead On Time (USA) — Majestic Kahala (USA) (Majestic Prince) (3238) 3427⁵

**Fragonard (IRE) 3** b g Pharly (FR) — Girl On A Swing (High Top) 432

**Fragrant Hackette 3** ch f Simply Great (FR) — Martin-Lavell News (Song) 1006

**Fragrant Hill 4** b f Shirley Heights — English Spring (USA) (Grey Dawn II) (854) 1211 1843⁶ 2461⁵ 2911 3571

**Fraise (USA) 4** b c Strawberry Road (AUS) — Zalataia (FR) (Dictus (FR)) 3648a² (3940a)

**Francis Ann 4** br f Balidar — Supper Party (He Loves Me) (660) 794⁵ 888 1130 1333⁶ 2875² (3154) 3341 3496⁶ 3916

**Franciscan 5** b g Godswalk (USA) — Athenian Primrose (Tower Walk) 354⁶ 426 593

**Frankie Goodman (IRE) 2** b c Colmore Row — Shukriaa (Busted) 907

**Frankus 3** b g Nicholas Bill — Sigh (Highland Melody) 833 1159 3690

**Frasers Hill (IRE) 2** b f Tate Gallery (USA) — Sybaris (Crowned Prince (USA)) 1541 2055

**Freaky Deaky 5** b g Prince Tenderfoot (USA) — Maylands (Windjammer (USA)) 866 1130⁵ 1317

**Freckenham 2** br f Rousillon (USA) — Screenable (USA) (Silent Screen (USA)) 2649 3181 3694

**Freddie Jack 2** b c Midyan (USA) — Sule Skerry (Scottish Rifle) 2897

**Freddie Lloyd (USA) 3** ch g Barrera (USA) — Shredaline (USA) (Shredder (USA)) 254³ 445⁶ (559) 714² (819) (1350a) (2448) 2851⁵

**Free At Last 5** b m Shirley Heights — Brocade (Habitat) 20a³

**Freebyjove 2** ch f King Among Kings — London Chimes (London Bells (CAN)) 584 782 1429 2195 3685 3926

**Free Dancer 2** b f Shareef Dancer (USA) — Free Touch (Kris) 2248⁴ 2551⁵ 3498

**Free Expression 7** b m Kind of Hush — Liberation (Native Prince) 1404 1721

**Free Flyer (IRE) 3** b c Bluebird (USA) — Lassalia (Sallust) 341² 1876⁴ 2507a⁴ 3322a

**Free Market 2** br g Crowning Honors (CAN) — Market Rose (Most Secret) 1071 1291⁵ 1694

**Free Minx 6** b g Free State — Musical Minx (Jukebox) **1991:** 4062 4083⁴ **1992:** 76 893

**Free Mover (IRE) 3** br g Rousillon (USA) — Free Dance (FR) (Green Dancer (USA)) 1069³ 1758³ (2089) 3007

**Freephone (CAN) 3** b g Phone Trick (USA) — Flying Aristocrat (USA) (Prince John) 242 728⁵ 972³ 1528⁶ 1772 2084

**Free Transfer (IRE) 3** b c Dara Monarch — Free Reserve (USA) (Tom Rolfe) **1991:** 4010 4053⁶ 4085⁶ **1992:** 487³ 1395² 1940⁵ 3282 3377⁶ 3536 3755 3875⁶

**Freewheel (USA) 3** ch f Arctic Tern (USA) — Dinner Surprise (USA) (Lyphard (USA)) (2282)

**French Flair (USA) 3** ch f Bering — Princess Cariole (Jaazeiro (USA)) 841a³

**French Heiress 2** b f Caerleon (USA) — Kereolle (Riverman (USA)) 3179

**French Ivy (USA) 5** ch g Nodouble (USA) — Lierre (USA) (Gummo (USA)) 718

**Frenchpark 2** b c Fools Holme (USA) — Piffle (Shirley Heights) 2887a² (3735a) 3975a⁵

**French Revolution (FR) 3** ch f Midyan (USA) — French Beauty (FR) (Jim French (USA)) **1991:** 4053⁵ **1992:** 94⁴ 3056⁴ 3306 3609

**Freni 3** b f Primo Dominie — F Sharp (Formidable (USA)) 347⁵ 408 1085 1160

**Frescade (USA) 2** b c Green Dancer (USA) — Breeze Me (USA) (Best Turn (USA)) 2799³ 3272⁵ (3775)

**Frescobaldo 6** b g Run The Gantlet (USA) — Voice of The River (USA) (Speak John) **1991:** 4073 4100⁴ **1992:** 25² 673 (88) DEAD

**Fret (USA) 2** b c Storm Bird (CAN) — Windy And Mild (USA) (Best Turn (USA)) 1610² (1899) 3446⁶

**Friendly Brave (USA) 2** b c Well Decorated (USA) — Companionship (USA) (Princely Native (USA)) 1161³ 1457 1709³ 1873⁴ 2456⁵

**Friendly Claim (IRE) 4** b g Petorius — Pitaka (Pitskelly) **1991:** 4047² (4077) 4103² **1992:** 874 1402

**Friendly House (IRE) 3** b c Fools Holme (USA) — Perle's Fashion (Sallust) 1746 1919² 2691⁵ 2870⁵

**Friendly Knight 2** b c Horage — Be A Dancer (Be Friendly) 2818 3498⁴ 3760 3913

**Friendlypersuasion (IRE) 4** b g Legend of France (USA) — Waladah (Thatch (USA)) **1991:** 4038⁶ **1992:** 277⁴ 364 422⁶ 469 875 962 1150 1294 2394³ 2630⁵ 3101⁴ 3302⁵ (3827) 3947

**Friendly Smile 2** b f Vin St Benet — Elfin Smile (Be Friendly) 3892

**Friendly Song 4** ch f Song — Friendly Jester (Be Friendly) 194

# G

**Gallery Artist (IRE) 4** ch c Tate Gallery (USA) — Avec L'Amour (Realm) *(1001)* 1266 1685 2201⁶ 2785⁵ *(3378)* 3595

**Gallery Note (IRE) 3** b f Tate Gallery (USA) — Thank You Note (What A Guest) 302 *2366⁶* 3383³ 3849⁶

**Galley Gossip 3** b g Dunbeath (USA) — Mother Brown (Candy Cane) 2813 375 448⁵ 1919⁵ 2088 2237⁶ 2539 2694 2931 3251 3592

**Gallop to Glory 2** b c Petong — Merchantmens Girl (Klairon) 3018 3179

**Game Germaine 2** b f Mummy's Game — Coppice (Pardao) 2459 2758

**Gan Awry 5** b m Kabour — Wedded Bliss (Relko) *1005*

**Ganeshaya 3** gr g Formidable (USA) — Lammastide (Martinmas) 508 948 1278 1570³ 1776⁴ 2063² *(2279)* 2548 2599² *(2821)* [3068W] [3103W] 3196 3397⁵ [3499W]

**Ganges (USA) 4** gr c Riverman (USA) — Paloma Blanca (USA) (Blushing Groom (FR)) 284⁴ 2626a⁴

**Gangleader 2** gr c Petong — Good Woman (Good Times (ITY)) 1208⁶ 1728² 2932 3285 (3410) 3606³ 3723 3867

**Gant Bleu (FR) 5** ch g Crystal Glitters (USA) — Gold Honey (Artaius (USA)) 962 1089³ 1193 1449³ 1564² *(1629)* 1793⁶ *(1961)* 2183⁶ 2668³ *(3086)* 3198⁵ 3417 *(3545)* 3612 3714

**Garabagh (IRE) 3** b c Darshaan — Glowing Halo (Grundy) 840a³

**Garachico (USA) 3** b g Green Dancer (USA) — Little Lady Luck (USA) (Jacinto) 857 2137³ 2549³ 2749⁴ 3021 3236

**Garah 3** b f Ajdal (USA) — Abha (Thatching) *(428)* *(601)* *(851)* 982⁴ 3528² 3731⁵ 3957³

**Garda's Gold 9** b g Garda's Revenge (USA) — Mielee (Le Levanstell) 1292³ 1430⁴ 1922⁵

**Garden District 3** b c Celestial Storm (USA) — Rose Chanelle (Welsh Pageant) 566² (1139) (1592) (1765) 1834² (2455)

**Garden of Heaven (USA) 3** ch c Arctic Tern (USA) — Garden of Eden (Exbury) 531² 1933² (2133) 3429³ (3814a)

**Garendare 3** br f Vacarme (USA) — Girouette (USA) (Nodouble (USA)) 379a³ (837a) 1498a 3658a

**Garnock Valley 2** b c Dowsing (USA) — Sunley Sinner (Try My Best (USA)) 874³ 1689⁵ 2223² 2444³ 3347

**Garp (FR) 2** b c Lead On Time (USA) — Copy Cat (FR) (King of Macedon) 1915⁴ (2335) 2841 3199 3508

**Garth 4** gr g Petong — Doppio (Dublin Taxi) 624² 1014⁴ 1247 1614 2060³ 3002⁴ 3417⁴ 3673 3905 3952

**Gate Lodge (IRE) 2** b f Last Tycoon — Tigeen (Habitat) 2093a⁶

**Gate of Heaven 2** b f Starry Night (USA) — Halatch (Habat) 3719

**Gaveko (USA) 3** b g Al Nasr (FR) — Corolina (USA) (Nashua) 1287 1919³ 2720

**Gay Glint 5** b g Glint of Gold — Gay Hellene (Ela-Mana-Mou) 632⁵ 861⁴ (1381) 1938 (2339) 2899 3666

**Gay Ming 3** b f Gay Meadow — Miss Admington (Double Jump) **1991:** *4066* **1992:** 502 603 (1052) *1548⁵* 1735² 1977² 2211² 2470³ 2736⁴ 3603⁵ 3705³ 3876⁴

**Gaynor Goodman (IRE) 2** ch f Fayruz — Sassess (Sassafras (FR)) 297 339³ 402⁴ 971⁴ 1638 1764⁴ 2005⁵ 2238 3218 3420⁶ 3590

**Gaynor's Boy (IRE) 3** ch c Hatim (USA) — Corista (Tudor Music) 1519 3583 3743⁵

**Gay Ruffian 6** b g Welsh Term — Alcinea (FR) (Sweet Revenge) 1331⁵

**Gdansk's Honour (USA) 3** b f Danzig (USA) — Royal Honoree (USA) (Round Table) (540a) 841a² 1097a 2760a² 2888a² 3226a⁵

**Geisway (CAN) 2** br c Geiger Counter (USA) — Broadway Beauty (USA) (Chompion (USA)) 828² (1017) 1457⁵ 1939⁴ 2175² (3272) 3446²

**Gemdoubleyou 4** b f Magnolia Lad — Amber Windsor (Windjammer (USA)) *158* 333 696 1034 1294 1624

**Gemini Bay 3** b c Petong — Deux Etoiles (Bay Express) 472 1107 1379 1636 3417 3766 *3931*

**Gemini Fire 8** br g Mansingh (USA) — Sealady (Seaepic (USA)) 1829⁵ 2073 2280 2741 3120⁶ 3464 3960

**Genair (FR) 7** ch h General Assembly (USA) — Metair (Laser Light) 768² 1018² 1480 1619 DEAD

**General Brooks (IRE) 2** b g Governor General — Choral Park (Music Boy) 543² 7515 1524 1788³ 2207³ 2965⁶ 3165

**General Chase 2** ch f Scottish Reel — Make A Signal (Royal Gunner (USA)) 721⁶ 968 1748⁴ 2409³ 2695 (3173) 3260⁴ 3574

**General Dixie (USA) 3** b g Dixieland Band (USA) — Bold Example (Bold Lad (USA)) [440W] 627⁵ 693⁴ [1577W]

**General John (IRE) 3** br g Cyrano de Bergerac — Hill's Realm (USA) (Key To The Kingdom (USA)) **1991:** *4044* **1992:** *(37)* 401⁵

**General Link 2** b c Governor General — City Link Lass (Double Jump) 3312⁵ 3626³ 3750

**Generally 2** b f Governor General — Long Valley (Ribero) 995⁶ 1170 1541 1601 3179

**General Mouktar 2** ch c Hadeer — Fly The Coop (Kris) 3525 3775

**General Polo 2** b g Governor General — Madam Chesty (English Prince) [2425W]

**Generous Ben 2** b g Myjinski (USA) — Playtex (Be Friendly) *2802* 2951

**Genesis Four 2** b c Dreams To Reality (USA) — Relma (Relko) 231 425⁵ 1140 1764

**Genio 2** br c Glow (USA) — Maxi Girl (My Swanee) 3519

**Genseric (FR) 2** br c Groom Dancer (USA) — Green Rosy (USA) (Green Dancer (USA)) 1701⁵ 2398 3297⁴

**Gentle Hero (USA) 6** ch g Hero's Honor (USA) — Tender Camilla (Prince Tenderfoot (USA)) 403 629 813 1403 1487⁵ 1943 2520⁶ 2839 3088 3355 3469 3620² 3866 3910

## H

**Hostess Quickly** 5 b m Hotfoot — Linda Dudley (Owen Dudley) **1991:** 4023 4032 DEAD

**Hostile Act** 7 b g Glenstal (USA) — Fandetta (Gay Fandango) (USA) 31744

**Hostile Witness (IRE)** 2 br c Law Society (USA) — No Time To Dance (Shareef Dancer (USA)) 26533 3000 34195 3665

**Host (IRE)** 3 b c Be My Guest (USA) — Take Your Mark (USA) (Round Table) 481 (1383) 21744 28385 33634 3663 (3835)

**Hotaria** 2 b f Sizzling Melody — Fair Eleanor (Saritamer (USA)) 770 8864 12335 27402 29603 (3077) 3187 3347 37236

**Hotel California (IRE)** 2 b f Last Tycoon — Rained Off (Welsh Pageant) 17153 2233 2544 2842 (3301) 3587

**Hot Favourite (FR)** 3 b f Fast Topaze (USA) — Beraude (FR) (Kenmare (FR)) 1815a3 2096a4

**Hotfoot Hannah (IRE)** 4 b f Anita's Prince — Serendip (Sing Sing) 3002 407 506 7525 (1162) 12825 1904 (2206) DEAD

**Hot Lavender (CAN)** 3 b f Shadeed (USA) — Wind Spray (Mill Reef (USA)) 3994 582 6904 9062 11134 17023 18713 19945 22796

**Hot Off the Press** 2 gr g Chilibang — Printafoil (Habat) 574 9734 11122 12993 1526 3071 3301 34973 3611 3843

**Hot Prospect** 3 b f Damister (USA) — Smelter (Prominer) 18395 19863 30285 33504 3601

**Hot Punch** 3 ch g Dara Monarch — Glebehill (Northfields (USA)) 366 1075 12813 14404 21605 25316

**Hotsocks** 2 ch f Hotfoot — Renira (Relkino) 3712 3844

**Hot Sound** 3 b f Hotfoot — Sound Type (Upper Case (USA)) 356 448

**Hot Star** 6 b g Hotfoot — La Camargue (Wollow) 35155 36212

**Hot Storm** 2 b f Celestial Storm (USA) — Canvas Shoe (Hotfoot) (2374) 25726 2696 3407 3623

**Hot Tip** 3 b f Beldale Flutter (USA) — Summer's Darling (Final Straw) 14385 1922

**Hot Tootsie** 5 b m Hotfoot — Lady of The Isle (Pitskelly) **1991:** 4005

**Houlston's Will** 3 ch f Nicholas Bill — Falcrello (Falcon) 235 3742 4933 671 1025 (2935) 3203 (3342) 3346 39084

**How's Yer Father** 6 b g Daring March — Dawn Ditty (Song) 344 4144 5963 (731) 8534 (1028) 1201 16142 17555 26182 27523 2945 30672 (3355) 3680 3729 38476

**Hoy-Liegh-Rag** 2 b c Glow (USA) — Wuthering Falls (Wind And Wuthering (USA)) 2024 23352 25682 3399

**Hthaal (USA)** 4 b or br g Caro — Endurable Heights (USA) (Graustark) 1518 1894 20715 3152

**Hubbers Favourite** 4 ch f Anfield — Printafoil (Habat) **1991:** 4032 **1992:** 13232 1550 16822 1847 20996 2785 3180 3251 3395 3481

**Hudud (USA)** 3 ch f Vaguely Noble — Belle Forbes (USA) (Bold Forbes (USA)) 38015 39665

**Huesca** 2 gr f Aragon — Houston Belle (Milford) 255 3296 588 782

**Huffa (USA)** 2 b g Ziggy's Boy (USA) — Science Hill (USA) (Cox's Ridge (USA)) (571) 7093 10674

**Hugging** 3 b f Beveled (USA) — Pillowing (Good Times (ITY)) 2525 4066 4902 6892 9384 (1209) 15335 21402 31355 3269 34393 3695

**Hula Bay (USA)** 2 ch g Lord At War (ARG) — Osculate (USA) (Forli (ARG)) 23643

**Hullo Mary Doll** 3 br f Lidhame — Princess Story (Prince de Galles) 16814 19865 3022 3416 3690

**Humam (IRE)** 2 ch c Nijinsky (CAN) — Passamaquoddy (USA) (Drone) (1249) (1471) 19393 24452

**Humber's Supreme (IRE)** 2 b f Digamist (USA) — Raise A Princess (USA) (Raise A Native) 18545 2551 2745

**Humour (IRE)** 3 b f Sadler's Wells (USA) — Princess Tracy (Ahonoora) 3024 3564 7883 908 12425 1739

**Hundred Hours (IRE)** 3 b c Pennine Walk — Santa Ana Wind (Busted) 175a3

**Hung Hing (IRE)** 2 b g Cyrano de Bergerac — Turbo Lady (Tumble Wind (USA)) 2986 3512

**Hung Over** 6 b m Smackover — Passionate (Dragonara Palace) 2946

**Hung Parliament** 2 gr f Sharrood (USA) — Session (Reform) 3394 4763 7213 9732 (2285) 2462 28413 31872 3530 (3786)

**Hunted** 5 ch g Busted — Madam Cody (Hot Spark) 3351

**Hunting Ground** 4 b c Dancing Brave (USA) — Ack's Secret (USA) (Ack Ack (USA)) 22872 36976 3950

**Hurricane Toke (IRE)** 3 gr c Kenmare (FR) — Believer (Blakeney) 633 2549 2780 3177

**Hush Baby (IRE)** 2 b f Ballacashtal (CAN) — Kind Lady (Kind of Hush) 2557 31156 34075 36236 3871

**Huso** 4 ch g Sharpo — Husnah (USA) (Caro) **1991:** 4052 **1992:** 2813 2926 3149 3302

**Hyde's Happy Hour** 2 b c Primo Dominie — Ixia (I Say) 2024 2277 27003 30296 3199

**Hydro Calido (USA)** 3 b f Nureyev (USA) — Coup de Folie (USA) (Halo (USA)) (380a) 958a2 1357a2 (2624a) 2892a 3738a

**Hymn Book (IRE)** 3 b f Darshaan — Divina (GER) (Alpenkonig (GER)) 3563 583 9025 26206

**Hymne D'Amour (USA)** 4 b f Dixieland Band (USA) — La Francaise (USA) (Jim French (USA)) 2054 24152 36876

**Hynes Torpedo** 2 b c Today And Tomorrow — Be Cool (Relkino) 1489

**Hypnotist** 5 b g High Top — Tamilian (Tamerlane) 358

**Hy Wilma** 2 b f Jalmood (USA) — Hymettus (Blakeney) 2005 (2238) 25586 2883 3218 3553

**I**

**Ian's Ace** 2 ch g Aragon — Rose And The Ring (Welsh Pageant) 729 856⁵ 3768

**Ibn Sina (USA)** 5 b g Dr Blum (USA) — Two On One (CAN) (Lord Durham (CAN)) 1361 1521

**Ibraz (USA)** 2 b c Cox's Ridge (USA) — Perfect Example (USA) (Far North (CAN)) (2286) 2679² 3127³

**I Broke the Rules (IRE)** 3 b f Montekin — Dar-A-Meter (Dara Monarch) 300 594 906 1030

**Ibsen** 4 b c Gorytus (USA) — State of Mind (Mill Reef (USA)) **1991:** 4074² **1992:** 799³ 2711⁵ 3021 3732 3882

**Ibtikar (USA)** 2 b f Private Account (USA) — Anne Campbell (USA) (Never Bend) 3430⁶ 3683³ 3848

**Ice Rebel** 2 br c Robellino (USA) — Ice Chocolate (USA) (Icecapade (USA)) 3018⁶ 3181 3419 3843⁵

**Ice Strike (USA)** 3 b c Eskimo (USA) — Gama Tres (USA) (El Pitirre (USA)) 3258 3609

**Ice Walk** 3 gr f Kalaglow — Krishnagar (Kris) 3306 3513⁶

**Icterina (USA)** 2 b f Secreto (USA) — Sugar And Spice (USA) (Key To The Mint (USA)) 3360

**Icy South (USA)** 2 b or br c Alleged (USA) — Arctic Eclipse (USA) (Northern Dancer) 817³ 1017³ (2002) 2918⁴ 3127⁵ 3891a⁴

**Ideal Candidate** 3 b f Celestial Storm (USA) — Rising Star (St Paddy) 1102⁴ 1175 1385⁶ (1572) 1679³ 1914³ (2007) (2014) 2156² 2407² 2682² (2915) 2992⁴ (3219) (3244) 3316⁴

**Idefix (USA)** 6 ch h Nureyev (USA) — Rose du Boele (FR) (Rheffic (FR)) 13a³

**Idir Linn (IRE)** 4 b g Camden Town — Dippy Girl (Sandford Lad) **1991:** 4057 **1992:** 731 830 1160² 1343² 1685² 2040⁶ (2366) 2689⁴ 3245 3391³ 3605

**I Do Care** 2 ch c Absalom — Oxide (USA) (Our Native (USA)) 1489⁴ 1779³ 2205 2812

**Idoni** 3 b c Bustino — Miranda Julia (Julio Mariner) 1207³ 1464

**If it Suits** 2 b c Local Suitor (USA) — If (FR) (Kashmir II) 1658⁶

**Iftakhaar (USA)** 3 b c Private Account (USA) — Old Goat (USA) (Olden Times) 440 710³ 1505³ 1953³ 3713 (3804)

**Ignatius (USA)** 2 b c Danzig (USA) — Royal Honoree (USA) (Round Table) 3113a⁵

**Ignited** 2 b c Colmore Row — Flame Up (Bustino) 2482 3289 3552

**I Have to Say (IRE)** 2 b f Jareer (USA) — Say Something (Reform) 3735a

**Ihsaas** 5 b h Niniski (USA) — Justicia (Nonoalco (USA)) **1991:** 4007 4023 4050

**Ihtiraz** 2 ch c Soviet Star (USA) — Azyaa (Kris) 1196² 1469 2269² (2947) 3205 3791²

**Ijab (CAN)** 2 b c Ascot Knight (CAN) — Renounce (USA) (Buckpasser) 3693 3844

**Ikhtiraa (USA)** 2 b c Imperial Falcon (CAN) — True Native (USA) (Raise A Native) 3525 3764⁴

**Ikhtisas (USA)** 2 gr f Woodman (USA) — Lettre d'Amour (USA) (Caro) 2190⁵ 2501 2674⁵ 3295³ 3502 3683²

**Ikteshaf** 4 b g Green Desert (USA) — Colourful (FR) (Gay Mecene (USA)) 225 398⁴ 887³ (1110) 2945³ 3002 3344² (3495) 3680

**Il Corsair (IRE)** 4 b c Horage — Corozal (Corvaro (USA)) 3661a³

**Ile de Chypre** 7 b h Ile de Bourbon (USA) — Salamina (Welsh Pageant) 343³ 557 2220⁴ 2846³ 3138⁵ 3368

**Ilewin** 5 br g Ile de Bourbon (USA) — City Swinger (Derrylin) 3426

**Illogical** 5 br m Ile de Bourbon (USA) — Modern Romance (Dance In Time (CAN)) 225⁵

**I'Ll Risk it** 2 b f Risk Me (FR) — Gymnopedie (Jaazeiro (USA)) 1264 1554 2363 3033

**I'Ll Soon Know** 5 ch m Known Fact (USA) — Soolyn (Dominion) **1991:** 4034 4068

**Illuminating** 3 ch f Electric — Jarama (Amber Rama (USA)) 230⁴ 376⁵ 497⁶ 1070

**Ilmenite** 2 gr f Petong — Irenic (Mummy's Pet) 3047 3295 3749

**Il Moro Di Venezia (IRE)** 2 b c Fairy King (USA) — Rosmarita (Sallust) 3240 3410 3517⁴ 3768

**I'M a Dreamer (IRE)** 2 b g Mister Majestic — Lady Wise (Lord Gayle (USA)) 1046⁶ 2776³ 2842 3746³ 3899

**Imafifer (IRE)** 2 b c Mazaad — Zareeta (Free State) 2031 2773⁴ 2826 3049⁶ 3218 3508 3685

**Imaginary (IRE)** 2 b f Dancing Brave (USA) — Bold Fantasy (Bold Lad (IRE)) 3684²

**Ima Red Neck (USA)** 3 b c Dixieland Band (USA) — Bright Reply (Gleaming (USA)) 1906 2200⁵

**Imco Double (IRE)** 4 ch g Double Schwartz — Cupids Hill (Sallust) **1991:** 4021² (4063) 4078⁵ **1992:** 2786² 2974 3559

**I'M Curious** 3 b f Kirchner — The Dupecat (Javelot) 3238 3425 3604 3771 3827

**I'M Electric** 5 b g Electric — Mouletta (Moulton) 364 521⁶ 913² 1106³ (1150) (1292) 3174³ 3279²

**Imhotep** 5 gr g Claude Monet (USA) — Miss Melmore (Nishapour (FR)) 1961 2351⁴ (2607)

**I'M No Fool** 2 b g Alias Smith (USA) — Duchy (Rheingold) 3146

**Impair (USA)** 2 b c Jade Hunter (USA) — Stitz (USA) (Crimson Satan) 1809³ 2629

**Impeccable Charm (USA)** 3 b f Lyphard (USA) — Island Charm (USA) (Hawaii) 1478² 1770⁶ 3425³

**Imperial Ballet (IRE)** 3 b c Sadler's Wells (USA) — Amaranda (USA) (Bold Lad (IRE)) (1672) (2056) 2464⁵

**Imperial Bid (FR)** 4 b g No Pass No Sale — Tzaritsa (USA) (Young Emperor) 879⁵ 1436³ 1618³ 2202 2637⁶ 2898 3759

**Imperial Flight** 7 b g Pampabird — Queen of Time (Charlottown) 3522

**Jinga 7** b g Castle Keep — Eldoret (High Top) 3273

**Jinsky's Jewel 4** b g Myjinski (USA) — Song of Pride (Goldhills Pride) 3042 3251 3605 3827

**Jinxy Jack 8** b g Random Shot — True Or False (Varano) 234 2877⁶

**Jitterbugging 3** b c Try My Best (USA) — Dancing Sally (Sallust) 549² 744a⁴ 1227a³

**Jive Music 6** b m Music Boy — Swift To Conquer (Solinus) 752⁴ 888 1020⁵ 1271 1310⁵ 1522 *1853* 1892³ 2046⁵ 2466 2936 3166

**Jizyah 2** b f Green Desert (USA) — Kawkeb (USA) (Vaguely Noble) 3247³ 3619⁴

**Jobie 2** b c Precocious — Lingering (Kind of Hush) 3011 (3268)

**Jocks Joker 2** b g Germont — Kaymay (Maystreak) *1321* 1782⁴ 3115 *3376³*

**Jodie Bobs 3** ch f Adonijah — Lunaria (USA) (Twist The Axe (USA)) *179*

**Jody's Gamble 3** b g Scorpio (FR) — Forgets Image (Florescence) 2084

**Joellise 2** b f Glint of Gold — Carolside (Music Maestro) 3480 3704

**Joe Sugden 8** b g Music Boy — Sum Star (Comedy Star (USA)) **1991:** *4006⁴* **1992:** *2094* 236 996⁶ 1199 1415⁶ 2548⁴ 2821³ 2919⁶ 3103 (3294) 3559² 3596 3783⁴

**Johanna Thyme 5** b m Reesh — Sea Thyme (Persian Bold) **1991:** *4063* **1992:** 752 1111 1310⁴ 1570 1924⁴ *2786* 2942⁶ *3373*

**Johann Quatz (FR) 3** b c Sadler's Wells (USA) — Whakilyric (USA) (Miswaki (USA)) *(959a)* 1356a⁴ 1823a 2890a 3329a

**John O'Dreams 7** b g Indian King (USA) — Mississipi Shuffle (Steel Heart) 2032 2127 2227³ 2752 2881 3098⁴ 3257³ 3400⁶ (3596) 3783 3879

**John Rose 3** b c Tina's Pet — City Link Lass (Double Jump) 556 722⁴ 959a⁵ 1229a 2464² (2943) 3229a 3542³ 3721

**Johns Act (USA) 2** b c Late Act (USA) — Deluxe Type (USA) (Singh (USA)) 2901³ 3320³ 3624²

**John Shaw (USA) 4** b c L'Emigrant (USA) — Ivory Wings (USA) (Sir Ivor) **1991:** *4007* **1992:** *2443* 272 773⁵ 1784 1922 2204 2734⁶ 2944² 3075 (3409) 3504⁵ (3761) 3922

**Johns Joy 7** b g Martin John — Saybya (Sallust) 3667 3769

**Johnston's Express (IRE) 4** b or br c Petorius — Siberian Princess (Northfields (USA)) 300 327 448 1338⁴ 1905⁴ 1961³ (2325) 2570⁴ 2816 3481³ 3916⁶

**Joie de Patina 3** ch f Forzando — Joie d'Or (FR) (Kashmir II) 1484 1865⁵ 1918 3119

**Join the Clan 3** ch f Clantime — Joint Reward (Netherkelly) 2862⁵ 3042⁵ 3252 3412

**Jokers Patch 5** ch g Hotfoot — Rhythmical (Swing Easy (USA)) 937 2867 2970³ *3930*

**Jokist 9** ro g Orchestra — What A Picture (My Swanee) 997⁴ 1203 1421 1799³ *2013* 3105⁶ 3365 3481 3785 3870⁶

**Jolie's Halo (USA) 5** b h Halo (USA) — Jolie Jolie (USA) (Sir Ivor) 3941a

**Jolis Absent 2** b f Primo Dominie — Jolimo (Fortissimo) 2501 3181 3414 3606

**Joli's Great 4** ch f Vaigly Great — Jolimo (Fortissimo) 273³ 409 565² (663) 1150³ 3140 3215³ 3873³ 3961

**Jolizal 4** ch f Good Times (ITY) — New Central (Remainder Man) 277 422 1009 1172² 1421⁶ 2729 3017

**Jolly Fisherman (IRE) 4** ch g Montekin — Ruby Relic (Monseigneur (USA)) **1991:** *4009*

**Jolly Jester 3** b g Jester — Casbar Lady (Native Bazaar) **1991:** *4092*

**Jolto 3** b c Noalto — Joytime (John de Coombe) 2496 2881² (3048) 3245 3963⁶

**Jolypha (USA) 3** b f Lyphard (USA) — Navajo Princess (USA) (Drone) 1098a² (1498a) (3330a) 3657a 3941a³

**Jo N Jack (IRE) 4** ch g Gorytus (USA) — Dancing Song (Ridan (USA)) *(3180)* 3311

**Jonsalan 2** gr g Robellino (USA) — Nelly Do Da (Derring-Do) 581⁴ 703⁴ 1899⁶ 2973⁶ 3044²

**Jood (USA) 3** b f Nijinsky (CAN) — Kamar (CAN) (Key To The Mint (USA)) 553³

**Jordywrath 2** ch g Efisio — Hedonist (Mandamus) *1547⁵* 1804³ *(2363)* 2973

**Jorrocks 3** ch g Risk Me (FR) — Rosana Park (Music Boy) 585 899 1086⁶ 1306

**Joseph's Wine (IRE) 3** b g Smile (USA) — Femme Gendarme (USA) (Policeman (FR)) 1964 2291 (2729) 3073⁵ 3149³ *(3705)*

**Joshua John (IRE) 3** br g Nashamaa — Nectareous (Tutankhamen) 1975⁶ 2493 3592

**Jotra 2** ch c Clantime — Branston Express (Bay Express) 3165 3484 3921

**Jovial Kate (USA) 5** gr m Northern Jove (CAN) — Flashy Feet (USA) (Pretense) **1991:** *4090* *4091⁴* **1992:** *43⁶* *57* *80⁴* *95²* *119* *(180)* *217* 285 541 613² 819 918⁵ 1050⁵ 1778⁵ 2040⁵ 2099² *2366* *(2481)* *2689²* 2936 3079

**Jovial Man (IRE) 3** b g Ela-Mana-Mou — Jovial Josie (USA) (Sea Bird II) 1319 1577 1917 2632

**Joyful Escapade 2** ch f Precocious — Mischiefmaker (Calpurnius) 2005

**Joyful Thought 3** b f Green Desert (USA) — Happy Thought (FR) (Kauai King) 522 949 1075⁵ 1514³

**Joy of Freedom 2** b or br f Damister (USA) — Debach Delight (Great Nephew) *3924*

**Joyofracing 2** b c Petoski — Lady Bequick (Sharpen Up) 446³ 555² (1573) 1868² (1979) 2176⁴ 3753² 3867

**J P Morgan 4** b or br g Law Society (USA) — Queen of The Brush (Averof) 405 663³ 916³ 1119 1239⁴ 1437⁴ 1562³ 1863 2048 2218⁴ 2699 2815 (2968) 3352⁵ 3493³ 3687 3761⁴ (3917)

**Jubal Early (IRE) 3** b g The Noble Player (USA) — Miss Galwegian (Sandford Lad) **1991:** *4037* 4097⁶ **1992:** 369 520⁵ 594 614

**Jubilata (USA) 4** ch f The Minstrel (CAN) — All Gladness (USA) (Alydar (USA)) 3141 3380⁵ 3493

**Luks Akura** 4 b g Dominion — Pacificus (USA) (Northern Dancer) *154 1925 2106* 249 *3154* 358 951 (1274) (1337) *14376 14524 15013 16916 17332* 18664 23292 2605 3273 3493 *37555* 3896

**Lumberjack (USA)** 8 b g Big Spruce (USA) — Snip (Shantung) *8936*

**Luna Bid** 9 b g Auction Ring (USA) — Moonscape (Ribero) 344 *4552* 624 *7752* 853 *10283* 1167 1343 *19526* *20325* *22035* (2290) 2520 2861 2942 3183 3400 3700

**Lunagraphe (USA)** 4 ch f Time For A Change (USA) — Lightship (USA) (Majestic Light (USA)) *206* 919 *1323 1550 21034 2784*

**Lunar Risk** 2 b c Risk Me (FR) — Moonlight Princess (Alias Smith (USA)) *3175 348906* 3691

**L'Uomo Classics** 5 b g Indian King (USA) — Sperrin Mist (Camden Town) *24156 28063* (3094) *3279 35225*

**Lupescu** 4 ch f Dixieland Band (USA) — Keep Me Posted (USA) (Stage Door Johnny) (3894)

**Lure (USA)** 3 b c Danzig (USA) — Endear (USA) (Alydar (USA)) (3938a)

**Lust of Love** 6 b m Sallust — Aridje (Mummy's Pet) 1013 1157

**Lute and Lyre (IRE)** 3 b f The Noble Player (USA) — Kool For Kats (Malinowski (USA)) *3326a*

**Luthier Enchanteur (USA)** 5 b h General Holme (USA) — Margis Lute (FR) (Luthier) *3938a6*

**Luthior (FR)** 6 gr g Carwhite — Luthiana (FR) (Luthier) *71*

**Luzum** 8 ch g Touching Wood (USA) — Velvet Habit (Habitat) *494* 63 89 *101*

**Lycian Moon** 3 b f Norwick (USA) — Brigannie Moon (Brigadier Gerard) 1319 *17585* 3258

**Lyford Cay (IRE)** 2 ch c Waajib — Island Goddess (Godswalk (USA)) *30352* *33552* (3631)

**Lyndon's Linnet** 4 b g Prince Sabo — Miss Rossi (Artaius (USA)) **1991:** *4028* **1992:** *32783* 3400 3777

**Lyn's Return (IRE)** 3 b c Nordico (USA) — Salmas (FR) (Right Royal V) *3665 4975* (603) *6945* (1102) *11655 16555 17723 19032 19766 24636* 2712 *31614* (3246) *33842 34665 35774 38635*

**Lyphantastic (USA)** 3 b c Lyphard's Wish (FR) — Tango Five Juliet (USA) (Fappiano (USA)) (1158) (1632)

**Lyphard's Song (IRE)** 4 b f Lyphard's Special (USA) — Supreme Song (Supreme Sovereign) *15605* 19884 *22616* 2565

**Lyric Fantasy (IRE)** 2 b f Tate Gallery (USA) — Flying Melody (Auction Ring (USA)) (584) (1067) (1461) (2176) (2851) *35292*

**Lys (IRE)** 2 ch f Don't Forget Me — Lycia (Targowice (USA)) 2338 (2683) 3001 3716

**Lysirra (USA)** 3 ch f Lyphard (USA) — Hopespringsforever (USA) (Mr Prospector (USA)) 434 699

# M

**Maamur (USA)** 4 gr g Robellino (USA) — Tiger Trap (USA) (Al Hattab (USA)) *(222)* 3543 *31185* 36682

**Maastricht** 2 b g Common Grounds — Awatef (Ela-Mana-Mou) 3717 3880

**Mabaadi (USA)** 2 b or br c Kris S (USA) — Faultless Too (USA) (Tudor Grey) 3820

**Ma Bella Luna** 3 b f Jalmood (USA) — Macarte (FR) (Gift Card (FR)) (546) *20183* *26013* 3958

**Mabonne** 3 b f King of Spain — Monsarah (Monsanto (FR)) *4086* 587 1159 *20063* 2198 2684 3037 *3557*

**Mabthul (USA)** 4 b g Northern Baby (CAN) — Persuadable (USA) (What A Pleasure (USA)) 422 586 799

**Macfarlane** 4 br c Kala Shikari — Tarvie (Swing Easy (USA)) *3862* *5503* 723 *12476* 1445 *18784* 3803

**Mack the Knife** 3 b c Kris — The Dancer (FR) (Green Dancer (USA)) 443 *7113* (3022) *32115* (3697) *38344*

**Macquarie Ridge (USA)** 4 ch f Cox's Ridge (USA) — Ocean's Answer (USA) (Northern Answer (CAN)) **1991:** *40453*

**Mac Rambler** 5 b g Hotfoot — Arkengarthdale (Sweet Story) 893 *27754* *30543*

**Macrobian** 8 b g Bay Express — White Domino (Sharpen Up) *3113 8192* *13932*

**Macs Bid (CAN)** 3 b c Summing (USA) — Hope She Does (USA) (Mr Leader (USA)) **1991:** *(4022)*

**Mac's Fighter** 7 ch h Hard Fought — Geoffrey's Sister (Sparkler) **1991:** *40654 40754* (4096) **1992:** *534 922 1273 2013 2072* 629 *8606 11163*

**Mac's Princess (USA)** 4 b f Sovereign Dancer (USA) — Jungle Princess (USA) (Jungle Road) **1991:** *40083 40392* 4057 *40683* **1992:** *284 502 632 1176 1243 1812*

**Mac the Lad** 3 ch g Rabdan — Halkissimo (Khalkis) 878

**Mac Tomb** 2 b c Valiyar — Elaine Ann (Garda's Revenge (USA)) 1161 1442 1675 2306

**Madagans Grey** 4 gr g Carwhite — Cheri Berry (Air Trooper) 435 2401 *26605* 3009

**Madam Caprice** 2 b f Salse (USA) — Maiden Pool (Sharpen Up) 2185 *27284* 3871

**Madam Cyn's Risk** 2 b f Risk Me (FR) — Very Special Lady (Mummy's Game) *7724 9002* *10073 12644* 14424 *23744* 26493 (2719) 2910 3173 3472

**Madame Cresson** 2 b f Petong — Sunley Stars (Sallust) 339 588

**Madam Petoski** 3 b f Petoski — Proper Madam (Mummy's Pet) 506 *7643* 885

**Mad March Hare** 2 ch c Jester — Maleiha (Martinmas) 1652 2225 2563

**Mad Martingan** 2 b or br c Alleging (USA) — Be My Lady (Be My Guest (USA)) *3945a2*

**Mad Militant (IRE) 3** b c Vision (USA) — Ullapool (Dominion) *(141) (177) (216)* 395 4643 7164 921 (1252) 25536 (2908) 31163 3461 36754 37885

**Mad Mytton 2** b c Crowning Honors (CAN) — Vynz Girl (Tower Walk) 4632 828 1424 16054 2675 30506 3115

**Maelkar (FR) 8** b g Maelstrom Lake — Karabice (Karabas) 3352

**M a El-Sahn 2** b c Presidium — Hoonah (FR) (Luthier) 3503 37925

**Maestroso (IRE) 3** b c Mister Majestic — That's Easy (Swing Easy (USA)) 3956 5994 8023 12104 15745 (2334) 25474 26984 29346 34155

**Magadeer (USA) 3** b f Mogambo (USA) — Star Silhouette (USA) (Dancer's Profile (USA)) 8046 1175 29225 *3184*5 33983 37062 38534 39093

**Magdalene Heights 4** ch g All Systems Go — Carreg-Wennol (Dublin Taxi) 2957

**Magdalene (USA) 4** b f Runnett — Grattan Princess (Tumble Wind (USA)) 532 660

**Maggie Siddons 4** b f Night Shift (USA) — Sarah Siddons (Reform) 240 610 7794

**Maggies Lad 4** b g Red Johnnie — Busted Love (Busted) 234

**Magical Maiden (USA) 3** b f Lord Avie (USA) — Gils Magic (USA) (Magesterial (USA)) *3937*a3

**Magical Queen (IRE) 2** ch f Magical Wonder (USA) — Lough Graney (Sallust) 24384 27282 30362

**Magical Retreat (USA) 2** b f Sir Ivor — Known Charter (Known Fact (USA)) 3904 39643

**Magication 2** b f Nomination — Gundreda (Gunner B) 13842 16682 20245 2695 3716

**Magic Carr (USA) 3** b c Carr de Naskra (USA) — Majestic Nature (USA) (Majestic Prince) 3327a

**Magic Fan (IRE) 2** b c Taufan (USA) — Magic Gold (Sallust) 2932 3262 3579

**Magic Night (FR) 4** b f Le Nain Jaune (FR) — Pin Up Babe (Prominer) 10a2 1231a 14972 1984a2 (2766a) (3332a) 3657a 3814a5

**Magic Orb 2** b f Primo Dominie — Tricky (Song) 7014 11206 20446 (3049) 3162 35906

**Magic Pearl 2** gr f Belfort (FR) — Oyster Gray (Tanfirion) 237 3652 7212 11862 1472 26365 28973 30515 34704 35902 37866

**Magic Penny 3** b f Sharrood (USA) — Bluebell (Town Crier) 1315 *1540*6

**Magic Ring (IRE) 3** b c Green Desert (USA) — Emaline (FR) (Empery (USA)) 391

**Magic Secret 4** b g Local Suitor (USA) — Meissarah (USA) (Silver Hawk (USA)) **1991:** *4026*2 *(4062)* **1992:** *25*3 *67*2 *(83)* 1073 19384 (2217) 2339 28206 29575

**Magic Steps 3** b f Nomination — Magic Tower (Tower Walk) 3014 3439 3787

**Magic Street 2** ch f Magical Wonder (USA) — Pushkinia (FR) (Pharly (FR)) 23383 26463 2986

**Magique Rond Point (USA) 2** b f Greinton — Petit Rond Point (USA) (Round Table) 19373 (2438) 34446

**Magirika (IRE) 2** br g Magical Wonder (USA) — Minarika (FR) (Djakao (FR)) 17445 23356 2633

**Magnetic Point (USA) 3** ch f Bering — Nonoalca (FR) (Nonoalco (USA)) 707 10124 12874 1528 19115 21282 22663 25313 26095 3576 3806 *3929*

**Magnetic Prince 3** b g Tina's Pet — Miss Magnetism (Baptism) 355 806 1294 1568

**Magnificent 3** b g Damister (USA) — Tantalizing Song (CAN) (The Minstrel (CAN)) (332) (464) 983 2795 2990 34754 3622

**Magnificent Star (USA) 4** b f Silver Hawk (USA) — Gulanar (Val de Loir) 2766a 2843 3190

**Magnified (USA) 3** br g Known Fact (USA) — Mofida (Right Tack) 6462 (1035) 24476 2852

**Magsood 7** ch g Mill Reef (USA) — Shark Song (Song) 9874 13614 1534 19516

**Mahaasin 4** b f Bellypha — Dame Ashfield (Grundy) 590 726 951 1248 14526 1572

**Mahairy (USA) 3** b c Theatrical — Papamiento (USA) (Blade (USA)) 12456 14476 19146 25243 2867 3054 3556

**Mahasin (USA) 3** b f Danzig (USA) — Icing (Prince Tenderfoot (USA)) 631 (989) (1148) 14026 24365

**Mahfil 4** b g Head For Heights — Polavera (FR) (Versailles II) 926 (1132) 13873 (1768) 2451 28602

**Mahogany Light (USA) 2** b c Woodman (USA) — Antique Lamp (USA) (Seattle Slew (USA)) 2456 33073 37094 3809

**Mahong 4** gr g Petong — Balearica (Bustino) 3021 3192 (3403) 35103

**Mahool (USA) 3** b c Alydar (USA) — Tax Dodge (USA) (Seattle Slew (USA)) 6714

**Mahrajan 8** b h Dominion — Dame Julian (Blakeney) 342 7086 8316 13183 17435 (2054) 22414 2827 3021 3273 3572

**Mahsul (IRE) 4** br c Ela-Mana-Mou — Afrah (USA) (Our Native (USA)) 438 7054 936 13035 15044 (1637) 20356 2184 (2415) 26602 28853 3139 32794 3708

**Mahzooz 3** ch g Crystal Glitters (USA) — Gandoorah (Record Token) 1661 2066 2536 2984

**Maid of Ice 3** b f Siberian Express (USA) — Kalorama (FR) (Bold Lad (IRE)) 5464 736

**Maid Welcome 5** br m Mummy's Pet — Carolynchristensen (Sweet Revenge) **1991:** *4058 4077*3 **1992:** *58 (132) 217*5 236 23015 2618

**Main Bid (IRE) 3** b g Auction Ring (USA) — Annabella (Habitat) 17123 2447 2852

**Main Caster (JPN) 6** ch f Northern Taste (CAN) — Nichido Queen (JPN) (Marino) 10a

**Mainly Me 3** b f Huntingdale — Mainmast (Bustino) 4062 5776 7154 16612 2066 23933 25862 2946 3245 3365 3511

**Mai Pen Rai 4** ch g All Systems Go — Jersey Maid (On Your Mark) **1991:** *4088* **1992:** *88 111 134 210*5 598 702

**Majal (IRE) 3** b g Caerleon (USA) — Park Special (Relkino) 2903 558 767 11752 13715 24633 26474 29202 32346 34664 37014

**Majboor (IRE) 3** b c Wassl — Mashteen (USA) (Majestic Prince) 3943 (511) 5852 1941 22822 3014 3241 3428

**Majed (IRE) 4** b c Wolverlife — Martin Place (Martinmas) 2145 (250) (373) 4314 5323 657 7995 1705 26445 29063 (3468) (3634) 37185 (3864)

**Majestic Boy (NZ) 6** b g Noble Bijou (USA) — Lili (NZ) (Royal Ridge (FR)) 24a3

**Majestic Hawk (USA) 2** br g Silver Hawk (USA) — Rose of The Sea (USA) (The Minstrel (CAN)) (1485) 19364 2445 2918 31274

**Majestic Image 6** ch m Niniski (USA) — Regal Twin (USA) (Majestic Prince) 18742 2339 (2921) 3728

**Majestic Maybe (IRE) 3** b f Mister Majestic — Lady Wise (Lord Gayle (USA)) **1991:** 4010

**Majestic Melody 4** ch f Crooner — Royal Birthday (St Paddy) 2476 2698 [3052W] 3418

**Majestic Sinclair (IRE) 3** b c Mister Majestic — Katie's Delight (Relko) 30806 33863 35835 36865

**Maji 3** b f Shareef Dancer (USA) — Majoritat (GER) (Konigsstuhl (GER)) 5002 7372 10792 13303 16025 19624 (2720) 29083 2985 33813 3556 3745

**Majira (USA) 3** b c Danzig (USA) — Private Colors (USA) (Private Account (USA)) 693 (1839) 2403

**Major Bugler (IRE) 3** b c Thatching — Bugle Sound (Bustino) 3876 6263 8586 29204 30402 3279 (3436) 36754

**Major Impact (USA) 3** b c Roberto (USA) — Convenienty (USA) (In Reality) 3645a2

**Majority Holding 7** b g Mandrake Major — Kirkby (Midsummer Night II) 3140

**Majority (IRE) 2** b c Dancing Brave (USA) — Majoritat (GER) (Konigsstuhl (GER)) 38183

**Major Ivor 7** ch h Mandrake Major — Double Birthday (Cavo Doro) 617 10513 1284 15272 17973

**Major Mouse 4** ch g All Systems Go — Tzu-Hsi (Songedor) (768) 10185 (1193) (1480) 2846 3069 3310

**Major Risk 3** ch g Risk Me (FR) — Brampton Grace (Tachypous) 1675 191 5193 806 1850 20875 25334 2682 33924

**Major's Law (IRE) 3** b c Law Society (USA) — Maryinsky (USA) (Northern Dancer) 242 395 5586 7163 12202 1466 26606 2992 32932 3415 37942

**Major Yaasi (USA) 2** b c Arctic Tern (USA) — Dimant Rose (USA) (Tromos) 36024 37752

**Make it Happen (IRE) 2** b c Fayruz — Genzyme Gene (Riboboy (USA)) 4913 654 9172 (1435) 21523 2960 31555 3482

**Make Me Proud (IRE) 3** b f Be My Native (USA) — Miami Life (Miami Springs) 1150 13725 21565 26926 29705

**Make Mine a Double 2** ch c Sharpo — My Fair Orchid (Roan Rocket) 491 6193 (1489) 17384 26694 2928 3155

**Makeminemusic 3** ch g Music Boy — Ultra Vires (High Line) 2517 2984 3513

**Make Or Mar 8** b or br m Daring March — Martelli (Pitskelly) 14516 16185 1853 22014 2234 26036

**Malaia (IRE) 2** b f Commanche Run — Spartan Helen (Troy) 34895

**Malcesine (IRE) 3** b f Auction Ring (USA) — Vain Deb (Gay Fandango (USA)) 854 177 2164 2953 5224 7494 9142 1992 2531 3052 31535 3383 37596 3849

**Maledetto (IRE) 3** b c Double Schwartz — Croglin Water (Monsanto (FR)) 1096a2 1350a2 1467 2092a2 2762a

**Malenoir (USA) 4** b g Solford (USA) — Viewed (USA) (Alydar (USA)) **1991:** 4059 4087 **1992:** 46 762 1032 (122) 138 (518) 6833 893 1002 3823

**Maligned (IRE) 3** b f Alzao (USA) — Place Royale (Pall Mall) 1505 17704 23023 2774 2934

**Malunar 7** gr g Mummy's Pet — Tranquility Base (Roan Rocket) 2533 344 4496 7943 10132 2570

**Malvernico (IRE) 4** b c Nordico (USA) — Malvern Beauty (Shirley Heights) 1495a3 1817a 2763a3 2889a5 3327a5

**Malzeta (IRE) 2** b f Alzao (USA) — Place of Honour (Be My Guest (USA)) 852 1279 2438 2951 3606

**Mamalama 4** ch f Nishapour (FR) — Gauloise (Welsh Pageant) 736 1044 11633 14234 15726 1810 2014

**Mamdooh 3** b g Green Desert (USA) — Shore Line (High Line) (2654) (3013) 3292 3527 3713

**Mamma's Too 3** b f Skyliner — Maple Syrup (Charlottown) 4542 8344 1535 (2061) 2406 (2663) 29092 30142 3212 34396 37145 3828

**Mam'zelle Angot 2** b f Balidar — Ragirl (Ragusa) 22773 28183 31152 32912 37125 38374

**Mamzooj (IRE) 3** br f Shareef Dancer (USA) — Inshirah (USA) (Caro) 502

**Manaarah (USA) 2** ch f Slew O' Gold (USA) — Edgewater (USA) (Verbatim (USA)) 2864 31472 34712 (3776)

**Manadel 2** b f Governor General — Manabel (Manado) 2606

**Manair (IRE) 3** b c Elegant Air — Romantic Overture (USA) (Stop The Music (USA)) 451 603

**Manaolana 4** b f Castle Keep — Ladysave (Stanford) 206 331 525 776

**Manbaa (IRE) 3** ch f Doulab (USA) — Dayajeer (Shirley Heights) 370 482 8846 17505

**Mandalay Prince 8** b g Nishapour (FR) — Ops (Welsh Saint) 3625 683

**Man From Eldorado (USA) 4** b c Mr Prospector (USA) — Promising Girl (USA) (Youth (USA)) 2395 390 929

**Mango Manila 7** b h Martinmas — Trigamy (Tribal Chief) 2336 (438) 6103 11334 1943 3359

**Mangrove Mist (IRE) 4** b f Nishapour (FR) — Antiguan Cove (Mill Reef (USA)) 3152 3351

**Manila Bay (USA) 2** b c Manila (USA) — Betty Money (USA) (Our Native (USA)) 13484 23562 30056

**Man of the Season (USA) 3** ch g Naked Sky (USA) — Kizzie (USA) (Naskra (USA)) **1991:** 40315 4079 **1992:** 3532 5103 734

**Manoftheyear 5** b h Sayf El Arab (USA) — Vexed Voter (Pontifex (USA)) 740a

**Mistic Glen (IRE) 3** b f Mister Majestic — Northern Glen (Northfields (USA)) 3384 3761

**Mist of the Marsh (USA) 3** b f Seattle Slew (USA) — Shywing (USA) (Wing Out (USA)) 989 1956 2236⁶ 3073 3177 3610³

**Mistress Minx 3** b f Faustus (USA) — Arctic Jewel (Mandamus) 2780 2995

**Misty Goddess (IRE) 4** gr f Godswalk (USA) — Silent Sail (Agloj) **1991:** 4033 **1992:** 56 120 505² 575⁴ (1034) 1255⁶ (1759) (2372) 2757⁴ 2937²

**Misty Jenni (IRE) 2** b f Night Shift (USA) — Mousil (Moulton) 2792 (3217) 3390⁶

**Misty Night 4** gr f Grey Desire — Maha (Northfields (USA)) 327

**Misty Silks 2** b f Scottish Reel — Silk St James (Pas de Seul) 3570 3684 3871

**Misty View 3** gr f Absalom — Long View (Persian Bold) 1123⁶ (1385) (1643) 2182² 2453 3066⁶ 3829

**Misunderstanding (IRE) 3** b g Wolverlife — Wallpark Princess (Balidar) 242 485³ 670³ 816⁶ 985³

**Mithi Al Gamar (USA) 2** ch f Blushing Groom (FR) — Raahia (CAN) (Vice Regent (CAN)) 3892

**Mithi Al Hawa 2** b f Salse (USA) — Moon Drop (Dominion) 3011² (3414) 3679² 3867

**Mitsubishi Centre (IRE) 3** gr f Thatching — Checkers (Habat) 3947

**Mitsubishi Video (IRE) 4** gr f Doulab (USA) — Checkers (Habat) 87 349⁶ 860 1021 1258⁶

**Mittenoski Pet 3** b f Petoski — Runabay (Run The Gantlet (USA)) 835 1003⁵ 1404

**Mizaaya 3** ch c Riverman (USA) — Exclusive Order (USA) (Exclusive Native (USA)) (235) 341 (725) (825) 1197 1460 2447

**Miznah (IRE) 3** b f Sadler's Wells (USA) — La Dame du Lac (USA) (Round Table) 429 2318a³ 3451a²

**Mizoram (USA) 3** ch c Miswaki (USA) — Ask Me How (USA) (Secretariat (USA)) 658 (1012) (1412) 1856² 2433

**Mizyan (IRE) 4** b g Melyno — Maid of Erin (USA) (Irish River (FR)) 1150⁴ 1324² (2101) 3875⁴

**Mma International (IRE) 3** ch g Milk of The Barley — Serena Maria (Dublin Taxi) 509 623 1213

**Model Nurse 5** b m Exhibitioner — Majestic Nurse (On Your Mark) 504 93 100³ 115³ 137

**Modern Art (IRE) 4** b g Tate Gallery (USA) — Fair Flutter (Beldale Flutter (USA)) 1682 1949 2545

**Modern Dance (USA) 3** b f Nureyev (USA) — Remedia (Dr Fager) 3416

**Modernise (USA) 3** ch c Known Fact (USA) — Modena (Roberto (USA)) 554² 816⁴ 983³ 3131⁶ (3645a)

**Modest Hope (USA) 5** b g Blushing Groom (FR) — Key Dancer (USA) (Nijinsky (CAN)) 422⁵ 525⁵ 875⁶ 1172 (3806) 3961³

**Modesto (USA) 4** b g Al Nasr (FR) — Modena (USA) (Roberto (USA)) **1991:** 4094 **1992:** 41⁴ (56) 81³ 111² (115) (146) 165⁴ (187) (190) 246³ 342 422 (713) 1132⁴ 1324³ 3256 3487

**Modhish (IRE) 3** b c Sadler's Wells (USA) — Arctique Royale (Royal And Regal (USA)) 635a² 843a⁵ 1356a⁵ (3111a) 3458a²

**Modi (USA) 2** b f Deputy Minister (CAN) — Katie Cochran (USA) (Roberto (USA)) 3132⁵ 3424²

**Mofador (GER) 8** br h Esclavo (FR) — Mantilla (GER) (Frontal) 158 3736 456 1018 1329³ 1449⁶ 1911 3239

**Mogwai (IRE) 3** b c Alzao (USA) — Maltese Pet (Dragonara Palace (USA)) 387 576⁵ 801³ 1412³ 2945⁵ 3133⁶ 3400⁴ 3700 3766 3931⁵

**Mohana 3** br f Mashhor Dancer (USA) — The Ranee (Royal Palace) 583 1165²

**Mohican Brave (IRE) 2** ch g Salt Dome (USA) — Mrs Tittlemouse (Nonoalco (USA)) 1017 1251 (1549) 2060² 2543 2938

**Mohican Girl 4** b f Dancing Brave (USA) — Unsuspected (Above Suspicion) 557⁵ 1197⁵ (1613) 2461³

**Mojave 3** b c Green Desert (USA) — Out of Shot (Shirley Heights) 1043² 1253 (2789) 3654a 3901

**Molly Splash 5** b m Dunbeath (USA) — Nelly Do Da (Derring-Do) 250⁴ 335 (505) 586³ 773 1257⁵ 1810⁵ 1976 (2253) 2416² 2600⁶ 2705² 2946⁵ 3045² 3387 3500³

**Molten Copper (IRE) 3** ch g Pennine Walk — Danger Signal (Red God) 401 456 604 1320 1548 3806

**Moment of Truth 8** b g Known Fact (USA) — Chieftain Girl (USA) (Chieftain II) 312 2677³ 2877⁵ 3351

**Monaafis 3** b c Kris — Mangayah (USA) (Spectacular Bid (USA)) 451

**Monarda 5** ch g Pharly (FR) — Emaline (FR) (Empery (USA)) 926⁴ (1081) (1543) 1766⁴ (2226) 2715³ 3057 3572

**Monastic Flight (IRE) 2** ch g Carmelite House (USA) — Short Stay (Be My Guest (USA)) 1670 2719³ 2901 3148

**Monazite 2** b c Damister (USA) — Princely Maid (King's Troop) 3959

**Monday At Three 2** ch c Absalom — Angel's Sing (Mansingh (USA)) 2619⁶ 3250

**Monde Bleu 4** b c Last Tycoon — Make Plans (USA) (Go Marching (USA)) (656) (1352a) 1475 2767a² 3450a² 3738a⁵

**Mondova (IRE) 3** b f Lomond (USA) — Padova (USA) (Forli (ARG)) 2165⁴ 2479⁴ 3374 3705

**Mondragon 2** b c Niniski (USA) — La Lutine (My Swallow) 2212² 2675 3631³ 3954

**Monet Monet Monet 2** ch f Claude Monet (USA) — Delta Wind (Tumble Wind (USA)) 2207 2428⁴ 2661³ 2863⁵ 3218 3472

**Monet Order 2** ch f Claude Monet (USA) — Surely Great (Vaigly Great) 803 1915 2055 2506⁶

**Money Spinner (USA) 3** b f Teenoso (USA) — Silver Dollar (Shirley Heights) (179) 788 2547

**Most Interesting** 7 b m Music Boy — Quick Glance (Oats) 1248

**Most Surprising (IRE)** 3 b g Runnett — Blue Elver (Kings Lake (USA)) 885² 1050⁶ 1791² 3383

**Mothers Day Magic** 6 ch m Kabour — Gay Walk (Farm Walk) 291

**Motley** 4 br f Rainbow Quest (USA) — Sans Blague (USA) (The Minstrel (CAN)) 536⁶ 663⁶ 891

**Mouchez le Nez (IRE)** 2 b f Cyrano de Bergerac — Gale Force Seven (Strong Gale) 1103 1384 2948 3218 3754

**Mougins (IRE)** 3 ch c Ela-Mana-Mou — Western Goddess (Red God) 7a⁴ 862⁴ 1136² 1476 2433 2711⁴

**Moujeeb (USA)** 2 b c Riverman (USA) — Capricorn Belle (Nonoalco (USA)) 3276 3593³ 3809

**Moumayaz (USA)** 2 b c Nureyev (USA) — Foreign Courier (USA) (Sir Ivor) 3326a⁵

**Mountain Ash** 3 b f Dominion — Red Berry (Great Nephew) (2322a) 3334a²

**Mountain Cat (USA)** 2 b c Storm Cat (USA) — Always Mint (CAN) (Key to the Mint (USA)) 3939a⁵

**Mountain High (FR)** 2 b c Lashkari — Lady River (FR) (Sir Gaylord) 3200⁵ 3512⁵ 3709

**Mountain Kingdom (USA)** 8 b h Exceller (USA) — Star In The North (USA) (Northern Dancer) 826 981⁶

**Mountain Retreat** 6 br g Top Ville — Tarrystone (So Blessed) 2226⁶

**Mountain Spring** 2 b c Myjinski (USA) — Flying Glory (Flying Mercury) 3719

**Mountain Willow** 2 b f Doyoun — Mountain Lodge (Blakeney) 3619³ 3855⁴ 3953

**Mount Helena** 3 b f Danzig (USA) — Helen Street (Troy) 1124⁴ 1928

**Mount Nelson** 6 ch g Morston (FR) — Doogali (Doon) 2267 2759 3118

**Mount Rose** 2 ch c Blushing Groom (FR) — Outstandingly (USA) (Exclusive Native (USA)) 3893

**Moussahim (USA)** 2 ch c Riverman (USA) — Abeesh (USA) (Nijinsky (CAN)) 3593⁵ 3917³ 3911³

**Move a Minute (USA)** 3 b c Al Nasr (FR) — Call Me Goddess (USA) (Prince John) 2133² 2464⁶

**Move Smartly (IRE)** 2 b c Smarten (USA) — Key Maneuver (USA) (Key To Content (USA)) 2675⁵ 3465⁶ 3631⁶ 3832 3954⁵

**Moving Force** 5 b g Muscatite — Saint Simbir (Simbir) 997⁶ 1366 1718⁵ 2077 2251² 2576⁵ 2705 2952 3045⁶ 3500

**Moving Image (IRE)** 2 b f Nordico (USA) — Aunty Eileen (Ahonoora) 476 1233² 1506² (1969) 2242³ 3012 3275 3590

**Moving Out** 4 b c Slip Anchor — New Generation (Young Generation) **1991:** (4050) **1992:** 385⁵ (507) 718 1331³ 1866² 1938⁶ 2373⁴ 3034 3351⁴

**Mow Waal (USA)** 2 ch f Shadeed (USA) — Bambee T T (Better Bee) 3904

**Mr Brooks** 5 b h Blazing Saddles (AUS) — Double Finesse (Double Jump) 827² 1475² (1942) (2767a) 2851² 3124² (3656a) 3935a

**Mr Butch** 2 b c Aragon — Kittycatoo Katango (USA) (Verbatim (USA)) 1913 2195³ 2428³ 2649² 2857³ 2973 3242⁵ (3394) 3550² 3642⁴ 3807

**Mr Confusion (IRE)** 4 b c Kafu — Mrs Foodbroker (Home Guard (USA)) (225) (422) (1295) (2028) (3122)

**Mr Copyforce** 2 gr c Sharrood (USA) — Cappuccilli (Lorenzaccio) 1873 2947⁴ 3186 3574 3926⁶

**Mr Cube (IRE)** 2 ch c Tate Gallery (USA) — Truly Thankful (CAN) (Graustark) 2118² 3410 3551 3837 3925²

**Mr Dingle** 2 ch c Music Boy — Toot Toot (Alias Smith (USA)) 772³ 3117 3376

**Mr Elk** 3 gr g Bellypha — Shuteye (Shirley Heights) 810 1048⁵ 1234³ 1491 1893³ 2045

**Mr Flood (USA)** 3 gr c Al Nasr (FR) — Flood (USA) (Riverman (USA)) 458² 633² 911² (1088) 1501

**Mr Geneaology (USA)** 2 b c Procida (USA) — Que Mona (USA) (Ribot) 2208⁴ 2733 3100⁶ 3758⁵

**Mr Kewmill** 9 b g Homing — Muninga (St Alphage) 2917

**Mr Martini (IRE)** 2 b c Pennine Walk — Arab Art (Artaius (USA)) (1405) 1472 2010³ 2193² (3325a)

**Mr Nevermind (IRE)** 2 b c The Noble Player (USA) — Salacia (Seaepic (USA)) 470 703 1171² 2257⁴ 2437 2706⁶ 2973 3283⁴ 3394² (3508)

**Mr News (IRE)** 3 b c Trojan Fen — Princess Biddy (Sun Prince) 369⁵ 457 1438 1783⁶ 1907⁶ 2250⁴ 2569 2701⁴ 2957 3141 3384 3752⁶

**Mr Optimistic** 5 ch g King Persian — Saybya (Sallust) 3351

**Mr Poppleton** 3 ch c Ballacashtal (CAN) — Greenstead Lady (Great Nephew) 497⁴ 694³ 932² 1260⁵ 1882⁶ 2455 3219

**Mrs Barton (IRE)** 4 gr f Faustus (USA) — Phar Lapa (Grundy) 552 1697 1988⁶ 2373 3244⁶ 3409² (3745) 3823⁵

**Mrs Claypool** 4 br f Petong — Rare Legend (Rarity) 3045

**Mrs Dawson** 2 gr f Sharrood (USA) — Faraway Grey (Absalom) 361 543⁶ 2058³ 2695⁴ 2938 3173

**Mrs Fisher (IRE)** 3 b f Salmon Leap (USA) — Amboselli (Raga Navarro (ITY)) (1523) 1928² (2140) 2436³ 2911⁶ (3433)

**Mrs Jawleyford (USA)** 4 b f Dixieland Band (USA) — Did She Agree (USA) (Restless Native) 3578⁵

**Mrs Jekyll (IRE)** 2 ch f Sure Blade (USA) — Grey Walls (Habitat) 3295 3617⁵ 3760³

**Mr Smiley** 5 b g Pharly (FR) — Yelming (Thatch (USA)) 3251 3423 3842

**Mrs Mouse** 4 ch f Formidable (USA) — Mary Mary Mouse (USA) (Valdez (USA)) 2754 3161

**Mr Snuggs (IRE)** 3 b c Nordico (USA) — Kilboy Concorde (African Sky) 472 216⁵

**Mr Sunny** 3 b g Revolutionary (USA) — Paddy's Widow (Paddy Boy) 2744⁴ 3078 3398

**Mrs West (USA)** 2 b f Gone West (USA) — Mrs Hat (Sharpen Up) 1259 (1553) 2657⁵ 3096 (3457a) 3739a⁵

**Native Lass (IRE) 3** ch f Be My Native (USA) — Fun Frolic (Sexton Blake) *194* 488

**Native Magic 6** ch m Be My Native (USA) — Tuyenu (Welsh Pageant) **1991:** *4040* **1992:** *1543* 2042 2295² 2731⁴ 3075

**Native Trio (USA) 2** b c Our Native (USA) — Ransomed Captive (USA) (Mr Leader (USA)) 2426⁵ 3100⁵ 3424

**Native Worth 2** b g Uncle Pokey — Jenavia (Krayyan) 1191 3147 3303 3474

**Natral Exchange (IRE) 3** b c Natroun (FR) — Aladja (Mill Reef (USA)) 268³ 597 1234² 1719³ 2122² 2677

**Naughty Charlotte 2** ch f Farajullah — Miss Sanur (Mummy's Pet) 2591⁴ 2863 3156 3291

**Navaresque 7** b m Raga Navarro (ITY) — Esquinade (Silly Season) 1338⁶ 1589⁶ 1756⁵ 2060⁵ 2582² 2770⁵ 2881

**Navarone (USA) 4** ch c Irish River (FR) — Wind Spirit (USA) (Round Table) 3940a

**Nawaaya (USA) 2** b f Fappiano (USA) — Skeeb (USA) (Topsider (USA)) 3549

**Nawwar 8** ch h Thatching — Priceless Pin (Saint Crespin III) 344 2634⁶ 2750⁶ 3037 3239⁵

**Nazare Blue 5** b h Absalom — Top Stream (Highland Melody) *109* *127* 830⁴ 967 1278⁶ 1339 1813⁵ 1978 2209 2698

**Nbaat (USA) 3** ch c El Gran Senor (USA) — Antartica (FR) (Arctic Tern (USA)) 924⁴ 2015³ 2419³ 2659⁵ 2831⁴ 3710² 3781

**Nectar Collector 3** b c Natroun (FR) — Mirkan Honey (Ballymore) 511 695⁵ 999² 1371 *2156⁶* 3073 3387

**Nedaarah 2** b f Reference Point — Shining Eyes (USA) (Mr Prospector (USA)) 2519 3172

**Ned's Bonanza 3** b g Green Ruby (USA) — Miss Display (Touch Paper) 559⁵ 690³ 949³ 1117⁴ (1669) 1871 2663 2741 2848 3144 3207

**Needle Gun (IRE) 2** b or br c Sure Blade (USA) — Lucayan Princess (High Line) 1349² 3205² 3446⁴

**Needwood Muppet 5** b g Rolfe (USA) — Sea Dart (Air Trooper) (312) 593³ 805⁴ 3504³ 3621 3877³

**Needwood Nugget 2** ch c Rolfe (USA) — Needwood Nut (Royben) 3948

**Needwood Poppy 4** b f Rolfe (USA) — Needwood Nap (Some Hand) 328³ 377 494 3500 3917

**Negative Pledge (USA) 3** b f Alleged (USA) — Laredo Lass (USA) (Bold Ruler) 1737⁵ 2043⁵

**Negatory (USA) 5** ch g Secreto (USA) — Negation (USA) (Mongo) **1991:** *4083* **1992:** *103*

**Neieb (USA) 3** b f Alleged (USA) — Victoria Star (CAN) (Northern Dancer) 2869³ 3025³ 3221 3306 3504² (3773) 3917⁵

**Neither Nor 3** ch f Norwich (USA) — Leap In Time (Dance In Time (CAN)) 624³ 808³ 1368⁶ (3252) 3554 3781

**Nellie Dean 3** ch f Song — Pubby (Doctor Wall) *1268²* *1852²* 2803 3042 *3375* (3747)

**Nellie Hen 2** b f Vaigly Great — Janlarmar (Habat) 3338 3626

**Nellie's Gamble 2** b f Mummy's Game — Harmonious Sound (Auction Ring (USA)) 2315 286 682 1121⁴ *1321⁶* 1559⁶ (3611) 3821 3913⁴

**Neltegrity 3** b g Neltino — Integrity (Reform) 451 (1109) 1255 1604⁴ 1986² 2237² 2430⁴ 3466

**Nemea (USA) 2** b f The Minstrel (CAN) — Donna Inez (USA) (Herbager) 1396⁴ 2901² 3191 3655a

**Nemir 3** b c Rainbow Quest (USA) — Orange Hill (High Top) 3114³ 3282² 3616² 3773³

**Neo-Classical 3** b f Primo Dominie — Musical Sally (USA) (The Minstrel (CAN)) 432

**Neologist 6** b or br g Bold Owl — Neophyte II (Never Say Die) 622⁶

**Neptune's Pet 4** b c Tina's Pet — Abalone (Abwah) 626 931⁵ 1032 1542² (1747) (1947) (2457) 2593² 3061 (3277) 3673 3732

**Neroli 4** b f Nishapour (FR) — Norska (Northfields (USA)) *53* *113* 273 515

**Nessun Dorma 2** b c Night Shift (USA) — Scala di Seta (Shantung) 2873⁴ 3289⁴ 3602²

**Nest 3** ch f Sharpo — Sanctuary (Welsh Pageant) 363 678⁵ *1320* 2950² 3119² 3365² 3582² 3898

**Nevada Mix 8** gr h Alias Smith (USA) — Northern Empress (Northfields (USA)) 420⁶ 542 885 1054⁶ 1326² 1512⁶ 1618⁴ 2816

**Never a Care (USA) 3** b f Roberto (USA) — Imperturbable Lady (CAN) (Northern Dancer) 607² 934⁴ 2748³

**Never Cry Wolf 4** b c Little Wolf — Ma Belle Amie (Never Say Die) **1991:** *4101*

**Never in the Red 4** b g Wattlefield — Swing Gently (Swing Easy (USA)) 723⁴ 1199 1688 2019² 2215² 2376³ 2642 2902⁵ 3059³ 3437 3633⁴

**Never in Touch 2** b f Never So Bold — Yelney (Blakeney) 263⁵ 423 574 1307⁵ *1375* 1526

**Never Late 3** b f Never So Bold — New Edition (Great Nephew) 668 949⁶ 1562 2117³ 2466⁶

**Never so Brave 2** ch g Never So Bold — Another Move (Farm Walk) 3307⁶ 3512

**Never so Lost 2** ch c Never So Bold — Lost In France (Northfields (USA)) 654⁶ 2456

**Never so Sure 4** br g Never So Bold — Amerella (Welsh Pageant) 236³ 311² 542² 712 872⁶ 1508⁶ *(1685)* *(2003)* 2214³ 2898 2997³ *(3083)* 3188 3356 3633² 3680

**Neviskia (USA) 3** ch f Arctic Tern (USA) — Water Dance (USA) (Nijinsky (CAN)) 857

**Newark Antiquefair 4** b g Rolfe (USA) — Sea Dart (Air Trooper) 664 951 1190⁶ 1419 2120⁵ 2737 2877

**New Beginning 9** b or br h Persian Bold — Bumble-Bee (High Line) 2148 2517⁶ 2966 3383 3919

**Notorious Pleasure (USA)** 6 b c Mr Pleasure (USA) — Lookie Cookie (USA) (Vague Image (USA)) (15a)

**Notrella (IRE)** 3 b f Trojan Fen — Recline (Wollow) 2778⁴

**Not so Generous (IRE)** 2 b f Fayruz — Ribero's Overture (Ribero) 297³ 416⁶ 7914 (1077) (1579) 1886² 2390³

**Not Yet 8** b g Connaught — Ritratto (Pinturischio) 267⁶ 4174 606 875⁵ 965⁴ 1184² 1331⁴ 1622⁴ 1894² 2047⁴ 2484² 2692⁵ 27271⁶ 337⁹³ 3479 3761⁵

**Noushy 4** ch f Ahonoora — Bolkonskina (Balidar) 27³ 278⁴ 505 1034 1184 3045

**Now Boarding 5** b m Blazing Saddles (AUS) — Strictly Swing (Swing Easy (USA)) 508 774 948 1338 1404² 1680³ (1945) 2413³ 2621⁶

**Noyan 2** ch c Northern Baby (CAN) — Istiska (FR) (Irish River (FR)) 1549² (2102) (2578) (2841) 3091 3830⁵

**Nuclear Express 5** b g Martinmas — Halka (Daring March) **1991:** 4008 **1992:** 1030 1235⁶ 1339 2061³ 2234⁴ 2617² 2752 3264²

**Nucleus (USA) 4** b c Nureyev (USA) — Nellie Forbes (USA) (Secretariat (USA)) 15a

**Nuez 3** b c Shareef Dancer (USA) — Nuas (GER) (Aspros (GER)) (512)

**Nun the Wiser (IRE) 3** b f Commanche Run — Welsh Abbey (Caerleon (USA)) 353 567 1145

**Nur (USA) 3** ch f Diesis — Shicklah (USA) (The Minstrel (CAN)) 719 1289 1994

**Nuryandra 2** b f Reference Point — Nuryana (Nureyev (USA)) 650² (995) 1471³ 2132² 3443

**Nu Shan (IRE) 2** b g Shareef Dancer (USA) — Nutria (GER) (Tratteggio) 2398⁵ 2629⁵ 2879⁶ 3274

**Nutacre 7** b m Julio Mariner — Misacre (St Alphage) 2929⁶ 3075

**Nut Bush 2** ch c Aragon — Divissima (Music Boy) 867 1039⁵ 1178⁶ 1579² 1749⁶ 1989⁵ 3712 (3925)

**Nutmeg Lass 3** br f Shanekite (USA) — Indian Flower (Mansingh (USA)) 3873

**Nutty Brown 2** b g Primitive Rising (USA) — Nuthill (Derrylin) 1071² 1322³ 1549³ 2076 2724⁶ 3642² 3792²

# O

**Oak Apple (USA) 3** ch f Theatrical — Virginia Hills (USA) (Tom Rolfe) 587⁴ 904 1242² 1740² 3306⁶ (3556)

**Oakmead (IRE) 2** b f Lomond (USA) — Amazer (USA) (Vaguely Noble) 3881⁶

**Oare Sparrow 2** b f Night Shift (USA) — Portvasco (Sharpo) 2459⁵ 3414⁴ 3684⁴ 3852

**Obeliski 6** b g Aragon — Pasha's Dream (Tarboosh (USA)) **1991:** 4083 **1992:** 26² 46⁶ 60 328⁶

**Obereggen (ITY) 3** ch c Be My Master (USA) — Vinalia (ITY) (Shamsan) 844a²

**Obsidian Grey 5** gr h Lyphard's Special (USA) — Marcrest (On Your Mark) 124⁶ 178 277 534² 684⁴ 809

**Ocara (USA) 2** b f Danzig Connection (USA) — Relevant (USA) (Hold Your Peace (USA)) 3011

**Ocean Lad 9** b g Windjammer (USA) — Elixir (Hard Tack) 301

**Oco Royal 3** b c Tinoco — Queen's Royale (Tobrouk (FR)) 256⁵ 330⁴ 597⁵ 2014 2228⁵

**October Brew (USA) 2** ch c Seattle Dancer (USA) — Princess Fager (USA) (Dr Fager) 1709 3000 3525

**Odoen (USA) 3** b g Capitol South (USA) — Charbon Risque (USA) (Bold Reason) 334 394 524 728 806 1741

**O'Donnell's Folly 3** b g Beveled (USA) — Silk Imp (Imperial Fling (USA)) 863³ 1918 DEAD

**Oeightnineeight (USA) 3** b f Phone Trick (USA) — Kazankina (Malinowski (USA)) 1453 DEAD

**Officer Cadet 5** b g Shernazar — Selection Board (Welsh Pageant) 990 3877

**Oh so Handy 4** b g Nearly A Hand — Geordie Lass (Bleep-Bleep) 2281 2705

**Oh so Risky 5** b g Kris — Expediency (USA) (Vaguely Noble) 390⁶

**Oh so Rosy 3** gr f Lomond (USA) — Red Rose Bowl (Dragonara Palace (USA)) 408² 727 DEAD

**Oka Flow 4** b c Vaigly Great — Atoka (March Past) 198 222 328

**Okaku 5** b g Be My Guest (USA) — Be My Darling (Windjammer (USA)) 1326⁵

**Okaz (USA) 7** b g Temperence Hill (USA) — She Is Gorgeous (USA) (Drop Volley) 232

**Ok Bertie 2** b c Interrex (CAN) — Rockery (Track Spare) 2388⁵ 3262⁴ 3523 3719 3867

**Ok Guv 2** gr g Governor General — Debbie Do (Absalom) 1579

**O K Kealy 2** gr c Absalom — Constanza (Sun Prince) 3474

**Ok Records 5** b g Cure The Blues (USA) — Last Clear Chance (USA) (Alleged (USA)) 3778

**Olanthe (USA) 3** ch c Blushing Groom (FR) — Olamic (USA) (Nijinsky (CAN)) 1823a⁶ 2509a²

**Old Comrades 5** ch g Music Boy — Miss Candine (King Emperor (USA)) 515³ 731³ 941 1343⁶ 1588³ (1811) 2254 2582⁴ 2953⁴ 3245² 3422⁴ 3595⁶ 3766² 3963³

**Old Fox (FR) 3** b g In Fijar (USA) — Warning Bell (Bustino) 1505 1852 3557 3747

**Old Glory 4** ch g Valiyar — Old Kate (Busted) 3317 3488 3698

**Old Peg 4** b f Reach — Lizarra (High Top) 1248

**Old Speckled Hen 4** ch f The Noble Player (USA) — Making Tracks (Sagaro) **1991:** 4056 **1992:** 1971

**Olej (USA) 3** b c Danzig Connection (USA) — Smarted (USA) (Smarten (USA)) 789 3877

**Olette 3** b f Rousillon (USA) — Royal Loft (Homing) 401⁴ (1363) 1928 (2588) 3058⁴ 3135⁶ 3433² (3667)

**Olicana (IRE) 2** ch c Persian Bold — Maniusha (Sallust) 3193 3402 3856

**Pleasuring** 3 ch f Good Times (ITY) — Gliding (Tudor Melody) 408⁵ 2753 3056³ 3252⁶ 3412⁶

**Plectrum** 4 b f Adonijah — Cymbal (Ribero) **1991:** 403² 4074⁴ **1992:** 71² 131² 155 354 777

**Pluck** 2 b f Never So Bold — Tahilla (Moorestyle) 3008² (3255) 3411⁶

**Plume Magique** 3 b f Kenmare (FR) — Pencil Sharpener (USA) (Sharpen Up) 461a³ 958a

**Plum First** 2 b c Nomination — Plum Bold (Be My Guest (USA)) 226 323⁶ 423² 574³ 1191⁵ 1321³ (1448) 2030⁴ 2360² 2543⁶ 2779⁶ 2842³ 3023²

**Pocket Piece (USA)** 2 ch f Diesis — Secret Asset (USA) (Graustark) 3372⁶

**Poco Pierna (IRE)** 2 ch f Ahonoora — Flaunting (Kings Lake (USA)) 548 782 1178² 1902 2578⁵ 2910 3063

**Podrida** 6 gr m Persepolis (FR) — Pot Pourri (Busted) 409 507 2083³ 2834³

**Poets Cove** 4 b g Bay Express — Miss Milton (Young Christopher) 686⁶ 935⁶ (1212) 1487² 2179⁴ 2435 2925 3067

**Poinciana** 3 b c Big Spruce (USA) — Andrushka (USA) (Giboulee (CAN)) 384⁵ 848² 1346 2798² 3090⁶ 3724

**Point the Way (IRE)** 2 b f Reference Point — Tender Loving Care (Final Straw) 3959³

**Poker Chip** 2 ch f Bluebird (USA) — Timely Raise (USA) (Raise A Man (USA)) 811³ (2171) 3096 (3210) 3529³

**Pokey's Pride** 9 b g Uncle Pokey — Strawberry Ice (Arctic Storm) 3504 3823

**Polanie (CAN)** 2 ch f Danzig Connection (USA) — Sister Shu (USA) (Nashua) 3549⁶ 3704 3904

**Polar Moon** 2 b f Damister (USA) — Almitra (Targowice (USA)) 721⁴ 1038²

**Polar Storm (IRE)** 2 b f Law Society (USA) — Arctic Winter (CAN) (Briartic (CAN)) 1259⁴ (1658) 2437 3019 3606

**Polar Wind** 3 ch c El Gran Senor (USA) — Tundra Goose (Habitat) 539a³

**Poleden (USA)** 2 b c Danzig (USA) — Paradise (FR) (Brigadier Gerard) 3892 3946

**Polish Blue (USA)** 3 b c Danzig (USA) — Office Wife (USA) (Secretariat (USA)) 394 511² (680) (823) 1401² 2220 3089³ 3204³ 3571⁶

**Polish Style (USA)** 3 b f Danzig (USA) — Family Style (USA) (State Dinner (USA)) 2322a³

**Polistatic** 5 br m Free State — Polyandrist (Polic) 271³ 831 1125 2033 2241³ 2397² 2759² 2934³ 3097

**Polity Prince** 2 b g Dominion — Chiming Melody (Cure The Blues (USA)) 255⁴ (345) 988

**Pollen Count (USA)** 3 b c Diesis — Apalachee Honey (USA) (Apalachee (USA)) (341) (556) 1198 1823a (2316a) 3652a 3730

**Polly Leach** 2 b f Pollerton — Come On Gracie (Hardiran) 1342 1867

**Pollys Glow (IRE)** 3 b f Glow (USA) — Suspicious Polly (Above Suspicion) 1353a² 2977a⁴ 3736a⁵

**Polonez Prima** 5 ch g Thatching — Taiga (Northfields (USA)) 1181⁶ 1295 1799⁴ 1930² (2183) 2447³ (2898) 3182² 3543 3732

**Polyplate** 4 b f Song — Countless Countess (Morston (FR)) 48 291⁵ 675 DEAD

**Polyroll** 6 b h Kampala — Hail To Feathers (USA) (Hail To All) **1991:** 403⁴ **1992:** 50

**Poly Snip** 3 b f Executive Man — Wild Jewel (Great Heron (USA)) 833⁵ 938

**Polytain (FR)** 3 ch c Bikala — Paulistana (USA) (Pretense) 1094a³ (1356a) 3329a 3657a

**Poly Vision (IRE)** 2 b c Vision (USA) — Beechwood (USA) (Blushing Groom (FR)) 1630⁴ 1873⁶ 2068³ 2285³ 2681⁴ 2802² 2910 2972⁵ 3044⁴ 3199 3301⁵

**Pompion (USA)** 3 b or br c Mr Prospector (USA) — Midnight Pumpkin (USA) (Pretense) 440 1746⁴ 2549⁶ 3459³ 3801

**Pondered Bid** 8 b or br g Auction Ring (USA) — Ponca (Jim French (USA)) 84 103⁶ 125 193 220 426 501 1065 1125⁴ 1419 1566² 1671 2235⁶ 2267 3540

**Pondering** 2 br c Another Realm — Fishpond (Homing) 1202 1370⁵ 1657⁵ 2008 2826 2961 3173⁴ 3574 3685³

**Ponds** 2 b f Slip Anchor — Pomade (Luthier) 3871

**Ponsardin** 3 b c Petoski — Premiere Cuvee (Formidable) (USA) (275) 445 1576² 1698⁴ 2194² 2472³ 2804³ 3495⁴

**Ponte Cervo** 3 b g Hadeer — Pontevecchio Due (Welsh Pageant) 749

**Pontenuovo** 7 b g Kafu — Black Gnat (Typhoon) 1061

**Pontevecchio Moda** 2 b f Jalmood (USA) — Pontevecchio Due (Welsh Pageant) 2491⁴ 2713² 3055⁶ (3291) 3611² (3837)

**Poolesta (IRE)** 3 b f Hero's Honor (USA) — Radiant (USA) (Foolish Pleasure (USA)) 1495a² 2318a² 2762a² 3326a³

**Poppet Plume** 2 b f Governor General — Sparkling Hock (Hot Spark) 1782⁵ 2067⁴ 2428 2740 3071

**Poppy Charm** 5 b m Star Appeal — Pop Music (FR) (Val de Loir) 1163⁵ 1419⁶

**Poppyland** 2 b f Blakeney — Sunderland (Dancer's Image) (USA) 3818

**Pop to Stans** 3 b g Gold Crest (USA) — Lady of Camelot (FR) (Bolkonski) (29) 61² 68² (98) (135) 160⁴ 195³ 215 397⁶ 570³ (614) 1219⁴ 1368³ 1525⁴ 2866

**Porick** 4 b g Marching On — Natina-May (Mandrake Major) 64⁶ 120⁴ 142⁶ 169

**Portico (USA)** 3 ch c El Gran Senor (USA) — Thorough (Thatch (USA)) (539a) 953a⁶ 1817a⁴ 2383⁵

**Port in a Storm** 3 b c Blakeney — Crusader's Dream (St Paddy) 370 1505 2146² 2600² 2860⁶ 3177 3577⁵ 3827⁴

**Port Lucaya** 2 ch c Sharpo — Sister Sophie (USA) (Effervescing (USA)) 1135³ (1370) 1639³ (1915) 2177² 2445 2981a 3541⁵ 3799³

**Portree** 3 b f Slip Anchor — Rynechra (Blakeney) 737⁴ 2200⁴ 3306⁴ 3756² 3853⁶

**Port Sunlight (IRE)** 4 ch g Tate Gallery (USA) — Nana's Girl (Tin Whistle) 479⁴ 705³ (931)

**Princess Nana** 3 b f Bellypha — Alys (Blakeney) (845a)

**Princess Nebia** 2 br f King of Spain — Nebiha (Nebbiolo) 1762 2719 3291

**Princess Oberon (IRE)** 2 b or br f Fairy King (USA) — Flash of Gold (Pardao) 548³ 867³ (1057) 1186⁴

**Princess of Alar** 2 b f Bold Owl — Krafty Kate (Klairon) 1120 1442 2058 2428

**Princess of Orange** 3 ch f Master Willie — Outward's Gal (Ashmore (FR)) 395⁴ 599⁶ 806² 932 2128⁶ 2372² *2685⁶* 2937 3263 3500⁶ 3601⁶ 3876

**Princess Proudfoot** 3 b f Hotfoot — Farandella (English Prince) 603

**Princess Roxanne** 5 b m Prince Tenderfoot (USA) — Godwyn (Yellow God) **1991:** *(4033)* 4060³ 4094⁵ **1992:** *(81)* 111³ 232³ 340³ 469⁵ 777³ 1509⁴ 1840 (2312) 2354² 2896⁴

**Princess Tamar** 3 gr f Absalom — Alkion (Fordham (USA)) 457 1052

**Princess Tara** 4 br or gr f Prince Sabo — La Magna (Runnymede) 992⁵ 1212 1504

**Princess Tateum (IRE)** 2 b f Tate Gallery (USA) — Church Mountain (Furry Glen) 3360⁵ 3617³ 3744³

**Principal Player (USA)** 2 br g Chief Singer — Harp Strings (FR) (Luthier) 266³ 323⁴ 447⁴ 619⁴ 826⁶ 1112⁰ 1027² 1524⁴ 2066 3165⁴ 3343⁶

**Print Finisher** 6 ch m Mandrake Major — Chubby Ears (Burglar) *901* 1084

**Priok** 9 b g Monsanto (FR) — Aracara (Prince Tenderfoot (USA)) *1544* 2036

**Private Bank (USA)** 3 b c Private Account (USA) — Lady Ice (CAN) (Vice Regent (CAN)) 2769³ 3062³ 3804⁵ 3906

**Private Liner** 2 b c Skyliner — Private Sue (Brigadier Gerard) 619 769 920⁶ 1151 1526 *2098²* 2363

**Private Practice** 3 gr f Kalaglow — Lady Gaylass (USA) (Sir Gaylord) [481W] 2137⁶ 2495⁵ 3062 3403 3769

**Probation** 3 b c Nomination — Ballagarrow Girl (North Stoke) 341 599

**Procada** 2 b g Damister (USA) — Smelter (Prominer) 3399⁶ 3631⁶

**Prolific** 7 b h Ballacashtal (CAN) — Sea Charm (Julio Mariner) 570² 629 813 1014⁵ 1474 1837⁴ 2003⁴ 2214⁶ 2262³ 2637⁵ 2898⁴ 3068⁶ 3088 3310⁶ 3696 3751 3828

**Profit a Prendre** 8 b g Tina's Pet — Brave Ballard (Derring-Do) 706 774 1054⁵ 1338³ 1527 1756³ 1905² 2032² (2254) 2458 2476² 2650⁶ 2807⁴ 2881

**Profit Stream** 3 ch g Adonijah — River Reem (USA) (Irish River (FR)) **1991:** *4043* *4067⁵* **1992:** *514* 264 353

**Profusion** 3 b c Rainbow Quest (USA) — Pauvresse (FR) (Home Guard (USA)) (500) 722² 927⁶ 1225a² (1537) 1972³ 3956

**Prosequendo (USA)** 5 b g Robellino (USA) — Allegedly (USA) (Sir Ivor) (586) *(773)* 1065³ 1163² 1381² 2129⁵ 2295⁴ (2774) 2921⁵ 3221⁴ 3946

**Prospective Ruler (USA)** 4 b c Northern Prospect (USA) — Swan Song (USA) (Ribot) 2628a³ 3979a²

**Protektor (GER)** 3 b c Acatenango (GER) — Prioritat (FR) (Frontal) 3659a³

**Proud Brigadier (IRE)** 4 b g Auction Ring (USA) — Naughty One Gerard (Brigadier Gerard) **1991:** *4090³* *4095⁴* **1992:** *57⁵* 738 1343⁴ 1590³ 2141⁵ 2589² 3067 3264⁵ 3391² 3605² 3766³

**Proud Moment (BAR)** 2 b f Bentom (USA) — Proud Performance (Owen Anthony) 3360 3486

**Proud Panther (FR)** 6 br h Blakeney — Pink Panther (FR) (Val de Loir) 644a² 3650a

**Prove It's Gold** 3 b f Alleging (USA) — Goldyke (Bustino) 200⁴ 804 *1540⁵* 1812⁵

**Prudent Manner** 5 ch h Cure The Blues (USA) — Prudent Girl (Primera) 24a²

**Ptolemy (FR)** 5 gr g Persepolis (FR) — Rivoltade (USA) (Sir Ivor) 1280⁴ 1477 2136⁵ 2373

**Public Appeal** 3 b g Law Society (USA) — Vacherin (USA) (Green Dancer (USA)) 3609

**Public Way (IRE)** 2 b c Common Grounds — Kilpeacon (Florescence) 491⁴ 751³ 3077 3385 3482⁴ 3587 3746 (3754) 3913⁵

**Puenta Aguila** 2 gr g Belfort (FR) — Sarah's Venture (Averof) 365³ 665 DEAD

**Puff Puff** 6 b m All Systems Go — Harmonious Sound (Auction Ring (USA)) 1137⁶ 1318 1430⁵ 1686⁴ 2083⁴ 2267

**Puffy** 5 ch g Wolverlife — Eskaroon (Artaius (USA)) 315⁶ 5724 768 965² 1090 3759

**Puget Dancer (USA)** 2 b f Seattle Dancer (USA) — Basin (USA) (Tom Rolfe) 3171³ 3480

**Punch N'Run** 4 b c Forzando — Wrangbrook (Shirley Heights) 13a² 3978a²

**Purbeck Centenary** 2 b c Lidhame — Double Stitch (Wolver Hollow) 231 786 2396 2994 3580 3702

**Purchased by Phone (IRE)** 2 b f Wolverlife — Gerise (Nishapour (FR)) (371) (769) (1191) 2067³ 3033

**Pure Bliss** 5 b m Idiot's Delight — Julie Emma (Farm Walk) **1991:** *4088* **1992:** *41*

**Pure Formality** 3 b f Forzando — Sharp Celine (Sharpo) 503³ 851⁴ 1166 2755 3095

**Pure Madness (USA)** 2 b c Northern Prospect (USA) — Icy Oddsmaker (USA) (Icecapade (USA)) 1569⁵ 2044⁴ 2897⁴ 3267

**Pure Misk** 2 b f Rainbow Quest (USA) — Miller's Creek (USA) (Star de Naskra (USA)) 2185

**Puritan (CAN)** 3 b c Alleged (USA) — Conform (CAN) (Blushing Groom (FR)) 1891² (2228) 2524² 2793² 3046⁴ 3244³ 3515⁶ (3808)

**Pursuit of Love** 3 b c Groom Dancer (USA) — Dance Quest (FR) (Green Dancer (USA)) (437) 655³ 991² 1460² 1942² (2626a) 2789² (3195) 3738a⁶

**Pusey Street Boy** 5 ch g Vaigly Great — Pusey Street (Native Bazaar) **1991:** *4035* *4089⁵* **1992:** *50* 1721² 1971⁴ 3403³ 3555⁴

**Quick Silver Boy 2** gr c Kalaglow — Safidar (Roan Rocket) 514 847 1571² 2277 2932

**Quick Steel 4** b g Alleging (USA) — Illiney Girl (Lochnager) 774⁵ 1261³ 2009⁶ 3105² 3183 3605⁴

**Quick Victory 2** b f Sharpo — In Triumph (USA) (Hoist The Flag (USA)) 2842 3308

**Quietly Impressive (IRE) 4** b f Taufan (USA) — Way Ahead (Sovereign Path) 277 456⁵ 626⁴ 866 1284 1637⁵ 2596⁴ 2860 3060⁴ 3174

**Quiet Miss 3** b f Kind of Hush — Miss Acrow (Comedy Star (USA)) **1991:** 4046³ (4076) (4097) **1992:** 474 995 1252 1885 2198 3554

**Quiet Riot 10** b g Hotfoot — Tuyenu (Welsh Pageant) 800 1009 1239³ 1640 1810 2705⁶

**Quiet Victory 5** b m Never So Bold — Les Saintes (Kris) **1991:** 4045⁴ 4069 **1992:** 1013³ 1070⁵ 1243⁴ (1365) 1570⁶ 1793 1961⁵ 2502⁶ 2668 2958 3101 3264 3481

**Quinsigimond 2** ch f Formidable (USA) — Quillotern (USA) (Arctic Tern (USA)) 2501² 3338⁵ 3480⁵ 3744⁵ 3848² 3948³

**Quinta (IRE) 4** b g Truculent (USA) — Feliscoa (FR) (Royal Ascot) 962

**Quinta Royale 5** b g Sayyaf — Royal Holly (Royal Buck) 86 120 1009⁴ 1143 1366⁶ 2570² 3245⁶

**Quinzii Martin 4** b g Song — Quaranta (Hotfoot) **1991:** 4009 4054⁵ **1992:** 27² 56³ (112) 143⁵ 199⁴ 515 738 (903) 1032 1550 1847 2040³ 2159⁶ 2481⁵ 3373

**Quip 7** ch g High Line — Sans Blague (USA) (The Minstrel (CAN)) 880⁶ 987 1190 1452⁵ 1530⁴ 1968⁴ 2045 2166⁴ 2420⁵ 2701

**Quixotic 3** gr c Bellypha — Pushy (Sharpen Up) 693 2704⁵ 2995³ 3119⁵ 3520

# R

**Raawi 4** b g Be My Guest (USA) — Fast Motion (Midsummer Night II) 232

**Raaya 3** b f Be My Guest (USA) — Fast Motion (Midsummer Night II) 136³ 157 179³

**Rabbit's Foot 4** b f Touching Wood (USA) — Royal Custody (Reform) 1766⁶

**Rabsha (IRE) 4** b f Taufan (USA) — Serraj (USA) (Seattle Slew (USA)) 3352

**Racecall Gold Card 5** ch g Camden Town — Polly Royal (Music Boy) **1991:** 4081

**Race to Time (IRE) 4** b g Runnett — Plunket's Choice (Home Guard (USA)) **1991:** 4094⁶ **1992:** 246 DEAD

**Rachelly 2** b f Faustus (USA) — Linda's Design (Persian Bold) 1675

**Racing Raskal 5** b g Dunphy — Raskaska (Aureole) **1991:** 4050³ 4101⁶ **1992:** 291⁶ (951) 1108³ 1337² 1789³ 2045⁵ 2513⁴ 2964²

**Racing Telegraph 2** b c Claude Monet (USA) — Near Enough (English Prince) 1769⁴ 2124² 2274⁴ 2965³ (3285) 3723

**Rad 2** b c Valiyar — Phlox (Floriana) 3160 3411⁵ 3719

**Radar Knight 4** b c Beldale Flutter (USA) — Eurynome (Be My Guest (USA)) 2565⁵ 2834

**Radio Caroline 4** b g All Systems Go — Caroline Lamb (Hotfoot) 508 592 696⁵ 1008

**R a Express 7** b g Bay Express — Pinaka (Pitcairn) 279 357 752 1263 1427 1752 1999⁵ 2808⁴ 2936

**Rafah 3** b f Dominion — Lys River (FR) (Lyphard (USA)) (699) 1062² 1533 2778³ 3003² 3058² 3269 3695⁴

**Ragamuffin Romeo 3** b g Niniski (USA) — Interviewme (USA) (Olden Times) 427

**Ragazzo (IRE) 2** b g Runnett — Redecorate (USA) (Hatchet Man (USA)) 3474

**Rage 5** ch g Final Straw — Nasty Niece (CAN) (Great Nephew) 915⁵ 2966 3759

**Raggerty (IRE) 2** b g Prince Rupert (FR) — Princess Martina (English Prince) 1375 1623 3200

**Raging Thunder 2** b g Taufan (USA) — Nasty Niece (CAN) (Great Nephew) 1259 1524² 1762⁴ 2883 3123 3716

**Ragtime 5** b g Pas de Seul — Boldella (Bold Lad (IRE)) 362 578⁵ 805

**Rag Time Belle 6** b m Raga Navarro (ITY) — Betbellof (Averof) 232 (615) 696 1013 1143 1339

**Ragtime Song 3** b c Dunbeath (USA) — Kelowna (USA) (Master Derby (USA)) 896

**Raheena (USA) 3** b f Lyphard (USA) — Hard Knocker (USA) (Raja Baba (USA)) 2399³ 2780 3072² 3398² 3609⁵ 3906

**Rahif 4** b c Shirley Heights — Vaguely (Bold Lad (IRE)) 1705 1958³ 2218² 2678⁶

**Rahon (IRE) 2** ch f Ahonoora — Carillon Miss (USA) (The Minstrel (CAN)) 701² 886⁵ 2225⁶ 2669⁵

**Rainbow Corner 3** b c Rainbow Quest (USA) — Kingscote (Kings Lake (USA)) (636a) 842a² 1198 2506a² 3721² 3894³

**Rainbow Fleet 4** b f Nomination — Olderfleet (Steel Heart) 1167² (1368) 2861 3183⁶ (3296) 3700

**Rainbow Stripes 5** ch g Rainbow Quest (USA) — Pampas Miss (USA) (Pronto) 3808 3922

**Rain Brother (USA) 2** b c Lear Fan (USA) — Ritualism (USA) (Exclusive Native (USA)) 3005³ (3240) (3390) (3679) 3891a⁶

**Rain Rider 3** b c Fools Holme (USA) — Moon Parade (Welsh Pageant) 481² (1176) (1633) (1940) (2996) 3211

**Rainridge 3** b c Rainbow Quest (USA) — Beveridge (USA) (Spectacular Bid (USA)) 433 680⁵ (1079) (1414) 3319³

**Rain Splash 2** gr f Petong — Bargouzine (Hotfoot) 476⁴ (650) 1536 2055⁴ 2342⁴ 2683² 3550⁵ 3716

**Raith Pc 3** ch g Aragon — All Fine (Fine Blade (USA)) 2720

**Rajai (IRE) 3** br c Last Tycoon — Flame of Tara (Artaius (USA)) 394⁵ 562² 864⁴ (1720) 1882³ (2391) 2734⁵ 3116⁴ 3434⁵

**Rajanpour (USA) 7** ch h Riverman (USA) — Rajpoura (Kashmir II) 1290 1534 3007 3745 3841³ 3930

**Rajaya (USA) 4** b c Nureyev (USA) — Don't Sulk (USA) (Graustark) 274⁴ 46

**Rakis (IRE) 2** b or br c Alzao (USA) — Bristle (Thatch (USA)) 3314 3551⁵ (3782) 3893³

**Ramaas (USA) 3** b c Danzig (USA) — Milliardare (USA) (Alydar (USA)) 658

**Ramble (USA) 5** ch m Highland Park (USA) — Hill Pleasure (USA) (What A Pleasure (USA)) *169⁵* 226⁶ 2723 409

**Rambo Express 5** b or br h New Express — Saul Flower (Saulingo) **1991:** *4005⁶ 4047⁵*

**Rambo's Hall 7** b g Crofthall — Murton Crags (No Argument) 1255² 2406⁵ (2644) (3125) (3428) (3547) 3903⁴

**Rami (USA) 5** br h Riverman (USA) — Ancient Regime (USA) (Olden Times) (1495a) 1817a³ 2789⁴

**Ramiya 2** b f Dancing Brave (USA) — Nouvelle Star (AUS) (Luskin Star (AUS)) 3904⁵

**Rampal (IRE) 3** b g Dancing Brave (USA) — Zinzara (USA) (Stage Door Johnny) 2122⁴ 2869 3246³ 3403⁵ 3763⁶

**Rancho Mirage 5** ch g Superlative — Que Sera (Music Boy) **1991:** *4028 4049⁵ 4080* **1992:** *33 66*

**Randama 5** b m Akarad (FR) — Ramanouche (FR) (Riverman (USA)) *26*

**Randybay 7** b g Bay Express — Kiara (Great Nephew) 962 1976 2116

**Raneen Alwatar 2** b f Sadler's Wells (USA) — Samya's Flame (Artaius (USA)) 3904

**Ranger (FR) 2** b c Un Desperado (FR) — Reine Caroline (FR) (Pharly (FR)) 3737a³ 3975a⁴

**Range Rider (IRE) 2** b c Bold Arrangement — Top Fille (FR) (Top Ville) 1709⁶ 2269⁵ 2918 3160² 3372 3665 3792³ 3954

**Ranunculus 2** b g Music Boy — Preziosa (Homing) 3030 3512 3704

**Rapid Lad 14** b g Rapid River — Seacona (Espresso) 422 504 766 965³ 1739⁴ 2602⁶

**Rapid Mover 5** ch g Final Straw — Larive (Blakeney) 1329⁴ 1441⁶ 1562 1733³ 1894

**Rapid Repeat (IRE) 2** b f Exactly Sharp (USA) — Silver Echo (Caerleon (USA)) 1937⁴ (3683)

**Rapid Rosie 4** ch f Noalto — Cora (Current Coin) 2051 2251 2545 2754 2944 3388

**Rapid Success (USA) 2** ch c Sort (USA) — Golden Rhyme (Dom Racine (FR)) (2346) 2756³ 3272⁶

**Rapporteur (USA) 6** b g His Majesty (USA) — Sweet Rapport (USA) (Round Table) **1991:** *4018 4060² 4089²* **1992:** *(74) (110) 146³ 202² 2971 3234⁴ 3555 3675³ 3763² 3928*

**Rap Up Fast (USA) 3** b g Eskimo (USA) — Naomi's Flash (USA) (Ray Jeter (USA)) 375 1962 3073 3380

**Rare Detail (IRE) 4** ch f Commanche Run — Sharp Dresser (USA) (Sharpen Up) 342² 513⁶ 831⁴ 1147 1318⁵ 3139 3244⁴

**Rare Occurance 2** b c Damister (USA) — Superior Quality (Star Appeal) 1424 2901 3593

**Rarfy's Dream 4** b c Dreams To Reality (USA) — Elbandary (Shirley Heights) *154* 273 1037⁶ 2413

**Rasan 5** ch h Dominion — Raffle (Balidar) 7784

**Rasco 3** gr g Natroun (FR) — Kabylia (FR) (Dancer's Image (USA)) 606 1018 1154 1737

**Rashita 5** b m Alzao (USA) — Apapa Port (My Swanee) 2110⁶ 2373 2731

**Ravecino 3** ch f Ballacashtal (CAN) — Lemelasor (Town Crier) 1130 1624³ 1896⁵ 2539 2966 3168

**Raven Runner (USA) 3** b f Storm Bird (CAN) — Simple Taste (USA) (Sharpen Up) 989⁵ 1315⁴ (1683)

**Rawaan (FR) 5** b g Labus (FR) — Rose Ness (Charlottesville) 315

**Raw Health 2** b c Sizzling Melody — Upholder (Young Generation) 581

**Rayon Bleu (FR) 5** b h Bellypha — Blue River (FR) (Riverman (USA)) (284a) 1352a⁵

**Rays Mead 4** gr f Tremblant — Free Range (Birdbrook) 506 735 1162⁵ 1427 (1552) 1727³ 1987² 2206³ 2599⁴ 3423

**Razaroo (USA) 2** b g Buckaroo (USA) — Mislop (USA) (Our Hero) (924) 1291³ 1690⁴ 3091 3482

**Reach for Glory 3** b g Reach — Carlton Glory (Blakeney) 366 457 1052² 1188² (1438) 1626⁵ 2533³ 3350² 3485 3577 3752 3876⁵

**Reach Forward 3** b f Reach — Good Woman (Good Times (ITY)) 594 1030

**Reach Me Not (IRE) 3** ch f Reach — Injaz (Golden Act (USA)) **1991:** *4092* **1992:** *396 945*

**Ready to Draw (IRE) 3** ch c On Your Mark — Mitsubishi Art (Cure The Blues (USA)) **1991:** *4051⁵* **1992:** *512 685 107² 355² 448² (567) 666² 8065 3149⁴ 3350³ 3494⁵ (3629) 3705*

**Realities (USA) 2** ch c Cozzene (USA) — Alquizar (USA) (Star de Naskra (USA)) (2124) (2710) 2847⁵ 3390² 3672⁵

**Really Honest 11** b g He Loves Me — Whitethorn (Gulf Pearl) 962

**Real Stunner 5** ch m Chief Singer — Real Party (Realm) 311⁵ 613⁵ 685⁴ 1187⁴ 1483³ 1707⁵ 1828³ 2117⁴

**Reasons for Love (IRE) 2** ch f Common Grounds — Fodens Eve (Dike (USA)) 361³ 3163³ 3338⁴ 3635 3754 (3821)

**Rebel Call 3** b g Never So Bold — Supper Time (Shantung) 238² 394² 628² 823⁵ 12075 1634⁶

**Recent Therm 3** b f Persian Bold — Maiden's Walk (Tower Walk) 2975a²

**Receptionist 3** b f Reference Point — Ever Genial (Brigadier Gerard) **1991:** *4053²* **1992:** *902³ 1722² 2089³ (2497) (2793) 3118³ (3298) 3538*

**Recipdico Mist (IRE) 2** ch f Digamist (USA) — Repicado Rose (USA) (Repicado (CHI)) 2256⁶ 2474⁵ 2832 3606 3768

**Recit D'Argent 2** b c Legend of France (USA) — Shiny Penny (Glint of Gold) 1378 1991 2832 3255⁵

**Recording Contract 4** b g Song — Port Na Blath (On Your Mark) 3909

**Record Lover (IRE) 2** b c Alzao (USA) — Spun Gold (Thatch (USA)) 3552⁴ 3844

**Red Admiral 2** b g Formidable (USA) — Dancing Meg (USA) (Marshua's Dancer (USA)) 2346 3946

**Saif Al Adil (IRE)** 3 b c Reference Point — Hardihostess (Be My Guest (USA)) 376² 547⁶ 7985 1102³ 1255⁴ 1655² *1850* 2477⁴ 2731³ 2867 3158 3282⁶ 3601

**Saifan** 3 ch g Beveled (USA) — Superfrost (Tickled Pink) 997 1417 (3288) 3520 3771 3870³

**Sailor Boy** 6 b g Main Reef — Main Sail (Blakeney) **1991:** 4059² 4072 4093 **1992:** 40 244² 331 362 605 1239 1802⁵

**Saint Bene't (IRE)** 4 b g Glenstal (USA) — Basilea (Frere Basile (FR)) *211* 291 (327) 453 469 575 891 1109 1441 1527

**Saint Ciel (USA)** 4 b c Skywalker (USA) — Holy Tobin (USA) (J O Tobin (USA)) 354⁵ 504 880 3955³

**Sainted Sue** 2 ch f Aragon — Nosey (Nebbiolo) 1959 2661 3472 3760

**Saint Express** 2 ch g Clantime — Redgrave Design (Nebbiolo) (1071) 1192² (1664) 2176⁶ 2528² 2847² 3210²

**Saintry (USA)** 3 ch c Groom Dancer (USA) — Sainte Croix (Nijinsky (CAN)) 7a³

**Saint Systems** 6 b m Uncle Pokey — Fire Mountain (Dragonara Palace (USA)) 1138 1282 1651² 1888

**Saint Vending** 4 br c Grey Desire — Girdle Ness (Pitskelly) 590 796⁴

**Saja (USA)** 2 b f Ferdinand (USA) — Summer Silence (USA) (Stop The Music (USA)) 3295⁴ 3617⁶

**Sakbah (USA)** 3 b f Al Nasr (FR) — Delray Dancer (USA) (Chateaugay) 922⁵ 1156³ 1565⁵

**Sakharov** 3 b g Bay Express — Supreme Kingdom (Take A Reef) 3596 3751⁵ 3849

**Salaam (SPA)** 4 b f Vacarme (USA) — Tomyris (FR) (Abdos) 641a³

**Saladan Knight** 7 b g Dalsaan — Exciting Times (Windjammer (USA)) *31⁶* 70² *87³* (121) 140⁴ 173² 265 888 918 *1377*

**Salar's Spirit** 6 ch g Salmon Leap (USA) — Indigine (USA) (Raise A Native) 2240 2416

**Salatin (USA)** 2 b c Seattle Dancer (USA) — Ivory Wings (USA) (Sir Ivor) 817⁴ (2340) 2835²

**Salbus** 2 b c Salse — Busca (USA) (Mr Prospector (USA)) 3693

**Salbyng** 4 b c Night Shift (USA) — Hsian (Shantung) 340⁵ 508² 626 936⁴ 1106⁶ (2707) 2935² 2990³ 3236³ 3488² 3698

**Salda** 3 b g Bustino — Martinova (Martinmas) 5214 1326⁴ [1391W] 1516⁵ (2647) 2852 3026 [3349W] (3514) 3640

**Salik (IRE)** 2 b or br c Doyoun — Safe Home (Home Guard (USA)) 2646

**Salinger** 4 b g Rousillon (USA) — Scholastika (GER) (Alpenkonig (GER)) 1975 2427 3045³ 3239 3479⁴ 3601

**Salisong** 3 gr c Song — Sylvanecte (FR) (Silver Shark) 387 472 792² 898 1219⁶ (2882) 3133⁵ 3241 3365 3781⁶

**Sally Fast** 3 ch f Legend of France (USA) — Strip Fast (Virginia Boy) 787⁶ 1611 1974⁶ 2209 (2545) 2882 3017 3159 3254

**Sally Fay (IRE)** 4 b f Fayruz — Trust Sally (Sallust) **1991:** 4077 **1992:** 293 364 684 809⁶ 1018 1747 2929³ 3026 3161

**Sally Forth** 6 b g Sallust — Sally Knox (Busted) 358 606 3215

**Sally Saad** 4 gr f Green Desert (USA) — Biding (Habat) 1570

**Sally's Son** 6 b g Beldale Flutter (USA) — Sally Chase (Sallust) **1991:** 4009⁵ 4028 **1992:** 42³ (57) (80) 130² 152² 185⁴ 209² 351² 515 2804⁵ 3375⁴ 3842³

**Sally Tadpole** 3 b f Jester — Sorata (FR) (Sodium) 310⁴ 454

**Salman (USA)** 6 b g Nain Bleu (FR) — H M S Pellinore (USA) (King Pellinore (USA)) *137* 358 905 (2896) 3311⁵

**Salmon Dancer (IRE)** 3 b c Salmon Leap (USA) — Welsh Walk (Welsh Saint) 512 603 806 2087 3251 3692

**Salt Lake (USA)** 3 b c Deputy Minister (CAN) — Take Lady Anne (USA) (Queen City Lad (USA)) 3647a³ 3843 3935a

**Salt N Vinegar (IRE)** 2 ch c Salt Dome (USA) — Karissima (Kalamoun) 807 2489² 3709

**Salu** 3 br f Ardross — String of Beads (Ile de Bourbon (USA)) 268² 547³ 810 1152⁶ 1784⁴ 2069³ 2533² 2613² (2701) 2985⁶ 3141³ 3266³ 3309⁶ (3494) (3863) (3920)

**Saluting Walter (USA)** 4 b c Verbatim (USA) — Stage Hour (USA) (Stage Director (USA)) 438 800

**Salvatore Giuliano** 2 ch c Superlative — Bonny Bright Eyes (Rarity) 3581⁶

**Samain (USA)** 5 ch m Caerleon (USA) — Samarta Dancer (USA) (Marshua's Dancer (USA)) 377⁴ 606⁵ *905* (964) (1119) 1290⁴ 1419³ (1740) 2071² 2267⁴ 2605²

**Samakatan (IRE)** 2 b c Assert — Samata (FR) (Rheffic (FR)) 3975a⁶

**Samanthas Joy** 2 b f Marching On — Sister Racine (Dom Racine (FR)) 402⁵ 1307⁶ *1373²* *1547* 2690² 3071 *3558⁵* 3754⁵ *3927⁴*

**Samjamalifran** 3 b f Blakeney — Royal Shoe (Hotfoot) 2751⁶ 2882 *3373* 3601

**Sammy Slew (USA)** 3 br g Tsunami Slew (USA) — Big Sparkle (USA) (The Big Boss (USA)) 363⁶ 576 725⁶ 1050⁴ 1154⁴ 1310 3710⁶ 3914⁵

**Samsolom** 4 b g Absalom — Norfolk Serenade (Blakeney) 407 613⁴ 876⁶ 1522⁵ 1987 2163 2404⁵ 2642 2813 3207³ 3537

**Samson-Agonistes** 6 b h Bold Fort — Hello Cuddles (He Loves Me) 1583² (1727) 1920 (2234) 2395² 2618⁵ (3144) 3207 (3397) 3585 3805⁶

**Sam the Man** 5 b g Aragon — First Temptation (USA) (Mr Leader (USA)) 738 1087 1341 3426

**Samurai Gold (USA)** 4 b c Golden Act (USA) — Taipan's Lady (USA) (Bold Hour) **1991:** 4019³ 4033⁵ **1992:** 56² *1152* 2112 342 606³ 1063² (1721) 2033 2413⁵ 2885 3066 3393 3468 3770

**Sanawi** 5 b g Glenstal (USA) — Russeting (Mummy's Pet) 1009⁵ 1143⁴ 1284⁴ 1488⁵ 1747³ 1794⁴ 2326⁶ (2394) 2775 2896⁵ 3052³ 3101 3668

**Sand Castle** 11 ch g Tap On Wood — Pacific Sands (Sandford Lad) 76 166⁵ *205* 244⁵ 340

**Sit Alkul (USA)** 2 br f Mr Prospector (USA) — Lypatia (FR) (Lyphard (USA)) 3904⁴

**Siwaayib** 2 b f Green Desert (USA) — Ma Petite Cherie (USA) (Caro) (3848)

**Sixofus (IRE)** 4 b or br g Glenstal (USA) — Grace Darling (USA) (Vaguely Noble) 2305 2545 2712 *2974*

**Sizzling Affair** 3 b c Sizzling Melody — Vivchar (Huntercombe) 1745 2493 2616

**Sizzling Rose** 3 b f Sizzling Melody — Garnette Rose (Floribunda) **1991:** *4024* **1992:** *148* 366 734 1950⁴

**Sizzling Saga (IRE)** 4 b or br c Horage — Alsaizia (FR) (Bolkonski) 1253 1467 (1829) 2169 3124⁶ 3699⁴

**Sizzling Sarah** 3 b f Sizzling Melody — Gundreda (Gunner B) 495 *902* 922

**Sizzling Thoughts** 3 b g Sizzling Melody — Palace Guest (Be My Guest (USA)) 627 784⁵ 969 1172

**Ski Captain** 8 b g Welsh Captain — Miss Nelski (Most Secret) **1991:** *4021* **1992:** *1493* *163* 236 480² 550 872 996 1138 2199² (2301) 2465 2499³ 3294⁶

**Ski Chief (USA)** 4 b c Chief's Crown (USA) — Ski Goggle (USA) (Royal Ski (USA)) 1352a

**Skimble (USA)** 3 ch f Lyphard (USA) — Nimble Folly (Cyane) 429 631 (818) 1058

**Skimmer Hawk** 3 b g Buzzards Bay — Song To Singo (Master Sing) 3104 3258 3752 3875

**Ski Paradise (USA)** 2 gr f Lyphard (USA) — Ski Goggle (USA) (Royal Ski (USA)) 3230a³

**Skipper to Bilge** 5 b g Night Shift (USA) — Upper Deck (Sun Prince) 373 532⁵ 832³ (1258) 1500⁵ *(3375)* 3514³ 3701 3797

**Skip Tracer** 4 b g Balliol — Song To Singo (Master Sing) *1186* *154* 333

**Skisurf** 6 b g Niniski (USA) — Seasurf (Seaepic (USA)) 937 1179² 14074 1988² 2172³ 2439 2731

**Skullcap** 2 b g Sharrood (USA) — Falaka (Sparkler) 988⁶ 1161⁵ (1804) 2418 2696⁴ 2916⁶ 3218⁵ *3315²*

**Sky Burst** 2 ch f Gunner B — Sky Bonnet (Sky Gipsy) 3414 3780 3953

**Sky Cat** 8 b g Skyliner — Spring Kitten (Pitcairn) 1673 1961 2379⁴ 2517³ 2607 2814⁶

**Sky Classic (CAN)** 5 ch h Nijinsky (CAN) — No Class (USA) (Nodouble (USA)) 3229a² (3648a) 3940a²

**Sky Hunter (USA)** 3 b c Star de Naskra (USA) — Hunt The Thimble (USA) (Turn And Count (USA)) 235⁶ (274) 499³ (653) 825² 1062

**Sky Record** 3 b g Skyliner — On The Record (Record Token) 2666

**Sky Train (IRE)** 3 gr f Siberian Express (USA) — Karietta (Wollow) 910³ 1371⁴ 1555⁴ (1812) 2305 3256 3510⁵ 3763

**Sky Wish** 2 b g Skyliner — On The Record (Record Token) 1251 2264 2534² 3077 3303³

**Slades Hill** 5 b h Lochnager — Mephisto Waltz (Dancer's Image (USA)) *2196* (407) 613⁶

**Slanderinthestrand (IRE)** 3 b g Millfontaine — Eccentric Lady (London Bells (CAN)) 693 1172⁵ 1385⁵ 1572⁵ 1772

**Sleepline Fantasy** 7 ch g Buzzards Bay — Sleepline Princess (Royal Palace) 285

**Sleet Skier** 5 b h Niniski (USA) — Fleet Girl (Habitat) 3223a³ (2503a)

**Slight Risk** 3 b f Risk Me (FR) — Sarah Gillian (USA) (Zen (USA)) **1991:** *4046* **1992:** *(91)* *(116)* *168²* 256 *350²* *[2407W]* 2805⁶ 2993 3185 3845 3929²

**Slip-a-Snip** 5 b m Wolverlife — Stramenta (Thatching) **1991:** *4058³* *4086³* **1992:** *954* *130⁶* 414 506⁴ 735 1199 2209³ 2617⁵ 2752 2830

**Slivovitz** 2 b c Petoski — Hiding (So Blessed) 3519⁶ 3818⁶

**Slumber Thyme (IRE)** 3 ch f Burslem — Chive (St Chad) 669 1070⁴ 1750 2162⁶

**Sly Prospect (USA)** 4 ch g Barachois (CAN) — Miss Sly (USA) (Diamond Prospect (USA)) 1090 1193⁶ 1718 1905 3157

**Smadoun (FR)** 2 gr c Kaldoun (FR) — Mossma (FR) (Tip Moss (FR)) 2510a³ 3324a³

**Smarginato (IRE)** 2 gr c Simply Great (FR) — Aldern Stream (Godswalk (USA)) 2233⁶ 3181 3411²

**Smart Daisy** 2 b f Elegant Air — Michaelmas (Silly Season) 2438 3099⁵ 3489³

**Smartie Lee** 5 ch m Dominion — Nosy Parker (Kashmir II) **1991:** *4026* 4072³ **1992:** 2135 2412⁴ 2759 2934

**Smart Performer** 7 b h Formidable (USA) — Brilliant Rosa (Luthier) **1991:** *4098*

**Smart Teacher (USA)** 2 b or br c Smarten (USA) — Finality (USA) (In Reality) 2024 2323 2746

**Smiles Ahead** 4 ch g Primo Dominie — Baby's Smile (Shirley Heights) 2827 3116⁶ 3641

**Smilingatstrangers** 4 b f Macmillion — My Charade (Cawston's Clown) 426 1419 1719² (1988) *(2278)* 2664⁴ 3046⁵ 3244 3406² 3621⁵ 3728⁵ 3950

**Smiling Chief (IRE)** 4 ch g Montelimar (USA) — Victa (Northfields (USA)) *206²* 777² 987⁵ 1390² 1612 1686³ 2059 2408³ (2754) *(2805)* 2971 3236

**Smiling Sun (IRE)** 4 ch g Thatching — Charites (Red God) 2785

**Smith N'Allan** 2 b c Tina's Pet — Mertola (Tribal Chief) 3285 3704

**Smith's Peak** 8 gr g Alias Smith (USA) — Sacred Mountain (St Paddy) **1991:** *4033⁴* **1992:** *81⁴* *211⁵*

**Smocking** 2 ch f Night Shift (USA) — Sue Grundy (Grundy) 3848

**Smoke** 6 gr m Rusticaro (FR) — Fire-Screen (Roan Rocket) 267 405 533³ 766⁶ 923² 1108⁵ 1248 1859² 2065⁴ 2423² 2734

**Smudgemupum** 3 b c Green Ruby (USA) — Cloudless Sky (He Loves Me) *72⁶* *148⁶* *164* 1214 1572 *(1912)* 2053 2131⁵ 2303 2949 3281 3507 *3842*

**Snaadee (USA)** 5 br h Danzig (USA) — Somfas (USA) (What A Pleasure (USA)) 430⁴ 478⁶ (1060)

**Snappy Landing (USA)** 3 b c Northrop (USA) — Tempest Tost (USA) (First Landing) 538a⁴

# T

**Tahdeed (USA)** 2  ch  c  Shadeed (USA) —
Widaad (USA) (Mr Prospector (USA))
(952a) 1457 DEAD

**Tahdid** 2  b  f  Mtoto — Yaqut (USA)
(Northern Dancer) 3360 3780³

**Tahitian** 3  b  g  Precocious — Pacificus
(USA) (Northern Dancer) 235 296 498
884 1072⁵ 1146 1294² 1449⁵ 1700² 1890
2814 (2941) 3203² (3396) 3732²

**Tajarib (IRE)** 2  gr  f  Last Tycoon — Turkish
Treasure (USA) (Sir Ivor) 2459³ 2948⁴
3164⁴ 3508 3843

**Tajdid (IRE)** 2  ch  c  Caerleon (USA) —
Tarib (Habitat) 1536⁴ 2398³ 3030 3408
3587

**Tajdif (USA)** 2  br  c  Storm Cat (USA) —
Hankow Willow (USA) (No Robbery)
1283 (2108) (2528) 2841 3123⁴ 3642

**Tajfehn (USA)** 3  ch  f  Chief's Crown
(USA) — Capay (USA) (Sir Ivor) 1830⁵
2542⁵

**Tajhiz (USA)** 2  b  c  Woodman (USA) —
Princess Ivor (USA) (Sir Ivor) 3820²

**Tajigrey** 3  gr  f  Grey Desire — Taj Singh
(Mansingh (USA)) 302⁶ 370 498 698
1500³ (1885) 2198⁶

**Take by Storm (IRE)** 3  b  c  Bluebird (USA)
— Laurel Express (Bay Express) 1849³
(2362) (2692) 2836 3357² 3641

**Take Issue** 7  h  g  Absalom — Abstract
(French Beige) 76³

**Take it in Cash** 3  ch  f  Ballacashtal (CAN) —
Soft Secret (Most Secret) 2343 2922
3777 3854³ 3879² 3924⁴

**Takenhall** 7  b  g  Pitskelly — Great Dora
(Great Nephew) 610 832 1061 1303
1504⁴ 1706⁴ 1954 2656⁴ (3088) 3209
3370⁵ 3673⁵ 3726 (3819)

**Take One** 6  b  h  Teenoso (USA) — Old Kate
(Busted) 362 533 1518 1691

**Take Risks (FR)** 3  gr  c  Highest Honor (FR)
— Baino Bluff (Be My Guest (USA))
842a⁶ (1493a) (2090a) 2892a 3231a

**Take the Mick** 2  b  g  Hello Sunshine —
Avenmore Star (Comedy Star (USA))
1443 1610 3181 3491

**Take Two** 4  b  g  Jupiter Island — Dancing
Daughter (Dance In Time (CAN)) 240
(799)

**Take Your Partner (IRE)** 2  b  f  Dance of
Life (USA) — Kentucky Belle (Glint of
Gold) 286 371⁴ 782³ 2247³ 2694⁴
2983² 3394 3760⁵ 3899

**Talaton Flyer** 6  b  g  Kala Shikari — Pertune
(Hyperion's Curls) 1143⁶ 1640

**Talb (USA)** 3  b  or  br  c  Caro — Go March
(USA) (Go Marching (USA)) 441³
(3016) 3201³ 3427² 3591² 3729 3957

**Talented** 2  b  f  Bustino — Triple Reef (Mill
Reef (USA)) 3881⁴

**Talented Ting (IRE)** 3  ch  g  Hatim (USA) —
An Tig Gaelige (Thatch (USA)) **1991:**
4043² 4048 **1992:** 767 884 (1072) 1528³
(2147) (2355) 2571³ (2670)

**Talent (USA)** 4  b  g  Clever Trick (USA) —
Contralto (Busted) (1104) (1431) 1755⁴
2457² (2714) 3370 3800⁶

**Tales of Wisdom** 3  br  f  Rousillon (USA) —
New Generation (Young Generation)
**1991:** 4022 **1992:** 1700⁴ (1909) 2296²
2692² 2784⁴ 3010 3577

**Talish** 4  br  g  Persian Bold — Baheejah
(Northfields (USA)) **1991:** 4073 4098
**1992:** 27⁶ 405 518 617 880⁵ 1274
1311⁵ 1482 1731 1896² 1964 2160 2517

**Tallino** 2  b  f  Robellino (USA) — Labista
(Crowned Prince (USA)) 2932 3051³

**Tamarpour (USA)** 5  b  g  Sir Ivor — Tarsila
(High Top) 234³ 718⁴ 937⁶ 1459⁶

**Tamasha** 3  b  f  Hotfoot — Polonaise
(Takawalk II) 104 141⁵ 1276 1903 2754
3849

**Tamim (USA)** 3  gr  c  Topsider (USA) —
Passamaquoddy (USA) (Drone) 465⁶
8794 2214 2559 3473⁴ 3640⁵ 3793

**Tamrah (IRE)** 3  gr  f  Lomond (USA) —
Turkish Treasure (USA) (Sir Ivor)
[2659W]

**Tanagome (USA)** 2  gr  g  Procida (USA) —
Tasha Two (USA) (Cougar (CHI))
665⁴ 793³ 1524⁶ 2038³ 3164² 3784⁴

**Tanana** 3  b  f  Teenoso (USA) — La
Nureyeva (USA) (Nureyev (USA)) 1276
2100⁴ 2785⁶ 3159

**Tancred Grange** 3  ch  g  Prince Sabo —
Carpadia (Icecapade (USA)) 1153
1516⁶ 1960⁵ (2326) 2554 3170 3513⁵

**Tanegrus** 4  b  g  Dunbeath (USA) —
Tanagrea (Blakeney) [41W] 53

**Tanfith (CAN)** 5  b  h  Chief's Crown
(USA) — Foxy Olympia (USA) (Stage
Door Johnny) (202) 230⁷ 670³ 929⁵

**Tango Charlie (USA)** 3  b  f  Cure the Blues
(USA) — La Vie (USA) (Le Fabuleux)
3322a³

**Tango Time** 4  ch  g  Music Boy — Liberty
Tree (Dominion) (1064) [1380W] 1829
1999² 2201

**Tanoda** 6  b  m  Tyrnavos — Anoda (FR)
(Amber Rama (USA)) **1991:** 4026
**1992:** 225³ 299 469² 565⁶ 1037² 1324⁵
1691⁵ 2086⁵ 2693² 2968³ 3346⁶ 3627

**Taos (IRE)** 2  b  c  Sadler's Wells (USA) —
Tenea (Reform) (3202) (3462) (3669)

**Tapestry Dancer** 4  b  g  Lidhame — Royal
Bat (Crowned Prince (USA)) **1991:**
4081 **1992:** 41 152⁵ 333⁴ 448 1366
1682 1945

**Tapis Rouge (IRE)** 3  ch  c  Irish River (FR)
— Marie Noelle (FR) (Brigadier Gerard)
(384) 781² (2933) (3319) 3535⁶ 3686³

**Tarakana (USA)** 2  ch  f  Shahrastani (USA)
— Tarata (Akarad (FR)) 3563a⁵

**Tara's Delight** 5  b  m  Dunbeath (USA) —
Tickton Bridge (Grundy) **1991:** 403³²
4081⁴ 4094² **1992:** 41³ (64) (79) 127²
178⁵ 190³ 903² 1114⁶ 1376 (1682) 2040
2159

**Tara's Girl** 5  b  m  Touching Wood (USA)
— Esquire Lady (Be My Guest (USA))
508 592 909 1093 1434 2561 3170

**Tarda** 5  ch  m  Absalom — Ixia (I Say)
617⁶ 8294 1153⁴ 1488³ 1966⁴ 2150²
(2379) 2670⁴ 3174

**Target Line** 2  b  g  Skyliner — Tree Breeze
(Farm Walk) 2002 2606

**Target Time** 2  b  f  Faustus (USA) — Alicia
Markova (Habat) 2776⁶ 3115 3471
3625⁵

**Target Zero (USA)** 2  ch  c  Star de Naskra
(USA) — Clouhalo (USA) (Halo (USA))
3588 3953

**Tarmon (IRE)** 4  ch  g  Whistling Deer —
Royal Performance (Klairon) 3409 3600

Tenayestelign 4 gr f Bellypha — Opale (Busted) *81 131⁴ 155² 166³ 273 565 777⁵ 2805 2828 3097

Tenby 2 b c Caerleon (USA) — Shining Water (Kalaglow) (2456) (2790) (3651a)

Tender Look (IRE) 3 b f Prince Tenderfoot (USA) — Piercing Glances (Patch) 355 666⁵ 1145

Tender Moment (IRE) 4 b f Caerleon (USA) — Cannon Boy (USA) (Canonero II (USA)) 277 411⁶ (515) 610⁵ 941² 1403 2183 2684³ 2958² 3095 3359 3766

Tender Monarch (IRE) 3 br c Tender King — Loving Cup (He Loves Me) 1040 1294 1855⁶

Tender Reach 4 b f Reach — Betty's Bid (Auction Ring (USA)) 40

Tendresse (IRE) 4 b f Tender King — Velinowski (Malinowski (USA)) 340 411 587 912 1797⁴ 2291⁵ 2729 3395² (3487) 3510⁴ 3601²

Tenga (USA) 2 b f Mr Prospector (USA) — Royal Strait Flush (USA) (Seattle Slew (USA)) 3331a⁶

Ten High (IRE) 3 b f Leap High (USA) — Another Decade (Daring Display (USA)) 1157 1440⁶ 2896 3086⁶ 3395 3827

Ten to Six 2 b f Night Shift (USA) — Nigel's Dream (Pyjama Hunt) 1056² (1396) 3642

Tequila Gold 4 b g Green Ruby (USA) — Diamante (Sparkler) 269 328 419⁴

Tequila Twist (IRE) 2 br f Midyan (USA) — Mexican Two Step (Gay Fandango (USA)) 1913 2052⁶ 2557

Terimon 6 gr h Bustino — Nicholas Grey (Track Spare) 10a 1205³ 1455⁴ 1876 2345⁶ 2837

Ternimus (USA) 5 ch h Arctic Tern (USA) — Lustrious (USA) (Delaware Chief (USA)) 3054 3500

Terrhars 4 b c Anita's Prince — Clodianus (Bay Express) 236⁶ 550² 813⁶ 1199 1474 1875⁶ 2179³ 3188 3437⁵ 3671

Tertian (USA) 3 b c Danzig (USA) — Tertiary (USA) (Vaguely Noble) 655⁶ 1222a³ 2626a

Teslemi (USA) 3 b f Ogygian (USA) — Martha Queen (USA) (Nijinsky (CAN)) (493) 607⁴ 1152 1594⁶

Tetradonna (IRE) 4 b f Teenoso (USA) — Miss Bali Beach (Nonoalco (USA)) 929⁴ 1168³ 1710³ 2446 3248⁴ 3578⁴

Texan Clamour (FR) 4 b g Vacarme (USA) — Texan Maid (FR) (Targowice (USA)) 249⁵ 912 2281⁵

Texan Tycoon 4 b g Last Tycoon — High Move (High Top) 2012 2473³ 3137 (3426) (3572) 3956

Texas Cowgirl (IRE) 2 ch f Salt Dome (USA) — Cloven Dancer (USA) (Hurok (USA)) 2771 3283² 3472 3606² 3965

Thakawah 3 br g Green Desert (USA) — Index To Forli (USA) (Forli (ARG)) 394 512 762³ 1195 (1491) 1667³ 1866³

Thaleros 2 b c Green Desert (USA) — Graecia Magna (USA) (Private Account (USA)) 3531 3727³

Thames Glow 3 gr f Kalaglow — Thamesfield Lady (Stanford) 938⁵ 3016² (3216) 3582⁶ 3701

Thamestar (IRE) 3 b g Al Nasr (FR) — Star River (FR) (Riverman (USA)) 394⁴ 693² (1049) 1275 3270 3627⁵ (3829) 3956

Tharsis 7 ch g What A Guest — Grande Promesse (FR) (Sea Hawk II) 1991: 4083

Thatchenne 7 b m Thatching — Enterprisor (Artaius (USA)) 143

Thawakib (IRE) 2 b f Sadler's Wells (USA) — Tobira Celeste (USA) (Ribot) 2338⁵ (3093) (3440)

The Atheling (IRE) 2 b c Taufan (USA) — Shady Glade (Sun Prince) 528⁴ 645⁵ 3874 3964

The Auction Bidder 5 b h Auction Ring (USA) — Stepping Gaily (Gay Fandango (USA)) 2a 241 403⁶ 629 813 3787 3828 3957

The Bethanian 2 b c Absalom — Jose Collins (Singing Bede) 1991² 2264³

The Can Can Man 5 br g Daring March — Dawn Ditty (Song) 449 670 941⁵ 1021⁵ 1254⁵ 1365 1529

The Country Dancer 2 br f Mashhor Dancer (USA) — Slip The Ferret (Klairon) 3410

The Cuckoo's Nest 4 b c Precocious — Troy Moon (Troy) 2830 3088 3264 3947

The Cut 2 ch f Sharpo — Penultimate (Final Straw) 362 422 882

The Dandy Don (IRE) 3 ch g On Your Mark — Balacco (Balidar) 374⁴ 662³ 767 1122³ 1438 2142⁵ 2249² 2814³ 2941² 3149⁶ 3476

The Devil's Music 8 ch h Music Boy — Obergurgl (Warpath) 269³ 364 419 1013 1093

The Dominant Gene 3 gr c Dominion — Judy's Dowry (Dragonara Palace (USA)) 448 524 1052⁵ 1486² 1890 2685

The Dream Maker (IRE) 3 b f Cyrano de Bergerac — Bermuda Princess (Lord Gayle (USA)) 591 1075 1364⁶ 1550⁶ 2041 2365⁴ 2481³ (2786) 2936⁵ 3079⁶ 3413

The Executor 2 ch c Vaigly Great — Fee (Mandamus) 1259 2598⁶ 2799 3035³ 3260⁵

The Fed 2 ch g Clantime — Hyde Princess (Touch Paper) 1283³ 1779² 2388³

The Golden Sport 2 ch g Risk Me (FR) — Golden Guilder (Sonnen · Gold) 2826 3181 3580 3685

The Gold Souk (IRE) 2 b c Wassl — Gaelic Jewel (Scottish Rifle) 2208⁶ 2584³ 2947⁵ 3173³ 3407 3754²

The Goofer 5 b g Be My Native (USA) — Siliferous (Sandy Creek) 3864³ (3907) 3958

The Gorrock 3 b g Petoski — Aquarula (Dominion) 3053

The Grey Texan 3 gr c Nishapour (FR) — Houston Belle (Milford) 2549 2801

The Huyton Lady 4 ch f Brotherly (USA) — The Huyton Girls (Master Sing) 162

The Informer (USA) 2 b c Slew O' Gold (USA) — Comicus (USA) (Northern Jove (CAN)) 581³ 828³ 3100² 3362² 3531³ 3672

The Institute Boy 2 b c Fairy King (USA) — To Oneiro (Absalom) 1092³ 1409⁶ 1835³ 2232 2863 3283 3315³ 3590 3750³ 3949⁶

**Vaganova (IRE) 3** b c Where To Dance (USA) — Modena (Sassafras (FR)) 640a³

**Vagrancy 3** br f Dancing Brave (USA) — Trampship (High Line) 440 1079³ 3259

**Vague Dancer 6** b g Vaigly Great — Step You Gaily (King's Company) 233 368 533 688⁴ 829⁵ 1143 (2609) (2777) (3009) 3547

**Vague Nancy (IRE) 4** b f Mazaad — Noble Nancy (Royal And Regal (USA)) *1550* 3510

**Vaigly Sunthyme 2** br f Vaigly Great — Red Roses (FR) (Roi Dagobert) 3307 3614 3856⁴

**Vailmont (USA) 3** ch f Diesis — Annie Edge (Nebbiolo) (691) (834) 1117 1717³

**Vain Prince 5** b h Sandhurst Prince — Vain Deb (Gay Fandango (USA)) 2535³ (2737) (2934) (3034)

**Valatch 4** ch g Valiyar — Love Match (USA) (Affiliate (USA)) 225 *905*

**Val des Bois (USA) 6** gr h — 3938a⁴

**Valere Knight (IRE) 2** b c Heraldiste (USA) — Kix (King Emperor (USA)) 1297⁴ 1923⁵ 2758 2932

**Valgrija (FR) 4** ch f Big John (FR) — Val Griette (FR) (Val de Loir) 3734a³

**Valiant Commander 2** b g War Hero — Polola (Aragon) 3776⁴

**Valiant Warrior 4** br g Valiyar — Jouvencelle (Rusticaro (FR)) 292⁷ 3076 347⁷

**Valiant Words 5** br g Valiyar — Wild Words (Galivanter) 1063 1203 1716⁵ 2012 3061

**Valkyrie Reef 3** ch f Miramar Reef — Private Sue (Brigadier Gerard) [2146W]

**Vallance 4** b c Top Ville — Kindjal (Kris) 229 354 565 (2012) (2202) (2529) 2791² 3292² 3634³

**Valley of Fire 3** b f Dancing Brave (USA) — Glowing Embers (Nebbiolo) (502) 1210³ 2182⁴ (2920) 3436 3836

**Valley of Time (FR) 4** br f ln Fijar (USA) — Vallee Sarthoise (FR) (Val de Loir) 326 913³ (1564) 1731⁴ 2216⁴ 2966 3759

**Valseur (USA) 3** ch c Lyphard (USA) — Vachti (FR) (Crystal Palace (FR)) 1346⁴ 1914

**Valued Friend (USA) 4** b g Ziggy's Boy (USA) — Tuvalu (USA) (Our Native (USA)) **1991:** 4087⁶ **1992:** *90* 831

**Vanart 3** b g Precocious — Red Spider (Red God) 878³ 1055⁶ 1862³ 2165³ 3908⁶

**Vanborough Lad 3** b g Precocious — Lustrous (Golden Act (USA)) 387³ 471 783² 1206 1412⁶ 2173⁵ 2410⁶ 3137 3241² 3564² 3584⁴ 3781⁵

**Vanda's Girl 4** br f Noalto — Concorde Lady (Hotfoot) *48*

**Vandervally 3** ch g Van Der Linden (FR) — Sannavally (Sagaro) 2469 3003 3477⁴

**Vanille (USA) 3** ch f Diesis — Valhalla (FR) (New Chapter) 2765a²

**Vaniski 5** b g Niniski (USA) — Voltigeuse (USA) (Filiberto) *114⁴*

**Vanroy 8** b g Formidable (USA) — Princess Tavi (Sea Hawk II) **1991:** 4038⁵ (4054) *4075* **1992:** 580³ 800² 1201 (1203) 1413⁵ 1916⁴ 2240² (2416) 2600⁴ 3060 3066 3418

**Vanuatu (IRE) 3** b f Orchestra — Owey (Sovereign Gleam) 1956 2823⁴ 3062⁵ 3249⁵

**Vardy (IRE) 2** ch g King Persian — Jolie Brise (Tumble Wind (USA)) 571 759 889⁴ 2572

**Vasarelli (IRE) 3** b c Last Tycoon — Wedgewood Blue (USA) (Sir Ivor) 1823a

**Vasiliev 4** b g Sadler's Wells (USA) — Poquito Queen (CAN) (Explodent (USA)) 405 518² 688 880² 3206 3467⁶ 3687 3829⁴ 3906

**Va Utu 4** b g Balliol — Flame (Firestreak) *35*

**Vayavaig 2** b f Damister (USA) — Dervaig (Derring-Do) 3414³ (3626) 3867

**Velasco (IRE) 2** b g Nordico (USA) — Donnarella (Dom Racine (FR)) 2568⁶ *2781* 2986 3179

**Vellandrucha 3** b f Cragador — Shadha (Shirley Heights) 1425⁴ 1885 2757 3252⁵ 3412 3963

**Veloce (IRE) 4** b g Kafu — Joanns Goddess (Godswalk (USA)) 364⁴ 456 592³ 684² 1018 1193⁵ 1379³ 1833³ 1992 3002² 3126³ 3344⁵ 3496⁴ 3620⁶ 3793 3879

**Velveteen Boy 4** b g Enchantment — Penny Bazaar (Native Bazaar) 531 579⁶

**Vendredi Treize 9** b or br g Lucky Wednesday — Angel Row (Prince Regent (FR)) 1282 1570⁵ 1905 1978 2564

**Ventiquattrofogli (IRE) 2** b c Persian Bold — India Atlanta (Ahonoora) 1658² (1946) (2328) (2572) (3233a) (3567a) 3891a

**Venture Capitalist 3** ch g Never So Bold — Brave Advance (USA) (Bold Laddie (USA)) 428³ 620² (727) 870⁵ 1698² 2029⁶ 2280⁴ (2493) 2848³ (3031) 3188² 3356 3729

**Venture Fourth 3** b c Hotfoot — Four Lawns (Forlorn River) 1245 1581³ 2088⁵ 2680⁴ 2941 3595

**Venture Prints 2** b c Presidium — Bar Gold (Lucky Brief) 968 1944⁶ 2414 3129 3821

**Venturina (IRE) 3** b f Taufan (USA) — Love Resolved (Dan Cupid) 473³ 780³

**Venturist (USA) 5** b h Al Nasr (FR) — Sleek Lassie (USA) (Northern Prospect (USA)) **1991:** *4018³*

**Venus Observed 4** ch f Sharpo — Fair And Wise (High Line) (692) 1061 1930 2852 3359 3543

**Verdant Boy 9** br g Green Dancer (USA) — Favorite Prospect (USA) (Mr Prospector (USA)) *903⁶* 1129⁵ *1266* 1451⁵ 2163⁵ 2352⁶ 2421³ 2966⁶ 3151² 3342 3476⁶ 3632³ 3759 3916

**Verde Alitalia (IRE) 3** ch c Fayruz — Soul of Discretion (Tumble Wind (USA)) 559 690⁶

**Vermont Magic 4** b g Elegant Air — Jove's Voodoo (USA) (Northern Jove (CAN)) 3763

**Vernonia 3** b f Bustino — Neenah (Bold Lad (IRE)) 553 784⁴ 1025 3238 3690

**Verro (USA) 5** ch h Irish River (FR) — Royal Rafale (USA) (Reneged) **1991:** 4032 4081⁶ **1992:** *42 70 119⁴ 143⁴ 184 351* 357³ 496³ *(661) 752 1266⁴ 1278 1544* 3595 3879 3916⁴

**Versailles Treaty (USA) 4** b f Danzig (USA) — Ten Cents a Dance (USA) (Buckpasser) 3937a²

# W

**Waaree (USA) 2** ro c Risen Star (USA) — Flight Dancer (USA) (Misty Flight) 3193 3465

**Waaza (USA) 3** b c Danzig Connection (USA) — Nishig (USA) (Naskra (USA)) 1734 1906⁴ 2200 2775 2959 3161² 3258⁴ 3706⁶

**Wabwom 3** b g Dunbeath (USA) — Lunar Shamal-Gal (Tumble Wind (USA)) [2432W]

**Waders Dream (IRE) 3** b g Doulab (USA) — Sea Mistress (Habitat) 576⁶ 1391² 1500 2411³ 3284⁶

**Wafi (USA) 3** b c Lyphard (USA) — Dictina (FR) (Dictus (FR)) 440 698³ 1807³ 2871 3016³ 3153 3511 3747⁶ 3810²

**Wahem (IRE) 2** b c Lomond (USA) — Pro Patria (Petingo) 446 564⁴ 659² 3019 3063³ (3199) 3830

**Wainwright (USA) 3** ch c Bering — Crystal Bright (Bold Lad (IRE)) 3016⁵

**Wajd (USA) 5** ch m Northern Dancer — Dahlia (USA) (Vaguely Noble) 10a⁶

**Wajeeb (USA) 3** b c Majestic Light (USA) — Reham (Mill Reef (USA)) 1280³

**Wakil (IRE) 3** br c Tate Gallery (USA) — Arena (Sallust) 394 695 972 1890⁴ 2496³ 2707² (2828)

**Wakt 2** b f Akarad (FR) — Nasara (FR) (Home Guard (USA)) 3871

**Walid's Princess (IRE) 2** b f Waajib — Glomach (USA) (Majestic Light (USA)) 561³ 703 1121 1989⁴ 2389 (2563) 2696⁵ 3694⁴

**Walimu (IRE) 3** b f Top Ville — Summer Impressions (USA) (Lyphard (USA)) 1956³ (2399) 2647³ 2913⁵ (3270) 3527⁵ (3713) 3896

**Wali (USA) 2** b c Lomond (USA) — Magic Slipper (Habitat) 3662⁴ 3802

**Walking on Water 3** ch g Celestial Storm (USA) — Maiden Pool (Sharpen Up) 432 653 1382 1634³ 1914 2069⁴ 2580 3057

**Walking Possession 3** b c Faustus (USA) — Pepeke (Mummy's Pet) 445 714⁴ 996² 1204 1576⁵ 2188 (2424) (2603) 2650 2909 3065³

**Walking Saint 5** b m Godswalk (USA) — Saintly Tune (Welsh Saint) 504 696 1147⁶ 1372 1653⁴ 1971 2391

**Walking the Plank 3** b g Daring March — Pirate Maid (Auction Ring (USA)) 482

**Walk in the Park 3** ch f Valiyar — Tripolitaine (FR) (Nonoalco (USA)) 413⁴ 472 690⁵ 939² 998² 1104³ 1314 1717² 1952² 2179² (2265) 2443⁴ 2642 (2909) 2997⁶ 3188⁴ 3361⁴

**Walkonthemoon 3** ch f Coquelin (USA) — Lunar Eclipse (Hot Spark) **1991:** 4036⁴ 4070⁶ **1992:** 104⁵ 135³ (182) 295 1085³ 2079 2303 2712⁴ 3003 3254 3421

**Walk That Walk 3** b f Hadeer — Che Gambe (USA) (Lyphard (USA)) 482

**Walk the Beat 2** b c Interrex (CAN) — Plaits (Thatching) 3608⁶ (3921)

**Walnut Burl (IRE) 2** b c Taufan (USA) — Hay Knot (Main Reef) 1039⁴ 1457 1769³ 2450⁵ 3581⁴ 3839

**Walsham Witch 2** b f Music Maestro — Makinlau (Lauso) 1038⁴ (1170) 2193⁶ (2612) 3001⁴ 3267 3394⁶

**Walstead (IRE) 3** b c Fairy King (USA) — Tecmessa (Home Guard (USA)) 559 678 939⁶ 2192⁵ 2411⁶ 2787⁴ 2795 3133 3284 3803⁶ 3879 3963

**Walters Wonder 2** b c Welsh Captain — Romana (Roman Warrior) 803 1007

**Wanda 5** b m Taufan (USA) — Pitaka (Pitskelly) 349*d 480

**Wandering Stranger 3** gr f Petong — Doppio (Dublin Taxi) 1683³ 2131³ (2419) 3004

**Wand (IRE) 3** b f Reference Point — Fairy Dancer (USA) (Nijinsky (CAN)) 529³ 2116² 2635⁴ (3114)

**Wanza 2** b c Petoski — Lovers Light (Grundy) 2606⁴ 2924 3147⁴ 3474 3832

**War Beat 4** b g Wolver Heights — Branitska (Mummy's Pet) **1991:** 4026 **1992:** 1566⁴ 1789⁵ 2059⁶

**Warkworth (USA) 2** ch c Tejano (USA) — Plum Quick (USA) (Terresto) 396 571² 877 2903⁵ 3148 3385⁴ 3712³

**Warm Spell 2** b g Northern State (USA) — Warm Wind (Tumble Wind (USA)) 1573 (1900) 2462 2578 3218⁴ 3385² (3574)

**War Requiem (IRE) 2** b c Don't Forget Me — Ladiz (Persian Bold) 7726 803 2577² 2000 3030⁵ 3242 3364 3508⁵ 3574 3837⁶

**Warrior Prince 4** b g Prince Sabo — Choral Park (Music Boy) **1991:** 4068 **1992:** 70

**Warspite 2** b c Slip Anchor — Valkyrie (Bold Lad (IRE)) 3531 3880⁶

**Waseela (IRE) 3** b f Ahonoora — Wassl's Sister (Troy) 699⁴ 878⁴ 1175 1449² (1620) 1863⁴ (2107) (2384) 2554 2987⁶ 3269

**Washington Red 3** ch g Tickled Pink — Apple Queen (Behistoun) 511 901 1139⁴

**Wassl This Then (IRE) 3** b f Wassl — Dancing Decoy (Troy) 858³ 1105² 1594² 1948³ (2241) 2547² 3013

**Watch Me Go (IRE) 3** b c On Your Mark — Nighty Night (Sassafras (FR)) 535⁵ 767 2123⁵ 2384⁴ (2662) 2813 2941 3170 3380 3476 3615³ 3751 3882

**Watch Tower Bay (IRE) 4** ch g Kings Lake (USA) — Noon Bells (Ballymore) 125⁵ DEAD

**Water Diviner 2** b g Dowsing (USA) — Prudence (Grundy) 735⁵ 1071 1208 1442 1675 (2058) 2389⁶ 2649 2782

**Waterfowl Creek (IRE) 3** b or br f Be My Guest (USA) — On Show (Welsh Pageant) (302) 473⁴ 2523² 3038⁵ (3265) 3591³ 3826⁴ 3902²

**Waterlord (IRE) 2** b c Bob Back (USA) — Ringtail (Auction Ring (USA)) 339 968² 1296⁴ 2037 2225² 2418 2900² 3129 3275 3792⁴

**Waterlow Park 10** ch g Wollow — Caraquenga (USA) (Cyane) 831

**Watermill Girl 4** b f Blakeney — Absurd (Absalom) 1266 1376 1543 2291⁶ 2427 2937⁶ 3017 3152

**Water Skier 2** b c Nishapour (FR) — Wave Dancer (Dance In Time (CAN)) 3531

**Watersong 3** b f Lochnager — Sonoco (Song) **1991:** 4022³ 4061 DEAD

**Wathik (USA) 2** ch c Ogygian (USA) — Copper Creek (Habitat) 1944² (2519) 3435⁴ (3824)

**Waveband 3** br f Thatching — Waveguide (Double Form) 503⁶ 801 3009 3460

**Wave Hill 3** b c Sizzling Melody — Trikymia (Final Straw) 454⁶ 870 1213² (1708) 2191² 2348² 2527 2852 3428⁶ 3547

**Wave Master 5** b g Chief Singer — Sea Fret (Habat) *112* 2576³ 2705⁴ *3180* 3406

**Waverley Star 7** br g Pitskelly — Quelle Blague (Red God) 1263⁴ 1451³ *1551³* (3423) 3703⁴ *3931*

**Wave to Me 3** ch g Risk Me (FR) — Songs Jest (Song) *1849* 2362

**Wayward Son 3** gr g Risk Me (FR) — Mummy's Chick (Mummy's Pet) 998 1214 1708 1978 2291 2583⁵ *2685²* 2806⁴ 2944

**Wealthywoo 2** ch f Rich Charlie — Woomargama (Creetown) 595 786³ 928 1442⁶ 1775³ 2080⁵ *(2257)* 2546⁵ 2824 3049

**Weapon Exhibition 5** ch m Exhibitioner — Weapon (Prince Ippi (GER)) *224* 335 *776⁴* 2416

**We Are Doomed 2** ch c Primo Dominie — Divetta (Ribero) 1887⁴ 2398 2771 2916 3407 3611

**Weaver Bird 2** b f Master Willie — Sweet Snow (USA) (Lyphard (USA)) 2758³ (2932)

**Weaver George (IRE) 2** b g Flash of Steel — Nephrite (Godswalk (USA)) 1249 1479⁴ 1623² 1860² 2543 3173 3301

**Wedding of the Sea (USA) 3** ch f Blushing Groom (FR) — Sweet Mover (USA) (Nijinsky (CAN)) 1352a³ *(1983a)* 3223a³

**Wedding Ring (IRE) 3** ch f Never So Bold — Fleur d'Oranger (Northfields (USA)) *(175a)* 381a² 3658a

**Wedding Vow (USA) 4** b f Nijinsky (CAN) — Wedding Picture (USA) (Blushing Groom (FR)) 535⁵

**Wednesdays Auction (IRE) 4** b c Mazaad — Happy Always (Lucky Wednesday) 2856 2937 3054

**Weeheby (USA) 3** ch c Woodman (USA) — Fearless Dame (USA) (Fearless Knight) 1033 1158⁵ 1426² 1643 (1981) 2160 2422³ 2708 2946³ 3140 3215 3434²

**Weekday Cross (IRE) 4** b g Taufan (USA) — Isoldes Tower (Balliol) 299 422 1008

**Weekend Girl 3** b f Vorvados — Mrs Scattercash (Northfields (USA)) *218* 278 468 594 *1001* 1128⁴ 2931 3413 3507

**Welcoming Arms 5** b m Free State — The Guzzler (Behistoun) **1991:** *4083* **1992:** 683

**Well Ahead 3** b f Last Tycoon — Sistabelle (Bellypha) 1287 1958² 2515² 2720⁶ 3087² 3169

**Well Beyond (IRE) 3** ch f Don't Forget Me — Mariakova (USA) (The Minstrel (CAN)) *(3038)* 3213⁵ *(3664)* 3901

**Well Bought (IRE) 3** b f Auction Ring (USA) — Knighton House (Pall Mall) *94²* *136* *182⁵*

**Well Directed (IRE) 3** b c Sadler's Wells (USA) — So Directed (Homing) 3459 3609 3801

**Wellington Rock (USA) 3** ch c Lyphard's Wish (FR) — Cuz's Star (USA) (Galaxy Libra) 869³ (1334) (1628) 1941⁵

**Well Saddled (IRE) 3** b c Sadler's Wells (USA) — Ukraine Girl (Targowice (USA)) 930⁵ 1198 3527 3697

**Well Suited 2** b g Elegant Air — Gay Appeal (Star Appeal) 935⁵

**Wellsy Lad (USA) 5** ch g El Baba (USA) — Iwishiknew (USA) (Damascus (USA)) **1991:** *4005³* 4027 *(4049)* *(4080)* 4103⁶ **1992:** *45²* *87* *132* *180* 201⁴ 221⁴ 325³ 496 *903* 1266² *1377⁴* *1550³* 2099⁵ 2366⁵ 2785 3378 3879 3910² 3963⁵

**Well Tried (IRE) 2** b f Thatching — Good Effort (Try My Best (USA)) 2897⁶ 3156 3399

**Welsh Heritage (IRE) 2** b f Slip Anchor — Mohibbah (USA) (Conquistador Cielo (USA)) 3360⁶

**Welshman 6** ch g Final Straw — Joie de Galles (Welsh Pageant) 229² 475⁴ (718) 2899⁵ 3128 3431 3666 3728

**Welsh Mill (IRE) 3** b c Caerleon (USA) — Gay Milly (FR) (Mill Reef (USA)) (1447) 2788² 3057² 3369² 3798³

**Welsh Pet 2** b f Petong — Glyn Rhosyn (Welsh Saint) 995³ 2758 3410 *3558*

**Welsh Secret 4** b f Welsh Captain — Bridge of Gold (Balidar) 449

**Wentbridge Lad (IRE) 2** b c Coquelin (USA) — Cathryn's Song (Prince Tenderfoot (USA)) 682⁶ 1202 1299⁶ 1660⁵ *(1860)* 2058⁴

**We're All Game 3** b f Mummy's Game — Swynford's Pride (Rapid River) 276³ 415⁵ 591² 3103 3220⁶ *(3341)* 3464 3596

**Wesaam (USA) 3** b c Riverman (USA) — Share The Fantasy (USA) (Exclusive Native (USA)) 474⁶ 722⁶ 1061 1504⁵ *(1856)* 2433² 2755³ 3212 3527

**Wessex Milord 7** ch g Stanford — Miss Osprey (Sea Hawk II) 967⁶ 1343 1564³ 2276⁵ 2634 3037 3418

**Wesshaun 2** b f Shaunicken — Wessex Flyer (Pony Express) 3683

**West Auckland 3** br g Silly Prices — Elitist (Keren) 3078 3384

**West by West (USA) 3** b c Gone West (USA) — West Turn (Cox's Ridge (USA)) 538a²

**West End Girl 2** b f Absalom — City Ditty (Camden Town) 2649⁵ 3178 3303 3623

**Westering 2** b f Auction Ring (USA) — Westerlake (Blakeney) 1937⁶

**Western Approach (USA) 3** b f Gone West (USA) — Devon Diva (USA) (The Minstrel (CAN)) *(1364)* *(1707)* 2448 *(2848)* 3731

**Western Cape (USA) 2** b c Gone West (USA) — Blue Bell Pearl (FR) (Pharly (FR)) 3005⁴

**Western Dancer 11** b g Free State — Polyandrist (Polic) 507² 790⁶ 2759

**Western Dynasty 6** ch g Hotfoot — Northern Dynasty (Breeders Dream) **1991:** 4026⁵ *4040⁵* **1992:** *(342)* 479 681⁵ 831 1612² 2086² 2451³ 2853 3139⁴ 3279³ 3572⁴ 3675 3851

**Western Valley 2** ch f Valiyar — Another Western (Good Times (ITY)) 2859 3414⁵

~~~~~~~~~~

# CORRECTIONS

**RACEFORM ANNUAL 1990**

    **Race 2654:** **Flown** has been disqualified (prohibited substance (hydroxycamphor) in urine. The second, third, fourth and fifth have been promoted.

**RACEFORM ANNUAL 1991**

    **Race 2912:** **Gentle Hero (USA):** has been disqualified (prohibited substance (trimethoprim) in urine). The third, fourth and fifth have been promoted.

    **Race 2974:** **The Right Time** has been disqualified (prohibited substance (testosterone) in urine. The second, third, fourth and fifth have been promoted.

**RACEFORM ANNUAL 1992**

    **Race 742a:** **Symphorino (USA):** should read Symphorine (USA)

    **Race 958a:** **Symphorino (USA)** should read: Symphorine (USA)

    **Race 1169:** Speed figures should read: 30/–/–/29/3/–

    **Race 1394:** **Rosgill:** side reference should read: 342

    **Race 1816a:** Going allowance should read: minus 0.40 sec per fur (F)

    **Race 1817a—1821a:** Going allowance should read: 5f-8f: minus 0.20 sec Rnd: minus 0.35 sec per fur (F)

    **Race 2749:** Speed Figures should read: 49/41/51/–

# RACEFORM RECORD TIMES

As recorded by "Raceform" since 1936. Courses with
electrical timing apparatus are indicated—(Electric).

## ASCOT (Electric)

| Distance | Time | Age | Weight | | Going | Horse | Date | |
|---|---|---|---|---|---|---|---|---|
| 5f | 59·1 | 3 | 8 | 8 | Firm | Orient | June 21, | 1986 |
| 5f | 59·72 | 2 | 8 | 8 | Firm | Lyric Fantasy (IRE) | June 17, | 1992 |
| 6f | 1. 12·53 | 4 | 9 | 4 | Firm | Shalford (IRE) | June 17, | 1992 |
| 6f | 1. 13·63 | 2 | 8 | 8 | Firm | Minstrella (USA) | June 19, | 1986 |
| 7f | 1. 25·94 | 3 | 9 | 1 | Firm | Prince Ferdinand | June 17, | 1992 |
| 7f | 1. 27·3 | 2 | 8 | 11 | Firm | Tour D'Or (USA) | Sept. 28, | 1984 |
| 8f (rnd) | 1. 38·8 | 3 | 9 | 0 | Firm | Shadeed | Sept. 28, | 1985 |
| 8f (rnd) | 1. 40·92 | 2 | 8 | 7 | Fast | Untold | Sept. 26, | 1985 |
| 8f (st) | 1. 38·07 | 4 | 7 | 8 | Firm | Colour Sergeant | June 17, | 1992 |
| 10f | 2. 3·31 | 4 | 9 | 1 | Firm | Trepan (disq.) | June 15, | 1976 |
| 12f | 2. 26·95 | 5 | 8 | 9 | Firm | Stanerra | June 17, | 1983 |
| 16f 45y | 3. 25·29 | 3 | 9 | 3 | Firm | Landowner (IRE) | June 17, | 1992 |
| 20f | 4. 15·67 | 5 | 9 | 0 | Firm | Royal Gait (disq) | June 16, | 1988 |
| 22f 34y | 4. 51·32 | 4 | 8 | 8 | Firm | Otabari | June 20, | 1986 |

## AYR (Electric)

| Distance | Time | Age | Weight | | Going | Horse | Date | |
|---|---|---|---|---|---|---|---|---|
| 5f | 57·68 | 7 | 7 | 7 | Firm | Red Desire | July 21, | 1972 |
| 5f | 57·80 | 2 | 8 | 0 | Hard | Monte Christo | May 17, | 1946 |
| 6f | 1. 9·36 | 3 | 8 | 10 | Good | Sarcita | Sept. 20, | 1991 |
| 6f | 1. 9·73 | 2 | 7 | 10 | Good | Sir Bert | Sept. 17, | 1969 |
| 7f | 1. 24·97 | 5 | 7 | 11 | Firm | Sir Arthur Hobbs | June 19, | 1992 |
| 7f | 1. 26·08 | 2 | 8 | 11 | Good | Soiree (IRE) | Sept. 19, | 1991 |
| 8f | 1. 36 | 4 | 7 | 13 | Firm | Sufi | Sept. 16, | 1959 |
| 8f | 1. 39·21 | 2 | 9 | 0 | Firm | Kribensis | Sept. 17, | 1986 |
| 9f | 1. 55·25 | 3 | 7 | 10 | Firm | Virkon Venture (IRE) | Sept. 21, | 1991 |
| | (hand-timed) | | | | | | | |
| 10f | 2. 6·03 | 3 | 8 | 6 | Good | Sharpitor (IRE) | July 20, | 1992 |
| 10f 192y | 2. 13·31 | 4 | 9 | 0 | Good | Azzaam (USA) | Sept. 18, | 1991 |
| 13f 13y | 2. 46·53 | 5 | 9 | 9 | Firm | Beau Quest | June 20, | 1992 |
| 15f | 3. 13·16 | 3 | 9 | 4 | Good | Romany Rye | Sept. 19, | 1991 |
| 17f 105y | 3. 45 | 4 | 6 | 13 | Good | Curry | Sept. 16, | 1955 |
| 20f 90y | 4. 33·86 | 4 | 8 | 6 | Good | Charles Stuart (FR) | July 8, | 1983 |

## BATH

| Distance | Time | Age | Weight | | Going | Horse | Date | |
|---|---|---|---|---|---|---|---|---|
| 5f 11y | 1. 0·3 | 3 | 8 | 9 | Hard | Katie's First (USA) | May 21, | 1990 |
| 5f 11y | 1. 0·9 | 2 | 8 | 4 | Fast | Mamma's Too | July 6, | 1991 |
| 5f 161y | 1. 8·1 | 6 | 9 | 0 | Firm | Madraco | May 22, | 1989 |
| 5f 161y | 1. 10·0 | 2 | 8 | 13 | Fast | Morocco (IRE) | July 22, | 1991 |
| 7f 8y | 1. 27·8 { | 4 | 8 | 3 | Firm | Diplomatic Cloak | Sept. 2, | 1961 |
| | | 3 | 8 | 4 | Firm | Star Flare | July 28, | 1980 |
| 7f 8y | 1. 28·6 | 2 | 9 | 0 | Firm | Hunting Tower | Aug. 3, | 1970 |
| 8f 5y | 1. 38·9 | 4 | 10 | 0 | Hard | Neptune's Pet | July 8, | 1992 |
| 8f 5y | 1. 40·7 | 2 | 8 | 11 | Firm | Myhamet | Oct. 2, | 1989 |
| 10f 46y | 2. 7 | 3 | 8 | 13 | Fast | Golden Wave | April 26, | 1988 |
| 11f 144y | 2. 26·3 { | 3 | 9 | 0 | Firm | Mubarak of Kuwait | April 27, | 1982 |
| | | 3 | 8 | 11 | Firm | Cypria Sacra (USA) | June 1, | 1987 |
| 13f 22y | 2. 47·3 | 4 | 10 | 0 | Firm | Flown | Aug 13, | 1991 |
| 17f 34y | 3. 43·9 | 6 | 7 | 9 | Fast | Patroclus | July 10, | 1991 |

# BEVERLEY

| Distance | Time | Age | Weight | Going | Horse | Date | |
|---|---|---|---|---|---|---|---|
| 5f | 1. 0·3 | 4 | 9 11 | Firm | Eager Deva | April 25, | 1991 |
| 5f | 1. 2 | 2 | 8 11 | Firm | Persian Breeze | June 13, | 1974 |
| | | 2 | 8 8 | Firm | Fimi | Aug. 27, | 1981 |
| 7f 100y | 1. 29·4 | 3 | 7 8 | Firm | Who's Tef (IRE) | July 30, | 1991 |
| 7f 100y | 1. 30·9 | 2 | 9 0 | Firm | Majal (IRE) | July 30, | 1991 |
| 8f 100y | 1. 42·3 | 3 | 8 4 | Firm | Legal Case | June. 14, | 1989 |
| 8f 100y | 1. 43·3 | 2 | 9 0 | Firm | Arden | Sept. 24, | 1986 |
| 9f 207y | 2. 1·6 | 3 | 9 7 | Firm | Rose Alto | July 5, | 1991 |
| 11f 216y | 2. 30·6 | 3 | 8 1 | Hard | Coinage | June 18, | 1986 |
| 16f 35y | 3. 30·1 | 4 | 7 7 | Firm | Between The Sheets | Sept. 21, | 1989 |
| 19f 100y | 4. 21·5 | 3 | 8 9 | Firm | Mandalay Prince | July 14, | 1987 |

# BRIGHTON

| Distance | Time | Age | Weight | Going | Horse | Date | |
|---|---|---|---|---|---|---|---|
| 5f 59y | 1. 0 | 3 | 9 2 | Firm | Access Flyer | May 29, | 1991 |
| | | 3 | 8 1 | Firm | Cheshire Annie (IRE) | May 27, | 1992 |
| 5f 59y | 1. 0·8 | 2 | 8 12 | Firm | Rio Tejo (USA) | June 26, | 1990 |
| 5f 213y | 1. 7·8 | 8 | 10 0 | Firm | Green Dollar | May 30, | 1991 |
| 5f 213y | 1. 8·5 | 2 | 8 9 | Firm | Holetown | Sept. 4, | 1991 |
| 6f 209y | 1. 19·4 | 4 | 9 3 | Firm | Sawaki | Sept. 4, | 1991 |
| 6f 209y | 1. 19·9 | 2 | 8 11 | Hard | Rain Burst | Sept. 15, | 1988 |
| 7f 214y | 1. 30·9 | 5 | 8 12 | Hard | Chase The Door | July 26, | 1990 |
| 7f 214y | 1. 32·8 | 2 | 9 7 | Firm | Asian Pete | Oct. 3, | 1909 |
| 9f 209y | 1. 57·2 | 3 | 9 0 | Firm | Get the Message | April 30, | 1984 |
| 11f 196y | 2. 25·8 (flag) | 4 | 8 2 | Firm | New Zealand | July 4, | 1985 |

# CARLISLE

| Distance | Time | Age | Weight | Going | Horse | Date | |
|---|---|---|---|---|---|---|---|
| 5f | | 4 | 9 0 | Hard | Brisas | Sept 10, | 1991 |
| 5f | 59·8 | 4 | 8 3 | Firm | Miss Taurus | July 15, | 1971 |
| | | 3 | 9 3 | Firm | Bollin Emily | July 5, | 1984 |
| 5f | 1. 0·2 | 2 | 8 9 | Hard | Metal Boys | June 1, | 1989 |
| 5f 207y | 1. 11·8 | 6 | 8 13 | Firm | Night Patrol | Aug. 27, | 1970 |
| 5f 207y | 1. 12·9 | 2 | 8 9 | Hard | Parfait Amour | Sept. 10, | 1991 |
| 6f 206y | 1. 25·7 | 3 | 9 1 | Firm | Kestrel Forboxes (IRE) | July 26, | 1991 |
| 6f 206y | 1. 26·6 | 2 | 9 4 | Hard | Sense of Priority | Sept. 10, | 1991 |
| 7f 214y | 1. 38·1 | 5 | 9 9 | Firm | Spanish Verdict | June 6, | 1992 |
| 7f 214y | 1. 44·6 | 2 | 8 8 | Firm | Blue Garter | Sept. 9, | 1980 |
| 9f 80y | 1. 56·4 | 3 | 8 2 | Firm | Desert of Wind (USA) | July 3, | 1986 |
| 12f | 2. 30·3 | 3 | 9 10 | Firm | Persian Fantasy | July 24, | 1992 |
| 14f 32y | 3. 2·7 | 3 | 8 10 | Hard | Ernie | Sept 10, | 1991 |

# CATTERICK

| Distance | Time | Age | Weight | Going | Horse | Date | |
|---|---|---|---|---|---|---|---|
| 5f | 57·1 | 4 | 8 7 | Fast | Kabcast | July 7, | 1989 |
| 5f | 57·7 | 2 | 9 0 | Fast | Verde Alitalia (IRE) | Sept 21, | 1991 |
| 5f 212y | 1. 10·4 | 3 | 8 8 | Firm | Triad Treble | May 31, | 1984 |
| | | 6 | 8 10 | Firm | Mendick Adventure | April 29, | 1987 |
| 5f 212y | 11·4 | 2 | 9 4 | Firm | Captain Nick | July 11, | 1978 |
| 7f | 1. 23 | 4 | 7 12 | Firm | Royal Ziska | June 9, | 1973 |
| | | 4 | 9 7 | Firm | Maazi | July 25, | 1985 |
| 7f | 1. 24·1 | 2 | 8 11 | Firm | Lindas Fantasy | Sept. 18, | 1982 |
| 12f 44y | 2. 33·4 | 3 | 8 3 | Firm | Watet Khet | June 4, | 1982 |
| 13f 175y | 2. 54·8 | 3 | 8 5 | Firm | Geryon | May 31, | 1984 |
| 15f 177y | 3. 20·8 | 4 | 7 11 | Firm | Bean Boy | July 8, | 1982 |

# CHEPSTOW

| Distance | Time | Age | Weight | Going | Horse | Date | |
|---|---|---|---|---|---|---|---|
| 5f 16y | 56·8 | 3 | 8 4 | Firm | Torbay Express | Sept. 15, | 1979 |

# CHEPSTOW - cont'd

| | | Age | Weight | Going | Horse | Date | |
|---|---|---|---|---|---|---|---|
| 5f 16y | 57·6 | 2 | 8 11 | Firm | Micro Love | July 8, | 1986 |
| 6f 16y | 1. 8·8 | 4 | 8 6 | Firm | African Rex (FR) | May 12, | 1987 |
| 6f 16y | 1. 9·4 | 2 | 9 0 | Fast | Royal Fi Fi (USA) | Sept. 9, | 1989 |
| 7f 16y | 1. 19·9 | 3 | 9 10 | Firm | Prince Titian | Aug. 29, | 1978 |
| 7f 16y | 1. 21·4 | 2 | 8 11 | Hard | Dijla | Aug. 31, | 1981 |
| 8f 14y | 1. 31·8 { | 6 | 9 6 | Firm | Traditional Miss | June 27, | 1981 |
| | | 6 | 9 6 | Hard | Traditional Miss | Aug. 31, | 1981 |
| 8f 14y | 1. 34·6 | 2 | 8 11 | Fast | Glowing Ardour | Aug 27, | 1990 |
| 10f 36y | 2. 4·1 { | 5 | 8 9 | Hard | Leonidas (USA) | July 5, | 1983 |
| | | 5 | 7 9 | Fast | Its Varadan | Sept. 9, | 1989 |
| 12f 23y | 2. 31 { | 5 | 8 11 | Hard | The Friend | Aug. 29, | 1983 |
| | | 7 | 9 6 | Hard | Maintop | Aug. 22, | 1984 |
| | | 3 | 8 9 | Fast | Spritsail | July 13, | 1989 |
| 16f 49y | 3. 27·7 | 4 | 9 0 | Fast | Wizzard Artist | July 1, | 1989 |
| *18f 33y | 4. 6·9 | 5 | 11 3 | Fast | Glenstal Priory | July 9, | 1992 |

*Distance remeasured July 1992

# CHESTER (Electric)

| Distance | Time | Age | Weight | Going | Horse | Date | |
|---|---|---|---|---|---|---|---|
| 5f 16y | 59·20 | 3 | 10 0 | Firm | Althrey Don | July 10, | 1964 |
| 5f 16y | 1. 0·40 | 2 | 8 11 | Firm | Cynara | May 3, | 1960 |
| 6f 18y | 1. 12·80 | 4 | 7 5 | Good | Welsh Warrior | July 27, | 1968 |
| 6f 18y | 1. 13·40 | 2 | 9 3 | Good | Stung | July 27, | 1968 |
| 7f 2y | 1. 25·27 | 3 | 9 3 | Fast | Mizaaya | May 7, | 1992 |
| 7f 2y | 1. 26·28 | 2 | 8 4 | Fast | By Hand | Aug. 31, | 1991 |
| 7f 122y | 1. 32·06 | 4 | 8 3 | Fast | Piquant | Aug. 31, | 1991 |
| 7f 122y | 1. 35 | 2 | 9 0 | Firm | Double Value | Sept. 1, | 1972 |
| 10f 75y | 2. 8·60 | 3 | 8 12 | Firm | Sir Harry Lewis (USA) | May 7, | 1987 |
| 11f 79y | 2. 23·71 | 4 | 8 11 | Fast | Braiswick | May 10, | 1989 |
| 12f 66y | 2. 34·21 | 3 | 8 11 | Fast | Old Vic | May 9, | 1989 |
| 13f 89y | 2. 45·43 | 5 | 8 11 | Firm | Rakaposhi King | May 7, | 1987 |
| 15f 195y | 3. 25 | 3 | 8 6 | Firm | Seacourt | Sept. 1, | 1972 |
| 18f 117y | 3. 57·26 | 4 | 9 8 | Firm | Just David | May 6, | 1987 |

# CURRAGH

| Distance | Time | Age | Weight | Going | Horse | Date | |
|---|---|---|---|---|---|---|---|
| 5f | 57·6 | 3 | 8 4 | Firm | Racefield | June 30, | 1979 |
| 5f | 58·1 | 2 | 8 11 | Firm | Ausone | May 20, | 1970 |
| 6f | 1. 10·1 | 3 | 8 4 | Good | Joy St Clair | Aug. 17, | 1991 |
| 6f | 1. 10·6 | 2 | 9 0 | Firm | London Bells | July 4, | 1979 |
| 6f 63y | 1. 12·4 | 4 | 9 8 | Firm | Bold Tack (disq) | June 11, | 1975 |
| 6f 63y | 1. 15·0 { | 2 | 8 7 | Firm | Gay Challenger | Sept. 2, | 1961 |
| | | 2 | 8 0 | Firm | Blue Nose | July 21, | 1979 |
| 7f | 1. 22·2 | 7 | 9 3 | Good | Smokey Lad | Aug. 17, | 1991 |
| 7f | 1. 23·1 | 2 | 9 0 | Fast | Heart Of Darkness | Sept. 8, | 1990 |
| 8f Old | 1. 35 | 3 | 9 0 | Good | Arctic Storm | May 16, | 1962 |
| 8f Old | 1. 45 | 2 | 8 12 | Yielding | Pontifex | Oct. 6, | 1962 |
| 8f New | 1. 34·3 | 4 | 9 4 | Good | Llyn Gwynant | July 19 | 1989 |
| 8f New | 1. 37·3 | 3 | 8 7 | Yielding | Mukaddamah (USA) | June 30, | 1991 |
| 9f | 1. 55·8 { | 3 | 8 13 | Good | Alberta Rose | Oct. 20, | 1992 |
| | | 4 | 9 11 | Yielding | Popular Glen | Sept. 23, | 1992 |
| 10f | 2. 0·6 | 3 | 8 6 | Good | Market Booster (USA) | June 27, | 1992 |
| 11f | 2. 21·0 | 3 | 8 13 | Fast | Montefiore | June 25, | 1988 |
| 12f | 2. 26·6 (unofficial) | 3 | 9 0 | Good | St Jovite (USA) | June 28, | 1992 |
| 13f | 2. 49·9 | 3 | 8 7 | Fast | Esprit D'Etoile | May 21, | 1988 |
| 14f | 2. 55·4 { | 3 | 8 7 | Good | Arrikala | June 28, | 1992 |
| | | 3 | 8 7 | Fast | Thetford Forest | July 15, | 1990 |
| 16f | 3. 25·8 | 3 | 8 6 | Yielding | Sinntara | Oct. 10, | 1992 |

# DONCASTER (Electric)

| Distance | Time | Age | Weight | Going | Horse | Date | |
|---|---|---|---|---|---|---|---|
| 5f | 58·20 | 3 | 8 8 | Firm | Sir Gatric | Sept. 10, | 1959 |

## DONCASTER - cont'd

| Distance | Time | Age | Weight | | Going | Horse | Date | |
|---|---|---|---|---|---|---|---|---|
| 5f | 58·40 | 2 | 9 | 5 | Firm | Sing Sing | Sept. 11, | 1959 |
| | | 2 | 9 | 0 | Good | D'Urberville | Sept. 13, | 1967 |
| 5f 140y | 1. 6·20 | 3 | 9 | 2 | Good | Welsh Abbot | Sept. 12, | 1958 |
| | | 6 | 7 | 3 | Firm | New World | Sept. 11, | 1959 |
| 5f 140y | 1. 8 | 2 | 8 | 10 | Good | Crown Flatts | Oct. 25, | 1947 |
| 6f | 1. 10·20 | 4 | 7 | 9 | Firm | Ryecroft | May 16, | 1959 |
| 6f | 1. 11·20 | 2 | 8 | 11 | Firm | Paddy's Sister | Sept. 9, | 1959 |
| 6f 110y | 1. 20·87 | 2 | 8 | 9 | Good | Nazoo | Sept. 13, | 1990 |
| 7f | 1. 22·60 | 3 | 9 | 4 | Hard | Pinolli | June 3, | 1963 |
| 7f | 1. 24·40 | 2 | 9 | 0 | Good | Chebs Lad | Sept. 12, | 1967 |
| 8f (st) | 1. 38·37 | 5 | 9 | 2 | Firm | Sky Cloud | Sept. 14, | 1991 |
| 8f (st) | 1. 39·08 | 2 | 7 | 13 | Firm | Wahem (IRE) | Sept. 10, | 1992 |
| 8f (rnd) | 1. 35·60 | 4 | 8 | 1 | Hard | Old Tom | June 3, | 1963 |
| 8f (rnd) | 1. 38·32 | 2 | 9 | 0 | Firm | Sandy Creek | Oct. 28, | 1978 |
| 10f 60y | 2. 6·40 | 4 | 8 | 7 | Firm | Silver Cloud | Sept. 12, | 1963 |
| 10f 60y | 2. 13·47 | 2 | 8 | 8 | Good | Yard Bird | Nov. 6, | 1981 |
| 12f | 2. 29·95 | 3 | 9 | 4 | Firm | Sheriffmuir | June 26, | 1992 |
| 14f 132y | 3. 2·22 | 3 | 8 | 3 | Firm | Brier Creek | Sept. 10, | 1992 |
| 16f 110y | 3. 34·44 | 4 | 9 | 12 | Fast | Farsi | June 12, | 1992 |
| 18f | 3. 55·60 | 6 | 9 | 3 | Firm | Further Flight | Sept. 10, | 1992 |

## EDINBURGH

| Distance | Time | Age | Weight | | Going | Horse | Date | |
|---|---|---|---|---|---|---|---|---|
| 5f | 57·4 | 4 | 7 | 2 | Firm | Palm Court Joe | July 4, | 1977 |
| 5f | 58·2 | 2 | 9 | 0 | Fast | Premier Developer | May 22, | 1989 |
| 7f 15y | 1. 26 | 6 | 9 | 0 | Firm | Show Of Hands | April 19, | 1982 |
| 7f 15y | 1. 27·5 | 2 | 9 | 1 | Firm | Mubdi (USA) | Oct. 6, | 1986 |
| 8f 16y | 1. 38·3 | 4 | 8 | 13 | Firm | Churchillian | July 11, | 1977 |
| 8f 16y | 1. 40·9 | 2 | 8 | 11 | Firm | Trompe D'Oeil | Oct. 6, | 1986 |
| 11f 32y | 2. 19·7 | 3 | 8 | 10 | Firm | Old Court | July 4, | 1977 |
| 12f 31y | 2. 32·2 | 5 | 7 | 9 | Good | Glengrigor | April 15, | 1946 |
| 15f 16y | 3. 10·4 | 3 | 8 | 0 | Good | Cunningham | Sept. 21, | 1953 |

## EPSOM (Electric)

| Distance | Time | Age | Weight | | Going | Horse | Date | |
|---|---|---|---|---|---|---|---|---|
| 5f | 53·60 | 4 | 9 | 5 | Firm | Indigenous | June 2, | 1960 |
| 5f | 55·20 | 2 | 8 | 9 | Firm | Cerise | June 4, | 1954 |
| | | 2 | 8 | 2 | Hard | Kerrabee | June 3, | 1960 |
| 6f | 1. 7·91 | 5 | 7 | 7 | Firm | Moor Lane | June 7, | 1973 |
| 6f | 1. 7·85 | 2 | 8 | 11 | Fast | Showbrook (IRE) | June 5, | 1991 |
| 7f | 1. 20·15 | 4 | 8 | 7 | Firm | Capistrano | June 7, | 1972 |
| 7f | 1. 22·40 | 2 | 8 | 8 | Fast | Goodnight Moon | Aug. 29, | 1988 |
| | | 2 | 9 | 0 | Hard | Leonardo | Sept 5, | 1964 |
| 8f 114y | 1. 40.75 | 3 | 8 | 6 | Fast | Sylva Honda | June 5, | 1991 |
| 8f 114y | 1. 42·80 | 2 | 8 | 5 | Fast | Nightstalker | Aug 30, | 1988 |
| 10f 18y | 2. 3·50 (unofficial) | 5 | 7 | 13 | Good | Crossbow | June 7, | 1967 |
| 12f 10y | 2. 33·31 | 4 | 9 | 0 | Firm | Bustino | June 7, | 1975 |

## FOLKESTONE

| Distance | Time | Age | Weight | | Going | Horse | Date | |
|---|---|---|---|---|---|---|---|---|
| 5f | 58·8 | 3 | 6 | 10 | Good | Tammany | Aug. 12, | 1963 |
| 5f | 58·6 | 2 | 8 | 11 | Good | Saque | Oct. 9, | 1990 |
| 6f | 1. 10·5 | 4 | 8 | 5 | Firm | Zipperdi-Doo-Dah | Mar. 31, | 1976 |
| 6f | 1. 11 | 2 | 7 | 13 | Hard | Fashion Model | Aug. 31, | 1970 |
| 6f 189y | 1. 21·3 | 3 | 8 | 9 | Fast | Cielamour (USA) | Aug. 9, | 1988 |
| 6f 189y | 1. 24·1 | 2 | 9 | 7 | Fast | Woodman's Mount (USA) | Sept. 24, | 1990 |
| 9f 149y | 1. 57·8 | 4 | 8 | 11 | Firm | Lord Raffles | June 2, | 1980 |
| 12f | 2. 33·3 | 4 | 8 | 8 | Hard | Snow Blizzard | June 30, | 1992 |
| 15f 92y | 3. 23·1 | 3 | 9 | 11 | Firm | Mata Askari | Sept. 12, | 1991 |
| 16f 93y | 3. 32·5 | 6 | 7 | 13 | Firm | North West | July 21, | 1981 |
| | | 3 | 8 | 5 | Firm | On Her Own | Aug. 11, | 1981 |

## GOODWOOD (Electric)

| Distance | Time | Age | Weight | | Going | Horse | Date | |
|---|---|---|---|---|---|---|---|---|
| 5f | 56·31 | 6 | 7 | 9 | Fast | Jondebe Boy | May 24, | 1990 |
| 5f | 57·53 | 2 | 8 | 12 | Fast | Poets Cove | Aug 3, | 1990 |
| 6f | 1. 10·71 | 3 | 8 | 10 | Fast | Milagro | May 20, | 1992 |
| 6f | 1. 10·25 | 2 | 8 | 11 | Fast | Mac's Imp (USA) | Aug 1, | 1990 |
| 7f | 1. 25·6 | 3 | 8 | 9 | Fast | Alidiva | July 31, | 1990 |
| 7f | 1. 25·97 | 2 | 8 | 11 | Fast | Maroof (USA) | July 30, | 1992 |
| 8f | 1. 36·06 | 4 | 9 | 7 | Fast | Distant Relative | Aug 1, | 1990 |
| 8f | 1. 39·44 | 2 | 8 | 11 | Fast | Seattle Rhyme (USA) | Sept. 13, | 1991 |
| 9f | 1. 54·36 | 4 | 8 | 8 | Fast | Neptunes Pet | July 31, | 1992 |
| 10f | 2. 4·96 | 3 | 8 | 6 | Firm | Kartajana | Aug 4, | 1990 |
| 12f | 2. 31·84 | 4 | 8 | 7 | Fast | Black Monday | Aug 1, | 1990 |
| | | 3 | 8 | 6 | Firm | Hajade | Aug 3, | 1990 |
| 14f | 2. 58·80 | 3 | 8 | 10 | Firm | Secret Waters | Aug 2, | 1990 |
| 16f | 3. 24·04 | 6 | 9 | 5 | Fast | Further Flight | July 30, | 1992 |
| 20f | 4. 11·75 | 3 | 7 | 10 | Firm | Lucky Moon | Aug 2, | 1990 |

## HAMILTON

| Distance | Time | Age | Weight | | Going | Horse | Date | |
|---|---|---|---|---|---|---|---|---|
| 5f 4y | 58 | 5 | 8 | 6 | Firm | Golden Sleigh | Sept. 6, | 1972 |
| 5f 4y | 58 | 2 | 7 | 8 | Firm | Fair Dandy | Sept. 25, | 1972 |
| 6f 5y | 1. 9·3 | 4 | 8 | 7 | Firm | Marcus Game | July 11, | 1974 |
| 6f 5y | 1. 10·1 | 2 | 7 | 5 | Hard | Yoohoo | Sept. 8, | 1976 |
| 8f 65y | 1. 42·7 | 6 | 7 | 7 | Firm | Cranley | Sept. 25, | 1972 |
| 8f 65y | 1. 45·8 | 2 | 8 | 11 | Firm | Hopeful Subject | Sept. 24, | 1973 |
| 9f 36y | 1. 54·2 | 3 | 8 | 2 | Hard | Fairman | Aug. 20, | 1976 |
| 11f 16y | 2. 20·5 | 3 | 9 | 3 | Firm | Wang Feihoong | July 21, | 1983 |
| 12f 17y | 2. 32 | 4 | 7 | 4 | Firm | Fine Point | Aug. 24, | 1981 |
| | | 4 | 10 | 0 | Firm | Hold Tight | Aug. 22, | 1983 |
| 13f 9y | 2. 46·4 | 4 | 7 | 0 | Firm | Luks Akura | June 11, | 1992 |

## HAYDOCK (Electric)

| Distance | Time | Age | Weight | | Going | Horse | Date | |
|---|---|---|---|---|---|---|---|---|
| 5f | 58·90 | 3 | 7 | 5 | Firm | Fish and Chips | June 6, | 1970 |
| 5f | 59·20 | 2 | 9 | 4 | Firm | Money For Nothing | Aug. 12, | 1964 |
| 6f | 1. 10·72 | 4 | 9 | 13 | Firm | Sizzling Saga (IRE) | July 2, | 1992 |
| 6f | 1. 11·95 | 2 | 8 | 3 | Fast | X My Heart | July 5, | 1991 |
| 7f 30y | 1. 27·21 | 4 | 9 | 4 | Firm | Indian King | June 5, | 1982 |
| 7f 30y | 1. 30·57 | 2 | 8 | 11 | Hard | Go Grandly | Sept. 30, | 1972 |
| 8f 30y | 1. 40·35 | 3 | 7 | 7 | Firm | Cashtal Dazzler | May 26, | 1990 |
| 8f 30y | 1. 41·42 | 2 | 9 | 5 | Firm | Suhailie (USA) | Oct. 4, | 1986 |
| 10f 120y | 2. 11·14 | 3 | 8 | 2 | Hard | Hill Top | Sept. 29, | 1972 |
| 11f 200y | 2. 26·40 | 5 | 8 | 2 | Firm | New Member | July 4, | 1970 |
| 14f | 3. 1·08 | 3 | 9 | 0 | Firm | Castle Cavalier | Sept. 6, | 1991 |
| 16f 45y | 3. 27·09 | 4 | 8 | 13 | Firm | Prince of Peace | May 26, | 1984 |
| 17f 130y | 3. 55·03 | 3 | 8 | 12 | Good | Crystal Spirit | Sept. 8, | 1990 |
| 19f | 4. 21·09 | 3 | 8 | 1 | Heavy | Nomadic Way (USA) | Sept 3, | 1988 |

## KEMPTON (Electric)

| Distance | Time | Age | Weight | | Going | Horse | Date | |
|---|---|---|---|---|---|---|---|---|
| 5f | 58·07 | 3 | 8 | 1 | Firm | Silent Majority | June 25, | 1986 |
| 5f | 58·30 | 2 | 9 | 7 | Firm | Schweppeshire Lad | June 3, | 1978 |
| 6f | 1. 10·04 | 7 | 7 | 10 | Firm | Jokist | April 6, | 1990 |
| 6f | 1. 10·80 | 2 | 8 | 10 | Good | Zabara | Sept. 22, | 1951 |
| 7f Jubilee | 1. 23·79 | 3 | 8 | 11 | Firm | Swiss Maid | Aug. 19, | 1978 |
| 7f Jubilee | 1. 24·92 | 2 | 8 | 11 | Firm | Silver Hawk | Sept. 5, | 1981 |
| 7f (rnd) | 1. 25·7 | 4 | 7 | 11 | Firm | Gaykart | July 14, | 1971 |
| | | 3 | 7 | 9 | Good | Glen Na Smole | May 7, | 1984 |
| 7f (rnd) | 1. 27·52 | 2 | 8 | 6 | Good | Duke of Ragusa | Sept. 1, | 1972 |
| 8f (rnd) | 1. 35·81 | 4 | 9 | 1 | Firm | County Broker | May 23, | 1984 |
| 8f (rnd) | 1. 43·40 | 2 | 7 | 0 | Good | Fascinating | Nov. 3, | 1956 |
| 8f Jubilee | 1. 35·91 | 3 | 9 | 1 | Firm | Mukddaam | April 6, | 1990 |
| 8f Jubilee | 1. 42·50 | 2 | 7 | 4 | Good | Bantanolius | Oct. 19, | 1962 |

## KEMPTON - cont'd

| | | Age | Weight | | Going | Horse | Date | |
|---|---|---|---|---|---|---|---|---|
| 9f (rnd) | 1. 50·56 | 3 | 8 | 12 | Fast | Sky Conqueror | June 29, | 1988 |
| 10f Jubilee | 1. 59·53 | 4 | 9 | 6 | Firm | Batshoof | April 6, | 1990 |
| 11f 30y | 2. 16·20 | 4 | 9 | 2 | Firm | Shernazar | Sept. 6, | 1985 |
| 12f | 2. 30·18 | 6 | 8 | 5 | Firm | Going Going | Sept. 7, | 1985 |
| 14f | 2. 59·12 | 3 | 8 | 0 | Good | Clare Court | Sept 7, | 1990 |
| 16f | 3. 30·23 | 4 | 9 | 4 | Good | Shambo | March 30, | 1992 |

## LEICESTER

| Distance | Time | Age | Weight | | Going | Horse | Date | |
|---|---|---|---|---|---|---|---|---|
| 5f 2y | 58·6 | 3 | 9 | 2 | Firm | Rapid River | Sept. 24, | 1973 |
| 5f 2y | 58·4 | 2 | 9 | 0 | Firm | Cutting Blade | June 9, | 1986 |
| 5f 218y | 1. 9·4 | 3 | 8 | 12 | Fast | Lakeland Beauty | May 29, | 1990 |
| 5f 218y | 1. 10·2 | 2 | 8 | 11 | Firm | Native Twine | Oct. 16, | 1989 |
| 7f 9y | 1. 20·8 | 3 | 8 | 7 | Firm | Flower Bowl | June 9, | 1986 |
| 7f 9y | 1. 23·3 | 2 | 8 | 11 | Firm | Noble Destiny | Oct. 16, | 1990 |
| 8f 8y | 1. 34·4 | 3 | 8 | 3 | Hard | Marlapolis | Sept. 19, | 1961 |
| 8f 8y | 1. 35·8 | 2 | 9 | 0 | Firm | Missionary Ridge | Oct. 17, | 1989 |
| 9f 218y | 2. 2·4 | 3 | 8 | 11 | Firm | Effigy | Nov. 4, | 1985 |
| 9f 218y | 2. 7·2 | 2 | 8 | 13 | Firm | Hardly Fair | Oct. 21, | 1985 |
| 11f 183y | 2. 28·5 | 4 | 7 | 11 | Hard | Gyroscope | Sept. 21, | 1964 |
| | | 3 | 9 | 3 | Firm | Summer Ridge (USA) | Oct. 21, | 1985 |

## LINGFIELD (Electric)

### TURF TRACK

| Distance | Time | Age | Weight | | Going | Horse | Date | |
|---|---|---|---|---|---|---|---|---|
| 5f | 56·80 | 3 | 8 | 9 | Firm | Marguerite | Oct. 7, | 1964 |
| 5f | 57·27 | 2 | 9 | 6 | Fast | Batzushka | Sept. 21, | 1989 |
| 6f | 1. 8·20 | 6 | 9 | 10 | Firm | Al Amead | July 2, | 1986 |
| 6f | 1. 8·60 | 2 | 9 | 3 | Firm | The Ritz | June 11, | 1965 |
| 7f | 1. 20·20 | 8 | 7 | 10 | Hard | Polar Jest | Aug. 19, | 1955 |
| 7f | 1. 21·34 | 2 | 7 | 6 | Firm | Mandav | Oct. 3, | 1980 |
| 7f 140y | 1. 26·73 | 3 | 8 | 6 | Firm | Hiaam (USA) | July 11, | 1987 |
| 7f 140y | 1. 29·93 | 2 | 8 | 12 | Firm | Rather Warm | Nov. 7, | 1978 |
| 9f | 1. 53 | 3 | 9 | 7 | Fast | Pay Homage | Sept 19, | 1991 |
| 10f | 2. 5·79 | 3 | 9 | 3 | Firm | Aromatic | July 14, | 1990 |
| 11f 106y | 2. 23·95 | 3 | 8 | 5 | Firm | Night-Shirt | July 14, | 1990 |
| 14f | 3. 3·63 | 3 | 8 | 9 | Firm | Arrastra | Aug. 17, | 1991 |
| 16f | 3. 28·96 | 3 | 9 | 0 | Firm | Lothian | Sept 20, | 1990 |

### ALL-WEATHER TRACK

| Distance | Time | Age | Weight | | Going | Horse | Date | |
|---|---|---|---|---|---|---|---|---|
| 5f | 58·16 | 4 | 7 | 8 | Std | Ever so Artistic | Jan. 5, | 1991 |
| 5f | 59·27 | 2 | 9 | 2 | Std | Fort Knox | July 12, | 1991 |
| 6f | 1. 10·58 | 4 | 9 | 4 | Std | J. Cheever Loophole | Nov. 23, | 1989 |
| 6f | 1. 11·65 | 2 | 9 | 7 | Std | Time's Arrow (IRE) | July 10, | 1992 |
| 7f | 1. 22·99 | 3 | 9 | 3 | Std | Confronter | July 18, | 1992 |
| 7f | 1. 24·0 | 2 | 8 | 12 | Std | Scottish Castle | Nov 2, | 1990 |
| 8f | 1. 36·32 | 5 | 9 | 5 | Std | Vanroy | Nov. 30, | 1989 |
| 8f | 1. 36·50 | 2 | 9 | 5 | Std | San Pier Niceto | Nov.30, | 1989 |
| 10f | 2. 2·93 | 4 | 9 | 3 | Std | Rapporteur | Nov. 2, | 1990 |
| | | 3 | 7 | 7 | Std | Dr Maccarter | Nov. 8, | 1990 |
| 12f | 2. 29·30 | 4 | 8 | 6 | Std | Puff Puff | Nov. 8, | 1990 |
| 13f | 2. 44·86 | 5 | 9 | 12 | Std | Go South | Nov. 23, | 1989 |
| 16f | 3. 20·09 | 3 | 9 | 0 | Std | Yenoora (IRE) | Aug. 8, | 1992 |

## NEWBURY (Electric)

| Distance | Time | Age | Weight | | Going | Horse | Date | |
|---|---|---|---|---|---|---|---|---|
| 5f 34y | 59·80 | 3 | 8 | 12 | Good | Minstrels Gallery | June 18, | 1955 |
| 5f 34y | 1. 0·60 | 2 | 8 | 7 | Firm | Zuccherene | June 25, | 1959 |
| 6f 8y | 1. 10·79 | 3 | 8 | 9 | Good | Dancing Dissident | May. 19, | 1989 |
| 6f 8y | 1. 11·61 | 2 | 8 | 6 | Firm | Bright Crocus | June 10, | 1982 |
| 7f (st) | 1. 24·40 | 3 | 9 | 7 | Firm | Firestreak | May 29, | 1959 |
| 7f (st) | 1. 25·93 | 2 | 9 | 0 | Good | Zoffany | Aug. 14, | 1982 |

# NEWBURY - cont'd

| | | Age | Weight | | Going | Horse | Date | |
|---|---|---|---|---|---|---|---|---|
| 7f 64y (rnd) | 1. 26·80 | 4 | 7 | 1 | Firm | Bucktail | June 25, | 1959 |
| 7f 64y (rnd) | 1. 29·12 | 2 | 9 | 7 | Firm | Kalaglow | Sept. 19, | 1980 |
| 8f 7y (rnd) | 1. 34·91 | 3 | 8 | 9 | Fast | Philidor | May 16, | 1992 |
| 8f 7y (rnd) | 1. 37·29 | 2 | 8 | 11 | Firm | Master Willie | Oct. 1, | 1979 |
| 8f (st) | 1. 36·21 | 4 | 9 | 7 | Firm | Kris | May 17, | 1980 |
| 8f (st) | 1. 39·65 | 2 | 8 | 11 | Fast | Zinaad | Sept. 20, | 1991 |
| 9f | 1. 52·25 | 3 | 9 | 7 | Firm | Port Sunlight (IRE) | Sept. 20, | 1991 |
| 10f 6y | 2. 2·76 | 3 | 8 | 4 | Fast | Monastery | Sept. 23, | 1989 |
| 10f 6y | 2. 2 | 3 | 8 | 9 | Firm | Sudden Love (FR) | May 13, | 1988 |
| | (hand timed) | | | | | | | |
| 11f 5y | 2. 17·51 | 4 | 9 | 0 | Fast | Hateel | May 19, | 1990 |
| 12f 5y | 2. 29·20 | 4 | 8 | 9 | Hard | Vidi Vici | June 21, | 1951 |
| 13f 61y | 2. 45·15 | 5 | 8 | 11 | Fast | Endoli (USA) | May 16, | 1992 |
| 16f | 3. 26·41 | 3 | 7 | 13 | Good | Sunyboy | Sept. 8, | 1973 |

# NEWCASTLE (Electric)

| Distance | Time | Age | Weight | | Going | Horse | Date | |
|---|---|---|---|---|---|---|---|---|
| 5f | 58·27 | 3 | 8 | 1 | Firm | Dublin Lad | June 27, | 1986 |
| 5f | 59·20 | 2 | 8 | 2 | Good | Dunce Cap | Aug. 6, | 1962 |
| 6f | 1. 11·21 | 3 | 9 | 2 | Good | Tadwin | June 30, | 1990 |
| 6f | 1. 12·67 | 2 | 9 | 0 | Firm | Sundance Kid (USA) | Oct. 3, | 1989 |
| 7f (st) | 1. 23·53 | 3 | 8 | 5 | Firm | Beaudelaire (USA) | July 23, | 1983 |
| 7f (st) | 1. 26·82 | 2 | 8 | 8 | Firm | Nice Balance | Aug. 10, | 1976 |
| 8f | 1. 38·96 | 3 | 8 | 12 | Firm | Jacamar | July 27, | 1989 |
| 8f | 1. 39·97 | 2 | 9 | 0 | Firm | Laxey Bay | Oct. 3, | 1989 |
| 9f 9y | 1. 52·30 | 3 | 6 | 3 | Good | Ferniehurst | June 23, | 1936 |
| 10f 32y | 2. 6·59 | 3 | 8 | 11 | Fast | Missionary Ridge | July 29, | 1990 |
| 12f 93y | 2. 38·26 | 6 | 8 | 9 | Firm | Daisy Girl | June 26, | 1992 |
| 16f 19y | 3. 22 | 4 | 7 | 12 | Good | Nectar II | June 23, | 1937 |

# NEWMARKET (Electric)

## ROWLEY MILE COURSE

| Course | Dist. | Time | Age | | Weight | Going | Horse | Date | |
|---|---|---|---|---|---|---|---|---|---|
| Rous | 5f | 57·40 | 5 | 8 | 9 | Firm | Knight's Armour | April 6, | 1938 |
| Rous | 5f | 58·78 | 2 | 8 | 13 | Good | Clifton Charlie | Oct. 4, | 1990 |
| Bretby Stakes | 6f | 1. 10·66 | 5 | 7 | 12 | Firm | Welsh Blossom | Oct. 1, | 1980 |
| Bretby Stakes | 6f | 1. 10·14 | 2 | 9 | 0 | Good' | Lyclus (USA) | Oct. 4, | 1990 |
| Dewhurst Stakes | 7f | 1. 22·24 | 4 | 9 | 5 | Fast | Perfolia (USA) | Oct. 18, | 1991 |
| Dewhurst Stakes | 7f | 1. 23·45 | 2 | 9 | 0 | Fast | Dr Devious (IRE) | Oct. 18, | 1991 |
| Rowley Mile | 8f | 1. 35·80 | 3 | 9 | 0 | Hard | My Babu | April 28, | 1948 |
| Rowley Mile | 8f | 1. 36·74 | 2 | 9 | 0 | Fast | Bold Pursuit (IRE) | Oct. 18, | 1991 |
| Cambdgshire | 9f | 1. 47·45 | 3 | 8 | 3 | Firm | Sin Timon | Oct. 1, | 1977 |
| A.F. | 10f | 2. 1·04 | 3 | 8 | 10 | Good | Palace Music (USA) | Oct. 20, | 1984 |
| A.F. | 10f | 2. 4·65 | 2 | 9 | 4 | Good | Highland Chieftain | Nov.2, | 1985 |
| Cesarewitch | 12f | 2. 27·67 | 3 | 8 | 5 | Fast | Kiveton Kabooz | Oct. 17, | 1991 |
| Cesarewitch | 14f | 2. 56·19 | 3 | 8 | 7 | Fast | Chief Minister (IRE) | Oct. 16, | 1992 |
| Cesarewitch | 16f | 3. 23·12 | 3 | 8 | 4 | Fast | Kikam | Oct. 2, | 1991 |
| Cesarewitch | 18f | 3. 47·50 | 3 | 7 | 12 | Hard | Whiteway | Oct. 15, | 1947 |

## JULY COURSE

| Course | Dist. | Time | Age | | Weight | Going | Horse | Date | |
|---|---|---|---|---|---|---|---|---|---|
| Chesterfield | 5f | 58·68 | 3 | 8 | 6 | Firm | Light Grey | July 3, | 1962 |
| Chesterfield | 5f | 58·52 | 2 | 8 | 10 | Good | Seductress | July 10, | 1990 |
| Bunbury Mile | 6f | 1. 9·82 | 4 | 9 | 6 | Good | Cadeaux Genereux | July 13, | 1989 |
| Bunbury Mile | 6f | 1. 10·61 | 2 | 8 | 10 | Fast | Multahid (USA) | July 11, | 1990 |
| Bunbury Mile | 7f | 1. 23·60 | 5 | 7 | 8 | Hard | Ti-Chin | June 17, | 1944 |
| Bunbury Mile | 7f | 1. 24·93 | 2 | 8 | 7 | Firm | Sexton Blake | July 30, | 1977 |
| Bunbury Mile | 8f | 1. 36·80 | 4 | 9 | 7 | Hard | Pink Flower | June 6, | 1944 |

## NEWMARKET - cont'd

| Distance | Time | Age | Weight | | Going | Horse | Date | |
|---|---|---|---|---|---|---|---|---|
| Bunbury Mile | 8f | 1. 40·28 | 2 | 9 4 | Fast | Lear Fan (USA) | Aug. 27, | 1983 |
| Suffolk Stks | 10f | 2. 2·31 | 4 | 9 1 | Fast | Vallance | Aug. 1, | 1992 |
| Suffolk Stks | 12f | 2. 28·39 | 3 | 10 5 | Fast | Cunning | Aug. 1, | 1992 |
| Summer | 14f 175y | 3. 10·21 | 3 | 8 9 | Good | Encore Une Fois (IRE) | Aug. 28, | 1992 |
| Summer | 16f 24y | 3. 24·97 | 4 | 9 13 | Good | Gay Glint | Aug. 9, | 1991 |

## NOTTINGHAM

| Distance | Time | Age | Weight | | Going | Horse | Date | |
|---|---|---|---|---|---|---|---|---|
| 5f 13y | 58·4 | 6 | 8 8 | | Good | Minstrel King | Mar. 29, | 1960 |
| | | 4 | 7 7 | | Firm | Vilgora | Apr. 12, | 1976 |
| 5f 13y | 58·6 | 2 | 8 11 | | Firm | Al Sylah | May 1, | 1984 |
| 6f 15y | 1. 10 | 4 | 9 2 | | Firm | Ajanac | Aug. 8, | 1988 |
| 6f 15y | 1. 11·4 | 2 | 8 11 | | Firm | Jameelapi (USA) | Aug. 8, | 1983 |
| 8f 54y | 1. 39·6 | 4 | 8 2 | | Fast | Blake's Treasure | Sept 3, | 1991 |
| 8f 54y | 1. 40·8 | 2 | 9 0 | | Fast | King's Loch | Sept. 3, | 1991 |
| 9f 213y | 2. 2·3 | 3 | 8 8 | | Firm | Ayaabi | July 21, | 1984 |
| 9f 213y | 2. 5·6 | 2 | 9 0 | | Firm | Al Salite | Oct. 28, | 1985 |
| 14f 15y | 2. 57·8 | 3 | 8 10 | | Firm | Buster Jo | Oct. 1, | 1985 |
| 16f 9y | 3. 24 | 5 | 7 7 | | Firm | Fet | Oct. 5, | 1936 |
| 18f 18y | 3. 55·1 | 9 | 9 10 | | Fast | Pearl Run | May 1, | 1990 |

## PONTEFRACT

| Distance | Time | Age | Weight | | Going | Horse | Date | |
|---|---|---|---|---|---|---|---|---|
| 5f | 1. 1·1 | 5 | 7 7 | | Hard | Regal Bingo | Sept. 29, | 1971 |
| 5f | 1. 1·4 | 2 | 8 9 | | Firm | Breakaway | Aug. 6, | 1987 |
| 6f | 1. 12·6 | 3 | 7 13 | | Firm | Merry One | Aug. 29, | 1970 |
| 6f | 1. 14 | 2 | 9 3 | | Firm | Fawzi | Sept. 6, | 1983 |
| 8f 4y | 1. 41·4 | 5 | 8 12 | | Firm | Nevison's Lad | May 14, | 1965 |
| | | 4 | 8 6 | | Firm | Effulgence | Aug. 29, | 1970 |
| | | 3 | 7 13 | | Firm | Whealden | Aug. 5, | 1970 |
| | | 4 | 7 12 | | Firm | Paddy's Amour | June 29, | 1970 |
| 8f 4y | 1. 42·8 | 2 | 9 13 | | Firm | Star Spray | Sept. 6, | 1983 |
| 10f 6y | 2. 8·2 | 3 | 7 13 | | Hard | Tom Noddy | Aug. 21, | 1972 |
| | | 4 | 7 8 | | Hard | Happy Hector | July 9, | 1979 |
| 10f 6y | 2. 15·5 | 2 | 8 3 | | Firm | One-Cal | Oct. 10, | 1977 |
| 12f 8y | 2. 34·3 | 4 | 8 9 | | Hard | Ezra | June 23, | 1975 |
| 17f 22y | 3. 42·1 | 3 | 9 2 | | Firm | Night Eye (USA) | Sept. 6, | 1983 |
| 17f 216y | 3. 51·1 | 3 | 8 8 | | Firm | Kudz (USA) | Sept. 9, | 1986 |
| 21f 122y | 4. 47·8 | 4 | 8 4 | | Firm | Physical (USA) | May 14, | 1984 |

## REDCAR

| Distance | Time | Age | Weight | | Going | Horse | Date | |
|---|---|---|---|---|---|---|---|---|
| 5f | 56·5 | 3 | 9 7 | | Firm | Nazela | Aug 10, | 1990 |
| 5f | 57·2 | 2 | 9 2 | | Firm | Captain Nick | July 27, | 1978 |
| | | 2 | 7 8 | | Firm | English Star | Sept. 24, | 1982 |
| 6f | 1. 8·6 | 3 | 9 2 | | Fast | Sizzling Saga (IRE) | June 21, | 1991 |
| 6f | 1. 9·8 | 2 | 8 11 | | Firm | Futuh | Aug. 11, | 1990 |
| 7f | 1. 22·1 | 3 | 8 2 | | Firm | Marston | July 25, | 1978 |
| | | 3 | 8 11 | | Fast | Susanna's Secret | Sept 28, | 1990 |
| | | 5 | 8 11 | | Fast | Super Benz | Oct 9, | 1991 |
| 7f | 1. 21·9 | 2 | 8 11 | | Firm | Nagwa | Sept. 27, | 1975 |
| 8f | 1. 34·8 | 5 | 8 12 | | Firm | Genair | Aug. 11, | 1990 |
| 8f | 1. 36·7 | 2 | 8 8 | | Firm | Carbonate | Sept. 15, | 1987 |
| | | 2 | 9 0 | | Fast | Cumbrian Challenge (IRE) | Aug.28, | 1991 |
| 9f | 1. 48·5 | 5 | 8 12 | | Firm | Mellottie | July 25, | 1990 |
| 9f | 1. 54·7 | 2 | 8 11 | | Firm | Cri De Coeur (USA) | Oct. 20, | 1983 |
| 10f | 2. 1·5 | 5 | 9 3 | | Firm | Inaad | May 29, | 1989 |
| 11f | 2. 17·0 | 3 | 8 9 | | Firm | Photo Call | Aug. 7, | 1990 |
| 12f | 2. 30·1 | 3 | 9 0 | | Firm | High Tension | June 22, | 1985 |
| 13f 135y | 2. 54·6 | 6 | 9 10 | | Firm | Brodessa | June 20, | 1992 |
| 14f 19y | 2. 59·9 | 3 | 8 6 | | Firm | Trianglot | July 25, | 1990 |
| 16f 4y | 3. 24·9 | 3 | 9 3 | | Fast | Subsonic (IRE) | Oct. 8, | 1991 |
| 19f | 4. 10·2 | 5 | 7 4 | | Fast | Seldom In | Aug. 9, | 1991 |

# RIPON

| Distance | Time | Age | Weight | Going | Horse | Date | |
|---|---|---|---|---|---|---|---|
| 5f | 57·7 | 3 | 9 5 | Firm | Fangio | June 17, | 1992 |
| 5f | 57·8 | 2 | 8 8 | Firm | Super Rocky | Aug, 5, | 1991 |
| 6f | 1. 9·8 | 5 | 7 0 | Firm | Quolt | July 23, | 1966 |
| 6f | 1. 11 | 2 | 8 11 | Fast | Colway Bold | Aug. 26, | 1991 |
| 8f | 1. 37 | 4 | 7 10 | Firm | Crown Witness | Aug. 25, | 1980 |
| 8f | 1. 41·2 | 2 | 7 2 | Good | Roanstreak | Sept. 5, | 1970 |
| 9f | 1. 50·8 | 4 | 8 3 | Firm | Tarda | Aug. 5, | 1991 |
| 10f | 2. 2·7 | 3 | 9 4 | Firm | Swift Sword | July 20, | 1991 |
| 12f 60y | 2. 32·2 | { 6 | 8 7 | Firm | Cholo | Sept. 27, | 1941 |
| | | 7 | 8 3 | Firm | Crusader's Horn | Aug. 8, | 1950 |
| 16f | 3. 28·5 | 3 | 9 7 | Firm | Thakawah | June 18, | 1992 |
| 17f 203y | 3. 51·3 | 3 | 7 8 | Firm | Beechwood Seeker | Sept. 1, | 1981 |

# SALISBURY (Electric)

| Distance | Time | Age | Weight | Going | Horse | Date | |
|---|---|---|---|---|---|---|---|
| | | { 5 | 7 12 | Fast | Loft Boy | Sept. 8, | 1988 |
| 5f | 59·78 | 3 | 9 3 | Firm | Fangio | June 9, | 1992 |
| | | { 3 | 9 2 | Firm | Iron King | Sept. 7, | 1989 |
| 5f | 59·89 | 2 | 8 11 | Firm | Blue Tango | June 25, | 1986 |
| 6f | 1. 11·54 | 4 | 8 7 | Firm | Prince Sky | June 25, | 1986 |
| 6f | 1. 12·41 | 2 | 9 1 | Fast | Basma (USA) | Sept. 6, | 1991 |
| 6f 212y | 1. 25·63 | 3 | 8 9 | Firm | Below Zero | June 26, | 1986 |
| 6f 212y | 1. 26·33 | 2 | 9 0 | Firm | Bartat | Oct. 4, | 1989 |
| 8f | 1. 39·25 | 3 | 8 11 | Firm | Schh-You-Know-Who | Oct. 4, | 1989 |
| 8f | 1. 43·86 | 2 | 9 3 | Fast | Carocrest | Sept. 1, | 1983 |
| 9f 209y | 2. 4·46 | 4 | 7 7 | Firm | Kala Nashan | June 25, | 1986 |
| 12f | 2. 32·42 | 3 | 8 4 | Fast | Buzzbomb | Sept. 8, | 1988 |
| 14f | 2. 58·01 | 4 | 10 0 | Fast | Dancing Affair | Aug. 16, | 1984 |

# SANDOWN (Electric)

| Distance | Time | Age | Weight | Going | Horse | Date | |
|---|---|---|---|---|---|---|---|
| 5f 6y | 59·24 | 3 | 8 6 | Fast | Lyndseylee | July 25, | 1990 |
| 5f 6y | 59·48 | 2 | 9 3 | Firm | Times Time | July 22, | 1982 |
| 7f 16y | 1. 26·36 | 3 | 9 0 | Firm | Mawsuff | June 14, | 1986 |
| 7f 16y | 1. 28·15 | 2 | 9 1 | Firm | Attempt | Aug. 19, | 1983 |
| 8f 14y | 1. 39·08 | 3 | 8 8 | Firm | Linda's Fantasy | Aug. 19, | 1983 |
| 8f 14y | 1. 41·14 | 2 | 8 11 | Firm | Reference Point | Sept. 23, | 1986 |
| 9f | 1. 54·23 | 3 | 8 13 | Firm | Lovealoch (IRE) | Aug. 30, | 1991 |
| 9f | 1. 57·74 | 2 | 8 7 | Firm | Marius (IRE) | Sept. 15, | 1992 |
| 10f 7y | 2. 2·14 | 4 | 8 11 | Firm | Kalaglow | May 31, | 1982 |
| 11f 91y | 2. 21·61 | 4 | 8 3 | Fast | Aylesfield | July 7, | 1984 |
| 14f | 3. 0·89 | 5 | 9 7 | Firm | Gay Glint | June 13, | 1992 |
| 2m 78y | 3. 29·93 | 6 | 9 2 | Fast | Sadeem | May 29, | 1989 |

# SOUTHWELL

**ALL-WEATHER TRACK**

| Distance | Time | Age | Weight | Going | Horse | Date | |
|---|---|---|---|---|---|---|---|
| 5f | 57·7 | 3 | 9 6 | Std | Case Law | Aug. 15, | 1990 |
| 5f | 59·1 | 2 | 7 7 | Std | Today's Fancy | Nov. 3, | 1990 |
| 6f | 1. 13·3 | 3 | 9 2 | Std | Rambo Express | Dec. 18, | 1990 |
| 6f | 1. 13·9 | 2 | 9 0 | Std | Superstrike | July 31, | 1991 |
| 7f | 1. 26·8 | 5 | 8 4 | Std | Amenable | Dec 13, | 1990 |
| 7f | 1. 27·0 | 2 | 8 4 | Std | Rejoice (IRE) | Nov 30, | 1990 |
| 8f | 1. 37·2 | 3 | 8 6 | Std | Valira | Nov. 3, | 1990 |
| 8f | 1. 38·0 | 2 | 8 9 | Std | Alpha Rascal | Nov. 13, | 1990 |
| 11f | 2. 21.5 | 4 | 9 7 | Std | Tempering | Dec. 5, | 1990 |
| 12f | 2. 34·1 | 4 | 9 12 | Std | Fast Chick | Nov. 8, | 1989 |
| 13f | 2. 52·9 | 4 | 9 2 | Std | Kenilworth Castle | Jan. 11, | 1990 |
| 14f | 3. 1·6 | 3 | 7 7 | Std | Qualitair Aviator | Dec. 1, | 1989 |
| 16f | 3. 37·8 | 4 | 9 12 | Std | Megan's Flight | Dec. 6, | 1989 |
| 18f | 4. 5·3 | 4 | 9 1 | Std | Ceciliano (USA) | Aug. 16, | 1990 |

## SOUTHWELL - cont'd

TURF

| Distance | Time | Age | Weight | Going | Horse | Date | |
|---|---|---|---|---|---|---|---|
| 6f | 1. 14·2 | 4 | 7 9 | Firm | Spanish Realm | Sept. 7, | 1991 |
| 6f | 1. 16·3 | 2 | 9 0 | Fast | Ghalyoon (USA) | Sept. 20, | 1991 |
| 7f | 1. 27·1 | 3 | 8 3 | Firm | Orient Air | Aug. 14, | 1991 |
| 7f | 1. 29·4 | 2 | 8 9 | Firm | Star of Albion | Sept. 7, | 1991 |
| 1m 3f | 2. 21.9 | 3 | 8 5 | Firm | Pims Gunner (IRE) | Aug. 15, | 1991 |
| 12f | 2. 34·4 | 5 | 9 3 | Firm | Corn Lily | Aug. 10, | 1991 |
| 2m | 3. 34·1 | 5 | 9 1 | Fast | Triplicate | Sept. 20, | 1991 |

## THIRSK

| Distance | Time | Age | Weight | Going | Horse | Date | |
|---|---|---|---|---|---|---|---|
| 5f | 56·9 | 4 | 8 6 | Fast | Singing Star | Aug. 3, | 1990 |
| 5f | 57·4 | 2 | 9 1 | Firm | Nifty Fifty (IRE) | July 19, | 1991 |
| 6f | 1. 9·6 | 3 | 8 10 | Firm | Cedar Grange | Sept. 3, | 1977 |
| 6f | 1. 9·9 | 2 | 9 5 | Firm | Daarlk | July 29, | 1989 |
| 7f | 1. 22·6 | 5 | 6 11 | Firm | Tuanwun | May 29, | 1970 |
| 7f | 1. 24·6 | 2 | 8 12 | Firm | Man of Harlech | Aug. 2, | 1975 |
| 8f | 1. 34·8 | 4 | 8 13 | Firm | Yearsley | May 5, | 1990 |
| 8f | 1. 39·1 | 2 | 9 0 | Fast | Wild Fire | Sept. 7, | 1991 |
| 12f | 2. 30 | 4 | 8 2 | Firm | Casting Vote | Aug. 1, | 1964 |
| 16f | 3. 22·3 | 3 | 8 11 | Firm | Tomaschek | July 17, | 1981 |

## WARWICK

| Distance | Time | Age | Weight | Going | Horse | Date | |
|---|---|---|---|---|---|---|---|
| 5f | 58·6 | 5 | 8 9 | Good | Iron King | Oct. 7, | 1991 |
| 5f | 59 | 2 | 9 3 | Good | Prompting | Oct. 7, | 1991 |
| 6f | 1. 11·8 | 4 | 9 5 | Firm | Pride of Kilmallock | July 1, | 1960 |
| 6f | 1. 12·1 | 2 | 7 7 | Firm | Sum Mede | July 14, | 1989 |
| 7f | 1. 23·8 | 6 | 7 12 | Hard | Blackshore | May 19, | 1956 |
| 7f | 1. 24·8 | 2 | 9 4 | Firm | Nocino | July 28, | 1979 |
| 8f | 1. 36 | 3 | 9 0 | Firm | Academic World | Aug. 25, | 1975 |
| 8f | 1. 37·5 | 2 | 9 3 | Firm | Perfect Stranger | Oct. 14, | 1986 |
| 10f 169y | 2. 13·2 | 3 | 8 8 | Firm | Classic Tale | July 7, | 1987 |
| 12f 115y | 2. 37·2 | 5 | 8 12 | Hard | Noirmont Buoy | June 19, | 1967 |
| 14f 194y | 3. 8·9 | 4 | 9 1 | Firm | Chucklestone | July 7, | 1987 |
| | | 4 | 8 3 | Firm | Ile de Reine | May 26, | 1990 |
| 16f 20y | 3. 25·8 | 4 | 9 7 | Fast | Sanamar (disq) | Aug. 29, | 1988 |
| | | 5 | 8 7 | Firm | Tilly Tavi | Aug 31, | 1987 |
| 18f 214y | 4. 3·9 | 5 | 9 10 | Fast | Fitzpatrick | Aug. 27, | 1984 |

## WINDSOR

| Distance | Time | Age | Weight | Going | Horse | Date | |
|---|---|---|---|---|---|---|---|
| 5f 10y | 59·2 | 3 | 9 7 | Fast | La Tuerta | July 15, | 1985 |
| | | 3 | 9 7 | Good | Possedyno | July 7, | 1986 |
| 5f 10y | 58·9 | 2 | 9 0 | Firm | Strictly Private | July 22, | 1974 |
| | | 2 | 7 0 | Firm | Miss Merlin (disq) | Sept. 11, | 1978 |
| 5f 217y | 1. 10·1 | 3 | 8 4 | Firm | Sweet Relief | Sept. 11, | 1978 |
| 5f 217y | 1. 10·1 | 2 | 9 3 | Firm | Rosier | Aug. 17, | 1981 |
| 8f 67y | 1. 41·5 | 4 | 7 2 | Firm | Blowing Bubbles | July. 16, | 1984 |
| 10f 7y | 2. 3.0 | 3 | 9 1 | Firm | Moomba Masquerade | May 19, | 1980 |
| 11f 135y | 2. 21·5 | 3 | 9 2 | Firm | Double Florin | May 19, | 1980 |

## WOLVERHAMPTON

| Distance | Time | Age | Weight | Going | Horse | Date | |
|---|---|---|---|---|---|---|---|
| 5f | 56·6 | 3 | 7 13 | Firm | Balvima | Sept. 17, | 1979 |
| 5f | 57·1 | 2 | 9 0 | Good | Soverena | July 3, | 1967 |
| 7f | 1. 26·4 | 3 | 9 3 | Firm | Mata Cara | July 1, | 1991 |
| 7f | 1. 26·0 | 2 | 8 11 | Firm | Marillette (USA) | June 29, | 1992 |
| 8f | 1. 37·3 | 3 | 8 8 | Firm | Tender Sovereign | July 4, | 1983 |

## WOLVERHAMPTON - cont'd

| 8f | 1. 39·1 | 2 8 8 | Fast | Ivory Tower | Sept. 12, | 1988 |
|---|---|---|---|---|---|---|
| 8f 200y | 1. 47·4 | 3 8 8 | Firm | Mailman | May 18, | 1982 |
| 8f 200y | 1. 51·8 | { 2 8 12 | Firm | Connaught Bridge | Oct. 9, | 1978 |
| | | 2 8 11 | Firm | River Jig (USA) | Oct. 7, | 1986 |
| 11f | 2. 20 | 3 7 13 | Firm | Sno Marque | July 1, | 1991 |
| 12f 70y | 2. 30·9 | 3 9 0 | Firm | Salient | July 8, | 1985 |
| 14f 134y | 3. 5·6 | 3 9 7 | Firm | Sanchi Steeple | July 8, | 1985 |
| 16f 201y | 3. 36·3 | 4 9 0 | Firm | Dark Proposal | May 17, | 1982 |

## YARMOUTH

| Distance | Time | Age Weight | Going | Horse | Date | |
|---|---|---|---|---|---|---|
| 5f 43y | 1. 0·2 | 3 8 11 | Fast | Charm Bird | Sept. 15, | 1988 |
| 5f 43y | 1. 0·9 | { 2 8 8 | Firm | Aberbevine | June 14, | 1967 |
| | | 2 8 10 | Fast | Sam's Wood | July 13, | 1983 |
| 6f 3y | 1. 10·4 | { 4 8 4 | Good | Denikin | July 4, | 1951 |
| | | 3 7 7 | Firm | Gold Prospector | Sept. 19, | 1978 |
| 6f 3y | 1. 10·4 | 2 9 0 | Fast | Lanchester | Sept. 15 | 1988 |
| 7f 3y | 1. 22·2 | 3 8 7 | Fast | Cielamour (USA) | Sept. 15 | 1988 |
| 7f 3y | 1. 22·2 | 2 9 0 | Fast | Warrshan (USA) | Sept. 14, | 1988 |
| 8f 3y | 1. 34·4 | 3 8 11 | Fast | Alderney | Sept. 14, | 1988 |
| 8f 3y | 1. 36·3 | 2 8 2 | Fast | Outrun | Sept. 15, | 1988 |
| 10f 21y | 2. 4·2 | { 3 8 1 | Firm | On The Foan | Aug. 17, | 1983 |
| | | 3 9 3 | Fast | Aunt Mabel | Aug. 3, | 1988 |
| 11f 101y | 2. 23·8 | { 3 9 0 | Firm | Lakenheath | June 10, | 1981 |
| | | 3 9 0 | Firm | His Turn | June 9, | 1982 |
| 14f 17y | 2. 57·8 | 3 8 2 | Fast | Barakat | July 24, | 1990 |
| 17f 170y | 3. 56 | 6 9 2 | Firm | Dolben Lad | Sept. 21, | 1978 |
| 18f 51y | 4. 14 | 3 9 2 | Fast | Receptionist | Sept. 17, | 1992 |

## YORK (Electric)

| Distance | Time | Age Weight | Going | Horse | Date | |
|---|---|---|---|---|---|---|
| 5f | 56·16 | 3 9 3 | Fast | Dayjur (USA) | Aug. 23, | 1990 |
| 5f | 57·39 | 2 7 8 | Firm | Lyric Fantasy (USA) | Aug. 20, | 1992 |
| 6f | 1. 8·82 | 4 9 4 | Fast | Shalford (IRE) | May 14, | 1992 |
| 6f | 1. 9·84 | 2 9 0 | Fast | Sharp N'Early | Aug. 17, | 1988 |
| 6f 214y | 1. 22·31 | 4 8 6 | Fast | Duckington | Oct. 8, | 1988 |
| 6f 214y | 1. 23·48 | 2 8 8 | Firm | Angelic Note (USA) | Oct. 6, | 1988 |
| 7f 202y | 1. 35·85 | 3 8 2 | Firm | Rosie Potts | May 17, | 1989 |
| 7f 202y | 1. 38·51 | 2 8 11 | Firm | Bocatower (disq) | Oct. 8, | 1986 |
| 8f 205y | 1. 48·90 | 3 8 5 | Fast | Jalmusique | May 16, | 1989 |
| 8f 205y | 1. 52·43 | 2 8 1 | Firm | Oral Evidence | Oct. 6, | 1988 |
| 10f 85y | 2. 6·35 | 3 8 10 | Fast | Persian Heights (disq) | Aug. 16, | 1988 |
| 11f 195y | 2. 25·79 | 3 9 0 | Fast | Diminuendo (USA) | Aug. 16, | 1988 |
| 13f 194y | 2. 52·92 | 5 8 9 | Firm | Mountain Kingdom | May 18, | 1989 |
| 15f 195y | 3. 18·49 | 3 8 0 | Fast | Dam Busters (USA) | Aug. 16, | 1988 |

**Raceform UPDATE**

**YOUR COMPLETE WEEKEND BETTING GUIDE**

# RACEFORM STANDARD TIMES

## REVISED UP TO 1991 INCLUSIVE

The following represent the standard true-run race times for the varied distances and courses brought to 9st.

## ASCOT

| | | |
|---|---|---|
| 5f.....................60.5s | 1m (rnd).....................1/39.6s | 2m 45yds.....................3/26.5s |
| 6f.....................1/13.6s | 1¼m.....................2/4.3s | 2½m.....................4/16s |
| 7f.....................1/26.5s | 1½m.....................2/29.5s | 2¾m 34yds.....................4/47s |
| 1m (st).....................1/39.4s | | |

## AYR

| | | |
|---|---|---|
| 5f.....................58s | 1m 1f.....................1/50s | 1m 7f.....................3/12.5s |
| 6f.....................1/10.4s | 1¼m.....................2/5.3s | 2m 1f 105yds.....................3/45.5s |
| 7f.....................1/24s | 1¼m 192yds.....................2/13.7s | 2½m 90yds.....................4/27s |
| 1m.....................1/37.2s | 1m 5f 13yds.....................2/46.2s | |

## BATH

| | | |
|---|---|---|
| 5f 11yds.....................60.5s | 1m 5yds.....................1/39.3s | 1m 5f 22yds.....................2/47.7s |
| 5f 161yds.....................1/9.3s | 1¼m 46yds.....................2/7.7s | 2m 1f 34yds.....................3/44s |
| 7f 8yds.....................1/27.8s | 1m 3f 144yds.....................2/26.7s | |

## BEVERLEY

| | | |
|---|---|---|
| 5f.....................61.5s | 1m 1f 207yds.....................2/2s | 2m 35yds.....................3/30.7s |
| 7f 100yds.....................1/30.2s | 1m 3f 216yds.....................2/31.6s | 2m 3f 100yds.....................4/16s |
| 1m 100yds.....................1/42.7s | | |

## BRIGHTON

| | | |
|---|---|---|
| 5f 59yds.....................60.3s | 6f 209yds.....................1/20s | 1m 1f 209yds.....................1/58s |
| 5f 213 yds.....................1/8.4s | 7f 214yds.....................1/32.2s | 1m 3f 196yds.....................2/27s |

## CARLISLE

| | | |
|---|---|---|
| 5f.....................60.2s | 7f 214yds.....................1/38.7s | 1½m.....................2/29.5s |
| 5f 207yds.....................1/12.3s | 1m 1f 80yds.....................1/57s | 1¾m 32yds.....................2/57s |
| 6f 206yds.....................1/25.2s | | |

## CATTERICK

| | | |
|---|---|---|
| 5f.....................57.5s | 7f.....................1/23.2s | 1m 5f 175yds.....................2/55.2s |
| 5f 212yds.....................1/10.5s | 1½m 44yds.....................2/34s | 1m 7f 177yds.....................3/21s |

## CHANTILLY

| | | |
|---|---|---|
| 5f.....................59.7s | 1m 1f.....................1/49.7s | 1½m.....................2/28s |
| 5½f.....................65.7s | 1¼m.....................2/2.3s | 1m 7f.....................3/9.7s |
| 6f.....................1/11.8s | 1¼m 110yds.....................2/8.7s | 2¼m.....................3/54s |
| 7f.....................1/24.5s | 1m 3f.....................2/15.4s | 2½m.....................4/20.5s |
| 1m.....................1/36.7s | | |

## CHEPSTOW

| | | |
|---|---|---|
| 5f 16yds.....................57s | 1m 14yds.....................1/32.5s | 1½m 23yds.....................2/31.3s |
| 6f 16yds.....................1/9s | 1¼m 36yds.....................2/4.3s | 2m 49yds.....................3/28s |
| 7f 16yds.....................1/20.5s | | |

## CHESTER

| | | |
|---|---|---|
| 5f 16yds.....................60.6s | 1¼m 75yds.....................2/10s | 1m 5f 89yds.....................2/49.4s |
| 6f 18yds.....................1/13.3s | 1m 3f 79yds.....................2/24s | 1m 7f 195yds.....................3/25s |
| 7f 2yds.....................1/26.2s | 1½m 66yds.....................2/36.6s | 2¼m 117yds.....................3/59s |
| 7f 122yds.....................1/32.7s | | |

## CURRAGH

| | | |
|---|---|---|
| 5f............58.5s | 1m (both courses).......1/37s | 1½m............2/30.3s |
| 6f............1/10.6s | 1m 1f............1/49.3s | 1m 5f............2/43.3s |
| 6f 63yds............1/14.5s | 1¼m............2/3s | 1¾m............2/56s |
| 7f............1/23.2s | 1m 3f............2/16.3s | 2m............3/23.3s |

## DEAUVILLE

| | | |
|---|---|---|
| 5f............56.6s | 1m (st)............1/36.6s | 1m 5f 110yds............2/50.5s |
| 6f............1/9s | 1m (rnd)............1/36s | 1m 7f............3/11s |
| 6f 110yds............1/15.5s | 1¼m............2/2.3s | 2m............3/24.6s |
| 7f............1/23s | 1½m 110yds............2/37.5s | 2¼m............3/51s |
| 7f 110yds............1/29s | | |

## DONCASTER

| | | |
|---|---|---|
| 5f............58.7s | 7f (st)............1/23.4s | 1½m............2/30.6s |
| 5f 140yds............1/7s | 1m (st)............1/36.5s | 1¾m 132yds............3/3.6s |
| 6f............1/11s | 1m (rnd)............1/36.3s | 2m 110yds............3/29s |
| 6f 110yds............1/17.2s | 1¼m 60yds............2/7s | 2¼m............3/52.7s |

## EDINBURGH

| | | |
|---|---|---|
| 5f............57.7s | 1m 16yds............1/38.6s | 1½m 31yds............2/32.5s |
| 7f 15yds............1/26.2s | 1m 3f 32yds............2/19.7s | 1m 7f 16yds............3/10.5s |

## EPSOM

| | | |
|---|---|---|
| 5f............54.5s | 7f............1/20.5s | 1¼m 18yds............2/4.5s |
| 6f............1/8s | 1m 114yds............1/41s | 1½m 10yds............2/35s |

## EVRY

| | | |
|---|---|---|
| 5f............58.5s | 1m (Moyenne)............1/37s | 1¼m 110yds (Moy.)............2/10s |
| 5f 110yds............64.4s | 1m (Grande)............1/37.4s | 1½m (Interior)............2/29.5s |
| 6f............1/10s | 1m 1f (Moyenne)............1/50s | 1½m (Grande)............2/29.6s |
| 6f 110yds............1/15.7s | 1m 1f (Grande)............1/50.3s | 1¾m (Grande)............2/57s |
| 7f............1/24.3s | 1¼m (Moyenne)............2/3.2s | 1m 7f............3/11s |
| 7f 110yds (Moy.)............1/31.3s | 1¼m (Grande)............2/3s | 1m 7f 110yds............3/18s |

## FOLKESTONE

| | | |
|---|---|---|
| 5f............58.8s | 1m 1f 149yds............1/57.7s | 1m 7f 92yds............3/19s |
| 6f............1/10.7s | 1½m............2/33.5s | 2m 93yds............3/32.5s |
| 6f 189yds............1/21.6s | | |

## GOODWOOD

| | | |
|---|---|---|
| 5f............57.6s | 1m 1f............1/50.7s | 1¾m............2/59s |
| 6f............1/10.4s | 1¼m............2/5s | 2m............3/26.6s |
| 7f............1/24.7s | 1½m............2/31.7s | 2½m............4/15s |
| 1m............1/37.6s | | |

## HAMILTON

| | | |
|---|---|---|
| 5f 4yds............58.3s | 1m 1f 36yds............1/54.3s | 1½m 17yds............2/32s |
| 6f 5yds............1/10s | 1m 3f 16yds............2/19s | 1m 5f 9yds............2/45.7s |
| 1m 65yds............1/43.3s | | |

## HAYDOCK

| | | |
|---|---|---|
| 5f............59s | 1¼m 120yds............2/11.7s | 2m 45yds............3/27.2s |
| 6f............1/11.7s | 1m 3f 200yds............2/28s | 2m 1f 130yds............3/47s |
| 7f 30yds............1/27.3s | 1¾m............2/58.5s | 2m 3f............4/6s |
| 1m 30yds............1/40.4s | | |

## KEMPTON

| | | |
|---|---|---|
| 5f.................................59s | 1m (rnd).....................1/37.2s | 1m 3f 30yds ..............2/17.6s |
| 6f................................1/11.3s | 1m (Jubilee) ..............1/36.6s | 1¹⁄₂m.........................2/30.2s |
| 7f (rnd)......................1/24s | 1m 1f (rnd)................1/50s | 1³⁄₄m.........................2/56.6s |
| 7f (Jubilee) ...............1/24.2s | 1¹⁄₄m (Jubilee) ...............2/2s | 2m............................3/24.4s |

## LEICESTER

| | | |
|---|---|---|
| 5f 2yds......................58.7s | 7f 9yds.....................1/22.3s | 1m 1f 218yds ..............2/2.7s |
| 5f 218yds...................1/10s | 1m 8yds.....................1/35s | 1m 3f 183yds ............2/28.8s |

## LEOPARDSTOWN

| | | |
|---|---|---|
| 5f.................................59s | 1m 1f ......................1/50.5s | 1³⁄₄m.........................2/56.3s |
| 6f................................1/11.2s | 1¹⁄₄m.............................2/4s | 2m............................3/24s |
| 7f................................1/25s | 1¹⁄₂m........................2/30s | 2¹⁄₄m........................3/50s |
| 1m...............................1/38s | 1m 5f ........................2/43s | 2¹⁄₂m........................4/17s |

## LINGFIELD (TURF)

| | | |
|---|---|---|
| 5f.................................57s | 7f 140yds.................1/28.5s | 1m 3f 106yds ...........2/22s |
| 6f................................1/8.6s | 1m 1f ......................1/49.3s | 1³⁄₄m.........................2/55.3s |
| 7f................................1/21.3s | 1¹⁄₄m............................2/3s | 2m............................3/24s |

## LINGFIELD (AWT)

| | | |
|---|---|---|
| 5f.................................58.2s | 1m............................1/36.7s | 1m 5f ........................2/43.5s |
| 6f................................1/10.6s | 1¹⁄₄m............................2/3s | 2m............................3/23s |
| 7f................................1/24s | 1¹⁄₂m........................2/29.4s | |

## LONGCHAMP

| | | |
|---|---|---|
| 5f.................................57s | 1m 1f 110yds (Moy.)....1/57s | 1¹⁄₂m (Grande) ..............2/30s |
| 7f................................1/20s | 1m 1f 165yds (Grd.)...1/59.5s | 1¹⁄₂m 110yds (Grd.) ...2/36.6s |
| 1m (Moyenne)..........1/37.4s | 1¹⁄₄m (Grande)...........2/3.2s | 1m 5f 110yds (Petite).2/50.5s |
| 1m (Grande)..............1/37.7s | 1¹⁄₄m (Moyenne)............2/3s | 1m 7f (Grande)..........3/12.3s |
| 1m 110yds (Petite).......1/45s | 1¹⁄₄m 110yds (Grande) 2/9.6s | 1m 7f (Moyenne) ..........3/12s |
| 1m 110yds (Moyenne)..1/44s | 1¹⁄₄m 110yds (Moy.)....2/9.3s | 1m 7f 110yds (Grande).3/19s |
| 1m 1f (Moyenne) .......1/50.4s | 1m 3f (Grande)...........2/16.3s | 2m 110yds (Grande)..3/32.4s |
| 1m 1f 55yds (Grd.).....1/53.3s | 1m 3f 110yds (Grande).2/23s | 2¹⁄₂m (Grande) .............4/18s |

## MAISONS-LAFFITTE

| | | |
|---|---|---|
| 4f 110yds (st)................53s | 1m (CD)......................1/37s | 1m 3f 110yds (CG) .....2/21.8s |
| 5f (st)...........................59s | 1m 110yds (CD) .........1/43.3s | 1m 3f 110yds (CD) .....2/22.6s |
| 5f 110yds (st)..............1/5.2s | 1m 1f (st)...................1/49s | 1¹⁄₂m (CG) ................2/28.3s |
| 6f (st)..........................1/10.5s | 1m 1f (CD) ................1/50.2s | 1¹⁄₂m 110yds (CD) .....2/35.7s |
| 6f 110yds (st)..............1/16.4s | 1¹⁄₄m (st)......................2/2.2s | 1¹⁄₂m 110yds (CD) .....2/34.5s |
| 7f (st)..........................1/22.7s | 1¹⁄₄m (CD) ...................2/2.5s | 1m 5f (CD) .................2/41.7s |
| 7f (CG)........................1/23.4s | 1¹⁄₄m 110yds (CG) .......2/8.5s | 1m 7f (CD) .................3/8s |
| 1m (st).........................1/35.3s | 1¹⁄₄m 110yds (CD) ......2/9.3s | 2m (CD) ....................3/22.2s |
| 1m (CG) ......................1/36.2s | 1m 3f (CG) ................2/15.4s | |

## NAAS

| | | |
|---|---|---|
| 5f.................................58s | 1m 1f ......................1/51s | 1¹⁄₂m.........................2/31s |
| 6f................................1/9.4s | 1¹⁄₄m........................2/4.5s | 2m............................3/26s |
| 7f................................1/24s | 1m 3f ........................2/17.4 | |

## NEWBURY

| | | |
|---|---|---|
| 5f 34yds.....................60.7s | 1m st.........................1/37s | 1m 3f 6yds....................2/16s |
| 6f 8yds.......................1/11.8s | 1m 7yds (rnd)..............1/36s | 1¹⁄₂m 5yds.................2/29.7s |
| 7f (st)..........................1/24.5s | 1m 1f ......................1/49.2s | 1m 5f 61yds ..............2/45.7s |
| 7f 64yds (rnd)............1/27.3s | 1¹⁄₄m 6yds.....................2/3s | 2m............................3/26.7s |

## NEWCASTLE

| | | |
|---|---|---|
| 5f...................................58.4s | 1m.....................................1/39s | 1¹/₂m 93yds................2/38.5s |
| 6f...................................1/11.5s | 1m 1f 9yds...................1/52.3s | 2m 19yds........................3/25.5s |
| 7f...................................1/24.3s | 1¹/₄m 32yds.................2/6.7s | |

## NEWMARKET
### (ROWLEY MILE COURSE)

| | | |
|---|---|---|
| 5f...................................59.4s | 1m 1f.............................1/50s | 2m.....................................3/23.3s |
| 6f...................................1/11.4s | 1¹/₄m.............................2/2.6s | 2¹/₄m.................................3/50s |
| 7f...................................1/24s | 1¹/₂m.............................2/29.3s | 2¹/₂m.................................4/17s |
| 1m.................................1/37.3s | 1³/₄m.............................2/56s | |

### (JULY COURSE)

| | | |
|---|---|---|
| 5f.....................................59s | 1m.................................1/37.7s | 1³/₄m 175yds..................3/6s |
| 6f...................................1/11.5s | 1¹/₄m.............................2/2.6s | 2m 22yds.......................3/23s |
| 7f...................................1/24.4s | 1¹/₂m.............................2/28.7s | 2¹/₂m.................................4/18s |

## NOTTINGHAM

| | | |
|---|---|---|
| 5f 13yds.........................58.7s | 1m 1f 213yds...............2/2.5s | 2m 9yds..........................3/24.4s |
| 6f 15yds.........................1/11s | 1³/₄m 15yds..................2/58.5s | 2¹/₄m 18yds...................3/51.5s |
| 1m 54yds......................1/39.6s | | |

## PONTEFRACT

| | | |
|---|---|---|
| 5f...................................61.5s | 1¹/₄m 6yds...................2/8.3s | 2m 1f 216yds...............3/52.2s |
| 6f...................................1/14s | 1¹/₂m 8yds...................2/34.5s | 2m 5f 122yds.............4/39.5s |
| 1m 4yds........................1/41.6s | 2m 1f 22yds.................3/40s | |

## REDCAR

| | | |
|---|---|---|
| 5f...................................56.7s | 1m 1f.............................1/49s | 1m 5f 135yds...............2/51s |
| 6f...................................1/9.3s | 1¹/₄m.............................2/2.5s | 1³/₄m 19yds...................2/57.6s |
| 7f...................................1/22.2s | 1m 3f.............................2/15.7s | 2m 4yds..........................3/25s |
| 1m.................................1/35s | 1¹/₂m.............................2/30.2s | 2m 3f.................................4/5s |

## RIPON

| | | |
|---|---|---|
| 5f...................................58.6s | 1m 1f.............................1/50.2s | 2m.....................................3/25s |
| 6f...................................1/11.7s | 1¹/₄m.............................2/3.5s | 2m 1f 203yds.............3/51.3s |
| 1m.................................1/37.7s | 1¹/₂m 60yds................2/34s | |

## SAINT-CLOUD

| | | |
|---|---|---|
| 4f 110yds.......................54s | 7f 110yds.....................1/31.7s | 1¹/₂m.................................2/30.3s |
| 6f...................................1/13s | 1m.................................1/38.6s | 1¹/₂m 110yds................2/37s |
| 6f 110yds.......................1/19.4s | 1¹/₄m.............................2/4s | 1³/₄m.................................2/56s |
| 7f...................................1/25.2s | 1¹/₄m 110yds...............2/10.3s | 1³/₄m 110yds................3/2.6s |

## SALISBURY

| | | |
|---|---|---|
| 5f.....................................60s | 1m.................................1/39.3s | 1¹/₂m.................................2/32.6s |
| 6f...................................1/12.3s | 1m 1f 209yds...............2/4.7s | 1³/₄m.................................2/58.2s |
| 6f 212yds.......................1/25.7s | | |

## SANDOWN

| | | |
|---|---|---|
| 5f 6yds...........................59.5s | 1m 1f.............................1/51.4s | 1³/₄m.................................2/54.7s |
| 7f 16yds.........................1/27s | 1¹/₄m 7yds...................2/4.3s | 2m 78yds........................3/30s |
| 1m 14yds......................1/39.2s | 1m 3f 91yds.................2/21.7s | |

## SOUTHWELL (AWT)

| | | |
|---|---|---|
| 5f..................................58s | 1m............................1/39.3s | 1m 5f.........................2/47.2s |
| 6f..............................1/13.4s | 1m 3f..........................2/21.5s | 1¾m.............................2/59.3 |
| 7f..............................1/26.6s | 1½m............................2/34.2s | 2m.................................3/26s |

## SOUTHWELL (TURF)

| | | |
|---|---|---|
| 6f..............................1/14.3s | 1m 3f.............................2/22s | 2m.................................3/26s |
| 7f..............................1/27.2s | 1½m............................2/34.6s | |

## THIRSK

| | | |
|---|---|---|
| 5f................................57.7s | 1m................................1/36s | 2m 1f.............................3/36s |
| 6f..............................1/10.2s | 1½m.............................2/30s | 2¼m............................3/49.3s |
| 6f 216yds..................1/23.3s | 2m.................................3/23s | |

## WARWICK

| | | |
|---|---|---|
| 5f..................................58s | 1m................................1/37s | 1¾m 194yds.................3/9s |
| 6f.................................1/12s | 1¼m 169yds.............2/13.5s | 2m 20yds.....................3/26s |
| 7f..............................1/24.2s | 1½m 115yds..............2/37.5s | 2¼m 214yds..................4/4s |

## WINDSOR

| | | |
|---|---|---|
| 5f 10yds.........................59s | 1m 67yds....................1/41.6s | 1m 3f 135yds.............2/22.5s |
| 5f 217yds..................1/10.5s | 1¼m 7yds.......................2/3s | |

## WOLVERHAMPTON

| | | |
|---|---|---|
| 5f................................57.3s | 1m 200yds..................1/48.5s | 1¾m 134yds.................3/6s |
| 7f..............................1/24.3s | 1m 3f...........................2/15s | 2m 201yds..................3/36.7s |
| 1m.............................1/37.3s | 1½m 70yds.................2/31.7s | |

## YARMOUTH

| | | |
|---|---|---|
| 5f 42yds.......................60.3s | 1m 3yds......................1/35.3s | 1¾m 17yds...................2/58s |
| 6f 3yds.......................1/10.6s | 1¼m 21yds..................2/4.4s | 2m 1f 170yds...............3/56s |
| 7f 2yds......................1/22.8s | 1m 3f 101yds................2/24s | |

## YORK

| | | |
|---|---|---|
| 5f................................57.5s | 7f 202yds......................1/36s | 1m 3f 195yds................2/27s |
| 6f..............................1/10.2s | 1m 205yds.....................1/49s | 1m 5f 194yds.............2/53.6s |
| 6f 214yds..................1/22.4s | 1¼m 85yds..................2/7.5s | 1m 7f 195yds................3/20s |

---

---

# TOP SPEED FIGURES
# RECORDED 1992

### TWO-YEAR-OLDS

#### COLTS

1. Zafonic (USA) ............................... 74
2. Armiger ..................................... 73
3. Tenby ....................................... 73
4. Up And At 'em .............................. 73
5. Ardkinglass ................................ 70

#### FILLIES

1. Lyric Fantasy (IRE) ........................ 82
2. Gold Splash (USA) .......................... 73
3. Kindergarten ............................... 72
4. Creaking Board ............................. 70
5. Love of Silver (USA) ....................... 70

### SPRINTERS

#### 5f–6f

##### 3-Y-O

1. Western Approach (USA) .................. 87
2. Hamas (IRE) ................................ 86
3. Pursuit of Love ............................ 86
4. Freddie Lloyd (USA) ........................ 85
5. Paris House ................................ 84

##### OLDER HORSES

1. Mr Brooks .................................. 96
2. Shalford (IRE) ............................. 96
3. Sheikh Albadou ............................ 96
4. Dream Talk ................................. 93
5. Bold Lez ................................... 91

### MILERS

#### 7f–9f

##### 3-Y-O

1. Rainbow Corner ............................. 93
2. Lion Cavern (USA) .......................... 91
3. Steinbeck (USA) ............................ 89
4. Alnasr Alwasheek ........................... 88
5. Culture Vulture (USA) ...................... 88

##### OLDER HORSES

1. Lahib (USA) ................................ 97
2. Selkirk (USA) .............................. 97
3. Exit to Nowhere (USA) ...................... 95
4. Second Set (IRE) ........................... 95
5. Sikeston (USA) ............................. 93

### MIDDLE DISTANCE

#### 10f–12f

##### 3-Y-O

1. Rodrigo de Triano (USA) .................. 96
2. St Jovite (USA) ............................ 95
3. Dr Devious (IRE) ........................... 92
4. All At Sea (USA) ........................... 91
5. Seattle Rhyme (USA) ........................ 88

##### OLDER HORSES

1. Pistolet Bleu (IRE) ....................... 102
2. Kooyonga (IRE) ............................. 99
3. Opera House ................................ 99
4. Subotica (FR) .............................. 98
5. Sapience ................................... 96

### STAYERS

#### 13f–20f

##### 3-Y-O

1. Sought Out (IRE) ........................... 84
2. User Friendly .............................. 78
3. Brier Creek (USA) .......................... 74
4. Sonus (IRE) ................................ 74
5. Bonny Scot (IRE) ........................... 73

##### OLDER HORSES

1. Mashaallah (USA) ........................... 96
2. Snurge ..................................... 95
3. Drum Taps (USA) ............................ 93
4. Further Flight ............................. 91
5. Witness Box (USA) .......................... 85

# FLAT SPEED FIGURES 1992

The following list, based on Standard Times, shows speed figures of 40 and upwards, returned on British and selected Irish and French tracks. All the ratings are given at 9st. after allowances for going and distance behind winners. Additional information in parentheses following the speed figure shows the distance of the race in furlongs, course, state of going and the date on which the figure was recorded. Going abbreviations are: H (hard), F (firm), Fs (fast), G (good), Std (standard), Y (yielding), Sl (slow), S (soft), Hvy (heavy).

## THREE-YEAR OLDS AND UPWARDS

Aahsaylad 67 (15f, Ayr, F, July 20)
Aardvark 41 (10f, Bev, F, June 4)
Abbey Strand (USA) 45 (7f, Nby, G, Aug 15)
Abingdon Flyer (IRE) 51 (10f, Asc, F, June 20)
Able Lassie 57 (10½f, Hay, Y, Sep 6)
Abso 47 (7f, Chep, S, Aug 31)
Absolutely Nuts 50 (5f, Hay, G, Oct 7)
Absolution 66 (5f, Yrk, F, June 12)
Absonal 54 (7f, Sal, F, June 9)
Absurde (FR) 83 (8f, Lon, F, May 17)
Access Ski 49 (20f, Gwd, F, July 29)
Acrobate (USA) 50 (12f, Nmkt, G, Apr 14)
Across The Bay 60 (7f, Gwd, F, June 12)
Acteur Francais (USA) 67 (8f, Lon, S, Oct 4)
Adam Smith 81 (9f, Nmkt, G, Apr 15)
Addicted To Love 41 (11½f, Yar, G, Oct 28)
Adieu Au Roi (IRE) 67 (12f, Chan, G, June 7)
Adjamiya (USA) 42 (6f, Naas, F, July 4)
Admirals Seat 43 (10½f, Hay, S, Apr 18)
Adwick Park 65 (6f, Nmkt, G, Aug 7)
Afaladja (IRE) 70 (12f, Lon, F, June 28)
Affordable 40 (7f, Red, F, June 20)
Afif 42 (6f, Rip, S, Apr 16)
African Chimes 65 (5f, Pon, F, Sep 21)
African Peace (USA) 61 (10½f, StCl, G, May 8)
Africanus (FR) 68 (7f, Lon, G, May 28)
Agnes Flemming (USA) 62 (8f, Nmkt, F, July 17)
Ahbab (IRE) 48 (6f, Nmkt, F, Oct 2)
Ain'tlifelikethat 42 (7f, Bri, G, Aug 26)
Air Speed (IRE) 44 (9f, Cur, G, Oct 20)
Aitch N'Bee 59 (8f, Bth, F, Aug 11)
Ajaad (USA) 61 (7f, Hay, Y, May 2)
Ajo (IRE) 54 (10½f, Hay, G, June 6)
Akiko (USA) 63 (10f, Lon, G, Sep 20)
Akkazao (IRE) 45 (8f, San, F, June 13)
Albemine (USA) 53 (8f, Pon, Y, Oct 5)
Alberta Rose (IRE) 42 (9f, Cur, G, Oct 20)
Al Fitzao (IRE) 58 (10f, Cur, Y, Oct 11)
Alflora (IRE) 74 (10f, Ayr, F, July 20)
Al Guswa 68 (10f, Cur, Y, Oct 11)
Alhaajib (USA) 47 (8f, Nby, G, Sep 19)
Alhamad 69 (12f, Nmkt, F, July 17)
Alhijaz 80 (8f, Lon, S, Oct 4)
Aljadeer (USA) 81 (10f, San, G, Apr 25)
Alkarif (USA) 63 (10f, Don, F, Sep 9)
Al Karnak (IRE) 55 (14½f, Don, F, Sep 10)
All At Sea (USA) 91 (10f, Yrk, G, Aug 18)
Allegan (USA) 65 (14f, Gwd, Y, Aug 29)
Allinson's Mate (IRE) 65 (5f, Tsk, F, Sep 5)
Allthruthenight (IRE) 70 (5f, Eps, G, June 4)

Almuhtarama (IRE) 54 (10f, San, G, Sep 15)
Al Mutahm (USA) 77 (16f, Asc, Y, Apr 29)
Alnasr Alwasheek 88 (8f, Nmkt, G, Apr 16)
Alphard 57 (12f, Asc, F, June 16)
Alqairawaan 44 (14½f, Don, G, Oct 23)
Al Ramis (IRE) 40 (8f, Nmkt, G, June 19)
Al Sadi 52 (7f, Nmkt, G, May 2)
Altermeera 50 (10f, San, G, July 16)
Alto Jane 49 (10f, Nmkt, F, Oct 15)
Alum Bay 40 (10f, San, G, May 26)
Always Friendly 94 (12f, Eps, G, June 4)
Alyafill (USA) 42 (10f, Chep, G, July 16)
Amaze 55 (8f, San, G, May 5)
Amazing Feat (IRE) 80 (7f, Red, S, Oct 27)
Amazon Express 44 (11½f, Yar, G, Oct 28)
Amber Mill 58 (5f, Ches, F, June 24)
Ambiguously Regal (USA) 46 (16f, Asc, F, June 17)
American Hero 43 (8f, Don, F, May 23)
Amigo Menor 76 (6f, Deau, Y, Aug 19)
Amron 72 (5f, Nwc, Y, Mar 30)
Amwag (USA) 71 (8f, San, Y, Aug 21)
Anchorite 46 (12f, Don, F, Sep 11)
Andrath (IRE) 70 (10f, Yrk, F, May 14)
Andros Bay (USA) 69 (12f, Cur, Y, Oct 11)
Anguish (IRE) 44 (12f, Nmkt, G, Oct 30)
Annabelle Royale 59 (7½f, Lin, G, July 27)
Annacurragh (IRE) 45 (10f, Bth, F, Aug 6)
Anna of Saxony 54 (14f, Gwd, F, July 31)
Anne Bonny 62 (10f, San, G, Sep 16)
Annonay (IRE) 59 (10f, Cur, Y, Sep 5)
Another Episode (IRE) 63 (5f, Eps, Y, Sep 1)
Antiguan Flyer 57 (13f, Ayr, S, Sep 19)
Appealing Bubbles (IRE) 51 (12f, Leo, F, June 10)
Appealing Times (USA) 43 (7f, Lin, Fs, July 11)
Appledorn 62 (6f, Don, G, Oct 24)
Apple Tree (FR) 84 (12f, Lon, G, Sep 13)
Approach The Bench (IRE) 80 (10f, Leo, G, Aug 8)
A Prayer For Wings 62 (6f, Kem, G, July 8)
Aquamarine 57 (11f, Ches, F, May 6)
Arabellajill 68 (6f, Gwd, G, Sep 12)
Arabian Bold (IRE) 51 (12f, Tsk, F, Aug 1)
Arak (USA) 58 (10f, Don, F, June 26)
Arany 67 (8f, Rip, Y, Aug 31)
Arazi (USA) 86 (8f, Lon, S, Oct 4)
Arboretum (IRE) 50 (7f, Lin, F, Aug 15)
Arbusha (USA) 64 (8f, Asc, Y, Apr 29)
Arcadian Heights 82 (16f, Gwd, F, July 30)
Arcangues (USA) 88 (12f, Lon, G, May 31)
Arc Lamp 45 (5f, Wol, F, June 22)

Arctic Appeal (IRE) 49 (6f, Yrk, G, July 11)
Ardisia (USA) 53 (10f, Not, G, May 29)
Aremef (USA) 68 (12f, Don, F, June 26)
Arlington Heights (IRE) 62 (10f, Leo, Y, Sep 13)
Armarama 66 (10f, Nmkt, G, Apr 30)
Army of Stars 51 (12f, Nby, G, July 18)
Arrikala (IRE) 66 (12f, Cur, Y, Oct 11)
Art Bleu 83 (10½f, Lon, G, May 3)
Art Form (USA) 57 (16f, Gwd, F, May 20)
Artic Tracker (USA) 67 (7f, Nmkt, F, Apr 15)
Artistic Reef 71 (5f, Nmkt, F, Sep 30)
Asaasy (USA) 71 (9f, Yrk, G, May 12)
Ashdren 64 (7f, Nmkt, G, July 9)
Ashtina 71 (5f, Nmkt, F, Oct 17)
Asian Punter (IRE) 43 (11f, San, Y, July 3)
Assessor (IRE) 71 (10f, San, G, Apr 25)
Assignment 66 (6f, Ayr, Y, Sep 19)
Asterix 42 (7f, Chep, F, June 27)
Athar (IRE) 46 (12f, Sal, Y, Sep 30)
A-To-Z (IRE) 49 (8f, Nmkt, G, Apr 30)
Aude La Belle (FR) 45 (16f, Asc, F, July 24)
Aughfad 73 (5f, Nmkt, F, July 7)
Avice Caro (USA) 54 (10f, San, G, Sep 15)
Avro Anson 42 (16f, Red, Y, Oct 6)
Awesome Power 48 (10f, Lin, Fs, Mar 10)
Awol 58 (12f, Don, F, June 26)
Ayr Raider 53 (6f, Not, Y, July 4)
Azureus (IRE) 50 (10f, Ayr, F, June 19)

Badawiah 44 (10f, Lin, Fs, Nov 5)
Badawi (USA) 80 (9f, Yrk, F, Aug 19)
Badie (USA) 67 (8f, Nmkt, G, Apr 16)
Bahi (IRE) 69 (10f, Leo, G, Oct 24)
Bakari (IRE) 71 (6f, Deau, Y, Aug 19)
Baligay 62 (6f, Kem, F, Aug 19)
Ballad Dancer 54 (5f, Ayr, F, Aug 8)
Balla Jidaal (USA) 52 (7f, Nmkt, G, May 15)
Ballasecret 61 (5f, Gwd, Y, Aug 28)
Ballerina Bay 49 (7f, Yar, F, Sep 16)
Ballykett Prince (IRE) 74 (8f, Cur, S, Sep 5)
Balnibarbi 43 (10f, Don, F, May 23)
Baluga 58 (8f, Gwd, F, May 19)
Banbury Flyer 44 (5f, Bri, F, May 7)
Banham College 44 (5f, Bev, F, Sep 17)
Barahin (IRE) 45 (8f, Nmkt, G, Apr 15)
Barbary Reef (IRE) 64 (10f, San, G, May 25)
Bardolph (USA) 69 (18½f, Ches, F, May 6)
Barford Lad 58 (10f, Nmkt, F, June 26)
Barr Na Coille (IRE) 44 (10f, Leo, Y, Oct 26)
Barrys Gamble 66 (5f, Tsk, F, May 15)
Basie Noble 57 (7f, Cur, Y, Aug 30)
Batabanoo 50 (10½f, Don, F, Sep 9)
Battle Colours (IRE) 54 (7f, San, G, May 25)
Bayaireg (USA) 56 (10f, Don, F, May 25)
Bayrouge (IRE) 70 (16f, Cur, G, Oct 10)
Baysham (USA) 49 (5f, Kem, G, Apr 20)
Beatle Song 48 (7f, Chep, F, May 25)
Beau Quest 54 (13f, Ayr, F, June 20)
Beau Venture (USA) 76 (5f, Hay, G, Aug 8)
Beebob 43 (18½f, Ches, F, May 6)
Belated 72 (5f, Gwd, G, Oct 2)
Beldi (USA) 42 (10f, Gwd, F, May 19)
Belfort Ruler 56 (7f, Ches, F, Aug 21)
Belgran (USA) 56 (12f, Nby, F, May 15)
Belle Isis (USA) 46 (10f, Eps, G, Sep 1)
Bells of Longwick 56 (5f, Nby, G, Sep 18)
Belmartin 48 (7f, Naas, Y, May 2)
Belmoredean 51 (10f, Lin, Fs, Aug 15)
Be My Hope (IRE) 51 (10f, Cur, Y, Oct 11)

Be My Hostage (IRE) 57 (11f, Naas, F, June 18)
Bengal Tiger (IRE) 40 (9f, Ham, F, May 29)
Bentico 53 (10f, Don, F, July 26)
Berceau (USA) 78 (12f, StCl, S, June 8)
Berlin Wall (IRE) 40 (8f, Nby, Y, Apr 11)
Bernstein Bette 58 (7f, Lei, Y, Oct 12)
Bertie Wooster 70 (6f, Yrk, Y, Oct 10)
Bescaby Boy 53 (10½f, Hay, G, July 4)
Besotted 50 (10f, San, G, Sep 16)
Best Effort 53 (5f, Ayr, F, Aug 8)
Beware of Agents 60 (7f, Yrk, F, May 14)
Beyton (USA) 71 (12f, Asc, F, June 16)
Bezelle 59 (5f, Lon, S, Oct 4)
Bid For Six (USA) 58 (8f, Nby, F, May 16)
Big Blue 43 (8f, Yrk, F, Aug 20)
Big Easy (IRE) 45 (10f, Eps, G, June 5)
Big Hand (IRE) 53 (6f, Ayr, F, July 18)
Bighayir 44 (10f, Ches, S, Oct 20)
Big Leap (IRE) 65 (8f, Nmkt, G, July 9)
Bigwheel Bill (IRE) 51 (12f, Yrk, Y, Oct 8)
Bill Moon 47 (6f, Chep, G, Oct 13)
Billy Blazer 60 (10f, Don, F, July 26)
Bineyah (IRE) 59 (12f, Cur, G, July 11)
Binkhaldoun (USA) 73 (12f, Chan, G, June 7)
Bit of A Lark 85 (5f, Hay, G, Aug 8)
Bit On The Side (IRE) 49 (12f, Lei, G, Sep 8)
Blacktrench Lady (IRE) 46 (6f, Cur, G, Aug 15)
Blake End (USA) 69 (5f, Nmkt, F, May 16)
Blanc Seing (FR) 41 (12f, Ham, Y, Sep 28)
Blazing Glory (IRE) 59 (5f, Cur, Y, Aug 22)
Bletchley Park (IRE) 62 (5f, Hay, F, Aug 7)
Blockade (USA) 64 (8f, Nmkt, F, Aug 1)
Blue Grit 41 (7f, Edn, G, Oct 19).
Blue Is True (IRE) 41 (5f, Wol, Y, Sep 28)
Blue Marine 42 (7f, Tsk, F, Sep 5)
Blue Topaze 48 (5½f, Bth, G, July 20)
Blushing Storm (USA) 56 (12f, Hay, G, July 4)
Blyton (USA) 95 (5f, Nmkt, F, Sep 30)
Bobzao (IRE) 67 (10f, Yrk, F, June 17)
Bodari 65 (5f, Gwd, F, July 29)
Bog Trotter (USA) 82 (7f, Lon, F, June 27)
Bo Knows Best (IRE) 50 (12f, Sal, Y, Sep 30)
Bold Angel 74 (7f, Lin, F, May 30)
Bold Boss 66 (7f, Hay, F, Aug 7)
Bold Elect 52 (12f, Rip, F, July 18)
Bold Habibti 62 (10f, Leo, Y, Sep 12)
Bold Habit 66 (5f, San, G, July 15)
Bold Lez 91 (6f, Lin, G, May 9)
Bold Memory 59 (7f, Nmkt, F, Oct 2)
Bold Pursuit (IRE) 60 (8f, Asc, G, Oct 9)
Bold Resolution (USA) 44 (16f, Asc, S, Sep 24)
Bold Stroke 67 (10f, San, G, Apr 24)
Bollin Patrick 40 (12f, Hay, S, Apr 18)
Boloardo 50 (10f, Yrk, F, June 13)
Bonny Scot (IRE) 75 (12f, Asc, S, Sep 24)
Boogie Bopper (IRE) 47 (10f, Rip, Y, Aug 31)
Booming (FR) 51 (8f, StCl, S, July 17)
Bourree 54 (5f, Leo, Y, Apr 18)
Boursin (IRE) 47 (7f, Cat, Y, June 5)
Bowden Boy (IRE) 51 (8f, Lin, Fs, May 9)
Boy Martin 53 (6f, Lin, Fs, Nov 5)
Brandon Prince (IRE) 56 (16f, Asc, F, July 24)
Branston Abby (IRE) 81 (5f, Don, G, Nov 7)
Bravura 51 (7f, Nmkt, G, May 2)
Break Bread (USA) 74 (10f, Lon, G, May 21)
Breezed Well 49 (8f, Nmkt, F, July 17)

Breezy Day 59 (5f, Hay, G, Sep 25)
Brief Truce (USA) 87 (8f, Asc, Y, Sep 26)
Brier Creek (USA) 74 (14½f, Don, F, Sep 10)
Briggsmaid 46 (13f, Ham, F, July 23)
Brightness 43 (7f, Bev, G, Mar 27)
Bright Paragon (IRE) 41 (6f, Tsk, G, Aug 28)
Brilliant 52 (9f, Yrk, G, Sep 2)
Broad Appeal 40 (8f, Gwd, Y, Sep 11)
Brodessa 41 (12f, Pon, F, Sep 21)
Brown Fairy (USA) 52 (10½f, Don, F, Sep 9)
Bryan Station (USA) 60 (10f, Leo, Y, May 9)
Buddy's Friend (IRE) 48 (8f, Chep, F, June 27)
Bunty Boo 70 (5f, Nmkt, F, Oct 17)
Burdur 59 (8f, Deau, Y, Aug 29)
Busted Rock 69 (10f, Yar, F, July 2)
Buzzards Bellbuoy 59 (8f, Don, G, Oct 23)
By Hand 58 (7f, Ches, F, May 7)

Cabochon 47 (16f, Asc, F, July 24)
Cachou (USA) 51 (8f, Kem, G, May 23)
Caerlina (IRE) 74 (8f, Deau, G, Aug 1)
Caleman 56 (7f, Nmkt, F, Oct 2)
Calling Collect (USA) 76 (9f, Nmkt, F, Oct 16)
Call To The Bar (IRE) 43 (5f, Wol, Y, Sep 28)
Calounia (IRE) 40 (10f, Leo, F, June 10)
Calpella 63 (8f, Asc, F, June 20)
Cambrian 70 (8f, Nmkt, G, Oct 31)
Cambrian Hills (IRE) 46 (8f, Don, G, Sep 12)
Camden's Ransom (USA) 40 (0f, Asc, Y, Sep 24)
Canaan Valley 41 (7f, Nwc, F, May 29)
Canny Chronicle 49 (10f, Asc, G, Oct 9)
Canon Kyle (IRE) 40 (1f, Cat, F, July 24)
Cantoris 79 (5½f, Don, G, Sep 9)
Cape Pigeon (USA) 69 (7f, Ches, F, Aug 21)
Captain Horatius (IRE) 49 (10f, Nmkt, F, May 1)
Cardinal Point (USA) 44 (7f, Cur, S, Apr 11)
Cardmania (USA) 73 (5f, San, G, May 25)
Cardoun (FR) 84 (8f, Deau, Y, Aug 16)
Cariboo Gold (USA) 42 (12f, Pon, G, Oct 22)
Carlingford (USA) 41 (12f, Ham, G, Aug 17)
Caroles Express 46 (7f, Lin, F, June 27)
Caromish (USA) 50 (6f, Bri, F, May 28)
Case Law 75 (6f, Nmkt, G, Apr 14)
Caspian Beluga 51 (12f, Sal, F, July 30)
Caspian Tern (USA) 41 (10f, Bth, G, Sep 14)
Casteddu 80 (7f, Nwc, G, July 27)
Castilian Queen (USA) 41 (7f, Nmkt, F, July 7)
Castillet 43 (11½f, Yar, G, Oct 28)
Castle Courageous 68 (14f, Nmkt, G, May 15)
Castlerea Lad 54 (6f, Hay, F, May 23)
Castoret 65 (11f, Nby, S, Oct 24)
Catalani 40 (5f, Lin, F, May 16)
Catherines Well 60 (5f, Don, F, Sep 11)
Causley 67 (7f, Don, G, Nov 6)
Cee-En-Cee 59 (6f, Kem, F, May 23)

Cee-Jay-Ay 48 (7f, Swl, Fs, July 25)
Central City 82 (6f, Mai, G, Sep 17)
Cezanne 48 (10f, San, G, May 26)
Chandigarh 45 (7f, Chep, S, Aug 31)
Change The Will 40 (7f, Nmkt, G, Aug 28)
Chaplins Club (USA) 47 (7f, Red, G, July 9)
Charlo 83 (10f, Asc, F, June 20)
Charmed Knave 48 (7f, Chep, F, May 25)
Charming Gift 50 (8f, Nmkt, F, May 16)
Chateau Nord 47 (5f, Car, H, June 25)
Chatham Island 61 (10f, Don, F, Sep 9)
Chatino 40 (7f, Bri, F, June 15)
Chatterer (USA) 46 (16f, Not, F, Aug 3)
Checkpoint Charlie 47 (12f, Pon, F, Aug 5)
Cherry Grove Lad (IRE) 70 (9f, Leo, G, July 25)
Chesa Plana 62 (10½f, StCl, S, Oct 31)
Cheshire Annie (IRE) 40 (5f, Eps, F, July 29)
Cheveux Mitchell 72 (7f, Lin, F, May 30)
Cheviot Amble (IRE) 75 (6f, Leo, G, Aug 29)
Chicarica (USA) 49 (6f, Nmkt, G, Aug 28)
Chief Minister (IRE) 54 (12f, Sal, Y, Apr 30)
Chief of Staff 47 (10f, Sal, Y, Sep 30)
Chobe Park (USA) 57 (6f, Cur, S, Sep 19)
Choir Practice 54 (6f, Yrk, G, May 12)
Choppy Choppy (USA) 50 (10f, Bth, S, May 9)
Chucklestone 47 (13f, Bth, F, Aug 11)
Cindora (IRE) 54 (5f, Don, G, Mar 19)
Citiqueen (IRE) 71 (10f, Nwc, G, Aug 31)
Clandolly (IRE) 73 (5f, Leo, G, May 20)
Clare Heights 66 (16f, Asc, Y, Apr 29)
Clare Kerry Lass 54 (7f, Eps, G, June 6)
Classical Affair (IRE) 56 (7f, Cur, G, Oct 20)
Claybank (USA) 64 (6f, Nmkt, G, Apr 14)
Clever Tiger (USA) 48 (8f, StCl, S, June 8)
Clifton Charlie (USA) 68 (6f, Nmkt, G, Aug 7)
Cloud of Dust 71 (8f, Cur, S, Sep 5)
Clurican (IRE) 44 (10f, Wind, G, July 13)
Coastal Express 47 (7f, Swl, Fs, May 23)
Co-Chin (IRE) 51 (8f, Nmkt, F, Aug 1)
Code Breaker (FR) 48 (8f, StCl, S, June 8)
Cold Shower (IRE) 48 (10f, Nmkt, F, Oct 15)
Coleridge 44 (16f, Gwd, F, May 20)
Colossus 57 (7f, Bev, G, Mar 27)
Colour Sergeant 79 (8f, Asc, G, July 25)
Colway Bold 70 (6f, Yrk, G, Sep 2)
Combative (IRE) 64 (8f, Nmkt, G, June 19)
Command 'n Control 41 (10f, Leo, Y, Sep 13)
Committed Dancer (USA) 63 (8f, Asc, F, June 17)
Common Council 55 (8f, Gwd, F, May 19)
Company Cash 47 (7f, Swl, Slw, Feb 28)
Comstock 66 (12f, Tsk, G, Apr 11)
Confronter 60 (7f, Lin, Fs, June 27)
Congress (IRE) 63 (10f, Don, F, July 26)
Coniston Lake (IRE) 46 (7f, Bri, G, Aug 26)
Coniston Water (USA) 40 (8f, Nmkt, G, Apr 15)
Consigliere 74 (7f, Yrk, F, Aug 20)

### SCALE OF CONVERSION

| 5 & 6 furs. | | 7-9 furs. | | 10-14 furs. | | 15 furs. & over | |
|---|---|---|---|---|---|---|---|
| 1 len... | = 4pts | 1 len... | = 3pts | 1 len... | = 2pts | 1 len... | = 1pt |
| ¾ len... | = 3pts | ¾ len... | = 2pts | ¾ len... | = 2pts | ¾ len... | = 1pt |
| ½ len... | = 2pts | ½ len... | = 2pts | ½ len... | = 1pt | ½ len... | = 1pt |
| nk, hd | | nk, hd | | nk, hd | | | |
| or sh-hd | = 1pt | or sh-hd | = 1pt | or sh-hd | = 1pt | | |

Constructivist (IRE) 40 (10f, Chep, G, July 16)
Consulate 54 (5f, Ayr, F, July 20)
Contested Bid (USA) 82 (12f, Lon, G, Sep 13)
Coolaba Prince (IRE) 48 (6f, Ayr, G, July 25)
Cooley's Valve (IRE) 61 (10f, Nmkt, G, May 2)
Cool Luke (IRE) 55 (7f, Yrk, F, June 14)
Cool Society (USA) 49 (10f, Sal, F, May 22)
Coppermill Lad 45 (6f, Gwd, F, June 12)
Coral Flutter 54 (7f, Lin, F, Aug 8)
Corcina 62 (10f, Nwc, F, July 25)
Corn Futures 48 (6f, Yrk, F, June 12)
Corn Lily 57 (12f, Tsk, F, Sep 5)
Corrupt (USA) 74 (10f, Deau, S, Aug 15)
Cottonwood 44 (10f, Nby, F, June 11)
Courageous Knight 44 (8f, Gwd, G, July 28)
Courtline Jester 57 (10½f, Hay, Y, May 2)
Court Minstrel 42 (7f, Bri, F, June 15)
Crack Regiment (USA) 72 (6½f, Deau, G, Aug 2)
Cradle Days 75 (5f, Nmkt, F, July 18)
Cranfield Comet 59 (5f, Nwc, G, Sep 29)
Creche 52 (5f, Swl, Slw, Mar 18)
Crept Out (IRE) 41 (7f, Cat, F, July 1)
Cristofori (USA) 49 (10½f, Lon, G, Apr 26)
Croft Valley 72 (7f, Don, G, Oct 24)
Cronk's Courage 60 (5½f, Don, G, July 26)
Crossillion 46 (11f, Swl, Slw, Jan 24)
Croupier 41 (8f, San, G, May 25)
Cruachan (USA) 41 (9f, Nmkt, G, Apr 15)
Cru Exceptionnel 52 (9f, Nmkt, G, Oct 3)
Crystal Cross (USA) 48 (12f, Eps, G, June 6)
Crystal Heights (FR) 53 (7f, Nmkt, F, Aug 8)
Crystal Jack (FR) 64 (5f, Ches, F, Aug 22)
Crystal Path (FR) 79 (8f, Deau, G, Aug 1)
Cultured 52 (12f, Swl, Slw, Aug 8)
Culture Vulture (USA) 88 (8f, Lon, F, May 17)
Cumbrian Challenge (IRE) 75 (8f, Nwc, F, Aug 29)
Cumbrian Waltzer 88 (6f, Yrk, G, May 12)
Cunning 85 (12f, Lon, G, Sep 13)
Currency Basket (IRE) 53 (16f, Asc, F, June 17)
Cutleaf 46 (10½f, Hay, F, July 2)
Cutting Reef (IRE) 50 (15f, Lon, S, Oct 3)

Daaris (USA) 44 (7f, Wol, F, June 22)
Dabtiya (IRE) 60 (10f, Leo, G, Aug 9)
Daisy Girl 60 (12f, Nwc, F, June 26)
Dajraan (IRE) 66 (12f, Chan, G, June 7)
Dancing Boy (USA) 45 (6f, Not, G, Apr 28)
Danzarin (IRE) 49 (10f, Ches, F, Aug 22)
Darakah 45 (7f, Don, F, May 23)
Daros 51 (8f, Don, Y, Mar 21)
Darussalam 63 (6f, Kem, F, Aug 19)
Daru (USA) 72 (12f, Don, G, Nov 7)
Dashing Colours (IRE) 65 (6f, Leo, G, Aug 29)
Dashing Rose 42 (10f, Cur, Y, June 6)
Daswaki (CAN) 56 (8f, San, G, May 25)
Dauberval (USA) 61 (5f, Lon, Y, Oct 25)
Dawahri (USA) 64 (9f, Nmkt, G, Oct 3)
Dawes of Nelson 43 (5f, Wind, F, Aug 1)
Dawn Bird (IRE) 51 (5f, Cur, G, June 6)
Dawning Street (IRE) 51 (8f, Kem, G, May 13)
Dawn Success 49 (10f, Yrk, F, May 14)
Dazzle The Crowd (IRE) 49 (10f, Bri, F, May 28)
Dazzling Fire (IRE) 43 (10f, Nby, Y, July 17)
Dear Doctor (FR) 90 (10f, San, G, Apr 25)
Deb's Ball 40 (13f, Ayr, F, June 20)
Debsy Do (USA) 43 (7f, Wol, G, Apr 27)

Decided Air (IRE) 58 (12f, Evry, F, July 18)
Dedicated Lady (IRE) 56 (7f, Cur, Y, Aug 30)
Deduce 50 (12f, Pon, G, Oct 22)
Deer Hunt 54 (10f, Nmkt, F, Sep 30)
Deja (USA) 64 (10f, Lon, G, Sep 30)
Delve 60 (10f, Sal, F, Aug 12)
Democratic (USA) 62 (8f, Don, Y, Mar 21)
Densben 72 (6f, Yrk, Y, Oct 10)
Deposki 45 (14f, Yrk, F, Aug 19)
Deprecator (USA) 80 (8f, Yrk, F, Aug 20)
Desert Calm (IRE) 43 (7f, Cur, Y, Aug 30)
Desert Excuse 59 (8f, Leo, Y, Mar 17)
Desert Force (IRE) 40 (12f, Don, F, June 26)
Desert Splendour 56 (8f, Asc, G, July 25)
Desert Sun 78 (8f, San, G, Apr 24)
Desert Thunder (IRE) 71 (6f, Naas, F, July 4)
Diaco 48 (8f, Bri, F, July 2)
Diamonds Galore (CAN) 90 (5f, Yrk, F, Aug 20)
Diamond Wedding (USA) 41 (10f, Nby, Y, July 17)
Dickens Lane 45 (5f, San, Y, Aug 22)
Diet 52 (6f, Ham, F, May 29)
Dilum (USA) 88 (7f, Lon, F, June 27)
Dime Bag 53 (16f, Lin, Fs, Nov 5)
Discord 52 (12f, Kem, F, June 24)
Dissimulateur (FR) 50 (12f, Lon, Y, Oct 18)
Distinct Thatcher (USA) 52 (8f, San, G, Apr 24)
Dive For Cover (USA) 63 (12f, Cur, F, June 27)
Divine Pet 52 (5½f, Bth, G, Sep 14)
Doctor Roy 51 (8f, Yrk, G, July 11)
Doesyoudoes 43 (5f, Lin, Fs, Feb 22)
Dokkha Oyston (IRE) 53 (7f, Edn, G, Oct 19)
Domicksky 61 (7f, Nmkt, G, Apr 15)
Dominos Ring (IRE) 50 (10f, Leo, F, June 1)
Dominuet 73 (5f, Nmkt, F, July 7)
Donnasoo (IRE) 47 (6f, Cur, S, Sep 19)
Don't Forsake Me 42 (10f, Not, F, Aug 4)
Don't Smile 42 (6f, Kem, S, Apr 18)
Dorking Lad 43 (7f, Chep, S, Sep 12)
Dorset Duke 73 (8f, Asc, F, June 17)
Double Blue 68 (6f, Yrk, G, Sep 2)
Double Echo (IRE) 61 (8f, Don, G, Sep 12)
Double Entendre 69 (8f, Don, G, Sep 12)
Double Feature 44 (6f, Rip, Y, Aug 31)
Double Flutter 58 (10f, Nwc, G, Aug 31)
Doulab's Image 70 (8f, Yrk, F, Aug 20)
Douraj (IRE) 42 (7f, War, F, June 20)
Dovale 41 (10f, Ayr, Y, Sep 18)
Dowland (USA) 66 (9f, Leo, G, July 25)
Draft Board 51 (6f, War, S, Oct 5)
Dr Devious (IRE) 92 (10f, Leo, Y, Sep 13)
Dream Carrier (IRE) 55 (7f, San, G, July 22)
Dreams End 63 (10f, Asc, F, July 25)
Dream Talk 93 (5f, Lon, G, May 7)
Dress Sense (IRE) 51 (8f, Nmkt, F, Oct 17)
Drummer Hicks 65 (10f, Don, F, July 26)
Drum Sergeant 54 (5f, Nmkt, F, May 16)
Drum Taps (USA) 93 (14f, Cur, Y, Sep 19)
Dry Point 42 (6f, Nmkt, G, Apr 30)
Dublin Indemnity (USA) 46 (8f, Swl, Fs, Jan 15)
Duc de Berry (USA) 52 (12f, Tsk, F, Aug 1)
Duckington 52 (7f, Nwc, F, June 27)
Duharra (IRE) 54 (12f, Leo, G, Aug 8)
Duke of Eurolink 59 (12f, Don, F, Sep 11)
Duke of Paducah (USA) 73 (16f, Gwd, F, July 30)
Dune River 45 (8f, Car, F, Sep 8)
Duplicity (IRE) 80 (6f, Yrk, G, May 12)

Durneltor 47 (7f, Bri, F, June 23)
Durshan (USA) 51 (10f, Leo, G, Oct 24)

Eager Deva 64 (5f, Pon, F, May 4)
Eagle Feather (IRE) 67 (10½f, Hay, Y, Sep 5)
Easy Line 67 (6f, Nmkt, F, July 31)
Ebaziya (IRE) 64 (12f, Cur, Y, Oct 11)
Ebony And Ivory (IRE) 64 (10f, Cur, Y, Sep 5)
Echo-Logical 68 (5f, Ayr, G, July 25)
Eclipsing (IRE) 65 (9f, Yrk, G, Sep 2)
Ecliptic (IRE) 62 (9f, Yrk, G, May 12)
Eden's Close 49 (10½f, Don, F, Sep 9)
Ednego Bay (IRE) 40 (7f, Lin, F, May 16)
Educated Pet 65 (5f, Nmkt, F, July 18)
Efharisto 65 (8f, Asc, F, June 19)
Efra 41 (7f, Lin, F, May 23)
Eid (USA) 43 (10f, Bev, F, May 19)
Elaine Tully (IRE) 55 (13f, Bth, G, July 20)
Elanmatina (IRE) 52 (8f, Lei, G, June 1)
Elbio 90 (5f, Asc, F, June 19)
El Dominio 43 (10f, Lin, Fs, Jan 4)
Elegant Friend 46 (9f, Kem, G, Sep 5)
Elegant Touch 41 (10f, Bev, Y, July 3)
El Nido 53 (12f, Nwc, G, Apr 20)
El Prado (IRE) 67 (8f, Deau, Y, Aug 16)
Elsals 47 (7f, Chep, Y, Oct 20)
Elsurimo (GER) 81 (16f, Gwd, F, July 30)
El Volador 48 (7f, Lin, Fs, Jan 4)
El Yasat (IRE) 87 (5f, Asc, F, June 19)
Emir Albadou (USA) 40 (8f, Yrk, G, Sep 2)
Empire Blue 51 (16f, Gwd, F, May 20)
En Attendant (FR) 72 (8f, Yrk, Y, Oct 8)
Encore Une Fois (IRE) 52 (12f, Hay, F, Aug 7)
Endoli (USA) 50 (13f, Nby, F, May 16)
Environment Friend 68 (12f, Nmkt, F, Oct 1)
Equal Eloquence (USA) 70 (8f, Cur, Y, Sep 27)
Equity Card (IRE) 43 (16f, Red, Y, Oct 6)
Erins Colleen 58 (5f, Leo, G, May 20)
Ernestan 44 (7f, Wol, G, May 11)
Erris Express 40 (5f, Not, G, Aug 4)
Esprit Fort (USA) 47 (10f, Rip, Y, Aug 31)
Eternal Flame 45 (8f, Bth, F, Aug 11)
Euphonic (USA) 82 (8f, Lon, F, May 17)
Euroblake 57 (7f, Cat, F, July 2)
Euro Festival 61 (7f, San, G, July 15)
Eurotwist 44 (12f, Ham, S, Nov 3)
Everglades (IRE) 66 (6f, Don, G, Oct 24)
Exclusion 45 (8f, Nmkt, G, Apr 30)
Execution Only (IRE) 47 (10f, Ayr, F, June 19)
Exit To Nowhere (USA) 95 (8f, Deau, Y, Aug 16)
Explosive Speed (USA) 46 (11f, Edn, G, July 21)
Ezzoud (IRE) 74 (8f, Asc, F, June 16)

Fabulous Hostess (USA) 77 (10½f, StCl, G, Apr 25)
Fair Average 69 (10f, Nby, G, June 2)
Fair Cop (USA) 71 (7f, Asc, F, June 17)
Fair Crack (IRE) 66 (7f, Nmkt, F, Apr 15)
Fair Flyer (IRE) 43 (12f, Tsk, G, Aug 28)
Fairy Express (IRE) 65 (5f, Leo, G, May 20)
Fangio 62 (5f, Sal, F, June 9)
Farat (USA) 65 (15f, Ayr, F, July 20)
Farfelu 74 (5f, Nmkt, F, Sep 30)
Faribole (IRE) 70 (10f, Deau, S, Aug 8)
Farmer's Pet 55 (16f, Nmkt, F, Oct 2)
Farsi 69 (20f, Gwd, F, July 29)

Fascination Waltz 53 (6f, Gwd, G, Sep 12)
Fast Manouvre (FR) 70 (10f, Asc, F, July 24)
Father Hayes (USA) 51 (11f, San, F, June 13)
Faugeron 44 (14f, Gwd, F, July 31)
Favagello (IRE) 64 (12f, Lon, Y, Apr 5)
Fawz (IRE) 45 (8f, Lei, G, Oct 13)
Faydini (IRE) 42 (6f, Naas, F, June 13)
Fay's Song 54 (6f, Nmkt, F, July 31)
Feminine Wiles (IRE) 79 (10f, Nmkt, G, Oct 3)
Fen Dance (IRE) 42 (7f, Don, F, July 22)
Ferdia (IRE) 42 (8f, Swl, Fs, Jan 15)
Fermoy (USA) 45 (10f, Yar, F, Sep 17)
Fetish 59 (10½f, Hay, Y, May 2)
Fiala (IRE) 40 (14f, Swl, Fs, Jan 15)
Field of Honour 56 (8f, Kem, G, May 4)
Fieldridge 41 (10f, Bth, G, Sep 14)
Filicaia 41 (6f, Rip, F, July 6)
Finjan 67 (6f, Yrk, G, Aug 18)
Firefighter 41 (10½f, Hay, G, June 6)
Fire Top 88 (10f, Eps, G, June 3)
Firing Line (IRE) 75 (10f, Cur, Y, June 6)
First Bid 42 (12f, Don, G, Oct 24)
First Century (IRE) 47 (8f, Nmkt, G, June 19)
First Fling (IRE) 40 (10f, Ches, F, Aug 22)
First Victory 60 (16f, Nby, Y, July 17)
Fivesevenfiveo 66 (5f, Gwd, F, May 21)
Five To Seven (USA) 57 (13f, Ayr, S, Sep 18)
Flaming Arrow 68 (10f, Nby, G, June 2)
Flashfoot 73 (8f, Yrk, G, Apr 15)
Flashy's Son 45 (6f, Rip, F, Aug 15)
Fleuretta (USA) 68 (7f, Cur, G, Oct 20)
Flight Lieutenant (USA) 55 (11f, San, G, May 26)
Floating Line 49 (10f, Bev, G, July 13)
Flourishing (IRE) 43 (7f, Chep, F, May 25)
Flowing (USA) 83 (5f, Asc, F, June 19)
Flustered (USA) 64 (14f, Leo, Y, Sep 13)
Flute (USA) 58 (6f, Yrk, F, June 13)
Fly Away Soon (USA) 46 (10f, Kem, F, June 24)
Flying Brave 50 (8f, Nby, F, May 15)
Flying Speed (USA) 51 (10f, Bth, H, July 8)
Folia 57 (12f, Yrk, G, July 10)
Food of Love 59 (5f, San, F, June 12)
Foolish Eclipse (CAN) 61 (8f, Deau, G, Aug 1)
Foolish Touch 50 (8f, Nmkt, F, July 17)
Forelino (USA) 40 (10½f, Hay, G, June 5)
Forest Concert (IRE) 43 (8f, Cur, S, Sep 5)
Forest Fairy 44 (5f, Pon, F, Aug 5)
Forest Tiger (USA) 45 (7f, Nmkt, F, June 27)
Forever Diamonds 62 (8f, Yrk, Y, Oct 8)
For Mog (USA) 53 (16f, Nby, G, Aug 14)
For Reg (IRE) 54 (8f, San, G, Sep 16)
Fortune's Wheel (IRE) 87 (10½f, Lon, G, May 3)
Foursingh 47 (10f, Lin, Fs, Feb 18)
Fraam 50 (7f, Asc, Y, Sep 24)
Fragrant Hill 58 (10f, Gwd, F, Aug 1)
Freddie Lloyd (USA) 85 (5f, Yrk, F, Aug 20)
Free Flyer (IRE) 84 (10f, San, Y, July 4)
Free Mover (IRE) 44 (10f, San, G, May 26)
Frescobaldo (USA) 43 (11f, Swl, Slw, Jan 24)
Friendly Claim (IRE) 56 (6f, Swl, Slw, Feb 14)
Funny Baby (FR) 75 (9f, Lon, G, May 31)
Furiella 53 (6f, Cat, Y, June 5)
Further Flight 91 (16f, Gwd, F, July 30)
Fusion (USA) 40 (8f, Chep, F, May 25)
Fylde Flyer 68 (6f, Lin, F, May 30)

Gabbiadini 42 (7f, Edn, G, Oct 19)
Gaelic Myth (USA) 69 (12f, Leo, Y, Apr 18)
Gai Bulga 62 (10f, Gwd, F, May 19)
Galactic Miss 47 (8f, Lei, G, Oct 13)
Gallant Hope 44 (5f, Bth, F, Aug 6)
Ganges (USA) 78 (6½f, Deau, G, Aug 2)
Gant Bleu (FR) 45 (5f, Yrk, G, Sep 2)
Garabagh (IRE) 66 (10f, Leo, Y, May 9)
Garachico (USA) 41 (10f, Chep, G, July 16)
Garah 79 (5f, Nmkt, F, Sep 30)
Garden District 47 (14f, Gwd, F, July 31)
Garden of Heaven (USA) 75 (12f, Asc, S, Sep 24)
Garendare 71 (10½f, StCl, G, May 8)
Garth 47 (7f, Gwd, Y, Aug 29)
Gay Glint 64 (16f, Asc, F, July 24)
Gdansk's Honour (USA) 57 (7f, Leo, Y, Apr 18)
Gdansk Victory (USA) 54 (10f, Cur, Y, Oct 11)
Gentle Hero (USA) 51 (6f, Nmkt, G, Apr 30)
Ghalyoon (USA) 54 (5½f, Bth, S, May 9)
Ghurrah (IRE) 47 (8f, Gwd, Y, Aug 28)
Gilderdale 62 (10f, Lin, Fs, Nov 5)
Gilt Dimension 54 (7f, Cur, G, Oct 20)
Gipsy Fiddler 76 (5f, Hay, G, Aug 8)
Gizlaan (USA) 43 (8f, Edn, G, July 21)
Glaisdale (IRE) 51 (12f, Nmkt, G, Apr 14)
Glendower (IRE) 71 (7f, Cur, G, Oct 20)
Glenfield Greta 42 (7f, Wol, G, July 18)
Glide Path (USA) 53 (10f, San, G, Sep 15)
Gliding Beauty (IRE) 46 (5f, Leo, F, Aug 9)
Glity (USA) 77 (10½f, Lon, G, May 3)
Gloria Mundi 66 (10½f, StCl, G, Apr 25)
Glowing Devil 42 (11f, Ham, F, June 11)
Glowing Touch (IRE) 45 (6f, Leo, G, Aug 3)
Gods Express (IRE) 45 (5f, Leo, F, Aug 9)
Go Executive 58 (7f, Eps, G, June 3)
Golden Chip (IRE) 55 (8f, Yrk, G, July 11)
Golden Torque 47 (10f, Pon, F, July 7)
Goldsmiths' Hall 67 (12f, Nmkt, F, July 17)
Gondo 66 (5f, Don, G, Mar 20)
Gondolier 60 (20f, Gwd, F, July 31)
Gone Savage 76 (5f, Nby, S, Oct 22)
Gong 59 (10f, San, G, July 22)
Good For A Loan 43 (11½f, Bth, G, Sep 14)
Good Hand 60 (18½f, Ches, F, May 6)
Good Hand (USA) 67 (20f, Gwd, F, July 29)
Goodniteout (IRE) 54 (10f, San, G, July 22)
Good To Dance (IRE) 69 (10½f, Chan, F, June 14)
Goofalik (USA) 71 (8f, Mai, Y, July 7)
Googly 47 (10f, Sal, G, Aug 13)
Gorgeous Dancer (IRE) 60 (14f, Leo, Y, Sep 13)
Gorinsky (IRE) 62 (5f, Yrk, F, June 12)
Go South 47 (18½f, Ches, F, May 6)
Gotcha (BAR) 46 (10f, Sal, G, Aug 20)
Grade A Star (IRE) 45 (10f, Leo, F, June 1)
Grand Guignol 50 (7f, Swl, Slw, Feb 26)
Grand Hawk (USA) 61 (10f, Nmkt, G, Apr 14)
Grand Master (IRE) 55 (9f, San, Y, Aug 21)
Grand Princess (IRE) 54 (6f, Cur, G, Aug 15)
Grand Prix 47 (5f, Yrk, G, July 10)
Grand Vitesse (IRE) 57 (8f, Gwd, S, Oct 3)
Granny Mc 42 (6f, Pon, F, Aug 6)
Great Lord (IRE) 42 (8f, Don, G, Oct 23)
Great Marquess 47 (20f, Lon, S, Oct 3)
Great Max (IRE) 56 (12f, Eps, G, Sep 1)
Great Palm (USA) 83 (10f, Deau, S, Aug 15)
Greek Gold (IRE) 50 (10½f, Hay, G, June 5)
Greek Tycoon (IRE) 50 (11f, Nby, Y, Apr 10)
Green Dollar 78 (6f, Nmkt, G, Apr 30)

Green Glen (USA) 41 (10f, Cur, Y, Aug 30)
Green Lane (USA) 52 (14f, Sal, Y, Aug 13)
Green's Ferneley (IRE) 75 (8f, Gwd, Y, Aug 28)
Greenwich Bambi 41 (14f, Sal, Y, Aug 13)
Grey Power 46 (12f, Ham, S, Nov 3)
Grog (IRE) 41 (12f, Sal, F, Aug 12)
Gueca Solo 52 (10f, Chep, S, Aug 31)
Guilty Secret (IRE) 49 (12f, Yrk, F, Aug 19)
Gulf Palace (USA) 53 (12f, Don, G, Mar 19)
Gulf Sailor (IRE) 64 (10f, Asc, F, July 25)
Gunner's Daughter 49 (8f, War, F, Aug 31)
Gussy Marlowe 63 (8f, Nmkt, G, July 8)
Gymcrak Premiere 82 (8f, Asc, F, June 17)
Gymcrak Tycoon 44 (7f, Red, F, Aug 26)

Habeta (USA) 48 (8f, Rip, F, July 6)
Haitham 54 (20f, Gwd, F, July 29)
Hajaim (IRE) 66 (12f, Asc, F, July 25)
Half A Tick (USA) 76 (10f, Deau, S, Aug 16)
Halkopous 63 (10½f, Hay, Y, Sep 5)
Hamadryad (IRE) 51 (7f, Gwd, F, July 31)
Hamas (IRE) 86 (5f, Nmkt, F, Oct 17)
Hameem (IRE) 54 (7f, Kem, G, Sep 4)
Hand On Heart (IRE) 40 (7f, Car, G, Sep 8)
Happy Bliss (IRE) 44 (12f, Leo, G, Aug 3)
Happy Rover 51 (6f, Leo, G, Aug 3)
Happy Smile (IRE) 62 (9f, Leo, G, July 25)
Harcliff 41 (7f, Lin, Fs, Oct 1)
Hard To Figure 82 (6f, Gwd, G, Sep 12)
Harry's Coming 58 (6f, Not, F, June 22)
Harvest Girl (IRE) 69 (5f, Nmkt, F, Sep 30)
Hashar (IRE) 88 (10f, Eps, G, June 3)
Hateel 79 (16f, Asc, Y, Apr 29)
Hatoof (USA) 80 (8f, Nmkt, G, Apr 30)
Hatta's Mill 44 (10f, Gwd, F, May 19)
Hawaii Storm (FR) 52 (7f, Swl, Fs, July 17)
Hawait Al Barr 63 (16f, Nwc, F, June 27)
Hawa Layaam (IRE) 48 (7f, Cat, F, July 2)
Hazaaf (USA) 44 (12f, Pon, F, Aug 5)
Hazaam (USA) 80 (7f, Gwd, Y, Oct 2)
Hazm (USA) 71 (6f, Hay, G, Sep 26)
Heart of Darkness 79 (7f, War, S, Oct 5)
Heather Bank 73 (6f, Gwd, Y, Aug 29)
Heaven-Liegh-Grey 59 (5f, Yrk, F, June 12)
Hebridean 43 (13f, Nby, F, May 16)
Helawe 44 (7f, Lin, Fs, Apr 4)
Helios 62 (7f, Eps, F, July 29)
Hemsworth Lad (IRE) 40 (5f, Cat, F, May 21)
Hereafter (USA) 61 (12f, Cur, Y, Oct 11)
Here Comes A Star 58 (5f, Nmkt, F, Oct 1)
Her Honour 56 (12f, Nmkt, G, Oct 30)
Herora (IRE) 51 (7f, War, S, Oct 5)
He's A Flyer 44 (5f, Cur, G, June 6)
Hester Stanhope 46 (10f, Sal, F, May 22)
Hidden Laughter (USA) 42 (10f, Nmkt, F, Oct 15)
Hidden Light (IRE) 53 (12f, Nmkt, G, Apr 14)
Hideyoshi (USA) 43 (16f, Eps, G, July 1)
Hierarch (USA) 46 (10f, Asc, F, July 24)
High Beacon 44 (16f, Nby, Y, July 17)
Highbrook (USA) 62 (10f, Ayr, Y, Sep 18)
Highest Ody (FR) 83 (8f, Lon, G, May 10)
Highflying 52 (14f, Hay, G, June 6)
Highland Dress 54 (10f, Nby, S, Oct 22)
Highland Fantasy (USA) 47 (16f, Nmkt, F, Oct 2)
Highland Magic (IRE) 68 (7f, Don, G, Nov 6)
High Low (USA) 71 (8f, Asc, F, June 17)
High Premium 51 (8f, Tsk, G, May 2)
High Principles 41 (6f, Ham, H, July 23)
High Sevens 54 (7f, Gwd, F, July 30)

Hinari Video 46 (5f, Lin, Fs, Mar 3)
Hi-Tech Honda (IRE) 49 (5f, Don, F, June 27)
Hit The Fan 45 (14f, Hay, Y, Sep 4)
Hob Green 49 (7f, Nmkt, F, Oct 15)
Holetown 43 (5f, Eps, G, Sep 1)
Holiday Island 53 (10f, Bev, G, Aug 13)
Holy Zeal 44 (14f, Yrk, F, Aug 19)
Home Counties (IRE) 54 (10f, Cur, Y, June 6)
Homme de Loi (IRE) 73 (9f, Lon, Y, Apr 16)
Honey Heather (IRE) 42 (6f, Ayr, G, July 25)
Honorary Prince (IRE) 43 (5f, Leo, G, May 20)
Horizon (IRE) 44 (12f, Swl, Slw, Mar 6)
Host (IRE) 63 (9f, Nby, S, Oct 24)
Hot Lavender (CAN) 56 (5f, San, Y, July 3)
Houlston's Will 40 (8f, Not, G, Aug 24)
How's Yer Father 74 (6f, Ayr, Y, Sep 19)
Hydro Calido (USA) 87 (8f, Deau, G, Aug 1)

Ideal Candidate 49 (16f, Gwd, G, Sep 12)
Idefix (USA) 74 (6½f, Evry, S, Jan 27)
Idoni 40 (10f, Eps, G, June 4)
Iftakhaar (USA) 52 (12f, Pon, G, Oct 22)
Ikteshaf 58 (7f, Ayr, S, Sep 17)
Ile de Chypre 86 (9f, Yrk, F, Apr 19)
Imco Double (IRE) 41 (5f, Swl, Fs, Aug 14)
I'm Electric 47 (11f, San, G, Sep 16)
Imperial Ballet (IRE) 57 (10f, Wind, G, July 13)
Imperial Bid 59 (7f, Hay, F, Aug 7)
Imperial Bri 59 (7f, Hay, F, Aug 7)
Inchcailloch (IRE) 67 (12f, Nby, F, June 11)
Incola 53 (12f, Eps, G, Sep 1)
Indian Quest 44 (14f, Not, G, Oct 19)
Indian Slave (IRE) 47 (8f, Don, G, Sep 12)
Ingenuity 42 (6f, Red, G, Oct 14)
Inherent Magic (IRE) 66 (5f, Nmkt, G, Aug 29)
Inner City (IRE) 85 (8f, Nmkt, F, Oct 2)
In The Money (IRE) 49 (12f, Tsk, G, Aug 28)
In The Picture (IRE) 53 (11f, San, G, May 26)
Invigilate 46 (5f, Car, H, June 25)
Invocation 54 (6f, Lin, G, May 9)
Ionian Sea 68 (12f, Lon, G, Sep 13)
I Perceive 54 (10f, Don, G, Mar 20)
Irek 48 (8f, Nmkt, F, July 18)
Irish Memory 78 (7f, Cur, Hvy, Apr 25)
Irish Shoal (USA) 65 (5f, Chan, F, June 4)
Iron Baron (IRE) 43 (14f, Not, S, Oct 29)
Iron King 59 (5f, Bri, F, May 7)
Isaiah 63 (6f, Lin, S, Oct 26)
Isdar (USA) 57 (5f, Hay, G, Sep 25)
Island Heather (IRE) 42 (6f, Leo, F, June 10)
Itqan (IRE) 61 (15f, Ayr, F, July 20)
Ivana (IRE) 53 (7f, Nmkt, G, Apr 30)
Ivor's Flutter 52 (12f, Asc, G, Oct 9)
Iywaan (IRE) 59 (12f, Nmkt, G, Apr 14)

Jack Button (IRE) 48 (16f, Nmkt, F, Oct 2)
Jackson Flint 40 (16f, Nmkt, G, Apr 30)
Jade Vale 58 (8f, Lei, G, Sep 8)
Jaffa Line 58 (10f, San, G, Apr 25)
Jahafil 68 (12f, Nmkt, F, June 27)
Jahangir (IRE) 72 (8f, Gwd, Y, Aug 28)
Jaldi (IRE) 51 (7f, Nmkt, F, June 26)
Jalmusique 78 (7f, Nwc, F, May 29)
Jamshid (JPN) 56 (15f, Lon, S, Oct 3)
Janaat 44 (12f, Sal, G, Aug 20)
Jape (USA) 66 (7f, San, G, Apr 25)
Jazilah (FR) 54 (10f, Bev, G, July 13)
Jdaayel 68 (8f, Nmkt, G, Oct 31)
Jefferson Davis (IRE) 48 (7f, Lin, Fs, Jan 18)

Jess Rebec 49 (5f, War, G, July 10)
Jeune 67 (12f, Asc, F, June 16)
Jezebel Monroe (USA) 56 (10f, Nby, F, June 11)
Jigsaw Boy 70 (5f, Lei, S, Oct 26)
Jimlil 53 (8f, San, G, May 5)
Jitterbugging 48 (8f, San, G, Apr 24)
Joe Sugden 47 (5f, Wind, F, Aug 1)
Johann Quatz (FR) 78 (12f, Chan, G, June 7)
John Rose 57 (8f, Nmkt, F, Oct 2)
Jokist 49 (7f, Lin, F, May 23)
Jolypha (USA) 86 (12f, Lon, G, Sep 13)
Jornel Amou (USA) 42 (14f, Leo, Y, Sep 13)
Jood (USA) 53 (10f, San, G, Apr 24)
Jovial Kate (USA) 41 (6f, Swl, Fs, July 29)
Joy of Glory (USA) 40 (9f, Evry, F, July 25)
J P Morgan 40 (13f, Ayr, S, Sep 19)
Jubran (USA) 53 (9f, Rip, F, Aug 3)
Judge And Jury 44 (14f, Not, S, Oct 29)
Judgement Call 49 (6f, Kem, F, May 23)
Jumaira Shark (CAN) 68 (10f, Don, F, Sep 9)
Jumaira Star (USA) 42 (7f, Kem, G, Sep 4)
Jungle Dancer (IRE) 66 (16f, Asc, F, Sep 24)
Juniper Berry (IRE) 56 (8f, Gwd, G, July 28)
Jupiter Moon 50 (12f, Nby, F, June 11)
Jura 66 (10f, Gwd, F, May 19)
Jurran 41 (8f, Nmkt, F, May 16)
Just A Mirage 47 (8f, Asc, Y, Apr 29)
Just A Step 50 (7f, Nwc, Hvy, Apr 18)

Kabayil 43 (11f, San, G, Sep 16)
Kadari 43 (10f, Nwc, G, Apr 18)
Kadi (GER) 47 (10f, Cur, Y, Aug 30)
Kaisar (GER) 43 (10f, Nwc, Y, Apr 18)
Kalita Melody 68 (8f, Mai, Y, July 7)
Kansk 70 (12f, Asc, F, June 17)
Kanvass 52 (12f, Rip, F, Aug 3)
Karamoja 48 (8f, Lei, G, June 1)
Karen Louise 46 (7f, Lei, F, July 28)
Karinga Bay 56 (10f, Asc, F, June 16)
Kasikci 47 (10f, Leo, G, Oct 24)
Kasmayo 65 (10f, Asc, F, July 24)
Katakana (USA) 53 (8f, Asc, F, June 17)
Kateb (IRE) 43 (7f, Bev, F, June 10)
Katie-A (IRE) 43 (5f, Car, G, Sep 8)
Katy's Lad 49 (11f, War, Y, Apr 20)
Kausar (USA) 43 (12f, Nwc, Hvy, Nov 2)
Kayfa (IRE) 57 (8f, Leo, Y, Oct 26)
Kayvee 70 (6f, Sal, F, June 24)
Keen Hunter (USA) 85 (5f, Lon, Y, Oct 25)
Keep Your Word 48 (8f, Gwd, Y, Sep 11)
Kenbu (FR) 77 (8f, Nmkt, G, Apr 30)
Ken de Saron (USA) 55 (10½f, StCl, S, Oct 31)
Kentucky Coffee (FR) 66 (6f, Mai, G, Sep 17)
Kenyatta (USA) 42 (11f, Edn, G, July 21)
Key Suspect (USA) 47 (7f, Chep, Y, Oct 20)
Khanata (USA) 72 (10f, Cur, F, June 27)
Khazari (USA) 48 (10f, Leo, G, May 20)
Khizarabad (IRE) 63 (8f, Cur, S, Sep 5)
Khrisma 43 (10f, Don, F, May 25)
Killy 52 (7f, Don, G, Nov 6)
Kimberley Park 68 (7f, Lin, F, May 30)
Kimbers (IRE) 59 (16f, Asc, Y, Apr 29)
Kinematic (USA) 74 (10f, Nmkt, F, Aug 8)
King Al 61 (7f, Nwc, G, Aug 29)
Kinglow (USA) 56 (12f, Yrk, G, July 10)
King of Chance (USA) 55 (7f, Nmkt, G, Apr 15)
King Olaf (IRE) 57 (7f, Nmkt, G, May 15)
King's Guest (IRE) 40 (9f, Red, Y, Oct 6)
King's Loch (IRE) 68 (12f, Gwd, Y, Oct 2)
King's Signet (USA) 73 (6f, Yar, G, Sep 15)

Kinoko 50 (12f, Tsk, F, Sep 5)
Kirsten 41 (12f, Cat, Y, June 6)
Kissavos 46 (7f, Chep, S, Aug 31)
Kitwood (USA) 69 (9f, Lon, Y, Apr 16)
Kiveton Kabooz 75 (14½f, Don, G, Oct 23)
Kiveton Tycoon (IRE) 41 (8f, Don, F, May 23)
Knifebox (USA) 92 (10f, Mai, G, Sep 21)
Knight of Mercy 82 (7f, Nmkt, G, Aug 1)
Knock Knock 69 (10f, Asc, F, July 25)
Knock To Enter (USA) 64 (8f, Nwc, F, Aug 29)
Kooyonga (IRE) 99 (10f, San, Y, July 4)
Kristianstad 67 (8f, Nby, F, June 23)

La Bamba 64 (7f, Don, G, Nov 6)
La Belle Vie 46 (7f, Chep, H, June 11)
Laburnum 68 (12f, Kem, G, Sep 5)
La Dama Bonita (USA) 51 (7f, Lin, F, June 27)
Lady Debra Darley 63 (8f, Lei, G, Oct 13)
Lady of Persia (USA) 62 (10½f, StCl, G, Apr 25)
Lady Sabo 55 (5f, San, Y, July 3)
Lahib (USA) 97 (8f, Asc, Y, Sep 26)
Lahoob (USA) 43 (9f, Yrk, Y, Oct 10)
La Kermesse (USA) 41 (7f, Cat, F, July 1)
Lambada (USA) 44 (9f, Lon, G, May 3)
Lamore Ritorna 41 (8f, Asc, Y, Apr 29)
Landowner (IRE) 72 (16f, Gwd, F, July 30)
Langtonian 53 (5f, Ayr, F, Aug 8)
Langtry Lady 55 (7½f, Ches, F, May 5)
Languedoc 46 (6f, Hay, G, Sep 25)
Lap of Luxury 73 (8f, Nby, G, Sep 19)
Lara's Baby (IRE) 45 (11f, Swl, Slw, Jan 24)
Larnaca 50 (10f, Leo, G, Oct 24)
Larrikin (USA) 40 (10f, Yrk, G, Sep 2)
Last Drama (IRE) 52 (10f, Lon, Y, Oct 18)
Last Embrace (IRE) 59 (10f, Pon, F, July 24)
Latour 52 (10f, Nmkt, G, Apr 14)
Latvian 64 (12f, Nwc, F, June 26)
Laughsome 42 (10f, San, F, June 12)
Laundry Maid 68 (7f, Nby, G, Aug 15)
Laurel Queen (IRE) 51 (7f, Nwc, G, Aug 29)
Lavinia Fontana (IRE) 64 (7f, Naas, G, Oct 17)
Lawnswood Junior 50 (8f, Edn, Y, Nov 5)
Layaali (USA) 42 (8f, Leo, Y, Apr 18)
Lead The Dance 67 (8f, Yrk, G, July 10)
Leap In The Dark (IRE) 45 (8f, Don, G, Oct 23)
Leariva (USA) 67 (8f, StCl, S, Nov 8)
Leave It To Lib 49 (7f, Cat, F, July 16)
Lech 69 (9f, Yrk, G, Sep 3)
Le Corsaire (USA) 70 (16f, Gwd, F, July 30)
Lee Artiste 49 (6f, Tsk, F, May 15)
Legal Adviser 41 (12f, Leo, Y, Apr 18)
Legal View (USA) 45 (9f, Yrk, F, June 13)
Leif The Lucky (USA) 41 (8f, Gwd, Y, Sep 11)
Ler Cru (IRE) 41 (7f, Bri, F, Sep 29)
Le Temeraire 40 (13f, Lin, Fs, Mar 21)
Let It Ride (IRE) 46 (10f, Leo, Y, Sep 13)
Letsbeonstaboutit 53 (6f, Kem, G, July 8)
Let's Get Lost 40 (10f, Eps, G, July 1)
Level Up 40 (7f, Lin, Fs, Jan 21)
L'Hermine 41 (8f, Wind, F, Aug 10)
Liability Order 50 (10f, Don, F, July 26)
Libk 83 (12f, Don, F, Sep 11)
Lifetime Fame 43 (6f, Hay, F, May 23)
Lifewatch Vision 57 (10f, San, G, July 3)
Liffey River (USA) 47 (5f, Pon, G, Oct 22)
Lift And Load (USA) 62 (12f, Asc, Y, Sep 26)
Light Hand 62 (10½f, Ham, Y, Sep 5)
Lincstone Boy (IRE) 57 (5f, Rip, G, Sep 1)
Line Drummer (USA) 57 (18½f, Ches, F, May 6)

Linnga (IRE) 71 (12f, Lon, G, Sep 13)
Linpac West 76 (12f, Yrk, G, May 12)
Lion Cavern (USA) 91 (8f, Lon, G, May 9)
Little Bean 72 (7f, Asc, Y, Sep 26)
Littledale (USA) 44 (10f, Lin, Fs, Jan 21)
Little Rousillon 56 (8f, Nmkt, F, July 17)
Little Saboteur 55 (5f, Flk, F, Sep 10)
Lobilio (USA) 64 (10f, Asc, F, July 24)
Lobinda 47 (12f, Sal, F, June 9)
Lochsong 82 (5½f, Don, G, Sep 9)
Loft Boy 43 (5f, Nwc, G, Sep 29)
Loki (IRE) 59 (10f, Nmkt, F, Oct 15)
Lookingforarainbow (IRE) 41 (14f, Not, G, May 29)
Lord Chickney (USA) 58 (7f, Ayr, Y, Sep 24)
Lord Hastie (USA) 50 (12f, Rip, F, May 27)
Lord High Admiral (CAN) 63 (6f, Nmkt, G, Apr 30)
Lord Noble (IRE) 77 (16f, Cur, G, Oct 10)
Lord Oberon (IRE) 53 (8f, Wol, G, July 18)
Lord Vivienne (IRE) 62 (7f, Nmkt, G, Aug 28)
Lost Reputation (IRE) 45 (10f, Ches, F, Aug 22)
Lots of Luck 47 (10f, Bev, F, July 28)
Louisville Belle (IRE) 47 (7f, Nby, G, Aug 15)
Louve Romaine (USA) 55 (10½f, StCl, G, Apr 25)
Lovealoch (IRE) 73 (8f, San, G, Apr 24)
Love Jazz (USA) 63 (6f, Ayr, Y, Sep 19)
Love Legend 61 (5f, Yrk, F, May 13)
Love Returned 60 (5f, Gwd, G, Oct 2)
Lucedeo 72 (5f, Yrk, F, June 12)
Luchiroverte (IRE) 78 (12f, Asc, F, June 19)
Lucknam Dreamer 63 (7½f, Lin, F, May 30)
Lucky Guest 81 (10f, Don, F, June 26)
Lucky Lindy (IRE) 79 (5f, Nmkt, G, May 2)
Lucky Noire 49 (8f, Nwc, Hvy, Nov 2)
Lucy Dancer (IRE) 48 (5f, Gwd, F, June 26)
Luna Bid 46 (6f, Rip, S, Apr 16)
L'Uomo Classics 54 (12f, Sal, Y, Sep 30)
Lute And Lyre (IRE) 67 (5f, Cur, Y, Aug 22)
Luthier Enchanteur (USA) 71 (8f, StCl, G, Apr 21)
Lyphantastic (USA) 50 (12f, Sal, F, June 24)

Maamur (USA) 51 (12f, Asc, G, Oct 9)
Ma Bella Luna 44 (8f, Kem, F, Aug 5)
Macfarlane 52 (5f, San, G, Apr 24)
Mack The Knife 67 (12f, Nby, S, Oct 24)
Macrobian 79 (5f, Yrk, F, May 13)
Madagans Grey 54 (10f, Nmkt, F, Aug 8)
Mad Militant (IRE) 53 (10½f, Hay, G, June 6)
Maestroso (IRE) 50 (12f, Pon, F, July 24)
Maggie Siddons 65 (6f, Lin, G, May 9)
Magic Carr (USA) 48 (8f, Cur, G, July 11)
Magic Night (IRE) 89 (12f, StCl, G, July 14)
Magic Secret 45 (12f, Ham, G, Aug 17)
Magnified (USA) 61 (8f, Yrk, F, Aug 20)
Mahasin (USA) 67 (8f, Kem, G, May 23)
Mahfil 49 (12f, Eps, G, July 1)
Mahool (USA) 42 (10½f, Hay, Y, May 2)
Mahsul (IRE) 49 (10f, Nmkt, F, Aug 8)
Maid Welcome 41 (5f, Swl, Slw, Feb 12)
Main Bid (IRE) 41 (8f, Nmkt, F, June 27)
Majal (IRE) 43 (8f, Hay, G, Aug 8)
Majboor (IRE) 46 (8f, War, G, Apr 21)
Majed (IRE) 53 (10f, Nmkt, F, Oct 15)
Major Bugler (IRE) 43 (10f, Asc, S, Sep 25)
Major Mouse 43 (8f, Don, F, May 23)
Major's Law (IRE) 42 (11f, Yar, F, Sep 16)

Malama (IRE) 45 (12f, Cur, G, July 11)
Maledetto (IRE) 70 (5f, Leo, F, June 1)
Malunar 51 (7f, Don, F, May 23)
Malvernico (IRE) 76 (10f, Don, G, Aug 9)
Mamdooh 61 (10f, Nmkt, F, Aug 29)
Mamma's Too 62 (8f, Don, G, Sep 12)
Man From Eldorado (USA) 48 (8f, Don, Y, Mar 21)
Mango Manila 73 (7f, Nmkt, G, Apr 15)
Manuleader 41 (6f, Tsk, F, Aug 10)
Marabella Star (USA) 57 (7f, Nmkt, G, Apr 14)
Maramouresh (IRE) 43 (10f, Cur, F, May 23)
Maratha (USA) 69 (6f, Evry, F, June 18)
Marble Maiden 83 (8f, Deau, G, Aug 1)
Marchman 44 (12f, Sal, F, June 25)
Marcus Thorpe (USA) 68 (12f, Nwc, F, Aug 29)
Maria Cappuccini 48 (5f, Lin, F, July 18)
Marignan (USA) 80 (12f, Chan, G, June 7)
Marine Diver 56 (8f, Don, G, Sep 12)
Market Booster (USA) 82 (12f, Lon, G, Sep 13)
Marling (IRE) 86 (8f, Gwd, F, July 29)
Martina 55 (5f, Nmkt, F, May 16)
Martini Executive 60 (8f, Lin, Fs, Jan 25)
Martinosky 53 (5f, Gwd, F, Aug 1)
Masad (IRE) 81 (10f, Yrk, G, Aug 18)
Mashaallah (USA) 96 (14f, Cur, Y, Sep 19)
Mashakel (USA) 44 (10f, Nmkt, F, May 10)
Masnun (USA) 66 (5f, San, G, July 15)
Massiba (IRE) 69 (6f, Hay, G, July 3)
Masskana (IRE) 51 (8f, StCl, G, July 17)
Master Copy (IRE) 49 (10f, Ayr, Y, Aug 20)
Master Foodbroker (IRE) 63 (20f, Gwd, F, July 29)
Master of Passion 71 (5f, Gwd, F, July 29)
Master Planner 81 (6f, Yrk, G, Aug 18)
Master Swordsman (USA) 49 (16f, Leo, F, Oct 26)
Matador (USA) 77 (12f, Asc, F, June 17)
Mawara (IRE) 58 (10f, Leo, G, Aug 8)
Mayaasa (USA) 48 (10f, Bri, F, Sep 29)
Mbulwa 44 (10f, Rip, G, Aug 22)
McA Below The Line 47 (7f, Swl, Fs, Jan 29)
Medaille d'Or 82 (5f, San, Y, July 4)
Meeson Times 40 (5f, Lin, Fs, Jan 25)
Mellaby (USA) 73 (12f, Asc, F, June 19)
Mellottie 90 (8f, Don, G, Sep 12)
Melpomene 71 (8f, San, Y, Aug 21)
Mel's Rose 50 (7f, Nmkt, G, June 19)
Memsahb 67 (5f, Bev, G, July 4)
Mendocino (USA) 70 (10f, StCl, G, July 14)
Merlins Wish (USA) 58 (7f, Kem, Y, Sep 22)
Merryhild Maid (IRE) 54 (6f, Nmkt, G, Apr 30)
Merseyside Man 46 (10f, Lin, Fs, Feb 18)
Merton Mill 47 (16f, Red, Y, Oct 6)
Mesleh 73 (10f, Nby, G, Aug 14)
Metal Boys 64 (5f, Pon, G, July 7)
Metal Storm (FR) 76 (8f, Mai, Y, July 7)
Michel Georges 56 (10f, Lon, Y, Apr 5)
Michelozzo (USA) 78 (15f, Deau, S, Aug 23)
Midnight Air (USA) 68 (10f, Nwc, G, Aug 31)
Milagro 66 (6f, Gwd, F, May 20)
Milanese 41 (10f, Lei, F, May 10)
Milieu 69 (7f, Naas, Y, May 2)
Military Fashion 78 (9f, Yrk, F, Aug 19)
Millfit (USA) 40 (7f, Wol, G, Apr 27)
Millie's Choice (IRE) 77 (8f, Leo, G, Aug 8)
Million In Mind (IRE) 45 (12f, Nby, G, Aug 14)
Millsolin (IRE) 56 (7f, Wol, G, Sep 3)
Milzig (USA) 58 (10f, Asc, S, Sep 25)

Mimique 49 (12f, Don, G, Oct 24)
Mingus (USA) 55 (10f, Don, F, Sep 9)
Mining Tycoon (IRE) 74 (10f, Leo, G, Oct 24)
Mirana (IRE) 47 (10f, Cur, G, June 3)
Misako Togo (USA) 57 (10f, Cur, Y, Oct 11)
Misdemeanours Girl (IRE) 57 (5f, San, Y, Aug 21)
Misil (USA) 72 (8f, Lon, G, Sep 6)
Miss Bluebird (IRE) 50 (6f, Lin, F, July 11)
Miss Doody 47 (7f, Wol, G, Apr 27)
Miss Haggis 48 (7f, Nmkt, F, July 7)
Miss Movie World 46 (5f, Nmkt, F, Oct 1)
Miss Nosey Parker (IRE) 72 (5f, Nmkt, F, Sep 30)
Miss Pin Up 42 (12f, Kem, F, Aug 5)
Miss Vaxette 58 (5f, Bri, G, Sep 23)
Misterioso 46 (8f, Kem, G, May 23)
Mister Jolson 44 (5f, Gwd, G, Oct 2)
Misty Goddess (IRE) 43 (10f, Sal, G, Aug 13)
Misunderstanding (IRE) 56 (7f, Nwc, Hvy, Apr 18)
Mizaaya 70 (7f, Ches, F, May 7)
Miznah (IRE) 68 (7f, Cur, S, Sep 19)
Mizyan (IRE) 41 (12f, Swl, Fs, July 15)
Modernise (USA) 75 (9f, Yrk, G, May 12)
Modest Hope (USA) 42 (10f, Pon, G, Oct 22)
Modesto (USA) 47 (10f, Lin, Fs, Feb 4)
Modhish (IRE) 74 (12f, Chan, G, June 7)
Mogwai (IRE) 48 (7f, Kem, G, Sep 4)
Mohican Girl 66 (10f, Gwd, F, Aug 1)
Mojave 57 (7f, Nby, G, Aug 14)
Monarda 56 (12f, Lin, Fs, June 20)
Monde Bleu 90 (6f, Mai, G, Sep 17)
Monte Bre 44 (7f, Bri, F, July 2)
Montello 59 (15f, Lon, Y, July 12)
Montendre 73 (6f, Don, G, Nov 7)
Montpelier Boy 71 (9f, Nmkt, G, Oct 3)
Moonlight Quest 51 (10f, Nmkt, G, Apr 14)
Moon Spin 45 (10f, Sal, G, Aug 13)
Morgannwg (IRE) 53 (6f, Chep, F, May 25)
Morocco (IRE) 58 (7f, Kem, G, Sep 4)
Morsun 57 (8f, Don, G, Oct 23)
Mossy Rave 44 (7f, Lin, F, Aug 9)
Mot de France (FR) 75 (6f, Mai, G, Sep 17)
Mougins (IRE) 58 (7½f, Lin, F, May 30)
Moving Out 45 (15f, War, F, July 25)
Mr Brooks 96 (5f, Yrk, F, Aug 20)
Mr Confusion (IRE) 68 (10½f, Hay, Y, Sep 5)
Mr Flood (USA) 56 (8f, Nmkt, G, Apr 30)
Mrs Barton (IRE) 46 (14f, Not, Y, Sep 22)
Mrs Fisher (IRE) 56 (7f, Gwd, G, July 28)
Much Sought After 46 (12f, Yrk, Y, Oct 8)
Mudaffar (IRE) 75 (8f, San, Y, July 4)
Muhayaa (USA) 55 (10f, Nby, G, Aug 14)
Muhit (USA) 51 (7f, Eps, G, June 6)
Muhtarram (USA) 76 (12f, Eps, G, June 3)
Mukaddamah (USA) 64 (8f, Kem, G, Sep 4)
Mull House 53 (15f, Nmkt, G, Aug 28)
Murray's Mazda (IRE) 47 (5f, Ayr, F, June 20)
Muse 42 (16f, Asc, S, Sep 24)
Musicale (USA) 68 (7f, Nby, Y, Apr 10)
Music Dancer 48 (6f, Hay, G, Sep 25)
Mustahil (IRE) 45 (8f, Bth, G, July 20)
Mutabahi (CAN) 59 (8f, Asc, F, June 19)
Myfontaine 53 (10f, Nmkt, G, Apr 14)
My Memoirs 62 (10f, Ches, F, May 7)
My Sovereign (USA) 48 (5f, Red, G, July 7)
Mystery Lad (IRE) 43 (11f, Yar, F, July 23)
Mystery Play (IRE) 67 (10f, Nmkt, G, Oct 3)
Mystiko (USA) 49 (8f, Nby, F, May 15)

Nadjati (USA) 49 (12f, Leo, F, June 10)

Nagida 61 (6f, Nmkt, F, Oct 2)
Nashville Blues (IRE) 70 (8f, Asc, F, June 20)
Nassau 72 (10f, Cur, Y, Sep 5)
Native Idol (USA) 56 (7f, Nmkt, G, June 19)
Ned's Bonanza 56 (5f, Don, F, June 27)
Neieb (USA) 40 (14f, Not, G, Oct 19)
Nellie Dean 41 (7f, Cat, G, Oct 16)
Nemir 42 (14f, Not, G, Oct 19)
Neptune's Pet 60 (8f, Bth, H, July 8)
Never A Care (USA) 59 (8f, Asc, Y, Apr 29)
Never In The Red 77 (5f, Eps, Y, Aug 31)
Never So Sure 82 (6f, Yrk, G, Sep 2)
Newton Point 42 (12f, Nby, G, June 2)
Nicely Thanks (USA) 44 (7f, Bev, G, Mar 28)
Nifty Fifty (IRE) 47 (7f, Red, G, Sep 25)
Night Asset 42 (6f, Eps, G, June 6)
Night Clubbing (IRE) 46 (6f, Leo, Y, May 9)
Night Jar 62 (7f, Hay, Y, May 2)
Night Manoeuvres 75 (8f, Kem, G, Sep 4)
Nijmegen 44 (16f, Asc, G, Oct 9)
Nile Delta (IRE) 50 (8f, Red, F, Aug 7)
Ninja Dancer (USA) 43 (10f, Gwd, F, May 19)
Niodini (USA) 62 (12f, Hay, G, July 4)
Nobby Barnes 42 (7f, Yar, F, Aug 19)
Noble Pet 66 (8f, Yrk, F, Aug 20)
Noble Power (IRE) 56 (5f, Kem, F, Aug 5)
Noble Vienna (USA) 42 (10f, Ches, F, June 24)
Non Partisan (USA) 77 (10f, StCl, G, July 14)
No Quarter Given 64 (5f, Wol, S, Apr 6)
Nordic Brave 63 (7f, Nwc, F, June 27)
Nordic Brief (IRE) 69 (5f, Cur, Y, June 6)
Nordic Display (IRE) 48 (10f, Cur, Y, Sep 5)
Nordic Oak (IRE) 73 (5f, Cur, Y, Aug 22)
Nordic Pageant (IRE) 67 (7f, Naas, G, Oct 17)
Nordic Soprano (IRE) 47 (10f, Cur, G, May 16)
Norfolkiev (FR) 42 (7f, Lin, Fs, July 11)
Northern Bluebird (IRE) 50 (5f, Leo, Y, Mar 14)
Northern Crystal 80 (8f, StCl, S, Nov 8)
Northern Graduate (USA) 48 (10f, Nwc, F, Aug 29)
Northern Park (USA) 61 (12½f, StCl, Y, Oct 5)
Northern Rainbow 71 (8f, Nmkt, G, June 19)
Northern Spark 41 (6f, Hay, G, June 5)
Northern Sprite 53 (10½f, Lon, Y, Apr 5)
North Esk 40 (10f, Pon, F, July 24)
North of Watford 44 (5f, Lei, F, July 6)
North Russia (CAN) 49 (10f, Chep, G, July 16)
Norton Challenger 80 (8f, Yrk, G, July 10)
Norwich 83 (5f, Cur, S, Sep 19)
No Submission (USA) 56 (10f, Kem, G, Apr 20)
Notley 75 (5f, Don, G, Sep 9)
Nuclear Express 40 (5f, Wol, Y, July 13)

Olanthe (USA) 63 (10f, Lon, F, June 28)
Oleari 41 (10f, Leo, G, July 18)
Olette 60 (8f, Asc, G, Oct 9)
Olifantsfontein 73 (5f, Kem, G, Apr 20)
Onesixnine (IRE) 76 (10f, Cur, G, Oct 10)
Only Royale (IRE) 65 (10f, Nby, Y, July 17)
On The Edge 59 (5f, Don, F, Sep 11)
On Tiptoes 65 (5f, Yrk, F, May 13)
On Y Va (USA) 46 (8f, Wol, S, Mar 26)
Open Market (USA) 55 (11f, Naas, G, June 13)

Opera Ghost 74 (12f, Nby, G, July 18)
Opera House 99 (10f, San, Y, July 4)
Optical (IRE) 56 (5f, San, F, June 13)
Orient Air 44 (6f, Swl, Slw, Feb 21)
Ormsby (IRE) 50 (12f, Cur, F, June 28)
Orthorhombus 75 (6f, Yrk, F, June 19)
Oumaldaaya (USA) 68 (10½f, Chan, F, June 14)
Our Aisling 42 (18½f, Ches, F, May 6)
Our Occasion 50 (7f, Nby, G, Aug 15)
Our Rita 47 (6f, Nwc, Hvy, Nov 2)
Overpower 50 (10½f, Hay, G, July 4)
Owner's Dream (USA) 57 (7f, Yrk, F, June 12)

Pabouche (USA) 48 (10f, Asc, Y, Apr 29)
Paddy Chalk 76 (5f, Gwd, F, Aug 1)
Pageboy 64 (5f, Nmkt, F, July 7)
Paix Blanche (FR) 70 (10½f, StCl, G, May 8)
Palacegate King 46 (7f, Swl, Fs, Jan 17)
Palacegate Racing 50 (5f, Swl, Fs, June 5)
Paley Prince (USA) 62 (9f, Pon, F, Aug 5)
Pallium (IRE) 57 (5f, Bev, F, Sep 16)
Palomelle (FR) 76 (12f, Lon, G, Sep 13)
Panikin 74 (5f, Don, G, Mar 20)
Paper Dance 40 (13f, Bth, G, July 20)
Paris House 84 (5f, Hay, S, Apr 18)
Park Dream (IRE) 75 (6f, Leo, G, Aug 8)
Parking Bay 43 (10f, Nmkt, F, Oct 15)
Parliament Piece 73 (8f, Don, G, Sep 12)
Parting Moment (USA) 70 (16f, Asc, Y, Apr 29)
Party Cited (USA) 69 (10f, Gwd, F, July 31)
Passing Sale (FR) 78 (10½f, Lon, Y, May 3)
Pater Noster (USA) 51 (7f, Asc, F, June 17)
Pay Homage 71 (8f, San, G, May 25)
Pearl Angel 47 (8f, Nmkt, G, Apr 30)
Peerage Prince 43 (5f, Not, G, Oct 19)
Pelargonia 47 (8f, Wind, G, July 20)
Pelorus 51 (10f, Gwd, F, Aug 1)
Pendor Dancer 44 (5f, Chep, F, May 25)
Pennine Music (IRE) 51 (8f, Leo, Y, Mar 17)
Pennine Star (IRE) 42 (12f, Lei, G, Oct 12)
Penny Drops 58 (7f, Nby, S, Oct 22)
Penny Hasset 64 (5f, Ham, F, July 30)
Percy's Girl (IRE) 64 (12f, Yrk, F, Aug 20)
Perfect Circle 75 (8f, Nmkt, G, Apr 30)
Perpendicular 82 (10f, Asc, F, June 16)
Per Quod (USA) 53 (12f, Hay, G, July 4)
Persian Creek (IRE) 73 (6f, Leo, G, Aug 29)
Persian Dynasty 41 (7f, Chep, F, May 25)
Persian Fantasy 54 (12f, Car, F, July 24)
Pesidanamich (IRE) 53 (7f, Swl, Slw, Feb 14)
Petal Girl 63 (7½f, Ches, F, May 6)
Petavious 59 (12f, Bev, F, May 8)
Petite-D-Argent 66 (7f, Eps, G, June 6)
Petite Sonnerie 47 (7f, Nmkt, G, May 2)
Peto 47 (10f, Pon, S, Apr 15)
Petraco (IRE) 66 (6f, Nmkt, G, Apr 30)
Pfalz 51 (10f, Kem, F, June 24)
Pharaoh's Dancer 53 (5f, Pon, Y, Oct 5)
Pharly Dancer 53 (5f, Pon, Y, Oct 5)
Pharly Story 71 (10f, Nmkt, G, Apr 14)
Philgun 43 (10f, Nwc, Y, Apr 18)
Philidor 63 (8f, Nby, Y, May 16)
Pia Bride (USA) 66 (8f, Deau, G, Aug 1)
Pica 49 (12f, Nmkt, G, Oct 30)
Pink Turtle (USA) 68 (10f, Mai, G, Sep 21)
Pipsqueak 64 (7f, Lon, G, May 28)
Piquant 55 (7f, Sal, F, June 9)
Pistolet Bleu (IRE) 102 (12f, StCl, G, July 4)
Plain Fact 74 (5f, San, G, July 15)
Plan Ahead 45 (11f, Nby, S, Oct 24)

**FLAT SPEED FIGURES — continued**

Playful Poet 57 (5f, Ayr, F, July 20)
Plume Magique 58 (8f, Lon, F, May 17)
Poets Cove 56 (6f, Eps, Y, June 5)
Polar Wind 43 (6f, Cur, Y, Oct 10)
Polish Blue (USA) 66 (9f, Yrk, G, Sep 3)
Polish Style (USA) 74 (6f, Evry, F, June 18)
Political Fact (USA) 62 (10f, Leo, G, Aug 29)
Pollen Count (USA) 82 (10f, San, G, Apr 25)
Pollys Glow (IRE) 48 (12f, Cur, Y, Oct 11)
Polonez Prima 67 (7f, Ches, F, Aug 21)
Polyxena (USA) 61 (10f, Lon, Y, Oct 18)
Ponsardin 56 (7f, Lin, Fs, July 18)
Pontenuovo 50 (8f, San, G, May 25)
Poolesta (IRE) 71 (6f, Leo, G, Aug 29)
Pop To Stans 52 (7f, Swl, Slw, Feb 12)
Portico (USA) 60 (8f, Cur, F, June 28)
Port In A Storm 42 (10f, Kem, F, Aug 5)
Port Sunlight (IRE) 51 (8f, San, G, May 5)
Post Impressionist (IRE) 44 (12f, Lei, G, Sep 8)
Powerful Edge 52 (7f, Hay, G, June 6)
Power Lake 41 (5f, Kem, G, May 13)
Precentor 40 (5f, Ches, F, Aug 22)
Precious Wonder 44 (7f, Flk, S, Oct 19)
Pre-Eminent 54 (8f, Cur, F, June 27)
Premier Prince 41 (7f, Chep, F, May 25)
Prenonamoss 67 (7f, Yrk, Y, Oct 10)
Pretonic 47 (5f, Bev, F, Sep 17)
Pridian (IRE) 42 (7f, Cat, G, Apr 22)
Prince Belfort 50 (5f, Oat, F, July 20)
Prince Ferdinand 83 (7f, Gwd, Y, Oct 2)
Prince Hannibal 53 (10f, Nmkt, G, Apr 14)
Prince Mercury 40 (16f, Asc, G, Oct 9)
Prince of The Sea (IRE) 44 (7f, San, G, July 22)
Prince Ole (IRE) 57 (10f, Cur, Y, June 6)
Prince Pericles (IRE) 42 (12f, Nmkt, G, Apr 14)
Prince Rodney 45 (8f, Nmkt, G, May 15)
Prince Russanor 62 (10f, Don, F, July 26)
Prince Sobur 49 (16f, Nby, Y, July 17)
Princess Moodyshoe 46 (11½f, Bth, G, Sep 14)
Princess Roxanne 51 (10f, Lin, Fs, Jan 21)
Princess Tara 49 (8f, Nmkt, G, June 19)
Private Guy (IRE) 42 (10f, Leo, F, June 10)
Profilic 62 (6f, Yrk, G, May 12)
Profusion 57 (10f, Ches, F, May 7)
Prosequendo (USA) 53 (12f, Flk, F, Sep 10)
Pure Formality 45 (6f, Nby, F, May 15)
Puritan (CAN) 49 (16f, Gwd, G, Sep 12)
Pursuit of Love 86 (6f, Nmkt, G, July 9)
Pytchley Night 61 (7f, Lin, Fs, Feb 18)

Quadrireme 41 (11½f, Bth, F, July 4)
Queen Caroline (USA) 40 (10f, Ches, F, Aug 22)
Queen of Shannon (IRE) 53 (7f, Yar, F, July 30)
Queen Warrior 57 (7f, Yrk, F, May 13)
Quick Ransom 58 (12f, Eps, Y, June 5)
Quinzii Martin 40 (8f, Lin, Fs, Feb 1)

Rafah 56 (7f, Eps, G, Aug 31)
Rahif 43 (8f, Ayr, F, July 20)
Rainbow Corner 93 (8f, Lon, G, May 9)
Rainbow Fleet 55 (6f, Gwd, F, June 12)
Rain Rider 70 (14f, Gwd, Y, Aug 29)
Rajai (IRE) 40 (13f, Bth, F, July 4)
Rambo's Hall 88 (9f, Nmkt, G, Oct 3)
Rami (USA) 74 (8f, Cur, F, June 27)
Rapporteur (USA) 63 (10f, Lin, Fs, Jan 18)

Rare Chic (IRE) 53 (7f, Naas, Y, May 2)
Rare Detail (IRE) 53 (12f, Kem, Y, Apr 3)
Rayon Bleu (FR) 53 (5f, Chan, F, June 4)
Rays Mead 45 (5f, War, G, July 10)
Real Stunner 40 (5f, Rip, H, June 17)
Rebel Call 51 (10f, Nmkt, G, Apr 30)
Receptionist 49 (16f, Nby, G, Aug 17)
Recollection (IRE) 47 (5f, Cur, Y, Aug 22)
Red Archer 46 (7f, San, F, June 13)
Red Bishop (USA) 83 (12f, Asc, S, Sep 24)
Rednet 47 (5f, Not, F, June 8)
Red Rosein 78 (6f, Rip, F, July 6)
Red Slippers (USA) 80 (10f, Nmkt, G, Oct 3)
Regal Lover (USA) 54 (12f, Nwc, F, July 27)
Regal Racer 49 (6f, Kem, G, June 10)
Regal Scintilla 64 (5f, Nmkt, F, Sep 30)
Regent Lad 55 (8f, Nmkt, F, June 19)
Regent's Folly (IRE) 74 (12f, Asc, F, June 17)
Reilton 43 (7f, Cat, F, July 1)
Remany 40 (10f, Bev, F, Sep 16)
Reported (IRE) 75 (7f, Yrk, F, Aug 20)
Requested 51 (16f, Asc, F, July 24)
Resolute Bay 58 (7f, Nmkt, F, July 31)
Respectable Jones 67 (7f, Lin, Fs, Jan 25)
Resplendent 40 (11f, Yar, F, July 24)
Retender (USA) 43 (10f, Yar, F, Aug 11)
Retouch 64 (20f, Gwd, F, July 29)
Revif (FR) 75 (9f, Nmkt, G, Oct 3)
Rhoman Ruby (IRE) 41 (10f, Leo, G, Aug 8)
Rhythmic Dancer 56 (5f, Kem, F, Aug 5)
Ringland (USA) 60 (7f, Red, F, June 1)
Rinja (USA) 60 (12f, Yrk, G, May 12)
Rise Up Singing 58 (7f, Nmkt, F, July 31)
Rising Tempo (IRE) 53 (10f, San, G, May 25)
Risk Master 44 (10f, Asc, S, Sep 25)
Risk Zone 46 (7f, Don, F, Sep 10)
Riszard (USA) 55 (10f, Asc, Y, Apr 29)
Rival Bid (USA) 46 (10f, Wind, F, Aug 10)
Rive-Jumelle (IRE) 52 (10f, Nmkt, G, Apr 14)
Riverbeam (IRE) 43 (8f, Cur, S, Sep 5)
River Defences (USA) 51 (8f, Nmkt, F, Oct 2)
River Falls 60 (7f, Nby, Y, Apr 11)
Riverillon 53 (10f, Leo, F, June 10)
River Jet (USA) 59 (10½f, StCl, G, Apr 25)
River Rhythm (USA) 57 (10f, StCl, Y, Mar 17)
Riviera Vista 61 (10f, Nmkt, F, Aug 8)
Roberty Lea 49 (12f, Eps, Y, June 5)
Robin des Pins (USA) 84 (7f, Lon, G, May 28)
Robingo (IRE) 57 (11f, Nby, S, Oct 24)
Rocality 60 (7f, Eps, G, Aug 31)
Roca Murada (IRE) 46 (7f, Kem, G, Sep 4)
Rockawhile (IRE) 42 (10f, Don, G, Nov 7)
Rock Hopper 91 (12f, Eps, G, June 4)
Rock Opera (IRE) 48 (5f, Lei, S, Oct 26)
Rocky Waters (USA) 60 (7f, Gwd, F, July 30)
Rocton North (IRE) 70 (7f, Don, F, Sep 10)
Rodrigo de Triano (USA) 96 (10f, Yrk, G, Aug 18)
Roll A Dollar 69 (12f, Kem, G, Sep 5)
Roly Wallace 42 (8f, Sal, F, June 25)
Roman Prose 72 (7f, Lon, G, May 28)
Rose Alto 66 (11f, Yar, F, Sep 16)
Roseate Lodge 52 (8f, Kem, G, May 4)
Rose Elegance 40 (10f, Nmkt, F, Sep 30)
Rosefinch (USA) 77 (10½f, Chan, F, June 14)
Rose Gem (IRE) 40 (7f, Edn, F, July 13)
Rose Glen 43 (10f, Ches, F, June 24)
Rose Indien (FR) 68 (6f, Yrk, G, Aug 18)
Rosina Mae 51 (12f, Hay, F, Aug 7)
Rougeur (USA) 55 (12f, Evry, F, July 18)
Rousitto 45 (10f, Bev, F, Apr 23)

Royal Dartmouth (USA) 49 (7f, Nby, S, Oct 22)
Royal Girl 44 (6f, Rip, H, June 17)
Royal Seaton 61 (9f, Nby, S, Oct 24)
Royal Theatre (USA) 64 (12f, Cur, Y, Oct 11)
Ruby Tiger 91 (10f, Cur, F, June 27)
Rudimentary (USA) 88 (8f, Nby, Y, Apr 11)
Ruhr (IRE) 60 (7f, Nmkt, G, Oct 31)
Running Glimpse (IRE) 65 (5f, Eps, Y, Aug 31)
Runyon (IRE) 77 (10½f, Lon, Y, July 12)
Rushanes 51 (5f, Lin, Fs, Feb 22)

Saafend 53 (8f, Nmkt, F, Oct 17)
Sabotage (FR) 48 (8f, Asc, F, July 24)
Saddlehome (USA) 63 (5f, Gwd, F, July 29)
Saddlers' Hall (IRE) 93 (12f, Eps, G, June 4)
Sadler's Way 54 (12f, Nby, F, June 11)
Safa 51 (12f, Yrk, F, June 13)
Saffaah (USA) 51 (12f, Sal, F, May 6)
Saganeca (USA) 83 (12f, Lon, S, Oct 4)
Sagebrush Roller 63 (7f, Nwc, Hvy, Apr 18)
Sahara Star 51 (5f, Yrk, G, July 10)
Sahel (IRE) 75 (8f, Asc, G, July 25)
Saint Ciel (USA) 43 (10f, Don, G, Nov 7)
Salbyng 50 (8f, Gwd, Y, Aug 28)
Salda 49 (8f, Hay, G, Aug 8)
Salisong 47 (7f, Kem, G, Sep 4)
Sally's Son 54 (7f, Lin, Fs, Jan 4)
Salmon Eile (IRE) 59 (9f, Leo, G, July 18)
Samsolom 48 (5f, Don, F, Sep 11)
Samson-Agonistes 64 (5f, Pon, F, Sep 21)
Samurai Gold (USA) 42 (10f, San, G, May 25)
Sandmoor Denim 46 (7f, Swl, Fs, July 25)
Sand Table 54 (5f, Nmkt, F, Oct 17)
Santana Lady (IRE) 40 (10f, Wind, F, Aug 10)
Santi Sana 41 (7f, Wol, G, July 13)
Sapience 96 (10f, San, Y, July 4)
Sapphirine 42 (12f, Cat, F, Aug 11)
Sarah-Clare 42 (10f, San, G, July 16)
Saratoga Source (USA) 57 (9f, Evry, G, July 9)
Sarawat 69 (14½f, Don, G, Oct 23)
Sartigila 47 (5f, Lei, S, Oct 26)
Sarum 45 (8f, Lin, Fs, May 9)
Sasparella 49 (5f, Nmkt, F, Oct 1)
Sastago (USA) 43 (12f, Ches, F, May 6)
Satin Lover 58 (16f, Nwc, F, June 27)
Savoyard 66 (7f, Don, G, July 26)
Sayh 42 (10f, Nmkt, G, Apr 14)
Scala Milano 43 (6f, Yar, F, July 24)
Scales of Justice 56 (8f, Chep, G, Oct 13)
Scandalmonger (USA) 40 (8f, Chep, F, May 25)
Scarlatine (IRE) 64 (7½f, Ches, F, May 6)
Scenic Dancer 43 (11f, San, F, June 13)
Scottish Bambi 49 (11f, War, F, May 23)
Scottish Park 41 (7f, Cat, G, Oct 17)
Scrutineer (USA) 61 (10f, Kem, G, July 8)
Sea-Deer 41 (5f, Bri, F, Aug 6)
Sea Devil 76 (6f, Nmkt, G, Apr 30)
Sea Dune 49 (7f, Lin, F, May 16)
Sea Goddess 58 (12f, Yrk, F, June 13)
Seal Indigo (IRE) 76 (12f, Nby, G, July 18)
Seamere 65 (5½f, Don, G, July 26)
Seattle Rhyme (USA) 88 (10f, Yrk, G, Aug 18)
Sebosan 47 (7f, Yar, F, June 23)
Second Set (IRE) 95 (8f, Asc, F, June 16)
Secret Haunt (USA) 63 (10f, San, G, Apr 25)
Secret Society 66 (12f, Don, F, Sep 11)
Secret Thing (USA) 43 (7f, Chep, F, May 25)

Secret Treaty (IRE) 42 (10½f, Don, F, Sep 9)
Seek The Faith (USA) 41 (7f, Leo, G, Aug 9)
Selaah 58 (7½f, Ches, F, May 5)
Self Expression 59 (10f, Bev, F, July 28)
Selkirk (USA) 97 (7f, Nmkt, F, Oct 15)
Seneca Reef (IRE) 70 (6f, Kem, F, May 23)
Serious Hurry 55 (5f, Ayr, F, Aug 8)
Shabanaz 60 (10½f, Hay, G, Oct 8)
Shades of Jade 50 (5f, Lin, F, July 18)
Shadideen (USA) 50 (13f, Ham, F, July 23)
Shadows of Silver 40 (12f, Pon, F, Sep 21)
Shaffaaf (USA) 54 (8f, Yrk, Y, Oct 8)
Shahaamh (IRE) 51 (10f, Bth, F, Aug 6)
Shahdjat (IRE) 57 (16f, Nby, Y, July 17)
Shakanda (IRE) 47 (14f, Leo, Y, Sep 13)
Shake Town (USA) 40 (7f, Red, F, Aug 26)
Shalabia 40 (7f, Chep, F, July 9)
Shalford (IRE) 96 (6f, Asc, F, June 18)
Shamawna (IRE) 73 (12f, StCl, S, June 8)
Shambo 86 (12f, Asc, F, June 17)
Shannkara (IRE) 46 (9f, Lon, G, May 3)
Sharastamina (USA) 57 (10f, Cur, Y, Sep 5)
Sharpalto 82 (7f, Asc, Y, Sep 26)
Sharp Dream 57 (9f, Kem, G, Sep 5)
Sharpitor (IRE) 82 (10f, Deau, S, Aug 15)
Sharp N' Smooth 54 (8f, Kem, G, May 4)
Sharp Review (IRE) 54 (7f, Cur, G, Aug 15)
Shati (IRE) 67 (8f, Asc, G, Oct 10)
Shawar (IRE) 56 (11f, Naas, G, June 13)
Shawiya (IRE) 41 (11f, Naas, F, June 13)
Sheikh Albadou 96 (6f, Hay, G, Sep 5)
She Looks On High (USA) 46 (7f, Nmkt, F, Apr 30)
Sheriffmuir 74 (12f, Don, F, June 26)
Sheringa 52 (12f, Sal, Y, Sep 3)
Shikari's Son 52 (6f, Bri, F, July 2)
Shining Jewel 51 (7f, Yar, F, Aug 11)
Ships Lantern 54 (7f, Chep, S, Aug 31)
Shirley Valentine 58 (10f, San, G, Apr 24)
Shivaree (FR) 75 (6f, Evry, F, June 18)
Shoehorn 43 (10f, Wind, F, Apr 27)
Shoofe (USA) 45 (16f, Kem, Y, Apr 18)
Showbrook (IRE) 77 (5f, Chan, F, June 4)
Showgi (USA) 52 (7f, Nmkt, G, Apr 14)
Shrewd Partner (IRE) 51 (10f, Kem, G, July 8)
Shuailaan (USA) 71 (14½f, Don, G, Sep 12)
Side Winger (USA) 59 (6f, Leo, Y, May 9)
Sie Amato (IRE) 58 (10f, Ayr, Y, Aug 20)
Sigama (USA) 66 (5f, Nmkt, G, Aug 29)
Sikeston (USA) 93 (8f, Asc, F, June 16)
Silca-Cisa 80 (5f, Gwd, F, July 29)
Silicon Bavaria (FR) 78 (7f, Lon, Y, Oct 11)
Sillery (USA) 74 (10f, Lon, S, Oct 3)
Silver Kite (USA) 52 (10½f, Lon, G, Apr 26)
Silvernesian (USA) 52 (12f, Sal, Y, Apr 30)
Silver Samurai 40 (10f, Ches, F, Aug 22)
Silver Wisp (USA) 83 (12f, Eps, G, June 4)
Simmie's Special 49 (5f, Pon, F, Sep 21)
Simonov 51 (12f, Don, G, Oct 24)
Simply Amber (IRE) 59 (5f, Leo, G, Aug 9)
Simply-H (IRE) 41 (11½f, Bth, G, Sep 28)
Sinclair Lad (IRE) 55 (10f, Bev, G, Aug 13)
Singers Image 42 (8f, Don, G, Oct 23)
Singing Star 53 (5f, Red, F, May 26)
Sinntara (IRE) 67 (16f, Cur, G, Oct 10)
Sir Arthur Hobbs 47 (7f, Ayr, F, June 19)
Sir Boudle (IRE) 56 (6f, Asc, F, July 24)
Sir Harry Hardman 71 (5f, Hay, S, Apr 18)
Sir Mark Sykes (IRE) 43 (8f, Car, G, May 7)
Sir Tasker 60 (5f, Lin, Fs, Feb 15)
Sirtelimar (IRE) 40 (8f, Swl, Fs, July 29)
Siwana (IRE) 54 (5f, Cur, G, June 6)

Sizzling Saga (IRE) 85 (6f, Hay, F, July 2)
Ski Captain 51 (5f, Yar, F, July 24)
Ski Chief (USA) 80 (5f, Lon, G, May 7)
Skimble (USA) 47 (10f, Yrk, F, May 13)
Skipper To Bilge 54 (7f, Nmkt, G, June 19)
Sky Hunter (USA) 61 (7f, Yrk, F, May 14)
Sky Train (IRE) 40 (10f, Bri, F, July 2)
Slades Hill 52 (5f, Tsk, G, Apr 11)
Sleet Skier 63 (14f, Cur, F, June 28)
Slight Risk 52 (12f, Lin, Fs, Nov 5)
Slip-A-Snip 42 (5f, Lin, Fs, Jan 25)
Smiling Chief (IRE) 46 (10f, Sal, G, Aug 13)
Snaadee (USA) 87 (5f, San, G, May 25)
Snow Blizzard 48 (12f, Lin, Fs, Nov 5)
Snowgirl (IRE) 40 (6f, Nmkt, F, Oct 2)
Snurge 95 (14f, Cur, Y, Sep 19)
Soba Guest (IRE) 54 (5f, Ham, Y, Nov 3)
Societies Lover 57 (16f, Cur, G, Sep 27)
Soiree (IRE) 65 (8f, Cur, S, Sep 5)
Solar Star (USA) 45 (10f, Nby, F, June 11)
Soleil Dancer (IRE) 55 (7f, Bri, F, Apr 13)
Sonderise 46 (6f, Hay, G, May 4)
Song of The Woods 54 (8f, Leo, G, Aug 8)
Sonus (IRE) 74 (14½f, Don, G, Sep 12)
So Rhythmical 69 (6f, Gwd, Y, Aug 29)
So Superb 54 (5f, Lin, F, June 13)
Sought Out (IRE) 84 (15f, Deau, S, Aug 23)
Source of Light 65 (12f, Asc, F, June 18)
Southwold Air 41 (8f, Bri, F, July 2)
Sovereign Page (USA) 48 (10f, Rip, F, July 18)
Sovereign Rock (IRE) 64 (7f, Kem, G, Sep 4)
Spaniards Close 91 (5f, Asc, Y, Sep 25)
Spanish Express 41 (7f, Swl, Fs, Aug 14)
Spanish Miner (USA) 59 (7f, Nmkt, G, Apr 14)
Spanish Storm (IRE) 56 (6f, Asc, F, June 18)
Spanish Verdict 51 (10f, Rip, G, Aug 22)
Spartan Shareef (IRE) 84 (9f, Yrk, G, Sep 3)
Speaker's House (USA) 60 (9f, Yrk, G, July 10)
Specificity (USA) 70 (12f, Evry, S, Nov 13)
Spectacular Dawn 48 (10f, Bev, Y, July 3)
Spectacular Rise (USA) 47 (7f, Naas, S, Mar 21)
Spencer's Revenge 42 (7f, Kem, G, Sep 22)
Spikenard 62 (13f, Nby, G, July 18)
Spinning 84 (12f, Asc, F, June 17)
Splice 72 (6f, Nmkt, F, Oct 2)
Spray of Orchids 50 (10f, Rip, Y, Aug 31)
Spring 69 (12f, Nby, S, Oct 24)
Spring High 52 (5f, Yar, F, Sep 16)
Springs Welcome 41 (12f, Lin, Fs, June 20)
Spring To The Top 43 (10f, Don, F, Sep 9)
Stack Rock 74 (5f, Hay, S, Apr 18)
Standiford 73 (10f, Lon, G, May 21)
Standing Cast (IRE) 72 (8f, Leo, G, Aug 8)
Stani (USA) 52 (12f, Nby, F, June 11)
Stapleton (IRE) 59 (12f, Tsk, F, Sep 5)
Star Connection 58 (8f, Tsk, G, May 2)
Star Goddess (USA) 45 (7f, Kem, G, June 10)
Starlight Flyer 86 (8f, San, Y, July 4)
Star of Cozzene (USA) 79 (8f, Gwd, F, July 29)
Star of Gdansk (USA) 90 (8f, Deau, Y, Aug 16)
Star Player 64 (18½f, Ches, F, May 6)
Star Quest 67 (16f, Kem, Y, Apr 18)
Star Sent (IRE) 46 (12f, Leo, G, Aug 8)
Statajack (IRE) 57 (10f, San, Y, Aug 21)
State Dancer (USA) 69 (8f, Don, G, Sep 12)
State Flyer 42 (7f, Nwc, Hvy, Apr 18)

State Governor 44 (7f, Swl, Fs, Jan 1)
Staunch Friend (USA) 55 (13f, Ayr, S, Sep 19)
Steerforth (IRE) 82 (10f, Yrk, G, July 11)
Steinbeck (USA) 89 (8f, Gwd, Y, Aug 29)
St Jovite (USA) 95 (12f, Cur, F, June 28)
St Ninian 73 (8f, Yrk, F, May 14)
Stormbuster 40 (6f, Tsk, G, Aug 28)
Storm Crossing (USA) 51 (12f, Nmkt, F, Oct 15)
Storm Dove (USA) 78 (7f, Gwd, G, July 28)
Storm Melody (USA) 43 (5f, San, Ga, Sep 15)
Straw Thatch 49 (8f, Nmkt, F, Aug 1)
Street Rebel (CAN) 83 (6f, Leo, G, Aug 29)
Striking Image (USA) 44 (10f, Sal, G, Aug 13)
Strong Suit (IRE) 57 (7f, Nmkt, F, July 31)
Stubass (IRE) 45 (9f, Evry, F, July 25)
Stylish Aristocrat (USA) 47 (6f, Naas, F, July 4)
Suave Dancer (USA) 88 (10½f, Lon, G, May 3)
Subotica (FR) 98 (12f, Lon, S, Oct 4)
Subsonic (IRE) 61 (16f, Kem, Y, Apr 18)
Sugemar 42 (7f, Sal, F, June 9)
Sunday's Hill 67 (6f, Hay, G, Sep 26)
Sunderland Echo 49 (12f, Nwc, Hvy, Nov 2)
Sun Seeker (IRE) 41 (10f, Kem, G, Apr 20)
Super Benz 54 (7f, Yrk, G, Sep 3)
Superbrave 64 (7f, Nwc, F, June 27)
Supermec (USA) 60 (8f, StCl, S, Apr 7)
Superoo 57 (7f, Nmkt, G, July 9)
Super Rocky 51 (5f, Don, F, June 27)
Super Sally 66 (8f, Lin, Fs, Feb 22)
Super Serenade 44 (7f, Sal, F, June 24)
Super Summit 45 (8f, Nwc, G, Aug 29)
Supertop 46 (10f, Don, F, July 22)
Supportive (IRE) 68 (5f, Cur, G, June 6)
Supreme Choice (USA) 76 (16f, Asc, Y, Apr 29)
Sure Lord (IRE) 41 (6f, Bri, G, Aug 25)
Sure Sharp (USA) 86 (9f, Nmkt, G, Apr 15)
Surf 44 (10f, Don, F, May 23)
Surrealist (IRE) 58 (12f, Gwd, F, July 31)
Surrey Dancer 54 (9f, Nby, S, Oct 24)
Surrey Racing 48 (7f, Wol, G, July 18)
Susurration (USA) 88 (8f, Yrk, G, July 10)
Swallowcliffe 46 (8f, Yrk, F, May 13)
Swing Low 71 (7f, Gwd, Y, Oct 2)
Sword Master 59 (10½f, Hay, G, Oct 8)
Sylva Honda 81 (8f, Yrk, F, May 14)
Sylvan Breeze 67 (5f, Eps, F, July 29)
Sylvan (IRE) 52 (9f, Yrk, Y, Oct 10)
Sylvan Sabre (IRE) 59 (6f, Kem, F, Aug 19)
Symphorine (USA) 66 (8f, Lon, F, May 17)

Tactical Mission (IRE) 42 (16f, Kem, Y, Apr 18)
Tahaddi (USA) 51 (16f, Cur, G, Sep 27)
Tahitian 41 (8f, Nmkt, F, Oct 17)
Take By Storm (IRE) 47 (12f, Swl, Slw, Aug 8)
Takenhall 51 (7f, Nmkt, G, June 19)
Take Two 50 (8f, Wind, F, May 11)
Talb (USA) 74 (7f, War, S, Oct 5)
Talented Ting (IRE) 53 (10f, Ayr, F, July 24)
Talent (USA) 72 (8f, Bth, F, Aug 11)
Tales of Wisdom 41 (12f, Swl, Slw, Aug 8)
Tamarpour (USA) 59 (18½f, Ches, F, May 6)
Tamim (USA) 59 (8f, Yrk, Y, Oct 8)
Tanfith (CAN) 67 (8f, Don, Y, Mar 21)
Tango Time 53 (5f, San, F, May 26)
Tapis Rouge (IRE) 54 (10f, Not, G, Aug 24)

Tara's Delight 42 (10f, Lin, Fs, Jan 4)
Tarwiya (IRE) 67 (7f, Cur, Y, Sep 19)
Tashkourgan (IRE) 57 (10f, StCl, Y, Mar 17)
Tate Dancer (IRE) 56 (6f, Lin, Slw, July 27)
Tauber 46 (5f, Lin, F, May 16)
Taufan Blu (IRE) 69 (6f, Asc, F, June 20)
Taylor Quigley (USA) 62 (7f, Nmkt, F, Apr 15)
Taylors Prince 48 (12f, Flk, F, Sep 10)
Tbab (IRE) 81 (5f, San, Y, July 4)
Tea Dust (IRE) 52 (7f, Lin, F, May 23)
Teanarco (IRE) 46 (6f, Ayr, Y, Sep 19)
Teddy's Play (USA) 49 (16f, Asc, F, June 17)
Tell No Lies 77 (10f, Ayr, Y, Sep 18)
Tel Quel (FR) 74 (9f, Lon, G, May 31)
Temple Fortune (USA) 49 (6f, Eps, G, Sep 1)
Tender Moment (IRE) 56 (7f, Lin, F, Aug 8)
Terimon 89 (12f, Eps, G, June 4)
Terrhars (IRE) 82 (6f, Yrk, G, May 12)
Tertian (USA) 73 (7f, Lon, G, May 28)
Teslemi (USA) 42 (8f, Asc, Y, Apr 29)
Tetradonna (IRE) 66 (16f, Gwd, F, July 30)
Texan Tycoon 40 (12f, Don, G, Nov 7)
Thakawah 40 (16f, Rip, F, June 18)
Thames Glow 41 (8f, Nmkt, G, Aug 29)
Thamestar (IRE) 52 (12f, Don, G, Oct 24)
The Cuckoo's Nest 40 (7f, Yrk, G, Sep 3)
The Dandy Don (IRE) 41 (8f, Edn, G, July 21)
The Goofer 49 (9f, Nwc, Hvy, Nov 2)
The Man From Cooks (IRE) 43 (9f, Cur, G, Oct 20)
The Noble Oak (IRE) 64 (5f, Gwd, G, June 5)
The Old Chapel 48 (6f, Rip, S, Apr 16)
The Poachers Lady (IRE) 64 (10f, Cur, Y, June 6)
The Right Time 43 (5f, Rip, G, Sep 1)
The Shanahan Bay 42 (5f, Swl, Fs, July 3)
Thewaari (USA) 53 (7f, Don, F, June 24)
Thinking Twice (USA) 40 (8f, Wind, G, July 6)
Thornberry (USA) 53 (10f, Cur, Hvy, Apr 25)
Thornton Gate 47 (7f, Edn, G, Aug 27)
Thourios 83 (7f, Nmkt, F, Oct 15)
Threepence 49 (5f, Hay, G, Oct 7)
Three Wells 51 (14f, Gwd, F, July 31)
Thrie-Na-Helah (IRE) 49 (7f, Ayr, F, June 19)
Thyer (USA) 77 (8f, Leo, G, Aug 8)
Tiffany's Case (IRE) 41 (8f, Yar, Y, Aug 20)
Tigani 48 (5f, Tsk, F, Sep 6)
Tijara (IRE) 54 (8f, Cur, Y, Sep 27)
Tik Fa (USA) 65 (8f, Nby, G, Sep 19)
Time It Right (IRE) 51 (10f, Leo, G, Aug 29)
Timurid (FR) 54 (10f, Don, F, July 26)
Tissisat (USA) 51 (9f, Yrk, G, July 10)
Title Roll (IRE) 74 (15f, Gwd, F, July 30)
Toast And Honey (IRE) 40 (11f, Naas, G, June 13)
Tongue Tied 60 (5f, Nmkt, F, May 16)
Tony's Delight (IRE) 54 (8f, Leo, Y, Oct 26)
Tony's Fen 57 (12f, Leo, G, Aug 3)
Top Register (USA) 55 (10f, Yrk, F, May 13)
Top Royal 44 (12f, Gwd, Y, Aug 28)
Top Spin 42 (12f, Don, F, Sep 11)
Top Table 44 (12f, Nwc, F, July 27)
Torchon 51 (12f, Bev, F, June 4)
Torrey Canyon (USA) 71 (8f, Kem, G, May 23)
Toshiba Comet 51 (6f, Swl, Slw, Feb 14)
Touch Above 49 (10f, Bev, F, July 28)
Touch of White 58 (5f, Nmkt, F, July 7)
Touch Paper (USA) 63 (10½f, Don, F, Sep 9)
Toulon 63 (12f, Evry, F, June 13)
Toussaud (USA) 83 (7½f, Lin, F, July 11)

Track Twenty Nine (IRE) 58 (7f, Naas, S, Mar 21)
Tradition 54 (11f, Ches, F, May 6)
Trafalgar Boy (USA) 61 (9f, Yrk, G, May 12)
Travelling Light 42 (16f, Rip, G, Apr 25)
Treasure Hope (IRE) 46 (7f, Leo, Y, Mar 17)
Treasure Time (IRE) 41 (5f, Bri, F, Aug 6)
Triennium (USA) 53 (10½f, Hay, G, Aug 14)
Triple Tiara (USA) 76 (12f, StCl, S, June 8)
Trishyde (USA) 81 (12f, Lon, G, Sep 13)
Trojan Lancer 53 (12f, Nwc, F, June 26)
Trooping (IRE) 65 (8f, Gwd, Y, Aug 28)
Tropicarr (USA) 55 (10f, Cur, S, Apr 11)
Troupe 45 (7½f, Ches, F, May 5)
Trove 55 (5f, Don, G, Mar 19)
Truben (USA) 42 (12f, Nmkt, G, Oct 30)
Trump 40 (10f, Nwc, Y, Apr 18)
Trumpet 47 (12f, Nby, G, June 2)
Truthful Image 48 (5f, Gwd, G, Oct 2)
Try Leguard (IRE) 49 (8f, Lin, Fs, Feb 15)
Tudor Island 54 (12f, Don, F, Sep 11)
Tunbridge Wells (IRE) 48 (10f, Nby, G, Oct 22)
Turgenev (IRE) 70 (12f, Don, G, Nov 7)
Turgeon (USA) 73 (15f, Deau, S, Aug 23)
Turret Gates 42 (7f, Nmkt, G, May 2)
Tusky 65 (7f, Ayr, F, June 19)
Twafeaj (USA) 76 (6f, Deau, Y, Aug 19)
Twilight Falls 50 (6f, Car, Y, Apr 24)
Twist And Turn 83 (10f, San, Y, July 4)
Two Left Feet 85 (8f, Rip, Y, Aug 31)
Tyrian Purple (IRE) 42 (7f, Swl, Fs, June 20)
Tyrone Bridge 75 (16f, Gwd, F, July 30)
Tyrone Flyer 42 (7f, Swl, Fs, Sep 18)

Uccello 54 (6f, Eps, G, June 6)
Unforgiving Minute 46 (10f, Red, G, Oct 14)
United Kingdom (USA) 45 (10f, Nmkt, G, July 8)
Up Anchor (IRE) 71 (12f, Nby, S, Oct 24)
Up The Punjab 46 (8f, Swl, Fs, Jan 15)
Urban Sea (USA) 86 (10f, Deau, S, Aug 22)
Usa Dollar 52 (7f, Lin, Fs, July 11)
Usaidit 41 (10f, Nmkt, F, Oct 15)
User Friendly 87 (12f, Lon, S, Oct 4)
Ushba (FR) 45 (6f, Pon, F, Aug 6)

Vague Dancer 42 (10f, Yrk, F, May 14)
Vailmont (USA) 56 (6f, Kem, G, May 4)
Vallance 62 (10f, Yar, F, Sep 16)
Valseur (USA) 49 (12f, Nby, F, June 11)
Vanille (USA) 71 (10f, Deau, S, Aug 8)
Vanroy 45 (8f, Wind, G, July 6)
Vasiliev 49 (12f, Don, G, Oct 24)
Venture Capitalist 83 (5½f, Don, G, Sep 9)
Venus Observed 68 (8f, Kem, G, May 4)
Vert Amande (FR) 93 (12f, Lon, S, Oct 4)
Verveine (USA) 83 (12f, Lon, G, Sep 13)
Very Dicey 64 (5f, Lin, Fs, Sep 17)
Via Borghese (USA) 62 (10f, Cur, F, June 27)
Viardot (IRE) 52 (10½f, Hay, G, May 4)
Viceroy 87 (5f, Nwc, G, July 25)
Victoire Bleue 57 (16f, Asc, Y, Apr 29)
View From Above 42 (12f, Don, G, Oct 24)
Villandry (USA) 68 (12½f, Mai, F, July 24)
Vintage 50 (12f, Kem, G, Sep 5)
Vintage Crop 84 (14f, Cur, Y, Sep 19)
Virkon Venture (IRE) 41 (10½f, Hay, G, Oct 8)
Vratislav (USA) 59 (10f, Wind, G, July 20)

Waders Dream (IRE) 55 (7f, Yrk, F, June 12)

Walimu (IRE) 49 (10f, San, G, Sep 15)
Walking On Water 40 (7f, Nmkt, G, Apr 14)
Walking Possession 55 (5f, Bev, F, July 28)
Walk In The Park 70 (5f, Gwd, F, July 29)
Wanda 55 (5f, Lin, G, Apr 4)
Wandering Stranger 43 (5f, San, G, July 16)
Wand (IRE) 45 (14f, Hay, Y, Sep 4)
Wassl This Then (IRE) 42 (8f, Gwd, G, May 29)
Waterfowl Creek (IRE) 61 (7f, Nmkt, G, Oct 31)
Wave Hill 66 (8f, Asc, G, July 25)
Waverley Star 45 (5f, Bri, G, Sep 23)
Wedding of The Sea (USA) 78 (6f, Evry, G, July 2)
Weeheby (USA) 43 (10f, Bev, F, July 28)
Well Beyond (IRE) 59 (7f, Chep, S, Aug 31)
Wellington Rock (USA) 41 (8f, Nmkt, G, July 9)
Well Saddled (IRE) 52 (8f, Gwd, F, May 19)
Wellsy Lad (USA) 41 (7f, Swl, Fs, June 20)
Welshman 53 (18¹/₂f, Ches, F, May 6)
Welsh Mill (IRE) 53 (12f, Eps, G, Aug 31)
We're All Game 43 (5f, Ayr, Y, Sep 17)
Wesaam (USA) 68 (8f, Gwd, G, July 28)
West Chazy (USA) 54 (8f, Cur, Y, Nov 4)
Western Approach (USA) 87 (5f, Yrk, F, Aug 19)
Western Dynasty 52 (11f, San, G, Sep 16)
Westfield Moves (IRE) 44 (10f, Pon, F, July 7)
Westholme (USA) 55 (12f, Rip, F, Aug 15)
West Stow 40 (10f, Nwc, Y, Apr 18)
Whippet 40 (7f, Wol, G, July 18)
Whirl 50 (10¹/₂f, Hay, G, Aug 14)
Whitechapel (USA) 57 (12f, Sal, F, May 6)
Who's Tef (IRE) 43 (8f, Car, F, July 24)
Widyan (USA) 63 (10f, Nmkt, G, Apr 14)
Wiedniu (USA) 65 (7f, Nby, Y, Apr 10)
Wild And Loose 56 (7f, Don, G, Nov 6)

Wilde Rufo 74 (7f, Nmkt, G, Apr 15)
Wild Fire 61 (10f, Yar, F, Sep 16)
Wild Honour (IRE) 62 (5f, Nmkt, F, June 26)
Wild Prospect 48 (7f, Cat, F, July 16)
Wild Sable (IRE) 43 (10f, Kem, G, Apr 20)
Wilkins 47 (14f, Sal, Y, Aug 13)
Will of Steel 57 (6f, Yrk, Y, Oct 10)
Will Soon 40 (9f, Kem, G, Sep 5)
Windpower (IRE) 47 (6f, Kem, S, Apr 18)
Winnetka (USA) 66 (12f, StCl, S, June 8)
Winning Heart 71 (8f, Cur, S, Sep 5)
Wiorno 83 (10¹/₂f, Lon, Y, July 12)
Witness Box (USA) 85 (16f, Gwd, F, July 30)
Wolfhound (USA) 82 (5f, Asc, F, June 19)
Woodurather 45 (11f, War, Y, Apr 20)

Yenoora (IRE) 41 (16f, Lin, Fs, Aug 8)
Yes 41 (5f, San, Y, Aug 22)
Yildiz 59 (10f, Nby, F, June 11)
Yorkshire Holly 41 (20¹/₂f, Pth, G, Sep 24)
Young Buster (IRE) 81 (10f, Asc, F, June 16)
Young Freeman (USA) 53 (10f, Nby, G, Sep 19)
Young George 44 (11f, Red, F, Apr 30)
Young Senor (USA) 65 (9f, Nmkt, G, Apr 16)
Young Shadowfax 40 (5f, Not, F, June 8)
Yours Or Mine (IRE) 45 (6f, Tsk, G, Aug 28)
Yousefia (USA) 46 (8f, Yrk, F, May 13)
Yukon Gold (IRE) 59 (10f, Leo, G, Oct 24)

Zaahi (USA) 88 (8f, Lon, G, May 9)
Zalon (IRE) 61 (9f, Yrk, G, May 12)
Zamirah (USA) 49 (10f, Ayr, Y, Sep 5)
Zawaahy (USA) 51 (10¹/₂f, Hay, Y, Sep 5)
Zeboim 62 (7f, Nby, S, Oct 22)
Ziggy's Power (USA) 42 (6f, Naas, G, June 13)
Zinaad 68 (12f, Nby, S, Oct 24)
Zoman (USA) 93 (10f, San, Y, July 4)

# TWO-YEAR-OLDS

Abbey's Gal 55 (6f, Wind, F, July 13)
Aberdeen Heather 44 (7f, Gwd, S, Oct 3)
Abergele 51 (6f, Nmkt, F, Oct 16)
Abtaal 51 (6f, Asc, G, July 25)
After The Last 46 (7f, Ches, F, Aug 22)
Ajfan (USA) 51 (8f, Asc, Y, Sep 26)
Alalija (IRE) 45 (6f, Cur, Y, Aug 22)
Alasib 40 (5f, Pon, F, June 29)
Alderney Prince (USA) 45 (7f, Nmkt, G, Aug 7)
Aljazzaf 40 (6f, Asc, F, June 18)
Alouette 57 (8f, Leo, Y, Sep 13)
Alyreina (USA) 42 (7f, Cur, G, Oct 20)
Anaheim (IRE) 46 (7f, Kem, F, Aug 5)
Ancestral Dancer 56 (5f, Nmkt, F, Apr 15)
Anonymous 47 (5f, Eps, G, June 6)
Anselman 67 (5f, Don, G, Oct 24)
Arabic Treasure (USA) 42 (6f, Naas, G, Oct 17)
Aradanza 53 (5f, Pon, Y, Oct 5)
Ardkinglass 70 (7f, Nmkt, G, July 19)
Area Girl 46 (5f, Wind, F, June 15)
Arkendale Diamond (USA) 41 (6f, Nmkt, G, Oct 31)
Armiger 73 (8f, Don, G, Oct 24)
Asema (USA) 63 (8f, Leo, Y, Sep 13)

Athens Belle (IRE) 48 (7f, Kem, G, Sep 4)
Austral Jane 43 (7f, Chep, Y, Oct 20)
Auvergne (CAN) 47 (9f, Lon, Y, Oct 11)
Awestruck 40 (6f, Eps, F, July 29)

Bangles 46 (5f, Nmkt, G, Oct 30)
Barathea (IRE) 69 (7f, Nmkt, F, Oct 17)
Baron Ferdinand 45 (7f, Kem, G, Sep 4)
Bashayer (USA) 53 (8f, Nmkt, F, Oct 15)
Basim (USA) 68 (6f, Cur, Y, Aug 22)
Beggarman Thief (USA) 66 (7f, Nby, S, Oct 22)
Bene Merenti (IRE) 48 (6f, Cur, G, Oct 20)
Benevolent 47 (7f, Nby, S, Oct 24)
Benzoe (IRE) 50 (6f, Nmkt, F, Oct 16)
Berdansk (USA) 56 (8f, Lon, Y, Sep 16)
Berinsfield 44 (5¹/₂f, Mai, F, July 19)
Bezique (USA) 52 (7f, Lin, S, Oct 26)
Bin Ajwaad (IRE) 60 (7f, Nby, S, Oct 22)
Birchwood Sun 45 (6f, Yrk, S, Oct 8)
Black Dragon (IRE) 46 (7f, Yrk, G, Sep 3)
Black Mischief 42 (7f, Yrk, Y, Oct 8)
Blow Dry (IRE) 46 (5f, Red, Y, Sep 26)
Blue Blazer 40 (8f, Hay, Y, Oct 7)
Blues Traveller (IRE) 46 (7f, Nmkt, F, Oct 16)
Blush Rambler (USA) 65 (8f, Lon, S, Oct 3)

Bobbie Dee 52 (10f, Nmkt, G, Oct 31)
Bob's Return (IRE) 59 (10f, Nmkt, G, Oct 31)
Bold County 45 (5f, Don, G, Nov 6)
Bold Pousse (IRE) 45 (5f, Lon, G, July 1)
Bonjour 44 (6f, Hay, G, Aug 8)
Borodislew (USA) 63 (8f, Lon, S, Oct 25)
Brigante di Cielo 50 (7f, Asc, G, Oct 9)
Brigg Fair 61 (5f, Nby, G, Sep 19)
Bright Generation (IRE) 46 (7f, Cur, S, Sep 5)
Bristol Fashion 47 (7f, Ches, Y, July 11)
Brockton Dancer 44 (5f, Nby, Y, July 17)
Brown's (FR) 48 (7f, Nmkt, F, Oct 1)
Burooj 49 (7f, Asc, G, Oct 9)

Canaska Star 55 (6f, Nmkt, G, July 8)
Carbon Steel (IRE) 42 (5f, Hay, Y, Sep 4)
Carelaman 43 (7f, Wol, G, Sep 19)
Carnbrea Snip 59 (5f, Ayr, Y, Sep 19)
Carranita (IRE) 59 (6f, Wind, F, July 13)
Carrnassier (USA) 42 (7f, Naas, F, July 22)
Cashell 48 (7½f, Lin, S, Oct 26)
Catrail (USA) 56 (7f, Nmkt, G, Oct 31)
Certain Prospect 40 (7f, Cur, G, July 11)
Chaddleworth (IRE) 41 (6f, Nby, F, June 11)
Chain Dance 56 (7f, Asc, G, Oct 9)
Charlie Bigtime 44 (10f, Nmkt, G, Oct 31)
Chatterberry 40 (5f, Sal, F, June 24)
Chevrotain 46 (8f, Yrk, G, Sep 3)
Chili Heights 43 (7f, Don, G, Nov 7)
Cissbury Ring 46 (7f, Sal, F, July 11)
City Rocket 45 (5f, Asc, F, June 19)
Classic Storm 45 (5f, Bev, Y, July 13)
Classic Story (USA) 54 (5f, Gwd, F, July 28)
Clear Honey (USA) 47 (7f, Edn, G, July 21)
Cliburnel News (IRE) 41 (6f, Wind, G, Aug 29)
Colour Party (USA) 49 (7f, Cur, G, July 11)
Colway Rock (USA) 41 (7f, Ayr, S, Sep 19)
Colyan (IRE) 65 (5f, Asc, F, June 19)
Commanche Gold (IRE) 49 (8f, Kem, Y, Sep 22)
Complete Madness 43 (6f, Nby, S, Oct 22)
Coneybury (IRE) 44 (7f, Bri, F, Sep 29)
Cons Prince 40 (7f, Cur, G, Oct 20)
Costa Verde 46 (5f, Lei, G, July 14)
Coy Boy (IRE) 46 (6f, Kem, F, June 24)
Creaking Board 70 (5½f, Mai, Y, July 19)
Criquette 44 (7f, Nby, S, Oct 24)
Cynic 42 (5f, Yrk, G, May 12)

Dahliz (IRE) 40 (5f, Bev, G, July 3)
Dahyah (USA) 46 (7f, Don, G, Oct 23)
Dalalah 48 (6f, Wind, F, July 13)
Dancing Bloom (IRE) 48 (6f, Asc, F, July 24)
Darbonne (USA) 60 (6f, Leo, G, Aug 9)
Darecliff (USA) 47 (7f, Asc, F, July 24)
Dawnsio (IRE) 41 (6f, Cur, Y, Aug 22)
Dayflower (USA) 48 (7f, Nmkt, F, July 17)
Dayjuz (IRE) 43 (5f, Hay, G, June 6)
Declassified (USA) 56 (8f, Asc, G, Oct 10)
Defenceless 50 (5f, Nmkt, F, Apr 15)
Desert Secret (IRE) 59 (8f, Asc, Y, Sep 26)
Desert Shot 51 (6f, Nmkt, F, Aug 1)
Devilry 47 (8f, Yrk, G, Sep 3)
Double Bass (USA) 56 (7f, Nmkt, F, June 27)
Dowreyna 44 (7f, Edn, G, July 21)
Dutosky 43 (5f, Yrk, S, Oct 7)

Earl of Barking (IRE) 44 (7f, Cur, G, Aug 15)
Eleusis (FR) 40 (8f, Bth, G, Sep 28)
Elle Shaped (IRE) 53 (5f, Gwd, F, May 21)
Embankment (IRE) 48 (7f, Nmkt, F, Oct 15)

Emperor Jones (USA) 40 (7f, Asc, Y, Sep 25)
Empire Pool 49 (7f, Yrk, F, Aug 18)
Enjoy Plan (USA) 46 (9f, Evry, G, Sep 26)
Eurolink Thunder 49 (8f, Asc, G, Oct 10)
Expo Mondial (IRE) 51 (7f, Asc, G, Oct 9)

Factual (USA) 52 (6f, Nmkt, F, Oct 1)
Faez 49 (7f, Lin, S, Oct 26)
Fairy Story (IRE) 40 (7f, Lin, G, Aug 27)
Falsoola 45 (5f, Rip, F, Aug 3)
Fatherland (IRE) 63 (7f, Cur, Y, Aug 30)
Felawnah (USA) 50 (7f, Nmkt, F, Oct 16)
Felucca 50 (6f, Nmkt, F, Oct 16)
Field of Stars 45 (7f, Don, G, Oct 23)
Finmental (IRE) 58 (5f, Gwd, F, July 28)
Firm Friend (IRE) 59 (6½f, StCl, F, Oct 5)
Firm Pledge (USA) 61 (7f, Nmkt, F, Oct 16)
First Option 50 (5f, Ayr, Y, Sep 19)
First Veil 52 (6f, Asc, G, July 25)
Fitzcarraldo (USA) 54 (7f, Don, F, Sep 11)
Flashfleet 48 (7f, Kem, G, Sep 4)
Forest Wind (USA) 60 (6f, Gwd, F, Aug 1)
Formaestre (IRE) 42 (5f, Not, G, May 29)
Fortensky (USA) 49 (7f, Nmkt, F, Oct 15)
Fortune Cay (IRE) 59 (5f, Wind, F, June 29)
Frenchpark 60 (8f, Cur, Y, Oct 10)
Fret (USA) 45 (6f, Kem, F, June 24)
Friendly Brave (USA) 46 (7f, Nmkt, F, June 27)
Futurballa 46 (8½f, Eps, G, Sep 1)
Fyfield Flyer (IRE) 69 (5f, Don, G, Oct 24)

Gabr 55 (7f, Nmkt, F, Oct 1)
Galaxy Star (IRE) 41 (5f, Leo, G, Mar 17)
Geisway (CAN) 57 (8f, Asc, Y, Sep 26)
Glowing Jade 42 (6f, Yrk, G, July 11)
Glowing Value (IRE) 53 (7f, Ches, F, Aug 22)
Gold Splash (USA) 73 (8f, Lon, S, Oct 4)
Gone Prospecting (USA) 48 (8f, Gwd, Y, Oct 2)
Grand Dancer (IRE) 45 (5f, Wind, F, Aug 1)
Great Steps 49 (7f, Yrk, Y, Oct 8)
Greenlet (IRE) 45 (5f, San, F, June 13)
Green's Bid 55 (6f, Yrk, F, Aug 19)
Greenwich Chalenge 49 (6f, Nmkt, F, Oct 15)
Greystoke 43 (8f, Gwd, Y, Oct 2)
Gymcrak Tiger (IRE) 55 (6f, Rip, Y, Aug 31)

Hamsah (IRE) 51 (5f, Nmkt, F, Oct 1)
Hawayah (IRE) 42 (5f, Nmkt, F, Apr 15)
Hazy Kay (IRE) 41 (5f, Asc, F, June 19)
Heathfield (USA) 56 (7f, Nby, F, May 15)
Heathyards Boy 48 (7f, Ches, S, Oct 21)
Hello Hobson's (IRE) 46 (5f, Flk, F, Aug 14)
Hesketh Hope (IRE) 40 (7f, Naas, F, July 22)
High Tycoon (IRE) 42 (6f, Asc, F, June 20)
Holly Golightly 41 (5f, Asc, F, June 17)
Home From The Hill (IRE) 40 (8f, Red, F, Aug 26)
Hostile Witness (IRE) 40 (7f, Nmkt, G, Aug 7)
Huffa (USA) 48 (5f, Ches, F, May 5)
Humam (IRE) 62 (7f, Nmkt, G, July 9)

Icy South (USA) 52 (7f, Ches, Y, July 11)
Ihtiraz 43 (7f, San, G, July 22)
In Case (USA) 50 (6f, Don, G, Sep 12)
Inchinor 62 (7f, Nmkt, F, Oct 16)
Infant Protege (USA) 41 (6f, Kem, G, Sep 4)
Infrasonic 65 (10f, StCl, S, Nov 8)
Iron Merchant (IRE) 54 (6f, Kem, F, June 24)
Isotonic 47 (5f, Swl, Slw, Aug 8)

Ivanka (IRE) 56 (8f, Asc, Y, Sep 26)
Iviza (IRE) 49 (8f, Asc, G, Oct 10)
Ivory Frontier (IRE) 58 (6f, Leo, G, Aug 9)
Ivory Palm (USA) 45 (7f, Chep, Y, Oct 20)

Jarena (IRE) 43 (5f, Nby, Y, July 17)
John Peel (IRE) 56 (7f, Cur, G, Oct 20)
Joyofracing 54 (6f, Cat, G, Oct 16)
Just Speculation (IRE) 54 (8f, Leo, Y, Sep 13)

Kahellan (FR) 53 (5f, Lin, F, May 30)
Kamaatera (IRE) 56 (5f, Gwd, F, July 31)
Kariniyd (IRE) 46 (7f, Cur, G, Oct 20)
Kar Or 45 (7f, Naas, F, July 4)
Kassab 42 (7f, Nmkt, F, July 31)
Katiba (USA) 60 (6f, Gwd, Y, Aug 29)
Kelly Mac 45 (5f, Red, Y, Sep 26)
Key To My Heart (IRE) 43 (6f, Tsk, F, May 15)
Kharaj 50 (5f, Asc, Y, Apr 29)
Khattat (USA) 44 (6f, Asc, G, Oct 9)
Khoraz (USA) 45 (6f, Cur, Y, Aug 22)
Kimberley Boy 42 (7½f, Ches, Y, Oct 20)
Kindergarten 72 (8f, Lon, S, Oct 4)
Kingmambo (USA) 54 (6f, Deau, S, Aug 23)
King Paris (IRE) 62 (7f, Nmkt, G, Aug 7)
Kusamba (USA) 46 (7f, Yrk, G, Sep 3)

Lady Ounavarra (IRE) 48 (8f, Leo, Y, Sep 13)
Lake Pleasant (IRE) 46 (6f, Asc, G, July 25)
Land O'Lakes (IRE) 41 (6f, Flk, S, Nov 9)
Laurel Delight 45 (5f, Wol, G, Sep 7)
Law Commission 53 (7f, Nmkt, F, Oct 15)
Lindon Lime (USA) 49 (7f, Ches, F, June 24)
Little Too Much (IRE) 51 (7f, Gwd, F, July 30)
Liyakah (USA) 40 (6f, Kem, G, Sep 5)
Look Who's Here (IRE) 47 (6f, Hay, G, Sep 5)
Lord Olivier (IRE) 59 (5f, Nmkt, F, Oct 1)
Lord President (USA) 51 (6f, Asc, F, June 18)
Lost Soldier (USA) 49 (8f, Asc, Y, Sep 26)
Love of Silver (USA) 70 (8f, Lon, S, Oct 4)
Lt Welsh (USA) 41 (7f, Gwd, F, July 31)
Lucky Parkes 58 (5f, Rip, F, Aug 15)
Lyford Cay (IRE) 40 (7f, Ayr, S, Sep 19)
Lyric Fantasy (IRE) 82 (5f, Nby, G, July 18)

Magique Rond Point (USA) 49 (7f, Gwd, G, July 28)
Majestic Hawk (USA) 49 (7f, Gwd, F, July 30)
Marastani (USA) 41 (7f, Lin, S, Oct 26)
Marchand de Sable (USA) 66 (10f, StCl, S, Nov 8)
Marchwell Lad 45 (6f, Gwd, G, June 5)
Marco Magnifico (USA) 49 (8f, Nmkt, F, Oct 15)
Margaret's Gift 41 (5f, Hay, G, Aug 14)
Marillette (USA) 66 (8f, Lon, S, Oct 4)
Marina Park 62 (6f, Deau, S, Aug 23)
Marius (IRE) 44 (7½f, Lin, S, Oct 26)
Maroof (USA) 62 (7f, Gwd, F, July 30)
Massyar (IRE) 43 (8f, Cur, Y, Oct 10)
Mhemeanies 46 (7f, Don, G, Nov 7)
Millyant 68 (5f, Gwd, F, July 31)
Mistertopogigo (IRE) 55 (5f, Hay, G, Aug 14)
Mithl Al Hawa 50 (6f, Yrk, Y, Oct 10)
Moon Over Miami 51 (6f, Wind, F, Aug 29)
Moumayaz (USA) 43 (5f, Leo, G, Sep 13)
Mr Martini (IRE) 48 (7f, Nmkt, F, July 18)
Mukhamedov 55 (8f, Asc, G, Oct 10)
Mullitover 44 (7f, War, Y, Oct 6)
My Bonus 48 (5f, Lei, G, July 14)
My Patriarch 43 (7f, Asc, G, Oct 9)

Mystic Goddess (USA) 60 (5f, Asc, F, June 17)

Na-Ayim (IRE) 43 (6f, Nby, F, June 23)
Nafuth (USA) 49 (6f, Nmkt, F, Oct 16)
Nectarine (IRE) 52 (8f, Lon, Y, Sep 16)
Needle Gun (IRE) 55 (7f, Don, F, Sep 11)
Newton's Law (IRE) 58 (7f, Cur, Y, Aug 30)
Nicea (IRE) 47 (7f, Cur, Y, Oct 10)
Niche 61 (5f, Gwd, F, July 31)
Nico Mike 46 (7f, Gwd, S, Oct 3)
Night Melody (IRE) 59 (5f, Sal, Y, Aug 20)
Nominator 54 (6f, Rip, Y, Aug 31)
Nordic Fox (IRE) 54 (6f, Naas, G, Oct 17)
No Reservations (IRE) 50 (7f, Asc, G, Oct 9)
Northern Bird 43 (6f, Nmkt, G, Oct 3)
Noyan 44 (7f, Bri, F, Aug 4)
Nutty Brown 40 (6f, Yrk, S, Oct 8)

Palacegate Episode (IRE) 64 (5f, Gwd, F, July 31)
Palacegate Touch 50 (6f, Nmkt, G, Oct 3)
Pamzig (USA) 43 (7f, Don, G, Oct 23)
Pembroke (USA) 50 (7f, Kem, G, Sep 4)
Peperonata (IRE) 51 (5f, Don, G, Sep 12)
Perfect Halo (USA) 51 (6f, Nby, F, June 11)
Persian Brave (IRE) 51 (7f, Nwc, G, July 25)
Persian Charmer (IRE) 43 (8f, Red, F, Aug 26)
Persian Revival (IRE) 50 (7f, Don, G, Nov 7)
Petardia 68 (5f, Asc, F, June 16)
Pinta (IRE) 42 (5f, Naas, Y, May 2)
Pips Pride 65 (6f, Red, S, Oct 27)
Pistol (IRE) 50 (6f, Kem, G, Sep 4)
Piston (IRE) 50 (7f, Nmkt, F, Oct 15)
Pizza Connection 53 (6f, Rip, F, Aug 22)
Placerville (USA) 57 (7f, Nmkt, F, Oct 1)
Planetary Aspect (USA) 46 (8f, Asc, Y, Sep 26)
Poker Chip 65 (5f, Don, G, Sep 12)
Port Lucaya 51 (7f, Nby, S, Oct 22)
Power of Polly (USA) 57 (6f, Yrk, F, May 13)
Premium 44 (6f, Rip, F, July 6)
Preponderance (IRE) 53 (5f, Gwd, F, July 31)
Press Gallery 43 (7f, Nmkt, F, Oct 1)
Prevene (IRE) 61 (7f, Nmkt, F, June 27)
Princely Favour (IRE) 47 (5f, Sal, G, July 11)
Princess Oberon (IRE) 48 (5f, San, G, May 25)

Queen's View (FR) 63 (7f, Nmkt, F, Oct 16)

Rain Brother (USA) 58 (6f, Yrk, Y, Oct 10)
Rapid Success (USA) 52 (6f, Asc, G, July 25)
Realities (USA) 56 (5f, Asc, F, Oct 10)
Redenham (USA) 45 (6f, Nby, F, June 11)
Regal Aura (IRE) 46 (7½f, Lin, S, Oct 26)
Reine de Neige 42 (7f, Nmkt, F, July 17)
Revelation (IRE) 64 (6f, Red, S, Oct 27)
Ribbonwood (USA) 40 (7f, Gwd, Y, Aug 28)
Ribhi (USA) 45 (7f, Yrk, S, Oct 7)
Richard of York 64 (9f, Evry, G, Sep 26)
Right Win (IRE) 55 (7f, Nby, G, Aug 14)
Risk Me's Girl 49 (5f, Ches, F, May 5)
Rocket To The Moon (IRE) 52 (5f, Nby, F, May 15)
Rockover 45 (7f, Gwd, S, Oct 3)
Rock Symphony 51 (5f, Bev, G, June 4)
Roger The Butler (IRE) 63 (5f, Asc, F, Oct 10)
Rouquette 67 (8f, Lon, S, Oct 4)
Royal Deed (USA) 47 (5f, Don, G, Nov 6)
Rustic Craft (IRE) 50 (6f, Asc, G, Oct 3)

Sabaya (USA) 48 (6f, Naas, G, Oct 17)

## FLAT SPEED FIGURES — continued

Sabre Rattler 59 (5f, Yrk, G, July 11)
Saint Express 67 (5f, Don, G, Sep 12)
Salatin (USA) 64 (7f, Yrk, F, Aug 18)
Samakatan (IRE) 50 (10f, StCl, S, Nov 8)
Saseedo (USA) 43 (5f, Nmkt, G, Oct 30)
Satank (USA) 66 (5f, Don, G, Sep 12)
Satin Dancer 55 (8f, Gwd, Y, Oct 2)
Sayyedati 53 (6f, Nmkt, F, Sep 30)
Scottish Peak (IRE) 43 (7f, San, Y, July 4)
Scribe (IRE) 59 (8f, Cur, Y, Oct 10)
Sea Gazer (IRE) 59 (6f, Cat, G, Oct 17)
Seaton Delaval (USA) 57 (8f, Lon, Y, Sep 16)
Second Chance (IRE) 44 (5f, Don, G, Nov 6)
Self Assured (IRE) 60 (8f, Don, F, Sep 9)
Shadow Jury 40 (5f, Bev, F, May 9)
Shahik (USA) 61 (6f, Leo, G, Aug 9)
Shamam (USA) 45 (9f, Asc, G, Oct 9)
Shamisen 41 (6f, Yrk, F, Aug 20)
Shandon Lake (IRE) 44 (8f, Cur, Y, Oct 10)
Sharjah (USA) 52 (10f, Nmkt, G, Oct 31)
Sharp Prod (USA) 58 (5f, Lin, F, July 11)
Shebl (USA) 54 (7f, Gwd, F, July 30)
Sheila's Secret (IRE) 63 (5f, Nmkt, F, Oct 1)
Shemaka (IRE) 61 (9f, Lon, Y, Oct 11)
Shiro 52 (6f, Asc, Y, Sep 24)
Shrewd Idea 44 (8f, Hay, Y, Sep 5)
Silverdale (USA) 50 (8f, Nmkt, F, Oct 15)
Silverlocks 43 (6f, Ayr, Y, Sep 18)
Silver Wizard (USA) 67 (6f, Kem, G, Sep 5)
Simmering 43 (6f, Not, G, Aug 3)
Simply Sooty 43 (5f, Bth, G, Sep 28)
Snowy River (FR) 40 (6f, Not, G, Sep 22)
Soaking 47 (6f, Nmkt, F, Oct 15)
Sober Lad (IRE) 48 (5f, Tsk, G, Apr 11)
Society Lady (USA) 46 (7f, Kem, G, Sep 4)
So Factual (USA) 67 (6f, Asc, F, June 16)
Son Pardo 56 (6f, Gwd, F, July 29)
Sooty Swift (IRE) 40 (5f, Asc, F, Oct 10)
So So 40 (7f, Don, G, Oct 24)
Special One 45 (6f, Wind, F, Aug 10)
Specified (USA) 44 (5f, Red, G, Oct 14)
Splash of Salt (IRE) 40 (6f, Nmkt, G, Oct 31)
Splendent (USA) 56 (5f, Yrk, F, Aug 19)
Spring To Action 43 (8f, Kem, Y, Sep 22)
Star Family Friend (IRE) 60 (6f, Rip, Y, Aug 31)
Stepanov (USA) 46 (5f, Don, G, Oct 24)
Storiths (IRE) 52 (6f, Nmkt, G, Oct 3)
Storm Canyon (IRE) 61 (7f, Nmkt, F, Oct 17)
Sueboog (IRE) 55 (7f, Nmkt, F, Oct 16)
Sumoto 61 (6f, Asc, F, June 20)
Sumy 50 (6f, Cur, G, Oct 20)
Surprise Offer 60 (5f, Asc, F, Oct 10)

Tahdeed (USA) 54 (5f, Cur, S, Apr 11)
Tajdif (USA) 46 (6f, Yar, G, July 15)
Tajhiz (USA) 45 (7f, Don, G, Oct 23)
Take No Chances (IRE) 53 (5f, Cur, Y, Oct 11)
Tales of Hearsay (GER) 43 (7f, Cur, G, Oct 20)
Taos (IRE) 65 (8f, Asc, G, Oct 10)
Tarakana (USA) 51 (8f, Leo, G, Oct 24)
Tbaareeh (USA) 45 (8f, Leo, Y, Sep 13)

Tenby 73 (8f, Lon, S, Oct 3)
Thaleros 40 (7f, Nmkt, F, Oct 17)
Thawakib (IRE) 50 (7f, Sal, Y, Sep 3)
The Informer (USA) 48 (5f, Asc, F, Oct 10)
The Little Ferret 46 (6f, Nby, S, Oct 22)
The Sharp Bidder (IRE) 44 (6f, Don, G, Sep 12)
Time's Arrow (IRE) 50 (6f, Lin, Fs, July 10)
Tinners Way (USA) 49 (7f, Don, G, Nov 7)
Tioman Island 57 (7f, Nmkt, F, Aug 1)
Tom Piper 43 (5f, Pon, G, June 8)
Toocando (IRE) 54 (5f, Asc, F, June 17)
Top Pet (IRE) 49 (6f, Asc, Y, Sep 24)
Trentesimo (IRE) 44 (5f, Bri, G, Sep 23)
Triple 42 (7f, Lin, G, Sep 17)
Troon 56 (5f, Nmkt, F, Oct 30)
Tropical 47 (5f, Cur, G, July 11)
True Hero (USA) 44 (7f, Lei, F, Sep 14)
True Story (IRE) 43 (6f, Wind, F, Aug 10)
Ttyfran 41 (6f, Rip, F, July 6)
Tuscan Dawn 41 (5f, Ham, F, July 16)
Two Moves In Front (IRE) 45 (5f, Ham, F, July 16)
Two Times Twelve (IRE) 43 (5f, Wind, G, July 6)

Ukud (USA) 47 (7f, Naas, F, July 4)
Up And At 'em 73 (5f, Asc, F, Oct 10)
Urgent Request (IRE) 61 (7f, Lin, G, Sep 8)
Urry Urry Urry 51 (6f, Yrk, G, July 11)

Ventiquattrofogli (IRE) 40 (6f, Bth, F, July 8)
Via Parigi (IRE) 40 (6f, Cur, G, June 3)
Viscardo (IRE) 47 (6f, Cur, Y, Aug 30)
Visto Si Stampi (IRE) 45 (8f, Hay, Y, Sep 5)

Wangola (IRE) 58 (7f, Naas, F, July 4)
Warkworth (USA) 43 (6f, Nmkt, F, Oct 15)
Wathik (USA) 43 (7f, Nmkt, F, July 31)
Wharf (USA) 56 (6f, Nmkt, G, July 8)
White Crown (USA) 66 (7f, San, Y, Aug 21)
White Muzzle 53 (7f, Nmkt, F, Oct 1)
White Shadow (IRE) 45 (6f, Nmkt, G, Aug 29)
Willshe Gan 45 (5f, Yrk, G, Sep 2)
Windrush Boy 50 (5f, Flk, F, Aug 14)
Wintering (IRE) 41 (5f, Flk, Y, Oct 6)
Woodchat (USA) 65 (7f, Yrk, F, Aug 18)
Woodenville (USA) 50 (7f, Gwd, F, July 30)
Wootton Rivers (USA) 45 (8f, Cur, Y, Oct 10)
Wufud (USA) 46 (7f, Nwc, G, July 25)
Wynona (IRE) 51 (7f, Nmkt, G, Aug 7)

Yajeed (USA) 46 (7f, Nmkt, G, Aug 7)
Yawl 65 (7f, Nmkt, F, Oct 16)
Young Ern 51 (6f, Red, S, Oct 27)
Yours By Right 49 (6f, Wind, F, Aug 29)

Zafonic (USA) 74 (7f, Nmkt, F, Oct 16)
Zany Zanna (IRE) 46 (5f, Hay, G, Oct 8)
Zarani Sidi Anna (USA) 44 (6f, Nby, S, Oct 22)
Zenith 45 (7f, Sal, Y, Sep 3)
Zieten (USA) 68 (6f, Evry, F, June 13)
Zind (IRE) 49 (7f, Nmkt, F, Oct 16)
Zuno Warrior 53 (7f, Bri, F, Aug 4)

# WINNING TRAINERS, (Turf only) 1992

| | Races Won | Stakes £ | Per Cent | Last Year |
|---|---|---|---|---|
| 1. HANNON, R. | 146 | 1,147,651 | 13.2% | 2 |
| 2. CHAPPLE-HYAM, P. W. | 41 | 989,495 | 17.0% | 16 |
| 3. BRITTAIN, C. E. | 63 | 974,550 | 10.8% | 4 |
| 4. STOUTE, M. R. | 73 | 861,996 | 16.4% | 3 |
| 5. CECIL, H. R. A. | 109 | 735,347 | 28.6% | 5 |
| 6. GOSDEN, J. H. M. | 111 | 727,766 | 21.8% | 12 |
| 7. DUNLOP, J. L. | 75 | 524,207 | 15.0% | 6 |
| 8. BALDING, I. A. | 36 | 499,091 | 11.4% | 13 |
| 9. WRAGG, G. | 39 | 489,430 | 19.8% | 15 |
| 10. COLE, P. F. I. | 75 | 411,768 | 17.7% | 1 |
| 11. LORD HUNTINGDON | 50 | 374,070 | 17.3% | 14 |
| 12. CUMANI, L. M. | 54 | 357,571 | 18.4% | 8 |
| 13. HILLS, B. W. | 59 | 324,487 | 14.4% | 7 |
| 14. BERRY, J. | 94 | 297,230 | 12.8% | 9 |
| 15. JOHNSTON, M. | 45 | 294,003 | 12.8% | 45 |
| 16. REVELEY, Mrs G. R. | 68 | 267,916 | 20.7% | 25 |
| 17. BOLGER, J. S. (Ireland) | 1 | 261,216 | 4.5% | 29 |
| 18. CHARLTON, R. | 43 | 253,691 | 25.9% | 44 |
| 19. SCOTT, A. A. | 35 | 227,391 | 11.4% | 23 |
| 20. LEWIS, G. | 54 | 227,178 | 15.7% | 28 |
| 21. FABRE, A. (France) | 4 | 192,211 | 20.0% | 11 |
| 22. ELSWORTH, D. R. C. | 29 | 182,822 | 9.4% | 10 |
| 23. WELD, D. K. (Ireland) | 2 | 166,308 | 22.2% | – |
| 24. GLOVER, J. A. | 21 | 155,461 | 15.6% | – |
| 25. EASTERBY, M. H. | 38 | 154,128 | 10.2% | 19 |
| 26. KAUNTZE, M. (Ireland) | 1 | 152,356 | 14.3% | 42 |
| 27. HOLLINSHEAD, R. | 42 | 149,818 | 8.2% | 50 |
| 28. HANBURY, B. | 39 | 144,668 | 12.8% | 31 |
| 29. BELL, M. | 34 | 143,930 | 11.2% | 27 |
| 30. AKEHURST, R. | 26 | 138,244 | 10.5% | 21 |
| 31. TOMPKINS, M. H. | 41 | 132,920 | 12.1% | 22 |
| 32. FANSHAWE, J. | 27 | 121,323 | 11.0% | 18 |
| 33. CECIL, Mrs J. | 27 | 121,297 | 17.8% | – |
| 34. MOUBARAK, M. | 17 | 118,223 | 13.7% | 20 |
| 35. PRESCOTT, Sir MARK | 44 | 115,389 | 19.3% | 36 |
| 36. McMAHON, B. A. | 29 | 112,815 | 10.6% | – |
| 37. HEAD, Mrs C. (France) | 1 | 111,387 | 100.0% | – |
| 38. THOMSON JONES, H. | 26 | 109,444 | 13.9% | 26 |
| 39. McCORMACK, M. | 15 | 105,182 | 9.4% | – |
| 40. NORTON, S. G. | 18 | 101,539 | 11.6% | – |
| 41. JARVIS, W. | 18 | 99,409 | 10.6% | 43 |
| 42. STEWART, A. C. | 21 | 97,816 | 16.4% | 34 |
| 43. CYZER, C. A. | 21 | 97,127 | 13.6% | – |
| 44. WATTS, J. W. | 17 | 90,824 | 10.6% | – |
| 45. CAMACHO, M. J. | 20 | 88,037 | 18.8% | – |
| 46. LEE, F. H. | 24 | 86,980 | 8.4% | 46 |
| 47. HARWOOD, G. | 27 | 86,212 | 11.8% | 17 |
| 48. HILLS, J. W. | 21 | 86,186 | 10.1% | – |
| 49. HODGES, R. J. | 20 | 86,086 | 5.6% | – |
| 50. WHITAKER, R. M. | 23 | 85,648 | 8.0% | 48 |

# WINNING JOCKEYS, (Turf only) 1992

| | 1st | 2nd | 3rd | Unplaced | Total | Last Year |
|---|---|---|---|---|---|---|
| 1. ROBERTS, M. | 197 | 143 | 112 | 590 | 1042 | 3 |
| 2. EDDERY, PAT | 177 | 118 | 76 | 356 | 727 | 1 |
| 3. CARSON, W. | 125 | 120 | 107 | 504 | 856 | 2 |
| 4. CAUTHEN, S. | 107 | 85 | 72 | 292 | 556 | 4 |
| 5. DUFFIELD, G. | 103 | 64 | 53 | 435 | 655 | 17 |
| 6. QUINN, T. | 100 | 114 | 80 | 444 | 738 | 9 |
| 7. DETTORI, L. | 97 | 80 | 75 | 416 | 668 | 7 |
| 8. REID, J. | 95 | 76 | 88 | 439 | 698 | 10 |
| 9. COCHRANE, R. | 90 | 77 | 93 | 439 | 699 | 5 |
| 10. DARLEY, K. | 86 | 82 | 61 | 313 | 542 | 15 |
| 11. RYAN, W. | 86 | 89 | 82 | 371 | 628 | 16 |
| 12. SWINBURN, W. R. | 80 | 84 | 73 | 276 | 513 | 14 |
| 13. HILLS, M. | 74 | 68 | 53 | 298 | 493 | 20 |
| 14. EDDERY, PAUL | 72 | 63 | 70 | 426 | 631 | 13 |
| 15. MUNRO, A. | 71 | 80 | 83 | 426 | 660 | 6 |
| 16. CARROLL, J. | 63 | 53 | 47 | 343 | 506 | 8 |
| 17. CARTER, G. | 61 | 52 | 53 | 378 | 544 | 19 |
| 18. HOLLAND, D. | 59 | 57 | 56 | 330 | 502 | 11 |
| 19. RAYMOND, B. | 52 | 61 | 49 | 426 | 588 | 12 |
| 20. ROBINSON, P. | 51 | 46 | 47 | 303 | 447 | – |
| 21. HILLS, R. | 50 | 61 | 50 | 290 | 451 | 18 |
| 22. McKEOWN, D. | 49 | 48 | 47 | 319 | 463 | 21 |
| 23. HARRISON, D. | 48 | 54 | 41 | 276 | 419 | – |
| 24. WILLIAMS, J. | 42 | 54 | 65 | 449 | 610 | 25 |
| 25. WEAVER, J. | 41 | 56 | 34 | 197 | 328 | – |
| 26. FALLON, K. | 41 | 36 | 50 | 292 | 419 | 31 |
| 27. BIRCH, M. | 38 | 46 | 53 | 334 | 471 | 22 |
| 28. QUINN, J. | 37 | 38 | 45 | 497 | 617 | 34 |
| 29. PIGGOTT, L. | 34 | 45 | 35 | 212 | 326 | 24 |
| 30. BIGGS, D. | 33 | 26 | 32 | 269 | 360 | 38 |
| 31. FANNING, J. | 33 | 38 | 43 | 373 | 487 | 28 |
| 32. LOWE, J. | 32 | 32 | 50 | 448 | 562 | 23 |
| 33. CONNORTON, N. | 28 | 19 | 24 | 170 | 241 | 37 |
| 34. NORTON, F. | 26 | 55 | 39 | 333 | 453 | 29 |
| 35. ROUSE, B. | 22 | 21 | 26 | 253 | 322 | – |
| 36. SPRAKE, T. | 21 | 17 | 21 | 177 | 236 | – |
| 37. FORTUNE, J. | 20 | 33 | 30 | 238 | 321 | 30 |
| 38. DAY, N. | 19 | 20 | 17 | 134 | 190 | 40 |
| 39. BARDWELL, G. | 19 | 15 | 11 | 279 | 324 | – |
| 40. CARLISLE, N. | 19 | 29 | 24 | 272 | 344 | 35 |
| 41. NEWNES, W. | 18 | 19 | 27 | 207 | 271 | 41 |
| 42. MALONEY, S. | 18 | 29 | 30 | 229 | 306 | 49 |
| 43. TEBBUTT, M. | 17 | 15 | 13 | 146 | 191 | – |
| 44. TUCKER, A. | 17 | 26 | 20 | 176 | 239 | 42 |
| 45. MOFFATT, DARREN | 16 | 10 | 11 | 105 | 142 | – |
| 46. GARTH, A. | 16 | 16 | 21 | 155 | 208 | – |
| 47. BAXTER, G. | 16 | 12 | 20 | 166 | 214 | 45 |
| 48. CULHANE, A. | 16 | 27 | 25 | 173 | 241 | 32 |
| 49. HIND, G. | 16 | 20 | 27 | 215 | 278 | 36 |
| 50. CHARNOCK, L. | 16 | 15 | 23 | 280 | 334 | – |

# WINNING OWNERS, (Turf only) 1992

| | Races' Won | Stakes' £ | Last Year |
|---|---|---|---|
| 1. SHEIKH MOHAMMED | 185 | 1,194,344 | 1 |
| 2. HAMDAN AL-MAKTOUM | 103 | 694,928 | 3 |
| 3. SANGSTER, Mr R. E. | 46 | 674,117 | 6 |
| 4. ABDULLA, Mr K. | 76 | 620,342 | 4 |
| 5. MAKTOUM AL MAKTOUM | 33 | 430,837 | 5 |
| 6. GREDLEY, Mr W. J. | 9 | 415,920 | 10 |
| 7. CRAIG, Mr S. H. | 1 | 355,000 | – |
| 8. LORD WEINSTOCK | 21 | 295,228 | 17 |
| 9. LORD CARNARVON | 14 | 265,165 | 36 |
| 10. KRAFT PAYSON, Mrs V. | 1 | 261,216 | – |
| 11. SALMAN, Mr FAHD | 48 | 251,579 | 2 |
| 12. SHEIKH AHMED AL MAKTOUM | 34 | 213,181 | 39 |
| 13. LORD HOWARD DE WALDEN | 15 | 208,896 | 43 |
| 14. LODER, Mr E. J. | 4 | 194,170 | 21 |
| 15. SMITH, Mr J. C. | 11 | 190,177 | – |
| 16. SIR PHILIP OPPENHEIMER | 20 | 163,961 | 47 |
| 17. COCK, Mr D. F. | 6 | 157,841 | 18 |
| 18. HAGA, Mr M | 1 | 152,356 | 26 |
| 19. MORRISON, Mr J. S. | 4 | 143,674 | – |
| 20. STRAWBRIDGE, Mr GEORGE | 6 | 143,623 | 8 |
| 21. ASAKAWA, Mr YOSHIO | 3 | 140,825 | – |
| 22. SALEM, Mr HILAL | 4 | 136,493 | 27 |
| 23. SAEED, Mr ALI | 5 | 127,075 | – |
| 24. SAVILL, Mr P. D. | 42 | 122,609 | 20 |
| 25. THE QUEEN | 21 | 121,263 | – |
| 26. FUSTOK ECURIE | 18 | 120,409 | 9 |
| 27. MOYGLARE STUD FARMS LTD. | 1 | 118,188 | – |
| 28. MELLON, Mr PAUL | 12 | 110,848 | 46 |
| 29. OBAIDA, Mr MOHAMED | 5 | 107,992 | – |
| 30. GREEN, Mr PAUL | 2 | 101,837 | – |
| 31. GRANT, Mrs V. S. | 3 | 97,818 | – |
| 32. WINGFIELD DIGBY, Mr S. | 6 | 95,000 | 28 |
| 33. CYZER, Mr R. M. | 19 | 88,378 | – |
| 34. MOLLERS RACING | 5 | 86,561 | 37 |
| 35. DIXON, Mr B. | 4 | 82,301 | – |
| 36. A. F. BUDGE (Equine) LTD. | 16 | 80,000 | 12 |
| 37. OLLEY, Mr C. T. | 3 | 75,168 | – |
| 38. LADY BEAVERBROOK | 9 | 70,047 | 7 |
| 39. SIR ROBIN McALPINE | 9 | 67,869 | – |
| 40. N. T. C. (Racing) LTD. | 5 | 67,681 | – |
| 41. WINCH, Miss J. | 4 | 59,953 | – |
| 42. FENWICK-GIBSON, Mr R. | 5 | 59,034 | – |
| 43. CLAREMONT MANAGEMENT | 10 | 56,182 | – |
| 44. VALENTINE, Mrs A. | 3 | 55,142 | – |
| 45. FACCHINO, Mrs B. | 16 | 54,549 | – |
| 46. PREW, Mr T. J. | 2 | 54,351 | – |
| 47. HIGSON, Mr K. | 16 | 53,928 | – |
| 48. SUHAIL, Mr SAEED | 11 | 52,800 | – |
| 49. BLACKER, Mrs PHILIP | 1 | 50,980 | – |
| 50. BRITTAIN, Mrs C. E. | 3 | 50,280 | – |

# WINNING BREEDERS, (Turf only) 1992

| | Races Won | Stakes £ | Last Year |
|---|---|---|---|
| 1. SWETTENHAM STUD (in USA) | 12 | 576,089 | 7 |
| 2. STETCHWORTH PARK STUD LTD | 15 | 429,786 | 6 |
| 3. LYONSTOWN STUD (in Ireland) | 3 | 359,791 | 11 |
| 4. BALLYMACOLL STUD FARM LTD (in Ireland) | 24 | 302,597 | 36 |
| 5. JUDDMONTE FARMS INC. (in USA) | 27 | 265,755 | 47 |
| 6. HAMDAN AL MAKTOUM (in USA) | 2 | 263,311 | – |
| 7. KRAFT PAYSON, VIRGINIA (in USA) | 1 | 261,216 | – |
| 8. JUDDMONTE FARMS | 31 | 253,586 | 4 |
| 9. GAINSBOROUGH STUD MANAGEMENT LTD | 17 | 233,938 | 9 |
| 10. SHEIKH MOHAMMED | 42 | 229,783 | 31 |
| 11. LODER, E. J. (in Ireland) | 11 | 215,852 | 21 |
| 12. HIGHCLERE STUD LTD | 9 | 210,974 | 17 |
| 13. LITTLETON STUD | 13 | 188,950 | – |
| 14. MINCH BLOODSTOCK (in Ireland) | 5 | 185,604 | – |
| 15. CHEVELEY PARK STUD LTD | 34 | 171,782 | 14 |
| 16. SWETTENHAM STUD (in Ireland) | 31 | 162,886 | 18 |
| 17. OVIDSTOWN BLOODSTOCK LTD (in Ireland) | 1 | 152,356 | 29 |
| 18. HASCOMBE & VALIANT STUDS | 16 | 150,723 | – |
| 19. BENHAM STUD | 5 | 145,514 | – |
| 20. MEON VALLEY STUD | 6 | 143,077 | 30 |
| 21. POWELL, W & NEWTON, B. (in USA) | 2 | 137,745 | 43 |
| 22. LORD HOWARD DE WALDEN | 11 | 137,203 | – |
| 23. STRAWBRIDGE Jnr., GEORGE (in USA) | 5 | 133,128 | 5 |
| 24. DARLEY STUD MANAGEMENT LTD (in USA) | 13 | 127,700 | 1 |
| 25. MOYGLARE STUD FARM LTD (in USA) | 1 | 118,188 | – |
| 26. STACKALLAN STUD (in Ireland) | 6 | 116,894 | – |
| 27. GAINSBOROUGH FARM INC. (in USA) | 2 | 113,319 | – |
| 28. WINGFIELD DIGBY, S. | 10 | 104,861 | 27 |
| 29. POPELY, R. A. & J. H. | 4 | 103,071 | – |
| 30. MELLON, PAUL | 7 | 93,594 | – |
| 31. ROSSDALE, Mrs J. R. | 1 | 92,619 | – |
| 32. THE QUEEN | 15 | 88,594 | – |
| 33. LODGE PARK STUD | 8 | 88,582 | – |
| 34. BARRETT, SQDN-LDR FRANK | 4 | 82,301 | – |
| 35. O'BRIEN, D. P. (in Ireland) | 6 | 81,903 | – |
| 36. HESMONDS STUD LTD | 20 | 78,570 | 2 |
| 37. DICK, D. M. (in Ireland) | 4 | 75,062 | 35 |
| 38. SIDE HILL STUD & FLOORS FARMING (in USA) | 2 | 73,815 | – |
| 39. BUCKRAM OAK FARM (in USA) | 11 | 71,598 | 8 |
| 40. WATSON, R. T. and Mrs | 6 | 71,365 | – |
| 41. HIGHFIELD AND GLEN ANDRED STUDS | 3 | 71,287 | – |
| 42. DERRY MEETING FARM (in USA) | 3 | 70,379 | – |
| 43. BADGER, E. A. | 6 | 69,636 | – |
| 44. SOMERIES STUD | 4 | 66,318 | – |
| 45. SIR ROBIN McALPINE | 7 | 60,087 | – |
| 46. GREENSWARD RACING LTD | 4 | 59,953 | – |
| 47. LORD HOWARD de WALDEN (in USA) | 2 | 57,953 | – |
| 48. BARRONSTOWN BLOODSTOCK (in Ireland) | 13 | 56,209 | – |
| 49. SHEIKH MOHAMMED (in Ireland) | 8 | 55,450 | – |
| 50. WHITSBURY MANOR STUD | 15 | 54,669 | – |

# WINNING SIRES, (Turf only) 1992

| | Races Won | Stakes £ | Last Year |
|---|---|---|---|
| 1. EL GRAN SENOR (USA) | 19 | 564,052 | 10 |
| 2. SADLER'S WELLS (USA) | 49 | 563,042 | 8 |
| 3. SLIP ANCHOR | 29 | 529,299 | 37 |
| 4. AHONOORA | 26 | 516,228 | 3 |
| 5. RIVERMAN (USA) | 15 | 353,530 | 17 |
| 6. GREEN DESERT (USA) | 42 | 350,497 | 2 |
| 7. PERSIAN BOLD | 27 | 281,583 | 12 |
| 8. RAINBOW QUEST (USA) | 34 | 264,927 | – |
| 9. LOMOND (USA) | 23 | 263,102 | 18 |
| 10. PLEASANT COLONY (USA) | 1 | 261,216 | – |
| 11. IRISH RIVER (FR) | 11 | 258,700 | – |
| 12. TATE GALLERY (USA) | 16 | 239,518 | – |
| 13. NUREYEV (USA) | 21 | 235,252 | 9 |
| 14. PETONG | 36 | 226,564 | 29 |
| 15. DANZIG (USA) | 29 | 223,469 | 6 |
| 16. THATCHING | 37 | 205,135 | 14 |
| 17. SHADEED (USA) | 15 | 194,022 | 26 |
| 18. SHAREEF DANCER (USA) | 20 | 180,536 | 15 |
| 19. SONG | 10 | 180,465 | – |
| 20. AJDAL (USA) | 20 | 174,807 | – |
| 21. ALLEGED (USA) | 19 | 164,488 | – |
| 22. DIXIELAND BAND (USA) | 5 | 159,059 | – |
| 23. DIESIS | 28 | 158,484 | – |
| 24. EFISIO | 17 | 153,624 | 40 |
| 25. HOSTAGE (USA) | 6 | 149,819 | – |
| 26. SHARPEN UP | 5 | 148,957 | 5 |
| 27. GONE WEST (USA) | 11 | 148,577 | – |
| 28. SHIRLEY HEIGHTS | 27 | 147,138 | 36 |
| 29. DANCING BRAVE (USA) | 14 | 143,514 | – |
| 30. SHARPO | 34 | 139,573 | – |
| 31. RISK ME (FR) | 27 | 132,992 | – |
| 32. ARAGON | 28 | 125,905 | 22 |
| 33. KING OF SPAIN | 23 | 125,866 | – |
| 34. LAST TYCOON | 30 | 122,648 | 27 |
| 35. KRIS | 21 | 119,984 | 42 |
| 36. GLINT OF GOLD | 13 | 118,967 | – |
| 37. COMMANCHE RUN | 13 | 117,703 | – |
| 38. KALAGLOW | 24 | 117,062 | 33 |
| 39. PHARLY (FR) | 14 | 113,554 | 28 |
| 40. CAERLON (USA) | 23 | 110,649 | 1 |
| 41. NINISKI (USA) | 15 | 110,647 | 39 |
| 42. ROUSILLON (USA) | 20 | 108,069 | – |
| 43. NIJINSKY (CAN) | 12 | 107,713 | 43 |
| 44. NEVER SO BOLD | 27 | 105,133 | – |
| 45. TINA'S PET | 24 | 102,225 | – |
| 46. CROFTHALL | 9 | 100,759 | – |
| 47. BLAZING SADDLES (AUS) | 4 | 99,990 | – |
| 48. ABSALOM | 29 | 99,925 | – |
| 49. PETORIUS | 25 | 92,699 | – |
| 50. PRIMO DOMINIE | 19 | 92,398 | 21 |